Infinite Loop

INFINITE LOOP

HOW THE WORLD'S MOST INSANELY GREAT COMPUTER COMPANY WENT INSANE

MICHAEL S. MALONE

AURUM PRESS

To everyone who ever believed the Dream

First published in Great Britain 1999 by Aurum Press Limited, 25 Bedford Avenue, London WC1B 3AT by arrangement with Doubleday, a division of Random House, Inc.

A catalogue record for this book is available from the British Library.

ISBN 1 85410 638 4

Book design by Leah S. Carlson

Printed in the United States of America

FOREWORD

It has often been written that Silicon Valley is merely a very large and very wealthy small town in which everyone at some time has worked for, with or against everyone else.

If that is the case, then Apple Computer for me has always been the curious neighborhood just down the street. I have encountered it in some way almost every day of the last quarter century—sometimes just passing by, on other occasions stopping for a visit, but never out of my life. Indeed, so ever present, for good and bad, has Apple been in my life that I gave a second thought to ever beginning this book. The prospect of having to relive the Apple story, with all its hopes and heartbreaks, hypocrisies and disasters, was almost too exhausting to contemplate.

My dealings with Apple Computer began two decades before the company was even founded. I saw a nine-year-old Steve Jobs on the playground of our elementary schoolyard in Mountain View. I even found one of his homework assignments in my papers.

A few years later, having coincidentally moved to Sunnyvale at the same time as Jobs, I watched Steve Wozniak ride up Bernardo Drive on his way home from swim practice. I looked over Woz's primitive adder at the local science fair. For a short time, I was part of the Boy Scouts Explorer post that was one of the roots of the Homebrew Computer Club. And I saw, but didn't recognize, Woz, Jobs and Bill Fernandez (whose father was my Sunday school teacher) as they shopped for parts in Owen Whetzel's hobby shop. A year after that, I saw a lonely—and apparently unremarkable—Apple I on a shelf at the first Byte Shop.

When I was just out of college and working in public relations at Hewlett-Packard, one of my divisions was APD, Woz's employer. And during that period, handling publicity for Dave Barram and Dianne McKenna in their run for Sunnyvale City Council, I stood in the Wozniak living room as Mr. Wozniak cornered Regis McKenna over his concerns about his son and Steve

Jobs. Ten years later, I sat in Barram's office at Apple just days before he was nominated to the Commerce Department.

When I began my journalism career at the *San Jose Mercury News* at the end of 1979, one of my first assignments was to profile a new young company with the absurd name of Apple Computer. I interviewed Jobs and Woz in their chaotic offices just days after their move to Bandley Drive. There I found two bright, if eccentric, young men whom I nevertheless recognized as fellow children of Silicon Valley.

I visited Apple many times in subsequent years, writing about it for the *Mercury News*, the *New York Times* and the *Boston Globe*. I was in the audience, as a stringer for *The Economist*, at the extraordinary Macintosh introduction. Then, broke and hungry, I quit reporting on Apple for several years and went to work writing for it. Writing on an Apple III given to me by Mike Markkula in exchange for ghostwriting an article, I authored one of the many drafts of the notorious 1984 Apple annual report—and saw firsthand both the eerie bond between John Sculley and Steve Jobs and the emotional damage that Jobs was wreaking on the company. I heard the grumbles of the Apple II group as their product was eclipsed by the Mac.

Having been a reporter and a contractor, my third relationship with Apple was as a beggar—that sophisticated version known as an entrepreneur. In the middle of the Sculley era, I spent some time as part of the start-up team of a new Valley company. Like many such teams of the period, we imagined the answer to all our prayers was to convince Apple to become a customer, an investor or a strategic partner (these days, such teams dream of the same deal with Microsoft). For two years, we used every connection we had—Barram, Del Yocam, Debi Coleman and dozens of others—to no avail. Most of the problem lay with our company—it is only now preparing to go public after a decade—but as we sat through endless meetings, being ignored by Apple executives as they jockeyed for power among themselves, it became apparent to us that this was a company in serious trouble, one that had lost the edginess and drive that had once made it great.

In 1996, the world saw what we had seen during those long, posturing meetings: a hollow company that had lost its purpose, a company searching for a charismatic figure to save it. And so, once again a reporter, I found myself in the crush of true believers in a ballroom in San Francisco to hear Gil Amelio describe his plans to turn Apple around—and more important, to see the return of Steve Jobs. Sitting there on the floor, I thought about the distance we had traveled in three decades. We were all now middle-aged fathers, some rich, some mythical, some still just trying to cover their mortgage—as old as our own fathers had been when the personal computing revolution began. Now that revolution seemed to be coming to an end, replaced by new technologies and new products that rightly belong to a younger generation. It had been thrilling and degrading, noble and base—and it would ring down through history.

That was when I knew I had to write the Apple story. The true story that lay beneath the accretion of thirty years of legends and lies. I figured getting all the truth was probably impossible, but at least I could make a start. Apple had defeated every other attempt to capture its story, so I had no illusions. But at least I could stake out a path for that definitive Apple biography that waits to be written by some future generation. For now, here is a look, from inside and outside, at a deeply human institution that is unlike any other, yet is somehow emblematic of America at the end of the twentieth century.

Having covered Apple for a quarter century, I find it impossible to list all the individuals, named and anonymous, who helped in the creation of this book. The sources (see Notes on Sources at the end of the text) number literally in the hundreds. However, I would like to acknowledge several individuals who made important contributions to the actual production of this manuscript.

First and foremost is Roger Scholl, my editor at Doubleday, and his staff. *Infinite Loop* was originally Roger's idea, and during the many long months of waiting for me to meet one missed deadline after the next, he no doubt often wondered what had possessed him. Roger's suggestions were always insightful, and his patience awe-inspiring. Also at Doubleday, I'd like to acknowledge the hard work of attorney Kathy Trager in legal fact-checking.

As always, my agent Don Congdon brought his wisdom and experience to the project, keeping me on track. This time, however, I had the added pleasure of working with Michael Congdon.

In Silicon Valley, my vital right hand was Geoff Baum, columnist for *Forbes ASAP*, co-founder of garage.com and world-class researcher, interviewer and fact-checker. Among Geoff's many contributions were the interviews of everyday Apple employees that provided much of the versimilitude and texture in this book. He also cast his legendary cold eye over my hyperbolics. Eleventh-hour research was provided by David Raymond of *Forbes ASAP*.

Finally, and most importantly, at home I enjoyed tremendous support from my family. Of my seven books, this one was easily the most difficult: endless 3 A.M. nights and groggy days. Through it all my wife, Carol, and my two boys, Tad and Skipper, stood by me, propping me up and keeping me going. To them, as usual, I owe my deepest gratitude.

A final note on technology, because my experience with computers seems to match that of the rest of the consuming public. I wrote my first books, and launched my freelancing career, with an Apple III. Despite its infamy, I loved that computer, using it long after Apple had orphaned it, even after I'd worn away the tops of some of the keys. It was venture capitalist Bill Davidow, when we were writing *The Virtual Corporation*, who finally convinced me to upgrade: to a Macintosh IIsi. I used that computer for three years, but as I began *Infinite Loop*, it started to fall apart. I borrowed an Apple Duo Dock for a while, but that only delayed the decision. It was a dilemma being faced by millions of Apple owners during that dark period in the company's history: Should I spend above-market prices for an inferior Apple machine just out of perhaps misguided loyalty to a company that hadn't really cared about me for a long time? Or should I go over to the dark side, accept the cynical compromises of Windows 95 and do my part to line Bill Gates's already well-gilded pockets?

It was a painful decision. In good times and bad, I had always aligned myself with Apple, the maverick company fighting the good fight against the bureaucratization of personal computers.

But I was tired of passing those endless aisles of Windows programs at Fry's just to get to the few shelves of Apple products. I was tired of paying too much for too little computing power. Most of all, I was tired of being loyal to a company that was so self-centered and arrogant that it seemed to have lost all interest in me as a customer. And so, even as I was writing about the glory days of Apple Computer, I was abandoning the Mac for a Toshiba laptop. It was on this Windows computer that, ironically, I wrote this book.

And yet . . .

These days I find myself again eyeing Apple computers, this time with envy. Not the iMac, Steve Jobs's triumph of image over reality, but the G3 machines—fast, powerful and only a little overpriced. Most of all, I find I miss the excitement of the Little Kingdom . . . especially now that Apple seems to have gotten the magic back. After all, it was always about magic.

—Michael S. Malone
Sunnyvale, California

CONTENTS

Can any poet re-create
a worthy portrait of the great?

—Horace, *Odes* 1:6

1.0 ROOTS

Before and after everything, companies are about character.

Before the first idea, the first money, the first employees, the first distributor, retailer and customer, before the creation of the company itself, there is the character of the founders. Their ambition, talent, creativity and will to succeed are what make them successful entrepreneurs and distinguish them from the millions of people who only dream of creating their own company. Character also distinguishes these rare individuals from the thousands who try to create their own companies but are defeated by the market, competition, bad luck and an unwillingness to do whatever it takes to win.

After the company has grown rich and safe and mature, character tells as well. After the founders have left or died, after the excitement has moved elsewhere along with the best employees, after the company's products and logo and image have grown synonymous with staid and predictable. After hot new firms have appeared on the scene, start-ups that most resemble the company of old, and begin to carve away great chunks of the market. Then once more it is character, in the company's institutional memory, its community and in the philosophy with which the founders imbued it, that may spell the difference between another generation of success, or a slow, ugly corporate death.

Good companies have strong characters. Great companies have heroic characters. The greatest companies of the twentieth century all had extraordinary characters: Royal Dutch Shell, De Beers, Ford, General Motors, IBM, Hewlett-Packard, General Electric, Intel, Microsoft. They weren't necessarily "good" characters. One need only think of De Beers and Shell and their rape of underdeveloped nations, Ford and its crushing of workers early in this century, Microsoft and its alleged monopolistic destruction of the software industry. But they were bold, fearless and consistent. And it was this inner strength that enabled these companies not only to win their early competitive battles but to survive wounds that would (and did) kill their lesser counterparts.

Ford, battered first by GM, and then by the Japanese in the 1980s, struggled and regained its leadership in the 1990s with a new family of brilliantly innovative cars. IBM suffered one of the worst business collapses in the century at the end of the 1980s, then restored itself in just five years. HP slid into complacency and inertia, then somehow righted itself in the 1990s to become the most innovative large company on the planet. During this same period, Microsoft missed the most important technological revolution of the era, the Internet, then accomplished a breathtaking turnabout and gained the leadership of that industry.

Of all the great companies of recent memory, there is only one that seemed to have *no* character, but only an attitude, a style, a collection of mannerisms. It constructed a brilliant simulacrum of character, in the way a man without empathy or conscience can pretend to have those traits. But it was never really there—even though two generations of employees convinced themselves otherwise. It was only when that character was finally tested did the essential hollowness of the enterprise finally stand exposed, and the employees and customers shrieked with betrayal.

This was Apple Computer Inc., and there has never been a company like it. It was founded by two young men, one a genius with no allegiance to any institution but his own mind; the other a protean, inconstant figure who seemed composed of nothing but charm and a pure will to power. The company they built seemed to have everything: great technology, superb products, talented employees, rabidly loyal customers, an arresting vision, even a lock on the zeitgeist. But, like its founders, it lacked character. And because of that, from the first minute of the first meeting of Steve Jobs and Steve Wozniak, a decade before the company's founding, Apple Computer was set on a path from which it could not escape, even after those founders were gone. And that path would in time lead to the company's destruction.

More than any other great company, the seeds of Apple's future glory and its subsequent humiliation were planted long before the company ever began. And bend and prune as it might, Apple Computer could never free itself of its roots.

2.0 SEED

It was Regis McKenna, the Silicon Valley marketing guru, who first saw the horrible truth: "The mistake everyone makes is assuming that Apple is a real company. But it is not. It never has been."

He was too much of a businessman (after all, Apple could prove to be a once and future client) to draw the final inference: "And it never will be."

Nobody alive knew Apple better than Regis McKenna—at least nobody who had been affected by the notorious "reality distortion field" that emanated from Steve Jobs. After fifteen years of handling the company, Regis had remained unwarped and unconverted because no matter how successful Regis McKenna Inc. had become, and no matter how far it had left the publicity game behind for the more rarefied climes of marketing and business development, Regis still remained a PR man at heart. He still upheld the flack's first law: never, ever believe the hot air you put out about your client.

Not that it was easy. When you watched your client land on the cover of *Time* magazine and knew you got the credit for getting him there; when you stood in the convention centers and giant auditoriums and felt the waves of adoration rolling around you; and when the calls came late at night and you heard Jobs the Seducer telling you how much he depended upon you, it would have been so simple to surrender to the undertow, to lose yourself in the Apple Will.

But every time Regis thought of doing so there would be a meeting to remind him that Apple was a kind of collective madness. He would bring in an expert on marketing, or branding, or organizational theory—anything that might give the company some order, some strategic planning, some simulation of real business discipline—and he would watch in dismay as that person was humiliated, ignored or driven away. As for his own advice—well, nobody blew off the mighty Regis McKenna. Instead, they'd listen intently, nodding, foreheads pinched in concentration, even the seraphic Jobs himself making those unreadable and delicate motions with his fingers on the tabletop as if he was taking seriously what Regis was saying . . . and then the Apple Corps would leave the room and never think about Regis's message again.

In the end, after fifteen years advising the company he'd helped to create, McKenna walked away from Apple Computer. And not just from Apple, but from PR itself. Henceforth, the most successful publicist in the history of high technology would dedicate his firm to marketing. "It got to be my cross to bear," he said, looking back at the story of Apple Computer. "I helped create much of the image of Apple. Then I realized that I could help make people famous and have them assume the mantle of greatness, but that I couldn't do anything about the reality behind the story—the flaws and the insecurities and the egos. It just got to the point where I couldn't do it anymore. If it wasn't real, I didn't want to construct it."

So McKenna understood first. And in the years that followed, others, typically after they left the Cupertino kindergarten, caught on as well. Yet what they had learned was somehow inexplicable. It was like coming out of a coma and trying to describe where you've been. Some were bitter, a few amused, most just dazed in a way that could never be brought to focus. Even Regis, a man who had become rich and famous explaining technology and the companies that built it, would hit a wall when describing Apple. After twenty years, he could tell you what Apple was not, but he was at a loss for words telling you what it was. The best he could come up with was "a corporate Woodstock"—which explained everything, and nothing.

Others tried. Michael Moritz, who in 1984 wrote the first and best-known book about Apple, entitled it *The Little Kingdom,* suggesting at once the attractive preciousness of the place, its essential unreality, and the imperial nature of its organization. A few years later, Steven Levy, in his book about the Macintosh, would choose a memorable Jobs phrase, *Insanely Great,* that captured in its near-oxymoronic form two essential characteristics of the company. The pseudonymous Robert X. Cringely, in his entertaining (if suspect) *Accidental Empires,* compared Apple to an episode of *Bonanza,* the Bagwan's Rancho Rajneesh in Oregon and even the suicidal Jonestown.

Yet none of these descriptions, witty as they were, were sufficient to capture the true nature of Apple. It was only later, as the deep undercurrents in the company finally broke the surface that it became apparent that Apple Computer was, in fact, a beautifully constructed story, an elaborate fiction that mixed comedy with tragedy, piled irony upon irony, and then finally, bizarrely, looped back on itself.

And once that became clear, so did the author. Steve Jobs. The truth had always been there in Jobs's knowing little smile.

There are thousands of successful entrepreneurs at work right now, from

Bill Gates to the men and women meeting right now with a start-up team at Denny's, and none of them have written a tale as soaring and arresting as that of Apple. Perhaps no company in history has ever provoked such intense interest, loyalty, love and hate. For the richness of the plot, for the endless dramas, for the sheer *aesthetics* of its story, Apple is unique.

Trip Hawkins, himself an important entrepreneur, and a former Apple manager of market planning, told Cringely, "Steve never knew his parents. He makes so much noise in life, he cries so loud about everything, that I keep thinking he feels that if he just cries loud enough, his real parents will hear and know that they made a mistake giving him up."

That cry was Steve Jobs's hidden goad. With it alone he might have become a poet like his natural sister, or, quite easily, given the pathological parts of his personality, gone into crime—which, in fact, for a short time he did. His great luck was to find himself on the perfect playground for his gifts: the world of Silicon Valley in the 1970s.

2.0.1 Collision

Silicon Valley in 1965, at the time when Steve Jobs was attending Monte Loma elementary school in Mountain View, was a tense combination of opposing demographic forces.

Strictly speaking, Silicon Valley didn't yet exist. Sure, Fairchild was there, but it became mythic only in retrospect. If you were to drive down Ellis Street in Mountain View past its headquarters you never would have known that this little company was already changing the world.

Hewlett-Packard, of course, was there. By 1965 it was already more than twenty-five years old. At night, driving up El Camino Real in Palo Alto heading to the young Stanford Shopping Center, you could see its sawtooth roof glowing atop the hill up Page Mill Road. But HP was, and is, as hermetic as a church. If your father worked there, you were embraced within the HP family, you met Bill and Dave and attended the company picnic, and lived in an Eichler home in Palo Alto. Your neighbors were college professors from Stanford, other HPers or engineers and scientists who worked near HP in the Stanford Industrial Park at companies like Varian Corp., Watkins Johnson or Syntex.

But more important than HP was Lockheed Missiles & Space (LMSC), a city in itself rising alongside the Bay next to the Moffett Naval Air Station and NASA's Ames Research Center. Each day at 7 A.M., Lockheed's 25,000 employees would leave their homes in Mountain View, Sunnyvale, Cupertino and Santa Clara—from housing developments that had been built specifically for them by smart developers—and crowded the streets heading east into the morning sun toward the two LMSC gates. And each day at 3:30 P.M., the process would reverse, giving the Valley a distinct work cycle that would dominate the area for twenty years.

More than any other force, Lockheed was the dynamo that made Santa Clara County (the western cities of the South San Francisco Bay from Palo Alto to San Jose) the fastest-growing place in America. Young men, new families in tow, arrived by the scores each day, armed with a GI Bill degree in aeronautical, electrical or mechanical engineering, and looking for a piece of the aerospace future. They bought their ranch-style house—or, if they were adventurous, a Bauhaus-for-everyman Eichler with an atrium—and drove off every morning to build ICBMs for Lockheed.

Those who now call that world stultifying, conformist or retrograde weren't there. It was, in fact, as progressive in its way as any place on earth. The men and women who populated Silicon Valley in the 1960s were optimists. They believed that they were not only constructing the future but creating a perfect world for themselves and their families in the process. They would be famous and rich, have beautiful children and live in a Winterless Paradise and own a modernistic house and collect fine wines—all at the same time.

The betrayal, the depression and the self-doubt only came later, after Lockheed laid off at least one breadwinner on every residential block, after their kids grew their hair long and despised them and, worst of all, after these young men and women of infinite promise became divorced, career-stalled middle-aged men and women with a ceiling on their hopes.

It came after the counterculture revolution, Vietnam and recession, and after Silicon Valley had become a single monolithic urban stretch of high-tech communities thirty miles long and ten miles wide. In 1965, though, these professional communities were still tiny enclaves of (mostly) white, (mostly) Protestant, (mostly) engineers embedded in vast stretches of old Santa Clara Valley: blue-collar, rural, orchard-based, seasonal, immigrant, Catholic.

Mountain View was one of the oldest of Valley communities. Originally the Castro family land grant from Mexico, it was a well-developed farming community by the beginning of the twentieth century. The children and grandchildren of these farmworkers were enjoying the postwar prosperity by moving up to the new suburban housing developments, like the square mile of ersatz Eichlers built by Mackay Homes on the edge of Mountain View along Alma and San Antonio roads hard by the southern tip of Palo Alto.

For the local families that moved into this development in the early 1960s, these homes were the culmination of an assimilationist dream that in some cases reached back a century. It was the family's first toehold in the middle class, thanks to new jobs in auto repair shops, assembly lines and retail stores. Yet they soon found their shiny dreams tarnished by the arrival of new neighbors from the East Coast or the Midwest; arrivistes who drove their foreign cars every Friday night to San Francisco in search of real culture, and who owned not just college diplomas but graduate degrees in unimaginable disciplines like solid-state physics and semiconductor electronics.

For these newcomers, the neighborhood was not a culmination but a flagstone on the path to bigger houses in nicer neighborhoods in Sunnyvale or Cupertino, and then, with luck and some stock options, Los Altos Hills or Saratoga. For now, they merely demanded that the schools improve their facilities, that local stores offer more diverse merchandise and that the constabulary protect their children from the predations of the tougher working-class kids down the street.

It was a situation guaranteed to provoke friction and hostility. The upwardly mobile new Silicon Valleyites saw the natives as uneducated, unsophisticated and slightly dangerous, and the old Santa Clara Valleyites saw the newcomers as arrogant, pushy and, worst of all, a threat to their hard-fought prosperity.

2.1 Mockingbird

It was in this tense milieu that nine-year-old Steven P. Jobs found himself in 1965. And within this sensitive and often irritating boy the schisms went even deeper.

His father, Paul Jobs, grew up on a farm in Germantown, Wisconsin, dropped out of high school, then knocked around the Midwest in search of work. After Pearl Harbor he made the odd decision, for someone at the landlocked center of the country, to join the Coast Guard. As the war ended, he found himself in San Francisco on a decommissioning ship, and in yet another one of the compulsive moves that would characterize his life, Jobs bet a shipmate that on one of their upcoming leaves he would find himself a wife.

He did just that, on a blind date. Feckless he might be, but Paul Jobs was also a persuasive man; a natural salesman. Unfortunately, he had one disastrous flaw for a salesman. He hated kowtowing to customers. He talked his new wife, Clara, into moving back with him to the Midwest, a decision that ran precisely counter to the great migration of ex-GIs. Needless to say, it was a bad strategy, and after struggling as a machinist and then a used-car salesman, Paul finally, in 1952, caught on to the spirit of the era and he and Clara headed back to San Francisco.

Despite the fact that California wasn't as golden as he expected, and Paul jumped from one lousy job to another—bad-debt collector, car repossessor, loan checker—he and Clara were now feeling suitably stable and settled to start a family. In 1956, they adopted a baby boy, Steven. Five months later, before the adoption legalities were even complete, the family moved to South San Francisco.

There was in Paul Jobs an unusual, though not rare, combination of romanticism, unreality, hard work, ego and self-doubt. He was, in a sense, an entrepreneur who missed his calling, a lone wolf who chafed in every organization in which he worked, who resented being subordinate to anyone, who felt he was destined for important things but always arrived at the station just as the train pulled away, and who was perpetually ashamed about his lack of success. No sooner did he construct a new hopeful reality than it would crash around him and he would set off again.

In 1960, the finance company Paul was working for transferred him to Palo Alto. It was a good place for a man approaching middle age. The economy was booming and jobs were waiting unfilled. As they moved into their new home in Mountain View, it seemed that Paul Jobs had finally made it. Marking this new phase in their lives, Paul and Clara adopted a daughter, Patricia.

Now the Jobs family was in the very embodiment of a Postwar Upward Mobile community. It was as diverse a neighborhood as any the Valley would ever know. On a single block one might find a psychiatrist working at Agnews State Mental Hospital, a high school janitor, a naval officer flying P-3 sub chasers out of Moffett Field, a gardener from the Philippines who worked for the city, a Pakistani PhD in geology analyzing moon rills at NASA-Ames Research Center and a computer scientist who would one day be a vice president of Hewlett-Packard.

In the midst of all this was a brilliant little boy, often distracted, something of a discipline problem and accustomed to being the center of attention. He was the inevitable star of neighborhood home movies, birthday parties and picnics. Not only was young Steven doted upon by his parents but as the years went on he increasingly became the surrogate for his father's frustrated career desires.

The result would likely have been an arrogant chronic overachiever, the kind of obnoxious personality type that fills the senior, but not top, management ranks of Silicon Valley. But there were two other factors at work as well. One was that young Steven, the adopted child, was simply *different* from his family. Where his old man was tough and gregarious, the kind of guy who could repossess cars all week, then spend the weekend rooting around junkyards for parts for the classic cars he rebuilt in his garage, his son was sensitive and withdrawn. The boy was a discipline problem at school, while still managing to have few friends. He would go with his dad to the junkyards, obviously enjoying the dickering, but once they returned home he showed no interest in getting his hands dirty bolting on carburetors and fenders.

Worse, Steven was also a whiner. When he took swim lessons at the Mountain View Dolphins Swim club, one of his classmates, Mark Wozniak (yet more evidence that Silicon Valley has always been a very large small town) would recall: "He was pretty much of a crybaby. He'd lose a race and go off and cry. He didn't quite fit in with everybody else. He wasn't one of the guys." In fact, he was one of the boys, found in every class, who get the stuffing knocked out of them on a regular basis.

Out of place at home and at school, Steven turned to others in the neighborhood for friendship. It was possible in those days to walk down the street on a Saturday morning, past all the open, well-stuffed one-car garages and see the neighborhood men at work on their hobbies. And these extracurricular activities were as diverse as their careers. For every two Paul Jobses installing new lifters on engines there was at least one man surrounded by used oscilloscopes, multimeters, waveform generators, oscillators and all the other detritus of the vacuum-tube age of electronic instruments. Many of these obsolete devices had been lifted out of Dumpsters at the office and were now being put to use on televisions, stereos and, identified by the telltale antenna masts swaying over the house, ham radios.

Steven had just such a neighbor, a Hewlett-Packard engineer. One Saturday, while the boy was desultorily working with his father on a car, this engineer hauled a carbon microphone, a battery and an old stereo speaker out on the driveway, hooked them up and shook the street. Steven's eyes lit up. How does that work? he asked his father. Paul Jobs shrugged. He didn't know. So Steven ran to the engineer's house to ask. From then on, almost every Saturday, Steven stood in a new garage, peppering his new role model with questions.

His son's attention wasn't the only thing Paul Jobs lost. His job, he was convinced, was going nowhere. It didn't help that one by one the professionals among his neighbors began to move away to smarter, more expensive neighborhoods in Palo Alto and Los Altos. Unhappy and desperate, Paul Jobs decided once again to make a career shift. He took courses in his off-time and earned his realtor's license.

It was, in fact, a brilliant move. With the economy surging, the cost of living starting to climb, and one more old cherry orchard being covered by a new housing tract almost by the week, real estate was one of the most lucrative professions in the Valley. Had he stuck with it, Paul Jobs, like many others, might have made himself wealthy over the next twenty years.

Instead, he detested the work, a fact he might have realized long before he got into it. He didn't like making nice to every idiot with a buck in his pocket, he despised the whole phony nature of the profession and, most of all, he really hated not knowing when the next check was coming in. And they came in less and less frequently as his attitude spilled into his work and scared away clients.

The family was now caught in a downward spiral, made worse by the success of everyone around them. To stay afloat, the Jobses had to mortgage their house. Clara even took a part-time job. And when Steven took up swimming, she added babysitting to pay for his fees. Vacations were canceled. The car grew old. And in perhaps the ultimate statement of defeat in 1960s California, when the Jobses' color TV broke it was replaced with a black-and-white version. Eventually, to everyone's relief, Paul Jobs bailed out of real estate. But his only career choice now was to go back to work as a machinist with no seniority. He managed to find a job twenty miles away in San Carlos and the family struggled on.

Steven, now nine years old, watched in despair as the world around him, *his* world, began to crumble. Already alienated from his parents and his schoolmates, he was now, in a way he couldn't fully appreciate, also losing touch with his social class. It came to a head one day in school when his teacher asked a simple astronomy question: "What is it in this universe you don't understand?"

Little Steven Jobs, hovering over a cosmic abyss the teacher couldn't understand, answered abjectly: "Why is my family so broke?"

2.2 Revenge

Although the smartest kid in his class, Jobs became so difficult and obnoxious that he was thrown out of his fourth-grade class. Luckily, another, better, teacher took him in. Years later, Jobs would recall that the teacher found a quick motivational tool for the young man: bribes. Especially money. With the prospect of a payoff down the line, Steven Jobs could do amazing things. So amazing that he skipped fifth grade altogether.

But skipping a grade was both an honor and a curse, because the troubled, socially awkward boy was now a year younger than his classmates. Worse, jumping to sixth grade brought Steven one year closer to Crittenden Junior High School.

Monte Loma was paradise compared to Crittenden. Located in a poor neighborhood a half mile closer to the Bay, drawing from the middle class all the way down to the bottommost economic strata, Crittenden was a school where the daughter of an astrophysicist might sit at a desk next to the deeply disturbed son of a parolee. Fights were a daily occurrence; as were shakedowns in the bathrooms. Knives were regularly brought to school as a show of macho. The year before Steven arrived a group of eighth-grade boys had gone to jail for gang rape. During Steven's seventh-grade year the school lost a wrestling match to Sunnyvale's Mango Junior High and proceeded to demolish that school's team bus.

Among the students, there were two ruling elites: the hoods, mostly Hispanic, in pointed high-heel shoes, pegged black pants, white shirts, DAs; and a small number of surfers, with long blond hair, knit shirts, baggy pants and deck shoes. Everyone else cowered in fear. And Steven Jobs, a year younger than his classmates and thus the youngest kid in school, a pariah even among the pariahs, was in the sorriest spot of all.

That summer, Steven dreaded September more than anything he'd ever known. Finally, he couldn't stand it any longer. He told his parents that if he had to go back to Crittenden, he would quit school.

What happened then was a turning point in Steven Jobs's life. He wasn't alone in fearing his school. In his neighborhood scores of families, worried about the quality of education and the threat to their children represented by Crittenden, had picked up stakes and moved elsewhere. But these were upwardly mobile families; most had planned to leave for months, even years, and the quality of schooling proved to be the trip wire.

An even greater number of kids in the neighborhood, when they expressed the same fear, or came home with a split lip and missing lunch money, were told by their less affluent parents to buck up and not be pushed around.

But when Steven Jobs made his ultimatum, the most amazing thing happened: his parents agreed. His family *moved* to a safer, and more expensive, neighborhood in Sunnyvale—despite the fact that they were working extra jobs trying just to stay solvent, despite the fact that it meant an even longer commute for his father and pulled his sister out of elementary school.

This was power. And Steven Jobs learned its lesson.

2.3 Suburbia's Child

Sunnyvale, though it abutted Mountain View, was a very different town. Younger than its neighbor, it was part of the giant landholdings of Martin Murphy, Jr., one of the first American pioneers of California.

Sunnyvale had largely grown up north (on the Bay side) of El Camino Real, and many of these older neighborhoods of bungalows and tiny homes were as rough and troubled as the one in Mountain View. Until after World War II, the land south of El Camino consisted of several square miles of orchards and farmland. It was this land that was flattened, asphalted and covered with tract homes, mostly Eichlers, to house the workers of Silicon Valley.

This section of Sunnyvale was one of the first neighborhoods to become part of the new Silicon Valley. The streets were wide, the shopping centers and light poles and sidewalks brand-new, and, because all of the newly planted trees were still saplings, everything was brilliantly lit in a sharp intense light. The city government was progressive, the public safety officers switched back and forth between being cops and firemen and crime was almost nonexistent. Even thirty years later, Sunnyvale would be named the safest city of more than 100,000 citizens in the entire United States.

This was Stephen Wozniak's world. Born in 1952, he had grown up in the stablest of families in the safest of neighborhoods. That very security, while it might temper his ambition, even when the opportunity was put in his hands, would also make him one of the few entrepreneurs in high-tech history to emerge contented from great success.

If Steven Jobs was an odd child who imposed his vision of normalcy upon the world through sheer force of will, Stephen Wozniak was the opposite: a normal kid turned odd by the power of obsession.

It didn't begin that way. Contrary to his later reputation as a nerd, Wozniak was a typical, even athletic, boy. His father had played football while earning an electrical engineering degree at Caltech; and then had spent a year as an entrepreneur, working with a partner in a failed venture to design and sell an automatic stacking machine. After that, now married and with a son, Jerry Wozniak sought out more stable corporate work. Drawn to the aerospace boom, he first found work in San Diego designing weapons, then with Lear in Santa Monica perfecting autopilots. Finally, following the path of thousands of other young engineers, he went to work at Lockheed. The family moved to an Eichler on the Sunnyvale-Cupertino border in a neighborhood that had once been the farm of an entrepreneur of a previous generation, William Wright, Jr., who had pioneered the artesian wells and orchards that transformed Santa Clara Valley from cattle ranches into a sea of fruit trees.

Even as he played Little League baseball and golf on the former orchards with his dad, the zeitgeist was already stalking Stephen Wozniak. History, in the form of computers and Steven Jobs, was about to catch him by the tail.

There is an intersection in Sunnyvale that a cynical person might say embodies everything wrong with life in postwar suburban America. The intersection, of Fremont and Bernardo avenues, is flanked on one side by freeway on- and off-ramps and an overpass which covers a once beautiful stretch of Stevens Creek. The other two corners of the intersection are blank walls hiding two housing developments. Fremont Avenue at this intersection is four lanes wide, with a divider filled with stones. In summer this intersection of cement and asphalt bakes under an unrelenting sun. Except for the crush of cars waiting for lights or racing along the ramps, this intersection is almost completely devoid of life.

And yet, on a given evening in the late 1960s, two men and a boy would have passed one another at this intersection. One was Robert Noyce, racing home from his new company, Intel Corp., to his home in Los Altos. The other man was one of Noyce's employees, Ted Hoff, who happened to live at the intersection in a house directly behind one of those walls. The boy was a teenaged Stephen Wozniak, returning home on his bike from swim practice, his left arm scraped and sore from always having to swim the butterfly stroke in the outside lane.

Thus, the inventors of three of the most important technology products of the century, the integrated circuit, the microprocessor and the personal computer—each made possible by the one that came before—regularly converged on this anonymous and bleak intersection in a seemingly unremarkable suburban city on the edge of a continent.

2.4 Obsession

If the electronics revolution was in the air in Steven Jobs's Mountain View neighborhood, it was the very soil of Stephen Wozniak's corner of Sunnyvale. Essentially everybody in northwestern Sunnyvale and Cupertino worked in the high-tech industry or in a profession that supported it. Jerry Wozniak was a prime example: each morning he drove off to Lockheed to work on a top secret defense project. The other fathers on the street were also engineers, some at Lockheed or NASA. But as the years passed more and more worked for the new local electronics companies that had sprung up after the disintegration of Fairchild.

In this world, the neighborhood children, if they showed any aptitude, soon found themselves immersed in the world of electronics. There were odd jobs they could do for neighborhood men on weekends, such as soldering or helping to test new semiconductor devices bought at local specialty shops. A few of the more ambitious and talented boys (and it was always boys) built simple devices of their own.

And no neighborhood kid showed more aptitude than Stephen Wozniak. By the time he was ten, the neighborhood men recognized that little Stephen was a natural, even a savant, at electronics. In fifth grade, as part of this informal apprenticeship, he was given a voltmeter kit and built it beautifully. A year later, thanks to long hours spent hanging around a neighbor, Stephen built his own 100-watt ham radio station and qualified for an operator's license. He also interconnected his home with those of nearby friends in a crude communications network.

By the time Stephen entered Cupertino Junior High he was so lost in the grip of an obsession with electronics that it resembled a kind of autism. "I was all alone," he would later say. His mother, Margaret Wozniak, a strong-willed, outspoken woman who in later years would call and berate reporters if they wrote anything less than positive about "my Stephen," would remember going into his bedroom and finding the boy so intent on a new project or trade magazine article that she would have to rap him on top of the head to get his attention.

If such behavior wasn't healthy, it sure beat stealing cigarette lighters at Payless or smoking reefers or hiding under the headphones listening to the Rolling Stones or any of the other forms of teen rebellion of the day. "I was lucky," he would later tell *Wired* magazine. "Keys to happiness came to me that would keep me happy for the whole of my life. It was just accidental. I don't know how many people get it. It's like a religion or something that just popped into my head, walking home from school."

Stephen loved what he was doing. Working in the cramped kitchen, making a disaster of the standard Eichler Formica breakfast table, Stephen built an electronic tic-tac-toe game like the one he'd seen in one of his endless electronics magazines. Next he built a prototype robot.

Then came a breakthrough. Stephen had begun a new project: a basic two-function calculator circuit that had become the hot new build-at-home fad among electronics hobbyists. The actual circuit was called an adder-subtractor, which, though Wozniak didn't know it yet, was a board-level version of the same kind of transistor "gate" circuitry on the surface of the new semiconductor logic chips.

With the kind of maniacal focus that now characterized his daily encounter with the world of electronics, Stephen studied the diagram in the magazine over and over . . . until he understood not only how the circuit worked but its underlying *metaphysics*. And with that understanding came the flash of an epiphany.

Now Stephen understood. Electronics could be more than just the manipulation of electricity or radio waves to achieve some physical result. It could create the world itself; becoming thought and memory. It could inhabit a universe of its own devising. And if you knew these basic components, like the adder-subtractor, you could treat them the way a conductor would a string section, calling up this instrument or that or all together. You could create a symphony of effects, a harmony—a music of digital life.

Stephen was so excited that he decided to vault the one-bit adder-subtractor described in the diagram and build a ten-bit parallel (that is, it would carry) adder-subtractor. He built it out of spare parts and with a soldering gun. There were two rows of switches on the bottom, one for addition, the other for subtraction, and a row of lights at the top from which you could read the results of the computation.

Not surprisingly, the adder-subtractor won the Cupertino school district science fair. Thirteen-year-old Stephen Wozniak, on his own, from his own design, had built a computer as powerful as any in the nonmilitary world just twenty-five years before. That alone was incredible, but more important for the future, his design exhibited uncanny elegance and conservation of parts and board space. Young Steve announced to his father that he wanted a Data General Nova, a hot new minicomputer that featured 4K of onboard memory. Jerry Wozniak informed his crestfallen son that such a machine "cost as much as a house." "Well, I'll live in an apartment," Steve replied.

Woz's childhood enchantment wasn't unique. When his protocomputer was entered in the Bay Area Science Fair that year, it earned only third place. This was an era when first place went to teenagers who built homemade Van de Graaff atomic particle accelerators. Even in his neighborhood, Wozniak was hardly alone. Walking the halls of Cupertino Junior High in that era one would have seen perhaps a half dozen kids just like him. Some were ham radio fanatics. Others built nasty electric shockers that could send arcs of blue light from every door of a bank of student lockers.

The luckiest kids were the ones whose fathers had jobs that allowed them to bring home printer-terminals. These heavy, typewriter-sized machines could, with the help of an acoustic coupler into which the family telephone receiver was jammed, talk to a distant mainframe computer. This was heaven itself, especially when you could "talk" to one of those programs that, in rehearsal for some future Turing test, would converse with you by riffing off your own statements. If your dad worked for NASA-Ames you could even sit in the lobby of one of the buildings there and talk to a computer this way for hours—for free! It was amazing. You could feel the power of digital reality, a new life form, through your fingertips.

Each year it seemed there were more and more of these boys who had been inhabited by electronic dreams. Anywhere else—say, up the road in Steven Jobs's neighborhood—they might have been tortured by fellow students for their strangeness. Even at Sunnyvale High School, across town, this was still true. But not in Cupertino, and not at Homestead High. Homestead, upper-middle-class, almost exclusively white and Asian, was instead a kind of sanctuary for the brilliantly dysfunctional. Not only was it among the best schools in the South Bay, it also had the resources to respond to this influx of odd newcomers.

In particular, there was a class at Homestead in electronics taught by John McCollum. It would prove as important to the computer age as Fred Terman's electronics class at Stanford had been for Bill Hewlett and David Packard three decades before. There, at last, Stephen Wozniak's private love and public education could become one.

2.5 HOMESTEADING

From the moment he arrived in McCollum's class, in which he quickly became the shining star, Wozniak's life seemed to take a sidetrack from the rest of mankind. In an obvious way, he seemed to stop developing emotionally like his peers, but instead drifted on in pursuit of his Cyber Circe. The rest of his studies suffered, as did his social life. His classmates would see him all day, in homeroom and other classes, sketching out new circuit designs, absent-mindedly drifting off to conduct rondos and sonatas with the brass, woodwinds and strings of logic chips, memory devices and linear circuits. By the time he finished high school, Woz had designed fifty computers on paper.

Stephen Wozniak, the boy who played golf and swam competitively and watched television, the typical suburban boy, had now become the Woz. The great achievements were still years ahead; and for now the new persona, unadorned by fame, was not a pretty sight.

One characteristic of the new Woz was a singular lack of understanding of human behavior and the boundaries of social etiquette. And nowhere was this more evident than in his practical jokes—a lifelong predilection that took on twisted new forms in the hands of the Woz.

The most celebrated example of this was the bomb scare. Using some old-fashioned, stick-shaped dry cell batteries, some wire and an oscillator chip to produce a reliably loud clicking sound, Woz constructed a pretty good simulacrum of a dynamite device. He put it in a friend's locker and gleefully awaited the result.

He got more than he bargained for: the bomb squad. Evacuated buildings. Hysteria. And the crowning touch: William Byrd, the school principal, rushing up, grabbing the "bomb" and sprinting with it—sweat flying, tie flapping, leather shoes clicking on the cement hallway—out to the football field. There, expecting death at any second, he yanked out the wires.

By most measures, Byrd was a hero. Except one: Stephen Wozniak had made a complete fool of him. Woz somehow never anticipated any of this. He trotted off to the principal's office later that day expecting to receive a math award—and instead was arrested and thrown into juvenile hall overnight. But what is perhaps most telling about this episode is that Margaret Wozniak bailed out her son the next day, all the while screaming at the cops and anyone else in earshot that her son was the suburban equivalent of a political prisoner, that she was surprised he hadn't had a number tattooed on his chest and thrown into San Jose's equivalent of Bergen-Belsen. Stephen's sister Leslie got into the act too, writing an exposé on the affair of the faux bomb in the school newspaper she helped edit.

Despite the troubles at school, which included not just the bomb prank but falling grades in other courses as electronics took over more and more of his life, Woz was also becoming one of the more celebrated students at Homestead. Single-mindedness is not a common trait in high schoolers, and single-mindedness combined with genius appears rarely indeed. Stephen Wozniak was that student. Often those students are hated by their classmates, but the Woz was too friendly (if distracted) to have enemies.

Instead, his classmates mostly just stood back in amazement as the Woz devoured every bit of knowledge in McCollum's class and then begged for more. One of the glories of Silicon Valley, then and now, was the proximity of some of the best minds and technology in the world. McCollum wisely found a school credit internship for the boy at GTE Sylvania, a microwave telephony research facility in Mountain View. Joining Woz there was his closest friend, Allen Baum, the only other kid at school who could remotely keep up with him in electronics.

The two boys were lucky to have landed at Sylvania. In Silicon Valley at this time there were perhaps a dozen mainframe computers. Some, like those at NASA-Ames and Lockheed, were largely inaccessible. Others, like those at Hewlett-Packard, were simply too busy doing payroll and engineering simulations. But Sylvania was a looser place, an R&D lab whose fiberglass bubble dome rose over the surrounding orchards as a South Bay icon.

The mainframe used by Sylvania was nothing special, an IBM 1130 that in the words of one author "was about the size of a refrigerator, shook the floor when it operated, and was so loud that shouting replaced normal conversation." It required punched computer cards for input and had about the same computing power as a modern fifty-dollar handheld video game. But Stephen Wozniak would have sawed off his arm to own it.

High school technical internships in the late 1960s and early 1970s are a rarely noticed factor in the creation of the modern Silicon Valley. Yet these programs, at Ames, Lockheed, Sylvania, the Stanford Linear Accelerator and elsewhere, were of incalculable value to the founders of personal computing; and it is no coincidence that the early organizations in this field had their beginnings at these sites.

Certainly the internship at Sylvania, with the mainframe at hand and friendly scientists more than happy to help a young kindred soul, had a profound effect upon the Woz. He arrived an electrical technician of native genius and left a computer scientist of nearly infinite potential.

Until now, Woz had dealt with electronics as a hardware exercise. You had a problem to be solved and you did so using some configuration of the hardware tools of electronics: the old linear devices like capacitors, oscillators, resistors; discrete devices of more recent vintage like diodes; and the new digital integrated circuits, including ROMs, RAMs and TTL logic. The obvious difficulty in this method—the only method the engineering world had known until recently—was that the more complex the problem, the more complicated the hardware setup needed to address it. In this world, the most gifted engineers were those who could puzzle out novel ways to reduce the number of components by, say, 10 percent. And it was in this particular type of simplification that Woz had shown almost supernatural talent.

The encounter with the Sylvania computer changed Wozniak's life because, thanks to helpful explanations from the scientists and time spent playing with the machine itself, Woz saw, literally in a flash of lights, another, *better* way.

What the scientists showed him was how the compiler of the 1130 worked. Thirty years later, the millions who use a personal computer, whether they know it or not, have a good idea of how a compiler works. When you type in a command, or drag a window across the screen with a mouse, you know that the computer is actually taking this information, converting it in software to a series of instructions in the ones and zeros of binary code, then performing the requisite operations in hardware, then translating the results through software—moving the window, erasing a word, drawing a shape—back onto the screen.

We understand this because Woz taught us. But the teacher himself had to be taught; and the education of Stephen Wozniak took place during those days at Sylvania. The lesson wasn't self-evident. As with most electrical engineers of the era, Woz's notion of data processing was computation, and his image of a computer was a calculator. Thus, the music of electronics he heard in his head, complicated as it was, remained merely a melody, a string of distinct events leading toward a conclusion.

What transformed Wozniak at Sylvania was the realization that there was another world in electronics, *software*, that would make the music infinitely richer and more ambitious through counterpoint, minor chords and repetitive refrains. He learned one of the early computer languages, FORTRAN, and began programming the 1130 to do things he had never before imagined possible. From now on, he would create symphonies.

Again, Woz wasn't the only teenager in Silicon Valley learning about computers. All those boys tapping into distant mainframes through the acoustic modem and terminal Dad brought home from work every Friday night were doing the same thing. Out at NASA-Ames, Foothill Community College taught a course in programming on Saturday mornings that was jammed with students ranging from high schoolers to pensioners. But what made Woz almost unique among the young budding programmers was his already vast experience in circuit design. And even as he was finishing his Sylvania internship, Ted Hoff, that neighbor he passed in the intersection, was working a few miles away at the Intel Corp. plant in Cupertino to create the microprocessor, the electronic device that would bring Woz's two great skills together.

2.6 LIAISON

Woz was a junior at Homestead High when Steven Jobs arrived for his eighth-grade year at Cupertino Junior High four blocks away. There, Jobs soon found a friend and kindred spirit in Bill Fernandez. Fernandez would say, "For some reason the kids in eighth grade didn't like [Jobs] because they thought he was odd." Fernandez didn't follow suit, largely because he and Jobs shared a common passion for electronics.

The two boys would hang out together in Steven's garage, listen to rock and roll, build simple electronics devices and put on cool light shows by ricocheting laser beams off bottles and cans. This garage would later become an object of myth, the spiritual descendant of that most sacred of Silicon Valley sites: the Packard garage in Palo Alto—as if a garage beginning conferred a certain mystical advantage to high-tech companies. In fact, given the mild winters of the Bay Area, the thin sound insulation of most houses and the high flammability of Eichlers in particular, garages were typically the most comfortable, safest and most soundproof places for teenage experimenters to build stuff and crank the music up loud.

Jobs and Fernandez never built anything of importance in that garage—that would come later. Neither, in fact, had much technical acumen. Jobs in particular was just too mercurial to develop any real skill—though he would sometimes show flashes of brilliance.

Fernandez, for all of his shyness, nevertheless was well connected to the neighborhood nerd network. Woz, of course, was already a local legend, and Fernandez knew him slightly. It was Fernandez, halfway in age between Woz and Jobs, who would first bring the two future partners together—creating a friendship that would soon leave him behind.

Steve Jobs's sojourn at Homestead was marked by what can only be called a singular combination of conventional failures and unforgettable victories. Like Woz two years earlier, he took John McCollum's electronics class. But whereas Wozniak had become a class legend, Jobs alienated everyone, then dropped out of the class. Despite this, he still managed to perform one indelible act: unable to get a part he needed at school to finish one of his projects, Jobs simply placed a collect call to the PR department of computer giant Burroughs in Detroit and asked for it. When told by McCollum that a collect call wasn't proper, Jobs reportedly replied, "I don't have the money for the phone call. They've got plenty of money."

Jobs's act of rebellion was well timed. This was the first moment in history that a kid could learn about computers without a classroom or a rich dad. The minicomputer revolution was now in full bloom throughout Silicon Valley. Mainframes were becoming more numerous too, and using them becoming less expensive. It was possible now for a kid to get cheap computer time at numerous locations all over the Valley, including Homestead High's electronics club. Despite having dropped McCollum's class, Jobs maintained a steady attendance at the club. Ames Research Center was doing more educational work all the time; not the least of which was hosting a new Boy Scout Explorer Post dedicated to high tech. The Post would be one of the farm teams of what would be called the Homebrew Computer Club.

Hewlett-Packard too was helping teach young people about electronics.

Stanford professor Fred Terman had trained Bill Hewlett and Dave Packard; now they returned the favor by enabling their engineers to take Stanford graduate courses in HP facilities. Some of these courses and lectures were open to the public, and they regularly drew a young and increasingly scruffy (Fremont Union High School District had by now abandoned its dress code) Steve Jobs. Jobs, as was characteristic of him, was fearless about going up to the speakers afterward and peppering them with questions.

But the most significant event that occurred at this time happened in Santa Clara in a laboratory to which only a handful of people had access. In 1968, Fairchild Semiconductor of Mountain View, the preeminent computer chip company in the world, exploded. A half dozen key employees, all of them in their late twenties and early thirties, walked out, furious at the company's unwillingness to award them stock options and let them get rich off their success. This core group teamed up with the very first high-tech venture capitalists and founded a group of new companies. Their success in turn convinced other Fairchildren to walk out, some to try their own hand at entrepreneurship.

By the mid-1970s the Valley had been seeded with more than fifty new semiconductor companies. Their success turned Santa Clara Valley into Silicon Valley. Then these new firms in turn blew up and scattered even more new companies across the landscape, making Silicon Valley the world's leading technology center.

A few of these firms became very successful and survive to this day, notably Advanced Micro Devices, National Semiconductor (which had the revenge of buying and bulldozing the Fairchild building into dust) and, greatest of all, Intel Corp. Intel was founded by the general manager and the chief technologist of Intel, Robert Noyce and Gordon Moore, respectively, and the two had quickly hired a third, Andrew Grove, Fairchild's top applications scientist.

Intel took off quickly, moving fast to dominate the memory chip market with a new type of semiconductor design called MOS (metal on silicon). In 1970, about the time Stephen Wozniak was graduating from high school, Intel was approached by a Japanese calculator company—calculators being the hottest and most fiercely contested consumer electronics market of the era—named Busicom to develop a new chip set to run its calculators.

Intel was still young enough, and cash poor enough, that it took on the contract, even though it didn't fit with the company's business. The project took so long, more than a year, that Busicom eventually gave up and sold the rights to Intel. And when the finished chip set, called the 4004, finally appeared in 1971, even Intel wasn't sure it wanted to deal with a whole new technology and brand-new market. Eventually, thanks to some strong lobbying by, among others, outside PR consultant Regis McKenna, Noyce, Moore and Grove decided to give the 4004 (which had begun to be called a "microprocessor") a few months' tryout. The rest was history.

But as important as the microprocessor was as a digital electronics device, perhaps even more important was the way it behaved economically. Just about the time his company was announcing the 4004, Gordon Moore took out a sheet of graph paper and plotted out the performance of each of Intel's random-access memory chips to date. To his amazement, the plot points made a straight line, doubling in complexity (speed, performance, etc.) every two years. Moore realized that the line might continue its upward path for decades to come. He was looking at the future of electronics.

His discovery, called Moore's Law ever since, is the defining rule of the chip age, and the metronome of modern life. In accord with that law, the Intel Pentium chip of 1996 was 10,000 times as powerful as the 4004 from twenty-five years before—yet carried the same price.

This performance-to-price curve, unprecedented in the history of commerce, worked the other way as well—and that would prove to be of crucial importance to Steven Jobs and Stephen Wozniak. Moore's Law meant that the same chips of a given performance would also *halve* in price every two years. So the most powerful microprocessor or memory chip in the world in one era would be reduced in price from a few hundred dollars to a few hundred cents in just a few years. And that would make it available to even the poorest Sunnyvale schoolboy.

At this time, the high-end effect of Moore's Law was being felt in the new computer-based "smart" instruments (like programmable mass spectrometers) and the new minicomputers from HP, DEC and Digital Equipment that the two Steves were now encountering in their sojourns around Silicon Valley.

By comparison, the low-end impact of Moore's Law was only now beginning to show sparks. The first consumer product made possible by Moore's Law was the pocket four-function calculator, first introduced by Canon in 1970, but made into a market phenomenon by Texas Instruments two years later. Soon more than forty companies would be vying for that market. Three years after that, TI, Japanese companies Casio and Seiko, and even Intel, kicked off another fad with the introduction of the first digital watches. Millions were sold in a matter of months.

Both of these consumer booms proved fleeting. By the end of the decade, bloody shakeouts had taken place in both industries, prices had been slashed and just a few survivors remained. It was the first glimpse of a pattern of boom and bust that would characterize all hot new consumer electronics businesses thereafter.

But there was a third consumer electronics explosion during this period that would prove far more enduring. About the time Steven Jobs was graduating from Homestead High, a twenty-six-year-old engineer from Ampex was working late nights in his home in Santa Clara in a shop made from the borrowed bedroom of one of his daughters. With $500 in capital, this engineer, Nolan Bushnell, set out to re-create a game he had played on a mainframe computer while a student at the University of Utah.

Bushnell's great breakthrough, the lesson he taught Silicon Valley and the rest of electronics, was that Moore's Law was a design tool. Since you knew where price and performance were going, you could design a product early and then wait, ready to jump, for the curves to cross and the market opportunity to open up. And that's exactly what he did—though not without a few sleepless nights.

The result was Pong. In 1972, Bushnell set up the first of his arcade-type video games in Andy Capp's, a bar operating along the main drag of El Camino Real in one of Sunnyvale's oldest buildings. He prayed as only a good lapsed Mormon can. God apparently listened, but not without playing a practical joke. The next day, the bar's owner called and, to Bushnell's dismay, told him that the damn game had already busted. Bushnell sent his partner, Al Alcorn, down to the joint, prepared to pack it in. He was out of money and out of hope.

But once Alcorn got there, he almost laughed out loud when he saw the cause of the problem: the cardboard box he'd used to collect the players' money was so jammed with quarters that it had backed up into the coin slot. From that moment, Nolan Bushnell realized he was going to become very, very rich.

2.7 Cream Soda

The years after Wozniak's graduation from high school have always been a difficult time for computer industry fanatics and Apple Computer public relations people to deal with. In the early 1980s, when the excesses of the 1970s were still freshly shared and the myths not yet exposed, it was possible to think of the late-adolescent Woz and Jobs as heroic—or, better yet, antiheroic—mavericks.

Certainly an increasingly mature Apple liked to use that angle, as it justified the various felonies committed by its founders. In fact, the pairing of an increasingly socially retarded genius with a frighteningly precocious narcissist was a dangerous combination. Four years apart in age, the two were, for the next few years, almost equals in emotional development.

Woz, now bearded and long-haired, grew chunkier and more stooped. He was becoming the very embodiment of what happens to a human being who spends his life hunched over a printed circuit board and survives on junk food. Jobs, by comparison, though also long-haired and with the wisps of a beard, was whippet-thin, with all the intensity and mystery of a medieval fanatic.

Wozniak had finished Homestead High in glory. The capstone was scoring a perfect 800 on the math portion of the SAT, the first official recognition of his brilliance. But, as is often the case, the beginning of college also signaled the beginning of payback time for all of the other parts of life Woz had neglected in high school. His father sensed what was coming, and asked his son to stay closer to home, but Woz wanted to go away to school.

Having failed in his dream of going to Caltech, Woz accepted the fallback of the University of Colorado in Boulder. But within months of enrolling there, he dropped out just before flunking out, his only noteworthy accomplishment a series of characteristically juvenile practical jokes: jamming closed-circuit classroom televisions during lectures, blacking out a dorm TV just before the finish of the Kentucky Derby, programming a school computer to print out thousands of lines of FUCK NIXON. Unhitched from a larger purpose, Wozniak became a tiresome jerk.

Finally he returned home, to the relief of his parents, and enrolled at De Anza Community College in Cupertino, a half mile from his old high school. Safe again, Woz buried himself in electronics, haunting local electronics stores and chip "schlockers" who sold obsolete or slightly flawed circuits. With a structure again surrounding his life, Woz also managed to complete the school year with (barely) passing grades.

That summer was one of the best of Wozniak's youth. Baum was back from his first year at MIT and between them the two talked endlessly about electronics. They even found a job together as programmers at a start-up called Tenet, one of the scores of short-lived Valley computer companies of the era. When Baum went back to school, Woz stayed at Tenet, content that he had at last found a place to put all of his private skills to work.

And by this point those skills were formidable. Ever since GTE Sylvania, Woz's heart had been stolen by computers. At night, while still in high school, he would read trade magazines like *Datamation* and *Electronics*, or scrutinize the schematics in manuals like DEC's *Small Computer Handbook*, and then fall asleep dreaming of building his own minicomputer.

But the dream proved difficult to realize. During high school, using the schematics of a minicomputer designed by Varian Corp. up the road in Palo Alto, Woz tried to build one of his own using his growing hoard of chips. He couldn't do it. He understood computer architecture now, but not how to create that architecture using integrated circuits. And though he'd glimpsed the power of software, he still couldn't speak its language.

Then came graduation and the disastrous trip to Colorado. But if Woz's brief sojourn in Boulder had been an academic failure, it was not a technological one. Instead of cutting class to ski like the rest of his classmates, Woz hung around the computer labs, perfecting his fluency in computer languages, especially FORTRAN, and picking up design clues.

Now back at California, working at Tenet, Woz had access to computers every day. Moreover, Allen Baum was sending him photocopies of anything interesting in his classes at MIT. And, most important, there was the charged environment of Silicon Valley itself. Here he could attend trade shows and conferences and science fairs. It was at one such fair that Woz had his next breakthrough. He saw on display a working electromechanical calculator that could perform multiple operations in sequence, emitting intermediate results as it did.

For the era, the calculator was truly kid stuff. But in Woz it awakened a new understanding of how a low-cost computer, built with a microprocessor and other integrated circuits, could perform a string of functions on command. Just to check, Woz converted the design of the device he saw into an electronic schematic.

There it was. The missing philosophical gap in his understanding. He tested his new wisdom against the design of the Data General Nova minicomputer, one of the most powerful machines of the era. He saw it now: a direct cognitive link between that first simple adder-subtractor he'd built six years before and this cutting-edge computer used to design satellite trajectories and track subatomic particles.

It was all of a piece now. The symphony in his head now echoed across the vault of heaven. Woz knew he could do it. He would build a computer of his own. He began to lay out the schematics for one imaginary computer after another, each of them better, more elegant and more efficient than the one that came before. He dreamed of building each one, but the chips he needed were still too expensive to buy on his Tenet salary.

Then, drowned by the recession of 1972, Tenet went belly-up. At the time it seemed the worst thing that could have happened to Stephen Wozniak. After all, there went his daily access to computers. And a salary. But had Tenet survived, Woz might well have stayed on, becoming a lifer, just like his dad at Lockheed. Instead, he was forced out on his own. Now he had not only time to build his computer but the financial incentive to come up with a design that used as few chips as possible.

Toward that end, Jerry Wozniak made his own commitment to his son's obsession—a tacit, and no doubt painful, admission that this was Stephen's destiny in life—by connecting the boy with an old friend who designed integrated circuitry for Fairchild. From this man Stephen learned just which portions of his circuit board design could now be reproduced with silicon at a much lower cost.

With Baum a continent away, Woz settled for another neighborhood kid as a partner: Bill Fernandez, Steven Jobs's friend. It was Fernandez's unlucky fate to be the bridesmaid to history. For now, though, he was just happy to work with a neighborhood legend—so happy in fact that he offered his own family's garage for the work area. Then the two set out in search of parts.

The project took several months. In every spare moment the pair would head for the Fernandez garage, crank up the rock and roll, down endless cans of Shasta cream soda that Mrs. Fernandez bought by the case and worked on the computer. Woz did almost all of the work, laying out the printed circuit board, soldering the chips and testing the circuits. Fernandez's official duty was to construct the timing circuits for the computer's flashing output lights. But his real job was to be a sounding board and companion to the older genius hunched over the table next to him. And his greatest talent was neatness, something Wozniak at this embryonic stage needed more than anything else.

In 1973 the machine, which the two had dubbed the Cream Soda Computer in honor of their life-sustaining refreshment, was nearly completed. Fernandez, knowing he was part of a great event, was ecstatic. So ecstatic that he brought his young friend Steve Jobs over to the garage to see the project.

There is no record of that first meeting in the Fernandez garage. Even the two principals don't recall what they were wearing (though probably T-shirts and jeans) or what they said. But before that chance encounter was over an hour later, Woz and Jobs had already embarked on a fateful partnership.

What was the chemistry? For his part, Jobs would say years later, "He was the only person I met who knew more about electronics than me." This, of course, was utter bullshit, said at a time when Jobs was feeling under assault and had the reality distorter at full throttle. The fact was that there were probably a half dozen men and boys on Steve Jobs's *block* who knew more about electronics than he did.

No, the connection was far more complex than that. The key lay in an odd feature of the relationship that few observers have ever remarked upon: Stephen Wozniak was *four* years older than Steve Jobs; Jobs was just a junior at Homestead while Woz was two years beyond graduation. This was unusual pairing to say the least.

What it does suggest, from Wozniak's side, was how far emotionally he had already fallen behind his contemporaries. Now, in this sixteen-year-old he finally found a peer who could also, if not as deeply, hear the music that played in Woz's own head twenty-four hours a day.

Jobs's perspective was more subtle and, as usual, manipulative. Once again, he had found that helpful engineer down the street—only this time it was even better, because now he could dominate his emotionally underdeveloped partner, pulling him firmly into the Steven Jobs universe.

Mrs. Wozniak called the community newspaper, the *Sunnyvale Scribe/ Cupertino Courier*, and convinced it to send out a reporter and a photographer. Woz and Fernandez prepared a demonstration of their invention. But as the reporter scratched out notes and the photographer focused his lens, the Cream Soda Computer, in a shower of sparks and a puff of smoke, blew up.

So did the story. Woz had missed his chance. The next time a Woz computer would meet the press, its inventor would have to more than share the credit.

2.8 Countercultural Schlock

The sixteen-year-old Steven Jobs that Stephen Wozniak met that day in the Fernandez garage had a remarkable combination of childlike selfishness and grown-up bravado. Jobs would later say that had he not become a business tycoon he probably would have been a criminal—an opinion that would not be disputed by many of his old classmates.

Steven Jobs was simply not like anyone else you knew in high school in the early 1970s. There were druggies, there were gifted manipulators of others and there were unbelievably gutsy con men. But no one had all three traits in one person—except Steven Jobs.

The call Jobs made to Burroughs for parts was just the beginning. Not long thereafter, he called Bill Hewlett to hustle parts. Hewlett, a great engineer and an even greater entrepreneur, was at this point one of the most powerful businessmen in America and on the way to becoming a multibillionaire. Forty thousand people reported to him from HP divisions and sales offices in nearly a hundred countries.

It speaks volumes that, even as a teenager, Steven Jobs could detect a soft touch in Hewlett and then contact him directly (and even more volumes that Hewlett would answer the call). Once he had Hewlett on the line, Jobs made his pitch. Remarkably, though also characteristically, Hewlett agreed. The man who would one day give some $50 million to build an engineering building at Stanford in the name of his old professor, was never one to turn down a student. But once Steve Jobs scored, he wasn't about to stop there. He then pitched Hewlett for a summer job at HP. He got that too, ending up on an assembly line at HP's plant in Cupertino building computers. The experience was so compelling that Steven even tried to design a computer of his own—a notion he quickly abandoned as too difficult.

There were other after-school jobs, notably working at an electronics store in Sunnyvale. This job taught Steven the real value of electronic components: how little squares of silicon sand, once etched with a maplike grid of circuitry, could leap in value from a few cents of materials to a hundred dollars or more in market value. He also learned the rhythms of the chip industry—how the periodic cycles of boom and bust created distortions between chip demand and supply that sent prices skyrocketing; how companies would pay outrageous sums for that one obsolete chip that kept their expensive machinery running; and, most of all, how the inefficient distribution process of the semiconductor industry created a lucrative market for middlemen who could find the right chips and bring them together with the right customer.

Long before he graduated from high school, Jobs had already become a journeyman "schlocker," one of the small army of men—some of them legitimate, some criminal, nearly all slightly shady—who brokered rare old chips and popular (and sometimes hot) new ones. Before long, Jobs became something of a phenomenon within this small community as the kid who could wander through the warrens of the big Haltek chip warehouse and score that one critical part, or wander among the broken toasters and bicycle frames of the San Jose Flea Market and find that apparently worthless circuit board that yielded a rare, and profitable, chip when sold to an electronics shop. It was a talent Jobs had developed touring the junkyards with his father, and it put him in good stead with Stephen Wozniak. At this point in his work, with his computer burning itself up, Woz needed Jobs's procuring skills even more than he needed Fernandez's neatness—or even his garage.

Besides, Jobs had a garage too. And soon Wozniak's equipment moved three blocks across the city limits into Los Altos and the Jobs garage. Now Jobs could not only help Woz but keep an eye on him. Woz, happy to have a place to work and a source of parts, couldn't have been happier.

Jobs also appealed to Woz's puerile sense of humor. Woz was always willing to go along on any adventure or practical joke his young friend could devise. And Woz would sometimes enlist Allen Baum, when he was home from school, into the scheme as well. Once, the three persuaded Baum's mother to paint a giant hand giving the finger—they told her it was a Brazilian good-luck symbol—on a sheet tie-dyed in the Homestead colors, which they then hung at the school. Jobs, the only student of the three, was eventually caught and hauled before the principal. Steven's father got him off the hook.

By this point, Woz had enrolled at Berkeley. He would stay less than a year before again dropping out. But his presence at the university gave Jobs an excuse to regularly drive up to the campus. Soon, he was also visiting friends at Stanford as well. Needless to say, Berkeley and Stanford in 1972 were singular places, where predators and purists lived side by side in a kaleidoscope of sin, pharmaceuticals, study and sedition. Despite his now long hair, beard and tie-dyed clothes, the hermitlike Woz, with his 1980s view of technology and 1960s flower power beliefs about human nature, fit in poorly in 1970s Berkeley.

But for high schooler Steven Jobs it was paradise. He might be a pariah in Cupertino, but in Berkeley his behavior was barely eccentric. He could smoke dope and talk the usual epistemological blather all night long with confused undergraduates and sinister grad students. He even took to walking around smoking a pipe, a nice beatnik touch that connected him behaviorally with an even older group of outcasts. It was in this period that Jobs took on the manner, the vocabulary and the mores that would seem paradoxical in later years, when people would ask how someone his age, properly an early yuppie, could have so assimilated the hippie persona, an era he was too young to fully know.

Paul Jobs once found a bag of ground leaves in his son's car and asked what it was. "It's marijuana," Steve replied blithely. Needless to say, his father did nothing. The day when he might have drawn a line, or at least boxed his son's ears, was long past.

The Berkeley experiences proved good for young Steven back at high school as well. His new worldliness got him a girlfriend; pretty, if a bit of a druggie. She met Steven while they were working on a semisecret animated movie that classmates assumed was pornographic. Wozniak never quite understood what Jobs saw in her; but it may have been because he didn't recognize elements of himself. She was a lonely, vulnerable girl trying to make sense of her parents' impending divorce. And Steve Jobs was there to give her life direction.

As for the girl (she has preferred to remain anonymous), she would later say that Jobs "was kind of crazy. I think that's why I was attracted to him."

Jobs's later description of this relationship would sound like the screenplay for a bad psychedelic movie. They would cut class, drink wine and talk about higher things. They dropped acid together for the first time and Jobs found himself standing in one of the area's many piedmont meadows of dried straw grass, conducting the waving stalks as they exploded into a Bach fugue.

2.9 NOTES FROM THE UNDERGROUND

At the beginning of 1972, while Woz was distractedly making his way through Berkeley and Jobs was exploring the delectations of his new girlfriend, an engineer at National Semiconductor named John Draper took the little plastic whistle from a box of Cap'n Crunch cereal, glued closed the third sound hole, then held the device to a telephone mouthpiece.

The first sound he heard was an earsplitting, 2,600-cycle, high A note from the whistle. The second sound was a click on the other end of the phone. From that moment on, the telephone call was free.

Draper, soon to call himself Cap'n Crunch in honor of the source of his little discovery, had been following a hunch. He knew that when the phone company, AT&T, first developed the direct dial system after World War II it had chosen to use multifrequency tones to direct the call and turn tolls on and off. Furthermore, Draper knew that, to save money, Ma Bell had combined these tones and callers' voices on the same circuit. What this told Draper—and a number of other budding phone phreakers around the country—was that if he could duplicate the right tone, *he,* and not the phone company, would be in charge of the call.

It was illegal, of course. But it was also 1972, and Draper, who had done a hitch in the Army working sophisticated radar systems, didn't have much respect for large corporations or their shareholders. Besides, when he left the Army the phone company had offered him a job with a starting salary—$650 per month—that he saw as insultingly low.

The whistle was just the beginning. Soon Draper made himself a celebrity among the growing crowd of fellow phone phreakers by building a "blue box" tone generator to mimic the whole palette of telephone tones. With it he could break through busy signals and pick up engaged conversations (a hobby he dropped after hearing his girlfriend flirt with another man). He could make calls around the world for free. He once even called President Nixon's private White House line to complain (snicker, snicker) about a toilet paper shortage in Southern California.

In late 1971, *Esquire* magazine, as always anxious to stay atop any new fad, wrote an article about Cap'n Crunch and his fellow phreakers. The article had two immediate consequences. First, it alerted the phone company (and scores of prospective phreakers) to this new and felonious phenomenon. Second, it was read by Margaret Wozniak, who, apparently oblivious to the fact that this behavior was criminal, saw kindred spirits among the phreakers to her own little Stephen. She showed the magazine to Woz and his new friend Steve Jobs.

Scales fell from their eyes. For the two boys, phone phreaking combined everything they loved: technology, practical jokes, insider status among the illuminati and an outlaw relationship to the rest of society. They immediately established for themselves two goals: one, find Cap'n Crunch, and two, build their own telephone blue box.

Despite the obvious obstacles, the second proved easier than the first. The phone company had read the *Esquire* article too and systematically set out to retrieve every telephone operating manual in every library in America. Unfortunately, it missed one such manual at the Sunnyvale library. Woz and Jobs found it and soon knew every page by heart.

But the manual only took them part of the way. From it, they learned how the tones worked, but not what they were or how to create them. An initial attempt, which involved building an audio oscillator and capturing the tones it produced on a tape recorder, failed. No matter how carefully the two tuned the oscillator, the combination of variation in its tone and distortion in the tape made the resulting note unreadable by the phone system.

Frustrated by his failure, Woz characteristically regrouped and set about developing a radically new design—this one designed to generate its own digital audio tone. This was an extraordinarily ambitious project for a twenty-year-old working in his dorm room, but it is a measure of Wozniak's genius that he completed the blue box in a matter of weeks. It ran off a 9-volt dry cell battery, and had a little speaker, so that the user merely had to hold it up to a phone and type on the calculator keyboard. On the first attempt, Woz tried to call his grandmother in Los Angeles, but managed instead to reach a wrong number—toll-free—in the small Southern California town of Angelino. Still, it worked.

Finding Cap'n Crunch was more problematic. Draper, like the other phone phreakers, preferred to fly low and out of sight of the authorities. The two boys, anxious to meet their hero, tried to locate him through *Esquire* and through a local radio station on which the Cap'n had appeared, but to no avail. The only way to find Cap'n Crunch was to become like him. Sure enough, as word spread about the Wozniak blue box, John Draper suddenly became accessible.

They met at Woz's dorm room at Cal. Draper, with his wild hair and even wilder eyes, bad teeth and dirty clothes, looked more like a mad monk than a king of electronic crime. "He looked absolutely horrid," Woz would say. But Draper also knew his place. When Woz asked, "Are you Cap'n Crunch?" Draper replied royally, "I am he."

And he was. The Jesus of Phreakdom. In the next couple of hours, Draper opened up the world of phreaking to the pair. Just for fun, Draper made a few toll-free long-distance calls. Next he made a free international call. He called weather forecasts in distant cities. Dial-A-Joke. Each time, he showed his mastery of the technology and, in his mind, of the phone company. Finally, with a showman's touch, Draper stacked a series of calls from one relay to the next, connected them in a single interconnected chain around the country, and rang the telephone across the hall from Woz's room.

After that Cap'n Crunch and his newly recruited apostles retired to a pizza parlor, where Draper studied Woz's blue box and gave some advice for boosting its tone, handed out phone numbers of other phreakers as well as a list of useful codes to unlocking the wonders of Ma Bell, and then warned them to always use a pay phone so as not to be traced. Then he disappeared into the darkness and, it would seem, to the empyrean of telephony.

On the way back to Jobs's house in Los Altos, Steven's worn-out Fiat, as usual, broke down. Abandoning it, the two finally found a pay phone and, in an unusual bit of logic, decided to use their blue box to call Cap'n Crunch and ask for help. Instead, an operator came on the line, and the boys, already jumpy from Draper's warning about being traced, panicked and hung up. Jobs stuffed the blue box in his pocket.

They were just beginning to make a legal phone call when a police car suddenly roared up, and two officers jumped out. Jobs managed to hand the blue box to Wozniak just before the two were run up against a wall and frisked. With their long hair and grungy clothes, Woz and Jobs no doubt looked like a couple of drug dealers taking orders from customers.

Perhaps remarkably in Jobs's case, the cops found no drugs. But they did find the blue box on Woz. When asked what it was, Wozniak replied, "A music synthesizer."

The other cop took the box and studied it. He pointed at an orange button. "What's this?"

"That's for calibration," said Jobs. Woz explained that the box was for synthesizing music via a computer.

"Too bad a guy named Moog beat you to it," said the cop.

"He's the guy who sent us the schematics," replied Steven Jobs.

Convinced that the boys weren't carrying any contraband, the policeman offered to give the two a ride to the nearest gas station.

In retrospect, the parable of the Cops and the Blue Box, a touchstone of the Apple legend, contains many of the defining features of the Jobs-Wozniak story. There is the meeting with a mysterious wizard who gives them the key to a new technology; the funky, breakdown-riven car to provide an earthy touch; the thrill of illicit behavior at the risk of being caught by the authorities; and, most important, *épater les bourgeois:* the clever technical insiders pulling a fast one on the ignorant rubes. The last would become an enduring attitude right up to today's computer hackers.

But on closer look the legend gives a more insightful picture. First there is the telling (and characteristic) moment when Jobs unloads the guilty object on poor Woz. Then there is the clever lying to the cops: Why do it at all? If they had said it was an automatic telephone dialer, the police would still have shrugged. And finally, there is that little comment by the one patrolman about the Moog synthesizer. Apparently, the cops weren't quite the ignorant fools the phreakers wanted them to be—something they would prove the next spring.

There was one other event that occurred that evening. After finally reaching Los Altos in the early hours of the morning, Woz climbed into his own car and drove back to Berkeley. On the way, he fell asleep at the wheel and crashed into a road barrier. Fortunately, he wasn't hurt.

2.10 Blue Oafs

Their dabble into the world of phone phreaking only made Jobs and Woz anxious for more. Having met the King Phreaker himself, the two began to model themselves after him. They affected code names—Woz was Berkeley Blue, Jobs was Oaf Tobark—and set about learning everything about their new hobby. They talked to other phreaks, read underground phreaker newsletters and experimented. Jobs used the blue box to set up a party at a London hotel; Wozniak showed off to Allen Baum by making a toll-free call to Baum's sister at an Israeli kibbutz.

But the most celebrated of these Adventures in Phreaking was Woz's call to the Pope. It was his first use of Cap'n Crunch's long-distance codes, and Wozniak went for the home run. Pretending to be Henry Kissinger, not only did he reach a papal secretary but that official actually offered to awaken the Pontiff. Terrified, Woz hung up.

Draper's recollection of the event is less factually accurate, but perhaps metaphorically truer: "Woz's first call was to the Pope. He wanted to make a confession."

In a pattern they would follow ever after, Wozniak soon returned to the challenge of improving his creation. Jobs, meanwhile, set out to find ways to sell Woz's creation. "He wanted to make money," Woz would say simply.

Jobs's strategy was a straightforward one: sell the service to students. For one thing, they didn't have enough money for all the calls they wanted to make; and second, they identified with the outlaw idea of blue-boxing. As he would show consistently throughout his career, Jobs was a brilliant marketing idea man—but he was not always a great implementer. With Woz's blue box he correctly identified the market, but had no idea how to reach it. As a result, he and Woz were reduced to knocking on dorm doors, hinting around to the resident what they had, and then inviting him to a demonstration. If this kind of shotgun marketing was hard enough with legal products, it was positively dangerous with felonious goods.

Nevertheless, the two were lucky enough not to get turned in to the feds, and in a few weeks they had enough of a customer base to abandon the high-risk approach and simply service the clients they already had—yet another useful lesson for the future. In short order, they were selling not only the $150 boxes, but a customized service of tape recordings of tones customers regularly used.

Meanwhile, Woz, when he wasn't building boxes, was perfecting their design—a lesson for him on the value of product upgrades. One of his most important innovations was an automatic dialer; thereby enhancing what would one day be called the user interface.

The two budding entrepreneurs also taped a handwritten guarantee on the bottom of each box. Customer service. Thus, Woz and Jobs, with almost no business experience, while breaking the law, managed to devise on their own most of the key operating units of the modern technology corporation.

There was only one problem with their business model: the more successful they became as a blue box manufacturer, the more likely they were to get arrested. Woz, as might be expected, was all but oblivious to the danger. He continued happily along, improving his product, adding upgrades to make it usable in almost any location, trying out new and more outrageous phreaks—such as tapping into an FBI call.

Jobs, on the other hand, was terrified. It was one thing to bluff some cops, another to run an ongoing criminal enterprise. He would always have a gift for sensing a shift in the culture, and he felt it now. The phreaker world, especially Cap'n Crunch itself, was getting too cocky and out of control. It had begun to read its own magazine clippings and convinced itself it was too clever and too cool to be ever taken down by the System. Though the blue box project had by now netted $6,000, and promised to make much more, Steven Jobs started backing away from it and from Stephen Wozniak.

He had good reason to be afraid. Woz's blue box was so good that everybody in the phreak underground knew about it, including the growing army of phone company undercover agents. Meanwhile, General Telephone, tracing Crunch's calls, had turned up, among others, Jobs's home number. The net was closing and Steven sensed it.

The end came, according to Jobs, when he was selling a Woz blue box to a prospective customer in a Sunnyvale pizza parlor parking lot and the other party pulled a gun and robbed him. One may choose whether or not to believe the account, but it was the story Jobs used to extricate himself from the business.

Woz soldiered on, eventually even hiring other people to sell the boxes, and jumping on planes himself to pitch his wares at other UC campuses. In his characteristically honest, touching and softheaded way, Woz continued to split his earnings with the partner who had abandoned him. Also characteristically, he often forgot to go to his nontech classes, and found himself on the brink of expulsion from Berkeley.

In May 1972, as he returned from a FORTRAN programming class, John "Cap'n Crunch" Draper was arrested by federal agents for wire fraud. Given probation, he returned to phreaking. Four years later he was arrested again on the same charges, convicted and sentenced to four months at the federal prison in Lompoc, California. He spent his hard time teaching phreaking to fellow inmates "so they would stop beating me up." By the time he emerged, the computer revolution was underway.

Draper, out of arrogance and enthusiasm, had made the mistake of being too early. In high technology, today's felony is next month's misdemeanor and next year's career path. Had he kept a lower profile he probably would have eventually been hired as a security consultant by the same phone company that busted him.

Instead, his place in history would be as the man who drew the heat off and spared Stephen Wozniak for bigger things.

3.0 SPROUT

About the time Woz was getting in trouble at Berkeley for his grades, Steven Jobs graduated from Homestead High.

In many respects, Jobs had outgrown high school long before. After all, not many high school seniors, even in those heady days, had already been involved in numerous felonies, been traced by the FBI and, by his own account, looked down the wrong end of a gun.

He informed his parents that he planned to rent a cabin in the Santa Cruz mountains for the summer and shack up with his girlfriend. His father, in an almost unprecedented display of determination toward his son, refused to allow him to go.

"Bye," said Steven Jobs, and he walked out of the house.

Like most postgraduation summers, for Steve Jobs the first few weeks of June were lit with a special glow. He and his girlfriend set up house, played guitar, wrote poetry, listened to Bob Dylan records and played host to their regular houseguest, the Woz. It was just like being grown up.

Then Steven's notorious Fiat caught on fire. Paul Jobs, ever willing to help, towed the car home. The young couple, now broke, were reduced to working as greeters at San Jose's decaying Valley Fair Shopping Center dressed in Alice in Wonderland costumes. Woz, also ever willing to help, joined them, despite the fact that his blue box business was quite lucrative. While his girlfriend played Alice, Jobs traded off with Woz the roles of White Rabbit and Mad Hatter, depending upon his mood.

It was the most degrading moment of Steve Jobs's life. He had organized his world like a kingdom, with himself as king and everyone from his parents to his best friend as vassals, and now here he was in a heavy, sweat-stinking, humiliating costume, acting like a damn fool for the entertainment of middle-class parents and their kids. Jobs would later say that after a few hours of this each day, he'd feel like murdering his young audience.

There was still a way out: college. Steven Jobs, who had professed a measure of contempt for higher education, now suddenly embraced it.

In his senior year, like most of his classmates, Jobs had leafed through a pile of college brochures and admission forms. Unlike most of his peers, however, Jobs was less than enthusiastic. He dismissed Cal and Stanford as being too big, too impersonal and, in Stanford's case, too haughty, for his tastes (though years hence he would pose for a collection of Silicon Valley leaders under an arch in Stanford's sandstone quad, thus looking forever like one of the school's most famous grads). He would later say, "Everyone [at Stanford] knew what they wanted to do with their lives. And I didn't know what I wanted to do with my life."

The school that did pique his interest was Reed College, outside of Portland, Oregon. As Steven confirmed during a visit there, Reed had the advantage of being small, five hundred miles from home, and the most radical liberal arts college on the West Coast. As it happened, Jobs was at Cal visiting Woz when his father called to say Reed had accepted him.

His parents preferred for him to get a more traditional education. Moreover, the tuition was prohibitively expensive, given Paul Jobs's salary. But this, of course, was not Steven's concern. Following his proven technique, he informed his parents that if he couldn't go to Reed, then he wouldn't go to college at all. They quickly caved in. They even drove him to Portland—and got into a fight with their son when Steven tried to keep them from taking him on campus. He wanted to create his own entrance, looking like an orphan who'd just arrived from years of bumming around the country and riding the rails.

3.1 Floater

Even among the radical schools of the West Coast, Reed was famous for being a kind of counterculture Lourdes. The campus and its environs were a way station for poets, counterculturalists and revolutionaries as they migrated out from the cities and back to the earth. And yet, even Reed College found Steven Jobs to be one of its weirder residents. The adult Steven Jobs, the enigmatic persona that would make him one of the most famous people in the world, was beginning to emerge. There was, as always, the infinite narcissism. But the creepy, off-putting behavior of high school was being transformed into a kind of beguiling willfulness.

This growing charisma was reflected in the people he sought out as friends. One, Dan Kottke, was the son of wealthy New York suburbanites and a National Merit Scholar who had chosen Reed only after being turned down by Harvard. Another was Jack Dudman, Reed's dean of students, and Jobs's latest surrogate father. With each, Jobs would spend long hours in deep conversation.

With Kottke, Jobs talked about Eastern mysticism. The two read endlessly from the corpus of books on Zen Buddhism and yoga then in vogue. Jobs, in particular, was drawn to Zen because of its emphasis upon surrendering the intellect to physical experience.

Steven also made a third friend at Reed, a parolee named Robert Friedland. The importance of Friedland to the creation of the Jobs mystique cannot be underestimated. Friedland had been a major manufacturer of LSD, producing an estimated 30,000 tabs of the hallucinogen before he was arrested and tried. During the trial, Friedland told the judge he shouldn't pass judgment until his honor had tried acid himself. The judge sentenced Friedland to two years in jail.

Paroled early, Friedland arrived at Reed with his counterculture hero's stripes and set about constructing a power base. Dressed in Indian robes, he ran for student body president. He failed, but thereafter cut a mighty figure on campus. He was admired, attended upon, and got to bed any number of pretty coeds.

He happened to be in the middle of doing the last when Steven Jobs knocked on his door selling a typewriter to make some quick cash. As an amazed Jobs looked on, Friedland calmly finished his immediate business, then sat down with the young man. Awestruck, Steven was smitten. He had found his first guru.

This was the education Steven Jobs had come to Reed for. With a few bizarre exceptions—like a dance class he took in hopes of meeting a more perfect mate than his present girlfriend—he slowly dropped each of his classes. This still being the early 1970s, Jobs was allowed to quit school without actually having to leave it. He became a "floater," moving from one unused dorm room to the next as they were occupied or emptied.

In his vision of himself, Jobs was becoming an ascetic, a holy man unencumbered by the burdens of the material world. It was a good strategy, especially after his angry parents finally cut back on their financial support for their college dropout. Steve's hair and beard grew long and ragged, his clothes worn and his feet usually bare. He spent his days reading religious books and meditating, and on Sundays he would hitchhike over to the Hare Krishna temple in Portland, eat the free vegetarian meal it proffered, then gave thanks by placing on the Krishna shrine flowers he'd stolen from neighborhood gardens.

Thanks to a horrifying diet, Jobs began to exhibit the emaciated, crazed look of a true shaman. To perfect that image, he took to staring at people, unblinking, for long minutes on end.

His friends, even Kottke, who shared many of Jobs's philosophical views, became worried about Steven's health and would regularly cook him vegetarian meals. Woz would occasionally drive up to Portland—a fifteen-hour drive in those pre-Interstate 5 days—for a long weekend (Woz wasn't going to class anyway) and come away concerned about his old friend. Jobs seemed not only distant and listless—spending all of his time meditating and reading—but also increasingly secretive. Everyone saw less and less of him, and to this day, there remain holes in this part of Steven Jobs's story.

At the end of the first year, Jobs moved off campus and took a $25-per-month room in town. All but cut off by his parents, he borrowed some money from Reed, then took a job there as a maintenance man for the electrical equipment used to experiment with animals—an interesting job choice for a young man who objected to the slaughter of animals for food.

But the job didn't pay much, and in that miserable, wet, cold, quintessentially Portland winter, huddled in a heatless room in an old down jacket, throwing the I Ching and slurping his Roman Meal, Steven suffered through the most physically difficult time he would ever know. The prince was sick and exhausted, his kingdom reduced to a single, cold rented room. The optimism of two years before was almost gone, but the inexhaustible ego remained.

Studying other primates, he determined, again without any scientific evidence, that mankind's natural diet was fruit. Thus he began a regime of fruit, fasting, occasional drugs and regular, endless lecturing of his friends about the wonderful changes taking place in his body. That Jobs never developed pellagra is a testament to the resilience of youth.

This odd fruitarian phase of Steven Jobs's life would be of interest only as an example of just how dumb college kids can be, if not for the fact that a few years later this fructophagia would prove historic when it came time for Jobs to name his new company.

Whereas Steven had staked his faith on fruit, Robert Friedland, the previous summer in India, had determined, a little more realistically, that the universe was composed of electricity—and nowhere, he claimed rhapsodically, was this "electric atmosphere of love" more charged than in the holy presence of the divine guru Neem Karolie Baba.

Throughout the story of Steven Jobs there are seemingly random events that lead him to change his life just when, pragmatically, it's a helluva good idea to do so. This time, the call of cosmic electricity arrived just as he was at a dead end in his life. And what better place to pursue this universal power grid than in the Mecca of Electricity itself, Silicon Valley? That it also happened to be the place where his best friend, his girlfriend, his parents' kitchen and a well-paying job were waiting was, of course, merely incidental. The goal was to loot the Valley for just long enough to pay for permanent expatriatism in India.

And so Steven Jobs came home.

3.2 The HP Way

If Steven Jobs was doing his best to spin out beyond the fringes of normal society, Steven Wozniak was trying to find his way back in.

It was a pattern that would last into middle age. Woz was a hedgehog to Jobs's fox; more stable, feeling deep responsibility for all of his actions and relationships—and, if not as brilliant as his friend, trapped in an obsession that had made him, for good and bad, a genius.

Even when he was breaking the law making blue boxes, Wozniak still included a money-back guarantee with each one. And, of course, he had split his take with the ever-inconstant Steven Jobs. There would always remain in him, whatever the distortions wrought by obsession, wealth and fame, a desire to return to a normal life, to be like his father and his brother, to be just another suburban kid turned suburban adult.

Toward this end, when Wozniak at last accepted the inevitable and dropped out of Berkeley in 1973, the place he went to find work was that most traditional, conservative and family-oriented of Silicon Valley companies, Hewlett-Packard. There he joined his old neighbor and Cream Soda Computer partner Bill Fernandez working at the company's handheld calculator division in Cupertino.

It was an inspired choice. The HP Advanced Products Division was, at the time, the most freewheeling and entrepreneurial of all HP operating units. Staffed by young men and women fresh out of college or from other Valley companies, it had a brashness and risk-taking style that made it something of a scandal within its staid parent company. Within four years all of that would begin to fade as the division moved to Corvallis, Oregon, and lost many of the wilder figures when they chose to stay in the Valley. But within that brief window of time, Woz managed to find the one part of Hewlett-Packard where he could easily fit in.

Just across the street from APD was HP's data systems group, the people who built the company's minicomputers. Though one might imagine that Woz might have been better off there, among the computers and the managers—Paul Ely (Convergent), Ed McCracken (Silicon Graphics), Bill Krause (3Com), and others—who would go on to lead the Silicon Valley computer and networking industry, he was, in fact, better off in calculators at that moment in technological history.

A year before, HP had introduced the HP-35, the world's first scientific calculator. It revolutionized scientific and engineering computation. And that was just the beginning. By the time Woz arrived, APD had introduced the HP-55, the world's first programmable calculator; and was preparing to introduce the company's flagship, the HP-65, programmable by magnetic strips and easily the most influential handheld calculator ever built.

Until the HP-65, calculators and computers, despite their apparent similarity to the layperson, were fundamentally different devices. The calculator's functions were essentially wired into its circuitry. It might do complex calculations blindingly fast, but that was all it could do. Computers, by comparison, were stupid until programmed with software, but then had almost infinite adaptability.

With the HP-65, calculators first moved into the middle ground between the two worlds. It was still a calculator, with a fixed set of functions, but now those functions could be strung together as a series of commands to perform calculations of enormous complexity. Moreover, by virtue of its tiny size, this handheld calculator, unlike its big desktop counterparts, forced a high level of integration of its electronics. In other words, semiconductor chips, including early forms of microprocessors. Thus, the HP-65 was the apotheosis of that multifunction calculator Woz had dreamed of a few years before.

Woz, who was naturally inclined toward finding the most economic and compact solution to any electronics design problem, found in the HP-65 a revelation. "It's got this little chip and serial registers and an instruction set," he would later recall thinking. "Except for its I/O [input/output] it's a computer, the love of my life." Studying the HP-65's design, he got his first clue that it might now be possible to enter that middle ground of computation from the other direction as well.

It was a happy time for Wozniak. He had a secure and legal job at a great company with an old friend, and he was working on an intriguing technology he could learn from. He rented an apartment and, not being a particularly social animal—a coffee shop just a block from his office was in fact one of the great high-tech watering hole/job hopping/technology transfer places of the era—spent his evening playing with a new project: Dial-A-Joke. Each morning as he left for work Woz would turn on his answering machine and read into it a joke using a thick accent.

Of all the businesses Stephen Wozniak started alone, Dial-A-Joke was the most successful. Unfortunately, it was also nonprofit—nobody having figured out a way yet to directly bill for services over the phone—but nevertheless it was a phenomenon. At its peak, Dial-A-Joke averaged 2,000 calls per day. It became the single most frequently called telephone number in the entire Bay Area, and on more than one occasion caused such switching snarls that the phone company asked him to shut it down.

Dial-A-Joke also drew the attention of other organizations as well, notably the Polish-American Congress, which, incensed by the jokes, sent Woz—himself of Polish extraction—a cease-and-desist letter. Woz switched to Italian jokes, waited until the furor died down, then went back to insulting Poles.

Dial-A-Joke would have been a footnote to Woz's career except that one caller, a young babysitter named Alice Robertson, proved so intriguing that the shy Woz, eavesdropping through a headset he often wore, impetuously picked up the receiver and said, "I bet I can hang up faster than you." He did just that—and the intrigued Alice called right back. Five calls and several weeks later, the two finally agreed to meet. Within a year they were married.

The Silicon Valley that Steven Jobs returned to from Oregon had changed subtly, but profoundly, in the two years he had been gone. Intel's microprocessor family had become the technological wonder of its time, the subject of numerous trade magazine articles and provoking a design frenzy across the electronics industry.

Meanwhile, the hottest new company in town was Nolan Bushnell's Atari. Video games were popping out in bars around the country, elbowing pinball machines out of the way and beginning to pull in millions of dollars in revenues, one quarter at a time. An even newer business was starting to make its first appearances on the scene: video game arcades, which eschewed booze or music or anything else to allow the growing population of young, male video game addicts to concentrate solely on their art.

In the meantime, Atari was learning something unexpected: consumer electronics was in many critical ways closer to Hollywood than to Hewlett-Packard. The public had a voracious appetite for video games, but also a short attention span. New and ever more technically impressive games had to be created every few months to keep this thirst slaked.

As a result, Atari and the growing number of firms chasing it were on a continuous search for new creative talent. Because the technology and the market were so new, almost any idea, no matter how off-the-wall, had the potential to be a new home run product . . . after all, who'd have thought electronic Ping-Pong and hungry little yellow dots would capture the minds of 50 million baby boomers?

No one was untouched by the video game wave. Even Woz, having spotted a Pong game in the Cherry Chase Bowling Alley, was hooked. He immediately had gone home and designed a game of his own. Of course, in typical Woz style, whenever a player missed, the words "OH SHIT" would flash on the screen—but the programming was brilliant. For fun, he even showed the game to Atari, which, not surprisingly, instantly offered him a job. Woz said no, thanks, he was happy at HP, and went back to his calculators.

Back in the Valley, Steven Jobs couldn't help but fall under Atari's spell. Soon after arriving in Los Altos, he spotted an employment ad in the *San Jose Mercury News* offering work at Atari designing video games. Though he knew little about the company, and had played no more than a handful of video games in his life, Jobs wanted the position. And when he wanted something, Steven Jobs got it, by whatever means necessary.

In this case, he had to lie through his teeth. When he arrived at the lobby of the Atari building, which happened to be just a couple of blocks from where Jerry Wozniak worked at his desk at Lockheed, Steven Jobs was not a likely candidate for a new job. He was scraggly, impossibly thin and, thanks to a philosophical disagreement with bathing, smelled. He also behaved like a methamphetamine addict, talking so fast—a technique he'd developed in Oregon to intellectually bully people—that he was nearly incoherent to an average human being. The receptionist called upstairs, saying, "We've got this kid in the lobby. He's either a crackpot or he's got something."

Being bizarre was not an impediment to becoming a game designer at Atari. The lab was full of people nearly as strange as Steven Jobs, though none quite as brazen. What did work against Jobs was that he had almost no job experience, much less any real training in electronics.

Still, Jobs had managed to talk his way into an interview with Al Alcorn, now the company's chief technologist. He would just have to bullshit the rest. As he had done in the past, he simply adopted Woz's career as his own. He told the credulous Alcorn that he worked at Hewlett-Packard, that he was part of the HP-35 team and that he could reprogram the HP-45 as a stopwatch.

Alcorn was so impressed he never even checked out Jobs's résumé, but hired him on the spot as a technician for ten bucks an hour.

Jobs's bluffing his way into Atari would later become part of his legend. But what is rarely asked is whether Jobs played the Woz card out of desperation or whether he already knew then that he would exploit his friend's skills.

Either way, Nolan Bushnell's Atari was perfectly suited for Steven Jobs—more so, in fact, than it was for Alcorn. As a lapsed Mormon who had worked the midway at amusement parks as a teenager, Bushnell seemed to be in a hurry to make up for past carnalities lost—and he was doing so in wealthy splendor by hustling millions of kids into his electronic games of chance.

Bushnell was himself a singular figure, the original of the swinging high-tech tycoon that dominated electronics until that archetype was replaced first by the ascetic hippie of Steven Jobs, then by the billionaire nerd of Bill Gates. Bushnell stood six foot four, but looked taller in his corona of curls and bespoke suit. He sported a beard and pipe, drove a Rolls-Royce, held dope-smoking executive staff meetings in hot tubs and code-named new company games after female staffers with the biggest breasts. Like many who followed, Bushnell was half con man, half visionary.

Such a swinging CEO might seem the very antithesis of the younger, self-denying Zen mystic Steven Jobs. But in fact they had much in common—enough so that, in a unique way, Nolan Bushnell served as Jobs's last great role model. After all, in the face of very long odds, Bushnell had managed to create and then successfully rule his own little, but rapidly growing corner of technology. He lived his life according to his own rules, some of them illegal in the surrounding society, and had not only escaped punishment but actually was both celebrated and amply rewarded for his moxie. Bushnell was arrogant, and the world admired him for it. He was mercurial, and people said that was genius. He lied with impunity—sometimes claiming orders he didn't have in order to spur Alcorn and the troops—and his people loved him for it. Bushnell lived his life exactly as he wished, and the world made him rich for doing so.

If Nolan Bushnell could do it, so could Steven Jobs.

3.3 Pariah

In the chaos that was Atari in the early 1970s, one might imagine that even as bizarre a character as Steve Jobs would have fit right in. In fact, it was just the opposite. His co-workers objected not only to Steve's smell—he still didn't believe in bathing—but to his attitude as well.

In a new start-up company, no matter what your lifestyle, experience or personality, your work must be subordinate to the team itself. This is the essential paradox of entrepreneurship: to become one you must be a rugged individualist, but to succeed as one you must be a team player. The infighting and purges must wait for better times.

Jobs was not, by any stretch, a team player. Worse, he was a backstabber. Bushnell would remember that Jobs was forever calling other Atari technicians and engineers "dumb shits" and claiming he could do their job better—despite the fact that he had little experience or skill, nor ever made much of a contribution to the company. In the end, he was so hated and reviled by his fellow workers, and caused so much workplace tension, that Alcorn moved him to the night shift.

It was, though Alcorn didn't appreciate it at the time, an inspired move. Left to his own devices, Jobs was capable of miracles. There on the night shift, Jobs had lots of time not only to bone up on his electronics—he was a mind-bogglingly fast learner—but to plot his escape. Eventually, an answer presented itself: the new Atari game machines being shipped to Europe were leaking radio waves at just the right frequency to interfere with the reception on European-standard televisions. The first place this problem had appeared was Germany. A call for help came in to Atari headquarters.

Jobs volunteered, knowing that once he got to Europe he could hop his way on to India and Neem Karolie Baba, Friedland's "divine guru." Alcorn, who had refused more bald-faced requests by Jobs for paid trips to India, agreed to let him go. Within days, Jobs had notified his old classmate Dan Kottke to meet him in the subcontinent, packed and was on his way.

In the first of what would be a series of legendary encounters between Steve Jobs and traditional business establishments, Jobs arrived in Germany to face a collection of stunned engineers. What kind of creature is this? they asked themselves. So incredulous were they that for a short time they assumed Jobs was an imposter; they even cabled Alcorn in Sunnyvale to see if there had been a mistake. No mistake, Alcorn replied. I know it's hard to believe, but he's our guy.

The punch line to this story, as to all the Steve versus the Straights stories, is that Jobs actually pulled the job off. Though he had no apparent natural aptitude for electronics, his mind was so quick that he could learn what he needed to know faster than anyone around him. Moreover, for the first time, he displayed a special gift for identifying the critical flaw within a larger working system. In short order, he fixed the problem.

And with that, Steven Jobs took leave of the dumbfounded German engineers and flew off to New Delhi.

Unfortunately, though Neem Karolie Baba may have been divine, he was not immortal. By the time Jobs and Kottke reached his home, having wandered around India and Tibet for a while, the guru was dead. To memorialize him, the two young men stayed in the guru's town, Kainchi, for a month in a rented hut that was happily right next to a marijuana field. They made their own burned offerings to the late guru, one joint at a time.

The one-room hut, though primitive, did come with daily meals prepared by the owners, a family of potato farmers. Soon, showing solidarity with poor Third World people, Jobs was accusing the farmer's wife of cheating him by diluting his water buffalo milk. The woman responded by calling Jobs a criminal.

And so went the summer of enlightenment, suffering from dysentery, haggling in the local market to deny poor farmers a few pennies, shaving his head and smearing himself with ashes.

Eventually, Kottke, whose parents apparently weren't interested in underwriting his subcontinental adventures, ran out of money. Jobs loaned him a few hundred bucks, which let his friend spend a month at a meditation center. Jobs meanwhile wandered about India a little longer, grew increasingly disenchanted with enchantment—he would later say that he learned that Thomas Edison had done more to improve the human condition than all the gurus that ever lived—and went home.

Disenlightenment, however, was not allowed to intrude on a good image. The Jobs who returned to Silicon Valley in late 1974 presented an even more singular appearance than the one who'd left. He was even more emaciated, and he still didn't bathe, but now he wore Indian clothes and his long hair was cut down to stubble. Most of the time his mind seemed a million miles away, as if the demands of quotidian reality could only barely penetrate his higher consciousness.

In time, he wandered back up to Oregon to where his old friend Robert Friedland was now running his newest shtick, the Oregon Feeling Center. There, Jobs signed up for a three-month course in primal scream therapy.

From the perspective of twenty years on, it's hard not to look at all of this quintessentially California-in-the-1970s crackpotism and laugh. But at the heart of all of Steve Jobs's posing, searching and dissembling seemed to be a sad emptiness. And it centered on his adoption and his sense of being unworthy, abandoned and a stranger to this life.

Three months later, Jobs returned once again to the Valley and Atari. He was not especially welcome by his old workmates, and Jobs was soon removed from the day-to-day activities of the firm by being made a consultant.

Why was Jobs rehired by Atari when he returned, more unpleasant than ever, after being gone most of the year? The answer was that Steve had the one champion that mattered: Nolan Bushnell. Entrepreneurs are a different breed, a fraternity of the possessed. They come in many different forms: libertines, ascetics, brainiacs, Scoutmasters and average Joes. But underneath they share a common desire to construct and then control their own world at any cost. As different as Steven Jobs was to Nolan Bushnell, the older man saw in the younger man a secret sharer. He saw in Jobs's bravado, his outlandish and impossible claims to get products ready in a fourth of the time, his dismissal of everyone else as incompetent, a mirror of his own self. And because of that, Bushnell chose to defend Jobs against the revilement of his own staff, even after there was no practical reason to do so.

Before that point was reached, however, Jobs was to make one real contribution to Atari. He did it, as usual, on the back of his friend Stephen Wozniak.

3.4 Nocturnal Inventions

Atari in the early days—in fact, right up to its big collapse in 1983—always had a room set up for people to try out its latest video games. It was a perfect market research tool, and on a given day one might find in there a couple of kids, a senior citizen, some young company executives on a lunch break and perhaps a designer enjoying playing his creation as much as any customer.

In all of his wanderings, Steven Jobs had never been out of touch with Stephen Wozniak. Now that he was back in town, he and Woz saw each other regularly. And Woz, not surprisingly, soon gravitated to Atari, where he could see his friend and play the newest games. He became such a fixture in the evenings that he was even allowed to play some of the games as they were being tested on the assembly line. And, as always, even as he played Woz studied each game, learning how it was built and programmed.

It was during this period that Bushnell, perpetually testing his young charge, finally decided to take Jobs up on his claims of superiority and offered him the chance to devise a game of his own, one that, Bushnell stipulated, involved a bouncing ball systematically knocking down a brick wall.

Bushnell, who has never been known as a great manager or motivator, nevertheless perfectly understood what made Steven Jobs tick. At the heart of his offer, Bushnell dangled a financial reward. Payment was to be based not upon delivery of the new game, but on how efficiently it could be manufactured. It is doubtful that Bushnell ever thought Jobs could do the job; but there is no doubt that Bushnell knew that Jobs would somehow get the job done. Jobs, who also understood exactly what Bushnell saw in him, made the outrageous claim that he would design the new game in just four days.

Jobs's counterparts at Atari knew this was impossible, and many secretly thrilled at the prospect of watching the cocky kid fail. But Jobs for his part knew he had an ace in the hole: after all, Jobs had gotten the Atari job impersonating Wozniak; now he would become a game designer by taking advantage of the real thing.

It helped that Woz was already a regular at Atari in the evenings. And it was not unusual for Jobs to call him away from the video game for a moment to help him on some technical problem or other. So the transition was easy. Now Woz spent only a few minutes each night at the games and the rest at Jobs's workstation. Woz needed no excuse to bury himself in a design project—especially one that put a premium on a solution using the fewest number of chips.

The two young men, as the future would certainly underscore, worked very well together despite all of their personality differences. Jobs was a natural "finder and minder," the guy who could identify and land the big projects and then seduce, cajole and threaten his partners (and later subordinates) to not only get the job done but accomplish far greater things than they could imagine. Wozniak was the critical third leg of the stool, the "grinder," the engineer of extraordinary gifts who was a perfect tool for Jobs, who could utterly submerge himself in the work until it was completed.

Both in recognition of Wozniak's critical (some would later say complete) contribution and no doubt in response to what Woz had done with the blue box profits, Jobs agreed to split the award for the new game, to be called Breakout, with his partner.

Wozniak, thrilled, stayed up for four consecutive nights, going from HP in the afternoon directly to Atari and then, after a short nap and a shower, back to HP in the morning. It was a heroic achievement. Each day, Jobs would look over the accomplishments of his partner from the night before, advance it forward as much as he could, then leave it for Woz to fix his errors and push on again the next night.

3.5 Betrayal

In the end, they did it. Wozniak had nearly broken his health and risked his job in the process, but Breakout was done. Jobs delivered it to Bushnell, listened to the chorus of praise and murmurs of resentment, and took it all upon himself with his trademark little smile that managed to combine wry bemusement and an arrogant smirk. And he never once mentioned the contribution of Stephen Wozniak.

Later, when he saw his partner, Jobs informed him about how happy Atari was with their work and counted out $350, Wozniak's half of the $700 bonus Jobs said Bushnell had awarded them for the project. Wozniak was thrilled.

There are moments, even with the most brilliant and carefully constructed personalities, when a single act, once exposed, opens a window into the essential character that lies underneath. And this was such a moment. Steven Jobs had taken advantage of his friend many times in the past. A sympathetic observer might even argue that some of these manipulations were in Wozniak's best interest; that the young man, in the grip of his obsession, needed someone to give him direction.

But this time was different. Jobs had lied. The payment was, in fact, $7,000. It had not been enough merely to exploit his friend, or even enough to take all the credit for the result. Jobs had then gone on to steal most of the award for Wozniak's herculean effort. It was a breathtaking betrayal; a glimpse into the dark center of Steven Jobs's soul.

It was also an extraordinarily risky and brazen move on Jobs's part. Woz was his meal ticket, not to mention one of his few friends, and now he had just put all of that on the line for a few thousand dollars. Until this point in Steve Jobs's story, it is easy to dismiss his behavior as that of a troubled, lonely, spoiled kid. But by the time he reached Atari, Jobs was twenty years old. He had traveled the world, and lived by himself for two years. He was a grown man and his character was established. Nonetheless, he had just betrayed, exploited and robbed his best friend.

One can muse on what would have happened if Jobs's fraud had failed—say, if he had found out a few months later when Alcorn learned who had really built Breakout and again offered Woz a job.

Woz again politely refused Alcorn's offer, saying he preferred to stay at HP. Alcorn, for his part, never knew of the financial deception. But had the $7,000 amount come up, would it have meant the end of the friendship and the stillbirth of Apple Computer?

Perhaps. But then again, if Steven Jobs had been so sure he could lie to and steal from his friend with such impunity, he must have also been sure that if he was caught he could lie his way out of that too. Apple would have happened, no matter what. Jobs would have made sure of it.

After Breakout, with his friend's money in his pocket as well as his own, Jobs again left Atari, to return to Oregon and the spiritual path. This time he landed at the All One Farm, an Oregon commune that specialized in growing organic apples. Here Steven pruned and picked apples and added bulimia to his growing portfolio of strange dietary habits.

Meanwhile, the Breakout experience, the ninety-six hours of pure kamikaze creativity, had rekindled in Wozniak his old spirit of invention. The job at Hewlett-Packard was interesting, paid pretty well ($24,000 per year) for a young man with a limited résumé. It even offered the occasional challenge. But Woz remained, at best, a glorified technician. Those nights at Atari he'd been the Man himself, the creator, who set his own standards and made his own rules. He set out to find something new and interesting to do.

He could not have picked a more perfect time. Something profound was happening out in Silicon Valley, a fundamental shift that Woz, tucked away in the notoriously cocoonlike Hewlett-Packard, had not even noticed.

The metronome of Moore's Law had clicked once again. Microprocessor prices had again fallen, while their power had increased. The hot new Intel chip was now the 8080, the first modern microprocessor and the founding member of what would be the Intel microprocessor family dynasty that dominates electronics to this day.

What made the 8080 particularly compelling was that, unlike its predecessors, the 4004 and 8008, it was not a collection of chips, but a single integrated circuit. That meant it could be designed into almost anything. And it was, from games to minicomputers.

Moreover, now Intel wasn't alone. In Austin, Texas, Motorola's design team had developed a competing chip, the 6800. Meanwhile, Federico Faggin and Masatoshi Shima, two of the men who'd built the first Intel microprocessor, had just left that company and were rumored to be designing their own competing chip at a new company called Zilog in Cupertino. A reborn Fairchild was apparently working on a microprocessor too, as was Texas Instruments. And, in the unlikely location of Norristown, Pennsylvania, a company called MOS Technologies had just announced its own microprocessor, the 6502.

Clearly a movement was underway. The microprocessor was no longer an expensive novelty, but the flagship device of the next high-tech wave—and the sheer number of players building them almost guaranteed prices would soon fall into a range affordable to the average tinkerer.

This wasn't the only movement afoot. Moore's Law worked on computers too. By the time Woz began to look around for a new challenge, Digital Equipment Corp. had cut the price of its PDP-8F minicomputer to just $6,000. That was still a lot of money in 1975, but it was just low enough to tantalize the growing numbers of people who dreamed of owning their own computers.

In the three years since Woz had built the Cream Soda Computer, much had changed in the world of personal computing. Now throughout the country there were scattered pockets of computing enthusiasts numbering perhaps a thousand individuals. They came from all sorts of backgrounds, from the military to the counterculture, the Explorer Post at NASA-Ames to the criminal underground of blue boxes. Even Cap'n Crunch was now playing with computers.

With a population of enthusiasts, personal computing reached its first critical mass: it now constituted a viable market for new products. And between 1972 and 1976 there was a rush of small businesses, typically run by inexperienced enthusiast/entrepreneurs, created to pursue this market.

About the time Jobs and Woz were selling blue boxes, the *People's Computer Company*, a computer enthusiast tabloid, was founded in the Bay Area. In Seattle, Paul Allen and sixteen-year-old Bill Gates founded Traf-O-Data to measure traffic patterns with computer software. And in Santa Cruz, programmer Gary Kildall devised PL/I, the first programming language for the Intel 4004.

By the time Woz finished Breakout, the electronics press was already beginning to talk about a new generation of companies—MITS, Altair, Cromemco, IMSAI—that were offering (or about to offer) hobbyists a whole new world of kits for building their own computers. Kildall, with John Torad, was now offering these same hobbyists a new kind of all-controlling "operating" software for these same machines. And, perhaps most portentous of all, the research arm of Xerox, the Palo Alto Research Center (PARC), was publicly describing a new prototype computer, the Alto, that featured such radical features as display graphics, a new handheld input device called a "mouse" and a technique for networking multiple machines called Ethernet.

Woz, for his part, knew almost nothing of this revolution for which he had been an unknown pioneer. But as he asked around, and read the new magazines, he became more and more intrigued. It was by chance that a workmate at HP learned of Woz's interest in computing and told him about a new group, the Homebrew Computer Club, that was meeting in a suburban garage in Menlo Park. Curious, Woz decided to attend.

The garage belonged to Gordon French, a mechanical engineer, slot car motor builder and budding computer hobbyist. He had been turned on to computers by Fred Moore, who had run a counterculture information service out of the Whole Earth Truck Store, located just a few blocks north of the Stanford campus in Menlo Park. Moore had in turn been introduced to computers by some of his clients, who asked him to help them meet other computerphiles.

The galvanizing event for the creation of Homebrew was the January 1975 issue of *Popular Electronics*. There, on the cover, for the first time anywhere, was a photograph of a true personal computer: the Altair. It was, in fact, an empty box, and a desperate gamble by the president of a fading Albuquerque calculator company called Micro Instrumentation Inc. MITS's president, Ed Roberts, had managed to convince *Popular Electronics* that by the time the issue appeared, his company would actually be able to deliver the $300, Intel 8080-based kit, named, on Roberts's daughter's suggestion, after the planetary destination of one episode of *Star Trek*. Altair made the deadline by a matter of weeks.

Meanwhile, this issue hit like a lightning bolt in computer hobbyist communities from coast to coast. A decade later, journalist T. R. Reid would describe its impact.

Here it finally was: the dream of every computerphile, blue boxer and programmer for nearly a decade. A computer anyone could own. Individual issues, increasingly battered and worn, were passed from one sweaty hand to the next, becoming a sacred text to join the seminal September 1973 issue of *Radio Electronics* that first described a "TV Typewriter."

Realizing the personal computer revolution had finally arrived, French and Moore sent out a flyer to Moore's wide network of computer junkies, phone phreaks, corporate hardware jockeys and anyone else anywhere near the Whole Earth Truck Store who'd ever mentioned computing. It read:

> Are you building your own computer? Terminal? TV Typewriter? I/O device? Or some other digital black box? Or are you buying time on a time-sharing service? If so, you might like to come to a gathering of people with like-minded interests. Exchange information, swap ideas, talk shop, help work on a project, whatever . . .

It was this flyer that was read by an engineer at Hewlett-Packard, who in turn told Stephen Wozniak. Woz contacted Allen Baum and the two agreed to go.

The first Homebrew meeting, held on March 5, 1975, drew thirty-two people from all over the Bay Area. All of them jammed into Gordon French's garage. The high point of that first meeting was a demonstration of a brand-new Altair that Berkeley's *People's Computer Company* had just received from MITS. The room was thrilled at the very sight of this marvel.

The low point came six weeks later with a presentation by Steve Dompier, a Berkeley building contractor who had sent MITS a check for $4,000 asking for "one of everything." What he got back was an apologetic note from the company secretary saying Altair "didn't have all that stuff yet." Dompier, not one to take no for an answer, caught the first flight to Albuquerque—only to discover that mighty MITS was in a little storefront next to a laundromat in a shopping center. Thanks to the *Popular Electronics* article, MITS had been buried in a blizzard of 4,000 orders, of which it had filled just 1,500, and might be able to ship 1,100 more in another month . . . though by then no doubt thousands of more orders would have poured in. In other words, said Dompier, who was the envy of nearly everyone because while at MITS he had spotted a box of parts and bought everything in it, the Homebrew members, even if they ordered today, might not get their Altair for months. And even then it might be incomplete. Later reports from those who did receive their Altairs suggested that the kit was not only very crude—basically a box and a handful of logic and memory boards—but that the Altair memory boards were unreliable.

One might imagine that this would have damped the spirits of the enthusiasts at Homebrew. Instead it did just the opposite. Had MITS produced a complete, reliable, and full-powered computer kit, it might well have scared everyone away. But by being maddeningly incomplete and limited, the Altair left open the door to every entrepreneur who had an idea how to finish it, or at least make it run better. It offered a furtive glimpse of what might be, without being that future itself.

3.6 Homebrewing

That first Homebrew meeting and the ones that came after were a revelation to Stephen Wozniak. Lost in the worlds of calculators and video games, he quickly discovered that a new computing subculture had been created since his departure, a world with its own language, heroes and sacred texts. He had a lot of catching up to do. And one of the best ways to do so was to attend the Homebrew meetings, which, thanks to the press of rapidly growing membership—numbering several hundred people by the third meeting—moved first to a nearby Victorian house, the Coleman Mansion, and then to an auditorium at the Stanford Linear Accelerator Center.

Though he was still catching up, Woz did enjoy a certain celebrity even in this group, thanks to his blue box career. And the meetings were great fun, thanks to Lee Felsenstein, something of a prophet of personal computerdom, its reigning philosopher, who had taken over as master of ceremonies and shown a surprising gift for running a chaotic but entertaining show. Felsenstein was also the perfect man for the moment; his distaste for structure led to meetings that were half formal presentations and half wild scrambles of people running around getting to know one another. In such an environment, new ideas were tossed about at electronic speed and even the oddest, youngest, or quietest person in the room could get noticed if he had something useful to share.

But even with Felsenstein's charisma, Homebrew soon grew so large that a second, San Francisco branch—which met, oddly, in the Lawrence Hall of Science in Berkeley—was formed. Now, a real computer enthusiast, which Woz had again become, could attend two different personal computing-oriented clubs, and swap ideas with more than a thousand of his peers.

Instead of just an Allen Baum or Steven Jobs off whom to bounce his ideas, Woz now had hundreds of people. As he attended the meetings of the subsequent months, and as he listened to the presentations and swapped ideas, Woz began to soak up not just the technology of personal computing but its gestalt, its wacky mix of Silicon Valley engineering for engineering's sake, Stanford technical phariseeism and Berkeley street Marxism. The personal computer of Homebrew's dreams would combine the coolest design features with the purest individuality, built by enterprises that undermined the predatory world of Big Business, and priced to liberate the common man. It would be not just a personal computer but a revolutionary act.

It wasn't long before Woz had not only caught up with the others but began to move beyond them. He was so quick and skilled with board-level design that soon other Homebrew members began to regard him with a certain awe. For example, one evening Homebrewer Harry Licht was talking to an acquaintance about some parts he had that neither of them knew much about. Harry picked up the phone and called Wozniak. As he listed each product number, Woz instantly responded with that chip's performance specs. When Licht hung up the phone, the amazed visitor asked: Who was that? Oh, said Licht, that's a young kid named Steve Wozniak. He keeps all that information in his head.

Despite its air of self-righteous radical purity, Homebrew contained many members who appreciated the real world of commerce and competition.

They were using Homebrew not only for market and product research but also to scout talent. And these individuals noticed Wozniak too.

The quickest recruiter off the mark was Alex Kamradt of Call Computer, the man looking for someone to build his video terminal with a keyboard. He asked around at one of the meetings who everybody thought was the smartest engineer in the hall. Just about everyone pointed at Stephen Wozniak.

Woz wasn't surprised to be approached. Before Jobs had left town he'd mentioned Call Computer to Woz as an interesting opportunity for their skills. Now here was Kamradt standing before him. But what did surprise Woz was Kamradt's offer: if Wozniak would build him a keyboard video terminal, Kamradt would pay him $12,000 and give him 30 percent ownership in a new subsidiary, Computer Converser, created just to manufacture and market the new invention. Woz didn't even have to quit his day job. And, of particular interest to Woz, he could even work with Call Computer's minicomputer.

This was serious money, half Woz's annual salary at HP. Playing with a real minicomputer was Woz's favorite hobby. And the stock was Wozniak's first glimpse at the real world of entrepreneurial equity. He liked it. A lot.

As he had with the Atari project, Woz quickly set aside every spare minute of his nonworking life to build the new terminal. In one respect, the project was actually retrograde to the events occurring at Homebrew. Whereas the Altair and the other new hobby computers in development were microprocessor-driven and designed to free their owners from dependence upon big computer iron, the purpose of Computer Converser terminal was to do just the opposite: to create a more efficient way for time-share users to communicate with mainframes and thus become even more dependent—and pay Alex Kamradt for that service.

Moreover, at a time when the rest of the hobbyist world was trying to learn more about using microprocessors, Woz was now getting paid to figure out how *not* to use those precious and expensive little chips.

In all, the whole project would have been a distraction to Woz's budding computer career . . . except for one crucial factor. It was that Woz, almost alone among his peers, was devoting his time to designing a complete *system.* The other Homebrewers were buying their Altairs—or, soon, their Cromemcos, IMSAIs and a half dozen others—soldering together the boards and then eagerly jumping into programming. Woz, by contrast, remained buried in the world of hardware, squeezing out every superfluous component to create the most elegant and inexpensive design. And, even more than the computer kit companies themselves, Woz was learning how to link together the main processor with peripherals such as a keyboard and video screen. By purposely not building a kit computer, Wozniak was making himself the best home computer designer in the world.

Woz finished his design and prototype by the end of the summer of 1975. Now he needed to test it. And, as an old blue box master, Woz knew exactly how to test a phone-based terminal. He called his old friend Cap'n Crunch and took his terminal over for a visit and tour of the world's telephone network.

Draper, on probation, but still a year away from his big bust and prison stretch, had taken phone phreaking on to even greater heights than the days when Woz and Jobs had been acolytes. Now he had discovered a target even more exciting than the phone company: the ARPAnet, the nationwide computer network of military, research and academic users. Draper showed Woz the way onto the network and Woz tested out his new design. It worked beautifully, the keyboard and VDT a distinct improvement over the traditional and awkward teletype machine. Woz logged off, thanked Draper and took off to deliver the terminal to Kamradt.

He would not log onto the network again for nearly twenty years, long after it had transformed into the Internet.

In the story of Apple Computer, each of the principal figures makes at least one dreadful mistake that will eventually prove disastrous to the company.

This was Woz's mistake. As it was the first, it was also the most forgivable.

Still, the moment is so tantalizing, the possibilities so infinite, that one just can't help thinking: what if, that day at Cap'n Crunch's, Stephen Wozniak had just played a few more minutes on the ARPAnet? Perhaps he would have seen in his mind's eye that moment, two decades off, when the paths of the Net and the personal computer would intersect. The day when the Net itself, driven by the PC, would create a social and commercial transformation far greater, and far more liberating, than anything imagined by the revolutionaries of the 1960s.

And, having glimpsed that future, perhaps Woz would have then gone home and tried to turn the Computer Converser terminal into a kind of pioneering Net Computer—or short of that, designed his own computers for the Internet Age to come—instead of creating an architecture that would resist the Internet until it was too late.

But that is asking an awful lot of a twenty-four-year-old. Changing the world once is enough to ask of anyone.

In the end, Wozniak delivered the keyboard video terminal to a thrilled Kamradt. But it wasn't long before the majority shareholder realized that only his junior partner understood how the terminal worked, even how to fix it. And when the prototype crashed, as prototypes will do, Kamradt quickly found that Woz, still working full-time at HP and contemplating marriage, wasn't always available to come over to fix the problem. Kamradt, knowing from experience that this was a recipe for disaster should the terminal ever be built in volume, killed the project. And Woz answered forever the question of whether he could have built a great company on his own.

Meanwhile, the young man who would do just that with Woz's help had just returned to Silicon Valley.

3.7 Conversant Computer

Jobs arrived in the Valley just as Woz was turning in the finished terminal. Kamradt, a pretty good judge of people, immediately recognized the power Steven Jobs had over his friend. Despite feeling that Jobs was "pretty unscrupulous," Kamradt approached the young man and asked for his help in handling Woz.

Jobs agreed, once again not telling his friend about the new role, and once again bringing his formidable negotiating skills to bear. Knowing he was the only person who could manipulate the young inventor, Jobs demanded from Kamradt not only money but title (director of the company's terminal division) and even stock.

It wasn't much, but it was a gig. And Jobs even had a subordinate, a contractor named Robert Way, whom he rode so hard that the man eventually quit the project—later calling Jobs "one of the weirdest people I ever met."

But Jobs wasn't concerned, even after Kamradt killed the project, because he'd learned a great truth in his time at Atari and Computer Converser: find a genius, ride his slipstream and wait for your chance. And Wozniak was, amazingly enough, proving to be just such a figure. The good side of that genius had made Jobs money at Atari, and the bad side of it had landed him a job at Computer Converser. Jobs couldn't lose.

The trick, then, was to keep an eye on Woz. Find out where his mind was roving next, then push and prod and cajole him toward that goal, demand the impossible from him and then look for ways to convert the results into money in Jobs's pocket.

It didn't take long for Woz, still bored by Hewlett-Packard, to cast off again on a new project. He was still a regular at Homebrew, and as the months passed, like all the others he could see a pecking order emerge. At the bottom were the computer curious, the gamma goofballs, the guys who'd heard about home kits and were carefully sticking a toe into the water. These were the consumers, the hobbyist hoi polloi who would ultimately buy the creations of others.

Next up the ladder were the bolt-on beta boys. These were the guys who bought the kits currently on the market, like the Altair, and had seen a way to make a buck building aftermarket hardware, such as memory boards, writing operating systems or applications software or selling their services to the gammas.

And at the very pinnacle of the Homebrew world were the alpha inventors. These were the guys who pissed on the Altair, believing they could build a better box. Felsenstein was an ersatz alpha; but his partner Bob Marsh was the real thing, as he would prove with his own new computer company, Processor Technology. So were two Stanford graduate students, Harry Garland and Roger Melen, who had just started Cromemco.

Wozniak looked at these alphas, and as shy as he was, knew he belonged with them. He had built the Cream Soda Computer, designed the greatest blue box, an Atari game, and now the Computer Converser terminal. Nobody at Homebrew had anything close to his credentials. Besides, he couldn't afford an Altair, anyway.

But he still hadn't built a computer that he could prove to the world actually worked. It was time.

So, while Jobs was off at Computer Converser trying to figure out Woz's last design, Wozniak once again went to ground to come up with a new invention. And once again, he took Allen Baum with him.

The first step for the two men was to bring themselves up to date. Almost a half decade had passed since their internship days at Sylvania, and both were convinced that they'd missed an entire technology revolution.

In fact, they were half right. In the years since they'd played on the big, noisy IBM 1130, the world of computing had indeed turned upside down. The new generation of minicomputers, exemplified by the DEC VAX, Data General Eclipse and the HP 3000, were as fast and nearly as powerful as the big iron mainframes, but much smaller and less expensive, and most important, they were real-time machines. You entered in the data, the internal program processed that data and the computer gave you back the results. No more stacks of punched cards awaiting one gigantic "batch" processing. The new minis took your call *right now*.

But the new minis were only half the story. At the other end of the spectrum, Moore's Law had done its work and the first generation of single-chip microprocessors were now on the scene in volume, their prices falling rapidly toward consumer levels. Just a hundred or so bucks now would buy you an Intel 8080 or its near relation, the Zilog Z80, or the exciting new Motorola 6800. And that was just the hottest name. In all, in 1975 there were sixteen major microprocessor manufacturers (including TI, National Semiconductor and Fairchild) selling on the open market, and perhaps an equal number (including IBM and HP) building proprietary microprocessors for their own equipment.

By picking the Intel 8080, Altair had made Intel the microprocessor supplier of choice for the Homebrewers. At the meetings, almost all the new designs were Intel chip-based. But the 8080 was expensive, one chip costing as much as a new stereo or an old Volkswagen. On Woz's salary, and with the prospect of marriage waiting around the corner, he couldn't afford that kind of investment on a device that might short itself out on a random burst of static electricity or a power surge when it was first turned on.

All of this—the prospect of relearning computer architecture, then trying to duplicate those operations with a microprocessor, then determining how to lay out all the supporting chips around that processor for input-output to the video screen, keyboard and memory, the memory boards themselves and a power supply, and *only then* addressing the problem of programming the finished box—was daunting even to the ever-ambitious Wozniak. Baum was even more doubtful.

Then Woz made a happy discovery: microprocessors *were* minicomputers. That might seem obvious; after all, from the beginning microprocessors had been called "computers on chips." But Woz had always assumed that meant that the two were alike only functionally. What he found instead was that organizationally, architecturally, the transistors on the surface of the silicon chip were laid out almost identically to the chips on the motherboards of the refrigerator-sized minis on which Woz and Baum had once played—and, by the same token, in the Cream Soda Computer itself.

What this meant, first of all, was that Woz didn't have to go back and relearn computer science, a task that might have driven away even Wozniak, who, for all his legendary focus, was increasingly being pulled in many different directions by love and work. But even more important, as Woz and only a few others understood, the microprocessor *gave you an architecture.*

This was a crucial breakthrough. Now you didn't have to completely design a new computer from the ground up, beginning with the central processing unit. The microprocessor could be your CPU, and your much simpler task then became finding the best way to construct all the interconnections that enabled the microprocessor to get electrical power and then to drive the external memory boards, disk drive or (in those days) cassette tape player, keyboard and display.

It is interesting to ask in retrospect why this understanding first arose among nerd hobbyists and not with the big established computer companies such as IBM, Burroughs or DEC. One answer is practical: the true microprocessor, in the form of the Intel 8080, was only a couple years old and still comparatively unproven. Giant corporations take longer than that to test new inventions for their usefulness. A second answer is philosophical: big-iron computer guys had built an entire epistemology around mainframe and minicomputers and the MIS departments that ran them. Personal computers in the control of individuals simply didn't fit into this reality. A third answer was technical: in an industry dedicated to constructing machines of ever-greater computing power, the personal computer represented a kind of surrender. Compared to a mainframe it was slow and unreliable, and it couldn't do a thousandth of the important applications—like process a 30,000-employee payroll—a mainframe could. Who needed it? A fourth answer was marketing: established computer companies sold to other companies, most of them manufacturers, and had little understanding of, or interest in, the consumer market. And a fifth answer was bureaucratic: these companies had made billions of dollars in large-scale computing. Many, like Burroughs and Univac, had resisted even minicomputers. Personal computing represented the ultimate apostasy. Most companies felt it was just a novelty, anyway, which would suck millions out of any foolish firm that pursued it, while acting as a distraction to the real business of building big iron. Better to just ignore it and hope it would go away.

In fact, there was one giant company at work building a personal computer: Xerox. The computer, designed between 1972 and 1974, was called the Alto and it was not only more advanced than anything being built anywhere else in the world, but with its use of a mouse, a sophisticated language called Smalltalk and a networking scheme called Ethernet, the Alto would remain the world's best personal computer for nearly a decade until the advent of the Macintosh, which more than a little resembled it. But it was the Alto's fate to be designed by Xerox's Palo Alto Research Center—and so, like many PARC inventions before and after, it was released commercially years too late (as the overpriced Star in 1981) and mainly served as useful carrion for other, more aggressive competitors to pick over.

Unlike the thousands of computer professionals at all of these giant firms, Stephen Wozniak understood what the microprocessor made possible. Now all he needed was to score one of those chips.

3.8 Revolution on the Cheap

Obtaining a microprocessor wasn't as easy as it might sound. Like everyone else in the Homebrew Computer Club, Woz coveted the Intel 8080. But not only were they expensive, but with everyone from NASA to Ford ordering them for testing and design, damn hard to get. There was also the year-old Motorola 6800, not as cool as the Intel chip but nevertheless being designed into the new MITS computer kit in Albuquerque and the Ohio Scientific mail-order computer kit. The 6800 was bigger than the 8080, but it was also 5-volt, which made it compatible with existing computer logic chips. Best of all, Woz could buy one for half the price of the Intel chip. Woz already knew the 6800—he'd used it with the Computer Converser terminal—and was comfortable with its design, which in some ways was even better than that of the 8080.

But the deciding factor was the decision by his employer, HP, at the time a major Motorola customer, to offer the 6800 to employees at discount. When Baum brought in that bit of good news, Woz quickly decided upon the Motorola chip.

But soon thereafter another piece of good news reached Woz. The Wescon computer show, at the time the largest gathering of computer manufacturers in the world, would be holding its annual event in San Francisco in just a matter of weeks. Wescon, with its big displays of big computing iron and sea of meandering computer engineers in white shirts, was just the kind of event the computer hobbyists despised and yet couldn't stay away from.

Woz was already planning to go. But what made the trip north an absolute necessity was the announcement that Chuck Peddle, a former Motorola chip guy now with MOS Technologies Inc. of Norristown, Pennsylvania, was planning on using the show to sell a limited number of new MOS 6502 microprocessors—basically a low-budget 6800, designed by some ex-Moto engineers—at the jaw-dropping price of *twenty dollars*. It was unbelievable! It was like selling a Ferrari for the price of a Chevy, a mansion for the price of its garage.

In those purer days before such free-for-alls as CES and Comdex, Wescon, which was held in the underground exhibit space called Brooks Hall in the City Hall plaza, did not allow the grubby business of retail selling on the exhibit floor. So Peddle set up shop, like a dope dealer, in a nearby hotel suite. And it was there that Wozniak found him, paid the twenty bucks to the lady at the door (who happened to be Mrs. Peddle) and dug the cherished 6502 chip out of a glass bowl. It was a brief, but fateful, meeting. Within two years, MOS would be bought by Commodore and Peddle would help that company build the Pet computer and make a serious, if brief, challenge to Apple.

Woz drove home to Sunnyvale with his prize, as excited as he'd ever been. In retrospect, he'd just made his second great mistake. By the time the magnitude of this mistake was apparent, it would be too late for Apple to turn back. Woz himself would be gone from the company as well.

Given what was to come, one can only look back in dismay and wonder what might have happened if Wozniak had not been too broke to buy anything but the 6502. What if he had the money—say, the $3,150 Jobs owed him—to have followed the lead of the other Homebrewers, as he wanted to, and bought an Intel 8080. Instead of building the first great personal computer around a chip from a troubled company that would soon disappear into the bowels of a competitor, Apple would have been working with one of the best-run companies in the world. Instead of being bludgeoned by the team of Intel and Microsoft in the years to come, Apple might have led it in an unbeatable troika. It's entirely possible that in cheating Woz out of thousands of dollars Steven Jobs robbed his own future of billions. He may have hamstrung Apple even before it began.

Woz began work almost from the instant he got home. For the next two months he would immerse himself in the last great solo act of invention in the twentieth century, and put himself in the company of the great lone inventors—Ford, Firestone, Tesla—who had begun it.

3.9 SMALL MIRACLE

There is something almost miraculous in the story of Woz's creation of the Apple I. For someone who until this point had seemed lost and undirected, Woz, perhaps because he was in the grip of the project of his dreams, was suddenly more surefooted in his actions than at any time before or after.

For example, despite what one would expect from a hardware guy with the critical part at last in hand, Woz instead kicked off the project by writing software. In fact, he wrote the first BASIC language program for the 6502. He would later say that he did so because he could "whip it out in a few weeks and zap the world with it"—which he certainly did with his admiring counterparts at Homebrew. But strategically it was exactly the right thing to do. BASIC validated the 6502; it showed not only that this microprocessor could run the kind of programming language needed for a good personal computer, but it also enabled Woz to work backward, designing the hardware to optimize for that language.

It was also a breathtaking achievement. In the entire history of digital electronics there are no more than a handful of examples of hardware designers crossing over to write code, or vice versa. It is the equivalent of a figure skater taking up water polo, and doing both at the Olympic level. And that is one reason why computer folks still speak with reverence and awe of Stephen Wozniak.

But he'd only just started. With the key software out of the way, Woz set to work building the hardware. As one might expect, in his own territory he was even more surefooted. He set about designing a motherboard to hold the central processor (including the 6502) with the minimum number of chips and the maximum number of interfaces to the outside world. Woz took on the board design challenge and passed much of the interface work to the ever-helpful Baum, who later described the experience of creating links for the keyboard, display and memory boards—all within the restrictions of a primitive 8-bit microprocessor—as having wrung the last bit of the fun for him out of computer design.

Woz, by comparison, was having the time of his life. The restrictions created by his limited budget had the same effect as a limited palette sometimes has on a painter: it forced him to find the most economical and most elegant solution to every problem. There was no place for anything extravagant or extraneous. And Woz, whose mind had always bent that way, rose to the challenge. One way he did so was to dip into his employer's supply of parts—not exactly legal, but, given the long-standing attitude of HP toward this behavior as well as the Advanced Products Division's own iconoclastic style, it was not a career-threatening infraction either. But even with these expropriated HP parts, Woz still was ruthless in his design economies.

This decisiveness seemed to spill out into Woz's private life as well—again for perhaps the only time in his life. In the midst of this design madness, trying to build a computer while still holding a full-time job, Woz suddenly decided to make up his mind about getting married to Alice Robertson.

Still, he wasn't so decisive as to simply make a stand. Instead, he decided to be mathematical about it: he would flip three coins. If all three came up heads (a one-in-eight likelihood) he would marry Alice. A rather cold-blooded way to make a decision about love and marriage . . . but a sweet story when one next learns that Woz kept flipping coins until those three heads finally came up. One cannot imagine his erstwhile best friend, or, for that matter, most of the future top executives of Apple, being caught in such a romantic act.

But marriage, once decided, would have to wait. The computer came first, and it was nearly done.

Woz himself, typically, cannot remember the exact date he finished the computer, though it was probably in late November 1975. But also typically, even today he can still describe its design in detail. In one respect, the computer was similar to the other computers being shopped around Homebrew. It was essentially a motherboard full of chips (though, of course, the use of the 6502 was a major departure), a keyboard and, less common, a video display (many computers demanded that the user buy a display somewhere else). To the modern user the computer would look like the remains of a PC ready to take to the recycler, not the beginning of a revolution.

Yet, for all of its similarities to other machines, the experienced homebrewer would have instantly noticed some fundamental differences in Woz's design. For one thing, it was simpler; Woz's genius for design had enabled him to endow his computer with the most elegant architecture anyone had ever seen. And simplicity meant greater reliability, because fewer chips reduced the likelihood of breakdown. It also meant it was cheaper: Woz's design meant not only greater profits at the market's typical selling price, but more important when the competitive crunch came, more room to cut prices while still dancing out of the red.

Of course, pricing strategy was about the furthest thing from Wozniak's mind, but there were people coming into his world who would know just what to do with it—for a while, at least.

The second obvious feature of Woz's computer was its neatness. Neatness, too, often manifested itself in reliability. Whereas many of his current colleagues/future competitors were selling motherboards that looked—with their externally attached wires and kluged together subsystems—less like finished products than like breadboarded prototypes, Wozniak's motherboard was clean; every chip and every other component was snipped and soldered into place. As such, Woz's computer was probably the very first kit machine that could actually be dropped and survive—not so important now with guys who spent their lives reconnecting wires and searching out shorts, but a very big deal when it came to the commercial market.

Finally, a third, and less obvious, feature of the Woz computer—one that would prove decisive in the long run—was that *it actually worked.* Working at HP, Woz had access to one of the company's minicomputers, with which—without HP's permission, of course—he simulated the operation of a 6502 and then ran his programs through it, checking for bugs, infinite loops (where the computation would stick in a logical cul-de-sac, unable to escape, repeating its action over and over again forever) and design flaws. Thus, poor in terms of cash on hand, Woz was incredibly rich when it came to test and measurement tools—richer in fact than all but his most established counterparts such as MITS. With his own native genius, backed by the laboratory resources of one of the electronics industry's greatest companies, Woz could run with the best of them.

By Christmas 1975, Wozniak had finished, tested and debugged his computer. And like a true engineer, the first thing he wanted to do was show everybody what he'd done. Then he wanted to be paid for it, forget it and move on to the next engineering challenge.

So for the next month he went about displaying his brilliance. The first place he showed it was to his own bosses at Hewlett-Packard. As it happened, he wasn't the only Homebrewer at the Advanced Products Division. In fact, he wasn't even the only designer working with the 6502: his workmate Myron Tuttle had also caught Woz's enthusiasm for personal computing, bought his own 6502 from Chuck Peddle and was also during this period racing to build a board-level computer.

But Woz's was finished first, and was clearly superior. So it was agreed that it would be Woz's machine that would be demonstrated to their superiors. So, on a day in early January 1976, Woz, Tuttle and one other young engineer had an informal meeting with their supervisor. The supervisor was impressed, but informed them that it was no go. Tuttle would later recall, "It was one of those informal meetings. It wasn't a big deal. We just sort of asked for five minutes and showed Woz's board. We were told, 'HP doesn't want to be in that kind of market.' "

Out of that meeting would come the myth that hidebound old HP had looked at Woz's revolutionary design and was either too unimaginative or too stupid to get it . . . leaving the brilliant young visionaries to make it on their own. Like most myths, however, anyone who was at APD during that era would have seen an entirely different situation.

HP's Advanced Products Division was, for the moment, as nonconformist and innovative as any place in Silicon Valley. Inside the company itself the division was seen as a collection of wild-eyed radicals not only by HP's very traditional instrument group but also by APD's compatriots across the street in the minicomputer group. Chartered to create perpetually innovative new calculator products, not just for engineers but also for businesspeople, students, even everyday consumers, APD had developed an internal culture that would not be seen again until, well, Apple Computer itself.

And this culture became even more anarchic after the announcement, soon after Woz arrived, that the division would be moving to Corvallis, Oregon. Half the division was excited about going, while the other half planned on staying in the Valley by transferring to another HP division or leaving the company. Either way, almost nothing substantive happened at the division while it awaited the move. Instead, APD's employees, Woz not least among them, spent much of their days playing with their own private projects.

So why turn down Woz's design? It probably had nothing to do with the inventor—HP had gotten into calculators, as well as LED displays, from outsiders with good ideas. More likely, HP was wary of anything purely targeted at consumers, a market that had sunk many an ambitious tech company and in which HP had no particular experience or skill. The company also had an unwritten (and, time would show, shortsighted) rule that there was no way it could make a profit on a computer priced less than $3,000. And if all that wasn't enough, there was the distraction at APD.

On April 28, 1976 (according to a copy in the HP Archives), Wozniak sent a memo to the company requesting a release of the technology. This was followed on March 1 by a carefully drawn schematic of a "Microprocessor System," with a footnote reading: "Apple Computer Co. is a partnership of myself and Steve Jobs founded to market PC boards." Four days later, HP granted the release.

Of course, plodding old HP would have the last laugh. Entering into the PC business late, it nevertheless managed to play off of its strengths—high quality and a strong connection to corporate offices and research labs—and slowly began accumulating market share. Taught by its successes with laser printers (which it also supplied to Apple under the latter company's LaserWriter title), HP even learned, after a few nasty missteps, how to mass-market to everyday computer owners. Moreover, because of HP's dominance in minicomputers, and later large computer servers and workstations, it was able to link its calculators, personal computers and large computers into giant networked client-server systems for corporations and other institutions.

As a result, in the end HP earned more revenues and profits from the personal computer it had originally turned down than Apple Computer ever did. Just as important, as Apple began to spiral down, HP, after its own stumble, righted itself and became the most successful large company of the era. In 1996, twenty years after Hewlett-Packard turned down what would be the Apple I, HP passed Apple in the personal computer market share. Two years later, Hewlett-Packard was the world's fourth-largest personal computer company, and planning to become the first.

All legends to the contrary, even in high tech the tortoise often beats the hare.

Since HP wasn't interested, in February 1976 Wozniak made the first public showing of his computer at the Homebrew Computer Club.

Despite yet another myth to the contrary, the reaction that night to Woz and his computer was relatively cool. Sure, everyone knew Wozniak was a hotshot computer designer and programmer. And yeah, as Woz handed out copies of the schematics, everyone was impressed by the elegance of the design. *But it was built around a 6502!* By now, everyone who was anyone had already adopted the Intel 8080 architecture, and Homebrew was rapidly turning into a user's group for computers built around Intel chips. What Woz had done was a work of genius, no doubt about it, but it was also a work of apostasy. Either you joined Woz or you joined everybody else—not a tough decision, no matter how slick Woz's computer. Still you could study his schematics and find some new design ideas to steal . . .

There was one person at the Homebrew meetings, though, who was willing to side with Woz. Steve Jobs had been an irregular and indifferent attendee at Homebrew almost from the beginning, more often than not going just to keep Woz company. But, as he buried himself deeper into Woz's terminal for Call Computer, Jobs began to appreciate just how extraordinary his friend really was.

It must have come as something of a shock to Jobs. After all, he had searched the world for a guru, a man of unique knowledge and vision—and that guy turned out to be his goofy childhood friend. Watching Woz at the meeting handing out schematics, Jobs saw what his friend did not: that though their design loyalties lay elsewhere, the Homebrew members held Woz in awe and were more than happy to get hold of his most recent design and deconstruct it for their own uses.

Jobs also knew something else as well: left to his own counsel, as he had been with the Computer Converser, Woz would happily design himself into a corner. But if properly managed and directed, as with Atari's Breakout, Woz could change the world.

So the first and most important step for Jobs was to get Woz back under his wing. The HP presentation, which Jobs had not been privy to, was a dodged bullet. Had HP said yes, Jobs would have been left in the cold. Now Woz, frustrated by the lack of universal acclaim for his invention, was talking about selling the machine to Call Computer. Kamradt, who had returned to the Homebrew meetings to find Wozniak and reenlist his help on the Computer Converser, was entranced by the new Woz design and was trying to recruit the young man back.

That would have to be stopped, and fast. Woz and Jobs were accustomed to talking on the phone nearly every day, usually about the computer and Woz's various pipe dreams for it. Now Jobs sat Woz down and told him what he really thought. It was a terrific invention, but Woz was being utterly unrealistic about it. Not only was he trying to sell it to the wrong people, but by giving away the schematics, Woz was essentially handing over his hard work for free to anyone willing to hold out a hand. It's time to turn this into a real business, said the young man who until recently had publicly eschewed all worldly things; and the first step is to start charging for the damn schematics.

Jobs was never a tactful person, but he had also never before called Woz a fool. Woz listened. Woz would say later, "Steve was the one who thought we could make money. I was the one who designed the computer. I was the one who had attended the Homebrew meetings and I had written the software, but Steve is the one who had the idea we could sell the schematics." He would later add, perhaps a bit ruefully, "Steve was the hustler, the entrepreneurial type."

And Jobs was about to give Woz a first lesson on what that meant.

3.10 Fast Learner

Jobs had before him five immediate tasks. One was to redirect Woz's attention away from Kamradt. The second was to convince Woz to join him, legally, in a new business. The third was to create a market for the new computer. The fourth was to build a manufacturing operation. And the fifth was to construct a supply and distribution channel to build and sell the new computer in volume.

This is not an easy task even for an experienced business entrepreneur. It requires a combination of charisma, leadership, promotional talent and salesmanship—not to mention basic business theory. Jobs, the rebel against Western Society, whose total (noncriminal) work experience at this point amounted to less than a couple of years and whose entire management experience consisted of supervising one employee for two months, had so far shown little business acumen beyond a capacity for hyperbole with his superiors.

And yet, within five months he had accomplished everything. It was the first indication that Woz was not the only member of the partnership with a kind of genius.

The first two steps were actually the hardest. Woz was happy at Hewlett-Packard. The mother firm of Silicon Valley, with its perfect job security, doughnuts in the morning and one big happy family atmosphere, had embraced the young engineer in its arms. And Stephen Wozniak, like 25,000 other employees, never wanted HP to let go. His father, after all, was a lifer at Lockheed, and it was with the idea of just such a career that Woz felt most comfortable. Thus, a deal with Kamradt offered the perfect scenario: Woz could keep designing new computers in his spare time, sell them to the Call Computers of the world—which would be more than happy to buy them—and use the bucks to supplement his HP salary.

Jobs used two levers on his old friend. First, he played the money angle, suggesting to Woz that he could make even more money going it alone. Next, he played on Woz's engineer's ego, arguing that Woz would enjoy far greater glory among his peers holding on to the machine. He even hinted darkly that if the computer was sold to Call, it would be mishandled and quickly disappear into the mists of computing history.

Desperate to reel in Woz, Jobs, in a beautiful bit of surrogation, enlisted an Atari engineer he knew named Ron Wayne. Wayne was two years older than Woz, and that maturity gave added weight to Jobs's argument. Wayne, a classic eccentric Silicon Valley bachelor who combined cranky survivalism with a belief in the transcendental power of engineering, tried to appeal to Woz's ego. He pointed out to the young man that few engineers ever made it on their own, that famous designers like Eiffel and Colt had always needed a good business mind behind them. It was, in fact, a very accurate argument, though the description of Steven Jobs as that crucial figure showed either incredible insight or craven self-interest on Wayne's part.

Still, Woz had hesitated. Ironically, it seemed that he had learned too well all those agrarian, proto-Marxist homilies Jobs had been spouting all these years. He was willing to let Jobs and Wayne build the new computer, but Woz wanted to be able to stay at HP and use whatever design tricks he'd learned with the computer as a leverage into a better job in a different division at the giant firm.

No way, thought Jobs and Wayne. The last thing they needed was Woz as their competitor. It took an all-out, and nearly all-night, assault on Woz before, at last—partly out of exhaustion, partly out of not wanting to disappoint his old friend and partly out of his own tangential ambitions—he signed on. The clincher was a compromise: Jobs agreed that Woz could stay at Hewlett-Packard, but he was not allowed to duplicate his computer work there. Wozniak was happy, but Jobs was even more so. That's because Jobs knew that if the new company failed, he wouldn't be responsible for his friend's career, and if it succeeded, Jobs could simply charm Woz into working for the company full-time. And, in the meantime, that was one less salary on the payroll.

In yet another too perfect bit of symbolism, the articles of incorporation for the new company were signed on April Fools' Day, 1976. The founders, who would forever be known as a duo, were in fact a troika.

With Woz, Jobs had the computer, but he still didn't have a business. First he needed to come up with a name. Exactly how he decided upon Apple, probably the most influential new business name of the century, remains, like many facts about the early days of the company, the subject of considerable speculation.

The best-known story, told by Michael Moritz in *The Little Kingdom,* is that the pair were driving up the Peninsula and Jobs, lost in reverie about his days at the commune picking apples, suddenly had a Paul-like epiphany on the road to Los Altos and realized that Apple Computer—rather than other proposed titles such as Executek and Matrix Electronics—was the perfect name for the firm. That's possible, though the stretch of 280 they were driving on hasn't a single fruit tree to spark such a memory. Another story, published elsewhere, says that the trio were sitting around Woz's apartment throwing out ideas and Jobs, in a neat piece of out-of-the-box brainstorming, threw out Apple and found that it trumped every other idea. Yet another story has it that Jobs, a Beatles fanatic, took the name Apple from the Apple Records label of the album he was playing (and it is known that the trio had a few days of worry about a trademark infringement suit from the Fab Four). And at least one old Homestead High classmate would later claim to remember a scurrilous publication by the two called "The Road Apple" (Homestead's nickname was the Mustangs), though naming his new company after horseshit is probably too flip and cynical even for Steven Jobs. This was, after all, about money.

Ultimately, the final decision to name the company Apple was determined by the United States government. In particular, the Securities and Exchange Commission required a name on its new company registration forms. So, finally, when the day came to mail in the form and the entry for company name was still blank, Jobs announced, "Come up with a better name than Apple by five P.M. or that's it."

Whatever the source, it was a brilliant name. Smart, funny, antiestablishment, unforgettable, friendly but hip, the very antithesis of not only the eponymous Fairchild and Hewlett-Packard but also the technophilic Intel and Intersil. Perhaps no company name has ever fit its era so perfectly. The Apple name may have been the Apple Company's biggest strength—and, ultimately, its biggest weakness. Because, like so many things that fit an era so precisely, it became at best an anachronism, and at worst a liability, when that era ended and a new one arrived.

But in 1976, Apple was a killer name. You laughed the first time you heard it, smiled the second time and fell in love with it thereafter. It wasn't just a name, it was the culmination of the Age of Aquarius. It said to tens of millions of baby boomers now cutting their hair and entering the corporate world that they weren't selling out after all, that every time they saw that logo on the computer before them they were still Woodstock warriors, undermining the suits around them, fomenting the revolution from within and, duplicating Steve Jobs's famous knowing smirk, secretly laughing at the absurdity of it all.

4.0 SAPLING

A modern venture capitalist looking at the Apple Computer of April 1976 as a possible investment would have tossed the business plan into the trash.

Sitting up on Sand Hill Road in Menlo Park overlooking the stretch of freeway where Steven Jobs first named Apple Computer, the venture capitalist would look at this motley team with its crude product and see it as just another of the hundreds of doomed new start-ups whose business plans cross his desk each year.

In the years since Apple was founded, Silicon Valley has become the most efficient new-company incubator the world has ever known. In a good year, more than one hundred new companies are founded and funded. In a great year such as 1996, thirty local companies, the creation of similar investments two or three years past, will go public with market valuations of $100 million or more. In such years, the cities of Sunnyvale, Mountain View and Santa Clara together are home to more newly public large companies than all the rest of the United States.

That kind of efficiency is the product of experience and the ongoing perfection of techniques. The modern venture capitalist uses not only a wealth of institutional experience but also highly sophisticated analytical tools to determine whether a new company will be successful, including measuring the quality of the entrepreneurial team, the innovativeness of the product and the potential growth and size of the market. And even with all of this wisdom and skill, a good venture capitalist is lucky to have one new company that eventually goes public out of every five investments. That's why the venture capitalist is very, very selective about the firms in which he or she will invest money.

It is interesting, and telling, that Apple Computer, one of Silicon Valley's greatest entrepreneurial success stories—the company that is emblematic of the power of entrepreneurs, venture capitalists and bankers working together synergistically—would have fit none of the modern investment templates. In fact, it would have fallen so far off the charts as to be unmeasurable.

The Valley's venture capital superstar of the 1990s, John Doerr of Kleiner Perkins Caufield & Byers, has said that the first thing he looks at in evaluating a new start-up is the quality of the team—in his words, each team member should look at the others and ask, "Are these the people I want to be in trouble with for the next five, ten, fifteen years of my life?" Among other features of a start-up team, Doerr looks for experience, a natural leader who is "ruthlessly, absolutely intellectually honest," a technical genius, an intelligent manufacturing and distribution strategy, a good understanding of the customer and a brand-new market with enormous upside potential.

In April 1976, Apple had none of these things. The company was three guys, none of them with much business—or any managerial—experience. The one founder with a real career, Wayne, gave no indication of any entrepreneurial acumen, nor exhibited any leadership skills. The apparent leader, Jobs, was a strange guy with an even stranger lifestyle who had a habit of walking away from employment to wander off to a commune or Indian ashram. He was reputed to have been involved with another of the partners in past criminal activity. And that confederate, the technical guy, while possibly a genius, wasn't even sure he wanted to be part of the company.

The product itself existed only in prototype, and the team didn't have a clue how to build it in volume. And even if they did, they didn't know how to sell it. And even if they knew how to sell the computer, the cold shoulder it had already earned from the largest single organization of potential stakeholders (Homebrew), suggested that the team completely misunderstood the market's desires.

Yet, four months later, that same, apparently doomed, little company had somehow transformed itself into a hot new firm that now easily met all of those criteria it had so recently failed. And the force behind this miraculous transformation was twenty-one-year-old Steve Jobs. The many later, and more public, achievements aside, it was Jobs's finest hour. In sixteen weeks, ferociously learning the rules of business as he lived them, Jobs leaped from a second-rate, indifferent low-level product manager to the most interesting young businessman of the era. And in the process he turned Apple from an impossibility to the early stages of a social phenomenon.

And most remarkable of all, Jobs did all this without for an instant surrendering his announced attitude that commerce would never tarnish his shining soul. That he was now spending his days down in the engine room of capitalism with all the hustlers, door-to-door salesmen and greedy shopkeepers never once seemed to smudge his persona. And this obvious exercise in public hypocrisy and (perhaps) personal delusion would prove to be Steve Jobs's—and Apple Computer's—critical competitive edge.

4.1 HIGH FINANCE

Just how Steve Jobs managed to accomplish so much in such a short time is worth a closer look.

His first step after getting Woz and Wayne to sign on was to divvy up the firm. Even the most inexperienced modern high-tech entrepreneur knows enough to establish a valuation for the firm, as well as the number of outstanding shares, then award some fraction of that to the founders and leave the rest for outside investors. It is a measure of just how primitive was Jobs's understanding of business and finance that he simply cut up the pie: 10 percent for Wayne, 45 percent each for himself and Wozniak.

Nevertheless, inexperienced as he was, Jobs wasn't stupid. The comparatively tiny percentage for Wayne was not just a recognition that he was little more than a contractor brought in to persuade Woz but also a signal that he was going to be a short-timer. The other two stakes were even more illuminating: Jobs, who had essentially contributed *nothing* to Apple Computer to that moment, nevertheless had made himself coequal to the man who had done *everything*. At first glance this might seem a supreme example of Jobs's characteristic selfishness, but as time would show, it was exactly right. Jobs knew that his critical contribution to the company lay ahead, that without it Apple Computer would be worth less than nothing, and he had the ego to cast that fact in equity right away.

With that little exercise in high finance out of the way, Jobs set to work figuring out how to build the damn machines without killing the three of them. Woz's original Apple I (as it was now called) was a beautiful piece of construction, but it also took sixty hours to get all those tiny solders and wiring interconnects just right. Obviously, taking that much time on each computer was unthinkable—to sell the results at anything near a competitive price would earn them less per hour than they did dressed as the White Rabbit and the Mad Hatter. The only practical solution was to take the basic wiring scheme and convert it into a printed circuit board (PCB) onto which the chips could be quickly attached.

But printed circuit boards weren't cheap. At least not the first one. There was a sizable up-front cost to lay out the wiring diagram artwork and create the silk screens needed to produce the finished board. Only in volume did this up-front cost eventually pay for itself, and more. Thus, in shifting to a PCB, the fledgling company was taking its first real financial risk.

Jobs may still have had as much as $5,000 left from the Atari deal, but he kept that hidden from his partner. He did so despite the fact that Woz, now married, was so broke that his landlord, tired of rubber checks, demanded Woz's rent in cash. Instead, Jobs proposed that the two of them each sell something of value, to raise the estimated $1,300 he figured it would cost to design the board. In the end, Woz sold his HP-65 calculator and Jobs his Volkswagen van.

The layout and silk-screening was done by an old officemate of Jobs's at Atari named Howard Cantin. Cantin did the work for the ever-persuasive Jobs at a discount, for cash. As a result, by not asking for a piece of the company, Cantin joined the legions of Silicon Valleyites who didn't take the piece of a new start-up that would turn out to be worth millions.

With the board in hand by mid-June, Jobs next set out to establish a market. By his estimation, the total potential business for the basic board was about one hundred units, most of them to be sold to Homebrewers. At $50 apiece retail, with a cost to produce of just $25, Jobs figured Apple could clear a neat $2,500.

The three men scrambled to build a handful of Apple I's to meet the expected demand. As all of them had other jobs, this meant evenings and weekends at the expense of just about everything else. Then, at the July Homebrew meeting, days after the nation's Bicentennial, Jobs and Woz took the podium at the Homebrew Computer Club and for the first time demonstrated the next great American invention.

The two young men were as simpatico again at this moment as they had been in their blue box days. They were again filling in each other's blanks; once more combining their personalities into a single character that would in time be the Apple business style. Woz took the technical explanation, as always racing through his talk in a nearly mumbled blur of technical data tinged with an inventor's obvious pride. Jobs, for the first time facing his future market, exhibited the irresistible combination of contempt and enthusiasm that would eventually lead millions to follow.

But not that night. The Homebrewers like and admired Woz—he was, after all, one of them—but almost from his first words it was obvious that the Apple I was a product so eccentric in its processor, its design and its software as to belong in an utterly different reality than the 8080/Engineers Only machines on which they had set their fortunes. This sense of difference was only exacerbated when Steve Jobs stepped up to give Apple's marketing presentation. They had noticed Jobs hanging around Homebrew meetings for a couple of months, and most knew he was chummy with Woz, but except for an odd personality and style, he was no doubt one of the multitude carpetbaggers that had recently popped up to cash in on the home computer fad.

It was circle-the-wagons time at Homebrew. Those members who managed to look up from their soldering irons now and then noticed that their precious little club was suddenly under assault from all sides. The Homebrewers had believed, as the Internet pioneers would two decades later, that they could somehow keep their new world free of ambition, greed, hierarchies and profit. They bought into Felsenstein's image of an engineering utopia.

Now that dream was melting fast. In February, a letter from Albuquerque had arrived at Homebrew signed by Bill Gates, listed as general partner of a new company called Micro-Soft. Entitled "An Open Letter to Hobbyists," Gates's missive blasted Homebrew members for copying Micro-Soft's BASIC software instead of paying for it. Copying had, of course, been a standard procedure in the Brave New Homebrew World, part of the easy ethics of the hobbyist universe. Now Gates, still in his teens, was calling them thieves: "As the majority of hobbyists must be aware, most of you steal your software."

This was not only outrageous but almost incoherent to the Homebrewers. How can you steal in a world where everything is shared? It was true, of course, but that didn't make any difference. Now standing in front of them were two guys presenting a nearly turnkey computer that was obviously designed more for Everyman than to impress one's peers.

There was a smattering of applause, a few questions, and then it was over. Lee Felsenstein would famously conclude, "Wozniak might very well be heading for a fall. I thought if he was going to fail he was going to fail big and I wasn't going to step in the way." And thus, as often happens, the intelligentsia, dreaming of touching the masses, turned away just as the tool for the task floated by.

And, once again, commerce, with the same goal but a different motive, kept a steady eye and put out a hand just in time.

4.2 Storefront

Steve Jobs wasn't the only carpetbagger trolling the July 1976 Homebrew meeting. Another was Paul Terrell.

Terrell was the rare combination, for that era, of a computer hobbyist with the soul of a shopkeeper. He has never gotten due credit as one of the greatest visionaries of the electronics age. While the rest of the hobbyists were wanking around selling computer boards to one another, Terrell had the crazy notion that just maybe you could sell these things to regular people. Consumers! And instead of selling fifty, maybe you could sell a thousand, someday maybe even two thousand. Terrell figured this out long before the people who usually get credit for the idea.

In mid-1976 Terrell knew he was on to something special. He had watched a demonstration of the Altair soon after it was introduced, saw the future in its front panel lights and quickly talked his way into a license as the computer's distributor for Northern California. Demand soon proved so strong that Terrell made the jump from distributor to retailer and set up a store on El Camino Real in Mountain View. He called it the Byte Shop—and he dreamed of running a national chain with hundreds of franchise stores.

The role of El Camino in the story of Silicon Valley has never really been described. The original path of the missionaries establishing missions in the late eighteenth century throughout California, El Camino was, by the early twentieth century, the business spinal cord of the San Francisco Peninsula. Well into the 1970s, nearly everything that happened in the electronics industry in Northern California occurred within shouting distance of El Camino Real. Stanford and Santa Clara universities, the Packard garage, Shockley Semiconductor, the first Fairchild building, all lay within blocks of the King's Highway.

By the 1970s and the rise of the great industrial parks of the modern Silicon Valley, the industrial heart of the community moved elsewhere, away from El Camino, which quickly reverted to its old form of small restaurants, car dealerships, bars and tiny retailers. And yet, El Camino still retained a vital role for Silicon Valley that it retains even to this day: as a test lab for the Valley's newest consumer products. It is no coincidence that Andy Capp's Tavern, where Nolan Bushnell first tested Pong, was located on El Camino in Sunnyvale, just across the street from a Radio Shack store and from Olson's Cherries, where Charlie Olson literally sold the fruits of the old Santa Clara Valley.

Where Terrell chose to site his first Byte Shop in Mountain View was no less symbolic. The shop was tucked between cocktail lounges and auto repair shops, across the street from a Mexican restaurant and a few blocks from Clark's hamburgers, where one could see above the fireplace an already fading photo of Steve Jobs's Monte Loma classmates on the 1964 Clark's team in the Mountain View Americans Little League.

Terrell's Byte Shop was impossibly crude by today's standards. A little store with a few shelves containing motherboards and a few Altairs, electric typewriters for printers, a couple of displays, a tiny rack bearing a handful of mimeographed hobbyist newsletters, it offered less merchandise than just the Mouse & Joystick aisle in a modern CompUSA or Fry's. But in the tiny, incestuous world of computer hobbyists in 1976, it was a revelation—*now you could actually go to a store and buy this stuff!*

Not surprisingly, that night at Homebrew, Terrell listened to the Woz and Jobs presentation more intently than did most of the rest of the audience. Here, after all, was a potentially brand-new product line for which the Byte Shop could be the sole distributor. So, as the rest of the crowd thinned out, Terrell went up and met the two entrepreneurs. Jobs in turn immediately did a second private demonstration of the computer, prefacing it with "Take a look at this. You're going to like what you see."

And Terrell did. That is, he liked the computer. He wasn't so sure about Jobs, who struck him as "a guy who could give you a hard time." Still, the computer had some potential. As he had done with others in the previous few months, Terrell told the two young men to stay in touch, gave them his card and left. Maybe they would call; but more likely, faced with the daunting prospect of building a new company, they wouldn't.

So it was with shock late the next morning that Terrell looked up from his work to see a barefoot Steve Jobs strolling into the store. "I'm keeping in touch," he said with his sardonic half smile. Terrell couldn't help but be impressed. The kid was strange, but he had guts. Terrell ordered fifty Apple I's in different configurations for $489 to $589 each, payment in cash on delivery.

Steve Jobs was more shell-shocked than cocky as he walked back out of the shop. The order represented almost $30,000, more than either he or Woz had ever earned in a year's work. He rushed home to tell Wozniak, who was even more overwhelmed. Later Woz would call it the single most important moment in Apple's history. "Nothing in subsequent years," he would say, "was ever so great or unexpected."

Then reality set in. The pair had assumed that Terrell would be buying the new PC boards. Instead, he had demanded assembled computers. Holy shit! How many hours would that take? And worse, how much would it cost to build them before the company saw a penny back?

The answer to the first question was the usual: they would just work their butts off day and night, and charm anyone else they could into helping. But the second question was more difficult to answer. After all, Woz and Jobs had originally planned to sell 100 boards. Now, Terrell's order had turned half of those boards into computers—and that was within less than twenty-fours after first demonstrating the new machine! If the computer was this hot, why not do them all? Jobs might not yet know much about business, but he had a native sense of both economies of scale and of catching a demand wave. He decided to convert all the boards to computers.

But a quick calculation told him that building those hundred Apple I's, including parts and labor, would run about $25,000. That meant a profit of as much as $5,000, or 20 percent pretax. A few years later Apple would walk away from products with a potential for twice that profit, but for now, to the neophyte businessmen, this seemed a spectacular return on their investment.

The only problem was the investment itself. Where were they going to find that kind of money? It was time for Steven Jobs to quickly teach himself yet one more skill: begging.

It didn't start well. A visit to a bank in Los Altos only got him tossed out, and convinced Jobs to try somewhere else besides banks. Next he tried his old employer, the parts warehouse Haltek. He offered owner Hal Elzig an equity participation in Apple (though it is not sure whose stock was to be given up since there were no outstanding shares) in exchange for parts. Elzig turned him down, saying later, "I didn't have any faith in those kids. They were running around barefoot"—an extraordinary remark from a man who employed some of the strangest technogeeks in the Valley.

Even Al Alcorn, Jobs's recent boss at Atari, refused to sell the pair parts unless they paid cash up front.

It is telling that Steven Jobs could not get credit with either of the two most important employers in his career to date. Perhaps they knew him too well. By the same token, in his visit to the bank he had been so many deviations from the norm that getting a loan beggared the imagination. As always a quick learner, Jobs realized he had to find a middle ground—that of people who knew electronics but didn't know him.

The perfect place for that was distributors. They had all the necessary parts, they were used to flaky customers and they had never heard of Steve Jobs or Apple Computer. Needless to say, it was here that Jobs struck gold. At three different parts houses, he was able to get past the initial resistance executives had to his style and manner by using the force of his personality to drive a deal. It took every trick Jobs knew or could improvise. Certainly he wasn't afraid to wave the Byte Shop contract and suggest the doubting supplier call Paul Terrell as a reference . . . which they did, once even interrupting Terrell in the middle of a conference.

All of this proved to be perfect training for Jobs as he went after the closer: Kierulff Electronics. Kierulff was one of the nation's largest electronic distributors, and its operation in Palo Alto was a major supplier to the companies of Silicon Valley. Like so many others, Bob Newton, Kierulff's division manager for the area, wasn't particularly impressed with Jobs ("He was just an aggressive little kid who didn't present himself very professionally"), yet still sat through a demonstration and made a deal with the young man: he would sell Jobs $20,000 in parts, net thirty days (a phrase Jobs didn't understand) without interest.

Had any other young man with Jobs's mannerisms—and there were more than a few of them in Palo Alto in 1976—walked into Bob Newton's office, would he have given them the same deal? Not likely. Steve Jobs had something. Charisma, perhaps, if that elusive word means a preternatural ability to enlist others in one's own single-mindedness. Throughout Steve Jobs's career there have been thousands who have done extraordinary things for him without ever being able later to explain why.

4.3 Paying the Price

With the Kierulff agreement, Jobs had it all nearly in place. He had a product, orders, suppliers, capital and a small staff. All that was left was manufacturing. He and Woz had originally thought they could do it the old way: no sleep and continuous work until they were done.

But life was beginning to intrude on the two Steves. In particular, Woz was a married man now, and couldn't just take off for a month with his pal anymore. Besides, the HP job could withstand four nights at Atari, but it would be hard to explain four weeks of sleeping at your desk all day.

They tried anyway, using Woz's apartment as the factory. This was a mistake. Alice Wozniak, understandably, was soon furious. Woz and Jobs would go off to Jobs's parents' house or someplace else and work on the Apple I design. Then in odd hours Woz would come home and build. As Alice later told Mike Moritz: "The Apple was consuming all of his time. I saw very little of him. He'd go off to HP and eat something at McDonald's on the way home. He wouldn't get home usually until after midnight. I was going nuts coming home from work and having things on the dining-room table that I couldn't touch."

Faced with this adamantine attitude, the pair for once retreated—this time to the one place that could never refuse them: Jobs's house. Jobs was back living with Mom and Dad, but there still was a spare room in the back that had once belonged to Steve's now married younger sister, Patty. Jobs and Woz took over the room, soon filling it with boxes of components arriving from the various suppliers. The pair built the computers in that bedroom and in Jobs's, where the endless soldering burned grooves into the top of Steve's desk.

But even with this new setup, the pair was falling behind. The thirty-day mark was approaching fast. The two were building computers so fast they were barely able to do much more testing than simply turning on the finished computer to make sure it didn't explode. And that still wasn't fast enough. It soon dawned on Jobs that what his manufacturing model lacked was sufficient labor: there were simply too many chips to stuff into too many slots on too many printed circuit boards for two assemblers to complete in the requisite time. So the ever-inventive Jobs went out and recruited a third worker: his sister Patty.

Patty was the perfect assembler: pregnant, stuck at home, looking to make a little extra money. Jobs offered his sister a buck a board and she soon was settled on the living-room couch of her apartment, the boards on the coffee table before her, the soaps on TV and a phone cradled on her shoulder talking to friends, jamming the rows of little caterpillar-shaped integrated circuits into the holes on the surface of the green place-mat-sized fiberglass printed circuit boards. She wasn't very good at it, with a tendency to jam the chips down when they didn't fit just right—thus bending their little gold legs and setting the stage for future short circuits—but she was cheap, methodical and, most of all, available.

As the thirty-day mark approached, the two Steves sat down to determine a price for a finished Apple I. A retail price, that is. Jobs was already thinking beyond the Byte Shop contract. Woz, ever the innocent, thought the computer should be priced at a fair markup over manufacturing costs. He suggested $300. Had that price stuck, Apple Computer would have been gone by the end of the summer.

Jobs's appraisal was more insightful. He understood, almost instinctively, though perhaps with a little of his Atari experience, what the rest of the electronics industry was only now beginning to appreciate: the market for new tech toys and tools was different from that for most other manufactured goods. You needed to charge a high initial price for the "early adopters," the hardcore techies who would try anything new, to get the profits you needed to pay back the high up-front development costs. Then, as volume went up you cut the price—almost to match Moore's Law—to capture market share and stay ahead of the growing body of competitors. Then you started the process all over again with the next product.

So Jobs essentially doubled Woz's suggested price, then tacked on top of that an 11 percent dealer markup. The result wasn't that much more than what Terrell had offered, so Jobs figured he was in the ballpark. (In fact, Terrell was selling his own brand of computer, the Byte 8, at a 50 percent margin.) And the number, with its satanic overtones, must have appealed to Jobs's sense of humor: $666.66.

4.4 First Team

On the thirtieth day, Steve Jobs walked back into the Byte Shop carrying a stack of finished Apple I motherboards, each in a pizza-sized box. The moment Terrell saw the boxes, he knew something was very wrong.

What he had ordered were finished computers. That meant a keyboard. A display. The BASIC programming language either encoded onto a chip on the board or downloadable from an attached cassette. And, if nothing else, for God sakes, it certainly meant a *box* to put the board in. "There was nothing," Terrell would later say.

Terrell at that moment had every right to say, "Are you nuts? Come back when you've fulfilled your end of the deal." After all, he didn't much trust Jobs in the first place and now it looked in every way like the kid was trying to pull a fast one. But then, as so often occurred inside Steve Jobs's reality distortion field, something happened. Terrell took delivery and, as promised, paid Steve Jobs in cash. Apple Computer was now a profit-making enterprise. The company would thank Terrell a year later by making it the first registered Apple retailer . . . then in 1980, when it stumbled trying to expand its franchise nationally, killed the Byte Shop chain by refusing to continue supplying it.

Jobs now had cash in Apple's account and fifty more computers to build and sell. He was still on a roll. Entrepreneurship is, at its heart, a kind of fraud. You begin with nothing more than an idea, and at every step thereafter you must convince employees, customers, supplier, investors and often even yourself that your enterprise is bigger and more sophisticated than it really is. You sell a fantasy of the future as if it was a reality of the present. To investors, your résumé is deeper than it really is, product development further along, customers hungrily lining up in legions, your finances so strong that you hardly need the added money. More than anything, even than the product itself, start-up entrepreneurship is playacting, constructing an elaborate persona in the belief that someday it will be indistinguishable from the real you.

For Steve Jobs, who had been trying on and tossing off images since childhood, this was the most intriguing and exciting role yet. And he took to it as well as anyone before or since. The summer of 1976 was his debut as an entrepreneur. He had begun the summer almost a stranger to personal computing; he would finish it as the best businessman in the industry.

From the day he walked out the Byte Shop with the money he was amazingly adroit. He rented a mail slot in Palo Alto to give Apple an HP-like address. He signed on to a telephone answering service to create the image of a busy corporate headquarters with a receptionist.

Now he needed talent. If Apple was going to keep growing, he needed to begin dividing up tasks and assigning them to new employees. First, after a perfunctory interview, he hired Woz's old friend Bill Fernandez, who'd not been invited to Corvallis with APD and wasn't excited about the prospect of working in the other old, boring divisions of HP. A veteran of the game already, Fernandez shrewdly asked for a contract. He was Apple's first true employee.

Fernandez proved valuable to Apple in those first few weeks in ways the two founders would never know. Owen Whetzel, now a reporter for the *San Jose Mercury-News*, at the time owned a hobby shop at the nearby little Westmoor Shopping Center. He often noticed the three longhairs in the back of the store buying alligator clips and other items. The parts were in fact for the Apple I. But Whetzel assumed they were buying drug paraphernalia (and perhaps dealing) and was preparing to call the cops when he noticed that one of the trio was Bill Fernandez. Since Bill's dad was not only the local Sunday school teacher but also mayor of Sunnyvale, Whetzel let them be.

Next, Jobs signed up an old Reed friend, Elizabeth Holmes, who'd been working as a gem cutter in San Francisco, to handle Apple's books. Holmes, who was paid four dollars per hour, would drive down to Jobs's house once a week and pick up the invoices and bills. She would describe Jobs at the time as "working very, very hard. He was very directed and not very sentimental." The ashramite had already become a hard-nosed businessman.

Finally, Jobs called his old friend Dan Kottke in Oregon and talked him down to Silicon Valley for the summer to help with assembly. The ever-dutiful Clara Jobs put Kottke up on the couch.

The team was now in place, but it was already beginning to splinter. Entrepreneurial teams are volatile aggregations, with often conflicting goals that aren't exposed until placed under stress. Fulfilling the Byte order was one thing: the money was already guaranteed. But now little Apple was embarking on a speculative venture that, should it fail, might place its founders under financial liability. Woz was willing to take that risk; he still had a job. Jobs was too, because Apple was now his company.

But Ron Wayne, fearful of his share of the company's growing financial liabilities, was unprepared to go any further. Steve Jobs and Apple scared him: "I had already learned what gave me indigestion and I was beginning to feel the months running by. If Apple had failed, I would have had bruises on top of bruises. Steve Jobs was an absolute whirlwind and I had lost the energy you need to ride whirlwinds."

It was the classic lament of the corporate soul trapped in an entrepreneurial start-up. It is still heard a hundred times each day in Silicon

Valley and other tech communities throughout the world. Wayne's remark about bruises was telling: a real entrepreneur is hardly slowed, much less bruised, by failure. Had Apple failed that summer, Jobs would have walked away without looking back and without remorse, leaving the broken hearts and angry debtors to work it out among themselves. And he would have been right to do so.

Wayne, stereotypically, wrote the company a heartfelt and exculpatory resignation letter and left to pursue other opportunities. His 10 percent ownership, even diluted by the time of the Apple initial public offering, would have been worth more than $100 million.

Jobs hardly noticed Wayne's departure. By now he had concluded that he could sell the next fifty machines and had decided to build a hundred more beyond that. It was a crazy notion, based on the fact that the Byte Shop had already bought twenty-five, and no doubt would buy many more—not to mention the huge direct sale market out there that Jobs was convinced was already waiting for the Apple Computer. He was, in fact, wrong on every count. Over at the Byte Shop, Terrell was having trouble selling the machines, even after he got a local cabinetmaker to fit the boards into koa-wood cases. And he didn't need the frustration: the Byte Shops, undergoing a rapid expansion, were suffering severe cash-flow shortages. Being stuck with $10,000 in unsalable inventory didn't help matters.

Terrell even went back to Woz and asked him to design an interface to the Apple I that would allow the user to download Woz's BASIC off a cassette player. Woz didn't have enough time to do it, so he contracted a fellow HP engineer in return for royalties. As it turned out, the finished design sucked—bad news for Apple in the short term, good news in the long term in that it might have had to pay millions in profits in perpetuity for that one-time engineering job. Instead, they paid the engineer off with $1,000—a devastating amount at the time—and Woz, with no experience, managed once again to come up with a brilliant solution on his own: an interface board, the size of a Post-it note, that connected from a cassette player into the Apple I motherboard.

Woz had performed another miracle, but it did little to help Apple's sales. The new generation of customers the Byte Shop was pulling in didn't give a damn about the elegance of Woz's design. Far more important was the fact that the Apple I used a 6502 processor instead of the 8080. And that difference was driven home by the week as new computers appeared on the scene and rumors spread that even big companies were now looking into the business.

The machine that exemplified the new competition was the IMSAI 8080, built by a team sixty miles to the north in Marin County. The IMSAI was almost everything the hobby computers were not. Its founder, Bill Millard, was not a techie, but an entrepreneur and a salesman, a man who had once sold IBM computers. Millard didn't give a damn about the nuances of computer hardware, or the Homebrew Computer Club. He just wanted to sell computers and build a healthy business doing so. And he surrounded himself with bright young men, most of them recruited from scary est graduates that populated Marin in that era. They all nodded appreciatively whenever Millard spoke his mantra: "Make a Miracle."

Or steal one. Millard's first idea was to buy MITS, but when Roberts refused, Millard simply hired a computer guru named Bill Killian, ordered some Altairs from Paul Terrell and had Killian reverse-engineer them and come up with an improved copy. That was the IMSAI 8080. It had all the strengths of the Altair—the 8080 chip, BASIC, all of the growing library of Altair software—and fixed some of the glaring weaknesses of the Altair, like a lousy power supply.

The result was a real computer, in a case, that the thousands of electronic engineers and mainframe computer programmers who weren't hobbyists could finally take home and crank up. Not surprisingly, IMSAI became the first personal computer company to sell (with a little book cooking) more than $1 million PCs in a single month.

This was what Apple Computer, with its four guys all but living with the founder's mom and dad in a suburban tract home, were up against. And all of the company's feeble promotional efforts—giving away the interface card and a BASIC cassette, crude ads that read "Byte into an Apple" and "A Little Cassette Board That Works" or a demonstration program on the display Apple I's that printed out on the screen THIS IS AN APPLE COMPUTER—did next to nothing to help. The Apple I's sat on the shelf while the IMSAIs flew out the door.

And the salespeople at the Byte Shops, many of whom thought Jobs was a jerk, didn't go out of their way to help. They watched as Jobs and Kottke, riding the bus up and down the Peninsula, would storm into their stores, making demands and pestering them with endless questions. To the salespeople, these two were a pain in the ass compared to the well-dressed, professional folks from IMSAI, who talked and acted like winners, rather than escapees from a Grateful Dead concert.

Computer consultant Darrell Chambers was working at the time as a clerk at the second Byte Shop, this one in San Jose. "Jobs and this other guy rode up on bikes. I remember the long hair. They were carrying this case made out of cardboard and foam. And they took out what we now call the Apple I and started showing it off to me. It was like 'Hey, this is really cool. Check it out.'

They were just kids like I was, hackers really, and they were absolutely convinced that people would just want to get into their computer.

"But all I saw was just a motherboard. There was nothing to it. Worse, it had a 6502 processor, a toy, when everybody else was using the Motorola 6800 or the Intel 8080, so it wasn't even compatible with what little software there was on the market.

"At the time, all the computers we were selling—the IMSAI, Altair, SWTP (which we called Southwest Toilet Paper)—at least came in a box. Most of them had an S100 interface bus, so they could also be expanded. The Apple didn't have anything going for it except, if I remember, a TV interface.

"So I told them to come back when they'd put the motherboard in a case, changed the processor and added a keyboard. They said, 'Thank you very much,' and left. I remember thinking as they walked away: Apple. What a strange name for a computer. All the other companies had such professional-sounding names. It stuck with me."

And so it went at one shop after the next. Steve Jobs began to panic. When things had been going well, the notion of being a businessman—a new kind of honorable, enlightened Buddhist businessman—had appealed to Jobs. But now after just three months, as the company seemed to be sliding toward oblivion, Jobs began to seriously doubt himself.

With the help of his old girlfriend, Jobs consulted a Zen monk, Kobin Chino, who lived on a ranch in the hills above Jobs's house, for advice. Wouldn't it be better, Jobs asked, if he were to drop this capitalist deceit and head for a monastery in Japan? The monk laughed and told Jobs that he would not find much difference between the two . . . a statement that showed the monk had incredible insight into either the nature of entrepreneurship or the personality of Steven Jobs. Afterward Jobs confided to his old girlfriend that he was afraid that Apple would turn him into a monster.

Jobs even flipped out with his most important client. As Terrell recounted to Moritz: "[Jobs] came flying into the Byte Shop, buzzing at a hundred miles per hour. 'It's the goddamn logo. People think it's horseshit. We've got to change the name. Nobody is going to take it seriously.' " Terrell wisely convinced the frantic young man not to abandon what would be the most famous logo on earth.

Trouble finds trouble in Silicon Valley. When you are on top, everything seems to break your way, but when you slip, the bad news piles on. As if the current marketing problems weren't enough, the too clever price tag began to create its own problems. First a group of Sikhs complained about the demonic nature of the $666.66. Then the hottest movie of the summer proved to be *The Omen*, with its explicit references to the Number of the Beast. Certain Christian Fundamentalist groups, already having convinced themselves that IBM bar code readers were part of a satanic conspiracy to read hidden 666s tattooed on American babies, went out in search of other electronic products bearing strings of sixes. Needless to say, soon the telephones at the answering service and the Jobs house were lit up with rabid callers.

Yet, even as he panicked under this pressure, Jobs once more showed a unique talent that set him in the company of the best executives. As much as he panicked to those outside Apple, inside the company he maintained his composure. When he expressed doubt, it was only about his own role, and then to the introverted and self-contained Fernandez during long walks away from the house. With the troops, he never wavered in his enthusiasm for the project or his apparent optimism that it would succeed. It was a fraud, but an *appropriate* fraud, of the type any successful leader must develop in tough times.

So it was that even as he was expressing doubt about the whole enterprise to others, inside Apple he was not only keeping production moving but even working to expand it. Toward that end, he even approached Allen Baum. Woz had long borrowed a few dollars here and there from Baum whenever he'd found himself in a cash crunch. Now Jobs, with Woz in tow, went to see Baum and his father, Elmer Baum, to ask for $5,000. It was one of those shameless experiences that test every new entrepreneur.

Once again with Steve Jobs, father and son agreed to make the loan over their own personal doubts about the borrower. Allen Baum said later, "I had no doubt it would be repaid. Steve Jobs had this silver tongue that could talk anyone into anything." Including Allen Baum. His father was even more skeptical and was in a worse position to invest. But he too went along, saying afterward, "I did it because he was Allen's friend. I was in pretty bad shape financially but Steve gave me a pitch. If I hadn't known him, I would have thought he was real good."

With the Baum money, Jobs had bought the survival of his little company into autumn. Now he turned, as always, to his ace in the hole: the Woz.

4.5 Local Color

A visitor to the Jobs house at the end of the summer of 1976 would have been amazed at its transformation. What had been a sleepy suburban house, with the kids gone and an aging middle-aged couple heading toward retirement, was now a hive of business activity. Apple had become too much for the bedrooms of the Jobs house, so it moved to the garage.

Once again, Steve's parents were more than willing to sacrifice for their boy. Paul Jobs surrendered not only the garage but temporarily his car restoration—he was working on a Nash Metropolitan at the time, creating a nice symmetry between one of the least successful consumer designs and one of the most. Jobs *père* even set up the garage for ersatz clean-room production, lining the walls with plasterboard, installing lights and adding an extra telephone line.

Paul Jobs also built for his son a "burn-in box," a wooden case about the size of a coffin, and fitted it with heat lamps. In that box, a dozen boards could be placed at one time and heated for several days to simulate months of real-world use. It was a sophisticated idea in a fairly crude form; nevertheless, about this time a few miles away in Santa Clara, National Semiconductor Corp., which owned millions of dollars of burn-in equipment, was secretly *not* testing millions of chips destined for spacecraft and missile guidance systems. Thus, Apple was doing a better job at product testing than one of the Valley's biggest firms.

Still recovering from gallbladder surgery, having to pick her way around parts and worktables just to get to the washing machine, Clara Jobs nevertheless served as a receptionist for the company, answering phone calls and serving coffee to customers and suppliers. She even calmed a distressed Alice Wozniak whenever she called in search of her missing husband.

For a young man so dismissive of traditional values, and so alienated from his adoptive milieu, Steve Jobs enjoyed an incredibly supportive family. And it was from this secure base that he could launch his assaults on the marketplace. Meanwhile, back in the garage, he kept up morale and, most important, kept Wozniak focused upon improving the Apple I.

Like some geniuses (though probably not as many as the cliché would suggest), Woz had little personal ego. But he had infinite, easily bruised supplies of professional pride. That night when he showed off the Apple I schematics at Homebrew had been one of the defining moments of his life. Now the attention had turned elsewhere. Sure, the Homebrewers admired Woz's talent . . . but what had he done lately? And worse, to Woz, were the whispers that, despite all his cleverness, Woz had blown the Apple I by going with the second-rate 6502, a microprocessor deemed fit only for toys.

By midsummer the disdain—and, worse, the indifference—was beginning to get to Woz. Just as Jobs was facing humiliation every time he walked into a Byte Shop, so too did Woz feel increasingly out of the conversation at Homebrew. And each month the parade moved further and further away. The Altair was now coming up on its first anniversary. The IMSAI 8080 was now the darling of gearheads everywhere. The company was even giving away a book about microcomputers, written by a Brit named Adam Osborne, with every computer it sold. A new company, Cromemco, was designing boards to fit into the Altair and enhanced that computer's performance. Even on the other side of little Los Altos from Jobs's house a company called Microcomputer Associates had announced a kit called Jolt that, like the Apple I, featured a 6502 processor. And adding insult to injury, MITS had added to the Altair line a new low-budget hobby computer kit called the KIM-1—also using the 6502.

That was just what was already on the market, jostling the Apple I for retail shelf space. MITS was also working on a new computer featuring the Motorola 6800 chip. So was Southwest Technical Products (SWTP). The big electronic mail-order houses, like Heath and Ohio Scientific, were either offering their own kits or preparing to do so. And coming up on the horizon was yet another new firm, Processor Technology, that threatened to have the best computer yet.

Processor Technology had been started in a Berkeley garage in 1975 by Bob Marsh, a founding Homebrewer, with more than a little help from Lee Felsenstein, the spiritual leader of Homebrew and the man who had publicly doubted Woz's design. Pro Tech had begun selling replacement boards for the unreliable early Altairs, but by the summer of 1976 it had grown into a full-blown computer company. In the first year of its existence, Pro Tech had also matured into a professional outfit, with a superb product vision: a complete, stand-alone personal computer that could be purchased by anyone. And by the end of the summer that vision was to be embodied in the Sol Terminal Computer, named after Les Solomon, the author of that seminal *Popular Electronics* article that had set the whole revolution in motion.

All this frenzy of activity only made Woz more anxious to plant his own flag once again out ahead of the pack. And he did so in the usual manner: he told his fellow Homebrewers he was going to attempt the impossible, then he went out and did it.

This time it was a color display. Color was the latest fantasy of the home computer makers and the hobbyists who bought their products. In this era before word processing, spreadsheets and the decade-long dominance of symbolic displays, it was assumed that the next big use of PCs beyond running numeric programs was graphics. But black-and-white doilies on the screen were still pretty dull. But color! Color was the Grail. Color would put home computers right up there with the minicomputers coming out of DEC and

Data General. Cromemco had shown off at Homebrew a new computer prototype, called the Dazzler, that sprayed color across its display. Woz had been transfixed at the sight.

The only problem was that most designers figured that to put color on a home computer would require another board, equal in size to the motherboard, containing forty or more chips. That would at least double the price of the computer, not to mention create all sorts of new problems with reliability, power consumption, cooling, etc.

It was the perfect challenge for Woz. Nobody alive could look at a chip design and simplify it by a factor of two or five or ten the way Woz could. And now, having announced his intentions, he set out to do it. And, being Woz, he also had his own silly, eccentric reason for doing the impossible: he wanted to play the game he'd devised for Atari, Breakout, on his own computer and not just on an arcade player.

Building a low-cost, small-chip-set, color computer was a bigger challenge than Wozniak assumed when he started. It would turn out to be not just a paring down of chips for ever-greater efficiency, but a revolutionary rethinking of the very nature of the computer itself.

In studying his own design, Woz well understood that the Apple I, like every other home computer of the era, had three areas of memory. One, the external tape drive, was out of bounds for anything but large-scale downloading and storage because it was so slow. That left two others with which to experiment. One of these memories, the cache, composed in the Apple I of chips capable of storing 8,000 bits, served only the main processor. The other memory, composed of simple shift registers designed to quickly pass on their data, served only the display. Woz decided that if there was some way to get around the design constraints of the registers and the processor's memory, he would not only save a considerable number of chips but also obtain the power he needed to drive a color display.

To make such a breakthrough, Woz thought back to an article in the Homebrew newsletter a year before. That article had asked: given the extraordinary speed of the microprocessor, and the fact that it didn't use its own memory cache for sometimes thousands of computation cycles, couldn't there be a way to tap into that memory for other tasks?

The idea was an outgrowth of what was being called, in the world of big-iron computers, "virtual" computing—the first application of that now ubiquitous term. Until the late 1960s, computers had been largely "batch-oriented"—that is, you dumped a whole bunch of raw data in and walked away for a few hours while the computer crunched it and then spit out the processed results. "On-line" computing replaced much of this with a continuous interaction between user, typically at a terminal, and the computer. On-line computing inevitably led to "distributed computing," in which multiple users, sitting at terminals in diverse locations, all talked to the computer at the same time. And this was possible only because the newest computers were designed to take advantage of the extraordinary speeds of the central processor in dealing with a single user *in between* its interactions with scores of others. The result, when everything worked, was that each user had the sensation of having the computer all to himself.

Not surprisingly, in the world of personal computers, where every inch of real estate on the motherboard was literally worth its weight in gold, virtual computing had considerable appeal. But no one yet had figured out how to do it.

Woz did it, and he did so by a twist of perspective and a clever piece of observation. Instead of another operator tapping into the microprocessor between beats, Woz instead made the display itself the user. The clever observation was in noticing that in operation a color television's three-gun raster scan works like a typewriter—sweeping out one line after another from left to right, then hopping back to start the next line. The twist was that Woz made *the display control the computer.* In particular, every time the raster swept across the screen, it had control over the main processor's memory. But the moment it stopped for its equivalent of a carriage return, the microprocessor regained control, doing all of its work literally in the blink of an eye before the next line was displayed. In fact, Woz even had to slow the microprocessor down a little to make the combination work.

It was a brilliant piece of mental gymnastics, as good as anything Woz did before or since. Today, when nine-year-olds can talk about 300 MHz PCs (machines capable of 300 million operations per second) as if they are discussing baseball cards, visualizing such a stunt is not too much of a stretch. But in 1976, even though personal computers were a thousand times less powerful than today, it was an amazing cognitive leap.

But it was also more than that, because in turning the process inside out and integrating the display driver into the microprocessor, Woz made possible the mass-market personal computer. Now you could put almost every part of the personal computer on a single board with a minimum number of chips. And that meant low power consumption, high speed, a small box and a low price. And on top of that, you could work in color.

Woz understood all of this. What he didn't appreciate—nor did anyone else—at the time was that in developing this new design he had also carved out a strong and defensible competitive niche for the entire personal computer industry. From this moment on, PCs would be a distinct business with a trajectory all its own.

4.6 Risk Aversion

Looking back from the perspective of a quarter century, it is hard, at first glance, to understand why no established companies roared into PCs and, with mass marketing, superior manufacturing and economies of scale, stole the business away from all these eccentric tyros.

They easily could have. But the story of the technology revolution (in fact, of all industrial revolutions) is that of misidentification, misunderstanding and misdirection.

Take Intel, for example. Owning the 8080, as well as being the world's leader in MOS memory chips, Intel could easily have added some circuitry and a box and owned the personal computing industry in a matter of months. In fact, Intel already had a PC, perhaps the very first one, in the form of an in-circuit emulator (a form of test equipment) for its chips. But Intel was still struggling to get the microprocessor established and was riven by an internal debate over whether to turn the company completely to microprocessors or abandon them and get back to memory. Moreover, it was still trying to get its new generation of microprocessor, the 8086, developed, and a whole host of competitors—including Zilog, Fairchild, National Semiconductor, Motorola and Texas Instruments—were challenging it for the business. Finally, Intel had just lost tens of millions in a failed attempt at digital watches so wrenching that for the next twenty years chairman Gordon Moore would wear an Intel/Microma watch to remind him to stay out of consumer products.

The same story was largely true for the other big chip companies. Those that had microprocessors, such as TI, HP, National Semiconductor and Motorola, were either so burned by or still so enmeshed in calculators, digital watches, video games or CB radio that they had no inclination to jump into yet another. Those that didn't build microprocessors weren't in computation, so they weren't even thinking about microcomputers.

Why weren't the little personal computers crushed from above by the big established computer companies? After all, certainly *they* could see the potential of microcomputers.

And they did. Sort of. But that didn't mean those companies did anything about it. At least not for a while. A mistake of hindsight is to assume that once microcomputers appeared on the scene it was self-evident that this would be a huge market. But nothing was further from the truth. The very first PCs, such as the Altair, required a hundred hours of soldering, chip stuffing, wiring and testing, just to get a box that really didn't do anything. You could program it to do some mathematics—but after a couple of hundred hours more work you basically ended up with a very, very large calculator. You could use it to do typewriting, but that was incredibly difficult because there were no word-processing programs yet. In fact, when you got right down to it, the first personal computers were essentially a fairly meaningless way for gearheads to show off their technical prowess. That's why so many Silicon Valley professionals walked into the Byte Shop, then walked right out again, unimpressed.

In 1976, the big computer companies were enjoying one of the great business booms tech had ever known. IBM, DEC, Data General, Wang, HP, Burroughs, Univac, Control Data—all were experiencing a period of both prosperity and great innovation. And much of this excitement was occurring at the minicomputer level. Small, powerful machines were opening brand-new markets in small businesses, academic institutions and the divisions of large companies.

Success is a great suppressor of risk. The computer companies were slamming away at their own established markets, using their exploding profits in new product development to try to race ahead and gain an edge on their competitors. Just about the last thing they needed was to launch off into a brand-new, unproven business. Better to spend the money on distribution channel development, more salespeople and software design and grow the current customer base rather than screw around with an unknown, and unproven, new one.

There was a cultural reason as well. Ever since ENIAC and the other pioneering mainframe computers of the late 1940s, computation had been the province of Computer Pharisees. You see it in the old photographs: giant computers, which were fragile and often required sophisticated air conditioning and water cooling, operated within special facilities, managed by a priesthood of electrical engineers, computer scientists and professional programmers, typically wearing lab coats.

By the 1960s, this postwar computing in universities, government agencies and military centers had largely given way to the payroll and management information computing of large corporations. The client changed, but not the culture. Amost every great company had its own data processing center, often in a modernist glass box and filled with the next generation of information mullahs, now in suits and skinny ties. The very nature of batch computing reinforced the exclusiveness of this caste. You sent in your reports or filled out punched cards (in No. 2 pencil only) and the wizards in DP performed their magic rites and, miraculously, back came your paycheck or printout. Nobody knew exactly what these people did, but it was obviously pretty damned important.

The appearance of both real-time processing and the minicomputer, which allowed that processing to be distributed, only slightly changed the status quo. Now there was not just one big computer center but also smaller ones located in each company division or factory—though they too were operated by the equivalent of parish priests. Despite the fact that some allowances were now made for the corporate hoi polloi—for example, an office might have a "dumb" terminal to send information directly to the mini—that access was carefully circumscribed, and unrestricted electronic contact with the big mainframe was never allowed to the nonclergy.

By 1976, the situation had become rather tense. The minicomputer companies, in their ferocious battle for the new market base, had found that there was a tremendous demand in the corporate world for distributed information systems that actually let different corporate operating units perform their own processing and run their own programs. In response, HP, DEC, Data General and the rest began to build new minicomputers that were smaller, cheaper and more accessible to everyday users. Looking ahead, these manufacturers could visualize a world (which they were happy to describe to customers) in which there might be a computer in every company building, perhaps on every floor, and each sprouting a profusion of terminals . . . perhaps someday so many that one could put a terminal on every desk!

The minicomputer people were so sold on the concept they even gave it a religious vision: the paperless office. And that extraordinarily seductive phantasm haunts the computer industry to this day.

It was all so perfect, so progressive, so democratic. But there was only one problem. It threatened the power, prestige and even the employment of the Data Templars. And since they were the folks who typically approved all computer purchases in the corporation, the DP directors typically did their best to veto or at least impede the adoption of distributed processing systems. The heresy had to be stopped at all costs.

The result was something of a war at many companies, with marketing and manufacturing arrayed for battle against data processing and accounting, with senior management caught in between. Luckily for most of these corporations, executive row despised the computer praetorians as much as everybody else and were happy to quash their growing power.

By the time Woz and Jobs were teaming up for the third time and starting Apple, this internecine war for control of corporate information was still far from over. But the end was in sight. The big-iron companies like Burroughs and Univac were essentially doomed, and the minicomputer firms on the road to triumph. Among the mainframers, only IBM, the biggest tech company of them all, was clever (and rich) enough to play both sides. Having introduced its own minicomputer line, while dissembling that it wasn't *really* in the minicomputer business, Big Blue managed to quickly become the leading supplier to this new world of data processing.

The new computing paradigm had won, the lesser nobles of minicomputing had brought King Mainframe to bay. But the minicomputer companies were exhausted. They had fought this battle during an economic depression, they had invested billions in product development and gained thousands of customers with great expectations who would need to be serviced. It was time now to focus on upgrading existing product designs, developing a library of software applications, building a service and support structure and starting to turn those investments into profits.

That was one reason why HP passed on Woz's prototype, a scenario repeated at other computer companies throughout the world. There would be enough time after the mop-up of minicomputing to worry about the next field of battle, personal computing by end users, if such a market even existed. And, when the time came, how hard would it be? Moore's Law already suggested that within eight or ten years it would be possible to put minicomputing power in a desktop box. Then it would be just a matter of scaling down the rest of the components. For now . . . well, you could tell it was too early just by looking at those half-baked, underpowered computers like IMSAI and Altair being sold to the (literally in Jobs's case) Great Unwashed.

It was here, on this critical question of scalability, that Stephen Wozniak, quietly and unseen, shut the door on the computer industry. With his design breakthrough of putting multiple functions on a single processor, he took the rule book away from its biggest players. From this point on, the game would be not, as the computer companies wanted it, how to dumb down big computers for the personal market, but instead how to add more power and performance to small, inexpensive PCs without changing their size or price.

It was not a game the big boys were philosophically or structurally prepared to play. They would eventually learn—but until they did, the minicomputer companies, to their dismay, would find themselves at the losing end of a war almost identical to the one they waged and won against mainframes. The lesser nobles had defeated the King only to see the serfs revolt.

Though no one knew it, Woz had bought his partners at Apple, his buddies at Homebrew and peers like Bill Gates in Albuquerque, five years of freedom in which to live out their entrepreneurial fantasies. They would have to live them very fast. The few that did survived.

4.7 Pro Tech in Check

By the end of the summer of 1976, as the Carter and Ford presidential campaigns kicked into high gear, and Americans sat in front of the television on hot August afternoons to watch Edwin Moses, Sugar Ray Leonard and Bruce Jenner win gold at the Montreal Olympics, Stephen Wozniak, working at home and in Steve Jobs's garage, was putting the final touches on his improved Apple I.

He was running out of time. On Labor Day weekend in an aging hotel in what was then the dying resort town of Atlantic City, there was to be a personal computer show, an imitation of the big computer shows like Wescon, and the prototype of what would become a multibillion-dollar personal computer industry show drawing hundreds of thousands of attendees to events like Comdex.

Needless to say, this show would be a lot more modest: two dozen exhibitors and a couple of hundred gearheads walking among the card tables looking for a good buy on memory boards. Nevertheless, it was the biggest thing the personal computer industry had yet seen, and everybody of importance was going to be there. Rumor was that Processor Technology was going to introduce the Sol at the show. If the Sol was everything it was reputed to be, it had a good chance of stealing away the entire industry. That's why Jobs not only had to be there but needed to be able to show Woz's new design.

Woz was still tweaking the prototype minutes before they left for the airport. But it was done. Armed with the computer, a suitcase full of Apple I boards and a sheaf of flyers, the two took off on the flight to Philadelphia, excited but filled with apprehension.

As has happened a thousand times since, the flight to the show was filled with competitors. And, as always, each of these little teams was smug in the knowledge that it had the edge over all the others—and at the same time nervously eavesdropping on those others to make sure it was true.

But one group on this flight was more smug than the rest. This was the team from Processor Technology. In fact, they were downright arrogant about it. Pro Tech was the worst nightmare of all the garage teams. First, with Lee Felsenstein on board, it had the pedigree. Next, it was like a real company: it had salespeople, and executives who wore suits and ties. But most of all, it had the Sol, and the Sol was beautiful. It had a keyboard, and motherboard and tape drive and display like (almost) everybody else, but *it had them all together in a sleek, magnificent sheet-metal case.* It not only ran like a computer but it even *looked* like one . . . well, at least like a real computer terminal. It certainly made all the other computers look like, well, what they really were: kluges soldered together by amateurs with no understanding of manufacturing, marketing or product design.

You had only to look at the slick Pro Tech boys and their even slicker computer and see the future of personal computing. This was a computer a corporate suit would be proud to walk into a Byte Shop and buy and not feel he was skulking into a porn shop to buy illicit goods (fittingly, the original Byte Shop building is now home to just such a business). You could put the Sol on your desk at the office and it would be all but indistinguishable from the Honeybee and HP terminals down the hall. The Pro Tech team had a winner and everybody on the plane knew it.

The absolute antithesis of that team sat, by coincidence, in the row of seats just in front of them. Scruffy and unprofessional, Jobs and Woz looked already like the ghost of Homebrew past. For Lee Felsenstein, sitting right behind the two, it was vindication. After all, he had dismissed the Apple I as a dead end. Now, as he peeked over Woz's seat, he could see the two young men poring over a crude mock-up mounted in an equally crude case typically used by amateur engineers. He would later say, "It was thoroughly unimpressive. These two guys just had a cigar box. What the hell did they know?"

He had in fact seen the future. And the end of his own company.

In Atlantic City, Woz and Jobs were joined by Dan Kottke, who'd since his couch days earlier in the summer had moved to New York City. They set up a card table and sold the older Apple boards and parts throughout the day to sparse crowds of young East Coast technophiles. At night they played with the new machine on the color TV screen in their room, dazzling select visitors with rainbows of arching color. Those who saw the demonstration, and then the little box it emanated from, came away convinced they'd seen the real winner at the show.

The pair came home from Atlantic City with a few dollars in their pockets, some promises for orders and, most of all, a sense that they could take this market within the year. They also needed some help. This time from grown-ups.

4.8 Mixed Signals

For all the successes in the final weeks, the summer of 1976 had not been a happy one for Jobs and Woz.

Entrepreneurial start-ups are like submarines. Detached from the outside world, under continuous pressure and facing the perpetual risk of obliteration, start-up teams very quickly begin to crack. Resentments form, personalities clash, the idiosyncrasies of others become unbearable. The story of Silicon Valley is filled with broken friendships, fistfights in hallways and nervous breakdowns among the team members of the thousands of start-ups that built that community. Feuds still fester between Valley pioneers decades after the original blowup in some tiny storefront. And it is a standard rule that by the time a tech company becomes successful it will have lost at least one of its founders.

Apple had already lost that co-founder in Ron Wayne. But during the ramp-up to Atlantic City, the two principals themselves came shockingly close to a breakup. And the reason was, of all things, Woz's pride.

Those merely acquainted with Wozniak during that era would have been surprised to learn this slovenly figure was deeply proud. But those who spent time with him at Homebrew knew better. What else could have compelled him to risk marriage, career and health over the last year devising one technological miracle after another? Woz wanted his peers to recognize him as the best among them; later he would expect the same from history.

But now, for the first time, Steve Jobs was beginning to intrude on Woz's private obsession. It was Jobs who was out there representing the product, who was becoming synonymous with Apple I—and for all Woz knew (and he wasn't far from the mark), getting the credit for its invention. Even worse, as the summer progressed Jobs was even beginning to intrude upon Woz's designs. They had a blowup over how many slots to put into the back of the color computer. Woz, dreaming of all that he wanted the computer to do, wanted eight slots. Jobs, thinking about price and about market targeting, wanted only two.

After Atlantic City, the situation only got worse. Woz, having stared into the eye of the Sol, was ready to give up. The Processor Technology guys obviously knew what they were doing. They weren't amateurs like Steve Jobs. Woz began to harbor notions of jumping ship. In particular, he seriously considered selling the color computer to Pro Tech. *They* would know what to do with it. And Woz also knew he was within his rights to make such a sale: the original Apple agreement allowed him to retain all rights to his invention.

Wozniak's family backed him in the mutiny. His wife wanted him home.

And his parents and siblings at last voiced the concerns they'd always had about Steve's questionable choice of best friend. His sister Leslie would later say that Jobs had always been described as "this schlunky-looking guy with bare feet and dirty hair." Woz's parents had long wanted him to abandon this distracting pipe dream and get back to settling down in his marriage and career. So, as work continued at the Jobs house, at the Wozniak house and apartment the prayers were for the worst.

If Woz had caved at the sight of the Sol, Jobs was thrilled. He'd gone against the best the industry had and, technologically at least, defeated it. The Sol didn't frighten him now at all; rather, he saw a wealth of good ideas to steal. Jobs knew he could build a better Sol, but Pro Tech couldn't build a better Apple. Not as long as he had Woz.

Sure, Woz balked when Jobs pressed him, but hell, Woz always got upset when he actually had to deal with the real world. Left to his own devices, Woz would have turned the Apple I into yet another Homebrew Wonder of interest to nine guys with empty wallets. Jobs knew it was he, and he alone, who could keep Woz aimed in the right direction. And if Woz didn't understand that, too bad. He would someday. In the meantime, Jobs could handle him—or so he thought.

There were other, more important things to worry about. One was to get the Apple computer into some sort of Sol-like box. And to do that required more than just bending sheet metal; it involved completely rethinking the problem of power supply and cooling. Jobs had noticed that many of the new enclosed designs were noisy as hell thanks to cheap built-in cooling fans. The Zen meditator appreciated the value of silence.

There was no more complete silence in a computer than to have no fan at all. But getting rid of the fan meant you needed a great power supply, a transformer so small and so well designed that it could run nearly forever without external cooling while still not turning red-hot and melting the case and motherboard.

While the public has always understandably focused upon the digital processing side of electronics, within the profession success or failure has often been decided by the quality of the supporting analog circuitry. After all, as clever as the Cream Soda Computer had been, it had still been burned up by a bad power supply. Analog circuitry, especially in the form of linear chips like capacitors and resistors, had long been the most invisible, yet most rarefied, of all the semiconductor design professions.

Whereas microprocessors were designed by committees, analog circuits were typically created by lone geniuses, often eccentric wild men, who were living legends in the industry. The most famous of these, Bob Widlar, became renowned at Fairchild and National Semiconductor for picking drunken fights at industry conferences, chopping down company trees when frustrated and, once, bringing a sheep to National Semi in the trunk of his Mercedes to chew the grass on an unmown lawn. Yet Widlar, who spent the last twenty years of his life in Mexico like a character in a Malcolm Lowry novel, still regularly would fly up to Santa Clara to deliver some splendid new design to National Semi or, later, Linear Technologies.

Woz had already proven he was no analog guy, so Jobs set out to find someone else to do the job. With almost no Valley contacts, he was reduced to going back to Atari, where he was not exactly the most popular guy around. Yet, in typical Jobs fashion, he managed to get in with Al Alcorn and talk his old boss into recommending an Atari employee to work as a consultant. Even more amazing, Alcorn recommended the best he had, Rod Holt.

Even in the cranky world of analog design, Holt was one of a kind. A middle-aged chain smoker, he had a raw voice and a drawn face that looked as if he'd slept in it. He had been variously a radical activist, treasurer of the National Coalition Against the War in Vietnam, the author of a book on Marxism, a leader of the Revolutionary Socialist Party, a manufacturer of stereo systems and a builder of racing motorcycles. He talked endlessly about everything, much of it cast in terms of the struggle of the proletariat. And like most revolutionaries, he knew the value of the dollar. When he told Jobs his high consulting rate, Jobs merely replied, "No problem."

"He just conned me into working," Holt said later.

Holt's work would prove critical in the years ahead. For now, he unwittingly played an equally important role: He was a grown-up. A strange, rather unlikely one perhaps, but a grown-up nevertheless. Jobs had seen what grown-ups could do, first at Atari in the form of Al Alcorn, then at Sol, and now Holt. They might not have the inspired creativity or boundless energy of the young people with whom Jobs had surrounded himself until now, but they countered that with discipline, gravity and, most of all, experience. And Steve Jobs needed all the experience he could get. He was headed into a dangerous and mysterious country now, of large-scale manufacturing, corporate finance, law and marketing, and he knew that without experienced guides he'd never survive.

Jobs also needed grown-ups in Apple for another reason: to help control the children, whose numbers were growing by the day. At Homebrew, Woz had already gained two teenaged acolytes, Randy Wigginton and Chris Espinosa. One was a former juvenile delinquent, the other a budding political activist; both were now born-again computerphiles. They followed Woz everywhere, acting as his gofer, his cheering section and his protégés.

And their Pied Piper was himself becoming a handful. Woz's first attempted mutiny may have been quelled, but worse was to come—and it would come at a time when Jobs, over his head in business negotiations, was most vulnerable.

4.9 The Scariest Man Alive

If the big computer and semiconductor companies were too distracted to chase the personal computer market, there was still one mysterious and sinister company willing to take a shot: Commodore. And it was just down the road in Santa Clara.

Well, sort of. It was hard to know exactly where Commodore was. The company was registered in the Bahamas, incorporated in Canada, listed its headquarters as Santa Clara, but at times appeared to be run out of Norristown, Pennsylvania. And the company's pedigree was equally suspicious. Ten years before, its chairman, Powell Morgan, had died suspiciously as he was about to be investigated for defrauding investors of millions of dollars through an investment firm called Atlantic Acceptance. It was one of the biggest financial scandals in Canada to that time and the resulting Ontario Supreme Court report implicated Commodore.

A few years later, Commodore sprang up in Silicon Valley, a major player in adding machines, then calculators, backed with money from its new chairman, financier Irving Gould. But it was the company's CEO who drew the most attention. His name was Jack Tramiel, a bald, tough Holocaust survivor who was already becoming legendary for his aphorisms ("Business is war"), his risk taking and his willingness to kill off suppliers by holding back payment for his own cash-flow needs. Tramiel was something of a terrifying figure, a role he relished. In a room of intellectuals he would wait until the right moment to say, "Yes, I went to university too. I went to the University of *Auschwitz!*"

Needless to say, Tramiel played for keeps, and he had no patience with human shortcomings or delays, which made working for Commodore a pretty horrible experience. But Tramiel was a winner. He had come late to calculators, but with a line of brilliantly conceived, shoddily built, low-cost models, he carved out a sizable market share. Then the market crunch came in 1974 and he was forced to write off a worthless inventory of chips. Tramiel swore he'd never be put in such a position again, and two years later he went out and bought a failing semiconductor company at a budget price.

The firm he bought just happened to be MOS Technologies, the makers of the 6502. And with MOS came Chuck Peddle, the 6502's creator and the man who had sold one of those chips to Woz nearly a year before and set Apple in motion. Tramiel was never afraid of a new business opportunity, and Peddle gave him one: home computers. Even better, suggested Peddle, go out and find the best new start-up company building a 6502-based computer and buy it while it's still cheap. With a good design already established and Commodore's financial strength we can own the market before any other real potential competitor even notices it.

Peddle knew what company he wanted too. He'd been to the conferences and shows and seen in what kind of awe the industry held Steve Wozniak's design. Best of all, the outfit appeared to be little more than two guys in a garage with absolutely no business experience. They ought to jump at the sight of real greenbacks.

So it was that a few weeks after Woz and Jobs returned from Atlantic City, two suits arrived at the Jobs garage. One was Peddle, with gray wavy hair and aviator glasses, the other Andre Souson, Commodore's vice president of engineering. Peddle, in fact, had visited Apple once before, when MOS was still independent, to demonstrate a kind of microcomputer called an in-circuit emulator to help engineers develop products around the 6502.

This time the two men had come for the company. They explained their intentions and asked Jobs to come up with a price. The numbers Jobs returned with were reasonable: $100,000, plus some Commodore stock, for Apple, plus guaranteed $36,000-per-year jobs for him and Woz. Peddle and Souson agreed to take the offer to their boss.

If the numbers Jobs threw out were appropriate for Apple, they were utterly outrageous for its two principals. Once again, this time faced with a giant potential competitor, Jobs had shown incredible cool. He and Woz were looking at a nearly $90,000 payoff in the first year, and that didn't even count the stock—more money than either of them (or their fathers) had ever seen in a single year. Yet when Jobs set his price, he barely blinked.

After the emissaries left, Jobs spent the next few days doing due diligence on his potential new employer. He called everyone he knew who had ever worked for Commodore, sold anything to the company or bought one of its calculators. And with each conversation, his optimism faded. Everybody hated Commodore. Their calculators were shit; clever functionality in a lousy package. You could park a car on an HP calculator and still use it; with a Commodore calculator you had to worry about punching the keys too hard. Working there was a nightmare, with everyone from the vice presidents to the janitors in terror of Jack Tramiel. And nobody worked *with* Commodore—instead you delivered according to the terms of the contract and then prayed you'd get paid someday. Finally, to a person, everybody who had ever dealt with Commodore warned Jobs about the pending negotiations.

"The more I looked into Commodore," Jobs would say later, "the sleazier they were. I couldn't find one person who had made a deal with them and was happy. Everyone felt they had been cheated."

In the end, Jobs withdrew his price. It was a brave call to walk away from a deal that would have put him on the Sunnyvale equivalent of Easy Street after just a summer of hard work. But as it happened, there never would have been a deal: when Peddle and Souson presented the proposal to Tramiel and chairman Gould they were quickly vetoed. Commodore didn't want to spend money for two freaks in some suburban garage. Rather, the company would design its own computer.

Faced with his first great business challenge, Jobs had made the right choice. But others thought differently. Woz in particular, saw the Commodore offer as the solution to all of his problems. He could bury his debts with the big cash-out, get out of the madness of this start-up company, see his baby turned into a real mass-market product sold by a major corporation *and* get a high-paying job in the process. He didn't want to hear Jobs's second thoughts about Tramiel and Commodore.

His father agreed. Until now, Jerry Wozniak had stayed on the sidelines, worried that his son was again mixed up with the ever-dangerous Steve Jobs, and at the same time proud of his son's brilliant new invention. For this Lockheed veteran, a Commodore deal would kill two birds with one stone: it would not only get Stephen out from under Jobs's controlling personality but also establish him in a corporate setting as an important engineering visionary.

There was more. Commodore's impending counteroffer also brought to a head the old issue of ownership. The original agreement had given Woz all rights to the technology. And what was Commodore buying, after all, but the design of the Apple I? They certainly weren't buying the Jobs garage or Apple's crude distribution system. So didn't that mean Woz deserved the lion's share of any payout?

Jerry Wozniak fretted over the threat posed by his son's new partner for weeks. By one of those strange coincidences that are a reminder that the Valley is a small town, his wife, increasingly involved in local politics, had offered their house for a neighborhood "meet the candidates" tea. The guests of honor were two candidates for the Sunnyvale city council. Both were members of the new city liberal splinter group, Orchards, and both lived in the neighborhood: Dianne McKenna and Dave Barram.

Regis came along to support his wife. Recognizing him, Jerry Wozniak took him aside and slowly began to pour out his heart. I'm worried about my boy, he told McKenna. He's gotten himself mixed up with this strange young man who seems to have some kind of power over him. Now he wants my boy to leave a great job at HP and join him in some crazy new company. What should I do?

Regis didn't know what to say.

It all came to a head one evening in September, as the Apple narrative shifted momentarily from the Jobs's house to the Wozniaks'. Jerry Wozniak confronted Steve Jobs. He had told his son Mark that he "was going to make the little son of a bitch cry and that'd be the end." And that was what he did. He told Jobs, as Mark overheard, "You don't deserve shit. You haven't produced anything. You haven't done anything." Jobs burst into tears. He told Jerry Wozniak that the veteran engineer didn't appreciate all that he, Steve Jobs, had done for the company. Then the tearful young man turned to his partner and said, "Woz, if we're not fifty-fifty you can have the whole thing."

Whether Steve Jobs cried out of betrayal, surprise or calculation is impossible to know. But even though he cried, as Jerry Wozniak had predicted, it was not the end. Through the tears, he had called the bluff of this rather unusual pairing of a middle-aged man fighting in the place of his grown-up son. And when it was over, Steve Jobs was still in charge, and he still killed the Commodore deal.

It had been the classic high-tech confrontation of engineering and marketing, writ small. As a lifelong engineer in a giant corporation, Jerry Wozniak was as naive about the true nature of business as his son. He was a good man and a good father, but a lousy businessman. R&D always believes that it makes the real contribution to a company's success, while management merely follows behind sweeping up the credit. Management knows better, but is forever embarrassed about not being clever enough to work on new inventions in the lab.

In that odd three-way argument in the Wozniak living room, it was Steven Jobs, with the least amount of work experience, who was right. His 50 percent share might be stretching things a bit after the first six months, but it would be low in light of things to come. He had, after all, built the company. In the ever-repeating story of high tech, engineering leads only for the first few months of a new revolution and thereafter marketing is king. Wozniak's design was brilliant, but it never would have happened without Jobs's prodding.

Moreover, if there hadn't been Wozniak, Jobs would have found someone else. Without Jobs, Wozniak would still be a low-grade engineer at Hewlett-Packard.

Jobs, his cheeks glistening with tears, had won the debate. But something had been torn in the friendship that would never again be fully mended. In another year, this friendship would be world-famous, in another decade it would be legend. But already, while Apple Computer was still known only to a few hundred computer hobbyists, Stephen Wozniak and Steven Jobs began to slowly drift apart. And though the tear would often be stitched together, usually for public occasions, the patch would never again be seamless or strong.

4.10 Searching for Daddy

Steve Jobs now knew more than ever that he needed the help of grown-ups. But finding them was a different matter entirely.

Of the few he knew well, some, like Holt, were too odd. Others, like his workmates at Atari, hated him. Even his partner's father thought he was a conniver. And the businessman he most admired, Nolan Bushnell, was busy with his own company.

So Jobs decided to start cold. Leafing through electronics magazines, he'd been struck by Intel's advertisements. In an era when chip and instrument companies were still selling their wares through impenetrable tombstone ads or using women with big breasts, Intel's ads were stylish and abstract.

Intel has always been known as a great technical innovator; but in fact its technology has rarely been triumphant. The real key to Intel's success, in 1976 and now, has been its marketing. In the mid-1970s, before almost anyone in tech, Intel recognized that in the new world of electronics, the user experience would matter more than product specifications. The result was a celebrated series of ads that used race cars to symbolize speed, a hamburger for customization and a meat cleaver for cost cutting. This was followed by stylish ads composed of illustrations of elegant people. It was microprocessors as lifestyle; and the ads were a decade ahead of their time.

Jobs saw these ads and was entranced. Alone among the players in his industry, he saw the value of this type of advertising. And if chips could be sold as fashion, just think what you could do with a personal computer. And Jobs also knew that only such ads could top the expensive five-page color ads now being placed in computer magazines by his nemesis, Pro Tech.

Somewhere behind those Intel ads, Jobs decided, was the grown-up he needed. Jobs called Intel's marketing department—and Intel referred him to a public relations and advertising agency in Palo Alto called Regis McKenna Inc. A few years hence, after he became famous, Jobs would be notorious for not returning phone calls. But now, when the agency's director of new business development, Frank Burge, proved unresponsive, Jobs refused to accept the silence and simply hounded the man with calls until he got a reply. Worn down by the assault, Burge agreed to visit the Jobs household.

Almost from the moment he agreed, Burge had doubts. PR agencies in Silicon Valley were, and are, constantly approached by new start-up firms with big ambitions and little money. A few turn out to be industry giants; most turn out to be bankruptcies that pay their contractors pennies on the dollar, if anything. "As I was driving over to the garage," Burge would say later, "I was thinking: Holy Christ, this guy is going to be something else. What's the least amount of time I can spend with this clown without being rude and then get back to something more profitable?"

But Burge, like so many others, came away a changed man. Though he still wasn't convinced Apple was a viable company, he was impressed by Jobs's personality and the sophistication of the product. Just to make sure he wasn't crazy in his optimistic evaluation, he called Paul Terrell over at the Byte Shop. Terrell told him that Apple was both financially and organizationally over its head, and that Jobs wasn't a very comfortable marketing man, but that nevertheless Apple had something there.

That was enough to keep the ball rolling. There were other meetings. The agency finally proposed taking on Apple's entire marketing campaign in exchange for a percentage of the company's profits—an unusual arrangement, as agencies usually would bill for hours, set a monthly retainer or, with the most interesting companies, work for equity. The most likely reason for this deal was that RMI had serious doubts about the long-term viability of the company, not to mention its short-term ability to meet its bills, so decided to take its money right off the top.

A few years later, while writing *The Little Kingdom*, Michael Moritz would uncover an early agency memo that read, in part: "Though he moved a quantity into retail distribution, there is as yet no evidence that the retailer(s) are successful in finding customers." It went on to note that "Steve is young and inexperienced" but that "[Nolan] Bushnell was young when he started Atari. And he claims to be worth $10 million now."

Jobs had, for the moment, made the cut. And that meant a meeting with Regis McKenna Himself (as the man's business card famously said).

Regis was a small, delicate-looking man, with a soft voice and an air of fragility about him that was largely due to a lifetime of battling the diabetes that had already killed one of his six brothers. But appearances were illusory, because McKenna was tough as nails, with an Irish temper that would explode when ignited. Like almost every Silicon Valley success story—and McKenna's was one of the most unusual because of the tangential path he had chosen—Regis was arrogant, shockingly brilliant, and suffered fools not one bit.

Yet for all the hobnobbing he did with Valley executives, and despite the fact that his name would eventually be synonymous with theirs, McKenna was not like the rest of Silicon Valley's elite. Like them, he came from humble beginnings—in his case a working-class family in Pittsburgh—but unlike them he had never graduated from college, much less gone on to grad school. He was also a true-blue Democrat when much of the rest of the Valley's leadership was Republican—a fact which cost him some business in the early years (his vindication came twenty-five years later, when a now Democratic Valley watched in envy as President Clinton had dinner at the McKenna house). Moreover, while the rest of the Valley's winners typically used their first real money to move off the Valley floor and up into the hills of Los Altos, Saratoga or Woodside, McKenna stayed in his surburban house in Sunnyvale, just blocks from the Wozniak home, where Dianne could pursue the political career that ultimately made her a county supervisor.

But what most distinguished Regis McKenna from his peers was that he was an aesthete in a world of gearheads. He had begun his career at Fairchild during its golden age, then jumped to National Semiconductor, where he did an impossibly good job for a company composed largely of hard-nosed, unimaginative chip builders. McKenna then broke out on his own in 1970, just in time for the first big Fairchild explosion, the one that created the modern Silicon Valley. Having worked with all of these Fairchildren, he had a superb network of contacts when they all became entrepreneurs and started their own Valley chip companies.

Not surprisingly, the chip company McKenna took on as a client was the most gilt-edged of the bunch: Intel, founded by the man who ran Fairchild semiconductor, Robert Noyce; Fairchild's top scientist, Gordon Moore; and its chief applications specialist, Andrew Grove. Regis would ride Intel to glory—a glory, even Intel would admit, that was in large part due to Regis McKenna's efforts.

For a guy trained in mass advertising, Intel posed a difficult challenge: how do you make silicon memory chips exciting? The fact is, you couldn't. But within months, fortune dropped into Regis's lap the biggest opportunity in high-tech history. The microprocessor.

It is to Regis's eternal credit that he understood the value of the microprocessor to Intel even before its founders did. While Noyce, Moore and especially Grove were hemming and hawing about the dangers of spreading the company's already thin resources on a whole new product line, Regis lobbied for the microprocessor in every way he could think of. Recognizing that nobody at Intel could figure out what to use this new invention for, McKenna hurriedly prepared a white paper offering scores of potential microprocessor applications. While some of the ideas were wacky (airport marijuana-sniffing machines) and others well beyond the capabilities of the chips at the time (blood analyzers, automatic toilet flushers), the white paper did, more than any other study of the time, accurately predict the extraordinary breadth of applications that would eventually appear for the microprocessor as it became the signal invention of the postwar world. McKenna's efforts played a critical role in convincing a doubtful Intel to stick with its new invention.

That was only the beginning. By 1976, McKenna was beginning to formulate in his mind a radically new model for high-tech marketing. The off-center Intel ads were a clue. What Regis realized before anyone else was that digital electronics, as it moved outward from laboratories to offices to daily life, would increasingly be sold not from the top down in the form of performance specifications and hard technical detail, but from the bottom up in terms of applications, user experiences and the complete *system* of not only product but software, packaging, design tools and customer service.

This in turn would require a new kind of marketing communications that went beyond merely mailing press releases to trade magazines. Instead, the goal would be consumer publications such as *Time* and *Newsweek* and business magazines such as *Fortune* and *Business Week*. But to get to these publications and their readers would require the cultivation of key industry "opinion makers" whose learned judgment on new products would be taken as gospel by both mainstream reporters and consumers.

Needless to say, this would be pretty tough sledding with a product as arcane as a microprocessor. In 1976 there were still chip company executives who didn't understand how the damn things worked. It wouldn't be until 1980 that McKenna's ideas of a system approach to chips would be made manifest in Intel's Operation Crush. Crush would be the seminal event of modern high-tech marketing and the antecedent of "Intel Inside" a decade later, which would prove to be one of the most successful marketing programs in modern business history.

Now, serendipitously, this funny little computer company with the even funnier name had dropped into Regis's lap. It was the perfect test bed for his new ideas. After all, unlike chips, home computing was something the average consumer actually might be able to understand. Regis had already experimented with some of his ideas using the Byte Shop, which happened to be another of his clients. But retailing was a different game—this was now manufacturing, with its opportunity to create brand identification. And a cute name like Apple certainly wasn't a bad way to start.

However, before anything could get underway there was the matter of the founders themselves. And Regis's doubts about these two neophytes weren't eased by their first conversation. Regis prided himself on his professionalism, his erudition and his ability to be comfortable around business Brahmins. Now across the desk from him were these shaggy near-juveniles without an ounce of tact or gracefulness between them.

Even the small talk went to hell. Regis asked the pair about how they were promoting their product. Woz mentioned that he was working on a technical article about the Apple I for a trade magazine. "Oh really?" asked Regis, who had spent a decade using just such articles to make unknown engineers into industry gurus. "I'd like to see it." Then he offered some free (and very useful) advice to the Woz: keep the article relatively untechnical and you'll reach a larger audience of not only your peers but also potential customers.

Woz visibly bristled. "I don't want any PR man touching my copy." Regis, understandably proud of his achievements, was not going to take this from some long-haired troll.

"I think you both better get out," Regis said very slowly, trying to restrain himself. For once, Steve Jobs dropped his usual role as troublemaker and played peacemaker between his resident genius and the adult who was to guide them out into the big world. It only partially worked. The pair left Regis having apparently blown their first shot at professional help.

4.11 Valentine's Day

Apple still needed money, serious money, if it was ever going to ramp up to catch Pro Tech or MITS now or prepare itself for the inevitable arrival of the big players in the months to come.

The only guy he knew who had ever raised that kind of money was Nolan Bushnell, so Jobs went back to visit his old boss and mentor. They were an interesting sight in Bushnell's office: Nolan with a beard, permed hair and pin-striped suit and Jobs with his own beard, lank hair and jeans; one of them the most celebrated name in consumer electronics, the other preparing to supplant him.

Bushnell still had a soft spot for his young apprentice, and spent more than an hour giving Jobs a tutorial on how venture capital worked. In 1976 it was a relatively new profession, having made its first important appearance in Silicon Valley just seven years before when Art Rock had helped fund the creation of Intel. Now there were perhaps a dozen venture capitalists investing in Silicon Valley, a number of them congregating in an industrial park in Menlo Park on Sand Hill Road, just behind Stanford University.

As Bushnell explained it, venture capitalists managed funds of money formed from private and institutional investors willing to take a sizable risk on new start-up companies. The venture capitalists identified those firms with potential, and then invested some of the fund's money in a series of rounds—seed, second, third, mezzanine—in exchange for equity, at founders stock prices, in the company. Sometimes a round was covered entirely by one venture firm, though more often it was a consortium. The amount of equity they took varied with the round. Typically an early round investment would be small—say, $200,000—but since the value of the company was also low, that would buy 20 percent or more of the company's total stock. If the company was successful, later investment rounds might be higher, often in the millions of dollars. But since the company would also have a higher value by then, the actual percentage of ownership lost would be smaller than in earlier rounds.

Nevertheless, it was probable that by the time the company was fully invested, these venture capital firms would own a majority of the firm . . . and that ownership, combined with the usual demand by these investors for one or more seats on the board of directors, would mean that the founders, who started down the road to have control over their own lives, would end up not even in control of the company they built. But then again, they might also be multimillionaires. So would be the venture capitalists and their fund investors. The payoff would come when the company, now successful, had its initial public offering, "going public" with its first open sale of stock and a listing on a stock exchange.

That, of course, was if everything worked right. And it rarely did. A venture capitalist who managed to get one public company out of every five investments was something of a star, and the one winner would usually more than cover all the losses of the others. But it was precisely because of these low odds that venture capitalists were notorious for exercising their control during tough times and booting the very entrepreneurs who'd built the company in the first place, replacing them with more experienced hands and, sometimes, personal friends.

This, in so many words, is what Bushnell told Steve Jobs. It was both an invitation and a warning: come join the game of big-time entrepreneuring, but don't be surprised if you lose it all.

Jobs was undaunted. He asked Bushnell to recommend a venture capitalist. Bushnell—and it is hard to know whether he was trying to help or teach Jobs a lesson, or both—gave him the name of one of Atari's investors: Don Valentine. The name wasn't new to Jobs, despite his limited knowledge of Silicon Valley. In fact, Regis had given him the same name a few weeks before.

One of the longest-standing myths in Silicon Valley is that when you go in to see Don Valentine, you come out either a tycoon or with a new asshole—and either way, the experience is not pleasant. Valentine was, and remains, the man with the golden gut. From Atari to Cisco, his masterpiece, he has had an uncanny ability to spot a potential winner, build it into a hot company (even if he has to fire all of the founders) and then take it public at exactly the right moment.

But to be on the other end of the process, as an entrepreneur, is akin to a ride through a wood chipper.

A truck driver's son, Valentine was a founder of Silicon Valley. At Fairchild, where he first met McKenna, Valentine served brilliantly as marketing manager and sales manager, in both roles putting in place organizations that held the company together for years to come. An imposing figure, variously described as "the straightest guy in the world" and a "real taskmaster," Valentine had enormous intelligence and integrity. Fairchild was essentially a drunken, skirt-chasing brawl, but Valentine would have none of it. In one respect that was to his credit, but it also pointed to a weakness: Valentine lacked the ability to deal with clever (as opposed to brilliant) people—in the most celebrated case, treating a subordinate named Jerry Sanders so crudely that the two men maintained a thirty-year feud that lasted long after Valentine had become a famous venture capitalist and Sanders the even more famous CEO of Advanced Micro Devices.

From Fairchild, Valentine had gone to National, where his toughness was a match for Charlie Sporck, then moved on to create his own venture firm, Sequoia Capital (he also sat on the board of Regis McKenna Inc.). Hard as nails, a master business strategist, wary of cleverness, dressed like a banker, it was hard to imagine anyone less suited to deal with a trickster like Steve Jobs. Even when Valentine made friendly conversation there was something threatening in his words. And when he smelled a deal, Valentine could be as terrifying as God Almighty.

And yet, on a bright autumn morning in 1976, Valentine drove down to the Jobs garage. Being a business community, Silicon Valley has very few classic visual images. But this is one of them: Don Valentine, thick head of hair, rugged good looks, in a rep tie and dark suit, climbing out of his Mercedes and warily trudging up the walk into the Apple Fairyland and wondering just what in God's name he was doing there.

As one might expect, it did not go well. Valentine would later call McKenna and ask, "Why did you send me these renegades from the human race?" But Valentine could live, albeit uneasily, with that. What bothered him much more was that the duo had no business strategy. They basically demonstrated the product, told Valentine that the market was going to be big and suggested that Apple could do very well on just a fraction of that business. This was heresy to Don Valentine, and just about the stupidest thing you could possibly say. He would recall thinking, "Neither one knew anything about marketing. Neither one had any sense of the size of the potential market. They weren't thinking anywhere near big enough."

Valentine didn't invest in entrepreneurs and their companies to be in fourth place in a market; he invested in companies that would do anything to *own* that market, to set the standards, steal the biggest customers and crush the opposition. His companies did not take prisoners. Time has shown he was right. Every new tech industry quickly fills with players, then experiences a devastating shakeout that leaves one clear winner, a couple also-rans and a bunch of corporate corpses. The only strategy in such a world is to play to win everything; to aim for second place is a form of business suicide.

End of meeting. Yet Valentine's golden gut told him that these goofballs had a diamond in the rough. He gave them some advice: get an experienced marketing guy and I might think about investing.

Once again, Steve Jobs's native brashness led him to do the right thing at the right moment. Know anyone? he asked Valentine, when a more veteran entrepreneur might have merely gulped. Lemme think about it, Valentine replied. Even the mighty Don Valentine could be momentarily disoriented by the Reality Distortion Field.

Back at Sequoia, Valentine dug up three names of marketing guys he'd worked with in his chip days. He called around to see what they were up to. Only one was currently free: an old Fairchild subordinate named Armas Clifford Markkula, known to everybody as Mike. The latest word on Markkula was that he had gone to Intel, made a few million in founders stock when Intel went public, retired at age thirty-three when someone was promoted ahead of him and was now spending his days with his family at home in Cupertino, going swimming, playing guitar and polishing his gold Corvette. Valentine gave him a call and suggested he go visit a garage just a few blocks away.

4.12 Mike Marketing

Mike Markkula was an interesting combination of tight-ass and show-off rarely seen in Silicon Valley. Raised in Southern California, he had come to Fairchild from Hughes Aircraft. Jumping to Intel, he had made something of a name for himself in the company for his skill at the details of marketing: customer relationships, order processing, pricing. Even at hard-nosed Intel, Markkula was, in a word, boring. A tinkerer, secretive in his moves and notorious for being negative about every new idea he heard ("You wouldn't get three words out of your mouth before he'd say, 'No, that's not the way it is,' " recalled one workmate), Markkula was the kind of middle manager on whom great companies are built but who never see the inside of executive row except to make a presentation. He managed to reach the job of product marketing manager for memory chips, and though he dreamed of greater things, no one else was surprised when he was passed over (Jack Carsten was promoted instead) for the job of corporate marketing director.

Away from the office, Markkula was, to all appearances, pure of heart, a dedicated family man and a loyal employee. There were only three things he hated. One was jokes about his hair, which he combed straight forward in a bang (a decade after one reporter called it a "Dutch boy haircut," the reporter understood Markkula blackballed him from the Santa Clara University Ethics Center he'd funded). Another was the use of his real Christian names. And a third was conflict with the employees he managed. Otherwise, he was as plain vanilla as Silicon Valley gets.

But sometimes within such a corporate Bartleby there is wild man just waiting for the chance to kick out the jams. Markkula had that beast, and thanks to some judicious purchases of company stock, when Intel went public Markkula surprised everyone by checking out. He wasn't a tycoon, but he was rich enough never to have to work again. In the process, the drone became a peacock; now set free, the wild man took to living the high life, with expensive clothes and a fast car.

Real entrepreneurs are start-up junkies. No matter how much money they make, they can't keep away from the next deal, even if it costs them their fortune. Markkula, by comparison, showed little interest in getting back into the game. It is possible he never would have returned to corporate life were it not for Don Valentine's call.

So it was that Mike Markkula drove over to the Jobs house and became richer and more powerful than he'd ever dreamed.

What Markkula saw in the Jobs garage was not a bunch of long-haired amateurs, but a wonderful little toy, a personalized version of the big computers Markkula had worked with when developing Intel's order entry system. The Apple I, he would later say, "was what I had wanted since I left high school." It was better than a Corvette.

Markkula walked out in the daze of a teenage crush. He called Valentine, told him he was interested and asked for a meeting. The two met. Valentine expressed his concerns, but Markkula wasn't worried. He was convinced that a nice little company could be built around this product given a mature hand at the helm, an intelligent marketing strategy and a real organization. Valentine, knowing well that the enthusiasm of the CEO was half the game, agreed.

With Valentine's words of support still in his ears, Markkula went home and told his wife that he was going to jump into a new start-up. Mrs. Markkula, who, like many Valley wives of the era, had been down this road before, made Mike promise not to give the company more than four years of his life. Next Markkula called Regis, told him that he was investing in Apple and asked the PR guru to forgive the kids and come on board. McKenna, who was in the business of forgiving slights, agreed.

Then Markkula called the boys and made their dreams come true: he would join Apple and support the development of the company's next product by underwriting a bank loan of as much as $250,000.

Apple Computer finally had its own in-house grown-up.

4.13 ANNIVERSARY

As 1976 ended, Steven Jobs had done nearly the impossible. In less than a year, starting with little business and no management experience, he had assembled a new company team, prototyped and tested a first product, built it in volume, established a distribution channel, improved that product and, finally, located both professional management and a seed round investment. Nine out of every ten new start-up companies in Silicon Valley never get this far, even though many are composed of teams of industry veterans with a hundred times the combined work experience of Jobs and Wozniak.

Little Apple Computer wasn't out of the woods yet, but it was on the way. There were still much larger competitors already in the market, and even bigger ones now just weeks away from entering the market. But, thanks to Wozniak, Apple had the best product design. And thanks to Jobs it now had on board the best marketer in high tech in Regis McKenna and, in Mike Markkula, a man who could give the fledgling company the marketing infrastructure of a giant corporation. With this combination, Apple could hold its own against anyone—at least for a while. Soon it would need a follow-up product, a second winner even better than the Apple I. The good news was that Woz was already at work on it.

But Steve Jobs had done something else in that first year that was not as apparent. He had stamped the company forever with his personality. And that was good news and bad. Companies that bear their founder's personality must live with the strengths and weaknesses of that personality even after that founder is gone. Hewlett and Packard were great men, and they had built a great company. Nolan Bushnell was an exciting, but mercurial, man, and Atari would prove to be a thrilling place to work right up until the moment it disintegrated. Jack Tramiel was a brilliant, but controlling figure, whose companies could never grow beyond his reach.

Steve Jobs was as talented an entrepreneur as any of these celebrated figures. But he was also more deeply flawed. He was now embarked on creating a company that wasn't just a business, but a children's crusade. Apple was to be the Krupp of a social revolution. And for nearly a decade, Jobs's personality gave Apple enough momentum to live out that dream.

But even as he founded Apple, Jobs was embedding into its personality the flaws of his own character. He had a company, but it had been built with a technical genius who no longer quite trusted him, a marketing man who didn't want to work anymore and hated the rough-and-tumble of management and a staff held together not by management or leadership, but by charisma and manipulation. Most dangerous of all, the company philosophy was steeped in self-actualization. In the HP Way, the first rule, before all the nice stuff about community service and management by objective, was *profit.* In the unwritten Apple Code, the first rule was *self,* and all selves were subordinate to, and existed in the reflection of, the Supreme Self, Steve Jobs. The Jobs Reality Distortion Field now enveloped all of Apple Computer, and from there would encompass millions.

These other, disturbing character flaws, would be buried under the extraordinary success of Apple's first two decades. But they would never disappear. Rather, they would grow in the dark, eating away at the company's heart, biding their time and waiting for a moment of weakness to emerge.

But that moment was still many years and many billions of dollars away. At the moment, it was moving day at the Jobs garage.

5.0 BLOSSOMS

As the new year began, the duo had become a troika. Now each set about inventing their corner of the business.

For Wozniak, the task at hand was to create the new computer, to be called the Apple II. For Markkula, it was to create a real company out of the ragtag pieces at hand. And for Jobs, it was to re-create himself. Thus, each set about to do what he did best.

But before they could begin there was the matter of ownership. The first step was to incorporate. That officially occurred on January 3, 1977. In mid-March the company bought out the original partnership for $5,308.96. This second move accomplished two things at once: it reconfigured ownership to allow for the presence of Markkula and those key employees who would follow, and it finally got Ron Wayne out of the picture.

By all accounts, Wayne, who had spent months dreading the inevitable call from Apple's creditors, was thrilled to get a check for $1,700. Given that his stock would one day be worth tens of millions, Wayne might appear to be the greatest loser in the Apple story; but seen from another perspective, he was a winner, because that check put him in the select ranks of Valleyites who ever made money from a start-up.

Having killed off the old Apple, Markkula now had to construct a new one to take its place. And the first step was to redivvy up ownership. This is a painful moment in any new start-up. Typically, the founders have spent months, even years, devoting their life to building the firm. Then along comes some Daddy Warbucks, who has done nothing for the company except write a check, and he demands the lion's share of ownership—in the process diminishing the ownership of everyone else. And though the total value of those diminished shares may actually be greater, it is still a bitter pill; one that further stresses the already tense relationship between the players.

That was certainly the case at Apple, turning long-standing fissures into fractures. The restructuring meetings took place during succeeding evenings in the cabana by the pool at Markkula's house in Cupertino—showing that while he didn't like confrontation, he didn't mind controlling the setting to his advantage. There, in the setting of a rich man's backyard ("See?" it whispered. "You can have all this too."), Markkula dropped the bomb: he wanted one-third of the company. And that, in turn, meant that he wanted to be the largest shareholder.

The grown-up had spoken. The reaction of the two founders was as diverse as their personalities. Jobs accepted the proposal; he was beginning to understand that this was what it took to build a real company, and the fantasy of being a powerful, albeit progressive and benevolent, business tycoon was taking over his dreams.

Woz was agreeable too, but for entirely different reasons. He had frankly been amazed that anyone would put big money into Apple, and already predicted to his parents that Markkula would lose it all. But Markkula's folly wasn't really his concern, because Woz had no intention of staying with the company. His wife was dead set against the financial riskiness of a start-up and she was pressuring him to stay with HP and move to Corvallis. Woz's workmates tried to talk him into going as well.

Only Rod Holt appraised the offer with a hard eye. Markkula, he saw more clearly than the rest, "had a certain arrogant bearing and the subtle self-confidence of those people who have a lot of money and believe that somehow or other they have a birthright to it. I was suspicious." Nevertheless, like many revolutionaries when they encounter real money, Holt went for the gold: even a few percent ownership of a big successful company would make him a rich man.

But acceptance wasn't enough. Markkula was smart enough also to demand commitment. With Jobs that was easy: he was already in with both feet. As for Holt, Markkula was largely indifferent, except that he wanted to make sure the sardonic anarchist could be trusted. So he personally checked all of Holt's references for the last twenty years. There were to be no revolutions at Apple except those of Mike Markkula's choosing.

But the real commitment Markkula wanted was Wozniak's. Not part-time either. Woz had to quit HP and join Apple. No new tech company ever becomes great without a resident engineering guru. Though Markkula had great expectations for Jobs, he also believed the young man could be replaced. But Woz was a different matter. Without him, at least until an engineering department was created, Apple could not go on.

Moreover, the guileless Woz was completely transparent; Markkula knew he was hesitating about committing himself to such a risky venture. It was obvious in Woz's behavior. He griped about Jobs getting too much of the company, suggesting that his old partner would never make it in the real working world the way he, Steve Wozniak, had. He prevaricated every time the conversation turned to his future with Apple.

If Markkula had a sense that Woz was hesitating, Jobs knew his old friend well enough to realize that Wozniak, and thus the whole enterprise, were at great risk of being lost. He told that to Markkula and Holt at secret meetings. And he set out to do what he had done so well all these years: turn Woz's head and heart.

Getting people who *want* to be part of a start-up to stick around is hard enough; convincing someone to give up everything and stick around when they believe the enterprise is doomed, is almost impossible. But, of course, Jobs had faced those odds with Woz before. Only now his partner was an adult with a solid career, a wife and parents who no longer believed in the good intentions of Steven Jobs.

Faced with this, Jobs put on a full-court press the likes of which Woz had never before experienced. He cajoled Woz, he begged, he threatened. He had mutual friends call Woz and try to convince him. He even went to the amazing length of entering the lion's den—the home of Woz's parents—to solicit their help . . . bursting again into tears (hey, it worked the first time). Holt joined in too, telling Woz of the magnificent technical opportunity of creating his own product line.

But it was Markkula who proved decisive. Emotionally beaten down and exhausted, Wozniak was ready for a lifeline. Markkula threw it to him, telling the young man that only at Apple would he be able to take his genius and convert it to real wealth. For Woz, who had never been that concerned about money, the world suddenly became crystal clear. It was so simple now to say yes. "Once I decided I was doing it to make money," he said later, "it made the rest of the decision easy."

To the disbelief of his parents and his wife, Woz quit Hewlett-Packard and joined the fledgling, and to his mind doomed, company.

But if Markkula demanded enormous sacrifices of time and energy from his new partners, he was unwilling to make them himself. In what would become characteristic of his tenure at Apple, the longest of any employee, when the time came to step up, Markkula backed off. He told the others he had no intention of running Apple on a day-to-day basis. Rather, he would do it by remote control—or, as he said it more colorfully, he would put in the money, and find someone else to mind the pennies.

5.1 Commander Scott

The man Markkula picked to be Apple's first CEO wasn't far away. A thirty-two-year-old bachelor, Mike Scott was obese (a situation he made worse by usually wearing a too tight T-shirt), wore aviator glasses and was perpetually tense. He burned off most of his nervousness by walking around with clenched fists and twisting his short hair around his finger. And when that wasn't sufficiently pacifying, he sometimes went ballistic.

Yet, on other occasions, Scott could be stunningly sentimental, delivering bouquets of flowers, taking staffers—usually the lowest-level employees—en masse to a movie or cruise.

On first glance, Scott would seem the very antithesis of the cool, debonair Mike Markkula, yet the two had an unusual bond. Both had been hired by Fairchild on the same day in September 1967. They had adjoining offices. For a few months Markkula had even worked for the younger Scott. But most amazing of all to the two men was the discovery that they had the same birthday, February 11. They made it an annual ritual, even after their careers took them in separate directions, to have their birthday lunch together.

During his tenure at Fairchild, Scott not only worked with Markkula but also reported to Gene Carter, Don Valentine and Charlie Sporck—all of whom would play a role during his tenure at Apple.

As Markkula's career took him deeper into marketing and eventually to Intel, Scott's talents led him to manufacturing and to National Semiconductor. And whereas Markkula's proved to be a mixed career success but a huge financial victory, Scott, though he never became rich, showed he could not only rise above the pressure cooker of life under Charlie Sporck but become a rising star at National. Starting in marketing, he in time moved over to manufacturing, becoming overall director of the company's hybrid circuit family.

But then his career hit a wall. As he recalls: "In 1976, after three years at the company, I turned down the chance to head National Semiconductor in Hong Kong. And that was not the thing to do if I wanted to keep advancing through the ranks." So, by the time his annual birthday lunch with Markkula rolled around a year later, Scott was looking for a way out. "That's when Mike told me about the two Steves and this intelligent terminal they had called an Apple I. He also told me they had a follow-up machine, the Apple II, in prototype.

"Mike also showed me the preliminary business plan. Apparently, the two Steves had not only never written such a plan, but when Valentine visited them and mentioned one, Jobs replied, 'What's a business plan?' We laughed about that."

Then Markkula made his pitch. Recalls Scott, "Mike said to me, 'I can sell more of these computers than you can make. Why not come over and run Apple? Right now it's run by a couple of inexperienced kids, but it's got a great product, and a market that's about to take off.' He wanted me on board to handle the details, which he never liked to do. Mike never liked to do the dirty work." Turn it into a real company, Markkula told Scott, and you may find yourself president of a company even bigger than Fairchild or National.

In the days that followed, Scott sat in his office at National and played out scenarios in his head. "It's like a chess game," he would say a few years later, "except the moves continue to happen. The challenge is to put together a system that works without being minded and has its own checks and balances. I wanted to see if I could build [such] a system from scratch."

He told Markkula he was in.

Adding the first new employee at the newly reorganized Apple, especially since this new arrival was also the CEO, was a potentially risky maneuver. But it all seemed to go swimmingly. Markkula, in his usual diplomatic/passive way, didn't force Scott on his partners, but merely suggested him as a possible candidate. Woz and Jobs agreed. And that was that.

But beneath the surface, things were much more complicated. Woz initially welcomed Scott, pleased that the company would finally have a pro who would get his next design built on time and in volume. But Woz would also soon learn that same professionalism also expected some discipline from the notoriously flighty chief technologist. And once Mike Scott put that pressure on Steve Wozniak, Woz would turn on him.

Jobs meanwhile, at late-night meetings with Woz and Holt at Bob's Big Boy in Cupertino, played Hamlet. Holt would recall, "Jobs didn't know whether he wanted to run the show or not." He had been intellectually mature enough to accept the idea of professional management, but emotionally unready to accept the reality of it. He saw the brief interval between Markkula's suggestion and the final vote on Scott as his last chance to decide to run the company himself. To others he couched his doubts in concern about how well Scott's meat-and-potatoes style would fit with Apple's antiestablishment philosophy—but it was really about power.

In the end, Jobs voted for Scott. He accepted that his apprenticeship as a business executive was not yet over and that Scott was the best man to lead Apple. For now. But Jobs also knew that one day his training would be complete and he would be ready. And when that day came, Mike Scott would be in Steve Jobs's crosshairs—and not even his birthday pal would fight to save him.

Mike Scott, thrilled at the challenge facing him, had a dim premonition: "I wondered whether I could really get anything done or whether we would argue all the time. My biggest concern was whether Jobs and I could get along. He was concerned that I wasn't doing consumer stuff. I was concerned that he didn't know what he was doing." But that was all. He failed to neutralize his greatest threat while he still had the chance.

Mike Scott joined Apple for some stock and a salary of $20,001, which was a fraction of what he had been making at National, but a dollar more than anyone else at Apple. But as everyone in Silicon Valley knows, it's the stock that matters—and here Scott was in a dangerous position. "I realized pretty quickly," he says, "that as president I was over the two Steves and Markkula—yet all three of them had far more ownership of the company, and thus more power, than I did."

Scott's first task as Apple president was to tell Jobs to bathe. Steve had only marginally improved his hygiene since his Atari days and it was now becoming a problem within the crowded confines of company headquarters. It was Scott's first test: could he stand up to the young founder?

Oh yeah. Twenty years later, Mike Scott laughs. "I think I'm *still* the only person who can stand up to Steve Jobs. I told him. And he did listen, but always, as I learned with Jobs, he had to get something back. In this case, I had to agree to read a book by some Indian guru that argued—obviously against the evidence at hand—that eating only fruits and nuts was so purifying that you never had to take another bath."

Scott came away from this encounter, and the many that followed, with considerable respect for the young founder. "The great thing about Jobs was that you always understood where you stood with him. He *never* said what he thought you wanted to hear. His positions were always well thought out, and he always told you where he was coming from. It could be very stressful, but the trick was not to take it personally."

Wozniak was a different matter. Like everyone else, Scott thought Woz a genius; but unlike the rest, he was less forgiving of the young man's eccentricities. "Woz was very, very creative, but it came in spurts. And he would cover himself during the in-between times. He'd never say he wasn't making progress on a project. Instead, he'd say everything was coming along just fine, and meanwhile he would be waiting for the little light in his brain to switch on and save him."

Scott's frustrations working with Wozniak were a warning of what was to come as Apple hired more and more computer whizzes. And to his credit, Scott heeded that warning, ultimately creating "a parallel management structure in engineering just to make sure the engineers got their annual reviews, their laundry done, etc." In the near term, it was clever strategy, freeing first Wozniak, then those who followed him, to devote themselves to innovation—and produce the great Apple products of the next seven years. But in the long run, well after Scott was gone, it created an environment at Apple that led to failed or misdirected projects that never rose above their own self-indulgence.

5.2 Undressed for Success

The biggest challenge faced by Scott and his growing team immediately after its incorporation in early 1977 was getting the Apple II ready for introduction. Since his design breakthrough at the end of the summer, Woz had been perfecting his design. It was now nearly ready.

Holt too had come through as promised. He'd had his own design breakthrough, abandoning the traditional linear power supply used by the other personal computers for a more sophisticated switching power supply normally found in advanced instruments. The result, in what was historically the Achilles' heel of personal computers, was a major improvement in reliability, efficiency and, best of all, size.

Thanks to the efforts of these two, the finished Apple II would contain just 62 chips (other personal computers had more than 100) and weigh less than 12 pounds (compared to 20). In fact, the II was so light that the company even considered putting lead weights inside to give it a more "serious" heft.

Jobs, meanwhile, had gone back to Howard Cantin at Atari and hired him to design, as he had with the Apple I, the printed circuit board for the II. As was becoming his signature, Jobs wanted a world-class design. So when Cantin returned with a merely adequate first design, Jobs sent him back to the drawing board to produce a crisper (and thus more reliable) design. Cantin grumbled that he would never work for Jobs again, but Steve Jobs got his board.

But there was still something missing. A case. The personal computing world had changed radically in six months. Ever since the appearance of the Pro Tech machine, no computer company with any hope of survival dared to introduce a new model not encased in steel. On top of that, rumor had it that a Commodore machine, the Pet, was about to be introduced. Tandy was reported to have something in the works as well—and it was bound to produce a slick machine to sell to all its loyal customers at the thousands of Radio Shack stores.

So the Apple II needed a box. But not just any box. As was his gift, Jobs had visions of merchandising grandeur. The II, he decided, would not have a heavy, crimped metal enclosure like the Pro Tech machine, but instead a smoothly curved hard plastic case. Said Jobs, "I got a bug up my rear that I wanted the computer in a plastic case." His exemplar was the Hewlett-Packard calculator family, as well as the cool new European-derived appliances that were showing up each week in the Macy's advertising supplement in the local paper. Jobs visited the Macy's store in San Francisco just to hang out in the kitchen department and study the toasters and mixers.

As for what the actual design would look like, Jobs only knew what he didn't want: neither the concept designs he had solicited from a guy he knew at Atari nor those from the departed co-founder Ron Wayne. The Atari design was way too space age, full of complicated—and probably expensive—curves. Wayne's design was a clunker, with a Plexiglas cover and a tambour front that looked like a cross between a record turntable and a rolltop desk.

Jobs was at his wit's end when an old workmate of Wozniak's at Hewlett-Packard suggested a designer. Jerry Mannock had worked as a case designer at HP, grew bored with the endless stream of identical instrument boxes, left to design products for a company that made devices for the handicapped, felt unappreciated, quit, sold cars, traveled and finally set up his own struggling design firm in his house.

In January 1977, about the time the new Apple team was organizing itself, Jobs called Mannock and invited him to the next Homebrew meeting. Mannock arrived to find Jobs holding court, amazingly keeping up three conversations at one time. "I'd never run into anybody who did this," he later said. Mannock was impressed, especially when Jobs made him the fourth.

What I need, Jobs told him, are three plastic cases for my new computer. And I need them in twelve weeks. He offered Mannock $1,500 to complete the mechanical drawings of those cases, payable on acceptance. Mannock refused; he wanted his money up front. "These were flaky-looking customers and I didn't know if they were going to be around when the case was finished." Jobs, flush with the new deal with Markkula, assured him that money was not a problem.

Mannock took three weeks to come up with a design, but it was a beauty, one of the classic designs of the electronics age. Thanks to Mannock's brilliant amateurishness (he'd never designed a computer case before) and Holt's low-profile power supply, the Apple II case was smooth, simple and elegant—best of all, it made all the other computer designs of the next five years look like tractors beside a Duesenberg. Mannock even made a foam mock-up of the design. It wowed everyone who saw it. He got his $1,500; but Jobs refused to pay him the additional $300 for the mock-up.

Jobs brought a similar sense of quality to the company's new logo. Until now, the Apple logo had been a rather complicated ink illustration of Sir Isaac Newton sitting in a wide landscape reading a book, his back resting against a tree. Above him, hanging from a branch, was a glowing apple, presumably about to fall and impress the famous noggin. Wrapped around this image, which was in a crest shaped like a car radiator, was a windswept banner reading "Apple Computer Co."

It was not a bad logo for a head shop, but it was all wrong for a computer company that wanted to be the class of its field.

This time Jobs got what he wanted on the first try. At Regis McKenna's outfit there was a young art director named Rob Janov who had an intuitive feel for what Jobs was looking for: simple, graphic and knowing. "Steve always wanted a high-quality look," he recalled. "He wanted something that looked expensive and didn't look like some chunky model airplane." Janov drew the simplest and most iconic apple shape possible, then tried to identify it even more by having a leaf sprout from the top and cutting a deep cleft into the bottom.

Still, to Janov's mind the image still looked too much like a cherry tomato. So to give it scale, as well as to make a sly play on "bytes," he carved away a bite mark on the right side of the apple.

Now it needed color. Janov chose a rainbow effect in stripes from the top to the bottom of the apple. For the main body of stripes he chose a spectrum from yellow through red to violet. But the top stripe was to be different. In a brilliant stroke, he made it and the leaf the same brilliant apple green—a color so uncommon in industrial graphics, even in that postpsychedelic era, as to be unforgettable.

Being a professional, Janov realized that printing such a logo would be expensive because of the problem of bleeding between the colors. So he proposed that thin lines be drawn between the stripes to separate them. Jobs, who had been hovering over the project from the beginning, bugging Janov by day and Regis by night, wisely nixed the idea. Apple was going to go first class.

Mike Scott would later say, "That damned logo was an endless headache. Nonstandard colors, seven separate print runs and then varnish on top of everything to keep the colors from bleeding. God knows how much it cost Apple over the years."

5.3 Happy Days

Like a good field general, during this period Jobs seemed to be everywhere at once. For a short while yet, until Scott came on board and learned the company, Apple was still Jobs's playground, and he intended to make the best use of every second.

Meanwhile, Apple couldn't wait around for its new CEO. A signal event in the personal computer story was coming up fast. Steve Jobs, perhaps more than anyone in the industry, realized that this was a point of inflection, a dividing line between the players in this industry and the also-rans. And Steve Jobs was going to be a player, whatever it took.

The event was the first West Coast Computer Faire, slated for May in the underground Brooks Hall across from City Hall in downtown San Francisco. There had been several other personal computer shows in the preceding year, including that one Jobs, Woz and Kottke had attended in Atlantic City the previous summer. But most had been held in technology backwaters like Trenton, New Jersey. This time the Computer Faire would be in the Homebrew Heartland, and could be expected to draw not only every one of the 1,500 club members but thousands of influential Silicon Valleyites. After years of sandlot ball, this was the big leagues.

Jobs also assumed, correctly, that this would be the first show where the major players, such as Commodore, would roll out their new models. Jobs had seen what it was like to stand with the rest of the losers at a card table with a paper sign taped on the wall behind you and watch real professionals like Pro Tech in their flashy booths with smoked Plexiglas displays and carpeting and stacks of brochures. He was never going to let that happen again.

Yet, as he was doing all of this preparation, Jobs still had to run a real company. Apple needed to move out of the garage, ramp up for production of the Apple II and start hiring employees. Every day presented a new and seemingly insurmountable distraction to getting ready for the Faire.

The first step was to get the money. That is, establish Markkula's line of credit. Don Cviestusa, who was with Bank of America at the time, remembers seeing Jobs and Woz shambling into the B of A building in San Jose to meet the corporate loan officers. "To those professional bankers," he recalls, "Jobs and Wozniak couldn't have looked any stranger than if they'd just landed from Mars."

But with Markkula's collateral they got the credit line.

The next step was to find a new home for the company. They located an office suite on Stevens Creek Boulevard on the other side of Cupertino. Suite E-3 was just 2,000 square feet, neighbored by a weight-loss clinic and an employment agency, in a shingled building all but indistinguishable from the thousands of other Silicon Valley concrete tilt-ups. But to the young Apple team it was miraculous, especially after a year in the Jobs garage. And, like new start-up teams before and since, they reacted to their new home by behaving like six-year-olds. In the evening, Jobs, Woz, Espinosa and Wigginton would sit in different parts of the office and try to ring each other's phones first.

The suite itself was divided in two by a plaster wall. One side was administration (desks) and the other the laboratory and factory (lab tables). Several times each day, the entire crew would troop across the parking lot to the Good Earth restaurant and eat tofu and fruit smoothies and share their dreams. So important did the Good Earth become to the Apple gestalt that in the years to come all of the headquarters facilities it would either lease or build would be within a few blocks of the restaurant.

In the modern Silicon Valley, where high-tech parks stretch for fifty miles in every direction, populated by 5,000 companies and 750,000 workers, it can be hard to remember the isolation in which the early Apple operated. Most of the rest of the major Valley companies, such as Fairchild, Amdahl, Intel and National Semiconductor, were five miles away, on the other side of the Valley floor near the San Francisco Bay. HP and the Stanford Industrial Park were ten miles to the north. The closest tech enclaves were tiny clusters of three or four companies a mile away to the west on Bubb Road (Zilog, Measurex) or east (Four-Phase, Timeshare) on Sunnyvale-Saratoga Road. The businesses surrounding Apple's little office suite included a Chevrolet dealership, Cali Bros. grain and feed, Cupertino Nursery, the Old West Steakhouse (a popular breakfast place for bikers) and United Auto Parts (a favorite among street racers). In the modern Silicon Valley one can walk into any coffee bar, supermarket or restaurant and hear conversations about field programmable gate arrays and Internet search engines; but in this era Silicon Valley was still crowded into a few enclaves buried in the still regnant Santa Clara Valley—and none of those tech communities were anywhere near Apple.

Perhaps because of that, this was in many ways the happiest time in the Apple story. No fame, no glory, no bureaucracy, not even much money, just the little band working day and night against enormous odds. Everybody took on whatever job needed to be done. Every decision was meaningless, yet momentous. And at night, long, deeply felt discussions at the Good Earth, making plans that—incredibly—came true.

While Jobs and soon Scott were constructing the skeleton of the company, Woz and his team of hippies and teenagers were trying to get the Apple II built. Their deadline was even earlier than the Faire. An ad placed by Jobs in the Homebrew newsletter had set the II's introduction date as April 30. Given the Valley's history of product slippage, lags between introductions and actual shipments, that was awfully soon.

Moreover, Woz was running into the realities of working at the cutting edge of technology. For example, other companies were misrepresenting shipment dates and product specifications as well. Thus, Woz had planned to put in the II a hot new read-only memory chip from American Microsystems Inc., located just down the street. But when the time came to order, AMI just couldn't deliver and Woz had to settle for a lesser chip from Synertek. Similarly, a linear chip in the II's new keyboard proved to be hypersensitive to static electricity and crashed the keyboard every twenty minutes.

But these were technical problems and technical problems could be fixed—especially once the engineering team learned how to work with one another and around Woz's eccentricities. In particular, one of the traits that distinguished Woz from most technical (but not artistic) geniuses was his combination of lassitude and a need for acclaim. It was Holt, the only adult in the group, who made this discovery. Woz loved to come up with new ideas, but would then do the minimum required to prove it could be done. He was content to merely breadboard a working demonstration; after that, in his mind, the actual process of turning that design into a clean, reliable working prototype was scut work, mere window dressing, to be done by lesser mortals. Worse, Woz wouldn't even do that much if he didn't have someone to watch what he was doing and be impressed by his genius.

"I hardly ever trusted Woz's judgment," Holt said later.

The solution, Holt quickly realized, was to constantly stay on Woz's ass, demanding that he establish benchmarks, prepare diagrams and demonstrate results—and to keep the young genius constantly surrounded by acolytes before whom he could show off. For his part, Holt took on the quality-control job, using multimeters and oscilloscopes to test every part as it arrived and every computer as it was finished. The Apple II was not going to be another Altair.

Hardware was only half (well, three-quarters) of the story. Both Markkula and Scott, when he arrived, were convinced that the success of the next generation of personal computers would depend upon a systems approach. This was the Intel marketing model applied to consumer products. It wouldn't be enough, they agreed, to simply ship Apple II's in a box with a few instructions, leaving customers to figure it out by themselves—not if they were going to reach beyond the Homebrew types to mainstream markets.

Scott and Markkula had an idea of just who those new customers would be. Almost from the day he joined the company, Markkula had been working on a more sophisticated business plan. It was just the type of organized structural activity that was natural to him but alien to the two Steves. What slowly dawned on Markkula as he prepared this document was that, for the near term at least, personal computers had essentially three markets.

To date, only one of these markets had been developed: computer hobbyists, a group distinguished by deep, almost obsessive understanding of computers, a pride in the technology for its own sake and a near-messianism about particular hardware models and software programs. This was an ardent market, but a comparatively small one. And it was being fought over by what would soon be scores of competitors.

But Markkula also saw two other, infinitely larger markets that were still unprospected. One was professionals, especially doctors, who had a native curiosity about any new technical gizmo and the disposable income to purchase it. With this group, which would eventually merge with the hobbyists, Markkula first identified what would eventually be known as *early adopters*, a sizable and growing population that every tech company would depend upon to pay the high prices needed to cover the high development costs of emerging technologies. In the process, Markkula, who had always been known as more of a detail than a visionary marketing man, proved he could run with the best marketing seers.

The third market Markkula identified was even bigger—and more ambitious. This was the fata morgana of high tech in the 1970s: the home. The home consumer market tantalized with its millions of customers and billions in potential sales. But it only looked easy. One giant electronics company after another had been badly bruised (or dashed to pieces) trying to crash its way through the front door of suburban America. Still, the Apple II might be the product to do it. Markkula, the happy tinkerer, mused that maybe the computer could control operations around the house, like the sprinkler system.

For a guy who had made his reputation as a stickler for detail, this was a pretty wacky business strategy. There were no market figures for total size or estimated demand or just about anything else. It was mostly wishful thinking—*very* wishful, as it would turn out, given that doctors would prove to be among the last groups to buy personal computers, and the home controller would still not be a household feature twenty years later.

At least Markkula knew he was dreaming. John Hall, a group controller at the pharmaceutical outfit Syntex up the road in Palo Alto, didn't have that option. Markkula brought in Hall, a casual acquaintance, to turn those fantasies into hard numbers. It was work Hall had performed for many start-ups in the past. Scott was now on the scene, and he also enlisted Hall to help construct a bill of materials and project manufacturing costs for the II.

Markkula hoped to pull Hall in as Apple's vice president of finance, but after two weeks of vacation time constructing Apple's revenue predictions, Hall decided to steer wide of the little start-up. "I didn't believe the business plan and Mike Markkula didn't believe it. I felt it was a weak plan strategically." Nevertheless, because hope springs eternal, in exchange for his work Hall asked for some founders stock. Markkula turned him down, so Hall took $4,000 and went back to Syntex.

As a Valley veteran Markkula knew that, pipe dream or not, a written business plan was a crucial first step to building a company. Everybody knew most business plans were fantasies. But that didn't matter—what counted was the spirit of the company as conveyed in the plan: the moxie of the business strategy, the technical acumen of the staff and the chutzpah of the management. That was the key to raising money. It also helped in recruiting talent. And, what the hell, they could always rewrite it.

Amazingly enough, Apple never really had to. Probably the most famous business plan in Silicon Valley history (if you don't count the ones, like MIPS, so technically brilliant that they were funded from notes written on place mats) was that of James Treybig, who walked out of HP, sat down for six months at Mayfield Fund venture capital and produced a plan so prescient that the company it created, Tandem Computers, hit every one of Treybig's sales and profit predictions for the next five years.

Apple's plan, though much less celebrated, was nearly as remarkable. In the details Markkula was wrong, but in the larger predictions it was dead on. For more than a decade (critics would say even longer), Apple's three markets remained early adopters, professionals and home users. That was the good part. The bad was that, in being such an accurate prognosticator, Markkula also made his first big mistake. The fourth market, bigger than all the rest, the one he neglected to list, was corporate customers. Obviously, during this era of minicomputer hegemony, it was hard to imagine a PC ever sitting in an office. Yet that day came, and Apple, so identified with the other three markets, would spend the rest of its history trying and failing to reach this new market. Meanwhile, johnny-come-lately competitors, not tied to this installed base of consumers, grew fat and rich off the business market.

5.4 Making a Show

The Computer Faire was just days away and Apple still wasn't ready. There were the usual little things, such as the business cards not being back yet from the printers.

But there was also one very big thing; a deal breaker: no enclosure cases for the computers. Working with Mannock, Jobs had learned that there were basically two ways to mold a plastic enclosure for electronic equipment: reaction injection or structural foam. Reaction injection, which filled an epoxy mold with polyurethane via an expansive chemical reaction, was the cheaper method because of the lower setup costs. But its weakness was that the reaction didn't always produce enough pressure inside the mold to fill all the edges uniformly.

By comparison, structural foam used metal molds to hold hot, pressurized plastic as it was injected into the form. The result was more reliable and smoother, but much more expensive up front for the tooling.

For once, Jobs's inclination toward quality abandoned him. The rationale was that since the business plan predicted no more than 5,000 Apple II's would ever be built and sold there was no way to justify in volume the tooling costs of the better method. Since that had never stopped Jobs before, he either got a temporary case of the cheaps, didn't care or was overruled by Markkula.

Whatever the cause, it was a dumb decision. The first cases came back a disaster: bowed lids, pockmarked and uneven surfaces, incomplete edges flashing, filled voids—just about everything that could go wrong with molded plastic. But now there was no going back. The whole team spent the final days slicing off overpourings, sanding down lumps, puttying holes and, ultimately, spraying the crude cases with beige paint. They left for the Faire knowing that some of the machines had no air vents and, if left on too long, would burn themselves up.

The team spent the night in Union Square at the St. Francis Hotel—a big deal for guys who usually slept in dingy apartments or on the office floor—then got up early in the morning to head across town to Brooks Hall, where just eighteen months before Woz had purchased his first 6502.

In an age when a show like Comdex can draw 200,000 people to three giant halls in Las Vegas to see thousands of personal computer vendors, it is hard to capture the pocket-sized thrill of that first West Coast Computer Faire. Even with the spate of new personal computers on the market, as well as the rise of the first home computer retailers, to own a personal computer in 1977 was to still feel isolated, a pioneer, unsure if there really was anyone else out there.

But 13,000 people walked down the ramp into the underground hall that weekend. It was the gathering of a tribe that had little idea it even existed. Jobs had been right: this was a turning point, the galvanizing event that pushed personal computing from being a mere novelty into a real product with a real market. No computer company of any size could now look at those 13,000 souls and still dismiss home computing as a marginal business.

By the same token, those thousands of engineers, computer buffs, teenagers and the simply curious who entered the hall, past the messy stacks of mimeographed advertisements and flyers announcing show-only sales, had little trouble distinguishing the real companies from the fly-by-nighters. The Faire was set up as a central body of larger and more elaborate booths leased by the big companies like Commodore and Processor Technology, surrounded by a ring of smaller booths filled with people selling everything from manuals to T-shirts to loose chips. This was the slums of the personal computing industry, populated by quick-buck artists, one-shots, poor up-and-comers and folks who sold stuff on the periphery of every electronics show.

The amateurishness of these little outfits was evident in their pathetic little displays. Form followed dysfunction: long-haired guys in glasses and T-shirts with limited business experience talking to equally inexperienced business owners selling arcane, usually undocumented products ("You don't know what 8K ROM DIP packaging is?") and hawking their wares out of torn-open boxes and paper bags. Most didn't take checks, much less credit cards, could rarely make change and looked surly when you asked for a receipt. And that was only if you managed to get their attention as they talked to one another, old friends or their neighbors in unintelligible technogook. These were obviously people who still believed it was about technology, despite the evidence from the center of the hall. They were so utterly doomed that they didn't even know it.

And there, amid this detritus of the first personal computer revolution, Jobs and Wozniak, as they toured the Faire, could see the sorry booth of Computer Converser Corporation, with Alex Kamradt selling Woz's box and already fading into history.

Kamradt wasn't alone. Much of Homebrew lined that outside wall. Its day was almost over. From the instant you walked into the Faire you knew a sorting had already taken place between the early winners and the never-gonna-bes. The eye and mind gravitated to the center of the hall, where you could see the big booths, with their professional-looking displays and their even more professional signs: Cromemco, Altair, Processor Technology, Tandy. But, most of all, you saw Apple. It was right in front. By identifying the importance of the Faire early, Jobs had been able to sign up the best booth site in the show. And if the company's display was small compared to some of the others, the $5,000 that had been spent on location, professionally printed business cards, signage and flyers and black draping for the tables had a dramatic effect.

So did the team of Apple employees, all dressed in suits behind the tables. Markkula had wisely ordered everyone to dress up. So Regis took Jobs to the elegant Wilkes Bashford haberdashery in the city to buy him a suit. It was the beginning of Jobs's noted sartorial style. (Years later, when the pair were walking through San Francisco past that same store, Jobs turned to Regis and said, "Did I ever tell you about the first time I shopped here?" Regis, knowing Jobs too well, suppressed a smile and replied, "No, Steve, you didn't." Jobs then launched into a long, convoluted story featuring a blind man who gave him directions and a host of other phantasms. When he finished, Regis said, "Actually, Steve, I brought you here. Remember?" "Oh. Yeah," Jobs said, and walked on.)

When you walked up to the Apple booth that first day of the Faire, you sensed you were in the hands of pros. And you knew you were when you saw the sleek beige computer with the brown keys and the color image on its screen. Now *this* was what a personal computer should look like. It was an impressive enough of a presentation that Apple would field more than 300 orders in the next few days—more than 2 percent of the show's attendance, half again as many orders as the Apple I enjoyed in its year of existence. For weeks after, people would walk into Apple's offices off the street, having found the address on the show brochure, count out twelve $100 bills and walk away with a machine.

In later years, when Apple became a success, the first West Coast Computer Faire was presented not just as a turning point in the company's history but as an unalloyed triumph over the competition. This wasn't quite true. The show's organizer would later say that Apple wasn't the strongest exhibitor. The issue of *Byte* magazine covering the show never even mentioned Apple. And there was a host of anecdotal remembrances from attendees that other companies had better exhibits.

But that revisionism missed the point. Apple had no dreams of taking the Faire; there were simply too many big, experienced players in contention to ever accomplish that. For now, Apple only wanted to be seen as a real company, to make the cut, to leave the ranks of the losers in their crude booths on the periphery and be seen as a real player out in the middle of the floor. In that, Apple more than succeeded.

There was one other lesson to come out of the Computer Faire. In the midst of all the hard work, Woz decided to play a practical joke. Exactly where he found time to do it is anybody's guess, but Woz had always had found that extra little bit of energy for a joke. It was fun, it built morale and it made him feel superior to the straights. It was also Woz's little revenge on Markkula, Scott and, most of all, Steve Jobs for having stolen his pure little computer, forced him out of his dream job and made him against his will into a tainted entrepreneurial capitalist.

It was a simple joke. Woz spent $400 printing up (secretively, in Los Angeles) a bunch of lime-green broadsides announcing a new computer: the Zaltair, an Altair using the hot new Z-80 microprocessor and featuring "BAZIC" programming language. It was a pretty crude joke, but an effective one, because it separated the illuminati, who caught the joke instantly, from the unenlightened, who stood in slack-jawed acceptance of every bit of news from the industry, and most of all from the poseurs, who pretended they knew what they were talking about.

Woz and his techie confederates distributed the flyers around the show, then awaited the response. There wasn't much. The pros laughed and everyone else dutifully stuffed it into their plastic shopping bags with the scores of other promotional sheets, never to look at it again. Only MITS got angry, especially when it noticed that the flyer included a money-back guarantee on all Altairs. For a company suffering from quality problems this was not a joke. Soon an ad hoc Altair SWAT team was racing around the show floor stamping NOT REAL or FRAUD on every Zaltair flyer it found. As it turned out, they were in a race with Woz and his crew, who belatedly realized they might be liable for all those returned Altairs and were in a panicked search for the papers as well.

But the practical joke nevertheless managed to hook the biggest fish in the pond. Woz showed the flyer to Jobs, who bought the story completely, shouting, "Oh my God! This thing sounds great," and expressing relief that the performance chart on the back showed the Apple II a close third.

It was the first salvo in what would be an ongoing war at Apple, sometimes cold but more often hot, between the techies and the suits. The techs would always believe themselves intellectually (and thus morally) superior to management; and management would be forever convinced that the techies were brilliant children, forever plotting puerile games, and rarely to be trusted with responsibility.

Meanwhile, Wozniak had gotten his revenge. He had put into place the first brick of the countermyth that Steve Jobs was not really a technologist at all, but a brilliant fake, a parasite on real geniuses like Stephen Wozniak. This contrary image, regularly fed by just enough evidence to seem true, would haunt Jobs for twenty years.

But Jobs too got his revenge. Never again would Wozniak be trusted by Apple management. Never again would he be given decision-making power. And never again would he be allowed to run loose. The day would come when Woz would need that influence—and would find that he had long ago frittered it away.

5.5 Sandbox's End

The Apple Computer that came out of the West Coast Computer Faire was different from the one that went in.

It had a new product. It had orders. But, most of all, it had Mike Scott. As Scott saw it, his job was to turn Apple from a day-care center into a real company . . . fast. There was no time to delay. Scott knew well what happened to companies with fast growth. It took everything those firms had just to keep from blowing up under the stress of success. One tiny crack in the operations of one department could open up under pressure and split the company in two. That's what had happened at Fairchild, where too much talent and too little discipline had set off a devastating chain reaction. Markkula's former company, Intel, was emerging from just such a crisis.

Scott knew that he had to move fast. He had to staff up the administrative offices, construct a financial department, organize production in such a way that it could scale up to tens of thousands of units per month, build a marketing department, establish national distribution channels, stay on the engineering department for product upgrades and meanwhile find funding for the next round of company growth. And while he was doing all of this, he also had to control the founding children, who had little idea what it took to create a real company and who resented him for trying to do so.

Woz was the immediate problem. He refused to take anything but his own work seriously. And even on his own projects he was notoriously mercurial, working feverishly one moment, blocked the next, and forever at risk of going off on some technical tangent that momentarily appealed to him. Sometimes Scott couldn't move Woz at all, and then he had to bring in the big artillery of Markkula—who, for example, had to convince Woz to remove the word BULLSHIT from the Breakout game he was adapting for the Apple II.

Jobs was another matter altogether. Here Scott faced a dangerous, potentially fatal dilemma. In so many ways, Jobs *was* Apple. Rod Holt might say that "Scotty could fire anybody. But it was hard to imagine Apple without Steve Jobs." From the first confrontation, Mike Scott had prided himself on his ability to handle Jobs. But there was another side to the coin. Scott knew as much as anybody at Apple that Steve Jobs was too great a talent to lose (and, given his stockholdings, almost impossible to fire). The young man had extraordinary vision and an amazing capacity to make those visions real. But he was also a tyro, who believed he could do any job better than the person doing it, no matter how experienced. That included Mike Scott. Jobs also was indifferent to organization charts, ignored job boundaries and, depending upon the situation, treated employees, suppliers and customers like lovers or like dogshit.

He even disrupted board meetings. As an appalled Scott watched, at one such meeting, Jobs put his smelly sandaled feet up on the table. "Get your dirty stinking feet off the table!" bellowed Markkula. "Then put out your disgusting cigarette!" Jobs shouted back, demanding that the room be divided in half between smokers and nonsmokers.

Jobs was the most dangerous man in any organization: the irreplaceable destroyer. Scott had seen other characters like Jobs in his Silicon Valley career, but none so magnificent in this combination. Almost from the first day, Scott knew that "Jobs cannot run anything. He doesn't know how to manage people. After you get something started he causes lots of waves. He likes to fly around like a hummingbird at ninety miles per hour. He needs to be sat on."

A CEO can sit on the largest shareholder, but he cannot crush him. Jobs had to be given work and some responsibility. And every time he saw wiggle room, Jobs stirred up trouble. In setting up the company offices, Jobs got into a shouting match with Scott because he wanted the more expensive white desks for engineers while Scott wanted the cheaper gray models. They clashed over the layout of workflow. When Scott implemented a badge security system and gave Woz badge number 1 for having invented the computer, Jobs number 2 for creating the company and Markkula number 3 for being the first chairman (the rest were Fernandez #4, Holt #5, Wigginton #6, Scott #7 and Espinosa #8), only Jobs objected. He, in fact, threw a tantrum.

The exchange, as remembered by the other employees, went like this:

Jobs: "Am I number one?"

Scott: "No. Woz is number one. You're number two."

Jobs: "I want to be number one. Can I be number zero? Woz can be number one. I want to be number zero."

It was at such moments that Scott wondered why he'd ever left National.

And it only got worse. Put in charge of purchasing, Jobs created chaos. When IBM accidentally delivered blue typewriters instead of the beige ones he wanted, Jobs went crazy, demanding they be returned and replaced. The same thing happened with the phone company. Worst of all, Jobs mistreated key suppliers, driving down prices and high-handing salespeople as if Apple was a Fortune 500 company and not some little storefront operation that would be swiftly dropped if it got to be too much trouble. As Gary Martin, a new employee, observed: "We were all asking, 'How can you treat people like that?' "

Jobs could, and he did. And he got away with it.

The problems with the two founders aside, Scott was having the time of his life as the CEO of Apple. While history would record Woz and Jobs as great entrepreneurs, the one true, classic entrepreneur in the early days of Apple was Mike Scott.

"It was so exciting," he recalls. "For the first time in my life I got to build from scratch the complete organization of a company. Up until then, I'd always had a corporate umbrella over me, protecting me. This time, I was completely on my own."

In this hothouse entrepreneurial environment, Mike Scott thrived. Despite its outrageous numbers, Scott's Apple during its first five years met all the revenue figures in its business plan. When he wasn't putting information-reporting structures into place at the company, or managing Jobs and Woz, Scott was browbeating suppliers into better deals. He instituted a program to collect debts in fifteen days, but only paying bills every forty-five days, in the meantime putting the liquidity to use. "At least we *did* pay in forty-five days—most companies promised thirty days and delivered in ninety," he says.

When Finis Conor, the CEO of Santa Clara disk drive giant Shugart, suddenly jacked up the price of its drives—of which Apple represented half of all purchases—from $30 to $120, Scott was ready. Rod Holt merely had to ask, "Should I use the plane ticket?" Scott nodded and Holt was off to Japan and the disk drive maker Alps with a $20 million purchase order in his pocket. (Shugart's owner, Xerox, was so mortified that a few years later it bought a piece of Apple—which Apple sold in exchange for a look at that company's research. And that is what led Steve Jobs to Xerox PARC.)

When Digital Equipment was late delivering a second PDP-ll minicomputer that Apple needed for its internal information network—perhaps because, as DEC CEO Ken Olsen had told Scott during an earlier visit: "Personal computers will never be big"—Scott ordered a sixteen-foot white rose wreath sent to DEC's lobby bearing a note reading: "This is what I think about your delivery commitments." The computer was on an airplane that night.

In those early years, Mike Scott ricocheted around the company. Not trusting Woz's assurances about the environmental toughness of the Apple II, Scott had a Sunnyvale neighbor, a carpenter, build him a wooden test chamber. To impact-test the machine, Scott threw it off the roof of his house.

This eccentric, sometimes poignant, personal touch was also in evidence in the early days of Scott's management. He maintained a small slush fund just for wacky expenses, such as an Apple hot-air balloon and a mainsail emblazoned with the Apple logo for Holt's yacht. One Christmas, when things had settled to a dull roar, Scott put on a Santa Claus suit and walked around the office dispensing gifts. When Randy Wigginton wanted to quit to make more money for school, Mike Scott offered to have Apple pay for the young man's college education.

Scott drove a battered Pinto to work for months until Apple, fearful of losing its president to an exploding car, ordered him to stop. For fun ("I wanted to make the day memorable for Steve") he ordered a white rose wreath with the inscription "RIP" and a note reading: "From somebody watching over your shoulder," signed "Anonymous," delivered to Jobs's office on his birthday. Scott today laughs at the memory. "Jobs threatened everybody, trying to find out who did it. It was five years before he learned the truth."

Thanks to a Hollywood connection, Scott had read a script of *Raiders of the Lost Ark* long before the movie went into production. So, when the film hit the theaters, Scott booked San Jose's Century Theater for a preview showing and invited all five hundred Apple employees. They arrived through two arbors of white roses (by now a Scott trademark) and then, as they entered the theater, were handed a single white silk rose by Mike Scott.

5.6 A House Divided

Like all new start-ups, Apple initially ramped up its employment by hiring friends and compatriots. Jobs, for example, hired Jim Martindale, an old workmate from Atari, to run production, Dan Kottke, home from college, and

Allen Baum. Woz hired his teenaged acolytes, Chris Espinosa and Randy Wigginton, the latter in turn hiring a high school pal, Don Breuner, as a part-time technician.

Mike Scott, as might be expected, hired pros. Gene Carter, who had worked with him at Fairchild (and, for a time, was his boss), signed on as head of sales and distribution. Sherry Livingston, from National Semiconductor, was hired as receptionist and secretary. She would gain Silicon Valley immortality as the secretary who made a million dollars when Apple went public—thus making her a model for staff workers everywhere. But, at the time, the only thing that convinced her to take a job at the unproven little company was Mike Markkula pulling open a desk drawer and showing her that it was filled with orders.

But the most important Scott hire, at least at the beginning, was Gary Martin, an accountant who had worked for Scott at National. Martin, on first seeing the Apple II, thought, "Who the hell is going to want this thing? I felt so sorry for Scott I tried to buy him lunch." But, no matter how dicey, new start-ups with their potential for founders stock, are the brass ring of Silicon Valley life. And since the Valley was and is one of the few places on earth that rewards rather than punishes entrepreneurial failure, there was every incentive for Martin to take the leap. The decision was made even easier by his current boss at National, who agreed not to let National know until Martin had given Apple a month's tryout.

Martin never went back.

Besides Woz's disciples, Jobs's contacts and Scott's workmates, there was a fourth type of new employee hired by Apple: the walk-ons. This group was exemplified by Wendell Sander, a Fairchilder who had been playing with an early Apple I for more than a year, designing his own memory boards and even programming a video game, based on *Star Trek*, for his kids. He walked out of a thirteen-year career at Fairchild to join Apple, later telling Michael Moritz, "If they had folded I could have gotten a job the next day. There wasn't much personal risk apart from the chance of getting a bruised ego. My career would not have vanished."

Sander's attitude was typical of many of Apple's professional hires. After 1974 and the worst recession the Valley had ever known, the local economy, driven by the rise of video games, minicomputers and consumer electronics, was on its way back. Experienced professionals were again becoming valuable, and well-paid, assets to local electronics companies.

With the arrival of these pros, the schism between the vets and the kids that had begun at Apple with the arrival of Scott now grew even more pronounced. Apple was now a company of both people who could get a job anywhere and people who probably couldn't get a job anywhere but Apple.

It was an impossible combination. But Apple did the impossible in 1977. The unlikely, and volatile, pairing of Steve Jobs and Mike Scott created a razor's edge of discipline mixed with creative license. The suits could for the first time take off their ties and be their weekend selves all week; while the freaks could at last function in a viable setting that channeled their talents. It worked so well—except for the occasional shouting matches—that soon the Apple corps began to believe it had created a whole new business philosophy.

5.7 Cutting Corners

A fact that has gone unremarked about Apple Computer is that it was Silicon Valley's first native company. Jobs, Fernandez and Wozniak were all hometown boys.

They weren't alone. Gary Martin was also a local, though, unlike the others, his roots reached back into old Santa Clara Valley. His parents had come to the Valley before the war and for years had run Martin's Market & Bar in downtown Santa Clara and delivered bread for Wilson's Jewel Bakery, still a Valley landmark.

Gary had grown up in the grocery store, attended local Catholic schools and then gone on for an accounting degree at San Jose State. In the meantime, he had also become a world-class judo expert, twice winning the NCAA championship, and at one point was ranked second in the world.

Few old Valley types ever made the crossover to the new Silicon Valley. And Martin's career might have taken a typical path had not the air freight company he was working for gone bankrupt at the end of the 1960s. Desperate for work as the economy was sliding into a recession, Martin took the bold step of signing on with National Semiconductor, a $99 million manufacturer of products he didn't understand.

He was at National Semi for five years, and for much of that time he served as a controller under a brilliant product group manager named Mike Scott. National Semi, Martin would recall, was as wild a place as its legend suggests: "It was completely wide open. Whatever it took to ship, we did." But within that madhouse, Martin could see that Scott was something special: a cultured man, who not only could run the business side of the operation but also could contribute to the technology. "The design freaks loved Mike because he was one of them. He'd studied nuclear physics at Caltech. I remember at one point Mike came in on weekends and wrote elegant programs for one of our devices. Not many managers could do that."

Martin was there the day a stunned and red-faced Scott stormed out of his office shouting in disbelief, "Mike Markkula just retired from Intel!" And he was there in April 1977 when Scott announced he was leaving National to join Markkula's new company. But three months later, when Scott telephoned and suggested they meet for lunch, Martin still knew next to nothing about that company.

By the end of that lunch, he not only had a better idea but also a job offer. "I was thirty years old. I remember going home and talking to my wife about it. We finally decided that if this Apple thing didn't work out, I could always go back to National. Besides, it would be a good way to meet venture capitalists if I ever wanted to start my own company." Martin also took the job because, the founders aside, Apple by now had a "very credible team," with Markkula, Scott and Holt. Thus, in the summer of 1977, Martin found himself in the Good Earth facility. "They gave me a box of papers and told me to get the company's books together."

Martin had expected the usual problems putting a company like Apple on a strong financial foundation. He assumed it would be the standard three-part process: first, hand off bookkeeping and accounting to professionals; second, reconcile payables with receivables; a third, establish a financial measurement cycle that worked to the company's benefit. In this endeavor, he had the full support of Mike Scott.

The immediate task was to find the pros. Scott had already hired Bank of America (the standard quid pro quo for a line of credit) to implement a payroll and withholding program for Apple. It would be B of A that wrote Apple's payroll checks. Martin, looking down the road to the day when Apple might be a publicly traded company with extensive reporting requirements, got the bluest-beribboned accounting firm in town, Arthur Young, to run Apple's annual audit. It was a nice side benefit that Arthur Young, trying to woo new Silicon Valley start-ups, offered a discount on the first year's work to rookie customers.

Duplicating National Semi, Martin put Apple on a weekly, "Sporckian" calendar—which, with its 53-week year, gave Apple an extra week each year to stick in where it would do the most good. Meanwhile, studying the balance sheet, Martin also concluded that the company would cross the break-even point in late September—so, in order to take advantage of a loophole on estimated tax (it offered the equivalent of a fifteen-month loan by the government in the form of taxes not yet paid), Martin chose to set the fiscal year at September 30. "I had no idea I was setting the rhythm for the whole company for all the years to come," Martin said later. In fact, the timing was perfect, because henceforth money could then be reinvested in manufacturing each winter in what was proving to be the busiest time of the year for personal computer purchases.

But by setting such a near date for the fiscal year close, and then bringing in Arthur Young, Martin had also set Apple up for a legal nightmare.

Apple, it seemed, already had a skeleton in its closet. Several times each week, a station wagon driven by a Los Altos housewife Hildy Licht (wife of Woz's old Homebrew friend, Harry Licht) would pull up to Apple to deliver stacks of finished, stuffed printed circuit boards and power supplies, and pick up a new order. From there she would select the proper number of boards and components stored in her own home and drop them off at houses and apartments throughout Silicon Valley.

It was a nice deal for Apple, because it was cheap, delivery was prompt and orders could be quickly modified without complaint. There was only one problem: it was illegal. Inside many of those houses and apartments were rooms crowded with women, some of them newly arrived Southeast Asian immigrants, as well as a few Mexican illegals. These ladies would sit there all day, stuffing boards, gossiping and watching soaps. They were happy to be paid piece rates. No one ever mentioned minimum wage, or Social Security, or workplace safety laws. And thus, for more than a year, the Apple II, promoted as the machine to liberate people from the slavery of bureaucracies and office work, was in fact being partially assembled in sweatshops.

No one outside Apple knew of the arrangement. But with this first audit, Martin realized, the accountants were about to learn everything. He later recalled, "The auditor from Arthur Young was this little Jewish guy named Fred, and he was very diligent. He didn't just want reports, he wanted to tally *everything*. At the time, the motherboards were being stuffed by a legit outfit in town, but the power supplies were being built by Hildy Licht and her little band of housewives. He wanted to see it.

"So we piled into a little BMW—me, Fred and in the back seat a new hire at Apple, an ex-cop named Brian Fitzgerald [later vice president of Intuit]. As we're driving over, I introduce Brian by telling Fred that Brian was kicked out of the police department for killing too many suspects. Fred starts to sweat.

"We get to Hildy's, our second manufacturing center. It's a house in Los Altos, and all Hildy's got to show is a box of parts. Fred asks, 'Where's the rest?' and Hildy walks over to a closet, flings open the door and points at a blackboard listing apartments all over the Valley. 'There they are!' Hildy says.

"We passed the audit."

"Looking back, the whole place was hysterical," recalled Martin. "And by that I mean both fun and insane."

There were also numerous shouting matches. The biggest were between Scott and Jobs. Jobs had a habit of purchasing equipment and not deigning to fill out the purchase order. Says Martin, "We were always surprised when the stuff would show up and we didn't have it in our budget.

"Finally, Mike Scott couldn't take it anymore. Right there in the middle of this thirty-foot-square room he started screaming at Jobs: 'Goddamnit! I'm calling an emergency board meeting. Either you straighten up or I'm out of here!' Of course, between him, Jobs, Markkula and Woz, you could say that the board was meeting all the time."

Unlike some of the others, Martin wasn't bothered by the shouting matches. "Hey, I grew up in a family store working with relatives. This was nothing." But what Martin encountered in the other room at the Good Earth office was unlike anything he'd ever seen. There in the laboratory, he'd see Woz, in a kind of communion with the Apple II. "What most people don't realize is that in the earliest days of the II there was no way for it to store its own code. We also didn't have a paper tape machine to download onto every night. So each morning, when Woz started up the machine, he would have to reload the entire operating code. That was hundreds of lines of code, and as near as I can tell, he did it all from memory. He *thought* in code.

"And that wasn't the strangest part. I remember walking in more than once and seeing Wozniak *talking* to the II. He would say something to it, while he typed, and then the II would reply on its screen in hex[adecimal] code. Then Woz would talk and type some more. It was as if they were carrying on a conversation, like a patient father teaching a dutiful child."

5.7.1 Breaking the Mold

When the numbers came in, it turned out that Apple had made $775,000 for the 1977 fiscal year. That was about Hewlett-Packard's annual budget for coffee and cinnamon rolls, but in the still tiny world of personal computing it was proof that Apple was now a serious competitor. Even better, orders were tripling by the month, with no sign of slowing for months, even years.

Meanwhile, Scott was scrambling. In one respect, he was the best kind of start-up company president because he had no sense of protocol when it came to getting things done. He would scrub the toilets, deliver boxes to UPS, pick up lunch for employees, whatever it took. In Wigginton's words: "Scott's motto was let's make some money. Let's get something out the door." It was a good philosophy, but it ran into resistance.

One was staffing. Given the pace of orders, there was no way the little company could ramp up manufacturing, especially board stuffing, fast enough to keep up with demand. Scott's solution, a not uncommon one, was to contract the work out. But outsourcing was expensive and Apple didn't have much money. So Scott cut corners by using Hildy Licht—in the process putting himself in some bad company. He later justified it by saying that he only hired Hildy, and how she chose to do the assembly work was her business—but that wasn't enough, especially not from a company that claimed to have cornered enlightenment.

The other obstacle, as usual, was Steven Jobs. With his usual sense of grandeur, Jobs wanted to create a professional-looking manual to be placed in the box with the Apple II. Such a manual was seen as a perfect project to keep Jobs out of the way. After all, how could he screw that up?

By being late, actually. Before long, deliveries of the company's computers were being held up waiting for Jobs's literary masterpiece. Finally, exasperated, Scott cut through the Jobsian knot and ordered the waiting II's to be sent out with simple data sheets (xeroxed in the shopping center across the street) showing the computer's features and describing how to set it up. Now it was Woz's turn to object. He argued that serious users would want information on subroutines, source codes, even a copy of Sander's *Star Trek* game. Fine, said Scott, just to end the conversation. If anybody asks, we'll send him the stuff you want. Henceforth, that collection of hard-core Apple II material would be known as the Wozpack.

Without knowing it, Scott had set a pattern for lousy manuals that would haunt Apple for years. Both Jobs and Woz had been right: users really did want extensive, professionally prepared documentation. Yet even the manual for the Apple III at the beginning of the 1980s would leave users dumbfounded with its kiss-off opening: We will assume you already know how to use a computer . . .

In the end, the only thing that saved Apple on the documentation front was that the manuals and user packets created by its competitors were even more awful.

But sweatshops and miserable manuals were minor compared to what came next. The punishment for Jobs's uncharacteristic decision to go with cheaper packaging wasn't over yet. In September, about the time the first audit was taking place at Apple, the tooling for the Apple II's enclosure broke down at the contractor. No plastic box, no computer. Scott was already running as lean as he could within the company's limited resources; this breakdown threatened to shut Apple down through the end of the year. That was enough to kill the company.

"It was life or death for us," Scott would remember. Unanswered orders backed up, as did the finished boards from the sweatshops. Meanwhile, new employees, crucial for the company's growth projections for 1978, were put on hold. Apple prayed they'd still be around when Apple could at last afford to hire them.

At a time when the slightest flicker in a struggling young computer company's reputation could scare off its entire market, word was out in the incestuous Homebrew world that Apple was in trouble and might not last out the year.

Steve Jobs was the person who got the company into this mess, and it fell upon him to get the company out. He was also the perfect man for the job. Fear turned the dials up high on his reality distorter. He jumped on a plane for Seattle to visit the same plastic molding company, Tempress, that made hundreds of thousands of HP calculator cases each year. It was a long shot that such a company would take a risk on such a small order from a financially desperate firm. Robert Reutimann, Tempress's vice president said later, "I thought to myself, 'Does he know what he's doing?' I was a little afraid of going ahead with the project. I thought, 'Here comes another guy with big ideas.' "

But Steve Jobs had talked his way past such skepticism before. He did it again. He talked Reutimann into taking the contract, then, in a new twist that showed he was already learning something about management, sweetened the deal with an incentive of $1,000 for every week that the new mold was delivered before the deadline. Apple was back in production in less than eight weeks—a nasty financial hit still, but not a crippling one. By December, orders were not only being filled but once more tripling by the month.

Jonathon Martin, the first Apple baby, was born in 1978 to Gary Martin and his wife. He was followed soon after by a child born to secretary Jean Richardson. The company was still so young and new that it had no medical coverage for pregnancies. So Martin and Richardson simply established a new employee program—a "baby bonus"—and awarded the first ones to themselves.

5.8 Lost Boy

As usual, the vagaries of daily business at Apple barely touched Woz. He already had most of his staffers, as well as a regular supply of walk-ons who had stopped by to see what was up and stayed to help.

Thus, at least on the job, Woz could happily hide in his hermetic world and play with his technology toys. He was content to work all hours of the night, drag himself home in the morning, work on the computer he kept there, then race back to work.

Unfortunately, try as he might, real life kept impinging on Stephen Wozniak. His wife, Alice, had long since grown tired of playing a distant second to silicon chips and cathode-ray tubes. And if she felt excluded from her husband and his friends during the garage days, the situation had only grown worse as Apple became a real company. Now Markkula and Scott, sensing what was coming, were keeping her at arm's length. "Steve was told not to bring me to Mike Markkula's house in case they discussed company business," she said later.

Finally, unable to take any more, she threw Woz out. He took to sleeping on a couch at the office, where he was happiest anyway. Meanwhile, as the trial separation moved inexorably toward divorce, Woz suddenly and suspiciously (one can hear the whispers of others) got interested in not giving Alice any stock as part of a possible settlement. In the end, Markkula intervened, at the request of Woz, and connected the young genius with a lawyer. Alice Wozniak, after seventeen lonely months of marriage, nevertheless managed to walk away with 15 percent of Woz's stock.

Meanwhile, for Woz it was like being free to live on the Island of Lost Boys. He could now spend all of his time at Apple playing with brilliant teenagers to his heart's content. Sure, there was always some grumpy grown-up like Holt or Scott to make them clean up the work they'd started, but that wasn't much of a sacrifice for all the fun in between.

The walk-ons saw all this fun and wanted to play too. And Woz, with his legendary lack of discrimination, let them stay. It was the perfect setting for disaster. And that disaster arrived in the eccentric form of Cap'n Crunch himself. John Draper was now out of Lompac prison, and looking for work. Contacting Woz, Draper proposed designing a new board for the Apple II that would turn the machine into a powerful automatic telephone dialer.

Only a fool would hire a convicted felon to go back into his old line of work. But Woz, in fact, was thrilled with the idea, dreaming of programming his computer to harass a friend by dialing his phone a thousand times. "It would have been one of the great products of all time," he said.

Others at Apple were terrified. And with good reason. Chris Espinosa looked at the card—called the Charlie Board—and instantly saw that it was in fact the ultimate blue box. With a little research he concluded that a dozen Apple II's equipped with Charlie Boards and networked together could pull down the entire U.S. telephone system. With other Apple engineers, and without Draper's knowledge, he secretly tried to modify the board to remove its hacking capabilities. Jobs too, when he found out about Draper, went nuts.

Luckily, relief came from a not wholly unexpected source. Draper, who had decided that Apple management, especially Jobs, "were chickenshit and paranoid about having me on the premises," pulled up stakes and disappeared. Not long after, he was arrested in Pennsylvania and charged with stealing $50,000 worth of telephone calls. Once again, Cap'n Crunch was thrown in jail. But he would be back.

Meanwhile, one of the items found in Draper's possession during his arrest was an Apple II with a Charlie Board mounted inside. Apple wasn't charged, but the police inquiry finally brought the news to Scott that his resident technical guru had been risking the company on an illegal project. Scott was understandably furious. He went to Markkula and the newly constituted Apple board of directors and asked that Woz be fired. Woz, who got wind of this, was worried. "Scotty is the only guy that would [dare] fire me. That guy could do anything," he later recalled with a shudder.

Somehow, the directors managed to calm Scott down. Woz was too important for Apple to lose . . . especially now that he had turned his attention to a bigger (and more legal) series of technology challenges.

5.9 OUTSIDERS

The Charlie Board may have been a fool's errand, but it pointed to where Woz's head was going: continuously adding new capabilities to the Apple II via add-in cards. And for the next eighteen months, Woz and his crew kept the attention of the home computer industry riveted with one new hardware enhancement announcement after another. There was a ROM card, which quickly added more core memory (16,000 bits!) to the computer. A communications card, which made possible limited networking. A serial interface card, which took advantage of the newly emerging industry (IEEE) standard for linking together instruments, computers and peripherals. And a printer card, to allow the II to output to the newly introduced, low-cost thermal dot matrix and typewriter-like daisy wheel printers.

But that was just a warm-up. Input and output interface cards were useful, even valuable, but they weren't revolutionary. Memory was. Already, just a couple of years into personal computing, PC owners were discovering to their chagrin one of the fundamental maxims of computing: no matter how much memory you have, it ain't enough. That was because every leap in information storage soon led to a commensurate jump in the size of the applications and files using that memory. Pretty soon you were full up on stored memory, with no place to put new files unless you wanted to start purging out important stuff to make room.

Moreover, in 1977 you didn't have to be a computer genius to appreciate that the days of cassette memory were numbered. Cassettes were designed for audio, where inherent weaknesses such as tape stretch and flutter were nearly invisible. If a note in "Stairway to Heaven" bent a little more than it used to, your ears couldn't tell the difference. But have that same tape stretch while downloading the millions of ones and zeros in BASIC or the *Star Wars* video game and the whole system crashed. The microprocessor inside a computer like the Apple II used that flow of binary digits not just for information to process, but also to synchronize the entire chip with the cycles of electricity flowing through it. Slip a millisecond-long half-beat and it was like having motion-picture film jump out of its sprocket holes or, more precisely, like skipping a line on the answer sheet of a very long multiple-choice test.

And that was only part of the problem with tape. The other was that it was just too slow. Downloading a big program, such as BASIC, took so long you could literally go out to lunch and come back just as it was finishing. Like personal computers, cassette drives were a descendant of much larger and more powerful machines. Unfortunately, in the case of cassettes a lot more had been lost in translation. The long banks of big-reeled tape drives that were providing much of the storage for mainframe computers had the benefit of wide (thus faster information transfer), high-density (again, plus more accuracy), and thick (no stretching) Mylar tape, as well as multiple drive wheels to adjust tape speed with precision. By comparison, the cassette players used with machines like the Apple II were indistinguishable from the ones teenaged girls used to play Carpenters tapes.

But a solution was already waiting in the wings. Disk-drive technology was nothing new in mainframes, having been around since the late 1950s—and, coincidentally, invented just down the road from Apple at IBM in San Jose—but its implementation was. The disk drives of 1976 were giant spinning metal platters covered by iron oxide with read/write heads flicking back and forth on cantilevered arms across the disk's surface reading millions of bits of data off thousands of tracks in a matter of seconds. They were a technological marvel, but also a tough technology to get into reliable, mass-producible form.

Yet, by the early 1970s, most of the world's mainframe computers had switched over to a combination of disk and tape memory (a third form, drum memory, was abandoned). The minicomputer revolution gave an added impetus to the creation of smaller, less costly versions. Once again, it was the IBM San Jose crew that came up with a solution. They used a new design for the read/write head and arm—code-named Winchester technology, after nearby Winchester Boulevard (and the mall where Woz and Jobs were at the time playing Alice in Wonderland), which in turn was named after the famous Winchester Mystery House. With Winchester technology, the IBM team had a semiconductor-based technique for building disk drives that let mass memory tap into the magic of Moore's Law.

Soon the platters got smaller, as did prices, while capacity held its own. Adventurous little companies, such as Shugart, sprang up to license this technology and experiment with new formats.

The most fruitful of these formats (discovered first by IBM in 1972) proved to be a revisit to Mylar tape—only this time not a ribbon, but a flexible disk the size of an LP record, etched with rings of magnetized dots. One had only to pick up one of these pizza-sized, razor-thin sheets out of its case to appreciate how it got the name "floppy disk."

The Homebrewers, as always keeping tabs on the big-iron boys, had watched disk memory coming for as long as the club had been in existence. Everyone in the industry knew that floppies were the future of personal computer memory. But as many of them well knew, it was a long way from a sexy dream to the real thing. Still, being computer freaks, they were not inclined to wait.

There were a number of private attempts to bolt a floppy drive onto an existing Altair, IMSAI or even Apple, but the resulting jury rig was usually a slow, unreliable kluge. These failures became particularly frustrating when companies like Shugart took the process to the next step and began offering drives for 5¼-inch disks. If ever there was a disk drive *made* for personal computing, this was it. The drive would even fit *in* the box!

But like every other big step in the personal computer story, it only looked easy. One of the first companies to try to put a floppy drive into its computer was—no surprise—Processor Technology. Pro Tech teamed up with another company, Diablo, to build a disk drive with the necessary accompanying controller. Before the whole mess was over, Diablo had tried to back out, the drives proved unreliable and Pro Tech, having promised a disk drive for the Sol, finally had to offer a more expensive version no one wanted. It was the beginning of the end for Processor Technology. Two years later, Apple's first great competitive threat was gone.

But if the failure to offer a reliable disk drive killed some of the early players, successful designs opened the door to the arrival of hot new companies, such as Morrow, Vector Graphics and NorthStar—the last in an especially good position as the leading Shugart licensee.

Obviously, if Apple was going to stay in the game, it would need its own disk drive. And just as obviously, the only person to do the job was Woz.

5.10 Discopolis

Wozniak officially first learned of this new company strategy at a company executive board meeting in early December 1977. But he must have known of it ex officio for several months, because Rod Holt, who was also at the meeting, was already pissed at Woz for being his usual procrastinating self.

"Woz," he later told Moritz, "would take a product right up to the crisis point and do it." It was almost as if he needed the adrenaline spike of approaching disaster in order to create. Holt apparently wasn't the only member of Apple's staff to appreciate this feature of Woz's, because at the meeting Markkula walked up to the board and listed Apple's product goals for the next couple of years and put "Disk drive" at the top. Then he turned and pointedly informed Woz that he was to have such a drive ready by the January Consumer Electronics Show . . . that is, in four weeks.

Woz knew about disk drives, of course. He had thumbed through a Shugart manual during his HP days. He'd even momentarily played in his mind with a circuit that could control such a drive. But other events had intervened. Now Woz realized he didn't have a clue how disk drives actually worked—and he was going to have to find out, fast.

Over the next two weeks he pored over every manual and reverse-engineered every drive he could get his hands on. IBM. Shugart. NorthStar. The deeper he dove, the more Woz realized he was back to the same problem he faced with the color display: synchronization, this time between the computer and the read/write head. More research showed him a second problem, standardization, which he came to realize might be turned into an opportunity.

The synchronicity problem initially seemed a deal breaker. Understanding why it was so complex requires a little background on computer operation. A computer's CPU, in this case its microprocessor, performs a series of operations as defined by the software program under which it is operating. Each step of that program typically has two components: the operation it is supposed to perform and the data upon which that operation is to work. That data is waiting in a temporary holding area on the chip called the cache. But to get it to the cache can be a convoluted process, because that data can be sitting on a memory chip on the motherboard or it may be sitting at some address out on the disk.

The problem is finding that data and getting it to the cache before the processor calls for it, and getting it there at the proper moment to match up with the right operation to work on it—and do it accurately a million (these days, 400 million) times per second.

To accomplish this, the engineers at IBM devised an elaborate disk-drive controller that essentially put the CPU and the disk drive on the same clock, a system comparable to having two traffic lights working together a thousand miles apart. It worked, but it was enormously complicated and expensive.

The more Woz studied the design of this controller, the more he recognized its sheer superfluousness. Once again, his genius lay in being a maverick, in throwing out the received view and having the hubris to start over from first principles.

He cast back to his old design for the Shugart drive. Back then, without really understanding how disk-drive controllers worked, he had nevertheless come up with an elegantly simple solution. All that it lacked was synchronicity.

And that's when Woz made yet another legendary cognitive leap. *What if you just ignored synchronicity?* After all, why did the disk drive have to operate in perfect tandem with the CPU? Let 'em go their own ways. Let the disk drive self-synch. When the microprocessor wants something, it merely has to call for it, the disk drive will send it in and the cache will hold it in queue until it's needed. The data would behave like cars reaching the tollgate on the Bay Bridge. The commuters didn't all have to leave their houses in Oakland and Berkeley at exactly the same moment; rather they merely had to wait their turn through the tollgate before entering the bridge. On the far end of the bridge, San Francisco saw only a continuous, even flow of traffic.

As for the problem of standardization, the good news was that there wasn't any. IBM, which made the earth shake every time it moved, had forced its disk interface standards on the industry at every step of the way. Thus, you either played by Armonk's rules or you didn't play at all.

Except in the 5¼-inch format. That market was so new that it hadn't fully consolidated yet, much less standardized. Woz therefore had a brief window of opportunity to come up with his own design and, with brilliance and luck, convince the rest of the industry to follow. He made the best of his chance.

IBM had spent millions of dollars and tied up scores of engineers for months designing its disk drive interface. Wozniak did the same thing alone—and better—in two weeks. And he knew what he had done. He had outwitted Big Blue. It made Cap'n Crunch's escapades look like petty vandalism . . . and on top of it all, it was legal. Woz knew he was about to wow his peers in ways he'd only dreamed of.

But first he had to build it. And he had two weeks to do it in, including Christmas and New Year's. But then again, he no longer had a wife or a home. What else was there to do but work day and night?

That's what he did. Even on Christmas Day, he left his parents' house after opening presents and went into the office to work for ten hours. Throughout this banzai run he kept young Randy Wigginton by his side, trusting the kid to take on any tasks he handed off to him with a minimum of explanation. Day after day they worked on the disk drive. Woz constructing the board, Wigginton writing the code for the disk formatter, Woz creating the read/write software.

Woz at these moments became both superhuman in his creativity and animal-like in his focus and endurance. Holt, whose job it was to ride herd on the pair and make sure they did not leave any loose ends, actually began to worry that Woz might go crazy staying so deeply immersed. Jean Richardson, who usually unlocked the office in the morning, would often let an exhausted and delirious Woz out the door as she came in. "He was a ghost who came and went at odd hours," she would recall. "He worked through the night . . . Eating and sleeping didn't seem to matter."

By New Year's, the pair were testing the controller by storing and downloading data to and from a Shugart disk drive. It worked faster and more accurately than any personal computer disk drive to date. It wasn't finished, but it was near enough to risk showing to the world. They had run out of time. With Apple's management team, the pair jumped on a plane for Las Vegas.

They arrived in the evening. The show was to open in the morning. Woz and Wigginton helped set up the booth, then went back to their room to finish the drive. They worked through the night, taking breaks to cruise the excitement of the casino floors below. For Wigginton, just seventeen, Vegas was a revelation. He even had the typical adolescent thrill of sneaking his way into various games of chance. So, while he was helping change the world upstairs, his real excitement that day came from winning thirty-five dollars at craps.

So excited was Wigginton that when he returned to work he managed to erase the entire disk. It took him and Woz most of the predawn hours to reconstruct the lost data. At 7:30 A.M., once again finished, they tried to crash for the couple of hours before the show started—but they were too wired to sleep.

That morning, the Consumer Electronics Show threw its doors open to nearly 100,000 attendees. Hot-air balloons, hookers waiting outside, car radios booming out hundred of watts of sound, CB radios, screaming video games, porn stars signing autographs, $10,000 stereo systems, electronic toys—the whole panoply of human entertainment and desire, all filtered through the wonderful world of electronics.

The decision to exhibit at CES was a canny one by Markkula, the marketing man. Showing at the West Coast Computer Faire was one thing. Everybody in personal computing did that. But to show at CES was a statement; it said that the personal computer was no longer just a toy for phreaks, but an important new *consumer* product, one that would soon be sold to everybody who now owned a Pioneer receiver or a Sony television set. And to be there first among its PC competitors was a way for Apple to say that it best understood this future and was already prepared for it.

In that respect, Woz's efforts on the disk drive controller were superfluous to the event. Most of the people wandering the floors of CES had little idea of how a computer worked, much less the radical innovation of a self-synchronizing disk-drive controller. But it *had* served the purpose of giving Woz the deadline he needed to focus his brain . . . and guaranteed that Apple would be ready to show off the controller to the group that really mattered three months later at the second Computer Faire.

Now the basic design was done. Thanks to Markkula's artificial deadline, Woz and Wigginton (with Holt, as always, riding herd) had time to perfect their creation. In particular, after Howard Cantin proved too busy (and too angry at Jobs) to lay out the circuit board for the controller, Woz took on the job himself. For two weeks, Woz worked until two o'clock each morning, teaching himself circuit board design as he went.

It seemed to go smoothly until near the end, when, just as he was completing the design, Woz noticed a problem. It was a crossover between a couple of the conductor lines on the board. That junction had the potential to create a "feedthrough" of signals between the two lines and wreck everything. In just twenty marathon hours, Woz redesigned the entire board around a relocated connector and fixed the problem.

He really didn't have to do so. Feedthrough was an unpleasant, though seemingly inevitable, part of electronic life, and finding a way to reroute the wires around such a crossover was usually a daunting, if not impossible, problem of topology. But Woz not only fixed that feedthrough but then found yet another and redesigned the board a second time.

The result was an engineering masterpiece, one of the last great works of solo electronic design in the century. Even Woz knew he had done something amazing, later saying, "It's something you can *only* do if you're [both] the engineer and the PC board person yourself. That was an artistic layout. The board has virtually no feedthroughs." In years to come he would call it "the favorite design of my life."

Woz liked an admiring audience, and this time he got it in spades. Word had already leaked out about Apple's disk-drive introduction at CES. At the West Coast Computer Faire, the company that had used every artifice the year before to be seen as a major competitor now had no trouble being the star. *Everyone* went by the Apple booth to see the new floppy drive for the II. The hard-core techies came away dumbstruck by the beauty and simplicity of Woz's design. Even Lee Felsenstein, who never had anything good to say about Apple, would remember seeing the Apple disk controller for the first time: "I nearly dropped my pants. It was so clever. I thought: We'd better keep out of the way of these guys."

In two years, in a series of extraordinary creative bursts, Stephen Wozniak had designed one of the world's first personal computers, then built the first practical home computer complete with color display; he had also written the programming language for those computers, and now he had brought mass memory to the average computer user. Hardware, software, display and storage: Woz had pulled off an engineering hat trick that has not been matched. He was already a legend.

Yet Woz was still just twenty-five. For the next decade, his face, with its beard, bangs and glasses, would become synonymous with the new generation of computing whizzes. *California* magazine would cement that image forever with a cover story declaring him "The King of the Nerds," in the process adding a new term to everyday language. Woz's odd little obsession had changed the world, and given its happy victim a kind of immortality.

So there was every reason to assume that he was not yet at his creative peak and that even greater inventions lay ahead. But the disk controller would prove to be Woz's last great contribution not only to Apple but to high technology.

5.11 Persona

While Woz was secreted away working on the disk drive, Jobs was making a nuisance of himself. But a good nuisance this time. At a moment when the organization was beginning to consolidate into a real company, complete with the endless compromising and corner cutting that comes with bureaucratization, Jobs still held out for the impossible, but thrilling combination of "insanely great" solutions and world-class style.

It didn't make him popular with Apple's growing army of employees, but Jobs, given his character, didn't much care. And in sticking to his principles, he assured that Apple didn't, like so many hot tech companies, take its success and fall into early middle-aged complacency.

On top of being the corporate conscience within Apple, Jobs also played an equally important role outside the company. The metamorphosis of Steven P. Jobs was now nearly complete. His hair cut, but still fashionably long, his beard trimmed, wearing his finely cut suits, Jobs was no longer the unkempt hippie with questionable hygiene. As the confused 1970s turned into the materialist 1980s, Jobs was becoming *cool.* His unique blend of Buddhist obscurantism, vegetarianism, cold calculation and handsome raptor looks was capturing the imagination of a whole generation. To the early baby boomers, he was the hippie who hadn't sold out, who could spout koans and talk revolution while hawking an electronic appliance. To the late boomers, he was a proto-yuppie, sleek and predatory, still a kid but able to run with the Brahmins of Corporate America.

Jobs could never supplant Wozniak in the hearts of technology buffs; they would always see Jobs as a usurper and poseur. But Woz could have that crowd; its days were already numbered. The real audience now was the millions of young business professionals: middle managers, doctors, government bureaucrats, advertising copywriters, lawyers, college professors. They were the future of the personal computer. And Steve Jobs had their number. When the time came to buy a computer, and that day was coming soon, they would look at the Commodore Pets, the NorthStars and the Tandys, see only faceless corporations, and turn away. But then they would see a smirking Steve Jobs, smooth and maybe a little vicious, and the Apple ads that bore his stamp, with their sly balance of cheekiness, warmth and boomer sensibility—Regis's first Apple II ad showed a couple in their kitchen, the wife preparing a meal and the husband pounding away at the computer—and they would know where they belonged.

Here, from 1984, is an early appraisal (by this author) of how the Jobs Reality Distortion Field began to emanate out over the entire consumer world:

> Jobs's youthful pluck and hipness obviously struck a responsive chord not just among hackers and long-haired computer engineers, but also among the millions of young business people who had grown up in the sixties and early seventies, the flower children, the Woodstock Generation, the baby boomers who had sworn themselves to an alternative lifestyle, to the Amerikan revolution, good dope and com-

munity—but who instead cut their hair, put on business suits, grabbed their MBAs and dove into the capitalist world with more selfish greed than the forefathers they had once derided. No matter what they said to each other over quiche and white wine and lines of coke, they knew in their bones that they had sold out in a big way, and they hated themselves for it. As they drove home in their BMWs and Volvos to their singles apartments or single-parent kids, these [aging] children knew that they had become just like their parents—but without the family or the patriotism or religious faith or any of the other fascist institutions that made these sacrifices worthwhile.

Jobs reached these people better than anybody else because he seemed to be *one of them.* As they sat in their offices, with the dwindling mementos of their youth and their dreams, they would turn to an enormous photo of Jobs in his beard and wicked smirk and think, "That bastard did it. He stuck by his principles and still can tell the establishment to kiss his ass." Then they'd get a little thrill of excitement mixed with envy. The revolution hadn't been lost after all, their lives weren't a sham. The campus guerillas had merely evolved into corporate freedom fighters.

And in their hearts they wished they were Steve Jobs.

Regis McKenna understood better than anybody in high tech that while a good product can make a company successful, corporate immortality only comes when a client begins to personify an era. McKenna knew what he had in Jobs and played that card for all it was worth. Jobs, for his part, was clever enough not only to go along for the ride but to add his own odd, but shrewdly entertaining, twists.

By the time Apple moved to a new and much bigger facility a couple of blocks away on Bandley Drive, Jobs had nearly perfected his new persona. The new facility, hard by the Cupertino nursery and a few doors from the Donut Wheel, a longtime hangout for dating teenagers and swing-shift cannery workers, was fifteen times larger than its predecessor. In moving there Apple began the inevitable process of physically separating its operations.

Walking into the building, the first impression was one of considerable unused space. The second was one of anarchy. There were boxes and papers everywhere. Desks were piled with books or hardware parts or computer magazines. And nowhere was the mess greater than in Wozniak's cubicle, which, with its stacks of printed circuit boards, wiring harnesses and test equipment, looked like an unoccupied storage area for broken parts.

At the other end of the building, Steve Jobs was carefully constructing his own reality. The office itself wasn't as interesting as the ideas with which Jobs was perpetually filling the space. Almost from the moment he arrived—usually late, an insulting habit that grew longer with the years—Jobs would pepper the visitor with an overwhelming, and seemingly unconnected, array of questions, typically about whatever he had most recently learned about. "Have you read Kuhn's *The Structure of Scientific Revolutions*? No? I'll get you a copy." "What the Apple computer really is is a fractional horsepower motor. Or, rather, it's a bicycle." It was the conversation of a brilliant autodidact; wildly enthusiastic about today's intellectual discovery. Jobs never seemed to care if you understood what he was talking about—only that you understood that *he did.*

It was all crazy and narcissistic, the clever offense of an emotional bully who preferred that the people who faced him be on their heels. Long or short, the meeting would always end abruptly, as if what seemed like a budding relationship had suddenly, inexplicably, turned into a royal audience . . . and that audience had just ended. The visitor came away feeling intellectually and spiritually molested, thrilled that this already legendary figure should so appreciate the visitor's intelligence, not sure whether he had just been hustled, and mostly, just exhausted. But later, when you recovered and pondered what Jobs had said, you were struck that it was not only correct but sometimes even profound. It is the megalomaniacs who control the symbols and thus our imaginations. Jobs was, in fact, trying out new metaphors for the personal computer revolution, playing Pied Piper to anyone who came near, searching for the tune that would make them follow.

And once you the target had taken a first step in pursuit, Jobs had his answer and moved on. The Steven Jobs Reality Distortion Field—more accurately now a zone, as Apple itself began to manifest his personality—quickly became the most exciting, and terrifying, experience in Silicon Valley. You approached it at your peril.

But if Jobs was brilliantly transforming time and space at work, he wasn't so successful at home. About the time of the Second Faire, Jobs, his old high school girlfriend, and Dan Kottke had set up house in a suburban ranch home in Cupertino. They tried to be ironic about the process—nicknaming the style of the house they rented Rancho Suburbio Special, denigrating their square neighbors—but they were in fact playing out the same game as all of their other Homestead High counterparts, embracing the bourgeois lifestyle of their parents without admitting they were doing so.

It was all pretty conventional. Jobs and girlfriend played mom and dad, and Kottke was the man who came to dinner. He took to sleeping in the living room, while filling the spare bedroom with foam shards for the neighborhood kids to play in. Kottke was trying to be antic, but it was also a little creepy.

The relationship between Jobs and his girlfriend, for all the meditation and radical talk, was also conventional. Jobs went off to work at Apple each day, and his girlfriend stayed home and slowly went mad. She would later say, "I was really insecure and young men in their early twenties are not very good with women. They need to prove themselves. I was afraid to go out. I didn't have any money." Instead, she trashed the house, punching holes in the wall, knocking down shelves, writing obscenities on the wall with charcoal. And when she wasn't being destructive, she was pleading for help, calling Jobs at the office at all hours, demanding he come home to fix some small item like a broken light socket.

But there was one way to shatter Jobs's carefully constructed reality. His girlfriend became pregnant. Steve Jobs's reaction was predictable, but unconscionable: he refused to accept paternity. "Steve didn't care that I was pregnant," said the woman later. In a terrible expression of his own selfishness, the abandoned child had now abandoned his own.

But the woman didn't give up easily. Desperate, and increasingly without support, she took a job on the assembly line at Apple. Feeling sorry for her, Holt tried both to advise Jobs about his responsibilities and to get his girlfriend to take some training in drafting. Both efforts failed. Finally, the woman moved out—"I had to get away from Steve, Apple and people's opinions"—and, on Jobs's advice, headed to Oregon and the farm of that old drug-dealing con man from Reed, Robert Friedland.

There, in May 1978, about the time Woz was showing off the new disk drive in San Francisco, the child, a girl, was born. Jobs drove up a few days later and, in one of their last encounters for years, named the little girl Lisa. Then Jobs, unencumbered by such messy matters as fatherhood or marriage, returned to ever-growing fame at Apple. Lisa's mother, meanwhile, struggled to raise Lisa through odd jobs such as waitressing and housecleaning. Eventually she moved back to the Bay Area and the Peninsula.

During this period, Jobs exhibited some paternal responsibility by voluntarily paying a modicum of child support. Lisa's mother finally asked for a $20,000 settlement, and though Markkula suggested Steve should pay four times that amount, the young man balked at what he considered a shakedown. Soon the child-care payments became fewer and farther between. Increasingly desperate, little Lisa on government relief, her mother turned to the legal system for remedy. It worked. Whenever a payment was late, Lisa's mother, with the help of her family, would bring in a lawyer. And Jobs would pay.

Finally the mother played her trump card. Lisa was now a year old. Her mother asked Jobs to submit to a blood test to finally establish paternity. For some inexplicable reason—perhaps he believed he was now above the laws of organic chemistry—Jobs agreed.

The test, conducted by UCLA, established a 94.41 percent likelihood that Jobs was the father. Jobs still refused to accept the inevitable. By multiplying all the error margins, he was able to convince himself that the real likelihood was just 72 percent. And that is what he told the world: "Twenty-eight percent of the male population of the United States could be the father." It was exceptionally cruel phrasing. For having betrayed his vision of himself, Jobs wasn't content to merely deny the fatherhood of the child, he had to intimate that her mother was a whore as well.

It would be two more years before Jobs, now a famous public figure with a reputation to protect—and faced with the possibility of a $10 million lawsuit—agreed to a court-ordered settlement. It was a pitiful amount for this now multimillionaire: $385 per month and $5,856 to pay back the welfare administrators of San Mateo County for having helped raise his child. As with everything else to that point in his life, Jobs got off easy.

5.12 Ground Zero Cool

As noted, in September 1977, Apple had revenues of $775,000 for the fiscal year, with a dozen employees and enough profits to buy a few fried tofu meals at the Good Earth. The company was located in a single rented office. Three years later, Apple was a publicly traded corporation, valued at more than $1 billion, with sales of $118 million, profits of $11.7 million . . . and more than 1,000 employees. These employees were based in thirteen buildings, including eleven along Bandley Drive in Cupertino and others in locations as diverse as Texas, Holland, Ireland and Singapore. Apple was also the most famous new company in the world.

Covering that extraordinary distance in that extraordinary brief amount of time had less to do with Steve Jobs's vision or Stephen Wozniak's inventive genius than with the chaotic, but ultimately successful, infrastructure built by Mike Scott. It was a herculean task, and in the end it destroyed him.

It has been said that Silicon Valley's greatest contribution to modern business is its willingness to accept failure, and thus to celebrate entrepreneurial endeavors no matter how doomed. But its other great contribution is the endless résumé: the establishment of career paths that have nothing to do with longevity or seniority and everything to do with the perpetual hunt for a spot on the leading edge. The result is a gypsy workforce, hopping from job to job, sometimes staying less than six months, rarely sticking around for more than three years, before moving on to the next big opportunity.

Here is where the long-standing comparison to the Forty-niners of the Gold Rush really does hold true. When one claim begins to dry up, you abandon it and move on to the next diggings in hopes of striking a rich new vein. And in modern Silicon Valley that perpetual flow of talent is as diverse as assembly-line workers spending lunch breaks at recruitment fairs hoping for another dollar per hour, to top managers and engineers hopscotching from one hot new company to the next in search of fame and founders stock.

By the beginning of 1979 Apple had bubbled to the surface of the Valley's consciousness. The word was out that this strange little outfit, with its unlikely founders, was the biggest new deal in town. It wasn't long before talented people, most of them young, were converging on Bandley Drive, résumés in hand.

The only thing more difficult than failure for a new start-up is great success. And Apple was a supreme success. Within a couple of months after Apple had moved into the first Bandley building, it had to add two more. The newly hired employees moved in while structural modifications (without a city permit) were still being made. Soon those buildings too were filled.

In every way it was an exhilarating, terrifying mess. Every decision was made with the knowledge that it might prove fatal to the company—and yet those same decisions were often made on the fly, with little consideration or consultation, sometimes by people who had no responsibility for the result. Apple had no facilities manager, no legal officer, no corporate communications manager, some buildings didn't even have a receptionist. Security was a disaster, the organizational chart was only intermittently observed, and when all else failed, work was contracted out.

And yet, one of the miracles of entrepreneurial start-ups is that despite (some would say because of) this confusion they thrive. When employees don't have precise job responsibilities but only enthusiasm and loyalty, they often migrate to the work they do best. So, precisely because there are no rigid walls, employees in start-ups tend to self-sort by talent and desire.

Like Jobs, Apple was becoming cool. Because of that it increasingly attracted bright young people coming out of college. Apple was also beginning to dominate its market. While the other early contenders began, one after another, to stumble and disappear, Apple continued to gain market share. And that in turn made the company more interesting to other companies, big and small, who saw a market in designing software and aftermarket hardware for the Apple II. Soon there were scores of interesting new companies working to make Apple a success.

This external activity proved critical to Apple during this difficult period. First, it filled in the blanks—and there were a hell of a lot of them in the company's organization and catalog. But just as important, these outsiders could help grow Apple's market faster than the company, with limited capital and staff, could by itself.

Two examples illustrate what these other players could do.

Jef Raskin had been on the periphery of the home computer revolution from the beginning and with computers long before that. He had run a computer center at UC San Diego, working with the people who would later invent the Pascal computer language. He had been a visiting scholar at Stanford and worked with the crowd at Xerox PARC. He and his friends had also build Altairs and IMSAI.

Raskin had finally landed at *Dr. Dobb's Journal of Computer Calisthenics and Orthodontia* (Running Light without Overbyte), a hobbyist magazine that exists to this day as a technical journal. Raskin was an odd guy—he had resigned from UC San Diego by ascending in a hot-air balloon, playing his soprano recorder and proclaiming his departure—so when he was sent by the magazine to interview two guys building a computer in a Cupertino garage, he felt an instant bond with the company. He would recall, "I loved the name Apple instead of the techie names everybody else was using; it fit my iconoclastic spirit." He even helped the pair write a section of the Apple I manual.

Two years later, he was contracted by Apple to manage the company's documentation. Apple was in desperate need of help in that department, as a letter kept by Markkula from an angry customer of that era suggests:

> You fucking bastards. I bought an Apple with floppy and nobody, I mean nobody, in L.A. or San Diego knows how to use the sonuvabitch for random access files. I really feel "ripped off." Everybody talks about this great manual in the sky that is coming out soon??? Shit! Shit! Shit! I need this computer now in my business, not next year. Fuck you. I hope your dog dies.

This wasn't the only such customer "testimonial." In moving to the consumer market from the gearheads business, Apple had taken on the task of supporting these computer neophytes. It was failing badly. Obviously, Raskin had his work cut out for him. Unfortunately, as he quickly discovered, the one guy at the company who knew enough about the Apple II to write such a manual was leaving. Chris Espinosa, Woz's teenage acolyte, was off to Berkeley for his freshman year. Despite this, Raskin somehow talked Espinosa into writing a manual for the II that would once and for all explain to the neophyte how the computer really worked.

What happened next is a testament to the kind of loyalty Apple could instill in its employees, ex-employees and users. Espinosa worked on the manual all through the term, somehow managing to do his classwork as well. When the term ran out and his dorm room closed, Espinosa still wasn't finished with the manuscript. So, all his belongings stuffed into a backpack, he slept in computer labs on campus when he wasn't caught and in a nearby park when he was. Since he was also writing eighteen hours each day, the amount of time he actually slept was thankfully small. He typeset the finished manual on school equipment and delivered it to Apple just as the new term began. The finished "red book" proved a great success at soothing the customers.

Jef Raskin went on to give Apple's publications their celebrated look: clean, white, with splashes of color (Apple was the first of the home computer companies with color publications) and a witty style. By the end of the 1970s, Apple had hired Raskin to work inside the company. Three years later, he would lead the team that invented the Macintosh.

Dan Fylstra, by comparison, was an Apple enthusiast who never joined the company. Tall, with owlish glasses, and a long, blond premature comb-over, Fylstra had earned a Harvard MBA (at the same time Bill Gates was a freshman) while running a small personal computer software company called Personal Software.

Personal Software was, in its own way, a pioneer. It didn't design software, but licensed and marketed the creations of others. One of those creations was from a fellow MBA candidate, Dan Bricklin. Bricklin had an idea for a program to perform financial forecasting on a personal computer, and despite ridicule from one of his professors (*another* financial forecasting program, the professor said) Bricklin managed to get in touch with Fylstra, who'd been another of that professor's students.

Fylstra, who had researched the personal computer software market as part of his degree, recognized a good product idea when he saw one. He supported Bricklin's project, even lending him the one computer Personal Software had on hand, an Apple II. Bricklin in turn hooked up with a brilliant mathematician named Bob Frankston, and the two, creating their own company called Software Arts, worked long winter nights in a cold attic devising the program.

The result, marketed by Fylstra as VisiCalc, wasn't just a stunner, it was the first *fundamentally new* piece of software for the personal computer. Word processing programs, games, everything until then designed for the personal computer was essentially a watered-down version of a program already done, better, on mainframes or minis. But VisiCalc was sui generis; it was the world's first electronic spreadsheet. You could sit down and type in your indices and the computer would draw out a vast array, of which only a part appeared on your computer screen and the rest existed in virtual space. Then, when you typed in your data, the computer would automatically fill up the table. Then you could navigate around this giant matrix, checking out the results at the coefficient you desired—the motion itself providing a clue about personal computing to come.

But even more amazing, you could play 'What if?' with Visicalc. You could change an entry with the flick of a key and the *whole damn grid would recalculate itself.* Today, when spreadsheets are routinely bundled with word processing and other office productivity tools, it is hard to imagine the stunning effect of watching that recalculation occur for the first time. Calculations would take days to do by hand, so nobody ever did them. Even on big computers, processing time was far too expensive for everyday users to futz around with alternative scenarios. But VisiCalc was a reminder that the Apple II belonged to *you.* You could sit and play all night with different numbers. What happens if we raise prices by 4 percent? What if I hire the new controller for $4,000 a year less? What happens over the next eight years if I can cut the cost of goods sold by 3 percent per year and invest those savings?

For the very first time, the personal computer had an application that was all its own. Better yet, that application was the lifelong dream of every small business and new start-up company on the planet.

Not that Apple appreciated what Fylstra had. Moving his company to Sunnyvale, Fylstra showed up at Markkula's office with a prototype of VisiCalc and offered to give a demonstration. Markkula watched, unimpressed, and then showed the visitor a checkbook-balancing program of his own devising. Fylstra left, stunned but undeterred.

One person at Apple who did appreciate Fylstra was Jef Raskin. He too tried to convince Markkula and Jobs to buy VisiCalc, but when he was also turned down, he managed at least to get a leave of absence from Apple to join the fledgling software company. There he played an important role writing the tutorial section of the VisiCalc's manual.

In October 1979, Fylstra formally introduced VisiCalc. It was initially priced at $100, but soon was raised to $150 when Fylstra saw the market would accept that price with nary a blink. Even at its new price, VisiCalc took off like a rocket, within two years selling more than 12,000 copies per month, making it the first great personal computer software best-seller.

More than that, because it was initially available only for the Apple II, VisiCalc also legimitized Apple Computer. Now, for the first time, the average user had a reason, besides novelty, to buy a personal computer; it was a productivity tool, an investment that might pay for itself many times over. In the end, despite being turned down by Markkula, VisiCalc, as much as the Apple II or Woz's disk-drive controller, made Apple Computer. Mike Scott estimated that VisiCalc alone sold more than 25,000 Apple II's by the end of fiscal 1980, almost 20 percent of Apple's total unit sales.

Fylstra, Raskin and Espinosa weren't the only outsiders helping to turn Apple into a business and social phenomenon. There were hundreds of other manufacturers and programmers throughout the world working on Apple II-related products. Most were newcomers to the playground, but others, like ghosts, reemerged from the shady past. One of these ghosts, remarkably, was John Draper, back out of prison. This time Cap'n Crunch played it straight, designing a simple, but popular, word-processing program called EasyWriter that sold through Information Unlimited Software in Berkeley. It too helped the sale of Apple II's, Draper at last in some way paying back the two boys for all the times he'd led them astray.

It was through the efforts of all of these people that the Apple II soon had the largest software library of any personal computer—more programs, in fact, than the Commodore Pet, the Morrow Designs Inc. Adam, Vector Graphics and all the others combined. All these programs represented millions of hours of work by thousands of individuals, far more than Apple could ever have mustered alone. Moreover, in hopes of their own big score, these designers took all the risk, while Apple sold the box. And that in turn was why, as early as mid-1978, Regis could run ads proclaiming that the Apple II "is the world's best-selling personal computer" without indulging in too much misrepresentation.

5.13 Antibodies

Of course, you couldn't just wait for talented people to show up in the lobby with job applications. Knowing what slots needed to be filled and having no time to waste, Apple's veterans went out searching for talent. Not surprisingly, the places they chose to raid were also the ones they used to work for. Thus, Markkula chased employees at Intel, Scott at National Semiconductor and Jobs, still working out his lifelong obsession with Bill and Dave's company, went after Hewlett-Packard.

The good news was they were successful. The bad news was they were successful. Raiding top-notch companies for their best minds was a time-honored Valley tradition, and Apple went about it more honorably than, say, National Semiconductor had a decade before. But in raiding companies with strong corporate cultures, Apple also ran the risk of infecting itself with those same sensibilities.

That was what had happened to Intel just a few years before when a contingent from Texas Instruments had acted like a tumor within the body of its new employer. Eventually the group was either fired or absorbed into Intel's own special culture—but not before grinding the company to a near-halt and damaging employee morale.

Apple was now growing much faster than Intel ever had. Mike Scott, overburdened, had little time to extend his will over the organization, Jobs was too quixotic to do so and Markkula, ever retiring, would never have considered such a thing. So, lacking any structure imposed from above, these new employees fell back on what they knew: how things were done at their last job. The result was that by 1979 Apple was quickly dividing into fiefdoms, the largest of them ruled by the people hired by the troika. And each of these duchies had its own territory and culture.

There was a Hewlett-Packard contingent, characterized by endless, tiresome niceness and consensus building. Its strength was attention to details and quality. The HP crowd was exemplified by Tom Whitney, who came from HP's desktop calculator division (he was Woz's old boss) and took over Apple's engineering. Whitney, in typical HP fashion, quickly organized Apple's new product development under specific guidelines, each with its own forms and subcommittees. Project teams were created, each with its own leader. It was all so organized and enlightened and decent that it made everyone want to puke, but for the moment it worked.

The Intel crowd—and there were enough of them so that Andy Grove, a major Apple shareholder, even complained to Markkula about Apple's raiding—not surprisingly congregated in the technical operations, where it installed Intel's legendary engineering arrogance and "creative confrontation" (shouting). The best-known ex-Intel employee at Apple was Ann Bowers, the personnel director, who just happened to be Bob Noyce's wife. According to secretary Sherry Livingston: "Everything had to be done the Intel way. [Bowers] wouldn't go to the left or right." One of Bowers's first decisions was that everyone in the company would henceforth drink only decaffeinated coffee. The result was a general mutiny. "My biggest hiring mistake," Mike Scott would later say.

But the most outrageous enclave at Apple belonged to the recruits from National Semiconductor. Chip guys are notoriously savvy, crazy and mean, but National Semi employees were, as the company's promotion said, "The animals of Silicon Valley." They were the true spiritual descendants of Fairchild, without the sense of humor. Charlie Sporck, National's president, was the toughest of all. He ran National as if it was a billion-dollar factory floor and he was the world's greatest shop foreman. The assembly lines were dangerous, the administrative offices spartan when they weren't jammed with boxes and the sales force did whatever it took, from misrepresentation to borrowing a competitor's designs. And all of this took place under eerie, strobing sodium vapor lights that made daily life at National even more disorienting, strange and unhealthy than it already was. Years later it would turn out that during this period National was intentionally undertesting millions of chips destined to be used in military weapons systems and the space program. It was scary and depressing, but it worked: in the depth of the chip wars, only National Semi met the Japanese head-on and survived.

One might think that National would be the very antithesis of Apple Computer in the late 1980s. But, in fact, that's what made its people appealing to the new company, especially in the two departments where the hippie-gearhead mentality ran smack into the reality of running a serious business: sales and manufacturing. If the HP people were Scoutmasters and church deacons, the National Semi boys were thugs, who bullied suppliers, padded their expense accounts and lied to customers. Where the HP contingent said, "Why can't we all get along? Good products and good service are the best way to keep customers for life," the National Semi crowd's philosophy was "Fuck 'em. We can always find another customer."

As one Apple employee would later describe the contingent to Moritz: "There was a real sense that they were going to ship this shit one way or another and they were going to get the dealers to fix it. They more or less said, 'We're going to ship this sucker, to hell with the customer.' "

But there was another side to the National culture at Apple, and it was best represented by Roy Mollard, whose résumé included not only National but Fairchild before that. Mollard was from Liverpool, just like his old Fairchild boss Wilf Corrigan, after Tramiel the second-scariest man in Silicon Valley, and they both shared the same single-mindedness.

What Mollard brought to Apple, as its director of manufacturing, was a different facet of adulthood. Not the talent and maturity of Markkula, but the other side of being a grown-up, the hard-assed, no bullshit, "crack a few heads to make things happen" kind of adulthood. The adulthood of the guy who ran the graveyard shift at the cannery or led young recruits out of foxholes or who wore a title like "warden."

Mollard had no patience for the airy-fairy manufacturing line he inherited. Here was a company on the cutting edge of a new technology and it ran its manufacturing line as if it was building headlamps for Hupmobiles. Critical records, such as purchase orders and production rates, were kept by hand, division of labor appeared to be made up by the day and a single supervisor controlled twenty-eight assemblers. Other Apple employees felt free to wander in and out of manufacturing, asking questions, hanging out, getting their own orders taken care of first.

It was no wonder that Apple was barely able to build 150 computers and just fifteen disk drives per week. And senior management not only acquiesced in this mess but even contributed to it. Jobs, for example, had found a great deal on plastic, bought about two years' worth of inventory and had it stacked in the assembly area, where it took up nearly half the room.

This kind of undisciplined behavior was a drawing-and-quartering offense at National, and Mollard brought that attitude to Apple. In Mollard's memorable phrasing, his task, and that of his department, was "to hose out computers." In his mind, Apple's manufacturing department was the Augean stables, and he was there to clean it out, to get the computers on the loading dock and get them sold. And Mollard wasn't going to let anything stop him or his people.

One way he did this was to put the fear of God into his own staff. Out went the luncheon Ping-Pong games, in went hidden microphones and alarms. He hired security guards and fired anyone who wouldn't get with the program, including the quality-assurance manager. He reorganized the assembly floor into work teams, each with its own supervisor; and he removed every storage device, from drawers to cabinets, to make sure that no inventory could be hidden away.

And Mollard was just as tough on those outside his team. Jobs believed in an open company, in which employees could walk anywhere. Mollard, who had seen millions of dollars of National's inventory walk out in pockets, briefcases and salted scrap, quickly put the nix on that. Before long, the security guards were checking the names of every visitor for clearance. Steve Jobs complained, but ultimately deferred to Mollard. In the end, not surprisingly, Apple's manufacturing became a lot less fun and a lot more productive.

As incompatible as these three groups might seem, as long as Mike Scott (and the Apple dream) could hold them together they gave Apple extraordinary strength and resilience. The combination of Intel technology arrogance, HP's class and integrity and National's hardball attitude was every CEO's dream team. Better yet, Scott supplemented this triple play with individuals from across society, from academics like Raskin to outsiders like Wendell Sander.

It didn't always work. For example, in its rush to take some of the load off an increasingly overworked Holt, Apple managed to hire two people for the same senior position of running the engineering lab. One, as already noted, was HP's Tom Whitney. The other was Chuck Peddle, the man who had sold the 6502 chip to Woz and had once tried to buy Apple for Commodore; now he was just trying to join the company. Instead, he found himself redundant in the job for which he had been hired, and quit after a few weeks to return to Commodore and lead the attack against Apple. He should have stuck around, because Whitney's obsession with organization soon began to grind his operation to a halt in an HP-like blizzard of reports and reorganizations.

But despite such occasional snafus, Scott somehow managed to hold the whole snarling, infighting mob together long enough to tame most of its members into a coherent team. And those who couldn't give up their former allegiances either cracked or were driven out.

It was a virtuoso performance by a remarkable manager. Scott, because of what was to come, has never been given proper credit for his achievements at Apple. Successful Silicon Valley companies are like the old Soviet encyclopedias. Once you are purged, you become a nonperson, lost down the memory hole, and your entry in the company story is pasted over with a new, official history—in Apple's case, one that rewards the leadership of Steven Jobs . . . not the fact that much of the success of the early years occurred in spite of him.

The real credit is Scott's. Scott was neither as brilliant as Wozniak nor as charismatic as Jobs. Instead, to those foxes he played the role of hedgehog. The one thing this hedgehog knew was that if you didn't get products out the door, then you didn't have a company. And it was from this obsession to ship units that Scott's style arose.

Mike Scott could be a bully (he sometimes began memos with YOU ALL BETTER READ THIS), a Captain Queeg (one memo ordered employees not to talk in the hallways or while standing up) and a technocrat (he not only put into place a management information system that finally organized Apple's operations but also used it to run his own private spy system). But there was also that sweet side. Wigginton's tuition and the Santa Claus visit were just two examples. A year or two later, when the *Star Wars* trilogy first appeared, Scott rented the local Century Theater and took the entire company to see it, first sending them engraved invitations, then meeting them at the door with white roses. When some employees missed one of these movie outings because they were at a trade show, he called them to his office and escorted them to the theater in a bus tended by liveried waiters.

Scott was a CEO who could terrorize you one moment and at the next throw you a party. He would object to first-class travel for executives, then blow thousands on company entertainment at Christmas. He was alternately shy and in your face, cruel and embracing, a public man at the office and invisible in his private life. He was a man on a tightrope, and for three years he managed to keep from falling. He also made Apple into a real company; but in the process he divided the company into his enemies and his friends. Unfortunately for Mike Scott, his enemies were far more powerful.

5.14 Moolah

While Mike Scott was turning Apple into a real company, Mike Markkula was looking for money. And though he would remain at Apple longer than anyone else, it was his accomplishments in this search over the first three years of the company that would be his greatest achievement.

Markkula's first money search began in the fall of 1977, during the plastic case disaster. The company spent so much time patching bad cases, losing revenues during the shutdown and then ramping up to make up for lost time that it exhausted its cash reserves. That time, Markkula and Scott dipped into their own pockets for a one-time cash injection of nearly $200,000.

Neither, understandably, was willing to do that again. The next time Apple needed money it would have to come from pros. As it happened, even as he was writing the check Markkula already was talking to potential investors. He did so with trepidation. Even before 1977 a pattern had emerged with venture capital that had not been lost on entrepreneurs: the earlier you allowed in venture capital, the more you gave up control of your firm. Take their money early enough—say soon after the company's founding—and before they were done the venture capitalists would own your company. They might even throw you and the other founders out and put in their own guys to protect their investments.

So the strategy was to hold off accepting outside capital for as long as possible. Typically, in a successful start-up there were about four rounds of investment. The first, usually called the seed round, was the funding that set up the company and got the first product designed and built. Apple, with Markkula's money and Bank of America's line of credit (banks, by law, couldn't take a stock position), had made it through that round without outside investment. But ahead lay the second round, typically used to set up the company's manufacturing operations and distribution channels, a third round, often used to launch the follow-up product, and a final mezzanine round to prepare the company for the Big Payday: the initial public offering (IPO) of stock.

The Going Public Day of the IPO, if it ever occurred (and it did for only about 10 percent of all high-tech start-ups), was the reward to everyone—founders, employees and investors—who had helped make the company a success. Tens, even hundreds, of millions of dollars in stock wealth would be distributed that day to holders of founders stock.

Unfortunately, by then most of that stock would be in the hands of the venture capitalists and their funders, because in each of those rounds, in exchange for ever more money, the company would have given away 10 percent to 40 percent of its total value. Thus, it was not unusual for a company at the IPO to have given up 70 to 90 percent of its total worth to venture capital firms. One study, done in the early 1980s, found that in the typical start-up that went public, only the founder(s) and the first four employees realized more financial gain than they would have if they'd stayed at their old jobs.

By escaping the seed round, Apple had saved perhaps 30 percent of its stock for its employees—a fact that would be celebrated three years hence. But the plastic case debacle, a tiny Steve Jobs mistake that was now taking on enormous proportions, signaled the end of Apple's independence. The company would never be able to bootstrap its financing again.

For all the costs of venture capital, there were also some enormous advantages. Venture capitalists, because they had independent control of giant funds of $50 million or more, could provide a lot of fast cash. Moreover, they were not constrained by law from collusion, so it was not unusual for multiple venture capital firms to team up on an investment, especially the big-money later rounds. Most of the high-tech venture capitalists worked alongside one another in the 3000 Sand Hill Road industrial park on a hill above Stanford, and many joint investment deals were worked out over lunch at the Sun Deck restaurant there.

A second advantage of venture capitalists was their experience. Many of the best venture capitalists were former high-tech company executives, such as Don Valentine, who had already successfully been down the path their young charges were now facing. They knew what came next and how to get through it. These industry veteran venture capitalists, and their numbers grew by the year as each generation of talent got rich and then retired to play with their investments, combined with bright young things fresh out of Harvard and Stanford. This latter group offered endless reservoirs of energy to crunch financials and study industry reports. Together, old and experienced with young and energetic, venture capitalists represented an asset to a new start-up nearly as great as the money they proffered. For Apple, with its senior management ranks utterly lacking in anyone with CEO experience, this was a critical need.

The final, and least tangible, advantage offered by venture capitalists was the legitimacy they conferred. The right venture capitalist on your board of directors (and the big investors always took a board seat, sometimes the chairmanship) told the world that your company had been tapped as the Next Big Thing, that it was gilt-edged, that it was a place where winners wanted to work. Ultimately, it also signaled to the best underwriting firms that this was a company to keep track of, to one day represent in its IPO.

Mike Markkula understood all this very well. He also knew that the trick was to find the most respected and influential venture capitalists possible to invest in and advise Apple Computer—while at the same time not give them the whole store in compensation. An immediate obstacle was that, like most corporate types, Markkula didn't really know any venture capital firms. However, Silicon Valley being what it was—a very large and wealthy small town in which everybody at one time works for or against everybody else—this impediment was quickly vaulted.

As it turned out, Markkula had worked at Fairchild and Intel with a guy named Hank Smith. Smith had moved to New York and was now a general partner at Venrock. Venrock was a big deal, not just because it was the venture capital wing of the Rockefeller family but also because it had one of the best reputations in Silicon Valley for making smart investments (it would soon invest in VisiCalc as well). It would be good bait for other venture capitalists too. And the good news was that, unlike many of the other big names, Venrock hadn't yet invested in a personal computer company.

But one didn't just show up at Venrock's offices in Manhattan and ask for money. Getting venture money from a top-line firm, especially for an established company, is a very carefully choreographed process, with lots of mating dances, mutual sniffing and invasive procedures. So, though the initial contact between Markkula and Smith occurred in the spring of 1977, about the time of the Computer Faire, it wasn't until autumn, after Smith had visited the company several times, that Apple's executives were invited to New York to make a presentation.

Even then, Venrock exhibited some of the disdain for funky little start-ups that would cost it industry leadership in the years to come. As Smith would say later: "We probably would not have looked at Apple had I not known Mike Markkula."

Of course, Apple did nothing to help its image. Markkula, working with Gary Martin, put together an investor prospectus larded with wild speculations. Sherry Livingston, who watched the process, would tell Moritz, "It was a joke the way they came up with projections. There were so many projections they'd almost flip a coin." Bullshit financials were hardly uncommon in new start-ups, where the market is usually new and unknown, but by now Apple was an established company. To make up numbers at this point suggested that the company was almost flying blind.

But equally amateurish was the production of the document. While Markkula and Jobs flew on to Manhattan, Scott and most of his staff stayed up eating increasingly stale pizza and collated, stapled and bound the dozen prospectuses. Then Scott caught the red-eye flight out of San Francisco and joined his partners for the morning meeting at Venrock. The whole thing might have been a disaster, but plastic cases aside, this was the era when Apple could do no wrong. Venrock signed on.

Markkula knew enough not to hit up just one venture capitalist. The idea was to get multiple players in order to maximize the investment, dilute control and get as much prestige and experience on board as possible. The one guy Markkula wanted on board was Andy Grove, president of Intel. Bright, terrifyingly intense and a man who would battle failure to the death, Hungarian immigrant Grove was already on his way to becoming one of the great businessmen of the century. He was the dream corporate director, the man who not only could tell you how to run a billion-dollar company and set up the most sophisticated manufacturing plants ever known, but also just happened to be the world's leading supplier of microprocessors. But Andy's heart, as always, belonged to Intel. Still, having until recently worked for him, Markkula thought he might have a chance.

Grove's response was unvintage Andy: he bought 15,000 shares. That was the good part. The bad was that he refused a board position, saying that his time was devoted to Intel. That was a huge loss, because Andy Grove's money was much less important than his wisdom. One can only imagine that when the dark days came for Apple, what a difference it might have made to have the insights of the CEO of Intel Corp. Instead, Grove's role in this part of the Apple story was to telephone Mike Scott regularly over the next few months to ask to buy more stock and to bitterly complain about Apple stealing his employees.

But the Grove gambit did have one unexpected payoff. Markkula's demonstrations of the Apple II hadn't just occurred in front of Andy alone, but also before the Intel board of directors. And one of those directors just happened to be the Patriarch of Venture Capital: Arthur Rock.

Rock was a slim man who resembled, in his glasses and his piercing look, an IRS examiner. He was dignified, even courtly, but also often cold and reserved. And he had a mind as precise and as sharp as a laser beam. More even than Hewlett and Packard, it could be said of Rock that without him there would have been no Silicon Valley. It had been Rock who had taken the risk to invest in eight renegade scientists from Shockley Semiconductor when they'd decided to break out and form their own company, Fairchild. Then, a decade later, when three of those Fairchildren (including two of the original founders) had decided to break away again, it was Rock who put up their seed money for Intel. Along the way, he had put money into a company called Scientific Data Systems, which, when it sold to Xerox in 1969, netted him $60 million. Now with Intel humming away at the top of the microprocessor business—Rock had played a key role in getting the company to stay in that market—he was on his way to being worth ten times that.

Markkula hadn't gone to Rock because, well, you just didn't go to *Arthur Rock* on a whim. But there he was at the demonstration. And soon, something even more amazing occurred: he called Apple to inquire about an investment. It was if Zeus himself had reached down from the clouds and touched Apple, making it glow with a golden light.

Regis McKenna, Andy Grove, Art Rock. This wasn't just the hat trick of Silicon Valley, this was like owning the arena itself. And there was still one more name to go. Markkula, Jobs and Hank Smith were dining one night at the Villa Felice, an old Los Gatos restaurant catering to veteran Valleyites. They were discussing the Venrock investment when a bottle of wine appeared at the table with a note attached. It was from Don Valentine: "Don't lose sight of the fact that I'm planning on investing in Apple."

Valentine. Who just a year before had come away shocked after visiting the freaks in the garage. Now he wanted to play. And even though Apple's management assumed the man's motives were cynical, they too were cynical enough to take his money. As with the Patriarch of Venture Capital, nobody turns down the Man with the Golden Gut.

Ultimately, the investments, totaling $517,500 and formally completed in January 1978, included the following: Venrock $288,000, Valentine $150,000 and Rock $57,600. Apple was now valued at $3 million. Woz and Jobs were now, at least on paper, well on the way to becoming millionaires. Not bad for two kids who only wanted to sell a few computers over the summer.

That was just the beginning. As expected, the presence of this Investor

Murderers Row quickly caught the attention of the rest of the investment community. In June, while running a booth at the Consumer Electronics Show in Chicago, the Apple team was contacted by Continental Illinois Bank, located nearby. Continental wanted in, to the tune of $500,000. But in the intervening six months, Apple had become a much more valuable commodity. Woz had introduced the disk drive, the plastic problem was solved and orders were coming in fast. Apple was now valued at about $9 million—so Continental's half million bought only as many shares (about 5 percent) of the company as Valentine had purchased at the beginning of the year.

Meanwhile, another player, this time a friend of Rock's named Henry Singleton, also anted up a little more than $100,000. It wasn't huge money, but Singleton was also chairman of Teledyne Inc., the legendary conglomerate that had its fingers in everything from dental waterpicks to military tank motors. With his investment, Singleton accepted a board position—something he had never done—and thus further added to Apple's financial luster.

Treating this cluster of investments as the equivalent of another round, Markkula then went back to his original investors and gave them the opportunity to purchase more shares at the new price. Only Valentine refused, angrily complaining that at $9 per share Apple's stock was absurdly overpriced.

5.15 Game Plan

With the completion of the second round of investments, Apple had the funding to match its products and talent. Now it needed three other factors to make it into a major corporation.

The first was distribution. Apple already had a deal with the Byte Shops, but that chain was beginning to stumble. So the company began to look elsewhere. One growing phenomenon that was hard to miss was the rise of independent personal computer shops. Most of these were tiny, with limited inventories, and run by hobbyists who'd decided to make their obsession pay for itself. But there were also scores of these shops springing up just in Northern California, and hundreds more around the rest of the country. For now, at least until the big retail chains like Sears began to sell computers—and no one knew how far off that day might be—these little shops would be the point of entry for most first-time computer buyers.

And these little shops needed all the help they could get. An antisocial longhair who spoke in assembly code behind the counter and a bunch of shelves bearing complicated electronic boxes and old issues of *Dr. Dobb's* was no way to make computer neophytes feel secure in their first purchase. These shops needed sexy displays, appealing point-of-sale materials, colorful flyers and other collateral to hand out, and computers that didn't look like something left over from a Flash Gordon serial.

Jobs, who had wandered these aisles long before any of his peers at Apple or his competitors in the industry, understood this need better than anyone. So, while Commodore and the other major players played hardball with the stores, treating them like expendable serfs, Jobs and Apple romanced the shopkeepers. With Regis's help, Apple flooded the little stores with flashy sales support items. And, in the most inspired marketing move of the company's early years, Apple became the first personal computer company to enter into co-op advertising deals with its retailers.

Co-op in this case also meant co-opt. By agreeing to share the cost of advertising with the little stores, Apple not only helped to locally promote its products everywhere it had a store, but at the same time the resulting ads made it appear to all the world that the shop was dedicated to Apple. Commodore and Atari seethed, because their products were more properly targeted at consumers than Apple's more premium-priced machines, but Apple got all the attention.

Yet Apple could also be a demanding lover. It expected the shops to act more professionally, even to the point of changing their names. Ultimately, this was to the good, as the stores named after, and with clerks that looked like, Tolkien characters had little chance of survival. But not so heartwarming was Apple's treatment of those same stores when, like the Byte Shops, they were no longer up to snuff. Then Apple cut them off.

Inevitably, all of this petty entrepreneurship would toss up one figure of vision who would begin the process of consolidating the market. That turned out to be Ed Faber, founder of Computerland. And as Computerland began to open one store after another across the United States, Apple's spadework with small shops began to pay off big. Faber, faced with the huge cash-flow demands of opening a new store every few weeks, was more than happy to join Apple's co-op program. He would later say, "It frightened other manufacturers. They thought we were so closely allied with Apple that they wouldn't get any recognition in our stores."

By 1979 Apple had in place the best distribution system of any personal computer maker, one extensive enough to hold its own against Tandy's own string of Radio Shack stores. Just as important, it had, in Computerland, close ties to a retail chain that was as innovative and sophisticated in its style as Apple itself. Said Faber, "It was one of those mutually advantageous relationships. Apple had a product; we had the beginnings of a retail distribution system. The more success we had, the more success they had. The more success they had, the more success we had."

The second factor Apple needed to become a real corporation was public recognition. It was one thing to be respected in the world of personal computing and to be the coolest thing around to guys who wore plastic pocket protectors; it was another to be an object of interest and affirmation by the world's leading business executives, politicians and investors. The first group bought your products, but the second bought your stock. And if Apple was planning to go public, this second group would be even more important than the first.

This would be where Regis McKenna's theory of opinion makers faced its ultimate test. Could you take a comparatively small company in a still largely unknown business, a company still just a few years away from two hairy scofflaws in a garage, and capture the imagination first of institutional investors and underwriters, then of society itself?

Regis had done a little of this work at Intel. But despite his best efforts, microprocessors wouldn't really be sexy for another fifteen years. And at Apple, until now, his agency had done some clever work, but it still wasn't far removed from the same old high-tech PR scam of taking credit for articles that advertising-hungry trade press editors would have written anyway. The same was true for the company's advertising, which, though smart, essentially echoed the bloviating claims of the competition.

And there was more competition than ever. Now the field included not only Cromemco, Atari and Commodore but also Mattel, the idiotically named Kentucky Fried Computers (which changed its name, too late, to NorthStar), Ohio Scientific, Tandy and now the biggest gorilla of them all, Texas Instruments.

TI scared the bejesus out of everybody. And with good reason. Not only was it a billion-dollar company but it also made its own chips. On top of that, it had just spent five years conducting, in pocket calculators, one of the harshest scorched-earth marketing campaigns the electronics industry had ever seen. TI was at the time the leading proponent of "learning curve pricing," a theory propounded by the Boston Consulting Group (BCG), which argued that all new high-tech products followed a life cycle from high prices for early adopters at the beginning to heavy discounting and commoditization for the masses at the end of the product's career. Knowing this curve, BCG argued, meant that, as with Moore's Law, you could predict the future and leapfrog your competition to get there. Texas Instruments read that to mean you priced today at the lower future price, snatched up all the market share from your competitors and then held on with a near-monopoly for the big payoff.

TI had tried this strategy on pocket calculators and nearly destroyed the industry. Except for HP, which, though singed, still managed to cling to the premium market, almost everyone else was soon run out of calculators by TI's aggressive pricing. That TI crippled itself with losses in the process didn't matter; everyone assumed in 1979 that the company's payoff for owning the calculator market would soon come.

And now the behemoth of Richardson, Texas, was turning its sights on personal computers, and everyone expected it to once more leave a charred wasteland as it passed.

Now was the time for Regis to prove himself. Like many Valleyites, he usually worked best during the big moments and grew bored during the successful lulls that came afterward. With Intel cruising along, still a couple of years away from the collapse that would lead to Operation Crush, Regis was in just such a lull. But the arrival of TI, combined with the announcement by Apple's board that the company was preparing to ramp up for an IPO, set Regis's heart beating again. He knew what he had to do.

It was a four-pronged plan, much of it driven by public relations. Advertising would continue to play up Apple's strengths, especially vis-à-vis the competition. For example, the Commodore Pet was in many ways a technically better computer. But it was also shoddy, with a little calculator-quality keyboard, a bent metal case and a tiny black-and-white display. So Apple would play up the elegance of its computer. Atari's machine wasn't great, but it wasn't bad either. The company was equated with video games and thus not taken seriously. Apple played up its reputation, as one magazine called it, of being "the Cadillac of home computers." Tandy, with its massive distribution but questionable quality, was met with the co-op campaign and advertisements promoting the II's quality and reliability.

But TI was a different story. Its machines, the 99/4 and the soon to appear 99/6 were top-notch. They were also, as might be expected, competitively priced. But TI had one big weakness: Everybody *hated* those cutthroat bastards, especially the press. And the feeling was mutual.

That's where the PR side of Regis's plan came in. Advertising could help, especially by emphasizing the playful, friendly side of Apple (with its implicit comparison with the nasty, cold-blooded company in Texas). But the heart of the campaign against TI would have to be fought in the press. This would in turn have the long-term advantage of positioning Apple before the readership—that is, potential Apple shareholders—of those publications.

Thus, the other three prongs of Regis's strategy were aimed at influencing different segments of the Fourth Estate. The first of these was the trade magazines, the verticals. This was a pretty malleable group, eager to please advertisers and thrilled to be noticed by industry leaders. Regis fed them with a continuous stream of "loaner" computers, press releases, exclusive interviews and visits. Embraced by Apple and thrown crumbs by TI, the magazines soon reflected their loyalties in their editorial pages.

The second PR target was key opinion makers. These were the folks whose judgment determined for thousands of customers, analysts and developers whether a product or a company was perceived as a winner (with the attendant success) or a loser (decline and death). In an industry as young as personal computing there really weren't any such thought leaders—except perhaps Lee Felsenstein and he was tainted by his corporate connections.

But there was such an opinion maker in the world of microprocessors and Regis knew him well: Benjamin Rosen. Rosen was a small, almost elfin man, with delicate Southern manners. But he also had a powerful intellect, nerves of steel and, best of all, a beautiful style. In just a year he had turned his personal newsletter into the most influential voice in the microprocessor industry. One word from him in the newsletter could make or break a company's reputation, sending its stock value shooting up or down in increments of millions of dollars.

From microprocessors it was only a small jump to personal computers. And Regis set out to help Rosen across. It turned out to be easier than anyone imagined: Rosen, in fact, already owned and admired an Apple II. And he was already at work becoming a personal computer pundit.

But getting Rosen to write about computing was one thing, getting him to write positively about Apple was another. Unlike the craven trade press editors, Rosen could not be bought. And his newsletter took no advertising. Moreover, since he was more clever than anyone he dealt with, he was almost impossible to charm. He had made his reputation (and growing wealth) by telling the truth, no matter whom it hurt, and he was not going to abandon that principle just because some little computer company in Cupertino winked at him.

But, like all pundits, Rosen had one weakness: he was only as good as his information. He needed that information both to render his considered judgment and to offer his subscribers inside stuff they couldn't get elsewhere. Being nearly as clever as Rosen, Regis understood this. The rest of the computer industry, suffering from either the technomumbles or paranoid gigantism, clearly did not. So Regis played this card for all it was worth.

Before long Rosen was being constantly fed the latest insider news about Apple. When he needed help with his computer, he had only to call Apple to get the best possible service. And Apple executives cleared their calendars whenever Ben was in town, devoting long hours to deep discussions about technology and markets.

The point man for much of this was Mike Markkula, who had first met Rosen years before at National Semiconductor, and in one of those sweet Silicon Valley ironies, had been taught by Rosen how to operate a programmable calculator. Now Markkula, the chairman of Apple, was always there at Rosen's beckoning, even taking phone calls at home to answer Ben's technical questions. Markkula became such a close friend of Rosen's that he nearly destroyed the whole campaign by offering Ben stock. Luckily, Rosen politely refused.

The strategy paid off in spades. Rosen never lost his objectivity, he still called them as he saw them, but that didn't matter. It was too early in the game for the major players to really screw up anyway. What mattered was the quality and quantity of copy. And in that game Apple won hands down. Rosen gave Apple so much attention that venture capitalist Hank Smith would later say that Ben was "one of Apple's best salesmen."

But it was even better than that, because Rosen was also Apple's entree into the fourth prong of Regis's strategy: the mainstream press. These were the guys Apple had to seduce if it was to have a successful IPO. And Ben Rosen opened the doors for Apple to that world.

Almost from the beginning, personal computer companies had been trying to break into the general press. They mailed out press releases, held events, toured product demonstrations, mailed out gifts—and all they had to show for it was a few brief mentions in the *San Jose Mercury News* and *Business Week*. Regis had done his share of this kind of low-rent flackery for Apple.

But the support of Ben Rosen changed everything. Based in New York, he was becoming the world's leading tech guru and a quote source for the nation's leading media. And when reporters read Rosen's newsletter, they couldn't help but notice the attention he paid to a wacky little computer company in California. And when they visited his office they couldn't miss the fact that he was working on an Apple II. Soon Apple's name was starting to appear in publications such as the *New York Times* and *Fortune*.

Then, remarkably, Rosen went one step further. He began to play matchmaker between Apple and the press. He organized luncheons to introduce the company to publications like *Time*. Apple was now on its way to becoming a business phenomenon. In Markkula's words: "We were carrying the corporate image far out in front of the size and reputation of the corporation."

Regis had proven his theory.

There was one more matter before Apple could go public. It needed a new product.

In the late 1970s, personal computers were still so new that no one was really sure how long a product generation ought to last. A new generation of mainframes, dragging along their ever-growing burden of software, might last nearly a decade. But pocket calculators were as evanescent as mayflies. In between, microprocessors and other semiconductor chips turned over every couple of years according to the dictates of Moore's Law.

It would seem, then, that personal computers, dependent as they were upon the latest generation of microprocessors, would also have a middling life expectancy—shorter if the model was a dog, longer if it had an active base of users, programmers and aftermarket hardware designers.

The Apple II certainly seemed to fit into this latter category. Not only was it a best-seller but it had a very popular software library with the likes of VisiCalc, EasyWriter and a superb new word-processing program, called AppleWriter, written by an Apple fan named Paul Lutus in a tiny log cabin in the wilds of Oregon. Programmers liked Apple for the same reason journalists did: it was approachable. You could show up at the Bandley Drive headquarters, ask for Steve Jobs, show him your new program and if he liked it he might very well count up your lines of code and pay you on the spot. A few weeks later you'd be in the catalog of the world's best-known personal computer. Who could pass by such an opportunity? Especially when almost everybody else treated you like a carpetbagger and an intruder.

As for hardware, it seemed as if every mechanical engineer who bought an Apple II ended up building some add-on for it. Already there were electrical surge protectors, screen filters, specialty keyboards, drawing tablets, high-speed bolt-on cooling fans, even furniture for the Apple II. One enthusiast even carved a *wooden* Apple II, as if it was some totemic object, and presented it to the company.

But even given all that activity, Apple had to assume that by 1980 the Apple II would simply be obsolete. After all, hadn't the Apple I been competitive for only a year? By the end of the decade, the II would be four years old, ancient in small computer terms.

There were two ways to deal with this problem, and Apple chose to pursue both. The least of the two was to simply let the increasingly insular and eccentric Woz play with II and see if he could find some wrinkle to give it extra life. Woz, in fact, did have a notion about improving the machine's performance with the use of custom chips.

Being the great Woz, he was funded and left alone to follow his muse. Unfortunately, that muse had grown increasingly mute. In the end, Woz, working with an assistant, mainly futzed around, never really completing a new design. It would be others who would take some of his ideas, add their own and build the Apple IIe almost five years later.

Apple's management, recognizing this was a dead end, tried desperately to find an activity that would reanimate the company's resident genius. So a second project was begun, this one to create a new type of personal computer that would use "bit-slice" technology to divide up processing between multiple microprocessors. But Woz lost interest in that as well. He complained about having to attend too many distracting meetings, so many that he "was lucky to have two hours a day to myself." That project, after many incarnations, would become Lisa.

The fact was that Woz was tanking. Whatever it was that had caught him in its grip fifteen years before was finally sated and had moved on. Woz still had the genius, but he no longer had the heart. He was much more excited about playing practical jokes, such as sneaking Alka-Seltzer tablets labeled "for your convenience" into the menus at Bob's Big Boy or dousing fellow employees with green slime or putting a live mouse (another bit of technological irony) in another programmer's machine. He also lost himself in mindless activities like computing transcendental numbers on his computer, and in gambling away his salary at the casino tables in Reno.

His fellow employees weren't sympathetic. One programmer would say, "Woz lost the challenge. People stopped telling him that what he was doing was bullshit. He acquired the status of being a wizard and after a while he believed it. He knew better in his heart, but he loved the role." Randy Wigginton, his onetime disciple, was even tougher: "He preferred being the Messiah."

With Woz disintegrating, Apple's other-product strategy moved front and center, soon consuming most of the company's precious time and resources. This was the creation of a radically new computer design, a replacement for the Apple II.

Apple was nothing if not ambitious: three distinct product designs, as well as a new disk drive, were to be pursued concurrently. Like Woz's project, each was given a code name: Lisa, Mac, Sara and Twiggy. Twiggy was a low-profile ("skinny") double disk drive, so named because, in the loutish world of computer engineers, the two mini-floppies made them think of the famous model. Lisa and Mac were further off into the future. In the near term, Apple's next big play would be Sara, a direct replacement for the II. Ultimately, and unimaginatively, it would be named the Apple III (Apple played with the actual logo using symbols from the keyboard: thus, the Apple II was presented as][, and the Apple III as ///).

The III was to be Apple's proof that it was not a one-hit wonder. It was also to be the company's first shot at the business market. And finally, it was to serve as a financial bridge to the more innovative Lisa and Mac, which weren't expected to appear until the mid-1980s.

In the end, the Apple III accomplished none of these. But at least its failure was well timed.

Tom Whitney, at that time the new head of engineering, gave the Apple III project to his old Iowa State classmate Wendell Sander. Sander seemed the perfect choice: he was a fine engineer, disciplined and widely respected within the company. He was also intensely loyal to Apple. It was just the kind of choice most established companies make when choosing a product manager, especially a company sick of nursing prima donnas. But there was one thing Sander was not: a person who would fight his superiors for the integrity of his product. And at this point in the company's history, this was the skill the Apple III manager needed more than any other.

Because Sander was a good soldier, he accepted almost without complaint the product requirements set for him by senior management. At first glance, they didn't seem onerous. The III, unlike the stock II, was to have a 80-character-wide screen and upper- and lowercase characters. It was to feature some basic graphics and offer an improved operating system. And it was to have an internal electronic clock.

So far so good. These were *engineering* enhancements, derived from the needs of the market, from the experience with the Apple II and from a recognition of the improved technologies now available. But then management tacked on two other requirements that had nothing to with engineering, but with the company's own *marketing* needs.

The first was that the III must run the Apple II software library—the logic being that the III would thus be introduced already possessing the largest body of software in the personal computer market. That would give Apple users a smooth upward migration path requiring only the expense of new hardware.

The second management requirement was that the first III prototype be ready in one year. The ostensible reason for this speeded-up development cycle was that the II was getting old and that newer, more competitive machines were coming onto the market. But, in fact, the II was doing better than ever. In the fiscal year ended September 30, 1979, Apple sold 35,100 of the machines, four times that of the year before. And in 1980 that number doubled again, passing the unit market leader, Radio Shack, and regaining its position as the best-selling personal computer in the world. The real reason to rush the III to market was to have a hot new model out just before the legal "quiet period" began for the Apple IPO.

The end result of these two extratechnical requirements, as Sander soon discovered, was that he was boxed in. One reason for the extraordinary success of the II was that Woz had begun with a blank slate, unconstrained by a corporate structure. Egged on by Jobs, he had built the best machine imaginable. Sander, by comparison, had to fight a bureaucracy all the way, while dragging the Apple II emulation requirement behind him like an anchor. He could not build the best machine imaginable, only the best machine possible under the circumstances.

Not that he didn't give it his best shot. With Dan Kottke as his assistant, Sander spent each day designing some new part of the motherboard, then handed the drawing over to Kottke, who would make a clean drawing, then work into the night, usually under headphones, wiring that design into a real board. It was a very effective partnership, and one that met its deadlines, but in the end it still couldn't overcome the underlying limitations of the design.

The biggest of those limitations was the II emulation. Sander knew it, Kottke knew it, the whole engineering staff knew it. But marketing wanted the feature, and marketing prevailed. The problem with emulation is that it requires a translation function in software. Pumping programs through this emulation mode feature slows everything down. And the problem becomes especially acute if the translation must bridge between two entirely different microprocessors.

No problem, said Apple management, we'll use the same processor in the III as we had in the II. But that was the 6502, the underpowered microprocessor that Woz had compromised on originally because it was all he could afford; a processor that was never designed for a task as complicated as running a personal computer. So now an obsolete chip was going to run Apple's new flagship computer as it entered the 1980s. Worse, it was going to have to run a computer with two or three times the 64K core memory of the II.

Sander knew this was a mistake and proposed adding a second processor.

That was nixed by management because a dual-processor machine would have to be priced above the company's target for the III.

Now Sander was in a box. But still he didn't complain. Instead he came up with a severely compromised design. The III would still have the larger memory, but it would be divided up into banks, each of them no larger in capacity than the memory of the II—that is, at the functional limits of the 6502. In this new design, the computer would use some of its processing power to keep track of which bank a particular piece of data was in and shuttle back and forth to reach it. This meant the III could have internal memory as great as 256K or more, but would grow less efficient with each jump in capacity.

It was an ugly solution made even uglier by the fact that all this Apple II emulation ultimately precluded the III from offering any better graphics than its predecessor. Woz might have helped overcome this difficulty, or at least used his pull at the executive level to get a more practical set of product specifications. And, in fact, Sander sometimes went to Woz for advice. But Wozniak stayed away, played his practical jokes and repeated that Sander was the best man for the job. Later, however, he was one of the loudest critics of the III's emulator, saying, "Apple claims they've got it and they don't," and announcing that he would have found a better solution.

Still Sander soldiered on. Now the unrealistic time requirement took its toll. Sander hit his deadline, but at a cruel price: between the time the prototype was completed and manufacturing was to begin, National Semiconductor informed Apple that it would not be able to deliver the clock chip in the volumes needed. Those that did arrive usually failed after three hours. Jobs screamed at Sporck—a remarkably brave thing in itself, given that the six-foot-four Charlie could have broken the young man in two with his hands—but it had no effect. Apple was not going to get its chips.

One could think of this as Charlie Sporck's revenge for having Apple raid his people, and Sporck certainly played for keeps. But revenues meant more to Sporck than revenge, especially in 1980, when the regular-as-clockwork four-year business cycle was hitting the chip industry hard. In truth, late and unreliable chip deliveries were standard procedure for the U.S. chip industry during this era—and for this lassitude the American semiconductor companies would soon be taught a nasty lesson by their Japanese competitors.

Meanwhile, Apple was without a clock chip for its new computer—a capability already being promoted by the company's overanxious marketing department. Needless to say, engineering got the blame . . . and the resulting distrust by both sides set in motion a feud between the two camps that would haunt the rest of Apple's history. For now, however, with the IPO just six months away, and with the III already trumpeted in the company's prospectus, Apple decided to go ahead with the clockless computer and take any publicity hits that might result.

As Raskin later told Moritz: "It was the classic story of people at the bottom saying, 'Things aren't working here. We're in trouble.' Then the next level up would say, 'We're in some trouble with this,' and the level above would say, 'We're getting around the trouble,' and the people at the top would say, 'It will be okay. Let's ship.' "

And Sander wasn't the only person forced by the deadline to make compromises on the Apple III. The need to make the III fully compatible with the II, combined with the entirely different hardware layout of the III from keyboard to memory, meant that nearly every single operation on the new computer had to be modified. That in turn meant most of Apple's programming team spent every second it had just trying to make the III work, much less work well or feature any new functions. It would be a year after the III's introduction before Apple's programmers had a version of the Pascal language to run on it.

With software running this far behind, it was inevitable that Apple's outside developers would be even further behind. After all, with nothing available for them to design for, they could hardly begin. Even Fylstra at VisiCorp, the single most important outside developer for the III, didn't receive his first III prototype until two weeks before the computer's formal introduction.

But perhaps the most compromised group of all was Apple's publications group. Apple, after all, had pulled itself head and shoulders above its competitors largely by the quality of the support it gave its users. The Apple II manual, when it finally appeared, helped thousands of neophytes smoothly enter the world of personal computing. In creating such documentation for the II, Apple had set the bar higher for everyone, including itself. From now on, any new computer would have to come with a well-written, in-depth library of support documents.

But with the III so late, with its final lineup of features apparently changing by the day, the publications team was paralyzed. As a result, the final documents were rushed, and new Apple III owners, many of them first-time computer operators, found themselves with badly written and poorly organized manuals, some describing capabilities that weren't even in the computer.

Still, for all of its flaws, the Apple III was introduced on time, gathered some good initial reviews from the slack-jawed press and it accomplished what it was designed to do. It gave Apple a follow-up product to prove that the company was not a one-hit wonder, propped up the stock at the IPO and gave the company a bridge, albeit a creaky one, to the business market in preparation for the more interesting Apple machines to come.

5.16 The Little Magic Kingdom

The Apple III was introduced at the May 1980 National Computer Conference in Anaheim. Apple stole the show. The company rented Disneyland for an evening and drove 20,000 attendees over to the Magic Kingdom in red double-decker buses.

The sheer brazenness of the act stoked the imagination of the computer industry. Babes in evening gowns and bathing suits, sure. Maybe a TV star to sign autographs or a pop band to cover their hits or even a cocktail party in the best restaurant in town, *but take over Disneyland!* That was righteous; that was flash!

It was an eerie experience to walk through Disneyland that evening just before the party began. Disneyland on a warm night at the edge of summer . . . empty. Just a few Apple employees scurrying about, some Disney employees waiting to operate the rides. The Magic Kingdom seemed strangely small and old. A light misty rain, rare in May in the Los Angeles basin, was an augury of what was to come if anyone had stopped to notice.

Then the London buses rolled up and spit out their riders, long-haired programmers, junior marketing execs in suits, salesmen eyeing both a good time and a clever close. The event was a huge success, lasting until the wee hours. It was a metaphor both for Apple and for the Apple generation. Grown men and women acting like children, in an amusement park built for children, on a night when real children weren't allowed. There were echoes of the past—Jobs and Woz working as the Mad Hatter and the White Rabbit; the Disney science documentaries that had captured the imaginations of a whole generation of future engineers; and the Tomorrowland of rockets and plastic houses that had managed to miss the biggest revolution of all in information. And there were glimpses of the future—of product introductions that were cultural events, of marketing style hiding failures of engineering substance and of a generation that would refuse to ever be adults. And at the very center of it all, the King of the Lost Boys, a Peter Pan who would soon be rich enough to never have to grow up, was Steve Jobs.

The Disneyland party was more than just a celebration of the Apple III; it would also prove to be the kickoff for the Apple IPO in December. And from that night, Apple never looked back.

Today, nearly two decades later, after hundreds of IPOs by high-tech start-ups, some of them of even greater financial magnitude, many of Apple's antics in the next six months would be cause for the SEC to suspend the stock sale. Just a decade later, MIPS Computer's IPO was nearly stopped at the eleventh hour because a harmless article about the company unexpectedly appeared in *USA Today*.

If the Securities and Exchange Commission, the cops of the stock market, eventually grew wary of hyperbole and price manipulation surrounding high-tech IPOs, it was because Apple had set the pattern that every company tried to follow. And if Apple got away with it, it was because there was no precedent for what happened in the weeks preceding the company's Going Public Day.

Some of the credit for this success went to Regis McKenna and his crew. Beginning with the early ads and press tours, Regis & Company had carefully built interest in Apple toward a crescendo. He had made for the company the right contacts in the press and the analyst community, he had trained Apple's management in how to be public figures and then controlled their accessibility to just the right people. And now, as the mainstream press finally began to notice Apple, he was ready. Soon stories about the growing excitement over the Apple IPO began appearing in newspapers and magazines such as *Time*. And for the first time ever, average people began take an interest in the first public sale of a company's stock.

But Regis's success also carried with it failure. Because just as the ramp-up to the IPO began, Apple went out and hired an internal PR director to help manage investor relations. And this wasn't just some flack out of the Fortune 500; this was Fred Hoar, the only publicist in the Valley considered Regis's equal. If Regis was Mr. Outside, the ultimate agency man, Hoar was Mr. Inside, the prince of corporate PR managers. Big, blond-haired and square-jawed, perpetually hail-fellow-well-met, his words littered with classical allusions, Hoar was a corporate spokesman out of central casting. Once again, Apple, for all its public posturing as a new kind of company, had, when the crunch came, gone out to Old Valley for help.

Hoar's arrival did not set well with Regis & Company. Before, Regis McKenna Inc. had essentially been Apple's marketing and marketing communications wing. Now Hoar controlled the latter, and with it access in one direction to the press and in the other to Apple's management. It was months before the edges of the respective territories were established.

But for all that tension, the double play of Hoar and McKenna worked beautifully. Both men were pros, and both knew that the most important task of the moment was to get Apple successfully public. Moreover, Hoar offered many talents Regis lacked. Regis was something of pharisee: serious, ironic, always slightly embarrassed by the sordidness of PR, he preferred to sit above the fray and develop strategy. Fred Hoar, by comparison, loved the sweat and funk and fraud of good old-fashioned flackery. He knew it was all bullshit, but he reveled in it. And he winked to let you know he knew that you knew it was bullshit too.

It was a great combination, the strategist and the tactician. Regis devised the big campaign and Hoar went out into the mud and the blood and executed it. Regis organized the receptions for newspaper editors and presidents of investment funds; Fred made sure the Apple executives got to the event on time, then went out and slapped the backs and pumped the hands of everyone in the room.

The decision to go public was not the usual result of careful corporation consideration. On the contrary, in typical Apple form, the company found itself in crisis, and rushed out to make the best of it. This time the catalyst was another naive blunder by Woz.

Recalls Mike Scott: "At the June board meeting I had to report that Mr. Steve Wozniak, even though he was not allowed to sell stock, was nevertheless giving away 1,000-share blocks to relatives, friends, acquaintances and just about anybody else he could think of.

"That wasn't all. The real problem was that with Woz doing this, Apple was rapidly heading toward the SEC threshold of having more than five hundred shareholders. And when that happened, we would have to begin filing a 10K report." In other words, Apple was about to be a public company whether it wanted to or not. "So," says Scott, "we elected to pull the trigger."

By late summer the Going Public Campaign was picking up speed. By autumn it had taken on a momentum of its own. A year before, the company had gone out for a final, "mezzanine" round of venture investment to reward its friends, to line up new blue-chip investors and to fund the final drive to the IPO. That round raised $7.3 million from shares priced at $10.50 apiece. Among the sixteen investors were some of the big venture capitalists, including LF Rothschild and Brentwood Capital; Xerox Corp., both a potential competitor and a source of new technologies; and a private investor named Fayez Sarofim, who was a friend of Art Rock's. Mezzanines are also times when founders get a last easy and nearly painless chance to sell some of their own holdings for cash. That's exactly what Markkula and Jobs did, selling about $1 million worth apiece. For Markkula it was no big deal, but for Jobs it was a stunning accomplishment: in five years he had gone from starving in a rented room to being a millionaire. He would be able to go into the IPO already looking like a success.

But not everything went smoothly. Don Valentine, claiming a financial restructuring created by the closeout of one of his partnerships, used the mezzanine to sell all of his Apple holdings. It was an unwelcome act. To lose a major investor, especially one of Valentine's stature, in the mezzanine round might be read by the market as a signal of impending disaster. Luckily, it went by almost unremarked—so much so that Valentine is still often miscredited with being Apple's key investor.

But the loss of Valentine created another problem: with his departure, Apple had lost the man with the golden gut about the perfect date to go public. Luckily, Art Rock was still around, and if he didn't have Valentine's clairvoyance at picking IPO dates, he still had as much experience at going public as anyone else in tech. It was Rock who helped Apple select the underwriters for the IPO—hometown boys Hambrecht & Quist for the action, gray-suited Morgan Stanley for the stability (Morgan Stanley screamed; it was the first time it had to share underwriting)—and then worked with them to ultimately set the date as December 12, 1980.

Now, more than a year after the mezzanine, with the press giving more coverage by the day to the upcoming Apple IPO, hysteria began to form both inside and outside the company.

Initial Public Offerings are times of paralysis for companies. "It was a three-month paperwork nightmare," Scott recalls. For one thing, management is divided in two; with half preparing the prospectus, meeting with underwriters, then racing about the world holding investor road shows. Meanwhile, the other half is trying to keep a dynamic, fast-moving company growing at the same pace without missing a step. And down in the bowels of the company those with stock daydream about what to do with their new riches, and those without stock spend their days scheming to find out who does have stock, how much they have, and then hating them for it.

Founders stock, equity, in a new start-up is never handed out equitably. Draw a cartoon for the company's first flyer when the firm is just three people and you may end up paid with more stock than the executive vice president who is hired ten years later when the company has a billion dollars in annual sales. Inevitably, on Going Public Day managers discover they have less stock than their subordinates, secretaries have more than their bosses, and, of two equally qualified people sitting side by side, one will become a tycoon and retire while the other can only look forward to another thirty years of mortgage payments.

Even in the most sobersided company the new start-up equity game is built on luck, timing and connections. In a company as chaotic and improvised as Apple, the situation was bound to be even more arbitrary and explosive. Once again, the presence of an arbitrary, punitive and mercurial Steve Jobs only made matters worse. One engineer would later say, "The amount of stock that people were given had nothing to do with their ability to work. It had everything to do with their ability to get stock." Rod Holt was philosophical: "The fact that a turkey who is worth a million and a half doesn't deserve to have an office in the building is a quirk of fate."

There were three ways to get Apple stock options. One was to be an investor—and that was a game for millionaires in search of more millions. Another was to make stock options part of your employment contract with Apple's management—but that only went to senior managers.

A third was to play on a major shareholder's conscience or soft heart. Needless to say, the softest of those hearts (and some would say heads when it came to money) belonged to Woz. Some stock Woz sold because he was asked—to Rock's friend Sarofim (that's where he got the stock in the mezzanine round), to one of Rock's partners and to personnel director Ann Bowers. Another buyer was Stephen Vidovich, the scion of a local orchard family grown rich leasing out most of the business districts of Cupertino. Vidovich happened to own the De Anza Racquet Club, where Apple had a corporate membership. He bought 25,000 shares.

Those who took advantage of Woz's sympathy included more than thirty Apple employees whom Woz felt had not been given a fair shake. They got it, 80,000 shares worth $7.50 apiece. As Jobs would say: "Woz couldn't say no. A lot of people took advantage of him."

Perhaps, but at least Woz was selling stock to make Apple more equitable to its people, not to mention giving his parents more than enough shares to buy financial independence. By comparison, Job was using his shares as a bludgeon. When it was learned that Dan Kottke, who had shared Jobs's house and helped him build the first Apple I's, was ineligible for stock because he was still merely a technician, Rod Holt went to Jobs and suggested they both chip in equal amounts for their old friend. "Great!" said Jobs. "I'll give him zero." When Kottke's supervisor approached the board of directors with a proposal to give him stock, Jobs shot the proposal down again.

Others were screwed too. Elmer Baum, who had lent the money to help found the company; Bill Fernandez, the childhood friend and first company employee; Chris Espinosa, who'd slept in the park while writing the Apple II manual—all were left out of the big payoff for Apple's success. Espinosa would tell Moritz, "We missed out on the American dream because we were too nice to grab part of it. Kottke was too nice. Fernandez was too Buddhist and I was too young . . . We all realized to some degree we weren't heavy enough. We weren't obnoxious enough to make ourselves millionaires."

At the same time, there were some unlikely beneficiaries, including Sherry Livingston, the mythmaking millionaire secretary. Other shareholding employees sold their stock to everybody from Caribbean investment funds to the HP pension fund to Charlie Finley, owner of the Oakland A's (who would later sue over the stock price).

As December approached, the hysteria seemed to grow by the day. Inside Apple, the company became increasingly paralyzed as rumors flew back and forth about who had stock and how much, and as those with holdings drifted off into reverie about how their lives were about to change. Even reports that the early shipments of Apple III's were DOA didn't seem to faze the company.

Meanwhile, Apple's various support entities, from Venrock to the underwriters to Regis McKenna Inc.—nearly all of them standing to make millions in the IPO—were scrambling to keep the whole process from derailing. Even in that permissive era of the SEC, there was still such a thing as too much publicity for an IPO. Apple likely passed that point by late October. McKenna and Hoar did their parts, honoring the prescribed "quiet period" and killing ads, publicity campaigns and interviews.

But there was no dampening the hysteria. By November, the Apple IPO was on its way to becoming the most famous, and popular, initial stock offering in American business history. By the first week of December, it had all gone completely nuts. It seemed as if everyone in America wanted a piece of Apple, and if they hadn't before, the nation's newspapers and newsmagazines convinced them they should. In the newsroom of the *San Jose Mercury News*, the technology reporter was besieged at his desk, in the cafeteria, even in the lavatory by other reporters, ignoring rules about conflict of interest, trying to find out how to get a few shares.

Big IPO fortunes sometimes go to those who are shameless enough to play on any connection to the company, no matter how tenuous, to beg for a few shares. If you ever delivered a pizza to Bandley Drive or lent Woz a soldering iron in high school or worked with Mike Scott for a week at Fairchild, you felt you were a key contributor to Apple's current success and deserved to be compensated for it. There was no penalty for being pushy or obnoxious or self-degrading—after all, Apple's own employees were doing the same thing.

For weeks before the big day, bags of pleading letters poured into the underwriters, Apple employees were accosted by relatives, neighbors, even strangers. Every public statement (not to mention private remarks) by Apple executives was deconstructed for clues about how to get stock.

It seemed as if everybody in the capitalist world (and probably many in the Communist world as well) wanted shares of Apple stock, believing that it would shoot sky high the instant it began trading on Nasdaq.

They were correct. In August, during a private placement with Hambrecht & Quist, Apple's stock was valued at $5.44 per share. When Apple published its prospectus on the sale on November 6, it formally predicted that the stock would be priced between $14 and $17 at the IPO. That, as everybody knew, was standard underwriter palaver. *Every* high-tech IPO seemed to be priced at $14 to $17. What counted was how high the stock would go in the hours immediately after the opening bell.

Just how high was anyone's guess, and everyone's fantasy. Certainly the signs were good: Genentech, the hottest biotech firm around, had gone out in October at an opening of $35, jumped to $89 by afternoon and settled back at $71 by the end of the first day. That was a different company in a different industry, but it hinted that the market for new tech issues was strong—as if the madness surrounding Apple didn't scream that already.

5.17 LOCUS

Finally, the day came. On the morning of December 12, 1980, Apple went public. There was so much pent-up demand for the stock (listed as AAPL, the letters picked by Hoar) that it opened at $22. That was already 50 percent above the expected opening price. But any early morning speculation that demand had already been sated evaporated as the stock price began to climb.

Every company freezes on the day it goes public. And Apple was no exception, especially since much of America froze with it. In the buildings along Bandley, employees were alternately giddy and sober, vocal and contemplative. There were spontaneous parties and speeches, hugs and tears. Meanwhile, through these various incarnations of a life-changing event, every eye was on the many computers around the company hooked up to the Dow Jones ticker.

When the market closed at 1 P.M. P.S.T., Apple's stock was selling for $29 per share, nearly double the original estimated opening price. It was one of the great Going Public Days, the biggest since Ford went public in 1956, and everyone and everything it touched was changed forever. Apple itself had raised $82.8 million—money it didn't really think it needed, but would soon want badly.

As for individual shareholders, the numbers were even more staggering. Even before the IPO one Apple clerk had quit because she couldn't emotionally deal with the kinds of numbers she was seeing processing stock options. And the real numbers were even bigger. Jobs came away with $256.4 million for his 15 percent ownership. Markkula made $239 million, Woz $135 million, Scott $95.5 million. Among the outside investors, Art Rock made $21.8 million, Venrock $129.3 million and Teledyne's Henry Singleton $40.8 million.

But even among lesser lights the sums were astonishing. Rod Holt was worth $67 million. John Couch, who'd demanded stock in exchange for joining the company and running the Lisa project, made $13.6 million. Jef Raskin and Sherry Livingston also became millionaires.

And, this being Apple, there were the oddball stories as well. Alice Robertson, Woz's ex, made $42.4 million on her settlement stock—then complained she'd not gotten enough. But driving around in a new gold Mercedes with a license that read 24 CARAT seemed to calm her down. And Tom Whitney, Woz's old boss, the guy who'd beaten out Chuck Peddle for a job at Apple, then proved a disaster, came away with $48.9 million.

It was sheer madness. Mike Scott calculated the number of new millionaires that day at 104. In a single day, people who'd been working for $40,000 per year, people just a half dozen years out of college, were suddenly worth tens of millions of dollars. Some were now among the richest people in the United States. It was so much money they couldn't imagine it; they couldn't even figure out how to spend it all.

The only proper thing to do was to celebrate. Some went to the Good Earth; others went home as soon as they could to try to understand what had just happened. The big winners were gathered for a celebration around a speaker phone hooked up to Morgan Stanley's offices in New York. Mike Scott, never one to miss an excuse for a party, brought in some champagne, but even he seemed dazed through all the toasts and handshakes.

Only one man appeared unaffected by all of this success: the husband of Ann Bowers, the human resources director. But then, he was Robert Noyce of Intel, who was still (barely) the richest person in the room. He was kind enough to keep his own counsel and not spoil the moment by warning the others of what was to come.

Jef Raskin, who was also in the room, said it suddenly struck him that "all the people in the room were millionaires. The forceful thing was the world had shifted. I hadn't seen that happen before."

The world had indeed shifted. Apple Computer, just five years before nothing more than two antisocial postadolescents and a pile of parts in a dingy suburban garage, was now a billion-dollar company, its founders on their way to becoming living legends, its products transforming the home, the school and the office. Apple was now the first great company of the new age in electronics, the first great enterprise created by children of the baby boom. As such it would forever be the benchmark for any accomplishment of that generation, and the paradigm for the thousands of companies to follow. The kid who once neglected to bathe had become the voice of a new high-tech generation.

That night, after the parties finally faded out, the children of Apple went home to their new lives. IPOs are convergences. In the run-up to Going Public Day, companies often enjoy the greatest morale and cohesiveness in their histories. For five years, Apple had been a great crusade—a Children's Crusade, with all the attendant grandiosity, immaturity, posturing, missteps, victories and boundless enthusiasms—all working toward the common goal of making this foundling company a success.

Now that success had come. All the career trajectories had finally intersected on a sunny December day. And from now on, they would diverge. There would be other convergences, including an even greater one four years hence. But that, with a few exceptions, would be for a new group of Apple employees, not for this one. Even as they finally fell asleep that night, the lives of Apple's first round of winners were already heading off on different tangents that would take many far from Bandley Drive.

For some, that departure would come much sooner than expected. Having reached such a lofty pinnacle of success, Apple was now about to fall into the abyss. But at least it would have a full wallet for the trip.

6.0 BEARING FRUIT

High-tech companies nowadays go to great lengths to control the impact of going public. They try to stop employees from burning up their new wealth on wasteful and ostentatious toys. They try to keep the celebrations down to a controlled riot. They sometimes bring in financial managers to teach the new tycoons how to deal with their overnight riches and to understand that stock (which many hold for the first time) is a volatile and temperamental instrument that can suffer wild swings in price. And they try, though it can be very difficult, to keep their senior executives from either walking away with their incredible wealth or staying and doing something selfish and stupid that pulls down the company.

They do these things because Silicon Valley has learned its lessons about IPOs. And two of the biggest of these lessons came in the early 1980s, during the Valley's first great going-public boom. One of these warnings came from Eagle Computer, a short-lived personal computer company that managed to go public at just the right moment in June 1983. On that day, the company's forty-year-old CEO, Dennis Barnhart, celebrated his new wealth—$9 million—by having lunch with a yacht salesman, getting drunk, then driving his new Ferrari off a cliff.

The moral wasn't lost on other CEOs who could easily imagine themselves in Barnhart's expensive shoes. To this day, IPO boardroom celebrations remain comparatively sober affairs.

The second lesson taught to the high-tech world about IPOs came from Apple Computer. No company had ever flown so high in such a short time, and no company ever screwed up in so many ways in the weeks and months thereafter. What actually happened to Apple after its IPO is largely forgotten by Valleyites, but to this day both employees and executives of newly public companies are obsessed with the fear that their company will now begin to fall apart. Yet, even armed with that knowledge, many still do.

When Apple went public, it had neither of these warnings. Nor, with the arrogance and narcissism that had characterized the company from the beginning, would it likely have listened if it had. So instead, the company devoted its days for the next few months tracking the roller-coaster ride of the company's stock. If the stock had a good day, so did Apple—employees were happy and motivated, work got done, products were shipped. If the stock faltered, dark clouds formed over Cupertino, the staff grew moody and sullen and nothing got done.

Meanwhile, employees who owned company stock devoted a considerable amount of the day to figuring out how to protect those shares from the government—and how to spend them on themselves. This was when local banks around Silicon Valley first learned how to make loans by accepting stock options as collateral. One group of employees even flew out of the country to Vancouver, British Columbia, on April 15 in order to legally file for an extension on their 1980 taxes.

Even to the outsider, the transformation of Apple was obvious within a week after the IPO. Where the parking lot had been Volkswagen vans, Volvos and beat-up American clunkers, suddenly, almost overnight, the same slots were filled with Mercedeses and Porsches.

Executive row was no more immune to this than any other department at Apple. A conversation about business was likely to devolve into a discussion about relative merits of private airplanes, the amount of time needed to get a multiengine license and the relative difficulty of getting a good space at San Jose Airport.

Bill Atkinson, at the time an Apple programmer, said with dismay, "Some people spent half their waking hours counting their stock options." And it was even worse than that, because once they finished counting, many of these same employees realized that in a couple of years when the stock fully vested, they could sell out, quit Apple and retire forever.

The loss of key employees after an IPO is a common problem. But Steve Jobs only made matters worse at Apple. Before the IPO, he had used options as a bludgeon against enemies and former friends; now he used it as a test of loyalty. That Markkula had taken some of his money, bought a used Learjet and paid two pilots to operate it, or that Woz, caught up in Markkula's flying fever, had bought his own Beechcraft, didn't seem to bother Jobs—in fact, it pleased him, because it increased his comparative ownership. But let a lesser mortal at Apple try to sell his stock and Jobs saw it as a betrayal to the cause.

Jef Raskin landed on Jobs's enemy list for just such a sale. This was especially ironic because Raskin sold his stock precisely because he didn't want to have to worry about it anymore and because he wanted to focus again on his work for Apple. Nevertheless, Jobs would never fully trust Raskin again, a change in attitude that would have enormous implications for the company.

To Jobs's credit, when it came to stock he lived his philosophy. His quality of clothes improved a little—he was already becoming a noted fashion plate—as did his lifestyle, which now included an expensive, but famously spartan, home, a Mercedes and a motorcycle. But in light of his fabulous new wealth, this was pocket change. He didn't need to touch his stockholdings. And Jobs expected no less from anybody else at Apple.

Admirable as this asceticism might be, it also signaled that Jobs was just as obsessed about his stock as everyone else at Apple. Nobody but resentful nonshareholding employees was minding the store.

That might have been okay for a little while, except for a growing high-tech tumor in the corpus of the company: the Apple III. It was still being shipped DOA or ready to blip off within hours of being turned on. And nobody knew why. While everyone was watching the stock ticker, Apple was sliding toward a PR disaster that could turn all those stock certificates into wallpaper.

It wasn't until January, luckily while the world was still in Apple IPO afterglow, that the cause of the III's electronic aneurism was finally isolated. One person had actually discovered the cause weeks before: Dan Kottke, the founder who'd been refused stock options by a vengeful Jobs. Kottke had been working with a III that would unexpectedly die. One day, furious, he picked the machine up a couple of inches and then slammed it down on his worktable. The III jumped back to life. A faulty connector, Kottke decided. But he told no one. Later he would say that, as a lowly engineer, he didn't feel in a position to bring his concerns to his superiors. "Lowly engineer," of course, was a phrase Jobs had used in explaining why he wouldn't give Kottke stock. It was Kottke's revenge.

Sander's boss, Tom Whitney, assuming that everything was fine with production, told Mike Scott that all was well and III's would soon be rolling off the manufacturing line. Then, despite Mike Scott's request that he stay in Cupertino in case of an emergency, he left on a business trip to Europe. Whitney returned to be fired. He left with his millions.

In the end, the bad connection proved to be the one to the Apple III's heart. Sander, trapped by the impossible performance and design demands made on the product, had been forced to build the III using two printed circuit boards full of chips: the motherboard and a smaller board containing all the memory chips stacked precariously atop one another. Even worse, that memory board had to be made out of the thinnest printed circuit material on the market.

It was a perfect recipe for disaster. Some machines actually ran until they were bolted into their enclosures, then the memory board flexed and shorted out. In other III's, the problem was on the motherboard. To protect the all-important microprocessor chip in this dense layout, it was mounted in a pit within a raised platform for the connector. Unfortunately, the pit itself wasn't much bigger than the chip, leaving no clearance for the assembler's fingers to line up the little lead wire "legs" of the chip to fit into the proper slots. In shades of Jobs's sister building the Apple I, Apple III assemblers were reduced to pushing down the chip with their thumb and hoping for the best.

Still other machines shorted out the moment they were turned on because the metal conductors plated on the surface of the printed circuit boards were so close that they exceeded the tolerances of the PC industry. And in still others, the wiring was so close to screw holes holding everything together that the act of assembly would drive the screws through the wiring insulation and either short the machine out or threaten to set it on fire.

The whole situation was so absurd that Kottke's "bounce" test temporarily became a recommended manufacturing step. Each III was to be picked up three inches and dropped to knock some sense into it. And even that wasn't easy, since the damn computer, thanks to a heavy metal case (used because of fears the FCC would soon rule against excessive RF—radio frequency—leakage), weighed about as much as a microwave oven. That weight, combined with the fact that the III was unbalanced by a heavy power supply against its rear wall, made it literally a backbreaker for assembly workers and owners performing the Kottke Bounce. So a visitor to the III manufacturing line in early 1981 would have met the astonishing sight of employees smacking the brand-new Apple III's with rubber mallets.

At any other time, Apple would simply have bitten the bullet and stopped production of the III until the design and manufacturing problems were worked out. But the company was stuck. It had announced the delivery date of the III in its stock prospectus and didn't dare back off. So now, the product that was to replace the aging Apple II, the killer computer that was to smash the existing competition, scare off potential new ones and forever position Apple in the corporate market, was proving for many buyers little more than a $5,000 paperweight. And even when it worked it lacked its most promoted, and anticipated, design feature.

For all that, the Apple III was not a bad computer. Just a benighted one. It had a sophisticated operating system (which was called just that: SOS), a full-sized 80-character screen, as much as 512K of memory, and a magnificent keyboard. In time it would be the first mass-market personal computer with an optional hard disk drive, the Profile. But none of that mattered, because the horrible launch of the III had already doomed it.

As bad as the hardware problem was for the III, it masked a deeper, and ultimately more far-reaching failure in the machine. Because of that, Apple never learned what should have been the real lesson of the III debacle. In an executive meeting several months before the III introduction, Jobs and Markkula got into a long conversation about the incredible number of new companies—board builders, software developers, hardware makers—that had sprung up surrounding the Apple II. According to an attendee at the meeting, the two executives then began to ask each other, "Why should we allow people to make money off of us? Off of our innovations?"

"It was a turning point," recalled that individual fifteen years later. "From that moment on, Apple fought all third-party development. All the way down the line. It even killed Radius, a $300-million monitor company that was doing a great job. Over time it got worse, and it became not just about money but ego. This attitude developed at Apple that nobody could do anything better than Apple could. That's why the company kept building its own keyboards and everything else—and why Apple computers became so much more expensive than everyone else."

6.1 III Be Gone

By the end of 1980, after all the attention over the IPO ended, the first in-depth reviews of the III appeared, and they were almost uniformly negative. The press had wanted to love the Apple III, and they had shown their ardor at Disneyland. But there was no mistaking that the machine was a beauty on the surface but a dog at heart. And a dog without a brain—two months after its introduction, the III had only three software programs available for it, one of them a mail management program written by Markkula himself . . . and few new ones expected for another six months. The III also had a terrible habit, especially for a journalist on deadline in the middle of writing a story about it, of simply crapping out, responding to a SAVE command with that most depressingly final of technology phrases: SYSTEM FAILURE.

So bad were the reviews that Apple finally accepted (but never publicly admitted) failure, and pulled the III. On Regis's advice, the company stopped all advertising and promotion of the III and went back to the drawing boards. The guts were redesigned for greater reliability, more memory (to a total of 512K) was added, the clock chip was finally put in, new manuals were prepared, and a complete software library was rushed to completion. Existing III owners with a dead or malfunctioning machine (sometimes the second or third one) were allowed, without cost, to swap it for the new, more powerful machine.

Finally, at the end of 1981, as if nothing had ever happened, the Apple III was formally relaunched.

It was a bit of chutzpah on Apple's part, but it wasn't unique for the industry. Throughout the 1970s, Hewlett-Packard had to reintroduce its 3000 minicomputer three times before it finally got the technology right. It went on to become one of the best-selling computers in industry history.

Apple, however, wasn't so fortunate. The fixed III was a fine computer, a fact recognized by hundreds of businesses, which bought them by the dozens each, and by thousands of individuals who, even after the misery they had been through, became rabid Apple III loyalists. But by 1983 only 65,000 Apple III's had been sold—a figure only a little higher than Apple had expected in sales the first year.

Still, some Apple marketers and engineers wanted to stick with the III. After all, its wrinkles had been smoothed out, it had penetrated the all-important business market and the company had some obligation to the III's user base. But one figure was adamant about burying the III like a dead cat: Regis McKenna. He saw the III as a living reminder of Apple's ability to screw up, and an enduring symbol of the company's arrogance. Regis wanted to clear the decks for the new computer families to come. He refused to promote the III and it quickly died.

It was a mistake. Until then, Apple, in its style, its carefully crafted image and its public pronouncements, had always presented itself as different from other companies. It was the people's computer company . . . as the ads would say in a few years, the maker of "computers for the rest of us." A company like that didn't abandon its loyal customers, it didn't summarily kill a computer line and make orphans of its users. Apple wasn't supposed to do things like that . . . but now it had, and those thousands of III owners (and many more thousands of II owners who were watching) would never completely trust Apple again. Even at Apple, it seemed, business was still just business.

Pissed off III owners were only part of Regis's mistake. The full implications of his error wouldn't be known for years. Unwittingly, by killing the III early, McKenna never allowed its real flaw—limited third-party hardware and software—to be fully felt. Had he let the Apple III limp on for another year, its internal problems fixed, but its software library still bare, Apple might have learned the one big lesson about open systems that would have later saved it. Instead, Regis killed the patient when it began to cough, before the cancer made itself known. Now, Apple could convince itself that the real problem had been a procedural problem, a bug, and not a systemic collapse.

6.2 Shattered Genius

One measure of just how interesting new wealth was at Apple right after the IPO—and, conversely, how boring the daily business of cranking out II's and fixing III's was by comparison—was to talk to Markkula or Wozniak during the early months of 1981.

Markkula, accustomed to wealth, was a little more discreet, but nevertheless was delighted to get off business and talk about skiing, vacation home and, most of all, flying his Learjet.

A conversation with Wozniak during this period was much more disconcerting. There in his office, surrounded by the detritus of the computing revolution he'd helped to spark, Woz too would drift off into discussions about flying, about how he'd bought a Beechcraft Bonanza back before Thanksgiving with some of the proceeds of his private stock sales, how he was finishing up his pilot's license and his dreams of getting a multiengine license and eventually working his way up to pilot his own jet.

It was wildly disorienting. Here was a young man just pushing thirty, who just a couple of years before had been so indifferent to the material world beyond his computer screen that he regularly forgot where he was. Now he was behaving like a spoiled prince. It was as if Woz, struggling to resurface in the world after all those years lost in the fun house of computer technology, had suddenly been shaken awake by all the excitement around the IPO. Now he found himself not only back in the world but richer than God. His father once discovered $250,000 in uncashed checks in his son's new Porsche and said mournfully, "A person like him shouldn't have that much money."

And with the emotional development of a teenager who had never grown up, Woz set out to indulge as many experiences and buy as many toys as he could. To hell with computers, now it was time to live.

That explained the gambling at Lake Tahoe and the fast car. And when his lawyers advised him to expand his portfolio, Woz went out and bought a movie theater in the Hispanic barrio of East Side San Jose. The theater soon showed the provocative gang film *The Warriors*, which provoked a small riot, and Woz soon found himself attending community meetings and apologizing to angry residents.

He also became engaged again. Candi Clark, the daughter of a contractor from the East Bay, was an Apple employee. According to her childhood friends, she had always wanted, from an early age, to find a wealthy husband. And one fine day she found him, a man so wealthy it would be hard to ever burn up his money and so innocent as to fall in love at first sight, on the other side of a water-gun fight. And in that little vignette—childish play, a shrewd companion and a naive Woz—could be seen the pattern for the next decade of Stephen Wozniak's life.

There was about Woz during this period and ever after the sense of an innocent fool, caught up in situations more complicated and more sinister than he could ever understand. He was the Candide of the computer age, doing everything wrong, but earnestly and with good intentions . . . then somehow managing to emerge, alive, from the resulting rubble.

Alive, but not always intact. In the future it would be his bank account that would take a beating. But not now. On February 7, 1981, Woz, Clark and two friends drove up into the nearby Santa Cruz mountains to the airport at Scotts Valley and climbed into Woz's Beechcraft.

It was a strange time for Woz. Personally, his life couldn't be better. He was rich, engaged and a living legend. But professionally, his life had not been happy. His workmates, many of them his greatest fans and former apostles, were getting sick of his unproductiveness. And nobody was more annoyed at Woz's apparent goldbricking than Mike Scott.

Angry that Fylstra and Personal Software had begun to design VisiCalc for Apple's competitors, Scott decided to get even by rendering the software company irrelevent. His strategy was to have Apple design its own spreadsheet program and have it bundled in with every II or III. But Scott also knew that pushing such a project through Apple's growing bureaucracy would take forever. Atypically, he circumvented his own organization chart and assigned the project to Randy Wigginton, Woz's erstwhile acolyte. Scott reasoned that Wigginton would undoubtedly enlist Woz, and that might in turn get the resident genius off his butt and back to creating.

But it didn't quite work out as planned. Wigginton did convince Woz to help work out some math routines. But then Woz wandered off, figuring he had lots of time to get to it. Meanwhile, Wigginton tore through the code writing and suddenly found himself ready for Woz's routines and Woz hadn't even begun.

Wigginton was pissed, but not nearly as much as Mike Scott. From the beginning Scott's job had been that of not only running a high-profile, fast-growing corporate superstar but also babysitting the two founders. That meant controlling Jobs and motivating Woz. Jobs, perpetually wandering off the reservation to make pronouncements outside the company and interfering with the work of departments within, had initially been the greater challenge. But Woz's deepening inertia in the months leading up the IPO had been increasingly worrisome.

Now it was threatening Mike Scott's own authority within the company. Before it was too late, he set out to make an example to other slugs coasting along at the newly rich company. He decided to put the screws to Woz.

Throughout January 1981 Scott made Wozniak's life a living hell, hectoring him, buffaloing him, ragging his ass almost every day. In response, Woz seemed to return to his old form. He worked day and night constructing the routines. As always, once he set his mind to it, he made amazing progress.

Through it all, Woz did manage to retain his sense of humor. He even managed the classic Wozniak revenge of pulling a practical joke on Scott. Knowing Mike was a George Lucas fanatic—Scott had mentioned his dream of inviting the movie director onto the Apple board—Woz talked a friend into calling Scott's office when he knew Mike wasn't in. Impersonating Lucas, the caller left a message saying he'd call back. Scott nearly swooned when he heard the message, and became so obsessed with being on hand for the call that he stayed off Wozniak's back for nearly a week.

By the first week of February an exhausted Woz had the routines completed except for a final check. He decided to celebrate by getting away and doing some flying. And that's what found him with his fiancée and two other friends at the Scotts Valley airport. He likely had the routines with him in the plane when it took off, planning on putting on the finishing touches later that day.

Even before takeoff, Woz had been nervous and jumpy, complaining about headphone interference. At takeoff, the plane had climbed just fifty feet in the air, bounced down again off the tarmac, then careened off at an angle through two fences and into an embankment.

Exactly what happened is a matter of speculation. The first reports had it that Woz and company were practicing touch-and-go landings as part of Woz's training for his next-level pilot's license. If so, it was an incredibly stupid and reckless act on Woz's part: an unskilled pilot performing high-risk maneuvers with a plane full of people. Later the story was that the group was actually leaving for Southern California to pick up Woz and Candi's wedding rings. It may even have been both.

The National Transportation Safety Board never found a mechanical cause for the crash. But, pilot error or not, the result was nearly catastrophic—

the plane came to rest just two hundred feet from a roller-skating rink jammed with teenagers.

If the skaters were spared, the passengers in the plane were not. Candi Clark suffered severe enough cuts on her face to need plastic surgery. The back-seat passengers were battered and bruised.

But it was Woz, slammed into the controls and dashboard, who took the worst of it. He bit through his upper lip, fractured the socket of his right eye and took a bump on the head sufficient to cause double vision. But he was conscious and, all things considered, seemed normal on the trip to El Camino Hospital in Mountain View, the facility nearest his home and his parents.

But he wasn't all right. The blow had caused amnesia. He retained his long-term memory, remembering events up to a day before the accident, but could not recall the day of the crash itself. Nor, it seemed, could he form any new short-term memories. The near-present seemed perpetually lost. He was a computer with a disk drive but no internal memory.

Then, most frightening of all, as he lay in his hospital room waves of paranoia swept over Woz. He refused to eat, acting as if it might be poisoned. He announced in conspiritorial tones that the government was plotting to take his money and, presumably with him in it, blow up the hospital.

The paranoia was obvious to his friends and family, but the deeper neural injuries were not. After a few days, Woz seemed on the mend. He awoke one night to tell Candi that he dreamed he'd been in a plane crash, and was stunned to find it had actually happened. He began to regain the present. Finally, after a week in the hospital, he was released. If he seemed any different from the experience, it was, some noticed, that he seemed slower, as if his mind had to wind itself up before it could render a judgment.

At Apple, paralyzed and in shock over its beloved founder, resident genius and mascot being nearly killed, there was a sigh of relief that Woz was okay. And when he left the hospital, it was generally agreed that after a brief rest he would soon be back to work at Apple.

But Woz wouldn't come back for five years. Sitting at home, he was as lost and confused as he'd ever been in his life.

6.3 Black Wednesday

It was to be a season of losses and betrayals. The failure of the III demanded its pound of employee flesh. Mike Scott, displaying the hard side of his personality that was always there with his sweetness, set out to do the butchering.

In the months leading up to and just after the IPO, Scott had grown convinced that Apple had become too bloated with employees who were either superfluous or not up to their jobs. In most companies growing as fast as Apple, this temporary excess could easily have been remedied by some transfers, a few pointed suggestions about finding work elsewhere and a temporary hiring slowdown.

But Scott, an offspring of Fairchild and National Semiconductor, decided instead to do all in one swift, brutal stroke. The result, known forever after at Apple as Black Wednesday, came in late February less than three months after the IPO. As with the day of the introduction of the Apple III, it was rainy; but this time it was miserably dark and cold as well. It was a good day for slaughter.

Companies almost never have layoffs so soon after an initial public stock offering. For one thing, they are usually too rich and growing too fast to worry about a little deadwood. The natural attrition of people wealthy enough not to have to work anymore also helps solve the problem. And finally, management is usually too obsessed with its newest challenge—keeping tens of thousands of new stockholders happy—to risk bad publicity for a while.

But Mike Scott didn't care about any of these things. He believed the III mess called for extreme measures if Apple was ever going to get back into fighting trim. "Apple had been doubling its employment almost every quarter," he recalls. "We had grown from 500 to 1,500 in just the previous year. What started it was one guy we had running peripherals who was a real turkey, and I made up my mind to fire him. I starting wondering how many others at the company were out of their depth.

"So I brought it up at a staff meeting. I said, 'Maybe we've made some mistakes. Go back and look over your list of new hires and determine who should be laid off.' "

He had his supporters in this move. Gary Martin for one: "I was in the meeting with Scott and Don Bryson of the III group before the III's introduction. I said, 'Hey, are we ready to go with the product?' He said, 'Yes.'

"Then Scott asked, 'Would you bet the company on it?'

" 'Yes.'

" 'Would you bet your job on it?'

" 'Yes,' Bryson said.

"But they weren't ready. They screwed it up, and they deserved to be fired."

It was to be a ritual purging to purify Apple for the battles to come. At least that was Scott's plan. Just three weeks after Woz's accident, while the company was still in shock, Scott circulated to the department heads a list of eighty people to be canned and asked if any should be kept around. The shocked managers acted like managers everywhere when faced with such an edict: they protected their friends by marking them off the list or transferring them to other departments, and got rid of their enemies, including not only incompetents but goldbricks, malcontents and contenders for their jobs. As a result, some good people, many who'd recently been awarded raises or good performance reviews, or who were accidentally in the wrong place on the organization chart were hauled into Scott's office with all the rest, given a month's severance and summarily fired. The final tally was forty employees laid off. Scott, setting a pattern for future Apple CEOs, filled Whitney's slot by naming himself director of engineering.

The newly laid-off employees were also forced to endure another humiliation before they left. After the ugly mass layoffs in Silicon Valley of a few years before, many local firms had abandoned the old policy of mass firing and out the door the same day that had ruled at places like Fairchild during the previous two decades. The new procedure was to announce the layoff as much as a month in advance, bring in employee placement experts and handle the transition as delicately as possible. Mike Scott neither understood nor adopted this new policy. "I did it my way. The Charlie Sporck way. No pre-notice. We handed out the checks and escorted the employees out the door. I've always thought that was the most humane way, instead of paralyzing the company for weeks and leaving people worrying if they were on the list. I know a lot of people don't agree."

Forty employees. A small number, but it had a devastating impact. Mike Scott had expected the company to react to the layoffs by bearing down and becoming more disciplined, and for the market to applaud the move. Instead, both recoiled with horror. This wasn't the Apple each group thought it knew. Apple was *family*, it was caring, it was the antithesis of mean old capitalism. Apple didn't just throw people out on the street. That's why you came to work at Apple, that's why you invested in the company—because it was *special*. Besides, wasn't it the most successful new company in the world? Hadn't its employees done superhuman things to make it so? And this was their payoff?

Scott, of course, saw it differently. He had weeded out the incompetents—*after* many of them had been amply rewarded by the IPO. He had done it swiftly and precisely. "And I even tried to soften the blow by calling it a layoff," he says. "I didn't realize how loaded that word had become. If I had known that, I would have just called it what it was: forty individual firings."

From the beginning, Steve Jobs had said that he wanted to build Apple on the same principles as Hewlett-Packard's philosophy, the famous HP Way—but without being as staid and boring. But in more than forty years, through wars and recessions, good times and bad, Bill Hewlett and David Packard, retrograde and old-fashioned as they seemed to Steve Jobs, had never laid off a single employee. Now, after just five years in business Apple had already shattered its avowed philosophy.

Steve Jobs, powerless as a manager, but with veto power as the leading shareholder, had done nothing. A furious Chris Espinosa found him and hissed, "This is no way to run a company." A disconsolate Jobs (who, with Markkula, had approved the layoffs) gave only the Pontius Pilate reply, "How do you run a company?"

Apple couldn't, and wouldn't, be quite the same again. From this point on, employees knew that management not only carried a meat ax but was willing to use it. A decade later, when the first of the giant layoffs came, thousands of fired Apple people would again howl, but they couldn't honestly claim they'd been betrayed. After all, they'd been warned by Black Wednesday.

But perhaps the worst of it was that Black Wednesday had exactly the opposite effect anticipated. The market price of the stock didn't appreciably change. Customers weren't left more trusting of Apple's business acumen, but wondering why the company had so many incompetents that it had to resort to such extreme measures. And most devastating, at a time when the company itself needed to recoup from the failure of the III, hold on to its now wealthy best employees and get to work on new products to consolidate its control of the market, Apple collapsed into a dispirited, paranoid funk. Woz was hurt and perhaps gone forever, Jobs was sullen and depressed and the once bright company, the hope of a generation, now seemed in the hands of a heartless slavemaster.

"All of a sudden," said Fred Hoar, "Apple values were tanked and in its place we had ruthlessness." Another employee, Phil Roybal, told Mike Moritz, "A lot of people always assumed that sort of thing couldn't happen at Apple. Th[is] was the first sign of grim reality. People didn't know what the world was coming to. Their values had been turned upside down. Suddenly we were a company just like any other." Added Bruce Tognazzini, "It was the end of a lot of things. It was the end of innocence. It was the end of loyalty. It ushered in an era of incredible fear."

All of that from the layoff of just forty people; departures that could have easily been handled one at a time over a period of several months.

Mike Scott had blown it.

There had been about Scott in the year leading up to Black Wednesday a growing sense that he was beginning to crack under the pressure of running Apple. His behavior, always erratic, had grown even more unpredictable and even, contrary to his nature, cruel. He stomped on those around him, as even one of his admirers later admitted, "in the way a gorilla enjoys raw, unabated power." He left requisitions hanging, awaiting his signature, just to remind underlings who had the power. He cut off subordinates both in person and in memos. And at times he seemed completely out of control, marching around the company aisles, looking in over the tops of cubicles and demanding, "Are you working your ass off?"

By the beginning of 1981 Scott was acting paranoid, muttering dark threats about setting things straight, saying, "I'm not going to put up with things I don't like." Even his body began to succumb to the stress. Years of overwork, combined with his weight problem, had already given him diabetes. Now he developed a viral eye infection so severe that it threatened his sight. Eyeless in Cupertino, he bluffed his way through the day and then at night secretly had all of his communications read aloud to him by his secretary.

To his credit, Mike Scott knew as much as anyone that he was beginning to succumb to the stress. He had worn himself out over the previous two years building the company and taking it public. And looking ahead, he saw no break: the Mac, the impending attack by IBM, the problems with the Apple III, a second major stock offering in May 1981. His one relief, and great love, was opera, and he had long planned to attend the Wagner *Ring* cycle at the Seattle opera. But when he looked at his schedule, "I suddenly realized that I had every day booked for the next year. I was trapped."

Scott approached Markkula and asked him to help run half the company. It was both a strategic decision and a cry for help. Apple's engineering group was in disarray and in desperate need of close management attention. Scott had already moved his desk to the center of the III group building in Sunnyvale. The proposed plan was for Scott to take over engineering and straighten it out, while Markkula, as CEO, would run the rest of the company.

It was a solid plan, and Scott assumed that Markkula, both as a good businessman and as one of his closest friends, would readily accept.

But Markkula, with one foot already out the door in happy anticipation of a second retirement, refused. As Gary Martin recalled: "Markkula was always retired. He was always saying, 'I'm retired. I'm just doing this for fun. Scott's in charge.' "

"It was all on me now," recalled Scott. "I asked Mike for help and he turned me down. That's what hurt the most." They would never again be good friends.

By Black Wednesday, Scott was both a frightening and a sad figure. That afternoon he called a company meeting in hopes of getting the company past the layoffs and focused on a bright new beginning. But with the gloom over the company as dark as the leaden skies outside, the meeting, appropriately held in a company basement, didn't have the least chance of succeeding. The employees desultorily drank a little beer and sneaked disgusted or fearful looks at one another. Finally, Scott got up and gave a little speech designed to restore morale and regain the old Apple spirit. It was disjointed, uninspired and terribly inappropriate. Every figure in the room, even the Mike Scott fans, even the people who agreed that Apple needed a little downsizing, at that moment resented the man who had built their company.

In the grim weeks that followed, it was obvious that only another sacrifice could expiate Apple's sin. There were even anonymous memos passed around calling for concerted action. One such memo, signed by the Computer Professionals Union, read in part: "The thing they fear most is concerted employee action; the tactics they use are divide and conquer, and threats of economic reprisal. They can't get away with it if we unite! Apple was once a good place to work; management preaches to us about the 'Apple Spirit'; let's show them what a little bit of real spirit is like and ram it down their throats."

This was unionization—the bottommost circle of hell in the Silicon Valley theology. There would have to be blood for blood. And everyone knew whose blood it should be. But even then top management hesitated. It was only when Scott began to mutter darkly about Black Wednesday being only the first of several rounds of layoffs that he sealed his fate. He had to go. "I got scapegoated," says Scott. "Every v.p. in the company had contributed to the layoff list. Now it was all my fault."

Since the president is the highest-ranking line officer of a company, the only way he can be fired is by a vote of the board. In this case, that really meant a decision by the chairman, Mike Markkula, both because of his massive stockholdings and because of his daily involvement with the firm. And Markkula did it in the characteristic Markkula manner: he waited until Scott was out of town.

Scott, his eye problems now matched by a nasty and unresponsive case of sinusitis, planned to recover his health with a long weekend in Hawaii. While he was gone, Markkula convened a meeting of senior Apple managers—although some of Scott's strongest supporters were intentionally left out—to discuss what to do about the company's president, the man who had taken them, in one of the most extraordinary business trajectories, from a garage to international fame and $300 million in annual sales. In a single voice vote, the managers ruthlessly ended Scott's Apple career.

Scott returned to a message from Markkula asking to see him. Their conversation began with a little forced chitchat, and then Markkula cut it off by saying, "Scotty, the executive staff has voted to ask for your resignation." He added that he wanted that resignation, in writing, by morning.

Traditionally, a company's first era, its corporate adolescence, ends with the first public offering of stock. But Apple's adolescence, appropriately, was attenuated. It ended the next morning with Mike Scott's resignation. Officially, he was promoted to vice-chairman, Jobs to chairman, and Markkula assumed Scott's old role as president. In doing that, Apple set yet another pattern—the ritual purging of CEOs by management mutiny—that would haunt the company for years to come.

The transition could have been handled more smoothly, after a search for a new and experienced CEO. Certainly there was no shortage of talented veteran executives with Fortune 500 experience who would have killed to take the wheel of Apple Computer. Instead, the reins would now go to a marketing man who only dreamed of ski slopes and his second retirement and to an immature global celebrity whose managerial experience, because no one trusted him as a boss, was still essentially zero.

Scott's departure was cheered by many of the troops. To them, the ogre was gone at last. And the transition occurred so quietly, the subsequent rewriting of history so complete, that Mike Scott essentially fell down the memory hole. The public barely noticed his departure then, and barely remembers him now at all. It was all done so smoothly that Art Rock, who knew from experience what good and bad executive executions were like, complimented Apple on its handling of the whole affair. In fact, in the press, Scott's firing was treated as comparable to the regular and benign job rotation Intel performed every few years among Noyce, Moore and Grove.

But Mike Scott's resignation was anything but benign. Against almost impossible odds he had performed a business miracle. Under his command, Apple had grown into a $300 million company growing at nearly 200 percent per year, with a market capitalization of more than $1 billion and an astonishing productivity rate of $200,000 in revenues per employee. At the end of his tenure, Apple employed hundreds of people based not only in Cupertino but at manufacturing plants in San Jose, Dallas, Los Angeles and Cork, Ireland, sold its products through 3,000 dealers and dominated the profitable corner of the fastest-growing new industry in the world.

Mike Scott had taken a manufacturing operation that consisted of a handful of people in a garage backed by a few dozen immigrants doing illegal piecework and converted it into a state-of-the-art assembly plant supported by one of the best computerized corporate information systems of any company its size. And finally, of course, Scott had managed the company through the most difficult of all challenges to a young business, an IPO, and pulled off one of the greatest stock sales ever recorded. Don Valentine, no mean judge of executive talent, would call it one of the best executive performances he'd ever seen.

Against all that, from twenty years' perspective, Scott's occasional cruelties, his arbitrariness and his increasingly erratic behavior seem minor. If the Apple Corps wanted to see what tough looked like, they merely had to drive down the street to National Semiconductor or Commodore. And if they wanted a close-up look at executive capriciousness, they merely had to spend a day visiting Atari . . . or the Apple that was about to be created by the newly unleashed Steve Jobs.

But the deed was now done. Scott was out. Meanwhile, Apple, as it scapegoated Scott, turned Black Wednesday into a far bleaker event than it had ever been. Now, inculcated into its culture would be the vow to never allow such a terrible layoff to ever happen again. And for the next decade, the company would keep that promise—as it grew bloated, unmanageable and top-heavy with employees and managers who had no reason for being there. And Apple would hold to its vow right up to the moment, too late, when it would spectacularly shatter it.

From the perspective of two decades, Regis McKenna would conclude that Scott's firing, as welcome as it seemed at the time, was in fact a horrible mistake. "Intel was just a few years older than Apple, yet by this point it had already developed a body of distinct management processes. Decisions were no longer made by someone's flip idea of the moment.

"Mike Scott was a tough and demanding boss. But he was also intent on putting some sort of systematic decision-making process into place at Apple. And Apple got rid of him. Looking back, he was Apple's last chance to institute some kind of order. After that, the culture became so overwhelming that even the toughest manager would come in to shake things up—and instead find himself two months later lounging on a beanbag chair."

There has always been something suspicious about the official story of Mike Scott's firing. Why would a public company, so soon after its IPO, toss out the CEO who had done such an extraordinary job getting it there? For being stressed out and mercurial? That's why leaves of absences were invented. HP and Intel already had established programs for exhausted executives. Three months on a beach and a diet and Mike Scott would have been renewed and back at the helm of Apple Computer.

For Black Wednesday? Against the recession of a few years before, in which electronics companies had laid off thousands, or the aerospace crash of 1970, in which Lockheed had fired 10 percent of the Valley's adult males, the Apple layoff wasn't even a blip. Sure it was traumatic to the utopians at Apple, but they would have gotten over it, just as they had rationalized their other ethical lapses.

In fact, there was one other, decisive, reason why Mike Scott was driven out: he was homosexual. It was hardly a secret, and Scott, though discreet, had never tried to hide the fact—certainly not from his old friend Mike Markkula. But what had been a matter of indifference when Apple was a small private company suddenly loomed large in many minds when Apple was a publicly traded giant. It didn't fit with the profile of a Fortune 500 CEO; and especially not the tough cowboy world of Silicon Valley.

But Mike Scott today is forgiving: "Great people sometimes make thoughtless mistakes. Great companies do too. I like to think this was one of those times."

At first, Mike Scott seemed to take his impeachment well. As a consolation prize he was asked to manage the expansion of his beloved management information system. He lasted a month, long enough to make one presentation to his former lieutenants. Then he cracked. He wrote a bitter and sad memo, saying (in an ironic echo of the Computer Professionals Union memo) that he was through forever with the "hypocrisy, yes-men, foolhardy plans, a 'cover your ass' attitude and empire builders." In defense of his own autocratic style, he added: "A company's quality of life is not and cannot be set by a committee."

Then he was gone. Now rich enough to never work again, Scott began his retirement by flying off to the Seattle Wagner Festival.

But life without Apple wasn't as easy as he had imagined. "It was like a death in the family," he says. He returned to become a lonely hermit, hiding in his suburban house for days at a time, listening to Wagner, sleeping during the day, sitting alone with his cats and watching TV or playing the organ. When he went out, it was often to the city dump to fire off model rockets. He rarely had visitors, but when he did, they usually found him heartbroken, living over and over his fall from grace. One visitor reported that Scott's spirits only lifted once: when he found he could still remember the model numbers for all the parts in the Apple II.

He had loved Apple Computer—"my baby" he called it—and assumed that his love would be requited. Unfortunately, as he should have known from the beginning, he didn't have enough stock for that.

As the weeks turned into months and Scott showed no signs of recovering, and did not respond to entreaties for him to get reinvolved in the company, many of his old compatriots began to worry. Even Steve Jobs was haunted by Scott's plight. Four years later Jobs would admit, "I was always afraid that I'd get a call to say that Scotty had committed suicide."

But Mike Scott never did away with himself. In time, he pulled himself together and went on with his life. He started a rocket company, visited Africa numerous times, rented a square rigger and took many of his old Apple associates on a weeklong cruise. He turned his house into a garden spot atop its Los Altos Hills ridge. And be became a leading expert on color gems and minerals, eventually assembling one of the world's great private collections.

Mike Scott was happy again. And, on special occasions, he still sent white roses to secretaries and receptionists at Apple.

6.4 Bloodshed

With the Apple III back on the drawing board, the Apple II somehow managed not just to hold its own but to leap even higher in sales. As a result, Apple believed it could breathe easy. The months after an IPO are almost always a letdown, but at Apple they had been the very nadir. It was as if after flying so high the company had to find a balance by hitting rock bottom. But now, with sales still holding strong, it seemed as if Apple had truly dodged a bullet.

TI and Radio Shack, though their PC sales were strong, had never caught the market's imagination. TI's TRS-80 had been nicknamed the "Trash 80" because it was so crudely built. And Radio Shack, because it sold its computers through its own stores, was limited to selling only to the kind of people who shopped at Radio Shack.

Commodore was also selling a lot of computers—it would be the first, in 1983, to reach a billion dollars in sales, Apple's claims to the contrary—but its Pet computer and its successor, the VIC, ultimately reflected the personality of Jack Tramiel. That is, they were made to reach the widest possible audience at the lowest possible production cost. Thus, they were simultaneously brilliant in conception and cheesy in execution, innovative in technology and out of date in design. It was the kind of computer bought by people who didn't know anything about computers, worried that they needed one, didn't want to spend much money and were willing to admit all that to anyone. Commodore played on this by running a brilliant ad showing a child returning from school, apparently having flunked out for not having a computer.

If Commodore's market was at the low end of the business, it wasn't alone. Everybody was there. And as expected, as the smaller players faded away, the big boys arrived. Most of them came in through the back door, via video games, their goal to profit off cheap game players, then ratchet their customers up through more and more functions and add-ons. It was a sound strategy: after all, then as today, the microprocessors in game players were as powerful as those in low-end personal computers.

Thus, by the early 1980s Commodore was running into Mattel and Atari, both of them offering proprietary game machines and inching their way upward. Mattel never quite got there, but Atari made it, and in a big way, with a line of attractive, graphics/game-oriented computers that were as impressive as anything on the market.

This was a different Atari than Jobs had left four years before. Nolan Bushnell was now long gone, having made himself rich selling Atari to Warner Communications. Now he was building a new start-up, the Chuck E. Cheese robotic Pizza Time Theaters. The new Atari was a much different company. Indeed it was different from any other company in Silicon Valley. Whereas the old Atari was like an endless dorm party at San Jose State, the new Atari was like a lawn party in the Hamptons. The president, Ray Kassar, a former rug merchant who kept a copy of a recent *National Geographic* issue about Silicon Valley in his desk so he could understand what was going on, ate in an executive dining room (a Valley first) and lived in a penthouse in San Francisco with beautiful furnishings. He was chauffeured each day to Sunnyvale in a Rolls-Royce. When Warner chairman Steve Ross visited Atari from his skyscraper in New York City, Ross wouldn't even stay in the Valley, the local inns being too déclassé, but would helicopter down from San Francisco to the company parking lot, where he would be met by a limousine to drive him the three hundred feet to the door.

Meanwhile, slaving in the kitchen at this big Atari party were the programmers themselves. Under Bushnell, they'd been the revelers. Now they were considered a necessary, if annoying, evil. Kassar even called them glorified towel designers and emotional prima donnas. But in high tech, only a fool pisses on his programmers. By the early 1980s, Atari was bleeding its best game designers to a new company, Activision, which not only gave them credit for their work but treated them as superstars.

The impact from all that lost talent wouldn't be felt for a couple more years, especially after Atari had the foresight to acquire the home rights to the phenomenal Pac-Man game from the Japanese company Taito Ltd. In the meantime, the company had money to burn. And what better place to burn it than on computers? They were, after all, the logical future of game machines.

Atari had a resident guru to tell it where computers were going. Alan Kay was a brilliant young man who played classical piano as he formulated the most compelling vision of the personal computer era: the Dynabook, the book-sized work slate with enough computer power to configure itself to any application the user desired. So compelling was the Dynabook's siren call that any computer executive who heard it, from Ray Kassar to John Sculley, was instantly seduced and driven onto the nearest set of rocks.

Kay had first made his name at Xerox's research laboratory, where he had invented an intuitive, graphics-oriented user interface for computers called Smalltalk. Smalltalk pointed the way to future products such as Macintosh and, in theory, the Dynabook. As a result, Atari snapped Kay up. Though it never did anything with his ideas, Atari seemed content to just have Kay around.

For now, Atari's strategy was to build a personal computer that would run the usual crude word-processing programs, along with VisiCalc and, most importantly, Atari games. The resulting model 2600, did just that, but little more. It sold a lot of computers, largely because of the game function, but it could have done much more had not the company been completely distracted by the home video game boom. Three years hence, when the video game business collapsed into a five-year bust, more powerful computers might have saved Atari. But it was too late.

In early 1981, as Apple surveyed the competitive landscape, the Atari debacle was still years away. But even against the formidable Atari of the era, Apple could only be pleased. Each of the major players, Radio Shack, TI, Atari and Commodore, had deep structural flaws, either in products, management, distribution or orientation. Moreover, the high-end machines, the ones that should be its competitors, were either junk (TI) or hard to get (Tandy), while the good machines (Commodore and Atari) were targeted at the low end of the market, far from the Apple II and III.

Thus, despite all the problems facing the III, Apple still held the high, profitable ground all to itself. In his memoirs of his years as Jack Tramiel's assistant, Michael S. Tomczyk would write of the envy he felt for Apple's position: "Apple had chosen not to enter the low-priced computer market, wisely deciding to stay upscale and make more money per unit. Apple sold fewer physical units than Commodore, but for several years had higher dollar sales." Apple, he added, never had to slug it out against bargain basement competitors at places like the Consumer Electronics Show, but could do classy things like show at Wescon and rent Disneyland.

As the 1980s began, more and more companies dove into the personal computer market. But all went either the budget route (Sinclair) or toward video game players (Coleco). The only radically new products were the first "portable" computers—which were still heavy enough to induce sciatica in owners trying to lug them through airports. The first of these, from Osborne Computer, created a small sensation, but it was the next competitor in that market, Compaq, that would last.

With all these competitors squabbling over the low-end market, Apple could float above the fray, with the computers everybody wanted but only the serious could afford. The company seemed invulnerable, with a clear pathway ahead to dominate quality personal computing for at least the rest of the decade.

But it was all an illusion. In losing two years to the debacle of the III, Apple had missed its one and only opportunity to close the door on the upper half of the personal computer market. Had the III been the killer machine it was meant to be—had Woz been more involved, or Jobs not dumped on his old colleagues, or had the IPO been held off for another six months—Apple might have had time to both drive a defensible beachhead into the corporate market and set the standard for quality consumer machines.

But it had failed on both fronts. And now, the biggest, scariest computer company of them all was preparing to hit Apple head-on.

IBM.

6.5 CRUSH

In the story of Apple, it is hard to keep from tripping over all the ironies. One of the biggest had to do with Regis McKenna and his legendary work with his other big client. In late 1979, while Apple was buried in the latter stages of developing the III and plotting the Disneyland party, Intel Corp. was in trouble.

Intel, the Valley's newest giant, had known hard times before. Its heavy investment in new product research sometimes left its coffers empty when the chip industry went through one of its quadrennial busts. But these were comparatively minor stumbles; in the mongrel world of semiconductors, Intel was the one true thoroughbred. It had the finest management, the top engineers and, always, the best technology. Intel had been the first to make a mark in

MOS circuit electronics, in memory chips and, most important, in microprocessors. Everybody else paddled in its wake.

Now Intel was in trouble in the one area no one would have imagined possible: technology. Just eighteen months before, in June 1978, Intel had introduced its fourth-generation microprocessor. Called the 8086 it was created in just two years and was destined to be the ancestor of every Intel microprocessor to this day. Its announcement advertisement, "The Birth of a New Era," was not an exaggeration. Intel soon ran over the market.

But one competitor was not willing to admit defeat. Motorola had long given Intel a run for its money and it had its own new microprocessor waiting in the wings. The 68000, like the 8086 a 16-bit device, was introduced in mid-1979. It was a beautiful piece of work, with an elegant architecture that displayed the extra year Motorola had to study the weaknesses of the Intel chip and improve upon it.

Even the executives at Intel had to admit that Moto now had the better chip. In fact, as Intel's director of microprocessor marketing at the time, William Davidow, later admitted, it was becoming obvious that not only was Motorola now the first-place company in the market, but that Zilog's Z80 was second and Intel was third and fading. The market recognized this too, and by autumn 1979 Intel was experiencing for the first time in nearly a decade the regular loss of new design wins to a competitor.

By December, the situation had become critical. A meeting was hastily called by Andy Grove on December 4. Davidow was there, as were several other Intel managers. So was Regis McKenna.

What came out of that meeting and those that followed was the realization that not only was Intel at risk of becoming an also-ran with the 8086 but there was no new product in the pipeline to come to the rescue. Instead, the company would have to use its wits and work with the inferior product it had.

The product of this desperation was Operation Crush, the seminal marketing program of modern electronics. What the Crush team did was invent a brand-new product entirely from what it already had. The 8086 alone might not be as good a chip as the 68000, but if you thought of it as only the most important component of a total package that included design tools, peripheral chips such as math co-processors, in-circuit emulators, documentation, software and Intel's service and support operations . . . in other words, if you looked beyond mere performance stats to what it actually took to *use* one of these microprocessors, the 8086 compared mighty well indeed with the Motorola and Zilog offerings.

It took just three intense days for the Crush team to come up with this new marketing strategy. Yet it changed electronics forever. Henceforth, all successful tech products would have to be sold not as stand-alone products, but as complete *systems*. And once the systems approach was in place, it was a mere step to giving this system an identity—"branding" in marketing parlance—of its own, even if it was merely a component of an even larger system. Thus, Crush begat "Intel Inside," one of the most successful and influential product branding campaigns in any industry in modern times.

Having identified what it believed to be a truly competitive product, the Crush team then had to sell it, first to Andy Grove and then to the sales force. Andy, willing to try anything at this point, signed off just two days later. Convincing field sales was a little more complicated. The team set about preparing, under Regis's leadership, a collection of sales materials emphasizing Intel's new, integrated systems approach. There were new advertisements and new data sheets. Even customers were invited to write glowing articles about their experiences with Intel chips. Within months, Davidow's team put on more than fifty technical seminars throughout the world.

Goals were set too (though with Grove's signature on the mission statement, it was more of a command): one new customer design win per salesperson per month in 1980—2,000 new users.

Operation Crush was brilliant. It was also largely a sleight of hand, asking customers to ignore what they saw with their own eyes and accept instead a new point of view. But it worked, brilliantly, partly because the biggest convert to this new worldview was a panicked Motorola. As Davidow would later say: "Had Motorola chosen to remain aloof from our challenge, I think Intel would have been in deep trouble." Instead, Motorola, caught off guard, tried to hurriedly construct its own systems-oriented sales program. In doing so, Motorola validated Intel's concept; in doing a half-assed job of it, Moto gave the game away to its biggest competitor. In the end, Intel landed 2,500 design wins for the year, made the 8086 the de facto 16-bit standard for microprocessors and gained a near-monopoly on the microprocessor business it has never relinquished.

But that wasn't the end of the story. One of those Intel salespeople, Earl Whetstone, under the gun one month to land a sales win and having no obvious prospects, took a crazy chance and called Big Blue. It was an impossibly long shot because IBM made all of its own chips, including microprocessors. But Whetstone was desperate . . . and, as it turned out, the luckiest man alive.

IBM was ready. It had played with personal computing now longer than anybody, with some projects dating back to the 1960s. But every one had failed, mostly because Big Blue couldn't get out of its own way. It couldn't help but approach this new market as if it was merely an extension of its existing mainframe and minicomputer businesses. Every new idea, every design, every marketing strategy had to be vetted over and over by corporate bureaucrats to make sure that it met the IBM style, that it didn't overlap other products or that it didn't interfere with the sales force's primary focus of selling computer mainframes.

It was no wonder that IBM couldn't make a start in the chaotic, improvisational world of personal computing. What was a wonder, though, was that Big Blue actually understood what it was doing wrong. It had watched Apple closely almost from the beginning, and had come to appreciate that if it was ever going to compete with such an agile, quick-witted company, it would have to cultivate some of those characteristics in itself.

Since that was never going to happen in a company that still wore white shirts, IBM took the unprecedented step of creating a separate, independent division in Boca Raton, Florida—as far from Armonk, New York, as you could get without going to California. This division was not only given the charter to produce the first true IBM personal computer, Project Chess, but, most remarkably, given the unprecedented freedom to purchase components *anywhere.*

And it was at this moment, to this division, that Earl Whetstone made his telephone call. Instead of getting the door slammed in his face, Whetstone was all but dragged across the threshold like a traveling salesman by a lonely housewife. Why yessss, purred IBM, we would be interested in a demonstration of your hardware.

If Whetstone's experiences started out like a stag film, they ended up a Hitchcock movie. The Manhattan Project had less secrecy than Project Chess. When Whetstone and his people were called in to give technical support, they often found themselves in a room on one side of a black curtain, while IBM's technical people hid on the other side with a prototype of their new machine. Said Whetstone, ". . . they'd tell us what was happening and we'd have to try to solve the problem literally in the dark. If we were lucky, they'd let us reach a hand through the curtain and grope around a bit to try to figure out what the problem was."

It may have been weird, but if that's what the world's largest manufacturing company wanted, Intel was more than happy to oblige. In the end, IBM chose to buy not the cutting edge 8086, but the safer Intel 8088. The 8088 was an entry-level, budget chip created by Intel to help current 8-bit users make the transition to 16-bit. It had many of the features of the 8086, but instead of being a true 16-bit processor, the 8088 had a 16-bit central processor unit, but only an 8-bit bus. This compromise in performance would make IBM PC users gnash their teeth for years.

But that didn't matter to Intel. Big Blue was now committed to the Intel architecture. It would mean, Whetstone would exult, that in a business where 10,000 units was major victory, Intel had landed a contract for tens of *millions* of units annually.

With the IBM contract, Intel won the microprocessor wars. And the victory was due to Operation Crush. Intel had been lucky, but it had made that luck. Regis McKenna, the PR man who dreamed of being a great marketer, had now earned his wings. He was deservedly now high tech's most famous marketing guru. But he had achieved his greatest victory at the cost of his most famous client. He had hooked up Apple's newest and biggest competitor with the best chip company on earth. He would now spend the next decade trying to help Apple survive the onslaughts from the partnership he'd just helped to create.

6.6 Chess Games

For Apple, an Intel and IBM partnership was scary enough. But Boca Raton still needed one more piece to the puzzle of building its new PC: software, especially programming languages and an operating system.

Boca knew where to go for the former: a little software company in Redmond, Washington, called Microsoft. Big Blue had contacted Microsoft once before about buying a product, but nothing had come of it. Now, the unleashed Personal Computer group was ready to play ball.

In comparison with Apple, Microsoft had not come very far from its hobbyist roots. Bill Gates and Paul Allen had made enough money in both hardware design (notably an interface card for the Apple II to run software for Intel 8080-based and Zilog Z80-based computers) and software (BASIC language) to employ a dozen people. The pair made a strong, if combustible, team. Gates was a driven and fearless competitor willing to take on any assignment, no matter how unprepared his company was for the job, in order to build sales and beat the competition. But he was also an abrasive, unpleasant individual, whose personality (intellectual arrogance, spitefulness and contempt for others), mannerisms (a strange autistic-like rocking) and personal hygiene (he appeared to never brush his teeth) often got in the way of his talent as a businessman.

Allen, by comparison, was bearish, professorial and kindhearted. More than once he calmed the business waters roiled by Gates's behavior. Thanks to Allen, you wanted to do business with Microsoft; thanks to Gates, you had to.

In mid-1980 Microsoft, though far from the leading player in personal computer software, set out to claim that leadership by making its various software products universally compatible with all personal computers, no matter the microprocessor. It was a massive undertaking for such a tiny company. But strategically it was a brilliant stroke, because it would give Microsoft economies of budget from having to develop only a single program for all platforms and economies of scale by enabling it to market to all PC users. And that, in turn, would position Microsoft software as the first industry-wide standard—a novel idea in such an anarchic business.

It wasn't easy to pull off. The Microsoft team had to first perform the equivalent of translating all of its programs into Latin, then retranslating that into the different Romance languages and dialects. This was accomplished by rewriting all the company's programs (more than a quarter million lines of code) in a "neural" language that could run on a DEC mainframe. Once in there, it could then be translated out in microprocessor-specific versions.

The task would consume the company for many months. In the meantime, Microsoft still had to make money. So Allen set to work improving the company's BASIC for the 8086, and Gates took a contract from Atari to convert that same language to Atari machines.

They were buried in these projects when, in July, a call came from a representative of IBM Corp. Would Gates be willing to meet with some representatives from Big Blue to talk about a project?

A year before, another rep from Big Blue had contacted Microsoft about possibly buying a product. The deal had fallen through, but not before raising expectations throughout the little company, then dashing them. But Gates was always game. Sure, he said. "How about next week?"

"We'll be on a plane in two hours," said the IBMer, adding that he was bringing some researchers from Boca Raton.

As it happened, Gates had an appointment the next day with Atari's chairman, Ray Kassar. It came down to a deal in the hand with a billion-dollar company or one still in the air with a thirty-billion-dollar company. Gates blew Kassar off.

Bill knew enough about himself to appreciate that it might not be in Microsoft's best interests to face IBM alone. So he turned to his other partner, Steve Ballmer, an old friend from Harvard who'd done a spell at Procter & Gamble before joining Microsoft a year before. Ballmer was the practical side to Gates's vision, the orthodox, friendly businessman to Allen's absentminded professor and Gates's smart-ass kid. Gates asked Ballmer to sit in on the meeting.

The IBM team arrived to find Ballmer and a cleaned-up Gates in suit and tie. In the hours before the meeting, the normally cool Gates had been unusually excited. Though he had no real evidence, Bill sensed something big was in the works. He hoped that IBM, like Atari before it, had come to buy Microsoft BASIC.

The meeting proved to be more tantalizing than decisive. Before it began, the IBMers asked Gates and Ballmer to sign a nondisclosure agreement. No problem, they said, without giving it a second thought. Then, as Gates would recall, the IBM reps asked "a lot of crazy questions" about what Microsoft was up to, and, curiously, what Gates thought were the crucial features in a competitive home computer. That was it. Gates and Ballmer told Allen what had happened; everybody shrugged and went back to work.

Then, a month later, another call from Big Blue. "What you said was real interesting," the IBMer told Gates. How about another meeting? This time we'd like to send five people, including one of our lawyers. Cool, Gates and Ballmer said and, as before, set out to counter the IBM team with equivalent firepower. The IBM team was met by Gates, Ballmer, two Microsoft employees and the company's own hired attorney. The IBM crew, which included such hitters as the chief of corporate public relations, were impressed: these were people they could deal with.

Another, even more restrictive release to be signed by one and all. Before IBM began, the PR chief gave a nervous little prologue, "This is the most unusual thing the corporation has ever done." And then the Big Blue team set about describing Project Chess. Bill Gates saw for the first time the technology that would make him a billionaire.

He was not particularly impressed. He began to grill the IBMers about the computer, especially its processor. It appeared to be an 8-bit device. That wouldn't do Microsoft, or IBM, any good. So Gates argued vehemently for a 16-bit chip. Big Blue, to his amazement, listened. By the end of the meeting, Microsoft had a consulting agreement with IBM, with the goal of producing a report advising IBM on not only software but hardware.

Before they left, the IBM team had one more question for Gates. They had heard about a terrific new operating system software for personal computers called CP/M. Did Microsoft own that too? Would they be willing to sell it?

Well, *no*, Gates told them. CP/M belonged to a little software company called Digital Research Inc., located down in a California beach town near Monterey. But, Gates added quickly, he knew the founder, Gary Kildall, quite well and would be happy to get him on the phone.

At this point, history becomes shrouded in a fog of claims and counter-claims. Gates says that when he reached Kildall he impressed upon his counterpart that "important customers" were coming down to visit Digital Research and that Kildall should "treat them right."

But that obviously was not the message that Kildall received. When the IBM team arrived in Pacific Grove at Digital Research headquarters, Kildall wasn't even there. Instead the team was met by Dorothy McEwen, who was in charge of DRI's hardware accounts. The IBMers frowned at not meeting the founder, but decided to proceed anyway.

Where was Kildall? Gates, who liked to believe that all those he defeated suffered from the moral handicap of insufficient seriousness, would later say dismissively, "Gary went flying," as if Kildall was out joyriding in his plane instead of meeting with IBM. For the rest of his life (he would die in 1994 in a drunken fall in a saloon), Kildall would protest that he was flying to a business appointment and that Gates had not fully explained the importance of the meeting.

Meanwhile, back at DRI it only got worse. The IBM team pulled out the same disclosure release they'd used with Microsoft. McEwen balked, fearing she was putting her company in a vulnerable position. She called in the company lawyer, Jerry Davis. He read the release and agreed: Digital Research would not sign. The meeting ended before it began; and the IBM team flew back to Redmond to see if Gates would help them with an operating system. Digital Research was doomed.

Gates and Microsoft now had a shot at the brass ring of personal computing software. And unlike Kildall, Gates showed up at the next meeting ready to give Big Blue anything it wanted.

Unfortunately, what IBM wanted Microsoft didn't have: an operating system. But Microsoft had a neighbor in Seattle, Seattle Computer Products, that had an operating system for the Intel 8086 called SCP-DOS, designed by Tim Paterson, a friend of Paul Allen. So Gates met the disgruntled IBM team, expressed shock at their ill treatment by Kildall, then soothed their concern by noting that IBM didn't really need the 8-bit CP/M anyway. And as long as the business was up for grabs, why not look elsewhere? Say, at Microsoft?

In making such an offer, Gates for the first time displayed a part of his personality that would come to dominate the Microsoft legend. As software pioneer Gordon Eubanks, then at DRI, would say later to Robert Cringely: "The unstated rule around Digital Research was that Microsoft did languages, while we did operating systems. It was never stated emphatically, but I always thought that Gary assumed he had an agreement with Bill Gates about this separation and that as long as we didn't compete with Microsoft, they wouldn't compete with us." Digital Research was the first in a long line of companies to learn to its regret that there are no unstated rules with Bill Gates.

The IBMers were agreeable to Microsoft's proposal, but the final decision would have to be made at the top. And that meant the upcoming report by the team to IBM senior management had top priority.

It was finished in September, and Gates, Ballmer and another Microsoft employee (again, not Allen) caught the red-eye to Boca Raton. The daylong meeting was an almost continuous interrogation by the Chess team. IBM had set a one-year target for the entire project, an almost unprecedented pace for Big Blue, and the team was making sure it wouldn't be derailed by one of its suppliers. Intel had run the same gauntlet.

Gates would later say that by noon he figured he had the contract. He also admitted that the critical factor may have been that IBM's chairman, John Opel, recognized his name, having served with Bill's mother, Mary Gates, on the board of the United Way.

Whatever the deciding factor, Gates's noontime hunch was correct. Microsoft got the contract, signing the papers in November.

By then Gates & Company were already underway, establishing—to meet IBM's paranoid security requirements—a skunk works within the hot, windowless heart of the ancient National Bank building in downtown Seattle. The two companies even set up a pioneering private e-mail system to swap information . . . a lesson for the future not lost on Bill Gates.

Despite being told that "we were three months behind schedule before we started," Gates promised Big Blue that he would have both the new operating system and the translated BASIC ready by March 1981, just five months off. He was prepared to put the screws on both himself and his employees to get there.

Gates himself, along with Allen, took on the BASIC conversion. But the operating system was a different story. For this Microsoft had to depend upon the outsider Paterson and his Seattle Computer Products. That created considerable vulnerability: since Microsoft's languages were going to have to run with that operating system, if Seattle Computer Products screwed up or was incomplete on the specs, Microsoft would be stuck.

So Gates simply hired Paterson—and the operating system, SCP-DOS (for Seattle Computer Products—Digital Operating System), became Microsoft's: MS-DOS.

6.7 Apprentice Antichrist

In the midst of all of those proto-e-mails flying back and forth from Seattle to Boca Raton, Gates began to broach with his IBM handlers the possibility that the new computer might feature an open architecture. That is, unlike the thirty years of proprietary, closed IBM computers before it, the Chess personal computer would allow independent hardware and software developers to design products for it.

After all, Gates argued, the new computer was already a precedent setter at Big Blue, as it featured off-the-shelf chips from the likes of Intel, as well as MS-DOS, Fylstra's VisiCalc and the EasyWriter word-processing software designed by, of all people, Cap'n Crunch himself, John Draper. The message was: If IBM's greatest fear about open systems was letting every riffraff garage inventor offer add-on products and programs, well then, was there anybody out there scruffier and more menacing than the ex-felon they were already working with?

But the clincher to Gates's argument was, in yet another painful irony, the example of Apple Computer itself. After all, hadn't Apple outrun its competitors precisely because the Apple II was open? Hadn't that very openness given Apple the equivalent of a worldwide design army that no competitor—not even IBM—could match with an in-house R&D lab? And hadn't this army of designers also given Apple a global sales and marketing team as well?

Gates's Apple argument proved the clincher because the head of the Chess project, Don Estridge, happened to be an enthusiastic Apple II owner. IBM went for the open architecture, and the history of personal computing was changed forever.

Thus, thanks to chance, serendipity, guile and ambition, IBM found itself completely out of character with a new personal computer made out of off-the-shelf parts and featuring an open architecture. In other words, the perfect machine for the moment. But, what was even more important—and dangerous—Big Blue had also linked itself to Andy Grove and Bill Gates, perhaps the two best businessmen of the age. Had it made any other choice, had only one of these figures entered the narrative at this point, the story of personal computing likely would have been completely different.

But just like Apple two years before, IBM's Boca Raton division was blessed with uncommon luck during this period. It made all the best choices—at least for the near term. In the long term, those same choices would carry a sting. It didn't know it yet, but for all its size and strength, IBM was the least of the three partners. By both opening its architecture for

Microsoft and tying itself to the Intel 8086 chip family, Big Blue had already unwittingly preordained its own fate.

But if IBM was in a vulnerable position, at least it was at the table. Apple's position was much worse. It wasn't even in the room. The honeymoon, in which it had owned a billion-dollar market by itself, was over. Now it was facing the world's biggest computer company, the world's largest microprocessor company and the world's most competitive software company. A single misstep would be fatal. And coming off the Woz crash, the Scott purge and the Apple III failure, a sudden return of Apple's surefootedness was pretty damn unlikely.

And yet the unlikely, even the impossible, was exactly what Apple did for the next two years. It was a business miracle not seen by the electronics industry before or since. Good companies produce one brilliant, industry-transforming product; great companies invent two. Apple became immortal because it not only invented that second product but did so at the moment it needed most to do so.

Tim Bajarin, director of Creative Strategies Inc. and the most veteran of Apple watchers (he began in 1977) and consultants, also had the unique opportunity to be invited to consult the Estridge group at IBM Boca Raton at the time of the PC introduction.

"I was struck by two things at Boca," he later recalled. "The first was how limited the group's expectations were. The business plan only called for IBM to sell only 240,000 units in the entire lifetime of the PC. They ended up doing that in a matter of a few months.

"The second was the utter disregard with which they held Apple. They saw Apple as little more than a toy—an opinion that didn't change until 1988. One IBM executive there had a daughter who was married to an early employee and so had a chance to buy Apple stock. He passed on the opportunity. That's how little they thought of their new competitor."

IBM introduced the Chess computer on August 12, 1981. Big Blue may have changed its rules for product creation but it hadn't forgotten its old arrogance. The new computer was called, simply, the IBM Personal Computer, as if it was the only one of its kind in the world, having sprung from the void. Henceforth it would be called the PC, creating endless confusion between the product name and the general term for all the industry's products.

Against the monolith of IBM marketing, even Bill Gates couldn't win every argument. Thus, MS-DOS became PC-MOS—though it did remain the PC's primary operating system, consigning Kildall's CP/M to the ash heap of history.

But the zenith of IBM's arrogance regarding the PC was its advertising campaign. It featured an actor playing Charlie Chaplin as the Little Tramp. It was designed to be charming and cute and help potential customers overcome their fear of computers: after all, if the childlike man in the derby and baggy pants could run a PC, why couldn't you? Thus, the biggest capitalist company on the planet had co-opted the image of the world's most popular Marxist, whose most famous movie image (from *Modern Times*) was of being crushed between the giant gears of industry, in order to sell expensive boxes to the proletariat.

Of course, it worked. By December, IBM had shipped 13,000 PCs, and for years thereafter, the demand curve ramped up almost hyperbolically. By the end of 1993, more than a half million machines had been sold.

Needless to say, Apple had known for months, even years, that IBM was coming—according to Mike Scott, it was even predicted in the company's original business plan. And in the weeks before the August 12 introduction, the greatest fear among Big Blue's future competitors was that the PC would contain some extraordinary new technology that would make every other computer on the market look like a paperweight.

But that fear aside—and many in personal computing were skeptical that IBM could even be that innovative—it was generally assumed that Chess would be, in typical IBM style, a solid but uninteresting box priced too high that would sell to the legions of IBM lovers. That, the industry decided, would be good news: the very presence of IBM would validate the personal computer market for the first time. Big Blue would make personal computing something more than the perceived land of geeks, hippies and nerds, turning it into a legitimate and growing sector of the computer industry. Armonk might take a big slice of that pie, but it would make the pie so big that everyone would win.

This was cockiness crossed with whistling through the graveyard. It had its purest expression in the famous Apple ad that appeared in *The Wall Street Journal* the day of the PC introduction:

Welcome IBM
seriously.

Welcome to the most exciting and important marketplace since the computer revolution began 35 years ago . . . We look forward to responsible competition in the massive effort to distribute this American technology to the world.

It was a classic bit of cheekiness, almost unique in U.S. business history—actually welcoming your biggest, scariest competitor, a firm forty times your size, into your market.

But the confusion and dismay that day at Apple didn't match the self-confidence of the ad. Jobs and company were relieved that the IBM PC didn't contain any great technological breakthroughs. In fact, it contained no breakthroughs at all. Its sheer prosaicness was disconcerting: off-the-shelf parts, a competitive price. What the hell was going on here? This wasn't the Big Blue everybody knew. Should they be relieved or terrified that this new computer was so uninteresting?

They got their answer as the world's attention suddenly shifted away from Apple, which had grown accustomed to the limelight, and toward Big Blue. Apple, its management having grown up either in the world of semiconductors or hacking, had never really experienced the true force of IBM. This was a company that had more cash on hand than Apple had sales. It had an advertising budget bigger than the rest of the computer industry, from mainframes to micros, combined. Whereas most personal computers had dozens of salespeople, IBM had thousands.

But it was more than that. Since the late 1950s IBM had owned three-quarters of the world's computer business. It was the sun and all the other companies mere planets. Most companies, large and small, banks or brokerages, car makers or fast-food suppliers, didn't just have computer departments, the had *IBM* computer departments. IBM established industry standards around its products and architectures by the sheer mass of its presence in the marketplace.

This had been the case for twenty years and several generations of computer center directors. You used IBM equipment because your company's first computer purchase had been from IBM—and so had every purchase since. To even considering buying, in their day, a Burroughs mainframe or a DEC mini or an Apple II was heresy. And everyone knew what happened to heretics. As the phrase went in corporate offices throughout the world: "No one ever got fired for buying from IBM."

This was the behemoth that Apple and the other personal computer companies now faced. Within months it became apparent that Big Blue was almost effortlessly penetrating the corporate market, slipping across the barrier that Apple and the others had banged up against for years. Worse, IBM was also, for the first time ever, successfully reaching out to the small business and consumer markets as well. After all, if you were buying your first computer, wouldn't you feel better ordering from the World's Greatest Computer Company? The one that put the mainframe in your company's computer center and the mini down the hall and the Selectric on your desk?

Like a mob elbowing its way backward after suddenly looking down the barrel of a cannon, the low-end computer and video game companies began scurrying down the price-performance chart to get out of IBM's way. Crushed together at the bottom of the market, Commodore, Texas Instruments, Atari and Coleco were reduced to scrabbling for a dwindling market share. An explosion was inevitable.

And who better to light the match than Jack Tramiel? "I guess we started the price wars when we introduced the VIC for under $300 when everyone else was selling computers for $600," wrote Mike Tomczyk. By August 1982, just one year after the IBM announcement, the low-end computer companies, particularly Commodore and TI, were in a battle to the death. That month TI announced a $50 rebate on its budget machine, the 99/4, bringing its retail price down to just $200. Commodore responded in kind. It even stopped publishing suggested retail prices to let them float. "Capitalism in its purest form," according to Tomczyk. Pure suicide too.

By December 1982 Atari had slashed the price of its budget machine, the 400, to under $200. Meanwhile, the model 800 was cut to $500. That was a 20 percent price drop, yet it was still not enough to keep it in the game. Meanwhile, Atari had much bigger problems to worry about. At the beginning of the year, the company had celebrated passing the $1 billion sales mark, and there was every reason to expect 1982's sales to double that. Waiting in the wings for the prime Christmas retail season was a new video game of *E.T.*, the all-time movie moneymaker still showing in theaters around the country. Sure, the game was derivative, but how could it fail?

But fail it did. Before Atari could blame the game's design, suddenly the entire video game industry began to stall. After a thrilling, decade-long run, a period in which Atari became one of the most successful companies of all time, it seemed that a generation of children had finally grown tired of playing video games. Nobody was buying the product that Christmas, nor would they again until a new generation arrived at the beginning of the 1990s. Atari, which had undersupported its fine computers in lieu of much more profitable video games, now found itself burying millions of unsold game cartridges in the Arizona desert and looking to those computers to bail out the company . . . only to find that a price war was squeezing all the margins out of that business as well.

So Atari disintegrated. As early as September, the company secretly began planning layoffs. In December, Ray Kassar and executive vice president David Groth sold some of their stockholdings not long after hyping the company's earnings predictions (the SEC would get Kassar for this later). Then, in January, the bomb was dropped. The response was so ugly that Atari stock was temporarily suspended on the New York Stock Exchange.

Then, on a Friday afternoon in February, without any warning or support, Atari summarily laid off 1,700 people. It would prove to be one of the biggest quarterly losses in modern business history—and the biggest layoff Silicon Valley had ever seen, and would not see again until . . . Apple Computer. By June, a total of 3,000 employees were gone and Atari was on its way to losing $500 million for the year. By December 1993, the once great company of Nolan Bushnell, Steve Jobs's old employer, was little more than an empty shell.

It was one of the biggest business meltdowns of all time. It was also a harbinger of things to come. In the rest of the low-end personal computer business, the price war was only growing hotter. In January 1983, even as Atari was dying, Commodore cut the retail price of its top-end Commodore 64 to $400 and started selling it in Kmarts. TI responded a month later by cutting the 99/4 to $150. There were almost no profits left. *Home Furnishings Daily* ran a cartoon of Tramiel dressed as a real Commodore, using his cutlass to slash through price tags.

In February, TI announced that there was a problem with the power packs in their computers—they could set the machine on fire—and froze production for a month to fix both new and old machines. Commodore used that opportunity to announce that it would give a $100 rebate on any computer turned in to purchase a Commodore 64—which led to a run on little $50 Timex computers in department stores around the country.

Terrified, TI preannounced its own price cut, saying it would make the announcement in June, then panicked again and announced it in May.

It was almost over. At the June 1983 Consumer Electronics Show, Commodore finally killed the industry. It cut the price of the Commodore 64, its flagship, to $200—a machine that nine months before had retailed for three times that much. On top of that, Commodore cut the price of its software library in half.

Within a few weeks, TI announced a $100 million loss, the president of its computer operations resigned and TI left the personal computer business forever. Commodore, with its superior manufacturing economies and ruthless style, had won the war for the low end of the computer market. But what had it won? Sales, certainly. As the last survivor, Commodore finished 1983 as the first company with personal computer sales of more than $1 billion. That represented 3 million computers and 600,000 related books. The company held a press conference to celebrate.

Then, one week later, after a falling-out with the chairman, Jack Tramiel resigned. He had been too harsh, his health was at risk, the company now needed to move past the warrior stage and be run by sober, professional managers—there were many explanations. But the bottom line was that the toughest son of a bitch the market had ever seen was gone, having taken most of the rest of the industry down with him. And without Jack Tramiel, Commodore was soon gone as well.

6.8 GRUDGE MATCH

Thus ended the second generation of personal computer companies. The first generation, the hobbyists, had been annihilated by the arrival of the professionals. Now the pros had been taken out by an industry consolidation driven by the arrival of the first of the behemoths. It was the archetypical story of a high-tech industry.

All that was left now was Apple, IBM and debris. The victor of the first era was now about to meet the second in a grudge match. Jobs had already predicted this: "When you have nothing to lose you can shoot for the moon. So we shot for the moon, and we knew that if we were successful it would come down to Apple and IBM. And that's exactly what's going to happen."

The personal computer industry was now eight years along from the first Homebrew meeting. Perhaps fifty computer companies had now come and gone, 10 million personal computers had been sold, more than $10 billion had been made, *Time* magazine had named the personal computer its "Man of the Year" for 1983 (it would have been Jobs, but the IBM PC introduction ruined it) and the little hobby machine made out of wood and hand-soldered boards was now the heart of a new zeitgeist sweeping the classrooms, offices and dens of the industrial world.

Technology industries rarely learn from success, but always learn from failure. The runaway success of personal computing in the mid-1980s was entirely due to the lessons learned from all the individual and corporate disasters that had preceded it. From the disasters, the industry had learned a number of important lessons:

• *The right processor is everything.* Those companies that had built their computers around the wrong microprocessor doomed themselves from the start. Apple alone had hooked up with the wrong chip and survived, thanks to a superior design. Henceforth, any company that attempted to build around anything but an Intel or Motorola microprocessor had no chance.

• *It takes brawn, brains and balls.* The best personal computer and software companies had a combination of a market visionary, an experienced businessman and a technical guru. Those firms that were run only by technologists (IMSAI, Cromemco and most of the first generation of companies) could not compete once the market matured and customers demanded quality, service, competitive pricing and documentation.

By comparison, the companies that were run by good businessmen typically fulfilled those tasks, but eventually zigged when they should have zagged in adopting a new technology. By the mid-1980s, as demand reached millions of units, the game increasingly went to the company that could best get a new model out of prototype and into full production, then down the best distribution channels. Tandy had solid machines, but sold them only through Radio Shacks. Atari killed TI by being so much more efficient a manufacturer that it could price its biggest competitor out of business.

Still, even these advantages weren't enough. For a personal computer company to survive over the long run it also needed a vision of where the industry was going and the influence to turn the company in that direction. Atari lacked that vision, so did Mattel and TI. Commodore had it fitfully, but Tramiel lost the support of his board.

By comparison, Apple had managed to cover all the bases with its team of Markkula, Wozniak, Scott and Jobs. But now half that team was gone, and the company would have to move fast to replace them. IBM had the combination too, but its makeup was even more unusual: while its in-house manufacturing and business management were unequaled, its visionary and software guru, Bill Gates, worked for another company, as did its hardware expert, Andrew Grove. Thus, whereas Apple had to reconstitute its damaged team, IBM had the best team in the land—but one with divided loyalties.

• *The less control the more command.* Apple had taught this lesson to the rest of the computer industry. By not only allowing but actively supporting third-party software developers to design applications for its machines, Apple effectively multiplied its corporate manpower and collective intelligence without having to spend a dime. Personal computers were only as good as their use, and no single company—not even IBM—could dream up all the possible uses for personal computing. But several thousand computer buffs, coming from all walks of life, could. Dan Fylstra and Cap'n Crunch had been as important to Apple as any of its employees. And if VisiCalc made millions in the process for somebody else, so what? It also sold thousands of Apple II's . . . and that meant not only revenues for Apple, but ever-precious market share.

Hewlett-Packard, for all of its technical prowess, missed that lesson. But thanks to Gates, who had learned from Apple, IBM got it. Now it would be Gates's turn to teach Apple a final lesson about the power of open systems and standardization.

• *It ain't just hardware and software.* For sheer performance for the price, the Commodore VIC was probably the best personal computer in the world in its day. Had the market judged the new machines solely on their performance, Commodore would have won. But it didn't, because Commodore never captured the imaginations of more than a fraction of the total market—mostly third-generation hobbyists and techie eccentrics without much money. It wasn't cool to own a VIC, even less so to own an Atari 2600. You weren't serious; you weren't part of a movement. Not like you were when you bought an Apple II and proudly put the rainbow apple decal in the rear window of your car.

Regis McKenna understood this and geared Apple's marketing campaign toward precisely that image. Members of the Apple Corps were rebels, they were hip and sardonic and sly, they were contemptuous of suits. And most of all, they were out to make the world a better, freer place through personal computing. Apple was a style, an attitude, a *movement.* And all those traits were personified in a single figure, Steve Jobs.

Jobs understood this too and, at least publicly, he played the role brilliantly. And why not? The world now saw him as he always saw himself: special, golden, selected for some higher calling. Regis's ads and Steve Jobs's personality; it was a perfect combination.

IBM, by comparison, perfectly filled a niche antithetical to Apple. It represented security, predictability and strength in a market until now characterized by insecurity, mercurial figures and fly-by-night storefront companies. It even took the industry's nomenclature as its own branding—as if nothing in this industry had been real until Big Blue arrived. IBM induced the kind of fear that could best be assuaged by submitting to it. Jump on board before you are run over. When you joined IBM you too became part of the juggernaut. And if Apple positioned itself against IBM, IBM merely ignored Apple as superfluous.

It was to be the establishment versus the counterculture. The social wars of the 1960s were now about to play themselves out in the computer wars of the 1980s.

The only trouble was that it looked as if the war would be over almost before it began. IBM had a hot new computer notching up ever more market share by the month. It had already crushed a half dozen of the most successful companies in the personal computer business, and it had both invaded and occupied an enormous market of its own in personal office computers. Apple, meanwhile, had fired its president and replaced him with a guy who only wanted to retire, made a postadolescent its chairman, lost its technical genius to a plane crash, introduced a botched product that nobody wanted and was living off another aging computer design.

Yet, within a year, Apple would recapture the world's imagination, and then hold it with almost religious fervor for a dozen more years thereafter in one of the great corporate Second Acts. And it would accomplish this with a product it did everything to kill.

6.9 The Great Myth

The personal computer industry has many stories, anecdotes and tales. But it has only one legend:

> As part of its agreement to let Xerox Corp. invest in it before the IPO, Apple demanded and got the right to visit Xerox's famous Palo Alto Research Center, where, rumor had it, Xerox was developing some of the most interesting new computers around.
>
> Steve Jobs, relentless in his quest for innovative new ideas, took advantage of the deal as soon as possible and in late 1979 or early 1980 (the stories vary) took a tour of Xerox PARC with some other Apple technical types, including Bill Atkinson. What he saw there changed the course of computing.
>
> Like Paul on the road to Damascus, Jobs saw his own brilliant burst of light—in this case, a demonstration of the Xerox Star, Alto and several other prototype personal computer models. Each model featured one or more of the most creative new ideas about personal com-

puting. For example, the Star not only had a detached keyboard but also used a small external device—a "mouse," the descendant of the original devised by Douglas Engelbart more than a decade before—to control the motion of the cursor on the screen. The Star and Alto also had a unique and intuitive way of presenting information in the form of "windows" that could be arrayed across the screen and accessed by pointing the mouse. Integrated with these windows was a collection of "icons," representational images for common commands. Finally, though sadly Jobs didn't notice, the computers were also able to talk to each other through a new networking scheme.

Jobs and his group were so impressed by what they saw that they began to press their tour guide, PARC director Larry Tesler, with one question after another. Tesler would later tell Jobs biographer Jeffrey Young, "What impressed me was that their questions were better than any I had heard in the seven years I had been at Xerox . . . Their questions showed that they understood the implications and the subtleties . . ." Tesler was so impressed that he quit PARC and joined Apple.

Jobs returned to Apple literally with Stars in his eyes. He had seen the future and it computed. Better yet, he knew Xerox would never get the product to market. So he made it his crusade to do so, even if he had to steal Xerox's ideas.

The first Apple project to incorporate all of these new ideas was the Lisa, a project directed by John Couch, but really driven by Jobs's enthusiasm. When completed, the Lisa was a remarkable computer, one that proved the appeal of the new Apple interface, but at $10,000 was just too expensive. What the world really needed, as only Jobs fully understood, was a computer that incorporated all of these new features but carried a price affordable to Everyman. A Volkswagen of personal computing.

The result was a second, complementary development project called Macintosh. It was originally run by Apple veteran Jef Raskin, but when he proved unable to bring the project to completion, Jobs stepped in and, using all of his skills at threatening, cajoling and seducing, drove the Mac team to a heroic effort.

The finished Macintosh was introduced in 1984 and quickly became the most famous personal computer ever, turning Apple's fortunes around and proving forever that Steve Jobs was both a great visionary and, putting old doubts finally to rest, a true technologist.

This legend, promulgated for years by Apple's PR department (one of the most successful PR campaigns ever in high tech, not just because it succeeded, but because no one knew any better), has been picked up and repeated in almost every history ever written about Steve Jobs or Apple. In the uplifting versions, say Steven Levy's *Insanely Great,* Jobs is presented as the one person who could see what Xerox PARC had and then make it real for the masses. The cynical versions, such as Cringely's *Accidental Empires,* suggest that Jobs essentially stole the ideas from Xerox, ramrodded them through Apple, drove the Lisa team until he saw that it wasn't going to be a winner and then hijacked the Mac project, elbowing Raskin out of the way.

But whatever the approach, all of them have missed one fundamental fact about the legend: *it isn't true.* It endures because we want it to be true. And we want it to be true because it fits the form of a good legend: it is simple, and it involves a superhuman individual, a latter-day Prometheus, heroically stealing a magical secret from the gods and delivering it to mankind.

Real life is much more random and tawdry. This need for myth explains, but it certainly doesn't forgive, Cringely's written reply when told the real story by Jef Raskin: "As for all the business of what project started when, whether the Lisa started before or after Steve visited PARC, whether the Mac had already begun or not, well I don't think that matters very much. My attempt was to EXPLAIN (I say that at the front of my book), not to be a historian."

So much for facts.

The evidence has always been there. Had any journalist, author or historian actually *used* a Xerox Star or Alto, he or she would have quickly discovered that the look and feel of their primitive interfaces, while certainly pointing the way to the Mac Operating System, were far from it. That would have been obvious the first time they grabbed the three-button mouse and tried to drag an unmovable window across the screen.

There is also the evidence of Xerox's belated lawsuit against Apple. Xerox had read the same books and convinced itself that the Mac violated PARC's intellectual property protections. So, the case should have been a slam dunk. Instead, Xerox lost.

Meanwhile, in the intervening years, no one ever publicly asked exactly when, in those years after the Apple II, Jobs suddenly became a technology savant. A brilliant young man, certainly. Probably a genius at product packaging, positioning and branding. But a guy capable of walking into one of the leading research institutions in the world, seeing a collection of radically new technologies whose implications weren't even fully understood by their inventors and then, like the young Jesus before the rabbis, extemporaneously peppering the director of that institution with questions so penetrating and knowing that even the experts were taken aback? Please.

And finally, the most obvious clue that something wasn't right with the story had always been available in the Apple archives: a chronology that showed that both the Macintosh and Lisa projects were proposed in the spring of 1979 and were approved and begun in September—*at least three months before Job's visit to PARC.*

Jobs, it seems, had only managed to discover the obvious. He had been set up.

But he would have his revenge in the history books.

6.10 Macintosh

If Jobs didn't "discover" the Macintosh, who did?

Here again, neither Apple nor the people who rewrote its press releases are much help. Apple did hint that it knew a deeper truth in later years, after Jobs had not only left the company but become a competitor. Then the official story was rewritten to give credit to Bill Atkinson and Andy Hertzfeld, two Mac development team members. This Soviet encyclopedia-style revisionism was not particularly original, especially in a town where a company's value is often judged by the quality of its in-house creative talent. Intel had set the pattern in the 1970s by giving Ted Hoff complete credit for inventing the microprocessor, and all but erasing the equally important role of Federico Faggin, who had inconveniently gone off to Zilog. Jobs too might have gone down the memory hole, had he not been already too big to stuff through.

It was not until mid-1996, in an obscure journal called *The Analytical Engine*, the journal of the Computer History Association of California, that another version of the Macintosh story appeared. It was the memoirs of Jef Raskin, the Apple pioneer who had led the Mac team until purged by Jobs. Raskin was no more humble than Jobs, but he was a real technologist. And once one filtered out Raskin's own self-promotion, the story that remained had the ring of truth. It was messy, ugly, tossed about by greed, ambition and mutual loathing, and best of all, it explained all those obvious contradictions in the official legend.

Most companies, when flush with a successful IPO, come down with a bad case of grandiosity and embark on the killer product about which it has always dreamed but could never before afford. This is the fantasy product that incorporates every feature of every fantasy and is designed to conquer the market once and forever.

Many companies wisely abandon this pipe dream early on. Those that continue to pursue it usually end up compromising it so much that what finally is introduced to the world is either a mess (the Intel iAPX 432, the HP-01 digital watch) or just another incremental and disappointing improvement over what came before (the Apple Newton). A few tragic companies (Triad, Dynabook) pursue their vision all the way into oblivion.

Apple's story is almost unique because its pipe-dream product not only came true but really did all that was claimed for it. It revolutionized computing. And, though this seemed the least likely of possibilities at the beginning, it also saved the company.

In 1979, Apple was rich with Apple II profits and looking at even greater riches from the impending IPO. And so great was the company's imagination (and hubris) that within a matter of months it set out to create not one, but *three* new killer machines.

One of these, the Apple III, was to be a safe, incremental product. But it ended up so compromised and crippled that it suffered through a few miserable years and was mercifully destroyed.

The second, the Lisa, was to be Apple's golden machine. A premium computer that would be so awe-inspiring that it would not only give Apple the high ground in personal computing but also begin carving up the underside of the minicomputer market. John Couch was given control of that project.

The third product was the most fantastic and unlikely of them all. Aimed directly at the newly emerging low-end game/computer market, it was to be so user-friendly as to be irresistible; more a home appliance than a data processing machine. This was to position Apple as the industry's leading consumer mass marketer.

A brainchild of Markkula, this third product, which he designated Annie, was to cost $500 and be primarily used for games. In other words, a player much like those being offered by Atari, Coleco, Commodore and TI. In March 1979, he called Raskin in, asked him to study the Annie project and consider running the team.

But Raskin wasn't interested in something as pedestrian as a game machine. "So I counterproposed a general-purpose, low-cost computer based on my own ideas—and dreams—for an interface."

Raskin had been dreaming for a long time. As far back as 1965, when he was still a grad student at Penn State, Raskin found himself frustrated with the needless complexities of working with computers. His thesis two years later even made the then radical proposal of developing computer displays based on graphics, rather than characters. The thesis itself was written in a multiple-font format that presaged desktop publishing twenty years later. At one point, frustrated by the problem of getting all this graphic data into a computer, Raskin tried to build a device to do the job—a failed early attempt at a mouse.

Tired of Pennsylvania and Penn State, Raskin turned in his thesis, jumped into a car with his wife, Karen, and lit out for the territories. He ended up at the University of California at San Diego, where Karen took a job at the Institute of Geophysics and Planetary Physics and he got a job at the University Computer Center.

Within a couple of years, frustrated with both the bureaucracy of the main computer center and its allegiance to big mainframes, Raskin had opened his own minicomputer-based computer center elsewhere on campus. Raskin would later say that a visitor to the center in 1972 would have seen the purcursor to the Mac in the "low tables with small rectangular monitors and detached keyboards," all linked to a pair of Data General Nova minis.

Summers, Raskin would take one of the Novas home and use it as his own personal computer, even once carrying it into a restaurant to compute the bill and tip. "These experiences with a 'portable' computer system gave me a foretaste of what it would be like to own a personal computer," wrote Raskin. "Like the crocodile in Peter Pan, I would never forget that taste, and craved it for years."

Wozniak, of course, was coming to personal computers at the same time. But as much respect as the two computer geniuses had for the other, it is important to note that they arrived at this new world from different directions. Woz came from below; his goal was to figure out a way to own a minicomputer, even if he had to build it. Raskin came from above. He had begun with mainframes, then moved to minicomputers the moment he got a chance—and by the mid-1970s he was trying to get away from the constraints of minis as well. This difference in perspective would be made manifest in their inventions.

Summer wasn't only a time for Raskin to play with his computer at home. It was also a time to travel, especially north, to Stanford University. In the summer of 1973, Raskin visited SAIL, the Stanford Artificial Intelligence Laboratory—and while there was given a tour of Xerox PARC a mile down the road. He was mightily impressed. The next summer, when he was invited back to SAIL as a visiting scholar, "I found myself gravitating more and more toward the beanbag chairs at PARC."

It was there, more than five years before Jobs's fateful visit, that Raskin learned for the first time about the work of people like Doug Englebart. He saw the beginning stages of the finished work Apple would ultimately draw upon. And if that wasn't enough, back at SAIL, Raskin learned to send proto-e-mails on the ARPAnet, the precursor of the Internet. He was standing at a crossroads in the history of technology, watching the two great movements of the rest of the century as they formed and converged.

Raskin never forgot what he had seen at Xerox PARC. And when, a couple of years later, he visited the garage to interview the two Steves for *Dr. Dobb's* he knew he was seeing the future. He joined Apple as its thirty-first employee on the day it incorporated in early 1977.

So, by 1979, when Markkula approached him about building the $500 game machine, Raskin knew exactly what he wanted to do instead. He duly mulled over Markkula's proposal, then came back with his radical counterproposal.

The choice of Markkula, then chairman and not considered a hard-core technologist, as champion might seem odd. But Raskin knew what he was doing. After two years of working with Apple, first as a contractor, then as an employee, Raskin had come to some unsettling conclusions about Woz and Jobs, whom he characterized as "a strange mix of the radical and the conservative. They wanted to create personal computers, but expected them to work much like the hard-to-use minicomputers from DEC, HP and Data General. Dragging the two Steves into the interface future was like preaching in an unknown tongue . . ."

But Markkula was a marketer, a consumer guy and a tinkerer. He might just understand. Besides, as chairman he could also trump the two Steves. So Raskin made his pitch: How about instead of a game player I build you an easy-to-use consumer computer for the same price? I've got some ideas for a new interface . . .

Markkula was enthusiastic. He agreed to present the plan with his backing to the executive board. In the meantime, Raskin wrote down his ideas in a paper presciently entitled "Computers by the Millions" and distributed it around the company. The paper, which proved to be the philosophical foundation of the Mac (and, by extension, the future of personal computing) dealt not only with the design and manufacture of a new generation of computers but also with the potential effect of those computers on society itself. Apple management found it so insightful that it refused to allow Raskin to disseminate it outside the company until 1982.

But he could pass it around inside Apple—and in doing so, Raskin unknowingly set the stage for his own demise at Apple three years hence. That's because one of the readers was Steve Jobs. Raskin: "Jobs, unaccountably, did not at all agree with my views of the future, nor with my distributing them internally at Apple, even though I was doing so at Markkula's request. By proposing new strategic ideas and products independently of Jobs, I began to get on his 'wrong' side."

While waiting for company approval, Raskin joined the Lisa team. The Lisa had actually been proposed after, but approved before, the Macintosh. In his short tenure there, Raskin managed his usual combination of making important contributions while simultaneously stirring up trouble. His biggest contribution was to recruit one of his former UCSD students named Bill Atkinson, who ultimately would prove to be the central and enduring figure in the Mac story.

But the trouble came when Raskin managed to convince the first Lisa team leader, an ex-HPer named Ken Rothmuller, to adopt the distinctive bit-mapped display for the Lisa, thus making the computer more graphics-friendly and establishing the stunning print-on-paper look of the next generation of Apple (and all other) machines. Raskin had tried the same argument with Woz and Jobs three years before and had been brushed off. Now Raskin had a victory—a short-lived one, at least for Rothmuller, who was soon fired by Jobs for being too difficult to work with.

In September, just before the Annie project was finally approved, Raskin talked the Lisa team—now managed by another, more politically astute former HPer, John Couch—to join him on a tour of PARC. There, the Lisa team, watching the demonstration of the Alto, the Star, the mouse and the Crosstalk network, had its own epiphany. For Raskin, who had seen it all before and who had long ago determined exactly where the Xerox technology could be improved or revised, the trip held no revelations. He even told Tesler as he left, "We don't need this, but I'm glad they saw it."

But in fact, the Lisa team decided this was exactly what they needed and embarked on a program to build the most powerful personal computer yet. Raskin, with his Everyman philosophy, was soon left on the sidelines. But it didn't matter, because literally within days Markkula finally gave Raskin the Annie project, and let him take it in the new direction.

Jobs was not happy. He told anyone who asked (and many who didn't) that the new project was the "dumbest idea" he'd ever heard of. Raskin remembered, "He would often recite a list of imagined advantages that the Lisa project had over the Mac and put obstacles in the way of my obtaining staff or supplies." Jobs would, in fact, despise the Mac project almost until the day he took it over, when he would declare it so great that it "would make a dent in the universe."

Still, Apple's third, and least, new-product program was finally underway. But with the company's most powerful figure its sworn enemy, few gave it any hope.

With its three new products in the works, Apple was heading toward a defining moment. The only problem was that the company didn't know that it was.

With the Apple I and II, the strategy had been straightforward. The personal computer industry was then still largely monolithic, so the task was narrow: build the best machine possible and then market the hell out of it. But by 1982 the PC business had sufficiently matured to begin segmenting into distinct submarkets with identifiable customers and product specifications. Apple, by embarking upon its three-pronged new-product strategy, seemed to be targeting these different markets. But that was mostly an illusion. The real market divisions emerging were between consumer (including home computers and games), professional (including professional offices and small businesses) and corporate products.

Conceivably, at this early point in the game, a company could produce two types of products—consumer and business—and have sufficient product breadth to still cover the industry. That was what IBM was rumored to be doing.

Apple too seemed to be moving in that direction. The company had a consumer machine, the II. It also had, largely by default, an extensive business software library and corporate customer base. Now Apple was developing two new computers, the III and the Lisa, both aimed essentially at the business market, where the Lisa would hit the corporate market, while the III would be appealing to professionals and small businesses. Finally, there was Raskin's Macintosh, the volkscomputer, which would target the personal and home markets.

It all might have worked if Apple had maintained this segmentation, worked on intercompatibility among the different product lines and moved the four product lines forward in a combined front. But that required corporate discipline: four different product groups operating in coordination toward a common purpose, giving up common markets for the common good. Needless to say, that wasn't Apple Computer.

In fact, even at the most elemental level, the company seemed organically incapable of sticking to a single business model. It didn't help that, with only a couple exceptions, there wasn't a single business veteran in the whole management team. And those who were, such as Floyd Kvamme, came out of chips, not corporate or consumer marketing. Regis McKenna once sat in a senior staff meeting at Apple, and was stunned to realize that he had more big-business experience than anyone in the room. And he wasn't even an employee. How, he asked himself, do these people even *presume* to know what the corporate world wants, much less sell to it? The veterans consistently tried to tell the youngsters that Apple had to decide upon an overall business strategy; that if it wanted to sell to the corporate world it had to bring in experienced marketers who understood it; that, whether it decided upon the consumer or corporate market, it *had* to link up with a giant company that knew how to market, sell and distribute there.

As early as 1983, Regis put together a white paper for Apple that was prescient in its understanding of the distinct personalities of the two markets. It clearly showed that the corporate market would increasingly move toward networking, large central computers, electronic communications, sophisticated information management software and a demand for strong service and support. Conversely, consumer computers would be open systems linked to hundreds of third-party developers, sold retail and via mail order and be highly price-sensitive.

"I kept saying, 'There's a split here. You need to make a decision. Whether you want to be a Sony or an IBM. You can't be both,' " recalls Regis. "I gave that presentation for years. I wrote papers; I drew diagrams. 'You have to decide what company you want to be. This path [corporate] goes toward systems, and systems are different things than stand-alone computers. They need heavy support, infrastructure. You can't just sell *things.* If you want to sell things, then go the other way. Be like Sony. There's certainly nothing wrong with Sony. *But you've got to decide!*' "

But Apple didn't want to decide. It wanted both markets, products and systems, consumer and corporate, Sony and IBM. It thought that it could cut through these divisions by sheer technological brilliance. And Apple believed this because most of the people making those marketing decisions had very little sense of how great the gulf was between these two markets—*no* single computer would ever again be able to vault it.

So, with no division in its strategy, Apple embarked on its second generation with fragile firewalls between its products. The result was that whenever one of the products hit a snag in one market, it simply crashed sideways through the wall into the Apple product already there. The Lisa, which was to be a corporate product, was also marketed as a consumer product, and later as an enterprise server. The Mac, the people's computer, became a premium office product. Apple's new computers were soon being marketed as all things to all people.

And the poor Apple II got hit from every direction.

6.11 DREAMS TEAM

The first thing Raskin did when given approval for the new project was to change its name. He hated the code word "Annie" because "I felt that the trend in the company to give new products feminine names was sexist—and if you had spoken to the namers you would agree." Instead, keeping with the Apple motif, he chose "Macintosh" because it was his favorite variety of the fruit. He intentionally misspelled it, instead of McIntosh, in hopes of avoiding legal problems with the well-established stereo component company. (He failed: Apple eventually had to reach a settlement not only with McIntosh Ltd. but also with a British raincoat company.)

The second thing Raskin did was to embark on a journal, *The Book of Macintosh*, which contained not only all the documents from the project but also regular updates by team members and even Raskin's own musings. It would eventually reach 400 pages.

Years later, Steven Levy would get a chance to peruse *The Book*. In an entry from January 1980, he found a note from Raskin that read: "The purpose of this design is to create a low-cost portable computer so useful that its owner misses it when it is not around . . ." A month later, Raskin wrote: "The personal computer will come of age when it goes the way of the calculator or the telephone, or probably both . . . it will become a nearly indispensable companion." It was probably the earliest statement of a mature philosophy for the personal computer.

Raskin's words are uncannily like those Steve Jobs would use a few years later in his public flights of hyperbole about the finished Macintosh. By then, of course, he'd read *The Book of Macintosh*. For now, though, he hated the very idea of the Mac. The Lisa was his baby, and with it he intended to rule the computer world forever. Toward that end, he made of himself a general nuisance around the Lisa group, dropping surprise visits on poor programmers and designers to alternately tell them their work was shit or pure gold in his patented motivational technique. He made life a living hell for John Couch, second-guessing the latter's every decision despite having only a limited understanding of what was going on.

Meanwhile, the Mac team continued to grow. It now included programmers Bud Tribble, a former medical student, and Brian Howard, an old friend of Raskin; hardware designer Burrell Smith, a brilliant programmer plucked out of Apple's repair department, and UC computer department dropout Andy Hertzfeld. Raskin also hired an ex-PARC tester named Bruce Horn; Steve Clark, one of Raskin's old UCSD students (and brother of Woz's future bride); technical writer Donald Reed; and, in marketing, Joanna Hoffman, an MIT anthropology student. Chosen as much for their musical skills (Raskin was an ardent musician) as their programming were two old SAIL colleagues, Gareth Loy and Bill Schottstaedt; and, most unlikely, Bana Witt, a poet and former music student of Raskin who would go on to marry yet another team member, Bruce Tognazzini. As a licensed minister, Raskin performed the ceremony.

There was one other, secret, member of the Mac team, who would later prove to be vital: Bill Atkinson. Despite being a member of the Lisa team, Atkinson had fallen in love with the idea of the Macintosh. So when Jobs forbade him to join Raskin's group, he secretly worked under the table.

Even by personal computer industry standards, it was a remarkably eclectic group. Insular too. Before long Jobs had become so obnoxious and interfering that Mike Scott, then still CEO, moved the Mac group to an office building behind a Texaco station, next to an old Catholic social hall, and across the road from the rest of Apple. Jobs would later claim the move was his idea to protect the brilliant team from industrial spies and interference by Apple itself.

During this period, Jobs's greatest contribution to Apple was to make himself into a shared problem for the two product teams, thus forcing natural opponents to make common cause against a shared enemy. According to Raskin: "By the end of 1979 it was clear to many people that unless Jobs had a better understanding of what was being attempted on both the Lisa and the Mac, he would continue to inadvertently sabotage the former and be antagonistic to the latter."

So they set him up.

A year earlier, Raskin had tried to talk both Woz and Jobs into visiting Xerox PARC, but neither was interested. Jobs told Raskin that it wasn't possible for a giant company like Xerox to create anything innovative and exciting. For his part, Woz saw his own turndown at the hands of HP as proof of just such corporate myopia. Raskin also knew that anything he recommended to Jobs would be dismissed out of hand. So the trick was to find two messengers Jobs trusted who could encourage him to go. It fell to Atkinson, the double agent, and Raskin and Couch's boss, Tom Whitney.

Jobs bought it—and the rest, one might say, was rewritten history. When one knows the truth, the events of that visit to PARC become a lot clearer: The fact that Raskin was pointedly not invited. The brilliant questions with which Jobs's group peppered Tesler (of course, they'd been working on the same stuff for seven months). And why, on the way out of PARC, when Jobs famously turned to Atkinson and asked, "How long will it take to duplicate all of this?" Atkinson calmly replied, "About six months." Only a fool or a man who thought he was already halfway done would give such an answer.

6.12 WINDOWS ON THE PAST

The 1970s ended with Apple on top of the world. A year later, the company was gloriously wealthy, thanks to the IPO, and also in serious trouble, thanks to the Apple III, the Woz crash and the Scott coup d'état.

Atkinson's prediction had proven to be wildly optimistic. The Lisa team's love affair with the Alto and Smalltalk hadn't faded after the team left PARC that first day, but had grown into an obsession. Almost from the hour they returned to Apple, Jobs sat down with one of his top people, Trip Hawkins (who would later have his five minutes of fame as founder of Electronic Arts), and they defined all the new parameters of the Lisa, including windows, mouse and an icon-driven interface. Soon, Larry Tesler quit PARC and joined the Lisa team. Later, inevitably, Alan Kay joined Apple as well, as an in-house guru and founding Apple Fellow.

But all this resident talent didn't accelerate the Lisa's development, but rather slowed it down. Not just duplicating, but actually improving upon, all those features of the Alto (which was, after all, a multimillion-dollar prototype) proved not only more time-consuming but more expensive than anyone had imagined. And an ambitious operating system wasn't the only problem. The initial design also called for the ill-advised use of the company's own proprietary Twiggy 5¼-inch disk drives, whose software-controlled automatic ejection and micro-stepping head technology were too advanced for the era and led to endless quality problems. Working out the bugs in these new drives further ate up precious time.

One group within the Lisa team that never fully bought into the PARC philosophy were the old HPers, including Couch. But if this group didn't have the Xerox obsession, it had the next-worse thing: the Hewlett-Packard disease. This was HP's worst era; Hewlett and Packard had pulled away from the daily activities of the firm, and their company, now in the hands of John Young, was growing richer but more bloated, somehow producing overpriced, overengineered and overdue products in between seemingly endless meetings. The HPers, who should have brought a measure of discipline to the Lisa project, instead contributed their own portfolio of failings.

Finally, there was the ever-present Jobs. Jobs's perpetual yo-yoing of employees between seduction and humiliation often produced great results, but it was hugely stressful and horrifically time-consuming. Months of work would be lost in a single morning when Steve would suddenly and capriciously change his mind. Trapped in their secure team area, never knowing what to expect from their mercurial and arbitrary captor, many Lisa team members, like other Apple employees before them, exhibited something like the Stockholm Effect in relation to Jobs. They feared him, despised him, protected him and worshipped him all at the same time. The real lesson of the PARC visit, team members quickly learned, was to first present the new idea to Jobs, have him reject it, then wait a week for him to convince himself that it had been his idea all along and announce it as the team's new strategy. It usually worked, but it wasted time and emotional energy to regularly enact such a charade.

Jobs knew the effect he had on subordinates and played it to the hilt. Raskin had his own ax to grind with Jobs, but his description is accurate to anyone who ever worked with Steve Jobs: "By this time Jobs had begun to have people who were 'in' and those who were 'out'; if you were 'in,' everything you did was golden; if you were 'out,' everything you did was rotten. . . . Most people worked around him or sucked up to him or were in awe of him. In fact, he was no genius; he resembled a planet shining by reflecting the light of others. Yet he thought of himself as the Sun King. He could not abide someone who was unimpressed by Steve Jobs."

Cringely has provided one of the most memorable descriptions of Jobs in action:

> Coming up to an Apple employee, he'd say, "I think Jim [another employee] is shit. What do you think?"
>
> If the employee agrees that Jim is shit, Jobs went to the next person and said, "Bob and I think Jim is shit. What do you think?"
>
> If the first employee disagreed and said that Jim is not shit, Jobs would move on to the next person, saying, "Bob and I think that Jim is great. What do you think?"

The Jobs Reality Distortion Field was now complete and running at full wattage. He might, on a given day, make the lives of Lisa team members a living hell. But to outsiders—especially members of the increasingly beleaguered Apple II group—it looked like paradise, especially after Black Wednesday left the Lisa team untouched.

All successful breakthrough products have a technical genius behind them somewhere. And if that genius is lucky, he can overcome almost every other problem associated with the product. The Lisa, it turned out, had its own

Woz in Bill Atkinson. Having shot his mouth off with Jobs and set the whole PARC play going, he now performed a miracle by making the fantasy real.

Atkinson had come out of the University of Washington's neurobiochemistry department and had joined Apple in 1978 after falling in love with Woz's Apple II design (as he would a few years later with the Mac). Atkinson went on the PARC tour having a pretty good idea what the Alto, Star and Smalltalk were all about, and was well on his way to developing his own version of each of their novel functions.

But in his visit to PARC, Atkinson had experienced a dangerous misapprehension. Watching a brief demonstration of Smalltalk, Atkinson was struck by what seemed to him a working version of an operation called clipping. This was the effect, when windows overlap on the computer screen, of not actually constructing the entire screen(s) peeking out underneath the top one. This saved considerable processing power by the computer, but it also required some unprecedented software. In seeing Smalltalk do just that, Atkinson came away convinced that it could be done and dedicated himself to the task.

The trouble was, Atkinson only *thought* he saw clipping. What he actually saw was much closer to a side-by-side tiling of windows of predetermined size, with some slow simulation of overlap. In other words, the clipping technology Atkinson assumed had already been developed had in fact not yet been proven.

Atkinson began to realize his mistake just about the time he went nuts trying to figure out how Xerox did it. He spent months trying to duplicate the process—even getting up in the middle of the night to jot down notes from his dreams. And little by little, Atkinson began to solve the puzzle, developing algebraic equations to quickly describe the cutout pieces as a window "disappeared" behind another.

So focused did Atkinson become on the project that, nearing completion, while driving his little Mazda RX-7 to work, he failed to notice that the semitrailer truck he was preparing to cross behind was in fact *parked.* He drove right under it, tearing the roof completely off his car and nearly decapitating himself. In the end, he was only knocked unconscious, awakening in the hospital to see a worried Steve Jobs looking down at him, fearful of a Woz II. "Don't worry, Steve," he told him, "I still know how to do regions."

Atkinson knew how to do other things as well. He took the iconography that he saw at PARC and combined it with Raskin's one-button mouse technique, which he'd seen on his secret forays to the Mac building, and came up with a method of using the mouse to drag both icons and windows around the computer screen. This, along with the clipping technology, enabled Atkinson to create a revolutionary user interface that brought together the familiar experience of moving papers around a desktop with every messy person's fantasy of being able to instantly uncover that crucial buried item.

The Lisa was on its way. But before it could go much further, one last bottleneck had to be removed. With some very careful diplomacy that landed the support of Mike Markkula, Jobs was tossed—gingerly—out of the Lisa project. The rationale, which he eventually accepted, was that the chairmanship was in itself sufficient responsibility, even for a man of his caliber. The Lisa team took a collective sigh of relief and went back to work.

But it would still take longer than anyone imagined. Even after the hardware configuration and packaging were established, the Lisa's wildly ambitious software proved endlessly troublesome. One unexpected problem popped up after another.

It became like a burlesque routine. The software engineers would see a problem and present an innovative solution. The marketers (especially the HPers) would argue that it would take too long to complete. The software engineers, often Atkinson, would pull all-nighters to prove them wrong. Then Tesler would take the solution and try it out on new, inexperienced Apple employees. He would find that it worked, but that the process had identified a whole new problem—and the cycle would begin again.

There was also the matter of the name. Lisa just wasn't a proper name for a computer, especially with its rumored connection to Jobs's daughter. Here once again the underlying tension between the suits and the freaks at Apple reared its head. The marketing and business types, looking to the corporate market, wanted to call the new computer something sober and formal, like the Apple IV or the TI-like Apple 400. The hackers screamed *no, no,* the whole point of the Lisa was to be different from all the others. It was supposed to be a friendly, approachable computer, a tool to enhance your lifestyle, not just crank out spreadsheets. Their candidates included Esprit (already taken) and Applause. The result was the type of deadlock that in a few years would characterize all of Apple.

In the end, the company just swallowed hard and went with the status quo, praying that the Jobs paternity connection wouldn't come out. It did, in *Time,* of course. So much for secrecy.

By now 1980 had turned into 1981, then 1982. Finally, in mid-1982, the Lisa at last approached completion. Physically, it was as impressive a machine as the computer industry had yet seen. An elegant, beige box whose rectangular face contained on one side a twelve-inch black-and-white screen and on the other the stacked slots for two Twiggy disk drives. But that wasn't the first thing you noticed. Rather, your eyes instantly went to the keyboard. It wasn't built in! Instead, it was connected to the central processor box by a looped, telephone-like electrical wire. And then, next to the keyboard was another, tinier satellite, also connected by a wire to the computer. With its single giant button, it was like a kid's toy . . . a mouse.

But there was still something wrong. The hardware was fine, as were the special functions. But something was unsettling about the user interface. When you first fired up the Lisa, on-screen there appeared a Filer program that welcomed you and asked you what you wanted to do. The problem was this questioning process was akin to an interrogation. Some Lisa group members jokingly called it the "20 Questions Program." Others inflated that to "100." It is always a bad sign when the inventors begin making black jokes about their own creation.

Yet as late as mid-1982 the Filer was still slated to be the standard front-end interface for the Lisa. Luckily, that potential disaster was averted by the Wife Test. Doing a little field testing of his own, Dan Smith, the designer of the Filer, took it home and asked his wife to use it. Try as she might, Mrs. Smith couldn't figure the Filer out.

That did it. Smith was brave enough to admit he had made a mistake. He went to Atkinson and told him the problem, convinced that Apple would never allow such an expensive revision so near introduction. But Atkinson, who by now was getting accustomed to stealth, had a better idea. He proposed that he, Smith and a third engineer named Frank Ludoloph meet in an extended secret cram session at Atkinson's house and come up with an alternative. Atkinson even tried to tell his plan to his boss, Wayne Rosing, director of engineering for the Lisa project. Rosing replied, "Don't tell me what you're working on, but good luck."

Weeks later, the trio reemerged with a new Filer interface, now called the Desktop Manager. And of all the amazing new features on the Lisa, this one would prove the most memorable, and the one most associated with Apple Computer.

Now, instead of being bombarded with questions, the owner was met with a simulated desktop, complete with folders bearing labels. These folders merely had to be tapped by the mouse to open and display an array of files, each designated by both a name and an icon of its type (application program, word processing file, etc.). The file was then opened by tapping the single button on the mouse twice. When you were done with that file you merely tapped once on a square in the upper corner. You could put the file back into its folder, create a new one or, coolest of all, drag the file's icon down to the lower right-hand corner of the screen and throw it into a trash-can icon—an act so cute and so lifelike that it was usually the first thing most new Apple users tried.

6.13 Flacking, Flogging and Floundering

The Lisa was slated for a January 1983 introduction. Apple's publicity machine kicked into overdrive. Both Regis McKenna and Fred Hoar were intent upon making this the biggest product introduction in electronics history.

They succeeded. The Lisa was the high water mark for Silicon Valley flackery. The national press had all but ignored the introduction of the Valley's other great products, the HP-35, the Intel 8080 microprocessor, the Amdahl and Tandem computers, even Pong. Now it seemed to be atoning for this past indifference by treating the Lisa introduction as if it were the Salk vaccine. The result was the most successful new-product introduction since the Boeing 707, the Ford Mustang or pull tabs for beer cans. Hoar, having done his job with the IPO and the Lisa, left soon after. Fifteen years later, as Apple stumbled, he would still be a Valley heavyweight, and would tell Apple jokes as part of his famous introductions at industry gatherings.

Jobs, the man who had to be thrown out of the Lisa project for it to go forward, finally got his *Time* cover (complete with halo) in the yearlong ramp-up to the introduction. Meanwhile, the Brahmins of high-tech business reporting (Andy Pollack of the *New York Times*, Dick Shaffer of *The Wall Street Journal*, Ben Rosen) were given an early glimpse of the machine and dubbed it more than worthy. They lauded its packaging, its interface, the company's decision to go with the new Motorola 68000 processor, its megabyte of memory and its remarkable Lisa Office System suite of seven powerful software programs (LisaWrite, LisaDraw, LisaCalc, LisaGraph, LisaProject, LisaList and LisaTerminal). And when the Lisa finally appeared for public viewing and coverage by the lesser lights of the press, it was hailed as Apple's Great Comeback, its answering shot to IBM.

But it wasn't. Even as Apple geared up for the Lisa introduction, there was a gnawing sense that something was wrong. For all of its revolutionary attributes, the Lisa was also so freighted with features and overwritten new programs that it had become painfully slow in operation and, at a typical price of $12,000 (almost ten times the price of a basic Apple II), was shockingly expensive. It had to be to recoup the $50 million invested in creating it, $20 million of that in software alone. The Apple II, by comparison, had cost just 1 percent of that, $500,000.

For the early reviewers, folks who would never have to buy one of these computers for themselves (or hundreds of them for their companies), the price was easily rationalized away by noting that the only computers currently available with the Lisa's power were $40,000 minicomputers. That was true, but consumers and small businesses weren't buying minis.

What the Lisa team had invented was the first computer workstation. Unfortunately, that market wouldn't appear for another six years. And when it did, in the hands of Sun Microsystems, Silicon Graphics and Hewlett-Packard, these new workstations would shrewdly be designed for engineering applications, where all that computing firepower could immediately be put to use—not for business, where all this power needed sophisticated (and as yet unwritten) software to prove its worth.

In the end, the Lisa was a great product without a market. It was one of those rare products that manage to do everything right, while also doing everything wrong. It couldn't help but fire the first shot of a new era, and then be the first casualty of the resulting revolution. Even as it sat in the lobby of the new Apple headquarters building, its smooth sides dully reflecting the neon decorative elements of the surrounding lobby, the exotic bit-mapped images bursting on its screen, you couldn't help but admire the Lisa for its brilliance and yet secretly sense that it was the Edsel of computers.

But if Lisa was an Edsel, Apple at least still had the Volkswagen. By the end of 1982, the company had sold 600,000 Apple II's, by far the largest installed base in the personal computer industry. Even the fast-growing PC had sold only a third as many machines. Moreover, the II had the best software library in the industry, with Apple and third-party developers coming up with dozens of new titles each month. Woz's little boxes were now the driving share of Apple's $583 million in revenues. And they showed little signs of fading.

That was good news. But IBM was still coming on fast. By mistakenly, but serendipitously, losing control over its architecture and operating system, Big Blue had left a very big door open. Copycat manufacturers were free to jump into the market with "clone" machines that imitated the PC's performance and ran its software. By the end of 1983, more than a hundred such clone companies were in the market, many with only a fraction of the PC's functionality, but some so close to perfect compatibility that it made no difference to the average user. Using off-the-shelf parts, manufacturing that was sometimes superior even to IBM's and prices that were often half that of the PC, these third-wave clone makers very quickly became a market force in themselves. Ultimately, they played as great a role as Big Blue in destroying Atari and the second wave of personal computer makers.

In all the hoopla about the Lisa, less noticed was the simultaneous introduction of a new, more powerful Apple II, called the IIe. The annual meeting/press conference, when the two products were rolled out, was entitled "evolution/revolution." But it was obvious to everyone present that the one person whose views counted, Steve Jobs, didn't give half a damn about the IIe. Revolutionaries don't like incremental change.

Ironically, both on the Apple balance sheet and in the hearts of millions of schoolkids, the IIe was by far the more important product. It was a gutsy little machine that Apple, thanks to the increasing power and miniaturization of chips, would eventually build for under $100 and sell for more than ten times that amount. The IIe would not only prop up Apple's market share and give it the capital it needed to launch the Mac, but would also create a generation of Apple fanatics that would buoy the company for the next decade. Most important, it gave Apple an enduring share of the market's heart long after it lost most of its share of the market. Unheralded, but beloved, the Apple IIe may well have been the greatest personal computer ever built. And it didn't even get top billing at its own introduction.

Still, in one respect, Jobs was right: without a new breakout product, Apple was destined to slowly fade away. The Apple II, no matter what its form, would never be the future. Though he had already turned against it, Jobs had no choice for now but to put heart and soul behind the Lisa. That the world considered it his baby was only added motivation.

Apple predicted sales of 10,000 Lisas in the second half of 1983 (when deliveries would begin in volume) and 40,000 in 1984. In the end, the company sold 80,000 of the machines, or 13,000 per each quarter of its short life—a figure not far from the company's projections, and one that was ramping up toward the end. But almost from the beginning, it was obvious that the Lisa, while not a disaster like the III, was also not going to save Apple.

Now it was up to the Macintosh. Lisa's ill-treated and disreputable baby brother had now become Apple's last hope.

6.14 Headless Hunting

Even as the Lisa was being introduced, Steve Jobs was in negotiations for a new company CEO. Markkula was ready again for one of his regular retirements. Jobs, both because he was chairman and because, having been booted from the Lisa project, he needed something important to do, made it his project to find someone to run the new, more mature Apple.

Using headhunters to help in the search, Jobs began looking in October 1982. By Christmas he had narrowed the list to two individuals: One was Don Estridge, the guy from Boca Raton who had given IBM the PC. The other was John Sculley of Pepsi-Cola, reputedly the best marketing guy of his generation, the man who'd done for Pepsi's market share what generations of his predecessors had failed to accomplish. The guy who invented "The Pepsi Generation."

Estridge would have been a great choice. He was Apple's kind of maverick executive (and he'd done it inside the most conformist corporation of them all). As a former software engineer he knew more about computers than Jobs and Markkula combined. And, as icing on the cake, his departure would rob Apple's biggest competitor of its leadership.

But if Estridge seemed made for Apple, there was one problem: he wasn't made for Steve Jobs. Author Frank Rose would write about Estridge that "like Jobs, he was full of energy and intelligence and charisma," but, unlike Jobs, "he also had a remarkable generosity of spirit. He could give you an idea and make you think it was your own, and he could put so much trust in you that you'd break down walls to get your job done."

It is said that a con job works only on people with a little larceny already in their hearts. One of the interesting features rarely remarked about Steve Jobs's Reality Distortion Field is that it too worked most effectively on people whose personalities shared some of its attributes. Not being a natural self-mythologizer, Estridge not only resisted Jobs's blandishments but was actually repelled by them. When Jobs tried to seduce him with conspiratorial stories about his felonious activities of old, Estridge was disgusted: I'm going to work for a kid who is *proud* of being a criminal?

But there was more than that. Estridge believed in traditional notions long in disrepute in Silicon Valley. Like loyalty. Estridge was proud he worked for IBM; and he was even more proud of his team at Boca. Going to work for Apple would betray them both.

So in the end, despite being offered millions in salary, bonus and stock—more money than he would ever make at IBM—Estridge turned Steve Jobs down. When an IBM vice president later asked him why, Estridge explained simply that when he was talking to a stranger on a plane and was asked where he worked, he wanted to say, "IBM."

Now Steve Jobs had two choices. Either go with the number two choice or start over. He chose the former. It was, after his little larceny with Woz, Jobs's second big mistake. Until that point, Jobs had done the right things in his recruitment program. He had not only accepted that he wasn't yet ready to run a corporation (not an easy thing for him to admit) but had consciously gone out in search of a grown-up, for someone who combined corporate experience with a maverick style, a technology background mixed with proven marketing skill, and, most importantly, someone who was smart enough and secure enough to see through Steven P. Jobs.

Unfortunately, Jobs had found somebody better than himself, only to run him off. If he had been brave enough or patient enough, Jobs would have started over. He should have repeated what he did so brilliantly with Apple's computers by refusing to settle for anything but the very best. In time he would have found that perfect individual, because Apple was the biggest lure in American business.

Instead he settled for John Sculley. Why? Perhaps because he felt he was running out of time. Or maybe he really did believe that Sculley was the best man for the job and that any additional searching would find no better candidate. Maybe it was just because in Sculley he found a talented man he could still intellectually seduce. Once again, with Steve Jobs it may have been all three. But whatever the reason, Jobs had made his second great mistake. It wasn't as venal as the petty theft from Woz, but it was nearly as devastating. Steve had understood the need for an experienced CEO, but when he went looking he settled only on variations of himself: Estridge the entrepreneur, Sculley the marketing legend. But Apple already had those positions filled—by Steve Jobs. What the company needed now was a more experienced and emotionally stable Mike Scott, an executive who could keep the company's books in order, negotiate strategic partnerships and get products out on budget and on time. Jobs never liked such people, and didn't hire one.

6.15 Moles

The Mac group had taken good advantage of its years of isolation. Raskin had assembled his team quickly and thoughtfully. He could be insufferably arrogant, but he also recognized and supported talent when he saw it. Never was this more the case than with Burrell Smith, the kid from the repair department. Atkinson had found Smith, took him to Raskin's house one evening and announced, "Here's the guy who's going to design your machine for you."

Raskin was dubious, but he quickly came to respect the little man's talents. And it didn't hurt that Smith quickly became a true believer in Raskin's vision of the Mac as Everyman's companion, the Swiss Army knife of computers. Still, it took an extraordinary leap of faith that December for Raskin to turn over the assignment of building the first prototype to the kid.

Smith didn't let him down. For the next month, Burrell hunkered down in the Mac area, working day and night through Christmas, scrounging parts whenever he needed them (an advantage of being a former repairman was knowing where to look) and constantly keeping in mind Raskin's seemingly impossible goal of a $1,000 machine that nevertheless featured bit-mapping and built-in keyboard, display and mass memory. This stringent price goal led to some distressing compromises—for example, the prototype had to settle for the lame little Motorola 6809, a microprocessor hardly more powerful than the II's now obsolete 6502, as well as a rotten cassette player instead of the current industry-standard floppy disk—but Smith soldiered on.

He finished right after New Year's, putting the motherboard and other subsystems into an Apple II box. That last night, as he finished, Smith sent a note to Andy Hertzfeld, apprising him of what he'd accomplished and challenging Hertzfeld to come make it work.

Hertzfeld took the challenge, working most of the night. In the morning, Smith arrived to see the computer's display glowing, appropriately, with an image of Scrooge McDuck and the words "Hi, Burrell!"

Smith got his display, Atkinson got a real role at last in the Mac group and, most important, Raskin got his prototype. And all of them would soon be working for the 1980s version of McDuck, a figure rich enough to even buy history.

6.16 The Prince of Thieves

Nineteen eighty was Macintosh's year in the wilderness.

Three times in the course of the year, the project teetered on the brink of cancellation. The third time, in October, it was officially canceled—only to be saved at the last moment by Raskin successfully begging Mike Scott for a three-month extension. The team somehow struggled on. But the writing was on the wall: come the first of the year, if the Mac didn't show something spectacular it was gone.

Then a miracle, the last miracle in the Apple story. And like the other Apple miracles, it managed also to be a little tawdry. Steve Jobs, tossed out of the Lisa project and wandering about looking for something to do, came upon Raskin's *Book of Macintosh.* Jobs was enough of an ersatz technical visionary to recognize the real thing when he saw it. There it was, the insanely great idea Jobs always talked about. In his characteristic way, Jobs adopted the vision as his own—and since it was he, not Raskin, in the public eye, fielding press interviews and giving industry speeches, the Macintosh soon became synonymous with Steven Jobs. Henceforth it would be his idea.

But co-opting Jef Raskin's ideas was only the beginning. The ideas were, after all, being made manifest in a real product. The Mac group had by now moved to its little rented office behind the Texaco station. The team members named its hole-in-the-wall the Texaco Towers, set up a Ping-Pong table and styled themselves rebels—pirates—from the rest of Apple.

And it wasn't long before Steve Jobs started hanging around, talking to the team behind Raskin's back. It was hard to resist his charms. Apple was public now, and Jobs was the richest young entrepreneur in the world. He was more famous than most rock stars. The public considered him a business genius. And he could talk the talk. He'd read *The Book of Mac;* he could spout the liturgy almost as well as Raskin. But, unlike Raskin, Jobs could also make things happen at Apple. Pirates they might be, but not by choice. With Steve Jobs in the building, all of Apple—hell, the entire world—would be looking their way.

Meanwhile, at the II and Lisa groups (and, rumor had it, on executive row) everyone was glad to have Jobs distracted and buried off in some dead-end corner of the company where he couldn't do much damage.

But to focus solely on the deceits and petty cruelties of Steve Jobs during this period would be a mistake. Because if his methods were often improper, even on occasion despicable, there is no denying that Steve was still the preeminent market visionary and product positioner of his generation. And for all the damage he was about to do to the lives of everyone connected with the Mac project, he also gave them a little share of immortality. He would take a little, dreamy, probably doomed new-product idea and turn it into, as Steven Levy would later claim, the commercial product of the century.

Despite his later protestations, Jef Raskin could never have done that. He may have been the father of the Mac, but he was a difficult parent. He was not a martinet like Jobs (he was in fact a very supportive manager), but Raskin had a character weakness nearly as damaging as Jobs's: he was a dogmatist. The Mac of his dreams had little memory, a cassette drive, no mouse and none of the Xerox software innovations. In a first prototype, these weren't huge flaws; rather they proved the concept of a $1,000 computer at a time when most machines cost three times that much.

But Raskin was unyielding. Left to him, future Macs would likely have perpetuated those flaws. Jobs was different; he was attached to an idea only as long as it worked, then would compromise it or abandon it (and pretend he'd never been part of it) if it failed. And it certainly didn't hurt to be chairman, rather than merely a product manager, when it came to making such unilateral decisions.

Raskin was well liked as a manager, but his ideological narrow-mindedness was wearing thin. The team would build his machine, with its puny microprocessor, but they craved a chance to blow out the spit valves. So when Steve Jobs began to lurk around making suggestions, plying his charms, offering the team members a chance to prove what they could do, they met his mutiny halfway.

Jobs's first move was to work on the team's version of Woz, Burrell Smith. It was a technique he knew well. He dared Smith to build a Mac with the hottest chip then on the market, the Motorola 68000. Smith couldn't help himself—and there went another Christmas vacation spent on all-nighters and a new prototype.

The result was a dragster among PCs. It hadn't been easy to build. Putting the 68000 in the econobox of the Mac was the digital equivalent of stuffing a big-block Chevy engine into the back of a Volkswagen: if you didn't find a way to control and channel all that horsepower it would simply twist the transmission into a pretzel and tear the wheels off the car. Smith's comparable problem was that the 68000 was processing information so fast, blasting off bursts of data, that it would simply overwhelm the keyboard, display and every other peripheral device. Smith's solution, an elegant way of queuing and managing the transmission of data off the processor called "bus multiplexing," would be a hallmark of all PCs in the years to come.

Smith's 68000 Mac was the death knell not just for Raskin but, as time would show, for the Lisa as well. The new Mac did everything the Lisa did at a tenth the retail price, and a twentieth the development cost. In this new prototype Jobs saw the future of computing, and Apple. Now if the new Mac could just run some of those Xerox programs he'd seen that day at PARC . . .

By the end of January, Jobs had attached himself fully to the Mac team. As Joanna Hoffman would tell Levy: "When Steve started coming over, Jef's dream was shattered on the spot. It was difficult on everybody and there was an air of allegiance to Jef, but Steve had his own competing aura. He immediately started talking about what it would look like, feel like, how we would sell it . . ."

It wasn't long before Jobs started complaining that Raskin was a poor manager, and worse, that he was too slow. The Mac was never going to get to market in another year as Raskin claimed, Jobs said, so the project needed a firmer hand at the tiller. (Needless to say, it would in fact take Jobs three years.)

The confrontation peaked on February 17, when Raskin was scheduled to give an informal lunchtime "brown bag" seminar on his vision of the personal computer. Other Apple employees were anxious to know about the topic, and Raskin had agreed not to give out any trade secrets about the Macintosh. Jobs had already canceled one such event by Raskin in January. Now, just two hours before the talk, he called Raskin and told him the seminar was canceled once again.

But Jobs, perhaps because he had forgotten or perhaps because he wanted to injure Raskin's reputation by making him look unreliable, never told the seminar's organizer. As a result, when in a spur-of-the-moment decision just after noon, Raskin decided to stroll over to the seminar site, he found a hundred Apple employees waiting for his talk. So, not above a little deviousness himself, Raskin got up, announced the cancellation, then launched into a different talk on his current work at Apple. He didn't mention Macintosh by name, but everyone in the room knew what he was describing.

Jobs was furious. He called Raskin into his office the next morning and fired him. Raskin knew better; he told Jobs he'd come back later in the day. When he did, Jobs had changed his mind: Raskin wasn't fired, but he was put on an extended paid leave.

Jef Raskin was many things, but he was not a fool. He knew what was coming. But he had no intention of giving up easily the most important creation of his life. So, even as he was being purged by Jobs, Raskin fired off a memo to Markkula. He would later claim that the rest of the Mac team was going to sign the letter with him, but chickened out.

For whatever reason—exhaustion, a recognition of his own limitations, or, as he presented it, the need to focus on the technical side of the project—Raskin had already spoken of the possibility of getting a professional manager to run the business side of the project. It was a big mistake, as he now realized to his horror, because by admitting weakness he had allowed his biggest enemy in through the front door.

In his memo to Markkula, currently the CEO, Raskin made a last-ditch attempt to ward off the specter of Jobs. As Raskin described it later:

> I didn't want Steve to be in charge. The memo specified, in detail and in my judgment, Jobs's many and egregious failings as a manager . . .
>
> The memo reflected the running joke that the way to get Jobs to agree to something was to tell him about it, let him reject it and wait a week; when he came running to tell you about "his new" idea, you'd exclaim, "Great, Steve, we'll do it right away!" In the memo, I also made the prediction that was to prove exact: "Jobs was wrong on his Apple III schedule, wrong on the Lisa schedule, wrong on the cost and price estimates, and he will be wrong on Macintosh. He is a prime

> example of a manager who takes the credit for his optimistic schedules and then blames the workers when deadlines are not met.

That wasn't all:

> While Mr. Jobs's stated positions on management techniques are all quite noble and worthy, in practice he is a dreadful manager. . . . He was late for appointments, he attacked other people's work without understanding it, he sowed divisiveness and discontent, he played favorites, he had no idea of realistic scheduling . . .

Raskin asked that the memo be kept secret. But somehow Jobs got a copy. Markkula would later suggest that, Apple being an open company, it had been taken off his desk. Just as likely, he showed it to Jobs. Either way, Raskin would never touch the Mac project again. While on leave, he bought a plot of land in the Santa Cruz mountains and restored the old house on it. When he returned, Apple offered him the job of head of the company's research division, a job he'd taken once before, only to see his staff slowly bled away to other projects. "In those days, Apple didn't know what research meant, and looked at the talented people I hired as resources wasted if they weren't working on current products. Besides, there was the matter of personal integrity. Steve Jobs had become impossible for me to work with . . . [and] the only alternatives left for me were to leave or learn to toady to Steve Jobs."

So Raskin quit Apple. Later, Canon of Japan would hire him to build the computer of his dreams. The result, the Cat, combined Raskin's strength in design (it was perhaps the easiest-to-use computer ever built) with his weaknesses in corporate politics (it was marketed as a secretarial tool and never allowed to operate at full performance). It failed miserably.

Looking back at his Apple experiences, Raskin would write:

> Steve had chutzpah in the extreme . . . And you can explain Jobs with another Yiddish word, mensch. It is high praise to say of a person that he (or in these enlightened days, she) is a mensch or "a real mensch." A mensch is cultivated without losing the common touch, upholds high principles while remaining practical, is kind and generous without shortchanging himself, and is attentive to his responsibilities to himself, his family, his business, his associates, his community and the world. If you understand the qualities that make a man a mensch, then you understand a lot about Steve Jobs. Everything a mensch is, he isn't.

Perhaps, but Steve Jobs had also won. He now had his hands on the greatest product of the age.

6.17 We Lucky Few

Steve Jobs once bet John Couch $5,000 the Macintosh would beat the Lisa to market.

It was a bet he was lucky to lose. The success of the Lisa as an invention, and its failure as a product, proved invaluable lessons for Jobs and the Mac team. It suggested the right path for the product: a combination of Raskin's budget computer for the masses, the Xerox/Lisa interface, and Jobs's own flair for packaging and design.

That mix alone would take time; but added to it was Jobs's own mercurial style, his endless flip-flops about one feature or another that ran the Mac team ragged. On top of this was Jobs's own paranoid style in a volatile mix with his thirst for revenge against all those who drove him out of the Lisa group or who suggested that he was little more than a con man who'd hooked on to Woz.

All this came together in a symbolic event: Jobs had a pirate flag (with Apple logo eyes) raised above the Mac team's building, where it could be seen by the rest of Apple. The message wasn't lost. Jobs was symbolically giving the finger to the rest of the company. But what has been little remarked about this little Peter Pan moment is that Jobs was at this time also *chairman of the board* of Apple. It was as if the founder and governor of a colony had suddenly rowed out to command a pirate ship to attack his own home. It is hardly surprising that Jobs wanted it both ways, rebel and pillar of the corporate establishment, but what is amazing is that he pulled it off. "Chutzpah" almost isn't a strong enough term.

Jobs's arrival also meant some radical changes to the work environment of the Mac team. No more scrimping and praying the project wouldn't be canceled. The Dauphin was now in charge, and nothing was too good for the team. Before long, the Mac group was ensconced in Bandley 3, right smack in the middle of the Apple campus. Now, besides the old Ping-Pong table, the lobby featured a Bösendorfer grand piano, Jobs's BMW racing motorcycle and a Defender video arcade game. Rock and classical music boomed day and night from giant studio-quality speakers. There was even a masseuse on staff to rub and Rolf bodies back into celestial harmony.

It was a building you entered with both trepidation and delight. Trepidation because everything screamed at you that here were special people performing special tasks to which you were not privy; but thrilling, because it looked like the coolest place to work in America. Bandley 3 would prove to be the prototype of every product design shop in Silicon Valley and Seattle for the next quarter century. And, like those that followed, Bandley 3 was in fact a very well-appointed sweatshop, whose inhabitants worked days that would have been illegal had they been paid by the hour.

Thanks to Burrell Smith, Jobs had his hardware prototype, a supercharged version of Raskin's box. Now he needed the Lisa interface. That task fell to Andy Hertzfeld, and he knew just what to do. Unconstrained by the bureaucracy and the compromise of working on a large, expensive team, Hertzfeld simply raided the Lisa interface for the pieces he liked best. And, having little respect for most of the Lisa team, Hertzfeld took almost exclusively from a single source, Bill Atkinson. As he told Levy: "Anything Bill Atkinson did, I took, and nothing else."

Hertzfeld didn't work in a vacuum. From the beginning, partly because of Raskin's loose management style, the Mac team worked democratically. New features were often put to a vote by the entire team, and typically those that won were selected because they were interesting or fun. Jobs's arrival didn't change that. Rather it amplified it. Now added to the mix was Jobs's goal of an "insanely great" product. That was a license to pursue the cool.

Meanwhile, the team slowly learned to deal with the mercurial Jobs, playing the game Raskin described of waiting out his goofier ideas, allowing the young chairman to take credit for ideas that weren't his and, most important, letting him run cover for the team in the rest of Apple. With Jobs in the Mac group, the rest of the company might pray he would fall on his face, but no one would dare take him on.

Jobs was more than just a champion and a nuisance. What he brought to the group was what he had provided Apple from the beginning: an aesthetic. Cringely would later say that Jobs was the most dangerous man in Silicon Valley because he didn't care about money. Others would say that Jobs was dangerous because he didn't care about any other living thing. But whatever the truth of those statements, they missed an essential fact about Steve Jobs: he was dangerous because he was important. And he was important because he was essential. And he was essential because he was the only person in the entire personal computer industry who operated at the nexus between the digital revolution and the artistic one that preceded it. If he was a monster, he was a monster like Picasso, not like Rockefeller. He had stolen the Macintosh from its creator, but now he made it his canvas, adding new ideas, then painting them over and trying something else until he got it right.

One thing he got right the first time was the box. Jobs wanted the Mac to be a memorable object in itself and the only person he knew up to that standard was the man who'd designed the Apple II, Jerry Mannock. Jobs told Mannock (who, one will remember, had said he'd never work for Jobs again) that he wanted a design that would get into the Museum of Modern Art. That swashbuckling ambition was a hallmark of Steve Jobs in this era. He also said that he wanted Tom Wolfe to write his biography. And he would, in time, hire I. M. Pei to design his New York apartment (so much for his austerity).

But it was more than name-dropping, or affiliating himself with famous names. Jobs simply wanted the best, and those were the people he was most likely to get it from, artists who were the greatest living masters of their craft. As Jobs once explained: "When you're a carpenter making a beautiful chest of drawers, you're not going to use a piece of plywood on the back, even though it faces the wall and nobody will ever see it. *You'll* know it's there, so you're going to use a beautiful piece of wood on the back. For you to sleep well at night, the aesthetic, the quality, has to be carried all the way through."

This comment (though betraying a lack of experience with real antique furniture) nevertheless showed Jobs's deep, Zen-like sense of purity when it came to the design of his products. Sometimes this obsession would lead him astray; for example, he spent a couple of weeks hanging around Macy's appliance department convinced that the Mac should resemble a Cuisinart. But throughout his career, from the Apple II to the NeXT computer to *Toy Story*, when the moment of truth came Jobs had an almost perfect eye for the right look.

Thus, when he saw Mannock's design for a friendly little upright box with a facelike display, a floppy-disk slot like an off-kilter mouth, a detachable keyboard and a footprint no bigger than a piece of stationery, Jobs knew he had the design of his dreams. It was Raskin's Swiss Army knife computer crossed with the cool elegance Jobs dreamed for himself and his machines. Even more important, the Mac's design was *friendly*. Its anthropomorphic shape, similar to the little robots seen padding around the background of *Star Wars*, made it appear like one of the Seven Dwarfs, or Sancho Panza. It was the companion that Raskin had written about four years before.

Jobs's perfect eye came through for him one more time during the Mac project. Chiat/Day of Los Angeles had the reputation as the hottest and most innovative television advertising agency of the day. Needless to say, Jobs was drawn to it and was instrumental in hiring the agency to represent Apple. But the partnership had not begun well. The agency's first ad for the Lisa was entitled "Alone Again." It was a lifestyle ad, rich in texture (music by Wyndham Hill, a dreamlike floating room featuring a young man at work on his Lisa)—but also unintentionally funny. In view of the few Lisas being sold, if you did buy one you certainly would be alone.

But what Chiat/Day did have going for it was the director Ridley Scott, a Brit who was making himself famous in feature films directing *Blade Runner* and *Alien.* Scott had begun in advertising and had escaped the stigma of his roots so well that he was able to return to them without fear. He would direct a series of Apple ads, "Apple People," featuring slice-of-life images (the lunch-time basketball game, etc.) that were well received less because of their clichéd content than for the filmlike quality of their production.

Now, with the prospect of a revolutionary new product like Macintosh, Scott wanted to cut loose and make an equally revolutionary commercial of the likes American television had never seen. If the Mac was to be introduced in 1984, then by God, let's give the audience a vision of Orwell's *1984.* IBM would be Big Brother and Apple a Winston Smith who really does defeat the regime. Scott wanted the look to be a cross between the gray Eastern Europe at the time of the Hungarian uprising, the worn-out machinery of his own *Alien* and the Deco cities of *Metropolis* and *Things to Come.* The only sound-track would be Stalinist gibberish emanating from Big Brother on a giant screen.

The original plan was to have a beautiful woman enter the scene and, in a play on old Stalinist socialist realist filmmaking, throw a sledgehammer that shatters Big Brother's image and frees the workers. However, during an audition in Hyde Park, the model trying out for the part lost control of the heavy implement, threw it the wrong way and nearly brained a little old lady walking by. So Scott and company switched to an athletic young woman, her brilliant red running shorts the only saturated color in the entire commercial.

When Jobs saw the storyboards, he wasn't impressed. But he also knew that Scott was the best, and when the director announced that he would do the other planned Apple commercials only if he could do "1984," Jobs quickly agreed. Later, when Jobs saw the rough cut, he knew he had one of the most amazing commercials ever shot.

It was all there: the philosophy, the hardware, the software, the look and now the promotional campaign. Every part of the Mac was a breakthrough over what had come before. Jobs could now sleep at night knowing that "the aesthetic, the quality, had been carried all the way through" and that even the back was beautiful.

6.18 Dr. Jekyll and Mr. Jobs

With Steve Jobs, the brilliant always came with the beastly. And because the Mac project was in many ways the highest point of his extraordinary career, this was also the period when his behavior was often at its most destructive, cruel and just plain difficult even for the people he supported.

For all the perquisites that came with it, being on Jobs's side during these years was not a particularly enviable place to be. There might be a grand piano in the lobby at Bandley, but that didn't mean the centimillionaire who ran the Mac group was willing to pay his team a decent salary. Some of the Mac team members made little more than $30,000 per year. In view of the hundred-hour workweeks, they would have made more money picking cherries at one of the few remaining Valley orchards.

Moreover, just as Jobs was perfectly willing to send the team off for weeks on some tangential project, then change his mind, recall the troops and then send them off in a different direction on his latest brainstorm, so too did he sometimes get so fixated on an idea that no amount of reason or evidence could move him. The preeminent example of this was the Mac's core memory. Raskin, trapped in his own ideology, had decreed that the Macintosh would be shipped with 64K, the same as the seriously underpowered (and ungraphic) IBM PC.

Jobs had his own biases. He held to the 64K memory size until long after it was obvious that the Mac would never work as planned without a lot more memory. And even then, Jobs grudgingly only let the capacity double to 128K, despite the fact that, thanks to Moore's Law, the new doubled capacity was actually *less* expensive than the original. The Mac team nodded agreement with Jobs's decision and then, in secret, designed the computer for the inevitable 512K the market would demand.

That one could be fixed. Other Jobs decisions could not. When Jobs had visited Xerox PARC he had seen not only the graphical user interface but also computer networking and even a primitive version of the Internet. He ignored them. In the hermetic world of Steven Jobs one didn't share information with others, so why would one need to wire computers together? Thus, the Mac would be designed as a stand-alone system, solitary and self-contained in its operation and its philosophy. It couldn't even multi-task—that is, perform multiple operations at the same time—because the solitary user rarely needed that kind of performance. As a result, a decade later, when the world linked itself up in one gigantic networked daisy chain, as users wanted to simultaneously receive e-mail, work spreadsheets and print out a word processing file, the Mac would find itself almost paralyzed and mute before such overwhelming demands.

Jobs could be nasty and demeaning with his teammates in order to motivate them. But when they succeeded, he would shower them with praise that was both absurd and irresistible. Meanwhile, Jobs saved his real cruelty for his enemies, both inside and outside the company. There was one story, likely apocryphal, that went around the computer industry during this era that Jobs, while on a trip to Massachusetts, had taken the time to visit Ken Olsen, the formidable CEO of Digital Equipment. DEC, still a minicomputer giant, had been struggling trying to acquire a beachhead in PCs.

As the story went, Jobs strolled into Olsen's office, put his feet up on the man's desk and informed him that Apple was going to kick DEC's ass in personal computers. True or not, the story was accepted by the industry, cheered by those (usually young newcomers) who admired Jobs for his cockiness and guts, decried by others (usually veterans) who thought only a damned fool would antagonize the lion in his lair.

But Jobs could be just as cruel to his own people, even though he was chairman of the board, if they were not, like the Mac team, part of his praetorian guard. And he was not above the nastiest sort of revenge. After the Lisa introduction, that product's design team and development group closed shop and readied themselves for the next project. Some of these three hundred employees even harbored fantasies of joining the Mac team as it now raced toward its own product introduction.

Standing before the assembled throng, Jobs looked down with contempt. "I see only B and C players here. All the A players work for me in the Macintosh division. I might be interested in hiring two or three of you. Don't you wish you knew which ones I'll choose?"

This was the most despicable type of bullying, the schoolyard behavior of a spoiled nine-year-old. Jobs had been kicked off the Lisa team and now he was going to get even, the company be damned. Those employees he had just spat upon had given years (and sometimes their families, their youth and their good health) to realize what had been Steve Jobs's onetime dream. They had done all he had asked of them and more. If the Lisa had proven to be only a moderate success, it wasn't their fault, but that of the men who had first visualized the Lisa, including Jobs himself. Now he dumped his own culpability on them.

Until that moment, many of those Apple employees had admired, even loved, Steve Jobs. Now he had created a cohort of enemies. Within months he would need their help. And they would return the favor.

Jobs knew that his reputation at Apple and increasingly in the computer industry was tanking. Once, over a sushi dinner, he leaned across the table and asked a writer, "People think I'm an asshole, don't they?"—using precisely the vulgarity most commonly associated with him. There was no hurt in the question, or embarrassment or dismay. It was simply asked out of curiosity.

It was not a problem he saw as needing remedy. On the contrary, he got even worse.

By 1983, even getting to see Jobs was a crapshoot. He was notorious for leaving subordinates, reporters, investors—everyone but celebrities—waiting for an hour or more in the reception area. Then at last he would arrive without apology. Depending upon his mood, Jobs could be vicious and belittling ("Your magazine/newspaper/work/report is shit") or, alternately, charming, inviting you for a ride in his new Mercedes, playing tracks from a tape of the new and unreleased album by his girlfriend at the time, Joan Baez, discussing great metaphysical topics with you and all in all making you feel that the most famous young man of his generation had at last found in you a soul mate. Most disorientingly, sometimes he would be both characters at once.

But if Jobs's personal stock was falling in the computer industry, it continued to rise in the outside world. On recruiting tours to major universities, he was treated like a rock star (just as among rock stars he was treated as an intellectual genius). The national press and its readers couldn't get enough of his enigmatic remarks and the anecdotes about his wealth and lifestyle. Readers especially liked the stories about the empty home and Jobs's gruesome habit of massaging his feet at the office by putting one foot, then the other in a flushing toilet (relaxed toes apparently being more important than *E. coli*) and the rumors about the ultracool new computer he was creating in a not very well-hidden secret project. And Jobs never let them down. He charmed the college kids ("How many here are still virgins?"), he seduced the press and, if now as much through fear and hatred as love and admiration, he kept the cult of his personality alive at Apple.

Yet, even as his fame approached a peak, Steve Jobs was already becoming an anachronism. A late baby boomer, he had nevertheless adopted the philosophy of his near-elders. He was one of the last creations of the 1960s. But now it was the 1980s, a less romantic but more pragmatic age. And not many months after his own appearance on the cover of *Time*, the face of another young computer tycoon appeared in the same spot. A few years before, at a dinner at Arnaud's in New Orleans at the Ben Rosen Conference, the assembled industry leaders had feted, and roasted, Steve Jobs. Sitting at a table in the back, the youngest person in the room by far, this future cover boy had been all but ignored. He had watched the entertainment with a tiny smile, his arms folded. Now Bill Gates was the heir apparent to Jobs's throne. And Gates was a 1980s character through and through.

Still, for the moment, Jobs had the spotlight to himself and he was prepared to put on a show. It was an extraordinary juggling act, and a glimpse into the sheer complexity of Steve Jobs's soul. And it was in the midst of this madness that the darkest corner of that soul suddenly was illuminated. Thanks to his new fame, Steve learned the answer to the question he had asked all of his life: Who am I?

Through a process that has never been publicly disclosed, at age twenty-seven Steve Jobs finally contacted his natural parents. His father, it turned out, was a respected political science professor, his mother a speech therapist. They had married and settled in Green Bay, Wisconsin, not long after Steve was born and put up for adoption. The marriage had produced a daughter two years later, Steve's sister, Mona Simpson, who grew up to become a successful novelist (*Anywhere But Here, The Lost Father*).

Nothing is known of a reunion with his parents, but Jobs did become close to his natural sister, visiting her often in Manhattan. "We're family," he would later say. "She's one of my best friends in the world." Simpson for her part published a novel in 1996, *A Regular Guy*, about a Silicon Valley entrepreneur. The first public acknowledgment of the relationship came at a book party for Simpson, put on by George Plimpton and *The Paris Review*, at which Jobs arrived with his birth sister and birth mother.

The adoptive parents of many children born before 1960 were told by the adoption agency or foundling home that their child's birth parents were successful professionals. "College professors" was a common story. And a generation of adopted children, like Steve Jobs, grew up believing that story, dreaming that they had been denied a richer, more fulfilling life than the one in which they had found themselves. But only Steve Jobs would grow up to find the story to be true. He *was* special; everything he had dreamed on those lonely days in a tract home in Mountain View had come true.

The realization that he had indeed been blessed in this life, that he had been lucky in both heredity and circumstance, might have induced in Jobs a certain humility, a thankfulness for all his blessings. But instead, it had no discernible effect on his behavior. It was too late. The news was no longer big enough to fill the hole.

Ken Krugler was one of those few "B and C players" on the Lisa who made the cut to the Mac group. He had just earned a degree in computer science from MIT and while still in school had worked for both IBM and Data General. "I decided I didn't want to work in cubes all my life. So I talked with my adviser and she suggested some West Coast companies that had a more relaxed atmosphere." He found Apple, joining the firm in July 1983, as employee number 4788.

It wasn't quite the relaxed atmosphere he expected—in fact, within a year he would be diagnosed with high blood pressure ("I thought it was strange since I had always had low pressure before") and told by his doctor to take a leave of absence.

After finishing his work on the Lisa project, Krugler was assigned by the Mac team to several projects, including preparing the now dying Lisa to run Mac software, then on development tools and an operating system code for future Mac models.

One of the first things that struck Krugler as different at his new employer, compared with Data General and especially IBM, was its size. "I was amazed at how small Apple was at the time. When I got there, there were just ten people in the Macintosh system software group." And that in turn meant considerable freedom: "If you had a good idea and pitched it to the right person, you could do it. You could find someone who agreed with your concept and they'd give you the go-ahead.

"That was both a blessing and a curse for Apple. It allowed people to be creative and develop innovative new technology, but it also created an environment where no one had a clear concept of all the different technologies being developed and how they worked together."

Lurking about in all this chaos was Jobs himself. "Jobs was around a lot. He always approached developers with a challenging demeanor. He'd come up to you and say something like 'Have you done anything great for the company today? Have you made a difference for Apple today?'

"Jobs used to see things in black and white. You were either really great or you were a complete bozo. Then, as the project progressed, he changed a little. Now he had four stages of evaluation: bozo, okay, good, great. We used to joke that it was a big improvement."

Returning after his leave of absence, Ken Krugler took an offer from Apple Japan and left the country for three years. There was chaos at the Japanese office as well, but at least it was far from headquarters and it had a solid new boss named Michael Spindler.

6.19 ROYAL AUDIENCE

The final run-up to the Macintosh, originally planned to take a few months, instead took two years. Even the compromise introduction date of March

1983 slipped ten months. The sheer complexity of the project grew by the week. The interface had to be perfected, including the title bar, the icons and the many built-in typefaces that would give the Mac an unprecedented "print-shop" capability. So too the handful of programs that the team planned to bundle into each computer—MacPaint, MacWrite—had to be created.

Most important for the long-term sales of the Mac, armies of outside software developers had to be enlisted and cultivated to provide the Macintosh with a large and growing library of applications.

Jobs and the Mac team had learned their lesson. They may have held the Lisa group in contempt, but they had enormous respect for the Apple II—and not just because it paid the bills. Woz's brilliant design had only carried that computer a couple of years; the II's miraculous six-year reign at the top of personal computing had been almost entirely due to the legions of independent programmers still busily cranking out scores of new programs for the II each month. Technically almost obsolete, the II survived now on sheer momentum, on the triumph of its usefulness.

The goal for the Mac, then, would be to introduce not just an amazing new piece of hardware but a platform for a plethora of programs. It wouldn't be just Apple up there onstage, but Microsoft and VisiCorp and all the other big names in personal computer software.

But there was a problem. Jobs was pissed off at VisiCorp—with some reason, as that company was busily developing its own (ultimately doomed) Xerox-like operating system. And, of course, Gates was happily making himself and IBM a lot of money with MS-DOS.

Jobs wasn't ready to make nice with VisiCorp, but Microsoft was too big a force to be ignored. So Jobs flew to Redmond to try to work some of his magic on his old friend.

Gates, as might be expected, was immune to Jobs's blandishments—he found his elder's behavior boorish when it wasn't annoying—but he *was* interested in the Mac. In later years, when wealth and the complexities of running a multibillion-dollar corporation would distract him, Gates would become sluggish identifying hot new trends, most famously the Internet. But in 1982 he was not only the smartest man in the computer industry but also the quickest. He looked right past Jobs's blather and saw the computer of his own dreams. *This* was the computer the world had been waiting to experience, this was the synthesis of hardware and interface and ergonomics that he had tried to describe to others for years.

When Steven Levy went to visit him a few months later, Gates first described how irritating and hyperbolic Jobs had been on that visit, but then stopped and said, "People concentrate on finding the guy's flaws. Why? He's in the center of things. They ask, 'Does he know the instruction set of the 68000?' I don't think that's super-important. There's no way there would be anything like that Macintosh without Jobs."

It was the sympathetic appraisal of one giant for another. And, like the great corporate field general he was, once Gates recognized the potential for the Macintosh, he threw every available soldier he had at it—until by the time of the Mac's introduction, Microsoft was fielding a larger Mac team than Apple itself. And the presence of Microsoft Word for the Mac would prove a key factor in the computer's success.

Meanwhile, of course, Gates made other plans. He had not yet gained his reputation as the High-Tech Python, whose embrace was always fatal. The world still saw him as a lesser Jobs. But, in fact, the two young men were almost perfect opposites. Steve Jobs, the last child of the 1960s, really did want to save the world—but only if he could be the Savior. Gates, was far more pragmatic: he didn't want to save the world, only to own it. It was an equally impossible goal, but it had the advantage of being realistic in the short term.

Gates had now seen the Mac interface close up and knew he wanted it. Even as his people were at work on applications for this new operating system, Gates was also setting others to work to destroy it. This new, graphical operating system, to be called Windows, was too late to beat the Mac to market, but Gates figured it could at least meet head-on a more immediate concern, VisiCorp's new software. With that threat out of the way, he could then devote months and millions to undermining his old acquaintance and new partner, Steve Jobs.

6.20 Lust Object

With the industry leader now in the stable, Apple set out to scoop up the rest of the software industry. To do so, it embarked on a unique program that, in its own way, was as innovative and far-reaching in its influence as the Mac itself. The Mac group had hired a new marketing manager, Mike Murray, with a charter to use any trick he knew to round up third-party developers. The best gimmick he came up with was to hire people for the sole purpose of being true believers in the Macintosh and in Apple. They would be "evangelists," and the most famous was the third one Murray hired (and who devised the name): Guy Kawasaki.

Kawasaki would not only prove to be a brilliant evangelist for the Mac; he would take those skills (he had a unique talent at being both supremely sincere and ironic at the same time—"I know this is bullshit and so do you, but it's also the truth"—that was like St. Paul giving you a knowing wink as he ushered you through the Pearly Gates) and turn them into a philosophy of marketing. He wrote a best-selling book on the subject, *The Macintosh Way*, and went on to become one of the most popular business speakers of the 1990s. The *San Jose Mercury News* would write that Kawasaki had achieved the final breakthrough in high-tech business: from selling almost nothing (semiconductors) to nothing (software) and now less than nothing—enthusiasm!

But in 1983 software evangelism was an unknown profession trying to sell an unknown product to a skeptical market. That the evangelists succeeded, and brilliantly, is a testament to both their skills and the Mac itself. The patter of the evangelists almost always fell on deaf ears until the developers finally sat down in front of a Mac prototype . . . at which point all the extravagant claims almost seemed too humble. As the first evangelist would say after a few months of successful pitching, "People were uniformly blown away. I remember one guy who had just designed what he thought was a good accounting program. After seeing the Mac, he felt like he had just designed the best propeller in the world, then saw a jet fly by."

Even Apple competitors, such as software companies committed to the PC world, tipped their hats at what they saw. Mitch Kapor, the founder of Lotus Development Corp. in Cambridge, Massachusetts, whose spreadsheet product, Lotus 1-2-3, would soon wipe out VisiCalc and dominate the PC world, met the Apple representatives with "I'd sell my mother to get a Mac." A few weeks later he would give Levy the definitive epigram of the era:

"The IBM is a machine you can respect. The Macintosh is a machine you can love."

Lotus immediately set to work designing a spreadsheet program, to be called Jazz, for the Mac.

Kapor wasn't alone. Scores of other software developers fell in love with the Mac the moment they saw it. It was a glimpse of what would come when the first Macs hit retail stores. Two of those developers were independently pursuing their own visions of what the computer of the future should be. One, legendary programmer John Warnock, had founded in Silicon Valley a collegelike company called Adobe to develop fonts and typefaces that would give computer output a more professional, printshop-like appearance.

The other, Paul Brainerd, driven and difficult where Warnock was professorial and avuncular, was chasing a complementary idea: software that would allow the user to mix text and graphics on the personal computer in a format that would look the same on the printed page as it did on the display. This "what you see is what you get" (WYSIWYG) technology was dependent upon the advent of low-cost laser printers—and Brainerd was betting his company, Aldus, that Moore's Law would deliver those printers to him in time.

Like the many others, Warnock and Brainerd saw in the Mac the launch pad for their dreams. They would be too late for the Mac introduction. But within a year, the pair would return the gift of the Mac by being the answer to Steve Jobs's prayers. Together, they gave the Mac its desperately needed Killer Application, *desktop publishing*. And that in turn would forever change the relationship between owners and their computers.

6.21 Chiclets

After endless delays, the Macintosh introduction was formally set for Tuesday, January 24, 1984. The Ridley Scott commercial, which alone had cost $500,000, was to be placed, for another $1 million, in the third quarter of the broadcast of the Los Angeles Raiders–Washington Redskins Super Bowl.

There was no going back now. For three years, Jobs had driven the team on using every gambit he knew. He had even been reduced to that cliché of every second-rate manager: the slogan. These slogans would appear, sometimes unannounced, sometimes part of a pep talk, on an easel in the Mac offices. The first, "*It's better to be a pirate than join the Navy,*" was his final co-option of the Raskin philosophy. Another, "*The journey is the reward,*" was Jobs's old Buddhism at work (and the title of his biography). Another, written a year before the introduction, was a reminder that the time for innovation was over and the time for completing the project had begun: "*Real artists ship.*"

Of course it was pure hokum. Jobs knew it and so did the Mac team members. They might joke that it was hard to be a pirate when you worked for the Admiral of the Navy; that it was easy to say the journey was the reward when your net worth was $300 million, not $30,000; and that the real artists would have shipped a year ago if Jobs hadn't changed his mind so many times—but even as they joked, they also believed the truths behind those slogans. One of Steve Jobs's greatest traits was that he was willing to be absurd, and he never used that skill better than now.

The final three months leading up to the introduction were madness. First there was the Finder program. That solved, Apple itself suddenly became an impediment. The company had smugly predicted $1 billion in sales for the Lisa and had geared up its corporate infrastructure accordingly. Manufacturing capacity was increased with a new factory, 3,000 new employees were hired and millions were spent on point-of-sale materials, advertising and sales support. So convinced was the group that the Lisa would run over both the business market and the rest of Apple that it even held meetings at nearby De Anza Junior College to discuss whether Apple should change its name to something "a little more corporate."

In the first few months after the Lisa's introduction, as the orders poured in and exceeded the company's backlog, it seemed as if all the predictions for the product's success were coming true. There seemed no need to rein in.

But by June 1983, disaster appeared on the horizon as quickly as a summer storm. Lisa orders slumped. The new factory, now with overcapacity, was forced to sit idle. New hirings were frozen and a few employees with bad performance reviews were fired. For the fourth quarter ended September 30, Apple's profits plunged 80 percent, from $25 million to $5 million, and the company's stock went with it, falling from $31.50 (reflecting a two-for-one split) per share in June to $23 in October.

IBM, for once with perfect timing, dropped a bomb that summer: the introduction of the IBM PC XT, a more powerful second-generation machine. The PC XT was ideally suited to run Lotus 1-2-3, the now preeminent business spreadsheet program. Small and large businesses flocked to IBM. By autumn the company had passed Apple in total personal computer market share, 28 percent to 23 percent. The Intel-Microsoft architecture had now taken the industry leadership from Apple . . . and would never give it back.

Apple responded as best it could with an old beloved computer and a young unwanted one. It redoubled its marketing of the II and hurried development of a new generation, the IIc. It also expanded the dealer base, unbundled the software and slashed the price of the Lisa. It only helped a little. The company went into the critical Christmas season praying that its old workhorse, the Apple II, still had enough momentum to keep the company profitable. If it failed, the big Macintosh introductory splash would have to be canceled. And no one wanted to say it but that might be the beginning of the end of the company.

There was no shortage of skeptics. Soon after the PC XT introduction, several trade magazines (presaging the flood to come) called upon Apple to admit the jig was up, abandon its new operating system and join the growing army of IBM clone makers. The company could still win, they said, on marketing, software and design.

Though Apple never seriously accepted that possibility (not with the Mac waiting in the wings), even the more thoughtful minds in the company had to agree with the industry observers that a turning point had occurred with

IBM's rise to industry leadership. And everyone in the industry waited for what was generally agreed would be the final, decisive battle in October. Then, it was rumored, Big Blue would introduce a new budget consumer computer that would do to the low end of the market what the PC XT was now doing to the high end. With that victory, IBM would enjoy complete industry hegemony.

As autumn rolled around, everyone held their breath. Was the game already over?

No. The new computer, the IBM PCjr, was . . . a turd. It was so awful, the press actually ridiculed it, something that never before happened with an IBM product. Underpowered, with a mediocre screen, not enough software and a horrifyingly inept keyboard full of cheap and barely functional keys—"chiclets" one industry wag described them (and, to IBM's horror, the nickname stuck).

But Big Blue wasn't used to failure. It was used to power. So the company spent $50 million promoting its new machine, complete with ads featuring the now tiresome Little Tramp. The campaign and the product failed miserably. The PCjr became synonymous with condescending product design.

The game was still on.

It was, for Apple, the first good news in a long time. The PCjr had not stolen the Mac's thunder or the II's market—instead, it had created a void, a hunger, for truly *personal* computers that were both powerful and easy to use.

Just as important, the cratering of the PCjr also gave Regis McKenna one last lesson. Operation Crush had taught him the value of selling a complete experience, as opposed to merely a product. The II and the Lisa had shown him the new power of key industry opinion leaders. Now, with the PCjr he was given a demonstration that, unlike, say, selling Pepsi-Cola, in PCs no amount of company prestige or money spent on mass promotion could counter the power of those opinion leaders. Dick Shaffer and Ben Rosen, as well as a new generation of cocky trade press reporters like John Dvorak, were now more powerful than all the advertising in the world. Regis would remember that as the Mac introduction approached.

But even as the auguries pointed toward a major Mac introduction, the company hesitated. Would there be enough money? Had the failure of the PCjr sufficiently sullied IBM to make the mainstream market take a second look at the II? Or had it simply scared everyone off?

Then a second roadblock. The executive team showed the new Macintosh "1984" commercial to the Apple board of directors. The opinion was unanimous: they hated it. Worse, several of the outside directors thought that it was the single worst television commercial they had ever seen.

The response was probably not surprising. Dr. Henry Singleton, the legendary founder of the conglomerate Teledyne; venture capital giant Arthur Rock; Peter O. Crisp, managing partner of Venrock Associates venture capital; and Philip S. Schlein, CEO of Macy's California were not exactly young men weaned in the Age of Television. What was amazing was the extraordinary vehemence with which this notoriously passive board expressed itself. (The following conversation was recorded by John Sculley.)

"Steve," one board member asked, "you're not really going to run that thing, are you?"

"We haven't made a final decision on it yet, but we had planned to run it on the Super Bowl."

"How much does that cost?"

"About a million dollars," said Mike Murray, the Mac's new marketing manager."

"Oh my God!"

Apple's management finally agreed to tell Chiat/Day to try to sell the Super Bowl spot. And that if it couldn't be sold *and* if the II had a good Christmas season, *then* Apple would go ahead and run the ad.

In the end the company could only sell the spot for half price and the II, perhaps benefiting from the combination of the incredible amount of promotion for the PCjr and the bad reviews for the product itself, had a terrific Christmas—110,000 computers sold for a total of $160 million. The Mac commercial and the big kickoff event were given the green light. The Macintosh era of Apple would get the roaring start it deserved.

6.22 IGNORANCE IS STRENGTH

The "1984" commercial ran as scheduled for the one and only time to a wide audience (it was actually shown to a small midwestern audience in December to make it eligible for awards) during the third quarter of the Super Bowl.

Wozniak, with characteristic naiveté, nearly wrecked the plan. Invited to appear on *Good Morning America* a few days before the Super Bowl, he decided to take a copy of the commercial with him to show on the air. Luckily, he was caught in time.

Apple had wanted to make a splash with "1984." What it got was Eniwetok. The biggest single splash in the history of television advertising. Only one other commercial had ever had such an impact from a single showing, and that was the infamous Johnson political attack ad against Barry

Goldwater showing a little girl pulling petals off a daisy as the voice-over began the countdown to a nuclear explosion.

On this Sunday afternoon in the winter of 1984, 43 million Americans saw the corporate analog of that infamous commercial. The bleak, gulag-like world. Big Brother on the screen intoning:

> "My friends, each of you is a single cell in the great body of the State. And today, that great body has purged itself of parasites. We have triumphed over the unprincipled dissemination of fact. The thugs and wreckers have been cast out. And the poisonous weeds of disinformation have been consigned to the dustbin of history. Let each and every cell rejoice! For today we celebrate the first, glorious anniversary of the Information Purification Directive. We have created, for the first time in all history, a garden of pure ideology, where each worker may bloom secure from the pests of contradictory and confusing truths. Our Unification of Thought is a more powerful weapon than any fleet or army on earth. We are one people. With one will. One resolve. One cause. Our enemies shall talk themselves to death. And we will bury them with their own confusion . . ."

If it was gibberish, it was also just coherent enough for the audience to understand. Never before had a major U.S. corporation been described in such a way: evil, brainwashing, antidemocratic, totalitarian. Hundreds of thousands of jaws across America dropped in unison.

And then the Avenging Angel ran on-screen in her tank top and gym shorts. She flung her hammer, shattering the projected visage of Big Brother, unleashing a windstorm of shattered glass—stunning and awakening the sleepwalking prisoners like a shaft of sunlight bursting into Plato's Cave.

Then the final voice-over: "On January 24, Apple Computer will introduce Macintosh. 1984 won't be like *1984*."

In ten million households from coast to coast there was a collective gasp, then, echoing the on-air words of one of the sports announcers, "Wow, what was *that?*"

6.23 The Most Famous Company in the World

The next day, the world was still talking about it. It was on the evening news. Millions of unfortunate people who had been in the kitchen or bathroom at the moment still claimed they saw it, so as not to be left out. In one minute's time, Apple, still a cult company to much of the consuming world, had become the coolest place on earth.

It was, indeed, insanely great. The commercial, which would never be broadcast again, thus adding to its legend, would go on to be the first American commercial to win a Grand Prix award at Cannes.

Now Apple needed a closer: the formal introduction on Tuesday. The commercial had primed the marketplace. It had done everything Jobs had wanted for it. Now he had the chance to capture the culture itself.

With the help of Regis McKenna, a willing press and a perfect historical window, he did it. The Mcintosh introduction was the great set piece of the digital age. All others that aspire to the title are in some way deeply flawed. The Windows 95 introduction eleven years later drew thousands to all-night vigils in computer store parking lots around the world. But it was an act of submission: desperate users awaiting the largesse of a monopoly. The Intel Pentium Bug debacle certainly shook the electronics world and beyond, reminding the semiconductor industry that it was now a global consumer force, with all the responsibilities that flowed from that role—but it was also essentially a boneheaded screwup.

The Macintosh introduction, by comparison, was uplifting, transcendent. Sitting there in the Flint Center auditorium on the De Anza College campus, just a block from Apple's first office, there was the sense of being part of history, of being present at a thrilling discontinuity in the story of computing. *This* was what a computer was supposed to be. Plucky little Apple, already being written off by industry cynics, had somehow managed to jump to its feet and throw a fast one right into the chin of the biggest, baddest corporate goliath of all. You couldn't help but laugh, it was so outrageous. And then the computer itself turned out to be so goddamned *cute*.

It really was a turning point. Before the Macintosh, electronics companies were institutions that aspired to the stature and gravity of their manufacturing counterparts. When they introduced products, it was almost always at a staid press conference before an audience of tech insiders who looked at the spec sheet before they looked at the product itself. After Macintosh, every tech company, to prove that its product was important, was forced to create some sort of extravaganza, develop a unique logo and motif and try to link its product to the train of history.

But they would never pull it off. They couldn't, because no matter how great the product or how elaborate the promotion, those later companies could never recapture the delirious shock of experiencing such a moment for the first time. Even Apple would fail in the years to come to conjure up the old magic, until near the end its big events became only sad, forced parodies of the past.

Flint Center could hold two thousand people, but the event drew only about half that—less than attended a travelogue a few days before. But the empty balcony was nearly invisible, so the room seemed full. Of the crowd, fully half were Apple employees serving as shills. But that was still more people than any comparable event before, and those non-Appleites who were there were the cream of high-tech investment, analysis and reporting. Regis had seen to that, and he had made sure that each had received a packet containing not only a press kit but other freebies, notably a T-shirt with a cleverly simplified (and groundbreaking) graphic of the Mac.

The day before, during rehearsals, the dark side of Steve Jobs had emerged. He belittled the hardworking stagehands, yelling at their every mistake while flubbing his own lines over and over. He changed his speech, tossed out and reinserted slides and generally cast a pall over the proceedings. More than one Apple employee left Flint that night praying the next day wouldn't be a complete disaster.

But it was the other Steve who stood behind the curtains the next day. He privately confessed, "This is the most important moment of my entire life. I can't tell you how I feel. It's the most incredible thing I've ever had to go through and I'm really nervous."

Then he walked out from behind the curtains, apparently calm, with the smirk so tiny that it seemed less contemptuous than ironic at the sheer unlikeliness of it all. This was the new Steve Jobs, only a decade but a million years from the smelly ascetic, now sleek and chic, wearing a double-breasted, European-cut charcoal-gray suit and a bright red bow tie that managed to look at once intellectual, revolutionary and arch. He cut a striking figure, one that was nearly as significant to the audience as the product he was about to introduce: *Jobs is going for it!*

There was a murmur of expectation. Then Jobs, the last child of the 1960s, began to recite Bob Dylan's famous lines about "the times they are a-changing" for the last famous time.

It was a tocsin to the Woodstock generation: *Don't sell out! Don't forget the dream! Stay free!* And in that hall filled with boomers, both from Apple and from the press, most of them now with babies and first mortgage payments, receding hairlines and business suits, a thrill shot through a thousand hearts. *Yes! We've been sleepwalking. Wake us up!* There was a hush of expectation. Where will the Pied Piper lead us?

But Jobs had already slipped backstage. The audience, ready to rise up and rush the stage, instead had to sit impatiently through the company's annual meeting. Quarterly earnings and announcements of new facilities and joint ventures. Yeah yeah yeah blah blah blah. Even the reporters put down their notebooks. They could get all this financial garbage off the press release. *Where's Steve?*

Then, as suddenly as he had disappeared, he was back, gleaming in the white spotlight. He spoke with the disarming, confiding earnestness he used for his biggest seductions. His head was cocked just slightly, his body rigid, but his arms and hands punctuated every sentence. He began almost lightly, but, feeding off the embrace of the audience, seemed to grow more confident and powerful with each paragraph. He was twenty-nine years old and this was the greatest moment of his life:

> "It is 1958. IBM passes up the chance to buy a young, fledgling company that has just invented a new technology called xerography. Two years later, Xerox is born, and IBM has been kicking itself ever since.
>
> "It is ten years later, the late 1960s. Digital Equipment Corporation and others invent the minicomputer. IBM dismisses the minicomputer as too small to do serious computing and, therefore, unimportant to its business. DEC grows to become a multi-hundred-million dollar corporation before IBM finally enters the minicomputer market.
>
> "It is now ten years later, the late 1970s. In 1977, Apple, a young fledgling company on the West Coast, invents the Apple II, the first personal computer as we know it today. IBM dismisses the personal computer as too small to do serious computing and therefore unimportant to its business.
>
> "The early 1980s—1981. Apple II has become the world's most popular computer, and Apple has grown to a $300 million corporation, becoming the fastest-growing company in American business history. With over fifty companies vying for a share, IBM enters the personal computer market in November of 1981 with the IBM PC.
>
> "1983. Apple and IBM emerge as the industry's strongest competitors, each selling approximately $1 billion worth of personal computers in 1983.
>
> ". . . The shakeout is in full swing. The first major firm goes bankrupt, with others teetering on the brink. Total industry losses for 1983 overshadow even the combined profits of Apple and IBM for personal computers.
>
> "It is now 1984. It appears IBM wants it all. Apple is perceived to

> be the only hope to offer IBM a run for its money. Dealers, initially welcoming IBM with open arms, now fear an IBM-dominated and -controlled future. They are increasingly turning back to Apple as the only force that can ensure their future freedom . . ."

Jobs paused, as if steeling himself for the enormity of the task ahead. He looked out at the audience, as if asking them to join him at the battlements of computing freedom. Then his voice dropped a half octave, as if at the sheer magnitude of corporate evil. Oh the humanity . . .

> "IBM wants it all and is aiming its guns on its last obstacle to industry control, Apple. Will Big Blue dominate the entire computer industry, the entire information age? Was George Orwell right?"

"No!" shouted the audience. "No!" shouted the first five rows, filled with the Apple team. "No!" shouted the other Apple employees and the analysts and the distributors and dealers and retailers and shareholders. No! said the assembled journalists secretly to themselves.

Steve Jobs smiled. Enough with that Zen bullshit about the "journey being the reward." *This* was the reward.

He walked over to a table bearing an ominous-looking bag. With a flourish, Jobs unzipped it . . . and there, the color of brown stone, like a little primitive totem, a friendly phallus, was the Macintosh. An appreciative murmur went up from the crowd. It was instantly drowned out by the amplified theme from the movie *Chariots of Fire*. It was corny, but nevertheless spine-tingling.

"Today," intoned Steve Jobs, "for the first time ever, I'd like to let Macintosh speak for itself." That couldn't be true: Apple had never actually tested speech synthesis on the Mac until this moment. But what the hell, go with the flow. It was all too exciting to quibble.

Jobs touched a key, and in a quivering little voice—its very crudeness perfect in its antithesis to Big Brother—the Mac announced:

> "Hello, I am Macintosh. It sure is great to get out of that bag. Unaccustomed as I am to public speaking, I'd like to share with you a thought that occurred to me the first time I met an IBM mainframe. Never trust a computer you can't lift. But right now I'd like to sit back and listen. So it is with considerable pride that I introduce a man who has been like a father to me, Steve Jobs."

"Like a father" was the appropriate phrase, as Mac's real father was at that moment living in the Santa Cruz mountains. And it was a bit cheesy to even steal Jef Raskin's line about not trusting computers you can't lift. But it didn't matter. The crowd laughed and cheered—even those in the front row who knew better.

It went on like this for another twenty minutes, losing momentum by the minute. After all, how could you top the introduction of one of the greatest products of the century? Still, those final depleted minutes did manage to establish a second turning point in the history of personal computing: this was the day the press, especially the computer trade press, formally and publicly, sold out.

It was hard to resist. After all, Apple was now the underdog, and the press loves underdogs. And the Macintosh represented such an unbelievable comeback. And IBM was a tight-assed pain to deal with, with its PR department keeping a database on every reporter and firing off angry notes every time you suggested the company was bigger than the corner drugstore—while Apple was young and brash and answered the phone and was always good for a quote. And almost everybody in the press owned an Apple at home even though they had to use IBMs in the newsroom. And, not least, Apple bought a lot of advertising pages, especially in the last month.

It was just so easy to succumb. And never more so than at this moment of triumph for Apple. Onstage, the company introduced the publisher of a new, purportedly independent magazine called *MacWorld*, dedicated entirely to the Macintosh. It was an amazing moment in modern journalism, and nobody seemed to notice. On the contrary, the reporters reminded themselves to get subscriptions.

If the electronics trade magazines, dependent upon Apple advertising revenues, finally revealed themselves as lickspittles at the Mac introduction, the general press was only slightly more reserved. Esther Dyson, who had taken over Ben Rosen's newsletter and was on her way to becoming the preeminent opinion maker in personal computing, actually sat through the event wearing her free Mac T-shirt. The story passed around that she had changed into it while driving down from the San Francisco Airport—to the entertainment of men in nearby cars. Other writers were discreet enough to wait until they got home before putting on, literally and journalistically, Mac shirts of their own.

Then it was over. Jobs, drained and tearfully happy, made his way back behind the curtain. "It's really happened," he said. "Mac is a real product now."

The press rushed the stage, where Apple representatives, from publicists to Art Rock, held forth in little clusters of reporters. When will the Mac be available? What different configurations are available? How much market share do you think you can take back from IBM?

In one of the largest of these clusters, Regis McKenna held forth. "Where are the cursor keys?" asked a reporter. "It doesn't have any cursor keys." "I know," said Regis, reliving an argument he'd had a few months before. "I tried to talk them into it. But they wanted a mouse and a mouse alone." He shrugged and smiled, as if to say: I know it's nuts, but what are you going to do? It's Apple.

By now, the January afternoon had turned gray. The reporters rushed off to file their stories. The Apple staffers wandered back down the street to their offices. And no one had the slightest doubt that a new era had begun.

7.0 EARLY HARVEST

7.1 Enigma

There was one other figure onstage at the Macintosh launch. A protean figure so elusive that everyone in the computer industry had already invested him with their hopes and fears for Apple Computer. And they were right to do so, because unbeknownst to them (and to himself) he had already made a series of decisions that would guide Apple's future and seal its fate.

John Sculley had been with Apple now for nine months—nearly a year if you included his rounds of job interviews. He had even been with Jobs at the Chiat/Day premiere of the 1984 commercial. Yet he still remained largely an enigma both inside and outside of the company.

It was Sculley who shook Jobs's hand just before he stepped out from behind the curtain, and it was Sculley, Apple's new CEO, who took over the middle of the presentation to talk to the assembled shareholders about the company's financials. And it was John Sculley, now in the cockpit of, for the moment, the most exciting corporation in the world, who broke from his prepared text to say, "The most important thing that has happened to me in these nine months has been the chance to develop a friendship with Steve Jobs. The two of us have had tremendous challenges together in leading this company, and the rapport and friendship that have developed between us mean an awful lot."

At the time, the comment was a minor note in the major chord of the Mac introduction. Most people assembled weren't really listening. Rather, for many it was a first public glimpse of the East Coast businessman Jobs had lured to run Apple. They noted his thin runner's form, so skinny that his clothes seemed to hang from his skeleton, and his face—hawkish like Jobs's, but less bland, pale and Yankee. A chicken hawk to Jobs's falcon.

Yet, in retrospect, those first, ostensibly impromptu remarks were vintage John Sculley. Sensitive and personal to the brink of tears, unexpectedly passive for a corporate executive and, behind it all, calculating. The hidden message of the remark, unexpected even to the people running the cue cards, was: *I am now Steve Jobs's equal in this company. I am his new friend. I may be new, but I have more power than anyone here.* And to Jobs, standing behind the screen, who amazingly said to Sculley at the rehearsal the night before, "I think of you just like Woz and Markkula. You're like one of the founders of the company. They founded the company, but you and I are founding the future," the comment carried a personal message: *"See, I think so highly of our new friendship that I'm willing to tell the world about it."*

The greatest corporate politician in American business had just given a brilliant lesson in his craft, and the audience, being largely Silicon Valleyites, was too inexperienced and naive to notice.

7.2 CHALLENGE

It was the day before Thanksgiving 1982 when John Sculley received a call from a headhunter.

Sculley had gotten these calls many times before and rarely returned them. But this one was from the best in the business, Gerry Roche, chairman of Heidrick & Struggles. Roche had called before, each time with an intriguing offer: the presidency of Norton Simon cosmetics, chairmanship of NBC, CEO of Warner-Amex. But Sculley had always passed. "Pepsi," he would later write in his memoirs, "was my life . . . I made the company my extended family. The mere thought of entertaining another job would have provoked the angst of a personal separation or divorce." And he wasn't kidding: Sculley had once even been married to the chairman's daughter.

John Sculley's life to that point had been one of great success, but also of competing, and opposing, forces. His father was a stern and demanding Wall Street lawyer, his mother a free-spirited native Bermudan with an artistic bent. Each contributed to their son's character. As a toddler, Sculley had enjoyed the tropical freedom of trips to Bermuda, but as a boy he had been sent first to the prestigious Buckley School in Manhattan, then as a teenager to board at St. Mark's in Southboro, Massachusetts.

The struggle of countervailing forces in John Sculley's life, and increasingly in his personality, probably made its first appearance in a painful stammer the young man developed as a child. He was cured as a teenager by hypnosis. But without a doubt the tension was still there when the time came for young John to choose a college. When he told his father he wanted to attend an art school, the old man was furious. "I sent you to one of the finest preparatory schools in the country. I sacrificed everything. You've had every advantage in life and you don't even want to go to college. You want to study design. I can't believe it."

If Steve Jobs's father had given him almost infinite latitude, John Sculley's old man brought down the whole weight of family tradition and parental guilt to constrain his son. And young John, having long since learned to defuse a challenge by diplomacy and compromise, agreed to go to Brown University, but only if he could attend the nearby Rhode Island School of Design at night. Then he did it again by earning an MBA from Wharton, but afterward going into advertising.

Alongside the battle between good son and renegade aesthete, there was a second one taking place in John Sculley's soul between business and science. Although this other part of his youth was considerably exaggerated once Apple's PR department got its hands on the story, it was a fact that as a boy John had been a bit of an electronics bug. He apparently got it from his maternal grandfather, a wild inventor and adventurer. Sculley would later claim, Woz-like, that as a boy he would wake up early in the morning to read *The Radio Amateur's Handbook* until it became dog-eared. If that seems dubious, there is the fact that by ten he was rewiring radios, by eleven was a ham radio operator and by fourteen (in 1954) had designed a single-gun television tube not unlike what would become the Sony Trinitron. His father helped him apply for a patent, but the boy was beaten out by only a few weeks by Ernest Lawrence, of Lawrence Livermore Laboratories fame.

But by the time he departed for Brown and RISD, John Sculley had left electronics far behind. Like his two brothers (who would later make their names as president of H. J. Heinz USA and senior vice president of Morgan Guaranty), John abandoned the passions of his youth to make his way in the business world. While still at Brown he met and married the stepdaughter of Don Kendall, soon to be Pepsi's CEO. It was Kendall who convinced Sculley to abandon his dream of a graduate degree from the Penn School of Architecture and go to Wharton.

After a four-year stint at an advertising agency doing competitive research for Coca-Cola (he neglected to tell anyone that he was the son-in-law of the head of Pepsi) and a divorce (which didn't seem to dent his relationship with Kendall), John finally went to work for his ex-father-in-law's company.

He thrived, soon gaining a reputation as the company's hottest new star—and also one of its most devious corporate politicians and hatchet men. At thirty, he was the youngest vice president in the company's history. He was not well liked, and as he would himself admit, was lousy at handling people.

But even those at Pepsi who disliked him had to admit that John Sculley was some kind of demon marketing man. Over the next few years he would prove himself one of the best American industry had ever seen.

No battle in American business history has been as protracted or vicious as that between Coca-Cola and Pepsi. For nearly a century, the two companies have beaten up each other in the marketplace, cheering a percentage point shift in market share as either a magnificent victory or a crushing defeat.

In this competitive marketplace, Pepsi had always been the also-ran. And it didn't look like the status quo would change for another century—not when Pepsi's current ad slogan, "The taste that beats the others cold," was up against Coke's landmark "The Real Thing."

But Sculley had his own ideas. For a start, he committed the ultimate marketing sin of revivifying a marginally successful marketing campaign the company had abandoned a few years before—"The Pepsi Generation." Next, he added the incoherent, but catchy tag line "You've got a lot to live and Pepsi's got a lot to give."

This was lifestyle marketing just at the moment baby boomers became independent consumers. Coke, still playing off its history and tradition, was caught with its pants down. And Sculley didn't stop. He spent millions on advertising filled with vignettes of the youth culture. And he backed up this fluff with some hard reengineering of point-of-sale presentations, a reorganization of the company's reporting structure and a redirected emphasis on important new retail channels, such as drugstore chains. The result, beginning in 1970, was a record three and half years of continuous gains in market share.

It was a remarkable achievement, though in the process Sculley had become notorious in the company for tearing through one subordinate after another. So, for this combination of ruthlessness and creative brilliance, Sculley was "rewarded" (many in the company thought it a demotion) with the job of running Pepsi's screwed-up and unprofitable international foods division.

He then spent nearly four years traveling the world, putting out fires everywhere he went. He shut down some operations and rebuilt others. In some countries, he focused on manufacturing, in others on marketing and brand awareness. It was exciting stuff. And in the process, Sculley built a kind of SWAT team of talented people who traveled with him, ready to deal with anything they encountered. Over the months this team became very tight-knit, and Sculley, for the first time submerging his personality into a team, was enthralled.

Once again he succeeded brilliantly, turning an $83 million business with annual losses of $16 million into a $300 million business turning an annual pretax profit of $40 million. Sculley himself was so happy where he was that he repeatedly turned down entreaties from headquarters to come home.

Finally he relented. "The thought of having to be confined in the United States was terribly demoralizing. It just wasn't what I wanted to do with my life." But he was a company man, so he came home. He politely endured a comment from Kendall about getting his hair cut. He married again (for the third time), to Leezy Hersh, the divorced wife of a senior Pepsi marketing executive.

It was not a happy time for John Sculley. He missed the globe-trotting, the independence of making his own decisions. He missed being part of a close-knit group. His new wife was the target of a hissing campaign by other company wives, who saw her as trading her way up from a vice president to a company president. And worst of all, he was trapped in the backstabbing political life of corporate headquarters—a world in which he was a master, but now found distasteful.

So, the answer was to go back to his first love: marketing.

Before he left for International, Sculley had commissioned some studies comparing the responses to Pepsi and Coca-Cola in a taste test. The results were stunning: Pepsi not only won the majority of these tests, it came close to winning them all. Time would show this had as much to do with a momentary reaction to the greater sweetness of Pepsi, but as raw data this was dynamite. Unfortunately, the company only saw it as a firecracker. While Sculley was overseas, the company used this data to construct a last-ditch marketing campaign for Pepsi in its weakest domestic market, Texas, where Pepsi had just a 7 percent market share. Even then, the campaign was a largely renegade effort, driven by the company's executive vice president for bottling and his own vice president of marketing, the future Mrs. Sculley's ex-husband. They even hired a local advertising agency.

The result was the Pepsi Challenge, in which local residents, seemingly live on television, were invited to blind-test the two major colas. Pepsi, as expected, nearly always won. That much wasn't particularly new—competitors in different industries had advertised similar tests for decades. The real innovation was that the Pepsi Texas team then took the Challenge out to the streets, inviting anyone and everyone to taste tests at local fairs, supermarkets and other public locations.

It was a smashing success. Pepsi gained market share wherever the Challenge was held. So pleased was the company that it expanded the Challenge to several other southern states where Pepsi had nothing to lose. But there it stopped. After all, the reasoning went, it was one thing to use the Pepsi

Challenge in markets where the company had nothing to lose, but why would you risk the company's market share on the vox populi in regions where Pepsi was the leader? What if you held the Challenge in, say, Illinois and everybody picked Coke?

That likely would have been the end of it, except that John Sculley had come home from the world to PepsiCo headquarters in Purchase, New York, as Pepsi's youngest president. He saw in the Challenge a way not just to build sales in losing markets but to expand them in winning ones.

It was a dangerous strategy. Wiser heads at headquarters objected. Bottlers, fearing kicking off a price war that would undermine with falling profits whatever was gained in market share, complained angrily. But Sculley had a sense that America had changed. Watergate, Vietnam and the 1960s were behind it; now the consuming public wanted wide-open, honest competition. He pushed ahead, forming SWAT teams that raced around the country (usually followed by camera crews) holding Challenges. Only once did Sculley make a mistake—he took the Challenge himself at the Daytona 500 and picked Coke—but luckily no camera crews were present that day.

The Pepsi Challenge was one of the great marketing successes. For months, it was a hot topic throughout the country, a fad that was also a marketing program. One reason for its success, Sculley would admit later, was that it blurred the line between news and public relations. "Event publicity" it was called, a technique that Steve Jobs, working with Regis McKenna, would discover on his own a few years later. There was another factor as well: although, thanks to the Challenge, Pepsi enjoyed a remarkable market-share jump in an industry that was considered all but frozen in the status quo, most of those gains came not from Coca-Cola but from lesser brands. Against mighty Coke, a situation comparable to Apple against IBM, Pepsi could still barely make a dent. Coke drinkers were unshakable in their loyalty.

But what the Challenge did accomplish against Coke was to throw the venerable giant off its game. Coke's public reaction to the Challenge was almost hysterical. It accused Pepsi of trying to destroy the industry; it tried to distract the market with various forms of advertising chaff; it called for a moratorium on taste tests. Basically, Coke went nuts—and just how nuts would not be known for several years. That's because Coke executives, obsessed with the Challenge, ordered a newer, sweeter Coca-Cola that could win the challenge. The result was New Coke, easily the worst new-product marketing debacle of modern times, greater even than the PCjr. Thus, the Pepsi Challenge almost, but not quite, destroyed one of the world's most successful consumer companies. It was a near-victory not lost on the rest of the world, even on the young chairman of a computer company in Silicon

Valley facing the same competitive scenario. Jobs thought that if IBM could similarly be knocked off balance, there still might be a chance to reorder the industry.

7.3 ODYSSEY

In 1978, after decades of ferocious competition and pitched battles around the world, Pepsi for the first time passed Coca-Cola as the market leader. It was an extraordinary moment, and much of the success could be credited to the Pepsi-Cola's young president John Sculley. He was now a celebrated figure on the business scene. A marketing legend in his own time. A cover story in *Business Week*. An object of awe within his company. He was even on good terms with his ex-father-in-law, PepsiCo CEO Don Kendall, considered one of the toughest bosses anywhere.

He had it all. And for the next four years he stayed at the top of his game: extending the Challenge, beating Coke to market with a caffeine-free product, carving into Coca-Cola's ownership of beverage sales to fast-food chains. His third marriage also appeared to be going well.

But, like the clichéd plot of some midlife-crisis novel of the era, beneath it all John Sculley was restless and unhappy. Entering his forties, he found the old conflict was still there. He was a thinker, an artist, a creator, not just a businessman. Sure, he could devise amazing marketing campaigns, but was that all he was put on this earth to do?

It was an existential crisis faced by many middle-aged business executives at the peak of their careers. Some cure it with new mansions, new wives or new hobbies that scare the bejesus out of insurance underwriters. But in the end, most get over it. John Sculley would have likely done the same by, say, underwriting a PBS series on technology, and gone on to a distinguished career at the company that had been his life. Instead, at his most vulnerable moment, when he himself didn't yet know what was wrong, the young piper appeared at the gates of Pepsi and lured him away.

Sculley paid his first visit to Apple in December, a week before Christmas, not realizing that was always an important time for the company. This was, in fact, the same period when Burrell Smith was preparing to squirrel himself away on the new Macintosh design.

In *Odyssey*, his earnest and opportunistically self-effacing autobiography (now even more risible in light of subsequent events), Sculley describes that first visit with the Sturm und Drang of a man meeting his fate—an event even more symbolic than he would know:

> With a map and a Hertz car, I navigated my way south on Route 280 to Silicon Valley in a downpour so heavy it caused mudslides in the landscape. The strong winds pushed my rented Datsun around the freeway. It was a thirty-mile drive through fog and rain to Apple Computer in Cupertino. . . .
>
> As I came off the freeway exit onto De Anza Boulevard in Cupertino, the first building I saw with the Apple logo in front was the three-story glass-and-concrete Mariani Building. I thought this must be Apple's headquarters building because it was the only large building around. It wasn't.
>
> Instead, the company was headquartered in a much smaller, more modest building on Bandley Drive, which cut through the middle of Apple's hodgepodge campus. At one end of Bandley was the Any Mountain Ski Shop, at the other end a supermarket. In between were a spate of flat, one-story huts from the Taco Bell school of architecture. At each entrance was a redwood sign carved with the company's rainbow-striped Apple emblem.
>
> I was taken aback when I found that Jobs and Markkula were ensconced in a two-story wood-frame building with a shingled roof. It seemed more appropriate as a branch office of an insurance company than the executive office of a fast-rising corporation. Outside the building hung a small employment sign. As I parked the car, I noticed a surprising number of Mercedeses and Porsches in the adjacent parking lot. One sported a license plate with the letters THX APPL . . .

With that storm as a warning, Sculley began his own odyssey. But in his case there would be no return to Ithaca. He was about to fall under the spell of Steve Jobs, the Circe of Computing.

It was a typical Apple day of that era. Everyone was nearly too busy to talk. The Lisa announcement was only a month away, and the place was boiling with nervous anticipation. Sculley had a brief meeting with Markkula, then was taken in to see the *enfant terrible.* Jobs played his role to perfection. He was dressed like a college student, his manner alternately distracted, curt and messianic. At lunch, he was apparently bored by much of what Sculley had to say, then suddenly would focus like a laser beam on his tablemate and launch into a monologue about how Apple would change the world.

It was disorienting stuff, but thrilling to a man who was the ultimate corporate infighter, yet styled himself as a rebel. A cynic might say that even at that first meeting Sculley had seen enough of the flaws in Steve Jobs's character to know how to handle him. But that is probably not true. A more likely explanation was that Jobs, with his amazing intuition, unwittingly and more by what he didn't say, struck John Sculley's most vulnerable point.

Here was a middle-aged man, a great success in his field, who was looking ahead at his career and seeing only more years of the same old thing, trying not to screw up and waiting for the CEO's job to be handed to him like an award for perfect attendance. He was the colonel growing tired of long road to a brigadier's star.

Just as bad, John Sculley had Marketing Man's disease, a syndrome common among marketing professionals, who come to believe that (a) marketing is the key to a corporation's success and (b) therefore no one but the top marketing guy is worthy of becoming CEO. Generations of marketing CEOs screwing up companies because they didn't understand manufacturing, personnel or R&D, had done nothing to cure this illness. And John Sculley had a serious case. Sure, he was president of Pepsi-Cola, but Kendall and PepsiCo still hung over him like an unyielding father. He had come to Apple that December day already with his own notions about how Apple should be run—that is, how it should improve its marketing. A visit to a computer store during the stopover in Los Angeles had convinced him that neither Apple nor any of its competitors really knew how to present computers at the point of sale. And his own frustrating experiences as an Apple II+ owner—"At Pepsi, I found the Apple to be more work to us than it was worth"—further convinced him that he understood the needs of the company's new corporate market better than anyone at Apple did. In fact, so pumped was Sculley when he left the luncheon that on the flight home he drafted an eight-page letter to Jobs outlining just how traditional corporate hierarchies worked and how they presented obstacles to the adoption of personal computers.

A third and final reason Jobs struck home with Sculley had to do with the technology itself. In Jobs's youthful success Sculley saw a chance to rev up his old excitement about his career. And in Jobs's callowness about corporate life Sculley saw a chance to put his awesome marketing skills to work in an exciting new field. But it was in Jobs's enthusiasm about the Lisa (ironically, the project he was no longer part of) that Sculley saw the chance to reignite his own childhood love affair with technology. In the end, Apple was the antithesis of Pepsi, and to his own surprise, that was exactly what John Sculley discovered he wanted.

But wanting and taking are two different matters. And a great corporation politician like John Sculley doesn't make it to the near-summit of corporate life by instantly chasing every dream that catches his fancy. Like a married man in love with a younger woman, Sculley at first denied his obsession even as his days turned increasingly to thoughts of Apple. More and more in his mind Apple came to represent lost youth, the thrill of starting out again, a return to the team spirit of Pepsi International.

It was also fame. Sculley thought he knew what business fame looked like. But Apple was something else. Before his first visit to the company, he had told his stepdaughter that he was meeting with Steve Jobs. She reacted as if he was visiting a rock star. This too was something Pepsi could never provide.

Still, he resisted. On January 12 he agreed to meet with Jobs again, this time in New York City, where Jobs was conducting the Lisa preview tour for the press. Sculley met with Jobs and two other Apple executives for an evening meeting at the Carlyle Hotel. By making Sculley feel like an insider to a secret project, and even more important to Sculley, part of a high-spirited team again, Jobs further set the hook. At the same time, Sculley was sufficiently acute to recognize the simmering tension between John Couch and Jobs, though he as yet didn't know their history. He also noticed that Paul Dali, one of the general managers of the Apple II group and the man on the tour charged with demonstrating the new Apple II+, was all but ignored. Thus, in a matter of a half hour, being the politician he was, Sculley deduced most of the underlying dynamics of Apple Computer.

From the Carlyle, the group made its way to the Four Seasons for dinner. Now it was Sculley's turn to seduce. For more than three hours he conducted a near-monologue on the marketing lessons of Pepsi and how they might apply to high technology. He talked about the positive message of the Pepsi Generation and how it had endured one of the most turbulent eras of American history by conveying a comforting message of optimism. He talked about the Pepsi Challenge and how it complemented that long-standing campaign by adding a personal, empirical dimension. He talked about how the Challenge also represented a new hybrid of advertising, PR and news. That's exactly what we're trying to do with the Lisa, said Jobs and Couch in rare agreement.

Finally, in the crowning moment, Sculley suggested that, if there could be a Pepsi Generation, why couldn't there now be an *Apple Generation*? A silent shock wave rolled around the table.

It was nearly midnight, the restaurant closed and the bored waiters pacing around, when the little group finished and strolled out into the cold night. On the walk back to the hotel, Jobs suddenly turned to Sculley and announced, "This has been one of the most exciting evenings in my whole life. I just can't tell you how much fun I've had tonight." It was a perfect Steve Jobs moment. What made it remarkable was that he wasn't the only one who felt that way. John Sculley too was in a near-swoon. For a few hours he was back in Mexico and Brazil and Sweden with the Pepsi International team. "In some queer way, I felt more kinship with these young renegades from Apple than I did with many of the people I had been working with at Pepsi-Cola for years."

He went back to Pepsi, but now he was a changed man. As he would later write, in an extraordinary admission: "I was one of Kendall's most competitive soldiers, yet after sixteen years of being constantly tested, I was discovering that I didn't enjoy competing, I enjoyed building."

Had Steve Jobs known at the time that these were John Sculley's real feelings, the subsequent history of Apple, Pepsi, Sculley and Jobs might have been entirely different. Sculley, it seems, had a completely misguided view of the personal computer industry—because beneath the teamwork and the innovation and the youthful energy lay one of the most competitive business landscapes of all. The cola battles only *seemed* more competitive; yet so established was the marketplace that even the biggest executive screwup in that business might mean the loss of a point or two of market share. In personal computing, by comparison, you could appear to make all the right decisions and be dead tomorrow. What John Sculley saw as a youthful adventure, a creative experience, was in fact a bloody life-or-death struggle.

Thus, at the very moment when they seemed most simpatico, Jobs and Sculley were actually a world apart. And this mutual lack of understanding foretold disaster.

For now, though, Sculley played hard to get. This wasn't college anymore. He couldn't cut it down the middle, being a buttoned-down Pepsi man during the day and play at Apple at night. He had to choose. And each day that choice got more painful, yet easier to make.

Apple, needless to say, nudged him along. The day after the dinner, headhunter Gerry Roche called to say how thrilled Jobs was about the evening before. Then, every few days thereafter, Roche, Jobs or Markkula, tag-teaming, would call to check in, ask for advice, plumb his feelings about joining Apple—anything to capture Sculley's frame of mind.

After a few weeks, Markkula jumped in his jet and paid a visit to Sculley's imperial offices in an effort to get him to sign on. It was a precipitous moment: the Lisa had just been introduced to acclaim, the computer was *Time*'s Man of the Year and Jobs was on the cover of *Fortune*. Apple, it seemed, had caught the tide of history. Markkula's visit all but screamed: What better time to join the company?

But again Sculley put him off. He would love to advise Apple, be a friend of the company, but he just couldn't imagine ever leaving Pepsi.

Then it was Jobs's turn again. He visited New York a couple of weeks later, on the pretext of getting Sculley's advice on buying an apartment. It was a Sunday afternoon, so the visit began at Sculley's exquisite modern home in

Greenwich. Jobs toured the grounds, met Leezy Sculley, then the pair retired to the library to talk. "Why are you talking to me?" Sculley asked. "Why don't you go talk to somebody at IBM or Hewlett-Packard? Why do you want somebody out of the soft-drink industry? I don't know anything about computers."

A lot of people would ask the same question in the years to come. In reply, Jobs said, "What we're doing has never been done before. We're trying to build a totally different kind of company, and we need really great people. . . . My dream is that every person in the world will have their own Apple computer. To do that, we've got to be a great marketing company."

It was a magnificent answer. A Steve Jobs answer: full of sweeping gestures, flattery, perfectionism and bravado. But it was also a silly, flip answer to a very serious question, the answer of a young man in love with his own romantic poses. Sculley was right to ask: in the history of the electronics industry, no nontechnie had ever successfully taken over the reins of a major company. Hewlett and Packard were technologists, as were Charlie Sporck, Bill Gates, Robert Noyce, Gordon Moore, Ken Olsen, Andy Grove, Jerry Sanders, even Regis McKenna, Nolan Bushnell and Jack Tramiel. The sole exception was Irwin Federman, who successfully ran the midsized Valley chip company Monolithic Memories—but though a finance guy, Federman had spent years at MMI before being given the top spot. Why indeed wasn't Jobs looking for the new Apple CEO at IBM, DEC, HP or one of the hundreds of other computer-oriented technology companies? But if Sculley, to his credit, recognized the flaw in Jobs's approach, it was to his discredit that chose to ignore it and be flattered instead.

The rest of the afternoon took on all the characteristics of teen love. The pair jumped in Sculley's car and raced out to look at PepsiCo's magnificent headquarters building. Jobs acted like a wide-eyed first date as Sculley toured him through the building with its world-class sculptures, fountains and sprawling office suites. Young Steve charmed the older man by being both in awe of and contemptuous of all this corporate ostentatiousness. Then they jumped in the car again and raced over to look at IBM's headquarters, much more anonymous than PepsiCo, but chilling in its excruciating perfection. Sculley explained to Jobs that IBM even sterilized the surrounding trees so that they would blossom but not bear fruit that might rot on the ground. "Rotten fruit are forbidden fruit at world headquarters." The too obvious metaphor was not lost on his young charge, who jokingly suggested that Apple ought to rent a jet to fly in the whole Macintosh division to look at this corporate monstrosity (as if the group had not already seen a corporate monster up close).

Then it was back to Sculley's house, where a limousine was waiting to take Jobs back to Manhattan. Once again, Sculley suggested that Apple ought to make a more focused search in electronics for its new CEO. Once again Jobs ignored him. Back in the house, Sculley asked his wife what she thought of Steve Jobs. "I just don't know," said Leezy Sculley. A thrice-married man should have heard warning signals coming from such a noncommittal answer. But John Sculley's mind was already in the clouds.

7.4 AERIE

A week later, Sculley was in Hawaii to give the keynote speech at the annual convention of several thousand Pepsi bottlers. He had done such a speech many times before at similar events. But this time would be different. As a test, he decided to devote the speech to the computer revolution and its impact on the future of the soft-drink business.

The ostensible subject was how personal computers could improve the productivity of independent bottlers. But the real purpose was for Sculley to see if he really could stand up in front of an audience—as he would every week as Apple CEO—and talk both compellingly and knowledgeably about PCs. The speech was a success. Afterward, the producer of the event found Sculley standing in the wings, crying.

On the way back East, Sculley stopped again in Cupertino. This time Jobs took him to Bandley 3, and there gave Sculley his first look at the Macintosh and the group that had built it. This was the team within the team—Atkinson, Hertzfeld, all the others—a group so eccentric that it left Sculley disoriented. This was beyond anything he had ever known at Pepsi. That too should have been a warning.

Before he left, Sculley stopped by Markkula's office. There, the current CEO made his potential replacement a formal offer: $300,000 in salary and options for 500,000 shares of stock. It was a classic Silicon Valley offer—take a salary cut, but bet on the success you'll help create. Even at the current market price of $36 per share those options (assuming Sculley stayed around long enough for vestment) were worth $18 million.

But for an East Coaster, Markkula's offer came as a rude shock. Almost an insult. Pepsi was currently paying Sculley a $500,000 per year salary. What kind of fool would take a *40 percent* pay cut? And that wasn't half of it: all the assorted pensions and bonuses at Pepsi came close to doubling that salary figure. Apple didn't give bonuses *and it didn't have a pension plan!* Why should it? This was Silicon Valley; this was a children's game. Nobody expected to be around long enough to get a ten-year pin from the company, much less a gold watch. Markkula tried to explain the facts of Valley life, that if Apple continued to grow as it had the stock would be worth $100 million or more. But Sculley wasn't listening. Only an idiot would choose to speculate on the prospect of future wealth rather than nail down a firm salary commitment.

Sculley went home deeply disappointed. He called Gerry Roche and told him there was no way he was going to work for Apple at such a salary, especially as part of a contract that contained no long-term deferred compensation. And, he added, he would never take Leezy to California unless they could move into a home equal to the one they enjoyed in Greenwich. Roche said he'd tell Markkula.

Not surprisingly, Steve Jobs soon called and requested another meeting with Sculley. They met on another Sunday, March 20, this time at the Carlyle. They had lunch, then went for a walk in Central Park. Sculley would later remember how chagrined he was by all the people recognizing Jobs—it was hardly the anonymous meeting Sculley had hoped for.

"I want you to come and work with me," said Jobs. "I can learn so much from you."

They walked through the Metropolitan Museum of Art. Sculley explained to the young man the differences between Archaic and Periclean Greek sculpture. "Apple wants to stand for great design," said Steve Jobs. "Anything that Apple does, we want to be the best. It has to be the best."

As they walked, Sculley began to imagine himself as the teacher of a brilliant student, an Aristotle, say, to Alexander—or perhaps just John Sculley to his younger self. Sculley told Jobs how he vacationed in Paris, drawing in his sketchbook and visiting the Louvre. He confessed that if he hadn't been a businessman he probably would have become an artist. Jobs, in a remarkable coincidence, said that if he hadn't become a technologist, he would have been a poet in Paris. The birds twittered in the trees.

They walked up the West side, stopping to look at jazz records, then on to the twin-spired San Remo apartment building. As it turned out, Jobs was considering buying the two-story penthouse apartment in one of those spires, an apartment fomerly owned by Jacob Rothschild.

The younger man led the older man out onto the terrace of the penthouse, thirty stories above the great city. Sculley, who suffered from vertigo, hugged the wall as Jobs pointed out the extraordinary view. Sculley's head swam. He would later write, "It seemed as if the two of us were standing out there above the world, above the world of New York that I knew and that Steve was now trying to discover, and above the world he was going to change."

It was a scene out of an Ayn Rand novel. The young superman, fearlessly looking out over the landscape from his skyscraper aerie, challenging the older, less immortal man to join him. Now it needed a climax. Jobs asked Sculley if he intended to join Apple. Sculley recapitulated his concerns about salary, home and deferred compensation. It was oh so prosaic. Jobs waved it away. "Even if I have to pay for it out of my own pocket, I want you to come to Apple. We'll have to solve those problems because you're the best person I've ever met. I know you're perfect for Apple, and Apple deserves the best."

Scully protested weakly one last time. Couldn't he just be an adviser to Apple?

Jobs dropped his head until his chin rested on his chest, as if the burden of his thoughts were too great. He stared down at the distant sidewalk and street. Then he said in measured words, "Do you want to spend the rest of your life selling sugared water or do you want a chance to change the world?"

It was the single most famous moment in Steve Jobs's life. Just twenty-eight years old, he had fully learned not only the part of business tycoon but also the mythology. The scene, the words, the style, all had their effect. Jobs's question tore right through John Sculley's guts. As he stumbled off into the early evening, "I realized for the first time in four months that I couldn't say no."

7.5 Premature Maturity

It was a magnificent seduction, orchestrated by a master. Steve Jobs had proven that he could work his charm and will not only on lesser mortals under his command but even on the cream of American business Brahmins. On that rooftop high over Metropolis, Jobs had reduced John Sculley from a figure who easily commanded the destiny of thousands, and who controlled the flow of billions of dollars, to a befuddled, fawning disciple.

But like many seducers, Jobs was more in love with the chase than the object. He had accomplished something extraordinary in luring John Sculley from Pepsi to Apple. But did Apple really need John Sculley?

Certainly the company needed a CEO. Markkula, in his usual manner, had never wanted the job in the first place, and now was anxious to get off the hot seat. Jobs too, to his great credit, recognized that he was still too young and inexperienced to become the chief executive officer of a billion-dollar corporation.

With the usual arrogance, Jobs also concluded that no one beneath him in the company was sufficiently qualified for the job. Yet, in fact, there was a new arrival to the firm who was so qualified that everyone else at Apple assumed he had joined as the heir apparent. This was Floyd Kvamme. As one of the youngest Fairchildren, Kvamme had been the junior member of the group that left with Charlie Sporck to take over National Semiconductor. Handsome, brilliant, multilingual, Kvamme was like a swan amidst the tough, ugly ducklings at National Semi. He was not only the nice face Sporck liked to put on the company for public events but also the company's best marketing man.

In a departure from its usual chip business, National had been a major supplier of IBM-compatible mainframe computers to the giant leasing company Itel Corp. When Itel began to totter, instead of renegotiating the contract, Sporck simply pulled the plug, leaving Itel to crash in one of the biggest financial meltdowns of the era (it almost took Lloyd's of London with it), and took over Itel's computer-leasing operation. Renamed National Advanced Systems, the subsidiary was given to Kvamme to run. If NAS's greatest success was a perverse one—IBM used it for the big FBI sting that nearly drove its two biggest Japanese competitors, Hitachi and Fujitsu, out of the computer business—the subsidiary still was well run and proved a neat little business for National for more than a decade.

Kvamme himself came out of the deal with his reputation stronger than ever. Now he knew not only chips but computers—and IBM. He also showed he could run a company. So when he decamped for Apple it was generally assumed that he would spend a few months learning the business, then step into Markkula's shoes.

But it never happened. Jobs already had decided that what the company needed now in a CEO was a veteran of large corporations who had the skills to take a still raw and volatile Apple Computer and turn it into a smooth-running, competent, *stable* enterprise. He was looking beyond Apple now, and never seemed to glance in Kvamme's direction.

Jobs's moves were entirely justifiable in strategic terms. Yet they were also profoundly wrongheaded. They were based on two assumptions on Jobs's part—assumptions about which, as an industry founder, he should have known better.

The least dangerous of these was that Apple needed to grow up. Certainly, as a major industry player, the company needed to refine its processes, ramp up manufacturing while still improving both quality and service. It also needed to grow up in other ways; notably the ad hoc nature of the company's organization. A company with several thousand employees could no longer behave like a frat house. On the hand, those problems were largely of Jobs's own doing. In fact, in the Apple II area, in marketing communications and in sales, the company was becoming quite professional. It was Jobs himself who was jumping around the firm, interfering with operations, setting up skunk works such as the Mac team, overruling standard procedures. He'd also helped drive off Mike Scott, who'd made the first real attempt to give the company structure.

The more dangerous assumption that Jobs made was that the industry was about to grow up as well. This was no doubt a reaction—after all, executive search began not long after the Apple III introduction—to IBM's arrival. Faced with this juggernaut of a corporation, the largest manufacturer in the world, the embodiment of corporate maturity and hierarchy, Jobs tried to be clever by trying to beat Big Blue at its own game. If the personal computer industry was about to settle down into a premature middle age, then why not beat the competition to the punch? Why not turn Apple into an HP with spark? And the only way to do that was to find a guy who knew his way around a Fortune 500 boardroom, a big-time CEO who knew how to sell to his own kind.

But in thinking this way, Steve Jobs betrayed his own inexperience—and the dangers of being too clever by half. In fact, the personal computer had not settled into a comfortable maturity. The shakeout it had just seen was only the first round, taking out the incompetent pioneers. Even with IBM in the market, there was still extraordinary room to maneuver—as the growing number of IBM cloners proved. Moreover, Moore's Law said that the next generation of microprocessors was due any day, and that would start the game all over again. And if none of these facts convinced Jobs that the personal computer industry was still young, then he needed to look only as far as his own Lisa and Macintosh design teams. Wasn't it Steve Jobs himself who went around proclaiming that these two computers were going to change the world? If he really believed that, why wasn't he looking for a feisty CEO/technologist prepared to deal with, and triumph over, change?

But Jobs was playing from his own rule book. A big-time corporation needed a big-time CEO. He and Markkula approached a local headhunter, Ed Winters, who'd proven an effective recruiter for Apple in the past, and gave him orders to look for the best CEO candidate in the country. It was Winters who led them to Don Estridge of IBM.

When Estridge turned down the offer, Jobs in his usual manner set out to find the best headhunter in the business. He ended up at the doorstep of Heidrick & Struggles and Gerry Roche. Roche, as was his standard procedure, asked Jobs and Markkula to come up with a list of attributes they wanted to see in the new CEO. The list they provided was telling: the new CEO needed to have consumer marketing experience, be interested in high tech, serve as a mentor to Jobs, adjust quickly to the unusual Apple culture and act as a visionary in the industry. It was not your typical set of CEO job requirements, especially the part about mentoring the corporate dauphin.

This need for a CEO with consumer marketing experience betrayed a dangerous shift in Jobs's thinking, encouraged by Markkula, the marketing man. They had decided that the future of personal computing was not as a technology business (hence that amazing second requirement of only an *interest* in technology), but as a consumer business—and that the key to managing that transition would be brilliant marketing. It was an extraordinary philosophical shift by the leadership of Apple and it occurred at the worst possible moment. There was no evidence that personal computers were becoming consumer products—quite the contrary, the game computer business was a wreck, while the successful companies like IBM and Apple were selling to schools, professionals and corporations.

And why marketing? Apple already had a marketing expert in Markkula, a legend in marketing communications in Regis McKenna and a budding marketing genius in Steve Jobs. If anything, Apple had too much marketing for its own good. What it needed was a firm and experienced hand in manufacturing or sales and distribution or administration.

Taking his orders, Roche set about creating a list of potential Apple CEOs. At one point it ran to almost 150 names, including most of the leading lights in American industry, such as Charles Brown, chairman of AT&T; Buck Rodgers, IBM's senior marketing vice president; and, of course, John Sculley. But as the search went to the contact phase, nearly all of the blue-chip names turned Apple down. Increasingly the list came down to John Sculley as the last major figure who fit the criteria yet had not peremptorily dismissed the Apple job.

This was the critical moment in Apple's middle years. The search for a CEO had stalled. The one remaining solid candidate not only was reluctant to take the job but had no computer, even electronics, industry experience. This was the moment when a wise executive would have stopped to take stock. A billion-dollar company was on the line. Jobs needed to ask himself, in a variant, the same question he would pose to Sculley: Am I willing to turn my computer company over to a man who has spent his entire career selling sugared water? Can I trust Apple to a man who has operated in a largely static market; and who has never really had to bring a new product through design and into large-scale manufacturing in a matter of months?

But Jobs never asked himself any of these questions in a systematic way. Once he had John Sculley in his sights he went after him with the relentlessness of a stalker. If anything, the prospect of landing a CEO from another world appealed to Jobs's romantic sense of himself. He would do something so daring no one else in the industry would dare try it. And when Sculley succeeded, Jobs's genius would again be acclaimed.

That was only part of it. The criterion about mentoring Jobs was a clue: Steve didn't want someone who would triumph in this new job and become synonymous with the company; rather, Jobs wanted someone to run Apple competently *until he could succeed him.* That may have been one reason why Kvamme, who far better fit Jobs's requirements, was passed over. By comparison, one of the things that made Sculley so appealing as time went on was that he was apparently in complete thrall to Jobs. Sculley was a great businessman whom he could handle, and Jobs liked that.

Jobs got what he wanted. But his luck, so remarkable until now, had finally turned. Because in John Sculley what Jobs got was a new Apple CEO who would run him out of the firm, lose the company's image as the industry thought leader, wasn't fully grounded in the underlying technology and would be unable to introduce a successful new product line for the next decade. John Sculley—in Steve Jobs's words that day in the Manhattan penthouse, "the best person I ever met"—would do the one thing worse than killing Apple Computer: he would make it boring.

7.6 Blind Date

John Sculley's acceptance of the chief executive's post stunned the rest of Apple, not least the senior management team. Only a couple of executives even knew of Jobs's recruitment efforts. The rest assumed that Kvamme was the man and were too busy with the III and the Lisa to give it much more attention.

Then on the morning of Friday, April 8, 1983, Mike Markkula called a meeting of the executive staff in the Bandley 6 boardroom. There he announced the hiring of John Sculley. It was a classic Apple moment. Markkula gave a quick biography of the new CEO: forty-four years old, president of Pepsi-Cola Company, senior vice president of PepsiCo Inc., MBA from

Wharton, third wife Leezy, etc. Then, attempting to prepare the team for Sculley's atypical personality, and perhaps for the only time to show his own doubts, Markkula added that the new CEO was an outstanding individual, if somewhat uncharismatic.

At that point, Steve Jobs jumped up to say that he thought Sculley was very charismatic. The others in the room were left to their own opinions, most deciding to wait until they met the man. But it was hardly a propitious beginning. After all this searching for the perfect CEO, the current CEO and the chairman couldn't even agree what he was like?

Pepsi made the announcement later that day. Kendall had accepted Sculley's resignation well, albeit with considerable amazement. It was too late for the dailies and for television news to carry more than the headline. But by Monday, the first of the "Who is John Sculley?" articles began to appear, notably in *The Wall Street Journal.* That's when the real industry talk began. The appointment itself had been a shocker—nobody in tech had ever tried something this outré. But then as the industry learned more about this buttoned-down Yankee corporate type who'd been married to the boss's daughter, the shock was replaced by stunned disbelief: Was this genius, or had Apple finally gone nuts?

The nature of the deal got out as well. Sculley had been hired for a salary of $1 million per year, *plus* another $1 million first-year bonus, *plus* a $1 million severance package, *plus* options on 350,000 shares of stock, *plus* a $2 million loan to buy a house (what they didn't know was that John and Leezy had gone to real estate people in the wealthy enclaves of Atherton and Woodside and told them to look for a house priced at *exactly* $2 million—no less, they wanted the best they could get, but no more, because they had no intention of putting up their own cash).

It was an amazing employment contract—the kind of deal that impresses outsiders and pisses off insiders. The last time anybody in Silicon Valley had cut such a deal was when Dr. Les Hogan was recruited from archrival Motorola to take over Fairchild after Noyce's departure. Hogan's salary was henceforth derisively used as a standard Valley salary measure (one Hogan, two and half Hogans, etc.) and brought up every time Fairchild stumbled thereafter. By cutting a comparable deal, Sculley guaranteed that henceforth he would be a target.

In the meantime, it was obvious that Kvamme was the odd man out. He would be gone in a year, off to a long and respectable career as a venture capitalist at Kleiner Perkins. A decade later his son would get a measure of family revenge by buying a crippled Apple's television studios and using them as the centerpiece of his very successful multimedia production company, CKS Inc. CKS would go public in a wildly successful IPO at the same time that Apple was losing hundreds of millions of dollars.

Yet the management team had still not met their new boss. That encounter occurred on Wednesday, April 13, when Sculley held his first executive staff meeting.

If Apple's management had been confused about the situation before, they weren't left much better off by meeting's end. On the one hand, Sculley was reassuring. He told them he wanted to preserve Apple's unique entrepreneurial style, not allow it to sink into the bureaucratic inertia he'd seen at the big eastern corporations. He even used a Steve Jobs phrase, "leveraging Apple's critical mass," a nebulous, but meaningful phrase that meant that Apple, while it still had the most popular personal computer (the II), the largest installed base and the market's imagination, must combine all of these advantages into a single, monolithic marketing strategy.

There were other things Sculley said that day that also gave the executive team reason to be both surprised and optimistic. One was that he wanted Apple to shift from a single-product to a multi-product company. On the surface that was not a startling remark, given that Apple now had the II family, the III, the Lisa and the impending Macintosh. But on reflection, it was a powerful statement, especially as Steve Jobs seemed to be doing everything he could to kill the II, ignore the III and humiliate the Lisa team. *Hey, maybe this guy isn't Jobs's patsy after all!*

And that was just the beginning. Later in the meeting, which lasted hours, Sculley bowled over the room by announcing that if Apple was to succeed in selling to the business world—one of his goals—then it would have to move away from selling individual computers and begin selling a "total systems environment." In other words, the company would have to move into networks: PCs that acted like terminals, data communications systems, large central computers, the whole shebang. This was amazing stuff; Sculley was actually proposing that Apple start acting like IBM.

It was a gutsy call for Sculley, to take the war back into IBM's territory. But just as gutsy was his proclaiming this strategy in the presence of Steve Jobs, the young man who had built Apple on the old Homebrew antiestablishment policy of "one person, one computer." Even as Sculley was saying these words, Jobs had the Mac team hard at work on a computer that would be the very embodiment of solitary use, that would be specifically designed *not* to network with other computers.

As Sculley's words sank in, there were surreptitious glances at Jobs, expecting a blowup at any moment. But instead, in the words of author Frank Rose, who was covering Apple at the time, "Steve sat through all of this like the proud owner of an ingenious new toy. It was the first clue to the executive staff that the relationship between the new CEO and the young tycoon was going to be different from anything they'd ever seen with Steve Jobs."

But if Sculley's words assuaged the team's worries *(Hey, he understands this stuff more than you'd think)*, his manner did not. Later observers would make much of the fact that John Sculley wore a suit and tie in a world of jeans and (sometimes) sport coats. But that is reversing the cliché a little too much. Silicon Valleyites were not that alienated by business clothes; after all, the Valley's founders had all looked like IBM refugees. Some of the veterans at the meeting, such as Kvamme, still wore ties. At places like Apple, it was more of a game than anything else for the more casual baby boomers to get their elders to shed their business uniforms

No, what made Sculley seem so out of place was his manner. He seemed perpetually nervous, even frightened, and when he spoke (perhaps as a residue of his old stutter) he often sputtered as though he was fighting to get the words out. First-time encounters were the strangest: in the years to come, at Valley social events, more than one person walked away from meeting John Sculley saying, as a woman was overheard muttering at a fund-raiser in Menlo Park, "*That* is the president of a billion-dollar company?" She, like many others, had been met with averted eyes, a limp and cold handshake and a whispered greeting.

The Apple executives, seeing this, first said to themselves, *Jesus, Markkula was right about this guy. He has no charisma at all. What was Jobs thinking?* Then they asked themselves how this nervous, shrinking figure before them was going to represent Apple Computer on the world stage. Could he face down top-flight journalists, giant investors and sly competitors? Could he go on television and convince you to buy an Apple computer because he was a great technological visionary or because he was more clever than his counterparts in the industry or, most important, because he was a tough, take-no-prisoners businessman? Could John Sculley really present himself to the world as a *winner?*

There was something else as well, an undertone that only the most subtle in the room could detect. It lay beneath the phrases Sculley used, such as "power curve" and "vision." Everybody at Apple, in emulation of Jobs, threw terms like that around. Hyperbole and imprecision were the very air you breathed at Apple. Even the veterans who really ran the place occasionally tossed out these stock phrases in their conversations to prove they were fellow travelers. But they also knew it was bullshit, that what really counted was moving iron. Talk all you want about a cosmic revolution in consciousness, but first you've got to build and sell the goddamn boxes.

Now here was Sculley using some of these same airy phrases. He was supposed to be from the hard-knuckle soda-pop business; where did he learn the lingo so fast? Was he always like this? Was he just sandbagging Jobs or, God forbid, did he actually believe it?

As they would discover, the answer to the last was: a little of both.

7.7 BABEL

To the outsider, the first few months of the Sculley era at Apple were largely indistinguishable from what had come before it. Nevertheless, for someone coming from a giant corporation he moved with amazing alacrity. What was even more impressive was the subtlety with which he did so. To those he met, Sculley professed to be in a "learning-curve mode," which meant that he followed Steve Jobs around the company or wandered about on his own, asking questions and writing notes in notebooks. He said he had a lot to learn—not just about Apple but about computers and the industry. And by the end of the year he would fill up twenty notebooks.

But, in fact, Sculley was using his naiveté as a cover for some very serious analysis of the business, the organization and the culture of Apple. From the beginning, he knew enough to take Jobs's point of view about Apple and its competitors with skepticism. Sculley noticed immediately that under the Jobs regime the Apple II group was being screwed. Here was the heart of the company's balance sheet and the chairman referred to its members as bozos. The II group had been exiled to a rented triangular building overlooking the freeway four miles away in Santa Clara. Jobs had also publicly suggested that the Lisa team, the people behind the most important new company product in a decade, were a collection of second-raters and losers. Meanwhile, Jobs's pets, the Macintosh team members, were treated like pampered rock stars, right down to their own masseuse.

Having identified this early, Sculley was more dismayed than surprised to find that Apple had become a collection of opposing camps, each with its own culture, style and business strategy. The II, III and Lisa lines all had their own advertising and promotional campaigns—and as Sculley found out when he visited Chiat/Day with Jobs, the Mac group was about to embark on yet another. They also had redundant marketing teams, R&D operations, manufacturing groups and staff positions.

Having come from such a world, Sculley knew well the dangers of a company divided against itself. But for now he kept his counsel—so well that his lieutenants assumed that he had bought Jobs's point of view hook, line and sinker. John Couch shuddered one day to hear Sculley describe Jobs as "my boy genius," figuring it meant the apotheosis of his worst enemy.

Sculley identified troubling features about Apple's products as well. For example, the Lisa and the Macintosh, though they had overlapping markets, were utterly incompatible—and as long as the two product groups despised each other, they would remain so forever. The Lisa itself had already been introduced by the time of Sculley's arrival at Apple, so he had no control over its design or packaging. But he could still revamp its market and certainly could change the direction of follow-up products. He chose to do both.

As for organization, even Apple veterans recognized the company was turning into Babel. New operating divisions had proliferated under Mike Scott, but exploded under Markkula. There were now *thirteen* autonomous divisions at Apple, most of them with redundant staffs. And it was precisely this autonomy that allowed the II, III, Lisa and Mac groups to remain at each other's throats. Sculley, who had enjoyed the pleasures of autonomy during his overseas sojourn, also knew well its dangers. He also knew that to pull the diverse groups together would require the glue of a common management and of shared information systems.

Finally, Sculley was deeply disturbed by Apple's (that is, Jobs's) attitude toward its competitors and its target customers. As he would later write in his autobiography:

> [In] October, a *Business Week* cover story declared IBM the "winner" in the microcomputer race. I was furious, but no one at Apple seemed to notice. If it had appeared in *Computer Currents*, a freebie street paper in the Valley, the story probably would have had more impact. Apple people didn't really read business magazines. So absorbed in what they were doing at the company, many had no touch with the outside business world.

In other words, Apple was planning to take on the business computing market without understanding either the customer or the largest manufacturer in that industry. To Sculley, this was flabbergasting. You might despise Coca-Cola, even deride it, but never for a moment did you forget that it was the largest and most venerable company in your industry. The same was even more true for IBM. Big Blue's share of the business PC market in 1984 would be more than 36 percent, compared with less than 13 percent for Apple. And while

Apple had screwed up the III and taken forever on the Lisa and the Mac, big, slow IBM had shown itself to be surprisingly nimble: now in the summer of 1983 it was preparing to introduce a brilliant new machine, the PC XT, aimed right at the heart of the office workplace.

The buzz was everywhere, already burying the coverage of the Lisa. It seemed that the old minicomputer line about never getting fired for buying IBM, so derided by the personal computing crowd, was proving true after all. Corporate directors of management information systems, who for years had refused purchase requests for computers with that funny name from those hippies in California, were now at last caving before the inevitability of the PC revolution and allowing purchases—as long as they were from IBM. Average office workers, though surveys found the majority preferred Apple, bowed too before the inevitable. Why fight the power (and pay out of one's own pocket for an Apple) when the company would pick up the tab for a PC? Even before the Lisa, Apple's sales team had discovered that most of its "corporate" sales were in fact small orders from renegade offices.

As Sculley knew all too well, corporate sales was Lisa's target market. And Apple understood that market so little that it was going after it with *lifestyle* ads—precisely the thing to reach those office renegades, while confirming to corporate officers that this was an artsy-fartsy outsider company too flaky to deal with.

Along with a handful of chip-industry veterans like Markkula and Kvamme, Sculley did understand the corporate marketplace, with its intense desire for predictability, security and the need for everyone involved with a decision at every level to be able to cover his or her ass if anything went wrong. That's why *Business Week*'s prediction of IBM's victory over Apple was so terrifying: no corporate purchasing officer in his right mind would ever buy from a company that didn't appear to have a future.

It went deeper than that. The corporate world, especially the world of giant Fortune 500 companies, had very distinct structural requirements. Like the military, it bought in giant volumes—a purchase order for PCs might run to the hundreds, even thousands of machines, the order totaling millions of dollars. Reaching that decision point could be a long and arduous process. But given the sheer size of the order, anything less would be irresponsible. Moreover, in making that decision, dozens of signatories up and down the organization chart might be required. That was the dark side of corporate bureaucracies, and what ultimately killed many big firms. Finally, before making the deal, the large corporate buyer exerted due diligence to confirm that the supplier was viable, trustworthy and able to provide service and support effectively for years to come.

That was the bad part. The good part was that once the order was made, the supplier didn't simply fulfill that order but entered into an enduring relationship with the company. The initial checkout complete, dealing could now be made more quickly—sometimes even automatically—and might continue for decades. Thus, the enormous front-end expenditure in time and money to land one of these big corporate whales was often paid back many times over in generations of sales.

IBM knew this process well. It had cut its teeth selling computers to big companies back in the 1950s, and was even now enjoying the payoff with the PC. HP had learned the lesson too, as had DEC. Sculley had learned it at Pepsi. But now he was running a company that not only did not understand this fact but had a culture consciously designed to be the antithesis of that corporate world. How were you going to sell to General Mills or General Motors or General Electric when your own founder proudly discussed his days as a drug-abusing felon and the company currently flew a pirate flag over one of its buildings?

Within Apple, the conviction, even among those who despised Steve Jobs, was that if you created a product that was truly insanely great, then everything else would follow. It was a classic Silicon Valley point of view, one which explained not only why so many great technical innovations had come out of this small community but (though no one at Apple seemed to notice) why the Valley was littered with the wreckage of so many dead companies.

Nevertheless, a small amount of reality had managed to penetrate Apple's fantasyland. Having projected the Lisa to become a $1 billion business by itself, the company had scrambled to put in place enough infrastructure to handle that kind of load. New salespeople were added, bringing the total Lisa sales force to 100; new dealers were also signed up. Apple itself was hiring at the rate of 250 people per month. But was this enough to drive a young company, and a disreputable one at that, into the loving arms of corporate America? Was it enough to supplant IBM, which had more salespeople than Apple had employees? And most of all, was Apple stable enough and organized enough to maintain the consistent marketing and sales contacts the Fortune 500 expected of its suppliers?

So, in the end, Sculley saw empirically what Steve Jobs already sensed: Apple could never hope to maintain its current growth or its industry leadership, or successfully penetrate its new target markets unless it streamlined its operations, formed linkages between its competing product lines, developed a coherent and relevant message and committed itself completely not just to designing great products but also to getting them sold. In other words, Apple had to grow up and get its act together. It had to become a real company.

7.8 On the Beach

How John Sculley reacted to his analysis of Apple Computer is a glimpse of both his character and his understanding (or lack thereof) of the new industry in which he found himself. Whether he knew it yet or not, the exciting, successful company he had jumped ship to join turned out to be in very great danger of hitting the rocks. This wasn't the soda-pop industry, where success or failure might be a century-long process. In Silicon Valley even the most robust-appearing companies could die overnight. He had only to look at Atari, the toast of American industry three years before, now in straitened circumstances and facing oblivion.

In retrospect, the decisions John Sculley made in the first six months after his arrival at Apple, during his so-called honeymoon, helped to determine the story of Apple ever after. Though the effects of those decisions in some cases might not be known for a decade, by the time Sculley stood onstage at the Macintosh introduction and introduced his own self to the world, the die had already been cast. The fate of the most exciting company in the world had been placed in the hands of a man who understood neither company nor its world.

Nevertheless, if one can fault Sculley for taking the job, one can hardly accuse him of being indecisive during those first few months. All of that walking around and all of those filled notebooks had given him a plan and he didn't waste any time putting it into motion. One reason for this decisiveness was Sculley's recognition that he had only a brief window of market opportunity to position Apple for the future before IBM shut it. But just as important, Sculley shrewdly appreciated that any moves he might make against Jobs had to occur now while the young founder was still doting upon, and forgiving the mischievous behavior of, his new protégé.

The immediate concern was the Lisa, and if there was little Sculley could do now about the machine itself—beguiling in its interface, but too slow in its performance and way too expensive for its market—he could at least do something about its marketing. As Jobs had reminded him that day on the rooftop, computers weren't soda pop. Lifestyle advertising worked best with undifferentiated products, like sugared water, precisely because they were a minor part of an overall pattern of living.

Personal computers, by comparison, were highly differentiated, complex and a major part of the life of anyone who used them. They didn't reflect a current lifestyle, they helped *define a new lifestyle.* With only one out of every twenty people in the United States actually using a computer, and most of the rest wary of the complexity and cost of these new machines, potential customers still had to be taught to like personal computing. Nowhere was this more true than at the executive level in corporations. It was about this time that a new magazine, *Personal Computing,* actually spiked a cover story on how CEOs were using personal computers because it discovered that most of them *weren't.* Word processing was something their secretaries did; spreadsheets were for accountants.

This world of hard-nosed businessmen was precisely the target market for Lisa. Yet the Lisa ads—themed "Alone Again" and featuring images such as a solitary man playing a flute—were almost a parody of the worst kind of insufferably cute lifestyle advertising. Sculley, the man who had virtually invented lifestyle advertising at Pepsi, positively hated the ads. They were in fact his worst nightmare of how not to sell to executive row. One Apple dealer had it right when he described the ads as "nice foreign movies."

So Sculley killed them. It was a smart tactical stroke, but Sculley flinched from the much more difficult strategic campaign his action implied. If Apple really was determined to drive the Lisa into the world's corporate offices, then it would have to make the necessary commitment in time and resources. Sculley hedged, perhaps wisely given the Lisa's flaws, and the product built to save Apple was doomed.

Sculley quickly moved to streamline Apple's operations, forcing out three redundant vice presidents and cutting thirteen autonomous divisions into three. He pulled the Lisa and the Macintosh together into what he called Apple's thirty-two-bit family—an optimistic call to say the least, given that the Lisa and the Mac were utterly incompatible and the two product groups despised each other. Still, it was a gutsy move, one at odds with Sculley's already growing reputation for being Jobs's patsy. So was his next move, of forcing Jobs to make the Mac compatible, if not with the Lisa, then with its planned follow-up, the Lisa 2. By gutting out the center of Apple's management with these moves, Sculley effectively flattened the organization a decade before downsizing became a national trend. In doing so, he cut overhead, streamlined operations and, most important for Apple, forced the unfriendly parties to work with one another.

But all of this flattening had unanticipated results. By removing the intermediaries, Sculley knew that he was increasing the number of people reporting directly to him. He welcomed that, in the belief that it would speed decision making and provide him with a superb vantage point on the company's day-to-day operations. It also appealed to his paranoia that somehow the techies were pulling a fast one on him. But in time it all but buried him in raw information and the entreaties of corporate courtiers.

In the years to come Sculley would try to overcome the first by instituting sophisticated management information systems (MIS), some of them quite innovative, to reduce the mountains of raw data to manageable summaries—in the process putting into place computer networks that ironically undermined Apple's (especially Jobs's) own argument for the role of unlinked personal computers in corporate life. Yet even with all of this MIS firepower, Sculley never did get fully on top of the data flood. Moreover, none of these systems overcame the lack of an official decision-making process in the company—in fact, they worked against its creation.

This endless parade of Apple employees trying to catch John Sculley's ear only grew worse with the years. Ultimately, John Sculley would discover to his rue that by radically expanding his span of control without countering it with firm rules of access, he had not reduced factionalism at Apple but increased it. Apple stopped being a body of warring camps and, over the next decade, became an anarchy of everyone for themselves.

Sculley's other organizational move during this period was equally ambiguous in its results: he named himself head of the Apple II group. Little noticed at the time, this was a telling move in several ways. For one thing, despite his image both inside and outside of Apple of being joined to Jobs at the hip, Sculley almost from the first day began positioning himself *against* Jobs. He had forced the Mac group to integrate with the rest of the company and then he had taken over the product group that formed the greatest impediment to Jobs's strategy for the company. Sculley would later present these moves as the inevitable outgrowth of events at the time—but they show that Sculley hadn't left his political gifts at Pepsi. Certainly it was good for the morale of the II group in its exile down the freeway in the triangular building: *At least the new CEO appreciates us!*

But if his clever maneuvering at the start of his tenure, moving fast while Jobs still had stars in his eyes, showed Sculley at his best, his decision to take over the II group was the new boss at his worst. Just as, during his final days at Apple, he would take over as the company's chief technology officer, Sculley showed that when he couldn't trust anyone else to do the job he would do it himself, even when he was manifestly unqualified for the job.

This flurry of executive activity on Sculley's part culminated at the beginning of May in a weeklong Apple executive team retreat at Pajaro Dunes, a gated community on the beach near Monterey that in years to come would become best known as the site of Tom Peters's Skunk Works seminars. Though the attendees didn't realize it at the time, it would prove to be one of the most important events in Apple history.

Pajaro, a collection of homes embedded in the sand, by its very nature supported small, informal gatherings, campfires and long, meditative walks.

But that same detachment from everyday life can also lead to disassociation from reality. More than one group has left Pajaro Dunes over the years armed with disastrous strategies that seemed just brilliant at a 2 A.M. bull session.

The week began with a presentation by Chiat/Day of the new Apple commercials for each of the company's product lines. It culminated in plans for the Macintosh. The agency was understandably concerned that everything the Mac claimed to be—friendly, easy to use, affordable, etc.—had already been co-opted by competitors for machines that were manifestly unfriendly, hard to use, expensive, etc. So what Apple needed to do, creative director Lee Clow proposed, was to come up with a kickoff ad as groundbreaking and unforgettable as the Mac itself. He offered two storyboards. The first played off the scene in *King Kong* in which the giant ape bursts through the two-hundred-foot-tall iron gates that protect the tribal village. In this version, the gates would open only a crack to let a few little people through—the same tiny opening the Apple II had made in the monolithic world of computing. Then the gates would burst open, freeing nine thousand people—all thanks to the Mac, the "computer for the rest of us."

It was a terrific story line, but an expensive one, given the legions of extras. The second ad idea was expensive too, but at least it was manageable. This was "1984," stepchild of a year-old essay by a Chiat/Day copywriter named Steve Hayden entitled "Why 1984 Won't Be Like *1984*," which had been planned to run in *The Wall Street Journal* as part of a series of institutional ads. The ad was spiked, but the idea was reborn on Clow's storyboard. Sculley and Jobs loved this second theme, and Chiat/Day was sent off to create it.

Among the other topics addressed that fateful week in the dunes was products. Here, once again, the main topics were the Lisa and the Mac. The III was forgotten and the II all but ignored. The news on the Lisa was mixed. First shipments had originally been targeted for April, but like most new tech products, had slipped—in the Lisa's case until June, three weeks hence. That wasn't so bad, and it might have given Sculley the opportunity to redouble his support of the product's drive into the business market. But back orders were now approaching 20,000 units and the projections were still holding steady at nearly 60,000 Lisas to be sold in the next year. That represented more than a half billion dollars in revenues, tracking right along with the $1 billion targeted sales for Lisa during its two-year life span . . . and better yet, enough to push Apple to fiscal 1984 revenues of as great as $3 billion.

The Macintosh news was just as encouraging. The commitment to the 1984 campaign meant that the Mac had to be ready for introduction by no later than January, when George Orwell would be on everyone's mind. After that, Big Brother would be old, and overworked, news. But the Mac, which had already slipped from August, was still no gimme for January. The big problem was the floppy-disk drive. Jobs had originally wanted the Macintosh to contain the Twiggy drive. Twiggy was a godchild of Woz's classic design of a disk controller, created during his great marathon effort in 1977. So clever had been Woz's design, reducing seventy chips on multiple boards to just eight on a single board, that Apple began to get ideas of becoming a disk drive maker.

The original plan, after Scott's showdown with Shugart, had been to buy the new 5¼-inch floppy drives from Shugart—or, better yet, just use Shugart's design—add Woz's controller and have Alps Electric Co. in Japan put it all together. It was the incredible profit potential that turned Apple's head: the whole package would cost less than a hundred bucks, yet could be sold to Apple II owners for $500—and still be more than competitive with the kluges being sold at the time by Shugart and the rest.

The result, officially designated the Disk II, proved to be a great success not just for Apple, which made a lot of money, but for the Apple II computer. The added mass memory made the Apple II a true computer in the traditional sense. Arguably, the Disk II did as much to set off the personal computer revolution as did the computer to which it was attached.

But now Apple, swellheaded from having pulled a fast one on the disk memory industry, made the dangerous mistake of believing that it was a disk drive *designer*. Vice president of engineering Rod Holt, the guy who had made the slick move with the Disk II, decided to embark on a wholly new disk drive project, capable of even greater feats of storage, speed and reliability than the Disk II. This project, called Twiggy, proved to be a disaster almost from the start, not least because nobody at Apple actually knew how to design a disk drive.

As Frank Rose would write in *West of Eden*, his book about this era at Apple:

> [An official] Apple Value might have been "We work here, so we must be brilliant." Twiggy was the most visible result of this hubris, but the attitude itself was pervasive. Everybody at Apple seemed to think he was Woz. And the result was Twiggy, an engineering project that had turned into a nightmare.

Four years later, the result—expensive and unreliable—appeared on the Lisa, and played a major role in compromising that already compromised machine. John Vennard, who now ran the mass storage division (he was an old National Semi buddy of Mike Scott) after having run off Holt, continued to promise that Twiggy's problems would be cured in time for the Mac's first shipments.

Luckily, just as happened in the early days of the Mac project, members of the Lisa and Macintosh teams were quietly (that is, without Jobs knowing about it) talking. In particular, in February, Wayne Rosing, the Lisa engineering manager, dropped a few ugly facts on Bob Belleville, his Mac counterpart.

What Rosing said left Belleville in shock: Twiggy was proving to be a disaster. Apple's disk manufacturing plant in San Jose could not produce the drives anywhere fast enough to meet demand, primarily because most of the finished drives were defective and had to be rebuilt. And of those few that did trickle out to the Lisa manufacturing plant, many later blew up anyway. If you depend upon Twiggy, Rosing warned Belleville, you won't get the Mac out on time—maybe never. "Wayne," Belleville yelped, "there's no possible way!"

Needless to say, Belleville immediately ran to Jobs. Jobs, in fact, had been partly responsible for the problems with Twiggy: his rule, laid down for aesthetic reasons, that Apple computers not have noisy cooling fans had made the creation of Twiggy nearly impossible from the outset. Disk drives, with their electric motors, spinning platters and moving armatures, produce a lot of heat. In the uncooled heart of an Apple computer, a high-speed, advanced drive like Twiggy simply cooked, burning out its own chips and melting or distorting the Mylar diskette.

Jobs dashed off an angry letter to Markkula saying he'd lost faith in the mass storage division, then grabbed Belleville and took off for the San Jose plant. There, a furious Jobs interviewed the workers. The factory, a potential bottleneck for all Apple manufacturing, was a disaster. Most of the workers not only were temps but had never built disk drives before. The workers further admitted that it was a rare event—sometimes it didn't occur for scores of machines—when a Twiggy drive came off the assembly line for the first time and actually worked. And even many of those had to be sent back for minor repair. In other words, the initial yield of usable Twiggy drives, the guts of the Lisa, and soon the Mac, was *zero*.

At that news, Jobs nearly became unhinged. He threatened to fire everyone in the place. Belleville all but had to drag him out of the building to the parking lot, reminding him over and over that these were just foot soldiers, that the man he wanted was Vennard.

That showdown occurred at a Valentine's Day party. It was cinematic. The event was the announcement by the company of its newest Apple Fellows, Rich Page and Bill Atkinson of the Lisa group. Under a huge white tent, the Stanford marching band played, the company executives made speeches, employees drank from champagne glasses etched with Apple logos . . . and out at the far end of the parking lot, Steve Jobs verbally reamed out John Vennard.

But deep-sixing Twiggy only created the added challenge of coming up with a new disk drive system on the shortest possible notice. Mac team members flew in every direction, searching for a solution. The search centered on Japan; and it wasn't long before an anxious Jobs joined them.

The first stop was Alps. There, Jobs, Belleville, Holt and Dave Vaughan, head of Mac manufacturing, were given a presentation by company executives desperate to keep Apple's business. The Disk II had gotten Alps into the mass memory business and had made this second-tier company into a major player. So the company had gone all out in preparation for the meeting. The pièce de résistance was a mock-up, in milled aluminum, of the drive. It was gorgeous. Jobs and Holt were sold.

Belleville wasn't. He had a reputation for pessimism, but in a fairyland like Apple that was an important trait to have. Where Jobs saw a sleek new design and Holt saw the continuance of a happy business relationship with a strategic partner, Belleville rightly identified an unproven new design that might take years to perfect. Needless to say, he was pleased the group decided to continue its tour of Japanese manufacturers, even though Jobs thought it would be all but pro forma.

The rest of the trip was pure Jobs. Here's how Rose described it:

> For the next three days they visited other companies and looked at other drives. They weren't impressed by anything. They'd be ushered into a room and rafts of engineers would come out to show them their drives and Steve would pick one up and examine it for a minute with a look of extreme distaste and cry, "What are you showing me *this* for? This is a piece of crap! *Anybody* could build a better drive than this." . . . It was Steve's first trip to Japan, and he was indifferent to the niceties of doing business there. He'd show up wearing blue jeans at formal meetings with the heads of major corporations. The underlings were flabbergasted, but the corporate chieftains loved it. They'd all heard about this brash young California millionaire industrialist who'd started in a garage, and to meet him in person was—well, it was almost as good as going to Disneyland. And then, when he explained that the only reason he was holding their products up to ridicule was because he admired their company and he wanted their products to be the best

in the world—when he did that, with that riveting intensity that turned his eyes into magnets, they nearly swooned.

The team's final visit was to the venerable Sony Corp. Sony was building its drives by hand a few hundred units at a time and selling them to Hewlett-Packard. In other words, the drive was still essentially in the beta stage, still being checked out by customers, and so Sony had it located in a slummy skunk works outside Tokyo in the industrial town of Atsugi. Visiting the Gary, Indiana, of Japan was already guaranteed to put Jobs in a foul mood. Then, actually seeing the product, a messy kluge that looked half assembled, only made things worse. Jobs, and Holt with him, left Japan having decided to go with Alps. The lone dissenting vote was cast by Vaughan; as a manufacturing man, he could look past the clutter and see the quality of the Sony design. He was voted down.

Belleville, knowing better than to confront Jobs directly, kept his own counsel. He waited until the time was right and then went to Markkula. Markkula told Belleville to do what he had to do to get the Macintosh out in time. (It is interesting to note that this time Markkula didn't tell Jobs, which suggests a change in the relationship between the two.) And from that moment on, Belleville played double agent. He secretly met with a representative from Sony America, apprised him of the situation, and within days Hidetoshi Komoto, the Purdue-trained engineer who'd invented the drive, was flown over from Japan and sneaked into Apple. For the next week, Bandley 6 resembled a French farce, with Komoto whisked away into a far cubicle whenever Jobs appeared, then dragged out for hurried meetings whenever Jobs was gone. Komoto for his part never seemed to have understood why he was regularly yanked into corners.

Indeed, this farce even had a climax, which occurred when Jobs stopped off at a local drugstore to check out the magazine rack and ran into Komoto doing the same thing. Back at the office, Jobs wondered aloud what Komoto from Sony was doing in town. He was met with shrugs and blank stares.

In the end it was just as Belleville had feared. Alps couldn't get the drive right. Weeks slipped into months. The planned August introduction for Mac evaporated and now everyone at Pajaro knew that January was at risk. And if Apple missed January, especially with the still unknown PCjr, waiting in the wings, it could be disastrous.

The magnitude of that disaster was underscored by Floyd Kvamme. In one of his last contributions to the company, he ran the assembled executives through a thought problem—"target analysis process" was the formal gobbledygook—he'd often used at National Semiconductor. He drew a bull's-eye on a blackboard and solicited nearly forty answers to the question: What is the most important thing Apple has to accomplish in the next year? Then, with the group, he spent the next hour culling out the least important goals. In the end there was only one goal left in the center: "Successfully introduce the Macintosh."

There it was. Even the II and Lisa people agreed: everything depended now upon the Mac. And the Mac wasn't ready. This opened the gates. The assembled group turned on Jobs, who could only retreat. He offered them projected sales figures, but the group dismissed them. Everyone knew that all that mattered now was whether the Mac would be ready in January. Would the drives be ready?

Jobs, taken aback, could only prevaricate. In sixty to ninety days, he said, we'll know. That would be September, and everyone knew that left no margin for even the slightest slip. Moreover, they no longer trusted Jobs's pronouncements. They turned now to Belleville, the man immediately in charge of the drive problem. "Well, Bob?" asked Sculley.

Belleville was the only man in the room who knew that Komoto would be in town the next week with a working prototype designed exclusively for the Mac. He had betrayed his boss, but likely saved the company. Now he was about to be exposed. "In thirty days," he said, "we'll know for sure."

Jobs stared at him. How? In thirty days you could only test a finished . . . Then it hit him. He laughed. "You son of a bitch!" Once again, he had been saved from himself.

7.9 Copycat Fight

There were other events at that pivotal Pajaro meeting. Some were silly: for example, like two kids at Scout camp who can't get along, Jobs and Couch were sent out one evening on a walk along the beach to work out their differences. The walk was predictably futile. In a few months, buried under the Lisa collapse, Couch would be gone.

Another meeting proved much more fruitful. Apple's vice president of sales, Gene Carter, wanted full software compatibility between the Lisa and the Mac. That was understandable if the sales force was going to really offer the corporate world a full family of products. Jobs was adamant in his refusal: to make the Mac compatible with the Lisa would result in a much more expensive machine. They compromised on a special window on the Lisa screen where a user could run Mac software.

But it was another small gathering, one of such little moment at the time that Sculley didn't even mention it in his autobiography, that would ultimately determine the fate of Apple Computer. Sculley himself served up the notion that if Apple really wanted to succeed in the corporate world, then it should make its computers compatible not just with one another but with IBM too. This was, of course, heresy of the highest order. It was also the right thing to do. Sculley's instincts, trained in the Cola wars, were telling him the right thing. Just as Pepsi had copied Coke, ridden its coattails to riches, then used its superior innovation to pull ahead, so too might Apple, instead of trying to slow the IBM juggernaut in the workplace, join it, use its muscle to penetrate the market, then pull ahead with better products.

But having gone that far, Sculley stumbled. Apple was paying now for hiring a man without technical expertise. His proposal was quickly attacked by everyone. They pointed out the incompatibility between the Intel 8086 microprocessor and the II's 6502 and the Lisa/Mac's 68000. They argued that MS-DOS was optimized for the 8086, that it simply couldn't be carried over to the Apple machines.

But Sculley asked, now less forcibly, can't we add an Intel chip to our machines via one of the card slots? No, was the unanimous reply. Well, actually, yeah, except on the Mac, which had no card slots. But why do that? the group asked. If we play IBM's game they'll price-bomb us into dust. And besides—and this Jobs argued most vehemently—the whole meaning of Apple is to be the alternative to IBM, not its copycat. We've gone this far, succeeded this well, by setting our own standards. Why should we now imitate our own imitator?

At that, Sculley caved. He had his chance, but he had neither the will nor the knowledge to force it. The Apple management team, caught up in their own world, insular in their illusions about the business market, convinced of their own brilliance by the early success of the Lisa, closed their minds. The pirates, proud of their risk-taking bravery, had cowered from taking the biggest chance of all. There was only one person in the room who alone could have changed Apple's history by siding with Sculley: Steve Jobs. He wasn't afraid of risking everything. Moreover, he'd seen the Mac user interface and knew that nothing in the IBM arsenal could match it.

It would have been the visionary's greatest vision. And looking back over the intervening years and the rise of giant IBM clone companies that would dwarf even Big Blue in PCs, the mind swims. Imagine Apple in 1984 as a combination of Dell, Compaq and Gateway 2000, all with the Mac operating system. A world without the hegemony of Bill Gates and Microsoft.

But beating IBM at its own game wasn't an aesthetic that suited Steve

Jobs. He preferred to go his own way. And for now John Sculley couldn't stop him.

7.10 STUMBLE

The Pajaro meeting ended on a happy note. The distant storm clouds were obscured by the glow of the immediate good news. Lisa orders were strong, the Mac's problems seemed to be resolved, compatibility issues had been addressed and the new Apple II, the IIe, would be ready for the January launch event. Sculley even got caught up in the excitement. He boldly announced that he hadn't come to Apple to take it from a $1 billion to a $2 billion company. He was here to make it a $10 billion company. Everybody cheered. It was like the last day of summer camp.

The team returned to Cupertino energized and ready to tackle the hard but exciting months ahead. But by August, all hell had broken loose in the Lisa group as the 15,000 orders slumped to 12,000, and falling. Worse, the latest forecasts showed demand and production converging. Then they crossed. By September, estimated demand was 6,400 Lisas per month. Instead of the anticipated overdemand, there was overcapacity. Apple had invested in infrastructure for a demand of 11,000 Lisas per month. Now it was approaching the point where it would lose money on every computer it sold.

There were a number of reasons for this change of fortune, none of them good. The initial burst of demand had come from a new class of customers, still only barely understood, called *early adopters*. This group would buy anything new in technology, merely for the sake of being there first. This was not a large group, especially for $10,000 computers, but it temporarily inflated sales. Lisa went through that crowd in just three months. Now it was facing the real market of cold-blooded corporate MIS directors who looked askance at expensive, non-IBM computers from offbeat companies.

On top of that, even mainstream consumers quickly divided into two camps: those who wanted the Lisa but couldn't afford one, and those who were initially excited by the machine in concept but were disappointed by its reality.

Other factors were at work as well. The personal computing bubble had indeed burst, and the same shakeout that killed the game machine makers was now spreading up the ranks. More than a billion dollars would be collectively lost by the computer industry. Consumers, already overwhelmed by the Babel of different computers and operating systems, were now, having seen some major players fold, frightened to buy anything. Many decided to hold their purchases until the shakeout was over—when they would not only know who the winners were but could get a better deal. Those who *had* to buy now typically went to the safest vendor: IBM. Even the Apple II, the Iron Horse of personal computing, suddenly experienced a slump in sales.

The wreck of the PCjr didn't help anything but Apple's morale. In the company's eyes, there was now nothing in the path of the Mac. But in reality, IBM had not really been wounded: it actually gained a little market share. And, worse for Apple, consumers were now even more wary (even IBM can't be trusted!) of buying radically new computer designs.

This industry-wide recession was not the triumph John Sculley had in mind. Instead he was reduced to damage control. Apple's rapid hiring was stopped, its employment frozen at 5,500. Sculley slashed the price of the Lisa, while at the same time expanding its dealer network from a controlled collection of 150 top-notch stores to just about anyone who wanted it (the final number was about 350 dealers). But still he couldn't stanch the bleeding. For the fourth quarter ended September 30, 1983, Apple's profits fell 80 percent from $25 million to $5 million. The stock tumbled too. Sculley had been justifiably proud that, under his brief tenure, Apple's stock had hit a historic high of $63 per share. That was in June; by October it had collapsed to just $23, a bottom it wouldn't reach again until the crisis of 1997.

It got so bad that Don Kendall called from Pepsi and joked that at a recent board meeting someone had calculated that Sculley had already made and lost $9 million in personal wealth in little more than a half year at Apple. That was a little reminder of Sculley's treason to the Old Guard by going out West for stock options. Then to rub it in, Kendall, laughing the whole time, asked his ex-son-in-law if he'd like his old job back.

Sculley would later write:

> How could we introduce a revolutionary new product like Macintosh from a failing company? Momentum and timing are everything in marketing. Few people would want to buy a computer from a company that isn't doing well. We had to get the momentum back.

7.11 Rescue

In the end, of course, it was the Apple II, the Little Computer That Could, that pulled a sidetracked Apple over the mountain. Treated with contempt by the spiritual leader of its own company, perpetually reduced at Apple family gatherings to the role of maiden aunt who refuses to die, Woz's creation nevertheless had become a cult object to millions of computer owners. Like the Model T, it could be adapted for a hundred different tasks and do all of them, if not brilliantly, then with predictable pluck.

After a half decade, the II was no longer merely an Apple product. It was instead an industry, an extended family, and a religion. It was also a money machine that had financed the III, the Lisa and the Mac. Apple sold it to dealers at three times the manufacturing cost, then the dealers themselves added their own sizable markup—and customers *still* saw it as a bargain. Scores of little companies had sprung up to offer special internal boards and external support machines for the II. Hundreds of others, from large companies like Microsoft to solitary programmers with a clever idea, had designed a well-stocked library of application programs for the II—the first such library of its kind for a personal computer and the model for every important computer that came after. And Apple II's, new and old, stock or so stuffed with custom Input/Output boards they nearly ignited, could be found in professional offices, household dens and, perhaps most of all, classrooms throughout the world. More than any other machine, the Apple II had created the personal computer revolution dreamed of by the idealists at Homebrew. It had also brought computers to education. And, though unacknowledged and often sneaked in through the back door, the II had also cut the path for Apple into the corporate world.

But Steve Jobs no longer cared about the II. He publicly derided it, saying the II group was the dull and boring division, that it had "shitty" ideas, and calling its engineers "Clydesdales" because they were little more than dull draft horses. Even worse, Jobs undermined sales by broadly hinting to the world that once the Mac arrived on the scene the II would be obsolete.

Sculley's assumption of the leadership of the II group, so celebrated at the time, did nothing to help. When he asked his question at Pajaro about IBM compatibility, not even he mentioned the II as a possible vehicle. And while the executives were living it up at the beach, the II group (with the III team) were meeting in the cramped quarters of Rickey's Hyatt House in Palo Alto in one of the tiny rooms stuck in the parking lot behind the hotel. The III team didn't even know its presence was superfluous: at Pajaro the top brass had decided to kill their product. The new-product manager, Dave Fradin, readying a follow-up machine, the Apple III+, found out his fate through a roundabout series of calls even as the meeting was taking place.

But if the II group was starved for love within Apple, it drew strength from its loyal customers. Every time the II seemed to fade the team managed to perform another miracle. The original II had been supplanted by the II+, then most recently by the brilliant IIe, the last in many ways the apotheosis of the first generation of personal computing.

Now there was a new II in the works, the IIb, which would ultimately see life as the IIc. But its introduction was still a long way off—it wouldn't help Apple in the desperate months to come. To get the Mac introduced right, Apple would have to depend upon the III it despised and the current II it ignored.

Both came through. Even as it was being discontinued, the III was still selling 2,000 machines per month. Moreover, thanks to an automatic order system in the accounting department, the previous December Apple accidentally ordered the equivalent of a year's worth of new III parts. That meant Apple had enough machines still in inventory (about 6,000) and enough parts (the equivalent of about 12,000 machines) to keep selling III's into the spring of 1994. Even at the current rate, that meant $30 million or more in unexpected revenues that otherwise would have to be written off. It was perhaps the last time Apple would successfully screw up.

Dave Fradin, having seen the plugs pulled on his project just weeks before, now was thrilled to find the patient still breathing. In a heroic bit of planning and hard work—the kind of thing Apple project managers and team members were becoming famous for—Fraden and his III team put together in two weeks a complete plan for the future of the III, including a rollout of the III+ as a niche-oriented product for legal, medical and real estate professionals complete with specialty software. The plan succeeded so well that in the end Apple sold off most of its inventory of III's. After that, the III's user base of 120,000 owners proved so loyal to their machines that they continued to buy III's and develop software among themselves into the early 1990s . . . long after Apple had effectively erased the III from its official history.

The Apple II, on the other hand, was very much alive, even if its sales had taken a momentary stumble in the face of the PCjr. Sculley became a true believer—and in the autumn of 1983 he at last shone as a II lover. It may have been, less than one year into his ten-year tenure, Sculley's finest hour at Apple. The II slump played to his strengths: it was a marketing problem, the public was confused and resistant and the biggest competitor was preparing to unveil a new killer campaign. Sculley had been down this road many times. He immediately boosted the ad money for the II, and at the same time slashed prices, offered dealer incentives and rebates to buyers—all in the face of the expected PCjr onslaught.

It was a slick play, a lesson from a master of consumer marketing.

Christmas now approached. Consumers, still wary after the PCjr, took a second look at the II, with its great reputation and new low price . . . and decided to buy.

As noted, in December 1983, the last month for Apple to turn around its fortunes, Apple sold 110,000 Apple II's, for total company revenues of $160 million. It was the biggest single month's sales in the II's history. The Apple II had pulled it off one last time. Even the Lisa's sales temporarily improved. Apple was now positioned to charge into the Mac introduction with flags flying.

7.12 Woz Redux

One of the most satisfying aspects of the II's last great hurrah was that its creator was on hand to see it. One morning in June, a few weeks after the Pajaro gathering, the greatest inventor of the PC era quietly strolled into the Triangle Building, walked up to the receptionist and inquired about a job.

In anybody else, this might have been a clever bit of role playing, the "humble genius." But with Steve Wozniak, it was genuine. He had no appointment. He didn't really know who was running the Apple II division now. The stunned receptionist sent him to Dave Paterson, one of the general managers of the division. There, Woz announced that he wanted to work on the II project.

He got the job.

It had been a long, strange two-year trip for Steve Wozniak since the plane crash. He had officially remained an Apple employee at a minimal salary, but in fact he had been far away. Coming out of the semi-coma had been like flipping a reset switch in Woz's brain. It was as if in his thirty-year old body he had regained the mind he'd had at eighteen before all the computer madness had begun. And when that happened, Woz found he had little interest in engineering or design. Rather, in an odd sort of way, he wanted to start over fresh.

But, of course, that was impossible. He was famous, rich, twice married and a public figure. Yet, in a poignant way, Woz still tried. He went back to Berkeley, this time attending under an assumed name, "Rocky Clark" (derived from his dog's and wife's names) and took classes in subjects like economics and psychology, with a little computer science thrown in. No one was fooled. His classmates and teachers humored him, but almost from the first day the word was out that he was the Great Woz.

Even playing poor student, Woz couldn't escape the charms of his own great wealth, the legions of hangers-on willing to turn whims to reality. One of those whims hit Woz while he was driving from class to his home in Scotts Valley. He was listening to music on the car radio when it suddenly struck him: Why not put on a concert? And not just any concert, but a Woodstock for the 1980s! With computers and bands and New Age ideas and all the rest!

A lot of other people were probably musing on the same idea at the same time, this having been the proper interval from the 1960s to call for a regathering of the tribes. But none of the others were as rich as Steve Wozniak. It wasn't long before Woz, via the conduit of a Santa Cruz nightclub owner (of course) was connected with Peter Ellis, a Santa Cruz businessman, est graduate and promoter (of course) and they hooked up in turn with the San Francisco rock impresario Bill Graham (of course, of course).

The result was the US festival, a production of UNUSON (unite us in song), an organization founded and financed by Woz. The event itself, which took place in a hot desert valley in the San Bernardino Mountains east of Los Angeles, drew 200,000 people and featured such acts as Tom Petty, the Police and Fleetwood Mac. If the music wasn't particularly memorable, the activities surrounding the show were. There were laser shows, a giant video screen showing the performers, an inflated "Sensonics Theater" dome featuring videos and high-quality sound, a hot-air balloon with the Apple logo and air-conditioned booths exhibiting the latest computers and other equipment. Woz sat in his headquarters, an old house on the hilltop above the madness, listening to the music and occasionally venturing down into the throng.

Ever loyal to its favorite founder, Apple was there too, with a booth showing off its wares. The company had been involved with the event from the beginning—though not without reservations. UNUSON's management was filled with unusual characters—sharp-eyed figures who talked the New Age talk but walked like used-car salesmen. The Apple folks, many of them est graduates themselves in the 1970s, recognized the look and silently prayed for Woz. They were secretly relieved when the festival went off without a major hitch.

Woz himself was out $12.5 million for his little vanity Woodstock, an amount more than offset by the $18 million he made that summer on his Apple stock. In fact, he was so happy about the event that, despite the warnings of friends and acquaintances, he announced he was going to do it again the next year. Once was eccentric; twice was stupid. This time, Apple bowed out, as did most of the other honorable people involved with the project, leaving USII in the hands of every con artist, sleazeball and sharpie who could figure out a way to get their hands on the multimillionaire's wallet. The Candide of computers had now become the patsy of the pop world.

USII, held on Memorial Day weekend in 1983, just days after Sculley and crew were meeting at Pajaro, drew an equally enormous crowd, but of a wholly different demographic. This mob came to party. The result was a disaster: 145 people in jail, 120 hurt, one dead from an overdose, another beaten to death with a tire iron.

The dead, the hospitalized, the jailed, the feuding bands, the trashed site—all were merely prelude to Ellis and the other organizers rewarding themselves with hundreds of thousands of dollars for a job well done. Everyone, from the est devotees to the musicians to the promoters, took Steve Wozniak's money and went home. Woz, having burned up $25 million in just two weekends, ignored the world's laughter, pronounced the two US Festivals a great success ("I think the fans got their money's worth. I know I got mine") and within a month was standing in the reception area of the Triangle Building. In October 1998, co-hosting a Bay Area rock radio station, Woz would make the extraordinary remark that he had fully anticipated that the US Festivals would be profitable, "because, after all, profitability is the real test of whether an idea is good or not."

Woz arrived at Apple in time for a late summer meeting of Apple III engineers, convened by Sculley to tell them that their product was dead. Woz came away impressed that Sculley was a real businessman. Sculley didn't even recognize Woz.

As summer turned into fall, and as Apple started to ramp up for the Macintosh introduction, Woz devoted his time to making a mouse work on the Apple II. He succeeded, but not without the endless distractions that came with fame. Once the world heard he was back at a desk at Apple, the phone perpetually rang with requests for interviews, advice, speeches and connections. Woz's very presence improved the II group's morale in this dispiriting period, but any hopes the group had that Woz would become its champion on executive row were soon dashed. Woz wanted nothing to do with headquarters or managing; he wanted to once again hide in his cubicle and design.

7.13 Epiphany

The great revenue figures in December brightened the first days of January 1984. Apple owned the buzz again. By the first week of January, as rumors about not only the Mac but the 1984 ad began to swarm, Apple became the focus of every eye in high tech.

There were many doubters. After all, Apple had promised the moon a year before and all it delivered was the Lisa, which everyone now knew was a failure. Add to that the fiasco of the PCjr and there was some question not just whether Apple could come out with a fundamentally new computer but if anyone could at this point in the industry's history.

The day after the Macintosh introduction even the hardest skeptics had to admit that Apple had pulled off an unprecedented coup in personal computing. On first glance, Apple seemed to have done *everything* right. The Mac had all the innovations of the Lisa (and more), the sturdiness and low price of the II and a charm all its own. Jobs got his wish: the Mac design was simple, yet elegant—a true classic. Even the graphics in the ads and documents supporting the Mac were superb: the vast white spaces, the lean and elegant typeface so reminiscent of Jobs himself, the simple slashes of color that effortlessly captured the form of the Mac box and screen. If the IBM PC was your lawn mower, and the Apple II was the nice kid down the street, the Mac was your pet, even your child. The bond was instant and visceral. Thousands of people loved the Macintosh the first time they saw it, and more than a decade later were still deep in that affair.

Everyone interested in personal computers—and by 1984 that numbered in the tens of millions in the United States alone—was anxious to see a real Macintosh in person, to put their fingers on the keyboard and slide the mouse around (still a very new sensation) and see if the image on the little screen was as precise as it appeared in the big *Newsweek* advertising supplement. And when the first Macs started showing up in local computer shops—and they arrived quickly, thanks to a magnificent new $20 million automated Mac factory across the Bay from Cupertino in Fremont—people lined up for the chance to see it. Even the most cynical IBM PC loyalist took a moment to sneak over and play with the little Mac.

The experience was electrifying. From the first-time computer user to Bill Gates, everyone who walked into a computer store and experienced the Macintosh knew that it was touched by magic. The experienced programmers dismissively tapped a few keys, then, blown away by the sharpness of the bit-mapped display and by the versatility of the windowed interface, sat down for an hour of intense experimentation. The graphic artist who neither liked nor used computers, played with the mouse—then suddenly drew a bouquet of flowers. The middle-aged couple stepped in from the sidewalk out of curiosity, took their first look at the New Digital World and concluded that these computers were easier than they thought. The boomers listened knowingly to the Wyndham Hill background music on the instructional cassette and concluded that computers were no longer just the province of freaks, but *cool.*

Steve Jobs had done what he set to do when he hijacked the Mac project. He had created the first true *personal* computer, a masterpiece of form and function.

7.14 The Peopleless Computer

And nobody bought it.

Before the Mac was introduced, Jobs had confidently predicted two million would be sold the first year. Even the realists within the company were wildly optimistic. An early estimate predicted monthly sales of the Mac at 80,000 per month, or one million units per year. Kvamme had managed to cool that ardor somewhat by pointing out that a million Macs represented $2.5 billion in revenues, a mark reached in the first year by only one product in history, the Boeing 727, a product with a wholly different market and pricing structure. So the figure was lowered to 425,000 units in 1984—still a billion dollars, and equal to Apple's total sales in 1983. But the Mac launch was so strong, the product so well received by both the public and the press, the Mac marketers saw no reason to doubt their predictions.

But even as Jobs and the gang were setting off on the road show to pitch the product, the Mac's weaknesses were beginning to show. One of those mistakes was Sculley's, and it was evident the first time you saw the Mac: its price tag. Raskin's $995 People's Computer had become, under Jobs, a computer with a target price of $1,995. Given all the added features, that was still a tremendous bargain. To sit down at the Mac for the first time, give it a test drive, then look up and see it was all available for under two grand . . . that would have been exhilarating. Jobs knew it better than anyone; by now he had an intuitive sense of how the market valued new computers.

But the decision wasn't his. And John Sculley, coming out of the soda-pop world, operated under a more rigorous and traditional pricing model. You priced high up front to cover development and initial marketing costs, then systematically cut prices to gain market share. It was a good model for video games, calculators and even minicomputers. But it was wrong for a still immature business like personal computing. There, the game was still to maximize market share in order to control the industry standard. The big profits would then be made on the back end in software and future generations of hardware. That's why, a decade later, Microsoft, running late behind Netscape and trying to capture the standard for Internet browsers, gave away its first generation of products. Sculley didn't understand any of this yet. He looked at the multimillion-dollar ad campaign (including twenty-page ad inserts in *News-*

week, Time, Forbes, Fortune and *Business Week)*, the $20 million factory and the tens of millions spent on developing the Mac, and—after neatly juking Jobs into believing the $1,995 price would hold—announced that the Macintosh would sell for $2,495.

The announcement did more than break the Mac team's heart. It also forever removed the Mac from being the People's Computer. At $1,995 it was a no-brainer; but at $2,495 it became a premium product you thought twice about before buying. Some began to have doubts. For example, on the matter of software application programs, there was a word processing program—but you couldn't write more than eight pages at a time. There was a slick little spreadsheet program—but it was slow. Macpaint, a graphics program, was thrilling—but it quickly raised expectations beyond what the Apple could give. And Apple was willing to sell you a modem to put the Mac on a network—but it didn't have a telecommunications program to run that modem. What other software was available for the Mac was usually buggy and slow, the former due to the rush to market, the latter to the huge memory requirements for that nifty screen.

But these were minor problems compared to the Big Mistake. If the price was Sculley's error, the Mac's tiny memory was Jobs's. Jef Raskin had originally wanted to put on 64K of memory in the Mac, a tribute to his own dogmatism (people don't need more than that) and the era (memory was expensive in 1980). But Moore's Law and rising consumer expectations had done their part, and even from the most conservative perspective the 64K of 1980 should have been 256K by 1984. A progressive view would have realized not only that memory was becoming essentially free but that demand for it (thanks to ever-larger files and programs) was becoming insatiable. From that perspective, any new computer should have had a 1Meg of core memory at the time of the Mac introduction.

But Jobs saw things differently. Half of him was still stuck with the vision for the Mac he'd co-opted from Raskin. The other half, like the senior citizen who still secretly believes that houses should cost $25,000 and cars $1,000, was still trapped in the Homebrew world, where 4K of memory was not only horribly expensive but more than enough to do anything you could imagine. Being also incredibly facile, Jobs managed to rationalize all this—and convince those around him—by wrapping his prejudices in contemporary philosophy: in this case, Joseph Schumpeter's "Small is Beautiful." Anyone who disagreed with him, as Mac marketer Joanna Hoffman did in 1982 when she proposed a hard disk for the Mac, got verbally abused and accused of being a Xerox bigot or a minicomputer lover.

As a result, the Macintosh hit the streets in 1984 with only 128K of memory (the same as the PCjr), a single floppy and no hard disk drive. By then even Jobs should have known better: that legendary verbal greeting from the Mac at the product's introduction had been possible only because the machine on display was a fake—it had been custom-built with beefed-up memory to do the job.

A 128K memory wouldn't have been too bad if the Mac had been an ordinary machine. Thousands of PCs with that much memory were still being sold every month. But the fancy bit-mapped display on the Mac was a giant memory black hole. Once you turned on the display there wasn't much memory space left to do anything. The nightmare really began when you attempted to engage in some memory-intensive activity on the Mac, such as copying a disk. Then, because the machine could hold only small chunks of data at a time, you were forced to pull out the original diskette, put in the copy, then pull it out and put in the original . . . over and over again endlessly. One test put the number of diskette reinsertions at fifty times per copy. It was enough to kill an afternoon, tear apart your elbow and drive you insane.

Yet, for many, even that limitation wasn't enough to keep them from achieving congress with the Mac. Author Douglas Adams (as quoted by Steven Levy) explained it this way:

> I can remember when . . . a group of people [were] crowded around a small beige-colored box that looked like a toy . . . I watched, at first with mild curiosity, then gradually I began to feel that kind of roaring, floating sensation which meant I had my first experience with MacPaint. But what I (and I think everybody else who bought the machine in the early days) fell in love with was not the machine itself, which was ridiculously slow and underpowered, but a romantic idea of the machine. And that romantic idea had to sustain me through the realities of actually working on the 128K Mac.

But for every romantic like Adams, there were a dozen others who loved the Mac, wished they owned one, but decided against making a purchase. For them, the Mac became the perfect computer to play with at your friend's house.

And "play" was the operative term. Underpowered and overpriced, with a tiny software library and with an arrogance that manifested itself in everything from the single diskette drive to the missing cursor keys to the lack of add-in board slots, the Mac, which seemed at first to announce a new consumer revolution, now seemed little more than a clever novelty, a toy for the techno-obsessed. Certainly that was the angle many tech writers now took, their message pushed along behind the scenes by an IBM that feared the Mac much more than it let on. Sales began to plummet. By late summer, there were months when Apple sold only 5,000 Macs, a tenth of its goal and no better than the Lisa. Apple was very close to having a second disaster in two years.

But there was one crucial difference. This time, the world wanted the Mac to succeed. Part of this (nonbuying) support came from the charms of the computer itself, but much also derived from the growing fear of IBM hegemony. With the shakeout now over and most of the other corporate players dead or crippled, Apple was now seen as the last best hope for a personal computer industry free from Big Blue's control. The media pressed Jobs for a solution: Was there a more powerful "Fat Mac" in the offing? Sure, said Jobs, vamping, and we'll have it ready by early 1985.

Once again, Steve Jobs was unexpectedly saved from himself by one of his subordinates. This time it was Burrell Smith. From the beginning, Smith had disapproved of Jobs's decision to put only 128K of memory in the Mac. Smith simply went around Jobs and secretly designed the machine to hold four times that much memory without any major redesign. As a result, the 512K Fat Mac proved ready to ship by September 1984. It cost the early adopters a thousand bucks to upgrade to the new memory size; but grumble as they might, they had no choice. Not if they wanted to run any of the tardy applications programs that were just now coming out for the Mac. Throw in another $400 and you could add a second disk drive that plugged into the back of the computer. In other words, for just under $4,000 (not including software) you could now own the Mac that should have been.

7.15 FOLLIES

The upgrades silenced the detractors, but did little for sales. Meanwhile, a kind of collective madness seemed to descend upon Apple Computer, beginning at the very top, then spreading first to the Mac group and then to the entire company.

Jobs's behavior, always quixotic, had become bizarre in the year before the Mac introduction. In February 1983 he put on an appropriately late Christmas party for the Mac team. It was a formal dinner-dance at San Francisco's St. Francis Hotel; black tie with music provided by two orchestras. That nobody else on the team even owned a tuxedo (or wanted to), that few were familiar with ballroom dancing and that most had little experience with an evening in a grand hotel seemed to have no impact on Steve Jobs. This was the kind of event a world-class team like the Mac group should have, and by God, they were going to have it.

Jobs's date that night was Joan Baez, whom he had been seeing lately. Baez had been a hero of Jobs's in high school, and this burgeoning relationship had caused considerable talk. Anyone who rode in Jobs's big new Mercedes was treated to a hearing of Baez's unreleased new album. That Baez, almost old enough to be Jobs's mother, knew nothing about computers and was as much out of place with the Mac crowd as they were with her, didn't seem to matter to Jobs either. In his black tux, he was Jay Gatsby putting on a swank party and dancing with the Daisy of his teenage dreams.

The weirdness only increased as the months passed. One rich source of it was the relationship between Jobs and Sculley. They seemed almost inseparable, the bonds greater than mere mutual respect. Sometimes they even seemed to finish each other's sentences. They spent weekends together, and there were even shots of the pair in the woods, shirtless, looking part father and son and part lovers. And to sit through a meeting in the boardroom with the two, as they carried on a private dialogue with each other, reinforcing each other's views, ending each other's thoughts, smiling knowingly at each other's code words and refusing to allow disagreements to stick, was to realize that no lovers or family members were ever *this* simpatico. Then you understood that what you were really seeing was two boys, two best pals, so deeply involved in a game and each other that they had lost track of the rest of the world. They were deaf to their mothers calling them home for dinner.

As Sculley would later recall: "He was the only person I ever met whom I could speak with on multiple levels. We felt we were living life on several different planes at all times. We spoke, thought and worked in synchronization."

Jobs, now playing FDR facing the Depression, publicly announced that the Mac would be made or broken in the first Hundred Days. Soon that became the rallying cry for the entire company—and the benchmark set for Apple by both industry analysts and the press. Meanwhile, exactly what constituted true success was unclear: Jobs was quoted at saying he expected to sell a half million Macs the first year; Sculley publicly cut that number in half. Meanwhile, the internal memos predicting a million units sold by the end of 1985 had also been made public.

Jobs responded to this challenge by hitting the road armed with Macs to give away to every faddish artist, image maker and trendsetter he could find. It was a jetted-up version of his old days riding the bus around Silicon Valley trying to line up computer shops. And the group he took with him was remarkably similar: Wozniak, his old friend Dan Kottke, Andy Hertzfeld and Burrell Smith. Hard-core freaks and techies, pulled together again as if they were good-luck charms, on the road once more selling Bibles to believers.

They crossed the country visiting computer clubs to give demonstrations, and, when they could find them, celebrities on whom to bestow free Macs. It should have been a great time, a celebration of Apple's first decade by the geniuses who'd built its great products. But it was the opposite. Smith and Hertzfeld, coming off their herculean labors on the Mac, were exhausted and showing the first signs of battle fatigue and depression.

But Wozniak was far worse. Hertzfeld had taken along on the trip a copy of a new book about Atari. Finishing it, he handed the book to Woz. And there, on the plane, in perhaps the most poignant moment in the Apple story, Woz finally read the real story of the computer game Breakout: how Jobs had taken advantage of him, suckered him into doing the design work, and worst of all, then cheated him out of nearly all the money he had earned. As he sat there, stunned, rereading the words, the truth of what had happened rolled over Woz like a wave. All those years of trusting his friends, the company they'd built together, *everything* was based on a lie.

He cried. No one on the plane knew what to say.

It was a miserable time for Steve Wozniak. He had wasted a fortune on a boondoggle, learned of the betrayal of his best friend and in a few months would be publicly humiliated around the world when his wife was arrested in Los Angeles trying to scalp the free tickets to the Summer Olympics she'd been given by Apple. Within a year, increasingly embittered, unable to focus on the design of a new Apple II, Wozniak again walked out of Apple Computer. "Poor Woz," said Steve Jobs.

Meanwhile, Jobs was in his element. The program to hand out Macs to the famous, a more cynical version of Apple's 1982 "Kid's Can't Wait" program to get corporations to donate Apple II's—for a tax write-off—to elementary school classrooms, had been mischievously dubbed "Stars Can't Wait." Jobs took to it with abandon. He was in his element. He flew across America to deliver a Mac to Mick Jagger (whose daughter proved more interested than he was). He sat on the floor of Yoko Ono's apartment at Julian Lennon's birthday party and demonstrated the Mac to Andy Warhol, who shouted with uncharacteristic excitement, "My God! I drew a circle!" (and a year later did ads for the Commodore Amiga).

Meanwhile, Jobs's personal life was taking on a similar celebrity sheen. He had become an overnight sex symbol among the chattering classes, and his social calendar was filled with high-profile partnerings. Some of these relationships, like that with architect Maya Lin, of Vietnam memorial fame, appeared to be serious, then quickly cooled. He was a global figure now, one of the most famous people in the world, a torch carrier of his generation.

And when he wasn't out chasing stars or being one himself, Jobs was back at Apple obsessing over his own latest fantasies.

The most emblematic of these was the Apple 1984 annual report. Annual reports are among the greatest paradoxes of modern business. All public companies are required by the SEC to make an annual report to shareholders of their earnings or losses and of their assets and liabilities. Theoretically, this could be done in about five pages of an earnings statement, balance sheet and footnotes. But companies almost never settle for that. Instead, they produce a slick booklet that typically contains a collection of vanity photos of the company's executives, a few thousand words about the company's operations that are so vetted by lawyers as to be meaningless, color photos of company operations that show exactly nothing and a letter to shareholders from the CEO that is a small miracle of euphemism, cliché and evasion. The company proudly hands the reports out by the thousands to people who never read them. And every twelve months the cycle begins again.

It was just this fragile and worthless vehicle upon which Steve Jobs chose to waste his precious time and energy. The 1984 Apple annual report, he decided, would be not just any annual report, but the greatest annual report of all time, a document for the ages, a masterpiece of design and content that would be a touchstone for anyone in years to come curious about the wellsprings of Apple's greatness. It was as if Jobs had decided to create the finest owner's warranty in business history, the greatest and most beautiful power cord. In choosing the annual report, Jobs was making a devastating statement about himself as a manager: unable to distinguish between things of importance and mere trifles, he was a young man without perspective.

It was a magnificent folly. Three succeeding teams of professional writers prepared drafts of the body copy. None of them met Jobs's approval—though all received handsome checks. In the end the copy was written in-house by the same person who'd written the more pedestrian (and more realistic) 1983 annual report. For the photos in the annual report, Jobs hired, at $50,000 per day, the team that had shot the classic black-and-white photos for Fleetwood Mac albums. The assignment was to record the members of all of Apple's product teams (with emphasis on the Mac). When the first round of shots didn't meet Jobs's standards, the camera crew was brought back—to the tune of $100,000. Finally, the capper of the report was to be a photo-essay showing all those famous stars Jobs had contacted proudly using their free Macs to change the Course of History. But it didn't quite work out that way. Sure, there were famous folks—the photo of Jim Henson was particularly striking, but more for his puppeteer's fingers than anything to do with computers). But with the exception of Kurt Vonnegut, who'd written the first two pages of his new novel *Galapagos* on his Mac, most of the applications were impressive only in how pedestrian they were. Dianne Feinstein, for example, wrote business letters on her Mac, a task she could have performed a lot better at that moment on an IBM PC.

This was Jobs as Ozymandias. The thousands who received their 1984 Apple annual report looked at it, were impressed, then threw it away. The shrewder shareholders asked how much this little vanity project had cost and wondered what kind of company would be this needlessly extravagant with its profits. In fact, the annual report had cost between $5 million and $10 million, according to inside reports. In the end, the editor on the project, who'd slept on his office floor for most of two months and who had bowed before Jobs's every changing whim, was scapegoated and fired.

But before that happened, one writer got an unexpected glimpse of the turmoil roaring at the heart of the company. Late one night, sitting with a company vice president in a conference room at Apple headquarters, struggling with the fourth draft of the second iteration of the copy, this writer was stunned to watch the vice president (later a key figure in the Sculley era) suddenly lose it. Frustrated and tired, the executive suddenly began to rant about everything that was wrong with Apple: the prima donnas, the little fiefdoms, but most of all, the unpredictability of Steve Jobs. Then the executive leaped to his feet, marched over to a poster on the wall—it showed a still from the "1984" commercial—and punched it to the floor. "You want to know where Big Brother really is?" he shouted. "It's not at IBM. It's right here!"

At the end of 1984, Joanna Hoffman, back marketing the Mac in the United States after international duty, was asked to prepare a forecast of Mac sales for a meeting with Jobs. As she studied the numbers covering Macintosh sales to date, she realized to her shock that these weren't real sales numbers, but estimates dating back to the weeks just after the Mac introduction back in January. The entire company was operating off fake numbers. As she told Steven Levy: "Nobody had the guts to tell Steve that his original forecasts were stupid." Instead, Jobs, tucked deep in his psychic bunker, heard only good news from the front.

As the real sales numbers began to leak out to insiders, they could no longer ignore the depressing truth: They had built the greatest computer in history, an invention that was supposed to change the world, and nobody wanted it. One by one the team began to drift away. Bruce Horn, who had been part of the heroic last-minute fix of the Filer program, felt he hadn't gotten enough credit or money for his contribution and quit. His partner on the Filer project, Steve Capps, moved to Paris and tried to write music-related third-party software for the Mac. Randy Wigginton, who kept himself distracted for months working on a cleanup version of MacWrite, collapsed and spent much of the next year in bed watching television. He later said, "Everyone who worked there identified totally with their work—we all believed we were on a mission from God. When people didn't buy it, we were majorly depressed."

In the autumn of 1984, frustrated by the inertia in the Mac design program and tired of waiting for orders from above, Burrell Smith set out on his own initiative to restart the lab. Gathering together other Mac veterans, he created his own skunk works, "Turbotown," to build a new, more powerful Turbo Macintosh. This new Mac would feature a pair of new custom chips that would make the machine not only more powerful but less expensive, a crisp, photographic-quality black-and-white screen and, most important, a built-in hard disk drive. It was an engineer's dream computer, and Turbotown would be an engineer's dream work environment, free from all the suits and rules and memos, just as the Mac operation had been in its early days.

But that was the problem. The new Apple, the one being built by Sculley with the tacit approval of Jobs, didn't want unruly Turbotowns anymore. It also didn't want the Turbo Mac either, at least as it was configured. And as Smith bogged down in chip design, the ever-skeptical Bob Belleville made his move. At yet another off-site meeting at Pajaro, Belleville made his case: Apple could not afford two new Mac projects: the Turbo Mac and the one he believed more salable, a modular Mac with a full-sized screen and an optional disk drive. In the meeting, Jobs held out for the Turbo Mac, but afterward in the hallway he changed his mind. And by the time he returned to Cupertino on Monday, he had decided to kill the Turbo Mac and with it Turbotown. He informed Smith, in the ultimate insult to a man who hated bureaucracies, that the design of the new Mac would have to be left to a committee.

In retrospect, Belleville and Jobs were probably right for that time. They got their modular, big-screen Mac—though it would soon also hold a hard disk. But their heavy-handedness, Jobs's inexplicable failure to use his wiles, cost them Burrell Smith. Smith went on to co-found Mac display maker Radius Inc. with Mike Boich, the first Macintosh evangelist. But he was so bitter that for years he refused even to drive by Apple's headquarters.

That left one last founding figure on the Mac team, Andy Hertzfeld, who had been there from the Texaco Tower era. These days, Hertzfeld seemed an anachronism, the last designer with the old Homebrew sensibility in a company that was trying every day to be more like IBM. Hertzfeld had a running feud with Belleville, whom he believed personified everything wrong with the new Apple. When he heard that Smith was leaving, Hertzfeld snapped. Hertzfeld's dream was even more ambitious than Smith's: he saw Turbotown as the core of a new design team that would set out to create the next insanely great Apple project, the true successor to the Mac. And Smith was crucial to the plan.

Now that dream was dying fast. In desperation, Hertzfeld took his case to Sculley. As Sculley listened, he dumped out all of his frustrations with Belleville, with the new Apple, with the death of the dream. Receiving no response, Hertzfeld grew desperate. The situation is so bad, Hertzfeld told Sculley, that Apple is now about to lose the man who created the Macintosh: Burrell Smith himself! The name hardly seemed to register with Sculley. Lab guys were lab guys. Sculley thanked Hertzfeld for stopping by.

Andy Hertzfeld walked out of the meeting and out of Apple. He kept up a good front, but later admitted that for a month thereafter he cried himself to sleep every night.

7.16 Blue Bust

By early 1985, there was no denying that sales of the Macintosh were nowhere near predictions and that the company was in serious trouble.

Apple had managed to keep up a good front through the previous year. By the summer of 1984, it could still proclaim terrific sales figures, but a sizable chunk of that (50,000 machines) came from a single group, the Apple University Consortium, a group of twenty-four schools, including Stanford and Harvard, which offered the Macs to students at discount prices. Thanks to that order, Apple could announce on Day 101 that it had shipped 70,000 Macs. That was a little less than the internal projection, but a lot more than the public one. As a result, Apple could claim the Mac was a huge success, profitable in its very first quarter.

Unfortunately, the company began to believe its own press releases. Now it predicted 80,000 units for the month of September alone. August saw only 15,000 Macs shipped. In desperation, the Mac sales force, realizing that the business market wasn't panning out fast enough, began trying to sell the machine to schools—thus poaching on the II's territory and further aggravating the hatred between the two groups.

In October, the company had its second annual sales meeting in Hawaii. The 1983 meeting had been a wild success and Apple, now addicted to Big

Events, decided to make this year's even more spectacular. It would prove to be Apple's biggest party ever, complete with laser shows, Don Ho, banquets, lei-making seminars and endless quantities of booze and sun.

Given the location, the incongruous theme of the meeting was "Bluebusters," a play on the previous summer's hit movie *Ghostbusters*, with a touch of *The Blues Brothers*. It seemed that everywhere you looked there was a figure in blue suit, fedora, sunglasses, briefcase and ceramic mask cakewalking to the Bluebusters' theme song:

When the big machine
Wants to take control
Who ya gonna call?
Bluebusters!

Zaniness is, of course, the rule at sales meetings, but usually it is in direct proportion to the success of the preceding fiscal year. With the Lisa and the III dead or dying, and the Mac not hitting projections, this was not exactly the time for this kind of party.

In fact, the Big Blue that Apple was pretending to bust was growing stronger by the month. In May, IBM dropped a bomb by announcing that it would soon be possible to link up all of its computers, from mainframes to PCs, in vast, company-wide networks. This announcement, which shocked everyone in the computer business, proved to be more vaporware than anything else. But a few weeks later, IBM made a second announcement, and this one wasn't smoke: a new "PC Cluster" networking scheme that would enable users to link as many as five machines (four PCs and one PC XT with hard disk) into a self-contained network capable of carrying electronic mail, swapping files and storing common documents. At $2,500, PC Cluster was no bargain—customers were already buying cheaper networks with comparable performance from the likes of 3Com—but it was a reminder to the corporate world of IBM's commitment to the workplace.

Given all this, one might have presumed that the Hawaiian sales meeting would have emphasized the real reason for such gatherings: to prepare the field sales force for the challenges of the next year, provide them with sales tools for fighting the competition and preintroducing them to the new products they would sell. The Apple sales staff especially needed this kind of help because the company had added more than 200 new salespeople just to the Mac. Instead, the sales force, new and old, got piña coladas and dancing Bluebusters. Jobs and Sculley, meanwhile, made the cover of *Business Week* together ("The Dynamic Duo") wearing luau shirts.

Soon after the hungover salespeople returned, Apple kicked off a new, $12 million promotional campaign, "Test Drive a Macintosh," which appeared as a forty-page special supplement in the election issue of *Newsweek*. Test Drive was the brainchild of Mike Murray and his Mac marketing group. Once one got past the overblown and alarming *(How much did Apple pay for this?)* supplement, the idea of the campaign was rather clever: everyone was invited to walk into any computer store of their choice that sold Macs, plunk down a credit card for deposit and take a Macintosh home for the night to play with. The Test Drive was meant to be the solution to the growing opinion inside Apple (confirmed by watching customers in stores) that if people would just sit down and try the Mac for a few minutes, they'd be sold forever.

There was only one problem with the idea: Apple apparently did not hear the grumbles of the dealers who were forced to sign on to the idea. It didn't seem to notice that the Test Drive, guaranteed to create chaos even in a slow month, was being dropped right into the middle of the Christmas rush, the year's biggest selling period for personal computers. Thus the dealers responded to the Test Drive in a predictable way: they sabotaged it through neglect . . . *Sorry, our loaner's out. Come back after the first of the year.*

7.17 APPLE II FOREVER

By the end of 1984, Apple had sold 250,000 Macintoshes. It was not, in fact, a bad figure by any measure, except Apple's own expectations. And those expectations continued to grow.

In a most extraordinary move, Apple's senior management decided in October—against all evidence to the contrary—to adopt a business plan that called for Apple to sell 80,000 Macs per month for the next fiscal year. A million Macs, just as Sculley and Jobs had dreamed ten months before. Combined with the Apple II's revenue predictions, this gave Apple predicted revenues in fiscal 1985 of $3 billion. That meant a doubling of Apple's size in the next twelve months. It was sheer madness, partly brought on by Jobs's emotional need for the Mac's business to be the equal of the II's.

Obviously these numbers couldn't stand, but because Jobs wouldn't budge unless the II group backed off as well, company planners raced back and forth between the two groups to pound out a compromise. They finally reached it at $2 billion in revenues, with equal contributions from each group.

For revenues to be that big, Apple would need to have a $1 billion Christmas season. Not only was that unprecedented; it was probably impossible. And if Apple was going to have a billion-dollar quarter, then its factories and suppliers were going to have to gear up for full-scale production. And so, to mollify one man, an entire corporation put itself on the line, risking its fiscal health and the livelihoods of all the people who worked for it and their families.

Of course it failed. Though, thankfully, not horribly. It proved to be a $700 million quarter, enough to keep Apple afloat but also awash in unsold inventory. The company now had 250,000 Sony disk drives on hand, a year's supply, just as Sony was about to introduce a new model. When Apple begged the company to stop production, Sony refused.

Now looming ahead was January, traditionally the month when Apple displayed itself to the world. Two years ago it had been the Lisa, last year the Mac. Now the world had come to expect miracles from Apple at Super Bowl time. But this year Apple had little to show. The II group had been given its own moment in the sun the previous April when it had introduced the IIb (for "book"), almost renamed the Pippin in response to the Macintosh, and finally called the IIc (for "compact"). The IIc was designed to be an entry-level machine, a small miracle of redesign that put the IIe into a box the size of a large book. The IIc had been targeted for $995 (without monitor), a price point perfect for housewives, students and other first-time users.

Unfortunately, at introduction the machine was priced at $1,295 retail, with another $200 bucks for an Apple display. Even worse, the company announced at the same time that the IIe, with one disk drive and no display, would now be priced at just $995. Thus, in one stroke, Apple undermined its own new product. The introduction itself didn't help.

Planned to be the latest in Apple's new "event" publicity style, the II's introduction took place at San Francisco's Moscone Center. It was an early glimpse of all that would go wrong with Apple events in the years to come. First, it was ridiculously overblown, from the hagiographics of replicating the Jobs garage to the bombast of giant television screens to the silliness of II engineers arriving in tuxedos. There was a sense of desperation, obvious in the theme "Apple II Forever." Then the event was momentarily hijacked by Jobs, who came onstage to discuss the status of the Mac Hundred Days (60,000 shipped!) program. Finally, and most pathetically, Steve Wozniak came out onstage and played stand-up comedian. It was embarrassing: "I ran into Ronald Reagan downstairs [the Democratic convention was to be held at Moscone in a few months] and I asked him what he thought of the PCjr. He told me he was against abortions!" Behind Woz, Jobs covered his face with his hands.

It ended, mercifully, with Sculley. His words would be recalled later with some irony:

> Apple is going to become a great marketing company. McDonald's and Burger King are great marketing companies in their industries, just as Pepsi and Coke are in theirs. The Apple challenge is built on great foundations—that product innovation and marketing innovation can play the major role in shaping this dynamic growth industry. If we are right—and we believe we are—Silicon Valley will never be the same again.

There was yet another II in the works, the IIx. It might have been the greatest Apple II of all. Certainly it had the right pedigree: its microprocessor was to be a new and more powerful second generation of the original 6502 chip, this time to be developed by the Western Design Center in Phoenix; and its design leader was to be Wozniak himself. The IIx was to be the Super II, and its most interesting feature was to be a second processor slot in which the user could plug in everything from the Intel 8088 (to make the IIx fully IBM-compatible) to the Motorola 68000 (to make it a pseudo-Mac). But the IIx ran into a host of problems. A few of those problems were technical—the first chips from WDC arrived four months late and DOA. But most were political. The IIx had no champions. Woz, the erstwhile design leader, was growing more erratic and distracted by the week. By early 1984 he seemed to lose interest in the project altogether. Meanwhile, the Macintosh group, especially Jobs, hated the very idea of the IIx, which threatened to out-Mac the Mac to an audience of millions of loyal II users.

With the September introduction date lost, the product design still incomplete, the support for the product within the company fading, the coup de grace to the IIx came in March. That's when the IIx's own product manager, Ida Cole, circulated to management her prediction that the machine would sell only 25,000 units per month. Nine months later, Apple would have killed for a product with those sales figures, but in early spring the company was still dreaming of 80,000-unit months for the Mac and 100,000 for the IIc. Thus, even before the Moscone event, the computer that might have bridged the gap between the II and the Mac, as well as taken Apple into the IBM clone world, was quietly killed.

So the II group was out of the picture for the big January 1985 extravaganza. That left only the Mac team. But the 512K Mac had already been introduced. The only new product left on the horizon was something called the Mac XL, which was basically a Lisa with a hard disk drive. It was something, but hardly earthshaking. In response to the IBM network threat, the team had also been working on a new idea called the Macintosh Office.

In developing the Office, Apple knew it had no chance of competing technologically against the enterprise-wide networking scheme being proposed by IBM. It could not even compete directly against the new PC Cluster. But Apple knew it might succeed with an alternative tack: a very low-cost ($50 per node) network that would tie together up to six Macs with a common printer and a disk drive-based FileServer to create a kind of computing "work team."

With no little irony, Apple even knew where to go for the networking model: back to the old days of Xerox PARC and the Ethernet networking system developed there. A lot of Valley companies were experimenting with Ethernet at this time, so it wasn't an outrageous notion that Apple could create a slow-speed networking scheme that might handle the transfer of files and other data.

Laser printers too, though horribly expensive ($10,000 was a typical entry-level price), were becoming common. So it was not too difficult a task for Apple to establish a repackaging agreement with the leading laser printer engine manufacturer, Canon, and then build its own custom box around it.

But convincing Apple to make such a commitment was another matter.

"Desktop publishing totally saved Apple," said Tim Bajarin, "and the laser printer made desktop publishing possible. So even though Steve Jobs didn't think up the Mac, he certainly deserves credit for standing behind laser printing. Everybody else wanted to forget it. But Steve—coached by John Warnock—stuck with it. Even Apple's board wanted no part of it. Steve nearly had to stage a hissy-fit to keep it. I think it was Jobs's biggest decision at Apple."

Office automation software was equally problematic, but that obstacle was breached when Lotus agreed to create Jazz, a Mac-oriented version of the wildly popular Lotus 1-2-3 suite of programs.

The FileServer was yet another problem. Apple was not a hard disk drive designer. And it soon found itself at sea just coming to an agreement on what such a server should do. The marketing department, of course, wanted it to do everything, from electronic mail to full work team collaboration. The designers, by comparison, weren't even sure where to start. No one had been down this path before. There was no e-mail software yet. And how did you deal with two people working on the same file at the same time? How did you protect private files, while leaving others wide open? And how did you link up with other networks in the organization, including those with IBM computers? The answers might eventually be found, but not before the January announcement.

7.18 Lemmings

And so Apple went into the January gauntlet with a new product missing its critical component.

As in the year before, the extravaganza kicked off at the Super Bowl. The good news was that the game was being held at Stanford Stadium just up the road and that one of the contending teams was the San Francisco 49ers. This was seen as a good omen: the first Silicon Valley Super Bowl featuring Silicon Valley's home team.

The promotion had two parts. First, nearly 85,000 seat cushions bearing the Apple logo were placed in the stands. It made an impressive sight, one noted by the announcers and seen by millions of viewers when they were waved by fans. Second, in the final time slot of the game, Apple was to premiere its new commercial—a fact it heralded in newspaper ads across the country warning people not to go to the bathroom during the fourth quarter.

The moment finally came. Thanks to an exciting game, America was glued to the TV. The commercial was entitled "Lemmings" and featured a line of blindfolded businessmen in suits marching across a blasted landscape singing, like middle management dwarfs, a weary and heartless "Heigh-ho, heigh-ho." Then, as the camera pulled back, the viewer saw that each man in turn was stepping off a cliff. Only the last businessman in line stopped at the brink, pulled up his blindfold and thus, illuminated, saved himself from certain death.

The commercial was a complete disaster. Dreary, obvious and unpleasant, it not only lacked the sense of freedom and liberation that had made the "1984" ad so thrilling, but, in its death-filled way, managed to insult the very businesspeople Apple was trying to reach. It was unbelievably misguided and inappropriate. Like the "1984" ad, but for entirely different reasons, it was never shown again.

"Lemmings" was an augury of things to come. The annual meeting/new product extravaganza proved an equal disaster. It was again held at Flint Center, and this time the place was overflowing. In a metaphor for the year before, the Mac group was warned to be there early, so they filled all the best seats, while the II group was told nothing at all—so many had to watch the event from across the street at the movie theater in the Oaks Shopping Center. Their place, out of sight and mind, may explain why someone called in a death threat against Jobs. Some Mac group members responded by painting bull's-eyes on the backs of their T-shirts and calling themselves "bullet blockers." Whatever the source of the threat, prank or real, the place swarmed with security men.

The event kicked off with "Lemmings." Jobs tried to riff off the ad by coming out onstage wearing a blindfold. It went over great with the Apple folks, like a lead balloon with everyone else. Having essentially accused IBM and all of its customers of being blind and suicidal, Jobs then held out what he called "a hand of peace":

> When we spoke of a two-horse race in personal computers in 1984 it might have seemed like we were on a collision course with IBM. But in 1985, as the smoke clears from the '84 shakeout, many of those large corporations are telling us that they're going to use both Apple and IBM workstations, or that they want to use Macintoshes to talk with their IBM mainframes. It's imperative that we talk with the IBM part of the world, that we exchange information and have frequent discourse. So, for 1985, Apple proposes détente with IBM.

As he said this, a mock-up image of the front page of *The Wall Street Journal* was beamed overhead. The unlikely headline read: "Apple Declares Détente with IBM."

In just a few words, Steve Jobs voided the entire previous year's marketing campaign, beginning with "1984." Moreover, his ex cathedra declaration ignored one important question: Was IBM willing to declare détente with Apple? The entire event reeked of desperation and confusion—meaning that it did an excellent job of portraying Apple at this very moment. This, of course, was not what the company had in mind: it preferred the press to come away with the story Jobs told of a letter from a six-year-old boy who was doing a crossword puzzle and substituted "computer" for "pie" in the phrase "As American as Apple . . ." That Steve Jobs, of all people, was resorting to the last refuge, patriotism, was a hint of how bad things really were.

With all the fanfare the company could muster, the components of the Mac Office were introduced: the Mac XL, the LaserWriter printer, Lotus Jazz, and the AppleTalk network. They each were applauded, but everyone in the house couldn't help but think of the missing guest of honor, the FileServer. It was promised for autumn, along with e-mail software and the plug-in cards for linking up PCs. Members of the press muttered to one another: Apple has just introduced a nonproduct.

Afterward, as Jobs came out to meet the Mac team, Bob Belleville burst into tears. "We've got so much to do!" he sobbed. "And it's all such a mess!"

The board of directors meeting that afternoon was worse. Markkula and the others had been hearing a lot of complaints, on the record and off, about what was going on at the company. They took both Sculley and Jobs to task.

Sculley was told to start taking charge and acting like a CEO. That's what he was being paid for. Jobs, conversely, was told to *stop* acting like a CEO, leave the II group alone, stop playing petty monarch and start focusing on running the Mac group properly. Sculley took the criticism like a professional. Jobs, pouting, went back to his office and began typing on the computer like a schoolboy kept after school, "I will not criticize the rest of the organization. I will not criticize the rest of the organization. . . ."

The meeting with stock analysts was held the following morning. Underscoring the fact that this was not an Apple-controlled production, the meeting took place in San Jose, in the more dour confines of the big, anonymous Red Lion Inn next to the Bayshore Freeway. These weren't shareholders, but the people who made the market on Apple stock, and as such they demanded much more inside financial information.

In particular, they had some tough questions to ask about the apparently contradictory nature of the recently released quarterly results. Even if Apple had not met its own internal projections, it had more than met those of these analysts. It had indeed been a killer quarter: just short of $700 million, and almost a 100 percent jump from the previous Christmas. Coming at the end of a tough year for the Lisa, an industry-wide shakeout and the depredations of IBM, this was impressive stuff.

That was the good news. The bad news was that Sculley, having been informed that orders for both the Mac and the IIc had collapsed right after New Year's and that thousands of unsold machines were piling up at dealers, distributors and Apple's own warehouses, was obliged to add in the release a warning that the next few quarters' revenues would be much lower. Those words alone dropped the stock by two points. Now the analysts wanted to know more. They asked Sculley and Jobs to break out the revenues by product group, something Apple had not been required to do in its public filing. This was the moment of truth. For a year, Apple had been covering up the reality of the Mac's disappointing sales not only from the world but from itself. Now it had to fess up.

The Mac, Jobs admitted to the group, had been "left out in the cold" over the Christmas season. Sales were just $200 million—meaning that the II, the forgotten Apple, had contributed nearly $500 million. And, Jobs added, he didn't expect the Mac's sales to pick up anytime soon.

There it was: the truth at last. Eyebrows lifted around the room. But the analysts weren't done. Now they peppered the pair about the Mac Office. Why wasn't it complete? Where was the FileServer?

Then an extraordinary thing happened, something few of the analysts had ever seen: in response to a whispered message from an Apple staffer, Sculley got up and left the room, leaving the meeting in the hands of Steve Jobs. The analysts glanced at each other inquisitively: what would pull Sculley out of an analyst meeting?

The "third-largest shareholder in the company." That was how Steve Wozniak introduced himself when Sculley picked up the telephone. Woz had taken this moment of all moments to lodge a bitter complaint. Sculley, recognizing the legal and voting power behind that self-introduction, listened politely.

Woz was furious, a rare emotion for him even in those difficult days. He was calling from the Triangle Building representing, he said, the entire Apple II group. Sculley, Wozniak continued, had presented a fraudulent view of the company the day before at the shareholders' meeting. If the stock remark hadn't already set off alarms in Sculley's ear, Woz's words certainly did. *Lawsuit!*

How so? Sculley politely asked. Well, said Woz bitterly, you failed to give adequate time to the successes of the Apple II. In particular, we had a demonstration showing that not only the Mac but the II worked with the new LaserWriter. But that demonstration was pulled at the last moment. Woz was on a roll now. I'm used to this kind of treatment, he continued, I've watched as the II has taken a back seat to every new company computer, from the III to the Lisa and now to the Mac. But the new people in my group aren't and it makes me angry to see them hurt and demoralized like this. Now they're talking about writing a mass protest letter to you. I decided to call you first.

Sculley relaxed. *Is that all?* He would just calm Woz down and get back to the meeting. Listen, Steve, Sculley told Woz, the II got its own event back in April; besides, the Mac Office was the only new product available in time for the annual meeting.

But we didn't get the April event, Woz replied. Jobs hijacked it to give a presentation on the status of the Mac. Why wasn't the II given the same courtesy yesterday? We weren't even allowed to make a presentation at the business session.

Well, Sculley replied, you're getting your moment right now. When you called I was presenting the II's financials to the . . .

But Woz had already hung up on him. A few days later, Wozniak quit Apple Computer, slamming the company as he left: "Apple's direction has been horrendously wrong for five years," he told the press. Woz, seething in anger and resentment, had timed the moment perfectly to stick a knife in the company and Steve Jobs.

With Wozniak's departure the technical disintegration of Apple Computer was now complete. In just one year's time, the company had managed to drive off the last of its first generation of technical geniuses. To Jef Raskin's name could now be added Burrell Smith, Bill Atkinson and now the greatest of all, Steve Wozniak. There was now only one founding visionary left.

7.19 Sugar Daddies

Where was John Sculley during all of this? Obviously not running the company with an iron fist. Even the board recognized that. Nor was he fighting to make peace among the company's feuding factions. That had been the message of Woz's angry telephone call.

Sculley was, in fact, having a helluva good time living out a dream of empire building. With the Mac successfully launched and the numbers apparently terrific, he embarked on a grand strategic campaign of transforming Apple from a clever upstart into a corporate titan—and if not that, then finishing the Apple story with a glorious climax. After all, what would be a better capstone to his career than either to grow Apple through mergers and acquisitions into an IBM-like giant or, better yet, to walk away to the cheers of shareholders and his peers after having sold the company to the highest corporate bidder?

Sculley's plan was not entirely selfish. Unlike many of his lieutenants, he had a very good idea of what it would take to compete against a corporation as huge and well established as IBM. For all of its successes to date, Apple was still just a Tokyo citizen trying to survive against Godzilla. The success of the Mac and the failure of the PCjr had merely stubbed the monster's toes. IBM would recover—then sooner or later Apple would be squished underfoot. The only solutions were:

- *Get out of IBM's way.* Almost impossible unless the home or other as yet unknown computer market suddenly took off.
- *Grow Apple big enough to hold its own against Big Blue.* Nearly impossible through internal growth (especially in a slow market), but conceivable using the more than $100 million in cash on hand to make intelligent acquisitions.
- *Hook up with another corporate Godzilla.* The most likely scenario: Sell Apple now, while it was America's darling and about to have its best quarter ever, at a premium price to a big company wanting to expand into consumer electronics. Short of that, sell off a minority of the firm to one of these companies for enough money to fund a massive expansion.

This buyout scenario had the added advantage of enabling Sculley to walk away a corporate hero, cheered by Apple shareholders and his peers (if not by employees) before he had to deal with the hard work of coming up with new products, building existing machines and dealing with a mutinous rank and file. So why should he worry too much about the nasty details of daily corporate life? After all, soon they would be somebody else's problem.

Besides, it was fun. Throughout 1984, during their evenings and weekends together, Sculley and Jobs happily tossed business scenarios at one another. Nothing was too crazy to imagine—especially not in that era of corporate excess, leveraged buyouts and junk bonds.

Author Frank Rose, inside Apple during this period, describes it best:

> During the day they might quarrel and snap at each other, but alone together in the boardroom, late at night, they sensed no limit to the things they could do together. They could get a billion-dollar loan from GM or GE or AT&T and float enough junk bonds to take over Xerox and dominate the office automation market. They could run for president together and take turns being vice president and run the country between them for sixteen years.

In fact, GE, AT&T and Xerox were just the companies Sculley was looking at, along with Ford and, through its newly acquired computer services company EDS, General Motors. As Sculley saw it, each had a reason to be interested in Apple, from computer phones for AT&T to computerized factories for Ford and GM, to desktop office automation for Xerox. And each had billions of dollars on hand to burn.

So, throughout the summer and fall of 1984, often unbeknownst even to other top executives at Apple, the company was visited by delegations representing each of these corporate giants. Apple was on the block.

Roger Smith of General Motors stopped by to tour the Macintosh plant. EDS head H. Ross Perot came out to Cupertino too, representing GM. The little Napoleon, now thanks to the GM buyout "the third-craziest billionaire in Texas" (Molly Ivins's phrase), showed perhaps just how crazy he was by coming away from the visit powerfully impressed by not only Apple but Steve Jobs. In fact, he recommended that GM consider Apple only if Jobs agreed to stay.

AT&T sniffed around Apple too, as did some smaller players, such as workstation maker Wang, then at the height of its success. But the most serious discussions took place between Apple and General Electric. Jack Welch, whom many considered the best (and scariest) businessman of his generation, had restored GE from a declining dinosaur back to a vital business powerhouse. He'd done so through scores of mergers and acquisitions, followed by ruthless reorganizations. Neutron Jack was the one top businessman in America who not only could understand what Apple was about but could also knock some sense back into it. And GE's computer-leasing company already had a contract with Apple. Pretty soon, visitors from GE corporate were regularly flying out to Cupertino, and Sculley and Jobs were returning the favor by flying back to Fairfield, Connecticut.

With all of this activity and interest, it seemed inevitable that Apple would find a Sugar Daddy. But in the end, it all proved to be sound and fury, signifying nothing more than the fact that Apple was Corporate America's Playmate of the Month.

In the midst of all this, one other business opportunity also presented itself. Once again the uncelebrated Floyd Kvamme played a key role as facilitator. The proposal was brought in by Apple's old friend Ben Rosen. Rosen, the shrewdest of high-tech journalists, had shown just how clever he was by selling off his newsletter to Esther Dyson and going into the venture capital business. In time, his investments would make him nearly as rich as Steve Jobs, but for now, Sevin-Rosen Partners was struggling. Its biggest investment had been in a new IBM computer clone company based in Texas called Compaq.

Compaq had just enjoyed one of the most amazing first years in business history—$111 million in revenues—but it was cash-poor and, thanks to IBM price bombing, short on profits. Would Apple be interested, Rosen asked, in acquiring Compaq? The deal would cost just $100 million, well within Apple's budget. This was Sculley's first scenario—growth by acquisition—but Sculley was far more distracted by the third. Why waste time on acquiring a little Texas computer company when General Electric was knocking on the door? As for Jobs: Compaq was in the IBM business. Enough said.

And so a golden opportunity to beat IBM at its own game was ignored. In a few years, Compaq would be bigger than IBM in personal computers. It would also be bigger than Apple. By 1998, having bought Tandem and Digital Equipment, it would be the third-largest computer company on earth.

7.20 Coup d'Etat

Apple had bet everything and lost. It had wagered that it would have a huge Christmas, that the Mac would take off and that a White Knight would arrive to save it from the Armonk dragon.

Now it was adrift, demasted and rudderless. In a year's time the company had gone from the most celebrated new-product introduction in high-tech history, a historic collection of talent, a charismatic leader of worldwide celebrity and the prospect of huge financial success—to a disorganized and squabbling collection of fiefdoms, its technical heroes scattered to the winds, one founder gone and the other under assault and warehouses filled with unsold products. Everyone working within the company and watching it from without knew that some sort of terrible reckoning was due. And most had a good idea on whose neck the ax would, and should, fall.

The 1985 Steve Jobs was even more eccentric and infuriating than ever. Before the board had warned him off interfering with other company operations, he had tried to destroy Apple's distribution system by suggesting (on the basis of a casual conversation with the founder of Federal Express) that Apple should entirely replace its current infrastructure with, say, FedEx jets landing on a private runway next to the Milpitas plant. That guaranteed that one more department in the company hated him. He also talked about moving the entire company to a campus site in the hills south of San Jose—as if the company wasn't already isolated and introverted enough. Now Jobs wanted to make it Super Turbotown, the Anaconda Copper of Computing. That terrified just about everybody. Even members of the Mac group were now growing tired of Jobs's mercurial and high-handed style.

They weren't alone. One local reporter took an informal poll of everyone he knew—reporters, Apple employees, suppliers, customers, etc.—who had dealt with Steve Jobs. They were asked to use one word to describe Jobs. The vote was almost unanimous: "asshole." The same word was whispered by a few attendees at Jobs's thirtieth birthday party in late February (the St. Francis again, this time with Ella Fitzgerald) after he walked away leaving their carefully chosen gifts behind.

Other outsiders noticed too, especially the analysts and industry observers who established the market for Apple products and stock. Said Doug Cayne with the Gartner Group, "Jobs tends to decide where he thinks the personal computer ought to go, which isn't always where the market thinks it wants to go." Said Joan McKay of Kidder, Peabody, "People either think Jobs is a brainchild or they hate him. He's not a personality you're neutral on." Most influential, though, was Esther Dyson, who would announce as a postscript to the episode, "Clearly something had to be done, and it seems Jobs was in the way of things happening."

In the midst of all this, *Time* reporter Michael Moritz published *The Little Kingdom*, the first (and best) book about Apple. It was devastating, because for once a reporter had looked past the well-polished myths about the company and its beginnings and simply told the truth about Steve Jobs.

Suddenly, unexpectedly for many people still, it became possible to imagine an Apple Computer without Jobs, or at least one without him in a position of authority. After all, Woz had gone and come and gone again without the sky falling. And once that taboo thought became imaginable, it slowly became practical.

Steve Jobs, who had lived by his unique personality, now began to die by it. As Jobs himself, with his love of philosophy, would appreciate, his subordinates, minions, acolytes and admirers underwent a gestalt shift. Now, his endless reversals of opinion were no longer seen as symptomatic of his brilliance, but of his inconstancy. His charm was no longer soulful, but manipulative. And his eccentricities, like his disgusting foot massages, were no longer the mark of a rebel, but a crank. And when Jobs, the day after the party, sent around a memo, "Rough Sailing Ahead," suggesting the Apple employees give up their free juice, first-class tickets and off-site retreats, most employees just laughed. They had seen Jobs pull his scapegoat routine before, and they knew who really was to blame.

By March, Jobs was prone to explosive outbursts. The worst came when he visited frogdesign, the brilliant designers of the Mac box, and discovered the team there was also designing a product for Wozniak's new company, CL9. Jobs lost it. He warned the designers they would have to choose between him and Woz—then for good measure called Woz and threatened to destroy his company.

All that was left to destroy was the perfect partnership. For a couple of months after the annual meeting fiasco, Sculley and Jobs had been staying pretty much apart. But Sculley never fully escaped the shock waves Jobs was creating. At one seminar, he found himself confronted by several middle managers, one of whom asked him bluntly, "Who's running this company anyway? If you're running the company, why is Steve Jobs going around telling us what to do?" Now as the Macintosh problem deepened, as Sculley learned that no one was even working on a second-generation machine—and as he began to hear reports of Jobs bad-mouthing him on the sly—Sculley decided it was time for a confrontation. He feared it was too late. "I had given Steve greater power than he had ever had and I had created a monster." Jobs's little group had now swollen to more than 1,000 employees.

The meeting took place on a rainy evening in Jobs's crowded office. They were joined by Jay Elliot, Apple's human resources director, who during this period often seemed to be the only person holding the company together.

Elliot had long been pushing for this meeting, rightly believing that only Sculley could handle Jobs. But Sculley, for his part, wasn't even sure of that—he still remembered the seduction in the Manhattan aerie. Sculley began the conversation by saying that no one admired Jobs's "brilliance and vision more than I do." Nevertheless, he continued, "I have lost confidence in your ability to run the Macintosh division."

Jobs was stunned, but still clever enough to take an unexpected tack. As he had done when recruiting Sculley, he became the student at the foot of the master. "Well," he said, "you've got to spend more time with me."

That, as intended, confused Sculley, but he pressed on. "I want you to know that I'm going to bring this up with the board and I'm going to recommend that you step down from your operating job of running the Macintosh division. And I want you to know that ahead of time."

Jobs said he didn't believe it. But Sculley held firm. At that point, Jobs leaped to his feet, paced the room and began a tirade against Sculley. "If you do that, you're going to destroy this company! I'm the only one who understands enough around here about manufacturing and operations, and I don't think you understand these things yet. You're too far removed from the actual day in, day out operations, and if I'm not overseeing this, we're not going to get any new products out and we're not going to succeed!"

That was only the start of the argument. Before it was over, Sculley was more convinced than ever of the need to remove Jobs from line responsibility. Jobs, for his part, appeared to believe that Sculley wouldn't have the guts to follow through on his threat.

But Jobs was wrong. At the April 10 board of directors meeting, Sculley announced that he was asking Steve Jobs to step down from running the Mac group. He also informed the directors that if they weren't willing to back him on this, they could find a new CEO.

The board meeting ran the entire evening, and all of the next day. Separately, the directors called in Sculley and Jobs to grill them. At three-thirty, the board unanimously voted to back Sculley.

Outside, waiting in the hallway, it was at last Steve Jobs's turn to cry.

7.21 ABDICATION

In the weeks that followed, Jobs tried to play the good son. He worked on Sculley, promising to behave himself if only he could get his old job back. But Sculley refused to cave. So Jobs took a different tack and assaulted his ego. "I think you really lost your stride," he told Sculley. "You really were great the first year and everything went wonderful. I can't pin it down, but it was sometime during the end of 1984 . . ."

It was all very petty, but behind the scenes Jobs was playing a bigger, more dangerous game. After the board meeting, Jobs hid out for a few days away from Apple, then took off on a scheduled trip to Japan. There, with Bob Belleville, he hatched a coup plot. The plan (along with a nasty late night call he made to Sculley) so thrilled Jobs that he seemed to come out of his depression. In fact, he felt so good that when he ran into Wayne Rosing, engineering director of the Apple II division, Jobs so belittled him that Rosing decided that Jobs was back in charge of Apple . . . and quit the company.

On May 23, on the eve of his executive staff meeting, Sculley and his executive team were having dinner at the home of Apple vice president Al Eisenstat. During the evening, Sculley was pulled aside by Jean-Louis Gassée for a private word. Gassée, who had been a sensation running Apple France, where he had defeated even IBM, had been brought over to be Jobs's replacement in the Mac group. For the moment, he was the group's marketing manager, having replaced Mike Murray, whose days had been numbered ever since the Test Drive.

It was, for the first time in a long month, a happy evening. Sculley had been invited to China for a celebration of a big order for Apple computers. There was to be a major ceremony in the Great Hall in Beijing, and after months of misery, Sculley was excited about going. Besides, it might mean billions in future sales.

But Gassée had a dangerous message to convey. Don't go to China, he told Sculley. "John, you should be aware that there are real forces going on to try to throw you out of the company." It seemed that Jobs had decided to spring the coup while Sculley was halfway around the world. But in his typically impatient way, Jobs had done almost everything wrong. He just wasn't subtle enough to be devious. For example, he didn't even try to regain the trust of the board—which meant that even if the coup had succeeded it wouldn't have been ratified. Then, unwilling to wait, he began rounding up confederates for the coup even before Sculley's departure. That's how Gassée heard. And knowing that Jobs hated him for taking his job, Gassée, no minor corporate politician himself, had gone to Sculley.

Sculley canceled the trip.

At the Friday morning meeting, which was ostensibly about developing a new action plan for the company, Sculley waited until Jobs arrived, then dispensed with formalities. "Steve . . . it has come to my attention that you'd like to throw me out of the company, and I'd like to ask if that's true."

The room froze. Jobs's knew this was his one chance. "I think you're bad for Apple and I think you're the wrong person to run this company. You really should leave this company. I'm more worried about Apple than I have ever been. I'm afraid of you. You don't know how to operate and never have.

"John, you manage by monologue! You have no understanding of the product development process. You don't know how manufacturing works. You're not close to the company. The middle managers don't respect you. . . ."

The worst of it was that everything Jobs said was true. Jobs may have been incapable of truthfully judging himself, but he had nailed Sculley perfectly. Sculley, for his part, was so disturbed by the words that he reverted to his childhood stutter. The other executives sat around the table in stricken silence. They had all been party to Jobs's conspiracy, but now they weren't sure whom they'd pick if forced to choose between someone they didn't respect but admired and someone they respected but didn't admire.

Then Sculley threw down the gauntlet, "If I left, who would run the company?"

"I think I could run the company," Jobs replied.

It was a galvanizing moment. Suddenly the executives around the table could see in sharp relief what they had almost done. Sculley knew it too. He called for a vote, asking each man and woman in turn to state their views. Most told Jobs that they loved him, but they all voted for Sculley. Perhaps the most devastating vote came from Regis McKenna, who was sitting in on the meeting. Regis, who'd been there with Jobs before everyone else, who had seen him grow this company from a garage, told him straight: You shouldn't run this company.

Jobs rose wobbily to his feet. "I guess I know where things stand," he said, and ran from the room.

No one followed.

8.0 BLIGHT

8.1 Pastoral

One of the problems facing any history of Apple Computer is how to deal with the Sculley era. Apple's first decade is a straightforward and exciting tale of genius, heroism, ego and venality. It is the epic of Steve Jobs; an updated, funkified tale out of Dreiser in which the ambitious young man makes it to the top and is then destroyed. It is an adventure yarn, a mystery and a cautionary tale all in one—with a few touches out of Dostoyevsky and Kafka.

But the Sculley era, especially after the cleanup of the corporate wreck in 1985, is a different kind of story altogether. Suddenly the headlong rush of the Jobs era comes to a screeching halt and the narrative suddenly goes nonlinear and expansive. In the Sculley era at Apple, time seems to stop. New products are regularly introduced, some marvelous, some rotten, but none ever again has the impact of the original II or Mac. There are big promotions and events, but none fix in the mind years later.

Instead, we are left with a different type of story, the kind that fills up shelves of endless, boring authorized corporate biographies. A sequence of minor events that seem to start nowhere, meander around and end up nowhere. If there are none of the deep horrifying troughs of the Jobs era, neither are there the dizzying, exalting peaks. The screaming roller-coaster ride becomes a Sunday afternoon drive: mildly interesting, sleepy and largely eventless. The narrative is now a novel of manners, Trollope with a shot of *Buddenbrooks,* in which apparently minor decisions made in distraction take on a life of their own, and eventually lead to the downfall of what seemed impregnable. It is a pastoral, where, though nothing ever seems to happen, great forces are forming just over the horizon that will one day blow this peaceful Little Kingdom to bits.

8.2 DEAD ZONE

Pax Apple didn't begin calmly. By the time of the vote that forced Jobs to step down from the Mac group, Apple was a company in serious trouble. The Great Bet of 1984—run at full capacity, break all sales records over the Christmas quarter to cover past mistakes, then sell off the tarted-up company to the highest bidder—had failed. Now Apple, its distributors and its retailers were awash in unsold Macs and IIc's. The company had too many employees on the payroll, had spent too much on advertising and had no new products in the pipeline. There was no hiding from the truth now: Apple was going to have to take its punishment—and nothing less than a huge hit would do the job.

Meanwhile, Jobs had only been demoted, not fired. And his intuition told him that he still had a chance, if he moved fast, at wrenching the controls back away from Sculley. He was, after all, just thirty years old and he owned 11.3 percent of all Apple stock—a voting block worth nearly $120 million. He had youth and equity on his side.

The next four days were as crazy as any in Apple's crazy history. Immediately after the vote, both Sculley and Jobs had to attend a meeting downstairs for representatives from all company departments to discuss what to do about the impending business crisis. Nothing was said about what had just happened, but everyone in the room knew something was wrong. Jobs came into the room like a wraith, unexpectedly took a chair in the back and sat with his arms folded and head down. Sculley, who had called the meeting, looked equally worn and exhausted. The crowd had come expecting marching orders; what it got was platitudes, calls for reducing expenses and the creation of "study teams" to report on the problem. As they watched, Sculley seemed to evaporate before their eyes. He began by standing in the middle of the room, then, as he started to crumple, he leaned against a nearby pillar. By the end of the meeting, as he took the final questions, Sculley slumped against the *back* of the pillar, almost hidden from the room.

Both men stumbled out of Apple that day in shock. Sculley told Al Eisenstat he was ready to quit, and even put in a call to Gerry Roche, the headhunter who'd brought him there. Leezy Sculley, who had disliked Jobs from the very first day, was so pissed off when she heard the news she drove down to Cupertino in search of Steve. She caught him in front of the Sun & Soil natural foods restaurant a block from Apple. She had been waiting for him in her Mercedes, and when he walked up with a group of Macolytes she jumped out and called him over. For a moment Leezy thought about slugging Jobs, but she chose to yell instead. She hadn't planned her words, but once she started they came roaring out.

"Do you have any idea what a privilege it has been even to know someone as fine as John Sculley? He has been a real friend to you, but you'll never know it until the day you're on your deathbed."

Jobs hung his head.

"Steve," she yelled, "can't you even look me in the eyes when I'm talking to you?"

"You don't understand," said Jobs. "You don't understand."

"Look at me when I talk to you," Leezy demanded. Jobs finally looked up.

"No," said Leezy, "Never mind. Don't look at me. When I look into most people's eyes, I see a soul. When I look into your eyes, I see a bottomless pit, an empty hole, a dead zone."

"You don't understand."

"I think I understand everything there is to understand, Steve. I feel sorry for you." Then she turned on her heel and marched off. Leezy Sculley had proven she had more guts facing Steve Jobs than her husband did. And in the annals of Silicon Valley, in which there is no shortage of strange and bizarre anecdotes, this is the only time a CEO's wife ever kicked the ass of a company founder in a public parking lot.

Meanwhile, back at Apple, everything was confusion along executive row. Just that morning, the company's executives had sworn fealty to Sculley—and now the word was out that he was thinking about quitting. Jesus! Did that mean Jobs would take over now—and have their heads for betraying him? Loyalists to both Sculley and Jobs began to crack under the stress. Bob Belleville, who'd played his hand with Jobs, scribbled out a resignation note, packed his stuff and marched out. Jay Elliot, the human resources director who'd sided with Sculley, stormed out as well, saying, "Fuck this."

Eventually, with nothing better to do, the management of Apple finally drifted off into the night and the three-day Memorial weekend. Most were exhausted and depressed. Only Jobs, recognizing that his time was short, managed to pull himself into action the next day. He called around, polled his supporters, then called Sculley to arrange a walk in the mountains the next day, and called Markkula to set up a meeting after that down at Markkula's spread near Big Sur. Then, to pump himself up, he set out to watch the movie *Patton* with Mike Murray, but failing to find his own copy or one at the video store, watched a Hitchcock film instead. It was the perfect choice.

The Sunday walk was up Dish Hill behind Stanford University. At the top Sculley and Jobs could look down the back slope to the west and see the stretch of Interstate 280 where Jobs and Woz had first come up with the name of their little company. That was the beginning. And this was to be the end.

Jobs gave it his best shot. He proposed running the new combined R&D operation that Sculley was planning to create out of the II and Mac groups. Or he could be Sculley's coequal and run product development while Sculley directed corporate sales and marketing. Neither received a response. So Jobs pulled out the big one: what if Sculley were to move up to chairman and let him become the new CEO.

It was completely nuts and completely Jobs. Booted out of one job, he took a shot at landing an even better one. Once again, high above the landscape, Jobs tried to seduce and overwhelm John Sculley. And the mere fact that Sculley had foolishly agreed to such a rendezvous suggested to Jobs he had a chance. But it was too late. As Sculley would later write: "When I joined Apple, I had come to terms with what I was going to be in life. I believed that the blithe spirit in fading jeans and Velcro sneakers was one of the important figures in our country during this century. I was going to help him succeed. I never imagined that I would run the company by myself someday. Now that was the reality and our friendship was over." The selflessness of the first part of that remark is a little hard to believe, but certainly the final words were accurate.

Jobs's visit to Markkula fared no better. Markkula was key to the board. Only he could smooth over the feathers Jobs had ruffled in the preceding months. But Markkula wasn't listening—at least to Jobs. As soon as Jobs and the others arrived, Markkula announced that everyone but Jobs would be allowed to talk and make the case for keeping him. It was over before it began.

Sculley went back to the office on Monday, while Apple was largely deserted, and had a series of private meetings with his lieutenants on what role they thought Jobs should have at Apple in the months and years to come. He was amazed to find that most of them were aghast at the very question. Most wanted Jobs out of all positions of responsibility at Apple *forever.* Better yet: out of the company. Sure, it would hurt the company's image to lose the face most people attached to Apple, but it sure beat the alternative.

So on May 31, exactly one week after receiving the warning from Gassée, John Sculley signed the papers that officially booted Steve Jobs out of any line responsibilities at Apple. The founder was now a man without a job in his own company. Sculley met Jobs for breakfast to tell him that the chances of him having line authority at Apple were now thin, then drove up to Markkula's house in Woodside to learn his own fate.

Mike Markkula had every reason to be furious. Since the beginning of the year, his net worth had dropped by $200 million. After five years of hard work he had at last pulled away from the day-to-day operations of the company, believing he had left the running of Apple Computer—and the care and feeding of Steve Jobs—in the hands of a pro. Now it was obvious that through incompetence, distraction and a failure of will, John Sculley had brought the company to the brink of chaos, had allowed the feuds between the different product groups turn into all-out war and had allowed Steve Jobs to run amok while giving him more and more power. "There was a lack of respect for Sculley because he wasn't managing Jobs," said one Apple manager who quit during this period. ". . . It was a very destructive environment."

In April, the board had given Sculley the green light to deal with Jobs—and in response he had done worse than nothing. Now, at the worst possible moment in terms of vulnerability, Apple was about to have its second founder, one of the most famous people in the world, also make an angry and noisy exit. Though Apple had consistently grown during Sculley's tenure, at no time had it ever met any of the revenue targets he had set for it. Employees were demoralized, business partners angry and customers confused and concerned. And IBM was still gaining market share and now owned the corporate market for personal computers.

Markkula told most of these things to John Sculley, and those he didn't Sculley announced against himself. In fact, for much of the four-hour meeting, Markkula didn't say a word. Instead it turned into a monologue by Sculley, soaked in sweat, struggling to save his career and reputation. He took the blame upon himself, promised (uncannily like Jobs a few days before) to do better and offered a strategy for getting Apple out of its current mess. It was a courageous play by Sculley, though that courage would have been better used in the months before.

Markkula listened, and then in the end did an extraordinary thing: he kept Sculley on as the pilot of Apple Computer. "You've got my support," he told Sculley, "but I'm very disappointed Apple is in this position." Incredibly forgiving words from a man who held ultimate responsibility for the livelihoods of 6,000 employees and for the investments of hundreds of thousands more.

It was Mike Markkula's biggest mistake. But he was only the most powerful figure at Apple to make this decision. The same conclusion had been reached by those senior managers around the table the previous Friday. No one at Apple still believed that John Sculley was either a great businessman or a great leader of men. Rather, the consensus was that he was a superb marketing man who'd been Peter Principled to the top. Yet, bizarrely, there was also an agreement that Sculley remained the best choice for the helm. During this time of crisis it would be too much for Apple to take off on yet another CEO search and risk finding a replacement who knew even less about computers than Sculley. Sculley wasn't much, it was quietly agreed, but he was their guy.

But was this really the case? Was there really no one out there in electronics suited to take charge of Apple, clean out the rot at headquarters and rev up product development? Nobody checked. Instead, Markkula in the lead, Apple stayed with a man almost everyone agreed was not up to the job, and who, just the day before, had proved his loyalty by threatening to quit. Steve Jobs's crimes were legion, but one thing he had never done in his tenure at Apple was to settle for anything but the best. With his departure, Apple seemed to revert to what it would have been without him: a company that was content with the merely adequate.

Resurrected and revivified, Sculley left Markkula's house that evening and went back to the office. There he polled his managers, then called Steve Jobs to tell him his fate: He was out. They couldn't fire the company's second-largest shareholder, but he had been stripped of not only the Mac division but every other possible operational role in the company. Steve Jobs was now merely a figurehead, with no power within the company.

Jobs did not take the news well. Instead he spent the rest of the evening calling everyone he knew, from Mac team members to family members and sobbed into the phone. He cried, rambled, at times became nearly incoherent in his grief. As even a company spokesperson admitted to the press, Steve "lives and eats and breathes Apple. It's very difficult for him to admit that somebody else runs it."

Steve Jobs had created himself through Apple Computer; it had been the centerpiece of his entire adult life. But his creation had turned on him, declared him worthless, made him for the second time an orphan. Now he was calling everyone he cared about to tell them goodbye.

One of the calls was to Mike Murray. In a shattered voice, Jobs thanked him for the best years of his life, told him goodbye and hung up. Murray was sufficiently frightened by what he heard that he jumped in his car and raced over to Jobs's house. Murray worried that he would find Jobs dead on the bare floor of the bare house. The giant front door was open—an awful sign. Murray raced through the house, finding nothing. Then he spotted a tiny light in Jobs's bedroom. He burst in, expecting the worst.

Instead he found Jobs, his face swollen from crying, wrapped in a blanket on the mattress on the floor. "Oh, hi," said Jobs distractedly, as if from far away. Mike joined him on the mattress, held his former boss in his arms, and the two cried together.

"This is not a power play," Regis McKenna told the newspapers the next day.

8.3 Aftermath

The future of Apple Computer was now officially in the hands of John Sculley.

Jobs was now not only out of the organization chart but out of sight. When he was in Cupertino he had the only office in a nearly empty building, the Little Napoleon on St. Helena. But most of the time he was on the road. *What do we do with Steve?* stopped being a question asked in desperation and instead became a subject for after-hours bullshit sessions. One rumor, quickly quashed, was that Jobs was considering a run for the U.S. Senate.

Another possibility, that of being one of the first of the new civilian astronauts on the Space Shuttle, did appeal to Jobs for its manifold glories, but he dropped it after learning of the months of training involved. It is interesting to speculate what would have happened to the Jobs myth if he had stayed with the program and become, instead of schoolteacher Christa McAuliffe, the civilian astronaut on *Challenger*. Would he have become the Elvis Presley or Princess Diana of high tech?

Finally, there were even rumors that Jobs was plotting yet another coup, this time by accumulating other shareholders to create a powerful voting block. But that seemed an unlikely bet, as, in the words of Valley veteran Jan Lewis of InfoCorp.: "Most of the finance community, by and large, [sees] Jobs as a negative to the community and Sculley a positive. Under those conditions, it will be hard to get financing." A counter-rumor was that Jobs was preparing to sell off his Apple shareholdings. That one would prove to be the most accurate.

Meanwhile, the career plans of Steven Jobs were of little consequence to John Sculley and his team. They had much bigger problems to worry about. Sculley had somehow caught a break with Markkula and the board. But it would not happen again: everyone on executive row knew that if Apple wasn't turned around in six months, Sculley would be only the first to go.

There were huge problems facing the company. It had to get itself organized, revive morale in the II group and restore the momentum to the Mac team. It had to regain control over its finances. And most of all, Apple had to reaffix itself to the Myth now that the Great Mythmaker was gone. Said Anton Bruehl, an analyst and onetime competitor as head of Atari International,

"Apple employees need to get behind the company again. It will take a lot of work to bring it back. With the combination of old and new employees, some loyal to Jobs, it's not going to be an easy task for Sculley [when] the market isn't helping him."

The market, in fact, was nearly in free fall. After the Christmas boom at the end of 1984, sales of computers for homes—including the IIe and IIc—fell 58 percent in the first quarter of 1985. Business computer sales did better—a drop of just 8 percent—but it was IBM PCs that made up most of that market, not Macintoshes. With nothing new to offer, Apple could only fall back on slogans. Having already described the Mac as an "appliance" and "the computer for the rest of us," the company now tried feebly to court industry professionals with "power tool for the mind." It didn't work.

On June 5, 1985, Bill Gates sent a special three-page memo to John Sculley and Jean-Louis Gassée entitled "Apple Licensing of Mac Technology." It would remain hidden from the public eye until 1996, when Jim Carlton, writing a book about the Sculley era at Apple discovered it.

The ideas within the memo were not originally Gates's, but belonged to a twenty-seven-year-old marketing manager at Microsoft named Jeff Raikes. Raikes had worked at Apple for a year after graduating from Stanford, then left to join Microsoft in 1981 ("Microsoft will go out of business," Jobs reportedly warned him when he quit). Thus, this early in the game, Raikes was one of the few people in personal computing with experience on both sides of the hardware-software fence.

Because of this, Raikes had come to realize early what the rest of the world would only come to five years hence: in personal computing, software (and processors) drove hardware, not the other way around. From the perspective of fifteen years on, when Windows and Pentium own the world, that might seem obvious. Even at the time there was already considerable evidence of this truth: witness how VisiCalc and the Mac operating system (OS) had saved the Apple II and Mac. But in that world, where tangible, physical assets ruled the day, the idea that lines of code could triumph over steel, copper and plastic was completely counterintuitive.

Whether Gates fully understood Raikes's vision or was merely indulging in some self-aggrandizing wishful thinking is a matter of speculation. But the memo was amazingly prescient.

The memo began with a brief overview of Apple's current situation:

> . . . Apple must make Macintosh a standard. But no personal computer company, not even IBM, can create a standard without independent support. Even though Apple realized this, they have not been able to gain the independent support required to be perceived as a standard. . . . IBM architecture continues to receive huge investment and gains additional momentum. . . . Any deficiencies in the IBM architecture are quickly eliminated by independent support. . . . The closed architecture prevents similar independent investment in the Macintosh. The IBM architecture, when compared to the Macintosh, probably has more than 100 times the engineering resources applied to it when investment of compatible manufacturers is included.

For all of these reasons, Gates concluded, "the industry has reached the point where it is now impossible for Apple to create a standard out of their innovative technology without support from, and the resulting credibility of, other personal computer manufacturers. Thus, Apple must open the Macintosh architecture to have the independent support required to gain momentum and establish a standard."

Gates then went on to list six reasons why the Mac had not become a standard, including that customers weren't secure buying from a sole source, Apple had a rep for being slow to market, recent bad publicity and a small sales force. He then went on to list a score of companies, both domestic and international, from TI and HP to Kodak, Xerox, Siemens and Sony, that would significantly enhance the Mac OS's reputation and distribution. Finally, Gates concluded with a half dozen reasons why these companies would be good strategic partners, ending with:

"Licensing Mac compatibles will enhance Apple's image as a technological innovator. Ironically, IBM is viewed as being a technological innovator. This is because compatible manufacturers are afraid to innovate too much and stray from the standard."

Gates and Microsoft pledged "to help Apple implement this strategy."

Jim Carlton would declare this "one of the most important documents in Silicon Valley history," and certainly if Apple had followed Bill's advice it would have become a much different—and perhaps more successful—company. But the subsequent fate of Gates and of Apple puts a little more of a luster on this memo than it probably deserves.

In fact, during this era Apple was getting advice from every quarter about what to do with the Mac OS, much of it having to do with licensing. Regis, for one, had been arguing the case since 1983. Even at the time Gates was drafting his letter, one could read calls in the trade press for Apple to license the Mac OS. Dealers, recognizing the need for multiple vendors, were calling for it too. In the midst of all of this, Bill Gates, still a comparatively small player and erstwhile competitor, was just one voice (albeit particularly perceptive) out of many—all of them doomed to be ignored.

Regis McKenna made the same case over and over again for the rest of the decade, begging, pleading and even demanding that Apple choose between being a consumer products company and being a manufacturer of information tools for corporations. But Apple Computer was of no mind to make a choice—not when it meant abandoning one market or the other. Instead it tried to finesse a path in between, never giving either market quite what it wanted.

As for Gates and the growing chorus calling for licensing the OS, Apple's top management, especially after the recent purge of Jobs, was simply too unstable and too unsure of itself to make a move with such enormous implications. On top of that, there was the long-standing attitude, shared by Jobs and Sculley, that any money made by anyone else off an Apple idea was essentially *stolen*. It was like giving away the formula to Coca-Cola.

And if all that wasn't enough to scare Apple away from licensing, watching IBM's troubles over the next few years with cloners sealed it. Regis's memos, Bill Gates's letter and the dozens of other documents with similar conclusions generated within Apple itself were merely filed away, awaiting future postmortems.

In the meantime, technology—and entrepreneurship—moved on. In 1988, Roger Pelton, a market development expert, was sitting in a meeting at a new Valley company, called Sun Microsystems, that had been founded to prospect a new kind of low-cost, graphics-oriented minicomputer called an engineering workstation. Sun had chosen to go with Unix as its operating system, and there was considerable concern within the company about competition from above (mainframe computers) and below ("super" PCs) squeezing out the market even before it formed. An even greater threat, the group agreed, was from another operating system setting a standard different from Unix.

"We finally concluded," Pelton recalls, "that the biggest danger we faced would come from Apple if it decided to license the Mac OS. That would *really* hurt us.

"Then we all looked at each other and said, 'Naah. Apple will never do it.' "

Little noticed in the larger world at the time was the impact the Apple binge and purge had on John Sculley's reputation in Silicon Valley. His arrival at Apple in 1983 had been seen by Valley veterans as an enormous risk. Could a nontechie really run a tech company? His initial success, culminating in the Macintosh introduction, had made the Valley safe for CEOs without EE degrees. Headhunters were now told to cast wider nets beyond electronics, to search for John Sculley-like figures.

All that changed in June 1985. Old-timers began to nod that they had been right in the first place, that the Valley was no place for amateurs. Hungry executives from the automotive, retailing and consumer goods industries, anxious to get into the Silicon Valley gold rush, suddenly found doors slammed in their faces. "That's because the John Sculley model has become suspect," said employment psychologist Richard Hagberg. It would remain so ever after.

Amid all this misery, the good news was that Sculley had gathered around him a team that not only was supremely talented but, in such a young business, could be classified as seasoned veterans. Some, like Del Yocam and Debi Coleman, were survivors of the Jobs era. Others, like Jean-Louis Gassée, had made a name at Apple far away from Cupertino. And still others, like Dave Barram, had just come to Apple after years elsewhere in high tech. This was John Sculley's team, and for good or ill they would define the company for the rest of his tenure.

It was a team as bright and talented—if not necessarily as capable—as any Silicon Valley had ever seen. The same, in fact, might be said for the entire company. Because of the big hiring rush the company conducted throughout 1984 and into 1985, much of the best young talent around found its way into the company, where its effects would be felt for years to come.

The operations side of the company was run by Del Yocam. But for the beard, he was a kind of Dickensian figure—pudgy, congenial, a devoted family man, the very embodiment of organization and attention to details. Sculley, noting how Yocam kept meticulous notes in a maroon notebook he always carried under his arm, was even reminded of Bob Cratchit. Yocam even walked carefully, as if making sure each fastidious step was properly placed. If Yocam had any enemies it was only among those who found him too agreeable, too willing to accept out of politeness whatever was being said to him, then ignoring it later. If Yocam lacked anything, it was a burning fire in his guts. After Jobs, that missing component in Yocam was welcomed.

Yocam joined Apple in 1979, another member of the Fairchild diaspora. His initial job was as director of materials. But he proved so competent that he was soon put in charge of the Apple II group. There he had kept the group alive and its morale as strong as possible through the endless push-pull of being either ignored by the rest of the company or assaulted by Steve Jobs.

It was a measure of Yocam's personality, being the absolute antithesis of Jobs, that he was always able to get along with Apple's *enfant terrible*. Coming out of that April board meeting where he had just been eviscerated by Apple's directors, Jobs had cried on Del's shoulder. Even as he was nursing Jobs, Yocam was also supporting Sculley, showing him the ropes at Apple, making decisions Sculley was too distracted to make himself. He was the perfect lieutenant, and in the end Sculley rewarded Yocam for that trait by giving him the perfect lieutenant's job: director of operations, in charge of R&D, the factories and distribution.

Needless to say, Yocam's promotion was welcomed by the II group, which saw at last a hope for true appreciation by top brass. And Yocam certainly cheered them by publicly announcing that "the pendulum swung too far on Macintosh."

The cheering quickly stopped. With Sculley's approval, one of Yocam's first moves was to finally end the internal feud that had torn Apple in two for three years—he merged the Macintosh and II divisions into a single product group organized by functions (such as manufacturing and product development) instead of products. "We are switching from being product-driven to being market-driven," said Yocam the day after Jobs was booted from daily management. It sounded easy, but behind the words was the touchy task of melding together one strong but humiliated team with another, arrogant one in disarray. As one insider complained at the time: "It's not clear who works where. Exactly where the line is is not a hundred percent clear."

Immediately under Yocam, the two most important figures were Debi Coleman and Jean-Louis Gassée. Both were more talented than Yocam, but neither had the experience yet for his job. And both were unusual even by Valley standards.

Gassée's nickname was "the King of France." Coming from Exxon Office Systems, Data General and Hewlett-Packard, he had made a name for himself within Apple by running Apple France so brilliantly that it even led IBM in market share. Back home he'd been a model for Yves Saint Laurent clothes (in *Vogue*), spokesperson for Vittel mineral water, talk-show regular and a poet (but not an engineer), and even was once listed as one of France's ten best-dressed men. In Frank Rose's memorable words, "he was the technocrat as café revolutionary, spouting existential mumbo jumbo about personal computers and the future." In France, wearing black leather, Gassée looked like a character out of an early Godard film. In California, wearing jeans, he looked like a Gallic Carl Sagan.

Gassée's sophistication (he once famously described IBM using the old Nazi phrase *"ein Volk, ein Bund, ein Führer")* buffaloed the press and instilled a cultlike worship by many of his subordinates. But there were others who listened closely to Gasséeisms, like the one that the Apple II "smelled like infinity," and concluded he was full of shit. Gassée only abetted this suspicion with brazen public remarks . . . like the one to the audience at a product introduction when he announced that Apple's slogan at the time, "The Power to Be Your Best," should really be "The Power to Beat Your Chest."

More than one person came away from dealing with Gassée struck by how much he was like Steve Jobs, if not in ruthlessness then certainly in grandiosity. But whereas Jobs fixated on a single project to the point of madness, Gassée was scattered, pursuing a score of different projects at the same time, making hundreds of decisions every day. Apple thanked him by paying him $800,000, more than the salary of most Valley CEOs.

Debi Coleman, by comparison, cultivated no such flourishes, yet she was a far more unusual and eccentric individual. She may have been the most versatile businessperson Silicon Valley has ever known. Overweight to the point of obesity, and childlike in her lack of any social graces, she also had a devastating intellect and a natural ability to attract a small army of powerful protectors and people as awkward as she. This made Coleman both formidable and unthreatening. She could be tough one moment and delicate the next. Watching her gnaw on candy bars while holding a staff meeting that was like a support group, it was at first hard to imagine what this individual was doing inside a billion-dollar corporation. But if you listened closely, you realized that this was a kind of genius all its own, and that Coleman might be as great a visionary as Jobs himself.

Debi had begun her career at Apple as a Macolyte and Jobs functionary. She was his secret weapon. The daughter of a Rhode Island machine-tool shop owner, Coleman had gone to Brown and dreamed of a career in manufacturing—even one day running General Electric. Instead she got an MBA at Stanford and found herself in Silicon Valley working at HP improving production. By a fluke, she ran into an old business school classmate at the Good Earth one lunchtime in September 1981 and soon found herself applying for a controller's job at Apple. Given the choice between taking that job in the established Lisa group and working for the Bandley Pirates of the Mac group, Coleman took the latter.

She did the job brilliantly, though it was a long leap from production to finance. But most important, she learned how to handle Steve Jobs. Her gift for comforting tortured souls had found its perfect recipient. In return, Jobs adored her, and shrewdly gave her his most difficult assignments. To Debi's delight, the biggest of these proved to be manufacturing. Jobs had shown that when he had almost gone berserk that day in the Fremont plant. Not long after that, in May 1984, with Apple still predicting skyrocketing Mac sales, he made his move. At the Pajaro retreat, he took a walk on the beach with Debi and offered her the manufacturing manager position.

Coleman, who had prayed for just such a chance, took it and ran. She even had a replacement ready for the controller's job, Susan Barnes. Then, with a decisiveness usually associated at Apple only with Jobs, she made the gutsy call of shutting the plant down for a month. During the interval she tore the place apart. She threw out nearly $10 million worth of obsolete equipment, fired every deadbeat she could find, scrubbed the place out and repainted the walls and then hired people who knew what they were doing. When the factory reopened in July it was a showpiece of modern American manufacturing. Even GM's Roger Smith stopped by for a look. At 43,000 units, the plant produced more than double May's figure—meaning that by the old standard not a single production day had been lost.

Coleman had remained a Jobs loyalist right up to the end. She had even been with him that day when Leezy Sculley reamed him out. But she had never turned on Sculley—Debi was too awkward and obvious to be a good corporate politician. She had simply gone about her work within her self-contained world. Sculley admired her for that. But nobody appreciated Debi more than Del Yocam, who put her by his side (as he would do again a decade later at Tektronix).

So operations was in good shape. Next, Sculley bolted together sales and marketing—always a dangerous move—and put it in the hands of Bill Campbell, the first person Sculley had recruited to Apple and at the time the head of the company's U.S. sales. Campbell was also an interesting character. Tall, robust, with a powerful voice, he appeared every inch the jock he'd once been. In fact, before working at Eastman Kodak (where Sculley found him), Campbell had been the football coach at Columbia University. Campbell had never lost his take-charge style, and it had served him well trying to rebuild the workforce he'd inherited from Gene Carter, getting 300 new salesmen in position to relieve the existing army of manufacturer's representatives, then dealing with the roller-coaster experience of the Mac launch, the summer doldrums, the Test Drive, the resurgent II and now the prospect of layoffs. Among Apple's dealers, Campbell's arrival was welcomed with cheers. Said one, "He's the kind of guy who gets things done."

Reporting to Campbell as director of marketing was Michael Lorelli, promoted from marketing manager of the II group. Like Sculley, Lorelli had come from consumer products, in his case from Playtex, where he'd promoted tampons and Clairol shampoo. Apple's image was now in the hands of two men with almost no experience marketing computers.

In human resources, Jay Elliot, the bearded surfer, had returned from his march-out and was back in position. Overseas, a taciturn, hard-driving German named Michael Spindler, who'd done good work as European marketing manager, was put in charge of international operations. Al Eisenstat, chief counsel and secretary to the board, also stayed in position and was promoted to a company directorship. He had been a Sculley loyalist, and now, in thanks for that loyalty, he was given the most dangerous task of all: playing chaperone to Jobs. Eisenstat had been Apple's point man on international deals, especially those involving embargoed countries, such as China. Now he explored the possibility of sales to the Soviet Union. Sculley, meanwhile, needed to get Jobs out of the company for a few weeks to conduct this reorganization without internal interference or snide remarks to the press. Take Jobs with you to Russia, he told Eisenstat. Keep him busy, keep him out of sight, and make sure he doesn't do anything crazy that hurts the company.

On the finance side, with the departure of Joe Graziano, who'd resigned earlier in the year when Sculley expressed a lack of confidence in his work, the newest team member was Dave Barram. Barram had spent a long career at Hewlett-Packard, eventually working his way up to corporate controller, then followed that with a brief stint at Silicon Graphics. As such, he carried the cachet of doing the books for the most financially respected company in high tech. Sculley made him chief financial officer and gave him the added responsibility of inventory control. Barram himself was an interesting character. The son of a Baptist minister, he talked in a low, sardonic voice that always sounded on the brink of a knowing chuckle. Though he was a competent finance man, Barram's real love was Democratic Party politics. Five years before he had run for the Sunnyvale city council on a shared ticket with Regis McKenna's wife, Dianne. She won, in time becoming a Santa Clara County supervisor. He lost, despite having walked to every home in the city. But he still managed to stay in politics through his wife, Joan, who was elected a few years later to the school board.

Barram, the McKennas and Sunnyvale mayor Larry Stone (later county assessor) composed a tight little coterie of yellow dog Democrats in a community where most of the corporate executives were Republican and even the local Dems often voted for GOP candidates out of fiscal prudence. The little group created something of a machine that ran Sunnyvale politics for nearly two decades. Through this connection and that of his wife, Barram found his way into various national education groups, as well as the Democratic Leadership Council. There he became fast friends with an up-and-coming young Arkansas governor and his attorney wife.

That was Sculley's crew. As even he admitted, it wasn't yet a team: "Trust and respect establish the basis of any good working team. Yet there wasn't much trust in the beginning. We didn't know one another very well; we hadn't worked together as a team before, partly because Steve and I called all the shots."

Still, Sculley was thrilled by the group. Its diversity appealed to him: this was what a real California high-tech company team should look like! As he crowed later in his autobiography:

> What a group to lead Apple out of its quagmire: a soda-pop executive from the East; a solid, though untested, Apple II manager; an Ivy League football coach; a French intellectual; a German conceptual thinker; an English literature major; a seasoned attorney; a Baptist philosopher; and a laid-back surfer!

It sounded nice, but there were two types of people missing from this walking diversity cliché.

The first missing party, to use Guy Kawasaki's term, was a *high priest* of technology. Not just a tech intellectual, like Gassée, but that elusive combination of visionary and evangelist, who could make everyone share his dream, then pull them along into it. Just about all who'd held that role, from cardinals like Woz, Jobs and Raskin to archbishops like Burrell Smith, were gone. And it was a dangerous glimpse into the holes in Sculley's knowledge of high tech that he didn't seem to know he needed such a figure. In time he would understand, but then he would make a disastrous choice.

The second empty chair at the executive table belonged to an even more unnoticed type: the industry veteran. Despite all the brilliance of Coleman and Gassée, and the business experience of Sculley and Campbell, there was nobody in the room who could be called a veteran of the computer industry. Here was a company that presumed to establish a wide line of computer products, from educational computers up to the brink of minicomputers; that planned, in large part, to sell its computers to the corporate world; and that knew eventually it would have to link its products in networks to the large and small systems of other computer companies . . . and yet, there was nobody at the very top of Apple Computer who had *any* experience selling computers to industry.

This was indicative of Sculley's ignorance and arrogance; his attitude from the start that selling personal computers wasn't really fundamentally different than selling soda pop, once you understood the nomenclature. It was a devastating position to hold, because ultimately selling PCs really *was* different, especially to the corporate world, and especially as part of larger enterprise solutions with other computer companies.

A few others saw it as well. One consultant, after a staff meeting at a Santa Clara Hotel, caught up with Sculley in the parking lot. Gassée had just been appointed director of engineering. Please, pleaded the consultant, don't turn Gassée into another Jobs (that is, the sole technologist who buffaloes all the amateurs, especially Sculley himself). You'll only be re-creating the same problem you just solved.

"How can I avoid that?" Sculley asked.

For one thing, said the consultant, by naming more technical people to the executive staff and to the board of directors as a balance. He even offered some names.

Sculley nodded, but in the end did nothing. Before long, Apple was in the thrall of the musings of the King of France. And when the time came—and it came within months—when Apple had to decide in which direction to go, there was no one at the table to offer the wisdom of experience.

8.4 Madness

There were many different explanations as to why Apple suddenly found itself in deep financial trouble, with products stacked up in warehouses, the founder impeached and a new executive team in command. At the time, most observers put the blame at the feet of Steve Jobs. Later, when the outlines of the Sculley era became clear, Jobs underwent a rehabilitation of sorts *(yeah, he was nuts, but he had the right idea)* and Sculley became the goat.

A valid case could in fact be made for either view. Jobs did go on a rampage. He behaved not like an executive but like a bully taking revenge on everyone who had slighted him. He'd also held hostage the careers of thousands of employees to live out, despite mounting evidence to the contrary, his little fantasy of success.

On the other hand, Jobs was *supposed* to be out of control. He was the corporate shaman, the cheerleader, the charismatic. He made the impossible real. Sculley, by comparison, was hired to be the mature grown-up. He was supposed to control Jobs and command the company. But he had done neither. Instead, he had bet the company on a foolish risk, then had covered his failure by first blaming Jobs, then giving him the boot.

There was also a third explanation for Apple's troubles: the company simply went mad. It was all just too much, too heady an experience for any company, much less such a new one filled with young and inexperienced people. This was how Guy Kawasaki saw it when he sat down in 1990 to write *The Macintosh Way*. Kawasaki was, of course, a paid Apple cheerleader, yet it was precisely that enthusiasm for Apple, its people and, most of all, its products that enabled him to put the positive parts of the story in proper perspective to the negative:

> This is what actually happened:
>
> Steve, the Macintosh division, and Apple blew a hole in the side of the invincible IBM ship. Along the way, we suffered through calamities, infighting, and strife.
>
> After the introduction, we were physically and emotionally exhausted. Bringing Macintosh to market was an impossible act to follow, and this, combined with our physical and emotional fragility, caused us to stumble and fall. Nevertheless, a core of true believers—Apple employees, developers, and early Macintosh owners—sustained Macintosh, and made it successful.

To Kawasaki, the real lesson to be learned from the episode was that

> [a] small team of bright, fearless and ambitious punks led by a charismatic high priest trying to do the right thing can defeat mediocrity and the status quo. The battle can cost a lot (even the life of the high priest), but it is so magnificent that the toll almost doesn't matter.

Well, perhaps. But the hole in IBM wasn't big enough to sink that dreadnought. And if Sculley or Jobs had kept their eye on the ball—and on the declining spirits of the Mac team—that talent need never have been lost. Finally, Apple would never have stumbled and fallen had the high priest just for a moment stopped deluding himself or bullying those around him into a silent co-conspiracy to deny the reality of the situation.

Kawasaki is right to see Apple's disaster in mid-1985 as the by-product of its huge success the year before, but he is wrong to assume it was inevitable.

And it *was* a disaster. Kawasaki was there; he saw it up close:

> We brought our org charts to a large conference room in De Anza 2, the Apple building that housed most of the Apple executive staff, and wrote names on a white board. The people whose names weren't on the board at the end of two days of meetings were laid off. It was like being a master of ceremonies at a massive funeral, and I never want to go through an experience like that again.

The same scenario occurred in Apple offices and factories throughout the world. When it was over, and the layoffs were formally announced on Friday, June 14, just twenty days after the final Jobs-Sculley confrontation, fully one-fifth of Apple's total workforce—1,200 employees—had been laid off. As is almost always the case, the blow fell hardest not upon headquarters among the managers and executives who had been party to Apple's mistakes, but upon the factory workers. "The mood is very down," said one employee. "Even among people who kept their jobs, there's no rejoicing here today." A factory near Los Angeles, one in Dallas and one in Ireland were shut down. The IIc's assembly was moved to Fremont, the IIe's to Singapore.

"What happened to Atari can happen [at Apple]," Woz told reporters from his outsider's perch. "It's a time of desperation."

Back in Cupertino, 250 people were laid off at headquarters. In many ways, their shock was even greater. These were professional people who'd signed on to a skyrocketing company. They weren't accustomed to failure in either their careers or their employers. Worse, because of the unique nature of Apple, many had moved to Silicon Valley, bought homes or condos near Apple headquarters in what had become de facto company villages and socialized almost exclusively with Apple people. For them, being laid off meant losing not only their careers but their personal lives. They worked with Apple people, played with Apple people and slept with Apple people. Now they were pariahs, stripped of friends and lovers, marooned in the most expensive real estate market in America and facing a depressed job market.

8.5 Regroup

The company swallowed its bad medicine all at once. On the same day as the layoffs, Apple also announced the first quarterly loss in its history. It would prove to be $17 million. The company had actually shown a profit on sales, but decided to take the negative news all at once by factoring in an anticipated cost of reorganization of $40 million.

It didn't help much. The stock quickly went into free fall with the news, bottoming out at $14.75 within the week—and even after the analysts made their reappraisal of the company's comeback efforts, it still managed only a feeble climb back to $16. The question all the analysts were asking was: Can Apple find sales for the Macintosh?

Sculley and his team were asking the same thing. They were in a crisis mode, meeting every day, determining the next move, then rushing off to implement it. Meanwhile, the shock waves from the purge were still rolling across the company, setting off new explosions at unexpected locations. Two of these were near the top. Bob Belleville had resigned during the excitement, but had been talked into staying by Markkula. Now, a few weeks later, he found himself squeezed out by Gassée.

Mike Murray was next. In the reorganization, the II and Macintosh marketing teams had been pulled together under Campbell's aegis. Given their bitter history, there was bound to be a clash. Then into this mix was added a new marketing director, Mike Lorelli, who had recently joined Apple from Playtex. Campbell and Murray had fought in the past; Lorelli's marketing style, right out of consumer products, was antithetical to that which had grown up around the Mac group; Murray was given a space-filler job reporting to both of them. It wasn't long before he too packed up his stuff and moved over into the empty building. Steve Jobs now had his first team member for the new era.

On Tuesday, July 23, 1985, at a black-tie-optional event for 2,200 reporters and dignitaries at Lincoln Center in New York City, Commodore International announced its new computer, the $1,295 Amiga. Industry analyst Tim Bajarin, usually known as an Apple fan, pronounced the event "the most impressive demonstration I've seen in microcomputers. Amiga sets a standard, not just in its price range, but in personal computers."

In many important ways, the Amiga was the rest of Raskin's volkscomputer. It had superb stereo sound and bright graphics. Andy Warhol, betraying the Mac in a heartbeat, showed up to use the machine to draw a portrait of rocker Deborah Harry—having just learned how to use the machine the day before. "It's everything the Mac should be," said Richard Matlack of InfoCorp.

The Amiga was multimedia, and it was cheap. That was the best. On the downside, it had little software, its user interface paled next to the Mac OS and there was always Commodore's lousy reputation for quality. But still, at the lowest moment in Apple's story, the Amiga suddenly now presented the first real challenge to the Mac on its own turf. And this attack had come from below, right there at Jobs's original price point. Now Apple could no longer even take its own market base for granted.

Almost the same day as the Amiga introduction, Andy Hertzfeld was a featured guest on a panel put on by the new subscription on-line service Compuserve.

Having left Apple several months before, Hertzfeld felt unconstrained by any confidentiality rules. In unprecedented detail, he told the audience about the projects Apple had in the works—and the problems the company was having with those projects.

One was the urgent matter of getting the Finder program of the operating system, the traffic cop of the Mac interface, off the disk and into the Mac's core memory. Until that happened, Hertzfeld said, the interface would continue to be frustratingly slow. The trouble, said Hertzfeld, was that the Finder program was too big for the Mac's current complement of read-only core memory. It would be 1986, he warned, before the Mac had enough ROM capacity to move the Finder to where it belonged.

Responding to the threat of the Amiga, Hertzfeld warned that Apple wouldn't have a color Mac ready until late 1986, and a portable Mac, Apple's response to the success of a now surging Compaq in the PC world, wouldn't be available until long after that.

But it was to numerous questions about an "open" Mac architecture—a greater capacity for hooking up to third-party printers, disk drives and monitors—that Andy Hertzfeld made his most devastating appraisal. "It's certain," he said, "that the next Mac will be more open hardware-wise, but I'm not sure how much." What about software? The operating system itself? These questions were so far out of the realm of possibility that Hertzfeld didn't even address them. The underlying message was: no IBM compatibility, not even any Mac clones, for the rest of the 1980s. Apple was going to go it alone.

Six months later, John Sculley underscored the point. At the next analysts meeting, he agreed that IBM "will be the major force in defining most systems standards," but still argued that Apple "can be the leader in bringing together a superior human interface with real functionality in an IBM-defined systems world." It was Apple's first public admission that Big Blue had won that standards war.

And Apple's solution? It had none, only the counterargument that as long as Apple computers could be hooked up to IBM networks it didn't matter anyway. "We've always done everything ourselves," said Sculley. "Compatibility is no longer a barrier to entry."

He was utterly wrong.

Throughout the summer of 1985, Apple was haunted by the specter of Steve Jobs. He was the crazy aunt in the attic, the one nobody talked about, but no one ever forgot was there. And as long as he was there, the hermit of Apple, glimpsed as he entered and left the building, Jobs's very presence tore Apple in two. Half the company, including the Apple II group and most of senior management, was pleased to have him out of power and wished there was a way to get him out of the company without killing morale and gutting the stock. The other half of the company, mostly the Mac group and all the people in the far reaches of the company who saw him only as a distant star, ached at his loss from the firmament and prayed for his return. Some put on T-shirts with barely disguised double entendres like "We Want Our Jobs Back" (subtlety never being a company strong point). Others, less brave, silently prayed for the return of their champion. Sure, they'd heard the stories about him, but they also knew this: when Jobs had been in charge, Apple had been an exciting, successful, *vital* place. The only thing of importance that had occurred on Sculley's watch was the Macintosh . . . and whose idea was that?

Jobs, for his part, remained elusive. Intentional or not, it was an effective strategy. Everyone, from Sculley on down, was thinking about the peripatetic founder. Where is he now? What's he doing? What is he plotting?

After Russia, Jobs went to Italy with his girlfriend. Then Paris. While there, he called Susan Barnes to apologize for forgetting a dinner they'd planned. As an aside he mentioned that he was having such a good time in Europe he might stay there permanently. Barnes, beside herself in frustration at what was going on at Apple, began to cry. She told Jobs that if he was planning any new venture, she wanted to be part of it . . . and thus Apple got a new rumor and Jobs yet another mutineer.

Then, in late August, he returned. Once again, his timing was perfect. While Sculley and his team had spent the summer cleaning up the mess with moves that had left the company bitter and fearful, Jobs had been off taking the high-profile Grand Tour. Now he returned, unsullied by all that had happened. *He* hadn't announced the loss. *He* hadn't laid off all those wonderful Apple people. In fact, the rumors were that he felt terrible about it, that *he* would never have done such a thing were *he* still in charge.

It was a perfect play. Jobs may have made the mess, but Sculley had to clean it up. Jobs was still fun, which was more than you could say for the increasingly sullen and defensive John Sculley. Sculley knew it, and the realization that Jobs not only had left him holding the bag but now was winning the PR battle merely by doing nothing seemed to drive him to distraction.

Scariest of all, Jobs still owned 11 percent of the company. Sculley may have declawed the lion, but he still had teeth. With these holdings, Jobs as chairman could raise hell with Apple at annual meetings and directors gatherings and on proxy votes. And the presence of that sword, wielded by his jilted former pal, took its toll on Sculley. At the dreary analysts meeting, following the bombshells of the previous weeks, including the Commodore Amiga announcement the night before, Sculley, the man who hadn't blinked in the face of mighty Coca-Cola, finally lost his vaunted self-control. During the questions at the end of his presentation, Sculley was asked what operational role Jobs would now have at Apple. None, said Sculley testily. "There is no role for Steve Jobs in the operations of this company either now or in the future."

That was it. Sculley had finally been goaded into saying his real feelings. If Jobs wanted to stay at Apple, his role would be strictly ceremonial. He would be just like Woz had been in the latter days: a figurehead carted out for public appearances, well supervised so as not to say anything controversial, and kept far away from doing anything of substance within the company.

Even Jobs, back from Russia, could not romanticize or willfully misconstrue the message. "That was about as black-and-white as you need to make things," Jobs would later say.

But where to go? Jobs toyed for a while with the idea of running for the Senate, that perpetual fantasy of wealthy men who imagine themselves both wise and beloved. There were other ideas as well. An encounter with Stanford biochemist and Nobel laureate Paul Berg had left Jobs enamored with biology. And, like a good autodidact, Jobs quickly turned that curiosity into a small obsession. He read everything he could on the subject and even, like Woz, contemplated going back to school to study it. And, like computer scientists everywhere, Jobs also began developing elaborate theories about the relationship between electronics and living organisms.

Biochemistry wasn't the only topic that captured Jobs's wide-ranging imagination. He contemplated the creation of educational charities, outgrowths of Apple's existing programs to put computers in schools.

He was also being pulled in the direction of entrepreneurship. The massive reorganizations and the rampant confusion at Apple had left many of the old Mac team despondent and ready to resign. Just a short time before they had been heroes of the company, celebrities in the world of personal computing. Now they were being blamed for the company's financial straits. But the last straw was the arrival of the arrogant Gassée, who treated them as if they were incompetent, when, after all, they had designed the greatest computer of all time. Gassée lectured them as if they were children, and, in the ultimate apostasy, seemed to be planning to make the Mac into a high-end computer, almost a workstation, instead of sticking with Raskin's (compromised) People's Computer.

This wasn't what they signed on to Apple to do. And it didn't help that they weren't being spoiled and pampered anymore under the new regime. They wanted out. They came to Jobs individually and in groups: George Crow, an experienced analog engineer from the Mac group. Rich Page, an Apple Fellow in charge of the next-generation Mac. Bud Tribble, back from medical school and now running the Mac's software engineering department. Susan Barnes, senior controller for U.S. sales and marketing. Daniel Lewin, marketing manager for higher education. Andy Hertzfeld. Bob Belleville. Each had his own ax to grind. Whatever their motives, each had the same message for Jobs: Start another company and let us join you. We'll re-create the thrill and success of the Mac project.

Jobs, tucked away in his empty building, bitter at the mutiny of his staff, listened closely. And with his unique skill at synthesizing multiple and diverse notions into a single idea, it slowly came to him: What if he, not Apple, built the Big Mac? That is, a powerful, graphics-based workstation targeted primarily at higher education and capable of performing such tasks as Berg's complex biochemical equations? And what if he didn't compromise on any part of the machine, but simply made it into the most elegant computer in the world? It would be the Mac Redux, without the Mac's flaws—and better, it would be the true successor to the Apple II in the education market. The idea hit all of Jobs's hot buttons—not least of which was revenge.

In one respect, and perhaps only in that respect, was Steve Jobs like Steve Wozniak: once a big idea captured his imagination he was incapable of letting it go. It took over his life, and he pursued it ardently and obsessively, caring only fleetingly about the consequences. That was Jobs with this new project, as it had been with the Mac and before it the Apple I. It was what made him one of the greatest figures of his time, as well as one of its most flawed.

But if Jobs's strength was his ruthless single-mindedness, his weakness was his transparency. As with the coup attempt, he seemed incapable of not telegraphing his next pitch. He signaled his plan beginning on July 22 by filing, with the Securities and Exchange Commission, his intention to sell 100,000 shares valued at $1.7 million. The next day, he filed again, this time for 250,000 shares, worth $4.2 million. Two days after that, he filed for another 500,000 shares worth $8.1 million. The total came to 850,000 shares worth $14 million—14.2 percent of his Apple holdings of 6 million shares.

In the end, he would sell 782,000 of those shares, for a total of $11.2 million. Then, in late August, he again filed with the SEC, for 500,000 more shares, worth $7.4 million. After this, he would be down to 5.5 million shares, 8.9 percent of the company. He would still be the company's largest shareholder, but the sale was hardly a show of faith.

Needless to say, there was considerable speculation about the play. Apple officially declared it a "private transaction," but others, notably securities analyst John Dean, had other ideas. "I have a feeling he is out there putting a company together," perhaps obtaining the liquidity from the sale to "buy out someone who is distressed. If he has cash available, he can do some tough deals."

John Sculley, with his sixth sense for corporate politics, tried to contact Jobs. He wrote him a note suggesting the two get together on the morning of Friday, September 13. Jobs didn't deign to reply. Instead, to everyone's great curiosity, he added to the agenda of the September 12 board meeting a final entry, "Chairman's Report." As the board filed into the boardroom, the expectation—especially by Sculley—was that Jobs would use his soapbox to harangue the assembled about the reorganization, the state of the company, the loss of key employees and everything else about the Sculley regime—the subtext being that things would be different were Steven Jobs in charge. Sculley wasn't worried: the board had made its decision, the die was cast, the reorganization was underway; there was no way the directors would rescind their decision now.

This time Jobs didn't telegraph his next surprise. Instead, he calmly got up and said dispassionately, "I've been thinking a lot and it's time for me to get on with my life. It's obvious to me that I've got to do something. I'm thirty years old."

He's quitting! Jobs went on as calmly as before, reading from a prepared script. He had, he said, done a lot of thinking over the summer about what he wanted to do with his life. Politics. School. Entrepreneurship. In the end he had looked back on his career and realized that the most satisfying experience had been his work getting computers into schools. For that reason he had decided to start a new venture aimed at the high end of the education market.

There were murmurs. Jobs quickly added that this new venture would not compete in any way with Apple, but would be complementary. And though a few Apple employees would be leaving with him, they would not be critical to

Apple's future plans. Jobs went on to suggest that ultimately Apple might be interested in becoming a distributor to whatever product was to be built by this company. And, on top of that, Jobs & Co. might want to license Macintosh software—an unusual twist from the guy most viscerally against any Apple clones.

If Jobs expected the Apple board to react in the same low-key manner in which he had made the announcement, he was mistaken. These were old pros, and red lights were going off everywhere. Quitting? New venture? Complementary? *Taking employees?! What the hell is going on here?*

No one was more agitated than Mike Markkula. He had taken this aggressive, brilliant, difficult kid and built a billion-dollar corporation around him. He had retreated to the shadows, pushing Jobs forward into the limelight until the young man had become synonymous not only with Apple Computer but with his entire generation. He had defended Jobs during the hard times and coddled him during the good; he had spent thousands of hours calming down the angry employees and putting out the wildfires that Jobs left in his wake. Now he was not only walking out in a snit but starting another computer company—and taking Apple employees with him.

It was the last that especially annoyed Markkula. "Why would you take anyone at all?" he demanded of the young man.

"Don't get upset," said Jobs, defensively, to his old mentor. "These are very low-level people that you wouldn't miss. And they will be leaving anyway. Don't look at this as a big issue."

If anyone in the room thought he was lying, they didn't say so until a few moments later after Jobs was asked to leave the room. Instead, the discussion revolved around the new company Jobs planned to build. As always with Steve Jobs, there was that contradictory feeling that he was utterly incapable of running a company, yet that he was clever enough to figure out how to do it anyway. And if so, what would that company be like? With the II covering the low end of the education market and Gassée already talking about making the next-generation Mac a more sophisticated and powerful machine, how could any product be *complementary* to Apple? Where would you go in that market without competing directly with an Apple product? But would Steve Jobs really compete with the company he had built, that he professed to love, in which he was a leading shareholder?

It was suggested, and agreed upon by the board, that Apple should take a position in Jobs's new company—as much as 10 percent. That would maintain the link with Jobs while retaining a defensive position in any decisions by the company that might go against Apple. And, if the new company really was complementary, and if it was successful, Apple would be in a perfect position to buy it out and bring Jobs & Co. back into the fold.

Sculley, of all people, was given the task of telling Jobs the news: "All of us have appreciated what you have done for Apple and we recognize you want to get on with your life. On the assumption that your business is complementary and not competitive, and that you're not taking key people from Apple, we want you to reconsider your decision to resign from the board." Sculley then offered the investment deal.

Jobs replied that he would like to consider both offers. They agreed to meet again in a week.

It never happened. The next morning, Friday the 13th, Jobs dropped his bomb. Knowing that Sculley had a regular staff meeting at 7:30 A.M., Jobs called at 7:10 and asked if he could come right over. When he arrived, he handed Sculley ("sheepishly," Sculley would later claim) an envelope containing a typewritten note. It said:

> Dear John,
>
> Today these five employees of Apple Computer will be resigning to join me in my new venture.

Then the names: Page, Lewin, Tribble, Barnes and Crow. It was the ultimate corporate Dear John (literally) letter. Jobs was not only leaving; he was taking with him the guts of the Mac team in education. As Sculley would later write:

> Together, they knew our internal schedules, our costs, the focus of Apple's next products, the schedule of when we would introduce them, how they would be used, and which individuals and universities we would work with to ensure their success. Their accumulated knowledge would give Steve a decided advantage to compete directly with Apple in terms of marketing opportunities and technical and product know-how.

"Steve, these aren't low-level people," a stunned Sculley told Jobs.

"Well," Jobs replied, "these people were going to resign anyway. They are going to be handing in their resignations by nine this morning, so I wanted to give you and the executive staff the courtesy of knowing that beforehand because I know you have your meeting this morning."

Silicon Valley had been built on teams of talented employees (though rarely by a founder/chairman) walking out to start new companies. And some degree of subterfuge had been involved in all of them—secret meetings at Denny's, coordinated resignations, etc. But this was ugly. Less than twenty-four hours earlier Jobs had blithely treated his new company as if it was just a notion still being developed and mentioned that he might be taking some minor Apple foot soldiers with him. He had lied about almost everything but the fact that he was leaving.

Furious, Sculley pressed him on his words before the board. *All* of this had happened since yesterday? Yes, said Jobs, we all met last night and agreed to resign together this morning.

It was bullshit. Sculley knew it. Every executive at Apple would soon know it. And if Steve would lie about that, what about the rest?

A few minutes later, an ashen Sculley marched in to his staff meeting. He gave the note to Eisenstat, then turned and told the others. There was an uproar. Bill Campbell reportedly announced, "We should expose him for the fraud that he is so that people here stop regarding him as the Messiah."

But, with consequences unimaginable at the time, Apple did nothing of the sort. The news of Jobs's resignation broke on September 17. In keeping with the sordidness of the entire affair, the press got a copy of Jobs's resignation letter to Markkula even before Markkula and Apple did. It was classic Steve Jobs: arrogant, self-pitying, and with one eye cocked on the publicity angle.

"Dear Mike," the letter began. "This morning's papers carried suggestions that Apple is considering removing me as Chairman. I don't know the source of these reports but they are both misleading to the public and unfair to me." Jobs went on to recount his version of the events of the previous week, portraying himself as sincerely presenting his plans to the board and encountering only "a hostile posture towards me and my new venture."

Then came the self-pity: "I find myself saddened and perplexed by the management's conduct in this matter, which seems to me contrary to Apple's best interests. . . . I continue to hope that calmer voices within the Company may yet be heard. . . . I am but thirty and want still to contribute and achieve. . . . I would wish our parting to be both amicable and dignified."

The result was a predictable media storm. If Apple had any plans for a concerted demolition of Jobs's reputation, they were quickly abandoned in the panic to maintain some sort of PR control on the frenzy. Apple could only react, and by the time it had a chance to recoup, the story was already stale. On the critical day after, a furious, frustrated Mike Markkula was reduced to releasing a terse formal statement saying that Jobs had implied that "he would not recruit any key Apple personnel."

At least in his exit, Jobs had checkmated Apple. And he had done so on the day the company planned to introduce several new products for the Mac and the II. Said one Apple executive, "He always gets even. That's the way he is." Said a former Apple manager, "This is one of the best soap operas in America."

But if Steve had hoped to wound his old company on the way out, he failed. His reputation now preceded him, at least among business leaders and technologists. Apple's stock actually went up a dollar per share with his departure. Still, there were thousands of Apple employees and millions of consumers around the world who still saw him, in Campbell's words, as the Messiah. That guaranteed him a willing audience whenever his new company decided to make an announcement—and scores of talented Appleites who secretly watched with envy and made plans to follow him.

John Sculley, in his autobiography, would claim that when Jobs's office was cleaned out, a worker found a framed photo of Jobs and Sculley, huddled together in one of their endless private conversations, taken just seven months before. On the back Sculley had written, "Here's to Great Ideas, Great Experiences and a Great Friendship." The glass on the picture was shattered, as if it had been smashed against a wall.

For his part, Jobs, reached at his home soon after the news of his resignation broke, would only say about his relationship with John Sculley that "it is surprising to me that John Sculley doesn't say anything" and "I'm more worried about Apple than I am about him."

In fact, Sculley called Jobs the next day, saying later only that the two had "agreed to set aside our friendship." He added, "I'm disappointed someone so big a contributor to the industry and such a shaper to Apple's success would get himself into this predicament." A few days later, he would add defensively, "I didn't come to Apple to take it away from Steve Jobs."

In its first decade, Apple Computer had slowly learned that it couldn't live with Steve Jobs; now it would spend the next decade coming to the realization that it couldn't live without him either. Other executives, and Sculley more than anyone, would make terrible business mistakes. But in the end, it was Steve Jobs who had placed Apple in this terrible dilemma.

Jobs, of course, didn't see it this way. It was he who had been betrayed. It was he who was the victim. He likened his experiences at Apple to "the first woman you've fallen in love with. . . . This has been such an awful thing." He said it felt as if someone had "punched you in the stomach and it knocks the wind out of you and you can't breathe."

Now he would go off and try to make himself famous and important once again. He would continue to raid Apple for talent, and he would find in

Canon and Ross Perot investors still bedazzled by his image. The result would be NeXT Computer, the most dysfunctional company family in Silicon Valley. NeXT was a glimpse of what Apple would have been under Jobs alone. It produced a magnificent, stylish computer—the most beautiful machine in industry history—out of equally stylish offices in Menlo Park. The press lauded the machine after its big showcase launch in 1988, but no one bought it. Instead, as Apple was about to enter the most successful and profitable era in its history, Steve Jobs sat in his glass box, a high-tech Heathcliff, terrorizing everyone around him from employees to caterers, watching lesser mortals like Bill Gates and Larry Ellison become even richer and more famous than he, and praying for his moment of redemption to come.

Looking back from the perspective of nearly fifteen years, Regis McKenna would say, "The biggest mistake we ever made was letting Steve leave the company. There had to have been some way to keep him; there must have been *some* role he could have played. Because after he left, the company was never again the same."

8.6 Angels in the Printshop

Apple remained a deeply troubled company. For the year ended September 27 the company's net income fell 4 percent to $61.2 million, much of that drop due to the fourth quarter. Sales had picked up—27 percent to $1.9 billion—but the company was still losing market share and still was not penetrating the corporate market in anywhere near the manner it needed. The II was getting older by the day and without a major redesign would be obsolete soon. Any new Mac was still in the distant future, the lost year of the Mac team now starting to tell.

The capper, one guaranteed to damage the company's already fragile morale, came on Halloween, when *Electronic Business* magazine announced that John Sculley, despite Apple's dreary year, the layoffs and the ousting of Jobs, was the highest-paid executive in electronics: $2.1 million in salary and bonuses.

In the midst of all this, there was one piece of bright news. Somewhere beneath all the dross, there hid a sterling company. Years of fame had brought to Apple an enormous number of talented people, and most had survived the layoffs. In fact, firing 20 percent of the workforce not only had not slowed Apple down but seemed to make it more efficient, if not more innovative. Also, despite the losses, the company's financial reserves had increased to

$254.6 million in cash with no debt—enough to finance several new product ventures. And, just as vital, there remained a loyal, even rabid, customer base. And there were superb products, from the IIe to the Turbo Mac to the Apple LaserWriter printer.

By the end of 1985, it was dawning on Sculley and the leadership team that merely by maintaining and growing the current product catalog and cutting out the gross inefficiencies, Apple could return to its former levels of profitability *without* any great new product breakthroughs or improved Mac unit sales. For a guy like Sculley, who always kept one eye on the stock price, this was wonderful news.

For the medium term, perhaps as much as three years, it also meant that Apple didn't have to run around and try to change the world yet again. The new team could take some time to get it right, rather than race against a declining bank account. But in the long term, the old problem had not changed: Apple was running out of room to maneuver. IBM and the army of clone makers following in its wake were slowly, inexorably gobbling up market share. Each percentage point gain increased the likelihood that the IBM-Intel-Microsoft architecture would become the universal (it was already the dominant) standard in personal computing, while reducing the interest by software developers in creating products for Apple machines.

The last year had shown that, despite exhausting efforts by the sales and marketing staffs, Apple was never going to dislodge IBM from the office market. Apple would always be a renegade, an outsider, in that world. So what did that leave? The home market might someday be vast, but prognosticators had been predicting that market to take off ever since Apple had been founded. Many good companies had died waiting for consumers to come around. Education? The II had that market sewn up. But how long could Apple depend upon that old workhorse? And though schools might covet the Macintosh, it was way too expensive. That presented the dangerous possibility that one day in the near future the II would suddenly become obsolete and the educational community, if it didn't find a low-cost Mac waiting in the wings, would turn forever to the far-cheaper IBM clones.

So it seemed at that moment, in late 1985, that Apple was trapped. Having lived on its image, it had now lost its chief image maker. Having created the mass market for personal computers, it now found itself either squeezed out of every submarket within that world or holding on to one of those submarkets with a geriatric machine. Unless some new market came along—which seemed utterly unlikely—the best Apple could do would be to run a tighter ship, introduce occasional product upgrades and try to slow as much as possible a long, inevitable decline to oblivion. That was a hard reality for the management of Apple to take: after all, despite the recent problems, the company was still the toast of the computing world.

So who was buying Macintoshes, besides early adopters, nonconformist corporate types and the wealthy curious? It turned out to be an interesting group, composed mostly of people in graphics-oriented fields: advertising agencies, designers, publishers, owners of newsletters. These were people for whom the computer culture had until recently seemed as remote as Siberia. But the Mac was something entirely different, a graphics-based computer, and the visual world understood it immediately. In this motley collection of customers, Apple might have gotten a clue to its future success. But nobody besides the sales force really noticed this group, or the interesting fact that many were also buying the Apple LaserWriter.

The LaserWriter, Apple's laser printer, had enjoyed a typically checkered history at Apple. Jobs had initially been against it, though by the time it was ready to appear he had turned into its greatest proponent. The goal of the LaserWriter team had been to create the functional equivalent of the wonderful new $30,000 laser printers, now being used with mainframes, in a $7,000 box that would work with the Macintosh. The team achieved its goal, using the combination of a Canon printer engine and a powerful motherboard (designed by Burrell Smith himself) that featured a new microprocessor, the Motorola 68020, that was actually more powerful than the one in the Macintosh. Thus, those in the know realized that the LaserWriter was in fact a computer in which the display and keyboard had been replaced by a printer mechanism.

It was a masterpiece of design, yet another in Apple's growing list, but within the company doubts were loudly expressed right up to the day of the LaserWriter's introduction. I don't care how good the printout looks, said the doubters, who the hell is going to pay for a printer that costs twice as much as the computer it serves?

And yet, month by month, the number of LaserWriters Apple sold increased. So solid was this business that during the dark months of mid-1985 one could have made a strong case for Apple being not a computer, but a printer company. And that was only the beginning. Because what happened next may be the best confirmation of the notion, held by some Apple fanatics even now, that Apple is a blessed place where lifesaving miracles regularly occur.

This miracle, for once, came not from inside, but from outside the company. Two young companies converged, seemingly out of the blue, at the moment of Apple's greatest need. And, like angels, these two companies helped Apple back on its feet and then off into the most prosperous period of its history.

One of these companies was the creation of an eccentric, bespectacled and unemployed engineer named Paul Brainerd, who, coincidentally, hailed from the Seattle area in Microsoft's backyard. Brainerd had a unique résumé for someone in high tech: he actually had real-life experience in a different field—in Brainerd's case, publishing. He had once been a newspaper editor. In January 1984, at the time of the Macintosh introduction, Brainerd was working for Atex, a company familiar to journalists everywhere as a purveyor of terminals to newsrooms. These were expensive and sophisticated systems, but they still offered Brainerd invaluable training in the relationship between computer technology and the physical process of composing, layout and printing newspapers and magazines.

When Atex was bought by Kodak, Brainerd, golden parachute in hand, hired four of his old engineers and set about building a new company.

Brainerd had a vision that computing technology had passed a threshold in price and performance that made it possible to stand an established industry on its head, revolutionize it and then dominate it. For Brainerd, this sleeping industry ripe for attack was printing—not just books, magazines and newspapers, but brochures, newsletters, flyers; all the various projects currently handled by printing shops and small presses. These industries were only now being touched by technology in the form of very expensive, computerized composing machines. Brainerd was convinced he could duplicate all but the most sophisticated forms of this work on low-cost personal computers, especially those equipped with the new laser printers. He called his idea "desktop publishing" and his company, Aldus, after the Renaissance printer Aldus Manutius, creator of the first low-cost pocket books.

Brainerd and the team spent the winter and spring of 1984 perfecting their product, which they called Pagemaker. And as soon as a crude prototype was ready on a stack of disks, Brainerd grabbed them and hit the road in search of investors, customers and, most of all, the right machine on which to run the product. So improvised was this tour that Brainerd actually showed up unannounced at Apple's sales office in Beaverton, Oregon, and asked to see one of the new Macintoshes he'd heard about. Luckily, the local rep was a shrewd judge of software—even though it was still so buggy that it rarely ran all the way through—and he not only promised to show Brainerd a Mac as soon as he had one available, but actually drove up to Seattle with the machine in his trunk and left it at Aldus for more than a month.

Needless to say, Brainerd and the boys were entranced. This was just the computer interface they needed to draw out the full measure of Pagemaker.

They decided to go with the Mac. Imagine, then, their thrill when a couple of months later, now being received at Apple as true business partners, they were given an early glimpse of the LaserWriter.

There it was. Everything Paul Brainerd had dreamed of: a composing room, a printshop, all in a personal computer and an accompanying printer with a total price of only $10,000. He was ready now to conquer an industry.

Brainerd not only had a great product but also had perfect timing. He had come to Apple just at the moment that Sculley and his team had reached the terrifying conclusion that the Mac had no markets it could call its own; and, just as bad, that in those markets where it needed most to be taken seriously—the office, the laboratory—it was still seen as a clever toy. It didn't help that the killer app software that was supposed to legitimize the Mac in the workplace, Lotus's Jazz, turned out to be not only a dud but an insult. Jazz was so elementary that it *confirmed* the shallowness of the Mac.

But Brainerd had the answer. With the help of a champion inside Apple, a young Harvard MBA with the bad luck to be named John Scull, the Aldus story was taken right to the top. Scull had asked Brainerd to prepare a document describing Pagemaker and its philosophy, and when Brainerd delivered a twenty-page white paper, Scull took it directly to Sculley. As Brainerd later told Steven Levy: "Apple was desperate to differentiate Macintosh from the IBM PC. Desktop publishing was the only option."

Sculley proved willing to throw some of the company's tight resources behind Aldus. It was Apple, not Aldus, that took out ads for Pagemaker in major magazines—and that subsidized Brainerd on a national press tour timed with Pagemaker's July 15, 1985, introduction.

There was a third player in this nexus. Adobe had been founded by a group of former Xerox PARC researchers led by John Warnock, who just happened to be one of the few people in the world Steve Jobs looked up to. Cringely would even claim that Warnock, with his programming genius, intellectual arrogance and personal dignity was "the father that Steve Jobs always wished for."

Warnock had his own vision of how personal computer technology could be put to use to create compelling graphics. He began this work at the University of Utah, then moved on to Xerox PARC. There he created a graphics programming language with fellow researcher Martin Jewell. Called JaM (for "John and Martin"), this language was further refined into a Xerox laser printer-compatible language called Interpress in the hopes that the mother company would adopt it as its own. But Xerox, keeping its streak perfect for stupid decisions in personal computing, spent two years hemming and hawing. Meanwhile, Warnock and his PARC boss, Chuck Geschke, who was Interpress's biggest supporter, finally said to hell with it and quit to start their own company.

Even more than Aldus, Adobe—named after a creek in Warnock's backyard in Los Altos—had a rocky start. The new start-up first contemplated building high-end printers, then computer workstations, then finally settled on what it knew best, software. In software, Adobe's initial business thrust was to use Warnock's understanding of graphics to generate typefaces on computer screens—type ultimately being just another form of graphics. The result was Postscript, perhaps the most influential software program in personal computing history.

Postscript enabled computer users to at last escape from a world of a single typeface in only a single point size that could only be capitalized and underlined for emphasis. By encoding fonts and typefaces into mathematical equations, Postscript allowed computer owners to pick from scores of typefaces, adjust character size as needed and switch to italic or bold or shadow at the press of a key. It all happened effortlessly, instantaneously and without any degradation of the image. You could even add graphics generated by the computer or inputted through a scanner.

In its own way, Postscript was as exciting as Pagemaker, and it had many times the potential user base. And, like Pagemaker, Postscript needed a crisp, bit-mapped display and a precise laser printer to really show its stuff. Postscript made the Mac special, not just clever, and that would prove the critical difference. Apple, recognizing a good thing, bought 15 percent of Adobe, for $2.5 million. It was Jobs's last great act of his first tenure at Apple, and it was a reminder of just how valuable to the company he could be.

The marvelous thing about Pagemaker and Postscript was that they dovetailed together beautifully—and, in turn, they could only work well on the Macintosh. It was a three-way synergy of a kind rarely seen in business. And the combination of desktop publishing and a graphical user interface sent waves of delight and terror, respectively, through the market and the competition.

Customers adored desktop publishing. Here, at last, was the first great new application for computers since spreadsheets. And better yet, it could be used by anybody. Graphic artists and printers loved the technology because it drastically simplified their work (working so well, in fact, that it put many out of business). In short order, even the magazines that had predicted the imminent demise of Apple were laying out their issues on Mac systems. Moreover, AppleTalk, that nearly forgotten linchpin of the Mac Office, now suddenly made sense. At seven grand, a LaserWriter was a lot of bucks for use with a single computer, but not with a dozen or more Macs scattered around a company.

For consumers professionals and small businesspeople, Mac desktop publishing was just as exciting. Ten thousand dollars might be a hunk of change, but it was justified for a machine that could not only maintain mailing lists and do payroll but also create mailers, newsletters, posters and invitations. It quickly became a status symbol to send out an invoice or flyer that was a riot of fonts and faces. By mid-1986, in a measure of how quickly desktop publishing was adopted as a standard in the corporate world, it was a rare day when you didn't pass a bulletin board or kiosk or receive an interoffice memo or a piece of mail that didn't look like an explosion in a type factory.

Almost overnight, Apple once again commanded the awe of the computer industry. *It* had the new killer app, and the penumbra from desktop publishing seemed to wrap the Mac in its warm light. Apple salesmen and evangelists found themselves welcomed into the halls of giant corporations. The same MIS managers who had looked upon the Mac as an expensive novelty now clamored to know all about desktop publishing.

And not just desktop publishing. The glow also extended to the Mac's graphical user interface and to any third-party software that took advantage of it. "Graphics" was the new buzzword and everybody wanted it. And for good reason. After sitting down at a Macintosh and constructing a cover page for a newsletter, complete with masthead, illustrations and multiple typefaces—all in a WYSIWYG ("what you see is what you get") format that looked just like the finished result—using an IBM/DOS computer ("C:load file") was like switching off half of your brain.

Desktop publishing made manifest what had always been Steve Jobs's dream. It made the Macintosh so cool that to own anything else was humiliating. The company for the first time had the attention and respect of creative types, small business owners, educators *and* the Fortune 500. This was the moment for Steve Jobs to shine; to bring his charisma, enthusiasm and risk taking to bear on this brief moment of opportunity and blow it open with new products, new promotions and a new attitude. But Jobs was gone, and there was no one at Apple now capable of assuming his mantle.

Just a few days after his resignation Jobs had a confrontation with Mike Markkula. Feeling it proper, for old times' sake, to formally put his letter of resignation in Markkula's hands (even though he already leaked it to the press), Jobs had driven with Tribble and Barnes over to Mike's house. He entered the home alone, with the condition that the other two retrieve him if he hadn't returned in fifteen minutes. What he encountered inside was not just Markkula but Eisenstat and Mike Brown, the attorney Apple had just hired to sue Jobs's new company. Before Susan Barnes ran in and dragged him off, Jobs found himself in a shouting match with Markkula. And in the midst of this, Markkula at last let his true feelings be known: If you had only waited, he told Jobs, if you'd only been willing to stand in the corner for a year, everything might have been worked out.

And it wouldn't even have been a year. It would have been only a few months before Jobs would likely have been given desktop publishing. Sculley & Co. would have grinned and bore it, because Jobs was the only person up to the task. It would have been the perfect vindication, not just of the Mac but of Steve Jobs's judgment. Instead he chose to pout and betray Apple. Apple in turn would make billions off desktop publishing, but it would take Sculley years to fully appreciate its importance—and by then it was too late, the opportunity to regain dominance of the market had been lost.

8.7 SILICON SYMPHONY

One person who did understand the import of desktop publishing was Bill Gates, and it scared him every way but witless. As with his arm's-length partner at Intel, Andy Grove, one of Gates's greatest skills was that he responded to every real or imagined attack with an instant, all-out counteroffensive. He never allowed his more inventive competitors to consolidate their gains. And he never showed this skill more brilliantly than in response to the threat from Mac desktop publishing. Gates had been smart enough to get a forewarning of what was to come thanks to the November 1983 introduction by VisiCorp of a new graphical user interface (GUI) for IBM PCs called VisiOn.

VisiOn proved to be a disaster, partly for design problems and partly because VisiCorp did just about everything to alienate applications developers, but its impending arrival had lit a fire under Gates. DOS, after all, was the franchise at Microsoft, and there was no way Bill Gates was ever going to allow a usurper to even get on the field. So he flogged the company to build its own GUI, called the Interface Manager, to be ready for introduction by the time of the VisiOn announcement. It wasn't, but Gates simply announced it anyway, preempting VisiCorp.

It would take him two years to fulfill that product announcement, and when the new operating system arrived, now called Windows, it proved to be a kluge—slow, unwieldy, ugly and counterintuitive where the Mac OS was elegant and self-evident. Having been built on top of the DOS core, it was compromised from the start—a weakness that would haunt Windows upgrades right to the present. But none of that mattered. What counted was that when the Macintosh finally took off, abashed IBM PC owners had a graphical operating system of their own, albeit profoundly flawed, that they could turn to instead of switching to Macintosh.

Of course, Gates didn't stop there. Once he saw the Mac, and then watched it break out with desktop publishing, he knew his franchise would only be secure when he could match Apple step by step on the IBM PC. To that end, he held the Windows development group to the fire, while at the same time began developing applications programs for the Mac (Microsoft would eventually be the Mac's largest software developer) and even licensed those parts of the Mac interface that Apple made available. In other words, he helped Apple (and made a tidy profit in the process) while learning enough to crush it. And John Sculley's Apple was happy for the help. Faced with the very last opportunity it would have to regain market leadership, Apple instead chose to embrace its most dangerous competitor.

And what was the company doing during this critical period? Redoubling its effort to consolidate its new market gains? No, celebrating its restored profitability at the annual sales meeting. On the last night, which happened to fall on Halloween, the Apple assembled threw a costume party. John Sculley showed up in long underwear, his face painted silver with multicolored stars for eyes, dressed as the "Spirit of Apple." But the real spirit of Apple was running a company called NeXT. Sculley only looked like a fool.

Now in the driver's seat at Apple, and despite being warned once by the board, Sculley was quickly reverting to his passive-aggressive ways. Not long after Jobs's departure, Sculley flew to San Diego to address Bill Campbell's sales team, ostensibly to thank the group for having kept its act together in the face of apparent chaos back at headquarters. Instead, Sculley reamed out the room. He told the sales force—the same people who had just brought in Apple's biggest new business partners—that they weren't even the best sales organization in their corner of the industry. That they paled against their counterparts at IBM and Compaq. He further warned them against cruising on their recent successes and slacking off in the months ahead.

The reaction was predictable. The staff was furious. Campbell was so hurt and humiliated that he was ready to quit. In the end, though there was a core of hard truth in what he said, Sculley backed off. Writing about that experience later, Sculley would say that, unlike Pepsi, where "toughness counted," such behavior by a CEO at Apple was "a terrible mistake" because it "created tremendous anxiety." In response, Sculley sentenced himself to reeducation and sensitivity training:

> The image of the chief executive as a tough, aloof, nearly macho hero is an anachronism in today's world. The New Age leaders will lead not with toughness but powerful ideas. My natural instincts were to be authoritative, cool and distant. I was too consumed with solving a problem instead of the building for the future.

The New Age leader, he went on to write, "has to show his fallibility. Making mistakes is a very real and important part of succeeding."

Apple Computer was in the hands of a chief executive undergoing a midlife spiritual crisis, and the timing couldn't be worse. Thousands of lives were to be held hostage to the on-the-job self-actualization training of the CEO. Even worse, a company unequaled for its tiny fiefdoms, internecine battles, unmanageable prima donnas and runaway new-product development programs was now to be managed by a man who no longer believed in interfering or banging heads. John Sculley, the tough marketing genius who had been brought in to bring some rigor and maturity to Apple, had instead become, indeed, the Spirit of Apple in silver lamé tights. In his person, he embodied almost everything wrong with the company, while lacking most things right.

It was all there in that eyes-averted, limp handshake. But it also could be found in almost every action, every day, at Apple with John Sculley. And here too Steve Jobs had left his mark. When you heard an Apple vice president say to Sculley, "What's the matter, John? You seem sad. Have you meditated yet today?" you couldn't be sure, after Jobs, whether you were seeing a company careening toward disaster or were getting a lucky first glimpse of the enlightened CEO of the twenty-first century. After all, Jobs was crazy and he'd built Apple into a billion-dollar corporation, so if Sculley sometimes acted like he should be turning pottery and pouring candles instead of running a computer company, who was to say he was wrong? The press—and even analysts—gave him the benefit of the doubt.

Had John Sculley sold off Apple right after the Macintosh introduction, he might have been a hero. He had a second chance after the financial turnaround in 1985. Now he could take credit for fixing Apple *without* Jobs. He could have walked away an industry legend, his mysterious persona still intact, his reputation untarnished.

Instead, he stayed. Apple, like every other company in the personal computer industry, lived in a state of perpetual crisis and desperation. But behind this steady hiss of near-term problems and opportunities, there were larger market forces at work, sensed only as a deep, almost inaudible rumble under the chatter of today's news. The great industry leaders and innovators—from Hewlett and Packard to Gates—had always been attuned to that hidden sound. Other successful entrepreneurs and executives, such as Nolan Bushnell, Gene Amdahl and Tandem's Jimmy Treybig, had heard it once and built giant companies, but never heard it again. Woz had heard it too, in 1975, but as the failure of his new universal remote control company, CL9, proved, he now had a tin ear. Woz even ran off to Hawaii in search of isolation and inspiration—only to discover after four weeks that, according to *Wired* magazine, "He couldn't recapture that loneliness and the idealism that had once been the source of his prodigious concentration. He came back and hired other engineers to finish the job." Jobs, by comparison, heard the sound all the time, but in his arrogance thought that he was making it, and could control it, even change it.

Sculley never heard it. Perhaps it was impossible for him to do so. Perhaps you need to *live* the high-tech revolution, and fight in its trenches, not join up as a brigadier general. That was why the number of successful nontechnical business executives in electronics could almost be counted on one hand—and on close inspection every one of them was a special case. Sure, Irwin Federman, a finance guy, had largely succeeded at MMI, but he was a strong-willed boss of legendary personal integrity running a chip business in a mature industry. And in time, even MMI would get caught flat-footed during a technological shift and wind up selling out to a technologist with almost perfect pitch: Jerry Sanders of Advanced Micro Devices.

A similar story could be told about most of the other nontech businessmen running high-tech companies. Either they were in older industries in which most of the innovation had already been wrung out or they had at their right hand a genius chief technologist. Or they were living on borrowed time.

If John Sculley had ever heard the deep waves of technological change, it was only for a moment as a child. But twenty years at Pepsi had left him utterly tone deaf. So his only choice was to depend upon the talents of others. But he was too out of touch to choose the right mentors. Jean-Louis Gassée, with good Cartesian logic, could postulate those deep waves, even turn them into poetry, but he couldn't hear them . . . and he was Apple's chief technologist.

Instinctively, Sculley turned elsewhere in the company. But many of the most creative souls in the company had moved on during the failure of the III and the Lisa, or the collapse of the Mac, or the abandonment of the II. They had been replaced by the kind of people always attracted to highly visible, public corporations: risk-averse, highly competent professionals, typically from the very best schools. These were bright, talented people who, when faced with the choice of risking everything on a big stock payoff or merely taking a good salary in a secure job, would always choose the latter. Most swaggered like entrepreneurs, but in the end they were merely bureaucrats in mufti. Their mission—to the relief of many, because life in a start-up is brutal and exhausting—was to kill the entrepreneurial spirit and replace it with an organization built to last.

By the end of the 1980s, Apple's executive row looked more like Savile Row. The pirate days were gone, surviving only in company histories and advertisements. The more dangerous elements in Apple's past—the hacking, the sweatshops, the rip-offs—were now either buried or gelded into a nice, safe mischievousness that gave a little shiver of rakish frisson to the new legions of well-scrubbed, double-breasted young professionals who now roamed the company's halls.

The January 1986 Apple annual shareholders meeting was special, precisely because it was not.

For years, especially in 1984, Apple had used the occasion as the proscenium for its biggest product announcements. It was the moment when Steve Jobs would stride out onstage and announce Apple's newest insanely great creation, whether it lived up to that title or not.

But Jobs was history—and as if to remind the world of that fact—Apple decided *not* to use the event again as anything but a meeting of folks holding company stock. "We're going to be more discreet and less predictable in product announcement and not march to the dates we have had before. Our January shareholders meetings will be just that—a shareholders meeting."

The subtext was: *This is no longer a juvenile company run by Steve Jobs. We are now a mature corporation led by grown-ups.* But the fact was that Apple would never again have a new product introduction that riveted the world's attention.

The Apple being built by the new executive team was infinitely more efficient than the one it replaced. New products now mostly came out on time, neatly packaged and stocked with the right software and the crisply designed manuals. The company's advertisements and commercials were now cute and housebroken, as reinforcing of the values of yuppie boomers as those produced by Honda and, of course, Pepsi. Apple Computer was now sold in computer stores, department stores and even stereo stores using the most sophisticated point-of-sale tools, demos and promotions. And when new products were introduced, the company still held media events, now much more sophisticated and choreographed than the original Lisa and Mac announcements—and instead of taking place in the theater of a community college, these events now were put on at Apple's own trade show, MacWorld Expo, held each year in Boston and San Francisco, before tens of thousands of true believers.

Apple under John Sculley quickly became a satisfying (if not wonderful) place to work. The company that had no retirement plan because nobody figured to stay that long, got one. It got a day-care center too. And an employee store. And a real, honest-to-God working budget. Unlike in the Steve Jobs era, you could arrive in the morning and know that today would be much like yesterday. It was like a college campus with older, but better-dressed students. PhDs were everywhere: they filled the offices of the Mac educational group, of Apple University and the labs. As a boomer facing middle age, you could go to work at Apple and feel good about helping teach kids and fighting the totalitarian Intel-Microsoft monolith and sitting in meetings where important people talked about the philosophical challenge of making the world a better place. Then that night, at the Little League game, you could feel the countercultural, superior thrill of saying you worked for Apple Computer.

Boring as it was, the new Apple business model seemed to work. For the first quarter ended December 27, 1985, Apple announced record earnings far above even Wall Street's estimates. They were, in fact, the best quarterly numbers in the company's history. That morning the stock jumped two points to 22⅝.

It seemed a validation of everything Apple had done over the previous year: Jobs's ouster, the arrival of the new team, the layoffs, the reorganization, even the decision to remain PC-incompatible. Most of all, it was a testament to the wisdom of John Sculley. He had taken a troubled company run by a troubled founder and turned it into a lean, mean moneymaking machine. "Apple Computer is healthy and strong," he crowed in the announcement. The long corporate nightmare was over. Let the era of normalcy begin.

The company was feeling so cocky that Sculley felt safe to sell off 125,000 shares of his own without anyone reading anything into it but a CEO's justly earned reward.

Apple used its new public platform, the AppleWorld Conference in San Francisco, to introduce the $2,599 Macintosh Plus and LaserWriter Plus to 2,000 product developers and dealers. At the event, John Sculley announced that it would use some of its $441.5 million in cash on hand to create a $25 million venture capital fund to help found new Apple-oriented start-up companies. This was the classic move of a company that believes it now owns its market and is setting out to consolidate it. It compounded this image of business maturation by announcing it was embarking on strategic partnerships with, among others, Northern Telecom and 3Com.

At that moment, coming off a miserable year, Apple looked more than ever on top of its game. The theme song of the conference was Patti LaBelle's "New Attitude" and the title seemed to fit. Apple's Golden Age had begun.

Buried in all this good news, though, there were eerie signs of things to come. For all the glowing pronouncements about the Apple Computer to come, details were vague. Campbell, for example, once again mentioned a portable Mac, but declined to give a delivery date.

Meanwhile, copies of Sculley's speech announcing the new Mac Plus/LaserWriter Plus combination, the heart of Apple's desktop publishing strategy, were so freighted with typographical and spelling errors as to be a parody of the perils of word processing.

Sculley used the occasion to publicly pitch Apple's board for the company to buy a $15 million Cray computer, ostensibly for advanced modeling of future company hardware and software products. It sounded impressive, but as Regis McKenna and others who lobbied against it well knew, the Cray was little more than a vanity project, a fancy gift to R&D that had little to contribute to the company's creativity beyond helping to design plastic enclosures for the computers. In the end, Sculley wanted the Cray because he wanted the biggest, most powerful computer on earth. It was a warning of things to come.

But strangest of all were the "exhibits" lining the walk journalists and analysts took between the convention center and the speech in the ballroom of a nearby building. These were Plexiglas display cases containing real human beings in frozen poses using Apple computer products. Meant to be compelling, these tableaus were instead disturbing, partly because the cases were so narrow that the performers seemed in danger of suffocation. Thus, instead of the planned image of liberation through Apple computers, the result was the unforgettable metaphor of people trapped by a technology and in desperate need of liberation.

Apple culminated this celebration with the deification of its new leader. On January 29, John Sculley was named chairman of Apple Computer, officially replacing Steve Jobs. At age forty-six, three years out of "selling sugar water," he was now the most famous—and one of the most powerful—figures in high technology.

On March 15, almost five years to the day after the firing of Mike Scott, Steve Jobs officially sold the last of his Apple stock . . . all except for one symbolic share. That solitary remaining share, the last of his 6.5 million ($120 million) shares, was more than a mere memento of his former life: it also gave Jobs a ticket to all future Apple shareholder meetings.

The second quarter ended March 28, 1986, only brought more good news. Sales were down 6 percent, but they were off 11 percent for the industry as a whole. At the same time, profits had *tripled*; gross margins were 56.6 percent, the highest in the company's history. Three months later, the numbers were even better: compared to the $17 million loss the year before, Apple saw a profit of $32 million. And sales for the quarter had jumped 20 percent to $448 million.

The company was now feeling so upbeat that it fired its advertising agency, Chiat/Day, creator of the magnificent but dour "1984" ad, and replaced it with BBDO, Sculley's old agency at Pepsi, and famous for its upbeat campaigns.

"I'm having a ball," said Sculley. "I can't think of anything I'd rather do in the world." He had now traded in his suits for chinos, plaid shirts and deck shoes. Now, padding around Apple's offices, he looked more like the company psychologist than the CEO.

Apple employees, wary at first because of Sculley's lack of technical credentials and his history of snuggling with Jobs, slowly began to warm up to their boss as well. Not surprisingly, the first to come around was the beleaguered II group. As one of its members told the *San Jose Mercury News*, "Things have gotten better. No one has to hide anything anymore from other Apple engineers. When Jobs was around, if the II group had done a project he hadn't okayed, he'd just cancel it." Said another, "More people are happier at Apple than they were before."

Sculley himself would proudly say, with considerable justification, "Apple is a more disciplined, grown-up company today. People have grown to recognize that discipline is not a threat to innovation. . . . I know what it takes to be a success."

One of those ways, Sculley decided, was to promote Del Yocam to the post of chief operating officer. Henceforth, Bill Campbell and Mike Spindler would report to Yocam, not Sculley, the chairman/president/CEO. In one respect, this was standard operating procedure. Sculley, like any person running a multibillion-dollar publicly traded corporation, was being pulled in many ways, from captain of the corporate ship, to public advocate on industry issues, to liaison to Apple's millions of shareholders, to company figurehead. In the face of all this, now that the immediate crisis threatening the company appeared past, John Sculley needed a first lieutenant to take over the daily operations of Apple Computer.

He said as much in the news release announcing the appointment: "With Apple now set on a clear and positive course for the future, this was the right time to create this position."

Yet, as proper as the move sounded, it rested on a flawed assumption: that Apple's crises were now behind it; that having righted itself and enjoyed a few quarters of good news, the company now could look forward to years of smooth sailing.

But this was not the soda-pop industry. Changes didn't arrive slowly, with considerable advance warning that gave you time to prepare your response. In computers, just the opposite was true. Radical, life-threatening change more often than not arrived overnight, seemingly from nowhere. Sculley might have learned that lesson from the almost instantaneous appearance of desktop publishing—but then, he was the beneficiary of that revolution, not, like thousands of printing companies, its victim.

To run a high-tech company you had to be *engaged* at all times. Even while you were taking on all the other ancillary tasks. That's why Apple was paying John Sculley millions of bucks each year. The company was decidedly *not* on a "clear and positive course for the future," but only for the moment. And by stepping away like some East Coast corporate Brahmin, John Sculley not only abrogated his duties as much as Jobs had six months before but placed himself in the position of being perpetually disappointed by lieutenants who found it impossible to maintain the company on the sunny upward trajectory Sculley believed he'd set for it.

8.8 Messiahs

Now that success—the company saw profits rise another 47 percent in the fourth quarter—had freed Sculley to think higher thoughts, those thoughts turned to the task of restoring Apple's lost market mojo. In time he became convinced that he could resurrect the Old Spirit of Apple by finding a new visionary and a new figurehead to replace Steve Jobs. And for that task he found a most unlikely (and more manageable) pair: Steve Wozniak and Alan Kay.

Sculley was working on Woz's return even before Jobs left. Wozniak's huffy departure had been a minor distraction in the madness that was Apple in 1984. He had never actually quit Apple, but merely gone off with the company's modest blessings to start Cloud Nine (CL9), a maker of universal remote controls. There, he proved that as a CEO he was a good lab technician. He even reverted to his old ways: his secretary, echoing his mother, had to pull him away from his soldering gun and clean him up to attend company board meetings. The company was doomed from the start.

Woz was unruffled. In truth, he seemed happier up at his big home in the Santa Cruz mountains, putting on elaborate birthday parties and building cave mazes under the house for his kids. He continued to indulge the childlike side of his own personality—to often magnificent results. The greatest of these was as the lead benefactor of the Children's Discovery Museum in San Jose. Like all such projects, it had gotten off to a slow start in fund-raising. Then, like a bolt from the blue, Woz put up $2 million, nearly 10 percent of the funding goal. He posed for photographers putting handprints on a wall while kneeling with a group of kids. When asked by reporters why he had made such a remarkable gift, Woz harked back to his childhood, to reading Scrooge McDuck comic books and deciding that if he ever got that rich he would use his money to help people. It was charming, fixing forever the image of Steve Wozniak as a childlike saint/genius. And when the museum was finished, the name of the road leading to it was rechristened Woz Way.

But it was not all happy news. His second marriage broke up, with Candi Wozniak claiming that, in a heated argument, he had thrown her down the stairs at CL9. There was never any proof. Still, all was obviously not perfect with Woz. And so, when Sculley invited him back to replace Jobs as the face of Apple, Woz was happy to oblige. He told Sculley he had some great new ideas for the Apple II.

Wozniak turned out to be a terrific public speaker, and his eccentricities, like buying dollar bills by the sheet and simply cutting off whatever he needed for payment, were ingratiating. But with the decision not to clone IBM, the rise of desktop publishing on the Mac and the Internet still four years away, the II was nothing more than a winning antique, a holding pen for future Mac converts. Sculley didn't want it because it wasn't part of his regime, and he couldn't imagine a future for it. Gassée didn't want the II either, because it didn't fit his strategy of high-end, elegant machines. And Del Yocam, the II's last great champion, had been promoted away.

The only people who still wanted the Apple II were the folks who bought a billion dollars' worth of them every year, as well as twice that amount or more in software.

For them, the first generation of true Apple loyalists, the Apple II line was allowed a swan song. And it was a doozy: the 1986 Apple IIGS (for "graphics and sound"), perhaps the high-water mark of the computer maker's art and, in terms of quality, price and performance, the best computer Apple ever built. It featured an elegant box filled with the simplest componentry imaginable—all superfluity having been winnowed out over the previous nine years—a color display and stereo sound. It was a computer designed from the start to appeal to schools, which needed a reliable computer of considerable power at a reasonable price . . . yet so inexpensive to build that it was like a license for Apple to print money. Moreover, the IIGS actually outperformed the Macintosh on the Mac's own turf. It was the II group's last hurrah.

Hundreds of thousands of IIGS's were sold, used by a generation of kids right up to the mid-1990s, when they were finally junked—most of them still working as well as the day they were bought.

But as Apple support dried up, as the new products disappeared and third-party developers moved on, the customer base gradually eroded. It was a testament to the Apple myth that most bought Macs.

And as the II slowly faded away, so once more did Steve Wozniak.

But Sculley had a second guru waiting in the wings. Besides his tenure at Atari, Alan Kay had one of the finest minds and most distinguished résumés in personal computing. He arrived in the world of computing armed with degrees in math, computer science and biology. He was also a disciple of MIT's Marvin Minsky, the computers-in-education pioneer. This alone should have been a red flag to everyone thereafter: MIT is notorious—witness the Media Lab there—for coming up with brilliant, seductive ideas about the future of computing that never find practical application. Kay would be MIT's Typhoid Mary, bringing the pox of impracticality to Silicon Valley.

From MIT, Kay's career took him to the Utah operations of ARPA, that great government seeding ground of U.S. technology, most notably the Internet. There, Kay had his vision that would haunt personal computing forever. Watching a demonstration of a flat panel display, Kay suddenly realized that, with Moore's Law at work, this expensive form of output would within a decade be affordable to everybody. So too would the big mainframe computers he was working with. Put the two together you had something amazing: an affordable, book-sized computer with a thin display and the ability to be configured to any user.

When ARPA fell into disarray, Kay fortuitously landed at Xerox PARC, where he perfected his vision of this new portable computer, which he called the Dynabook: it would have the power of a minicomputer, with vast amounts of memory, yet be so simple and self-evident in its operation that a young child could play with it.

It was the single most compelling vision of the future that the personal computing world had ever seen. And it sucked into the crusade everyone who ever heard about it. Even among the arrogant engineers at PARC it proved irresistible. Soon the entire computer lab was dreaming of Dynabooks. Kay's vision had everything going for it: it was coherent, imaginable and years away from being practical. And that just spurred the scientists on.

The effect, at least at PARC, was both galvanizing and salutary. The group not only had a goal but had a template with which to select which new inventions were useful and which were not. Thus, the mouse was good because it reduced the need for punching keys. By the same token, graphic interfaces were superior to textual ones because they required less typing, less memorization of commands, and were more universal in application. The use of icons, such as garbage cans, helped simplify matters even further. And bit-mapped displays were good because they made the computer's operations transparent.

Kay had his own team at PARC, and just when the rest of the computer group would catch up with his current research, Kay would launch off in a new product direction. The best of these inventions was Smalltalk (named after the simplicity of conversations at cocktail parties), a programming language designed to be so simple that even children with their limited vocabularies could use it. Kay actually brought in a group of kids to test it.

It was largely Kay's work (combined with Douglas Engelbart's mouse) that Jef Raskin had studied before going to Apple, and that Jobs saw on his fateful tour. And it was Kay's vision of the Dynabook that underscored the Mac project—the idea that someday it too would be a handheld machine. In fact, along with Jobs's other mottoes that he put up in the Mac offices, one was dedicated to the Dynabook: "Mac in a book by 1986."

By 1983 Kay found his way to Apple. There, he was named a company Fellow, able to live elsewhere, play Bach on his grand piano and send ex cathedra missives full of his brilliance to company headquarters. His most irritating habit was dismissing almost every new idea he heard of as being little more than an outgrowth of his work at PARC. This was not guaranteed to make him many friends at Apple. But by constantly holding back his approval, and by suggesting that even the greatest breakthroughs were merely baby steps toward a greater goal, Kay managed to gain considerable influence among those in the company who knew the least about technology.

The most famous Kay memo even managed to piss off Jobs, his greatest champion, and the man who recruited him to Apple. The memo, sent to his other great champion, John Sculley (who thought him a genius) was entitled "Have I Got a Deal for You: A Honda with a One-Quart Gas Tank." In the memo, Kay argued that having such limited memory and a single disk drive in the Mac was a terrible mistake. It was classic Kay: arrogant, supercilious and painfully accurate. Kay reacted to the resulting outcry by professing surprise: after all, he had only criticized the Macintosh because it was the first personal computer worthy of criticism.

That remark didn't make him any friends either. But it did capture John Sculley's attention. And a few years later, when Sculley was casting about for a new tech guru, it was Kay who came to mind. Soon they were nearly as inseparable as Sculley and Jobs had been. Sculley would write, ominously, in 1987:

> After my breakup with Steve Jobs in the summer of 1986, I found a new teacher. Apple Fellow Alan Kay. He led me on an extraordinary journey by sharing with me many of his unique and inventive ideas. It was Alan, perhaps more than anybody else, who expanded my range of viewpoints. We have regularly held weekly discussions which are usually accompanied by his suggestion of a new book or two for me to read. When I trace the origins of the most exciting and outrageous ideas behind the personal computer revolution, most paths lead directly to Alan. He has been both a friend and mentor on this journey.

There was nothing wrong with Kay's ideas; on the contrary, they are vindicated every day now with the rise of "thin clients" and "software agents." But the Dynabook was a concept too dangerous for anyone without the industry experience to put it into perspective, who didn't appreciate that it was not a computer generation, but a *human* generation away; and that there were a thousand technological problems, none of them trivial, in between. And that to try to jump one of those steps was a recipe for disaster.

There were no philosophers of soda pop at Pepsi, so Sculley had no resistance to their charms. People like Don Valentine or Mike Markkula or even Steven Jobs, who had listened to a new theory of organization, technology or management every week for the last twenty years, were largely indifferent to their blandishments. They had seen hundreds of brilliant new theories come and go, and the most exciting ones were always the ones most likely to fail. Like every successful Valley veteran, they knew better than to jump on board the latest fad theory, but instead to steal what was immediately applicable and remain skeptical of the rest.

Even Jobs fell for Kay's theory—at least for a time. He even made some moves to co-opt the Dynabook. But eventually, recognizing the enormity of the task, he moved on.

But Sculley didn't just adopt Kay's Dynabook; he wanted to make it his own. He'd almost invented the Trinitron television, hadn't he? Why couldn't he be the inventor of the second-generation Dynabook as well? It was the perfect combination of glossy high theory and dim technological underpinnings to appeal to an amateur technologist.

The result was the Knowledge Navigator. And it stole John Sculley's heart like nothing since Steve Jobs. The KN was Kay's Dynabook with enough added wrinkles for Sculley to make it his own. It was to be, in Sculley's New Age hyperbole:

> . . . a discoverer of worlds, a tool as galvanizing as the printing press. Individuals could use it to drive through libraries, museums, databases, or institutional archives. This tool wouldn't just take you to the doorstep of these great resources as sophisticated computers do now; it would invite you deep inside its secrets, interpreting and explaining—converting vast quantities of information into personalized and understandable knowledge.

As Sculley described it, the actual product would be Kay's Dynabook (portable, flat screen, networked, full motion video, adaptive keyboard or perhaps just speech recognition) with the addition of a pair of joysticks on either side so that the user could "fly" like the Wilbur Wright of cyberspace through empyreans of knowledge.

8.9 FELLOW

This last idea was courtesy of a recent invention by Bill Atkinson, the creator of the Lisa user interface, inventor of the single-button mouse and, unlike the more publicized Kay, Apple's true technological guru and the one worthy successor to Woz.

Atkinson, thirty-five, an Apple Fellow now and struggling to keep from succumbing to the post-Mac depression facing most of his peers, was a typical Apple techno-eccentric. For example, he was convinced that mankind would one day soon be replaced by silicon-based entities descended from the work being done right now on computers. In other words, he was God—not a unique attitude among programmers. And Atkinson was one hell of a programmer, one of the two or three best in the history of personal computers.

It was his gift for programming, combined with his unmatched understanding of how mere humans dealt with the complexities of information, that enabled him to develop Apple's last truly great contribution to the computer revolution.

Atkinson had spent the months after Mac trapped in Kay's fantasy too. Atkinson's version of the Dynabook was to be called the Magic Slate, and it was to feature many of the traits ultimately found in Newton: flat display, touch screen and handwriting recognition. It was also to be so cheap as to be nearly disposable.

That Atkinson thought he could pull off the Magic Slate at that moment in history was a testament to how deeply he had internalized the old Jobs bravado. But it was also a reminder that even great programmers and designers must be supported by enlightened management. Apple no longer had that type of leadership. The project was killed. The irony was that just as John Sculley was dreaming about the Knowledge Navigator he was denying support to his best programmer for the intermediate step to his goal.

Atkinson was heartbroken, but he still hadn't given up. Amazingly, he had another, equally brilliant invention up his sleeve. It was called Wildcard, and it was a new way of linking information in a manner never possible before the computer. Wildcard was the first step in the realization of computer visionary Ted Nelson's dream, called Xanadu, of a worldwide interlinkage of the world's knowledge into a single metanarrative—a "hypertext," as Nelson called it. Atkinson's Wildcard literally represented a new way of thinking—an achievement that can be claimed by only a handful of people in history.

At the heart of Wildcard was Atkinson's realization that, unlike the world of printed pages and libraries, computer information was largely unconstrained by time or space. In the world of print, both the author and the reader are limited by the linear nature of narrative. Try to stuff too much information into that narrative and the meaning is lost and the text becomes impenetrable. In four thousand years of printed books, only a handful of ways around this intrinsic obstacle had been developed—footnotes, indexes, bibliographies, etc. But each of those had their own weaknesses, notably the lost time and energy spent flipping through pages or running to the library, and the resulting lost connection with the core text.

Until Atkinson, text on computers was still trapped in this old print paradigm. The biggest breakthrough until now had been the "search" function. What Atkinson recognized was that in the digital realm, text size wasn't important. If you chose, you could have a thousand pages of footnotes appended to a single paragraph. In fact, thanks to Moore's Law, you could soon make that one million or one billion pages. And you could append those thousand pages and then simply call them up from anywhere in the world with the push of a button.

This was powerful enough, but Atkinson, with his remarkable three-dimensional mind, took it even further. If you could append a thousand pages behind that single paragraph, why not link a thousand separate documents, all of them related to the topic at hand? And to those documents, why not be able to append a thousand more documents—some just sentences, others lengthy tomes—and on and on. One of these underlying documents, a dozen layers down, might even in fact be the original document—thus closing the loop, and tying together in a vast web all the relevant information on a topic. This was the medieval memory theater in binary form, but evanescent, created in real time according to the immediate desires of the user. You could state your interest and be led down and down deeper into that topic, until you finally got the bends, or, if you were sufficiently patient, broke through the bottom and found yourself back on the surface.

Atkinson's creation, renamed Hypercard, was so amazing that, almost uniquely in the world of high tech, everyone who saw it instantly knew it was great. Meanwhile, computer theorists talked about how, as computers became more powerful and communications faster and broader, it might be possible to hyperstack not only text but sounds, images, even moving pictures.

But Hypercard had one serious weakness: It was a networked product in a world of stand-alone machines. Nelson's Xanadu was still far off. Hypertexts were clever in a Mac or a PC, but profoundly limited. So what if you could link a half dozen of your different files together? You could count the uses for that—unless perhaps you were a teacher—on one hand. But what if a bunch of computers were linked together? What if thousands were, or millions? Personal computers and mainframes, giant databases and high-speed communications lines?

Just such a network was already in place: the ARPAnet, the linkup of thousands of computers at universities and defense contractors, all under the aegis of the Department of Defense. By the time Atkinson invented Hypercard, the ARPAnet was already fifteen years old, with nearly a million users, and already developing its own culture. Within another four years, the ARPAnet would be privatized into the Internet, and a vast organizing grid, the

World Wide Web, would be overlaid atop it. A year after that, Marc Andreeson and some fellow students at the University of Illinois would develop Mosaic, the first search engine for the Web, and the spark that would turn the Internet into the greatest global phenomenon of its time.

Ten years after Atkinson first began handing out test copies of Hypercard to his friends at Apple, one hundred million people each day would call up Web pages, then dive into the mountains of data stacked behind them, or tap on hot (hyper) links and zip around the world, surfing other sites—an entire world built upon Atkinson's new way of thinking.

It was all there in 1986 in Hypercard. Atkinson had given Apple an unequaled glimpse into the future. And with the Macintosh and its graphical operating system, Apple had the unmatched machine for exploring this new world. But to do that, Apple first had to proliferate the use of personal computers to millions of people through easy-to-use, low-cost machines—Raskin Revisited. It had to develop computers that performed more than one function at a time—multitasking. And most of all, it had to reorient the company away from stand-alone, isolated personal computers and toward machines designed for maximum utility in networked settings.

John Sculley's Apple did none of these things. Atkinson had hesitated to even show Hypercard to Apple, figuring the company would screw him. Instead, he considered quitting. But Alan Kay heard of his plans and went to Sculley to tell him to give Atkinson a hearing. Sculley did as he was told and even he was thrilled by what he saw. He wanted Hypercard. Atkinson, shrewdly, cut a deal: Hypercard would henceforth be bundled into every Apple computer sold—and if it wasn't, the rights to the invention would revert to Atkinson. Sculley agreed. Meanwhile, he also incorporated its implications into his growing model of the Knowledge Navigator.

With Kay's Dynabook and Atkinson's Hypercard, Sculley had nearly a turnkey vision of the future he could call his own. The final step was to bolt on the potentialities of the ARPAnet and a brand-new theory called software agency, in which "agents" created by software would interact on the screen with the user and do that user's bidding.

8.10 Surrogates

The whole package made Sculley dizzy with excitement. Here was his Trinitron; his own personal Unified Field Theory of computing, the idea that would place him among not only the great executives but the great *thinkers* of computing. And it wasn't enough to merely give speeches about it or dwell on it in endless, breathless depth over the final third of his autobiography. Sculley wanted to make the Knowledge Navigator *real.* And since that was impossible—almost everything about the KN, from its color flat panel display to speech recognition, full motion video and high-speed broadband data links were at least a decade away—Sculley decided to simply *pretend* it was real.

He hired Lucasfilm, fresh from its *Star Wars* trilogy triumph, to create a series of expensive, Hollywood-quality videos, each five minutes long, of futuristic scenarios involving the Knowledge Navigator. The most famous of these was the first, which Apple showed to the world on every occasion it could think of for the next two years.

It was a homey, beautifully filmed, yet oddly sterile little infomercial that featured a Berkeley professor preparing a lecture for a class he is to teach later that day on the destruction of the rain forest. The tool he uses for this work is an intriguing little laptop/notebook computer that appears to be no more than an inch thick with an elegant Art Deco design: the Knowledge Navigator. The professor opens the Navigator and up on the screen pops the image of a young man wearing a bow tie. For viewers in 1989, it took a moment to realize that this young man was not real, but a creation of the computer—an anthropomorphized software agent who can understand what the professor says to him, reply and serve as the professor's surrogate by going out into the electronic world and gathering information from databases. The agent also attends to other matters in the professor's life, such as keeping his appointments (about which he gently hectors his boss), his phone list and personal records.

In the course of this interaction between biological master and software servant, the professor has the agent search the world's databases for movies and animations that vividly show the damage being done to the world's rain forests. These are quickly displayed on the screen, then melded together into a complete multimedia presentation with charts and graphics and video windows. The professor then orders the servant to get hold of Jill, another professor, who has recently written a paper on the same subject. The agent has already anticipated (!) this request, and already placed the call. Jill appears on the screen, she and the professor have a conversation and they sign off. The professor and the servant have a few more words, then he shuts off the Navigator and departs, no doubt to change the lives of his students forever and in the process save Mother Earth.

An impressive production, with tonalities as much High Spielberg as Lucas. And the video had the desired effect, especially upon first-time viewers with little computer experience. With this group, the typical response was "Wow! When can we get something like that?"

But upon multiple viewings, an uneasiness developed, especially if you knew something about personal computing and about Apple. Then the video became a banquet of subtexts, a picnic for deconstructionists. For one thing, the professor was something of a pompous jerk—apparently John Sculley's image of enlightenment. Then there was the matter of the servant. Prissy, impeccable and wearing a bow tie, the software agent became even more irritating with each viewing. Was the bow tie some kind of clue? Was this digital eunuch a stand-in for a castrated Steve Jobs? And, to take the allegory further, was this master-servant relationship, which Steven Levy accurately compared to slavery—"If for some reason he got out of line, his owner could drag him to the trash can and replace him with a more obsequious icon"—also a kind of wish fulfillment for Sculley?

Finally, there was Jill, the professional associate. Again, Levy, normally a staunch defender of Apple during this era, sounding the proper alarm: Was Jill a real person? After all, she didn't seem any more substantial than the eunuch. Or perhaps she was Jill's servant, in this case designed to look just like its master. And if the latter was true, what kind of hall of mirrors was the Knowledge Navigator getting us into? What would it mean if we couldn't tell the difference between what was real and what was a digital representation?

Luckily for Apple, most people didn't ask themselves these larger ontological questions. Instead, the video worked its magic all too well. After watching it, your own personal computer, even a Mac, seemed like an archaic piece of junk. Newcomers watched the video and wondered why they couldn't find anything like it at the electronics store. Veterans asked if this constituted a commitment by Apple to embark on a long-term project to build the Knowledge Navigator, and what that meant for company products between now and then.

But beyond promoting the idea of the Knowledge Navigator, Apple had nothing much to say. Even Sculley stopped talking about it after a couple of years, suggesting that it was little more than a vanity project, something to earn him his tech spurs. But in unexpected ways, the Knowledge Navigator campaign cost Apple enormously. When, in 1989, Apple finally introduced its first laptop, the Macintosh Portable, underpowered, oversized, heavy and with a short battery life, the outcry was in no small part due to the market's disappointment over the gap between these products and the ones they'd been trained to expect from the Knowledge Navigator.

But the real damage came a couple of years later with the introduction in 1992 of the Newton.

8.11 Abdication II

The Dynabook wasn't the only thing that rushed in to fill the void in John Sculley's attention as he pulled away from the daily running of Apple Computer.

The other was the game of moving executives about on the organization chart. For the rest of the decade after the 1985 shake-up, senior managers came and went under Sculley's rule, rising up through the ranks until they approached the throne itself, only to be ritually beheaded and their corpse cast out of the company.

As befit a corporate monarch, Sculley kept his court in constant turmoil. In his creepy passive-aggressive style, with its spooky combination of thoughtful altruism and scheming pragmatism, he regularly promoted managers into positions of unprecedented (and often undeserved) authority, at the same time pulling the rug out from under those veterans who got too close to the throne.

The game began with a flurry of hirings and appointments. Larry Tesler, the old Xerox PARC leader, was promoted from the directorship of advanced technology development to the new position of first vice president of advanced technology and membership on Sculley's seven-person executive staff. Kevin Sullivan arrived from DEC to become vice president of human resources. Allan Loren came from the Philadelphia insurance company Cigna to help Apple set up a management information system, a field in which he was an acknowledged expert. Then, inexplicably, he was moved sideways and put in charge of Apple's sales and marketing. Fred Forsythe, who'd done a fine job of running manufacturing at Apple, was made head of engineering.

Nearly every one of these moves would prove misguided.

But if unlikely promotion was the order of the outer rings of John Sculley's empire, being a long-standing member of his inner circle was akin to belonging to the Politburo in 1937. Sooner or later, almost everyone was purged.

The first to go was a surprise. Jean-Louis Gassée.

The fall came fast. In May 1987, Gassée, who was heading Apple's research and development team, was given management of the company's advanced technology research group. In June 1988, product marketing was placed under his control. By August, he had also been handed Apple's worldwide marketing operations. He was now Sculley's heir apparent. "It's clear Gassée's star is still rising," said Bruce Lupatkin, analyst at Hambrecht & Quist. Industry watcher Stewart Alsop was even more enthusiastic: "They've essentially handed Gassée the company." But then he added the foreboding words: "He and Sculley are clearly identifying with each other. It's one of those situations where one guy is finishing the other guy's sentence."

As Steve Jobs had proven, this was the kiss of death. By early 1990, stung by accusations that he wasn't getting enough hot new products out the door, Gassée resigned. The announcement stunned the Apple rank and file, especially in Gassée's own group. In what would soon be a standard response to any unpopular move at the company, a small contingent of a hundred employees staged a protest outside a company building a mile from Apple headquarters (it was chosen because it had a lawn). They sang "Louie, Louie, oh baby, THEY gotta go," waved signs and wore black berets out of solidarity with Gassée. They tried to chant the letters of Jean-Louis's name, but forgot how to spell it. After a half hour, they gave up and went back to work. "We're too old for real protesting," one of the employees said.

Rory O'Connor, the computing editor of the *San Jose Mercury News,* responded to the news with one of the first blistering public attacks on Sculley's presidency:

> In a dozen years, Apple has managed to take the ideas of a couple eccentric kids working in their garage and parlay them into a $5 billion company.
>
> Yet, despite all that has come before, the company that brought computers to individuals is now in danger of losing every semblance of influence and innovation in computing. For that, I blame Chairman, President and chief executive John Sculley, from whom the company derives little real leadership. . . . Charisma may not be vital to the chief executive of every company, but it is the coin of the realm at Apple, the stuff needed to motivate a company that resembles a religion more than a business.
>
> Even ignoring that unique aspect of Apple, Sculley also has failed in another aspect of leadership: clearly articulating a strategy for the company's future. I've seen Apple's endless stream of videotapes of what computers will be like in 20 years. What I can't fathom is what Apple computers will be like in two.
>
> The products Sculley's company has brought to market in the last year or two have been less than innovative. They seem designed simply to offer current customers faster, more expensive computers, not to broaden the appeal of the product line. As a result, Apple's growth rate is declining—now below both Wall Street's and Apple's own estimates—and its market share relative to the IBM world is shrinking.

> Without . . . leadership, without a clear plan for the future . . . Apple's star will surely plummet as fast as the fortunes of its top executives.

Debi Coleman, the most brilliant of Sculley's lieutenants, actually left Apple twice. Obese, manic to the point of hysteria, so driven by work that she barely had time for a social life, emotionally involved in the lives of everyone who worked for her, Debi was a time bomb waiting to explode. Having brilliantly run Apple's manufacturing; having learned to deal with both Steve Jobs and John Sculley; and most of all having played a crucial role in getting Apple through the tough times after the Mac introduction, Coleman was promoted to chief financial officer at Apple in August 1987.

She was only thirty-four years old and now one of the hottest stars in Apple. But already the pressures of her lifestyle had pushed Coleman to a state of near-collapse and, medically, at risk for her life.

At Apple, admitting weakness, especially in the form of a few tears, was acceptable, even admirable, among male executives. But taking a leave of absence due to stress was not acceptable in a fat woman executive—especially when that story was splattered all over the front page of *The Wall Street Journal* and a subject for discussion in boardrooms across America.

Debi took her five-month leave in February 1988 and lost thirty pounds. She returned that summer to find a different Apple—at least different in its attitude toward her. She took a post running the administrative side of Apple's headquarters—MIS, the television studio, etc.—and once again became a kind of star, with her own coterie of supporters inside the company. That was getting too close to the throne. Within a couple of years, she was gone for good, joining another former Sculley lieutenant, Del Yocam, in Oregon.

In terms of power the closest employee to Sculley, Del Yocam was also the most experienced senior manager in the company, especially when it came to personal computers. The combination of this experience and his conciliatory personality would seem to make Yocam the perfect Apple COO.

He lasted only two years in the job. In the same reorganization that made Gassée heir apparent, Yocam found himself stripped of the COO duties to become head of the education and Pacific divisions. At that point, said one analyst, "it became very apparent Yocam was not going to run the company some day. . . . Yocam is the last bastion of the old regime."

By early 1989, he too was gone. Yocam took over the CEO job at the venerable, and fading, Beaverton, Oregon, instrument company Tektronix, and immediately set about stripping down the company, divesting it of all the peripheral operations Tek had created over the previous half century. When

Debi arrived, he told her to take her pick of one of Tek's divisions, spin it off as an independent company, and the parent company would help out as a minority investor.

Coleman chose the most unlikely operation of all: Merix, a manufacturer of printed circuit boards. The PC board business was easily the dreariest and most retrograde industry in all of high technology, and Debi's choice, combined with her move to Oregon, signaled to Silicon Valley veterans a final admission of defeat.

In fact, it was just the opposite. Coleman had found the weakest and most vulnerable link on the electronics food chain, one filled with boring old companies content with their little corner of the market. Now she set out to turn it upside down. Within a year, she had taken Merix public, experimented with innovative new relationships with suppliers and was stealing market share from everybody. Meanwhile, Yocam eventually left Tek to tackle the turnaround of Borland, a software company in the Santa Cruz mountains that had flown high and then crashed under the spell of Philippe Kahn.

The saddest, and most costly, of Sculley's Peter Principled protégés was Michael Spindler. As head of Apple Europe, he'd done a superb job of holding on to Apple's market leadership. Taciturn, earnest and infinitely careful, he was a brilliant defensive businessman and probably Sculley's best lieutenant. But, because of his success, and perhaps because he posed the least threat to the throne, Sculley appointed Spindler president of Apple Computer, with Sculley himself remaining as chief executive. It was a cynical and ultimately cruel move disguised as a thoughtful gesture. A poor politician, a man with little flash and artifice and a businessman unaccustomed to going on the attack, Spindler, with his broken English, was a fish out of water in Cupertino. But, ever loyal, he gave it everything he had.

There were several other lesser-known figures hired, fired or shifted in John Sculley's great management shake-up of 1987.

Dave Barram, Regis McKenna's pal, had proven not to be a true CFO (ironic, since he would one day be the director of the U.S. Office of Management and Budget), so when he was replaced by Coleman, Barram was transferred to a new job, director of government affairs, which more accurately fit his abilities.

Ralph Russo, director of international operations, was moved over into Coleman's old manufacturing job. Chuck Boesenberg was named vice president of sales, then quickly joined MIPS Computer Systems in one of the celebrated Silicon Valley IPOs of the late 1980s. Bud Colligan, director of higher educational marketing and sales, resigned to join Authorware Inc. John Scull, in charge of Apple's desktop publishing business, quit to become president of Macromind Inc. Joe Schoendorf, marketing vice president, quit to pursue personal interests.

After executing or exiling most of his first team, and then promoting congenial second-tier players into the wrong positions, Sculley had no choice but to recruit real executive talent from outside. The best-known of these was Joe Graziano himself, who had quit Apple during the Jobs purge and gone to work at Sun Microsystems as chief financial officer. Sculley lured him back as CFO of Apple with a big salary and an even bigger signing bonus: $1.5 million, enough for Graziano to buy a couple of the vintage Ferraris (he'd graduated from Corvettes) that he collected, as well as the profits on another $1.35 million in stock options. The bonus package quickly became known inside Apple as "one Graz," a common measure by which all future bonuses would be measured. And there were a lot of Graz's and half Graz's flying around: Sculley needed management people badly, and talent was no longer flocking to Apple. Meanwhile, a few years later Graziano thanked Apple for this kind gesture by attempting to hijack the company.

The biggest winner in this management rondelle appeared to be Allan Loren, the new marketing and sales chief. About the shake-up, Loren would say smugly, "Our growth means we have to make some changes. Sometimes guys like it, sometimes they don't. Sometimes guys get promoted, sometimes they don't."

Within months, and much more deservedly than the others, Loren's head would be on the chopping block too.

Meanwhile, on April 22, 1987, Apple split its stock and announced a dividend. In May, Sculley was again named Silicon Valley's top-paid executive ($2.2 million). In July, company profits were up 66 percent. In December, the company announced that it would put up astronaut Sally Ride for a company directorship. In January 1988, company profits again doubled, as Apple raced to finish the year as a $4 billion company.

Meanwhile, after five years on the job, and tired from his herculean labors, John Sculley rested. He spent the summer on a nine-week leave of absence. The next winter, he bought a legendary mansion and estate in Woodside.

8.12 Sequel

Beyond these flights of fancy, both good and bad, Apple Computer mostly spent the end of the 1980s and the beginning of the 1990s in the business of settling down and designing and building products.

From now on, just as Jobs had wanted, Apple would be a Macintosh company. And now it was time for that company to take all that it had painfully learned from the first generation of Macs and apply it to a second generation.

It wasn't easy. The preliminary work on a new Mac had been started by Wayne Rosing and his team back in 1985. But Rosing had quit when he thought Jobs might win the feud with Sculley, leaving, with much of his team, for Sun Microsystems. Gassée and his team then took up the project, which by now was two:

- an upgrade to the 512K Mac, to be called the Mac SE ("system extended") featuring considerably more power and memory, as well as a circuit board slot for added functions;
- and the new-generation Mac II, with a larger display, more core memory, some added networking capabilities and a built-in hard disk drive.

The SE was designed to be a bridge product, bringing first-generation Mac users up to the brink of the II. It would also give them enough computing power to run the hottest software around, Microsoft's Excel for Mac, a Macintosh-compatible version of the best-selling bookkeeping software.

The Mac II, on the other hand, was something altogether new. It was to be the basic design of all Macintosh models well into the new decade.

The Mac II was Gassée's baby, and like so many products in Apple's history, it deeply reflected the personality of its creator. Despite the deep reservations of many inside Apple and out about Gassée's character and technical acumen—doubts reinforced by the man's affected style and woolly pronouncements—everyone agreed that the man was not afraid to follow his own opinions wherever they took him. Even if they collided with Apple's shibboleths. And, even though he ran his team like a pompous seminar instructor at the Sorbonne, Gassée still managed to retain the allegiance, even the respect, of notoriously freewheeling individualists like Guy Kawasaki.

Given his ego, his equating of computers with the infinite and, well, his Frenchness, Gassée managed to both worship the Mac and dislike almost everything about it. He didn't want to destroy the Mac, only help it find its destiny, to become its inner Platonic ideal: a high-powered business computer that would wow the corporate computer czars and stomp the PC and its clones into dust. That this lofty goal was also congruent with Gassée's own desire for respect as a hard-ass computer gunsel by these same MIS managers was, of course, only a coincidence.

The actual creation of the Mac II was yet another of those numerous recurring stories that make up Apple—in this case, the renegade that flies under the corporate radar screen, then surfaces at just the right moment to save the company. The hero on this occasion was a veteran of the Macintosh Office project named Mike Dhuey.

After the Macintosh introduction and the product's subsequent collapse, those Mac team members who still remained with the firm slowly shook off their depression and began to rouse themselves for what would come next. First came Burrell Smith's machine and Rich Page's Big Mac. To this was added a third project that never really got off the ground, code-named Jonathan.

But there was also a fourth Mac project, a solo venture undertaken by Dhuey simply because he believed his vision was correct and wanted to prove that fact to the world. That vision was for a modular computer, with a color display and, most important, slots for added function boards offered by both Apple and third-party suppliers. But this was still the Jobs era, and Dhuey well knew that to even suggest slots in the Mac constituted heresy and was grounds for excommunication. The Mac, in Jobs's eyes, was to always be a sealed, "closed" box.

So Dhuey kept his ideas to himself, working secretly with a hardware designer named Brian Berkeley. So fearful were they of Jobs's wrath that in their memos to one another they didn't even use the word "slot."

Then a series of events thrust Dhuey into the limelight. First, Jobs quit; then Gassée took over the group. And Gassée was not only open to openness, he was a fanatic about it—even his 240Z had vanity license plates that read OPEN MAC. Then all the other Mac projects began to fade out one at a time. Smith quit. Page joined NeXT Computer. And the Jonathan was stillborn. That left Dhuey's project, dubbed the Little Big Mac.

Needless to say, Gassée loved it, not least because it was the last interesting new Mac design left standing with its original creator. He had heard about it not long after taking over and had allowed it to continue with his tacit support. Dhuey thanked him by ultimately code-naming the project Paris, replacing its earlier names: Milwaukee (where Dhuey hailed from), Reno (slots, of course—good engineering humor) and Uzi (bad engineering humor).

Underground through the first phases of the project, Dhuey had been free from toeing the company design line. And that in turn left him open to the best solutions for the task at hand. Adding slots was only one example. Another was his choice of the Motorola 68020, a new high-performance 16-bit microprocessor, as Little Big Mac's brains, instead of the older 68000 used in earlier Macs.

In the end, Gassée selected the Little Big Mac as the Mac II not just because it was the only machine left (after all, he could have gone on upgrading the Mac I), or because it fit his own strategic model, but because it was a beautifully designed machine. To his credit, Gassée rewarded Dhuey for his efforts by promoting the young man into a leadership role on the project. Then Gassée gutted all the other Mac II projects and shifted their staffs to the Little Big Mac.

The Macintosh II was introduced in March 1987 and was an immediate sensation, in its various incarnations selling billions of dollars' worth of computers—and at last giving the Mac sales to match its reputation. But if the Mac II validated the Mac architecture, it undermined it as well. The Mac philosophy, promulgated by Raskin and elucidated by Jobs, was to produce the computer for Everyman: cheap, comparatively low-powered and turnkey. But the Mac II was almost the exact opposite. It was expensive, high-powered and configurable. All it really had in common with the original Mac was the user interface—no minor thing, of course—while its real counterpart was, ironically, the IBM PC. In that respect, the Mac II was Apple's first great surrender to the "Wintel" (Windows & Intel) world: it accepted the IBM paradigm for personal computer architecture, then set out to distinguish itself from the IBM clones (and demand a 50 percent higher price) through the uniqueness of its operating system.

The press loved it. It resolved much of the schizoid nature of the reporting that had always afflicted the industry. From the beginning there had always been the problem of having to report on a single industry that was divided into two self-contained worlds. You had to report on IBM and Apple not only separately but differently. It was as if the two companies appealed to opposite sides of the reader's brain. But now that Apple was building IBM-type boxes, you could at last compare Apples and oranges. And in such comparisons, Apple's ineffable edge in style and user experience played less well than IBM's tangible advantages in price, in libraries of applications and in the most obvious measures of performance. The Mac's sheer strangeness had been an important distinguishing feature, and now Gassée had taken that advantage away.

Once the Mac began playing the same game as the PC, the race suddenly came down to five very distinct factors: price, applications, third-party support, processor and operating system.

Price was a field of competition that Apple seemed almost determined to lose. The first-time buyer walked into a Fry's or Computerland or some other electronics chain store and tried out the various machines. Overwhelmingly, that person was drawn to the Mac. It was infinitely easier to learn to use. Then that person looked at the price tag—and decided it made better sense to spend a lot less money and devote a few extra hours to learning Windows.

Despite this lesson in price elasticity taking place a thousand times each day at stores around the world, Sculley and his team exhibited no inclination to compete with the PC world on price. For Sculley, showing his East Coast roots, high prices meant high profit margins, and high profit margins meant a good balance sheet—and that meant a strong stock price on Wall Street.

Filled with self-doubt, Sculley had submitted to years of training in technology by the best minds at Apple. He even grudgingly admitted, after the financial disaster of 1985, that he also had much to learn about the cyclical nature of the personal computer industry. But one thing he never would believe was that he also didn't understand the basic rules of business—after all, wasn't that what he'd been hired for?—in the digital realm. In personal computers (as well as software, semiconductors and just about everything else) the name of the game was, if necessary, to sacrifice short-term profits for market share. If you could dominate the market and set the standard you could make your fortune on volume and higher-priced upgrades. Bill Gates understood this, as did the clone makers. But Sculley and Gassée did not. Pressed by the media, they even grew surly. Steven Levy, attending one Apple press conference, heard Gassée reply to a question about high prices: "We don't want to castrate our computers to make them inexpensive. We make Hondas, we don't make Yugos."

Thanks to this pricing policy, the war in **applications software** was over before it began. With millions of IBM PC and clones now out in the marketplace, with the Wintel architecture the dominant industry standard, and with hundreds of software developers racing to develop new programs to tap into the wealth of this market, Apple didn't stand a chance. Increasingly, it had to wait in line while the biggest developers produced DOS and Windows versions first, then, sometimes a year or more later, a Macintosh-compatible version. The smaller developers didn't write Mac versions at all; they were able to sustain lively businesses on the giant PC world alone.

Thus, inexorably, the slower-growing Apple applications library became but a tiny fraction of its gigantic, and faster-growing, PC counterpart. This wasn't lost on customers. It became even harder to justify a Mac: not only was it more expensive but sometimes it didn't even run the one program you were buying a computer for. The modest Apple applications software collection was increasingly buried by the seemingly endless applications library for the PC. And that growing gap was as obvious at the computer store: the single wall of Mac programs and the aisles of DOS and Windows offerings.

Ironically, the one company that consistently (albeit tardily) produced Mac versions of all of its major products was Microsoft. Gates & Co. sold billions of dollars' worth of Word and Excel for Macintosh, the profits from which Microsoft used to develop new products that would ultimately undermine the Mac.

Responding to this situation, in 1987 Apple founded an "independent" (it retained 85 percent control) software company called Claris. Claris was initially created to help Apple overcome a problem that plagued much of the computer industry: every time you created a new piece of software and bundled it into your computer, you inevitably pissed off a score of developers working on or selling competitive products. So Apple initially decided to sell these programs as stand-alone products, and, in order to disguise their source, parked them under the Claris label. Nobody was fooled, especially since, as Guy Kawasaki would later point out, Microsoft salespeople ran around reminding developers of the cozy Apple-Claris connection.

But in its second role, that of creating major new software products to keep Apple in the game, Claris fared much better. In particular, Claris Works, a suite of office productivity programs (word processing, spreadsheet, desktop publishing), proved to be an effective argument for many professionals and small business owners to go with the Mac. But whatever its victories, Claris was just one company, part of a small cohort of Apple software designers, up against an army of PC developers. There was no way it could ever keep up.

Software developers were only one group of **third-party developers** upon which Apple depended. Just as important was a second constituency, Apple licensees. Unfortunately, they didn't exist. Repeatedly through the last years of the 1980s, the call went out, from developers, the trade press, analysts and even employees, for Apple to license its operating system. But Sculley refused every time. A decade later he would justify his decision by saying that such licensing would have damaged Apple's profit margins, turning the company at best into just one of a host of price-bombing clone makers and at worst into a software-only developer. In Sculley's reasoning, diminished margins meant diminished stock prices, and in the John Sculley cosmology, that was the worst of all fates. He simply could not imagine how Apple could be helped by low-cost products from competitors.

But the fact was, they could. Clones might give the Mac architecture a bigger market share (attracting more third-party developers) while at the same time forcing Apple to build better products. But Sculley wasn't hearing it.

Margins and stock price were the Gog and Magog of his business faith. Coke and Pepsi didn't sell their secret recipes, did they? And if that argument wasn't decisive, Sculley had only to point at IBM and its sudden shocking business collapse to show the dangers of allowing clones at the company picnic.

But Sculley missed the point. IBM had lost control over its own PC architecture to the likes of Dell, Compaq, Hitachi and HP not because it had allowed the licensing of its operating system, but because it never owned it in the first place—Microsoft did. Apple, in comparison, owned its OS. It would make money on every Mac clone sold. But more than that, IBM got into trouble because it fell down on the job—its new computers were ugly, overpriced and mediocre in performance. Clones kept you on your toes, and the big dinosaur of Armonk proved to be flat-footed.

So there would be no licensing of the Mac OS, at least not during John Sculley's tenure. Apple would have to go it alone against an ever-growing number of PC clone makers, some of them huge with vast distribution networks (such as HP), others with enormous manufacturing skills and low labor costs (Leading Edge, Acer, Fujitsu, NEC), and still others that were young, hungry and brilliantly managed (like Dell, Compaq and Gateway 2000).

As for the **processor,** Sculley would also later privately admit that one of his worst mistakes running Apple was not to switch from the Motorola 68000 family to the far more popular Intel 80×86 family, which by the end of the 1980s already owned nearly seven-eighths of the microprocessor business. On first glance, like so much about Apple, this judgment seems reasonable. But it really isn't. Apple's problem was not that it wasn't more like the PC world, but that it wasn't impressively *different* from it. The world had gone with the Intel-based machines not because of "Intel Inside" but because they liked the computer outside. All that counted was that the processor ran the DOS and Windows applications library. And that only mattered because Apple had let the PC become the industry standard. Andy Grove was a great businessman, but had IBM originally gone with Motorola, it would have been the same story with a different chip. The fact was that during this period, Motorola's microprocessors were consistently better designed and better performing than their Intel counterparts. Motorola didn't let Apple down; if anything, the reverse was true. A dominant Apple might not have made the Motorola microprocessor dominant, but it certainly would have kept Intel from becoming a near-monopoly.

That left only the **operating system** as the one competitive factor where Apple had a distinct advantage over the competition. The Mac OS was so clearly superior to DOS and even Windows 1.0 that its presence alone, in the minds of millions, completely trumped every other consideration. But by

1990, the Mac OS was as old as the Apple II had been when the Lisa and Mac projects had set out to replace it. Six years had passed, and though still magnificent, the Mac OS had not appreciably changed. There were some new projects in the works to come up with a replacement, but they might take years. In essence, Apple decided it had a great hand and chose to stand pat.

But across the table was a player extraordinaire, Bill Gates. The most relentless competitor in high tech, Gates had seen the future with the introduction of the Mac and had unceasingly chased this threat ever since. Windows 1.0 was a crude botch, but Gates, as always, learned from his mistakes and redoubled his efforts. In his peculiar and dangerous manner, Gates didn't look upon the Mac OS as competition, but as an intruder into a world that was rightfully his. As Gates saw it, the graphical user interface of the later Windows products wasn't a copy of the Mac, but his all along. Monomania combined with megalomania is a powerful thing.

Apple should have gotten a clue to Gates's attitude when, not long after the Macintosh introduction, the company sued Microsoft for copyright infringement. According to one of his biographers, when Gates was accused by Jobs of ripping off the Mac interface, Gates angrily replied, "No, Steve, I think it's more like we both have this rich neighbor named Xerox, and you broke in to steal the TV set, found I'd been there first, and said, 'No fair, I wanted to steal the TV set!' "

Leaving aside the fact that the Mac OS (unlike the Lisa) wasn't really a Xerox copy, what is breathtaking about Gates's comment is that it rewrites history to suggest that not only did Microsoft chance upon graphical user interfaces first but it had been so successful that there had been nothing left for Apple to use. Given the brilliance of the Mac OS and the ineptness of Windows 1.0, this is a glimpse into a mind more subtle, but no less solipsistic than Jobs's own.

The difference was that Bill Gates didn't alienate his own staff, behave inconsistently from day to day or refuse to understand the basic rules of commerce. While Apple fluttered about, Microsoft moved relentlessly forward in a straight line. And by 1990 it had its answer to the Mac OS ready, Windows 3.0. It was still inelegant, and, being built on top of the old DOS core, rather crude, but it looked a little like the Mac OS—and that was good enough. The tens of millions of Wintel computer users would never again have to hang their heads in embarrassment when comparing their machines with the Mac . . . and Apple zealots could never again be fully comfortable claiming uniqueness for their products. By 1993, Microsoft had sold 25 million copies of 3.0, more than the Mac OS and DOS combined.

And it didn't stop there. Windows 3.0 was just a way station for Bill Gates.

His other awesome trait was that once he took the war to an enemy he never stopped attacking until he'd won. Bill Gates was the Ulysses S. Grant of high tech; he was relentless in his assaults. Even before 3.0 was announced, Microsoft was hard at work on its follow-up, code-named Chicago and targeted on paper to eventually become Windows 93.

Apple, finally awakening from its five-year slumber, at last geared up to respond. But in a manner typical of the company in that era, it set off in several different directions, meandered about and frittered away all of its precious time. The most straightforward of these projects was an upgrade of the existing OS. It alone would actually see the light of day, appearing as Mac OS 7.0 in 1991. It was an adequate piece of work, but no earthshaker. Moreover, its solutions to many of the growing problems with the Mac OS in the new world of computing—for example, the graphical metaphor of files in folders was becoming obsolete when users now had hundreds of such files—were so jury-rigged (in this case the use of a system of aliases to let one file be filed multiple ways) that they not only didn't really solve the problems but made them more obvious. Windows 3.0 screamed for a powerful response from Apple, one that pulled the Mac as far ahead as the original Mac OS had been from DOS. Instead, 7.0 was a move *toward* Microsoft. It seemed that they were converging on some common middle—and on that killing ground, the victor was predestined.

Sitting behind the 7.0 was another project, this one Apple's real response to Windows. This one wasn't an imitation of anything from the past; a balls-out project to build a brand-new operating system as innovative as the Mac OS had been. Code-named Copland, it picked up speed at the beginning of the 1990s and slowly began to gobble up company resources from almost everything else. By the mid-1990s, as Apple's troubles grew deadly, Copland would become the symbol of Apple's deliverance, the next magical product that would pull the company out of its doldrums and put Apple back on top. In the end, it *did* become a symbol, but of a different kind.

8.13 Predictability

What Apple did manage to do well during the late 1980s was build new products. Those new products in turn masked a greater loss. With the exception of Atkinson's Hypercard, Apple seemed to lose its ability to innovate. The company could still do a damn good job at improvement—the new Macs demonstrated that—but the days of radical, earthshaking creation were now suddenly, inexplicably behind it. Month after month, year after year, the world awaited the next great invention from Apple, but it never came.

Partly this was the environment created by John Sculley, which looked upon the discontinuities forced by major inventions (except, of course, Sculley's own Newton) as a threat to the orderly business of the company. But even more, this loss of imagination at Apple was a validation of the 80–20 rule of high tech: All the really interesting stuff in electronics is accomplished by 20 (some would say 2) percent of the people. All the other people—some brilliantly, some poorly, most adequately—perform the task of elucidating upon, upgrading, packaging, marketing, promoting and selling those good ideas.

That's why Silicon Valley's best journalists, investors and analysts identify the few important players in each market and track their movements. If those players suddenly converge on one company, as they did upon Apple in 1981, you can assume that company will soon be hot and a major innovator. If then you see those same players leaving the company in dribs and drabs—no matter how reasonable their explanations (I want to spend more time with my family, I want to pursue other interests, it's a time in my life when I'm ready for a major change)—the bottom line is that the company has lost its edge. It may look financially strong, have a good product portfolio and be hailed by the rest of the world—but without those key innovators, it is a hollow shell, a dead company walking.

And that is exactly what happened to Apple in the decade after the Mac introduction. One by one the 20 percenters had quit, abandoned or been driven out of the company. Del Yocam had recognized this loss as early as the layoff of 1985, saying, "This is very difficult for us. We are losing people who are great performers and are part of this family." But there was nothing he could do to stanch the flow.

The places where these special employees eventually settled—General Magic, Sun, Silicon Graphics—became the hot new companies. Sun and SGI were especially interesting because they pioneered a whole new computer field, graphics workstations, that essentially put a ceiling on Apple's business. These workstations, priced about as much as the original Lisa, but with hundreds of times the power and the ability to construct special-effects imagery, were the darlings of high tech in the early 1990s. The world's attention turned to these companies as they grew even faster than their personal computing predecessors. Because their machines could do everything from model weather to create computer animation to develop three-dimensional MRI scan images, they soon became the investment focus of everyone from Hollywood studios to stock market analysts. They drew the best talent too. The migration of expensive new cars that once headed west toward Cupertino now headed east toward Mountain View and Palo Alto, where Sun and SGI made their headquarters.

Sun and SGI now had the spark and the talent and everybody knew it. Steve Jobs certainly did. Presiding over NeXT, he had, as part of a larger strategy of buying content producers for his computers, acquired Pixar from George Lucas. Pixar, based across the Bay from San Francisco in Pt. Richmond, succeeded far better in its field, computer-generated animation for the motion-picture industry, than NeXT did in academic computing. One reason was that it managed to capture the best talent in the field and keep it. Another was that Jobs, distracted by NeXT, had only enough time at Pixar to be inspiring, not interfering. Having made several award-winning shorts, Pixar found itself in the early 1990s with a deal to make a feature-length film, *Toy Story*, for Disney. It set to work not with Apples or Windows or even NeXT computers, but with banks of the latest workstations from SGI, Hewlett-Packard and Sun.

Yet if Apple had lost its premier talent, (or, even worse, made them into Apple Fellows) it still had thousands of other employees, the cream of the previous decade of college grads and young industry up-and-comers. If these multitudes couldn't come up with revolutionary new products, they could reconfigure and enhance the hell out of the ones they had.

The result was an explosion of new products coming out of Apple that continued well into the new decade. Below is a list of Mac models introduced during Sculley's tenure:

Model	*Date of Introduction*	*Date of Retirement*
128K	1/84	4/86
512K	9/84	4/86
Plus	1/86	10/90
512E	4/86	8/86
SE	3/87	10/90
II	3/87	10/90
IIx	10/88	10/90
SE/80	1/89	10/91
IIcx	3/89	3/91
IIci	9/89	3/91
Portable	9/89	10/91
IIfx	3/90	4/92
Classic	10/90	9/92

IIsi	10/90	3/95
LC	11/90	3/92
Classic II	10/91	9/95
Quadra 700	10/91	3/95
Quadra 900	10/91	5/92
PowerBook 100	10/91	8/92
PowerBook 140	10/91	8/92
PowerBook 170	10/91	10/92
LC II	3/92	3/93
Quadra 950	5/92	present
PowerBook 145	8/92	6/95

With a few exceptions (the horrible Portable was kept around until a replacement, the superb PowerBook, could be found) the life span of each of these models is a clue to their quality. And on this list were a few beauties, including the Mac Classic, the IIsi and the first three PowerBooks.

After the embarrassment of the Portable, and a long frustrating wait by customers, Apple finally introduced its PowerBook series in October 1991. Sleek, solidly built, though a bit underpowered for their price (as was almost everything else at Apple) and with a miserable battery life, the PowerBooks—models 100, 140 and 170—were a revelation, if not a revolution. In those intervening years, Apple had taken the time to figure out what the experience of using a laptop computer should be like, and how it differed from working on a desktop. The result was a keyboard that didn't fill the whole lower wing of the computer, but only the top half of it. The lower half consisted of a place to rest your hands and, when the user's thumbs landed, a trackball mouse. Laptops were never the same again. So many people rushed to buy this first generation of PowerBooks that they were perpetually out of stock.

In fact, a lot of Apple computers were out of stock. As noted earlier, Allan Loren had been promoted from Apple's MIS department and put in charge of Apple's sales and marketing. One reason for the move was that Loren thought just like Sculley, especially about the primacy of profit margins over every other business consideration. Apple's profits had been slipping, partly because of the competitive pressure from the PC world that forced Apple to discount with retailers and partly because Apple had not been introducing new products innovative enough to keep up with Moore's Law. So Loren raised prices.

Robert Cringely, with his usual hyperbole, would call the move Apple's single greatest disaster and compare it to "asking the earth to reverse its direction of rotation." But one thing was for sure. Apple's extraordinary ramp-up over the last four years was now suddenly, jarringly over. Sales of high-end machines, now wildly (instead of merely) overpriced, slid. The low end was far worse: thanks to Gassée, Apple's budget machines had long been neglected. Now obsolete *and* overpriced, their sales plummeted. During the all-important Christmas season of 1988, sales of the Macintosh Plus and SE barely moved. And the market for the Apple II "almost disappeared," one shop owner told the *New York Times*. It was the end of the II; what Jobs couldn't do intentionally, Allan Loren accomplished through incompetence.

All told, Apple's market share fell. But the margins increased. Wrote Cringely, "Any momentum that Apple had was gone, maybe for years."

Well, two years. After hamstringing the company, Loren suddenly discovered he was no longer completing John Sculley's sentences. He was replaced by David Hancock, whom everybody at Apple but Sculley thought was a jerk. He in turn reorganized the department so many times (nine reorganizations in two years) that he threw the place into chaos, drove off the best talent and left the company in the crucial years of 1989 and 1990 effectively without a marketing operation.

8.14 Amateurs

Having driven off Yocam, Coleman and Gassée, John Sculley now found himself with an executive team almost completely devoid of anyone with computer industry experience.

Sculley responded in a predictable manner. He hired Australian Ian Diery to replace Yocam as head of Apple Pacific. Diery came from minicomputer maker Wang, where he had been caught up in (and took some of the blame for) one of the biggest corporate craterings in computer history.

Next, Sculley recalled Michael Spindler from Europe and named him chief operating officer.

Finally, Sculley put himself in Gassée's job, in charge of all new-product development in the company. It was reminiscent of Mike Markkula's regular returns in the early years of the company to take over the reins of the company and straighten things out.

But this situation was entirely different, and one fraught with perils John Sculley seemed incapable of noticing.

For one thing, with the exception of Spindler, who would be distracted by having to adapt to life at headquarters, there were no longer any real personal computer technologists at the top of Apple. That created a dangerous power vacuum waiting to be filled by anyone with ambition.

Unfortunately for Apple, the three most ambitious men on the executive team were not technologists, but staff executives: CFO Joe Graziano, human resources director Kevin Sullivan and chief counsel Al Eisenstat. Before long, they had assembled their power blocs and taken de facto control of Apple's decision making. Recalled one individual who was in those meetings: "It was incredible. I'd never seen anything like it: here was a computer company that now was mostly being run by legal, personnel and finance. There was nobody there to say, 'Shut the fuck up and get out of here. Let real businesspeople and technologists run this company.' "

What power these three camps could not obtain proactively, they held through veto. None used that power more than Graziano, who could quash almost any new idea by announcing that it would hurt Apple's bottom line.

The lone voice of experience, the only person out in the field seeing what was *really* going on in the computer industry was Bill Campbell. But Campbell was running Claris now, so he wasn't *really* Apple anymore, and besides, Claris at the moment was taking shots for not having gotten more products to market sooner. So his comments were largely ignored.

Thus, at the moment when Apple was about to announce its best collection of new products ever, when its biggest competitor, IBM, was rumored to be in deep trouble and the head of the largest software company on earth was giving it thoughtful advice, Apple was not only lost but convinced that it knew where it was going. In fact, it was plunging deeper into the woods.

And into all this was dropped Apple's last true believer, Mike Spindler, the last line guy standing.

Unlike the rest of the executive team, Spindler really did understand the technology, manufacture and marketing of personal computers. Recalls one observer, "I remember when Spindler took over. There was this meeting at Apple with all the senior people. Mike stood up at the board and outlined Microsoft's strategy. Then he outlined all the clone companies and what they were doing. Then operating systems and their kernels. Then all the microprocessor strategies. Then he compared all of that with what Apple was doing. It was an incredible performance. It seemed almost to be incoherent when he started—and then as he went along it all came together. It was breathtaking.

"Then, when he'd filled the entire board up, Mike turned around and looked at the audience: forty blank faces. All Apple senior people, and none of them had a clue. Finally, after a few moments of silence, one British guy, a marketing vice president from Procter & Gamble, said, 'Brilliant, Mike,' and they went on with the meeting."

But Spindler plunged on. If he couldn't find internally the resources that he needed to turn Apple around, he'd look outside the company for strategic partners. And what better place than the biggest resource warehouse of them all?

IBM. It was a crazy idea, but what better time to do it than when Big Blue was wounded and desperate? Just imagine: the Mac OS on IBM PCs, sold by the best sales force in the industry.

He ran the idea past Regis McKenna. McKenna happened to know Jack Kuehler, IBM's president: the two had served together on a board at Santa Clara University. "So I literally jumped on a plane and flew back and proposed the alliance to Jack. He just smiled and said, 'That's a really great idea, but I don't think so right now.'

"But three months later he called Mike and said, 'I think now is the time to talk.' "

But now Spindler had a dilemma. He hadn't told Sculley anything about the IBM contact, because, as he told others, "he wants in on everything." Spindler had learned what other top managers at headquarters had known for years: Sculley, perpetually paranoid about threats to his position as well as deeply sensitive about his lack of technology credentials, didn't want any high-level meetings taking place inside or outside Apple without his involvement. Most of all, he didn't want his senior execs doing anything without him, Sculley, present.

Now Spindler had to tell him. Sculley took the news well . . . so well, in fact, that while Mike was off on a sabbatical, Sculley announced the new joint venture with IBM and took credit for creating it.

The joint venture between the two historic enemies was called Taligent, and it was chartered, as a test of the mutual chemistry of the relationship, to write a new kind of operating system based on the influential new theory of object-oriented programming. The appeal of object-oriented programming was that it enabled the programmer to skip the endless task of writing thousands of lines of code, and instead string together blocks of existing applications and then write only the connecting tissue of code. It was faster, more flexible and easier to upgrade. If 7.0 was a move toward Microsoft, and Copland was the big swing for the fences, Taligent was a challenge to Steve Jobs's NeXT computer. NeXT may have built a computer that nobody wanted, but in that computer was an object-oriented operating system, NeXTStep, that everybody admired.

But if NeXT was all cleverness and not much business sense, Taligent combined two companies that were all business and that had left their cleverness behind. It also smacked of desperation: two multibillion-dollar companies, one of them left behind by the market, the other squeezed into a corner by superior competition, now teaming up in an effort to get back into the game. Apple had, in fact, been working on object-oriented software for years with little to show for it.

It fell to Bill Gates to point out that the emperor had no clothes. "If the software is so important," he asked, "why did Apple give away half of it?" A poll of industry leaders found that most believed Microsoft, the deal's biggest competitor, would end up the winner.

It was a victory by default. Taligent was a bust. And the world assumed that the fault was entirely IBM's. After all, how could a slow dinosaur like Big Blue *ever* work with a jackrabbit like Apple? But the truth was just the opposite. Throughout the Taligent story, IBM executives involved with the project regularly complained that it was Apple that was impeding progress. Recalled one Valley executive, "IBM was saying to Apple, 'What's wrong? We want to work with you and now you don't want to work with us? What's going on here? You came to us. We're supposed to be the company that's hard to work with.'

"What it came down to was that old latent attitude of Apple emerging again. You know: 'It's IBM. The enemy. And nothing IBM does is right.' It wrecked the venture."

8.15 Masks

John Sculley's need to participate in everything his lieutenants were doing betrayed a deeper desperation. Seven years at the top of the most famous technology company in the world had done little to resolve the schism within this divided man.

The passive-aggressiveness, the New Age/old guard and all the other obvious contradictions were merely symptoms of something much more elemental in the man. As early as 1984 the men and women in his inner circle had already noticed it. One confided privately at the time, "I often wonder who John Sculley is when he goes home and takes off the mask. And I have this terrible feeling that when he takes off that mask, all there is underneath is another mask."

Many people who worked with Sculley on a daily basis never felt they knew the man; he so rarely let down his guard. Even going out to dinner was usually a public event, complete with entourage. Said one Apple employee later, "Only once, at a sales meeting, did I ever see him relaxed and happy. I never saw him that way again."

Much of his dualism derived from Sculley's fear: Though the world increasingly saw him as a high-tech visionary, Sculley himself was forever afraid of being exposed as a nontechnologist. And no amount of tutoring by the likes of Alan Kay or covers of *Fortune* and *Business Week* could allay that fear.

That explained why, inside Apple, John Sculley was comfortable with an executive team of nontechnologists and among those scientists so brilliant and arrogant that they treated *everyone* like idiots. It also helped explain why Sculley was so obsessed with new inventions and fresh ideas—not just because they represented new opportunities for Apple but because they did so for *him*. With new markets and products, nobody was yet an expert.

Meanwhile, within the quotidian world of Apple, Sculley, perpetually afraid of being left behind, or made a fool, or simply exposed as an outsider, demanded to know everything going on around him. It wasn't, as some thought, a lack of trust in others, but a lack of trust in himself.

Outside Apple, the schism was even deeper. In a prepared setting, where he was presenting a new idea to a known audience, John Sculley was often magnificent. Those who went expecting the nervous Nellie with the halting voice were usually amazed. "When he was rested and armed with a good script," recalled one Apple employee, "Sculley could bring an audience to its feet. He could be extraordinary." But force him to improvise, say on television, before an audience he didn't know, and all the fears and flaws would come rushing in and John Sculley would splutter and stumble and look like a trapped animal.

Odd as they were in the CEO of a multibillion-dollar corporation, none of these personality tics were especially damaging as long as Apple was a successful company sailing alone in the economic sea. Apple's PR staff was more than adept at creating controlled settings in which John Sculley could shine, and protect him from those occasions when he would not.

But as the 1980s turned into the 1990s, the business climate changed. The age of the stand-alone personal computer was nearly over. Now, most of the world's business computers were being linked up into vast corporate networks centered on powerful mainframe servers. Tiny, unknown companies that supplied this new market—Cisco, 3Com, Sybase, Oracle—were now becoming giants. Meanwhile, in the home computer market, users were beginning to buy millions of modems in order to link up with the new information services, such as Compuserv and America Online, or visit chat rooms in the new "cyberspace" sites such as the Well. And waiting in the wings was the promise of a technology revolution as great as PCs—the Internet.

That was only part of it. In the personal computer industry itself, the once monolithic world of personal computer builders and software designers had now exploded into thousands of submarkets, each with hundreds of competitors. And all were racing to build better, faster, more powerful and cheaper products. This proliferation was so vast and all-encompassing, penetrating every niche business imaginable, that the ambitious user didn't even need to buy a finished computer anymore—rather, you could just order exactly the components you wanted and build a customized machine of your own. And soon even that market was filled with giant competitors, notably Dell and Gateway 2000, offering customized computers you could order over the phone and receive in three days.

Against this efflorescence in the PC world, Apple's strategy of verticalization, of owning every component possible, and of selling stand-alone machines, was increasingly untenable. The days of going it alone were over; and Apple, once the most progressive of companies, was now looking anachronistic. By the beginning of the 1990s, most people at Apple knew the company would have to enter into joint ventures with some of its erstwhile enemies, license its technology or get bought.

But there was the rub. The company was simply unprepared to do any of those things. Taligent was a microcosm of everything that was wrong: the glory-hogging CEO who is yet too full of self-doubt to give a project the freedom it needs to succeed and a contingent of inflexible true believers determined to make it fail.

And so it went with other such deals. A few (with DEC, IBM) actually became real enterprises, only to shuffle along weakened, unsupported and underpowered, then finally fade away. Many others never even made it that far. Once, Apple had the opportunity to discuss a joint effort with its Cupertino neighbor Tandem Computers. Tandem was also a billion-dollar company, its super-reliable "fail-safe" computers were the heart of thousands of sensitive data processing operations (banks, stock exchanges, newspapers, hospitals) throughout the world.

But Tandem was now being challenged by the new generation of client-server companies such as Sun. So a joint venture, even a merger, between Apple and Tandem made great sense: Tandem would give Apple the hub of the network, and Apple would give Tandem the nodes. And Tandem's CEO, Jimmy Treybig, a brilliant good old boy whose hobby was setting up ham radio stations on remote atolls, was known to be honest, fair and an enlightened executive of the HP school.

It seemed perfect. Contact with Tandem was made: they were interested. But at the last moment, Sculley balked. He was overheard bewailing to an adviser, "Does Treybig know *I'm not a technologist?*"

8.16 Bonus Babies

Spindler's arrival at Cupertino and Gassée's departure in early February 1990 signaled the end of Gassée's strategy, which had dominated Apple for five years, of chasing the high end of the computer market. No more "I want to build ze perfect machines." No more pedantic lectures about how the world was composed of "passengers" (most people) and "sailors" (people who bought Macintoshes). That strategy would only have worked with a company that could still regularly create great product breakthroughs and owned a market—namely, corporations—that could afford them.

Since Apple could do neither, it now found itself with overpriced products that were perceived by most computer owners as not being worth their much publicized advantages. From this point forward, Apple would be pulled in two directions: trying to support its current customers (and high margins) at the high end, while chasing the low-end market with computers that usually were never quite cheap or distinctive enough. The damage was done. Thanks to overpriced products and a marketing operation that had been demoralized and disemboweled by company politics and Allan Loren, Apple was already boxed in. The Christmas season had been a nightmare. Instead of the usual jump in sales, Apple had seen revenues rise by only 6 percent. Meanwhile, profits slumped 11 percent.

The stock market, which had already seen this coming, sent Apple's stock into crash dive. From a fifty-two-week high in 1989 of $50 per share, the stock price dropped nearly 40 percent to $30. The only thing that kept it from falling further was the safety cushion of the company's $900 million in cash reserves.

On February 21, Apple announced the layoff of 400 employees, 280 of them in Cupertino. From the Night of the Long Knives, as it became known, to Gil Amelio's great purges in 1996, Apple would suffer more layoffs in a shorter time than any other successful company of its size. All were bitter, but none more than this one.

The heart of this bitterness was resentment over the growing inequality in a company that had once symbolized equality. It was no secret that Apple executives were paid well above the industry average. That was accepted: after all, Apple was a hot company filled with the fastest-trackers in high tech, and you paid top dollar for top talent. But the burst of outside executive recruitment over the last couple years had distorted those salary figures even more—40 percent higher than warranted by the company's performance, one shareholders' rights group had determined.

The newly laid-off employees, rightly, saw all this as a betrayal. They had done their jobs, they had built beautiful new products, orders were going through the roof—and they still found themselves on the street. Those who were fired and those who remained would never forgive John Sculley.

Overpriced executives were still forgivable if those bonus babies did their job. But what the Apple rank and file saw was an environment in which the hardworking employees had produced one fine new product after another, month after month, and in the process had restored the company's old glory—and the revolving door of senior management ("An Apple vice president has the life expectancy of an armadillo on a Texas highway," wrote one Apple middle manager) had managed to screw it all up with long-term strategies that seemed to be revised weekly, idiotic pricing programs, endless reorganizations and misdirected marketing.

At the same time, Apple decided to cancel the expensive parties that employees had assumed were part of the company's culture, revised (that is, all but killed) the profit-sharing program that had enabled employees to take home thousands of dollars more each year and promised not to use security guards to escort newly terminated employees from their offices (thanks!). The company also said it would realign *all* salaries to bring them more in line with industry averages—a move certain to materially impact workers more than executives. This last claim was undermined by the word leaking out that Apple had given new hires William B. Coldrick (senior vice president for sales) and Donald P. Case (vice president for networking and communications) $2.1 million and $1.2 million, respectively, in future severance golden parachutes . . . and may have given Allan Loren several times that.

There had always been the sneaking suspicion among employees—aggravated by the man's manner and his big-business background—that Sculley never really cared about them. This was just the opposite of the truth, say former Sculley insiders. But this layoff, so close on the heels of a three-year boom in which Apple had grown as fast as any large company in history, seemed to confirm cold-bloodedness at the top. Killing profit sharing—"Looks to me like we all just took a ten to fifteen percent pay cut," one employee told the *Mercury News*—just underscored that belief.

It wasn't long before the company's electronic bulletin boards were awash with angry employee comments. "I've been at this company seven and a half years," wrote one employee. "Never have I seen the discord that is now running rampant." About the profit sharing, another employee wrote, "How about tying executive bonuses into the exact same formula?"

Apple's climate of shared values "may be beginning to break down," intoned Berkeley organizational behaviorist Charles O'Reilly with a scholar's gift for the obvious.

8.17 Inconsolation

On June 28, 1990, John Sculley announced that Claris, Apple's software subsidiary, would be folded back into the parent company.

"Claris has exceeded our expectations in establishing an independent brand identity and a competitive presence in the applications software business," he said. "While its spin-off market value would certainly be considerable, Claris has greater strategic value for Apple shareholders by remaining part of Apple."

He added, "Apple's goal is to significantly increase our unit growth. Developers should view our decision on Claris as a key indicator that Apple is very serious about this goal."

If Sculley had hoped to kick-start Apple's slumping stock, he failed. Company shares fell 25 cents to $42.75.

But the real loss was much greater than that. In folding the energetic and thriving Claris back into Apple Computer, Sculley cost the company two of its biggest assets: Claris itself and Bill Campbell.

In its three years of independent existence, Claris had become one of the shiniest jewels in Apple's diadem. After a rough start it had gone on to do exactly what Sculley had wanted of it: become a successful satellite that enhanced the value of Apple itself. Recalled Bill Joos, Claris's vice president of sales, "We all went there to become an independent company, on the belief that when it was spun off we'd have some skin in the game. Campbell created an aggressive culture. We were a group of rebels. The attitude was: Let's kick ass. Let's go out there and do things."

By June 1990, Claris was second only to Microsoft as the leading supplier of Apple software. Claris Works, its suite of office productivity tools, had pulled tens of thousands of new customers into Apple's orbit.

Much of the success of Claris was due to Bill Campbell. The old coach had proven himself to be one of the best business executives, and one of the best leaders, in the company's history. Now he was on the brink of fulfilling the dream with which he had started Claris: to take it public.

But he had made a terrible miscalculation. Campbell had strayed too far away. He threatened to become an even more successful and dynamic company than the one he was supporting. Moreover, says Joos, "Apple was scared that if Claris went independent it would have to start developing for Windows and Apple would lose control over its biggest software developer." So Sculley reeled Campbell in.

When Bill Campbell got the news that Claris was not only not going public but being folded back into Apple, he did something common among Apple believers, but uncharacteristic for him: he cried.

A few months later, he was gone . . . to found the software company Intuit, and to teach the world a lesson about how to tackle Bill Gates.

8.18 A BIG BLUE CRATER

Despite all these shuffles and reshuffles of management, employee layoffs and roller-coaster financials, Apple continued to design and build new products.

Every few months there was a new product announcement, or two, or three. And that meant that if you didn't like what you saw in the company catalog right now, wait a few minutes and you might find something new you liked. That in turn did a nice job of winnowing out the product line. New products that didn't get good reviews or a strong response from the market were allowed to die, while those that met with a positive response were kept around until interest faded. And there were always new candidates in the wings awaiting their audition.

But most important, newspaper headlines aside, all of this activity gave Apple the image of a glowing, healthy, prospering, lively company—an image that belied the gloomy predictions and the falling market share reports. The resulting cognitive dissonance was only to Apple's advantage. You might occasionally hear reports that the company was in a dangerous, vulnerable position—that was the perceived view in Silicon Valley by 1990—but a trip to the computer store or a glance at retail ads or an upbeat thirty-second spot on television seemed to contradict that image. How could Apple be a troubled company? Look at all their new products!

But Apple *was* a troubled company. It had missed one great chance after another to recapture its early market leadership. And now it was running out of chances. The introduction of Windows 3.0 effectively closed off the operating system software market forever. Copland, still a glowing possibility in 1991, would now, no matter how terrific, be little more than a stopgap in Apple's plunge.

There might still be an opportunity for some landmark new application program on the order of VisiCalc, Postscript or Hypercard, but it seemed unlikely that Apple would be the one to create it. And, of course, when those NeXT killer apps did appear, in the form of Lotus Notes and Netscape Navigator, they were, in fact, Windows-compatible. Claris might have come up with something extraordinary, but now it too was embedded in Apple bureaucracy.

That left only hardware. And here, remarkably, a window of opportunity opened up early in Sculley's tenure and only grew wider by the year. Somehow, IBM, generally considered at the time to be the best-run company in the world, managed to come down with a serious case of stupidity. In March 1982, Intel announced its newest-generation microprocessor, the 80286. It was the first of the "modern" 80×86 architecture processors that continue to define personal computing to this day. The 286 was a superb processor—and that presented Big Blue with a problem: the PCs that would be built with the 286 would be powerful enough to rival IBM's larger and more expensive family of minicomputers.

The rest of IBM had been jealous of Boca Raton for a long time. It was the renegade division in the buttoned-down company and it had to be stopped.

And it was. The division was stripped of its independence and assimilated back into mainstream Big Blue.

IBM then tried to hold back its clone makers by making proprietary the one part of the computer it hadn't given away to Intel or Microsoft: the wiring ("bus") that carried data around the computer's motherboard. By controlling the bus, Lowe believed, he could control the cloners, crush them when he wanted to and make them pay fealty until then.

Instead, it was IBM that was crushed. Big Blue could not order back the waves. Compaq Computer simply designed its own busing scheme and did an end run around IBM. The rest of the cloners soon followed. Two years later, Moore's Law (as well as Moore himself) did its work, and Intel introduced the 80386, the defining chip of the Windows 3.0 era. IBM was left behind. Within a few years it would suffer one of the most crushing business collapses ever. And even after it recovered, it would never again dominate personal computers.

For the rest of the 1980s, the personal computer market had been essentially leaderless as scores of companies, including Compaq, Dell, HP and the Japanese (NEC, Fujitsu, Hitachi) and Taiwanese (Acer, Leading Edge) scrambled to fill the IBM void. Apple alone had the name and the reputation. Had it produced an IBM-compatible computer—say, a new Apple II—or introduced a brand-new product family as innovative as the Mac, it might have owned the world. But, of course, it did nothing of the sort.

Only as the decade ended, as the clone industry began to firm up not around a particular box but around the Intel and Microsoft standards, did Apple finally begin to do something on the hardware front besides selling upgraded machines to its current customers. There were, in fact, two programs, one for a new product family capable of running both Mac and DOS-based programs; the other for a new kind of handheld consumer device.

The new computer family was to be the product of a consortium of three companies: Apple, IBM and Motorola. Like Taligent, this too smacked of desperation. The good news was the presence of Motorola, the one company of the three that still seemed capable of getting interesting things done. Thanks in no small part to Apple, Moto had never been a serious threat to Intel in processors. But it had always been an innovator. Meanwhile, in its other businesses, from microcontrollers (lower-powered processors used to manage automobile engines, streetlights and literally a million other applications) to cell phones, Motorola had become one of the most successful and respected companies in high tech. Now it proposed to take one last big shot at the computer processor business: the PowerPC, a family of high-powered, very fast processors that would use an alternative architecture called RISC (reduced instruction set computing)—Intel's chips were CISC (complex instruction set computing)—and be capable of running both Mac OS and DOS/Windows programs.

The idea was that Motorola would finally get a chip that could compete directly with Intel, Apple could build a new generation of computers, and IBM would once again be able to distinguish itself from the pack of clones. It was a great idea, and Motorola more than held up its end of the bargain. The first PowerPC chip, the 301, introduced in late 1992, was a beauty. In its *slowest* version, it was still as fast as the fastest new Intel chip, the Pentium. And within a year, the company introduced three even more powerful and faster models. It was as fast a creation of a new processor family as the semiconductor industry had ever seen.

But there was only one problem: the PowerPC was five years too late. By the time Apple introduced its first PowerPC-based PowerMac computers in 1994, they were no more than a welcome offering to Apple's own market base. By then, there were nearly one billion microprocessors in use in the world—and of those, nearly 900 million were Intel chips. It was just too great a market dominance for even Motorola to overcome. And Apple didn't help the cause: the Mac OS actually slowed the PowerPC chips to lower speeds in real-life use than the Pentium. Meanwhile, stumble-footed IBM announced that its PowerPC-based computers would be at least a year late. Through all this, Intel, kept running at ramming speed by Andy Grove, continued cranking out a new and more splendid ×86 chip (286, 386, 486, Pentium, Pentium Pro) every couple of years to make sure that Motorola would never catch up.

The second Apple hardware project, a consumer product, was the Newton, an electronic tablet, the size of a paperback book, designed to read handwriting on its screen, store sizable quantities of data and communicate with personal computers—all at a price that could be afforded by the average professional.

Pen-based computing, with a computer capable of using sophisticated algorithms to interpret handwriting, was the hottest new computer market idea of the early 1990s. Some of the best venture capitalists in the business, such as John Doerr of Kleiner Perkins, invested millions of fund dollars into new pen computing start-ups. In every way it appeared to be the Next Big Thing. And Newton, a handheld pen computer with an Apple logo in front and Apple's giant distribution network behind, looked like a surefire winner.

Apple certainly treated it that way. Compared to the skunk works of the early Apple team, whose members were shunned as corporate lepers, the Newton project was granted instant stardom. Its progress was treated like a royal caravan moving through the countryside.

Newton was an extraordinarily self-conscious production. The team even allowed itself to be photographed through the project in preparation for a celebratory book to be published with the Newton's introduction. In so many ways, Newton was not a new-product development project, but a simulation of one, an acting out of the process with one eye cocked backward at famous projects of the past.

But if the history of the personal computer industry teaches anything, it is that ritual re-creations of the past don't guarantee an equally glorious present. The Newton was the most anxiously awaited new Apple product since the Mac. But when it was finally introduced in 1993, it proved to be a bitter disappointment. Not that it was a bad little machine, but it fell vastly below expectations. And this was John Sculley's fault. He had spent years promoting the idea of his Dynabook, the Knowledge Navigator. He even had the temerity to claim that the Newton would be the centerpiece of a $3.5 *trillion* new market in personal information tools.

To paraphrase the absent Jean-Louis Gassée, that smelled a little like infinity.

Not surprisingly, when people first heard of the Newton, they thought it would be the KN dream incarnate. Instead, in the plastic, it turned out to be a little device of limited application that didn't even read handwriting that well. It quickly tanked, and Apple, showing the same loyalty to its products as it did to its employees, couldn't back far enough away from it. Ironically, later improvements on the Newton proved it to be a useful device. But the damage was already done. Descendants of the Newton, such as 3Com's Palm Pilot, inferior in technology (at least at first) but superior in meeting market expectations, captured the now booming field. The Palm Pilot in fact sold one million units in a single year. The Newton, which was to be the next Macintosh, became only a tragic footnote to the Apple story.

8.19 Profitless Endeavors

In late 1990 Apple announced yet another new plan: to bombard the market with a portfolio of brand-new desktop and portable computer models, slash prices across the board and sacrifice profits (current margins were 54 percent) for added volume and market share. "This plan has no sacred cows," Sculley told the press.

Publicly, Sculley talked about Apple becoming a $10 billion company in the early 1990s, but in the executive offices at Apple, the discussions were a lot more pessimistic. This new announcement was the first public admission (though few noticed at the time) that Apple was losing market share so fast that it was in danger of losing control of its destiny. Somewhere up ahead—a 5 percent market share, a 3 percent market share, perhaps even less—was a point of no return, beyond which Apple and its operating system would become superfluous, where developers would no longer be interested in building for it, stores would stop selling it and even the most loyal users would begin to fade away. And to keep from reaching that point Apple was now willing to sacrifice its profits—and, inevitably, the value of its stock.

The announced goal was a market share jump of three percentage points in 1991—an amazingly ambitious target for a company with only a 10.7 percent market share the year before. Apple threw everything it had into the campaign. "We're pulling out all the stops," announced Spindler.

It was the best multiple-new-product introduction in company history. First, and most celebrated, was the $999 Mac Classic. It was at long last the realization of Jef Raskin's now generation-old dream of the Everyman computer: a full-blown Mac I costing less than $1,000. With the even better Classic II that followed a year later, the Mac Classic finally set Apple on a path to build affordable full-power machines.

The second product, the Mac LC was even more impressive. At $2,499, it was the lowest-priced color Macintosh to date, evidence that Apple could compete even with the clone makers on price. It also offered, as an option, a $199 add-in board, that enabled the LC to run old Apple II software. Targeted at schools, this option was the last lifeline to be thrown out to the old Apple II fanatics.

Finally, at the Mac II level, Apple introduced the third machine, the mid-range IIsi. It wasn't as interesting as the other two, but time would prove it to be one of the company's most enduring and reliable products.

It was an impressive collection. It had to be. As industry analyst and long-time Apple adviser Tim Bajarin said: "Apple is going back to its roots. It has to get the lowest-cost Macintosh into the hands of as many people as possible. It has to get more people addicted to the Mac." Then, ominously: "If they don't have this one right, they're in trouble."

The strategy worked almost as well as planned. It also produced as many bad consequences as good ones.

Almost from the beginning, Apple's new market share strategy provoked an outcry. Apple's 1,700 dealers read (correctly) into the news a hidden plan by Apple to expand its distribution network to superstores and other retailers. They went nuts. Said one Valley dealer pointedly, "Apple's problems have not been due to a lack of distribution."

The shareholders weren't any happier. The company's stock dropped $2.75 to $25 on the news—and the expectation that the company was about to suffer another bad quarter. But John Sculley wasn't deterred. He trumpeted the news that the three new computers had received more initial orders than any computers in the company's history.

He wasn't kidding. By January and the end of the next quarter, Apple's revenues had jumped 12 percent (to $1.68 billion) and profits leaped 21 percent (to $150.5 million, or $1.28 per share). And there was more good news: Apple had forestalled the expected drop in margins through greater manufacturing efficiencies: it had fallen only 0.6 percentage point from the year before, to 51.4 percent.

Some of that good news had already leaked out during the intervening months—so that by the January 18 announcement, Apple's stock was back up to more than $51.

It seemed as if Apple had once again turned itself around. Once again, acting as if he'd finally put the company on the right track, John Sculley announced that he was pulling away from the daily activities of Apple to focus on "breakthrough projects"—in this case, the Newton. And, once again, his assessment of the company's competitive condition was completely wrong. Meanwhile, with $16.7 million in salary and stock in 1990, John Sculley was the second-highest-paid chief executive in the United States.

8.20 Overlap

Meanwhile, the new-product announcements continued unabated. In May, Apple finally introduced System 7.0, the long-awaited upgrade to the Mac OS. System 7.0 was powerful and graphic, an adequate answer to Windows 3.0. Yet it was also obviously merely a step up for the Mac OS, not a quantum leap. The product also proved to be buggy, which scared off many users, already nervous about messing around with operating system upgrades. Others were put off by the $99 price Apple put on the product, the company in the past having given away software upgrades for free. The result was that Apple had to devote considerable time and resources on getting its user base to adopt a product that should have been met with a stampede. Meanwhile, the marketplace, fed on Copland rumors for years, waited for the big announcement.

Then, in October, there was another mass hardware introduction. And once again, some home runs.

The biggest of these was a new family of laptops: the PowerBooks. After the embarrassment of the Portable, and the long, frustrating wait by customers (some of whom finally gave up and crossed over to the numerous Wintel laptops), Apple finally had in the PowerBook a great laptop computer.

On the same day, Apple introduced the first pair (Models 500 and 700) of a new family of consumer Macs, called the Performa. Marketwise, these were the descendants of the Apple II, the Mac Classic, the Classic II and the LC. The Performas were nice, only slightly overpriced computers featuring a strong library of bundled software and a number of built-ins such as a CD-ROM drive.

All in all, an appealing package. But the Performa line, which grew like ivy, in many places overlapped the Mac II line. This was an inevitable result of crossing an entrenched bureaucracy with a program that yields good performance reviews for everyone involved. The good news was that such a proliferation of Apple models countered the growing skepticism in the press and among analysts that Apple could still compete against the Windows world. It made customers feel better about buying Apple products, it made developers more comfortable designing Mac-compatible products and it made analysts more willing to suggest the purchase of Apple stock.

But the bad news came when those same people actually decided to purchase an Apple. Now all that abundance looked more like chaos. Should I buy a high-end Performa or a II, or, starting the next year, a low-end Quadra? They're both the same price, so which is better? Apple didn't help matters by regularly yanking one product off the shelf and quickly replacing it with the other. Should I buy this one or wait a year? Didn't Apple just announce a replacement?

It wasn't long before this shell-game affliction also infected PowerBooks. Just as the first generation of PowerBooks were reaching excited customers, Apple proceeded to declare them obsolete and announced a second generation. Even the model numbers were confusing. Then a couple of years later, before the market had fully recovered, Apple announced a third generation with a whole new numbering scheme. And this third generation of PowerBooks was so shoddily built and, occasionally, so dangerous as to make users pine for the simpler days of the early PowerBooks.

It was as if Apple, having lost its way in new-product development in the late 1980s, had suddenly decided to make up for lost time in the first half of the 1990s. It had become a binge developer. The problem with all these new products was not their design, or even their price, but their orientation. Apple was now selling only to Apple people. By now, five years after IBM's stumble, PC owners had learned to live without an industry standard setter in hardware. Now they merely looked to Intel and Microsoft for validation of their purchases of Gateway 2000, Dell or Compaq computers. Apple, meanwhile, could look back on the previous five years and see an incredible profusion of new products for its existing customers—and a series of blown chances to do anything more. The company was again growing in revenues but it was also still shrinking in market share. The 1991 cost-cutting campaign managed to gain a couple of points of market share, but after that it began to fall once more—this time even faster.

Apple's fate was now set. From this point on Apple would be selling only within its 3.5 million-member family: schoolkids, art directors, graphic artists, writers. The young and the old and the computer-illiterate. Apple's only hope now would be that it could keep these groups constantly turning over and upgrading their equipment and that all those schoolkids learning now on Macs would grow up to become a new army of Apple fanatics.

In other words, Apple could only pray for a miracle—and that miracle was not a computer, but a human, generation away. In the meantime, it would have to pay for its latest strategy du jour.

8.21 MIDDLE-AGE SPREAD

As it passed its fifteenth anniversary, Apple, with its 12,000 employees and 3,000 contractors, spilled out of Bandley Drive to sites all over Silicon Valley and the world. Its very presence had transformed both the economy and the society of Cupertino. Employees still ate at the Good Earth and Bob's Big Boy and occasionally transgressed from correct dietary behavior by sneaking doughnuts at the ancient Donut Wheel. But now at the corner of Stevens Creek and Homestead, great changes were afoot. On one side, the Wagon Wheel restaurant, a 1940s remnant that catered to both bikers and programmers, was replaced by a red-brick building that housed Apple's educational group. Much more obvious, though, were the events taking place on the diagonal corner. There for forty years had stood R. Cali Bros. Feed Co., an anachronistic collection of dusty buildings and storage silos out of a 1930s precisionist painting. Now it had been bulldozed and was busily being replaced by the green lawns and tall glass towers of Apple's new corporate headquarters.

There is an old law in Silicon Valley that when a company builds a new corporate headquarters the shrewd investor shorts the stock. It is an investment strategy that has held for companies as diverse as Apple, Silicon Graphics and even Hewlett-Packard (though not Intel, which wisely continues to shrink from the very idea of a headquarters), and it comes from an understanding of entrepreneurship and human behavior. When a company grows big enough and wealthy enough to finally move out of the warren of rented buildings it has grown up in, it has also usually grown so staid and self-obsessed that it will soon lose track of its customers, its products and its markets. Moreover, once such a facility is announced, everyone with any authority in the company quickly becomes obsessed with getting the right office on the right floor with the best parking place, while minor matters like running the company are put on the back burner.

This, of course, is precisely what happened at Apple, though the company was moving toward that attitude long before the cardboard boxes full of office supplies were shipped over to the new building. But what made the Apple headquarters move not just the latest example of a dispiriting trend but also a classic tragedy was that, with the exception perhaps of Oracle's glass tubes, no office buildings in Silicon Valley more resembled those IBM and PepsiCo buildings Jobs had ridiculed that night seven years before.

In the ten-year reign of John Sculley, Apple's ersatz philosopher king, Apple had aged from the Little Kingdom to the Middle Kingdom. It shared many traits with dynastic China: isolation and insularity, contempt for outsiders, an elegant but decadent culture at the top, endless palace intrigue and indifference to the fate of average citizens. As the Khans looked upon Westerners, Apple looked upon Wintel users as either dupes or idiots, and certainly blind. And at the top of this cultish society was the Emperor himself, coolly detached from harsh reality. Fittingly, his glass-walled office in the new headquarters faced not outward at the big, ugly world, but inward, toward the not so little Kingdom.

Gary Martin, leaving Apple in 1992, was "amazed just how big the IBM-compatible world was. Inside Apple, we were so completely insulated from the vast non-Apple computing world outside."

In the Apple cosmology, Mac users were the true illuminati. They sported Apple logo stickers in their car windows and crowded into MacExpo to look at the newest products and read *MacWorld* or *MacUser* magazines for the latest dope. It was a beautifully self-contained world. And when everyone was talking to one another at the same time, it was almost loud enough to drown out the roar of Wintel barbarians just outside the walls, pounding on the gates.

At the center of it all was John Sculley himself. He had come to Cupertino to escape the politics and bureaucracies of Pepsi and the East Coast establishment corporations. He wanted to be an agent for change at Apple, and God was cruel enough to give him his wish: he managed to change everything for the worse.

Apple was also opening a giant new R&D facility a half mile down De Anza Boulevard, overlooking the freeway. The huge complex of buildings had once been the headquarters of Four-Phase Inc., a benighted computer terminal and network company that had been bought out years before. Now Apple turned it into a glass-and-steel metaphor of itself. The renovated facility had green lawns for employees to play Frisbee upon and a cafeteria that served everything from cappuccino to sushi. And all the buildings faced inward.

Even more telling was the name of the driveway leading into the complex. As a joke, the company had named it Infinite Loop, after the mistake in programming code that causes a program to repeat the same mistake over and over. Nobody seemed to notice that the name also was a devastating comment on the New Apple itself. Fittingly, this new facility along Infinite Loop was the home of the Copland team.

Narcissism had always been at the heart of the Apple way. It had once enabled the company to overcome enormous obstacles to success. It was also why the company could be so insufferably smug. But now, as they looked in the mirror, many Apple employees didn't like what they saw. Cringely, writing at the time, caught it perfectly:

> Today, the sense of anomie—alienation, disconnectedness—at Apple is major. The difference between the old Apple, which was crazy, and the new Apple is anomie. People are alienated. Apple still gets the bright young people. They come into Apple, and instead of getting all fired up about something, they go through one or two reorgs and get

> disoriented. I don't hear people who are really happy to be at Apple anymore. They wonder why they are there, because they've had two bosses in six months, and their job has changed twice.

What Cringely didn't have to say was that the difference between the Old Apple and the New Apple was John Sculley. The pirate flag could now be found in the Apple museum, alongside stills from the "1984" ad and all the other crazy, thrilling, psycho things the young Apple had done. Now, at the Hapsburg Apple, wearing jeans to the executive offices was the height of bohemianism. Just about everything that had made Apple special had been driven off, gelded or packed away. Apple's republican days were now long gone, replaced by its Augustan age. Sculley had traded everything for maximum profits and stock price. Apple was now literally trapped on Infinite Loop.

There were stories of a kind of imperial arrogance taking over Apple's executive offices. Worried by what he was seeing, Regis brought in a series of consultants and speakers to try to teach Sculley & Co. how a corporation can both grow and endure, yet still remain vital and dynamic. "They would listen attentively to the speaker," Regis recalled with dismay. "Then when he was done they would walk out and go right back to what they were doing before." It wasn't long before McKenna, not without a little mourning for the company he'd helped create, began to back away from Apple.

Apple next decided it wanted a corporate jet. Despite the area's wealth, there were few such aircraft in the Valley. HP had a couple, but any employee could hop a ride to get to an outlying division. But at Apple, this would not be the Aircraft for the Rest of Us. Management only. But when the jet finally arrived, the executives were aghast to see that the Apple logo on the tail did not have the exact tonality in its colors. So, at a cost of tens of thousands of dollars, they had it scraped off and repainted.

But the last straw came when John Sculley had declared himself, in March 1990, Apple's new chief technology officer. The little inventor was at long last going to be a real engineer—even if he had to award the title himself. Outside Apple, the news was met with laughter and endless jokes. Whenever Sculley's name came up in conversation, the other person was bound to raise an eyebrow and ask solemnly, "You mean, Apple's *chief technology officer?*" followed by general laughter.

Inside Apple, it wasn't so funny. Down in the ranks of *real* engineers, nobody was laughing. They hadn't worked eighty-hour weeks for years to have to take this kind of insult. As Apple graphics engineer Konstantin Othmer told Jim Carlton of *The Wall Street Journal:* "Every engineer should have walked out when he did that. You're taking an executive from the soda industry and making him CTO of one of the best technology companies in the world."

From that moment, the technical ranks of Apple, the heart of the company, turned its back on John Sculley forever. They would cheer his departure and, even then, hold a grudge against him for years. Sculley, meanwhile, thought the decision one of the best he ever made at Apple.

8.22 SLAUGHTER

On May 20, 1991, via a morning voice mail message to Apple employees, John Sculley announced the layoff of 1,600 (it would eventually be 1,500) employees.

Rumors had been swirling for days. Experts had predicted anywhere from 500 to 2,000 layoffs. So it wasn't as bad as it might have been, although close. The number represented 10 percent of Apple's total workforce, including temps and contractors.

The layoff was described as the inevitable consequence of Apple's new strategy. The first quarter's strong sustained profits had been an illusion; now the arithmetic was taking its revenge. Reduced margins had to be matched with reduced overhead. For the quarter ended March 31, revenues had jumped 19 percent, driven by the new low-cost Macs. But earnings hadn't budged from the year before.

"Obviously, we don't like having to do this," said Sculley. "It will be hard for all of us to see some wonderful and talented employees leave the company." But, he added, "our industry has gone through a tremendous change very rapidly and these changes are affecting all major competitors, not just Apple."

Yet most of the cuts came in the distribution change and through a reorganization of the field sales force into fewer offices. This was bizarre . . . and illuminating. As observers noted at the time, Apple was one of the most productive companies per capita in its industry. Its $440,000 in annual sales per employee was the best in the industry, twice that of most of its competitors. Profits per employee—$37,400—were second only to Compaq.

In other words, the line operations of Apple were more than paying for its keep. On the other hand, Apple's management and administrative costs were also at the top of the industry—31.7 percent. Maintaining the palace and court were a real bloated cost on Apple's balance sheet.

It was Apple's biggest layoff to date. The pink slips arrived on June 20. Once again, there was a small lunch-hour protest. One hundred twenty employees showed up for the rally. They waved copies of Sculley's biography and called for Sculley to live up to his own enlightened management advice. One employee read a selection from the book:

> Let's say we stop judging business and planning in the future by the balance sheet. Every way we currently look at business has been financially focused. Instead, let's look at the creative value of a corporation.

Some wanted to burn the books in a bonfire. But in the end the group decided to mail the copies back to its author. The sole protest sign, carried by newly laid-off networking engineer Suzy Brown, read: "I used to have the spirit and passion for Apple. Now I'm just 'collateral damage.' "

But it was all meaningless. The protesters were just some of the last true believers. As they put on their pathetic show, the rest of Apple watched quietly from the company cafeteria. These hundreds understood now that Apple was no longer a dream or a family. Now it was just a business—and what mattered now was holding on to your job.

8.23 Divine Intervention

Incredibly, even as hope was fading, Apple was given one last chance to get out of its Catch-22.

By now it was apparent to almost everyone that Apple's major operating system efforts, first envisioned at an off-site conference in March 1988, and now having sucked up hundreds of millions of dollars of Apple R&D money, were in trouble.

The three original projects had been code-named Pink, Red (being pinker than pink) and Blue. Pink was to be the revolutionary new object-oriented operating system. It would dead-end in Taligent. Red, which was to be even more outré than Pink, passed through a second phase, called Raptor, then mutated into the hydra of Copland and took on a life of its own. It would never be completed. Only Blue, the Mac OS upgrade, and thus the least ambitious of the three, ever made it to market.

Now, in February 1992, the new OS upgrade, System 7, completed, its project manager, Gifford Calenda, walked into the office of his boss, vice president for software development Roger Heinen, with a proposal. "Bill Gates is going to kill us because we are sitting at maybe eight percent market share," he told Heinen. It was only going to get worse unless Apple got the

Mac OS to work on another platform. Calenda asked for permission to give it a shot.

His timing was perfect. A week later, Heinen was contacted by a vice president of Novell Inc., the Utah computer network software giant. The representative, Darrell Miller, was speaking for Novell CEO Ray Noorda, Bill Gates's most single-minded antagonist. Noorda, looking for yet another end run around Microsoft, wanted to know if Apple would like to team up with Novell to create an Intel-compatible version of the Mac OS? And if not, would Apple sue if Novell went ahead without it?

Apple didn't need to do the calculations. Novell had twelve *million* customers. Heinen called Calenda back and told him to assemble a team and go for it. The project, in perfect techie style, was code-named Star Trek, because its charter was to "boldly go where no one has gone before."

But Apple and Novell still needed one more player: Intel, the guys who owned the microprocessor standard. And this was when it got interesting—because Intel was not only interested but got involved at the very top. So did Apple. In late 1991, John Sculley was interviewed by David Yoffie, a Harvard Business School professor and Intel director, when Yoffie was preparing a case study on Apple. Like most interviews, the conversation took off on its own, in this case about the Apple/Intel-Microsoft-PC war. "I don't think you have a prayer," Yoffie told Sculley. Why? Sculley asked. Yoffie explained that the growing power and performance of Windows atop Intel chips was rapidly closing the gap with the Mac and its OS and demolishing Apple's sole marketing advantage.

Sculley didn't buy the argument. So Yoffie offered to bring to Apple someone who could make the case far better than he. And so, in early 1992, a small, trim Hungarian emigrant with a look of infinite authority walked through the lobby of De Anza 7 for a meeting with John Sculley.

Apple's flacks had spent years molding the image of Sculley as a great manager, business titan and technology visionary. But Andrew S. Grove was the real thing. Unlike Apple in personal computers, Intel had started in the middle of the pack in a far rougher business and not only emerged as the leader but demolished the competition. It owned 90 percent of the market for microprocessors, the most important product in the world. And that made Andy Grove the most powerful business executive in high technology.

Grove was fearless, tough and brilliant. In five years, Intel would be worth more than the entire U.S. auto industry. On one occasion, its good quarterly earnings report would pull the world's stock markets back from the brink of a crash.

But Intel had an Achilles' heel: for all of its power, wealth and influence, it was married to Gates's Microsoft. And in this marriage, Intel did all the heavy lifting. It was no secret that Windows, built in layers atop the now ancient DOS core, was a kluge that depended for much of its performance upon Intel coming out with a new, more powerful chip every couple of years. Grove well knew he was being forced to put a race-car engine in a Buick, but he had little choice unless he could find another OS.

And that was why he was here at Apple Computer. The message Grove delivered in Sculley's fourth-floor office was a simple one. He presented Sculley with Intel's forecast for microprocessor shipments to PC companies in the year to come. It was far above anything Apple had imagined. Then Grove leaned forward with the look that drained the blood out of the faces of lesser mortals, and said, "John, you are going to get killed by Microsoft. You have to put your technology on Intel."

John Sculley, dazed, nodded. "I guess you're right."

Star Trek was given a bright green light.

One by one, Apple had been visited by the three Magi of PCs. Gates, IBM and now Grove. All offered salvation. Apple had blown the first two chances, dismissing Gates's advice and wrecking the IBM joint venture even before it began. Grove had come calling with one last chance.

This time, Apple seemed determined to follow. Calenda quickly pulled together a team of seven engineers, four marketers and two administrative assistants from Apple, along with four representatives from Novell. The project was so sensitive (being a greater apostasy inside Apple than outside) that the team moved out of Apple and set up shop at Novell in Santa Clara—ironically, just across the way from Grove's office at Intel.

It was like the old pirate days on the Mac team. The refrigerator was filled with Sierra Nevada beer, courtesy of the company. When someone joked about needing an arcade video game, it was delivered. The team even put on the door a joke company name: WE ARE ARROGANT BASTARDS & ASSOCIATES—which mortified Novell's largely Mormon staff and was eventually removed. Instead the team put up a new fake business title every week.

It was a wonderful experience, the last of its kind in the Apple story. The Star Trek team got a brief glimpse of what their predecessors had known a decade before. No company politics, no suits from headquarters looking over their shoulders. Just long days and nights, sitting at a pair of computers—one a Mac, the other a PC—writing code for one, then translating it for the other. When they didn't understand something about the chip (in this case the Intel 80486), a technician was always waiting at Intel to take their call.

Five years before, when Dan Eilers had suggested just such a translation project, Jean-Louis Gassée had declared it impossible. Gassée was partly right: the existing Mac OS code, some of it dating back to 1983, resisted conversion. But that didn't stop this team; they just rewrote the old code so it would work. And even that wasn't enough. The team was only chartered to translate the critical Finder program of the OS, but the members went on and converted the hot new graphics feature, QuickDraw, to DOS as well. Then, for fun, they even made the DOS version boot up with the same sound and the same happy face icon as the Mac. If you didn't look down from the screen, it would be impossible to tell whether you were working on a Macintosh or a Compaq computer.

It was not only an incredible achievement but an extraordinarily prodigious one. By November 1992, less than six months after they'd begun, the team held a demonstration of Star Trek for some Apple and Novell brass.

The demonstration was simple—the Mac OS tool bar, spinning dice, bouncing balls, the letters A-P-P-L-E floating in space, finishing with a QuickTime video of a rocket taking off as the audio announced, "Liftoff. We have liftoff"—but it was historic. The first-ever bridge between the two worlds of personal computing. One Novell executive began giggling with joy.

On December 4, in De Anza 7, the Star Trek team was asked to give a demonstration of their achievement to the Apple executive team. They were all there, including Sculley, Graziano, Spindler, Sullivan and Eisenstat. As the presentation progressed, the team grew more and more optimistic. *Maybe they won't kill us like they did all the others.* Sculley was grinning. Graziano was so excited he couldn't stay in his seat.

When the demonstration finished, the execs began to pepper the team with questions, interrupting each other, repeating each other's questions. It was so chaotic that one Star Trek team member asked himself if these were really the men who ran Apple Computer. But it didn't matter. What was important was the enthusiasm. They were going for it! Star Trek was going to happen.

Then Fred Forsythe, head of Apple's engineering, said quietly, "This will mean a whole new business model."

Forsythe was concerned that Apple was already committed to the PowerPC joint venture and that any distraction might upset the partners and confuse the marketplace. That was the end of Star Trek. In the end, Apple chose the safer path. Though the executive team voted to continue funding and ramping up Star Trek, it was already over. A few weeks later, during the Christmas break, Heinen quit Apple to join, in the ultimate insult, Microsoft.

And so ended Apple's last chance to avert disaster.

8.24 Distractions

"Ironically, the times when I had the most power [were] when Apple was in trouble," Sculley told reporter Jim Carlton. By end of the summer of 1991, the layoffs completed, the company having eaten a horrific $224 million to cover its restructuring—giving it its first quarterly loss, $53.1 million, since 1985—John Sculley found himself without an immediate crisis and hungry for a new crusade.

In November, the world got its first clue that Sculley's mind was wandering when he filed with the SEC to sell up to 100,000 of his 165,000 shares in hand (he had options on almost 600,000 more).

On top of that, Silicon Valley and the rest of high tech were finally, begrudgingly, beginning to accept the outsider who had now run one of its biggest companies through thick and thin for nearly a decade. The occasion for this reappraisal was the introduction of the Newton at the Consumer Electronics Show in Chicago at the end of May 1992. Its future as yet unknown, and apparently shining, the Newton was seen as a kind of culmination to Sculley's tenure after Jobs. "[Newton] represents perhaps the first tangible glimpse of a vision of technology's future," wrote the *Mercury News*, "a vision now shared by many of the world's biggest high-technology companies. Many people now credit Sculley with shaping that vision." Industry researcher Dataquest was even more ebullient; wrote one of its analysts, "Sculley is the leading visionary in the computer industry today."

It was true. His ideas might be derived from others, the Newton might not succeed as a product, but there was no denying that John Sculley had single-mindedly driven a new technology from a mere daydream into a real product that would soon set into motion a real industry. He had proven that he could duplicate what Steve Jobs had done—and do it in the much more demanding environment of a multibillion-dollar company with thousands of employees. Whatever happened from this point, no one could ever take that away from John Sculley.

Sculley's reputation, like that of so many business leaders, only increased the further away you went from company headquarters. He was disrespected by his own engineers, but lionized on the East Coast. After all, here was one of them, a clubby Brahmin, who had gone out West with the savages and who, like Kurtz, managed to become their ruler. For a while, Sculley was even short-listed to become the new chief executive of IBM. But there were even bigger ponds for John Sculley now to swim in.

In Silicon Valley, once you reach the top, the only place to go is inside the Beltway. As with so many things, David Packard had cut the path in the late

1960s, when he had accepted a job as Deputy Secretary of Defense. By the 1980s there was a continuous stream of Valley CEOs making the trip to lobby, testify and dole out contributions in the name of the American Electronics Association, the Semiconductor Industry Association and various legislative campaigns.

It was also great fun to go inside the Beltway, because unlike among one's peers back in San Jose, Valley executives were treated like visiting royalty in Washington—after all, electronics was now America's largest manufacturing employer, the key to its balance of trade and, the politicos hoped, a source for millions in campaign contributions. The nexus of Silicon Valley's curiosity about Washington, and Washington's lust for Silicon Valley, reached its peak in the 1992 presidential election campaign.

Despite their liberal credentials, the players in Silicon Valley, being bootstrap entrepreneurs and fiscal conservatives, had almost universally voted for the GOP for thirty years. But 1992 was going to be different. Most of the Valley's leaders were frustrated with George Bush's Rust Belt orientation and intrigued (and secretly thrilled) by Bill Clinton's apparent understanding of tech. Suddenly, it was okay to be a liberal in Silicon Valley, and closet Democrats started popping up everywhere. John Sculley teamed up with Ed McCracken, CEO of Silicon Graphics, and a number of other local Valley execs and venture capitalists to draft Clinton's technology white paper. The Clinton campaign thanked Sculley by leaking word that, until the selection of Senator Al Gore, Sculley had been a contender for Clinton's vice presidential running mate.

When Clinton finally made his way out to Silicon Valley, it was Sculley and the other execs who met him, wrote him sizable checks and then set up what was likely the most important single event of the entire campaign: a press conference in which a dozen of the Valley's top CEOs came out onstage to give their support to candidate Clinton. Cameras rolled, sending the image around the world. Later, one CEO would say he had been duped into the appearance: Gil Amelio of National Semiconductor.

The Valley press conference was a galvanizing moment for the Clinton campaign. The top executives of America's most important industry, guys who really knew the future and how America could best get there, born leaders who had single-handedly changed the modern world . . . and they had dubbed Bill Clinton their choice. It was no wonder that Clinton returned to the Valley again and again, not just during the campaign but throughout his first term as President. And as the election results rolled in that November night, hands were rubbed together in boardrooms all over the Valley—not least in Cupertino. Now the Valley had its own pipeline right into the Oval Office.

But at Apple, the connection went even deeper, thanks to Dave Barram, whose enduring friendship with that Arkansas governor and his wife had turned into a career Lotto jackpot. There was growing talk of Barram coming to Washington. Barram, being a loyal lieutenant, put in a good word for his boss. Soon John Sculley was being talked about as well for a job in Washington, or perhaps an ambassadorship. Sculley, it was rumored, had begun quietly campaigning for the job of Secretary of Education as early as the Bush Administration.

It was a perfect moment for Sculley to make such a move. As he saw it, he was at his very peak in power and prestige at Apple. Moreover, he knew the future looked bleak. Company stock had fallen 3¼ to $45.25 on news that the quarter ended July 31 had seen flat earnings from the quarter before—and it was only going to get worse as product prices fell and R&D rose to get Copland out to meet the newest Windows. Now was the time to get the hell out—*après moi le déluge*—while his reputation was still intact and, at age fifty-three, step up to an even greater role on the world stage. Meanwhile, to position Apple neatly, Sculley entered into conversations with Ray Noorda of Novell about a possible merger to take on Microsoft directly.

So, in every way, the fix seemed to be in. Barram was called back to D.C. for an appointment as Deputy Secretary of Commerce. Though he denied it, Sculley looked to be next. Certainly Washington insiders thought so: even conservative William Schneider of the American Enterprise Institute said that the Clinton White House considered Sculley to be "the very model of the modern business person." *Financial World* magazine named him CEO of the Year. And then came the appearance during the State of the Union address. John Sculley seemed poised on the brink of greatness . . .

Then months passed. Whether it was because the Clinton administration, notoriously slow in making appointments, never got around to him; or because it wanted him to stay where he was in Silicon Valley; or whether it didn't want him at all, the call never came for John Sculley. Once again, as had happened during the attempted sell-off of Apple after the Mac introduction, Sculley had devised the perfect exit strategy only to see it fade away. The Novell deal collapsed as well.

Meanwhile, the Sculleys had purchased a home in Connecticut and Leezy was spending much of her time there. Sculley himself, who had never hidden his preference for the East, began to talk increasingly about going back, maybe even opening an office in New York City and running Apple from there. More than one board member grumbled that the CEO seemed distracted and out of touch.

Then on June 9, 1993, Apple publicly projected a sizable drop in earnings for the rest of the year. Gross margins, well over 50 percent when Apple had embarked on its new strategy the year before, were now in the high 30s—and falling. Worse, analysts determined that in order to pump up volume enough to sustain its current earnings, Apple would have to cut prices. But that would slash margins. The new strategy had put Apple Computer into a dangerous downward spiral; yet another infinite loop. Another massive layoff was now inevitable.

At last, the board of directors, somehow rediscovering the spine it had been missing for a decade, decided that Sculley had been too attentive to his own career back East to mind the store at home. It asked for his resignation as CEO and as chief technology officer. He would be left with the chairmanship.

John Sculley was shocked by the news, both because he assumed he was secure in the job until he was ready to abandon it and because it also meant the end of his political career. But he didn't show his dismay to the world. Instead, he put a positive spin on the move, "The strategy Apple has been pursuing for three years, which Michael [Spindler] and I designed, is coming to fruition. We decided the CEO position is a full-time job." He was correct on both counts.

Though Sculley and Apple put the best face on the firing, the real story came out three months later in one of the strangest episodes in John Sculley's strange tenure at Apple. In late September, Al Eisenstat, Apple's veteran (thirteen years) executive vice president and secretary, furious for having just been squeezed out of the company, filed suit against Apple and its new CEO, Michael Spindler. According to the suit, Eisenstat and Kevin Sullivan, those two hidden powers on the executive team, had secretly spent months preparing Spindler to depose Sculley.

Eisenstat claimed that he had been approached by several outside Apple directors and asked to sound out Spindler about taking over the CEO post. According to Eisenstat, those directors felt Sculley "was not focused on the day-to-day operations of Apple, other than on its technology" and wanted help removing him. Eisenstat did as he was asked, and when Spindler proved amenable, he and Sullivan worked with him to grease the transition. As Sculley's chief adviser, Eisenstat was particularly well placed for treachery. But tied to that service was a quid pro quo—or at least Eisenstat thought. Maybe an employment guarantee. A promotion. Stock.

So the ax fell on Sculley. And Eisenstat, who had sided with Sculley nine years before against Jobs, was in the front row for the execution, knitting his own future Apple. Then—surprise!—Mike Spindler, apparently with little trust for traitors, even his own, concluded that since Al's primary job was as John Sculley's adviser, and since Sculley was gone, Eisenstat was now superfluous. Eisenstat, who had made $911,831 in salary and stock the year before, and who held $6.5 million in company stock, would just have to get by somehow on the gilded executive severance package he'd helped Sculley devise a few years before.

Eisenstat would have none of it. He sued for emotional distress, conspiracy (!), age discrimination and wrongful termination under California "whistle blower" laws. His case was dismissed.

8.25 Exit Strategy

Some optimists predicted that leaving Apple would at last free Sculley to take on Washington; the number two job in Commerce was currently vacant. But the call still didn't come, especially now that he was damaged goods.

Meanwhile, Sculley's old Pepsi skills returned to him one last time. After having done the same for his lieutenants over the years, he held out for the biggest golden parachute he could get, a reward for the quality of his stewardship. The negotiations dragged on, the board trying to get out of this ugly situation with the minimum of bad publicity, Sculley knowing he had the board over a barrel for exactly the same reason. In the midst of this, Art Rock, the grand old man of high-technology venture capital and, in the words of one Apple manager, "the one really adult adult in the whole place," abruptly resigned after thirteen years on the board. He claimed a potential conflict of interest between his directorship at Intel and Apple's involvement with the PowerPC chip. But the timing suggested there was more to it. Certainly the results were far-reaching. With Rock's departure, the board caved, and John Sculley walked away from Apple with a lucrative parting gift: $1 million in severance, $750,000 in "consultant fees" and immediate vesting of all unearned stock options, worth $2.4 million—$4.1 million in all. Sculley also got the rest of his 1993 salary ($1.059 million, plus a bonus of $412,000). Apple agreed to buy Sculley's house in Woodside ($3.95 million) and his Lear 55 jet for "fair market value." It was a deal so munificent that the next day the SEC announced a plan to give shareholders more control over executive bonuses and severance packages. Nothing was too good for *Financial Week*'s CEO of the Year.

For Eric Krugler, a six-year Apple veteran who went on to become CEO of Orbital Concepts Inc., the John Sculley era was bracketed by two company meetings.

The first all-hands meeting, taking place at the Flint Center within days of Krugler's arrival in 1989, was a celebration. "Everybody loved to go. There were demonstrations of great new technologies, then afterward there'd be a party with good food and music. Everybody seemed really excited.

"But I also remember that at that first meeting they showed a videotape of employees talking about the company and their work and how exciting it was. But all through the video they kept cutting to a guy holding up a sign saying 'No More Reorgs.' It was a running joke, which I didn't really get. Then three weeks later, sure enough, there was another reorganization."

Krugler remembers, "Apple in those days was a great place to work. Apple had great furniture, a great work environment, great office space. But it was no way to run a company. There were no financial controls. The audit department couldn't keep up because the rest of the company was simply out of control."

By the autumn of 1993, the high life had finally caught up with Apple and John Sculley. There was yet another company meeting. This time, said Krugler, "instead of talking to the employees, they videotaped a joint speech between Sculley and Spindler in a studio and broadcast it to us. The spin was that John was leaving and handing over the reins to Michael—a kind of amicable separation. But it didn't work because on the tape John was so obviously uncomfortable that it was obvious he wasn't giving up power willingly. We all knew he was being forced into it."

8.26 POSTMORTEM

The Sculley era at Apple was finally over. But how to judge it? On the one hand, in his decade-long tenure, Apple had grown from $800 million in sales to $6 billion. It had also introduced a score of impressive, if not remarkable products. Yet, at the same time, the company had almost continuously lost market share. It had lost the technical leadership of the industry that it had once carried so effortlessly. It had lost the attention of 90 percent of the marketplace and the dreams of the best talents in the industry. And, having begun his stewardship when it was the most dynamic and innovative computer corporation on earth, Apple at the time of his departure had been reduced to a bureaucratic, bloated organization with no obvious direction and no apparent ability to convert a new idea into a real product. The sleek panther roaming the jungle of personal computing had become a fat snail darter in a tiny, and evaporating, puddle.

"John Sculley was extremely bright," said Tim Bajarin afterward. "And when he first arrived at Apple John wisely knew he wasn't a technologist. But toward the end he started thinking of himself as a technical futurist. He got so involved in the future that he lost his effectiveness as a company manager. Then add politics on top of that and a wife who hated being in California. He took his eye off the ball."

There are in the story of high technology a number of men who grew great companies into even bigger companies, but because of mistakes and missed opportunities, ultimately destroyed them, leaving them rotting, sinking hulks. John Young at Hewlett-Packard, John Akers at IBM, Ken Olsen at DEC—and John Sculley at Apple. For them is reserved a special fate. The brilliance of Silicon Valley is that it honors most types of failures. The ambitious start-ups that never get it together, the companies that take enormous risks and lose, the pioneers who cut a new path and are sacrificed in the process—the executives of these companies are held in great esteem and backed in their next business ventures. But not the men who snuff out the spark of great companies. Their fate is to become invisible. Their public comments, the speeches and participation on panels, their honorary positions, are all politely ignored.

In John Sculley's case, he made the right move and headed back East. There he hid out in Maine and Manhattan.

In mid-October, he joined an unknown 200-person Long Island telecom company called Spectrum Information Technologies as its chairman and CEO. Spectrum had only a few million in sales and hadn't turned a profit in five years. Its stock had fallen as low as \$1 per share. Days after Sculley's arrival, Spectrum was awarded a major patent. The company's stock jumped \$3½ to \$11⅛. The result was that, just three weeks after joining his new company, John Sculley had made nearly \$63 million on paper. Even high-rolling Silicon Valley was boggled.

Then the little Spectrum house of cards collapsed. Three executives resigned. Then it was discovered that the company had backdated \$3.8 million in patent license fees to pump its quarterly financials and give itself a profit. Meanwhile, Spectrum's president had made \$8 million in profits selling a million shares of company stock while it was plumped. The SEC announced an investigation.

Innocent, but humiliated, turned into a chump and a dupe, Sculley resigned. This commentary on his skills at judging businesses and people made him the subject of even more derision.

Eventually, he joined up with his brothers to create a venture fund to invest in technology companies. In an effort to rehabilitate himself, he also started an annual conference on the future of technology held each summer in Maine. Slowly, he worked his way back into electronics. He invested in companies in Israel, where his name still had some cachet, and eventually in a multimedia company located just south of Silicon Valley.

But Silicon Valley was not ready to either forgive or forget. There, his name connected with any enterprise was still poison. Still, when Apple was in extremis in 1997, Sculley offered the press his own suggestions about what Apple should do, notably hire Del Yocam. He was ignored.

At the end of 1997, interviewed by *Forbes ASAP*, John Sculley said that he was happier than ever, that people came up to him now and told him how great he looked. But the words were belied by the cadaverous picture of him on the facing page. He closed the interview by saying that in the future "I will continue doing what I've always done. Help people."

Mike Moritz had a different view. In the years since writing *The Little Kingdom*, Moritz had become a successful venture capitalist and, thanks to a brilliant investment in the Internet company Yahoo!, became as rich as Apple's founders. Looking back over the intervening thirteen years, having watched Apple disintegrate and Microsoft take over the computing world, he had his own bitter judgment on John Sculley's career:

"For what he did to Apple, John Sculley deserves to be in the cell next to Charlie Manson."

9.0 STUMP

9.1 Diesel

If ever a company fit William Carlos Williams's observation about the pure products of America going crazy, it was Apple Computer. And now this most idiosyncratic of American firms was in the hands of a fifty-year-old German CEO with a thick accent whose experience with daily life in the United States could be counted in months.

Even for Apple, it was a reckless move. Sculley's tenure ultimately had been a failure, but at least in hiring him Jobs had set out to find the best marketer in the world to run what he believed was the best company in the world. This time, the board of directors, after a moment of courage in toppling Sculley, reverted to type. As if royal succession was the rule rather than the exception in Silicon Valley, as if the preceding five years at Apple had been a smashing success rather than prelude to disaster, the board simply promoted the president and COO to the top spot. Mike Markkula, the perpetual custodian of the status quo, was named company chairman. John Sculley couldn't have picked a better combination to take the fall.

History, in the fickle form of Apple fanatics, reviles Spindler as at best an incompetent and at worst a cowardly fool. But history is wrong. Spindler is more a tragic figure. And if he made mistakes—and he made many—his biggest was in being, like Mike Scott, Jef Raskin, Burrell Smith and several million customers, a true believer in the Apple myth. Few people have ever given so much for a company and, at least at the executive level, been rewarded with such calumny.

Michael Spindler's short unhappy reign stands as one more reminder of the old saw that no good deed ever goes unpunished. By giving his all to Apple, he inherited the Furies. In Europe, Spindler had thrived. In fact, in terms of market share, customer satisfaction, share of mind and almost every other competitive measure, Apple was more successful in Europe than in the

United States. Spindler had succeeded partly because he was more entrepreneurial than most of his fellow Europeans and partly because he was like a provincial governor: close enough to get the products, marketing tools and support from headquarters, but far enough away to be independent of all the political bullshit that encased Cupertino.

But once at headquarters, Spindler's strengths became his weaknesses. He was wholly unprepared to deal with Cupertino's court intrigue. As president, he could be shielded from much of this by being relatively impotent. As CEO, there was no escape.

It began well enough. Apple employees, investors and even customers were relieved to get the Sculley years behind them, especially with the stock price now having fallen from a high of $70 in 1991 to a low of $22 in mid-1993. The Sculley era was one of those experiences that, while you live it, seems eminently reasonable, but once it's over you suddenly look around and ask, "What the hell were we thinking?" After Jobs's psychoses and Sculley's neuroses, Spindler perversely seemed the perfect antidote to all that was wrong with Apple. No more vainglorious, egomaniacal or self-conscious CEOs risking other people's dreams to fulfill their own.

Spindler was just a meat-and-potatoes kind of guy, without any apparent artifice or hidden emotional problems. He was the Diesel—and though that unfortunate moniker didn't catch the gentleness of the man, he was nevertheless a head-down-and-charge-forward kind of guy who didn't care who got the credit as long as the ball moved forward. It was such a great relief to have somebody prosaic in the top spot that nobody seemed to notice that Spindler was, in his own, wholly different way, utterly unsuited for the job.

Having dealt with the ethereal Sculley for a decade, no group was more thrilled with Spindler's arrival than the press. *Forbes* magazine hailed him as "Mr. Pragmatic":

> That his feet are firmly planted, Spindler has left no doubt. "Pragmatist" is one of his favorite words. He sprinkles his conversation with it. Being pragmatic means dealing with the world as it is rather than as you would like it to be. . . . When speaking in his native German, he frequently uses the word *Mut.* The word means courage, which is what it took to cancel projects and fire thousands of people. But *Mut* also means spirit, which is what Steve Jobs had. Spindler promises to combine the two kinds of *Mut.*
>
> Scrambling his metaphors but speaking with great sincerity, Spindler sums up: "I won't mortgage the company's future by amputating the things that Apple stands for." He leaves his listeners in little doubt

> about his determination to keep in Apple that magic mixture of imagination and pragmatism that made it great.

The only problem with this appraisal was that it missed three crucial facts.

First, Apple had lost that "magic mixture" of imagination and pragmatism in about 1989. It was still full of imagination, but pragmatism was hard to find—and those pockets (such as the Star Trek project) in which it survived were well fire-walled to keep them from contaminating the rest of the company.

The second mistake was to believe that even if both traits were still available in equal proportions, Spindler had anywhere near the talent needed to mix them.

And the third mistake was in believing that Spindler's feet were "firmly planted." He was, in fact, at this point in his life, a deeply divided and distracted man. Perhaps at another time he might have been ready to run Apple Computer, Inc. successfully, as he had Apple Europe and Apple Japan. But not now.

The years of devoting himself to Apple's success had taken their toll. Spindler was tired. His blood pressure was elevated. He was frustrated by corporate politics, by Sculley's micromanagement and self-promotion and by Apple's financial roller coaster. In 1987, not long after coming to Cupertino, he'd been talked out from under his desk. Two years later he had a stress attack and his secretary had found him on the floor of his office. On another occasion, he was found passed out at his desk. In the years thereafter, he occasionally had to be raced by ambulance to the hospital—always taken out of the building by the back door, and in an ambulance with the siren off.

Spindler knew that the chief executive's job would be infinitely more stressful. So when Eisenstat and Sullivan approached him about the prospective coup d'état, Mike Spindler should have said no. But his hands were already dirty from having helped boot Yocam years before. Besides, who could turn down a dream of more than fifteen years, the chance to correct all the wrongs that have haunted you for much of your professional career? To justify all your scheming and backstabbing and corporate climbing?

Spindler should have said no. If not during the coup, then right after he took the CEO job, when his wife was diagnosed with lymph cancer and he spent most of the time he needed to rest at Stanford Hospital taking care of her. Or a year after that, when his daughter was in a major car crash that seriously injured the other driver, put her parents into a nasty lawsuit and drove her away to a distant boarding school. Or when his blood pressure kept climbing and he stopped sleeping and eating, and when the waves of depression paralyzed him at his desk. Or when his doctor wrote him that Christmas and warned him that if he didn't quit he'd die.

But most of all Mike Spindler should have quit when he realized that he wasn't the man for the job. That Apple needed some radical decisions that he wasn't healthy enough to make. When he realized that the management techniques that worked out in the field, like leaving subordinates alone and trusting them to do their jobs, didn't work anymore in Cupertino.

But Michael Spindler didn't quit. Even after Regis, now all but out of Apple, warned him, "Quit, or you'll end up dead at your desk and two weeks from now no one will remember who you are."

9.2 Tunnel Vision

What Mike Spindler *did* have was a profound understanding of everything that had gone wrong with Apple since he had joined the firm. It was the perfect example of the obsessive outsider who has a very precise idea of where a company has made mistakes, and a commitment to fix them, but not a clue about what to do after that. Spindler merely set out to follow his plan, no matter how devastating its effects, no matter how cold-blooded it seemed to everyone else, and worst of all, without ever looking around to see if the world had changed and the strategy still worked. Thus, Mike Spindler's worst moves were often better than his best moves because both were so ill timed.

It was the classic behavior of an engineer. And Spindler, unlike Markkula, Jobs or Sculley, really was an engineer, a graduate of Rheinische Fachhochschule. He couldn't have been more different in terms of personality, than Mike Scott, his only engineering predecessor in the executive office, and yet they had much in common, especially their belief in a rational approach to business leadership. And both suffered the same fate of having their irrational hearts broken (in Spindler's case, literally) by the company.

The Apple Computer that Spindler inherited was in serious trouble. The new Windows-based PCs were coming on fast. Heavy competition was driving down costs in that market, each month making more dramatic the growing gap in price between Macs and everyone else. In some cases PC clones with power comparable to Macs' were selling at half the price. No matter how great the Mac operating system, that was a pretty wide gap to overcome. Apple had to cut prices, further.

But that only underscored the essential dilemma that now lay across the company's path to a viable future. As the sole "other" architecture in the personal computing business (Unix aside), Apple had to go alone against the combined efforts of scores of Wintel machines. The fact that these other companies were competing ferociously among themselves only heightened their push to be more innovative, more powerful and more price-competitive. So, though Apple might see itself as competing piecemeal against Dell, Compaq, Acer and all the rest, it was in fact competing against a single monolithic entity called the Windows PC Market, with hundreds of thousands of employees, a hundred billion dollars in annual revenues and R&D expenditures totaling perhaps $20 billion. Even if many of these efforts were redundant, even contradictory, nevertheless they still totaled far more than anything that could be put together by Apple, an $8 billion company with just $90 million in profits to reinvest.

The company was showing the strain. New competitors, new products and new ideas were busting out all over in the Wintel world—Compaq was becoming an unequaled manufacturer, Dell had put into place a superb distribution system, every month IBM and HP were coming up with new designs for laptops, graphical workstations and peripherals, Gateway 2000 was establishing a new system for fast custom manufacturing and the Japanese and Koreans were bombing the hell out of prices. Wintel trade shows, especially Comdex, which drew 200,000 engineers, executives and reporters to Las Vegas every winter, now dwarfed MacExpo. Hundreds of new applications programs were being introduced every month, all of them for Windows, a few with a token tag line in the announcement release promising to introduce a Mac-compatible version sometime in the next year. And up in Redmond, Gates & Co. were readying a new operating system, code-named Chicago, that was rumored to be its Mac buster. It was slated for introduction in 1993.

So it came down to this: there was no possible way that Apple could keep up with the Wintel world. The company's one hope had been to set the pace and force the others to follow, always remaining far enough ahead to command the maximum price. But Sculley had blown that opportunity. Now Apple was trapped forever selling to its own customer base. But even that infinitely suffering, infinitely loyal base wasn't going to buy such obviously overpriced products as a $5,000 Quadra that didn't have any more speed or memory than a $2,300 Compaq PC.

So prices had to come down. But, once again, when prices fell, margins fell as well. And that in turn meant that the company wouldn't have enough money for R&D to stay in the race. The only solution was to cut costs—and the only way to do that in a knowledge-intensive company was to lay off people. It was a cruel equation. But it was also inescapable, as not only Spindler but his successor would learn to their dismay.

Making matters worse, Spindler's own lieutenants screwed him. They gave him optimistic unit sales projections, which he dutifully presented to the board of directors, then turned around a few days later and revised those numbers down by *100,000* units for the quarter.

So within weeks after taking over Apple, Spindler was forced to announce the layoff of 2,100 employees, bringing the company rolls down to fewer than 11,000. Like all smart new CEOs dealt a bad hand, he quickly consolidated the company's financial problems into a single big $188 million one-time quarterly loss.

If the great Sculley era layoff had been a devastating and traumatic shock to both Apple and the electronics industry, the Spindler era layoff was just ugly. There was a growing sense now that this would be Apple's future: an endless whittling away until there was nothing left. In yet another bit of Apple symbolism, this layoff round took Bill Fernandez, Apple's first employee, the guy whose family name had given Woz and Jobs cover when they'd shopped at Owen Whetzel's store, the young man whom Jobs had refused to reward with stock before the IPO. In the face of everything he'd been through, Fernandez had been a loyal Apple employee for almost twenty years. This was his thanks.

Spindler made no excuses. "When you're hit with something like this," he said, "you have to take action very swiftly." And he was right. To stay competitive, some Apple computer prices were cut by 20 percent or more. That in turn had a devastating effect upon gross profit margins, which fell from 43 percent to 26 percent in a single year. Spindler knew that these weren't enough profits to keep Apple competitive in the long term. Moreover, it seriously hurt the company's stock price, which had shown some signs of renewal with Spindler's arrival and the subsequent layoff. By collapsing again to the mid-20s, the market all but closed the doors on another source of investment capital for Apple.

So, as Spindler saw it, Apple was on the brink of being stuck in a downward spiral of falling prices, tumbling profits and stock prices and endless rounds of layoffs driving away the company's best talent and loyal customers. There were only two ways out of this spin. One was to again produce products so obviously superior to the competition that the company could command high prices once more. The other way was to increase market share by any means necessary and thus capture greater influence with developers and customers, with the resulting jump in revenues (and drop in profits). Best of all would be to do both at the same time.

Spindler set out to do the latter. His first step was to do the unthinkable . . . at least to his predecessors. He licensed the Mac OS. It was the key move John Sculley should have made almost a decade before. Spindler had believed in licensing for years, but his had been a lonely voice at Apple headquarters.

The argument for licensing was straightforward: clones would not only generate licensing revenues for Apple, money it needed desperately for new-product development, but would also create the same competitive fervor that had driven the DOS/Windows world to leadership. That in turn would grow overall Mac OS market share, capture more shelf space for products and draw back the prodigal applications designers.

There was only one downside to this strategy. It was the IBM lesson: if you are going to cede ownership of your market, then you'd better be damn sure you can control it through other means. Big Blue had come down with a bad case of stupidity at the time of the 80286 computers and had surrendered its leadership in innovation, manufacturing, packaging and distribution to its clones. Now it was still playing catch-up. But still, the overall strategy had worked: setting the PC free had enabled it to rule the world. So the trick would be to free the Mac OS while still remaining the strongest competitor in its market.

Spindler thought he had the answer to that too. After all, he was an engineer. All those prima donnas in the labs might have been able to blow fast ones past John Sculley, who never turned down a project he liked and never killed one that was underway, but they weren't going to fool Mike Spindler. He was fully prepared to cancel new products and boot the design team if they couldn't prove their worth.

So, as Apple reeled from the big layoff and the price per share began to climb once again, Spindler took stock of what products he had in his portfolio to begin his assault on the future. Well, for one thing, there was the benighted Newton. As he told *Forbes:* "I won't mortgage the company's future by amputating the things that Apple stands for." And Newton, failure that it was, *was* what Apple stood for: independence, innovative technology, personal creativity. If it had sold just 80,000 units in its first six months, that could be blamed on its price (at $750, it was 50 percent more than the public thought it was worth), the flaws in its first-generation handwriting-recognition software and, most of all, because Sculley and his damn Knowledge Navigator campaign had wildly oversold the technology. Spindler was convinced that Newton could be redeemed through improved software, discounting and better market positioning.

If it worked, Newton would be a safety valve, a market away from the computer wars (and Microsoft) where Apple could hide if things got too hot. But in the meantime, Apple was a personal computer company, fighting the good fight against a giant, many-headed competitor. And here too Spindler thought he had a roster of powerful new weapons in the form of the soon to be introduced PowerPC Macintoshes, the "PowerMacs."

The PowerMacs seemed to have everything going for them. The Motorola PowerPC 601 processor, a 32-bit RISC chip, was not only as fast as Intel's Pentium but less than half the price. And waiting in the wings were some new PowerPCs—the 603, 604, and 620—that outperformed anything Intel had to offer. The 620 was the real beast, a 64-bit processor capable of screaming along at 300 MHz—twice as fast as Intel's best. It also could not only emulate the PC world but actually execute Intel instructions at the chip level. In other words, as Mike Spindler's strategy saw it, with the new line of PowerMacs, Apple would be able to offer computers that were more powerful than their PC counterparts, at about the same price, *and* able to run the entire DOS/ Windows applications software library.

Spindler predicted one million PowerMacs sold in the first year, and the numbers to skyrocket thereafter as popular applications programs were rewritten by their developers in order to take full advantage of the PowerPC's speed.

This was heady stuff. For the first time in a decade, Apple would be able to take the battle to the Wintel universe, carving out new market share, instead of trying to defend what it already had. Then, once Apple had regained its market momentum, it would be able to shift into overdrive through the object-oriented software tools in development at subsidiaries Taligent and Kaleida. These tools would allow for quick custom software updates, thus giving Apple the same edge with software designers it expected to soon have in hardware. And that in turn, by the late 1990s, would position Apple to consolidate its gains by advancing its user interface through new versions of the Mac OS (starting with Copland), new functions such as speech recognition and new media such as set-top boxes to turn TVs into computers. Newton was one step in this direction, but much more important was the company's line of PowerBooks. Having screwed up its first laptop, Apple now had a winner in this line. The key was to keep improving the high end, first with a color display, then with the PowerMac processor, all the while dropping prices on the low end to bring in new users.

It was a sound business plan. But it depended upon one crucial factor: Apple had to be able to execute Spindler's strategy. The company had to be able to move fast enough and with enough decisiveness to stay a step ahead of its new clone-maker competitors. That didn't seem too hard, especially given Apple's size, lead and technological prowess. Spindler himself had proven he had the mettle for the job not just with his work in Europe but also as Apple's COO. In his three years as the company's chief operations guy, Spindler had driven the company's notoriously lax product development cycle times down from twenty-four months to just nine months. In any company that would be amazing; at Apple it was nothing short of a miracle. And if the Diesel could do that in product development, just think what he could do with the entire company given the chance.

But if the strategy looked good, it also was very, very fragile. Nobody knew this better than Spindler. One mistake—a delay in the next generation of PowerPC chips from Motorola, a bad distribution or pricing strategy on a major product in Apple's catalog, too many slips or bugs in the new software tools—and the whole edifice could collapse like a house of cards. And if that happened, the company would stall quickly and fall back into its downward spin, a vicious cycle of plummeting prices, margins, market share and stock prices, a growing inability to hire new talent and an abandonment of new-product development projects.

Spindler knew that he was walking on a high wire. The problem was: Did the rest of Apple know it was too? And there lay the mortal flaw in Spindler's plan. After a decade of John Sculley, Apple had become its own worst nightmare: arrogant, bloated, introverted, balkanized, obsessed with office politics and trapped in its own myth. Down in its foxhole Apple had embarked on an extended conversation with itself, its suppliers and its customers and seemed to have forgotten that there was still a war going on.

Rousing Apple out of its lassitude and inertia would require a brilliant leader. Worse, the legacy of Steve Jobs was such that it wasn't enough to *lead* Apple. Now it took *charisma* to awaken the sleeping company. Sculley may have had the charisma of a nervous Unitarian minister, but he was also a demon marketing man. He could fake charisma with theatrically staged events, appeals to the corporate myth and, when all else failed, the Knowledge Navigator video. He could be Virtual Steve for an hour at a time. And, after a few years, he was content to let Apple slumber.

But Spindler no longer had that option. He had to put the company on the march. And no one was less suited for the task. The taciturn Diesel not only hated the limelight; he hid from it at every opportunity. His self-consciousness with the English language only made matters worse. He ducked press interviews, rarely appeared at public events and under the spotlights in front of Apple employees he couldn't have looked more uncomfortable than if he'd been a janitor plucked from backstage and pushed out through the curtains.

So why was Mike Spindler, of all people, thrust into this impossible role? The answer went back to Apple's board of directors and most of all to Mike Markkula. Though the sheer inadequacy of the board wouldn't be brought into harsh relief for another few years, it was already woefully ill prepared to advise a company like Apple Computer. Just the list of members should have been enough of a clue: Katherine Hudson, president and CEO of W. H. Brady, a clothing manufacturer; Delano Lewis, president and CEO of National Public Radio; French packaging company executive B. Jurgen Hintz; investment banker Bernard Goldstein of Broadview Associates; venture capitalist Peter Crisp of Venrock Associates (filling for Art Rock); Gil Amelio, CEO of National Semiconductor; and Markkula. It was a dream lineup for a CEO who never wanted to be second-guessed. Sculley had done a masterful job: with the exception of Amelio, all the experienced managers knew nothing about technology, and all the directors who knew anything about technology knew little about management. Divide and conquer. And presiding over it all was Markkula, back as chairman with Sculley's departure.

This toothless board had rubber-stamped Spindler's promotion and now didn't have the insight to recognize that he was the wrong man to direct his own strategy. Besides, there were too many dazzling products to enjoy. And it was so much fun to be part of a such a cool and famous company.

There was another problem as well. By now, Apple had lost just about every talented senior executive who might have taken over Apple's reins. A new generation was now in place: Dan Eilers, who was running Claris; Ian Diery, executive vice president; Joe Graziano, the bonus baby lured back from Sun to become chief financial officer; and Dave Nagel, head of software. None had the experience to run a company the size of Apple, but at least one, Graziano, secretly believed he deserved the top spot and was already plotting to get it. Thus, the board would have had to go outside Apple for a new CEO—something it was unprepared to do.

Like most disasters, the Spindler era started out promising. The new PowerPCs were hailed as impressive new machines, proof that Apple could still do it. Licensing plans moved forward. And even the Newton began to get a little respect. By mid-1994, Apple seemed to be back on its feet. The market was strong and the company's stock price was climbing beyond $40 again for the first time in nearly two years. At the same time, Spindler held hiring down, kept staffing steady at about 11,000 full-time employees and made up the added demand for staffers with contract workers.

Then a huge market break: Microsoft's Mac killer, Chicago software, now generally known as Windows 93, had begun to slip. There was talk of it becoming Windows 94—then, as the new year dawned, word leaked out that it would now be Windows 95.

It was a chance for Apple's survival. The Mac OS had fumbled along now for a decade, being upgraded every couple of years, blowing breakout chances like Pink and Star Trek. Meanwhile, Gates had been laying on the whip hand at Microsoft, driving Windows ever closer to the Mac ideal. He didn't need to catch Apple, only come close, and Microsoft would seal up the market forever. Now was the moment for Copland, years in the works, to roar across the finish line first, steal Microsoft's thunder and put Apple once again a decade ahead of the Boys from Redmond.

But Copland wasn't ready. It wasn't ready in 1993. Or in 1994. Or in 1995. The company had spent hundreds of millions of dollars and it had nothing to show for it. Copland forever remained just around the corner.

Hardware too began to explode. Literally. At a trade show in March 1995, the new model 5300 PowerBooks were a hit . . . until a new type of battery caused them to overheat so much they ignited. An embarrassed Apple had to halt production and order a recall just as the machines were taking off in the marketplace.

That problem fixed, an even greater one emerged. Spindler had entered 1995 forecasting a year of good, but not spectacular growth. It was an uncharacteristically conservative position for the usually wildly optimistic Apple. And it turned out to be the worst possible year to turn careful. In fact, 1995 proved to be one of the greatest years in personal computing history—and Apple, with its new strategy and hot new products, was wonderfully positioned to take advantage of it. Expecting 15 percent market growth, instead of what proved to be twice that, the company terribly underproduced. As a result, by October and the end of its fiscal year, Apple had a $1 *billion* backlog. That meant there were nearly a million customers out there—small companies, giant corporations, loyal private users—who wanted a Mac and now faced the prospect of waiting months to get one. In the already dwindling floor space in computer stores devoted to Apple products, the shelves were stripped bare. Spindler had had his chance to fulfill his strategy and regain five years of lost market share—and he'd blown it.

Spindler well understood his predicament. So did the market, which began to kill Apple's stock value. But no one *understood* Apple's problems more acutely than the CFO, Joe Graziano. In one respect, Graziano was now the key executive at Apple. Since his return, he had forced the company to develop a new and more realistic set of metrics to evaluate its performance. Before, all of Apple's measurement schemes had been, typically, self-centered. The company set its own internal performance goals and tried to meet them. R&D expenditures were held sacred. The company was, in Graziano's accurate description, a fiscal "monastery." Apple, he told *CFO* magazine, "had this belief that it wouldn't be affected by what these other people did."

Graziano, with the power that comes from being not only chief financial officer but the only other employee director besides Spindler, instituted a new, more pragmatic program, one that demanded such market comparison metrics as market share and return on capital employed. "People thought I had my head screwed on backward," Graziano said later. But it worked. "It was like they were monks who never read a newspaper, and all of a sudden they come out of the monastery and saw this new world." This was Graziano playing Plato, but it wasn't far from the truth.

And that truth wasn't a pleasant one for Apple's management team. But it had played a crucial role in moving Spindler to adopt his current strategy.

But for all his brilliance, and his undeniable contributions to the company, the flamboyant Graziano, with his thick curly hair and black mustache, trendy clothes and vintage Ferraris, was also the most dangerous lieutenant a CEO like Spindler could have. Graziano was brilliant enough to see the inadequacies in the company and its top executive, but not wise enough to see the flaws in himself.

Graziano had heard himself called Spindler's heir apparent long enough to actually believe it, not noticing that his vain style was as unlikely for corporate leadership as Spindler's inarticulateness. And now, as the troubles at Apple began to mount, there was no shortage of Apple people whispering in Graziano's ear confirmation of what he already deeply believed: that he was the only man who could save Apple.

At first, it was hard to argue with that appraisal. Graziano seemed to have an easygoing rapport with the press that Spindler could only dream of. He also seemed to have some of Steve Jobs's long-missed gift for turning a disaster into an apparent triumph. For example, way back in early 1985, when Apple was still going strong, the company announced first quarter profits of $73 million on sales of $2.7 billion. That was a fourfold improvement over the disastrous profits of a year before, but still a long way from analysts' predictions of as much as $120 million in profits. So where had the missing $50 million gone? Graziano had lost it in foreign currency hedging as the dollar dropped.

Yet, when the stories about his screwup appeared in the press, Graziano wasn't vilified but lionized. *Business Week* went so far as to applaud him for, of all things, his usually conservative fiscal management. The story went on to credit Graziano with cutting Apple's operating expenses from 36 percent to 19 percent of sales. It talked about him taking care of his dying brother, of growing up in a working-class family and of hauling meat and delivering potatoes to pay his way through college. And accompanying this exercise in hagiography were adoring quotes from peers and industry observers ("He has had a lot to do with making Apple a more competitive company," said Robert Saltmarsh, a former Apple vice president), and a photo of the Man Himself looking kicked back and casual, as if losing $50 million was the kind of thing pros did before lunch.

This was self-promotional genius of the highest order. It made Mike Spindler look like a guy who shoveled coal for a living. And it only made Graziano more certain of his destiny. What he couldn't yet know was that he had already peaked.

So had the company's stock. In the second week of June 1995, Apple stock reached $50 per share. Then it began to fall, slowly at first, then picking up speed with each round of bad news, until by October it sat at $35 per share. Spindler had been given two years to turn Apple's fortunes around. But his good strategy had combined with miserable execution. Some of it, like the inaccurate forecast, was his fault; some of it, like the exploding laptops and the endlessly unfinished Copland, were the fault of others, but his responsibility.

But the most pernicious problem Apple had, the declining quality of Apple employee talent, long preceded him. The 80-20 rule was starting to tell. Like so many successful companies before it, Apple, believing it would stay on top forever, was profligate with talent. Now there were scores of companies all over the Valley (not to mention scores of offices at Microsoft in Redmond) filled with ex-Apple people. They were everywhere you looked: General Magic, MIPS/Silicon Graphics, Sun, Radius, Adobe, HP, Macromedia, WebTV, Intuit, Pixar, Logitech, the venture capital firms in Menlo Park, the U.S. Department of Commerce—everywhere but Cupertino. Apple was beginning to compete with the legendary Fairchild Semiconductor as the mother firm of a whole new generation of Valley start-ups. By the Spindler era, there were more talented ex-Apple people than sterling employees still at the firm. And Apple no longer had the cachet to attract new ones. The best and brightest now were lining up to become Microserfs. And that imbalance in talent was now about to become obvious to the world.

Spindler had not taken this loss into account. No high-tech executive ever does. After all, how do you quantify the fact that your employees aren't as clever as they used to be? If anything, Apple employees now had more advanced degrees than ever before, so how could you test for loss of magic? You can dumb down a machine tool factory, but not a high-tech company. You have to go with your best strategy and hope your staff can pull it off. And Spindler, feeling the growing resentment of the rank and file, was unwilling to leave the tower to visit the troops.

Spindler's plan was good, but Apple could no longer execute. It would be the same frustration felt by his successor. The brain still sent out commands, but the body no longer responded.

Midway through Mike Spindler's tenure as CEO at Apple, one of the company's directors received a visitation from a ghost.

As Gil Amelio would later recount in his memoirs, he was in his office at National Semiconductor, where he was CEO, when he got an unexpected phone call. It was Steve Jobs.

Amelio, of course, knew of the legendary figure, now much in the news with the success of the film *Toy Story*, but had never met him. He took the call.

"I want to come over and see you," said Jobs.

The younger man arrived exactly on time in a long-sleeved sport shirt, dress slacks and, in Amelio's words, "grungy tennis shoes."

After a few minutes of small talk, Jobs cut to the chase. "Apple is on its way out of business. The only thing that can save it is a strong leader, somebody who can rally employees, the press, users and developers."

Amelio was taken aback. But he was also curious. After all, this was Steve Jobs.

Jobs continued his pitch: "The world has changed, the Mac has outlived its usefulness, it's time to go on to something else."

Now Amelio was amazed. After all, the Mac was Jobs's greatest creation. He asked, "If the Mac is dead, what's going to replace it?"

To that Jobs had no real answer. Nor did he have good answers to the questions Amelio then posed, such as "What would you do if you were CEO tomorrow? What would your first decision be?" Instead, according to Amelio, Jobs replied in clichés and evasions. He recalled, "His pitch added up to 'Apple should make a change, I can lead the change, but I don't know what the change will be.' " Nevertheless, Amelio found him charming.

Once Jobs realized that his pitch was going nowhere, the visit began to fall apart. He grew visibly irritated, snapping, "Maybe you have some better ideas." Finally, the conversation lapsed into a long silence, and the meeting was over.

Recalled Eric Krugler, "My boss was trying to get in good with Spindler, so one morning I got called in at 7 A.M. to fix some problems and add software to Spindler's computer.

"I get there and turn the machine on. Nothing comes on the monitor. I checked . . . *and it wasn't even plugged in.* Spindler was obviously embarrassed that he'd called somebody in to fix a problem that was so obvious. But he still asked me to come over to his house and set up his home system.

"I was starting to get annoyed. I politely suggested he get someone else.

"But that day, while I was working on Spindler's machine, I noticed something amazing. There was absolutely no security on the main corporate computers. There wasn't even security on the file servers containing all the corporate contacts. *Anybody* could have gone into the corporate files, even Spindler's personal files. It was so indicative of the atmosphere at Apple, even at that late date. There was just a complete lack of control."

9.3 SUITABLE SUITORS

There was one other piece in Mike Spindler's grand strategy. That was to set the turnaround in motion, pump up the stock . . . and then sell off the company. Obviously, he wasn't the first person running Apple to come up with this idea. In fact, it is infinitely telling that, after Mike Scott, *every* Apple CEO tried to unload the company. Protestations to the contrary, big speeches at trade shows announcing that Apple was here to stay, great plans for new products and markets—all fell before the inescapable fact that neither Jobs nor Sculley nor Spindler (and soon Amelio and Jobs again) ever really believed that Apple could survive on its own. Everything else was a pose, a fraud, a worst-case contingency. The company that never really was was also forever the company that wasn't to be.

Spindler had embarked on his search for a sugar daddy almost from the day he arrived at Cupertino. The company he focused on a second time as his savior was none other than IBM, still smarting from its wounding at the hands of Gates and Grove. It was not a bad pick: the courtship of Taligent and foreplay of the PowerPC joint venture both pointed toward a consummation of the relationship he had once initiated. Apple, as it had seven years before, desperately needed IBM's financial firepower, distribution channels and business market cachet. IBM, conversely, would gain from Apple a PowerPC architecture that worked better than its own abortive efforts, and better yet, the jewel in the crown, the Mac OS. Put that baby on the Intel chip, and Microsoft, Compaq, Dell and all the other jumped-up pretenders to the throne could watch Big Blue's dust. IBM would be back on top where it belonged.

At least that was the case that Spindler intended to make with the white-shirt boys in Armonk. And it seemed to work. By the late summer of 1994, negotiations between IBM and Apple were heating up. Finally, IBM was ready to deal. It offered $50 per share for Apple, then selling at about $45. It was a good offer, but not a great one. In retrospect, Spindler should have jumped on the deal and dropped to his knees to thank God for his deliverance. But he was worshipping before a different altar. As one associate would say: "The Macintosh is a religion to Mike, and he wants to see it sustained."

Now Spindler would pay the cost of being Apple's last true believer. The IBM deal would have been perfect for any CEO but one who believed the Mac's true destiny was to rule. But selling to Big Blue would have been consorting with a onetime enemy of the Mac, giving the product to a buyer that would likely junk the beautiful box and tinker with the operating system until it was just another of the tens of thousands of products in the IBM catalog. This wasn't the fate Mike Spindler had worked for all those long years flogging Apple products all over Europe.

Even then, Spindler might have sold, but for the fact that in late 1994 Apple was still on a tear. It was as if the Diesel had developed a strategy whose end play was the sale of the company, then performed the first part of the plan so brilliantly that he forgot why he'd embarked on the strategy in the first place. Apple could no longer survive on its own. In a world where Windows machines held more than 90 percent of the market, Apple was now little more than a rounding error on a pure monopoly.

But the numbers were so damn good that Spindler began to feel some of the old magic again. He grew cocky. Maybe, he asked himself, I really can save this company. And as the quarters of 1994 passed, each of them showing ever-increasing sales growth—5 percent in the first quarter, 17 percent in the second, 27 *percent* during the Christmas selling season—and with profits hovering between 25 percent and 30 percent, and even market share beginning to rise, Spindler stopped wondering and began to believe. He was going to save Apple. He would be Apple's savior and redeemer.

Recalled Tim Bajarin of Creative Strategies, who consulted Apple at the time, "Mike's nickname may have been the Diesel, but he had to be motivated by something to drive himself into the ground the way he did. I couldn't figure out what it was—until one day I had to leave a meeting to go make a phone call. Mike followed me and pulled me into a private conference room. 'Listen,' he said, 'This next generation of Mac OS is so good that Bill Gates will want it.'

"That's when I finally realized what was motivating Spindler. He wanted to beat Bill Gates at his own game. In operating systems. That's what had destroyed Ray Noorda (of Novell). And that's what almost killed Mike Spindler. Fighting Bill Gates is always bad for your health."

One person who knew better was Graziano. He was the man who ran the meters, and what those gauges showed him was a whole different story. What Graziano saw was that nothing had really changed; the good news of the last year was just a blip, a bit of momentary relief in what was still a growing tragedy. With overpriced products, declining distribution, fewer third-party software and hardware developers and a dwindling share of mind among consumers, Apple was still racing toward oblivion. Apple had merely benefited from a cusp year in the Wintel juggernaut. Microsoft had momentarily stumbled, the world was awaiting the arrival of the new Intel Pentium chips and no radically new boxes had appeared on the scene. That wouldn't last for long.

So Graziano watched in horror as the deal with IBM collapsed. Then a deal Spindler nearly brokered with Philips missed by a single vote of the Philips board. Another deal, with Sun Microsystems (yet another contact brokered by Regis McKenna), was intermittently on and off because Spindler didn't seem to have respect for Sun's boss, Scott McNealy. Then Spindler began to behave as if Apple was no longer interested in a merger or buyout. There were rumors on the street that one hot firm after another—Silicon Graphics, Oracle—was eyeing Apple. Oracle's CEO, Larry Ellison, not known for either subtlety or sanity, almost acted like a humble suitor when he announced that "if Apple should want to merge, we would be honored." But Spindler didn't follow up on any of these hints. Instead, he seemed to dismiss them, saying that, short of an "indecent" proposal, "there's no strategic fit that makes sense." *What?* Anybody who read the newspaper could identify a half dozen companies that could make good use of Apple—and even if they couldn't, who cared? Apple wasn't buying, it was *selling*. The employees would get some job security, the technology would survive, customers would, at least for a while, see some product stability and investors would get a nice payoff. Who would lose?

But Spindler plunged on. And glorious 1994 became disastrous 1995. The exploding PowerBooks, the wrong forecast, the missing new operating system. Then the capstone: on August 24, 1995, Microsoft, two years late, finally introduced its second-generation Windows product. It was now called Windows 95, and its formal introduction—taking place with its arrival on computer store shelves throughout the world at exactly midnight—was the biggest media event the personal computing industry had seen since . . . the Macintosh introduction. Hundreds of thousands of PC owners queued up in late-night parking lots in Manhattan, Paris, Bombay, Jakarta and a thousand other sites around the world. Soft-drink and fast-food distributors vied for the right to sell to these masses. It was the single most important mass cultural event between the Gulf War and the death of Princess Diana.

This is what it had come to, two decades after Steve Jobs's perhaps apocryphal moment getting robbed selling blue boxes in a Sunnyvale parking lot. Now it was a kind of robbery on a global scale, not the least of which at the supermarket-sized Fry's department store on the other side of Sunnyvale. Like all mythic occasions, the Windows 95 introduction captured the zeitgeist of the era: unembarrassed millions lining up Soviet style for the chance to buy a second-rate product two years late from the world's richest private citizen . . . and thankful for the opportunity.

Windows 95, the apotheosis of Bill Gates, was inevitable. Until now, the electronics industry had known many great entrepreneurs, a few of them saints, many of them monsters, who had driven their companies to great success and industry dominance. But at some point, all of these men had stopped because they were bored, or distracted by the lure of other types of fame, or exhausted, or just hungry to enjoy their new wealth. But in Bill Gates, high tech had at last met the incorruptible man. Power was Bill Gates's greatest love, and his hunger for it seemed insatiable. The great guessing game of Silicon Valley (and eventually the world) in the 1990s was: What does Bill Gates want? And the terrifying answer was always the same: He wants everything. And one thing Bill Gates had wanted since he was little more than a teenager, was the Apple magic.

Every company bears the stamp of its founder, and Microsoft was no exception. It was filled with young people, many of them made wildly rich by the company, the others hoping to do the same, and all of them without any doubt that Microsoft's success, its endless bullying of every industry near it, was a just cause. Even if it meant destroying the electronics revolution in the process. Microsoft stultified every technology it touched, but it also gave that technology to the world at a low price with a promise of perpetual, if slowed, innovation, and offered the security of knowing that it came from a company that knew how to win.

It was a devil's pact each customer made when signing on with Windows, but that was the point. Unlike Apple, Microsoft seemed to know what it was doing. If it wasn't exciting, it also wasn't unpredictable. Join Microsoft and you joined the Great Mass: designers developed for you; stores set aside their aisles for you; you could swap files with the employee down the hall; and most of all, you didn't have to be a rebel anymore and suffer all the discomforts and humiliations that came with rebellion.

But if Microsoft's run-up to the Windows 95 introduction was predictable—late, arrogant, offering less than it seemed to promise, but available everywhere in good quality at a low price backed by whole libraries of new applications—Apple's response was not. At least not to anyone who still believed the myth. Faced with the biggest single competitive threat in its history, an operating system that duplicated much of what the Mac OS could do and yet offered many things (multiprocessing) it could not, Apple did . . . nothing. Well, almost nothing: there were those pissy bumper stickers seen all over Cupertino that read "Windows 95, Macintosh 84." Cute, accurate, but utterly meaningless because it wasn't 1984 anymore, but 1995, and Microsoft had just produced a perfect cubic zirconium copy of Apple's crown jewel.

In the decade since his departure, Steve Jobs's loss was never felt more acutely than in those days when Microsoft was making front pages all over the world. Since 1990, *five* years, Apple had known Microsoft was coming. It didn't take a rocket scientist to appreciate that, faced with this upcoming event, Apple Computer had only one real priority: come up with its next-generation operating system. If it didn't, relentless Microsoft would eventually catch up and, having achieved parity with Apple in the only place Apple still had an advantage, would quickly crush it with its superior manufacturing, marketing and enormous market base.

Everybody knew that was true. Fourth graders knew it. And yet Apple wasted those years on Newton and upgrades to the current OS, endless hardware permutations, education programs, sponsorships of concerts and television shows . . . everything but getting the damn operating system ready. Copland, the hope of Apple, had turned into a black hole, sucking up money and talent and producing nothing.

Steve Jobs may have been an executive horror and spoiled brat, but nobody ever accused him of missing an opportunity. And as Windows 95 rolled out with totalitarian irresistibility, you couldn't help musing what Apple under Jobs would have done in response. One thing for sure, there would have been a new OS not only in the works but already introduced. And even if it wasn't ready, Jobs would still have announced it just to steal Gates's thunder. One could almost imagine the full-page ad in *The Wall Street Journal* and the *New York Times:* "You Waited Five Years for a Second-Rate Product, How About Waiti ng Six Months More for the Greatest Operating System in History?" in Apple's unmistakable typeface on a white background. That was what playing to win looked like. That was what had made Jobs's Apple, for all of its manifold flaws, so magnificent. Apple had long forgotten what the burn of that fire felt like.

9.4 Iago

At the October board meeting in Austin, Graziano made his move. He knew that Apple was headed for the rocks; both his business sense and his financial indicators told him so. The company was resting its bloated hulk on a foundation of sand. No one could save Apple but him, and he had spent months building support within the company, finding allies in the likes of Dan Eilers.

Eilers was now the number two man at Apple, having joined the firm as part of the Lisa project way back in 1982—and he had been one of the happiest to see Jobs go. After that, he'd been vice president for strategic planning, president of Claris and, since April, senior vice president for worldwide marketing. Eilers, who had as much institutional memory as anyone left at Apple, also had a bad feeling about the direction in which the company was heading. And despite being the ultimate Apple team player, he too secretly threw in his lot with the CFO.

Now was Graziano's chance to capture the support of his fellow board members. He had the perfect venue—a board of directors meeting, with CEO/director Spindler in attendance—and what he was convinced was a compelling case.

As the board members, and not least Spindler himself, listened with growing uneasiness, Graziano presented his argument: the year-to-year gains Apple was enjoying right now were a smoke screen hiding deep and perhaps mortal problems in the company. Disaster was waiting around the corner. Apple had made a terrible mistake in not selling out to IBM, and it would be making an even greater mistake if it didn't land another corporate buyer right away.

The room was silent, though as the other directors listened they began to twist in their chairs, some even to tremble with anger. One director would say that "the body language was incredible."

Graziano thought he was getting his point across. He never raised his voice, but spoke in measured, intimate, almost funereal tones—as if Apple, enjoying one of the most successful years in its history, was ready to be fitted for a shroud. Over and over during the presentation, Graziano repeated that this was not meant to be a coup against Mike Spindler and that he, Graziano, didn't want the CEO job. When it was over, Graziano thanked his fellow directors and, on Markkula's orders, left the room (as did Spindler) convinced that he had saved Apple and turbocharged his own career. The hero had met his greatest challenge—*veni, vidi, vici!*

But the moment the door closed behind Graziano, the board members caught their breath, then turned to one another with raised eyebrows and shaking heads. A couple even made the thumbs-down sign. Graziano thought he had won over the room, but what the room saw was an ambitious vice president making a devious run at the top job by playing Cassandra. The men in the room saw Graziano's behavior as cowardly, his voice "whining." "If you're there saying you've got to throw the guy out, you've got to throw the guy out," said one.

Katherine Hudson was a bit more sympathetic. She told *CFO* magazine, "He felt morally and ethically obligated to make this pitch because he was a member of the board. I can sympathize with this." But notice that she too said "pitch." Nobody was fooled by Graziano's protestations of his own disinterest.

And there was one thing all the board members agreed upon. It was that Graziano had come woefully unprepared to make his case. He was the CFO for Christ sakes! Where was his evidence? The only financials the directors saw were glowing. Did Graziano have other figures to support his argument? And if he did, had he shown them to Spindler? Had he tried to help Apple or only himself? And how could you trust a guy with the reins of a giant corporation if he couldn't even run a coup d'état without fumbling it?

It was one of those moments, much more common in literature than in real-life business, when a person's greatest moment is also his worst. When Graziano walked out of the boardroom, he was on top of the world. A few hours later that world had fallen on him.

The irony—one more for the long Apple list—is that both sides were right. The message Graziano brought that day was an accurate one, as the board and the world would soon learn. But he also wore his ambition on his sleeve. Given a decision between Spindler, who honestly seemed to put the company first and who had achieved a measurable level of success, and Graziano, who seemed to be leveraging off the company's potential misfortune to improve his own résumé, the decision was clear. Graziano was gone. And if Apple's board of directors shot the messenger, well, some messengers deserve it.

But Graziano was also telling the truth. Had he been more generous and presented his case more selflessly, or more professional and proved his point with charts and graphs, or more cynical and waited until the troubles began, he might have saved Apple. But instead, he had forced the board to stand forthright behind Spindler at the worst possible moment. Now they were committed to keeping the Diesel behind the wheel as the bus went off the cliff. And who better to do the driving than a man heading for a crash himself?

Remarkably, having just been handed his head, Graziano asked Markkula if he might hitch a ride on Mike's jet back to Silicon Valley. Equally remarkably, the third passenger was another director, Gil Amelio.

It was a very strained trip. No one knew what to say. As Amelio remembered: "He must have convinced himself of being right and figured at least a fifty-fifty chance of succeeding. But he had failed miserably, to a degree he must not have foreseen as a possibility. Though he didn't lack for money, he was flying home to no job, no income and, it must have seemed a clouded future."

Inevitably, the stilted conversation came around to what had just happened, and as it did, Graziano became more and more upset. Finally he began to sob. Had any other company caused so many tears?

Mortified, Amelio tried to change the subject. He knew Graziano was a Ferrari fiend, so he asked, "Joe, I've been thinking about buying a sports car. What do you think? Can you give me a recommendation?"

Relieved, Graziano dried his tears and launched into a monologue about the relative merits of different Ferraris.

9.5 Aerie

Graziano's Last Stand, as it came to be called, did more than rob Apple of its smartest internal analyst. It also broke Mike Spindler.

It had been a year of unbearable contradictions, apogees and nadirs. The company had record sales and profits. It had the hottest new products in the industry. But it couldn't get its laptops to work for much of the year. It had made inaccurate market forecasts that had cost it a magnificent opportunity. The company's second tier of top managers had embarked on a failed mutiny that had now cost Apple its superb CFO and soon, thanks to a "reorganization" that was in a fact a punishment for disloyalty, its number two executive, Dan Eilers. Add that to the departure early in the year of Ian Diery and the director of Apple Japan and Spindler had either lost, turned on or been betrayed by and then fired much of his inner circle. And, of course, Microsoft had now introduced a product that essentially negated Apple's last real technological advantage.

Spindler was now left alone in his Cupertino tower, knowing his Grand Strategy had failed. Even at the top of his game, Spindler had been a brusque, isolated, socially inept manager. But now the situation grew bizarre. In public, he ran from reporters, even well-wishers. And there were stories of him hiding behind his desk, ducking unwelcome visitors. He still talked a good game when forced to. But Michael Spindler knew what was coming, and he could only hold on and await its impact.

He didn't have to wait long. The unraveling of high-tech companies usually occurs at a stunning pace. Great companies appear to be rolling along just fine, their employees bustling about, new products in the works, conferences being held, users groups holding meetings—and then everything suddenly implodes. It happened at Wang, Digital Equipment and Atari before Apple, and at Borland, Conner Peripherals and Silicon Graphics after. In an industry where success and technological leadership are worshipped above all and loyalty is an archaic notion among employers, employees and customers, once a great firm stumbles or shows weakness it is quickly abandoned by friends and devoured by enemies.

In personal computing, the situation was only marginally better, primarily because the amount of intellectual and financial capital that users had to invest in hardware, software and training was high enough to make them dread the prospect of switching computer architectures. Also working to Apple's advantage was the growing dread and resentment of the hegemony of Bill Gates and Microsoft. The Windows 95 introduction would prove to be the high-water mark of Microsoft's reputation. From now on, fearful (with good reason) of the rule of a monopoly in computer software—and soon the Internet—the world would begin to turn on Microsoft.

And there was one other factor as well working in Apple's favor as it entered its greatest crisis. There were millions of people who still believed in Apple. Not the company, nor even its products, but the myth of Apple itself. More than the Mac, more than the Apple II and certainly more than the reality of the company itself, Apple had created a vision of a new kind of enterprise, a new way of approaching the world that had resonated now with generations of computer owners. It had proved to be only a minority view, but that only cemented its case. This myth was Jobs's and Woz's greatest invention and it had now long outlived them at the company they founded.

If there weren't enough of these true believers to keep Apple strong, there were enough to keep it alive. And in a few months, Apple, which had turned down a multibillion-dollar offer from IBM just a year before, would be happy to settle for staying alive.

"Apple always had a good athletic program run by the employees and held at Foothill [Junior] College," recalled Eric Krugler, "I played on some softball and volleyball teams there. One person I met there from Apple was a junior financial analyst. He told me that Apple was heading to profit margins under twenty percent. At the time, our margins were thirty-five percent.

"But sure enough, by the next year the margins were twenty percent. I've always wondered: Why did some junior financial analyst know this and senior management didn't?

"There was some critical information being filtered somewhere at Apple. Valuable information that was being ignored or not getting through."

9.6 Unraveling

By Christmas, the nightmare scenario Graziano described and Spindler feared was beginning to play itself out.

It went like this: Following the poor forecasts at the beginning of the year, Apple pumped up production by 30 percent in an effort to catch up during the usually strong Christmas season. But the Windows 95 announcement, and the run-up to that announcement, temporarily slowed the company's sales. Faced with the prospect of excess inventory, and simultaneously caught in an unexpected price war on personal computers in Japan, Apple then did what Spindler had feared: it cut prices, reducing the price difference between Macs and comparable PCs from $1,000 to just $320. That made Macs more desirable, but those cuts came at the expense of profit margins.

The cuts were across the board, on nearly every company model, and in some cases were as great as 30 percent. Unfortunately, this discounting didn't have its desired effect—it didn't sell enough entry and mid-level models to new customers. Instead, recognizing a temporary bargain, both new customers and Apple's veteran customers used the opportunity to pick up high-end Macs. Before long, instead of a surplus, there was a shortage of these high-end models, the most profitable computers in the company's catalog. So now, having slashed prices and profits, Apple could no longer make up the difference through volume.

There was no turning back. Graziano's indicators were now going crazy.

The good news was that, for the first time in many years, Apple's market share jumped—from just less than 8 percent in mid-1995 to nearly 10 percent by year's end. Unfortunately, capturing that added market share so quickly had devastated all of the company's other financials. Gross profit margins fell from their 1994 high of nearly 30 percent to just 20 percent, and revenue growth slumped from 28 percent to just 15 percent. Apple was growing, but killing itself in the process. Cash reserves were sinking fast—so low ($200 million) that a week before Christmas both Standard & Poor's and Moody's started reviews of the company's credit.

Needless to say, the stock was in free fall as well. From just kissing $50 per share at the middle of the year, Apple stock by year's end had slumped to less than $30—a figure not much above the company's book value of $23.50 per share. That made the company takeover bait; but at a selling price far less than what it had turned down fifteen months before. To no one's surprise, by year's end rumors were racing around Silicon Valley that Sun Microsystems, that hot-dog computer workstation maker up the road that'd almost run itself into the ground until it all but tripped over the Java programming language for the Internet, was in serious negotiations about purchasing Apple with some of its newfound riches.

Sun was, in fact, in play. But it was a measure of Apple's predicament that Sun's opening bid, when it came in, was in the high 20s—less than Apple's market price!

This was an insult. But it was not made flippantly. The opening bid reflected a sober—and, as would soon be apparent, accurate—appraisal of Apple's future. With Spindler's Grand Strategy in shambles, and no killer hardware or software products waiting in the wings, Apple now had no choice but to become a different company, one that competed on price, manufacturing and product quality—everything the company wasn't good at. Sun's offer said that Apple might not yet be in the commodity business, but it was on its way. Everything had hinged on Apple maintaining its high prices and margins through product differentiation, and now that difference was gone. It would now have to slug it out in the mud with everyone else, and given the company's character and history, few gave it much hope of being able to do so.

And even as all this was happening, Apple had no choice but to keep building market share by undercutting profits. The only chance now was a paradoxical strategy of having to dig a deep enough hole to be able to regain its destiny and climb out. Thus, by the end of the year, Apple was offering added discounts to its largest resellers and slashing prices still further on its PowerBooks and on the top-of-the-line PowerPC Macs it could still deliver in a reasonable time.

9.7 Whiplash

There are few things more devastating to a company than to abruptly switch its business model. The torque of that change is felt in every office, and in every career, in the company. Suddenly, nothing works quite right. Every piece of paper the company produces is out of synchronization with where the company is now going. Employees whose skills and talents were uniquely suited to the company now find themselves horribly out of place and disoriented. Meanwhile, some marginal employees who never really fit in the organization, whose jobs were perpetually precarious, now find themselves the ideal people to help lead the company in its new direction. Power shifts back and forth and up and down. Rules of behavior and notions of best business practices are thrown out or revised. The entire process is so dislocating, so unproductive and so destructive that few companies that ever attempt it survive the process. And those that do, emerge as such vastly different enterprises from the ones that entered the tunnel that, but for the logo and name, they might as well be new companies.

Apple went into that tunnel in December 1995, with no idea of how or when it would come out. It entered as the manufacturer of a proprietary computer family sold at a premium. Some, perhaps all, of those characteristics were now untenable. Some, perhaps all, would have to be jettisoned. But how? And what would replace them? After twenty years of intense competition, almost every market niche in personal computing was filled. In every direction, a giant company, many of them as big as Apple, squatted directly in the company's path. Mass-market a Windows clone and Compaq would crush you. Custom-build budget machines and you ran into Dell and Gateway 2000. Laptops? IBM, Toshiba, NEC, Compaq, Hitachi and Acer had every market segment sewn up. Peripherals? Network computers? Hello Hewlett-Packard.

Apple seemed checkmated. And that proximate predicament argued then for an even more radical move. Perhaps specialty machines for education or graphics design, Apple's last two market strengths. But would schools train their kids on computers they wouldn't use as adults? And were there any margins left in that market? As for graphics, going after that tiny market was like declaring yourself a permanent bit player.

There was another market emerging, the Internet, that supposedly was going to explode. And early reports were that all the good Web page designers were doing their development work on Macs. But who knew where that was going?

Then how about something *really* radical? Like getting out of computers altogether. But then where would Apple go? Software? But it had no Copland. Consumer products? Like the *Newton?* There was talk of a new class of hardware emerging, the so-called network computer being stumped by Oracle's Larry Ellison, that would be a low-cost (under $1,000) half-empty box (no disk memory) optimized for cheaply surfing the Internet. An interesting notion, and certainly the talk of that year's Comdex, but no one knew whether it could be built at that price and make any money—or if anyone would even buy it with full-blown PC prices already down to $1,500 and falling.

But as Apple entered 1996 and prepared for its annual meeting, all of those considerations would have to wait. Even if the company made a strategic decision, the impact of that choice wouldn't be felt for a year or more. Right now, the company had to deal with the consequences of the past. It would now have to endure the purifying fire of failure.

9.8 PLUMMET

When the numbers appeared, they were breathtakingly bad. Worse than anyone outside the company had imagined. Sales for the first quarter ended December 31 amazingly were up to $3.15 billion. But it meant next to nothing, because margins had utterly collapsed amid all the discounting. For the quarter, Apple lost $69 million, or 56 cents per share. That was compared to profits of $188 million ($1.55 per share) the year before. This was a quarter-billion-dollar swing in profits for a company with sales of just $9 billion.

And that wasn't even the worst of it. Apple might have been able to justify some of these losses in the name of capturing market share. But Windows 95 had taken care of that. Thus, Apple's market share, which had climbed back to nearly 9 percent in the fourth quarter ended the previous September, had now slumped back to 7.4 percent, two percentage points less than when Spindler had taken over the company. And it wasn't going to get any better. Apple had no important new software or hardware products in the works for at least a year. And this was just the first broadside—it had pulled down a mast and chewed up some sails. The next financial blast, three months from now, would be aimed at Apple's hull.

Spindler now had no real strategy but to react with damage control. He ordered another round of layoffs, the second in his brief career as CEO. This time it was 1,300 people, though everyone knew that would not be enough. Literally risking death, reading the calumny directed toward him in the press and in the eyes of his fellow Apple employees, Spindler soldiered on. He convinced himself that he could still save Apple.

But first he had to save himself. The annual meeting and the board of directors meeting lay dead ahead.

9.9 PILLORY

Everyone was worried about Michael.

It was one thing to fire a guy, another to kill him. And sitting there at the long board table in the Venrock offices on the fifty-fifth floor of Manhattan's Rockefeller Center, his heavy face pale and melted, Michael Spindler looked like a dying man. Word was that on January 8, three weeks before, Spindler had checked into the hospital with heart palpitations.

It wasn't supposed to happen this way. Sure, everybody believed the Apple Computer myth. The users did, the programmers did, even the senior managers. But it was like all childhood myths; one day when harsh reality just became too self-evident, you gave up the fantasy and moved on to a more realistic adulthood. Nobody ever martyred themselves for the Tooth Fairy.

Steve Jobs certainly didn't believe the myth and he invented it. If Jobs believed anything, it was in his own glory. And Sculley believed only in his career. Both were perfectly happy to let the Apple cult thrive so long as it reflected upon them.

But Spindler was supposed to be the businessman, the technology guy, the Diesel. The Teutonic salesmeister who'd turned Apple Europe into a powerhouse. Spindler was the guy who always talked about pragmatism. When he told Forbes, "I'm as much of a dreamer as anyone else, but I'm also a realistic businessman," everybody thought he was just kidding about the first part. He wasn't supposed to believe in the myth.

The nightmare had begun on Tuesday, January 23, 1996, the day of Apple's annual meeting. Behind the scenes, the company had once more been negotiating with Sun Microsystems—and Sun, despite having been blown off by Spindler, was once more acting interested in getting its hands on Apple to fill out the bottom of its product line. Even Sun's chief technologist, Eric Schmidt, one of the canniest press manipulators in Silicon Valley, had been quoted as saying that Apple was a "strong brand."

Negotiating teams were meeting every day now up in Palo Alto in the offices of Valley überlawyers Wilson Sonsini Goodrich & Rosati. Larry Sonsini was a player—the man who had so many IPO Lucite cubes on his shelves that they nearly demolished his office and killed a secretary when they fell during the Loma Prieta quake, the man who saved the MIPS's IPO with a single telephone call to the SEC—so something was going to happen.

Sun would play, and soon. No doubt about it. The company had recently offered $33 a share for Apple stock. Still not enough, of course, but just a few bucks light from where it ought to be at, say, $40 a share. So the trick was to spend a couple of hours doing duck-and-cover with the angry shareholders at the annual meeting, look thoughtful, answer their complaints sincerely and not say anything that might scare off Sun and queer the deal. Just run the gauntlet and keep telling yourself that all will be forgiven and forgotten in a few days when Sun buys everybody's problems away.

The Diesel was the biggest worry. It was he who would have to sit there on the dais and answer for the company's falling margins (down to 15 percent from a peak of 42 percent a decade before ago), slipping market share and $69 million loss in the fourth quarter.

The Copland operating system, the erstwhile savior of Apple, the Windows 95 killer, was still not ready—and now there were rumors it might never be ready.

Worst of all, there was a potential bombshell hiding in warehouses all over the world: $1 *billion* in unsold inventory; computers and peripherals that were supposed to be sold off during the Christmas season, and now might very well end up in that notorious Arizona landfill where Atari bulldozed all of its obsolete products just before that company crashed.

Spindler was a man of enormous pride. He blamed himself for this debacle. And though PR had thoroughly coached him to stay cool as the shareholder lynch mob roared over him, there was grave concern that he might crack under the stress.

But he didn't, even though the meeting was a howling storm of shareholder fury. These were, after all, not just investors in some company from which they expected a predictable return. Those people invested in Compaq or Dell. No, the people who came to the Apple annual meeting to wave their six or fifty or 20,000 shares were stakeholders in the revolution, they had bought into the dream of the Little Kingdom . . . and now not only their bankbooks but their faith had been betrayed.

An hour later, the board's pro forma commitment to a shareholders meeting complete, the gathering was adjourned and the management team staggered off to a nearby meeting room for a press conference. There, at the front table, fielding not only tough questions from the mainstream press but even zingers from the normally lapdog computer magazines, were ex-chairman and co-founder Mike Markkula and Mike Spindler, peeking with frightened eyes around his hands as they folded as if in prayer against his face, looking ready to disintegrate at any moment.

But again, the Diesel, through sheer force of will, survived. Under the pressure, his heart didn't explode. Then word came that the Sun offer had just arrived. Right in front of the assembled press, a relieved Markkula even put his hand on Spindler's shoulder and declared, "I like this guy. He's a very good person."

The directors retired to Apple's boardroom in a state of excitement to review Sun's offer. *God bless Scott McNealy.* An Apple-Sun combination would strike fear into the heart of IBM (again), Hewlett-Packard, Silicon Graphics and just about anyone else who put chips in a box.

The offer was read. Before it was half completed, the board knew that redemption had decided to bump its appointment. *Twenty-five* bucks a share, seven dollars off their offer of just a few days before. Twenty-five bucks! That was the goddamn *book* value. That was what Sun was offering for Apple in a stock swap. They didn't have to read the stock tables in the newspapers beside them to know that Apple that day was selling for a tick over $31. It was an insult. Scott McNealy was trying to fire-sale them. The shareholders, that angry mob just getting into their cars outside, were never going to go for it.

"The board really thought they would come out with a deal and all would be forgiven," an insider told *Business Week.*

Not this time. Now they were stuck with the place. The board called an emergency evening session and the parade began. One manager after another—from sales, from manufacturing, from international, from education, from the labs—marched in and did a core dump of everything that was wrong. Some were defensive, some tried to be optimistic, others were glad to finally get a hearing and blow off.

And the board members just sat stupefied, barely saying a word. *My God, it's even worse than we figured,* each of them thought in one manner or another. *How are we going to fix this and get out alive?*

It was nearly midnight when the board at last adjourned to stagger off to limousines and hotel suites and corporate jets. But even as they did they knew this was no "Thanks for the dinner, see you next quarter" board meeting. This was not going to go away. Whatever their manifold other commitments, the Little Kingdom was going to be foremost in their minds in the weeks to come.

It didn't even take that long. By the next morning, the denunciations had begun. First in the press, and then among major shareholders. It came in waves. First up were the newspapers, which pilloried Spindler and Apple for not only doing nothing about the company's plight but not even having a clue about what to do next.

The rest of the industry took its shot as well. Venture capitalist John Doerr, bitter that his ally in the two-front war against Microsoft was blowing up and abandoning his litter of new Internet start-ups, said with uncharacteristic rancor, "Apple's management ought to be tried for war crimes." Most devastating of all, because of its precise and chilly description by Apple's most veteran reporter of everything that had gone wrong at the Little Kingdom over the last five years, was Kathy Rebello's cover story in *Business Week*. Its devastating title was "The Fall of an American Icon."

Then came the shareholders, especially the big institutional investors. Rumors of the negotiations with Sun had leaked out, and the big shareholders, who had assumed that Apple would take the low-ball offer, were hopping mad. Faxes were coming in. Letters. Phone calls. E-mails. Everybody was shrieking for the board not to take Sun's offer. Well, hell, that was easy: the board didn't want it either. No, we stick with Spindler; Markkula likes him, he says he's got a plan. What other choice is there?

Each day for the rest of the week, new reports of disasters from the front poured in. From every sales region, stories were flying back to Cupertino that key customers weren't reordering, but instead were waiting to see if Apple was going to pull itself out of this newest swamp. Pissed-off shareholders you could deal with—give them good financial news and all is forgiven. But when customers start complaining, then you're on the fast slide to corporate death.

After a long weekend trying to recover, the board was hit with an even harder body blow first thing Monday morning, the 29th: Standard & Poor downgraded a bunch of Apple's debt to junk. In other words, S&P, the arbiter of corporate value, had just announced to every Apple distributor, consultant, supplier and contractor that Apple IOUs were all but worthless. Standard & Poor had just made Apple a corporate leper.

That did it. It was time to forget friendships and start throwing bodies overboard. Time to say adios, Michael Spindler. The Diesel would be making no more long hauls for Apple.

Markkula called an emergency board meeting for Tuesday, January 30, at the St. Regis Hotel and the Venrock offices in Manhattan. Spindler was invited too. He brought his wife along and seemed unaware of the fate awaiting him.

The board members rode together from the St. Regis to Rockefeller Center, no one giving the slightest hint to Spindler of what was to come. Once there, fearful of making Spindler's termination the penultimate one, the board members broke the news gently. Markkula, who had approved the Diesel's hiring sixteen years before and watched as the promising young German salesman had risen up through the ranks, led the meeting. It was touching. Spindler fought heroically to stay on. He had made some mistakes, he said, but his overall strategy had been right. It still was. The key was to focus on the execution.

But the board was firm in its resolve. He was out. Markkula walked his shattered, but proud ex-CEO to the door, then left him to wander back to his wife and home to global humiliation. Apple's last boardroom romantic was gone.

Apple needed a new CEO, and it needed him *now*. With the company's business imploding there was no time to go on a multimonth star search for talent. Nor, given the company's current reputation for management incompetence, was there any possibility of promoting up from inside. Besides, the only Apple executive qualified for the job had been Dan Eilers, head of worldwide marketing. But he had sided with Graziano and Spindler had canned him.

No, it would have to be some near-insider, somebody the chairman already knew, respected and could work with. It would be Markkula's call. Markkula, always invisible, but always there for the big purges. He already knew whom he wanted in the job.

That man, sitting there at the same table, looking like a middle-aged refrigerator repairman, was Gil Amelio.

Amelio, fifty-two, the current CEO of National Semiconductor Corp., was everything Apple wasn't. And that was part of his appeal. He was a friendly, badly dressed, socially awkward, honest, plain-spoken engineer, and thus the very antithesis, in some ways, of every Apple CEO who had come before him.

Amelio also had a reputation as a turnaround artist. He had come out of the second, Les Hogan–Wilf Corrigan, era of Fairchild—a nice little irony when one remembered that Jobs built Apple as a rebuttal to the old Fairchild-Valley way of doing business. Then Gil had spent a dozen years running the semiconductor operations at Rockwell, where he'd turned an obsolete operation into an industry player. And for the last half decade he'd taken on the turnaround of National Semi, an old Valley chip dinosaur with an unsavory reputation. Amelio had pulled that company up from losses of $151.4 million in 1991 to a record profit of $264.2 million by streamlining operations, abandoning old product lines and focusing the firm on peripheral processors and microcontrollers rather than continuing to beat itself to death trying to knock down the impregnable walls of Intel in microprocessors.

Amelio was also a working engineer, with sixteen patents to his credit. He was even a certified jet pilot, just like Mike Markkula, a topic the two discussed nearly as much as Apple on their flight home together in Markkula's plane. Still, they talked enough about business for Markkula to offer Amelio the job. Amelio, despite having been given three warnings about the cost of joining Apple—Graziano's tears, Jobs's scheming visit and Spindler's disintegration—accepted the job.

By 8 A.M., when A Clean Well-Lighted Place for Books opened its doors just a mile down the road from Apple headquarters, employees were already waiting to rush in and buy Amelio's new book, *Profit from Excellence,* a typically dreary, self-congratulations-disguised-as-sober-advice, CEO business tome that had gone largely unnoticed. Now it was flying off the shelves. After all, if you are going to suck up to the new boss, it certainly couldn't hurt to have a suitably well-worn copy of *PFE* on your shelf when the old man happens to walk by.

Both of Apple's CEOs, the newly minted and the newly deposed, went that morning to their respective offices, as if nothing had changed. This, of course, was the traditional Executive Quadrille. *You* knew everything had changed. Everyone around you knew everything had changed. By tomorrow morning the press would be reporting rumors that everything had changed. But until the Securities and Exchange Commission and Nasdaq were properly notified, *nothing* had changed.

That afternoon, Amelio notified National's board—in particular, Charlie Sporck—that he was resigning. The meeting took twenty minutes. Gil told the board that he had not sought the Apple job, but having been offered it, he was going to take it. For America's sake.

The news, to put it mildly, was not taken well.

Charlie had never much liked Amelio. Part of it was that Amelio was from the wrong family of Fairchildren. He wasn't first-generation, like Sporck and Noyce and Sanders, the men who built high tech's most mythical company, then tore it apart to build Silicon Valley. Amelio had been a minor player in Fairchild's second generation, the apostasy of Hogan and Corrigan, the Motorola cabal that had taken over Fairchild and had systematically, and arrogantly, driven it into the ground.

But it went deeper than that. Sporck had run National as his own fiefdom for twenty-five years, taken it from a falling-down little outfit based in New Jersey, moved it to Santa Clara, turned it into a billion-dollar giant, taken the Japanese invasion head-on and, though the company was crippled in the process, managed to hold the place together long enough for the good times. Then Amelio comes along, does a solid job in a rising market and the next thing you know he's a turnaround genius.

The old Valley vets gnawing on steaks and sucking on Camels in Mac's Tea Room in Los Altos laughed at that one. Months later one semiconductor demi-legend would take a pull on his gin on the rocks and say, "How the fuck did Gil Amelio ever get a rep as a turnaround artist. I mean, what did he do? Turn a piece-of-shit, third-rate chip house like Rockwell into a piece-of-shit, second-rate chip house? And all he had to do at National was not fuck it up while the U.S. chip industry came back." He laughed. "Apple thought in Gil Amelio it was getting the second coming."

Publicly, Sporck was polite. Older now, but still more than six feet tall, and still wearing the Zapata mustache of his early National days, his eyes hard as gravel, Sporck managed to say, "I was shocked and annoyed. I'm disappointed that he decided to bag it." For Charlie Sporck, that was diplomatic. Privately, he was furious. At Mac's he would say through gritted teeth, "I cannot believe a professional would behave in such a manner."

National had no choice but to accept Amelio's resignation. By then it was early afternoon. The stock exchanges had closed. Having considerable practice in such matters, the company chose to spend the rest of the day preparing a terse press release, vetted by the board and the corporate lawyers into shaved ice, and then sent it out the next morning.

Thus, at 8:30 A.M. on Friday, February 2, 1996, the world officially learned that Amelio had left National Semiconductor. And though, thanks to CNN, the *New York Times* and the Associated Press, everybody knew where he was going, the announcement of his hiring never appeared.

The day went on. No news. The markets closed for the weekend, and still no news. One by one the key newspapers on the East Coast, the Midwest and finally on the West Coast passed their deadlines and were put to bed. Apple, the company that had invented big-event tech publicity now couldn't even get a simple press release out on time—and when it did the story would already be old news.

The apparent reason for the delay, though Apple refused to comment in reply to the increasingly anxious press calls, was that Spindler and Markkula hadn't come to final agreement on the size of the Diesel's golden parachute. Why compensation negotiations would hold up an exit announcement was never clear. But little about Apple was clear anymore.

While this was going on, Spindler had time to compose and e-mail a message to those embattled survivors he'd left behind.

"Dear Colleagues: The end of a long voyage. A page in my life has turned," it began, followed by a rambling reminiscence of his years at Apple, of the good times and the bad. He blamed himself for all that had gone wrong—a noble sentiment, but exactly the wrong message for the legions of screwups, malcontents, myopics and empire builders at Apple who collectively bore at least as much responsibility for the current disaster as the Diesel.

Then the big, chest-baring finish: "So it's time for me to go! Mistakes or misjudgments made? Oh yes—even plenty. Both in business and personal judgment terms. I take personal responsibility for things that didn't work and should have worked. I tried to give it my best—both intellectually and physically in every corner of the world to carry this cause and its color."

It was just the kind of loopy, overwrought message to remind everybody that Michael Spindler was exactly the wrong person to have run Apple.

At last, at 6:45 P.M., in the closing darkness of the worst business week in Apple's history, the company finally sent out a missive. Michael Spindler had officially resigned as Apple's chief executive officer, replaced by Gilbert Amelio. Then a surprise: Amelio would also assume the title of Apple chairman, with A. C. "Mike" Markkula stepping down to his old title of vice-chairman. Markkula had retired again—and his move signaled that the play was now Gil's. Amelio and Apple would rise and fall together . . . and alone.

9.10 Gone to Ground

And alone was how Gil Amelio would play it for the next fourteen weeks. The world, or at least the dwindling part of the world that still shared or cared about Apple's fate, waited for a sign.

But the real sign was that there were no signs. No big press conferences. No massive layoffs. No sweeping pronouncements about the future. Amelio remained out of sight, by all reports quietly and systematically surveying the company, taking technical presentations, talking to outside observers.

No one before had ever been so apparently unaffected by the most famous bully pulpit in high technology. But no one who had run Apple before had been this much of an adult. It was comforting now to come to work in the morning and look up at the big glass double tower with its microprocessor motif on the top floors and know that behind the glass Gil Amelio was working to fix everything.

And the weeks passed. Business, such as it was, went on as usual. The middle managers read and reread and deconstructed *Profit from Excellence,* all the while looking for a puff of white smoke from the tower. The programmers went back to throwing the Frisbee on the lawn at Infinite Loop, eating sushi in the cafeteria and working on their own hermetic corner of the endlessly late Copland operating system. Occasionally a new rumor would pop up on their computer screen and they would laugh or momentarily freeze with dread. Then they would pass it on.

Some of the rumors were fantastic—that Jobs, Ellison and Lotus's Jim Manzi had made an accepted buyout offer—and would be proven untrue. Other rumors that were equally fantastic—that Copland would be killed and its design team fired *(Impossible! We've already spent too much)*—would in time prove true. And still others—the negotiations with Sun had permanently broken down—were quickly confirmed by the press.

But still, there was no word from Gil Amelio. Within hours of his appointment, he had asked for a hundred days to study the company and its problems, and amazingly enough, he actually meant it. For Apple, this consistency was almost breathtaking. Only in late April did he have a serious interview with the press, and then he merely outlined his long-term plans. No grandstanding. No posing. It was almost as if the man didn't have an ego.

Not that he was doing nothing. Like all smart CEOs, before his honeymoon with the public ended, Amelio dumped every obsolete piece of inventory he could find, thus sticking the blame where it belonged, on his predecessors. It was ugly: a $740 million loss in the first quarter of 1996—an amount big enough, had it been profits, to make Apple one of the hundred most successful companies in America. But even this devastating announcement was done ex cathedra, the press release sent out and Gil not available for interviews.

During his disappearance, Amelio also made a bold move: he met with Bill Gates. After six weeks as CEO, Gil decided he knew enough about Apple's predicament to meet with the man largely responsible for it.

Amelio had worked with Gates before, during his National Semiconductor days, so he knew a little of what to expect. Gates even offered to fly down to Cupertino, but Amelio preferred to fly with a small Apple contingent on his own jet to Redmond.

Gates met them graciously like old friends. Then, as the meeting began, and Gates launched into a long presentation on his long relationship with Apple—including old photos of him with Jobs—it seemed clear to the visitors that America's richest man was pained by the turn that relationship had taken in recent years. And since with Bill Gates the personal was also the commercial, part of the pain came from the fact that Microsoft's billion-dollar Mac software business was declining along with the fortunes of Apple.

When he and Gates retreated to the latter's office for a private conversation, Amelio was convinced that he was close to a deal—one in which Microsoft would agree to design its key programs (like Office) specifically for the Mac, not just translate them over from Windows in forms that were slow and unwieldy to load and use.

Gates refused, insisting instead that Amelio and Apple adopt Microsoft's new Web browser, Explorer—without a quid pro quo. The conversation ended there. For the rest of Amelio's time at Apple, the two would continue to talk and negotiate. But it went nowhere. In time, Amelio concluded: "Once he's explained his position, Bill sincerely can't understand why you don't want to do what he wants you to. On the other hand, when you make the point that the best deals are 'I'll scratch your back, you scratch mine,' he's ready with a list of excuses and reasons why that isn't possible in this case. I rapidly came to realize that Bill found it difficult to meet another person halfway."

Amelio came down from the tower on May 14, 1996, almost exactly five-score days since he had arrived at Apple. To a gathering of employees Amelio gave a sort of State of the Company address, which was to be part of the annual Apple Worldwide Developers Conference—a group even more important than Apple's own employees. The venue was to be the quarter-mile-long neo-Quonset hut of the San Jose McEnery Convention Center.

The hall was standing room only as Amelio stepped up to the podium. His chunky, avuncular image, projected on the giant screen above him, drew an audible murmur from large regions of the audience. Was this Apple's new image? Sure, Spindler had been heavyset and sloppily dressed, but at least he was German. An exotic. But think of Sculley and Jobs—both of them lean as whippets, bony and drawn as if the purity of their purpose had mortified their flesh to parchment.

And now . . . *this.* Gil Amelio, with his red tie, his square meat-and-potatoes face, his short wavy hair brushed straight back, looked like a high school shop teacher. Worse, in an era when nine-year-olds practice news bites in front of the mirror, and when corporate CEOs are as smooth in public as movie stars, Amelio behaved like an assistant plant supervisor at Dow Chemical in 1956 giving a presentation to the Wilmington Rotary Club. His hands shook with nerves and adrenaline as he made his first gesture. His voice wavered momentarily at the sight of thousands of anxious faces.

Then something happened. A gravity came into Amelio's face. It was if an iron weight settled into his jaw. Gil smiled. Not a warm grin, but a smile of power. "Can you believe all the press on this thing?" he asked. "You'd think I was going to part the Red Sea." Yes, yes, laughed the audience. That's exactly what we expect you to do.

Another smile. "Actually, it's kind of intimidating to be here in front of four thousand people, all of whom know more about the technical details of our computers than I do." A roar. Was this real humility by the CEO?

A heckler in the audience, no doubt one of those legions of employees who still believed Apple was a philosophy and not a moneymaking enterprise, shouted, "Take off your tie!" to the titters of hundreds of the like-minded throughout the hall. Gil ignored them, but for a millisecond his look said: Laugh now, clown. You are going to disappear long before my tie does.

Like good children, the audience sat up a little straighter in its folding chairs.

After that, the rest of the speech was anticlimax. Copland, the troubled new operating system that had been the Mac's long-awaited savior, would no longer wait to be presented in final form. Instead it would be chopped up, the best pieces currently ready would be part of the upcoming Mac OS 7.6. No more "insanely great" products of the Jobs era. Now we go for revenues whenever anything is ready to sell.

There was also to be a major simplification of Apple's incoherent eighty-product Mac family, a list so convoluted and redundant that few company employees, much less customers, could understand it.

There was also to be a reorganization—SOP for new CEOs—dividing the company into "independently competitive" hardware and software groups. The audience had heard that bullshit many times before and always ignored it. Much better, except to middle managers, was Amelio's announcement that henceforth the company would abandon its tradition of promoting only from within and would seek talent elsewhere: "In order to get the depth we want, we'll have to go outside."

Then even better news. Amelio announced that Apple's new focus for its products would be on the two hottest markets in computing: the Internet and multmedia. *Finally,* thought every developer in the room. Three years late on the former, five on the latter, but at last Apple is finally committing to two industries it helped create. Had the company done this when it should have, Apple would now *own* computing. No Netscape, no Silicon Graphics and only half a Microsoft.

By now the developers were getting aroused. Employees too. The dogs of the press were scribbling furiously. This might be it! The Apple Messiah, disguised as the head of the paint department at Orchard Supply Hardware. Amelio's unslickness, laughable at the beginning, was now a reason for celebration. Here was one guy too boring to lie to us. And too plodding to be anything but consistent.

It had come to this: Apple had sunk so low that the only person anyone believed was the one who obviously didn't belong there.

Feeling the crowd's growing support, Amelio responded by becoming ever more earnestly pedantic as the speech went on. And that only increased the crowd's ardor—until, by the trademark Amelio attenuated dead finish, the convention center had become a giant lovefest. Old Silicon Valley and New had bonded around their two common passions: technology and money.

It was a beautiful thing.

And that meant something was wrong. By this time the hall should have filled with wailing and the gnashing of teeth as the Apple dream died in its thousands of incarnations. Instead, there was applause and cheers. Gil was visibly heartened by this response, the absolutely wrong one from a company that desperately needed the corporate equivalent of shock therapy.

Had Gil Amelio looked down to his left, he would have seen a warning, an omen of the past and future. Sitting on the carpet between the front row and the speaker's platform, was Ben Weiss, Macintosh programming guru, his hair and beard falling on his chest, wearing a sleeveless, low-cut sarong shirt, brown corduroys and Birkenstocks, scrutinizing every bump on Gil's face through a little monocular telescope.

Weiss, like hundreds, maybe thousands, of others scattered throughout the hall, was a ghost of Apple Past. In the months to come, these ethereal keepers of the flame would haunt Amelio and bollix his attempts at change, sometimes by ignoring him, sometimes by fighting him, but most of all by embracing him.

But in the end, the greatest role of these wraiths would be incantatory: summoning back the greatest Apple ghost of them all: Steven Jobs.

On Tuesday, March 26, 1996, while Amelio and Apple were in their self-imposed quiet period, David Packard, Silicon Valley's patriarch, died quietly at age eighty-three.

A deep sadness fell over the Valley. In a rare tribute to a businessman, the news made headlines throughout the world. Thousands filled Stanford Chapel and the Quad for the funeral. The *San Jose Mercury News* devoted an entire special section in tribute.

It is the strange fate of business titans, the absolute value of their power in life often so much greater than that of entertainers or politicians or novelists, to be forgotten far sooner in death. But not David Packard. If every CEO stands in the shower each morning and dreams of immortality, Packard in life and death gave them a glimpse of what it really looked like. The greatest businessman in the history of the electronics revolution. And, if the sum of an enterprise's success, innovation and respect is the true measure, co-founder of the greatest American company of modern times.

The death of David Packard, and the effusions of tributes that followed, only threw Apple's latest troubles into sharper relief.

If Apple always talked revolution, HP actually lived it. Profit sharing, flex-time, tuition support, telecommuting . . . all HP organizational innovations that had changed the world as completely as its calculators, instruments and computers. In the end, it was always about character at HP, that secret ingredient that Apple had always lacked. And that character, made manifest in the famous HP Way, had its roots in the lives of David Packard and Bill Hewlett. Like Woz and Jobs, Bill and Dave had also met in their late teens, drawn together by a mutual interest in technology, in their case electronic test and measurement instruments.

But Bill and Dave were not only business partners but also best friends. They worked together, and played together, for sixty years. In all of those years, neither ever betrayed the other. In fact, there is no record of them ever having fought. Their respect for each other was boundless, and they shared that respect with everyone with whom they worked. In the words of ex-HPer and Valley entrepreneur Bill Krause, Packard was a hardhearted businessman who demanded perfection from everyone in the company, but when it came to his employees' lives, he was the most softhearted of men. In six decades, David Packard was never seen to belittle or humiliate an employee—or anyone else, for that matter. And to cap their magnificent careers, Bill and Dave, now among the richest men in America, joined their wives in creating two of the nation's largest philanthropies.

At the heart of Packard's greatness, of his character, was a rock-hard integrity. He did not lie. He did not assume credit for others' work—on the contrary, he was comfortable giving credit and authority to people he thought more talented or more brilliant than he. And most of all, he was a man of his word, and his word was literally as good as gold. David Packard had always behaved maturely, gravely and with a deep sense of responsibility to those who worked for him and those who bought his products. Largely for these reasons, he and Bill had built a real company, with mass and form, a proud past and a hopeful future—all of the things Apple never had.

There was one other decisive difference between Hewlett and Packard and Wozniak and Jobs. It was that at HP, the founders never left. For a half century, Bill and Dave stayed at their posts, through good times and bad, protecting their people, maintaining the company's philosophy and myths, and defending HP from anyone who would put themselves before the company.

It was this combination of integrity, trust and commitment that led to the extraordinary final act of these two remarkable men. At the beginning of the

1990s, HP, like Apple, was sinking into a decadence of executive perquisites, bloated bureaucracies, departmental fiefdoms and endless meetings. Bill and Dave were now in their eighties and increasingly in ill health. They had long since retired from the daily operations of the company and were now on the brink of retiring from the HP board of directors. But a memo changed all of that: a secretary, buried deep in the bowels of the company, wrote to Packard to tell him what was going wrong at his company.

Only a man like David Packard would have ever gotten such a note from an employee so far down the organization chart, and only a man like David Packard would have read the memo, understood its underlying meaning and taken action. Within a year, Packard and Hewlett had turned HP upside down, reorganized it, slashed away at the fat and replaced deadwood managers with dynamic ones. Two old men in their last hurrah, one of them literally just months away from the end. It was one of the most heroic accomplishments in business history. By Packard's death, Hewlett-Packard not only had regained its old energy but was growing as fast as any company of its size had ever done.

So, on that March day at Stanford, it was easy for one's heart to go out to Bill Hewlett, as he sat feebly in a wheelchair saying goodbye to his lifelong friend, and to the crowds of current and ex-HPers as they mourned the greatest human being they would ever meet. And it was hard to feel much sympathy for the predicament of the arrogant little tribe down the road in Cupertino.

9.11 Reemergence

The Apple that emerged from Amelio's hundred days was a vastly different one from the company that began it. It was already on its way to becoming, if Amelio's strategy worked, a new company.

Amelio, to his credit, went about this reconstruction systematically and relentlessly. First, he changed the company's relationship with its shareholders. On February 12, he suspended the company's program, first begun in 1987, of awarding quarterly stock dividends. This had been a classic bit of Sculley's East Coast mentality. Silicon Valley companies, even wildly successful ones like Intel, didn't give out dividends. You wanna invest in a high-tech company, then you gotta play venture capitalist. You make your money on the stock appreciation; we reinvest the dividends for growth. Done.

Next up, the senior management. On February 29, Amelio announced the new title of chief administrative officer and hired corporate enforcer George

Scalise away from National. Sporck howled. So, soon, would Apple employees. Then, on March 7, Amelio announced the hiring of Fred Anderson, formerly CFO of Automatic Data Processing of Roseland, New Jersey, to take on the same post at Apple. Anderson had a rep for being able, and loyal. Then Amelio hired Ellen Hancock, who had quit National on the morning of Amelio's hundred-day speech. Hancock was one of the highest-ranking women scientists in American industry.

With his new team in place, Amelio turned to the company's operations.

In finance, Amelio recognized that for his turnaround plan to succeed—the process he publicly predicted at the May gathering would take three years—he would need a lot of cash. Cash flow, never a big concern at Apple, now became something of an obsession. And the company was burning cash fast: reserves fell almost by half in the first three months of 1996, from $1.1 billion to $592 million. This wasn't very much money for a company that needed to drive new-product development on multiple fronts *and* was still running in the red.

Next, Amelio went after Apple's products, software in particular. By the time of the speech, he had already killed the pathetic Copland, picking through its entrails for bits he could bolt onto the current System 7 Mac OS. He pushed for the speeded-up development of System 8, with added emphasis on its Internet capabilities. That still left all the pissed-off and alienated developers. As a bone to them, Apple hired, or more accurately, rehired Heidi Roizen. Roizen had been the best developer relations manager Apple had ever known. But like so many others, she had drifted off to try her hand at entrepreneurship. She had successfully co-founded T/Maker Co. in Mountain View, which published clip art programs and children's software.

Roizen knew what it was like to deal with a troubled Apple from within and without—especially without. When T/Maker began to move away from the Mac platform, Roizen had been amazed that Apple never even noticed. Nobody drove the five miles from Cupertino to find out what was going wrong at T/Maker. For a company that had always treated its developers like part of the family, this was like having your parents suddenly stop returning your phone calls.

Needless to say, having been abandoned gave Roizen a special understanding of the needs of the developers she was to manage and motivate. Her friendship with Bill Gates gave her a special understanding of the competition. Roizen's return as vice president for developer relations signaled that Apple was again serious about the $1 billion in Mac software sold annually. As Roizen was willing to admit at the time of her hiring, "In many ways, Apple has been its own worst enemy . . . [it] has forgotten at times to treat developers as a business community and treated them more as religious followers."

Hardware too came under Amelio's scrutiny. Besides moving to consolidate the company's confused Mac desktop line, he also began to knock heads in other parts of the catalog. At about the time of his public reemergence, Apple had to once again suspend production and recall its PowerBooks. This time the problem was buggy software, cracked cases and an often experienced but little reported tendency for the display lid to fall off. The days when Steve Jobs would demand the highest-quality packaging for Apple products was a distant memory. Now, despite being elegant and powerful, Apple's portables were gaining a reputation for being shoddy.

The recall could not have come at a more damaging time. In the first quarter of 1994, Apple PowerBooks had reached a 9 percent market share in an extremely competitive market—then collapsed in the second and third quarters thanks to the exploding keyboards. By the fourth quarter, though, the problem solved, PowerBook market share had climbed back up to 7.5 percent, with shipments reaching a record 200,000 units. And the demand was only expected to get bigger as summer approached and the PowerBook's image got a big goose from its appearance in two blockbuster movies, *Mission: Impossible* and *Independence Day*. In the former the PowerBook did everything but provide the movie with a coherent plot, and in the latter it saved all of mankind.

Even before the recall, the PowerBook division was in trouble. In a market where most competitors rolled out a new model every six months, Apple was still hanging on to its 1995 models as they approached their first birthday. After putting out too many models when the market didn't want it, now Apple wasn't introducing enough when the market did. Not surprisingly, by April, a month before the recall, PowerBook retail sales dropped 31 percent. They fell another 27 percent in May. Then came the recall, and suddenly Apple wasn't selling *any* of the product that accounted for 15 percent—$1.5 billion—of its annual revenue. The company promised to have the machines back on the shelves in a month. But two months went by and still no PowerBooks. Then, to make matters worse, the company quietly announced that it might not have any new models ready until late 1996 at the earliest.

In losing the PowerBook, Apple lost not only its sexiest product but also the allegiance of many of the developers for the PowerBook—the people Heidi Roizen had been hired to hold on to. One of these angry developers was Global Village Communication Inc., a leading supplier of computer modems. When Apple stopped selling its PowerBooks, Global Village's

PowerBook modem business stopped dead. To stay healthy, the company responded by switching its emphasis to the laptop platform that *was* still shipping. "It has certainly caused us to increase investment in the Windows products we do," company president Neil Selvin told the *San Jose Mercury News*. "We took a lot of risks [in launching our PowerBook modem] and decided to do things that were cutting-edge. In the last two years, with all the problems [at Apple], they got cautious. We're not seeing the kind of aggressive risk taking that we'd like to see."

This was the first nonfinancial crisis of Amelio's tenure. He handled it with a welcome decisiveness. The head of the PowerBook division was booted and replaced with Brodie Keast, who had run the division during its good times the year before and had been promoted to corporate marketing. Six weeks later, when the problem still wasn't solved, Amelio allowed Keast to quietly take a two-month sabbatical long due him.

Before he left, Keast uttered a comment that stood not only for the PowerBook division but for Apple Computer itself—and, as time would show, Gil Amelio as well: "If there's anything we've learned over the last year or two, it's that we need to be more humble."

Amelio replaced Keast temporarily with Fred Forsythe, Keast's boss and Apple's vice president for Macintoshes. Eventually the problem resolved itself and PowerBooks began to reappear in stores. But not before the product's reputation and market dominance had been lost. The PowerBook, like the Macintosh before it, had been a trendsetter. It had defined the future of portable computing. Now, like the Mac, it was reduced to a niche product used by a small population of true believers.

The PowerBook division, though its crisis took up considerable portions of his time, wasn't the only hardware operation that Amelio targeted during his first Hundred Days and the weeks thereafter. In the company's bread-and-butter business, he began hacking up the Macintosh's eighty-product catalog, emphasizing especially the overlap between the Performa and Quadra families. When he was done, the Mac had half as many models.

Next came the Newton. There had been considerable talk about unloading the Newton division to a consumer electronics company or other hardware manufacturer, or in the worst case, simply jettisoning it. Jobs was advising the company to get rid of it. Amelio would later say that he spent weeks pondering at what price to sell off the operation, which was generating $200 million per year, but costing $250 million. The sale price, Amelio concluded, was $50 million, but despite serious negotiations with Samsung and Ericsson, neither company's offer was close to that amount.

So, eyeing the (finally) growing market for personal digital assistants, and the lively interest in the future of "thin clients" in the global telecommunications grid, Amelio surprised Apple watchers by sticking with the product synonymous with Apple's current disasters. The Newton, he announced, would become yet another Apple subsidiary.

Amelio also hung in with Pippin, a new $600 television set-top box that combined CD-ROM player technology with Internet search capabilities—a device not far, in theory at least, from Larry Ellison's budget network computer. Helping this decision was the advice of Wozniak, who made a strong case for Apple refocusing on education and young people. Pippin was targeted for late 1997.

That left the matter of clones. Needless to say, licensing the Mac OS had been a decision faced by every Apple CEO except Mike Scott. Jobs and Sculley made the wrong decision for the right reasons. Spindler made the right decision for the wrong reasons. Now the crisis Apple faced pretty much resolved the matter. Jobs and Sculley had, thoughtfully and against the best advice to the contrary, chosen not to clone out of simple arithmetic: why make $85 on every licensed Mac sold when you can make $1,500 selling your own machine? Especially when you lose market share in the process? Only in the latter years of the Sculley era did the equation change and the reclamation of lost market share become first priority for Apple's survival. But by then the anticloning philosophy had locked in.

Spindler, fighting the last war, had decided to license the cloners in the belief that market share rather than profits was now most critical. But by now the marketplace had changed. It had settled in rigid boundaries, in which there was little Apple could do to make serious market share gains. The window (literally) of opportunity for Apple to regain market dominance had closed. Now the best strategy for Apple was to hold on to its unique OS and try to compete against the Wintel world by attacking it on the corners and by diversifying into brand-new markets, such as Internet-dedicated machines. And for that, the company would need the money generated by profits, not licenses. But Spindler, fulfilling a dream, went ahead and licensed anyway. The one consolation was that, typical for Apple in the 1990s, he did it so badly—forcing prospective cloners to use Apple, their chief competitor, as their only source of supply—that clones barely made a dent in the market under his leadership.

When Amelio arrived, the situation had once again changed. Apple was now so deep in extremis that it needed revenues, even licensing fees, anywhere it could find them. That made Amelio's decision easier. By February 19, less than three weeks after his takeover, Apple announced that Motorola had signed a sublicensing agreement that made it a second supplier to clones of Macintosh technology. In May, IBM signed an agreement to license the Mac OS.

The result was an explosion of growth and an efflorescence of exciting new products in the clone community. For the first time in a dozen years, Mac owners now had a choice. In the dark days ahead, the clone companies, notably Power Computing, would become more effective advocates for Apple than Apple itself.

Stock, senior management, developers, hardware and software. Three months into his tenure, Amelio had taken on every part of the company but one: the employees. Until the big coming-out party on May 14, Amelio's only real mass interaction with Apple's staff had been a negative one done by remote control. Like all smart new CEOs, he took the gall with the vinegar as early as possible in his tenure to minimize personal blame: in April, as he announced Apple's $740 million loss for the quarter, Amelio also announced—ex cathedra, of course, the layoff of another 1,500 employees. The first figure was big enough to annihilate 98 percent of the businesses in America; so big that the sidetracking of more than a thousand careers and families was scarcely noticed. After two years of Spindler, Apple employees were becoming used to having their departments regularly purged and to regularly upgrading their own résumés for quick use.

Now, having emerged from his lair, Amelio set about restoring the morale of his people. His results were perversely mixed. Amelio, the corporate dinosaur, proved to have greater rapport with the rank and file at Apple than with management. Senior managers, used to being on the inside of the endless feel-good consensus building at the top of Apple during the Sculley years, were now shocked to find themselves locked out of Amelio's inner circle. Amelio was willing to give them more latitude and freedom to run their operations than ever before. But what Gil gave he also took away: *he* decided what the goals of each operation would be. Managers were now free to get to those targets any way they liked, but by God, they better hit those targets or they were gone.

Not that some senior executives didn't try to skirt the new paradigm and convert Amelio to the Apple Way. Jim Buckley, president of Apple America, gave it a shot. At a staff meeting of the Apple Leadership Team, he suggested to Amelio that the company write letters to all of its customers asking them to hang in with Apple during these tough times. Great, said Amelio, prepare the letters and I'll sign them personally. Buckley disagreed, saying that those are *my* customers, so the letter should come from me. No, said Amelio with finality, the letters will come from *me*.

It was a minor matter, and the participants later insisted it had little importance, but the story of Amelio stomping Buckley sent shock waves through Apple. Here was a real boss, who understood the perquisites and responsibilities of command . . . and did not accept disagreement on the boundaries of his control. From that point on, Apple's managers privately complained about being left out of the loop and not knowing where the company was going, but at the office they deferred to Number One. "He doesn't appear to be into management by committee," gulped Frank Casanova, director of the company's advanced prototyping laboratory.

Upon his arrival, George Scalise, National's enforcer, underscored the difference between the old order and the new, between those in the circle and those outside it, by marching into City Center 3 and taking over the office of Kevin Sullivan, vice president for human resources and the most powerful member of the Old Guard. Sullivan meekly accepted the new rules. He would later claim he offered the office to Scalise, but few believed him.

By comparison, the Apple workforce seemed happy with Amelio's presence. After years of endless reorganizations, misdirected new-product developments and, most of all, flip-flopping management strategies, most were frankly relieved just to have as boss a guy who seemed to have the same consistent plan from one day to the next. "The challenge," said George Everhart, former Apple vice president for U.S. sales, who left to run Fujitsu America, "is if you don't have a feeling where you are headed, it tends to drain energy. It tires out people who are working hard. When you boil it down, that's been the company's problem over the past year."

Amelio seemed to offer the hope that now Apple would have a direction. That even now he was formulating a plan, and then would order the troops to march on the objective. As one engineer told the *San Jose Mercury News:* "Everyone is certainly willing to work around the clock for him, but we want to know on what."

Even the "Skirt Man," engineer Jeremy Bornstein in the advanced technology group, who got his moniker from his choice of skirts and sarongs as work clothes, gave Amelio a thumbs-up: "When I met [him], I could see there were some wheels turning in there. I heard later he talked about doing something about the dress code around here."

9.12 Indian Summer

As summer turned to autumn in 1996, there was a renewed sense that Apple could indeed be restored to its glory days. Just the fact that there was little news coverage about the company that fall was a welcome relief from the endless run of bad news over the previous eighteen months.

What news there was was mostly good. Morale was up. So was demand, with the company's traditionally strong market sectors—education, desktop publishing, Europe and Japan—showing renewed strength. Good news even came from unexpected quarters. Microsoft, fearing further antitrust actions by the Justice Department of the type that led it to sign a recent consent decree, suddenly showed new interest in helping its old friend.

Microsoft had long been in the odd position of being not only Apple's greatest competitor but the leading independent third-party supplier for Macintosh—to the tune of more than a billion dollars each year. In fact, the combination of Microsoft Word and Microsoft Office for Mac usually led to Microsoft making more money per Macintosh sold than Apple did.

Microsoft was doubly motivated to help its old enemy. Apple was now reduced to the humiliating position of having its triumphant opponent giving it life support. In 1995, as the troubles began, Gates had dispatched a team to Silicon Valley to establish a liaison with Apple. By 1996, as Apple began to collapse, Microsoft strengthened the operation, assigning it the task of helping small software companies write Internet programs for Apple. Since Microsoft was using every machination to crush Netscape and control access to the Net, it could afford to spend millions to help prop up Apple as a cover for its activities. Don Bradford, head of the operation, even admitted that his assignment was to "help make sure that Apple's market share stays between 8 percent and 11 percent"—in other words, not enough to be in any way threatening to Microsoft's hegemony, but yet enough to make Apple a credible competitor Microsoft could point to the next time it was called a monopoly.

Some of the more prescient observers saw in this deal a future quid pro quo: "How would this conversation be any different if I was talking to Satan?" asked Mark Kriegsman, president of ClearWay Technologies Inc. in Boston. "They're saying, 'I'm your friend, here's some money, but don't worry, we'll figure out later how you can help me?' " Apple wouldn't learn what that quid was for another year. But already the company was Bill Gates's cat's-paw.

By the end of 1996, the Microsoft operation in Silicon Valley had several dozen employees. And, at a time when Microsoft bashing by Apple reached a hysterical pitch, the Apple faithful could still attend Mac Expo and see a Microsoft booth filled with arrogant, but nervous people.

So Apple now had an unlikely patron. Further support came from another, equally unexpected direction: the clone makers. The changed rules on licensing had unfettered Mac copycats around the world. The best of these companies, such as Power Computing and Umax, were now starting to bring their products to market. The new machines were everything Apple hoped for—and feared—from clones. They were only adequately designed in terms of packaging, but they were fast, as powerful as their Apple counterparts, and about 30 percent cheaper . . . in other words, about the price the average consumer thought Macs should carry.

But the best thing about the new clone builders was that they were cheeky bastards; brash, full of themselves, willing to take wild risks. In other words, they were Apple back when Apple was the hottest company in the world. None captured that style better than Power Computing Corp.

Power Computing had been founded in the Silicon Valley city of Milpitas in 1993 by a born entrepreneur named Stephen "King" Kahng. Kahng had gotten his nickname as a pioneer in the cloning of IBM PCs a decade before, but he had always seen the Mac as a terrific business opportunity. As Apple began to show signs under Spindler of licensing the Mac OS, Kahng made his move. He incorporated Power Computing in November 1993 and by the spring of 1994 he was deep in negotiations with Apple. He finally got the license in November. By February 1995, with backing from Olivetti, he opened a factory in Austin, Texas, and by May 1995 was shipping his first clones, called the Power family. The Power machines were as powerful as their Apple counterparts and a lot less expensive—as much as 25 percent. By October 1995, Power Computing was shipping its second, more powerful product family, called the PowerWave line.

Umax was a different story. Formed from the purchase of Radius's clone line, Umax was a division of a $3 billion Taiwanese corporation. It got into the business largely to protect its scanners, most of which were used with Macs, but soon found low-cost cloning of the expensive Apple line to be a lucrative business. The vice president for engineering, Peter Mehring, who had come from Radius, argued that "we don't even compete directly with Apple. Rather, we complement its sales. Apple doesn't sell a machine priced at under $1,800. We don't sell anything priced above that. And we sell in places where Apple is now weak, like Taiwan, Japan and Western Europe. I don't see how we can do anything but help Apple."

Amelio knew the key to managing clones was to stay on top of them. They were going to be innovative and audacious—that was the point of having them—but the trick was to never let them get too far ahead. But once they took the risk of finding a price point that generated the best sales and profit margins, the smart big company could then roll in after them and stake out that territory. If the clones came up with a new wrinkle in hardware and software, you watched the market's response. If it was strong, then you adopted the new idea. Clone companies were outliers; you gave them their lead, allowed them good strong growth, you worked with them when it was useful—but you always stayed in command of the market. IBM had forgotten that, and its clones had simply broken their reins, run off and grown rich.

But once again, knowing what had to be done and actually doing it with a self-centered and unwieldy organization were two different things. Power Computing dazzled the Mac world, and infuriated Apple by producing not just better machines but designs a generation ahead of anything being done by the crowd in Cupertino. Thus, the Power line was the first to feature Motorola's new 120 MHz PowerPC chip. Then, as Apple struggled to keep up, Kahng brought out the 150 MHz PowerWave. Six months later, as Apple was bringing out its own 150 MHz models, Power Computing announced its first Power Tower, with 180 MHz speed. Combine that with lower prices, and if you were willing to sacrifice some swanky packaging and the little rainbow logo in the corner, Power Computing looked like a far better buy. Apple didn't even have the traditional advantage of stability. Apple might be shipping 5 million computers per year compared with Power Computing's 50,000. But in May 1996, Power Computing had $250 million in annual revenues, while $11 billion Apple was in the midst of *losing* three times that much. So much for the security of a large, established company.

The same thing happened at the low end of the market. Umax, by producing computers that were the equal of Apple's but at half the price, not only found new customers but (because Apple didn't sufficiently advance its own machines to be worth the premium price) began to carve away at the low end of Apple's business. By 1997, it had global Mac clone sales estimated at $300 million.

Said Umax chairman Frank Huang, "The industry today is very different than it was ten years ago. There are price segments where companies compete on price alone. Apple is a symbol of the American computing industry. They still have a big media and PR presence, but their marketing power has dwindled and they don't have the compelling technological lead they once had. Their advantage is diminishing faster than we can imagine. Our existence makes them more powerful."

Ten years after the success of Compaq and Dell, clones didn't bear the stigma they once had. Even Rush Limbaugh, with the largest radio audience in history and one of the last highly visible Apple fanatics, would proudly announce to his listeners that he had just bought a Power Computing clone.

Kahng was also creating a competing myth for Power Computing. Whereas Apple under Sculley would blow tens of thousands of dollars on airplane logos and its executive would stay in the poshest hotel suites, Kahng's staff became famous for attending a Boston trade show and staying in a $49-per-night motel.

At the January 1996 MacWorld Expo in San Francisco, Power Computing pulled off a coup the industry hadn't seen since Apple hijacked the West Coast Computer Faire in 1977. Apple, in the midst of the Spindler crisis, had all but pulled out of the event. In response, several other companies bailed as well. Power Computing made its move: picking up an abandoned $170,000 booth for just $30,000. Power Computing stole the show. Luck, mixed with audacity, was on Power Computing's side.

And the little company, now with 300 employees, just got more interesting and lovable. Perhaps nothing better captured the style of this brash new start-up than an advertisement run by Power Computing. It was an imitation Roy Lichtenstein comic book painting showing in close-up an All-American blonde in front of an American flag holding a smoking .45 automatic and saying in a talk balloon, "You can take my Mac when you pry my cold, dead fingers off the mouse!" The caption shouted: "Refuse to be a victim! Fight back for the Mac!"

It was thrilling. Power Computing offered a vision for the Macintosh in the 1990s and a road map for Apple to follow, if it dared. And Power Computing wasn't alone. Other clone makers were signing licenses with Apple and building their own Mac knockoffs. It was an interesting, if motley group, including Umax, with it refugees from monitor maker Radius, DayStar Digital, a small workstation builder, Japanese giant Pioneer Electronics Corp., which proposed to sell to the Japanese market, and two American giants, Motorola and IBM.

The last were particularly interesting. Motorola, bigger than Apple, was not only the supplier of the microprocessor for Macs, but also one of the world's best manufacturers of consumer electronics. Thus, it seemed to have Apple bracketed. IBM, meanwhile, under a historic turnaround by Lou Gerstner, had more than regained its old glory. It remained the leading computer maker, but had also become a very aggressive marketer. With these two behemoths on one side, and a plucky start-up like Power Computing and a price bomber like Umax on the other, it wasn't hard to look out a few years into the future and see a sluggish Apple slowly being crushed between them.

But in the meantime, the cloners served Amelio's purpose nicely. During the hard times of 1996, the Macintosh line was in very great danger of simply being buried in all the gossip and speculation about Apple's financial predicament. If Apple really was in danger of dying, what difference did it make how good its new products were? No sane person ever bought an orphan computer. But the clones offered a welcome cognitive dissonance. If the Mac was doomed, why were all these big companies and intriguing start-ups so anxious to build it? Did they know something the rest of the world didn't?

At least for the short term, the Mac clones did what Spindler and Apple's critics had always said they would: raise product visibility, enlarge retail shelf space, open new distribution and marketing channels and ultimately improve market share. They could also (via Motorola and hopefully in time IBM) sell to the corporate world in ways Apple had never been able to duplicate. And they could provide a marketing counterpoint—techie or abrasive or sternly corporate—to Apple's increasingly predictable sleek New Age style.

But in the long term, there was still the question that had scared off Sculley and haunted Spindler. Could Apple still keep up with its copycats? Could it still set the agenda for the market? Was Apple still clever and competent enough to allow the cloners to prospect new territories, then enable Apple to overrun them and consolidate the success?

The thrilling answer came in October. Just six months after Amelio predicted it would take three years for Apple to rise from its woes, the company announced a profit for the final quarter of fiscal 1996. Twenty-five million bucks, 20 cents per share. It wasn't much for an $11 billion company, but it was nevertheless a bombshell. A year before, Apple had enjoyed a $60.1 million profit on revenues of 48 cents per share, but everything in between had been a nightmare. Even with this little profit, losses for fiscal 1996 were $816 million ($6.59 per share), compared to a profit of $424 million ($3.45 per share) in fiscal 1995.

These losses had taken their toll in customer loyalty. In the fourth quarter of 1995, Apple had enjoyed a run rate of a $12 billion company. Now, at the end of the fourth quarter of fiscal 1996, Apple had shrunk to just a $9.3 billion company. There weren't enough clones in the world yet to make up that difference in lost market share. Commensurately, during the fourth quarter, Apple shipped only 932,000 units, down 26 percent from the year before.

Nevertheless, shipments were up 11 percent from the third quarter. And there was no denying the reality that Apple was again profitable. It seemed a miracle. On the day of the announcement, company stock jumped $2.25 to $28, the highest it had been in many months. As for employees, the good news meant that layoffs would now be stopped at just 1,500, instead of the planned 2,800.

Two days later, Apple followed with a counterpunch. It slashed prices on its Performa family, top to bottom. The high-end 6400/200 with 200 MHz speed, 16 megabytes of RAM and a 2.4 gigabyte hard drive had been announced just two months before at $2,799. It was now reduced in price by 20 percent to just $2,199. So it went down the line. But the capper was the introduction at the high end of a 6400/200 model with built-in video editing circuitry for $2,699—proof that Apple understood who its premium customers were—and better yet, a new low-end machine, the Performa 5360 (160 MHz, 16 Mb RAM, 1.6 Gb disk) for just $1,499.

This last was a real breakthrough: now, for probably the first time in its history, Apple had the lowest-price computer for its power on the market. The news was like a blast of trumpets. Apple, which had spent twenty years charging its customers a premium for the right to use the products of the company's genius, was now going to compete on price! It was if the aging heavyweight champ, knocked around for ten rounds and left for dead, had somehow risen off the canvas just before the bell and landed a roundhouse on the stunned opponent. For a company that just a few months before had been given up as doomed, Apple now looked like the supplier to beat during the Christmas buying season.

The hero of the hour was Gilbert Frank Amelio. The retro chip guy with the shy manner and will of iron seemed godlike. Two months before, at the Mac Expo in Boston, one unabashed fan had even run up after his keynote speech and planted a kiss on him. Millions of shareholders were ready to do the same. Amelio, for his part, looked proudly presidential when he added to the financial goodies by saying he "remained confident" that Apple would achieve sustainable profitability by the end of the second quarter of fiscal 1997. The reason, he said proudly, was that under his watch Apple had accomplished two critical goals: increasing revenues from the third quarter and strengthening the company's financial position.

It seemed that Gil Amelio had fixed everything.

9.13 *VANITAS*

But not everyone was so enraptured by Amelio's apparently successful turnaround of Apple.

Some senior managers at Apple had privately complained, almost from the moment of Amelio's arrival, that they were being left in the dark about company plans and strategies, and that there were no clear lines to Amelio. Others darkly noted that Amelio's technique for team building among his senior managers—bringing them together at places like the Claremont Hotel in Berkeley to create task forces and meet with management training specialists—was just more of the same old "talk about it endlessly, then do nothing" Apple style.

Again, the rank-and-file Apple employees were much more enthusiastic. They loved it when Amelio said, "I'll never be as charismatic as Steve Jobs. And Steve will never be as accomplished an operations manager as I am." Finally, Apple seemed oriented toward results, not good intentions.

Soon after Amelio arrived, one enthusiastic employee told the *San Jose Mercury News*, "People [are] letting him know, 'We are with you.' He has a big magnifying glass and is going around to everyone and looking at everything. We are not going to get the knee-jerk stuff we were expecting. We are going to get a cure."

In the first few months, Amelio reinforced his image of a decisive, competent, employee-oriented CEO by regularly trying to get out and meet employees. He held regular meetings with employees, with his leadership team and one-on-one encounters throughout the company. It was hard work for a man who was obviously awkward and shy, but Amelio seemed intent upon being a people-oriented boss. But tellingly, what proved to be his most effective communications tool with employees was electronic mail. Once employees learned that he was diligent about answering these missives, Amelio was quickly flooded with mountains of crisp complaints, rambling monologues and thoughtful suggestions.

All that changed with the arrival of George Scalise. Scalise had been known at National as Amelio's hatchet man, but like most such reputations, the relationship was much more complex. Scalise was Amelio's alter ego and, at times, his demonic. Extravagant (he once wore a cravat to a "casual dress" meeting at Apple) and voluble, Scalise enjoyed contact with people, whether it was to praise or kick butt. He could be what Gil was not: smooth, glib and fearless in public. Scalise could shout and pound his fist so that Amelio would never have to raise his voice or his hand.

Needless to say, before Scalise had been at Apple more than a few weeks, Amelio began to retreat from the public life at Apple. National Semi folks had called this the good cop/bad cop routine, but it was closer to Mr. Inside/Mr. Outside. As Scalise would later describe it: "I spent a lot of time [at Apple] meeting and talking to people. Gil would spend a lot of time in his office, thinking."

This was not a good sign. And it became even less so once the world realized what Gil Amelio was thinking about.

Behind the hosannahs about Amelio's performance as Apple CEO there had always been an undercurrent of resentment and concern. For one thing, there was his supposedly sterling record at National Semiconductor. Charlie Sporck would later say, "His main drive is an ego drive and money. His biggest legacy [at National] was a corporate jet and that book." But Sporck was bitter. Yet Amelio's reply—"That's bullshit. If you look at that place when I left compared to when I got there, it's obvious. There's not a person on Wall Street who would say I didn't do a terrific job"—had the odd ring of a man judging himself by others' perceptions.

Sporck wasn't alone. Others from the National days noted the difference between what they saw at National under Amelio and the legend he had subsequently created for himself. As National's CEO, Amelio—*Doctor* Amelio, he insisted on being called, even though his doctorate was in solid-state physics—had been a corporate climber who talked a good management game, but who rarely lived up to his own bromides. He was insulated, intensely self-conscious, and on the business side emphasized short-term gains over long-term market power . . . in all, a man who some might say was more interested in his own career success than in the company he worked for, or the people who worked for him.

Narcissism is no stranger to Silicon Valley, and certainly not to Apple Computer. But Amelio was something different. Most of the great egos of high tech are flamboyant, preening or loquacious. Amelio was none of these things. He was the old-fashioned chip nerd who fooled the new cybernerds. And beneath the avuncular, slightly amusing exterior—the moussed hair, the monogrammed custom shirts, the pimpy Cadillac Seville, the uneasy air of a man who thinks he looks great but isn't quite sure—was the soul of a man of enormous ambition.

One member of Apple's executive offices, who watched three CEOs come and go, when asked about why such apparently competent and successful men were so distorted by the presidency of Apple, replied in Latin: "*Vanitas!* The office of CEO is a strange animal anywhere, but at Apple it is especially bizarre. All the publicity, the attention, the fame. If you don't know where you are vulnerable, the office will show you very quickly."

Gilbert Amelio had been a painfully shy child, the son of a contractor, who had found success in the perfectible world of science and mathematics. Through sheer force of will he made himself into a top student. By forcing himself to join social groups and clubs as well as learn public speaking, Amelio made himself into a successful, if uncomfortable, member of the outside world. Like many self-created success stories, Amelio was obsessed with success; it defined his value as a person. As he would recall in his book: "I needed to be a credit to my family, my university and my science."

He was. He earned his undergraduate degree from the Georgia Institute of Technology, then a master's in physics and a PhD in solid-state physics. He was a good enough scientist to land his first job at AT&T Bell Labs in New Jersey, where the transistor had been invented, and the Lourdes of commercial electronics research. He felt unworthy and terrified to be there, but his fear of failure was even greater—"Anything short of success would have been humiliating" he would write. Ultimately, he earned sixteen patents while at Bell.

Crushing self-doubt often is a paradoxical partner with grand illusions. Thus, the frightened young man who joined Bell Labs became, at age thirty-five, an angry veteran annoyed that he hadn't won—and likely never would win—a Nobel Prize. So he decided to play his hand for greatness on a different table: management. If young nineteenth-century romantics threw away their lives, often literally, after reading Goethe's *Young Werther*, engineers and physicists in the 1960s and 1970s often decided to abandon their careers and pursue corporate management after reading Peter Drucker. In Drucker's works they found a mix of scientific reasoning and heroic entrepreneurial independence that appealed to ambitious young men with advanced degrees, like Gil Amelio, stuck in prestigious but unrewarding laboratory jobs.

Fairchild, Rockwell, National Semiconductor. Amelio had risen to the top with a string of successes. Even landing the Apple job was a clever piece of maneuvering. Unlike Graziano, Amelio had waited to hear the cries of distress before he offered to save the day. Now he had the glittering prize: the most visible corporate presidency in the world, the friendship of the famous, the press hanging on his every word.

So overwhelming was his success that Amelio even maintained the pretense of humility for several months. The man of the people, the new Apple CEO who was honest enough to admit that he knew less about technology than his employees. Who joked about being such a square.

But he couldn't maintain the guise for long. Scalise's arrival signaled as well the debut of the real Gil Amelio. He began to be much less accessible not just to managers but to the rank and file. Apple's executive offices became much less accessible too. Those who did get access to Amelio's office quickly noticed a growing shrine to one man's success. There was the framed *Forbes* cover of himself and the embarrassing tendency to hand reporters copies of glowing articles about himself. As Mark Leibovitch of the *Mercury News* recounted about one such occasion, Amelio, in the middle of an interview, handed him a printout of a *Hot Wired* article in which the headline "Amelio Cheered" was highlighted in yellow.

Even Amelio's old friends noticed the change. The old Gil had been a hail-fellow-well-met kind of guy, down to earth, comfortable in his traditional, conservative lifestyle. A jokester. And a man proud to be a scientist. One lifelong, but increasingly estranged friend, Bill Sweet, remembered the two of them taking their kids and a carload of guns up into the mountains and having fun shooting at everything in sight. The "New Gil," as Sweet described him, would never do such a thing. "He would worry about having to read about the CEO of Apple shooting up pinecones in the *San Jose Mercury News.*" When it was discovered that Amelio had bought for his father a replica of George Patton's pearl-handled revolvers, Amelio took great pains to announce on the record that he himself did not own a handgun.

As the year ended, there was a growing disquiet within Apple that instead of a savior, Apple had managed to find yet another martinet. And this time one without any style or charisma. The more cynical suggested that the unexpectedly profitable quarter had merely been a puff job to give Amelio the maximum personal bonus—and a rumor that grew teeth in December, when an SEC filing showed that Apple had awarded him a total of $3 million, just for the interval between February and September. A $655,061 salary and a $2.3 million bonus. Amelio, who already had a house in Silicon Valley, also received from Apple a $5 million loan and, most bizarre of all, the company leased his airplane at $1,695 per hour, for a total of $108,000. The fuddy-duddy hardware store clerk was beginning to look more and more like Cash McCall.

These numbers might have provoked more of a scandal had they not already been ameliorated by the profitable quarter. But what residual resentment remained was quickly forgotten in an even bigger, brasher move by Amelio. Having convinced himself that he had already saved Apple, Amelio did the one thing that would have put a stab of fear in the hearts of his two predecessors:

He brought back Steve Jobs.

9.14 Prodigal

In December 1996, Steve Jobs had been out of Apple Computer for more than eleven years. He was no longer the *enfant terrible* of high tech. Now, at forty-one, he was still a striking figure, with an affection for European suits with waist-length jackets and shirts with banded collars—a kind of hybrid between a Nehru jacket and executive power suit in *Blade Runner.* But though he retained his old panache, he was not a young man anymore. His wire-rimmed glasses no longer reflected rebellion but astigmatism. His straight hair was still long and black, but it had noticeably thinned in the front. And his familiar hawklike profile had softened slightly, giving him the look less of a raptor than a Cheyenne chief.

Jobs's decade in the wilderness had, after a rocky start, given him considerable wealth, but not fame. When he had stormed off to get his revenge on Apple by founding NeXT, the entire world watched. It waited for NeXT to bring out its own computer and for the battle with Apple to begin.

But the NeXT computer was a dud. Not that it wasn't a good machine. In fact, it was beautiful, smoky black and sleek, easily the best-looking computer ever built. It had the usual Jobs quirky touch: in this case an optical memory system that was quickly abandoned. But, beginning in 1989, it also had a new object-oriented operating system, NeXTStep, that was even more magnificent than the box. It had a user interface, OpenStep, that was light-years ahead of both the Mac OS and, still in the distant future, Microsoft Windows. With the NeXT computer and operating system, Jobs had proven once again that he was the greatest design team leader in the history of electronics.

But Jobs was trapped in his own infinite loop. The NeXT computer, like the Macintosh before it, failed because a good design was no longer enough. NeXT didn't have the size or distribution to drive the new computer into the marketplace. In a world where MS-DOS was dominant, where Jobs's own Mac OS covered all the lower fringes and Unix-based computers held the high end, there just wasn't any room for a fourth operating system. Especially one being promulgated by a little company, no matter how famous the guy running it. Had Jobs cut a deal with Apple, or gone into the IBM clone business, his high profile and brilliant design sense might have made NeXT into a giant. He might even have beat Gates at his own game by coming out with a DOS-based NeXTStep that would have been five years ahead of Windows 95. But Jobs was already showing his age. Whereas the real visionaries in personal computing now recognized that the future lay in software and microprocessors, Jobs, like an old factory supervisor, still believed success lay in Big Iron.

Meanwhile even as Jobs was embroiled in the Apple/NeXT soap opera, he was still casting about for other business opportunities. So distracting was the bigger story that Jobs's purchase in February 1986 of a little computer graphics company called Pixar Inc. was barely noticed by the public. Computer graphics in those days was still more a wish than a reality, and George Lucas's founding of the firm to help create movie special effects was viewed as a secondary effort, a way to park some of his *Star Wars* money, to his much more famous Industrial Light & Magic.

Pixar slipped out of the public's imagination almost from the day Jobs bought it. Unfortunately, NeXT soon did as well. Once it became apparent that NeXT had not produced the home run everybody expected from Jobs, that the company's orders were a fraction of predictions, the world turned away. NeXT seemed to be the corporate crypt for Steve Jobs's career.

What attention the company did get was almost uniformly negative. Gossips shook their heads to stories about Jobs yelling at caterers and contractors, belittling employees, making arbitrary decisions and acting like the same old jerk they loved to hate. And they clucked when rumors leaked out about the pampered but degraded NeXT employees slowly going mad in such an autocratic, dysfunctional work environment. It served them right for going to work for a lunatic megalomaniac. As for Jobs, let him stay forever in his self-created, elegantly appointed purgatory.

As he sensed impending failure, the darker sides of Steve Jobs began to dominate his personality. When *Upside* magazine published a devastating story about NeXT, its editor, Rich Karlgaard, received a phone call at home one Saturday morning what years later he still recalled as one of the strangest he'd ever experienced. "It was Steve Jobs. He started by telling me how he was going to destroy me. Then how much he liked me. Then what a worthless magazine *Upside* was. Then how he was my friend. And sometimes he would say both things *in the same sentence*. It was eerie."

By 1992, NeXT had fallen down the Silicon Valley memory hole. If its name was mentioned, it was usually accompanied by a knowing snicker. Jobs had gotten his comeuppance. And when, in February 1993, NeXT announced that it was getting out of the hardware business and laying off 500 employees—having burned up an estimated $200 million in the process, the general reaction was: Are they still in business?

But great software never really dies. It just waits for a good application. And great operating systems are like gold—they never really lose their value. Even as NeXT was pulling out of hardware, it was licensing NeXTStep to Sun and to Hewlett-Packard, two firms fighting one another for control of the workstation market. Thus, while most of the world forgot it, NeXT found itself in the unlikely position of having the only personal computer operating system that was fully compatible with five of the world's major computer architectures: Hewlett-Packard's PA-RISC, Sun's SPARCstation, Intel-based PCs, NeXT's own computer . . . and Macintosh.

Meanwhile, with NeXT running itself, Jobs began to spend more time in the East Bay with his other little company, Pixar. Without anyone really noticing, mainly because its products appeared under the Disney label, Pixar had become the world's leading computer animator. Though the image was one of computers doing all the work, the reality of a Pixar film was experienced illustrators working tens of thousands of hours designing images on banks of powerful graphic workstations to produce a few minutes of film stock. The results, awkward at first, grew increasingly beautiful and Pixar began to pick up Oscars and critical raves.

As Jobs was neither an animator nor a programmer, there was little he could do in the actual production process—to the relief of the folks at Pixar, who knew all too well Jobs's reputation. Thus, Steve was reduced to doing what he did best: cheerleading, making connections, creating visions, motivating, building team confidence. It was an almost perfect setting for Jobs. He could lead without managing, direct without running. He excelled.

The result was *Toy Story*, one of the most popular feature cartoons ever, a landmark in the history of animation as the first full-length computer-generated movie—not to mention a terrific story with memorable characters. This time the world wanted to look past the Disney label—and Pixar was happy to oblige, especially since it was ramping up toward its initial public offering of stock.

The happy glow remained all through Pixar's quiet period before the IPO. The company didn't have to promote itself. Its advertisements were on every junior sheet, pair of underpants, lunch box and Halloween costume in the world. And so, in January 1995, Pixar stock opened on its first day in the teens and, buoyed by a strong market, quickly rose to $49 per share. It soon slumped a little as the irrational exuberance calmed to a pragmatic appraisal. Nevertheless, for a few days in January, Steve Jobs was officially a billionaire. Though his net worth wilted with the stock price, the mantle remained. From now on, Jobs would be listed in the Billionaire's Valhalla with his enemy/friend Bill Gates and his new best buddy, Larry Ellison of Oracle.

Interviewed on PBS's *Charlie Rose*, a professorial Jobs would profess to "not really following the computer industry much anymore," and claim that he was dedicated now to the future endeavors of Pixar. It was a convincing act for people in Manhattan, New York, and Manhattan, Kansas. But few believed it in Silicon Valley. They knew that Steve Jobs would burn forever for vindication at Apple. A more accurate clue to how little the Apple wound had healed could be found in a revealing interview with *Wired* magazine soon after the Pixar IPO. There, asked about Apple, Jobs testily replied, "Microsoft dominates . . . That's over. Apple lost."

Meanwhile, though he had all but fallen off the technology world's radar screen, Jobs had never fully left the public eye. Every few years his name popped up—as on the list of key contributors to the Clinton campaign who had spent a night in the Lincoln bedroom. When *Time* ran a list of the 100 most important baby boomers, there he was in the top ten, with the likes of

Steven Spielberg and Gates. When the same magazine ran a cover story on the new young tycoons of Silicon Valley, there was the obligatory sidebar on the most famous young tycoon of them all, telling how he had become a more introspective person, less flamboyant, and best of all, how he had learned to become a loving father to Lisa, now a bright teenager. Neighbors often saw them walking or Rollerblading together. Those who worshipped Jobs during his Apple days had always had to admit that his denial of paternity damned him. Now, even those who despised Jobs had to admit that this quiet rapprochement with his daughter redeemed him.

Even megalomaniacs grow older and wiser. Neighbors reported that Jobs still regularly reamed out caterers and other hired help. But he had mellowed. The suicidal brashness that had destroyed him at Apple in 1985 had been replaced by a more careful, thoughtful style. He was a husband now, having married in 1990. The courtship was classic Steve Jobs: romantic, impulsive and unique. While waiting to give a lecture at the Stanford Business School, he struck up a conversation with the student sitting next to him. By the time he took the stage he had her phone number—but later, rushing to his car to get to a business dinner, he stopped in his tracks: "I was in the parking lot, with the key in the car, and I thought to myself, 'If this is my last night on Earth, would I rather spend it at a business meeting or with this woman?' I ran across the parking lot, asked her if she'd have dinner with me. She said yes, we walked into town and we've been together since."

Steve and Laurene Jobs had two children (Lisa also lived with them until leaving for college), with a third child born in late 1998. He had fully settled into a domestic life as a burgher of Palo Alto, restoring a 1930's house, and this new domesticity seemed to improve his management style. Tom Carlisle, who had left Apple with Jobs and had followed him to NeXT, then Pixar, would say, "At Apple [Jobs] had a difficult time hearing what he didn't want to hear. Now, he's very much more open. He'll say, 'Don't tell me what I want to hear. Tell me the truth.' In reality, it's not always so clear-cut. But he's trying so much harder."

Still, no one believed that the New Steve Jobs was profoundly different than the Old one. So only a naive fool or someone utterly convinced of his own abilities *and* career invulnerability would embrace the most dangerous viper of all to his breast. Gil Amelio was a little of the former and a lot of the latter. He believed his recent success in turning around Apple, combined with superior management skills and Jobs's reputation, would protect him. And if all else failed, there was always the board of directors, especially Markkula, who had an understandable fear of the return of the prodigal son.

But Amelio had one very strong reason for inviting Jobs back: he needed NeXT.

With the collapse of Copland, Amelio faced a serious problem. The Mac OS was getting archaic. And though it still had an almost religious appeal to everyday users, in the cutting-edge applications, Apple's bread-and-butter graphics business, the OS's lack of multitasking and multithreading—the ability to run several different programs, or several different operations within one program, at the same time—was slowly driving long-standing customers into the arms of Microsoft. With the rise of the Internet, with millions of people running Java applets or constructing their own Web pages, this flaw in the Mac OS would soon become pandemic to Apple's entire customer base.

So the company needed a new operating system, fast. The lesson of Copland was that Apple couldn't do the job itself. So that meant licensing. A survey of the market showed there were four candidates: Windows NT, Sun Solaris, Be Inc. and NeXT. Amelio talked with Gates about moving the NT onto the Mac while keeping the Mac user interface—a combination that would give the Mac access to the whole world of Windows. Gates, seeing before him the chance of a complete monopoly of the desktop, was, needless to say, enthusiastic. But Ellen Hancock argued against it, saying that despite Gates's claims to the contrary, such a combination would be extremely difficult to pull off. She, instead, fought for Solaris, a solid, Unix-based operating system with a weak user interface. In the end Amelio turned against both, the former because of the complexity of the task, and the latter because Apple would have to create a whole new interface. With that decision, Apple now turned its full attention to the other two candidates. And with that decision, Apple went back into the irony business, because Be Inc. was founded and run by Jean-Louis Gassée and NeXT by Steve Jobs.

Be Inc. was the most likely candidate. Its Be OS not only worked on the PowerPC chip but had all the advanced features Apple desired. Scalise made the initial approach to Gassée in June 1996. By autumn, the negotiations were taking place in earnest.

But right from the start there was one very big obstacle to a deal. Gassée was greedy. He understood Apple's predicament as well as anyone—after all, he had helped create it. Now he was convinced he had his old company over a barrel. He was almost right. Still, Gassée overplayed his hand. He asked for $400 million for the rights to the Be OS—throwing in the added incentive of his rejoining Apple to run the software program. Apple, stunned (it had concluded that Be's market value was just $50 million), offered $120 million, then slowly lifted the offer to $200 million. But Be, believing it had time on its side, dragged its feet. Bad poker. While Gassée thought he was forcing a desperate Apple to the table, he was instead driving the company into the arms of another. Apple was indeed desperate for a solution, but at that price it was willing to even consider the unimaginable.

Though in many ways the Be OS was a superior, and more modern, operating system, NeXTStep did have its advantages. For one thing, it was more mature; there were hundreds of developers out there who knew how to write for it. There was also that nice connection with Sun and HP, as well as the crossover to the PC world. It would be harder to port NeXTStep over to the Mac OS world, but once you did, a whole universe opened up in the area of enterprise—that is, large-scale corporate network computing. Apple had never been good in that sphere and, seeing the success of companies such as Oracle, coveted some of that business. Finally, one other appealing thing about NeXT was its founder. As Gassée said later: "I think putting [Steve Jobs] back into the company subliminally has a value we should not underestimate."

But the presence of Jobs posed a problem. *He* would never consider approaching Apple. And who at Apple would have the guts to suggest contacting Steven Jobs? Given all the historical bad blood, how could contact between NeXT and Apple be accomplished?

The answer was through a little skulduggery. The people at NeXT were convinced that they held the solution to Apple's software dilemma, if only Apple would listen. The word was out about the Be Inc. negotiations, so time was running short. The move was ultimately initiated by John Landwehr, a product manager, who convinced Mitch Mandich, NeXT's vice president for sales, that it was now or never to approach Apple. But Mandich, reacting like most people at NeXT when discussing fraternization with a blood enemy, decided not to make the call himself, but directed a marketing manager to do it. That manager passed the buck too, to Garrett Rice, NeXT's channel marketing manager.

Rice at last made the call to an engineering contact at Apple—who in turn passed him upward to Hancock, Apple's chief technical officer. This was the week of November 18. By the 26, representatives of both companies met via a conference call. "They wanted to come down here right away and see what we had," said Landwehr. The next day, November 27, the Apple contingent arrived at NeXT. Steve Jobs, busy at Pixar, was told nothing.

The meeting went well. Then, in the middle of it, by eerie coincidence, a call came in from Jobs on some minor business matter. It was only then that he learned what was going on.

He wasn't angry. On the contrary, he told the NeXT wheeler-dealers that he too had been thinking about Apple lately, and had even placed a call to an Apple executive he knew.

After that, things moved quickly. The two teams, now sometimes numbering thirty people, met almost every day, usually on neutral ground, such as at the offices of the Valley law firm of Wilson, Sonsini, Goodrich & Rosati or at the Garden Court Hotel across from the Stanford Shopping Center. There were some tough technical questions to be addressed; in particular, could NeXTStep, which had shown itself well suited for high-end video and graphic applications, also run the prosaic little programs that were the province of most everyday Mac users? The answer seemed to be yes.

Meanwhile, other parts of Apple raced around doing due diligence on the prospective new business partner. With the kind of care for superfluous details that bureaucracies are gifted at, Apple called nearly everyone who had ever worked for or with NeXT: developers, contractors, current and former customers, past and present employees, trying to find that one fatal bit of evidence that would nix the deal. "They gave us a very thorough scrubbing," said Jobs. But Apple never found that fatal flaw—like all bureaucracies, it devoted massive amounts of time and resources in pursuit of minutiae, while no one seemed to ask the one simple big question: Do we really want Steve Jobs back inside Apple?

The deal came down to a series of CEO blind dates. Jobs and Amelio had met before, first at that strange encounter at National Semi, then at a party held soon after Amelio took over Apple. Now it was time for them to meet more formally. At the first meeting, Jobs performed one of his classic product demonstrations, this time showing how NeXTStep could play five movie clips at the same time. Even for a computer veteran, this was an impressive demonstration. For a neophyte like Amelio, it was enthralling. Jobs too came away in a good mood about Gil Amelio. "He seems like an awfully nice guy," Jobs said. Soon, Amelio was visiting Jobs at his home. It wasn't a Manhattan aerie this time, but then again, Amelio was a more anxious buyer. Amelio would later say, scarily, that his relationship with Jobs was "like a flower blossoming."

Meanwhile, the financial negotiations continued to pick up speed. Curious to see them up close, Jobs paid a visit to one of the meetings. It just happened to be taking place at Apple itself. And thus, for the first time in many years, Steve Jobs walked on the grounds of the company he had founded. It was a historic moment noticed by only a few people. And it must have been disorienting, if satisfying, for Jobs. The Apple he visited, with its giant twin-towered headquarters and multi-acre research center, was only a block, but also a lifetime, away from the cluster of little buildings he had left behind in 1985. The company that had obsessed him for so many years, the people who had betrayed him, the maverick corporate culture that he had created through the force of his personality—all were gone now, or nearly so. He was the Rip van Winkle of the computer age, and now returning after a long absence to his old village, he found few recognizable touchstones beyond the logo on the wall. To those who saw him that day, Jobs was a myth unexpectedly made incarnate, a Founding Father suddenly emerging out of the misty past.

He was back.

It wasn't long before Be Inc. got wind of the negotiations with NeXT. Realizing that their bluff had been called, Gassée and his team rushed back to Apple with a final counteroffer: $210 million. But it was too late. In its greed, Be had left the door wide open, and now the NeXT deal had taken on enough momentum to be unstoppable. "*C'est la vie*," said Gassée, showing why he would never be a true Silicon Valley player. He would later rationalize that he had been lucky to have been spared from "hijacking the *Titanic*."

The week before Christmas 1996, the figures were finalized: $425 million, not just for NeXTStep but for the outright purchase of NeXT Inc. Apple would pay $350 million for NeXT, plus assume that company's $50 million debt.

It was an amazing amount—with the added coincidence that this was the same amount that Be Inc. had first proposed and Apple found outrageous. The difference, apparently, was that Apple was not just licensing the NeXT OS but buying the whole company.

But that too raised a disturbing question: What exactly was Apple getting for all that money? Well, there was the NeXTStep operating system. It had the potential to take the Mac into the wide world of multimedia, enterprise computing and Internet development. But it would not be an easy hybridization: at best, it would still take the Mac its usual thirty seconds to boot up (compared with five seconds with Be OS) and even then the question of its being able to run the basic Mac software library wasn't fully resolved. Then there was the user interface for NeXTStep, called OpenStep. It was impressive, but largely redundant to the much more popular Mac icons.

Perhaps it was the company itself. But, a decade old, and with only $50 million in annual revenues and 350 employees, NeXT was hardly an up-and-comer. In fact, it was in bad shape. Despite hundreds of millions of dollars spent, and the support of IBM, HP and Sun, NeXTStep had never caught on with the mass market. By early 1996, the firm was running out of capital to invest in new product enhancements to make NeXTStep more efficient on the Internet. The situation became sufficiently desperate that as late as August, NeXT was shopping NeXTStep around to competitors.

Thus, to the objective observer, NeXT seemed less a hot company with an even hotter product than an aging firm on its last legs looking for a Sugar Daddy to save it. In that light, one could only wonder why Apple didn't wait and force NeXT's hand—or at least bargain as hard as it did with Be Inc.

Jobs had always enjoyed a lot of fans, but he never had as many enthusiastic true believers as he did that day among the NeXT employees. Like the good entrepreneur he was, Jobs had distributed most of NeXT's stock to its employees and now, after years of frustration and hard work, they were about to get the payoff of their lives. Many were now millionaires. It was one promise that Steve Jobs more than fulfilled.

9.15 ODYSSEUS

The news of Steve Jobs's return to Apple rocked the high-tech world. The Beatles were never all going to get back together, but at least one great boomer era estrangement was now about to be mended.

Jobs tried to dampen the cheering, reminding the world that "my job is not savior . . . I'm just a part-time consultant," but no one believed him. Damnit, his job *was* savior. Jobs knew it too, which was why he smiled when he said, "Gil asked me to give him some advice . . . I'd love to help Apple." All Jobs's pretending not to care, of acting indifferent to the company's fate through the years, was shown to be the defensive, hurt lie it had always been. It was great to be back, to know that your predictions about the company without you had all come true. To return even richer than when you left. To still be a household word when all of your enemies were now forgotten. To save Apple as the great third act of your young life.

At the news of the NeXT purchase and Jobs's return, Gil Amelio received a call from Bill Gates. "Do you really think Steve Jobs has got anything there?" Amelio recalled Gates asking. "I know his technology, it's nothing but warmed-over UNIX, and you'll never be able to make it work on your machines." Then Gates grew even angrier: "Don't you understand that Steve doesn't know anything about technology? He's just a supersalesman. I can't believe you're making such a stupid decision."

The rant went on for twenty minutes. "Damnit, Gil," Gates said at one point, "Steve is a pure salesman, that's all he is. He's not an engineer, he doesn't know anything about engineering, and 99 percent of everything he thinks and says is wrong. What the hell are you buying that garbage for?"

Jobs's return was the talk of Silicon Valley through the Christmas holidays. It was such big news that it buried the other big Apple story taking place on store shelves throughout the United States and Europe: despite the profitable quarter, the new pricing policy, the return of the founder, Apple computers weren't selling. A clue that things weren't as good as portrayed could have been found as far back as the beginning of September. Then, *The Wall Street Journal* had kicked off its second-section front, the most widely read newspaper page in high tech, with the headline "Companies Dump Macs as Loyalists Lose Faith." The story went on to recount Apple Computer's worst nightmare, that one by one its big corporate accounts were giving up supporting Macs and surrendering to the comfortable hegemony of Windows. The examples were devastating: 9,000 Macs dropped at Dow Chemical, 3,000 at Northern Telecom Ltd., 7,000 at Eli Lilly & Co., 2,000 at Ernst & Young and on and on. That was just the tip of the iceberg, because for every one of these office Macs dropped, there was at least one compatible home machine that would likely soon be dropped too, as well as thousands of Macs at suppliers and distributors that had been bought to be compatible with the giant corporate client.

It wasn't just the big boys either; the abandonment of Macs was also occurring at those key pivot points and opinion leaders, where the number of computers lost was minuscule, but the influence was enormous. Thus, when Kleiner Perkins, the world's hottest venture capital firm, decided to convert from Apple to Windows, the message to every entrepreneur in Silicon Valley was: Apple is dead; Windows is the future.

The only thing scarier than these facts were the quotes from people who'd made those decisions. All had once been Mac fanatics. They had suffered risks to their careers, censure and jeers from their peers in their lonely missionary work for the Mac. They had fought to bring the maverick Macs into giant companies where the inertia and conservatism had naturally led top management to prefer IBM clones. They had finally won their case . . . and now years later, they seemed to speak for millions of weary, heartbroken Mac owners when they said they were tired of fighting for a company that had been too busy in the last few years dealing with its own arrogance, mismanagement and bureaucratic incompetence to fight for them. Their words were devastating:

"Buy a PC. They're cheaper. And the Mac is going to disappear. . . . It's just not worth fighting for anymore," said Jeffrey Bade of Dow Chemical.

"Once [Windows] NT came out, that was it. . . . I used to tell my bosses that the Mac was like a Ferrari and the PC was a Model T. . . . Now it's the reverse," said Seth Gersch of Montgomery Securities.

"I used to say that it didn't matter if there were more programs available for Windows machines," explained computer consultant Darren Starr, "as long as there was at least one of what I needed running on the Mac. But now there isn't even that."

Throughout the world, not just in great clusters at big corporations and other institutions, but one by one in dens and family rooms, Mac users were making the painful decision to divorce their Mac mate. It was typically an awful experience, because the Macintosh was not just another appliance. It wasn't even the equivalent, say, of a good reliable toaster that had been a trusty tool for twenty years. It was deeper than that. At some point in every Mac owner's career, you made the decision to turn your back on the main parade of the personal computer revolution and follow another, smaller, quirkier group heading off in a different direction. And the cost of making that decision was remeasured almost every day. The seemingly endless stream of Windows users who mocked your use of a "dying" architecture, the long waits for Mac versions of Windows-based applications that sometimes never appeared, the vast mass of exciting new low-cost hardware, peripherals and software for Wintel machines and the volumes of stories about the success of Microsoft and the matching counterpoint stories of the growing disaster at Apple. The hundreds of magazines devoted to the Wintel world, the thousands of creative companies developing new products for it. The millions of people in users groups. The repair shops. The consultants. The aisles and aisles of Windows products at the computer store, compared to the single pathetic, half-empty shelf of Mac products.

Worst of all was the gnawing sense, growing by the year, that you had made the wrong choice, and that history was passing you by.

And then one day, the loyalty, the dissonance and the thousands of hours of experience with the Mac were no longer enough. It often happened the day your old Mac broke down or became too obviously underpowered and you decided it was time to buy a new computer. Then you realized that while it was painful to stay with Apple, it would be madness to re-up with it. Then, though you hated it, though it made you feel like a Quisling, a traitor to your youth and your beliefs, you held your nose and bought a Wintel computer. And after it was over, and you sat there with your new Micron Millennium or Toshiba Satellite Pro, you had the satisfaction of smugly pronouncing to your friends that the Windows 95 interface was "crap" compared to the Mac OS . . . while secretly inside feeling relieved that it was all over and that you would never have to depend upon Apple again.

9.16 Denial

It wasn't just among key customers where Apple's cracks began to show in the autumn and winter of 1996. Inside the company there were warning signs as well. In his supreme self-confidence about his management skills, Gil Amelio convinced himself that he really had turned Apple around. An engineer at heart, he knew he had put in place the right systems and that those systems in turn guaranteed that a structural change was now occurring in Apple. It was already, Amelio was certain, a different company.

But he was wrong, fatally so. The systems approach to high-tech management works only if you already have changed the hearts and minds of the people involved. Only then can you use reorganizations, new communications networks and new command and control systems to bring out the best of the staff, clear away bureaucratic roadblocks and streamline and supercharge operations.

Amelio's techniques had largely worked at National Semi because the company he inherited was merely exhausted from fighting the Japanese and frustrated from living under a reactionary, autocratic administration. But the people at National Semiconductor were still "the animals of Silicon Valley," as that ad had once claimed; they were still the tough-minded, hard-charging sumbitches that had taken on everybody from Intel to NEC and lived to tell about it. By opening up the chain of command, clearing away deadwood and establishing a new, more orderly system of communication and measurement, Amelio had allowed the best parts of National to again come to the fore.

But Apple was a different story. Its unique perversity, the greatest legacy of both Jobs and Sculley, was that there was no great gleaming company beneath the tarnish waiting to emerge. The trick was not to let Apple be Apple. It already was, in spades. The trick was to force Apple to become something else, to eradicate those features that Apple thought best about itself—the cleverness, the triumph of image over content, the eminence of philosophy over results—and replace them with those traits, like pragmatism, raw competitiveness and dissatisfaction with anything but results, that many Apple people now considered crass, even evil. This would have taken a great leader, and Gil Amelio was merely a good executive when put in the proper setting.

Even more insidious was the office of the chief executive itself. Steve Jobs had created in the Apple CEO's position a job only he could handle—and even he didn't do it well. Everyone who followed was even less suited to the task. So even as Gil Amelio was working to fix Apple, the Apple CEO position was undoing him.

Amelio never really understood the magnitude of the task before him. If he had, he never would have taken the job. By the autumn of 1996, he had largely revamped Apple's executive team, filling it with the kind of folks who got things done. But there he stopped, convinced that this part of the task was done. He made the mistake of believing the e-mail he got from the rank and file, never realizing that Apple's uniformly brilliant employees were now masters at flimflamming the executive office. They were sabotaging his efforts and reestablishing the old destructive status quo, all while convincing Gil that they had been transformed by his leadership.

A visit to the Infinite Loop campus of Apple early that winter only underlined the stories being whispered around the Valley. Here, in the home of Copland, nearing the end of a year in which the company would lose nearly $900 *million*, nothing seemed to have changed. No one was panicking. On the contrary, there appeared to be ample time to sip lattes, nosh sprouts and throw Frisbees out on the lawn. There was chatter everywhere—Apple people being legendary talkers—but little about the company.

Employees played at Microsoft too, but only because Microsoft was winning; and when they talked it was almost always about Microsoft. Were Gates or Grove running Apple at that moment, there would have been bread and water in the cafeteria, the espresso machines would have been sold off and programmers' heads would have been on poles along the driveway.

But not at Amelio's Apple. It was as if it was 1987 and all was well, not the brink of 1997 and the shadow of death lurking in every corner. It was the Eloi in H. G. Wells's *The Time Machine*—beautiful people gamboling on green lawns, ignoring the fact that Morlocks occasionally appear from underground to drag off some of their numbers for food.

Amidst this surrealistic contentment, the only source of nervous energy in sight was Guy Kawasaki, the prodigal son brought back to help save Mother Apple. But even Kawasaki, who would remain optimistic if the sun went supernova, seemed disoriented. His patented rap about the glories of Apple and the evils of Microsoft contained an unexpected undertone of irony. It was as if he still believed in Bill Gates as the Antichrist, but it was getting tougher and tougher each day to look around him and still believe in his own company as the savior and redeemer of personal computing.

He was interrupted mid-rap by two company managers, who bent his ear for twenty minutes seeking advice on how best to play the politics of getting approval for a project by not really telling top management what they were doing. When Kawasaki got back to the first conversation, he had the look of a man who had returned home to find that nothing had changed, except that his family had become more insincere, backstabbing and incompetent than ever. "This is what it's like here now," he said with a shrug and a touch of sadness. Then he went back to slamming Microsoft.

Chris Braun joined Apple in mid-1996 as an assistant to the director of international marketing. "The first question that I was asked in my interview was 'Are you allergic to dogs?' I said 'No,' which was good because my boss had a German shepherd named Gretyl that followed her everywhere.

"Those I associated with at Apple were some of the most talented, well-traveled and exceptionally intelligent people I have ever been around. There was a lot of stress during those ten months because there were so many reorganizations."

In the end, Braun found himself enlisted in one of the strangest stress-reduction programs Apple ever invented: "Every Friday I would escort an ice-cream deliveryman named Uncle Tommy through four floors of the engineering building. Apparently the idea was to build morale."

In November 1996, at a glitzy Los Angeles press conference, Apple Computer announced a new, and paradoxical, marketing thrust.

With a British firm called Mega Bytes BVI International, Apple planned to create a chain of Mac-based cyber-cafes on the lines of Planet Hollywood and the Hard Rock Cafe. Mega Bytes had already hired the Landmark Entertainment Group to design the eateries, and the first 20,000-square-foot restaurant/Internet surf shop, in L.A., was slated for late 1997. If all went according to plan, future stores would open in San Francisco, New York, London, Paris, Tokyo and Sydney.

The news, meant to thrill the market, instead landed with a nasty thud. What was Apple doing in the restaurant business? Didn't it have enough problems already? And wasn't this just the kind of goofy, tangential activity that Amelio was brought in to stop?

It was a first glimpse that Gil Amelio's Apple Computer was not as clear-headed or as disciplined as the world had been made to think. Nor its judgment in selecting business partners: within a couple of months, Mega Bytes stopped returning phone calls. Nor did it ever make a licensing payment. The project was quietly buried.

9.17 Premonition

On December 17, Gil Amelio allowed ten reporters into Apple headquarters for an informal ninety-minute discussion on the state of the company. There he announced that Apple was on the road to recovery. Nineteen ninety-six, he said, had been phase one of the turnaround, fixing the infrastructural problems in the company. Nineteen ninety-seven, he predicted, would be a year spent overhauling all of the company's product lines. Nineteen ninety-eight would then be phase three. "At that point, I think, we'll be ready to start growing again and maybe even getting some market share back." The reporters had heard this before.

Amelio also mentioned that Pippin, the little consumer CD/ROM player/Internet box for the TV set that many hoped would be Apple's new breakout consumer product, was now dead. Apple had decided not to manufacture the device, but had licensed it to the Japanese company Bandai, which would begin shipping it in March 1997. With that news, Apple essentially admitted that it had failed once again. It had the core of Larry Ellison's $500 Network Computer ready a year before the competition and it had once again failed to follow through.

It didn't go down as well as Gil expected. Desperate, Amelio tried another spin: "There is still enormous sentiment in support of Apple," he argued. "I've had more than one corporate executive tell me that when we have an offering for the purpose of corporate computing . . . they'd be delighted to consider another option." In other words, a maybe on top of a chance of a possibility. Pathetic stuff. And through it all, Amelio nervously twisted his wedding ring and rolled a Styrofoam cup in his hands, like a man sitting on top of a bomb.

It was a bizarre moment. Why call such a gathering at all? One answer is that Amelio already knew what the numbers for the quarter would be, he had already heard the bad news coming from retailers about the disastrous Christmas season—and so now he was trying to do some quick dampening of the expectations raised by the previous quarter's success. But it was already too late for that. He had set the marketplace up for rising expectations with that profitable quarter. Now, no talk of going back to the old three-year plan would be sufficient.

The real answer may have been that Gil Amelio, consciously or not, had a premonition about what was coming and was making one last attempt to tell his own story his own way. In three weeks, unless a miracle happened—and miracles almost never happen in big business—Apple was going to announce quarterly losses of $150 million dollars. This time, especially after the turnaround quarter and his own big bonus, there would be no one to blame but

Amelio himself. That would be ugly enough. But now, the NeXT deal was in the bag. That meant, no matter what his protestations, the return of Steve Jobs. And that spelled doom for the career of Gil Amelio at Apple Computer. Even before the founder arrived, Gil had handed Steve Jobs the fiscal club with which to beat him to death.

9.18 Nadir

The bad financial news arrived on Friday, January 3, 1997, after the close of the market. Analysts had expected a loss, but in the range of $15 million. At ten times that amount, this loss was a slap in the face, a magnitude of error guaranteed to set off cries of fraud and misrepresentation.

It was a long two days that weekend. Was Amelio's reputation sufficient to mitigate the bad news?

The answer was no. As the market opened on Monday, millions of sell orders were already in place. By the end of the day, Monday, January 6, Apple shares had fallen $3.88 to $17.88, a plunge of nearly 20 percent. During that single session, 16.8 million shares were traded—one in every eight outstanding shares of Apple stock—making it the single most active stock that day on Nasdaq. Even Jobs couldn't escape the blast: his 1.5 million shares of Apple stock from the NeXT sale fell $5.8 million in value that day to $26.8 million. Luckily, he had held out for $150 million in cash from the deal as well. Asked about the bad news, an annoyed Jobs replied curtly, "I'm not interested in commenting on that."

Apple's stock was now once again in free fall. It had started 1996 at more than $34 per share and had slumped during the worst of the financial news the following July to just over $17 per share. Since then, the stock had recovered nearly half the loss, peaking at about $27 per share in November. Now it was again heading straight down. The next day it would fall again, to $17.50 per share.

As it happened, that next day, January 7, was the opening of MacWorld Expo in San Francisco. The year before, during the Spindler crisis, Apple had been a wraith at the show, backing off at the last moment from most of its commitments. But this year, to prove that it was alive and still vital, Apple planned to come steaming into Moscone Hall and, dangling a new operating system and Steve Jobs as bait, hold the world's attention for at least a few hours. It was to be a watershed event in Apple's history, the official turning point of the company's fortunes, the moment of inflection between the Old Apple and the New.

In that, Apple succeeded. The January 1997 MacWorld Expo proved to be the second great set piece of the Apple story. It was the other bookend to the Macintosh introduction almost exactly thirteen years before. It bracketed the company's story. Before the 1984 Mac introduction, Apple was a hungry young company struggling for survival and respect. After the 1997 MacWorld Expo, Apple would no longer be Apple, but a kind of Restoration comedy of grand gestures, pompous players and a convoluted plot.

As profoundly different as the two events were, both nevertheless uncannily captured the essence of Apple at that particular moment in its history. The Mac introduction had been improvisational, intimate and cocky. Before that comparatively small crowd, Steve Jobs had set off a revolution. On that day, Apple could do no wrong. Even its mistakes were brilliant. Its attempts at creating an "event" were so crude they were endearing. This was a company that knew it had everything to win and went for it. With just days to prepare, Jobs & Co. constructed a masterpiece, the model for every corporation, private institution and government agency ever after.

If the Mac intro was Jobs as Cortez, the tiny band with nothing to lose capturing an empire, MacWorld Expo was Amelio at the breaching of the Berlin Wall, a bloated, decadent empire knowing it is in collapse but unable to muster even the will to do anything about it. Nine-billion-dollar Apple Computer, with 11,000 employees and access to the best designers, producers and writers on earth, and given six months to prepare for an event upon which the fate of the entire corporation might rest, managed to produce a hollow, overwrought, disjointed and endless extravaganza that was less of a call to arms than a horrifying and unwelcome glimpse into the soul of a dying company. The worst hack journalist in the hall didn't have to work hard to spot the symbolism.

It began well enough. Given all the attention focused on the resurgent Apple, Moscone Hall was jammed to the rafters with 80,000 excited visitors, hundreds of companies showing off their wares, camera crews racing about covering the event for an anxious world.

Be Inc. took its best shot at conquering the show. Its booth was the most crowded at the event, as people swarmed around demonstrations of the losing Mac operating system. Many were blown away, and more than one viewer asked rhetorically, "Why can't my Mac do that?" Power Computing also took its best shot. Its employees in their camos and Humvee would have stolen any other show but this one.

The imminent presentation was the talk at every booth, and in every hallway conversation and pressroom interview. Was Apple doomed? Could

Jobs save the company, or was he an even bigger menace? This was the conversation between two industry veterans:

"So, are you of the school that believes Steve Jobs is a visionary? Or the one that thinks he is a sociopath?"

"I don't think the two are mutually exclusive."

They weren't the only ones who were both thrilled and frightened by the founder's return. A few months before, in a private conversation, one Silicon Valley analyst, when it was suggested that the best thing Apple could do would be to bring back Steve Jobs, rolled his eyes and said, "Good God! That'd be the last thing Apple needs right now." But he was quoted in the paper that morning saying that Apple had made a brilliant move bringing Steve back.

At the appointed time, the crowd of 8,000 true believers and curiosity seekers, as well as those who made a living reporting on both, hurried across the street to the grand ballroom of a nearby hotel. They jammed into a narrow hallway awaiting admission. When at last the doors opened, the crowd swarmed and filled the several thousand seats, and then, in violation of fire marshal restrictions, the believers squeezed into every square inch of floor space in the aisles and wings.

"If Gil doesn't give the speech of his life," muttered the editor of *Mac Home Journal*, "I'll give it for him."

The show literally began with a bang. The giant screen showed the clip from *Independence Day* in which Jeff Goldblum, riding in Air Force One, looks at his Apple PowerBook and realizes that the alien countdown has ended and the White House is about to be destroyed. Then an explosion and a glare of lights . . . and suddenly the spotlight focused on the real actor Jeff Goldblum standing at the podium. The crowd roared and cheered.

Then Gil Amelio stepped out onstage. Wearing chinos and a sport coat, he had made the unbelievable fashion mistake of putting on a collarless dress shirt. Thirty seconds earlier, Apple had once again looked like the coolest company on the planet. And now here stood the CEO, looking exactly like your newly divorced uncle on his first date. The crowd tried to stay pumped up, but Apple's old panache, its legendary hipness, invoked for that one thrilling moment, was now slipping away before their eyes.

It went downhill from there. Amelio's presentation didn't even have the attribute of brevity. Instead it went on for a disastrous, butt-breaking three hours.

Two hours into this marathon, the moment everyone had been waiting for finally arrived. "I'd like to bring a friend out," Amelio said casually, with more showmanship than he'd exhibited in the previous 120 minutes. The expectant rumble rose to a full-throated cry.

Steven Jobs, imperially slim in his dark, tailless suit, emerged from the wings to the explosion of a hundred camera flashes. He winced at the glare. "You guys are going to have to stop making me blind or I'm going to fall off the stage." He responded to the cheers with his little smile—and that set off another round of cheering. There he was. The legend. The one solipsist of his generation who had actually been proven right. At that moment, everyone was indeed merely an agent of his desires. And one suddenly realized the shocking possibility that the entire history of Apple Computer, twenty years of glory and ignominy, brilliant success and embarrassing failure, the parade of fallen captains on the Ship of Fools, even Jobs's passion, crucifixion and now resurrection, had been planned all along by Steven Jobs. And all of us—Apple employees, customers, suppliers, even casual observers—were merely characters in a gigantic epic novel, a *Bildungsroman* Jobs had been writing since he was nineteen years old. Perhaps that had always been the secret behind that ironic little smile.

And this was the latest brilliant chapter. Before the adoring audience, the constituency he needed to fulfill his plans, Jobs managed to accomplish in ten minutes what Apple had been trying to do all day. He gave the company a sense of purpose, a history (". . . that day I went to Xerox PARC"), and, through the new NeXT/Mac hybrid, to be called Rhapsody, a reason to believe in the company's future. That was awesome enough, but even more breathtaking was how he did it. Though he effortlessly owned the hall, Jobs presented himself humbly, as if he was just one more presenter, another, say, director of Pippin keyboard development. It was so disarming, such an unexpectedly clever new form of seduction, that the audience melted. Even those who knew better. And when he left the stage, Jobs left an aching void in the audience's heart.

Amelio should've ended the extravaganza right there, on the perfect emotional note, with the audience ready to climb out of the trenches and attack. But Gil Amelio couldn't stop. He still had a half dozen items on the agenda. Another hour, as the audience, already spent and happy, groaned and begged to be left alone in its afterglow.

Yet, amazingly, in that last hour there was one more transcendent, signifying moment. It came at the end, almost like an afterthought. Jobs was called back onstage, this time with Steve Wozniak. It was their first time together onstage in many years. The old best friends, separated by time, success and betrayals, but forever linked by history. If Jobs was a sleeker version of his old self, Woz was a more avuncular version of his. Rotund now, and dressed in a baggy, violently loud sweater, this middle-aged legend looked uncannily like Norm Abram on *This Old House*.

In the most obvious ways, Wozniak's Wilderness Years had been far less productive and yet more successful than his old partner's. He had not become a billionaire—in fact, he had less money than ever. Nor had he founded a successful company or slept in the White House. On the contrary, these days he was better known for being a has-been and an eccentric—a guy who paid for small items by cutting dollar bills from sheets purchased from the mint. He had become a well-known philanthropist too, his timely gift to the Children's Discovery Museum only the best-known of his donations.

In subtle ways, Woz's victory had been the most satisfying and complete of all. In the intervening years he had followed his own inner compass. It had not begun well, with the failure of CL9 and his second divorce. Bill Graham also reentered his life, this time taking $600,000 of Woz's money for a rock concert in Moscow—to interview the ferocious Graham and the trusting Woz sitting side by side was a chilling experience. Graham later confided to his associates that he thought Wozniak was "a simpleton."

Still, even the predator-prey relationship with Graham eventually bore fruit for Wozniak. The two became partners in the Shoreline Amphitheater, the largest concert venue between San Francisco and San Jose—and for years Woz attended almost every concert, sometimes bringing along a toy laser to draw squibbles on the theater's vast tent roof.

Meanwhile, Woz also learned something about finances: he knew nothing about how to handle his wealth. As he once famously said, "I don't feel attached to my money in normal ways." In the late 1980s, he took the small fraction of what was left of his once-great wealth and put it into tax-free municipal bonds—"safe," wrote *Wired*, "from the depredations of wise guys." The move at last freed Woz to grow up.

He married again, to Suzanne Mulkern, and the marriage seemed a happy one. He shared custody of his three children with Candy Clark. And if he paid too much for his big house in the Los Gatos hills, at least he didn't lose it. Instead, it sat nearly empty, as Woz and Mulkern moved elsewhere in town.

In a *Wired* profile of Woz in 1998, the magazine told how, in true style, Woz had spent years trying to get a phone number with matching digits—impossible in the Bay Area. Then came a new cell phone exchange, 888, and Woz quickly grabbed 888-8888 as his own number. He was soon buried in hundreds of phone calls each day, nearly all of them dead air, the sound of a TV in the background, or gurgles. It turned out to be babies, playing with the phone and endlessly tapping the number eight. As *Wired* noted with irony about the old phone hacker: "The children of America were making their first prank call. And the person who answered the phone was Woz."

It might have all ended badly, except that in 1990 Woz at last found something he could care about as much as he had personal computers: teaching. Using his own money to hire teachers, he volunteered with the Los Gatos school district to teach computers to fifth through eighth graders. The classroom was the three-car garage of the empty mansion, the latest-model computers sharing space with unopened cases of Jolt Cola.

By all accounts, Woz was a wonderful teacher, changing the lives of his young students. The man whose own life had gone sideways into unimaginable worlds when he was thirteen was now dedicating his time left to helping other children through that moment. The legacy of his middle years might not be *Toy Story* and NeXT Computer, but the street leading into the Children's Discovery Museum was officially titled Woz Way. Even Steve Jobs didn't have a city street named for him. And it was Woz who drew the biggest applause of the afternoon.

Wozniak didn't say a word. He didn't have to. His life had now taken him away from the ongoing soap opera of Apple and of Silicon Valley. There was now nothing for him to add to the Apple story—except one fact, revealed without the need for explication. As incredible as it seemed, Woz had won. Like David Packard, he now stood as a model for how not just to succeed in Silicon Valley but how to triumph. The lesson was missed by the assembled cheering thousands, because if Packard's path to victory was impossible, Wozniak's was utterly improbable. He didn't *fit* the image of high-tech success in the 1990s. He didn't look like Larry Ellison or Steve Jobs. He wasn't obsessed with the defeat of everyone else like Bill Gates.

The audience cheered Woz for his technical genius and at the same time pitied him for his irrelevance—and got it exactly backward. He was just a frumpy, poorly dressed middle-aged man who happened to be a legend. That he might also have found happiness in the same way Packard did—through loyalty, integrity, concern for others and doing what he loved most—did not fit the equation. And if he acted sometimes like a child, Woz had nevertheless become more of an adult than the superannuated adolescents who now wrote the narrative of Valley life . . . including the former friend with whom he now shared the stage. For Woz at least, the loop had not been closed, but shattered.

Having reassembled the founding duo, Amelio then announced that he was awarding them the first two models of a special version of the Macintosh. Out they came atop a rolling table, two exquisite machines that looked like a cross between a crystal Baccarat award and a Bang & Olufsen stereo. An upright, rearing flat box bearing a flat panel display, a pair of equally rampant stereo speakers, brushed chrome and Lucite. In their elegance, the two computers were as stunning and standard-setting as the original Macintosh had been all those years before.

Then, in a flicker, they were gone, leaving more than one reporter to ask, *"What the hell was that?"*

It was the visual highlight of the three hours. It seemed to cast in the shade everything in the presentation that came before it. And in perfect symmetry with the rest of the debacle, Amelio had brought it onstage like an afterthought, teased the audience and pulled it away. Computatis Interruptus. Months later, the magnificent box that would have been Apple's new hardware style, if Apple still had style or courage, appeared as the overpriced and rare Mac Special Edition.

Apple, it seemed, could still design interesting products. It could just no longer build them or market them. It really was time for Steve Jobs's return.

The Amelio marathon (or, as *Upside* cheekily called it, Gil Aid '97) ended as it had run, in a minor key on the downbeat. The crowd gleefully tore their free videos of *Independence Day* from under their chair seats and ran. But onstage there was one last telling moment. Wozniak walked to the edge of the stage to meet his friends and admirers. So did Gil Amelio, to accept false congratulations for his unfortunately unforgettable performance. (It was so bad that one attendee on the way out of the hall asked an Apple employee if Amelio had suffered a stroke.)

But the moment the lights came up, Steve Jobs slipped away, refusing to be part of a joint photograph with his old partner. The Wizard stepped behind the curtain and was gone—as if to remind everyone that he was merely a presenter, a *guest*, and that this travesty was not his creation. Thus, while Woz and Amelio stayed behind, Steve Jobs was already racing into the future.

10.0 GREEN SHOOTS

10.1 Serpent's Teeth

With the arrival of Steve Jobs, Gil Amelio found himself holding the devil by the tail—and realized that was the worst place to hold him. Not only was the most dangerous threat to his dreams of glory now by his side, but Amelio had invited him there. Steve Jobs not only believed he was brighter than Amelio, that he better understood both Apple and the personal computer industry, but, thanks to the success of a cartoon, appeared to be a better businessman than Amelio too.

This was lethal. The two times in the past, with Scott and Sculley, when Jobs had decided that his apprenticeship was over and that he now knew more than the CEO, a career homicide soon followed. And since Jobs had been the victim the last time, it was a sure bet that he would now strike first.

In the meantime, Amelio was Jobs's Toy Story. Jobs merely had to wait for the right moment. In the meantime, he let Amelio take the fall.

It didn't take long—though it seemed forever to the growing numbers of Macolytes who were convinced that Apple's only hope was for Steve Jobs to take over the company *right now*. For his part, Amelio was in the purgatory of doing exactly what he said he'd do, a strategy which drew cheers just three months before, and now being told that he was a disaster as CEO. That meant that from now on even his successes would be counted as failures. A more pragmatic or clever man might have pumped up the next quarter's profits, declared a victory and bailed out. But Amelio hadn't reached this pinnacle in his career to give it up so easily. He read the reports of his miserable performance at MacWorld Expo, but he dismissed them. After all, everybody knew he was awkward in public. What really mattered wasn't image but results.

No. After Jobs's appearance, Apple lovers everywhere suddenly decided that what they craved most was, in fact, image—and the rush of excitement that came with it. Gil Amelio was in the tragic position of being the only person in that crowded hall who didn't fall for Steve Jobs's charms. Thus, he couldn't even feel the weather changing around him.

The irony in this, a new one for the Apple archives, was that now that he had destroyed his image, Amelio suddenly discovered how to put on a tight, compelling show. The occasion was the Apple annual meeting, held once again at Flint Center at De Anza Junior College, site of the Mac introduction. Everyone walked into the hall that day, February 5, one month after the MacWorld Expo debacle, knowing the news was bad. Not only had Apple lost $120 million for the quarter, but there was an added wrinkle. Apple was now falling even further behind the rest of the personal computer industry. The precise amount had been made public a week earlier by the market research firm Dataquest: while worldwide PC shipments had increased by nearly 18 percent in 1996, Apple's had fallen by 22 percent. Apple's domestic slump was even greater, 30 percent, the biggest drop-off occurring during the Christmas season. That fourth quarter also marked the first time since records had been kept that Apple was not among the top five PC vendors in the United States. "Apple may have a rebound this year," predicted Dataquest, then added dolefully, "What that doesn't mean is that the underlying problems have been fixed."

And the stock kept sliding. By January 28, it had fallen from $26.56 the previous October to just $16.63. In the greatest bull market of modern times, Apple's stock couldn't even hold its value. Meanwhile, the company's business continued to slide, as did its market share. In *The Wall Street Journal*, columnist Walter Mossberg, perhaps the most influential journalist in high tech—and a longtime Apple advocate—stunned the computer world by announcing: "After carefully reading the plan and interviewing top Apple executives, I believe the strategy makes buying a Mac a relatively risky investment for [consumers and small business owners], compared with buying a computer running Microsoft's Windows 95 or Windows NT operating systems."

If Regis McKenna was correct, that only a handful of key opinion makers guided the thinking and buying habits of the entire electronics industry, then this one column was as damaging as the $120 million loss. When it came to making a computer purchase, Mossberg was the Man, and now he had turned his face against Apple. His words echoed millions of other once loyal Macintosh owners.

> I don't say this with any glee. It was Apple's computers that got me into computing, and I still own two Macs. . . . Only last year I advised

> that it was still safe to buy a Mac, despite Apple's troubles. But this new operating system plan asks for too much waiting and too much blind faith on the part of consumers.

At the heart of Mossberg's rejection was his concern not that the new Rhapsody operating system wouldn't work, but that it would work too well. After all, the NeXT OS had always been a product for large corporate users. No consumer applications library had ever been written for it, and there appeared to be no one signing up for that opportunity now that NeXT was part of Apple. Thus, as Mossberg saw it, there was a very great danger that the Mac's key customers—consumers, small businesses, graphics houses and schools—would find themselves trapped between an obsolete System 7 Mac OS and an unusable Rhapsody. Those who chose the former would end up abandoned by Apple, while those who chose the latter would discover that Rhapsody was in fact Threnody, a hymn for the dead.

It was certainly not a good time for the Apple CEO to be facing the company's shareholders, especially in light of what those same shareholders had done to Mike Spindler at the same event and location a year before. The employees on hand wouldn't be happy either, having received a memo the week before preparing them for even more layoffs. The crowd rumbled and grumbled into the hall loaded for bear.

But then, unexpectedly, amazingly, Amelio rose to the occasion. Commanding and self-assured, he faced the surly crowd.

> As you know, I've dealt with troubled companies before. I am well acquainted with what it takes to bring them back to health. When I joined Apple, I said the journey would take about three years. Today, we're a third of the way there. We're working hard to move faster, but unfortunately there are no shortcuts, no magic bullets.
>
> That aside for a moment, let me confess that I have never felt comfortable meeting with shareholders at a time when the stock is declining. I am no happier about that than you. And you have my word, for both institutional and personal reasons, that I am highly motivated to take all the necessary corrective steps to reverse our downward plunge.

Amelio went on to list "five crises" facing Apple when he joined the company and the strategies he had taken to "help the 'patient' get better." It was one of the best overviews of the company ever given:

1. *Liquidity.* "When I came on board, Apple's cash position was precari-

ous. . . . Today we are in much better shape. We ended the first quarter with $1.8 billion in cash. We slashed inventory by 75 percent."

2. *Quality*. "Faulty products were undermining Apple's greatest asset, its loyal customer base. . . . These quality issues, by the end of the year, would cost the company hundreds of millions of dollars. . . . Our PowerBook line was so severely faulted that we had to halt distribution. [Now] the data to date show a 90 percent decrease in warranty claims on our current PowerBook 1400 models."

3. *Copland*. "Our customers and developers demanded—and deserved—a clear road map for how we planned to bring them into the future with System 7 upgrades and with a new, state-of-the-art OS. And we didn't have one. Until we put a viable OS strategy in place, with [a] clear transition path for customers, we could not have a viable future. . . . With regard to Mac OS 7, our response was to plan releases every six months and to have at least three such releases defined at any given time. With regard to a new OS, our response was to identify and define a new architecture and implement that architecture in a timely fashion. We did a thorough and careful exploration of options. NeXT proved to be the answer."

4. *Culture*. "The fourth crisis involved Apple's internal culture. When margins were over 50 percent, the company seemed to move forward on sheer exuberance. But in today's world of competitive pressures and lower or even nonexisting margins, the lack of cohesiveness and discipline was killing us. Apple acted less like a coherent organization than a loose coalition of projects; a collection of tribes instead of a modern industrial enterprise. And perhaps that is a generous description. My response was to build a seasoned management team. . . . We instituted management training at all levels. We welcomed back Steve Jobs and Steve Wozniak in advisory roles. . . . My aim in this is to harness Apple's culture, not stifle it. I want to be clear that there is much I value—and much that you should value here: the incredible passion and resilience of our employees. Our insistence on creativity. And, yes, our sometimes evangelical fervor for the social value of our work. These are jewels you cannot create in management training seminars. I'm confident that they'll shine even brighter with the kind of mature management attention and nurturing we're giving them."

5. *Fragmentation*. "The company was simply doing too much, moving in too many directions—and not enough of it was profitable. . . . [That crisis] is still largely in front of us. And it is the most urgent near-term management issue we face. The lesson we are striving to teach is that the totality of our business is much greater than its individual parts. . . . We have made significant headway over the past year: lowering our break-even point by more than

a billion dollars, reducing head count by 3,565 and selling off facilities. But as our first quarter indicated, we continue to deliver unacceptable results. It will be necessary to be even more disciplined in narrowing our focus. We plan to make further cutbacks in expenses to bring us to a sustainable financial position."

It was both a magisterial presentation and the best argument Gil Amelio had yet mustered for his own continuing tenure as head of Apple Computer. But for all of its understanding of Apple's predicament, on closer inspection it also showed the weaknesses of his approach. For example, unanswered were the doubts about the NeXT OS, and thus about Rhapsody, as a consumer product. And then there was the matter of just how efficiently System 7 users would be able to migrate to Rhapsody. Amelio presented a chart showing a smooth transition from 7.6 to Tempo (late 1997) to new products code-named Allegro (early 1998) and Sonata (late 1998)—but, despite the melodic titles, no intersection with Rhapsody. Did that mean Apple would carry *two* operating systems through the end of the century? Wasn't this fragmentation?

Next there was the matter of corporate culture. The impressiveness of Amelio's acute and honest appraisal of Apple's internal problems was matched only by his breathtaking self-delusion that the problem had been solved by a new executive team, management training and bringing Jobs and Woz back for a cup of coffee. Apple's cultural problems were so vast they even scared the people who worked there and were part of that problem.

Finally, on the matter of fragmentation, the phrase "more disciplined in narrowing our focus" was code for: layoffs. Lots of them. Apple still needed to cut its overhead by another $400 million. And you couldn't do that by cutting back on sashimi and travel budgets. But to the shareholders, Amelio would only say that he would be more precise on the matter in a few days.

So there it was. Financially, the company appeared in worse shape than ever. But against that, Dr. Amelio posited the counternotion that such bad financial news was merely the painful symptom of a company in the process of healing and growing stronger by the day.

"It was pretty damn impressive," said one shareholder, Joe Shane, afterward. "I didn't know Gil had it in him." He immediately placed an order for more shares—and made money on the brief two-point bounce—then sold them. Within a few days, the stock was sliding again.

On the day of the annual meeting, Apple announced yet one more in its endless history of reorganizations. This one divided R&D into hardware and software, and pulled all marketing under one organization, headed by Guerrino De Luca, former chief of Claris. Then, on February 10, the company announced that it expected "substantial" losses in the current, second quarter, in large part because the $400 million deal with NeXT had now risen to about $430 million. Apple added that it also did not expect to be profitable until the fourth quarter. Meanwhile, Apple employees waited for the other shoe, layoffs, to drop.

But before that, there were two more blows. The next day, February 11, Apple's canary decided to fly off before the coal mine collapsed on her. Heidi Roizen resigned, citing a desire to spend more time with her children. No one really believed her explanation. And, in fact, when pressed, Roizen admitted that the reorganization had played a major part in her decision. The departure of Apple's "barometer" warned of a major storm ahead. (In May 1998, she joined Microsoft as a part-time consultant to burnish that company's image in Silicon Valley.)

The same day Roizen resigned, CalPERS, the California Public Employees' Retirement System, a $108 billion pension fund that was one of the most influential investors in America, put Apple at the very bottom of its annual list of America's ten leading "Financial Underperformers." This meant that Apple was now targeted by the organization for close monitoring and governance. And that meant regular meetings with Apple's managers and directors, and demands for structural changes or risk losing the fund's investment—in Apple's case, 710,000 shares. That was less than 1 percent of Apple's outstanding stock, but such was CalPERS's influence that should it pull out an avalanche of other departing investors would soon follow.

CalPERS slammed Apple for the "high salaries" of its top managers at a time of "poor performance and mounting layoffs"; an executive staff that "has not articulated a clear-cut strategy" for financial recovery and too many directors who sat on too many other boards, "thereby diminishing their ability to help the company." In a final insult, Kayla Gillan, chief counsel for CalPERS, said she'd sent a certified letter to Amelio way back in November noting these problems and requesting a meeting, "but they lost the letter."

On February 25, Steve Jobs and Pixar signed a ten-year deal with Disney to provide five more animated films. On the news, Pixar's stock jumped nearly 50 percent in value in a single day, to $21. Newspapers around the country carried the AP photo of him joking with Disney chief Michael Eisner—two titans of American industry having a private laugh over Eisner's Snow White tie. Reading those papers, a million Macolytes, awaiting the impending bombshell from Apple, saw the look of a winner, of the man who might lead them out of this slough of despond.

On March 6, with his inimitable timing, Joe Graziano, now advising new start-ups (and sitting on the board of Pixar), used the moment to kick Apple while it was down. In two long telephone interviews with the *Mercury News*, he recapitulated how, if only Apple's board had listened to him that day in Texas in 1995, he might have saved Apple. Then he savaged everything about the current company, especially Amelio, whom he said "hasn't a clue what he's dealing with." He particularly slammed Amelio's bonus package. As for the profitable quarter, Graziano claimed it was an accounting scam that involved taking back $28 million of previously booked charges. "Only in corporate America can anyone get away with that stuff. It's theft on a grand scale, only it's legal." Finally, with the NeXT deal, Graziano claimed, Apple was now "grasping at straws," adding, "It's good for Steve, and I'm glad for him. But I think it's too late even for Steve to save it. I don't see any scenario where Apple becomes a profit-making company."

For the second time in his strange relationship with Apple, Graziano delivered a message with the ring of truth about it. And once again, he wasted his shot by undermining the point he was trying to make.

The bomb, which had been whistling down over everyone's head for weeks, finally hit on March 14, a Friday—that being the traditional day for layoffs so everyone can be run out of the facility and given a weekend to cool off. Four thousand one hundred jobs cut. That was 31 percent of the company's total payroll. And though the layoffs were fairly equally distributed around the world, 4,100 jobs was almost equal to the number of employees Apple had in Silicon Valley. It was also among the largest mass firings the Valley had ever experienced. From a high of more than 17,500 full- and part-time employees in early 1995, Apple's employment rolls had now slumped to just 9,300.

At the same time, Amelio announced that the company was abandoning a number of new projects, notably OpenDoc, a Java-like framework for building software out of modular software pieces, Cyberdog, a Web browser, and QuickDraw GX, a graphics program. Since most of these were available in alternative, often better versions from other vendors, they weren't a great loss. But two other abandoned projects were much more disturbing. One was Open Transport, the networking software for the Mac, which was to be replaced by the networking system in Rhapsody; the other was any future development of tools—the programs used to write other programs—for the Mac OS. As one software vendor complained: "This is strictly the NeXT mafia trying to wrest control of the operating system from Apple." The news was chilling to Mac customers, especially big corporate customers that purchased hundreds, even thousands, of Apple computers. The announcement said: no matter what it publicly professes, Apple was not going to support its installed base of older machines.

And even with all that, Amelio wasn't yet done with the bad news. He also hinted that, financially, the current quarter was going to be bad. Very bad. Unbelievably, it might even be as bad as the horror of early 1995. The inflated NeXT price was just the start. Sales were still tanking—perhaps for losses as great as $150 million. Now to that the company would have to add another $155 million in severance costs. This suggested losses for the quarter of more than $700 million dollars. If true, that would mean that Apple would have lost, in just eighteen months, a total of nearly $2 *billion*—a loss so vast that a person couldn't count it in two lifetimes; a loss so big that if it were revenues it would make the Fortune 1000. At the same time, Apple's revenues were down by 25 percent, its staff by nearly a third and its total share of the world's personal computer market under 5 percent.

And yet, for all that, there was no indication that Gil Amelio had made Apple into a better company. It was easy simply to blame him—as many did. But the answer lay elsewhere, in a possibility that no one wanted to admit. It was that Amelio's real problem was a lack of imagination. He had followed all the traditional rules of business turnaround: pare back products to those that are or can soon be made profitable. Cut back employment to a central core of productive talent. Hold on to your supply and distribution channels for dear life.

But what if there was no core at Apple? What if the entire company was like a collection of Chinese boxes or Russian nested dolls? What if you kept peeling away layer after layer of superfluousness and then found, to your dismay, that there was nothing left—and that in the process you had turned a hollow, but enticing package into a pile of empty shells?

10.2 PROGENY

That Friday afternoon of the layoff was different from times past. Before, as far back as the Night of the Long Knives, Apple layoffs had been a time of bitterness, acrimony and a seething sense of betrayal. Not this time. The only people now at Apple who were surprised were the ones who *weren't* laid off. Everyone had seen it coming for weeks and had prepared themselves. Work in the offices had nearly stopped. Like soldiers pinning names on themselves before an attack, fresh résumés were copied and secreted into briefcases. And in many offices the prayer was not to keep one's job, but to get a great severance package that would let one hang out for a few months. The prayer even had a name: DSP, for Desperately Seeking Package.

When the pink slip did arrive, many met the news with relief. Apple, the "Graduate School of Silicon Valley" as one employee called it, was no longer seen as a career, much less a calling. It was now where you worked off the last fantasies of adolescent idealism before you moved on to the real-life world of work. Everyone knew there was no future at Apple. But like many young people leaving home for the first time, some needed a push. The layoff did just that. Meanwhile, beyond the lobby, Silicon Valley was enjoying its Golden Age, the most successful period of its already remarkable history. By one estimate, every single day of 1996 minted an average of sixty-four new millionaires. At start-ups like Yahoo! and Siebel Systems, generous stock options meant that *everybody* got rich.

Burke Tyree had just been hired by Apple as a temp. His first job was to go through the many offices of the newly fired and help them clean out their rooms. "They had about an hour to get their things and separate usable office supplies from personal junk. Some people who had just been fired were in shock. But mostly, even people who hadn't been fired were moping around.

"So many people had been laid off that the company seemed empty. There were now something like five hundred empty offices. So we consolidated the people that were still there, moved them closer together, so there wouldn't be so many empty offices between them."

Those who were soon to be fired and those who would soon be unexpectedly still employed walked out of Apple that afternoon and gathered in local restaurants and watering holes. Few were concerned. Many had been fielding calls from headhunters for days. Others found business cards from Aerotek Data Services Group, a recruiting firm, under the windshield wipers of their cars. In a Valley desperate for warm bodies, more so talented computer types, the ex-Apple employees knew they could have a new job in the morning.

So, for the sheer irony of it, they sat in places like the Peppermill, a retro lounge-restaurant full of retirees and waitresses forced to dress like tarts, and raised glasses in a toast to their old employer. As you looked at them, with their ironic smiles and knowing glances, long hair and grunge clothes, you suddenly realized that this entire generation was the bastard child of Steve Jobs. And if, as it was said, Jobs had set out to change the world, while Bill Gates had set out with the more prosaic goal of putting MS-DOS in every computer—then both had, in fact, achieved their goal.

The Apple children laughed the evening away. Some wore Apple decals on their faces. They joked about taking jobs at Microsoft, or having everyone gather around and drink, Jonestown style, a poison Kool-Aid in the colors of the Apple logo—not realizing that was a decade-old joke about working for Steve Jobs. Then, after drinks and appetizers, they broke up and wandered off into their separate lives. Summer camp was over.

For the older, truer believers, the end was much more touching. Said one assistant to a senior executive, "I had my very identity, my social life, my intellectual life, my whole sense of well-being wrapped up in the fabric of the Apple culture. It was a privilege to be part of a society so erotic, so liberating. I'd wake up in the morning and didn't feel I was going to work because I had this incredible sense of excitement. It was like being back in college.

"Then it was like the whole value system of the place shifted. I started to lose respect for the company. It wasn't the same place after Sculley left, and worse after Spindler. Finally one morning, it started to be work.

"I cried the day I quit."

10.3 AUTOPSY

Giving advice on how to save Apple Computer had become something of a cottage industry—one more profitable than its subject. As early as January, at the time of MacWorld Expo, industry leaders, academics, former employees, business theorists and, ultimately, anybody famous who owned a Macintosh was called upon to enlighten mankind on what should be done to turn around Apple's fortunes.

What was intriguing about these considered opinions, and they numbered in the hundreds, was (1) how contradictory they were, suggesting that none of these "experts" really had a clue; and (2) how passionate they were, a reminder that Apple may have lost its market share, but still enjoyed a truly spectacular share of mind. Nobody wept when Compaq had a bad quarter.

The first round of opinion makers, and the advice they gave, was fairly predictable: venture capitalist John Doerr ("Make a major contribution, with NeXT technology, to the development of the Java tsunami"), Esther Dyson ("Support what's already being done on the Mac") and Marc Andreeson ("Concentrate on building and demonstrating momentum"). As if Amelio & Co. hadn't at least considered every one of these platitudes. What was far more interesting was the realization of how the tables had turned. Most of these individuals had been made by Apple or the revolution it kicked off. Now these progeny were as famous as and much more influential than their progenitor.

By March and the big layoff, the Apple opinion factory was running at full capacity on all three shifts. You couldn't turn on the new wave of television business and computer shows on CNBC, MSNBC, CNN and Fox without hearing someone bloviate on Apple's problems and how they could be cured.

The apogee of all this opinion making came with the June 1997 edition of *Wired* magazine. *Wired*, having blown its own IPO a few months earlier, knew a lot about failing companies, and this newfound wisdom gave its article on Apple an edge. The cover was a classic: the Roman Catholic Sacred Heart, beloved in Latin American churches, with its wrapping of thorns dripping blood and starry spikes bursting behind it. Only this time it wasn't the *sacré coeur* within the barbs, but the Apple logo. And a one-word headline: *Pray.*

Inside, *Wired*'s editors had compiled "101 Ways to Save Apple." Some were tough ("1. Admit it. You're out of the hardware game." "6. Apologize." "76. Make damn sure that Rhapsody runs on an Intel chip.") Some were thoughtful ("2. License the Apple name/technology to appliance manufacturers." "9. Fire the people who forecast product demand." "15. Dump, or outsource, the Newton, eMate, digital cameras and scanners." "20. Sell yourself to IBM or Motorola." "36. Clone the PowerBook." "50. Give Steve Jobs as much authority as he wants in new product development.") And some—deservedly—were facetious and cruel: ("32. Advice to Gil Amelio: shorter speeches, tighter pants." "57. Bring back John Sculley. He would provide a convenient whipping boy." "69. Change your name to Snapple and see if you can dupe Quaker Oats into buying you.")

Surrounding these suggestions was the collected advice of experts and celebrities, ranging from MIT's Marvin Minsky to film critic Roger Ebert. Even Jef Raskin, now a bald graybeard, weighed in with the same advice of fifteen years before: "[Apple] never rethinks the whole proposition. Throw out the old and clumsy desktop, along with its operating-system-and-applications paradigm, and go for true task-centered design."

But amid all these pronouncements, there was one comment different from the rest. It was devastating in its accuracy. And, in an irony of ironies, it came from Nathan Myhrvold, chief technologist at Microsoft:

> At a certain critical point—perhaps five years ago—Apple stopped investing time, effort, brainpower and money in continuing to make a better product. Instead, it dissipated its energy on everything *but* the Macintosh—on Newton, Sweet Pea, Kaleida, Taligent. Meanwhile, the rest of the world caught up. The last great engineering task accomplished on the Mac was the switch to PowerPC. However, no new features went in. The company that had been the leader in operating systems found that it could no longer write an operating system—Copland was a disaster that never shipped. It had to suffer the ultimate ignominy of buying one outside. The NeXT purchase is too little too late. The Apple of the past was an innovative company that used software and hardware technology together to redefine the way people experienced computing. That Apple is already dead. Very adroit moves

> might be able to save the brand name. A company with the letters *A-P-P-L-E* in its name might survive, but it won't be the Apple of yore.

It was the epitaph of Apple Computer, written, perhaps appropriately, by its greatest competitor. *Apple is already dead.* It was what Valley veterans had been privately saying to each other for months. No company could emerge the same after what Apple had just been through.

If the death of Apple didn't fit the image of a traditional corporate death—broken men shuffling off into the darkness, padlocks on the gates, boarded windows and weeds in the parking lot—it was because nothing ever really died in high technology. Rather it was sold off in pieces or whole or its patents were licensed away. Even Fairchild, the founding company of modern Silicon Valley, still existed, even though it had been extinguished as a corporation for a decade. It was now a division of National Semiconductor. And even as Apple was laying off its thousands, National Semiconductor, now even more prosperous than it had been under Amelio, sold off the Fairchild division to an East Coast concern—which immediately announced it was bringing the firm back to the Valley.

Technology never really died either. Within most of the major software programs on the market were the kernels, sometimes just a few lines of code, of scores of long-forgotten programs that preceded them from decades past. It was the same with semiconductors. Inside of every new Pentium Plus chip from Intel was the tiny core of the original 8086 microprocessor. And even the little MOS 6502, the processor around which Wozniak had built the Apple I, still survived. Its design, having been licensed to one manufacturer after another over the course of a quarter century—including Synertek and Rockwell—was still regularly upgraded and redesigned by a little ten-person company called Western Design Center of Mesa, Arizona. Now a low-powered microcontroller chip sold for just pennies, the 6502 nevertheless was still being used by the millions by such giants as AT&T, ITT, Sanyo and Siemens.

For the same reason, a great company like Apple could die, and yet still be operating, even selling billions of dollars' worth of products. It could still have buildings and grounds and factory automation equipment and even thousands of employees showing up each day. But it would be a ghost, a phantasm.

The March 1997 layoff was that crossing over, that point of no return—as Apple's young employees instinctively understood. The Children's Crusade was over, ending, a lot like the original, in a massacre. The narrative itself might still go on, but it was now self-reflexive. Henceforth the Apple story would be only about the Apple story. A new company might climb out of the crater, it might even use the same name and logo, sell a few of the same products, even have a familiar face on the first page of the annual report. But it would be a different company. The infinite looping of Apple Computer had finally blown up the machine. Whether the new company would repeat the same deadly cycle was something only the future could tell. In the meantime, a lot of people would fight over Apple's corpse.

10.4 EXILE

In the months that followed, senior management at Apple behaved like a deposed royal family. Still going through the motions, still keeping up appearances, convincing themselves that the blade would never fall, the firing squad would never arrive at the door. And no one was more lost in this self-delusion than the king himself. Gil Amelio, convinced that his strategy was still sound, albeit unfinished, that he had saved Apple and was, as predicted, halfway through the turnaround, acted as if it was business as usual.

But it obviously wasn't. Now events began to pick up speed. On a single day, June 30, Apple's biggest Mac distributor to schools, Education Access, abruptly ended its relationship with Apple and switched to IBM, Compaq and Power Computing. Then Power Computing added to the damage by announcing that it would begin making Windows computers, claiming that to grow it needed to expand beyond the limited Apple market. It added that it was increasingly frustrated by the delays in its dealings with Apple.

Yet, in spite of this, so secure did Amelio feel in his position that, bizarrely, he devoted much of the board of directors meetings to endless discussions of what options and appointments he should have on his new jet.

But this was a different board than the rubber stamp of years past. In response to criticism, a fire breather had been added to the placid body: Edgar S. Woolard, Jr., chairman of E. I. Du Pont de Nemours & Co. Silver-haired, with an elegant nose, Woolard may have looked like a Delaware aristocrat, but he was tough as Kevlar. He'd done his own successful turnaround at Du Pont—his sell-off of $1.8 billion in assets and layoffs of 40,000 employees made even Amelio's efforts seem puny—so he was not a man to be fooled by CEO bombast. So, not surprisingly, it was Woolard who finally had enough and organized a vote over the Fourth of July weekend to remove Gil Amelio. And it was Woolard who delivered the news by phone to Amelio on Saturday, July 5, that the board wanted his resignation. Amelio quickly mounted a flurry of phone calls to press his case, but soon realized he had no chance. On Sunday, after telling his wife the news, he formally tendered his resignation.

He also learned that Steve Jobs had been asked to advise the company during the transition.

To his credit, Amelio not only took the news well but even faced the press a few days later. He was unrepentant, refusing to admit any errors. Instead, Amelio reasoned, the board had decided that he, having successfully completed 90 percent of the task at hand, now needed to get out of the way for someone with a different set of skills to take Apple across the finish line. It sounded good, and let him preserve his dignity.

"I know that I've rescued this company," Amelio said. "This company would not be here at this point in time had I not intervened when I did and done the things I've done. And I have done enough of the right things to lay a foundation so that they can realistically talk about a future that was impossible a year and a half ago. So I leave with the greatest sense of accomplishment that you can have for having done an awful lot in a very short period of time."

Others were not so kind. Pieter Hartsook, a former Apple vice president, said simply, "He was not a visionary leader and he never had the confidence of the employees."

"Gil never got his hands around Apple's culture," said Tim Bajarin afterward. "He didn't penetrate and motivate. His model was Lou Gerstertner of IBM. Gerstertner had started his turnaround of IBM by staying out of the public eye and touring around talking to employees and customers. Gil tried the same thing. But Amelio was no Gerstertner, and Apple was no IBM."

But columnist Mike Barnicle of the *Boston Globe,* speaking for the many nontech Mac owners, was much harsher—and probably more accurate about history's judgment. The column was entitled "Road Kill on the Information Highway":

> . . . Today, as a huge MacWorld convention begins in Boston, Apple is nearly extinct. It is at the edge of existence for a lot of reasons. First, some cement head from Pepsi decided that Apple was so great it didn't have to make its technology compatible with other computers because foolish start-up operations like Microsoft were pathetic pretenders and would soon die.
>
> The stupid soft drink guy was succeeded by someone with a funny name who was afraid to emerge from his office as long as the stock market was open. After he got fired, the Apple board of directors ran right out and got somebody else with a weird name and narrow perspective.
>
> . . . How can these nitwits still draw a paycheck when they took the only computer that didn't frighten people while getting the job

done and turned it into the technological equivalent of the 1987 Red Sox bullpen?

And so Gil Amelio, the rising turnaround star, who saw Apple as his launchpad to fame, who had rushed out to meet the movie stars and powerful politicians almost from the moment he took the job and who dreamed of business immortality, became merely a footnote, a nitwit with "a weird name and a narrow perspective." Apple had done it again.

Meanwhile, many inside Apple and out, saw the hidden hand of Steve Jobs in this latest coup d'état—and predicted that Jobs would soon be running Apple outright. But on that there was only silence . . . except for a denial by Gil Amelio, deluded about Jobs right to the end. Steve, said Gil, is my friend. And he added that one of his finest accomplishments at the helm of Apple was bringing Jobs home.

The next day, another ghost from Apple's past appeared from the mists of history to render his opinion on the matter. Happily out of sight now for nearly three years, Sculley decided to use this inauspicious moment to weigh in. It was his belief that the best person Apple could hire to replace Amelio was Sculley's old number two, Del Yocam, currently running a turnaround at another crippled company, Borland International. "While we will never know," Sculley continued, "I believe if Del had been made CEO seventeen months ago, Apple wouldn't be in its current precarious position." He went on to suggest that Jobs be made Apple's "non-executive chairman of the board"—note the first term. "Together, Steve and Del are a creditable team."

Sculley went on to explain that he was making this suggestion now because "this way it's harder for Apple's board to ignore, since time has run out for more absurdity." But of course, the board did ignore him. Who gave half a fuck what John Sculley thought? He made this mess. Besides, Yocam wasn't interested.

Not to be outdone, Jean-Louis Gassée distributed an essay entitled "I like Apple so much I want two of them," in which he recommended that Apple be split into a hardware company, run by Steve Kahng of Power Computing, and a software business run by current Apple marketing vice president Guerrino De Luca. It received about as much attention as Sculley's idea had.

Meanwhile, in the midst of all this management reshuffling, Apple's stock had now fallen to less than $14 per share. The company, it seemed, was now worth as much for its buildings and capital equipment as it was for its business.

On July 16, Apple announced that its losses for the third quarter were just $56 million. It was a measure of how far the company had fallen that this was welcomed as terrific news. After all, the final tally on the previous quarter had been a $708 million loss. And many analysts were half expecting a similar catastrophe, this one likely fatal for Apple as a corporation. "[It's] not good, but everybody was braced for a Greek tragedy," said J. P. Morgan analyst Daniel Kunstler.

Meanwhile, Apple's revenues fell by 20 percent to $1.7 billion. That meant the company had sold 140,000 fewer computers than it had during the same quarter in 1996. It also meant that Apple had shrunk, since the second quarter of 1996—in order by quarter—by 17 percent, 15 percent, 23 percent, 32 percent, 27 percent, and now 20 percent. It was now a $6 billion company—though it could not break even at anything less than $8 billion. For the quarter, it sold fewer than 700,000 computers. And, showing how its market was changing, half of those computers were entry-level products sold to schools and consumers. Server sales accounted for only 1 percent of the business. And sales of that old standby, the PowerBook, were slumping.

10.5 Dicing

Amelio's initial claims to the contrary, it was hard not to see the hand of Steve Jobs in the ouster. Vast conspiracies had been rumbling away in the background at Apple for months now, and though the mechanism still remained hidden, the increasingly Felliniesque nature of the players could only have been the work of one man.

Two of the players were especially intriguing. The first was, of all things, a Saudi Arabian prince. Prince Al-Waleed bin Talai bin Abdul-Azil al-Saud, forty-one, was one of the world's wealthiest and lowest-profile investors. Al-Waleed over the years had shrewdly built a $11.7 billion portfolio, and a $2 billion war chest, largely through a strategy of buying positions in large, struggling retailers (Saks Fifth Avenue), entertainment companies (Euro Disney) and luxury hotels. Those who knew anything about him agreed that Al-Waleed was known for his patience in holding an investment for a long-term recovery.

They also agreed that Al-Waleed's April 1997 investment in Apple—a 5 percent stake (6.25 million shares) for $115 million—was nearly unprecedented. He had never before shown much interest in playing the high-stakes game of technology investment. Now, after American Express, Al-Waleed was Apple's largest shareholder.

There was another departure from Al-Waleed's past investments. Typically he bought a piece of the action based upon a positive impression of the company's management. With Apple, however, his motives seemed to be different. Though in his official statement, he wrote, "I believe there is serious potential for Apple to provide large returns to its stockholders once again, as it did in the past," he privately made it known that if Amelio didn't turn the company around soon, he would support any outside group that could.

So it was not a friendly investment. As the prince told *Business Week*, "Gilbert Amelio extended an invitation to me to go to Apple, to be introduced to management and hear their objectives and see what they're doing. . . . He's saying publicly that recovery is only two, three, four quarters away. But he has to assure me in private that this is the case. Apple has to focus on areas it is strong in. Their biggest problem is that they expanded too much and are fighting on too many fronts. They've got to focus and cut costs."

But why choose Apple? The real clue was an aside by the prince that he was friends with Oracle's Larry Ellison, the man who called Steve Jobs his "best friend."

If the high-tech revolution had produced a few noble billionaires, such as Hewlett, Packard and Moore, it had also produced more than its share of venal, eccentric and scary ones. And the scariest, perhaps most demented of all was Larry Ellison.

Ellison, with his preternaturally smooth skin and Armani suits at the office, his obsession with Japanese samurai (and the kimonos he wore at his Japanese-style home), his yacht and Russian MiG, was like the worst-case scenario of the poor kid who got rich. Success only seemed to ignoble him. Along with his flamboyance, Ellison also had a reputation as a rake, of using Oracle as his private harem. But there was no denying he was a bold, creative and very smart businessman.

When Ellison sprang the $500 Internet computer, the NC, on the assembled throng at the Fall 1996 Comdex in Las Vegas, he managed the unprecedented act of hijacking the show. It was the talk of everyone assembled, instantly rendering obsolete everything on display, and even forcing Bill Gates to devote his speech to a rebuttal. In fact, so compelling was the NC idea that Ellison took the uncharacteristic step of actually following up on it. By Christmas, he had assembled a consortium of major companies committed to build the NC.

But what he didn't have was a real personal computer company, a company with both experience in building and selling computers to consumers and instant brand recognition. In Apple, he saw the perfect opportunity: a struggling company in need of a new product/market thrust and the most famous technology brand name on earth. And in his best friend Steve Jobs (interestingly, Jobs didn't say the same of his relationship with Ellison) found a receptive, if more careful, co-conspirator.

There were two things everyone, even his most loyal fans, agreed was true about Larry Ellison. He was incredibly bright . . . and he was almost inhumanly vain. The first enabled him to come up with brilliant ideas like the NC and superb strategies for implementing it. The second made him organically incapable of not blabbing about his plans the first chance he got.

That chance came on a hike with, incredibly enough, a reporter for the *Mercury News*. Yes, he told her, Steve and I, with the help of the prince and some others, are planning a buyout of Apple.

Needless to say, the story ran on the front page of the newspaper the next morning—complete with disavowals from Jobs. I don't know what Larry's talking about, said Steve defensively. But a few days later, at an informal "fireside chat" with a thousand Mac software developers in San Jose, Jobs, acting as if he now had nothing to lose, proceeded to lay into Apple, especially Amelio's management. He told the crowd what he said he'd already told Gil: Apple should sell off the Newton, make the cloning of Apple software easier but more expensive and, most of all, get into network computers. "Apple has suffered from lousy engineering management," he told the crowd. "I think Apple has had its head in the sand for . . . many years." The audience, which had already nicknamed the event the "pyreside chat" and expressed dread of having to endure the Jobs Reality Distortion Field at 9 A.M., ended up giving him a standing ovation.

But even as he appeared to be closing the door on his relationship with Apple, Jobs still took the time to keep a hand in and tidy up some loose ends. "I still have enough faith in Apple's management," he told the crowd, "that I told Larry Ellison not to try to take over Apple." That took care of the historical record.

A few weeks later, Jobs, his plan apparently exposed, sold off all but one share of the 1.5 million Apple shares he earned in the NeXT buyout. When Amelio demanded to know if the rumors of the sale (Jobs's name was not on the transaction) were true, whether Jobs had broken his promise, made at the time of the NeXT buyout, of not selling his shares, Jobs lied.

Jobs would later say that he prevaricated because he was embarrassed and depressed and that now he felt bad about it. His take, at the depressed price of $15 per share, was just $22 million. Apple was destined to be run by a man who had so much faith in it that he sold off his stock in the company.

Then fortune, which had ignored him for months, once again smiled on its mischievous child. As Jobs watched, the board of directors, led by the swift and efficient Edgar Woolard, did the job for him and tossed Amelio out on his ear. Jobs suddenly found himself in the power seat at Apple without spending a dime or getting a drop of blood on his hands. Even the press, loving the sheer theatricality of it, cheered him on. The past was nearly forgotten, and what little was remembered was treated as a mark of character. A characteristic swoon appeared in the *San Francisco Examiner:*

> Is Steve Jobs really about to hop back into the fray? Is this the case of the simultaneously headstrong and heartfelt fireman who, even as his cohorts warn that running in there means two dead rather than one, just can't stand by idly and watch his baby go up in flames?
>
> Certainly if this weren't playing itself out before our very eyes, it would make awfully good drama—actually the stuff of Greek mythology. How far mighty Apple has fallen. And who better to come to the rescue than its own—spurned—progenitor?

Said Tim Bajarin, "I think Jobs knew from the beginning that Amelio was going to fail."

But the most accurate comment was that of Steve Wozniak, who said simply, "Gil Amelio meets Steve Jobs. Game over."

Having been lurking around Apple now for a half year, privy to all of its inside information on products and markets, combined with the larger strategic planning that came with plotting the aborted coup, put Jobs in a superb position to take over his old company. He was already running; now he merely had to step onto the track. Doing so, Jobs moved so fast that he almost seemed to pull Apple—and the attentive world—along in his wake. Though he was still ostensibly merely an adviser to the company and current head of Pixar—and though Fred Anderson, former chief financial officer, was now officially the interim Apple CEO—there was no question that Steve Jobs was running Apple. He attended meetings, made decisions in the company's name and established the company's new strategy. Memos to employees were signed "Steve and the Executive Team." He also began cleaning house of the entire executive team brought in by Amelio. Scalise, a master of the Silicon Valley game, had left in May, skipping out just before the blast. But Jobs took care of the rest. By mid-September, when marketing chief Guerrino De Luca, the last of the Amelio team, quit, Jobs had run off eight top executives, including Ellen Hancock (she reportedly made the mistake of telling Jobs to stop acting like a child), and replaced them with people of his own. Now he would turn his sights on the board.

Executives weren't the only talented veterans leaving Apple. Even with the excitement created by Jobs's return, Apple was still bleeding good people from every department. Even the coddled Apple Fellows began to flee.

Jobs tried to stanch the flow of talent by completing a project Amelio had begun but never put into action: boosting the value of employee stock options through repricing. It was a good idea, but too late. The Thoroughbreds were already out of the barn. In a devastating appraisal of the company's current condition, executive recruiter Igor Still of Geneva Group International said, "Apple today is not viewed by other companies as having especially innovative technology or executives with superior management skills. Their best people have left over the past 24 months. There is no great interest in their remaining people."

Meanwhile, speculation about a corporate buyer for Apple slowly evaporated. This was despite the fact that the entire company could now be purchased (given the current record low stock price of $13.25) for just $2 billion—and that included the $1.3 billion Apple had in cash on hand. Yet even at this bargain basement price, there were no takers. "It's not as though it hasn't been shopped," said Andrew Neff of Bear, Stearns. Apple was now there for Steve Jobs's asking. It was generally assumed that he would take both jobs, as chairman and CEO, as soon as it was tendered by the board.

Yet, three weeks after Amelio's departure, when that offer finally was made, Jobs turned it down. His explanation was that he had a commitment to Pixar and wanted to spend more time with his family. Instead, he would manage the search to fill those positions. However, it escaped nobody that, title or not, Steve Jobs was running Apple Computer. In fact, even as he made the announcement, Jobs was busily approving Apple's final plans for the next week's MacWorld Expo in Boston—and preparing his own keynote speech.

10.6 In Vitro

The Boston MacWorld Expo, which began on Wednesday, August 6, 1997, was the first major event of Jobs's second term, the first gathering of the post-Apple era. Jobs, with his magnificent sense of occasion, understood that more than anyone, and from the moment he took control again of Apple, he focused everything the company had on that moment. Sensing even that wouldn't be enough, he also arranged to drop a bombshell so big that no one would be able to ignore it.

Apple may have never really been a company, but now it was no longer even an idea. It had lost its technology, its philosophy and most of its market. All it had left was its outsized grip on the popular imagination—and that came from its story and the symbolism that attached to it. Jobs appreciated the power of that story and those symbols. After all, he had helped create both. But even he must have been amazed by their potency, their seductiveness. What, after all, did Larry Ellison want but to append his own increasingly sordid story to Apple's, and thus elevate it in the process?

Now there was an even greater figure who wanted to be in on the story; someone who had coveted Apple even longer than Steve Jobs. And that man, the most powerful private citizen on earth, wanted to close his own loop with Apple Computer.

MacWorld Expo, like any good Steve Jobs event, began with a crisis. Meeting with a few hundred corporate computer buyers, Power Computing's COO, Joel Kocher, called for a protest at Jobs's keynote speech. The reason was Apple's apparent stalling in signing a deal to let clone makers sell their products equipped with Apple's new OS 8 operating system upgrade. The $99 OS 8 had earned raves from *The Wall Street Journal*'s Walter Mossberg and was helping move Apple computers . . . but not clone machines, which were still forced to use OS 7.6. Only Umax had managed to squeeze out an OS 8 license. It seemed that the clones, which now owned 30 percent of the Mac market, had been a little too successful. And the era of good feelings under Amelio had ended with Jobs's arrival.

There had been considerable speculation in the days before about what Jobs was going to discuss. Some insiders predicted that he would formally dedicate the company to the until now secret Zephyr project, an under $1,000 network computer that would run both Macintosh and Java applications. Other insiders contradicted this by predicting Jobs would talk about Apple's new commitment to high-end servers that would combine multiple Intel processors with the Rhapsody operating system.

Just on these rumors, Apple stock jumped to $19 per share, half again its worth just a month before. Jobs would have made a lot of money had he not sold his stock.

But these product announcements were just news flashes compared to what Jobs had planned for his keynote. He ordered a huge proscenium stage built, complete with a full-sized movie screen and a bank of computer monitors. *Time* magazine, warned about what was coming, sent a photographer and a reporter with hopes for a cover story. The photographer was even allowed into the hall early to scout sight lines. And Jobs, to keep the big mystery intact, even ordered up multiple finishes for his speech.

"He's Hamlet," said one observer at the show. "This is the way Steve Jobs likes it. He's the drama king."

By the morning of August 6, the consensus among the thousands of attendees at the Boston Castle was that Jobs would use the big close to announce Apple's new board of directors, including Larry Ellison. But a few, knowing even this wouldn't be enough for Jobs, still argued that he had something even bigger planned.

Within days after Amelio's exit, Jobs recognized that Apple might well collapse before he could even start fixing it if he didn't make some radical moves and find some cash. He knew where the answer to both lay: in Redmond. He called Bill Gates, and within days a barefoot Jobs was walking around Palo Alto in deep negotiations with Gates's emissary, Microsoft CFO Gregory Maffei.

Maffei had come expecting the worst. Just a year before, on Robert Cringley's popular PBS miniseries *Revenge of the Nerds*, Jobs had looked into the camera and said, "The only problem with Microsoft is they just have no taste. I don't mean that in a small way. I mean that in a big way, in the sense that they don't think of original ideas and they don't bring much culture into their products. I have no problem with their success—they've earned their success for the most part. I have a problem with the fact that they just make really third-rate products."

But Jobs, Maffei told *Time*, was expansive and charming: "We had spent a lot of time with Amelio, and they had a lot of ideas that were nonstarters. Jobs had a lot more ability. He didn't ask for 23,000 terms. He looked at the whole picture, figured about what he needed. And we figured he had the credibility to bring the Apple people around and sell the deal." Thus, Steve Jobs not only got credit for the deal with Microsoft that Gil Amelio had initiated but had given Bill Gates everything he had originally wanted—for only money, not the crucial quid pro quo in software.

If this was a different Steve Jobs and Apple, it was also a different Bill Gates and Microsoft. No one in American history, not even the Gilded Age robber barons like Rockefeller, Vanderbilt and Carnegie whom schoolchildren were taught to revile, had ever owned so complete a monopoly on a major U.S. industry. Even his counterpart, Andy Grove at Intel, had to fight Motorola and the Intel cloners. But Gates essentially owned the operating system of the half billion personal computers on the planet. Even the few computers that didn't run Windows, like Macs, most likely used Microsoft Word or Microsoft Excel as their main application.

Now, in the mid-1990s, Microsoft was moving outward from its secure center, using its mountains of cash and the implied (and sometimes not so implied) blackmail of Windows to envelop and absorb whole new markets.

Windows itself had moved up, as Windows NT, to slowly take over the server software business, and down, as Windows NX, to begin to swallow up the consumer electronics market.

Gates was anything but a fool. He knew his history. Whenever a company was on top in American business, it became a magnet for every antagonism in American life. Companies organized to defeat it, unions and activists plotted against it, columnists used it as a metaphor for all that was wrong in society, psychotics targeted it as the source of their demons—and worst of all, the government used its power under antitrust laws to shatter it. It had happened, each in their turn, to Standard Oil, Ford, IBM and AT&T. Now, Gates knew, it was happening to Microsoft. Venture capitalist John Doerr set up a $200 million investment fund just to create companies to attack Microsoft. Gates himself had stormed out of an interview with Connie Chung when it became too ugly—then had his PR people paint it over the next day by announcing that he planned to someday become a great philanthropist. Most ominously, Microsoft had to sign a consent decree with the U.S. Justice Department not to use the monopoly it held with Windows to force its way into other markets. Now Netscape and others were howling that Microsoft had done just that with the Explorer browser. It would not be surprising if the Justice Department made a major move, perhaps brought suit, very soon. For Gates, whose only goal in life had been to win, victory was turning to ashes.

And then, like the answer to a prayer, Steve Jobs called. For Gates, the offer had everything going for it. By investing just $150 million to prop up Apple, Microsoft, as the largest Apple software developer, would be protecting its $1 billion-plus-per-year Mac software business. And it would get nonvoting shares in the company to boot. There was also an agreement, for an undisclosed amount, to settle Apple's claims against Microsoft for violating its patents. That removed that tiresome little problem.

Gates had also gotten his own concession from the deal: all future Macintosh computers would come bundled with the Microsoft Internet Explorer. And Apple would join with Microsoft to help drive Microsoft's own version of Java. Netscape and Sun were to be left at the altar. Now every PC in the world would be sold with the Microsoft browser and run Microsoft's Java. Each of those concessions alone was worth more than a piddling $150 million to Microsoft.

But the agreement was far more than just the paperwork and the exchange of cash and equity. By keeping his enfeebled last competitor alive, Gates strengthened his argument against the Justice Department. How can you say I'm a monopoly? Apple remains a mighty competitor! Conversely, if Apple nevertheless were to shut its doors, no one could now blame Microsoft. Hey, we helped those guys stay alive!

And there was one other reason, much subtler than the rest. Like Larry Ellison, Bill Gates coveted the Apple story, the love and fidelity it enjoyed not only from its customers but from the general public. The world might buy Windows 95, but it did so without love. Since the Homebrew days, Gates had watched Apple longingly from afar. That was why he wrote the letter, why he hung in with Apple software even though he could easily have pulled out, killed Apple overnight and forced its customers to migrate to Wintel. In 1984, at the time of the Mac's introduction, he had gushed in *MacWorld*'s first issue: ". . . the Mac heralds a major change in how people view and interact with applications programs. That's why I'm so excited about it. There's no question that I'll let my mom try it out."

The toughest businessman of his era was a closet Macolyte, a secret romantic in love with the Apple myth. That wasn't the only reason why he was willing to help the company one more time; but it certainly was why he was willing to come out of his secure bunker in Redmond and make a live television appearance before an audience that was certain he was Satan incarnate. Bill Gates was closing his own loop with Apple Computer.

The final arrangements for the keynote were made the day before. As caught by the *Time* photographer, Jobs paced the stage, making last-minute decisions about the presentation (to be run by Jobs's IBM Thinkpad laptop), all the while talking with Gates in Redmond over a cell phone. The epiphany, the image *Time* put on its cover, came at the end of the conversation: Jobs, dressed all in black like a famous fashion designer, squatting on the stage, signing off on the phone to the world's richest man by saying, "Bill, thank you for your support of this company. I think the world's a better place for it." It was beautiful. Steve Jobs had attached his dead company to the most successful firm in America and somehow made it look not like he'd managed a desperate bailout but instead had performed a selfless act to save all of humanity. He said it was "a little like Nixon going to China. It's the right thing to do." In the process, Jobs had given a mini-lesson in self-promotion to his old friend and enemy. Of course, it was just for such lessons that Bill Gates had signed on.

The keynote itself was as earthshaking as Jobs had planned it to be. And it seemed so effortless—why hadn't he done it with NeXT or Pixar during the last decade? His talk was that unique mix of cockiness, false (and perhaps now even some real) humility and change-the-world optimism that had always been uniquely persuasive. It was a multimedia extravaganza as well, the computers themselves providing their own show—a measure of how far technology had come since the crowd had applauded the first Mac's ability to talk.

Then the first—as it turned out, minor—climax. Apple introduced its new board of directors. Conspicuously evident were Jobs and Larry Ellison. Conspicuously absent was Mike Markkula. His twenty-year side career at Apple was, mercifully, at an end. Jobs had finally taken his last bit of revenge.

On-screen, newly anointed director Larry Ellison, caught on video by a camera crew at the San Jose airport, described his feelings about Apple. He spoke from the heart, and his words unknowingly also captured the feelings of the surprise guest who would soon appear. "Apple is the only lifestyle brand in the industry," said Ellison. "It's the only company people feel passionate about. My company, Oracle, is huge; IBM is huge; Microsoft is huge; but no one has incredible emotions with our companies."

Then, unbelievably, on the giant screen appeared the live image of Bill Gates. The crowd, utterly stunned, was momentarily silent. Then it exploded into cheers, as much for Jobs as for Gates. My God! He even got *Bill Gates* to show up!

But in the midst of the cheers, there was also a chorus of boos. Someone yelled, "You've got to be kidding!" Gates heard this and for an instant was taken aback. He made a small smile of recognition. Normally he had an army of flacks to protect him from this exposure to the real world, and the smile was his acknowledgment that this was the cost of coming out in the open. Jobs was visibly annoyed at what, with no trace of irony, he later called "childish behavior." He added, "I'm sure some people want to cling to old identities. I was a little disappointed at the unprofessional reaction. On the one hand, people are dying to get the latest release of Microsoft Office on their Macs, and on the other hand, they're booing the CEO of the company that puts it out. It seems really stupid to me."

But to the stunned crowd, Jobs was more diplomatic. He told them, "We have to let go of the notion that for Apple to win, Microsoft needs to lose. The era of competition between Microsoft and Apple is over, as far as I'm concerned."

Gates himself spoke in the careful platitudes of a man who knew that nearly $200 billion of stock rested on his every word. "It's very exciting to renew our commitment to Macintosh," etc. etc. But what the crowd saw was something entirely different. It took a few moments, but soon whispers were racing through the multitudes. It was déjà vu. Where had they seen all this before?

Of course.

The famous "1984" commercial. The bespectacled Big Brother on the screen, spouting gibberish. How did it go?

> Each of you is a single cell in the great body of the state. And today, that great body has purged itself of parasites . . . The thugs and wreckers have been cast out . . . our unification of thought is more powerful a weapon than any fleet or army on earth. *We are one people. With one will. One resolve. One cause . . .*

The crowd gasped in realization that it had always been wrong. The "1984" commercial was not an allegory about IBM. It was a *prophecy.* And now that prophecy had come true.

10.7 Fan Dance

The Gates-Jobs reconciliation stunned and amazed the world. It ran in every newspaper on the planet. It led television news stories. And if *Time* had the exclusive on the story, *Newsweek* countered by devoting its cover story to a feverish debate on whether Microsoft was good for Apple. Only editor Allan Sloan, like the one sober grouch at a really fun drunken party, was churlish enough to note that it didn't really matter. Microsoft had won. And Apple was now too small and too dead to matter anymore except as an antitrust shield for Bill Gates. "Why a company with less than a 4 percent market share gets so much ink is one of life's mysteries," he wrote.

Meanwhile, Jobs, knowing the truth in those comments, but also understanding that now once again, as at the beginning, image meant more than reality, did his best to keep the delirium going—and keep the press focused upon Apple.

The new board quickly got kudos from analysts everywhere. Finally, Apple had a collection of directors with both technical and business experience—and enough reputation not to be buffaloed. There remained two holdovers from the past, both of whom had shown themselves capable of making decisions: Woolard and Gareth C. C. Chang, senior marketing vice president of Hughes Electronics. Then the impressive new four: Jobs (who finally got some Apple stock options again); Ellison; Jerry York, the former CFO of Chrysler and IBM; and Bill Campbell, the onetime head of Apple USA and Claris and now chairman of Intuit, one of the few companies that had ever taken on Microsoft and lived.

It was an amazing collection of names for such a little company, a credit to both Apple's image and Jobs's charms. But the personal dynamics were impossible. Ellison, for example, hated Gates to the point of obsession. How was that supposed to jibe with the new Apple-Microsoft love affair? Then there was the matter of how two giant egos like Jobs and Ellison were going to fit in the same room, much less come to an agreement. And what about all the baggage from the past being brought back by Campbell?

That kept Apple watchers occupied for days. And when that story faded, Jobs had another: Who would Apple choose as its interim CEO? The answer, of course, was a foregone conclusion. But Jobs strung it out for all that it was worth, finally accepting the job only after repeating that he didn't want to be the real CEO because his commitments lay elsewhere.

Then another bombshell. Jobs began to shut down all of Apple's support for its clone makers. Jobs hadn't liked the idea of licensing the OS in 1985 and he still didn't like it. The bitter cloners were left high and dry, scrambling for new survival strategies. Then Jobs drove home his point—*there will be no other Macs before me*—by buying back Power Computing's Apple license for $100 million. Power Computing's management, knowing it had no real choice, gulped and took the offer. As one Macolyte wrote on the Web: "In one fell swoop [Jobs] has alienated the hundreds of thousands of Mac clone buyers." Too bad.

Even as that story was filling the business pages of daily newspapers, Jobs played another card: the search for a new CEO. As early as the end of September there was rumored to be a short list of candidates who had been scrutinized and interviewed. They included, among others, Campbell, IBM senior vice president Samuel Palmisano, Sun senior executive Ed Zander, Pacific Bell CEO/SBC Communications vice president David Dorman, Autodesk CEO Carol Bartz and Cadence Design chief Joe Costello. But Dorman privately told others that the newspaper coverage was the first he'd heard of it, that Apple had never interviewed him and that in his conversations with some of the other candidates they said the same. Besides, said Dorman, "Good God, can you imagine taking a job where you've got Steve Jobs and Larry Ellison looking over your shoulder? You'd have to be out of your mind." Instead, Dorman took over hot little Internet company Pointcast.

The CEO campaign, planned as a nice publicity bridge, now began to backfire. Jobs publicly hinted that the CEO search was not going as well as expected. He said that he had turned the company over "to a bozo" once before, and he was not going to do it again. He told attendees at a Macromedia User Conference that he was considering dropping "interim" from his title at Apple.

It all smelled like a setup. Especially when Jobs announced that he was going to Hawaii—Mount Ararat apparently being too far—to walk on the beach and ponder his future. Everyone was surprised when he did just that, then returned to announce that . . . no, he wasn't going to take the CEO job. Instead, he would direct the interviews of his potential replacement.

The months rolled on. On October 15, 1997, Apple announced a larger than expected $24 million loss. Worse, company sales fell by 31 percent. The stock market, seeing these numbers and watching Apple's market share continue to fall, all the while noting the blank slot in the permanent position at the top of the company's organization chart, began to bail out. On December 23, Apple's stock hit a low of $12.94 per share. For a while, it was rumored that Apple would be able to announce a new CEO—apparently it had settled on a candidate—at the usual big venue of the January MacWorld Expo. But January 1998 passed without any news. Apparently the candidate had balked. The rainy El Niño winter of 1998 turned into a cold spring. Still no word. When asked about the search on CNBC, Jobs announced that there had been an agreement beforehand not to discuss that (there wasn't) and stormed off the set.

"One can only hope," joked the *San Francisco Chronicle*, "that they'll burn white smoke over Cupertino when the blessed event occurs."

Commenting on his now lifelong nemesis/partner Bill Gates, Jobs said, "I wish him the best, I really do. I just think he and Microsoft are a bit narrow. He'd be a broader guy if he had dropped acid once or gone off to an ashram when he was younger"—a responsible quote from a parent and role model.

John Dvorak, now an industry old-timer, wrote in his column that the best joke around was as follows: Bill Gates and Steve Jobs were playing a friendly game of Frisbee at the Gates estate on the shore of Lake Washington. At one point, Bill accidently sends the Frisbee over Steve's head, and the Frisbee lands in the lake. Steve walks out onto the surface of the lake and retrieves the Frisbee.

The next day, the newspapers report:

GATES' THROW EXCEEDS EXPECTATIONS
APPLE CEO UNABLE TO SWIM

In the last week of December 1997, after eighteen years at the company's headquarters, Apple packed up his museum, with its complete collection of Apple Computers dating back to Woz's Apple I, manuals, photos from company parties and coffee mugs, and shipped it to Stanford University for the school's Silicon Valley archives.

10.8 Resprouting

Then, on January 7, 1998, Jobs thrilled the crowd at MacWorld Expo—and shareholders everywhere—by announcing that though revenues for the quarter would be down slightly (to $1.575 billion), the company would show a $47 million *profit!* Nobody expected Apple to be in the black for another year or two, if ever again. And now Steve Jobs had pulled it off in a matter of months. Given that the company had spent the previous year losing $1 billion, this was a turnaround of almost historic proportions.

That was only the beginning. The company had already introduced a new PowerMac product family, the G3, and it seemed to be doing well. But hardware had never been Apple's problem—it had always been everything else. And so everywhere else was where Jobs attacked next.

He fired 300 workers at the Claris subsidiary, renamed the place FileMaker Inc. and folded it back into Apple. He also blew up Apple's shrinking distribution system, pulling out of every computer retailer except one, CompUSA, which had continued to aggressively sell Apple products. From now on, Jobs announced, Apple would direct-sell over the Internet, a technique successfully pioneered by Michael Dell. "We're coming to get you, buddy," Jobs warned Dell at a public event, talking to a giant poster of the Texas billionaire. Dell's reply was brief: "Having our picture on the wall isn't going to help them with the problem of their legacy."

Apple sold $30 million in computers the first day of its new Web retail site. Meanwhile, the company's share of the education market, the historic heart of Apple's business, dropped to 27 percent, compared with 61 percent four years before.

In January 1998, Gordon Thygeson, a one-time Apple contract employee, published *Apple T-Shirts: A Yearbook of History at Apple Computer.*

Thygeson explained the book by saying that he had been looking for a compelling way to tell the Apple story "when it hit me one day that it really was T-shirts."

There in the pages, was the other side of the Apple story. Not the great events and great men and women who led the company through them, but the witty voices of the Apple employees, T-shirt warriors for the great crusades, cannon fodder for the disasters. It was all there: from psychedelia (a photo of Steve Jobs: "This is Apple"; a photo of John Sculley: "This is Apple on drugs . . . any questions?") to power business in the 1990s (from the Power Macintosh group: "I helped save the company and all I got was this lousy T-shirt."). It was a reminder that no technology company had ever been so identified with the culture, had so changed the culture, or been changed by it in return, than Apple Computer.

Jonathon Martin, the first Apple baby, was now twenty years old. His father, Gary Martin, after serving as company treasurer and controller, had left Apple in 1982 and gone on to a successful career at several high-tech companies. He still stayed in touch with Mike Scott and looked back on his Apple days fondly as "the best of times and the worst of times."

Young Jonathon, a third-generation Valleyite, not surprisingly was a computer fan. His machine of choice was a Compaq.

Geoff Chatterton joined Apple in 1994 after graduating from MIT and a stint in the Navy. In his three years at Apple, most of them spent in a software engineering group for high-end Macs, Chatterton had worked for three different CEOs and suffered through six reorganizations. "I once spent eight months trying to put together some specs on a licensing deal, only to have them thrown out when Apple changed its strategy."

Chatterton had initially put a lot of hope in Gil Amelio straightening out the mess at Apple. But he was quickly disappointed. "Amelio went through an MBA 101 book to figure out how to run Apple. Everybody trusted him at first because he was a real engineer. But he turned out to have less charisma even than Spindler, had no insight into the business and ultimately added no value to the firm." As for Ellen Hancock: "Everybody was singing praises about her technical ability, but she understood broad concepts—that was all. People cheered when she left."

Now the boss was Steve Jobs. Chatterton admired his style, if he wasn't quite sure of his character. "Some people think he is good for Apple; others don't trust him," Chatterton said. What he liked was the man's decisiveness. "If he sees something that's screwed up, he makes a decision."

Decisiveness, and the consistency it created, had long been the missing factor in his time at Apple. His group, though it had been a major contributor to Apple's bottom line, had long been a victim of changing corporate strategies, especially in licensing. "It distracted a lot of time and energy from our work. Every time Apple licensed its technology to cloners, and they came up with some little improvement, Apple then felt compelled to respond to it. It was an incredible time sucker."

So why did he stay at Apple? Because he loved the Mac, the autonomy and most of all the camaraderie of his group. "A lot of people have been here a long time. They don't care about the CEO—they've seen them come and go. At one time, the three levels of management above us were all vacant. It didn't make any difference. They just keep doing their work."

Lubricating that camaraderie was plentiful quantities of beer. For a while, Apple bought the beer to stock the group's refrigerators. "It's not unusual to see people drink at any time of the day," says Chatterton. "You see guys drinking at 10 A.M. As long as we get our work done."

But, as an austerity measure during the hard times at the end of Amelio's term, Apple stopped supplying the beer, forcing the employees to bring their own. "That's their way of cutting costs."

10.9 GHOSTS

On March 2, 1998, Apple killed the Newton. Steve Jobs had now eliminated every trace of John Sculley from Apple. The explanation was that in its current condition Apple needed to focus on a much more narrow product line. Personal digital assistants were no longer in the business strategy.

The tragedy of the Newton was that, at the end, it was a superb little machine, better than anything on the market. But it still bore the stigma of its disappointing beginnings, and it had never escaped that curse. Apple might have been able to burnish that image. But it had been too distracted by two years of nightmares to pay much attention.

On the day after the announcement, the standard Apple protest crowd of a hundred appeared on the company lawn. Few knew the grass they walked on had been well trod. The group waved a few signs and spoke to a few bored reporters, but mostly they swapped business cards and programs and promised to stay in touch. Then they went on with their lives.

On the day the Newton was exterminated, John Sculley was invited to be Neil Cavuto's guest on the Fox news channel.

The segment was entitled "The Perils of Being Ahead of the Technological Curve." John Sculley had finally gotten his wish—at least on the East Coast, he was seen now as a great technological visionary, and, in Cavuto's words, "one of the classiest acts in corporate America."

In his eulogy for the Newton, Sculley described one of the most expensive failures in high-tech history (though far short of his disastrous Copland) as a noble failure. "In retrospect," he said, "the Newton shot too high," whereas the wildly successful Palm Pilot was "more pragmatic." Still, Sculley added wistfully, "the DNA of Apple is to be out on the leading edge of invention. The first versions [of Apple's products] were often not successful, but the second versions always were . . . [We] had to keep improving on them."

In other words, the Newton wasn't a multihundred-million-dollar disaster that had contributed to the meltdown of one of the most successful companies in America, but a great product on the brink of a magnificent victory . . . if only given a second chance.

Sculley was then asked about the return of Steve Jobs. "He should," Sculley replied. "It's his company. Only he can run it."

A few weeks later, yet another Apple ex-CEO was heard from. Gil Amelio was promoting his new book, *On the Firing Line,* subtitled *My 500 Days at Apple.* It was one of the oddest, and most memorable, memoirs ever written by the head of a major U.S. corporation, and tangible proof of the adage that nobody ever left Apple the same person.

Amelio's argument, presented as a Shakespearean tragedy (even the chapter heads were quotes from *Hamlet, Macbeth,* etc.) was that he had done a great job at Apple and had been in full command of the situation. As with Sculley's Newton, Amelio argued he needed only a little more time to turn things around.

But then he supported his case by, perversely, showing that he was neither competent nor in control of the company. In essence, CEOs have two tasks: make the company successful and identify any competitive threats to the company when they appear. Under Amelio's command, Apple had lost $1.6 billion and thousands of employees. Moreover, he had invited into the executive offices a dangerous and brilliant individual that everybody but Amelio (despite more than fair warning) knew would soon hijack the firm.

Thus, instead of the triumphant revisionism Gil Amelio imagined his book to be, it was in fact a revealing—and pathetic—look into the life of a successful businessman lost in a cultural phenomenon he still didn't understand. Slate.com called it "a work of colossal petulance."

In the book, Amelio whined about how he lost precious time because the CEO didn't have a reserved parking place (then noted that Jobs merely parked in the handicapped zone). He dropped celebrity names ("Michael Crichton's carefully expressed contribution was memorable and Richard Dreyfuss poignantly described the importance of saving Apple . . ."). He carefully blamed himself for what happened, but then accused subordinates of stupidity, cupidity or selfishness. He kvetched about the size of his golden parachute. He attacked some of the best reporters in the business for being inaccurate, cynical, disrespectful or irresponsible—then lauded some of the most notorious softballers in the media. In all, it was, in the words of one Valley veteran, "the kind of kiss-off book you write when you've got enough money not to worry about ever working again."

But Amelio saved most of his bile for Steve Jobs. In that meeting at National, Jobs had not only warned Amelio he wanted the CEO's seat again at Apple, but let him know what he would do to get it. Now, after Jobs had done exactly that, Amelio was bitter. "Betrayal, assassination, [and] trashing of reputations are part of the everyday tool kit of a person obsessed with power, control, or revenge," he wrote. "I was in Steve's way and had to be eliminated."

At a book-signing party in Silicon Valley after the publication of the book, Gil Amelio showed up in his standard dress suit. Looking around the room at the casual crowd, he ended his story with Apple perhaps as he might have begun.

He took off his tie.

10.10 Going Home

As the weeks of Jobs's return turned into months, observers increasingly began to complain that there appeared to be no rhyme or reason to Steve Jobs's leadership of Apple, that he seemed to be making it up as he went along, changing his mind almost every time he changed his socks.

But that was the point: Jobs *was* making up Apple as he went along. He always had. Then and now he understood that until the company found solid ground (if it ever did) he would have to keep dancing, bluffing, fighting for attention. Because if the world ever stopped looking or, more accurately, stopped believing in the fantasy, Apple would shrivel away to its true self: a tiny, dead company trying desperately to reincarnate itself. For fiscal 1997, Apple's total share of the world personal computer market was just 3.1 percent, down from 5.2 percent the year before. By February 1998, and the end of the company's first quarter, that number had slumped to just 2.6 percent.

But there was an even more mysterious question behind the first one. What does Steve Jobs want? Why was he back at Apple? He was already rich, famous beyond imagining, involved with another highly successful, wildly popular company. He hobnobbed with the rich and famous of Hollywood, Washington and Silicon Valley. He was reconciled with his daughter, happily married and blessed with two new children. He could have let Apple fade away and the blame would have fallen on Sculley, Spindler and Amelio. He seemed to have nothing to gain and much to lose by returning to the blasted remains of his former glory. What did Steve Jobs want with Apple?

A clue appeared not long after the Boston MacExpo. Steve Jobs requested a permit from the city of Palo Alto to allow him to purchase the property next door to his own, bulldoze the house and plant a fruit tree orchard.

The request provoked considerable mirth in Silicon Valley. But at its heart was a devastating image. The man who had probably done more than anyone else to bury verdant Santa Clara Valley, the "Valley of Heart's Delight," under the steel, asphalt and concrete of Silicon Valley, was now trying to restore a tiny corner of that lost world of his childhood. As any old orchardist could have told him, it wouldn't work. Fruit trees need virgin soil. But that probably still wouldn't have stopped him. The man with all the success any person could ever dream of was now looking back to that strange little boy who had begun this journey.

Then in October it became clear. The occasion was to announce a new advertising campaign for Apple. Its ungrammatical title was "Think Different" and it featured old black-and-white footage of famous mavericks: Einstein, Gandhi, Hitchcock, Bob Dylan, Martha Graham, Cassius Clay, the Dalai Lama (the last cravenly pulled in the Far East when China objected), and Ansel Adams. In downtown New York, on Fifth Avenue, a four-story-tall image of Joan Baez, Jobs's old girlfriend, appeared on the side of a building in all her folk era glory.

It was the whole pantheon of boomer heroes: the authors of the Penguin paperbacks you carried in your knapsack in 1969, the famous faces on the posters in your dorm room and at the art film house you hung out at in Palo Alto. The images would soon appear on billboards, in giant posters hung from the sides of the Infinite Loop facility and in television commercials featuring a voice-over by Richard Dreyfuss that sounded uncannily like Steve Jobs. It was a strange campaign, anachronistic in the 1980s and seemingly ill-suited for Apple at this moment in its history. As Umax Fred Huang said, "Apple's campaign is exactly wrong at this moment in history. In computing, nobody wants to think differently anymore. They want standardization. They all want to think the same way."

Huang was exactly wrong, for all the right reasons. If "Think Different" was preaching to the choir, it was also uniquely Steve Jobs. And these were his heroes. Once again, he was mapping his own inner world on to the one he was forced to share with the rest of us. The message was: These were the people you dreamed of growing up to be. And now, even if you have grown up to be only a department IT manager or an ad agency art director, you can still own the computer most of these people might have used if they weren't dead.

This oddly compelling campaign held yet another clue. Standing at the press conference before a giant projected image of Picasso—one sacred monster paying tribute to another—Steve Jobs looked as happy as he'd been in years. It was all there now, a recreation of the best days of his life: the tiny band, facing impossible odds, living by wit and pluck, fighting nobly to convince the world to dream its dream, and Steve Jobs standing before them, leading them on by the sheer force of his personality.

The journey is the reward, Steve Jobs had once famously said. And that reward had proved to be a second chance, a repeat journey. The opportunity to do it all over. And maybe not to just do it well this time, but also to do it right. No betrayals, no deceits, no victories at any cost.

10.11 Semper Fi

As before, Steve Jobs found his fanatical followers. His return was a catalyst for all the true believers, the Macolytes, to finally release all the pent-up frustration of years of apology and shame.

In early 1998, Rich Karlgaard, now the editor of *Forbes ASAP*, included an article on Apple in the issue about "Failure." Recalled Karlgaard, "Within days we were buried in dozens of e-mails calling us traitors and stooges for Microsoft and all kinds of obscenities. And most of them came from members of something called 'the Mac Marines.' "

Forbes ASAP responded in a later issue by running a parody of the "Think Different" ad, showing a picture of "Do," the leader of the suicidal Heaven's Gate cult.

10.12 Revisit

Could Steve Jobs regain the future by recreating the past?

The world had, after all, changed profoundly since he was touring computer stores along El Camino trying to sell the Apple I. Almost every person he had worked with or competed against in those days was now either dead, retired or long out of the industry. That too had been the seventies, with its economic recessions, antiestablishment hangover from the sixties, contempt for corporate life and its cult of individual satisfaction. It was the last hurrah of the baby boomers as a youth movement, and perhaps the last time small undercapitalized entrepreneurial start-ups could carve out a new hardware industry.

This was the nineties, one of the most prosperous epochs in American economic history. Corporate success stories, not lone rebels, were now the heroes of the age.

Technology, following the dictates of Moore's Law, had profoundly changed as well—so much that it belonged in a different universe from that of the Homebrew years. On March 17, 1998, Apple introduced a new PowerMacintosh G3 model. With 400 megahertz processing speed, more than a billion bits of disk memory, a built-in modem and stereo sound, a single one of these new computers was as powerful as all the computers in America when Jobs and Wozniak were first learning about data processing at Homestead High.

When Woz built the Apple I, the entire U.S. electronics industry was smaller than just Hewlett-Packard in 1998. Electronics was now, in fact, America's largest industrial employer, the linchpin of the current economic boom. Not only was Bill Gates, at $50 billion in personal worth, the richest private citizen in the world, but one company now had a market capitalization greater than the entire U.S. automobile industry. By century's end, it was predicted that one billion people would regularly be surfing the Internet. From David Packard's garage, and Steve Wozniak's garage and the halls of Fairchild Semiconductor had emerged one of the great social and economic revolutions in human history.

Could Steve Jobs really do it all again?

Certainly his luck seemed to have returned. Just six months before, Microsoft had seemed an unstoppable juggernaut—so dominant in high tech that new start-ups were now putting "sell to Microsoft" as the last step in their business plans. Now Microsoft found itself embroiled in one of the nastiest antitrust battles of the century. Bill Gates was appearing before congressional subcommittees, touring the country doing good PR works and marshalling support from cowed customers.

But arrayed against him was a Justice Department SWAT team and half the country's state attorney generals. There was talk of stopping the sale of the new Windows 98. Even of breaking up the company. Microsoft, which had never been defeated by a competitor, had now met the one force even greater than itself: the law and its enforcers.

That was only half of it. Despite its near-monopoly, until now Gates and Co. had escaped the calumny that usually surrounds monopolies. Until an extraordinarily late date, Bill was still seen by the general public as a benign nerd and his company an asset to modern life. That was crucial because Microsoft depended upon that reputation to recruit the best, brightest young people to become self-sacrificing "microserfs," to overrun new markets without fear of government interference and to sell its products to happy millions of eager customers.

Now all of that was at risk. Even if Microsoft survived the legal challenge, it was obvious that the image of the company would never be the same again. Microsoft was now the Evil Empire in many minds, a pernicious force in high tech—and perhaps soon in every other part of daily life. Against this backdrop, Apple suddenly once again seemed appealing. It was no longer an anachronism, a remnant of the past, but a refreshing alternative to Microsoft's totalitarianism.

Suddenly and serendipitously, Steve Jobs was back in vogue.

For those who believed he had changed over the previous two decades, they were soon disabused of that notion by reports coming out of Apple. Jobs, it seemed, was as manipulative and unpredictable as ever. If Jobs had intended to be different this time around, he had already failed. Jim Carlton presented a memorable image of the new/old Jobs on the cover of *The Wall Street Journal.*

In the profile, Jobs arrives at an interview with five prospective new engineering hires. He is wearing shorts and a T-shirt. One of the engineers asks what, after selling his stock and refusing to take the permanent CEO's post, is Jobs own commitment to Apple?

"Mr. Jobs starts out by tensely explaining how he is devoting so much time to Apple that he is sacrificing his family life. 'I'm working here eighteen hours a day,' he says. Then he quickly builds up to an obscenity-laced tirade, thundering, 'To the people who ask me that question, I say, "Fuck you! Fuck you!" ' "

When asked a similar question on a cable news show, Jobs announced,

"We agreed not to discuss that," yanked off his microphone and stormed off the set. The stunned reporter then informed the viewers there had been no such agreement.

The belittlement and abuse portions of the Jobs Reality Distortion Field were also back in regular use. Sculley and Amelio were publicly pronounced "bozos," with Amelio getting the added honor of having a stupidity gauge—the "Gil-o-meter"—named after him by Jobs: "two Gils" being twice as stupid as the man who had brought Jobs back to Apple. Wozniak, meanwhile, was informed he was no longer welcome.

The sweeping indictment was also restored. Not only did Jobs obviously favor his old NeXT employees at Apple, but even told visitors that Apple had "10,000 mediocre employees that have to be cleaned out." And, as always, there was the vengeance. After Jobs took over, he sent out a series of company-wide e-mails announcing everything from austerity measures to a new rule against bringing pets to work. When some employees, harkening back to the first Jobs era, responded by sending around a fake Jobs e-mail denouncing all Apple employees as lazy and reserving the handicapped parking only for himself, Jobs sent out yet one more e-mail making fake company e-mails a firing offense.

It was as if, after the decade-long absence, marriage, parenthood and independent success, Steve Jobs had not changed. He was as awful as ever. Yet, the same behavior that had driven him out of the company in 1985 was now met with a shrug, even a cheer. What had changed? One answer was Apple: The arrogant but troubled company of 1985, though now several times larger, was humbled and deeply in trouble. Even among the true believers there was a sense that this was the company's last chance. That it had nothing to lose by taking a final fling with the greatest, but most frightening, figure of its past.

There was also the myth itself. After ten years, there was almost no one left at Apple who recalled the Jobs era as it really had been. Rather, they remembered it from once-removed, from the stories they had heard and read of that time . . . and those tales had a frisson of excitement and danger. Better to reign in a thrilling corporate Hell than serve in a boring, dying Heaven.

They made the right choice—as had everyone who ever had the patience, the courage and the masochism to stick with Steve Jobs all the way through to the end. Somehow, as inexplicably as the first time, Apple Computer once again began to act like a winner—then became one. On April 15, the company announced yet another profitable quarter: $55 million. Sales were again down, $1.4 billion for the quarter, compared to $1.6 billion the year before, but operating expenses were also down (despite the new advertising campaign) and profit margins were up. The market responded by pushing Apple stocks to $28 per share, its highest point since the Sculley era, and adding $1.6 billion to the company's value. Better yet, the newest surveys showed Apple's market share back above 4 percent.

Profits up, market share up, stock up, hot new products rolling out the door, customer pride once again strong, Steve Jobs had once again pulled off a miracle at Apple Computer. The company was back from the dead.

And yet, like a new shoot from an old stump, the odds were against Apple this time ever becoming but a poor imitation of its former self. As much as one might cheer the company doubling its market share, that share was still less than 5 percent of the market—and the rest was almost entirely owned by the Wintel standard. The new G3's might be great machines, but the vast majority of the hardware and software was still being designed for Windows computers. Even if the Justice Department broke up Intel and Microsoft, that reality would not change.

Way back in the early 1980s, Mike Markkula had privately told Dave Martin, the Apple CFO, that the company had to maintain a 50 percent market share or it would lose control over its own destiny. Markkula had been prescient. When Apple crossed that line the year before the introduction of the Macintosh, its fate had been sealed. And no matter how many great new products the company introduced, how much attention it received in the press, how loyal its camp followers, the subsequent fifteen years had been one long slide.

In that light, for all of his success, all Steve Jobs had really accomplished was a temporary pause in Apple's long-term decline. Valley watchers understood this, seeing the recent two quarters of good news from Apple not as a rebirth, but as a perfect time to sell—for Jobs to repeat the successful final act of NeXT, the big payoff for loyal employees and shareholders—this time with his most famous creation. He had brought Apple into the world; now he was on hand to take it out.

Rumors ricocheted around the Valley in May 1998. Some thought the perfect buyer would be a content provider, such as Disney. Others guessed an appliance maker, such as GE. Still others suggested an infrastructure firm, such as cable giant TCI. Chris Nolan, tech gossip columnist at the *Mercury News*, reported rumors from inside Apple that the most ardent suitors were Japanese: Sony and Fujitsu. But the company denied any such reports.

10.13 Infinite Loop

But before the final fate of Apple Computer was determined, Steve Jobs still had one more unfinished item left on his agenda.

On May 7, 1998, Apple put on one more new product introduction. It was held, as long ago, at Flint Center on the campus of De Anza College. It was a disorienting sight. It seemed the same adoring crowd, the same press corps and camera crews as at the original Macintosh introduction 172 months before. Yet only Steve Jobs was the same. This was no longer a bid to control the future, but a long shot to save the past.

As on that first rainy afternoon, Jobs appeared onstage in a suit beside an object hidden beneath a velvet drape. With a flourish, Steve Jobs pulled away the cloth to reveal: the iMac, a stylish new G3 in a self-contained box of translucent "Bandai blue" plastic. In design, it was the sum of all of Steve Jobs's experiences in his first tenure at Apple, a cross between the Apple II, the Mac and the old Beehive terminals on which he and Woz had first learned about minicomputers. In style it was, like so much about Jobs's life, sixties redux, Jetsons meets the new Volkswagen Beetle. It was throwback artful enough to be cool. Some reviewers, including the reviewer for the online magazine *Salon*, hated it, suggesting that it looked like a sixties Japanese plastic toy. But he was buried in a tidal wave of adoration for the cute new Apple computer.

For ninety days, the world waited anxiously for the iMac to hit the shelves. With a mastery not seen in the computer industry since, well, the Macintosh, Apple nurtured the hysteria. Thanks to a $150 million advertising campaign (NOT AVAILABLE IN BEIGE read one Menlo Park billboard just a mile from the site of the first Homebrew meeting), consumers were brought to a near-frenzy of anticipation.

Amid the excitement, it was hard to get past the noise and spin and note that the iMac was, in fact, a pretty mediocre computer by the standards of the day. On the plus side, it did have a 233 MHz PowerPC G3 chip that made Jobs crow, "Faster than the fastest Pentium II money can buy"—an accurate statement for a few weeks at least. It also had a 4 GB hard disk, stereo speakers and a 33.6 modem—everything you needed for surfing the Net—all for just $1,299.

But it also didn't have a floppy disk drive, a decision made by Jobs to save money and justified by his belief that in the age of e-mail people didn't need floppies anymore. (As with the Mac and the Next computer, memory had always been Steve Jobs's biggest blind spot.) Adding an external floppy drive boosted the price a couple hundred bucks—a much less impressive price tag in a world where equivalently powered PCs (with 56K modems) were selling for $999.

Finally there was the design itself. Cute as a button, but the fixed screen and the circular mouse were a denial of fifteen years of accumulated experience in the ergonomics of personal computing. The iMac screamed repetitive stress injuries.

But none of that mattered in the least. What really mattered was that, in a dreary world of predictable, boring beige personal computers, Steve Jobs had brought style back to the computer industry. He had regained the perfect pitch in PCs he had enjoyed so many years before. Once more, he knew what the market wanted before the market itself knew.

If the iMac was more of a price and packaging breakthrough than a technological revolution, well, damn it, these weren't revolutionary times. If it represented a triumph of style over substance, so, it seemed in that dreary summer and autumn, did most things, including the U.S. presidency, the stock market and, in light of the impending Year 2000 Crisis, the technology revolution itself. Now that we knew that computers weren't going to save the world, why not just buy a cute one?

On August 14, 1998, the iMac was officially shipped to the world. The Apple I had made its first appearance in the little Mountain View Bytes Shop, one of a half-dozen computers in a store the size of a tract house living room. Twenty-two years later the iMac arrived in Silicon Valley at places like Fry's Electronics in Sunnyvale, giant 180,000-square-foot high-tech supermarkets that were commercial temples to the new religion invented by Woz and Jobs.

The iMac's arrival wasn't as earthshaking as Windows 95 had been—no midnight riots this time—but it was impressive nevertheless. All through the day, and for many days thereafter, customers parked in the giant parking lot and made their way past a huge inflated iMac balloon beside the front door and on into the noisy maw of Fry's in its full retail frenzy. Once inside, with scores of others, they crossed the crowded floor, past the espresso shop and the racks of hundreds of trade magazines, to the single aisle that offered Apple products.

Usually a lonely afterthought in the sea of PCs, the Apple aisle was now the target of all eyes. One after another, boxes bearing the blue iMac image were loaded into shopping carts and proudly rolled to the fifty checkout registers at the front of the store. And as the iMacs and their proud new owners made the transit across the store, they passed a small lucite pyramid, a museum in miniature, containing an original Apple I, the printed circuit board still bearing Woz's original solders.

Thousands of shopping carts were filled with iMacs in the next few weeks.

At the end of August, the iMac was declared the second bestselling personal computer in the world (behind the budget HP Pavilion 6330) during the month—despite the fact that it had been available only for two of the four weeks. The iMac had captured 7.1 percent of total sales for the month, despite being the most expensive of the top five (the other three were Compaq Presario versions). Analysts were now predicting that Apple might sell 400,000 to 600,000 iMacs by year's end—spiking Apple's sales by 120 percent in August alone and adding a predicted $400 million to the company's sales for the quarter on a base of $1.5 billion.

And the news only got better. Of the iMac's purchasers, only 82 percent were current Apple owners—meaning that the new computer was hardly cannibalizing the company's current customer base. Meanwhile, an incredible 16 percent of iMac buyers were either first-time computer purchasers or owners of Windows machines—the first serious turnaround in Apple's downward market share slide in twenty years. Better yet, one in five iMac purchasers were fifty years or older—meaning that the iMac was now penetrating markets even Microsoft couldn't reach. In the graphics and publishing world, the gains were even more significant, as the trade press for those industries reporting that firms were junking their multi-PC networks for comparable iMac configurations. By late September, to the world's appreciation but Silicon Valley's chagrin, even the unlamented old Apple arrogance could be seen in cafes and shops around Cupertino. On October 14, 1998, the company announced its first profitable year since 1995.

It was, by any measure, an extraordinary coup for Apple, perhaps the last great victory in the story of personal computing. Steve Jobs had kicked off the personal computer revolution, and now he had likely pulled down the curtain on the final act. For all the excitement generated by the iMac, it had about it the air of a twilight act.

The personal computer industry, long the embodiment of youthful enterprise, was growing old. Worse, it was growing stable. Despite the tiny revolts in the provinces, Bill Gates and Microsoft had won. The market itself, once unstoppable, had begun to plateau, the battle now largely between the big price-bombing mass manufacturers like Compaq, Dell and Gateway. By Christmas 1998, the world would likely see the first $600 PCs. As early as October, a Korean firm had announced a $995 laptop. In this low-budget, commodity computer world Apple could never compete. Even as the iMac was setting sales records, rumors were rife in Silicon Valley that Apple would soon surrender at last and introduce a Windows-based computer.

What once seemed heresy now seemed merely good business. Even reports that Apple was moving out of computers and seeking a Japanese game maker as a strategic partner in the marketing of a new TV set-top Web-surfer/ game machine—code-named Columbus—didn't set off any anguished cries. It was enough that Steve Jobs had brought back the magic one last time.

And he certainly did. Once more he had drawn the world's attention to Apple, the company he had formed out of sheer will. Once more he had asserted his personality, his style, upon the entire computing world—a world that now stretched around the globe and numbered 500 million people.

Whatever came next in the Apple story, for good or bad, Steve Jobs would always have this moment, the capstone of the great second act of his career. He would forever have that moment, before the crowd at the iMac introduction. Standing there, Steve Jobs had grinned—not the twisted, ironic, but a true and sincere grin of joy—as the crowd watched and cheered. And then, on the iMac's screen, like a punchline that had been waiting fourteen years, appeared the words

hello
AGAIN

And with that, Steve Jobs closed the greatest and most enduring Apple loop of them all.

NOTES ON SOURCES

There is no shortage of source material on the story of Apple. On the contrary, for nearly twenty years we have been awash in it. Even with the recent attention afforded Microsoft, it can still reasonably be claimed that no company in history has earned such intense press and public scrutiny over the entire course of its existence.

The real challenge is to wade through these mountains of reporting, commentary and gossip, and try to extract the true story of Apple Computer. It isn't easy, not in the least because Apple itself has been an effective co-conspirator in this myth-making. Nowhere is the fog of myth thicker than in the official stories about the beginnings of the company, that shadowy world in which the young Steve Jobs and Stephen Wozniak skirted back and forth across the boundaries of the law.

All successful companies attempt to rewrite their histories, promoting those who stayed and erasing others who left, downrating losers in corporate purges and honoring the often ignoble winners. But always there is a patina of glory that is gilded onto these official histories. Every decision made was brilliant, every victory heroic, and every failure due to forces beyond the company's control. That's why official corporate histories are so excruciatingly awful. Not a whiff of failure, of human complexity or cupidity, is ever allowed to arise from the endless empty pages.

But Apple Computer is different. In its official story, the principals often seem to vie for the most outrageous story, for the behavior most deviant from the traditional business norm. And when they aren't boasting of their antisocial behavior, as in the case of the founders, they seem to be acting out their deepest psychological impulses and fears. Looking back over the manuscript of this book, I was struck by how many grown men, when faced with a serious career obstacle, collapse into tears. It's hard to imagine a book about Bethlehem Steel or Boeing Aircraft or Dow Chemical containing so many lachrymose moments.

Yet, all of this corporate soul-bearing is itself a form of propaganda—especially in the hands of we baby boomers. And especially at Apple Computer, the emblematic company of that generation. In the story of Apple, sensitivity has often been used as a bludgeon, and heady talk of changing the world as a smokescreen for the exploitation of employees, customers and outsiders.

Yet, opposed to this, there is always that other, larger, more magical story. Of the little company founded in a garage by kids with a dream—that went on to change the world and turn thousands of people into multimillionaires. It is the seminal entrepreneurial myth of our time, and one that will be told for generations.

When writing about Apple, you must approach the subject warily, because nothing—good or bad—is what it seems. Nothing. Read an expose about some corporate misadventure or stunning success, and with a little digging you're likely to find a "true" story behind it that presents the opposite conclusion. Then, six months later you'll encounter another company veteran who'll tell you the "real inside story" that somehow contradicts both.

Having grown up with Apple and its founders, and at times in its history having been inside the company, I at least knew enough not to trust any of the accepted stories, nor to believe anything I heard just once. It proved to be a good strategy.

I also faced another challenge. Every book ever written about Apple has been obsolete from the day it arrived on the bookstands. Inevitably, the company has gone sideways right after the latest corporate history has gone to press. This was true for *The Little Kingdom* (1984), the first major Apple history, which appeared just after the Macintosh was introduced and paled its story, right up to Jim Carlton's *Apple* (1997), which ended just before Steve Jobs hijacked the company and turned it around.

That last turn nearly caught me as well. Luckily I was running behind—and thus have been able to capture all of Jobs's great turnaround year, as well as the introduction of the watershed iMac. Nevertheless, I have little doubt that between the time I write this at the end of October 1998 and the time you read it, Apple will have surprised us again.

As I noted in the Foreword, I chose not to footnote *Infinite Loop*. Some of my books, especially those of business theory, have included hundreds of notes. But I felt they would be distracting to this kind of narrative. Moreover, the Internet has transformed the very nature of research by allowing high-speed quote checking.

Nevertheless, I want to use this Note to recognize all of those authors and reporters on whose hard work this book rests. I truly stand on the shoulders of dozens of giants. I will begin with listing key texts, then magazines and newspapers, and then individual sources. I have tried to cite individual sources in the text itself; what follows are sources for dozens of quotes and facts.

Books

One of the impressive things about the books written on Apple is their universally high quality. One reason, no doubt, is that the Apple story is just so crazy that it almost writes itself. On top of that, the company is also such a big story that it attracts the very best business writers. Finally, I think the overachieving nature of the company, especially in its early years, has brought out the best talents in those covering the firm.

Here, in chronological order, are some of the most useful books on Apple:

1. *The Little Kingdom* by Michael Moritz (Morrow, 1984)—Though long out of print (and out of date), still the best book ever written about Apple. Good reporting teamed with fine writing and filtered through a tough reporter's sensibility. Almost no factual errors—an amazing achievement given the corporate smokescreen the author had to cut through. At the time, Moritz was the San Francisco bureau chief for *Time.* Afterward, he became a very successful venture capitalist. His lead investment in Yahoo! made him richer (except for Jobs) than anyone at Apple he wrote about.
2. *Fire in the Valley* by Paul Freiberger and Michael Swaine (Osborne, 1984)—A paperback that has become something of a Silicon Valley cult classic. The seminal text on the early, early years of the personal computing industry. Identifies all the players. Great photos, too. A great reminder that there was a personal computer industry before the Apple II.
3. *Odyssey* by John Sculley (Harper & Row, 1987)—A standard self-promoting executive autobiography; in light of subsequent events almost amusing. Yet the first half of the book is an unusually revealing memoir of a Steve Jobs seduction, the second half a glimpse of Sculley's obsession with coming up with the Next Big Thing (the Knowledge Navigator).
4. *West of Eden* by Frank Rose (Viking, 1989)—Rose had the misfortune of having one tiny factual error (the location of a room in an Apple exec's

house) blown up into a scandal by Guy Kawasaki in the latter's book. *West of Eden* didn't deserve that fate, nor its subsequent disappearance from memory. It is, in fact, a terrific piece of reporting, covering the purge of Jobs from Apple. A crucial text.

5. *The Macintosh Way* by Guy Kawasaki (Doubleday, 1990)—Kawasaki is one of the Valley's more memorable characters—a human dynamo, a brilliant speaker and a tongue-in-cheek true believer. No one read this book expecting anything but a cheerleading session about Apple Computer. Yet, the book is surprisingly tough-minded about many of the company's flaws. As always, Guy is full of surprises.
6. *Accidental Millionaires* by Robert X. Cringely (Addison-Wesley, 1992)—The pseudonymous Cringely is notorious for his sloppy way with facts (and his lifting, without credit, of other reporters' stories). No sane person would ever use this book—or to a lesser degree the popular PBS miniseries, *The Revenge of the Nerds*, based upon it—as a sole source of information. But if Bob often gets the little stuff wrong, he gets the big stuff right more often than anybody in tech reporting. And, he is one hell of an entertaining writer. The Apple section of this book can make you laugh out loud.
7. *Insanely Great* by Steven Levy (Viking, 1994)—Essentially a paen to the Macintosh on its tenth anniversary, this book does a good job at capturing the milieu into which the Mac exploded. A real weakness to researchers is the book's lack of an index. Levy, who was writing for *MacWorld* at the time, has gone on to the prestigious and influential post of top computer writer at *Newsweek*.
8. *Apple* by Jim Carlton (Times Books, 1997)—Carlton, a terrific reporter at *The Wall Street Journal*, is the unluckiest of all the Apple historians. His topic is the Spindler/Amelio era—the least interesting part of the entire Apple story. Moreover, as noted, the book appeared just as Jobs took over and rendered his two predecessors superfluous. Despite this, the book is the critical missing link in the Apple canon, and Carlton's reporting is the best ever done about Apple—almost too much, some reviewers complained, the facts all but burying the narrative. Perhaps, but for researchers it is a dream.
9. *On the Firing Line* by Gil Amelio (Harper Business, 1998)—A rather sad attempt at explanation and revenge by Apple's ousted CEO. Amelio attempts to justify his tenure and trash Jobs as a Judas, but instead undermines his own case. After all, if Amelio was as clever as he claims to be, how come he didn't see Jobs coming? Everybody else sure did. Still, a good source for gossip about the great Apple collapse.

Needless to say, there are dozens of other books about Apple, ranging from hardcore tech manuals to coffee-table design books to novelty items such as a book on company T-shirts. The serious fan or student will find useful material in nearly all of them. A few of particular interest are *The Mac Bathroom Reader* and *The Macintosh Reader*, two compendia of trivia about that momentous product; Jeffrey Young's biography *Steve Jobs: The Journey Is the Reward*, a look at Jobs during the Next era; and Doug Garr's *Woz*.

Magazines

Apple Computer has led the march of technology stories out of the trade press, where such coverage began in the late 1960s, into business magazines and then into general interest magazines. It is telling these days that such publications as *Newsweek* and *Time* not only have computer and technology sections, but regularly devote covers to the topic. The revolution is now over; technology won. We all live in Woz's world.

A number of magazines were important sources in the preparation of *Infinite Loop*. The following is a list of them, and, in parentheses, the names of especially influential reporters:

Among the mainstream business magazines, the most important were *Business Week* (Kathy Rebello, perhaps the best—and most enduring—of all the journalists covering Apple), *Fortune* (Brent Schlender), and *Forbes* (Julie Pitta). One often overlooked magazine, but one that I have always found incredibly useful for any technology story, is *Industry Week*.

Among technology business magazines, the most important source has long been *Upside* (Eric Nee, Richard Brandt, Tish Williams, Dave Coursey, Paulina Borsook, and numerous others), which has covered Apple in almost every issue since the magazine's founding a decade ago. *Upside* has never been popular with Apple, and it is despised by Steve Jobs—which underscores the fine job it has done. Other useful tech-business sources on Apple include *Forbes ASAP*, *Red Herring*, and most of all, *Wired* (James Daly), whose June 1997 sacred Apple heart cover is one of the classics of the genre.

The electronics trade magazines that have educated me about Apple over the course of the last quarter-century are too numerous to mention, and include the various Apple-related magazines (*MacWorld*, etc.), PC magazines (*PC*, *Dr. Dobbs*, *Infoworld*), and newsletters (*Release 1.0*). I would like to note, though, two unlikely but very useful sources. First, *Computer Currents* is a thick, free publication handed out in Silicon Valley at places like Fry's. It offers a surprisingly extensive level of editorial coverage on computer-related topics. Second, the source for Jef Raskin's myth-demolishing memoir is Kip Crosby's *The Analytical Engine*, the journal of the Computer History Association of California.

NEWSPAPERS

The primary source for this book, especially from 1984 to the present, was daily newspapers. Several generations of newsies have covered the Apple beat, most of it through hard work under tight deadlines with little lasting recognition. The phrase about journalists writing "the first draft of history" was never more accurate.

The three national newspapers that have done the best job covering Apple are *USA Today* (especially Kathy Rebello, in an earlier incarnation), the *New York Times* (the two veterans Andrew Pollack and John Markoff), and *The Wall Street Journal* (Walter Mossberg, Jim Carlton and G. Pascal Zachary). All have done an excellent job over the last decade in keeping the Apple story in its proper perspective.

But the real heavy lifting in the daily coverage of Apple has always been done by the newspapers of the San Francisco Bay Area: the *San Francisco Examiner*, the *San Francisco Chronicle* (Peter Sinton, Herb Greenberg, Tom Abate, Jon Swartz, David Einstein) and most of all, the *San Jose Mercury News*. Over the years, an army of Merc reporters have given Apple almost unprecedented attention, capturing nearly every nuance of that company's operations. At least one hundred quotes in this book come from the *Mercury News*'s twenty-plus year coverage of Apple. Here are the names of some of the reporters who did the work: Bruce Entin, Mike Cassidy, David Plotnikoff, G. Pascal Zachary, Nancy Marx Better, Ron Wolf, Jim Bartimo, Steve Kaufman, Evelyn Richards, Jim Mitchell, Rory O'Connor, Kathy Holub, Mark Shwanhausser, Lee Gomes, Alex Barnum, Mary A. C. Fallon, Kathleen Parker, Jodi Mardesich, Miranda Ewell, David Sylvester, Lisa Raleigh, Debra Hauser, Jonathan Greer, Ray Alvareztorres, Denis Collins, Leigh Weimers, Valerie Rice, Tom Schmitz, Christopher Pummer, Laurie Flynn, Michelle Levander, Dan Gillmor, Chris Nolan, Miguel Helft, Oanh Ha, Mark Leibovich, Tom Quinlan, Adam Lashinsky and Mike Langberg.

To all of these folks, history (and I) owe an enormous debt of gratitude.

INDEX

ABOUT THE AUTHOR

Michael S. Malone grew up in Silicon Valley and joined the *San Jose Mercury News* as one of the nation's first daily high-tech reporters. He has written for *The Wall Street Journal*, the *New York Times* and other national publications. He is currently editor of *Forbes ASAP*. Among his books are *The Big Score*, *The Virtual Corporation* and *Intellectual Capital*. He also hosts *Malone*, an interview series now in its ninth season on public television.

Taxes Consolidation Act 1997

Finance Act 2014

Editor Kimberley Rowan
General Editor Brian Keegan

Chartered Accountants Ireland

Published by
Chartered Accountants Ireland
Chartered Accountants House
47-49 Pearse Street
Dublin 2
www.charteredaccountants.ie

ISBN: 978-1-910374-26-9

Printed in the UK by CPI William Clowes

TABLE OF CONTENTS

PROVISIONAL COLLECTION OF TAXES ACT, 1927

WAIVER OF CERTAIN TAX, INTEREST AND PENALTIES ACT, 1993

INCOME TAX (EMPLOYMENTS) (CONSOLIDATED) REGULATIONS, 2001 (S.I. 559/2001)

PART 1
GENERAL

PART 2
REGISTER OF EMPLOYERS AND REGISTERS OF EMPLOYEES

PART 3
TAX CREDITS AND STANDARD RATE CUT-OFF POINT

PART 4
DEDUCTION AND REPAYMENT OF TAX

PART 5
PAYMENT AND RECOVERY OF TAX, ETC

PART 6
ASSESSMENT

PART 7
CONTRIBUTIONS BY EMPLOYEES TO CERTAIN SUPERANNUATION FUNDS AND SCHEMES

PART 8
SPECIAL PROVISIONS WHERE EMPLOYEES ARE IN RECEIPT OF OR ARE ENTITLED TO RECEIVE CERTAIN BENEFITS PAYABLE UNDER THE SOCIAL WELFARE ACTS

PART 9
MISCELLANEOUS

TAXES (OFFSET OF REPAYMENTS) REGULATIONS 2002 (S.I. 471/2002)

PART 1
GENERAL

PART 2
OFFSETTING

PART 3

MISCELLANEOUS

INTERPRETATION ACT 2005

PART 1

PRELIMINARY AND GENERAL

PART 2

MISCELLANEOUS RULES

PART 3

CITATION AND OPERATION OF ENACTMENTS

PART 4

MEANING AND CONSTRUCTION OF WORDS AND EXPRESSIONS

PART 5

POWERS AND DUTIES

PART 6

AMENDMENT OF ENACTMENTS, ETC.

TAX RETURNS AND PAYMENTS (MANDATORY ELECTRONIC FILING AND PAYMENT OF TAX) REGULATIONS 2008 (S.I. 341/2008)

TAX RETURNS AND PAYMENTS (MANDATORY ELECTRONIC FILING AND PAYMENT OF TAX) REGULATIONS 2011 (S.I. 223/2011)

UNIVERSAL SOCIAL CHARGE REGULATIONS 2011 (S.I. 658/2011) Amended by S.I. No 614 of 2014

PART 1

GENERAL

PART 2

RATE CUT-OFF POINTS

PART 3

DEDUCTION AND REPAYMENT OF USC

PART 4

PAYMENT AND RECOVERY OF USC

PART 5

ASSESSMENT

TAX RETURNS AND PAYMENTS (MANDATORY ELECTRONIC FILING AND PAYMENT OF TAX) REGULATIONS 2012 (S.I. 156/2012)

RETURNS OF PAYMENT TRANSACTIONS BY PAYMENT SETTLERS (MERCHANT ACQUIRERS) REGULATIONS 2012 (S.I. 324/2012)

INCOME TAX AND CORPORATION TAX (RELEVANT CONTRACTS TAX) REGULATIONS 2012 (S.I. 576/2012)

PART 1
GENERAL

PART 2
REGISTRATION

PART 3
NOTIFICATIONS TO REVENUE

PART 4
DEDUCTION AUTHORISATIONS AND DEDUCTION SUMMARIES

PART 5
RETURNS AND ADJUSTMENT TO LIABILITY

PART 6
MISCELLANEOUS

AGREEMENT TO IMPROVE TAX COMPLIANCE AND PROVIDE FOR REPORTING AND EXCHANGE OF INFORMATION CONCERNING TAX MATTERS (UNITED STATES OF AMERICA) ORDER 2013 (S.I. NO. 33/2013)

SCHEDULE

FINANCIAL ACCOUNTS REPORTING (UNITED STATES OF AMERICA) REGULATIONS 2014 (S.I. NO. 292/2014)

TAX RETURNS AND PAYMENTS (MANDATORY ELECTRONIC FILING AND PAYMENT OF TAX) REGULATIONS 2014 (S.I. NO. 572 OF 2014)

TAXES CONSOLIDATION ACT, 1997

PART 1

INTERPRETATION

PART 2
THE CHARGE TO TAX

CHAPTER 1
Income Tax

CHAPTER 2
Corporation Tax

CHAPTER 3
Capital Gains Tax

PART 3
PROVISIONS RELATING TO THE SCHEDULE C CHARGE AND GOVERNMENT AND OTHER PUBLIC SECURITIES

CHAPTER 1
Principal Provisions Relating to the Schedule C Charge

CHAPTER 2

GOVERNMENT AND OTHER PUBLIC SECURITIES: INTEREST PAYABLE WITHOUT DEDUCTION OF TAX

CHAPTER 3

GOVERNMENT AND OTHER PUBLIC SECURITIES: EXEMPTIONS FROM TAX

CHAPTER 4

MISCELLANEOUS PROVISIONS

PART 4

PRINCIPAL PROVISIONS RELATING TO THE SCHEDULE D CHARGE

CHAPTER 1

SUPPLEMENTARY CHARGING PROVISIONS

CHAPTER 2

Foreign Dividends

CHAPTER 3

Income Tax: Basis of Assessment Under Cases I and II

CHAPTER 4

Income Tax: Basis of Assessment Under Cases III, IV and V

CHAPTER 5

Computational Provisions: Corporation Tax

CHAPTER 6

Computational Provisions: General

CHAPTER 7

Special Measures on Discontinuance of, and Change of Basis of Computation of Profits or Gains of, a Trade or Profession

CHAPTER 8

Taxation of Rents and Certain Other Payments

CHAPTER 9

Miscellaneous Provisions

PART 5
PRINCIPAL PROVISIONS RELATING TO THE SCHEDULE E CHARGE

CHAPTER 1
Basis of Assessment, Persons Chargeable and Extent of Charge

CHAPTER 2
Computational Provisions

CHAPTER 3
Expenses Allowances and Provisions Relating to the General Benefits in Kind Charge

CHAPTER 4
Other Benefit in Kind Charges

CHAPTER 5
Miscellaneous Charging Provisions

PART 6

COMPANY DISTRIBUTIONS, TAX CREDITS, FRANKED INVESTMENT INCOME AND ADVANCE CORPORATION TAX

CHAPTER 1

Taxation of Company Distributions

CHAPTER 2

Meaning of Distribution

CHAPTER 3

Distributions and Tax Credits — General

CHAPTER 4

Distributions Out of Certain Exempt Profits or Gains or Out of Certain Relieved Income

CHAPTER 5

DISTRIBUTIONS OUT OF CERTAIN INCOME OF MANUFACTURING COMPANIES

CHAPTER 6

DISTRIBUTIONS—SUPPLEMENTAL

CHAPTER 7

FRANKED INVESTMENT INCOME

CHAPTER 8

ADVANCE CORPORATION TAX

CHAPTER 8A

Dividend Withholding Tax

CHAPTER 9

Taxation of Acquisition by a Company of Its Own Shares

PART 7

INCOME TAX AND CORPORATION TAX EXEMPTIONS

CHAPTER 1

INCOME TAX

CHAPTER 2

Corporation Tax

CHAPTER 3

Income Tax and Corporation Tax

PART 8

ANNUAL PAYMENTS, CHARGES AND INTEREST

CHAPTER 1

Annual Payments

CHAPTER 2

Charges on Income for Corporation Tax Purposes

CHAPTER 3

Principal Provisions Relating to the Payment of Interest

CHAPTER 4

Interest Payments by Certain Deposit Takers

CHAPTER 5

Dividend Payments by Credit Unions

CHAPTER 6

Implementation of Council Directive 2003/49/EC of 3 June 2003 on a Common System of Taxation Applicable to Interest and Royalty Payments Made between Associated Companies of Different Member States

CHAPTER 7

Certain Interest from Sources [Outside the State]

PART 8A

SPECIFIED FINANCIAL TRANSACTIONS

CHAPTER 1

Interpretation

CHAPTER 2

Credit Return

CHAPTER 3

Deposit Return

CHAPTER 4

Investment Certificates and Returns

CHAPTER 5

Reporting

CHAPTER 6

Application

PART 9

PRINCIPAL PROVISIONS RELATING TO RELIEF FOR CAPITAL EXPENDITURE

CHAPTER 1

Industrial Buildings or Structures: Industrial Building Allowances, Writing-Down Allowances, Balancing Allowances and Balancing Charges

CHAPTER 2

Machinery or Plant: Initial Allowances, Wear and Tear Allowances, Balancing Allowances and Balancing Charges

CHAPTER 3

Dredging: Initial Allowances and Annual Allowances

CHAPTER 4

Miscellaneous and General

PART 10

INCOME TAX AND CORPORATION TAX: RELIEFS FOR RENEWAL AND IMPROVEMENT OF CERTAIN URBAN AREAS, CERTAIN RESORT AREAS AND CERTAIN ISLANDS

CHAPTER 1

Custom House Docks Area

CHAPTER 2

Temple Bar Area

CHAPTER 3

Designated Areas, Designated Streets, Enterprise Areas and Multi-Storey Car Parks in Certain Urban Areas

CHAPTER 4

Qualifying Resort Areas

CHAPTER 5

Designated Islands

CHAPTER 6

Dublin Docklands Area

CHAPTER 7

Qualifying Areas

CHAPTER 8

Qualifying Rural Areas

CHAPTER 9

Park and Ride Facilities and Certain Related Developments

CHAPTER 10

Designated Areas of Certain Towns

CHAPTER 11

Reliefs for Lessors and Owner-Occupiers in Respect of Expenditure Incurred on the Provision of Certain Residential Accommodation

CHAPTER 12

Mid-Shannon Corridor Tourism Infrastructure Investment Scheme

CHAPTER 13

Living City Initiative

PART 11

CAPITAL ALLOWANCES AND EXPENSES FOR CERTAIN ROAD VEHICLES

PART 11A

INCOME TAX AND CORPORATION TAX: DEDUCTION FOR EXPENDITURE ON CONSTRUCTION, CONVERSION AND REFURBISHMENT OF CERTAIN RESIDENTIAL ACCOMMODATION FOR CERTAIN STUDENTS

PART 11B

INCOME TAX AND CORPORATION TAX: DEDUCTION FOR EXPENDITURE ON REFURBISHMENT OF CERTAIN RESIDENTIAL ACCOMODATION

PART 11C

EMISSIONS-BASED LIMITS ON CAPITAL ALLOWANCES AND EXPENSES FOR CERTAIN ROAD VEHICLES

PART 11D

INCOME TAX AND CORPORATION TAX: RELIEFS FOR THE REMOVAL AND RELOCATION OF CERTAIN INDUSTRIAL FACILITIES

PART 12

PRINCIPAL PROVISIONS RELATING TO LOSS RELIEF, TREATMENT OF CERTAIN LOSSES AND CAPITAL ALLOWANCES, AND GROUP RELIEF

CHAPTER 1

Income Tax: Loss Relief

CHAPTER 2

Income Tax: Loss Relief—Treatment of Capital Allowances

CHAPTER 3

Corporation Tax: Loss Relief

CHAPTER 4

Income Tax and Corporation Tax: Treatment of Certain Losses and Certain Capital Allowances

CHAPTER 4A

Termination of Carry Forward of Certain Losses

CHAPTER 5

Group Relief

PART 13

CLOSE COMPANIES

CHAPTER 1

Interpretation and General

CHAPTER 2

Additional Matters to be Treated as Distributions, Charges to Tax in Respect of Certain Loans and Surcharges on Certain Undistributed Income

PART 14

TAXATION OF COMPANIES ENGAGED IN MANUFACTURING TRADES, CERTAIN TRADING OPERATIONS CARRIED ON IN SHANNON AIRPORT AND CERTAIN TRADING OPERATIONS CARRIED ON IN THE CUSTOM HOUSE DOCKS AREA

CHAPTER 1

Interpretation and General

CHAPTER 2

Principal Provisions

PART 15
PERSONAL ALLOWANCES AND RELIEFS AND CERTAIN OTHER INCOME TAX AND CORPORATION TAX RELIEFS
CHAPTER 1
Personal Allowances and Reliefs

CHAPTER 2

Income Tax and Corporation Tax: Reliefs Applicable to Both

CHAPTER 2A

Limitation on Amount of Certain Reliefs Used by Certain High Income Individuals

CHAPTER 3

Corporation Tax Reliefs

PART 16

INCOME TAX RELIEF FOR INVESTMENT IN CORPORATE TRADES — EMPLOYMENT AND INVESTMENT INCENTIVE AND SEED CAPITAL SCHEME

PART 17

PROFIT SHARING SCHEMES AND EMPLOYEE SHARE OWNERSHIP TRUSTS

CHAPTER 1

Profit Sharing Schemes

CHAPTER 2

Employee Share Ownership Trusts

CHAPTER 3

Approved Savings-Related Share Option Schemes

CHAPTER 4

Approved Share Option Schemes

PART 18

PAYMENTS IN RESPECT OF PROFESSIONAL SERVICES BY CERTAIN PERSONS AND PAYMENTS TO SUBCONTRACTORS IN CERTAIN INDUSTRIES

CHAPTER 1

Payments in Respect of Professional Services by Certain Persons

CHAPTER 1A

Payments in Respect of Non-resident Artistes by Companies Qualifying for Relief for Investment in Films

CHAPTER 2

Payments to Subcontractors in Certain Industries

PART 18A

INCOME LEVY

PART 18B

PARKING LEVY IN URBAN AREAS

PART 18C
DOMICILE LEVY

PART 18D
UNIVERSAL SOCIAL CHARGE

PART 19
PRINCIPAL PROVISIONS RELATING TO TAXATION OF CHARGEABLE GAINS

CHAPTER 1
Assets and Acquisitions and Disposals of Assets

CHAPTER 2
Computation of Chargeable Gains and Allowable Losses

CHAPTER 3

Assets Held in a Fiduciary or Representative Capacity, Inheritances and Settlements

CHAPTER 4

Shares and Securities

CHAPTER 5

Life Assurance and Deferred Annuities

CHAPTER 6

Transfer of Business Assets

CHAPTER 7

Other Reliefs and Exemptions

PART 20
COMPANIES' CHARGEABLE GAINS

CHAPTER 1
General

CHAPTER 2
Provisions Where Companies Cease to be Resident in the State

PART 21
MERGERS, DIVISIONS, TRANSFERS OF ASSETS AND EXCHANGES OF SHARES CONCERNING COMPANIES OF DIFFERENT MEMBER STATES

PART 22

PROVISIONS RELATING TO DEALING IN OR DEVELOPING LAND AND DISPOSALS OF DEVELOPMENT LAND

CHAPTER 1

Income Tax and Corporation Tax: Profits or Gains From Dealing in or Developing Land

CHAPTER 2

Capital Gains Tax: Disposals of Development Land

PART 23
FARMING AND MARKET GARDENING

CHAPTER 1
Interpretation and General

CHAPTER 2
Farming: Relief for Increase in Stock Values

CHAPTER 3
Milk Quotas

CHAPTER 4

Taxation of Stallion Profits and Gains

PART 24

TAXATION OF PROFITS OF CERTAIN MINES AND PETROLEUM TAXATION

CHAPTER 1

Taxation of Profits of Certain Mines

CHAPTER 2

Petroleum Taxation

CHAPTER 3
Profit Resource Rent Tax

PART 24A
SHIPPING: TONNAGE TAX

PART 25
INDUSTRIAL AND PROVIDENT SOCIETIES, BUILDING SOCIETIES, AND TRUSTEE SAVINGS BANKS

CHAPTER 1
Industrial and Provident Societies

CHAPTER 2
Building Societies

CHAPTER 3
Trustee Savings Banks

PART 25A
REAL ESTATE INVESTMENT TRUSTS

PART 26
LIFE ASSURANCE COMPANIES

CHAPTER 1
General Provisions

CHAPTER 2
Special Investment Policies

CHAPTER 3
Provisions Applying to Overseas Life Assurance Companies

CHAPTER 4
Taxation of Assurance Companies — New Basis

CHAPTER 5
Policyholders — New Basis

CHAPTER 6
Certain Foreign Life Policies — Taxation and Returns

PART 27

UNIT TRUSTS AND OFFSHORE FUNDS

CHAPTER 1

Unit Trusts

CHAPTER 1A

Investment Undertakings

CHAPTER 2

Offshore Funds

CHAPTER 3

Offshore Funds: Supplementary Provisions

CHAPTER 4

Certain Offshore Funds — Taxation and Returns

CHAPTER 5

Relevant UCITS and Relevant AIF

PART 28

PURCHASE AND SALE OF SECURITIES

CHAPTER 1

Purchase and Sale of Securities

CHAPTER 2

Purchases of Shares by Financial Concerns and Persons Exempted from Tax, and Restriction on Relief for Losses by Repayment of Tax in Case of Dividends Paid Out of Accumulated Profits

PART 29

PATENTS, SCIENTIFIC AND CERTAIN OTHER RESEARCH, KNOW-HOW AND CERTAIN TRAINING

CHAPTER 1

Patents

CHAPTER 2
Scientific and Certain Other Research

CHAPTER 3
Know-How and Certain Training

CHAPTER 4
Transmission Capacity Rights

PART 30
OCCUPATIONAL PENSION SCHEMES, RETIREMENT ANNUITIES, PURCHASED LIFE ANNUITIES AND CERTAIN PENSIONS

CHAPTER 1
Occupational Pension Schemes

CHAPTER 2

Retirement Annuities

CHAPTER 2A

Personal Retirement Savings Accounts

CHAPTER 2B

Overseas Pension Plans: Migrant Member Relief

CHAPTER 2C

Limit on Tax-Relieved Pension Funds

CHAPTER 3
Purchased Life Annuities

CHAPTER 4
Miscellaneous

PART 31
TAXATION OF SETTLORS, ETC., IN RESPECT OF SETTLED OR TRANSFERRED INCOME

CHAPTER 1
Revocable Dispositions for Short Periods and Certain Dispositions in Favour of Children

CHAPTER 2
Settlements on Children Generally

PART 32
ESTATES OF DECEASED PERSONS IN COURSE OF ADMINISTRATION AND SURCHARGE ON CERTAIN INCOME OF TRUSTEES

CHAPTER 1
Estates of Deceased Persons in Course of Administration

CHAPTER 2
Surcharge on Certain Income of Trustees

PART 33
ANTI-AVOIDANCE
CHAPTER 1
Transfer of Assets Abroad

CHAPTER 2
Miscellaneous

CHAPTER 3
Mandatory Disclosure of Certain Transactions

CHAPTER 4

Payment Notices and Scheme Participants

PART 34

PROVISIONS RELATING TO THE RESIDENCE OF INDIVIDUALS

PART 35

DOUBLE TAXATION RELIEF

CHAPTER 1

Principal Reliefs

CHAPTER 2
Miscellaneous

PART 35A
TRANSFER PRICING

PART 36
MISCELLANEOUS SPECIAL PROVISIONS

PART 36A
SPECIAL SAVINGS INCENTIVE ACCOUNTS

PART 36B
PENSIONS: INCENTIVE TAX CREDITS

PART 37

ADMINISTRATION

PART 38

RETURNS OF INCOME AND GAINS, OTHER OBLIGATIONS AND RETURNS, AND REVENUE POWERS

CHAPTER 1

Income Tax: Returns of Income

CHAPTER 2

Corporation Tax: Returns of Profits

CHAPTER 3

Other Obligations and Returns

CHAPTER 3A

Implementation of Council Directive 2003/48/EC of 3 June 2003 on Taxation of Savings Income in the Form of Interest Payments and Related Matters

CHAPTER 4
Revenue Powers

CHAPTER 5

Capital Gains Tax: Returns, Information, etc.

CHAPTER 6

Electronic Transmission of Returns of Income, Profits, etc., and of Other Revenue Returns

PART 39
ASSESSMENTS [DELETED]

PART 40
APPEALS

CHAPTER 1
Appeals Against Income Tax and Corporation Tax Assessments

CHAPTER 2
Appeals Against Capital Gains Tax Assessments

CHAPTER 3
Miscellaneous

PART 41
SELF ASSESSMENT [DELETED]

PART 41 A
ASSESSING RULES INCLUDING RULES FOR SELF ASSESSMENT

CHAPTER 1
Interpretation (Part 41A)

CHAPTER 2
Assessments: General Rules

CHAPTER 3
Chargeable Persons: Returns

CHAPTER 4
Chargeable Persons: Self-Assessments

CHAPTER 5
Revenue Assessments and Enquiries and Related Time Limits

CHAPTER 6
Appeals

CHAPTER 7
Chargeable Persons: Preliminary Tax and Dates for Payment of Tax

PART 42
COLLECTION AND RECOVERY

CHAPTER 1
Income Tax

CHAPTER 1A
Interpretation

CHAPTER 1B
Collection of Tax, etc.

CHAPTER 1C
Recovery Provisions, Evidential Rules, etc.

CHAPTER 1D

CHAPTER 2
Corporation Tax

CHAPTER 3
Capital Gains Tax

CHAPTER 4

Collection and Recovery of Income Tax on Certain Emoluments (PAYE System)

CHAPTER 5

Miscellaneous Provisions

PART 43

PARTNERSHIPS AND EUROPEAN ECONOMIC INTEREST GROUPINGS (EEIG)

PART 44

MARRIED, SEPARATED AND DIVORCED PERSONS

CHAPTER 1

Income Tax

CHAPTER 2

Capital Gains Tax

PART 44A

TAX TREATMENT OF CIVIL PARTNERSHIPS

CHAPTER 1

Income Tax

CHAPTER 2

Capital Gains Tax

PART 44B

TAX TREATMENT OF COHABITANTS

CHAPTER 1

Income Tax

CHAPTER 2

Capital Gains Tax

PART 45

CHARGING AND ASSESSING OF NON-RESIDENTS

CHAPTER 1

Income Tax and Corporation Tax

CHAPTER 2
Capital Gains Tax

PART 46
PERSONS CHARGEABLE IN A REPRESENTATIVE CAPACITY
CHAPTER 1
Income Tax and Corporation Tax

CHAPTER 2
Capital Gains Tax

PART 47
PENALTIES, REVENUE OFFENCES, INTEREST ON OVERDUE TAX AND OTHER SANCTIONS

CHAPTER 1
Income Tax and Corporation Tax Penalties

CHAPTER 2

Other Corporation Tax Penalties

CHAPTER 3

Capital Gains Tax Penalties

CHAPTER 3A

Determination of Penalties and Recovery of Penalties

CHAPTER 3B

Income Tax, Corporation Tax and Capital Gains Tax: Penalties for False Returns, etc.

CHAPTER 4

Revenue Offences

CHAPTER 5
Interest on Overdue Tax

CHAPTER 6
Other Sanctions

PART 48
MISCELLANEOUS AND SUPPLEMENTAL

PART 49
COMMENCEMENT, REPEALS, TRANSITIONAL PROVISIONS, ETC.

Number 7 of 1927

PROVISIONAL COLLECTION OF TAXES ACT, 1927

AN ACT TO GIVE STATUTORY EFFECT FOR A LIMITED PERIOD TO RESOLUTIONS OF THE COMMITTEE ON FINANCE OF DÁIL EIREANN IMPOSING, RENEWING, VARYING, OR ABOLISHING TAXATION, AND TO MAKE PROVISION WITH RESPECT TO PAYMENTS, DEDUCTIONS, ASSESSMENTS, CHARGES, AND OTHER THINGS MADE OR DONE ON ACCOUNT OF ANY TEMPORARY TAX IN ANTICIPATION OF THE RENEWAL OF THE TAX BY THE OIREACHTAS.

[19*th March,* 1927.]

BE IT ENACTED BY THE OIREACHTAS OF SAORSTÁT EIREANN AS FOLLOWS:—

1 Definitions

In this Act—

the expression "*Committee on Finance*" means the Committee on Finance of Dáil Eireann when and so long as such Committee is a committee of the whole House;

[the expression "*new tax*" when used in relation to a resolution under this Act means a tax which was not in force immediately before the date on which the resolution is expressed to take effect or, where no such date is expressed, the passing of the resolution by Dáil Éireann;][1]

the expression "*permanent tax*" means a tax which was last imposed or renewed without any limit of time being fixed for its duration;

the expression "*temporary tax*" means a tax which was last imposed or renewed for a limited period only;

the expression "*normal expiration*" when used in relation to a temporary tax means the end of the limited period for which the tax was last imposed or renewed;

[the word "*tax*" means any customs duty, excise duty, income tax, value-added tax, capital gains tax, corporation tax, gift tax, inheritance tax, residential property tax, stamp duty, parking levy or any other levy or charge for the purposes of this Act, for the benefit of the Exchequer.][2]

Amendments

[1] Substituted by FA02 s139(a)

[2] Substituted by FA10 s160

2 Certain resolutions to have statutory effect

Whenever a resolution (in this Act referred to as a resolution under this Act) is passed by [Dáil Éireann][1] resolving—

(a) that a new tax specified in the resolution be imposed, or

(b) that a specified permanent tax in force [immediately before the date on which the resolution is expressed to take effect or, where no such date is expressed, the passing of the resolution by Dáil Éireann][2] be increased, reduced, or otherwise varied, or be abolished, or

(c) that a specified temporary tax in force [immediately before the date on which the resolution is expressed to take effect or, where no such date is expressed, the passing of the resolution by Dáil Éireann][3] be renewed (whether at the same or a different rate and whether with or without modification) as from the date of its normal expiration or from an earlier date or be discontinued on a date prior to the date of its normal expiration,

and the resolution contains a declaration that it is expedient in the public interest that the resolution should have statutory effect under the provisions of this Act, the resolution shall, subject to the provisions of this Act, have statutory effect as if contained in an Act of the Oireachtas.

Amendments

[1] Substituted by FA74 s85

[2, 3] Substituted by FA02 s139(b)

3 Application of general taxing enactments

(1) Whenever a new tax is imposed by a resolution under this Act and such resolution describes the tax as a duty of customs or as a duty of excise or as an income tax [...][1], the enactments which [immediately before the date on which the resolution is expressed to take effect or, where no such date is expressed, the passing of the resolution by Dáil Éireann][2] were in force in relation to customs duties generally, or excise duties generally, or income tax generally, [...][3] (as the case may require) shall, subject to the provisions of this Act, apply to and have full force and effect in respect of such new tax so long as the resolution continues to have statutory effect.

(2) Whenever a permanent tax is increased, reduced, or otherwise varied by a resolution under this Act, all enactments which were in force with respect to that tax immediately before the end of the previous financial year shall, so long as the resolution continues to have statutory effect and subject to the provisions of this Act, have full force and effect with respect to the tax as so increased, reduced, or otherwise varied.

(3) Whenever a temporary tax is renewed (whether at the same or a different rate and whether with or without modification) by a resolution under this Act, all enactments which were in force with respect to that tax immediately before the end of the previous financial year shall, so long as the resolution continues to have statutory effect and subject to the provisions of this Act, have full force and effect with respect to the tax as renewed by the resolution.

Amendments

[1] Repealed by FA74 sch2

[2] Substituted by FA02 s139(b)

[3] Repealed by FA74 sch2

4 Duration of statutory effect of resolution

[A resolution under this Act shall cease to have statutory effect upon the happening of whichever of the following events first occurs, that is to say:

[(a) subject to section 4A of this Act, if a Bill containing provisions to the same effect (with or without modifications) as the resolution is not read a second time by Dáil Eireann—

(i) where Dáil Eireann is in recess on any day between the eighty-second and the eighty-fourth day after the resolution is passed by

Dáil Eireann, within the next five 35 sitting days of the resumption of Dáil Eireann after that recess,

(ii) in any other case, within the next eighty-four days after the resolution is passed by Dáil Eireann,][1]

(b) if those provisions of the said Bill are rejected by Dáil Éireann during the passage of the Bill through the Oireachtas;

(c) the coming into operation of an Act of the Oireachtas containing provisions to the same effect (with or without modification) as the resolution;

(d) [subject to section 4A of this Act][2] the expiration of a period of four months from the date on which the resolution is expressed to take effect or, where no such date is expressed, from the passing of the resolution by Dáil Éireann.][3]

Amendments

[1] Substituted by Appropriation Act 1991 s2(a)

[2] Inserted by Appropriation Act 1991 s2(a)

[3] Substituted by FA74 s85(b)

4A Dissolution of Dail Eirean

[Where Dáil Éireann, having passed a resolution under this Act, has been dissolved on the date the resolution was so passed or within four months of that date, then the period of dissolution shall be disregarded for the purposes of calculating any period to which paragraph (a) or (d) of section 4 of this Act relates.][1]

Amendments

[1] Section inserted by the Appropriation Act 1991 s2(b), but replaced in its entirety by FA92 s250

5 Repayment of certain payments and deductions

(1) Whenever a resolution under this Act ceases to have statutory effect by reason of the happening of any event other than the coming into operation of an Act of the Oireachtas containing provisions to the same effect (with or without modification) as the resolution, all moneys paid in pursuance of the resolution shall be repaid or made good and every deduction made in pursuance of the resolution shall be deemed to be an unauthorised deduction.

[...][1]

(3) Whenever an Act of the Oireachtas comes into operation containing provisions to the same effect with modifications as a resolution under this Act and such resolution ceases by virtue of such coming into operation to have statutory effect, all moneys paid in pursuance of such resolution which would not be payable under such Act shall be repaid or made good and every deduction made in pursuance of such resolution which would not be authorised by such Act shall be deemed to be an unauthorised deduction.

Amendments

[1] Section 5, subsection 2 was deleted by FA74s85

6 Certain payments and deductions deemed to be legal

(1) Any payment or deduction on account of a temporary tax to which this section applies made within two months after the expiration of such tax in respect

of a period or event occurring after such expiration shall, if such payment or deduction would have been a legal payment or deduction if the tax had not expired, be deemed to be a legal payment or deduction subject to the conditions that—

(a) if a resolution under this Act renewing the tax (with or without modification) is not passed by [Dáil Éireann][1] within two months after the expiration of the tax, the amount of such payment or deduction shall be repaid or made good on the expiration of such two months, and

(b) if (such resolution having been so passed) an Act of the Oireachtas renewing the tax (with or without modification) does not come into operation when or before such resolution ceases to have statutory effect, the amount of such payment or deduction shall be repaid or made good on such cesser, and

(c) if (such Act having been so passed) the tax is renewed by such Act with such modifications that the whole or some portion of such payment or deduction is not a legal payment or deduction under such Act, the whole or such portion (as the case may be) of such payment or deduction shall be repaid or made good on the coming into operation of such Act.

(2) This section applies only to a temporary tax which was last imposed or renewed for a limited period not exceeding eighteen months and was in force immediately before the end of the financial year next preceding the financial year in which the payment or deduction under this section is made.

Amendments

[1] Substituted by FA74 s85(1)(d)

7 Repeal

The Provisional Collection of Taxes Act, 1913, is hereby repealed.

8 Short title

This Act may be cited as the Provisional Collection of Taxes Act, 1927.

Number 24 of 1993

WAIVER OF CERTAIN TAX, INTEREST AND PENALTIES ACT, 1993

AN ACT TO WAIVE CERTAIN TAX AND INTEREST AND PENALTIES ON CERTAIN TAX, TO AMEND THE PROVISIONS OF THE INCOME TAX ACT, 1967, BY AMENDING SECTION 512 AND SCHEDULE 15 TO THAT ACT AND BY SUBSTITUTING A NEW PROVISION FOR SECTION 516 OF THAT ACT, TO PROVIDE FOR THE FURNISHING OF CERTAIN INFORMATION BY FINANCIAL INSTITUTIONS TO INSPECTORS OF THE REVENUE COMMISSIONERS AND TO PROVIDE FOR CONNECTED MATTERS.

[14*th July*, 1993]

BE IT ENACTED BY THE OIREACHTAS AS FOLLOWS:

1 Interpretation

(a) In this Act, except where the context otherwise requires—

"*arrears of tax*", subject to *section 2 (5) (a)*, has the meaning assigned to it by *section 3 (2)*;

"*Chief Special Collector*" has the meaning assigned to it by *section 7 (3)*;

"*the declared amounts*" has the meaning assigned to it by *section 2 (3) (a) (iii)*;

"*estimate*" means an estimate of, or an assessment to, tax made in accordance with the provisions of—

(i) section 7 or 8 of the Finance Act, 1968,

(ii) section 17 of the Finance Act, 1970, and the regulations made thereunder, or

(iii) section 22 or 23 of the Value-Added Tax Act, 1972,

as the case may be;

"*functions*" includes powers and duties;

"*inspector*" means an inspector of taxes appointed under section 161 of the Income Tax Act, 1967;

"*the Minister*" means the Minister for Finance;

"*relevant interest*" means interest payable in accordance with the specified provisions;

"*the relevant period*" means any period ending on or before the 5th day of April, 1991;

"*relevant tax*" has the meaning assigned to it by *section 2 (2)*;

"*settlement amount*" has the meaning assigned to it by *section 2 (3) (b)*;

"*the specified period*" means the period beginning with the passing of this Act and ending on the [21st day of December, 1993][1];

"*the specified provisions*" means any provision of the Acts (within the meaning of *section 2* or *3*, as the case may be) pursuant to which a person may be liable—

(i) to interest in respect of tax (within the aforesaid meaning) which is unpaid, including interest on an undercharge of such tax which is attributable to fraud or neglect, or

(ii) to a fine or other penalty in respect of an offence or default.

(b) References in this Act to tax (within the meaning of *section 2* or *3*, as the case may be) being due and payable by a person include references to such tax which would have been due and payable by him if any return, statement or declaration (being a return, statement or declaration, as the case may be, which should have, but had not, been made by him in accordance with any provision of the Acts (within the aforesaid meaning)) had been so made and if that tax had been contained in an assessment made on the person or in an estimate issued to the person.

Amendments

[1] Substituted by FA94 s163(1)

Cross References

From Section 1

Section 2 Waiver of certain tax and related interest and penalties.
Section 3 Waiver of certain interest and penalties in respect of certain tax.
Section 7 Confidentiality.

2 Waiver of certain tax and related interest and penalties

(1) In this section—

"*the Acts*" means—

(a) the Income Tax Acts (other than Chapter IV of Part V of the Income Tax Act, 1967, and section 17 of the Finance Act, 1970),

(b) the Capital Gains Tax Acts,

(c) section 16 of the Finance Act, 1983,

(d) the Health Contributions Act, 1979, and

(e) the Youth Employment Agency Act, 1981,

and any instruments made thereunder;

"*income*" means total income from all sources as estimated in accordance with the provisions of the Income Tax Acts after deducting from the income so much of any deduction allowed by virtue of the provisions referred to in section 33 of the Finance Act, 1975, as is to be deducted from or set off against that income in charging it to income tax;

"*tax*" means any tax, levy or contributions payable in accordance with any provision of the Acts.

(2) This section applies to an individual who, for the relevant period, was in receipt of income or had chargeable gains in respect of which any tax (referred to in this Act as "*relevant tax*") due and payable by him in accordance with any provision of the Acts has not been paid:

Provided that—

(a) this section shall not apply to an individual if, before the 25th day of May, 1993 (hereafter in this proviso referred to as "*the designated date*"), he had been notified in writing by an inspector—

(i) that the inspector intended to make any enquiries or take any actions as are specified in section 15 of the Finance Act, 1988, in relation to the liability to tax of the individual for the relevant period, or

(ii) that any matter which occasions or may occasion a liability or further liability to tax of the individual for the relevant period is under investigation or enquiry by the inspector,

and such enquiries or actions, or investigation or enquiry, as the case may be, had not been concluded on or before the designated date, and for the purposes of this paragraph the aforesaid enquiries or actions, or investigation or enquiry, shall be deemed not to have been concluded unless an agreement has been reached between the individual and the inspector as to the liability to tax of the individual for the relevant period,

(b) relevant tax shall not include any sum—

(i) which, before the designated date, was certified in a certificate issued, and not withdrawn, under section 485 of the Income Tax Act, 1967,

(ii) which, before the designated date, was the subject of proceedings initiated, and not withdrawn, as a debt due to the Minister, in any court of competent jurisdiction,

(iii) which was tax contained in an assessment which was on the designated date the subject of an appeal to which the provisions of Part XXVI of the Income Tax Act, 1967, apply,

(iv) which, before the designated date, was entered as a specified amount in a notice of attachment issued, and not revoked, under section 73 of the Finance Act, 1988,

(v) which was not paid on or before the designated date by virtue of an arrangement or scheme the main purpose, or one of the main purposes, of which was the avoidance of liability to tax,

(vi) which, following enquiries made, or action taken, by an inspector pursuant to section 15 of the Finance Act, 1988, or any other investigation by an inspector, had been agreed before the designated date by an individual and an inspector as being the individual's tax liability,

(vii) being tax in respect of income or chargeable gains which arose from, or by reason of, an illegal source or activity (other than the evasion of tax or the non-compliance with the provisions relating to exchange control), or

(viii) paid or remitted in accordance with the provisions of *section 3* in respect of arrears of tax.

(3) An individual to whom this section applies shall—

(a) within the specified period give a declaration in writing to the Chief Special Collector which—

(i) is made and signed by the individual,

(ii) is in a form prescribed by the Revenue Commissioners and approved of by the Minister,

(iii) contains, in relation to the individual, a full and true statement of the respective amounts (referred to in this Act as "*the declared amounts*") of—

(I) the income, and

(II) the chargeable gains,

referred to in *subsection (2)*, and

(iv) declares that neither the declared amounts nor any part of those amounts arose from, or by reason of, an unlawful source or activity (other than the evasion of tax or the non-compliance with the provisions relating to exchange control), and

(b) not earlier than the giving of the declaration referred to in *paragraph (a)* but on or before the 14th day of January, 1994, remit to the Chief Special Collector an amount (referred to in this Act as "*the settlement amount*") equal to 15 per cent. of the declared amounts.

(4) On receipt by him of the declaration referred to in *subsection (3)* and the settlement amount, the Chief Special Collector shall give to the individual concerned—

(a) a certificate, in a form prescribed by the Revenue Commissioners and approved of by the Minister, stating, in relation to that individual—

(i) his name and address,

(ii) the settlement amount paid by him, and

(iii) the respective amounts of the declared amounts, and

(b) evidence, in a form prescribed by the Revenue Commissioners and approved of by the Minister, that such a certificate has been given.

(5) Notwithstanding any other provision of the Acts but subject to *section 4*, where an individual to whom this section applies complies with the provisions of *subsection (3)*—

(a) his liability to relevant tax in respect of the declared amounts—

(i) shall be deemed to be satisfied by the settlement amount, and

(ii) shall not be arrears of tax,

(b) any amount of relevant interest which the individual may have become liable for in relation to relevant tax in respect of the declared amounts shall be waived, and

(c) proceedings shall not be initiated or continued for the recovery of any fine or penalty to which the individual may be liable under any of the specified provisions in relation to relevant tax in respect of the declared amounts, nor shall the Revenue Commissioners seek or demand from the individual payment of any sum in lieu of such fine or penalty.

Cross References

From Section 2

Section 3 Waiver of certain interest and penalties in respect of certain tax.
Section 4 Non-application of sections 2 (5) and 3 (4).

To Section 2

Section 1 Interpretation.
Section 3 Waiver of certain interest and penalties in respect of certain tax.
Section 4 Non-application of sections 2 (5) and 3 (4).
Section 5 Enquiries or action by inspector or other officer.
Section 6 Demands or other requests for payment.
Section 7 Confidentiality.
Section 8 Remittances.
Section 9 Penalty for failure to comply with section 2 (3)(a) or 3 (6)(b).

3 Waiver of certain interest and penalties in respect of certain tax

(1) (a) In this section—

"*the Acts*" means—

(i) the Acts within the meaning of *section 2*,

(ii) Chapter IV of Part V of the Income Tax Act, 1967,

(iii) section 17 of the Finance Act, 1970,

(iv) the Corporation Tax Acts,

(v) Part V of the Finance Act, 1920, and the enactments amending or extending that Part,

(vi) the Value-Added Tax Act, 1972, and the enactments amending or extending that Act,

(vii) the Capital Acquisitions Tax Act, 1976, and the enactments amending or extending that Act,

(viii) the Stamp Act, 1891, and the enactments amending or extending that Act, and

(ix) Part VI of the Finance Act, 1983, and the enactments amending or extending that Part,

and any instruments made thereunder;

"*the due date*" means, in relation to an amount of tax, the date on which a person becomes liable to interest under any of the specified provisions in respect of the late payment of that tax;

"*tax*" means any tax, duty, levy or contributions payable in accordance with any provision of the Acts.

(b) The reference in *subsection (2)* to an amount of tax due and payable shall, in a case where tax is assessed or estimated in an assessment or estimate against which an appeal has been made, be construed as a reference to the amount of tax which becomes due and payable on the determination of the appeal (within the meaning of section 550 (2A) (*c*) of the Income Tax Act, 1967) or, pending such determination, the tax as assessed or estimated.

(2) This section applies to a person who had not paid or remitted before the due date an amount of tax (in this Act referred to as "*arrears of tax*") due and payable by him, or chargeable, in accordance with any provision of the Acts in respect of or during the relevant period.

(3) Where a person to whom this section applies has unpaid arrears of tax on the passing of this Act, he shall on or before the 14th day of January, 1994, and subject to the provisions of *subsection (6)*, pay or remit those arrears of tax.

(4) Notwithstanding any other provision of the Acts but subject to the provisions of *subsection (5)* and *section 4*, where a person has paid or remitted, on or before the 14th day of January, 1994, his arrears of tax—

(a) any amount of relevant interest to which the person may be liable in relation to arrears of tax and which is unpaid at the date of the payment or remittance referred to in *subsection (3)* shall be waived,

(b) any amount of relevant interest in relation to arrears of tax which is paid by the person on or after the 26th day of May, 1993, shall be refunded to him, and

(c) proceedings shall not be initiated or continued for the recovery of any fine or penalty to which the person may be liable under any of the specified provisions in relation to arrears of tax, nor shall the Revenue Commissioners seek or demand from the person payment of any sum in lieu of such fine or penalty.

(5) This section shall not apply to any interest, fine or other penalty that—

(a) in the case of a fine or other penalty, is imposed by a court under any of the Acts,

(b) in the case of interest, is ordered by a court in any proceedings for the recovery of tax or interest to be paid by a person, or

(c) in any case, is included in a specified sum such as is referred to in subsection (2) (*c*) of section 23 of the Finance Act, 1983, where the full amount of the specified sum was not paid on or before the 25th day of May, 1993.

(6) (a) Where a payment or remittance in accordance with the provisions of *subsection (3)* is made by an individual who also remits a settlement amount, then, without prejudice to the amount of that payment or remittance, so much of that payment or remittance as is referable to value-added tax may be remitted to the Chief Special Collector.

(b) Where, in accordance with *paragraph (a)*, an individual makes a remittance to the Chief Special Collector, the individual by whom the remittance is made shall on the earlier of—

(i) the date of payment, or

(ii) a date within the specified period,

give a declaration in writing to the Chief Special Collector which—

(I) is made and signed by the individual,

(II) is in a form prescribed by the Revenue Commissioners and approved of by the Minister, and

(III) contains, in relation to that individual, a full and true statement of the amount of value-added tax comprised in the arrears of tax.

(c) On receipt by him of the declaration referred to in *paragraph (b)* and the remittance referred to in *paragraph (a)*, the Chief Special Collector shall give to the individual by whom the remittance is made—

(i) a certificate, in a form prescribed by the Revenue Commissioners and approved of by the Minister, stating, in relation to that individual—

(I) his name and address, and

(II) the amount of the said remittance, and

(ii) evidence, in a form prescribed by the Revenue Commissioners and approved of by the Minister, that such a certificate has been given.

(7) Section 23 (4) of the Finance Act, 1983, is hereby amended by the substitution of the following paragraph for paragraph (*aa*) (inserted by section 72 of the Finance Act, 1988):

"(*aa*) the provisions of section 72 of the Finance Act, 1988, or *section 3* of the *Waiver of Certain Tax, Interest and Penalties Act, 1993*, apply, or".

Cross References

From Section 3

Section 2 Waiver of certain tax and related interest and penalties.

Section 3 Waiver of certain interest and penalties in respect of certain tax.

Section 4 Non-application of sections 2 (5) and 3 (4).

To Section 3

Section 1 Interpretation.
Section 2 Waiver of certain tax and related interest and penalties.
Section 3 Waiver of certain interest and penalties in respect of certain tax.
Section 4 Non-application of sections 2 (5) and 3 (4).
Section 5 Enquiries or action by inspector or other officer.
Section 6 Demands or other requests for payment.
Section 7 Confidentiality.
Section 8 Remittances.
Section 9 Penalty for failure to comply with section 2 (3)(a) or 3 (6)(b).

4 Non-application of sections 2 (5) and 3 (4)

(1) The provisions of *sections 2 (5)* and *3 (4)* shall not apply, and those provisions shall be deemed never to have applied, to a person where—

(a) such person fails—

(i) if he is an individual, for the year of assessment 1992-93, or

(ii) in any other case, for any accounting period ending in the year beginning on the 1st day of January, 1993, and ending on the 31st day of December, 1993,

to duly deliver a return of income on or before the specified date in relation to that return, or

(b) (i) a declaration given by such person to the Chief Special Collector under *subsection (3) (a)* of *section 2*—

(I) did not contain a full and true statement of the kind referred to in *subparagraph (iii)* of the said subsection, or

(II) is proven to be false in so far as the requirements of *subparagraph (iv)* of the said subsection are concerned,

or

(ii) a declaration given by him to the Chief Special Collector under *subsection (6) (b)* of *section 3* did not contain a full and true statement of the kind referred to in *subparagraph (III)* of the said subsection, or

(c) the amount paid or remitted by him in respect of arrears of tax was less than the arrears of tax due and payable by him,

and any certificate issued to that person pursuant to *section 2 (4)* or *section 3 (6) (c)* shall be null and void.

(2) Where, by virtue of this section, *section 2 (5)* does not apply and is deemed never to have applied to an individual, the amount paid by him as the settlement amount shall be treated as a payment on account of relevant tax.

(3) (a) In *subsection (1)* "*return of income*" and "*specified date*" have the meanings assigned to them by section 48 of the Finance Act, 1986.

(b) The provisions of subsection (1) (*b*) of section 48 of the Finance Act, 1986, shall apply for the purposes of *subsection (1) (a)* of this section as they apply for the purposes of that section.

Cross References

From Section 4

Section 2 Waiver of certain tax and related interest and penalties.
Section 3 Waiver of certain interest and penalties in respect of certain tax.

To Section 4

Section 2 Waiver of certain tax and related interest and penalties.
Section 3 Waiver of certain interest and penalties in respect of certain tax.
Section 6 Demands or other requests for payment.

5 Enquiries or action by inspector or other officer

(1) Where, in relation to any liability to tax (within the meaning of *section 2* or *3*, as the case may be) of an individual for the relevant period, being tax which has been remitted to the Chief Special Collector, an inspector or other officer of the Revenue Commissioners commences to make such enquiries, or take such action, as are within his powers, or gives a notice in writing to an individual of his intention to make such enquiries or take such action in relation to such liability to tax and the individual produces to the inspector or other officer, not later than 30 days from the commencement of the said enquiries or the taking of the said action, or the giving of the notice as aforesaid, a certificate referred to in *section 2 (4)* or *3 (6) (c)*, as the case may be, in respect of such liability to tax given to him by the Chief Special Collector, the inspector or other officer shall, on production to him of the said certificate and on validation of that certificate in accordance with the provisions of *paragraph (a)* of the proviso to *section 7 (4)*, be precluded from continuing with or commencing the said enquiries or continuing with or commencing the said action unless, on application by him to the Appeal Commissioners, he shows to the satisfaction of those Commissioners that—

(a) enquiries made or action taken in relation to the liability to tax (within the aforesaid meaning) of the individual for any period commencing on or after the 6th day of April, 1991, indicate, or

(b) there are other reasonable grounds which indicate,

that a declaration made by the individual to the Chief Special Collector under *section 2 (3) (a)* or *3 (6) (b)* did not contain a full and true statement of the declared amounts or the amount of value-added tax comprised in the [arrears of tax, as the case may be, or that the declaration made by the individual under section 2 (3) (a) (iv) is false][1].

(2) (a) An application by the inspector or other officer under *subsection (1)* shall be made by him by notice in writing to the Appeal Commissioners within 30 days of the receipt by him from the individual concerned of the certificate referred to in *section 2 (4)* or *3 (6) (c)*, as the case may be, given to that individual by the Chief Special Collector, and a copy of the application shall be furnished as soon as practicable by the inspector or other officer to the individual concerned.

(b) An application under *subsection (1)* shall, with any necessary modifications, be heard by the Appeal Commissioners as if it were an appeal against an assessment to income tax.

(c) Any action required to be taken by the individual and any further action proposed to be taken by the inspector or other officer pursuant to the inspector's or other officer's enquiry or action shall be suspended pending decision by the Appeal Commissioners on the application.

(d) Where, on the hearing of the application by an inspector or other officer under *subsection (1)*, the Appeal Commissioners—

(i) decide that there are no reasonable grounds to suggest that the declaration made by the individual to the Chief Special Collector under *section 2 (3) (a)* or *3 (6) (b)* did not contain a full and true statement of the declared amounts or the amount of value-added tax comprised in the arrears of tax, as the case may be, then the individual shall not be required to take any action pursuant to the inspector's or other officer's enquiry or action and the inspector or other officer shall be prohibited from pursuing his enquiry or action,

or

(ii) decide that there are such reasonable grounds, then the inspector or other officer may continue with his enquiry or action.

Amendments

[1] Substituted by the Criminal Assets Bureau Act 1996 s25

Cross References

From Section 5

Section 2 Waiver of certain tax and related interest and penalties.
Section 3 Waiver of certain interest and penalties in respect of certain tax.
Section 7 Confidentiality.

To Section 5

Section 7 Confidentiality.

6 Demands or other requests for payment

Where, in relation to an individual—

(a) the Revenue Commissioners, the Collector-General or any of their or his officers authorised in that behalf, have demanded or otherwise requested the payment of any tax—

(i) in respect of which a settlement amount has been remitted to the Chief Special Collector, or

(ii) which is value-added tax in respect of which a remittance has been made to the Chief Special Collector in accordance with *section 3 (6) (a)*, and

(b) the individual has been given a certificate as is referred to in *section 2 (4)* or *3 (6) (c)* in respect of such tax,

the individual shall produce to the Revenue Commissioners, the Collector-General or the authorised officer, as the case may be, within 30 days of—

(i) the date of the making of the demand or request, or

(ii) if later, the date he received the certificate,

the evidence referred to in *section 2 (4) (b)* or *section 3 (6) (c)*, as the case may be, and the demand or request shall be withdrawn and the amount of tax specified in the demand or request shall be discharged:

Provided that, where *subsection (5)* of *section 2* and *subsection (4)* of *section 3* do not apply by virtue of the provisions of *section 4*—

(i) the amount of tax discharged shall be reinstated, and

(ii) any additional assessments or estimates necessary to give effect to this proviso shall be made.

Cross References

From Section 6

Section 2 Waiver of certain tax and related interest and penalties.
Section 3 Waiver of certain interest and penalties in respect of certain tax.
Section 4 Non-application of sections 2 (5) and 3 (4).

To Section 6

Section 7 Confidentiality.

7 Confidentiality

(1) In this section—

"*declaration of confidentiality*" means the declaration of confidentiality contained in the Schedule to this Act;

"*special collection function*" means any function or duty related to—

(a) the receipt and retention of declarations referred to in *section 2 (3) (a)* or *3 (6) (b)*,

(b) the receipt, recording and lodgement of—

(i) settlement amounts, or

(ii) so much of any payment or remittance referred to in *section 3 (6) (a)* as is referable to value-added tax, or

(c) the issue and recording of certificates referred to in *section 2 (4)* or *3 (6) (c)*,

which could result in the person or persons discharging that function or performing that duty acquiring, or having access to, any information in respect of such declarations, amounts or certificates, and a reference to the discharge of a special collection function shall be construed as a reference to the discharge of such a function or performance of such a duty;

"*special collector*" means any officer or employee of the Revenue Commissioners who—

(a) has been nominated by the Revenue Commissioners to discharge a special collection function, and has not had his nomination revoked, and

(b) has made and subscribed the declaration of confidentiality.

(2) (a) Special collection functions may only be discharged by special collectors.

(b) Every person nominated by the Revenue Commissioners to be a special collector shall, upon making and subscribing to the declaration of confidentiality, become a special collector.

(c) Declarations of confidentiality shall be made before a peace commissioner or other person duly authorised to take and receive statutory declarations.

(3) (a) Special collection functions shall be under the control and direction of a special collector, to be known as and is referred to in this Act as "*the Chief Special Collector*", who is designated to be such by the Revenue Commissioners.

(b) Whenever there is no Chief Special Collector, the Revenue Commissioners shall designate as soon as is practicable thereafter a special collector to be the Chief Special Collector and all other special collectors shall observe and follow the orders, instructions and directions of the Chief Special Collector in relation to any special collection function:

Provided that nothing in *paragraph (b)* shall be construed so as to affect the proviso to *subsection (6)*.

(c) For the purposes of the receipt of any declaration, amount or remittance, or the issue of any certificate or evidence, in accordance with *section 2* or *3*, references to the Chief Special Collector shall be construed as including a reference to any other special collector acting on behalf of the Chief Special Collector in that matter.

(d) If and so long as the Chief Special Collector is unable through illness, absence or other cause to fulfil his duties, another special collector designated in that behalf by the Revenue Commissioners shall act as Chief Special Collector, and any reference in this Act to the Chief Special Collector shall be construed as including, where appropriate, a reference to a special collector designated under this paragraph.

(4) A special collector shall be deemed to have contravened his declaration of confidentiality if he discloses, or causes to be disclosed, to a person who is not a special collector, any information which he could have acquired, or had access to, only by virtue of being a special collector:

Provided that a special collector shall not be deemed to have contravened his declaration of confidentiality where—

(a) having been requested to validate a certificate or evidence referred to in *section 2 (4)* or *3 (6) (c)* by an officer of the Revenue Commissioners to whom that certificate or evidence has been produced for the purposes of *section 5* or *6*, as the case may be, he informs that officer whether or not that certificate or evidence, as the case may be, was given by a special collector,

(b) he provides to the Minister or the Revenue Commissioners such information, in the form of aggregates and in that form only, as the Minister or the Commissioners, as the case may be, may request in relation to—

(i) the total amount of—

(I) the declared amounts,

(II) settlement amounts, or

(III) such amounts of any payments or remittances referred to in *section 3 (6) (a)* as are referable to value-added tax remitted to the Chief Special Collector,

and

(ii) the total respective numbers of individuals who remitted amounts to the Chief Special Collector in respect of income, chargeable gains or value-added tax,

or

(c) he provides to the Comptroller and Auditor General or the Accounting Officer of the Revenue Commissioners such information as the Comptroller and Auditor General or that Accounting Officer, as the case may be, may request and reasonably require to ensure that any special collection function has been discharged in accordance with this Act.

(5) Any information acquired by the Comptroller and Auditor General or the Accounting Officer of the Revenue Commissioners by virtue of *paragraph (c)* of the proviso to *subsection (4)* shall be used by the Comptroller and Auditor General or that Accounting Officer, as the case may be, only for the purpose of ensuring that any special collection function has been discharged in accordance with this Act:

Provided that the foregoing provisions of this subsection shall not prevent the Comptroller and Auditor General from carrying out his functions, including exercising his reporting duty to Dáil Éireann.

(6) The Revenue Commissioners may make such nominations as are required for the purposes of this section and may at any time also revoke any such nomination:

Provided that the Revenue Commissioners may only revoke at any time the nomination of the special collector who is the Chief Special Collector where they also designate, with effect from that time, a special collector to be his successor as Chief Special Collector.

Cross References

From Section 7

Section 2 Waiver of certain tax and related interest and penalties.
Section 3 Waiver of certain interest and penalties in respect of certain tax.
Section 5 Enquiries or action by inspector or other officer.
Section 6 Demands or other requests for payment.

To Section 7

Section 1 Interpretation.
Section 5 Enquiries or action by inspector or other officer.
Section 14 Care and management.

8 Remittances

Any remittance made to the Chief Special Collector under *section 2 (3) (b)* or *3 (6) (a)* shall—

(a) where it is made otherwise than in cash, be made payable to the Revenue Commissioners, and

(b) be lodged to the General Account of the Revenue Commissioners in the Central Bank of Ireland as soon as prompt recording, and secure transmission to that account, of that remittance permits.

Cross References

From Section 8

Section 2 Waiver of certain tax and related interest and penalties.
Section 3 Waiver of certain interest and penalties in respect of certain tax.

9 Penalty for failure to comply with section 2 (3)(a) or 3 (6)(b)

(1) Where an individual, being an individual to whom *section 2* applies, or a person to whom *section 3* applies—

(a) (i) has knowingly or wilfully failed to comply with any provision of the Acts requiring—

(I) the furnishing of a return of income, profits or gains, or of sources of income, profits or gains, for the purposes of any tax,

(II) the furnishing of any other return, certificate, notification, particulars, or any statement or evidence, for the purposes of any tax, or

(ii) has knowingly or wilfully delivered any incorrect return, statement or accounts or knowingly or wilfully furnished any incorrect information in connection with any tax,

in respect of the relevant period, and

(b) (i) fails to give a declaration required by *section 2 (3) (a)*, or

(ii) gives such a declaration as aforesaid or a declaration under *section 3 (6) (b)* which is false or fails to comply with the requirements of *subparagraph (iii)* or *(iv)* of the said *section 2 (3) (a)* or *subparagraph (III)* of the said *section 3 (6) (b)* to the extent that any of the said subparagraphs apply to him,

he shall, without prejudice to any other penalty to which he may be liable, be guilty of an offence and shall be liable—

(I) on summary conviction where the amount of the specified difference is—

(A) less than £1,200, to a fine not exceeding 25 per cent. of the amount of the specified difference or, at the discretion of the court, to a term of imprisonment not exceeding 12 months or to both,

(B) equal to or greater than £1,200, to a fine not exceeding £1,200 or, at the discretion of the court, to a term of imprisonment not exceeding 12 months or to both,

or

(II) on conviction on indictment where the amount of the specified difference is—

(A) less than £5,000, to a fine not exceeding 25 per cent. of the amount of the specified difference or, at the discretion of the court, to a term of imprisonment not exceeding 2 years or to both,

(B) equal to or greater than £5,000 but less than £10,000, to a fine not exceeding 50 per cent. of the amount of the specified difference or, at the discretion of the court, to a term of imprisonment not exceeding 3 years or to both,

(C) equal to or greater than £10,000 but less than £25,000, to a fine not exceeding the amount of the specified difference or, at the discretion of the court, to a term of imprisonment not exceeding 4 years or to both,

(D) equal to or greater than £25,000 but less than £100,000, to a fine not exceeding twice the amount of the specified difference or, at the discretion of the court, to a term of imprisonment not exceeding 8 years or to both,

(E) equal to or greater than £100,000, to a fine not exceeding twice the amount of the specified difference and to a term of imprisonment not exceeding 8 years.

(2) Subsections (4), (6), (7) and (8) of section 94 of the Finance Act, 1983, shall, with any necessary modifications, apply and have effect for the purposes of this section as they apply and have effect for the purposes of that section.

(3) In this section—

"*the Acts*" and "*tax*" have the meanings assigned to them, respectively, by *section 2* or *3*, as appropriate;

"*the specified difference*" means the difference between—

(a) the amount of tax payable for the relevant period by the individual, and

(b) the amount which would have been so payable if—

(i) any return, certificate, notification or particulars or any statement of evidence, referred to in *subsection (1) (a) (i)*, not furnished by him, had, in fact, been so furnished and the details therein had been correct, or

(ii) any incorrect return, statement or accounts, or any incorrect information, referred to in *subsection (1) (a) (ii)*, in connection with any tax had, in fact, been correct.

Cross References

From Section 9

Section 2 Waiver of certain tax and related interest and penalties.

Section 3 Waiver of certain interest and penalties in respect of certain tax.

10 Amendment of Section 512 (mitigation and application of fines and penalties) of Income Tax Act, 1967 [Repealed]

Repealed by TCA97 Sch30

11 Penalty for false statement made to obtain allowance [Repealed]

Repealed by TCA97 Sch30

12 Amendment of Schedule 15 to Income Tax Act, 1967 [Repealed]

Repealed by TCA97 Sch30

13 Furnishing of certain information of financial institutions [Repealed]

Repealed by TCA97 Sch30

14 Care and management

Subject to *section 7 (3) (a)*, all matters relating to this Act are hereby placed under the care and management of the Revenue Commissioners.

Cross References

From Section 14

Section 7 Confidentiality.

15 Short title, construction and collective citation

(1) This Act may be cited as the Waiver of Certain Tax, Interest and Penalties Act, 1993.

(2) This Act shall be construed—

(a) so far as relating to income tax and sur-tax, together with the Income Tax Acts,

(b) so far as relating to corporation profits tax, together with Part V of the Finance Act, 1920, and the enactments amending or extending that Part,

(c) so far as relating to corporation tax, together with the Corporation Tax Acts,

(d) so far as relating to capital gains tax, together with the Capital Gains Tax Acts,

(e) so far as relating to value-added tax, together with the Value-Added Tax Acts, 1972 to 1993,

(f) so far as relating to stamp duty, together with the Stamp Act, 1891, and the enactments amending or extending that Act,

(g) so far as relating to capital acquisitions tax, together with the Capital Acquisitions Tax Act, 1976, and the enactments amending or extending that Act,

(h) so far as relating to residential property tax, together with Part VI of the Finance Act, 1983, and the enactments amending or extending that Part,

(i) so far as relating to income levy, together with section 16 of the Finance Act, 1983, and the enactments amending or extending that section,

(j) so far as relating to health contributions, together with the Health Contributions Act, 1979, and the enactments amending or extending that Act, and

(k) so far as relating to employment and training levy, together with the Youth Employment Agency Act, 1981, and the enactments amending or extending that Act.

(3) The collective citation "*the Value-Added Tax Acts, 1972 to 1993*" shall include this Act in so far as it relates to value-added tax.

(4) Any reference in this Act to any other enactment shall, except so far as the context otherwise requires, be construed as a reference to that enactment as amended by or under any other enactment including this Act.

(5) In this Act, a reference to a section is to a section of this Act, unless it is indicated that reference to some other enactment is intended.

(6) In this Act, a reference to a subsection, paragraph or subparagraph is to the subsection, paragraph or subparagraph of the provision in which the reference occurs, unless it is indicated that reference to some other provision is intended.

SCHEDULE

Form of declaration of confidentiality to be made by special collectors

Section 7.

"I, A.B., do solemnly declare that I have read and understand *section 7* of the *Waiver of Certain Tax, Interest and Penalties Act, 1993*, and that I will not disclose, or cause to be disclosed, to a person who is not a special collector (within the meaning of that section) any information which I acquire, or have access to, in the course of discharging special collection functions (within the meaning of the said section) save where the disclosure of such information is deemed, by virtue of the proviso to *subsection (4)* of the said *section 7*, not to be a contravention of this declaration.".

S.I. No. 559 of 2001

INCOME TAX (EMPLOYMENTS) (CONSOLIDATED) REGULATIONS, 2001

The Revenue Commissioners, in exercise of the powers conferred on them by section 986 of the Taxes Consolidation Act, 1997 (No. 39 of 1997), hereby make the following regulations:

PART 1

General

1 Citation and commencement

(1) These Regulations may be cited as the Income Tax (Employments) (Consolidated) Regulations, 2001.

(2) These Regulations shall come into operation on 1 January 2002.

2 Interpretation

(1) In these Regulations, except where the context otherwise requires—

"*the Act*" means the Taxes Consolidation Act, 1997;

"*authorised officer*" means an officer of the Revenue Commissioners authorised by them in writing for the purposes of these Regulations;

"*authorised person*" in relation to Regulations 29 and 30, means an employer who has been authorised in writing by the Collector-General for the purposes of Regulation 29 and, "*authorise*", "*authorised*" and "*authorisation*" shall be construed accordingly;

"*certificate of tax credits and standard rate cut-off point*" has the meaning specified in paragraph (2) of Regulation 11;

"*Collector-General*" means the Collector-General appointed under section 851 of the Act;

"*cumulative emoluments*" in relation to any date means the sum of all payments of emoluments made by the employer to the employee from the beginning of the year up to and including that date;

"*cumulative gross tax*" means the sum of cumulative tax due at the standard rate of tax and cumulative tax due at the higher rate of tax;

"*cumulative standard rate cut-off point*" in relation to any date means the sum of the standard rate cut-off point from the beginning of the year up to and including that date as specified on the employee's tax deduction card;

"*cumulative tax*" means cumulative gross tax less cumulative tax credits;

"*cumulative tax credits*" in relation to any date means the sum of the tax credits from the beginning of the year up to and including that date as specified on the employee's tax deduction card;

"*cumulative tax due at higher rate of tax*" in relation to any date means tax due at the higher rate of tax in respect of the cumulative emoluments to that date to the extent that they exceed the cumulative standard rate cut-off point to that date as specified on the employee's tax deduction card;

"*cumulative tax due at standard rate of tax*" in relation to any date means tax due by reference to the standard rate of tax for the year in respect of the cumulative emoluments, to that date, up to the amount of the cumulative standard rate cut-off point to that date as specified on the employee's tax deduction card;

"*domestic employee*" means an employee who is employed solely on domestic duties (including the minding of children) in the employer's private dwelling house;

"*domestic employment*" means employment by reference to which an employee is a domestic employee;

["*electronic communications*" has the meaning assigned to it by section 864A(1)(a) of the Act;][1]

"*emoluments*" means emoluments to which Chapter 4 of Part 42 of the Act applies;

"*employee*" means any person in receipt of emoluments;

"*employer*" means any person paying emoluments;

"*general tax credit*" has the same meaning as in section 3 of the Act;

"*higher rate of tax*" means the rate of income tax known by that description and provided for in section 15 of the Act;

"*income tax month*" means a calendar month;

["*inspector*" means an inspector of taxes; taxes or other officer of the Revenue Commissioners;][2]

["*notional payment*" has the meaning assigned to it by subsection (2) of section 985A (inserted by the Finance Act 2003) of the Act; and;][3]

"*personal public service number*" has the same meaning as in section 223 of the Social Welfare (Consolidation) Act, 1993;

"*personal tax credit*" has the same meaning as in section 3 of the Act;

"*prescribed*" means prescribed by the Revenue Commissioners;

"*reliefs from income tax*" means allowances, deductions and tax credits;

"*standard rate cut-off point*" in relation to an employee, means the standard rate cut-off point advised by the inspector on the certificate of tax credits and standard rate cut-off point;

"*standard rate of tax*" means the rate of income tax known by that description and provided for in section 15 of the Act;

"*tax credits*" in relation to an employee means the appropriate amount of personal tax credits and general tax credits to which the employee is entitled under the Act;

["*tax deduction card*" means a tax deduction card in the form prescribed by the Revenue Commissioners or such other document corresponding to a tax deduction card as may be authorised by the Revenue Commissioners in any particular case;][4]

["*temporary tax deduction form*" means any form as may be prescribed on which particulars of emoluments paid and the aggregate of—

(i) tax deducted from those emoluments and,

(ii) tax which was not so deducted, but which was remitted by the employer under section 985A(4) of the Principal Act in relation to notional payments,

are to be recorded by the employer pending receipt of a tax deduction card;

"*total net tax deducted*" means, in relation to the emoluments paid to any employee during any period, the aggregate of—

(i) the total tax deducted from those emoluments, and

(ii) tax which was not so deducted but which was remitted by the employer for that period under section 985A(4) of the Principal Act in relation to notional payments,

less any tax repaid to the employee;][5]

"*year*" means year of assessment;

[(1A) In these Regulations, except where the context otherwise requires—

(a) references to a payment of emoluments shall include references to notional payments in respect of emoluments, and

(b) references to tax deducted or to be deducted, or to a requirement to deduct tax, from a payment of emoluments shall include references to—

(i) tax deducted or to be deducted, or to a requirement to deduct tax, from the payment, and

(i) tax remitted or to be remitted, or a requirement to remit tax, under section 985A(4) of the Principal Act,

in respect of notional payments, as the circumstances may require,

and cognate words shall be construed accordingly.][6]

(2) A word or expression that is used in these Regulations and is also used in the Income Tax Acts has, except where the context otherwise requires, the same meaning in these Regulations that it has in those Acts.

Amendments

[1, 4] Inserted by the Income Tax (Employments) Regulations 2008, with effect from 1 January 2009

[2] Substituted by the Income Tax (Employments) Regulations 2008, with effect from 1 January 2009

[3] Inserted by the Income Tax (Employments) Regulations 2003, with effect from 1 January 2004

[5] Substituted by the Income Tax (Employments) Regulations 2003, with effect from 1 January 2004

[6] Inserted by the Income Tax (Employments) Regulations 2003, with effect from 1 January 2004

3 Intermediate employers

(1) Where an employee works under the general control and management of a person who is not his or her immediate employer, that person (referred to hereafter in this Regulation as the "*principal employer*") shall be deemed to be the employer for the purposes of these Regulations, and the immediate employer shall furnish the principal employer with such particulars of the employee's emoluments as may be necessary to enable the principal employer to comply with the provisions of these Regulations.

(2) If the employee's emoluments are actually paid to him or her by the immediate employer—

(a) the immediate employer shall be notified by the principal employer of the amount of tax to be deducted or repaid when the emoluments are paid to the employee, and shall deduct or repay accordingly the amount so notified, and

(b) the principal employer shall make a corresponding deduction or addition on making to the immediate employer the payment out of which the said emoluments will be paid.

4 Liability for payment of deduction and entitlement to payment of repayment

Persons who are required to make any deduction or repayment referred to in these Regulations shall, in the case of a deduction (whether or not made), be accountable for the amount of the tax, and liable to pay that amount, to the Revenue Commissioners and shall, in the case of a repayment, be entitled, if it has been made, to be paid it, or given credit for it, by the Revenue Commissioners.

5 Powers of inspector

Anything which is authorised or required by these Regulations to be done by the inspector shall be done by such inspector as the Revenue Commissioners may direct.

6 Service by post or electronic communications

[Any notice, notification, certificate, requirement or tax deduction card which is authorised or required to be given, served, made, sent or issued under these Regulations may be sent by post or by electronic communications.][1]

Amendments

[1] Substituted by the Income Tax (Employments) Regulations 2008, with effect from 1 January 2009

PART 2

Register of Employers and Registers of Employees

7 Register of employers

[(1) (a) Every employer who makes a payment of emoluments to or on behalf of an employee at a rate exceeding a rate equivalent to a rate of €8 a week, or in the case of an employee with other employment, €2 per week, shall, for the purposes of these Regulations—

(i) send or cause to be sent to the Revenue Commissioners, by such electronic means or otherwise as the Revenue Commissioners may require, a notification of his or her name and address and of the fact that he or she is paying such emoluments, and

(ii) register with the Revenue Commissioners in such manner, including by electronic means, as the Revenue Commissioners may require.

(b) In the case of an employee paid monthly or at longer intervals, the references in *subparagraph (a)* to a rate of €8 a week and a rate of €2 a week shall be treated as references to a rate of €36 a month and a rate of €9 a month respectively.

(2) Where a change occurs in a name or address which has been notified under this regulation, the employer shall send or cause to be sent to the Revenue Commissioners, by such electronic means or otherwise as the Revenue Commissioners may require, a notification of the change.

(3) (a) An employer who is liable under this Regulation to send a notification shall send or cause to be sent such notification within the period of 9 days beginning on the day on which the employer becomes so liable.

(b) An employer who is liable under this Regulation to register with the Revenue Commissioners shall register with them within the period of 9 days beginning on the day on which the employer becomes so liable.

(4) The Revenue Commissioners shall keep and maintain a register in electronic form in which names and addresses notified to them under this Regulation shall be registered and, when any name or address has been registered, they shall

give notice of the registration to the employer in writing or by means of such electronic system as the Revenue Commissioners may make available.][1]

Amendments

[1] Substituted by the Income Tax (Employments) Regulations 2012, comes into operation on 18 July 2012.

8 Registers of employees

[(1) Every employer who in any year makes to an employee or employees any payments of emoluments referred to in Regulation 7 shall keep and maintain in respect of such employee or employees employed throughout the year (or employed throughout the part or parts of a year during which such payments of emoluments are made) a register (to be known as the 'Register of Employees') for that year.

(2) The employer shall, in relation to each employee concerned, enter in the Register of Employees–

(a) the name and address of each such employee,

(b) the personal public service number of each such employee, and

(c) the date of commencement of employment and, where relevant, the date of cessation of employment, in respect of each such employee.

(3) The employer shall—

(a) keep and maintain the Register of Employees (or a copy of it)—

(i) at the normal place of employment of each employee, or

(ii) at the main place of business of the employer,

and

(b) on being required to do so by an officer of the Revenue Commissioners and within the period specified by that officer, produce the Register of Employees (or a certified copy of it) or an extract from it to any officer of the Revenue Commissioners.

(4) The Register of Employees may be kept in an electronic format.][1]

Amendments

[1] Substituted by the Income Tax (Employments) Regulations 2012, comes into operation on 18 July 2012.

9 Domestic employments

Regulations 7 and 8 shall not apply to an employer (being an individual) who pays emoluments to an employee engaged by that employer in a domestic employment where—

(a) the emoluments from that employment are less than €40 per week, and

(b) the employer has only one such employee.

PART 3

Tax Credits and Standard Rate Cut-off Point

10 Determination of appropriate tax credits and standard rate cut-off point by inspector

(1) The amount of the tax credits and standard rate cut-off point appropriate to an employee for any year shall be determined by the inspector who for that purpose may have regard to any of the following matters, namely—

(a) the reliefs from income tax to which the employee is entitled for the year in which the amount of the tax credits and standard rate cut-off point is determined, so far as the employee's title to those reliefs has been established at the time of the determination, but, where the amount of the tax credits and standard rate cut-off point is determined before the beginning of the year for which it is to have effect, the inspector shall disregard any such relief from income tax if he or she is not satisfied that the employee will be entitled to it for that year;

(b) the emoluments of the employee;

(c) where the employee has income (other than emoluments in relation to which the amount of the tax credits and standard rate cut-off point is being determined) the tax credits and standard rate cut-off point appropriate to that employee may be adjusted as necessary to collect the tax due on such income;

(d) where the employee is entitled to reliefs from income tax at the higher rate of tax, the tax credits and standard rate cut-off point appropriate to that employee may be adjusted as necessary to give effect to the relief;

(e) any tax overpaid for any previous year which has not been repaid;

(f) any tax remaining unpaid for any previous year which is not otherwise recovered;

(g) such other adjustments as may be necessary to secure that, so far as possible, the tax in respect of the employee's emoluments for the year to which the tax credits and standard rate cut-off point relate shall be deducted from the emoluments paid during the year.

(2) When an employee requests the inspector to disregard any particular relief or income referred to in subparagraph (a) or (c) of the foregoing paragraph, the inspector shall disregard it for the purposes of that paragraph.

(3) The inspector may disregard part or all of any expenses in respect of which the employee may be entitled to relief from income tax if it is impracticable to take account of all those expenses in determining the appropriate amount of tax credits and standard rate cut-off point, and, where he or she does so, shall direct the employer to disregard an equivalent amount of the employee's emoluments in calculating the tax to be deducted or repaid when any payment of emoluments is made to the employee.

11 Notice of determination of tax credits and standard rate cut-off point

(1) After the inspector has determined the amount of the tax credits and standard rate cut-off point for any year in accordance with Regulation 10, he or she shall [send, make available or cause to make available][1] notice of his or her determination to the employee.

[(2) The inspector shall send to the employer of the employee either a certificate (in these Regulations referred to as a "*certificate of tax credits and standard rate cut-off point*"), or a tax deduction card incorporating a certificate of tax credits and standard rate cut-off point, certifying—

(a) the amount of the tax credits and standard rate cut-off point of the employee as determined by the inspector, and

(b) where appropriate, details of total emoluments and total tax deducted in respect of the employee's previous employment or employments for the year; and such details shall be taken into account by the employer for the purposes of calculating the cumulative tax in respect of the cumulative emoluments of the employee in accordance with Regulation 17.][2]

(3) If it appears to the inspector that the employee has more than one employment, he or she shall send, in respect of each employment, to the employer a separate certificate of tax credits and standard rate cut-off point or a separate tax deduction card, as appropriate, showing the tax credits and standard rate cut-off point applicable to the particular employment, but the aggregate amount of the tax credits and standard rate cut-off point on the separate certificates of tax credits and standard rate cut-off point or separate tax deduction cards, as the case may be, shall not exceed the total amount of the tax credits and standard rate cut-off point of the employee for the year.

Amendments

[1] Substituted by the Income Tax (Employments) Regulations 2009, with effect from 1 January 2010

[2] Substituted by the Income Tax (Employments) Regulations 2008, with effect from 1 January 2009

12 Objection and appeal against amount of tax credits and standard rate cut-off point

(1) If the employee is aggrieved by the inspector's determination, he or she may give notice in writing of his or her objection to the inspector, stating the grounds of the objection, within 21 days of the date on which the determination was notified to him or her.

(2) On receipt of the notice of objection, the inspector may amend his or her determination by agreement with the employee, and in default of such agreement the employee, on giving notice in writing to the inspector, may appeal to the Appeal Commissioners.

(3) The Appeal Commissioners on appeal shall determine either or both the amount of tax credits and standard rate cut-off point having regard to the same matters as the inspector may have regard to when the amount of the tax credits and standard rate cut-off point is determined by the inspector, and, subject to the provisions of Regulation 13, their determination shall be final.

(4) Where either or both the amount of the tax credits and standard rate cut-off point is amended, either by the inspector or by the Appeal Commissioners, the inspector shall [send, make available or cause to make available][1] to the employee a notice of the new determination.

(5) A certificate of tax credits and standard rate cut-off point or a tax deduction card appropriate to the amount of the tax credits and standard rate cut-off point of an employee as determined by the inspector may be issued to the employer, notwithstanding that the inspector's determination is the subject of an objection or appeal.

(6) An appeal under this Regulation may be heard and determined by one Appeal Commissioner.

Amendments

[1] Substituted by the Income Tax (Employments) Regulations 2009, with effect from 1 January 2010

13 Amendments of amount of tax credits and standard rate cut-off point

(1) If either or both the amount of tax credits and standard rate cut-off point is found not to be appropriate because the actual circumstances are different from the circumstances by reference to which it was determined by the inspector or the Appeal Commissioners, the inspector may, and if so required by the employee

shall, by reference to the actual circumstances, amend, by way of increase or reduction, the previous determination.

(2) After the inspector has amended the determination of the amount of tax credits and standard rate cut-off point, he or she shall [give, make available or cause to make available][1] notice of the new determination to the employee not later than the date on which a new certificate of tax credits and standard rate cut-off point or new tax deduction card, as the case may be, is sent to the employer under Regulation 14.

(3) The provisions of Regulation 12 regarding objections and appeals shall apply in relation to the amended determination as they applied in relation to the previous determination.

Amendments

[1] Substituted by the Income Tax (Employments) Regulations 2009, with effect from 1 January 2010

14 Notice to employer of amended amount of tax credits and standard rate cut-off point

Where a determination of the inspector or of the Appeal Commissioners is amended after a certificate of tax credits and standard rate cut-off point or tax deduction card has been issued, the inspector shall send to the employer, and the employer shall thereafter use, such new certificate of tax credits and standard rate cut-off point or tax deduction card, as may be appropriate.

15 Special provisions for notices and certificates

(1) A determination of the amount of the tax credits and standard rate cut-off point appropriate to an employee for any year under paragraph (1) of Regulation 10 shall, if the inspector deems it proper, have effect for each subsequent year as if a separate determination had been duly made for each such year.

(2) Where the inspector has made a determination of the amount of the tax credits and standard rate cut-off point and the determination is to have effect for each subsequent year under the provisions of paragraph (1) of this Regulation, the notice of determination and the certificate or certificates of tax credits and standard rate cut-off point shall state that the amount of tax credits and standard rate cut-off point indicated thereon shall have effect for that year and for each subsequent year.

(3) The provisions of paragraph (2) of this Regulation shall not preclude an employee from requiring the inspector to determine the amount of the tax credits and standard rate cut-off point for any of the years after the first year included in a notice issued in accordance with the provisions of that paragraph and to [send, make available or cause to make available][1] to the employee concerned a notice of such determination, and the provisions of Regulation 12 shall apply to any such determination.

(4) The provisions of Regulation 13 shall apply in relation to each year after the first year included in a notice, certificate or certificates [issued, made available or caused to have been made available][2] under paragraph (2) of this Regulation as they apply in relation to the first year.

(5) The provisions of paragraphs (3) and (4) of this Regulation shall, with the necessary modifications, apply to any new determination of the amount of the tax credits and standard rate cut-off point for any year under Regulation 12 or Regulation 13 as if it were a determination under paragraph (1) of Regulation 10.

Amendments

[1, 2] Substituted by the Income Tax (Employments) Regulations 2009, with effect from 1 January 2010

PART 4

Deduction and Repayment of Tax

16 General provision for deductions and repayments

On payment of emoluments referred to in Regulation 7, deductions or repayments of tax shall be made subject to, and in accordance with, the subsequent provisions of this Part of these Regulations.

16A Deduction of tax in respect of notional payments

[The obligation on an employer to deduct tax in respect of a notional payment shall have effect as an obligation to deduct tax due on that payment from any payment or payments of emoluments actually made by the employer to or on behalf of the employee on—

(a) the day the notional payment is made, or

(b) if there is no actual payment of emoluments made to the employee on that day, the next pay day following the time when the notional payment is made,

and where, by reason of an insufficiency of payments of emoluments actually made to or on behalf of the employee, the employer is liable to remit under section 985A(4) of the Principal Act an amount of income tax which the employer was unable to deduct from such payments, the employer shall be liable to remit that amount of tax to the Revenue Commissioners as if the amount to be remitted had been deducted in accordance with this Regulation.][1]

Amendments

[1] Inserted by the Income Tax (Employments) Regulations 2003, with effect from 1 January 2004

16B Tax borne by the employer in respect of notional payments

[Where tax in respect of a notional payment is remitted by the employer in accordance with subsection (4) of section 985A of the Principal Act and subsection (5) of that section applies, the notional payment in respect of the emolument referred to in that subsection (5) shall be treated as if it were made on 31 March in the year of assessment in which the emolument is treated as arising.][1]

Amendments

[1] Inserted by the Income Tax (Employments) Regulations 2003, with effect from 1 January 2004

17 Calculation and making of deduction or repayment where tax deduction card held

(1) On any payment of emoluments to or on behalf of an employee in respect of whom the employer holds a tax deduction card, the employer, except where these Regulations otherwise provide, shall ascertain—

(a) firstly, the cumulative emoluments of that employee at the date of the payment,

(b) secondly, by reference to the cumulative standard rate cut-off point specified on the tax deduction card corresponding to the date of payment, the cumulative gross tax in respect of the cumulative emoluments, and

(c) finally, by reference to the cumulative tax credits specified on the tax deduction card corresponding to the date of payment, the cumulative tax in respect of the cumulative emoluments.

(2) If the cumulative tax ascertained in accordance with paragraph (1) of this Regulation, exceeds the cumulative tax corresponding to the employee's cumulative emoluments at the date of the last preceding payment of emoluments (hereafter in this Regulation referred to as the "*previous cumulative tax*"), the employer shall deduct the excess from the emoluments on making the payment in question.

(3) If the cumulative tax as so ascertained is less than the previous cumulative tax, the employer shall repay the difference to the employee on making the payment in question.

(4) If the cumulative tax is equal to the previous cumulative tax, no tax shall be either deducted or repaid when the payment in question is made.

(5) Where the payment in question is the first payment in the year, paragraphs (2), (3) and (4) of this Regulation shall not apply, but the employer shall deduct the cumulative tax as ascertained in accordance with paragraph (1) of this Regulation from the emoluments on making the payment in question.

(6) The employer shall record, either on the tax deduction card or in such other form as may be authorised by the Revenue Commissioners, the following particulars regarding every payment of emoluments which the employer makes to or on behalf of the employee, namely-

(a) the date of the payment;

(b) the gross amount of the emoluments;

(c) in relation to the date of payment—

(i) the cumulative emoluments;

(ii) the cumulative tax due at the standard rate of tax;

(iii) the cumulative tax due at the higher rate of tax; and

(iv) the cumulative gross tax;

(d) the corresponding cumulative tax; and

(e) the amount of tax, if any, deducted or repaid on making the payment.

17A Deduction of tax in respect of certain notional payments

[(1) This Regulation applies to emoluments being—

(a) the benefit of the private use of a car which is chargeable to tax by virtue of section 121 of the Act,

(b) the benefit of the private use of a van which is chargeable to tax by virtue of section 121A of the Act,

(c) the benefit arising from a preferential loan which is treated as a perquisite for the purposes of section 112 by virtue of section 122 of the Act, or

(d) a benefit arising from an asset which belongs to the employer and the valuation of which is determined in accordance with subsection (3) of section 119 of the Act.

(2) Where, a notional payment for a year is in respect of an emolument to which this Regulation applies—

(a) the amount of the notional payment for the year in relation to the emolument shall be apportioned over the period (referred to in subparagraph (b) as the "*period of benefit*") for which the benefit is available in that year, and

(b) the employer shall deduct tax in accordance with this Part of these Regulations or remit tax under section 985A(4) of the Principal Act by reference to the part of the notional payment for the year apportioned to each week, where the employee is paid weekly, or month, where the employee is paid monthly, in the period of benefit.][1]

Amendments

[1] Inserted by the Income Tax (Employments) Regulations 2003, with effect from 1 January 2004

18 Subsidiary emoluments of employee paid monthly, etc

(1) If the employer makes a payment in respect of overtime or other extra earnings to or on behalf of an employee whose main emoluments are paid monthly, and that payment is made at an earlier date in the income tax month than the date on which the main emoluments are paid, the employer shall repay no tax to the employee on the occasion of that payment, notwithstanding that tax may be repayable under the provisions of Regulation 17, but in such a case, that Regulation shall have effect as if that payment was made on the same date in that income tax month as the date on which the main emoluments are paid.

(2) The provisions of this Regulation shall apply with the necessary modifications to payments in respect of overtime or other extra earnings which are made to or on behalf of an employee whose main emoluments are paid at intervals greater than a month.

19 Deduction in special cases

[(1) This Regulation applies to—

(a) payments of emoluments made on 31 December in any year or, if that year is a leap year, on 30 or 31 December in that year, to an employee who is paid weekly, and

(b) any other payments of emoluments made to or on behalf of any employee to which the inspector directs that this Regulation shall apply.][1]

(2) Regulation 17 shall not apply to payments of emoluments to which this Regulation applies, and on making any such payment the employer shall deduct therefrom—

(a) by reference to the amount of the employee's tax credits and standard rate cut-off point, the amount of tax which would have been deductible therefrom if the payment had been made on the preceding 1 January or,

(b) [Where the employee has ceased to be employed by the employer and no tax deduction card or certificate of tax credits and standard rate cut-off point is held,][2] tax in accordance with paragraph (2) of Regulation 22.

(3) On making any such payment as mentioned in paragraph (1) of this Regulation, the employer shall record either on the tax deduction card or in such other form as may be authorised by the Revenue Commissioners—

(a) the date of the payment,

(b) the gross amount of the emoluments.

(c) the amount of the appropriate tax credits and standard rate cut-off point, and

(d) the amount of tax (if any) deducted on making the payment.

(4) Where the employee has ceased to be employed by the employer and no tax deduction card is held, the particulars referred to in paragraph (3) of this Regulation, except the amounts of the tax credits and standard rate cut-off point, shall be recorded on the emergency card referred to in Regulation 22.

Amendments

[1] Substituted by the Income Tax (Employments) Regulations 2008, with effect from 1 January 2009

[2] Substituted by the Income Tax (Employments) Regulations 2008, with effect from 1 January 2009

19A Arrears of pay

[(1) This Regulation applies to payments of emoluments made to or on behalf of an employee after he or she has ceased to be employed by the person making the payments.

(2) On making any such payment as mentioned in paragraph (1) of this Regulation, the employer shall deduct—

(a) in the case of an employee [who ceased in the current year and][1] in respect of whom the employer holds a certificate of tax credits and standard rate cut-off point or a tax deduction card, by reference to the amount of the employee's tax credits and standard rate cut-off point, the amount of tax which would have been deductible therefrom if the payment had been made on the date the employee ceased to be employed by the employer and Regulation 17 had applied, or

(b) [in the case of an employee who ceased to be employed by the employer—

(i) in the current tax year and in respect of whom no certificate of tax credits and standard rate cut off point or tax deduction card is held by the employer, or

(ii) in any tax year before the tax year in which the payment is made, tax in accordance with paragraph (2) of Regulation 22.][2]

(3) On making any such payment as mentioned in paragraph (1) of this Regulation, the employer shall record either on the tax deduction card or in such other form as may be authorised by the Revenue Commissioners—

(a) the date of the payment,

(b) the gross amount of the emoluments,

(c) the amount of the appropriate tax credits and standard rate cut-off point, and

(d) the amount of tax (if any) deducted on making the payment.

(4) Where the employee has ceased to be employed by the employer and no certificate of tax credits and standard rate cut-off point or tax deduction card is held, then the particulars referred to in paragraph (3) of this Regulation, except the amounts of the tax credits and standard rate cut-off point, shall be recorded on the emergency card referred to in Regulation 22.][3]

Amendments

[1] Inserted by the Income Tax (Employments) Regulations 2009, with effect from 1 January 2010

[2] Inserted by the Income Tax (Employments) Regulations 2009, with effect from 1 January 2010

[3] Inserted by the Income Tax (Employments) Regulations 2008, with effect from 1 January 2009

20 Change of employment where certificate of tax credits and standard rate cut-off point or tax deduction card held

(1) If an employer ceases to employ an employee in respect of whom a certificate of tax credits and standard rate cut-off point or tax deduction card has been issued to him or her, he or she shall immediately send to the inspector by whom the certificate of tax credits and standard rate cut-off point or tax deduction card was issued a certificate on the prescribed form containing the following particulars:

(a) the name of the employee;

(b) the date on which the employment ceased;

(c) the week or income tax month in respect of which the last payment of emoluments was recorded on the tax deduction card and the cumulative emoluments at the date of that payment;

and any other particulars as to tax credits and standard rate cut-off point, tax or any other matters which are indicated by such form as being required to be entered thereon.

(2) The employer shall make on the prescribed form [3 copies][1] of the certificate required by paragraph (1) of this Regulation and shall deliver them to the employee on the date the employment ceases.

(3) Immediately on commencing his or her next employment the employee shall deliver to the new employer [2 copies][2] of the certificate prepared by the former employer and, subject to the provisions of paragraph (4) of this Regulation, the following provisions shall have effect:

[(a) the new employer shall insert on one copy of the certificate—

(i) the address of the employee,

(ii) the date on which the new employment commenced,

(iii) the rate of payment of the emoluments and

(iv) the manner in which the payment of emoluments is made to the employee, that is to say, weekly, monthly or as the case may be some other period,

and immediately send that copy to the inspector by whom certificates of tax credit and standard rate cut-off point are ordinarily issued to the employee;][3]

(b) the inspector shall send to the new employer a certificate of tax credits and standard rate cut-off point or tax deduction card, as appropriate, for the employee;

(c) pending the receipt of the certificate of tax credits and standard rate cut-off point or tax deduction card from the inspector, the new employer shall prepare a temporary tax deduction form and, in relation to payments of emoluments by him or her, record on it—

(i) the date of payment,

(ii) the gross amount of emoluments, and

(iii) as respects each week or income tax month (as may be appropriate), the tax credits and standard rate cut-off point for Week 1 or Month 1 as specified on the copies of the certificate prepared by the former employer,

and having regard to the standard rate cut-off point as specified on the copies of the certificate prepared by the former employer, the new employer shall deduct tax on the aggregate amount of the emoluments for the week or income tax month (as may be appropriate) by reference to the tax due at the standard rate of tax and the higher rate of tax (as may be appropriate) on such emoluments reduced by the tax credits for Week 1 or Month 1 as specified on the copies of the certificate prepared by the former employer;

(d) when the new employer has received a certificate of tax credits and standard rate cut-off point or tax deduction card from the inspector, he or she shall, having ascertained the aggregate of the amounts of the emoluments and the aggregate of the amounts of the tax by reference to the relevant entries on the copies of the certificate prepared by the former employer and on the temporary tax deduction form (if any), record on the tax deduction card or such other record as may be authorised those aggregates, and those aggregates shall be deemed respectively to be the cumulative emoluments paid and the cumulative tax deducted by him or her.

(4) (a) Where the 2 copies of the certificate prepared by the former employer show that the last payment of emoluments was in the year preceding that in which the new employment commences, the new employer shall comply with the provisions of paragraph (3) of this Regulation with the modification that he or she shall not record, or have regard to, the cumulative emoluments and cumulative tax shown on the copies of the certificate.

(b) Where the 2 copies of the certificate prepared by the former employer show that the last payment of emoluments was in a year earlier than the year preceding that in which the new employment commences, the new employer shall comply with the provisions of subparagraph (a) of paragraph (3) of this Regulation but deduct tax from each payment of emoluments made by him or her to the employee, and keep records on the emergency card referred to in Regulation 22, as if those payments had been payments to which paragraph (2) of that Regulation applied.

(c) [where an employee has recommenced employment with the same employer in the same year and the 2 copies of the certificate referred to in paragraph (3) relate to that employment, then the employer shall comply with the provisions of paragraph (3) of this Regulation.][4]

(5) If the new employer ceases to employ the employee before he or she receives a certificate of tax credits and standard rate cut-off point or tax deduction card from the inspector, he or she shall comply with the provisions of paragraphs (1) and (2) of this Regulation as if a certificate of tax credits and standard rate cut-off point or tax deduction card in respect of the employee had been issued to him or her by the inspector, but—

(a) for the purposes of subparagraph (c) of paragraph (1) of this Regulation, the cumulative emoluments shall be taken to be the aggregate of the cumulative emoluments shown on the copies of the certificate prepared by the former employer and the gross emoluments paid by the new employer; and

(b) where, as respects the certificate on the prescribed form referred to in that paragraph (1), entry of particulars of the cumulative tax is required to be made thereon, that tax shall be taken for the purposes of that entry to be the aggregate of the cumulative tax shown on those copies and any tax deducted by the new employer.

(6) If the employee objects to the disclosure to the new employer of his or her cumulative emoluments, he or she may deliver the 2 copies of the certificate prepared by the former employer to the inspector before he or she commences his or her new employment, and the inspector shall send in respect of the employee to the new employer a certificate of tax credits and standard rate cut-off point or tax deduction card not stating the employee's cumulative tax credits and standard rate cut-off point or cumulative emoluments and direct that Regulation 19 shall apply to all payments of emoluments which the new employer makes to or on behalf of the employee.

(7) Retirement on pension shall not be treated as a cessation of employment for the purposes of this Regulation or of Regulation 19 if the emoluments are paid by the same person both before and after the retirement.

Amendments

[1, 2, 3] Substituted by the Income Tax (Employments) Regulations 2008, with effect from 1 January 2009

[4] Inserted by the Income Tax (Employments) Regulations 2008, with effect from 1 January 2009

21 Death of employee

(1) On the death of an employee in respect of whom an employer holds a certificate of tax credits and standard rate cut-off point or tax deduction card or in respect of whom a temporary tax deduction form has been prepared by the employer under subparagraph (c) of paragraph (3) of Regulation 20 or to whom the provisions of paragraph (2) of Regulation 22 apply, the employer shall immediately send to the inspector by whom certificates of tax credits and standard rate cut-off point or tax deduction cards are ordinarily issued to the employer the certificate (relating to cessation of employment) mentioned in paragraph (1) of Regulation 20 or in paragraph (6) of Regulation 22, as the case may require, and shall insert thereon the name and address of the personal representative of the deceased employee, if they are known to the employer.

(2) If any emoluments are paid by the employer after the date of the employee's death in respect of his or her employment with the employer, the employer shall, on making any such payment, deduct or repay tax as if the deceased employee was still in the employer's employment at the date of the payment, and—

(a) if the amount of those emoluments and the date on which they will be paid are known at the time the certificate mentioned in paragraph (1) of this Regulation is completed, the employer shall include thereon the amount of the emoluments, the date on which they will be paid, and the amount of tax which will be deducted or repaid, and

(b) in any other case, the employer shall indicate on the certificate that a further payment of emoluments will be made.

22 Emergency basis of deduction

(1) If the employer makes such payments of emoluments as are referred to in Regulation 7 to or on behalf of an employee in respect of whom the employer has not received either a certificate of tax credits and standard rate cut-off point, a tax deduction card or copies of a certificate made by a former employer under paragraph (2) of Regulation 20, the employer on the occasion of the first such payment, shall immediately send to the inspector, by whom certificates of tax credits and standard rate cut-off point or tax deduction cards are [ordinarily issued to the employee][1], a return stating the name and address of the employee, the date on which his or her employment commenced, and such other particulars as may be necessary to secure the issue to the employer of the appropriate certificate of tax credits and standard rate cut-off point or tax deduction card.

[(2) (a) Until a certificate of tax credits and standard rate cut-off point or a tax deduction card is received from the inspector, the employer, on making any payment of emoluments to or on behalf of an employee referred to in paragraph (1) of this Regulation, shall deduct tax from such payment in accordance with the following provisions of this paragraph.

(b) Subject to subparagraph (c) of this paragraph—

(i) during the period of 4 weeks, or in the case of an employee paid monthly, 1 month, from the day on which the employee first holds an employment with the employer in a year, or until the certificate of tax credits and standard rate cut-off point or a tax deduction card is received from the inspector, the employer shall deduct tax at the standard rate of tax and, where appropriate, the higher rate of tax and keep records on an emergency card on the basis that the amount of—

(I) the tax credits is an amount per week equal to one fifty-second of the basic personal tax credit specified in section 461 of the Act, as it applies for that year, or if the employee is paid monthly, an amount equal to one-twelfth of that tax credit, and

(II) the standard rate cut-off point is an amount per week equal to one fifty-second of the amount chargeable to tax at the standard rate specified in Part 1 of the Table to section 15 of the Act, as it applies for that year, or if the employee is paid monthly, one-twelfth of that amount,

and in determining the amount of any tax credits or the standard rate cut-off point under clause (I) or (II) of this subparagraph any part of a euro shall be treated as a whole euro,

(ii) if, within the period of 4 weeks or 1 month referred to in subparagraph (b)(i) of this paragraph, the employer has not received the certificate of tax credits and standard rate cut-off point or a tax deduction card, the employer shall, until a certificate of tax credits and standard rate cut-off point or a tax deduction card is received from the inspector, keep records on an emergency card and on the making of any payment of emoluments to or on behalf of the employee deduct tax on the basis that the employee's tax credits are nil and in accordance with the following provisions, that is to say—

(I) in the period of 4 weeks or, in a case where the employee is paid monthly, 1 month, commencing on the day after the end of the period mentioned in subparagraph (b)(i) of this paragraph, deduct tax at the standard rate of tax and, where appropriate, the higher rate of tax on the basis that the standard rate cut-off point is the amount referred to in subparagraph (b)(i)(II) of this paragraph, and

(II) thereafter deduct tax at the higher rate of tax

(c) In the case of an employee who first holds an employment with an employer on or after 1 January, 2003 and for whom the employer has not been provided with the employee's personal public service number, the provisions of subparagraph (b) of this paragraph shall not apply until such time as that number is provided to the employer and the employer shall, until such time, on making any payments of emoluments to or on behalf of the employee, deduct tax at the higher rate of tax and maintain records on an emergency card on the basis that the employee's tax credits are nil.

(2A) Where, for the purposes of this Regulation, an employee furnishes the employer with his or her personal public service number, the employer shall take all reasonable measures to establish that the number furnished is in fact the personal public service number of that employee.][2]

(3) For the purposes of paragraph 2 of this Regulation—

(a) all employments which the employee holds with the employer in a year of assessment shall be deemed to be one employment, and

(b) that employment, notwithstanding that for a part or parts of the year the employee does not hold an employment with the employer, shall be deemed to be held for a continuous period commencing on the day on which the employee first holds an employment with the employer in that year and ending on the day on which the employee last holds an employment with the employer in that year.

(4) Where the inspector sends a certificate of tax credits and standard rate cut-off point or tax deduction card the employer shall enter on the tax deduction card or such other record as may be authorised the particulars of emoluments and tax deducted as shown on the relevant emergency card.

(5) On making payments of emoluments to or on behalf of the employee after a certificate of tax credits and standard rate cut-off point or tax deduction card relating to the employee sent under paragraph (4) of this Regulation has been received, the following provisions shall have effect for the purposes of Regulation 17—

(a) any cumulative emoluments notified to the employer by the inspector shall be entered by the employer on the tax deduction card and shall be treated as if they represented emoluments paid by the employer, and

(b) the cumulative tax before the first of the said payments shall be taken to be the sum of any cumulative tax notified to the employer by the inspector and entered by the employer on the tax deduction card and any tax which the employer was liable to deduct from the employee's emoluments under paragraph (2) of this Regulation.

(6) (a) Where paragraph (2) of this Regulation applies and the employer ceases to employ the employee before a certificate of tax credits and standard rate cut-off point or tax deduction card in respect of the employee has been received, the employer shall immediately send to the inspector a certificate on the form prescribed for the purposes of paragraph (1) of Regulation 20 and shall make on the prescribed form [3 copies][3] of that certificate which the employer shall deliver to the employee on the date the employment ceases and the said certificate—

(i) shall not contain particulars of the cumulative emoluments or cumulative tax but shall contain particulars of the emoluments paid and tax deducted by the employer, and

(ii) shall indicate that an emergency card was in use when the employment ceased.

(b) [Immediately on commencing his or her next employment, the employee shall deliver to his or her new employer 2 copies of the certificate referred to above and the new employer shall—

(i) insert on one copy of the certificate the address of the employee, the date on which the new employment commenced, and the manner in which the payment of emoluments is made to the employee, that is to say, weekly, monthly or as the case may be some other period, and the rate of payment of the emoluments, and

(ii) immediately send that copy to the inspector by whom certificates of tax credit and standard rate cut-off point are ordinarily issued to the employee,

and paragraphs (2), (3), (4) and (5) of this Regulation shall apply as if the employee had not submitted to the new employer copies of a certificate by a former employer under paragraph (2) of Regulation 20.][4]

(7) This Regulation shall not apply where—

(a) the employee performs the duties of his or her employment wholly outside the State, or

(b) the employee is outside the State and the emoluments are paid outside the State.

(8) In this Regulation "*emergency card*" means a card in the form prescribed for the purposes of this Regulation.

Amendments

[1, 2, 3, 4] Substituted by the Income Tax (Employments) Regulations 2008, with effect from 1 January 2009

23 Emoluments not paid weekly or monthly

Where emoluments are paid at regular intervals other than regular intervals of a week or a month, any payment of such emoluments shall be deemed for the purposes of these Regulations to be made on the date on which it would have been made if a payment had been made on the last day of the preceding year, but the employer shall record the actual date of every such payment.

24 Aggregation of emoluments in non-cumulative cases

Where under these Regulations tax is deductible otherwise than by reference to cumulative emoluments and cumulative tax, the amount of tax to be deducted in any week or income tax month shall be calculated by reference to the aggregate of the emoluments paid to or on behalf of the employee in that week or month.

25 Tax-free emoluments

Where the employer makes a payment to or for the benefit of the employee in respect of his or her tax, the amount of the emoluments which the employer pays to or on behalf of the employee shall be deemed for the purposes of deduction and repayment of tax under these Regulations to be such a sum as will include the amount assessable on the employee in respect of the payment made by the employer in respect of the employee's tax.

26 Repayment during sickness and unemployment

(1) If, owing to the absence from work through sickness or other similar cause, the employee is entitled to receive no emoluments on the usual pay day, the employer shall, on application being made in person by the employee or his or her authorised representative, make such repayment of tax to the employee as may be appropriate, having regard to his or her cumulative emoluments at the date of the pay day in question and the corresponding cumulative tax.

(2) If, owing to absence from work otherwise than mentioned in paragraph (1) of this Regulation, the employee is entitled to receive no emoluments on the usual pay day, the employer either—

(a) shall make any such repayment of tax to the employee as would be appropriate under paragraph (1) if the absence from work was due to sickness, or

(b) not later than the first usual pay day on which no emoluments will be payable to the employee, shall send, to the inspector [by whom certificates of tax credits and standard rate cut-off point or tax deduction cards are ordinarily issued to the employee][1], a notification of the employee's absence from work and of the employer's intention to make no repayment to the employee under subparagraph (a) of this paragraph, together with a return containing the same particulars with respect to the employee as the employer would be liable to certify under paragraph (1) of Regulation 20 if the employment had ceased on the day on which emoluments were last paid to or on behalf of the employee.

(3) Where the notification and return referred to in subparagraph (b) of paragraph (2) of this Regulation are sent within the time limited by that subparagraph, the employer shall be relieved of the liability to make any repayment under the provisions of subparagraph (a) of that paragraph.

(4) On the employee's return to work the employer shall immediately notify the inspector and for the purpose of deducting or repaying tax on the occasion of any subsequent payment of emoluments to or on behalf of the employee during the year shall take into account the amount of any repayment which has been made under paragraph (5) of this Regulation of which he or she is notified by the inspector.

(5) In the case of a person who has ceased to be employed or with respect to whom a notification and return have been sent under the provisions of subparagraph (b) of paragraph (2) of this Regulation, any repayment which may be appropriate at any date, having regard to the person's cumulative emoluments at that date and the corresponding cumulative tax, shall be made to him or her by the Revenue Commissioners, and a person who has ceased to be employed shall, on applying for repayment, produce to the inspector the copies of the certificate mentioned in Regulation 20 and such evidence of his or her unemployment as the inspector may require.

Amendments

[1] Substituted by the Income Tax (Employments) Regulations 2008, with effect from 1 January 2009

27 Certificate of tax deducted

(1) Within 46 days from the end of the year the employer shall give to the employee a certificate showing the total amount of the emoluments paid by the employer to or on behalf of the employee during the year, the amount of the employee's tax credits and standard rate cut-off point and the total net tax deducted from the emoluments.

(2) In the case of an employee taken into employment after the beginning of the year, the certificate shall include any emoluments paid to the employee by any previous employer during the year and any tax deducted from those emoluments, being emoluments and tax which the employer giving the certificate was required to take into account for the purposes of deducting or repaying tax in the case of the emoluments paid by him or her.

(3) A certificate shall be given under this Regulation to every employee who is in the employer's employment on the last day of the year and from whose emoluments any tax has been deducted during the year.

PART 5

Payment and Recovery of Tax, etc

28 Payment of tax by employer

[(1) Within 14 days from the end of every income tax month the employer shall remit to the Collector-General the total of—

(a) all amounts of tax which the employer was liable under these regulations to deduct from emoluments paid by the employer during that income tax month, and

(b) any amount of tax that was not so deducted but which the employer was liable, in accordance with section 985A(4) of the Act, to remit, in respect of that income tax month, to the Collector-General in respect of notional payments made by the employer,

reduced by any amounts which the employer was liable under these Regulations to repay during that income tax month.][1]

[(1A) Where a remittance referred to in paragraph (1) is made by electronic means (within the meaning of section 917EA of the Act) as are required by the Revenue Commissioners, paragraph (1) shall apply and have effect as if the reference to "14 days" were a reference to "23 days"; but where the said remittance is not made on or before the date provided for in this paragraph, this Regulation shall apply and have effect without regard to the provisions of this paragraph.][2]

(2) On payment of tax, the Collector-General shall furnish the employer concerned with a receipt in respect of that payment which shall consist of whichever of the following the Collector-General considers appropriate, namely—

(a) a separate receipt on the prescribed form in respect of each such payment, or

(b) a receipt on the prescribed form in respect of all such payments that have been made within a period specified in the receipt.

[(3) If the amount which the employer is liable to remit to the Collector-General under paragraph (1) of this Regulation exceeds the amount of the total net tax deducted in relation to emoluments paid by the employer during the relevant income tax month, the Revenue Commissioners, on being satisfied that the employer took reasonable care to comply with the provisions of Chapter 4 of Part 42 of the Principal Act and these Regulations and that the under-deduction was due to an error made in good faith, may direct that the amount of the excess shall be recovered from the employee, and where they so direct, the employer shall not be liable to remit the amount of the excess to the Collector-General.

(4) If the amount which the employer is liable to remit to the Collector-General under paragraph (1) of this Regulation exceeds the amount of the total net tax deducted in relation to emoluments paid by the employer during the relevant income tax month and the Revenue Commissioners are of the opinion that an employee has received his or her emoluments knowing that the employer has wilfully failed to either deduct therefrom or to remit in respect thereof in accordance with section 985A(4) of the Principal Act an amount of tax which the employer was liable to deduct or so remit under these Regulations, the Revenue Commissioners may direct that the amount of the excess shall be recovered from the employee, and where they so direct, the employer shall not be liable to remit the amount of the excess to the Collector-General.][3]

(5) If a difference arises between the employer and the employee as to whether the employer has deducted tax, or having regard to Regulation 25 is deemed to have deducted tax, from emoluments paid to or on behalf of the employee, or as to the amount of the tax that has been so deducted or is so deemed to have been deducted, the matter shall, for the purposes of ascertaining the amount of any tax to be recovered from the employee under paragraph (3) or (4) of this Regulation, be determined by the Appeal Commissioners.

(6) If the total of the amounts which the employer was liable to repay during any income tax month exceeds the total of the amounts which the employer was liable to deduct during that income tax month, the employer shall be entitled to deduct the excess from any amount which he or she is subsequently liable to remit to the Collector-General under paragraph (1) of this Regulation or to recover it from the Revenue Commissioners.

(7) A determination under paragraph (5) of this Regulation may be made by one Appeal Commissioner.

Amendments

[1] Inserted by the Income Tax (Employments) Regulations 2003, with effect from 1 January 2004

[2] Inserted by the Income Tax (Employments) Regulations 2008, with effect from 1 January 2009

[3] Substituted by the Income Tax (Employments) Regulations 2003, with effect from 1 January 2004

29 Payment of tax for periods greater than one month but not exceeding one year

[(1) Notwithstanding the provisions of Regulation 28, the Collector-General may, from time to time, authorise, in writing, an employer (unless the employer objects) to remit to him or her within 14 days from the end of a period longer than an income tax month but not exceeding a year (which in this Regulation and in Regulation 30 is referred to as the "*accounting period*") the total of—

(a) all amounts of tax which the employer was liable under these regulations to deduct from emoluments paid by the employer during that accounting period, and

(b) any amount of tax that was not so deducted but which the employer was liable, in accordance with section 985A(4) of the Act, to remit, in respect of that accounting period, to the Collector-General in respect of notional payments made by the employer,

reduced by any amounts which the employer was liable under these Regulations to repay during that accounting period.][1]

[(1A) Where a remittance referred to in paragraph (1) is made by such electronic means (within the meaning of section 917EA of the Act) as are required by the Revenue Commissioners, paragraph (1) shall apply and have effect as if the reference to "14 days" were a reference to "23 days"; but where the said remittance is not made on or before the date provided for in this paragraph, this Regulation shall apply and have effect without regard to the provisions of this paragraph.][2]

(2) For the purposes of issuing an authorisation to an employer pursuant to this Regulation, the Collector-General shall, where he or she considers it appropriate, have regard to the following matters:

(a) he or she has reasonable grounds to believe that—

(i) the authorisation will not result in a loss of tax, and

(ii) the employer will meet all obligations imposed on the employer under the authorisation,

and

(b) the employer—

(i) has been a registered employer within the meaning of Regulation 7 during all of the period consisting of one year immediately preceding the year in which an authorisation for the purposes of this Regulation would, if it were issued, have effect, and

(i) has made all returns which the employer is required to make in accordance with the provisions of Regulation 31(1).

(3) An authorisation for the purposes of this Regulation may—

(a) be issued either without conditions or subject to such conditions as the Collector-General, having regard in particular to the matters set out in paragraph (2) of this Regulation, considers proper and specifies in writing to the employer concerned when issuing the authorisation, and

(b) without prejudice to the generality of the foregoing, require an authorised person to agree with the Collector-General a schedule of amounts of money which he or she undertakes to pay on dates specified by the Collector-General by direct debit from his or her account with a financial institution and the total of the amounts specified in that schedule shall be that person's best estimate of his or her total tax liability for his or her accounting period and he or she shall review on an ongoing basis whether the total of the amounts specified in that schedule is likely to be adequate to cover his or her actual liability for his or her accounting period and where this is not the case or is not likely to be the case, he or she shall agree a revised schedule of amounts with the Collector-General and adjust his or her direct debit amounts accordingly.

(4) The Collector-General may terminate an authorisation by notice in writing and, where an employer requests him or her to do so, the Collector-General shall terminate the authorisation.

(5) For the purposes of terminating an authorisation issued pursuant to this Regulation, the Collector-General shall, where he or she considers it appropriate, have regard to the following matters:

(a) he or she has reasonable grounds to believe that the authorisation has resulted or could result in a loss of tax,

(b) the employer—

(i) has failed to remit to the Collector-General within 14 days from the end of the preceding accounting period all amounts of tax which the employer was liable under these Regulations to deduct from emoluments paid by the employer during that accounting period, reduced by any amounts which the employer was liable under these regulations to repay during that accounting period, or

(ii) has furnished, or there is furnished on the employer's behalf, any incorrect information for the purposes of the issue to the employer of an authorisation, or

(iii) has failed to make within the required time limit all returns which the employer is required to make in accordance with the provisions of Regulation 31(1), or

(iv) has not complied with the conditions, if any, specified by the Collector-General under paragraph (3) of this Regulation in relation to the issue to the employer of an authorisation.

(6) In relation to each income tax month in respect of which he or she has not remitted an amount of tax in accordance with paragraph (1) of this Regulation or paragraph (1) of Regulation 28, an employer whose authorisation is terminated shall be deemed to have complied with paragraph (1) of Regulation 28 if he or she remits to the Collector-General, within 14 days of issue of a notice of termination, the amount of tax which he or she would have been required to remit in accordance with the provisions of paragraph (1) of Regulation 28 if he or she were an employer to whom an authorisation had not been issued.

(7) (a) An authorisation shall be deemed to have been terminated by the Collector-General on the date that an authorised person ceases to be an employer.

(b) An employer whose authorisation is deemed to have been terminated shall, in relation to any income tax month (or part of an income tax month) comprised in the accounting period which was in operation in his or her case on the date of such termination, comply with paragraph (1) of Regulation 29 as if he or she were an authorised person whose accounting period ended on the last day of the income tax month during which the termination occurred.

(c) The personal representative of a deceased employer shall be deemed to be the employer for the purposes of subparagraph (b)

(8) The provisions of paragraphs (2) to (7) of Regulation 28 shall apply to this Regulation as if references therein to "*income tax month*" were references to "*accounting period*".

Amendments

[1] Substituted by the Income Tax (Employments) Regulations 2003, with effect from 1 January 2004

[2] Inserted by the Income Tax (Employments) Regulations 2008, with effect from 1 January 2009

30 Employer failing to pay tax

(1) If within 14 days from the end of any income tax month or accounting period (as provided for in Regulation 29) the employer has remitted no amount of tax to the Collector-General under Regulation 28 or 29 for that income tax month or accounting period, as the case may be, and the Collector-General is unaware of the amount, if any, which the employer is liable so to remit, the Collector-General may give notice to the employer requiring him or her to send to the Collector-General, within the time limited in the notice, a return showing the name of every employee to whom or on behalf of whom he or she made any payment of emoluments or repayment of tax in the period from the preceding 1 January to the day (being the last day of an income tax month or of an accounting period) specified by the notice, together with such particulars with regard to each such employee as the notice may require, being particulars of—

(i) the amount of the tax credits and standard rate cut-off point appropriate to the employee's case;

(ii) the payments of emoluments made to or on behalf of him or her during that period, and

(iii) any other matter affecting the calculation of the tax which the employer was liable under these Regulations to deduct or to repay to the employee during that period,

and the employer shall comply with the requirements of the notice.

[(1A) Where a remittance referred to in paragraph (1) is made by such electronic means (within the meaning of section 917EA of the Act) as are required by the Revenue Commissioners, paragraph (1) shall apply and have effect as if the reference to "14 days" were a reference to "23 days".][1]

(2) In a case referred to in paragraph (1) of this Regulation the Collector-General shall ascertain, in like manner as the employer should, under these Regulations, have ascertained, the amount of tax which the employer should have deducted from the emoluments, and shall notify the amount to the employer.

(3) A notice given by the Collector-General under paragraph (1) of this Regulation may extend to two or more consecutive income tax months or two or more accounting periods, as the case may be.

(4) A notice may be given by the Collector-General under paragraph (1) of this Regulation notwithstanding that an amount of tax has been remitted to the Collector-General by the employer under Regulations 28 or 29 for any income tax month or accounting period, if the Collector-General is not satisfied that the amount so remitted is the full amount which the employer is liable to remit to him for that income tax month or accounting period, as the case may be, and the provisions of this Regulation shall have effect accordingly.

Amendments

[1] Inserted by the Income Tax (Employments) Regulations 2008, with effect from 1 January 2009

31 Return by employer at end of year

(1) Within 46 days from the end of the year, or from the date on which the employer ceases permanently to be an employer to whom Regulation 7(1) applies, whichever is the earlier, the employer shall send to the Collector-General—

[(a) in such form as the Revenue Commissioners may approve or prescribe, a return in respect of each employee showing the total amount of the emoluments, including emoluments in the form of notional payments, paid by the employer to or on behalf of the employee during the year and the total net tax deducted from the emoluments,][1]

(b) any temporary tax deduction form, or such other document corresponding to a temporary tax deduction form as may be authorised by the Revenue Commissioners, used by the employer during the year for an employee in respect of whom a tax deduction card was not received,

(c) any emergency card, or such other document corresponding to an emergency card as may be authorised by the Revenue Commissioners, used by the employer during the year for an employee in respect of whom a tax deduction card was not received, and

[(d) a statement, declaration and certificate in the prescribed form showing-

(i) the total amount of notional payments paid by the employer to or on behalf of every employee during the year, and

(ii) the total net tax deducted or repaid by the employer in respect of every employee during the year.][2]

(2) Where the employer is a body corporate, the declaration and the certificate referred to in subparagraph (d) of paragraph (1) of this Regulation shall be signed either by the secretary or by a director of the body corporate.

Amendments

[1,2] Substituted by the Income Tax (Employments) Regulations 2003, with effect from 1 January 2004

32 Inspection of employer's records

[(1) Upon request made to him or her at any premises of an employer by an authorised officer, any person, being the employer or a person employed by the employer at the premises, shall produce to the authorised officer for inspection all wages sheets, certificates of tax credits and standard rate cut-off point, tax deduction cards, and other documents and records whatsoever relating to the calculation or payment of the emoluments, including notional payments, of employees of the employer or the deduction of tax from, or the remittance of tax under section 985A(4) of the Principal Act in respect of, such emoluments as may be in that person's powers, possession or procurement.][1]

(2) Where in pursuance of this Regulation an authorised officer requests production of any documents or records, he or she shall, on request, show his or her authorisation for the purposes of this Regulation to the person concerned.

(3) The documents and records specified in paragraph (1) of this Regulation, other than certificates of tax credits and standard rate cut-off point and the temporary tax deduction forms, and emergency cards, and the documents corresponding to those forms and cards, referred to in Regulation 31, shall be retained by the employer for a period of six years after the end of the year to which they refer, or for such shorter period as the Revenue Commissioners may authorise by notice in writing to the employer.

Amendments

[1] Substituted by the Income Tax (Employments) Regulations 2003, with effect from 1 January 2004

33 Death of employer

If the employer dies, anything which the employer would have been liable to do under these Regulations shall be done by the employer's personal representative, or, in the case of an employer who paid emoluments on behalf of another person, by the person succeeding the employer or, if there is no such person, the person on whose behalf the employer paid emoluments.

34 Succession to a business, etc

(1) This Regulation applies where there has been a change in the employer from whom an employee receives emoluments in respect of his or her employment in any trade, business, concern or undertaking, or in connection with any property, or from whom an employee receives any annuity or pension.

(2) Where this Regulation applies, the change shall not be treated as a cessation of employment for the purposes of Regulation 20, but, in relation to any matter arising after the change, the employer after the change shall be liable to do anything which the employer before the change would have been liable to do under these Regulations if the change had not taken place.

(3) The employer after the change shall not be liable for the payment of any tax which was deductible from emoluments paid to the employee before the change took place.

PART 6

Assessment

35 Assessment of emoluments

(1) Nothing in these Regulations shall prevent an assessment under Schedule E being made on a person in respect of his or her emoluments (income assessed to tax) for any year.

(2) Any assessments on an employee in respect of emoluments may be made in any income tax district and shall be valid notwithstanding that the employee was not in that district, or in the State, during the year in which the assessment was made.

(3) All the emoluments of an employee may be included in one assessment.

36 Return of certain emoluments by employer

The inspector may give notice to the employer requiring the employer to send a return of any emoluments paid by the employer to or on behalf of any employee for any year, being emoluments which are not paid to or on behalf of the employee until after the end of that year, and any such return shall be sent to the inspector within the time limited in the notice.

37 Notification of liability

[The inspector may][1], in any case where he or she does not propose to make an assessment on an employee with respect to whom tax was deducted during a year, send to the employee, as soon as possible after the end of the year, a statement of his or her liability for the year and showing how it is proposed to deal with any overpayment or underpayment of tax.

Amendments

[1] Substituted by the Income Tax (Employments) Regulations 2008, with effect from 1 January 2009

38 Objections and appeals against assessment

The provisions of Part 40 of the Act shall, with any necessary modifications, apply in relation to an appeal by an employee against an assessment of emoluments.

39 Recovery of underpayments

(1) If the tax payable under the assessment exceeds the total net tax deducted from the employee's emoluments during the year, the inspector, instead of taking the excess into account in determining the appropriate amount of tax credits and standard rate cut-off point for a subsequent year, may require the employee to remit it to the Collector-General, and, where the inspector so requires, the employee shall remit the excess accordingly on demand made by the Collector-General.

(2) For the purposes of determining the amount of any such excess, any necessary adjustment shall be made to the total net tax in respect of any tax overpaid or remaining unpaid for any year.

40 Recovery of tax from employee

(1) Any tax which is to be remitted to the Collector-General by any employee may be recovered in the manner provided by the Income Tax Acts.

(2) Any tax which is to be remitted to the Collector-General under paragraph (1) of Regulation 39, shall be remitted within 14 days of the date on which the Collector-General first makes application therefore.

PART 7

Contributions by Employees to Certain Superannuation Funds and Schemes

41 Interpretation (Part 7)

[In this Part of these Regulations ["*allowable contribution*" means a contribution or a deduction][1] payable by an employee and deductible by an employer from emoluments of the employee and which is—

(a) by virtue of section 471 of the Act, allowable as a deduction from such emoluments for the purposes of assessment under Schedule E.

(b) an ordinary annual contribution, or any other contribution treated by the Revenue Commissioners, as respects the year in which it is paid, as an ordinary annual contribution paid in that year, allowable by virtue of section 774 or 776 of the Act, as a deduction from such emoluments for the purposes of assessment under Schedule E, [...][2]

(c) by virtue of section 787C (inserted by the Pensions (Amendment) Act 2002) of the Act, to be deducted from or set off against the employee's relevant earnings (within the meaning of section 787B (as so inserted) of the Act) for the year of assessment in which it is [[paid,][3]][4]][5]

(d) [by virtue of section 787 of the Act, to be deducted from or set off against the employee's relevant earnings (within the meaning of section 783 of the Act) for the year of assessment in which it is [paid, or][6]][7]

(e) [by virtue of section 790C of the Act (inserted by section 16 of the Financial Emergency Measures in the Public Interest Act 2009) allowable as a deduction from such emoluments for the purposes of assessment under Schedule E.][8]

Amendments

[1] Substituted by Financial Emergency Measures in the Public Interest Act 2009 s16(2)

[2] Deleted by the Income Tax (Employments) Regulations 2003, with effect from 1 January 2004 (the word "or")

[3] Substituted by the Financial Emergency Measures in the Public Interest Act 2009 s16(2) (punctuation change)

[4] Substituted by the Income Tax (Employments) Regulations 2003, with effect from 1 January 2004 (punctuation change)

[5] Substituted by the Income Tax (Employments) Regulations 2002

[6] Substituted by the Financial Emergency Measures in the Public Interest Act 2009 s16(2) (punctuation change)

[7] Inserted by the Income Tax (Employments) Regulations 2003, with effect from 1 January 2004

[8] Inserted by the Financial Emergency Measures in the Public Interest Act 2009 s16(2)

42 Deduction or repayment by reference to superannuation contribution

When making a deduction or repayment of tax in accordance with the provisions of Part 4 of these Regulations from or in respect of emoluments to which Chapter 4 of Part 42 of the Act, applies, an employer shall make such deduction or repayment as would require to be made if the amount of the emoluments were those emoluments reduced by the amount of the allowable contribution deductible from those emoluments.

PART 8

Special Provisions where Employees are in Receipt of or are Entitled to Receive Certain Benefits Payable Under the Social Welfare Acts

43 Interpretation (Part 8)

In this Part of these Regulations—

"*relevant period*" in relation to an employee who is absent from work and who in respect of any part of that absence receives, or is entitled to receive, a taxable benefit, means the period commencing with the date on which such taxable benefit first becomes payable to the employee and ending on the earliest of the following dates, that is to say:

(a) the date of cessation of employment,

(b) the 31 December following the employee's return to work, or

(c) such other date as the inspector may specify;

"*taxable benefit*", in relation to an employee, means any amount payable under the Social Welfare Acts in respect of—

(a) disability benefit, and

(b) injury benefit which is comprised in occupational injuries benefit,

which is chargeable to income tax by virtue of section 126 of the Act.

44 Tax due in respect of disability or injury benefit

Where, in respect of an absence from work, an employee receives or is entitled to receive a taxable benefit the following provisions shall, notwithstanding any other provision of these Regulations and unless the inspector otherwise directs, apply, that is to say:

(a) any payment of emoluments made by the employer to the employee in the relevant period shall be treated as if it were a payment to which Regulation 19 applies,

(b) (i) where the employee is entitled to receive payment of emoluments during such absence from work, the employer shall, in relation to such payments made by him or her to the employee during the relevant period, reduce the tax credits and standard rate cut-off point for Week 1 or Month 1, as may be appropriate, as specified on the tax deduction card held by the employer in respect of the employee by—

(A) such amount as the Revenue Commissioners, by general notice or otherwise, direct, or

(B) such other amount as the Minister for Social, Community and Family Affairs may notify to the employer in relation to the employee, and

(ii) the reduction of the employee's tax credits and standard rate cut-off point in accordance with the provisions of subparagraph (i) shall be treated as if it were a determination or, as the case may be, an amended determination of tax credits and standard rate cut-off point by the inspector but the inspector need not issue a notice of the determination or the amended determination, as may be appropriate, to the employee or a certificate of tax credits and standard rate cut-off point, an amended certificate of tax credits and standard rate cut-off point, a tax deduction card or an amended tax deduction card, as may be appropriate, to the employer,

and

(c) where, on any usual pay day during the period of absence from work which falls within the relevant period, the employee is not entitled to receive payment of emoluments from the employer, the provisions of Regulation 26 shall not apply in respect of such pay day.

PART 9

Miscellaneous

45 Revocations

The Regulations specified in the Schedule to these Regulations are revoked.

SCHEDULE

S.I. Number (1)	Regulations (2)
28 of 1960	Income Tax (Employments) Regulations 1960
166 of 1960	Income Tax (Employments) (No. 2) Regulations, 1960
223 of 1970	Income Tax (Employments) Regulations, 1970
182 of 1971	Income Tax (Employments) Regulations, 1971
260 of 1972	Income Tax (Employments) Regulations, 1972
86 of 1974	Income Tax (Employments) Regulations, 1974
292 of 1974	Income Tax (Employments) (No. 2) Regulations, 1974
170 of 1975	Income Tax (Employments) Regulations, 1975
368 of 1977	Income Tax (Employments) Regulations, 1977
377 of 1978	Income Tax (Employments) Regulations, 1978
284 of 1980	Income Tax (Employments) Regulations, 1980
67 of 1984	Income Tax (Employments) Regulations, 1984
148 of 1985	Income Tax (Employments) Regulations, 1985
270 of 1987	Income Tax (Employments) Regulations, 1987
58 of 1989	Income Tax (Employments) Regulations, 1989
77 of 1993	Income Tax (Employments) Regulations, 1993
231 of 1997	Income Tax (Employments) Regulations, 1997
66 of 1999	Income Tax (Employments) Regulations, 1999
35 of 2001	Income Tax (Employments) Regulations, 2001

Given this 12th day of December, 2001.

Frank M. Daly

Revenue Commissioner

EXPLANATORY NOTE

(This note is not part of the Instrument and does not purport to be a legal interpretation.)

These Regulations, which come into force on 1 January, 2002, revise and consolidate, subject to certain changes, the existing regulatory provisions which prescribe the manner in which the deduction of tax from salaries and wages under the "Pay As You Earn" system operates

The main changes made are—

(1) With effect from 1 January 2002, the special system for casual employees is abolished.

(2) With effect from 1 January 2003, employees who do not supply their employer with apersonal public service number (PPSN) will be subject to tax under the emergency system at the higher rate of tax.

(3) There will be an obligation on employers paying their liability by direct debit to review the adequacy of the payment from time to time and make adjustments as appropriate.

Part 1 of the Regulations contains definitions. It also covers the instance where an employee works under the management of a person who is not his or her immediate employer. In such circumstances the person under whose management the employee works is deemed to be his or her employer.

Part 2 provides for the maintenance of registers of employers and of employees. The register of employers is to be kept by the Revenue Commissioners and registers of employees by employers. In certain circumstances where an employer employs only one domestic employee there is no obligation to keep a register.

Part 3 requires inspectors of taxes to determine the amount of tax credits and standard rate cut-off point appropriate to the employee, to furnish the employee with a notice of this determination and with a certificate of tax credits and standard rate cut-off point and also to notify the employer of the amount of tax credits and standard rate cut-off point. An employee may appeal to the Appeal Commissioners any determination of tax credits and standard rate cut-off point made by an inspector. Certificates of tax credits and standard rate cut-off point for any particular year will have effect for each subsequent year for which taxpayers' personal circumstances and relevant tax credits and reliefs remain unchanged.

Part 4 concerns the deduction and repayment of tax under PAYE. Deductions and repayments are to be made by reference to cumulative emoluments and cumulative tax credits and standard rate cut-off point as specified on the employees tax deduction card. The required particulars are to be entered on the tax deduction cards on the occasion of every payment of emoluments. There are provisions regarding changes of employment and for deduction of tax on an emergency basis where the employee does not produce a certificate of tax credits and standard rate cut-off point or his or her personal public service number. At the end of each year employers are required to give every employee a certificate showing his or her emoluments, tax credits and standard rate cut-off point and the net tax deducted.

Part 5 deals with payment and recovery of tax deducted under PAYE. Employers are required within 14 days from the end of every income tax month to pay over to the Collector General all tax which they were liable to deduct under PAYE, less any tax which they were liable to repay, during the month.

The Collector General may authorise an employer to make remittances of PAYE/PRSI at longer intervals (not exceeding one year) than the normal monthly remittance basis. Where an authorised employer arranges to pay by direct debit he or she must ensure that the amounts paid are sufficient to cover ongoing liability. The Collector-General may also terminate such authorisation.

Within 46 days from the end of the year employers are to send to the Collector-General returns, in the appropriate form, showing total emoluments paid to the employee during the year and total net tax deducted.

Part 6 provides for the making of assessments on employees in special cases and, where assessments are not made, for supplying employees with statements of their liability. It also provides for an appeal by an employee against an assessment by an inspector; and for adjustment where underpayment of tax occurs.

Part 7, which provides for net pay arrangements, requires an employer when applying PAYE to an employee's earnings to make any necessary deduction or repayment of PAYE income tax by reference to the amount of the earnings reduced by the amount of any superannuation or Permanent Health Insurance contributions which relate to and are deducted from those earnings and which are allowable for income tax purposes.

Part 8 sets out the manner in which any tax due in respect of disability benefit and injury benefit is to be collected from recipients in employment.

Part 9 repeals all previous Regulations relating to the PAYE system.

S.I. No. 471 of 2002

TAXES (OFFSET of REPAYMENTS) REGULATIONS 2002

The Revenue Commissioners, in exercise of the powers conferred on them by section 1006A of the Taxes Consolidation Act 1997 (No. 39 of 1997), make the following regulations:

PART 1

General

1 Citation

These Regulations may be cited as the Taxes (Offset of Repayments) Regulations 2002.

2 Interpretation

(1) In these Regulations, unless the context otherwise requires—

"*Acts*", "*claim*", "*liability*", "*overpayment*" and "*tax*" have each the same meaning as they have, respectively, in the principal section;

"*Collector-General*" means the person appointed under section 851 of the Principal Act;

"*estimate*" means an estimate of tax made in accordance with the provisions of—

(a) section 989 of the Principal Act,

(b) Regulation 13 of the Income Tax (Relevant Contracts) Regulations 2000 (S.I. No. 71 of 2000), or

(c) section 110 of the Value-Added Tax Consolidation Act 2010;

"*current estimate*", in relation to any particular time, means an estimate in respect of either an income tax month or a taxable period, as the case may be, the due date for which is immediately prior to that time or the income tax month or taxable period immediately preceding that month or period;

"*due date*", in relation to a liability, means the date on which the liability is due and payable under the appropriate provision of the Acts and, in relation to an estimate, the date on which the period for the payment of the tax for the income tax month or taxable period, as the case may be, expires;

"*liability at enforcement*" means a liability which, at the time at which the repayment is to be made in respect of the claim or overpayment—

(a) was certified in a certificate issued, and not withdrawn, under section 962 of the Principal Act,

(b) was the subject of proceedings initiated, and not withdrawn, as a debt due to the Minister for Finance, in any court of competent jurisdiction, or

(c) was entered as a specified amount in a notice of attachment issued, and not revoked, under section 1002 of the Principal Act;

"*Principal Act*" means the Taxes Consolidation Act 1997 (No. 39 of 1997);

"*principal section*" means section 1006A of the Principal Act;

"*taxhead*" means-

(a) tax deductible under Chapter 2 of Part 18 of the Principal Act and any regulations made under it,

(b) income tax deductible under Chapter 4 of Part 42 of the Principal Act and any regulations made under it,

(c) corporation tax,

(d) an amount to be collected as income tax by the Collector-General in accordance with the provisions of the European Communities (Mutual Assistance for the Recovery of Claims relating to Certain Levies, Duties, Taxes and Other Measures) Regulations 2002 (S.I. No. 462 of 2002),

(e) income tax (other than that referred to in paragraphs (*b*) and (*d*) of this definition),

(f) capital gains tax,

(g) value-added tax,

(h) inheritance tax and gift tax,

(i) stamp duties,

(j) residential property tax,

(k) vehicle registration tax, or

(l) excise duties,

as the case may be.

(2) In these Regulations—

(a) a reference to a Regulation is to a Regulation of these Regulations, unless it appears that reference to some other provision is intended;

(b) a reference to a paragraph is to the paragraph of the provision in which the reference occurs, unless it appears that reference to some other provision is intended.

(3) Subject to paragraph (1), a word or expression that is used in these Regulations and is also used in any provision of the Acts has, except where the context otherwise requires, the same meaning in these Regulations as it has in that provision.

PART 2

Offsetting

3 Order of priority of offset against liabilities

Subject to Regulations 4, 5, 6 and 7, the amount of any repayment in respect of a claim or overpayment made by any person, which is, by virtue of subsection (2) of the principal section, to be set against any liability of that person, shall be set against—

(a) firstly, any liability, other than a current estimate or a liability at enforcement, in the following sequence:

(i) a liability arising under the same taxhead in respect of which the claim or overpayment is made,

(ii) a liability arising under the Value-Added Tax Consolidation Act 2010 and the enactments amending or extending that Act,

(iii) a liability arising under Chapter 4 of Part 42 of the Principal Act and the regulations made under it,

(iv) a liability arising under Chapter 2 of Part 18 of the Principal Act and the regulations made under it,

(v) a liability arising under the Corporation Tax Acts,

(vi) a liability arising under any provision (other than Chapter 4 of Part 42 of the Principal Act) of the Income Tax Acts,

(vii) a liability arising under the Capital Gains Tax Acts,

(viii) a liability arising under Part VI of the Finance Act 1983 (No. 15 of 1983) and the enactments amending or extending that Part,

(ix) a liability arising under the Capital Acquisitions Tax Act 1976 (No. 8 of 1976) and the enactments amending or extending that Act,

(x) a liability arising under the Stamp Duties Consolidation Act 1999 (No. 31 of 1999) and the enactments amending or extending that Act,

(xi) a liability arising under Chapter IV of Part II of the Finance Act 1992 (No. 9 of 1992),

(xii) a liability arising under the statutes relating to the duties of excise and to the management of those duties,

(b) secondly, any liability, being a liability at enforcement, in the sequence set out in paragraph (*a*), and

(c) finally, against any amount referred to in paragraph (*d*) of the definition of "*taxhead*".

4 Special arrangements regarding corporation tax, income tax and capital gains tax

Notwithstanding Regulation 3 but subject to Regulations 5, 6 and 7, in any case where a repayment in respect of a claim or overpayment made by any person, is under a taxhead referred to in paragraph (*c*), (*e*) or (*f*) of the definition of "*taxhead*", the amount of the repayment, which is, by virtue of subsection (2) of the principal section, to be set against any liability of that person, shall be set against—

(a) firstly, any liability, other than a current estimate or a liability at enforcement, in the following sequence:

(i) a liability arising under the same taxhead in respect of which the claim or overpayment is made,

(ii) a liability arising under the Corporation Tax Acts,

(iii) a liability arising under any provision (other than Chapter 4 of Part 42 of the Principal Act) of the Income Tax Acts,

(iv) a liability arising under the Capital Gains Tax Acts,

(v) a liability arising under the Value-Added Tax Consolidation Act 2010 and the enactments amending or extending that Act,

(vi) a liability arising under Chapter 4 of Part 42 of the Principal Act and the regulations made under it,

(vii) a liability arising under Chapter 2 of Part 18 of the Principal Act and the regulations made under it,

(viii) a liability arising under Part VI of the Finance Act 1983 and the enactments amending or extending that Part,

(ix) a liability arising under the Capital Acquisitions Tax Act 1976 and the enactments amending or extending that Act,

(x) a liability arising under the Stamp Duties Consolidation Act 1999 and the enactments amending or extending that Act,

(xi) a liability arising under Chapter IV of Part II of the Finance Act 1992,

(xii) a liability arising under the statutes relating to the duties of excise and to the management of those duties,

(b) secondly, any liability, being a liability at enforcement, in the sequence set out in paragraph (*a*), and

(c) finally, against any amount referred to in paragraph (*d*) of the definition of "*taxhead*".

5 Chronological order of priority of liabilities

For the purposes of Regulation 3 or 4, where, at any time, a repayment is to be set against more than one liability arising under a taxhead, it shall be set against any liability due for an earlier period or event in priority to a later period or event, as the case may be.

6 Nomination of liabilities by taxpayer

Notwithstanding Regulation 3 or 4, a person may, at any time but not later than 30 days after the issue of a notice to him or her under subsection (2A) of the principal section, by notice in writing to the Collector-General request that the repayment concerned be set against liabilities (other than any amount referred to in paragraph (*d*) of the definition of "*taxhead*") in an order nominated by the person and the Collector-General shall arrange accordingly.

7 Offset of interest

For the purposes of these Regulations, interest due and payable in relation to any liability to tax in respect of any period or event shall be deemed to be due and payable at the same time as the tax in respect of that period or event, as the case may be.

PART 3

Miscellaneous

8 Revocation

The Taxes (Offset of Repayments) Regulations 2001 (S.I. No. 399 of 2001) are revoked.

GIVEN under my hand,

2 October 2002.

Michael O'Grady,

Revenue Commissioner.

EXPLANATORY NOTE

(This note is not part of the Instrument and does not purport to be a legal interpretation.)

These Regulations are being made under subsection (3) of section 1006A (inserted by the Finance Act, 2000 and amended by the Finance Acts of 2001 and 2002) of the Taxes Consolidation Act, 1997. That section empowers the Revenue Commissioners to offset repayments due to a person against outstanding liabilities of the person.

They replace the existing regulations (Taxes (Offset of Repayments) Regulations, 2001 (S.I. No. 399 of 2001)) which set out an order of priority for such offsets.

Under the repealed regulations, liabilities were divided into 2 priority categories as follows:

(1) liabilities other than current estimates and liabilities at enforcement, and

(2) liabilities at enforcement.

Within each category, but subject to one special case, a repayment was set off in the following sequence—

(a) the taxhead giving rise to the repayment,

(b) value-added tax,

(c) employers PAYE,

(d) relevant contracts tax,

(e) corporation tax,

(f) income tax, other than at (c),

(g) capital gains tax,

(h) residential property tax,

(i) inheritance/gift taxes,

(j) stamp duties,

(k) vehicle registration tax, and

(l) excise duties.

The special case is where the repayment arises in the corporation tax, income tax capital gains tax grouping. In such a case liabilities within that same grouping are dealt with first before reverting to the order referred to above.

A third category of liability is now being introduced, that is, amounts which the Collector-General is to collect in accordance with the provisions of the European Communities (Mutual Assistance for the Recovery of Claims relating to Certain Levies, Duties, Taxes and Other Measures) Regulations 2002 (S.I. No. 462 of 2002)). A repayment may be set off against a liability in this category, when there are no outstanding liabilities in the other two categories.

The taxpayer will have the option to request the Collector-General, at any time but not later than 30 days after the issue of the notice of offset, to vary the offset as nominated by him/her. However, this right does not extend to liabilities in the new category referred to in the preceding paragraph.

Within a taxhead a claim or overpayment will be offset against older liabilities before younger ones.

For the purpose of offsetting against interest owed by the taxpayer, the "age" of the interest is determined by the "age" of the tax, etc. giving rise to it.

Number 23 of 2005

INTERPRETATION ACT 2005

AN ACT RESPECTING THE INTERPRETATION AND APPLICATION OF ACTS AND OF STATUTORY INSTRUMENTS MADE UNDER ACTS AND PROVIDING FOR THE REPEAL OF CERTAIN ENACTMENTS RELATING TO THOSE MATTERS.

[17*th October*, 2005]

BE IT ENACTED BY THE OIREACHTAS AS FOLLOWS:

PART 1

Preliminary and General

1 Short title and commencement

(1) This Act may be cited as the Interpretation Act 2005.

(2) This Act comes into operation on 1 January 2006.

2 Interpretation

(1) In this Act—

"*Act*" means—

(a) an Act of the Oireachtas, and

(b) a statute which was in force in Saorstát Éireann immediately before the date of the coming into operation of the Constitution and which continued in force by virtue of Article 50 of the Constitution;

"*enactment*" means an Act or a statutory instrument or any portion of an Act or statutory instrument;

"*repeal*" includes revoke, rescind, abrogate or cancel;

"*statutory instrument*" means an order, regulation, rule, bye-law, warrant, licence, certificate, direction, notice, guideline or other like document made, issued, granted or otherwise created by or under an Act and references, in relation to a statutory instrument, to "*made*" or to "*made under*" include references to made, issued, granted or otherwise created by or under such instrument.

(2) For the purposes of this Act, an enactment which has been replaced or has expired, lapsed or otherwise ceased to have effect is deemed to have been repealed.

Cross References

To Section 2

Section 5 Construing ambiguous or obscure provisions, etc.

3 Repeals and savings

(1) The following Acts are repealed:

(a) the Interpretation Act 1889;

(b) the Interpretation Act 1923;

(c) the Interpretation Act 1937;

(d) the Interpretation (Amendment) Act 1993.

(2) (a) The repeal by this Act of an Act which assigns a meaning to a word or expression in another enactment does not affect the meaning so assigned if—

(i) in the absence of that meaning in this Act, or

(ii) by the application to the other enactment of the meaning assigned by this Act to the same or a similar word or expression,

the other enactment would be changed in intent or become unclear or absurd.

(b) The repeal by this Act of an Act which provides for any matter (other than a matter to which *paragraph (a)* relates) in another enactment does not affect the matter so provided for if—

(i) in the absence of that matter being provided for in this Act, or

(ii) by the application to the other enactment of a matter provided for by this Act which corresponds to a matter provided for in the repealed Act concerned,

the other enactment would be changed in intent or become unclear or absurd.

4 Application

(1) A provision of this Act applies to an enactment except in so far as the contrary intention appears in this Act, in the enactment itself or, where relevant, in the Act under which the enactment is made.

(2) The provisions of this Act which relate to other Acts also apply to this Act unless the contrary intention appears in this Act.

PART 2

Miscellaneous Rules

5 Construing ambiguous or obscure provisions, etc

(1) In construing a provision of any Act (other than a provision that relates to the imposition of a penal or other sanction)—

(a) that is obscure or ambiguous, or

(b) that on a literal interpretation would be absurd or would fail to reflect the plain intention of—

(i) in the case of an Act to which *paragraph (a)* of the definition of "*Act*" in *section 2(1)* relates, the Oireachtas, or

(ii) in the case of an Act to which *paragraph (b)* of that definition relates, the parliament concerned,

the provision shall be given a construction that reflects the plain intention of the Oireachtas or parliament concerned, as the case may be, where that intention can be ascertained from the Act as a whole.

(2) In construing a provision of a statutory instrument (other than a provision that relates to the imposition of a penal or other sanction)—

(a) that is obscure or ambiguous, or

(b) that on a literal interpretation would be absurd or would fail to reflect the plain intention of the instrument as a whole in the context of the enactment (including the Act) under which it was made,

the provision shall be given a construction that reflects the plain intention of the maker of the instrument where that intention can be ascertained from the instrument as a whole in the context of that enactment.

Cross References

From Section 5

Section 2 Interpretation.

To Section 5

Section 7 Supplemental provision to sections 5 and 6.

6 Construing provisions in changing circumstances

In construing a provision of any Act or statutory instrument, a court may make allowances for any changes in the law, social conditions, technology, the meaning of words used in that Act or statutory instrument and other relevant matters, which have occurred since the date of the passing of that Act or the making of that statutory instrument, but only in so far as its text, purpose and context permit.

Cross References

To Section 6

Section 7 Supplemental provision to sections 5 and 6.

7 Supplemental provision to sections 5 and 6

(1) In construing a provision of an Act for the purposes of *section 5* or *6*, a court may, notwithstanding *section 18(g)*, make use of all matters that accompany and are set out in—

(a) in the case of an Act of the Oireachtas, the signed text of such law as enrolled for record in the Office of the Registrar of the Supreme Court pursuant to Article 25.4.5° of the Constitution,

(b) in the case of an Act of the Oireachtas of Saorstát Éireann, the signed text of such law as enrolled for record in the office of such officer of the Supreme Court of Saorstát Éireann as Dáil Éireann determined pursuant to Article 42 of the Constitution of the Irish Free State (Saorstát Éireann),

(c) in the case of any other Act, such text of that Act as corresponds to the text of the Act enrolled in the manner referred to in *paragraph (a)* or *(b)*.

(2) For the purposes of *subsection (1)*, it shall be presumed, until the contrary is shown, that a copy of the text of an Act that is required to be judicially noticed is a copy of the text to which *subsection (1)* relates.

Cross References

From Section 7

Section 5 Construing ambiguous or obscure provisions, etc.
Section 6 Construing provisions in changing circumstances.
Section 18 General rules of construction.

To Section 7

Section 18 General rules of construction.

8 Reading provisions together as one and summary proceedings for offences

Where—

(a) an Act or portion of an Act (whenever passed)—

(i) provides that summary proceedings for offences under it may be prosecuted by a specified person, and

(ii) is *subsequently* read together as one with any provision of another Act,

and

(b) an offence is created under that provision which can be prosecuted in a summary manner but no express power is given to the specified person to so prosecute,

then, the specified person may bring summary proceedings for an offence under that other provision unless some other person is authorised by that other Act to bring such proceedings.

9 References in enactments to Parts, etc

(1) A reference in an enactment to a Part, Chapter, section, Schedule or other division, by whatever name called, shall be read as a reference to a Part, Chapter, section, Schedule or other division of the enactment in which the reference occurs.

(2) A reference in an enactment to a subsection, paragraph, sub-paragraph, clause, subclause, article, subarticle or other division, by whatever name called, shall be read as a reference to a subsection, paragraph, subparagraph, clause, subclause, article, subarticle or other division of the provision in which the reference occurs.

10 Enactment always speaking

An enactment continues to have effect and may be applied from time to time as occasion requires.

11 References in enactments to examples

If under the heading—

(a) in the Irish language "Sampla" or "Samplaí", or

(b) in the English language "Example" or "Examples",

an enactment includes at the end of a provision or in a schedule relating to such provision an example of the operation of the provision, then the example—

(i) is not to be read as exhaustive of the provision, and

(ii) may extend, but does not limit, the meaning of the provision.

12 Deviation from form

Where a form is prescribed in or under an enactment, a deviation from the form which does not materially affect the substance of the form or is not misleading in content or effect does not invalidate the form used.

PART 3

Citation and Operation of Enactments

13 Judicial notice

An Act is a public document and shall be judicially noticed.

14 Citation and references to amended enactments

(1) An Act may be cited in any enactment or other document—

(a) by the long title or short title of the Act,

(b) where appropriate, by the consecutive number of the Act in the calendar year and by the calendar year in which it was passed, or

(c) where the Act was passed prior to the enactment of the Constitution of the Irish Free State (Saorstát Eireann) Act 1922, by its regnal year and chapter number and, where there was more than one parliamentary session in the same regnal year, by reference to the session concerned.

(2) A citation of or a reference to an enactment shall be read as a citation of or reference to the enactment as amended (including as amended by way of extension, application, adaptation or other modification of the enactment), whether the amendment is made before, on or after the date on which the provision containing the citation or reference came into operation.

(3) In citing—

(a) an Act by its short title, or

(b) any other enactment by its citation (if any),

a comma immediately before a reference to a year and a comma immediately after such a reference that is not required for the purpose of punctuation may be omitted.

15 Date of passing of Acts of Oireachtas

(1) The date of the passing of an Act of the Oireachtas is the date of the day on which the Bill for the Act is signed by the President.

(2) Immediately after the Bill for an Act of the Oireachtas is signed by the President, the Clerk of Dáil Éireann shall endorse on the Act immediately after the long title the date of the passing of the Act, and that date shall be taken to be part of the Act.

16 Commencement

(1) Subject to *subsection (2)*, every provision of an Act comes into operation on the date of its passing.

(2) Where an Act or a provision of an Act is expressed to come into operation on a particular day (whether the day is before or after the date of the passing of the

Act and whether the day is named in the Act or is to be fixed or ascertained in a particular manner), the Act or provision comes into operation at the end of the day before the particular day.

(3) Subject to *subsection (4)*, every provision of a statutory instrument comes into operation at the end of the day before the day on which the statutory instrument is made.

(4) Where a statutory instrument or a provision of a statutory instrument is expressed to come into operation on a particular day (whether the day is before or after the date of the making of the statutory instrument and whether the day is named in the instrument or is to be fixed or ascertained in a particular manner), the statutory instrument or provision comes into operation at the end of the day before the particular day.

17 Exercise of statutory powers before commencement of Act

Where an Act or a provision of an Act is expressed to come into operation on a day subsequent to the date of the passing of the Act, the following provisions apply:

(a) if the day on which the Act or the provision comes into operation is to be fixed or ascertained in a particular manner, the statutory instrument, act or thing whereby the day is fixed or ascertained may, subject to any restriction imposed by the Act, be made or done at any time after the passing of the Act;

(b) if, for the purposes of the Act or the provision, the Act confers a power to make a statutory instrument or do any act or thing, the making or doing of which is necessary or expedient to enable the Act or provision to have full force and effect immediately on its coming into operation, the power may, subject to any restriction imposed by the Act, be exercised at any time after the passing of the Act.

PART 4

Meaning and Construction of Words and Expressions

18 General rules of construction

The following provisions apply to the construction of an enactment:

(a) *Singular and plural.* A word importing the singular shall be read as also importing the plural, and a word importing the plural shall be read as also importing the singular;

(b) *Gender.*

(i) A word importing the masculine gender shall be read as also importing the feminine gender;

(ii) In an Act passed on or after 22 December 1993, and in a statutory instrument made after that date, a word importing the feminine gender shall be read as also importing the masculine gender;

(c) *Person.* "Person" shall be read as importing a body corporate (whether a corporation aggregate or a corporation sole) and an unincorporated body of persons, as well as an individual, and the subsequent use of any pronoun in place of a further use of "person" shall be read accordingly;

(d) *Adopted child.* A reference, however expressed, to a child of a person shall be read as including—

(i) in an Act passed after the passing of the Adoption Act 1976 a reference to a child adopted by the person under the Adoption Acts 1952 to 1998 and every other enactment which is to be construed together with any of those Acts, or

(ii) in an Act passed on or after 14 January 1988 (the commencement of section 3 of the Status of Children Act 1987), a child to whom *subparagraph (i)* relates or a child adopted outside the State whose adoption is recognised by virtue of the law for the time being in force in the State;

(e) *Distance.* A word or expression relating to the distance between two points and every reference to the distance from or to a point shall be read as relating or referring to such distance measured in a straight line on a horizontal plane;

(f) *Series description.* Where a consecutive series is described by reference to the first and last in the series, the description shall be read as including the first and the last in the series;

(g) *Marginal and shoulder notes, etc.* Subject to *section 7*, none of the following shall be taken to be part of the enactment or be construed or judicially noticed in relation to the construction or interpretation of the enactment:

(i) a marginal note placed at the side, or a shoulder note placed at the beginning, of a section or other provision to indicate the subject, contents or effect of the section or provision,

(ii) a heading or cross-line placed in or at the head of or at the beginning of a Part, Chapter, section, or other provision or group of sections or provisions to indicate the subject, contents or effect of the Part, Chapter, section, provision or group;

(h) *Periods of time.* Where a period of time is expressed to begin on or be reckoned from a particular day, that day shall be deemed to be included in the period and, where a period of time is expressed to end on or be reckoned to a particular day, that day shall be deemed to be included in the period;

(i) *Time.* Where time is expressed by reference to a specified hour or to a time before or after a specified hour, that time shall be determined by reference to the Standard Time (Amendment) Act 1971;

(j) *Offences by corporations.* A reference to a person in relation to an offence (whether punishable on indictment or on summary conviction) shall be read as including a reference to a body corporate.

Cross References

From Section 18

Section 7 Supplemental provision to sections 5 and 6.

To Section 18

Section 7 Supplemental provision to sections 5 and 6.

19 Construction of statutory instruments

A word or expression used in a statutory instrument has the same meaning in the statutory instrument as it has in the enactment under which the instrument is made.

20 Interpretation provisions

(1) Where an enactment contains a definition or other interpretation provision, the provision shall be read as being applicable except in so far as the contrary intention appears in—

(a) the enactment itself, or

(b) the Act under which the enactment is made.

(2) Where an enactment defines or otherwise interprets a word or expression, other parts of speech and grammatical forms of the word or expression have a corresponding meaning.

21 Interpretation of words and expressions in Schedule

(1) In an enactment, a word or expression to which a particular meaning, construction or effect is assigned in *Part 1* of the *Schedule* has the meaning, construction or effect so assigned to it.

(2) In an enactment which comes into operation after the commencement of this Act, a word or expression to which a particular meaning, construction or effect is assigned in *Part 2* of the *Schedule* has the meaning, construction or effect so assigned to it.

PART 5

Powers and Duties

22 Powers under enactments

(1) A power conferred by an enactment may be exercised from time to time as occasion requires.

(2) A power conferred by an enactment on the holder of an office as that holder shall be deemed to be conferred on, and may accordingly be exercised by, the holder for the time being of that office.

(3) A power conferred by an enactment to make a statutory instrument shall be read as including a power, exercisable in the like manner and subject to the like consent and conditions (if any), to repeal or amend a statutory instrument made under that power and (where required) to make another statutory instrument in place of the one so repealed.

23 Duties under enactments

(1) A duty imposed by an enactment shall be performed from time to time as occasion requires.

(2) A duty imposed by an enactment on the holder of an office as that holder shall be deemed to be imposed on, and shall accordingly be performed by, the holder for the time being of that office.

24 Rules of court

Where an enactment confers a new jurisdiction on a court or extends or varies an existing jurisdiction of a court, the authority having for the time being power to make rules or orders regulating the practice and procedure of the court has, and may at any time exercise, power to make rules or orders for regulating the practice and procedure of that court in the exercise of the jurisdiction so conferred, extended or varied.

25 Service by post

Where an enactment authorises or requires a document to be served by post, by using the word "*serve*", "*give*", "*deliver*", "*send*" or any other word or expression, the service of the document may be effected by properly addressing, prepaying (where required) and posting a letter containing the document, and in that case the service of the document is deemed, unless the contrary is proved, to have been effected at the time at which the letter would be delivered in the ordinary course of post.

PART 6

Amendment of Enactments, Etc.

26 Repeals and substitutions

(1) Where an enactment repeals another enactment and substitutes other provisions for the enactment so repealed, the enactment so repealed continues in force until the substituted provisions come into operation.

(2) Where an enactment ("*former enactment*") is repealed and re-enacted, with or without modification, by another enactment ("*new enactment*"), the following provisions apply:

(a) a person appointed under the former enactment shall continue to act for the remainder of the period for which the person was appointed as if appointed under the new enactment;

(b) a bond, guarantee or other security of a continuing nature given by a person under the former enactment remains in force, and data, books, papers, forms and things prepared or used under the former enactment may continue to be used as before the repeal;

(c) proceedings taken under the former enactment may, subject to *section 27(1)*, be continued under and in conformity with the new enactment in so far as that may be done consistently with the new enactment;

(d) if after the commencement of this Act—

(i) any provision of a former enactment, that provided for the making of a statutory instrument, is repealed and re-enacted, with or without modification, as a new provision, and

(ii) such statutory instrument is in force immediately before such repeal and re-enactment,

then the statutory instrument shall be deemed to have been made under the new provision to the extent that it is not inconsistent with the new enactment, and remains in force until it is repealed or otherwise ceases to have effect;

(e) to the extent that the provisions of the new enactment express the same idea in a different form of words but are in substance the same as those of the former enactment, the idea in the new enactment shall not be taken to be different merely because a different form of words is used;

(f) a reference in any other enactment to the former enactment shall, with respect to a subsequent transaction, matter or thing, be read as a reference to the provisions of the new enactment relating to the same subject-matter as that of the former enactment, but where there are no provisions in the new enactment relating to the same subject-matter, the former enactment shall be disregarded in so far as is necessary to maintain or give effect to that other enactment.

Cross References

From Section 26

Section 27 Effect of repeal of enactment.

27 Effect of repeal of enactment

(1) Where an enactment is repealed, the repeal does not—

(a) revive anything not in force or not existing immediately before the repeal,

(b) affect the previous operation of the enactment or anything duly done or suffered under the enactment,

(c) affect any right, privilege, obligation or liability acquired, accrued or incurred under the enactment,

(d) affect any penalty, forfeiture or punishment incurred in respect of any offence against or contravention of the enactment which was committed before the repeal, or

(e) prejudice or affect any legal proceedings (civil or criminal) pending at the time of the repeal in respect of any such right, privilege, obligation, liability, offence or contravention.

(2) Where an enactment is repealed, any legal proceedings (civil or criminal) in respect of a right, privilege, obligation or liability acquired, accrued or incurred under, or an offence against or contravention of, the enactment may be instituted, continued or enforced, and any penalty, forfeiture or punishment in respect of such offence or contravention may be imposed and carried out, as if the enactment had not been repealed.

Cross References

To Section 27

Section 26 Repeals and substitutions.

SCHEDULE
Interpretation of Particular Words and Expressions

Section 21.

PART 1

"*affidavit*", in the case of a person for the time being allowed by law to declare instead of swearing, includes declaration;

"*British statute*" means an Act of the Parliament of the former United Kingdom of Great Britain and Ireland;

"*Circuit Court*" means the Circuit Court as established and for the time being maintained by law;

"*commencement*", when used in relation to an enactment, means the time at which the enactment comes into operation;

"*Constitution*" means the Constitution of Ireland enacted by the people on 1 July 1937, as amended;

"*Dáil Éireann*" means the House of the Oireachtas to which that name is given by section 1 of Article 15 of the Constitution;

"*District Court*" means the District Court as established and for the time being maintained by law;

"*financial year*", in relation to an exchequer financial year, means the period which is coextensive with a calendar year;

"*Government*" means the Government mentioned in Article 28 of the Constitution;

"*Great Britain*" does not include the Channel Islands or the Isle of Man;

"*High Court*" means the High Court as established and for the time being maintained by law pursuant to Article 34 of the Constitution;

"*land*" includes tenements, hereditaments, houses and buildings, land covered by water and any estate, right or interest in or over land;

"*local financial year*" means a period which is coextensive with a calendar year;

"*midnight*" means, in relation to a particular day, the point of time at which the day ends;

"*Minister of the Government*" means a member of the Government having charge of a Department of State;

"*month*" means a calendar month;

"*oath*", in the case of a person for the time being allowed by law to affirm or declare instead of swearing, includes affirmation or declaration;

"*Oireachtas*" means the National Parliament provided for by Article 15 of the Constitution;

"*ordnance map*" means a map made under the powers conferred by the Survey (Ireland) Acts 1825 to 1870;

"*President*" means the President of Ireland or any Commission, or other body or authority, for the time being lawfully exercising the powers and performing the duties of the President;

"*pre-union Irish statute*" means an Act passed by a Parliament sitting in Ireland at any time before the coming into force on 1 January 1801 of the Act entitled "An Act for the Union of Great Britain and Ireland";

"*rateable valuation*" means the valuation under the Valuation Act 2001 of the property concerned;

"*rules of court*" means rules made by the authority for the time being having power to make rules regulating the practice and procedure of the court concerned;

"*Saorstát Éireann statute*" means an Act of the Oireachtas of Saorstát Éireann;

"*Seanad Éireann*" means the House of the Oireachtas to which that name is given by section 1 of Article 15 of the Constitution;

"*statutory declaration*" means a declaration made under the Statutory Declarations Act 1938;

"*Supreme Court*" means the Supreme Court as established and for the time being maintained by law pursuant to Article 34 of the Constitution;

"*swear*", in the case of a person for the time being allowed by law to affirm or declare instead of swearing, includes affirm and declare;

"*week*" means the period between midnight on any Saturday and midnight on the following Saturday;

"*week-day*" means a day which is not a Sunday;

"*writing*" includes printing, typewriting, lithography, photography, and other modes of representing or reproducing words in visible form and any information kept in a non-legible form, whether stored electronically or otherwise, which is capable by any means of being reproduced in a legible form;

"*year*", when used without qualification, means a period of 12 months beginning on the 1st day of January in any year.

PART 2

"*Companies Acts*" means the Companies Acts 1963 to 2001 and every other enactment which is to be read together with any of those Acts;

"*full age*", in relation to a person, means the time when the person attains the age of 18 years or sooner marries, or any time after either event;

"*functions*" includes powers and duties, and references to the performance of functions include, with respect to powers and duties, references to the exercise of the powers and the carrying out of the duties;

"*Member State*" means, where the context so admits, a Member State of the European Communities or of the European Union;

"*Minister of State*" means a person appointed under section 1 of the Ministers and Secretaries (Amendment) (No. 2) Act 1977 to be a Minister of State;

"*public holiday*" means a public holiday determined in accordance with the Organisation of Working Time Act 1997;

"*Social Welfare Acts*" means the Social Welfare (Consolidation) Act 1993 and every other enactment which is to be read together with that Act;

"*working day*" means a day which is not a Saturday, Sunday or public holiday.

S.I. No. 341 of 2008

TAX RETURNS AND PAYMENTS (MANDATORY ELECTRONIC FILING AND PAYMENT OF TAX) REGULATIONS 2008

ARRANGEMENT OF REGULATIONS

The Revenue Commissioners in exercise of the powers conferred on them by section 917EA (inserted by section 164 of the Finance Act 2003 (No. 3 of 2003)) of the Taxes Consolidation Act 1997 (No. 39 of 1997) make the following regulations:

1. Citation and commencement

(1) These Regulations may be cited as the Tax Returns and Payments (Mandatory Electronic Filing and Payment of Tax) Regulations 2008.

(2) These Regulations come into operation on 1 September 2008.

2. Interpretation and general

(1) In these Regulations—

"Acts" has the same meaning as it has in section 917D of the Principal Act;

"capacity" means access to the technology, including both hardware and software, by which either or both a specified return or the payment of any specified tax liabilities may be made by electronic means;

"Commissioners" means the Revenue Commissioners;

"Large Cases Division" means the division of the Office of the Revenue Commissioners known as Large Cases Division;

"Principal Act" means the Taxes Consolidation Act 1997;

"return"has the same meaning as it has in section 917D of the Principal Act.

(2) (a) Any return which a person is or may be required by the Acts to give to the Commissioners and which is specified for the purposes of Chapter 6 of Part 38 of the Principal Act by order made by the Commissioners under section 917E of that Act is specified as a specified return.

(b) Any liabilities to tax, including interest on unpaid tax, arising under any provision of the Acts, the payment of which is or will be accounted for, directly or indirectly, in a specified return, including any payment which is treated under the Acts as a payment on foot of, or on account of, any liabilities to tax, is specified as specified tax liabilities.

(c) Each person referred to in Schedules 1 and 2 is specified as a specified person for the purposes of paragraphs (a) and (b) of subsection (3) of section 917EA of the Principal Act and these Regulations.

3. Persons required to make returns and payments by electronic means from 1 January 2009

(1) Subject to paragraph (3), where, on or after 1 January 2009, any specified return falls due to be made by or on behalf of a specified person to whom Schedule 1 relates, then the return shall be made by electronic means and in accordance with Chapter 6 of Part 38 of the Principal Act.

(2) Subject to paragraph (3), where, on or after 1 January 2009, a payment of any specified tax liabilities falls due to be made by or on behalf of a specified person to whom Schedule 1 relates, then the payment shall be made by such electronic means as are required by the Commissioners.

(3) Where the specified person is a person to whom paragraph (1) or (2) relates and is a person whose tax affairs are dealt with by Large Cases Division, then the provisions of these Regulations shall only apply where the person has been notified in writing to that effect by the Commissioners.

4. Persons required to make returns and payments by electronic means from 1 January 2010

(1) Subject to paragraph (3), where, on or after 1 January 2010, any speci fied return falls due to be made by or on behalf of a specified person to whom Schedule 2 relates, then the return shall be made by electronic means and in accordance with Chapter 6 of Part 38 of the Principal Act.

(2) Subject to paragraph (3), where, on or after 1 January 2010, a payment of any specified tax liabilities falls due to be made by or on behalf of a specified person

to whom Schedule 2 relates, then the payment shall be made by such electronic means as are required by the Commissioners.

(3) The requirements placed by paragraphs (1) and (2) upon a specified person to whom paragraph 2 of Schedule 2 relates shall continue to apply, notwithstanding that the obligation on that person to append audited accounts to its annual return (under any provision of the Companies Acts) may no longer apply.

5. Repayment of tax by electronic means

(1) Where a repayment of any specified tax liabilities falls due to be made by the Commissioners—

(a) on or after 1 January 2009 to a specified person referred to in Schedule 1, or

(b) on or after 1 January 2010 to a specified person referred to in Schedule 2,

the repayment shall be made by electronic means.

6. Exclusion of certain specified persons

(1) A specified person may, by notifying the Commissioners in writing, request to be excluded from the provisions of these Regulations on the grounds that the person does not have the capacity to make a specified return or to pay the specified tax liabilities by electronic means and the notification shall include all information relevant to the consideration by the Commissioners of the request.

(2) Where the Commissioners receive a notification from a specified person in accordance with paragraph (1) or where the Commissioners otherwise consider it appropriate, they may exclude the person from the provisions of these Regulations only if they are satisfied that, in all of the circumstances, the person could not reasonably be expected to have the capacity to make a specified return or to make a payment in respect of specified tax liabilities by electronic means.

(3) A decision to exclude a specified person from the provisions of these Regulations by the Commissioners in accordance with paragraph (2) shall be made within 30 days of receipt of the notification from the specified person, and the Commissioners shall notify the specified person in writing of the decision.

7. Right of appeal to the Appeal Commissioners

(1) A person aggrieved by a failure of the Commissioners to exclude such person from the provisions of these Regulations in accordance with Regulation 6(2) may, by notice in writing to the Commissioners before the end of the period of 30 days beginning with the day on which notice of the decision was given to the person, apply to have such person's request to be excluded from the provisions of these Regulations heard and determined by the Appeal Commissioners.

(2) The Appeal Commissioners shall hear and determine an appeal made to them under paragraph (1) as if it were an appeal against an assessment to income tax, and the provisions of the Income Tax Acts relating to appeals shall apply accordingly.

(3) On the hearing of an appeal made under this Regulation, the Appeal Commissioners shall have regard only to those matters to which the Commissioners may or are required to have regard under these Regulations.

8. Provisions to amend exclusions

(1) If, at any time after a decision by the Commissioners in accordance with Regulation 6(2) or a determination by the Appeal Commissioners in accordance with Regulation 7(2) to exclude a specified person from the provisions of these Regulations, the Commissioners decide that, due to a material change in all of the circumstances, the specified person should not be so excluded, they shall notify the specified person in writing of that decision.

(2) The decision referred to in paragraph (1) shall be deemed to be a failure to exclude the specified person from the provisions of these Regulations and Regulation 7 shall apply accordingly.

9. Time at which payments and repayments made by electronic means are taken to be made

For the purpose of these Regulations—

(a) the time at which a payment of any specified tax liabilities by or on behalf of a specified person shall be taken as having been made shall be the later of the due date for that payment or the time at which the Commissioners receive authorisation to debit the amount of the payment from the account of the specified person in a financial institution, and

(b) the time at which a repayment of any specified tax liabilities to a specified person shall be taken as having been made shall be the time at which the Commissioners give authorisation to credit the amount of the repayment to the account of the specified person in a financial institution.

10. Presumptions

For the purposes of any dispute arising as to the time at which either or both a payment or a repayment of any specified tax liabilities to which these Regulations apply is to be taken as having been made, a certificate signed by an officer of the Commissioners which certifies that he or she has examined the relevant records and that it appears from them that the time at which the payment or the repayment is to be taken as having been made, is the time so specified in the certificate, shall be evidence until the contrary is proven that the payment or the repayment was made at the time so certified.

SCHEDULE 1

Specified Persons for the Purposes of Regulation 3

1. A Minister of the Government.

2. The Attorney General.

3. The Comptroller and Auditor General.

4. The Revenue Commissioners.

5. The Public Appointments Service.

6. The Commissioners of Public Works in Ireland.

7. The Houses of the Oireachtas Commission.

8. A company or other body whose tax affairs are dealt with by Large Cases Division at any time on or after 1 January 2009.

SCHEDULE 2

Specified Persons for the Purposes of Regulation 4

1. A person referred to in Schedule 13 to the Principal Act, other than one referred to in Schedule 1 to these Regulations.

2. A company which, at any time on or after 1 January 2010, is required under any provisions of the Companies Acts to append audited accounts to its annual return, other than one referred to in Schedule 1 to these Regulations.

GIVEN under my hand,
22 August 2008
MICHAEL O'GRADY,
Revenue Commissioner.

EXPLANATORY NOTE

Tax Returns and Payments (Mandatory Electronic Filing and Payment of Tax) Regulations 2008

These Regulations are made by the Revenue Commissioners under the provisions of section 917EA of the Taxes Consolidation Act 1997. This section was inserted by section 164 of the Finance Act 2003 and was made subject to a commencement order by the Minister for Finance. This order was signed on 28 July 2008.

The Regulations provide for mandatory electronic filing and paying of certain tax returns and tax liabilities by Government Departments and Offices, State Bodies and larger companies. These obligations are being introduced in 2 phases. Government Departments, certain named Government Offices and bodies whose tax affairs are dealt with by Large Cases Division of the Revenue Commissioners come within phase 1, with effect from 1 January 2009, while all other State agencies and companies who are obliged under the Companies Act to produce audited accounts come within phase 2, with effect from 1 January 2010.

In essence, any tax return to be made to the Revenue Commissioners, which can be made electronically under the provisions of Chapter 6 of Part 38 of the Taxes Consolidation Act 1997, is covered by these Regulations as well as the payment of all associated tax liabilities. Companies in phase 2 will continue to be obliged to pay and file electronically even if they subsequently become exempt from the obligation to produce audited accounts.

The Regulations also provide that, in all cases where a repayment is due to be made by the Revenue Commissioners, it will be made electronically.

The Revenue Commissioners may, on application, exclude a person from the obligations to pay and file electronically if they are satisfied that the person does not have the capacity to do so and in this context "capacity" is defined to mean access to the requisite technology, both hardware and software. A person aggrieved at a failure by the Revenue Commissioners to exclude them from the requirements may appeal that failure to the Appeal Commissioners. An excluded person may, if circumstances change, have that exclusion revoked and that decision may also be appealed to the Appeal Commissioners.

Finally, provision is made to determine the time at which payments and repayments made by electronic means are to be taken as having been made.

The bodies to which these Regulations apply are set out in Schedules 1 and 2 to these Regulations.

S.I. No. 223 of 2011

TAX RETURNS AND PAYMENTS (MANDATORY ELECTRONIC FILING AND PAYMENT OF TAX) REGULATIONS 2011

ARRANGEMENT OF REGULATIONS

The Revenue Commissioners in exercise of the powers conferred on them by section 917EA (inserted by section 164 of the Finance Act 2003 (No. 3 of 2003)) of the Taxes Consolidation Act 1997 (No. 39 of 1997) make the following regulations:

1. Citation and commencement

(1) These Regulations may be cited as the Tax Returns and Payments (Mandatory Electronic Filing and Payment of Tax) Regulations 2011.

(2) These Regulations come into operation on 1 June 2011.

2. Interpretation and general

(1) In these Regulations—

"capacity" means sufficient access to the Internet, by which either or both a specified return or the payment of any specified liabilities may be made by electronic means and, in the case of an individual, also means not prevented by reason of age, or mental or physical infirmity from either or both making a specified return or paying any specified liabilities by electronic means;

"Commissioners" means the Revenue Commissioners;

"Principal Act" means the Taxes Consolidation Act 1997;

"return" has the same meaning as it has in section 917D of the Principal Act;

"Regulations of 2008" means the Tax Returns and Payments (Mandatory Electronic Filing and Payment of Tax) Regulations 2008 (S.I. No. 341 of 2008);

"tax year" means a year of assessment.

(2) (a) Any return which a person is or may be required by the Acts to make to the Commissioners and which is specified for the purposes of Chapter 6 of Part 38 of the Principal Act by order made by the Commissioners under section 917E of that Act is specified as a specified return.

(b) Any liabilities to tax, including interest on unpaid tax, arising under any provision of the Acts, the payment of which is or will be accounted for, directly or indirectly, in a specified return, including any payment which is treated under the Acts as a payment on foot of, or on account of, any liabilities to tax, are specified as specified liabilities.

(c) Each person to whom these Regulations relate, other than the Commissioners, an officer of the Commissioners or the Appeal Commissioners, is specified as a specified person for the purposes of paragraphs (*a*) and (*b*) of subsection (3) of section 917EA of the Principal Act and these Regulations.

3. Persons required to make returns and payments by electronic means from 1 June 2011

(1) Subject to Regulation 6, where, on or after 1 June 2011, any specified return is required to be made by or on behalf of a specified person referred to in Schedule 1, that specified return shall be made by electronic means and in accordance with Chapter 6 of Part 38 of the Principal Act.

(2) Where, on or after 1 June 2011, a payment of any specified liabilities falls due to be made by or on behalf of a specified person referred to in Schedule 1, the payment shall be made by such electronic means as are required by the Commissioners.

4. High income individuals required to make returns and payments by electronic means from 1 June 2011

(1) Where any specified person is required to make a specified return in accordance with section 485FB(3) of the Principal Act for the tax year 2009 or any subsequent tax year, that specified person shall, on and from—

(a) 1 June 2011, or

(b) such later date by which that specified return is required to be made,

make that specified return and any other specified return that is required to be made by or subsequent to that date, by or on behalf of that specified person, by electronic means and in accordance with Chapter 6 of Part 38 of the Principal Act.

(2) Where, on or after the date from which paragraph (1) applies to a specified person, a payment of any specified liabilities falls due to be made by or on behalf of the specified person, the payment shall be made by such electronic means as are required by the Commissioners.

5. Persons in receipt of certain foreign income or claiming certain property-based reliefs, required to make returns and payments by electronic means from 1 June 2011

(1) Where any specified person, other than a specified person to which Regulation 4 applies, is required to make a specified return in accordance with section 951 of the Principal Act for the tax year 2009 or any subsequent tax year, being a specified return which includes either or both—

(a) income or gains to which any provisions of the Principal Act referred to in Schedule 2 applies, and

(b) a claim to any relief, allowance or deduction, or any amount which is deemed to have been received as rent under any provisions of the Principal Act referred to in Schedule 3,

that specified person shall, on and from—

(i) 1 June 2011, or

(ii) such later date by which that specified return is required to be made,

make any specified return that is required to be made by or subsequent to that date, by or on behalf of that specified person, by electronic means and in accordance with Chapter 6 of Part 38 of the Principal Act.

(2) Where, on or after the date from which paragraph (1) applies to a specified person, a payment of any specified liabilities falls due to be made by or on behalf of the specified person, the payment shall be made by such electronic means as are required by the Commissioners.

6. Companies subject to section 889 or 894 of the Principal Act, required to make returns by electronic means from 1 June 2011

Notwithstanding Regulation 3 and the Regulations of 2008, where any specified person, being a company within the meaning of section 4 of the Principal Act, is required to make a specified return in accordance with section 889 or 894 oif the Principal Act as respects—

(a) any accounting period, or

(b) any other period specified in a notice referred to in section 889 of that Act,

that specified return shall be made by or on behalf of that specified person by electronic means and in accordance with Chapter 6 of Part 38 of the Principal Act, only as respects a period ending on or after 1 January 2011.

7. Other persons subject to section 889 or 894 of the Principal Act, required to make returns and payments by electronic means from 1 June 2011

(1) Where, from any date arising on or after 1 June 2011, any specified person, other than a specified person to whom the Regulations of 2008 apply or Regulation 3, 4, 5 or 6 of these Regulations applies, is required to make a specified return in accordance with section 889 or 894 of the Principal Act, that specified person shall make that specified return and any other specified return that is required to be made by or subsequent to that date, by or on behalf of that specified person, by electronic means and in accordance with Chapter 6 of Part 38 of the Principal Act.

(2) Where, on or after the date from which paragraph (1) applies to a specified person, a payment of any specified liabilities falls due to be made by or on behalf of the specified person, the payment shall be made by such electronic means as are required by the Commissioners.

8. Persons required to make returns and payments by electronic means from 1 October 2011

(1) Where any specified person, other than a specified person to whom the Regulations of 2008 apply or Regulation 3, 4, 5, 6 or 7 of these Regulations applies, is required to make a specified return referred to in Regulation 31 of the Income Tax (Employments) (Consolidated) Regulations 2001 (S.I. No. 559 of 2001) for the year 2010 or any subsequent year and where that specified return relates to 10 or more employees, that specified person shall, on and from—

(a) 1 October 2011, or

(b) such later date by which that specified return is required to be made,

make any specified return that is required to be made by or subsequent to that date, by or on behalf of that specified person, by electronic means and in accordance with Chapter 6 of Part 38 of the Principal Act.

(2) Where, on or after the date from which paragraph (1) applies to a specified person, a payment of any specified liabilities falls due to be made by or on behalf of the specified person, the payment shall be made by such electronic means as are required by the Commissioners.

9. Exclusion of certain specified persons

(1) A specified person may, by notifying the Commissioners in writing, request to be excluded from the provisions of these Regulations on the grounds that the specified person does not have the capacity to make a specified return or pay the specified tax liabilities by electronic means and the notification shall include all information relevant to the consideration by the Commissioners of the request.

(2) Where the Commissioners receive a notification from a specified person in accordance with paragraph (1) or where the Commissioners otherwise consider it

SCHEDULE 3

Certain Reliefs, Allowances and Deductions Which May Be Claimed In A Specified Return For The Purposes Of Regulation 5

PART 1

Residential

1. Any deduction to which the person is entitled under the following provisions of the Principal Act:
   (*a*) section 372AP or 372AR,
   (*b*) section 372AP or 372AR, as either section is applied by section 372AU.
2. Any excess deficiency over any surplus, which may be carried forward in accordance with section 384(2) of the Principal Act and which is referable to any relief to which the person may be entitled under section 372AP of the Principal Act.
3. Any amount that is deemed to have been received as rent under section 372AP(7) of the Principal Act.

PART 2

Industrial and Commercial

4. Any area-based capital allowance, within the meaning of section 409F of the Principal Act, including any balancing allowance, within the meaning of that section, made under section 274 of the Principal Act.
5. Any specified capital allowance, within the meaning of section 409F of the Principal Act.

GIVEN under my hand,
11 May 2011.

MICHAEL O'GRADY,
Revenue Commissioner.

EXPLANATORY NOTE

(This note is not part of the Instrument and does not purport to be a legal interpretation).

Tax Returns and Payments (Mandatory Electronic Filing and Payment of Tax) Regulations 2011

These Regulations are made by the Revenue Commissioners under the provisions of section 917EA of the Taxes Consolidation Act 1997. This section was inserted by section 164 of the Finance Act 2003 and was made subject to a commencement order by the Minister for Finance. This order was signed on 28 July 2008.

These Regulations provide for mandatory electronic filing of certain tax returns and payment of tax liabilities by certain categories of taxpayers. The provisions are introduced in 2 stages.

With effect from 1 June 2011 the following categories of taxpayers are obliged to file their returns electronically:

- All companies, trusts, partnerships, collective investment undertakings and European Economic Interest Groupings.
- Individuals subject to the high earners restriction for the tax year 2009 or any subsequent tax year.
- Self-assessed individuals benefiting from or acquiring Foreign Life Poli-cies, Offshore Funds, other offshore products or claiming any of the property or area-based incentive reliefs for the tax year 2009 or any subsequent tax year.
- Self-assessed individuals filing a return of payments to third parties.

With effect from 1 October 2011 employers with more than 10 employees are required to file their returns electronically.

In all cases, the payment of any tax liability, which arises after the obligation to e-file returns commences, must be made electronically and in these circumstances this must continue for all subsequent returns and payments.

The Revenue Commissioners may, on application, exclude a person from the obligation to pay and file electronically if they are satisfied that the person does not have the capacity to do so and in this context "capacity" is taken to mean sufficient access to the Internet and in the case of an individual is not prevented by reason of age, physical or mental infirmity from filing and paying electronically. A person aggrieved at a failure by the Revenue Commissioners to exclude them from the requirements may appeal that failure to the Appeal Commissioners. An excluded person may, if circumstances change, have that exclusion revoked and that decision may also be appealed to the Appeal Commissioners.

Provision is also made to determine the time at which payments made by electronic means are to be taken as having been made.

S.I. No. 658 of 2011

UNIVERSAL SOCIAL CHARGE REGULATIONS 2011

ARRANGEMENT OF REGULATIONS

PART 1

GENERAL

PART 2

RATE CUT-OFF POINTS

PART 3

DEDUCTION AND REPAYMENT OF USC

The Revenue Commissioners, in exercise of the powers conferred on them by section 531AAB of the Taxes Consolidation Act 1997 (No. 39 of 1997), hereby make the following regulations:

PART 1

General

1. Citation and commencement

(1) These Regulations may be cited as the Universal Social Charge Regulations 2011.

(2) These Regulations shall come into operation as respects any payment of relevant emoluments made or to be made for the USC year 2012 and subsequent USC years.

2. Interpretation

(1) In these Regulations—

"the Act" means the Taxes Consolidation Act 1997 (No. 39 of 1997);

"certificate of rate cut-off points", in relation to an employee, means the certificate sent to an employer in respect of the employee for a USC year under Regulation 8(2) certifying—

(a) the rate cut-off points appropriate to the employee, and

(b) where appropriate, details of total relevant emoluments paid and total USC deducted in respect of the employee's previous employment or employments for the USC year;

"cessation certificate" means a certificate sent by an employer to the Revenue Commissioners under Regulation 19 or 20, as the case may be;

"Collector-General" means the Collector-General appointed under section 851 of the Act;

"cumulative rate cut-off points", in relation to an employee, any date and any rate, means, in respect of each rate, the sum of the rate cut-off points for that rate applicable to the employee and applied to each payment of relevant emoluments made to that employee from the beginning of the USC year up to and including such date;

"cumulative relevant emoluments", in relation to an employee and any date, means the total of all payments of relevant emoluments made to the employee from the beginning of the USC year up to and including such date;

"cumulative USC", in relation to an employee and any date, means the total of USC due at each of the rates from the beginning of the USC year up to and including that date;

"electronic means" has the same meaning as in section 917EA of the Act;

"employee" means any person in receipt of emoluments;

"employer" means any person paying emoluments;

"notional payment", in relation to an employee who is in receipt of relevant emoluments in the form of—

(a) perquisites and profits that are chargeable to USC by virtue of those perquisites and profits being chargeable to income tax under section 112 of the Act, or

(b) the benefit of the private use of a car or a van that is chargeable to USC by virtue of the benefit of that use being chargeable to income tax under section 121 or 121A, respectively, of the Act,

means an amount equal to the amount that, on the basis of the best estimate that can reasonably be made, is the amount of relevant emoluments likely to be chargeable to USC in respect of the emoluments referred to in subparagraph *(a)* or *(b)*;

"PAYE Regulations" means the Income Tax (Employments) (Consolidated) Regulations 2001 (S.I. No. 559 of 2001);

"personal public service number" has the same meaning as in section 262 of the Social Welfare Consolidation Act 2005 (No. 26 of 2005);

"principal employer" shall be construed in accordance with Regulation 3;

"rate" means any of the rates of USC specified in section 531AN of the Act;

"rate cut-off point", in relation to an employee and a rate, means the amount in respect of such employee and such rate determined by the Revenue Commissioners and included on the certificate of rate cut-off points;

"relevant emoluments" shall be construed in accordance with paragraph *(a)* of the Table to section 531AM(1) of the Act;

"relevant income" shall be construed in accordance with paragraph *(b)* of the Table to section 531AM(1) of the Act;

"return filing date" means—

(a) 14 days from the end of a month, or

(b) in the case of a remittance made by electronic means as required by the Revenue Commissioners, 23 days from the end of a month;

"Revenue officer" means an officer of the Revenue Commissioners;

"universal social charge" has the meaning assigned to it by section 531AM of the Act;

"USC" means universal social charge;

"USC year" means a year of assessment for the purposes of the Income Tax Acts.

(2) In these Regulations—

(a) references to the payment of relevant emoluments include references to notional payments in respect of relevant emoluments,

(b) references to USC deducted or to be deducted, or to a requirement to deduct USC from the payment of relevant emoluments, include references to USC remitted or to be remitted, or a requirement to remit USC in respect of notional payments,

(c) in relation to the period in respect of which relevant emoluments are paid, references to a week include references to a fortnight, 4 weeks, a month or any other longer interval or irregular interval at which relevant emoluments are paid, and

(d) references to any document, including a certificate, notice, notifi cation, form or return, authorised or required to be sent or given under these Regulations, include references to such a document otherwise made available or caused to be so sent, given or made available.

3. Intermediate employers

(1) Where an employee works under the general control and management of a person (in these Regulations referred to as the "principal employer") who is not his or her immediate employer, that person shall be deemed to be the employer

of the employee for the purposes of these Regulations, and the immediate employer shall give the principal employer such particulars of the employee's relevant emoluments as may be necessary to enable the principal employer to comply with these Regulations.

(2) If the employee's relevant emoluments are actually paid to him or her by the immediate employer—

(a) the immediate employer shall be notified by the principal employer of the amount of USC to be deducted or repaid when the relevant emoluments are paid to the employee, and shall deduct or repay accordingly the amount so notified, and

(b) the principal employer shall make a corresponding deduction or addition on making to the immediate employer the payment out of which the relevant emoluments are to be paid.

4. Liability for payment of deduction and entitlement to payment of repayment

Persons who are required to make any deduction or repayment of USC under these Regulations shall, in the case of a deduction (whether or not made), be accountable for the amount of USC, and be liable to pay that amount, to the Revenue Commissioners and shall, in the case of a repayment, be entitled, if it has been made, to be paid it, or given credit for it, by the Revenue Commissioners.

5. Delegation of functions of Revenue Commissioners

Any act to be performed or function to be discharged by the Revenue Commissioners that is authorised or required by these Regulations may be performed or discharged by any one or more of their officers acting under their authority.

6. Service by post or electronic means

Any document, including a certificate, notice, notification, form or return, authorised or required to be sent or given under these Regulations may be sent by post or by electronic means.

7. Combined documents for USC and income tax

Any document, including a certificate, notice, notification, form or return relating to USC may be combined with such a document relating to income tax and any document so combined may be modified by the Revenue Commis sioners accordingly in relation to its application to USC and income tax or to USC only or to income tax only, as the case may be.

PART 2

Rate Cut-off Points

8. Determination of rate cut-off points

(1) Subject to paragraph (2), the Revenue Commissioners shall cause the rate cut-off points appropriate to an employee for any USC year to be determined.

(2) Where the Revenue Commissioners have reason to believe that the relevant emoluments of an employee for a USC year will not exceed the amount specified in section 531AM(2) of the Act, no rate cut-off points appropriate to the employee for that USC year shall be determined.

(3) Any of the following matters may be taken into account in determining a rate cut-off point or points for an employee, namely—

(a) the relevant emoluments of the employee for the USC year, or any period within that year, whether for one employment or for more than one employment,

(b) the relevant income of the employee for the USC year,

(c) any request made by the employee under Regulation 10(4) in relation to the allocation of the rate cut-off points to different employments,

(d) the age of the employee,

(e) the full eligibility of the employee for services under Part IV of the Health Act 1970 (No. 1 of 1970), by virtue of sections 45 and 45A of that Act or Council Regulation (EC) No. 883/2004 of the European Parliament and of the Council of 29 April 2004* on the coordination of social security systems,

*OJ No. L166 30.4.2004, p.1

(f) any reliefs from USC to which the employee is entitled for the USC year,

(g) any USC overpaid for any previous USC year that has not been repaid,

(h) any USC remaining unpaid for any previous USC year that is not otherwise recovered,

(i) such other adjustments as may be necessary to secure that, so far as possible, USC in respect of the employee's relevant emoluments for the USC year to which the rate cut-off point or points relate shall be deducted from the relevant emoluments paid in that USC year.

9. Transitional arrangements concerning determination of rate cut-off points in absence of certificate of rate cut-off points

(1) In this Regulation "certificate of tax credits and standard rate cut-off point" has the same meaning as in the PAYE Regulations.

(2) This Regulation applies where—

(a) in relation to an employee, the employer does not have a certificate of rate cut-off points in respect of the employee, and

(b) in relation to the employee, the employer has a certificate of tax cred its and standard rate cut-off point that has effect for the USC year 2012.

(3) Where this Regulation applies the Revenue Commissioners shall be treated as having—

(a) determined the rate cut-off points applicable to the employee to be the amounts specified in column (1) of the Table to section 531AN of the Act and the rates applicable to those cut-off points to be the corresponding rates specified in column (2) of that Table,

(b) included those amounts and rates on a certificate of rate cut-off points, together with their weekly equivalents, and

(c) sent the certificate of rate cut-off points to the employer of the employee.

(4) Where this Regulation applies the employer of the employee shall on the payment of any relevant emoluments deduct USC from those emoluments—

(a) in accordance with Regulation 15, where the certificate of tax credits and standard rate cut-off point indicates that Regulation 17 of the PAYE Regulations applies, or

(b) in accordance with Regulation 21, where the certificate of tax credits and standard rate cut-off point indicates that Regulation 22 of the PAYE Regulations applies.

(5) Where—

(a) this Regulation applies, and

(b) in relation to an employee and the USC year 2012, a certificate of rate cut-off points appropriate to the employee has effect,

the employer shall disregard the certificate of rate cut-off points referred to in paragraph (3) and, instead, use the certificate sent to that employer under Regulation 10(2).

(6) This Regulation shall not apply or have effect on or after 31 December 2011.

10. Notification of determination of rate cut-off points

(1) After the rate cut-off points appropriate to an employee for any USC year have been determined in accordance with Regulation 8, the Revenue Commissioners shall send notice of the determination to the employee.

(2) The Revenue Commissioners shall send a certificate of rate cut-off points appropriate to an employee to the employer of the employee and, except where these Regulations otherwise provide, the details contained in the certificate shall be taken into account by the employer for the purposes of calculating the cumulative USC in respect of the cumulative relevant emoluments of the employee in accordance with Regulation 15.

(3) Where it appears to the Revenue Commissioners that an employee has more than one employment, the Revenue Commissioners shall, in respect of each employment, send to the employer a separate certificate of rate cut-off points showing the rate cut-off points applicable to the particular employment, but the aggregate amount of the rate cut-off points on each such certificate shall not exceed the total amount of rate cut-off points of the employee for the USC year.

(4) Before a determination for a USC year has been made in accordance with Regulation 8, an employee may request that a portion of the rate cut-off points be allocated to different employments in such a manner as the employee directs and where any such request is made, any determination shall take that request into account without prejudice to the other matters to be taken into account under Regulation 8.

11. Amendment of rate cut-off points

(1) If a determination of rate cut-off points under Regulation 8 is found not to be appropriate because the actual circumstances are different from the circumstances by reference to which the determination was made, the Revenue Commissioners may, and if so required by the employee shall, by reference to the actual circumstances, cause the previous determination to be amended.

(2) If an employee is aggrieved by a determination of rate cut-off points under Regulation 8, or by an amended determination under paragraph (1), he or she may give notice of his or her objection, stating the grounds of the objection, not later than 31 December in the USC year to which the determination relates.

(3) The Revenue Commissioners shall consider the employee's objection and either—

(a) send an amended determination of rate cut-off points to the employee, or

(b) notify the employee of their decision not to amend the determination of rate cut-off points.

(4) The employee concerned may appeal—

(a) an amended determination sent to the employee under paragraph (3)(*a*), or

(b) a decision of the Revenue Commissioners under paragraph (3)(*b*) not to amend a determination of rate cut-off points,

within 21 days of the date on which the amended determination is so sent, or as the case may be, the decision is so notified to the employee, and the appeal may be made to the Appeal Commissioners and may be heard and determined by one Appeal Commissioner.

(5) The Appeal Commissioners shall determine the rate cut-off points having regard to the matters set out in Regulation 8(3) and, subject to paragraph (1), their determination shall be final.

(6) (a) Where a determination of rate cut-off points under Regulation 8 is amended pursuant to paragraph (1) or (3)(*a*), as the case may be, the Revenue Commissioners shall send to the employer a new certificate of rate cut-off points that includes the amended determination and the employer shall then use the new certificate.

(b) The Revenue Commissioners shall send a notice of the amended determination referred to in subparagraph (*a*) to the employee not later than the date on which a new certificate of rate cut-off points is sent to the employer in accordance with that subparagraph.

12. Application of determinations of rate cut-off points for subsequent USC years

(1) A determination of the rate cut-off points appropriate to an employee for any USC year under Regulation 8, or an amended determination under Regulation 11, shall have effect for each subsequent USC year as if a separate determination had been made for each such year and the notice of determi nation and the certificate of rate cut-off points shall state that the rate cut-off points indicated on the notice and certificate shall have effect for that USC year and for each subsequent USC year.

(2) Paragraph (1) shall not preclude an employee from requesting a separate determination of rate cut-off points under Regulation 8 for any of the USC years after the first USC year and, where such a separate determination is made, a notice of such determination shall be sent to that employee.

(3) Regulation 11 shall, with the necessary modification, apply in relation to each USC year after the first USC year included in a notice or certificate sent under paragraph (1) as it applies in relation to the first USC year.

PART 3

Deduction and Repayment of USC

13. General provision for deductions and repayments

(1) Subject to paragraph (2), on payment of relevant emoluments, deductions or repayments of USC shall be made subject to, and in accordance with, the subsequent provisions of this Part.

(2) Paragraph (1) shall not apply where Regulation 8(2) applies.

14. Deduction of USC in respect of notional payments

(1) An employer shall deduct USC in respect of a notional payment from any payment of relevant emoluments actually made by the employer to or on behalf of an employee on—

(a) the day the notional payment is made, or

(b) if no actual payment of relevant emoluments is made to the employee on that day, the next pay day following the day on which the notional payment is made.

(2) Where, by reason of an insufficiency of payments of relevant emoluments actually made to or on behalf of the employee, the employer is unable to deduct the amount (or full amount) of USC required to be deducted by virtue of paragraph (1), the employer shall be liable to remit that amount of USC to the Collector-General as if the amount to be remitted had been deducted in accordance with this Regulation.

(3) This paragraph applies to relevant emoluments being—

(a) the benefit of the private use of a car or a van which is treated for the purposes of income tax as a benefit in kind by virtue of section 121 or 121A, respectively, of the Act,

(b) the benefit arising from a preferential loan which is treated for the purposes of income tax as a perquisite for the purposes of section 112 of the Act by virtue of section 122 of the Act, or

(c) the benefit arising from an asset which belongs to the employer and the valuation of which is for the purposes of income tax determined in accordance with section 119(4) of the Act.

(4) Where a notional payment for a USC year is in respect of relevant emolu ments to which paragraph (3) applies, the amount of that notional payment shall be apportioned over the period for which the benefit is available in that USC year and the employer shall deduct USC by reference to the part of that notional payment apportioned to each week in the period for which the benefit is avail able in that USC year.

15. Calculation and making of deduction or repayment where certificate of rate cutoff points held

(1) On any payment of relevant emoluments to or on behalf of an employee in respect of whom the employer holds a certificate of rate cut-off points, the employer, except where these Regulations otherwise provide, shall ascertain—

(a) the cumulative relevant emoluments of that employee at the date of payment, and

(b) by reference to the certificate of rate cut-off points in respect of that employee, the cumulative rate cut-off point for each rate corresponding to the date of payment,

and, by reference to the amounts referred to in subparagraph (*a*) and each of the amounts referred to in subparagraph (*b*), determine the amount of the cumulative USC in respect of the cumulative relevant emoluments in accordance with the formula in paragraph (2).

[(2) The cumulative USC shall be the amount represented by A in the formula–

$$A = (B \times 1.5\%) + (C \times 3.5\%) + (D \times 7\%) + (E \times 8\%)$$

where–

B is the amount (that may be nil) of the cumulative relevant emoluments chargeable to USC at the rate of 1.5% up to and including the rate cut-off point for that rate,

C is the amount (that may be nil) of the cumulative relevant emoluments chargeable to USC at the rate of 3.5% up to and including the rate cut-off point for that rate,

D is the amount (that may be nil) of the cumulative relevant emoluments chargeable to USC at the rate of 7% up to and including the rate cut-off point for that rate, and

E is the amount (that may be nil) of the cumulative relevant emoluments that exceeds the rate cut-off point referred to in the meaning of D.][1]

(3) If the cumulative USC determined in accordance with paragraph (2) exceeds the cumulative USC corresponding to the employee's cumulative relevant emoluments at the date of the last preceding payment of relevant emoluments (in this Regulation referred to as the "previous cumulative USC"), the employer shall deduct the excess from the relevant emoluments on making the payment of relevant emoluments.

(4) If the cumulative USC determined in accordance with paragraph (2) is less than the previous cumulative USC, the employer shall repay the difference to the employee on making the payment of relevant emoluments.

(5) If the cumulative USC determined in accordance with paragraph (2) is equal to the previous cumulative USC, the employer shall neither deduct nor repay USC when the payment of relevant emoluments is made.

(6) Where the payment of relevant emoluments is the first such payment in the USC year, the employer shall deduct the cumulative USC as determined in accordance with paragraph (2) from the relevant emoluments on making the payment of those relevant emoluments and paragraphs (3), (4) and (5) shall not apply.

(7) The employer shall record the following particulars in relation to every payment of relevant emoluments that the employer makes to or on behalf of the employee:

(a) the date of the payment;

(b) the amount of the relevant emoluments;

(c) in relation to the date of payment—

(i) the cumulative relevant emoluments,

(ii) the cumulative USC, that is, the amount represented by A in the formula in paragraph (2), and

(iii) the amount of USC, if any, deducted or repaid on making the payment of relevant emoluments.

16. Subsidiary relevant emoluments of employee

(1) If—

(a) an employer makes a payment of relevant emoluments in respect of overtime or other extra earnings to or on behalf of an employee whose main relevant emoluments are paid weekly, and

(b) that payment is made at an earlier date in the week than the date on which the main relevant emoluments are paid,

the employer shall repay no USC to the employee on the occasion of that payment, notwithstanding that USC may be repayable under Regulation 15.

(2) Regulations 15, 17, 21 and 22 shall have effect as if the payment of relevant emoluments referred to in paragraph (1)(*a*) is made on the same day in that week as the day on which the main relevant emoluments are paid.

17. Deduction where additional pay day in USC year

(1) This Regulation applies where—

(a) an employer paying relevant emoluments has received a certificate of rate cut-off points in respect of an employee from the Revenue Commissioners,

(b) relevant emoluments are paid on 31 December in any USC year or, if that year is a leap year, on 30 or 31 December in that year, to or on behalf of an employee who is paid weekly, and

(c) relevant emoluments are paid to or on behalf of an employee where the Revenue Commissioners send notice to the employer of that employee directing that this Regulation shall apply.

(2) Subject to paragraph (3), where this Regulation applies, Regulation 15 shall apply to payments of relevant emoluments to which this Regulation applies as if the reference in paragraph (1)(*b*) of Regulation 15 to the "date of payment" was a reference to the immediately preceding date on which relevant emoluments were paid.

(3) Where this Regulation and Regulation 22 apply, on making any payment of relevant emoluments to which this Regulation applies, the employer shall deduct USC from those emoluments, without regard to rate cut-off points, at the highest rate indicated on the certificate of rate cut-off points sent under Regulation 10(2) in respect of the employee referred to in paragraph (1).

(4) On making any such payment referred to in paragraph (1), the employer shall record—

(a) the date of the payment,

(b) the amount of the relevant emoluments,

(c) the rate cut-off points where a certificate of rate cut-off points is held,

(d) the cumulative relevant emoluments at the date of payment where the employee has not ceased to be employed by that employer,

(e) the rate applied to the relevant emoluments, and

(f) the amount of USC (if any) deducted on making the payment.

18. Arrears of pay

(1) This Regulation applies to payments of relevant emoluments made to or on behalf of an employee after he or she has ceased to be employed by the person making those payments.

(2) Where this Regulation applies, on making any such payment of relevant emoluments, the employer shall—

(a) in the case of an employee—

(i) who ceased to be employed by that employer in the same USC year in which those emoluments are paid, and

(ii) in respect of whom the employer holds a certificate of rate cutoff points,

deduct USC by reference to the rate cut-off points that would have applied to the payment if those emoluments had been paid on the date the employee ceased to be employed by the employer and Regulation 15 had applied,

or

(b) in the case of an employee who ceased to be employed by the employer—

(i) in the same USC year in which those emoluments are paid and in respect of whom no certificate of rate cut-off points is held by the employer, or

(ii) in any USC year before the USC year in which the payment is made,

deduct USC in accordance with Regulation 21(1).

(3) Where an employer pays such relevant emoluments as are referred to in paragraph (1) and details of those emoluments were not included on the cess ation certificate sent to the Revenue Commissioners in accordance with Regu lation 19(1), the employer shall immediately send to the Revenue Commis sioners a return, in a form approved by the Revenue Commissioners, showing—

(a) the date of the payment,

(b) the amount of the relevant emoluments,

(c) the amount of USC (if any) deducted on making the payment,

(d) the date on which the employee ceased to be employed, and

(e) any other particulars in relation to USC that are indicated by such form or by these Regulations as being required to be entered on that form.

(4) Where this Regulation applies, on making any such payment, the employer shall record—

(a) the date of the payment,

(b) the amount of the relevant emoluments,

(c) the rate cut-off points where a certificate of rate cut-off points is held,

(d) the cumulative relevant emoluments at the date of payment that would have applied if the employee had continued to be employed by that employer,

(e) the rate applied to the cumulative relevant emoluments,

(f) the amount of USC (if any) deducted on making the payment, and

(g) the amount of USC (if any) repaid on making the payment.

19. Change of employment where certificate of rate cut-off points held

(1) Where an employee, in respect of whom a certificate of rate cut-off of points is held by the employer, ceases employment with the employer, the employer shall, on the date the employment ceases, send to the Revenue Commissioners a certificate (in these Regulations referred to as a "cessation certificate") in a form approved by the Revenue Commissioners on which that employer has entered the following particulars—

(a) the name of the employee,

(b) the date on which the employment ceased,

(c) the week in respect of which the last payment of relevant emoluments was made,

(d) if appropriate, the cumulative relevant emoluments at the date of such payment, and

(e) any other particulars in relation to USC that are indicated by the cer-tificate or by these Regulations as being required to be entered on that certificate.

(2) The employer shall make 3 copies of the cessation certificate and send them to the employee on the date the employment ceases.

(3) Subject to paragraph (7), immediately on commencing his or her next employment the employee shall send to the new employer 2 copies of the cessation certificate prepared by the former employer.

(4) (a) The new employer shall insert on one copy of the cessation certificate prepared by the former employer—

(i) the address of the employee,

(ii) the date on which the new employment commenced,

(iii) the rate at which the relevant emoluments will be paid, and

(iv) the frequency with which the relevant emoluments will be paid,

and immediately send that copy to the Revenue Commissioners.

(b) On receipt of the copy of the cessation certificate from the new employer, the Revenue Commissioners, in accordance with Regulation 8, shall cause a determination of the rate cut-off points appropriate to the employee to be made and shall send a certificate of rate cut-off points to the new employer.

(c) Pending the receipt of the certificate of rate cut-off points referred to in subparagraph (*b*), the new employer—

(i) shall record—

(I) the date of payment of any relevant emoluments,

(II) the gross amount of the relevant emoluments, and

(III) as respects each date of payment of relevant emoluments, the rate cut-off points specified on the copies of the cessation certificate prepared by the former employer,

and

(ii) shall not deduct USC in accordance with Regulation 15 but, instead, shall deduct USC by reference to the aggregate of the relevant emoluments paid to or on behalf of the employee in that week by reference to the rate cut-off points specified on the cessation certificate prepared by the former employer.

(d) When the new employer receives the certificate of rate cut-off points referred to in subparagraph (*b*), he or she shall deduct USC in accord ance with Regulation 15 and, for this purpose—

(i) the aggregate of the cumulative relevant emoluments paid to or on behalf of the employee referred to in paragraph (1) from the beginning of the USC year to the date of commencement of employment with the new employer specified on that certificate

and the relevant emoluments paid by that new employer before receipt of the certificate, and

(ii) the aggregate of the cumulative USC deducted from the relevant emoluments referred to in clause (i) specified on the certificate and USC, if any, deducted by that new employer before receipt of the certificate,

shall be deemed, respectively, to be the cumulative relevant emoluments paid, and the cumulative USC deducted, by him or her.

(5) Where the copies of the cessation certificate prepared by the former employer show that the last payment of relevant emoluments was in the USC year preceding that in which the new employment commences, the new employer shall comply with paragraph (4) with the modification in relation to subparagraph (*d*) of that paragraph that he or she shall not record, or have regard to, the cumulative relevant emoluments and cumulative USC shown on the cessation certificate.

(6) Where the copies of the cessation certificate prepared by the former employer show that the last payment of relevant emoluments was in a USC year earlier than the year preceding that in which the new employment commences, the new employer shall comply with subparagraphs (*a*) and (*c*)(i) of paragraph (4) but—

(a) shall, instead, deduct USC from each payment of relevant emoluments made by him or her to the employee, and keep records, as if those payments had been payments to which Regulation 21 applied, and

(b) in relation to subparagraph (*d*) of paragraph (4), shall not record, or have regard to, the cumulative relevant emoluments and cumulative USC shown on the cessation certificate.

(7) If the new employer ceases to employ the employee before he or she receives the certificate of rate cut-off points referred to in subparagraph (*b*) of paragraph (4), he or she shall comply with paragraphs (1) and (2) as if that certificate of rate cut-off points had been sent to him or her, but, for the purposes of completing the cessation certificate—

(a) the cumulative relevant emoluments shall be taken to be the aggregate of the cumulative relevant emoluments shown on the cessation certificate prepared by the former employer and the gross relevant emoluments paid by the new employer, and

(b) where particulars of the cumulative USC are required, that USC shall be taken to be the aggregate of the cumulative USC shown on the cessation certificate prepared by the former employer and any USC deducted by the new employer.

(8) If the employee objects to the disclosure to the new employer of his or her cumulative relevant emoluments—

(a) paragraph (3) shall not apply,

(b) the employee shall provide 2 copies of the cessation certificate to the Revenue Commissioners before commencing his or her new employment, and

(c) the Revenue Commissioners shall send to the new employer a certifi-cate of rate cut-off points in respect of the employee not stating the employee's cumulative rate cut-off points or cumulative relevant emoluments and direct that Regulation 22 shall apply to all payments of relevant emoluments that the new employer makes to or on behalf of the employee.

(9) Retirement on pension shall not be treated as a cessation of employment for the purposes of this Regulation if the relevant emoluments are paid by the same employer both before and after the retirement.

20. Death of employee

(1) Where an employee dies while still employed by the employer, the employer shall immediately send to the Revenue Commissioners a cessation certificate on which the employer has entered the following details—

(a) the name of the employee,

(b) the date on which the employment ceased,

(c) the week in respect of which the last payment of relevant emoluments was made,

(d) if appropriate, the cumulative relevant emoluments at the date of such payment,

(e) any other particulars in relation to USC that are indicated by the cer-tificate or by these Regulations as being required to be entered on that certificate, and

(f) if they are known to the employer the name and address of the per-sonal representative of the employee.

(2) Where an employer makes any payment of relevant emoluments after the date of an employee's death in respect of his or her employment with the employer, the employer shall deduct or repay USC as if the deceased employee was still in the employer's employment at the date of the payment.

(3) If the amount of the relevant emoluments referred to in paragraph (2) and the date on which they will be paid are known at the time the cessation certificate is completed, the employer shall, when the cessation certificate referred to in paragraph (1) is sent to the Revenue Commissioners, notify the Revenue Commissioners of—

(a) the amount of the relevant emoluments,

(b) the date on which they will be paid, and

(c) the amount of USC that will be deducted or repaid.

(4) Where paragraph (3) does not apply, the employer shall indicate on the cessation certificate that a further payment of relevant emoluments will be made.

21. Emergency basis of deduction

(1) Until an employer receives a certificate of rate cut-off points in respect of an employee from the Revenue Commissioners, the employer shall, on making any payment of relevant emoluments to or on behalf of the employee, deduct USC from all such payments at the highest rate specified in [column (2) of Part 1 of the Table][2] to section 531AN of the Act unless Regulation 19(4)(c)(ii) applies.

(2) The employer shall record the following particulars in relation to every payment of relevant emoluments referred to in paragraph (1):

(a) the date of payment;

(b) the amount of relevant emoluments;

(c) the rate at which USC was deducted;

(d) the amount of USC deducted on making the payment.

(3) On making any payments of relevant emoluments to or on behalf of an employee after a certificate of rate cut-off points in respect of the employee has been received by the employer, the employer shall comply with Regulation 15 and, for this purpose—

(a) any cumulative relevant emoluments notified to the employer in the certificate of rate cut-off points shall be treated as if they represented relevant emoluments paid by that employer, and

(b) the cumulative USC before the first payment of relevant emoluments is made to or on behalf of the employee after the certificate of rate cut-off points is received shall be taken to be the aggregate of any cumulative USC notified to the employer in that certificate and any USC that the employer was liable to deduct from the employee's relevant emoluments under paragraph (1).

(4) Where paragraph (1) applies in respect of an employee and the employer ceases to employ the employee before a certificate of rate cut-off points in respect of that employee is received, the employer shall immediately send a cessation certificate to the Revenue Commissioners on which the employer has entered the following particulars:

(a) the name of the employee;

(b) the date on which the employment ceased;

(c) the week in respect of which the last payment of relevant emoluments was made;

(d) any other particulars in relation to USC that are indicated by the certificate or by these Regulations as being required to be entered on that certificate.

(5) The employer shall make 3 copies of the cessation certificate referred to in paragraph (4) and send them to the employee on the date the employment ceases.

(6) Immediately on commencing his or her next employment the employee shall send to the new employer 2 copies of the cessation certificate prepared by the former employer.

(7) On receipt of the copies of the cessation certificate the new employer—

(a) shall comply with subparagraph (*d*) of paragraph (4) of Regulation 19, and

(b) until the certificate of rate cut-off points is received from the Revenue Commissioners in respect of that employee, shall comply with the said paragraph (4).

(8) This Regulation shall not apply where—

(a) the employee performs the duties of his or her employment wholly outside the State, or

(b) the employee is outside the State and the relevant emoluments are paid outside the State.

22. Aggregation of relevant emoluments in non-cumulative cases

(1) Where, under these Regulations, USC is deductible by an employer otherwise than in accordance with Regulation 15, 17 or 21, the amount of USC to be deducted in any week in respect of an employee shall be calculated—

(a) by reference to the relevant emoluments paid to or on behalf of the employee in that week,

(b) by reference to the rate cut-off points on the certificate of rate cut-off points held by the employer in respect of that employee, and

(c) without regard to any cumulative relevant emoluments, cumulative rate cut-off points or cumulative USC in respect of the USC year in which the relevant emoluments are paid.

(2) The employer shall record the following particulars in relation to every payment of relevant emoluments referred to in paragraph (1)(a):

(a) the date of payment;

(b) the amount of relevant emoluments;

(c) the rate at which USC was deducted;

(d) the amount of USC deducted on making the payment.

23. USC paid by employer to or for benefit of employee

Where an employer makes a payment to or for the benefit of an employee in respect of the employee's USC, the amount of the relevant emoluments which the employer pays to or on behalf of the employee shall be deemed for the purposes of deduction and repayment of USC under these Regulations to be such an amount as will include the amount assessable on the employee in respect of the payment made by the employer in respect of the employee's USC.

24. Repayment during sickness and unemployment

(1) If, owing to the absence from work through sickness or other similar cause, the employee is entitled to receive no relevant emoluments on the usual pay day, the employer shall, on application being made in person by the employee or his or her authorised representative, make such repayment of USC to the employee, as may be appropriate, having regard to his or her cumulative relevant emoluments at the date of the pay day concerned and the correspond ing cumulative USC.

(2) If, owing to absence from work otherwise than as referred to in paragraph (1), the employee is entitled to receive no relevant emoluments on the usual pay day, the employer—

(a) shall make any such repayment of USC to the employee as would be appropriate under paragraph (1) if the absence from work was due to sickness, or

(b) not later than the first usual pay day on which no relevant emoluments will be payable to the employee, shall send to the Revenue Commissioners a notification of the employee's absence from work and of the employer's intention to make no repayment to the employee under subparagraph *(a)* together with a return containing the same particulars with respect to the employee as the employer would enter on a cessation certificate if the employment had ceased on the day on which relevant emoluments were last paid to or on behalf of the employee.

(3) Where the notification and return referred to in subparagraph *(b)* of paragraph (2) are sent within the period specified in that subparagraph, the employer shall be relieved of the liability to make any repayment under subparagraph *(a)* of that paragraph.

(4) The employer shall immediately notify the Revenue Commissioners when the employee returns to work and, for the purpose of deducting or repaying USC on the occasion of any subsequent payment of relevant emoluments to or on behalf of the employee during the USC year, shall take into account the amount of any repayment which has been made under paragraph (5) of which he or she is notified by the Revenue Commissioners.

(5) (a) The Revenue Commissioners shall make any repayment that may be appropriate at any date to a person who has ceased to be employed or with respect to whom a notification and return have been sent under paragraph (2)*(b)* and for this purpose shall have regard to the person's cumulative relevant emoluments at that date and the corresponding cumulative USC.

(b) On applying for a repayment to be made under subparagraph *(a)*, a person who has ceased to be employed shall provide the Revenue Commissioners with the copies of the cessation certificate referred to in Regulation 19(2) and such evidence of his or her unemployment as the Revenue Commissioners may require.

25. Particulars of USC deducted

(1) Within 46 days from the end of a USC year an employer shall give to every employee who is in the employer's employment on the last day of the USC year a certificate showing, in respect of that year—

(a) the total amount of the relevant emoluments paid by the employer to or on behalf of the employee during that USC year,

(b) the employee's rate cut-off points where a certificate of rate cut-off points is held, and

(c) the total USC deducted (that may be nil) from those relevant emoluments.

(2) (a) In the case of an employee taken into employment after the start of the USC year, the certificate referred to in paragraph (1) shall include any relevant emoluments paid to the employee by any previous employer during that USC year and any USC deducted from those relevant emoluments.

(b) The relevant emoluments and USC deducted referred to in subparagraph (*a*) are those that the employer giving the certificate was required to take into account for the purposes of deducting or repaying USC in the case of the relevant emoluments paid by that employer.

Amendments

1 Substituted by S.I. No. 614 s of 2014. Comes into operation on 01 January 2015.

2 Substituted by S.I. No. 614 s of 2014. Comes into operation on 01 January 2015.

PART 4

Payment and Recovery of USC

26. Payment of USC by employer

(1) An employer shall remit to the Collector-General by the return filing date the amount given by the formula—

$$A + B - C$$

where,

A is all amounts of USC that the employer is liable under these Regulations to deduct from relevant emoluments paid by the employer during the relevant month,

B is any amount of USC that was not so deducted but which the employer was liable to remit in respect of that month to the Collector-General in respect of notional payments made by the employer in accordance with Regulation 14, and

C is any amounts that the employer was liable under these Regulations to repay during that month.

(2) Where a remittance made by electronic means referred to in subparagraph (*b*) of the definition of "return filing date" in Regulation 2(1) is not made within 23 days from the end of the relevant month, the period referred to in subparagraph (*a*) of that definition shall apply and have effect for the purposes of this Regulation.

(3) (a) Where, under Regulation 29 of the PAYE Regulations, the Collector-General has authorised an employer to remit to the Collector-General, within 14 days or 23 days, as the case may be, from the end of a longer period than an income tax month (within the meaning of those Regulations), the employer shall also be authorised to remit the amounts given by the formula in paragraph (1) within 14 days or 23 days of the same longer period and this paragraph and paragraphs (4) to (8) shall apply in relation to such an authorisation.

(b) For so long as the authorisation referred to in subparagraph (*a*) remains in force, the schedule of amounts of money referred to in subparagraph (*b*) of paragraph (3) of Regulation 29 of the PAYE Regulations shall also include the employer's best estimate of his or her USC liability and the conditions referred to in the said subparagraph (*b*) shall, with any necessary modifications, apply to USC as they apply to income tax.

(c) Anything done under or in accordance with Regulation 29 of the PAYE Regulations in relation to income tax shall apply equally for the purposes of USC to which this Regulation applies.

(4) If the amount that the employer is liable to remit to the Collector-General under paragraph (1) exceeds the amount of the total USC deducted in respect of relevant emoluments paid by the employer during the relevant month, a Revenue officer—

(a) on being satisfied that the employer took reasonable care to comply with these Regulations and Part 18D of the Act and that the under-deduction was due to an error made in good faith, or

(b) where he or she is of the opinion that an employee has received his or her relevant emoluments knowing that the employer has willfully failed to either deduct from those emoluments or to remit in respect of those emoluments an amount of USC that the employer was liable to deduct or to remit in accordance with these Regulations,

may direct that the amount of the excess shall be recovered from the employee, and where he or she so directs, the employer shall not be liable to remit the amount of the excess to the Collector-General.

(5) If a difference arises between the employer and the employee as to—

(a) whether the employer has deducted USC, or in respect of Regulation 23 is deemed to have deducted USC, from relevant emoluments paid to or on behalf of the employee, or

(b) the amount of USC that has been so deducted or is so deemed to have been deducted,

the matter shall, for the purposes of ascertaining the amount of any USC to be recovered from the employee under paragraph (4), be determined by the Appeal Commissioners and such a determination may be made by one Appeal Commissioner.

(6) (a) If the total of the amounts that the employer was liable to repay during any month in a USC year exceeds the total of the amounts that the employer was liable to deduct during that month, the employer shall be entitled to deduct the excess from any amount that he or she is subsequently liable to remit to the Collector-General under paragraph (1).

(b) The excess referred to in subparagraph (*a*) may only be deducted from any amount that the employer is liable to remit to the Collector-General on or before the return filing date for the last month of that USC year and any part of that excess that is not so deducted may be recovered, on application, from the Revenue Commissioners.

(7) (a) On payment of USC, the Collector-General may send to the employer concerned a receipt in respect of the payment.

(b) The receipt referred to in subparagraph (*a*) may consist of—

(i) a separate receipt in respect of each such payment, or

(ii) a receipt for all such payments made within the period specified in the receipt.

27. Employer failing to pay USC

(1) (a) If, on or before the return filing date, or within such longer period as may be authorised under Regulation 26(3), as the case may be—

(i) the employer has remitted no amount of USC to the Collector-General under Regulation 26 for that month or longer authorised period, and

(ii) the Collector-General is unaware of the amount, if any, that the employer is liable to remit,

the Collector-General may give notice to the employer requiring him or her to send to the Collector-General, within the period specified in the notice, a return showing the name of every employee to whom or on behalf of whom he or she made any payment of relevant emoluments or repayment of USC in the period from the preceding 1 January to the date specified by the notice, and the employer shall comply with the requirements of the notice.

(b) The following particulars shall also be included in the return referred to in subparagraph (*a*) in respect of each employee—

(i) the rate cut-off points, where a certificate of rate cut-off points is held,

(ii) the payments of relevant emoluments made to or on behalf of the employee during that period, and

(iii) any other matter affecting the calculation of USC that the employer was liable under these Regulations to deduct or to repay during that period.

(2) In a case referred to in paragraph (1) the Collector-General shall ascertain, in like manner as the employer should, under these Regulations, have ascertained, the amount of USC that the employer should have deducted from the relevant emoluments, and shall notify the amount to the employer.

(3) A notice given by the Collector-General under paragraph (1) may extend to 2 or more consecutive months or 2 or more longer authorised periods, as the case may be.

(4) A notice may be given by the Collector-General under paragraph (1) notwithstanding that an amount of USC has been remitted to the Collector-General by the employer under Regulation 26 for any month or longer authorised period if the Collector-General is not satisfied that the amount so remitted is the full amount that the employer is liable to remit for that month or longer authorised period.

28. Return by employer at end of USC year

(1) Within 46 days from the end of a USC year, or from the date the employer ceases permanently to be an employer to whom Regulation 7(1) of the PAYE Regulations applies, whichever is the earlier, the employer shall send to the Collector-General—

(a) a return, in a form approved by the Revenue Commissioners, in respect of each employee to whom payment of relevant emoluments was made during that USC year showing—

(i) the total relevant emoluments paid to the employee in the USC year,

(ii) the total amount of USC payable as respects the employee in the USC year, and

(iii) the dates of commencement and cessation within the USC year of the employment of the employee, where applicable,

and

(b) a statement, declaration and certificate in a form approved by the Revenue Commissioners, showing the total amount of USC that the employer was liable to remit in respect of every employee to whom payment of relevant emoluments was made in the USC year.

(2) Where the employer is a body corporate, the statement, declaration and certificate referred to in paragraph (1)(*b*) shall be signed either by the secretary or by a director of the body corporate.

29. Death of employer

If an employer dies, anything that the employer would have been liable to do under these Regulations shall be done by the employer's personal rep resentative, or, in the case of an employer who paid relevant emoluments on behalf of another person, by the person succeeding the employer or, if there is no such person, the person on whose behalf the employer paid relevant emoluments.

30. Succession to a business, etc.

(1) This Regulation applies where there has been a change in the employer from whom an employee receives relevant emoluments in respect of his or her employment in any trade, business, concern or undertaking, or in connection with any property, or from whom an employee receives any annuity or pension.

(2) Where this Regulation applies, the change shall not be treated as a cessation of employment for the purposes of Regulation 19, but, in relation to any matter arising after the change, the employer after the change shall be liable to do anything that the employer before the change would have been liable to do under these Regulations if the change had not taken place.

(3) The employer after the change shall not be liable for the payment of any USC that was deductible from relevant emoluments paid to the employee before the change took place.

PART 5

Assessment

31. Assessment of relevant emoluments

(1) Nothing in these Regulations shall prevent an assessment to USC being made on a person in respect of his or her relevant emoluments for any USC year.

(2) Any assessment to USC on an employee in respect of relevant emoluments may be made by any Revenue officer and shall be valid notwithstanding that the employee is not in the State during the USC year in which the assessment to USC is made.

(3) All the relevant emoluments of an employee may be included in one assessment.

32. Return of certain relevant emoluments by employer

A Revenue officer may give notice to an employer requiring the employer to send a return of any relevant emoluments paid by that employer to or on behalf of any employee for any USC year, being relevant emoluments that are not paid to or on behalf of the employee until after the end of that USC year, and any such return shall be sent to that Revenue officer within the period specified in the notice.

33. End of year review and notification of liability

The Revenue Commissioners may, in any case where they do not propose to make an assessment to USC on an employee, send, as soon as possible after the end of the USC year, a statement of his or her liability for that year showing how it is proposed to deal with any overpayment or underpayment of USC.

34. Objections and appeals against assessments

Part 40 of the Act shall, with any necessary modifications, apply in relation to an appeal by an employee against an assessment of relevant emoluments.

35. Recovery of underpayments

(1) If USC payable under an assessment to USC exceeds the total USC deducted from an employee's relevant emoluments during a USC year, a Revenue officer, instead of taking the excess into account in determining—

(a) the appropriate rate cut-off points for a subsequent USC year,

(b) the amount of tax credits (within the meaning of the PAYE Regulations) for a subsequent USC year in accordance with section 531AY(4) of the Act, or

(c) the standard rate cut-off point (within the meaning of the PAYE Regulations) for a subsequent USC year in accordance with section 531AY(4) of the Act,

may require the employee to remit the excess to the Collector-General, and, where the Revenue officer so requires, the employee shall remit the excess accordingly on demand made by the Collector-General.

(2) For the purposes of determining the amount of any such excess, any necessary adjustment shall be made to the total USC in respect of any USC overpaid or remaining unpaid for any USC year.

(3) Any USC that is to be remitted to the Collector-General under paragraph (1) shall be remitted within 14 days of the date on which the Collector-General first makes application for payment of that USC.

(4) Any USC that is to be remitted to the Collector-General by any employee may be recovered in the manner provided by Part 42 of the Act.

Given under my hand,
16 December 2011.

MICHAEL O'GRADY,
Revenue Commissioner.

EXPLANATORY NOTE

(This note is not part of the Instrument and does not purport to be a legal interpretation)

These Regulations, which come into force on 1 January 2012, prescribe the manner in which universal social charge (USC) is to be deducted from salaries and wages and accounted for to the Revenue Commissioners under the "Pay As You Earn" (PAYE) system.

Part 1 contains definitions of several terms used in the Regulations. It also covers the instance where an employee works under the management of a person who is not his or her immediate employer. In such circumstances the person under whose management the employee works is deemed to be his or her employer. It allows responsibilities and functions of the Revenue Commissioners to be carried out by Revenue officers acting under their direction. It also allows for the same documents to be used for both income tax and USC purposes.

Part 2 requires the Revenue Commissioners to determine the rate cut-off points appropriate to an employee for a particular year of assessment and to make this determination available to the employee. The Revenue Commissioners are also required to furnish the employer of that employee with a certificate of those rate cut-off points. Determinations and certificates of rate cut-off points for any particular year of assessment will have effect for each subsequent year for which an employee's personal circumstances and USC rates and bands remain unchanged. There is provision for appealing a determination where an employee is aggrieved by the determination.

Part 3 concerns the deduction and repayment of USC under the PAYE system. There are special rules in relation to certain non-monetary benefits received by an employee. For the most part, deductions and repayments are to be made by reference to the cumulative emoluments paid to an employee and the cumulative rate cut-off points as specified on the certificate of rate cut-off points. There are provisions regarding changes of employment and for deduction of tax on an emergency basis where the employer does not hold a certificate of rate cut-off points. At the end of each year of assessment, employers are required to give every employee a certificate showing particulars of emoluments paid and USC deducted during that year.

Part 4 deals with payment and recovery of USC deducted under the PAYE system. Employers are required within 14 days from the end of every month to pay over to the Collector-General all USC that they were liable to deduct, less any USC that they were liable to repay, during the month. The Collector-General may authorise an employer to make remittances of USC at longer intervals (not exceeding one year) than the normal monthly basis. The Collector-General may also terminate such authorisation. Within 46 days from the end of a year of assessment, employers are to send to the Collector-General a return, in the appropriate form, showing total emoluments paid to the employee during the year and total net USC deducted.

Part 5 provides for the making of assessments on employees where insufficient USC has been deducted and, where assessments are not made, for supplying employees with statements of their liability. Underpayments of USC may also be recovered by adjusting rate cut-off points and income tax credits for subsequent years.

S.I. No. 156 of 2012

TAX RETURNS AND PAYMENTS (MANDATORY ELECTRONIC FILING AND PAYMENT OF TAX) REGULATIONS 2012

ARRANGEMENT OF REGULATIONS

The Revenue Commissioners in exercise of the powers conferred on them by section 917EA (inserted by section 164 of the Finance Act 2003 (No. 3 of 2003)) of the Taxes Consolidation Act 1997 (No. 39 of 1997) make the following regulations:

1. Citation and commencement

(1) These Regulations may be cited as the Tax Returns and Payments (Mandatory Electronic Filing and Payment of Tax) Regulations 2012.

(2) These Regulations come into operation on 1 June 2012.

2. Interpretation and general

(1) In these Regulations—

"capacity" means sufficient access to the Internet by which either or both a specified return or the payment of any specified liabilities may be made by electronic means and, in the case of an individual, also means not prevented by reason of age or mental or physical infirmity from either or both making a specified return or paying any specified liabilities by electronic means;

"Commissioners" means the Revenue Commissioners;

"Principal Act" means the Taxes Consolidation Act 1997 (No. 39 of 1997);

"Regulations of 2011" means the Tax Returns and Payments (Mandatory Electronic Filing and Payment of Tax) Regulations 2011 (S.I. No. 223 of 2011);

"return" has the same meaning as it has in section 917D of the Principal Act;

"tax year" means a year of assessment.

(2) (a) Any return which a person is or may be required by the Acts to make to the Commissioners and which is specified for the purposes of Chapter 6 of Part 38 of the Principal Act by order made by the Commissioners under section 917E of that Act is specified as a specified return.

(b) Any liabilities to tax, including interest on unpaid tax, arising under any provision of the Acts, the payment of which is or will be accounted for, directly or indirectly, in a specified return, including any payment which is treated under the Acts as a payment on foot of, or on account of, any liabilities to tax, are specified as specified liabilities.

(c) Each person to whom these Regulations relate, other than the Commissioners, an officer of the Commissioners or the Appeal Commissioners, is specified as a specified person for the purposes of paragraphs (a) and (b) of subsection (3) of section 917EA of the PrincipalAct and these Regulations.

3. Persons in receipt of certain income or claiming certain reliefs required to make returns and payments by electronic means

(1) Where any specified person, other than a specified person to whom the Regulations of 2011 apply, is required to make a specified return in accordance with section 951 of the Principal Act for the tax year 2010 or any subsequent tax year, being a specified return which includes either or both—

(a) income, profits or gains to which any provision of the Principal Act referred to in Schedule 1 applies, and

(b) a claim to any deduction or relief under any provision of the Principal Act referred to in Schedule 2,

that specified person shall, on and from—

(i) 1 June 2012, or

(ii) such later date by which that specified return is required to be made,

make any specified return that is required to be made by or subsequent to that date, by or on behalf of that specified person, by electronic means and in accordance with Chapter 6 of Part 38 of the Principal Act.

(2) Where, on or after the date from which paragraph (1) applies to a specified person, a payment of any specified liabilities falls due to be made by or on behalf of the specified person, the payment shall be made by such electronic means as are required by the Commissioners.

4. Persons registered for VAT required to make returns and payments by electronic means

(1) Where any specified person, other than a specified person to whom the Regulations of 2011 apply—

(a) is an accountable person for the purposes of section 65 of the Value Added Tax Consolidation Act 2010 (No. 31 of 2010) on 1 June 2012, or

(b) becomes an accountable person for those purposes on any date subsequent to 1 June 2012,

that specified person shall, on and from—

(i) where subparagraph (a) applies, 1 June 2012, or

(ii) where subparagraph (b) applies, the date the specified person becomes an accountable person,

make any specified return that is required to be made by or subsequent to that date, by or on behalf of that specified person, by electronic means and in accordance with Chapter 6 of Part 38 of the Principal Act.

(2) Where, on or after the date from which paragraph (1) applies to a specified person, a payment of any specified liabilities falls due to be made by or on behalf of the specified person, the payment shall be made by such electronic means as are required by the Commissioners.

5. Exclusion of certain specified persons

(1) A specified person may, by notifying the Commissioners in writing, request to be excluded from the provisions of these Regulations on the grounds that the specified person does not have the capacity to make a specified return or pay the specified tax liabilities by electronic means and the notification shall include all information relevant to the consideration by the Commissioners of the request.

(2) Where the Commissioners receive a notification from a specified person in accordance with paragraph (1) or where the Commissioners otherwise consider it appropriate, they may exclude the specified person from the provisions of these Regulations only if they are satisfied that, in all of the circumstances, the specified person could not reasonably be expected to have the capacity to make a specified return or to make a payment of specified tax liabilities by electronic means.

(3) A decision to exclude a specified person from the provisions of these Regulations by the Commissioners in accordance with paragraph (2) may be made at any time but where a notification has been received from a specified person in accordance with paragraph (1) the decision shall be made within 30 days of receipt of the notification, and the Commissioners shall, in all cases, notify the specified person in writing of the decision.

6. Right of appeal to Appeal Commissioners

(1) A specified person aggrieved by a failure of the Commissioners to exclude the specified person from the provisions of these Regulations in accordance with Regulation 5(2) may, by notice in writing to the Commissioners before the end of the period of 30 days beginning with the day on which notice of the decision was given to the specified person, apply to have such specified person's request to be excluded from the provisions of these Regulations heard and determined by the Appeal Commissioners.

(2) On the hearing of an appeal under this Regulation, the Appeal Commissioners shall have regard only to those matters to which the Commissioners may or are required to have regard under these Regulations.

7. Provision to amend exclusions

(1) If, at any time after a decision by the Commissioners in accordance with Regulation 5(2) or a determination by the Appeal Commissioners in accordance with Regulation 6(2) to exclude a specified person from the provisions of these Regulations, the Commissioners decide that, due to a material change in all of the circumstances, the specified person should not be so excluded, they shall notify the specified person in writing of that decision.

(2) The decision referred to in paragraph (1) shall be deemed to be a failure to exclude the specified person from the provisions of these Regulations and Regulation 6 shall apply accordingly.

8. Time at which payments made by electronic means are taken to be made

For the purpose of these Regulations, the time at which a payment of any specified liabilities by or on behalf of a specified person shall be taken as having been made shall be the later of the due date for that payment and the time at which the Commissioners receive authorisation to debit the amount of the payment from the account of the specified person in a financial institution.

9. Presumptions

For the purposes of any dispute arising as to the time at which a payment of any specified liabilities to which these Regulations apply is to be taken as having been made, a certificate signed by an officer of the Commissioners which certifies that he or she has examined the relevant records and that it appears from them that the time at which the payment is to be taken as having been made, is the time so specified in the certificate, shall be evidence until the contrary is proven that the payment was made at the time so certified.

SCHEDULE 1

Regulation 3

Provisions of the Principal Act Which Relate to Certain Income, Profits or Gains in a Specified Return for the Purposes of Regulation 3

Section 140

Section 141

Section 195

Section 232

Section 234

SCHEDULE 2

Regulation 3

Certain Deductions or Reliefs Which May Be Claimed in a Specified Return for the Purposes of Regulation 3

1. Any deduction to which the individual is entitled under the following provisions of the Principal Act:
   (a) section 248;
   (b) section 250;
   (c) section 253;
   (d) section 480A;
   (e) section 481;
   (f) section 489;
   (g) section 493;
   (h) section 774;
   (i) section 776;
   (j) section 787;
   (k) section 787C;
   (l) section 787N.

2. Any relief to which the individual is entitled under the following provisions of the Principal Act:
   (a) section 482;
   (b) section 825A.

GIVEN under my hand,
18 May 2012.

NIALL CODY,
Revenue Commissioner.

EXPLANATORY NOTE

(This note is not part of the Instrument and does not purport to be a legal interpretation).

Tax Returns and Payments (Mandatory Electronic Filing and Payment of Tax) Regulations 2012

These Regulations are made by the Revenue Commissioners under the provisions of section 917EA of the Taxes Consolidation Act 1997. This section was inserted by section 164 of the Finance Act 2003 and was made subject to a commencement order by the Minister for Finance. This order was signed on 28 July 2008.

The Regulations underpin Phase 4 of Revenue's programme to establish the use of electronic channels as the normal way of conducting tax business by providing for the mandatory electronic filing of certain tax returns and payment of tax liabilities by certain categories of taxpayers.

With effect from 1 June 2012 the following categories of taxpayers are obliged to file their returns electronically (if they are not already obliged to do so):

- Self-assessed individuals claiming certain income exemptions (Artists Exemption, Woodlands Exemption, Patent Income Exemption).
- Self-assessed individuals claiming certain retirement related reliefs: (relief for Retirement Annuity Contract payments, relief for PRSA contributions, relief in relation to Overseas Pension Plans (migrant member relief), Retirement Relief for Sportspersons, relief for Superannuation Contributions/Additional Voluntary Contributions).
- Self-assessed individuals claiming certain other income tax reliefs (BES relief, Employment and Investment Incentive relief, Seed Capital relief, Film relief, Interest relief on loans applied in acquiring an interest or share in certain companies or partnerships, Transborder relief, Significant Buildings/Gardens relief).
- All taxpayers who are registered for VAT.

In all cases, the payment of any tax and duty liabilities and the filing of any returns, which arise after the obligation to electronically file commences, must be made electronically and must continue for all subsequent returns and payments.

The Revenue Commissioners may, on application, exclude a taxpayer from the obligation to pay and file electronically if they are satisfied that the taxpayer does not have the capacity to do so and in this context "capacity" is taken to mean sufficient access to the Internet and in the case of an individual is not prevented by reason of age, physical or mental infirmity from filing and paying electronically. A taxpayer aggrieved at a failure by the Revenue Commissioners to exclude them from the requirements may appeal that failure to the Appeal Commissioners. An excluded taxpayer may, if circumstances change, have that exclusion revoked and that decision may also be appealed to the Appeal Commissioners.

Provision is also made to determine the time at which payments made by electronic means are to be taken as having been made.

S.I. No. 324 of 2012

RETURNS OF PAYMENT TRANSACTIONS BY PAYMENT SETTLERS (MERCHANT ACQUIRERS) REGULATIONS 2012

The Revenue Commissioners, in exercise of the powers conferred on them by section 891D (inserted by section 122 of the Finance Act 2012 (No. 9 of 2012)) of the Taxes Consolidation Act 1997 (No. 39 of 1997), hereby make the following regulations:

1. Citation

These Regulations may be cited as the Returns of Payment Transactions by Payment Settlers (Merchant Acquirers) Regulations 2012.

2. Definitions

In these Regulations–

"Commissioners" means the Revenue Commissioners;

"fees" include all fees, costs and charges charged to a merchant in relation to payment card transactions;

"return" means a return made electronically–

(a) using such technology as may be approved or provided by the Commissioners, and

(b) in such form or format as may be required by the Commissioners;

"terminal" means any electronic device used by a merchant that initiates a point of interaction whereby payment card details can be submitted to the merchant acquirer and any other device to like effect.

3. Returns of payments

(1) Subject to these Regulations, every merchant acquirer who makes a payment to a merchant in settlement of payment card transactions in the year 2010 or a subsequent year, shall make and deliver to the Commissioners, within the time specified in Regulation 4, a return of all such payment card transactions, or the aggregate of the payment card transactions, in the year concerned by the merchant acquirer.

(2) The return referred to in paragraph (1) shall include, as respects–

(a) the merchant acquirer, the details set out in paragraph (3),

(b) each merchant to whom the merchant acquirer makes a payment to which paragraph (1) relates, the details set out in paragraph (4), and

(c) the amount of the payment card transaction, or the aggregate of the payment card transactions, made by the merchant acquirer to the merchant, the details of which are set out in paragraph (5) or (6).

(3) The details relating to the merchant acquirer to be provided by him or her are as follows:

(a) name;

(b) address;

(c) tax reference number.

4. The details relating to the merchant to be provided by the merchant acquirer are as follows:

(a) the reference number used by the merchant acquirer to identify the merchant;

(b) name;

(c) address;

(d) any trading name used in dealings with the merchant acquirer,

(e) any email address and website used in connection with dealings between the merchant and the merchant acquirer;

(f) name of any duly designated contact person and telephone number used in connection with dealings between the merchant and the merchant acquirer;

(g) the unique reference code assigned to the merchant by the merchant acquirer to identify the principal nature of the merchant's business;

(h) whether or not online or internet trading has occurred during the calendar year concerned that relates to the contractual obligation of the merchant acquirer to make payments to the merchant;

(i) where payment card transactions with the merchant acquirer first commenced after 1 January 2010, the date from which such transactions so commenced;

(j) where payment card transactions with the merchant acquirer ceased on or after 1 January 2010, the date from which payment card transactions so ceased;

(k) the number of terminals provided to the merchant by the merchant acquirer which are subject to a rental or lease agreement on the last day of the year to which the return relates;

(l) the bank account number of the merchant and national sort code relating to that bank account to and from which funds are transferred by the merchant acquirer;

(m) the number to which Regulation 5(1) relates.

5. Subject to paragraph (6), the details required for each payment card transaction are–

(a) the amount, and

(b) the fees associated with the transaction.

(6) Subject to paragraph (7), a merchant acquirer may provide the following information, broken down on a monthly basis, in place of that required in paragraph (5)–

(a) the aggregate monetary amount, net of refunds, attributable to payment card transactions before deducting any fees,

(b) the fees which relate to the amount referred to in paragraph (*a*), and

(c) the aggregate monetary amount of refunds attributable to payment card transactions before deducting any fees.

(7) Where the information included in a return is made in accordance with paragraph (6), an authorised officer may at any time thereafter serve a notice on the merchant acquirer requiring the submission of a further return within 14

days from the date of the notice, in respect of a merchant specified in the notice, setting out the details specified in paragraph (5) by reference to the period of the return, or a shorter period or periods.

(8) Where a reportable payment transaction is made in a currency other than the euro, the payment shall be stated as the euro amount for which it might reasonably be exchanged by persons dealing at arm's length.

4. Time by which returns are to be made

Returns under these Regulations shall be made—

(a) in relation to returns for the years 2010, 2011 and 2012, not later than 30 April 2013, and

(b) in relation to any year subsequent to the year 2012, not later than 30 April following the end of the year concerned.

5. Obligation to seek and provide tax reference numbers, etc.

(1) With effect on and after the making of these Regulations and for the purposes of a merchant acquirer making a return under these Regulations to the Commissioners, the merchant acquirer shall, from each merchant with whom the merchant acquirer has a contractual obligation to make payments in settlement of payment card transactions, request details of–

(a) the tax reference number of the merchant, or

(b) where the merchant is a charity, the reference number assigned to the payee by the Commissioners and known as the charity (CHY) number,

and each such merchant shall provide to the merchant acquirer the relevant number for that purpose.

(2) A request under paragraph (1) shall be made as soon as practicable after the making of these Regulations.

Given under my hand,
20 August 2012.

LIAM IRWIN,
Revenue Commissioner.

EXPLANATORY NOTE

(This note is not part of the Instrument and does not purport to be a legal interpretation)

These Regulations require merchant acquirers (financial institutions that process debit and credit card transactions) to make returns of information to the Revenue Commissioners.

Returns are required for all years from 2010 and the information to be included in the returns relates to the value of debit and credit card transactions processed on behalf of merchants.

S.I. No. 576 of 2012

INCOME TAX AND CORPORATION TAX (RELEVANT CONTRACTS TAX) REGULATIONS 2012

ARRANGEMENT OF REGULATIONS

PART 1

GENERAL

PART 2

REGISTRATION

PART 3

NOTIFICATIONS TO REVENUE

PART 4

DEDUCTION AUTHORISATIONS AND DEDUCTION SUMMARIES

PART 5

RETURNS AND ADJUSTMENT TO LIABILITY

PART 6

MISCELLANEOUS

The Revenue Commissioners, in exercise of the powers conferred on them by sections 530B, 530C, 530D, 530F, 530J, 530K, 530M, 530R and 530S (all inserted by section 20 of the Finance Act 2011 (No. 6 of 2011)) of the Taxes Consolidation Act 1997 (No. 39 of 1997), hereby make the following regulations:

PART 1

General

1. Citation

1. These Regulations may be cited as the Income Tax and Corporation Tax (Relevant Contracts Tax) Regulations 2012.

2. Interpretation

(1) In these Regulations—

"Act" means Taxes Consolidation Act 1997 (No. 39 of 1997);

"deduction summary" has the meaning assigned to it by section 530(1) of the Act;

"payment notification" means a notification by a principal under section 530C(1) of the Act of a principal's intention to make a relevant payment;

"PPS number", in relation to an individual, means that individual's personal public service number within the meaning of section 262 of the Social Welfare Consolidation Act 2005 (No. 26 of 2005);

"principal" has the meaning assigned to it by section 530(1) of the Act;

"RCT service" means the electronic system made available by the Revenue Commissioners to allow principals to fulfil their obligations under sections 530A to 530V of the Act and under any Regulations made thereunder, and to allow for electronic communication between the Revenue Commissioners, principals, subcontractors and others pursuant to those obligations and includes any enhancements or other changes made to that system and any replacement system;

"Regulations of 2011" mean Income Tax and Corporation Tax (Relevant Contracts Tax) Regulations 2011 (S.I. No. 651 of 2011);

"relevant contract" has the meaning assigned to it by section 530(1) of the Act;

"relevant operations" has the meaning assigned to it by section 530(1) of the Act;

"relevant payment" has the meaning assigned to it by section 530(1) of the Act;

"return period" has the meaning assigned to it by section 530(1) of the Act;

"Revenue officer" has the meaning assigned to it by section 530(1) of the Act;

"subcontractor" has the meaning assigned to it by section 530(1) of the Act;

"tax reference number" means—

(a) in the case of an individual, that individual's PPS number or his or her registration number for the purposes of value-added tax, or

(b) in the case of a company, the reference number stated on any return of profits form or notice of assessment issued to that company by the Revenue Commissioners, or the registration number of the company for the purposes of value-added tax.

"technology systems failure" has the meaning assigned to it by section 530(1) of the Act.
["unreported payment notification" has the meaning assigned to it by section 530(1) of the Act.][1]

Amendments

[1] Inserted by S.I. No. 5 s of 2015.

PART 2

Registration

3. Register of principals

(1) Each principal required to register under section 530J(2) of the Act shall do so before providing the information and declaration required under section 530B(1) of the Act and Regulation 4.

(2) For the purposes of paragraph (1), each principal shall provide the Revenue Commissioners with all particulars required by the Revenue Commissioners for the purposes of registering the person as a principal.

(3) A person who ceases to be a principal to whom section 530A of the Act applies shall notify the Revenue Commissioners of such cessation by written or electronic means and shall specify the date of the cessation in the notification.

(4) Where, in the opinion of a Revenue officer, a person has ceased to be a principal to whom section 530A of the Act applies, the Revenue officer shall, by written or electronic means, notify that person of the intention to cancel that person's registration as a principal and such cancellation shall be effected as on and from 21 days from the date of the notification, unless, within that period, the person satisfies the Revenue officer that he or she is still a principal.

(5) Where—

(a) a person has made a notification under paragraph (3), or

(b) a person's registration under section 530J of the Act has been cancelled under paragraph (4),

requirements in relation to any future registration under section 530J shall apply as if that person had never previously been registered as a principal.

PART 3

Notifications to Revenue

4. Contract notification and declaration by principal

(1) The information and declaration required to be provided by a principal to the Revenue Commissioners under section 530B(1) of the Act shall be provided using the appropriate portal of the RCT service.

(2) Where the Revenue Commissioners are unable to verify the identity of a subcontractor by reference to the name and tax reference number supplied by a principal, the RCT service shall require the principal to inform the subcontractor

in writing within 7 days or before making a relevant payment to the subcontractor, whichever is the earlier, that—

(a) the Revenue Commissioners were unable to verify the identity of the subcontractor,

(b) tax at 35 per cent will be deducted from payments to the subcontractor, and

(c) the subcontractor should contact the Revenue Commissioners with a view to clarifying his or her identity.

(3) Where a principal does not indicate that the principal is satisfied that a contract is not a labour only contract, the principal shall provide the Revenue Commissioners with such other information, in relation to the contract, as may be required by the RCT service.

(4) On receipt of the information referred to in paragraph (1), the RCT service shall provide an acknowledgement to the principal, which communication shall be deemed to be an acknowledgement issued by the Revenue Commissioners. The acknowledgement shall include, for information purposes only, the rate of tax last notified to the subcontractor concerned under section 530I of the Act. This rate shall not be taken as the rate of RCT applicable to payments to be made under the contract concerned.

(5) Where the information referred to in section 530B(1)(a) of the Act changes in relation to—

(a) the estimated contract value,

(b) the contract duration, or

(c) the location or locations at which relevant operations under the contract are to take place,

the principal shall, using the appropriate portal of the RCT service, notify the Revenue Commissioners of each such change to the contract.

(6) Where a principal notifies the Revenue Commissioners of a contract under section 530B(1) of the Act and the Revenue Commissioners are satisfied as to the identity of the subcontractor, the Revenue Commissioners shall, by electronic or other means, notify the subcontractor of the details of the contract as supplied by the principal. The notification shall include the rate of tax notified to the principal under paragraph (4).

(7) Where a principal notifies the Revenue Commissioners under paragraph (5), the Revenue Commissioners shall, by electronic or other means, notify the subcontractor in relation to any changes referred to in that paragraph.

5. Notification of relevant payment by principal

(1) A payment notification shall be made to the Revenue Commissioners using the appropriate portal of the RCT service.

(2) For the purposes of paragraph (1) and subject to paragraph (3), details of the following matters shall be included in a payment notification:

(a) the identity of the subcontractor, including name and tax reference number;

(b) identification of the contract to which the payment relates;

(c) such other information as may be required by the RCT service.

[(3) Where a principal has entered into more than one relevant contract with a subcontractor, the principal shall associate the payment notification with any current contract for the subcontractor, or the principal may—

(a) where the payment to be made is in respect of a single contract, in giving a payment notification, identify the contract in respect of which the payment will be made, or

(b) where the payment to be made is in respect of more than one contract with that subcontractor, give separate payment notifications each identifying only that part of the payment that refers to the related contract.][1]

(4) Where a principal anticipates that a relevant payment is not going to be made before the end of the return period in which the payment notification is given, the principal shall, before the end of the return period, cancel the payment notification using the appropriate portal of the RCT service, and the payment notification concerned shall be deemed not to have been given.

(5) Where a principal cancels a payment notification under paragraph (4), and where tax was due to be deducted from the payment, the Revenue Commissioners shall, by electronic or other means, notify the subcontractor of the cancellation of the payment notification by the principal.

Amendments

[1] Substituted by S.I. No. 412 of 2013.

PART 4

Deduction Authorisations and Deduction Summaries

6. Deduction authorisations

(1) For the purposes of issuing a deduction authorisation under section 530D(1) of the Act, the Revenue Commissioners shall cause the RCT service to make available a deduction authorisation to the principal concerned.

(2) A deduction authorisation shall only be valid until—

(a) the making by the principal concerned of the payment concerned,

(b) the due date relating to the return period within which the deduction authorisation was issued,

(c) the making by the principal concerned of the return for the return period within which the deduction authorisation was issued, or

(d) the cancellation of the related payment notification in accordance with Regulation 5(4),

whichever is the earliest.

(3) A deduction authorisation shall be valid only in respect of the subcontractor named on it and the relevant payment to which it relates.

(4) On accessing a deduction authorisation, the principal concerned shall examine its contents to ensure that the subcontractor named on the deduction authorisation is a party to the relevant contract to which it relates.

(5) The Revenue Commissioners may, by electronic or other means, make available to a subcontractor details of the information contained in deduction authorisations relating to that subcontractor.

7. Deduction summaries

(1) For the purposes of section 530D(3) of the Act, the Revenue Commissioners shall, at the end of each return period, cause the RCT service to issue a deduction summary to a principal.

(2) A deduction summary in respect of a return period shall include—

(a) details in relation to all relevant payments, if any, notified by that principal, which are the subject of a valid deduction authorisation at the time of issue of the deduction summary (in these Regulations, the details on a deduction summary in relation to each such relevant payment shall be referred to as a "line item"),

(b) details of any relevant payment of which, during the return period, the principal has notified the Revenue Commissioners under section 530F(7) of the Act,

(c) details of any relevant payment to which Regulation 8(5) relates,

(d) the aggregate amount of tax that is, based on the details in the deduction summary, payable by the principal in respect of the return period, and

(e) information on how to accept, amend or supplement the information in the deduction summary for the purpose of making a return referred to in Regulation 8.

PART 5

Returns and Adjustment to Liability

8. Returns

(1) A return required under section 530K(1) of the Act and a return referred to in sections 530M(1) and 530N(7)(a) of the Act shall only be made using the RCT service.

(2) Where a deduction summary is issued to a principal under section 530D(3) of the Act and the details on that deduction summary do not accurately reflect all relevant payments made by the principal relating to the return period concerned or the liability of the principal to tax on those payments, the principal shall ensure that all relevant payments relating to the return period and the associated tax liability are accurately reflected on the return required under section 530K(1) of the Act, and paragraphs (3) to (9) shall apply.

(3) Subject to paragraph (4) and Regulation 5(4), where a payment notified to the Revenue Commissioners during a return period under section 530C of the Act is not made by the earlier of—

(a) the due date relating to the return period within which it was notified, and

(b) the making by the principal concerned of the return for the return period in which the payment was notified, the principal shall cancel the line item concerned and reflect the fact that the payment has not been made on the return for that return period.

(4) Where a payment is made to a subcontractor for relevant operations in respect of which a payment notification is given, and the amount of the payment differs from the amount specified in the payment notification due to exceptional circumstances unforeseen at the time of the notification, the principal shall, if the principal has deducted tax from the full amount of the payment at the rate specified on the related deduction authorisation, amend the line item concerned and declare the correct amount of the payment on the return to be made for the return period concerned.

(5) (a) Where a payment is made, in accordance with the terms of a valid deduction authorisation, in the return period following the return period during which that deduction authorisation was issued and before the making of the return by the principal in respect of the return period during which that deduction authorisation was issued, the principal shall ensure that this fact is reflected on that return.

(b) The liability of a principal relating to payment under subparagraph (a) shall be a liability of the return period following the return period in which the deduction authorisation concerned was issued.

(6) All line items on a deduction summary which are not cancelled under paragraph (3), or amended under paragraph (4), or to which paragraph (5) does not apply, shall form part of the return under section 530K(1) of the Act.

(7) A principal shall not be entitled to—

(a) cancel a line item under paragraph (3),

(b) amend a line item under paragraph (4), or

(c) take action under paragraph (5),

after the principal makes a return in respect of a relevant return period, or is deemed to have made such a return in accordance with section 530K(2) of the Act.

(8) A principal shall declare the aggregate amount of all relevant payments to which section 530F(2) of the Act applies, but excluding any payments referred to in paragraph (4), on the return for the return period during which the payments were made.

(9) Where a line item is cancelled under paragraph (3) or amended under paragraph (4), and where the relevant deduction authorisation indicated that tax was to be deducted from the relevant payment, the Revenue Commissioners shall, by electronic or other means, notify the relevant subcontractor of such cancellation or amendment.

9. Adjustment to liability

[(1) "An unreported payment notification" required to be provided by a principal to the Revenue Commissioners under Section 530F(3) of the Act shall be provided using the appropriate portal of the RCT service.

(2) For the purposes of paragraph (1) details of the following matters shall be included in an unreported payment notification:

(a) the identity of the subcontractor, including name and tax reference number;

(b) identification of the contract to which the payment relates;

(c) the amount of the relevant payment;

(d) the date the relevant payment was made;

(e) such other information as may be required by the RCT service.][1]

Amendments

[1] Substituted by S.I. No. 5 s of 2015.

PART 6

Miscellaneous

10. Partnerships, etc

(1) The details to be given to the Revenue Commissioners under section 530R(2) of the Act shall be given by using the appropriate portal of the RCT service or, where the person concerned cannot access the RCT service for reasons other than a technology systems failure, the details shall be given in writing.

(2) On receipt of details referred to in paragraph (1), the Revenue Commissioners shall cause each member of the gang, group or partnership concerned to be notified in writing or by electronic means of the amount of income tax or corporation tax treated as having been paid by him or her under section 530P.

11. Records

(1) A principal shall keep and maintain records in relation to—

(a) the information and declaration required to be provided to the Revenue Commissioners under section 530B of the Act,

(b) relevant payments which are required to be notified to the Revenue Commissioners under section 530C of the Act, including the tax deducted from each such payment,

(c) registration details required by the Revenue Commissioners under section 530J of the Act,

(d) the details included on a return made or required to be made under Chapter 2 of Part 18 of the Act,

(e) the details required to be included on a return under Chapter 2 of Part 18 of the Act, and

(f) tax due and payable under Chapter 2 of Part 18 of the Act.

(2) Records required to be kept or retained by virtue of section 530S of the Act and paragraph (1) shall—

(a) (i) be kept in written form in an official language of the State, or

(ii) subject to section 887(2) of the Act, be kept by means of any electronic, photographic or other process, and

(b) be retained by the person required to keep the records—

(i) for a period of 6 years after the completion of the transactions, acts or operations to which they relate, or

(ii) in the case of a person who fails to comply with section 530K(1) of the Act, until the expiry of a period of 6 years from the end of the return period in which the relevant return has been delivered.

(3) Where a principal, acting in accordance with any provision of Chapter 2 of Part 18 of the Act or these Regulations, creates or causes to be created any record, including records as defined in section 886 of the Act, the obligation of that principal to keep or retain that record, or cause that record to be kept or retained, shall exist notwithstanding the fact that a similar or identical record may be kept by the Revenue Commissioners.

12. Revocation

(1) The Regulations of 2011 are revoked.

(2) Notwithstanding the revocation in paragraph (1)—

(a) a payment within the meaning of Regulation 2 of the Income Tax (Relevant Contracts Tax) Regulations (S.I. No. 71 of 2000) made before 1 January 2012 shall be dealt with under those Regulations as if those Regulations had not been revoked under the Regulations of 2011, and

(b) a relevant payment made between 1 January 2012 and the date of the coming into operation of these Regulations shall be dealt with under the Regulations of 2011 as if those Regulations had not been revoked.

GIVEN under my hand,
24 December 2012.

NIALL CODY,
Revenue Commissioner.

EXPLANATORY NOTE

(This is note is not part of the Instrument and does not purport to be a legal interpretation.)

The purpose of these Regulations is to reflect changes made to the legislation governing the operation of relevant contracts tax (RCT) as provided for under section 22 of Finance Act 2012. The Regulations replace the Income Tax and Corporation Tax (Relevant Contracts Tax) Regulations 2011 (S.I. 651 of 2011). The main change from those Regulations involves enhanced engagement with subcontractors in relation to the application of RCT to contracts and payments under those contracts.

S.I. No. 33 of 2013

AGREEMENT TO IMPROVE TAX COMPLIANCE AND PROVIDE FOR REPORTING AND EXCHANGE OF INFORMATION CONCERNING TAX MATTERS (UNITED STATES OF AMERICA) ORDER 2013

WHEREAS it is enacted by *section 826(1B)* (as substituted by *section 35* of the Finance Act 2007 (No. 11 of 2007)) of the Taxes Consolidation Act 1997 (No. 39 of 1997) that where the Government by order declare that arrangements specified in the order have been made with the government of any territory outside the State in relation to exchanging information for the purposes of the prevention and detection of tax evasion in the case of taxes of any kind or description imposed by the laws of the State or by the laws of that territory, and that it is expedient that those arrangements should have the force of law, and that the order so made is specified in *Part 3* of *Schedule 24A* of the Taxes Consolidation Act 1997, then subject to *section 826* of that Act, the arrangements shall, notwithstanding any enactment, have the force of law as if such order were an Act of the Oireachtas on and from the date of the insertion of a reference to the order into *Part 3* of *Schedule 24A*;

AND WHEREAS it is further enacted by *section 826(6)* of the Taxes Consolidation Act 1997 that where such an order is proposed to be made, a draft of the order shall be laid before Dáil Éireann and the order shall not be made until a resolution approving of the draft has been passed by Dáil Éireann;

AND WHEREAS a draft of the following Order has been laid before Dáil Éireann and a resolution approving of the draft has been passed by Dáil Éireann;

NOW, the Government, in exercise of the powers conferred on them by *section 826(1B)* (as substituted by *section 35* of the Finance Act 2007) of the Taxes Consolidation Act 1997, hereby order as follows:

1. This Order may be cited as the Agreement to Improve Tax Compliance and Provide for Reporting and Exchange of Information concerning Tax Matters (United States of America) Order 2013

2. It is declared that—

   (*a*) the arrangements specified in the Agreement, the text of which is set out in the Schedule, have been made with the Government of The United States of America in relation to exchanging information for the purposes of the prevention and detection of tax evasion, and

   (*b*) it is expedient that those arrangements should have the force of law.

SCHEDULE

Agreement Between the Government of Ireland and the Government of the United States of America to Improve International Tax Compliance and to Implement FATCA

Whereas, the Government of Ireland and the Government of the United States of America (each, a "Party") have a longstanding and close relationship with respect to mutual assistance in tax matters and desire to conclude an agreement to improve international tax compliance by further building on that relationship,

Whereas, Article 27 of the Convention between the Government of Ireland and the Government of the United States of America for the Avoidance of Double Taxation and the Prevention of Fiscal Evasion with Respect to Taxes on Income and Capital Gains, signed at Dublin on July 28, 1997 ("the Convention"), authorizes exchange of information for tax purposes, including on an automatic basis,

Whereas, the United States of America enacted provisions commonly known as the Foreign Account Tax Compliance Act ("FATCA"), which introduce a reporting regime for financial institutions with respect to certain accounts,

Whereas, the Government of Ireland is supportive of the underlying policy goal of FATCA to improve tax compliance,

Whereas, FATCA has raised a number of issues, including that Irish financial institutions may not be able to comply with certain aspects of FATCA due to domestic legal impediments,

Whereas, the Government of the United States of America collects information regarding certain accounts maintained by U.S. financial institutions held by residents of Ireland and is committed to exchanging such information with the Government of Ireland and pursuing equivalent levels of exchange,

Whereas, the Parties are committed to working together over the longer term towards achieving common reporting and due diligence standards for financial institutions,

Whereas, the Government of the United States of America acknowledges the need to coordinate the reporting obligations under FATCA with other U.S. tax reporting obligations of Irish financial institutions to avoid duplicative reporting,

Whereas, an intergovernmental approach to FATCA implementation would address legal impediments and reduce burdens for Irish financial institutions,

Whereas, the Parties desire to conclude an agreement to improve international tax compliance and provide for the implementation of FATCA based on domestic reporting and reciprocal automatic exchange pursuant to the Convention and subject to the confidentiality and other protections provided for therein, including the provisions limiting the use of the information exchanged under the Convention,

Now, therefore, the Parties have agreed as follows:

Article 1
Definitions

1. For purposes of this agreement and any annexes thereto ("Agreement"), the following terms shall have the meanings set forth below:

   a) The term **"United States"** means the United States of America, including the States thereof, and, when used in a geographical sense, means the territory of the United States of America, including inland waters, the air space, the territorial sea thereof and any maritime area beyond the territorial sea within which the United States may exercise sovereign rights or jurisdiction in accordance with international law; the term, however, does not include the U.S. Territories. Any reference to a **"State"** of the United States includes the District of Columbia.

   b) The term **"U.S. Territory"** means American Samoa, the Commonwealth of the Northern Mariana Islands, Guam, the Commonwealth of Puerto Rico, or the U.S. Virgin Islands.

   c) The term **"IRS"** means the U.S. Internal Revenue Service.

   d) The term **"Ireland"** includes any area outside the territorial waters of Ireland which has been or may hereafter be designated, under the laws of Ireland concerning the Exclusive Economic Zone and the Continental Shelf, as an area within which Ireland may exercise such sovereign rights and jurisdiction as are in conformity with international law.

   e) The term **"Partner Jurisdiction"** means a jurisdiction that has in effect an agreement with the United States to facilitate the implementation of FATCA. The IRS shall publish a list identifying all Partner Jurisdictions.

   f) The term **"Competent Authority"** means:

      (1) in the case of the United States, the Secretary of the Treasury or his delegate; and

      (2) in the case of Ireland, the Revenue Commissioners or their authorised representative.

   g) The term **"Financial Institution"** means a Custodial Institution, a Depository Institution, an Investment Entity, or a Specified Insurance Company.

   h) The term **"Custodial Institution"** means any entity that holds, as a substantial portion of its business, financial assets for the account of others. An entity holds financial assets for the account of others as a substantial portion of its business if the entity's gross income attributable to the holding of financial assets and related financial services equals or exceeds 20 percent of the entity's gross income during the shorter of: (i) the three-year period that ends on December 31 (or the final day of a non-calendar year accounting period) prior to the year in which the determination is being made; or (ii) the period during which the entity has been in existence.

   i) The term "**Depository Institution"** means any entity that accepts deposits in the ordinary course of a banking or similar business.

   j) The term **"Investment Entity"** means any entity that conducts as a business (or is managed by an entity that conducts as a business) one or more of the following activities or operations for or on behalf of a customer:

(1) trading in money market instruments (cheques, bills, certificates of deposit, derivatives, etc.); foreign exchange; exchange, interest rate and index instruments; transferable securities; or commodity futures trading;

(2) individual and collective portfolio management; or

(3) otherwise investing, administering, or managing funds or money on behalf of other persons.

This *subparagraph 1j)* shall be interpreted in a manner consistent with similar language set forth in the definition of "financial institution" in the Financial Action Task Force Recommendations.

k) The term **"Specified Insurance Company"** means any entity that is an insurance company (or the holding company of an insurance company) that issues, or is obligated to make payments with respect to, a Cash Value Insurance Contract or an Annuity Contract.

l) The term **"Irish Financial Institution"** means (i) any Financial Institution resident in Ireland, but excluding any branches of such Financial Institution that are located outside Ireland, and (ii) any branch of a Financial Institution not resident in Ireland, if such branch is located in Ireland.

m) The term **"Partner Jurisdiction Financial Institution"** means (i) any Financial Institution resident in a Partner Jurisdiction, but excluding any branches of such Financial Institution that are located outside the Partner Jurisdiction, and (ii) any branch of a Financial Institution not resident in the Partner Jurisdiction, if such branch is located in the Partner Jurisdiction.

n) The term **"Reporting Financial Institution"** means a Reporting Irish Financial Institution or a Reporting U.S. Financial Institution, as the context requires.

o) The term **"Reporting Irish Financial Institution"** means any Irish Financial Institution that is not a Non-Reporting Irish Financial Institution.

p) The term **"Reporting U.S. Financial Institution"** means (i) any Financial Institution that is resident in the United States, but excluding any branches of such Financial Institution that are located outside the United States, and (ii) any branch of a Financial Institution not resident in the United States, if such branch is located in the United States, provided that the Financial Institution or branch has control, receipt, or custody of income with respect to which information is required to be exchanged under *subparagraph 2b)* of Article 2 of this Agreement.

q) The term **"Non-Reporting Irish Financial Institution"** means any Irish Financial Institution, or other entity resident in Ireland that is identified in Annex II as a Non-Reporting Irish Financial Institution or that otherwise qualifies as a deemed-compliant FFI, an exempt beneficial owner, or an excepted FFI under relevant U.S. Treasury Regulations.

r) The term **"Nonparticipating Financial Institution"** means a nonparticipating FFI, as that term is defined in relevant U.S. Treasury

Regulations, but does not include an Irish Financial Institution or other Partner Jurisdiction Financial Institution other than a Financial Institution identified as a Nonparticipating Financial Institution pursuant to *paragraph 2* of Article 5.

s) The term **"Financial Account"** means an account maintained by a Financial Institution, and includes:

(1) in the case of an entity that is a Financial Institution solely because it is an Investment Entity, any equity or debt interest (other than interests that are regularly traded on an established securities market) in the Financial Institution;

(2) in the case of a Financial Institution not described in *subparagraph 1(s)(1)* above, any equity or debt interest in the Financial Institution (other than interests that are regularly traded on an established securities market), if (i) the value of the debt or equity interestis determined, directly or indirectly, primarily by reference to assets that give rise to U.S. Source Withholdable Payments, and (ii) the class of interests was established with a purpose of avoiding reporting in accordance with this Agreement; and

(3) any Cash Value Insurance Contract and any Annuity Contract issued or maintained by a Financial Institution, other than a noninvestment-linked, nontransferable immediate life annuity that is issued to an individual and monetizes a pension or disability benefit provided under an account, product, or arrangement identified as excluded from the definition of Financial Account in Annex II.

Notwithstanding the foregoing, the term "Financial Account" does not include any account, product, or arrangement identified as excluded from the definition of Financial Account in Annex II.

t) The term **"Depository Account"** includes any commercial, checking, savings, time, or thrift account, or an account that is evidenced by a certificate of deposit, thrift certificate, investment certificate, certificate of indebtedness, or other similar instrument maintained by a Financial Institution in the ordinary course of a banking or similar business. A Depository Account also includes an amount held by an insurance company pursuant to a guaranteed investment contract or similar agreement to pay or credit interest thereon.

u) The term **"Custodial Account"** means an account (other than an Insurance Contract or Annuity Contract) for the benefit of another person that holds any financial instrument or contract held for investment (including, but not limited to, a share or stock in a corporation, a note, bond, debenture, or other evidence of indebtedness, a currency or commodity transaction, a credit default swap, a swap based upon a nonfinancial index, a notional principal contract, an Insurance Contract or Annuity Contract, and any option or other derivative instrument).

v) The term **"Equity Interest"** means, in the case of a partnership that is a Financial Institution, either a capital or profits interest in the partnership. In the case of a trust that is a Financial Institution, an Equity Interest is considered to be held by any person treated as a settlor or beneficiary of all or a portion of the trust, or any other natural person exercising ultimate effective control over the trust. A Specified U.S. Person shall be treated as being a beneficiary of a foreign trust if such Specified U.S. Person has the right to receive directly or indirectly (for example, through a nominee) a mandatory distribution or may receive, directly or indirectly, a discretionary distribution from the trust.

w) The term **"Insurance Contract"** means a contract (other than an Annuity Contract) under which the issuer agrees to pay an amount upon the occurrence of a specified contingency involving mortality, morbidity, accident, liability, or property risk.

x) The term **"Annuity Contract"** means a contract under which the issuer agrees to make payments for a period of time determined in whole or in part by reference to the life expectancy of one or more individuals. The term also includes a contract that is considered to be an Annuity Contract in accordance with the law, regulation, or practice of the jurisdiction in which the contract was issued, and under which the issuer agrees to make payments for a term of years.

y) The term **"Cash Value Insurance Contract"** means an Insurance Contract (other than an indemnity reinsurance contract between two insurance companies) that has a Cash Value greater than $50,000.

z) The term **"Cash Value"** means the greater of (i) the amount that the policyholder is entitled to receive upon surrender or termination of the contract (determined without reduction for any surrender charge or policy loan), and (ii) the amount the policyholder can borrow under or with regard to the contract. Notwithstanding the foregoing, the term "Cash Value" does not include an amount payable under an Insurance Contract as:

(1) a personal injury or sickness benefit or other benefit providing indemnification of an economic loss incurred upon the occurrence of the event insured against;

(2) a refund to the policyholder of a previously paid premium under an Insurance Contract (other than under a life insurance contract) due to policy cancellation or termination, decrease in risk exposure during the effective period of the Insurance Contract, or arising from a redetermination of the premium due to correction of posting or other similar error; or

(3) a policy holder dividend based upon the underwriting experience of the contract or group involved.

aa) The term **"Preexisting Account"** means a Financial Account maintained by a Reporting Financial Institution as of December 31, 2013.

bb) The term **"Reportable Account"** means a U.S. Reportable Account or an Irish Reportable Account, as the context requires.

cc) The term **"Irish Reportable Account"** means a Financial Account maintained by a Reporting U.S. Financial Institution if: (i) in the case of a Depository Account, the account is held by an individual resident in Ireland and more than $10 of interest is paid to such account in any given calendar year; or (ii) in the case of a Financial Account other than a Depository Account, the Account Holder is a resident of Ireland, including entities that certify that they are resident in Ireland for tax purposes, with respect to which U.S. source income that is subject to reporting under *chapter 3* or *chapter 61* of subtitle A of the U.S. Internal Revenue Code is paid or credited.

dd) The term **"U.S. Reportable Account"** means a Financial Account maintained by a Reporting Irish Financial Institution and held by one or more Specified U.S. Persons or by a Non-U.S. Entity with one or more Controlling Persons that is a Specified U.S. Person. Notwithstanding the foregoing, an account shall not be treated as a U.S. Reportable Account if such account is not identified as a U.S. Reportable Account after application of the due diligence procedures in Annex I.

ee) The term **"Account Holder"** means the person listed or identified as the holder of a Financial Account by the Financial Institution that maintains the account. A person, other than a Financial Institution, holding a Financial Account for the benefit or account of another person as agent, custodian, nominee, signatory, investment advisor, or intermediary, is not treated as holding the account for purposes of this Agreement, and such other person is treated as holding the account. In the case of a Cash Value Insurance Contract or an Annuity Contract, the Account Holder is any person entitled to access the Cash Value or change the beneficiary of the contract. If no person can access the Cash Value or change the beneficiary, the Account Holders are any person named as the owner in the contract and any person with a vested entitlement to payment under the terms of the contract. Upon the maturity of a Cash Value Insurance Contract or an Annuity Contract, each person entitled to receive a payment under the contract is treated as an Account Holder.

ff) The term **"U.S. Person"** means a U.S. citizen or resident individual, a partnership or corporation organized in the United States or under the laws of the United States or any State thereof, a trust if (i) a court within the United States would have authority under applicable law to render orders or judgments concerning substantially all issues regarding administration of the trust, and (ii) one or more U.S. persons have the authority to control all substantial decisions of the trust, or an estate of a decedent that is a citizen or resident of the United States. This *subparagraph 1(ff)* shall be interpreted in accordance with the U.S. Internal Revenue Code.

gg) The term **"Specified U.S. Person"** means a U.S. Person, other than: (i) a corporation the stock of which is regularly traded on one or more established securities markets; (ii) any corporation that is a member of the same expanded affiliated group, as defined in *section 1471(e)(2)* of the U.S. Internal Revenue Code, as a corporation described in clause (i); (iii) the United States or any wholly owned agency or instrumentality thereof; (iv) any State of the United States, any U.S. Territory, any political subdivision of any of the foregoing, or any wholly owned agency or instrumentality of any one or more of the foregoing; (v) any organization exempt from taxation under *section 501(a)* or an individual retirement plan as defined in *section 7701(a)(37)* of the U.S. Internal Revenue Code; (vi) any bank as defined in *section 581* of the U.S. Internal Revenue Code; (vii) any real estate investment trust as defined in *section 856* of the U.S. Internal Revenue Code; (viii) any regulated investment company as defined in *section 851* of the U.S. Internal Revenue Code or any entity registered with the Securities Exchange Commission under the Investment Company Act of 1940 (15 U.S.C. 80a-64); (ix) any common trust fund as defined in *section 584(a)* of the U.S. Internal Revenue Code; (x) any trust that is exempt from tax under *section 664(c)* of the U.S. Internal Revenue Code or that is described in *section 4947(a)(1)* of the U.S. Internal Revenue Code; (xi) a dealer in securities, commodities, or derivative financial instruments (including notional principal contracts, futures, forwards, and options) that is registered as such under the laws of the United States or any State; or (xii) a broker as defined in *section 6045(c)* of the U.S. Internal Revenue Code.

hh) The term **"Entity"** means a legal person or a legal arrangement such as a trust.

ii) The term **"Non-U.S. Entity"** means an Entity that is not a U.S. Person.

jj) The term **"U.S. Source Withholdable Payment"** means any payment of interest (including any original issue discount), dividends, rents, salaries, wages, premiums, annuities, compensations, remunerations, emoluments, and other fixed or determinable annual or periodical gains, profits, and income, if such payment is from sources within the United States. Notwithstanding the foregoing, a U.S. Source Withholdable Payment does not include any payment that is not treated as a withholdable payment in relevant U.S. Treasury Regulations.

kk) An Entity is a **"Related Entity"** of another Entity if either Entity controls the other Entity, or the two Entities are under common control. For this purpose control includes direct or indirect ownership of more than 50 percent of the vote or value in an Entity. Notwithstanding the foregoing, Ireland may treat an Entity as not a Related Entity of another Entity if the two Entities are not members of the same expanded affiliated group as defined in *section 1471(e)(2)* of the U.S. Internal Revenue Code.

ll) The term **"U.S. TIN"** means a U.S. federal taxpayer identifying number.

mm) The term **"Irish TIN"** means a number used by the Revenue Commissioners to identify an Irish taxpayer for taxation purposes.

nn) The term **"Controlling Persons"** means the natural persons who exercise control over an entity. In the case of a trust, such term means the settlor, the trustees, the protector (if any), the beneficiaries or class of beneficiaries, and any other natural person exercising ultimate effective control over the trust, and in the case of a legal arrangement other than a trust, such term means persons in equivalent or similar positions. The term "Controlling Persons" shall be interpreted in a manner consistent with the Recommendations of the Financial Action Task Force.

2. Any term not otherwise defined in this Agreement shall, unless the context otherwise requires or the Competent Authorities agree to a common meaning (as permitted by domestic law), have the meaning that it has at that time under the law of the Party applying the Agreement, any meaning under the applicable tax laws of that Party prevailing over a meaning given to the term under other laws of that Party.

Article 2
Obligations to Obtain and Exchange Information with Respect to Reportable Accounts

1. Subject to the provisions of Article 3, each Party shall obtain the information specified in *paragraph 2* of this Article with respect to all Reportable Accounts and shall annually exchange this information with the other Party on an automatic basis pursuant to the provisions of Article 27 of the Convention.
2. The information to be obtained and exchanged is:
   a) In the case of Ireland with respect to each U.S. Reportable Account of each Reporting Irish Financial Institution:
      (1) the name, address, and U.S. TIN of each Specified U.S. Person that is an Account Holder of such account and, in the case of a Non-U.S. Entity that, after application of the due diligence procedures set forth in Annex I, is identified as having one or more Controlling Persons that is a Specified U.S. Person, the name, address, and U.S. TIN (if any) of such entity and each such Specified U.S. Person;
      (2) the account number (or functional equivalent in the absence of an account number);
      (3) the name and identifying number of the Reporting Irish Financial Institution;
      (4) the account balance or value (including, in the case of a Cash Value Insurance Contract or Annuity Contract, the Cash Value or surrender value) as of the end of the relevant calendar year or other appropriate reporting period or, if the account was closed during such year, immediately before closure;
      (5) in the case of any Custodial Account:
         (A) the total gross amount of interest, the total gross amount of dividends, and the total gross amount of other income generated with respect to the assets held in the account, in each case paid or credited to the account (or with respect to the account) during the calendar year or other appropriate reporting period; and
         (B) the total gross proceeds from the sale or redemption of property paid or credited to the account during the calendar year or other appropriate reporting period with respect to which the Reporting Irish Financial Institution acted as a custodian, broker, nominee, or otherwise as an agent for the Account Holder;
      (6) in the case of any Depository Account, the total gross amount of interest paid or credited to the account during the calendar year or other appropriate reporting period; and
      (7) in the case of any account not described in *subparagraph (5)* or *(6)* of this paragraph, the total gross amount paid or credited to the Account Holder with respect to the account during the calendar year or other appropriate reporting period with respect to which

the Reporting Irish Financial Institution is the obligor or debtor, including the aggregate amount of any redemption payments made to the Account Holder during the calendar year or other appropriate reporting period.

b) In the case of the United States, with respect to each Irish Reportable Account of each Reporting U.S. Financial Institution:

(1) the name, address, and Irish TIN of any person that is a resident of Ireland and is an Account Holder of the account;

(2) the account number (or the functional equivalent in the absence of an account number);

(3) the name and identifying number of the Reporting U.S. Financial Institution;

(4) the gross amount of interest paid on a Depository Account;

(5) the gross amount of U.S. source dividends paid or credited to the account; and

(6) the gross amount of other U.S. source income paid or credited to the account, to the extent subject to reporting under *chapter 3* or *61* of subtitle A of the U.S. Internal Revenue Code.

Article 3
Time and Manner of Exchange of Information

1. For purposes of the exchange obligation in Article 2, the amount and characterization of payments made with respect to a U.S. Reportable Account may be determined in accordance with the principles of the tax laws of Ireland, and the amount and characterization of payments made with respect to an Irish Reportable Account may be determined in accordance with principles of U.S. federal income tax law.

2. For purposes of the exchange obligation in Article 2, the information exchanged shall identify the currency in which each relevant amount is denominated.

3. With respect to *paragraph 2* of Article 2, information is to be obtained and exchanged with respect to 2013 and all subsequent years, except that:

a) In the case of Ireland:

(1) the information to be obtained and exchanged with respect to 2013 and 2014 is only the information described in *subparagraphs a)(1)* to *a)(4)*;

(2) the information to be obtained and exchanged with respect to 2015 is the information described in *subparagraphs a)(1)* to *a)(7)*, except for gross proceeds described in *subparagraph a)(5)(B)*; and

(3) the information to be obtained and exchanged with respect to 2016 and subsequent years is the information described in *subparagraph a)(1)* to *a)(7)*;

b) In the case of the United States, the information to be obtained and exchanged with respect to 2013 and subsequent years is all of the information identified in *subparagraph b)*.

4. Notwithstanding *paragraph 3* of this Article, with respect to each Reportable Account that is a Preexisting Account, and subject to *paragraph 4* of Article 6, the Parties are not required to obtain and include in the exchanged information

the Irish TIN or the U.S. TIN, as applicable, of any relevant person if such taxpayer identifying number is not in the records of the Reporting Financial Institution. In such case, the Parties shall obtain and include in the exchanged information the date of birth of the relevant person, if the Reporting Financial Institution has such date of birth in its records.

5. Subject to *paragraphs 3* and *4* of this Article, the information described in Article 2 shall be exchanged within nine months after the end of the calendar year to which the information relates. Notwithstanding the foregoing, the information that relates to calendar year 2013 shall be exchanged no later than September 30, 2015.

6. The Competent Authorities of Ireland and the United States shall enter into an agreement under the mutual agreement procedure provided for in Article 26 of the Convention, which shall:
    a) establish the procedures for the automatic exchange obligations described in Article 2;
    b) prescribe rules and procedures as may be necessary to implement Article 5; and
    c) establish as necessary procedures for the exchange of the information reported under *subparagraph 1b)* of Article 4.

7. All information exchanged shall be subject to the confidentiality and other protections provided for in the Convention, including the provisions limiting the use of the information exchanged.

Article 4
Application of FATCA to Irish Financial Institutions

1. **Treatment of Reporting Irish Financial Institutions**. Each Reporting Irish Financial Institution shall be treated as complying with, and not subject to withholding under, section 1471 of the U.S. Internal Revenue Code if Ireland complies with its obligations under Articles 2 and 3 with respect to such Reporting Irish Financial Institution, and the Reporting Irish Financial Institution:
    a) identifies U.S. Reportable Accounts and reports annually to the Irish Competent Authority the information required to be reported in *subparagraph 2a)* of Article 2 in the time and manner described in Article 3;
    b) for each of 2015 and 2016, reports annually to the Irish Competent Authority the name of each Nonparticipating Financial Institution to which it has made payments and the aggregate amount of such payments;
    c) complies with the registration requirements applicable to Financial Institutions in Partner Jurisdictions;
    d) to the extent that a Reporting Irish Financial Institution is (i) acting as a qualified intermediary (for purposes of *section 1441* of the U.S. Internal Revenue Code) that has elected to assume primary withholding responsibility under *chapter 3* of subtitle A of the U.S. Internal Revenue Code, (ii) a foreign partnership that has elected to act as a withholding foreign partnership (for purposes of both *sections 1441* and *1471* of the U.S. Internal Revenue Code), or (iii) a foreign trust that has elected to act as a withholding foreign trust (for purposes of both *sections 1441* and 1471 of the U.S. Internal Revenue Code), withholds 30 percent of any U.S. Source Withholdable Payment to any Nonparticipating Financial Institution; and

e) in the case of a Reporting Irish Financial Institution that is not described in *subparagraph d*) of this paragraph and that makes a payment of, or acts as an intermediary with respect to, a U.S. Source Withholdable Payment to any Nonparticipating Financial Institution, the Reporting Irish Financial Institution provides to any immediate payor of such U.S. Source Withholdable Payment the information required for withholding and reporting to occur with respect to such payment.

Notwithstanding the foregoing, a Reporting Irish Financial Institution with respect to which the conditions of this paragraph are not satisfied shall not be subject to withholding under *section 1471* of the U.S. Internal Revenue Code unless such Reporting Irish Financial Institution is identified by the IRS as a Nonparticipating Financial Institution pursuant to *subparagraph 2b*) of Article 5.

2. **Suspension of Rules Relating to Recalcitrant Accounts**. The United States shall not require a Reporting Irish Financial Institution to withhold tax under *section 1471* or *1472* of the U.S. Internal Revenue Code with respect to an account held by a recalcitrant account holder (as defined in *section 1471(d)(6)* of the U.S. Internal Revenue Code), or to close such account, if the U.S. Competent Authority receives the information set forth in *subparagraph 2a*) of Article 2, subject to the provisions of Article 3, with respect to such account.

3. **Specific Treatment of Retirement Plans**. The United States shall treat as a deemed-compliant FFI or exempt beneficial owner, as appropriate, for purposes of *section 1471* of the U.S. Internal Revenue Code Irish retirement plans described and identified in Annex II. For this purpose, an Irish retirement plan includes an entity established or located in and regulated in Ireland, or a predetermined contractual or legal arrangement, operated to provide pension or retirement benefits or earn income for providing such benefits under the laws of Ireland and regulated with respect to contributions, distributions, reporting, sponsorship, and taxation.

4. **Identification and Treatment of Other Deemed-Compliant FFIs and Exempt Beneficial Owners.** The United States shall treat each Non-Reporting Irish Financial Institution as a deemed-compliant FFI or as an exempt beneficial owner, as appropriate, for purposes of *section 1471* of the U.S. Internal Revenue Code.

5. **Special Rules Regarding Related Entities That Are Nonparticipating Financial Institutions.** If an Irish Financial Institution, that otherwise meets the requirements of *paragraph 1* of this Article or is described in *paragraph 3* or *4* of this Article, has a Related Entity or branch that operates in a jurisdiction that prevents such Related Entity or branch from fulfilling the requirements of a participating FFI or deemed-compliant FFI for purposes of *section 1471* of the U.S. Internal Revenue Code, such Irish Financial Institution shall continue to be in compliance with the terms of this Agreement and shall continue to be treated as a deemed-compliant FFI or exempt beneficial owner for purposes of *section 1471* of the U.S. Internal Revenue Code, provided that:

a) the Irish Financial Institution treats each such Related Entity or branch as a separate Nonparticipating Financial Institution for purposes of all the reporting and withholding requirements of this Agreement and each such Related Entity or branch identifies itself to withholding agents as a Nonparticipating Financial Institution;

b) each such Related Entity or branch identifies its U.S. accounts and reports the information with respect to those accounts as required under section 1471 of the U.S. Internal Revenue Code to the extent permitted under the relevant laws pertaining to the Related Entity or branch; and

c) such Related Entity or branch does not specifically solicit U.S. accounts held by persons that are not resident in the jurisdiction where such Related Entity or branch is located or accounts held by Nonparticipating Financial Institutions that are not established in the jurisdiction where such branch or Related Entity is located, and such branch or Related Entity is not used by the Irish Financial Institution or any other Related Entity to circumvent the obligations under this Agreement or under *section 1471* of the U.S. Internal Revenue Code, as appropriate.

Article 5
Collaboration on Compliance and Enforcement

1. **Minor and Administrative Errors.** Subject to any further terms set forth in a competent authority agreement executed pursuant to *paragraph 6* of Article 3, a Competent Authority can make an inquiry directly to a Reporting Financial Institution in the other jurisdiction where it has reason to believe that administrative errors or other minor errors may have led to incorrect or incomplete information reporting or resulted in other infringements of this Agreement. The competent authority agreement may provide that a Competent Authority shall notify the Competent Authority of the other Party when the first-mentioned Competent Authority makes such an inquiry of a Reporting Financial Institution in the other jurisdiction regarding the Reporting Financial Institution's compliance with the conditions set forth in this Agreement.

2. **Significant Non-compliance.**

   a) A Competent Authority shall notify the Competent Authority of the other Party when the first-mentioned Competent Authority has determined that there is significant non-compliance with the obligations under this Agreement with respect to a Reporting Financial Institution in the other jurisdiction. The Competent Authority of such other Party shall apply its domestic law (including applicable penalties) to address the significant non-compliance described in the notice.

   b) If, in the case of a Reporting Irish Financial Institution, such enforcement actions do not resolve the non-compliance within a period of 18 months after notification of significant non-compliance is first provided, the United States shall treat the Reporting Irish Financial Institution as a Nonparticipating Financial Institution. The IRS shall make available a list of all Reporting Irish Financial Institutions and other Partner Jurisdiction Financial Institutions that are treated as Nonparticipating Financial Institutions pursuant to this paragraph.

3. **Reliance on Third Party Service Providers.** Each Party may allow Reporting Financial Institutions to use third party service providers to fulfill the obligations imposed on them by a Party, as contemplated in this Agreement, but these obligations shall remain the responsibility of the Reporting Financial Institutions.

4. **Prevention of Avoidance.** The Parties shall implement as necessary requirements to prevent Financial Institutions from adopting practices intended to circumvent the reporting required under this Agreement.

Article 6
Mutual Commitment to Continue to Enhance the Effectiveness of Information Exchange and Transparency

1. Reciprocity. The Government of the United States acknowledges the need to achieve equivalent levels of reciprocal automatic information exchange with Ireland. The Government of the United States is committed to further improve transparency and enhance the exchange relationship with Ireland by pursuing the adoption of regulations and advocating and supporting relevant legislation to achieve such equivalent levels of reciprocal automatic exchange.
2. **Treatment of Passthru Payments and Gross Proceeds.** The Parties are committed to work together, along with other partners, to develop a practical and effective alternative approach to achieve the policy objectives of foreign passthru payment and gross proceeds withholding that minimizes burden.
3. **Development of Common Reporting and Exchange Model.** The Parties are committed to working with other partners, the Organisation for Economic Cooperation and Development, and the European Union, on adapting the terms of this Agreement to a common model for automatic exchange of information, including the development of reporting and due diligence standards for financial institutions.
4. **Documentation of Accounts Maintained as of January 1, 2014.** With respect to Reportable Accounts that are Preexisting Accounts maintained by a Reporting Financial Institution:
   a) The United States commits to establish, by January 1, 2017, for reporting with respect to 2017 and subsequent years, rules requiring Reporting U.S. Financial Institutions to obtain and report the Irish TIN of each Account Holder of an Irish Reportable Account as required pursuant to *subparagraph 2b)(1)* of Article 2; and
   b) Ireland commits to establish, by January 1, 2017, for reporting with respect to 2017 and subsequent years, rules requiring Reporting Irish Financial Institutions to obtain the U.S. TIN of each Specified U.S. Person as required pursuant to *subparagraph 2a)(1)* of Article 2.

Article 7
Consistency in the Application of FATCA to Partner Jurisdictions

1. Ireland shall be granted the benefit of any more favorable terms under Article 4 or Annex I of this Agreement relating to the application of FATCA to Irish Financial Institutions afforded to another Partner Jurisdiction under a signed bilateral agreement pursuant to which the other Partner Jurisdiction commits to undertake the same obligations as Ireland described in Articles 2 and 3 of this Agreement, and subject to the same terms and conditions as described therein and in Articles 5 through 9 of the Agreement.
2. The United States shall notify Ireland of any such more favorable terms and shall apply such more favorable terms automatically under this Agreement as if they were specified in this Agreement and effective as of the date of the entry into force of the agreement incorporating the more favorable terms.

Article 8
Consultations and Amendments

1. In case any difficulties in the implementation of this Agreement arise, either Party may request consultations to develop appropriate measures to ensure the fulfillment of this Agreement.
2. This Agreement may be amended by written mutual consent of the Parties. Unless otherwise agreed upon, such an amendment shall enter into force through the same procedures as set forth in *paragraph 1* of Article 10.

Article 9
Annexes

The Annexes form an integral part of this Agreement.

Article 10
Term of Agreement

1. The Parties shall notify each other in writing when their necessary internal procedures for entry into force have been completed. The Agreement shall enter into force on the later of January 1, 2013, or the date of the later of such notifications, and shall continue in force until terminated.
2. Either Party may terminate the Agreement by giving notice of termination in writing to the other Party. Such termination shall become effective on the first day of the month following the expiration of a period of 12 months after the date of the notice of termination.
3. The Parties shall, prior to December 31, 2016, consult in good faith to amend this Agreement as necessary to reflect progress on the commitments set forth in Article 6.

In witness whereof, the undersigned, being duly authorized thereto by their respective Governments, have signed this Agreement.

Done at Dublin, Ireland in duplicate, in English, this 21st day of December, 2012.

FOR THE GOVERNMENT OF THE UNITED STATES OF AMERICA:	FOR THE GOVERNMENT OF IRELAND:
John Hennessey-Niland	Michael Noonan

ANNEX I

DUE DILIGENCE OBLIGATIONS FOR IDENTIFYING AND REPORTING ON U.S. REPORTABLE ACCOUNTS AND ON PAYMENTS TO CERTAIN NONPARTICIPATING FINANCIAL INSTITUTIONS

I. General

A. Ireland shall require that Reporting Irish Financial Institutions apply the due diligence procedures contained in this Annex I to identify U.S. Reportable Accounts and accounts held by Nonparticipating Financial Institutions.

B. For purposes of the Agreement,

1. All dollar amounts shall be read to include the equivalent in other currencies.

2. The balance or value of an account shall be determined as of the last day of the calendar year or other appropriate reporting period.

3. Where a balance or value threshold is to be determined as of the last day of a calendar year under this Annex I, the relevant balance or value shall be determined as of the last day of the reporting period that ends with or within that calendar year.

4. Subject to *paragraph II.E (1)*, an account shall be treated as a U.S. Reportable Account beginning as of the date it is identified as such pursuant to the due diligence procedures in this Annex I.

5. Unless otherwise provided, information with respect to a U.S. Reportable Account shall be reported annually in the calendar year following the year to which the information relates.

C. As an alternative to the procedures described in each section of this Annex I, Ireland may allow its Reporting Irish Financial Institutions to rely on the procedures described in relevant U.S. Treasury Regulations to establish whether an account is a U.S. Reportable Account or an account held by a Nonparticipating Financial Institution.

II. **Preexisting Individual Accounts.** The following rules and procedures apply for identifying U.S. Reportable Accounts among Preexisting Accounts held by individuals ("Preexisting Individual Accounts").

A. **Accounts Not Required to Be Reviewed, Identified, or Reported.** Unless the Reporting Irish Financial Institution elects otherwise, where the implementing rules in Ireland provide for such an election, the following accounts are not required to be reviewed, identified, or reported as U.S. Reportable Accounts:

1. Subject to *subparagraph E.2* of this section, Preexisting Individual Accounts with a balance or value that does not exceed $50,000 as of December 31, 2013.

2. Subject to *subparagraph E.2* of this section, Preexisting Individual Accounts that are Cash Value Insurance Contracts and Annuity Contracts with a balance or value of $250,000 or less as of December 31, 2013.

3. Preexisting Individual Accounts that are Cash Value Insurance Contracts or Annuity Contracts, provided the law or regulations

of Ireland or the United States effectively prevents the sale of Cash Value Insurance Contracts or Annuity Contracts to U.S. residents, such as if the relevant Financial Institution does not have the required registration under U.S. law, and the law of Ireland requires reporting or withholding with respect to insurance products held by residents of Ireland.

4. Any Depository Account with a balance or value of $50,000 or less.

B. **Review Procedures for Preexisting Individual Accounts With a Balance or Value as of December 31, 2013, that Exceeds $50,000 ($250,000 for a Cash Value Insurance Contract or Annuity Contract), But Does Not Exceed $1,000,000 ("Lower Value Accounts")**

1. **Electronic Record Search**. The Reporting Irish Financial Institution must review electronically searchable data maintained by the Reporting Irish Financial Institution for any of the following U.S. indicia:

a) Identification of the Account Holder as a U.S. citizen or resident;

b) Unambiguous indication of a U.S. place of birth;

c) Current U.S. mailing or residence address (including a U.S. post office box or U.S. "in-care-of" address);

d) Current U.S. telephone number;

e) Standing instructions to transfer funds to an account maintained in the United States;

f) Currently effective power of attorney or signatory authority granted to a person with a U.S. address; or

g) An "in-care-of" or "hold mail" address that is the ***sole*** address the Reporting Irish Financial Institution has on file for the Account Holder. In the case of a Preexisting Individual Account that is a Lower Value Account, an "in-care-of" address outside the United States shall not be treated as U.S. indicia.

2. If none of the U.S. indicia listed in *subparagraph B.1* of this section are discovered in the electronic search, then no further action is required until there is a change in circumstances described in *subparagraph C.2* of this section with respect to the account that results in one or more U.S. indicia being associated with the account.

3. If any of the U.S. indicia in *subparagraph B.1* of this section are discovered in the electronic search, then the Reporting Irish Financial Institution must treat the account as a U.S. Reportable Account unless it elects to apply subparagraph B.4 of this section and one of the exceptions in such subparagraph applies with respect to that account.

4. Notwithstanding a finding of U.S. indicia under *subparagraph B.1* of this section, a Reporting Irish Financial Institution is not required to treat an account as a U.S. Reportable Account if:

   a) Where Account Holder information unambiguously indicates a ***U.S. place of birth,*** the Reporting Irish Financial Institution obtains or has previously reviewed and maintains a record of:

      (1) a self-certification that the Account Holder is neither a U.S. citizen nor a U.S. resident for tax purposes (which may be on an IRS Form W-8 or other similar agreed form);

      (2) a non-U.S. passport or other government-issued identification evidencing the Account Holder's citizenship or nationality in a country other than the United States; ***and***

      (3) a copy of the Account Holder's Certificate of Loss of Nationality of the United States or a reasonable explanation of:

         (a) the reason the Account Holder does not have such a certificate despite renouncing U.S. citizenship; ***or***

         (b) the reason the Account Holder did not obtain U.S. citizenship at birth.

   b) Where Account Holder information contains a ***current U.S. mailing or residence address, or one or more U.S. telephone numbers that are the only telephone numbers associated with the account***, the Reporting Irish Financial Institution obtains or has previously reviewed and maintains a record of:

      (1) a self-certification that the Account Holder is not a U.S. citizen or resident for tax purposes (which may be on an IRS Form W-8 or other similar agreed form); ***and***

      (2) a non-U.S. passport or other government-issued identification evidencing the Account Holder's citizenship or nationality in a country other than the United States.

   c) Where Account Holder information contains ***standing instructions to transfer funds to an account maintained in the United States,*** the Reporting Irish Financial Institution obtains or has previously reviewed and maintains a record of:

      (1) a self-certification that the Account Holder is not a U.S. citizen or resident for tax purposes (which may be on an IRS Form W-8 or other similar agreed form); ***and***

(2) documentary evidence, as defined in paragraph VI.D of this Annex I, establishing the Account Holder's non-U.S. status.

d) Where Account Holder information contains ***a currently effective power of attorney or signatory authority granted to a person with a U.S. address, has an "in care of" address or "hold mail" address that is the sole address identified for the Account Holder, or has one or more U.S. telephone numbers (if a non-U.S. telephone number is also associated with the account),*** the Reporting Irish Financial Institution obtains or has previously reviewed and maintains a record of:

(1) a self-certification that the Account Holder is not a U.S. citizen or resident for tax purposes (which may be on an IRS Form W-8 or other similar agreed form); ***or***

(2) documentary evidence, as defined in paragraph VI.D of this Annex I, establishing the Account Holder's non-U.S. status.

C. **Additional Procedures Applicable to Preexisting Individual Accounts That Are Lower Value Accounts**

1. Review of Preexisting Individual Accounts that are Lower Value Accounts for U.S. indicia must be completed by December 31, 2015.

2. If there is a change of circumstances with respect to a Preexisting Individual Account that is a Lower Value Account that results in one or more U.S. indicia described in *subparagraph B.1* of this section being associated with the account, then the Reporting Irish Financial Institution must treat the account as a U.S. Reportable Account unless *subparagraph B.4* of this section applies.

3. Except for Depository Accounts described in *subparagraph A.4* of this section, any Preexisting Individual Account that has been identified as a U.S. Reportable Account under this section shall be treated as a U.S. Reportable Account in all subsequent years, unless the Account Holder ceases to be a Specified U.S. Person.

D. **Enhanced Review Procedures for Preexisting Individual Accounts With a Balance or Value That Exceeds $1,000,000 as of December 31, 2013, or December 31 of Any Subsequent Year ("High-Value Accounts")**

1. **Electronic Record Search**. The Reporting Irish Financial Institution must review electronically searchable data maintained by the Reporting Irish Financial Institution for any of the U.S. indicia identified in *subparagraph B.1* of this section.

2. **Paper Record Search.** If the Reporting Irish Financial Institution's electronically searchable databases include fields for and capture all of the information identified in *subparagraph D.3* of this section, then no further paper record search is required. If the

electronic databases do not capture all of this information, then with respect to High Value Accounts, the Reporting Irish Financial Institution must also review the current customer master file and, to the extent not contained in the current customer master file, the following documents associated with the account and obtained by the Reporting Irish Financial Institution within the last five years for any of the U.S. indicia identified in *subparagraph B.1* of this section:

a) the most recent documentary evidence collected with respect to the account;

b) the most recent account opening contract or documentation;

c) the most recent documentation obtained by the Reporting Irish Financial Institution pursuant to AML/KYC Procedures or for other regulatory purposes;

d) any power of attorney or signature authority forms currently in effect; and

e) any standing instructions to transfer funds currently in effect.

3. <u>Exception Where Databases Contain Sufficient Information.</u> A Reporting Irish Financial Institution is not required to perform the paper record search described in *subparagraph D.2* of this section if the Reporting Irish Financial Institution's electronically searchable information includes the following:

a) the Account Holder's nationality or residence status;

b) the Account Holder's residence address and mailing address currently on file with the Reporting Irish Financial Institution;

c) the Account Holder's telephone number(s) currently on file, if any, with the Reporting Irish Financial Institution;

d) whether there are standing instructions to transfer funds in the account to another account (including an account at another branch of the Reporting Irish Financial Institution or another Financial Institution);

e) whether there is a current "in care of" address or "hold mail" address for the Account Holder; ***and***

f) whether there is any power of attorney or signatory authority for the account.

4. <u>Relationship Manager Inquiry for Actual Knowledge.</u> In addition to the electronic and paper record searches described above, the Reporting Irish Financial Institution must treat as U.S. Reportable Accounts any High Value Accounts assigned to a relationship manager (including any accounts aggregated with such account) if the relationship manager has actual knowledge that the Account Holder is a Specified U.S. Person.

5. <u>Effect of Finding U.S. Indicia</u>

a) If none of the U.S. indicia listed in *subparagraph B.1* of this section are discovered in the enhanced review of High Value

Accounts described above, and the account is not identified as held by a Specified U.S. Person in *subparagraph D.4* of this section, then no further action is required until there is a change in circumstances described in *subparagraph E.4* of this section.

b) If any of the U.S. indicia listed in *subparagraph B.1* of this section are discovered in the enhanced review of High Value Accounts described above, or if there is a subsequent change in circumstances that results in one or more U.S. indicia being associated with the account, then the Reporting Irish Financial Institution must treat the account as a U.S. Reportable Account unless *subparagraph B.4* of this section applies.

c) Except for Depository Accounts described in *paragraph A.4* of this section, any Preexisting Individual Account that has been identified as a U.S. Reportable Account under this section shall be treated as a U.S. Reportable Account in all subsequent years, unless the Account Holder ceases to be a Specified U.S. Person.

E. **Additional Procedures Applicable to High Value Accounts**

1. If a Preexisting Individual Account is a High Value Account as of December 31, 2013, the Reporting Irish Financial Institution must complete the enhanced review procedures described in *paragraph D* of this section with respect to such account by December 31, 2014. If based on this review such account is identified as a U.S. Reportable Account, the Reporting Irish Financial Institution must report the required information about such account with respect to 2013 and 2014 in the first report on the account. For all subsequent years, information about the account should be reported on an annual basis.

2. If a Preexisting Individual Account is not a High Value Account as of December 31, 2013, but becomes a High Value Account as of the last day of a subsequent calendar year, the Reporting Irish Financial Institution must complete the enhanced review procedures described in *paragraph D* of this section with respect to such account within six months after the last day of the calendar year in which the account becomes a High Value Account. If based on this review such account is identified as a U.S. Reportable Account, the Reporting Irish Financial Institution must report the required information about such account with respect to the year in which it is identified as a U.S. Reportable Account and subsequent years on an annual basis.

3. Once a Reporting Irish Financial Institution applies the enhanced review procedures set forth above to a High Value Account, the Reporting Irish Financial Institution shall not be required to re-apply such procedures, other than the relationship manager inquiry in *subparagraph D.4* of this section, to the same High Value Account in any subsequent year.

4. If there is a change of circumstances with respect to a High Value Account that results in one or more U.S. indicia described in *subparagraph B(1)* of this section being associated with the account, then the Reporting Irish Financial Institution must treat the account as a U.S. Reportable Account unless *subparagraph B.4* of this section applies.
5. A Reporting Irish Financial Institution must implement procedures to ensure that a relationship manager identifies any change in circumstances of an account. For example, if a relationship manager is notified that the Account Holder has a new mailing address in the United States, the Reporting Irish Financial Institution shall be required to treat the new address as a change in circumstances and shall be required to obtain the appropriate documentation from the Account Holder.

III. **New Individual Accounts**. The following rules and procedures apply for identifying U.S. Reportable Accounts among accounts held by individuals and opened on or after January 1, 2014 ("New Individual Accounts").

A. **Accounts Not Required to Be Reviewed, Identified or Reported**. Unless the Reporting Irish Financial Institution elects otherwise where the implementing rules in Ireland provide for such an election:

1. A New Individual Account that is a Depository Account is not required to be reviewed, identified, or reported as a U.S. Reportable Account unless the account balance exceeds $50,000 at the end of any calendar year or other appropriate reporting period.
2. A New Individual Account that is a Cash Value Insurance Contract is not required to be reviewed, identified, or reported as a U.S. Reportable Account unless the Cash Value exceeds $50,000 at the end of any calendar year or other appropriate reporting period.

B. **Other New Individual Accounts.** With respect to New Individual Accounts not described in *paragraph A* of this section, upon account opening (or within 90 days after the end of the calendar year in which the account ceases to be described in *paragraph A* of this section), the Reporting Irish Financial Institution must obtain a self-certification which may be part of the account opening documentation, that allows the Reporting Irish Financial Institution to determine whether the Account Holder is resident in the United States for tax purposes (for this purpose, a U.S. citizen is considered to be resident in the United States for tax purposes, even if the Account Holder is also a tax resident of another country) and confirm the reasonableness of such self-certification based on the information obtained by the Reporting Irish Financial Institution in connection with the opening of the account, including any documentation collected pursuant to AML/KYC Procedures.

C. If the self-certification establishes that the Account Holder is resident in the United States for tax purposes, the Reporting Irish Financial Institution must treat the account as a U.S. Reportable Account and obtain a self-certification that includes the Account Holder's U.S. TIN (which may be an IRS Form W-9 or other similar agreed form).

D. If there is a change of circumstances with respect to a New Individual Account that causes the Reporting Irish Financial Institution to know or have reason to know that the original self-certification is incorrect or unreliable, the Reporting Irish Financial Institution cannot rely on the original self-certification and must obtain a valid self-certification that establishes whether the Account Holder is a U.S. citizen or resident for U.S. tax purposes. If the Reporting Irish Financial Institution is unable to obtain a valid self-certification, the Reporting Irish Financial Institution must treat the account as a U.S. Reportable Account.

IV. **Preexisting Entity Accounts.** The following rules and procedures apply for purposes of identifying U.S. Reportable Accounts and accounts held by a Non-participating Financial Institutions among Preexisting Accounts held by entities ("Preexisting Entity Accounts").

A. **Entity Accounts Not Required to Be Reviewed, Identified or Reported.** Unless the Reporting Irish Financial Institution elects otherwise, where the implementing rules in Ireland provide for such an election, Preexisting Entity Accounts with account balances that do not exceed $250,000 as of December 31, 2013, are not required to be reviewed, identified, or reported as U.S. Reportable Accounts until the account balance exceeds $1,000,000.

B. **Entity Accounts Subject to Review.** Preexisting Entity Accounts that have an account balance or value that exceeds $250,000 as of December 31, 2013, and Preexisting Entity Accounts that initially do not exceed $250,000 but the account balance of which later exceeds $1,000,000 must be reviewed in accordance with the procedures set forth in *paragraph D* of this section.

C. **Entity Accounts With Respect to Which Reporting is Required.** With respect to Preexisting Entity Accounts described in *paragraph B* of this section, only accounts that are held by one or more entities that are Specified U.S. Persons, or by Passive NFFEs with one or more Controlling Persons who are U.S. citizens or residents shall be treated as U.S. Reportable Accounts. In addition, accounts held by Nonparticipating Financial Institutions shall be treated as accounts for which aggregate payments as described in *paragraph 1b)* of Article 4 of the Agreement are reported to the Irish Competent Authority.

D. **Review Procedures for Identifying Entity Accounts With Respect to Which Reporting is Required.** For Preexisting Entity Accounts described in paragraph B of this section, the Reporting Irish Financial Institution must apply the following review procedures to determine whether the account is held by one or more Specified U.S. Persons, by Passive NFFEs with one or more Controlling Persons who are U.S. citizens or residents, or by a Nonparticipating Financial Institution:

1. **Determine Whether the Entity is a Specified U.S. Person.**

a) Review information maintained for regulatory or customer relationship purposes (including information collected pursuant to AML/KYC Procedures) to determine whether the information indicates that the entity Account Holder is a U.S. Person. For this purpose, information indicating that the entity is a U.S. Person includes a U.S. place of incorporation or organization, or a U.S. address.

b) If the information indicates that the entity Account Holder is a U.S. Person, the Reporting Irish Financial Institution must treat the account as a U.S. Reportable Account unless it obtains a self-certification from the Account Holder (which may be on an IRS Form W-8 or W-9, or a similar agreed form), or reasonably determines based on information in its possession or that is publicly available, that the Account Holder is not a Specified U.S. Person.

2. **Determine Whether a Non-U.S. Entity is a Financial Institution.**

a) Review information maintained for regulatory or customer relationship purposes (including information collected pursuant to AML/KYC Procedures) to determine whether the information indicates that the entity Account Holder is a Financial Institution.

b) If the information indicates that the entity Account Holder is a Financial Institution, then the account is not a U.S. Reportable Account.

3. **Determine Whether a Financial Institution is a Nonparticipating Financial Institution Payments to Which Are Subject to Aggregate Reporting Under *Paragraph 1(b)* of Article 4 of the Agreement.**

a) Subject to *subparagraph b)* of this paragraph, if the Account Holder is an Irish Financial Institution or other Partner Jurisdiction Financial Institution, then no further review, identification, or reporting is required with respect to the account.

b) An Irish Financial Institution or other Partner Jurisdiction Financial Institution shall be treated as a Nonparticipating Financial Institution if it is identified as such by the IRS as described in *paragraph 2* of Article 5 of the Agreement.

c) If the Account Holder, is not an Irish Financial Institution or other Partner Jurisdiction Financial Institution, then the Reporting Irish Financial Institution must treat the entity as a Nonparticipating Financial Institution payments to which are reportable under *paragraph 1(b)* of Article 4 of the Agreement, unless the Reporting Irish Financial Institution:

(1) Obtains a self-certification (which may be on an IRS Form W-8 or similar agreed form) from the entity that it is a certified deemed-compliant FFI, an exempt beneficial owner, or an excepted FFI, as those terms are defined in relevant U.S. Treasury Regulations; ***or***

(2) In the case of a participating FFI or registered deemed-compliant FFI, verifies the entity's FATCA identifying number on a published IRS FFI list.

4. **Determine Whether an Account Held by an NFFE Is a U.S. Reportable Account.** With respect to an Account Holder of a Preexisting Entity Account that is not identified as either a U.S. Person or a Financial Institution, the Reporting Irish Financial Institution must identify (i) whether the entity has Controlling Persons, (ii) whether the entity is a Passive NFFE, and (iii) whether any of the Controlling Persons of the entity is a citizen or resident of the United States. In making these determinations the Reporting Irish Financial Institution should follow the guidance in *subparagraphs a)* through *d)* of this paragraph in the order most appropriate under the circumstances.

   a) For purposes of determining the Controlling Persons of an entity, a Reporting Irish Financial Institution may rely on information collected and maintained pursuant to AML/KYC Procedures.

   b) For purposes of determining whether the entity is a Passive NFFE, the Reporting Irish Financial Institution must obtain a self-certification (which may be on an IRS Form W-8 or W-9, or on a similar agreed form) from the Account Holder to establish its status, unless it has information in its possession or that is publicly available, based on which it can reasonably determine that the entity is an Active NFFE.

   c) For purposes of determining whether a Controlling Person of a Passive NFFE is a citizen or resident of the United States for tax purposes, a Reporting Irish Financial Institution may rely on:

      (1) Information collected and maintained pursuant to AML/KYC Procedures in the case of a Preexisting Entity Account held by one or more NFFEs with an account balance that does not exceed $1,000,000; ***or***

      (2) A self-certification (which may be on an IRS Form W-8 or W-9, or on a similar agreed form) from the Account Holder or such Controlling Person in the case of a Preexisting Entity Account held by one or more NFFEs with an account balance that exceeds $1,000,000.

   d) If any Controlling Person of a Passive NFFE is a citizen or resident of the United States, the account shall be treated as a U.S. Reportable Account.

E. **Timing of Review and Additional Procedures Applicable to Preexisting Entity Accounts**

1. Review of Preexisting Entity Accounts with an account balance or value that exceeds $250,000 as of December 31, 2013, must be completed by December 31, 2015.

2. Review of Preexisting Entity Accounts with a balance or value that does not exceed $250,000 as of December 31, 2013, but exceeds $1,000,000 as of December 31 of a subsequent year, must be

completed within six months after the end of the calendar year in which the account balance exceeds $1,000,000.

3. If there is a change of circumstances with respect to a Preexisting Entity Account that causes the Reporting Irish Financial Institution to know or have reason to know that the self-certification or other documentation associated with an account is incorrect or unreliable, the Reporting Irish Financial Institution must re-determine the status of the account in accordance with the procedures set forth in *paragraph D* of this section.

V. **New Entity Accounts**. The following rules and procedures apply to accounts held by entities and opened on or after January 1, 2014 ("New Entity Accounts").

A. The Reporting Irish Financial Institution must determine whether the Account Holder is: (i) a Specified U.S. Person; (ii) an Irish Financial Institution or other Partner Jurisdiction Financial Institution; (iii) a participating FFI, a deemed-compliant FFI, an exempt beneficial owner, or an excepted FFI, as those terms are defined in relevant U.S. Treasury Regulations; or (iv) an Active NFFE or Passive NFFE.

B. A Reporting Irish Financial Institution may determine that an Account Holder is an Active NFFE, an Irish Financial Institution, or other Partner Jurisdiction Financial Institution if the Reporting Irish Financial Institution reasonably determines that the entity has such status on the basis of information that is publicly available or in the possession of the Reporting Irish Financial Institution.

C. In all other cases, a Reporting Irish Financial Institution must obtain a self-certification from the Account Holder to establish the Account Holder's status.

1. If the entity Account Holder is ***a Specified U.S. Person***, the Reporting Irish Financial Institution must treat the account as a U.S. Reportable Account.

2. If the entity Account Holder is ***a Passive NFFE***, the Reporting Irish Financial Institution must identify the Controlling Persons as determined under AML/KYC Procedures, and must determine whether any such person is a citizen or resident of the United States on the basis of a self-certification from the Account Holder or such person. If any such person is a citizen or resident of the United States, the account shall be treated as a U.S. Reportable Account.

3. If the entity Account Holder is: (i) a U.S. Person that is not a Specified U.S. Person; (ii) subject to *subparagraph C.4* of this section, an Irish Financial Institution or other Partner Jurisdiction Financial Institution; (iii) a participating FFI, a deemed-compliant FFI, an exempt beneficial owner, or an excepted FFI, as those terms are defined in relevant U.S. Treasury Regulations; (iv) an Active NFFE; or (v) a Passive NFFE none of the Controlling Persons of which is a U.S. citizen or resident, then the account is not a U.S. Reportable Account and no reporting is required with respect to the account.

4. If the entity Account Holder is a Nonparticipating Financial Institution (including an Irish Financial Institution or other Partner Jurisdiction Financial Institution that is identified by the IRS as a Nonparticipating Financial Institution as described in *paragraph 2* of Article 5 of the Agreement), then the account is not a U.S. Reportable Account, but payments to the Account Holder must be reported as contemplated in *paragraph 1b)* of Article 4 of the Agreement.

VI. **Special Rules and Definitions**. The following additional rules and definitions apply in implementing the due diligence procedures described above:

A. **Reliance on Self-Certifications and Documentary Evidence**. A Reporting Irish Financial Institution may not rely on a self-certification or documentary evidence if the Reporting Irish Financial Institution knows or has reason to know that the self-certification or documentary evidence is incorrect or unreliable.

B. **Definitions.** The following definitions apply for purposes of this Annex I.

1. **AML/KYC Procedures**. "AML/KYC Procedures" means the customer due diligence procedures of a Reporting Irish Financial Institution pursuant to the anti-money laundering or similar requirements of Ireland to which such Reporting Irish Financial Institution is subject.

2. **NFFE.** An "NFFE" means any Non-U.S. Entity that is not an FFI as defined in relevant U.S. Treasury Regulations, and also includes any Non-U.S. Entity that is resident in Ireland or other Partner Jurisdiction and that is not a Financial Institution.

3. **Passive NFFE.** A "Passive NFFE" means any NFFE that is not (i) an Active NFFE or (ii) a withholding foreign partnership or withholding foreign trust pursuant to relevant U.S. Treasury Regulations.

4. **Active NFFE.** An "Active NFFE" means any NFFE that meets any of the following criteria:

a) Less than 50 percent of the NFFE's gross income for the preceding calendar year or other appropriate reporting period is passive income and less than 50 percent of the assets held by the NFFE during the preceding calendar year or other appropriate reporting period are assets that produce or are held for the production of passive income;

b) The stock of the NFFE is regularly traded on an established securities market or the NFFE is a Related Entity of an Entity the stock of which is traded on an established securities market;

c) The NFFE is organized in a U.S. Territory and all of the owners of the payee are bona fide residents of that U.S. Territory;

d) The NFFE is a non-U.S. government, a government of a U.S. Territory, an international organization, a non-U.S. central bank of issue, or an Entity wholly owned by one or more of the foregoing;

e) Substantially all of the activities of the NFFE consist of holding (in whole or in part) the outstanding stock of, and providing financing and services to, one or more subsidiaries that engage in trades or businesses other than the business of a Financial Institution, except that an NFFE shall not qualify for this status if the NFFE functions (or holds itself out) as an investment fund, such as a private equity fund, venture capital fund, leveraged buyout fund or any investment vehicle whose purpose is to acquire or fund companies and then hold interests in those companies as capital assets for investment purposes;

f) The NFFE is not yet operating a business and has no prior operating history, but is investing capital into assets with the intent to operate a business other than that of a Financial Institution; provided, that the NFFE shall not qualify for this exception after the date that is 24 months after the date of the initial organization of the NFFE;

g) The NFFE was not a Financial Institution in the past five years, and is in the process of liquidating its assets or is reorganizing with the intent to continue or recommence operations in a business other than that of a Financial Institution;

h) The NFFE primarily engages in financing and hedging transactions with or for Related Entities that are not Financial Institutions, and does not provide financing or hedging services to any Entity that is not a Related Entity, provided that the group of any such Related Entities is primarily engaged in a business other than that of a Financial Institution; ***or***

i) The NFFE meets all of the following requirements:

   i. It is established and maintained in its country of residence exclusively for religious, charitable, scientific, artistic, cultural, or educational purposes;

   ii. It is exempt from income tax in its country of residence;

   iii. It has no shareholders or members who have a proprietary or beneficial interest in its income or assets;

   iv. The applicable laws of the Entity's country of residence or the Entity's formation documents do not permit any income or assets of the Entity to be distributed to, or applied for the benefit of, a private person or non-charitable Entity other than pursuant to the conduct of the Entity's charitable activities, or as payment of reasonable compensation for services rendered, or as payment representing the fair market value of property which the Entity has purchased; ***and***

   v. The applicable laws of the Entity's country of residence or the Entity's formation documents require that, upon the Entity's liquidation or dissolution, all of its assets be distributed to a governmental Entity or other non-profit organization, or escheat to the government of the Entity's country of residence or any political subdivision thereof.

C. **Account Balance Aggregation and Currency Translation Rules**

1. **Aggregation of Individual Accounts**. For purposes of determining the aggregate balance or value of accounts held by an individual, a Reporting Irish Financial Institution shall be required to aggregate all accounts maintained by the Reporting Irish Financial Institution, or Related Entities, but only to the extent that the Reporting Irish Financial Institution's computerized systems link the accounts by reference to a data element such as client number or taxpayer identification number, and allow account balances to be aggregated. Each holder of a jointly held account shall be attributed the entire balance or value of the jointly held account for purposes of applying the aggregation requirements described in this paragraph.

2. **Aggregation of Entity Accounts.** For purposes of determining the aggregate balance or value of accounts held by an Entity, a Reporting Irish Financial Institution shall be required to take into account all accounts held by Entities that are maintained by the Reporting Irish Financial Institution, or Related Entities, to the extent that the Reporting Irish Financial Institution's computerized systems link the accounts by reference to a data element such as client number or taxpayer identification number and allow account balances to be aggregated.

3. **Special Aggregation Rule Applicable to Relationship Managers.** For purposes of determining the aggregate balance or value of accounts held by a person to determine whether an account is a High Value Account, a Reporting Irish Financial Institution shall also be required, in the case of any accounts that a relationship manager knows or has reason to know are directly or indirectly owned, controlled, or established (other than in a fiduciary capacity) by the same person, to aggregate all such accounts.

4. **Currency Translation Rule.** For purposes of determining the balance or value of accounts denominated in a currency other than the U.S. dollar, a Reporting Irish Financial Institution must convert the dollar threshold amounts described in this Annex I into such currency using a published spot rate determined as of the last day of the calendar year preceding the year in which the Reporting Irish Financial Institution is determining the balance or value.

D. **Documentary Evidence.** For purposes of this Annex I, acceptable documentary evidence includes any of the following:

1. A certificate of residence issued by an appropriate tax official of the country in which the payee claims to be a resident.
2. With respect to an individual, any valid identification issued by an authorized government body (for example, a government or agency thereof, or a municipality), that includes the individual's name and is typically used for identification purposes.
3. With respect to an Entity, any official documentation issued by an authorized government body (for example, a government or agency thereof, or a municipality) that includes the name of the Entity and either the address of its principal office in the country (or U.S. Territory) in which it claims to be a resident or the country (or U.S. Territory) in which the Entity was incorporated or organized.
4. With respect to an account maintained in a jurisdiction with anti-money laundering rules that have been approved by the IRS in connection with a QI agreement (as described in relevant U.S. Treasury Regulations), any of the documents other than a Form W-8 or W-9 referenced in the jurisdiction's attachment to the QI agreement for identifying individuals or entities.
5. Any financial statement, third-party credit report, bankruptcy filing, or U.S. Securities and Exchange Commission report.

ANNEX II

NON-REPORTING FINANCIAL INSTITUTIONS AND PRODUCTS

General

This Annex II may be updated by a mutual agreement entered into between the Competent Authorities of Ireland and the United States:

(1) to include additional entities, accounts, and products that present a low risk of being used by U.S. Persons to evade U.S. tax and that have similar characteristics to the entities, accounts, and products identified in this Annex II as of the date of entry into force of the Agreement; or

(2) to remove entities, accounts, and products that, due to changes in circumstances, no longer present a low risk of being used by U.S. Persons to evade U.S. tax.

Procedures for reaching such a mutual agreement may be included in the mutual agreement described in *paragraph 6* of Article 3 of the Agreement.

I. **Exempt Beneficial Owners.** The following categories of institutions are Non-Reporting Irish Financial Institutions that are treated as exempt beneficial owners for purposes of *section 1471* of the U.S. Internal Revenue Code:

A. **The Irish Government, any political subdivision of the Irish Government or any wholly owned agency or instrumentality of any one or more of the foregoing including:**

1. The National Treasury Management Agency,
2. The National Pensions Reserve Fund and the National Pensions Reserve Fund Commission, and
3. The National Asset Management Agency

B. **Central Bank**

The Central Bank and Financial Services Authority of Ireland as established under The Central Bank and Financial Authority of Ireland Acts 2003 and 2004 together with the Central Bank Reform Act 2010 and the Central Bank Act 1942.

C. **International Organisations**

The office in Ireland of any institution of the European Union, of the European Investment Bank, the European Bank for Reconstruction and Development, or of any organisation to which the Diplomatic Relations and Immunities Acts 1967–2006 apply.

D. **Retirement Funds**

A pension trust and any other organisation, as referred to in Article 4(1)(c) (Residence) of the Convention, established in Ireland and maintained exclusively to administer or provide retirement or employee benefits.

II. **Deemed-Compliant Financial Institutions**

The following categories of institutions are *Non-Reporting Irish Financial Institutions* that are treated as *deemed-compliant FFIs* for purposes of *section 1471* of the U.S. Internal Revenue Code:

A. **Non-Profit Organisations**

- Charitable organisations that qualify for exemption from tax in accordance with *section 848A* and *Schedule 26A* of the Taxes Consolidation Act 1997.

- A body established for the promotion of athletic or amateur games or sports that has been granted exemption from tax in accordance with *section 235* of the Taxes Consolidation Act 1997 by the Revenue Commissioners.

B. **Financial Institutions with a Local Client Base**

An Irish Financial Institution that meets all of the following requirements:

(a) The Financial Institution must be licensed and regulated under the laws of Ireland;

(b) The Financial Institution must have no fixed place of business outside of Ireland;

(c) The Financial Institution must not solicit account holders outside of Ireland. For this purpose, a Financial Institution shall not be considered to have solicited account holders outside of Ireland merely because it operates a website, provided that the website does not specifically indicate that the Financial Institution provides accounts or services to non-residents, or otherwise target or solicit U.S. customers;

(d) The Financial Institution must be required under the tax laws of Ireland to perform either information reporting or withholding of tax with respect to accounts held by residents of Ireland;

(e) At least 98 per cent of the accounts by value provided by the Financial Institution must be held by residents (including residents that are entities) of Ireland or another Member State of the European Union;

(f) Subject to *subparagraph (g)* below, beginning on January 1, 2014, the Financial Institution does not open accounts for (i) any Specified U.S. Person who is not a resident of Ireland (including a U.S. Person that was a resident of Ireland when the account was opened but subsequently ceases to be a resident of Ireland), (ii) a Nonparticipating Financial Institution, or (iii) any Passive NFFE with Controlling Persons who are U.S. citizens or residents;

(g) On or before January 1, 2014, the Financial Institution must implement policies and procedures to monitor whether it provides any account held by a person described in *subparagraph (f)*, and if such an account is discovered, the Financial Institution must report such account as though the Financial Institution were a Reporting Irish Financial Institution or close such account;

(h) With respect to each account that is held by an individual who is not a resident of Ireland or by an entity, and that is opened prior to the date that the Financial Institution implements the policies and procedures described in *subparagraph (g)* above, the Financial Institution must review those accounts in accordance with the procedures described in Annex I applicable to Preexisting Accounts to identify any U.S. Reportable Account or account held by a Nonparticipating Financial Institution, and must close any such accounts that were identified, or report on such accounts as though the Financial Institution were a Reporting Irish Financial Institution;

(i) Each Related Entity of the Financial Institution must be incorporated or organised in Ireland and must meet the requirements set forth in this paragraph; and

(j) The Financial Institution must not have policies or practices that discriminate against opening or maintaining accounts for individuals who are Specified U.S. Persons and who are residents of Ireland.

C. **Certain Collective Investment Vehicles**

In the case of an Investment Entity that is a collective investment vehicle regulated under the laws of Ireland:

a) if all of the interests in the collective investment vehicle (including debt interests in excess of $50,000) are held by or through one or more Financial Institutions that are not Nonparticipating Financial Institutions, such collective investment vehicle will be treated as a deemed-compliant FFI for purposes of *section 1471* of the U.S. Internal Revenue Code, and the reporting obligations of any Investment Entity (other than a Financial Institution through which interests in the collective investment vehicle are held) will be deemed fulfilled with respect to interests in the collective investment vehicle; or

b) if the collective investment vehicle is not described in *paragraph a*), consistent with *paragraph 3* of Article 5 of the Agreement, and if the information required to be reported by the collective investment vehicle under the Agreement with respect to interests in the collective investment vehicle is reported by the collective investment vehicle or another Investment Entity, the reporting obligations of all other Investment Entities which have an obligation to report with respect to the interests in the collective investment vehicle will be deemed fulfilled with respect to such interests.

III. **Exempt Products**

The following categories of accounts and products established in Ireland and maintained by an Irish Financial Institution shall not be treated as Financial Accounts, and therefore shall not be U.S. Reportable Accounts or accounts held by a Nonparticipating Financial Institution, under the Agreement:

A. **Certain Retirement Accounts or Products**

- A Retirement Benefit Scheme, within the meaning of *section 771* of the Taxes Consolidation Act 1997, approved by the Revenue Commissioners for the purposes of *Chapter 1* of *Part 30* of that Act.
- An annuity contract or a trust scheme or part of a trust scheme approved by the Revenue Commissioners under *Chapter 2* of *Part 30* of the Taxes Consolidation Act 1997.
- A PRSA contract in respect of a PRSA product, approved by the Revenue Commissioners under *Chapter 2A* of *Part 30* of the Taxes Consolidation Act 1997.
- An Approved Retirement Fund or an Approved Minimum Retirement Fund provided for under a Retirement Benefit Scheme, an

annuity contract or a PRSA as approved under *Chapters 1, 2* or *2A* of Part 30 of the Taxes Consolidation Act 1997.

- Those Irish approved pension schemes or contracts under *Part 30* of the Taxes Consolidation Act 1997 or Approved Retirement Funds or Approved Minimum retirement Funds that are excluded from the definition of Financial Account pursuant to Article 1(s)(3).
- An account or product excluded from the definition of Financial Account under an agreement between the United States and another Partner Jurisdiction to facilitate the implementation of FATCA, provided that such account or product is subject to the same requirements and oversight under the laws of such other Partner Jurisdiction as if such account or product were established in that Partner Jurisdiction and maintained by a Partner Jurisdiction Financial Institution in that Partner Jurisdiction.

B. **Certain Other Tax-Favoured Accounts or Products**

- **Save As You Earn Share Option Schemes** — approved by the Revenue Commissioners under *Chapter 3*, *Part 17* and *Schedule 12A* Taxes Consolidation Act 1997.
- **Profit Sharing Schemes** — approved by the Revenue Commissioners under *Chapter 1*, *Part 17* and *Schedule 11* Taxes Consolidation Act 1997.
- **Employee Share Ownership Trusts** — approved by the Revenue Commissioners under *Chapter 2*, *Part 17* and *Schedule 12* Taxes Consolidation Act 1997.

L.S.

GIVEN under the Official Seal of the Government,
5 February 2013.

ENDA KENNY,
Taoiseach.

S.I. No. 292 of 2014

FINANCIAL ACCOUNTS REPORTING (UNITED STATES OF AMERICA) REGULATIONS 2014

INDEX

Regulation

The Revenue Commissioners, in exercise of the powers conferred on them by *section 891E* (inserted by *section 32* of the Finance Act 2013 (No. 8 of 2013)) of the Taxes Consolidation Act 1997 (No. 39 of 1997), with the consent of the Minister for Finance, hereby make the following regulations:

1. Citation and commencement

(1) These Regulations may be cited as the Financial Accounts Reporting (United States of America) Regulations 2014.

(2) These Regulations come into operation on 1 July 2014.

2. Interpretation

(1) In these Regulations—

"Act" means Taxes Consolidation Act 1997 (No. 39 of 1997);

"account balance or value" includes—

(*a*) a nil or negative balance or value, and

(*b*) in the case of a cash value insurance contract or an annuity contract, the cash value or surrender value of that contract;

"account number" includes, in addition to the account number, any code or codes used generally in the financial services industry to identify a reporting financial institution or a branch of a reporting financial institution, and "bank code", "branch code", "sorting code" and any other similar terms used to identify a reporting financial institution or a branch of a reporting financial institution shall be construed accordingly;

"Agreement" means the Agreement Between the Government of Ireland and the Government of the United States of America to Improve International Tax Compliance and to Implement FATCA, done at Dublin on 21 December 2012;

"authorised officer" means an officer of the Revenue Commissioners authorised by them in writing to exercise the powers conferred by these Regulations;

"deposit" has the same meaning as it has in *section 256* of the Act;

"entity" means an entity that is not a natural person;

"FATCA" means the provisions commonly known as the Foreign Accounts Tax Compliance Act in the enactment of the United States of America known as Hiring Incentives to Restore Employment Act 2010;

"financial group", in relation to a relevant company, means a group of entities consisting of the relevant company and the related entities of that company where one or more of those related entities is a custodial institution, depository institution, investment entity or specified insurance company;

"financing or refinancing facilities" has the same meaning as it has in *section 488* of the Act;

"G.I.N." means the Global Intermediary Identification Number allocated to a financial institution by the Internal Revenue Service of the United States of America for the purpose of identifying the institution as one whose FATCA obligations are modified by reason of the Agreement;

"high value pre-existing individual account" means a pre-existing individual account which on, or before, 30 June 2014 has an account balance or value that exceeds $1,000,000;

"investment entity" has the meaning given to it in Article 1(1)(j) of the Agreement;

"investment undertaking" means—

(*a*) an investment undertaking within the meaning of *section 739B(1)* of the Act,

(*b*) a common contractual fund within the meaning of *section 739I*(1)(a) of the Act, or

(*c*) an investment limited partnership within the meaning of *section 739J*(1)(a) of the Act;

"low value pre-existing individual account" means a pre-existing individual account which on, or before, 30 June 2014 has an account balance or value that—

(*a*) in the case of a cash value insurance contract, or annuity contract, is greater than $250,000 but does not exceed $1,000,000, or

(*b*) in any other case, is greater than $50,000 but does not exceed $1,000,000;

"new entity account" means a financial account maintained by a reporting financial institution which—

(*a*) is opened on, or after, 1 July 2014, and

(*b*) is beneficially owned by an entity;

"new individual account" means a financial account maintained by a reporting financial institution which—

(*a*) is opened on, or after, 1 July 2014, and

(*b*) is beneficially owned by a natural person;

"pre-existing account" means a financial account maintained by a reporting financial institution on 30 June 2014;

"pre-existing entity account" means a financial account that is beneficially owned by an entity and is maintained by a reporting financial institution on 30 June 2014;

"pre-existing individual account" means a financial account that is beneficially owned by a natural person and is maintained by a reporting financial institution on 30 June 2014;

"qualifying activities", in relation to a relevant treasury company, means activities carried on by that company which consist of one, or more, of the following:

(*a*) the making, or receiving, of deposits and the management of those deposits;

(*b*) the provision, or management, of financing or refinancing facilities;

(*c*) the acquisition of, or the holding of shares in, another company that is a custodial institution, depository institution, investment entity or specified insurance company;

(*d*) investing in securities;

(*e*) the entering into, or management of, specified agreements;

"registered financial institution", for the purpose of these Regulations and *section 891E* of the Act, means a financial institution that registers with the Internal Revenue Service of the United States of America in accordance with Regulation 5(1);

"relevant company" means a relevant holding company or a relevant treasury company, as the case may be;

"relevant holding company" means a person whose business consists wholly or mainly of—

(*a*) holding, directly or indirectly, any shares or securities in a related entity that is a custodial institution, depository institution, investment entity or specified insurance company, or

(*b*) holding shares or securities where the person has a qualifying relationship with an investment entity;

"relevant treasury company" means a company which exists wholly or mainly for the purpose of carrying on qualifying activities on behalf of—

(a) a financial group, or

(b) an investment entity with which it has a qualifying relationship;

"return date", in relation to a tax year, means a date that is not later than 30 June of the tax year following the tax year for which a return is required;

"specified agreement" has the same meaning as it has in *section 110(1)* of the Act;

"tax reference number" means a U.S. TIN;

"tax year" means—

(a) a year of assessment, or

(b) subject to *paragraph (3)*, where a financial institution has an established practice for the periodic valuation of accounts of a particular description otherwise than at the end of a year of assessment, another appropriate reporting period of 12 months;

"U.S." means United States of America.

(2) For the purposes of *paragraph (1)*, a person has a qualifying relationship with an investment entity where—

(a) the investment entity is a related entity, or

(b) the person provides services to, or holds investments on behalf of, that investment entity.

(3) In the definition of "tax year" in *paragraph (1)*, "another appropriate reporting period" means a period of 12 months ending with the date (or, if more than one, the latest date) in the year of assessment on which the institution has an established practice of valuing accounts of that description.

(4) Subject to *paragraph (1)*, and unless the context otherwise requires, a word or expression used in these Regulations that is also used in the Agreement shall have the same meaning as it has in the Agreement.

(5) For the purposes of these Regulations—

(a) where an investment undertaking is constituted by a person (other than a trustee) who carries on business in the State, that person is the reporting financial institution in the case of the undertaking and is to be regarded as an investment entity,

(b) where an investment undertaking is constituted as a trust and the trustee of the trust is a person who carries on business in the State, the trustee is the reporting financial institution in the case of the undertaking and is to be regarded as an investment entity, and

(c) where an investment undertaking is constituted otherwise than as described in *subparagraph (a)* or *(b)* and the manager of the undertaking is a person who carries on business in the State, that person is the reporting financial institution in the case of the undertaking and is to be regarded as an investment entity.

(6) Where a person is required under these Regulations to—

(*a*) deliver a return, or

(*b*) make a declaration or election,

the return, declaration, or election shall be delivered, made or given electronically—

(i) using such technology as may be approved or provided by the Revenue Commissioners, and

(ii) in such form as the Revenue Commissioners may require.

3. Reporting financial institutions

(1) Subject to *paragraph (2)*, any person that carries on business in the State as—

(*a*) a custodial institution,

(*b*) a depository institution,

(*c*) an investment entity,

(*d*) a specified insurance company,

(*e*) a relevant holding company, or

(*f*) a relevant treasury company,

shall be a reporting financial institution.

(2) Subject to Regulations 4 and 5, *paragraph (1)* shall not apply to a deemed compliant financial institution.

4. Deemed compliant financial institutions

(1) Where a financial institution—

(*a*) is a deemed compliant FFI referred to in Article 1(1)(q) of the Agreement, and

(*b*) is required to submit a return of information in relation to an account maintained by it,

the institution shall be a reporting financial institution for the purpose of returning information on that account.

(2) (*a*) A financial institution within the meaning of *paragraph II.B* of *Annex II* to the Agreement shall not, on or after 1 July 2014, open an account for—

(i) any specified U.S. person who is not a resident of Ireland,

(ii) any non-participating financial institution, or

(iii) any passive entity which has a controlling person who is a U.S. person.

(*b*) A financial institution referred to in *subparagraph (a)* shall on, or before, 1 July 2014 implement policies and procedures to monitor whether it maintains an account for—

(i) any specified U.S. person who is not a resident of Ireland,

(ii) any non-participating financial institution, or

(iii) any passive entity which has a controlling person who is a U.S. person.

(*c*) Where an account referred to in *subparagraph (b)* is identified, the financial institution concerned shall close the account or report the account as though the institution was a reporting financial institution.

5. Obligation of a reporting financial institution to register

(1) Every reporting financial institution shall, for the purposes of complying with Article 4(1)(c) of the Agreement, register with the Internal Revenue Service of the United States of America for the purposes of FATCA in such manner, including by electronic means, as the Internal Revenue Service may require.

(2) An application for registration shall be made by the reporting financial institution not later than 31 December 2014 or, where the institution is not a reporting financial institution on that date, not later than 30 days following the date on which the institution becomes a reporting financial institution.

6. Reportable accounts

(1) Subject to *paragraph (2)*, and notwithstanding—

(*a*) *paragraph A* of *section II*,

(*b*) *paragraph A* of *section III*, or

(*c*) *paragraph A* of *section IV*,

of Annex I to the Agreement, a reportable account, in relation to a reporting financial institution, means a U.S. reportable account that is maintained by that institution in the State for the purposes of its business as—

(i) a custodial institution,

(ii) a depository institution,

(iii) an investment entity,

(iv) a specified insurance company,

(v) a relevant holding company, or

(vi) a relevant treasury company,

and that is not an excluded account to which *paragraph (3)* applies.

(2) (*a*) Where a reporting financial institution so elects, an account shall not be a reportable account where it satisfies one of the following conditions:

(i) it is a pre-existing individual account—

(I) that is a cash value insurance contract, or annuity contract, with an account balance or value that does not exceed $250,000,

(II) that is a cash value insurance contract or annuity contract, where the sale of such contracts to U.S. residents is effectively prevented by law and the contract is maintained by a specified insurance company that is—

(A) subject to tax under, and

(B) subject to the reporting requirements of,

Part 26 of the Act, or

(III) that is not a cash value insurance contract, or annuity contract, which has an account balance or value that does not exceed $50,000;

(ii) it is a new individual account that is a depository account the account balance or value of which does not exceed $50,000 at the end of the tax year concerned;

(iii) it is a new individual account that is a cash value insurance contract, which has an account balance or value that does not exceed $50,000 at the end of the tax year;

(iv) it is a pre-existing entity account the account balance or value of which does not exceed $250,000.

(*b*) An election under this paragraph shall be made on, or before, the return date for the tax year in respect of which the return is required to be made and shall be in such form as the Revenue Commissioners may require.

(*c*) The account balance aggregation and currency translation rules set out in *paragraph C* of *section VI* of Annex I to the Agreement shall be used to determine whether an account satisfies one of the conditions set out in *paragraph* (*a*).

(3) This Regulation applies to exempt products within the meaning of *section III* of *Annex II* to the Agreement.

7. Identification of reportable accounts

(1) Subject to this Regulation, a reporting financial institution shall apply the due diligence rules and procedures specified in Annex I to the Agreement in order to identify the account holder of the reportable accounts maintained by the institution.

(2) The review of low value pre-existing individual accounts to be carried out by a reporting financial institution in accordance with the procedures set out in *paragraph B* of *section II* of *Annex I* to the Agreement shall be completed on, or before, 30 June 2016.

(3) Where an account is not a low value pre-existing individual account on 30 June 2014 but has an account value or balance greater than the relevant thresholds set out in the definition of "low value pre-existing individual account" in Regulation 2 on the last day of any subsequent tax year, the review of that account shall be completed not later than 6 months of the end of that tax year.

(4) The review of high value pre-existing individual accounts to be carried out by a reporting financial institution in accordance with the procedures set out in *paragraph D* of *section II* of Annex I to the Agreement shall be completed on, or before, 30 June 2015.

(5) Where an account is not a high value pre-existing individual account on 30 June 2014 but has an account balance or value that exceeds $1,000,000 on the last day of any subsequent tax year, the review of that account shall be completed not later than 6 months of the end of that tax year.

(6) The review of pre-existing entity accounts to be carried out by a reporting financial institution in accordance with the procedures set out in *paragraph D* of *section IV* of *Annex I* to the Agreement shall be completed on, or before, 30 June 2016 where the account balance or value of that account exceeds $250,000 on 30 June 2014.

(7) Where the account balance or value of a pre-existing entity account does not exceed $250,000 on 30 June 2014 but exceeds $1,000,000 in a subsequent tax year, the review of that account shall be completed not later than 6 months after the end of the tax year in which the account balance exceeds $1,000,000.

(8) A reporting financial institution may treat a new account opened by a natural person as a pre-existing individual account where—

(*a*) on the account opening date, the institution maintains a pre-existing account for that individual, and

(*b*) the institution returns the aggregate account balance or value of—

(i) the new account, and

(ii) the pre-existing account referred to in *subparagraph (a)*,

and for this purpose the account balance aggregation and currency translation rules set out in *paragraph C* of *section VI* of *Annex I* to the Agreement shall be used to determine the aggregate account balance or value of such accounts.

(9) Notwithstanding the requirements set out in Annex I to the Agreement, where—

(*a*) in the case of a low value pre-existing individual account, a reporting financial institution—

(i) has established the account holder's status as neither a U.S. citizen nor a U.S. resident (in this paragraph referred to as the "account holder's non-U.S. status") from the documentary evidence referred to in *paragraph D* of *section VI* of *Annex I* to the Agreement, and

(ii) has done so in order to meet its obligations under a QI agreement, as referred to in that paragraph,

the due diligence rules and procedures referred to in *paragraph (1)* in the case of that account shall not include the requirement to carry out the electronic search described in *paragraph B.1* of *section II* of *Annex I* to the Agreement.

(*b*) in the case of a high value pre-existing individual account, a reporting financial institution—

(i) has established the account holder's non-U.S. status from the documentary evidence referred to in *paragraph D* of *section VI* of *Annex I* to the Agreement, and

(ii) has done so in order to meet its obligations under a QI agreement as referred to in that paragraph,

the due diligence rules and procedures referred to in paragraph (1) in the case of that account do not include the requirement to—

(I) carry out the electronic searches described in *paragraph B.1* or *D.1* of *section II* of *Annex I* to the Agreement, or

(II) carry out the paper record search described in *paragraph D.2* of that section.

(10) (*a*) The due diligence rules and procedures referred to in *paragraph (1)* shall not apply in relation to a financial account where—

(i) the reporting financial institution concerned maintains the account as a result of a merger with, or acquisition of, a qualifying financial institution which had established whether the account holder and any controlling person of the account holder is a U.S. citizen or a U.S. resident (in this subparagraph referred to as the "U.S. status of the account holder or any controlling person of the account holder"), and

(ii) the institution has no reasonable cause to believe that the U.S. status of the account holder or any controlling person of the account holder has changed.

(*b*) For the purpose of this paragraph, "qualifying financial institution", in relation to a financial institution, means another financial institution—

(i) which has not previously been a related entity of the institution, and

(ii) which immediately before the merger or acquisition was a partner jurisdiction financial institution but was neither a registered deemed compliant FFI nor a non-participating financial institution.

(11) (*a*) Subject to *subparagraph (b)*, where the due diligence rules and procedures referred to in *paragraph (1)* require a person to submit evidence of their identity or residence, such evidence shall be in such form as the institution considers reasonable.

(*b*) Notwithstanding *subparagraph (a)* and where requested to do so by an authorised officer, the reporting institution shall obtain such other evidence of the identity or residence of the account holder as may be required by that officer.

(12) For the purposes of this Regulation, references to the documentary evidence set out in *paragraph D* of *section VI* of *Annex I* to the Agreement are to be treated as if "other than a Form W-8 or W-9" were omitted.

8. Obligation to submit returns of reportable accounts

(1) A reporting financial institution shall—

(*a*) as respects the tax year 2014 and each subsequent tax year, make and deliver to the appropriate Revenue officer on, or before, the return date, a return in respect of all reportable accounts maintained by the institution in that year, and

(*b*) as respects the tax years 2015 and 2016, make and deliver to the appropriate Revenue officer on, or before, the return date, a return of payments made to non-participating financial institutions in those years.

(2) The return referred to in *paragraph (1)(a)* shall include, as respects—

(*a*) the financial institution, the details set out in *paragraph (3)*, and

(*b*) each reportable account, the details set out in *paragraph (4)*.

(3) The details relating to the financial institution referred to in *paragraph (2)* are the following:

(*a*) the name of the institution;

(*b*) the address of the registered office of the institution;

(*c*) the G.I.I.N. allocated to the institution.

(4) Subject to *paragraph (5)*, the details relating to each reportable account referred to in *paragraph (2)* are the following:

(*a*) the name, address, and tax reference number of—

(i) each specified U.S. person that is an account holder,

(ii) each passive entity that is the holder of a reportable account, and

(iii) each specified U.S. person that controls the passive entity referred to in clause (ii);

(*b*) the account number or, where there is no account number, information capable of identifying the asset giving rise to the payment;

(*c*) the account balance or value as of the end of the tax year or, if the account was closed during such year, the account balance or value on the day on which the account was closed;

(*d*) in the case of any custodial account—

(i) the total gross amount of interest,

(ii) the total gross amount of dividends,

(iii) the total gross amount of other income arising from the assets held in the account, and

(iv) the total gross proceeds from the sale or redemption of any property where the financial institution acted as a custodian, broker, nominee, or otherwise as an agent, for the account holder in relation to that sale or redemption,

which has been paid or credited in respect of such account during the tax year;

(*e*) in the case of any depository account, the total gross amount of interest paid or credited to the account during the tax year;

(*f*) in the case of any account not described in *subparagraph (d)* or *(e)*, the total gross amount paid or credited to the account holder with respect to the account during the tax year, where the financial institution is the obligor or debtor including the aggregate amount of any redemption payments made to the account holder during the tax year.

(5) The return, referred to in *paragraph (1)(a)*, shall include the following:

(*a*) for the tax year 2014, the details set out in *subparagraphs (a)* to *(c)* of *paragraph (4)*;

(*b*) for the tax years 2015 and 2016, the details set out in *subparagraphs (a)* to *(f)* of *paragraph (4)* (other than the details set out in *subparagraph (d)(iv)*);

(*c*) for the tax year 2017 and all subsequent tax years, the details set out in *subparagraphs (a)* to *(f)* of *paragraph (4)*.

(6) In the case of a pre-existing account of a specified U.S. person (in this paragraph referred to as the "account holder"), where the tax reference number of the account holder is not available from the records of the financial institution, the financial institution shall, in the return referred to in *paragraph (1)(a)*, report the date of birth of the account holder where this information is available from the records of the financial institution.

(7) An account balance that has a negative value shall be treated as having a nil value for the purpose of applying *paragraph C* of *section VI* of *Annex I* to the Agreement.

(8) The return, referred to in *paragraph (1)(b)*, shall include the following:

(*a*) as regards the reporting financial institution, the details set out in *paragraph (3)*;

(*b*) the name and address of each non-participating financial institution;

(*c*) the aggregate amounts of payments made to the non-participating financial institution in the tax year or, where no such payments were made in a tax year, a statement to that effect.

9. Obligation to submit returns where there are no reportable accounts

(1) Where a reporting financial institution has no reportable accounts in a tax year, the institution shall make and deliver a nil return for that year.

(2) The return referred to in *paragraph (1)* shall include the details set out in Regulation 8(3).

10. Appointment of third parties

(1) A reporting financial institution may appoint another person as its agent to carry out the duties and obligations imposed on it by these Regulations or the Agreement.

(2) Where another person is appointed, in accordance with paragraph (1)—

(*a*) the financial institution shall, at all times, have access to and be able to produce, where so requested by an authorised officer, the records and documentary evidence used to identify and report on reportable accounts, and

(*b*) the financial institution is responsible for any failure of that other person to carry out its obligations and *subsections (7)* and *(8)* of *section 891E* of the Act will apply to the institution notwithstanding that—

(i) the actions were the actions of that other person, or

(ii) the failure to act was the failure by that other person to act.

11. Obligations of reporting financial institutions to obtain tax reference numbers

(1) A reporting financial institution shall implement arrangements to obtain the tax reference number of every U.S. Specified Person who is the account holder of a reportable account.

(2) Paragraph (1) has effect—

(*a*) from 1 January 2017, in the case of pre-existing accounts, and

(*b*) from 1 July 2014, in the case of new accounts opened on, or after, that date.

The Minister for Finance consents to the making of the foregoing Regulations.

L.S.

GIVEN under my Official Seal,
20 June 2014.

MICHAEL NOONAN,
Minister for Finance.

L.S.

GIVEN under my hand,
20 June 2014.

NIALL CODY,
Revenue Commissioner.

S.I. No. 572 of 2014

TAX RETURNS AND PAYMENTS (MANDATORY ELECTRONIC FILING AND PAYMENT OF TAX) REGULATIONS 2014

ARRANGEMENT OF REGULATIONS

The Revenue Commissioners in exercise of the powers conferred on them by section 917EA (inserted by section 164 of the Finance Act 2003 (No. 3 of 2003)) of the Taxes Consolidation Act 1997 (No. 39 of 1997) make the following regulations:

1 Citation and commencement

(1) These Regulations may be cited as the Tax Returns and Payments (Mandatory Electronic Filing and Payment of Tax) Regulations 2014.

(2) These Regulations come into operation on 1 January 2015.

2 Interpretation and general

(1) In these Regulations—

"capacity" means sufficient access to the Internet by which either or both a specified return or the payment of any specified liabilities may be made by electronic means and, in the case of an individual, also means not prevented by reason of age or mental or physical infirmity from either or both making a specified return or paying any specified liabilities by electronic means;

"Commissioners" means the Revenue Commissioners;

"Principal Act" means the Taxes Consolidation Act 1997 (No. 39 of 1997);

"registered with the Commissioners" means, with regard to a specified person, identified in any register, list, database or other record, maintained by the Commissioners in electronic or any other form, as a person who is required to make a return of income and gains in accordance with section 959I of the Principal Act;

"Regulations of 2008" means the Tax Returns and Payments (Mandatory Electronic Filing and Payment of Tax) Regulations 2008 (S.I. No. 341 of 2008);

"Regulations of 2011" means the Tax Returns and Payments (Mandatory Electronic Filing and Payment of Tax) Regulations 2011 (S.I. No. 223 of 2011);

"Regulations of 2012" means the Tax Returns and Payments (Mandatory Electronic Filing and Payment of Tax) Regulations 2012 (S.I. No. 156 of 2012);

"return" has the same meaning as it has in section 917D of the Principal Act;

"tax year" means a year of assessment.

(2) (a) Any return which a person is or may be required by the Acts to make to the Commissioners and which is specified for the purposes of *Chapter 6* of *Part 38* of the Principal Act by order made by the Commissioners under *section 917E* of that Act is specified as a specified return.

(b) Any liabilities to tax, including interest on unpaid tax, arising under any provision of the Acts, the payment of which is or will be accounted for, directly or indirectly, in a specified return, including any payment which is treated under the Acts as a payment on foot of, or on account of, any liabilities to tax, are specified as specified liabilities.

(c) Each person to whom these Regulations relate, other than the Commissioners, an officer of the Commissioners or the Appeal Commissioners, is specified as a specified person for the purposes of *paragraphs (a)* and *(b)* of *subsection (3)* of *section 917EA* of the Principal Act and these Regulations.

3 Certain individuals required to make returns and payments by electronic means

(1) Subject to paragraph (2), where any specified person, other than a specified person to whom the Regulations of 2008, the Regulations of 2011 or the Regulations of 2012 apply, is a chargeable person (within the meaning of section 959A of the Principal Act) as respects any tax year commencing on or after 1 January 2015, that specified person shall, for that tax year and all subsequent tax years, make any specified return that is required to be made, by or on behalf of that specified person, by electronic means and in accordance with Chapter 6 of Part 38 of the Principal Act.

(2) Subject to *paragraph (3)*, *paragraph (1)* shall not apply if the specified person was registered with the Commissioners on 31 December 2014.

(3) *Paragraph (2)* shall not apply if the specified person referred to in that paragraph has notified the Commissioners, that he or she is not a chargeable person as respects any tax year commencing on or after 1 January 2015 and subsequent to that notification becomes a chargeable person as respects any subsequent tax year.

(4) Where any specified person, other than a specified person to whom the Regulations of 2008, the Regulations of 2011 or the Regulations of 2012 apply, or to whom *paragraph (1)* applies, is required to make a specified return in accordance with *section 959I* of the Principal Act for the tax year 2015 or any subsequent tax year, being a specified return which includes a claim to a deduction under *section 372AAB* of the Principal Act, that specified person shall, on and from the date by which that specified return is required to be made, make any specified return that is required to be made by or subsequent to that date, by or on behalf of that specified person, by electronic means and in accordance with *Chapter 6* of Part 38 of the Principal Act.

(5) Where, on or after the date from which *paragraph (1)* or *(4)* applies to a specified person, a payment of any specified liabilities falls due to be made by or on behalf of the specified person, the payment shall be made by such electronic means as are required by the Commissioners.

4 Exclusion of certain specified persons

(1) A specified person may, by notifying the Commissioners in writing, request to be excluded from the provisions of these Regulations on the grounds that the specified person does not have the capacity to make a specified return or pay the specified tax liabilities by electronic means and the notification shall include all information relevant to the consideration by the Commissioners of the request.

(2) Where the Commissioners receive a notification from a specified person in accordance with *paragraph (1)* or where the Commissioners otherwise consider it appropriate, they may exclude the specified person from the provisions of these Regulations only if they are satisfied that, in all of the circumstances, the specified person could not reasonably be expected to have the capacity to make a specified return or to make a payment of specified tax liabilities by electronic means.

(3) A decision to exclude a specified person from the provisions of these Regulations by the Commissioners in accordance with *paragraph (2)* may be made at any time but where a notification has been received from a specified person in accordance with *paragraph (1)* the decision shall be made within 30 days of receipt of the notification, and the Commissioners shall, in all cases, notify the specified person in writing of the decision.

5 Right of appeal to Appeal Commissioners

(1) A specified person aggrieved by a failure of the Commissioners to exclude the specified person from the provisions of these Regulations in accordance with Regulation 4(2) may, by notice in writing to the Commissioners before the end of the period of 30 days beginning with the day on which notice of the decision was given to the specified person, apply to have such specified person's request to be excluded from the provisions of these Regulations heard and determined by the Appeal Commissioners.

(2) The Appeal Commissioners shall hear and determine an appeal made to them under *paragraph (1)* as if it were an appeal against an assessment to income tax, and the provisions of the Income Tax Acts relating to appeals shall apply accordingly.

(3) On the hearing of an appeal under this Regulation, the Appeal Commissioners shall have regard only to those matters to which the Commissioners may or are required to have regard under these Regulations.

6 Provision to amend exclusions

(1) If, at any time after a decision by the Commissioners in accordance with Regulation 4(2) or a determination by the Appeal Commissioners in accordance with Regulation 5(2) to exclude a specified person from the provisions of these Regulations, the Commissioners decide that, due to a material change in all of the circumstances, the specified person should not be so excluded, they shall notify the specified person in writing of that decision.

(2) The decision referred to in *paragraph (1)* shall be deemed to be a failure to exclude the specified person from the provisions of these Regulations and Regulation 5 shall apply accordingly.

7 Time at which payments made by electronic means are taken to be made

For the purpose of these Regulations, the time at which a payment of any specified liabilities by or on behalf of a specified person shall be taken as having been made shall be the later of the due date for that payment and the time at which the Commissioners receive authorisation to debit the amount of the payment from the account of the specified person in a financial institution.

8 Presumptions

For the purposes of any dispute arising as to the time at which a payment of any specified liabilities to which these Regulations apply is to be taken as having been made, a certificate signed by an officer of the Commissioners which certifies that he or she has examined the relevant records and that it appears from them that the time at which the payment is to be taken as having been made, is the time so specified in the certificate, shall be evidence until the contrary is proven that the payment was made at the time so certified.

GIVEN under my hand,

16 December 2014.

NIALL CODY,

Revenue Commissioner.

EXPLANATORY NOTE

(This note is not part of the Instrument and does not purport to be a legal interpretation.)

Tax Returns and Payments (Mandatory Electronic Filing and Payment of Tax) Regulations 2014

These Regulations are made by the Revenue Commissioners under the provisions of *section 917EA* of the Taxes Consolidation Act 1997. This section was inserted by *section 164* of the Finance Act 2003 and was made subject to a commencement order by the Minister for Finance. This order was signed on 28 July 2008.

With effect from 1 January 2015 the following categories of taxpayers are obliged to file their returns electronically (if they are not already obliged to do so):

- All individual taxpayers who register (or who are obliged to register) for income tax under self-assessment from 1 January 2015 onwards, including individuals who deregister after that date and who subsequently recommence business activities.
- Any self-assessed individuals claiming the owner/occupier residential relief under the Living City Initiative (when it is commenced).

In all cases, the payment of any tax and duty liabilities and the filing of any returns, which arise after the obligation to electronically file commences, must be made electronically and must continue for all subsequent returns and payments.

The Revenue Commissioners may, on application, exclude a taxpayer from the obligation to pay and file electronically if they are satisfied that the taxpayer does not have the capacity to do so. In this context "capacity" is taken to mean having sufficient access to the Internet and, in the case of an individual, not prevented by reason of age, physical or mental infirmity from filing and paying electronically. A taxpayer aggrieved by a failure of the Revenue Commissioners to exclude them from the requirements may appeal that failure to the Appeal Commissioners. An excluded taxpayer may, if circumstances change, have that exclusion revoked and that decision may also be appealed to the Appeal Commissioners.

Provision is also made to determine the time at which payments made by electronic means are to be taken as having been made.

Number 39 of 1997

TAXES CONSOLIDATION ACT, 1997

AN ACT TO CONSOLIDATE ENACTMENTS RELATING TO INCOME TAX, CORPORATION TAX AND CAPITAL GAINS TAX, INCLUDING CERTAIN ENACTMENTS RELATING ALSO TO OTHER TAXES AND DUTIES.

[30*th November,* 1997]

BE IT ENACTED BY THE OIREACHTAS AS FOLLOWS:

INTERPRETATION AND BASIC CHARGING PROVISIONS

PART 1

Interpretation

1 Interpretation of this Act

[ITA67 s3; FA74 s86 and Sch2 PtI; CTA76 s155(1) and (2); CGT(A)78 s1(1); FA80 s9]

(1) In this Act, except where the context otherwise requires, "*repealed enactments*" has the meaning assigned to it by *section 1098*.

(2) In this Act and in any Act passed after this Act, except where the context otherwise requires—

"*the Capital Gains Tax Acts*" means the enactments relating to capital gains tax in this Act and in any other enactment;

"*the Corporation Tax Acts*" means the enactments relating to corporation tax in this Act and in any other enactment, together with the Income Tax Acts in so far as those Acts apply for the purposes of corporation tax;

"*the Income Tax Acts*" means the enactments relating to income tax in this Act and in any other enactment;

"*the Tax Acts*" means the Income Tax Acts and the Corporation Tax Acts.

(3) References in this Act to any enactment shall, except where the context otherwise requires, be construed as references to that enactment as amended or extended by any subsequent enactment.

(4) In this Act a reference to a Part, section or Schedule is to a Part or section of, or Schedule to, this Act, unless it is indicated that reference to some other enactment is intended.

(5) In this Act a reference to a subsection, paragraph, subparagraph, clause or subclause is to the subsection, paragraph, subparagraph, clause or subclause of the provision (including a Schedule) in which the reference occurs, unless it is indicated that reference to some other provision is intended.

Cross References

From Section 1

Section 1098 Repeals.

To Section 1

Section 747 Deduction of offshore income gain in determining capital gain.
Section 1078 Revenue offences.
Schedule 20 Offshore Funds: Computation of Offshore Income Gains
Schedule 24 Relief from Income Tax and Corporation Tax by Means of Credit in Respect of Foreign Tax
Schedule 31 Consequential Amendments

2 Interpretation of Tax Acts

[ITA67 s1(1); CTA76 s155(3) to (5) and s171; F(MP)A68 s3(2) and Sch PtI; FA74 s1; FA75 s33(1); FA77 s41(1); FA97 s146(1) and Sch9 PtI par1(1)]

(1) In the Tax Acts, except where otherwise provided or the context otherwise requires—

"*Appeal Commissioners*" has the meaning assigned to it by *section 850*;

['*appropriate inspector*' in relation to a person, means—

(a) the inspector or other officer of the Revenue Commissioners (in this definition referred to as 'officer') who has last given notice in writing to the person that he or she is the inspector or officer to whom the person is required to deliver an account, declaration, list, particular, return, statement or other item,

(b) in the absence of an inspector or officer referred to in *paragraph* (*a*), the inspector or officer to whom it is customary for the person to deliver such an account, declaration, list, particular, return, statement or other item,

(c) in the absence of an inspector or officer referred to in *paragraph* (*a*) or (*b*), the inspector or officer in charge of the Revenue district which deals with the tax affairs of persons located in the city or county (or the part of the city or county) in which the person is located, or

(d) in any case where the person is directed to deliver an account, declaration, list, particular, return, statement or other item to the inspector of returns, the inspector of returns;][1]

"*body of persons*" means any body politic, corporate or collegiate, and any company, fraternity, fellowship and society of persons, whether corporate or not corporate;

"*capital allowance*" means any allowance (other than an allowance or deduction to be made in computing profits or gains) under—

(a) Part 9,

[(b) *Part 23*,][2]

(c) *Chapter 1* of *Part 24*, or

(d) *Part 29*,

and "*capital allowances*" shall be construed accordingly;

"*Clerk to the Appeal Commissioners*" means the person for the time being authorised by the Appeal Commissioners to act as such;

["*child of the civil partner*", in relation to an individual, means a child of the individual's civil partner who was born before the registration of their civil partnership or during their civil partnership;

"*civil partner*" means a civil partner within the meaning of the Civil Partnership and Certain Rights and Obligations of Cohabitants Act 2010;

"*civil partnership*" means—

(a) a civil partnership registration referred to in section 3(*a*) of the Civil Partnership and Certain Rights and Obligations of Cohabitants Act 2010, or

(b) a legal relationship referred to in section 3(*b*) of that Act;

"*cohabitant*" means a cohabitant within the meaning of section 172(1) of the Civil Partnership and Certain Rights and Obligations of Cohabitants Act 2010;][3]

"*Collector-General*" means the Collector-General appointed under *section 851*;

["*decree of dissolution*" means a decree under section 110 of the Civil Partnership and Certain Rights and Obligations of Cohabitants Act 2010;][4]

['*inspector*' means—

(a) an inspector of taxes appointed under *section 852*,

(b) an officer of the Revenue Commissioners who as part of his or her duties in that capacity carries out duties similar to those of an inspector of taxes appointed under *section 852*, including (but not limited to) the making and amending of assessments, the making of determinations and dealing with notices of appeal against assessments and determinations, or

(c) an officer of the Revenue Commissioners who is employed or acts in the execution of the Tax Acts or the Capital Gains Tax Acts;

'*inspector of returns*' means the inspector nominated under *subsection (1A)* by the Revenue Commissioners to be the inspector of returns;][5]

['*local authority*' means a local authority for the purposes of the Local Government Act 2001 (as amended by the *Local Government Reform Act 2014*);][6]

["*nominated civil partner*" has the meaning assigned to it by *section 1031A*;][7]

"*ordinary share capital*", in relation to a company, means all the issued share capital (by whatever name called) of the company, other than capital the holders of which have a right to a dividend at a fixed rate, but have no other right to share in the profits of the company;

["*other civil partner*" has the meaning assigned to it by *section 1031A*;][8]

"*profession*" includes vocation;

"*resident*" and "*ordinarily resident*", in relation to an individual, shall be construed in accordance with *Part 34*;

"*statute*" has the same meaning as in section 3 of the Interpretation Act, 1937;

["*surviving civil partner*", in relation to 2 individuals who were civil partners of each other until the death of one of them, means the civil partner other than the civil partner who died;][9]

[...][10]

["*year of assessment*" means—

(a) in relation to a period prior to 6 April 2001, a year beginning on 6 April in one year and ending on 5 April in the next year,

(b) the period beginning on 6 April 2001 and ending on 31 December 2001, which period is referred to as the "year of assessment 2001", and

(c) thereafter, a calendar year and, accordingly, the "year of assessment 2002" means the year beginning on 1 January 2002 and any corresponding expression in which a subsequent year of assessment is similarly mentioned means the year beginning on 1 January in that year;][11]

"*the year 1997–98*" means the year of assessment beginning on the 6th day of April, 1997, and any corresponding expression in which 2 years are similarly mentioned means the year of assessment beginning on the 6th day of April in the first-mentioned of those 2 years;

a source of income is within the charge to corporation tax or income tax if that tax is chargeable on the income arising from it, or would be so chargeable if there were any such income, and references to a person, or to income, being within the charge to tax, shall be similarly construed.

[(1A) (a) The Revenue Commissioners may nominate an inspector to be the inspector of returns.

(b) The inspector of returns shall take delivery of any account, declaration, list, particular, return, statement or other item which, under the Tax Acts or the Capital Gains Tax Acts, is required to be delivered to him or her.

(c) Where an inspector is nominated under *paragraph (a)*, the name of the inspector so nominated, and the address to which anything referred to in *paragraph (b)* is to be directed, shall be published in the *Iris Oifigiúil*;][12]

(2) Except where the context otherwise requires, in the Tax Acts, and in any enactment passed after this Act which by an express provision is to be construed as one with those Acts, "*tax*", where neither income tax nor corporation tax is specified, means either of those taxes.

(3) *Subsection (2)* is without prejudice to *section 76* (which applies income tax law for certain purposes of corporation tax), and accordingly the use of "*income tax*" rather than "*tax*" in any provision of the Income Tax Acts is not a conclusive indication that that provision is not applied to corporation tax by *section 76*.

[(3A) In the Tax Acts, a reference to a tax credit, in relation to a distribution, shall be construed as a reference to a tax credit as computed in accordance with those Acts as they applied at the time of the making of the distribution.][13]

[...][14]

Amendments

[1] Inserted by FA12 sched5(1)(a).

[2] Substituted by FA00 s61(a).

[3, 4, 7, 8, 9] Inserted by F(No.3)A11 sched1(1).

[5] Inserted by FA12 sched5(1)(b).

[6] Substituted by LGRA14 sched2(part5).

[10, 14] Deleted by FA00 sched2.

[11] Substituted by FA01 s77(1)(a).

[12] Inserted by FA12 sched5(1)(c).

[13] Inserted by FA00 sched2(a).

Cross References

From Section 2

Section 76 Computation of income: application of income tax principles.
Section 754 Interpretation (Chapter 1).
Section 818 Interpretation (Part 34).
Section 850 Appeal Commissioners.
Section 851 Collector-General.
Section 852 Inspectors of taxes.

To Section 2

Section 5 Interpretation of Capital Gains Tax Acts.
Section 591 Relief for individuals on certain reinvestment.

Section 628 Postponement of charge on deemed disposal under section 627.
Section 787 Nature and amount of relief for qualifying premiums.
Section 787B Relevant earnings and net relevant earnings.
Schedule 12 Employee Share Ownership Trusts
Schedule 19 Offshore Funds: Distributing Funds
Schedule 31 Consequential Amendments

3 Interpretation of Income Tax Acts

[ITA67 s1(1) and s2; FA69 s65 and Sch5; FA74 s1; CGTA75 s2(5); FA91 s2(3) and Sch1 PtI par1; FA93 s2(2) and Sch1 PtI; FA94 s2(2); FA96 s132(1) and Sch5 PtI par1(1)]

(1) In the Income Tax Acts, except where otherwise provided or the context otherwise requires—

["*chargeable tax*", in relation to an individual for a year of assessment, means the amount of income tax to which that individual is chargeable for that year of assessment under section 15 in respect of his or her total income for that year including, in the case of an individual assessed to tax in accordance with the provisions of *section 1017* or *1031C*, the total income, if any, of the individual's spouse or civil partner, as the case may be;][1]

["*general tax credit*", in relation to an individual for a year of assessment, means any relief (other than a credit under *section 59*) applicable for that year of assessment, not by way of deduction from income, but by way of reduction of or deduction from the chargeable tax or by way of repayment thereof when paid, other than a personal tax credit, and such credit shall be determined by reference to the amount of the reduction, deduction or repayment as the case may be;][2]

"*higher rate*", in relation to tax, means the rate of tax known by that description and provided for in *section 15*;

"*incapacitated person*" means any minor or person of unsound mind;

["*income tax payable*", in relation to an individual for a year of assessment, means the chargeable tax less the aggregate of the personal tax credits and general tax credits;

"*personal tax credit*", in relation to an individual for a year of assessment, means a tax credit specified in *sections 461, 461A, [462B]*[3]*, 463, 464, 465, 466, 466A, 468* and *472*;][4]

"*relative*" includes any person of whom the person claiming [relief][5] had the custody and whom he or she maintained at his or her own expense while that person was under the age of 16 years;

"*standard rate*", in relation to tax, means the rate of tax known by that description and provided for in *section 15*;

"*tax*" means income tax;

"*taxable income*" has the meaning assigned to it by *section 458*;

"*total income*" means total income from all sources as estimated in accordance with the Income Tax Acts;

"*trade*" includes every trade, manufacture, adventure or concern in the nature of trade.

(2) (a) Subject to *subsection (3)*, in the Income Tax Acts, "*earned income*", in relation to an individual, means—

[(i) any income arising in respect of any remuneration from any office or employment of profit held by the individual, or in respect of any pension, superannuation or other allowance, deferred pay, or compensation for loss of office, given in respect of the past services of the individual or of the individual's husband, civil partner, parent or parent's civil partner in any office or employment of profit, or given to the individual in respect of the past services of any deceased person, whether or not the individual or the individual's husband, civil partner, parent or parent's civil partner shall have contributed to such pension, superannuation allowance or deferred pay,][6]

(ii) any income from any property which is attached to or forms part of the emoluments of any office or employment of profit held by the individual, and

(iii) any income charged under Schedule D and immediately derived by the individual from the carrying on or exercise by the individual of his or her trade or profession, either as an individual or, in the case of a partnership, as a partner personally acting in the partnership.

[(b) In cases where the profits of a wife are deemed to be profits of the husband, or the profits of a civil partner are deemed to be the profits of his or her civil partner, any reference in this subsection to an individual includes the husband or the wife, or either civil partner.][7]

(3) Without prejudice to the generality of *subsection (2)*, in the Income Tax Acts, except where otherwise expressly provided, "*earned income*" includes—

(a) any annuity made payable to an individual under the terms of an annuity contract or trust scheme for the time being approved by the Revenue Commissioners for the purposes of *Chapter 2* of *Part 30* to the extent to which such annuity is payable in return for any amount on which relief is given under *section 787*, and

(b) any payment or other sum which is or is deemed to be income chargeable to tax under Schedule E for any purpose of the Income Tax Acts.

(4) References to profits or gains in the Income Tax Acts shall not include references to chargeable gains within the meaning of the Capital Gains Tax Acts.

Amendments

[1] Substituted by F(No.3)A11 sched1(2).

[2] Inserted by FA01 sched1(1)(a)(i). Applies as respects the year of assessment 2001 and subsequent years of assessment.

[3] Substituted by F(No.2)A13 s7(1)(a). Applies for the year of assessment 2014 and subsequent years of assessment.

[4] Inserted by FA01 sched1(1)(a)(ii). Applies as respects the year of assessment 2001 and subsequent years of assessment.

[5] Substituted by FA00 sched1(1).

[6] Substituted by F(No.3)A11 sched1(3).

[7] Substituted by F(No.3)A11 sched1(4).

Revenue Briefings

Tax Briefing

Tax Briefing October 2004 – Issue 57 pg 10 – Classification of Activities as Trading

Cross References

From Section 3

Section 15 Rate of charge.
Section 59 Charge to tax of income from which tax has been deducted.
Section 458 Deductions allowed in ascertaining taxable income and provisions relating to reductions in tax.
Section 461 Basic personal tax credit.
Section 461A Additional tax credit for certain widowed persons.
Section 462 One-parent family tax credit.
Section 463 Widowed parent tax credit.
Section 464 Age tax credit.
Section 465 Incapacitated child tax credit.
Section 466 Dependent relative tax credit.
Section 466A Home carer tax credit.
Section 468 Blind person's tax credit.
Section 472 Employee tax credit.
Section 783 Interpretation and general (Chapter 2).
Section 787 Nature and amount of relief for qualifying premiums.
Section 1017 Assessment of husband in respect of income of both spouses.

To Section 3

Section 188 Age exemption and associated marginal relief.
Section 191 Taxation treatment of Hepatitis C compensation payments.
Section 434 Distributions to be taken into account and meaning of "distributable income", "investment income", "estate income", etc.
Section 485FA Adaptation of provisions relating to taxation of married persons.
Section 530E Rates of tax.
Section 595 Life assurance policy or deferred annuity contract entered into or acquired by company.
Section 738 Undertakings for collective investment.
Section 739B Interpretation and application.
Section 1077E Penalty for deliberately or carelessly making incorrect returns, etc.
Schedule 31 Consequential Amendments

4 Interpretation of Corporation Tax Acts

[CTA76 s1(5)(a) to (d), s155(5), (9), (10), (11), (12) and (13); FA86 s57(1); FA90 s29(4); FA93 s42; FA97 s37(1)]

(1) In the Corporation Tax Acts, except where the context otherwise requires—

"*accounting date*" means the date to which a company makes up its accounts, and "*period of account*" means the period for which a company does so;

"*allowable loss*" does not include, for the purposes of corporation tax in respect of chargeable gains, a loss accruing to a company in such circumstances that if a gain accrued the company would be exempt from corporation tax in respect of the gain;

"*branch or agency*" means any factorship, agency, receivership, branch or management;

"*chargeable gain*" has the same meaning as in the Capital Gains Tax Acts, but does not include a gain accruing on a disposal made before the 6th day of April, 1976;

"*charges on income*" has the meaning assigned to it by *section 243(1)*;

"*close company*" has the meaning assigned to it by *sections 430* and *431*;

"*company*" means any body corporate and includes a trustee savings bank within the meaning of the Trustee Savings Banks Act, 1989, but does not include—

(a) [the Health Service Executive][1],

(b) a grouping within the meaning of *section 1014*,

[(c) an education and training board][2]

(d) a committee of agriculture established under the Agriculture Act, 1931, or [(e) a local authority for the purposes of the Local Government Act 2001 (as amended by the Local Government Reform Act 2014) and includes a body established under the Local Government Services (Corporate Bodies) Act 1971;][3]

"*distribution*" has the meaning assigned to it by *Chapter 2* of *Part 6* and [*sections 436* and *437*, and *subsection (2)(b)* of *section 816*][4];

"*the financial year*" followed by a reference to the year 1996 or any other year means the year beginning on the 1st day of January of such year;

"*franked investment income*" and "*franked payment*" shall be construed in accordance with *section 156*;

["generally accepted accounting practice" means—

(a) in relation to the affairs of a company or other entity that prepares accounts (in this section referred to as "*IAS accounts*") in accordance with international accounting standards, generally accepted accounting practice with respect to such accounts;

(b) in any other case, Irish generally accepted accounting practice;][5]

"*group relief*" has the meaning assigned to it by *section 411*;

"*interest*" means both annual or yearly interest and interest other than annual or yearly interest;

["*international accounting standards*" means the international accounting standards, within the meaning of Regulation (EC) No. 1606/2002 of the European Parliament and the Council of 19 July 2002 on the application of international accounting standards (in this section referred to as "the Regulation");

"*Irish generally accepted accounting practice*" means generally accepted accounting practice with respect to accounts (other than IAS accounts) of companies incorporated or formed under the laws of the State, being accounts that are intended to give a true and fair view;][6]

"*preference dividend*" means a dividend payable on a preferred share or preferred stock at a fixed rate per cent or, where a dividend is payable on a preferred share or preferred stock partly at a fixed rate per cent and partly at a variable rate, such part of that dividend as is payable at a fixed rate per cent;

"*profits*" means income and chargeable gains;

["*SE*" means a European public limited-liability company (Societas Europaea or SE) as provided for by Council Regulation (EC) No. 2157/2001 of 8 October 2001, on the Statute for a European Company (SE)*;

* OJ No. L294, 10.11.2001, p.1

"*SCE*" means a European Cooperative Society (SCE) as provided for by Council Regulation (EC) No. 1435/2003 of 22 July 2003 on the Statute for a European Cooperative Society (SCE)*;][7]

* OJ No. L207, 18.8.2003, p.1

["*standard credit rate*" for a year of assessment means—

(a) for the year of assessment 1997-98—

(i) 21 per cent where it has application in relation to a distribution made or treated as having been made by a company before the 3rd day of December, 1997, and

(ii) 11 per cent where it has application in relation to a distribution made or treated as having been made by a company on or after the 3rd day of December, 1997,

and

(b) for the year of assessment 1998-99, 11 per cent,

and, accordingly, "*standard credit rate per cent*" for the year of assessment 1997-98 means 21 or 11, as the case may be, and for the year of assessment 1998-99 means 11;][8]

"*standard rate per cent*" for a year of assessment means 26 where the standard rate for that year is 26 per cent and similarly as regards any reference to the standard rate per cent for a year of assessment for which the standard rate is other than 26 per cent;

"*trade*" includes vocation and includes also an office or employment.

(2) Except where otherwise provided by the Corporation Tax Acts and except where the context otherwise requires, words and expressions used in the Income Tax Acts have the same meaning in the Corporation Tax Acts as in those Acts; but no provision of the Corporation Tax Acts as to the interpretation of any word or expression, other than a provision expressed to extend to the use of that word or expression in the Income Tax Acts, shall be taken to affect its meaning in those Acts as they apply for the purposes of corporation tax.

(3) References in the Corporation Tax Acts to distributions or payments received by a company apply to any distributions or payments received by another person on behalf of or in trust for the company but not to any distributions or payments received by the company on behalf of or in trust for another person.

(4) References in the Corporation Tax Acts to—

(a) profits brought into charge to corporation tax are references to the amount of those profits chargeable to corporation tax before any deduction from those profits for charges on income, expenses of management or other amounts which can be deducted from or set against or treated as reducing profits of more than one description,

(b) total income brought into charge to corporation tax are references to the amount, calculated before any deduction mentioned in *paragraph (a)*, of the total income from all sources included in any profits brought into charge to corporation tax, and

(c) an amount of profits on which corporation tax falls finally to be borne are references to the amount of those profits after making all deductions and giving all reliefs that for the purposes of corporation tax are made or given from or against those profits, including deductions and reliefs which under any provision are treated as reducing them for those purposes.

(5) For the purposes of the Corporation Tax Acts, except where otherwise provided, dividends shall be treated as paid on the date when they become due and payable.

(6) Except where otherwise provided by the Corporation Tax Acts, any apportionment to different periods to be made under the Corporation Tax Acts shall be made on a time basis according to the respective lengths of those periods.

[(7) For the purposes of this section, where the European Commission in accordance with the Regulation adopts an international accounting standard with modifications, then as regards matters covered by that standard—

(a) generally accepted accounting practice with respect to IAS accounts shall be regarded as permitting the use of the standard either with or without the modifications, and

(b) accounts prepared on either basis shall be regarded as prepared in accordance with international accounting standards.][9]

Amendments

[1] Substituted by FA05 sched6(1)(a). Applies as on and from 25 March 2005.

[2] Substituted by EATBA13 sched6(24).

[3] Substituted by LGRA14 sched2(part5).

[4] Substituted by FA98 s43(1)(b). This section shall apply as respects shares issued by a company on or after the 3rd day of December, 1997.

[5] Inserted by FA05 s48(1)(a)(i)(I). This section applies as respects any period of account beginning on or after 1 January 2005.

[6] Inserted by FA05 s48(1)(a)(i)(II). This section applies as respects any period of account beginning on or after 1 January 2005.

[7] Inserted by FA06 s60(a).

[8] Substituted by FA98 s51(1). This section shall apply with effect as on and from the 3rd day of December, 1997.

[9] Inserted by FA05 s48(1)(a)(ii). This section applies as respects any period of account beginning on or after 1 January 2005.

Case Law

In Cronin v Youghal Carpets 1985 III ITR 229 it was held that the phrase 'total income brought into charge to corporation tax' had to be constructed as being analogous to the phrase 'profits or gains brought into charge to tax'.

Revenue Information Notes

Guidance Note on Section 48 of the Finance Act 2005 – Generally Accepted Accounting Standards

Cross References

From Section 4

Section 129 Irish resident company distributions not generally chargeable to corporation tax.
Section 130 Matters to be treated as distributions.
Section 156 Franked investment income and franked payments.
Section 243 Allowance of charges on income.
Section 411 Surrender of relief between members of groups and consortia.
Section 430 Meaning of "close company".
Section 431 Certain companies with quoted shares not to be close companies.
Section 436 Certain expenses for participators and associates.
Section 437 Interest paid to directors and directors' associates.
Section 816 Taxation of shares issued in place of cash dividends.
Section 1014 Tax treatment of profits, losses and capital gains arising from activities of a European Economic Interest Grouping (EEIG).

To Section 4

Section 10 Connected persons.
Section 110 Securitisation.
Section 128 Tax treatment of directors of companies and employees granted rights to acquire shares or other assets.
Section 250A Restriction of relief to individuals in respect of loans applied in acquiring interest in companies.
Section 268 Meaning of "industrial building or structure".
Section 270 Meaning of "expenditure on construction of building or structure".
Section 296 Balancing allowances and balancing charges: wear and tear allowances deemed to have been made in certain cases.
Section 409E Income tax: ringfence on use of certain capital allowances on certain industrial buildings and other premises.
Section 448 Relief from corporation tax.
Section 486C Relief from tax for certain start-up companies.
Section 660 Farming: wear and tear allowances deemed to have been made in certain cases.

Section 665 Interpretation (Chapter 2).
Section 730F Deduction of tax on the happening of a chargeable event.
Section 730H Interpretation and application.
Section 738 Undertakings for collective investment.
Section 739E Deduction of tax on the occurrence of a chargeable event.
Section 747B Interpretation and application.
Section 787G Taxation of payments from a PRSA.
Section 892 Returns by nominee holders of securities.

5 Interpretation of Capital Gains Tax Acts

[CGTA75 s2(1), (3) and (4); CTA76 s140(2) and Sch2 PtII par1; FA80 s61(a); FA90 s29(3); FA97 s146(1) and Sch9 PtI par9(1)]

(1) In the Capital Gains Tax Acts, except where the context otherwise requires—

"*Appeal Commissioners*" has the meaning assigned to it by *section 850*;

['*appropriate inspector*' has the same meaning as in *section 2*;][1]

"*body of persons*" has the same meaning as in *section 2*;

"*branch or agency*" means any factorship, agency, receivership, branch or management, but does not include the brokerage or agency of a broker or agent referred to in *section 1039*;

['*local authority*' means a local authority for the purposes of the Local Government Act 2001 (as amended by the *Local Government Reform Act 2014*) and includes a body established under the Local Government Services (Corporate Bodies) Act 1971;][2]

"*local authority*" has the meaning assigned to it by section 2(2) of the Local Government Act, 1941, and includes a body established under the Local Government Services (Corporate Bodies) Act, 1971;

"*allowable loss*" has the meaning assigned to it by *section 546*;

"*capital allowance*" means any allowance under the provisions of the Tax Acts which relate to allowances in respect of capital expenditure, and includes an allowance under *section 284*;

"*chargeable gain*" has the same meaning as in *section 545*;

"*charity*" has the same meaning as in *section 208*;

["*child of the civil partner*", in relation to an individual, means a child of the individual's civil partner who was born before the registration of their civil partnership or during their civil partnership;

"*civil partner*" means a civil partner within the meaning of the Civil Partnership and Certain Rights and Obligations of Cohabitants Act 2010;

"*civil partnership*" means—

(a) a civil partnership registration referred to in section 3(*a*) of the Civil Partnership and Certain Rights and Obligations of Cohabitants Act 2010, or

(b) a legal relationship referred to in section 3(*b*) of that Act;][3]

"*class*", in relation to shares or securities, means a class of shares or securities of any one company;

"*close company*" has the meaning assigned to it by *section 430*;

"*company*" means any body corporate, but does not include a grouping within the meaning of *section 1014*;

"*control*" shall be construed in accordance with *section 432*;

['*inspector*' has the same meaning as in *section 2*;

'*inspector of returns*' has the same meaning as in *section 2*;][4]

"*land*" includes any interest in land;

"*lease*"—

(a) in relation to land, includes an underlease, sub-lease or any tenancy or licence, and any agreement for a lease, under-lease, sub-lease or tenancy or licence and, in the case of land outside the State, any interest corresponding to a lease as so defined, and

(b) in relation to any description of property other than land, means any kind of agreement or arrangement under which payments are made for the use of, or otherwise in respect of, property,

and "*lessor*", "*lessee*" and "*rent*" shall be construed accordingly;

"*legatee*" includes any person taking under a testamentary disposition or an intestacy or partial intestacy or by virtue of the Succession Act, 1965, or by survivorship, whether such person takes beneficially or as trustee, and a person taking under a donatio mortis causa shall be treated as a legatee and such person's acquisition as made at the time of the donor's death and, for the purposes of this definition and of any reference to a person acquiring an asset as legatee, property taken under a testamentary disposition or on an intestacy or partial intestacy or by virtue of the Succession Act, 1965, includes any asset appropriated by the personal representatives in or towards the satisfaction of a pecuniary legacy or any other interest or share in the property devolving under the disposition or intestacy or by virtue of the Succession Act, 1965;

"*market value*" shall be construed in accordance with *section 548*;

"*minerals*" has the same meaning as in section 3 of the Minerals Development Act, 1940;

"*mining*" means mining operations in the State for the purpose of obtaining, whether by underground or surface working, any minerals;

"*part disposal*" has the meaning assigned to it by *section 534*;

"*personal representative*" has the same meaning as in *section 799*;

"*prescribed*" means prescribed by the Revenue Commissioners;

"*profession*" includes vocation;

"*resident*" and "*ordinarily resident*", in relation to an individual, shall be construed in accordance with *Part 34*;

"*settled property*" means any property held in trust other than property to which *section 567* applies, but does not include any property held by a trustee or assignee in bankruptcy or under a deed of arrangement;

"*settlement*" and "*settlor*" have the same meanings respectively as in *section 10*, and "*settled property*" shall be construed accordingly;

"*shares*" includes stock, and shares or debentures comprised in any letter of allotment or similar instrument shall be treated as issued unless the right to the shares or debentures conferred by such letter or instrument remains provisional until accepted and there has been no acceptance;

"*trade*" has the same meaning as in the Income Tax Acts;

"*trading stock*" has the same meaning as in *section 89*;

"*unit trust*" means any arrangements made for the purpose, or having the effect, of providing facilities for the participation by the holders of units, as beneficiaries under a trust, in profits or income arising from the acquisition, holding, management or disposal of securities or any other property whatever;

"*units*", in relation to a unit trust, means any units (whether described as units or otherwise) into which are divided the beneficial interests in the assets subject to the trusts of a unit trust;

"*unit holder*", in relation to a unit trust, means a holder of units of the unit trust;

"*wasting asset*" has the meaning assigned to it by *section 560* and *paragraph 2* of *Schedule 14*;

["*year of assessment*" means—

(a) in relation to a period prior to 6 April 2001, a year beginning on 6 April in one year and ending on 5 April in the next year,

(b) the period beginning on 6 April 2001 and ending on 31 December 2001, which period is referred to as the "year of assessment 2001", and

(c) thereafter, a calendar year and, accordingly, the "year of assessment 2002" means the year beginning on 1 January 2002 and any corresponding expression in which a subsequent year of assessment is similarly mentioned means the year beginning on 1 January in that year;][5]

"*the year 1997–98*" means the year of assessment beginning on the 6th day of April, 1997, and any corresponding expression in which 2 years are similarly mentioned means the year of assessment beginning on the 6th day of April in the first-mentioned of those 2 years.

(2) [(a) References in the Capital Gains Tax Acts to a married woman living with her husband or a civil partner living with his or her civil partner shall be construed in accordance with *section 1015(2)* or *1031A(2)*, as the case may be.][6]

(b) For the purposes of *paragraph (a)*, the reference in *section 1015(2)* to a wife shall be construed as a reference to a married woman.

(3) Any provision in the Capital Gains Tax Acts introducing the assumption that assets are sold and immediately reacquired shall not imply that any expenditure is incurred as incidental to the sale or reacquisition.

Amendments

[1] Inserted by FA12 sched5(1)(d).

[2] Substituted by LGRA14 sched2(part5).

[3] Inserted by F(No.3)A11 sched1(5).

[4] Inserted by FA12 sched5(1)(e).

[5] Substituted by FA01 s77(1)(b).

[6] Substituted by F(No.3)A11 sched1(6).

Case Law

Young v Pearce 1996 STC 73 considered the meaning of "settlor".

Cross References

From Section 5

Section 2 Interpretation of Tax Acts.
Section 10 Connected persons.
Section 89 Valuation of trading stock at discontinuance of trade.
Section 208 Lands owned and occupied, and trades carried on by, charities.
Section 284 Wear and tear allowances.
Section 430 Meaning of "close company".
Section 432 Meaning of "associated company" and "control".
Section 534 Disposals of assets.
Section 545 Chargeable gains.
Section 546 Allowable losses.

Section 548 Valuation of assets.
Section 560 Wasting assets.
Section 567 Nominees, bare trustees and agents.
Section 799 Interpretation (Chapter 1).
Section 818 Interpretation (Part 34).
Section 850 Appeal Commissioners.
Section 852 Inspectors of taxes.
Section 1014 Tax treatment of profits, losses and capital gains arising from activities of a European Economic Interest Grouping (EEIG).
Section 1015 Interpretation (Chapter 1).
Section 1039 Restrictions on chargeability.
Schedule 14 Capital Gains Tax: Leases

To Section 5

Section 219A Income of credit unions.
Section 701 Transfer of shares held by certain societies to members of society.

6 Construction of references to child in Tax Acts and Capital Gains Tax Acts

[FA77 s36; FA92 s16]

For the purposes of the Tax Acts and the Capital Gains Tax Acts, except where the contrary intention appears—

(a) references in any of those Acts to a child (including references to a son or a daughter) include references to—

(i) a stepchild, and

[(ii) a child who is adopted under an adoption order within the meaning of *section 3(1)* of the *Adoption Act 2010* or the subject of an intercountry adoption effected outside the state and recognised under that Act,][1]—

(I) adopted under the Adoption Acts, 1952 to 1991, or

(II) thesubjectof aforeignadoption(withinthemeaningof section1 of the Adoption Act, 1991) which is deemed to have been effected by a valid adoption order made under the Adoption Acts, 1952 to 1991,

and

(b) the relationship between a child referred to in *paragraph (a)(ii)* and any other person, or between other persons, that would exist if such child had been born to the child's adoptor or adoptors in lawful wedlock, shall be deemed to exist between such child and that other person, or between those other persons, and the relationship of any such child and any person that existed prior to the child being so adopted shall be deemed to have ceased,

and "*adopted child*" shall be construed in accordance with this section.

Amendments

[1] Substituted by AA10 s174(a). With effect from 1 November 2010 as per S.I. No 511 of 2010.

Cross References

To Section 6

Section 499 Value received by persons other than claimants.

7 Application to certain taxing statutes of Age of Majority Act, 1985

[FA86 s112(1) and (2)]

(1) Notwithstanding *subsection (4)* of section 2 of the Age of Majority Act, 1985 (in this section referred to as "the Act of 1985"), *subsections (2)* and *(3)* of that

section shall, subject to *subsection (2)*, apply for the purposes of the Income Tax Acts and any other statutory provision (within the meaning of the Act of 1985) dealing with the imposition, repeal, remission, alteration or regulation of any tax or other duty under the care and management of the Revenue Commissioners, and accordingly *section 2(4)(b)(vii)* of the Act of 1985 shall cease to apply.

(2) Nothing in *subsection (1)* shall affect a claimant's entitlement to [relief][1] under [*section 462B*][2] or *465*.

Amendments

[1] Substituted by FA00 sched1(2).

[2] Substituted by F(No.2)A13 s7(1)(b). Applies for the year of assessment 2014 and subsequent years of assessment.

Cross References

From Section 7

Section 462 One-parent family tax credit.
Section 465 Incapacitated child tax credit.

To Section 7

Section 908D Order to produce evidential material.
Section 1104 Short title and construction.
Schedule 31 Consequential Amendments

8 Construction of certain taxing statutes in accordance with Status of Children Act, 1987

[FA88 s74(1) and (2)]

(1) In this section, "*the Acts*" means—

(a) the Tax Acts,

(b) the Capital Gains Tax Acts,

(c) the Capital Acquisitions Tax Consolidation Act 2003, and the enactments amending or extending that Act, and

(d) the statutes relating to stamp duty

and any instruments made thereunder.

(2) Notwithstanding any provision of the Acts or the dates on which they were passed, in deducing any relationship between persons for the purposes of the Acts, the Acts shall be construed in accordance with section 3 of the Status of Children Act, 1987.

Cross References

To Section 8

Section 908D Order to produce evidential material.
Section 1104 Short title and construction.

9 Subsidiaries

[CTA76 s156]

(1) For the purposes of the Tax Acts, except where otherwise provided, a company shall be deemed to be—

(a) a "*51 per cent subsidiary*" of another company if and so long as more than 50 per cent of its ordinary share capital is owned directly or indirectly by that other company,

(b) a "*75 per cent subsidiary*" of another company if and so long as not less than 75 per cent of its ordinary share capital is owned directly or indirectly by that other company,

(c) a "*90 per cent subsidiary*" of another company if and so long as not less than 90 per cent of its ordinary share capital is directly owned by that other [company,][1]

[(d) a "wholly-owned subsidiary" of another company if and so long as 100 per cent of its ordinary share capital is directly owned by that other company.][2]

(2) In *paragraphs (a)* and *(b)* of *subsection (1)*, "*owned directly or indirectly*" by a company means owned whether directly or through another company or other companies or partly directly and partly through another company or other companies.

(3) In this section, references to ownership shall be construed as references to beneficial ownership.

(4) For the purposes of this section, the amount of ordinary share capital of one company owned by a second company through another company or other companies, or partly directly and partly through another company or other companies, shall be determined in accordance with *subsections (5)* to *(10)*.

(5) Where, in the case of a number of companies, the first directly owns ordinary share capital of the second and the second directly owns ordinary share capital of the third, then, for the purposes of this section, the first shall be deemed to own ordinary share capital of the third through the second and, if the third directly owns ordinary share capital of a fourth, the first shall be deemed to own ordinary share capital of the fourth through the second and third, and the second shall be deemed to own ordinary share capital of the fourth through the third, and so on.

(6) In this section—

(a) any number of companies of which the first directly owns ordinary share capital of the next and the next directly owns ordinary share capital of the next but one and so on, and, if there are more than 3, any 3 or more of them, are referred to as a "*series*";

(b) in any series—

(i) that company which owns ordinary share capital of another through the remainder is referred to as "*the first owner*";

(ii) that other company the ordinary share capital of which is so owned is referred to as "*the last owned company*";

(iii) the remainder, if one only, is referred to as an "*intermediary*" and, if more than one, are referred to as "*a chain of intermediaries*";

(c) a company in a series which directly owns ordinary share capital of another company in the series is referred to as an "*owner*";

(d) any 2 companies in a series of which one owns ordinary share capital of the other directly, and not through one or more of the other companies in the series, are referred to as being directly related to one another.

(7) Where every owner in a series owns the whole of the ordinary share capital of the company to which it is directly related, the first owner shall be deemed to own through the intermediary or chain of intermediaries the whole of the ordinary share capital of the last owned company.

(8) Where one of the owners in a series owns a fraction of the ordinary share capital of the company to which it is directly related, and every other owner in the series owns the whole of the ordinary share capital of the company to which it is directly related, the first owner shall be deemed to own that fraction of the ordinary share capital of the last owned company through the intermediary or chain of intermediaries.

(9) Where—

(a) each of 2 or more of the owners in a series owns a fraction, and every other owner in the series owns the whole, of the ordinary share capital of the company to which it is directly related, or

(b) every owner in a series owns a fraction of the ordinary share capital of the company to which it is directly related,

the first owner shall be deemed to own through the intermediary or chain of intermediaries such fraction of the ordinary share capital of the last owned company as results from the multiplication of those fractions.

(10) Where the first owner in any series owns a fraction of the ordinary share capital of the last owned company in that series through the intermediary or chain of intermediaries in that series, and also owns another fraction or other fractions of the ordinary share capital of the last owned company, either—

(a) directly,

(b) through an intermediary which is not a member, or intermediaries which are not members, of that series,

(c) through a chain or chains of intermediaries of which one or some or all are not members of that series, or

(d) in a case where the series consists of more than 3 companies, through an intermediary which is a member, or intermediaries which are members, of the series, or through a chain or chains of intermediaries consisting of some but not all of the companies of which the chain of intermediaries in the series consists,

then, for the purpose of ascertaining the amount of the ordinary share capital of the last owned company owned by the first owner, all those fractions shall be aggregated and the first owner shall be deemed to own the sum of those fractions.

Amendments

[1] Substituted by FA01 s79(a)(i).

[2] Inserted by FA01 s79(a)(ii).

Case Law

On entering liquidation (whether voluntary or compulsory) the company ceases to qualify as a parent company, as it is no longer the beneficial owner of its assets, even though the legal title may remain in its name. Ayerst v C & K (Construction) Ltd 1975 STC 1

Cross References

To Section 9

Section 23A Company residence.

Section 153 Distributions to certain nonresidents.

Section 172D Exemption from dividend withholding tax for certain non-resident persons.

Section 250 Extension of relief under section 248 to certain individuals in relation to loans applied in acquiring interest in certain companies.

Section 400 Company reconstructions without change of ownership.

Section 403 Restriction on use of capital allowances for certain leased assets.

Section 411 Surrender of relief between members of groups and consortia.
Section 412 Qualification for entitlement to group relief.
Section 450 Double taxation relief.
Section 479 Relief for new shares purchased on issue by employees.
Section 591 Relief for individuals on certain reinvestment.
Section 598 Disposals of business or farm on "retirement".
Section 616 Groups of companies: interpretation.
Section 626B Exemption from tax in the case of gains on disposals of shares.
Section 675 Exploration expenditure incurred by certain bodies corporate.
Section 908D Order to produce evidential material.
Schedule 9 Change in Ownership of Company: Disallowance of Trading Losses
Schedule 24 Relief from Income Tax and Corporation Tax by Means of Credit in Respect of Foreign Tax
Schedule 31 Consequential Amendments

10 Connected persons

[FA96 s131(1) to (8)]

(1) In this section—

"*close company*" has the meaning assigned to it by *sections 430* and *431*;

"*company*" has the same meaning as in *section 4(1)*;

"*control*" shall be construed in accordance with *section 432*;

"*relative*" means brother, sister, ancestor or lineal descendant and, for the purposes of the Capital Gains Tax Acts, also means uncle, aunt, niece or nephew;

"*settlement*" includes any disposition, trust, covenant, agreement or arrangement, and any transfer of money or other property or of any right to money or other property;

"*settlor*", in relation to a settlement, means any person by whom the settlement was made, and a person shall be deemed for the purposes of this section to have made a settlement if the person has made or entered into the settlement directly or indirectly and, in particular (but without prejudice to the generality of the preceding words), if the person has provided or undertaken to provide funds directly or indirectly for the purpose of the settlement, or has made with any other person a reciprocal arrangement for that other person to make or enter into the settlement.

(2) For the purposes of the Tax Acts and the Capital Gains Tax Acts, except where the context otherwise requires, any question whether a person is connected with another person shall be determined in accordance with *subsections (3)* to *(8)* (any provision that one person is connected with another person being taken to mean that they are connected with one another).

[(3) A person shall be connected with an individual if that person is the individual's husband, wife or civil partner, or is a relative, or the husband, wife or civil partner of a relative, of the individual or of the individual's husband, wife or civil partner.][1]

(4) A person in the capacity as trustee of a settlement shall be connected with—

(a) any individual who in relation to the settlement is a settlor,

(b) any person connected with such an individual, and

(c) a body corporate which is deemed to be connected with that settlement, and a body corporate shall be deemed to be connected with a settlement in any accounting period or, as the case may be, year of assessment if, at any time in that period or year, as the case may be, it is a close company (or only not a close company because it is not resident in the State) and the participators then include the trustees of or a beneficiary under the settlement.

(5) Except in relation to acquisitions or disposals of partnership assets pursuant to bona fide commercial arrangements, a person shall be connected with any

person with whom such person is in partnership, and with the spouse [or civil partner][2] or a relative of any individual with whom such person is in partnership.

(6) A company shall be connected with another company—

(a) if the same person has control of both companies, or a person (in this paragraph referred to as "*the first-mentioned person*") has control of one company and persons connected with the first-mentioned person, or the first-mentioned person and persons connected with the first-mentioned person, have control of the other company, or

(b) if a group of 2 or more persons has control of each company, and the groups either consist of the same persons or could be regarded as consisting of the same persons by treating (in one or more cases) a member of either group as replaced by a person with whom such member is connected.

(7) A company shall be connected with another person if that person has control of the company or if that person and persons connected with that person together have control of the company.

(8) Any 2 or more persons acting together to secure or exercise control of, or to acquire a holding in, a company shall be treated in relation to that company as connected with one another and with any person acting on the direction of any of them to secure or exercise control of, or to acquire a holding in, the company.

Amendments

[1] Substituted by F(No.3)A11 sched1(7). Shall have effect from 27 July 2011.

[2] Inserted by FA14 sched3(1)(a). Has effect on and from 23 December 2014.

Case Law

In Steele v EVC 1996 STC 785 it was held that two parties operating under a shareholders' agreement were acting together to exercise voting control over the company concerned.

Revenue Precedents

A daughter-in-law or son-in-law is connected with his/her father-in-law. IT 96 3504

Cross References

From Section 10

Section 4 Interpretation of Corporation Tax Acts.
Section 430 Meaning of "close company".
Section 431 Certain companies with quoted shares not to be close companies.
Section 432 Meaning of "associated company" and "control".

To Section 10

Section 5 Interpretation of Capital Gains Tax Acts.
Section 21B Tax treatment of certain dividends.
Section 81 General rule as to deductions.
Section 81A Restriction of deductions for employee benefit contributions.
Section 89 Valuation of trading stock at discontinuance of trade.
Section 98A Taxation of reverse premiums.
Section 118 Benefits in kind: general charging provision.
Section 122A Notional loans relating to shares, etc.
Section 129A Dividends paid out of foreign profits.
Section 186 Connected persons.
Section 189A Special trusts for permanently incapacitated individuals.
Section 192A Exemption in respect of certain payments under employment law.
Section 193 Income from scholarships.
Section 234 Certain income derived from patent royalties.
Section 247 Relief to companies on loans applied in acquiring interest in other companies.

Section 250 Extension of relief under section 248 to certain individuals in relation to loans applied in acquiring interest in certain companies.
Section 268 Meaning of "industrial building or structure".
Section 288 Balancing allowances and balancing charges.
Section 343 Capital allowances in relation to construction or refurbishment of certain buildings or structures in enterprise areas.
Section 372K Non-application of relief in certain cases and provision against double relief.
Section 372T Non-application of relief in certain cases and provision against double relief.
Section 372V Capital allowances in relation to construction or refurbishment of certain park and ride facilities.
Section 372W Capital allowances in relation to construction or refurbishment of certain commercial premises.
Section 372AJ Non-application of relief in certain cases and provision against double relief.
Section 372AZ Restrictions on relief, non-application of relief in certain cases and provision against double relief.
Section 409C Income tax: restriction on use of losses on approved buildings.
Section 433 Meaning of "participator", "associate", "director" and "loan creditor".
Section 530G Zero rate subcontractor.
Section 531 Payments to subcontractors in certain industries.
Section 531R Provision of parking space by employer.
Section 591A Dividends paid in connection with disposals of shares or securities.
Section 669G Interpretation (Chapter 4).
Section 669I Provisions as to deductions.
Section 730BA Personal portfolio life policy.
Section 739BA Personal portfolio investment undertaking.
Section 766 Tax credit for research and development expenditure.
Section 768 Allowance for know-how.
Section 783 Interpretation and general (Chapter 2).
Section 806 Charge to income tax on transfer of assets abroad.
Section 808 Power to obtain information.
Section 843A Capital allowances for buildings used for certain childcare purposes.
Section 848G Acquisition of qualifying assets.
Section 882 Particulars to be supplied by new companies.
Section 906A Information to be furnished by financial institutions.
Section 960H Offset between taxes.
Section 985C PAYE: payment by intermediary.
Section 985D PAYE: employee of non-resident employer, etc.
Section 985E PAYE: employment not wholly exercised in State.
Section 997A Credit in respect of tax deducted from emoluments of certain directors.
Section 1094 Tax clearance certificates in relation to certain licences.
Schedule 12A Approved Savings-Related Share Option Schemes
Schedule 12C Approved Share Option Schemes

11 Meaning of "*control*" in certain contexts

[CTA76 s158]

For the purposes of, and subject to, the provisions of the Corporation Tax Acts which apply this section, "*control*", in relation to a company, means the power of a person to secure—

(a) by means of the holding of shares or the possession of voting power in or in relation to that or any other company, or

(b) by virtue of any powers conferred by the articles of association or other document regulating that or any other company,

that the affairs of the first-mentioned company are conducted in accordance with the wishes of that person and, in relation to a partnership, means the right to a share of more than 50 per cent of the assets, or of more than 50 per cent of the income, of the partnership.

Cross References

To Section 11

Section 89 Valuation of trading stock at discontinuance of trade.
Section 110 Securitisation.
Section 130 Matters to be treated as distributions.
Section 173 Interpretation (Chapter 9).
Section 424 Effect of arrangements for transfer of company to another group, etc.
Section 453 Transactions between associated persons.
Section 492 Individuals qualifying for relief.
Section 505 Application to subsidiaries.
Section 511 The period of retention, release date and appropriate percentage.
Section 697LA Transactions between associated persons and between tonnage tax trade and other activities of same company.
Section 835A Interpretation.
Schedule 10 Relief for Investment in Corporate Trades: Subsidiaries

PART 2

The Charge to Tax

CHAPTER 1

Income Tax

12 The charge to income tax

[ITA67 s4; FA80 s55]

Income tax shall, subject to the Income Tax Acts, be charged in respect of all property, profits or gains respectively described or comprised in the Schedules contained in the sections enumerated below—
Schedule C — *Section 17*;
Schedule D — *Section 18*;
Schedule E — *Section 19*;
Schedule F — *Section 20*;
and in accordance with the provisions of the Income Tax Acts applicable to those Schedules.

Cross References

From Section 12

Section 17 Schedule C.
Section 18 Schedule D.
Section 19 Schedule E.
Section 20 Schedule F.

To Section 12

Section 472 Employee tax credit.
Section 739G Taxation of unit holders in investment undertakings.Taxation of unit holders in investment undertakings.
Section 747 Deduction of offshore income gain in determining capital gain.
Schedule 2 Machinery for Assessment, Charge and Payment of Tax under Schedule C and, in Certain Cases, Schedule D

13 Extension of charge to income tax to profits and income derived from activities carried on and employments exercised on the Continental Shelf

[FA73 s33(1)(a), (b) and (c), (2) to (5) and (7)]

(1) In this section and in *Schedule 1*—

"*designated area*" means an area designated by order under section 2 of the Continental Shelf Act, 1968;

"*exploration or exploitation activities*" means activities carried on in connection with the exploration or exploitation of so much of the sea bed and subsoil and their natural resources as is situated in the State or in a designated area;

"*exploration or exploitation rights*" means rights to assets to be produced by exploration or exploitation activities or to interests in or to the benefit of such assets.

(2) Any profits or gains from exploration or exploitation activities carried on in a designated area or from exploration or exploitation rights shall be treated for income tax purposes as profits or gains from activities or property in the State.

(3) Any profits or gains arising to any person not resident in the State from exploration or exploitation activities carried on in the State or in a designated area or from exploration or exploitation rights shall be treated for income tax purposes as profits or gains of a trade carried on by that person in the State through a branch or agency.

[(4) Where exploration or exploitation activities are carried on by a person on behalf of the holder of a licence or lease granted under the Petroleum and Other Minerals Development Act, 1960, such holder shall, for the purpose of an assessment to income tax, be deemed to be the agent of that person.][1]

(5) Any emoluments from an office or employment in respect of duties performed in a designated area in connection with exploration or exploitation activities shall be treated for income tax purposes as emoluments in respect of duties performed in the State.

(6) *Schedule 1* shall apply for the purpose of supplementing this section.

Amendments

[1] Substituted by FA01 s44(a).

Cross References

From Section 13

Schedule 1 Supplementary Provisions Concerning the Extension of Charge to Tax to Profits and Income Derived from Activities Carried On and Employments Exercised on the Continental Shelf

To Section 13

Section 23 Application of section 13 for purposes of corporation tax.
Section 29 Persons chargeable.
Section 627 Deemed disposal of assets.
Section 980 Deduction from consideration on disposal of certain assets.
Schedule 1 Supplementary Provisions Concerning the Extension of Charge to Tax to Profits and Income Derived from Activities Carried On and Employments Exercised on the Continental Shelf

14 Fractions of a pound and yearly assessments

[ITA67 s5 and s6; FA70 s3]

(1) The due proportion of income tax shall be charged for every fractional part of [one euro][1], but no income tax shall be charged on a lower denomination than [one cent][2].

[(2) Every assessment and charge to income tax shall be made for a year of assessment.][3]

Amendments

[1, 2] Substituted by FA01 sched5.

[3] Substituted by FA01 s77(1)(c).

15 Rate of charge

[FA91 s2; FA97 s2(1) and (2)]

(1) Subject to *subsection (2)*, income tax shall be charged for each year of assessment at the rate of tax specified in the Table to this section as the standard rate.

[(2) Where a person who is charged to income tax for any year of assessment is an individual (other than an individual acting in a fiduciary or representative capacity), such individual shall, notwithstanding anything in the Income Tax Acts but subject to *section 16(2)*, be charged to tax on such individual's taxable income—

(a) in a case in which such individual is assessed to tax otherwise than in accordance with [*section 1017* or *1031C*][1] and is not an individual referred to in *paragraph (b)*, at the rates specified in Part 1 of the Table to this section, or

(b) in a case in which the individual is assessed to tax otherwise than in accordance with [*section 1017* or *1031C*][2] and is entitled to a reduction of tax provided for in [*section 462B*][3], at the rates specified in Part 2 of the Table to this section, or

(c) subject to *subsections (3)* and *(5)*, in a case in which such individual is assessed to tax in accordance with [*section 1017* or *1031C*][4], at the rates specified in Part 3 of the Table to this section,

and the rates in each Part of that Table shall be known respectively by the description specified in *column (3)* in each such Part opposite the mention of the rate or rates, as the case may be, in *column (2)* of that Part.

(3) Subject to *subsections (4)* and *(5)*—

(a) where an individual is charged to tax for a year of assessment in accordance with [*section 1017* or *1031C*][5], and

(b) both the individual and his or her [spouse or civil partner][6] are each in receipt of income in respect of which the individual is chargeable to tax in accordance with that section,

the part of his or her taxable income chargeable to tax at the standard rate specified in *column (1)* of *Part 3* of the Table to this section shall be increased by an amount which is the lesser of—

(i) [€24,800][7], and

(ii) the specified income of the individual or the specified income of the individual's [spouse or civil partner][8], whichever is the lesser.

[(4) For the purposes of *subsection (3)*, "*specified income*" means total income after deducting from such income any deduction attributable to a specific source of income and any relevant interest within the meaning of *Chapter 4* of *Part 8*.][9]

(5) Where all or any part of an increase under *subsection (3)* in the amount of an individual's taxable income chargeable to income tax at the standard rate is attributable to emoluments from which tax is deductible in accordance with the provisions of *Chapter 4* of *Part 42* and any regulations made thereunder, then, the full amount of the increase, or that part of the increase, as may be appropriate in the circumstances, shall only be used in accordance with the provisions of that Chapter and those regulations in calculating the amount of tax to be deducted from those emoluments.][10]

[TABLE

PART 1

Part of taxable income (1)	Rate of tax (2)	Description of rate (3)
The first €33,800	20 per cent	the standard rate
The remainder	40 per cent	the higher rate

PART 2

Part of taxable income (1)	Rate of tax (2)	Description of rate (3)
The first €37,800	20 per cent	the standard rate
The remainder	40 per cent	the higher rate

PART 3

Part of taxable income (1)	Rate of tax (2)	Description of rate (3)
The first €42,800	20 per cent	the standard rate
The remainder	40 per cent	the higher rate][11]

Amendments

[1, 2, 4, 5] Substituted by F(No.3)A11 sched1(8).

[3] Substituted by F(No.2)A13 s7(1)(c). Applies for the year of assessment 2014 and subsequent years of assessment.

[6, 8] Substituted by F(No.3)A11 sched1(9).

[7] Substituted by FA14 s3(a). Applies as respects the year of assessment 2015 and subsequent years of assessment.

[9] Substituted by FA01 s3(a). Applies as respects the year of assessment 2001 and subsequent years of assessment.

[10] Substituted by FA00 s3(a). Applies as respects the year of assessment 2000-2001 and subsequent years of assessment.

[11] Substituted by FA14 s3(b). Applies as respects the year of assessment 2015 and subsequent years of assessment.

Cross References

From Section 15

Section 16 Income tax charged by deduction.
Section 237 Annual payments payable wholly out of taxed income.
Section 256 Interpretation (Chapter 4).
Section 462 One-parent family tax credit.
Section 960 Date for payment of income tax other than under self assessment.
Section 983 Interpretation (Chapter 4).
Section 1017 Assessment of husband in respect of income of both spouses.

To Section 15

Section 3 Interpretation of Income Tax Acts.
Section 126 Tax treatment of certain benefits payable under Social Welfare Acts.
Section 261B Taxation of specified interest.
Section 267M Tax rate applicable to certain deposit interest received by individuals.
Section 466A Home carer tax credit.
Section 730J Payment in respect of foreign life policy.
Section 747D Payment in respect of offshore funds.
Section 747E Disposal of an interest in offshore funds.
Section 1024 Method of apportioning reliefs and charging tax in cases of separate assessments.

16 Income tax charged by deduction

[FA74 s5(2) and (3)]

(1) In estimating under the Income Tax Acts the total income of any person, any income chargeable with tax by means of deduction at the standard rate in force for any year shall be deemed to be income of that year, and any deductions allowable on account of sums payable under deduction of tax at the standard rate in force for any year out of the property or profits of that person shall be allowed as deductions in respect of that year, notwithstanding that the income or sums, as the case may be, accrued or will accrue in whole or in part before or after that year.

(2) Where a person is required to be assessed and charged with tax in respect of any property, profits or gains out of which such person makes any payment in respect of any annual interest, annuity or other annual sum, or any royalty or other sum in respect of the user of a patent, such person shall, in respect of so much of the property, profits or gains as is equal to that payment and may be deducted in computing such person's total income, be charged at the standard rate only.

Cross References

To Section 16

Section 15 Rate of charge.
Section 244 Relief for interest paid on certain home loans.
Section 458 Deductions allowed in ascertaining taxable income and provisions relating to reductions in tax.

Section 469 Relief for health expenses.
Section 470 Relief for insurance against expenses of illness.
Section 470B Age-related relief for health insurance premiums.
Section 472C Relief for trade union subscriptions.
Section 473 Allowance for rent paid by certain tenants.
Section 473A Relief for fees paid for third level education, etc.
Section 476 Relief for fees paid for training courses.
Section 477 Relief for service charges.
Section 477A Relief for energy efficient works.
Section 478 Relief for payments made by certain persons in respect of alarm systems.
Section 825A Reduction in income tax for certain income earned outside the State.
Schedule 31 Consequential Amendments

17 Schedule C

[ITA67 s47 and s51]

(1) The Schedule referred to as Schedule C is as follows:

SCHEDULE C

1. Tax under this Schedule shall be charged in respect of all profits arising from public revenue dividends payable in the State in any year of assessment.
2. Where a banker or any other person in the State, by means of coupons received from another person or otherwise on that other person's behalf, obtains payment of any foreign public revenue dividends, tax under this Schedule shall be charged in respect of the dividends.
3. Where a banker in the State sells or otherwise realises coupons for any foreign public revenue dividends and pays over the proceeds of such realisation to or carries such proceeds to the account of any person, tax under this Schedule shall be charged in respect of the proceeds of the realisation.
4. Where a dealer in coupons in the State purchases coupons for any foreign public revenue dividends otherwise than from a banker or another dealer in coupons, tax under this Schedule shall be charged in respect of the price paid on the purchase.
5. Nothing in *paragraph 1* shall apply to any annuities which are not of a public nature.
6. The tax under this Schedule shall be charged for every [one euro][1] of the annual amount of the profits, dividends, proceeds of realisation or price paid on purchase charged.

(2) *Section 32* shall apply for the interpretation of Schedule C.

[(3) *Subsection (1)* shall not apply to a banker by virtue only of the clearing of a cheque, or the arranging for the clearing of a cheque, by the banker.][2]

Amendments

[1] Substituted by FA01 sched5.

[2] Inserted by FA05 s46(1)(a). This section applies as respects any payment on or after 25 March 2005.

Cross References

From Section 17

Section 17 Schedule C.
Section 32 Interpretation (Chapter 1).

To Section 17

Section 12 The charge to income tax.
Section 17 Schedule C.
Section 19 Schedule E.
Section 32 Interpretation (Chapter 1).
Section 33 Method of charge and payment.
Section 54 Interest, etc. paid without deduction of tax under Schedule C.
Section 59 Charge to tax of income from which tax has been deducted.
Section 189 Payments in respect of personal injuries.
Section 189A Special trusts for permanently incapacitated individuals.
Section 192 Payments in respect of thalidomide children.
Section 207 Rents of properties belonging to hospitals and other charities.
Section 211 Friendly societies.
Section 213 Trade unions.
Section 485G Miscellaneous (Chapter 2A).
Section 812 Taxation of income deemed to arise from transfers of right to receive interest from securities.
Section 814 Taxation of income deemed to arise from transactions in certificates of deposit and assignable deposits.
Section 821 Application of sections 17 and 18(1) and Chapter 1 of Part 3.
Section 918 Making of assessments under Schedules C, D, E and F.
Schedule 2 Machinery for Assessment, Charge and Payment of Tax under Schedule C and, in Certain Cases, Schedule D

18 Schedule D

[ITA67 s52 and s53; FA69 s33(1) and Sch4 Pt I, s65(1) and Sch5 Pt I]

(1) The Schedule referred to as Schedule D is as follows:

SCHEDULE D

1. Tax under this Schedule shall be charged in respect of—
   (a) the annual profits or gains arising or accruing to—
      (i) any person residing in the State from any kind of property whatever, whether situate in the State or elsewhere,
      (ii) any person residing in the State from any trade, profession, or employment, whether carried on in the State or elsewhere,
      (iii) any person, whether a citizen of Ireland or not, although not resident in the State, from any property whatever in the State, or from any trade, profession or employment exercised in the State, and
      (iv) any person, whether a citizen of Ireland or not, although not resident in the State, from the sale of any goods, wares or merchandise manufactured or partly manufactured by such person in the State,

   and
   (b) all interest of money, annuities and other annual profits or gains not charged under Schedule C or Schedule E, and not specially exempted from tax,

   in each case for every [one euro][1] of the annual amount of the profits or gains.

2. Profits or gains arising or accruing to any person from an office, employment or pension shall not by virtue of *paragraph 1* be chargeable to tax under this Schedule unless they are chargeable to tax under Case III of this Schedule.

(2) Tax under Schedule D shall be charged under the following Cases:

Case I — Tax in respect of—

(a) any trade;

(b) profits or gains arising out of lands, tenements and hereditaments in the case of any of the following concerns—

(i) quarries of stone, slate, limestone or chalk, or quarries or pits of sand, gravel or clay,

(ii) mines of co al, tin, lead, copper, pyrites, iron and other mines, and

(iii) ironworks, gasworks, salt springs or works, alum mines or works, waterworks, streams of water, canals, inland navigations, docks, drains or levels, fishings, rights of markets and fairs, tolls, railways and other ways, bridges, ferries and other concerns of the like nature having profits from or arising out of any lands, tenements or hereditaments;

Case II — Tax in respect of any profession not contained in any other Schedule;

Case III — Tax in respect of—

(a) any interest of money, whether yearly or otherwise, or any annuity, or other annual payment, whether such payment is payable in or outside the State, either as a charge on any property of the person paying the same by virtue of any deed or will or otherwise, or as a reservation out of it, or as a personal debt or obligation by virtue of any contract, or whether the same is received and payable half-yearly or at any shorter or more distant periods, but not including any payment chargeable under Case V of Schedule D;

(b) all discounts;

(c) profits on securities bearing interest payable out of the public revenue other than those charged under Schedule C;

(d) interest on any securities issued, or deemed within the meaning of *section 36* to be issued, under the authority of the Minister for Finance, in cases where such interest is paid without deduction of tax;

(e) income arising from securities outside the State except such income as is charged under Schedule C;

[(f) income arising from possessions outside the State except, in the case of income from an office or employment (including any amount which would be chargeable to tax in respect of any sum received or benefit derived from the office or employment if the profits or gains from the office or employment were chargeable to tax under Schedule E), so much of that income as is attributable to the performance in the State of the duties of that office or employment;][2]

Case IV — Tax in respect of any annual profits or gains not within any other Case of Schedule D and not charged by virtue of any other Schedule;

Case V — Tax in respect of any rent in respect of any premises or any receipts in respect of any easement;

and subject to and in accordance with the provisions of the Income Tax Acts applicable to those Cases respectively.

(3) This section is without prejudice to any other provision of the Income Tax Acts directing tax to be charged under Schedule D or under one or other of the Cases mentioned in *subsection (2)*, and tax so directed to be charged shall be charged accordingly.

Amendments

[1] Substituted by FA01 sched5.

[2] Substituted by FA06 s15. Applies as respects the year of assessment 2006 and subsequent years of assessment.

Case Law

Trading?

In Ransom v Higgs 1974 STC 539 it was decided that an individual who procured other persons to carry out a complex scheme, designed to realise a profit, could not be said to be personally trading.

The infinite variety of possible factual circumstances means that no fixed formula can be applied to determine whether or not an activity should be classified as trading or non-trading. Erichsen v Last 1881 4 TC 422

Stewardess of a golf club provided catering services to the club. Profits were Schedule D rather than Schedule E. McManus v Griffiths 1997 STC 1089

Exploitation of copyright and trademark of a fictional character was held to be a trade in Noddy Subsidiary Rights Co. Ltd 1966 43 TC 458.

In Reed v Nova Securities 1985 STC 724 it was held that the acquisition of property which had no resale value and was thus inherently incapable of producing a profit could not form part of a trading transaction.

Isolated transactions do not constitute a trade. Jenkinson (HM Inspector of Taxes) v Freedland 1961 39 TC 636

In Neenan Travel Limited v Minister for Social and Family Affairs 2011 IEHC 458, the court in this case were asked to determine whether or not a proprietary director was liable to PRSI as a Class A or a Class S contributor. The issues of employed versus self employed for income tax purposes were also examined.

In Brightwater Selection [Ireland] Ltd v Minister for Social and Family Affairs 2011 IEHC 510, this case examined whether an agency worker for Brightwater was engaged under a contract of service and thereby insurable at the PRSI Class A rate of contribution.

Badges of Trading

Subject matter of the realisation

In IRC v Fraser 24 TC 498, a taxpayer who bought and sold a large quantity of whiskey, was held to be trading.

Length of ownership

In Kirby v Hughes 1993 STC 77 the fact that a building contractor constructed a property and occupied it for a short period did not rule out an intention to acquire it for the purpose of his trade.

Frequency of transactions

A taxpayer who systematically purchased endowment policies and held them to maturity was said to be trading. Smith Barry v Cordy 28 TC 250

Supplementary work

In Martin v Lowry 1926 11 TC 297 the taxpayer rented offices and hired employees in order to sell off a large stock of surplus linen to various customers. The taxpayer was held to be trading.

Three individuals who converted a cargo vessel into a steam drifter and then sold it were held to be trading. IRC v Livingston 11 TC 538

Circumstances responsible for the realisation

In Spa Estates v O'hArgain 1975 HC it was held that an intending land developer who sold off land before any development activities commenced, was not engaged in an 'adventure' in the nature of trade.

Motive

Accounting treatment of a transaction is evidence of intention. Shadford v Fairweather 1966 43 TC 291

Accounting Treatment

Profits should be based on historical cost accounting and not on current cost accounting. Carroll Industries plc (Formerly PJ Carroll & Co Ltd) and PJ Carroll & Co Limited v S O'Culachain (Inspector of Taxes) 1988 IV ITR 135

Ordinary accountancy treatment applied, in calculating the loss on sale of a lease, by a company to a shareholder. Cronin (Inspector of Taxes) v Cork and County Property Company Ltd 1986 III ITR 198

Lands may be treated as trading stock of a developer even if it does not yet have possession. In deciding whether the lands qualified as trading stock, the accounting treatment was held to be strong evidence of the 'commercial reality' of the situation. Murnaghan Bros v J O Maoldhomhnaigh (Inspector of Taxes) 1990 IV ITR 304

Advance payments made to a company, whose business consisted of the hiring of motor vehicles, and related to periods after the sale of the company to a third party, were part of the company's profits in the accounting period in which the business was sold. Tapemaze Ltd v Melluish (HM Inspector of Taxes) 2000 STC 189

Revenue or Capital Receipts

The distinction between a capital profit made on the disposal of an investment and a trading profit made as the result of a 'deal' was expressed in California Copper Syndicate v Harris 1904 5 TC 159.

A payment for the cancellation of the company's future rights under an agreement, which constituted a capital asset of the company, was a capital receipt. Van den Berghs Limited v Clark (H.M. Inspector of Taxes) 1935 19 TC 390

The taxpayer set aside funds to meet future liabilities of its business. It was claimed that the interest arising on investment of those funds should be treated as trading income. This was rejected. Nuclear Electric plc v Bradley 1979 STC 750

An inducement payment made to a lessee for undertaking an onerous lease was a capital payment. CIR v Wattie and anor 1998 STC 1160

A payment received in return for the sale of an income stream, was a capital receipt. IRC v John Lewis Properties plc 2001 STC 1118

Able (UK) Ltd v Revenue & Customs Commissioners 2007 STC 1738 considered whether compensation received for losses and expenses arising out of the giving and withdrawal of a CPO notice to a taxpayer was income or capital in nature.

Taxable Receipts

In Wain v Cameron 1995 STC 555 it was held that the sale of property rights created in the course of a profession were taxable receipts.

Training grants and other contributions towards expenditure should normally be taxable O'Cleirigh (Inspector of Taxes) v Jacobs International Ltd 1985 III ITR 165

Investment in silver bullion by loans with a high rate of interest held to be an adventure in the nature of trade. Wisdom v Chamberlain (H.M. Inspector of Taxes) 1969 45 TC 92

The proposition that 'any profit made by a bank on the realisation of an investment is part of the bank's taxable profits' was rejected in Guinness & Mahon Limited v Browne (Inspector of Taxes) 1985 III ITR 373.

Income generated from the purchase of sweepstake tickets was trading income. HH v MJ Forbes (Inspector of Taxes) 1974 II ITR 614.

Goods and services provided for consideration to non-members of a club, any surplus arising will be taxable. Carlisle & Silloth Golf Club v Smith 1913 6 TC 198

The selling off of whiskey stocks over a period after the liquidator had ceased to trade was not trading. IRC v Old Bushmills Distillery Co Ltd 1928 12 TC 1148

In N Cohan's Executors v IRC 12 TC 602, executors were held not to be trading when they completed the purchase of a contract to buy a ship entered into by the taxpayer before his death and when they resold the ship.

Trade Carried On Exclusively Abroad

A warehousing business carried on entirely by managers in Toronto was not carried on wholly abroad as the UK proprietor had oversight of the business from the UK. Ogilive v Kitton 1908 5 TC 338

In Colquhoun v Brooks 1889 2 TC 490 it was held that Case I applied to "a trade carried on partly abroad and partly in Great Britain" but that it "was not intended to apply to a trade carried on exclusively abroad".

A trade is carried on exclusively abroad and taxed under Case III only if all activities are carried on outside the State and such activities are not controlled and directed from the State. San Paulo (Brazilian) Railway Company v Carter 1896 3 TC 407

Revenue Briefings

Tax Briefing

Tax Briefing April 1998 – Issue 31 pg 21 – Prompt Payment Act – Treatment of Interest Payments

Tax Briefing September 1998 – Issue 33 pg 24 – Employed or Self-Employed

Tax Briefing April 2001 – Issue 43 pg 3 – Report of the Employment Status Group and Code of Practice

Tax Briefing June 2001 – Issue 44 Part 2 pg 24 – Deposit Interest – Whether a Trading Receipt?

Tax Briefing April 2002 – Issue 47 pg 32 – Share Fishing

Tax Briefing October 2004 – Issue 57 pg 10 – Classification of Activities as Trading

Tax Briefing September 2010 – Issue 12 – Share Farming

Revenue Information Notes

Deposit Interest – Whether a Trading Receipt?

Guidance on Revenue Opinions on Classification of Activities as Trading

Revenue Precedents

In determining whether video tapes in use in video rental shops should be classed as fixed assets or stock in trade, the ordinary rules of commercial accounting apply. It is necessary to examine the facts of each case to determine whether video tapes are fixed assets or stock in trade. IT923002

In the case of tapes owned by a video library it was agreed that tapes could be treated as trading stock. IT912005

It was agreed to concessionally exempt from tax certain allowances paid to Agency for Personnel Services Overseas (APSO) volunteers. IR 10470/406/93

Disability Benefits receivable by Irish Residents under US Insurance Policies are taxable here under Schedule D Case III. IT903513

Court interest chargeable to income tax in the hands of the recipient under Schedule D Case III. IT913520

Income earned abroad by Irish resident entertainers is taxable in Ireland under Schedule D Case II. IT903501

The special seller's prize paid by the national lottery to lotto agents who sell winning lotto tickets is taxable under Schedule D Case 1. GD94027

Payments made under the Emergency Aid Grant, paid by an Bord Iascaigh Mhara to compensate fishermen for poor earnings during adverse weather conditions, are taxable receipts liable to Income Tax. IT953549

Payments made to foster parents in Ireland, where the foster parents are not employees of the German paying authorities, under German Rehabilitation Programmes, to board/accommodate German youths, are chargeable to tax under Schedule D Case 1. IT952520

In general, where the recipient is a sportsperson who engages in the sport purely for recreational purposes i.e. is not carrying on a trade or profession as a sportsperson or is not an employee of the club etc which provides the gift, it would be regarded as a gift which would not give rise to an Income Tax liability. However, the circumstances of each case would need to be considered, before giving a definitive answer. IT962011

Revenue accepts CCJ decision that payment over and above the fee charged was not a receipt of the profession but a personal gift. 4265/83

Credit for US tax shown in a Lloyds account is given against the tax for the year of assessment for which the accounts form the basis of assessment. If there are losses, the effective rate of Irish tax is nil. In these circumstances the amount of the US tax is allowed as a deduction. IT923078

A bookmaker's stand/patch at a racecourse constitutes a permanent establishment. IT952546

Boarding Out Allowances paid under Statutory Instrument 225 of 1993 by Health Boards to people who board out elderly persons are taxable. There is no exempting provision. IT972515

Where a company acts as a trustee and the settlors are not resident, ordinarily resident or domiciled in Ireland and funds upon the trust are settled in currencies other than Irish pounds and/or property situated outside Ireland, the trust is treated as non resident. IT913510

The rate of exchange applied for the purpose of converting dividend income to Irish Pound is the rate of exchange which applied to the dividend on encashment. IT913539

Cross References

From Section 18

Section 36 Government securities.

To Section 18

Section 12 The charge to income tax.
Section 56 Tax on quarries, mines and other concerns chargeable under Case I(b) of Schedule D.
Section 77 Miscellaneous special rules for computation of income.
Section 104 Taxation of certain rents and other payments.

19 Schedule E

[ITA67 s109 and Sch2 rule2]

(1) The Schedule referred to as Schedule E is as follows:

SCHEDULE E

1. In this Schedule, "*annuity*" and "*pension*" include respectively an annuity which is paid voluntarily or is capable of being discontinued and a pension which is so paid or is so capable.
2. Tax under this Schedule shall be charged in respect of every public office or employment of profit, and in respect of every annuity, pension or stipend payable out of the public revenue of the State, other than annuities charged under Schedule C, for every [one euro][1] of the annual amount thereof.
3. Tax under this Schedule shall also be charged in respect of any office, employment or pension the profits or gains arising or accruing from which would be chargeable to tax under Schedule D but for *paragraph 2* of that Schedule.
4. *Paragraphs 1* to *3* are without prejudice to any other provision of the Income Tax Acts directing tax to be charged under this Schedule, and tax so directed to be charged shall be charged accordingly.
5. *Subsection (2)* and *sections 114*, *115* and *925* shall apply in relation to the tax to be charged under this Schedule.

(2) Tax under Schedule E shall be paid in respect of all public offices and employments of profit in the State or by the officers respectively described below—

(a) offices belonging to either House of the Oireachtas;

(b) offices belonging to any court in the State;

(c) public offices under the State;

(d) officers of the Defence Forces;

(e) offices or employments of profit under any ecclesiastical body;

(f) offices or employments of profit under any company or society, whether corporate or not corporate;

(g) offices or employments of profit under any public institution, or on any public foundation of whatever nature, or for whatever purpose established;

(h) offices or employments of profit under any public corporation or local authority, or under any trustees or guardians of any public funds, tolls or duties;

(i) all other public offices or employments of profit of a public nature.

Amendments

[1] Substituted by FA01 sched5.

Case Law

The definition of an office given in Great Western Railway v Bater 1922 8 TC 231 was "a subsisting permanent substantive position which had an existence independent of the person who filled it, which went on and was filled in succession by successive holders."

The meaning of 'office' was also considered by the Court of Appeal in Edwards v Clinch 1980 STC 438 and by the House of Lords Edwards v Clinch 1981 STC 617.

Schedule E includes fees earned in the year but paid subsequently. MacKeown (Inspector of Taxes) v Patrick J Ros 1927 I ITR 214

The head clerkship of a barrister's chambers was held, on the facts, not to constitute an office. McMenamin v Diggles 1991 STC 419

Revenue Briefings

Tax Briefing

Tax Briefing September 1998 – Issue 33 pg 24 – Employed or Self-Employed

Tax Briefing April 2001 – Issue 43 pg 3 – Report of the Employment Status Group and Code of Practice

Tax Briefing August 2006 – Issue 64 pg 12 – PAYE – Foreign Employments

eBrief

eBrief No. 43/2005 – PAYE and Foreign Employments

eBrief No. 09/2006 – 2005 Bonuses, Temporary Assignees, and Pension Contributions

eBrief No. 28/2006 – PAYE Foreign Employments

eBrief No.48/2007 – Foreign Employment Income

eBrief No. 05/2010 – Clarification of certain matters relating to employment vs. self employment status

Revenue Information Notes

Tax Treatment of Remuneration of Members of State and State Sponsored Committees and Boards. SP-IT/1/04

Employee Payroll tax deductions in relation to non-Irish Employment Exercised in the State. SP-IT/3/07

Cross References

From Section 19

Section 17 Schedule C.
Section 18 Schedule D.
Section 114 General rule as to deductions.
Section 115 Fixed deduction for certain classes of persons.
Section 925 Special rules relating to assessments under Schedule E.

To Section 19

Section 12 The charge to income tax.

20 Schedule F

[CTA76 s83(2) and (3)]

(1) The Schedule referred to as Schedule F is as follows:

SCHEDULE F

1. In this Schedule, "*distribution*" has the meaning assigned to it by *Chapter 2* of *Part 6* and [*sections 436*, *436A*, *437*, *816(2)(b)* and *817*][1].

2. Income tax under this Schedule shall be chargeable for any year of assessment in respect of all dividends and other distributions in that year of a company resident in the State which are not specially excluded from income tax and, for the purposes of income tax, all such distributions shall be regarded as income however they are to be dealt with in the hands of the recipient.

[…][2]

(2) No distribution chargeable under Schedule F shall be chargeable under any other provision of the Income Tax Acts.

Amendments

[1] Substituted by FA11 s29(a). Deemed to have come into force and takes effect as on and from 1 January 2011.

[2] Deleted by FA00 sched2.

Cross References

From Section 20

Section 129 Irish resident company distributions not generally chargeable to corporation tax.
Section 130 Matters to be treated as distributions.
Section 436 Certain expenses for participators and associates.
Section 436A Certain settlements made by close companies
Section 437 Interest paid to directors and directors' associates.
Section 816 Taxation of shares issued in place of cash dividends.

To Section 20

Section 12 The charge to income tax.
Section 172A Interpretation.

CHAPTER 2

Corporation Tax

21 The charge to corporation tax and exclusion of income tax and capital gains tax

[CTA76 s1(1), (2) and (3); FA97 s59(1)]

[(1) Corporation tax shall be charged on the profits of companies at the rate of—

(a) 32 per cent for the financial year 1998,

(b) 28 per cent for the financial year 1999,

(c) 24 per cent for the financial year 2000,

(d) 20 per cent for the financial year 2001,

(e) 16 per cent for the financial year 2002,

(f) 12½ per cent for the financial year 2003 and each subsequent financial year.][1]

[(1A) (a) In this subsection—

"*qualifying shipping activities*" and "*qualifying shipping trade*" have the same meanings respectively as in *section 407*;

(b) Notwithstanding *subsection (1)*, for the financial year 2001 and 2002, in relation to a company carrying on a qualifying shipping trade, profits from qualifying shipping activities carried on in the course of the qualifying shipping trade shall be charged to corporation tax at the rate of 12½ per cent.][2]

[(c) Notwithstanding *subsection (1)*, for the financial year 2002, in relation to a tonnage tax company (within the meaning of *Part 24A*), tonnage tax profits shall be charged to corporation tax at the rate of 12½ per cent.][3]

(2) The provisions of the Income Tax Acts relating to the charge of income tax shall not apply to income of a company (not arising to it in a fiduciary or representative capacity) if—

(a) the company is resident in the State, or

(b) the income is, in the case of a company not so resident, within the chargeable profits of the company as defined for the purposes of corporation tax.

(3) Subject to *section 649*, a company shall not be chargeable to capital gains tax in respect of gains accruing to it so that it is chargeable in respect of them to corporation tax.

Amendments

[1] Substituted by FA99 s71(1). Shall have effect for the purposes of supplementing this section.

[2] Inserted by FA01 s82(1)(a). This section applies as on and from 1 January 2001.

[3] Inserted by FA02 s53(3). Per FA03 s62(2) comes into operation on and from the date of passing of Finance Act 2003; 28 March 2003.

Revenue Briefings

Tax Briefing

Tax Briefing October 2004 – Issue 57 pg 10 – Classification of activities as trading

Revenue Information Notes

Guidance on Revenue Opinions on Classification of Activities as Trading

Cross References

From Section 21

Section 407 Restriction on use of losses and capital allowances for qualifying shipping trade.
Section 649 Companies chargeable to capital gains tax in respect of chargeable gains accruing on relevant disposals.
Section 697A Interpretation (Part 24A).

To Section 21

Section 21A Higher rate of corporation tax.
Section 22A Reduction of corporation tax liability in respect of certain trading income.
Section 78 Computation of companies' chargeable gains.
Section 243B Relief for certain charges on income on a value basis.
Section 396B Relief for certain trading losses on a value basis.
Section 420B Group relief: Relief for certain losses on a value basis.
Section 487 Corporation tax: credit for bank levy.
Section 707 Management expenses.
Section 711 Chargeable gains of life business.
Section 713 Investment income reserved for policyholders.
Section 738 Undertakings for collective investment.
Section 739 Taxation of unit holders in undertakings for collective investment.
Section 747E Disposal of an interest in offshore funds.
Section 864 Making of claims, etc.
Section 1009 Partnerships involving companies.
Section 1044 Bodies of persons.
Schedule 24 Relief from Income Tax and Corporation Tax by Means of Credit in Respect of Foreign Tax

21A Higher rate of corporation tax

[(1) In this section—

"*construction operations*" means operations of any of the descriptions referred to in the definition of "*construction operations*" in *section 530(1)*, other than operations referred to in *paragraph (f)* of that definition;

"*dealing in or developing land*" shall be construed in accordance with *Chapter 1* of *Part 22*;

"*excepted operations*" means any one or more of the following operations or activities—

[(a) dealing in or developing land, other than such part of that operation or activity as consists of—

(i) construction operations, or

(ii) dealing by a company in land which, in relation to the company, is qualifying land,][1]

[(b) (i) working scheduled minerals, mineral compounds or mineral substances (within the meaning of *section 2* of the Minerals Development Act 1940), or

(ii) working minerals (other than those specified in *subparagraph (i)*) other than so much of working such minerals as is manufacturing,

and,][2]

(c) petroleum activities;

"*excepted trade*" means a trade consisting only of trading operations or activities which are excepted operations or, in the case of a trade consisting partly of excepted operations and partly of other operations or activities, the part of the trade consisting only of excepted operations which is treated as a separate trade by virtue of *subsection (2)*;

["*exempt development*" means a development within Class 1 of Part 1 of the Second Schedule to the Local Government Planning and Development Regulations, 1994 (S.I. No. 86 of 1994), which complies with the conditions and limitations specified in column 2 of that Part which relate to that Class;][3]

"*land*" includes foreshore and land covered with water, and "*dry land*" means land not permanently covered by water;

"*minerals*" means all substances (other than the agricultural surface of the ground and other than turf or peat) in, on or under land, whether obtainable by underground or by surface working, and includes all mines, whether or not they are already opened or in work, and also includes the cubic space occupied or formerly occupied by minerals;

"*petroleum*" has the same meaning as in section 2(1) of the Petroleum and Other Minerals Development Act, 1960;

"*petroleum activities*" means any one or more of the following activities—

(a) petroleum exploration activities,

(b) petroleum extraction activities, and

(c) the acquisition, enjoyment or exploitation of petroleum rights;

"*petroleum exploration activities*" means activities carried on in searching for deposits of petroleum, in testing or appraising such deposits or in winning access to such deposits for the purposes of such searching, testing or appraising;

"*petroleum extraction activities*" means activities carried on in—

(a) winning petroleum from any land, including searching in that land and winning access to such petroleum,

(b) transporting as far as dry land petroleum so won from a place not on dry land, or

(c) effecting the initial treatment and storage of petroleum so won from any land;

"*petroleum rights*" means rights to petroleum to be extracted or to interests in, or to the benefit of, petroleum;

["*qualifying land*", in relation to a company, means land which is disposed of at any time by the company, being land—

(a) on which a building or structure had been constructed by or for the company before that time, and

(b) which had been developed by or for the company to such an extent that it could reasonably be expected at that time that no further development (within the meaning of *section 639*) of the land would be carried out in the period of 20 years beginning at that time (other than a development which is not material and which is intended to facilitate the occupation of, and the use or enjoyment of, the building or structure for the purposes for which it was constructed) and for those purposes a development of land on which a building or buildings had been constructed shall not be material if it consists of one or both of the following—

(i) an exempt development, and

(ii) a development, not being an exempt development, if the total floor area of the building or buildings on the land after such development is not greater than 120 per cent of the total floor area of the building or buildings on the land calculated without regard to that development;][4]

"*working*", in relation to minerals, includes digging, searching for, mining, getting, raising, taking, carrying away and treating minerals and the sale or other disposal of minerals.

(2) For the purposes of this section, where a trade consists partly of excepted operations and partly of other operations or activities, the part of the trade consisting of excepted operations and the part of the trade consisting of other operations or activities shall each be treated as a separate trade, and there shall be apportioned to each such part such proportion of the total amount receivable from sales made and services rendered in the course of the trade, and of expenses incurred in the course of the trade, as is just and reasonable.

[(3) (a) Notwithstanding *section 21*, [but subject to *subsection (4)* and *section 21B*][5], corporation tax shall be charged on the profits of companies, in so far as those profits consist of income chargeable to corporation tax under Case III, IV or V of Schedule D or of income of an excepted trade, at the rate of 25 per cent for the financial year 2000 and subsequent financial years.

(b) For the purposes of *paragraph (a)*, the profits of a company for an accounting period shall be treated as consisting of income of an excepted trade to the extent of the income of the trade for the accounting period after deducting from the amount of that income the amount of charges on income paid in the accounting period wholly and exclusively for the purposes of that trade.

[(4) This section shall not apply to the profits of a company for any accounting period to the extent that those profits consist of income which arises in the course of any of the following trades—

(a) non-life insurance,

(b) reinsurance, and

(c) life business, in so far as the income is attributable to shareholders of the company.][6]

and

[...][7]

(5) (a) Notwithstanding *subsection (1)*, as respects an accounting period ending before 1 January 2001, operations carried out in relation to residential development land (within the meaning of *section 644A*) shall be treated for the purposes of this section as not being construction operations if they consist of—

(i) the demolition or dismantling of any building or structure on the land,

(ii) the construction or demolition of any works forming part of the land, being roadworks, water mains, wells, sewers or installations for the purposes of land drainage, or

(iii) any other operations which are preparatory to residential development on the land other than the laying of foundations for such development.

(b) For the purposes of this subsection, where an accounting period of a company begins before 1 January 2001 and ends on or after that day, it shall be divided into two parts, one beginning on the day on which the accounting period begins and ending on 31 December 2000 and the other beginning on 1 January 2001 and ending on the day on which the accounting period ends, and both parts shall be treated for the purpose of this section as if they were separate accounting periods of the company.][8]][9]

Amendments

[1] Substituted by FA00 s75(1)(a)(i). This section shall apply for the financial year 2000 and subsequent financial years.

[2] Substituted by FA12 sched1(2)(a).

[3] Inserted by FA00 s75(1)(a)(ii). This section shall apply for the financial year 2000 and subsequent financial years.

[4] Inserted by FA00 s75(1)(a)(iii). This section shall apply for the financial year 2000 and subsequent financial years.

[5] Substituted by FA08 s43(1)(a). This section shall be deemed to have applied as respects a dividend received on or after 1 January 2007.

[6] Substituted by FA12 sched1(2)(b).

[7] Deleted by FA12 sched1(2)(c).

[8] Substituted by FA00 s75(1)(b). This section shall apply for the financial year 2000 and subsequent financial years.

[9] Inserted by FA99 s73.

Revenue Information Notes

Deposit Interest – Whether a Trading Receipt?

Guidance on Revenue Opinions on Classification of Activities as Trading

Notes for Guidance – Finance Act 2008. Chapter 4 of Part 1. – Tax treatment of certain dividends

Cross References

From Section 21A

Section 21 The charge to corporation tax and exclusion of income tax and capital gains tax.

Section 21B Tax treatment of certain dividends.

Section 442 Interpretation (Part 14).

Section 448 Relief from corporation tax.

Section 530 Interpretation (Chapter 2).

Section 639 Interpretation (Chapter 1).

Section 644A Relief from income tax in respect of income from dealing in residential development land.

To Section 21A

Section 21B Tax treatment of certain dividends.
Section 22A Reduction of corporation tax liability in respect of certain trading income.
Section 243A Restriction of relevant charges on income.
Section 396A Relief for relevant trading losses.
Section 420A Group relief: relevant losses and charges.
Section 448 Relief from corporation tax.
Section 486C Relief from tax for certain start-up companies.
Section 541C Tax treatment of certain venture fund managers.
Section 644C Relief from corporation tax for losses from dealing in residential development land.
Section 696C Charge to profit resource rent tax.
Section 835G Elimination of double counting.
Schedule 24 Relief from Income Tax and Corporation Tax by Means of Credit in Respect of Foreign Tax

21B Tax treatment of certain dividends

[(1) (a) In this section—

"*profits*", in relation to a company for a period, means—

(i) where the profit and loss account, or income statement, of the company for that period is required to be laid before the annual general meeting of the company, the amount of profits, after taxation, as shown in that profit and loss account, or that income statement, and

(ii) in any other case, the amount of profits, after taxation, as shown in the profit and loss account, or income statement, of the company which is prepared in accordance with an accounting framework that, in the territory in which the company is incorporated, is generally accepted as presenting a fair view of the profit for that period;

['*relevant territory*' means—

(i) a Member State of the European Communities,

(ii) not being such a Member State, a territory with the government of which arrangements having the force of law by virtue of *section 826(1)* have been made,

(iii) not being a territory referred to in *subparagraph (i)* or *(ii)*, a territory with the government of which arrangements have been made which on completion of the procedures set out in *section 826(1)* will have the force of law, or

(iv) not being a territory referred to in *subparagraph (i)*, *(ii)* or *(iii)*, a territory the government of which has ratified the Convention referred to in *section 826(1C)*;][1]

"*trading profits*", in relation to a company for a period, means the aggregate of so much of the profits of the company for that period as are, on a just and reasonable basis, attributable to—

(i) the carrying on by the company of a trade, and

(ii) the amount of dividends received by the company which are treated as trading profits by virtue of this section,

but does not include amounts attributable to profits, or to dividends received by a company which are paid out of profits, of an excepted trade (within the meaning of *section 21A*).

(b) For the purposes of this section—

[(i) references to a company by which a dividend is paid apply only to a company, where throughout the period out of the profits of which the dividend was paid—

(I) the company was, by virtue of the law of a relevant territory, resident for the purposes of tax in such a relevant territory, and for this purpose "tax", in relation to a relevant territory, means any tax imposed in the relevant territory which corresponds to corporation tax in the State, or

(II) the principal class of shares of the company or, where the company was a 75 per cent subsidiary of another company, the principal class of shares of that other company, was substantially and regularly traded on a stock exchange in the State, on one or more than one recognised stock exchanges in a relevant territory or territories or on such other stock exchange as may be approved of by the Minister for Finance for the purposes of *Chapter 8A* of *Part 6*,][2]

(ii) so much of a dividend received by a company (in this subparagraph referred to as the "*first-mentioned company*") which is paid by another company out of trading profits, or an amount treated by this section as trading profits, of the other company shall be treated as trading profits of the first-mentioned company,

(iii) subject to subparagraph (iv), the period out of the profits of which a dividend is paid by a company shall be—

(I) if the dividend is paid by the company for a specified period, that period,

(II) if the dividend is not paid for a specified period but is paid out of specified profits, the period in which those profits arise, or

(III) if the dividend is not paid by the company for a specified period nor out of specified profits, the last period for which accounts of the company were made up and which ended before the dividend became payable,

and

(iv) where, as respects a period identified in accordance with subparagraph (iii) or this subparagraph, the total dividend exceeds the profits available for distribution for that period, then so much of the dividend as is equal to the excess shall be treated as paid out of profits of the preceding period (other than profits of that period which were, or were treated for the purposes of this subparagraph as, previously distributed), and such period shall be treated as a period identified by subparagraph (iii) for the purposes of the further application of this subparagraph where required.

[(c) For the purposes of *paragraph (b)(i)(II)*, *sections 412* to *418* shall apply as those sections would apply for the purposes of *Chapter 5* of *Part 12* if *section 411(1)(c)* were deleted.][3]

(2) For the purposes of this section—

[(a) subject to *paragraph (b)*, the amount of a dividend to be treated as paid out of trading profits of a company shall be—

(i) where the dividend is paid out of specified profits, so much of the dividend, as bears to the amount of that dividend the same proportion as the amount of trading profits of the company contained in the specified profits bears to the amount of those specified profits of the company, and

(ii) where the dividend is not paid out of specified profits so much of the dividend, as bears to the amount of that dividend the same proportion as the amount of trading profits of the company for the period out of which the dividend is paid bears to the total profits of the company for that period, and][4]

(b) a dividend received by a company (in this paragraph referred to as the "*receiving company*") within the charge to corporation tax in the State which is paid by a company (in this paragraph referred to as the "*paying company*") out of the profits of a period shall be treated as paid out of trading profits of the paying company for that period if—

(i) not less than 75 per cent of the total profits of the paying company for the period are trading profits, and

(ii) the value at the end of the accounting period in which the dividend is received by the receiving company of assets (other than specified assets) used by the receiving company, and each company of which the receiving company is the parent company (within the meaning of *section 626B*), during that period for the purposes of the carrying on by those companies of a trade or trades is not less than 75 per cent of the value at the end of that period of the assets (other than specified assets) of those companies, and for this purpose an asset shall be treated as a specified asset if it consists of—

(I) shares of one of those companies held by another of those companies, or

(II) loans made by one of those companies to another of those companies.

(3) Subject to *subsection (4)*, this section applies as respects an accounting period of a company where the company receives a dividend chargeable under Case III of Schedule D from another company and the dividend is paid by the other company out of trading profits of the other company.

[(4) (a) This subsection applies to a dividend paid to a company (in this subsection referred to as the "*first-mentioned company*") by another company and the first-mentioned company—

(i) does not own, directly or indirectly, either alone or together with a person who is connected (within the meaning of *section 10*) with the first-mentioned company, more than 5 per cent of the share capital of the other company, and

(ii) does not hold more than 5 per cent of the voting rights in the other company.

(b) Where the income of a company which is chargeable to tax under Case III of Schedule D includes a dividend, being a dividend to which this subsection applies, paid to the company by another company then the dividend shall be treated for the purposes of *subsection (3)* as a dividend paid by the other company out of trading profits of the other company.

(c) Where the income of a company which is income chargeable to tax under Case I of Schedule D would, but for this paragraph, include a dividend to which this subsection applies, then, except where otherwise expressly provided by the Corporation Tax Acts, corporation tax shall not be chargeable on the dividend, nor shall the dividend be taken into account in computing income for corporation tax.][5]

(5) Where a company proves that this section applies as respects an accounting period of the company and makes a claim in that behalf, then *subsection (3)* of *section 21A* shall not apply to so much of any income of the company chargeable under Case III of Schedule D as consists of a dividend received by the company from another company if the dividend is paid by the other company out of trading profits of the other company.

(6) A claim by a company under this section as respects an accounting period of the company shall be included with the return under [*Chapter 3* of *Part 41A*][6] which falls to be made by the company for the accounting period.][7]

Amendments

[1] Substituted by FA12 s53(1). Applies to dividends received on or after 1 January 2012.

[2] Substituted by FA10 s50(1)(a). This section shall apply to dividends received on or after 1 January 2010.

[3] Inserted by FA10 s50(1)(b). This section shall apply to dividends received on or after 1 January 2010.

[4] Substituted by FA10 s50(1)(c). This section shall apply to dividends received on or after 1 January 2010.

[5] Substituted by FA10 s50(1)(d). This section shall apply to dividends received on or after 1 January 2010.

[6] Substituted by FA12 sched4(part 2)(g).

[7] Inserted by FA08 s43(1)(b). This section shall be deemed to have applied as respects a dividend received on or after 1 January 2007.

Revenue Information Notes

Notes for Guidance – Finance Act 2008. Chapter 4 of Part 1. – Tax treatment of certain dividends

Cross References

From Section 21B

Section 10 Connected persons.
Section 21A Higher rate of corporation tax.
Section 129 Irish resident company distributions not generally chargeable to corporation tax.
Section 381 Right to repayment of tax by reference to losses.
Section 410 Group payments.
Section 411 Surrender of relief between members of groups and consortia.
Section 412 Qualification for entitlement to group relief.
Section 418 Beneficial percentage.
Section 626B Exemption from tax in the case of gains on disposals of shares.
Section 826 Agreements for relief from double taxation.
Section 951 Obligation to make a return.

To Section 21B

Section 21A Higher rate of corporation tax.
Section 243A Restriction of relevant charges on income.
Section 396A Relief for relevant trading losses.
Section 420A Group relief: relevant losses and charges.
Section 644C Relief from corporation tax for losses from dealing in residential development land.

22 Reduced rate of corporation tax for certain income [Repealed]

Repealed by FA99 s72(2) with effect from the 1st day of January, 2000.

22A Reduction of corporation tax liability in respect of certain trading income [Deleted]

Deleted by FA12 sched1(3).

23 Application of section 13 for purposes of corporation tax

[CTA76 s140(1) and Sch2 PtI par34]

Section 13 shall apply for the purposes of corporation tax as it applies for the purposes of income tax.

Cross References

From Section 23

Section 13 Extension of charge to income tax to profits and income derived from activities carried on and employments exercised on the Continental Shelf.

To Section 23

Schedule 1 Supplementary Provisions Concerning the Extension of Charge to Tax to Profits and Income Derived from Activities Carried On and Employments Exercised on the Continental Shelf

23A Company residence

[(1) Subject to *subsection (2)*, a company which is incorporated in the State shall be regarded for the purposes of the Tax Acts and the Capital Gains Tax Acts as resident in the State.

(2) Notwithstanding *subsection (1)*, a company which is regarded for the purposes of any arrangements, having the force of law by virtue of *section 826(1)*, as resident in a territory other than the State and not resident in the State shall be regarded for the purposes of the Tax Acts and the Capital Gains Tax Acts as not resident in the State.

(3) Nothing in *subsection (1)* shall prevent a company that—

(a) is not incorporated in the State, and

(b) is centrally managed and controlled in the State, being resident in the State for the purposes of the Tax Acts and the Capital Gains Tax Acts.][1]

Amendments

[1] Substituted by FA14 s43(1)(a).

Note:

Per FA14 s43(2) certain important conditions apply with reference to the company's ownership and date of incorporation. FA14 s43(2) cannot be consolidated but is reproduced here in full. References to the "Principal Act" are to TCA 97.

(a) Subject to *paragraph (b)*, this section shall have effect from 1 January 2015. (b) As respects a company incorporated before 1 January 2015, this section shall have effect— (i) after 31 December 2020, or (ii) from the date, after 31 December 2014, of a change in ownership of the company where there is a major change in the nature or conduct of the business of the company within the relevant period, whichever is the earlier. (c) In *paragraph (b)* "relevant period" means a period— (i) beginning on the later of— (I) 1 January 2015, or (II) the date which occurs one year before the date of the change in ownership of the company referred to in that paragraph, and (ii) ending 5 years after the date of that change of ownership. (d) For the purposes of the references in *paragraphs (b)* and *(c)* to a change in ownership of a company, Schedule 9 (other than paragraph 4 of that Schedule) to the Principal Act shall apply as if references in that Schedule to section 401 or 679(4) of the Principal Act were references to the said *paragraphs (b)* and *(c)*. (e) For the purposes of *paragraph (b)*, "a major change in the nature or conduct of the business of the company" means— (i) a major change in the nature or conduct of a trade (within the meaning of section 401(1)(a) or (b) of the Principal Act) carried on by the company, (ii) the commencement by the company of a new trade, or (iii) a major change arising from the acquisition by the company of property or of an interest in, or right over, property.

23B Residence of SE or SCE

[(1) An SE or an SCE which has its registered office in the State shall, subject to section 23A, be treated for the purposes of the Tax Acts and the Capital Gains Tax Acts as resident in the State.

(2) (a) An SE which transfers its registered office out of the State in accordance with Article 8 of Council Regulation (EC) No. 2157/2001 on the Statute for a European Company (SE), and

(b) an SCE which transfers its registered office out of the State in accordance with Article 7 of Council Regulation (EC) No. 1435/2003 of 22 July 2003 on the Statute for a European Cooperative Society (SCE),

shall not cease to be resident in the State by virtue only of that transfer.][1]

Amendments

[1] Inserted by FA06 s60(b).

24 Companies resident in the State: income tax on payments made or received

[CTA76 s3]

(1) No payment made by a company resident in the State shall by virtue of this section or otherwise be treated for any purpose of the Income Tax Acts as paid out of profits or gains brought into charge to income tax, nor shall any right or obligation under the Income Tax Acts to deduct income tax from any payment be affected by the fact that the recipient is a company not chargeable to income tax in respect of the payment.

(2) Subject to the Corporation Tax Acts, where a company resident in the State receives any payment on which it bears income tax by deduction, the income tax on that payment shall be set off against any corporation tax assessable on the company by an assessment made for the accounting period in which that payment is to be taken into account for corporation tax (or would be taken into account but for any exemption from corporation tax), and accordingly in respect of that payment the company, unless wholly exempt from corporation tax, shall not be entitled to a repayment of income tax before the assessment for that accounting period is finally determined and it appears that a repayment is due.

(3) References in this section to payments received by a company apply to any payments received by another person on behalf of or in trust for the company, but not to any payments received by the company on behalf of or in trust for another person.

Cross References

To Section 24

Section 239 Income tax on payments by resident companies.
Section 372AU Saver for relief due, and for clawback of relief given under, old schemes.
Section 372AV Continuity.
Section 697M Exclusion of reliefs, deductions and set-offs.
Section 864 Making of claims, etc.

25 Companies not resident in the State

[CTA76 s8(1), (2) and (3)]

(1) A company not resident in the State shall not be within the charge to corporation tax unless it carries on a trade in the State through a branch or agency, but if it does so it shall, subject to any exceptions provided for by the Corporation Tax Acts, be chargeable to corporation tax on all its chargeable profits wherever arising.

(2) For the purposes of corporation tax, the chargeable profits of a company not resident in the State but carrying on a trade in the State through a branch or agency shall be—

(a) any trading income arising directly or indirectly through or from the branch or agency, and any income from property or rights used by, or held by or for, the branch or agency, but this paragraph shall not include distributions received from companies resident in the State, and

(b) such chargeable gains as but for the Corporation Tax Acts would be chargeable to capital gains tax in the case of a company not resident in the State;

but such chargeable profits shall not include chargeable gains accruing to the company on the disposal of assets which, at or before the time when the chargeable gains accrued, were not used in or for the purposes of the trade and were not used or held or acquired for the purposes of the branch or agency.

(3) Subject to *section 729*, where a company not resident in the State receives any payment on which it bears income tax by deduction, and that payment forms part of, or is to be taken into account in computing, the company's income chargeable to corporation tax, the income tax on that payment shall be set off against any corporation tax assessable on that income by an assessment made for the accounting period in which the payment is to be taken into account for corporation tax, and accordingly in respect of that payment the company shall not be entitled to a repayment of income tax before the assessment for that accounting period is finally determined and it appears that a repayment is due.

Case Law

The meaning of "income from property or rights used by, or held by or for, the branch or agency" was considered in Murphy V Dataproducts (Dublin) Ltd 1988 IV ITR 12.

Revenue Briefings

Tax Briefing

Tax Briefing April 1997 – Issue 26 pg 11 – Criteria and Guidelines on Permanent Establishment

Cross References

From Section 25

Section 729 Income tax, foreign tax and tax credit.

To Section 25

Section 247 Relief to companies on loans applied in acquiring interest in other companies.
Section 590 Attribution to participators of chargeable gains accruing to non-resident company.
Section 697M Exclusion of reliefs, deductions and set-offs.
Section 729 Income tax, foreign tax and tax credit.
Section 745 Charge to income tax or corporation tax of offshore income gain.
Section 864 Making of claims, etc.

26 General scheme of corporation tax

[CTA76 s6(1) to (3); FA97 s59(2) and Sch6 PtI par1]

(1) Subject to any exceptions provided for by the Corporation Tax Acts, a company shall be chargeable to corporation tax on all its profits wherever arising.

(2) A company shall be chargeable to corporation tax on profits accruing for its benefit under any trust, or arising under any partnership, in any case in which it would be so chargeable if the profits accrued to it directly, and a company shall be chargeable to corporation tax on profits arising in the winding up of the company, but shall not otherwise be chargeable to corporation tax on profits accruing to it in a fiduciary or representative capacity except as respects its own beneficial interest (if any) in those profits.

(3) Corporation tax for any financial year shall be charged on profits arising in that year; but assessments to corporation tax shall be made on a company by reference to accounting periods, and the amount chargeable (after making all proper deductions) of the profits arising in an accounting period shall where necessary be apportioned between the financial years in which the accounting period falls.

(4) *Subsection (3)* shall apply as respects accounting periods ending on or after the 1st day of April, 1997, as if—

(a) the period beginning on the 1st day of January, 1996, and ending on the 31st day of March, 1997, and

(b) the period beginning on the 1st day of April, 1997, and ending on the [31st day of December, 1997][1],

were each a financial year.

Amendments

[1] Substituted by FA98 sched6(1).

Case Law

The receiver was not liable to corporation tax on the interest earned on monies coming into his possession or control. Wayte (Holdings) Ltd (in receivership) Alex Burns v Edward N Hearne 1986 III ITR 553

Cross References

To Section 26

Section 22A Reduction of corporation tax liability in respect of certain trading income.
Section 448 Relief from corporation tax.
Schedule 24 Relief from Income Tax and Corporation Tax by Means of Credit in Respect of Foreign Tax

27 Basis of, and periods for, assessment

[CTA76 s9]

(1) Except where otherwise provided by the Corporation Tax Acts, corporation tax shall be assessed and charged for any accounting period of a company on the full amount of the profits arising in that period (whether or not received in or remitted to the State) without any deduction other than one authorised by the Corporation Tax Acts.

(2) An accounting period of a company shall begin for the purposes of corporation tax whenever—

(a) the company, not then being within the charge to corporation tax, comes within it whether by the coming into force of any provision of the Corporation Tax Acts, or by the company becoming resident in the State or acquiring a source of income, or otherwise, or

(b) an accounting period of the company ends without the company then ceasing to be within the charge to corporation tax.

(3) An accounting period of a company shall end for the purposes of corporation tax on the first occurrence of any of the following—

(a) the expiration of 12 months from the beginning of the accounting period,

(b) an accounting date of the company or, if there is a period for which the company does not make up accounts, the end of that period,

(c) the company beginning or ceasing to trade or to be, in respect of the trade or (if more than one) of all the trades carried on by it, within the charge to corporation tax,

(d) the company beginning or ceasing to be resident in the State, and

(e) the company ceasing to be within the charge to corporation tax.

(4) For the purposes of this section, a company resident in the State, if not otherwise within the charge to corporation tax, shall be treated as coming within the charge to corporation tax at the time when it commences to carry on business.

(5) Where a company carrying on more than one trade makes up accounts of any of those trades to different dates and does not make up general accounts for the whole of the company's activities, *subsection (3)(b)* shall apply with reference to the accounting date of such one of the trades as the Revenue Commissioners may determine.

(6) Where a chargeable gain or allowable loss accrues to a company at a time not otherwise within an accounting period of the company, an accounting period of the company shall then begin for the purposes of corporation tax and the gain or loss shall accrue in that accounting period.

(7) (a) Notwithstanding anything in *subsections (1)* to *(6)*, where a company is wound up, an accounting period shall end and a new one shall begin with the commencement of the winding up, and thereafter an accounting period shall not end otherwise than by the expiration of 12 months from its beginning or by the completion of the winding up.

(b) For the purposes of *paragraph (a)*, a winding up shall be taken to commence on the passing by the company of a resolution for the winding up of the company, or on the presentation of a winding up petition if no such resolution has previously been passed and a winding up order is made on the petition, or on the doing of any other act for a like purpose in the case of a winding up otherwise than under the Companies Act, 1963.

(8) Where it appears to the inspector that the beginning or end of any accounting period of a company is uncertain, he or she may make an assessment on the company for such a period, not exceeding 12 months, as appears to him or her appropriate, and that period shall be treated for all purposes as an accounting period of the company unless—

(a) the inspector on further facts coming to his or her knowledge sees fit to revise it, or

(b) on an appeal against the assessment in respect of some other matter, the company shows the true accounting periods,

and, if on an appeal against an assessment made by virtue of this subsection the company shows the true accounting periods, the assessment appealed against shall, as regards the period to which it relates, have effect as an assessment or assessments for the true accounting periods, and such other assessments may be made for any such periods or any of them as might have been made at the time when the assessment appealed against was made.

Case Law

A new accounting period commenced when a company which ceased to trade became liable to pay Advance Corporation Tax. Walker (HMIT) v Centaur Clothes Group 2000 STC 324

Cross References

To Section 27

Section 127 Tax treatment of restrictive covenants.
Section 495 Specified individuals.
Section 665 Interpretation (Chapter 2).

CHAPTER 3

Capital Gains Tax

28 Taxation of capital gains and rate of charge

[CGTA75 s3(1) to (3); FA92 s60(1)(a)]

(1) Capital gains tax shall be charged in accordance with the Capital Gains Tax Acts in respect of capital gains, that is, in respect of chargeable gains computed in accordance with those Acts and accruing to a person on the disposal of assets.

(2) Capital gains tax shall be assessed and charged for years of assessment in respect of chargeable gains accruing in those years.

(3) Except where otherwise provided by the Capital Gains Tax Acts, the rate of capital gains tax in respect of a chargeable gain accruing to a person on the disposal of an asset shall be [33 per cent][1], and any reference in those Acts to the rate specified in this section shall be construed accordingly.

Amendments

[1] Substituted by FA13 s43(1)(a). Applies to disposals made on or after 6 December 2012.

Revenue Information Notes

Tax & Duty Manuals – Section 16 [2.3.1A] Capital gains tax – rate of charge (S.28)

Cross References

To Section 28

Section 541C Tax treatment of certain venture fund managers.
Section 594 Foreign life assurance and deferred annuities: taxation and returns.
Section 649A Relevant disposals: rate of charge.
Section 711 Chargeable gains of life business.
Section 732 Special arrangements for qualifying unit trusts.
Section 737 Special investment schemes.
Section 738 Undertakings for collective investment.
Section 747A Capital gains tax: rate of charge.
Section 978 Gifts: recovery of capital gains tax from donee.
Section 1042 Charging and assessment of persons not resident or ordinarily resident: modification of general rules.

29 Persons chargeable

[CGTA75 s4(1) to (4) and (6) to (8), s51(1) and Sch4 par2(2); FA77 s54(1)(a) and Sch2 PtI]

(1) In this section—

"*designated area*" means an area designated by order under section 2 of the Continental Shelf Act, 1968;

"*exploration or exploitation rights*" has the same meaning as in *section 13*;

"*shares*" includes stock and any security;

"*security*" includes securities not creating or evidencing a charge on assets, and interest paid by a company on money advanced without the issue of a security for the advance, or other consideration given by a company for the use of money so advanced, shall be treated as if paid or given in respect of a security issued for the advance by the company;

references to the disposal of assets mentioned in *paragraphs (a)* and *(b)* of *subsection (3)* and in *subsection (6)* include references to the disposal of shares deriving their value or the greater part of their value directly or indirectly from those assets, other than shares quoted on a stock exchange.

(2) Subject to any exceptions in the Capital Gains Tax Acts, a person shall be chargeable to capital gains tax in respect of chargeable gains accruing to such person in a year of assessment for which such person is resident or ordinarily resident in the State.

(3) Subject to any exceptions in the Capital Gains Tax Acts, a person who is neither resident nor ordinarily resident in the State shall be chargeable to capital gains tax for a year of assessment in respect of chargeable gains accruing to such person in that year on the disposal of—

(a) land in the State,

(b) minerals in the State or any rights, interests or other assets in relation to mining or minerals or the searching for minerals,

(c) assets situated in the State which at or before the time when the chargeable gains accrued were used in or for the purposes of a trade carried on by such person in the State through a branch or agency, or which at or before that time were used or held or acquired for use by or for the purposes of the branch or [agency,][1] [(d) assets situated outside the State of an overseas life assurance company (within the meaning of *section 706(1)*), being assets which were held in connection with the life business (within the meaning of *section 706(1)*) carried on by the company, which at or before the time the chargeable gains accrued were used or held by or for the purposes of that company's branch or agency in the State.][2]

(4) *Subsection (2)* shall not apply in respect of chargeable gains accruing from the disposal of assets situated outside the State […][3] to an individual who satisfies the Revenue Commissioners that he or she is not domiciled in the State; but—

(a) the tax shall be charged on the amounts received in the State in respect of those chargeable gains,

(b) any such amounts shall be treated for the purposes of the Capital Gains Tax Acts as gains accruing when they are received in the State, and

(c) any losses accruing to the individual on the disposal of assets situated outside the State […][4] shall not be allowable losses for the purposes of the Capital Gains Tax Acts.

(5) For the purposes of *subsection (4)*, all amounts paid, used or enjoyed in or in any manner or form transmitted or brought to the State shall be treated as received in the State in respect of any gain, and *section 72* shall apply as it would apply if the gain were income arising from possessions outside of the State.

[(5A) (a) This subsection shall apply where an individual referred to in *subsection (4)* transfers outside the State, to his or her spouse or civil partner, any of the proceeds of the disposal of any assets on which chargeable gains accrue, as referred to in that subsection.

(b) Where this subsection applies, any amounts received or treated, under *subsection (5)*, as received in the State on or after 24 October 2013 which derive from any transfer referred to in *paragraph (a)* shall be treated, for the purpose of *subsection (4)*, as amounts received in the State by the individual in respect of chargeable gains referred to in *subsection (4)*.][5]

(6) Any gains accruing on the disposal of exploration or exploitation rights in a designated area shall be treated for the purposes of the Capital Gains Tax Acts as gains accruing on the disposal of assets situated in the State.

(7) Any gains accruing to a person who is neither resident nor ordinarily resident in the State on the disposal of assets mentioned in *subsections (3)(b)* and *(6)* shall be treated for the purposes of capital gains tax as gains accruing on the disposal of assets used for the purposes of a trade carried on by that person in the State through a branch or agency.

(8) Any person aggrieved by a decision of the Revenue Commissioners on any question as to domicile or ordinary residence arising under the Capital Gains Tax Acts may, by notice in writing to that effect given to the Revenue Commissioners within 2 months from the date on which notice of the decision is given to such person, make an application to have such person's claim for relief heard and determined by the Appeal Commissioners.

(9) Where an application is made under *subsection (8)*, the Appeal Commissioners shall hear and determine the claim in the like manner as an appeal made to them against an assessment, and the provisions of the Income Tax Acts relating to such an appeal (including the provisions relating to the rehearing of an appeal

and to the statement of a case for the opinion of the High Court on a point of law) shall apply accordingly with any necessary modifications.

Amendments

[1] Substituted by FA05 s41(1)(a). This section applies as respects accounting periods ending on or after 1 March 2005.

[2] Inserted by FA05 s41(1)(b). This section applies as respects accounting periods ending on or after 1 March 2005.

[3, 4] Deleted by F(No.2)A08 s42(1). Applies to disposals made on or after 20 November 2008.

[5] Substituted by F(No.2)A13 s41. Comes into operation on 1 January 2014.

Revenue Precedents

A Diplomatic Agent is exempt in respect of gains on assets other than investments made in commercial undertakings in the State. In practice, this exemption will be treated as covering a period of up to one year after the end of their posting. If the disposal is at a later date, the gains will be apportioned. G54(1)

The OTC Bulletin Board is not a Stock Exchange for the purpose of section 29 TCA 1997. However, where a company has applied for a full listing on NASDAQ, its ADR's will be treated as "shares quoted on a Stock Exchange" for the purpose of the said section 29. G.160(1)

Cross References

From Section 29

Section 13 Extension of charge to income tax to profits and income derived from activities carried on and employments exercised on the Continental Shelf.
Section 72 Charge to tax on sums applied outside the State in repaying certain loans.
Section 706 Interpretation and general (Part 26).

To Section 29

Section 533 Location of assets.
Section 546 Allowable losses.
Section 549 Transactions between connected persons.
Section 590 Attribution to participators of chargeable gains accruing to non-resident company.
Section 620A Deemed disposal in certain circumstances.
Section 626B Exemption from tax in the case of gains on disposals of shares.
Section 726 Investment income.
Section 745 Charge to income tax or corporation tax of offshore income gain.

29A Temporary non-residents

[(1) (a) In this section—

"*intervening year*", in relation to an individual, means any year of assessment falling within the period commencing with the first day of the year of assessment immediately following the year of his or her departure and ending with the last day of the year of assessment immediately preceding the year of his or her return;

"*relevant assets*", in relation to an individual, means shares in a company, or rights to acquire shares in a company, being shares or rights which he or she beneficially owned on the last day of the year of his or her departure and the market value of which on that day—

(i) is equal to, or exceeds, 5 per cent of the value of the issued share capital of the company, or

(ii) exceeds €500,000;

"*year of departure*", in relation to an individual, means the last year of assessment before the year of return, for which the individual is resident in the State, and references to year of his or her departure shall be construed accordingly;

"*year of return*", in relation to an individual, has the meaning assigned to it by *subsection (2)*, and references to year of his or her return shall be construed accordingly.

(b) References in this section to an individual being resident in the State for a year of assessment shall be construed as references to an individual—

(i) who is resident in the State for the year of assessment, and

(ii) who could be taxed in the State for that year in respect of gains on a disposal, on each day of that year, of his or her relevant assets, if such a disposal were made by the individual on that day and gains accrued on the disposal.

(c) References in this section to an individual being not resident in the State for a year of assessment shall be construed as references to an individual who could not be taxed in the State for that year in respect of gains on a disposal in that year, or part of that year, of his or her relevant assets, or part of those assets, if the individual had made such a disposal in that year, or, as the case may be, that part of that year, and gains accrued on the disposal.

(2) This section applies to an individual where—

(a) the individual has relevant assets,

(b) the individual is resident in the State for a year of assessment (in this section referred to as the "*year of return*"),

(c) the individual was not resident in the State for one or more years of assessment immediately preceding the year of his or her return; but there is a year of assessment before the year of return for which the individual was resident in the State and, at any time during that year, the individual was domiciled in the State, and

(d) there are not more than 5 years of assessment falling between the year of his or her departure and the year of his or her return.

(3) Where an individual to whom this section applies, disposes of his or her relevant assets or any part of them (as the case may be) in one or more intervening years, the individual shall, for the purposes of the Capital Gains Tax Acts, be deemed to have disposed of and immediately reacquired, the relevant assets or that part of them (as the case may be), on the last day of the year of his or her departure, for a consideration equal to their market value on that day.

[(3A) Notwithstanding *subsection (3)*, where the market value of the relevant assets on the day they were disposed of is greater or less than the market value of those assets on the last day of the year, referred to in that subsection, that greater or lesser market value shall be substituted for the market value on that last day of the year.][1]

(4) Where by virtue of *subsection (3)*, an individual is chargeable to capital gains tax in respect of a deemed disposal of his or her relevant assets or any part of them (as the case may be), credit shall be allowed against such tax in respect of tax (in this section referred to as "*foreign tax*") payable on the subsequent disposal by the individual of those relevant assets or that part of them (as the case may be) under the law of any territory outside the State, the government of which has entered into arrangements having the force of law by virtue of [*826(1)*][2], and the amount of such credit—

(a) shall be calculated having regard to the provisions of *Schedule 24*, and

(b) notwithstanding those provisions, shall not exceed the amount by which capital gains tax payable by the individual would be reduced if the individual had not been deemed to have disposed of relevant assets or that part of them (as the case may be).

(5) Where by virtue of *subsection (3)* a chargeable gain accrues to an individual, the provisions of [*Part 41A*][3] shall apply in relation to the chargeable gain, as if the year of his or her departure were the year of his or her return.][4]

Amendments

[1] Inserted by FA14 s46(1). Applies to disposals made on or after 23 December 2014.

[2] Substituted by FA07 sched2(1)(b). Has effect as on and from 2 April 2007.

[3] Substituted by FA12 sched4(part 2)(g).

[4] Inserted by FA03 s69.

Note:

The amendment made by FA03 s69(1) is amplified by FA03 s69(2). FA03 s69(2) cannot be directly consolidated, and reads as follows: (2) (a) Subject to paragraph (b), subsection (1) applies as respects an individual who ceases to be resident in the State for the year of assessment 2003, or a subsequent year of assessment. (b) Subsection (1) does not apply as respects an individual who before 24 February 2003 ceases to be resident in the State for the year of assessment 2003, but who would not have so ceased, if paragraph (c)(ii) had not been enacted. (c) For the purposes of paragraphs (a) and (b), an individual is resident in the State for a year of assessment so long as he or she— (i) is resident in the State for the year of assessment, and (ii) could be taxed in the State for that year in respect of gains on a disposal, on each day of that year, of his or her relevant assets, if such a disposal were made by the individual on that day and gains accrued on the disposal.

Revenue Briefings

Tax Briefing

Tax Briefing May 2003 – Issue 52 pg 14 – Finance Act 2003

Cross References

From Section 29A

Section 826 Agreements for relief from double taxation.
Section 950 Interpretation (Part 41).
Schedule 24 Relief from Income Tax and Corporation Tax by Means of Credit in Respect of Foreign Tax

30 Partnerships

[CGTA75 s4(5)]

Where 2 or more persons carry on a trade, business or profession in partnership—

(a) capital gains tax in respect of chargeable gains accruing to those persons on the disposal of any partnership assets shall be assessed and charged on them separately, and

(b) any partnership dealings in assets shall be treated as dealings by the partners and not by the firm as such.

Revenue Information Notes

Tax & Duty Manuals – Section 16 [2.3.3] Partnerships (S.30)

Cross References

To Section 30

Section 549 Transactions between connected persons.
Section 745 Charge to income tax or corporation tax of offshore income gain.
Section 1014 Tax treatment of profits, losses and capital gains arising from activities of a European Economic Interest Grouping (EEIG).

31 Amount chargeable

[CGTA75 s5(1)]

Capital gains tax shall be charged on the total amount of chargeable gains accruing to the person chargeable in the year of assessment, after deducting—

(a) any allowable losses accruing to that person in that year of assessment, and

(b) in so far as they have not been allowed as a deduction from chargeable gains accruing in any previous year of assessment, any allowable losses accruing to that person in any previous year of assessment (not earlier than the year 1974-75).

Cross References

To Section 31

Section 78 Computation of companies' chargeable gains.
Section 538 Disposals where assets lost or destroyed or become of negligible value.
Section 546 Allowable losses.
Section 579 Non-resident trusts.
Section 579A Attribution of gains to beneficiaries.
Section 591 Relief for individuals on certain reinvestment.
Section 594 Foreign life assurance and deferred annuities: taxation and returns.
Section 601 Annual exempt amount.
Section 653 Restriction of relief for losses, etc. in relation to relevant disposals.
Section 697N Chargeable gains.
Section 711 Chargeable gains of life business.
Section 737 Special investment schemes.
Section 738 Undertakings for collective investment.
Section 746 Offshore income gains accruing to persons resident or domiciled abroad.
Section 751B Exchange of Irish Government bonds.
Section 838 Special portfolio investment accounts.
Section 980 Deduction from consideration on disposal of certain assets.
Section 1028 Married persons.
Section 1042 Charging and assessment of persons not resident or ordinarily resident: modification of general rules.

INCOME TAX AND CORPORATION TAX: THE MAIN PROVISIONS

PART 3

Provisions Relating to the Schedule C Charge and Government and Other Public Securities

CHAPTER 1

Principal Provisions Relating to the Schedule C Charge

32 Interpretation (Chapter 1)

[ITA67 s51]

In this Chapter—

"*banker*" includes a person acting as a banker;

"*coupons*" and "*coupons for any foreign public revenue dividends*" include warrants for or bills of exchange purporting to be drawn or made in payment of any foreign public revenue dividends;

"*dividends*", except in the phrase "*stock, dividends or interest*", means any interest, annuities, dividends or shares of annuities;

"*foreign public revenue dividends*" means dividends payable elsewhere than in the State (whether they are or are not also payable in the State) out of any public revenue other than the public revenue of the State;

"*public revenue*", except where the context otherwise requires, includes the public revenue of any Government whatever and the revenue of any public authority or institution in any country outside the State;

"*public revenue dividends*" means dividends payable out of any public revenue.

Cross References

From Section 32

Section 17 Schedule C.

To Section 32

Section 17 Schedule C.

Section 64 Interest on quoted Eurobonds.

Section 697O Capital allowances: general.

Section 821 Application of sections 17 and 18(1) and Chapter 1 of Part 3.

Schedule 2 Machinery for Assessment, Charge and Payment of Tax under Schedule C and, in Certain Cases, Schedule D

33 Method of charge and payment

[ITA67 s48]

(1) Tax under Schedule C [...][1] shall be paid on behalf of the persons entitled to the profits, dividends, proceeds of realisation or price paid on purchase which are the subject of the tax—

(a) in the case of tax charged under *paragraph 1* of that Schedule, by the persons and bodies of persons respectively entrusted with payment;

(b) in the case of tax charged under *paragraph 2*, *3* or *4* of that Schedule, by the banker or other person, or by the banker or by the dealer in coupons, as the case may be.

(2) *Schedule 2* shall apply in relation to the assessment, charge and payment of tax under Schedule C.

Amendments

[1] Deleted by FA12 s38(1)(a). With effect from 1 January 2013 per S.I. No. 561 of 2012.

Cross References

From Section 33

Section 17 Schedule C.

Schedule 2 Machinery for Assessment, Charge and Payment of Tax under Schedule C and, in Certain Cases, Schedule D

To Section 33

Section 141 Distributions out of income from patent royalties.

Schedule 2 Machinery for Assessment, Charge and Payment of Tax under Schedule C and, in Certain Cases, Schedule D

34 Stock, dividends or interest belonging to the State

[ITA67 s49(1) and (2); F(MP)A68 s3(3) and Sch PtII]

(1) No tax shall be chargeable in respect of the stock, dividends or interest transferred to accounts in the books of the Bank of Ireland in the name of the Minister for Finance in pursuance of any statute, but the Bank of Ireland shall transmit to the Revenue Commissioners an account of the total amount of such stock, dividends or interest.

(2) No tax shall be chargeable in respect of the stock, dividends or interest belonging to the State in whatever name they may stand in the books of the Bank of Ireland.

35 Securities of foreign territories

[ITA67 s50; F(MP)A68 s3(2) and Sch PtI]

(1) (a) No tax shall be chargeable in respect of the dividends on any securities of any territory outside the State which are payable in the State, where it is proved to the satisfaction of the Revenue Commissioners that the person owning the securities and entitled to the dividends is not resident in the State; but, except where provided by the Income Tax Acts, no allowance shall be given or repayment made in respect of the tax on the dividends on the securities of any such territory which are payable in the State.

(b) Where the securities of any territory outside the State are held under any trust, and the person who is the beneficiary in possession under the trust is the sole beneficiary in possession and can, by means either of the revocation of the trust or of the exercise of any powers under the trust, call on the trustees at any time to transfer the securities to such person absolutely free from any trust, that person shall for the purposes of this section be deemed to be the person owning the securities.

(2) Relief under this section may be given by the Revenue Commissioners either by means of allowance or repayment on a claim being made to them for that purpose.

(3) Any person aggrieved by a decision of the Revenue Commissioners on any question as to residence arising under this section may, by notice in writing to that

effect given to the Revenue Commissioners within 2 months from the date on which notice of the decision is given to such person, make an application to have such person's claim for relief heard and determined by the Appeal Commissioners.

(4) Where an application is made under *subsection (3)*, the Appeal Commissioners shall hear and determine the claim in the like manner as an appeal made to them against an assessment, and the provisions of the Income Tax Acts relating to such an appeal (including the provisions relating to the rehearing of an appeal and to the statement of a case for the opinion of the High Court on a point of law) shall apply accordingly with any necessary modifications.

Cross References

To Section 35

Section 809 Saver.

Section 845 Corporation tax: treatment of tax-free income of non-resident banks, insurance businesses, etc.

CHAPTER 2

Government and Other Public Securities: Interest Payable without Deduction of Tax

36 Government securities

[ITA67 s466; FA97 s146(1) and Sch9 PtI par1(31)]

(1) The Minister for Finance may direct that any securities already issued or to be issued under that Minister's authority shall be deemed to have been, or shall be, issued subject to the condition that the interest on those securities shall be paid without deduction of tax.

(2) The interest on all securities issued, or deemed to have been issued, subject to the condition referred to in *subsection (1)* shall be paid without deduction of tax, but all such interest shall be chargeable under Case III of Schedule D and, where any funds under the control of any court or public department are invested in any such securities, the person in whose name the securities are invested shall be the person so chargeable in respect of the interest on those securities.

(3) Where interest on any security is paid under this section without deduction of tax, every person by whom such interest is paid, every person who receives such interest on behalf of a registered or inscribed holder of the security, and every person who has acted as an intermediary in the purchase of the security, shall, on being so required by the Revenue Commissioners, furnish to them—

(a) the name and address of the person to whom such interest has been paid, or on whose behalf such interest has been received, and the amount of the interest so paid or received, or, as the case may require,

(b) the name and address of the person on whose behalf such security was purchased and the amount of such security.

Cross References

To Section 36

Section 18 Schedule D.

Section 37 Securities of certain State-owned companies.

Section 38 Certain State-guaranteed securities.
Section 39 Securities of certain European bodies.
Section 40 Securities of International Bank for Reconstruction and Development.
Section 41 Securities of designated bodies under the Securitisation (Proceeds of Certain Mortgages) Act, 1995.
Section 246 Interest payments by companies and to non-residents.
Section 751B Exchange of Irish Government bonds.
Schedule 32 Transitional Provisions

37 Securities of certain State-owned companies

[FA97 s144]

(1) In this section, "*securities*" means any bonds, certificates of charge, debentures, debenture stock, notes, stock or other forms of security.

(2) The securities specified in the Table to this section shall be deemed to be securities issued under the authority of the Minister for Finance under *section 36*, and that section shall apply accordingly.

(3) Notwithstanding anything in the Tax Acts, in computing for the purposes of assessment under Schedule D the amount of the profits or gains of a company (being a company referred to in the Table to this section) for any accounting period, the amount of the interest on any securities which, by direction of the Minister for Finance given under *section 36*, as applied by *subsection (2)*, is paid by the company without deduction of tax for such period shall be allowed as a deduction.

TABLE

[…][1]

Securities issued on or after the 13th day of July, 1954, by the Electricity Supply Board.

Securities issued on or after the 13th day of July, 1954, by Córas Iompair Éireann.

Securities issued on or after the 18th day of July, 1957, by Bord na Móna.

[…][2]

Securities issued on or after the 2nd day of July, 1964, by [Dublin Airport Authority][3].

[…][4]

[…][5]

[…][6]

Securities issued on or after the 24th day of May, 1989, by Radio Telefís Éireann.

[…][7]

Securities issued on or after the 28th day of May, 1992, by Bord Gáis Éireann.

[Securities issued on or after the 23rd day of October 2014 by the company established pursuant to *section 5* of the Gas Regulation Act 2013.][8]

[Securities issued on or after the 24th day of October 2013 by Irish Water.][9]

Amendments

[1] Repealed by ACC BA 01 s12. With effect from 28 February 2002 per S.I. 69 of 2002.

[2] Deleted by FA08 sched8(1)(a)(i). Has effect as on and from 31 January 2008.

[3] Substituted by FA08 sched8(1)(a)(ii). Has effect as on and from 31 January 2008.

[4] Deleted by FA08 sched8(1)(a)(iii). Has effect as on and from 31 January 2008.

[5, 6] Deleted by FA01 s241(1)(a). Has effect as respects any securities issued by Bord Telecom Éireann or Irish Telecommunications Investments plc. on or after 15 February 2001.

[7] Repealed by ICC BA 00 s7 and ICC BA00 (Sections 5 and 7) (Commencement) Order 2001. With effect from 12 February 2001 per S.I. 46 of 2001.

[8] Inserted by FA14 s25(1)(a). Comes into operation on 1 January 2015.

[9] Inserted by F(No.2)A13 s29(1)(a). Comes into operation on 1 January 2014.

Cross References

From Section 37

Section 36 Government securities.

To Section 37

Section 38 Certain State-guaranteed securities.
Section 48 Exemption of premiums on certain securities.
Section 49 Exemption of certain securities.

38 Certain State-guaranteed securities

[FA70 s59(1), (2) and (3); FA97 s146(1) and Sch9 PtI par4(3)]

[(1) This section applies to any securities which are issued by a body corporate and in respect of which the payment of interest and the repayment of principal are guaranteed by a Minister of the Government under statutory authority; but does not apply [to securities specified in the Table to section 37.][1]][2]

(2) Any securities to which this section applies shall be deemed to be securities issued under the authority of the Minister for Finance under *section 36*, and that section shall apply accordingly.

(3) Notwithstanding anything in the Tax Acts, in computing for the purposes of assessment under Case I of Schedule D the amount of the profits or gains of a body corporate by which the securities to which this section applies are issued, for any period for which accounts are made up, the amount of the interest on such securities which, by direction of the Minister for Finance under *section 36*, as applied by this section, is paid by the body corporate without deduction of tax for such period shall be allowed as a deduction.

Amendments

[1] Deleted and Substituted by NTMA(A)A14 part4(1).

[2] Substituted by FA03 s43(1)(a). This section applies on and from 6 February 2003.

Cross References

From Section 38

Section 36 Government securities.
Section 37 Securities of certain State-owned companies.

To Section 38

Section 49 Exemption of certain securities.

39 Securities of certain European bodies

[FA73 s92(1) and (2)(a); FA89 s98(1)]

(1) This section shall apply to any stock or other form of security issued in the State by the European Community, the European Coal and Steel Community, the European Atomic Energy Community or the European Investment Bank.

(2) Any stock or other form of security to which this section applies shall be deemed to be a security issued under the authority of the Minister for Finance under *section 36*, and that section shall apply accordingly.

Cross References

From Section 39

Section 36 Government securities.

To Section 39

Section 49 Exemption of certain securities.

40 Securities of International Bank for Reconstruction and Development

[FA94 s161(1) and (2)(a)]

(1) This section shall apply to any stock or other form of security issued by the International Bank for Reconstruction and Development.

(2) Any stock or other form of security to which this section applies shall be deemed to be a security issued under the authority of the Minister for Finance under *section 36*, and that section shall apply accordingly.

Cross References

From Section 40

Section 36 Government securities.

To Section 40

Section 49 Exemption of certain securities.

41 Securities of designated bodies under the Securitisation (Proceeds of Certain Mortgages) Act, 1995

[FA96 s39(1) and (3)]

Any stock or other form of security issued by a body designated under section 4(1) of the Securitisation (Proceeds of Certain Mortgages) Act, 1995, shall be deemed to be a security issued under the authority of the Minister for Finance under *section 36*, and that section shall apply accordingly.

Cross References

From Section 41

Section 36 Government securities.

To Section 41

Section 49 Exemption of certain securities.

CHAPTER 3

Government and Other Public Securities: Exemptions from Tax

42 Exemption of interest on savings certificates

[(1) In this section—

"*EEA Agreement*" means the Agreement on the European Economic Area signed at Oporto on 2 May 1992, as adjusted by the Protocol signed at Brussels on 17 March 1993;

"*EEA state*" means a state which is a contracting party to the EEA Agreement;

"*relevant State*" means—

(i) a Member State of the European Union, or

(ii) not being such a Member State, an EEA state which is a territory with the government of which arrangements having the force of law by virtue of *section 826(1)* have been made.

(2) The accumulated interest payable in respect of any savings certificate issued by the Minister for Finance, or savings certificates or other similar securities issued by the Government of a relevant State pursuant to rules and conditions which correspond to the rules and conditions contained in regulations issued by the Minister for Finance, under which the purchaser, by virtue of an immediate payment of a specified sum, becomes entitled after a specified period to receive a larger sum consisting of the specified sum originally paid and accumulated interest on that specified sum, shall not be liable to tax so long as the amount of such certificates held by the person who is for the time being the holder of the certificate does not exceed the amount which that person is for the time being authorised to hold under regulations made by the Minister for Finance.][1]

Amendments

[1] Substituted by FA10 s35(1)(a).This section comes into force and takes effect as on and from 4 February 2010.

Cross References

From Section 42

Section 826 Agreements for relief from double taxation.

To Section 42

Section 898E Interest payment.

43 Certain securities issued by Minister for Finance

[ITA67 s464; FA92 s42(1)(a); FA97 s45]

(1) Any security which the Minister for Finance has power to issue for the purpose of raising any money or loan may be issued with a condition that neither the capital of nor the interest on such security shall be liable to tax so long as it is shown in the manner to be prescribed by the Minister for Finance that such security is in the beneficial ownership of a person who is not, or persons who are not, [resident][1] in the State, and accordingly every security issued with such condition shall be exempt from tax.

(2) (a) Notwithstanding *subsection (1)*, where a security has been issued with the condition referred to in that subsection and the security is held by or for a branch or agency through which a company carries on a trade or business in the State, which is such a trade or business, as the case may be, that, if the security had been issued without that condition, interest on, or other profits or gains from, the security accruing to the company would be chargeable to corporation tax under Case I or, as respects interest and other profits or gains accruing on or after the 21st day of April, 1997, from the security, Case IV of Schedule D, or in accordance with *section 726*, then, such interest and profits or gains shall be charged to tax as if the security had been issued without such condition.

(b) *Paragraph (a)* shall apply as respects securities acquired by a company after the 29th day of January, 1992, whether they were issued before or after that date.

Amendments

[1] Substituted by FA10 s35(1)(b). This section comes into force and takes effect as on and from 4 February 2010.

Cross References

From Section 43

Section 726 Investment income.

To Section 43

Section 398 Computation of losses attributable to exemption of income from certain securities.
Section 718 Foreign life assurance funds.
Section 809 Saver.
Section 845 Corporation tax: treatment of tax-free income of non-resident banks, insurance businesses, etc.
Schedule 19 Offshore Funds: Distributing Funds

44 Exemption from corporation tax of certain securities issued by Minister for Finance

[FA85 s69]

(1) In this section—

"*control*" shall be construed in accordance with *subsections (2)* to *(6)* of *section 432*, with the substitution in *subsection (6)* of that section for "*5 or fewer participators*" of "*persons resident in a relevant territory*";

"*foreign company*" means a company which is—

(a) not resident in the State, and

(b) under the control of a person or persons resident in a relevant territory;

"*qualifying company*" means a company—

(a) (i) which is resident in the State and not resident elsewhere,

(ii) whose business consists wholly or mainly of—

(I) the carrying on of a relevant trade or relevant trades, or

(II) the holding of stocks, shares or securities of a company which exists wholly or mainly for the purpose of the carrying on of a relevant trade or relevant trades,

and

(iii) of which not less than 90 per cent of its issued share capital is held by a foreign company or foreign companies, or by a person or persons directly or indirectly controlled by a foreign company or foreign companies,

or

(b) which is a foreign company carrying on a relevant trade through a branch or agency in the State;

"*relevant territory*" means the [...][1] a territory with the government of which arrangements having the force of law by virtue of [*826(1)*][2] have been made;

"*relevant trade*" means a trade carried on wholly or mainly in the State, but does not include a trade consisting wholly or partly of—

(a) banking within the meaning of the Central Bank Act, 1971,

(b) assurance business within the meaning of section 3 of the Insurance Act, 1936,

(c) selling goods by retail, or

(d) dealing in securities,

but goods shall be deemed for the purposes of this definition not to be sold by retail if they are sold to—

(i) a person who carries on a trade of selling goods of the class to which the goods so sold to such person belong,

(ii) a person who uses goods of that class for the purposes of a trade carried on by such person, or

(iii) a person, other than an individual, who uses goods of that class for the purposes of an undertaking carried on by such person.

(2) Any security which the Minister for Finance has power to issue for the purpose of raising any money or loan may be issued with a condition that any interest arising on such security shall not be liable to corporation tax so long as the security is held continuously from the date of issue in the beneficial ownership of a qualifying company to which the security was issued.

Amendments

[1] Deleted by FA98 sched3(1).

[2] Substituted by FA07 sched2(1)(c). Has effect as on and from 2 April 2007.

Revenue Precedents

Profit or loss arising on the disposal of foreign currency under a hedging contract linked to Section 44 securities is not exempt from CGT by virtue of Section 607. The section 44 securities and the foreign currency are separate assets. CTF377

Cross References

From Section 44

Section 432 Meaning of "associated company" and "control".

Section 826 Agreements for relief from double taxation.

45 Exemption of non-interest-bearing securities

[ITA67 s465; FA74 s86 and Sch2 PtI; FA84 s28 and FA90 s138]

(1) The excess of the amount received on the redemption of a unit of non-interest-bearing securities issued by the Minister for Finance under section 4 of the Central Fund Act, 1965, over the amount paid for the unit on its issue shall, except where the excess is to be taken into account in computing for the purposes of taxation the profits of a trade, be exempt from tax.

(2) *Subsection (1)* shall not apply to issues of securities to which *subsection (3)* applies made after the 25th day of January, 1984, unless a tender for any such securities was submitted on or before that date.

(3) The securities to which this subsection applies are—

(a) non-interest-bearing securities issued by the Minister for Finance at a discount, including Exchequer Bills and Exchequer Notes, and

(b) Agricultural Commodities Intervention Bills issued by the Minister for Agriculture and Food.

(4) (a) In this subsection, "*owner*", in relation to securities, means at any time the person who would be entitled, if the securities were redeemed at that time by the issuer, to the proceeds of the redemption.

(b) Notwithstanding *subsection (2)*, where the owner of a security to which *subsection (3)* applies—

(i) sells or otherwise disposes of the security, or

(ii) receives on redemption of the security an amount greater than the amount paid by such owner for that security either on its issue or otherwise,

then, any profit, gain or excess arising to the owner from such sale, disposal or receipt shall be exempt from tax where the owner is not [resident][1] in the State; but this subsection shall not apply in respect of corporation tax chargeable on the income of an Irish branch or agency of a company not resident in the State.

Amendments

[1] Substituted by FA10 s35(1)(c). This section comes into force and takes effect as on and from 4 February 2010.

Cross References

To Section 45

Section 48 Exemption of premiums on certain securities.
Section 530A Principal to whom relevant contracts tax applies.

46 Exemption of premiums on Investment Bonds

[F(No.2)A68 s8; FA74 s86 and Sch2 PtI]

The excess of the amount received on the redemption of a unit of securities created and issued by the Minister for Finance under the Central Fund (Permanent Provisions) Act, 1965, and known as Investment Bonds, over the amount which was paid for the unit on its issue shall, except where the excess is to be taken into account in computing for the purposes of taxation the profits of a trade, be exempt from tax.

Cross References

To Section 46

Section 48 Exemption of premiums on certain securities.

47 Certain securities of ACC Bank plc [Repealed]

Repealed by ACC BA 01 s12. With effect from 28 February 2002 per S.I. 69 of 2002.

Cross References

To Section 47

Section 809 Saver.

48 Exemption of premiums on certain securities

[FA69 s63; FA70 s59(1) and (6); FA73 s92(1) and (2)(b); FA74 s86 and Sch2 PtI; FA84 s28; FA89 s98(1); FA90 s138; FA94 s161(1) and (2)(b); FA97 s34]

(1) The securities to which this subsection applies are—

(a) securities created and issued by the Minister for Finance under the Central Fund (Permanent Provisions) Act, 1965, or under any other statutory powers conferred on that Minister, and any stock, debenture, debenture stock, certificate of charge or other security issued with the approval of the Minister for Finance given under any Act of the Oireachtas and in respect of which the payment of interest and repayment of capital is guaranteed by the Minister for Finance under that Act, but excluding securities to which section 4 of the Central Fund Act, 1965, or *section 45(1)* or *46* applies,

(b) securities (other than securities specified in the Table to *section 37*) issued by a body corporate and in respect of which the payment of interest and the repayment of principal is guaranteed by a Minister of the Government under statutory authority,

(c) any stock or other form of security issued in the State by the European Community, the European Coal and Steel Community, the European Atomic Energy Community or the European Investment Bank, and

(d) any stock or other form of security issued by the International Bank for Reconstruction and Development.

(2) The excess of the amount received on the redemption of a unit of securities to which *subsection (1)* applies over the amount paid for the unit on its issue shall, except where the excess is to be taken into account in computing for the purposes of taxation the profits of a trade, be exempt from tax.

(3) *Subsection (2)* shall not apply to issues of securities to which *subsection (4)* applies made after the 25th day of January, 1984, unless a tender for any such securities was submitted on or before that date.

(4) The securities to which this subsection applies are—

(a) non-interest-bearing securities issued by the Minister for Finance at a discount, including Exchequer Bills and Exchequer Notes,

(b) Agricultural Commodities Intervention Bills issued by the Minister for Agriculture and Food, and

(c) strips within the meaning of section 54(10) of the Finance Act, 1970 (inserted by section 161 of the Finance Act, 1997).

(5) (a) In this subsection, "*owner*", in relation to securities, means at any time the person who would be entitled, if the securities were redeemed at that time by the issuer, to the proceeds of the redemption.

(b) Notwithstanding *subsection (3)*, where the owner of a security to which *subsection (4)* applies—

(i) sells or otherwise disposes of the security, or

(ii) receives on redemption of the security an amount greater than the amount paid by the owner for that security either on its issue or otherwise,

any profit, gain or excess arising to the owner from such sale, disposal or receipt shall be exempt from tax where the owner is not [resident][1] in the State; but this subsection shall not apply in respect of corporation tax chargeable on the income of an Irish branch or agency of a company not resident in the State.

Amendments

[1] Substituted by FA10 s35(1)(d). This section comes into force and takes effect as on and from 4 February 2010.

Cross References

From Section 48

Section 37 Securities of certain State-owned companies.
Section 45 Exemption of non-interest-bearing securities.
Section 46 Exemption of premiums on Investment Bonds.

49 Exemption of certain securities

[ITA67 s474; FA92 s42(1)(c); FA97 s47, s146(1) and Sch9 PtI par1(32)]

(1) This section shall apply to any stock or other security on which interest is payable without deduction of tax by virtue of a direction given by the Minister for Finance in pursuance of *section 37, 38, 39, 40* or *41*.

[(2) Any stock or other security to which this section applies may be issued with a condition that neither the capital of nor the interest on the stock or other security shall be liable to tax so long as it is shown in the manner directed by the Minister for Finance that the stock or other security is in the beneficial ownership of persons who are not resident in the State, and accordingly as respects every such stock or other security issued, exemption from tax shall be granted.][1]

(3) (a) Notwithstanding *subsection (2)*, where a security to which this section applies has been issued with either or both of the conditions referred to in that subsection and the security is held by or for a branch or agency through which a company carries on a trade or business in the State, which is such a trade or business, as the case may be, that, if the security had been issued without either of those conditions, interest on, or other profits or gains from, the security accruing to the company would be chargeable to corporation tax under Case I or, as respects interest and other profits or gains accruing on or after the 21st day of April, 1997, from the security, Case IV of Schedule D, or in accordance with *section 726*, then, such interest and profits or gains shall be charged to tax as if the security had been issued without either of those conditions.

(b) *Paragraph (a)* shall apply as respects securities acquired by a company after the 15th day of May, 1992, whether they were issued before or after that date.

Amendments

[1] Substituted by FA10 s35(1)(e). This section comes into force and takes effect as on and from 4 February 2010.

Cross References

From Section 49

Section 37 Securities of certain State-owned companies.
Section 38 Certain State-guaranteed securities.
Section 39 Securities of certain European bodies.
Section 40 Securities of International Bank for Reconstruction and Development.
Section 41 Securities of designated bodies under the Securitisation (Proceeds of Certain Mortgages) Act, 1995.
Section 726 Investment income.

To Section 49

Section 398 Computation of losses attributable to exemption of income from certain securities.
Section 718 Foreign life assurance funds.
Section 809 Saver.
Section 845 Corporation tax: treatment of tax-free income of non-resident banks, insurance businesses, etc.
Schedule 19 Offshore Funds: Distributing Funds
Schedule 32 Transitional Provisions

50 Securities of Irish local authorities issued abroad

[ITA67 s470; FA92 s42(1)(b); FA97 s46]

(1) In this section, "*local authority*" includes any public body recognised as a local authority for the purpose of this section by the Minister for the Environment and Local Government.

(2) Securities issued outside the State by a local authority in the State for the purpose of raising any money which the local authority is authorised to borrow, if issued under the authority of the Minister for Finance, shall not be liable to tax, except—

(a) where they are held by persons domiciled in the State or ordinarily resident in the State, or

(b) as respects securities acquired by a company after the 15th day of May, 1992, whether they were issued before or after that date, where they are held by or for a branch or agency through which a company carries on a trade or business in the State which is such a trade or business, as the case may be, that, if this section had not been enacted, interest on, or other profits or gains from, the securities accruing to the company would be chargeable to corporation tax under Case I or, as respects interest and other profits or gains accruing on or after the 21st day of April, 1997, from the securities, Case IV of Schedule D, or in accordance with *section 726*.

Cross References

From Section 50

Section 726 Investment income.

To Section 50

Section 398 Computation of losses attributable to exemption of income from certain securities.

Section 809 Saver.

Section 845 Corporation tax: treatment of tax-free income of non-resident banks, insurance businesses, etc.

Schedule 19 Offshore Funds: Distributing Funds

CHAPTER 4

Miscellaneous Provisions

51 Funding bonds issued in respect of interest on certain debts

[ITA67 s475;CTA76 s140(1) and Sch2 PtI par 26]

(1) In this section, "*funding bonds*" includes all bonds, stocks, shares, securities and certificates of indebtedness.

(2) This section shall apply to all debts owing by any government, public authority or public institution whatever or wherever and to all debts owing by any body corporate whatever or wherever.

(3) Where any funding bonds are issued to a creditor in respect of any liability to pay interest on a debt to which this section applies, the issue of those bonds shall be treated for the purposes of the Tax Acts as if it were the payment of an amount of the interest equal to the value of the bonds at the time of the issue of the bonds, and the redemption of the bonds shall not be treated for any of the purposes of the Tax Acts as payment of the interest or any part of the interest.

PART 4

Principal Provisions Relating to the Schedule D Charge

CHAPTER 1

Supplementary Charging Provisions

52 Persons chargeable

[ITA67 s105]

Income tax under Schedule D shall be charged on and paid by the persons or bodies of persons receiving or entitled to the income in respect of which tax under that Schedule is directed in the Income Tax Acts to be charged.

Revenue Precedents

What regime of tax should apply to payments by individuals to a trust for funeral expenses? Arrangements have been agreed for the taxation and administration of trusts established by funeral directors to hold payments made in advance by individuals to meet their future funeral costs. The conditions for the operation of these trusts are as follows: a) 18% tax to be applied to all gross income of the trust with credit for DIRT allowed. No refund of DIRT is available; b) the individual has no further tax liability; c) no individual may invest more than 4,000 (this limit is subject to review); d) no individual may have more than one investment; e) details need not be included in the individuals tax return; f) the scheme is subject to review to ensure that it is operating satisfactorily. 5068/95

Cross References

To Section 52

Section 284 Wear and tear allowances.
Section 324 Double rent allowance in respect of rent paid for certain business premises.
Section 333 Double rent allowance in respect of rent paid for certain business premises.
Section 339 Interpretation (Chapter 3).
Section 351 Interpretation (Chapter 4).
Section 372A Interpretation and application (Chapter 7).
Section 372L Interpretation (Chapter 8).
Section 372AA Interpretation and application (Chapter 10).
Section 372AK Interpretation (Chapter 11).
Section 372AO Qualifying lease.
Section 372AP Relief for lessors.
Section 384 Relief under Case V for losses.
Section 639 Interpretation (Chapter 1).
Section 655 Farming and market gardening profits to be charged to tax under Schedule D.
Section 657 Averaging of farm profits.
Section 658 Farming: allowances for capital expenditure on construction of buildings and other works.
Section 664 Relief for certain income from leasing of farm land.
Section 812 Taxation of income deemed to arise from transfers of right to receive interest from securities.
Section 831 Implementation of Council Directive No. 90/435/EEC concerning the common system of taxation applicable in the case of parent companies and subsidiaries of different Member States.
Section 879 Returns of income.
Section 888 Returns, etc. by lessors, lessees and agents.
Section 918 Making of assessments under Schedules C, D, E and F.
Schedule 2 Machinery for Assessment, Charge and Payment of Tax under Schedule C and, in Certain Cases, Schedule D
Schedule 14 Capital Gains Tax: Leases
Schedule 31 Consequential Amendments

53 Cattle and milk dealers

[FA69 s19; FA96 s132(1) and Sch5 PtI par4]

(1) In this section—

"*farm land*" means land in the State wholly or mainly occupied for the purposes of husbandry, other than market garden land within the meaning of *section 654*;

"*occupation*", in relation to any land, means having the use of that land.

(2) The occupation by a dealer in cattle, or a dealer in or a seller of milk, of farm land which is insufficient for the keep of the cattle brought on to the land shall be treated as the carrying on of a trade, and the profits or gains thereof shall be charged under Case I of Schedule D.

Cross References

From Section 53

Section 654 Interpretation (Part 23).

54 Interest, etc. paid without deduction of tax under Schedule C

[ITA67 s55]

(1) This section shall apply to all interest, dividends, annuities and shares of annuities payable out of any public revenue of the State or out of any public revenue of Great Britain or of Northern Ireland or of Great Britain and Northern Ireland.

(2) Where any interest, dividends, annuities or shares of annuities to which this section applies or the profits attached to any such interest, dividends or annuities are to be charged under the provisions applicable to Schedule C but are in fact not assessed for any year under that Schedule, tax on such interest, dividends, annuities, shares of annuities or profits may be charged and assessed on and shall be payable by the person entitled to receive such interest, dividends or other annual payments for that year under the appropriate Case of Schedule D.

Cross References

From Section 54

Section 17 Schedule C.

55 Taxation of strips of securities

[FA97 s33]

(1) In this section—

"*chargeable period*" has the same meaning as in *section 321(2)*;

"*market value*" shall be construed in accordance with *section 548*;

"*nominal value*", in relation to a unit of a security, means—

(a) where the interest on the unit of the security is expressed to be payable by reference to a given value, that value, and

(b) in any other case, the amount paid for the unit of the security on its issue;

"*opening value*", in relation to a unit of a security from which at any time strips of the unit have been created by a person, means—

(a) in the case of a person who is carrying on a trade which consists wholly or partly of dealing in securities of which the unit of the security is an asset in respect of which any profits or gains are chargeable to tax under Case I of Schedule D, an amount equal to the market value of the unit of the security at the time the strips were created, and

(b) in the case of any other person, an amount equal to the lesser of—

(i) the market value of the unit of the security at the time the strips were created, and

(ii) the nominal value of the unit of the security;

"*relevant day*", in relation to a person who holds a strip, means—

(a) where the person is not a company within the charge to corporation tax, [31 December][1] in a year of assessment, and

(b) where the person is a company within the charge to corporation tax, the day on which an accounting period of the company ends;

"*securities*" has the same meaning as in *section 815(1)*, and a unit of a security shall be construed accordingly;

"*strip*", in relation to a unit of a security, means an obligation of the person who issued the security to make a payment, whether of interest or of principal, which has been separated from other obligations of that person to make payments in respect of the unit of the security.

(2) Where at any time a person who owns a unit of a security creates strips of that unit—

(a) the unit of the security shall be deemed to have been sold at that time by that person for an amount equal to its market value at that time,

(b) that person shall be deemed to have acquired at that time each strip for the amount which bears the same proportion to the opening value of the unit of the security as the market value of the strip at that time bears to the aggregate of the market value at that time of each of the strips of the unit of the security, and

(c) each strip shall be deemed to be a non-interest-bearing security any profits or gains arising on a disposal or redemption of which shall, subject to *subsection (5)*, be chargeable to tax under Case III of Schedule D unless charged to tax under Case I of that Schedule.

(3) Where a person, other than a person carrying on a trade which consists wholly or partly of dealing in securities in respect of which any profits or gains are chargeable to tax under Case I of Schedule D, acquires a strip in respect of a unit of a security referred to in *section 607*, otherwise than in accordance with *subsection (2)*, the person shall be deemed to have acquired the strip for an amount equal to the lesser of—

(a) the amount which bears the same proportion to the nominal value of the unit of the security as the market value of the strip at the time of issue of the security would have borne to the aggregate of the market value at that time of each of the strips of the unit of the security if the strip had been created at the time of issue of the security, and

(b) the amount paid by the person for the acquisition of the strip.

(4) Where at any time strips of a unit of a security are reconstituted into a unit of the security by any person—

(a) each of the strips shall be deemed to have been sold at that time by that person for an amount equal to its market value at that time, and

(b) that person shall be deemed to have acquired at that time the unit of the security for an amount equal to the aggregate of the market value at that time of each of the strips.

(5) Where a person holds a strip on a relevant day, that person shall on that day be deemed to have disposed of and immediately reacquired the strip at the market value of the strip on that day.

(6) Where under *subsection (5)* a person is deemed to have disposed of a strip on a relevant day, the amount to be included in the profits or gains chargeable to tax under Case III of Schedule D for the chargeable period in which the relevant day falls shall be the aggregate of the amounts of any profits or gains arising on such deemed disposals in the chargeable period after deducting the aggregate of the amounts of any losses arising on such deemed disposals in that chargeable period and, in so far as they have not been allowed as a deduction from profits or gains in any previous chargeable period, any losses arising on such deemed disposals in any previous chargeable period.

Amendments

[1] Substituted by FA01 sched2(1).

Cross References

From Section 55

Section 321 Provisions of general application in relation to the making of allowances and charges.
Section 548 Valuation of assets.
Section 607 Government and certain other securities.
Section 815 Taxation of income deemed to arise on certain sales of securities.

To Section 55

Section 719 Deemed disposal and reacquisition of certain assets.
Section 738 Undertakings for collective investment.
Section 898B Interpretation (Chapter 3A).

56 Tax on quarries, mines and other concerns chargeable under Case I(b) of Schedule D

[ITA67 s56(1) to (3)]

(1) Subject to this section, *Chapter 3* of this Part and *section 108* shall apply in relation to the concerns which by virtue of *section 18* are chargeable under Case I(*b*) of Schedule D.

(2) Tax under Case I of Schedule D shall be assessed and charged on the person or body of persons carrying on such concern or on the agents or other officers who have the direction or management of the concern or receive the profits of the concern.

(3) (a) The computation in respect of any mine carried on by a company of adventurers shall be made and stated jointly in one sum, but any adventurer may be assessed and charged separately if that adventurer makes a declaration of that adventurer's proportion or share in the concern for that purpose.

(b) Any adventurer so separately assessed and charged may set off against that adventurer's profits from one or more of such concerns the amount of that adventurer's loss sustained in any other such concern as certified by the inspector.

(c) In any such case one assessment and charge only shall be made on the balance of profit and loss, and shall be made in the assessment district where the adventurer is chargeable to the greatest amount.

Cross References

From Section 56

Section 18 Schedule D.

Section 65 Cases I and II: basis of assessment.
Section 108 Statement of profits.

To Section 56

Section 73 Income from certain possessions in Great Britain or Northern Ireland.
Section 623A Transitional provisions in respect of section 623

57 Extension of charge to tax under Case III of Schedule D in certain circumstances

[FA76 s22]

(1) This section shall apply to any sum received or benefit derived by an employee in respect of which there would be a charge to tax by virtue of *Chapter 3* of *Part 5* if the office or employment held by the employee were one the profits or gains from which were chargeable to tax under Schedule E.

(2) Where a person holds an office or employment and—

(a) the profits or gains arising to the person from that office or employment are chargeable to tax under Case III of Schedule D by virtue of *section 18*, and

(b) the person receives a sum in respect of expenses or derives a benefit, being a sum or benefit to which this section applies,

the profits or gains from that office or employment assessable to tax shall include the specified amount and shall be charged to tax accordingly.

(3) The specified amount referred to in *subsection (2)* shall be the amount which by virtue of *Chapter 3* of *Part 5* would be chargeable to tax in respect of the sum or benefit to which this section applies if the profits or gains from the office or employment referred to in that subsection were chargeable to tax under Schedule E.

Cross References

From Section 57

Section 112 Basis of assessment, persons chargeable and extent of charge.
Section 116 Interpretation (Chapter 3).

To Section 57

Schedule 12 Employee Share Ownership Trusts

58 Charge to tax of profits or gains from unknown or unlawful source

[FA83 s19(1) and (2); DITPA96 s11]

(1) Profits or gains shall be chargeable to tax notwithstanding that at the time an assessment to tax in respect of those profits or gains was made—

(a) the source from which those profits or gains arose was not known to the inspector,

(b) the profits or gains were not known to the inspector to have arisen wholly or partly from a lawful source or activity, or

(c) the profits or gains arose and were known to the inspector to have arisen from an unlawful source or activity,

and any question whether those profits or gains arose wholly or partly from an unknown or unlawful source or activity shall be disregarded in determining the chargeability to tax of those profits or gains.

(2) Notwithstanding anything in the Tax Acts, any profits or gains charged to tax by virtue of *subsection (1)* or charged to tax by virtue of or following any investigation by any body (in this subsection referred to as "*the body*") established by or under

statute or by the Government, the purpose or one of the principal purposes of which is—

(a) the identification of the assets of persons which derive or are suspected to derive, directly or indirectly, from criminal activity,

(b) the taking of appropriate action under the law to deprive or to deny those persons of the assets or the benefit of such assets, in whole or in part, as may be appropriate, and

(c) the pursuit of any investigation or the doing of any other preparatory work in relation to any proceedings arising from the purposes mentioned in *paragraphs (a)* and *(b)*,

shall be charged under Case IV of Schedule D and shall be described in the assessment to tax concerned as "*miscellaneous income*", and in respect of such profits and gains so assessed—

(i) the assessment—

(I) may be made solely in the name of the body, and

(II) shall not be discharged by the Appeal Commissioners or by a court by reason only of the fact that the income should apart from this section have been described in some other manner or by reason only of the fact that the profits or gains arose wholly or partly from an unknown or unlawful source or activity,

and

(ii) (I) the tax charged in the assessment may be demanded solely in the name of the body, and

(II) on payment to it of the tax so demanded, the body shall issue a receipt in its name and shall forthwith—

(A) lodge the tax paid to the General Account of the Revenue Commissioners in the Central Bank of Ireland, and

(B) transmit to the Collector-General particulars of the tax assessed and payment received in respect of that tax.

Case Law

The Irish Courts have held that the profits from a trade or business that is wholly illegal cannot be assessed to tax as resulting from a trade or an adventure in the nature of trade. Hayes v Duggan 1929 I ITR 195 and Collins v Mulvey 1956 31 TC 151. However, the UK Courts rejected the Hayes v Duggan decision and in Mann v Nash 1932 16 TC 523 it was held that once transactions were considered trading, the fact that the trade was illegal could not prevent assessment to tax.

Cross References

To Section 58

Section 859 Anonymity of authorised officers in relation to certain matters.

59 Charge to tax of income from which tax has been deducted

[FA74 s4; CTA76 s 140(1) and Sch2 PtI par41 and s164 and Sch3 PtI; FA96 s132(2) and Sch5 PtII]

Where income (in this section referred to as "*the relevant income*")—

(a) from which tax is deductible by virtue of [provisions relating to][1] Schedule C or D, or

(b) from which tax is deductible by virtue of *section 237* or *238*, is to be taken into account in computing the total income of an individual for any year of assessment, then, for the purpose of charging that total income to tax at the rate or rates of tax charged for that year of assessment, the following provisions shall apply:

(i) the relevant income shall be regarded as income chargeable to tax under Case IV of Schedule D and shall be charged accordingly, and

(ii) in determining the amount of tax payable on that total income, credit shall be given for the tax deducted from the relevant income and the amount of the credit shall be the amount of tax deducted from the relevant income.

Amendments

[1] Inserted by FA12 sched6(1)(a). Has effect as on and from 31 March 2012.

Revenue Precedents

Credit for DIRT under section 59 is available only in computing tax payable on total income and is not available for set off against PRSI liability. IT932006

Cross References

From Section 59

Section 17 Schedule C.
Section 237 Annual payments payable wholly out of taxed income.
Section 238 Annual payments not payable out of taxed income.

To Section 59

Section 3 Interpretation of Income Tax Acts.
Section 189 Payments in respect of personal injuries.
Section 189A Special trusts for permanently incapacitated individuals.
Section 192 Payments in respect of thalidomide children.
Section 261 Taxation of relevant interest, etc.
Section 439 Effect of release, etc. of debt in respect of loan under section 438.
Section 926 Estimation of certain amounts.

CHAPTER 2

Foreign Dividends

60 Interpretation (Chapter 2)

[ITA67 s459]

In this Chapter—

"*dividends to which this Chapter applies*" means any interest, dividends or other annual payments payable out of or in respect of the stocks, funds, shares or securities of any body of persons not resident in the State, but does not include any payment to which *section 237* or *238* applies, and references to dividends shall be construed accordingly;

"*banker*" includes a person acting as a banker;

references to coupons in relation to any dividends include warrants for or bills of exchange purporting to be drawn or made in payment of those dividends.

Revenue Briefings

Tax Briefing

Tax Briefing December 2005 – Issue 62 – Encashment Tax – Notice to Bankers and Brokers

Cross References

From Section 60

Section 237 Annual payments payable wholly out of taxed income.

Section 238 Annual payments not payable out of taxed income.

To Section 60

Section 812 Taxation of income deemed to arise from transfers of right to receive interest from securities.

Section 831 Implementation of Council Directive No. 90/435/EEC concerning the common system of taxation applicable in the case of parent companies and subsidiaries of different Member States.

Section 918 Making of assessments under Schedules C, D, E and F.

Schedule 2 Machinery for Assessment, Charge and Payment of Tax under Schedule C and, in Certain Cases, Schedule D

61 Dividends entrusted for payment in the State

[ITA67 s460; F(MP)A68 s 3(3) and Sch PtII]

Where dividends to which this Chapter applies are entrusted to any person in the State for payment to any persons in the State—

(a) the dividends shall be assessed and charged to tax under Schedule D by the Revenue Commissioners, and

(b) *Parts 1*, *4* and *5* of *Schedule 2* shall extend to the tax to be assessed and charged under this section.

Cross References

From Section 61

Schedule 2 Machinery for Assessment, Charge and Payment of Tax under Schedule C and, in Certain Cases, Schedule D

To Section 61

Schedule 2 Machinery for Assessment, Charge and Payment of Tax under Schedule C and, in Certain Cases, Schedule D

62 Dividends paid outside the State and proceeds of sale of dividend coupons

[ITA67 s461]

[(1)][1]Where—

(a) a banker or any other person in the State, by means of coupons received from another person or otherwise on that other person's behalf, obtains payment of any dividends to which this Chapter applies elsewhere than in the State,

(b) a banker in the State sells or otherwise realises coupons for any dividends to which this Chapter applies and pays over the proceeds of such realisation to or carries such proceeds to the account of any person, or

(c) a dealer in coupons in the State purchases coupons for any dividends to which this Chapter applies otherwise than from a banker or another dealer in coupons,

then, the tax under Schedule D shall extend—

(i) in the case mentioned in *paragraph (a)*, to the dividends,

(ii) in the case mentioned in *paragraph (b)*, to the proceeds of the realisation, and

(iii) in the case mentioned in *paragraph (c)*, to the price paid on such purchase,

and *Parts 1*, *4* and *5* of *Schedule 2* shall apply in relation to the assessment, charge and payment of the tax.

[(2) This section does not apply to a banker by virtue only of the clearing of a cheque, or the arranging for the clearing of a cheque, by the banker.][2]

Amendments

[1] Renumbered by FA05 s46(1)(b)(i). This section applies as respects any payment on or after 25 March 2005.

[2] Inserted by FA05 s46(1)(b)(ii). This section applies as respects any payment on or after 25 March 2005.

Cross References

From Section 62

Schedule 2 Machinery for Assessment, Charge and Payment of Tax under Schedule C and, in Certain Cases, Schedule D

To Section 62

Section 64 Interest on quoted Eurobonds.

Section 486B Relief for investment in renewable energy generation.

Schedule 2 Machinery for Assessment, Charge and Payment of Tax under Schedule C and, in Certain Cases, Schedule D

63 Exemption of dividends of non-residents

[ITA67 s462; F(MP)A68 s3(2) and Sch PtI]

(1) (a) No tax shall be chargeable in respect of dividends to which this Chapter applies which are payable in the State where it is proved to the satisfaction of the Revenue Commissioners that the person owning the stocks, funds, shares or securities and entitled to the income arising from those stocks, funds, shares or securities is not resident in the State but, except where provided by the Income Tax Acts, no allowance shall be given or repayment made in respect of the tax on dividends to which this Chapter applies which are payable in the State.

(b) Where the dividends referred to in *paragraph (a)* are from stocks, funds, shares or securities which are held under any trust, and the person who is the beneficiary in possession under the trust is the sole beneficiary in possession and can, by means either of the revocation of the trust or of the exercise of any powers under the trust, call on the trustees at any time to transfer the stocks, funds, shares or securities to such person absolutely free from any trust, such person shall for the purposes of this section be deemed to be the person owning the stocks, funds, shares or securities.

(2) Relief under this section may be given by the Revenue Commissioners either by means of allowance or repayment on a claim being made to them for that purpose.

(3) Any person aggrieved by a decision of the Revenue Commissioners on any question as to residence arising under this section may, by notice in writing to that effect given to the Revenue Commissioners within 2 months from the date on which notice of the decision is given to such person, make an application to have such person's claim for relief heard and determined by the Appeal Commissioners.

(4) Where an application is made under *subsection (3)*, the Appeal Commissioners shall hear and determine the claim in the like manner as an appeal made to them against an assessment, and the provisions of the Income Tax Acts relating to such an appeal (including the provisions relating to the rehearing of an appeal and to the statement of a case for the opinion of the High Court on a point of law) shall apply accordingly with any necessary modifications.

Cross References

To Section 63

Section 64 Interest on quoted Eurobonds.
Section 809 Saver.
Section 845 Corporation tax: treatment of tax-free income of non-resident banks, insurance businesses, etc.
Schedule 19 Offshore Funds: Distributing Funds

64 Interest on quoted Eurobonds

[ITA67 s462A; FA94 s15]

(1) In this section—

["*appropriate officer*" means an officer of the Revenue Commissioners authorised by them for the purposes of this section;][1]

"*quoted Eurobond*" means a security which—

(a) is issued by a company,

(b) is quoted on a recognised stock [exchange, and][2]

[…][3]

(d) carries a right to interest;

[…][4]

"*relevant foreign securities*" means—

(a) any such stocks, funds, shares or securities as give rise to dividends to which this Chapter applies, or

(b) any such securities as give rise to foreign public revenue dividends within the meaning of *section 32*;

"*relevant person*" means—

(a) the person by or through whom interest is paid, or

(b) a banker or any other person, or a dealer in coupons, referred to in *section 62*,

as the case may be.

[(1A) The definition of "*recognised clearing system*" in *section 246A(2)* applies for the purposes of this section as it applies for the purposes of *section 246A*.][5]

(2) *Section 246(2)* shall not apply to interest paid on any quoted Eurobond where—

(a) the person by or through whom the payment is made is not in the State, or

(b) the payment is made by or through a person in the State, and—

(i) the quoted Eurobond is held in a recognised clearing system, or

(ii) the person who is the beneficial owner of the quoted Eurobond and who is beneficially entitled to the interest is not resident in the State and has made a declaration of the kind mentioned in *subsection (7)*.

(3) In a case within *subsection (2)(b)*, the person by or through whom the payment is made shall deliver to the [appropriate officer][6]—

(a) on demand by the [appropriate officer][7], an account of the amount of any such payment, and

(b) not later than 12 months after making any such payment and unless within that time that person delivers an account with respect to the payment under *paragraph (a)*, a written statement specifying that person's name and address and describing the payment.

(4) Where by virtue of any provision of the Tax Acts interest paid on any quoted Eurobond is deemed to be income of a person other than the person who is the beneficial owner of the quoted Eurobond, *subsection (2)(b)(ii)* shall apply as if it referred to that other person.

(5) *Sections 62* and *63* and, in so far as it relates to *section 62*, *Schedule 2* shall apply in relation to interest on quoted Eurobonds as they would apply in relation to dividends to which this Chapter applies—

(a) if in *paragraph (a)* of *section 62* the following were substituted for "applies elsewhere than in the State":

"applies and—

(i) the payment of those dividends was not made by or entrusted to any person in the State, or

(ii) the stocks, funds and securities in respect of which those dividends are paid are held in a recognised clearing system",

(b) if in *section 63* the following were substituted for *subsection (1)(a)*:

"(1) (a) No tax shall be chargeable in respect of dividends to which this Chapter applies which are payable in the State where the person who is the beneficial owner of the stocks, funds, shares or securities and who is beneficially entitled to the dividends is not resident in the State and has made a declaration of the kind mentioned in *section 64(7)*.",

and

[(c) if in *paragraph 1A* of *Part 1* of *Schedule 2*, *clauses (1)* and *(2)* of the definition of 'chargeable person' were deleted.][8]

[...][9]

(7) The declaration referred to in *subsection (2)(b)(ii)* or in *subsection (1)(a)* of *section 63* (as construed by reference to *subsection (5)(b)*) shall be a declaration in writing to a relevant person which—

(a) is made by a person (in this section referred to as "*the declarer*") to whom any interest in respect of which the declaration is made is payable by the relevant person, and is signed by the declarer,

(b) is made in such form as may be prescribed or authorised by the Revenue Commissioners,

(c) declares that at the time the declaration is made the person who is beneficially entitled to the interest is not resident in the State,

(d) contains as respects the person mentioned in *paragraph (c)*—

(i) the name of the person,

(ii) the address of that person's principal place of residence, and

(iii) the name of the country in which that person is resident at the time the declaration is made,

(e) contains an undertaking by the declarer that, if the person referred to in *paragraph (c)* becomes resident in the State, the declarer will notify the relevant person accordingly, and

(f) contains such other information as the Revenue Commissioners may reasonably require for the purposes of this section.

(8) (a) A relevant person shall—

(i) keep and retain for the longer of the following periods—

(I) a period of 6 years, and

(II) a period which ends not earlier than 3 years after the latest date on which interest in respect of which the declaration was made is paid,

and

(ii) on being so required by notice given in writing by an inspector [or appropriate officer][10], make available to the inspector [or appropriate officer][11] within the time specified in the notice,

all declarations of the kind mentioned in this section which have been made in respect of interest paid by the relevant person.

(b) The inspector [or appropriate officer][12] may examine or take extracts from or copies of any declarations made available under *paragraph (a)*.

Amendments

[1] Substituted by FA06 s57(1)(a)(i). This section applies from 2 February 2006.

[2] Substituted by FA06 s57(1)(a)(ii)(I). This section applies from 2 February 2006.

[3] Deleted by FA06 s57(1)(a)(ii)(II). This section applies from 2 February 2006.

[4] Deleted by FA03 s49(3)(a)(i). Applies as on or after 28 March 2003.

[5] Inserted by FA03 s49(3)(a)(ii). Applies as on or after 28 March 2003.

[6, 7] Substituted by FA06 s57(1)(b). This section applies from 2 February 2006.

[8] Substituted by FA12 s38(1)(b). With effect from 1 January 2013 per S.I. No. 561 of 2012.

[9] Deleted by FA03 s49(3)(a)(iii). Applies as on or after 28 March 2003.

[10, 11] Inserted by FA06 s57(1)(c)(i). This section applies from 2 February 2006.

[12] Inserted by FA06 s57(1)(c)(ii). This section applies from 2 February 2006.

Revenue Information Notes

Revenue's Information Leaflet "Recognised Clearing Systems" sets out a list of clearing systems for the purpose of this section.

Cross References

From Section 64

Section 32 Interpretation (Chapter 1).
Section 62 Dividends paid outside the State and proceeds of sale of dividend coupons.
Section 63 Exemption of dividends of non-residents.
Section 64 Interest on quoted Eurobonds.
Section 246 Interest payments by companies and to non-residents.
Section 246A Interest in respect of wholesale debt instruments.
Schedule 2 Machinery for Assessment, Charge and Payment of Tax under Schedule C and, in Certain Cases, Schedule D

To Section 64

Section 64 Interest on quoted Eurobonds.
Section 110 Securitisation.
Section 198 Certain interest not to be chargeable.
Section 243 Allowance of charges on income.
Section 246A Interest in respect of wholesale debt instruments.

CHAPTER 3

Income Tax: Basis of Assessment Under Cases I and II

65 Cases I and II: basis of assessment

[ITA67 s58(1) and s60; FA90 s14(1)(a) and s15; FA97 s146(1) and Sch9 PtI par1(2)]

(1) Subject to this Chapter, income tax shall be charged under Case I or II of Schedule D on the full amount of the profits or gains of the year of assessment.

(2) Where in the case of any trade or profession it has been customary to make up accounts—

(a) if only one account was made up to a date within the year of assessment and that account was for a period of one year, the profits or gains of the year ending on that date shall be taken to be the profits or gains of the year of assessment;

(b) if an account, other than an account to which *paragraph (a)* applies, was made up to a date in the year of assessment, or if more accounts than one were made up to dates in the year of assessment, the profits or gains of the year ending on that date or on the last of those dates, as the case may be, shall be taken to be the profits or gains of the year of assessment;

(c) in any other case, the profits or gains of the year of assessment shall be determined in accordance with *subsection (1)*.

(3) Where the profits or gains of a year of assessment have been computed on the basis of a period in accordance with *paragraph (b)* or *(c)* of *subsection (2)* and the profits of the corresponding period relating to the preceding year of assessment exceed the profits or gains charged to income tax for that year, then, [notwithstanding anything to the contrary in *section 66(2)*,][1] the profits of that corresponding period shall be taken to be the profits or gains of that preceding year of assessment and the assessment shall be amended accordingly.

[(3A) As respects the year of assessment 2001, *subsection (2)* shall apply as if in both *paragraph (a)* and *paragraph (b)* of that subsection "74 per cent of the profits or gains of the year ending on that date" were substituted for "the profits or gains of the year ending on that date".

(3B) For the purposes of *subsection (2)(a)*, an account made up for a period of one year to a date falling in the period from 1 January 2002 to 5 April 2002 shall, in addition to being an account made up to a date in the year of assessment 2002, be deemed to be an account for a period of one year made up to a date within the year of assessment 2001, and the corresponding period in relation to the year of assessment 2000-2001 for the purposes of *subsection (3)* shall be determined accordingly.

(3C) Notwithstanding *subsection (3)*, where the profits or gains of the year of assessment 2001 have been taken to be the full amount of the profits or gains of that year of assessment in accordance with *subsection (2)(c)*, and the full amount of the profits or gains of the year of assessment 2000-2001 exceed the profits or gains charged to income tax for that year of assessment, then, the profits or gains of the year of assessment 2000-2001 shall be taken to be the full amount of the profits or gains of that year of assessment and the assessment shall be amended accordingly.

(3D) Notwithstanding *subsection (3)*, where the profits or gains of a period of one year ending in the year of assessment 2002 have been taken to be the profits or gains of that year of assessment in accordance with *subsection (2)(b)*, and the profits or gains charged to income tax for the year of assessment 2001 are less than 74 per cent of the profits or gains of the corresponding period relating to the year of assessment 2001, then, the profits or gains of the year of assessment 2001 shall be taken to be 74 per cent of the profits or gains of that corresponding period and the assessment shall be amended accordingly.

(3E) For the purposes of *subsection (3D)*, where, apart from this subsection, a period (in this subsection referred to as the "relevant period") would not be treated as the corresponding period relating to the year of assessment 2001 by virtue of the fact that the relevant period ends on a date falling in the period from 1 January 2001 to 5 April 2001, the relevant period shall, notwithstanding any other provision of the Income Tax Acts, be treated as the corresponding period relating to that year of assessment.

(3F) Notwithstanding *subsection (3)*, where the profits or gains of the year of assessment 2002 have been taken to be the full amount of the profits or gains of that year of assessment in accordance with *subsection (2)(c)*, and the full amount of the profits or gains of the year of assessment 2001 exceed the profits or gains charged to income tax for that year of assessment, then, the profits or gains of the year of assessment 2001 shall be taken to be the full amount of the profits or gains of that year of assessment and the assessment shall be amended accordingly.][2]

(4) In the case of the death of a person who, if he or she had not died, would under this section have become chargeable to income tax for any year of assessment, the tax which would have been so chargeable shall be assessed and charged on such person's executors or administrators, and shall be a debt due from and payable out of such person's estate.

Amendments

[1] Inserted by FA03 s11.

[2] Inserted by FA01 sched2(2).

Case Law

The distinction between a capital profit made on the disposal of an investment and a trading profit made as the result of a 'deal' was expressed in California Copper Syndicate v Harris 1904 5 TC 159.

Goods and services provided for consideration to non-members of a club, any surplus arising will be taxable. Carlisle & Silloth Golf Club v Smith 1913 6 TC 198

Compensation paid in respect of revenue expenditure will itself be revenue in nature. Alliance & Dublin Consumers Gas Co v McWilliams 1927 I ITR 207

The selling off of whiskey stocks over a period after the liquidator had ceased to trade was not trading. IRC v Old Bushmills Distillery Co Ltd 1928 12 TC 1148

In N Cohan's Executors v IRC 12 TC 602, executors were held not to be trading when they completed the purchase of a contract to buy a ship entered into by the taxpayer before his death and when they resold the ship.

Income generated from the purchase of sweepstake tickets was trading income. HH v MJ Forbes (Inspector of Taxes) 1974 II ITR 614

Training grants and other contributions towards expenditure should normally be taxable. O'Cleirigh (Inspector of Taxes) v Jacobs International Ltd 1985 III ITR 165

In Tanfield v Carr 1999 STC (SCD) 213 exclusivity payment was held to be revenue and not capital.

Advance payments made to a company whose business consisted of the hiring of motor vehicles and related to periods after the sale of the company to a third party were part of the company's profits in the accounting period in which the business was sold. Tapemaze Ltd v Melluish (HM Inspector of Taxes) 2000 STC 189

Able (UK) Ltd v Revenue & Customs Commissioners 2007 STC 1738 considered whether compensation received for losses and expenses arising out of the giving and withdrawal of a CPO notice to a taxpayer was income or capital in nature.

A Building Society lent money to borrowers who were not members of the company. It was held the company was liable to tax on its profits as it was not carrying on a building society business by lending exclusively to its members. Property Loan and Investment Company Ltd v Revenue Commissioners 1945 II ITR 25

Revenue Briefings

Tax Briefing

Tax Briefing October 2001 Issue 45 pg 15 – Case I and Case II Basis of Assessment and the Calendar Tax Year

Tax Briefing September 2010 – Issue 12 – Share Farming

Revenue Information Notes

Preparation of Accounts for Revenue Purposes Treatment of Debtors

Revenue Precedents

Payments made under the Emergency Aid Grant, paid by an Bord Iascaigh Mhara to compensate fishermen for poor earnings during adverse weather conditions, are taxable receipts liable to Income Tax. IT953549

Payment received from the Department of agriculture in respect of the grubbing-up of orchards is not chargeable Case I. These appear to be capital in nature and would be chargeable under the Capital Gains Tax rules. IT953511

There are no special arrangements for the taxation of athletes. Athletes are taxable in the normal way i.e. the income earned from all sources, less expenses which have been incurred wholly and exclusively, is assessable. GD95010

Is the sale of copyright subject to Income Tax or Capital Gains Tax? The U.K. case of Nethersole v. Withers (28 TC 501) which was concerned with the sale of copyright in a play is relevant. It contains a useful summary of the case law on the point. To apply the decision to a case it would firstly be necessary to decide if the activities of the taxpayer are in the nature of a trade. If so, the payments are liable to Income Tax and there is no consideration for Capital Gains Tax Purposes. If not, they are capital and liable to Capital Gains Tax. IT933036

A farmer avails of the EC set-a-side scheme and instead of leaving the land fallow grows trees. Are the set-a-side payments in respect of that woodland, which is managed on a commercial basis and with a view to the realisation of profits, exempt from income tax? Payments under the EC schemes for set-aside of land are assessable under the rules of Case I of Schedule D. The payments are to reimburse the farmer for the loss of income which would have accrued had he continued to till the land. Where a farmer receives payments under the set-aside scheme, and afforests the set-aside land; the payments will not be derived from the occupation of woodlands. They will still represent loss of income which would have accrued had tillage continued, and are not therefore exempt under Section 232 Taxes Consolidation Act 1997. IT913022

Where a race horse trainer, who holds a license, trains horses which he or she owns or part owns, the activity is regarded as part of the trade of training. Accordingly, the expenses of training those horses may be allowed as a Case I deduction, and any income from prize money or the sale of horses is part of the income of that trade. IT963004

Revenue do not accept that income arising from holiday cottages registered with Bord Failte are Case I trading receipts. The question of whether the income arising from a particular scheme of holiday cottages is chargeable under the rules of Case I or Case V of Schedule D is one which can only be determined by reference to the facts of each case. IT953544

Statements of Practice

Creditors and Work-in-Progress in Professional Accounts – SP IT/2/92

Cross References

From Section 65

Section 66 Special basis at commencement of trade or profession.

To Section 65

Section 56 Tax on quarries, mines and other concerns chargeable under Case I(b) of Schedule D.
Section 520 Interpretation (Chapter 1).
Section 655 Farming and market gardening profits to be charged to tax under Schedule D.
Section 657 Averaging of farm profits.
Section 658 Farming: allowances for capital expenditure on construction of buildings and other works.
Section 668 Compulsory disposals of livestock.
Section 879 Returns of income.
Section 951 Obligation to make a return.

Section 958 Date for payment of tax.
Section 1008 Separate assessment of partners.
Schedule 31 Consequential Amendments

66 Special basis at commencement of trade or profession

[ITA67 s58(2), (3) and (4); FA90 s14(1)(b)]

(1) Where a trade or profession has been set up and commenced within the year of assessment, the computation of the profits or gains chargeable under Case I or II of Schedule D shall be made either on the full amount of the profits or gains arising in the year of assessment or according to the average of such period, not being greater than one year, as the case may require and as may be directed by the inspector.

[(2) Any person chargeable with income tax in respect of the profits or gains of any trade or profession which has been set up and commenced within one year preceding the year of assessment shall be charged—

(a) if only one account was made up to a date within the year of assessment and that account was for a period of one year, on the full amount of the profits or gains of the year ending on that date,

(b) if—

(i) an account, other than an account to which paragraph (*a*) applies, was made up to a date in the year of assessment or more accounts than one were made up to dates in the year of assessment, and

(ii) the trade or profession was set up and commenced not less than 12 months before the first-mentioned date in subparagraph (i) or, as the case may be, the last of the second-mentioned dates in that subparagraph,

on the full amount of the profits or gains of the year ending on that first-mentioned date or, as the case may be, the last of those second-mentioned dates, or

(c) in any other case, on the full amount of the profits or gains of the year of assessment.][1]

(3) Any person chargeable with income tax in respect of the profits or gains of any trade or profession which has been set up and commenced within the year next before the year preceding the year of assessment shall be entitled, [on including a claim in that behalf with the return required under [*Chapter 3* of *Part 41A*][2] for the year of assessment][3] reduced by the amount (if any) by which the amount of the assessment for the year preceding the year of assessment exceeds the full amount of the profits or gains of that preceding year; but, where the excess is greater than the amount of the assessment, the difference between the excess and the amount of the assessment shall be treated for the purposes of *section 382* as if it were a loss sustained in a trade in that year of assessment.

[(3A) As respects the year of assessment 2001, *subsection (2)* shall apply as if in both *paragraph (a)* and *paragraph (b)* of that subsection "74 per cent of the full amount of the profits or gains" were substituted for "the full amount of the profits or gains".

(3B) As respects the year of assessment 2002—

(a) *subsection (2)* shall apply as if "within the period from 6 April 2001 to 31 December 2001" were substituted for "within one year preceding the year of assessment", and

(b) *subsection (3)* shall apply as if "within the period from 6 April 2000 to 5 April 2001" were substituted for "within the year next before the year preceding the year of assessment".

(3C) As respects the year of assessment 2003, *subsection (3)* shall apply as if "within the period from 6 April 2001 to 31 December 2001" were substituted for "within the year next before the year preceding the year of assessment".][4]

Amendments

[1] Substituted by FA98 s8. Applies as respects the year of assessment 1998-99 and subsequent years of assessment.

[2] Substituted by FA12 sched4(part 2)(g).

[3] Substituted by FA01 s78(2)(a). Applies as respects the year of assessment 2001 and subsequent years and as respects accounting periods of companies ending on or after 1 April 2001.

[4] Inserted by FA01 sched2(3).

Case Law

In Birmingham District Cattle By-Products Co Ltd v IRC 1919 12 TC 92 a company commenced trading only at the point when it began to receive raw material and to turn out its product.

The cessation of one activity of the company does not necessarily denote the cessation of the trade. M Cronin v Lunham Brothers Ltd. 1985 III ITR 363

Revenue Briefings

Tax Briefing

Tax Briefing March 1999 – Issue 35 pg 8 – Income Tax Commencement Rules

Tax Briefing October 2001 – Issue 45 pg 17 – Income Tax Commencement Rules – Calendar Tax Year Changes

Revenue Information Notes

Tax & Duty Manuals – Section 16 – Part 4 [4.3.3] Trade or Profession – Commencement Rules, Basis of assessment at commencement of trade or profession 1998/99 et seq.

Revenue Precedents

Where a trade is set up and commenced on the 6th April the profits of the first year to 5th April represent the amount on which the person is charged for the first year of assessment and the second year of assessment. IT943515

Cross References

From Section 66

Section 382 Right to carry forward losses to future years.

To Section 66

Section 65 Cases I and II: basis of assessment.

Section 1084 Surcharge for late returns.

67 Special basis on discontinuance of trade or profession

[ITA67 s58(5) and (6); FA71 s3; FA90 s14(2); FA96 s132(2) and Sch5 PtII]

(1) (a) Where in any year of assessment a trade or profession is permanently discontinued, then, notwithstanding anything in the Income Tax Acts—

(i) the person charged or chargeable with income tax in respect of the trade or profession shall be charged for that year on the amount of the profits or gains of the period beginning on [the first day of the year of assessment][1] and ending on the date of the discontinuance, subject to any deduction or set-off to which such person may be entitled under *section 382* and, if such person has been charged otherwise than in accordance with this paragraph, any tax overpaid shall be repaid, or [an assessment made on or by such person may be amended][2], as the case may require;

[(ii) if the full amount of the profits or gains of the year of assessment preceding the year of assessment in which the discontinuance occurs exceeds the amount on which that person has been charged for that preceding year of assessment, or would have been charged if no such deduction or set-off to which such person may be entitled under *section 382* had been allowed, [an assessment on or by such person may be made or amended][3], so that such person shall be charged for that preceding year of assessment on the full amount of the profits or gains of that preceding year of assessment, subject to any such deduction or set-off to which such person may be entitled.][4]

(b) In the case of the death of a person who, if he or she had not died, would under this subsection have become chargeable to income tax for any year, the tax which would have been so chargeable shall be assessed and charged on such person's executors or administrators, and shall be a debt due from and payable out of such person's estate.

(2) The reference in *subsection (1)* to the discontinuance of a trade or profession shall be construed as referring to a discontinuance occurring by reason of the death while carrying on such trade or profession of the person carrying on the same, as well as to a discontinuance occurring in the lifetime of such person, and for the purposes of *subsection (1)* such death shall be deemed to cause a discontinuance and such discontinuance shall be deemed to take place on the day of such death.

Amendments

[1] Substituted by FA01 sched2(4)(a).

[2, 3] Substituted by FA12 sched4(part 2)(g).

[4] Substituted by FA01 sched2(4)(b).

Case Law

In Gordon & Blair Ltd v IRC 1962 40 TC 358 the company ceased its brewing operations and began to sell beer supplied to its own specifications by another brewery. It was held that this represented a discontuinance of the old trade and the commencement of a new trade.

In Rolls Royce Motors Ltd v Bamford 1976 STC 162 approximately 20 percent of the activities transferred to a new company. It was held that the transferred activities carried on by the new company represented a new trade.

Revenue Briefings

Tax Briefing

Tax Briefing June 1999 – Issue 36 pg 17 – Cessation of a Trade or Profession: basis of assessment

Tax Briefing April 2001 – Issue 43 pg 27 – Cessation of a Trade – tax treatment

Tax Briefing October 2001 – Issue 45 pg 17 – Cessation of a Trade – changes to assessment rules consequent on changeover to a calendar tax year

Cross References

From Section 67

Section 382 Right to carry forward losses to future years.

To Section 67

Section 68 Short-lived businesses.

Section 657 Averaging of farm profits.

68 Short-lived businesses

[ITA67 s58A; FA95 s19]

(1) This section shall apply to a trade or profession—

(a) which has been set up and commenced in a year of assessment,

(b) which is permanently discontinued within the second year of assessment following that year of assessment, and

(c) in respect of which the aggregate of the profits or gains on which any person has been charged, or would be charged to income tax, by virtue of any other provision of the Income Tax Acts, exceeds the aggregate of the profits or gains arising in the period beginning on the date of set up and commencement and ending on the date of permanent discontinuance of the trade or profession.

(2) Any person chargeable to income tax on the profits or gains of a trade or profession to which this section applies shall be entitled, on giving notice in writing to the inspector on or before the specified return date (within the meaning of [section 959A][1]) for the year of assessment in which the trade or profession is permanently discontinued, to have the assessment for the year of assessment immediately preceding that year reduced by the amount by which the amount of the assessment for that immediately preceding year exceeds the full amount of the profits or gains arising in that same year.

(3) *Subsection (2)* of *section 67* shall apply to this section as if references in that subsection to *subsection (1)* of that section included references to this section.

Amendments

[1] Substituted by FA12 sched4(part 2)(g).

Cross References

From Section 68

Section 67 Special basis on discontinuance of trade or profession.
Section 950 Interpretation (Part 41).

69 Changes of proprietorship

[ITA67 s59]

(1) Where at any time a trade or profession which immediately before that time was carried on by an individual (in this subsection referred to as "*the predecessor*") becomes carried on by another individual or by a partnership of persons (including a partnership in which the predecessor is a partner), the income tax payable for all years of assessment by the predecessor shall be computed as if the trade or profession had been permanently discontinued at that time.

(2) Where at any time an individual (in this subsection referred to as "*the successor*") succeeds to a trade or profession which immediately before that time was carried on by another individual or by a partnership of persons (including a partnership in which the successor was a partner), the income tax payable for all years of assessment by the successor shall be computed as if the successor had set up or commenced the trade or profession at that time.

(3) In the case of the death of a person who, if he or she had not died, would under this section have become chargeable to income tax for any year, the tax which

would have been so chargeable shall be assessed and charged on such person's executors or administrators, and shall be a debt due from and payable out of such person's estate.

Case Law

In Watson Bros v Lothian 1902 4 TC 441 it was held that the purchase of a ship from another trader, without the goodwill or rights over any particular route, did not constitute a succession to trade but merely the acquisition of assets.

Cross References

To Section 69

Section 313 Effect, in certain cases, of succession to trade, etc.
Section 388 Meaning of "permanently discontinued" for purposes of terminal loss.
Section 1010 Capital allowances and balancing charges in partnership cases.

CHAPTER 4

Income Tax: Basis of Assessment Under Cases III, IV and V

70 Case III: basis of assessment

[ITA67 s75 and s77(1), (2) and (5); FA90 s17(1)(a)(i) and (iii); FA97 s146(1) and Sch9 pt1 par1 (5)]

(1) Income or profits chargeable under Case III of Schedule D shall, for the purposes of ascertaining liability to income tax, be deemed to issue from a single source, and this section shall apply accordingly.

[(1A) (a) In this subsection "*excluded amount*" means the amount of the deficiency where—

(i) the computation of income arising in respect of a possession outside the State gives rise to a deficiency, and

(ii) income arising in respect of that possession would be chargeable under Case V of Schedule D if the possession was in the State.

(b) Nothing in *subsection (1)* shall be construed as meaning that an excluded amount can be taken into account in computing the income or profits chargeable under Case III of Schedule D.][1]

(2) Income tax under Case III of Schedule D shall be computed on the full amount of the profits or income arising within the year of assessment.

(3) Income tax shall, subject to *section 71*, be paid on the actual amount computed in accordance with *subsection (2)* without any deduction.

(4) *Subsection (2)* shall, in cases where income tax is to be computed by reference to the amount of income received in the State, apply as if the reference in that subsection to income arising were a reference to income so received.

Amendments

[1] Inserted by FA13 s16. Deemed to have come into force and takes effect on and from 1 January 2013.

Case Law

In the UK case Girvan v Orange Personal Communications Services 1985 STC 567 the line from previous UK cases that income is taxable on a receipts basis was upheld.

Revenue Precedents

Interest received by partnership should be returned on the strict basis i.e. on the basis of the year to 5 April (31 December for the short tax year and later tax years). IT912002

Cross References

From Section 70

Section 71 Foreign securities and possessions.

To Section 70

Section 71 Foreign securities and possessions.
Section 73 Income from certain possessions in Great Britain or Northern Ireland.
Section 234 Certain income derived from patent royalties.
Section 726 Investment income.

71 Foreign securities and possessions

[ITA67 s76(1),(2)(a), (3), (5) and (6); F(MP)A68 s3(2) and Sch PtI; FA74 s46; FA90 s17(1)(a)(ii); FA97 s146(1) and Sch9 PtI par1(4)]

(1) Subject to this section and *section 70*, income tax chargeable under Case III of Schedule D in respect of income arising from securities and possessions in any place outside the State shall be computed on the full amount of such income arising in the year of assessment whether the income has been or will be received in the State or not, subject to, in the case of income not received in the State—

(a) the same deductions and allowances as if it had been so received,

(b) the deduction, where such deduction cannot be made under, and is not forbidden by, any other provision of the Income Tax Acts, of any sum paid in respect of income tax in the place where the income has arisen, and

(c) a deduction on account of any annuity or other annual payment (apart from annual interest) payable out of the income to a person not resident in the State,

and the provisions of the Income Tax Acts (including those relating to the delivery of statements) shall apply accordingly.

[(2) *Subsection (1)* shall not apply to any person who satisfies the Revenue Commissioners that he or she is not domiciled in the State.][1]

(3) [In the case mentioned in *subsection (2)*][2], the tax shall, subject to *section 70*, be computed on the full amount of the actual sums received in the State from remittances payable in the State, or from property imported, or from money or value arising from property not imported, or from money or value so received on credit or on account in respect of such remittances, property, money or value brought into the State in the year of assessment without any deduction or abatement.

[(3A) (a) In this subsection "*foreign tax*" means a tax chargeable and payable under the law of a territory other than the State which corresponds to income tax or corporation tax.

(b) Where income arising outside the State is chargeable to tax under Case III of Schedule D and a payment is made under the law of a territory other than the State to the person in receipt of the income by reference to foreign tax paid by another person, then the amount of income so chargeable shall be increased by an amount equal to the amount of the payment.][3]

[(3B) (a) This subsection shall apply where a person referred to in *subsection (2)* applies, outside the State, any income arising from securities or possessions in any place outside the State, in the making of a loan, or the transfer of money to that person's spouse or civil partner, or in the acquisition of any property which is subsequently transferred to that person's spouse or civil partner.

(b) Where this subsection applies, any sums received in the State on or after 13 February 2013 from—

(i) remittances payable in the State,

(ii) property imported,

(iii) money or value arising from property not imported, or

(iv) money or value so received on credit or on account in respect of such remittances, property, money or value,

which derive from the loan, or transfer of money or property referred to in *paragraph (a)*, shall be treated, for the purpose of *subsection (3)*, as if the sums received in the State had been brought into the State by the person referred to in *subsection (2)*.][4]

(4) Income arising outside the State which if it had arisen in the State would be chargeable under Case V of Schedule D shall be deemed to be income to which *sections 75* and *97* apply, in so far as those sections relate to deductions to be made by reference to *section 97(2)(e)*.

[(4A) For the purposes of *subsection (4)*, *section 97* shall apply as if references to the 23rd day of April, 1998, in *subsections (2A)*, *(2B)*, *(2C)* and *(2E)* of that section, were references to the 7th day of May, 1998.][5]

[(4B) Income arising to a person from property situated outside the State which, if it had arisen from property in the State, would be chargeable under Case V of Schedule D shall include income from any such property outside the State transferred by that person to another person to hold in trust pursuant to the terms of a Debt Settlement Arrangement or a Personal Insolvency Arrangement entered into under the Personal Insolvency Act 2012.][6]

(5) Any person aggrieved by a decision of the Revenue Commissioners on any question [as to domicile][7] arising under *subsection (2)* may, by notice in writing to that effect given to the Revenue Commissioners within 2 months from the date on which notice of the decision is given to him or her, make an application to have his or her claim for relief heard and determined by the Appeal Commissioners.

(6) Where an application is made under this section, the Appeal Commissioners shall hear and determine the claim in the like manner as an appeal made to them against an assessment, and the provisions of the Income Tax Acts relating to such an appeal (including the provisions relating to the rehearing of an appeal and to the statement of a case for the opinion of the High Court on a point of law) shall apply accordingly with any necessary modifications.

Amendments

[1] Substituted by FA10 s9(a). As respects the year of assessment 2010 and subsequent years of assessment.

[2] Substituted by FA10 s9(b). As respects the year of assessment 2010 and subsequent years of assessment.

[3] Inserted by FA10 s41(1). This section applies to income and dividends received on or after 4 February 2010.

[4] Inserted by FA13 s6. Deemed to have come into force and takes effect on and from 1 January 2013.

[5] Inserted by FA98No2 s1(2).

[6] Inserted by FA13 s100(1)(a). Applies on and from 27 March 2013.

[7] Substituted by FA10 s9(c). As respects the year of assessment 2010 and subsequent years of assessment.

Case Law

Only remittances of income, as distinct from capital, are subject to income tax. Kneen v Martin 19 TC 33

Sums remitted under the Emergency Powers Orders were held to be taxable remittances since the fact of the compulsory transfer did not alter their essential character as foreign income. O'Sullivan v O'Connor 1947 II ITR 61

In the UK case Harmel v Wright 1974 49 TC 149 it was held that where a sum received in the UK, could be directly traced to the taxpayer's South African salary, he had remitted his income.

Revenue Briefings

eBrief

eBrief No. 43/2005 – PAYE and Foreign Employments

eBrief No. 09/2006 – 2005 Bonuses, Temporary Assignees, and Pension Contributions

eBrief No. 48/2007 – Foreign Employment Income

eBrief No. 11/2010 – The remittance basis of assessment as regards UK source income and chargeable gains

Cross References

From Section 71

Section 70 Case III: basis of assessment.
Section 75 Case V: basis of assessment.
Section 97 Computational rules and allowable deductions.

To Section 71

Section 70 Case III: basis of assessment.
Section 72 Charge to tax on sums applied outside the State in repaying certain loans.
Section 73 Income from certain possessions in Great Britain or Northern Ireland.
Section 76 Computation of income: application of income tax principles.
Section 128 Tax treatment of directors of companies and employees granted rights to acquire shares or other assets.
Section 201 Exemptions and reliefs in respect of tax under section 123.
Section 472B Seafarer allowance, etc.
Section 807A Liability of nontransferors.
Section 822 Split year residence.
Section 823 Deduction for income earned outside the State.
Section 825A Reduction in income tax for certain income earned outside the State.
Schedule 19 Offshore Funds: Distributing Funds

72 Charge to tax on sums applied outside the State in repaying certain loans

[FA71 s4(1) to (4) and (6); FA97 s15]

(1) For the purposes of this section—

(a) a debt for money loaned shall, to the extent to which that money is applied in or towards satisfying another debt, be deemed to be a debt incurred for satisfying that other debt, and a debt incurred for satisfying in whole or in part a debt within *subsection (2)(c)* shall itself be treated as within that subsection, and

(b) "*lender*", in relation to any money loaned, includes any person for the time being entitled to repayment.

(2) For the purposes of *section 71(3)*, any income arising from securities and possessions in any place outside the State which is applied outside the State by a person ordinarily resident in the State in or towards satisfaction of—

(a) any debt for money loaned to such person in the State or for interest on money so loaned,

(b) any debt for money loaned to such person outside the State and received in or brought to the State, or

(c) any debt incurred for satisfying in whole or in part a debt within *paragraph (a)* or *(b)*,

shall be treated as received by such person in the State and as so received from remittances payable in the State.

(3) Where a person ordinarily resident in the State receives in or brings to the State money loaned to such person outside the State, but the debt for that money is wholly or partly satisfied before such person does so, *subsection (2)* shall apply as if the money had been received in or brought to the State before the debt was so satisfied, except that any sums treated by virtue of that subsection as received in the State shall be treated as so received at the time when the money so loaned is actually received in or brought to the State.

(4) Where a person is indebted for money loaned to him or her, income applied by the person in such a way that the money or property representing the income is held by the lender on behalf of or to the account of the person in such circumstances as to be available to the lender for the purpose of satisfying or reducing the debt by setoff or otherwise shall be treated as applied by the person in or towards its satisfaction if, under any arrangement between the person and the lender, the amount for the time being of the person's indebtedness to the lender, or the time at which it is to be repaid in whole or in part, depends in any respect directly or indirectly on the amount or value so held by the lender.

(5) In relation to income applied in or towards satisfaction of a debt for money loaned on or after the 20th day of February, 1997, or a debt incurred for satisfying in whole or in part any such debt, this section shall apply as if the references to ordinarily resident in the State in *subsections (2)* and *(3)* were references to resident or ordinarily resident in the State.

Cross References

From Section 72

Section 71 Foreign securities and possessions.

To Section 72

Section 29 Persons chargeable.
Section 807A Liability of nontransferors.
Section 825B Repayment of tax where earnings not remitted.

73 Income from certain possessions in Great Britain or Northern Ireland

[ITA67 Sch6 PtIII par1; F(MP)A68 s3(2) and Sch PtI; FA69 s21; FA90 s17(1)(b); FA97 s146(1) and Sch9 PtI par1(36)]

(1) In this section, "*rents*" includes any payment in the nature of a royalty and any annual or periodical payment in the nature of a rent derived from any lands, tenements or hereditaments, including lands, tenements and hereditaments to which *section 56* would apply or would have applied if such lands, tenements and hereditaments were situate in the State.

(2) In respect of property situate and profits or gains arising in Great Britain or Northern Ireland—

(a) *sections 70* and *71* shall apply as if *section 71(2)* were deleted, and

(b) *subsection (3)* shall apply for the purposes of Case III of Schedule D, notwithstanding anything to the contrary in *section 70* or *71*.

(3) (a) Income tax in respect of income arising from possessions in Great Britain or Northern Ireland, other than stocks, shares, rents or the occupation of land, shall be computed either—

(i) on the full amount of such income arising in the year of assessment, or

(ii) on the full amount of such income on an average of such period as the case may require and as may be directed by the Appeal Commissioners,

so that according to the nature of the income the tax may be computed on the same basis as that on which it would have been computed if the income had arisen in the State, and subject in either case to a deduction on account of any annuity or other annual payment (apart from annual interest) payable out of the income to a person not resident in the State, and the provisions of the Income Tax Acts (including those relating to the delivery of statements) shall apply accordingly.

(b) The person chargeable and assessable in accordance with *paragraph (a)* shall be entitled to the same allowances, deductions and reliefs as if the income had arisen in the State.

[(4) This section ceases to have effect in respect of income arising on or after 1 January 2008.][1]

Amendments

[1] Inserted by FA08 s18(1)(a). Has effect as on and from 1 January 2008.

Revenue Briefings

eBrief

eBrief No. 11/2010 – The remittance basis of assessment as regards UK source income and chargeable gains

Cross References

From Section 73

Section 56 Tax on quarries, mines and other concerns chargeable under Case I(b) of Schedule D.
Section 70 Case III: basis of assessment.
Section 71 Foreign securities and possessions.

To Section 73

Section 832 Provisions in relation to Convention for reciprocal avoidance of double taxation in the State and the United Kingdom of income and capital gains.

74 Case IV: basis of assessment

[ITA67 s79; FA96 s132(1) and Sch5 PtI par1(2)]

(1) Income tax under Case IV of Schedule D shall be computed either on the full amount of the profits or gains arising in the year of assessment or according to the average of such a period, not being greater than one year, as the case may require and as may be directed by the inspector.

(2) The nature of the profits or gains chargeable to income tax under Case IV of Schedule D, and the basis on which the amount of such profits or gains has been computed, including the average, if any, taken on such profits or gains, shall be stated to the inspector.

(3) Every such statement and computation shall be made to the best of the knowledge and belief of the person in receipt of or entitled to the profits or gains.

Revenue Precedents

The taxpayer won the grand prize in a U.S. state lottery and under the U.S. tax code the winnings were treated as income. The winnings were to be paid to the taxpayer in 20 annual payments. How would these payments be treated if the taxpayer became resident here? On the basis of the information provided it appears that the taxpayers is receiving a series of income payment which would be liable to Income Tax here. IT953503

75 Case V: basis of assessment

[ITA67 s81(1), (2) and (3)(a) and s86; FA69 s22, s33(1) and Sch4 PtI and s65(1) and Sch5 PtI; FA90 s18(1)(a)]

(1) Without prejudice to any other provision of the Income Tax Acts, the profits or gains arising from—

(a) any rent in respect of any premises, and

(b) any receipts in respect of any easement,

shall, subject to and in accordance with the provisions of the Income Tax Acts, be deemed for the purposes of those Acts to be annual profits or gains within Schedule D, and the person entitled to such profits or gains shall be chargeable in respect of such profits or gainsunder Case V of that Schedule; but such rent or such receipts shall not include any payments to which *section 104* applies.

(2) Profits or gains chargeable under Case V of Schedule D shall, for the purposes of ascertaining liability to income tax, be deemed to issue from a single source, and *subsection (3)* shall apply accordingly.

(3) Tax under Case V of Schedule D shall be computed on the full amount of the profits or gains arising within the year of assessment.

(4) Neither this section nor *section 97* or *384* shall apply to a case in which the rent reserved under a lease (including, in the case of a lease granted on or after the 6th day of April, 1963, the duration of which does not exceed 50 years, an appropriate sum in respect of any premium payable under the lease) is insufficient, taking one year with another, to defray the cost to the lessor of fulfilling such lessor's obligations under the lease and of meeting any expense of maintenance, repairs, insurance and management of the premises subject to the lease which falls to be borne by such lessor.

(5) *Section 96* shall apply for the interpretation of this section as it applies for the interpretation of *Chapter 8* of this Part.

Case Law

A lump sum received in return for the right to receive future rents was capital in nature in the UK High Court case IRC v John Lewis Properties plc 2001 STC 1118. This followed the decision in Paget v IRC 1938 21 TC 677.

Revenue Briefings

Tax Briefing

Tax Briefing February 1997 – Issue 25 pg 11 – Accountancy Fees are an Allowable Deduction.

Revenue Information Notes

IT 70 – A Revenue Guide to Rental Income

Revenue Precedents

The milk quota is treated as attaching to the land. Income from leasing of the quota would be assessable under the rules of Case V of Schedule D, i.e. on the profits arising in the year of assessment, and not on the profits received. If the agreement provides that the full amount of the payment in respect of the lease will arise (i.e. become payable) in the first year, then it will be taxed in that year. If the agreement provides that the amount will become payable over each of the five years, then it will be taxed accordingly. IT903004

Whether rent paid as an up-front lump sum is taxable in year of receipt? On the basis that the up-front payment represents a single payment of rent, it is taxable in the year in which it is received. A trader making such a payment would be required to spread it in accordance with the matching principle in preparing accounts. IT972009

Cross References

From Section 75

Section 96 Interpretation (Chapter 8).
Section 97 Computational rules and allowable deductions.
Section 104 Taxation of certain rents and other payments.
Section 384 Relief under Case V for losses.

To Section 75

Section 71 Foreign securities and possessions.
Section 98 Treatment of premiums, etc. as rent.
Section 105 Taxation of rents: restriction in respect of certain rent and interest.
Section 232 Profits from occupation of certain woodlands.
Section 641 Computation under Case I of Schedule D of profits or gains from dealing in or developing land.
Schedule 14 Capital Gains Tax: Leases

CHAPTER 5

Computational Provisions: Corporation Tax

76 Computation of income: application of income tax principles

[CTA76 s11(1), (2)(b) and (3) to (8); FA96 s132(2) and Sch5 PtII]

(1) Except where otherwise provided by the Tax Acts, the amount of any income shall for the purposes of corporation tax be computed in accordance with income tax principles, all questions as to the amounts which are or are not to be taken into account as income, or in computing income, or charged to tax as a person's income, or as to the time when any such amount is to be treated as arising, being determined in accordance with income tax law and practice as if accounting periods were years of assessment.

(2) For the purposes of this section, "*income tax law*", in relation to any accounting period, means the law applying to the charge on individuals of income tax for the year of assessment in which that accounting period ends, but does not include such of the enactments of the Income Tax Acts so applying as make special provision for individuals in relation to matters referred to in *subsection (1)*.

(3) Accordingly, for the purposes of corporation tax, income shall be computed and the assessment shall be made under the like Schedules and Cases as apply for the purposes of income tax, and in accordance with the provisions applicable to those Schedules and Cases, but (subject to the Corporation Tax Acts) the amounts so computed for several sources of income, if more than one, together with any amounts to be included in respect of chargeable gains, shall be aggregated to arrive at the total profits.

(4) Nothing in this section shall be taken to mean that income arising in any period is to be computed by reference to any other period (except in so far as this results from apportioning to different parts of a period income of the whole period).

(5) Subject to *section 77* and to any enactment applied by this section which expressly authorises such a deduction, no deduction shall be made for the purposes of the Corporation Tax Acts in computing income from any source—

(a) in respect of dividends or other distributions, or

(b) in respect of any yearly interest, annuity or other annual payment or any other payments mentioned in *section 104* or *237(2)*, but not including sums which are, or but for any exemption would be, chargeable under Case V of Schedule D.

(6) Without prejudice to the generality of *subsection (1)*, any provision of the Income Tax Acts, or of any other statute, which confers an exemption from income tax, provides for the disregarding of a loss, or provides for a person to be charged to income tax on any amount (whether expressed to be income or not, and whether an actual amount or not), shall, except where otherwise provided, have the like effect for the purposes of corporation tax.

(7) This section shall not have effect so as to apply for the purposes of corporation tax anything in [*subsections (1), (2), (3), (4A), (5)* and *(6)* of][1] *section 71*.

(8) Where by virtue of this section or otherwise any enactment applies both to income tax and to corporation tax—

(a) that enactment shall not be affected in its operation by the fact that income tax and corporation tax are distinct taxes but, in so far as is consistent with the Corporation Tax Acts, shall apply in relation to income tax and corporation tax as if they were one tax, so that, in particular, a matter which in a case involving 2 individuals is relevant for both of them in relation to income tax shall in a like case involving an individual and a company be relevant for such individual in relation to income tax and for such company in relation to corporation tax, and

(b) for that purpose, references in any such enactment to a relief from or charge to income tax or to a specified provision of the Income Tax Acts shall, in the absence of or subject to any express adaptation, be construed as being or including a reference to any corresponding relief from or charge to corporation tax or to any corresponding provision of the Corporation Tax Acts.

Amendments

[1] Inserted by FA11 sched3(1)(a). Has effect as on and from 6 February 2011.

Cross References

From Section 76

Section 71 Foreign securities and possessions.
Section 77 Miscellaneous special rules for computation of income.
Section 104 Taxation of certain rents and other payments.
Section 237 Annual payments payable wholly out of taxed income.

To Section 76

Section 2 Interpretation of Tax Acts.
Section 77 Miscellaneous special rules for computation of income.
Section 79 Foreign currency: computation of income and chargeable gains.
Section 141 Distributions out of income from patent royalties.
Section 256 Interpretation (Chapter 4).
Section 267 Repayment of appropriate tax in certain cases.
Section 716 General annuity business.
Section 717 Pension business.
Section 730D Gain arising on a chargeable event.
Section 730E Declarations.

Section 739D Gain arising on a chargeable event.
Section 845 Corporation tax: treatment of tax-free income of non-resident banks, insurance businesses, etc.

76A Computation of profits or gains of a company – accounting standards

[(1) For the purposes of Case I or II of Schedule D the profits or gains of a trade or profession carried on by a company shall be computed in accordance with generally accepted accounting practice subject to any adjustment required or authorised by law in computing such profits or gains for those purposes.

(2) [*Schedule 17A* shall apply to a company as respects any matter related to the computation of income of the company where as respects that matter][1]—

(a) for an accounting period profits or gains of a trade or profession carried on by the company are computed in accordance with relevant accounting standards (within the meaning of that Schedule), and

(b) for preceding accounting periods profits or gains of a trade or profession carried on by the company are computed in accordance with standards other than relevant accounting standards (within the meaning of that Schedule).][2]

Amendments

[1] Substituted by FA06 s61(1)(a). This section shall be deemed to have applied as respects any period of account beginning on or after 1 January 2005.

[2] Inserted by FA05 s48(1)(b). This section applies as respects any period of account beginning on or after 1 January 2005.

Revenue Briefings

eBrief

eBrief No. 32/2006 – Guidance on Section 76A (as inserted by the Finance Act 2005) of the Taxes Consolidation Act 1997

Revenue Information Notes

Guidance Note on Section 48 of the Finance Act 2005 – Generally Accepted Accounting Standards

Cross References

From Section 76A

Schedule 17A Accounting Standards

To Section 76A

Section 76B Treatment of unrealised gains and losses in certain cases.
Section 76D Computation of income from finance leases.
Section 110 Securitisation.

76B Treatment of unrealised gains and losses in certain cases

[(1) (a) In this section and *paragraph 4* of *Schedule 17A*, "*fair value*", "*financial asset*" and "*financial liability*" have the meanings assigned to them by international accounting standards.

(b) For the purposes of this section, *section 76A* and *paragraph 4* of *Schedule 17A*—

(i) references to profits or gains include references to losses, and

(ii) the amount of a loss incurred in a trade or profession in an accounting period shall be computed in like manner as profits or gains from the trade or profession in the accounting period would have been computed.

(2) A profit or gain from a financial asset or a financial liability of a company that, in accordance with relevant accounting standards (within the meaning of *Schedule 17A*) is—

(a) calculated on the basis of fair values of the asset or the liability in an accounting period, and

(b) included in the profit or loss of the company for the accounting period,

shall be taken into account on that basis in computing profits or gains of the company for that accounting period for the purposes of Case I or II of Schedule D.][1]

Amendments

[1] Inserted by FA05 s48(1)(b). This section applies as respects any period of account beginning on or after 1 January 2005.

Cross References

From Section 76B

Section 76A Computation of profits or gains of a company – accounting standards.
Schedule 17A Accounting Standards

76C Use of different accounting policies within a group of companies

[(1) (a) In this section "*tax advantage*" means—

(i) a reduction, avoidance or deferral of any charge or assessment to tax, including any potential or prospective charge or assessment, or

(ii) a refund of or a payment of an amount of tax, or an increase in an amount of tax refundable or otherwise payable to a person, including any potential or prospective amount so refundable or payable.

(b) For the purposes of this section, a series of transactions is not prevented from being a series of transactions in relation to companies by reason only of the fact that one or more of the following is the case—

(i) there is no transaction in the series to which both those companies are parties;

(ii) that parties to any arrangement in pursuance of which the transactions in the series are entered into do not include one or both of those companies;

(iii) there are one or more transactions in the series to which neither of those companies is a party.

(2) Where—

(a) a company within the charge to tax under Case I or II of Schedule D prepares accounts in accordance with international accounting standards,

(b) another company within the charge to tax under Case I or II of Schedule D, being a company which is an associated company (within the meaning of *section 432*) of the company referred to in *paragraph (a)*, prepares accounts in accordance with Irish generally accepted accounting practice,

(c) there is a transaction between, or a series of transactions involving, those companies, and

(d) a tax advantage would, apart from this section, accrue to the company which prepares its accounts in accordance with international accounting standards compared with its position if it had prepared its accounts in accordance with Irish generally accepted accounting practice in relation to the transaction or series of transactions,

then the Corporation Tax Acts shall apply for the purposes of computing profits or gains of that company from that transaction or series of transactions as if that company prepared its accounts in accordance with Irish generally accepted accounting practice.][1]

Amendments

[1] Inserted by FA05 s48(1)(b). This section applies as respects any period of account beginning on or after 1 January 2005.

Cross References

From Section 76C

Section 432 Meaning of "associated company" and "control".

76D Computation of income from finance leases

[(1) In this section "*finance lease*" means a lease which, under generally accepted accounting practice, falls to be treated as a finance lease.

(2) Notwithstanding *section 76A* and subject to *section 80A*, for the purposes of computing income of a company from a trade of leasing, income of a lessor from a finance lease—

(a) shall not be the amount of income from the lease computed in accordance with generally accepted accounting practice, and

(b) shall be computed, subject to the provisions of the Corporation Tax Acts other than *section 76A*, by treating—

(i) lease payments receivable in respect of the lease as trading receipts of the trade, and

(ii) as trading expenses of the trade any disbursements or expenses laid out or expended for the purposes of earning those lease payments.][1]

Amendments

[1] Inserted by FA06 s61(1)(b). This section shall be deemed to have applied as respects any period of account beginning on or after 1 January 2005.

Cross References

From Section 76D

Section 76A Computation of profits or gains of a company – accounting standards.

Section 80A Taxation of certain short-term leases plant and machinery.

77 Miscellaneous special rules for computation of income

[CTA76 s12(1) to (7)]

(1) For the purposes of corporation tax, income tax law as applied by *section 76* shall apply subject to *subsections (2)* to *(7)*.

(2) (a) Where a company begins or ceases to carry on a trade, or to be within the charge to corporation tax in respect of a trade, the company's income shall be computed as if that were the commencement or, as the case may be, discontinuance of the trade, whether or not the trade is in fact commenced or discontinued.

(b) Notwithstanding *paragraph (a)*, where any provision of the Income Tax Acts is applied for corporation tax by the Corporation Tax Acts, this subsection shall not apply for any purpose of that provision if under any enactment a trade is not to be treated as permanently discontinued for the corresponding income tax purpose.

(3) In computing income from a trade, *section 76(5)(b)* shall not prevent the deduction of yearly interest.

(4) In computing a company's income for any accounting period from the letting of rights to work minerals in the State, there may be deducted any sums disbursed by the company wholly, exclusively and necessarily as expenses of management or supervision of those minerals in that period; but any enactments restricting the relief from income tax that might be given under *section 111* shall apply to restrict in the like manner the deductions that may be made under this subsection.

(5) Where a company is chargeable to corporation tax in respect of a trade under Case III of Schedule D, the income from the trade shall be computed in accordance with the provisions applicable to Case I of Schedule D.

(6) The amount of any income arising from securities and possessions in any place outside the State shall be treated as reduced (where such a deduction cannot be made under, and is not forbidden by, any provision of the Income Tax Acts applied by the Corporation Tax Acts) by any sum paid in respect of income tax in the place where the income has arisen.

[(6A) (*a*) In this subsection—

'*amount of the income referable to the relevant interest*' shall be construed in accordance with *paragraph 9D(1)(b)(ii)* of *Schedule 24*;

'*relevant foreign tax*' and '*relevant interest*' have the same meanings, respectively, as in *paragraph 9D(1)(a)* of *Schedule 24*.

(*b*) Where, as respects an accounting period of a company, the trading income of a trade carried on by the company includes an amount of relevant interest, the amount of the income referable to the relevant interest shall be treated as reduced (where such a deduction cannot be made under, and is not forbidden by, any provision of the Income Tax Acts applied by the Corporation Tax Acts) by [so much of the relevant foreign tax in relation to the relevant interest as does not exceed that amount of the income referable to the relevant interest][1]

(6B) (*a*) In this subsection—

'*amount of the income referable to the relevant royalties*' shall be construed in accordance with *paragraph 9DB(1)(b)(ii)* of *Schedule 24*;

'*relevant foreign tax*' and '*relevant royalties*' have the same meanings, respectively, as in *paragraph 9DB(1)(a)* of *Schedule 24*.

(*b*) Where, as respects an accounting period of a company, the trading income of a trade carried on by the company includes an amount of relevant royalties, the amount of the income referable to the relevant royalties shall be treated as reduced (where such a deduction cannot be made under, and is not forbidden by, any provision of the Income Tax Acts applied by the Corporation Tax Acts) by [so much of the relevant foreign tax in relation to the relevant royalties as does not exceed that amount of the income referable to the relevant royalties][2].][3]

(7) *Paragraphs (e)* and *(f)* of Case III of Schedule D in *section 18(2)* shall for the purposes of corporation tax extend to companies not resident in the State, in so far as those companies are chargeable to tax on income of descriptions which,

in the case of companies resident in the State, are within those paragraphs (but without prejudice to any provision of the Income Tax Acts specially exempting non-residents from income tax on any particular description of income).

Amendments

[1] Substituted by F(No.2)A13 s32(1)(a). Applies as respects accounting periods beginning on or after 1 January 2014.

[2] Substituted by F(No.2)A13 s32(1)(b). Applies as respects accounting periods beginning on or after 1 January 2014.

[3] Inserted by FA12 s50(1). Applies as respects accounting periods ending on or after 1 January 2012.

Cross References

From Section 77

Section 18 Schedule D.
Section 76 Computation of income: application of income tax principles.
Section 111 Allowance to owner of let mineral rights for expenses of management of minerals.

To Section 77

Section 76 Computation of income: application of income tax principles.
Section 729 Income tax, foreign tax and tax credit.
Schedule 19 Offshore Funds: Distributing Funds

78 Computation of companies' chargeable gains

[CTA76 s13(1), (1A), (1B), (1C), (2), (3)(a) and (c), (4) and (5); FA82 s31(1); FA88 Sch3 PtI par1(b); FA97 s59(2) and Sch6 PtI par1]

(1) Subject to this section, the amount to be included in respect of chargeable gains in a company's total profits for any accounting period shall be determined in accordance with *subsection (3)* after taking into account *subsection (2)*.

(2) Where for an accounting period chargeable gains accrue to a company, an amount of capital gains tax shall be calculated as if, notwithstanding any provision to the contrary in the Corporation Tax Acts, capital gains tax were to be charged on the company in respect of those gains in accordance with the Capital Gains Tax Acts, and as if accounting periods were years of assessment; but, in calculating the amount of capital gains tax, *section 31* shall apply as if the reference in that section to deducting allowable losses were a reference to deducting relevant allowable losses.

(3) (a) The amount referred to in *subsection (1)* shall be an amount which, if (before making any deduction from the amount) it were charged to corporation tax as profits of the company arising in the accounting period at the rate specified in *section 21(1)*, would produce an amount of corporation tax equal to the amount of capital gains tax calculated for that accounting period in accordance with *subsection (2)*.

(b) For the purposes of *paragraph (a)*, where part of the accounting period falls in one financial year (in this paragraph referred to as the "first-mentioned financial year") and the other part falls in the financial year succeeding the first-mentioned financial year and different rates are in force under *section 21(1)* for each of those years, "the rate specified in *section 21(1)*" shall be deemed to be a rate per cent determined by the formula—

$$\frac{(A \times C)}{E} + \frac{(B \times D)}{E}$$

where—

A is the rate per cent in force for the first-mentioned financial year,

B is the rate per cent in force for the financial year succeeding the first-mentioned financial year,

C is the length of that part of the accounting period falling in the first-mentioned financial year,

D is the length of that part of the accounting period falling in the financial year succeeding the first-mentioned financial year, and

E is the length of the accounting period.

(c) *Paragraph (b)* shall apply as respects accounting periods ending on or after the 1st day of April, 1997, as if—

(i) the period beginning on the 1st day of January, 1996, and ending on the 31st day of March, 1997, and

(ii) the period beginning on the 1st day of April, 1997, and ending on the [31st day of December, 1997][1],

were each a financial year.

(4) In *subsection (2)*—

"*chargeable gains*" does not include chargeable gains accruing on relevant disposals within the meaning of *section 648*;

"*relevant allowable losses*" means any allowable losses accruing to the company in the accounting period and any allowable losses previously accruing to the company while it has been within the charge to corporation tax in so far as they have not been allowed as a deduction from chargeable gains accruing in any previous accounting period.

(5) Except where otherwise provided by the Corporation Tax Acts, chargeable gains and allowable losses shall for the purposes of corporation tax be computed in accordance with the principles applying for capital gains tax, all questions as to the amounts which are or are not to be taken into account as chargeable gains or as allowable losses, or in computing gains or losses, or charged to tax as a person's gain, or as to the time when any such amount is to be treated as accruing, being determined in accordance with the provisions relating to capital gains tax as if accounting periods were years of assessment.

(6) Subject to *subsection (8)*, where the enactments relating to capital gains tax contain any reference to income tax or to the Income Tax Acts, the reference shall, in relation to a company, be construed as a reference to corporation tax or to the Corporation Tax Acts; but—

(a) this subsection shall not affect the references to income tax in *section 554(2)*, and

(b) in so far as those enactments operate by reference to matters of any specified description, for corporation tax account shall be taken of matters of that description which are confined to companies, but not of any such matters which are confined to individuals.

(7) The Capital Gains Tax Acts as extended by this section shall not be affected in their operation by the fact that capital gains tax and corporation tax are distinct taxes but, in so far as is consistent with the Corporation Tax Acts, shall apply in relation to capital gains tax and corporation tax on chargeable gains as if they were one tax, so that, in particular, a matter which in a case involving 2 individuals is relevant for both of them in relation to capital gains tax shall in a like case involving an

individual and a company be relevant for such individual in relation to capital gains tax and for such company in relation to corporation tax.

(8) Where assets of a company are vested in a liquidator, this section and the enactments applied by this section shall apply as if the assets were vested in, and the acts of the liquidator in relation to the assets were the acts of, the company (acquisitions from or disposals to the liquidator by the company being disregarded accordingly).

Amendments

[1] Substituted by FA98 sched6(2).

Cross References

From Section 78

Section 21 The charge to corporation tax and exclusion of income tax and capital gains tax.
Section 31 Amount chargeable.
Section 554 Exclusion of expenditure by reference to income tax.
Section 648 Interpretation (Chapter 2).

To Section 78

Section 79 Foreign currency: computation of income and chargeable gains.
Section 487 Corporation tax: credit for bank levy.
Section 571 Chargeable gains accruing on disposals by liquidators and certain other persons.
Section 595 Life assurance policy or deferred annuity contract entered into or acquired by company.
Section 633 Company reconstruction or amalgamation: transfer of development land.
Section 653 Restriction of relief for losses, etc. in relation to relevant disposals.
Section 697N Chargeable gains.
Section 711 Chargeable gains of life business.
Section 722 Benefits from life policies issued before 6th April, 1974.
Section 726 Investment income.
Section 732 Special arrangements for qualifying unit trusts.
Section 738 Undertakings for collective investment.
Section 739 Taxation of unit holders in undertakings for collective investment.
Schedule 18A Restriction on Set-off of Pre-entry Losses

79 Foreign currency: computation of income and chargeable gains

[CTA76 s12A; FA94 s56(a); FA96 s45(1)]

(1) (a) In this section—

"*profit and loss account*" means—

(i) in the case of a company (in this definition referred to as the "*resident company*") resident in the State, the account of that company, and

(ii) in the case of a company (in this definition referred to as the "*non-resident company*") not resident in the State but carrying on a trade in the State through a branch or agency, the account of the business of the company carried on through or from such branch or agency,

which, in the opinion of the auditor appointed under section 160 of the Companies Act, 1963, or under the law of the State in which the resident company or non-resident company, as the case may be, is incorporated and which corresponds to that section, presents a true and fair view of the profit or loss of the resident company or the business of the non-resident company, as the case may be;

"*rate of exchange*" means a rate at which 2 currencies might reasonably be expected to be exchanged for each other by persons dealing at arm's length or, where the context so requires, an average of such rates;

"*relevant contract*", in relation to a company, means any contract entered into by the company for the purpose of eliminating or reducing the risk of loss being incurred by the company due to a change in the value of a relevant monetary item, being a change resulting directly from a change in a rate of exchange;

"*relevant monetary item*", in relation to a company, means money held or payable by the company for the purposes of a trade carried on by it;

"*relevant tax contract*", in relation to an accounting period of a company, means any contract entered into by the company for the purpose of eliminating or reducing the risk of loss being incurred by the company due to a change in the value of money payable in discharge of a liability of the company to corporation tax for the accounting period, being a change resulting directly from a change in a rate of exchange of the functional currency (within the meaning of *section 402*) of the company for the currency of the State.

(b) The treatment of a contract entered into by a company as a relevant contract for the purposes of this section shall be disregarded for any other purpose of the Tax Acts.

[(c) For the purposes of this section a gain or loss arising to a company which results directly from a change in a rate of exchange shall include a gain or loss which results directly from an event which substitutes for the currency of a State another currency of that State where the other currency, as a result of the event, becomes the functional currency (within the meaning of *section 402*) of the company.][1]

(2) Notwithstanding *section 76*, for the purposes of corporation tax, the amount of any gain or loss, whether realised or unrealised, which—

(a) is attributable to any relevant monetary item or relevant contract of a company,

(b) results directly from a change in a rate of exchange, and

(c) is properly credited or debited, as the case may be, to the profit and loss account of the company,

shall be taken into account in computing the trading income of the company.

(3) (a) Notwithstanding *section 78*, for the purposes of corporation tax, where any gain or loss arises to a company in respect of—

(i) a relevant contract of the company, or

(ii) money held by the company for the purposes of a trade carried on by it,

so much of that gain or loss as results directly from a change in a rate of exchange shall not be a chargeable gain or an allowable loss, as the case may be, of the company.

(b) This subsection shall not apply as respects any gain or loss arising to a company carrying on life business within the meaning of *section 706(1)*, being a company which is not charged to corporation tax in respect of that business under Case I of Schedule D.

(4) Notwithstanding *section 78*, so much of the amount of any gain or loss arising to a company which carries on a trade in the State in an accounting period as—

(a) is attributable to any relevant tax contract in relation to the accounting period,

(b) results directly from a change in a rate of exchange, and

(c) (i) where it is a gain, does not exceed the amount of the loss which, if the company had not entered into the relevant tax contract, would have been incurred by the company, and

(ii) where it is a loss, does not exceed the amount of the gain which, if the company had not entered into the relevant tax contract, would have arisen to the company,

due to a change in the value of money payable in discharge of a liability of the company to corporation tax for the accounting period,

shall not be a chargeable gain or an allowable loss, as the case may be, of the company.

Amendments

[1] Inserted by FA98 sched2(1). With effect from 31 December 1998 per S.I. 502 of 1998.

Case Law

Foreign currency translation was considered in Pattison v Marine Midland Ltd 1984 STC 10.

Revenue Briefings

Tax Briefing

Tax Briefing April 1998 – Issue 31 pg 6 – Exchange Gains and Losses in Trading Companies

Cross References

From Section 79

Section 76 Computation of income: application of income tax principles.
Section 78 Computation of companies' chargeable gains.
Section 402 Foreign currency: tax treatment of capital allowances and trading losses of a company.
Section 706 Interpretation and general (Part 26).

To Section 79

Section 79A Matching of relevant foreign currency assets with foreign currency liabilities.
Section 79B Matching of foreign currency assets with certain foreign currency share capital.
Section 247 Relief to companies on loans applied in acquiring interest in other companies.
Section 402 Foreign currency: tax treatment of capital allowances and trading losses of a company.
Section 697C Calculation of profits of tonnage tax company.
Section 697J Relevant shipping income: foreign currency gains.
Section 697LB Treatment of finance costs.

79A Matching of relevant foreign currency assets with foreign currency liabilities

[(1) (a) In this section—

"*foreign currency asset*", in relation to a company, means an asset, not being a relevant monetary item (within the meaning of *section 79*), of the company the consideration for the acquisition of which consisted solely of an amount denominated in a currency other than the currency of the State;

"*foreign currency liability*", in relation to a company, means—

(i) a liability, not being a relevant monetary item (within the meaning of *section 79*), or

(ii) a sum subscribed for paid-up share capital or contributed to the capital,

of the company which is denominated in a currency other than the currency of the State;

"*rate of exchange*" has the meaning assigned to it by *section 79*.

(b) For the purposes of this section—

(i) a foreign currency asset is a relevant foreign currency asset in relation to a company if it consists of shares in another company acquired by the company and immediately after the acquisition by the company of the shares in the other company—

(I) the company owns not less than 25 per cent of the share capital of the other company, and

(II) the other company is a trading company or a holding company of a trading company,

(ii) where at any time a company disposes of a relevant foreign currency asset which has been matched with a corresponding foreign currency liability and the company does not discharge the liability at that time, the company shall be deemed to discharge the liability, and to incur a new liability equal to the amount of the liability, at that time,

(iii) where in accordance with *subsection (2)* a company specifies that a relevant foreign currency asset acquired by it at any time is to be matched with a corresponding foreign currency liability incurred by it before that time, the company shall be deemed to discharge the foreign currency liability, and to incur a new liability equal to the amount of the liability, at that time, and

(iv) the amount of a gain or loss on the discharge of a foreign currency liability shall be the amount which would be the gain accruing to, or as the case may be the loss incurred by, the company on the disposal of an asset acquired by it at the time the liability was incurred and disposed of at the time at which the liability was discharged if—

(I) the amount given by the company to discharge the liability was the amount given by the company as consideration for the acquisition of the asset, and

(II) the amount of the liability incurred by the company was the consideration received by the company on the disposal of the asset.

(2) (a) A company may, by giving notice in writing to the inspector, specify that a relevant foreign currency asset denominated in a currency other than the currency of the State shall be matched with such corresponding foreign currency liability denominated in that currency as is specified by the company.

(b) A notice under *paragraph (a)* shall be given within 3 weeks after the acquisition by the company concerned of the relevant foreign currency asset.

(3) Where in an accounting period a company disposes of a relevant foreign currency asset which has been matched by the company under *subsection (2)* with a foreign currency liability of the company, any chargeable gain or allowable loss on the relevant foreign currency asset shall be computed for the purposes of capital gains tax as if the consideration received for the disposal of the asset—

(a) where the company incurs a loss on discharge of the liability which loss results directly from a change in a rate of exchange, were reduced by an amount equal to the amount of that loss, but the amount of any such reduction shall not exceed the amount of so much of any gain on the disposal of the asset as results directly from a change in a rate of exchange, and

(b) where the company realises a gain on discharge of the liability which gain results directly from a change in a rate of exchange, were increased by an amount equal to the amount of that gain, but the amount of any such increase shall not exceed the amount of so much of any loss incurred on the disposal of the asset which loss results directly from a change in a rate of exchange.][1]

Amendments

[1] Inserted by FA03 s37(1). This section applies as respects accounting periods ending on or after 6 February 2003.

Cross References

From Section 79A

Section 79 Foreign currency: computation of income and chargeable gains.

79B Matching of foreign currency assets with certain foreign currency share capital

[(1) (a) In this section—

"*foreign currency asset*", in relation to a company, means an asset of the company—

(i) the consideration for the acquisition of which consisted solely of an amount denominated in a currency other than the [functional currency of the company][1], and

(ii) any gain on the disposal of which would be taken into account in computing income of the company chargeable to tax under Case I of Schedule D;

["*functional currency*" has the same meaning as in *section 402*;][2]

"*relevant foreign currency liability*", in relation to a company, means a liability, not being a relevant monetary item (within the meaning of *section 79*) which arises from a sum subscribed for paid-up redeemable share capital of the company which is denominated in a currency other than the [functional currency of the company][3];

"*rate of exchange*" has the meaning assigned to it by *section 79*.

(b) For the purposes of this section—

(i) where at any time a company disposes of a foreign currency asset which has been matched with a corresponding relevant foreign currency liability and the company does not discharge the liability at that time, the company shall be deemed to discharge the liability, and to incur a new liability equal to the amount of the liability, at that time,

(ii) where in accordance with *subsection (2)* a company specifies that a foreign currency asset acquired by it at any time is to be matched with a corresponding relevant foreign currency liability incurred by it before that time, the company shall be deemed to discharge the foreign currency liability, and to incur a new liability equal to the amount of the liability, at that time, and

(iii) the amount of a gain or loss on the discharge of a relevant foreign currency liability shall be the amount which would be the gain accruing to, or as the case may be the loss incurred by, the company on the disposal of an asset acquired by it at the time the liability was incurred and disposed of at the time at which the liability was discharged if—

(I) the amount given by the company to discharge the liability was the amount given by the company as consideration for the acquisition of the asset, and

(II) the amount of the liability incurred by the company was the consideration received by the company on the disposal of the asset.

(2) (a) A company may, by giving notice in writing to the inspector, specify that a foreign currency asset denominated in a currency other than the [functional currency of the company][4] shall be matched with such corresponding relevant foreign currency liability denominated in that currency as is specified by the company.

(b) A notice under *paragraph (a)* shall be given within 3 weeks after the acquisition by the company concerned of the foreign currency asset.

(3) [Where, in relation to an accounting period of a company, a foreign currency asset][5] has been matched by the company under *subsection (2)* with a relevant foreign currency liability of the company, then any gain or loss, whether realised or unrealised, on the relevant foreign currency liability shall be taken into account in computing the trading income of the company [for that accounting period][6].][7]

Amendments

[1] Substituted by FA07 s49(1)(a)(i). This section is deemed to have applied as on and from 1 January 2006.

[2] Inserted by FA07 s49(1)(a)(ii). This section is deemed to have applied as on and from 1 January 2006.

[3] Substituted by FA07 s49(1)(a)(iii). This section is deemed to have applied as on and from 1 January 2006.

[4] Substituted by FA07 s49(1)(b). This section is deemed to have applied as on and from 1 January 2006.

[5] Substituted by FA07 s49(1)(c)(i). This section is deemed to have applied as on and from 1 January 2006.

[6] Inserted by FA07 s49(1)(c)(ii). This section is deemed to have applied as on and from 1 January 2006.

[7] Inserted by FA06 s62(1).

Revenue Briefings

eBrief

eBrief No. 47/2006 – Section 79B Taxes Consolidation Act 1997 – matching a foreign currency asset with redeemable share capital denominated in the same currency.

Cross References

From Section 79B

Section 79 Foreign currency: computation of income and chargeable gains.

Section 402 Foreign currency: tax treatment of capital allowances and trading losses of a company.

79C Exclusion of foreign currency as asset of certain companies

[(1) In this section—

'*approved accounting standards*' means standards which are in accordance with generally accepted accounting principles in the State or in accordance with International Financial Reporting Standards (as promulgated by the International Accounting Standards Board);

'*net foreign exchange gain*' means the excess of foreign exchange gains over foreign exchange losses arising on the disposal of currency in a relevant bank deposit by a relevant holding company, but does not include such gains and losses which are chargeable to corporation tax under Case I of Schedule D;

'*net foreign exchange loss*' means the excess of foreign exchange losses over foreign exchange gains arising on the disposal of currency in a relevant bank deposit by a relevant holding company, but does not include such gains and losses which are chargeable to corporation tax under Case I of Schedule D;

'*profit and loss account*' has the same meaning as in *section 81C*;

'*relevant bank deposit*' means a sum standing to the credit of a relevant holding company in a bank and which is not [the currency of the State][2];

'*relevant holding company*' means a company—

(a) with at least one wholly-owned subsidiary and that subsidiary derives the greater part of its income from trading activities, or

(b) which acquires or sets up, within one year of a net foreign exchange gain being credited to its accounts, a wholly-owned subsidiary which derives the greater part of its income from trading activities.

(2) Currency in a relevant bank deposit shall not be an asset to which *section 532* applies.

[(3) An amount determined by the formula—

$$\frac{A \times C}{B}$$

where—

A is the net foreign exchange gain which is credited in the profit and loss account of a relevant holding company, as reduced by so much of any loss under *section 383* as is attributable to a net foreign exchange loss and which has not been deducted from any other amount of income,

B is the rate referred to in *section 21A(3)(a)*, and

C is the rate referred to in *section 28(3)*,

shall be income chargeable under Case IV of Schedule D.][3]

(4) This section shall not apply unless the accounts are drawn up in accordance with approved accounting standards.

(5) An allowable loss under *section 546* which is unused at the date this section comes into effect and which has arisen, or would have arisen, on the disposal of currency in a relevant bank deposit of a relevant holding company may be treated as an unused loss, at the same date, under *section 383*.

(6) An allowable loss under *section 546* to which *subsection (5)* applies may qualify for relief under *section 383* or *546*, but may not qualify for relief under both those provisions.][1]

Amendments

[1] Inserted by FA12 s65(1). Applies as respects accounting periods ending on or after 1 January 2012.

[2] Substituted by FA13 s27(1)(a). Applies in respect of accounting periods ending on or after 1 January 2013.

[3] Substituted by FA13 s27(1)(b). Applies in respect of accounting periods ending on or after 1 January 2013.

Revenue Briefings

Tax Briefing

Tax Briefing February 2014 – Issue 01 – Section 79C – Computation of amount to be brought into charge where there is a change in the rate of Capital Gains Tax during an accounting period

80 Taxation of certain foreign currencies

[FA93 s47(1) and (2)]

(1) In this section—

"*relevant liability*", in relation to an accounting period, means relevant principal—

(a) denominated in a currency other than the currency of the State, and

(b) the interest in respect of which—

(i) is to be treated as a distribution for the purposes of the Corporation Tax Acts, and

(ii) is computed on the basis of a rate which, at any time in that accounting period, exceeds 80 per cent of the specified rate at that time;

"*relevant principal*" means an amount of money advanced to a borrower by a company, the ordinary trading activities of which include the lending of money, where—

(a) the consideration given by the borrower for that amount is a security within *subparagraph (ii), (iii)(I)* or *(v)* of *section 130(2)(d)*, and

(b) interest or any other distribution is paid out of the assets of the borrower in respect of that security;

"*specified rate*" means—

[(a) the rate known as the 3 month European Interbank Offered Rate, or][1]

(b) where such a record was not maintained, the rate known as the Interbank market 3 month fixed rate as published in the statistical appendices of the bulletins and annual reports of the Central Bank of Ireland.

(2) Notwithstanding any other provision of the Tax Acts or the Capital Gains Tax Acts, a profit or loss from any foreign exchange transaction, being a profit or loss which arises in an accounting period—

(a) in connection with relevant principal which, in relation to the accounting period, is a relevant liability, and

(b) to a company which, in relation to that relevant liability, is the borrower,

shall for the purposes of those Acts be deemed to be a profit or gain or a loss, as the case may be, of the trade carried on by the borrower in the course of which trade the relevant liability is used.

Amendments

[1] Substituted by FA98 sched2(2). With effect from 1 January 1999 per S.I. 502 of 1998.

Cross References

From Section 80

Section 130 Matters to be treated as distributions.

To Section 80

Section 443 Meaning of "goods".

80A Taxation of certain short-term leases plant and machinery

[(1) In this section—

"*asset*" means machinery or plant;

"*fair value*", in relation to a leased asset, means an amount equal to such consideration as might be expected to be paid for the asset at the inception of the lease on a sale negotiated on an arm's length basis, less any grants receivable by the lessor towards the purchase of the asset;

["*group limit*" means an amount determined by the formula—

$$A + (B \times (C - D)/C)$$

where—

A is the threshold amount,

B is an aggregate amount computed in accordance with generally accepted accounting practice charged to the profit and loss account for all companies who are members of the group for the period of account which is the same as the specified period in respect of the amortisation or impairment of the cost of specified assets,

C is the cost of specified assets owned by all companies who are members of the group at the end of the specified period, and

D is the lesser of the cost of specified assets owned by all companies who are members of the group at the end of the threshold period or C;][1]

"*inception of the lease*" means the date on which the leased asset is brought into use by the lessee or the date from which lease payments under the lease first accrue, whichever is the earlier;

"*lease payments*" means the lease payments over the term of the lease to be paid to the lessor in relation to the leased asset, and includes any residual amount to be paid to the lessor at or after the end of the term of the lease and guaranteed by the lessee or by a person connected with the lessee or under the terms of any scheme or arrangement between the lessee and any other person;

"*lessee*" and "*lessor*" have the same meanings, respectively, as in *section 403*;

"*normal accounting practice*" means normal accounting practice in relation to the accounts of companies incorporated in the State;

"*predictable useful life*", in relation to an asset, means the useful life of the asset estimated at the inception of the lease, having regard to the purpose for which the asset was acquired and on the assumption that—

(a) its life will end when it ceases to be useful for the purpose for which it was acquired, and

(b) it will be used in the normal manner and to the normal extent throughout its life;

["*profit and loss account*", in relation to an accounting period of a company, has the meaning assigned to it by generally accepted accounting practice and includes an income and expenditure account where a company prepares accounts in accordance with international accounting standards;][2]

"*relevant period*" means the period—

(a) beginning at the inception of the lease, and

(b) ending at the earliest time at which the aggregate of amounts of the discounted present value at the inception of the lease of lease payments under the terms of the lease which are payable at or before that time amounts to 90 per cent or more of the fair value of the leased asset, and, for the purposes of this definition, relevant lease payments shall be discounted at a rate which, when applied at the inception of the lease to the amount of the relevant lease payments, produces discounted present values the aggregate of which equals the amount of the fair value of the leased asset at the inception of the lease;

"*relevant short-term asset*" in relation to a company means an asset—

(a) the predictable useful life of which does not exceed 8 years, and

(b) the expenditure on which is incurred by the company on or after the date referred to in *subsection (3)*;

"*relevant short-term lease*" means a lease—

(a) of a relevant short-term asset, and

(b) the relevant period in relation to which does not exceed [8 years;][3]

["*specified assets*" means [assets the predictable useful life of which does not exceed 8 years and which are][4] owned by a company which—

(a) in respect of those assets, is entitled to any allowance under *Part 9*, *section 670*, *Part 29* or any other provision of the Tax Acts relating to the making of allowances in accordance with *Part 9*, and

(b) leases those assets, other than by means of a relevant short-term lease, for a period which does not exceed 8 years;

"*specified period*" means—

(a) in the case of companies which are members of a group the respective ends of the accounting periods of which coincide, the period of 12 months throughout which one or more members of the group carries on a trade of leasing specified assets and ending at the end of the first accounting period which commences on or after 1 January 2010, and

(b) in the case of companies which are members of a group the respective ends of the accounting periods of which do not coincide, the period specified in a notice in writing made jointly by companies which are members of the group and given to the inspector on or before the specified return date for the chargeable period (within the meaning of [*section 959A*][5]) which is the same as the period so specified, being a period of 12 months throughout which one or more members of the group carries on a trade of leasing specified assets and ending at the end of the first accounting period of a company which is a member of the group which accounting period commences on or after 1 January 2010,

and each subsequent period of 12 months commencing immediately after the end of the relevant preceding specified period;

"*threshold amount*" in relation to a group of companies means the aggregate of allowances granted to all companies which are members of that group in respect of expenditure incurred on specified assets under *Part 9*, *section 670*, *Part 29* or any other provision of the Tax Acts relating to the making of allowances in accordance with *Part 9* for the threshold period;

"*threshold period*" in relation to a group of companies means an accounting period of one year ending on a date immediately preceding the date on which the first specified period commencing on or after 1 January 2010 begins.][6]

(2) Where a company makes a claim [under this subsection—][7]

(a) the amount to be included in the trading income of the company in respect of all relevant short-term leases is the amount of income from such leases computed in accordance with normal accounting practice,

(b) the company will not be entitled to any allowance in respect of expenditure incurred on assets which are the subject of relevant short-term leases under *Part 9*, *section 670*, *Part 29* or any other provision of the Tax Acts relating to the making of allowances in accordance with *Part 9*, and

(c) the income from relevant short-term leases will be treated for the purposes of *section 403* as if it were not income from a trade of leasing.

[(2A) Where a company makes a claim under this subsection in respect of specified assets—

(a) subject to *paragraph (c)*, *subsection (2)* of *section 284* shall be construed as if a reference in that section to an amount of wear and tear allowance to be made was a reference to an amount, computed in accordance with generally accepted accounting practice, charged to the profit and loss account of the company for the period of account which is the same as the specified period in respect of the amortisation or impairment of the cost of specified assets,

(b) the income from specified assets will be treated for the purposes of *section 403* as if it were not income from a trade of leasing,

(c) [for specified periods ending on or before 31 December 2014,][8] the amount of the wear and tear allowance to be made to the company in accordance with *paragraph (a)* for any accounting period shall not exceed an amount to be determined by the formula—

$$E \times F/G$$

where—

E is the group limit,

F is the cost of specified assets owned by the company at the end of the accounting period, and

G is the cost of specified assets owned by all companies who are members of the group, at the end of the accounting period,

(d) where the amount of wear and tear allowance, computed in accordance with generally accepted accounting practice, charged to the profit and loss account of the company for the period of account which is the same as the specified period in respect of the amortisation or impairment of the cost of specified assets, exceeds the amount of wear and tear to be made in accordance with *paragraph (c)*, the amount of the excess shall be added to the amount of wear and tear due, in accordance with *paragraph (a)*, for the following specified period, and deemed to be part of the amount so computed,

(e) the amount of the wear and tear allowance to be made to the company in accordance with *paragraph (a)*, attributable to each specified asset for any accounting period shall be such portion of the amount of the allowance to be made in accordance with *paragraph (a)* as bears to that amount the same proportion as the cost of the asset bears to the cost of all specified assets which belong to the company and are in use for the purposes of the trade at the end of that accounting period,

(f) where in respect of a company, which is a member of a group of companies no accounting period coincides with the threshold period, there shall be made in relation to allowances granted to that company, in the calculation of the threshold amount, such apportionment as is just and [reasonable][9],

(g) where, in respect of a group of companies, no specified period commences before 1 January 2011, the threshold amount shall be [nil, and][10].

[(h) for any specified period ending on or after 1 January 2015, the amount of the wear and tear allowance to be made to the company in accordance with *paragraph (a)* shall not exceed the amount of amortisation or impairment charged to the profit and loss account in that specified period.][11]

(2B) For the purposes of a claim under *subsection (2A)*—

(a) 2 companies shall be deemed to be members of a group if one company is a 51 per cent subsidiary of the other company or both companies are 51 per cent subsidiaries of a third company: but in determining whether one company is a 51 per cent subsidiary of another company, the other company shall be treated as not being the owner of—

(i) any share capital which it owns directly in a company if a profit on a sale of the shares would be treated as a trading receipt of its trade, or

(ii) any share capital which it owns indirectly and which is owned directly by a company for which a profit on a sale of the shares would be a trading receipt;

(b) *sections 412* to *418* shall apply for the purposes of this subsection as they would apply for the purposes of *Chapter 5* of *Part 12* if—

(i) "51 per cent subsidiary" were substituted for "75 per cent subsidiary" in each place where it occurs in that Chapter, and

(ii) *paragraph (c)* of *section 411(1)* were deleted;

(c) a company and all its 51 per cent subsidiaries shall form a group and, where that company is a member of a group as being itself a 51 per cent subsidiary, that group shall comprise all its 51 per cent subsidiaries and the first-mentioned group shall be deemed not to be a group: but a company which is not a member of a group shall be treated as if it were a member of a group which consists of that company;

(d) in determining whether a company is a member of a group of companies (in this paragraph referred to as the "*threshold group*") for the purposes of determining the threshold amount in relation to a specified period of a group of companies (in this paragraph referred to as the "*relevant group*"), the threshold group shall be treated as the same group as the relevant group notwithstanding that one or more of the companies in the threshold group is not in the relevant group, or vice versa, where any person or group of persons which controlled the threshold group is the same as, or has a reasonable commonality of identity with, the person or group of persons which controls the relevant group.][12]

(3) A claim by a company under this section shall be made by the time by which a return under [*Chapter 3 of Part 41A*][13] falls to be made for an accounting period of the company and shall apply as respects expenditure incurred on or after the date on which the accounting period begins.][14]

Amendments

[1] Inserted by FA10 s52(1)(a). Applies as respects accounting periods commencing on or after 1 January 2010.

[2] Inserted by FA10 s52(1)(b). Applies as respects accounting periods commencing on or after 1 January 2010.

[3] Substituted by FA10 s52(1)(c). Applies as respects accounting periods commencing on or after 1 January 2010.

[4] Substituted by FA12 s40(1). Applies as respects accounting periods commencing on or after 1 January 2012.

[5] Substituted by FA12 sched4(part 2)(g).

[6] Inserted by FA10 s52(1)(d). Applies as respects accounting periods commencing on or after 1 January 2010.

[7] Substituted by FA10 s52(1)(e). Applies as respects accounting periods commencing on or after 1 January 2010.

[8] Inserted by FA14 s36(a). Comes into operation on 1 January 2015.

[9] Substituted by FA14 s36(b). Comes into operation on 1 January 2015.

[10] Substituted by FA14 s36(c). Comes into operation on 1 January 2015.

[11] Inserted by FA14 s36(d). Comes into operation on 1 January 2015.

[12] Inserted by FA10 s52(1)(f). Applies as respects accounting periods commencing on or after 1 January 2010.

[13] Substituted by FA12 sched4(part 2)(g).

[14] Inserted by FA04 s35(1). This section applies as respects accounting periods ending on or after 4 February, 2004.

Revenue Briefings

Tax Briefing

Tax Briefing April 2004 – Issue 55 pg 7 – Short Term Leases of Plant and Machinery

Cross References

From Section 80A

Section 268 Meaning of "industrial building or structure".
Section 284 Wear and tear allowances.
Section 320 Other interpretation (Part 9).
Section 381 Right to repayment of tax by reference to losses.
Section 403 Restriction on use of capital allowances for certain leased assets.
Section 410 Group payments.
Section 411 Surrender of relief between members of groups and consortia.
Section 412 Qualification for entitlement to group relief.
Section 418 Beneficial percentage.
Section 670 Mine development allowance.
Section 754 Interpretation (Chapter 1).
Section 950 Interpretation (Part 41).
Section 951 Obligation to make a return.

To Section 80A

Section 76D Computation of income from finance leases.
Section 299 Allowances to lessees.

CHAPTER 6

Computational Provisions: General

81 General rule as to deductions

[ITA67 s57 and s61; FA69 s 65(1) and Sch 5 PtI; FA74 s42(1); FA97 s146(1) and Sch9 PtI par1(3)]

(1) The tax under Cases I and II of Schedule D shall be charged without any deduction other than is allowed by the Tax Acts.

(2) Subject to the Tax Acts, in computing the amount of the profits or gains to be charged to tax under Case I or II of Schedule D, no sum shall be deducted in respect of—

(a) any disbursement or expenses, not being money wholly and exclusively laid out or expended for the purposes of the trade or profession;

(b) any disbursements or expenses of maintenance of the parties, their families or establishments, or any sums expended for any other domestic or private purposes distinct from the purposes of such trade or profession;

(c) the rent of any dwelling house or domestic offices or any part of any dwelling house or domestic offices, except such part thereof as is used for the purposes of the trade or profession, and, where any such part is so used, the sum so deducted shall be such as may be determined by the inspector and shall not, unless in any particular case the inspector is of the opinion that having regard to all the circumstances some greater sum ought to be deducted, exceed two-thirds of the rent bona fide paid for that dwelling house or those domestic offices;

(d) any sum expended for repairs of premises occupied, or for the supply, repairs or alterations of any implements, utensils or articles employed, for the purposes of the trade or profession, over and above the sum actually expended for those purposes;

(e) any loss not connected with or arising out of the trade or profession;

(f) any capital withdrawn from, or any sum employed or intended to be employed as capital in, the trade or profession;

(g) any capital employed in improvements of premises occupied for the purposes of the trade or profession;

(h) any interest which might have been made if any such sums as aforesaid had been laid out at interest;

(i) any debts, except bad debts proved to be such to the satisfaction of the inspector and doubtful debts to the extent that they are respectively estimated to be bad and, in the case of the bankruptcy or insolvency of a debtor, the amount which may reasonably be expected to be received on any such debts shall be deemed to be the value of any such debts;

(j) any average loss over and above the actual amount of loss after adjustment;

(k) any sum recoverable under an insurance or contract of indemnity;

(l) any annuity or other annual payment (other than interest) payable out of the profits or gains;

(m) any royalty or other sum paid in respect of the user of a [[patent;][1]][2]

[(n) without prejudice to the preceding paragraphs any consideration given for goods or services, or to an employee or director of a company, which consists, directly or indirectly, of shares in the company, or a connected company (within the meaning of *section 10*), or a right to receive such shares, except to the extent—

(i) of expenditure incurred by the company on the acquisition of the shares at a price which does not exceed the price which would have been payable, if the shares were acquired by way of a bargain made at arm's length, […][3]

(ii) where the shares are shares in a connected company, of any payment by the company to the connected company for the issue or transfer by that company of the shares, being a payment which does not exceed the amount which would have been payable in a transaction between independent persons acting at arm's [length, or][4]][5]][6]

[(iii) of other—

(I) expenditure incurred, or

(II) payment made to the connected company,

by the company in connection with the right to receive such shares which is incurred or, as the case may be, made for *bona fide* commercial purposes and does not form part of any scheme or arrangement of which the main purpose or one of the main purposes is the avoidance of liability to income tax, corporation tax or [capital gains tax;][7]

[(o) any sum paid or payable under any agreement or understanding whereby a person is obliged to make a payment to a connected person resident in any territory outside the State for an adjustment made, or to be made, to the profits of the connected person for which relief may be afforded under the terms of an arrangement entered into by virtue of *subsection (1)* or *(1B)* of *section 826*, or for a similar adjustment made to the profits of a connected person resident in [a territory in respect of which there are not for the time being in force any arrangements providing for such relief.][8]][9][10]

[(3) (a) In respect of a company—

(i) interest payable by the company, and

(ii) expenditure on research and development incurred by the company,

shall not be prevented from being regarded for tax purposes as deductible in computing profits or gains of the company for the purposes of Case I or II of Schedule D by virtue only of the fact that for accounting purposes they are brought into account in determining the value of an asset.

(b) Any amount shall not be regarded by virtue of *paragraph (a)* as deductible in computing profits or gains of a company for the purposes of Case I or II of Schedule D for an accounting period to the extent that—

(i) a deduction has been made in respect of that amount in computing such profits or gains for a previous accounting period, or

(ii) the company has benefited from a tax relief under any provision in respect of that amount for a previous accounting period.][11]

Amendments

[1, 2, 5, 6] Substituted by FA05 s48(1)(c)(i). This section applies as respects any period of account beginning on or after 1 January 2005.

[3] Deleted by FA07 s37(1)(a). Applies as respects accounting periods ending on or after 1 February 2007.

[4] Substituted by FA07 s37(1)(a). Applies as respects accounting periods ending on or after 1 February 2007.

[7] Substituted by F(No.2)A08 s23(1). Applies in respect of any sum paid or payable in an accounting period ending on or after 20 November 2008, or in a basis period for a year of assessment where that basis period ends on or after 20 November 2008.

[8] Substituted by FA10 sched(4)(1)(a). Has effect as on and from 3 April 2010.

[9] Inserted by F(No.2)A08 s23(1). Applies in respect of any sum paid or payable in an accounting period ending on or after 20 November 2008, or in a basis period for a year of assessment where that basis period ends on or after 20 November 2008.

[10] Inserted by FA07 s37(1)(b). Applies as respects accounting periods ending on or after 1 February 2007.

[11] Inserted by FA05 s48(1)(c)(ii). This section applies as respects any period of account beginning on or after 1 January 2005.

Case Law

Expenses must be incurred before they can be deducted. Naval Colliery Co Ltd v IRC 1928 12 TC 1017

In Herbert Smith v Honour 1999 STC 173 the taxpayer was entitled to a deduction for a provision of future rental payments in respect of business premises which had become surplus to requirements.

The distinction between expenses and losses was discussed in Allen v Farquharson Bros & Co 1932 17 TC 59.

For the Purpose of the Trade

A bad debt arising on advances made by the taxpayer to its supplier, to ensure continuity of supplies, held not incurred for the purpose of its trade. English Crown Spelter Co Ltd v Baker 1908 5 TC 327.

"Wholly and Exclusively"

In Mallalieu v Drummond 1983 STC 665 the taxpayer was a practicing lady barrister who bought black clothing for her court appearances in conformity with the Bar Council's guidance notes on dress. She claimed the cost of replacing and laundering her court clothes. The Court held that the taxpayer's object was both to serve the purpose of her profession and also to serve her personal purposes.

In Murgatroyd v Evans Jackson 1966 43 TC 581 the taxpayer conducted his business from his hospital room. The taxpayer's claim for 60 per cent of the hospital charges as a business expense was rejected.

Regular annual subscriptions to a local hospital were allowed. Bourne & Hollingsworth Ltd v Ogden 1929 14 TC 349

In Norman v Golder 1944 25 TC 293 the taxpayer was a self-employed shorthand writer who claimed medical costs. The Court rejected his claim.

In Morgan v Tate & Lyle Ltd 1954 35 TC 367, the taxpayer claimed the costs of a campaign to prevent the confiscation of its entire trade under a proposed programme of nationalisation. The Revenue's argument that the expenditure was incurred by the taxpayer in the capacity as 'owner' rather than as 'trader' was rejected by the House of Lords.

The cost of insuring against workmen's compensation claims was held to be allowable since it served to mitigate a potential future expense. Thomas v R Evans & Co Ltd 11 TC 790

Capital or Revenue Expenditure?

The cost of forming a new holding company was held to be capital in Kealy v O'Mara 1942 1 ITR 642

The costs associated with a corporate restructuring were held to be capital in Watney Combe Reid & Co Ltd v Pike 1982 STC 733

Expenditure designed to achieve a capital outcome remains capital in nature, even if that outcome is not actually achieved. Pyrah v Annis 37 TC 163

In Walker v Joint Credit Card Co 1982 STC 427 a lump sum payment to a competitor to cease trading permanently was held to be capital.

Costs incurred by an investment company in evaluating potential future investments were capital. Hibernian Insurance Company Ltd v MacUimis 2000 V ITR 495

Annual payment for goodwill of a cinema business was a revenue expenses. Ogden v Medway Cinemas 1934 18 TC 691

Supplementary pension contributions to a trust fund on behalf of certain employees were revenue in nature. Jeffs v Ringtons Ltd 1985 STC 809 However, in British Insulated & Helsby Cables Ltd v Atherton 1926 10 TC 155 a single lump sum paid to establish a pension fund was capital. Subsequent contributions to the fund were held to be revenue.

In Southern v Borax Consolidated 1940 23 TC 597 the taxpayer incurred legal costs in protecting its title to land and buildings used for the purpose of its trade. Such costs were held to be revenue.

Costs of promoting a bill in the Oireachtas, to empower a gas undertaking to compensate employees dismissed as a result of improved efficiency, were revenue in nature. McGarry v Limerick Gas Co 1 ITR 375

In IRC v Carron Co 45 TC 18, the costs of amending the terms of a company's charter, in order that it could trade more efficiently, were held to be revenue in nature.

Revenue Briefings

Tax Briefing

Tax Briefing July 1993 – Issue 11 pg 3 – Allowability of Keyman Insurance Premia

Tax Briefing December 1997 – Issue 29 pg 13 – Tax Treatment of Subscriptions to Trade and Professional Associations

Tax Briefing April 1998 – Issue 31 pg 18 – Tax Treatment of Interest Paid under the Prompt Payment of Accounts Act 1997

Tax Briefing April 1998 – Issue 31 pg 23 – Schedule D – Case I & II – Food and Subsistence Expenses

Tax Briefing September 2000 – Issue 41 pg 14 – Accounting Rules & Taxation FRS 12

Revenue Information Notes

IT 52 – Taxation Treatment of Finance Leases

Revenue Precedents

Whether a deduction due in respect of a provision for a loss on a court case? In principle there is no statutory rule against charging a provision for a liability which has not materialised at the accounts date, provided such a provision will result in the accounts providing a true and fair view of the profits of the period and the amount of the provision can be estimated with reasonable accuracy. Where the claim includes a claim for a return of fees already earned, this aspect should be dealt with in the same manner as the rest of the claim. IT972004A

Registration fees/licence renewal fees which are required by law to be paid by a trader or professional are deductible provided they are laid out wholly and exclusively for the purposes of the trade. IT891143

Are legal fees incurred in connection with the ownership of a business property deductible in arriving at trading profits? The allowability of legal expenditure will depend on whether it is attributable to Revenue or Capital. This matter has been considered in a number of tax cases and the main findings appear to be that legal expenses incurred in acquiring a capital asset are treated as capital expenditure, yet expenditure incurred in protecting the title to a capital asset, when it has been acquired, may be deductible revenue expenditure. The case of Southern v Borax Consolidated Ltd. 23 TC 597 is relevant. IT943501

If a trader, who offers a "free gift" to a customer who purchases certain items, entitled to a deduction for the cost of the "free gift" or is the cost disallowed under Section 840? e.g. a trader starts a sales promotion whereby the purchaser of a washing machine will receive a radio to the value of 20. It appears that in these circumstances the contract between the customer and the trader involves both the washing machine and the radio. In effect the radio is not a "free gift" and as such would not come within the provisions of Section 840. It is the Revenue view that the cost of each radio is allowable in computing the profits of the trade. IT943520

Professional fees incurred in connection with a tax appeal are not deductible. Normal recurring professional fees incurred in preparing accounts or agreeing liabilities are allowable. IT952564

Interest on a loan to finance the payment of income tax is not allowable. It is not wholly and exclusively laid out for the purposes of the trade. IT952561

Whether, in a trade or profession, interest paid on borrowings used to fund drawings is allowable? Where a capital account is in a debit position and the debit balance arises from an excess of drawings over profits available to fund those drawings, the interest portion of the bank borrowings used to fund the deficit is not allowable. IT962501

Can a partnership claim a deduction for rent paid in respect of premises which is owned by the individual partners in the firm? It appears that the lease involved between the partnership and the partners has no legal standing. The case of Rye-v-Rye 1962 A.C. 496 is relevant. The issue is currently the subject of an appeal, which has not yet been finalised. However, the foregoing continues to represent Revenue thinking in the issue. It is considered that the fact that partners may share partnership profits on a basis which differs from the basis on which that rent on the premises is paid to the various partners does not affect the issue. IT953545

Is the super levy penalty collected by Co-ops from farmers for exceeding their milk quota allowed as a charge against farming profits? It is accepted that payments by farmers under the European Communities (Milk Levy) Regulations, 1985 are an expense of the trade. IT903106

Taxpayer claiming relief for foreign exchange loss on five year loan obtained to purchase plant for use in the taxpayer's trade. The exchange losses arose in respect of the balance outstanding on the loan and were claimed as a deduction in calaulating the taxpayer's trading profit. The question at issue was whether the exchange losses were on capital account. This in turn depended on whether borrowings are a means of temporary and fluctuating accommodation. Effect of decision in Mutual Enterprises Ltd case. The Supreme Court decision in Mutual Enterprises held that the question of whether borrrowings are a means of temporary and fluctuating accommodation is a question of fact rather than law. Even though the Circuit Court judge in the particular circumstances of the case held that the borrowings were on revenue account, the dicta in the High Court indicate that the High Court judge would have attached significance to the fact that money was borrowed with the intention of purchasing a capital asset. Revenue's view is that borrowings to purchase a capital asset for use in a trade is indicative that the borrowings are on fixed capital account and that any exchange loss incurred in relation to the borrowings should not be deducted in arriving at the taxable profits of the trade. IT972000

Refunds of a percentage of fees paid by self employed practitioners to the Medical Protection Society are made by Health Boards. Tax relief on the gross fees is estimated by the boards when they are calculating the refunds. Do these refunds have to be taken into account when preparing accounts and on what amounts is tax relief due to the practitioners? Refunds of fees received must be taken into account.

As a result tax relief will be due on the net amount paid in each case i.e. the gross payment made less the actual refund received. IT953548

Amateur sportsmen in receipt of payments from media are chargeable to tax and payment should be included in returns. IT892043

A deduction is not allowable in respect of "protection money". IT972501

Whether insurance premiums and insurance claims paid by a compensation fund which is a trade protection association are allowable as deductions against income of the fund? Both insurance premiums and insurance claims are allowable deductions. IT972510

Whether unbilled disbursements on behalf of clients can be deducted in the period in which paid? Where there are unbilled disbursements, there is no known liability in the majority of cases. The presumption is that the disbursement will be billed to the client on whose behalf it was incurred. In so far as it cannot be so billed or the client refuses to pay it the amount can be written off at that stage. IT972004B

Cross References

From Section 81

Section 10 Connected persons.
Section 826 Agreements for relief from double taxation.

To Section 81

Section 86 Cost of registration of trade marks.
Section 91 Receipts accruing after discontinuance of trade or profession.
Section 92 Receipts and losses accruing after change treated as discontinuance.
Section 104 Taxation of certain rents and other payments.
Section 127 Tax treatment of restrictive covenants.
Section 176A Purchase of own shares — supplementary.
Section 267H Application (Chapter 6).
Section 697LB Treatment of finance costs.
Section 758 Relief for expenses.

81A Restriction of deductions for employee benefit contributions

[(1) (a) In this section—

"*accident benefit scheme*" means an employee benefit scheme under which benefits may be provided only by reason of a person's disablement, or death, caused by an accident occuring during the person's service as an employee of the employer;

"*chargeable period*" has the same meaning as in *section 321*;

"*employee benefit scheme*" means a trust, scheme or other arrangement for the benefit of persons who are employees of an employer;

["*qualifying expenses*", in relation to a scheme manager and an employee benefit scheme, does not include expenses that, if incurred by the employer, would not be allowed as a deduction in calculating the profits or gains of the employer to be charged to tax under Case I or II of Schedule D but, subject to the foregoing, includes any expenses of a scheme manager (apart from the provision of benefits to employees of the employer) incurred in the operation of the employee benefit scheme;

"*scheme manager*" means a person who administers an employee benefit scheme or any person to whom an employer pays money or transfers an asset and such person is entitled or required, under the provisions of an employee benefit scheme to retain or use the money or asset for or in connection with the provision of benefits to employees of the employer.][1]

(b) For the purposes of this section—

[(i) an employee benefit contribution is made if, as a result of any act or omission—

(I) any assets are held, or may be used, under an employee benefit scheme, or

(II) there is an increase in the total value of assets that are so held or may be so used (or a reduction in any liabilities under an employee benefit scheme),][2]

(ii) qualifying benefits are provided where there is a payment of money or a transfer of assets, otherwise than by way of a loan, and the recipient or a person other than the recipient is or would, if resident, ordinarily resident and domiciled in the State, be chargeable to income tax in respect of the provision of such benefits, and

(iii) a reference to a person's employee includes a reference to the holder of an office under that person.

(2) (a) This section applies where—

(i) a calculation is made of the amount of a person's profits or gains to be charged to tax under Case I or II of Schedule D for a chargeable period beginning on or after 3 February 2005, and

(ii) a deduction would, but for this section, be allowed by the Tax Acts for that period in respect of employee benefit contributions made, or to be made, by that person (referred to in this section as the "employer").

(b) Notwithstanding *paragraph (a)*, this section does not apply in respect of a deduction referred to in *subsection (7)*.

(3) (a) A deduction in respect of employee benefit contributions referred to in *subsection (2)(a)* shall be allowed only to the extent that, during the chargeable period in question or within 9 months from the end of it—

(i) qualifying benefits are provided out of the contributions, or

(ii) qualifying expenses are paid out of the contributions.

(b) (i) For the purposes of *paragraph (a)*, any qualifying benefits provided or qualifying expenses paid by [a scheme manager][3] after the receipt by [the scheme manager][4] of employee benefit contributions shall be regarded as being provided or paid out of those contributions, up to the total amount of the contributions as reduced by the amount of any benefits or expenses previously provided or paid as referred to in *paragraph (a)*.

(ii) In the application of this paragraph, no account shall be taken of any other amount received or paid by [the scheme manager][5].

(4) (a) An amount which is disallowed under *subsection (3)* shall be allowed as a deduction for a subsequent chargeable period to the extent that qualifying benefits are provided out of the employee benefit contributions in question before the end of that subsequent chargeable period.

(b) (i) For the purposes of *paragraph (a)*, any qualifying benefits provided by [a scheme manager][6] after the receipt by [the scheme manager][7] of employee benefit contributions shall be regarded as being provided out of those contributions, up to the total amount of the contributions as reduced by the amount of any benefits or expenses previously provided or paid as referred to in *subsection (3)(a)* or *paragraph (a)* of this subsection.

(ii) In the application of this paragraph, no account shall be taken of any other amount received or paid by [the scheme manager][8].

(5) (a) This subsection applies where the provision of a qualifying benefit takes the form of the transfer of an asset.

[(b) The amount provided shall be taken for the purposes of this section to be the total of—

(i) (I) the amount, if any, expended on the asset by a scheme manager, or

(II) where the asset consists of new shares in a company connected (within the meaning of *section 10*) with the employer, or rights in respect of such shares, issued by the connected company, the market value of those shares or rights, as the case may be, at the time of the transfer,

and

(ii) in a case in which the asset was transferred to a scheme manager by the employer, the amount of the deduction that would be allowed as referred to in *subsection (2)* in respect of the transfer.][9]

(c) Where the amount calculated in accordance with *paragraph (b)* is greater than the amount (referred to in this paragraph as the "second-mentioned amount") in respect of which an employee is chargeable to income tax in respect of the transfer, the deduction to be allowed in accordance with *subsection (3)* or *(4)* shall not exceed the second-mentioned amount.

(6) In any case where the calculation referred to in *subsection (2)(a)* is made before the end of the 9 month period mentioned in *subsection (3)*—

(a) for the purposes of making the calculation, *subsection (3)* shall be construed as if the reference to that 9 month period were a reference to the period ending at the time when the calculation is made, and

(b) after the end of the 9 month period the calculation shall if necessary be adjusted to take account of any benefits provided, expenses paid or contributions made within that period but after the time of the calculation.

(7) This section does not apply in relation to any deduction that is allowable—

(a) in respect of anything given as consideration for goods or services provided in the course of a trade or profession,

(b) in respect of contributions under an accident benefit scheme,

(c) under *Part 17*, or

(d) under *Part 30*.][10]

Amendments

[1] Substituted by FA08 s25(1)(a). Applies as respects employee benefit contributions made on or after 31 January 2008.

[2] Substituted by FA08 s25(1)(b). Applies as respects employee benefit contributions made on or after 31 January 2008.

[3, 4] Substituted by FA08 s25(1)(c). Applies as respects employee benefit contributions made on or after 31 January 2008.

[5] Substituted by FA08 s25(1)(d). Applies as respects employee benefit contributions made on or after 31 January 2008.

[6, 7] Substituted by FA08 s25(1)(e). Applies as respects employee benefit contributions made on or after 31 January 2008.

[8] Substituted by FA08 s25(1)(f). Applies as respects employee benefit contributions made on or after 31 January 2008.

[9] Substituted by FA08 s25(1)(g). Applies as respects employee benefit contributions made on or after 31 January 2008.

[10] Inserted by FA05 s17. Has effect from 3 February 2005.

Cross References

From Section 81A

Section 10 Connected persons.
Section 321 Provisions of general application in relation to the making of allowances and charges.
Section 509 Interpretation (Chapter 1).
Section 770 Interpretation and supplemental (Chapter 1).

81B Equalisation reserves for credit insurance and reinsurance business of companies

[(1) In this section—

["*credit insurance risks*" means risks included in class 14 of Section A of the Annex to the First Council Directive 73/239/EEC of 24 July 1973*;

*OJ No. L228, 16 August 1973, p.3.

"*Principal Regulations*" means the European Communities (Non-Life Insurance) Regulations 1976 (S.I. No. 115 of 1976) as amended from time to time;][1]

"*Reinsurance Regulations*" means the European Communities (Reinsurance) Regulations 2006 (S.I. No. 380 of 2006);

"*relevant rules*" means the rules as set out in point D, as inserted by Council Directive 87/343/EEC of 22 June 1987*, to the Annex to the First Council Directive 73/239/EEC of 24 July 1973†.

* OJ No. L185, 4 July 1987, p.72
† OJ No. L228, 16 August 1973, p.3

[(1A) This section applies to—

(a) an insurance company whose business has at any time been, or included, business in respect of which it was required, by virtue of Regulation 24 of the Reinsurance Regulations, to establish and maintain an equalisation reserve, or

(b) an insurance company which is underwriting credit insurance risks and which is required by Article 14(8) of the Principal Regulations to set up an equalisation reserve.][2]

[(2) Subject to the following provisions of this section, full account shall be taken of all amounts in accordance with the rules in *subsection (3)* in making any computation, for the purposes of Case I of Schedule D, of the profits or losses for any accounting period of an insurance company to which this section applies.][3]

(3) The rules specified in this subsection are—

(a) amounts which, in accordance with the relevant rules, are transferred into the equalisation reserve in respect of the company's business in a period are to be deductible in that period,

(b) amounts which, in accordance with the relevant rules, are transferred out of the reserve in respect of the company's business in a period are to be treated as receipts of that business in that period, and

(c) it shall be assumed that all such transfers as are required by the Reinsurance Regulations [or the Principal Regulations][4]to be made into or out of the reserve in respect of the company's business for any period are made as required.

(4) Where an insurance company having any business in respect of which it is required, by virtue of Regulation 24 of the Reinsurance Regulations [or Article 14(8) of the Principal Regulations][5], to maintain an equalisation reserve ceases to trade—

(a) any balance which exists in the reserve at that time for the purposes of the Corporation Tax Acts shall be deemed to have been transferred out of the reserve immediately before the company ceases to trade, and

(b) that transfer out shall be deemed to be a transfer in respect of the company's business for the accounting period in which the company ceases and to have been required by virtue of the Reinsurance Regulations [or the Principal Regulations][6].

(5) To the extent that any actual or assumed transfer in accordance with the Reinsurance Regulations [or the Principal Regulations][7] of any amount into an equalisation reserve is attributable to arrangements entered into wholly or mainly for tax purposes—

(a) *subsection (2)* shall not apply to that transfer, and

(b) the making of that transfer shall be disregarded in determining, for the purposes of the Tax Acts, whether and to what extent there is subsequently any requirement to make a transfer into or out of the reserve in accordance with the Reinsurance Regulations [or the Principal Regulations][8],

and this subsection applies irrespective of whether the insurance company in question is a party to the arrangements.

(6) For the purposes of this section, the transfer of an amount into an equalisation reserve is attributable to arrangements entered into wholly or mainly for tax purposes to the extent that the arrangements to which it is attributable are arrangements—

(a) the sole or main purpose of which is, or

(b) the sole or main benefit accruing from which might, apart from *subsection (7)*, be expected to be,

the reduction by virtue of this section of any liability to tax.

(7) Where—

(a) any transfer made into or out of an equalisation reserve maintained by an insurance company is made in accordance with the Reinsurance Regulations [or the Principal Regulations][9] in respect of business carried on by that company over a period (in this subsection referred to as the "*equalisation period*"), and

(b) parts of the equalisation period are in different accounting periods,

then the amount transferred shall be apportioned for the purposes of this section between the different accounting periods in the proportions that correspond to the number of days in the equalisation period that are included in each of those accounting periods.][10]

Amendments

[1] Inserted by F(No.2)A08 s24(1)(a). This section is deemed to have effect as on and from 15 July 2006.

[2] Inserted by F(No.2)A08 s24(1)(b). This section is deemed to have effect as on and from 15 July 2006.

[3] Substituted by F(No.2)A08 s24(1)(c). This section is deemed to have effect as on and from 15 July 2006.

[4] Inserted by F(No.2)A08 s24(1)(d). This section is deemed to have effect as on and from 15 July 2006.

[5] Inserted by F(No.2)A08 s24(1)(e)(i). This section is deemed to have effect as on and from 15 July 2006.

[6] Inserted by F(No.2)A08 s24(1)(e)(ii). This section is deemed to have effect as on and from 15 July 2006.

[7, 8] Inserted by F(No.2)A08 s24(1)(f). This section is deemed to have effect as on and from 15 July 2006.

[9] Inserted by F(No.2)A08 s24(1)(g). This section is deemed to have effect as on and from 15 July 2006.

[10] Inserted by FA08 s37(1). This section is deemed to have effect as and from 15 July 2006.

81C Emissions allowances

[(1) In this section—

'Directive' has the same meaning as in *section 540A*;

'emissions allowance' means—

(*a*) an allowance within the meaning of Article 3 of the Directive,

(*b*) an emission reduction unit or ERU, within the meaning of Article 3 of the Directive, or

(*c*) a certified emission reduction or CER, within the meaning of Article 3 of the Directive;

'profit and loss account', in relation to an accounting period of a company, has the meaning assigned to it by generally accepted accounting practice and includes an income and expenditure account where a company prepares accounts in accordance with international accounting standards.

(2) Notwithstanding anything in *section 81*, any amount, computed in accordance with generally accepted accounting practice, charged to the profit and loss account of a company, for the period of account which is the same as the accounting period, in respect of expenditure, for the purposes of a trade carried on by the company, on the purchase of an emissions allowance shall be allowed to be deducted as expenses in computing the amount of the profits or gains of the company to be charged to tax under Case I of *Schedule D* for the accounting period.

(3) Subject to *section 540A*, where a company disposes of an emissions allowance which it purchased for the purposes of a trade carried on by it, the consideration for such disposal shall be treated as a trading receipt of the trade.][1]

Amendments

[1] Inserted by FA12 s44(1)(a). Deemed to have come into force and takes effect on and from 1 January 2012.

Revenue Briefings

Tax Briefing

Tax Briefing July 2012 – Issue No. 03/12 – EU Emissions Trading Scheme

82 Pre-trading expenditure

[FA97 s29(1) and (4) to (6)]

(1) This section shall apply to expenditure incurred for the purposes of a trade or profession set up and commenced on or after the 22nd day of January, 1997.

(2) Subject to *subsection (3)*, where a person incurs expenditure for the purposes of a trade or profession before the time that the trade or profession has been set up and commenced by that person, and such expenditure—

(a) is incurred not more than 3 years before that time, and

(b) is apart from this section not allowable as a deduction for the purpose of computing the profits or gains of the trade or profession for the purposes of Case I or II of Schedule D, but would have been so allowable if it had been incurred after that time,

then, the expenditure shall be treated for that purpose as having been incurred at that time.

[(3) The amount of any expenditure to be treated under *subsection (2)* as incurred at the time that a trade or profession has been set up and commenced shall not be so treated for the purposes of *section 381*, *396(2)* or *420*.][1]

(4) An allowance or deduction shall not be made under any provision of the Tax Acts other than this section in respect of any expenditure or payment which is treated under this section as incurred on the day on which a trade or profession is set up and commenced.

Amendments

[1] Substituted by FA12 sched1(4).

Case Law

Excessive service charges were held not to be allowable as managements expenses in Fragmap Developments v Cooper 44 TC 366.

"The making of investments" did not require the "turning over" of investments. CIR v Tyre Investment Trust Ltd 1924 12 TC 646.

A company formed to acquire, develop and manage a large estate was not an "investment company" in Howth Estate Co v Davis 1934 21 TC 74.

Expenses of a property owning company in advertising for tenants were held to be an expense of management in Southern v Aldwych Property Trust Ltd 1940 23 TC 707.

In Casey v Monteagle estate Co v Davis 1962 3 ITC 313 a company formed to acquire an estate in land was also held not to be an "investment company".

In the UK case Cook v Medway Housing Society Ltd 1997 STC 90, the society which made an investment in houses which it rented below market value, was held to be an investment company.

Due diligence costs incurred by a company in relation to a proposed investment acquisition were not management expenses. Hibernian Insurance Company Ltd v MacUimis 2000 V ITR 495

Revenue Briefings

Tax Briefing

Tax Briefing August 1997 – Issue 27 pg 2 – Relief for Pre-Trading Expenses

Cross References

From Section 82

Section 381 Right to repayment of tax by reference to losses.
Section 396 Relief for trading losses other than terminal losses.
Section 420 Losses, etc. which may be surrendered by means of group relief.
Section 455 Restriction of certain losses.
Section 456 Restriction of group relief.

83 Expenses of management of investment companies

[CTA76 s15]

(1) For the purposes of this section and of the other provisions of the Corporation Tax Acts relating to expenses of management, "*investment company*" means any company whose business consists wholly or mainly of the making of investments, and the principal part of whose income is derived from the making of investments, but includes any savings bank or other bank for savings.

(2) In computing for the purposes of corporation tax the total profits for any accounting period of an investment company resident in the State—

(a) there shall be deducted any sums disbursed as expenses of management (including commissions) for that period, except any such expenses as are deductible in computing income for the purposes of Case V of Schedule D; but

(b) there shall be deducted from the amount treated as expenses of management the amount of any income derived from sources not charged to tax, other than franked investment income.

(3) Where in any accounting period of an investment company the expenses of management deductible under *subsection (2)*, together with any charges on income paid in the accounting period wholly and exclusively for the purposes of the company's business, exceed the amount of the profits from which they are deductible, the excess shall be carried forward to the succeeding accounting period, and the amount so carried forward shall be treated for the purposes of this section […][1], including any further application of this subsection, as if it had been disbursed as expenses of management for that accounting period.

(4) For the purposes of *subsections (2)* and *(3)*, there shall be added to a company's expenses of management in any accounting period the amount of any allowances to be made to the company for that period by virtue of *section 109* or *774*.

[…][2]

Amendments

[1] Deleted by FA03 s41(1)(a)(i). This section applies as respects accounting periods ending on or after 6 February 2003.

[2] Deleted by FA03 s41(1)(a)(ii). This section applies as respects accounting periods ending on or after 6 February 2003.

Case Law

Dawsongroup Ltd v R & C Commrs 2010 EWHC 1061 (Ch) expenses incurred in de-listing from the stock exchange were not expenses of management.

Cross References

From Section 83

Section 109 Payments in respect of redundancy.
Section 774 Certain approved schemes: exemptions and reliefs.

To Section 83

Section 109 Payments in respect of redundancy.
Section 127 Tax treatment of restrictive covenants.
Section 375 Limit on renewals allowance for cars.
Section 396 Relief for trading losses other than terminal losses.
Section 420 Losses, etc. which may be surrendered by means of group relief.
Section 517 Payments to trustees of approved profit sharing scheme.
Section 518 Costs of establishing profit sharing schemes.
Section 519 Employee share ownership trusts.
Section 519B Costs of establishing savings-related share option schemes.
Section 519D Approved share option schemes.
Section 531W No relief for any payment in relation to parking levy.
Section 697LA Transactions between associated persons and between tonnage tax trade and other activities of same company.
Section 707 Management expenses.
Section 708 Acquisition expenses.
Section 710 Profits of life business.

Section 774 Certain approved schemes: exemptions and reliefs.
Section 787J Allowance to employer.
Section 840 Business entertainment.
Schedule 19 Offshore Funds: Distributing Funds
Schedule 32 Transitional Provisions

83A Expenditure involving crime

[(1) In computing any income chargeable to tax under Schedule D, no deduction shall be made for any expenditure incurred—

(a) in making a payment the making of which constitutes the commission of a criminal offence, or

(b) in making a payment outside of the State where the making of a corresponding payment in the State would constitute a criminal offence.

(2) Any expenditure specified in *subsection (1)* shall not be included in computing any expenses of management in respect of which relief may be given under the Tax Acts.][1]

Amendments

[1] Inserted by FA08 s41(1). Applies as respects any chargeable period (within the meaning of section 321(2)) ending on or after 31 January 2008.

84 Expenses in relation to establishment or alteration of superannuation schemes

[ITA67 s63; FA72 s13(4) and Sch1 PtIII par 1, and s46(2) and Sch4 PtII]

Where a superannuation scheme is established in connection with a trade or undertaking or a superannuation scheme so established is altered, and the person by whom the trade or undertaking is carried on makes a payment in respect of expenses (including a payment in respect of professional fees, but not including a payment by means of contribution towards the cost of providing the benefits payable under the scheme) in connection with such establishment or alteration, then, if the scheme or, as the case may be, the altered scheme is approved by the Revenue Commissioners under *section 772*, the amount of the payment shall be allowed to be deducted in the computation, for the purposes of assessment to tax, of the profits or gains of the trade or undertaking as an expense incurred when the payment is made.

Cross References

From Section 84

Section 772 Conditions for approval of schemes and discretionary approval.

85 Deduction for certain industrial premises

[ITA67 s67(1), (2), (3) and (3A); FA69 s31]

(1) In this section, "*premises*" means an industrial building or structure within the meaning of *section 268* which is not a building or structure to which *section 272* applies.

(2) In estimating the amount of annual profits or gains arising or accruing from any trade the profits of which are chargeable to tax under Case I of Schedule D, there shall be allowed to be deducted, as expenses incurred in any year on account of any premises owned by the person carrying on that trade and occupied by such person for the purposes of that trade, a deduction equal to five-twelfths of the rateable valuation of those premises.

(3) In estimating the profits for any year of any of the concerns which by virtue of *section 18(2)* are charged under Case I(*b*) of Schedule D, there shall be allowed to be deducted,

as expenses incurred in any year on account of any premises owned by the person carrying on the concern and occupied by such person for the purposes of that concern, a deduction equal to five-twelfths of the rateable valuation of those premises.

(4) (a) Where, in the case of property valued under the Valuation Acts as a unit, a part is and a part is not premises, the rateable valuation of each part shall be arrived at by apportionment of the rateable valuation of the property.

(b) Any apportionment required by this subsection shall be made by the inspector according to the best of his or her knowledge and judgment.

(c) An apportionment made under *paragraph (b)* may be amended by the Appeal Commissioners or by the Circuit Court on the hearing or the rehearing of an appeal against an assessment made on the basis of the apportionment; but, on the hearing or the rehearing of any such appeal, a certificate of the Commissioner of Valuation tendered by either party to the appeal and stating, as regards property valued under the Valuation Acts as a unit, the amount of the rateable valuation of the property attributable to any part of the property shall be evidence of the amount so attributable.

Cross References

From Section 85

Section 268 Meaning of "industrial building or structure".
Section 272 Writing-down allowances.

To Section 85

Section 670 Mine development allowance.
Section 765 Allowances for capital expenditure on scientific research.

86 Cost of registration of trade marks

[FA71 s5]

Notwithstanding anything in *section 81*, in computing the amount of the profits or gains of any trade, there shall be allowed to be deducted as expenses any fees paid or expenses incurred in obtaining for the purposes of the trade the registration of a trade mark or the renewal of registration of a trade mark.

Cross References

From Section 86

Section 81 General rule as to deductions.

87 Debts set off against profits and subsequently released

[FA70 s24(1) and (2)(a)]

(1) Where, in computing for tax purposes the profits or gains of a trade or profession, a deduction has been allowed for any debt incurred for the purposes of the trade or profession, then, if the whole or any part of that debt is thereafter released, the amount released shall be treated as a receipt of the trade or profession arising in the period in which the release is effected.

(2) If in any case referred to in *subsection (1)* the trade or profession has been permanently discontinued at or after the end of the period for which the deduction was allowed and before the release was effected, or is treated for tax purposes as if it had been so discontinued, *section 91* shall apply as if the amount released were a sum received after the discontinuance.

Cross References

From Section 87

Section 91 Receipts accruing after discontinuance of trade or profession.

To Section 87

Section 91 Receipts accruing after discontinuance of trade or profession.

87A Deductions for gifts to Foundation for Investing in Communities [Repealed]

Repealed by FA01 s84(3). Has effect from 6 April 2001.

87B Release of debts in certain trades

[(1) In this section—

"*specified debt*" means any debt incurred by an individual in respect of borrowed money employed in the purchase or development of land held as trading stock (within the meaning of *section 89*) of a specified trade;

"*specified trade*" means a trade, or a business which is deemed to be a trade by virtue of *section 640(2)(a)*, consisting of or including dealing in or developing land to which *Chapter 1* of *Part 22* applies;

"*tax year*" means a year of assessment.

(2) If at any time the whole or part of a specified debt of an individual who is engaged in a specified trade is released, the amount released shall be treated as a receipt of the specified trade arising in the tax year in which the release is effected.

(3) If, in any case referred to in *subsection (2)*, the specified trade has been permanently discontinued or is treated for tax purposes as if it had been so discontinued, in a tax year before the release was effected, *section 91* shall apply as if the amount released were a sum received after the discontinuance.

(4) For the purposes of this section, the release of the whole or part of a specified debt is treated as having been effected on the earliest of the following dates—

(a) the date when the lender has confirmed that release to the borrower,

(b) the date on which the lender and the borrower have first come to an agreement (whether formal or informal) that the debt or part of the debt is no longer required to be repaid,

(c) in a case in which the agreement under which the money was borrowed provides for any release or non-collection of the debt or part of the debt, the date when the conditions necessary for that release or non-collection are first satisfied, or

(d) in a case in which the release is a result of—

(i) a discharge from bankruptcy, or

(ii) a discharge from debt under the provisions of the Personal Insolvency Act 2012,

the date of that discharge.][1]

Amendments

[1] Inserted by FA13 s18(1)(a). Comes into operation in respect of any specified debt (within the meaning of section 87B) released on or after 13 February 2013.

Revenue Briefings

eBrief

eBrief No. 31/2014 – Debt Release – Land Dealers and Developers

88 Deduction for gifts to Enterprise Trust Ltd [Repealed]

Repealed by TCA97 s848A, as inserted by FA01 s45.

Cross References

To Section 88

Section 848A Donations to approved bodies.

88A Double deduction in respect of certain emoluments

[(1) In this section—

"*chargeable period*" has the same meaning as in *section 321(2)*;

"*emoluments*", "*employment*", "*employment scheme*", "*qualifying employment*", and "*qualifying individual*" have the same meanings, respectively, as in *section 472A*;

"*qualifying period*", in relation to a qualifying employment, means the period of 36 months beginning on the date when that employment commences.

(2) (a) Where in the computation of the amount of the profits or gains of a trade or profession for a chargeable period, a person is, apart from this section, entitled to a deduction (in this subsection referred to as "the first-mentioned deduction") on account of—

(i) emoluments payable to a qualifying individual in respect of a qualifying employment, and

(ii) the employer's contribution to the Social Insurance Fund payable, in respect of those emoluments, under the Social Welfare Acts,

that person shall be entitled in that computation to a further deduction (in this subsection referred to as "the second-mentioned deduction") equal to the amount of the first-mentioned deduction as respects that qualifying employment.

(b) Relief under this section, in respect of a qualifying employment, shall not be granted—

(i) in respect of a second-mentioned deduction which relates to a chargeable period or part of a chargeable period outside the qualifying period in relation to such qualifying employment, or

(ii) if the claimant or the qualifying individual is benefiting, or has benefited, under an employment scheme, whether statutory or otherwise.

(c) For the purposes of this section, an activity, programme or course mentioned in *section 472A(1)(b)(i)* shall be deemed not to be an employment scheme.][1]

[(3) This section shall cease to have effect in respect of all claims relating to—

(a) emoluments payable in respect of an employment commencing on or after such day as the Minister for Finance may by order appoint, and

(b) the employer's contribution to the Social Insurance Fund payable, in respect of those emoluments, under the Social Welfare Acts.][2]

Amendments

[1] Inserted by FA98 s16(a).

[2] Inserted by FA13 s7(1). With effect from 1 July 2013 per S.I. No. 229 of 2013.

Revenue Briefings

Tax Briefing

Tax Briefing April 1998 – Issue 31 pg 19 – Revenue Job Assist – New Tax Incentives

Revenue Information Notes

IT 58 Revenue Job Assist – Information for Employees

IT 59 Revenue Job Assist – Information for Employers

Cross References

From Section 88A

Section 321 Provisions of general application in relation to the making of allowances and charges.

Section 472A Relief for the long-term unemployed.

CHAPTER 7

Special Measures on Discontinuance of, and Change of Basis of Computation of Profits or Gains of, a Trade or Profession

89 Valuation of trading stock at discontinuance of trade

[ITA67 s62(1) (apart from proviso) and (2); FA70 s23(4)]

(1) (a) In this section, "*trading stock*" means, subject to *paragraph (b)*, property of any description, whether real or personal, which is either—

(i) property such as is sold in the ordinary course of the trade in relation to which the expression is used or would be so sold if it were mature or if its manufacture, preparation or construction were complete, or

(ii) materials such as are used in the manufacture, preparation or construction of property such as is sold in the ordinary course of that trade.

[(b) For the purposes of this section—

(i) "*trading stock*", in relation to a trade, includes any services, article or material which, if the trade were a profession, would be treated as work in progress of the profession for the purposes of *section 90*, and references to the sale or transfer of trading stock shall be construed accordingly;

(ii) two persons are connected with each other if—

(I) they are connected with each other within the meaning of *section 10*;

(II) one of them is a partnership and the other has a right to a share in the partnership;

(III) one of them is a body corporate and the other has control over that body;

(IV) both of them are partnerships and some other person has a right to a share in each of them; or

(V) both of them are bodies corporate or one of them is a partnership and the other is a body corporate and, in either case, some other person has control over both of them;

and in this subparagraph the references to a right to a share in a partnership are references to a share of the assets or income of the partnership and control has the meaning given by *section 11*.][1]

(c) References in this section to a trade having been discontinued or to the discontinuance of a trade shall be construed as not referring to or including any case where such trade was carried on by a single individual and is discontinued by reason of such individual's death (whether such trade is or is not continued by another person after such death), but shall be construed as referring to and including every other case where a trade has been discontinued or is, by virtue of any of the provisions of the Tax Acts, treated as having been discontinued for the purpose of computing tax.

(2) In computing the profits or gains of a trade which has been discontinued, any trading stock belonging to the trade at the discontinuance of the trade shall be valued in accordance with the following provisions:

(a) in the case of any such trading stock—

(i) which is sold, or is transferred for valuable consideration, to a person who carries on or intends to carry on a trade in the State, and

(ii) the cost of which to such person on such sale or transfer may be deducted by such person as an expense in computing for any purpose of the Tax Acts the profits or gains of the trade carried on or intended to be carried on by such person,

the value of such trading stock shall be taken to be [the amount determined in accordance with *subsections (3)* and *(4)*][2];

(b) in the case of any other such trading stock, the value of such other trading stock shall be taken to be the amount which it would have realised if it had been sold in the open market at the discontinuance of the trade.

[(3) Subject to *subsection (4)*, *paragraph 2(2)* of *Schedule 16* and *paragraph 4(2)* of *Schedule 17*, the value of any trading stock falling to be valued under *subsection (2)(a)* shall be taken—

(a) except where the person to whom it is sold or transferred is connected with the person who makes the sale or transfer, to be the amount (in this subsection and *subsection (4)* referred to as "*the price actually received for it*") realised on the sale or, as the case may be, which is in fact the value of the consideration given for the transfer, and

(b) if those persons are connected with each other, to be what would have been the price actually received for it had the sale or transfer been a transaction between independent persons dealing at arm's length.

(4) If—

(a) trading stock is sold or transferred to a person in circumstances where *subsection (3)(b)* would, apart from this subsection, apply for determining the value of stock so sold or transferred,

(b) the amount which would be taken in accordance with *subsection (3)(b)* to be the value of the stock sold or transferred to that person is more than the acquisition value of that stock and also more than the price actually received for it, and

(c) the person by whom the stock is sold or transferred includes in a return required to be delivered under [*Chapter 3* of *Part 41A*][3] for the chargeable period in which the trade is discontinued an election signed by both parties to the sale or transfer that this subsection shall apply, then the stock so sold or transferred shall be taken to have a value equal to whichever is the greater (taking all the stock so sold or transferred together) of its acquisition value and the price actually received for it or, in a case where they are the same, to either of them.

(5) In *subsection (4)* "*acquisition value*", in relation to any trading stock, means the amount which, in computing for any tax purposes the profits or gains of the discontinued trade, would have been deductible as representing the purchase price of that stock if—

(a) the stock had, immediately before the discontinuance, been sold in the course of the trade for a price equal to whatever would be its value in accordance with *subsection (3)(b)*, and

(b) the period for which those profits or gains were to be computed began immediately before the sale.

(6) Where any trading stock falls to be valued under *subsection (2)(a)*, the amount determined in accordance with *subsections (3)* and *(4)* to be the amount to be brought into account as the value of that stock in computing profits or gains of the discontinued trade shall also be taken, for the purpose of making any deduction in computing the profits or gains of any trade carried on by the purchaser, to be the cost of that stock to the purchaser.][4]

Amendments

[1] Substituted by FA01 s42(1)(a). This section applies from 6 December 2000.

[2] Substituted by FA01 s42(1)(b). This section applies from 6 December 2000.

[3] Substituted by FA12 sched4(part 2)(g).

[4] Inserted by FA01 s42(1)(c). This section applies from 6 December 2000.

Revenue Precedents

Does a transfer of stock at a grossly inflated price come within the provisions of Section 89(2)(a)? In order for a transaction to come within this provision the purchaser must be entitled to deduct the cost in computing his/her trading profits. Where the value at which stock is transferred does not come within the realms of being a bona fide transaction the purchaser would not be entitled to a deduction for such cost. IT953552

Natural love and affection does not constitute "valuable consideration" for the purposes of this section. IT953557

Cross References

From Section 89

Section 10 Connected persons.
Section 11 Meaning of "control" in certain contexts.
Section 90 Valuation of work in progress at discontinuance of profession.
Section 951 Obligation to make a return.
Schedule 16 Building Societies: Change of Status
Schedule 17 Reorganisation into Companies of Trustee Savings Banks

To Section 89

Section 5 Interpretation of Capital Gains Tax Acts.
Section 247 Relief to companies on loans applied in acquiring interest in other companies.
Section 615 Company reconstruction or amalgamation: transfer of assets.
Section 639 Interpretation (Chapter 1).
Section 656 Farming: trading stock of discontinued trade.
Section 665 Interpretation (Chapter 2).
Section 835G Elimination of double counting.
Section 840A Interest on loans to defray money applied for certain purposes.
Schedule 16 Building Societies: Change of Status
Schedule 17 Reorganisation into Companies of Trustee Savings Banks

90 Valuation of work in progress at discontinuance of profession

[FA70 s23(1) to (3) and (5); FA81 s9(d)]

(1) Where, in computing for any of the purposes of the Tax Acts the profits or gains of a profession which has been discontinued, a valuation is taken of the work of the profession in progress at the discontinuance, that work shall be valued as follows:

(a) if the work is transferred for money or any other valuable consideration to a person who carries on or intends to carry on a profession in the State, and the cost of the work may be deducted by that person as an expense in computing for any such purpose the profits or gains of that profession, the value of the work shall be taken to be the amount paid or other consideration given for the transfer;

(b) if the work is not to be valued under *paragraph (a)*, its value shall be taken to be the amount which would have been paid for a transfer of the work on the date of the discontinuance as between parties at arm's length.

(2) Where a profession is discontinued and the person by whom it was carried on immediately before the discontinuance so elects, by notice in writing sent to the inspector at any time within 24 months after the discontinuance, the amount, if any, by which the value of the work in progress at the discontinuance (as ascertained under *subsection (1)*) exceeds the actual cost of the work shall not be taken into account in computing the profits or gains of the period immediately before the discontinuance, but the amount by which any sums received for the transfer of the work exceed the actual cost of the work shall be included in the sums chargeable to tax under *section 91* as if it were a sum to which that section applies received after the discontinuance.

(3) *Subsections (1)* and *(2)* shall apply where a profession is treated for any of the purposes of the Tax Acts as permanently discontinued as they apply in the case of an actual discontinuance, but shall not apply in a case where a profession carried on by a single individual is discontinued by reason of such individual's death.

(4) References in this section to work in progress at the discontinuance of a profession shall be construed as references to—

(a) any services performed in the ordinary course of the profession, the performance of which was wholly or partly completed at the time of the discontinuance and for which it would be reasonable to expect that a charge would have been made on their completion if the profession had not been discontinued, and

(b) any article produced, and any such material as is used, in the performance of any such services,

and references in this section to the transfer of work in progress shall include references to the transfer of any benefits and rights which accrue, or might reasonably be expected to accrue, from the carrying out of the work.

Cross References

From Section 90

Section 91 Receipts accruing after discontinuance of trade or profession.

To Section 90

Section 89 Valuation of trading stock at discontinuance of trade.

Section 94 Conventional basis: general charge on receipts after change of basis.

91 Receipts accruing after discontinuance of trade or profession

[FA70 s20(1) to (4) and (5)(b), (c) and (d)]

(1) Subject to *subsection (2)*, this section shall apply to all sums arising from the carrying on of a trade or profession during any period before the discontinuance of the trade or profession (not being sums otherwise chargeable to tax), in so far as the amount or value of the sums was not taken into account in computing the profits or gains for any period before the discontinuance, and whether or not the profits or gains for the period were computed on an earnings basis or on a conventional basis.

(2) This section shall not apply to any of the following sums—

(a) sums received by a person beneficially entitled to such sums who is not resident in the State, or by a person acting on such person's behalf, which represent income arising directly or indirectly from a country or territory outside the State,

(b) a lump sum paid to the personal representatives of the author of a literary, dramatic, musical or artistic work as a consideration for the assignment by them, wholly or partially, of the copyright in the work,

(c) sums realised by the transfer of trading stock belonging to a trade at the discontinuance of the trade or, in a case in which the profits or gains of a profession were computed on an earnings basis at the discontinuance of the profession, sums realised by the transfer of the work of the profession in progress at the discontinuance, and

(d) sums arising to an individual from a work which is such that any profits or gains that might have arisen to the individual from its publication, production or sale, as the case might be, would in accordance with *section 195(3)* have been disregarded for the purposes of the Income Tax Acts if they had arisen before the discontinuance of that individual's profession.

(3) Where any trade or profession, the profits or gains of which are chargeable to tax under Case I or II of Schedule D, has been permanently discontinued, tax shall be charged under Case IV of that Schedule in respect of any sums to which this section applies received after the discontinuance subject to any such deduction as is authorised by *subsection (4)*.

(4) In computing the charge to tax in respect of sums received by any person which are chargeable to tax by virtue of this section (including amounts treated as sums received by such person by virtue of *section 87* [or *87B*][1]), there shall be deducted from the amount which apart from this subsection would be chargeable to tax—

(a) any loss, expense or debit (not being a loss, expense or debit arising directly or indirectly from the discontinuance itself) which, if the trade or profession had not been discontinued, would have been deducted in computing for tax purposes the profits or gains of the person by whom the trade or profession was carried on before the discontinuance, or would have been deducted from or set off against those profits or gains as so computed, and

(b) any capital allowance to which the person who carried on the trade or profession was entitled immediately before the discontinuance and to which effect has not been given by means of relief before the discontinuance.

(5) For the purposes of this Chapter—

(a) the profits or gains of a trade or profession in any period shall be treated as computed by reference to earnings where all credits and liabilities accruing during that period as a consequence of the carrying on of the trade or profession are taken into account in computing those profits or gains for tax purposes, and not otherwise, and "*earnings basis*" shall be construed accordingly,

(b) the profits or gains of a trade or profession in any period shall be treated as computed on a conventional basis where they are computed otherwise than by reference to earnings, and

(c) the value of any sum received in payment of a debt shall be treated as not taken into account in the computation to the extent that a deduction has been allowed in respect of that sum under *section 81(2)(i)*.

Amendments

[1] Inserted by FA13 s18(1)(b). Comes into operation in respect of any specified debt (within the meaning of section 87B) released on or after 13 February 2013.

Statements of Practice

Preparation of Accounts for Revenue Purposes – SP IT/02/92

Cross References

From Section 91

Section 81 General rule as to deductions.
Section 87 Debts set off against profits and subsequently released.
Section 195 Exemption of certain earnings of writers, composers and artists.

To Section 91

Section 87 Debts set off against profits and subsequently released.
Section 90 Valuation of work in progress at discontinuance of profession.
Section 92 Receipts and losses accruing after change treated as discontinuance.
Section 93 Cash basis, etc: relief for certain individuals.
Section 95 Supplementary provisions as to tax under section 91 or 94.

92 Receipts and losses accruing after change treated as discontinuance

[FA70 s22]

(1) This section shall apply in any case where, as a result of a change in the persons engaged in carrying on a trade or profession, the trade or profession is treated for any of the purposes of the Tax Acts as if it had been permanently discontinued and a new trade or profession set up and commenced.

(2) (a) *Sections 91* and *95* shall apply in the case of any such change as if the trade or profession had been permanently discontinued.

(b) Notwithstanding *paragraph (a)*, where the right to receive any sums to which *section 91* applies is or was transferred at the time of the change to the persons carrying on the trade or profession after the change, tax shall not be charged by virtue of that section, but any sums received by those persons by virtue of the transfer shall be treated for all purposes as receipts to be taken into the computation of profits or gains of the trade or profession in the period in which they are received.

(3) In computing for tax purposes the profits or gains of the trade or profession in any period after the change, there may be deducted a sum equal to any amount proved during that period to be irrecoverable in respect of any debts credited in computing for tax purposes the profits or gains for any period before the change (being debts the benefit of which was assigned to the persons carrying on the trade or profession after the change), in so far as the total amount proved to be irrecoverable in respect of those debts exceeds any deduction allowed in respect of them under *section 81(2)(i)* in a computation for any period before the change.

Cross References

From Section 92

Section 81 General rule as to deductions.
Section 91 Receipts accruing after discontinuance of trade or profession.
Section 95 Supplementary provisions as to tax under section 91 or 94.

93 Cash basis, etc: relief for certain individuals

[FA70 s25]

(1) In this section—

"*the net amount*" with which a person is chargeable to tax under *section 91* means the amount with which such person is so chargeable after making any deduction authorised by *section 91(4)* but before giving any relief under this section;

"*relevant date*" means—

(a) in relation to tax under *section 91*, the date of the permanent discontinuance, and

(b) in relation to tax under *section 94*, the date of the change of basis.

(2) Where an individual born before the 6th day of April, 1919, or the personal representative of such an individual, is chargeable to tax under *section 91* or *94* and—

(a) the individual was engaged in carrying on the trade or profession on the 4th day of August, 1970, and

(b) the profits or gains of the trade or profession were not computed by reference to earnings in the period in which the date specified in *paragraph (a)* fell, or in any subsequent period ending before or on the relevant date,

the net amount with which such individual is so chargeable to tax shall be reduced by multiplying that net amount by the fraction specified in *subsection (4)*.

(3) Where *section 94* applies in relation to a change of basis taking place on a date before the 4th day of August, 1970, then, in relation to tax chargeable by reference to that change of basis, *subsection (2)* shall apply as if—

(a) that earlier date were substituted for the date specified in *paragraph (a)* of that subsection, and

(b) *paragraph (b)* of that subsection were deleted.

(4) The fraction referred to in *subsection (2)* is—

(a) where on the 6th day of April, 1970, the individual had not attained the age of 52 years, nineteen-twentieths,

(b) where on that date the individual had attained the age of 52 years, but had not attained the age of 53 years, eighteen-twentieths, and so on, reducing the fraction by one-twentieth for each year the individual had attained, up to the age of 64 years,

(c) where on that date the individual had attained the age of 65 years or any greater age, five-twentieths.

Cross References

From Section 93

Section 91 Receipts accruing after discontinuance of trade or profession.
Section 94 Conventional basis: general charge on receipts after change of basis.

To Section 93

Section 95 Supplementary provisions as to tax under section 91 or 94.

94 Conventional basis: general charge on receipts after change of basis

[FA70 s26(1) to (4)]

(1) Where in the case of any trade or profession the profits or gains of which are chargeable to tax under Case I or II of Schedule D there has been—

(a) a change from a conventional basis to the earnings basis, or

(b) a change of conventional basis which may result in receipts dropping out of computation,

tax shall be charged under Case IV of Schedule D in respect of sums to which this subsection applies which are received after the change and before the trade or profession is permanently discontinued.

(2) *Subsection (1)* shall apply to all sums arising from the carrying on of the trade or profession during any period before the change (not being sums otherwise chargeable to tax) in so far as their amount or value was not taken into account in computing the profits or gains for any period.

(3) Where in the case of any profession the profits or gains of which are chargeable to tax under Case II of Schedule D—

(a) there has been a change from a conventional basis to the earnings basis, or a change of conventional basis, and

(b) the value of work in progress at the time of the change was debited in the accounts and allowed as a deduction in computing profits for tax purposes for a period after the change,

then, in so far as no counterbalancing credit was taken into account in computing profits for tax purposes for any period ending before or on the date of the change, tax shall be charged under *subsection (1)* in respect of that amount for the year of assessment in which the change occurred as if that amount were a sum to which *subsection (2)* applies and the change of basis were a change of the kind described in *subsection (1)*.

(4) In this section, references to work in progress at the time of a change of basis shall be construed in accordance with *section 90(4)* but as if references in that section to the change of basis were references to the discontinuance.

(5) There shall be a change from a conventional basis to the earnings basis at the end of a period, the profits or gains of which were computed on a conventional basis, if the profits or gains of the next succeeding period are computed by reference to earnings and, if the profits or gains of 2 successive periods are computed on different conventional bases, a change of conventional basis shall occur at the end of the earlier period.

Revenue Precedents

A farmer who has been on the profile basis can change to the accounts basis in his final year of trading. However a charge under Section 94(1) is likely to arise in respect of sums arising from the carrying on of the trade prior to the changeover which are not brought into the accounts in computing the profits of the trade. IT963526

Statements of Practice

Preparation of Accounts for Revenue Purpose – SP IT/02/92

Cross References

From Section 94

Section 90 Valuation of work in progress at discontinuance of profession.

To Section 94

Section 93 Cash basis, etc: relief for certain individuals.

Section 95 Supplementary provisions as to tax under section 91 or 94.

Section 95A Change of basis of computation of profits or gains of a trade or profession.

95 Supplementary provisions as to tax under section 91 or 94

[FA70 s21; CTA76 s164 and Sch3 PtII]

(1) In the case of a transfer for value of the right to receive any sums described in *section 91(1)* or *94*, any tax chargeable by virtue of either of those sections shall be charged in respect of the amount or value of the consideration (or, in the case of a transfer otherwise than at arm's length, in respect of the value of the right transferred as between parties at arm's length), and references in those sections to sums received shall be construed accordingly.

(2) Where an individual is chargeable to tax by virtue of *section 91* in respect of any sums received after the discontinuance of a trade or profession, and the profits or gains of the trade or profession to which such individual was entitled before the discontinuance fell to be treated as earned income for the purposes of the Income Tax Acts, those sums shall also be treated as earned income for those purposes but after any reduction in those sums under *section 93*.

(3) Where any sum chargeable to tax by virtue of *section 91* or *94* is received in any year of assessment beginning not later than [4 years][1] after the discontinuance or, as the case may be, change of basis by the person by whom the trade or profession was carried on before the discontinuance or change or by such person's personal representatives, such person or (in either case) such person's personal representatives may, by notice in writing sent to the inspector within 2 years after the end of that year of assessment, elect that the tax so chargeable shall be charged as if the sum in question were received on the date on which the discontinuance took place or, as the case may be, on the last day of the period at the end of which the change took place, and, in any such case, [an assessment made on or by such person shall (notwithstanding anything in *Chapter 5* of *Part 41A*) be amended accordingly][2] and, in connection with that assessment, no further deduction or relief shall be made or given in respect of any loss or allowance deducted in pursuance of *section 91(4)*.

(4) Where work in progress at the discontinuance of a profession, or the responsibility for its completion, is transferred, the sums to which *section 91* applies include any sums received by means of consideration for the transfer and any sums received by means of realisation by the transferee on behalf of the transferor of the work in progress transferred.

(5) No amount shall be deducted under *section 91(4)* if that amount has been allowed under any other provision of the Tax Acts.

(6) No amount shall be deducted more than once under *section 91(4)* and, as between sums chargeable for one year of assessment and sums chargeable for a subsequent year of assessment, any deduction in respect of a loss or capital allowance shall be made against sums chargeable for the earlier year of assessment but, in the case of a loss which by virtue of this subsection or *section 91(4)* is to be allowed after the discontinuance, a deduction shall not be made from any sum chargeable for a year of assessment preceding that in which the loss is incurred.

Amendments

[1] Substituted by FA13 s92 and sched1(part 2)(a).

[2] Substituted by FA12 sched4(part 2)(g).

Note:

FA13 s92 applies—

(a) in the case of a chargeable period (within the meaning of section 321(2)) which is an accounting period of a company, as respects chargeable periods that start on or after 1 January 2013, and

(b) in a case other than that referred to in paragraph (a), as respects the year of assessment (within the meaning of section 2(1)) 2013 and subsequent years of assessment.

Cross References

From Section 95

Section 91 Receipts accruing after discontinuance of trade or profession.
Section 93 Cash basis, etc: relief for certain individuals.
Section 94 Conventional basis: general charge on receipts after change of basis.
Section 924 Additional assessments.

To Section 95

Section 92 Receipts and losses accruing after change treated as discontinuance.

95A Change of basis of computation of profits or gains of a trade or profession

[(1) In this section—

"*Accounting Standards Board*" means the body known as the Accounting Standards Board established under the articles of association of The Accounting Standards Board Limited, a company limited by guarantee and registered in England;

"*chargeable period*" has the same meaning as in *section 321(2)*.

(2) Where—

(a) in a case to which *section 94(3)* does not apply there has been a change in the basis of valuing work in progress for the purposes of computing profits or gains of a trade or profession chargeable under Case I or II of Schedule D, and

(b) the amount (in this subsection referred to as the "*relevant amount*") of the value of work in progress at the time of the change is allowed as a deduction in computing profits or gains for tax purposes for a chargeable period after the change (in this section referred to as the "*relevant period*"),

then, in so far as the counterbalancing credit in connection with that work in progress, taken into account in computing profits or gains for tax purposes for the period preceding the relevant period, is less than the relevant amount, tax shall be charged under Case I or II of Schedule D for the relevant period on so much of the relevant amount as exceeds that credit.

(3) Where *subsection (2)* applies in respect of a partnership trade or profession, any amount chargeable to tax under *subsection (2)* shall be treated for the purposes of the Tax Acts as an amount of profits or gains of the partnership trade or profession.

(4) Where *subsection (2)* applies to a change in the basis of computing profits or gains for a chargeable period ending in the period of 2 years beginning on 22 June 2005 and the change arises by virtue only of the guidance issued on 10 March 2005 by the Urgent Issues Task Force of the Accounting Standards Board on Application Note G of Financial Reporting Standard 5 (known as "UITF Abstract 40"), then tax shall not be charged in respect of the excess amount in the relevant period but instead—

(a) where the person by whom the trade or profession is carried on is a person other than a company, tax shall be charged—

(i) on one-fifth of the excess amount for the relevant period, and

(ii) on a further one-fifth of the excess amount for each succeeding chargeable period until the whole amount has been accounted for, and

(iii) where any chargeable period referred to in *subparagraph (i)* or *(ii)* is the chargeable period in which the trade or profession was permanently discontinued, then tax shall be chargeable for that chargeable period on such fraction of the excess amount referred to in those subparagraphs as is required to ensure that the whole of that excess amount is accounted for,

and

(b) where the person by whom the trade or profession is carried on is a company—

(i) tax shall be charged on a part of the excess amount for each chargeable period falling wholly or partly into the period of 5 years beginning at the commencement of the relevant period referred to in *subsection (1)*: and the part of the excess amount on which tax is to be charged for any such chargeable period shall be such amount as bears to the excess amount the same proportion as the length of the chargeable period, or the part of the chargeable period falling into the period of 5 years, bears to 5 years, and

(ii) where any chargeable period referred to in *subparagraph (i)* is the last chargeable period in which the company carried on a trade or profession then tax shall be charged for that chargeable period on such part of the excess amount as is required to ensure that the whole of that amount is accounted for.][1]

Amendments

[1] Inserted by FA06 s56.

Cross References

From Section 95A

Section 94 Conventional basis: general charge on receipts after change of basis.

Section 321 Provisions of general application in relation to the making of allowances and charges.

CHAPTER 8

Taxation of Rents and Certain Other Payments

96 Interpretation (Chapter 8)

[ITA67 s80(1), (2), (4) and (5) and s81(1) (definition of "*the person chargeable*"); FA69 s27; FA75 s19 and Sch2 PtI par1 and 2]

(1) In this Chapter, except where the context otherwise requires—

"*easement*" includes any right, privilege or benefit in, over or derived from premises;

"*lease*" includes an agreement for a lease and any tenancy, but does not include a mortgage, and "*lessee*" and "*lessor*" shall be construed accordingly, and "*lessee*" and "*lessor*" include respectively the successors in title of a lessee or a lessor;

["*the person chargeable*" means the person entitled to the profits or gains arising from—

(a) any rent in respect of any premises, and

(b) any receipts in respect of any easement,

and for the purposes of this definition a debtor, within the meaning of *section 2* of the Personal Insolvency Act 2012, who transfers property to a person to hold in trust pursuant to the terms of a Debt Settlement Arrangement or a

Personal Insolvency Arrangement entered into under that Act, shall be treated as remaining entitled to such profits or gains arising during the period in which the property is held in trust by that person;][1]

"*premises*" means any lands, tenements or hereditaments in the State;

"*premium*" includes any like sum, whether payable to the immediate or a superior lessor or to a person connected with the immediate or superior lessor;

"*rent*" includes—

(a) any rentcharge, fee farm rent and any payment in the nature of rent, notwithstanding that the payment may relate partly to premises and partly to goods or services, and

(b) any payment made by the lessee to defray the cost of work of maintenance of or repairs to the premises, not being work required by the lease to be carried out by the lessee.

["*rented residential premises*" means a residential premises in respect of which any person is entitled to a rent or receipts from any easements;

"*residential premises*" means any building or part of a building used or suitable for use as a dwelling and any outoffice, yard, garden or other land appurtenant to or usually enjoyed with that building or part of a building.][2]

(2) (a) In ascertaining for the purposes of this Chapter the duration of a lease, the following provisions shall apply:

(i) where any of the terms of the lease (whether relating to forfeiture or to any other matter) or any other circumstances render it unlikely that the lease will continue beyond a date falling before the expiration of the term of the lease and the premium was not substantially greater than it would have been (on the assumptions required by *paragraph (b)*) if the term had been one expiring on that date, the lease shall not be treated as having been granted for a term longer than one ending on that date;

(ii) where the terms of the lease include provision for the extension of the lease beyond a particular date by notice given by the lessee, account may be taken of any circumstances making it likely that the lease will be so extended;

(iii) where the lessee or a person connected with the lessee is or may become entitled to a further lease or the grant of a further lease (whenever commencing) of the same premises or of premises including the whole or part of the same premises, the term of the lease may be treated as not expiring before the term of the further lease.

(b) *Paragraph (a)* shall be applied by reference to the facts which were known or ascertainable at the time of the grant of the lease or, in relation to tax under *section 98(4)*, at the time when the contract providing for a variation or waiver of a kind referred to in *section 98(4)* is entered into, and in applying *paragraph (a)*—

(i) it shall be assumed that all parties concerned, whatever their relationship, act as they would act if they were at arm's length, and

(ii) if by the lease or in connection with the granting of it—

(I) benefits were conferred other than vacant possession and beneficial occupation of the premises or the right to receive rent at a reasonable commercial rate in respect of the premises, or

(II) payments were made which would not be expected to be made by parties so acting if no other benefits had been so conferred,

it shall be further assumed, unless it is shown that the benefits were not conferred or the payments were not made for the purpose of securing a tax advantage in the application of this Chapter, that the benefits would not have been conferred nor the payments made had the lease been for a term ending on the date mentioned in *paragraph (a)*.

(3) Where the estate or interest of any lessor of any premises is the subject of a mortgage and either the mortgagee is in possession or the rents and profits are being received by a receiver appointed by or on the application of the mortgagee, that estate or interest shall be deemed for the purposes of this Chapter to be vested in the mortgagee, and references to a lessor shall be construed accordingly; but the amount of the liability to tax of any such mortgagee shall be computed as if the mortgagor was still in possession or, as the case may be, no receiver had been appointed and as if it were the amount of the liability of the mortgagor that was being computed.

(4) Where an inspector has reason to believe that a person has information relevant to the ascertainment of the duration of a lease in accordance with *subsection (2)*, the inspector may by notice in writing require such person to give, within 21 days after the date of the notice or such longer period as the inspector may allow, such information relevant to the ascertainment of the duration of the lease on the matters specified in the notice as is in such person's possession.

Amendments

[1] Substituted by FA13 s100(1)(b). Applies on and from 27 March 2013.

[2] Inserted by FA98No2 s1(1)(a). Applies as on and from the 23rd day of April, 1998.

Revenue Information Notes

IT 70 – A Revenue Guide to Rental Income

Cross References

From Section 96

Section 98 Treatment of premiums, etc. as rent.

To Section 96

Section 75 Case V: basis of assessment.
Section 98 Treatment of premiums, etc. as rent.
Section 248A Restriction of relief in respect of loans applied in acquiring interest in companies and partnerships.
Section 284 Wear and tear allowances.
Section 324 Double rent allowance in respect of rent paid for certain business premises.
Section 333 Double rent allowance in respect of rent paid for certain business premises.
Section 339 Interpretation (Chapter 3).
Section 351 Interpretation (Chapter 4).
Section 372A Interpretation and application (Chapter 7).
Section 372L Interpretation (Chapter 8).
Section 372AA Interpretation and application (Chapter 10).
Section 372AK Interpretation (Chapter 11).
Section 372AO Qualifying lease.
Section 372AP Relief for lessors.
Section 384 Relief under Case V for losses.
Section 639 Interpretation (Chapter 1).
Section 654 Interpretation (Part 23).
Section 664 Relief for certain income from leasing of farm land.

Section 888 Returns, etc. by lessors, lessees and agents.
Schedule 14 Capital Gains Tax: Leases
Schedule 31 Consequential Amendments

97 Computational rules and allowable deductions

[ITA67 s81(4), (5), (6), (7) and (8); FA69 s22; FA97 s146(1) and Sch9 PtI par1(6)]

(1) Subject to this Chapter, the amount of the profits or gains arising in any year shall for the purposes of Case V of Schedule D be computed as follows:

(a) the amount of any rent shall be taken to be the gross amount of that rent before any deduction for income tax;

(b) the amount of the profits or gains arising in any year shall be the aggregate of the surpluses computed in accordance with *paragraph (c)*, reduced by the aggregate of the deficiencies as so computed;

(c) the amount of the surplus or deficiency in respect of each rent or in respect of the total receipts from easements shall be computed by making the deductions authorised by *subsection (2)* from the rent or total receipts from easements, as the case may be, to which the person chargeable becomes entitled in any year.

(2) The deductions authorised by this subsection shall be deductions by reference to any or all of the following matters—

(a) the amount of any rent payable by the person chargeable in respect of the premises or in respect of a part of the premises;

(b) any sums borne by the person chargeable—

(i) in the case of a rent under a lease, in accordance with the conditions of the lease, and

(ii) in any other case, relating to and constituting an expense of the transaction or transactions under which the rents or receipts were received,

in respect of any rate levied by a local authority, whether such sums are by law chargeable on such person or on some other person;

(c) the cost to the person chargeable of any services rendered or goods provided by such person, otherwise than as maintenance or repairs, being services or goods which—

(i) in the case of a rent under a lease, such person is legally bound under the lease to render or provide but in respect of which such person receives no separate consideration, and

(ii) in any other case, relate to and constitute an expense of the transaction or transactions under which the rents or receipts were received, not being an expense of a capital nature;

(d) the cost of maintenance, repairs, insurance and management of the premises borne by the person chargeable and relating to and constituting an expense of the transaction or transactions under which the rents or receipts were received, not being an expense of a capital nature;

(e) interest on borrowed money employed in the purchase, improvement or repair of the premises.

[(2A) Notwithstanding *subsection (2)* but subject to the other provisions of this section, a deduction shall not be authorised by *paragraph (e)* of that subsection by reference to interest on borrowed money employed on or after the 23rd day of April, 1998, in the purchase, improvement or repair of a premises which, at any time during the year, is a residential premises.

(2B) Subject to *subsection (2C)*, *subsection (2A)* shall not apply in relation to interest on borrowed money employed—

(a) on or before the [31st day of March, 1999][1], in the purchase of a residential premises in pursuance of a contract which was evidenced in writing prior to the 23rd day of April, 1998, for the purchase of that premises,

(b) in the improvement or repair of a premises which on the 23rd day of April, 1998, or at any time during the 12 month period ending on that day, is or was a rented residential premises—

(i) in which the person chargeable had an estate or interest on that day, or

(ii) in respect of which the person chargeable is, or would be, entitled, by virtue of *paragraph (a)*, to a deduction authorised by *subsection (2)(e)* by reference to interest on borrowed money employed in its purchase,

(c) in the purchase, improvement or repair of premises which is—

(i) a building or structure to which *section 352* applies by virtue of the building or structure being a holiday cottage of the type referred to in *section 268(3)*, or

(ii) a building or structure which is a qualifying premises within the meaning of *section 353* by virtue of the building or structure being—

(I) a holiday apartment registered under Part III of the Tourist Traffic Act, 1939, or

(II) other self-catering accommodation specified in a list published under section 9 of the Tourist Traffic Act, 1957,

or

(iii) a qualifying premises within the meaning of *section 356*, *357* or *358*,

(d) in the purchase, improvement or repair of any premises, other than premises to which *paragraph (c)* applies, the site of which is wholly within a qualifying rural area within the meaning of Chapter 8 of Part 10 of the *Taxes Consolidation Act,* [*1997,*][2]

(e) in the purchase, improvement or repair of premises, other than premises to which *paragraphs (c)* and *(d)* apply, where—

(i) the premises is a holiday cottage, holiday apartment or other self-catering accommodation either registered under Part III of the Tourist Traffic Act, 1939, or specified in a list published under section 9 of the Tourist Traffic Act, 1957,

(ii) an application for planning permission for the development of the premises was received by a planning authority before the 23rd day of April, 1998, and

(iii) the terms under which planning permission in respect of the development of the premises was granted by the planning authority contain the condition that the premises may not be used by any person for residential use in excess of 2 consecutive calendar months at any one time and such condition is in force [during the year, or][3]

[(f) in the purchase, improvement or repair of a premises which complies with the conditions of *subsection (2F)*.][4]

(2C) (a) For the purposes of *subsections (2A)* and *(2B)*, borrowed money employed on or after the 23rd day of April, 1998, on the construction of a building or part of a building for use or suitable for use as a dwelling on land in which the person chargeable has an estate or interest shall, together with any borrowed money which that person employed in the acquisition of such land, be deemed to be borrowed money employed in the purchase of a residential premises.

(b) In any case where *paragraph (a)* applies, *subsection (2B)(a)* shall apply only where the money is employed on or before the [31st day of March, 1999][5] and the person chargeable—

(i) has before the 23rd day of April, 1998, either—

(I) an estate or interest in land, or

(II) entered into a contract evidenced in writing to acquire an estate or interest in land,

and

(ii) in respect of any building or part of any building for use or suitable for use as a dwelling to be contructed on that land, either—

(I) has entered into a contract evidenced in writing before the 23rd day of April, 1998, for the construction of that building or that part of that building, or

(II) if no such contract exists, satisfies the Revenue Commissioners that the foundation for that building or that part of that building was laid in its entirety before the 23rd day of April, 1998.

(2D) Where—

(a) any premises in respect of which the person chargeable is entitled to a rent or to receipts from any easement consists in part of residential premises and in part of premises which are not residential premises, and

(b) *subsection (2A)* applies,

then, the amount of the deduction which is authorised under *subsection (2)(e)* by reference to interest on borrowed money employed in the purchase, improvement or repair of those premises shall be the amount of interest on that part of the borrowed money which can, on a just and reasonable basis, be attributed to that part of the premises which are not residential premises.

(2E) Notwithstanding anything contained in this section, where a premises in respect of which the person chargeable is entitled to a rent or to receipts from any easement is at any time on or after the 23rd day of April, 1998, the sole or main residence of that person, a deduction shall not be authorised by *subsection (2)(e)* by reference to any interest payable for any year or part of a year commencing after the date on which the premises ceases to be the sole or main residence of that person.][6]

[(2F) (a) The conditions of this subsection are—

(i) the premises was converted into multiple residential units prior to 1 October 1964,

(ii) the premises was acquired by the chargeable person under a contract which was evidenced in writing on or after 5 January 2001,

(iii) subsequent to the acquisition by the chargeable person of the premises, the number of residential units is not, subject to *subparagraph (iv)*, reduced to less than 50 per cent of the total number of residential units contained in the premises at date of acquisition,

(iv) the premises consists throughout the year of a minimum of 3 residential units,

(v) at all times during the year (except for reasonable periods of temporary disuse between the ending of one lease and the commencement of another lease) not less than 50 per cent of the residential units in the premises are let under a lease where the lessee in the case of each such letting is either—

(I) a local authority, or a person nominated by a local authority under an agreement in writing between the lessor and that local authority, or

(II) a person who, at the commencement of the tenancy, is entitled to a payment under [section 198 of the Social Welfare Consolidation Act 2005,][7] in respect of rent,

and

(vi) all the requirements of the following Regulations—

(I) the Housing (Standards for Rented Houses) Regulations, 1993 (S.I. No. 147 of 1993),

(II) the Housing (Rent Books) Regulations, 1993 (S.I. No. 146 of 1993), and

(III) the Housing (Registration of Rented Houses) Regulations, 1996 (S.I. No. 30 of 1996), as amended by the Housing (Registration of Rented Houses) (Amendment) Regulations, 2000 (S.I. No. 12 of 2000),

are complied with in relation to the premises throughout the year,

and

(b) in this subsection—

"*local authority*", in relation to a premises, means the council of a county or the corporation of a county or other borough or, where appropriate, the council of an urban district in whose functional area the premises is located;

"*residential unit*" means a separately contained part of a residential premises used or suitable for use as a dwelling.][8]

[(2G) *Subsections (2A)* to *(2F)* shall not apply or have effect in relation to interest on borrowed money employed [in the purchase, other than from the [spouse or civil partner][9] of the person chargeable][10], improvement or repair of residential premises where that interest accrues on or after 1 January 2002 and, for the purposes of this subsection, interest on such borrowed money shall be treated as accruing from day to day.][11]

[(2H) The reference to 'spouse or civil partner' in subsection (2G) does not include—

(a) a spouse to a marriage—

(i) in which the spouses are separated under an order of a court of competent jurisdiction or by deed of separation, or

(ii) that has been dissolved under either—

(I) section 5 of the Family Law (Divorce) Act 1996, or

(II) the law of a country or jurisdiction other than the State, being a divorce that is entitled to be recognised as valid in the State,

or

[(b) a civil partner in a civil partnership—

(i) in which the civil partners are separated by a deed of separation, agreement, arrangement or any other act giving rise to a legally enforceable obligation and made or done in consideration or in consequence of living separately in the circumstances referred to in *section 1031A(2)*, or

(ii) that has been dissolved under *section 110* of the Civil Partnership and Certain Rights and Obligations of Cohabitants Act 2010 or deemed to have been so dissolved under *section 5(4)* of that Act.][12][13]

[(2I) (a) Notwithstanding *subsection (2)*, a deduction shall not be authorised by *paragraph (e)* of that subsection by reference to interest payable for a chargeable period (within the meaning of *section 321*) on borrowed money employed in the purchase, improvement or repair of a rented residential premises unless the person chargeable can show that the registration requirements of Part 7 of the Residential Tenancies Act 2004 have been complied with in respect of all tenancies which existed in relation to that premises in that chargeable period.

(b) For the purposes of *paragraph (a)*, a written communication from the Private Residential Tenancies Board to the chargeable person confirming the registration of a tenancy, relating to a rented residential premises to which *paragraph (a)* applies, shall be accepted as evidence that the registration requirement in respect of that tenancy (and that tenancy only) has been complied with.][14]

[(2J) (a) Notwithstanding subsection (2) but subject to the other provisions of this section (including paragraph (*b*) of this subsection), the deduction authorised by subsection (2)(*e*) shall not exceed 75 per cent of the deduction that would, but for this subsection, be authorised by subsection (2)(*e*) in respect of interest accrued on or after 7 April 2009 on borrowed money employed in the purchase, improvement or repair of a premises which, at the time the interest accrues, is a residential premises and, for the purposes of this subsection, interest on such borrowed money shall be treated as accruing from day to day.

(b) For the purposes of paragraph (*a*)—

(i) borrowed money employed on the construction of a residential premises on land in which the person chargeable has an estate or interest shall, together with any borrowed money which that person employed in the acquisition of such land, be deemed to be borrowed money employed in the purchase of a residential premises, and

(ii) where a premises consists in part of residential premises and in part of premises which are not residential premises, paragraph (*a*) shall apply to the interest accrued on the part of the borrowed money employed in the purchase, improvement or repair of the premises that is attributable, on a just and reasonable basis, to residential premises.][15]

(3) (a) The amount of the deductions authorised by *subsection (2)* shall be the amount which would be deducted in computing profits or gains under the provisions applicable to Case I of Schedule D if the receipt of rent were deemed to be a trade carried on by the person chargeable—

(i) in the case of a rent under a lease, during the currency of the lease, and

(ii) in the case of a rent not under a lease, during the period during which the person chargeable was entitled to the rent, and the premises comprised in the lease or to which the rent relates were deemed to be occupied for the purpose of that trade.

(b) For the purpose of this subsection, the currency of a lease shall be deemed to include a period immediately following its termination, during which the lessor immediately before the termination was not in occupation of the premises or any part of the premises, but was entitled to possession of the premises, if at the end of that period the premises have become subject to another lease granted by the lessor.

(4) (a) Where the person chargeable is entitled in respect of any premises (in this subsection referred to as "*the relevant premises*") to a rent or to receipts from any easement and a sum by reference to which a deduction is authorised to be made by *subsection (2)* is payable by such person in respect of premises which comprise the whole or a part of the relevant premises and other premises, the inspector shall make, according to the best of his or her knowledge and judgment, any appropriate apportionment of the sum in determining the amount of any deduction under that subsection.

(b) Where the person chargeable retains possession of a part of any premises and that part is used in common by persons respectively occupying other parts of the premises, *paragraph (a)* shall apply as if a payment made in respect of the part used in common had been made in respect of those other parts.

(5) Any amount or part of an amount shall not be deducted under *subsection (2)* if it has otherwise been allowed as a deduction in computing the income of any person for the purposes of tax.

Amendments

1, 5 Substituted by FA99 s31(1). This section shall be deemed to have come into force and shall take effect as on and from the 20th day of May, 1998.

2 Susbtituted by FA01 s34(a)(i).

3 Susbtituted by FA01 s34(a)(ii).

4 Inserted by FA01 s34(a)(iii).

6 Inserted by FA98No2 s1(1)(b). Applies as on and from the 23rd day of April, 1998.

7 Substituted by FA07 sched4(1)(b). Shall have effect as on and from 2 April 2007.

8 Inserted by FA01 s34(b).

9 Substituted by F(No.3)A11 sched1(10). Shall have effect from 27 July 2011.

10 Substituted by FA03 s16(1)(a)(i). Applies and has effect in relation to interest referred to in sections 97(2G) and 248A(2) which accrues on or after 6 February 2003 and, for the purposes of this subsection, such interest shall be treated as accruing from day to day.

11 Inserted by FA02 s17(a).

12 Substituted by F(No.2)A13 sched(1)(a). Has effect as if they had come into operation for the year of assessment (within the meaning of section 2) 2011 and each subsequent year of assessment.

13 Substituted by F(No.3)A11 sched1(11).

14 Inserted by FA06 s11(1)(a).

15 Inserted by FA09 s5. This section is deemed to have come into force and takes effect as on and from 1 January 2009.

Case Law

Letting and legal fees in relation to negotiating leases were deductible as expenses of management of the premises in respect of which the leases were made. Stephen Court Ltd v Browne 1983 III ITR 95

Revenue Briefings

Tax Briefing

Tax Briefing February 1997 – Issue 25 pg 11 – Accountancy Fees are an Allowable Deduction.

Tax Briefing April 1997 – Issue 26 pg 29 – Rental Income Computations

Tax Briefing April 1998 – Issue 31 pg 28 – Rental Income / Pre-Letting Expenses / Leasing

Tax Briefing October 1999 – Issue 37 pg 6 – Rental Income

Tax Briefing October 2002 – Issue 50 pg 13 – Rental Income – Deductibility of Loan Interest and Related Issues

Tax Briefing August 2003 – Issue 53 pg 16 – Mortgage Protection Policy Premiums

Tax Briefing August 2005 – Issue 60 pg 18 – Rent Pooling

Tax Briefing May 2006 – Issue 63 pg 1 – Rental Income – Interest Deduction

Tax Briefing December 2006 – Issue 65 – Registration of Tenancies and Property-based Incentive Schemes

Tax Briefing July 2007 – Issue 66 pg 5 – Interest Relief in Respect of Rental Property

Tax Briefing September 2009 – Issue 73 – 'Rent-to-Buy' (and similar) Schemes

eBrief

eBrief No. 54/2007 – Requirement to Register Tenancies – Reminder

eBrief No. 62/2009 – Rental Income – Treatment of Interest Rate Caps

eBrief No. 45/2009 – 'Rent-to-Buy' (and similar) Schemes

Revenue Precedents

A balancing charge made in charging a person's income under Case V of Schedule D is a Case V surplus for the purpose of section 97(1). IT913011

Interest on borrowed money employed in the purchase, repair or improvement of a rented premises is allowable. In certain situations, Revenue allows interest where the original loan is replaced by another loan. In determining whether such interest is to be allowed, the inspector will take into account all the circumstances of the case, including whether the transaction was a genuine commercial transaction. IT962509

Whether interest paid on a loan used to repay a loan for which relief allowable under section 97 would be allowed under section 97? Yes; provided the redemption of the earlier loan was for bona fide commercial reasons and not for the avoidance of tax, the interest could be allowed in computing profit rent. IT932019

Is pre-letting expenditure allowable under section 97(3) TCA 1997 given that pre-trading expenditure is allowable under section 82 TCA 1997? Pre-letting expenditure is not allowable under section 97(3). The only Case V deductions allowable are those set out in section 97(2). Under Section 97(3), the amount of the deductions authorised under section 97(2) is the amount which would be deducted under Case 1 if the receipt of rent were deemed to be a trade carried on during the currency of the lease or the period during which the recipient of the rent was entitled to that rent. In a pre-letting situation there is no receipt of rent. Accordingly, section 97(3) does not invoke section 82 for the purposes of authorising a deduction for pre-letting expenditure. IT972519

A deduction is allowable under section 97 sub-section (2) (e) where a loan which falls into the subsection is replaced by other borrowings for genuine commercial reasons only. CTF90/302A

Cross References

From Section 97

Section 268 Meaning of "industrial building or structure".

Section 321 Provisions of general application in relation to the making of allowances and charges.

Section 352 Accelerated capital allowances in relation to construction or refurbishment of certain industrial buildings or structures.

Section 353 Capital allowances in relation to construction or refurbishment of certain commercial premises.

Section 356 Rented residential accommodation: deduction for certain expenditure on construction.

Section 357 Rented residential accommodation: deduction for certain expenditure on conversion.

Section 358 Rented residential accommodation: deduction for certain expenditure on refurbishment.

To Section 97

Section 71 Foreign securities and possessions.
Section 75 Case V: basis of assessment.
Section 98 Treatment of premiums, etc. as rent.
Section 103 Deduction by reference to premiums, etc. paid in computation of profits for purposes of this Chapter.
Section 105 Taxation of rents: restriction in respect of certain rent and interest.
Section 106A Transfer of rent.
Section 109 Payments in respect of redundancy.
Section 267H Application (Chapter 6).
Section 372AM Grant of certain certificates and guidelines, qualifying and special qualifying premises.
Section 372AP Relief for lessors.
Section 384 Relief under Case V for losses.
Section 399 Losses in transactions from which income would be chargeable under Case IV or V of Schedule D.
Section 409E Income tax: ringfence on use of certain capital allowances on certain industrial buildings and other premises.
Section 485C Interpretation (Chapter 2A).
Section 664 Relief for certain income from leasing of farm land.
Section 700 Special computational provisions.
Schedule 25B List of Specified Reliefs and Method of Determining Amount of Specified Relief Used in a Tax Year
Schedule 25C Determination of Amount of Relief to be Treated as Referable to Specified Reliefs as Respects Relief Carried Forward from Tax Year 2006 to Tax Year 2007

98 Treatment of premiums, etc. as rent

[ITA67 s83; FA69 s33(1) and Sch4 PtI; FA75 s20 and Sch2 PtI pars1 and 2; CTA76 s140(1) and Sch2 PtI par3]

(1) Where the payment of any premium is required under a lease or otherwise under the terms subject to which a lease is granted and the duration of the lease does not exceed 50 years, the lessor shall be treated for the purposes of *section 75* as becoming entitled when the lease is granted to an amount as rent (in addition to any actual rent) equal to the amount of the premium reduced by 2 per cent of that amount for each complete period of 12 months, other than the first, comprised in the term of the lease.

(2) (a) Where the terms subject to which a lease of any premises is granted impose on the lessee an obligation to carry out any work on the premises, the lease shall be deemed for the purposes of this section to have required the payment of a premium to the lessor (in addition to any other premium) of an amount equal to the amount by which the value of the lessor's estate or interest immediately after the commencement of the lease falls short of what its then value would have been if the work had been carried out, but otherwise than at the expense of the lessee, and the rent were increased accordingly.

(b) Notwithstanding *paragraph (a)*, this subsection shall not apply in so far as the obligation requires the carrying out of work payment for which, if the lessor and not the lessee were obliged to carry it out, would be deductible from the rent under *section 97(2)*.

(3) Where under the terms subject to which a lease is granted a sum becomes payable by the lessee in place of the whole or a part of the rent for any period, or as consideration for the surrender of the lease, the lease shall be deemed for the purposes of this section to have required the payment of a premium to the lessor (in addition to any other premium) of the amount of that sum; but—

(a) in computing tax chargeable by virtue of this subsection in respect of a sum payable in place of rent, the term of the lease shall be treated as not including any period other than that in relation to which the sum is payable, and

(b) notwithstanding *subsection (1)*, rent treated as arising by virtue of this subsection shall be deemed to become due when the sum in question becomes payable by the lessee.

(4) Where as consideration for the variation or waiver of any of the terms of a lease a sum becomes payable by the lessee otherwise than as rent, the lease shall be deemed for the purposes of this section to have required the payment of a premium to the lessor (in addition to any other premium) of the amount of that sum; but—

(a) in computing tax chargeable by virtue of this subsection, the term of the lease shall be treated as not including any period which precedes the time at which the variation or waiver takes effect or falls after the time at which the variation or waiver ceases to have effect, and

(b) notwithstanding *subsection (1)*, rent treated as arising by virtue of this subsection shall be deemed to become due when the contract providing for the variation or waiver is entered into.

(5) Where a payment mentioned in *subsection (1)*, *(3)* or *(4)* is due to a person other than the lessor, *subsection (1)*, *(3)* or *(4)*, as the case may be, shall not apply in relation to that payment, but any amount which would have been treated as rent if the payment had been due to the lessor shall be treated as an annual profit or gain of that other person and chargeable to tax under Case IV of Schedule D; but, where the amount relates to a payment within *subsection (4)*, it shall not be so treated unless the payment is due to a person connected with the lessor.

(6) For the purposes of this section, any sum other than rent paid on or in connection with the granting of a lease shall be presumed to have been paid by means of a premium except in so far as other sufficient consideration for the payment is shown to have been given.

(7) Where *subparagraph (iii)* of *section 96(2)(a)* applies, the premium, or an appropriate part of the premium, payable for or in connection with any lease mentioned in that subparagraph may be treated as having been required under any other lease.

(8) Where an amount by reference to which a person is chargeable to income tax or corporation tax by virtue of this section is payable by instalments, the tax chargeable may, if the person chargeable satisfies the Revenue Commissioners that such person would otherwise suffer undue hardship, be paid at such person's option by such instalments as the Revenue Commissioners may allow over a period not exceeding 8 years and ending not later than the time at which the last of the first-mentioned instalments is payable.

(9) Reference in this section to a sum shall be construed as including the value of any consideration, and references to a sum paid or payable or to the payment of a sum shall be construed accordingly.

Case Law

The distinction between a capital sum and an advance payment of rent was considered in Flynn v Noone Ltd 1953 II ITR 222

Cross References

From Section 98

Section 75 Case V: basis of assessment.

Section 96 Interpretation (Chapter 8).

Section 97 Computational rules and allowable deductions.

To Section 98

Section 96 Interpretation (Chapter 8).
Section 99 Charge on assignment of lease granted at undervalue.
Section 102 Deduction by reference to premium, etc. paid in computation of profits for purposes of Schedule D, Cases I and II.
Section 103 Deduction by reference to premiums, etc. paid in computation of profits for purposes of this Chapter.
Section 274 Balancing allowances and balancing charges.
Section 275 Restriction of balancing allowances on sale of industrial building or structure.
Section 641 Computation under Case I of Schedule D of profits or gains from dealing in or developing land.
Section 918 Making of assessments under Schedules C, D, E and F.
Section 947 Appeals against determination under sections 98 to 100.
Schedule 14 Capital Gains Tax: Leases

98A Taxation of reverse premiums

[(1) (a) In this section—

"*chargeable period*" means an accounting period of a company or a year of assessment;

"*first relevant chargeable period*" means—

(a) the chargeable period in which a relevant transaction is entered into, or

(b) if a relevant transaction is entered into—

(i) by a person receiving a reverse premium, and

(ii) for the purposes of a trade or profession which that person is about to carry on,

the chargeable period in which the person commences to carry on the trade or profession;

"*relevant arrangements*" means a relevant transaction and any arrangements entered into in connection with it, whether before, at the same time or after it;

"*relevant transaction*" means a transaction under which a person is granted an estate or interest in, or a right in or over, land;

"*reverse premium*" means a payment or other benefit received by a person by way of inducement in connection with a relevant transaction being entered into by that person or by a person connected with that person;

"*sale and lease-back arrangement*" means an arrangement under which a person disposes of the full estate or interest held by that person in land to another person and the terms subject to which the disposal is made provide for the grant of a lease of an interest in or a right in or over the land concerned to the person by that other person.

(b) For the purposes of this section persons are connected with each other if they are connected within the meaning of *section 10* at any time during the chargeable period or periods when the relevant arrangements are entered into.

(2) A reverse premium shall, for the purposes of the Tax Acts, be regarded as a receipt of a revenue nature.

(3) Subject to *subsections (4)* and *(6)*, the amount or value of a reverse premium shall be treated as if it were an amount of rent.

(4) Where a relevant transaction is entered into—

(a) by a person receiving a reverse premium, and

(b) for the purposes of a trade or profession carried on or to be carried on by that person,

the amount or value of the reverse premium shall be taken into account in computing the profits or gains of that trade or profession under Case I or II of Schedule D, as the case may be, as if it were a receipt of that trade or profession.

(5) Where—

(a) two or more of the persons who enter into relevant arrangements are connected with each other, and

(b) the terms of those arrangements are not such as would reasonably have been expected if those persons had been dealing at arm's length,

the whole of the amount or value of the reverse premium shall, for the purposes of *subsections (3)* and *(4)* be treated as accruing in the first relevant chargeable period.

(6) Where a reverse premium is received by an assurance company (within the meaning of *section 706*) carrying on life business (within the meaning of *section 706*) in respect of which it is chargeable to tax otherwise than in accordance with the rules applicable to Case I of Schedule D, the amount or value of the reverse premium shall be deducted from the amount treated as the company's expenses of management for the chargeable period in which the reverse premium is received.

(7) This section does not apply to a payment or benefit—

(a) received by an individual in connection with a relevant transaction and the transaction relates to the grant of an estate or interest in, or a right in or over premises occupied or to be occupied by that individual as his or her only or main residence,

(b) to the extent that it is consideration for the transfer of an estate or interest in land which constitutes the sale in a sale and lease-back arrangement where the terms of that arrangement at the time the arrangement is entered into are on bona fide commercial terms, or

(c) to the extent that, apart from this section, it is taken into account in computing the profits or gains of a trade or profession under Case I or II of Schedule D, as the case may be, as a receipt of that trade or profession.][1]

Amendments

[1] Inserted by FA02 s18(1). This section applies as on and from 7 June 2001 in respect of a reverse premium received on or after that date.

Cross References

From Section 98A

Section 10 Connected persons.

Section 706 Interpretation and general (Part 26).

99 Charge on assignment of lease granted at undervalue

[ITA67 s84; FA69 s33(1) and Sch4]

(1) Where the terms subject to which a lease of a duration not exceeding 50 years was granted are such that the lessor, having regard to values prevailing at the time the lease was granted, and on the assumption that the negotiations for the lease were at arm's length, could have required the payment of an additional sum (in this section referred to as "*the amount forgone*") by means of a premium or an

additional premium for the grant of the lease, then, on any assignment of the lease for a consideration—

(a) where the lease has not previously been assigned, exceeding the premium (if any) for which it was granted, or

(b) where the lease has been previously assigned, exceeding the consideration for which it was last assigned,

the amount of the excess, in so far as it is not greater than the amount forgone reduced by the amount of any such excess arising on a previous assignment of the lease, shall, in the same proportion as the amount forgone would under *section 98(1)* have been treated as rent if it had been a premium under a lease, be treated as profits or gains of the assignor chargeable to the tax under Case IV of Schedule D.

(2) In computing the profits or gains of a trade of dealing in land, any trading receipts within this section shall be treated as reduced by the amount on which tax is chargeable by virtue of this section.

Cross References

From Section 99

Section 98 Treatment of premiums, etc. as rent.

To Section 99

Section 102 Deduction by reference to premium, etc. paid in computation of profits for purposes of Schedule D, Cases I and II.

Section 103 Deduction by reference to premiums, etc. paid in computation of profits for purposes of this Chapter.

Section 643 Tax to be charged under Case IV on gains from certain disposals of land.

Section 918 Making of assessments under Schedules C, D, E and F.

Section 947 Appeals against determination under sections 98 to 100.

Schedule 14 Capital Gains Tax: Leases

100 Charge on sale of land with right to reconveyance

[ITA67 s85]

(1) Where the terms subject to which an estate or interest in land is sold provide that it shall be, or may be required to be, reconveyed at a future date to the vendor or a person connected with the vendor, the vendor shall be chargeable to tax under Case IV of Schedule D on any amount by which the price at which the estate or interest is sold exceeds the price at which it is to be reconveyed or, if the earliest date at which in accordance with those terms it would fall to be reconveyed is a date 2 years or more after the sale, on that excess reduced by 2 per cent of that excess for each complete year (other than the first) in the period between the sale and that date.

(2) Where under the terms of the sale the date of the reconveyance is not fixed, then—

(a) if the price on reconveyance varies with the date, the price shall be taken for the purposes of this section to be the lowest possible under the terms of the sale;

[(b) notwithstanding any limitation in *section 865(4)* on the time within which a claim for a repayment of tax is required to be made—

(i) the vendor may, before the expiration of 4 years after the date on which the reconveyance takes place, claim repayment of any amount by which tax assessed on such vendor by virtue of this section exceeded the amount which would have been so assessed if that date had been treated for the purposes of this section as the date fixed by the terms of the sale, and

(ii) *section 865(6)* shall not prevent the Revenue Commissioners from repaying such an amount of tax where a timely claim has been made under this subsection and such a claim is a valid claim within the meaning of *section 865(1)(b)*.][1]

(3) Where the terms of the sale provide for the grant of a lease directly or indirectly out of the estate or interest to the vendor or a person connected with the vendor, this section shall apply as if the grant of the lease were a reconveyance of the estate or interest at a price equal to the sum of the amount of the premium (if any) for the lease and the value at the date of the sale of the right to receive a conveyance of the reversion immediately after the lease begins to run; but this subsection shall not apply if the lease is granted, and begins to run, within one month after the sale.

(4) In computing the profits or gains of a trade of dealing in land, any trading receipts within this section shall be treated as reduced by the amount on which tax is chargeable by virtue of this section; but where, on a claim being made under *subsection (2)(b)*, the amount on which tax is chargeable by virtue of this section is treated as reduced, this subsection shall be deemed to have applied to the amount as reduced, and such adjustment of liability to tax shall be made (for all relevant years of assessment), whether [by means of an amended assessment or otherwise][2], as may be necessary.

Amendments

[1] Substituted by FA08 sched6(1)(a). Applies as on and from 31 January 2008.

[2] Substituted by FA12 sched4(part 2)(g).

Cross References

From Section 100

Section 865 Repayment of tax.

To Section 100

Section 102 Deduction by reference to premium, etc. paid in computation of profits for purposes of Schedule D, Cases I and II.

Section 103 Deduction by reference to premiums, etc. paid in computation of profits for purposes of this Chapter.

Section 643 Tax to be charged under Case IV on gains from certain disposals of land.

Section 918 Making of assessments under Schedules C, D, E and F.

Section 947 Appeals against determination under sections 98 to 100.

Schedule 14 Capital Gains Tax: Leases

101 Relief for amount not received

[ITA67 s90; FA69 s28]

Where on a claim in that behalf the person chargeable proves—

(a) that such person has not received an amount to which such person is entitled and which is to be taken into account in computing the profits or gains on which such person is chargeable by virtue of this Chapter under Case IV or V of Schedule D, and

(b) (i) if the non-receipt of the amount was attributable to the default of the person by whom it was payable, that the amount is irrecoverable, or

(ii) if the person chargeable has waived payment of the amount, that the waiver was made without consideration and was reasonably made in order to avoid hardship, then, the person chargeable shall be treated for tax purposes for all relevant years of assessment as if such person had not been entitled to receive the amount, and such adjustment shall be made by repayment [(notwithstanding any limitation in *section 865(4)* on the time within which a claim for a repayment of tax is required to be made)][1] or otherwise, as the case may require; but, if all or any part of the amount is subsequently received, such person's liability to tax for all relevant years of assessment shall be appropriately readjusted [by amended assessment or otherwise][2].

Amendments

[1] Inserted by FA08 sched6(1)(b). Applies as on and from 31 January 2008.

[2] Substituted by FA12 sched4(part 2)(g).

Cross References

From Section 101

Section 865 Repayment of tax.

To Section 101

Section 1094 Tax clearance certificates in relation to certain licences.

102 Deduction by reference to premium, etc. paid in computation of profits for purposes of Schedule D, Cases I and II

[ITA67 s91; FA75 s22(3) and Sch 2 PtIII]

(1) In this section, "*the relevant period*" means—

(a) where the amount chargeable arose under *section 98*, the period treated in computing that amount as being the duration of the lease;

(b) where the amount chargeable arose under *section 99*, the period treated in computing that amount as being the duration of the lease remaining at the date of the assignment;

(c) where the amount chargeable arose under *section 100*, the period beginning with the sale and ending on the date fixed under the terms of the sale as the date of the reconveyance or grant, or, if that date is not so fixed, ending with the earliest date at which the reconveyance or grant could take place in accordance with the terms of the sale.

(2) Where in relation to any premises an amount (in this section referred to as "*the amount chargeable*")—

(a) has become chargeable to tax under *subsection (1), (2), (3), (4)* or *(5)* of *section 98* or under *section 99* or *100*, or

(b) would have become so chargeable but for *section 103(3)* or any exemption from tax,

and during any part of the relevant period the premises are wholly or partly occupied by the person for the time being entitled to the lease, estate or interest as respects which the amount chargeable arose for the purposes of a trade or profession carried on by such person, such person shall be treated, for the purpose of computing the profits or gains of the trade or profession for assessment under Case I or II of Schedule D, as paying in respect of the premises rent for any part of the relevant period during which the premises are occupied by such person (in addition to any rent actually paid) of an amount which bears to the amount chargeable the same proportion as that part of the relevant period bears to the whole, and such rent shall be taken as accruing from day to day.

(3) Where the amount chargeable arose under *section 98(2)* by reason of an obligation which included the incurring of expenditure in respect of which any allowance has been or will be made under *Part 9*, this section shall apply as if the obligation had not included the incurring of that expenditure and the amount chargeable had been calculated accordingly.

(4) Where the amount chargeable arose under *section 100* and the reconveyance or grant in question takes place at a price different from that taken in calculating that amount or on a date different from that taken in determining the relevant period, *subsections (1)* to *(3)* shall be deemed to have applied (for all relevant years of assessment) as they would have applied if the actual price or date had been so taken and such adjustments of liability to tax shall be made, [by means of amended assessment or otherwise][1], as may be necessary.

Amendments

[1] Substituted by FA12 sched4(part 2)(g).

Cross References

From Section 102

Section 98 Treatment of premiums, etc. as rent.

Section 99 Charge on assignment of lease granted at undervalue.

Section 100 Charge on sale of land with right to reconveyance.

Section 103 Deduction by reference to premiums, etc. paid in computation of profits for purposes of this Chapter.

Section 268 Meaning of "industrial building or structure".

To Section 102

Section 103 Deduction by reference to premiums, etc. paid in computation of profits for purposes of this Chapter.

103 Deduction by reference to premiums, etc. paid in computation of profits for purposes of this Chapter

[ITA67 s92; FA69 s33(1) and Sch4 PtI; FA75 s22 and Sch2 PtIII]

(1) In this section, "*the relevant period*" means, in relation to any amount—

(a) where the amount arose under *section 98*, the period treated in computing that amount as being the duration of the lease;

(b) where the amount arose under *section 99*, the period treated in computing that amount as being the duration of the lease remaining at the date of the assignment;

(c) where the amount arose under *section 100*, the period beginning with the sale and ending on the date fixed under the terms of the sale as the date of the reconveyance or grant, or, if that date is not so fixed, ending with the earliest date at which the reconveyance or grant could take place in accordance with the terms of the sale.

(2) Where in relation to any premises an amount has become or would have become chargeable to tax as mentioned in *section 102(2)* by reference to a lease, estate or interest, the person for the time being entitled to that lease, estate or interest shall, subject to this section, be treated for the purposes of *section 97(2)* as paying rent accruing from day to day in respect of the premises (in addition to any rent actually paid) during any part of the relevant period in relation to the amount for which such person is entitled to the lease, estate or interest and in all bearing to that amount the same proportion as that part of the relevant period bears to the whole.

(3) Where in relation to any premises an amount has become or would have become chargeable to tax as mentioned in *section 102(2)*, and by reference to a lease granted out of, or a disposition of, the lease, estate or interest by reference to which the amount (in this section referred to as "the prior chargeable amount") so became or would have so become chargeable, a person would apart from this subsection be chargeable under *section 98*, *99* or *100* on any amount (in this section referred to as "the later chargeable amount"), the amount on which the person is so chargeable shall be the excess, if any, of the later chargeable amount over the appropriate fraction of the prior chargeable amount or, where the lease or disposition by reference to which the person would be so chargeable extends to a part only of that premises, the excess, if any, of the later chargeable amount over so much of the appropriate fraction of the prior chargeable amount as on a just apportionment is attributable to that part of the premises.

(4) (a) In a case in which *subsection (3)* operates to reduce the amount on which apart from that subsection a person would be chargeable by reference to a lease or disposition, *subsection (2)* shall apply for the relevant period in relation to the later chargeable amount only if the appropriate fraction of the prior chargeable amount exceeds the later chargeable amount and shall then apply as if the prior chargeable amount were reduced in the proportion which the excess bears to that appropriate fraction.

(b) Notwithstanding *paragraph (a)*, where the lease or disposition extends to a part only of the premises mentioned in *subsection (3)*, *subsection (2)* and this subsection shall be applied separately in relation to that part and to the remainder of the premises, but as if for any reference to the prior chargeable amount there were substituted a reference to that amount proportionately adjusted.

(5) For the purposes of *subsections (3)* and *(4)*, the appropriate fraction of the prior chargeable amount shall be the sum which bears to that amount the same proportion as the length of the relevant period in relation to the later chargeable amount bears to the length of the relevant period in relation to the prior chargeable amount.

(6) Where the prior chargeable amount arose under *section 98(2)* by reason of an obligation which included the incurring of expenditure in respect of which any allowance has been or will be made under *Part 9*, this section shall apply as if the obligation had not included the incurring of that expenditure and the prior chargeable amount had been calculated accordingly.

(7) Where the prior chargeable amount arose under *section 100* and the reconveyance or grant in question takes place at a price different from that taken in calculating that amount or on a date different from that taken in determining the relevant period in relation to that amount, *subsections (1)* to *(6)* shall be deemed to have applied (for all relevant years of assessment) as they would have applied if the actual price or date had been so taken and such adjustments of liability to tax shall be made, [by means of amended assessment or otherwise][1], as may be necessary.

Amendments

[1] Substituted by FA12 sched4(part 2)(g).

Cross References

From Section 103

Section 97 Computational rules and allowable deductions.
Section 98 Treatment of premiums, etc. as rent.
Section 99 Charge on assignment of lease granted at undervalue.

Section 100 Charge on sale of land with right to reconveyance.
Section 102 Deduction by reference to premium, etc. paid in computation of profits for purposes of Schedule D, Cases I and II.
Section 268 Meaning of "industrial building or structure".

To Section 103

Section 102 Deduction by reference to premium, etc. paid in computation of profits for purposes of Schedule D, Cases I and II.
Schedule 14 Capital Gains Tax: Leases

104 Taxation of certain rents and other payments

[ITA67 s93(1) and (2); FA69 s29]

(1) (a) This section shall apply to the following payments—

(i) any rent payable in respect of any premises or easements where the premises or easements are used, occupied or enjoyed in connection with any of the concerns the profits or gains arising out of which are chargeable to tax under Case I(*b*) of Schedule D by virtue of *section 18(2)*, and

(ii) any yearly interest, annuity or other annual payment reserved in respect of, or charged on or issuing out of any premises, not being a rent or a payment in respect of an easement.

(b) In *paragraph (a)(i)*, the reference to rent shall be deemed to include a reference to a toll, duty, royalty or annual or periodical payment in the nature of rent, whether payable in money, money's worth or otherwise.

(2) (a) Any payment to which this section applies shall—

(i) in so far as it is not within any other Case of Schedule D, be charged with tax under Case IV of that Schedule, and

(ii) be treated for the purposes of *sections 81(2)(m)*, *237* and *238* as if it were a royalty paid in respect of the user of a patent.

(b) Notwithstanding *paragraph (a)*, where a rent mentioned in *subsection (1)(a)* is rendered in produce of the concern, this subsection shall apply as if *paragraph (a)(ii)* were deleted, and the value of the produce so rendered shall be taken to be the amount of profits or gains arising from that produce.

Cross References

From Section 104

Section 18 Schedule D.
Section 81 General rule as to deductions.
Section 237 Annual payments payable wholly out of taxed income.
Section 238 Annual payments not payable out of taxed income.

To Section 104

Section 75 Case V: basis of assessment.
Section 76 Computation of income: application of income tax principles.
Section 243 Allowance of charges on income.
Section 730K Disposal of foreign life policy.
Section 1087 Charge and deduction of income tax not charged or deducted before passing of annual Act.

105 Taxation of rents: restriction in respect of certain rent and interest

[FA74 s62(1) and (2)]

(1) This section shall apply to—

(a) rent in respect of premises, or

(b) interest on borrowed money employed in the purchase, improvement or repair of premises, payable by a person chargeable to tax in accordance with *section 75* on the profits or gains arising from rent in respect of those premises for a period before the date on which the premises are first occupied by a lessee for the purpose of a trade or undertaking or for use as a residence.

(2) No deduction shall be allowed for any year of assessment under *section 97(2)* in respect of rent or interest to which this section applies.

Cross References

From Section 105

Section 75 Case V: basis of assessment.

Section 97 Computational rules and allowable deductions.

106 Tax treatment of receipts and outgoings on sale of premises

[FA69 s26(1) to (4)]

(1) Where by virtue of a contract for the sale of an estate or interest in premises there is to be apportioned between the parties a receipt or outgoing in respect of the estate or interest which becomes due after the making of the contract but before the time at which the apportionment is to be made, and a part of the receipt is therefore receivable by the vendor in trust for the purchaser or, as the case may be, a part of the outgoing is paid by the vendor as trustee for the purchaser, the purchaser shall be treated for the purposes of tax under Case V of Schedule D as if that part had become receivable or payable on the purchaser's behalf immediately after the time at which the apportionment is to be made.

(2) Where by virtue of such a contract there is to be apportioned between the parties a receipt or outgoing in respect of the estate or interest which became due before the making of the contract, the parties shall be treated for the purposes of tax under Case V of Schedule D as if the contract had been entered into before the receipt or outgoing became due, and *subsection (1)* shall apply accordingly.

(3) Where on the sale of an estate or interest in premises there is apportioned to the vendor a part of a receipt or outgoing in respect of the estate or interest which becomes receivable or is paid by the purchaser after the making of the apportionment, then, for the purposes of tax under Case V of Schedule D—

(a) when the receipt becomes due or, as the case may be, the outgoing is paid, the amount of the receipt or outgoing, as the case may be, shall be treated as reduced by so much of that amount as was apportioned to the vendor, and

(b) the part apportioned to the vendor shall be treated as if it were of the same nature as the receipt or outgoing and had become receivable, or had been paid, directly by the vendor and, where it is a part of an outgoing, had become due, immediately before the time at which the apportionment is made.

(4) Any reference in *subsection (1)* or *(2)* to a party to a contract shall include a person to whom the rights and obligations of that party under the contract have passed by assignment or otherwise.

Cross References

To Section 106

Section 1094 Tax clearance certificates in relation to certain licences.

106A Transfer of rent

[(1) (a) In this section—

"*relevant transaction*" means any scheme, arrangement or understanding under which a person becomes entitled to receive a capital sum and the consideration given for the entitlement to receive the sum consists wholly or mainly of the direct or indirect transfer to another person of a right to receive rent which, in the absence of the scheme, arrangement or understanding, could reasonably have been expected to accrue to the first-mentioned person or to a person connected with that person;

"*rent*" includes any sum which—

(i) is chargeable to tax under Case V of Schedule D, or

(ii) would be so chargeable if the source of the sum were in the State.

(b) For the purposes of this section, a scheme, arrangement or understanding under which a person grants a lease in connection with which—

(i) the person is entitled to a capital sum,

(ii) rent is payable to another person, and

(iii) the consideration given for the entitlement to receive the capital sum consists wholly or mainly of the grant to the other person or a person connected with the other person of a right to rent under the lease,

shall be treated as a relevant transaction and this section applies as if the capital sum were a capital sum under the relevant transaction.

(2) (a) Subject to *paragraph (b)*, where a person other than a company becomes entitled to receive a capital sum under a relevant transaction, the capital sum shall be treated for the purposes of the Tax Acts as being an amount of income of the person chargeable to tax under Case IV of Schedule D for the year of assessment—

(i) in which the person becomes entitled to the capital sum, or

(ii) if it is earlier, in which the sum was received.

(b) *Paragraph (a)* does not apply to a person, other than an individual, if the consideration for the capital sum—

(i) was given by the person, and

(ii) is a qualifying asset (within the meaning of *section 110*) acquired by a qualifying company (within the meaning of that section) in the course of its business.

(3) Any profits or gains arising by virtue of a relevant transaction to the person to whom the right to receive rent was transferred shall be computed in accordance with *section 97*, and shall, notwithstanding any other provision of the Tax Acts, be chargeable to tax under Case V of Schedule D: but this subsection does not apply in relation to a person if—

(a) the consideration received by the person for the capital sum is a qualifying asset (within the meaning of *section 110*) acquired by a qualifying company (within the meaning of that section) in the course of its business, and

(b) the asset was acquired from a person other than an individual.][1]

Amendments

[1] Inserted by FA03 s36(1).

Cross References

From Section 106A

Section 97 Computational rules and allowable deductions.
Section 110 Securitisation.

CHAPTER 9

Miscellaneous Provisions

107 Apportionment of profits

[ITA67 s107; FA69 s65(1) and Sch5 PtI]

(1) Where in the case of any profits or gains chargeable under Case I, II or IV of Schedule D it is necessary, in order to determine the profits or gains or losses of any year of assessment or other period, to divide and apportion to specific periods the profits or gains or losses for any period for which the accounts have been made up, or to aggregate any such profits or gains or losses or any apportioned parts of such profits or gains or losses, it shall be lawful to make such division and apportionment or aggregation.

(2) Any apportionment under this section shall be made in proportion to the number of months or fractions of months in the respective periods.

Cross References

To Section 107

Section 1008 Separate assessment of partners.

108 Statement of profits

[ITA67 s68(1)]

Every statement of profits to be charged under Schedule D which is made by any person—

(a) on that person's own account, or

(b) on account of another person for whom that person is chargeable, or who is chargeable in that person's name,

shall include every source of income so chargeable.

Cross References

To Section 108

Section 56 Tax on quarries, mines and other concerns chargeable under Case I(b) of Schedule D.

109 Payments in respect of redundancy

[FA68 s37(1) and (3) to (7); FA74 s86 and Sch2 PtI; CTA76 s140(1) and Sch2 PtI par30; FA77 s42 and Sch1 PtIV par2]

(1) In this section, "*lump sum*" and "*rebate*" have the same meanings respectively as in the Redundancy Payments Act, 1967.

(2) Where a lump sum is paid by an employer in respect of employment wholly in a trade or profession carried on by the employer and within the charge to income tax or corporation tax, the amount of the lump sum shall (if not otherwise so allowable) be allowable as a deduction in computing for the purposes of Schedule D the profits or gains or losses of the trade or profession, but if it is so allowed by virtue of this section the amount of the rebate recoverable shall (if it is not otherwise to be so treated) be treated as a receipt to be taken into account in computing those

profits or gains and, if the lump sum was paid after the discontinuance of the trade or profession, the net amount so deductible shall be treated as if it were a payment made on the last day on which the trade or profession was carried on.

(3) Where a lump sum is paid by an employer in respect of employment wholly in a business carried on by the employer and expenses of management of the business are eligible for relief under [*section 83* or *707*][1], the amount by which the lump sum exceeds the amount of the rebate recoverable shall (if not otherwise so allowable) be allowable as expenses of management eligible for relief under that section and, if the lump sum was paid after the discontinuance of the business, the net amount so allowable shall be treated as if it were expenses of management incurred on the last day on which the business was carried on.

(4) Where a lump sum is paid by an employer in respect of employment wholly in maintaining or managing premises and the expenses of maintaining or managing the premises were deductible under *section 97*, the amount by which the lump sum exceeds the amount of the rebate recoverable shall (if not otherwise allowable under that section) be treated for the purposes of *section 97* as a payment made by the employer in respect of the maintenance or management of the premises and, if the payment was made after the latest time when it could be taken into account under *section 97* as a payment in respect of the maintenance or management of the property, it shall be treated as having been made at that time.

(5) Relief shall not be given under *subsections (2)* to *(4)*, or otherwise, more than once in respect of any lump sum and, if the employee was being employed by the employer in such a way that different parts of the employee's remuneration fell to be treated for income tax purposes in different ways, the amount (in this subsection referred to as "*the excess amount*") by which the lump sum exceeds the amount of the rebate recoverable shall be apportioned to the different capacities in which the employee was employed, and *subsections (2)* to *(4)* shall apply separately to the employment in those capacities, and by reference to the apportioned part of the excess amount, instead of by reference to the full amount of the lump sum and the full amount of the rebate.

(6) Where under section 32 of the Redundancy Payments Act, 1967, a payment of the whole or part of a lump sum is made by the Minister for Enterprise, Trade and Employment, the payment shall, in so far as the employer has reimbursed that Minister, be deemed for the purposes of this section to have been made by the employer.

Amendments

[1] Substituted by FA98 sched9(2).

Cross References

From Section 109

Section 83 Expenses of management of investment companies.

Section 97 Computational rules and allowable deductions.

Section 709 Companies carrying on life business.

To Section 109

Section 83 Expenses of management of investment companies.

110 Securitisation

[(1) In this section—

"*authorised officer*" means an officer of the Revenue Commissioners authorised by them in writing for the purposes of this section;

[“*carbon offsets*” means—

(a) an allowance, permit, licence or right to emit during a specified period, a specified amount of carbon dioxide or any other greenhouse gas as defined in Directive 2003/87/EC of the European Parliament and of the Council of 13 October 2003* establishing a scheme for greenhouse gas emission allowance trading within the Community and amending Council Directive 96/61/EC of 24 September 1996†, where such allowance, permit, licence or right is issued by a State or by an inter-governmental or supra-national institution pursuant to a scheme which—

*OJ No. L275 of 25.10.2003, p.32
†OJ No. L257 of 10.10.1996, p.26

(i) imposes limitations on the emission of such greenhouse gases, and
(ii) allows the transfer for value of such allowances, permits, licences or rights,

(b) an allowance, permit, licence or right to emit during a specified period, a specified amount of carbon dioxide or any other recognised greenhouse gas under a voluntary scheme sponsored by a State or by an inter-governmental institution, or regulated commercial enterprise, where such allowance, permit, licence or right is subject to recognised independent periodic verification, monitoring and [reporting][1]

[(ba) a forest carbon offset issued pursuant to the United Nations [Reducing][2] Emissions from Deforestation and Forest Degradation [process][3], or][4]

[(c) any right that is directly attributable to an offset, allowance, permit, licence or right to emit within *paragraph (a), (b)* or *(ba)*;][5]

"*commodities*" means tangible assets (other than currency, securities, debts or other assets of a financial nature) which are dealt in on a recognised commodity exchange;][6]

["*qualifying asset*" means an asset which consists of, or of an interest (including a partnership interest) in—

(a) a financial asset,
(b) commodities, or
(c) plant and machinery;][7]

"*financial asset*" includes—

(a) shares, bonds and other securities,
(b) futures, options, swaps, derivatives and similar instruments,
(c) invoices and all types of receivables,
(d) obligations evidencing debt (including loans and deposits),
(e) leases and loan and lease portfolios,
(f) hire purchase contracts,
(g) acceptance credits and all other documents of title relating to the movement of goods, [...][8]
(h) bills of exchange, commercial paper, promissory notes and all other kinds of negotiable or transferable [instruments,][9]
[(i) carbon offsets, and][10]
(j) contracts for insurance and contracts for reinsurance;][11]

[...][12]

"*qualifying company*" means a company—

(a) which is resident in the State,

(b) which—
(i) acquires qualifying assets from a person,
(ii) as a result of an arrangement with another person holds or manages qualifying assets, or
(iii) has entered into a legally enforceable arrangement with another person which arrangement itself constitutes a qualifying asset,

[(c) which carries on in the State a business of holding, managing or both the holding and managing of qualifying assets, including, in the case of plant and machinery acquired by the qualifying company, a business of leasing that plant and machinery,][13]

(d) which, apart from activities ancillary to that business, carries on no other activities,

(e) in relation to which company—
(i) the market value of all qualifying assets held or managed, or
(ii) the market value of all qualifying assets in respect of which the company has entered into legally enforceable arrangements,

is not less than €10,000,000 on the day on which the qualifying assets are first acquired, first held, or an arrangement referred to in *subparagraph (iii)* of *paragraph (b)* is first entered into, by the company, and

(f) which has notified in writing the authorised officer in a form prescribed by the Revenue Commissioners that it is or intends to be a company to which *paragraphs (a)* to *(e)* apply and has supplied such other particulars relating to the company as may be specified on the prescribed form [on or before the specified return date (within the meaning of [*section 959A*][14]) for the first accounting period, in relation to which it is such a company,][15]

but a company shall not be a qualifying company if any transaction or arrangement is entered into by it otherwise than by way of a bargain made at arm's length, apart from a transaction or arrangement where *subsection (4)* applies to any interest or other distribution payable under the transaction or arrangement unless the transaction or arrangement concerned is excluded from that provision [by virtue of *subsections (4A)* and *(5)*][16].

["*quoted Eurobond*" has the same meaning as in *section 64*;

"*return agreement*", in relation to a qualifying company, means a specified agreement whereby payments due under the specified agreement are dependent on the results of the company's business or any part of the company's business;

"*specified instrument*" means a quoted Eurobond or wholesale debt instrument;

"*specified person*", in relation to a qualifying company, means—

(a) a company which directly or indirectly—
(i) controls the qualifying company,
(ii) is controlled by the qualifying company, or
(iii) is controlled by a third company which also directly or indirectly controls the qualifying company,

where "*controls*" and "*controlled*" have the same meanings as they would have by the application of *section 11* to this paragraph, or

(b) a person, or persons who are connected with each other—
(i) from whom assets were acquired, or
(ii) to whom the qualifying company has made loans or advances, or

(iii) with whom the qualifying company has entered into specified agreements, where the aggregate value of such assets, loans, advances or agreements represents not less than 75 per cent of the aggregate value of the qualifying assets of the qualifying company;

"*specified agreement*" means any agreement, arrangement or understanding that—

(a) provides for the exchange, on a fixed or contingent basis, of one or more payments based on the value, rate or amount of one or more interest or other rates, currencies, commodities, securities, instruments of indebtedness, indices, quantitative measures, or other financial or economic interests or property of any kind, or any interest therein or based on the value thereof, and

(b) transfers to a person who is a party to the agreement, arrangement or understanding or to a person connected with that person, in whole or in part, the financial risk associated with a future change in any such value, rate or amount without also conveying a current or future direct or indirect ownership interest in an asset (including any enterprise or investment pool) or liability that incorporates the financial risk so transferred;

"*wholesale debt instrument*" has the same meaning as in *section 246A*.][17]

(2) For the purposes of the Tax Acts, profits arising to a qualifying company, in relation to activities carried out by it in the course of its business, shall, notwithstanding any other provisions of the Tax Acts, be treated as annual profits or gains within Schedule D and shall be chargeable to corporation tax under Case III of that Schedule, and for that purpose—

(a) the profits or gains shall be computed in accordance with the provisions applicable to Case I of that Schedule,

(b) there shall be deducted, in computing the amount of the profits or gains to be charged to tax, the amount, in so far as it is not—

(i) otherwise deductible, or

(ii) recoverable from any other person or under any insurance, contract of indemnity or otherwise,

of any debt which is proved to be bad and of a doubtful debt to the extent that it is estimated to be bad, and

(c) where at any time an amount or part of an amount which had been deducted under *paragraph (b)* is recovered or is no longer estimated to be bad, the amount which had been deducted shall, in so far as it is recovered or no longer estimated to be bad, be treated as income of the qualifying company at that time.

(3) (a) Notwithstanding *Chapter 5* of *Part 12*, a qualifying company shall not be eligible to surrender in accordance with that Chapter any amount eligible for relief from corporation tax.

(b) (i) Where in an accounting period a qualifying company incurs a loss, the company may make a claim requiring that the amount of the loss be set off against the amount of any profits of the company for any subsequent accounting period for so long as the company continues to be a qualifying company, and the company's profits for any accounting period shall be treated as reduced by the amount of the loss.

(ii) The claim referred to in *subparagraph (i)* shall be included with the return which the company is required to make under [*Chapter 3* of *Part 41A*][18] for the subsequent accounting period concerned.

(iii) The amount of a loss incurred by a qualifying company in an accounting period shall be computed for the purposes of this paragraph in the same way as any profits of the company in that period would have been computed under *subsection (2)*.

[(4) Subject to *subsections (4A)* and *(5)*, any interest or other distribution which is paid out of the assets of a qualifying company to another person and is so paid in respect of a security referred to in *section 130(2)(d)*(iii), shall not be a distribution by virtue only of the provisions of that section.][19]

[(4A) (a) For the purposes of this subsection "*relevant territory*" and "*tax*" have the same meanings as in *section 246*.

(b) Subject to *paragraph (c)*, as respects any interest or other distribution paid by a qualifying company to a person, other than—

[(i) a person who is resident in the State or, if not so resident, is otherwise within the charge to corporation tax in the State in respect of that interest or other distribution, or][20]

(ii) a person, (not being a specified person) who is a pension fund, government body or other person resident in a relevant territory who, under the laws of that territory, is exempted from tax which generally applies to profits, income or gains in that territory,

subsection (4) shall only apply to so much of such interest or other distribution—

(I) as under the laws of a relevant territory, is subject, without any reduction computed by reference to the amount of such interest or other distribution, to a tax which generally applies to profits, income or gains received in that territory, by persons, from sources outside that territory, or

(II) as is a payment from which tax has been deducted at the standard rate in force at the time of the payment in accordance with *section 246(2)*.

(c) Notwithstanding *paragraph (b)*, *subsection (4)* shall apply to any interest or other distribution paid by a qualifying company in respect of a specified instrument other than so much of such interest or other distribution as is paid to a specified person in respect of a specified instrument where, at the time the instrument was issued, the qualifying company was in possession, or aware, of information, including information about any arrangement or understanding in relation to ownership of the instrument after that time, which could reasonably be taken to indicate that interest or other distributions which would be payable in respect of that instrument would not be subject, without any reduction computed by reference to the amount of such interest or other distribution, to a tax in a relevant territory which generally applies to profits, income or gains received in that territory, by persons, from sources outside that territory.

(4B) Where any amount, paid out of the assets of a qualifying company under a return agreement, that is dependent on the results of that company's business or any part of that business, would not be deducted in computing profits or gains of that company if that amount were to be treated, for all the purposes of the Tax Acts, other than *subsection (2)* of *section 246*, as a payment of interest, in respect of securities of the company other than specified instruments, that was dependent on the results of the company's business, then that amount shall not be so deducted.][21]][22]

[(5) *Subsection (4)* shall not apply in respect of any interest or other distribution as is paid by a qualifying company where the qualifying company concerned is, at the time of the payment, in possession, or aware, of information that can reasonably be taken to indicate that the payment is part of a scheme or arrangement the main benefit or one of the main benefits of which is the obtaining of a tax relief or the reduction of a tax liability the benefit of which would be expected to accrue to a person who, in relation to the qualifying company, is a specified person.][23]

[(6) (a) Subject to *paragraph (b)*, *section 76A* shall have effect in relation to a qualifying company as it would if, in *section 4*, the following were substituted for the definition of generally accepted accounting practice:

"*generally accepted accounting practice*" means Irish generally accepted accounting practice as it applied for a period of account ending on 31 December 2004.

(b) A qualifying company may, as respect any accounting period, by notice in writing given to the inspector by the specified return date (within the meaning of [*section 959A*][24]) for the accounting period, elect that this subsection shall not apply as respects that or any subsequent accounting period; and any election under this paragraph shall be irrevocable.

(c) *Schedule 17A* shall apply with any necessary modifications to a company which makes an election under *paragraph (b)*.][25]

Amendments

[1] Substituted by FA12 s41(1)(a). Deemed to have come into force and takes effect on and from 1 January 2012.

[2,3] Substituted by FA13 sched2(1)(a). Has effect on and from 27 March 2013.

[4] Inserted by FA12 s41(1)(b). Deemed to have come into force and takes effect on and from 1 January 2012.

[5] Substituted by FA12 s41(1)(c). Deemed to have come into force and takes effect on and from 1 January 2012.

[6] Inserted by FA11 s40(1)(a).

[7] Substituted by FA11 s40(1)(b).

[8] Deleted by FA08 s36(1)(b)(i). This section applies on and from 13 March 2008.

[9] Substituted by FA08 s36(1)(b)(i). This section applies on and from 13 March 2008.

[10] Substituted by FA11 s40(1)(c).

[11] Inserted by FA08 s36(1)(b)(ii). This section applies on and from 13 March 2008.

[12] Deleted by FA11 s40(1)(d).

[13] Substituted by FA11 s40(1)(e).

[14] Substituted by FA13 s92 and sched1(part 2)(b).

[15] Inserted by FA12 s41(2). Deemed to have come into force and takes effect on and from 1 January 2012.

[16] Substituted by FA11 s40(1)(f).

[17] Inserted by FA11 s40(1)(g).

[18,24] Substituted by FA12 sched4(part 2)(g).

[19] Substituted by FA11 s40(2).

[20] Substituted by FA12 s41(3). Deemed to have come into force and takes effect on and from 1 January 2012.

[21] Inserted by FA11 s40(3).

[22] Substituted by FA03 s48(1). Applies as respects any asset on or after 6 February 2003.

[23] Substituted by FA11 s40(4).

[25] Inserted by FA05 s48(1)(d). This section applies as respects any period of account beginning on or after 1 January 2005.

Note:

FA13 s92 applies—

(a) in the case of a chargeable period (within the meaning of section 321(2)) which is an accounting period of a company, as respects chargeable periods that start on or after 1 January 2013, and

(b) in a case other than that referred to in paragraph (a), as respects the year of assessment (within the meaning of section 2(1)) 2013 and subsequent years of assessment.

Revenue Briefings

Tax Briefing

Tax Briefing April 2012 – Issue 02 – Securitisation Transactions

Tax Briefing October 2012 – Issue 06 – Tax Treatment of Debt Issuance Costs

eBrief

eBrief No. 01/2010 – Exemption from Encashment Tax for "Qualifying Company" within the meaning of section 110 of the Taxes Consolidation Act 1997

eBrief No. 48/2012 – Tax Treatment of Debt Issuance Costs

Cross References

From Section 110

Section 4 Interpretation of Corporation Tax Acts.
Section 11 Meaning of "control" in certain contexts.
Section 64 Interest on quoted Eurobonds.
Section 76A Computation of profits or gains of a company – accounting standards.
Section 130 Matters to be treated as distributions.
Section 246 Interest payments by companies and to non-residents.
Section 246A Interest in respect of wholesale debt instruments.
Section 381 Right to repayment of tax by reference to losses.
Section 410 Group payments.
Section 950 Interpretation (Part 41).
Section 951 Obligation to make a return.
Schedule 17A Accounting Standards

To Section 110

Section 106A Transfer of rent.
Section 198 Certain interest not to be chargeable.
Section 246 Interest payments by companies and to non-residents.
Section 446 Certain trading operations carried on in Custom House Docks Area.
Section 739D Gain arising on a chargeable event.
Section 739G Taxation of unit holders in investment undertakings.Taxation of unit holders in investment undertakings.
Section 840A Interest on loans to defray money applied for certain purposes.
Schedule 31 Consequential Amendments

111 Allowance to owner of let mineral rights for expenses of management of minerals

[ITA67 s553; F(MP)A68 s3(2) and Sch PtI and s3(5) and Sch PtIV; FA81 s9(c)]

(1) (a) Where for any year of assessment rights to work minerals in the State are let, the lessor shall be entitled on making a claim in that behalf to be repaid so much of the income tax paid by such lessor by deduction or otherwise in respect of the rent or royalties for that year as is equal to the amount of the tax on any sums proved to have been wholly, exclusively

and necessarily disbursed by such lessor as expenses of management or supervision of those minerals in that year.

(b) Notwithstanding *paragraph (a)*, no repayment of tax under that paragraph shall be made—

(i) except on proof of payment of tax on the aggregate amount of the rent or royalties, or

(ii) if, or to such extent as, the expenses of management or supervision have been otherwise allowed as a deduction in computing income for the purposes of income tax.

(2) Notice of any claim under this section together with the particulars of the claim shall be given in writing within 24 months after the expiration of the year of assessment in respect of which the claim is made, and where the inspector objects to such claim the Appeal Commissioners shall hear and determine the claim in the like manner as in the case of an appeal to them against an assessment under Schedule D, and the provisions of the Income Tax Acts relating to the statement of a case for the opinion of the High Court on a point of law shall apply.

Cross References

To Section 111

Section 77 Miscellaneous special rules for computation of income.

PART 5

Principal Provisions Relating to the Schedule E Charge

CHAPTER 1

Basis of Assessment, Persons Chargeable and Extent of Charge

112 Basis of assessment, persons chargeable and extent of charge

[ITA67 s110; FA90 s19(a); FA91 s6]

(1) Income tax under Schedule E [shall be charged for each year of assessment][1] on every person having or exercising an office or employment of profit mentioned in that Schedule, or to whom any annuity, pension or stipend chargeable under that Schedule is payable, in respect of all salaries, fees, wages, perquisites or profits whatever therefrom, and shall be computed on the amount of all such salaries, fees, wages, perquisites or profits whatever therefrom for the year of assessment.

(2) (a) In this subsection, "*emoluments*" means anything assessable to income tax under Schedule E.

(b) Where apart from this subsection emoluments from an office or employment would be for a year of assessment in which a person does not hold the office or employment, the following provisions shall apply for the purposes of *subsection (1)*:

(i) if in the year concerned the office or employment has never been held, the emoluments shall be treated as emoluments for the first year of assessment in which the office or employment is held, and

(ii) if in the year concerned the office or employment is no longer held, the emoluments shall be treated as emoluments for the last year of assessment in which the office or employment was held.

Amendments

[1] Substituted by FA01 sched2(5).

Case Law

Office

In Great Western Railway v Bater 1922 8 TC 231 the definition of 'office' was "a subsisting, permanent, substantive position, which had an existence independent of the person who filled it, which went on and was filled in succession by successive holders".

The meaning of the word 'office' was also considered in Edwards v Clinch 1980 STC 438. In this case it was held that an independent local inquiry inspector was not the holder of an 'office' within the meaning of the word as used in Schedule E.

Employment

In Market Investigations v Minister of Social Security 1969 2 QB 173, the fundamental test was 'is the person who has engaged himself to perform these services performing them as a person in business on his own account?'

A professional actress who had entered into separate contracts for each play, film, radio appearance etc. for which she was engaged, was held assessable under Schedule D. Davies v Braithwaite 1931 18 TC 198

In contrast to Davies v Braithwaite, in Fall v Hitchen 1972 49 TC 433 a professional dancer was required to work full-time, during specified hours, for a regular salary, and was not permitted to perform elsewhere without consent. It was held that the taxpayer acted under a contract of service and was assessable under Schedule E.

In Dolan (Inspector of Taxes) v K. National School Teacher 1943 I ITR 656 a nun worked as a qualified national school teacher in a school conducted by her order. She was obliged to the hand over her income to the order by virtue of her vows. She remained liable to tax under Schedule E.

An early Irish case, Roche v Kelly 1968 IR 100 held that the principal test is the right of the master to direct servants as to what is to be done and how it is to be done.

An insurance agent who had purchased his own collection book and was not subject to any restrictions was held to be in business on his own account. McDermott v Loy TL 118 (HC July 1982)

The case of Ready Mixed Concrete (SE) Ltd v Minister of Pensions and National Insurance 1968 2 QB 497 laid down three tests – work and skill, control over the worker, and financial risk. If these were met, a contract of service existed.

In O'Coindealbhain v Mooney 1988 IV ITR 45, the taxpayer acted as branch manager for the Department of Social Welfare. The Court found that a contract for services existed and that the features of the contract were inconsistent with a contract of service as they pointed to an independent contractor.

The case of Hall v Lorimer 1994 STC 23 indicates that it is necessary to consider the personal factors existing outside the terms of each individual contract. In this case, a vison mixer who worked under a series of one and two-day contracts for a wide range of paymasters, employed no staff and did not use his own equipment, was held to be self-employed.

In the leading Irish case of Henry Denny & Sons v Minister for Social Welfare 1997 V ITR 283 the High Court found that a supermarket demonstrator was engaged under a contract of service and the decision was upheld by the Supreme Court. Justice Keane, in his judgment, placed the emphasis on the substance of the contract over its form.

The findings in the Denny case were followed in Tierney v An Post 2000 1 IR 536, Castleisland Cattle Breeding Society Ltd v Minister for Social Affairs 2004 4 IR 150 and ESB v Minister for Social Community and Family Affairs 2006 IEHC 59

In McLoughlin v Director of Public Prosecutions 1986 III ITR 467, members of a fishing crew, who were entitled to a share of the proceeds of sale of the catch, were held not to be employees.

In the UK case of Barnett v Brabyn 1996 STC 716 it was held that Mr Barnett, who was engaged as a video and television technician without a written contract, was an independent contractor. This case emphasised an important point that there is little to be gained from comparing the facts of one case with another when the Judge said, " factors relevant in one situation may be irrelevant or of no weight in another" The same principle from the Barnett case was applied in Walls v Sinnett 1986 60 TC 150.

In Neenan Travel Limited v Minister for Social and Family Affairs 2011 IEHC 458, the court in this case were asked to determine whether or not a proprietary director was liable to PRSI as a Class A or a Class S contributor. The issues of employed versus self employed for income tax purposes were also examined.

In Brightwater Selection [Ireland] Ltd v Minister for Social and Family Affairs 2011 IEHC 510, this case examined whether an agency worker for Brightwater was engaged under a contract of service and thereby insurable at the PRSI Class A rate of contribution.

Emoluments and Perquisites

A teacher who took night classes under a separate contract with her employer was assessable under Schedule E. Fuge v Mc Clelland 36 TC 571

The main charging words of Schedule E are only applicable to tax money or money's worth. Tennant v Smith 1892 3 TC 158

In Wilkins v Rogerson 39 TC 44, an employer arranged for a tailor to provide certain employees with a suit up to the cost of £15, and the cost was covered by the employer. It was held that the emolument to be taxed was not the cost of the suit but the price the employee would get if he sold it.

In Connolly v McNamara 3 ITC 341 a company paid the weekly rent payable by its employee under a letting agreement with the council. The employee was not required to live in the house for the purpose of his employment. The High Court held that the employee was assessable under Schedule E on the rent paid.

In Shilton v Wilmshurst 1991 STC 88 a footballer was paid a large sum by his employer to induce him to sign for another club. The payment was held to be an emolument arising from employment.

Payments in respect of promotional rights, which did not relate to services required under the employment contract, were not liable as emoluments under general principles. Sports Club and others v Inspector of Taxes 2000 STC 443

A present of £400, given to a jockey who had just won a race, by the horse's owner, was held to be an emolument. Wing v O'Connell 1 ITC 170

In Jarrold v Boustead 41 TC 701 a lump sum paid by a Rugby League club to Mr. Boustead as a signing on fee was held to be an inducement payment to give up his amateur status and was not paid in consideration for undertaking to play football.

The transfer of shares to induce the taxpayer to give up his employment position after a fixed period was held not in the nature of a reward for future services. Pritchard v Arundale 1971 47 TC 680

In Teward v IRC 2001 STC 36, the payment by a new employer to a taxpayer, to compensate the taxpayer for no longer being able to participate in a previous employer's share option scheme, was a taxable emolument of the new employment.

Payment in lieu of notice pursuant to a contractual provision was an emolument of the employment. EMI Group Electronics v Coldicott 1997 STC 1372

Supplementary redundancy payments made irrespective of whether or not employee was actually made redundant, was held to be a taxable emolument. Allen v IRC 1995 STC 945

An ex gratia lump sum paid to employees for the loss of use of a company car was taxable. Bird v Martland 1982 STC 603

Revenue Briefings

Tax Briefing

Tax Briefing October 1997 – Issue 28 pg 18 – Taxation of Part-Time Lecturers / Teachers / Trainers

Tax Briefing April 1998 – Issue 31 pg 10 – Taxation of Individuals Engaged through Agencies

Tax Briefing June 1998 – Issue 32 pg 43 – Employment Inducement Payments

Tax Briefing December 2000 – Issue 42 pg 48 – Home Leave Travel for Expatriate Employees

Tax Briefing April 2001 – Issue 43 pg 3 – Report of Employment Status Group – Code of Practice for Determining Employment or Self-Employment Status of Individuals

Tax Briefing October 2002 – Issue 50 pg 7 – Directors' Remuneration

Tax Briefing January 2003 – Issue 51 pg 20 – Termination Payments and Legal Costs

Tax Briefing December 2004 – Issue 58 pg 13 – Third-party benefits

Tax Briefing August 2005 – Issue 60 pg 4 – Tax Treatment of Legal Fees

Tax Briefing May 2006 – Issue 63 pg 22 – Restricted Stock Units – Income Tax

Tax Briefing December 2009 – Issue 82 – Individuals described as 'locums' engaged in the fields of medicine, health care and pharmacy

eBrief

eBrief No. 05/2010 – Clarification of certain matters relating to employment vs. self employment status

eBrief No. 37/2012 – Changes to the treatment of taxable Illness Benefit paid to PAYE employees by the Department of Social Protection (DSP)

eBrief No. 69/2012 – Treatment of Restricted Stock Units by Payroll Operators

Revenue Information Notes

IT11 – Employees' Guide to PAYE

Employer's Guide to PAYE

Tax & Duty Manuals – Section 16 Part 5 – Principal Provisions Relating to the Schedule E Charges

Revenue Precedents

As the decision of the tribunal related to the re-instatement of the employee, the award is in respect of the earnings that he was entitled to and is chargeable as ordinary emoluments under section 112 TCA 1997. IT 97 1521

Employer lodges an allowance to the credit card account of an employee. Is it a perquisite or benefit? It is a perquisite. The payment ranks no differently from an employer lodging wages to his employees bank accounts. The PAYE system applies to such allowances. IT 95 1508

A payment to a member of staff, who introduces a potential employee, is taxable under section 112 TCA 1997, as the payment arises from the employment. IT 97 1537

Informal scheme operates which is funded jointly by employer and employees. Tax relief is not allowed for the employees contributions. Benefits received by employees are chargeable to tax to the extent that they represent the employer's contribution to the fund (under PAYE). Tax is not chargeable on the employees at the time the employer's contributions are made to the fund. IT 95 1572

Employer had a bonus scheme and the employees were obliged to expend their benefits under the bonus scheme in a particular way. The benefits form part of the gross emoluments of the employees. IT 97 1534

Statements of Practice

Tax treatment of Remuneration of Members of State and State Sponsored Committees and Boards – SP IT/1/04

Tax treatment of the reimbursement of Expenses of Travel and Subsistence to Office Holders and Employees – SP IT/2/07

PAYE System – Employee payroll tax deductions in relation to non-Irish employments exercised in the State – SP IT/3/07

Cross References

To Section 112

Section 57 Extension of charge to tax under Case III of Schedule D in certain circumstances.
Section 112A Taxation of certain perquisites.
Section 117 Expenses allowances.
Section 118 Benefits in kind: general charging provision.
Section 122 Preferential loan arrangements.
Section 124 Tax treatment of certain severance payments.
Section 125 Tax treatment of benefits received under permanent health benefit schemes.
Section 126 Tax treatment of certain benefits payable under Social Welfare Acts.
Section 127 Tax treatment of restrictive covenants.
Section 128C Tax treatment of directors and employees who acquire convertible shares.
Section 128D Tax treatment of directors of companies and employees who acquire restricted shares.
Section 128E Tax treatment of directors of companies and employees who acquire forfeitable shares.
Section 236 Loan of certain art objects.
Section 289 Calculation of balancing allowances and balancing charges in certain cases.
Section 470B Age-related relief for health insurance premiums.
Section 471 Relief for contributions to permanent health benefit schemes.
Section 479 Relief for new shares purchased on issue by employees.
Section 790AA Taxation of lump sums in excess of the tax free amount.
Section 823 Deduction for income earned outside the State.
Section 924 Additional assessments.
Section 985A Application of section 985 to certain perquisites, etc.

112A Taxation of certain perquisites

[(1) In this section—

(a) as respects so much of a payment that qualifies for relief under *section 470*, "*appropriate percentage*", "*authorised insurer*", "*relevant contract*" and "*relievable amount*" have the same meanings, respectively, as in *section 470*,

(b) as respects so much of a payment that qualifies for relief under *section 470B*, "*authorised insurer*" and "*relevant contract*" have the same meanings, respectively, as in *section 470B*,

(c) "*employee*" and "*employer*" have the same meanings, respectively, as in section 983, and

(d) "*qualifying insurer*" and "*qualifying long-term care policy*" have the same meanings, respectively, as in *section 470A*.][1]

(2) *Section 112* shall apply in relation to a perquisite comprising the payment to—

(a) an authorised insurer under a relevant contract, or

(b) a qualifying insurer under a qualifying long-term care policy as if any deduction authorised by—

(i) in a case in which *paragraph (a)* applies, *section 470(3)(a)*, or

(ii) in a case in which *paragraph (b)* applies, *section 470A(8)(a)*,

had not been made.

[(2A) Where, for any relevant year of assessment, an employer makes a payment of emoluments to an employee consisting of a perquisite in the form of a payment to an authorised insurer under a relevant contract, and such payment qualifies for relief under *section 470B* for that relevant year of assessment, *section 112* shall apply as if the perquisite were increased by the amount of the age-related tax credit or age-related tax credits, as the case may be, that the employee is entitled to under *section 470B* in respect of the payment.][2]

(3) Where, for any year of assessment, an employer [...][3]—

(a) makes a payment of emoluments consisting of a perquisite of the kind mentioned in *subsection (2)*, and

(b) deducts therefrom and retains in accordance with—

(i) *section 470(3)(a)*, an amount equal to the appropriate percentage for the year of assessment of the relievable amount in relation to the payment, or

(ii) *section 470A(8)(a)*, an amount equal to the appropriate percentage for the year of assessment of the payment,

the employer shall be assessed and charged to income tax in an amount equal to the amount so deducted and retained and that amount shall be allowable as a deduction in charging to tax the profits or gains of such employer.

(4) *Subsections (3)* to *(6)* of *section 238* shall apply, with necessary modifications, in relation to a payment referred to in *subsection (3)* as they apply in relation to a payment to which that section applies.][4]

Amendments

[1] Substituted by the Health Insurance (Miscellaneous Provisions) Act 2009 sec 19(a).

[2] Inserted by the Health Insurance (Miscellaneous Provisions) Act 2009 sec 19(b).

[3] Deleted by the Health Insurance (Miscellaneous Provisions) Act 2009 sec 19(c).

[4] Inserted by FA01 s21. Applies as respects the year of assessment 2001 and subsequent years of assessment.

Revenue Briefings

Tax Briefing

Tax Briefing August 2002 – Issue 49 pg 18 – Employer Paid Medical Insurance Premiums

Cross References

From Section 112A

Section 112 Basis of assessment, persons chargeable and extent of charge.

Section 238 Annual payments not payable out of taxed income.

Section 470 Relief for insurance against expenses of illness.

Section 470A Relief for premiums under qualifying long-term care policies.

Section 470B Age-related relief for health insurance premiums.

To Section 112A

Section 985A Application of section 985 to certain perquisites, etc.

CHAPTER 2

Computational Provisions

113 Making of deductions

[ITA67 s111(4) and s112; FA90 s19(b)(proviso)]

(1) In this section, "*emoluments*" means all salaries, fees, wages, perquisites or profits or gains whatever arising from an office or employment, or the amount of any annuity, pension or stipend, as the case may be.

(2) Any deduction from emoluments allowed under the Income Tax Acts for the purpose of computing an assessment to income tax under Schedule E shall be made by reference to the amount paid or borne for the year or portion of the year on the emoluments of which the computation is made.

Cross References

To Section 113

Section 121 Benefit of use of car.

Section 122A Notional loans relating to shares, etc.

114 General rule as to deductions

[ITA67 Sch2 rule3; FA96 s132(2) and Sch5 PtII]

Where the holder of an office or employment of profit is necessarily obliged to incur and defray out of the emoluments of the office or employment of profit expenses of travelling in the performance of the duties of that office or employment, or otherwise to expend money wholly, exclusively and necessarily in the performance of those duties, there may be deducted from the emoluments to be assessed the expenses so necessarily incurred and defrayed.

Case Law

Expenses incurred in travelling to the place of work not allowed in Ricketts v Colquhoun 10 TC 118. However travelling expenses incurred in the course of the duties of employment are allowed, Nolder v Walters 15 TC 388.

In Pook v Owen 45 TC 571, costs incurred by a doctor in travelling between his home and the hospital were allowed. The key in this case was that his duties as a doctor commenced as soon as he received a telephone call from the hospital. The Irish Revenue's interpretation of this case is set out in SP IT/2/07.

The cost of travelling from home to work where the taxpayer had volunteered to work from home was disallowed. Kirkwood v Evans 2002 STC 231

In Bennett v Revenue & Customs Commissioners 2007 SpC 576 travelling and accommodation expenses to various construction sites was not deductible as just ordinary commuting expenses.

In Brown v Bullock 40 TC 1 the test was whether the duties could be performed without incurring the expenses.

A fee paid to an employment agency for obtaining a job was held not to be incurred in the performance of duties. Shortt v McIlgorm 26 TC 262

The cost of suing for recovery of wages is not allowed. Eagles v Levy 19 TC 23

Gratuities paid where disallowed on the basis that there was no legal obligation to pay them. HF Kelly v H II ITR 460.

Cost of work clothing was disallowed. Hillyer v Leeke 1976 STC 490, Woodcock v IRC 1977 STC 405 and Ward v Dunn 1979 STC 178

In Emms v Revenue and Customs Commissioners 2008 STC (SCD) 618 a rugby player was not allowed a deduction for the cost of food, nutritional supplements and medicines. The relief was denied on the basis that the expenditure was not incurred exclusively and necessarily in the performance of his employment duties. The expense was incurred to enable him to perform his duties, but not "in the performance of the duties".

Expenses incurred in connection with training, contractually required, were not deductible for purposes of income tax. Revenue and Customs Commissioners v Decadt 2008 STC 1103

Agent's fees paid by the employer to negotiate terms of contract were held to be not deductible. Madeley and another v Revenue and Customs Commissioner 2006 SpC 547

Revenue Briefings

Tax Briefing

Tax Briefing May 2003 – Issue 52 pg 17 – Expenses

Tax Briefing May 2006 – Issue 63 pg 16 – Employees' travel expenses

Tax Briefing April 2009 – Issue 71 – Employees' Motoring & Subsistence Expenses

Tax Briefing Supplement June 2009 pg 42 – 49

eBrief

eBrief No. 6/2006 – Reimbursement of travel expenses to employees who are required to attend an emergency at their normal place of work outside their normal working hours

eBrief No. 19/2011 – Annual Membership Fees of a Professional Body – Employees and Office Holders

eBrief No. 61/2014 – Expenses of travel – Non-executive directors attending board meetings

Revenue Information Notes

IT 51 – Employees' Motoring Expenses

IT 54 – Employees Subsistence Expenses

IT 69 – eWorking and Tax

Statements of Practice

Tax treatment of the reimbursement of Expenses of Travel and Subsistence to Office Holders and Employees – SP IT/2/07

Cross References

To Section 114

Section 19 Schedule E.
Section 116 Interpretation (Chapter 3).
Section 117 Expenses allowances.
Section 118 Benefits in kind: general charging provision.
Section 196 Expenses of members of judiciary.
Section 531W No relief for any payment in relation to parking levy.
Section 836 Allowances for expenses of members of Oireachtas.
Section 840 Business entertainment.

115 Fixed deduction for certain classes of persons

[ITA67 Sch2 rule 4]

Where the Minister for Finance is satisfied, with respect to any class of persons in receipt of any salary, fees or emoluments payable out of the public revenue, that such persons are obliged to lay out and expend money wholly, exclusively and necessarily in the performance of the duties in respect of which such salary, fees or emoluments are payable, the Minister for Finance may fix such sum as in that Minister's opinion represents a fair equivalent of [the average amount for a year of assessment][1] so laid out and expended by persons of that class, and in charging the tax on such salary, fees or emoluments, there shall be deducted from the amount of such salary, fees or emoluments the sums so fixed by the Minister for Finance; but, if any person would but for this section be entitled to deduct a larger amount than the sum so fixed, that sum may be deducted instead of the sum so fixed.

Amendments

[1] Substituted by FA01 sched2(6).

Cross References

To Section 115

Section 19 Schedule E.
Section 196 Expenses of members of judiciary.
Section 836 Allowances for expenses of members of Oireachtas.

CHAPTER 3

Expenses Allowances and Provisions Relating to the General Benefits in Kind Charge

116 Interpretation (Chapter 3)

[ITA67 s119 and s122]

(1) In this Chapter—

"*business premises*", in relation to a body corporate, includes all premises occupied by that body for the purpose of any trade carried on by it and, except when the reference is expressly to premises which include living accommodation, includes so much of any such premises so occupied as is used wholly or mainly as living accommodation for any of the directors of the body corporate or for any persons employed by the body corporate in any employment to which this Chapter applies;

["*business use*", in relation to the use of an asset by a person, means the use of that asset by the person in the performance of the duties of the person's office or employment;][1]

"*control*", in relation to a body corporate, means the power of a person to secure—

(a) by means of the holding of shares or the possession of voting power in or in relation to that or any other body corporate, or

(b) by virtue of any powers conferred by the articles of association or other document regulating that or any other body corporate,

that the affairs of the first-mentioned body corporate are conducted in accordance with the wishes of that person;

"*director*" means—

(a) in relation to a body corporate the affairs of which are managed by a board of directors or similar body, a member of that board or body,

(b) in relation to a body corporate the affairs of which are managed by a single director or similar person, that director or person,

(c) in relation to a body corporate the affairs of which are managed by the members themselves, a member of the body corporate,

and includes any person in accordance with whose directions or instructions the directors of a body corporate, defined in accordance with the preceding provisions of this definition, are accustomed to act, but a person shall not, within the meaning of this definition, be deemed to be a person in accordance with whose directions or instructions the directors of a body corporate are accustomed to act by reason only that those directors act on advice given by the person in a professional capacity;

["*employee*" includes the holder of an office;][2]

"*employment*" means an employment such that any emoluments of the employment would be assessed under Schedule E, and references to persons employed by, or employees of, a body corporate include any person who takes part in the management of the affairs of the body corporate and is not a director of the body corporate.

["*premises*" includes lands;][3]

["*private use*", in relation to an asset, means use of the asset other than business use.][4]

(2) Any reference in this Chapter to anything provided for a director or employee shall, unless the reference is expressly to something provided for the director or employee personally, be construed as including a reference to anything provided for the

[spouse, civil partner, family, children of the civil partner, servants, dependants or guests][5] of that director or employee, and the reference in the definition of "*business premises*" to living accommodation for directors or employees shall be construed accordingly.

(3) (a) Subject to *subsection (4)* and *paragraphs (b)* and *(c)*, the employments to which this Chapter applies shall be employments the emoluments of which, estimated for the year of assessment in question according to the Income Tax Acts and on the basis that they are employments to which this Chapter applies, and without any deduction being made under *section 114* in respect of money expended in performing the duties of those employments, are [...][6][€1,905][7] or more.

(b) Where a person is employed in 2 or more employments by the same body corporate and the total of the emoluments of those employments for the year of assessment in question estimated in accordance with *paragraph (a)* is [...][8][€1,905][9] or more, all those employments shall be treated as employments to which this Chapter applies.

(c) Where a person is a director of a body corporate, all employments in which the person is employed by the body corporate shall be treated as employments to which this Chapter applies.

(4) All the directors of, and persons employed by, a body corporate over which another body corporate has control shall be treated for the purposes of *paragraphs (b)* and *(c)* of *subsection (3)* (but not for any other purpose) as if they were directors of that other body corporate or, as the case may be, as if the employment were an employment by that other body corporate.

Amendments

[1] Inserted by FA04 s8(1)(a)(i). This section is deemed to have come into force and taken effect as on and from 1 January 2004.

[2] Inserted by FA13 s13(a). Applies as respects the year of assessment 2013 and subsequent years of assessment.

[3] Inserted by FA05 s7.

[4] Inserted by FA04 s8(1)(a)(ii). This section is deemed to have come into force and taken effect as on and from 1 January 2004.

[5] Substituted by F(No.3)A11 sched1(12). Shall have effect from the passing of this Act 27 July 2011.

[6, 8] Substituted by FA01 sched2(7). Shall apply only as respects the year of assessment 2001.

[7] Substituted by FA01 sched5.

[9] Substituted by FA02 sched6(3)(a). Shall be deemed to have come into force and take effect as on and from 1 January 2002.

Cross References

From Section 116

Section 114 General rule as to deductions.

To Section 116

Section 57 Extension of charge to tax under Case III of Schedule D in certain circumstances.
Section 120 Unincorporated bodies, partnerships and individuals.
Section 121 Benefit of use of car.
Section 121A Benefit of use of van.
Section 236 Loan of certain art objects.
Section 591 Relief for individuals on certain reinvestment.
Section 629 Tax on non-resident company recoverable from another member of group or from controlling director.
Section 897 Returns of employees' emoluments, etc.

Section 924 Additional assessments.
Section 950 Interpretation (Part 41).
Section 1084 Surcharge for late returns.

117 Expenses allowances

[ITA67 s116; FA74 s86 and Sch2 PtI]

(1) Subject to this Chapter, any sum paid in respect of expenses by a body corporate to any of its directors or to any person employed by it in an employment to which this Chapter applies shall, if not otherwise chargeable to income tax as income of that director or employee, be treated for the purposes of *section 112* as a perquisite of the office or employment of that director or employee and included in the emoluments of that office or employment assessable to income tax accordingly; but nothing in this subsection shall prevent a claim for a deduction being made under *section 114* in respect of any money expended wholly, exclusively and necessarily in performing the duties of the office or employment.

(2) The reference in *subsection (1)* to any sum paid in respect of expenses includes a reference to any sum put by a body corporate at the disposal of a director or employee and paid away by him or her.

Revenue Briefings

Tax Briefing

Tax Briefing April 1998 – Issue 31 pg 11 – Removal/Relocation Expenses – Change in Procedures

Tax Briefing May 2006 – Issue 63 pg 16 – Employees' Travel Expenses

Tax Briefing April 2009 – Issue 71 – Employees' Motoring & Subsistence Expenses

Tax Briefing Supplement June 2009 pg 42 – 49

Tax Briefing July 2013 – Issue 03 of 2013 – Reimbursement of Travel and Subsistence Expenses by Intermediaries

eBrief

eBrief No. 6/2006 – Reimbursement of travel expenses to employees who are required to attend an emergency at their normal place of work outside their normal working hours

eBrief No. 61/2014 – Expenses of travel – Non-executive directors attending board meetings

Revenue Information Notes

IT 51 – Employees' Motoring Expenses

IT 54 – Employees' Subsistence Expenses

IT 69 – eWorking and Tax

Statements of Practice

Removal/Relocation Expenses – SP/IT/1/91

Tax treatment of the reimbursement of Expenses of Travel and Subsistence to Office Holders and Employees – SP IT/2/07

Cross References

From Section 117

Section 112 Basis of assessment, persons chargeable and extent of charge.
Section 114 General rule as to deductions.

118 Benefits in kind: general charging provision

[ITA67 s117; FA73 s41; FA74 s86 and Sch2 PtI; FA96 s131(9)(a)]

(1) Subject to this Chapter, where—

(a) a body corporate incurs expense in or in connection with the provision, for any of its directors or for any person employed by it in an employment to which this Chapter applies, of—

(i) living or other accommodation,

(ii) entertainment,

(iii) domestic or other services, or

(iv) other benefits or facilities of whatever nature, and

(b) apart from this section the expense would not be chargeable to income tax as income of the director or employee,

then, *sections 112, 114* and *897* shall apply in relation to so much of the expense as is not made good to the body corporate by the director or employee as if the expense had been incurred by the director or employee and the amount of the expense had been refunded to the director or employee by the body corporate by means of a payment in respect of expenses, and income tax shall be chargeable accordingly.

(2) *Subsection (1)* shall not apply to expense incurred by the body corporate in or in connection with the provision for a director or employee in any of its business premises of any accommodation, supplies or services provided for the director or employee personally and used by the director or employee solely in performing the duties of his or her office or employment.

(3) *Subsection (1)* shall not apply to expense incurred by the body corporate in or in connection with the provision of living accommodation for an employee in part of any of its business premises which include living accommodation if the employee is, for the purpose of enabling the employee properly to perform his or her duties, required by the terms of his or her employment to reside in the accommodation and either—

(a) the accommodation is provided in accordance with a practice which since before the 30th day of July, 1948, has commonly prevailed in trades of the class in question as respects employees of the class in question, or

(b) it is necessary in the case of trades of the class in question that employees of the class in question should reside on premises of the class in question;

but this subsection shall not apply where the employee is a director of the body corporate in question or of any other body corporate over which that body corporate has control or which has control over that body corporate or which is under the control of a person who also has control over that body corporate.

(4) *Subsection (1)* shall not apply to expense incurred by the body corporate in or in connection with the provision of meals in any canteen in which meals are provided for the staff generally.

[(5) *Subsection (1)* shall not apply to expense incurred by the body corporate in or in connection with the provision for a director or employee, or for [the director's or employee's spouse, civil partner, children or dependants, or the children of the director's or employee's civil partner][1], of any pension, annuity, lump sum, gratuity or other like benefit to be given on the death or retirement of the director or employee, other than an expense incurred by way of contribution by the body corporate to a PRSA (within the meaning of *Chapter 2A* of *Part 30*).][2]

[(5A) (a) *Subsection (1)* shall not apply to expense incurred by the body corporate in or in connection with the provision for a director or employee of a monthly or annual bus, railway or ferry travel pass issued by or on behalf of one or more approved transport providers [and which must be for a service for which the approved transport provider is contracted or licensed][2].

[(b) In this subsection "*approved transport provider*" means—

(i) a public transport operator within the meaning of section 2 of the Dublin Transport Authority Act 2008,

(ii) the holder of a licence in respect of a public bus passenger service under Part 2 of the Public Transport Regulation Act 2009, or

(iii) a person who provides a ferry service within the State, operating a vessel which holds a current valid—

(I) passenger ship safety certificate,

(II) passenger boat licence, or

(III) high-speed craft safety certificate,

issued by the Minister for Transport, Tourism and Sport.][4]][5]

(5B) (a) *Subsection (1)* shall not apply to expense incurred by the body corporate in or in connection with the provision, without any transfer of the property in it, for a director or employee of a mobile telephone for business use where private use of the mobile telephone is incidental.

(b) The mobile telephones to which the exemption provided by this subsection applies include any mobile telephone provided in connection with a car or van notwithstanding that the vehicle is made available as referred to in *section 121* or *121A*, as the case may be.

(c) In this subsection "*mobile telephone*" means telephone apparatus which—

(i) is not physically connected to a land-line, and

(ii) is not a cordless telephone.

(d) For the purposes of *paragraph (c)*—

"*cordless telephone*" means telephone apparatus designed or adapted to provide a wireless extension to a telephone, and used only as such an extension to a telephone that is physically connected to a land-line;

"*telephone apparatus*" means wireless telegraphy apparatus designed or adapted for the purposes of transmitting and receiving either or both spoken messages and information (being information for the same purposes as the Electronic Commerce Act 2000) and connected to a public telecommunications network (as defined in the European Communities (Telecommunications Services) Regulations 1992 (S.I. No. 45 of 1992)).

(5C) (a) *Subsection (1)* shall not apply to expense incurred by the body corporate in or in connection with the provision for a director or employee of a high-speed internet connection to the director's or employee's home for business use where private use of the connection is incidental.

(b) In this subsection "*high-speed internet connection*" means a connection capable of transmitting information (being information for the same purposes as the Electronic Commerce Act 2000) at a rate equal to or greater than 250 kilobits per second.

(5D) (a) *Subsection (1)* shall not apply to expense incurred by the body corporate in or in connection with the provision, without any transfer of the property in it, for a director or employee of computer equipment for business use where private use of the computer equipment is incidental.

(b) In this section "*computer equipment*", in addition to a computer, includes—

(i) a facsimile machine, and

(ii) printers, scanners, modems, discs, disc drives, and other peripheral devices designed to be used by being connected to or inserted in a computer and computer software to be used in such equipment.

(5E) (a) *Subsection (1)* shall not apply to expense incurred by the body corporate, or incurred by a director or employee and reimbursed by the body corporate, in or in connection with the payment on behalf of a director or employee of the annual membership fees of a professional body where membership of that body by the director or employee is relevant to the business of the body corporate.

(b) Membership of a professional body by a director or employee of a body corporate may be regarded as relevant to the business of that body corporate where—

(i) it is necessary for the performance of the duties of the office or employment of the director or employee, or

(ii) it facilitates the acquisition of knowledge which—

(I) is necessary for or directly related to the performance of the duties of the office or employment of the director or employee, or

(II) would be necessary for or directly related to the performance of prospective duties of the office or employment of the director or employee with that body corporate.

[(c) This subsection shall not apply as respects the year of assessment 2011 and each subsequent year of assessment.][6]

(5F) *Subsection (1)* shall not apply to expense incurred by the body corporate in or in connection with the provision, without any transfer of the property in it, for a director or employee of a mechanically propelled road vehicle which is—

(a) designed or constructed solely or mainly for the carriage of goods or other burden, and

(b) of a type not commonly used as a private vehicle and unsuitable to be so used.][7]

[(5G) (a) Subject to *paragraph (c)* of this subsection, *subsection (1)* shall not apply to expense of up to €1,000 incurred by the body corporate in, or in connection with, the provision for a director or employee of a bicycle or bicycle safety equipment, where—

(i) the bicycle and bicycle safety equipment provided is unused and not second-hand,

(ii) the director or employee uses the bicycle or bicycle safety equipment, or the bicycle and the bicycle safety equipment, as the case may be, mainly for qualifying journeys, and

(iii) bicycles or bicycle safety equipment, or bicycles and bicycle safety equipment, as the case may be, are made available generally to directors and employees of the body corporate.

(b) In this subsection—

"*bicycle*" means a pedal cycle;

"*bicycle safety equipment*" includes—

(i) bicycle bells and bulb horns,

(ii) bicycle helmets that conform to European product safety standard CEN/EN 1078,

(iii) bicycle lights, including dynamo packs,

(iv) bicycle reflectors and reflective clothing, and

(v) such other safety equipment as the Revenue Commissioners may allow;

"*normal place of work*" means the place where the director or employee normally performs the duties of his or her office or employment;

"*pedal cycle*" means—

(i) a bicycle or tricycle which is intended or adapted for propulsion solely by the physical exertions of a person or persons seated thereon, or

(ii) a pedelec,

but does not include a moped or a scooter;

"*pedelec*" means a bicycle or tricycle which is equipped with an auxiliary electric motor having a maximum continuous rated power of 0.25 kilowatts, of which output is progressively reduced and finally cut off as the vehicle reaches a speed of 25 kilometres per hour, or sooner if the cyclist stops pedalling;

"*qualifying journey*", in relation to a director or employee, means the whole or part of a journey—

(i) between the director's or employee's home and normal place of work, or

(ii) between the director's or employee's normal place of work and another place of work, where the director or employee is travelling in the performance of the duties of his or her office or employment.

(c) A director or employee shall not, by virtue of this subsection, be relieved from a charge to income tax under *subsection (1)* more than once in any period of 5 consecutive years of assessment, commencing with the year of assessment in which the director or employee concerned is first provided with a bicycle or bicycle safety equipment.][8]

(6) Any reference in this section to expense incurred in or in connection with any matter includes a reference to a proper proportion of any expense incurred partly in or in connection with that matter.

(7) Where expense is incurred by a person connected with a body corporate, being expense which if incurred by the body corporate would be expense of the kind mentioned in *subsection (1)(a)*, the body corporate shall be deemed for the purposes of this section to have incurred the expense, and *subsection (1)* shall apply accordingly in relation to any person, being a director or employee of the body corporate, in respect of whom the expense was incurred.

(8) A person shall be regarded as connected with a body corporate for the purposes of *subsection (7)* if the person is—

(a) a trustee of a settlement (within the meaning of *section 794*) made by the body corporate, or

(b) a body corporate,

and would be regarded as connected with the body corporate for the purposes of *section 10*.

Amendments

[1] Substituted by F(No.3)A11 sched1(13).

[2] Substituted by PAA02 s4(1)(a). With effect from 7 November 2002 per S.I. 502 of 2002.

[3] Inserted by FA13 s13(b). Applies as respects the year of assessment 2013 and subsequent years of assessment.

[4] Substituted by FA13 s13(c). Applies as respects the year of assessment 2013 and subsequent years of assessment.

[5] Substituted by FA05 s8.

[6] Inserted by FA11 s7(1)(a). Deemed to have come into force and takes effect as on and from 1 January 2011.

[7] Substituted by FA04 s8(1)(b). This section is deemed to have come into force and taken effect as on and from 1 January 2004.

[8] Inserted by F(No.2)A08 s7(1)(a). Applies in respect of expense incurred on or after 1 January 2009.

Case Law

A benefit is 'provided' at the point in time when it became available to be enjoyed by the taxpayer and not when the cost of providing the benefit was incurred. Templeton V Jacobs 1996 STC 991

A cash payment made by an educational trust, established by the taxpayer's employer, to the minor child of a taxpayer, was caught under the term 'benefits and facilities of whatsoever nature'. Wicks v Firth 1984 56 TC 318

The expression 'benefits and facilities of whatsoever nature' also covers a cash payment made directly to the taxpayer. Mairs v Haughey 1992 STC 495

Expenditure by a company on repairs of a house let to a director where such repairs are of a nature that usually fall on the tenant are assessable as a benefit-in-kind. Doyle v Davison 40 TC 140

However, in the UK case of IRC v Luke 40 TC 630, expenditure on repairs, being of a kind which would normally fall on an owner, were not a taxable benefit-in-kind.

Revenue Briefings

Tax Briefing

Tax Briefing April 1998 – Issue 31 pg 11 – Removal/Relocation Expenses – Change in Procedures

Tax Briefing September 2000 – Issue 41 pg 22 – Benefit-in-Kind (Bus and train passes/salary sacrifice)

Tax Briefing June 2002 – Issue 48 pg 14 – Taxation of Long Service Awards

Tax Briefing December 2004 – Issue 58 pg 13 – Third-party benefits

Tax Briefing August 2005 – Issue 60 pg 4 – Tax Treatment of Legal Fees

Tax Briefing December 2006 – Issue 65 – Mandatory Licence for Employees in Private Security

eBrief

eBrief No. 19/2011 – Annual Membership Fees of a Professional Body – Employees and Office Holders

Revenue Information Notes

IT 20A – Taxation (PAYE/PRSI) of Benefits from Employments from 1st January 2004

Employer's Guide to Benefit-in-kind

Employer's Guide to PAYE

Statements of Practice

Removal/Relocation Expenses – SP/IT/1/91

Cross References

From Section 118

Section 10 Connected persons.
Section 112 Basis of assessment, persons chargeable and extent of charge.
Section 114 General rule as to deductions.
Section 121 Benefit of use of car.
Section 121A Benefit of use of van.
Section 770 Interpretation and supplemental (Chapter 1).
Section 794 Interpretation and application (Chapter 2).
Section 897 Returns of employees' emoluments, etc.

To Section 118

Section 118A Costs and expenses in respect of personal security assets and services.
Section 118B Revenue approved salary sacrifice agreements.
Section 119 Valuation of benefits in kind.
Section 120A Exemption from benefit-in-kind of certain childcare facilities.

Section 236 Loan of certain art objects.
Section 436 Certain expenses for participators and associates.
Section 787E Extent of relief.
Section 823 Deduction for income earned outside the State.
Section 985A Application of section 985 to certain perquisites, etc.

118A Costs and expenses in respect of personal security assets and services

[(1) In this section—

"*asset*" includes equipment or a structure, but not any mode of transport or a dwelling or grounds appurtenant to a dwelling;

"*service*" does not include a dwelling or grounds appurtenant to a dwelling.

(2) This section applies where there is a credible and serious threat to a director's or an employee's personal physical security, which arises wholly or mainly because of the director's or employee's office or employment.

(3) This section applies to expense incurred by the body corporate, or incurred by a director or employee and reimbursed to the director or employee by the body corporate—

(a) in—

(i) the provision or use of, or

(ii) expenses connected with,

an asset or service for the improvement of personal security which is provided for or used by the director or employee to meet the threat to his or her personal physical security, and

(b) with the sole object of meeting that threat.

(4) Subject to *subsections (6)* and *(7)*, where this section applies, *section 118(1)* shall not apply to an expense to which this section applies.

(5) Where the body corporate intends the asset to be used solely to improve personal physical security, any use of the asset incidental to that purpose shall be ignored.

(6) Where the body corporate intends the asset to be used only partly to improve personal physical security, *subsection (4)* shall apply only to that part of the expense incurred in relation to the asset which is attributable to the intended use for that purpose.

(7) *Subsection (4)* shall only apply to an expense incurred in relation to a service referred to in *subsection (3)* where the benefit resulting to the director or employee consists wholly or mainly of an improvement of his or her personal physical security.

(8) In determining whether or not this section applies in relation to an asset or service, the fact that—

(a) the asset becomes fixed to land (whether the land constitutes a dwelling or otherwise), or

(b) the director or employee is, or becomes, entitled—

(i) to the property in the asset, or

(ii) if the asset is a fixture, to any estate or interest in the land concerned,

or

(c) the asset or the service improves the personal physical security of a member of the director's or employee's family or household, as well as that of the director or employee,

does not exclude the expense incurred by the body corporate from coming within *subsection (4)*.][1]

Amendments

[1] Inserted by FA05 s10.

Cross References

From Section 118A

Section 118 Benefits in kind: general charging provision.

118B Revenue approved salary sacrifice agreements

[(1) In this section—

"*approved transport provider*" has the same meaning as in *section 118(5A)*;

"*exempt employee benefit*" means a benefit specifically approved by the Revenue Commissioners which is referred to in subsection (2)(*a*)(i) and (ii);

" *[salary sacrifice arrangement]*[1] " means any arrangement under which an employee forgoes the right to receive any part of his or her remuneration due under his or her terms or contract of employment, and in return his or her employer agrees to provide him or her with a benefit;

"*approved profit sharing scheme*" shall be construed in accordance with *section 510*.

(2) (a) The amount of the remuneration forgone under any salary sacrifice arrangement specifically approved by the Revenue Commissioners in relation to—

(i) travel passes issued by an approved transport provider under *section 118(5A)*, [...][2]

(ii) shares appropriated to employees and directors under an approved profit sharing scheme within the meaning of Chapter 1 of Part 17, which are exempt from a charge to tax by virtue of [section 510(4), and][3]

[(iii) a bicycle or bicycle safety equipment provided to a director or employee and which is exempt from a charge to tax by virtue of *section 118(5G)*,][4]

shall be exempt from tax.

(b) Any amount of remuneration forgone by an individual under any salary sacrifice arrangement and not exempt from tax by virtue of paragraph (*a*) shall be deemed to be [the payment of emoluments by an employer][5] and income tax shall be chargeable accordingly.

(3) Where an exempt employee benefit is provided to the [spouse, civil partner or dependant][6] of, or a person connected with, the individual, being an individual who has entered into a salary sacrifice arrangement, then any such benefit shall be deemed to be [the payment of emoluments by an employer][7] and income tax shall be chargeable accordingly.

(4) Where—

(a) but for this subsection, *subsection (2)(a)* would apply, and

(b) there is an arrangement or scheme in place whereby the employee is recompensed, wholly or partly, by the provision of an exempt employee benefit together with a compensating payment,

then the provisions of *subsection (2)(a)* shall not apply and the remuneration foregone shall be treated as [the payment of emoluments by an employer][8] and income tax shall be chargeable accordingly.

(5) Where a [salary sacrifice arrangement][9] is entered into in respect of any right, bonus, commission or any other emolument which arises to an individual after

the end of the year of assessment, then subsection (2)(*a*) shall not apply and the remuneration foregone shall be treated as [the payment of emoluments by an employer][10] for that year and income tax shall be chargeable accordingly.

(6) This section has effect as on and from 31 January 2008.][11]

Amendments

[1] Substituted by F(No.2)A08 s7(1)(b)(i). Applies in respect of expense incurred on or after 1 January 2009.

[2] Deleted by F(No.2)A08 s7(1)(b)(ii)(I). Applies in respect of expense incurred on or after 1 January 2009.

[3] Substituted by F(No.2)A08 s7(1)(b)(ii)(I). Applies in respect of expense incurred on or after 1 January 2009.

[4] Inserted by F(No.2)A08 s7(1)(b)(ii)(II). Applies in respect of expense incurred on or after 1 January 2009.

[5] Substituted by FA13 s13(d). Applies as respects the year of assessment 2013 and subsequent years of assessment.

[6] Substituted by F(No.3)A11 sched1(14). Shall have effect from the passing of this Act 27 July 2011.

[7] Substituted by FA13 s13(e). Applies as respects the year of assessment 2013 and subsequent years of assessment.

[8] Substituted by FA13 s13(f). Applies as respects the year of assessment 2013 and subsequent years of assessment.

[9] Substituted by F(No.2)A08 s7(1)(b)(iii). Applies in respect of expense incurred on or after 1 January 2009.

[10] Substituted by FA13 s13(g). Applies as respects the year of assessment 2013 and subsequent years of assessment.

[11] Inserted by FA08 s21.

Revenue Briefings

Tax Briefing

Tax Briefing December 2008 – Issue 70 pg 24 – Salary Sacrifice

eBrief

eBrief No. 27/2008 – Revenue Approved Salary Sacrifice Agreements

Cross References

From Section 118B

Section 118 Benefits in kind: general charging provision.

Section 509 Interpretation (Chapter 1).

Section 510 Approved profit sharing schemes: appropriated shares.

119 Valuation of benefits in kind

[ITA67 s118(1), (2) and (4); FA69 s32(b) and (c)]

(1) Any expense incurred by a body corporate in the acquisition or production of an asset which remains its own property shall be disregarded for the purposes of *section 118*.

(2) Where the making of any provision mentioned in *section 118(1)* takes the form of a transfer of the property in any asset of the body corporate and, since the acquisition or production of that asset by the body corporate, that asset has been used or has depreciated, the body corporate shall be deemed to have incurred in the making of that provision expense equal to the value of that asset at the time of the transfer.

(3) Where an asset which continues to belong to the body corporate is used wholly or partly in the making of any provision mentioned in *section 118(1)*, the body corporate shall be deemed for the purposes of that section to incur (in addition to any other expense incurred by it in connection with the asset, not being expense to which *subsection (1)* applies) annual expense in connection with the asset of an amount

equal to the annual value of the use of the asset, but where any sum by means of rent or hire is payable by the body corporate in respect of the asset—

(a) if the annual amount of the rent or hire is equal to or greater than the annual value of the use of the asset, this subsection shall not apply, and

(b) if the annual amount of the rent or hire is less than the annual value of the use of the asset, the rent or hire shall be disregarded for the purposes of *section 118(1)*.

[(4) For the purposes of *subsection (3)*, the annual value of the use of an asset shall be taken to be—

(a) in the case of an asset being premises, the rent which might reasonably be expected to be obtained on a letting from year to year if the tenant undertook to pay all usual tenant's rates, and if the landlord undertook to bear the costs of repairs and insurance, and the other expenses, if any, necessary for maintaining the premises in a state to command that rent, and

(b) in the case of any other asset, 5 per cent of the market value (within the meaning of *section 548*) of the asset at the time when it was first applied by the body corporate in making any provision mentioned in *section 118(1)*.][1]

Amendments

[1] Substituted by FA03 s6(1)(a). This section applies and has effect as on and from 1 January 2004.

Case Law

In Pepper v Hart 1993 1 AL ER 42, the taxpayer was assessed to tax in respect of the additional costs incurred by his employer's school in providing places for his children at a heavily discounted price.

Cross References

From Section 119

Section 118 Benefits in kind: general charging provision.
Section 548 Valuation of assets.

To Section 119

Section 436 Certain expenses for participators and associates.

120 Unincorporated bodies, partnerships and individuals

[ITA67 s123]

(1) This Chapter shall apply in relation to unincorporated societies[, public bodies][1] and other bodies as it applies in relation to bodies corporate and, in connection with this Chapter, the definition of "*control*" in *section 116(1)* shall, with the necessary modifications, also so apply.

(2) This Chapter shall apply in relation to any partnership carrying on any trade or profession as it would apply in relation to a body corporate carrying on a trade if so much of this Chapter as relates to directors of the body corporate or persons taking part in the management of the affairs of the body corporate were deleted; but—

(a) "*control*", in relation to a partnership, means the right to a share of more than 50 per cent of the assets, or of more than 50 per cent of the income, of the partnership, and

(b) where a partnership carrying on any trade or profession has control over a body corporate to which this Chapter applies ("*control*" being construed for this purpose in accordance with the definition of that term in *section 116(1)*)—

(i) any employment of any director of that body corporate by the partnership shall be an employment to which this Chapter applies, and

(ii) all the employments of any person who is employed both by the partnership and by the body corporate (being employments by the partnership or the body corporate) shall, for the purpose of ascertaining whether those employments or any of them are employments to which this Chapter applies, be treated as if they were employments by the body corporate.

(3) *Subsection (2)* shall apply in relation to individuals as it applies in relation to partnerships, but nothing in this subsection shall be construed as requiring an individual to be treated in any circumstances as under the control of another person.

[(4) (a) This subsection applies where an expense, which if it had been incurred by a body corporate would be an expense of the kind mentioned in *subsection 118(1)(a)*, is incurred by a public body in relation to a person who holds an office or exercises an employment in that or in another public body.

(b) Where this subsection applies the expense shall be treated for the purposes of this Chapter as if it had been incurred by the public body in which the office is held or the employment is exercised and as if that public body was a body corporate.

(5) For the purposes of this section "*public body*" means—

(a) the Civil Service of the Government and the Civil Service of the State,

(b) the Garda Síochána, or

(c) the Permanent Defence Force.][2]

Amendments

[1] Inserted by FA13 s13(h). Applies as respects the year of assessment 2013 and subsequent years of assessment.

[2] Inserted by FA13 s13(i). Applies as respects the year of assessment 2013 and subsequent years of assessment.

Revenue Briefings

Tax Briefing

Tax Briefing October 1999 – Issue 37 pg 10 – Childcare facilities provided by employers for their employees

Cross References

From Section 120

Section 116 Interpretation (Chapter 3).

120A Exemption from benefit-in-kind of certain childcare facilities

[(1) In this section—

"*childcare service*" means any form of child minding service or supervised activity to care for children, whether or not provided on a regular basis;

"*qualifying premises*" means premises which—

(a) are made available solely by the employer,

(b) are made available by the employer jointly with other persons and the employer is wholly or partly responsible for financing and managing the provision of the childcare [service][1]

(c) are made available by any other person or persons and the employer is wholly or partly responsible for financing and managing the provision of the childcare service, [or][2] [(d) are made available by the employer jointly with other persons or are made available by any other person or persons and the employer is wholly or partly responsible for capital expenditure on the construction or refurbishment of the premises,][3]

and in respect of which it can be shown that the requirements of Article 9, 10 or 11, as appropriate, of the Child Care (Pre-School Services) Regulations, 1996 (S.I. No. 398 of 1996), have been complied with.

(2) *Subsection (1)* of *section 118* shall not apply to any expense incurred by a body corporate in or in connection with the provision of a childcare service in qualifying premises for a child of a director or employee.

[(3) In the case of a qualifying premises within the meaning of *paragraph (d)* of the definition of "*qualifying premises*", the exemption provided for in *subsection (2)* shall be limited to the amount expended by the employer on capital expenditure on the construction or refurbishment of the premises.][4]

[(4) This section shall not apply as respects the year of assessment 2011 and each subsequent year of assessment.][5][6]

Amendments

[1, 2] Substituted by FA01 s25(a).

[3] Inserted by FA01 s25(b).

[4] Inserted by FA01 s25(c).

[5] Inserted by FA11 s7(1)(b). Deemed to have come into force and takes effect as on and from 1 January 2011.

[6] Inserted by FA99 s34.

Cross References

From Section 120A

Section 118 Benefits in kind: general charging provision.

CHAPTER 4

Other Benefit in Kind Charges

121 Benefit of use of car

[FA82 s4(2) to (6) and (9)(a) and (b)(i), (ii) and (iv); FA92 s8(a),(b)(i) and (ii)(V) and Sch1 PtV; FA96 s6]

(1) (a) In this section—

"*business mileage for a year of assessment*", in relation to a person, means the total number of [whole kilometres][1] travelled in the year in the course of business use by that person of a car or cars in respect of which this section applies in relation to that person;

"*business use*", in relation to a car in respect of which this section applies in relation to a person, means travelling in the car which that person is necessarily obliged to do in the performance of the duties of his or her employment;

["*car*" means any mechanically propelled road vehicle designed, constructed or adapted for the carriage of the driver or the driver and one or more other persons other than—

(a) a motor-cycle,

(b) a van (within the meaning of *section 121A*), or

(c) a vehicle of a type not commonly used as a private vehicle and unsuitable to be so used;][2]

"*employment*" means an office or employment of profit such that any emoluments (within the meaning of *section 113*) of the office or employment would be charged to tax, and cognate expressions shall be construed accordingly;

["*motor-cycle*" means a mechanically propelled vehicle with less than four wheels and the weight of which unladen does not exceed 410 kilograms;][3]

"*private use*", in relation to a car, means use of the car other than business use;

"*relevant log book*", in relation to a person and a year of assessment, means a record maintained on a daily basis of the person's business use for the year of assessment of a car or cars in respect of which this section applies in relation to that person for that year of assessment which—

(i) contains relevant details of distances travelled, nature and location of business transacted and amount of time spent away from the employer's place of business, and

(ii) is certified by the employer as being to the best of the employer's knowledge and belief true and accurate.

(b) For the purposes of this section—

(i) (I) a car made available in any year to an employee by reason of his or her employment shall be deemed to be available in that year for his or her private use unless the terms on which the car is so made available prohibit such use and no such use is made of the car in that year;

(II) a car made available to an employee by his or her employer or by a person connected with the employer shall be deemed to be made available to him or her by reason of his or her employment (unless the employer is an individual and it can be shown that the car was made so available in the normal course of his or her domestic, family or personal relationships);

(III) a car shall be treated as available to a person and for his or her private use [if it is available to—][4]

[(A) a member or members of his or her family or household,

(B) his or her civil partner,

(C) a member or members of the family or household of his or her civil partner,

(D) any spouse or civil partner of a child of the person, or

(E) any spouse or civil partner of a child of the civil partner of the person;][5]

(IV) references to a person's family or household are references to the person's spouse, sons and daughters and their spouses, parents and servants, dependants and guests;

(ii) in relation to a car in respect of which this section applies, expenditure in respect of any costs borne by a person connected with the employer shall be treated as borne by the employer;

(iii) the original market value of a car shall be the price (including any duty of customs, duty of excise or value-added tax chargeable on the car) which the car might reasonably have been expected to fetch if sold in the State singly in a retail sale in the open market immediately before the date of its first registration in the State under section 6 of the Roads Act, 1920, or under corresponding earlier legislation, or elsewhere under the corresponding legislation of any country or territory.

(2) (a) In relation to a person chargeable to tax in respect of an employment, this section shall apply for a year of assessment in relation to a car which, by reason of the employment, is made available (without a transfer of the property in it) to the person and is available for his or her private use in that year.

(b) In relation to a car in respect of which this section applies for a year of assessment—

(i) *Chapter 3* of this Part shall not apply for that year in relation to the expense incurred in connection with the provision of the car, and

[(ii) there shall be treated for that year as emoluments of the employment by reason of which the car is made available, and accordingly chargeable to income tax, the amount, if any, by which the cash equivalent of the benefit of the car for the year exceeds the aggregate for the year of the amount which the employee is required to make good and actually makes good to the employer in respect of any part of the costs of providing or running the car.][6]

(3)

[(a) The cash equivalent of the benefit of a car for a year of assessment shall be 30 per cent of the original market value of the car.][7]

(b) Where a car in respect of which this section applies in relation to a person for a year of assessment is made available to the person for part only of that year, the cash equivalent of the benefit of that car as respects that person for that year shall be an amount which bears to the full amount of the cash equivalent of the car for that year (ascertained under *paragraph (a)*) the same proportion as that part of the year bears to that year.

[...][8]

[(d) This subsection is subject to subsection 5 (4B) for years of assessment 2009 and subsequent years.][9]

(4)

[(a) Where in relation to a person the business mileage for a year of assessment exceeds [24,000 kilometres][10] the cash equivalent of the benefit of the car for that year, instead of being the amount ascertained under *subsection (3)* shall be the percentage of the original market value of the car applicable to the business mileage under the Table to this subsection.][11]

(b) In the Table to this subsection, any percentage shown in *column (3)* shall be that applicable to any business mileage for a year of assessment which—

(i) exceeds the lower limit shown in *column (1)*, and

(ii) does not exceed the upper limit (if any) shown in *column (2)*,

opposite the mention of that percentage in *column (3)*.

[(c) Where a car in respect of which this section applies in relation to a person for a year of assessment is made available to the person for part only of that year, the cash equivalent of the benefit of that car as respects that person for that year shall be an amount determined by applying *paragraph (a)* as if—

(i) the figure [24,000][12] referred to in that paragraph were replaced by a figure (in this paragraph referred to as the "new figure") determined by the formula—

$$15{,}000 \times \frac{A}{365}$$

where—

A is the number of days in the part of the year, and

(ii) each figure in *columns (1)*, *(2)* and *(3)* of the [Table to this subsection][13] were reduced in the same proportion as the new figure bears to [24,000.][14]][15]

[TABLE

Business mileage lower limit (1)	Business mileage upper limit (2)	Percentage of original market value (3)
kilometres	kilometres	per cent
24,000	32,000	24
32,000	40,000	18
40,000	48,000	12
48,000	—	6][16]

[(d) This subsection is subject to subsection (4B) for years of assessment 2009 and subsequent years.][17]

[…][18]

[(4B) (a) Where a new car is provided for the first time for the year of assessment 2009 or any subsequent year, the cash equivalent of the benefit shall be an amount determined by the formula:

$$\text{Original market value} \times A$$

where—

A is a percentage, based on vehicle categories and business mileage, determined in accordance with column (3), (4) or (5), as the case may be, of Table A to this subsection.

(b) In Table A to this subsection, any percentage shown in column (3), (4) or (5), as the case may be, shall be the percentage applicable to any business mileage for a year of assessment which—

(i) exceeds the lower limit (if any) shown in column (1), and

(ii) does not exceed the upper limit (if any) shown in column (2),

opposite the mention of that percentage in column (3), (4) or (5), as the case may be.

(c) Any reference in this section to a vehicle in any of the vehicle Categories A to G as set out in the first column of Table B to this subsection is a reference to a vehicle whose CO_2emissions, confirmed by reference to the relevant EC type approval certificate or EC certificate of conformity, are set out in the corresponding entry in the second column of Table B to this subsection.

TABLE A

Business mileage		Vehicle Categories A, B and C	Vehicle Categories D and E	Vehicle Categories F and G
lower limit	upper limit			
(1)	(2)	(3)	(4)	(5)
kilometres	kilometres	per cent	per cent	per cent
—	24,000	30	35	40
24,000	32,000	24	28	32
32,000	40,000	18	21	24
40,000	48,000	12	14	16
48,000	—	6	7	8

TABLE B

Vehicle Category (1)	CO_2Emissions (CO_2g/km) (2)
A	0g/km up to and including 120g/km
B	More than 120g/km up to and including 140g/km
C	More than 140g/km up to and including 155g/km
D	More than 155g/km up to and including 170g/km
E	More than 170g/km up to and including 190g/km
F	More than 190g/km up to and including 225g/km
G	More than 225g/km.][19]

(5) (a) Where for a year of assessment—

(i) a person, in the performance of the duties of his or her employment, spends 70 per cent or more of his or her time engaged on such duties away from the place of business of his or her employer, and

(ii) in relation to that person, the business mileage exceeds [8,000 kilometres][20],

then, if the person so elects in writing to the inspector, the cash equivalent of the benefit of the car for that year of assessment in relation to the person shall, instead of being the amount ascertained under *subsection (3)* or *(4)*, as may otherwise be appropriate, be 80 per cent of the amount ascertained under *subsection (3)*.

(b) When requested in writing by the inspector, a person who makes an election under *paragraph (a)* for a year of assessment shall within 30 days of the date of such request furnish to the inspector a relevant log book in relation to that year of assessment.

(c) This subsection shall not apply as respects a year of assessment where—

(i) when requested to do so, a person fails to deliver to the inspector within the time specified in *paragraph (b)* a relevant log book in relation to that year of assessment, or

(ii) the time spent by a person in the performance of the duties of his or her employment in that year of assessment is on average less than 20 hours per week.

(d) *Subsection (7)(e)* shall apply for the purposes of this subsection as it applies for the purposes of *subsection (7).*

(e) Where a person makes an election under *paragraph (a)* for a year of assessment, such person shall retain the relevant log book in relation to that year of assessment for a period of 6 years after that end of that year or for such shorter period as the inspector may authorise in writing.

(6) (a) Where any amount is to be treated as emoluments of an employment under *subsection (2)(b)(ii)* for a year of assessment, it shall be the duty of the person who is chargeable to tax in respect of that amount to deliver in writing to the inspector, not later than 30 days after the end of that year of assessment, particulars of the car, of its original market value and of the business mileage and private mileage for that year of assessment.

(b) Where in relation to a year of assessment—

(i) a person makes default in the delivery of particulars in relation to—

(I) the original market value of a car in respect of which this section applies in relation to him or her,

(II) his or her business mileage for the year, or

(III) his or her private mileage for the year,

or

(ii) the inspector is not satisfied with the particulars which have been delivered by the person,

then, the original market value or business mileage or private mileage which is to be taken into account for the purpose of computing the amount of the tax to which that person is to be charged shall be such value or mileage, as the case may be, as according to the best of the inspector's judgment ought to be so taken into account and, in the absence of sufficient evidence to the contrary, the business mileage for a year of assessment in relation to a person shall be determined [by deducting 8,000 from the total number of kilometres travelled][21] in that year by that person in a car or cars in respect of which this section applies in relation to that person.

[...][22]

[...][23]

(d) A value or mileage taken into account under *paragraph (b)* may be amended by the Appeal Commissioners or the Circuit Court on the hearing or the rehearing of an appeal against an assessment in respect of the employment in the performance of the duties of which the business mileage is done.

(7) (a) This subsection shall apply to any car in the case of which the inspector is satisfied (whether on a claim under this subsection or otherwise) that it has for any year been included in a car pool for the use of the employees of one or more employers.

(b) A car shall be treated as having been so included for a year if—

(i) in that year the car was made available to and actually used by more than one of those employees and in the case of each of them was made available to him or her by reason of his or her employment but was not in that year ordinarily used by any one of them to the exclusion of the others,

(ii) in the case of each of them, any private use of the car made by him or her in that year was merely incidental to his or her other use of the car in the year, and

(iii) the car was in that year not normally kept overnight on or in the vicinity of any residential premises where any of the employees was residing, except while being kept overnight on premises occupied by the person making the car available to them.

(c) Where this subsection applies to a car, the car shall be treated under this section as not having been available for the private use of any of the employees for the year in question.

(d) A claim under this subsection in respect of a car for any year may be made by any one of the employees mentioned in *paragraph (b)(i)* (they being referred to in *paragraph (e)* as "*the employees concerned*") or by the employer on behalf of all of them.

(e) (i) Any person aggrieved by a decision of the inspector on any question arising under this subsection may, by notice in writing to that effect given to the inspector within 2 months from the date on which notice of the decision is given to that person, make an application to have his or her claim for relief heard and determined by the Appeal Commissioners.

(ii) Where an application is made under *subparagraph (i)*, the Appeal Commissioners shall hear and determine the claim in the like manner as an appeal made to them against an assessment, and the provisions of the Income Tax Acts relating to such an appeal (including the provisions relating to the rehearing of an appeal and to the statement of a case for the opinion of the High Court on a point of law) shall apply accordingly with any necessary modifications.

(iii) On an appeal against the decision of the inspector on a claim under this section all the employees concerned may take part in the proceedings, and the determination of the Appeal Commissioners or the Circuit Court, as the case may be, shall be binding on all those employees, whether or not they have taken part in the proceedings.

(iv) Where an appeal against the decision of the inspector on a claim under this subsection has been determined, no appeal against the inspector's decision on any other such claim in respect of the same car while in the same car pool and the same year shall be entertained.

Amendments

[1] Substituted by F(No.2)A08 s6(1)(a). This section comes into operation on such day or days as the Minister for Finance may by order or orders appoint and different days may be appointed for different purposes or different provisions.

[2] Substituted by FA03 s6(1)(b)(i)(I). This section applies and has effect as on and from 1 January 2004.

[3] Inserted by FA03 s6(1)(b)(i)(II). This section applies and has effect as on and from 1 January 2004.

[4, 5] Substituted by F(No.3)A11 sched1(15). Shall have effect from the passing of this Act 27 July 2011.

[6] Substituted by FA03 s6(1)(b)(ii). This section applies and has effect as on and from 1 January 2004.

[7] Substituted by FA03 s6(1)(b)(iii). This section applies and has effect as on and from 1 January 2004.

[8] Deleted by F(No.2)A08 s6(1)(b)(i). This section comes into operation on such day or days as the Minister for Finance may by order or orders appoint and different days may be appointed for different purposes or different provisions.

[9] Inserted by F(No.2)A08 s6(1)(b)(ii). This section comes into operation on such day or days as the Minister for Finance may by order or orders appoint and different days may be appointed for different purposes or different provisions.

[10] Substituted by F(No.2)A08 s6(1)(c)(i). This section comes into operation on such day or days as the Minister for Finance may by order or orders appoint and different days may be appointed for different purposes or different provisions.

[11] Substituted by FA03 s6(1)(b)(iv)(I). This section applies and has effect as on and from 1 January 2004.

[12] Substituted by F(No.2)A08 s6(1)(c)(ii)(I). This section comes into operation on such day or days as the Minister for Finance may by order or orders appoint and different days may be appointed for different purposes or different provisions.

[13, 14] Substituted by FA09 s30(4)(a).

[15] Inserted by FA03 s6(1)(b)(iv)(II). This section applies and has effect as on and from 1 January 2004.

[16] Substituted by F(No.2)A08 s6(1)(c)(ii)(II). This section comes into operation on such day or days as the Minister for Finance may by order or orders appoint and different days may be appointed for different purposes or different provisions.

[17] Inserted by F(No.2)A08 s6(1)(c)(iii). This section comes into operation on such day or days as the Minister for Finance may by order or orders appoint and different days may be appointed for different purposes or different provisions.

[18] Deleted by F(No.2)A08 s6(1)(d). This section comes into operation on such day or days as the Minister for Finance may by order or orders appoint and different days may be appointed for different purposes or different provisions.

[19] Inserted by F(No.2)A08 s6(1)(e). This section comes into operation on such day or days as the Minister for Finance may by order or orders appoint and different days may be appointed for different purposes or different provisions.

[20] Substituted by F(No.2)A08 s6(1)(f)(i). This section comes into operation on such day or days as the Minister for Finance may by order or orders appoint and different days may be appointed for different purposes or different provisions.

[21] Substituted by F(No.2)A08 s6(1)(g)(i). This section comes into operation on such day or days as the Minister for Finance may by order or orders appoint and different days may be appointed for different purposes or different provisions.

[22] Deleted by F(No.2)A08 s6(1)(g)(ii). This section comes into operation on such day or days as the Minister for Finance may by order or orders appoint and different days may be appointed for different purposes or different provisions.

[23] Deleted by FA03 s6(1)(b)(v). This section applies and has effect as on and from 1 January 2004.

Case Law

Arguments that the motor car benefit-in-kind provisions were unconstitutional were unsuccessful in Browne & Ors v AG 1991 IV ITR 323

Revenue Briefings

Tax Briefing

Tax Briefing March 1996 – Issue 21 pg 8 – Overseas duties and Car Benefit-in-Kind

Tax Briefing October 1997 – Issue 28 pg 13 – Benefit-in-Kind on Company Cars

Tax Briefing May 2003 – Issue 52 pg 8 – Income Tax Benefit-in-Kind

Tax Briefing December 2004 – Issue 58 pg 13 – Third-party benefits

Revenue Information Notes

IT 20A – Taxation (PAYE/PRSI) of Benefits from Employments from 1st January 2004

Employers Guide to Benefit-in-kind

Cross References

From Section 121

Section 113 Making of deductions.
Section 116 Interpretation (Chapter 3).
Section 121A Benefit of use of van.

To Section 121

Section 118 Benefits in kind: general charging provision.
Section 121A Benefit of use of van.
Section 122A Notional loans relating to shares, etc.
Section 531O Interpretation (Part 18B).
Section 823 Deduction for income earned outside the State.
Section 897 Returns of employees' emoluments, etc.
Section 985A Application of section 985 to certain perquisites, etc.
Schedule 29 Provisions Referred to in Sections 1052, 1053 and 1054

121A Benefit of use of van

[(1) In this section—

["*gross vehicle weight*", in relation to a vehicle, means the weight which the vehicle is designed or adapted not to exceed when in normal use and travelling on the road laden.][1]

"*van*" means a mechanically propelled road vehicle which—

(a) is designed or constructed solely or mainly for the carriage of goods or other burden,

(b) has a roofed area or areas to the rear of the driver's seat, […][2]

(c) has no side windows or seating fitted in that roofed area or [areas, and][3]

[(d) has a gross vehicle weight not exceeding 3,500 kilograms.][4]

(2) (a) In relation to a person chargeable to tax in respect of an employment, this section shall apply for a year of assessment in relation to a van which, by reason of the employment, is made available (without a transfer of the property in it) to the person and is available for his or her private use in that year.

(b) In relation to a van in respect of which this section applies for a year of assessment—

(i) *Chapter 3* of this Part shall not apply for that year in relation to the expense incurred in connection with the provision of the van, and

(ii) there shall be treated for that year as emoluments of the employment by reason of which the van is made available, and accordingly chargeable to income tax, the amount, if any, by which the cash equivalent of the benefit of the van for the year exceeds the aggregate for the year of the amounts which the employee is required to make good and actually makes good to the employer in respect of any part of the costs of providing or running the van.

[(2A) *Subsection (2)* shall not apply for a year of assessment in respect of the private use of a van made available to a person (in this subsection referred to as the "*employee*") as set out in that subsection where the following conditions are met—

(a) the van made available to the employee is necessary for the performance of the duties of the employee's employment,

(b) the employee is required by the person who made the van available to keep it, when not in use in the performance of the duties of the employee's employment, at or in the vicinity of the employee's private residence,

(c) apart from travel between the employee's private residence and workplace, other private use of the van is prohibited by the person making the van available and there is no such other private use, and

(d) in the performance of the duties of his or her employment, the employee spends at least 80 per cent of his or her time engaged on such duties away from the premises of the employer to which the employee is attached.][5]

(3) The cash equivalent of the benefit of a van for a year of assessment shall be 5 per cent of the original market value of the van.

(4) The provisions of *subsections (1)* (other than the definition of car in *paragraph (a)*), *paragraph (b)* of *subsection (3)*, *(6)* and *(7)* of *section 121* shall apply, with any necessary modifications in relation to a van, for the purposes of this section as they apply in relation to a car for the purposes of that section.][6]

Amendments

[1] Inserted by FA04 s8(1)(c)(i)(I). This section is deemed to have come into force and taken effect as on and from 1 January 2004.

[2] Deleted by FA04 s8(1)(c)(i)(II)(A). This section is deemed to have come into force and taken effect as on and from 1 January 2004.

[3] Substituted by FA04 s8(1)(c)(i)(II)(B). This section is deemed to have come into force and taken effect as on and from 1 January 2004.

[4] Inserted by FA04 s8(1)(c)(i)(II)(C). This section is deemed to have come into force and taken effect as on and from 1 January 2004.

[5] Inserted by FA04 s8(1)(c)(ii). This section is deemed to have come into force and taken effect as on and from 1 January 2004.

[6] Inserted by FA03 s6(1)(c). This section applies and has effect as on and from 1 January 2004.

Revenue Briefings

Tax Briefing

Tax Briefing May 2003 – Issue 52 pg 8 – Income Tax Benefit-in-Kind

Tax Briefing December 2004 – Issue 58 pg 13 – Third-party Benefits

Cross References

From Section 121A

Section 116 Interpretation (Chapter 3).

Section 121 Benefit of use of car.

To Section 121A

Section 118 Benefits in kind: general charging provision.

Section 121 Benefit of use of car.

Section 531O Interpretation (Part 18B).

Section 985A Application of section 985 to certain perquisites, etc.

122 Preferential loan arrangements

[ITA67 s195B(3) and (6); FA82 s8(1) to (5), (7) and (9); FA89 s6; FA93 s10(1); FA95 s9; FA97 s146(1) and Sch9 PtI par12(1)]

(1) (a) In this section—

["*employee*", in relation to an employer, means an individual employed by the employer in an employment—

(a) to which Chapter 3 of this Part applies, or

(b) the profits or gains of which are chargeable to tax under Case III of Schedule D, including, in a case where the employer is a body corporate, a director (within the meaning of that Chapter) of the body corporate;][1]

"*employer*", in relation to an individual, means—

[(i) a person of whom the individual or the [spouse or civil partner][2] of the individual is or was an employee,][13]

(ii) a person of whom the individual becomes an employee subsequent to the making of a loan by the person to the individual, and while any part of the loan, or of another loan replacing it, is outstanding, or

(iii) a person connected with a person referred to in *paragraph (i)* or *(ii)*;

"*loan*" includes any form of credit, and references to a loan include references to any other loan applied directly or indirectly towards the replacement of another loan;

"*preferential loan*" [means, in relation to an individual, a loan, in respect of which no interest is [paid][4] or interest is [paid][5] at a preferential rate, made directly or indirectly to the individual][6] or to the [spouse or civil partner][7] of the individual by a person who in relation to the individual or the [spouse or civil partner][8] is an employer, but does not include any such loan in respect of which interest is [paid][9] at a rate that is not less than the rate of interest at which the employer in the course of the employer's trade makes equivalent loans for similar purposes at arm's length to persons other than employees or their [spouses or civil partners][10];

"*preferential rate*" means a rate less than the specified rate;

["*qualifying loan*" has the meaning assigned to it by *section 244(1)(a)*;][11]

"*the specified rate*", in relation to a preferential loan, means—

[(i) in a case where the preferential loan is a qualifying loan, the rate of [4 per cent][12] per annum or such other rate (if any) prescribed by the Minister for Finance by regulations,][13]

(ii) in a case where—

(I) the preferential loan is made to an employee by an employer,

(II) the making of loans for the purposes of purchasing a dwelling house for occupation by the borrower as a residence, for a stated term of years at a rate of interest which does not vary for the duration of the loan, forms part of the trade of the employer, and

(III) the rate of interest at which, in the course of the employer's trade at the time the preferential loan is or was made, the employer makes or made loans at arm's length to persons, other than employees, for the purposes of purchasing a dwelling house for occupation by the borrower as a residence is less than [4 per cent][14] per annum or such other rate (if any) prescribed by the Minister for Finance by regulations,

the first-mentioned rate in *subparagraph (III)*, or

(iii) in any other case, the rate of [13.5 per cent][15] per annum or such other rate (if any) prescribed by the Minister for Finance by regulations.

(b) For the purposes of this section, a person shall be regarded as connected with another person if such person would be so regarded for the purposes of *section 250*.

(c) In this section, a reference to a loan being made by a person includes a reference to a person assuming the rights and liabilities of the person who originally made the loan and to a person arranging, guaranteeing or in any way facilitating a loan or the continuation of a loan already in existence.

[(2) Where, for the whole or part of a year of assessment, there is outstanding, in relation to an individual, a preferential loan, the individual shall, subject to *subsection (4)*, be treated for the purposes of *section 112* or a charge to tax under Case III of Schedule D, as having received in that year of assessment, as a perquisite of the office or employment with the employer who made the loan, a sum equal to—

(a) if no interest is payable on the preferential loan or loans, the amount of interest which would have been payable in that year, if interest had been payable on the loan or loans at the specified rate, or

(b) if interest is paid or payable at a preferential rate or rates, the difference between the aggregate amount of interest paid or payable in that year and the amount of interest which would have been payable in that year, if interest had been payable on the loan or loans at the specified rate,

and the individual or, [in the case of an individual—][16]

[(i) who is a wife whose husband is chargeable to tax for the year of assessment in accordance with the provisions of *section 1017*, the spouse of the individual, or

(ii) who is a civil partner whose civil partner is chargeable to tax for the year of assessment in accordance with the provisions of *section 1031C*, the civil partner of the individual,

shall be charged to tax accordingly.][17]][18]

(3) Where an individual has a loan made to him or her directly or indirectly in any year of assessment by a person who at the time the loan is made is, or who at a time subsequent to the making of the loan becomes, an employer in relation to the individual and the loan or any interest payable on the loan is released or written off in whole or in part—

(a) the individual shall be deemed for the purposes of *section 112* or, in a case where profits or gains from an employment with that person would be chargeable to tax under Case III of Schedule D, for the purposes of a charge to tax under that Case to have received in the year of assessment in which the release or writing off took place as a perquisite of an office or employment with that person a sum equal to the amount which is released or written off, and

(b) [the individual or, in the case of an individual—][19]

[(i) whose spouse is chargeable to tax for the year of assessment in accordance with *section 1017*, the spouse of the individual, or

(ii) whose civil partner is chargeable to tax for the year of assessment in accordance with *section 1031C*, that civil partner,

shall be charged to tax accordingly.][20]

(4) Where for any year of assessment a sum is chargeable to tax under *subsection (2)* in respect of a preferential loan or loans or under *subsection (3)* in respect of an amount of interest written off or released, the individual to whom the loan or loans was or were made shall be deemed for the purposes of *section 244* to have paid in the year of assessment an amount or additional amount of interest, as the case may be, on the loan or loans equal to such sum or the individual by whom the interest written off or released was payable shall be deemed for those purposes to have paid in the year of assessment the interest released or written off.

(5) This section shall not apply to a loan made by an employer, being an individual, and shown to have been made in the normal course of his or her domestic, family or personal relationships.

(6) Any amount chargeable to tax by virtue of this section shall not be emoluments for the purpose of *section 472*.

(7) Every regulation made under this section shall be laid before Dáil Éireann as soon as may be after it is made and, if a resolution annulling the regulation is passed by Dáil Éireann within the next 21 days on which Dáil Éireann has sat after the regulation is laid before it, the regulation shall be annulled accordingly, but without prejudice to the validity of anything previously done thereunder.

Amendments

[1] Substituted by FA05 s9(a)(i).

[2, 7, 8] Substituted by F(No.3)A11 sched1(16). Shall have effect from the passing of this Act 27 July 2011.

[3] Substituted by FA04 s10(1)(a). Applies as respects loans made on or after 4 February 2004.

[4, 5, 9] Substituted by FA11 s7(1)(c). Shall have effect as on and from 26 January 2011.

[6] Substituted by FA05 s9(a)(ii).

[10] Substituted by F(No.3)A11 sched1(17). Shall have effect from the passing of this Act 27 July 2011.

[11] Inserted by FA10 s4(a). Applies as respects the year of assessment 2010 and subsequent years of assessment.

[12, 14] Substituted by FA13 s13(j)(i). Applies as respects the year of assessment 2013 and subsequent years of assessment.

[13] Substituted by FA10 s4(b). Applies as respects the year of assessment 2010 and subsequent years of assessment.

[15] Substituted by FA13 s13(j)(ii). Applies as respects the year of assessment 2013 and subsequent years of assessment.

[16, 17] Substituted by F(No.3)A11 sched1(18). Shall have effect from the passing of this Act 27 July 2011.

[18] Substituted by FA05 s9(b).

[19, 20] Substituted by F(No.3)A11 sched1(19). Shall have effect from the passing of this Act 27 July 2011.

Case Law

A loan could not be transmuted into something else merely because it would be discharged by an amount greater or less than the sum originally borrowed. Harvey v Williams 1995 STC 329

The definition of a 'loan' covered an advance of salary repayable by instalment. Williams v Todd 1988 STC 676

Misappropriation of funds by a director was not a 'loan'. Stephens v T Pittas Ltd 1983 STC 576

Revenue Briefings

Tax Briefing

Tax Briefing September 2009 – Issue 77 – Tax Relief on Qualifying Home Loans / BIK on Preferential Loans

Revenue Information Notes

IT 20A – Taxation (PAYE/PRSI) of Benefits from Employments from 1st January 2004

Employers Guide to Benefit-in-kind

Revenue Precedents

Employer wished to provide loans to employees to enable them purchase computers. The loans would be repaid by salary deduction over a 12 month period. The employer sought to have the provisions in s122 TCA 1997 dispensed with, by concession. Concession not acceded to. IT 971522

Cross References

From Section 122

Section 112 Basis of assessment, persons chargeable and extent of charge.

Section 244 Relief for interest paid on certain home loans.

Section 250 Extension of relief under section 248 to certain individuals in relation to loans applied in acquiring interest in certain companies.
Section 472 Employee tax credit.
Section 1017 Assessment of husband in respect of income of both spouses.

To Section 122

Section 122A Notional loans relating to shares, etc.
Section 267P Treatment of credit transaction.
Section 823 Deduction for income earned outside the State.
Section 897 Returns of employees' emoluments, etc.
Section 985A Application of section 985 to certain perquisites, etc.
Section 1003A Payment of tax by means of donation of heritage property to an Irish heritage trust.

122A Notional loans relating to shares, etc

[(1) In this section—

"*connected person*" has the same meaning as in *section 10*;

"*emoluments*" has the same meaning as in *section 113*;

"*employee*" and "*employer*" have the same meanings, respectively, assigned to them by *section 122*;

"*employment*" has the same meaning as in *section 121*;

"*market value*" shall be construed in accordance with *section 548*;

"*preferential loan*" has the same meaning as in *section 122*;

"*shares*" includes securities within the meaning of *section 135* and stock.

(2) Where an employee, or a person connected with him or her, acquires shares in a company (whether the employing company or not) and those shares are acquired at an under-value in pursuance of a right or opportunity available by reason of his or her employment, he or she shall be deemed to have the benefit of a loan on which no interest is payable (in this section referred to as the "*notional loan*") made directly or indirectly to him or her by a person who at the time the loan is made is, or who at a time subsequent to the making of the loan becomes, an employer in relation to the individual and such notional loan shall be deemed to be a preferential loan to which *section 122* applies.

(3) This section shall apply, subject to *Chapter 1* of *Part 17*, for a year of assessment in which an individual has, in accordance with *subsection (2)*, a notional loan and in this section—

(a) references to shares being acquired at an under-value are references to shares being acquired either without payment for them at the time or being acquired for an amount then paid which is less than the market value of fully paid-up shares of that class (in either case with or without obligation to make payment or further payment at some later time), and

(b) any reference, in relation to any shares, to the under-value on acquisition is a reference to the market value of fully paid-up shares of that class less any payment then made for the shares.

(4) The amount initially outstanding of the notional loan shall be so much of the under-value on acquisition as is not chargeable to tax as an emolument of the employee, and—

(a) the loan shall remain outstanding until terminated under *subsection (5)*, and

(b) payments or further payments made for the shares after the initial acquisition shall go to reduce the amount outstanding of the notional loan.

(5) The notional loan shall terminate on the occurrence of any of the following events—

(a) the whole amount of it outstanding is made good by means of payments or further payments made for the shares;

(b) the case being one in which the shares were not at the time of acquisition fully paid up, any outstanding or contingent obligation to pay for them is released, transferred or adjusted so as no longer to bind the employee or any person connected with him or her;

(c) the shares are so disposed of by surrender or otherwise that neither he nor she nor any such person any longer has a beneficial interest in the shares;

(d) the employee dies.

(6) If the notional loan terminates in a manner referred to in *subsection (5) (b)* or *(c)*, the provisions of *section 122(3)* shall apply as if an amount equal to the then outstanding amount of the notional loan had been released or written off from a loan within that section.

(7) Where shares are acquired, whether or not at an under-value but otherwise as mentioned in *subsection (2)*, and—

(a) the shares are subsequently disposed of by surrender or otherwise so that neither the employee nor any person connected with him or her any longer has a beneficial interest in them, and

(b) the disposal is for a consideration which exceeds the then market value of the shares,

then, for the year in which the disposal is effected, the outstanding amount of the excess shall be treated as emoluments of the employee's employment and accordingly chargeable to income tax under Schedule D or Schedule E.

(8) If at the time of the event giving rise to a charge by virtue of *subsection (6)* the employment in question has terminated, that subsection shall apply as if it had not.

(9) No charge arises under *subsection (6)* by reference to any disposal effected after the death of the employee, whether by his or her personal representatives or otherwise.

(10) This section applies in relation to acquisition and disposal of an interest in shares less than full beneficial ownership (including an interest in the proceeds of sale of part of the shares but not including a share option) as it applies in relation to the acquisition and disposal of shares, subject to the following:

(a) reference to the shares acquired shall be construed as reference to the interest in shares acquired,

(b) reference to the market value of the shares acquired shall be construed as reference to the proportion corresponding to the size of the interest of the market value of the shares in which the interest subsists,

(c) reference to shares of the same class as those acquired shall be construed as reference to shares of the same class as those in which the interest subsists,

(d) reference to the market value of fully paid-up shares of that class shall be construed as reference to the proportion of that value corresponding to the size of the interest.

(11) In this section, any reference to payment for shares includes giving any consideration in money or money's worth or making any subscription, whether in pursuance of a legal liability or not.][1]

Amendments

[1] Inserted by FA98 s15(1).

Revenue Briefings

Tax Briefing

Tax Briefing June 1998 – Issue 32 pg 8 – Notional Loans relating to Shares

Cross References

From Section 122A

Section 10 Connected persons.
Section 113 Making of deductions.
Section 121 Benefit of use of car.
Section 122 Preferential loan arrangements.
Section 135 Distributions: supplemental.
Section 509 Interpretation (Chapter 1).
Section 548 Valuation of assets.

To Section 122A

Section 128C Tax treatment of directors and employees who acquire convertible shares.

CHAPTER 5

Miscellaneous Charging Provisions

123 General tax treatment of payments on retirement or removal from office or employment

[ITA67 s114(1) to (5) and (7)]

(1) This section shall apply to any payment (not otherwise chargeable to income tax) which is made, whether in pursuance of any legal obligation or not, either directly or indirectly in consideration or in consequence of, or otherwise in connection with, the termination of the holding of an office or employment or any change in its functions or emoluments, including any payment in commutation of annual or periodical payments (whether chargeable to tax or not) which would otherwise have been so made.

(2) Subject to *section 201*, income tax shall be charged under Schedule E in respect of any payment to which this section applies made to the holder or past holder of any office or employment, or to his or her executors or administrators, whether made by the person under whom he or she holds or held the office or employment or by any other person.

(3) For the purposes of this section and *section 201*, any payment made to the [spouse, civil partner, or any relative or dependant][1] of a person who holds or has held an office or employment, or made on behalf of or to the order of that person, shall be treated as made to that person, and any valuable consideration other than money shall be treated as a payment of money equal to the value of that consideration at the date when it is given.

(4) Any payment chargeable to tax by virtue of this section shall be treated as income received on the following date—

(a) in the case of a payment in commutation of annual or other periodical payments, the date on which the commutation is effected, and

(b) in the case of any other payment, the date of the termination or change in respect of which the payment is made,

and shall be treated as emoluments of the holder or past holder of the office or employment assessable to income tax under Schedule E.

(5) In the case of the death of any person who if he or she had not died would have been chargeable to tax in respect of any such payment, the tax which would have been so chargeable shall be assessed and charged on his or her executors or administrators, and shall be a debt due from and payable out of his or her estate.

(6) Where any payment chargeable to tax under this section is made to any person in any year of assessment, it shall be the duty of the person by whom that payment is made to deliver particulars of the payment in writing to the inspector not later than 14 days after the end of that year.

Amendments

[1] Substituted by F(No.3)A11 sched1(20). Shall have effect from the passing of this Act 27 July 2011.

Case Law

Redundancy payments made to disabled employees were taxable as the payments were not on account of their disabilities. Albert Harding and others v O'Cahill 1990 IV ITR 233

Pay in lieu of notice, as provided for under an employee's contract of service, was not a redundancy payment but an emolument of the employment. EMI Group Electronics Ltd v Coldicott (HMIT) 1999 STC 803

The transfer of shares for acceptance of employment was not an emolument. Pritchard v Arundale 1971 47 TC 680

Colquhoun v R&C Commrs 2010 UKUT (TCC) 431 considered whether a lump sum payment for a change to an employee's future contractual redundancy terms was a payment in respect of termination of employment and therefore qualified for exemption under UK legislation.

Revenue Briefings

Tax Briefing

Tax Briefing June 1996 – Issue 22 pg 14 – Redundancy Payments and Re-Engagement of Employee's

Tax Briefing October 1997 – Issue 28 pg 8 – Taxation Treatment of Redundancy / Termination Payments

Tax Briefing January 2003 – Issue 51 pg 20 – Termination Payments and Legal Costs

Tax Briefing December 2003 – Issue 54 pg 10 – Redundancy Payments

Tax Briefing August 2005 – Issue 60 – pg 4 – Tax Treatment of Legal Fees

Tax Briefing November 2007 – Issue 67 – Lump Sum Payments & Top Slicing Relief

eBrief

eBrief No. 28/2014 – Tax treatment of termination lump sum payments

Revenue Precedents

Payment of compensation arising from an unfair dismissals case is treated as a payment chargeable under section 123, with appropriate reliefs. Note: The award was not in respect of actual salary, which would be chargeable under section 112. IT 97 1507

Whether the item included in the severance agreement and described as "Damages" is liable to tax. A payment made in consideration or in consequence of, or otherwise in connection with the termination of an employment – however described – is chargeable to tax under section 123 TCA 1997, unless it is otherwise chargeable to tax. IT 97 1533

Cross References

From Section 123

Section 201 Exemptions and reliefs in respect of tax under section 123.

To Section 123

Section 192A Exemption in respect of certain payments under employment law.

Section 201 Exemptions and reliefs in respect of tax under section 123.

Section 202 Relief for agreed pay restructuring.

Section 289 Calculation of balancing allowances and balancing charges in certain cases.
Section 471 Relief for contributions to permanent health benefit schemes.
Section 479 Relief for new shares purchased on issue by employees.
Section 480 Relief for certain sums chargeable under Schedule E.
Section 531B Charge to income levy.
Section 823 Deduction for income earned outside the State.
Section 924 Additional assessments.
Schedule 3 Reliefs in Respect of Income Tax Charged on Payments on Retirement, Etc
Schedule 29 Provisions Referred to in Sections 1052, 1053 and 1054

124 Tax treatment of certain severance payments

[FA93 s7(2)]

(1) This section shall apply to the following payments—

(a) a termination allowance (other than that part of the allowance which comprises a lump sum) payable in accordance with section 5 of the Oireachtas (Allowances to Members) and Ministerial and Parliamentary Offices (Amendment) Act, 1992, and any regulations made under that section, and

(b) a severance allowance or a special allowance payable in accordance with Part V (inserted by the Oireachtas (Allowances to Members) and Ministerial and Parliamentary Offices (Amendment) Act, 1992) of the Ministerial and Parliamentary Offices Act, 1938.

(2) Notwithstanding any other provision of the Income Tax Acts, payments to which this section applies shall be deemed to be—

(a) profits or gains accruing from an office or employment (and accordingly tax under Schedule E shall be charged on those payments, and tax so chargeable shall be computed under *section 112(1)*), and

(b) emoluments to which *Chapter 4* of *Part 42* is applied by *section 984*.

Cross References

From Section 124

Section 112 Basis of assessment, persons chargeable and extent of charge.
Section 960 Date for payment of income tax other than under self assessment.
Section 983 Interpretation (Chapter 4).
Section 984 Application.

124A Tax treatment of payments made pursuant to an order under section 2B of Employment Permits Act 2003

[(1) Payments made pursuant to an order under *section 2B* of the Employment Permits Act 2003 shall be regarded as—

(a) profits or gains accruing from an office or employment (and accordingly tax under Schedule E shall be charged on those payments, and tax so chargeable shall be computed under *section 112(1)*), and

(b) emoluments to which *Chapter 4* of *Part 42* applies.][1]

Amendments

[1] Inserted by EP(A)A14 s37(a).

125 Tax treatment of benefits received under permanent health benefit schemes

[FA79 s8(1), (4), (4A) and (6); FA86 s7; FA92 s7]

(1) In this section—

"*benefit*" means a payment made to a person under a permanent health benefit scheme in the event of loss or diminution of income in consequence of ill health;

"*permanent health benefit scheme*" means any scheme, contract, policy or other arrangement, approved by the Revenue Commissioners for the purposes of this section, which provides for periodic payments to an individual in the event of loss or diminution of income in consequence of ill health.

(2) (a) A policy of permanent health insurance, sickness insurance or other similar insurance issued in respect of an insurance made on or after the 6th day of April, 1986, shall be a permanent health benefit scheme within the meaning of this section if it conforms with a form which, at the time the policy is issued, is either—

(i) a standard form approved by the Revenue Commissioners as a standard form of permanent health benefit scheme, or

(ii) a form varying from a standard form so approved in no other respect than by making such alterations to that standard form as are, at the time the policy is issued, approved by the Revenue Commissioners as being compatible with a permanent health benefit scheme when made to that standard form and satisfying any conditions subject to which the alterations are so approved.

(b) In approving a policy as a standard form of permanent health benefit scheme in pursuance of *paragraph (a)*, the Revenue Commissioners may disregard any provision of the policy which appears to them insignificant.

(3) (a) Any benefit received by a person under a permanent health benefit scheme, whether as of right or not, shall be deemed to be—

(i) profits or gains arising or accruing from an employment, and

(ii) emoluments within the meaning of *Chapter 4* of *Part 42*.

(b) Tax under Schedule E shall be charged on every person to whom any benefit referred to in *paragraph (a)* is paid in respect of all such benefits paid to such person, and tax so chargeable shall be computed under *section 112(1)*.

(4) The Revenue Commissioners may nominate any of their officers, including an inspector, to perform any acts and discharge any functions authorised by this section to be performed or discharged by them.

Cross References

From Section 125

Section 112 Basis of assessment, persons chargeable and extent of charge.
Section 960 Date for payment of income tax other than under self assessment.
Section 983 Interpretation (Chapter 4).

To Section 125

Section 471 Relief for contributions to permanent health benefit schemes.

126 Tax treatment of certain benefits payable under Social Welfare Acts

[ITA67 s224(1), (2) and (4); FA71 s12; FA92 s15; FA95 s10(1); FA97 s4]

[(1) In this section "*the Acts*" means the Social Welfare Acts.][1]

(2) (a) This subsection shall apply to the following benefits payable under the Acts—

(i) widow's (contributory) pension,

(ii) orphan's (contributory) allowance,

(iii) retirement pension, and

(iv) old age (contributory) pension.

(b) Payments of benefits to which this subsection applies shall be deemed to be emoluments to which *Chapter 4* of *Part 42* applies.

[(2A) (a) This subsection shall apply to the following benefits payable on or after 1 July 2013 under the Acts—

(i) maternity benefit,

(ii) adoptive benefit, and

(iii) health and safety benefit.

(b) Amounts to be paid on foot of the benefits to which this subsection applies shall be deemed—

(i) to be profits or gains arising or accruing from an employment (and accordingly tax under Schedule E shall be charged on every person to whom any such benefit is payable in respect of amounts to be paid on foot of such benefits, and tax so chargeable shall be computed under *section 112(1)*), and

(ii) to be emoluments to which *Chapter 4* of *Part 42* applies.][2]

[(2B) Notwithstanding the provisions of *section 112(1)*, where an increase in the amount of a pension to which *section 112, 113, 117* or *157*, as the case may be, of the Social Welfare Consolidation Act 2005 applies is paid in respect of a qualified adult (within the meaning of the Acts), that increase shall be treated for all the purposes of the Income Tax Acts as if it arises to and is payable to the beneficiary referred to in those sections of that Act.][3]

(3) (a) This subsection shall apply to the following benefits payable under the Acts—

(i) disability benefit,

(ii) unemployment benefit,

(iii) injury benefit which is comprised in occupational injuries benefit, and

(iv) pay-related benefit.

(b) Amounts to be paid on foot of the benefits to which this subsection applies (other than amounts so payable in respect of a qualified child within the meaning of [section 2(3) of the Social Welfare Consolidation Act 2005][4] shall be deemed—

(i) to be profits or gains arising or accruing from an employment (and accordingly tax under Schedule E shall be charged on every person to whom any such benefit is payable in respect of amounts to be paid on foot of such benefits, and tax so chargeable shall be computed under *section 112(1)*), and

(ii) to be emoluments to which *Chapter 4* of *Part 42* is applied by *section 984*.

[(c) (i) In this paragraph "*short-time employment*" has the same meaning as it has for the purposes of the Acts.

(ii) Notwithstanding *paragraphs (a)* and *(b)* and the Finance Act 1992 (Commencement of *Section 15*) (Unemployment Benefit and Pay-Related Benefit) Order 1994 (S.I. No. 19 of 1994), *paragraph (b)* shall not apply in relation to unemployment benefit paid or payable, to a person employed in short-time employment.][5]

(4) (a) In this subsection, "*income tax week*" means one of the successive periods of 7 days in a year of assessment beginning on the 1st day of that year, or on any 7th day after that day, and the last day of a year of assessment (or the last 2 days of a year of assessment ending in a leap year) shall be taken as included in the last income tax week of that year of assessment.

(b) Notwithstanding *subsection (3)*, the first [€13][6] of the aggregate of the amounts of unemployment benefit payable to a person in respect of one or more days of unemployment comprised in any income tax week (other than an amount so payable in respect of a qualified child within the meaning of section 2(3)(*a*) of the Social Welfare (Consolidation) Act, 1993) shall be disregarded for the purposes of the Income Tax Acts.

[...][7]

(6) (a) *Subsection (3)* shall come into operation on such day or days as may be fixed for that purpose by order or orders of the Minister for Finance, either generally or with reference to any particular benefit to which that subsection applies, or with reference to any category of person in receipt of any particular benefit to which that subsection applies, and different days may be so fixed for different benefits or categories of persons in receipt of benefits.

(b) Where an order is proposed to be made under this subsection, a draft of the order shall be laid before Dáil Éireann, and the order shall not be made until a resolution approving of the draft has been passed by Dáil Éireann.

(7)

[(a) The Revenue Commissioners may, in order to provide for the efficient collection and recovery of any tax due in respect of benefits [to which *subsections (2A)* and *(3)* apply][8], make regulations modifying the [Income Tax (Employments) (Consolidated) Regulations 2001 (S.I. No. 559 of 2001)][9], in their application to those benefits, the employees in receipt of those benefits, the reliefs from income tax appropriate to such employees, and employers of such employees or certificates of tax credits and standard rate cutoff point or tax deduction cards held by employers of such employees in respect of those employees.

(b) Without prejudice to the generality of *paragraph (a)*, regulations under that paragraph may include provision for the reallocation by the Revenue Commissioners (without the issue of amended notices of determination of tax credits and standard rate cut-off point, amended certificates of tax credits and standard rate cut-off point and amended tax deduction cards) of the reliefs from income tax appropriate to employees between the benefits [to which *subsections (2A)* and *(3)* apply][10] and other emoluments receivable by them.][11]

(c) Every regulation made under this subsection shall be laid before Dáil Éireann as soon as may be after it is made and, if a resolution annulling the regulation is passed by Dáil Éireann within the next 21 days on which Dáil Éireann has sat after the regulation is laid before it, the regulation shall be annulled accordingly, but without prejudice to the validity of anything previously done thereunder.

[…][12]

Amendments

[1] Substituted by FA07 s10(a).

[2] Inserted by FA13 s8(a). Deemed to have come into force and takes effect on and from 1 January 2013.

[3] Inserted by F(No.2)A13 s12. Comes into operation on 1 January 2014.

[4] Substituted by FA07 s10(b)(i).

[5] Inserted by FA07 s10(b)(ii).

[6] Substituted by FA00 sched2.

[7] Deleted by FA12 s7. Applies for the year of assessment 2012 and each subsequent year of assessment.

[8,10] Substituted by FA13 s8(b). Deemed to have come into force and takes effect on and from 1 January 2013.

[9] Substituted by FA02 sched6(3)(c). Shall be deemed to have come into force and take effect as on and from 1 January 2002.

[11] Substituted by FA01 sched1(1)(b). Applies as respects the year of assessment 2001 and subsequent years of assessment.

[12] Deleted by FA07 s10(c).

Revenue Briefings

Tax Briefing

Tax Briefing April 1997 – Issue 26 pg 21 – Taxation of Disability Benefit

eBrief

eBrief No. 19/2013 – Taxation of Maternity Benefit, Adoptive Benefit and Health & Safety Benefit

Revenue Information Notes

IT 22 – Taxation of Illness and Short-term Occupational Injury Benefits

IT 24 – Taxation of Jobseekers Benefit

Cross References

From Section 126

Section 15 Rate of charge.
Section 112 Basis of assessment, persons chargeable and extent of charge.
Section 960 Date for payment of income tax other than under self assessment.
Section 983 Interpretation (Chapter 4).
Section 984 Application.

127 Tax treatment of restrictive covenants

[ITA67 s525; FA92 s18(1) and (3); FA97 s146(1) and Sch9 PtI par1(35)]

(1) In this section—

"*accounting period*" means an accounting period determined in accordance with *section 27*;

"*basis period*" means the period on the profits or gains of which income tax is to be finally computed under Schedule D or, where by virtue of the Income Tax Acts the profits or gains of any other period are to be taken to be the profits or gains of that period, that other period;

"*office or employment*" means any office or employment whatever such that the emoluments of that office or employment, if any, are or would be chargeable to income tax under Schedule E or under Case III of Schedule D for any year of assessment;

references to the giving of valuable consideration shall not include references to the mere assumption of an obligation to make over or provide valuable property, rights or advantages, but shall include references to the doing of anything in or towards the discharge of such an obligation.

(2) Where—

(a) an individual who holds, has held or is about to hold an office or employment gives, in connection with the holding of the office or employment, an undertaking (whether absolute or qualified and whether legally valid or not), the tenor or effect of which is to restrict the individual as to his or her conduct or activities,

(b) in respect of the giving of that undertaking by the individual, or of the total or partial fulfilment of that undertaking by the individual, any sum is paid either to the individual or to any other person, and

(c) apart from this section, the sum paid would not be treated as profits or gains from the office or employment,

the sum paid shall be deemed—

(i) to be profits or gains arising or accruing from the office or employment, and accordingly—

(I) in a case where the profits or gains from the office or employment are or would be chargeable to tax under [Schedule E][1], tax under that Schedule shall be charged on that sum, and tax so chargeable shall be computed under *section 112(1)*, or

(II) in a case where the profits or gains from the office or employment are or would be chargeable to tax under Case III of Schedule D, tax under that Case shall be charged on that sum,

and

(ii) in a case within *paragraph (i)(I)*, to be emoluments to which *Chapter 4* of *Part 42* is applied by *section 984*,

for the year of assessment in which the sum is paid; but where the individual has died before the payment of the sum this subsection shall apply as if the sum had been paid immediately before the individual's death.

(3) Where valuable consideration otherwise than in the form of money is given in respect of the giving of, or of the total or partial fulfilment of, any undertaking, *subsection (2)* shall apply as if a sum had instead been paid equal to the value of that consideration.

(4) Notwithstanding *section 81(2)*, where any sum paid or valuable consideration given by a person carrying on a trade or profession is chargeable to tax in accordance with *subsection (2)*, the sum paid or the value of the consideration given, as the case may be, may be deducted as an expense in computing for the purposes of Schedule D the profits or gains of that person's trade or profession, as the case may be—

(a) in the case of a person chargeable to income tax, for the basis period, or

(b) in the case of a person chargeable to corporation tax, for the accounting period,

in which the sum is paid or valuable consideration is given.

(5) Where any sum paid or valuable consideration given by an investment company (within the meaning of *section 83*), or a company to which *section 83* applies by

virtue of *section 707*, is chargeable to tax in accordance with *subsection (2)*, the sum paid or the value of consideration given, as the case may be, shall for the purposes of *section 83* be treated as an expense of management for the accounting period in which the sum is paid or valuable consideration is given.

(6) This section shall apply in relation to any sum paid or consideration given in respect of the giving of, or the total or partial fulfilment of, any undertaking whenever given.

Amendments

[1] Substituted by FA05 sched6(1)(b). Applies as on and from 25 March 2005

Cross References

From Section 127

Section 27 Basis of, and periods for, assessment.
Section 81 General rule as to deductions.
Section 83 Expenses of management of investment companies.
Section 112 Basis of assessment, persons chargeable and extent of charge.
Section 707 Management expenses.
Section 960 Date for payment of income tax other than under self assessment.
Section 983 Interpretation (Chapter 4).
Section 984 Application.

To Section 127

Section 201 Exemptions and reliefs in respect of tax under section 123.
Section 644A Relief from income tax in respect of income from dealing in residential development land.
Section 823 Deduction for income earned outside the State.

127A Tax treatment of members of the European Parliament

[(1) Notwithstanding any other provision of the Tax Acts, income arising to any individual as a member of the European Parliament and payable out of moneys provided—

(a) by the Oireachtas, shall be chargeable to tax under Schedule E, or

(b) by the budget of the European Union, shall be chargeable to tax under Case III of Schedule D.

(2) Any income tax liability arising in the State in respect of any such income referred to in subsection (1) shall be reduced by the amount of tax, if any, paid for the benefit of the budget of the European Union in respect of such income.][1]

Amendments

[1] Inserted by the European Parliament (Irish Constituency Members) Act 2009 Sec 5. This Act comes into operation on the first day of the parliamentary term beginning in 2009.

127B Tax treatment of flight crew in international traffic

[(1) Income arising to any individual, whether resident in the State or not, from any employment exercised aboard an aircraft—

(a) that is operated in international traffic, and

(b) where the aircraft is so operated by an enterprise that has its place of effective management in the State,

shall be chargeable to tax under Schedule E.

(2) For the purposes of an arrangement to which this section and *section 826* applies, "*international traffic*", in relation to an aircraft, does not include an aircraft operated solely between places in another state.][1]

Amendments

[1] Inserted by FA11 s(16). Deemed to have come into force and takes effect as on and from 1 January 2011.

Revenue Briefings

eBrief

eBrief No. 27/2012 – Tax and Universal Social Charge (USC) treatment of employment income arising to flight crew members

Cross References

From Section 127B

Section 826 Agreements for relief from double taxation.

128 Tax treatment of directors of companies and employees granted rights to acquire shares or other assets

[FA86 s9(1)(a) and (b)(i) and (iii), and (2) to (11)(a)]

(1) (a) In this section, except where the context otherwise requires—

["*branch or agency*" has the same meaning as in *section 4*;][1]

"*company*" has the same meaning as in *section 4*;

"*director*" and "*employee*" have the meanings respectively assigned to them by *section 770(1)*;

"*right*" means a right to acquire any asset or assets including shares in any company;

"*market value*" shall be construed in accordance with *section 548*;

"*shares*" includes securities within the meaning of *section 135* and stock.

(b) In this section—

(i) references to the release of a right include references to agreeing to the restriction of the exercise of the right;

(ii) a person shall be regarded as acquiring a right as a director of a company or as an employee—

(I) if by reason of the person's office or employment it is granted to the person, or to another person who assigns the right to the person, and

(II) if *section 71(3)* does not apply in charging to tax the profits or gains of that office or employment,

and *clauses (I)* and *(II)* shall apply to a right granted by reason of a person's office or employment before the person has commenced to hold it or after the person has ceased to hold it as they would apply if the person had commenced to hold the office or employment or had not ceased to hold the office or employment, as the case may be.

(2) Where a person realises a gain by the exercise of, or by the assignment or release of, a right obtained by the person on or after the 6th day of April, 1986, as a director of a company or employee, the person shall be chargeable to tax under Schedule E for the year of assessment in which the gain is so realised on an amount equal to the amount of his or her gain as computed [and shall be so chargeable notwithstanding that he or she was not resident in the State on the date on which the right was obtained][2].

[(2A) Notwithstanding any other provision of the Tax Acts, where a person is, by virtue of this section, chargeable to tax under Schedule E for a year of assessment in respect of an amount equal to the gain realised from the exercise, assignment or release of a right, he or she shall be a chargeable person for that year for [the purposes of *Part 41A*][3], unless—

[…][4]

(b) the person has been exempted by an inspector from the requirements of [*Chapter 3* of *Part 41A* by reason of a notice given under *section 959N*][5].][6]

(3) Subject to *subsection (5)*, where tax may by virtue of this section become chargeable in respect of any gain which may be realised by the exercise of a right, tax shall not be chargeable under any other provision of the Tax Acts in respect of the receipt of the right.

(4) The gain realised by—

(a) the exercise of any right at any time shall be taken to be the difference between the market value of the asset or assets, as the case may be, at the time of acquisition and the aggregate amount or value of the consideration, if any, given for the asset or assets and for the grant of the right, and

(b) the assignment or release of any right shall be taken to be the difference between the amount or value of the consideration for the assignment or release and the amount or value of the consideration, if any, given for the grant of the right,

and for this purpose the inspector may make a just apportionment of any entire consideration given for the grant of the right or for the grant of the right and for something besides; but neither the consideration given for the grant of the right nor any such entire consideration shall be taken to include the performance of any duties in or in connection with an office or employment, and no part of the amount or value of the consideration given for the grant shall be deducted more than once under this subsection.

(5) (a) Where a right mentioned in *subsection (2)* is obtained as mentioned in that subsection and the right is capable of being exercised later than 7 years after it is obtained, *subsection (3)* shall not prevent the charging of tax under any other provision of the Tax Acts in respect of the receipt of the right; but where tax is charged under such provision it shall be deducted from any tax which under *subsection (2)* is chargeable by reference to the gain realised by the exercise, assignment or release of the right.

(b) For the purpose of any charge to tax enabled to be made by this subsection, the value of a right shall be taken to be not less than the market value at the time the right is obtained of the asset or assets which may be acquired by the exercise of the right or of any asset or assets for which the asset or assets so acquired may be exchanged, reduced by the amount or value (or, if variable, the least amount or value) of the consideration for which the asset or assets may be so acquired.

[(6) (a) Subject to subsection (7), a person shall, in the case of a right granted by reason of the person's office or employment, be chargeable to tax under this section in respect of a gain realised by another person—

(i) if the right was granted to that other person,

(ii) if the other person acquired the right otherwise than by or under an assignment made by means of a bargain at arm's length,

(iii) if the 2 persons are connected persons at the time when the gain is realised, or

(iv) if the person benefits directly or indirectly from the exercise, assignment or release of the right by the other person;

but in a case within subparagraphs (ii), (iii), or (iv), the gain realised shall be treated as reduced by the amount of any gain realised by a previous holder on an assignment of the right.

(b) For the purposes of this subsection, a gain realised by another person shall include a gain realised on the exercise of a right by the person in respect of whose office or employment the right was granted, where that person exercises the right as nominee or bare trustee of the other person, or otherwise on behalf of the other person.][7]

(7) A person shall not be chargeable to tax by virtue of [*subparagraph (ii) or (iii) of subsection (6)(a)*][8] in respect of any gain realised by another person if the first-mentioned person was divested of the right by operation of law on the first-mentioned person's bankruptcy or otherwise, but the other person shall be chargeable to tax in respect of the gain under Case IV of Schedule D.

[(8) (a) Where a right (referred to in this subsection as the "original right") is assigned or released and the whole or part of the consideration for the assignment or release consists of or comprises another right (referred to in this subsection as the "new right") the new right shall not be treated as consideration for the assignment or release; but this section shall apply in relation to the new right as it applies in relation to the original right and as if the consideration for its acquisition did not include the value of the original right but did include the amount or value of the consideration given for the grant of the original right in so far as that has not been offset by any valuable consideration for the assignment or release other than the consideration consisting of the new right.

(b) The operation of paragraph (a) shall not prevent a charge arising under this section on a gain realised by the exercise of the original right.][9]

(9) (a) Where as a result of 2 or more transactions a person ceases to hold a right and the person or a connected person comes to hold another right (whether or not acquired from the person to whom the other right was assigned) and any of those transactions was effected under arrangements to which 2 or more persons holding rights in respect of which tax may be chargeable under this section were parties, those transactions shall be treated for the purposes of *subsection (8)* as a single transaction whereby the one right is assigned for a consideration which consists of or comprises the other right.

(b) This subsection shall apply in relation to 2 or more transactions, whether they involve an assignment preceding, coinciding with, or subsequent to, an acquisition.

(10) Where a gain chargeable to tax under *subsection (2)* or *(6)* is realised by the exercise of a right, *section 552* shall apply as if a sum equal to the amount of the gain so chargeable to tax formed part of the consideration given by the person acquiring the shares for their acquisition by that person.

(11) Where in any year of assessment a person grants a right in respect of which tax may be chargeable under this section, or allots any shares or transfers any asset in pursuance of such a right, or gives any consideration for the assignment

or release in whole or in part of such a right, or receives written notice of the assignment of such a right, the person shall deliver particulars thereof [to the Revenue Commissioners, in an electronic format approved by them,][10] not later than [[31 March][11] in the year of assessment following][12] that year.

[(12) Where in relation to any right—

(a) the person referred to in *subsection (11)* is not resident in the State, and

(b) the person who obtains the right is a director or employee of a company which is either—

(i) resident in the State, or

(ii) not resident in the State but carries on a trade, profession or vocation in the State through a branch or agency in which the director or employee is employed,

subsection (11) shall, as regards a company referred to in *paragraph (b)(i)* apply to the company, and, as regards a company referred to in *paragraph (b)(ii)* apply to its agent, manager, factor or other representative.][13]

Amendments

[1] Inserted by FA02 s11(1)(a). Shall apply with effect from 25 March 2002.

[2] Substituted by FA05 s16(1). This section comes into operation on such day as the Minister for Finance may appoint by order. With effect from 5 April 2007 per S.I. 170 of 2007.

[3, 5] Substituted by FA12 sched4(part 2)(g).

[4] Deleted by FA03 s8(1)(b). Applies as respects the exercise, assignment or release of a right on or after 30 June 2003.

[6] Inserted by FA00 s27(a)(i).

[7] Substituted by F(No.2)A08 s10(1)(a). Applies as on and from 20 November 2008.

[8] Substituted by F(No.2)A08 s10(1)(b). Applies as on and from 20 November 2008.

[9] Substituted by F(No.2)A08 s10(1)(c). Applies as on and from 20 November 2008.

[10] Substituted by FA14 s4. Comes into operation on 1 January 2015.

[11] Substituted by FA02 s11(1)(b). Applies as respects the year of assessment 2002 and subsequent years of assessment.

[12] Substituted by FA00 s27(a)(ii).

[13] Substituted by FA02 s11(1)(c). Shall apply with effect from 25 March 2002.

Revenue Briefings

Tax Briefing

Tax Briefing April 1998 – Issue 31 pg 16 – Share Option Schemes – Residence

Tax Briefing June 1998 – Issue 32 pg 8 – Notional Loans Relating to Shares

Tax Briefing June 1999 – Issue 36 pg 16 – Unapproved Share Option Schemes – Returns and Assessments

Tax Briefing June 2000 – Issue 40 pg 27 – Share Options and Other Rights – Tax Treatment

Tax Briefing October 2002 – Issue 50 pg 4 – Release of Share Options

Tax Briefing May 2003 – Issue 52 pg 26 – Share Options – Payment of Tax

Tax Briefing April 2005 – Issue 59 pg 20 – Share Option Cases – Late Filing Surcharge

Tax Briefing May 2006 – Issue 63 – Restricted Stock Units – Income Tax

Tax Briefing May 2006 – Issue 63 – Unapproved Share Option Schemes Mansworth v Jelley

Tax Briefing April 2011 – Issue 02 – Share-Based Remuneration-Finance Act 2011 Changes

eBrief

eBrief No. 08/2010 – Employee share schemes – Extended date for filing returns of information

eBrief No. 22/2010 – Unapproved Employee Share Schemes – Return of Information 2009

eBrief No. 17/2011 – Share-Based Remuneration – Finance Act 2011 Changes

eBrief No. 69/2012 – Treatment of Restricted Stock Units by Payroll Operators

Revenue Information Notes

IT 72 – Tax Treatment of Shares Acquired by Employees and Directors under Unapproved Share Option Schemes

CG16 – Relevant Tax on a Share Option – Information Leaflet

A Guide to the new Approved Share Options Schemes introduced by Section 15, Finance Act, 2001

A Guide to Approved Savings Related Share Option Schemes

Explanatory Notes on the Completion of Form RSS1

Revenue Precedents

Income chargeable to tax under section 128 TCA 1997 should be included in the calculation of FED – section 823 TCA 1997. GM

Income chargeable to tax under section 128 TCA 1997 should be included as an emolument for the purposes of calculating SCSB. IT 96 1593

Statements of Practice

Tax Treatment of Share Options granted in respect of Employments and Directorships International Aspects – SP/IT/1/07

Cross References

From Section 128

Section 4 Interpretation of Corporation Tax Acts.
Section 71 Foreign securities and possessions.
Section 135 Distributions: supplemental.
Section 548 Valuation of assets.
Section 552 Acquisition, enhancement and disposal costs.
Section 770 Interpretation and supplemental (Chapter 1).
Section 950 Interpretation (Part 41).
Section 951 Obligation to make a return.

To Section 128

Section 128A Deferral of payment of tax under section 128.
Section 128B Payment of tax under section 128.
Section 128C Tax treatment of directors and employees who acquire convertible shares.
Section 128D Tax treatment of directors of companies and employees who acquire restricted shares.
Section 128E Tax treatment of directors of companies and employees who acquire forfeitable shares.
Section 823 Deduction for income earned outside the State.
Schedule 32 Transitional Provisions

128A Deferral of payment of tax under section 128

[(1) Subject to *subsection (2)*, in any case where—

(a) for any year of assessment a person is chargeable to tax under Schedule E, by virtue of *section 128*, on an amount equal to a gain realised by the exercise of a right to acquire shares in a company ("the relevant shares"), which right was exercised [in the period from 6 April 2000 to the date of the passing of the Finance Act 2003][1], and

(b) following an assessment for the year in which that right was exercised ("the relevant year") an amount of tax, chargeable by virtue of *section 128* in respect of the amount referred to in *paragraph (a)*, is payable to the Collector-General, and

(c) the person concerned makes an election in accordance with *subsection (3)*,

he or she shall be entitled to defer payment of the tax in accordance with *subsection (4)*.

(2) *Subsection (1)* shall not apply where the relevant shares are disposed of by the person concerned in the relevant year.

[(3) An election under this section shall be made by notice in writing to the inspector on or before—

(a) where the relevant year is the year of assessment 2000-2001, 31 January 2002, and

(b) where the relevant year is the year of assessment 2001 or any subsequent year of assessment, 31 October in the year of assessment following the relevant year.][2]

(4) Where an election has been made under this section the tax referred to in *subsection (1)(b)* shall, notwithstanding any other provision of the Income Tax Acts, but subject to the provisions of this section, be paid on or before the earlier of—

(a) [31 October][3] in the year of assessment following the year of assessment in which the relevant shares are disposed of, or

(b) [31 October][4] in the year of assessment following the year of assessment beginning 7 years after the relevant year.

[(4A) (a) Notwithstanding *subsection (4)*, where an election has been made in accordance with *subsection (3)* and—

(i) relevant shares are disposed of (in this subparagraph referred to as the "*first-mentioned disposal*"), and

(I) but for this subparagraph, tax would be payable, by reference to the first-mentioned disposal, in accordance with *subsection (4)(a)*, and

(II) the market value of those shares at the date of the first-mentioned disposal is less than the tax chargeable under *section 128*, by reference to the exercise of an option to acquire those shares,

then an amount, being an amount equal to that market value, shall be due and payable to the Collector-General within 30 days after the date of the first-mentioned disposal or, if later, on or before 30 June 2003, and the balance of the tax chargeable remaining unpaid after that payment shall be payable in the event of, and by reference to, disposals of any shares in a company in a year of assessment, in accordance with *paragraph (d)*, being disposals after the date of the first-mentioned disposal, or

(ii) relevant shares are held at 31 December in the year of assessment beginning 7 years after the relevant year (in this subparagraph referred to as the "*first-mentioned date*"), and

(I) but for this subparagraph, tax would be payable in accordance with *subsection (4)(b)*, and

(II) the market value of the relevant shares is, at the first-mentioned date, less than the tax chargeable under *section 128*, by reference to the exercise of an option to acquire those shares,

then an amount, being an amount equal to that market value, shall be due and payable to the Collector-General within 30 days after the date of the first-mentioned date and the balance of the tax chargeable remaining unpaid after that payment shall be payable in the event of, and by reference to, disposals of any shares in a company in a year of assessment, in accordance with *paragraph (d)*, being disposals after the first-mentioned date.

(b) Where a person who is entitled to make an election in accordance with *subsection (3)*, after 6 February 2003 and on or before 31 October in the year of assessment following the relevant year in respect of relevant shares, does not do so, or tax chargeable under *section 128*, in respect of any gain realised by the exercise before 6 February 2003 of a right to acquire shares, is due after 6 February 2003 but on or before 31 October in the year of assessment following the relevant year, and the market value of the shares on—

(i) that 31 October, or

(ii) where the shares are disposed of before that date, the date of the disposal (referred to in this paragraph as the "first-mentioned disposal") of the shares,

is less than the tax chargeable under *section 128*, then an amount, being an amount equal to that market value, shall be due and payable to the Collector-General within 30 days after the said 31 October, and the balance of the tax chargeable remaining unpaid after that payment shall be payable in the event of, and by reference to, disposals of any shares in a company in a year of assessment, in accordance with *paragraph (d)*, being disposals after the said 31 October or the date of the first-mentioned disposal of the shares, as the case may be.

(c) In all cases other than those referred to in *paragraph (a)* or *(b)*, where tax is chargeable under *section 128* on an amount equal to a gain realised by the exercise, at any time before 6 February 2003, of a right to acquire shares in a company, and the market value of the shares on—

(i) that date, or

(ii) where the shares are disposed of before that date, the date of the disposal of the shares,

is less than the tax chargeable under *section 128*, then an amount, being an amount equal to that market value, shall be due and payable to the Collector-General on or before 30 June 2003, and the balance of the tax chargeable remaining unpaid after that payment shall be payable in the event of, and by reference to, disposals of any shares in a company in a year of assessment, in accordance with *paragraph (d)*, being disposals after 6 February 2003.

(d) (i) A payment that is to be made in the event of, and by reference to, disposals of any shares in a year of assessment shall be a payment which is the lesser of—

(I) the aggregate of the balances of unpaid tax referred to in *paragraphs (a)*, *(b)* and *(c)*, as reduced by tax payable in accordance with this paragraph by reference to disposals of shares in a previous year of assessment, and

(II) [half of the aggregate][5] of the net gains (if any) arising in respect of disposals of shares in the year of assessment.

(ii) For the purposes of *subparagraph (i)(II)*, the net gain arising in relation to a disposal of shares shall be the market value at the date of disposal of those shares reduced by so much of the aggregate of—

(I) the amount of the consideration, if any, given for the shares (including, where relevant, the grant of a right to acquire the shares),

(II) (A) where this subsection does not apply to the payment of income tax chargeable under *section 128* by reference to the acquisition of the shares, the amount of the income tax so chargeable, or

(B) where this subsection does apply to the payment of income tax chargeable under *section 128* by reference to the acquisition of the shares, the total amount paid, before the date of the disposal, in respect of that income tax,

and

(III) capital gains tax chargeable by reference to the disposal of the shares,

as does not exceed that market value.

(iii) For the purposes of *subparagraph (ii)*, the income tax or capital gains tax, as the case may be, so chargeable shall be the amount by which the income tax or capital gains tax, as the case may be, chargeable on the taxpayer for the year of assessment would have been reduced if the acquisition or disposal of the shares, as the case may be, had not taken place.

(iv) Payments referred to in *paragraph (d)(i)* which are to be made by reference to disposals of shares shall be due and payable to the Collector-General on or before 31 October in the year following the year of assessment in which the disposal of those shares takes place.

(e) (i) A taxpayer who wishes to be entitled to avail of the provisions of this subsection shall so elect, by giving notice in writing to the inspector, on or before 1 June 2003 in a form prescribed or authorised by the Revenue Commissioners, and the notice shall contain details of—

(I) the date of exercise of the option,

(II) the number of shares acquired by exercise of the option,

(III) the market value of the shares at date of exercise of that option, and

(IV) such further particulars for the purposes of this subsection as may be required or indicated by the Revenue Commissioners.

(ii) The inspector or such other officer as the Revenue Commissioners shall appoint in that behalf may admit a late election under *subparagraph (i)* in circumstances where he or she is satisfied that the delay in making the election was due to absence, illness or other reasonable cause.

(f) In any case where, at any time, the requirements of this subsection have not been fully complied with, any amount of tax chargeable under *section 128* which is unpaid shall be due and payable as if this subsection had not been enacted.

(g) Any tax chargeable under *section 128* which is due and payable in accordance with *subsection (4)* or this subsection, which remains unpaid at the date of death of the chargeable person, shall be discharged by the Revenue Commissioners.

(h) Any amount paid before 6 February 2003 in respect of tax chargeable under *section 128* shall not be repaid by reference to any provision of this subsection.

(i) The reference in *paragraph (d)* to the disposal of shares includes a reference to the disposal of shares by the [spouse or civil partner][6] of the person chargeable—

(I) in a case where [*section 1017* or *1031C*, as the case may be,][7] applies, or

[(II) in a case where *section 1017* or *1031C*, as the case may be, does not apply, but the disposal—

(A) is a disposal by the spouse subsequent to a transfer, on or after 25 February 2003, of the shares from the other spouse, except where the spouses are separated in the circumstances referred to in paragraph (*a*) or (*b*) of *section 1015(2)*, or their marriage has been dissolved under either section 5 of the Family Law (Divorce) Act 1996, or the law of a country or jurisdiction other than the State, being a dissolution that is entitled to be recognised as valid in the State, or

(B) is a disposal by a civil partner subsequent to a transfer of the shares from his or her civil partner, except where the civil partnership has been dissolved either under section 110 of the Civil Partnership and Certain Rights and Obligations of Cohabitants Act 2010, or the law of a country or jurisdiction other than the State, being a dissolution that is entitled to be recognised as valid in the State.][8]

(j) A person shall not, at any time, be entitled to avail of the provisions of this subsection where, at that time, he or she has not paid, or agreed an arrangement acceptable to the Collector-General for the payment of, tax due and payable which is chargeable under *section 128* in respect of the exercise of a right to acquire shares to which this subsection does not apply.

(k) In this subsection—

"*market value*" shall be construed in accordance with *section 548*;

"*shares*" includes securities within the meaning of *section 135* and stock.

(4B) In any case where the provisions of *subsection (4A)* apply, the amount by which the market value of the shares at the time of acquisition exceeds the market value at the date of disposal of those shares, or any part of that amount, shall not be an allowable loss for the purposes of the Capital Gains Tax Acts until such time as the tax liability of the person under *section 128* has been paid in full to the Collector-General.][9]

(5) The reference in [*subsections (4)(a)* and *(4A)*][10] to the relevant shares being disposed of includes a part disposal of such shares, and in the case of a part disposal, the tax to be paid shall be determined in a manner that is just and reasonable.

(6) Subject to any other provision of the Income Tax Acts requiring income of any description to be treated as the highest part of a person's income, in determining for the purposes of *paragraph (b)* of *subsection (1)* what tax is chargeable on a person by virtue of *section 128* in respect of an amount referred to in *paragraph (a)* of that subsection, that amount shall be treated as the highest part of his or her income for the relevant year.

(7) Notwithstanding any other provision of the Income Tax Acts, the due date in relation to tax, the payment of which has been deferred by virtue of an election under this section, shall, for the purposes of *section 1080*, be the date

when the amount becomes due and payable under [*subsections (4)* and *(4A)* but notwithstanding any provisions of *subsection (4A)* that subsection shall have no effect as respects the payment of any tax in relation to a gain realised by the exercise on or after 6 February 2003 of a right to acquire shares.][11]][12]

Amendments

[1] Substituted by FA03 s7(a).

[2] Substituted by FA03 s34(1)(a). This section is deemed to have come into operation as on and from 6 April 2001.

[3, 4] Substituted by FA01 sched2(9)(b).

[5] Substituted by FA12 s4(1)(a). Deemed to have come into force and takes effect on and from 1 January 2012.

[6] Substituted by F(No.3)A11 sched1(21).

[7] Substituted by F(No.3)A11 sched1(22).

[8] Substituted by F(No.3)A11 sched1(23).

[9] Inserted by FA03 s7(b).

[10] Substituted by FA03 s7(c).

[11] Substituted by FA03 s7(d).

[12] Inserted by FA03 s8(1)(a). This section shall come into operation as on and from 30 June 2003.

Revenue Briefings

Tax Briefing

Tax Briefing June 1999 – Issue 36 pg 16 – Unapproved Share Option Schemes – Returns and Assessments

Tax Briefing June 2000 – Issue 40 pg 27 – Share Options and Other Rights – Tax Treatment

Tax Briefing September 2000 – Issue 41 pg 28 – Share Options – Deferral of Payment of income Tax

Tax Briefing December 2001 – Issue 46 pg 25 – Deferral of Payment of Income Tax under Section 128A TCA 1997

Tax Briefing June 2002 – Issue 48 pg 18 – Share Options – Deferral of Payment of income Tax

Tax Briefing October 2002 – Issue 50 pg 4 – Deferral of Income Tax on the exercise of Share Option(s)

Cross References

From Section 128A

Section 128 Tax treatment of directors of companies and employees granted rights to acquire shares or other assets.

Section 135 Distributions: supplemental.

Section 548 Valuation of assets.

Section 1015 Interpretation (Chapter 1).

Section 1017 Assessment of husband in respect of income of both spouses.

Section 1080 Interest on overdue income tax, corporation tax and capital gains tax.

128B Payment of tax under section 128

[(1) This section applies where, by virtue of *section 128*, a person (in this section referred to as a "*taxable person*") is chargeable to tax under Schedule E for a year of assessment on an amount equal to the gain realised by the exercise, on or after 30 June 2003, of a right to acquire shares (in this section referred to as "*relevant shares*") in a company.

(2) Where this section applies for a year of assessment, the taxable person shall pay an amount of tax (in this section referred to as "*relevant tax*") in respect of the gain realised by the exercise of the right to acquire relevant shares, and that amount of tax shall be determined by the formula—

A × B

where—

A is the amount of that gain computed in accordance with *section 128(4)*, and

B is the percentage which is equal to the higher rate in force for the year of assessment in which the taxable person exercises the right to acquire the relevant shares.

(3) Relevant tax shall be due and payable to the Collector-General within 30 days after the exercise of the right to acquire the relevant shares, and shall be so due and payable without the making of an assessment, but relevant tax which has become so due and payable may be assessed on the taxable person (whether or not it has been paid when the assessment is made) if the tax or any part of it is not paid on or before the due date.

(4) Each payment of relevant tax shall be accompanied by a return containing, in relation to the taxable person by whom the payment is made, details of the amount of the gain referred to in *subsection (1)* and of the relevant tax due in respect of that gain and such other particulars as may be required by the return.

(5) Every return under this section shall be in a form prescribed or authorised by the Revenue Commissioners, and shall include a declaration to the effect that the return is correct and complete.

(6) The Collector-General shall give the taxable person a receipt for the amount of relevant tax paid by the taxable person.

(7) Where it appears to an officer of the Revenue Commissioners that there is any amount of relevant tax which ought to have been but has not been included in a return under *subsection (4)*, or where such officer is dissatisfied with any such return, such officer may make an assessment on the taxable person concerned to the best of such officer's judgement, and any amount of relevant tax due under an assessment made by virtue of this subsection shall be treated for the purposes of interest on unpaid tax as having been payable at the time specified in *subsection (3)*.

(8) Where any item has been incorrectly included in a return under *subsection (4)* as a gain in respect of which relevant tax is required to be paid, an officer of the Revenue Commissioners may make such assessments, adjustments or set-offs as may in his or her judgement be required for securing that the resulting liability to relevant tax, including interest on unpaid tax, of the taxable person is, in so far as possible, the same as it would have been if the item had not been so included.

(9) (a) The provisions of the Income Tax Acts relating to—

(i) assessments to income tax,

(ii) appeals against such assessments (including the rehearing of appeals and the statement of a case for the opinion of the High Court), and

(iii) the collection and recovery of income tax,

shall, in so far as they are applicable, apply to the assessment, collection and recovery of relevant tax.

(b) Any amount of relevant tax payable in accordance with this section without the making of an assessment shall carry interest at the rate of 0.0322 per cent for each day or part of a day from the date when the amount becomes due and payable until payment.

(c) [*Subsections (3)* to *(5)* of *section 1080*][1] shall apply in relation to interest payable under *paragraph (b)* as they apply in relation to interest payable under that section.

(d) In its application to any relevant tax charged by any assessment made in accordance with this section, *section 1080* shall apply as if [*subsection (2)(b)*][2] of that section were deleted.

(10) Where a taxable person has paid relevant tax in respect of a gain realised by the exercise, in any year of assessment, of a right to acquire relevant shares, the taxable person may claim to have that relevant tax set against the income tax chargeable on the taxable person for that year of assessment and, where that relevant tax exceeds such income tax, to have the excess refunded to the taxable person.

(11) Relevant tax payable by a taxable person in respect of a gain realised by the exercise, in any year of assessment, of a right to acquire relevant shares shall not be regarded as a payment of, or on account of, preliminary tax for the purposes of [*Chapter 7* of *Part 41A*][3].

(12) Relevant tax payable by a taxable person in respect of a gain realised by the exercise, in any year of assessment, of a right to acquire relevant shares—

(a) shall not, for the purposes of [*section 959AN(2)*][4], form part of the income tax which in the opinion of the taxable person is likely to become payable by that person for that year of assessment, [and][5]

[...][6]

(c) shall not, for the purposes of [section 959AO(3)][7], be regarded as income tax payable by the taxable person for that year of assessment.

(13) Notwithstanding any other provision of this section, any gain realised by the exercise, in any year of assessment, of a right to acquire relevant shares and in respect of which relevant tax is payable by a taxable person shall be included in the return required to be delivered by that person under *section 951*.

(14) Where, on an application in writing having been made to them in that behalf, the Revenue Commissioners are satisfied that an individual is likely to be chargeable to income tax for a year of assessment at the standard rate only, the reference in the meaning of B in *subsection (2)* to the higher rate shall be construed for the purposes of the payment or payments required to be made by the individual for that year in accordance with *subsection (2)*, as a reference to the standard rate.][8]

Amendments

[1, 2] Substituted by FA05 sched5.

[3, 4, 7] Substituted by FA12 sched4(part 2)(g).

[5] Inserted by FA12 sched4(part 2)(a).

[6] Deleted by FA12 sched4(part 2)(a).

[8] Inserted by FA03 s8(1)(a). This section shall come into operation as on and from 30 June 2003.

Revenue Briefings

Tax Briefing

Tax Briefing August 2003 – Issue 53 pg 17 – Payment of Tax on Share Options – RTSO

Tax Briefing April 2004 – Issue 55 pg 14 – Share Options – Preliminary Tax

eBrief

eBrief No. 21/2009 – Employee Share Schemes – Extended date for filing returns of information

eBrief No. 08/2010 – Employee Share Schemes – Extended date for filing returns of information

eBrief No. 22/2010 – Unapproved Employee Share Schemes – Return of Information 2009

eBrief No. 17/2011 – Share-Based Remuneration – Finance Act 2011 Changes

Revenue Information Notes

IT 72 – Tax Treatment of Shares Acquired by Employees and Directors under Unapproved Share Option Schemes

CG 16 – Relevant Tax on a Share Option – Information Leaflet

Cross References

From Section 128B

Section 128 Tax treatment of directors of companies and employees granted rights to acquire shares or other assets.

Section 951 Obligation to make a return.

Section 952 Obligation to pay preliminary tax.

Section 958 Date for payment of tax.

Section 1080 Interest on overdue income tax, corporation tax and capital gains tax.

128C Tax treatment of directors and employees who acquire convertible shares

[(1) In this section—

"*chargeable amount*" has the same meaning as it has in subsection (6), computed in accordance with subsection (8);

"*chargeable event*" has the meaning given in subsection (7);

"*collective investment scheme*" means any scheme or arrangement made for the purpose, or having the effect, of providing facilities for the participation by persons, as beneficiaries, in profits or income arising from the acquisition, holding, management or disposals of assets;

"*convertible securities*" shall be construed in accordance with subsection (4);

"*director*" and "*employee*" have the meanings respectively assigned to them by *section 770(1)*;

"*interest*", in relation to securities, includes an interest in securities which is less than full beneficial ownership and an interest in the proceeds of the sale of them, but does not include a right to acquire securities;

"*market value*" shall be construed in accordance with *section 548*;

"*securities*" includes—

(a) shares,

(b) securities within the meaning of *section 135*,

(c) debentures, debenture stock, loan stock, bonds, certificates of deposit, and other instruments (including certificates and warrants) creating or acknowledging indebtedness, including certificates and other instruments providing for a share in the profits of a company,

(d) options (other than options to acquire securities, except where such options are acquired under arrangements of which the main purpose or one of the main purposes is the avoidance of income tax, corporation tax or capital gains tax) and financial and commodity futures (within the meaning of the Investment Intermediaries Act 1995),

(e) warrants and other instruments entitling their holders to subscribe for securities,

(f) certificates and other instruments conferring rights in respect of securities held by persons other than persons on whom the rights are conferred and the transfer of which may be effected without the consent of those persons, and

(g) units in a collective investment scheme,

but does not include cheques or other bills of exchange, bankers' drafts or letters of credit, statements showing balances in current, deposit or savings accounts, or leases and other dispositions of property;

"*shares*" includes securities (within the meaning of *section 135*) and stock.

(2) References in this section to an employee or director acquiring securities in a company as a director or employee of that company or of another company, includes references to securities acquired by any other person by reason of the director's or employee's office or employment, [and for this purpose "employment" includes a former or prospective employment, and "office" includes a former or prospective office.][1]

(3) This section applies where—

(a) an employee or director acquires securities in a company as a director or employee of that company or of another company (in this section referred to as "*employment-related securities*"), and

(b) at the time of acquisition, the securities are convertible securities or an interest in convertible securities.

(4) For the purposes of this section securities are convertible securities if—

(a) they confer on the holder an entitlement (whether immediate or deferred and whether conditional or unconditional) to convert them—

(i) into securities of a different description, or

(ii) into money or money's worth,

or

(b) a contract, agreement, arrangement or condition—

(i) authorises or requires the grant of such an entitlement as is referred to in paragraph (*a*) to the holder if certain circumstances arise or do not arise, or

(ii) provides for the conversion of the securities, otherwise than by the holder, into securities of a different description or into money or money's worth.

(5) (a) For the purposes of—

(i) any charge to income tax under Schedule E and computed in accordance with *section 112* or *128* on the acquisition of the employment-related securities, or

(ii) the operation of *section 122A*,

the market value of the employment-related securities shall be determined as if they were not convertible securities.

(b) Paragraph (*a*) does not apply if the employment-related securities are acquired under arrangements of which the main purpose or one of the main purposes is the avoidance of income tax, corporation tax or capital gains tax, unless the market value of the employment-related securities determined in accordance with paragraph (*a*) is greater than that determined under paragraph (*c*).

(c) Where paragraph (*a*) does not apply, the market value of the employment-related securities shall be determined—

(i) in the case of securities that fall within subsection (4)(*a*)(i) and the entitlement to convert is not both immediate and unconditional, as if it were both immediate and unconditional,

(ii) in the case of securities that fall within subsection (4)(*b*)(i), as if the circumstances are such that an entitlement to convert arises immediately,

(iii) in the case of securities that fall within paragraph (*a*)(ii) or (*b*)(ii) of subsection (4), as if provision were made for their immediate conversion,

and in each case, as if they were immediately and fully convertible.

(d) For the purposes of paragraph (*c*) "*immediately and fully convertible*" means convertible immediately after the acquisition of the employment-related securities so as to obtain the maximum gain that would be possible on a conversion at such time without giving any consideration for the conversion or incurring any expenses in connection with it.

(6) Subject to subsection (11), where, at a time when an employee or director (or any other person who acquired the employment-related securities by reason of the director's or employee's office or employment) has a beneficial interest in employment-related securities, a chargeable event occurs, then the employee or director shall be chargeable to income tax under Schedule E, in the year in which the chargeable event occurs, on an amount (referred to in this section as the "*chargeable amount*") computed in accordance with subsection (8).

(7) A "*chargeable event*" means—

(a) the conversion of the employment-related securities (or the securities in which they are an interest) into securities of a different description in circumstances in which the employee or director (or any other person who acquired the employment-related securities by reason of the director's or employee's office or employment) is beneficially entitled to the securities into which the employment-related securities are converted,

(b) the release for consideration of the entitlement to convert the employment-related securities (or the securities in which they are an interest) into securities of a different description,

(c) the disposal for consideration of the employment-related securities or any interestinthembythedirectororemployee(orbyanyotherpersonwhoacquired the employment-related securities by reason of the director's or vttttttth employee's office or employment), at a time when such securities are still convertible securities, or

(d) the receipt by the employee or director (or by any other person who acquired the employment-related securities by reason of the director's or employee's office or employment) of a benefit in money or money's worth in connection with the entitlement to convert (other than securities acquired on the conversion of the employment-related securities or consideration referred to in paragraphs (*b*) and (*c*)).

(8) (a) For the purposes of subsection (6), the chargeable amount is to be determined by the formula—

$$A - B$$

where—

A is the amount of any gain realised on the occurrence of a chargeable event, and

B is the total of any consideration given for the entitlement to convert the employment-related securities and the amount of any expenditure incurred by the holder of the employment-related securities in connection with the conversion, disposal, release of the entitlement to convert, or receipt of a benefit in connection with the entitlement to convert the employment-related securities, as the case may be.

(b) The amount of the gain realised on the occurrence of a chargeable event is—

(i) in the case of an event to which subsection (7)(*a*) applies, to be determined by the formula—

$$C - (D + E)$$

where—

C is the market value at the time of the chargeable event of the securities into which the employment-related securities are converted and where those securities are themselves convertible, the market value is to be determined as if they were not convertible; and where the employment-related securities are an interest in securities, then C is the same proportion of that market value as the market value of the interest in the securities in which the employment-related securities are an interest bears to the market value of those securities,

D is the market value of the employment-related securities at the time of the chargeable event, determined as if they were not convertible securities or an interest in convertible securities, and

E is the amount of the consideration given for the conversion of the employment-related securities,

(ii) in the case of a chargeable event to which subsection (7)(*b*) applies, the amount of the consideration received in respect of the release,

(iii) in the case of a chargeable event to which subsection (7)(*c*) applies, to be determined by the formula—

$$F - G$$

where—

F is the amount of consideration given on disposal of the employment-related securities, and

G is the market value of the employment-related securities at the time of the chargeable event, determined as if they were not convertible securities or an interest in convertible shares,

(iv) in the case of an event to which subsection (7)(*d*) applies, the amount or market value of the benefit received, as the case may be.

(c) If, because of paragraph (*b*) of subsection (5), paragraph (*a*) of that subsection did not apply in relation to employment-related securities, the chargeable amount is to be reduced by the amount determined by the formula—

$$H - I$$

where—

H is the amount by which the market value of the employment-related securities for the purposes specified in paragraph (a) of subsection (5), exceeded what it would have been had that paragraph applied, and

I is the aggregate of any amount by which the chargeable amount on any previous chargeable event relating to the employment-related securities has been reduced under this subsection.

(9) (a) For the purposes of calculating B in the formula in subsection (8)(*a*), consideration is to be treated as given for the entitlement to convert the employment-related securities only if the amount of any consideration given for the acquisition of the employment-related securities exceeds the market value of such securities (determined as if the employment-related securities were not convertible securities) at the time of their acquisition.

(b) Where the consideration is in excess of the market value, the amount of such excess shall be treated as the amount of consideration given for the entitlement to convert the employment-related securities.

(10) For the purposes of this section, any consideration given for the acquisition of employment-related securities and any consideration given for the entitlement to convert shall not be taken to include the performance of any duties in or in connection with the office or employment, and no part of the amount or value of the consideration shall be deducted more than once.

(11) (a) This section does not apply in relation to employment-related securities, where—

(i) the employment-related securities are shares in a company of a class,

(ii) all the company's shares of the class are convertible securities,

(iii) all the company's shares of the class are affected by an event similar to that which is a chargeable event in relation to the employment-related securities, and

(iv) immediately before the event that would, but for the provisions of this subsection, be a chargeable event, the majority of the company's shares of the class are not employment-related securities,

or,

(b) if, at the time of the acquisition of the employment-related securities, the emoluments from the office or employment are not within the charge to tax under Schedule E or Schedule D.

(12) For the purposes of subsection (11)(*a*)(iii), shares are affected by an event similar to that which is a chargeable event in relation to employment-related securities, if—

(a) in the case of a chargeable event to which subsection (7)(*a*) applies, they are converted into securities of a different class,

(b) in the case of a chargeable event to which subsection (7)(*b*) applies, the entitlement to convert them into securities of a different description is released,

(c) in the case of a chargeable event to which subsection (7)(*c*) applies, they are disposed of,

(d) in the case of a chargeable event to which subsection (7)(*d*) applies, a similar benefit is received in respect of the entitlement to convert them.

(13) Notwithstanding any other provision of the Tax Acts, where a person is, by virtue of this section, chargeable to tax under Schedule E for a year of assessment in respect of a chargeable amount computed in accordance with subsection (8), then he or she shall be a chargeable person for that year for [the purposes of *Part 41A*][2], unless the person has been exempted by an officer of the Revenue Commissioners from the requirement of [*Chapter 3* of *Part 41A* by reason of a notice given under *section 959N*][3].

(14) Where a person is charged to tax under this section on a chargeable amount computed in accordance with *subsection (8)*, then *section 552* shall apply as if a sum equal to the amount so charged formed part of the consideration given by the person acquiring securities for their acquisition by that person.

(15) Where in any year—

(a) a person awards employment-related securities to an employee or director (or to any other person by reason of the director's or employee's office or employment) to which this section applies, or

(b) a chargeable event occurs in relation to employment-related securities so awarded,

then the person shall deliver to the Revenue Commissioners on or before 31 March in the year following the year in which the award was made or the chargeable event occurred, as the case may be, particulars of the awards or the chargeable event, as the case may be.][4]

Amendments

[1] Substituted by F(No.2)A08 sched6(1)(a). This paragraph is deemed to have come into force and have taken effect as on and from 31 January 2008.

[2, 3] Substituted by FA12 sched4(part 2)(g).

[4] Inserted by FA08 s16(1). Applies as on and from 31 January 2008 in respect of employment-related securities acquired on or after that date.

Revenue Briefings

eBrief

eBrief No. 21/2009 – Employee Share Schemes – Extended date for filing returns of information

eBrief No. 08/2010 – Employee Share Schemes – Extended date for filing returns of information

eBrief No. 22/2010 – Unapproved Employee Share Schemes – Return of Information 2009

Revenue Information Notes

IT 72 – Tax Treatment of Shares Acquired by Employees and Directors under Unapproved Share Option Schemes

CG16 – Relevant Tax on a Share Option – Information Leaflet

Explanatory Notes on the Completion of Form RSS1

Cross References

From Section 128C

Section 112 Basis of assessment, persons chargeable and extent of charge.

Section 122A Notional loans relating to shares, etc.

Section 128 Tax treatment of directors of companies and employees granted rights to acquire shares or other assets.

Section 135 Distributions: supplemental.

Section 548 Valuation of assets.

Section 552 Acquisition, enhancement and disposal costs.
Section 770 Interpretation and supplemental (Chapter 1).
Section 950 Interpretation (Part 41).
Section 951 Obligation to make a return.

128D Tax treatment of directors of companies and employees who acquire restricted shares

[(1) In this section—

"*director*" and "*employee*" have the meanings, respectively, given to them by *section 770(1)*;

["*EEA Agreement*" means the Agreement on the European Economic Area signed at Oporto on 2 May 1992, as adjusted by all subsequent amendments to that Agreement;

"*EEA state*" means a state, other than the State, which is a Contracting Party to the EEA Agreement;][1]

"*employer*" means the company in which the director or employee holds his or her office or employment;

"*market value*" shall be construed in accordance with *section 548*;

"*restricted shares*" shall be construed in accordance with *subsection (3)*;

"*shares*" includes stock;

"*specified period*" has the same meaning as in [*subsection (3)(a)*;][2]

["*trust*" means a trust established in the State or in an EEA state and the trustees of which are resident in the State or in an EEA state.][3]

(2) Subject to *subsection (7)*, this section applies where—

(a) a director or employee acquires shares (including shares acquired on the exercise of a right to which *section 128* applies) in a company as a director or employee of that company or of another company,

(b) the shares are shares in the company in which the director or employee holds his or her office or employment or in a company which has control (within the meaning of *section 432*) of that company, and

(c) at the time of acquisition, the shares are restricted shares.

(3) For the purposes of this section, shares are restricted shares if—

(a) there is a written contract or agreement in place under the terms of which there is a restriction on the freedom of the director or employee by whom the shares are held to assign, charge, pledge as security for a loan or other debt, transfer, or otherwise dispose of the shares for a period of not less than one year (in this section referred to as the "*specified period*"),

(b) the contract or agreement is in place for bona fide commercial purposes and does not form part of a scheme or arrangement of which the main purpose or one of the main purposes is the avoidance of tax,

(c) the shares cannot be assigned, charged, pledged as security for a loan or other debt, transferred, or otherwise disposed of in any circumstances during the specified period, other than—

(i) on the death of the director or employee, or

(ii) as a consequence of the director or employee agreeing to—

(I) accept an offer for the shares (in this clause referred to as the "original shares") if the acceptance or agreement would result in a new holding (within the meaning of *section 584*) being equated with the original shares for the purposes of capital gains tax,

(II) a transaction affecting the shares or such of the shares as are of a particular class if the transaction would be entered into pursuant to a compromise, arrangement or scheme applicable to or affecting all the ordinary share capital of the company in question or, as the case may be, all the shares of the same class as the shares acquired by the director or employee, or

(III) accept an offer of cash, with or without other assets, for the shares if the offer forms part of a general offer made to holders of shares of the same class as the shares acquired by the director or employee or of shares in the same company and made in the first instance on a condition such that if it is satisfied the person making the offer will have control (within the meaning of *section 432*) of that company,

and

(d) during the specified period, the shares are held in a trust established by the employer for the benefit of employees and directors, or held under such other arrangements as the Revenue Commissioners may allow.

(4) Where this section applies—

(a) any [amount chargeable to income tax][4] under Schedule E (and computed in accordance with *section 112* or *128*, as the case may be), or under Schedule D, on the acquisition of the shares, shall be reduced by an amount determined by the formula—

$$A \times \frac{B}{100}$$

where—

A is the amount of [the income chargeable to tax][5] under Schedule E or Schedule D, as the case may be, and

B is—

(i) where the specified period is one year, 10,

(ii) where the specified period is 2 years, 20,

(iii) where the specified period is 3 years, 30,

(iv) where the specified period is 4 years, 40,

(v) where the specified period is 5 years, 50,

(vi) where the specified period is more than 5 years, 60,

(b) the [amount chargeable to income tax][6] referred to in paragraph (*a*) shall be computed by reference to the market value of the shares at the date of acquisition but without regard to the restriction on the freedom of the director or employee by whom the shares are held to assign, charge, pledge as security for a loan or other debt, transfer, or otherwise dispose of the shares.

(5) Where [an amount chargeable to income tax][7] under Schedule E or Schedule D on the acquisition of shares by a director or employee is reduced in accordance with subsection (4), and—

(a) the restriction on the freedom of the director or employee to assign, charge, pledge as security for a loan or other debt, transfer, or otherwise dispose of the shares acquired by him or her is subsequently removed or varied, or

(b) the shares are disposed of in any of the circumstances mentioned in subparagraphs (i) and (ii) of subsection (3)(*c*) before the specified period expires,

then, notwithstanding any limitation in the [Income Tax Acts][8] on the time within which assessments may be made, [the amount chargeable to income tax][9] on the acquisition of the shares shall be adjusted to take account of the actual period during which there was a restriction on the freedom of the director or employee to assign, charge, pledge as security for a loan or other debt, transfer or otherwise dispose of the shares. The adjustment of liability to tax as may be necessary for the purposes of this paragraph shall be made at any time, whether by means of an assessment, [an amended assessment or otherwise][10].

(6) Where this section applies and [an amount chargeable to income tax][11] on the acquisition of shares by a director or employee is, for the purposes of *section 552*, to be treated as forming part of the consideration given by the director or employee for the acquisition of the shares, then [the amount chargeable to income tax][12] to be so treated shall be the amount as reduced in accordance with subsection (4), together with any additional amount charged as a consequence of an adjustment made in accordance with subsection (5).

(7) This section does not apply to shares acquired by a director or employee under the terms of a scheme approved of by the Revenue Commissioners under Schedule 11, 12, 12A or 12C.

(8) Where in any year—

(a) a person awards restricted shares to a director or employee, or

(b) an event that comes within paragraph (*a*) or (*b*) of subsection (5) occurs in relation to restricted shares awarded,

then the person shall deliver to the Revenue Commissioners on or before 31 March in the year of assessment following the year in which the award was made or the event occurred, as the case may be, particulars of the award or the event, as the case may be.

(9) For the purposes of subsection (8), a person shall be deemed to award restricted shares to a director or employee where the director or employee acquires the restricted shares on the exercise of a right to which *section 128* applies, and the right was granted to the director or employee by the person.][13]

Amendments

[1] Inserted by FA10 s17(1)(a). Applies to shares acquired on or after 4 February 2010.

[2] Substituted by FA10 s17(1)(b). Applies to shares acquired on or after 4 February 2010.

[3] Inserted by FA10 s17(1)(b). Applies to shares acquired on or after 4 February 2010.

[4, 6] Substituted by FA10 s17(1)(c)(i). Applies to shares acquired on or after 20 November 2008.

[5] Substituted by FA10 s17(1)(c)(ii). Applies to shares acquired on or after 20 November 2008.

[7] Substituted by FA10 s17(1)(d)(i). Applies to shares acquired on or after 20 November 2008.

[8] Substituted by FA10 s17(1)(d)(iii). Applies to shares acquired on or after 20 November 2008.

[9] Substituted by FA10 s17(1)(d)(ii). Applies to shares acquired on or after 20 November 2008.

[10] Substituted by FA12 sched4(part 2)(g).

[11] Substituted by FA10 s17(1)(e)(i). Applies to shares acquired on or after 20 November 2008.

[12] Substituted by FA10 s17(1)(e)(ii). Applies to shares acquired on or after 20 November 2008.

[13] Inserted by F(No.2)A08 s12(1). Applies as on and from 20 November 2008 in respect of shares acquired on or after that date.

Revenue Briefings

Tax Briefing

Tax Briefing April 1998 – Issue 31 pg 17 – Restricted Shares

Tax Briefing March 1999 – Issue 35 pg 18 – Share Schemes – Clarification

eBrief

eBrief No. 21/2009 – Employee Share Schemes – Extended date for filing returns of information

eBrief No. 08/2010 – Employee Share Schemes – Extended date for filing returns of information

eBrief No. 22/2010 – Unapproved Employee Share Schemes – Return of Information 2009

Revenue Information Notes

IT 73 – Tax Treatment of Restricted Shares Acquired By Directors and Employees

Explanatory Notes on the Completion of Form RSS1

Cross References

From Section 128D

Section 112 Basis of assessment, persons chargeable and extent of charge.

Section 128 Tax treatment of directors of companies and employees granted rights to acquire shares or other assets.

Section 432 Meaning of "associated company" and "control".

Section 548 Valuation of assets.

Section 552 Acquisition, enhancement and disposal costs.

Section 584 Reorganisation or reduction of share capital.

Section 770 Interpretation and supplemental (Chapter 1).

128E Tax treatment of directors of companies and employees who acquire forfeitable shares

[(1) In this section'

"*director*" and "*employee*" have the meanings, respectively, given to them by *section 770(1)*;

"*market value*" shall be construed in accordance with *section 548*;

"*forfeitable shares*" shall be construed in accordance with subsection (3);

"*shares*" includes stock.

(2) This section applies where'

(a) a director or employee acquires shares (including shares acquired on the exercise of a right to which *section 128* applies) in a company as a director or employee of that company or of another company, and

(b) at the time of acquisition, the shares are forfeitable shares.

(3) Subject to subsection (4), for the purposes of this section, shares are forfeitable shares if'

(a) there is a written contract or agreement in place under the terms of which'

(i) there will be a forfeiture of the shares, if certain circumstances arise or do not arise,

(ii) as a result of the forfeiture, the director or employee will cease to have any beneficial interest in the shares, and

(iii) the director or employee will not be entitled to receive, directly or indirectly, consideration in money or money's worth in respect of the shares on their forfeiture in excess of the consideration given by the director or the employee for the acquisition of the shares,

and,

(b) the contract or agreement is in place for bona fide commercial purposes and does not form part of a scheme or arrangement of which the main purpose or one of the main purposes is the avoidance of tax.

(4) Shares shall not be forfeitable shares by reason only that the shares are unpaid or partly paid shares which may be forfeited for non-payment of calls.

(5) Where this section applies, any charge to income tax under Schedule E (and computed in accordance with *section 112* or *128*, as the case may be), or under Schedule D, on the acquisition of the shares, shall be computed by reference to the market value of the shares at the date of acquisition but without regard to provision in a contract or agreement referred to in subsection (3) for the forfeiture of the shares.

(6) If under the terms of a contract or agreement referred to in subsection (3) the shares are forfeited, then'

(a) the director or employee shall, [[...][1] the purposes of income tax, income levy and universal social charge][2], be treated, for the year of assessment in which the shares were acquired, as if he or she did not acquire the shares, and

(b) such adjustment shall be made by repayment or otherwise as the case may require, on receipt of a claim from the director or employee, which shall be made within 4 years from the end of the year of assessment in which the shares are forfeited.

(7) Subsection (6) applies notwithstanding any limitation in *section 865(4)* on the time within which a claim for a repayment of tax is required to be made. *Section 865(6)* does not prevent the Revenue Commissioners from repaying an amount of tax as a consequence of any adjustment made in accordance with subsection (6).

(8) Notwithstanding *section 546(2)*, where *subsection (6)* of this section applies, the amount of a loss accruing on the forfeiture of the shares shall not exceed the amount of consideration given by the director or employee for the acquisition of the shares less any amount received by the director or employee on the forfeiture of the shares.

(9) Where in any year'

(a) a person awards forfeitable shares to a director or employee, or

(b) shares awarded to a director or employee are forfeited,

then the person shall deliver to the Revenue Commissioners on or before 31 March in the year following the year of assessment in which the award was made or the shares were forfeited, as the case may be, particulars of the award or the forfeiture, as the case may be.][3]

Amendments

[1] Deleted by FA13 sched2(1)(b). Has effect on and from 27 March 2013.

[2] Substituted by FA12 s4(1)(b). Deemed to have effect as on and from (a) 1 January 2009 in the case of income levy, (b) 1 January 2011 in the case of universal social charge, and (c) 1 January 2012 in the case of income tax.

[3] Inserted by F(No.2)A08 s12(1). Applies as on and from 20 November 2008 in respect of shares acquired on or after that date.

Revenue Briefings

eBrief

eBrief No. 21/2009 – Employee Share Schemes – Extended date for filing returns of information

eBrief No. 08/2010 – Employee Share Schemes – Extended date for filing returns of information

eBrief No. 22/2010 – Unapproved Employee Share Schemes – Return of Information 2009

Revenue Information Notes

Explanatory Notes on the Completion of Form RSS1

Cross References

From Section 128E

Section 112 Basis of assessment, persons chargeable and extent of charge.

Section 128 Tax treatment of directors of companies and employees granted rights to acquire shares or other assets.

Section 546 Allowable losses.

Section 548 Valuation of assets.

Section 770 Interpretation and supplemental (Chapter 1).

Section 865 Repayment of tax.

PART 6

Company Distributions, Tax Credits, Franked Investment Income and Advance Corporation Tax

CHAPTER 1

Taxation of Company Distributions

129 Irish resident company distributions not generally chargeable to corporation tax

[CTA76 s2]

Except where otherwise provided by the Corporation Tax Acts, corporation tax shall not be chargeable on dividends and other distributions of a company resident in the State, nor shall any such dividends or distributions be taken into account in computing income for corporation tax.

Cross References

To Section 129

Section 4 Interpretation of Corporation Tax Acts.
Section 20 Schedule F.
Section 21B Tax treatment of certain dividends.
Section 129A Dividends paid out of foreign profits.
Section 172B Dividend withholding tax on relevant distributions.
Section 174 Taxation of dealer's receipts on purchase of shares by issuing company or by its subsidiary.
Section 250A Restriction of relief to individuals in respect of loans applied in acquiring interest in companies.
Section 434 Distributions to be taken into account and meaning of "distributable income", "investment income", "estate income", etc.
Section 487 Corporation tax: credit for bank levy.
Section 598 Disposals of business or farm on "retirement".
Section 701 Transfer of shares held by certain societies to members of society.
Section 712 Distributions received from Irish resident companies.
Section 714 Life business: computation of profits.
Section 717 Pension business.
Section 738 Undertakings for collective investment.
Section 1003 Payment of tax by means of donation of heritage items.
Section 1003A Payment of tax by means of donation of heritage property to an Irish heritage trust.
Section 1087 Charge and deduction of income tax not charged or deducted before passing of annual Act.
Schedule 2A Dividend Withholding Tax
Schedule 19 Offshore Funds: Distributing Funds
Schedule 22 Dividends Regarded as Paid Out of Profits Accumulated Before Given Date

129A Dividends paid out of foreign profits

[(1) (a) In this section "profits", in relation to a company for a period of account, means the amount of the profits after taxation as shown in the profit and loss account or income statement for that period as laid before the annual general meeting of the company.

(b) For the purposes of this section—

(i) any question whether a company is connected with another company shall be determined in accordance with *section 10* (as it applies for the purposes of the Tax Acts) and *subparagraph (ii)*,

(ii) where a company is party to a scheme or arrangement, the main purpose, or one of the main purposes, of which is the avoidance of the whole or part of a distribution being treated as a taxable distribution, then the company shall be treated as connected with any other company which is a party to that scheme or arrangement.

(c) For the purposes of *subsection (5)* "control" shall be construed in accordance with *subsections (2)* to *(6)* of *section 432* as if in *subsection (6)* of that section for "5 or fewer participators" there were substituted "persons resident in the State".

(2) Where—

(a) a company receives a distribution from another company (in this section referred to as the "*paying company*") resident in the State with which it is connected, and

(b) the paying company became resident in the State in the period—

(i) beginning on the date—

(I) 10 years before the date the distribution was made, or

(II) of passing of the *Finance Act 2010*,

whichever is the later, and

(ii) ending on the date the distribution is made, then, subject to *subsection (5)*, *section 129* shall not apply to such amount of the distribution as is paid out of profits arising before the paying company became resident in the State and that amount shall be treated as income chargeable to tax under Case IV of Schedule D.

(3) (a) For the purposes of this section, where the amount of a distribution made by the paying company on or after the date (or the last such date if there was more than one date) it became resident in the State exceeds the distributable profits of the company for the period (in this subsection referred to as the "*specified period*")—

(i) beginning on the date (or the last such date if there was more than one date) the company became resident in the State, and

(ii) ending on the last day of the accounting period of the company immediately preceding the accounting period in which the distribution is made,

then the excess shall be treated as paid out of profits arising before the company became resident in the State.

(b) For the purposes of this subsection—

(i) the distributable profits of the paying company for a specified period shall, subject to *subparagraph (ii)*, be taken to be the aggregate of the profits of the periods of account (in this subsection referred to as "*corresponding periods*") which fall wholly or partly within the specified period, as reduced by the aggregate of so much of the amounts of any distributions made in the specified period as were amounts to which section 129 applied,

(ii) where a corresponding period falls partly within a specified period, the amount to be included in the distributable profits for the specified period in respect of the profits of that corresponding period shall be the profits of that corresponding period reduced by applying the fraction—

$$\frac{A}{B}$$

where—

A is the length of the period common to the specified period and the corresponding period, and

B is the length of the corresponding period.

(4) Where, by virtue of *subsection (2)*, *section 129* does not apply to the whole or part of a distribution (such whole or part, as the case may be, in this section referred to as the "*taxable distribution*") received by a company (in this subsection referred to as the "*first-mentioned company*") from another company resident in the State then the first-mentioned company shall be entitled to reduce the corporation tax attributable to the taxable distribution by the amount of the credit for foreign tax that would have been applied, under the provisions of Schedule 24, in reducing the corporation tax chargeable in respect of a dividend of an amount equal to the taxable distribution received by the first-mentioned company from the other company on the day before the day (or the last such day where there was more than one) the other company became resident in the State.

(5) *Subsection (2)* shall not apply where the paying company was at all times before the date it became resident in the State (or the last such date where there was more than one date) not controlled by persons resident in the State.][1]

Amendments

[1] Inserted by FA10 s49(1). Has effect for distributions made as on and from 3 April 2010.

Cross References

From Section 129A

Section 10 Connected persons.

Section 129 Irish resident company distributions not generally chargeable to corporation tax.

Section 432 Meaning of "associated company" and "control".

CHAPTER 2

Meaning of Distribution

130 Matters to be treated as distributions

[CTA76 s84]

(1) The following provisions of this Chapter, together with [*sections 436*[, *436A*][1] and *437*, and *subsection (2)(b)* of *section 816*][2], shall, subject to any express exceptions, apply with respect to the meaning in the Corporation Tax Acts of "*distribution*" and for determining the persons to whom certain distributions are to be treated as made; but references in the Corporation Tax Acts to distributions of a company shall not apply to distributions made in respect of share capital in a winding up.

(2) In relation to any company, "*distribution*" means—

(a) any dividend paid by the company, including a capital dividend;

(b) any other distribution out of assets of the company (whether in cash or otherwise) in respect of shares in the company, except, subject to *section 132*, so much of the distribution, if any, as represents a repayment of capital on the shares or is, when it is made, equal in amount or value to any new consideration received by the company for the distribution;

(c) any amount met out of assets of the company (whether in cash or otherwise) in respect of the redemption of any security issued by the company in respect of shares in, or securities of, the company otherwise than wholly for new consideration, or in the redemption of such part of any such security so issued as is not properly referable to new consideration;

(d) any interest or other distribution out of assets of the company in respect of securities of the company (except so much, if any, of any such distribution as represents the principal thereby secured, and, without prejudice to *section 135(9)*, for this purpose no amount shall be regarded as representing the principal secured by a security in so far as it exceeds any new consideration received by the company for the issue of the security), where the securities are—

(i) securities issued as mentioned in *paragraph (c)*, but excluding securities issued before the 27th day of November, 1975,

(ii) securities convertible directly or indirectly into shares in the company or securities carrying any right to receive shares in or securities of the company, not being (in either case) securities quoted on a recognised stock exchange nor issued on terms which are reasonably comparable with the terms of issue of securities so quoted,

(iii) securities under which—

(I) the consideration given by the company for the use of the principal secured is to any extent dependent on the results of the company's business or any part of the company's business, or

(II) the consideration so given represents more than a reasonable commercial return for the use of that principal; but this shall not operate so as to treat as a distribution so much of the interest or other distribution as represents a reasonable commercial return for the use of that principal,

(iv) securities issued by the company and held by a company not resident in the State, where—

(I) the company which issued the securities is a 75 per cent subsidiary of the other company,

(II) both companies are 75 per cent subsidiaries of a third company which is not resident in the State, or

(III) except where 90 per cent or more of the share capital of the company which issued the securities is directly owned by a company resident in the State, both the company which issued the securities and the company not resident in the State are 75 per cent subsidiaries of a third company which is resident in the State,

or

(v) securities connected with shares in the company, where "*connected with*" means that, in consequence of the nature of the rights attaching to the securities or shares, and in particular of any terms or conditions attaching to the right to transfer the shares or securities, it is necessary or advantageous for a person who has, or disposes of or acquires, any of the securities also to have, or to dispose of or acquire, a proportionate holding of the shares;

(e) any amount required to be treated as a distribution by *subsection (3)* or by [section 131;][3]

[(f) any qualifying amount (within the meaning of *subsection (2C)*) paid to an individual who at the time that amount is paid—

(i) is a beneficiary under the terms of a trust deed of an employee share ownership trust approved of by the Revenue Commissioners under *Schedule 12* and for which approval has not been withdrawn and which trust deed contains provision for the transfer of securities to the trustees of a scheme approved of by the Revenue Commissioners under *Schedule 11* and for which approval has not been withdrawn, and

(ii) would be eligible to have securities appropriated to him or her, had such securities been available for appropriation, under the scheme referred to in *subparagraph (i)*.][4]

[(2A) For the purposes of *subsection (2)(d)(iii)(I)*, the consideration given by the company for the use of the principal received shall not be treated as being to any extent dependent on the results of the company's business or any part of the company's business by reason only of the fact that the terms (however expressed) of the security provide—

(a) for the consideration to be reduced in the event of the results improving, or

(b) for the consideration to be increased in the event of the results deteriorating.][5]

[(2B) *Subsection (2)(d)(iv)* shall not apply as respects interest, other than interest to which *section 452* or *845A* applies, paid to a company which is a resident of a Member State of the European Communities other than the State and, for the purposes of this subsection, a company is a resident of a Member State of the European Communities if the company is by virtue of the law of that Member State resident for the purposes of tax (being any tax imposed in the Member State which corresponds to corporation tax in the State) in such Member State.][6]

[(2C) Notwithstanding *section 519(6)* and *paragraph 13(4)* of *Schedule 12*, "*qualifying amount*" means an amount paid solely out of income consisting of dividends received in a chargeable period (within the meaning of *section 321*) in respect of securities (within the meaning of *Schedule 12*) held by the trustees of the employee share ownership trust referred to in *subsection (2)(f)(i)*, but only to the extent that such income exceeds the aggregate of—

(a) any sum or sums spent to meet expenses of the trust,

(b) any interest paid on sums borrowed by the trust,

(c) any sum or sums paid to the personal representatives of a deceased person who was a beneficiary under the terms of the trust deed,

(d) any amount spent on the repayment of sums borrowed including any amount capable of being so spent, having regard to the conditions referred to in *paragraph 11(2B)(d)* or *11A(5)(d)* of *Schedule 12*, and

(e) any amount spent on the acquisition of securities (within the meaning of *Schedule 12*) including any amount capable, at any particular time, of being so spent on such securities at their market value (within the meaning of *section 548*) at that time,

in the chargeable period.][7]

(3) (a) Where on a transfer of assets or liabilities by a company to its members or to a company by its members the amount or value of the benefit received by a member (taken according to its market value) exceeds the amount or value (so taken) of any new consideration given by the member, the company shall be treated as making a distribution to the member of an amount equal to the difference (in *paragraph (b)* referred to as "*the relevant amount*").

(b) Notwithstanding *paragraph (a)*, where the company and the member receiving the benefit are both resident in the State and either the former is a subsidiary of the latter or both are subsidiaries of a third company[, being a company which, by virtue of the law of a [relevant Member State][8], is resident for the purposes of tax in such a Member State][9], the relevant amount shall not be treated as a distribution.

[(c) For the purposes of this subsection and *subsection (4)*, "*tax*", in relation to a [relevant Member State][10] other than the State, means any tax imposed in the Member State which corresponds to corporation tax in the State.][11]

[(d) For the purposes of this subsection and *subsection (4)*—

"*EEA Agreement*" means the Agreement on the European Economic Area signed at Oporto on 2 May 1992, as adjusted by the Protocol signed at Brussels on 17 March 1993;

"*EEA State*" means a state which is a contracting party to the EEA Agreement;

"*relevant Member State*" means—

(i) a Member State of the European Communities, or

(ii) not being such a Member State, an EEA State which is a territory with the government of which arrangements having the force of law by virtue of [*section 826(1)*][12] have been made.][13]

(4) The question whether one company is a subsidiary of another company for the purpose of *subsection (3)* shall be determined as a question whether it is a 51 per cent subsidiary of that other company, except that that other company shall be treated as not being the owner of—

(a) any share capital which it owns directly in a company, if a profit on a sale of the shares would be treated as a trading receipt of its trade,

(b) any share capital which it owns indirectly and which is owned directly by a company for which a profit on the sale of the shares would be a trading receipt, or

(c) any share capital which it owns directly or indirectly in a company[, not being a company which, by virtue of the law of a [relevant Member State][14], is resident for the purposes of tax in such a Member State][15].

(5) (a) No transfer of assets (other than cash) or of liabilities between one company and another company shall constitute, or be treated as giving

rise to, a distribution by virtue of *subsection (2)(b)* or *(3)* if they are companies—

(i) both of which are resident in the State and neither of which is a 51 per cent subsidiary of a company not so resident, and

(ii) which neither at the time of the transfer nor as a result of it are under common control.

(b) For the purposes of this subsection, 2 companies shall be under common control if they are under the control of the same person or persons, and for this purpose "*control*" shall be construed in accordance with *section 11*.

(c) Any amount which would be a distribution by virtue of *subsection (3)(a)* shall not constitute a distribution by virtue of *subsection (2)(b)*.

Amendments

[1] Inserted by FA11 s29(b). Deemed to have come into force and takes effect as on and from 1 January 2011.

[2] Substituted by FA98 s43(1)(d). This section shall apply as respects shares issued by a company on or after the 3rd day of December, 1997.

[3] Substituted by FA05 s18(1)(a). This section comes into operation on 3 February 2005.

[4] Inserted by FA05 s18(1)(b). This section comes into operation on 3 February 2005.

[5] Inserted by FA01 s85(1). Applies as on or after 15 February 2001.

[6] Inserted by FA03 s61(1). Applies as respects any interest paid or other distribution made on or after 6 February 2003.

[7] Inserted by FA05 s18(1)(c). This section comes into operation on 3 February 2005.

[8] Substituted by FA02 s39(a)(i).

[9] Substituted by FA99 s79(1)(a)(i). This section shall apply as respects accounting periods ending on or after the 1st day of July, 1998.

[10] Substituted by FA02 s39(a)(ii).

[11] Inserted by FA99 s79(1)(a)(ii). This section shall apply as respects accounting periods ending on or after the 1st day of July, 1998.

[12] Substituted by FA07 sched2(1)(d). Has effect as on and from 2 April 2007

[13] Inserted by FA02 s39(a)(iii).

[14] Substituted by FA02 s39(b).

[15] Substituted by FA99 s79(1)(b). This section shall apply as respects accounting periods ending on or after the 1st day of July, 1998.

Case Law

The case of First Nationwide v Commissioners for HMRC 2010 UKFTT 24 TC considered the meaning of "dividend" and the Court held that dividends paid out of the company's share premium account were income in nature.

Revenue Briefings

Tax Briefing

Tax Briefing October 2001 – Issue 45 pg 9 – Payments to Residents of Tax Treaty Countries and EU Member Countries.

eBrief

eBrief No. 39/2014 – Tax Treatment of Return of Value to Vodafone Shareholders

Revenue Precedents

Would interest payable by a qualified company within the meaning of section 446 TCA 1997 on borrowings from group companies in non-treaty countries be treated as a distribution under section 130(2)(d)(iv) TCA 1997? Interest would not be treated as a distribution under section 130(2)(d)(iv) TCA 1997 subject to the following conditions: a) the interest is charged at a commercial rate; b) the interest would otherwise be recognised (apart from the afore-mentioned section) as an expense to be set against income of the trade; c) the funds borrowed are used solely for qualifying activities certified by the Minister for Finance under section 446 TCA 1997; d) an application for this treatment must be made in letter form to the Revenue Commissioners, Direct Taxes: Incentives Branch, Dublin Castle, Dublin 2. 5049/97

The redemption of shares in stock exchange where stock broker retires would not be treated as a distribution under section 130 TCA 1997 but would be treated as a disposal for CGT purposes. IR892028

Cross References

From Section 130

Section 11 Meaning of "control" in certain contexts.
Section 132 Matters to be treated or not treated as repayments of share capital.
Section 135 Distributions: supplemental.
Section 321 Provisions of general application in relation to the making of allowances and charges.
Section 436 Certain expenses for participators and associates.
Section 436A Certain settlements made by close companies
Section 437 Interest paid to directors and directors' associates.
Section 452 Application of section 130 to certain interest.
Section 519 Employee share ownership trusts.
Section 548 Valuation of assets.
Section 816 Taxation of shares issued in place of cash dividends.
Section 826 Agreements for relief from double taxation.
Section 845A "Non-application of section 130 in the case of certain interest paid by banks.
Schedule 11 Profit Sharing Schemes
Schedule 12 Employee Share Ownership Trusts

To Section 130

Section 4 Interpretation of Corporation Tax Acts.
Section 20 Schedule F.
Section 80 Taxation of certain foreign currencies.
Section 110 Securitisation.
Section 132 Matters to be treated or not treated as repayments of share capital.
Section 133 Limitation on meaning of "distribution" — general.
Section 134 Limitation on meaning of "distribution" in relation to certain payments made in respect of "foreign source" finance.
Section 135 Distributions: supplemental.
Section 137 Disallowance of reliefs in respect of bonus issues.
Section 154 Attribution of distributions to accounting periods.
Section 175 Purchase of own shares by quoted company.
Section 176 Purchase of unquoted shares by issuing company or its subsidiary.
Section 267O Treatment of credit return.
Section 267Q Treatment of deposit return.
Section 267R Treatment of investment return.
Section 436 Certain expenses for participators and associates.
Section 437 Interest paid to directors and directors' associates.
Section 452 Application of section 130 to certain interest.
Section 514 Company reconstructions, amalgamations, etc.
Section 598 Disposals of business or farm on "retirement".
Section 690 Interest and charges on income.
Section 817 Schemes to avoid liability to tax under Schedule F.
Section 845A "Non-application of section 130 in the case of certain interest paid by banks.
Section 1087 Charge and deduction of income tax not charged or deducted before passing of annual Act.
Schedule 22 Dividends Regarded as Paid Out of Profits Accumulated Before Given Date
Schedule 31 Consequential Amendments

131 Bonus issues following repayment of share capital

[CTA76 s85]

(1) In this section—

"*ordinary shares*" means shares other than preference shares;

"*preference shares*" means shares—

(a) which do not carry any right to dividends other than dividends at a rate per cent of the nominal value of the shares which is fixed, and

(b) which carry rights in respect of dividends and capital which are comparable with those general for fixed-dividend shares quoted on a stock exchange in the State;

"new consideration not derived from ordinary shares" means new consideration other than consideration consisting of the surrender, transfer or cancellation of ordinary shares of the company or any other company or consisting of the variation of rights in ordinary shares of the company or any other company, and other than consideration derived from a repayment of share capital paid in respect of ordinary shares of the company or of any other company.

(2) Where a company—

(a) repays any share capital or has done so at any time on or after the 27th day of November, 1975, and

(b) at or after the time of that repayment, issues as paid up, otherwise than by the receipt of new consideration, any share capital,

the amount so paid up shall be treated as a distribution made in respect of the shares on which it is paid up, except in so far as that amount exceeds the amount or aggregate amount of share capital so repaid less any amounts previously so paid up and treated by virtue of this subsection as distributions.

(3) *Subsection (2)* shall not apply where the repaid share capital consists of fully paid up preference shares—

(a) if those shares existed as issued and fully paid preference shares on the 27th day of November, 1975, and throughout the period from that date until the repayment those shares continued to be fully paid preference shares, or

(b) if those shares were issued after the 27th day of November, 1975, as fully paid preference shares wholly for new consideration not derived from ordinary shares and throughout the period from their issue until the repayment those shares continued to be fully paid preference shares.

(4) Except in relation to a close company within the meaning of *section 430*, this section shall not apply if the issue of share capital mentioned in *subsection (2)(b)*—

(a) is of share capital other than redeemable share capital, and

(b) takes place more than 10 years after the repayment of share capital mentioned in *subsection (2)(a)*.

Cross References

From Section 131

Section 430 Meaning of "close company".

To Section 131

Section 132 Matters to be treated or not treated as repayments of share capital.

Section 137 Disallowance of reliefs in respect of bonus issues.

Section 514 Company reconstructions, amalgamations, etc.

132 Matters to be treated or not treated as repayments of share capital

[CTA76 s86]

(1) In this section, "*relevant distribution*" means so much of any distribution made in respect of shares representing the relevant share capital as apart from *subsection (2)(a)* would be treated as a repayment of share capital, but by virtue of that subsection cannot be so treated.

(2) (a) Where—

(i) a company issues any share capital as paid up otherwise than by the receipt of new consideration, or has done so on or after the 27th day of November, 1975, and

(ii) any amount so paid up is not to be treated as a distribution,

then, for the purposes of *sections 130* and *131*, distributions made afterwards by the company in respect of shares representing that share capital shall not be treated as repayments of share capital, except to the extent to which those distributions, together with any relevant distributions previously so made, exceed the amounts so paid up (then or previously) on such shares after that date and not treated as distributions.

(b) For the purposes of *paragraph (a)*, all shares of the same class shall be treated as representing the same share capital, and where shares are issued in respect of other shares, or are directly or indirectly converted into or exchanged for other shares, all such shares shall be treated as representing the same share capital.

(3) Where share capital is issued at a premium representing new consideration, the amount of the premium shall be treated as forming part of that share capital for the purpose of determining under this Chapter whether any distribution made in respect of shares representing the share capital is to be treated as a repayment of share capital; but this subsection shall not apply in relation to any part of the premium after that part has been applied in paying up share capital.

(4) Subject to *subsection (3)*, premiums paid on redemption of share capital shall not be treated as repayments of capital.

(5) Except in relation to a close company within the meaning of *section 430*, *subsection (2)(a)* shall not prevent a distribution being treated as a repayment of share capital if it is made—

(a) more than 10 years after the issue of share capital mentioned in *subsection (2)(a)(i)*, and

(b) in respect of share capital other than redeemable share capital.

Cross References

From Section 132

Section 130 Matters to be treated as distributions.
Section 131 Bonus issues following repayment of share capital.
Section 430 Meaning of "close company".

To Section 132

Section 130 Matters to be treated as distributions.
Section 135 Distributions: supplemental.
Section 137 Disallowance of reliefs in respect of bonus issues.
Section 514 Company reconstructions, amalgamations, etc.

133 Limitation on meaning of "distribution"—general

[CTA76 s84A, FA87 s28(5)(b); FA89 s21(1)(a) and (2), FA90 s41(4) and s46; FA91 s28; FA92 s40; FA93 s45; FA94 s50; FA97 s146(1) and Sch9 PtI par10(2)(b)]

(1) (a) In this section—

['*agricultural society*' means a society—

(i) in relation to which both the following conditions are satisfied:

(I) the number of the society's members is not less than 50, and

(II) all or a majority of the society's members are persons who are mainly engaged in and derive the principal part of their income from husbandry,

or

(ii) to which a certificate to which this subparagraph applies has been issued;

'*fishery society*' means a society—

(i) in relation to which both the following conditions are satisfied:

(I) the number of the society's members is not less than 20, and

(II) all or a majority of the society's members are persons who are mainly engaged in and derive the principal part of their income from fishing,

or

(ii) to which a certificate to which this subparagraph applies has been issued;][1]

"*relevant principal*" means an amount of money advanced to a borrower by a company which is within the charge to corporation tax and the ordinary trading activities of which include the lending of money, where—

(i) the consideration given by the borrower for that amount is a relevant security, and

(ii) interest or any other distribution is paid out of the assets of the borrower in respect of that security;

"*selling by wholesale*" means selling goods of any class to a person who carries on a business of selling goods of that class or uses goods of that class for the purposes of a trade or undertaking carried on by the person;

['*specified trade*' means, subject to *paragraphs* (*b*), (*d*) and (*e*), a trade which consists wholly or mainly of the manufacture of goods.][2]

(b) Where the borrower mentioned in *subsection (5)* is a 75 per cent subsidiary of—

(i) an agricultural society, or

(ii) a fishery society,

"*specified trade*", in that subsection, means a trade of the borrower which consists wholly or mainly of either or both of—

(I) the manufacture of goods within the meaning of the definition of "*specified trade*" in *paragraph (a)*, and

(II) the selling by wholesale of—

(A) where *subparagraph (i)* applies, agricultural products, or

(B) where *subparagraph (ii)* applies, fish.

(c) For the purposes of the definition of "*specified trade*" in *paragraph (a)* and of *paragraph (b)*, a trade shall be regarded, as respects an accounting period, as consisting wholly or mainly of particular activities only if the total amount receivable by the borrower from sales made in the course of those activities in the accounting period is not less than 75 per cent of the total amount receivable by the borrower from all sales made in the course of the trade in that period.

(d) A qualifying shipping trade (within the meaning of *section 407*) shall not be regarded as a specified trade for the purposes of this section.

[(da) A certificate to which *subparagraph (ii)* of the definition of *'agricultural society'* or *subparagraph (ii)* of the definition of *'fishery society'* in *paragraph (a)* applies is, as the case may be, a certificate given under—

(i) *paragraph (b)* or *(c)* of [*section 443(16)*][3],

(ii) *paragraph (a)* or *(b)* of *section 70(2)* of the Finance Act 1963,

(iii) *paragraph (a)* or *(b)* of *section 220(2)* of the Income Tax Act 1967, or

(iv) *paragraph (a)* or *(b)* of *section 18(2)* of the Finance Act 1978,

and not revoked.][4]

and

[...][5]

(2) Any interest or other distribution which—

(a) is paid out of assets of a company (in this section referred to as "*the borrower*") to another company within the charge to corporation tax, and

(b) is so paid in respect of a security (in this section referred to as a "*relevant security*") within *subparagraph (ii), (iii)(I)* or *(v)* of *section 130(2)(d)*,

shall not be a distribution for the purposes of the Corporation Tax Acts unless the application of this subsection is excluded by *subsection (3), (4)* or *(5).*

(3) *Subsection (2)* shall not apply where the principal secured has been advanced by a company out of money subscribed for the share capital of the company and that share capital is beneficially owned directly or indirectly by a person or persons resident outside the State.

(4) *Subsection (2)* shall not apply in a case where the consideration given by the borrower for the use of the principal secured represents more than a reasonable commercial return for the use of that principal; but, where this subsection applies, nothing in *subparagraph (ii), (iii)(I)* or *(v)* of *section 130(2)(d)* shall operate so as to treat as a distribution for the purposes of the Corporation Tax Acts so much of the interest or other distribution as represents a reasonable commercial return for the use of that principal.

(5) Subject to *subsections (6)* and *(7), subsection (2)* shall not apply to any interest paid by the borrower, in an accounting period of the borrower, to another company in respect of relevant principal advanced by that other company, where—

(a) in that accounting period the borrower carries on in the State a specified trade,

(b) the relevant principal in respect of which the interest is paid is used in the course of the specified trade—

(i) for the activities of the trade which consist of the manufacture of goods within the meaning of the definition of "*specified trade*" in *paragraph (a)* of *subsection (1)*, or

(ii) where *paragraph (b)* of *subsection (1)* applies, for the activities of the trade which consist of such selling by wholesale as is referred to in *paragraph (II)* of the definition of "*specified trade*" in that paragraph,

and

(c) the interest, if it were not a distribution, would be treated as a trading expense of that trade for that accounting period.

(6) *Subsection (5)* shall not apply to interest paid in respect of relevant principal to a company which on the 12th day of April, 1989, had no outstanding amounts of relevant principal advanced.

(7) Notwithstanding *subsection (5)*, where at any time after the 12th day of April, 1989, the total of the amounts of relevant principal (in this subsection referred to as "the current amounts of relevant principal") advanced by a company in respect of relevant securities held directly or indirectly by the company at that time is in excess of a limit, being a limit equal to 110 per cent of the total of the amounts of relevant principal advanced by the company in respect of relevant securities held directly or indirectly by the company on the 12th day of April, 1989, then, such part of any interest paid at that time to the company in respect of relevant principal as bears, in relation to the total amount of interest so paid to the company, the same proportion as the excess bears in relation to the current amounts of relevant principal shall not be treated as a distribution for the purposes of the Corporation Tax Acts in the hands of the company.

(8) (a) In this subsection and in *subsection (10)*, "*specified period*", in relation to relevant principal, means the period commencing on the date on which the relevant principal was advanced and ending on the date on which the relevant principal is to be repaid under the terms of the agreement to advance the relevant principal or, if earlier—

(i) in the case of relevant principal advanced before the 11th day of April, 1994, the 11th day of April, 2001, and

(ii) in any other case, a date which is 7 years after the date on which the relevant principal was advanced.

(b) Notwithstanding *subsection (5)*, where at any time on or after the 31st day of January, 1990, the total of the amounts of relevant principal (in this subsection and in *subsections (9)* and *(10)* referred to as "the current amounts of relevant principal") advanced by a company in respect of relevant securities held directly or indirectly by the company at that time is in excess of a limit, being a limit equal to 75 per cent of the total of the amounts of relevant principal advanced by the company in respect of relevant securities held directly or indirectly by the company on the 12th day of April, 1989, then, any interest paid to the company in respect of relevant principal advanced by the company on or after the 31st day of January, 1990, being relevant principal which is included in the current amounts of relevant principal, shall not be treated as a distribution for the purposes of the Corporation Tax Acts in the hands of the company.

(c) Where apart from this paragraph any part of any interest paid to a company in respect of relevant principal advanced by the company on or after the 31st day of January, 1990, would not be treated as a distribution for the purposes of the Corporation Tax Acts in the hands of the company by virtue only of *paragraph (b)*, then, that paragraph shall not apply in relation to so much of that interest as is paid for a specified period in respect of relevant principal advanced and which was, at the time the relevant principal was advanced, specified in the list referred to in *subparagraph (iv)* if—

(i) the relevant principal is advanced by the company to a borrower who was in negotiation before the 31st day of January, 1990, with any company for an amount of relevant principal,

(ii) the borrower had received before the 31st day of January, 1990, a written offer of grant aid from the Industrial Development Authority, the Shannon Free Airport Development Company Limited or Údarás na Gaeltachta in respect of a specified trade or a proposed specified trade for the purposes of which trade the relevant principal is borrowed,

(iii) the specified trade is a trade which the borrower commenced to carry on after the 31st day of January, 1990, or is a specified trade of the borrower in respect of which the borrower is committed, under a business plan approved by the Industrial Development Authority, the Shannon Free Airport Development Company Limited or Údarás na Gaeltachta, to the creation of additional employment,

(iv) before the 25th day of March, 1992, the specified trade of the borrower was included in a list prepared by the Industrial Development Authority and approved before that day by the Minister for Industry and Commerce and the Minister for Finance, being a list specifying a particular amount of relevant principal in respect of each trade which amount is considered to be essential for the success of that trade, and

(v) the borrower or a company connected with the borrower is not a company which commenced to carry on relevant trading operations (within the meaning of *section 446*) after the 20th day of April, 1990, or intends to commence to carry on such trading operations;

but this paragraph shall not apply to any interest in respect of any relevant principal advanced after the time when the total of the amounts of relevant principal to which this paragraph applies, advanced by all lenders who have made such advances, exceeds [€215,855,473.33][6].

(d) For the purposes of this subsection and *subsections (9)* and *(10)*—

(i) relevant principal advanced by a company at any time on or after a day includes any relevant principal advanced on or after that day to a borrower under an agreement entered into before that day,

(ii) where on or after the 6th day of May, 1993, a period of repayment of relevant principal advanced by a company is extended (whether or not the right to such an extension arose out of the terms of the agreement to advance the relevant principal), the company shall be treated as having—

(I) received repayment of the relevant principal, and

(II) advanced a corresponding amount of relevant principal,

on the date on which apart from the extension the relevant principal fell to be repaid, and

(iii) where at any time after an amount of relevant principal is specified in a list in accordance with *paragraph (c)(iv)* or *subsection (9)(c)(ii)* or *(10)(b)(ii)* a company advances, or is treated as advancing, to a borrower relevant principal the interest in respect of which is treated as a distribution by virtue only of *paragraph (c)* or *subsection (9)(c)* or *(10)(b)*, the amount of relevant principal specified in the list shall be treated as reduced by the amount of relevant principal so advanced, or treated as advanced, and the amount so reduced shall be treated as the amount specified in that list.

(e) For the purposes of this subsection and *subsections (9)* and *(10)*, where a company which has on or after the 31st day of January, 1990, advanced relevant principal to a borrower under the terms of an agreement and, under the terms of that or any other agreement, the company assigns to another company part or all of its rights and obligations under the first-mentioned agreement in relation to the relevant principal, such assignment shall be deemed not to have taken place.

(9) (a) Notwithstanding *subsections (5)*, *(7)* and *(8)*, where at any time on or after the 31st day of December, 1991, the current amounts of relevant principal advanced by a company in respect of relevant securities held directly or indirectly by the company at that time is in excess of a limit, being a limit equal to 40 per cent of the total of the amounts of relevant principal advanced by the company in respect of the relevant securities held directly or indirectly by the company on the 12th day of April, 1989, then, any interest paid to the company in respect of relevant principal advanced by the company on or after the 31st day of December, 1991, being relevant principal which is included in the current amounts of relevant principal, shall not be treated as a distribution for the purposes of the Corporation Tax Acts in the hands of the company.

(b) (i) Where the total of the amounts of relevant principal advanced by a company in respect of relevant securities held directly or indirectly by the company at any time on or after the 31st day of December, 1991, is less than the limit referred to in *paragraph (a)*, that paragraph shall apply as if that limit were the total of the amounts of relevant principal so advanced as at that time unless the company proves that it has as far as possible, at all times on or after the 31st day of December, 1991, advanced to borrowers relevant principal in respect of the interest on which *paragraph (a)* does not, or would not, apply by virtue of *paragraph (c)*.

(ii) Where at any time during the period commencing on the 18th day of April, 1991, and ending immediately before the 31st day of December, 1991, an amount of relevant principal which was advanced to a borrower, being a company which carries on one or more trading operations (within the meaning of *section 445(1)*), is repaid, this section shall apply as if—

(I) references in *subparagraph (i)* and in *paragraph (a)* to the 31st day of December, 1991, were references to the day on which the amount is repaid, and

(II) during that period—

(A) the reference in *subparagraph (i)* to relevant principal in respect of the interest on which *paragraph (a)* does not, or would not, apply by virtue of *paragraph (c)* were a reference to such principal in respect of the interest on which *paragraph (b)* of *subsection (8)* does not, or would not, apply by virtue of *paragraph (c)* of that subsection, and

(B) the reference in *paragraph (c)* of *subsection (8)* to *paragraph (b)* of that subsection were a reference to *paragraph (a)*.

(c) Where apart from this paragraph any part of any interest paid to a company in respect of relevant principal advanced by the company on or after the 31st day of December, 1991, would not be treated as a distribution for the purposes of the Corporation Tax Acts in the hands of the company by virtue only of *paragraph (a)*, then, subject to *subsection (11)*, that paragraph shall not apply in relation to so much of that interest as is paid if—

(i) the specified trade is a trade which the borrower commenced to carry on after the 31st day of January, 1990, or is a specified trade of the borrower in respect of which the borrower is committed, under a business plan approved by the Industrial Development Authority, the Shannon Free Airport Development Company Limited or Údarás na Gaeltachta, to the creation of additional employment,

(ii) the specified trade of the borrower was selected by the Industrial Development Authority for inclusion in a list, approved by the Minister for Industry and Commerce and the Minister for Finance, being a list specifying a particular amount of relevant principal in respect of each trade which amount is considered to be essential for the success of that trade, and

(iii) the borrower or a company connected with the borrower is not a company which commenced to carry on relevant trading operations (within the meaning of *section 446*) after the 20th day of April, 1990, or intends to commence to carry on such trading operations.

(10) (a) Notwithstanding *subsections (5)* and *(7)* to *(9)*, any interest paid to a company in respect of relevant principal advanced by the company on or after the 20th day of December, 1991, shall not be treated as a distribution for the purposes of the Corporation Tax Acts in the hands of the company.

(b) Where apart from this paragraph any interest paid to a company in respect of relevant principal advanced by the company on or after the 20th day of December, 1991, would not be treated as a distribution for the purposes of the Corporation Tax Acts in the hands of the company by virtue only of *paragraph (a)*, then, subject to *subsection (11)*, that paragraph shall not apply in relation to so much of that interest as is paid for a specified period in respect of relevant principal advanced and which was, at the time the relevant principal was advanced, specified in the list referred to in *subparagraph (ii)* if—

(i) the specified trade is a trade which the borrower commenced to carry on after the 31st day of January, 1990, or is a specified trade of the borrower in respect of which the borrower is committed, under a business plan approved by the Industrial Development Authority, the Shannon Free Airport Development Company Limited or Údarás na Gaeltachta, to the creation of additional employment,

(ii) before the 25th day of March, 1992, the specified trade of the borrower was included in a list prepared by the Industrial Development Authority and approved before that day by the Minister for Industry and Commerce and the Minister for Finance, being a list specifying a particular amount of relevant principal in respect of each trade which amount is considered to be essential for the success of that trade, and

(iii) the borrower is not a company which carries on relevant trading operations (within the meaning of *section 446*) or intends to carry on such trading operations.

(11) *Subsections (9)(c)* and *(10)(b)* shall not apply to any interest in respect of any relevant principal advanced after the time when the total of the amounts of relevant principal to which those subsections apply, advanced by all lenders who have made such advances, exceeds the aggregate of—

(a) [€317,434,519.61][7], and

(b) the excess, if any, of [€215,855,473.33][8] over the total of the amounts of relevant principal to which *subsection (8)(c)* applies advanced by all lenders who have made such advances.

(12) (a) In this subsection, "*scheduled repayment date*", in relation to any relevant principal, means the date on which that relevant principal is to be repaid under the terms of the agreement to advance that relevant principal.

(b) Where at any time before the 7th day of December, 1993—

(i) relevant principal (in this subsection referred to as "the first-mentioned relevant principal"), the interest in respect of which was treated as a distribution by virtue only of *subsection (8)(c)*, *(9)(c)* or *(10)(b)*, advanced by a company to a borrower was repaid by the borrower before the scheduled repayment date, and

(ii) a further amount or further amounts of relevant principal, the interest in respect of which is to be treated as a distribution by virtue only of *subsection (8)(c)*, *(9)(c)* or *(10)(b)*, was or were advanced to that borrower,

then, *subsection (8)(d)(iii)* shall not apply in relation to so much of—

(I) the further amount of relevant principal advanced as does not exceed the amount of relevant principal repaid, or

(II) where there are more further amounts advanced than one, the aggregate of the further amounts of relevant principal advanced as does not exceed the relevant principal repaid.

(c) Where by virtue of *paragraph (b) subsection (8)(d)(iii)* does not apply in relation to any amount of relevant principal advanced by a company, the company shall be treated as having—

(i) received a repayment of that amount of relevant principal, and

(ii) advanced a corresponding amount of relevant principal,

on the scheduled repayment date of the first-mentioned relevant principal.

(d) For the purposes of this subsection, where there are more further advances of relevant principal than one, the amount to which *subsection (8)(d)(iii)* does not apply shall be referable as far as possible to an earlier rather than a later such further advance.

(e) Notwithstanding *paragraphs (b)* to *(d)*, interest which but for this paragraph would not be treated as a distribution by virtue only of *subsection (8)(d)(iii)* may be treated as a distribution if it is paid in respect of relevant principal advanced before the 7th day of December, 1993.

(13) (a) In this subsection, "*relevant period*" means a period which commences at a time at which, in accordance with the terms of the agreement under which relevant principal secured by a relevant security is advanced, an amount representing the interest for the use of the relevant principal is to be paid, and ends at a time immediately before the next time at which such an amount is to be paid.

(b) Interest paid to a company in respect of—

(i) relevant principal denominated in a currency other than [the currency of the State][9], and

(ii) a relevant period which begins on or after the 30th day of January, 1991,

shall not be a distribution for the purposes of the Corporation Tax Acts in the hands of the company if, at any time during that period, the rate on the basis of which interest is computed exceeds 80 per cent of [the rate known as the 3 month European Interbank Offered Rate][10].

(c) *Paragraph (b)* shall not apply to any interest paid to a company in respect of relevant principal advanced by the company—

(i) before the 30th day of January, 1991, under an agreement entered into before that day if on that day the rate on the basis of which interest in respect of the relevant security is to be computed exceeds 80 per cent of [the rate known as the 3 month European Interbank Offered Rate][11]; but this subparagraph shall not apply as respects any relevant period commencing on or after the 20th day of December, 1991, if in that relevant period that rate exceeds the rate on the basis of which interest would have been computed if the relevant principal had continued to be denominated in the currency in which it was denominated on the 30th day of January, 1991,

(ii) on or after the 30th day of January, 1991—

(I) which is included in a list referred to in *subsection (8)(c)(iv), (9)(c)(ii)* or *(10)(b)(ii)*, and

(II) for the purposes of a specified trade of a borrower who is certified by the Minister for Enterprise, Trade and Employment as having received an undertaking that the interest would be treated as a distribution;

but this subparagraph shall not apply as respects any relevant period commencing on or after the 20th day of December, 1991, if in that relevant period the rate on the basis of which interest in respect of the relevant security is to be computed exceeds—

(A) a rate approved by the Minister for Finance in consultation with the Minister for Enterprise, Trade and Employment, or

(B) where it is lower than the rate so approved and the relevant principal was advanced on or after the 30th day of January, 1991, and before the 20th day of December, 1991, the rate which would have applied if the relevant principal had continued to be denominated in the currency in which it was denominated when it was advanced,

(iii) on or after the 18th day of April, 1991, where the rate on the basis of which that interest is computed exceeds 80 per cent of [the rate known as the 3 month European Interbank Offered Rate][12] by reason only that the relevant principal advanced is denominated in sterling, or

(iv) to a borrower which is a company carrying on one or more trading operations within the meaning of *section 445(1)*.

Amendments

[1, 2] Substituted by FA12 sched1(5)(a).

[3] Substituted by FA13 sched2(1)(c)(i). Has effect on and from 27 March 2013.

[4] Inserted by FA12 sched1(5)(b).

[5] Deleted by FA12 sched1(5)(c)

[6, 7, 8] Deleted by FA01 sched5.

[9] Substituted by FA13 sched2(1)(c)(ii). Has effect on and from 27 March 2013.

[10] Substituted by FA98 sched2(4)(a). With effect from 1 January 1999 per S.I. 502 of 1998.

[11] Substituted by FA98 sched2(4)(b)(i). With effect from 1 January 1999 per S.I. 502 of 1998.

[12] Substituted by FA98 sched2(4)(b)(ii). With effect from 1 January 1999 per S.I. 502 of 1998.

Revenue Precedents

Treatment of interest in accordance with section 133 of the Taxes Consolidation Act, 1997 (was s.84(2)(d)(iv) Corporation Tax Act, 1976) and the Ireland/Netherlands Double Taxation Convention. Interest paid to a Dutch parent company by its Irish subsidiary will be regarded as interest and will be allowed as trading expense to the paying company. DTX 7008/94

Conflict in the treatment of interest which is treated as a distribution within the meaning of section 133 Taxes Consolidation Act, 1997 (s.84(2)(d)(iv), Corporation Tax Act, 1976) and interest which is treated as such for the purposes of a Double Taxation Convention. Where a conflict arises the Double Taxation Convention provisions will apply unless a claim to the contrary is made by the company. IR 10407/339/95

Cross References

From Section 133

Section 130 Matters to be treated as distributions.
Section 407 Restriction on use of losses and capital allowances for qualifying shipping trade.
Section 442 Interpretation (Part 14).
Section 443 Meaning of "goods".
Section 445 Certain trading operations carried on in Shannon Airport.
Section 446 Certain trading operations carried on in Custom House Docks Area.

To Section 133

Section 271 Industrial building allowances.
Section 273 Acceleration of writing-down allowances in respect of certain expenditure on certain industrial buildings or structures.
Section 283 Initial allowances.
Section 285 Acceleration of wear and tear allowances.
Section 404 Restriction on use of capital allowances for certain leased machinery or plant.

134 Limitation on meaning of "*distribution*" in relation to certain payments made in respect of "*foreign source*" finance

[CTA76 s84A(1) to (6), (9) and (10); FA84 s41; FA86 s54; FA87 s28(5)(b); FA89 s21(2)(a); FA97 s146(1) and Sch9 PtI par10(2)(a)]

(1) (a) In this section—

"*agricultural society*" and "*fishery society*" have the meanings respectively assigned to them by [*section 133(1)(a)*][1];

"*selling by wholesale*" means selling goods of any class to a person who carries on a business of selling goods of that class or uses goods of that class for the purposes of a trade or undertaking carried on by the person;

"*specified trade*" means, subject to *paragraphs (b)* and *(d)* and to *subsection (6)*, a trade which consists wholly or mainly of—

(i) the manufacture of goods, including activities which, if the borrower were to make a claim for relief in respect of the trade under *Part 14*, would be regarded for the purposes of that Part as the manufacture of goods, or

(ii) the rendering of services in the course of a service undertaking in respect of which an employment grant was made by the Industrial

Development Authority under section 2 of the Industrial Development (No. 2) Act, 1981.

(b) Where the borrower mentioned in *subsection (5)* is a 75 per cent subsidiary of—

(i) an agricultural society, or

(ii) a fishery society,

"*specified trade*", in that subsection, means a trade of the borrower which consists wholly or mainly of either or both of—

(I) the manufacture of goods within the meaning of the definition of "*specified trade*" in *paragraph (a)*, and

(II) the selling by wholesale of—

(A) where *subparagraph (i)* applies, agricultural products, or

(B) where *subparagraph (ii)* applies, fish.

(c) For the purposes of the definition of "*specified trade*" in *paragraph (a)* and of *paragraph (b)*, a trade shall be regarded, as respects an accounting period, as consisting wholly or mainly of particular activities only if the total amount receivable by the borrower from sales made or, as the case may be, in payment for services rendered in the course of those activities in the accounting period is not less than 75 per cent of the total amount receivable by the borrower from all sales made in the course of the trade in that period.

(d) A qualifying shipping trade (within the meaning of *section 407*) shall not be regarded as a specified trade for the purposes of this section.

(2) This section shall apply only where the principal secured has been advanced by a company out of money subscribed for the share capital of the company and that share capital is beneficially owned directly or indirectly by a person or persons resident outside the State.

(3) Any interest or other distribution which—

(a) is paid out of assets of a company (in this section referred to as "*the borrower*") to another company within the charge to corporation tax, and

(b) is so paid in respect of a security (in this section referred to as a "*relevant security*") within *subparagraph (ii)*, *(iii)(I)* or *(v)* of *section 130(2)(d)*,

shall not be a distribution for the purposes of the Corporation Tax Acts unless the application of this subsection is excluded by *subsection (4)* or *(5)*.

(4) *Subsection (3)* shall not apply in a case where the consideration given by the borrower for the use of the principal secured represents more than a reasonable commercial return for the use of that principal; but, where this subsection applies, nothing in *subparagraph (ii)*, *(iii)(I)* or *(v)* of *section 130(2)(d)* shall operate so as to treat as a distribution for the purposes of the Corporation Tax Acts so much of the interest or other distribution as represents a reasonable commercial return for the use of that principal.

(5) *Subsection (3)* shall not apply to any interest paid by the borrower, in an accounting period of the borrower, to another company the ordinary trading activities of which include the lending of money, where—

(a) in that accounting period the borrower carries on in the State a specified trade, and

(b) the interest, if it were not a distribution, would be treated as a trading expense of that trade for that accounting period.

(6) (a) This subsection shall apply to any interest or other distribution which apart from this subsection would be a distribution for the purposes of the Corporation Tax Acts, other than any interest or other distribution which is paid by the borrower under an obligation entered into—

(i) before the 13th day of May, 1986, or

(ii) before the 1st day of September, 1986, in accordance with negotiations which were in progress between the borrower and a lender before the 13th day of May, 1986.

(b) *Subsection (5)* shall apply as respects any interest or other distribution to which this subsection applies as if *paragraph (ii)* of the definition of "*specified trade*" in *subsection (1)(a)* were deleted.

(c) For the purposes of *paragraph (a)*—

(i) an obligation shall be treated as having been entered into before a particular date only if before that date there was in existence a binding contract in writing under which that obligation arose, and

(ii) negotiations in accordance with which an obligation was entered into shall not be regarded as having been in progress before the 13th day of May, 1986, unless on or before that date preliminary commitments or agreements in relation to that obligation had been entered into between the lender referred to in that paragraph and the borrower.

Amendments

[1]Substituted by FA12 sched1(6).

Cross References

From Section 134

Section 130 Matters to be treated as distributions.

Section 407 Restriction on use of losses and capital allowances for qualifying shipping trade.

Section 442 Interpretation (Part 14).

Section 443 Meaning of "goods".

135 Distributions: supplemental

[CTA76 s87; FA91 s29]

(1) (a) In this Chapter, "*new consideration*" means consideration not provided directly or indirectly out of the assets of the company, but does not include amounts retained by the company by means of capitalising a distribution.

(b) Notwithstanding *paragraph (a)*, where share capital has been issued at a premium representing new consideration, any part of that premium applied afterwards in paying up share capital shall also be treated as new consideration for that share capital, except in so far as the premium has been taken into account under *section 132(3)* so as to enable a distribution to be treated as a repayment of share capital.

(2) (a) No consideration derived from the value of any share capital or security of a company, or from voting or other rights in a company, shall be regarded for the purposes of this Chapter as new consideration received by the company unless the consideration consists of—

(i) money or value received from the company as a distribution,

(ii) money received from the company as a payment which for those purposes constitutes a repayment of that share capital or of the principal secured by that security, or

(iii) the giving up of the right to that share capital or security on its cancellation, extinguishment or acquisition by the company.

(b) No amount shall be regarded as new consideration by virtue of *subparagraph (ii)* or *(iii)* of *paragraph (a)* in so far as it exceeds any new consideration received by the company for the issue of the share capital or security in question or, in the case of share capital which constituted a distribution on issue, the nominal value of that share capital.

(3) Where 2 or more companies enter into arrangements to make distributions to each other's members, all parties concerned may for the purposes of this Chapter be treated as if anything done by any of those companies had been done by any other, and this subsection shall apply however many companies participate in the arrangements.

(4) (a) In this Chapter and in *section 137*, "in respect of shares in the company" and "in respect of securities of the company", in relation to a company which is a member of a 90 per cent group, mean respectively in respect of shares in that company or any other company in the group and in respect of securities of that company or any other company in the group.

(b) Without prejudice to *section 130(2)(b)* as extended by *paragraph (a)*, in relation to a company which is a member of a 90 per cent group, "distribution" includes anything distributed out of assets of the company (whether in cash or otherwise) in respect of shares in or securities of another company in the group.

(c) Nothing in this subsection shall require a company to be treated as making a distribution to any other company which is in the same group and is resident in the State.

(d) For the purposes of this subsection, a principal company and all its 90 per cent subsidiaries form a 90 per cent group, and "*principal company*" means a company of which another company is a subsidiary.

(e) Nothing in this subsection shall require any company which is a subsidiary (within the meaning of section 155 of the Companies Act, 1963) of another company to be treated as making a distribution where it acquires shares in the other company in accordance with section 9(1) of the Insurance Act, 1990.

(5) A distribution shall be treated under this Chapter as made, or consideration as provided, out of assets of a company if the cost falls on the company.

(6) In this Chapter and in *section 137*, "*share*" includes stock and any other interest of a member in a company.

(7) References in this Chapter to issuing share capital as paid up apply also to the paying up of any issued share capital.

(8) For the purposes of this Chapter and of *section 137*, "*security*" includes securities not creating or evidencing a charge on assets, and interest paid by a company on money advanced without the issue of a security for the advance, or other consideration given by a company for the use of money so advanced, shall be treated as if paid or given in respect of a security issued for the advance by the company.

(9) Where securities are issued at a price less than the amount repayable on them and are not quoted on a recognised stock exchange, the principal secured shall not be taken for the purposes of this Chapter to exceed the issue price unless the securities are issued on terms reasonably comparable with the terms of issue of securities so quoted.

(10) For the purposes of this Chapter and of *section 137*, a thing shall be regarded as done in respect of a share if it is done to a person as being the holder of the

share, or as having at a particular time been the holder of the share, or is done in pursuance of a right granted or offer made in respect of a share, and anything done in respect of shares by reference to share holdings at a particular time shall be regarded as done to the then holder of the shares or the personal representatives of any shareholder then dead.

(11) *Subsection (10)* shall apply in relation to securities as it applies in relation to shares.

Cross References

From Section 135

Section 130 Matters to be treated as distributions.
Section 132 Matters to be treated or not treated as repayments of share capital.
Section 137 Disallowance of reliefs in respect of bonus issues.

To Section 135

Section 122A Notional loans relating to shares, etc.
Section 128 Tax treatment of directors of companies and employees granted rights to acquire shares or other assets.
Section 128A Deferral of payment of tax under section 128.
Section 128C Tax treatment of directors and employees who acquire convertible shares.
Section 130 Matters to be treated as distributions.
Section 174 Taxation of dealer's receipts on purchase of shares by issuing company or by its subsidiary.
Section 413 Profits or assets available for distribution.
Section 415 Meaning of "the notional winding up".
Section 440 Surcharge on undistributed investment and estate income.
Section 817 Schemes to avoid liability to tax under Schedule F.
Section 897B Returns of information in respect of awards of shares to directors and employees.

CHAPTER 3

Distributions and Tax Credits — General

136 Tax credit for certain recipients of distributions [Repealed]

Repealed by FA00 sched2.

137 Disallowance of reliefs in respect of bonus issues

[CTA76 s89]

(1) This section shall apply where any person (in this section referred to as "*the recipient*") receives an amount treated as a distribution by virtue of—

(a) *paragraph (c)* or *(d)* of *section 130(2)*,

(b) *section 131*, or

(c) *section 132(2)(a)*,

and, in this section, a distribution within *paragraph (a)*, *(b)* or *(c)* is referred to as a "*bonus issue*"[…][1].

(2) Subject to *subsection (5)*, where the recipient is entitled by reason of—

(a) any exemption from tax,

(b) the setting-off of losses against profits or income, or

(c) the payment of interest,

to recover tax in respect of any distribution which the recipient has received, no account shall be taken, for the purposes of any such exemption, set-off or payment of interest, of any bonus issue […][2] which the recipient has received.

(3) Subject to *subsection (5)*, a bonus issue [...][3] shall be treated as not being franked investment income within the meaning of *section 156*.

[...][4]

(5) Nothing in [*subsections (2)* and *(3)*][5] shall affect the proportion (if any) of any bonus issue made in respect of any shares or securities which, if that bonus issue were declared as a dividend, would represent a normal return to the recipient on the consideration provided by the recipient for the relevant shares or securities, that is, those in respect of which the bonus issue was made and, if those securities are derived from shares or securities previously acquired by the recipient, the shares or securities which were previously acquired[...][6].

(6) For the purposes of *subsection (5)*—

(a) if the consideration provided by the recipient for any of the relevant shares or securities was in excess of their market value at the time the recipient acquired them, or if no consideration was provided by the recipient for any of the relevant shares or securities, the recipient shall be taken to have provided for those shares or securities consideration equal to their market value at the time the recipient acquired them, and

(b) in determining whether an amount received by means of dividend exceeds a normal return, regard shall be had to the length of time before the receipt of that amount that the recipient first acquired any of the relevant shares or securities and to any dividends and other distributions made in respect of the relevant shares or securities during that time.

Amendments

[1, 2, 4, 6] Deleted by FA00 sched2.

[3] Deleted by FA03 s41(1)(b). This section applies as respects accounting periods ending on or after 6 February 2003.

[5] Substituted by FA00 sched2(b).

Cross References

From Section 137

Section 130 Matters to be treated as distributions.

Section 131 Bonus issues following repayment of share capital.

Section 132 Matters to be treated or not treated as repayments of share capital.

Section 156 Franked investment income and franked payments.

To Section 137

Section 135 Distributions: supplemental.

138 Treatment of dividends on certain preference shares

[FA84 s42(1), (2) and (3); FA 89 s26]

(1) In this section—

"*preference shares*" does not include preference shares—

(a) which are quoted on a stock exchange in the State,

(b) which are not so quoted but which carry rights in respect of dividends and capital comparable with those general for fixed-dividend shares quoted on a stock exchange in the State, or

(c) which are non-transferable shares issued on or after the 6th day of April, 1989, by a company in the course of carrying on relevant trading operations within the meaning of *section 445* or *446*, to a company—

(i) none of the shares of which is beneficially owned, whether directly or indirectly, by a person resident in the State, and

(ii) which, if this paragraph had not been enacted, would not be chargeable to corporation tax in respect of any profits other than dividends which would be so chargeable by virtue of this section;

"*shares*" includes stock.

(2) This section shall apply to any dividend which—

(a) is paid by a company (in this section referred to as "*the issuer*") to another company (in this section referred to as "*the subscriber*") within the charge to corporation tax, and

(b) is so paid in respect of preference shares of the issuer.

(3) Notwithstanding any provision of the Tax Acts—

[...][1]

(b) the dividend shall be chargeable to corporation tax under Case IV of Schedule D.

[(4) Where, but for the deletion of *sections 445* and *446*, shares issued by a company would not be preference shares for the purposes of this section then, notwithstanding the deletion of those sections, those shares shall be treated as not being preference shares for those purposes and this section shall apply with any modifications necessary to give effect to this subsection.][2]

Amendments

[1] Deleted by FA00 sched2.

[2] Inserted by FA12 sched1(7).

Cross References

From Section 138

Section 445 Certain trading operations carried on in Shannon Airport.
Section 446 Certain trading operations carried on in Custom House Docks Area.

To Section 138

Section 154 Attribution of distributions to accounting periods.

139 Dividends and other distributions at gross rate or of gross amount [Repealed]

Repealed by FA00 sched2.

CHAPTER 4

Distributions Out of Certain Exempt Profits or Gains or Out of Certain Relieved Income

140 Distributions out of profits or gains from stallion fees, stud greyhound services fees and occupation of certain woodlands

[CTA76 s93; FA96 s25(3); FA97 s146(1) and Sch9 par10(3)]

(1) In this section—

"*exempt profits*" means profits or gains which by virtue of *section 231*, *232* or *233* were not charged to tax;

"*other profits*" includes a dividend or other distribution of a company resident in the State, but does not include a distribution to which *subsection (3)(a)(i)* applies.

(2) Where a distribution for an accounting period is made by a company in part out of exempt profits and in part out of other profits, the distribution shall be treated as if it consisted of 2 distributions respectively made out of exempt profits and out of other profits.

(3) (a) So much of any distribution as has been made out of exempt profits—

(i) shall, where the recipient of that distribution is a company, be deemed for the purposes of the Corporation Tax Acts to be exempt profits of the company, and

(ii) shall not be regarded as income for any purpose of the Income Tax Acts.

[...][1]

[...][2]

(5) In relation to any distribution [...][3], including part of a distribution treated under *subsection (2)* as a distribution, made by a company out of exempt profits, *section 152* shall apply to the company so that the statements provided for by that section shall show as respects each such distribution, in addition to the particulars required to be given apart from this section, that the distribution is made out of exempt profits.

[...][4]

(7) Where a company makes a distribution for an accounting period, the distribution shall be regarded for the purposes of this section as having been made out of the distributable income (within the meaning of *section 144(8)*) of that period to the extent of that income and, in relation to the excess of the distribution over that income, out of the most recently accumulated income.

[(8) Where a period of account for or in respect of which a company makes a distribution is not an accounting period and part of the period of account is within an accounting period, the proportion of the distribution to be treated for the purposes of this section as being for or in respect of the accounting period shall be the same proportion as that part of the period of account bears to the whole of that period.

(9) Where a company makes a distribution which is not expressed to be for or in respect of a specified period, the distribution shall be treated for the purposes of this section as having been made for the accounting period in which it is made.][5]

Amendments

1, 2, 3, 4 Deleted by FA00 sched2.

5 Substituted by FA00 sched2(c).

Cross References

From Section 140

Section 144 Distributions out of profits from trading within Shannon Airport.
Section 152 Explanation of tax credit to be annexed to interest and dividend warrants.
Section 231 Profits or gains from stallion fees.
Section 232 Profits from occupation of certain woodlands.
Section 233 Stud greyhound service fees.

To Section 140

Section 141 Distributions out of income from patent royalties.
Section 142 Distributions out of profits of certain mines.

Section 143 Distributions out of profits from coal, gypsum and anhydrite mining operations.
Section 144 Distributions out of profits from trading within Shannon Airport.
Section 154 Attribution of distributions to accounting periods.
Section 155 Restriction of certain reliefs in respect of distributions out of certain exempt or relieved profits.
Section 172B Dividend withholding tax on relevant distributions.
Section 434 Distributions to be taken into account and meaning of "distributable income", "investment income", "estate income", etc.
Section 531B Charge to income levy.
Section 531AM Charge to universal social charge.
Section 531AS Universal social charge payable by chargeable persons (within the meaning of Part 41).
Section 669G Interpretation (Chapter 4).
Schedule 25B List of Specified Reliefs and Method of Determining Amount of Specified Relief Used in a Tax Year

141 Distributions out of income from patent royalties

[CTA76 s170; FA92 s19(2); FA96 s32(2) and (3)(b); FA97 s146(1) and Sch9 par10(9)]

(1) In this section—

"*disregarded income*" means—

(a) as respects distributions made out of specified income accruing to a company on or after the 28th day of March, 1996—

(i) income from a qualifying patent which by virtue of *section 234(2)* has been disregarded for the purposes of income tax, and

(ii) income from a qualifying patent which by virtue of *section 234(2)* and *section 76(6)* has been disregarded for the purposes of corporation tax,

but does not include income (in this section referred to as "*specified income*") from a qualifying patent (within the meaning of *section 234*) which would not be income from a qualifying patent if *paragraph (a)* of the definition of "*income from a qualifying patent*" in *section 234(1)* had not been enacted, and

(b) as respects any other distributions—

(i) income which by virtue of *section 234(2)* has been disregarded for the purposes of income tax, and

(ii) income which by virtue of *section 234(2)* and *section 76(6)* has been disregarded for the purposes of corporation tax;

"*eligible shares*", in relation to a company, means shares forming part of the ordinary share capital of the company which—

(a) are fully paid up,

(b) carry no present or future preferential right to dividends or to the company's assets on its winding up and no present or future preferential right to be redeemed, and

(c) are not subject to any different treatment from the treatment which applies to all shares of the same class, in particular different treatment in respect of—

(i) the dividend payable,

(ii) repayment,

(iii) restrictions attaching to the shares, or

(iv) any offer of substituted or additional shares, securities or rights of any description in respect of the shares;

"*other profits*" includes a dividend or other distribution of a company resident in the State, but does not include a distribution to which *subsection (3)(a)(ii)* applies.

(2) Where a distribution for an accounting period is made by a company in part out of disregarded income and in part out of other profits, the distribution shall be treated as if it consisted of 2 distributions respectively made out of disregarded income and out of other profits.

(3) (a) So much of any distribution as has been made out of disregarded income—

(i) shall, subject to *subsection (4)(a)*, not be regarded as income for any purpose of the Income Tax Acts, and

(ii) shall, where the recipient of that distribution is a company and the distribution is in respect of eligible shares, be deemed for the purposes of this section to be disregarded income.

[…][1]

(4) (a) *Subsection (3)(a)(i)* shall not apply to any distribution received by a person unless it is a distribution—

(i) in respect of eligible shares, or

(ii) made out of disregarded income, being income (in this subsection referred to in relation to a person as "*relevant income*") which is referable to a qualifying patent in relation to which the person carried out, either solely or jointly with another person, the research, planning, processing, experimenting, testing, devising, designing, development or other similar activity leading to the invention which is the subject of the qualifying patent.

(b) For the purposes of *paragraph (a)*, where a distribution for an accounting period is made by a company to a person in part out of relevant income, in relation to the person, and in part out of other disregarded income, the distribution shall be treated as if it consisted of 2 distributions respectively made out of relevant income and out of other disregarded income.

(5) (a) In this subsection—

"*the amount of aggregate expenditure on research and development incurred by a company in relation to an accounting period*" means the amount of expenditure on research and development activities incurred in the State by the company in the accounting period and the previous 2 accounting periods; but, where in an accounting period a company incurs expenditure on research and development activities and not less than 75 per cent of that expenditure was incurred in the State, all of that expenditure shall be deemed to have been incurred in the State;

"*the amount of the expenditure on research and development activities*", in relation to expenditure incurred by a company in an accounting period, means non-capital expenditure incurred by the company, being the aggregate of the amounts of—

(i) such part of the emoluments paid by the company to employees of the company engaged in carrying out research and development activities related to the company's trade as is laid out for the purposes of those activities,

(ii) expenditure incurred by the company on materials or goods used solely by the company in the carrying out of research and development activities related to the company's trade, and

(iii) a sum paid to another person, not being a person connected with the company, in order that such person may carry out research and development activities related to the company's trade,

but, where the company (in this definition referred to as "*the first company*") is a member of a group, then, for the purposes of this section, the amount of expenditure on research and development activities incurred in an accounting period by another company which in the accounting period is a member of the group shall, on a joint election in writing being made on that behalf by the first company and the other company, be treated as being expenditure incurred on research and development activities in the accounting period by the first company and not by the other company;

["*research and development activities*" has the meaning that it would have in *section 766* if *section 33* of the *Finance Act 2004* had not been enacted.][2]

(b) For the purpose of this subsection—

(i) 2 companies shall be deemed to be members of a group if both companies are wholly or mainly under the control of the same individual or individuals or if one company is a 75 per cent subsidiary of another company or both companies are 75 per cent subsidiaries of a third company and, in determining whether one company is a 75 per cent subsidiary of another company, the other company shall be treated as not being the owner of—

(I) any share capital which it owns directly in a company if a profit on sale of the shares would be treated as a trading receipt of its trade, or

(II) any share capital which it owns indirectly and which is owned directly by a company for which a profit on the sale of the shares would be a trading receipt;

(ii) a company shall be wholly or mainly under the control of an individual or individuals if not less that 75 per cent of the ordinary share capital of the company is owned directly or indirectly by the individual or, as the case may be, by individuals each of whom owns directly or indirectly part of that share capital;

(iii) *sections 412* to *418* shall apply for the purposes of this paragraph as they apply for the purposes of *Chapter 5* of *Part 12* and, where 2 companies are deemed to be members of a group by reason that both companies are wholly or mainly under the control of the same individual or individuals, those sections shall apply as they would apply for the purposes of that Chapter if the references in those sections to a parent company included a reference to an individual or individuals who hold shares in a company.

(c) Where for an accounting period a company makes one or more distributions out of specified income which accrued to the company on or after the 28th day of March, 1996 [and the specified income is income from a qualifying patent in respect of an invention which was patented for bona fide commercial reasons and not primarily for the purpose of avoiding liability to taxation][3], so much of the amount of that distribution, or the aggregate of such distributions, as does not exceed the amount of aggregate expenditure on research and development incurred by the company in relation to the accounting period shall be treated as a distribution made out of disregarded income.

(d) (i) Notwithstanding *paragraph (c)* but subject to *subparagraph (ii)*, if in an accounting period the beneficial recipient (in this paragraph referred to as "*the recipient*") of the specified income shows in writing to the satisfaction of the Revenue Commissioners that the specified income is income from a qualifying patent in respect of an invention which—

(I) involved radical innovation, and

(II) was patented for bona fide commercial reasons and not primarily for the purpose of avoiding liability to taxation,

the Revenue Commissioners shall, after consideration of any evidence in relation to the matter which the recipient submits to them and after such consultations (if any) as may seem to them to be necessary with such persons as in their opinion may be of assistance to them, determine whether all distributions made out of specified income accruing to the recipient for that accounting period and all subsequent accounting periods shall be treated as distributions made out of disregarded income and the recipient shall be notified in writing of the determination.

(ii) A recipient aggrieved by a determination of the Revenue Commissioners under *subparagraph (i)* may, by notice in writing given to the Revenue Commissioners within 30 days of the date of notification advising of the determination, appeal to the Appeal Commissioners and the Appeal Commissioners shall hear and determine the appeal made to them as if it were an appeal against an assessment to income tax, and the provisions of the Income Tax Acts relating to the rehearing of an appeal and to the statement of a case for the opinion of the High Court on a point of law shall apply accordingly with any necessary modifications.

(e) The Revenue Commissioners may nominate any of their officers to perform any acts and discharge any functions authorised by this subsection to be performed or discharged by the Revenue Commissioners, and references in this subsection to the Revenue Commissioners shall, with any necessary modifications, be construed as including references to an officer so nominated.

[(5A) (a) In this subsection—

"*arrangement*" means any arrangement, agreement, understanding, promise or undertaking whether express or implied;

"*relevant income*" means income to which *paragraph (b)* of the definition of "*income from a qualifying patent*" in *section 234* applies;

"*the amount of aggregate expenditure on research and development incurred by a company in relation to an accounting period*", "*the amount of the expenditure on research and development activities*", and "*research and development activities*" have the same meanings as they have in *subsection (5)(a)*;

"*payment in respect of the use of intellectual property*" means any payment made, directly or indirectly, in respect of—

(i) any franchise, trade mark, registered design, design right, invention or domain name,

(ii) any copyright or related right within the meaning of the Copyright and Related Rights Act 2000,

(iii) any licence or other right in respect of anything within *paragraph (i)* or *(ii)*,

(iv) any rights granted under the law of any country, territory, state or area, other than the State, or under any international treaty, convention or agreement to which the State is a party, that correspond to or are similar to those within *paragraph (i)*, *(ii)* or *(iii)*,

(v) goodwill to the extent that it is directly attributable to anything within *paragraph (i)*, *(ii)*, *(iii)* or *(iv)*.

(b) *Paragraph (b)* of *subsection (5)* shall apply for the purposes of this subsection as it applies for the purposes of that subsection.

(c) This subsection shall apply to a company for an accounting period if under any arrangement—

(i) (I) a person could become liable to make to the company any payment in respect of the use of intellectual property by virtue of the fact that any payment which is relevant income made by the person to the company could have been insufficient for the purposes of the arrangement, or

(II) a person becomes liable to make to the company any payment in respect of the use of intellectual property by virtue of the fact that any payment which is relevant income made by the person to the company was insufficient for the purposes of the arrangement,

or

(ii) (I) the company could become liable to make to any person any payment in respect of the use of intellectual property by the person by virtue of the fact that any payment which is relevant income made by the person to the company could have been excessive for the purposes of the arrangement, or

(II) the company becomes liable to make to any person any payment in respect of the use of intellectual property by the person by virtue of the fact that any payment which is relevant income made by the person to the company was excessive for the purposes of the arrangement.

(d) Where this subsection applies to a company for an accounting period and the company makes for that accounting period one or more distributions out of relevant income, then so much of the amount of that distribution, or the aggregate of such distributions, as does not exceed the amount of aggregate expenditure on research and development incurred by the company in relation to the accounting period shall be treated as a distribution made out of disregarded income; but a distribution shall not be treated as a distribution made out of disregarded income unless the relevant income is income from a qualifying patent in respect of an invention that was patented for bona fide commercial reasons and not primarily for the purpose of avoiding liability to tax.][4]

[…][5]

(7) In relation to any distribution […][6], including part of a distribution treated under *subsection (2)* as a distribution, made by a company out of disregarded income, *section 152* shall apply to the company so that the statements provided for by that section shall show as respects each such distribution, in addition to the particulars required to be given apart from this section, that the distribution is made out of disregarded income.

[…][7]

(9) Where a company makes a distribution for an accounting period, the distribution shall be regarded for the purposes of this section as having been made out of the distributable income (within the meaning of *section 144(8)*) of that period to the extent of that income and, in relation to the excess of the distributions over that income, out of the most recently accumulated income.

(10) [*Subsections (8)* and *(9)* of *section 140*][8] shall apply for the purposes of this section as they apply for the purposes of that section.

[(11) This section shall not apply to distributions made out of disregarded income on or after 24 November 2010.][9]

Amendments

1, 5, 6, 7 Deleted by FA00 sched2.

2 Substituted by FA04 s33(1)(b). This section comes into operation on such day as the Minister for Finance may appoint by order and has effect as respects expenditure incurred on or after that day.

3 Inserted by FA06 s55(1)(a). This section applies and has effect as respects any distributions made on or after 2 February 2006.

4 Inserted by FA06 s55(1)(b). This section applies and has effect as respects any distributions made on or after 2 February 2006.

8 Substituted by FA00 sched2(d).

9 Inserted by FA11 s26(a).

Case Law

The case of Revenue Commissioners v Wen-Plast (Research & Development) Ltd 2007 IEHC 66, considered whether the patented invention of a fire-resitant, hygienic door set, which included a fire resistant strip encased in a plastic material, 'involved radical innovation' within the meaning of section 141.

Revenue Briefings

Tax Briefing

Tax Briefing December 1999 – Issue 38 pg 18 - Patent Royalties – Income & Distributions

Cross References

From Section 141

Section 33 Method of charge and payment.

Section 76 Computation of income: application of income tax principles.

Section 140 Distributions out of profits or gains from stallion fees, stud greyhound services fees and occupation of certain woodlands.

Section 144 Distributions out of profits from trading within Shannon Airport.

Section 152 Explanation of tax credit to be annexed to interest and dividend warrants.

Section 234 Certain income derived from patent royalties.

Section 381 Right to repayment of tax by reference to losses.

Section 412 Qualification for entitlement to group relief.

Section 418 Beneficial percentage.

Section 766 Tax credit for research and development expenditure.

To Section 141

Section 144 Distributions out of profits from trading within Shannon Airport.

Section 154 Attribution of distributions to accounting periods.

Section 155 Restriction of certain reliefs in respect of distributions out of certain exempt or relieved profits.

Section 172B Dividend withholding tax on relevant distributions.
Section 434 Distributions to be taken into account and meaning of "distributable income", "investment income", "estate income", etc.
Section 472A Relief for the long-term unemployed.
Section 531B Charge to income levy.
Section 531AM Charge to universal social charge.
Section 531AS Universal social charge payable by chargeable persons (within the meaning of Part 41).
Schedule 25B List of Specified Reliefs and Method of Determining Amount of Specified Relief Used in a Tax Year

142 Distributions out of profits of certain mines

[CTA76 s81]

(1) In this section—

"*exempted income*" means income in respect of which a company has obtained relief under—

(a) the Finance (Profits of Certain Mines) (Temporary Relief from Taxation) Act, 1956, or

(b) Chapter II (Profits of Certain Mines) of Part XXV of the Income Tax Act, 1967;

"*other income*" means income of a company which is not exempted income.

(2) Where a distribution for an accounting period is made by a company wholly out of exempted income, the distribution shall not be regarded as income for any purpose of the Income Tax Acts [...][1].

(3) Where a distribution for an accounting period is made by a company in part out of exempted income and in part out of other income, the distribution shall be treated as if it consisted of 2 distributions respectively made out of exempted income and other income, and *subsection (2)* shall apply to such part of the distribution as is made out of exempted income as it applies to a distribution made wholly out of exempted income.

(4) Any distribution, including part of a distribution treated under *subsection (3)* as a distribution, made out of exempted income shall, where the recipient is a company resident in the State, be deemed for the purposes of this section to be exempted income of the company.

[...][2]

(6) *Subsections (7)* and *(8)* of *section 144* and [*subsections (8)* and *(9)* of *section 140*][3] shall apply for the purposes of this section as they apply for the purposes of those sections.

(7) In relation to any distribution [...][4], including part of a distribution treated under *subsection (3)* as a distribution, made out of exempted income, *section 152* shall apply so that the statements provided for by that section shall show, in addition to the particulars required to be given apart from this section, that the distribution is made out of exempted income.

Amendments

[1, 2, 4] Deleted by FA00 sched2.

[3] Substituted by FA00 sched2(e).

Cross References

From Section 142

Section 140 Distributions out of profits or gains from stallion fees, stud greyhound services fees and occupation of certain woodlands.

Section 144 Distributions out of profits from trading within Shannon Airport.
Section 152 Explanation of tax credit to be annexed to interest and dividend warrants.

To Section 142
Section 144 Distributions out of profits from trading within Shannon Airport.
Section 172B Dividend withholding tax on relevant distributions.
Section 434 Distributions to be taken into account and meaning of "distributable income", "investment income", "estate income", etc.
Section 531B Charge to income levy.
Section 531AM Charge to universal social charge.
Section 531AS Universal social charge payable by chargeable persons (within the meaning of Part 41).
Schedule 25B List of Specified Reliefs and Method of Determining Amount of Specified Relief Used in a Tax Year

143 Distributions out of profits from coal, gypsum and anhydrite mining operations

[CTA76 s82; FA77 s5(2) and Sch1 PtII; FA97 s37 and Sch2 par1]

(1) In this section, "*relieved income*" means the income of a company—

(a) on which income tax was paid at a reduced rate by virtue of—

(i) section 395(1) of the Income Tax Act, 1967,

(ii) section 7 or 8 of the Finance (Miscellaneous Provisions) Act, 1956, or

(iii) section 32 of the Finance Act, 1960,

(b) on which income tax was borne by deduction at a reduced rate under—

(i) section 396(1) of the Income Tax Act, 1967, or

(ii) section 9 of the Finance (Miscellaneous Provisions) Act, 1956, or

(c) which is franked investment income, [which consists of a distribution made out of relieved income][1].

[...][2]

(3) Where a distribution is made in part out of relieved income and in part out of other income, the distribution shall be treated as if it consisted of 2 distributions respectively made out of relieved income and out of other income[...][3].

(4) Any distribution, including part of a distribution treated under *subsection (3)* as a distribution, made out of relieved income shall, where the recipient is a company resident in the State, be deemed for the purposes of this section to be relieved income of the company.

[...][4]

(6) Where for a year of assessment the taxable income of an individual which is chargeable at the standard rate includes income represented by distributions made out of relieved income, the individual's liability to income tax in respect of the income represented by such distributions shall be an amount equal to the tax on that income calculated at 50 per cent of the standard rate for the year of assessment in which the distributions were made.

(7) Where for a year of assessment the taxable income of an individual which is chargeable at the higher rate includes income represented by distributions made out of relieved income, the individual's liability to income tax at the higher rate in respect of the income represented by such distributions shall be an amount equal to the tax, calculated at the higher rate for the year of assessment in which the distributions were made, on the income reduced by 50 per cent, [...][5].

[...][6]
[...][7]
(10) *Subsections (7)* and *(8)* of *section 144* and [*subsections (8)* and *(9)* of *section 140*][8] shall apply for the purposes of this section as they apply for the purposes of those sections.
(11) In relation to any distribution [...][9], including part of a distribution treated under *subsection (3)* as a distribution, made by a company out of relieved income, *section 152* shall apply so that the statements provided for by that section shall show, in addition to the particulars required to be given apart from this section, that the distribution is made out of relieved income [...][10].

Amendments

[1] Substituted by FA00 sched2(f)(i).

[2, 3, 4, 5, 6, 7, 9, 10] Deleted by FA00 sched2.

[8] Substituted by FA00 sched2(f)(ii).

Cross References

From Section 143

Section 140 Distributions out of profits or gains from stallion fees, stud greyhound services fees and occupation of certain woodlands.
Section 144 Distributions out of profits from trading within Shannon Airport.
Section 152 Explanation of tax credit to be annexed to interest and dividend warrants.

To Section 143

Section 531B Charge to income levy.
Section 531AM Charge to universal social charge.
Section 531AS Universal social charge payable by chargeable persons (within the meaning of Part 41).
Schedule 25B List of Specified Reliefs and Method of Determining Amount of Specified Relief Used in a Tax Year

144 Distributions out of profits from trading within Shannon Airport

[CTA76 s76(1), (2)(a)(ii) and (b) and (3) to (8); FA92 s35(b); FA97 s146(1) and (2), Sch9 PtI par10(1) and PtII]

(1) In this section—

"*exempted trading operations*" means trading operations which were exempted trading operations for the purposes for Part V of the Corporation Tax Act, 1976;

"*other profits*" includes a dividend or other distribution of a body corporate resident in the State, but does not include a distribution to which *subsection (3)(a)* applies.

(2) Where a distribution for an accounting period is made by a body corporate in part out of income from exempted trading operations and in part out of other profits, the distribution shall be treated as if it consists of 2 distributions respectively made out of income from exempted trading operations and out of other profits.

(3) (a) So much of any distribution as has been made out of income from exempted trading operations shall, where the recipient of that distribution is a body corporate, be deemed for the purposes of this section to be income from exempted trading operations.

[...][1]
[...][2]

(5) In relation to any distribution [...][3], including part of a distribution treated under *subsection (2)* as a distribution, made by a body corporate out of income from exempted trading operations, *section 152* shall apply to the body corporate so

that the statements provided for by that section shall show, as respects each such distribution, in addition to the particulars required to be given apart from this section, that the distribution is made out of income from exempted trading operations.

[...][4]

(7) Where a body corporate makes a distribution for an accounting period, the distribution shall be regarded for the purposes of this section as having been made out of the distributable income of that period to the extent of that income and in relation to the excess of the distribution over that income out of the most recently accumulated income.

(8) For the purposes of *subsection (7)*, the distributable income of a company for an accounting period shall be an amount determined by the formula—

$$(R - S) + T$$

[where—

[R is the amount of income of the company charged to corporation tax for the accounting period with the addition of any amount of income of the company which would be charged to corporation tax for the accounting period but for *section 231*, *232*, *233* or *234*, or section 71 of the Corporation Tax Act, 1976; and, for the purposes of this definition—

(a) the income of a company for an accounting period shall be taken to be the amount of its profits for that period on which corporation tax falls finally to be borne exclusive of the part of the profits attributable to chargeable gains, and

(b) the part referred to in *paragraph (a)* shall be taken to be the amount brought into the company's profits for that period for the purposes of corporation tax in respect of chargeable gains before any deduction for charges on income, expenses of management or other amounts which can be deducted from or set against or treated as reducing profits of more than one description,

S is the amount of the corporation tax which, before any set-off of or credit for tax, including foreign tax, and after any relief under *section 448* or *paragraph 16* or *18* of *Schedule 32*, or section 58 of the Corporation Tax Act, 1976, is chargeable for the accounting period, exclusive of the corporation tax, before any credit for foreign tax, chargeable on the part of the company's profits attributable to chargeable gains for that period; and that part shall be taken to be the amount brought into the company's profits for that period for the purposes of corporation tax in respect of chargeable gains before any deduction for charges on income, expenses of management or other amounts which can be deducted from or set against or treated as reducing profits of more than one description, and][5][6]

[T is the amount of the distributions received by the company in the accounting period which is included in its franked investment income of the accounting period with the addition of any amount received by the company in the accounting period to which *section 140(3)(a)*, *141(3)(a)*, *142(4)* or *144(3)(a)* applies.][7]

(9) [*Subsections (8)* and *(9)* of *section 140*][8] shall apply for the purposes of this section as they apply for purposes of that section.

Amendments

[1, 2, 3, 4] Deleted by FA00 sched2.

[5, 6] Substituted by FA00 sched2(g)(i).

[7] Substituted by FA03 s41(1)(c). This section applies as respects accounting periods ending on or after 6 February 2003.

[8] Substituted by FA00 sched2(g)(ii).

Cross References

From Section 144

Section 140 Distributions out of profits or gains from stallion fees, stud greyhound services fees and occupation of certain woodlands.
Section 141 Distributions out of income from patent royalties.
Section 142 Distributions out of profits of certain mines.
Section 144 Distributions out of profits from trading within Shannon Airport.
Section 152 Explanation of tax credit to be annexed to interest and dividend warrants.
Section 231 Profits or gains from stallion fees.
Section 232 Profits from occupation of certain woodlands.
Section 233 Stud greyhound service fees.
Section 234 Certain income derived from patent royalties.
Section 448 Relief from corporation tax.
Schedule 32 Transitional Provisions

To Section 144

Section 140 Distributions out of profits or gains from stallion fees, stud greyhound services fees and occupation of certain woodlands.
Section 141 Distributions out of income from patent royalties.
Section 142 Distributions out of profits of certain mines.
Section 143 Distributions out of profits from coal, gypsum and anhydrite mining operations.
Section 144 Distributions out of profits from trading within Shannon Airport.
Section 154 Attribution of distributions to accounting periods.
Section 155 Restriction of certain reliefs in respect of distributions out of certain exempt or relieved profits.

145 Distributions out of profits from export of certain goods [Repealed]

Repealed by FA00 sched2.

146 Provisions supplementary to section 145 [Repealed]

Repealed by FA00 sched2.

CHAPTER 5

Distributions Out of Certain Income of Manufacturing Companies

147 Distributions [Repealed]

Repealed by FA00 sched2.

Cross References

To Section 147

Section 154 Attribution of distributions to accounting periods.
Schedule 32 Transitional Provisions

148 Treatment of certain deductions in relation to relevant distributions [Repealed]

Repealed by FA00 sched2.

149 Dividends and other distributions at gross rate or of gross amount [Repealed]

Repealed by FA00 sched2.

150 Tax credit for recipients of certain distributions [Repealed]

Repealed by FA00 sched2.

151 Appeals [Repealed]

Repealed by FA00 sched2.

CHAPTER 6

Distributions—Supplemental

152 Explanation of tax credit to be annexed to interest and dividend warrants

[CTA76 s5 and s83(5)]

(1) Every warrant, cheque or other order drawn or made, or purporting to be drawn or made, in payment by any company of any dividend, or of any interest which is a distribution, shall have annexed to it or be accompanied by a statement in writing showing—

(a) the amount of the dividend (distinguishing a dividend or any part of it which is paid out of capital profits of the company) or interest paid, [and][1]

[…][2]

(c) the period for which that dividend or interest is paid.

[(2) Where a company fails to comply with any of the provisions of subsection (1), the company shall incur a penalty of €200 in respect of each failure, but the aggregate amount of the penalties imposed under this section on any company in respect of all such failures connected with any one distribution of dividends or interest shall not exceed €2,000.][3]

(3) (a) A company which makes a distribution (not being a distribution to which *subsection (1)* refers) shall, if the recipient so requests in writing, furnish to the recipient a statement in writing showing the amount or value of the distribution[…][4].

(b) The duty imposed by this subsection shall be enforceable at the suit or instance of the person requesting the statement.

Amendments

[1] Inserted by FA00 sched2(h).

[2, 4] Deleted by FA00 sched2.

[3] Substituted by F(No.2)A08 sched5(part2)(1)(a). The enactments specified in Schedule 5 are amended or repealed to the extent and manner specified in that Schedule and, unless the contrary is stated, shall come into effect after 24 December 2008.

Cross References

To Section 152

Section 140 Distributions out of profits or gains from stallion fees, stud greyhound services fees and occupation of certain woodlands.

Section 141 Distributions out of income from patent royalties.

Section 142 Distributions out of profits of certain mines.

Section 143 Distributions out of profits from coal, gypsum and anhydrite mining operations.
Section 144 Distributions out of profits from trading within Shannon Airport.
Section 172I Statement to be given to recipients of relevant distributions.
Section 174 Taxation of dealer's receipts on purchase of shares by issuing company or by its subsidiary.
Section 816 Taxation of shares issued in place of cash dividends.

153 Distributions to certain nonresidents

[(1) In this section—

["*qualifying non-resident person*", in relation to a distribution, means the person beneficially entitled to the distribution, being—

(a) a person, other than a company, who—

(i) is neither resident nor ordinarily resident in the State, and

(ii) is, by virtue of the law of a relevant territory, resident for the purposes of tax in the relevant territory,

or

(b) a company which is not resident in the State and—

(i) is, by virtue of the law of a relevant territory, resident for the purposes of tax in the relevant territory, but is not under the control, whether directly or indirectly, of a person or persons who is or are resident in the State,

(ii) is under the control, whether directly or indirectly, of a person or persons who, by virtue of the law of a relevant territory, is or are resident for the purposes of tax in the relevant territory and who is or are, as the case may be, not under the control, whether directly or indirectly, of a person who is, or persons who are, not so resident, or

(iii) the principal class of the shares of which, or—

(I) where the company is a 75 per cent subsidiary of another company, of that other company, or

(II) where the company is wholly-owned by 2 or more companies, of each of those companies,

is substantially and regularly traded on one or more than one recognised stock exchange in a relevant territory or territories or on such other stock exchange as may be approved of by the Minister for Finance for the purposes of this section;][1]

"*relevant territory*" means—

(a) a Member State of the European Communities other than the State, [...][2]

(b) not being such a Member State, a territory with the government of which arrangements having the force of law by virtue of [*section 826(1)*][3] [have been made, or][4]

[(c) not being a territory referred to in *paragraph (a)* or *(b)*, a territory with the government of which arrangements have been made which on completion of the procedures set out in *section 826(1)* will have the force of law;][5]

"*tax*", in relation to a relevant territory, means any tax imposed in that territory which corresponds to income tax or corporation tax in the State.

[(1A) For the purposes of *paragraph (b)(i)* of the definition of "qualifying non-resident person", "control" shall be construed in accordance with *subsections (2)* to *(6)* of *section 432* as if in *subsection (6)* of that section for "5 or fewer participators" there were substituted "persons resident in the State".][6]

(2) For the purposes of [*paragraph (b)(ii)* of the definition of "qualifying non-resident person"][7] in *subsection (1)*, "*control*" shall be construed in accordance with *subsections (2)* to *(6)* of *section 432* as if in *subsection (6)* of that section for "5 or fewer participators" there were substituted—

(a) in so far as the first mention of "*control*" in that paragraph is concerned, "persons who, by virtue of the law of a relevant territory (within the meaning assigned by *section 153*), are resident for the purposes of tax in such a relevant territory (within that meaning)", and

(b) in so far as the second mention of "*control*" in that paragraph is concerned, "persons who are not resident for the purposes of tax in a relevant territory (within that meaning)".

(3) For the purposes of [*paragraph (b)(iii)(I)* of the definition of "qualifying non-resident person"][8] in *subsection (1)*, *sections 412* to *418* shall apply as those sections would apply for the purposes of *Chapter 5* of *Part 12* if [...][9] *section 411(1)(c)* were deleted.

[(3A) For the purposes of *paragraph (b)(iii)(II)* of the definition of "qualifying non-resident person", a company (in this subsection referred to as an "aggregated 100 per cent subsidiary") shall be treated as being wholly-owned by 2 or more companies (in this subsection referred to as the "joint parent companies") if and so long as 100 per cent of its ordinary share capital is owned directly or indirectly by the joint parent companies, and for the purposes of this subsection—

(a) *subsections (2)* to *(10)* of *section 9* shall apply as those subsections apply for the purposes of that section, and

(b) *sections 412* to *418* shall apply with any necessary modifications as those sections would apply for the purposes of *Chapter 5* of *Part 12* if—

(i) *section 411(1)(c)* were deleted, and

(ii) the following subsection were substituted for *subsection (1)* of *section 412*:

"(1) Notwithstanding that at any time a company is an aggregated 100 per cent subsidiary (within the meaning assigned by *section 153(3A)*) of the joint parent companies (within the meaning so assigned), it shall not be treated at that time as such a subsidiary unless additionally at that time—

(a) the joint parent companies are between them beneficially entitled to not less than 100 per cent of any profits available for distribution to equity holders of the company, and

(b) the joint parent companies would be beneficially entitled between them to not less than 100 per cent of any assets of the company available for distribution to its equity holders on a winding-up.".][10]

(4) Where for any year of assessment the income of a person who for that year of assessment is a [...][11][qualifying non-resident person][12] includes an amount in respect of a distribution made by a company resident in the State—

(a) income tax shall not be chargeable in respect of that distribution, and

(b) the amount or value of the distribution shall be treated for the purposes of *sections 237* and *238* as not brought into charge to income tax.

[(4A) *Subsection (4)* shall not apply to a property income dividend (within the meaning of *section 705A*).][13]

(5) Where, by virtue of *section 831(5)*, Chapter 8A of Part 6 (other than *section 172K*) does not apply to a distribution made to a parent company (within the meaning of *section 831*) which is not resident in the State by its subsidiary (within the meaning of that section) which is a company resident in the State—

(a) income tax shall not be chargeable in respect of that distribution, and

(b) the amount or value of the distribution shall be treated for the purposes of *sections 237* and *238* as not brought into charge to income tax.

[(6) Where for any year of assessment the income of a person, being an individual who for that year of assessment is neither resident nor ordinarily resident in the State but is not a qualifying non-resident person, includes an amount in respect of a distribution made by a company resident in the State, then—

(a) notwithstanding *section 15(2)*, income tax shall not be chargeable in respect of that distribution at a rate in excess of the standard rate, and

(b) the amount or value of the distribution shall be treated for the purposes of *sections 237* and *238* as not brought into charge to income tax.][14][15]

Amendments

[1] Substituted by FA00 s31(a). Applies as respects distributions made on or after 6 April 2000.

[2] Deleted by F(No.2)A08 s33(b)(i). This section is deemed to have come into force and takes effect as on and from 1 January 2009.

[3] Substituted by FA07 sched2(1)(e). Has effect as on and from 2 April 2007.

[4] Substituted by F(No.2)A08 s33(b)(i). This section is deemed to have come into force and takes effect as on and from 1 January 2009.

[5] Inserted by F(No.2)A08 s33(b)(ii). This section is deemed to have come into force and takes effect as on and from 1 January 2009.

[6] Inserted by FA00 s31(b). Applies as respects distributions made on or after 6 April 2000.

[7] Substituted by FA00 s31(c). Applies as respects distributions made on or after 6 April 2000.

[8] Substituted by FA00 s31(d)(i). Applies as respects distributions made on or after 6 April 2000.

[9] Deleted by FA00 s31(d)(ii). Applies as respects distributions made on or after 6 April 2000.

[10] Inserted by FA00 s31(e). Applies as respects distributions made on or after 6 April 2000.

[11, 12] Substituted by FA00 s31(f). Applies as respects distributions made on or after 6 April 2000.

[13] Inserted by FA13 s41(b). Deemed to have come into force and takes effect on and from 1 January 2013.

[14] Inserted by FA00 s31(g). Applies as respects distributions made on or after 6 April 2000.

[15] Substituted by FA99 s28(1). This section shall apply as respects distributions made on or after the 6th day of April, 1999.

Cross References

From Section 153

Section 9 Subsidiaries.
Section 153 Distributions to certain nonresidents.
Section 172K Returns, payment and collection of dividend withholding tax.
Section 237 Annual payments payable wholly out of taxed income.
Section 238 Annual payments not payable out of taxed income.
Section 381 Right to repayment of tax by reference to losses.
Section 410 Group payments.
Section 411 Surrender of relief between members of groups and consortia.
Section 412 Qualification for entitlement to group relief.
Section 418 Beneficial percentage.
Section 432 Meaning of "associated company" and "control".
Section 826 Agreements for relief from double taxation.

Section 831 Implementation of Council Directive No. 90/435/EEC concerning the common system of taxation applicable in the case of parent companies and subsidiaries of different Member States.

To Section 153

Section 153 Distributions to certain nonresidents.

Section 712 Distributions received from Irish resident companies.

154 Attribution of distributions to accounting periods

[FA89 s25; FA92 s37; FA97 s38]

(1) (a) Notwithstanding *sections 140, 141*, [and *144*][1] but subject to *subsections (2)* and *(3)*, where a company which makes a distribution specifies, by notice in writing given to the inspector within 6 months of the end of the accounting period in which the distribution is made, the extent to which the distribution is to be treated for the purposes of *sections 140, 141*, [and *144*][2] as made for any accounting period or periods, the distribution shall be so treated for those purposes irrespective of the period of account for which it was made.

(b) A part of a distribution treated under *paragraph (a)* as made for an accounting period shall be treated for the purposes of *sections 140, 141* [and *144*][3], and [...][4] as a separate distribution.

(2) A company may specify in accordance with *subsection (1)* that only so much of a distribution, or more than one distribution, made on any day is made—

(a) for any accounting period, as does not exceed the undistributed income of the company for that accounting period on that day, and

(b) for an accounting period or accounting periods ending more than 9 years before that day, as does not exceed the amount by which the amount of the distribution or the aggregate amount of the distributions, as the case may be, exceeds the aggregate of the undistributed income of the company on that day for accounting periods ending before, but not more than 9 years before, that day.

(3) Except where a distribution made by a company is—

(a) an interim dividend paid before [1 January 2003][5], by the directors of the company, pursuant to powers conferred on them by the articles of association of the company, in respect of the profits of the accounting period in which it is paid,

(b) a distribution by virtue only of *subparagraph (ii), (iii)(I)* or *(v)* of *section 130(2)(d)*,

(c) a distribution made in respect of shares of a type referred to in *paragraph (c)* of the definition of *"preference shares"* in *section 138(1)*, or

(d) made in an accounting period in which the company ceases or commences to be within the charge to corporation tax,

the company shall not be entitled to specify in accordance with *subsection (1)* that the distribution is to be treated as made for the accounting period in which it is made.

[...][6]

[...][7]

[(6) For the purposes of this section, the amount of the undistributed income of a company for an accounting period shall be the amount determined by the formula—

$$(R - S) + T - W,$$

reduced by the amount of each distribution, or part of each distribution, made before [the day in question][8] and on or after 6 April 1989, which is to be treated under this section, or which was treated under *section 147*, as made for that accounting period,

where—

R, S and T have the same meanings respectively as in *section 144(8)*, and W is the amount of the distributions made by the company before 6 April 1989, which—

(a) were made for the accounting period,

(b) are, by virtue of *subsection (7)*, deemed to have been made for the accounting period, or

(c) would be deemed to have been made for the accounting period by virtue of *subsection (9)* of *section 140* if that subsection were treated as applying for the purposes of this section as it applies for the purpose of that section.

(7) For the purposes of this section—

(a) where the total amount of the distributions made by a company for an accounting period exceeds the amount determined by the formula—

$$(R - S) + T$$

for that accounting period (where R, S and T have the same meanings respectively as in *section 144(8)*), the excess shall be deemed for the purposes of this section to be a distribution for the immediately preceding accounting period, and

(b) where the total amount of the distributions made or deemed under *paragraph (a)* to have been made by a company for the immediately preceding accounting period referred to in *paragraph (a)* exceeds the amount determined for that accounting period in accordance with the formula mentioned in *paragraph (a)*, the excess shall be deemed to be a distribution for the immediately preceding accounting period and so on.][9]

Amendments

[1, 2, 3] Substituted by FA03 s41(1)(d)(i). This section applies as respects accounting periods ending on or after 6 February 2003.

[4] Deleted by FA00 sched2(i)(i)(II).

[5] Substituted by FA01 sched2(10).

[6, 7] Deleted by FA00 sched2.

[8] Substituted by FA03 s41(1)(d)(ii). This section applies as respects accounting periods ending on or after 6 February 2003.

[9] Substituted by FA00 sched2(i)(ii).

Cross References

From Section 154

Section 130 Matters to be treated as distributions.

Section 138 Treatment of dividends on certain preference shares.

Section 140 Distributions out of profits or gains from stallion fees, stud greyhound services fees and occupation of certain woodlands.

Section 141 Distributions out of income from patent royalties.

Section 144 Distributions out of profits from trading within Shannon Airport.

Section 147 Distributions.

155 Restriction of certain reliefs in respect of distributions out of certain exempt or relieved profits

[FA90 s34(1)(a) and (b)(ii), (2), (3), (5) and (6)]

(1) In this section, "*distribution*" has the same meaning as in the Corporation Tax Acts.

(2) (a) This section shall apply to shares in a company where any agreement, arrangement or understanding exists which could reasonably be considered to eliminate the risk that the person beneficially owning those shares—

(i) might, at or after a time specified in or implied by that agreement, arrangement or understanding, be unable to realise directly or indirectly in money or money's worth an amount so specified or implied, other than a distribution, in respect of those shares, or

(ii) might not receive an amount so specified or implied of distributions in respect of those shares.

(b) The reference in this subsection to the person beneficially owning shares shall be deemed to be a reference to both that person and any person connected with that person.

(c) For the purposes of this subsection, an amount specified or implied shall include an amount specified or implied in a foreign currency.

(3) Where any person receives a distribution in respect of shares to which this section applies and, apart from the application of this subsection to the distribution, *section 140(3)(a)*, *141(3)(a)*, [*144(3)(a)*][1] would apply to the distribution, then, notwithstanding any provision of the Tax Acts other than *subsection (4)* and for the purposes of those Acts—

(a) none of those sections shall apply to the distribution, [and][2]

[…][3]

(c) the distribution shall be treated as income chargeable to income tax or corporation tax, as the case may be, under Case IV of Schedule D.

(4) *Subsection (3)* shall not apply to a distribution received—

(a) by a company—

(i) none of the shares of which is beneficially owned by a person resident in the State, and

(ii) which, if this subsection had not been enacted, would not be chargeable to corporation tax in respect of any profits other than distributions which would be so chargeable by virtue of this section, or

(b) by a person not resident in the State.

(5) Notwithstanding *subsection (4)*, the liability to income tax or corporation tax of any person resident in the State, other than a company to which *paragraph (a)* of that subsection relates, shall be determined as if that subsection had not been enacted.

Amendments

[1] Substituted by FA03 s41(1)(e). This section applies as respects accounting periods ending on or after 6 February 2003.

[2] Inserted by FA00 sched2(k).

[3] Deleted by FA00 sched2.

Cross References

From Section 155

Section 140 Distributions out of profits or gains from stallion fees, stud greyhound services fees and occupation of certain woodlands.
Section 141 Distributions out of income from patent royalties.
Section 144 Distributions out of profits from trading within Shannon Airport.

CHAPTER 7

Franked Investment Income

156 Franked investment income and franked payments

[(1) Income of a company resident in the State which consists of a distribution made by another company resident in the State shall be referred to in the Corporation Tax Acts as "franked investment income" of the company, and the amount of the franked investment income of such a company shall be the amount or value of the distribution.

(2) A reference in the Corporation Tax Acts to a "franked payment" in relation to a company resident in the State which makes a distribution shall be construed as a reference to the amount or value of the distribution and references to any accounting or other period in which a franked payment is made are references to the period in which the distribution is made.][1]

Amendments

[1] Substituted by FA03 s41(1)(f)(i). This section applies as respects accounting periods ending on or after 6 February 2003.

Cross References

To Section 156

Section 4 Interpretation of Corporation Tax Acts.
Section 137 Disallowance of reliefs in respect of bonus issues.

157 Set-off of losses, etc. against franked investment income [Deleted]

Deleted by FA03 s41(1)(f)(ii). This section applies as respects accounting periods ending on or after 6 February 2003.

158 Set-off of loss brought forward or terminal loss against franked investment income in the case of financial concerns [Deleted]

Deleted by FA03 s41(1)(f)(ii). This section applies as respects accounting periods ending on or after 6 February 2003.

CHAPTER 8

Advance Corporation Tax

159 Liability for advance corporation tax [Deleted]

Deleted by FA03 s41(1)(g). This section applies as respects accounting periods ending on or after 6 February 2003.

Cross References

To Section 159

Section 487 Corporation tax: credit for bank levy.
Section 845B Set-off of surplus advance corporation tax.
Section 1003 Payment of tax by means of donation of heritage items.
Section 1003A Payment of tax by means of donation of heritage property to an Irish heritage trust.

160 Set-off of advance corporation tax [Deleted]

Deleted by FA03 s41(1)(g). This section applies as respects accounting periods ending on or after 6 February 2003.

Cross References

To Section 160

Schedule 30 Repeals

161 Rectification of excessive set-off of advance corporation tax [Deleted]

Deleted by FA03 s41(1)(g). This section applies as respects accounting periods ending on or after 6 February 2003.

162 Calculation of advance corporation tax where company receives distributions [Deleted]

Deleted by FA03 s41(1)(g). This section applies as respects accounting periods ending on or after 6 February 2003.

163 Tax credit recovered from company [Deleted]

Deleted by FA03 s41(1)(g). This section applies as respects accounting periods ending on or after 6 February 2003.

164 Restrictions as to payment of tax credit [Deleted]

Deleted by FA03 s41(1)(g). This section applies as respects accounting periods ending on or after 6 February 2003.

165 Group dividends [Repealed]

Repealed by FA00 sched2.

166 Surrender of advance corporation tax [Deleted]

Deleted by FA03 s41(1)(g). This section applies as respects accounting periods ending on or after 6 February 2003.

167 Change of ownership of company: calculation and treatment of advance corporation tax [Deleted]

Deleted by FA03 s41(1)(g). This section applies as respects accounting periods ending on or after 6 February 2003.

168 Distributions to certain non-resident companies [Repealed]

Repealed by FA00 sched2.

169 Non-distributing investment companies [Repealed]

Repealed by FA00 sched2.

170 Interest in respect of certain securities [Repealed]

Repealed by FA00 sched2.

171 Returns, payment and collection of advance corporation tax [Repealed]

Repealed by FA00 sched2.

172 Application of Corporation Tax Acts [Deleted]

Deleted by FA00 sched2.

Cross References

To Section 172

Section 1094 Tax clearance certificates in relation to certain licences.

Chapter 8A

Dividend Withholding Tax

172A Interpretation

[(1) (a) In this Chapter and in *Schedule 2A*—

"*American depositary receipt*" has the same meaning as in section 207 of the Finance Act, 1992;

["*approved body of persons*" has the same meaning as in *section 235*;][1]

["*approved minimum retirement fund*" has the same meaning as in *section 784C*;

"*approved retirement fund*" has the same meaning as in *section 784A*;][2]

"*auditor*", in relation to a company, means the person or persons appointed as auditor of the company for the purposes of the Companies Acts, 1963 to 1990, or under the law of the territory in which the company is incorporated and which corresponds to those Acts;

"*authorised withholding agent*", in relation to a relevant distribution, has the meaning assigned to it by *section 172G*;

["*collective investment undertaking*" means—

(i) a collective investment undertaking within the meaning of *section 734*,

(ii) an undertaking for collective investment within the meaning of *section 738*, […][3]

(iii) an investment undertaking within the meaning of *section 739B* (inserted by the Finance Act, 2000), [or][4]

[(iv) a common contractual fund within the meaning of *section 739I* (inserted by the Finance Act 2005),][5]

not being an offshore fund within the meaning of *section 743*;][6]

["*designated broker*" has the same meaning as in *section 838*;][7]

"*dividend withholding tax*", in relation to a relevant distribution, means a sum representing income tax on the amount of the relevant distribution at the standard rate in force at the time the relevant distribution is made;

["*electronic dividend voucher*" means a statement in electronic format that satisfies the requirements of *section 172I(1A)(a)*;

"*electronic number*" means a unique number on an electronic dividend voucher;][8]

"*excluded person*", in relation to a relevant distribution, has the meaning assigned to it by *section 172C(2)*;

"*intermediary*" means a person who carries on a trade which consists of or includes—

(i) the receipt of relevant distributions from a company or companies resident in the State, or

(ii) the receipt of amounts or other assets representing such distributions from another intermediary or intermediaries,

on behalf of other persons;

["*ISI Number*", in relation to a security issued by a company, means that security's unique International Securities Identification Number (ISIN) issued by the Irish Stock Exchange Limited or by an equivalent authority in a relevant territory;][9]

"*non-liable person*", in relation to a relevant distribution, means the person beneficially entitled to the relevant distribution, being an excluded person or a qualifying non-resident person;

"*pension scheme*" means an exempt approved scheme within the meaning of *section 774* or a retirement annuity contract or a trust scheme to which *section 784* or *785* applies;

["*PRSA administrator*" has the same meaning as in *section 787A*;

"*PRSA assets*" has the same meaning as in *section 787A*;][10]

"*qualifying employee share ownership trust*" means an employee share ownership trust which the Revenue Commissioners have approved of as a qualifying employee share ownership trust in accordance with *Schedule 12* and which approval has not been withdrawn;

["*qualifying fund manager*" has the same meaning as in *section 784A*;][11]

"*qualifying intermediary*", in relation to a relevant distribution, has the meaning assigned to it by *section 172E*;

"*qualifying non-resident person*", in relation to a relevant distribution, has the meaning assigned to it by *section 172D(3)*;

["*qualifying savings manager*" has the same meaning as in *section 848B* (inserted by the Finance Act, 2001);][12]

["*recipient ID code*", in relation to the recipient of a dividend, means the unique code on an electronic dividend voucher that identifies that recipient;][13]

"*relevant distribution*" means—

[(i) a distribution within the meaning of *paragraph 1* of Schedule F in *section 20(1)*, other than such a distribution made to—

(I) a Minister of the Government in his or her capacity as such a Minister,

[(IA) the National Treasury Management Agency,

(IB) a Fund investment vehicle (within the meaning of *section 37* of the *National Treasury Management Agency (Amendment) Act 2014*) of which the Minister for Finance is the sole beneficial owner,][14]

[…][15]

[…][16]][17]

[(IIIA) the Strategic Banking Corporation of Ireland or a subsidiary wholly owned by it or a subsidiary wholly owned by any such subsidiary,][18]

[(IV) the National Asset Management Agency, or a company referred to in section 616(1)(*g*), and][19]

(ii) any amount assessable and chargeable to tax under Case IV of Schedule D by virtue of *section 816*;

"*relevant person*", in relation to a relevant distribution, means—

(i) where the relevant distribution is made by a company directly to the person beneficially entitled to the distribution, the company making the relevant distribution, and

(ii) where the relevant distribution is not made by the company directly to the person beneficially entitled to the relevant distribution but is made to that person through one or more than one qualifying intermediary, the qualifying intermediary from whom the relevant distribution, or an amount or other asset representing the relevant distribution, is receivable by the person beneficially entitled to the distribution;

"*relevant territory*" means—

(i) a Member State of the European Communities other than the State, [...][20]

(ii) not being such a Member State, a territory with the government of which arrangements having the force of law by virtue of [*section 826(1)*][21] [have been made, or][22]

[(iii) not being a territory referred to in *subparagraph (i)* or *(ii)*, a territory with the government of which arrangements have been made which on completion of the procedures set out in *section 826(1)* will have the force of law;][23]

["*special portfolio investment account*" has the same meaning as in *section 838*;][24]

["*special savings incentive account*" has the same meaning as in *section 848M* (inserted by the Finance Act, 2001);][25]

"*specified person*", in relation to a relevant distribution, means the person to whom the relevant distribution is made, whether or not that person is beneficially entitled to the relevant distribution;

"*tax*", in relation to a relevant territory, means any tax imposed in that territory which corresponds to income tax or corporation tax in the State;

"*tax reference number*" has the same meaning as in *section 885*.

(b) In this Chapter and in Schedule 2A, references to the making of a relevant distribution by a company, or to a relevant distribution to be made by a company, or to the receipt of a relevant distribution from a company do not include, respectively, references to the making of a relevant distribution by a collective investment undertaking, or to a relevant distribution to be made by a collective investment undertaking, or to the receipt of a relevant distribution from a collective investment undertaking.

(2) For the purposes of this Chapter, the amount of a relevant distribution shall be an amount equal to—

(a) where the relevant distribution consists of a payment in cash, the amount of the payment,

(b) where the relevant distribution consists of an amount which is treated under *section 816* as a distribution made by a company, the amount so treated,

(c) where the relevant distribution consists of an amount which is assessable and chargeable to tax under Case IV of Schedule D by virtue of *section 816*, the amount so assessable and chargeable, and

(d) where the relevant distribution consists of a non-cash distribution, not being a relevant distribution to which *paragraph (b)* or *(c)* applies, an amount which is equal to the value of the distribution,

and a reference in this Chapter to the amount of a relevant distribution shall be construed as a reference to the amount which would be the amount of the relevant distribution if no dividend withholding tax were to be deducted from the relevant distribution.

(3) Schedule 2A shall have effect for the purposes of supplementing this Chapter.][26]

Amendments

[1, 24] Inserted by FA00 s30(1)(a)(i).

[2] Inserted by FA01 s43(1)(a)(i).

[3] Deleted by FA05 s44(a)(i).

[4] Inserted by FA05 s44(a)(ii).

[5] Inserted by FA05 s44(a)(iii).

[6, 7] Substituted by FA00 s59.

[8] Inserted by FA07 s38(1)(a)(i). Applies as respects any relevant distribution made on or after 1 February 2007.

[9] Inserted by FA07 s38(1)(a)(ii). Applies as respects any relevant distribution made on or after 1 February 2007.

[10] Inserted by FA05 s47(1)(a). This section shall apply as on and from 3 February 2005.

[11] Inserted by FA01 s43(1)(a)(ii).

[12] Inserted by FA01 s43(1)(a)(iii).

[13] Inserted by FA07 s38(1)(a)(iii). Applies as respects any relevant distribution made on or after 1 February 2007.

[14] Inserted by NTMA(A)A14 part4(2)(a).

[15] Deleted by NTMA(A)A14 part4(2)(b).

[16] Deleted by NTMA(A)A14 part4(2)(c).

[17] Substituted by the Investment of the National Pensions Reserve Fund and Miscellaneous Provisions Act 2009 s9(a). With effect from 30 March 2009 per S.I. No. 102 of 2009.

[18] Inserted by SBCoIA14 part7(1)(a). Does not apply in circumstances where the Minister does not hold all of the shares in the SBCI.

[19] Inserted by the National Asset Management Agency Act 2009 Sched 3 part 10.

[20] Deleted by F(No.2)A08 s33(c)(i). This section is deemed to have come into force and takes effect as on and from 1 January 2009.

[21] Substituted by FA07 sched2(1)(f). Has effect as on and from 2 April 2007.

[22] Substituted by F(No.2)A08 s33(c)(i). This section is deemed to have come into force and takes effect as on and from 1 January 2009.

[23] Inserted by F(No.2)A08 s33(c)(ii). This section is deemed to have come into force and takes effect as on and from 1 January 2009.

[25] Inserted by FA01 s43(1)(a)(iv).

[26] Inserted by FA99 s27(a).

Revenue Briefings

Tax Briefing

Tax Briefing June 1999 – Issue 36 pg 9 – Dividend Withholding Tax Update (on Issue 35)

Tax Briefing March 1999 – Issue 35 pg 10 – Dividend Withholding Tax

Tax Briefing September 2000 – Issue 41 pg 24 – Dividend Withholding Tax - Summary of Scheme/ Refunds

Tax Briefing July 2004 – Issue 56 pg 18 – Stapled Stock Arrangements

eBrief

eBrief No. 38/2005 – Dividend Withholding Tax Paper Returns

Revenue Information Notes

DWT Info 1 Dividend Withholding Tax – Information Leaflet

Refunds of Dividend Withholding Tax

Dividend Withholding Tax – A Guide to the Submission of Returns in Electronic Form Qualifying Intermediary Annual Return of Dividend Withholding Tax Information – a Guide to the Submission of Q.I Returns

CHY 1 – Applying for Relief from Tax on the Income and Property of Charities

Cross References

From Section 172A

Section 20 Schedule F.
Section 172C Exemption from dividend withholding tax for certain persons.
Section 172D Exemption from dividend withholding tax for certain non-resident persons.
Section 172E Qualifying intermediaries.
Section 172G Authorised withholding agent.
Section 172I Statement to be given to recipients of relevant distributions.
Section 235 Bodies established for promotion of athletic or amateur games or sports.
Section 734 Taxation of collective investment undertakings.
Section 738 Undertakings for collective investment.
Section 739B Interpretation and application.
Section 739I Common contractual funds.
Section 743 Material interest in offshore funds.
Section 774 Certain approved schemes: exemptions and reliefs.
Section 784 Retirement annuities: relief for premiums.
Section 784A Approved retirement fund.
Section 784C Approved minimum retirement fund.
Section 785 Approval of contracts for dependants or for life assurance.
Section 787A Interpretation and supplemental.
Section 816 Taxation of shares issued in place of cash dividends.
Section 826 Agreements for relief from double taxation.
Section 838 Special portfolio investment accounts.
Section 848B Interpretation.
Section 848M Taxation of gains.
Section 885 Obligation to show tax reference number on receipts.
Schedule 2A Dividend Withholding Tax
Schedule 12 Employee Share Ownership Trusts

To Section 172A

Section 172B Dividend withholding tax on relevant distributions.
Section 172D Exemption from dividend withholding tax for certain non-resident persons.
Section 242A Tax treatment of certain royalties.
Section 784A Approved retirement fund.
Section 790B "Exemption of cross-border scheme.
Section 831 Implementation of Council Directive No. 90/435/EEC concerning the common system of taxation applicable in the case of parent companies and subsidiaries of different Member States.
Section 904I Power of inspection: returns and collection of dividend withholding tax.

172B Dividend withholding tax on relevant distributions

[(1) Except where otherwise provided by this Chapter, where, on or after the 6th day of April, 1999, a company resident in the State makes a relevant distribution to a specified person—

(a) the company shall deduct out of the amount of the relevant distribution dividend withholding tax in relation to the relevant distribution,

(b) the specified person shall allow such deduction on the receipt of the residue of the relevant distribution, and

(c) the company shall be acquitted and discharged of so much money as is represented by the deduction as if that amount of money had actually been paid to the specified person.

(2) Except where otherwise provided by this Chapter, where, at any time on or after the 6th day of April, 1999, a company resident in the State makes a relevant distribution to a specified person and the relevant distribution consists of an amount referred to in *paragraph (b)* or *(c)* of *section 172A(2)* (being an amount equal to the amount which the specified person would have received if that person had received the relevant distribution in cash instead of in the form of additional share capital of the company), *subsection (1)* shall not apply, but—

(a) the company shall reduce the amount of the additional share capital to be issued to the specified person by such amount as will secure that the value at that time of the additional share capital issued to the specified person does not exceed an amount equal to the amount which the person would have received, after deduction of dividend withholding tax, if the person had received the relevant distribution in cash instead of in the form of additional share capital of the company,

(b) the specified person shall allow such reduction on the receipt of the residue of the additional share capital,

(c) the company shall be acquitted and discharged of so much money as is represented by the reduction in the value of the additional share capital as if that amount of money had actually been paid to the specified person,

(d) the company shall be liable to pay to the Collector-General an amount (which shall be treated for the purposes of this Chapter as if it were a deduction of dividend withholding tax in relation to the relevant distribution) equal to the dividend withholding tax which, but for this subsection, would have been required to be deducted from the relevant distribution, and

(e) the company shall be liable to pay that amount in the same manner in all respects as if it were the dividend withholding tax which, but for this subsection, would have been required to be deducted from the relevant distribution.

(3) Except where otherwise provided by this Chapter, where, on or after the 6th day of April, 1999, a company resident in the State makes a relevant distribution to a specified person and the relevant distribution consists of a non-cash distribution, not being a relevant distribution to which *subsection (2)* applies, *subsection (1)* shall not apply, but the company—

(a) shall be liable to pay to the Collector-General an amount (which shall be treated for the purposes of this Chapter as if it were a deduction of dividend withholding tax in relation to the relevant distribution) equal to the dividend withholding tax which, but for this subsection, would have been required to be deducted from the amount of the relevant distribution,

(b) shall be liable to pay that amount in the same manner in all respects as if it were the dividend withholding tax which, but for this subsection, would have been required to be deducted from the relevant distribution, and

(c) shall be entitled to recover a sum equal to that amount from the specified person as a simple contract debt in any court of competent jurisdiction.

(4) A company resident in the State shall treat every relevant distribution to be made by it on or after the 6th day of April, 1999, to a specified person as a distribution to which this section applies, but, where the company has satisfied itself that a relevant distribution to be made by it to a specified person is not, by virtue of the following provisions of this Chapter, a distribution to which this section applies, the company shall, subject to those provisions, be entitled to so treat relevant distributions to be made by it to the specified person until such time as it is in possession of information which can reasonably be taken to indicate that a relevant distribution to be made to the specified person is or may be a relevant distribution to which this section applies.

[(4A) (a) A company resident in the State shall keep and retain for the longer of the following periods—

(i) a period of 6 years, or

(ii) a period which, in relation to the relevant distributions in respect of which the declaration or notification is made or, as the case may be, given, ends not earlier than 3 years after the date on which the company has ceased to make relevant distributions to the person who made the declaration or, as the case may be, gave the notification to the company,

all declarations (and accompanying certificates) and notifications (not being a notice given to the company by the Revenue Commissioners) which are made or, as the case may be, given to the company in accordance with this Chapter and *Schedule 2A*.

(b) A company resident in the State shall, on being so required by notice in writing given to the company by the Revenue Commissioners, make available to the Commissioners, within the time specified in the notice—

(i) all declarations, certificates or notifications referred to in *paragraph (a)* which have been made or, as the case may be, given to the company, or

(ii) such class or classes of such declarations, certificates or notifications as may be specified in the notice.

(c) The Revenue Commissioners may examine or take extracts from or copies of any declarations, certificates or notifications made available to the Commissioners under *paragraph (b)*.][1]

(5) The provisions of the Tax Acts relating to the computation of profits or gains shall not be affected by the deduction of dividend withholding tax in relation to relevant distributions in accordance with this section and, accordingly, the amount of such relevant distributions shall, subject to *section 129*, be taken into account in computing for tax purposes the profits or gains of persons beneficially entitled to such distributions.

[(6) This section shall not apply to a relevant distribution where *section 831(5)* applies in relation to that distribution.][2]

[(7) This section shall not apply where a relevant distribution is made by a company resident in the State and that distribution is—

(a) a distribution made out of exempt profits within the meaning of *section 140*,

(b) a distribution made out of disregarded income within the meaning of *section 141* and to which *subsection (3)(a)* of that section applies, or

(c) a distribution made out of exempted income within the meaning of *section 142*.][3]

[(8) This section shall not apply where a relevant distribution is made by a company resident in the State to another company so resident and the company making the relevant distribution is a 51 per cent subsidiary of that other company.][4][5]

Amendments

[1] Inserted by FA00 s30(1)(b)(i).

[2] Substituted by FA00 s30(1)(b)(ii).

[3] Inserted by FA00 s30(1)(b)(iii).

[4] Inserted by FA01 s43(1)(b).

[5] Inserted by FA99 s27(a).

Cross References

From Section 172B

Section 129 Irish resident company distributions not generally chargeable to corporation tax.

Section 140 Distributions out of profits or gains from stallion fees, stud greyhound services fees and occupation of certain woodlands.

Section 141 Distributions out of income from patent royalties.

Section 142 Distributions out of profits of certain mines.

Section 172A Interpretation.

Section 831 Implementation of Council Directive No. 90/435/EEC concerning the common system of taxation applicable in the case of parent companies and subsidiaries of different Member States.

Schedule 2A Dividend Withholding Tax

To Section 172B

Section 172C Exemption from dividend withholding tax for certain persons.

Section 172D Exemption from dividend withholding tax for certain non-resident persons.

Section 172E Qualifying intermediaries.

Section 172F Obligations of qualifying intermediary in relation to relevant distributions.

Section 172G Authorised withholding agent.

Section 172H Obligations of authorised withholding agent in relation to relevant distributions.

Section 172K Returns, payment and collection of dividend withholding tax.

Section 1078 Revenue offences.

172C Exemption from dividend withholding tax for certain persons

[(1) *Section 172B* shall not apply where a company resident in the State makes a relevant distribution to an excluded person.

(2) For the purposes of this Chapter, a person shall be an excluded person in relation to a relevant distribution if the person is beneficially entitled to the relevant distribution and is—

(a) a company resident in the State which has made a declaration to the relevant person in relation to the relevant distribution in accordance with *paragraph 3* of *Schedule 2A*[, but this paragraph is without prejudice to the operation of *section 172B(8)*][1],

(b) a pension scheme which has made a declaration to the relevant person in relation to the relevant distribution in accordance with *paragraph 4* of *Schedule 2A*,

[(ba) a qualifying fund manager or a qualifying savings manager who—

(i) is receiving the relevant distribution as income arising in respect of assets held—

(I) in the case of a qualifying fund manager, in an approved retirement fund or an approved minimum retirement fund, and

(II) in the case of a qualifying savings manager, in a special savings incentive account,

and

(ii) has made a declaration to the relevant person in relation to the relevant distribution in accordance with *paragraph 4A* of *Schedule 2A*,][2]

[(bb) a PRSA administrator who is receiving the relevant distribution as income arising in respect of PRSA assets, and has made a declaration to the relevant person in relation to the relevant distribution in accordance with *paragraph 10* of *Schedule 2A*,][3]

(c) a qualifying employee share ownership trust which has made a declaration to the relevant person in relation to the relevant distribution in accordance with *paragraph 5* of *Schedule 2A*,

(d) a collective investment undertaking which has made a declaration to the relevant person in relation to the relevant distribution in accordance with *paragraph 6* of *Schedule 2A*, [...][4]

[(da) a person who—

(i) is entitled to exemption from income tax under Schedule F in respect of the relevant distribution by virtue of *section 189(2)*, *subsection (2)* or *(3)(b)* of *section 189A* or *section 192(2)*, and

(ii) has made a declaration to the relevant person in relation to the relevant distribution in accordance with *paragraph 6A* of Schedule 2A,][5]

[(db) a unit trust to which *section 731(5)(a)* applies and which has made a declaration to the relevant person in relation to the relevant distribution in accordance with *paragraph 11* of Schedule 2A,][6]

(e) a person who—

(i) is entitled to exemption from income tax under Schedule F in respect of the relevant distribution by virtue of *section 207(1)(b)*, and

(ii) has made a declaration to the relevant person in relation to the relevant distribution in accordance with *paragraph 7* of [Schedule 2A,][7]

[(f) an approved body of persons which—

(i) is entitled to exemption from income tax under Schedule F in respect of the relevant distribution by virtue of *section 235(2)*, and

(ii) has made a declaration to the relevant person in relation to the relevant distribution in accordance with *paragraph 7A* of *Schedule 2A*,

or

(g) a designated broker who—

(i) is receiving the relevant distribution as all or part of the relevant income or gains (within the meaning of *section 838*) of a special portfolio investment account, and

(ii) has made a declaration to the relevant person in relation to the relevant distribution in accordance with *paragraph 7B* of *Schedule 2A*.][8]

[(3) For the purposes of *subsection (2)* and *Schedule 2A*—

(a) a collective investment undertaking which receives a relevant distribution, [...][9]

(b) a designated broker who receives a relevant distribution as all or part of the relevant income or gains (within the meaning of *section 838*) of a special portfolio investment account,

[(c) a qualifying fund manager or a qualifying savings manager who receives a relevant distribution as income arising in respect of assets held—

(i) in the case of a qualifying fund manager, in an approved retirement fund or an approved minimum retirement fund, and

(ii) in the case of a qualifying savings manager, in a special savings incentive account,

and

[(ca) a PRSA administrator who receives a relevant distribution as income arising in respect of PRSA assets,

(cb) a unit trust to which *section 731(5)(a)* applies which receives a relevant distribution in relation to units in that unit trust,][10]

(d) the trustees of a qualifying trust (within the meaning of *section 189A*) who receive a relevant distribution as income arising in respect of the trust funds (within the meaning of that section),][11]

shall be treated as being beneficially entitled to the relevant distribution.][12]][13]

Amendments

[1] Inserted by FA01 s43(1)(c)(i)(I).

[2] Inserted by FA01 s43(1)(c)(i)(II).

[3] Inserted by FA05 s47(1)(b)(i)(I). This section shall apply as on and from 3 February 2005.

[4, 12] Deleted by FA00 s30(1)(c)(i)(I).

[5] Inserted by FA01 s43(1)(c)(i)(III).

[6] Inserted by FA05 s47(1)(b)(i)(II). This section shall apply as on and from 3 February 2005.

[7] Substituted by FA00 s30(1)(c)(i)(I).

[8] Inserted by FA00 s30(1)(c)(i)(II).

[9] Deleted by FA01 s43(1)(c)(ii)(I).

[10] Inserted by FA05 s47(1)(b)(ii). This section shall apply as on and from 3 February 2005.

[11] Inserted by FA01 s43(1)(c)(ii)(II).

[13] Inserted by FA99 s27(a).

Cross References

From Section 172C

Section 20 Schedule F.
Section 172B Dividend withholding tax on relevant distributions.
Section 189 Payments in respect of personal injuries.
Section 189A Special trusts for permanently incapacitated individuals.
Section 192 Payments in respect of thalidomide children.
Section 207 Rents of properties belonging to hospitals and other charities.
Section 235 Bodies established for promotion of athletic or amateur games or sports.
Section 731 Chargeable gains accruing to unit trusts.
Section 838 Special portfolio investment accounts.
Schedule 2A Dividend Withholding Tax

To Section 172C

Section 172A Interpretation.
Section 172F Obligations of qualifying intermediary in relation to relevant distributions.
Schedule 2A Dividend Withholding Tax

172D Exemption from dividend withholding tax for certain non-resident persons

[...][1]

(2) *Section 172B* shall not apply where, on or after the 6th day of April, 2000, a company resident in the State makes a relevant distribution to a qualifying non-resident person.

(3) For the purposes of this Chapter, a person shall be a qualifying non-resident person in relation to a relevant distribution if the person is beneficially entitled to the relevant distribution and is—

(a) a person, not being a company, who—

(i) is neither resident nor ordinarily resident in the State,

(ii) is, by virtue of the law of a relevant territory, resident for the purposes of tax in the relevant territory, and

(iii) has made a declaration to the relevant person in relation to the relevant distribution in accordance with *paragraph 8* of *Schedule 2A* and in relation to which declaration the certificate referred to in *subparagraph (f)* of that paragraph is a current certificate (within the meaning of *paragraph 2* of that Schedule) at the time of the making of the relevant distribution,

or

[(b) a company which is not resident in the State and—

(i) is, by virtue of the law of a relevant territory, resident for the purposes of tax in the relevant territory, but is not under the control, whether directly or indirectly, of a person or persons who is or are resident in the State,

(ii) is under the control, whether directly or indirectly, of a person or persons who, by virtue of the law of a relevant territory, is or are resident for the purposes of tax in the relevant territory and who is or are, as the case may be, not under the control, whether directly or indirectly, of a person who is, or persons who are, not so resident, or

(iii) the principal class of the shares of which, or—

(I) where the company is a 75 per cent subsidiary of another company, of that other company, or

(II) where the company is wholly-owned by 2 or more companies, of each of those companies,

[is substantially and regularly traded on a stock exchange in the State, on][2] one or more than one recognised stock exchange in a relevant territory or territories or on such other stock exchange as may be approved of by the Minister for Finance for the purposes of this Chapter,

and which has made a declaration to the relevant person in relation to the relevant distribution in accordance with *paragraph 9* of *Schedule 2A* and [where the declaration made is a current declaration (within the meaning of *paragraph 2A* of that Schedule)][3] at the time of the making of the relevant distribution.][4]

[(3A) For the purposes of *subsection (3)(b)(i)*, "*control*" shall be construed in accordance with *subsections (2)* to *(6)* of *section 432* as if in *subsection (6)* of that section for "5 or fewer participators" there were substituted "persons resident in the State".][5]

[(3B) *Subsections (2)* and *(3)* shall not apply to a property income dividend (within the meaning of *section 705A*).][6]

(4) For the purposes of [*subsection (3)(b)(ii)*][7], "control" shall be construed in accordance with *subsections (2)* to *(6)* of *section 432* as if in *subsection (6)* of that section for "5 or fewer participators" there were substituted—

(a) in so far as the first mention of "control" in [*subsection (3)(b)(ii)*][8] is concerned, "persons who, by virtue of the law of a relevant territory (within the meaning assigned by *section 172A*), are resident for the purposes of tax in such a relevant territory (within that meaning)", and

(b) in so far as the second mention of "control" in [*subsection (3)(b)(ii)*][9] is concerned, "persons who are not resident for the purposes of tax in a relevant territory (within that meaning)".

(5) For the purposes of [*subsection (3)(b)(iii)(I)*][10], *sections 412* to *418* shall apply as those sections would apply for the purposes of *Chapter 5* of *Part 12* if […][11] *section 411(1)(c)* were deleted.

[(6) For the purposes of *subsection (3)(b)(iii)(II)*, a company (in this subsection referred to as an "aggregated 100 per cent subsidiary") shall be treated as being wholly-owned by 2 or more companies (in this subsection referred to as the "joint parent companies") if and so long as 100 per cent of its ordinary share capital is owned directly or indirectly by the joint parent companies, and for the purposes of this subsection—

(a) *subsections (2)* to *(10)* of *section 9* shall apply as those subsections apply for the purposes of that section, and

(b) *sections 412* to *418* shall apply with any necessary modifications as those sections would apply for the purposes of *Chapter 5* of *Part 12*—

(i) if *section 411(1)(c)* were deleted, and

(ii) if the following subsection were substituted for subsection (1) of *section 412*:

"(1) Notwithstanding that at any time a company is an aggregated 100 per cent subsidiary (within the meaning assigned by *section 172D(6)*) of the joint parent companies (within the meaning assigned by that section), it shall not be treated at that time as such a subsidiary unless additionally at that time—

(a) the joint parent companies are between them beneficially entitled to not less than 100 per cent of any profits available for distribution to equity holders of the company, and

(b) the joint parent companies would be beneficially entitled between them to not less than 100 per cent of any assets of the company available for distribution to its equity holders on a winding-up.".][12]][13]

Amendments

[1] Deleted by FA01 s43(1)(d).

[2] Substituted by FA07 s38(1)(b). Applies as respects any relevant distribution made on or after 1 February 2007.

[3] Substituted by FA10 s33(1)(a). Has effect as on and from 3 April 2010.

[4] Substituted by FA00 s30(1)(d)(i).

[5] Inserted by FA00 s30(1)(d)(ii).

[6] Inserted by FA13 s41(b). Deemed to have come into force and takes effect on and from 1 January 2013.

[7, 8, 9] Substituted by FA00 s30(1)(d)(iii).

[10] Substituted by FA00 s30(1)(d)(iv)(I).

[11] Deleted by FA00 s30(1)(d)(iv)(II).

[12] Inserted by FA00 s30(1)(d)(v).

[13] Inserted by FA99 s27(a).

Revenue Briefings

eBrief

eBrief No. 26/2010 – Dividend Withholding Tax – Self-Certification for Non-Resident Companies

Cross References

From Section 172D

Section 9 Subsidiaries.
Section 172A Interpretation.
Section 172B Dividend withholding tax on relevant distributions.
Section 381 Right to repayment of tax by reference to losses.
Section 410 Group payments.
Section 411 Surrender of relief between members of groups and consortia.
Section 412 Qualification for entitlement to group relief.
Section 418 Beneficial percentage.
Section 432 Meaning of "associated company" and "control".
Schedule 2A Dividend Withholding Tax

To Section 172D

Section 172A Interpretation.
Section 172F Obligations of qualifying intermediary in relation to relevant distributions.
Schedule 2A Dividend Withholding Tax

172E Qualifying intermediaries

[(1) Subject to *section 172F(6)*, *section 172B* shall not apply where a company resident in the State makes a relevant distribution through one or more than one qualifying intermediary for the benefit of a person beneficially entitled to the relevant distribution who is a non-liable person in relation to the relevant distribution.

(2) For the purposes of this Chapter, a person shall be a qualifying intermediary in relation to relevant distributions to be made to the person by a company resident in the State, and in relation to amounts or other assets representing such distributions to be paid or given to the person by another qualifying intermediary, if the person is an intermediary who—

(a) is resident in the State or who, by virtue of the law of a relevant territory, is resident for the purposes of tax in the relevant territory,

(b) has entered into a qualifying intermediary agreement with the Revenue Commissioners, and

(c) has been authorised by the Revenue Commissioners, by way of notice in writing, to be a qualifying intermediary in relation to relevant distributions to be made to the person by companies resident in the State, and in relation to amounts or other assets representing such distributions to be paid or given to the person by another qualifying intermediary, for the benefit of other persons who are beneficially entitled to the relevant distributions, which authorisation has not been revoked under *subsection (6)*.

(3) A qualifying intermediary agreement shall be an agreement entered into between the Revenue Commissioners and an intermediary under the terms of which the intermediary undertakes—

[(a) to accept, and to retain for the longer of the following periods—

(i) a period of 6 years, or

(ii) a period which, in relation to the relevant distributions in respect of which the declaration or notification is made or, as the case may be, given, ends not earlier than 3 years after the date on which the intermediary has ceased to receive relevant distributions on behalf of the person who made the declaration or, as the case may be, gave the notification to the intermediary,

all declarations (and accompanying certificates) and notifications (not being a notice given to the intermediary by the Revenue Commissioners) which are made or, as the case may be, given to the intermediary in accordance with this Chapter and Schedule 2A,

(b) on being so required by notice in writing given to the intermediary by the Revenue Commissioners, to make available to the Commissioners, within the time specified in the notice—

(i) all declarations, certificates or notifications referred to in *paragraph (a)* which have been made or, as the case may be, given to the intermediary, or

(ii) such class or classes of such declarations, certificates or notifications as may be specified in the notice,][1]

(c) to inform the Revenue Commissioners if the intermediary has reasonable grounds to believe that any such declaration or notification made or given by any person was not, or may not have been, a true and correct declaration or notification at the time of the making of the declaration or the giving of the notification, as the case may be,

(d) to inform the Revenue Commissioners if the intermediary has at any time reasonable grounds to believe that any such declaration made by any person would not, or might not, be a true and correct declaration if made at that time,

(e) to operate the provisions of *section 172F* in a correct and efficient manner and provide to the Revenue Commissioners the return referred to in *subsection (7)* of that section within the time specified in that behalf in *subsection (8)* of that section,

[(f) to provide to the Revenue Commissioners, not later than 3 months after the end of the first year of the operation of the agreement by the intermediary, a report on the intermediary's compliance with the agreement in that year, which report shall be signed by—

(i) if the intermediary is a company, the auditor of the company, or

(ii) if the intermediary is not a company, a person who, if the intermediary were a company, would be qualified to be appointed auditor of the company,

and thereafter, on being required by notice in writing given to the intermediary by the Revenue Commissioners, to provide to the Commissioners, within the time specified in the notice, a similar report in relation to such other period of the operation of the agreement by the intermediary as may be specified in the notice,][2]

(i) if the intermediary is a company, the auditor of the company, or

(ii) if the intermediary is not a company, a person who, if the intermediary were a company, would be qualified to be appointed auditor of the company,

(g) if required by the Revenue Commissioners, to give a bond or guarantee to the Revenue Commissioners which is sufficient to indemnify the Commissioners against any loss arising by virtue of the fraud or negligence of the intermediary in relation to the operation by the intermediary of the agreement and the provisions of this Chapter,

(h) in the case where the intermediary is a depositary bank holding shares in trust for, or on behalf of, the holders of American depositary receipts—

(i) if authorised to do so by the Revenue Commissioners, to operate the provisions of *subsection (3)(d)* of *section 172F*, and

(ii) to comply with any conditions in relation to such operation as may be specified in the agreement,

and

(i) to allow for the verification by the Revenue Commissioners of the intermediary's compliance with the agreement and the provisions of this Chapter in any other manner considered necessary by the Commissioners.

[(3A) The Revenue Commissioners may examine or take extracts from or copies of any declarations, certificates or notifications made available to the Commissioners under *subsection (3)(b)*.][3]

(4) The Revenue Commissioners shall not authorise an intermediary to be a qualifying intermediary unless the intermediary—

(a) is a company which holds a licence granted under section 9 of the Central Bank Act, 1971, or a person who holds a licence or other similar authorisation under the law of any relevant territory which corresponds to that section,

(b) is a person who is wholly owned by a company or person referred to in *paragraph (a)*,

(c) is a member firm of the Irish Stock Exchange Limited or of a recognised stock exchange in a relevant territory, or

(d) is in the opinion of the Revenue Commissioners a person suitable to be a qualifying intermediary for the purposes of this Chapter.

(5) The Revenue Commissioners shall maintain a list of intermediaries who have been authorised by the Commissioners to be qualifying intermediaries for the purposes of this Chapter and whose authorisations have not been revoked under *subsection (6)*, and, notwithstanding any obligations as to secrecy or other restriction upon disclosure of information imposed by or under any statute or otherwise, the Revenue Commissioners may make available to any person the name and address of any such qualifying intermediary.

(6) Where, at any time after the Revenue Commissioners have authorised an intermediary to be a qualifying intermediary for the purposes of this Chapter, the Commissioners are satisfied that the intermediary—

(a) has failed to comply with the agreement referred to in *subsection (3)* or the provisions of this Chapter, or

(b) is otherwise unsuitable to be a qualifying intermediary,

they may, by notice in writing served by registered post on the intermediary, revoke the authorisation with effect from such date as may be specified in the notice.

(7) Notice of a revocation under *subsection (6)* shall be published as soon as may be in *Iris Oifigiúil.*

[(8) Without prejudice to the operation of *subsection (6)*, the authorisation by the Revenue Commissioners of an intermediary as a qualifying intermediary for the purposes of this Chapter shall cease to have effect on the day before the seventh anniversary of the date from which such authorisation applied; but this shall not prevent—

(a) the intermediary and the Revenue Commissioners from agreeing to renew the qualifying intermediary agreement entered into between them in accordance with *subsection (3)* or to enter into a further such agreement, and

(b) a further authorisation by the Revenue Commissioners of the intermediary as a qualifying intermediary for the purposes of this Chapter.][4]][5]

Amendments

[1] Substituted by FA00 s30(1)(e)(i)(I).

[2] Substituted by FA00 s30(1)(e)(i)(II).

[3] Inserted by FA00 s30(1)(e)(ii).

[4] Inserted by FA00 s30(1)(e)(iii).

[5] Inserted by FA99 s27(a).

Cross References

From Section 172E

Section 172B Dividend withholding tax on relevant distributions.

Section 172F Obligations of qualifying intermediary in relation to relevant distributions.

To Section 172E

Section 172A Interpretation.

Section 172F Obligations of qualifying intermediary in relation to relevant distributions.

Schedule 2A Dividend Withholding Tax

172F Obligations of qualifying intermediary in relation to relevant distributions

[(1) A qualifying intermediary which is to receive on behalf of other persons—

(a) any relevant distributions to be made by any company resident in the State, or

(b) from another qualifying intermediary amounts or other assets (in this section referred to as "*payments*") representing such distributions,

shall create and maintain, in relation to such distributions and payments, 2 separate and distinct categories to be known, respectively, as the "*Exempt Fund*" and the "*Liable Fund*", and the qualifying intermediary shall notify that company or that other qualifying intermediary, as the case may be, by way of notice in writing, whether the relevant distributions to be made to it by that company, or, as the case may be, the payments representing such distributions to be made to it by that other qualifying intermediary, are to be received by it for the benefit of a person included in the Exempt Fund or a person included in the Liable Fund.

(2) Subject to *subsections (3)* and *(5)*, a qualifying intermediary shall include in its Exempt Fund in relation to such distributions and payments only those persons on whose behalf it is to receive such distributions or payments, being—

(a) persons beneficially entitled to such distributions or payments who are non-liable persons in relation to such distributions, and

(b) any further qualifying intermediary to whom such distributions or payments (or amounts or other assets representing such distributions or payments) are to be given by the qualifying intermediary and are to be received by that further qualifying intermediary for the benefit of persons included in that further qualifying intermediary's Exempt Fund.

(3) (a) A qualifying intermediary shall not include a person referred to in *subsection (2)(a)* in its Exempt Fund unless it has received from that person—

(i) a declaration made by that person in accordance with *section 172C(2)*, or

[(ii) a declaration made by that person in accordance with *section 172D(3)*—

(I) in relation to which the certificate referred to in *paragraph 8(f)* of *Schedule 2A* is a current certificate (within the meaning of *paragraph 2* of that Schedule), or

(II) which is a current declaration (within the meaning of *paragraph 2A* of *Schedule 2A*),][1]

(b) A qualifying intermediary shall not include a further qualifying intermediary referred to in *subsection (2)(b)* in its Exempt Fund unless the qualifying intermediary has received from that further qualifying intermediary a notification in writing given to the qualifying intermediary by that further qualifying intermediary in accordance with *subsection (1)* to the effect that the relevant distributions made by the company resident in the State, or, as the case may be, the payments representing such distributions, which are to be given by the qualifying intermediary to that further qualifying intermediary are to be received by that further qualifying intermediary for the benefit of a person included in that further qualifying intermediary's Exempt Fund.

(c) Notwithstanding *paragraphs (a)* and *(b)*, a qualifying intermediary, being a depositary bank holding shares in trust for, or on behalf of, the holders of American depositary receipts, shall, if provided for in the qualifying intermediary agreement and subject to any conditions specified in that agreement, operate the provisions of *paragraph (d)*.

(d) Where this paragraph applies in relation to a qualifying intermediary, the qualifying intermediary shall include in its Exempt Fund—

(i) any person on whose behalf it is to receive any relevant distributions to be made by a company resident in the State, or on whose behalf it is to receive from another qualifying intermediary payments representing such distributions, being a person who is beneficially entitled to such distributions or payments, who is the holder of an American depositary receipt and whose address on the qualifying intermediary's register of depositary receipts is located in the United States of America, and

(ii) any specified intermediary to which such distributions or payments (or amounts or other assets representing such distributions or payments) are to be given by the qualifying intermediary and are to be received by that specified intermediary for the benefit of—

(I) persons who are beneficially entitled to such distributions or payments, who are the holders of American depositary receipts, whose address on that specified intermediary's register of depositary receipts is located in the United States of America, and who in accordance with *paragraph (e)(iii)(I)* are to be included in that specified intermediary's Exempt Fund, or

(II) any further specified intermediary to which such distributions or payments (or amounts or other assets representing such distributions or payments) are to be given by the first-mentioned specified intermediary and are to be received by that further specified intermediary for the benefit of persons who in accordance with *clauses (I)* and *(II)* of *paragraph (e)(iii)* are to be included in that further specified intermediary's Exempt Fund.

(e) [For the purposes of this section, but subject to *paragraphs (g)* and *(h)*][2], an intermediary shall be treated as a specified intermediary if the intermediary—

(i) is not a qualifying intermediary but is a person referred to in *paragraph (a)*, *(b)*, *(c)* or *(d)* of *section 172E(4)* who is operating as an intermediary in an establishment situated in the United States of America,

(ii) creates and maintains, in relation to such distributions or payments (or amounts or other assets representing such distributions or payments) to be received by it on behalf of other persons from a qualifying intermediary or another specified intermediary, an Exempt Fund and a Liable Fund in accordance with *subsections (1)* and *(5)*, but subject to *subparagraphs (iii)* and *(iv)*, as if it were a qualifying intermediary,

(iii) includes in its Exempt Fund in relation to such distributions or payments (or amounts or other assets representing such distributions or payments), only—

(I) those persons who are beneficially entitled to such distributions or payments, being persons who are the holders of American depositary receipts and whose address on its register of depositary receipts is located in the United States of America, and

(II) any further specified intermediary to which such distributions or payments (or amounts or other assets representing such distributions or payments) are to be given by the intermediary and are to be received by that further specified intermediary for the benefit of persons who in accordance with this subparagraph are to be included in that further specified intermediary's Exempt Fund,

(iv) includes in its Liable Fund in relation to such distributions or payments (or amounts or other assets representing such distributions or payments), all other persons (being persons who are the holders of American depositary receipts) on whose behalf such distributions or payments (or amounts or other assets representing such distributions or payments) are to be received by it from a qualifying intermediary or a further specified intermediary, other than those persons included in its Exempt Fund,

(v) notifies, [by way of notice in writing or in electronic format][3], the qualifying intermediary or, as the case may be, the further specified intermediary from whom it is to receive, on behalf of other persons, such distributions or payments (or amounts or other assets representing such distributions or payments), whether such distributions or payments (or amounts or other assets representing such distributions or payments) are to be so received by it for the benefit of persons included in its Exempt Fund or persons included in its [Liable Fund, and][4],

[(vi) enters into an agreement with the qualifying intermediary or further specified intermediary, as the case may be, under the terms of which it agrees that if and when required to comply with *subsection (7A)* it will do so.][5]

(f) Where, by virtue of the preceding provisions of this subsection, any person, being a person who, apart from this paragraph, would not be a non-liable person in relation to the distributions or payments (or amounts or other assets representing such distributions or payments) to be received on that person's behalf by a qualifying intermediary or a specified intermediary, is included in the Exempt Fund of the qualifying intermediary or, as the case may be, of the specified intermediary, that person shall, notwithstanding any other provision of this Chapter, be treated as a non-liable person in relation to such distributions.

[(g) Notwithstanding *paragraph (e)*, where the Revenue Commissioners are satisfied that an intermediary, being a specified intermediary or other specified intermediary referred to in *subsection (7A)*, has failed to comply with that subsection—

(i) the Commissioners may, by notice in writing given to the intermediary, notify it that it shall cease to be treated as a specified intermediary for the purposes of this section from such date as may be specified in the notice, and

(ii) notwithstanding any obligations as to secrecy or other restriction upon disclosure of information imposed by or under statute or otherwise, the Commissioners may make available to any qualifying intermediary (being a depositary bank holding shares in trust for, or on behalf of, the holders of American depositary receipts) or specified intermediary a copy of such notice.

(h) Where subsequently the Revenue Commissioners are satisfied that the intermediary has furnished the information required under *subsection (7A)* and will in future comply with that subsection if and when requested to do so, the Commissioners may, by further notice in writing given to the intermediary, revoke the notice given to the intermediary under *paragraph (g)* from such date as may be specified in the further notice, and a copy of that further notice shall be given to any person to whom a copy of the notice under *paragraph (g)* was given.][6]

(4) Subject to *subsection (5)*, a qualifying intermediary shall include in its Liable Fund in relation to relevant distributions to be made to it by a company resident in the State and payments representing such distributions to be made to it by another

qualifying intermediary all persons on whose behalf the qualifying intermediary is to receive such distributions or payments, other than those persons included in its Exempt Fund in relation to such distributions and payments.

(5) A qualifying intermediary shall update its Exempt Fund and Liable Fund, in relation to relevant distributions to be made to it by a company resident in the State and payments representing such distributions to be made to it by another qualifying intermediary, as often as may be necessary to ensure that the provisions of *section 172E(1)* and *subsections (2)* to *(4)* of this section are complied with, and shall notify the company or, as the case may be, that other qualifying intermediary, by way of notice in writing, of all such updates.

(6) Where at any time a company resident in the State makes a relevant distribution to a qualifying intermediary and, apart from this subsection, the relevant distribution would be treated as being made to the qualifying intermediary for the benefit of a person beneficially entitled to the relevant distribution who is a non-liable person in relation to that distribution, the distribution shall be treated as if it were not made to the qualifying intermediary for the benefit of such a person unless, at or before that time, the qualifying intermediary has notified the company in accordance with *subsection (1)* or *(5)*, as the case may be, that the relevant distribution is to be received by the qualifying intermediary for the benefit of a person included in the qualifying intermediary's Exempt Fund in relation to relevant distributions to be made to the qualifying intermediary by the company, and accordingly, in the absence of such a notification, *section 172B* shall apply in relation to the relevant distribution.

[(7) (a) A qualifying intermediary shall, on being so required by notice in writing given to the qualifying intermediary by the Revenue Commissioners, make a return to the Commissioners, within the time specified in the notice (which shall not be less than 30 days) and as respects such year of assessment as may be specified in the notice (being the year of assessment 1999-2000 or any subsequent year of assessment), showing—

(i) the name and address of—

(I) each company resident in the State from which the qualifying intermediary received, on behalf of another person, a relevant distribution made by that company in the year of assessment to which the return refers, and

(II) each other person from whom the qualifying intermediary received, on behalf of another person, an amount or other asset representing a relevant distribution made by a company resident in the State in the year of assessment to which the return refers,

(ii) the amount of each such relevant distribution,

(iii) the name and address of each person to whom such a relevant distribution, or an amount or other asset representing such a relevant distribution, has been given by the qualifying intermediary, and

(iv) the name and address of each person referred to in *subparagraph (iii)* in respect of whom a declaration under *section 172C(2)* or *172D(3)* has been received by the qualifying intermediary.

(b) A return required to be made by a qualifying intermediary under *paragraph (a)* may be confined to such class or classes of relevant distributions as may be specified in the notice given to the qualifying intermediary by the Revenue Commissioners under that paragraph.

(7A) (a) This subsection shall apply where a qualifying intermediary has been required to make a return to the Revenue Commissioners under *subsection (7)(a)* and a relevant distribution (or an amount or other asset representing a relevant distribution), the details of which are required to be included in that return, has been given by the qualifying intermediary to a specified intermediary.

(b) The qualifying intermediary shall, immediately on receipt of the notice referred to in *subsection (7)(a)*, request the specified intermediary, by way of notice in writing or in electronic format, to notify the qualifying intermediary or the Revenue Commissioners of the name and address of each person to whom the specified intermediary gave such a distribution (or an amount or other asset representing such a distribution) and of the amount of each such distribution.

(c) The specified intermediary shall, within 21 days of the receipt of a notice under *paragraph (b)*, furnish to the qualifying intermediary or, at the discretion of the specified intermediary, to the Revenue Commissioners, by way of notice in writing or in electronic format, the information required under that paragraph.

(d) Where the specified intermediary furnishes the information required under *paragraph (b)*—

(i) to the qualifying intermediary, the qualifying intermediary shall include that information in the return required to be made by it under *subsection (7)(a)*, or

(ii) to the Revenue Commissioners, the specified intermediary shall, by way of notice in writing or in electronic format, immediately advise the qualifying intermediary of that fact and the qualifying intermediary shall include in the return required to be made by it under *subsection (7)(a)* a statement to the effect that it has been so advised by the specified intermediary.

(e) If any person to whom a specified intermediary gave such a distribution (or an amount or other asset representing such a distribution) is another specified intermediary, the specified intermediary shall, immediately on the receipt of a notice under *paragraph (b)*, request the other specified intermediary, by way of notice in writing or in electronic format, to notify the specified intermediary or the Revenue Commissioners of the name and address of each person to whom it gave such a distribution (or an amount or other asset representing such a distribution) and of the amount of each such distribution.

(f) The other specified intermediary shall, within 21 days of the receipt of a notice under *paragraph (e)*, furnish to the specified intermediary or, at the discretion of the other specified intermediary, to the Revenue Commissioners, by way of notice in writing or in electronic format, the information required under that paragraph.

(g) Where the other specified intermediary furnishes the information required under *paragraph (e)*—

(i) to the specified intermediary, the specified intermediary shall, by way of notice in writing or in electronic format, immediately transmit that information to the person referred to in *paragraph (d)* (being the qualifying intermediary or the Revenue Commissioners, as the case may be) to whom it furnishes the information required under *paragraph (b)*, and—

(I) if that person is the qualifying intermediary, the qualifying intermediary shall include that information in the return required to be made by it under *subsection (7)(a)*, or

(II) if that person is the Revenue Commissioners, the specified intermediary shall, by way of notice in writing or in electronic format, immediately advise the qualifying intermediary of the fact that the information required to be furnished by the other specified intermediary under *paragraph (e)* has been furnished to the specified intermediary and transmitted by the specified intermediary to the Revenue Commissioners in accordance with this paragraph and the qualifying intermediary shall include in the return to be made by it under *subsection (7)(a)* a statement to the effect that it has been so advised by the specified intermediary,

or

(ii) to the Revenue Commissioners, the other specified intermediary shall, by way of notice in writing or in electronic format, immediately advise the specified intermediary of that fact, the specified intermediary shall in turn, by way of similar notice, immediately advise the qualifying intermediary of that fact and the qualifying intermediary shall include in the return required to be made by it under *subsection (7)(a)* a statement to the effect that it has been so advised by the specified intermediary.

(h) Where, in accordance with this subsection, the specified intermediary or the other specified intermediary furnishes information to the Revenue Commissioners in electronic format, such format shall be agreed in advance with the Revenue Commissioners.][7]

(8) Subject to *subsection (9)*, every return by a qualifying intermediary under *subsection (7)* shall be made[...][8] in an electronic format approved by the Revenue Commissioners and shall be accompanied by a declaration made by the qualifying intermediary, on a form prescribed or authorised for that purpose by the Revenue Commissioners, to the effect that the return is correct and complete.

(9) Where the Revenue Commissioners are satisfied that a qualifying intermediary does not have the facilities to make a return under *subsection (7)* in the format referred to in *subsection (8)*, the return shall be made in writing in a form prescribed or authorised by the Revenue Commissioners and shall be accompanied by a declaration made by the qualifying intermediary, on a form prescribed or authorised for that purpose by the Revenue Commissioners, to the effect that the return is correct and complete.][9]

Amendments

[1] Substituted by FA10 s33(1)(b). Has effect as on and from 3 April 2010.

[2] Substituted by FA00 s30(1)(f)(i)(I).

[3, 4] Substituted by FA00 s30(1)(f)(i)(II).

[5] Substituted by FA00 s30(1)(f)(i)(III).

[6] Inserted by FA00 s30(1)(f)(i)(IV).

[7] Substituted by FA00 s30(1)(f)(ii).

[8] Deleted by FA00 s30(1)(f)(iii).

[9] Inserted by FA99 s27(a).

Cross References

From Section 172F

Section 172B Dividend withholding tax on relevant distributions.
Section 172C Exemption from dividend withholding tax for certain persons.
Section 172D Exemption from dividend withholding tax for certain non-resident persons.
Section 172E Qualifying intermediaries.

To Section 172F

Section 172E Qualifying intermediaries.

172G Authorised withholding agent

[(1) Subject to *section 172H*, *section 172B* shall not apply where a company resident in the State makes a relevant distribution to an authorised withholding agent for the benefit of a person beneficially entitled to the relevant distribution, not being the authorised withholding agent.

(2) For the purposes of this Chapter, a person shall be an authorised withholding agent in relation to relevant distributions to be made to the person by a company resident in the State if the person is an intermediary who—

(a) (i) is resident in the State, or

(ii) if not resident in the State, is, by virtue of the law of a relevant territory, resident for the purposes of tax in the relevant territory, and carries on through a branch or agency in the State a trade which consists of or includes the receipt of relevant distributions from a company or companies resident in the State on behalf of other persons,

(b) has entered into an authorised withholding agent agreement with the Revenue Commissioners, and

(c) has been authorised by the Revenue Commissioners, by way of notice in writing, to be an authorised withholding agent in relation to relevant distributions to be made to the person by companies resident in the State for the benefit of other persons who are beneficially entitled to the relevant distributions, which authorisation has not been revoked under *subsection (6)*.

(3) An authorised withholding agent agreement shall be an agreement entered into between the Revenue Commissioners and an intermediary under the terms of which the intermediary undertakes—

[(a) to accept, and to retain for the longer of the following periods—

(i) a period of 6 years, or

(ii) a period which, in relation to the relevant distributions in respect of which the declaration or notification is made or, as the case may be, given, ends not earlier than 3 years after the date on which the intermediary has ceased to receive relevant distributions on behalf of the person who made the declaration or, as the case may be, gave the notification to the intermediary,

all declarations (and accompanying certificates) and notifications (not being a notice given to the intermediary by the Revenue Commissioners) which are made or, as the case may be, given to the intermediary in accordance with this Chapter and Schedule 2A,

(b) on being so required by notice in writing given to the intermediary by the Revenue Commissioners, to make available to the Commissioners, within the time specified in the notice—

(i) all declarations, certificates or notifications referred to in *paragraph (a)* which have been made or, as the case may be, given to the intermediary, or

(ii) such class or classes of such declarations, certificates or notifications as may be specified in the notice,][1]

(c) to inform the Revenue Commissioners if the intermediary has reasonable grounds to believe that any such declaration or notification made or given by any person was not, or may not have been, a true and correct declaration or notification at the time of the making of the declaration or the giving of the notification, as the case may be,

(d) to inform the Revenue Commissioners if the intermediary has at any time reasonable grounds to believe that any such declaration made by any person would not, or might not, be a true and correct declaration if made at that time,

(e) to operate the provisions of *section 172H* in a correct and efficient manner,

(f) to provide to the Collector-General the return referred to in *section 172K(1)*, and to pay to the Collector-General any dividend withholding tax required to be included in such a return, within the time specified in that behalf in that section,

[(g) to provide to the Revenue Commissioners, not later than 3 months after the end of the first year of the operation of the agreement by the intermediary, a report on the intermediary's compliance with the agreement in that year, which report shall be signed by—

(i) if the intermediary is a company, the auditor of the company, or

(ii) if the intermediary is not a company, a person who, if the intermediary were a company, would be qualified to be appointed auditor of the company,

and thereafter, on being required by notice in writing given to the intermediary by the Revenue Commissioners, to provide to the Commissioners, within the time specified in the notice, a similar report in relation to such other period of the operation of the agreement by the intermediary as may be specified in the notice,

and][2]

(i) if the intermediary is a company, the auditor of the company, or

(ii) if the intermediary is not a company, a person who, if the intermediary were a company, would be qualified to be appointed auditor of the company,

and

(h) to allow for the verification by the Revenue Commissioners of the intermediary's compliance with the agreement and the provisions of this Chapter in any other manner considered necessary by the Commissioners.

[(3A) The Revenue Commissioners may examine or take extracts from or copies of any declarations, certificates or notifications made available to the Commissioners under *subsection (3)(b)*.][3]

(4) The Revenue Commissioners shall not authorise an intermediary to be an authorised withholding agent unless the intermediary—

(a) is a company which holds a licence granted under section 9 of the Central Bank Act, 1971, or a person who holds a licence or other similar authorisation under the law of any relevant territory which corresponds to that section,

(b) is a person who is wholly owned by a company or person referred to in *paragraph (a)*,

(c) is a member of the Irish Stock Exchange Limited or of a recognised stock exchange in a relevant territory, or

(d) is in the opinion of the Revenue Commissioners a person suitable to be an authorised withholding agent for the purposes of this Chapter.

(5) The Revenue Commissioners shall maintain a list of intermediaries who have been authorised by the Commissioners to be authorised withholding agents for the purposes of this Chapter and whose authorisations have not been revoked under *subsection (6)*, and, notwithstanding any obligation as to secrecy or other restriction upon disclosure of information imposed by or under any statute or otherwise, the Revenue Commissioners may make available to any person the name and address of any such authorised withholding agent.

(6) Where, at any time after the Revenue Commissioners have authorised an intermediary to be an authorised withholding agent for the purposes of this Chapter, the Commissioners are satisfied that the intermediary—

(a) has failed to comply with the agreement referred to in *subsection (3)* or the provisions of this Chapter, or

(b) is otherwise unsuitable to be an authorised withholding agent,

they may, by notice in writing served by registered post on the intermediary, revoke the authorisation with effect from such date as may be specified in the notice.

(7) Notice of a revocation under *subsection (6)* shall be published as soon as may be in *Iris Oifigiúil*.

[(8) Without prejudice to the operation of *subsection (6)*, the authorisation by the Revenue Commissioners of an intermediary as a qualifying intermediary for the purposes of this Chapter shall cease to have effect on the day before the seventh anniversary of the date from which such authorisation applied; but this shall not prevent—

(a) the intermediary and the Revenue Commissioners from agreeing to renew the qualifying intermediary agreement entered into between them in accordance with *subsection (3)* or to enter into a further such agreement, and

(b) a further authorisation by the Revenue Commissioners of the intermediary as a qualifying intermediary for the purposes of this Chapter.][4]][5]

Amendments

[1] Substituted by FA00 s30(1)(g)(i)(I).

[2] Substituted by FA00 s30(1)(g)(i)(II).

[3] Inserted by FA00 s30(1)(g)(ii).

[4] Inserted by FA00 s30(1)(g)(iii).

[5] Inserted by FA99 s27(a).

Cross References

From Section 172G

Section 172B Dividend withholding tax on relevant distributions.

Section 172H Obligations of authorised withholding agent in relation to relevant distributions.

Section 172K Returns, payment and collection of dividend withholding tax.

To Section 172G

Section 172A Interpretation.

172H Obligations of authorised withholding agent in relation to relevant distributions

[(1) An authorised withholding agent which is to receive, on behalf of other persons, any relevant distributions to be made to it by any company resident in the State shall notify that company, by way of notice in writing, that it is an authorised withholding agent in relation to those distributions.

(2) Where an authorised withholding agent receives, on behalf of another person, a relevant distribution from a company resident in the State, and gives that distribution, or an amount or other asset representing that distribution, to that other person, this Chapter shall apply, with any necessary modifications, as if—

(a) the authorised withholding agent were the company which made the distribution, and

(b) the giving by the authorised withholding agent of the relevant distribution, or an amount or other asset representing that distribution, to that other person were the making of the relevant distribution by the authorised withholding agent to that other person at the time of the making of the relevant distribution to the authorised withholding agent by the company,

and accordingly, except where otherwise provided by this Chapter, *section 172B* shall apply in relation to that relevant distribution and the authorised withholding agent shall be obliged to pay and account for the dividend withholding tax (if any) due in relation to the relevant distribution.

(3) Where at any time a company resident in the State makes a relevant distribution to a person and, apart from this subsection, the relevant distribution would be treated as being made to an authorised withholding agent for the benefit of another person, the distribution shall be treated as if it were not made to the authorised withholding agent for the benefit of that other person unless, at or before that time, the authorised withholding agent has notified the company in accordance with *subsection (1)* that it is an authorised withholding agent in relation to the relevant distribution, and accordingly, in the absence of such a notification, *section 172B* shall apply in relation to the relevant distribution.][1]

Amendments

[1] Inserted by FA99 s27(a).

Cross References

From Section 172H

Section 172B Dividend withholding tax on relevant distributions.

To Section 172H

Section 172G Authorised withholding agent.
Section 172K Returns, payment and collection of dividend withholding tax.
Section 904I Power of inspection: returns and collection of dividend withholding tax.

172I Statement to be given to recipients of relevant distributions

[(1) Every person (in this section referred to as "*the payer*") who makes, or who (being an authorised withholding agent) is treated as making, a relevant distribution shall, at the time of the making of the relevant distribution or, in the case of an authorised withholding agent, at the time of the giving by the authorised withholding agent of the relevant distribution, or an amount or other asset representing that distribution, to another person, give the recipient of the relevant distribution or, as the case may be, that other person a statement in writing[, or by means of electronic communications,][1] showing—

(a) the name and address of the payer and, if the payer is not the company making the relevant distribution, the name and address of that company,

(b) the name and address of the person to whom the relevant distribution is made,

(c) the date the relevant distribution is made,

(d) the amount of the relevant distribution, and

(e) the amount of the dividend withholding tax (if any) deducted in relation to the relevant distribution.

[(1A) A statement delivered by means of electronic communications to an intermediary [or the recipient of a relevant distribution][2] shall satisfy the requirements of *subsection (1)* where—

(a) the statement [delivered to an intermediary][3] contains—

(i) an ISI Number,

(ii) a recipient ID code,

(iii) the information referred to in *paragraphs (c)* to *(e)* of *subsection (1)*, and

(iv) an electronic number,

(b) the intermediary [or the recipient of the relevant distribution][4] has consented to the statement being delivered by means of electronic communications and has not withdrawn that consent, and

(c) the Revenue Commissioners have agreed to accept the statement for the purposes of this Chapter.][5]

(2) The requirements of *subsection (1)* shall be satisfied by the inclusion of the information referred to in that subsection in a statement in writing made in relation to the distribution in accordance with *section 152(1)*.

(3) Where a person fails to comply with any of the provisions of *subsection (1)*, *subsection (2)* of *section 152* shall apply as it applies where a company fails to comply with any of the provisions of *subsection (1)* of that section.][6]

Amendments

[1] Inserted by FA10 s33(1)(c)(i). Has effect as on and from 3 April 2010.

[2] Inserted by FA10 s33(1)(c)(ii)(I). Has effect as on and from 3 April 2010.

3 Inserted by FA10 s33(1)(c)(ii)(II). Has effect as on and from 3 April 2010.

4 Inserted by FA10 s33(1)(c)(ii)(III). Has effect as on and from 3 April 2010.

5 Inserted by FA07 s38(1)(c). Applies as respects any relevant distribution made on or after 1 February 2007.

6 Inserted by FA99 s27(a).

Revenue Briefings

eBrief

eBrief No. 26/2010 – Dividend Withholding Tax – Electronic Vouchers

Cross References

From Section 172I

Section 152 Explanation of tax credit to be annexed to interest and dividend warrants.

To Section 172I

Section 172A Interpretation.

Section 172J Credit for, or repayment of, dividend withholding tax borne.

172J Credit for, or repayment of, dividend withholding tax borne

[(1) Where, in relation to any year of assessment, a person is within the charge to income tax and has borne dividend withholding tax in relation to a relevant distribution to which the person is beneficially entitled which tax is referable to that year of assessment, the person may claim to have that dividend withholding tax set against income tax chargeable for that year of assessment and, where that dividend withholding tax exceeds such income tax, to have the excess refunded to the person.

(2) Where, in relation to any year of assessment, a person is not within the charge to income tax and has borne dividend withholding tax in relation to a relevant distribution to which the person is beneficially entitled which tax is referable to that year of assessment, the person may claim to have the amount of that dividend withholding tax refunded to the person.

(3) [Where, in a year of assessment or in an accounting period of a company (as appropriate),][1] a person has borne dividend withholding tax in relation to a relevant distribution to which the person is beneficially entitled, and the person—

- (a) is a non-liable person in relation to the relevant distribution, or
- (b) would have been a non-liable person in relation to the relevant distribution if the requirement for the person to make the appropriate declaration referred to in *Schedule 2A* had not been necessary,

the person may claim to have the amount of that dividend withholding tax refunded to the person.

(4) A person making a claim under this section shall furnish, in respect of each amount of dividend withholding tax to which the claim relates, the statement [...][2] given to the person in accordance with *section 172I(1)* by the person who made, or who (being an authorised withholding agent) was treated as making, the relevant distribution in relation to which the dividend withholding tax was deducted.

(5) The Revenue Commissioners shall not authorise the setting-off of dividend withholding tax against income tax chargeable on a person for a year of assessment, or pay a refund of dividend withholding tax to a person, unless the Commissioners receive such evidence as they consider necessary that the person is entitled to that setting-off or refund.][3]

Amendments

[1] Substituted by FA07 s38(1)(d). Applies as respects any chargeable period ending on or after 1 February 2007.

[2] Deleted by FA10 s33(1)(d). Has effect as on and from 3 April 2010.

[3] Inserted by FA99 s27(a).

Revenue Briefings

eBrief

eBrief No. 68/2012 – Preliminary Tax Requirements for 2012 - Interaction with Credit for Withholding Taxes

Cross References

From Section 172J

Section 172I Statement to be given to recipients of relevant distributions.
Schedule 2A Dividend Withholding Tax

172K Returns, payment and collection of dividend withholding tax

[(1) Any person (in this section referred to as "*the accountable person*"), being a company resident in the State which makes, or an authorised withholding agent who is treated under *section 172H* as making, any relevant distributions to specified persons in any month shall, within 14 days of the end of that month, make a return to the Collector-General which shall contain details of—

(a) the name and tax reference number of the company which actually made the relevant distributions,

(b) if different from the company which actually made the relevant distributions, the name of the accountable person, being an authorised withholding agent, in relation to those distributions,

(c) the name and address of each person to whom a relevant distribution was made or, as the case may be, was treated as being made by the accountable person in the month to which the return refers,

(d) the date on which the relevant distribution was made to that person,

(e) the amount of the relevant distribution made to that person,

(f) the amount of the dividend withholding tax (if any) in relation to the relevant distribution deducted by the accountable person or, as the case may be, the amount (if any) to be paid to the Collector-General by the accountable person in relation to that distribution as if it were a deduction of dividend withholding tax, [...][1]

(g) the aggregate of the amounts referred to in *paragraph (f)* in relation to all relevant distributions made or treated under *section 172H* as being made by the accountable person to specified persons in the month to which the return [refers, and][2]

[(h) in a case where *section 172B* has not applied to a relevant distribution by virtue of the operation of *subsection (7)* of that section, whether the relevant distribution is a distribution within *paragraph (a)*, *(b)* or *(c)* of that subsection.][3]

(2) Dividend withholding tax which is required to be included in a return under *subsection (1)* shall be due at the time by which the return is to be made and shall be paid by the accountable person to the Collector-General, and the dividend withholding tax so due shall be payable by the accountable person without the

making of an assessment, but dividend withholding tax which has become so due may be assessed on the accountable person (whether or not it has been paid when the assessment is made) if that tax or any part of it is not paid on or before the due date.

(3) Where it appears to the inspector that there is any amount of dividend withholding tax in relation to a relevant distribution which ought to have been but has not been included in a return under *subsection (2)*, or where the inspector is dissatisfied with any such return, the inspector may make an assessment on the accountable person in relation to the relevant distribution to the best of the inspector's judgment, and any amount of dividend withholding tax in relation to a relevant distribution due under an assessment made by virtue of this subsection shall be treated for the purposes of interest on unpaid tax as having been payable at the time when it would have been payable if a correct return under *subsection (1)* had been made.

(4) Where any item has been incorrectly included in a return under *subsection (1)* as a relevant distribution in relation to which dividend withholding tax is required to be deducted, the inspector may make such assessments, adjustments or set-offs as may in his or her judgment be required for securing that the resulting liabilities to tax, including interest on unpaid tax, whether of the accountable person in relation to the relevant distribution or any other person, are in so far as possible the same as they would have been if the item had not been so included.

(5) Any dividend withholding tax assessed on an accountable person under this Chapter shall be due within one month after the issue of the notice of assessment (unless that tax is due earlier under *subsection (2)*) subject to any appeal against the assessment, but no such appeal shall affect the date when any amount is due under *subsection (2)*.

(6) (a) The provisions of the Income Tax Acts relating to—

(i) assessments to income tax,

(ii) appeals against such assessments (including the rehearing of appeals and the statement of a case for the opinion of the High Court), and

(iii) the collection and recovery of income tax,

shall, in so far as they are applicable, apply to the assessment, collection and recovery of dividend withholding tax.

[(b) Any amount of dividend withholding tax payable in accordance with this Chapter without the making of an assessment shall carry interest from the date when the amount becomes due and payable until payment—

(i) for any day or part of a day before 1 July 2009 during which the amount remains unpaid, at a rate of 0.0322 per cent, and

(ii) for any day or part of a day on or after 1 July 2009 during which the amount remains unpaid, at a rate of 0.0274 per cent.][4]

(c) [*Subsections (3)* to *(5)* of *section 1080*][5] shall apply in relation to interest payable under *paragraph (b)* as they apply in relation to interest payable under *section 1080*.

(d) In its application to any dividend withholding tax charged by any assessment made in accordance with this Chapter, *section 1080* shall apply as if [*subsection (2)(b)*][6] of that section were deleted.

(7) Subject to *subsection (8)*, every return by an accountable person under *subsection (1)* shall be made in an electronic format approved by the Revenue Commissioners and shall be accompanied by a declaration made by the accountable person, on a form prescribed or authorised for that purpose by the Revenue Commissioners, to the effect that the return is correct and complete.

(8) Where the Revenue Commissioners are satisfied that an accountable person does not have the facilities to make a return under *subsection (1)* in the format referred to in *subsection (7)*, the return shall be made in writing in a form prescribed or authorised by the Revenue Commissioners and shall be accompanied by a declaration made by the accountable person, on a form prescribed or authorised for that purpose by the Revenue Commissioners, to the effect that the return is correct and complete.][7]

Amendments

[1] Deleted by FA00 s30(1)(h)(i).

[2] Substituted by FA00 s30(1)(h)(i).

[3] Inserted by FA00 s30(1)(h)(ii).

[4] Substituted by FA09 s29(1)(a). Applies as respects any unpaid tax or duty, as the case may be, that has not been paid before 1 July 2009 regardless of whether that tax or duty became due and payable before, on or after that date.

[5, 6] Substituted by FA05 sched5.

[7] Inserted by FA99 s27(a).

Cross References

From Section 172K

Section 172B Dividend withholding tax on relevant distributions.
Section 172H Obligations of authorised withholding agent in relation to relevant distributions.
Section 1080 Interest on overdue income tax, corporation tax and capital gains tax.

To Section 172K

Section 153 Distributions to certain nonresidents.
Section 172G Authorised withholding agent.
Section 831 Implementation of Council Directive No. 90/435/EEC concerning the common system of taxation applicable in the case of parent companies and subsidiaries of different Member States.
Section 831A Treatment of distributions to certain parent companies.
Section 904I Power of inspection: returns and collection of dividend withholding tax.
Section 1078 Revenue offences.
Schedule 29 Provisions Referred to in Sections 1052, 1053 and 1054

172L Reporting of distributions made under stapled stock arrangements

[(1) For the purposes of this section, a distribution made to a person by a company which is not resident in the State (in this section referred to as "*the non-resident company*") shall be treated as made under a stapled stock arrangement where—

(a) the person has, under any agreement, arrangement or understanding, whether made or entered into on, before or after the 6th day of April, 1999, exercised a right, whether directly or through a nominee or other person acting on behalf of the person, to receive distributions from the non-resident company instead of receiving relevant distributions from a company resident in the State (in this section referred to as "*the resident company*"), and

(b) that right has not been revoked.

(2) Where on or after the 6th day of April, 1999, the non-resident company makes distributions to persons under a stapled stock arrangement, the resident company shall, within 14 days of the end of each month in which those distributions were made, make a return to the Revenue Commissioners which shall contain details of—

(a) the name and tax reference number of the resident company,

(b) the name and address of the non-resident company which made those distributions,

(c) the name and address of each person to whom such a distribution was made in the month to which the return refers,

(d) the date on which such distribution was made to that person, and

(e) the amount of such distribution made to that person.

(3) Subject to *subsection (4)*, every return by a company under *subsection (2)* shall be made in an electronic format approved by the Revenue Commissioners and shall be accompanied by a declaration made by the company, on a form prescribed or authorised for that purpose by the Revenue Commissioners, to the effect that the return is correct and complete.

(4) Where the Revenue Commissioners are satisfied that a company does not have the facilities to make a return under *subsection (2)* in the format referred to in *subsection (3)*, the return shall be made in writing in a form prescribed or authorised by the Revenue Commissioners and shall be accompanied by a declaration made by the company, on a form prescribed or authorised for that purpose by the Revenue Commissioners, to the effect that the return is correct and complete.][1]

Amendments

[1] Inserted by FA99 s27(a).

Revenue Briefings

Tax Briefing

Tax Briefing July 2004 – Issue 56 pg 18 – Stapled Stock Arrangements

Cross References

To Section 172L

Schedule 29 Provisions Referred to in Sections 1052, 1053 and 1054

172LA Deduction of dividend withholding tax on settlement of market claims

[(1) In this section, "*stockbroker*", means a member firm of the Irish Stock Exchange or of a recognised stock exchange in another territory.

(2) For the purposes of this section, a market claim shall be deemed to have arisen in relation to a relevant distribution where—

(a) a company resident in the State has made a relevant distribution to a person (in this section referred to as the "recorded owner") on the basis of the information on the share register of the company at a particular date,

(b) it subsequently transpires, as a result of an event (in this section referred to as the "specified event"), being—

(i) the sale or purchase of, or

(ii) the happening, or failure to happen, of another event in relation to, the shares or other securities in respect of which the relevant distribution was made, that another person (in this section referred to as the "proper owner") had actually been entitled to receive the relevant distribution, and

(c) a person (in this section referred to as an "accountable person"), being—

(i) the relevant stockbroker who has acted for the recorded owner in the specified event, or

(ii) if the recorded owner is a qualifying intermediary or an authorised withholding agent, that intermediary or agent,

is obliged to pay the relevant distribution to the proper owner or, as may be appropriate, to the relevant stockbroker who has acted for the proper owner in the specified event, which action is in this section referred to as the "settlement of the market claim".

(3) Notwithstanding any other provision of this Chapter, where a market claim arises, then, if dividend withholding tax had not already been deducted out of the amount of the relevant distribution made by the company resident in the State to the recorded owner—

(a) the accountable person shall, on the settlement of the market claim, deduct out of the amount of the relevant distribution dividend withholding tax in relation to the relevant distribution,

(b) the proper owner or, as may be appropriate, the relevant stockbroker who has acted for the proper owner in the specified event shall allow such deduction on the receipt of the residue of the relevant distribution, and

(c) the accountable person shall be acquitted and discharged of so much money as is represented by the deduction as if that amount of money had actually been paid to the proper owner or, as may be appropriate, to the relevant stockbroker who has acted for the proper owner in the specified event.

(4) Where *subsection (3)* applies, the accountable person shall, on the settlement of the market claim, give the proper owner or, as may be appropriate, the relevant stockbroker who has acted for the proper owner in the specified event a statement in writing showing—

(a) the name and address of the accountable person,

(b) the name and address of the company which made the relevant distribution,

(c) the amount of the relevant distribution, and

(d) the amount of the dividend withholding tax deducted in relation to the relevant distribution.

(5) Dividend withholding tax which is required to be deducted by the accountable person under *subsection (3)* shall be paid by the accountable person to the Collector-General within 14 days of the end of the month in which that tax was required to be so deducted, and the dividend withholding tax so due shall be payable without the making of an assessment, but dividend withholding tax which has become so due may be assessed on the accountable person if that tax or any part of it is not paid on or before the due date.

(6) Dividend withholding tax which is required to be paid in accordance with *subsection (5)* shall be accompanied by a statement in writing from the accountable person making the payment showing—

(a) the name and address of that accountable person,

(b) the name and address of the company or companies which made the relevant distribution or distributions to which the payment relates, and

(c) the amount of the dividend withholding tax included in the payment.

(7) An accountable person shall, as respects each year of assessment (being the year of assessment 1999-2000 or any subsequent year of assessment) in which *subsection (3)* applied in relation to the accountable person and not later than [15 February][1] following that year of assessment, make a return to the Revenue Commissioners showing—

(a) the name and address of the accountable person, and

(b) the following details in relation to each market claim to which *subsection (3)* applied in that year:

(i) the name and address of the company resident in the State which made the relevant distribution to which the market claim relates,

(ii) the amount of the relevant distribution concerned, and

(iii) the amount of the dividend withholding tax in relation to the relevant distribution deducted by the accountable person.

(8) Subject to *subsection (9)*, every return by an accountable person under *subsection (7)* shall be made in an electronic format approved by the Revenue Commissioners and shall be accompanied by a declaration made by the accountable person, on a form prescribed or authorised for that purpose by the Revenue Commissioners, to the effect that the return is correct and complete.

(9) Where the Revenue Commissioners are satisfied that an accountable person does not have the facilities to make a return under *subsection (7)* in the format referred to in *subsection (8)*, the return shall be made in writing in a form prescribed or authorised by the Revenue Commissioners and shall be accompanied by a declaration made by the accountable person, on a form prescribed or authorised for that purpose by the Revenue Commissioners, to the effect that the return is correct and complete.

(10) (a) An accountable person shall keep and retain for a period of 6 years the accountable person's documents and records relating to market claims arising from relevant distributions made by companies resident in the State.

(b) An accountable person shall allow the Revenue Commissioners to inspect such documents and records and to verify the accountable person's compliance with this section in any other manner considered necessary by the Commissioners.][2]

Amendments

[1] Substituted by FA01 sched2(11). Applies as respects the year of assessment 2001 and subsequent years of assessment.

[2] Inserted by FA00 s30(1)(i). Shall apply as on and from 10 February 2000.

172M Delegation of powers and functions of Revenue Commissioners

[The Revenue Commissioners may nominate any of their officers to perform any acts and discharge any functions authorised by this Chapter or *Schedule 2A* to be performed or discharged by the Revenue Commissioners.][1]

Amendments

[1] Inserted by FA99 s27(a).

Cross References

From Section 172M

Schedule 2A Dividend Withholding Tax

CHAPTER 9

Taxation of Acquisition by a Company of Its Own Shares

173 Interpretation (Chapter 9)

[FA91 s59; FA97 s39(1)(a)]

(1) In this Chapter—

"*chargeable period*" means an accounting period of a company or a year of assessment;

"*control*" shall be construed in accordance with *section 11*;

"*group*" means a company which has one or more 51 per cent subsidiaries together with those subsidiaries;

"*holding company*" means a company whose business, disregarding any trade carried on by it, consists wholly or mainly of the holding of the shares or securities of one or more companies which are its 51 per cent subsidiaries;

"*inspector*", in relation to any matter, means an inspector of taxes appointed under *section 852*, and includes such other officer as the Revenue Commissioners shall appoint in that behalf;

"*personal representative*" has the same meaning as in *section 799*;

"*quoted company*" means a company whose shares, or any class of whose shares, are listed in the official list of a stock exchange or dealt in on an unlisted securities market;

"*shares*" includes stock;

"*trade*" does not include dealing in shares, securities, land, futures or traded options, and

"*trading activities*" shall be construed accordingly;

"*trading company*" means a company whose business consists wholly or mainly of the carrying on of a trade or trades;

"*trading group*" means a group the business of whose members taken together consists wholly or mainly of the carrying on of a trade or trades.

(2) References in this Chapter to the owner of shares shall be treated as references to the beneficial owner except where the shares are held on trusts other than bare trusts, or are comprised in the estate of a deceased person, and in such a case shall be treated as references to the trustees or, as the case may be, to the deceased's personal representatives.

(3) References in this Chapter to a payment made by a company include references to anything else that is, or but for *section 175* or *176* would be, a distribution.

(4) References in this Chapter to a company being unquoted shall be treated as references to a company which is neither a quoted company nor a 51 per cent subsidiary of a quoted company.

Cross References

From Section 173

Section 11 Meaning of "control" in certain contexts.

Section 175 Purchase of own shares by quoted company.

Section 176 Purchase of unquoted shares by issuing company or its subsidiary.

Section 799 Interpretation (Chapter 1).

Section 852 Inspectors of taxes.

174 Taxation of dealer's receipts on purchase of shares by issuing company or by its subsidiary

[FA91 s60]

(1) In this section—

"*fixed-rate preference shares*" means shares which—

(a) were issued wholly for new consideration,

(b) do not carry any right either to conversion into shares or securities of any other description or to the acquisition of any additional shares or securities,

(c) do not carry any right to dividends other than dividends which are of a fixed amount or at a fixed rate per cent of the nominal value of the shares, and

(d) carry rights in respect of dividends and capital which are comparable with those general for fixed-dividend shares quoted on a stock exchange in the State;

"*new consideration*" has the meaning assigned to it by *section 135*.

(2) Where—

(a) a company purchases its own shares from a dealer, or

(b) a company, which is a subsidiary (within the meaning of section 155 of the Companies Act, 1963) of another company, purchases the other company's shares from a dealer,

the purchase price shall be taken into account in computing the profits of the dealer chargeable to tax under Case I or II of Schedule D, and accordingly—

(i) tax shall not be chargeable under Schedule F in respect of any distribution represented by any part of the price, [and][1]

[…][2]

(iii) *sections 129* and *152* shall not apply to the distribution.

(3) For the purposes of *subsection (2)*, a person shall be a dealer in relation to shares of a company if the price received on their sale by the person other than to the company, or to a company which is a subsidiary (within the meaning of section 155 of the Companies Act, 1963) of the company, would be taken into account in computing the person's profits chargeable to tax under Case I or II of Schedule D.

(4) Subject to *subsection (5)*, in *subsection (2)*—

(a) the reference to the purchase of shares includes a reference to the redemption or repayment of shares and the purchase of rights to acquire shares, and

(b) the reference to the purchase price includes a reference to any sum payable on redemption or repayment.

(5) *Subsection (2)* shall not apply in relation to—

(a) the redemption of fixed-rate preference shares, or

(b) the redemption, on binding terms settled before the 18th day of April, 1991, of other preference shares issued before that date,

if in either case the shares were issued to and continuously held by the person from whom they are redeemed.

Amendments

[1] Inserted by FA00 sched2(m).

[2] Deleted by FA00 sched2.

Cross References

From Section 174

Section 20 Schedule F.

Section 129 Irish resident company distributions not generally chargeable to corporation tax.

Section 135 Distributions: supplemental.

Section 152 Explanation of tax credit to be annexed to interest and dividend warrants.

175 Purchase of own shares by quoted company

[FA91 s60A; FA97 s39(1)(b) and (2)]

(1) Notwithstanding *Chapter 2* of this Part, references in the Tax Acts to distributions of a company shall be construed so as not to include references to a payment made on or after the 26th day of March, 1997, by a quoted company on the redemption, repayment or purchase of its own shares [where the redemption, repayment or purchase does not form part of a scheme or arrangement the main purpose or one of the main purposes of which is to enable the owner of the shares to participate in the profits of the company or of any of its 51 per cent subsidiaries without receiving a dividend][1].

[(1A) (a) Where in any accounting period a quoted company makes a payment on the redemption, repayment or purchase of its own shares, the company shall, not later than 12 months from the end of the accounting period, give notice to the Collector-General, or such other officer of the Revenue Commissioners as may be authorised by them for the purposes of this subsection, of—

(i) the payment, and

(ii) whether the payment is to be treated as not being a distribution by virtue of *subsection (1)*.

(b) A notice under *paragraph (a)* shall be given by a company—

(i) in the return required to be made under [*Chapter 3* of *Part 41A*][2] for the accounting period of the company in which the payment is made, or

(ii) in such manner and form as the Revenue Commissioners may prescribe.][3]

(2) References in [*subsections (1)* and *(1A)*][4] to a quoted company shall include references to a company which is a member of a group of which a quoted company is a member.

Amendments

[1] Inserted by FA10 s34(1)(a). This section applies to payments referred to in section 175 which are made on or after 4 February 2010.

[2] Substituted by FA12 sched4(part 2)(g).

[3] Inserted by FA10 s34(1)(b). This section applies to payments referred to in section 175 which are made on or after 4 February 2010.

[4] Substituted by FA10 s34(1)(c). This section applies to payments referred to in section 175 which are made on or after 4 February 2010.

Revenue Briefings

Tax Briefing

Tax Briefing August 2003 – Issue 53 pg 3 – First Active Plc – CGT

Tax Briefing August 2003 – Issue 53 pg 21 – Jefferson Smurfit Shares – CGT

Cross References

From Section 175

Section 130 Matters to be treated as distributions.

Section 951 Obligation to make a return.

To Section 175

Section 173 Interpretation (Chapter 9).

Section 176A Purchase of own shares — supplementary.

176 Purchase of unquoted shares by issuing company or its subsidiary

[FA91 s61]

(1) Notwithstanding *Chapter 2* of this Part, references in the Tax Acts to distributions of a company, other than any such references in *sections 440* and *441*, shall be construed so as not to include references to a payment made by a company on the redemption, repayment or purchase of its own shares if the company is an unquoted trading company or the unquoted holding company of a trading group and either—

(a) (i) the redemption, repayment or purchase—

(I) is made wholly or mainly for the purpose of benefiting a trade carried on by the company or by any of its 51 per cent subsidiaries, and

(II) does not form part of a scheme or arrangement the main purpose or one of the main purposes of which is to enable the owner of the shares to participate in the profits of the company or of any of its 51 per cent subsidiaries without receiving a dividend,

and

(ii) the conditions specified in *sections 177* to *181*, in so far as applicable, are satisfied in relation to the owner of the shares, or

(b) the person to whom the payment is made—

(i) applies the whole or substantially the whole of the payment (apart from any sum applied in discharging that person's liability to capital gains tax, if any, in respect of the redemption, repayment or purchase) to discharging—

[(I) on or before 31 October in the year in which inheritance tax is due to be paid in accordance with *section 46(2A)* of the Capital Acquisitions Tax Consolidation Act 2003 in respect of a taxable inheritance (within the meaning of *section 11* of that Act) of the company's shares taken by that person, a liability to inheritance tax in respect of that inheritance, or][1]

(II) within one week of the day on which the payment is made, a debt incurred by that person for the purpose of discharging that liability to inheritance tax,

and

(ii) could not without undue hardship have otherwise discharged that liability to inheritance tax and, where appropriate, the debt so incurred.

(2) Where *subsection (1)* would apply to a payment made by a company which is a subsidiary (within the meaning of section 155 of the Companies Act, 1963) of another company on the acquisition of shares of the other company if for the purposes of the Tax Acts other than this subsection—

(a) the payment were to be treated as a payment by the other company on the purchase of its own shares, and

(b) the acquisition by the subsidiary of the shares were to be treated as a purchase by the other company of its own shares,

then, notwithstanding *Chapter 2* of this Part, references in the Tax Acts to distributions of a company, other than references in *sections 440* and *441*, shall be construed so as not to include references to the payment made by the subsidiary.

Amendments

[1] Substituted by FA12 s19(1). Applies as on and from 8 February 2012.

Revenue Briefings

Tax Briefing

Tax Briefing February 1997 – Issue 25 pg 9 – Company Buy-Back of Shares – "Trade Benefit Test"

Cross References

From Section 176

Section 130 Matters to be treated as distributions.
Section 177 Conditions as to residence and period of ownership.
Section 181 Relaxation of conditions in certain cases.
Section 440 Surcharge on undistributed investment and estate income.
Section 441 Surcharge on undistributed income of service companies.

To Section 176

Section 173 Interpretation (Chapter 9).
Section 176A Purchase of own shares — supplementary.
Section 177 Conditions as to residence and period of ownership.
Section 181 Relaxation of conditions in certain cases.
Section 182 Returns.
Section 183 Information.
Section 185 Associated persons.
Section 186 Connected persons.
Section 598 Disposals of business or farm on "retirement".

176A Purchase of own shares—supplementary

[(1) Subject to *subsection (2)*, no sum shall be deducted in computing the amount of the profits or gains charged to tax under Case I or II of Schedule D in respect of any payment that is treated by virtue of *section 175* or *176* as not being a distribution.

(2) Subject to *section 81(2)(n)*, *subsection (1)* shall not apply to so much of any payment as consists of expenditure incurred by a company to the extent that it is incurred

on shares acquired by the company and given by it as consideration for goods or services, or to an employee or director of the company.][1]

Amendments

[1] Inserted by FA08 s48(1). Applies as respects accounting periods ending on or after 31 January 2008.

Cross References

From Section 176A

Section 81 General rule as to deductions.

Section 175 Purchase of own shares by quoted company.

Section 176 Purchase of unquoted shares by issuing company or its subsidiary.

177 Conditions as to residence and period of ownership

[FA91 s62]

(1) In this section and in *sections 178* to *181*—

"*the purchase*" means the redemption, repayment or purchase referred to in *section 176(1)(a)*;

"*the vendor*" means the owner of the shares immediately before the purchase is made.

(2) The vendor shall be resident and ordinarily resident in the State for the chargeable period in which the purchase is made and, if the shares are held through a nominee, the nominee shall also be so resident and ordinarily resident.

(3) The residence and ordinary residence of trustees shall be determined for the purposes of this section as they are determined under *section 574* for the purposes of the Capital Gains Tax Acts.

(4) The residence and ordinary residence of personal representatives shall be taken for the purposes of this section to be the same as the residence and ordinary residence of the deceased immediately before his or her death.

(5) The references in this section to a person's ordinary residence shall be disregarded in the case of a company.

[(6) The shares shall have been owned by the vendor throughout the period of—

(a) where the shares were appropriated to the vendor under an approved scheme (within the meaning of *Chapter 1* of *Part 17*), and to which the provisions of *subsections (4)* to *(7)* of *section 515* do not apply, 3 years, and

(b) in any other case, 5 years,

ending on the date of redemption, repayment or purchase, as the case may be.][1]

(7) Where at any time during that period the shares were transferred to the vendor by a person who was then the vendor's [spouse or civil partner][2] living with the vendor, then, unless that person is alive at the date of the purchase but is no longer the vendor's [spouse or civil partner][3] living with the vendor, any period during which the shares were owned by that person shall be treated for the purposes of *subsection (6)* as a period of ownership by the vendor.

(8) Where the vendor became entitled to the shares under the will or on the intestacy of a previous owner or is the personal representative of a previous owner—

(a) any period during which the shares were owned by the previous owner or the previous owner's personal representatives shall be treated for the purposes of *subsection (6)* as a period of ownership by the vendor, and

(b) that subsection shall apply as if it referred to 3 years instead of 5 years.

(9) In determining whether the condition in *subsection (6)* is satisfied in a case where the vendor acquired shares of the same class at different times—

(a) shares acquired earlier shall be taken into account before shares acquired later, and

(b) any previous disposal by the vendor of shares of that class shall be assumed to be a disposal of shares acquired later rather than of shares acquired earlier.

(10) Where for the purposes of capital gains tax the time when a person acquired shares would be determined under *section 584, 585, 586, 587* or *600*, then, unless the person is to be treated under *section 584(4)* as giving or becoming liable to give any consideration, other than the old holding, for the acquisition of those shares, it shall be determined in the same way for the purposes of this section.

Amendments

[1] Substituted by FA01 s35. Applies as respects a redemption, repayment or purchase of its own shares by a company to which section 176 applies on or after 15 February 2001.

[2, 3] Substituted by F(No.3)A11 sched1(24).

Cross References

From Section 177

Section 176 Purchase of unquoted shares by issuing company or its subsidiary.
Section 178 Conditions as to reduction of vendor's interest as shareholder.
Section 181 Relaxation of conditions in certain cases.
Section 509 Interpretation (Chapter 1).
Section 515 Excess or unauthorised shares.
Section 574 Trustees of settlement.
Section 584 Reorganisation or reduction of share capital.
Section 585 Conversion of securities.
Section 586 Company amalgamations by exchange of shares.
Section 587 Company reconstructions and amalgamations.
Section 600 Transfer of business to company.

To Section 177

Section 176 Purchase of unquoted shares by issuing company or its subsidiary.

178 Conditions as to reduction of vendor's interest as shareholder

[FA91 s63]

(1) Where immediately after the purchase the vendor owns shares in the company, the vendor's interest as a shareholder shall, subject to *section 181*, be substantially reduced.

(2) Where immediately after the purchase any associate of the vendor owns shares in the company, the combined interest as shareholders of the vendor and the vendor's associates shall, subject to *section 181*, be substantially reduced.

(3) The question whether the combined interests as shareholders of the vendor and the vendor's associates are substantially reduced shall be determined in the same way as is (under *subsections (4)* to *(7)*) the question whether a vendor's interest as a shareholder is substantially reduced, except that the vendor shall be assumed to have the interests of the vendor's associates as well as the vendor's own interests.

(4) Subject to *subsection (5)*, the vendor's interest as a shareholder shall be taken to be substantially reduced only if the total nominal value of the shares owned by the vendor immediately after the purchase, expressed as a percentage of the issued

share capital of the company at that time, does not exceed 75 per cent of the corresponding percentage immediately before the purchase.

(5) The vendor's interest as a shareholder shall not be taken to be substantially reduced where—

(a) the vendor would, if the company distributed all its profits available for the distribution immediately after the purchase, be entitled to a share of those profits, and

(b) that share, expressed as a percentage of the total of those profits, exceeds 75 per cent of the corresponding percentage immediately before the purchase.

(6) In determining for the purposes of *subsection (5)* the division of profits among the persons entitled to them, a person entitled to periodic distributions calculated by reference to fixed rates or amounts shall be regarded as entitled to a distribution of the amount or maximum amount to which the person would be entitled for a year.

(7) In *subsection (5)*, "*profits available for distribution*" has the same meaning as it has for the purposes of Part IV of the Companies (Amendment) Act, 1983, except that for the purposes of that subsection the amount of the profits available for distribution (whether immediately before or immediately after the purchase) shall be treated as increased—

(a) in the case of every company, by [€100][1], and

(b) in the case of a company from which any person is entitled to periodic distributions of the kind mentioned in *subsection (6)*, by a further amount equal to that required to make the distribution to which that person is entitled in accordance with that subsection,

and, where the aggregate of the sums payable by the company on the purchase and on any contemporaneous redemption, repayment or purchase of other shares of the company exceeds the amount of the profits available for distribution immediately before the purchase, that amount shall be treated as further increased by an amount equal to the excess.

(8) References in this section to entitlement are, except in the case of trustees and personal representatives, references to beneficial entitlement.

Amendments

[1] Substituted by FA01 sched5.

Cross References

From Section 178

Section 181 Relaxation of conditions in certain cases.

To Section 178

Section 177 Conditions as to residence and period of ownership.

Section 179 Conditions applicable where purchasing company is member of a group.

Section 180 Additional conditions.

Section 181 Relaxation of conditions in certain cases.

179 Conditions applicable where purchasing company is member of a group

[FA91 s64]

(1) Subject to *subsections (2)* to *(4)*, in this section, "*group*" means a company which has one or more 51 per cent subsidiaries but is not itself a 51 per cent subsidiary of any other company, together with those subsidiaries.

(2) Where the whole or a significant part of the business carried on by an unquoted company (in this section referred to as "*the successor company*") was previously carried on by—

(a) the company making the purchase, or

(b) a company which apart from this subsection is a member of a group to which the company making the purchase belongs,

the successor company and any company of which it is a 51 per cent subsidiary shall be treated as being a member of the same group as the company making the purchase, whether or not apart from this subsection the company making the purchase is a member of a group.

(3) *Subsection (2)* shall not apply if the successor company first carried on the business referred to in that subsection more than 3 years before the time of the purchase.

(4) For the purposes of this section, a company which has ceased to be a 51 per cent subsidiary of another company before the time of the purchase shall be treated as continuing to be such a subsidiary if at that time there exist arrangements under which it could again become such a subsidiary.

(5) Subject to *section 181*, where the company making the purchase is immediately before the purchase a member of a group and immediately after the purchase—

(a) the vendor owns shares in one or more other members of the group, whether or not the vendor then owns shares in the company making the purchase, or

(b) the vendor owns shares in the company making the purchase and immediately before the purchase the vendor owned shares in one or more members of the group,

the vendor's interest as a shareholder in the group shall be substantially reduced.

(6) Subject to *section 181*, where the company making the purchase is immediately before the purchase a member of a group, and at that time an associate of the vendor owns shares in any member of the group, the combined interests as shareholders in the group of the vendor and the vendor's associates shall be substantially reduced.

(7) Subject to *subsection (8)*, in *subsections (9)* to *(11)*, "*relevant company*" means the company making the purchase and any other company—

(a) in which the vendor owns shares, and

(b) which is a member of the same group as the company making the purchase,

immediately before or immediately after the purchase.

(8) The question whether the combined interests as shareholders in the group of the vendor and the vendor's associates are substantially reduced shall be determined in the same way as is (under this section) the question whether a vendor's interest as a shareholder in a group is substantially reduced, except that the vendor shall be assumed to have the interests of the vendor's associates as well as the vendor's own interests, and references in *subsections (9)* to *(11)* to a relevant company shall be construed accordingly.

(9) The vendor's interest as a shareholder in the group shall be ascertained by—

(a) expressing the total nominal value of the shares owned by the vendor in each relevant company as a percentage of the issued share capital of the company,

(b) adding together the percentages so obtained, and

(c) dividing the result by the number of relevant companies (including any in which the vendor owns no shares).

(10) Subject to *subsection (11)*, the vendor's interest as a shareholder in the group shall be taken to be substantially reduced only if it does not exceed 75 per cent of the corresponding interest immediately before the purchase.

(11) The vendor's interest as a shareholder in the group shall not be taken to be substantially reduced where—

(a) the vendor would, if every member of the group distributed all its profits available for distribution immediately after the purchase (including any profits received by it on a distribution by another member), be entitled to a share of the profits of one or more or them, and

(b) that share, or the aggregate of those shares, expressed as a percentage of the aggregate of the profits available for distribution of every member of the group which is—

(i) a relevant company, or

(ii) a 51 per cent subsidiary of a relevant company,

exceeds 75 per cent of the corresponding percentage immediately before the purchase.

(12) *Subsections (6)* and *(7)* of *section 178* shall apply for the purposes of *subsection (11)* as they apply for the purposes of *subsection (5)* of that section.

Cross References

From Section 179

Section 178 Conditions as to reduction of vendor's interest as shareholder.
Section 181 Relaxation of conditions in certain cases.

To Section 179

Section 180 Additional conditions.
Section 181 Relaxation of conditions in certain cases.

180 Additional conditions

[FA91 s65]

(1) In this section, "*group*" has the same meaning as in *section 179*.

(2) Subject to *section 181*, the vendor shall not immediately after the purchase be connected with the company making the purchase or with any company which is a member of the same group as that company.

(3) Subject to *section 181*, the purchase shall not be part of a scheme or arrangement which is designed or likely to result in the vendor or any associate of the vendor having interests in any company such that, if the vendor or any associate of the vendor had those interests immediately after the purchase, any of the conditions in *sections 178* and *179* and *subsection (2)* could not be satisfied.

(4) A transaction occurring within one year after the purchase shall be deemed for the purposes of *subsection (3)* to be part of a scheme or arrangement of which the purchase is also part.

Cross References

From Section 180

Section 178 Conditions as to reduction of vendor's interest as shareholder.

Section 179 Conditions applicable where purchasing company is member of a group.
Section 181 Relaxation of conditions in certain cases.

To Section 180

Section 181 Relaxation of conditions in certain cases.
Section 183 Information.

181 Relaxation of conditions in certain cases

[FA91 s66]

Where—

(a) any of the conditions in *sections 178* to *180* which are applicable are not satisfied in relation to the vendor, but

(b) the vendor proposed or agreed to the purchase in order to produce the result that the condition in *section 178(2)* or *179(6)*, which could not otherwise be satisfied in respect of the redemption, repayment or purchase of shares owned by a person of whom the vendor is an associate, could be satisfied in that respect,

then, if that result is produced by virtue of the purchase, *section 176(1)(a)* shall apply, as respects so much of the purchase as was necessary to produce that result, as if the conditions in *sections 178* to *180* were satisfied in relation to the vendor.

Cross References

From Section 181

Section 176 Purchase of unquoted shares by issuing company or its subsidiary.
Section 178 Conditions as to reduction of vendor's interest as shareholder.
Section 179 Conditions applicable where purchasing company is member of a group.
Section 180 Additional conditions.

To Section 181

Section 176 Purchase of unquoted shares by issuing company or its subsidiary.
Section 177 Conditions as to residence and period of ownership.
Section 178 Conditions as to reduction of vendor's interest as shareholder.
Section 179 Conditions applicable where purchasing company is member of a group.
Section 180 Additional conditions.

182 Returns

[FA91 s67]

(1) In this section, ["*prescribed form*" has the same meaning][1] as in [*Part 41A*][2].

(2) Where a company makes a payment which it treats as one to which *subsection (1)* or *(2)* of *section 176* applies, the company shall make a return in a prescribed form to the appropriate inspector of—

(a) the payment,

(b) the circumstances by reason of which that subsection is regarded as applying to it, and

(c) such further particulars as may be required by the prescribed form.

(3) A company shall make a return under this section—

(a) within 9 months from the end of the accounting period in which it makes the payment, or

(b) if, at any time after the payment is made, the inspector by notice in writing requests such a form, within the time (which shall not be less than 30 days) limited by such notice.

(4) *Section 1071* shall, with any necessary modifications, apply in relation to a return under this section as it applies in relation to a return under *section 884*.

Amendments

[1] Substituted by FA12 sched5(1)(l).

[2] Substituted by FA12 sched4(part 2)(g).

Cross References

From Section 182

Section 176 Purchase of unquoted shares by issuing company or its subsidiary.
Section 884 Returns of profits.
Section 950 Interpretation (Part 41).
Section 1071 Penalties for failure to make certain returns.

183 Information

[FA91 s68(1) to (3)]

(1) Where a company treats a payment made by it as one to which *subsection (1)(a)* or *(2)* of *section 176* applies, any person connected with the company who knows of any such scheme or arrangement affecting the payment as is mentioned in *section 180(3)* shall, within 60 days after that person first knows of both the payment and the scheme or arrangement, give a notice to the inspector containing particulars of the scheme or arrangement.

(2) Where the inspector has reason to believe that a payment treated by the company making it as one to which *subsection (1)(a)* or *(2)* of *section 176* applies may form part of a scheme or arrangement of the kind referred to in that section or in *section 180(3)*, the inspector may by notice require the company or any person connected with the company to furnish to the inspector within such time, not being less than 60 days, as may be specified in the notice—

(a) a declaration in writing stating whether or not, according to information which the company or that person has or can reasonably obtain, any such scheme or arrangement exists or has existed, and

(b) such other information as the inspector may reasonably require for the purposes of the provision in question and the company or that person has or can reasonably obtain.

(3) (a) The recipient of a payment treated by the company making it as a payment to which *subsection (1)(a)* or *(2)* of *section 176* applies shall, if so required by the inspector, state whether the payment in question is received on behalf of any person other than such recipient and, if so, the name and address of that person.

(b) Any person on whose behalf a payment referred to in *paragraph (a)* is received shall, if so required by the inspector, state whether the payment in question is received on behalf of any person other than that person and, if so, the name and address of that other person.

Cross References

From Section 183

Section 176 Purchase of unquoted shares by issuing company or its subsidiary.
Section 180 Additional conditions.

To Section 183

Section 185 Associated persons.

Section 186 Connected persons.

Schedule 29 Provisions Referred to in Sections 1052, 1053 and 1054

184 Treasury shares

[FA91 s70]

(1) For the purposes of the Tax Acts and the Capital Gains Tax Acts—

(a) any shares which are—

(i) held by the company as treasury shares, and

(ii) not cancelled by the company,

shall be deemed to be cancelled immediately on their acquisition by the company,

(b) a deemed or actual cancellation of shares shall be treated as giving rise to neither a chargeable gain nor an allowable loss, and

(c) a reissue by the company of treasury shares shall be treated as an issue of new shares by it.

(2) For the purposes of this section, a reference to treasury shares shall be a reference to treasury shares within the meaning of section 209 of the Companies Act, 1990.

185 Associated persons

[FA91 s71]

(1) Any question whether a person is an associate of another person in relation to a company shall be determined for the purposes of *sections 176* to *183* and *section 186* in accordance with the following provisions:

(a) [a husband and wife living together, or civil partners living together, shall be associates of one another, a person under the age of 18 shall be an associate of his or her parents and their spouses or civil partners, and his or her parents and their spouses or civil partners shall be the person's associates;][1]

(b) a person who has control of a company shall be an associate of the company and the company shall be the person's associate;

(c) where a person who has control of one company has control of another company, the second company shall be an associate of the first company;

(d) where shares in a company are held by trustees other than bare trustees, then, in relation to that company but subject to *subsection (2)*, the trustees shall be associates of—

(i) any person who directly or indirectly provided property to the trustees or has made a reciprocal arrangement for another person to do so,

(ii) any person who is by virtue of *paragraph (a)* an associate of a person within *subparagraph (i)*, and

(iii) any person who is or may become beneficially entitled to a material interest in the shares,

and any such person shall be an associate of the trustees;

(e) where shares in a company are comprised in the estate of a deceased person, then, in relation to that company, the deceased's personal representatives shall be associates of any person who is or may become beneficially entitled to a material interest in the shares, and any such person shall be an associate of the personal representatives;

(f) where one person is accustomed to act on the directions of another person in relation to the affairs of a company, then, in relation to that company, the 2 persons shall be associates of one another.

(2) *Subsection (1)(d)* shall not apply to shares held on trusts which—

(a) relate exclusively to an exempt approved scheme within the meaning of *Chapter 1* of *Part 30*, or

(b) are exclusively for the benefit of the employees, or the employees and directors, of the company referred to in *subsection (1)(d)* or of companies in a group to which that company belongs, or their dependants, and are not wholly or mainly for the benefit of directors or their relatives,

and for the purposes of this subsection "*group*" means a company which has one or more 51 per cent subsidiaries, together with those subsidiaries.

(3) For the purposes of *paragraphs (d)* and *(e)* of *subsection (1)*, a person's interest shall be a material interest if its value exceeds 5 per cent of the value of all the property held on the trusts or, as the case may be, comprised in the estate concerned, excluding any property in which the person is not and cannot become beneficially entitled to an interest.

Amendments

[1] Substituted by F(No.3)A11 sched1(25). Shall have effect from the passing of this Act 27 July 2011.

Cross References

From Section 185

Section 176 Purchase of unquoted shares by issuing company or its subsidiary.

Section 183 Information.

Section 186 Connected persons.

Section 770 Interpretation and supplemental (Chapter 1).

186 Connected persons

[FA91 s72; FA96 s131(9)(a)]

(1) Any question whether a person is connected with a company shall, notwithstanding *section 10*, be determined for the purposes of *sections 176* to *183* in accordance with the following provisions:

(a) a person shall, subject to *subsection (2)*, be connected with a company if the person directly or indirectly possesses or is entitled to acquire more than 30 per cent of—

(i) the issued ordinary share capital of the company,

(ii) the loan capital and issued share capital of the company, or

(iii) the voting power in the company;

(b) a person shall be connected with a company if the person directly or indirectly possesses or is entitled to acquire such rights as would, in the event of the winding up of the company or in any other circumstances, entitle the person to receive more than 30 per cent of the assets of the company which would then be available for distribution to equity holders of the company, and for the purposes of this paragraph—

(i) the persons who are equity holders of the company, and

(ii) the percentage of the assets of the company to which a person would be entitled,

shall be determined in accordance with *sections 413* and *415*, but construing references in *section 415* to the first company as references to an equity holder and references to a winding up as including references to other circumstances in which assets of the company are available for distribution to its equity holders;

(c) a person shall be connected with a company if the person has control of the company.

(2) Where a person—

(a) acquired or became entitled to acquire loan capital of a company in the ordinary course of a business carried on by the person, being a business which includes the lending of money, and

(b) takes no part in the management or conduct of the company,

the person's interest in that loan capital shall be disregarded for the purposes of *subsection (1)(a)*.

(3) References in this section to the loan capital of a company are references to any debt incurred by the company—

(a) for any money borrowed or capital assets acquired by the company,

(b) for any right to receive income created in favour of the company, or

(c) for consideration the value of which to the company was at the time when the debt was incurred substantially less than the amount of the debt, including any premium on the debt.

(4) For the purposes of this section—

(a) a person shall be treated as entitled to acquire anything which the person is entitled to acquire at a future date or will at a future date be entitled to acquire, and

(b) a person shall be assumed to have the rights or powers of the person's associates as well as the person's own rights or powers.

Cross References

From Section 186

Section 10 Connected persons.

Section 176 Purchase of unquoted shares by issuing company or its subsidiary.

Section 183 Information.

Section 413 Profits or assets available for distribution.

Section 415 Meaning of "the notional winding up".

To Section 186

Section 185 Associated persons.

PART 7

Income Tax and Corporation Tax Exemptions

CHAPTER 1

Income Tax

187 Exemption from income tax and associated marginal relief

[FA80 s1; FA81 s1(a)(i); FA89 s1(a); FA91 s1(a)(iii); FA94 s1(a); FA97 s1(a)]

[(1) In this section, "*the specified amount*" means, subject to subsection (2)—

(a) in a case where the individual would apart from this section be entitled to a tax credit specified in *section 461(a)* (inserted by the Finance Act, 2001), [€10,420][1], and

(b) in any other case, [€5,210][2].][3]

(2) (a) For the purposes of this section and *section 188*, where a claimant proves that he or she has living at any time during the year of assessment any qualifying child, then, subject to *subsection (3)*, the specified amount (within the meaning of this section or *section 188*, as the case may be) shall be increased for that year of assessment by—

(i) [€575][4] in respect of the first such child,

(ii) [€575][5] in respect of the second such child, and

(iii) [€830][6] in respect of each such child in excess of 2.

(b) Any question as to whether a child is a qualifying child for the purposes of this section or *section 188* shall be determined on the same basis as it would be for the purposes of *section 462*, but without regard to [*subsections (1)(b)*, *(2)* and *(3)* of that section.][7]

(3) Where for any year of assessment 2 or more individuals are, or but for this subsection would be, entitled under *subsection (2)* to an increase in the specified amount (within the meaning of this section or *section 188*, as the case may be) in respect of the same child, the following provisions shall apply:

(a) only one such increase under *subsection (2)* shall be allowed in respect of each child;

(b) where such child is maintained by one individual only, that individual only shall be entitled to claim the increase;

(c) where such child is maintained by more than one individual, each individual shall be entitled to claim such part of the increase as is proportionate to the amount expended on the child by that individual in relation to the total amount paid by all individuals towards the maintenance of the child;

(d) in ascertaining for the purposes of this subsection whether an individual maintains a child and, if so, to what extent, any payment made by the individual for or towards the maintenance of the child which that individual is entitled to deduct in computing his or her total income for the purposes of the Income Tax Acts shall be deemed not to be a payment for or towards the maintenance of the child.

(4) Where for any year of assessment—

(a) an individual makes a claim for the purpose, makes a return in the prescribed form of his or her total income for that year and proves that such total income does not exceed the specified amount, the individual shall be entitled to exemption from income tax, or

(b) an individual makes a claim for the purpose, makes a return in the prescribed form of his or her total income for that year and proves that such total income does not exceed a sum equal to twice the specified amount, the individual shall be entitled to have the amount of income tax payable in respect of his or her total income for that year, if that amount would but for this subsection exceed a sum equal to 40 per cent of the amount by which his or her total income exceeds the specified amount, reduced to that sum.

[(5) This section ceases to have effect on or after 1 January 2008.][8]

Amendments

[1, 2] Substituted by FA01 sched1(1)(d)(i). Applies as respects the year of assessment 2001 and subsequent years of assessment.

[3] Substituted by FA01 sched1(2)(a)(i). Applies as respects the year of assessment 2002 and subsequent years of assessment.

[4, 5, 6] Substituted by FA01 sched1(1)(d)(ii). Applies as respects the year of assessment 2001 and subsequent years of assessment.

[7] Substituted by FA02 sched6(3)(d). Shall be deemed to have come into force and take effect as on and from 6 April 2001.

[8] Inserted by FA08 s5(a).

Revenue Information Notes

IT8 – Income Tax Exemption & Marginal Relief for 2011

Revenue Precedents

Are the exemption limits available to a person who is not resident in Ireland. (section 187 and section 188 TCA 1997)? Yes. "Total Income" for these purposes includes income arising outside the State which is not chargeable to tax in the State. IT923063

Cross References

From Section 187

Section 188 Age exemption and associated marginal relief.
Section 461 Basic personal tax credit.
Section 462 One-parent family tax credit.

To Section 187

Section 485G Miscellaneous (Chapter 2A).
Section 1024 Method of apportioning reliefs and charging tax in cases of separate assessments.

188 Age exemption and associated marginal relief

[FA80 s2(1) to (4) and (6) and (7); FA81 s1(b)(i); FA89 s1(b); FA94 s1(b); FA96 s132 and Sch5 PtI par12; FA97 s1(b)]

[(1) In this section [...][1]—

"*income tax payable*" has the same meaning (inserted by the Finance Act, 2001) as in *section 3*, but without regard to any reduction of tax under *section 244*;

"*total income*" has the same meaning as in *section 3*, but includes income arising outside the State which is not chargeable to tax.

(2) In this section, "*the specified amount*" means, [subject to *subsection (2A)*][2]—

(a) in a case where the individual would apart from this section be entitled to a tax credit specified in *section 461(a)* (inserted by the Finance Act, 2001), [€36,000][3], and

(b) in any other case, [€18,000][4].][5]

[(2A) (a) For the purposes of this section, where a claimant proves that he or she has living at any time during the year of assessment any qualifying child then, subject to *subsection (2B)*, the specified amount (within the meaning of this section) shall be increased for that year of assessment by—

(i) €575 in respect of the first such child,

(ii) €575 in respect of the second such child, and

(iii) €830 in respect of each such child in excess of 2.

(b) Any question as to whether a child is a qualifying child for the purposes of this section shall be determined on the same basis as it would be for the purposes of [*section 462B*, but without regard to *subsections (1)(b), (1)(c), (3)* and *(5)*][6] of that section.

(2B) Where for any year of assessment 2 or more individuals are, or but for this subsection would be, entitled under *subsection (2A)* to an increase in the specified amount, (within the meaning of this section) in respect of the same child, the following provisions shall apply:

(a) only one such increase under *subsection (2A)* shall be allowed in respect of each child;

(b) where such child is maintained by one individual only, that individual only shall be entitled to claim the increase;

(c) where such child is maintained by more than one individual, each individual shall be entitled to claim such part of the increase as is proportionate to the amount expended on the child by that individual in relation to the total amount paid by all individuals towards the maintenance of the child;

(d) in ascertaining for the purposes of this subsection whether an individual maintains a child and, if so, to what extent, any payment made by the individual for or towards the maintenance of the child which that individual is entitled to deduct in computing his or her total income for the purposes of the Income Tax Acts shall be deemed not to be a payment for or towards the maintenance of the child.][7]

(3) This section shall apply for any year of assessment to an individual who makes a claim for the purpose, makes a return in the prescribed form of his or her total income for that year and proves that, at some time during the year of assessment, either the individual, or, in a case where the individual would apart from this section be entitled to [a tax credit specified in *section 461(a)*][8], the [spouse or civil partner][9] of the individual, was of the age of 65 years or over.

(4) Where an individual to whom this section applies proves that his or her total income for a year of assessment for which this section applies does not exceed the specified amount, the individual shall be entitled to exemption from income tax for that year.

(5) Where an individual to whom this section applies proves that his or her total income for a year of assessment for which this section applies does not exceed a sum equal to twice the specified amount, the individual shall be entitled to have the amount of income tax payable in respect of his or her total income for that year, if that amount would but for this subsection exceed a sum equal to 40 per cent of the amount by which his or her total income exceeds the specified amount, reduced to that sum.

(6) (a) *Subsections (1)* and *(2)* of *section 459* and *section 460* shall apply in relation to exemption from tax or any reduction of tax under this section [...][10] as they apply to any allowance, deduction, relief or reduction under the provisions specified in the Table to *section 458*.

(b) *Subsections (3)* and *(4)* of *section 459* and *paragraph 8* of *Schedule 28* shall, with any necessary modifications, apply in relation to exemption from tax or any reduction of tax under this section [...][11].

Amendments

[1] Deleted by FA08 s5(b)(i).

[2] Substituted by FA08 s5(b)(ii).

[3] Substituted by FA11 s5(a). As respects the year of assessment 2011 and subsequent years of assessment.

[4] Substituted by FA11 s5(b). As respects the year of assessment 2011 and subsequent years of assessment.

[5] Substituted by FA01 s4(a)(i). Applies as respects the year of assessment 2001 and subsequent years of assessment.

[6] Substituted by F(No.2)A13 s7(1)(d). Applies for the year of assessment 2014 and subsequent years of assessment.

[7] Inserted by FA08 s5(b)(iii).

[8] Substituted by FA01 s4(a)(ii). Applies as respects the year of assessment 2001 and subsequent years of assessment.

[9] Substituted by F(No.3)A11 sched1(26).

[10, 11] Deleted by FA08 s5(b)(iv).

Revenue Information Notes

IT8 – Income Tax Exemption & Marginal Relief for 2011

Revenue Precedents

Are the exemption limits available to a person who is not resident in Ireland. (section 187 and section 188 TCA 1997)? Yes. "Total Income" for these purposes includes income arising outside the State which is not chargeable to tax in the State. IT923063

Cross References

From Section 188

Section 3 Interpretation of Income Tax Acts.
Section 244 Relief for interest paid on certain home loans.
Section 458 Deductions allowed in ascertaining taxable income and provisions relating to reductions in tax.
Section 459 General provisions relating to allowances, deductions and reliefs.
Section 460 Rate of tax at which repayments are to be made.
Section 461 Basic personal tax credit.
Section 462 One-parent family tax credit.
Schedule 28 Statements, Lists and Declarations

To Section 188

Section 187 Exemption from income tax and associated marginal relief.
Section 244 Relief for interest paid on certain home loans.
Section 256 Interpretation (Chapter 4).
Section 261 Taxation of relevant interest, etc.
Section 263A Declarations to a relevant deposit taker relating to deposits of certain persons.
Section 459 General provisions relating to allowances, deductions and reliefs.
Section 485G Miscellaneous (Chapter 2A).
Section 644A Relief from income tax in respect of income from dealing in residential development land.
Section 739G Taxation of unit holders in investment undertakings. Taxation of unit holders in investment undertakings.
Section 787R Liability to tax and rate of tax on chargeable excess.
Section 790AA Taxation of lump sums in excess of the tax free amount.
Section 1024 Method of apportioning reliefs and charging tax in cases of separate assessments.

189 Payments in respect of personal injuries

[FA90 s5(1) and (2)]

(1) This section shall apply to any payment made—

(a) to or in respect of an individual who is permanently and totally incapacitated by reason of mental or physical infirmity from maintaining himself or herself, and

[(b) (i) pursuant to the issue of an order to pay under section 38 of the Personal Injuries Assessment Board Act 2003, or

(ii) following the institution by or on behalf of the individual of a civil action for damages,

in respect of personal injury giving rise to that mental or physical infirmity.][1]

[(2) (a) In this subsection—

"*relevant gains*" means chargeable gains (including allowable losses) within the meaning of the Capital Gains Tax Acts, which accrue to an individual, to or in respect of whom payments to which this section applies are made, from the disposal of—

(a) assets acquired with such payments,

(b) assets acquired with relevant income, or

(c) assets acquired directly or indirectly with the proceeds from the disposal of assets referred to in *paragraphs (a)* and *(b)*;

"*relevant income*" means income which arises to an individual, to or in respect of whom payments to which this section applies are made, from the investment—

(a) in whole or in part of such payments, or

(b) of income derived directly or indirectly from such payments,

being income consisting of dividends or other income which, but for this section, would be chargeable to tax under Schedule C or under Case III, IV (by virtue of [*section 59, 745* or *747E*][2]) or V of Schedule D or under Schedule F.

(b) Where for any year of assessment the aggregate of the relevant income arising to and the relevant gains accruing to an individual exceeds 50 per cent of the aggregate of the total income arising to and the total chargeable gains (including allowable losses) accruing to the individual for that year of assessment—

(i) the relevant income shall be exempt from income tax and shall not be reckoned in computing total income for the purposes of the Income Tax Acts, but the provisions of those Acts relating to the making of returns shall apply as if this section had not been enacted, and

(ii) the relevant gains shall be exempt from capital gains tax, but the provisions of the Capital Gains Tax Acts relating to the making of returns shall apply as if this section had not been enacted.

(c) For the purposes of computing whether a chargeable gain is, in whole or in part, a relevant gain, or whether income is, in whole or in part, relevant income, all such apportionments shall be made as are, in the circumstances, just and reasonable.][3]

Amendments

[1] Substituted by FA04 s6.

[2] Substituted by FA07 s11(a).

[3] Substituted by FA04 s17(1)(a). This section applies for the year of assessment 2004 and subsequent years of assessment.

Revenue Briefings

Tax Briefing

Tax Briefing June 2001 – Issue 44 pg 29 – Personal Injuries – Exemption of Income

Revenue Information Notes

IT 13 – Personal Injury Compensation Payments

Cross References

From Section 189

Section 17 Schedule C.
Section 20 Schedule F.
Section 59 Charge to tax of income from which tax has been deducted.
Section 745 Charge to income tax or corporation tax of offshore income gain.
Section 747E Disposal of an interest in offshore funds.

To Section 189

Section 172C Exemption from dividend withholding tax for certain persons.
Section 267 Repayment of appropriate tax in certain cases.
Section 730GA Repayment of appropriate tax.
Section 739G Taxation of unit holders in investment undertakings.Taxation of unit holders in investment undertakings.

189A Special trusts for permanently incapacitated individuals

[(1) In this section—

"*incapacitated individual*" means an individual who is permanently and totally incapacitated, by reason of mental or physical infirmity, from being able to maintain himself or herself;

"*public subscriptions*" means subscriptions, in the form of money or other property, raised, following an appeal made in that behalf to members of the public, for the benefit of one or more incapacitated individual or individuals, whose identity or identities is or are known to the persons making the subscriptions, being subscriptions that meet either of the following conditions, namely—

(a) the total amount of the subscriptions does not exceed [€381,000][1], or

(b) no amount of the subscriptions, at any time on or after the specified return date for the chargeable period for which exemption is first claimed under either *subsection (2)* or *(3)*, constitutes a subscription made by any one person that is greater than 30 per cent of the total amount of the subscriptions;

"*qualifying trust*" means a trust established by deed in respect of which it is shown to the satisfaction of the inspector or, on appeal, to the Appeal Commissioners, that—

(a) the trust has been established exclusively for the benefit of one or more specified incapacitated individual or individuals, for whose benefit public subscriptions, within the meaning of this section, have been raised,

(b) the trust requires that—

(i) the trust funds be applied for the benefit of that individual or those individuals, as the case may be, at the discretion of the trustees of the trust, and

[(ii) the undistributed part of the trust funds—

(I) where the individual or the last surviving individual, as the case may be, is survived by a child, spouse or civil partner, be appointed in favour of the estate of the deceased individual, or

(II) otherwise, be applied for charitable purposes or be appointed in favour of the trustees of charitable bodies,][2]

and

(c) none of the trustees of the trust is connected (within the meaning of *section 10*) with that individual or any of those individuals, as the case may be;

"*specified return date for the chargeable period*" has the same meaning as in [*section 959A*][3];

"*trust funds*" means, in relation to a qualifying trust—

(a) public subscriptions, raised for the benefit of the incapacitated individual or individuals, the subject or subjects of the trust, and

(b) all moneys and other property derived directly or indirectly from such public subscriptions.

(2) Income arising to the trustees of a qualifying trust in respect of the trust funds, being income consisting of dividends or other income which but for this section would be chargeable to tax under Schedule C or under Case III, IV (by virtue of *section 59* or *section 745*) or V of Schedule D or under Schedule F, shall be exempt from income tax and shall not be reckoned in computing total income for the purposes of the Income Tax Acts.

[(3) Gains accruing to trustees of a qualifying trust in respect of the trust funds shall not be chargeable gains for the purposes of the Capital Gains Tax Acts.

(4) (a) In this subsection—

"*relevant gains*" means chargeable gains (including allowable losses) within the meaning of the Capital Gains Tax Acts, which accrue to an incapacitated individual from the disposal of—

(a) assets acquired with payments made by the trustees of a qualifying trust,

(b) assets acquired with relevant income, or

(c) assets acquired directly or indirectly with the proceeds from the disposal of assets referred to in *paragraphs (a)* and *(b)*;

"*relevant income*" means income which—

(a) consists of payments made by the trustees of a qualifying trust to or in respect of an incapacitated individual, being a subject of the trust, or

(b) arises to such an incapacitated individual from the investment—

(i) in whole or in part of payments, made by the trustees of a qualifying trust, or

(ii) of income derived directly or indirectly from such payments,

being income consisting of dividends or other income which, but for this section, would be chargeable to tax under Schedule C or under Case III, IV (by virtue of [*section 59, 745* or *747E*][4]) or V of Schedule D or under Schedule F.

(b) Where for any year of assessment the aggregate of relevant income arising to and the relevant gains accruing to an individual exceeds 50 per cent of the aggregate of the total income arising to and the total chargeable gains (including allowable losses) accruing to the individual in that year of assessment—

(i) the relevant income shall be exempt from income tax and shall not be reckoned in computing total income for the purposes of the Income Tax Acts, but the provisions of those Acts relating to the making of returns shall apply as if this section had not been enacted, and

(ii) the relevant gains shall be exempt from capital gains tax, but the provisions of the Capital Gains Tax Acts relating to the making of returns shall apply as if this section had not been enacted.

(c) For the purposes of computing whether a chargeable gain is, in whole or in part, a relevant gain, or whether income is, in whole or in part, relevant income, all such apportionments shall be made as are, in the circumstances, just and reasonable][5]

(5) This section shall have effect as respects the year 1997-98 and subsequent years of assessment.][6]

Amendments

[1] Substituted by FA01 sched5.

[2] Substituted by FA14 s10. Comes into operation on 1 January 2015.

[3] Substituted by FA12 sched4(part 2)(g).

[4] Substituted by FA07 s11(b).

[5] Substituted by FA04 s17(1)(b). This section applies for the year of assessment 2004 and subsequent years of assessment.

[6] Inserted by FA99 s12(a).

Revenue Briefings

Tax Briefing

Tax Briefing December 1999 – Issue 38 pg 7 – Special Trusts – Permanently Incapacitated Individuals
Tax Briefing June 2001 – Issue 44 pg 29 – Personal Injuries – Exemption of Income

Cross References

From Section 189A

Section 10 Connected persons.
Section 17 Schedule C.
Section 20 Schedule F.
Section 59 Charge to tax of income from which tax has been deducted.
Section 745 Charge to income tax or corporation tax of offshore income gain.
Section 747E Disposal of an interest in offshore funds.
Section 950 Interpretation (Part 41).

To Section 189A

Section 172C Exemption from dividend withholding tax for certain persons.
Section 256 Interpretation (Chapter 4).
Section 263B Declarations to the Revenue Commissioners relating to deposits of certain persons.
Section 263C Notifications by the Revenue Commissioners relating to deposits of certain persons.
Section 267 Repayment of appropriate tax in certain cases.
Section 730GA Repayment of appropriate tax.

190 Certain payments made by the Haemophilia HIV Trust

[FA90 s7]

(1) In this section, "*the Trust*" means the trust established by deed dated the 22nd day of November, 1989, between the Minister for Health and certain other persons, and referred to in that deed as "the Haemophilia H.I.V. Trust" or "the HHT".

(2) This section shall apply to income consisting of payments made by the trustees of the Trust to or in respect of a beneficiary under the Trust.

(3) Notwithstanding any provision of the Income Tax Acts, income to which this section applies shall be disregarded for the purposes of those Acts.

191 Taxation treatment of Hepatitis C compensation payments

[FA96 s9]

[(1) In this section—

"*the Act*" means the Hepatitis C Compensation Tribunal Act, 1997;

"*the Tribunal*" means the Tribunal known as the Hepatitis C Compensation Tribunal established under *section 3* of the Act.

(2) This section shall apply to any payment in respect of compensation—

(a) by the Tribunal in accordance with the Act, or

(b) following the institution by or on behalf of a person of a civil action for damages in respect of personal injury,

to a person referred to—

(i) in subsection (1) of section 4 of the Act, in respect of matters referred to in that section, or

(ii) in any regulations made under section 9 of the Act, in respect of matters referred to in those regulations.][1]

(3) For the purposes of [the Income Tax Acts and the Capital Gains Tax Acts][2] and notwithstanding any provision of those Acts to the contrary—

(a) income consisting of payments to which this section applies shall be disregarded, and

(b) any payment by the Tribunal to which this section applies shall be treated in all respects as if it were a payment made following the institution, by or on behalf of the person to or in respect of whom the payment is made, of a civil action for damages in respect of personal injury.

Amendments

[1] Substituted by FA98 s8. Applies as on and from the 1st day of November, 1997.

[2] Substituted by FA04 s17(1)(c). This section applies for the year of assessment 2004 and subsequent years of assessment.

Revenue Briefings

Tax Briefing

Tax Briefing March 1999 – Issue 35 pg 6 – Hepatitis C Compensation Payments
Tax Briefing June 2001 – Issue 44 pg 28 – Hepatitis C Compensation Payments

Cross References

From Section 191

Section 3 Interpretation of Income Tax Acts.

192 Payments in respect of thalidomide children

[FA73 s19(1) and (2); FA78 s7]

(1) This section shall apply to any payment made by the Minister for Health and Children or by the foundation known as [Conterganstiftung für behinderte Menschen][1] to or in respect of any individual handicapped by reason of infirmity which can be linked with the taking by the individual's mother during her pregnancy of preparations containing thalidomide.

(2) Income which—

(a) consists of a payment to which this section applies, or

(b) arises to a person to or in respect of whom payments to which this section applies are made, from the investment in whole or in part of such payments or of the income derived from such payments, being income consisting of dividends or other income which but for this section would be chargeable to tax under Schedule C or under Case III, IV [(by virtue of [*section 59*, *745* or *747E*][2])][3] or V of Schedule D or under Schedule F,

shall be exempt from income tax and shall not be reckoned in computing total income for the purposes of the Income Tax Acts; but the provisions of those Acts relating to the making of returns of total income shall apply as if this section had not been enacted.

[(3) Gains which accrue to a person, to or in respect of whom payments to which this section applies are made, from the disposal of—

(a) assets acquired with such payments,

(b) assets acquired with income exempted from income tax under *subsection (2)*, or

(c) assets acquired directly or indirectly with the proceeds from the disposal of assets referred to in *paragraphs (a)* and *(b)*,

shall not be chargeable gains for the purposes of the Capital Gains Tax Acts.

(4) For the purposes of computing whether by virtue of this section a gain is, in whole or in part, a chargeable gain, or whether income is, in whole or in part, exempt from income tax, all such apportionments shall be made as are, in the circumstances, just and reasonable.][4]

Amendments

[1] Substituted by FA11 sched3(1)(b). Has effect as on and from 6 February 2011.

[2] Substituted by FA07 s11(c).

[3] Substituted by FA99 s13(b).

[4] Inserted by FA04 s17(1)(d). This section applies for the year of assessment 2004 and subsequent years of assessment.

Revenue Briefings

Tax Briefing

Tax Briefing June 2001 – Issue 44 pg 29 – Personal Injuries – Exemption of Income

Revenue Precedents

Where a rental property is financed partly by thalidomide compensation funds and partly by a mortgage, what is the treatment for tax purposes of the rental income from the property? Given the wide ranging nature of Section 192 TCA 1997, the full amount of the rental income is treated as exempt. IT972503

Cross References

From Section 192

Section 17 Schedule C.

Section 20 Schedule F.

Section 59 Charge to tax of income from which tax has been deducted.

Section 745 Charge to income tax or corporation tax of offshore income gain.

Section 747E Disposal of an interest in offshore funds.

To Section 192

Section 172C Exemption from dividend withholding tax for certain persons.

Section 267 Repayment of appropriate tax in certain cases.

Section 730GA Repayment of appropriate tax.

Section 739G Taxation of unit holders in investment undertakings.Taxation of unit holders in investment undertakings.

192A Exemption in respect of certain payments under employment law

[(1) In this section—

"*relevant Act*" means an enactment which contains provisions for the protection of employees' rights and entitlements or for the obligations of employers towards their employees; relevant authority' means any of the following—

(a) a rights commissioner,

(b) the Director of Equality Investigations,

(c) the Employment Appeals Tribunal,

(d) the Labour Court,

(e) the Circuit Court, or

(f) the High Court.

(2) Subject to *subsections (3)* and *(5)*, this section applies to a payment under a relevant Act, to an employee or former employee by his or her employer or former employer, as the case may be, which is made, on or after 4 February 2004, in accordance with a recommendation, decision or a determination by a relevant authority in accordance with the provisions of that Act.

(3) A payment made in accordance with a settlement arrived at under a mediation process provided for in a relevant Act shall be treated as if it had been made in accordance with a recommendation, decision or determination under that Act of a relevant authority.

(4) (a) Subject to *subsection (5)* and without prejudice to any of the terms or conditions of an agreement referred to in this subsection, this section shall apply to a payment—

(i) made, on or after 4 February 2004, under an agreement evidenced in writing, being an agreement between persons who are not connected with each other (within the meaning of *section 10*), in settlement of a claim which—

(I) had it been made to a relevant authority, would have been a *bona fide* claim made under the provisions of a relevant Act,

(II) is evidenced in writing, and

(III) had the claim not been settled by the agreement, is likely to have been the subject of a recommendation, decision or determination under that Act by a relevant authority that a payment be made to the person making the claim,

(ii) the amount of which does not exceed the maximum payment which, in accordance with a decision or determination by a relevant authority (other than the Circuit Court or the High Court) under the relevant Act, could have been made under that Act in relation to the claim, had the claim not been settled by agreement, and

(iii) where—

(I) copies of the agreement and the statement of claim are kept and retained by the employer, by or on behalf of whom the payment was made, for a period of six years from the day on which the payment was made, and

(II) the employer has made copies of the agreement and the statement of claim available to an officer of the Revenue Commissioners where the officer has requested the employer to make those copies available to him or her.

(b) (i) On being so requested by an officer of the Revenue Commissioners, an employer shall make available to the officer all copies of—

(I) such agreements as are referred to in *paragraph (a)* entered into by or on behalf of the employer, and

(II) the statements of claim related to those agreements,

kept and retained by the employer in accordance with *subparagraph (iii)* of that paragraph.

(ii) The officer may examine and take extracts from or copies of any documents made available to him or her under this subsection.

(5) This section shall not apply to so much of a payment under a relevant Act or an agreement referred to in *subsection (4)* as is—

(a) a payment, however described, in respect of remuneration including arrears of remuneration, or

(b) a payment referred to in *section 123(1)* or *480(2)(a)*.

[(5A) This section shall not apply to payments made pursuant to an order under *section 2B* of the Employment Permits Act 2003.][1]

(6) Payments to which this section applies shall be exempt from income tax and shall not be reckoned in computing total income for the purposes of the Income Tax Acts.][2]

Amendments

[1] Inserted by EP(A)A14 s37(b).

[2] Substituted by FA04 s7.

Revenue Information Notes

IT71 – Exemption from Income Tax

Cross References

From Section 192A

Section 10 Connected persons.

Section 123 General tax treatment of payments on retirement or removal from office or employment.

Section 480 Relief for certain sums chargeable under Schedule E.

192B Foster care payments etc

[(1) In this section—

"*carer*" means an individual who is or was a foster parent or relative or who takes care of an individual on behalf of the Health Service Executive;

"*foster parent*" has the meaning assigned to it in the Child Care (Placement of Children in Foster Care) Regulations 1995 (S.I. No. 260 of 1995);

"*relative*" has the meaning assigned to it in the Child Care (Placement of Children with Relatives) Regulations 1995 (S.I. No. 261 of 1995).

(2) This section applies to payments made—

(a) to a carer by the Health Service Executive in accordance with—

(i) article 14 of the Child Care (Placement of Children in Foster Care) Regulations 1995, or

(ii) article 14 of the Child Care (Placement of Children with Relatives) Regulations 1995,

(b) at the discretion of the Health Service Executive to a carer in respect of an individual—

(i) who had been in the care of a carer until attaining the age of 18 years,

(ii) in respect of whom a payment referred to in *paragraph (a)* had been paid until the individual attained the age of 18 years,

(iii) who since attaining the age of 18 years continues to reside with a carer, and

(iv) who has not attained the age of 21 years or where the person has attained such age, suffers from a disability or is in receipt of full-time instruction at any university, college, school or other educational establishment and such disability or instruction commenced before the person attained the age of 21 years,

or

(c) in accordance with the law of any other Member State of the European Communities which corresponds to the payments referred to in *paragraph (a)* or *(b)*.

(3) Payments to which this section applies are exempt from income tax and shall not be taken into account in computing total income for the purposes of the Income Tax Acts.][1]

Amendments

[1] Inserted by FA05 s11.

192C Exemption in respect of payments of State support

[(1) Notwithstanding any other provision of the Income Tax Acts, a person in receipt of care services shall be exempt from income tax in respect of any State support provided to the person under section 12(2) of the Nursing Homes Support Scheme Act 2009 and the payment shall not be reckoned in computing the person's income for the purposes of the Income Tax Acts.

(2) Notwithstanding any provision of the Income Tax Acts, any payment referred to in subsection (1) shall be paid without deduction of income tax.

(3) In this section "*care services*" and "*State support*" have the same meaning as in the Nursing Homes Support Scheme Act 2009.][1]

Amendments

[1] Inserted by the Nursing Homes Support Scheme Act 2009 Sec 48. This Act shall come into operation on such day or days as the Minister may appoint by order or orders either generally or with reference to any particular purpose or provision, and different days may be so appointed for different purposes and different provisions

193 Income from scholarships

[ITA67 s353; FA97 s11(1) and (2)]

(1) (a) In this section—

"*relevant body*" means a body corporate, unincorporated body, partnership, individual or other body;

"*relevant scholarship*" means a scholarship provision for which is made, either directly or indirectly, by a relevant body or a person connected with the relevant body and where payments are made, either directly or indirectly, in respect of such a scholarship to—

(i) an employee or, where the relevant body is a body corporate, a director of the relevant body, or

(ii) the [spouse, civil partner, family, dependants, servants or children of the civil partner][1] of such employee or director;

"*scholarship*" includes an exhibition, bursary or other similar educational endowment.

(b) A person shall be regarded as connected with a relevant body for the purposes of this subsection if that person is—

(i) a trustee of a settlement, within the meaning of *section 10*, made by the relevant body, or

(ii) a relevant body,

and that person would be regarded as connected with the relevant body for the purposes of that section.

(2) Income arising from a scholarship held by a person receiving full-time instruction at a university, college, school or other educational establishment shall be exempt from income tax, and no account shall be taken of any such income in computing the amount of income for the purposes of the Income Tax Acts.

(3) Nothing in *subsection (2)* shall be construed as conferring on any person other than the person holding the scholarship in question any exemption from a charge to income tax.

(4) Notwithstanding *subsection (3)*, a payment of income arising from a relevant scholarship which is—

(a) provided from a trust fund or under a scheme, and

(b) held by a person receiving full-time instruction at a university, college, school or other educational establishment,

shall be exempt from income tax if, in the year of assessment in which the payment is made, not more than 25 per cent of the total amount of the payments made from that fund, or under that scheme, in respect of scholarships held as mentioned in *paragraph (b)* is attributable to relevant scholarships.

(5) If any question arises whether any income is income arising from a scholarship held by a person receiving full-time instruction at a university, college, school or other educational establishment, the Revenue Commissioners may consult the Minister for Education and Science.

(6) Where a payment is made before the 6th day of April, 1998, in respect of a scholarship awarded before the 26th day of March, 1997, this section shall apply subject to *paragraph 2* of *Schedule 32*.

Amendments

[1] Substituted by F(No.3)A11 sched1(27). Shall have effect from the passing of this Act 27 July 2011.

Case Law

The UK equivalent of section 193, in its original form, granted a blanket exemption to scholarship income. Wicks v Firth 1984 56 TC 318

Cross References

From Section 193

Section 10 Connected persons.
Schedule 32 Transitional Provisions

To Section 193

Section 897 Returns of employees' emoluments, etc.
Schedule 32 Transitional Provisions

194 Child benefit

[ITA67 s354; FA97 s146(1) and Sch9 PtI par1(26)]

Child benefit payable under [Part 4 of the Social Welfare Consolidation Act 2005,][1] or any subsequent Act together with which that Act may be cited, shall be exempt from income tax and shall not be reckoned in computing income for the purposes of the Income Tax Acts.

Amendments

[1] Substituted by FA07 sched4(1)(c). Shall have effect as on and from 2 April 2007

194A Early childcare supplement

[Early childcare supplement payable under Part 4A (inserted by the *Social Welfare Law Reform and Pensions Act 2006*) of the Social Welfare Consolidation Act 2005 shall be exempt from income tax and shall not be reckoned in computing income for the purposes of the Income Tax Acts.][1]

Amendments

[1] Inserted by SWLRPA s47(1).

195 Exemption of certain earnings of writers, composers and artists

[FA69 s2; FA89 s5; FA94 s14; FA95 s173(2); FA96 s14; FA97 s146(1) and Sch9 PtI par18(1)]

[(1) In this section—

'*EEA Agreement*' means the Agreement on the European Economic Area signed at Oporto on 2 May 1992, as adjusted by all subsequent amendments to that Agreement;

'*EEA state*' means a state which is a contracting party to the EEA Agreement;

'*work*' means an original and creative work which is within one of the following categories:

(a) a book or other writing;

(b) a play;

(c) a musical composition;

(d) a painting or other like picture;

(e) a sculpture.][1]

(2) (a) This section shall apply to an individual—

[(i) who is—

(I) resident in one or more Member States, or in another EEA state, and not resident elsewhere, or

(II) ordinarily resident and domiciled in one or more Member States, or in another EEA state, and not resident elsewhere, and][2]

(ii) (I) who is determined by the Revenue Commissioners, after consideration of any evidence in relation to the matter which the individual submits to them and after such consultation (if any) as may seem to them to be necessary with such person or body of persons as in their opinion may be of assistance to them, to have written, composed or executed, as the case may be, either solely or jointly with another individual, a work or works generally recognised as having cultural or artistic merit, or

(II) who has written, composed or executed, as the case may be, either solely or jointly with another individual, a particular work which the Revenue Commissioners, after consideration of the work and of any evidence in relation to the matter which the individual submits to them and after such consultation (if any) as may seem to them to be necessary with such person or body of persons as in their opinion may be of assistance to them, determine to be a work having cultural or artistic merit.

(b) The Revenue Commissioners shall not make a determination under this subsection unless—

(i) the individual concerned duly makes a claim to the Revenue Commissioners for the determination, being (where the determination is sought under *paragraph (a)(ii)(II)*) a claim made after the publication, production or sale, as the case may be, of the work in relation to which the determination is sought, and

(ii) the individual complies with any request to him or her under *subsection (4)*.

(3) (a) An individual to whom this section applies and who duly makes a claim to the Revenue Commissioners in that behalf shall, [subject to *paragraphs* (*aa*) and (*b*)][3], be entitled to have the profits or gains arising to him or her from the publication, production or sale, as the case may be, of a work or works in relation to which the Revenue Commissioners have made a determination

under *clause (I)* or *(II)* of *subsection (2)(a)(ii)*, or of a work of the individual in the same category as that work, and which apart from this section would be included in an assessment made on him or her under Case II of Schedule D, disregarded for the purposes of the Income Tax Acts.

[(aa) The amount of the profits or gains for a year of assessment which an individual shall be entitled to have disregarded for the purposes of the Income Tax Acts by virtue of *paragraph* (*a*) [shall not exceed €50,000 for the year of assessment 2015][4] and each subsequent year of assessment.][5]

(b) The exemption authorised by this section shall not apply for any year of assessment before the year of assessment in which the individual concerned makes a claim under *clause (I)* or *(II)* of *subsection (2)(a)(ii)* in respect of which the Revenue Commissioners make a determination referred to in *clause (I)* or *(II)* of *subsection (2)(a)(ii)*, as the case may be.

(c) The relief provided by this section may be given by repayment or otherwise.

(4) (a) Where an individual makes a claim to which *subsection (2)(a)(ii)(I)* relates, the Revenue Commissioners may serve on the individual a notice or notices in writing requesting the individual to furnish to them within such period as may be specified in the notice or notices such information, books, documents or other evidence as may appear to them to be necessary for the purposes of a determination under *subsection (2)(a)(ii)(I)*.

(b) Where an individual makes a claim to which *subsection (2)(a)(ii)(II)* relates, the individual shall—

(i) in the case of a book or other writing or a play or musical composition, if the Revenue Commissioners so request, furnish to them 3 copies, and

(ii) in the case of a painting or other like picture or a sculpture, if the Revenue Commissioners so request, provide, or arrange for the provision of, such facilities as the Revenue Commissioners may consider necessary for the purposes of a determination under *subsection (2)(a)(ii)(II)* (including any requisite permissions or consents of the person who owns or possesses the painting, picture or sculpture).

(5) The Revenue Commissioners may serve on an individual who makes a claim under *subsection (3)* a notice or notices in writing requiring the individual to make available within such time as may be specified in the notice all such books, accounts and documents in the individual's possession or power as may be requested, being books, accounts and documents relating to the publication, production or sale, as the case may be, of the work in respect of the profits or gains of which exemption is claimed.

(6) (a) In this subsection, "*relevant period*" means, as respects a claim in relation to a work or works or a particular work, the period of 6 months commencing on the date on which a claim is first made in respect of that work or those works or the particular work, as the case may be.

(b) Where—

(i) an individual—

(I) has made due claim (in this subsection referred to as a "*claim*") to the Revenue Commissioners for a determination under *clause (I)* or *(II)* of *subsection (2)(a)(ii)* in relation to a work or works or a particular work, as the case may be, that the individual has written, composed or executed, as the case may be, solely or jointly with another individual, and

(II) as respects the claim, has complied with any request made to the individual under *subsection (4)* or *(5)* in the relevant period,

and

(ii) the Revenue Commissioners fail to make a determination under *clause (I)* or *(II)* of *subsection (2)(a)(ii)* in relation to the claim in the relevant period,

the individual may, by notice in writing given to the Revenue Commissioners within 30 days after the end of the relevant period, appeal to the Appeal Commissioners on the grounds that—

(A) the work or works is or are generally recognised as having cultural or artistic merit, or

(B) the particular work has cultural or artistic merit,

as the case may be.

(7) The Appeal Commissioners shall hear and determine an appeal made to them under *subsection (6)* as if it were an appeal against an assessment to income tax and, subject to *subsection (8)*, the provisions of the Income Tax Acts relating to such appeals and to the rehearing of an appeal and to the statement of a case for the opinion of the High Court on a point of law shall apply accordingly with any necessary modifications.

(8) (a) On the hearing of an appeal made under *subsection (6)*, the Appeal Commissioners may—

(i) after consideration of—

(I) any evidence in relation to the matter submitted to them by or on behalf of the individual concerned and by or on behalf of the Revenue Commissioners, and

(II) in relation to a work or works or a particular work, the work or works or the particular work,

and

(ii) after such consultation (if any) as may seem to them to be necessary with such person or body of persons as in their opinion may be of assistance to them,

determine that the individual concerned has written, composed or executed, as the case may be, either solely or jointly with another individual—

(A) a work or works generally recognised as having cultural or artistic merit, or

(B) a particular work which has cultural or artistic merit,

and, where the Appeal Commissioners so determine, the individual shall be entitled to relief under *subsection (3)(a)* as if the determination had been made by the Revenue Commissioners under *clause (I)* or *(II)* of *subsection (2)(a)(ii)*, as the case may be.

(b) This subsection shall, subject to any necessary modifications, apply to the rehearing of an appeal by a judge of the Circuit Court and, to the extent necessary, to the determination by the High Court of any question or questions of law arising on the statement of a case for the opinion of the High Court.

(9) For the purposes of the hearing or rehearing of an appeal made under *subsection (6)*, the Revenue Commissioners may nominate any of their officers to act on their behalf.

(10) For the purposes of determining the amount of the profits or gains to be disregarded under this section for the purposes of the Income Tax Acts, the Revenue Commissioners may make such apportionment of receipts and expenses as may be necessary.

(11) Notwithstanding any exemption provided by this section, the provisions of the Income Tax Acts regarding the making by the individual of a return of his or her total income shall apply as if the exemption had not been authorised.

(12) (a) An Comhairle Ealaíon and the Minister for Arts, Heritage, Gaeltacht and the Islands shall, with the consent of the Minister for Finance, draw up guidelines for determining for the purposes of this section whether a work within a category specified in *subsection (1)* is an original and creative work and whether it has, or is generally recognised as having, cultural or artistic merit.

(b) Without prejudice to the generality of *paragraph (a)*, a guideline under that paragraph may—

(i) consist of a specification of types or kinds of works that are not original and creative or that have not, or are not generally recognised as having, cultural or artistic merit, including a specification of works that are published, produced or sold for a specified purpose, and

(ii) specify criteria by reference to which the questions whether works are original or creative and whether they have, or are generally recognised as having, cultural or artistic merit are to be determined.

(13) (a) Where a claim for a determination under *subsection (2)* is made to the Revenue Commissioners, the Revenue Commissioners shall not determine that the work concerned is original and creative or has, or is generally recognised as having, cultural or artistic merit unless it complies with the guidelines under *subsection (12)* for the time being in force.

(b) *Paragraph (a)* shall, with any necessary modifications, apply to—

(i) a determination by the Appeal Commissioners under *subsection (8)* on an appeal to them under *subsection (6)* in relation to a claim mentioned in *paragraph (a)*, and

(ii) a rehearing by a judge of the Circuit Court of an appeal mentioned in *subparagraph (i)* and, to the extent necessary, to the determination by the High Court of any question of law arising on such an appeal or rehearing and specified in the statement of a case for the opinion of the High Court, by the Appeal Commissioners or, as the case may be, a judge of the Circuit Court.

(14) Where a determination has been or is made under *clause (I)* or *(II)* of *subsection (2)(a)(ii)* in relation to a work or works of a person, *subsection (3)(a)* shall not apply to any other work of that person that is in the same category as such work or works and is or was first published, produced or sold on or after the 3rd day of May, 1994, unless that other work is one that complies with the guidelines under *subsection (12)* for the time being in force and would qualify to be determined by the Revenue Commissioners as an original or creative work and as having, or being generally recognised as having, cultural or artistic merit.

(15) On application to the Revenue Commissioners in that behalf by any person, the Revenue Commissioners shall supply the person free of charge with a copy of any guidelines under *subsection (12)* for the time being in force.

[(16) (a) The Revenue Commissioners may publish, or cause to be published, the name of an individual who is the subject of a determination under *subsection (2)*.

(b) Publication under *paragraph (a)* may, as appropriate, include the title or category of the work of an individual.][6]

Amendments

[1] Substituted by FA14 s5(a). Comes into operation on 1 January 2015.

[2] Substituted by FA14 s5(b). Comes into operation on 1 January 2015.

[3] Substituted by FA11 s(17)(a). Deemed to have come into force and takes effect as on and from 1 January 2011.

[4] Substituted by FA14 s5(c). Comes into operation on 1 January 2015.

[5] Inserted by FA11 s(17)(b). Deemed to have come into force and takes effect as on and from 1 January 2011.

[6] Inserted by FA12 s132.

Case Law

In Gormley v EMI Records 1998 ILRM 124 the word 'original' was considered in respect of a claim to copyright.

A series of articles published by a journalist were not 'original and creative'. Healy v Breathnach 1986 III ITR 496

Revenue Briefings

Tax Briefing

Tax Briefing December 2000 – Issue 42 pg 17 – Artist Exemption – Questions and Answers

Tax Briefing July 2004 – Issue 56 pg 12 – 'Not Resident Elsewhere'

Tax Briefing October 2004 – Issue 57 pg 15 – 'Not Resident Elsewhere' – Correction (Tax Briefing 56)

eBrief

eBrief No. 56/2013 – New Guidelines for the Artists Exemption Scheme

Cross References

To Section 195

Section 91 Receipts accruing after discontinuance of trade or profession.

Section 531B Charge to income levy.

Section 531AM Charge to universal social charge.

Section 531AS Universal social charge payable by chargeable persons (within the meaning of Part 41).

Schedule 25B List of Specified Reliefs and Method of Determining Amount of Specified Relief Used in a Tax Year

Schedule 31 Consequential Amendments

195A Exemption in respect of certain expense payments

[(1) In this section—

"*body*" means an unincorporated body of persons or a body corporate, being—

(a) any board, council or committee, however expressed, or

(b) any body of persons exercising some or all of the functions of such a board, council or committee,

where the duties, other than incidental duties such as attendance at conventions or meetings as delegates on behalf of the body, of the office of members of the body are discharged in the course of meetings of the body concerned, or preparation for such meetings;

"*civil servant*" has the meaning assigned to it by section 1(1) of the Civil Service Regulation Act 1956;

"*member*", in relation to a body, means a person holding office as a member of that body—

(a) who has no other duties directly or indirectly, whether as an employee of the body or of a person connected with that body, in relation to that body, and

(b) whose annualised amount of the emoluments from the office for the year of assessment 2006 and for each subsequent year in which the person is a member of the body, other than payments to which this section applies, does not exceed—

(i) in the case of a member who is the chairperson of the body, not being a body referred to in *paragraph (b)* of the definition of "*body*", €24,000, and

(ii) in any other case, €14,000;

"*non-commercial body*" means a body—

(a) organised solely for purposes other than profit, where the declared purposes of the body can be ascertained from documents of record,

(b) which, in fact, operates solely for purposes other than profit and, for this purpose, any activity generating income carried on by the body—

(i) which is carried on for the purposes of assisting the body to achieve its purposes, and

(ii) the income of which is used for those purposes,

shall be regarded as operating for purposes other than profit, and

(c) any benefit, or part of the income or accumulated income, of which, cannot be paid to, or cannot otherwise be made available to, any officer, employee or member of the body for the personal benefit of that person or a person connected with that person other than—

(i) any wages, salaries, fees or honorariums for services rendered to the body but only if the amounts paid are no more than reasonable amounts that would be paid in a transaction at arm's length for similar services by a body organised solely for purposes other than profit, being a body operating in accordance with *paragraph (b)*,

(ii) any payment to which this section applies,

(iii) any payment made to officers, employees or members to assist in the covering of expenses to attend conventions or meetings as delegates on behalf of the body where such attendance is to further the purposes of the body, and

(iv) where the officer, employee or member concerned, or a person connected with such officer, employee or member, is also an object of the purposes of the body, a benefit which is in furtherance of the purposes of the body.

(2) This section applies to payments made by a non-commercial body to or on behalf of a member of the body in respect of expenses of travel and subsistence incurred by the member in the attendance by him or her at meetings of the body.

(3) So much of any payments to which this section applies, as does not exceed the upper of any relevant rate or rates laid down from time to time by the Minister for Finance in relation to the payment of expenses of travel and subsistence of a civil servant, shall be disregarded for all the purposes of the Income Tax Acts.][1]

Amendments

[1] Inserted by FA07 s12. Applies as respects the year of assessment 2007 and subsequent years of assessment.

Revenue Briefings

Tax Briefing

Tax Briefing July 2007 – Issue 66 – Finance Act 2007 – Income Tax

Statements of Practice

Tax Treatment of Remuneration of Members of State and State Sponsored Committees and Boards – SP/1/04

Tax Treatment of the reimbursement of Expenses of Travel and Subsistence to office Holders and Employees – SP/IT/2/07

196 Expenses of members of judiciary

[FA94 s164]

(1) In this section, "*a member of the Judiciary*" means—

(a) a judge of the Supreme Court,

(b) a judge of the High Court,

(c) a judge of the Circuit Court, or

(d) a judge of the District Court.

(2) An allowance payable by means of an annual sum to a member of the Judiciary in accordance with section 5 of the Courts of Justice Act, 1953, and which has been determined, in accordance with *subsection (2)(c)* of that section, by the Minister for Justice, Equality and Law Reform in consultation with the Minister for Finance to be in full settlement of the expenses which such a person is obliged to incur in the performance of his or her duties as a member of the Judiciary, and which are not otherwise reimbursed either directly or indirectly out of moneys provided by the Oireachtas, shall be exempt from income tax and shall not be reckoned in computing income for the purposes of the Income Tax Acts.

(3) *Sections 114* and *115* shall not apply in relation to expenses in full settlement of which an allowance referred to in *subsection (2)* is payable, and no claim shall lie under those sections in respect of those expenses.

Cross References

From Section 196

Section 114 General rule as to deductions.

Section 115 Fixed deduction for certain classes of persons.

196A State employees: foreign service allowances

[(1) Where any allowance to, or emoluments of, an officer of the State are certified by the Minister for Finance, having consulted with the Minister for Foreign Affairs, or with such Minister of the Government as the Minister for Finance considers appropriate in the circumstances, to represent compensation for the extra cost of having to live outside the State in order to perform his or her duties, that allowance, or those emoluments, shall be disregarded as income for the purposes of the Income Tax Acts.

(2) In this section—

"*emoluments*" means emoluments to which *section 985A* applies;

"*officer of the State*" means—

(a) a civil servant within the meaning of section 1(1) of the Civil Service Regulation Act 1956,

(b) a member of the Garda Síochána, or

(c) a member of the Permanent Defence Force.

(3) This section is deemed to have applied as on and from 1 January 2005.][1]

Amendments

[1] Inserted by FA05 s12.

Cross References

From Section 196A

Section 985A Application of section 985 to certain perquisites, etc.

196B Employees of certain agencies: foreign service allowances

[(1) (a) In this section "*emoluments*" means emoluments to which *section 985A* applies.

(b) The agencies to which this section applies are as follows:

(i) Enterprise Ireland;

(ii) An Bord Bia;

(iii) Tourism Ireland Ltd;

(iv) The Industrial Development Agency (Ireland).

(2) Where any allowance to, or emoluments of, employees of the agencies to which this section applies are certified by the Minister for Finance, having consulted with the Minister for Foreign Affairs, or with such Minister of the Government as the Minister for Finance considers appropriate in the circumstances, to represent compensation for the extra cost of having to live outside the State in order to perform his or her duties, that allowance, or those emoluments, shall be disregarded as income for the purposes of the Income Tax Acts.][1]

Amendments

[1] Inserted by FA07 s8(1). This section is deemed to have taken effect as on and from 1 January 2007.

Cross References

From Section 196B

Section 985A Application of section 985 to certain perquisites, etc.

197 Bonus or interest paid under instalment savings schemes

[FA70 s18]

Any bonus or interest payable to an individual under an instalment savings scheme (within the meaning of section 53 of the Finance Act, 1970) shall be disregarded for the purposes of the Income Tax Acts if, or in so far as, the bonus or interest is payable in respect of an amount not exceeding the amount permitted under the scheme to be paid by the individual.

198 Certain interest not to be chargeable

[FA95 s40]

[(1) (a) In this subsection—

["*arrangements*" means arrangements having the force of law by virtue of *section 826(1)* or arrangements made with the government of a territory which on completion of the procedures set out in *section 826(1)* will have the force of law;][1]

"*relevant territory*" means—

(i) a Member State of the European Communities other than the State, […][2] [or][3]

(ii) not being such a Member State, a territory with the government of which arrangements [have been][4][made;][5]

[…][6]

"*tax*", in relation to a relevant territory, means any tax imposed in that territory which corresponds to [income tax or corporation tax, as is appropriate,][7] in the State.

(b) For the purposes of this subsection, a [person][8] shall be regarded as being a resident of a relevant territory if—

(i) in a case where the relevant territory is a territory with the government of which arrangements have been made [and have effect in accordance with the provisions of those arrangements][9], the [person][10] is regarded as being a resident of that territory under those arrangements, and

(ii) in any other case, the [person][11] is by virtue of the law of the relevant territory resident for the purposes of tax in that territory.

(c) Notwithstanding any other provision of the Income Tax Acts but without prejudice to any charge under the Corporation Tax Acts on the profits of such a person—

(i) a company not resident in the State or a person not ordinarily resident in the State shall not be chargeable to income tax in respect of interest paid by—

(I) a company in the course of carrying on relevant trading operations (within the meaning of *section 445* or *446*), or

(II) a specified collective investment undertaking (within the meaning of *section 734*),

[…][12]][13]

[(ii) a company shall not be chargeable to income tax in respect of interest paid by a relevant person (within the meaning of *section 246*) in the ordinary course of a trade or business carried on by that person—

(I) if the company is not resident in the State but is regarded for the purposes of this subsection as being a resident of a relevant territory which imposes a tax that generally applies to interest receivable in that territory by companies from sources outside that territory, or

(II) where the interest—

(A) is exempted from the charge to income tax under arrangements made with the government of a territory outside the State having the force of law under the procedures set out in *section 826(1)*, or

(B) would be exempted from the charge to income tax if arrangements made, on or before the date of payment of the interest, with the government of a territory outside the State, that do not have the force of law under the procedures set out in *section 826(1)*, had the force of law when the interest was paid,][14]

[…][15]

[(iii) a person shall not be chargeable to income tax in respect of interest paid by a company—

(I) if the person is not a resident of the State and is regarded as being a resident of a relevant territory for the purposes of this subsection, or

(II) [if][16] the person is a company controlled in accordance with *section 172D(3)(b)(ii)*, or a company the principal class of shares of which are shares to which *section 172D(3)(b)(iii)* applies, and the interest is interest to which *section 64(2)* applies, an interest payment to which *section 246A* applies or interest paid in respect of an asset covered security within the meaning of *section 3* of the Asset Covered Securities Act 2001,][17]

[(iv) a person shall not be chargeable to income tax in respect of interest paid by a qualifying company (within the meaning of *section 110*) if the person is not a resident of the State and is regarded as being a resident of a relevant territory for the purposes of this subsection, and the interest is paid out of the [assets of the qualifying company, and][18].][19]

[(v) a person shall not be chargeable to income tax in respect of discounts arising on securities issued by a relevant person (within the meaning of *section 246*) in the ordinary course of a trade or business carried on by that person if the first mentioned person is not a resident of the State and is regarded as being a resident of a relevant territory for the purposes of this subsection.][20]

[(2) Where a company would not be chargeable to income tax in respect of interest paid in respect of a '*relevant security*' (within the meaning of *section 246*) in accordance with this section but for the fact that—

(a) *sections 445* and *446* have been deleted, and

(b) those sections referred to time limits in respect of certificates to which each section related,

then, notwithstanding those deletions and time limits, the company shall not be so chargeable and the other provisions of this section shall apply with any modifications necessary to give effect to this subsection.][21]

Amendments

[1] Substituted by FA10 s40(1)(a). Has effect as on and from 3 April 2010.

[2] Deleted by F(No.2)A08 s33(d)(i). This section is deemed to have come into force and takes effect as on and from 1 January 2009.

[3] Inserted by FA10 s40(1)(b)(i). Has effect as on and from 3 April 2010.

[4] Substituted by F(No.2)A08 s33(d)(i). This section is deemed to have come into force and takes effect as on and from 1 January 2009.

[5] Substituted by FA10 s40(1)(b)(ii). Has effect as on and from 3 April 2010.

[6] Deleted by FA10 s40(1)(b)(iii). Has effect as on and from 3 April 2010.

[7] Substituted by FA01 s36(1)(a). This section shall apply as respects interest paid on or after the date of 30 March 2001

[8, 10, 11] Substituted by FA01 s36(1)(b). This section shall apply as respects interest paid on or after the date of 30 March 2001

[9] Inserted by FA10 s40(1)(c). Has effect as on and from 3 April 2010.

[12] Deleted by FA01 s36(1)(c). This section shall apply as respects interest paid on or after the date of 30 March 2001

[13] Substituted by FA00 s34(1). This section shall apply as respects interest paid in the year of assessment 2000-2001 and subsequent years of assessment.

[14] Substituted by FA10 s40(1)(d). Has effect as on and from 3 April 2010.

[15] Deleted by FA03 s48(3)(a). Applies as respects interest paid on or after 6 February 2003.

[16] Inserted by FA13 sched2(1)(d). Has effect on and from 27 March 2013.

[17] Substituted by FA12 s39(1). Shall apply to interest paid on or after 31 March 2012.

[18] Substituted by F(No.2)A08 s25(1)(b). Applies as respects interest paid or discounts arising on or after 1 January 2009.

[19] Inserted by FA03 s48(3)(c). Applies as respects interest paid on or after 6 February 2003.

[20] Inserted by F(No.2)A08 s25(1)(c). Applies as respects interest paid or discounts arising on or after 1 January 2009.

[21] Substituted by FA12 sched1(8).

Revenue Briefings

eBrief

eBrief No. 43/2012 – Interest payments and section 246(3)(h)(I) of the Taxes Consolidation Act 1997

Cross References

From Section 198

Section 64 Interest on quoted Eurobonds.
Section 110 Securitisation.
Section 246 Interest payments by companies and to non-residents.
Section 246A Interest in respect of wholesale debt instruments.
Section 445 Certain trading operations carried on in Shannon Airport.
Section 446 Certain trading operations carried on in Custom House Docks Area.
Section 734 Taxation of collective investment undertakings.
Section 826 Agreements for relief from double taxation.

To Section 198

Section 817C Restriction on deductibility of certain interest.

199 Interest on certain securities

[ITA67 s345; FA74 s86 and Sch 2 PtI]

Income tax shall not be chargeable in respect of the interest on securities issued by the Minister for Finance for the purpose of being used in payment of income tax, and such interest shall not be reckoned in computing income for the purposes of the Income Tax Acts.

200 Certain foreign pensions

[F(MP)A68 s9; FA97 s146(1) and Sch9 PtI par3]

(1) In this section, "*tax*", in relation to any country, means a tax which is chargeable and payable under the law of that country and which corresponds to income tax in the State.

(2) This section shall apply to any pension, benefit or allowance which—

(a) is given in respect of past services in an office or employment or is payable under the provisions of the law of the country in which it arises which correspond to the provisions of [Chapter 15, 18 or 19 of Part 2 of, or Chapter 4 or 6 of Part 3 of, the Social Welfare Consolidation Act 2005,][1] or any subsequent Act together with which that Act may be cited, and

(b) if it were received by a person who, for the purposes of tax of the country in which it arises, is resident in that country and is not resident elsewhere, would not be regarded as income for those purposes.

[(2A) Notwithstanding *subsection (2)*, this section shall not apply to a pension to which *subparagraph (b)* of paragraph 1 of Article 18 (Pensions, Social Security, Annuities, Alimony and Child Support) of the Convention between the Government of Ireland and the Government of the United States of America for the Avoidance of Double Taxation and the Prevention of Fiscal Evasion with respect to Taxes on Income and Capital Gains signed at Dublin on the 28th day of July, 1997 applies.][2]

(3) In *section 18(2)*, the reference in *paragraph (f)* of Case III to income arising from possessions outside the State shall be deemed not to include a reference to any pension, benefit or allowance to which this section applies.

Amendments

[1] Substituted by FA07 sched4(1)(d). Shall have effect as on and from 2 April 2007

[2] Inserted by FA98 s18.

Revenue Briefings

Tax Briefing

Tax Briefing September 1998 – Issue 33 pg 18 – US Social Security Pensions – Taxation in Ireland

201 Exemptions and reliefs in respect of tax under section 123.

[ITA67 s115 and Sch3 pars 12 and 13; FA72 s13(4) and Sch1 PtIII par2; FA80 s10(1)(a) and (c); FA92 s18(2); FA93 s7(1) and s8(a); FA97 s12]

(1) (a) In this section and in *Schedule 3*—

"*the basic exemption*" means [€10,160][1] together with [€765][2] for each complete year of the service, up to the relevant date, of the holder in the office or employment in respect of which the payment is made;

"*foreign service*", in relation to an office or employment, means service such that—

(i) tax was not chargeable in respect of the emoluments of the office or employment,

(ii) the office or employment being an office or employment within Schedule E, tax under that Schedule was not chargeable in respect of the whole of the emoluments of that office or employment, or

(iii) the office or employment being regarded as a possession in a place outside the State within the meaning of Case III of Schedule D, tax in respect of the income arising from that office or employment did not fall to be computed in accordance with *section 71(1)*;

"*the relevant date*", in relation to a payment not being a payment in commutation of annual or other periodical payments, means the date of the termination or change in respect of which it is made and, in relation to a payment in commutation of annual or other periodical payments, means the date of the termination or change in respect of which those payments would have been made.

(b) In this section—

"*control*", in relation to a body corporate, means the power of a person to secure—

(i) by means of the holding of shares or the possession of voting power in or in relation to that or any other body corporate, or

(ii) by virtue of any power conferred by the articles of association or other document regulating that or any other body corporate, that the affairs of the first-mentioned body corporate are conducted in accordance with the wishes of that person and, in relation to a partnership, means the right to a share of more than 50 per cent of the assets, or of more than 50 per cent of the income, of the partnership;

references to an employer or to a person controlling or controlled by an employer include references to such employer's or such person's successors.

(c) For the purposes of this section and of *Schedule 3*, offices or employments in respect of which payments to which *section 123* applies are made shall be treated as held under associated employers if, on the date which is the relevant date in relation to any of those payments, one of those employers is under the control of the other or of a third person who controls or is under the control of the other on that or any other such date.

[(1A) (a) In this subsection—

"*eligible employee*" means an employee, being a person who is being made redundant, who, in relation to a full-time employment, has completed at least 2 years continuous service in that employment or is, for the purposes of the law relating to redundancy, deemed to have at least 2 years continuous service;

"*retraining*" means a training course, made available by an employer as part of a redundancy package, that is—

(i) designed to impart or improve skills or knowledge relevant to, or intended to be used in, obtaining gainful employment or in the setting up of a business,

(ii) primarily devoted to the teaching or practical application of such skills or knowledge, and

(iii) completed within 6 months of the termination of employment;

"*redundancy package*", in relation to an eligible employee, means any scheme of compensation offered to the employee on termination of his or her employment.

(b) Income tax shall not be charged by virtue of *section 123* in respect of the first €5,000 of the cost of retraining an eligible employee where—

(i) such training forms part of his or her redundancy package, and

(ii) the employer makes available such retraining for all eligible employees.

[(c) Paragraph (*b*) does not apply to any retraining provided to any or all of the spouse, civil partner and any dependant of the employer.][3]

(d) Paragraph (*b*) does not apply to an eligible employee where there is an arrangement or scheme in place whereby an employee may receive the cost of retraining in money or money's worth, wholly or partly, directly or indirectly, and such employee so receives that cost.][4]

[(2) (a) Income tax shall not be charged by virtue of *section 123* in respect of the following payments:

(i) an amount not exceeding €200,000 of any payment made—

(I) in connection with the termination of the holding of an office or employment by the death of the holder, or

(II) on account of injury to or disability of the holder of an office or employment;

(ii) any sum chargeable to tax under *section 127*;

(iii) a benefit provided pursuant to any retirement benefits scheme where, under *section 777*, the employee (within the meaning of that section) was chargeable to tax in respect of sums paid, or treated as paid, with a view to the provision of the benefit;

(iv) a benefit paid in pursuance of any scheme or fund described in *section 778(1)*.

(b) Where *paragraph (a)(i)* applies to any payment, or any part of a payment—

(i) the exemptions from income tax provided by virtue of any other provision of this section (other than *subsection (1A)*) and *Schedule 3*, or

(ii) any deduction in computing the charge to income tax under *paragraph 6* of *Schedule 3*,

shall not apply to the excess of any such payment.

(c) (i) Notwithstanding *subparagraph (i)* of *paragraph (a)* the amount of €200,000 referred to in that subparagraph shall be reduced by an amount equal to the aggregate amount of all payments, exempted from income tax by virtue of that subparagraph, which were paid before or at the same time as the making of the payment to which that subparagraph refers.

(ii) Where two or more payments to which *subparagraph (i)* of *paragraph (a)* applies are made to or in respect of the same person in respect of the same office or employment, or in respect of different offices or employments, for the purposes of that subparagraph this subparagraph shall apply as if those payments were a single payment of the aggregate amount of all such payments, and the provisions of *subparagraph (i)* of *paragraph (a)* shall apply to that single payment accordingly.][5]

[(2A) Where a payment[, or any part of a payment,][6] is not chargeable to tax under *section 123* by virtue of *subsection (2)(a)*, the person by whom the payment was made shall deliver to the inspector, not later than 46 days after the end of the year of assessment in which the payment was made, the following particulars—

(a) the name and address of the person to whom the payment was made,

(b) the personal public service number (within the meaning of [section 262 of the Social Welfare Consolidation Act 2005][7]) of the person who received the payment,

(c) the amount of the payment, and

(d) the basis on which the payment[, or part of the payment,][8] is not chargeable to tax under *section 123*, indicating, in the case of a payment made on account of injury or disability, the extent of the injury or disability, as the case may be.][9]

(3) [*Subsection (2)(a)(iv)*][10] shall not apply to the following payments—

(a) a termination allowance payable in accordance with section 5 of the Oireachtas (Allowances to Members) and Ministerial and Parliamentary Offices (Amendment) Act, 1992, and any regulations made under that section,

(b) a severance allowance or a special allowance payable in accordance with Part V (inserted by the Oireachtas (Allowances to Members) and Ministerial and Parliamentary Offices (Amendment) Act, 1992) of the Ministerial and Parliamentary Offices Act, 1938,

(c) a special severance gratuity payable under section 7 of the Superannuation and Pensions Act, 1963, or any analogous payment payable under or by virtue of any other enactment, or

(d) a benefit paid in pursuance of any statutory scheme (within the meaning of *Chapter 1* of *Part 30*) established or amended after the 10th day of May, 1997, other than a payment representing normal retirement benefits, which is made in consideration or in consequence of, or otherwise in connection with, the termination of the holding of an office or employment in circumstances—

(I) of redundancy or abolition of office, or

(II) for the purposes of facilitating improvements in the organisation of the employing company, organisation, Department or other body by which greater efficiency or economy can be effected,

and, for the purposes of this paragraph, "*normal retirement benefits*" means recognised superannuation benefits customarily payable to an individual on retirement at normal retirement date under the relevant statutory scheme, notwithstanding that, in relation to the termination of an office or employment in the circumstances described in this paragraph, such benefits may be paid earlier than the designated retirement date or may be calculated by reference to a period greater than the individual's actual period of service in the office or employment, and includes benefits described as short service gratuities which are calculated on a basis approved by the Minister for Finance.

(4) Income tax shall not be charged by virtue of *section 123* in respect of a payment in respect of an office or employment in which the holder's service included foreign service where the foreign service comprised—

(a) in any case, three-quarters of the whole period of service down to the relevant date,

(b) where the period of service down to the relevant date exceeded 10 years, the whole of the last 10 years, or

(c) where the period of service down to the relevant date exceeded 20 years, one-half of that period, including any 10 of the last 20 years.

[(4A) *Subsection (4)* ceases to have effect for payments made [on or after the date of the passing of the Finance Act 2013][11].][12]

(5) (a) Income tax shall not be charged by virtue of *section 123* in respect of a payment of an amount not exceeding the basic exemption and, in the case of a payment which exceeds that amount, shall be charged only in respect of the excess.

(b) Notwithstanding *paragraph (a)*, where 2 or more payments in respect of which tax is chargeable by virtue of *section 123*, or would be so chargeable apart from *paragraph (a)*, are made to or in respect of the same person in respect of the same office or employment, or in respect of different offices or employments held under the same employer or under associated employers, that paragraph shall apply as if those payments were a single payment of an amount equal to that aggregate amount, and the amount of any one payment chargeable to tax shall be ascertained as follows:

(i) where the payments are treated as income of different years of assessment, the amount of the basic exemption shall be deducted from a payment treated as income of an earlier year before any payment treated as income of a later year, and

(ii) subject to *subparagraph (i)*, the amount of the basic exemption shall be deducted rateably from the payments according to their respective amounts.

(6) The person chargeable to income tax by virtue of *section 123* in respect of any payment may, before the expiration of [4 years][13] after the end of the year of assessment of which that payment is treated as income, by notice in writing to the inspector claim any such relief in respect of the payment as is applicable to the payment under *Schedule 3* and, where such a claim is duly made and allowed, all such repayments and assessments of income tax shall be made as are necessary to give effect to such a claim.

(7) For the purposes of any provision of the Income Tax Acts requiring income of any description to be treated as the highest part of a person's income, that income shall be calculated without regard to any payment chargeable to tax by virtue of *section 123*.

[(8) (a) Notwithstanding the provisions of this section and *Schedule 3*, income tax shall be charged by virtue of *section 123* on the amount of the lump sum which exceeds the lesser of—

(i) that part of the lump sum which, apart from this subsection, would be exempt from income tax by virtue of this section and *Schedule 3*, including any deduction in computing the charge to income tax under *paragraph 6* of that Schedule, and

(ii) €200,000.

(b) The amount of €200,000 referred to in *subparagraph* (*a*)(ii) shall be reduced by an amount equal to the aggregate amounts exempted from income tax in respect of all payments to which *section 123* applied which were paid before or at the same time as the payment of the lump sum, and shall include any deduction in computing the charge to income tax under *paragraph 6* of *Schedule 3*.

(c) The amount determined in accordance with paragraphs (*a*) and (*b*) shall be determined without regard to *subsections (1A)* and *(2)*.

(d) Where 2 or more payments in respect of which tax is chargeable by virtue of *section 123* are made to or in respect of the same person in respect of the same office or employment, or in respect of different offices or employments, for the purposes of this subsection this paragraph shall apply as if those payments were a single payment of an amount equal to that aggregate amount, and the provisions of *paragraph* (*a*) shall apply to that amount accordingly.][14]

Amendments

[1, 2] Substituted by FA01 sched5.

[3] Substituted by F(No.3)A11 sched1(28). Shall have effect from the passing of this Act 27 July 2011.

[4] Inserted by FA08 s22(1). Has effect as respects retraining within the meaning of section 201(1A) made available on or after 13 March 2008.

[5] Substituted by FA13 s14(1)(a). Applies as respects payments made on or after 27 March 2013.

[6] Inserted by FA13 s14(1)(b). Applies as respects payments made on or after 27 March 2013.

[7] Substituted by FA07 sched4(1)(e). Shall have effect as on and from 2 April 2007.

[8] Inserted by FA13 s14(1)(c). Applies as respects payments made on or after 27 March 2013.

[9] Inserted by FA05 s19(1)(a)(i). Applies as respects payments made on or after 25 March 2005.

[10] Substituted by F(No.2)A13 sched(1)(b)(i). Deemed to have come into force and have taken effect on and from 27 March 2013.

[11] Substituted by F(No.2)A13 sched(1)(b)(ii). Deemed to have come into force and have taken effect on and from 27 March 2013.

[12] Inserted by FA13 s14(1)(d). Deemed to have come into force and takes effect on and from 1 January 2013.

[13] Substituted by FA05 s19(1)(a)(ii). Applies as respects payments made on or after 25 March 2005.

[14] Inserted by FA11 s8(1). This section shall apply as respects any payment made on or after 1 January 2011.

Revenue Briefings

Tax Briefing

Tax Briefing October 1997 – Issue 28 pg 7 – Taxation Treatment of Redundancy/Termination Payments
Tax Briefing June 1999 – Issue 36 pg 13 – Lump Sum Payments on Redundancy/Retirement Queries
Tax Briefing December 2003 – Issue 54 pg 10 – Redundancy Payments and Re-Engagement of Employees
Tax Briefing August 2005 – Issue 60 pg 23 – New Reporting Requirements for Certain Termination Payments
Tax Briefing November 2007 – Issue 67 – Lump Sum Payments & Top Slicing Relief

Revenue Information Notes

IT 21 – Lump Sum Payments on Redundancy / Retirement

Revenue Precedents

Whether an individual employed in the State by a non-resident employer (PAYE not operating) is entitled to the exemptions and reliefs in section 201 TCA 1997? The individual is entitled to the exemptions and reliefs as the charge under section 123 TCA 1997 depends on holding an office or employment. The basis of assessment of the emoluments is not the issue. IT 96 1514

Does the exemption in section 201(2)(a) TCA 1997 apply to a payment made in connection with the termination of an office or employment where the individual suffers from an injury or disability? To qualify for relief, the payment must be made on account of injury or disability of the holder of the office or employment and the disability must cause the termination. Where the payment is made on account of the termination of the office or employment, it does not qualify for exemption under section 201(2)(a) TCA 1997, unless the termination is due to injury or disability. IT 94 1509

Cross References

From Section 201

Section 71 Foreign securities and possessions.
Section 123 General tax treatment of payments on retirement or removal from office or employment.
Section 127 Tax treatment of restrictive covenants.
Section 770 Interpretation and supplemental (Chapter 1).
Section 777 Charge to income tax in respect of certain relevant benefits provided for employees.
Section 778 Exceptions to charge to tax under section 777.
Schedule 3 Reliefs in Respect of Income Tax Charged on Payments on Retirement, Etc

To Section 201

Section 123 General tax treatment of payments on retirement or removal from office or employment.
Section 202 Relief for agreed pay restructuring.
Section 531B Charge to income levy.
Section 531AM Charge to universal social charge.
Schedule 3 Reliefs in Respect of Income Tax Charged on Payments on Retirement, Etc
Schedule 12A Approved Savings-Related Share Option Schemes

202 Relief for agreed pay restructuring

[FA97 s14]

(1) (a) In this section—

"*basic pay*", in relation to a participating employee of a qualifying company, means the employee's emoluments (other than non-pecuniary emoluments) from the company in respect of an employment held with the company;

"*collective agreement*" means an agreement entered into by a company with, or on behalf of, one or more than one body representative of employees of the company where each such body is either the holder of a negotiation licence under the Trade Union Act, 1941, or is an excepted body within the meaning of section 6 of that Act as amended by the Trade Union Act, 1942;

"*control*", in relation to a qualifying company, means the power of a person to secure—

(i) by means of the holding of shares or the possession of voting power in or in relation to the qualifying company or any other qualifying company, or

(ii) by virtue of any power conferred by the articles of association or any other document regulating the qualifying company or any other qualifying company,

that the affairs of the first-mentioned qualifying company are conducted in accordance with the wishes of such person and, in relation to a partnership, means the right to a share of more than 50 per cent of the assets, or of more than 50 per cent of the income, of the partnership;

"*emoluments*" has the same meaning as in *section 472*;

"*employment*" means an office or employment of profit such that any emoluments of the office or employment of profit are to be charged to tax under Schedule E;

"*the Minister*" means the Minister for Enterprise, Trade and Employment;

"*participating employee*", in relation to a qualifying company, means a qualifying employee who is a participant in a relevant agreement with the company;

"*qualifying company*" means a company to which the Minister has issued a certificate under *subsection (2)* which has not been withdrawn under that subsection;

"*qualifying employee*", in relation to a qualifying company, means an employee of the company in receipt of emoluments from the company;

"*reduced basic pay*", in relation to a participating employee, means the basic pay of the employee as reduced by the substantial reduction provided for in the relevant agreement concerned;

["*relevant agreement*", in relation to a qualifying company, means a collective agreement—

(a) that applies to—

(i) more than 50 per cent of the total number of qualifying employees of the company, or

(ii) more than 75 per cent of a bona fide class or classes of qualifying employees of the company if the number of participating employees in the class or classes, as the case may be, comprises at least 25 per cent of the total number of qualifying employees of the company,

(b) that provides amongst other things for—

(i) a substantial reduction in the basic pay of the participating employees to which it relates,

(ii) the payment of the reduced basic pay to the participating employees to which it relates for the duration of the relevant period, and

(iii) the payment to them of a lump sum to compensate for that reduction,

and

(c) that is registered with the Labour Relations Commission;][1]

"relevant date", in relation to a relevant agreement, means the date the relevant agreement was registered with the Labour Relations Commission;

"relevant period", in relation to a relevant agreement, means the period of 5 years commencing on the relevant date in relation to that agreement;

[*"specified amount"*, in relation to a participating employee, means—

(a) in a case where the basic pay of the employee is subject to a reduction of at least 10 per cent but not exceeding 15 per cent, [€7,620][2] together with [€255][3] for each complete year of service (subject to a maximum of 20 years), up to the relevant date, of the employee in the service of the qualifying company,

(b) in a case where the basic pay of the employee is subject to a reduction exceeding 15 per cent but not exceeding 20 per cent, [€7,620][4] together with [€635][5] for each complete year of service (subject to a maximum of 20 years), up to the relevant date, of the employee in the service of the qualifying company, and

(c) in a case where the basic pay of the employee is subject to a reduction exceeding 20 per cent, [€10,160][6] together with [€765][7] for each complete year of service (subject to a maximum of 20 years), up to the relevant date, of the employee in the service of the qualifying company.][8]

(b) For the purposes of this section—

(i) a reduction in the basic pay of a participating employee shall not be regarded as substantial unless it amounts to at least 10 per cent of the average for one year of the employee's basic pay ascertained by reference to such pay for the 2 year period ending on the relevant date, and

(ii) employments in respect of which payments to which this section applies are made shall be treated as held with associated qualifying companies if, on the date of any of those payments, one of those companies is under the control of the other company or of a third person who controls or is under the control of the other company on that or any other such date.

[(c) In determining for the purposes of the definition of *"relevant agreement"* whether qualifying employees of a qualifying company are comprised in a bona fide class or classes, as the case may be, regard shall be had to matters such as common work practices, skills, established collective bargaining arrangements and the organisational structure and arrangements within the company.][9]

(2) (a) The Minister, on the making of an application in that behalf by a company, may, in accordance with guidelines laid down for the purpose by the Minister with the agreement of the Minister for Finance, give a certificate to a company stating that for the purposes of this section it may be treated as a qualifying company.

(b) The Minister may not grant a certificate to a company under this subsection unless the Minister is satisfied, on advice from the Labour Relations Commission, that—

[(i) the company is confronted with a substantial adverse change to its competitive environment which will determine its current or continued viability,

(ii) to accommodate that change and maintain its viability, it is necessary for it to enter into a relevant agreement with its qualifying employees, and.][10]

(iii) the relevant agreement into which it is proposed to enter is designed for the sole purpose of addressing, and can be reasonably expected to address, that change.

(c) An application under *paragraph (a)* shall be in such form as the Minister may direct and shall contain such information in relation to the company, its trade or business and the terms of the relevant agreement into which it proposes to enter with its qualifying employees as may be specified in the guidelines referred to in that paragraph.

(d) A certificate issued by the Minister under *paragraph (a)* shall contain such conditions as the Minister considers appropriate and specifies in the certificate.

(e) Any cost incurred by the Labour Relations Commission in providing advice to the Minister in accordance with *paragraph (b)* shall be reimbursed by the company concerned to the Commission.

(f) Where during the relevant period a qualifying company fails to comply with any of the conditions to which a certificate given to it under *paragraph (a)* is subject, the Minister may, by notice in writing to the company, revoke the certificate.

(g) The Minister may not give a certificate under *paragraph (a)* at any time on or after the [1 January 2004][11].

(3) (a) An agreement shall not be a relevant agreement for the purposes of this section unless and until it has been registered with the Labour Relations Commission.

(b) A qualifying company shall, within the period of one month from the date of each of the first 5 anniversaries of the relevant date or such longer period as the Labour Relations Commission may in writing allow, confirm to the Commission, in such form as the Commission shall direct, that all the terms of the relevant agreement, to the extent that they are still relevant, continue to be in force.

(4) Nothing in this section shall be construed as preventing a participating employee from receiving during the relevant period an increase in basic pay—

(a) which is—

(i) provided for under the terms of the agreement known as Partnership 2000 for Inclusion, Employment and Competitiveness entered into by the Government and the Social Partners in December, 1996, or any similar increase under an agreement, whether negotiated on a national basis or otherwise, which succeeds that agreement or which succeeds an agreement which succeeds the first-mentioned agreement, or

(ii) part of an incremental scale under the terms of the employee's contract of employment and which was in place 12 months before the relevant date,

and

(b) which is determined by reference to the employee's reduced basic pay or that pay as subsequently increased as provided for in *paragraph (a)*.

(5) (a) This section shall apply to a payment made to a participating employee by a qualifying company under a relevant agreement.

(b) A payment to which this section applies shall, to the extent that the payment does not exceed the specified amount, be exempt from any charge to income tax.

(c) Where 2 or more payments to which this section applies are made to or in respect of the same person in respect of the same employment or in respect of different employments held with the same qualifying company or an associated qualifying company, this subsection shall apply as if those payments were a single payment of an amount equal to the aggregate of those payments, and the amount of any payment chargeable to income tax shall be ascertained as follows:

(i) where the payments are treated as income of different years of assessment, the specified amount shall be deducted from a payment treated as income of an earlier year before any payment treated as income of a later year, and

(ii) subject to *subparagraph (i)*, the specified amount shall be deducted from a payment made earlier in a year of assessment before any payment made later in that year.

(6) Where during the relevant period—

(a) the Minister revokes, in accordance with *paragraph (f)* of *subsection (2)*, a certificate given to a company under *paragraph (a)* of that subsection,

(b) a qualifying company fails to meet the requirements of *subsection (3)(b)*, or

(c) a participating employee receives an increase in reduced basic pay other than as provided for in *subsection (4)*,

then, any relief granted under this section, where *paragraph (a)* or *(b)* applies, to all the participating employees of the company or, where *paragraph (c)* applies, to the participating employee concerned, shall be withdrawn by the making of an assessment to income tax under Case IV of Schedule D for the year of assessment for which the relief was granted.

(7) Where during the relevant period a participating employee receives a payment from a qualifying company, other than a payment to which this section applies, which is chargeable to tax by virtue of *section 123*, any relief from tax in respect of that payment under *section 201(5)* or *Schedule 3* shall be reduced by the amount of any relief given under this section in respect of a payment to which this section applies made in the relevant period.

(8) *Section 201* and *Schedule 3* and *section 480* shall not apply in relation to a payment to which this section applies.

Amendments

[1] Substituted by FA98 s10(a)(i).

[2, 3, 4, 5, 6, 7] Substituted by FA01 sched5.

[8] Substituted by FA00 s18(1)(a). Shall apply and have effect as respects payments made under a relevant agreement the relevant date of which is after 20 July 1999.

[9] Inserted by FA98 s10(a)(ii).

[10] Substituted by FA98 s10(b).

[11] Substituted by FA01 sched2(12).

Cross References

From Section 202

Section 123 General tax treatment of payments on retirement or removal from office or employment.
Section 201 Exemptions and reliefs in respect of tax under section 123.
Section 472 Employee tax credit.
Section 480 Relief for certain sums chargeable under Schedule E.
Schedule 3 Reliefs in Respect of Income Tax Charged on Payments on Retirement, Etc

203 Payments in respect of redundancy

[FA 68 s37(1) and (2)]

(1) In this section, "*lump sum*" and "*weekly payment*" have the same meanings respectively as in the Redundancy Payments Act, 1967.

(2) Any lump sum or weekly payment and any payment to or on behalf of an employed or unemployed person in accordance with regulations under section 46 of the Redundancy Payments Act, 1967, shall be exempt from income tax under Schedule E.

204 Military and other pensions, gratuities and allowances

[ITA67 s340(1), (2)(a), (b) and (c)]

(1) This section shall apply to—

(a) all wound and disability pensions, and all increases in such pensions, granted under the Army Pensions Acts, 1923 to 1980, or those Acts and any subsequent Act together with which those Acts may be cited; but, where the amount of any pension to which this paragraph applies is not solely attributable to disability, the relief conferred by this section shall extend only to such part as is certified by the Minister for Defence to be attributable to disability;

(b) all gratuities in respect of wounds or disabilities similarly granted under any enactment referred to in *paragraph (a)*;

(c) military gratuities and demobilisation pay granted to officers of the National Forces or the Defence Forces of Ireland on demobilisation;

(d) deferred pay within the meaning of any regulations under the Defence Act, 1954, which is credited to the pay account of a member of the Defence Forces;

(e) gratuities granted in respect of service with the Defence Forces.

(2) Income to which this section applies shall be exempt from income tax and shall not be reckoned in computing income for the purposes of the Income Tax Acts.

204A Exemption in respect of annual allowance for reserve members of the Garda Síochána

[The annual allowance payable under Regulation 15 of the Garda Síochána (Reserve Members) Regulations 2006 (S.I. No. 413 of 2006) shall be exempt from income tax and shall not be reckoned in computing income for the purposes of the Income Tax Acts.][1]

Amendment

[1] Inserted by F(No.2)A13 s10. Comes into operation on 1 January 2014.

204B Exemption in respect of compensation for certain living donors

[The compensation for donation of a kidney for transplantation payable to a living donor under conditions defined by the Minister for Health pursuant to Regulation 21(2) of the European Union (Quality and Safety of Human Organs Intended for Transplantation) Regulations 2012 (S.I. No. 325 of 2012) shall be exempt from income tax and shall not be reckoned in computing income for the purposes of the Income Tax Acts.][1]

Amendment

[1] Inserted by FA14 s6. Comes into operation on 1 January 2015.

205 Veterans of War of Independence

[FA82 s9(1) and (2)]

(1) In this section—

"*military service*" means the performance of duty as a member of an organisation to which Part II of the Army Pensions Act, 1932, applies, but includes military service within the meaning of that Part of that Act, military service within the meaning of the Military Service Pensions Act, 1924, and service in the Forces within the meaning of the Military Service Pensions Act, 1934;

"*relevant legislation*" means the Army Pensions Acts, 1923 to 1980, the Military Service Pensions Acts, 1924 to 1964, the Connaught Rangers (Pensions) Acts, 1936 to 1964, any Act amending any of those Acts and any regulation (in so far as it affects a pension, allowance, benefit or gratuity under any of those Acts or any other Act amending any of those Acts) made under the Pensions (Increase) Act, 1964, or under any of those Acts or any other Act amending any of those Acts;

"*relevant military service*" means military service during any part of a period referred to in section 5(2) of the Army Pensions Act, 1932, or, in the case of a qualified person within the meaning of the Connaught Rangers (Pensions) Act, 1936, the circumstances referred to in paragraphs (*a*), (*b*) and (*c*) of section 2 of that Act;

"*veteran of the War of Independence*" means a person who was—

(a) a member of an organisation to which Part II of the Army Pensions Act, 1932, applies, or a qualified person within the meaning of the Connaught Rangers (Pensions) Act, 1936, and

(b) engaged in relevant military service.

(2) A pension, allowance, benefit or gratuity, in so far as it is related to the relevant military service of a veteran of the War of Independence, or to an event which happened during or in consequence of such relevant military service, which is paid under the relevant legislation to—

(a) such veteran, or

(b) the wife, widow, child or other dependant or partial dependant of such veteran,

shall be exempt from income tax and shall not be reckoned in computing income for the purposes of the Income Tax Acts.

205A Magdalen Laundry Payments

[(1) In this section—

"*relevant individual*" means an individual to whom a relevant payment has been made;

"*relevant payment*" means a payment or payments made, directly or indirectly, to a relevant individual by or on behalf of the Minister for Justice, Equality and Defence, in accordance with the Table of Payments set out in Appendix A to the Magdalen Commission Report dated May 2013 on the establishment of an *ex gratia* scheme and related matters for the benefit of those women who were admitted to and worked in the Magdalen Laundries.

(2) This section applies to the following payments:

(a) a relevant payment;

(b) an amount equal to the State Pension (Contributory) as set out in column 2 of *Part 1* of *Schedule 2* of the Social Welfare Consolidation Act 2005 to a relevant individual;

(c) an amount equal to the State Pension (Non-Contributory) as set out in *Part 3* of the Social Welfare Consolidation Act 2005 to a relevant individual;

(d) any payment, other than a payment referred to in *paragraphs (a)* to *(c)*, made, directly or indirectly, by or on behalf of the Minister for Social Protection to a relevant individual, by virtue of that individual being a relevant individual.

(3) For the purposes of the Income Tax Acts, and notwithstanding any provision of those Acts to the contrary, a payment to which this section applies, made to a relevant individual, shall be disregarded.][1]

Amendment

[1] Inserted by F(No.2)A13 s77(1)(a). Applies to payments to which section 205A applies made on or after 1 August 2013.

206 Income from investments under Social Welfare (Consolidation) Act, 1993

[ITA67 s338]

[(1) The Minister for Finance shall be entitled to exemption from tax in respect of the income derived from investments made under [section 9][1] of the [Social Welfare Consolidation Act 2005][2].][3]

[(2) The Minister for Social Protection shall be entitled to exemption from tax in respect of the income derived from accounts held under *section 9* of the Social Welfare Consolidation Act 2005.][4]

Amendments

[1] Substituted by FA07 sched4(1)(f)(ii). Shall have effect as on and from 2 April 2007.

[2] Substituted by FA07 sched4(1)(f)(i). Shall have effect as on and from 2 April 2007.

[3] Renumbered by FA14 s21(a). Comes into operation on 1 January 2015.

[4] Inserted by FA14 s21(b). Comes into operation on 1 January 2015.

207 Rents of properties belonging to hospitals and other charities

[ITA67 s333 and s339(2) and (4); F(MP)A68 s3(4) and Sch PtIII; FA69 s65(1) and Sch5 PtI; CTA76 s140(1) and Sch2 PtI par13]

(1) Exemption shall be granted—

(a) from income tax chargeable under Schedule D in respect of the rents and profits of any property belonging to any hospital, public school or almshouse, or vested in trustees for charitable purposes, in so far as those rents and profits are applied to charitable purposes only;

(b) from income tax chargeable—

(i) under Schedule C in respect of any interest, annuities, dividends or shares of annuities,

(ii) under Schedule D in respect of any yearly interest or other annual payment, and

(iii) under Schedule F in respect of any distribution,

forming part of the income of any body of persons or trust established for charitable purposes only, or which, according to the rules or regulations established by statute, charter, decree, deed of trust or will, are applicable to charitable purposes only, and in so far as the same are applied to charitable purposes only;

(c) from income tax chargeable under Schedule C in respect of any interest, annuities, dividends or shares of annuities in the names of trustees applicable solely towards the repairs of any cathedral, college, church or chapel, or any building used solely for the purposes of divine worship, and in so far as the same are applied to those purposes.

(2) (a) This subsection shall apply to every gift (within the meaning of the Charities Act, 1961) made before the 1st day of July, 1961, which, if it had been made on or after that day, would by virtue of section 50 of that Act (which relates to gifts for graves and memorials) have been, to the extent provided in that section, a gift for charitable purposes.

(b) *Subsection (1)* shall apply in relation to a gift to which this subsection applies as if the gift had been made on or after the 1st day of July, 1961.

(3) Every claim under this section shall be verified by affidavit, and proof of the claim may be given by the treasurer, trustee or any duly authorised agent.

(4) A person who makes a false or fraudulent claim for exemption under this section in respect of any interest, annuities, dividends or shares of annuities charged or chargeable under Schedule C shall forfeit the sum of [€125][1].

Amendments

[1] Substituted by FA01 sched5.

Case Law

Four general categories of charitable purposes were established in the UK case of IT Comrs v Pemsel 1891 3 TC 53: 1. Relief of poverty, 2. Advancement of education, 3. Advancement of religion, 4. Other purposes beneficial to the community.

Exemption is only available to charities 'established' within the State. Dreyfus Foundation Inc v IRC 1955 36 TC 126.

A foreign charity with Irish activities held eligible for exemption. Revenue Commissioners v Sisters of Charity of the Incarnate Word 1998 VI ITR 7

The question of ancillary purposes was considered in the case Incorporated Council of Law Reporting for England and Wales v AG 3 All ER 1029.

The purpose of the body must be solely charitable. The main purpose of the society in the case of Pharmaceutical Society of Ireland v Revenue Commissioners 1938 1 ITR 542 was the protection and furtherance of the pharmaceutical profession, therefore the society did not qualify as a charity.

Revenue Information Notes

List of Bodies with Charitable Tax Exemption under the Tax Acts

Standardised Memorandum And Articles Of Association For A Company Limited By Guarantee And Seeking Tax Exemption As A Charity Under The Provisions Of Section 207, Taxes Consolidation Act, 1997.

CHY 1 – Applying for Relief from tax on the Income and Property of Charities

Non-resident Charities (resident in and operating in an EEA/EFTA state) Seeking a Determination

Revenue Precedents

A Lions Club is not considered charitable. CHY 9051

The provision of insurance is not a charitable object. APP 11332

Health Boards are charitable. There is no need for a Governing Instrument as they are set under the Health Act, 1970. CHY 11471

Local Authorities are not charitable; however, there is relief from income tax available to them, in accordance with section 13 of the Finance Act, 1990. GENERAL

Mutual Investment Funds are not charitable in law. APP 11990

Fisheries Societies are charitable in law and exemption is in order—per reference. CHY 11043

Per Revenue solicitor's opinion it is in order for a co-operative to be considered charitable as long as the possibility of any benefit to members is removed. CHY 11012

Christian Fellowships are charitable under the advancement of religion. CHY 11445

In the absence of a Deed of Variation a charitable trust cannot be amended or altered but as an alternative undertaking may be accepted from the charity. CHY 10863

The provision of advice, whether financial or legal, for the benefit of the community is charitable. CHY 11431

It is acceptable that a charity can accumulate funds for more than two years provided that it is for a specific charitable purpose approved by the charities section and accounts to be submitted and checked annually. CHY 9661

The promotion of a festival in itself is not a charitable objective, unless it is for the advancement of the Arts e.g. music, theatre etc. APP 11342

A case cannot proceed to Appeal if: (1) the applicant is not constituted i.e. no completed Governing Instrument (2) there is no income in respect of which exemption is being sought. It also has to prove that tax was suffered. CHY 11074

Generally, the promotion of tourism is not a charitable objective, however, each application with the promotion of tourism as a main object must be examined on its own merits. CHY 11294

A gift to a narrow class of persons for the relief of poverty is a valid charitable gift. But the gift must be one which is expressly for the relief of poverty and if an attention to relieve poverty is not expressed, the Courts will not infer same. APP 11269

The Co-operative Society or any other organisation should not have two Governing Instruments. However, under this society's rules it is possible to amend the Governing Instrument under Clause 15 of the Rules. CHY 11168

The Asst. Revenue solicitor agreed with the view that a trust for the benefit of individuals engaged in a particular industry is a trust which is for a sufficiently large section of the community to render it charitable in law. CHY 11381

Charitable exemption can be granted under the category of advancement of religion, where the main objects of an organisation are the relief of the infirm, sick and aged priests of a particular order (precedent case—Forster, Gellatly v. Palmer).CHY 11648

Tidy Towns are considered to be charitable under the fourth Pemsel category. CHY 8691 & CHY 13150

Charities are not entitled to claim a repayment of income tax/dirt suffered on the income during the administration of an estate. CHY 1333

Social Services Councils may or may not be charitable pending on their main objects (the co-ordination of charitable bodies in itself is not regarded as a charitable object). CHY 8815

A gift for the protection of lives or property of the community was held to be charitable e.g. lifeboat or a public fire brigade. APP 11802

A distribution to a charity by a unit trust which invested only in rental property would be regarded as rental income in the hands of the charity. IT922023

Cross References

From Section 207

Section 17 Schedule C.
Section 20 Schedule F.

To Section 207

Section 172C Exemption from dividend withholding tax for certain persons.
Section 208A Overseas charities.
Section 208B Charities — miscellaneous.
Section 209 Bodies for the promotion of Universal Declaration of Human Rights and the implementation of European Convention for the Protection of Human Rights and Fundamental Freedoms.
Section 256 Interpretation (Chapter 4).
Section 266 Deposits of charities.
Section 267 Repayment of appropriate tax in certain cases.
Section 520 Interpretation (Chapter 1).
Section 730D Gain arising on a chargeable event.
Section 730E Declarations.
Section 739D Gain arising on a chargeable event.
Schedule 26A Donations to approved bodies, etc.

208 Lands owned and occupied, and trades carried on by, charities

[ITA67 s334(1)(a) and (c), (2A) and (3); FA69 s33(1) and Sch4 PtI and s65(1) and Sch5 PtI; FA81 s11]

(1) In this section, "*charity*" means any body of persons or trust established for charitable purposes only.

(2) Exemption shall be granted—

(a) from income tax chargeable under Case I (*b*) of Schedule D by virtue of *section 18(2)* where the profits or gains so chargeable arise out of lands, tenements or hereditaments which are owned and occupied by a charity;

(b) from income tax chargeable under Schedule D in respect of the profits of a trade carried on by any charity, if the profits are applied solely to the purposes of the charity and either—

(i) the trade is exercised in the course of the actual carrying out of a primary purpose of the charity, or

(ii) the work in connection with the trade is mainly carried on by beneficiaries of the charity.

(3) *Subsection (2)(b)* shall apply in respect of the profits of a trade of farming carried on by a charity as if the words after "solely to the purposes of the charity" were deleted.

Case Law

In Davies v Superioress, Mater Misericordiae Hospital, Dublin 1933 1 ITR 387 a hospital granted charitable exemption was held taxable in respect of trading profits derived from private patients.

A business, which was donated to a society established for charitable purposes, and which had an employee who would otherwise have been an object of the society, was refused charitable exemption. Beirne v St Vincent de Paul Society, Wexford 1932 1 ITR 388

Revenue Information Notes

Non-resident Charities (resident in and operating in an EEA/EFTA state) Seeking a Determination

CHY 1 – Applying for Relief from Tax on the Income and Property of Charities

Cross References

To Section 208

Section 5 Interpretation of Capital Gains Tax Acts.

Section 208A Overseas charities.

Section 208B Charities — miscellaneous.

Section 745 Charge to income tax or corporation tax of offshore income gain.

208A Overseas charities

[(1) In this section and *section 208B*—

"*charity*" means any body of persons or trust established for charitable purposes only;

"*EEA Agreement*" means the Agreement on the European Economic Area signed at Oporto on 2 May 1992, as adjusted by all subsequent amendments to that Agreement;

"*EEA state*" means a state, other than the State, which is a contracting party to the EEA Agreement;

"*EFTA state*" means a state, other than an EEA state, which is a Member State of the European Free Trade Association.

(2) A person or trust established in an EEA state or in an EFTA state may on a claim being made to the Revenue Commissioners seek a determination to the effect that, if the person or trust were to have income in the State of a kind referred to in *section 207* or *208*, it would qualify for the exemptions provided for by those sections.

(3) A claim referred to in *subsection (2)* shall be determined by the Revenue Commissioners or such officer of the Revenue Commissioners (including an inspector) as they may authorise in that behalf.

(4) Where a claim referred to in *subsection (2)* has been determined in accordance with *subsection (3)* and the determination is to the effect that if the person or trust were to have income in the State of a kind referred to in *section 207* or *208* it would qualify for the exemptions provided for by those sections, the Revenue Commissioners, or such officer of the Revenue Commissioners as they may authorise in that behalf, shall issue the person or trust with a notice of that determination.

(5) Every claim made under this section shall be verified by a document corresponding to an affidavit sworn in the State or by an equivalent sworn statement, and proof of the claim may be given by the treasurer, trustee or any duly authorised agent.][1]

Amendments

[1] Inserted by FA10 s24(a). Deemed to have come into force and takes effect as on and from 1 January 2010.

Revenue Information Notes

Non-resident Charities (resident in and operating in an EEA/EFTA state) Seeking a Determination

Cross References

From Section 208A

Section 207 Rents of properties belonging to hospitals and other charities.
Section 208 Lands owned and occupied, and trades carried on by, charities.
Section 208B Charities — miscellaneous.

To Section 208A

Section 208B Charities — miscellaneous.
Schedule 26A Donations to approved bodies, etc.

208B Charities—miscellaneous

[(1) In this section—

"*charity trustee*" includes—

(a) in the case of a charity that is a company, the directors and other officers of the company, and

(b) in the case of a charity that is a body corporate (other than a company) or an unincorporated body of persons, any officer of the body or any person for the time being performing the functions of an officer of the body;

"*qualified person*" means—

(a) a person who, in accordance with section 187 of the Companies Act 1990, is qualified for appointment as an auditor of a company, or

(b) in relation to a person or trust that—

(i) has made a claim for a determination under *section 208A(2)*,

(ii) is established in an EEA state or in an EFTA state, and

(iii) does not have a principal place of business in the State,

a person who is qualified under the law of that EEA state or that EFTA state, as the case may be, to perform functions the same as or similar to those which may be performed in the State by a person referred to in *paragraph (a)*.

(2) A claim by a person or trust for—

(a) a determination under *section 864* in relation to a claim under *section 207* or *208*, or

(b) a determination under *section 208A*,

shall be supported by such information as the Revenue Commissioners may reasonably require for the purpose of determining the claim.

(3) A charity—

(a) who has been granted an exemption under *section 207* or *208*, or

(b) to whom a notice of determination has been issued in accordance with *section 208A(4)*,

shall, on request, provide such information to the Revenue Commissioners as they may require in respect of the activities of that charity in any financial year following the granting of an exemption or, as the case may be, the issuing of a notice of the determination.

(4) Any information to be provided to the Revenue Commissioners under *subsection (2)* or *(3)* shall be in an official language of the State.

(5) The Revenue Commissioners may appoint such qualified persons as they consider appropriate to verify any information provided to them under *subsection (2)* or *(3)*.

(6) The expenses incurred by any person appointed by the Revenue Commissioners under *subsection (5)* shall be recoverable by the Revenue Commissioners as a simple contract debt in any court of competent jurisdiction—

(a) from the charity trustees (who shall be jointly and severally liable for those expenses), or

(b) from the charity concerned, where it is not practicable to recover them from the charity trustees.][1]

Amendments

[1] Inserted by FA10 s24(a). Deemed to have come into force and takes effect as on and from 1 January 2010.

Revenue Information Notes

Non-resident Charities (resident in and operating in an EEA/EFTA state) Seeking a Determination

Cross References

From Section 208B

Section 207 Rents of properties belonging to hospitals and other charities.
Section 208 Lands owned and occupied, and trades carried on by, charities.
Section 208A Overseas charities.
Section 864 Making of claims, etc.

To Section 208B

Section 208A Overseas charities.

209 Bodies for the promotion of Universal Declaration of Human Rights and the implementation of European Convention for the Protection of Human Rights and Fundamental Freedoms

[FA73 s20]

Where any body of persons having consultative status with the United Nations Organisation or the Council of Europe—

(a) has as its sole or main object the promotion of observance of the Universal Declaration of Human Rights or the implementation of the European Convention for the Protection of Human Rights and Fundamental Freedoms or both the promotion of observance of that Declaration and the implementation of that Convention, and

(b) is precluded by its rules or constitution from the direct or indirect payment or transfer, otherwise than for valuable and sufficient consideration, to any of its members of any of its income or property by means of dividend, gift, division, bonus or otherwise however by means of profit, there shall, on a claim in that behalf being made to the Revenue Commissioners, be allowed, in the case of the body, such exemption from income tax as is to be allowed under *section 207* in the case of a body of persons established for charitable purposes only the whole income of which is applied to charitable purposes only.

Cross References

From Section 209

Section 207 Rents of properties belonging to hospitals and other charities.

To Section 209

Schedule 26A Donations to approved bodies, etc.

210 The Great Book of Ireland Trust

[FA91 s13]

(1) In this section, "*the Trust*" means "The Great Book of Ireland Trust" established by trust deed dated the 12th day of December, 1990, for the purposes of—

(a) making and carrying to completion and selling a unique manuscript volume (in this section referred to as "The Great Book of Ireland"), and

(b) using the proceeds of the sale of The Great Book of Ireland for the benefit of—

(i) a company incorporated on the 5th day of August, 1986, as Clashganna Mills Trust Limited, and

(ii) a company incorporated on the 1st day of March, 1991, as Poetry Ireland Limited.

(2) Notwithstanding any provision of the Income Tax Acts—

(a) income arising to the trustees of the Trust in respect of the sale by it of The Great Book of Ireland, and

(b) payments made to the companies referred to in *subsection (1)(b)* under the Trust by the trustees of the Trust,

shall be disregarded for the purposes of those Acts.

211 Friendly societies

[ITA67 s335 and s339(2) and (4); FA67 s7; F(MP)A68 s3(4) and Sch PtIII; FA73 s44; CTA76 s140(1) and Sch2 PtI par14]

(1) An unregistered friendly society whose income does not exceed [€205][1] shall be entitled to exemption from income tax, and a registered friendly society which is precluded by statute or by its rules from assuring to any person a sum exceeding [€1,270][2]by means of gross sum, or [€70][3]a year by means of annuity, shall be entitled to exemption from income tax under Schedules C, D and F.

(2) A registered friendly society shall not be entitled to exemption from tax under this section in relation to any year of assessment if the Revenue Commissioners determine, for the purposes of entitlement to exemption for that year, that the society does not satisfy the following conditions—

(a) that it was established solely for any or all of the purposes set out in section 8(1) of the Friendly Societies Act, 1896, and not for the purpose of securing a tax advantage, and

(b) that since its establishment it has engaged solely in activities directed to achieving the purposes for which it was so established and has not engaged in trading activities, other than by means of insurance in respect of members, with a view to the realisation of profits.

(3) In making a determination under this section in relation to a registered friendly society, the Revenue Commissioners shall consider any evidence in relation to the matter submitted to them by the society.

(4) In any case where a friendly society is aggrieved by a determination of the Revenue Commissioners under this section in relation to the society, the society shall be entitled to appeal to the Appeal Commissioners against the determination of the Revenue Commissioners and the Appeal Commissioners shall hear and determine the appeal as if it were an appeal against an assessment to income tax, and the provisions of the Income Tax Acts relating to the rehearing of an appeal and to the statement of a case for the opinion of the High Court on a point of law shall apply accordingly with any necessary modifications.

(5) Every claim under this section shall be verified by affidavit, and proof of the claim may be given by the treasurer, trustee or any duly authorised agent.

(6) A person who makes a false or fraudulent claim for exemption under this section in respect of any interest, annuities, dividends or shares of annuities charged or chargeable under Schedule C shall forfeit the sum of [€125][4].

Amendments

1, 2, 3, 4 Substituted by FA01 sched5.

Revenue Precedents

Charge to tax in respect of trade unions—income to which section 211 exemption does not apply is chargeable to income tax at the standard rate. IT912007

Cross References

From Section 211

Section 17 Schedule C.

Section 20 Schedule F.

To Section 211

Schedule 15 List of Bodies for Purposes of Section 610

212 Credit unions [Repealed]

Repealed by FA98 s58(2).

213 Trade unions

[ITA67 s336 and s339(2) and (4); F(MP)A68 s3(4) and Sch PtIII; CTA76 s140 and Sch2 PtI par15; FA80 s11]

(1) In this section, "*provident benefits*" includes any payment expressly authorised by the registered rules of the trade union and made to a member during sickness or incapacity from personal injury or while out of work, or to an aged member by means of superannuation, or to a member who has met with an accident, or has lost his or her tools by fire or theft, and includes a payment in discharge or aid of funeral expenses on the death of a member, or the [spouse or civil partner of a member, or as provision for the children of a deceased member or for the children of the civil partner of a deceased member.][1]

[(2) A registered trade union which is precluded by statute or by its rules from assuring to any persons a sum exceeding [€10,160][2] by means of gross sum or [€2,540][3] a year by means of annuity shall be entitled to exemption from income tax under

Schedules C, *D* and *F* in respect of its interest and dividends which are applicable and applied solely for one or more of the following purposes—

(a) provident benefits, and

(b) the education, training or retraining of its members and dependent children of members.

(3) Every claim under this section shall be verified in such manner (including by affidavit) as may be specified by the Revenue Commissioners and proof of the claim may be given by the treasurer, trustee or any duly authorised agent of the trade union concerned.][4]

(4) A person who makes a false or fraudulent claim for exemption under this section in respect of any interest, annuities, dividends or shares of annuities charged or chargeable under Schedule C shall forfeit the sum of [€125][5].

Amendments

[1] Substituted by F(No.3)A11 sched1(29).

[2, 3, 5] Substituted by FA01 sched5.

[4] Substituted by FA00 s74.

Revenue Precedents

The term "provident benefits" in section 213 includes dental, optical and legal benefits. IT903515

Cross References

From Section 213

Section 17 Schedule C.

Section 20 Schedule F.

214 Local authorities, etc

[FA90 s13]

[(1) In this section 'local authority' means a local authority for the purposes of the Local Government Act 2001 (as amended by the *Local Government Reform Act 2014*) and includes a body established under the Local Government Services (Corporate Bodies) Act 1971.][1]

(2) This section shall apply to each of the following bodies—

(a) a local authority;

(b) [the Health Service Executive][2];

[(c) an education and training board,][3]

(d) a committee of agriculture established under the Agriculture Acts, 1931 to 1980.

(3) Notwithstanding any provision of the Income Tax Acts, other than *Chapter 4* of *Part 8*, income arising to a body to which this section applies shall be exempt from income tax.

Amendments

[1] Substituted by LGRA14 sched2(part5).

[2] Substituted by FA05 sched6(1)(c). Applies as on and from 25 March 2005

[3] Substituted by EATBA13 sched6(24).

Cross References

From Section 214

Section 237 Annual payments payable wholly out of taxed income.

Section 256 Interpretation (Chapter 4).

215 Certain profits of agricultural societies

[ITA67 s348]

(1) In this section, "*agricultural society*" means any society or institution established for the purpose of promoting the interests of agriculture, horticulture, livestock breeding or forestry.

(2) Any profits or gains arising to an agricultural society from an exhibition or show held for the purposes of the society shall, if they are applied solely to the purposes of the society, be exempt from income tax.

Case Law

A committee comprised of trustees, which was set up to hold annual horse races was not a society established for the purpose of breeding livestock and therefore not an agricultural society. The Trustees of the Ward Union Hunt Races v Hughes 1937 I ITR 538.

Revenue Precedents

Trade Protection Association. The case did not qualify as an Agricultural Society but it may be considered as a trade protection association. An application for such recognition can be obtain from the Office of the Chief Inspector of Taxes. A.S.4

216 Profits from lotteries

[ITA67 s350]

Exemption from income tax shall be granted in respect of profits from a lottery to which a licence under Part IV of the Gaming and Lotteries Act, 1956, applies.

216A Rent-a-room relief

[(1) In this section—

"*qualifying residence*", in relation to an individual for a year of assessment, means a residential premises situated in the State which is occupied by the individual as his or her sole or main residence during the year of assessment;

"*relevant sums*" means all sums arising in respect of the use for the purposes of residential accommodation, of a room or rooms in a qualifying residence and includes sums arising in respect of meals, cleaning, laundry and other similar goods and services which are incidentally supplied in connection with that use;

"*residential premises*" means a building or part of a building used as a dwelling.

(2) (a) This subsection applies if—

(i) relevant sums, chargeable to income tax under Case IV or Case V of Schedule D, arise to an individual (regardless of whether the relevant sums are chargeable to income tax under Case IV or Case V or under both Case IV and Case V), and

(ii) the amount of the relevant sums does not exceed the individual's limit for the year of assessment.

(b) In ascertaining the amount of relevant sums for the purposes of this subsection no deduction shall be made in respect of expenses or any other matter.

(c) Where this subsection applies the following shall be treated as nil for the purposes of the Income Tax Acts—

(i) the profits or gains of the year of assessment, and

(ii) the losses of any such year of assessment, in respect of relevant sums arising to an individual.

(d) Where an individual has relevant sums chargeable to income tax under Case V of Schedule D and an election under *subsection (3)(a)* has not been made, an allowance under *section 284*, which would on due claim being made be granted, shall be deemed to have been granted.

(3) (a) *Subsection (2)* shall not apply for a year of assessment if an individual so elects by notice in writing to the inspector on or before the specified return date for the chargeable period (within the meaning of [*section 959A*][1]).

(b) An election under this subsection shall have effect only for the year of assessment for which it is made.

[(3A) *Subsection (2)* shall not apply for a year of assessment where the relevant sums arising to the individual are received from [a child of the individual or of the civil partner of the individual.][2]][3]

[(3B) (a) *Subsection (2)* shall not apply for a year of assessment to relevant sums arising to—

(i) an individual, or

(ii) a person connected with the individual,

where the individual is an office holder, or employee, of—

(I) the person making the payment, or

(II) a person connected with the person making the payment.

(b) This subsection shall apply irrespective of whether the relevant sums are paid directly or indirectly by the person referred to in clauses (I) and (II) of *paragraph (a)* to the individual or to a person connected with the individual.][4]

(4) The provisions of the Income Tax Acts relating to the making of returns shall apply as if this section had not been enacted.

(5) Subject to *subsections (6)* and *(7)*, the limit of an individual referred to in *subsection (2)* is [€12,000][5].

[…][6]

(7) Where relevant sums arise to more than one individual in respect of a qualifying residence the limits referred to in *subsections (5)* and *(6)* shall be divided by the number of such individuals.

(8) Where subsection (2) applies, the receipt of relevant sums shall not operate so as to restrict or reduce any entitlement to relief under *section 244* or *604*.][7]

Amendments

[1] Substituted by FA12 sched4(part 2)(g).

[2] Substituted by FA12 s134(1)(a). Applies to relevant sums (within the meaning of section 216A(1)) arising to an individual on or after 8 February 2012.

[3] Inserted by FA07 s14. Applies as respects the year of assessment 2007 and subsequent years of assessment.

[4] Inserted by FA10 s13. Deemed to have come into force and takes effect as on and from 1 January 2010.

[5] Substituted by FA14 s9. Applies as respects the year of assessment 2015 and subsequent years of assessment.

[6] Deleted by FA01 s32(2)(b). Applies as respects the year of assessment 2002 and subsequent years of assessment.

[7] Inserted by FA01 s32(1).

Revenue Briefings

Tax Briefing

Tax Briefing April 2001 – Issue 43 pg 17 – Rent a-Room Relief
Tax Briefing June 2001 – Issue 44 pg 41 – Rent-a-Room Relief – Topical Questions
Tax Briefing July 2007 – Issue 66 – Finance Act 2007 Amendments to section 216A

Cross References

From Section 216A

Section 244 Relief for interest paid on certain home loans.
Section 284 Wear and tear allowances.
Section 604 Disposals of principal private residence.
Section 950 Interpretation (Part 41).

To Section 216A

Section 477A Relief for energy efficient works.

216B Payments under Scéim na bhFoghlaimeoirí Gaeilge

[(1) This section shall apply, in the case of a qualified applicant under a scheme administered by the Minister for Community, Rural and Gaeltacht Affairs and known as Scéim na bhFoghlaimeoirí Gaeilge, to any income received under that scheme in respect of a person who is temporarily resident with the qualified applicant, together with any other income received in the ordinary course in respect of such temporary resident.

(2) Notwithstanding any provision of the Income Tax Acts, income to which this section applies shall be disregarded for the purposes of those Acts.][1]

Amendments

[1] Inserted by FA04 s12.

216C Childcare services relief

[(1) In this section—

"*childcare services*" means any form of childminding services or supervised activities to care for minors, whether or not provided on a regular basis;

"*qualifying residence*", in relation to an individual for a year of assessment, means a residential premises situated in the State which is occupied by the individual as his or her sole or main residence during the year of assessment and in which at any time in the year of assessment childcare services are provided to not more than 3 minors, excluding minors occupying the residential premises as their sole or main residence;

"*relevant sums*" means all sums arising in respect of the use for the purposes of the provision of childcare services other than sums arising from the provision of sch services to minors, any of whom is or are—

(a) the child or children of the individual providing those services, or

(b) occupying the qualifying residence as his or her sole or main residence,

of a room or rooms in a qualifying residence and includes sums arising in respect of meals, cleaning, laundry and other similar goods and services which are incidentally supplied in connection with that use;

"*residential premises*" means a building or part of a building used as a dwelling.

(2) (a) Subject to *subsection (3)(a)*, this subsection applies if—

(i) relevant sums, chargeable to income tax under Case I or Case IV of Schedule D, arise to an individual (regardless of whether the relevant sums are chargeable to income tax under Case I or Case IV or under both Case I and Case IV), and

(ii) the amount of the relevant sums does not exceed the individual's limit for the year of assessment.

(b) In ascertaining the amount of relevant sums for the purposes of this subsection no deduction shall be made in respect of expenses or any other matter.

(c) Where this subsection applies the following shall be treated as nil for the purposes of the Income Tax Acts—

(i) the profits or gains of the year of assessment, and

(ii) the losses of any such year of assessment,

in respect of relevant sums arising to an individual.

(d) Where an individual has relevant sums chargeable to income tax under Case I of Schedule D and an election under *subsection (3)(a)* has been made, an allowance under *section 284*, which would on due claim being made be granted, shall be deemed to have been granted.

(3) (a) *Subsection (2)* shall apply for a year of assessment if an individual so elects by notice in writing to the inspector on or before the specified return date for the chargeable period (within the meaning of [*section 959A*][1]) and shows to the satisfaction of the Revenue Commissioners evidence that the individual has notified the person, recognised by the Health Service Executive for the purposes of such notification, that childcare services are being, will be or have been provided by the individual in the year of assessment.

(b) An election under this subsection shall have effect only for the year of assessment for which it is made.

(4) The provisions of the Income Tax Acts relating to the making of returns shall apply as if this section had not been enacted.

(5) Subject to *subsection (6)*, the individual's limit referred to in *subsection (2)* is [€15,000][2].

(6) Where relevant sums arise to more than one individual in respect of a qualifying residence the limit referred to in *subsection (5)* shall be divided by the number of such individuals.

(7) Where *subsection (2)* applies, the receipt of relevant sums shall not operate so as to restrict or reduce any entitlement to relief under *section 244* or *604*.][3]

Amendments

[1] Substituted by FA12 sched4(part 2)(g).

[2] Substituted by FA07 s15.

[3] Inserted by FA06 s13.

Revenue Briefings

eBrief

eBrief No. 18/2014 – Exempt Childcare Services

Cross References

From Section 216C

Section 244 Relief for interest paid on certain home loans.

Section 284 Wear and tear allowances.

Section 604 Disposals of principal private residence.

Section 950 Interpretation (Part 41).

CHAPTER 2

Corporation Tax

217 Certain income of Nítrigin Éireann Teoranta

[FA88 s39; FA92 s57]

Notwithstanding any provision of the Corporation Tax Acts, income—

(a) arising to Nítrigin Éireann Teoranta in any accounting period ending in the period commencing on the 1st day of January, 1987, and ending on the 31st day of December, 1999, from the business of supplying gas purchased from Bord Gáis Éireann to Irish Fertilizer Industries Limited under a contract between Nítrigin Éireann Teoranta and Irish Fertilizer Industries Limited, and

(b) which but for this section would have been chargeable to corporation tax under Case I of Schedule D,

shall be exempt from corporation tax.

218 Certain income of Housing Finance Agency plc

[FA85 s24; FA90 s56]

Notwithstanding any provision of the Corporation Tax Acts, income arising to the Housing Finance Agency plc—

(a) from the business of making loans and advances under section 5 of the Housing Finance Agency Act, 1981, which income would but for this section have been chargeable to corporation tax under Case I of Schedule D, and

(b) which income would but for this section have been chargeable to corporation tax under Case III of Schedule D,

shall be exempt from corporation tax.

219 Income of body designated under Irish Takeover Panel Act, 1997

[FA97 s63]

Notwithstanding any provision of the Corporation Tax Acts, income arising in any accounting period ending after the 30th day of April, 1997, to the body designated by the Minister for Enterprise, Trade and Employment under section 3 of the Irish Takeover Panel Act, 1997, shall be exempt from corporation tax.

219A Income of credit unions

[(1) In this section "*the Act*" means the Credit Union Act, 1997.

(2) Income arising to a credit union which is—

(a) registered as such under the Act, or

(b) deemed to be so registered by virtue of *section 5(3)* of the Act,

shall, with effect from the date of the registration or the deemed registration, as the case may be, of the credit union under the Act, be exempt from corporation tax.][1]

Amendments

[1] Inserted by FA98 s58(1).

Cross References

From Section 219A
Section 5 Interpretation of Capital Gains Tax Acts.

219B Income of Investor Compensation Company Ltd

[(1) In this section, "*the company*" means the company incorporated on the 10th day of September, 1998, as The Investor Compensation Company Limited.

(2) Notwithstanding any provision of the Corporation Tax Acts, profits arising in any accounting period ending on or after the 10th day of September, 1998, to the company shall be exempt from corporation tax.][1]

Amendments

[1] Inserted by FA99 s76(1)(a).

220 Profits of certain bodies corporate

[FA83 s32; FA87 s34; FA91 s41; FA95 s44(1) and (2); FA97 s49(1) and (2)]

Notwithstanding any provision of the Corporation Tax Acts, profits arising to any of the bodies corporate specified in the Table to this section shall be exempt from corporation tax.

TABLE

[...][1]	
2.	A company authorised by virtue of a licence granted by the Minister of Finance under the *National Lottery Act, 1986*.
3.	The Dublin Docklands Development [Authority and any of its wholly-owned subsidiaries.][2]
4.	An Bord Pinsean—The Pensions Board.
5.	[Horse Racing Ireland][3].
6.	The company incorporated on the 1st day of December, 1994, as Irish Thoroughbred Marketing Limited.
7.	The company incorporated on the 1st day of December, 1994, as Tote Ireland Limited.
[8.	The Commission for Electricity Regulation.][4]

Amendments

[1] Deleted by FA99 s77. Applies as respects any accounting period beginning on or after 25 March 1999

[2] Substituted by FA01 s79(b). Applies as respects accounting periods ending on or after 6 April 2001.

[3] Substituted by HGRA01 s11(a), with effect from 18 December 2001.

[4] Inserted by FA00 s84(1). This section shall be deemed to have applied as on and from 14 July 1999.

221 Certain payments to National Co-operative Farm Relief Services Ltd and certain payments made to its members

[FA94 s52; FA95 s57]

(1) In this section—

"*the first agreement*" means the agreement in writing dated the 4th day of July, 1991, between the Minister for Agriculture, Food and Forestry and the National Co-operative for the provision of financial support for farm relief services, together with every amendment of the agreement in accordance with Article 9.1 of that agreement;

"*the second agreement*" means the agreement in writing dated the 16th day of May, 1995, between the Minister for Agriculture, Food and Forestry and the National

Co-operative for the provision of financial support for the development of agricultural services, together with every amendment of the agreement in accordance with Article 9.1 of that agreement;

"*a member co-operative*" means a society engaged in the provision of farm relief services which has been admitted to membership of the National Co-operative;

"*the Minister*" means the Minister for Agriculture and Food;

"*the National Co-operative*" means the society registered on the 13th day of August, 1980, as National Co-operative Farm Relief Services Limited;

"*society*" means a society registered under the Industrial and Provident Societies Acts, 1893 to 1978.

(2) Notwithstanding any provision of the Corporation Tax Acts—

(a) a grant made under Article 3.1 of the first agreement by the Minister to the National Co-operative,

(b) a transfer of moneys under Article 3.6 of the first agreement by the National Co-operative to a member co-operative,

(c) a payment made under Article 3.1(*a*) of the second agreement by the Minister to the National Co-operative, and

(d) a transmission of moneys under Article 3.4 in respect of payments under Article 3.1(*a*) of the second agreement by the National Co-operative to a member co-operative,

shall be disregarded for the purposes of those Acts.

[(3) This section does not apply to any grant, payment, transfer or transmission of moneys referred to in *subsection (2)* which is made on or after 1 January 2011.][1]

Amendments

[1] Inserted by FA11 s39(1). Deemed to have come into force and takes effect as on and from 1 January 2011.

222 Certain dividends from a non-resident subsidiary

[FA88 s41; FA91 s40]

(1) (a) In this section—

"*approved investment plan*" means an investment plan in respect of which the Minister has given a certificate in accordance with *subsection (2)* to the company concerned;

"*investment plan*" means a plan of a company resident in the State which is directed towards the creation or maintenance of employment in the State in trading operations carried on, or to be carried on, in the State and which has been submitted—

(i) before the commencement of its implementation, or

(ii) where the Minister is satisfied that there was reasonable cause for it to be submitted after the commencement of its implementation, within one year from that commencement,

to the Minister by the company for the purpose of enabling it to claim relief under this section;

"*the Minister*" means the Minister for Finance;

"*relevant dividends*" means dividends, received by a company resident in the State (being the company claiming relief under this section) from a foreign subsidiary of the company, which are—

(i) [specified in a certificate given before 15 February 2001 by the Minister][1] under *subsection (2)*, and

(ii) applied within a period—

(I) which begins one year before the first day on which the dividends so specified are received in the State, or at such earlier time as the Revenue Commissioners may by notice in writing allow, and

(II) which ends 2 years after the first day on which the dividends so specified are received in the State, or at such later time as the Revenue Commissioners may by notice in writing allow,

for the purposes of an approved investment plan;

"*relief under this section*", in relation to a company for an accounting period, means the amount by which any corporation tax payable by the company is reduced by virtue of *subsection (3)*.

(b) (i) The reference in the definition of "*relevant dividends*" to "*a foreign subsidiary*" means a 51 per cent subsidiary of a company where the company is resident in the State and the subsidiary is a resident [...][2] of a territory with the government of which arrangements having the force of law by virtue of [*section 826(1)*][3] have been made.

(ii) For the purposes of *subparagraph (i)*—

[...][4]

a company shall be regarded as being a resident of a territory [...][5] if it is so regarded under arrangements made with the government of that territory and having the force of law by virtue of [*section 826(1)*][6].

(2) Where an investment plan has been duly submitted by a company, and the Minister—

(a) is satisfied that the plan is directed towards the creation or maintenance of employment in the State in trading operations carried on, or to be carried on, in the State, and

(b) has been informed in writing by the company of the amount of dividends concerned,

the Minister may give a certificate to the company certifying that an amount of dividends specified in the certificate shall be an amount of relevant dividends.

(3) Subject to *subsection (4)*, where a company claims and proves that it has received in an accounting period any amount of relevant dividends, the amount of the company's income for the period represented by those dividends shall not be taken into account in computing the income of the company for that accounting period for the purposes of corporation tax.

(4) Where in relation to a certificate given to a company under *subsection (2)* the Minister considers that, as regards the approved investment plan concerned, all or part of the relevant dividends have not been applied within the period provided for in the definition of "*relevant dividends*", the Minister may, by notice in writing to the company, reduce the amount of the relevant dividends specified in the certificate by so much as has not been so applied, and accordingly where the amount of the relevant dividends specified in a certificate is so reduced—

(a) in a case where relief under this section has been granted in respect of the amount of the relevant dividends specified in the certificate before such a reduction of that amount, the inspector shall make such assessments [or amend such assessments][7] as are necessary to recover the relief given in respect of the amount of the reduction, and

(b) in a case where a claim for relief has not yet been made, relief shall not be due under this section in respect of the amount of the reduction.

(5) A claim for relief under this section shall be made in writing to the inspector and shall be submitted together with the company's return of profits for the period in which the relevant dividends are received in the State.

Amendments

[1] Substituted by FA01 s86.

[2] Deleted by FA04 sched3(1)(h). This section shall have effect as on and from 25 March 2004

[3, 6] Substituted by FA07 sched2(1)(h). Has effect as on and from 2 April 2007

[4] Deleted by FA98 sched3(3)(a).

[5] Deleted by FA98 sched3(3)(b)(i).

[7] Substituted by FA12 sched4(part 2)(g).

Cross References

From Section 222

Section 826 Agreements for relief from double taxation.

CHAPTER 3

Income Tax and Corporation Tax

223 Small enterprise grants

[FA93 s37]

(1) This section shall apply to a grant made under section 10(5)(*a*) of the Údarás na Gaeltachta Act, 1979, or section 21(5)(*a*) (as amended by the Industrial Development (Amendment) Act, 1991) of the Industrial Development Act, 1986, being an employment grant—

(a) in the case of section 10(5)(*a*) of the Údarás na Gaeltachta Act, 1979, under the scheme known as "Deontais Fhostaíochta ó Údarás na Gaeltachta do Thionscnaimh Sheirbhíse Idir-Náisiúnta" or the scheme known as "Deontais Fhostaíochta ó Údarás na Gaeltachta do Thionscail Bheaga Dhéantúsaíochta", or

(b) in the case of section 21(5)(*a*) of the Industrial Development Act, 1986 (as so amended), under the scheme known as "Scheme Governing the Making of Employment Grants to Small Industrial Undertakings".

(2) A grant to which this section applies shall be disregarded for the purposes of the Tax Acts.

224 Grants to medium and large industrial undertakings

[FA95 s43]

(1) This section shall apply to a grant made under section 10(5)(*a*) of the Údarás na Gaeltachta Act, 1979, or section 21(5)(*a*) (as amended by the Industrial Development (Amendment) Act, 1991) of the Industrial Development Act, 1986, being an employment grant—

(a) in the case of section 10(5)(*a*) of the Údarás na Gaeltachta Act, 1979, under the scheme known as "Deontais Fhostaíochta ó Údarás na Gaeltachta do Ghnóthais Mhóra/Mheánmhéide Thionsclaíocha", or

(b) in the case of section 21(5)(*a*) of the Industrial Development Act, 1986 (as so amended), under the scheme known as "Scheme Governing the Making of Employment Grants to Medium/Large Industrial Undertakings".

(2) A grant to which this section applies shall be disregarded for the purposes of the Tax Acts.

225 Employment grants

[FA82 s18; FA97 s146(1) and Sch9 PtI par12(2)]

(1) This section shall apply to an employment grant made under—

[(a) section 3 or section 4 (as amended by the Shannon Free Airport Development Company Limited (Amendment) Act, 1983) of the Shannon Free Airport Development Company Limited (Amendment) Act, 1970,

(b) section 25 of the Industrial Development Act, 1986, or

(c) section 12 of the Industrial Development Act, 1993.][1]

(2) A grant to which this section applies shall be disregarded for the purposes of the Tax Acts.

Amendments

[1] Substituted by FA99 s38(1). This section shall be deemed to have applied as respects a grant made on or after the 6th day of April, 1996.

226 Certain employment grants and recruitment subsidies

[FA96 s40(1) and (2); FA97 s40]

(1) This section shall apply to an employment grant or recruitment subsidy made to an employer in respect of a person employed by such employer under—

(a) the Back to Work Allowance Scheme, being a scheme established on the 1st day of October, 1993, and administered by the Minister for Social, Community and Family Affairs,

(b) any scheme which may be established by the Minister for Enterprise, Trade and Employment with the approval of the Minister for Finance for the purposes of promoting the employment of individuals who have been unemployed for 3 years or more and which is to be administered by An Foras Áiseanna Saothair,

(c) paragraph 13 of Annex B to an operating agreement between the Minister for Enterprise, Trade and Employment and a County Enterprise Board, being a board specified in the Schedule to the Industrial Development Act, 1995,

(d) as respects grants or subsidies paid on or after the 6th day of April, 1997, the Employment Support Scheme, being a scheme established on the 1st day of January, 1993, and administered by the National Rehabilitation Board,

[(dd) as respects grants or subsidies paid on or after the 1st day of September 2005, the Wage Subsidy Scheme, being a scheme administered by the Department of Social Protection,][1]

[...][2]

(f) the European Union Leader II Community Initiative 1994 to 1999, and which is administered in accordance with operating rules determined by the Minister for Agriculture and Food,

(g) the European Union Operational Programme for Local Urban and Rural Development which is to be administered by the company incorporated under the Companies Acts, 1963 to 1990, on the 14th day of October, 1992, as Area Development Management Limited,

(h) the Special European Union Programme for Peace and Reconciliation in Northern Ireland and the Border Counties of Ireland which was approved by the European Commission on the 28th day of July, 1995,

(i) the Joint Northern Ireland/Ireland INTERREG Programme 1994 to 1999, which was approved by the European Commission on the 27th day of February, 1995, […][3]

(j) any initiative of the International Fund for Ireland, which was designated by the International Fund for Ireland (Designation and Immunities) Order, 1986 (S.I. No. 394 of 1986), as an organisation to which Part VIII of the Diplomatic Relations and Immunities Act, 1967, [applies, or][4]

[(k) as respects payments made to employers on or after 1 July 2013, JobsPlus, being a scheme administered by the Department of Social Protection.][5]

(2) An employment grant or recruitment subsidy to which this section applies shall be disregarded for the purposes of the Tax Acts.

Amendments

[1] Inserted by FA13 s36(1)(a). Deemed to have come into force and takes effect on and from 1 January 2013.

[2] Deleted by FA13 s36(1)(b). Deemed to have come into force and takes effect on and from 1 January 2013.

[3] Deleted by F(No.2)A13 s2(a). Comes into operation on 1 January 2014.

[4] Substituted by F(No.2)A13 s2(b). Comes into operation on 1 January 2014.

[5] Inserted by F(No.2)A13 s2(c). Comes into operation on 1 January 2014.

227 Certain income arising to specified non-commercial state-sponsored bodies

[FA94 s32(1),(2),(3) and (4)]

(1) In this section, "*non-commercial state-sponsored body*" means a body specified in *Schedule 4*.

(2) For the purposes of this section, the Minister for Finance may by order amend *Schedule 4* by the addition to that Schedule of any body or the deletion from that Schedule of any body standing specified.

(3) Where an order is proposed to be made under *subsection (2)*, a draft of the order shall be laid before Dáil Éireann and the order shall not be made until a resolution approving of the draft has been passed by Dáil Éireann.

(4) Notwithstanding any provision of the Tax Acts other than the provisions (apart from *section 261(c)*) of *Chapter 4* of *Part 8*, income arising to a non-commercial state-sponsored body—

(a) which but for this section would have been chargeable to tax under Case III, IV or V of Schedule D, and

(b) from the date that such body was incorporated under the Companies Acts, 1963 to 1990, or was established by or under any other enactment,

shall be disregarded for the purposes of the Tax Acts; but a noncommercial state-sponsored body—

(i) which has paid income tax or corporation tax shall not be entitled to repayment of that tax, and

(ii) shall not be treated as—

(I) a company within the charge to corporation tax in respect of interest for the purposes of *paragraph (f)* of the definition of "*relevant deposit*" in *section 256*, or

(II) a person to whom *section 267* applies.

Cross References

From Section 227

Section 256 Interpretation (Chapter 4).

Section 261 Taxation of relevant interest, etc.

Section 267 Repayment of appropriate tax in certain cases.

Schedule 4 Exemption of Specified Non-Commercial State Sponsored Bodies from Certain Tax Provisions

To Section 227

Schedule 4 Exemption of Specified Non-Commercial State Sponsored Bodies from Certain Tax Provisions

228 Income arising to designated bodies under the Securitisation (Proceeds of Certain Mortgages) Act, 1995

[FA96 s39(1) and (2)]

Notwithstanding any provision of the Tax Acts, income arising to a body designated under section 4(1) of the Securitisation (Proceeds of Certain Mortgages) Act, 1995, shall be exempt from income tax and corporation tax.

229 Harbour authorities and port companies

[FA97 s60(1) and (3) to (5)]

(1) (a) In this section—

"*relevant body*" means—

(i) a harbour authority within the meaning of the Harbours Act, 1946,

(ii) a company established pursuant to section 7 of the Harbours Act, 1996, and

(iii) any other company which controls a harbour and carries on a trade which consists wholly or partly of the provision in that harbour of such facilities and accommodation for vessels, goods and passengers as are ordinarily provided by harbour authorities specified in *paragraph (i)*, and companies specified in *paragraph (ii)* which control harbours, situate within the State, in those harbours;

"*relevant profits or gains*" means so much of the profits or gains of a relevant body controlling a harbour situate within the State as arise from the provision in that harbour of such facilities and accommodation for vessels, goods and passengers as are ordinarily provided by—

(i) harbour authorities specified in *paragraph (i)*, and

(ii) companies specified in *paragraph (ii)*,

of the definition of "*relevant body*" which control harbours, situate within the State, in those harbours.

(b) For the purposes of this section, where an accounting period falls partly in a period, the part of the accounting period falling in the period shall be regarded as a separate accounting period.

(2) Exemption shall be granted from tax under Schedule D in respect of relevant profits or gains in the period beginning on the 1st day of January, 1997, and ending on the 31st day of December, 1998.

(3) *Subsection (2)* shall apply to a relevant body which is a harbour authority referred to in *paragraph (i)* of the definition of "*relevant body*" as if "in the period beginning on the 1st day of January, 1997, and ending on the 31st day of December, 1998" were deleted.

(4) Where a relevant body is chargeable to tax under Schedule D in respect of relevant profits or gains, the relevant profits or gains shall be reduced by an amount equal to—

(a) as respects accounting periods falling wholly or partly in the year 1999, two-thirds of those relevant profits or gains, and

(b) as respects accounting periods falling wholly or partly in the year 2000, one-third of those relevant profits or gains.

229A Shannon Commercial Enterprises Ltd.

[(1) In this section—

'*company*' means Shannon Commercial Enterprises Limited;

'*qualifying period*', in relation to an asset, means the period beginning on the date of the acquisition of the asset, or if the asset was held on 6 April 1974, that date, and ending on 31 December 2013;

'*period of ownership*', in relation to an asset, means the period beginning on the date of the acquisition of the asset, or if the asset was held on 6 April 1974, that date, and ending on the date of disposal of the asset;

'*relevant profits or gains*' means so much of the profits or gains of the company as are attributable to any rent in respect of any premises or any receipts in respect of any easement.

(2) Exemption shall be granted from tax chargeable under Case V of Schedule D in respect of relevant profits or gains in the period beginning 1 January 2014 and ending 31 December 2015.

(3) Where the company is chargeable to tax under Case V of Schedule D in respect of relevant profits or gains, the relevant profits or gains shall be reduced by an amount equal to—

(a) as respects accounting periods falling wholly or partly in the year 2016, two-thirds of those relevant profits or gains, and

(b) as respects accounting periods falling wholly or partly in the year 2017, one-third of those relevant profits or gains.

(4) For the purposes of the Capital Gains Tax Acts, where a gain accrues to the company from the disposal of an asset after 31 December 2013, such portion of the gain shall not be a chargeable gain as represents the same proportion of the gain as the length of the qualifying period bears to the length of the period of ownership.][1]

Amendments

[1] Inserted by SA(SG)A14 s36(a).

230 National Treasury Management Agency

[FA91 s20(1) and (3)]

(1) Notwithstanding any provision of the Corporation Tax Acts, profits arising to the National Treasury Management Agency in any accounting period shall be exempt from corporation tax.

[(1A) Notwithstanding any provision of the Corporation Tax Acts, profits arising to a Fund investment vehicle (within the meaning of *section 37* of the *National Treasury Management Agency (Amendment) Act 2014*) of which the Minister for Finance is the sole beneficial owner shall be exempt from corporation tax.][1]

(2) Notwithstanding any provision of the Tax Acts, any interest, annuity or other annual payment paid by the National Treasury Management Agency shall be paid without deduction of income tax.

Amendments

[1] Inserted by NTMA(A)A14 part4(3).

230A National Pensions Reserve Fund Commission [Repealed]

Repealed by NTMA(A)A14 part4(4).

230AA NAMA profits exempt from corporation tax

[Notwithstanding any provision of the Corporation Tax Acts, profits arising to the National Asset Management Agency shall be exempt from corporation tax.][1]

Amendments

[1] Inserted by the National Asset Management Agency Act 2009 Sched 3 part 10.

230AB National Development Finance Agency [Repealed]

Repealed by NTMA(A)A14 part4(5).

230AC Strategic Banking Corporation of Ireland

[Notwithstanding any provision of the Corporation Tax Acts, profits arising to the Strategic Banking Corporation of Ireland or a subsidiary wholly owned by it or a subsidiary wholly owned by any such subsidiary shall be exempt from corporation tax.][1]

Amendments

[1] Inserted by SBCoIA14 part7(1)(b). Does not apply in circumstances where the Minister does not hold all of the shares in the SBCI.

231 Profits or gains from stallion fees

[FA69 s18(2)(b); CTA76 s11(6); FA85 s14(1)]

[(1) The profits or gains arising—][1]

(a) (i) to the owner of a stallion, which is ordinarily kept on land in the State, from the sale of services of mares within the State by the stallion, or

(ii) to the part-owner of such a stallion from the sale of such services or of rights to such services, or

(b) to the part-owner of a stallion, which is ordinarily kept on land outside the State, from the sale of services of mares by the stallion or of rights to such services, where the part-owner carries on in the State a trade which consists of or includes bloodstock breeding and it is shown to the satisfaction of the inspector, or on appeal to the satisfaction of the Appeal Commissioners, that the part-ownership of the stallion was acquired and is held primarily for the purposes of the service by the stallion of mares owned or partly-owned by the part-owner of the stallion in the course of that trade,

[shall be exempt from income tax and corporation tax][2]

[(2) As respects the making of a return of income (being a return which a chargeable person, within the meaning of *section 950*, is required to deliver under *section 951*), the Tax Acts shall apply—

(a) as if *subsection (1)* had not been enacted,

(b) notwithstanding anything to the contrary in *Part 41*, as if a person to whom profits or gains referred to in *subsection (1)* arise for any chargeable period (within the meaning of *section 321(2)*) were, if such person would not otherwise be, a chargeable person (within the meaning of *section 950*) for that chargeable period,

(c) where a person to whom profits or gains referred to in *subsection (1)* arise for any chargeable period (within the meaning of *section 321(2)*) is a person to whom a notice under *section 951(6)* has been issued, as if such a notice had not been issued, and

(d) in so far as those Acts relate to the keeping of records (within the meaning of *section 886*) and the making available of such records for inspection, as if such profits or gains were chargeable to income tax or corporation tax, as the case may be.

(3) For the purposes of *subsection (2)*—

(a) profits or gains referred to in *subsection (1)* or a loss referred to in *paragraph (b)* shall be computed in accordance with the Tax Acts as if *subsection (1)* had not been enacted, and

(b) where a loss is incurred for any chargeable period (within the meaning of *section 321(2)*), the amount of that loss shall be included in the return of income referred to in *subsection (2)* for that chargeable period.][3]

[(4) *Subsections (1)* to *(3)* do not apply to any profits or gains arising after 31 July 2008 to an owner or a part-owner of a stallion.][4]

Amendments

1 Renumbered by FA03 s35(1)(a)(i). Applies as respects any chargeable period commencing on or after 1 January 2004.

2 Substituted by FA03 s35(1)(a)(ii). Applies as respects any chargeable period commencing on or after 1 January 2004.

3 Inserted by FA03 s35(1)(a)(iii). Applies as respects any chargeable period commencing on or after 1 January 2004.

4 Inserted by FA06 s22(a).

Revenue Briefings

Tax Briefing

Tax Briefing September 1998 – Issue 33 pg 30 – Stallions – "In the State"

Tax Briefing June 2002 – Issue 48 pg 18 – Dual Hemisphere or Shuttle Stallions

Cross References

From Section 231

Section 321 Provisions of general application in relation to the making of allowances and charges.

Section 886 Obligation to keep certain records.

Section 950 Interpretation (Part 41).
Section 951 Obligation to make a return.

To Section 231

Section 140 Distributions out of profits or gains from stallion fees, stud greyhound services fees and occupation of certain woodlands.
Section 144 Distributions out of profits from trading within Shannon Airport.
Section 531B Charge to income levy.
Section 669G Interpretation (Chapter 4).
Schedule 25B List of Specified Reliefs and Method of Determining Amount of Specified Relief Used in a Tax Year
Schedule 31 Consequential Amendments

232 Profits from occupation of certain woodlands

[FA69 s18(1) and (2)(c); CTA76 s11(6); FA96 s132(2) and Sch5 PtII]

(1) In this section—

"*occupation*", in relation to any land, means having the use of that land;

"*woodlands*" means woodlands in the State.

(2) Except where otherwise provided by *section 75*, the profits or gains arising from the occupation of woodlands managed on a commercial basis and with a view to the realisation of profits [shall be exempt from income tax and corporation tax.][1]

["(3) As respects the making of a return of income (being a return which a chargeable person, [within the meaning of *Part 41A*, is required to deliver under *Chapter 3* of that Part][2]), the Tax Acts shall apply—

(a) as if *subsection (2)* had not been enacted,

(b) notwithstanding anything to the contrary in [*Part 41A*][3], as if a person to whom profits or gains referred to in *subsection (2)* arise for any chargeable period (within the meaning of *section 321(2)*) were, if such person would not otherwise be, a chargeable person (within the meaning of [*Part 41A*][4]) for that chargeable period,

(c) where a person to whom profits or gains referred to in *subsection (2)* arise for any chargeable period (within the meaning of *section 321(2)*) is a person to whom a notice under [*section 959N*][5] has been issued, as if such a notice had not been issued, and

(d) in so far as those Acts relate to the keeping of records (within the meaning of *section 886*) and the making available of such records for inspection, as if such profits or gains were chargeable to income tax or corporation tax, as the case may be.

(4) For the purposes of *subsection (3)*—

(a) profits or gains referred to in *subsection (2)* or a loss referred to in *paragraph (b)* shall be computed in accordance with the Tax Acts as if *subsection (2)* had not been enacted, and

(b) where a loss is incurred for any chargeable period (within the meaning of *section 321(2)*), the amount of that loss shall be included in the return of income referred to in *subsection (3)* for that chargeable period.][6]

Amendments

[1] Substituted by FA03 s35(1)(b)(i). Applies as respects any chargeable period commencing on or after 1 January 2004.

[2, 3, 4, 5] Substituted by FA12 sched4(part 2)(g).

[6] Inserted by FA03 s35(1)(b)(ii). Applies as respects any chargeable period commencing on or after 1 January 2004.

Case Law

In the UK case of Jaggers v Ellis 1996 SpC 98, no exemption was available in respect of profits derived from the sale of Christmas trees as the term 'woodlands' suggests the production of timber.

Collins v Fraser 46 TC 143 implies that exemption applies in respect of profits up to the point at which normal exploitation of the woodlands ceases.

Revenue Precedents

Whether forestry premium income from occupation of woodlands on a commercial basis. Yes. IT892033

A person intends to plant a small area of holly. Small amounts of foliage can be harvested after 3 years but the main harvest will arise after 6 to 10 years. Is the profit arising from the sale of the holly exempt under section 232 Taxes Consolidation Act 1997? The profits from the sale of foliage from holly bushes are not regarded as profits arising from the occupation of woodlands and are therefore not exempt. IT933006

Profits from the planting and harvesting of Christmas trees are exempt under the section. IT 96 3506

Statements of Practice

Taxation of Farmers and Landowners – New Forest Premium Scheme – SP IT/1/90

Cross References

From Section 232

Section 75 Case V: basis of assessment.
Section 321 Provisions of general application in relation to the making of allowances and charges.
Section 886 Obligation to keep certain records.
Section 950 Interpretation (Part 41).
Section 951 Obligation to make a return.

To Section 232

Section 140 Distributions out of profits or gains from stallion fees, stud greyhound services fees and occupation of certain woodlands.
Section 144 Distributions out of profits from trading within Shannon Airport.
Section 488 Interpretation (Part 16).
Section 531B Charge to income levy.
Section 531AM Charge to universal social charge.
Section 531AS Universal social charge payable by chargeable persons (within the meaning of Part 41).
Schedule 25B List of Specified Reliefs and Method of Determining Amount of Specified Relief Used in a Tax Year
Schedule 31 Consequential Amendments

233 Stud greyhound service fees

[FA96 s25(1) and (2)]

(1) In this section—

"*greyhound bitches*" means female greyhounds registered in the Irish Greyhound Stud Book or in any other greyhound stud book recognised for the purposes of the Irish Greyhound Stud Book;

"*stud greyhound*" means a male greyhound registered as a sire for stud purposes in the Irish Greyhound Stud Book or in any other greyhound stud book recognised for the purposes of the Irish Greyhound Stud Book.

(2) The profits or gains arising—

(a) (i) to the owner of a stud greyhound, which is ordinarily kept in the State, from the sale of services of greyhound bitches within the State by the stud greyhound, or

(ii) to the part-owner of such a stud greyhound from the sale of such services or of rights to such services, or

(b) to the part-owner of a stud greyhound, which is ordinarily kept outside the State, from the sale of services of greyhound bitches by the stud greyhound or of rights to such services, where the part-owner carries on in the State a trade which consists of or includes greyhound breeding and it is shown to the satisfaction of the inspector, or on appeal to the satisfaction of the Appeal Commissioners, that the part-ownership of the stud greyhound was acquired and is held primarily for the purposes of the service by the stud greyhound of greyhound bitches owned or partly-owned by the part-owner of the stud greyhound in the course of that trade,

[shall be exempt from income tax and corporation tax][1]

[(3) As respects the making of a return of income (being a return which a chargeable person, within the meaning of *section 950*, is required to deliver under *section 951*), the Tax Acts shall apply—

(a) as if *subsection (2)* had not been enacted,

(b) notwithstanding anything to the contrary in *Part 41*, as if a person to whom profits or gains referred to in *subsection (2)* arise for any chargeable period (within the meaning of *section 321(2)*) were, if such person would not otherwise be, a chargeable person (within the meaning of *section 950*) for that chargeable period,

(c) where a person to whom profits or gains referred to in *subsection (2)* arise for any chargeable period (within the meaning of *section 321(2)*) is a person to whom a notice under *section 951(6)* has been issued, as if such a notice had not been issued, and

(d) in so far as those Acts relate to the keeping of records (within the meaning of *section 886*) and the making available of such records for inspection, as if such profits or gains were chargeable to income tax or corporation tax, as the case may be.

(4) For the purposes of *subsection (3)*—

(a) profits or gains referred to in *subsection (2)* or a loss referred to in *paragraph (b)* shall be computed in accordance with the Tax Acts as if *subsection (2)* had not been enacted, and

(b) where a loss is incurred for any chargeable period (within the meaning of *section 321(2)*), the amount of that loss shall be included in the return of income referred to in *subsection (3)* for that chargeable period.

[(5) *Subsections (1)* to *(4)* do not apply to any profits or gains arising after 31 July 2008 to an owner or a part-owner of a stud greyhound.][2]][3]

Amendments

[1] Substituted by FA03 s35(1)(c)(i). Applies as respects any chargeable period commencing on or after 1 January 2004.

[2] Inserted by FA06 s22(b).

[3] Inserted by FA03 s35(1)(c)(ii). Applies as respects any chargeable period commencing on or after 1 January 2004.

Cross References

From Section 233

Section 321 Provisions of general application in relation to the making of allowances and charges.
Section 886 Obligation to keep certain records.
Section 950 Interpretation (Part 41).
Section 951 Obligation to make a return.

To Section 233

Section 140 Distributions out of profits or gains from stallion fees, stud greyhound services fees and occupation of certain woodlands.

Section 144 Distributions out of profits from trading within Shannon Airport.

Section 531B Charge to income levy.

Schedule 25B List of Specified Reliefs and Method of Determining Amount of Specified Relief Used in a Tax Year

234 Certain income derived from patent royalties

[FA73 s34; CTA76 s140(1) and Sch2 PtI par35; FA81 s19; FA92 s19(1); FA94 s28; FA96 s32(1) and (3)(a) and s132(1) and Sch5 PtI par7; FA97 s146(1) and Sch9 PtI par6(2)]

(1) In this section—

["*EEA Agreement*" means the Agreement on the European Economic Area signed at Oporto on 2 May 1992, as adjusted by the Protocol signed at Brussels on 17 March 1993;

"*EEA state*" means a state which is a Contracting Party to the EEA Agreement;][1]

"*income from a qualifying patent*" means any royalty or other sum paid in respect of the user of the invention to which the qualifying patent relates, including any sum paid for the grant of a licence to exercise rights under such patent, where that royalty or other sum is paid—

(a) for the purposes of activities which—

(i) would be regarded, otherwise than by virtue of *paragraph (b)* or *(c)* of *section 445(7)* or *section 446*, as the manufacture of goods for the purpose of relief under *Part 14*, or

(ii) would be so regarded if they were carried on in the State by a company,

but, as respects a royalty or other sum paid on or after the 23rd day of April, 1996, where the royalty or other sum exceeds the royalty or other sum which would have been paid if the payer of the royalty or other sum and the beneficial recipient of the royalty or other sum were independent persons acting at arm's length, the excess shall not be income from a qualifying patent,

or

(b) by a person who—

(i) is not connected (within the meaning of *section 10* as it applies for the purposes of capital gains tax) with the person who is the beneficial recipient of the royalty or other sum, and

(ii) has not entered into any arrangement in connection with the royalty or other sum the main purpose or one of the main purposes of which was to satisfy *subparagraph (i)*;

"*qualifying patent*" means a patent in relation to which the research, planning, processing, experimenting, testing, devising, designing, developing or similar activity leading to the invention which is the subject of the patent was carried out [in an EEA state;][2]

"*resident of the State*" means any person resident in the State for the purposes of income tax and not resident elsewhere;

a company shall be regarded as a resident of the State if it is managed and controlled in the State.

(2) (a) A resident of the State who makes a claim in that behalf and makes a return in the prescribed form of his or her total income from all sources,

as estimated in accordance with the Income Tax Acts, shall be entitled to have any income from a qualifying patent arising to him or her disregarded for the purposes of the Income Tax Acts.

(b) In *paragraph (a)*, the reference to a return of total income from all sources as estimated in accordance with the Income Tax Acts shall apply for corporation tax as if it were or included a reference to a return under *section 884*.

(3) Notwithstanding *subsection (2)*, an individual shall not be entitled to have any amount of income from a qualifying patent arising to him or her disregarded for any purpose of the Income Tax Acts unless the individual carried out, either solely or jointly with another person, the research, planning, processing, experimenting, testing, devising, designing, developing or other similar activity leading to the invention which is the subject of the qualifying patent.

[(3A) (a) Notwithstanding *subsection (2)* but subject to *paragraphs (b)* to *(d)*, so much of the aggregate of the amounts of any income from qualifying patents arising to a person in a relevant period which would, apart from this subsection, be disregarded under *subsection (2)* for the purposes of income tax or corporation tax as exceeds €5,000,000 shall not be so disregarded.

(b) Where—

(i) in relation to a company, income from qualifying patents arising in a relevant period would, apart from this paragraph, be disregarded under *subsection (2)*, and

(ii) in relation to one or more persons who are connected (within the meaning of *section 10*) with the company referred to in *subparagraph (i)*, income from qualifying patents arising in that relevant period would, apart from this paragraph, be disregarded under *subsection (2)*,

then the aggregate of the amounts of income from qualifying patents, which is to be disregarded under *subsection (2)*, arising to the company and all of those persons in the relevant period shall not be greater than €5,000,000.

(c) Where the aggregate of the amounts of income from qualifying patents in a relevant period arising to a company and all of the persons referred to in *paragraph (b)* which would, apart from *paragraph (b)*, be disregarded under *subsection (2)* exceeds €5,000,000, the amount of any income from qualifying patents which is to be so disregarded for the relevant period in relation to the company or any person referred to in *paragraph (b)* shall be—

(i) so much of €5,000,000 as is allocated to the company or that person in the manner specified in a notice made jointly in writing to the appropriate inspector by the company and the connected persons on or before the time by which a return under *section 951* is to be made for the latest chargeable period (within the meaning of *section 321(2)*) of—

(I) the company, or

(II) any of those persons,

which falls wholly or partly into the relevant period: but the aggregate of the amounts allocated to the company and all of the persons referred to in *paragraph (b)* in relation to the relevant period shall not exceed €5,000,000, and

(ii) where no such notice is given, an amount determined by the formula—

$$€5,000,000 \times \frac{P}{T}$$

where—

P is the aggregate of the amounts of income from qualifying patents arising to the company, or as the case may be the person, in the relevant period, and

T is the aggregate of the amounts of income from qualifying patents arising to the company and all of the persons referred to in *paragraph (b)* in the relevant period.

(d) For the purposes of this subsection, where a relevant period does not coincide with an accounting period of a company—

(i) the amount of income from qualifying patents arising to the company in the relevant period shall be the aggregate of the amounts of income from qualifying patents arising to the company in any accounting period or part of an accounting period falling within the relevant period,

(ii) income from qualifying patents arising to a company in an accounting period shall be treated as arising in part of that accounting period on a time basis according to the respective lengths of the part and the whole of the accounting period, and

(iii) subject to the preceding provisions of this paragraph, income arising in a relevant period that is to be disregarded under *subsection (2)* shall be treated as representing income of an accounting period only to the extent that it cannot be treated as representing income of an earlier period, or part of such period.

(e) In this subsection—

"*income from qualifying patents*" means income from a qualifying patent or from more than one such patent;

"*relevant period*" means the period of 12 months commencing on 1 January 2008 and each subsequent period of 12 months.][3]

(4) Where, under section 77 of the Patents Act, 1992, or any corresponding provision of the law of any other country, an invention which is the subject of a qualifying patent is made, used, exercised or vended by or for the service of the State or the government of the country concerned, this section shall apply as if the making, user, exercise or vending of the invention had taken place in pursuance of a licence and any sums paid in respect of the licence were income from a qualifying patent.

(5) Where any income arising to a person is by virtue of this section to be disregarded, the person shall not be treated, by reason of such disregarding, as having ceased to possess the whole of a single source within the meaning of *section 70(1)*.

(6) For the purpose of determining the amount of income to be disregarded under this section for the purposes of the Income Tax Acts, the Revenue Commissioners may make such apportionments of receipts and expenses as may be necessary.

(7) The relief provided by this section may be given by repayment or otherwise.

(8) *Subsections (3)* and *(4)* of *section 459* and *paragraph 8* of *Schedule 28* shall, with any necessary modifications, apply in relation to exemptions from tax under this section.

[(9) This section shall not apply to income from a qualifying patent which is paid to a person on or after 24 November 2010.][4]

Amendments

[1] Inserted by FA07 s45(1)(a)(i). Applies as respects income from a patent in relation to which the research, planning, processing, experimenting, testing, devising, designing, developing or similar activity leading to the invention which is the subject of the patent is carried out on or after 1 January 2008.

[2] Substituted by FA07 s45(1)(a)(ii). Applies as respects income from a patent in relation to which the research, planning, processing, experimenting, testing, devising, designing, developing or similar activity leading to the invention which is the subject of the patent is carried out on or after 1 January 2008.

[3] Inserted by FA07 s45(1)(b). Applies as respects a relevant period beginning on or after 1 January 2008.

[4] Inserted by FA11 s26(b).

Case Law

In the case of Revenue Commissioners v Wen-Plast (Research & Development) Ltd 2007 IEHC 66 the Court concluded that "it is not necessary that radical innovation is capable of being demonstrated as part of the process leading to a patent but it is sufficient that a combination of known technology could, and did, result in an invention which involved radical innovation".

Revenue Briefings

Tax Briefing

Tax Briefing December 1999 – Issue 38 pg 18 – Patent Royalties Income and Distributions
Tax Briefing July 2004 – Issue 56 pg 12 – 'Not Resident Elsewhere'
Tax Briefing October 2004 – Issue 57 pg 15 – 'Not Resident Elsewhere' – Correction (Tax Briefing 56)
Tax Briefing July 2007 – Issue 66 pg 21 – Finance Act 2007

Revenue Precedents

Interaction of Ireland/UK Double Taxation convention and section 234. Where a person is a resident of Ireland and not a resident of the UK in accordance with the Irl/UK Double Taxation convention, that person is a resident of Ireland for the purposes of section 234. IT912011
Exempt income from patents has to be declared on a return of income Form 11. IT943527

Cross References

From Section 234

Section 10 Connected persons.
Section 70 Case III: basis of assessment.
Section 321 Provisions of general application in relation to the making of allowances and charges.
Section 442 Interpretation (Part 14).
Section 445 Certain trading operations carried on in Shannon Airport.
Section 446 Certain trading operations carried on in Custom House Docks Area.
Section 459 General provisions relating to allowances, deductions and reliefs.
Section 884 Returns of profits.
Section 951 Obligation to make a return.
Schedule 28 Statements, Lists and Declarations

To Section 234

Section 141 Distributions out of income from patent royalties.
Section 144 Distributions out of profits from trading within Shannon Airport.
Section 531B Charge to income levy.
Section 531AM Charge to universal social charge.
Section 531AS Universal social charge payable by chargeable persons (within the meaning of Part 41).
Section 766 Tax credit for research and development expenditure.
Schedule 25B List of Specified Reliefs and Method of Determining Amount of Specified Relief Used in a Tax Year

235 Bodies established for promotion of athletic or amateur games or sports

[ITA67 s349; FA84 s9; FA97 s146(1) and Sch9 PtI par1(25)]

(1) In this section, "*approved body of persons*" means—

(a) any body of persons established for and existing for the sole purpose of promoting athletic or amateur games or sports, and

(b) (i) any body of persons that, as respects the year 1983-84 or any earlier year of assessment, was granted exemption from income tax under section 349 of the Income Tax Act, 1967, before that section was substituted by section 9 of the Finance Act, 1984, or

(ii) any company that, as respects any accounting period ending before the 6th day of April, 1984, was granted exemption from corporation tax under section 349 (before the substitution referred to in *subparagraph (i)*) of the Income Tax Act, 1967, as applied for corporation tax by section 11(6) of the Corporation Tax Act, 1976;

but does not include any such body of persons to which the Revenue Commissioners, after such consultation (if any) as may seem to them to be necessary with such person or body of persons as in their opinion may be of assistance to them, give a notice in writing stating that they are satisfied that the body—

(I) was not established for the sole purpose specified in *paragraph (a)* or was established wholly or partly for the purpose of securing a tax advantage, or

(II) being established for the sole purpose specified in *paragraph (a)*, no longer exists for such purpose or commences to exist wholly or partly for the purpose of securing a tax advantage.

(2) Exemption from income tax or, as the case may be, corporation tax shall be granted in respect of so much of the income of any approved body of persons as is shown to the satisfaction of the Revenue Commissioners to be income which has been or will be applied to the sole purpose specified in *subsection (1)(a)*.

(3) Where a notice is given under *subsection (1)*, the exemption from income tax or, as the case may be, corporation tax accorded to the body of persons to which it relates shall cease to have effect—

(a) if the notice is a notice to which *paragraph (I)* of that subsection applies—

(i) as respects income tax, for the year of assessment in which the body of persons was established or the year 1984-85, whichever is the later, and for each subsequent year of assessment, or

(ii) as respects corporation tax, for the first accounting period of the body of persons which commences on or after the 6th day of April, 1984, and for each subsequent accounting period;

(b) if the notice is a notice to which *paragraph (II)* of that subsection applies—

(i) as respects income tax, for the year of assessment in which in the opinion of the Revenue Commissioners the body of persons ceased to exist for the sole purpose specified in *subsection (1)(a)* or the year in which it commenced to exist wholly or partly for the purpose of securing a tax advantage, whichever is the earlier, but not being a year earlier than the year 1984-85, and for each subsequent year of assessment, or

(ii) as respects corporation tax, for the accounting period in which in the opinion of the Revenue Commissioners the body of persons ceased to exist for the sole purpose specified in *subsection (1)(a)* or the accounting period in which it commenced to exist wholly or partly for the purpose of securing a tax advantage, whichever is the earlier, but not being an accounting period which ends before the 6th day of April, 1984, and for each subsequent accounting period.

(4) *Section 949* shall apply to a notice under *subsection (1)* as if the notice were a determination by the Revenue Commissioners of a claim to an exemption under the Income Tax Acts.

(5) Anything required or permitted to be done by the Revenue Commissioners or any power or function conferred or imposed on them by this section may be done, exercised or performed, as appropriate, by an officer of the Revenue Commissioners authorised by them in that behalf.

Revenue Briefings

Tax Briefing

Tax Briefing June 2001 – Issue 44 pg 20 – Games and Sports Bodies

Revenue Precedents

Whether a sporting body entitled to exemption under section 235 TCA 1997 would be entitled to receive interest without deduction of tax on the basis of a declaration under section 265 TCA 1997? No; since the sporting body would not be within the charge to corporation tax in respect of the interest, Also, the body in question could not complete a declaration to the effect that the interest will be included in the profits of the company on which it will be charged to Corporation Tax, as required by section 265. IT922034

Cross References

From Section 235

Section 949 Appeals against determinations of certain claims, etc.

To Section 235

Section 172A Interpretation.
Section 172C Exemption from dividend withholding tax for certain persons.
Section 847A Donations to certain sports bodies.
Schedule 15 List of Bodies for Purposes of Section 610

236 Loan of certain art objects

[FA94 s19(1) to (6)]

(1) In this section—

"*art object*" has the meaning assigned to it by *subsection (2)(a)*;

"*authorised person*" means—

(a) an inspector or other officer of the Revenue Commissioners authorised by them in writing for the purposes of this section, or

(b) a person authorised by the Minister in writing for the purposes of this section;

"*the Minister*" means the Minister for Arts, Heritage, Gaeltacht and the Islands;

"*relevant building*" means an approved building within the meaning of *section 482*;

"*relevant garden*" means an approved garden within the meaning of *section 482*.

(2) (a) In this section, "*art object*" means any work of art (including a picture, sculpture, print, book, manuscript, piece of jewellery, furniture or other similar object) or scientific collection which, on application to them in that behalf by a person who owns or occupies a relevant building or a relevant garden, as the case may be, is determined—

(i) by the Minister, after consideration of any evidence in relation to the matter which the individual submits to the Minister and after such consultation (if any) as may seem to the Minister to be necessary with such person or body of persons as in the opinion of the Minister may be of assistance to the Minister, to be an object which is intrinsically of significant national, scientific, historical or aesthetic interest, and

(ii) by the Revenue Commissioners, to be an object reasonable access to which is afforded, and in respect of which reasonable facilities for viewing are provided, to the public.

(b) Without prejudice to the generality of the requirement that reasonable access be afforded, and that reasonable facilities for viewing be provided, to the public, access to and facilities for the viewing of an art object shall not be regarded as being reasonable access afforded, or the provision of reasonable facilities for viewing, to the public unless—

(i) subject to such temporary removal as is necessary for the purposes of the repair, maintenance or restoration of the object as is reasonable, access to it is afforded and facilities for viewing it are provided for not less than 60 days (including not less than 40 days during the period commencing on the 1st day of May and ending on the 30th day of September) in any year and, on each such day, such access is afforded and such facilities for viewing are provided in a reasonable manner and at reasonable times for a period, or periods in the aggregate, of not less than 4 hours,

(ii) such access is afforded and such facilities are provided to the public on the same days and at the same times as access is afforded to the public to the relevant building or the relevant garden, as the case may be, in which the object is kept, and

(iii) the price, if any, paid by the public in return for such access is in the opinion of the Revenue Commissioners reasonable in amount and does not operate to preclude the public from seeking access to the object.

(c) Where the Revenue Commissioners make a determination under *paragraph (a)* in relation to an art object, and reasonable access to the object ceases to be afforded, or reasonable facilities for the viewing of the object cease to be provided, to the public, the Revenue Commissioners may, by notice in writing given to the owner or occupier of the relevant building or relevant garden, as the case may be, in which the object is kept, revoke the determination with effect from the date on which they consider that such access or such facilities for viewing so ceased, and—

(i) this subsection shall cease to apply to the object from that date, and

(ii) for the year of assessment in which this subsection ceases to apply to the object, *subsection (3)* shall cease to apply to any expense referred to in *paragraph (a)* of that subsection incurred or deemed to have been incurred by the body corporate concerned.

(3) Subject to this section, where—

(a) a body corporate incurs an expense solely in, or solely in connection with, or is deemed to incur an expense in connection with, the provision to an individual (being an individual who is employed by the body corporate in an employment to which *Chapter 3* of *Part 5* applies, or who is a director, within the meaning of that Chapter, of the body corporate) of a benefit or facility which consists of the loan of an art object of which the body corporate is the beneficial owner, and

(b) the object is kept in a relevant building or a relevant garden, as the case may be, owned or occupied by the individual,

then, *section 436(3)* shall not apply to any such expense and *section 118(1)* shall not apply to any such expense for any year of assessment for which a claim in that behalf is made by the individual to the Revenue Commissioners.

(4) (a) Where an individual makes an application under *subsection (2)* or a claim under *subsection (3)*, an authorised person may at any reasonable time enter the relevant building or relevant garden concerned for the purpose of inspecting the art object to which the application or claim relates.

(b) Whenever an authorised person exercises any power conferred on him or her by this subsection, the authorised person shall on request produce his or her authorisation to any person concerned.

(c) Any person who obstructs or interferes with an authorised person in the course of exercising a power conferred on the authorised person by this subsection shall be guilty of an offence and shall be liable on summary conviction to a fine not exceeding [€630][1].

(5) An application under *subsection (2)* or a claim under *subsection (3)*—

(a) shall be made in such form as the Revenue Commissioners may from time to time prescribe, and

(b) in the case of a claim under *subsection (3)*, shall be accompanied by such statements in writing as may be required by the prescribed form in relation to the expense in respect of which the claim is made, including statements by the body corporate which incurred the expense.

(6) *Section 606* shall not apply to an object which is an art object.

[(7) This section ceases to have effect for the year of assessment 2010 and subsequent years of assessment.][2]

Amendments

[1] Substituted by FA01 sched5.

[2] Inserted by FA10 s5(a). Deemed to have come into force and takes effect as on and from 1 January 2010.

Cross References

From Section 236

Section 112 Basis of assessment, persons chargeable and extent of charge.
Section 116 Interpretation (Chapter 3).
Section 118 Benefits in kind: general charging provision.
Section 436 Certain expenses for participators and associates.
Section 482 Relief for expenditure on significant buildings and gardens.
Section 606 Disposals of work of art, etc., loaned for public display.

PART 8

Annual Payments, Charges and Interest

CHAPTER 1

Annual Payments

237 Annual payments payable wholly out of taxed income

[ITA67 s433; FA69 s33 and Sch4 PtI; FA74 s5(1); CTA76 s164 and Sch4 PtI; FA89 s89(1); FA96 s132(1) and Sch5 PtI par1(19)]

(1) Where any annuity or any other annual payment apart from yearly interest of money (whether payable in or outside the State, either as a charge on any property of the person paying the same by virtue of any deed or will or otherwise, or as a reservation thereout, or as a personal debt or obligation by virtue of any contract, or whether payable half-yearly or at any shorter or more distant periods), is payable wholly out of profits or gains brought into charge to income tax—

(a) the whole of those profits or gains shall be assessed and charged with income tax on the person liable to the annuity or annual payment, without distinguishing the same,

(b) the person liable to make such payment, whether out of the profits or gains charged with tax or out of any annual payment liable to deduction, or from which a deduction has been made, shall be entitled on making such payment to deduct and retain out of such payment a sum representing the amount of the income tax on such payment at the standard rate of income tax for the year in which the amount payable becomes due,

(c) the person to whom such payment is made shall allow such deduction on the receipt of the residue of such payment, and

(d) the person making such deduction shall be acquitted and discharged of so much money as is represented by the deduction as if that sum had been actually paid.

(2) Where any royalty or other sum is paid in respect of the user of a patent wholly out of profits or gains brought into charge to income tax, the person paying the royalty or other sum shall be entitled on making the payment to deduct and retain out of the payment a sum representing the amount of income tax on the payment at the standard rate of income tax for the year in which the royalty or other sum payable becomes due.

(3) This section shall not apply to any rents or other sums in respect of which the person entitled to them is chargeable to tax under Case V of Schedule D or would be so chargeable but for any exemption from tax.

Case Law

'Profits brought into charge to tax' are the profits assessable for that year and on which tax is payable. Allchin v Corporation of South Shields 25 TC 445

Gross voluntary payments made under a mistake of law do not generally entitle the payer to recover the tax at a later stage. Warren v Warren 1895 72 LT 628

However, if the failure to deduct was due to a mistake of fact, the right to recover the under-deduction is not lost. Turvey v Dentons Ltd 1952 2 ALL ER 1025

An under-deduction of tax on instalment payments may be recovered against subsequent instalments of the same payment. Taylor v Taylor 1937 3 All ER 571

Revenue Precedents

Copyright royalties are not "annual payments" within the scope of Section 237 and 238. CTF189/DON

Cross References

To Section 237

Section 15 Rate of charge.
Section 59 Charge to tax of income from which tax has been deducted.
Section 60 Interpretation (Chapter 2).
Section 76 Computation of income: application of income tax principles.
Section 104 Taxation of certain rents and other payments.
Section 153 Distributions to certain nonresidents.
Section 214 Local authorities, etc.
Section 243 Allowance of charges on income.
Section 267H Application (Chapter 6).
Section 267P Treatment of credit transaction.
Section 267Q Treatment of deposit return.
Section 316 Interpretation of certain references to expenditure and time when expenditure is incurred.
Section 439 Effect of release, etc. of debt in respect of loan under section 438.
Section 690 Interest and charges on income.
Section 697LB Treatment of finance costs.
Section 731 Chargeable gains accruing to unit trusts.
Section 737 Special investment schemes.
Section 738 Undertakings for collective investment.
Section 739C Charge to tax.
Section 739I Common contractual funds.
Section 759 Spreading of revenue payments over several years.
Section 762 Application of Chapter 4 of Part 9.
Section 766 Tax credit for research and development expenditure.
Section 779 Charge to income tax of pensions under Schedule E.
Section 784A Approved retirement fund.
Section 789 Supplementary provisions (Chapter 3).
Section 817A Restriction of relief for payments of interest.
Section 838 Special portfolio investment accounts.
Section 847A Donations to certain sports bodies.
Section 848E Payment of tax credit.
Section 904A Power of inspection: returns and collection of appropriate tax.
Section 950 Interpretation (Part 41).
Section 1007 Interpretation (Part 43).
Section 1078 Revenue offences.
Schedule 22 Dividends Regarded as Paid Out of Profits Accumulated Before Given Date

238 Annual payments not payable out of taxed income

[ITA67 s434(1) to (5A) and (8); FA69 s33 and Sch4; FA74 s11 and Sch1 PtII; CTA76 s151(14); FA90 s51(3); FA96 s132(1) and Sch5 PtI par1(20)]

(1) In this section, "*the inspector*" means such inspector as the Revenue Commissioners may direct.

(2) On payment of any annuity or other annual payment (apart from yearly interest of money) charged with tax under Schedule D, or of any royalty or other sum paid in respect of the user of a patent, not payable or not wholly payable out of profits or gains brought into charge, the person by or through whom any such payment is made shall deduct out of such payment a sum representing the amount of the income tax on such payment at the standard rate of tax in force at the time of the payment.

(3) Where any such payment is made by or through any person, that person shall forthwith deliver to the Revenue Commissioners an account of the payment, or of so much of the payment as is not made out of profits or gains brought into charge, and of the income tax deducted out of the payment or out of that part of the payment, and the inspector shall assess and charge the payment of which an account is so delivered on that person.

(4) The inspector may, where any person has made default in delivering an account required by this section, or where he or she is not satisfied with the account so delivered, make an assessment according to the best of his or her judgment.

(5) The provisions of the Income Tax Acts relating to—

(a) persons who are to be chargeable with income tax,

(b) income tax assessments,

(c) appeals against such assessments,

(d) the collection and recovery of income tax,

(e) the rehearing of appeals, and

(f) cases to be stated for the opinion of the High Court,

shall, in so far as they are applicable, apply to the charge, assessment, collection and recovery of income tax under this section.

(6) *Subsections (3)* to *(5)* shall apply subject to *sections 239* and *241* with respect to the time and manner in which certain companies [...][1] are to account for and pay income tax in respect of—

(a) payments from which tax is deductible, and

(b) any amount deemed to be an annual payment.

(7) Except where provided by *section 1041(1)*, this section shall not apply to any rents or other sums in respect of which the person entitled to them is chargeable to tax under Case V of Schedule D or would be so chargeable but for any exemption from tax.

Amendments

[1] Deleted by FA12 s43(1). Deemed to have come into force and takes effect on and from 1 January 2012.

Case Law

In contrast to section 237, under-deductions of tax cannot be recovered against subsequent instalment of an annual payment. Tenbry Investments Ltd v Peugeot Motor Co Ltd 1992 STC 791

Revenue Precedents

Copyright royalties are not annual payments for the purposes of section 238 TCA 1997. IT952508

Interest paid on an award made by an arbitrator under section 34 of the Arbitrator's Act 1954 IS "interest of money" within the meaning of section 238 TCA 1997. IT923104

Are film royalties' annual payments? Generally, yes, since they are normally pure income profit. IT913560

Statements of Practice

Treatment of Certain Patent Royalties Paid to Companies Resident outside the State – SP – CT/01/10

Cross References

From Section 238

Section 239 Income tax on payments by resident companies.

Section 241 Income tax on payments by non-resident companies.

Section 1041 Rents payable to non-residents.

To Section 238

Section 59 Charge to tax of income from which tax has been deducted.

Section 60 Interpretation (Chapter 2).

Section 104 Taxation of certain rents and other payments.
Section 112A Taxation of certain perquisites.
Section 153 Distributions to certain nonresidents.
Section 239 Income tax on payments by resident companies.
Section 241 Income tax on payments by non-resident companies.
Section 242A Tax treatment of certain royalties.
Section 243 Allowance of charges on income.
Section 246 Interest payments by companies and to non-residents.
Section 267I Exemptions from tax and withholding tax.
Section 316 Interpretation of certain references to expenditure and time when expenditure is incurred.
Section 390 Amount of assessment made under section 238 to be allowed as a loss for certain purposes.
Section 410 Group payments.
Section 439 Effect of release, etc. of debt in respect of loan under section 438.
Section 516 Assessment of trustees in respect of sums received.
Section 644 Provisions supplementary to section 643.
Section 683 Charge to tax on sums received from sale of scheduled mineral assets.
Section 750 Persons entitled to exemption.
Section 751 Traders other than dealers in securities.
Section 752 Purchases of shares by financial concerns and persons exempted from tax.
Section 757 Charges on capital sums received for sale of patent rights.
Section 759 Spreading of revenue payments over several years.
Section 762 Application of Chapter 4 of Part 9.
Section 779 Charge to income tax of pensions under Schedule E.
Section 884 Returns of profits.
Section 950 Interpretation (Part 41).
Section 1041 Rents payable to non-residents.
Schedule 22 Dividends Regarded as Paid Out of Profits Accumulated Before Given Date
Schedule 29 Provisions Referred to in Sections 1052, 1053 and 1054

239 Income tax on payments by resident companies

[CTA76 s151(1) to (13) (apart from subsection (8)(c)); FA90 s49]

(1) In this section, "*relevant payment*" means—

(a) any payment from which income tax is deductible and to which *subsections (3)* to *(5)* of *section 238* apply, and

(b) any amount which under *section 438* is deemed to be an annual payment.

(2) This section shall apply for the purpose of regulating the time and manner in which companies resident in the State—

(a) are to account for and pay income tax in respect of relevant payments, and

(b) are to be repaid income tax in respect of payments received by them.

(3) A company shall make for each of its accounting periods in accordance with this section a return to the inspector of the relevant payments made by it in that period and of the income tax for which the company is accountable in respect of those payments.

(4) A return for any period for which a return is required to be made under this section shall be made within 9 months from the end of that period [, but in any event not later than day 21 of the month in which that period of 9 months ends][1].

[(4A) Where a return referred to in subsection (4) is made by electronic means and in accordance with Chapter 6 of Part 38, then subsection (4) shall apply and have effect as if "day 23 of the month" were substituted for "day 21 of the month"; but where that return is made after the day provided for in this subsection the Tax Acts shall apply and have effect without regard to the provisions of this subsection.][2]

(5) Income tax in respect of any payment required to be included in a return under this section shall be due at the time by which [corporation tax][3] (if any) for the accounting period for which the return is required to be made under *subsection (3)* is due and payable, and income tax so due shall be payable by the company [in accordance with [*Chapter 7* of *Part 41A*] and][5] without the making of any assessment; but income tax which has become so due may be assessed on the company (whether or not it has been paid when the assessment is made).

(6) Where it appears to the inspector that there is a relevant payment which ought to have been but has not been included in a return, or where the inspector is dissatisfied with any return, the inspector may make an assessment on the company to the best of his or her judgment, and any income tax due under an assessment made by virtue of this subsection shall be treated for the purposes of interest on unpaid tax as having been payable at the time when it would have been payable if a correct return had been made.

(7) Where in any accounting period a company receives any payment on which it bears income tax by deduction, the company may claim to have the income tax on that payment set against any income tax which it is liable to pay under this section in respect of payments made by it in that period, and any such claim shall be included in the return made under *subsection (3)* for the accounting period in question, and (where necessary) income tax paid by the company under this section for that accounting period and before the claim is allowed shall be repaid accordingly.

(8) (a) Where a claim has been made under *subsection (7)*, no proceedings for collecting tax which would be discharged if the claim were allowed shall be instituted pending the final determination of the claim, but this subsection shall not affect the date when the tax is due, and when the claim is finally determined any tax underpaid in consequence of this subsection shall be paid.

(b) Where proceedings are instituted for collecting tax assessed, or interest on tax assessed, under *subsection (5)* or *(6)*, effect shall not be given to any claim under *subsection (7)* made after the institution of the proceedings so as to affect or delay the collection or recovery of the tax charged by the assessment or of interest on that tax.

(9) Income tax set against other tax under *subsection (7)* shall be treated as paid or repaid, as the case may be, and the same tax shall not be taken into account both under this subsection and under *section 24(2)*.

(10) (a) Where a company makes a relevant payment on a date which does not fall within an accounting period, the company shall make a return of that payment within 6 months from that date, and the income tax for which the company is accountable in respect of that payment shall be due at the time by which the return is to be made.

(b) Any assessment in respect of tax payable under this subsection shall be treated as relating to the year of assessment in which the payment is made.

(c) *Subsection (11)* shall not apply to an assessment under this subsection.

(11) (a) Subject to *subsection (10)(b)*, income tax payable (after income tax borne by the company by deduction has been set, by virtue of any claim under *subsection (7)*, against income tax which it is liable to pay under

subsection (5)) in respect of relevant payments in an accounting period shall, for the purposes of the charge, assessment, collection and recovery from the company making the payments of that tax and of any interest or penalties on that tax, be treated and described as corporation tax payable by that company for that accounting period, notwithstanding that for all other purposes of the Tax Acts it is income tax.

(b) Tax paid by a company which is treated as corporation tax by virtue of this subsection shall be repaid to the company if it would have been so repaid under *subsection (7)* had it been treated as income tax paid by the company.

(c) Any tax assessable under one or more of the provisions of this section may be included in one assessment if the tax so included is all due on the same date.

(12) Nothing in this section shall be taken to prejudice any powers conferred by the Tax Acts for the recovery of tax by means of an assessment or otherwise.

(13) (a) The Revenue Commissioners may, by regulations made for the purposes mentioned in *subsection (2)*, modify, supplement or replace any of the provisions of this section, and references in the Corporation Tax Acts and in any other enactment to this section shall be construed as including references to any such regulations and, without prejudice to the generality of the foregoing, such regulations may, in relation to tax charged by this section, modify any provision of the Tax Acts relating to returns, assessments, claims or appeals, or may apply any such provision with or without modification.

(b) Regulations under this subsection may—

(i) make different provision for different descriptions of companies and for different circumstances, and may authorise the Revenue Commissioners, where in their opinion there are special circumstances justifying it, to make special arrangements as respects income tax for which a company is liable to account or the repayment of income tax borne by a company;

(ii) include such transitional and other supplemental provisions as appear to the Revenue Commissioners to be expedient or necessary.

(c) Every regulation made under this subsection shall be laid before Dáil Éireann as soon as may be after it is made and, if a resolution annulling the regulation is passed by Dáil Éireann within the next 21 days on which Dáil Éireann has sat after the regulation is laid before it, the regulation shall be annulled accordingly, but without prejudice to the validity of anything previously done thereunder.

Amendments

[1] Inserted by F(No.2)A08 s39(1)(a). This section has effect for accounting periods commencing on or after 14 October 2008.

[2] Inserted by F(No.2)A08 sched3(1)(a). Have effect as on and from 1 January 2009.

[3] Substituted by F(No.2)A08 s39(1)(b). This section has effect for accounting periods commencing on or after 14 October 2008.

[4] Substituted by FA12 sched4(part 2)(g).

[5] Inserted by F(No.2)A08 s39(1)(b). This section has effect for accounting periods commencing on or after 14 October 2008.

Revenue Briefings

eBrief

eBrief No. 28/2008 – Income Tax Payable under Section 239 TCA 1997 and Preliminary Tax for Small Companies

Cross References

From Section 239

Section 24 Companies resident in the State: income tax on payments made or received.
Section 238 Annual payments not payable out of taxed income.
Section 438 Loans to participators, etc.
Section 958 Date for payment of tax.

To Section 239

Section 238 Annual payments not payable out of taxed income.
Section 240 Provisions as to tax under section 239.
Section 243 Allowance of charges on income.
Section 243B Relief for certain charges on income on a value basis.
Section 396B Relief for certain trading losses on a value basis.
Section 420B Group relief: Relief for certain losses on a value basis.
Section 438 Loans to participators, etc.
Section 448 Relief from corporation tax.
Section 486C Relief from tax for certain start-up companies.
Section 644C Relief from corporation tax for losses from dealing in residential development land.
Section 710 Profits of life business.
Section 950 Interpretation (Part 41).
Section 958 Date for payment of tax.
Section 1075 Penalties for failure to furnish certain information and for incorrect information.
Schedule 32 Transitional Provisions

240 Provisions as to tax under section 239.

[CTA76 s152; FA78 s46(1)(f), (2) and (3); FA81 s22; FA90 s50; FA97 s146(2) and Sch9 PtII]

(1) *Subsections (2)* to *(4)* shall apply only in respect of a company to which *section 239(10)* relates.

(2) The provisions of the Income Tax Acts relating to—

(a) persons who are to be chargeable to income tax,

(b) income tax assessments,

(c) appeals against such assessments (including the rehearing of appeals and the statement of a case for the opinion of the High Court), and

(d) the collection and recovery of income tax,

shall, in so far as they are applicable, apply to the charge, assessment, collection and recovery of income tax under *section 239.*

(3) [(a) Any tax payable in accordance with *section 239* without the making of an assessment shall carry interest from the date when the amount becomes due and payable until payment—][1]

[(i) for any day or part of a day before 1 August 1978 during which the amount remains unpaid, at a rate of 0.0492 per cent,

(ii) for any day or part of a day on or after 1 August 1978 and before 1 April 1998 during which the amount remains unpaid, at a rate of 0.0410 per cent,

(iii) for any day or part of a day on or after 1 April 1998 and before 1 July 2009 during which the amount remains unpaid, at a rate of 0.0322 per cent, and

(iv) for any day or part of a day on or after 1 July 2009 during which the amount remains unpaid, at a rate of 0.0274 per cent.][2]

(b) [*Subsections (3)* to *(5)* of *section 1080*][3] shall apply in relation to interest payable under this subsection as they apply in relation to interest payable under *section 1080.*

(4) In its application to any tax charged by an assessment to income tax in accordance with *section 239*, *section 1080* shall apply as if [*subsection (2)(b)*][4] of that section were deleted.

(5) *Section 1081(1)* shall not apply where by virtue of *section 438(4)* there is any discharge or repayment of tax assessed under *section 239.*

Amendments

[1, 2] Substituted by FA09 s29(1)(b). Applies as respects any unpaid tax or duty, as the case may be, that has not been paid before 1 July 2009 regardless of whether that tax or duty became due and payable before, on or after that date.

[3, 4] Substituted by FA05 sched5.

Cross References

From Section 240

Section 239 Income tax on payments by resident companies.
Section 438 Loans to participators, etc.
Section 1080 Interest on overdue income tax, corporation tax and capital gains tax.
Section 1081 Effect on interest of reliefs given by discharge or repayment.

To Section 240

Schedule 12A Approved Savings-Related Share Option Schemes

241 Income tax on payments by non-resident companies

[FA90 s51(1) and (2)]

(1) This section shall apply in relation to an accounting period of a company not resident in the State if the company is—

(a) required by virtue of *section 238(3)* to deliver an account to the Revenue Commissioners, and

(b) within the charge to corporation tax in respect of the accounting period.

(2) Where this section applies in relation to an accounting period of a company, then—

(a) the company shall make a return to the inspector of—

(i) payments made by the company in the accounting period and in respect of which income tax is required to be deducted by virtue of [*section 238(2)* or *246(2)*][1], and

(ii) the tax deducted out of those payments by virtue of [*section 238(2)* or *246(2)*][2],

[...][3]

[(b) *section 239(5)* shall apply to income tax in respect of payments referred to in *paragraph (a)*, and

(c) income tax in respect of which a return is to be made under *paragraph (a)* shall, for the purposes of the charge, assessment, collection and recovery from the company making the payments of that tax and of any interest or penalties on that tax, be treated as if it were corporation tax chargeable for the accounting period for which the return is required under *paragraph (a)*.][4]

Amendments

[1] Substituted by FA12 s43(2)(a). Deemed to have come into force and takes effect on and from 1 January 2012.

[2] Substituted by FA12 s43(2)(b). Deemed to have come into force and takes effect on and from 1 January 2012.

[3] Deleted by FA12 s43(2)(c). Deemed to have come into force and takes effect on and from 1 January 2012.

[4] Substituted by FA12 s43(2)(d). Deemed to have come into force and takes effect on and from 1 January 2012.

Cross References

From Section 241

Section 238 Annual payments not payable out of taxed income.

To Section 241

Section 238 Annual payments not payable out of taxed income.
Section 243 Allowance of charges on income.
Section 243B Relief for certain charges on income on a value basis.
Section 396B Relief for certain trading losses on a value basis.
Section 420B Group relief: Relief for certain losses on a value basis.
Section 448 Relief from corporation tax.
Section 486C Relief from tax for certain start-up companies.
Section 644C Relief from corporation tax for losses from dealing in residential development land.
Schedule 32 Transitional Provisions

242 Annual payments for non-taxable consideration

[FA89 s89(2)]

(1) This section shall apply to any payment which is—

(a) an annuity or other annual payment charged with tax under Case III of Schedule D, other than—

(i) interest,

(ii) an annuity granted in the ordinary course of a business of granting annuities, or

(iii) a payment made to an individual under a liability incurred in consideration of the individual surrendering, assigning or releasing an interest in settled property to or in favour of a person having a subsequent interest,

and

(b) made under a liability incurred for consideration in money or money's worth, where all or any part of such consideration is not required to be taken into account in computing for the purposes of income tax or corporation tax the income of the person making the payment.

(2) Any payment to which this section applies—

(a) shall be made without deduction of income tax,

(b) shall not be allowed as a deduction in computing the income or total income of the person by whom it is made, and

(c) shall not be a charge on income for the purposes of corporation tax.

242A Tax treatment of certain royalties

[(1) In this section "*relevant territory*" has the meaning assigned to it in *section 172A*.

(2) This section applies to a payment of royalties—

(a) made by a company in the course of a trade or business carried on by the company,

(b) to a company (in this subsection referred to as the "*receiving company*") which—

(i) is not resident in the State, and

(ii) is, by virtue of the law of a relevant territory, resident for the purposes of tax in a relevant territory which imposes a tax that generally applies to royalties receivable in that territory by companies from sources outside that territory,

and

(c) which is made for *bona fide* commercial reasons and does not form part of any arrangement or scheme of which the main purpose or one of the main purposes is avoidance of liability to income tax, corporation tax or capital gains tax,

except where the royalties are paid to the receiving company in connection with a trade or business carried on in the State by the company through a branch or agency.

(3) Where, apart from this section, *section 238* would apply to a payment of royalties to which this section applies, that section shall not apply to that payment.

(4) A company shall not be chargeable to corporation tax or income tax in respect of a royalty payment to which this section applies where—

(a) the company—

(i) is not resident in the State, and

(ii) is, by virtue of the law of a relevant territory, resident for the purposes of tax in a relevant territory which imposes a tax that generally applies to royalties receivable in that territory by companies from sources outside that territory,

and

(b) the payment is made for *bona fide* commercial reasons and does not form part of any arrangement or scheme of which the main purpose or one of the main purposes is avoidance of liability to income tax, corporation tax or capital gains tax,

except where the royalty payment is made to the company in connection with a trade or business which is carried on in the State by the company through a branch or agency.][1]

Amendments

[1] Inserted by FA10 s55(1)(a). This section applies to a payment made on or after 4 February 2010.

Statements of Practice

Treatment of Certain Patent Royalties Paid to Companies Resident outside the State – SP – CT/01/10

Cross References

From Section 242A

Section 172A Interpretation.

Section 238 Annual payments not payable out of taxed income.

To Section 242A

Section 243 Allowance of charges on income.

CHAPTER 2

Charges on Income for Corporation Tax Purposes

243 Allowance of charges on income

[CTA76 s10; FA82 s23(3); FA83 s25(2); FA90 s43; FA97 s29(2), (5) and (6)]

(1) Subject to this section and to any other express exceptions, "*charges on income*" means, for the purposes of corporation tax, payments of any description mentioned in *subsection (4)*, not being dividends or other distributions of the company; but no payment deductible in computing profits or any description of profits for the purposes of corporation tax shall be treated as a charge on income.

[(1A) For the purposes of this section, "*bank*" [has the meaning assigned to it by *section 845A* and][1] includes building society within the meaning of *section 256(1)*.][2]

(2) In computing the corporation tax chargeable for any accounting period of a company, any charges on income paid by the company in the accounting period, in so far as paid out of the company's profits brought into charge to corporation tax, shall be allowed as deductions against the total profits for the period reduced by any other relief from corporation tax other than group relief [in accordance with *section 420*][3].

(3) (a) This subsection shall apply to expenditure incurred for the purposes of a trade or profession set up and commenced on or after the 22nd day of January, 1997.

(b) Where—

(i) a company pays any charges on income before the time it sets up and commences a trade, and

(ii) the payment is made wholly and exclusively for the purposes of that trade,

that payment, to the extent that it is not otherwise deducted from total profits of the company, shall be treated for the purposes of corporation tax as paid at that time.

(c) An allowance or deduction shall not be made under any provision of the Tax Acts, other than this subsection, in respect of any expenditure or payment treated under this section as incurred on the day on which a trade or profession is set up and commenced.

(4) Subject to *subsections (5)* to *(8)*, the payments referred to in *subsection (1)* are—

(a) any yearly interest, annuity or other annual payment and any other payments mentioned in *section 104* or *237(2)*, and

(b) any other [interest payable on an advance][4] from—

(i) a bank carrying on a bona fide banking business [in a Member State of the European Communities][5], or

(ii) a person who in the opinion of the Revenue Commissioners is bona fide carrying on business as a member of a stock exchange in the State or bona fide carrying on the business of a discount house [in a Member State of the European Communities][6],

and for the purposes of this section any interest payable by a company as is mentioned in *paragraph (b)* shall be treated as paid on such interest being debited to the company's account in the books of the person to whom it is payable.

(5) No payment mentioned in *subsection (4)(a)* made by a company to a person not resident in the State shall be treated as a charge on income unless it is a payment—

(a) from which, in accordance with—

(i) *section 238*, or

(ii) that section as applied by *section 246*,

[except where—

(I) the company has been authorised by the Revenue Commissioners to do otherwise, […][7]

[(II) the interest is interest referred to in *paragraph (a)*, *(b)* or *(h)* of *section 246(3)*, or

(III) the interest is interest to which *section 64(2)* applies,][8]

the company deducts income tax which it accounts for under *sections 238* and *239*, or under *sections 238* and *241*, [as the case may be,][9]][10]

(b) which is payable out of income brought into charge to tax under Case III of Schedule D and which arises from securities and possessions outside [the State, or][11]

[(c) to which *section 238* or *246(2)* do not apply by virtue of [*section 242A* or *267I*][12].][13]

(6) No such payment made by a company as is mentioned in *subsection (4)* shall be treated as a charge on income if—

[(a) the payment is not ultimately borne by the company, or

(i) in the case of any royalty or other sum in respect of the user of a patent, the payment is in respect of capital expenditure, and

(ii) in any other case, the payment is charged to capital,

or][14]

(b) the payment is not made under a liability incurred for a valuable and sufficient consideration and, in the case of a company not resident in the State, incurred wholly and exclusively for the purposes of a trade carried on by the company in the State through a branch or agency, and for the purposes of this paragraph a payment within *subparagraph (ii)* or *(iii)* of *section 792(1)(b)* shall be treated as incurred for valuable and sufficient consideration.

(7) Subject to *subsection (8)*, interest shall not be treated as a charge on income.

[(8) Subject to *subsection (9)*, *subsection (7)* shall not apply to any payment of interest on a loan to a company if—

(a) subject to *subsections (2A), (4), (4A)* and *(4E)* of that section, *subsection (2)* of *section 247* applies to the loan, and

(b) the conditions specified in *subsection (3)* of *section 247* are fulfilled.][15]

(9) *Section 249* shall apply for corporation tax as for income tax, and accordingly references in that section to *section 247*, to the investing company and to the borrower, to interest eligible for relief, and to affording relief for interest shall apply as if they were or included respectively references to *subsection (8)*, to such a company as is mentioned in that subsection, to interest to be treated as a charge on income, and to treating part only of a payment of interest as a charge on income.

Amendments

[1] Inserted by FA05 s49(1)(a). This section applies as respects accounting periods ending on or after 3 February 2005.

[2] Inserted by FA01 s37(1)(a)(i). This section shall apply as respects interest paid on or after 30 March 2001

[3] Inserted by FA05 s49(1)(b). This section applies as respects accounting periods ending on or after 3 February 2005.

[4] Substituted by FA05 s49(1)(c)(i). This section applies as respects accounting periods ending on or after 3 February 2005.

[5, 6] Substituted by FA05 s49(1)(c)(ii). This section applies as respects accounting periods ending on or after 3 February 2005.

[7] Deleted by FA01 s37(1)(a)(ii)(I). This section shall apply as respects interest paid on or after 30 March 2001

[8] Substituted by FA01 s37(1)(a)(ii)(II). This section shall apply as respects interest paid on or after 30 March 2001

[9] Substituted by FA05 s49(1)(d)(i). This section applies as respects accounting periods ending on or after 3 February 2005.

[10] Substituted by FA00 s65(1). This section shall apply as on and from 10 February 2000.

[11] Substituted by FA05 s49(1)(d)(ii). This section applies as respects accounting periods ending on or after 3 February 2005.

[12] Substituted by FA10 s55(1)(b). This section applies to a payment made on or after 4 February 2010.

[13] Inserted by FA05 s49(1)(d)(iii). This section applies as respects accounting periods ending on or after 3 February 2005.

[14] Substituted by FA06 s61(1)(c). This section shall be deemed to have applied as respects any period of account beginning on or after 1 January 2005.

[15] Substituted by FA11 s37(1)(a). Shall apply in respect of a loan made on or after 21 January 2011 other than any such loan made in accordance with a binding written agreement made before that date.

Revenue Briefings

Tax Briefing

Tax Briefing June 2001 – Issue 44 pg 39 – CT Losses, Charges and Group Relief Offset

Cross References

From Section 243

Section 64 Interest on quoted Eurobonds.

Section 104 Taxation of certain rents and other payments.

Section 237 Annual payments payable wholly out of taxed income.

Section 238 Annual payments not payable out of taxed income.

Section 239 Income tax on payments by resident companies.

Section 241 Income tax on payments by non-resident companies.

Section 242A Tax treatment of certain royalties.

Section 246 Interest payments by companies and to non-residents.
Section 247 Relief to companies on loans applied in acquiring interest in other companies.
Section 249 Rules relating to recovery of capital and replacement loans.
Section 256 Interpretation (Chapter 4).
Section 267I Exemptions from tax and withholding tax.
Section 420 Losses, etc. which may be surrendered by means of group relief.
Section 792 Income under dispositions for short periods.
Section 845A "Non-application of section 130 in the case of certain interest paid by banks.

To Section 243

Section 4 Interpretation of Corporation Tax Acts.
Section 243A Restriction of relevant charges on income.
Section 247 Relief to companies on loans applied in acquiring interest in other companies.
Section 267N Interpretation.
Section 397 Relief for terminal loss in a trade.
Section 410 Group payments.
Section 421 Relation of group relief to other relief.
Section 426 Partnerships involving companies: effect of arrangements for transferring relief.
Section 434 Distributions to be taken into account and meaning of "distributable income", "investment income", "estate income", etc.
Section 438 Loans to participators, etc.
Section 495 Specified individuals.
Section 690 Interest and charges on income.
Section 700 Special computational provisions.
Section 846 Tax-free securities: exclusion of interest on borrowed money.
Section 950 Interpretation (Part 41).
Section 1013 Limited partnerships.
Schedule 22 Dividends Regarded as Paid Out of Profits Accumulated Before Given Date

243A Restriction of relevant charges on income

[(1) In this section—

"*relevant trading charges on income*", in relation to an accounting period of a company, means the charges on income paid by the company in the accounting period wholly and exclusively for the purposes of a trade carried on by the company, other than so much of those charges as are charges on income paid for the purposes of an excepted trade within the meaning of *section 21A*;

"*relevant trading income*", in relation to an accounting period of a company, means the trading income of the company for the accounting period (not being income chargeable to tax under Case III of Schedule D) other than so much of that income as is income of an excepted trade within the meaning of *section 21A*.

(2) Notwithstanding *section 243*, relevant trading charges on income paid by a company in an accounting period shall not be allowed as deductions against the total profits of the company for the accounting period.

(3) [Where][1] a company pays relevant trading charges on income in an accounting period and, apart from *subsection (2)*, those charges would be allowed as deductions against the total profits of the company for the accounting period, those charges shall be allowed as deductions against—

[(a) income specified in *section 21A(4)*,][2]

(b) relevant trading [income, and][3]

[(c) income to which *section 21A(3)* does not apply by virtue of *section 21B*,][4]

of the company for the accounting period as reduced by any amount set off against that income under *section 396A*.][5]

Amendments

[1] Substituted by FA12 sched1(9)(a).

[2] Substituted by FA12 sched1(9)(b).

[3] Substituted by FA08 s43(1)(c)(i). This section shall be deemed to have applied as respects a dividend received on or after 1 January 2007.

[4] Inserted by FA08 s43(1)(c)(ii). This section shall be deemed to have applied as respects a dividend received on or after 1 January 2007.

[5] Inserted by FA01 s90(1)(a). Applies as respects an accounting period ending on or after 6 March 2001.

Revenue Briefings

Tax Briefing

Tax Briefing June 2001 – Issue 44 pg 39 – CT Losses, Charges and Group Relief Offset

Cross References

From Section 243A

Section 21A Higher rate of corporation tax.
Section 21B Tax treatment of certain dividends.
Section 243 Allowance of charges on income.
Section 396A Relief for relevant trading losses.
Section 454 Restriction of certain charges on income.

To Section 243A

Section 243B Relief for certain charges on income on a value basis.
Section 247 Relief to companies on loans applied in acquiring interest in other companies.
Section 420A Group relief: relevant losses and charges.
Section 448 Relief from corporation tax.
Section 644C Relief from corporation tax for losses from dealing in residential development land.
Section 713 Investment income reserved for policyholders.
Schedule 24 Relief from Income Tax and Corporation Tax by Means of Credit in Respect of Foreign Tax

243B Relief for certain charges on income on a value basis

[(1) In this section—

[...][1]

"*relevant corporation tax*", in relation to an accounting period of a company, means the corporation tax which, apart from this section and *sections 239, 241, 396B, 420B, 440* and *441*, would be chargeable on the company for the accounting period;

"*relevant trading charges on income*" has the same meaning as in *section 243A*.

[(2) Where a company pays relevant trading charges on income in an accounting period and the amount so paid exceeds an amount equal to the aggregate of the amounts allowed as deductions against the income of the company for the accounting period in accordance with *section 243A*, then the company may claim relief under this section for the accounting period in respect of the excess.][2]

(3) Where for any accounting period a company claims relief under this section in respect of the excess, the relevant corporation tax of the company for the accounting period shall be reduced—

(a) in so far as the excess consists of charges on income paid for the purpose of the sale of goods [...][3], by an amount equal to 10 per cent of those charges on income paid for the purpose of the sale of goods, and

[(3) Where for any accounting period a company claims relief under this section in respect of the excess, the relevant corporation tax of the company for the accounting period shall be reduced, in so far as the excess consists of relevant trading charges, by an amount determined by the formula—

$$C \times \frac{R}{100}$$

where—

C is the amount of the relevant trading charges on income, and

R is the rate per cent of corporation tax which, by virtue of *section 21*, applies in relation to the accounting period.]³

and

[(4) Where a company makes a claim for relief under this section in respect of any relevant trading charges on income paid in an accounting period, an amount (which shall not exceed the amount of the excess in respect of which a claim under this section may be made), determined by the formula—

$$T \times \frac{100}{R}$$

where—

T is the amount by which the relevant corporation tax for the accounting period is reduced by virtue of *subsection (3)*, and

R is the rate per cent of corporation tax which, by virtue of *section 21*, applies in relation to the accounting period,

shall be treated for the purposes of the Tax Acts as relieved under this section.]⁴]⁵

Amendments

[1] Deleted by FA12 sched1(10)(a).

[2] Substituted by FA06 sched2(1)(b)(ii). Shall apply to accounting periods ending on or after 2 February 2006.

[3] Substituted by FA12 sched1(10)(b).

[4] Substituted by FA12 sched1(10)(c).

[5] Inserted by FA02 s54(1)(a). This section applies as respects an accounting period ending on or after 6 March 2001.

Revenue Briefings

Tax Briefing

Tax Briefing January 2003 – Issue 51 pg 14 – Relief for Certain Losses on a Value Basis

Cross References

From Section 243B

Section 21 The charge to corporation tax and exclusion of income tax and capital gains tax.

Section 239 Income tax on payments by resident companies.

Section 241 Income tax on payments by non-resident companies.

Section 243A Restriction of relevant charges on income.

Section 396B Relief for certain trading losses on a value basis.

Section 420B Group relief: Relief for certain losses on a value basis.

Section 440 Surcharge on undistributed investment and estate income.

Section 441 Surcharge on undistributed income of service companies.

Section 448 Relief from corporation tax.

CHAPTER 3

Principal Provisions Relating to the Payment of Interest

244 Relief for interest paid on certain home loans

[FA97 s145]

(1) (a) In this section—

["*dependent relative*" in relation to an individual, means [any of the persons mentioned in *paragraph (a)* or *(b)* of *subsection (2)*, or in *paragraph (a)* or *(b)* of *subsection (2A)*, of *section 466*][1] in respect of whom the individual is entitled to a tax credit under that section.][2]

['*EEA Agreement*' means the Agreement on the European Economic Area signed at Oporto on 2 May 1992, as adjusted by all subsequent amendments to that Agreement;

'*EEA state*' means a state (including the State) which is a contracting party to the EEA Agreement;][3]

"*loan*" means any loan or advance or any other arrangement whatever by virtue of which interest is paid or payable;

"*qualifying interest*", in relation to an individual and a year of assessment, means the amount of interest paid by the individual in the year of assessment in respect of a qualifying loan;

"*qualifying loan*", in relation to an individual, means a loan or loans which, without having been used for any other purpose, is or are used by the individual solely for the purpose of defraying money employed in the purchase, repair, development or improvement of a qualifying residence or in paying off another loan or loans used for such purpose;

"*qualifying residence*", in relation to an individual, means a residential premises [situated in an EEA state][4] which is used as the sole or main residence of—

(i) the individual,

(ii) [a former or separated spouse of the individual, or a former civil partner or a civil partner from whom the individual is living separately [...][5] in circumstances where reconciliation is unlikely,][6] or

(iii) a person who in relation to the individual is a dependent relative,

and which is, where the residential premises is provided by the individual, provided rent-free and without any other consideration;

["*relievable interest*", in relation to an individual and a year of assessment, means—

(i) in the case of—

(I) an individual assessed to tax for the year of assessment in accordance with [*section 1017* or *1031C*,][7] or

(II) [a widowed individual or a surviving civil partner,][8]

the amount of qualifying interest paid by the individual in the year of assessment or, if less, [€6,000][9],

(ii) in the case of any other individual, the amount of qualifying interest paid by the individual in the year of assessment or, if less, [€3,000][10], but, notwithstanding the preceding provisions of this definition and subject to *paragraph (c)*, as respects the first [7 years][11] of assessment for which there is an entitlement to relief under this section in respect of a qualifying loan [taken out on or after 1 January 2004 and on or before 31 December 2012][12][13], "*relievable interest*", in relation to an individual and a year of assessment, shall mean—

(iii) in the case of—

(I) an individual assessed to tax for the year of assessment in accordance with *section 1017*, or

(II) [a widowed individual or a surviving civil partner,][14]

the amount of qualifying interest paid by the individual in the year of assessment or, if less, [€20,000][15],

(iv) in the case of any other individual, the amount of qualifying interest paid by the individual in the year of assessment or, if less, [€10,000][16];][17]

"*residential premises*" means—

(i) a building or part of a building used, or suitable for use, as a dwelling, and

(ii) land which the occupier of a building or part of a building used as a dwelling has for the occupier's own occupation and enjoyment with that building or that part of a building as its garden or grounds of an ornamental nature;

"*separated*" means separated under an order of a court of competent jurisdiction or by deed of separation or in such circumstances that the separation is likely to be permanent.

(b) For the purposes of this section, in the case of an individual assessed to tax for a year of assessment in accordance with [*section 1017* or *1031C*,][18] any payment of qualifying interest made by the individual's [spouse or civil partner][19], in respect of which the individual's [spouse or civil partner][20] would have been entitled to relief under this section if that [spouse or civil partner][21] were assessed to tax for the year of assessment in accordance with [*section 1016* (apart from *subsection (2)* of that section) or *section 1031B* (apart from *subsection (2)* of that section)][22] shall be deemed to have been made by the individual.

[(c) The number of years of assessment for which the amount of relievable interest is to be determined by reference to *subparagraph (iii)* or *(iv) of* the definition of "*relievable interest*" shall be reduced by one year of assessment for each year of assessment in which an individual was entitled to relief for a year of assessment before the year 1997-1998 under section 76(1) or 496 of, or paragraph 1(2) of Part III of Schedule 6 to, the Income Tax Act, 1967.][23]

[(1A) (a) This section shall not apply as respects interest paid on or after 1 May 2009.

[(b) Notwithstanding *paragraph (a)*, this section shall continue to apply for the year of assessment 2010 and subsequent years of assessment up to and including the year of assessment 2017 in respect of qualifying interest paid in respect of a qualifying loan taken out on or after 1 January 2004 and on or before 31 December 2012.][24]

(c) (i) Paragraph (*b*) shall not apply in respect of qualifying interest attributable to that part of a qualifying loan used to repay another qualifying loan (in this paragraph referred to as an "existing qualifying loan") unless the qualifying interest on that existing qualifying loan would, had the existing qualifying loan not been repaid, have been interest referred to in [*paragraph (b)*][25].

(ii) Where subparagraph (i) applies, the number of years of assessment for which there is an entitlement to relief under this section in respect of qualifying interest attributable to that part of a qualifying loan used to repay the existing qualifying loan shall not exceed the number of years of assessment for which relief would have applied had the existing qualifying loan not been repaid.

(d) As respects the year of assessment 2009 only, the definition of "relievable interest" is amended—

(i) in paragraph (i) by substituting "the amount of qualifying interest paid by the individual in the period 1 January 2009 to 30 April 2009 or, if less, €2,000 and the amount of qualifying interest paid by the individual in the period 1 May 2009 to 31 December 2009 or, if less, €4,000" for "the amount of qualifying interest paid by the individual in the year of assessment or, if less, €6,000", and

(ii) in paragraph (ii) by substituting "the amount of qualifying interest paid by the individual in the period 1 January 2009 to 30 April 2009 or, if less, €1,000 and the amount of qualifying interest paid by the individual in the period 1 May 2009 to 31 December 2009 or, if less, €2,000" for "the amount of qualifying interest paid by the individual in the year of assessment or, if less, €3,000".][26]

[(2) (a) In this subsection "*appropriate percentage*", in relation to a year of assessment, means—

(i) as respects qualifying interest to which [*subsection (1A)(b)*][27] applies—

(I) where relievable interest is determined by reference to *paragraph (i)* or *(ii)* of the definition of "*relievable interest*", 15 per cent for that year, and

(II) where relievable interest is determined by reference to *paragraph (iii)* or *(iv)* of the definition of "*relievable interest*":

(A) 25 per cent for the first and second years of assessment for which there is an entitlement to relief under this section,

(B) 22.5 per cent for the third, fourth and fifth years of assessment for which there is an entitlement to relief under this section, and

(C) a percentage equal to the standard rate of tax for the sixth and seventh years of assessment for which there is an entitlement to relief under this section,

and

[(ii) notwithstanding *subparagraph* (i), 30 per cent for the year of assessment 2012 and subsequent years of assessment up to and including the year of assessment 2017 as respects qualifying interest paid on a qualifying loan taken out on or after 1 January 2004 and on or before 31 December 2008 to purchase an individual's—

(I) first qualifying residence, or

(II) second or subsequent qualifying residence but only where the first qualifying residence was purchased on or after 1 January 2004.][28]

(b) Where an individual for a year of assessment proves that in the year of assessment such individual paid an amount of qualifying interest, then, the income tax to be charged, other than in accordance with *section 16(2)*, on such individual for that year of assessment shall be reduced by an amount which is the lesser of—

(i) the amount equal to the appropriate percentage of the relievable interest, and

(ii) the amount which reduces that income tax to nil.

(c) [Except for the purpose of *section 188*][29], no account shall be taken of relievable interest in calculating the total income of the individual by whom the relievable interest is paid.

(3)

[(a) Where the amount of relievable interest is determined by reference to [*paragraph*][30] *(iii)* or *(iv)* of the definition of "*relievable interest*", then, notwithstanding any other provision of the Tax Acts, in the case of an individual who has elected or could be deemed to have duly elected to be assessed to tax for the year of assessment in accordance with [*section 1017* or *1031C*][31], where either—

(i) the individual, or

(ii) the individual's [spouse or civil partner][32],

was previously entitled to relief under this section or under section 76(1) or 496 of, or paragraph 1(2) of Part III of Schedule 6 to, the Income Tax Act, 1967, and the other person was not so entitled—

(I) the relief to be given under this section, other than that part of the relief (in this subsection referred to as "*the additional relief*") which is represented by the difference between the relievable interest and the amount which would have been the amount of the relievable interest if this had been determined by reference to [*paragraph*][33] *(i)* or *(ii)* of that definition, shall be treated as given in equal proportions to the individual and that individual's [spouse or civil partner][34] for that year of assessment, and

(II) the additional relief shall be reduced by 50 per cent and the additional relief, as so reduced, shall be given only to the person who was not previously entitled to relief under this section or under section 76(1) or 496 of, or paragraph 1(2) of Part III of Schedule 6 to, the Income Tax Act, 1967.][35]

(b) *Paragraph (a)* shall apply notwithstanding that—

(i) [*section 1023* or *1031H*][36] may have applied for the year of assessment, and

(ii) the payments in respect of which relief is given may not have been made in equal proportions.

(4) (a) Notwithstanding anything in this section, a loan shall not be a qualifying loan, in relation to an individual, if it is used for the purpose of defraying money applied in—

(i) the purchase of a residential premises or any interest in such premises from an individual who is the spouse of the purchaser,

(ii) the purchase of a residential premises or any interest in such premises if, at any time after the 25th day of March, 1982, that premises or interest was disposed of by the purchaser or by his or her spouse or if any interest which is reversionary to the interest purchased was so disposed of after that date, or

(iii) the purchase, repair, development or improvement of a residential premises, and the person who, directly or indirectly, received the money is connected with the individual and it appears that the purchase price of the premises substantially exceeds the value of what is acquired or, as the case may be, the cost of the repair, development or improvement substantially exceeds the value of the work done.

(b) *Subparagraphs (i)* and *(ii)* of *paragraph (a)* shall not apply in the case of a husband and wife who are separated.

(5) Where an individual acquires a new sole or main residence but does not dispose of the previous sole or main residence owned by the individual and it is shown to the satisfaction of the inspector that it was the individual's intention, at the time of the acquisition of the new sole or main residence, to dispose of the previous sole or main residence and that the individual has taken and continues to take all reasonable steps necessary to dispose of it, the previous sole or main residence shall be treated as a qualifying residence, in relation to the individual, for the period of 12 months commencing on the date of the acquisition of the new sole or main residence.

(6) (a) In this subsection, "*personal representative*" has the same meaning as in *section 799*.

(b) Where any interest paid on a loan used for a purpose mentioned in the definition of "*qualifying loan*" by persons as the personal representatives of a deceased person or as trustees of a settlement made by the will of a deceased person would, on the assumptions stated in *paragraph (c)*, be eligible for relief under this section and, in a case where the condition stated in that paragraph applies, that condition is satisfied, that interest shall be so eligible notwithstanding the preceding provisions of this section.

(c) For the purposes of *paragraph (b)*, it shall be assumed that the deceased person would have survived and been the borrower and if, at the time of the person's death, the residential premises was used as that person's sole or main residence, it shall be further assumed that the person would have continued so to use it and the following condition shall then apply, namely, that the residential premises was, at the time the interest was paid, used as the sole or main residence of the deceased's [widow, widower or surviving civil partner, or of any dependent relative of the deceased][37].

[(7) This subsection shall apply to a loan taken out and used by an individual—

(a) on or after 1 January 2012 and on or before 31 December 2012 solely for the purpose of defraying money employed in the purchase of an estate or interest in the land referred to in *paragraph (b)* and in respect of which the permission in *subsection (10)* applies but only where a residential premises, which is a qualifying residence in relation to that individual, is constructed on that land, or

(b) on or after 1 January 2012 and on or before 31 December 2013 solely for the purpose of defraying money employed in the construction of a residential premises which is a qualifying residence in relation to that individual on land—

(i) in respect of which he or she has, on or after 1 January 2012 and on or before 31 December 2012, acquired an estate or interest, and

(ii) the acquisition of which was financed by way of the loan referred to in *paragraph (a)*.

(8) This subsection shall apply to a loan in respect of which there was in place, on or after 1 January 2012 and on or before 31 December 2012, an agreement evidenced in writing to provide that loan to an individual and—

(a) part of that loan is used in the period 1 January 2012 to 31 December 2012, and

(b) the balance of that loan is used in the period 1 January 2013 to 31 December 2013,

by that individual solely for the purpose of defraying money employed in the repair, development or improvement of a residential premises which is a qualifying residence in relation to that individual.

(9) Any loan to which *subsection (7)* or *(8)(b)* applies shall, for the purposes of this section, be deemed to be a qualifying loan taken out on or after 1 January 2012 and on or before 31 December 2012.

(10) Relief shall not be granted in respect of interest paid on any loan to which *subsection (7)* or *(8)* applies unless any permission required under the Planning and Development Act 2000 was granted on or before 31 December 2012 in respect of such construction, repair, development or improvement, as appropriate, and such permission has not ceased to exist.][38]

Amendments

[1] Substituted by F(No.3)A11 sched1(30).

[2] Substituted by FA02 sched6(3)(e). Shall be deemed to have come into force and take effect as on and from 6 April 2001.

[3] Inserted by FA14 s7(b). Comes into operation on 1 January 2015.

[4] Substituted by FA14 s7(a). Comes into operation on 1 January 2015.

[5] Deleted by F(No.2)A13 sched(1)(c). Has effect as if they had come into operation for the year of assessment (within the meaning of section 2) 2011 and each subsequent year of assessment.

[6] Substituted by F(No.3)A11 sched1(31).

[7] Substituted by F(No.3)A11 sched1(32).

[8, 14] Substituted by F(No.3)A11 sched1(33).

[9] Substituted by FA07 s6(a). Applies as respects the year of assessment 2007 and subsequent years of assessment.

[10] Substituted by FA07 s6(b). Applies as respects the year of assessment 2007 and subsequent years of assessment.

[11] Substituted by FA03 s9(1)(a).

[12] Substituted by FA12 s9(a). Applies as respects the year of assessment 2012 and each subsequent years of assessment.

[13] Inserted by FA10 s7(a). Applies as respects the year of assessment 2010 and each subsequent years of assessment.

[15] Substituted by FA08 s7(a). Applies as respects the year of assessment 2008 and subsequent years of assessment.

[16] Substituted by FA08 s7(b). Applies as respects the year of assessment 2008 and subsequent years of assessment.

[17] Substituted by FA00 s17(a)(ii). Applies as respects the year of assessment 2000-2001 and subsequent years of assessment.

[18] Substituted by F(No.3)A11 sched1(34).

[19, 20, 21] Substituted by F(No.3)A11 sched1(35).

[22] Substituted by F(No.3)A11 sched1(36).

[23] Substituted by FA00 s17(a)(iii). Applies as respects the year of assessment 2000-2001 and subsequent years of assessment.

[24] Substituted by FA12 s9(b). Applies as respects the year of assessment 2012 and each subsequent years of assessment.

[25] Substituted by FA12 s9(c). Applies as respects the year of assessment 2012 and each subsequent years of assessment.

[26] Inserted by FA09 s3. Applies as respects the year of assessment 2009 and each subsequent years of assessment.

[27] Substituted by FA12 s9(d). Applies as respects the year of assessment 2012 and each subsequent years of assessment.

[28] Substituted by FA12 s9(e). Applies as respects the year of assessment 2012 and each subsequent years of assessment.

[29] Substituted by FA08 s5(c).

[30, 33] Substituted by F(No.2) A08 s14(b). Applies as respects the year of assessment 2012 and each subsequent years of assessment.

[31] Substituted by F(No.3)A11 sched1(37).

[32, 34] Substituted by F(No.3)A11 sched1(38).

[35] Substituted by FA00 s17(b). Applies as respects the year of assessment 2000-2001 and subsequent years of assessment.

[36] Substituted by F(No.3)A11 sched1(39).

[37] Substituted by F(No.3)A11 sched1(40).

[38] Inserted by FA13 s9. Deemed to have come into force and takes effect on and from 1 January 2013.

Revenue Briefings

Tax Briefing

Tax Briefing December 1998 – Issue 35 pg 9 – Relief for Home Loan Interest – Rules & Guidelines
Tax Briefing September 2009 – Issue 77 – Tax Relief on Qualifying Home Loans / BIK on Preferential Loans

Revenue Precedents

What is regarded as "qualifying loan" where borrower of home improvement loan has option of insurance policy to cover himself against accident? Interest charged on insurance premium would not qualify for relief but element of loan relating solely to home improvement regarded as "qualifying loan". 8270/84

Cross References

From Section 244

Section 16 Income tax charged by deduction.
Section 188 Age exemption and associated marginal relief.
Section 446 Certain trading operations carried on in Custom House Docks Area.
Section 799 Interpretation (Chapter 1).
Section 1016 Assessment as single persons.
Section 1017 Assessment of husband in respect of income of both spouses.
Section 1023 Application for separate assessments.

To Section 244

Section 122 Preferential loan arrangements.
Section 188 Age exemption and associated marginal relief.

Section 216A Rent-a-room relief.
Section 216C Childcare services relief.
Section 244A Application of section 244 (relief for interest paid on certain home loans) of Principal Act.
Section 245 Relief for certain bridging loans.
Section 288 Balancing allowances and balancing charges.
Section 458 Deductions allowed in ascertaining taxable income and provisions relating to reductions in tax.
Section 1024 Method of apportioning reliefs and charging tax in cases of separate assessments.

244A Application of section 244 (relief for interest paid on certain home loans) of Principal Act

[(1) (a) In this section—

(i) "*qualifying dwelling*", in relation to an individual, means a qualifying residence situated in the State;

"*qualifying lender*" has the meaning assigned to it by *subsection (3)*;

"*qualifying mortgage interest*", in relation to an individual and a year of assessment, means the qualifying interest paid by the individual in the year of assessment in respect of a qualifying mortgage loan;

"*qualifying mortgage loan*", in relation to an individual, means a qualifying loan or loans secured by the mortgage of freehold or leasehold estate or interest in a qualifying dwelling, and

(ii) "*appropriate percentage*", "*qualifying interest*", "*qualifying loan*", "*qualifying residence*" and "*relievable interest*" have the same meanings, respectively, as they have in *section 244*.

(b) This section provides for a scheme whereby relief due under *section 244* shall, in certain circumstances, be given by way of deduction at source ("the tax relief at source scheme") under *subsection (2)(a)* and in no other manner.

(2) (a) Where an individual makes a payment of qualifying mortgage interest to a qualifying lender in respect of which relief is due under *section 244*, the individual shall be entitled in accordance with regulations to deduct and retain out of it an amount equal to the appropriate percentage, for the year of assessment in which the payment is due, of the relievable interest.

(b) A qualifying lender to which a payment referred to in *paragraph (a)* is made—

(i) shall accept in accordance with regulations the amount paid after deduction in discharge of the individual's liability to the same extent as if the deduction had not been made, and

(ii) may, on making a claim in accordance with regulations, recover from the Revenue Commissioners an amount equal to the amount deducted.

(3) The following bodies shall be qualifying lenders—

(a) a bank holding a licence under section 9 of the Central Bank Act, 1971;

(b) a building society incorporated or deemed to be incorporated under the Building Societies Act, 1989;

(c) a trustee savings bank within the meaning of the Trustee Savings Banks Act, 1989;

(d) ACC Bank plc;

(e) a local authority;

(f) a body which—

(i) (I) holds a licence or similar authorisation, corresponding to a licence referred to in *paragraph (a)*, or

(II) has been incorporated in a manner corresponding to that referred to in *paragraph (b)*,

under the law of any other Member State of the European Communities,

and

(ii) provides qualifying mortgage loans;

and

(g) a body which applies to the Revenue Commissioners for registration as a qualifying lender and in respect of which the Revenue Commissioners, having regard to the activities and objects of the body, are satisfied is entitled to be so registered.

(4) (a) The Revenue Commissioners shall maintain, and publish in such manner as they consider appropriate, a register for the purposes of subsection (3).

(b) If the Revenue Commissioners are satisfied that an applicant for registration is entitled to be registered, they shall register the applicant with effect from such date as may be specified by them.

(c) If it appears to the Revenue Commissioners at any time that a body which is registered under this subsection would not be entitled to be registered if it applied for registration at that time, the Revenue Commissioners may, by written notice given to the body, cancel its registration with effect from such date as may be specified by them in the notice.

(d) Any body which is aggrieved by the failure of the Revenue Commissioners to register it or by the cancellation of its registration, may, by notice given to the Revenue Commissioners before the end of the period of 30 days beginning with the date on which the body is notified of the Revenue Commissioners' decision, require the matter to be determined by the Appeal Commissioners and the Appeal Commissioners shall hear and determine the matter in like manner as an appeal.

(5) (a) The Revenue Commissioners shall make regulations providing generally as to administration of this section and those regulations may, in particular and without prejudice to the generality of the foregoing, include provision—

(i) that a claim under *subsection (2)(b)(ii)* shall be—

(I) made in such form and manner,

(II) made at such time, and

(III) accompanied by such documents,

as provided for in the regulations,

(ii) that, in circumstances specified in regulations, a claim may be made under *subsection (2)(b)(ii)* where a payment is due but not made;

(iii) for the making by qualifying lenders, in such form and manner as may be prescribed, of monthly returns containing particulars in relation to—

(I) each individual making payments of qualifying mortgage interest,

(II) the amount of qualifying mortgage interest paid or due by the individual to date in the year of assessment,

(III) the amount deducted by the individual, or the amount he or she would have been entitled to deduct, under *subsection (2)(a)*,

(IV) the estimated qualifying mortgage interest to be paid by the individual in the year of assessment,

(V) the total amount of qualifying mortgage loans of the qualifying lender outstanding at the date of the return,

(VI) the total amount claimed by the qualifying lender under *subsection (2)(b)(ii)* for the month to which the return relates,

(VII) qualifying mortgage loans repaid in full in that month, and

(VIII) such other matters as may be specified;

(iv) for the transmission by the Revenue Commissioners to qualifying lenders, on a monthly basis, of such details as may be specified in the regulations in relation to—

(I) qualifying mortgage loans, and

(II) individuals with qualifying mortgage loans,

which are necessary for the operation of this section;

(v) in relation to the obligations and entitlements of individuals with qualifying mortgage loans under the tax relief at source scheme;

(vi) in relation to the obligations and entitlements of qualifying lenders under the tax relief at source scheme;

(vii) for deeming of certain qualifying mortgage loans, in such circumstances as may be specified in the regulations, as being no longer entitled to relief under this section;

(viii) for the granting of appropriate relief in any case where inadequate or excessive relief has been granted under this section; and

(ix) for the implementation of this section where a qualifying lender disposes of all or part of its qualifying mortgage loans.

(b) Every regulation made under this section shall be laid before Dáil Éireann as soon as may be after it is made and, if a resolution annulling the regulation is passed by Dáil Éireann within the next 21 days on which Dáil Éireann has sat after the regulation is laid before it, the regulation shall be annulled accordingly, but without prejudice to the validity of anything previously done thereunder.

(6) (a) Where any amount is paid to a qualifying lender by the Revenue Commissioners as an amount recoverable by virtue of *subsection (2)(b)(ii)* but is an amount to which that qualifying lender is not entitled, that amount shall be repaid by the qualifying lender.

(b) There shall be made such assessments, adjustments or set-offs as may be required for securing repayment of the amount referred to in *paragraph (a)* and the provisions of this Act relating to the assessment, collection and recovery of income tax shall, in so far as they are applicable and with necessary modification, apply in relation to the recovery of such amount.

[(7) (a) Notwithstanding any other enactment, an officer of the Revenue Commissioners may request a qualifying lender to provide, in such form as the Revenue Commissioners may require, such information in relation to qualifying mortgage loans granted by the qualifying lender—

(i) as will or may assist an officer of the Revenue Commissioners to determine if relief is due under *section 244* for a particular year of assessment, and

(ii) as is necessary for the proper administration of this section.

(b) The qualifying lender shall comply with a request under paragraph (*a*) no later than—

(i) 30 days after receipt of such request, or

(ii) any extension of the period referred to in subparagraph (i) as may be agreed with an officer of the Revenue Commissioners.

(c) Information provided to the Revenue Commissioners under this subsection shall be used by them only for the purposes of *section 244* and this section and, notwithstanding *section 872*, shall be used for no other purpose.][1]][2]

Amendments

[1] Inserted by FA09 s4. Applies as respects the year of assessment 2009 and subsequent years of assessment.

[2] Inserted by FA01 s23(1). Applies as respects the year of assessment 2002 and subsequent years of assessment.

Revenue Briefings

Tax Briefing

Tax Briefing September 2009 – Issue 77 – Tax Relief on Qualifying Home Loans / BIK on Preferential Loans

Revenue Information Notes

Mortgage Interest Tax Relief at Source (TRS) – FAQs

Cross References

From Section 244A

Section 244 Relief for interest paid on certain home loans.
Section 872 Use of information relating to other taxes and duties.

To Section 244A

Section 904F Power of inspection: claims by qualifying lenders.
Schedule 29 Provisions Referred to in Sections 1052, 1053 and 1054

245 Relief for certain bridging loans

[FA74 s32; FA97 s146(1) and Sch9 PtI par8(1)]

(1) Where a person—

(a) disposes of such person's only or main residence and acquires another residence for use as such person's only or main residence,

(b) obtains a loan, the proceeds of which are used to defray in whole or in part the cost of the acquisition or the disposal or both, and

(c) pays interest on the loan (and on any subsequent loan the proceeds of which are used to repay in whole or in part the first-mentioned loan or any such subsequent loan or to pay interest on any such loan) in respect of the period of 12 months from the date of the making of the first-mentioned loan,

such person shall be entitled on proof of those facts to a reduction in tax under *section 244* on the amount of that interest as if no other interest had been paid by such person in respect of the period of 12 months from the date of the making of the first-mentioned loan.

(2) *Subsection (1)* shall not apply to a loan the proceeds of which are applied for some other purpose before being applied for the purpose specified in that subsection.

Revenue Briefings

Tax Briefing

Tax Briefing December 1998 – Issue 35 pg 23 – Bridging Finance Guidelines

Cross References

From Section 245

Section 244 Relief for interest paid on certain home loans.

To Section 245

Section 1013 Limited partnerships.

246 Interest payments by companies and to non-residents

[FA74 s31; CTA76 s140(1) and Sch2 PtI par42; FA88 s38; FA96 s33(1) and s132(2) and Sch5 PtII; FA97 s36]

(1) In this section—

["*bank*" includes building society within the meaning of *section 256(1)*;][1]

"*company*" means any body corporate;

["*investment undertaking*" means—

(a) a unit trust mentioned in *section 731(5)(a)*,

(b) a special investment scheme within the meaning given to it in *section 737*, […][2]

(c) an investment undertaking within the meaning given to it in [*section 739B*, [...][3]][4]

[(d) a common contractual fund within the meaning given to it in *section 739I* [(inserted by the Finance Act 2005), or][5]][6]

[(e) an investment limited partnership within the meaning of section 739J;][7]

"*relevant person*" means—

(a) a company, or

(b) an investment undertaking;][8]

"*relevant security*" means a security issued by a company [in the course of carrying on relevant trading operations within the meaning of section 445 or 446][9], on terms which oblige the company to redeem the security within a period of 15 years after the date on which the security was [issued;][10]

["*relevant territory*" means—

(a) a Member State of the European Communities other than the State, […][11]

(b) not being such a Member State, a territory with the government of which arrangements having the force of law by virtue of [*section 826(1)*][12] [have been made, or][13]][14]

[(c) not being a territory referred to in paragraph (*a*) or (*b*), a territory with the government of which arrangements have been made which on completion of the procedures set out in *section 826(1)* will have the force of law;][15]

["*tax*", in relation to a relevant territory, means any tax imposed in such territory which corresponds to income tax or corporation tax in the State.][16]

(2) Where any yearly interest charged with tax under Schedule D is paid—

(a) by a company, otherwise than when paid in a fiduciary or representative capacity, to a person whose usual place of abode is in the State, or

(b) by any person to another person whose usual place of abode is outside the State,

the person by or through whom the payment is made shall on making the payment deduct out of the payment a sum representing the amount of the tax on the payment at the standard rate in force at the time of the payment, and *subsections (1)* and *(3)* to *(5)* of *section 238* shall apply to such payments as they apply to payments specified in *subsection (2)* of that section.

(3) *Subsection (2)* shall not apply to—

(a) interest paid in the State on an advance from a bank carrying on a bona fide banking business in the State,

(b) interest paid by such a bank in the ordinary course of such business,

[(bb) interest paid in the State—

(i) by a company to another company, being a company to which *paragraph (a)* of *subsection (5)* applies, for so long as that other company is a company to which that paragraph applies, or

(ii) by a company (in this paragraph referred to as the 'first-mentioned company') to which *subparagraphs (i)* and *(ii)* of *subsection (5)(a)* apply to another company resident in the State where that other company is deemed to be a member of the same group of companies as the first-mentioned company and for this purpose the provisions of *subsection (1)* of *section 411* shall apply to determine whether companies are deemed to be members of the same group of companies as if references in that subsection to a 75 per cent subsidiary were references to a 51 per cent subsidiary,][17]

[(bbb) interest paid in the State to an investment undertaking within the meaning of *section 739B*,][18]

[(c) interest paid to a person whose usual place of abode is outside the State—

(i) in respect of a relevant security, or

(ii) by a specified collective investment undertaking within the meaning of *section 734*,][19]

[(cc) interest paid in the State to a qualifying company (within the meaning of *section 110*),

(ccc) interest paid by a qualifying company (within the meaning of *section 110*) to a person who, by virtue of the law of a relevant territory, is resident for the purposes of tax in the relevant territory, except, in a case where the person is a company, where such interest is paid to the company in connection with a trade or business which is carried on in the State by the company through a branch or agency,][20]

(d) interest paid by a company authorised by the Revenue Commissioners to pay interest without deduction of income tax,

[(da) interest paid to the Strategic Banking Corporation of Ireland or a subsidiary wholly owned by it or a subsidiary wholly owned by any such subsidiary,

(db) interest paid by the Strategic Banking Corporation of Ireland or a subsidiary wholly owned by it or a subsidiary wholly owned by any such subsidiary,][21]

(e) interest on any securities in respect of which the Minister for Finance has given a direction under *section 36*,

[(ea) interest paid to—

(i) the National Asset Management Agency or a company referred to in section 616(1)(*g*),

(ii) the State acting through the National Asset Management Agency or through a company referred to in section 616(1)(*g*), or

(iii) the National Treasury Management Agency by the National Asset Management Agency or by a company referred to in section 616(1)(*g*),][22]

[(eb) interest paid by—

(i) the National Asset Management Agency,

(ii) a company referred to in section 616(1)(*g*), or

(iii) the State acting through the National Asset Management Agency, or through a company referred to in section 616(1)(*g*),

to a person who, by virtue of the law of a relevant territory, is resident for the purposes of tax in the relevant territory, except, in a case where the person is a company, where such interest is paid to the company in connection with a trade or business which is carried on in the State by the company through a branch or agency,][23]

[(ec) interest paid to—

(i) the National Treasury Management Agency,

(ii) the State acting through the National Treasury Management Agency, or

(iii) a Fund investment vehicle (within the meaning of *section 37* of the *National Treasury Management Agency (Amendment) Act 2014*) of which the Minister for Finance is the sole beneficial owner,

(ed) interest paid by a Fund investment vehicle (within the meaning of *section 37* of the *National Treasury Management Agency (Amendment) Act 2014*) of which the Minister for Finance is the sole beneficial owner,][24]

(f) interest paid without deduction of tax by virtue of [*section 700*,][25]

[(fa) interest paid in the State to an exempt approved scheme within the meaning of *section 774*,][26]

(g) interest which under *section 437* is a [distribution, or][27]

[(h) interest, other than interest referred to in *paragraphs (a)* to *(g)*, paid by a relevant person in the ordinary course of a trade or business carried on by that person to a company—

(I) which, by virtue of the law of a relevant territory, is resident in the relevant territory for the purposes of tax and that relevant territory imposes a tax that generally applies to interest receivable in that territory by companies from sources outside that territory, or

(II) where the interest—

(A) is exempted from the charge to income tax under arrangements made with the government of a territory outside the State having the force of law under the procedures set out in *section 826(1)*, or

(B) would be exempted from the charge to income tax if arrangements made, on or before the date of payment of the interest, with the government of a territory outside the State, that do not have the force of law under the procedures set out in *section 826(1)*, had the force of law when the interest was paid,

except where such interest is paid to that company in connection with a trade or business which is carried on in the State by that company through a branch or agency.][28]

[...][29]

[(5) (a) This paragraph shall apply to a company—

(i) which advances money in the ordinary course of a trade which includes the lending of money,

(ii) in whose hands any interest payable in respect of money so advanced is taken into account in computing the trading income of the company, and

(iii) which—

(I) has notified in writing [the appropriate inspector][30] that it meets the requirements of *subparagraphs (i)* and *(ii)*, and

(II) (A) has notified the first company referred to in *subsection (3)(bb)* in writing that it is a company which meets those requirements and that it has made the notification referred to in *subparagraph (iii)(I)*, and

(B) has provided the first company referred to in *subsection (3)(bb)* with its tax reference number (within the meaning of *section 885*).

(b) A company which is no longer a company to which *paragraph (a)* applies shall, upon that paragraph ceasing to apply to it, immediately notify in writing the inspector referred to in *subparagraph (iii)(I)* of *paragraph (a)* and the company referred to in *subparagraph (iii)(II)* accordingly.][31]

Amendments

[1] Substituted by FA01 s37(1)(b)(i). This section shall apply as respects interest paid on or after 30 March 2001

[2] Deleted by FA05 s44(b)(i).

[3] Deleted by FA13 s42(1)(a). Applied in respect of an investment limited partnership that has been granted an authorisation under section 8 of the Investment Limited Partnerships Act 1994 on or after 13 February 2013.

[4] Substituted by FA05 s44(b)(ii).

[5] Substituted by FA13 s42(1)(a). Applied in respect of an investment limited partnership that has been granted an authorisation under section 8 of the Investment Limited Partnerships Act 1994 on or after 13 February 2013.

[6] Inserted by FA05 s44(b)(iii).

[7] Inserted by FA13 s42(1)(a). Applied in respect of an investment limited partnership that has been granted an authorisation under section 8 of the Investment Limited Partnerships Act 1994 on or after 13 February 2013.

[8] Substituted by FA01 s37(1)(b)(ii). This section shall apply as respects interest paid on or after 30 March 2001

[9] Substituted by FA99 s39(a)(iii)(I).

[10] Substituted by FA99 s39(a)(iii)(II).

[11] Deleted by F(No.2)A08 s33(e)(i). This section is deemed to have come into force and takes effect as on and from 1 January 2009.

[12] Substituted by FA07 sched2(1)(i). Has effect as on and from 2 April 2007

[13] Substituted by F(No.2)A08 s33(e)(i). This section is deemed to have come into force and takes effect as on and from 1 January 2009.

[14] Inserted by FA99 s39(a)(iv).

[15] Inserted by F(No.2)A08 s33(e)(ii). This section is deemed to have come into force and takes effect as on and from 1 January 2009.

[16] Inserted by FA00 s66(1)(a). This section shall apply as on and from 10 February 2000.

[17] Substituted by F(No.2)A13 s22(1). Applies to interest paid on or after 1 January 2014.

[18] Inserted by FA06 s47.

[19] Substituted by FA13 s29(1)(a). Applies to interest paid on or after 27 March 2013.

[20] Inserted by FA03 s48(2). Applies as respects interest paid on or after 6 February 2003.

[21] Inserted by SBCoIA14 part7(1)(c). Does not apply in circumstances where the Minister does not hold all of the shares in the SBCI.

[22, 23] Inserted by the National Asset Management Agency Act 2009 Sched 3 part 10.

[24] Inserted by NTMA(A)A14 part4(6).

[25] Substituted by FA99 s39(b)(i).

[26] Inserted by FA13 s29(1)(b). Applies to interest paid on or after 27 March 2013.

[27] Substituted by FA99 s39(b)(ii).

[28] Substituted by FA10 s40(2). Has effect as on and from 3 April 2010.

[29] Deleted by FA13 s29(1)(c). Applies to interest paid on or after 27 March 2013.

[30] Substituted by FA12 sched5(1)(l).

[31] Inserted by FA02 s19(1)(b). This section applies as respects interest paid on or after the date of the passing of the Finance Act, 2002.

Case Law

Goslings & Sharpe v Blake 2 TC 450 considered the distinction between yearly and short interest and described short loans as "loans for a period short of one year, loans which are not intended to be continued, and are not continued for a longer period".

CIR v Duncan Hay 8 TC 686 also looked at the characteristics of yearly interest.

Interest on a loan is yearly interest if the loan was made with the intention that it would be outstanding for longer than one year. Cairns v MacDiarmid 56 TC 556

Interest in respect of a loan which was repayable on demand in certain circumstances was held to be yearly interest in Corinthian Securities Ltd v Cato 46 TC 93

Revenue Briefings

Tax Briefing

Tax Briefing April 1998 – Issue 31 pg 18 – Tax Treatment of Interest Paid Under the Prompt Payment of Accounts Act 1997

Tax Briefing May 2003 – Issue 52 pg 25 – Late Payment in Commercial Transactions

Tax Briefing April 2004 – Issue 55 pg 14 – Interest Payment – Exemption from Withholding Tax

eBrief

eBrief No. 43/2012 – Interest payments and section 246(3)(h)(I) of the Taxes Consolidation Act 1997

Revenue Precedents

Whether interest payable on borrowings between companies carrying on relevant trading operations within the meaning of section 445 or 446 TCA 1997 may be paid without deduction of tax? Yes, provided that the following conditions are satisfied: a) the loan is in a foreign currency; b) the making of the loan is covered by the terms of the certificate of the lending company i.e. it's licensed trading operations include lending to other IFSC/Shannon companies (in this connection, the lender should provide written confirmation that this is the case and that it will remain so throughout the period of the loan); c) the loan is applied by the borrower for the purpose of it's own licensed trading operations; d) authorisations are granted on a case by case basis. Applications for exemption should be made in letter form to the Revenue Commissioners, Direct Taxes: Incentives Branch, Dublin Castle, Dublin 2. 5047/97

Whether obligation to deduct and account for tax applies where payment is made from taxed profits? Yes; section 246 treats a payment of interest as one to which section 238 TCA applies i.e. the payment is treated as made out of profits or gains not brought into charge to tax. 922017

Where a local authority is late in making a payment of an amount under a compulsory purchase order and is required to pay interest on such amount because it is late, the interest "yearly interest" is within the meaning of section 246 1997. IT952534

Cross References

From Section 246

Section 36 Government securities.
Section 110 Securitisation.
Section 238 Annual payments not payable out of taxed income.
Section 256 Interpretation (Chapter 4).
Section 437 Interest paid to directors and directors' associates.
Section 445 Certain trading operations carried on in Shannon Airport.
Section 446 Certain trading operations carried on in Custom House Docks Area.
Section 700 Special computational provisions.
Section 731 Chargeable gains accruing to unit trusts.
Section 734 Taxation of collective investment undertakings.
Section 737 Special investment schemes.
Section 739B Interpretation and application.
Section 739I Common contractual funds.
Section 826 Agreements for relief from double taxation.
Section 885 Obligation to show tax reference number on receipts.
Section 951 Obligation to make a return.

To Section 246

Section 64 Interest on quoted Eurobonds.
Section 110 Securitisation.
Section 198 Certain interest not to be chargeable.
Section 243 Allowance of charges on income.
Section 246A Interest in respect of wholesale debt instruments.
Section 257 Deduction of tax from relevant interest.
Section 261B Taxation of specified interest.
Section 267I Exemptions from tax and withholding tax.
Section 390 Amount of assessment made under section 238 to be allowed as a loss for certain purposes.
Section 410 Group payments.
Section 891A Returns of interest paid to non-residents.

246A Interest in respect of wholesale debt instruments

[(1) In this section—

"*approved denomination*", in relation to a wholesale debt instrument, means a denomination of not less than—

(a) in the case of an instrument denominated in euro, €500,000;

(b) in the case of an instrument denominated in United States Dollars, US$500,000; or

(c) in the case of an instrument denominated in a currency other than euro or United States Dollars, the equivalent in that other currency of €500,000;

and, for the purposes of this definition, the equivalent of an amount of euro in another currency shall be determined by reference to the rate of exchange—

(i) in the case of instruments issued under a programme, at the time the programme under which the instrument is to be issued is first publicised; or

(ii) in the case of all other instruments, on the date of issue of the instrument;

"*Revenue officer*" means an officer of the Revenue Commissioners;

"*certificate of deposit*" means an instrument, either in physical or electronic form, relating to money in any currency which has been deposited with the issuer or some other person, being an instrument—

(a) issued by a financial institution,

(b) which recognises an obligation to pay a stated amount to bearer or to order, with or without interest, and

(c) (i) in the case of instruments held in physical form, by the delivery of which, with or without endorsement, the right to receive the stated amount is transferable, or

(ii) in the case of instruments held in electronic form, in respect of which the right to receive the stated amount is transferable;

"*commercial paper*" means a debt instrument, either in physical or electronic form, relating to money in any currency, which—

(a) is issued by—

(i) a financial institution, or

(ii) a company that is not a financial institution,

(b) recognises an obligation to pay a stated amount,

(c) carries a right to interest or is issued at a discount or at a premium, and

(d) matures within 2 years;

"*financial institution*" has the same meaning as it has in *section 906A*;

"*relevant person*" means the person by or through whom a payment in respect of a wholesale debt instrument is made;

"*tax reference number*" has the meaning assigned to it by *section 885*;

"*wholesale debt instrument*" means a certificate of deposit or commercial paper, as appropriate.

(2) (a) In this section and in any other provision of the Tax Acts or the Capital Gains Tax Acts which applies this subsection, "*recognised clearing system*" means the following clearing systems—

(i) Bank One NA, Depository and Clearing Centre,

(ii) Central Moneymarkets Office,

(iii) Clearstream Banking SA,

(iv) Clearstream Banking AG,

(v) CREST,

(vi) Depository Trust Company of New York,

(vii) Euroclear,

(viii) Monte Titoli SPA,

(ix) Netherlands Centraal Instituut voor Giraal Effectenverkeer BV,

(x) National Securities Clearing System,

(xi) Sicovam SA,

(xii) SIS Sega Intersettle AG, and

(xiii) any other system for clearing securities which is for the time being designated, for the purposes of this section or any other provision of the Tax Acts or the Capital Gains Tax Acts which applies this subsection, by order of the Revenue Commissioners under *paragraph (b)* as a recognised clearing system.

(b) For the purposes of this section and *sections 64* and 739B, the Revenue Commissioners may, designate by order one or more than one system for clearing securities as a "recognised clearing system".

(c) An order of the Revenue Commissioners under *paragraph (b)* may—

(i) contain such transitional and other supplemental provisions as appear to the Revenue Commissioners to be necessary or expedient, and

(ii) be varied or revoked by a subsequent order.

(3) As respects any payment made in respect of a wholesale debt instrument—

(a) if either—

(i) the person by whom the payment is made, or

(ii) the person through whom the payment is made,

is not resident in the State and the payment is not made by or through a branch or agency through which a company not resident in the State carries on a trade or business in the State, and

(I) the wholesale debt instrument is held in a recognised clearing system, and

(II) the wholesale debt instrument is of an approved denomination,

then—

(A) *section 246(2)* shall not apply to that payment, and

(B) the wholesale debt instrument shall not be treated as a relevant deposit (within the meaning of *section 256*) for the purposes of Chapter 4 of this Part,

or

(b) (i) if either—

(I) the person by whom the payment is made, or

(II) the person through whom the payment is made,

is resident in the State or the payment is made either by or through a branch or agency through which a company not resident in the State carries on a trade or business in the State,

and

(ii) (I) the wholesale debt instrument is held in a recognised clearing system and is of an approved denomination, or

(II) the person who is beneficially entitled to the interest is a resident of the State and has provided the person's tax reference number to the relevant person, or

(III) the person who is the beneficial owner of the wholesale debt instrument and who is beneficially entitled to the interest is not resident in the State and has made a declaration of the kind described in *subsection (5)*,

then, subject to *subsection (4)* or *(5)*—

(A) *section 246(2)* shall not apply to that payment, and

(B) the wholesale debt instrument shall not be treated as a relevant deposit (within the meaning of *section 256*) for the purposes of *Chapter 4* of this Part.

(4) A relevant person who makes a payment in respect of a wholesale debt instrument shall as respects a case which is within *paragraph (b)(ii)(I)* or *(b)(ii)(II)*, as the case may be, of *subsection (3)* and which is not within *paragraph (a)* of that subsection—

(a) (i) be regarded as a person to whom *section 891(1)* applies as respects that case, if that provision would not otherwise apply to that person,

(ii) be regarded as a "relevant person" (within the meaning of *section 894*) for the purposes of that section as respects that case, if that person would not otherwise be a "relevant person" (within that meaning), and

(iii) in addition to the matters to be included in a return to be made under *section 891* for a chargeable period (within the meaning of *section 321(2)*), include on that return, in respect of that case, the tax reference number of the person to whom the payment was made,

and

(b) on being so required by notice given in writing by a Revenue officer, in relation to any person named by the officer in the notice, deliver an account in writing of the amount of any payment made in respect of a wholesale debt instrument to that person together with details of the person's name and address and tax reference number if such details have not been included in a return made by that person under *section 891*.

(5) The declaration referred to in *subsection (3)(b)(ii)(III)* is a declaration in writing to a relevant person which—

(a) is made by a person (in this section referred to as "*the declarer*") to whom any payment in respect of which the declaration is made is payable by the relevant person, and is signed by the declarer,

(b) is made in such form as may be prescribed or authorised by the Revenue Commissioners,

(c) declares that at the time the declaration is made the person who is beneficially entitled to the interest is not resident in the State,

(d) contains as respects the person mentioned in *paragraph (c)*—

(i) the name of the person,

(ii) the address of that person's principal place of residence, and

(iii) the name of the country in which that person is resident at the time that the declaration is made,

(e) contains an undertaking by the declarer that, if the person referred to in *paragraph (c)* becomes resident in the State, the declarer shall notify the relevant person accordingly, and

(f) contains such other information as the Revenue Commissioners may reasonably require for the purposes of this section.

(6) Where a relevant person is satisfied that any payment made by that person in respect of a wholesale debt instrument has been made to a person to whom *paragraph (b)(ii)(II)* or *(b)(ii)(III)*, as the case may be, of *subsection (3)* applies, the relevant person shall be entitled to continue to treat that person as a person to whom that paragraph applies until such time as the relevant person is in possession, or aware, of information which can reasonably be taken to indicate that that paragraph no longer applies to that person.

(7) (a) A relevant person shall—

(i) keep and retain for the longer of the following—

(I) a period of 6 years after the declaration is made, and

(II) a period which ends not earlier than 3 years after the latest date on which any payment in respect of which the declaration was made is paid,

and

(ii) on being required by notice given in writing by a Revenue officer, make available to that officer within the time specified in the notice,

all declarations of the kind mentioned in this section that have been made in respect of any payment made by the relevant person.

(b) A Revenue officer may examine or take extracts from or copies of any declarations made available under *paragraph (a)*.][1]

Amendments

[1] Inserted by FA03 s49(1). Applies as respects a wholesale debt instrument issued on or after such day as the Minister for Finance may appoint by order. With effect from 13 June 2003 per S.I. 245 of 2003.

Revenue Information Notes

List of Recognised Clearing Systems

Cross References

From Section 246A

Section 64 Interest on quoted Eurobonds.
Section 246 Interest payments by companies and to non-residents.
Section 256 Interpretation (Chapter 4).
Section 321 Provisions of general application in relation to the making of allowances and charges.
Section 885 Obligation to show tax reference number on receipts.
Section 891 Returns of interest paid or credited without deduction of tax.
Section 894 Returns of certain information by third parties.
Section 906A Information to be furnished by financial institutions.

To Section 246A

Section 64 Interest on quoted Eurobonds.
Section 110 Securitisation.
Section 198 Certain interest not to be chargeable.
Section 904A Power of inspection: returns and collection of appropriate tax.

247 Relief to companies on loans applied in acquiring interest in other companies

[FA74 s33 and s35(4) and (5); CTA76 s140(1) and Sch2 PtI par43; FA96 s131(9)(a)]

(1) (a) In this section and in *sections 248* and *249*—

"*control*" shall be construed in accordance with *section 432*;

"*material interest*", in relation to a company, means the beneficial ownership of, or the ability to control, directly or through the medium of a connected company or connected companies or by any other indirect means, more than 5 per cent of the ordinary share capital of the [company;][1]

["*trading stock*" has the same meaning as in *section 89*.][2]

(b) For the purposes of this section and *sections 248* and *249*, a company shall be regarded as connected with another company if it would be so regarded for the purposes of the Tax Acts by virtue of *section 10* and[, except for the purposes of [*subsections (4A)* and *(4E)*][3],][4] if it is a company referred to in *subsection (2)(a)*.

(2) This section shall apply to a loan to a company (in this section and in *section 249(1)* referred to as "*the investing company*") to defray money applied—

(a) in acquiring any part of the ordinary share capital of—

(i) a company which exists wholly or mainly for the purpose of carrying on a trade or trades or a company whose income consists wholly or mainly of profits or gains chargeable under Case V of Schedule D, or

(ii) a company whose business consists wholly or mainly of the holding of stocks, shares or securities of a company referred to in *subparagraph (i)*,

[(b) in lending to a company referred to in *paragraph (a)* money which is used wholly and exclusively—

(i) where the company is a company which exists wholly or mainly for the purpose of carrying on a trade or trades, for the purposes of that trade or those trades,

(ii) where the company is a company whose income consists wholly or mainly of profits or gains chargeable under Case V of Schedule D, in the purchase, improvement or repair of premises to which the profits or gains relate, or

(iii) where the company is a company whose business consists wholly or mainly of the holding of stocks, shares or securities of a company referred to in *paragraph (a)(i)*, for the purposes of holding such stocks, shares or securities,

(ba) in lending to a company referred to in *paragraph (a)* money which is used wholly and exclusively by a connected company—

(i) where the connected company is a company which exists wholly or mainly for the purpose of carrying on a trade or trades, for the purposes of that trade or those trades,

(ii) where the connected company is a company whose income consists wholly or mainly of profits or gains chargeable under Case V of Schedule D, in the purchase, improvement or repair of premises to which the profits or gains relate, or

(iii) where the connected company is a company whose business consists wholly or mainly of the holding of stocks, shares or securities of a company referred to in *paragraph (a)(i)*, for the purposes of holding such stocks, shares or securities, or][5]

(c) in paying off another loan where relief could have been obtained under this section for interest on that other loan if it had not been paid off (on the assumption, if the loan was free of interest, that it carried interest).

[(2A) *Subsection (2)* shall not apply to a loan to an investing company to defray money applied in subscribing for share capital of another company on the issue of share capital by that other company unless the capital is used by that other company or by a connected company wholly and exclusively—

(a) where the company which uses the capital is a company which exists wholly or mainly for the purpose of carrying on a trade or trades, for the purposes of that trade or those trades,

(b) where the company which uses the capital is a company whose income consists wholly or mainly of profits or gains chargeable under Case V of Schedule D, in the purchase, improvement or repair of premises to which the profits or gains relate, or

(c) where the company which uses the capital is a company whose business consists wholly or mainly of the holding of stocks, shares or securities of a company referred to in *paragraph (a)(i)*, [of *subsection (2)*][6] for the purposes of holding such stocks, shares or securities.][7]

(3) Relief shall be given in respect of any payment of the interest by the investing company on the loan if—

(a) when the interest is paid the investing company has a material interest in the company [and, where *subsection (2)(ba)* applies to the money lent in respect of which the interest is paid, in the connected company][8],

(b) during the period taken as a whole from the application of the proceeds of the loan until the interest was paid at least one director of the investing company was also a director of the company [and, where *subsection (2)(ba)* applies to the money lent in respect of which the interest is paid, of the connected company][9], and

(c) the investing company shows that in the period referred to in *paragraph (b)* it has not recovered any capital from the company or from a connected company apart from any amount taken into account under *section 249*.

(4) *Subsection (2)* shall not apply to a loan unless it is made in connection with the application of the money and either on the occasion of its application or within what is in the circumstances a reasonable time from the application of the money, and that subsection shall not apply to a loan the proceeds of which are applied for some other purpose before being applied as described in that subsection.

[(4A) (a) Subject to the following paragraphs of this subsection, *subsection (2)* shall not apply to a loan to the investing company to defray money applied—

(i) in acquiring any part of the ordinary share capital of, or

(ii) in lending to a company money which is used directly or indirectly for the purposes of acquiring any part of the capital of,

a company (from such company or another company, being in either case a company which, at the time of the acquiring of the capital or immediately after that time, was connected with the investing company) if the loan is made to the investing company by a person who is connected with the investing company.

(b) Where, as a part of, or in connection with, any scheme or arrangement for the making of a loan to the investing company by a person (in this paragraph referred to as the "*first-mentioned person*") who is not connected with the investing company, another person who is connected with the investing company directly or indirectly makes a loan to, a deposit with, or otherwise provides funds to the first-mentioned person or to a person who is connected with the first-mentioned person, then the loan made to the investing company shall be treated for the purposes of *paragraph (a)* as being a loan made to the investing company by a person with whom it is connected.

(c) *Paragraph (a)* shall not apply to interest on a loan (in this paragraph referred to as the "*original loan*") made to a company if—

(i) the original loan is used to defray money applied—

(I) in acquiring ordinary share capital of another company on the issue of the share capital by the other company, or

(II) in lending to a company money which is used directly or indirectly for the purposes of acquiring ordinary share capital of another company on the issue of the share capital by the other company,

and

(ii) the share capital is issued for the purposes of increasing the aggregate of the capital available to the other company for the use by the other company wholly and exclusively for the purposes of its trade or business and not as part of any arrangement or understanding, entered into in connection with the original loan, the purpose or one of the purposes of which is to provide moneys, directly or indirectly—

(I) to the person (referred to in clause (II) as the "*original lender*") who made the original loan and to thereby achieve directly or indirectly the effective repayment of the original loan or the greater part of it, or

(II) to another person who is connected with the original lender and to thereby achieve a provision of moneys that is, notwithstanding that the moneys are being provided (as part of the arrangement or understanding) to a person other than the original lender, equivalent to the achievement directly or indirectly of the effective repayment, referred to in clause (I), of the original loan or the greater part of it,

at a time before interest ceased to be payable by the investing company in respect of the original loan or such greater part of it.

(d) Where the use, whether direct use (in this paragraph referred to as the "*direct use*") by the investing company or subsequent indirect use (in this paragraph referred to as the "*indirect use*") through another company as investee or borrower or through a sequence of companies acting, in turn, as investees or borrowers, of a loan (in this paragraph and *paragraph (e)* referred to as the "*original loan*") received by an investing company involves lending or acquisition of shares so that such use results in—

(i) interest (which is not deductible in computing income or profits under any provision of the Corporation Tax Acts by the investing company or any company connected with it) being received in, or being receivable in respect of, an accounting period, so as to be income, or as the case may be an amount credited in computing income, chargeable to corporation tax for that period, or

(ii) dividends or other distributions chargeable to corporation tax being received in an accounting period,

and the interest mentioned in *subparagraph (i)* is, or the dividends or distributions mentioned in *subparagraph (ii)* are, income of the investing company or a company connected with the investing company, being income which would not have arisen but for the direct use or indirect use of the original loan, then that income shall be relevant income for the purposes of *paragraph (e)* and shall be referred to in that paragraph as "*relevant income*".

(e) If relief for interest paid (in this paragraph referred to as the "*relevant interest*") by the investing company in an accounting period (in this paragraph referred to as the "*relevant accounting period*") in respect of the original loan would, apart from this paragraph, be denied by virtue of *paragraph (a)*, relief shall not be denied in respect of so much of the relevant interest as does not exceed the relevant income of the investing company for the relevant accounting period and where—

(i) the relevant interest exceeds the relevant income of the investing company for the relevant accounting period, by an amount referred to in this paragraph as the "*relevant excess*",

(ii) apart from relief by virtue of an election under *subparagraph (iii)*, relief could not be claimed under the Corporation Tax Acts in respect of the relevant interest represented by the relevant excess,

(iii) the investing company and a company (in this paragraph referred to as the "*electing company*") connected with it jointly so elect and notify the inspector of that election in such form as the Revenue Commissioners may require, and

(iv) the aggregate value of relevant interest that may be deducted by virtue of elections under *subparagraph (iii)*, by one or more companies other than the investing company, does not exceed the relevant excess, then so much of the relevant interest represented by the relevant excess may be deducted from the total profits, reduced by any other relief from corporation tax, of the electing company, for the accounting period (in this paragraph referred to as the "*second-mentioned period*") for which the relevant income of the electing company is chargeable to corporation tax, as does not exceed the lesser of—

(I) the part of the relevant income of the electing company for the second-mentioned period which may be apportioned to the relevant accounting period (by reference to the proportion which the length of the period common to the relevant accounting period and the second-mentioned accounting period bears to the length of the second-mentioned accounting period), and

(II) the amount by which such part of that relevant income of the electing company exceeds the aggregate of any amounts, being—

(A) amounts of any relief, which is referable to the second-mentioned period, surrendered at any time by the electing company under *Chapter 5* of *Part 12*, or

(B) amounts, which are not amounts referred to in clause (A), of any losses which could have been set off under *section 396(2)* against profits of the second-mentioned period but which were not set off against those profits,

but relief, for interest paid by the investing company, which has been allowed by virtue of this paragraph shall be deemed for the purposes mentioned in *Paragraph 4(5)* of *Schedule 24* […][10] to have been allocated by the company concerned to the relevant income of the company by reference to which the relief for the interest was allowed, and the foreign tax in respect of that relevant income shall be disregarded for the purposes of *paragraph 9E* and *9F* of *Schedule 24*.

(f) Where, as a part of, or in connection with, any scheme or arrangement for the making of a loan to any company (in this paragraph referred to as the "*borrower*"), which is connected with the investing company, by a person (in this paragraph referred to as the "*first-mentioned person*") who is not connected with the investing company, another person who is connected with the investing company directly or indirectly makes a loan to, a deposit with, or otherwise provides funds to the first-mentioned person or to a person who is connected with the first-mentioned person, then interest payable by the first-mentioned person to the other person in respect of the loan, deposit or other funds shall be treated for the purposes of *paragraph (d)(i)* as interest which is deductible in computing income or profits under provisions of the Corporation Tax Acts by the investing company or a company connected with it.

(g) For the purposes of *paragraph (e)*, "*relevant income*" of a company shall be increased or reduced by any amount of profit or gain or, as the case may be, loss directly related to that income or to the source of that income which is an amount arising—

(i) by virtue of a change in a rate of exchange (within the meaning of *section 79*), or

(ii) from any contract entered into by the company for the purpose of eliminating or reducing the risk of loss being incurred by the company due to a change in a rate of exchange (within the meaning of *section 79*) or in a rate of interest.

(h) For the purposes of *paragraph (c)*, share capital shall not be treated as issued by a company as part of an arrangement or understanding of a type described in that paragraph, entered into in connection with an original loan (within the meaning of that paragraph), solely because that share capital is used directly or indirectly in paying off, to the person who made the original loan (within that meaning) or to a person connected with that person, a loan, advance or debt (in this paragraph referred to as the "*other loan*") other than the original loan where—

(i) the other loan was used wholly and exclusively for the purposes of a trade or business of the company and not as part of any arrangement or understanding, entered into in connection with the other loan, the purpose or one of the purposes of which was to provide moneys, directly or indirectly—

(I) to a person (referred to in clause (II) as the "*original lender*") who made, or directly or indirectly funded, the other loan and to thereby achieve directly or indirectly the effective repayment of the other loan or the greater part of it, or

(II) to another person who is connected with the original lender and to thereby achieve a provision of moneys that is, notwithstanding that the moneys are being provided (as part of the arrangement or understanding) to a person other than the original lender, equivalent to the achievement directly or indirectly of the effective repayment, referred to in clause (I), of the other loan or the greater part of it,

at a time before interest ceased to be payable by the company in respect of the other loan or such greater part of it, and

(ii) interest on the other loan, if that other loan had been made on or after 2 February 2006, would have been deductible in computing profits, or any description of profits, for the purposes of corporation tax—

(I) if the other loan had not been paid off, and

(II) on the assumption, if the other loan was free of interest, that it carried interest.][11]

[(4B) Where a loan, or part of a loan, to an investing company has been applied—

(a) to subscriptions for the share capital of another company on the issue of the share capital by the other company, or

(b) in lending moneys to another company,

and such other company (in this subsection and *subsection (4D)* referred to as the "*other company*") uses those subscriptions or moneys to provide specified intangible assets (within the meaning of *section 291A*) in respect of which allowances are to be made to it under *section 284* as applied by *section 291A*, then, notwithstanding *subsection (3)* and *section 243*, the amount of the relief to be given in respect of so much (in this subsection and *subsections (4C)* and *(4D)* referred to as the "*relevant interest*") of the interest paid in an accounting period by the investing company on the loan, or the part of the loan, as the case may be, as exceeds the sum of—

(i) any dividends or other distributions chargeable to corporation tax received by the investing company from the other company in that accounting period in respect of that share capital, and

(ii) any interest received by the investing company for that accounting period in respect of those moneys lent to the other company,

shall not exceed the amount of interest that would be—

(I) the amount of the relevant interest to be deducted for the corresponding accounting period (within the meaning of *subsection (4D)*) by the other company—

(A) if that relevant interest had been incurred by the other company in connection with the provision of a specified intangible asset by reference to which allowances were to be made to it under *section 284* as applied by *section 291A* in addition to any other interest so incurred by it, and

(B) notwithstanding *subsection (6)* of *section 291A*, if any additional restrictions of deductions, whether for allowances or interest, which would then be required by that subsection, were to be made solely by restriction of the deduction for that relevant interest,

or

(II) where the corresponding accounting period is not the same as the accounting period of the investing company or there is more than one corresponding accounting period, the aggregate of the amounts of relevant interest to be deducted for the corresponding period or periods by the other company if that relevant interest had been incurred by the other company, which amounts are computed by apportionment in accordance with *paragraph (d)* of *subsection (4D)* and are interest paid or treated as paid in the accounting period of the investing company.

(4C) The amount (in this paragraph referred to as the "*excess amount*") of the interest paid in an accounting period by the investing company in respect of which, in accordance with *subsection (4B)*, relief is not given under this section for that accounting period shall not be deducted or otherwise relieved for that period under any other provision of the Tax Acts but that excess amount of interest paid shall be carried forward and treated as an amount of relevant interest paid in the succeeding accounting period to be added to the relevant interest, if any, actually paid in that accounting period, for which, subject to *subsection (4B)*, relief can be given for that accounting period and any excess amount of interest paid or treated as paid in that next succeeding accounting period shall, in turn, be carried forward and treated as an amount of relevant interest paid in the next succeeding accounting period to be added to the relevant interest, if any, actually paid in that accounting period for which, subject to *subsection (4B)*, relief can be given for that accounting period and so on for each succeeding accounting period.

(4D) For the purposes of computing any restriction of relief to be given for an accounting period required by *subsection (4B)*—

(a) any accounting period (in this subsection referred to as the "*corresponding accounting period*") of the other company which falls wholly or partly within an accounting period of the investing company corresponds to the accounting period of the investing company,

(b) if an accounting period of the investing company and the corresponding accounting period of the other company are not the same relevant interest will be apportioned to corresponding accounting periods on a time basis according to the proportion which the period common to the accounting period of the investing company and the corresponding accounting period bears to the accounting period of the investing company,

(c) the total relevant interest referable to a corresponding accounting period shall be the aggregate of each of the amounts of relevant interest apportioned to that corresponding accounting period under *paragraph (b)*, and

(d) the amount of the total relevant interest referred to in *paragraph (c)* which, subject to *subsection (4B)(I)(A)* and *(B)*, would have been deducted if it had been incurred by the other company for the corresponding accounting period shall be apportioned to each of the amounts of relevant interest referred to in *paragraph (c)* by reference to the proportion which each of those amounts bears to that total relevant interest.][12]

[(4E) (a) In this subsection "*asset*" means any asset other than—

(i) share capital in a company,

(ii) an asset referred to in *subsection (4B)* which is treated by the provisions of *section 291A(2)* as plant and machinery for the purposes of *Chapters 2* and *4* of *Part 9*, or

(iii) an asset acquired as trading stock.

(b) Subject to *paragraphs (c)* to *(f)*, *subsection (2)* shall not apply to a loan to the investing company to defray money applied in lending to a company money which is used directly or indirectly for the purposes of acquiring an asset from a company which, at the time of the acquiring of the asset, was connected with the investing company if the loan is made to the investing company by a person who is connected with the investing company.

(c) (i) Where, in an accounting period, interest is paid by an investing company on a loan to defray money applied in lending to another company (in this paragraph referred to as the "*other company*") money which is used wholly and exclusively for the purposes of acquiring a trade (in this subsection referred to as an "*acquired trade*") which immediately before its acquisition by the other company was carried on by a company which was not within the charge to corporation tax, then *paragraph (b)* shall not apply to that loan and, notwithstanding *subsection (3)* and *section 243*, the amount of the relief to be given in respect of the interest paid in an accounting period by the investing company on the loan shall not exceed the amount of the profits or gains of the other company in respect of the acquired trade for the corresponding period.

(ii) This paragraph shall apply where a company acquires part of a trade as if that part were a separate trade.

(iii) Where the other company begins to carry on the activities of an acquired trade as part of its trade then that part of its trade shall, for the purposes of this subsection, be treated as a separate trade and any necessary apportionment shall be made so that profits or gains shall be attributed to the separate trade on a just and reasonable basis and the amount of those profits or gains shall not exceed the amount which would be attributed to a distinct and separate company, engaged in those activities, if it were independent of, and dealing at arm's length with, the investing company.

(d) (i) Where, in an accounting period, interest is paid by an investing company on a loan to defray money applied in lending to another company (in this paragraph referred to as the "*other company*") money which is used wholly and exclusively for the purposes of acquiring an asset (in this paragraph referred to as an "*acquired asset*") which is leased by the other company for that accounting period in the course of a trade (in this paragraph referred to as the "*first-mentioned trade*") then, if immediately before that asset was acquired by the other company it was not in use for the purposes of a trade carried on by a company which was within the charge to corporation tax, *paragraph* (*b*) shall not apply to that loan and, notwithstanding *subsection (3)* and *section 243*, the amount of the relief to be given in respect of the interest paid in the accounting period by the investing company on the loan shall not exceed the amount of the profits or gains of the first-mentioned trade for the corresponding period as is attributable to the acquired asset.

(ii) For the purposes of *subparagraph (i)*, in arriving at the profits or gains of a trade attributable to an acquired asset, any necessary apportionment shall be made of the expenses and receipts of the trade.

(e) For the purposes of computing any restriction of relief to be given for an accounting period required by *paragraphs* (*c*) and (*d*)—

(i) where an accounting period of the investing company and an accounting period of the other company coincide then the profits or gains of the other company in respect of the acquired trade for the corresponding period shall be the amount of the profits or gains of the acquired trade, for that accounting period, which are chargeable to tax under Case I of Schedule D, and

(ii) (I) any accounting period of the other company which, without coinciding with that accounting period, falls wholly or partly within an accounting period of the investing company shall correspond to that accounting period, and

(II) where an accounting period of the investing company and an accounting period of the other company do not coincide then the profits or gains of the other company in respect of the acquired trade for the corresponding period shall be the aggregate of the profits or gains in respect of the acquired trade which are chargeable to corporation tax under Case I of Schedule D for accounting periods of the other company that correspond to the accounting period of the investing company as reduced in each case by applying the fraction—

$$\frac{A}{B}$$

(if the fraction is less than unity)

where—

A is the length of the period common to the two accounting periods, and

B is the length of the accounting period of the other company.

(f) Where, as a part of, or in connection with, any scheme or arrangement for the making of a loan to the investing company by a person (in this paragraph referred to as the "*first-mentioned person*") who is not connected with the investing company, another person who is connected with the investing company directly or indirectly makes a loan to, a deposit with, or otherwise provides funds to the first-mentioned person or to a person who is connected with the first-mentioned person, then the loan made to the investing company shall be treated for the purposes of *paragraph (a)* as being a loan made to the investing company by a person with whom it is connected.

(4F) (a) In this subsection "*relevant period*", in relation to interest paid by an investing company, means the period to which that interest relates.

(b) Where a loan to an investing company, to which *subsection (2)* applies, has been applied in lending to another company (in this paragraph referred to as the "*other company*") not within the charge to corporation tax money which is used wholly and exclusively for the purposes of the trade or business of the other company then, notwithstanding *subsection (3)* and *section 243*, the amount of the relief to be given in respect of so much of the interest paid (referred to in this paragraph as the "*interest paid*") in an accounting period by the investing company on the loan, as exceeds the amount (including a nil amount) of any interest, arising to the investing company on the money lent to the other company, for the relevant period, shall not exceed the amount by which the interest paid exceeds the interest (if any) arising to the other company in that relevant period in respect of the money so used.

(c) Where a loan to an investing company, to which *subsection (2)* applies, has been applied in lending to another company (in this paragraph referred to as the "*other company*") money which is used wholly and exclusively for the purposes of the trade or business of a connected company not within the charge to corporation tax then, notwithstanding *subsection (3)* and *section 243*—

(i) where the other company is within the charge to corporation tax, the amount of the relief to be given in respect of so much of the interest paid (referred to in this subparagraph as the "*interest paid*") in an accounting period by the investing company on the loan, as exceeds the amount (including a nil amount) of any interest, arising to the investing company on the money lent to the other company, for the relevant period, shall not exceed the amount by which the interest paid exceeds the interest (if any) arising to the connected company in that relevant period in respect of the money so used, and

(ii) where the other company is not within the charge to corporation tax, the amount of the relief to be given in respect of so much of the interest paid (referred to in this subparagraph as the "*interest paid*") in an accounting period by the investing company on the loan, as exceeds the amount (including a nil amount) of any interest, arising to the investing company on the money lent to the other company, for the relevant period, shall not exceed the amount by which the interest paid exceeds the greater of—

(I) the interest (if any) receivable by the other company from the connected company (in respect of the use by the other company of the money lent to it by the investing company), and

(II) the interest receivable by the connected company in that relevant period in respect of the money so used.

(4G) Where a loan to an investing company, to which *subsection (2)* applies, has been applied in lending to a company money which is used wholly and exclusively for the purposes of the trade of the company or of a connected company, the interest on the loan shall be treated for the purposes of *Chapter 5* of *Part 12* as relevant trading charges on income within the meaning of *section 243A*.][13]

[(5) Interest eligible for relief under this section shall be deducted from or set off against the income (not being income referred to in *subsection (2)(a)* of *section 25*) of the borrower for the year of assessment in which the interest is paid and tax shall be discharged or repaid accordingly.

(6) Where relief is given under this section in respect of interest on a loan, no relief or deduction under any other provision of the Tax Acts shall be given or allowed in respect of interest on the loan.][14]

Amendments

[1] Substituted by FA11 s37(1)(b). Shall apply in respect of a loan made on or after 21 January 2011 other than any such loan made in accordance with a binding written agreement made before that date.

[2] Inserted by FA11 s37(1)(c). Shall apply in respect of a loan made on or after 21 January 2011 other than any such loan made in accordance with a binding written agreement made before that date.

[3] Substituted by FA11 s37(1)(d). Shall apply in respect of a loan made on or after 21 January 2011 other than any such loan made in accordance with a binding written agreement made before that date.

[4] Inserted by FA06 s65(1)(a). This section applies as respects a loan made on or after 2 February 2006.

[5] Substituted by FA11 s37(1)(e). Shall apply in respect of a loan made on or after 21 January 2011 other than any such loan made in accordance with a binding written agreement made before that date.

[6] Inserted by FA12 sched6(1)(b). Has effect as on and from 31 March 2012.

[7] Inserted by FA11 s37(1)(f). Shall apply in respect of a loan made on or after 21 January 2011 other than any such loan made in accordance with a binding written agreement made before that date.

[8] Substituted by FA11 s37(1)(g)(i). Shall apply in respect of a loan made on or after 21 January 2011 other than any such loan made in accordance with a binding written agreement made before that date.

[9] Substituted by FA11 s37(1)(g)(ii). Shall apply in respect of a loan made on or after 21 January 2011 other than any such loan made in accordance with a binding written agreement made before that date.

[10] Deleted by FA08 sched8(1)(b). Has effect as on and from 13 March 2008.

[11] Inserted by FA06 s65(1)(b). This section applies as respects a loan made on or after 2 February 2006.

[12] Inserted by FA09 s13(1)(a). Applies to expenditure incurred by a company after 7 May 2009.

[13] Inserted by FA11 s37(1)(h). Shall apply in respect of a loan made on or after 21 January 2011 other than any such loan made in accordance with a binding written agreement made before that date.

[14] Substituted by FA00 s67(1). This section shall be deemed to have applied as on and from 6 April 1997.

Revenue Briefings

eBrief

eBrief No. 11/2011 – Finance Act 2011 – Interest Payable on Loans

eBrief No. 48/2012 – Tax Treatment of Debt Issuance Costs

Revenue Precedents

A "company" for section 247 subsection (2) (a) (i) need not be resident in the State or within the charge to Irish tax. CTF89/3006

The cessation of a trading activity by the company in which shares have been acquired does not trigger withdrawal of the relief. CTF203

Cross References

From Section 247

Section 10 Connected persons.
Section 25 Companies not resident in the State.
Section 79 Foreign currency: computation of income and chargeable gains.
Section 89 Valuation of trading stock at discontinuance of trade.
Section 243 Allowance of charges on income.
Section 243A Restriction of relevant charges on income.
Section 248 Relief to individuals on loans applied in acquiring interest in companies.
Section 249 Rules relating to recovery of capital and replacement loans.
Section 284 Wear and tear allowances.
Section 291A Intangible assets.
Section 381 Right to repayment of tax by reference to losses.
Section 396 Relief for trading losses other than terminal losses.
Section 410 Group payments.
Section 432 Meaning of "associated company" and "control".
Schedule 24 Relief from Income Tax and Corporation Tax by Means of Credit in Respect of Foreign Tax

To Section 247

Section 243 Allowance of charges on income.
Section 248A Restriction of relief in respect of loans applied in acquiring interest in companies and partnerships.
Section 249 Rules relating to recovery of capital and replacement loans.

248 Relief to individuals on loans applied in acquiring interest in companies

[FA74 s34 and s35(4) and (5); FA92 s14(4)]

(1) This section shall apply to a loan to an individual to defray money applied—

(a) in acquiring any part of the ordinary share capital of—

[(i) a company which exists wholly or mainly for the purpose of carrying on a trade or trades, or][1]

(ii) a company whose business consists wholly or mainly of the holding of stocks, shares or securities of a company referred to in *subparagraph (i)*,

(b) in lending to a company referred to in *paragraph (a)* money which is used wholly and exclusively for the purpose of the trade or business of the company or of a connected company, or

(c) in paying off another loan where relief could have been obtained under this section for interest on that other loan if it had not been paid off (on the assumption, if the loan was free of interest, that it carried interest).

[(1A) *Subsection (1)(c)* shall not apply to a loan made after 7 December 2005 which is applied in paying off another loan applied in acquiring ordinary share capital in, or making a loan to, a company whose income consists wholly or mainly of profits or gains chargeable under Case V of Schedule D unless—

(a) the loan does not exceed the balance outstanding on, and

(b) the term of the loan does not exceed the balance of the term of,

the loan being paid off.][2]

(2) Relief shall be given in respect of any payment of interest by the individual on the loan if—

(a) when the interest is paid the individual has a material interest in the company or in a connected company,

(b) during the period taken as a whole from the application of the proceeds of the loan until the interest was paid, the individual has worked for the greater part of his or her time in the actual management or conduct of the business of the company or of a connected company, and

(c) the individual shows that in the period referred to in *paragraph (b)* he or she has not recovered any capital from the company or from a connected company, apart from any amount taken into account under *section 249*.

(3) Relief shall not be given in respect of any payment of interest by an individual on a loan applied on or after the 24th day of April, 1992, for any of the purposes specified in *subsection (1)* unless the loan is applied for bona fide commercial purposes and not as part of a scheme or arrangement the main purpose or one of the main purposes of which is the avoidance of tax.

(4) *Subsection (1)* shall not apply to a loan unless it is made in connection with the application of the money and either on the occasion of its application or within what is in the circumstances a reasonable time from the application of the money, and that subsection shall not apply to a loan the proceeds of which are applied for some other purpose before being applied as described in that subsection.

(5) Interest eligible for relief under this section shall be deducted from or set off against the income of the borrower for the year of assessment in which the interest is paid and tax shall be discharged or repaid accordingly, and such interest shall not be eligible for relief under any provision of the Income Tax Acts apart from this section.

[(6) Notwithstanding *subsection (5)*, the deduction authorised by that subsection shall not exceed—

(a) as respects the year of assessment 2011, 75 per cent of the deduction that would but for this subsection be authorised by that subsection,

(b) as respects the year of assessment 2012, 50 per cent of the deduction that would but for this subsection be authorised by that subsection,

(c) as respects the year of assessment 2013, 25 per cent of the deduction that would but for this subsection be authorised by that subsection, and

(d) as respects the year of assessment 2014 and each subsequent year of assessment, zero per cent of the deduction that would but for this subsection be authorised by that subsection.

(7) This section shall not apply to a loan made after 7 December 2010.][3]

Amendments

[1] Substituted by FA06 s9(a). Applies as respects a loan which is made after 7 December 2005.

[2] Inserted by FA06 s9(b).

[3] Inserted by FA11 s11.

Revenue Precedents

Whether interest on money advance to company allowable, where the company had been struck off the companies register? No; if the company was restored to the register, interest would be allowed for the periods during which it was struck off. IT932018

Whether cessation of the trade by the company would result in the relief being withdrawn? Not in itself, however unless trading was resumed within a reasonable period the individual would be unable to satisfy the requirements of subsection (2) (b) and relief would be withdrawn. CTF 203A1

Individuals borrowed money which was applied in acquiring an interest in a company. The company subsequently ceased to trade. Can the individuals still claim relief under S 248 TCA 1997? Relief is not due. The company no longer existed for the purposes set out in the section. Separately, at the time the interest was paid, the individuals did not have a material interest in the company or a connected company. IT 96 1560

Borrowings on a loan were used for 1) financing a qualifying home loan and 2) for a qualifying loan to a company. Subject to satisfying the necessary conditions, relief may be allowed on the interest paid under the relevant sections of the act, based on the appropriate percentage of the loan. IT 92 2021

Cross References

From Section 248

Section 249 Rules relating to recovery of capital and replacement loans.

To Section 248

Section 247 Relief to companies on loans applied in acquiring interest in other companies.

Section 248A Restriction of relief in respect of loans applied in acquiring interest in companies and partnerships.

Section 249 Rules relating to recovery of capital and replacement loans.

Section 250 Extension of relief under section 248 to certain individuals in relation to loans applied in acquiring interest in certain companies.

Section 250A Restriction of relief to individuals in respect of loans applied in acquiring interest in companies.

Section 251 Restriction of relief to individuals on loans applied in acquiring shares in companies where a claim for "BES relief" or "film relief" is made in respect of amount subscribed for shares.

Section 252 Restriction of relief to individuals on loans applied in acquiring interest in companies which become quoted companies.

Schedule 25B List of Specified Reliefs and Method of Determining Amount of Specified Relief Used in a Tax Year

248A Restriction of relief in respect of loans applied in acquiring interest in companies and partnerships

[(1) In this section—

"*chargeable period*" has the same meaning as in *section 321(2)*;

"*premises*" and "*rented residential premises*" have the same meanings, respectively, as in *section 96*.

(2) Where—

(a) a loan, being a loan to which *section 247*, *248* or *253* applies, is applied on or after the 7th day of May, 1998, to defray money for any of the purposes specified in those sections, and

(b) the money so defrayed is used, in whole or in part, directly or indirectly—

(i) in the purchase, improvement or repair of a premises, or

(ii) in paying off a loan used in the purchase, improvement or repair of a premises,

then, the relief to be given for a chargeable period under those sections in respect of that loan shall, for any chargeable period in which the premises is at any time a rented residential premises, be reduced by the interest attributable to so much of the money used for the purposes specified in *subparagraphs (i)* and *(ii)* of *paragraph (b)*.

[(3) This section shall not apply or have effect in relation to interest referred to in *subsection (2)* which accrues on or after 1 January 2002 and, for the purposes of this subsection, such interest shall be treated as accruing from day to day.][1]

[(4) Notwithstanding subsection (3), subsection (2) shall apply in relation to interest referred to in subsection (2) where the purpose of the loan is the purchase of a residential premises from the [spouse or civil partner][2] of the individual to whom relief is given under *section 248* or *253*.

[(5) The reference to 'spouse or civil partner' in *subsection (4)* does not include—

(a) a spouse to a marriage—

(i) in which the spouses are separated under an order of a court of competent jurisdiction or by deed of separation, or

(ii) that has been dissolved under either—

(I) section 5 of the Family Law (Divorce) Act 1996, or

(II) the law of a country or jurisdiction other than the State, being a divorce that is entitled to be recognised as valid in the State,

or

[(b) a civil partner in a civil partnership—

(i) in which the civil partners are separated by a deed of separation, agreement, arrangement or any other act giving rise to a legally enforceable obligation and made or done in consideration or in consequence of living separately in the circumstances referred to in *section 1031A(2)*, or

(ii) that has been dissolved under *section 110* of the Civil Partnership and Certain Rights and Obligations of Cohabitants Act 2010 or deemed to have been so dissolved under *section 5(4)* of that Act.][3]][4]][5]][6]

Amendments

[1] Inserted by FA02 s17(b).

[2] Substituted by F(No.3)A11 sched1(41). Shall have effect from 27 July 2011.

[3] Substituted by F(No.2)A13 sched(1)(d). Has effect as if they had come into operation for the year of assessment (within the meaning of section 2) 2011 and each subsequent year of assessment.

[4] Substituted by F(No.3)A11 sched1(42). Shall have effect from 27 July 2011.

[5] Inserted by FA03 s16(1)(b). Applies and has effect in relation to interest referred to in sections 97(2G) and 248A(2) which accrues on or after 6 February 2003 and, for the purposes of this subsection, such interest shall be treated as accruing from day to day.

[6] Inserted by FA98No2 s2.

Cross References

From Section 248A

Section 96 Interpretation (Chapter 8).

Section 247 Relief to companies on loans applied in acquiring interest in other companies.

Section 248 Relief to individuals on loans applied in acquiring interest in companies.

Section 253 Relief to individuals on loans applied in acquiring interest in partnerships.

Section 321 Provisions of general application in relation to the making of allowances and charges.

249 Rules relating to recovery of capital and replacement loans

[FA74 s35(1) to (3)]

[(1) (a) (i) In this section—

"*specified loan*", in relation to a company, means—

(I) any loan or advance made to the company before 6 February 2003 (other than a loan referred to in *paragraph (II)*), or

(II) any loan or advance in respect of which any interest paid is, or if charged would be, deductible if the company were within the charge to Irish tax—

(A) in computing the company's profits or gains for the purposes of Case I of Schedule D, or

(B) in computing the company's profits or gains for the purposes of Case V of Schedule D;

"*relevant period*", in relation to a loan to which *section 247* applies, means the period beginning 2 years before the date of application of the proceeds of the loan and ending on the date of application of the proceeds of the loan.

(ii) Where at any time in the relevant period in relation to a loan to which *section 247* applies the investing company recovered any amount of capital from the company concerned, other than a repayment in respect of a specified loan, the investing company shall immediately after the application of the loan to which *section 247* applies be treated for the purposes of this section as if the investing company had repaid out of the loan an amount equal to the amount of capital recovered and so that out of the interest otherwise eligible for relief and payable for any period after that time there shall be deducted an amount equal to interest on the amount of capital so recovered, but this subparagraph shall not apply to so much of the capital so recovered as was applied by the investing company—

(I) before the application of the loan to which *section 247* applies, in repayment of any other loan to which *section 247* applies, or

(II) in accordance with *paragraph (a)* or *(b)* of *section 247(2)*;

and, for the purposes of this section, the investing company shall not be treated as having repaid so much of an amount out of a loan as does not exceed the amount, if any, of capital so recovered which has been previously treated under this section as being in repayment of a loan.

(iii) Where at any time after the application of the proceeds of the loan to which *section 247* applies the investing company—

(I) has recovered any amount of capital from the company concerned or from a connected company, or

(II) is deemed, under *subsection (2)(aa)*, to have recovered any amount of capital from the company concerned,

without using the amount recovered or an amount equal to the amount deemed to have been recovered in repayment of the loan, the investing company shall be treated for the purposes of this section as if the investing company had at that time repaid out of the loan an amount equal to the amount of capital recovered or deemed to have been recovered and so that out of the interest otherwise eligible for relief and payable for any period after that time there shall be deducted an amount equal to interest on the amount of capital so recovered or so deemed to have been recovered.

(iv) Where, after the application of the proceeds of a loan to which *section 248* applies, the individual has recovered any amount of capital from the company concerned or from a connected company without using that amount in repayment of the loan, the individual shall be treated for the purposes of this section as if the individual had repaid that amount out of the loan and so that out of the interest otherwise eligible for relief and payable for any period after that time there shall be deducted an amount equal to interest on the amount of capital so recovered.][1]

(b) Where part only of a loan referred to in *paragraph (a)* fulfils the conditions in *section 247* or *248* so as to afford relief for interest on that part, the deduction to be made under this subsection shall be made wholly out of interest on that part.

[(2) (a) The investing company or the individual, as the case may be (in this paragraph referred to as the "*borrower*") shall be treated as having recovered an amount of capital from the company concerned or from a connected company if—

(i) the borrower receives consideration of that amount or value for the sale of any part of the ordinary share capital of the company concerned or of a connected company or any consideration of that amount or value by means of repayment of any part of that ordinary share capital,

(ii) the company concerned or a connected company repays that amount of a loan or advance from the borrower,

(iii) the borrower receives consideration of that amount or value for assigning any debt due to the borrower from the company concerned or from a connected company.

(aa) (i) Where the company concerned is a company to which *section 247(2)(a)(ii)* applies, the investing company shall be deemed to have recovered from the company concerned an amount equal to so much of any capital recovered by the company concerned from another company, being a company more than 50 per cent of the ordinary share capital of which was directly owned by the company concerned, as is not applied by the company concerned—

(I) in repayment of any loan or part of a loan made to it by the investing company,

(II) in redemption, repayment or purchase of any of its ordinary share capital acquired by the investing company,

(III) in accordance with *paragraph (a)* or *(b)* of *section 247(2)*, or

(IV) in repayment of a loan to which *section 247* applies.

(ii) The company concerned shall be treated as having recovered an amount of capital from another company if—

(I) the company concerned receives consideration of that amount or value for the sale of any part of the ordinary share capital of the other company or any consideration of that amount or value by means of repayment of any part of that ordinary share capital,

(II) the other company repays that amount of a loan or advance from the company concerned, other than a repayment in respect of a specified loan,

(III) the company concerned receives consideration of that amount or value for assigning any debt due to the company concerned from the other company.

(iii) Where *subparagraph (i)* applies and more than one investing company has either—

(I) made a loan to the company concerned, or

(II) acquired any part of its share capital,

the amount deemed to have been recovered under that subparagraph shall be apportioned between the investing companies in proportion to the aggregate amount of any loan made and any money applied in acquiring that share capital by each company, but if the companies concerned agree between them to such other apportionment of the amount as they may consider appropriate and jointly specify in writing to the inspector, then the amount deemed to have been so recovered shall be apportioned accordingly.][2]

[(ab) (i) Where—

(I) a company (in this paragraph referred to as the "*first-mentioned company*") issues shares to the company concerned in exchange for shares (in this paragraph referred to as the "*original shares*") in another company,

(II) *section 584* is applied or, but for *section 626B*, would be applied to the exchange by *section 586*, and

(III) the investing company, in the absence of an election under this subsection, would be deemed by *paragraph (aa)* to have, by virtue of the exchange, recovered an amount of capital from the company concerned,

then the investing company may elect that *paragraph (aa)* shall not so apply.

(ii) Where the investing company makes an election in accordance with *subparagraph (i)*, then the first-mentioned company shall be treated for the purposes of *paragraph (aa)* as if it were the company concerned if the effect of so treating it is that the investing company is deemed by *paragraph (aa)(i)* to have recovered an amount of capital equal to the amount of capital treated by *paragraph (aa)(ii)(I)* as recovered in respect of the original shares by that company.

(iii) An election under this paragraph shall be included by the investing company with the return required under [*Chapter 3* of *Part 41A*][3] for the accounting period in which the original shares are exchanged.][4]

(b) In the case of a sale or assignment otherwise than by means of a bargain made at arm's length, the sale or assignment shall be deemed to be for consideration of an amount equal to the market value of what is disposed of.

(3) *Sections 247(3)* and *248(2)* and *subsections (1)* and *(2)* shall apply to a loan referred to in *section 247(2)(c)* or *248(1)(c)* as if such loan and any loan it replaces were one loan, and as if—

(a) references in *sections 247(3)* and *248(2)* and in *subsection (1)* to the application of the proceeds of the loan were references to the application of the proceeds of the original loan, and

(b) any restriction under *subsection (1)* which applied to any loan which has been replaced applied also to the loan which replaces that loan.

Amendments

[1] Substituted by FA03 s46(1)(a). This section applies as respects any recovery of capital or deemed recovery of capital effected on or after 6 February 2003.

[2] Substituted by FA03 s46(1)(b). This section applies as respects any recovery of capital or deemed recovery of capital effected on or after 6 February 2003.

[3] Substituted by FA12 sched4(part 2)(g).

[4] Inserted by FA11 s37(1)(i). Shall apply in respect of a loan made on or after 21 January 2011 other than any such loan made in accordance with a binding written agreement made before that date.

Cross References

From Section 249

Section 247 Relief to companies on loans applied in acquiring interest in other companies.
Section 248 Relief to individuals on loans applied in acquiring interest in companies.
Section 584 Reorganisation or reduction of share capital.
Section 586 Company amalgamations by exchange of shares.
Section 626B Exemption from tax in the case of gains on disposals of shares.
Section 951 Obligation to make a return.

To Section 249

Section 243 Allowance of charges on income.
Section 247 Relief to companies on loans applied in acquiring interest in other companies.
Section 248 Relief to individuals on loans applied in acquiring interest in companies.

250 Extension of relief under section 248 to certain individuals in relation to loans applied in acquiring interest in certain companies

[FA78 s8; FA79 s9; FA96 s131(9)(a)]

(1) In this section—

"*90 per cent subsidiary*" has the meaning assigned to it by *section 9*;

"*full-time employee*" and "*full-time director*", in relation to a company, mean an employee or director, as the case may be, who is required to devote substantially the whole of his or her time to the service of the company;

"*holding company*" has the same meaning as in *section 411*;

"*part-time employee*" and "*part-time director*", in relation to a company, mean an employee or director, as the case may be, who is not required to devote substantially the whole of his or her time to the service of the company;

"*private company*" has the meaning assigned to it by section 33 of the Companies Act, 1963.

(2) Notwithstanding that an individual does not satisfy one or both of the conditions set out in *paragraphs (a)* and *(b)* of *section 248(2)*, the individual shall be entitled to relief under *section 248* for any interest paid on any loan to him or her applied for a purpose specified in *section 248(1)* if—

(a) the company part of whose ordinary share capital is acquired or, as the case may be, to which the money is loaned is—

(i) both a company referred to in *paragraph (a)(i)* of *section 248(1)* and a company in relation to which the individual was a full-time employee, part-time employee, full-time director or part-time director during the period taken as a whole from the application of the proceeds of the loan until the interest was paid, or

(ii) both a company referred to in *paragraph (a)(ii)* of *section 248(1)* and a private company in relation to which, or in relation to any company which would be regarded as connected with it for the purposes of *section 248*, the individual was during that period a full-time director or a full-time employee,

and

(b) the company or any person connected with the company has not, during the period specified in *paragraph (a)(i)*, made any loans or advanced any money to the individual or a person connected with the individual other than a loan made or money advanced in the ordinary course of a business which included the lending of money, being business carried on by the company or, as the case may be, by the person connected with the company.

(3) In relation to any payment or payments of interest on any loan or loans applied—

(a) in acquiring any part of the ordinary share capital of a company other than a private company,

(b) in lending money to such a company, or

(c) in paying off any other loan or loans applied for a purpose specified in *paragraphs (a)* and *(b)*,

no relief shall be given for any year of assessment by virtue of this section other than to a full-time employee or full-time director of the company and no such relief shall be given to such employee or director on the excess of that payment, or the aggregate amount of those payments, for that year of assessment over [€3,050][1].

(4) Where relief is given by virtue of this section to an individual and any loan made or money advanced to the individual or to a person connected with the individual is, in accordance with *paragraph (c)* of *subsection (5)* and by virtue of *subparagraph (ii)*, *(iii)*, *(iv)* or *(v)* of that paragraph, subsequently regarded as not having been made or advanced in the ordinary course of a business, any relief so given, which would not have been given if, at the time the relief was given, the loan or money advanced had been so regarded, shall be withdrawn [and assessments shall, as necessary, be made or amended][2] to give effect to this subsection.

(5) For the purposes of this section—

(a) any question whether a person is connected with another person shall be determined in accordance with *section 10* (as it applies for the purposes of the Tax Acts) and *paragraph (b)*,

(b) a person shall be connected with any other person to whom such person has, otherwise than in the ordinary course of a business carried on by such person which includes the lending of money, made any loans or advanced any money, and with any person to whom that other person has so made any loan or advanced any money and so on,

(c) a loan shall not be regarded as having been made, or money shall not be regarded as having been advanced, in the ordinary course of a business if—

(i) the loan is made or the money is advanced on terms which are not reasonably comparable with the terms which would have been applied in respect of that loan or the advance of that money on the basis that the negotiations for the loan or the advance of the money had been at arm's length,

(ii) at the time the loan was made or the money was advanced the terms were such that *subparagraph (i)* did not apply, those terms are subsequently altered and the terms as so altered are such that if they had applied at the time the loan was made or the money was advanced *subparagraph (i)* would have applied,

(iii) any interest payable on the loan or on the money advanced is waived,

(iv) any interest payable on the loan or on the money advanced is not paid within 12 months from the date on which it became payable, or

(v) the loan or the money advanced or any part of the loan or money advanced is not repaid within 12 months of the date on which it becomes repayable,

(d) the cases in which any person is to be regarded as making a loan to any other person include a case where—

(i) that other person incurs a debt to that person, or

(ii) a debt due from that other person to a third party is assigned to that person;

but *subparagraph (i)* shall not apply to a debt incurred for the supply by that person of goods or services in the ordinary course of that person's trade or business unless the period for which credit is given exceeds 6 months or is longer than normally given by that person,

(e) a company other than a private company shall be deemed to be a company referred to in *section 248(1)(a)(i)* if it is a holding company and is resident in the State, and

(f) an individual shall be deemed to be a full-time employee or full-time director of a company referred to in *paragraph (e)* if the individual is a full-time employee or full-time director of any company which is a 90 per cent subsidiary of that company.

Amendments

[1] Substituted by FA01 sched5.

[2] Substituted by FA12 sched4(part 2)(g).

Revenue Precedents

Whether relief is allowed where a holding company is also a trading company (subsections 5 (e) & (f))? Relief is allowed. 10407/5224/88

Can employees of a subsidiary company claim relief on loans acquired to buy shares in the holding Co.? Employees of a Co., which is a 100% subsidiary of a second Co., which in turn is a subsidiary of a third Co., can claim relief. 10407/5699/90

Would a registered Industrial & Provident Society be regarded as a private co. for relief under section 250? Such a society would not be regarded as a private company for the purposes of granting interest relief under section 250. 6835/86

Cross References

From Section 250

Section 9 Subsidiaries.
Section 10 Connected persons.
Section 248 Relief to individuals on loans applied in acquiring interest in companies.
Section 411 Surrender of relief between members of groups and consortia.

To Section 250

Section 122 Preferential loan arrangements.
Section 250A Restriction of relief to individuals in respect of loans applied in acquiring interest in companies.
Section 251 Restriction of relief to individuals on loans applied in acquiring shares in companies where a claim for "BES relief" or "film relief" is made in respect of amount subscribed for shares.
Section 252 Restriction of relief to individuals on loans applied in acquiring interest in companies which become quoted companies.
Section 488 Interpretation (Part 16).
Section 591 Relief for individuals on certain reinvestment.
Schedule 12A Approved Savings-Related Share Option Schemes
Schedule 25B List of Specified Reliefs and Method of Determining Amount of Specified Relief Used in a Tax Year

250A Restriction of relief to individuals in respect of loans applied in acquiring interest in companies

[(1) In this section—

"*distribution*" has the same meaning as it has for the purposes of the Corporation Tax Acts by virtue of *section 4*;

"*eligible loan*" in relation to an individual and a company, means a loan, being a loan to which *section 248* applies, to the individual to defray money applied for any of the purposes specified in that section;

"*relevant interest*" has the same meaning as in *section 269*;

"*residue of expenditure*" shall be construed in accordance with *section 277*;

"*specified amount*" in relation to an eligible loan, means the amount of the eligible loan or so much of the eligible loan where the money or, as the case may be, part of the money which was defrayed by that loan and which was applied by the individual—

(a) is used after 1 January 2003 by the company directly or indirectly—

(i) in the acquisition (whether by the company or by any other person) of the relevant interest in relation to any capital expenditure incurred or deemed to be incurred on the construction or refurbishment of a specified building,

(ii) in replacing money used in such acquisition of such an interest, or

(iii) in paying off a loan used in such acquisition of such an interest,

(b) pays off another eligible loan or so much of another eligible loan where the money or, as the case may be, part of the money which was defrayed by that other loan (or any previous loan or loans which it replaced) and which was applied by the individual was used after 1 January 2003 by the company directly or indirectly for any of the purposes referred to in *paragraph (a)*, or

(c) was applied in acquiring, on or after 20 February 2004, any part of the ordinary share capital of a company at least 75 per cent of whose income consists of profits or gains chargeable under Case V of Schedule D in respect of one or more specified buildings;

"*specified building*" means a building or structure, or a part of a building or structure—

(a) (i) which is or is to be an industrial *building or structure by reason of its use or deemed use for a purpose specified in section 268(1)* and in relation to which an allowance has been, or is to be, made to a company under *Part 9*, or

(ii) in relation to which an allowance has been, or is to be, so made to a company by virtue of *Part 10* or *section 843* or 843A,

in respect of—

(I) the capital expenditure incurred or deemed to be incurred on the construction or refurbishment of the building or structure or, as the case may be, the part of the building or structure, or

(II) the residue of that expenditure,

(b) in relation to which at any time beginning on or after 1 January 2003 the company referred to in *paragraph (a)* is entitled to the relevant interest in relation to the capital expenditure referred to in that paragraph, and

(c) in relation to which any other company (not being the company referred to in paragraph (a)) is entitled, at any time subsequent to the time referred to in paragraph (b), to an allowance under Part 9, in respect of the capital expenditure referred to in *paragraph (a)* or the residue of that expenditure, following the acquisition of the relevant interest or any part of the relevant interest in relation to that capital expenditure, whether or not, subsequent to the time referred to in *paragraph (b)*, any other person or persons had previously become entitled to that relevant interest or that part of that relevant interest;

"*specified provisions*" means *section 248* and that section as extended by *section 250*.

(2) Notwithstanding anything in the specified provisions, relief under *section 248* for any year of assessment in relation to any payment or payments of interest on the specified amount of an eligible loan by the individual concerned shall not exceed that individual's return from the company concerned in that year in relation to that specified amount.

(3) Subject to *subsection (4)*, an individual's return from a company in relation to a specified amount of an eligible loan in any year of assessment is—

(a) where the specified amount defrays an amount of money applied by the individual for the purpose specified in *section 248(1)(a)* or *(b)*, the amount, if any, of the distributions (before deduction of any dividend withholding tax under Chapter 8A of *Part 6*), or, as the case may be, the amount, if any, of the interest, received by the individual from the company in that year as a result of the application by the individual of that amount of money, or

(b) where the specified amount defrays an amount of money applied by the individual, directly or indirectly, in paying off the specified amount of another eligible loan where the earlier specified amount defrayed an amount of money (subsequently referred to in this paragraph as "*that earlier amount of money*") which was applied by the individual for the purpose specified in *section 248(1)(a)* or *(b)*, the amount, if any, of the distributions (before deduction of any dividend withholding tax under Chapter 8A of *Part 6*), or, as the case may be, the amount, if any, of the interest, received by the individual from the company in that year as a result of the application by the individual of that earlier amount of money.

(4) In determining for the purposes of this section—

(a) the amount of any payment or payments of interest by an individual on the specified amount of an eligible loan, or

(b) the amount of interest received by an individual as a result of the application by the individual of an amount of money which was defrayed by the specified amount of an eligible loan,

such apportionment, where necessary, of the total payments of interest by the individual on the eligible loan, or, as the case may be, the total amount of interest received by the individual as a result of the application of all the money defrayed by the eligible loan, shall be made in the same proportion which the specified amount of the eligible loan bears to the amount of the eligible loan.][1]

Amendments

[1] Inserted by FA04 s22(1).

Revenue Briefings

Tax Briefing

Tax Briefing April 2004 – Issue 55 pg 5 – Finance Act 2004 – Loans Applied in Acquiring Interest in Companies

Cross References

From Section 250A

Section 4 Interpretation of Corporation Tax Acts.

Section 129 Irish resident company distributions not generally chargeable to corporation tax.

Section 248 Relief to individuals on loans applied in acquiring interest in companies.

Section 250 Extension of relief under section 248 to certain individuals in relation to loans applied in acquiring interest in certain companies.

Section 268 Meaning of "industrial building or structure".

Section 269 Meaning of "the relevant interest".

Section 277 Writing off of expenditure and meaning of "residue of expenditure".

Section 322 Interpretation (Chapter 1).

Section 843 Capital allowances for buildings used for third level educational purposes.

251 Restriction of relief to individuals on loans applied in acquiring shares in companies where a claim for "BES relief" or "film relief" is made in respect of amount subscribed for shares

[FA90 s11; FA93 s6]

Notwithstanding *sections 248* and *250*, relief shall not be given under either section in respect of any payment of interest on any loan applied in acquiring shares (being shares forming part of the ordinary share capital of a company) issued—

(a) on or after the 20th day of April, 1990, if a claim for relief under *Part 16* is made in respect of the amount subscribed for those shares, or

(b) on or after the 6th day of May, 1993, if a claim for relief under *section 481* is made in respect of the amount subscribed for those shares.

Cross References

From Section 251

Section 248 Relief to individuals on loans applied in acquiring interest in companies.

Section 250 Extension of relief under section 248 to certain individuals in relation to loans applied in acquiring interest in certain companies.

Section 481 Relief for investment in films.

Section 488 Interpretation (Part 16).

252 Restriction of relief to individuals on loans applied in acquiring interest in companies which become quoted companies

[FA92 s14(1), (2) and (3); FA97 s10]

(1) In this section—

"*loan*" means a loan applied for any of the purposes specified in the principal section;

"*the principal section*" means *section 248* as extended by *section 250*;

"*quoted company*" means a company whose shares or any class of whose shares—

(a) are listed in the official list of the Irish Stock Exchange or any other stock exchange, or

(b) are quoted on an unlisted securities market of any stock exchange;

"*the specified date*", in relation to a loan, means—

(a) (i) in a case where the loan was applied on or before the 5th day of April, 1989, the 6th day of April, 1992,

(ii) in a case where the loan was applied on or after the 6th day of April, 1989, but on or before the 5th day of April, 1990, the 6th day of April, 1993, and

(iii) in a case where the loan was applied on or after the 6th day of April, 1990, the 6th day of April, 1994,

or

(b) if later, [1 January][1] in the second year of assessment next after the year of assessment in which the company, part of whose ordinary share capital was acquired or, as the case may be, to which the money was loaned, becomes a quoted company.

(2) Subject to *subsection (3)*, if the company, part of whose ordinary share capital was acquired or, as the case may be, to which the money was loaned, is, at the specified date in relation to the loan, a quoted company, entitlement to relief under the principal section in respect of interest paid on a loan shall be determined subject to the following provisions:

(a) as respects the year of assessment commencing with the specified date, relief shall not be given in respect of the excess of the amount, or of the aggregate amount, of the interest over 70 per cent of the amount, or of the aggregate amount, of the interest in respect of which apart from this paragraph relief would otherwise have been given under the principal section;

(b) as respects the next year of assessment, relief shall not be given in respect of the excess of the amount, or of the aggregate amount, of the interest over 40 per cent of the amount, or of the aggregate amount, of the interest in respect of which apart from this paragraph relief would otherwise have been given under the principal section;

(c) as respects any subsequent year of assessment, no relief shall be given under the principal section.

(3) Notwithstanding anything in *subsection (2)* or the principal section, the principal section shall not apply in relation to any payment of interest on a loan applied on or after the 29th day of January, 1992, if, at the time the loan is applied, the company, part of whose ordinary share capital was or is acquired or, as the case may be, to which the money was or is loaned, is a quoted company.

Amendments

[1] Substituted by FA01 sched2(15). Applies as on and from 1 January 2002.

Cross References

From Section 252

Section 248 Relief to individuals on loans applied in acquiring interest in companies.

Section 250 Extension of relief under section 248 to certain individuals in relation to loans applied in acquiring interest in certain companies.

253 Relief to individuals on loans applied in acquiring interest in partnerships

[FA74 s36]

(1) This section shall apply to a loan to an individual to defray money applied—

(a) in purchasing a share in a partnership,

(b) in contributing money to a partnership by means of capital or a premium, or in advancing money to the partnership, where the money contributed or advanced is used wholly and exclusively for the purposes of the trade or profession carried on by the partnership, or

(c) in paying off another loan where relief could have been obtained under this section for interest on that other loan if it had not been paid off (on the assumption, if the loan was free of interest, that it carried interest).

(2) Relief shall be given in respect of any payment of interest by the individual on the loan if—

(a) throughout the period from the application of the proceeds of the loan until the interest was paid the individual has personally acted in the conduct of the trade or profession carried on by the partnership as a partner therein, and

(b) the individual shows that in that period he or she has not recovered any capital from the partnership, apart from any amount taken into account under *subsection (3)*.

(3) (a) Where at any time after the application of the proceeds of the loan the individual has recovered any amount of capital from the partnership without using that amount in repayment of the loan, the individual shall be treated for the purposes of this section as if he or she had at that time repaid that amount out of the loan, and accordingly there shall be deducted out of the interest otherwise eligible for relief and payable for any period after that time an amount equal to interest on the amount of capital so recovered.

(b) Where part only of a loan fulfils the conditions in this section so as to afford relief for interest on that part, the deduction to be made under this subsection shall be made wholly out of interest on that part.

(4) (a) The individual shall be treated as having recovered an amount of capital from the partnership if—

(i) the individual receives a consideration of that amount or value for the sale of any part of his or her interest in the partnership,

(ii) the partnership returns any amount of capital to the individual or repays any amount advanced by the individual, or

(iii) the individual receives a consideration of that amount or value for assigning any debt due to the individual from the partnership.

(b) In the case of a sale or assignment otherwise than by means of a bargain made at arm's length, the sale or assignment shall be deemed to be for consideration of an amount equal to the market value of what is disposed of.

(5) *Subsections (2)* to *(4)* shall apply to a loan referred to in *subsection (1)(c)* as if such loan and any loan it replaces were one loan, and as if—

(a) references in *subsections (2)* to *(4)* to the application of the proceeds of the loan were references to the application of the proceeds of the original loan, and

(b) any restriction under *subsection (3)* which applied to any loan which has been replaced applied also as respects the loan which replaces that loan.

(6) *Subsection (1)* shall not apply to a loan unless it is made in connection with the application of the money and either on the occasion of its application or within what is in the circumstances a reasonable time from the application of the money, and that subsection shall not apply to a loan the proceeds of which are applied for some other purpose before being applied as described in that subsection.

(7) Interest eligible for relief under this section shall be deducted from or set off against the income of the individual for the year of assessment in which the interest is paid and tax shall be discharged or repaid accordingly, and such interest shall not be eligible for relief under any provision of the Income Tax Acts apart from this section.

[(8) Notwithstanding *subsection (7)*, the deduction authorised by that subsection shall not exceed—

(a) as respects the year of assessment 2014, 75 per cent of the deduction that would but for this subsection be authorised by that subsection,

(b) as respects the year of assessment 2015, 50 per cent of the deduction that would but for this subsection be authorised by that subsection,

(c) as respects the year of assessment 2016, 25 per cent of the deduction that would but for this subsection be authorised by that subsection, and

(d) as respects the year of assessment 2017 and each subsequent year of assessment, zero per cent of the deduction that would but for this subsection be authorised by that subsection.

(9) This section shall not apply to a loan made after 15 October 2013.

(10) *Subsections (8)* and *(9)* shall not apply to a loan referred to in *subsection (1)* where the partnership is a farming partnership within the meaning of *section 598A*.

(11) *Subsection (9)* shall not apply to a loan made after 15 October 2013 which is applied in paying off another loan to an individual used to defray money applied under *paragraph (a), (b)* or *(c)* of *subsection (1)*, provided—

(a) the loan does not exceed the balance outstanding on the loan being paid off, and

(b) the term of the loan does not exceed the balance of the term of the loan being paid off.][1]

Amendment

[1] Inserted by F(No.2)A13 s3. Comes into operation on 1 January 2014.

Revenue Briefings

eBrief

eBrief No. 23/2014 – Relief to individuals on loans applied in acquiring interest in partnerships

Cross References

To Section 253

Section 248A Restriction of relief in respect of loans applied in acquiring interest in companies and partnerships.

Schedule 25B List of Specified Reliefs and Method of Determining Amount of Specified Relief Used in a Tax Year

254 Interest on borrowings to replace capital withdrawn in certain circumstances from a business

[FA74 s37]

Where a person borrows money to replace in whole or in part capital in any form formerly employed in any trade, profession or other business carried on by the person in respect of the profits or gains of which tax is charged under Schedule D, being capital which within the 5 years preceding the date of replacement was withdrawn from such use for use otherwise than in connection with a trade, profession or other business carried on by the person, interest on such borrowed money shall not be regarded as interest wholly and exclusively laid out or expended for the purposes of a trade, profession or other business.

255 Arrangements for payment of interest less tax or of fixed net amount

[FA74 s39]

(1) Any agreement made, whether orally or in writing, for the payment of interest "less tax", or using words to that effect, shall be construed, in relation to interest payable without deduction of tax, as if the words "less tax" or the equivalent words were not included.

(2) In relation to interest on which the recipient is chargeable to tax under Schedule D and which is payable without deduction of tax, any agreement, whether orally or in writing and however worded, for the payment of interest at such a rate (in this subsection referred to as "*the gross rate*") as shall, after deduction of tax at the standard rate of tax for the time being in force, be equal to a stated rate, shall be construed as if it were an agreement requiring the payment of interest at the gross rate.

Cross References

To Section 255

Section 1013 Limited partnerships.

CHAPTER 4

Interest Payments by Certain Deposit Takers

256 Interpretation (Chapter 4)

[FA 86 s31; FA91 s11; FA92 s22(1)(a); F(No.2)A92 s3(a); FA93 s15(1)(a); FA95 s11(1) and s167]

(1) In this Chapter—

"*amount on account of appropriate tax*" shall be construed in accordance with *section 258(4)*;

["*appropriate tax*", in relation to a payment of relevant interest, means a sum representing income tax on the amount of the payment at the rate of 41 per cent;][1]

"*building society*" means a building society within the meaning of the Building Societies Act, 1989, or a society established in accordance with the law of any other Member State of the European Communities which corresponds to that Act;

["*credit union*" means a society registered under the Credit Union Act, 1997, including a society deemed to be so registered under section 5(3) of that Act;][2]

["*deposit*" means a sum of money paid to a relevant deposit taker on terms under which it, or any part of it, may be repaid with or without interest and either on demand or at a time or in circumstances agreed by or on behalf of the person making the payment and the person to whom it is made, notwithstanding that the amount to be repaid may be to any extent linked to or determined by changes in a stock exchange index or any other financial index;][3]

"*foreign currency*" means a currency other than the currency of the State;

["*interest*" means any interest of money whether yearly or otherwise, including any amount, whether or not described as interest, paid in consideration of the making of a deposit, and, as respects—

(a) a deposit, where the amount to be repaid may be to any extent linked to or determined by changes in a stock exchange index or any other financial index, includes any amount which is or is to be repaid over and above the amount of the deposit,

(b) a building society, includes any dividend or other distribution in respect of shares in the society,

[…][4],][5]

["*long term account*" means an account opened by an individual with a relevant deposit taker on terms under which the individual has agreed that each relevant deposit held in the account is to be held in the account for a period of not less than 5 years;

"*medium term account*" means an account opened by an individual with a relevant deposit taker on terms under which the individual has agreed that each relevant deposit held in the account is to be held in the account for a period of not less than 3 years;][6]

"*pension scheme*" means an exempt approved scheme within the meaning of *section 774* or a retirement annuity contract or a trust scheme to which *section 784* or *785* applies;

['*Personal Retirement Savings Account*' has the same meaning as in *section 787A*;][7]

["*PRSA provider*" has the same meaning as in Part X of the Pensions Act 1990;][8]

"*relevant deposit*" means a deposit held by a relevant deposit taker, other than a deposit—

(a) which is made by, and the interest on which is beneficially owned by—

(i) a relevant deposit taker,

(ii) the National Treasury Management Agency,

[(iia) a Fund investment vehicle (within the meaning of *section 37* of the *National Treasury Management Agency (Amendment) Act 2014*) of which the Minister for Finance is the sole beneficial owner,][9]

(iii) the State acting through the National Treasury Management Agency,

[...][10]

[...][11]

[...][12]

[(iiid) the National Asset Management Agency,

(iiie) the State acting through the National Asset Management Agency,][13]

[(iiif) the Strategic Banking Corporation of Ireland or a subsidiary wholly owned by it or a subsidiary wholly owned by any such subsidiary,][14]

[(iv) the Central Bank of Ireland,

(v) The Investor Compensation Company Limited, or

(vi) Icarom plc,][15]

(b) which is a debt on a security issued by the relevant deposit taker and listed on a stock exchange,

(c) which, in the case of a relevant deposit taker resident in the State for the purposes of corporation tax, is held at a branch of the relevant deposit taker situated outside the State,

(d) which, in the case of a relevant deposit taker not resident in the State for the purposes of corporation tax, is held otherwise than at a branch of the relevant deposit taker situated in the State,

(e) which is a deposit denominated in a foreign currency made—

(i) by a person other than an individual before the 1st day of January, 1993, or

(ii) by an individual before the 1st day of June, 1991,

but, where on or after the 1st day of June, 1991, and before the 1st day of January, 1993, a deposit denominated in a foreign currency is made by an individual to a relevant deposit taker with whom the individual had a deposit denominated in the same foreign currency immediately before the 1st day of June, 1991, such a deposit shall not be regarded as a relevant deposit,

(f) (i) which is made on or after the 1st day of January, 1993, by, and the interest on which is beneficially owned by—

(I) a company which is or will be within the charge to corporation tax in respect of the interest, or

(II) a pension scheme,

and

[(ii) in respect of which the company or pension scheme which is the beneficial owner of the interest has provided the relevant deposit taker with that person's tax reference number (within the meaning of *section 885*) or where, in the case of a pension scheme, there is no such number, with the number assigned by the Revenue Commissioners to the employer to whom that pension scheme relates,][16]

(g) in respect of which—

(i) no person resident in the State is beneficially entitled to any interest, and

(ii) a declaration of the kind mentioned in *section 263* has been made to the relevant deposit taker, […][17]

(h) (i) the interest on which is exempt—

(I) from income tax under *Schedule D* by virtue of *section 207(1)(b)*, or

(II) from corporation tax by virtue of *section 207(1)(b)* as it applies for the purposes of corporation tax under *section 76(6)*,

and

[(ii) in respect of which the beneficial owner of the interest has provided the relevant deposit taker with the reference number assigned to that person by the Revenue Commissioners in recognition of that person's entitlement to exemption from tax under *section 207* and known as the [charity (CHY) number,][18]][19]

[(i) which is a deposit referred to in *subsection (1A)*, […][20]

(j) which is a deposit referred to in [*subsection (1B)*, or][21]][22]

[(k) which is made by a PRSA provider and which is held for the purposes of a Personal Retirement Savings Account, where the PRSA provider has provided the relevant deposit taker with the number assigned to that provider by the Revenue Commissioners;][23]

"*relevant deposit taker*" means any of the following persons—

(a) a person who is a holder of a licence granted under section 9 of the Central Bank Act, 1971, or a person who holds a licence or other similar authorisation under the law of any other Member State of the European Communities which corresponds to a licence granted under that section,

(b) a building society,

(c) a trustee savings bank within the meaning of the Trustee Savings Banks Acts, 1863 to 1989,

[(ca) a credit union,][24]

[(cb) a specified intermediary in relation only to a specified deposit,][25]

[…][26]

[…][27]

(g) the Post Office Savings Bank;

["*relevant interest*" means, subject to *section 261A*, interest paid in respect of a relevant deposit;][28]

"*return*" means a return under *section 258(2)*;

"*special savings account*" means an account opened [on or after 1 January 1993 and before 6 April 2001][29], in which a relevant deposit or relevant deposits made by an individual is or are held and in respect of which—

(a) the conditions in *section 264(1)* are satisfied, and

(b) a declaration of the kind mentioned in *section 264(2)* has been made to the relevant [deposit taker;][30]

["*special term account*" means—

(a) a medium term account, or

(b) a long term account,

being an account in which a relevant deposit or relevant deposits made by an individual is or are held and in respect of which—

(i) the conditions specified in *section 264A(1)* are satisfied, and

(ii) a declaration of the kind mentioned in *section 264A(2)* has been made to the relevant deposit [taker;][31]][32]

["*special term share account*" has the same meaning as in [*section 267A*;][33]][34]

["*specified deposit*" means a deposit of a class designated by the Minister for Finance for the purposes of this definition;

"*specified intermediary*" means a person appointed by the National Treasury Management Agency for the purposes only of taking specified deposits.][35]

[(1A) A deposit shall be a deposit to which this subsection refers as respects any year of assessment if—

(a) (i) at any time in that year of assessment the individual beneficially entitled to the interest or the individual's [spouse or civil partner][36] has attained the age of 65 years, and

(ii) the total income of the individual for that year of assessment does not exceed the specified amount (within the meaning of *section 188(2)*) applicable to that individual,

and

(b) a declaration of the kind mentioned in *section 263A* has been made to the relevant deposit taker.

(1B) A deposit shall be a deposit to which this subsection refers as respects any year of assessment if—

(a) (i) the individual beneficially entitled to any interest paid in respect of that deposit in that year of assessment, or the individual's [spouse or civil partner][37], is a relevant person (within the meaning of *section 267(1)(b)*) and the individual would, in accordance with *section 267(3)*, be entitled to repayment of the whole of any appropriate tax if it had been deducted from that interest, or

(ii) the person entitled to any interest paid in respect of that deposit in that year of assessment is a person who is exempt from income tax by virtue of *section 189A(2)* and that person would, in accordance with *section 267(2)*, be entitled to repayment of the whole of any appropriate tax if it had been deducted from that interest,

(b) a declaration of the kind mentioned in *section 263B* has been made to the Revenue Commissioners,

(c) a notification of the kind mentioned in *section 263C* has been issued by the Revenue Commissioners to the relevant deposit taker that the deposit is a deposit to which this subsection refers and that notification is not cancelled in accordance with *section 263C(2)*, and

(d) the individual beneficially entitled to the interest is not an individual referred to in *subsection (1A)*, other than an individual who is a relevant person within the meaning of *section 267(1)(b)*,

and where, by virtue of *section 263C(2)*, a deposit is not a deposit to which this subsection refers as respects any year of assessment, then the Revenue Commissioners shall notify the deposit taker accordingly and where at any time the Revenue Commissioners have so notified the deposit taker, the deposit shall not be a deposit to which this subsection applies from that time.][38]

(2) For the purposes of this Chapter—

(a) any amount credited as interest in respect of a relevant deposit shall be treated as a payment of interest, and references in this Chapter to relevant interest being paid shall be construed accordingly,

(b) any reference in this Chapter to the amount of a payment of relevant interest shall be construed as a reference to the amount which would be the amount of that payment if no appropriate tax were to be deducted from that payment, and

(c) a deposit shall be treated as held at a branch of a relevant deposit taker if it is recorded in its books as a liability of that branch.

[(3) As respects any specified deposits, the relevant deposit taker shall obtain the tax reference number (within the meaning of *section 885*) of the person making the deposit and the person making the deposit shall provide the tax reference number.][39]

Amendments

[1] Substituted by F(No.2)A13 s23(1)(a). Applies to interest or dividends (within the meaning of Part 8) paid on or after 1 January 2014.

[2] Inserted by FA01 s57(1)(a)(i)(II). With effect from 1 January 2002 per S.I. 596 of 2001.

[3] Substituted by FA01 s55(a)(ii). Applies as respects a deposit made on or after 6 April 2001.

[4, 26] Repealed by ACCBA01 s12. With effect from 28 February 2002 per S.I. 69 of 2002.

[5] Substituted by FA01 s55(a)(iii). Applies as respects a deposit made on or after 6 April 2001.

[6] Inserted by FA01 s57(1)(a)(i)(III). With effect from 1 January 2002 per S.I. 596 of 2001.

[7] Inserted by FA12 s36(1)(b). Applies to any payment or crediting of relevant interest (within the meaning of Chapter 4 of Part 8) made on or after 1 January 2012.

[8] Inserted by FA10 s37(1)(a). Applies as respects any payment or crediting of relevant interest (within the meaning of Chapter 4 of Part 8) made on or after 3 April 2010.

[9] Inserted by NTMA(A)A14 part4(7)(a).

[10] Deleted by NTMA(A)A14 part4(7)(b).

[11] Deleted by NTMA(A)A14 part4(7)(c).

[12] Deleted by NTMA(A)A14 part4(7)(d).

[13] Inserted by the National Asset Management Agency Act 2009 Sched 3 part 10.

[14] Inserted by SBCoIA14 part7(1)(d). Does not apply in circumstances where the Minister does not hold all of the shares in the SBCI.

[15] Substituted by FA99 s76(1)(b). Shall be deemed to have come into operation on the 10th day of September, 1998.

[16] Substituted by FA02 s20(1)(a)(i). Applies as respects deposits made on or after 25 March 2002

[17] Deleted by FA07 s34(1)(a)(i)(I). Applies on and from 2 April 2007

[18] Substituted by FA07 s34(1)(a)(i)(I). Applies on and from 2 April 2007

[19] Substituted by FA02 s20(1)(a)(ii). Applies as respects deposits made on or after 25 March 2002

[20] Deleted by FA10 s37(1)(b). Applies as respects any payment or crediting of relevant interest (within the meaning of Chapter 4 of Part 8) made on or after 3 April 2010.

[21] Substituted by FA10 s37(1)(c). Applies as respects any payment or crediting of relevant interest (within the meaning of Chapter 4 of Part 8) made on or after 3 April 2010.

[22] Inserted by FA07 s34(1)(a)(i)(II). Applies on and from 2 April 2007

[23] Substituted by FA12 s36(1)(c). Applies to any payment or crediting of relevant interest (within the meaning of Chapter 4 of Part 8) made on or after 1 January 2012.

[24] Inserted by FA01 s57(1)(a)(i)(IV). With effect from 1 January 2002 per S.I. 596 of 2001.

[25] Inserted by FA07 s34(1)(a)(ii). Applies on and from 2 April 2007

[27] Repealed by ICCBA00. With effect from 12 February 2001 per S.I. 46 of 2001.

[28] Substituted by FA01 s57(1)(a)(i)(V). With effect from 1 January 2002 per S.I. 596 of 2001.

[29] Substituted by FA01 s55(a)(iv).

[30] Substituted by FA01 s57(1)(a)(i)(VI). With effect from 1 January 2002 per S.I. 596 of 2001.

[31] Substituted by FA02 s21(a)(i).

[32] Inserted by FA01 s57(1)(a)(i)(VII). With effect from 1 January 2002 per S.I. 596 of 2001.

[33] Substituted by FA07 s34(1)(a)(iii). Applies on and from 2 April 2007

[34] Inserted by FA02 s21(a)(ii).

[35] Inserted by FA07 s34(1)(a)(iv). Applies on and from 2 April 2007

[36] Substituted by F(No.3)A11 sched1(43).

[37] Substituted by F(No.3)A11 sched1(44).

[38] Inserted by FA07 s34(1)(b). Applies on and from 2 April 2007

[39] Inserted by FA10 s37(1)(e). Applies as respects any payment or crediting of relevant interest (within the meaning of Chapter 4 of Part 8) made on or after 3 April 2010.

Revenue Briefings

Tax Briefing

Tax Briefing April 2001 – Issue 43 pg 18 – Taxation of Credit Unions Dividends and Interest
Tax Briefing August 2002 – Issue 49 pg 1 – Bogus Non-Resident Accounts
Tax Briefing January 2003 – Issue 51 pg 7 – Bogus Non-Resident Accounts – Non Co-operation
Tax Briefing July 2007 – Issue 66 – Simplifying Tax Relief – Accounts Exempt from DIRT
Tax Briefing September 2008 – Issue 69 – Voluntary Disclosure Initiative – Deposit Interest Reporting

eBrief

eBrief No. 25/2008 – Revenue announces voluntary disclosure deadline for undisclosed income or funds held in Irish bank, building society or other accounts

eBrief No. 71/09 – Extension of Voluntary Disclosure Initiative for Interest Reporting to include Credit Unions.

Revenue Information Notes

DE1 – DIRT-free Deposit Accounts for those aged 65 or over

DE2 – DIRT-free Deposit Accounts for Permanently Incapacitated Individuals and Special Trusts for Permanently Incapacitated Individuals

Revenue Precedents

Double Taxation Conventions over-ride the DIRT provisions which preclude repayment of DIRT except in certain circumstances. Where deposit held in trust for non-resident such that the non resident had an absolute interest in the deposit, the interest retains its character as relevant interest when paid to her by the trustee. IT92050

Whether deposit held in the name of the EU commission is a relevant deposit within the meaning of section 256 TCA 1997? Deposit is not a relevant deposit, in view of the EC accession treaty and the protocol on privileges and immunities of the European community. IT932012

Whether notification of change of residence necessary to make a deposit in relation to which a non-resident declaration was completed a relevant deposit? No; where the person who is beneficially entitled to the interest becomes ordinarily resident (now resident) in the State, the deposit automatically becomes a relevant deposit, although we might not seek to penalise a relevant deposit taker who continued to treat such a deposit as not a relevant deposit in good faith. IT922026

Statements of Practice

"Underlying Tax" on Funds Deposited in Bogus Non-Resident Accounts – SP GEN/1/01

Cross References

From Section 256

Section 76 Computation of income: application of income tax principles.
Section 188 Age exemption and associated marginal relief.
Section 189A Special trusts for permanently incapacitated individuals.
Section 207 Rents of properties belonging to hospitals and other charities.
Section 258 Returns and collection of appropriate tax.
Section 260 Provisions supplemental to sections 258 and 259.
Section 261A Taxation of interest on special term accounts.
Section 263 Declarations relating to deposits of non-residents.
Section 263A Declarations to a relevant deposit taker relating to deposits of certain persons.
Section 263B Declarations to the Revenue Commissioners relating to deposits of certain persons.
Section 263C Notifications by the Revenue Commissioners relating to deposits of certain persons.
Section 264 Conditions and declarations relating to special savings accounts.
Section 264A Conditions and declarations relating to special term accounts.
Section 267 Repayment of appropriate tax in certain cases.
Section 267A Interpretation (Chapter 5).
Section 774 Certain approved schemes: exemptions and reliefs.
Section 784 Retirement annuities: relief for premiums.
Section 785 Approval of contracts for dependants or for life assurance.
Section 885 Obligation to show tax reference number on receipts.

To Section 256

Section 15 Rate of charge.
Section 214 Local authorities, etc.
Section 227 Certain income arising to specified non-commercial state-sponsored bodies.
Section 243 Allowance of charges on income.
Section 246 Interest payments by companies and to non-residents.
Section 246A Interest in respect of wholesale debt instruments.
Section 261 Taxation of relevant interest, etc.
Section 261B Taxation of specified interest.
Section 263 Declarations relating to deposits of non-residents.
Section 263A Declarations to a relevant deposit taker relating to deposits of certain persons.
Section 263B Declarations to the Revenue Commissioners relating to deposits of certain persons.
Section 263C Notifications by the Revenue Commissioners relating to deposits of certain persons.
Section 264 Conditions and declarations relating to special savings accounts.
Section 264A Conditions and declarations relating to special term accounts.
Section 265 Deposits of companies and pensions schemes.
Section 265A Deposits of certain persons.
Section 266 Deposits of charities.
Section 267A Interpretation (Chapter 5).
Section 267B Election to open a special share account or a special term share account.
Section 267F Supplementary provisions (Chapter 5).
Section 267M Tax rate applicable to certain deposit interest received by individuals.
Section 267N Interpretation.
Section 267Q Treatment of deposit return.
Section 409E Income tax: ringfence on use of certain capital allowances on certain industrial buildings and other premises.
Section 485G Miscellaneous (Chapter 2A).

Section 519C Interest, etc. under certified contractual savings schemes.
Section 730BA Personal portfolio life policy.
Section 731 Chargeable gains accruing to unit trusts.
Section 737 Special investment schemes.
Section 738 Undertakings for collective investment.
Section 739C Charge to tax.
Section 739I Common contractual funds.
Section 784A Approved retirement fund.
Section 790B "Exemption of cross-border scheme.
Section 838 Special portfolio investment accounts.
Section 839 Limits to special investments.
Section 847A Donations to certain sports bodies.
Section 848A Donations to approved bodies.
Section 848B Interpretation.
Section 848E Payment of tax credit.
Section 891 Returns of interest paid or credited without deduction of tax.
Section 898B Interpretation (Chapter 3A).
Section 904A Power of inspection: returns and collection of appropriate tax.
Section 904B Report to Committee of Public Accounts: publication etc.
Section 906A Information to be furnished by financial institutions.
Section 1078 Revenue offences.
Schedule 12 Employee Share Ownership Trusts

257 Deduction of tax from relevant interest

[FA 86 s32]

(1) Where a relevant deposit taker makes a payment of relevant interest—

(a) the relevant deposit taker shall deduct out of the amount of the payment the appropriate tax in relation to the payment,

(b) the person to whom such payment is made shall allow such deduction on the receipt of the residue of the payment, and

(c) the relevant deposit taker shall be acquitted and discharged of so much money as is represented by the deduction as if that amount of money had actually been paid to the person.

(2) A relevant deposit taker shall treat every deposit made with it as a relevant deposit unless satisfied that such a deposit is not a relevant deposit; but, where a relevant deposit taker has satisfied itself that a deposit is not a relevant deposit, it shall be entitled to continue to so treat the deposit until such time as it is in possession of information which can reasonably be taken to indicate that the deposit is or may be a relevant deposit.

(3) Any payment of relevant interest which is within *subsection (1)* shall be treated as not being within *section 246*.

Cross References

From Section 257

Section 246 Interest payments by companies and to non-residents.

To Section 257

Section 258 Returns and collection of appropriate tax.
Section 260 Provisions supplemental to sections 258 and 259.
Section 261A Taxation of interest on special term accounts.
Section 267C Taxation of dividends on special term share accounts.
Section 267I Exemptions from tax and withholding tax.
Section 519C Interest, etc. under certified contractual savings schemes.
Section 838 Special portfolio investment accounts.
Section 904A Power of inspection: returns and collection of appropriate tax.

Section 1078 Revenue offences.
Schedule 29 Provisions Referred to in Sections 1052, 1053 and 1054

258 Returns and collection of appropriate tax

[FA 86 s33(1) to (9)(d) and (10); FA97 s146(2) and Sch9 PtII]

(1) Notwithstanding any other provision of the Tax Acts, this section shall apply for the purpose of regulating the time and manner in which appropriate tax in relation to a payment of relevant interest shall be accounted for and paid.

(2) Subject to *subsection (5)*, a relevant deposit taker shall make for each year of assessment, within 15 days from the end of the year of assessment, a return to the Collector-General of the relevant interest paid by it in that year and of the appropriate tax in relation to the payment of that interest.

(3) The appropriate tax in relation to a payment of relevant interest which is required to be included in a return shall be due at the time by which the return is to be made and shall be paid by the relevant deposit taker to the Collector-General, and the appropriate tax so due shall be payable by the relevant deposit taker without the making of an assessment; but appropriate tax which has become so due may be assessed on the relevant deposit taker (whether or not it has been paid when the assessment is made) if that tax or any part of it is not paid on or before the due date.

(4)

[(a) Notwithstanding *subsection (3)*, a relevant deposit taker shall for each year of assessment pay an amount of appropriate tax to the Collector-General within 21 days of each of the following dates in that year of assessment—

(i) 31 March,

(ii) 30 June, and

(iii) 30 September.

(b) The amount to be paid—

(i) within 21 days of 31 March as referred to in *paragraph (a)(i)* shall not be less than the amount of appropriate tax which would be due and payable by the relevant deposit taker for the year of assessment concerned under *subsection (3)* if the total amount of the relevant interest which had accrued in the period commencing on 1 January and ending on 31 March,

(ii) within 21 days of 30 June as referred to in *paragraph (a)(ii)* shall not be less than the amount of appropriate tax which would be due and payable by the relevant deposit taker for the year of assessment concerned under *subsection (3)* if the total amount of the relevant interest which had accrued in the period commencing on 1 April and ending on 30 June, and

(iii) within 21 days of 30 September as referred to in *paragraph (a)(iii)* shall not be less than the amount of appropriate tax which would be due and payable by the relevant deposit taker for the year of assessment concerned under *subsection (3)* if the total amount of the relevant interest which had accrued in the period commencing on 1 July and ending on 30 September,

in that year of assessment on all relevant deposits held by the relevant deposit taker in that period (and no more) had been paid by it in that year of assessment.][1]

(c) Any amount on account of appropriate tax so paid by the relevant deposit taker for any year of assessment shall be treated as far as may be as a payment on account of any appropriate tax due and payable by it for that year of assessment under *subsection (3)*.

(d) For the purposes of *paragraph (b)*, interest shall be treated as accruing from day to day if not otherwise so treated.

(e) Where the amount on account of appropriate tax paid by a relevant deposit taker for any year of assessment under this subsection exceeds the amount of appropriate tax due and payable by it for that year of assessment under *subsection (3)*, the excess shall be carried forward and shall be set off against any amount due and payable under this subsection or *subsection (3)* by the relevant deposit taker for any subsequent year of assessment (any such set-off being effected as far as may be against an amount so due and payable at an earlier date rather than at a later date).

[(4A) For the purposes of this section and subject to *subsection (4B)*, interest payable by a relevant deposit taker in respect of a relevant deposit, other than interest which cannot be determined until the date of payment of such interest, notwithstanding that the terms under which the deposit was made are complied with fully, shall be deemed—

(a) to accrue from day to day, and

(b) to be relevant interest paid by the relevant deposit taker on 31 December in each year of assessment to the extent that—

(i) it is deemed to accrue in that year of assessment, and

(ii) it is not paid in that year of assessment,

and the relevant deposit taker shall account for appropriate tax accordingly.

(4B) (a) Where, apart from *subsection (4A)*, a relevant deposit taker makes a payment of relevant interest which is or includes interest (in *paragraph (b)* referred to as "*accrued interest*") which, by virtue of that subsection, is deemed to have been paid by the relevant deposit taker on 31 December in a year of assessment, the relevant deposit taker shall—

(i) deduct out of the whole of the amount of that payment the appropriate tax in relation to that payment in accordance with *section 257*, and

(ii) account for that appropriate tax under this section,

and that appropriate tax shall be due and payable by the relevant deposit taker in accordance with this section.

(b) So much of the appropriate tax paid by the relevant deposit taker by virtue of *subsection (4A)* as is referable to accrued interest included in a payment of relevant interest referred to in *paragraph (a)* shall be set off against any amount of appropriate tax due and payable by the relevant deposit taker for the year of assessment in which that payment of interest is made or against any amount, or amount on account of, appropriate tax due and payable by it for a year of assessment subsequent to that year (any such set-off being effected as far as may be against an amount so due and payable at an earlier date rather than a later date).][2]

(5) (a) Any amount on account of appropriate tax payable by a relevant deposit taker under *subsection (4)* shall be so payable without the making of an assessment.

(b) The provisions of this Chapter relating to the collection and recovery of appropriate tax shall, with any necessary modifications, apply to the collection and recovery of any amount on account of appropriate tax.

(c) A return required to be made by a relevant deposit taker for any year of assessment shall contain a statement of the amount of interest in respect of which an amount on account of appropriate tax is due and payable by the relevant deposit taker for that year of assessment and of the amount on account of appropriate tax so due and payable, and a return shall be so required to be made by a relevant deposit taker for a year of assessment notwithstanding that no relevant interest was paid by it in the year of assessment.

(6) Where it appears to the inspector that there is any amount of appropriate tax in relation to a payment of relevant interest which ought to have been but has not been included in a return, or where the inspector is dissatisfied with any return, the inspector may make an assessment on the relevant deposit taker to the best of his or her judgment, and any amount of appropriate tax in relation to a payment of relevant interest due under an assessment made by virtue of this subsection shall be treated for the purposes of interest on unpaid tax as having been payable at the time when it would have been payable if a correct return had been made.

(7) Where any item has been incorrectly included in a return as a payment of relevant interest, the inspector may make such assessments, adjustments or set-offs as may in his or her judgment be required for securing that the resulting liabilities to tax, including interest on unpaid tax, whether of the relevant deposit taker or any other person, are in so far as possible the same as they would have been if the item had not been so included.

(8) (a) Any appropriate tax assessed on a relevant deposit taker under this Chapter shall be due within one month after the issue of the notice of assessment (unless that tax or any amount treated as an amount on account of that tax is due earlier under *subsection (3)* or *(4)*) subject to any appeal against the assessment, but no such appeal shall affect the date when any amount is due under *subsection (3)* or *(4)*.

(b) On the determination of an appeal against an assessment under this Chapter, any appropriate tax overpaid shall be repaid.

(9) (a) The provisions of the Income Tax Acts relating to—

(i) assessments to income tax,

(ii) appeals against such assessments (including the rehearing of appeals and the statement of a case for the opinion of the High Court), and

(iii) the collection and recovery of income tax,

shall, in so far as they are applicable, apply to the assessment, collection and recovery of appropriate tax.

[(b) Any amount of appropriate tax or amount on account of appropriate tax payable in accordance with this Chapter without the making of an assessment shall carry interest from the date when the amount becomes due and payable until payment—

(i) for any day or part of a day before 1 July 2009 during which the amount remains unpaid, at a rate of 0.0322 per cent, and

(ii) for any day or part of a day on or after 1 July 2009 during which the amount remains unpaid, at a rate of 0.0274 per cent.][3]

(c) [*Subsections (3)* to *(5)* of *section 1080*][4] shall apply in relation to interest payable under *paragraph (b)* as they apply in relation to interest payable under *section 1080*.

(d) In its application to any appropriate tax charged by any assessment made in accordance with this Chapter, *section 1080* shall apply as if [*subsection (2) (b)*][5] of that section were deleted.

(10) Every return shall be in a form prescribed by the Revenue Commissioners and shall include a declaration to the effect that the return is correct and complete.

Amendments

[1] Substituted by FA10 s37(1)(f). With effect from 1 January 2011 per S.I. No. 115 of 2011.

[2] Inserted by FA01 sched2(16)(b). Applies as respects the year of assessment 2001 and subsequent years of assessment.

[3] Substituted by FA09 s29(1)(c). Applies as respects any unpaid tax or duty, as the case may be, that has not been paid before 1 July 2009 regardless of whether that tax or duty became due and payable before, on or after that date.

[4, 5] Substituted by FA05 sched5.

Revenue Briefings

eBrief

eBrief No. 14/2011 – Deposit Interest Retention Tax (DIRT) – Commencement Orders and New Pay & File Arrangements

Revenue Precedents

A nil deposit is not a relevant deposit for the purposes of section 257. IT913562

Where a parent gives money to a child to open a deposit account and enters into a verbal agreement that the child is to pay over to the parent the deposit interest arising on the deposit, who is beneficially entitled to the deposit interest? The parent is beneficially entitled to the deposit interest. IT952568

Cross References

From Section 258

Section 257 Deduction of tax from relevant interest.

Section 1080 Interest on overdue income tax, corporation tax and capital gains tax.

To Section 258

Section 256 Interpretation (Chapter 4).

Section 259 Alternative amount on account of appropriate tax.

Section 260 Provisions supplemental to sections 258 and 259.

Section 267F Supplementary provisions (Chapter 5).

Section 838 Special portfolio investment accounts.

Section 1078 Revenue offences.

259 Alternative amount on account of appropriate tax

[FA87 s7(1)(a) and (b), (2), (3) and (4)]

(1) For the purposes of this section—

(a) interest shall be treated, if not otherwise so treated, as accruing from day to day, and

(b) references to "*general crediting date*", as respects a relevant deposit taker, shall be construed as references to a date on which the relevant deposit taker credits to all, or to the majority, of relevant deposits held by it on that date interest accrued due on those deposits (whether or not the interest is added to the balances on the relevant deposits on that date for the purpose of calculating interest due at some future date).

(2) Where for any year of assessment the amount of appropriate tax due and payable by a relevant deposit taker for that year under *section 258* is less than the amount of appropriate tax which would have been so due and payable by the relevant deposit taker for that year if the total amount of the interest which had accrued, in the period of [12 months][1] ending on—

(a) the general crediting date as respects that relevant deposit taker falling in that year of assessment,

(b) if there is more than one general crediting date as respects that relevant deposit taker falling in that year of assessment, the last such date, or

(c) if there is no general crediting date as respects that relevant deposit taker falling in that year of assessment, [31 December][2] in that year,

on all relevant deposits held by the relevant deposit taker in that period (and no more) had been paid by it in that period, this section shall apply to that relevant deposit taker for the year of assessment succeeding that year of assessment and for each subsequent year of assessment.

(3) Notwithstanding anything in *section 258*, where this section applies to a relevant deposit taker for any year of assessment, *section 258(4)* shall not apply to the relevant deposit taker for that year of assessment but *subsection (4)* shall apply to that relevant deposit taker for that year and, as respects that relevant deposit taker for that year, any reference in the Tax Acts (apart from this section) to *section 258(4)* shall be construed as a reference to *subsection (4)*.

(4)

[(a) (i) Subject to *subparagraph (ii)* and notwithstanding *section 258(3)*, a relevant deposit taker shall for each year of assessment pay to the Collector-General, within 21 days of each of the dates referred to in *subparagraphs (i), (ii)* and *(iii)* of *section 258(4)(a)* (each of which dates, as the case may be, is referred to in the Table to this subparagraph as the "*relevant quarterly date*") in that year of assessment, an amount on account of appropriate tax which shall be not less than the amount determined by the formula set out in the Table to this subparagraph, and any amount on account of appropriate tax so paid by the relevant deposit taker for a year of assessment shall be treated as far as may be as a payment on account of any appropriate tax due and payable by it for that year of assessment under *section 258(3)*.

TABLE

$$\frac{A-(B-C)}{3}$$

where—

A is the amount of appropriate tax which would be due and payable by the relevant deposit taker for the year of assessment (in this Table referred to as "the relevant year") in accordance with *section 258(3)* if the total amount of the relevant interest which had accrued in the period of 12 months ending on the relevant quarterly date in the relevant year on all relevant deposits held by the relevant deposit taker in that period (and no more) had been paid by it in the relevant year,

B is the amount of appropriate tax which was due and payable by the relevant deposit taker for the year of assessment preceding the relevant year in accordance with *section 258(3)*, and

C is an amount equal to the lesser of the amount at B and the amount treated, in accordance with this subsection or *section 258(4)*, as paid by the relevant deposit taker on account of the appropriate tax due and payable by it for the year of assessment preceding the relevant year.

(ii) Notwithstanding *section 258(3)*, the aggregate of the amounts on account of appropriate tax due in accordance with *subparagraphs (i)* and *(iii)* shall not, in any event, be less than the amount determined by the formula set out in the Table to this subparagraph.

TABLE

A—(B—C)

where—

A is the amount of appropriate tax which would be due and payable by the relevant deposit taker for the year of assessment (in this Table referred to as "the relevant year") in accordance with *section 258(3)* if the total amount of the relevant interest which had accrued in the period of 12 months ending on 30 September in the relevant year on all relevant deposits held by the relevant deposit taker in that period (and no more) had been paid by it in the relevant year,

B is the amount of appropriate tax which was due and payable by the relevant deposit taker for the year of assessment preceding the relevant year in accordance with *section 258(3)*, and

C is an amount equal to the lesser of the amount at B and the amount treated, in accordance with this subsection or *section 258(4)*, as paid by the relevant deposit taker on account of the appropriate tax due and payable by it for the year of assessment preceding the relevant year.

(iii) Where, for any year of assessment the amount computed in accordance with *subparagraph (ii)* exceeds the aggregate of the amounts computed in accordance with *subparagraph (i)*, and without prejudice to the obligation to pay any amount computed in accordance with *subparagraph (i)*, that excess shall be paid by the relevant deposit taker to the Collector-General within 21 days of 30 September in that year of assessment and shall be treated as far as may be as a payment on account of any appropriate tax due and payable by it for that year of assessment under *section 258(3)*.][3]

(b) Where the amount on account of appropriate tax paid by a relevant deposit taker for any year of assessment under this subsection exceeds the amount of appropriate tax due and payable by it for that year of assessment under *section 258(3)*, the excess shall be carried forward and shall be set off against any amount due and payable under this subsection or *section 258(3)* by the relevant deposit taker for any subsequent year of assessment (any such set-off being effected as far as may be against an amount so due and payable at an earlier date rather than at a later date).

Amendments

[1] Substituted by FA01 sched2(17)(a). Shall apply only as respects the year of assessment 2001.

[2] Substituted by FA01 sched2(17)(b). Applies as respects the year of assessment 2001 and subsequent years of assessment.

[3] Substituted by FA10 s37(1)(g). With effect from 1 January 2011 per S.I. No. 115 of 2011.

Cross References

From Section 259

Section 258 Returns and collection of appropriate tax.

To Section 259

Section 260 Provisions supplemental to sections 258 and 259.
Section 838 Special portfolio investment accounts.

260 Provisions supplemental to sections 258 and 259

[FA86 s33A; FA96 s42; FA97 s146(1) and Sch9 PtI par14]

(1) In this section—

"*specified deposit*" means a relevant deposit made on or after the 28th day of March, 1996, in respect of which specified interest is payable other than such a deposit—

(a) which is held in a special savings account, or

(b) in respect of which—

(i) the interest payable is to any extent linked to or determined by changes in a stock exchange index or any other financial index,

(ii) arrangements were, or were being put, in place by the relevant deposit taker before the 28th day of March, 1996, to accept such a deposit, and

(iii) the deposit is made on or before the 7th day of June, 1996;

"*specified interest*" means interest in respect of a specified deposit, other than so much of the amount of that interest as—

(a) is payable annually or at more frequent intervals, or

(b) cannot be determined until the date of payment of such interest, notwithstanding that the terms under which the deposit was made are complied with fully.

(2) (a) Subject to this section, specified interest shall for the purposes of *section 258* be deemed—

(i) to accrue from day to day, and

(ii) to be relevant interest paid by the relevant deposit taker in each year of assessment to the extent that—

(I) it is deemed to accrue in that year of assessment, and

(II) it is not paid in that year of assessment,

and the relevant deposit taker shall account for appropriate tax accordingly.

(b) The amount of specified interest deemed to be relevant interest paid by a relevant deposit taker in any year of assessment by virtue of this subsection shall not be less than such amount as would be deductible in respect of interest or any other amount payable on the specified deposit in computing the income of the relevant deposit taker for the year of assessment if the year of assessment were an accounting period of the relevant deposit taker.

(3) (a) Where apart from *subsection (2)* a relevant deposit taker makes a payment of relevant interest which is or includes specified interest, the relevant deposit taker shall—

(i) deduct out of the whole of the amount of that payment the appropriate tax in relation to that payment in accordance with *section 257*, and

(ii) account for that appropriate tax under *section 258*,

and that appropriate tax shall be due and payable by the relevant deposit taker in accordance with *section 258*.

(b) So much of the amount of appropriate tax paid by the relevant deposit taker by virtue of *subsection (2)* as is referable to specified interest included in a payment of relevant interest referred to in *paragraph (a)* shall be set off against any amount of appropriate tax due and payable by the relevant deposit taker for the year of assessment in which that payment of interest is made or against any amount, or amount on account of, appropriate tax due and payable by it for a year of assessment subsequent to that year (any such set-off being effected as far as may be against an amount so due and payable at an earlier date rather than at a later date).

(4) *Subsection (2)* shall not apply for any year of assessment where, for that year of assessment and all preceding years of assessment—

[(a) in accordance with *section 258(4)* or *259(4)*, as may be appropriate, a relevant deposit taker makes a payment on account of appropriate tax in respect of specified interest as if, in relation to each specified deposit held by it, the references—

(i) in *section 258(4)*, to each of the periods referred to in *subparagraphs (i), (ii)* and *(iii)* of *paragraph (b)* of *section 258(4)* in the year of assessment, were a reference to the period beginning on the date on which the specified deposit was made and ending on each date referred to in *subparagraphs (i), (ii)* and *(iii)* of *section 258(4)(a)*, as the case may be, in the year of assessment,

(ii) in *section 259(4)(i)*, where it occurs in the meaning assigned to "A", to the period of 12 months ending on each of the dates referred to in *subparagraphs (i), (ii)* and *(iii)* of *section 258(4)(a)* in the relevant year, were a reference to the period beginning on the date on which the specified deposit was made and ending on each date referred to in *subparagraphs (i), (ii)* and *(iii)* of *section 258(4)(a)*, as the case may be, in the year of assessment, and

(iii) in *section 259(4)(ii)*, where it occurs in the meaning assigned to "A", to the period of 12 months ending on 30 September in the relevant year, were a reference to the period beginning on the date on which the specified deposit was made and ending on 30 September in the year of assessment,

and][1]

(b) the full amount payable on account of appropriate tax by the relevant deposit taker in that year of assessment in accordance with *section 258(4)* or *259(4)*, including any amount payable in accordance with those sections as modified by *paragraph (a)*, before the set-off of any amount on account of appropriate tax paid in an earlier year of assessment, does not exceed the appropriate tax payable by the relevant deposit taker for that year of assessment.

Amendments

[1] Substituted by FA10 s37(1)(h). With effect from 1 January 2011 per S.I. No. 115 of 2011.

Cross References

From Section 260

Section 257 Deduction of tax from relevant interest.
Section 258 Returns and collection of appropriate tax.
Section 259 Alternative amount on account of appropriate tax.

To Section 260

Section 256 Interpretation (Chapter 4).

261 Taxation of relevant interest, etc

[FA 86 s35(1)(a) to (cc); FA93 s15(1)(b); FA94 s12(1)(a)]

Notwithstanding anything in the Tax Acts—

(a) no part of any interest paid by a building society in respect of any shares in the society shall be treated for the purposes of the Corporation Tax Acts as a distribution of the society or as franked investment income of any company resident in the State;

(b) except where otherwise provided for in *section 267*, no repayment of appropriate tax in respect of any relevant interest shall be made to any person receiving or entitled to the payment of the relevant interest who is not a company within the charge to corporation tax in respect of the payment;

[(c) (i) the amount of any payment of relevant interest shall be regarded as income chargeable to tax under Case IV of Schedule D, and under no other Case or Schedule, and shall be taken into account in computing the total income of the person entitled to that amount, but, in relation to such a person (being an individual)—

(I) except for the purposes of a claim to repayment under *section 267(3)*, the specified amount within the meaning of [section 188][1] shall, as respects the year of assessment for which he or she is to be charged to income tax in respect of the relevant interest, be increased by the amount of that payment,

[(II) where the taxable income of that person includes relevant interest, the part of taxable income equal to that relevant interest shall be chargeable to tax at the rate at which tax was deducted from that relevant interest,][2]

[...][3]

and][4]

(ii) where the specified amount is so increased, references in [section 188][5] to—

(I) income tax payable shall be construed as references to the income tax payable after credit is given by virtue of *section 59* for appropriate tax deducted from the payment of relevant interest, and

(II) a sum equal to twice the specified amount shall be construed as references to a sum equal to the aggregate of—

(A) twice the specified amount (before it is so increased), and

(B) the amount of the payment of relevant interest;

(d) *section 59* shall apply as if a reference to appropriate tax deductible by virtue of this Chapter were contained in *paragraph (a)* of that section.

Amendments

[1] Substituted by FA08 s5(d)(i).

[2] Substituted by F(No.2)A13 s23(1)(b)(i). Applies to interest or dividends (within the meaning of Part 8) paid on or after 1 January 2014.

[3] Deleted by F(No.2)A13 s23(1)(b)(ii). Applies to interest or dividends (within the meaning of Part 8) paid on or after 1 January 2014.

[4] Substituted by FA00 s28(2).

[5] Substituted by FA08 s5(d)(ii).

Revenue Briefings

Tax Briefing

Tax Briefing August 2002 – Issue 49 pg 1 – Bogus Non-Resident Accounts

Statements of Practice

"Underlying Tax" on Funds Deposited in Bogus Non-Resident Accounts – SP GEN/1/01

Cross References

From Section 261

Section 59 Charge to tax of income from which tax has been deducted.
Section 188 Age exemption and associated marginal relief.
Section 256 Interpretation (Chapter 4).
Section 267 Repayment of appropriate tax in certain cases.

To Section 261

Section 227 Certain income arising to specified non-commercial state-sponsored bodies.
Section 261A Taxation of interest on special term accounts.
Section 261B Taxation of specified interest.
Section 264 Conditions and declarations relating to special savings accounts.
Section 267 Repayment of appropriate tax in certain cases.
Section 267F Supplementary provisions (Chapter 5).
Section 485C Interpretation (Chapter 2A).
Section 679 Exploration expenditure.

261A Taxation of interest on special term accounts

(1) Where interest is paid by a relevant deposit taker in respect of a relevant deposit held in a special term account [that is opened before 16 October 2013][1], such interest shall be relevant interest for the purposes of this Chapter only to the extent provided for in this section.

[(2) Interest paid in a year of assessment in respect of a relevant deposit held in a medium term account shall—

(a) be relevant interest only to the extent that such interest exceeds €480, and

(b) as respects the first €480 of such interest, be exempt from income tax and shall not be reckoned in computing total income for the purposes of the Income Tax Acts.

(3) Interest paid in a year of assessment in respect of a relevant deposit held in a long term account shall—

(a) be relevant interest only to the extent that such interest exceeds €635, and

(b) as respects the first €635 of such interest, be exempt from income tax and shall not be reckoned in computing total income for the purposes of the Income Tax Acts.][2]

(4) Where an individual opens a medium term account, the individual may subsequently make an election in writing to the relevant deposit taker to have the account converted to a long term account.

[(5) Where an election is made in accordance with *subsection (4)*, interest paid in a year of assessment which commences on or after the date the election is made shall—

(a) be relevant interest only to the extent that such interest exceeds €635, and

(b) as respects the first €635 of such interest, be exempt from income tax and shall not be reckoned in computing total income for the purposes of the Income Tax Acts.][3]

(6) Subject to *subsection (8)*, *section 261* shall apply in relation to any relevant interest paid in respect of a relevant deposit held in a special term account, as if the following paragraph were substituted for *paragraph (c)* of that section:

"(c) the amount of any payment of relevant interest paid in respect of any relevant deposit held in a special term account shall not, except for the purposes of a claim to repayment under *section 267(3)* in respect of the appropriate tax deducted from such relevant interest, be reckoned in computing total income for the purposes of the Income Tax Acts;".

(7) An account shall cease to be a special term account if any of the conditions specified in *section 264A(1)* cease to be satisfied, and where that occurs—

(a) all interest paid on or after the occurrence in respect of relevant deposits held in the account shall be relevant interest,

(b) all interest (in this paragraph referred to as "*past interest*") paid prior to the occurrence, in respect of relevant deposits held in the account, shall be treated by the relevant deposit taker as relevant interest to the extent that such interest has not already been treated as relevant interest, and—

(i) the provisions of *section 257(1)* shall apply as if the payment of past interest was being made on the date of the occurrence, and

(ii) where on that date the past interest has already been withdrawn from the account—

(I) the relevant deposit taker shall deduct from the relevant deposits held in the account on that date, an amount equal to the amount of the appropriate tax which would have been deducted from the past interest under *subparagraph (i)*, but for the withdrawal, and such amount shall be treated as appropriate tax, and

(II) the provisions of *paragraphs (b)* and *(c)* of *section 257(1)* shall apply to such deduction as they apply to a deduction from relevant interest.

(8) *Subsection (6)* shall not apply to any interest in respect of any relevant deposit held in the account which is paid, or by virtue of *subsection (7)* treated as paid, on or after the date on which the account ceases to be a special term account.

[(9) An account shall cease to be a special term account on a date which is—

(a) 3 years after the day on which the account was opened if the account is a medium term account, or

(b) 5 years after the day on which the account was opened if the account is a long term account, including an account which was opened as a medium term account but which was subsequently converted into a long term account.][4]

Amendments

[1] Inserted by F(No.2)A13 s23(1)(c)(i). Applies to interest or dividends (within the meaning of Part 8) paid on or after 1 January 2014.

[2] Substituted by FA02 s21(b)(i).

[3] Substituted by FA02 s21(b)(ii).

[4] Inserted by F(No.2)A13 s23(1)(c)(ii). Applies to interest or dividends (within the meaning of Part 8) paid on or after 1 January 2014.

Cross References

From Section 261A

Section 257 Deduction of tax from relevant interest.
Section 261 Taxation of relevant interest, etc.
Section 264A Conditions and declarations relating to special term accounts.
Section 267 Repayment of appropriate tax in certain cases.

To Section 261A

Section 256 Interpretation (Chapter 4).

261B Taxation of specified interest

[(1) In this section "*specified interest*" means interest arising to a person in respect of a deposit in relation to which a declaration has been made by the person under *subsection (1A)* or *(1B)* of *section 256* and which is not included in relevant interest for the purposes of *paragraph (c)(i)(II)* of *section 261*.

[(2) Notwithstanding *section 15*, where the taxable income of that person includes specified interest, the part of taxable income, equal to that specified interest, shall be chargeable to tax at the rate at which tax would have been deducted, from that interest, if a declaration under *subsection (1A)* or *(1B)* of *section 256* had not been made.][1]

(3) *Section 246(2)* does not apply to a payment of specified interest if it would otherwise apply.][2]

Amendments

[1] Substituted by F(No.2)A08 s26(1)(c). Applies for the year of assessment 2009 and subsequent years of assessment.

[2] Inserted by FA07 s34(1)(c). Applies on and from 2 April 2007

Cross References

From Section 261B

Section 15 Rate of charge.
Section 246 Interest payments by companies and to non-residents.
Section 256 Interpretation (Chapter 4).
Section 261 Taxation of relevant interest, etc.

To Section 261B

Section 485C Interpretation (Chapter 2A).

262 Statement furnished by relevant deposit taker

[FA86 s36]

A relevant deposit taker [shall furnish to every person entitled to any relevant interest on a relevant deposit held by the relevant deposit taker][1] as respects any payment of such relevant interest, a statement showing—

(a) the amount of that payment,

(b) the amount of appropriate tax deducted from that payment,

(c) the net amount of that payment, and

(d) the date of that payment.

Amendments

[1] Substituted by FA10 s37(1)(i). With effect from 1 January 2011 per S.I. No. 114 of 2011.

Revenue Briefings

eBrief

eBrief No. 14/2011 – Deposit Interest Retention Tax (DIRT) – Commencement Orders and New Pay & File Arrangements

263 Declarations relating to deposits of non-residents

[FA86 s37(1) (apart from paragraph (i) of the proviso) and (2); FA95 s167]

(1) The declaration referred to in *paragraph (g)(ii)* of the definition of "*relevant deposit*" in *section 256(1)* shall be a declaration in writing to a relevant deposit taker which—

(a) is made by a person (in this section referred to as "*the declarer*") to whom any interest on the deposit in respect of which the declaration is made is payable by the relevant deposit taker and is signed by the declarer,

(b) is made in such form as may be prescribed or authorised by the Revenue Commissioners,

(c) declares that at the time when the declaration is made the person beneficially entitled to the interest in relation to the deposit is not, or, as the case may be, all of the persons so entitled are not, resident in the State,

(d) contains as respects the person or, as the case may be, each of the persons mentioned in *paragraph (c)*—

(i) the name of the person,

(ii) the address of the person's principal place of residence, and

(iii) the name of the country in which the person is resident at the time the declaration is made,

(e) contains an undertaking by the declarer that if the person or, as the case may be, any of the persons mentioned in *paragraph (c)* becomes resident in the State, the declarer will notify the relevant deposit taker accordingly, and

(f) contains such other information as the Revenue Commissioners may reasonably require for the purposes of this Chapter;

and a declaration made before the 27th day of May, 1986, in a form authorised by the Revenue Commissioners under paragraph (22) of Financial Resolution No. 12 passed by Dáil Éireann on the 30th day of January, 1986, shall be deemed for the purposes of this Chapter to be a declaration of the kind mentioned in this subsection.

(2) (a) A relevant deposit taker shall—

(i) keep and retain for the longer of the following periods—

(I) a period of 6 years, and

(II) a period which, in relation to the deposit in respect of which the declaration is made, ends not earlier than 3 years after the date on which the deposit is repaid or, as the case may be, becomes a relevant deposit, and

(ii) on being so required by notice given to it in writing by an inspector, make available to the inspector, within the time specified in the notice,

all declarations of the kind mentioned in *subsection (1)* which have been made in respect of deposits held by the relevant deposit taker.

(b) The inspector may examine or take extracts from or copies of any declarations made available to him or her under *paragraph (a)*.

Revenue Precedents

Micro-film copies of non-resident declarations are not sufficient for Revenue Purposes. The original declarations should be maintained. IT922026

Cross References

From Section 263

Section 256 Interpretation (Chapter 4).

To Section 263

Section 256 Interpretation (Chapter 4).
Section 263A Declarations to a relevant deposit taker relating to deposits of certain persons.
Section 264 Conditions and declarations relating to special savings accounts.
Section 264A Conditions and declarations relating to special term accounts.
Section 267D Conditions and declarations relating to special term share accounts.
Section 784B Conditions relating to an approved retirement fund.
Section 784D Conditions relating to an approved minimum retirement fund.
Section 907 Application to Appeal Commissioners: information from financial institutions.
Section 908 Application to High Court seeking order requiring information: financial institutions.

263A Declarations to a relevant deposit taker relating to deposits of certain persons

[(1) The declaration referred to in *section 256(1A)* is a declaration in writing to a relevant deposit taker which—

(a) is made by an individual (in this section referred to as the "*declarer*") to whom any interest on the deposit in respect of which the declaration is made is payable by the relevant deposit taker and is signed by the declarer,

(b) is made in such form as may be prescribed, authorised or approved by the Revenue Commissioners,

(c) declares that at the time when the declaration is made—

(i) the individual beneficially entitled to the interest in relation to the deposit or his or her [spouse or civil partner][1] has attained the age of 65 years, and

(ii) the total income of the individual for the year of assessment in which the declaration is made will not exceed the specified amount (within the meaning of *section 188(2)*) applicable to that individual,

(d) contains as respects the individual, or as the case may be each of the individuals, mentioned in *paragraph (c)*—

(i) the name and address of the individual,

(ii) the date of birth of the individual who has attained the age of 65 years, and

(iii) the individual's PPS Number (within the meaning of *section 891B*),

(e) contains an undertaking by the declarer that if the individual or, as the case may be, any of the individuals mentioned in *paragraph (d)* no longer satisfies the conditions set out in *paragraph (a)* of *section 256(1A)* the declarer will notify the relevant deposit taker accordingly, and

(f) contains such other information as the Revenue Commissioners may reasonably require for the purposes of this Chapter.

(2) *Section 263(2)* applies as respects declarations of the kind mentioned in this section as it applies as respects declarations of the kind mentioned in that section.][2]

Amendments

[1] Substituted by F(No.3)A11 sched1(45).

[2] Inserted by FA07 s34(1)(d). Applies on and from 2 April 2007

Revenue Precedents

Where a certificate of interest which incorporates DIRT deductions at different rates (i.e. where the DIRT rate changed from one tax year to the next and the certificate is in respect of a calendar year) how is credit given for the purposes of a repayment of DIRT? The amount of DIRT for which credit is to be given is the actual amount of DIRT deducted. In circumstances, it may be necessary to gross up the DIRT at one of the two rates of tax in order to give effect to allowing the correct credit. IT962516

Whether renegotiation of interest rates on special savings accounts at two yearly intervals breaches the condition for SSA's that interest cannot be fixed for periods longer than 2 years? Whether the condition is breached will depend on the terms of an SSA product. If the interest rate is fixed for two years and genuinely reset after this time, the condition will not be regarded as breached. IT962514

In calculating tax payable under the 1993 Amnesty, whether account is to be taken of DIRT which has been or should have been deducted? No account is to be taken of DIRT which has been or should have been deducted. Tax due under amnesty is calculated on income – no credit for DIRT is given against such tax due. IT962513

Are disabled persons required to make & sign an SSA declaration themselves? Yes. But if mentally or physically incapable of doing so, another person may do it for them. Revenue requires a medical certificate & details of relationship. 1331/93

In the event of an SSA exceeding the £50,000 limit, time given in which to reduce account balance below the limit.(ceases to be SSA over £50,000). Three working days. 1331/93

Where joint SSA held by married couple and one spouse dies can surviving spouse convert the joint account into a single account? Yes. Provided that a single SSA declaration is made within a reasonable period and the single SSA limit is observed. 10407/1331/93

An SSA be transferred between branches of the same financial institution without triggering closure of the SSA provided no payment is made to the depositor. 1331/93

Cross References

From Section 263A

Section 188 Age exemption and associated marginal relief.

Section 256 Interpretation (Chapter 4).

Section 263 Declarations relating to deposits of non-residents.

Section 891B Returns of certain payments made by certain persons.

To Section 263A

Section 256 Interpretation (Chapter 4).

263B Declarations to the Revenue Commissioners relating to deposits of certain persons

[The declaration referred to in *section 256(1B)* is a declaration in writing to the Revenue Commissioners which—

(a) is made by the person (in this section referred to as the "*declarer*") to whom any interest on the deposit in respect of which the declaration is made is payable by the relevant deposit taker and is signed by the declarer,

(b) is made in such form as may be prescribed, authorised or approved by the Revenue Commissioners,

(c) declares that at the time when the declaration is made—

(i) (I) the individual beneficially entitled to the interest in relation to the deposit or his or her [spouse or civil partner][1] is permanently incapacitated by reason of mental or physical infirmity from maintaining himself or herself, and

(II) the individual beneficially entitled to any interest paid in respect of that deposit in any year of assessment or his or her [spouse or civil partner][2], is a relevant person (within the meaning of *section 267*) and the individual would, in accordance with *section 267(3)*, be entitled to repayment of the whole of any appropriate tax if it had been deducted from that interest,

or

(ii) (I) the person entitled to the interest in relation to the deposit is exempt from income tax by virtue of *section 189A(2)*, and

(II) the person entitled to any interest paid in respect of that deposit in any year of assessment is a person referred to in *section 189A(2)* and would, in accordance with *section 267(2)*, be entitled to repayment of the whole of any appropriate tax if it had been deducted from that interest,

(d) contains as respects the person, or as the case may be, each of the persons mentioned in *paragraph (c)*—

(i) the name and address of the person,

(ii) the person's PPS Number (within the meaning of *section 891B*) or where the person is not an individual, the person's tax reference number (within the meaning of *paragraphs (b)* and *(c)* of the definition of "*tax reference number*" in *section 885*),

(iii) the name and address of the deposit taker (including the name and address of the branch of the deposit taker, if any) who holds the deposit in respect of which the declaration is made, and

(iv) the account number or membership number, as the case may be, of the deposit in respect of which the declaration is made,

(e) contains an undertaking by the declarer that if the person or, as the case may be, any of the persons mentioned in *paragraph (d)* no longer satisfies the conditions set out in *paragraph (a)* of *section 256(1B)* the declarer will notify the Revenue Commissioners accordingly, and

(f) contains such other information as the Revenue Commissioners may reasonably require for the purposes of this Chapter.][3]

Amendments

[1] Substituted by F(No.3)A11 sched1(46).

[2] Substituted by F(No.3)A11 sched1(47).

[3] Inserted by FA07 s34(1)(d). Applies on and from 2 April 2007

Cross References

From Section 263B

Section 189A Special trusts for permanently incapacitated individuals.
Section 256 Interpretation (Chapter 4).
Section 267 Repayment of appropriate tax in certain cases.
Section 885 Obligation to show tax reference number on receipts.
Section 891B Returns of certain payments made by certain persons.

To Section 263B

Section 256 Interpretation (Chapter 4).

263C Notifications by the Revenue Commissioners relating to deposits of certain persons

[(1) The notification referred to in *section 256(1B)* is a notification—

(a) in writing by the Revenue Commissioners to a relevant deposit taker confirming that the account identified in the notification is to be treated as not being a relevant deposit unless and until the notification is cancelled in accordance with *subsection (2)*,

(b) which contains as respects the person beneficially entitled to, or the person (being one or more than one trustee) referred to in *section 189A(2)* entitled to, the interest in relation to the deposit mentioned in *paragraph (a)*—

(i) the name and address of the person,

(ii) the person's PPS Number (within the meaning of *section 891B*) or, where the person is not an individual, the person's tax reference number (within the meaning of *paragraphs (b)* and *(c)* of the definition of "*tax reference number*" in *section 885*), and

(iii) the account number of the deposit,

and

(c) which contains such other information as the Revenue Commissioners may reasonably decide for the purposes of this Chapter.

(2) The Revenue Commissioners may at any time cancel the notification and give notice in writing to that effect to both the relevant deposit taker and the person or persons mentioned in *subsection (1)(b)*. Where at any time the Revenue Commissioners have so notified the deposit taker, the deposit shall not be a deposit to which this section applies from that time.][1]

Amendments

[1] Inserted by FA07 s34(1)(d). Applies on and from 2 April 2007.

Cross References

From Section 263C

Section 189A Special trusts for permanently incapacitated individuals.
Section 256 Interpretation (Chapter 4).
Section 885 Obligation to show tax reference number on receipts.
Section 891B Returns of certain payments made by certain persons.

To Section 263C

Section 256 Interpretation (Chapter 4).

264 Conditions and declarations relating to special savings accounts

[FA86 s37A; FA92 s22(1)(c); F(No.2)A92 s3(b); FA93 s15(1)(c); FA94 s12(1)(b)]

(1) The following are the conditions referred to in *paragraph (a)* of the definition of "*special savings account*" in *section 256(1)*:

(a) the account shall be designated by the relevant deposit taker as a special savings account;

(b) the account shall not be denominated in a foreign currency;

(c) the account shall not be connected with any other account held by the account holder or any other person; and for this purpose an account shall be connected with another account if—

(i) (I) either account was opened with reference to the other account, or with a view to enabling the other account to be opened on particular terms, or with a view to facilitating the opening of the other account on particular terms, and

(II) the terms on which either account was opened would have been significantly less favourable to the account holder if the other account had not been opened,

or

(ii) the terms on which either account is operated are altered or affected in any way whatever because of the existence of the other account;

(d) no withdrawal of money shall be made from the account within the period of 3 months commencing on the date on which it is opened;

(e) the terms under which the account is opened shall require the individual to give a minimum notice of 30 days to the relevant deposit taker in relation to the withdrawal of any money from the account;

(f) all moneys held in the account shall be subject to the same terms;

(g) there shall not be any agreement, arrangement or understanding in existence, whether express or implied, which influences or determines, or could influence or determine, the rate (other than an unspecified and variable rate) of interest which is paid or payable, in respect of the relevant deposit or relevant deposits held in the account, in or in respect of any period which is more than 24 months;

(h) interest paid or payable in respect of the relevant deposit or relevant deposits held in the account shall not directly or indirectly be linked to or determined by any change in the price or value of any shares, stocks, debentures or securities listed on a stock exchange or dealt in on an unlisted securities market;

(i) the relevant deposit or the aggregate of the relevant deposits held in the account, including any relevant interest added to that deposit or those deposits, shall not at any time exceed [€63,500][1];

(j) the account shall not be opened by or held in the name of an individual who is not of full age;

(k) the account shall be opened by and held in the name of the individual beneficially entitled to the relevant interest payable in respect of the relevant deposit or relevant deposits held in the account;

(l) except in the case of an account opened and held jointly only by [2 individuals who are married to each other or who are civil partners of each other,][2] the account shall not be a joint account;

(m) except in the case of an account opened and held jointly only by [2 individuals who are married to each other or who are civil partners of each other,][3] either the same or any other relevant deposit taker shall not simultaneously hold another special savings account opened and held by an individual;

(n) in the case of an account opened and held jointly only by [2 individuals who are married to each other or who are civil partners of each other,][4] they shall not simultaneously hold (either with the same or any other relevant deposit taker) any other special savings account either individually or jointly other than one other such account opened and held jointly by them.

(2) The declaration referred to in *paragraph (b)* of the definition of "*special savings account*" in *section 256(1)* shall be a declaration in writing to a relevant deposit taker which—

(a) is made by the individual (in this section referred to as "*the declarer*") to whom any interest payable in respect of the relevant deposit or relevant deposits held in the account in respect of which the declaration is made is payable by the relevant deposit taker, and is signed by the declarer,

(b) is made in such form as may be prescribed or authorised by the Revenue Commissioners,

(c) declares that at the time when the declaration is made the conditions referred to in *paragraphs (j)* to *(n)* of *subsection (1)* are satisfied in relation to the account in respect of which the declaration is made,

(d) contains the full name and address of the individual beneficially entitled to the interest payable in respect of the relevant deposit or relevant deposits held in the account in respect of which the declaration is made,

(e) contains an undertaking by the declarer that, if the conditions referred to in *paragraphs (j)* to *(n)* of *subsection (1)* cease to be satisfied in respect of the account in respect of which the declaration is made, the declarer will notify the relevant deposit taker accordingly, and

(f) contains such other information as the Revenue Commissioners may reasonably require for the purposes of this Chapter.

(3) *Subsection (2)* of *section 263* shall apply as respects declarations of the kind mentioned in this section as it applies as respects declarations of the kind mentioned in that section.

(4) *Section 261* shall apply in relation to any relevant interest paid in respect of any relevant deposit held in a special savings account as if the following paragraph were substituted for *paragraph (c)* of that section:

"(c) the amount of any payment of relevant interest (being relevant interest paid in respect of any relevant deposit held in a special savings account) shall not, except for the purposes of a claim to repayment under *section 267(3)* in respect of the appropriate tax deducted from such relevant interest, be reckoned in computing total income for the purposes of the Income Tax Acts,".

(5) An account shall cease to be a special savings account if any of the conditions mentioned in *subsection (1)* cease to be satisfied, and *subsection (4)* shall not apply to any relevant interest in respect of any relevant deposit held in the account which is paid on or after the date on which the account ceases to be a special savings account.

Amendments

[1] Substituted by FA01 s233(1).

[2] Substituted by F(No.3)A11 sched1(48).

[3] Substituted by F(No.3)A11 sched1(49).

[4] Substituted by F(No.3)A11 sched1(50).

Cross References

From Section 264

Section 256 Interpretation (Chapter 4).
Section 261 Taxation of relevant interest, etc.
Section 263 Declarations relating to deposits of non-residents.
Section 267 Repayment of appropriate tax in certain cases.

To Section 264

Section 256 Interpretation (Chapter 4).
Section 838 Special portfolio investment accounts.
Section 839 Limits to special investments.

264A Conditions and declarations relating to special term accounts

[(1) The following are the conditions referred to in *subparagraph (i)* of the definition of "*special term account*" in *section 256(1)*:

(a) the account shall be opened and designated by the relevant deposit taker as a medium term account or, as the case may be, a long term account;

(b) the account shall not be denominated in a foreign currency;

(c) the account shall not be connected with any other account held by the account holder or any other person; and for this purpose an account shall be connected with another account if—

(i) (I) either account was opened with reference to the other account, or with a view to enabling the other account to be opened on particular terms, or with a view to facilitating the opening of the other account on particular terms, and

(II) the terms on which either account was opened would have been significantly less favourable to the account holder if the other account had not been opened,

or

(ii) the terms on which either account is operated are altered or affected in any way whatever because of the existence of the other account;

(d) all relevant deposits held in the account shall be subject to the same terms;

(e) there shall not be any agreement, arrangement or understanding in existence, whether express or implied, which influences or determines, or could influence or determine, the rate (other than an unspecified and variable rate) of interest which is paid or payable, in respect of the relevant deposit or relevant deposits held in the account, in or in respect of any period which is more than 12 months;

(f) interest paid or payable in respect of the relevant deposit or relevant deposits held in the account shall not directly or indirectly be linked to or determined by any change in the price or value of any shares, stocks, debentures or securities listed on a stock exchange or dealt in on an unlisted securities market;

(g) the account shall not be opened by or held in the name of an individual who is under 16 years of age;

(h) the account shall be opened by and held in the name of the individual beneficially entitled to the relevant interest payable in respect of the relevant deposit or relevant deposits held in the account;

(i) the account may be held jointly by not more than 2 individuals;

[(j) an individual shall not simultaneously hold whether solely or jointly—

(I) a special term share account, or

(II) subject to *paragraph (k)*, another special term account;][1]

(k) where the account is held jointly by [individuals who are married to each other or who are civil partners of each other][2] they may simultaneously hold one other such account jointly;

(l) subject to *paragraphs (m)* and *(n)*, the amount of a deposit or the aggregate amount of deposits which may be made to an account in any one month shall not exceed [€635][3];

(m) at the time an individual opens an account with a relevant deposit taker, a deposit consisting of all or part of the relevant deposits of the individual which are at that time held by the same relevant deposit taker, may be transferred to the account;

(n) otherwise than by way of a transfer under *paragraph (m)*, a deposit of not more than [€7,620][4] may be made by an individual once and only once to an account during the period in which the account is a special term account;

(o) any interest credited to the account by the relevant deposit taker shall not be treated as a deposit for the purposes of *paragraph (l)* or *(p)*, but such interest may not be withdrawn from the account, otherwise than in accordance with *paragraph (q)*, unless the withdrawal is made within the period of 12 months from the date it was so credited;

(p) subject to *paragraph (q)*, a deposit may not be withdrawn from an account held by an individual within—

(i) 3 years from the date the deposit was made, in the case of a medium term account, and

(ii) 5 years from the date the deposit was made, in the case of a long term account,

otherwise than on the death of the individual or, where the account is an account held jointly by 2 individuals, on the death of one of them;

(q) one and only one withdrawal may be made from an account by an individual who is 60 years of age or over on the date of the withdrawal, provided that the account was opened when the individual was under that age.

(2) The declaration referred to in *subparagraph (ii)* of the definition of "*special term account*" in *section 256(1)* shall be a declaration in writing to a relevant deposit taker which—

(a) is made by the individual (in this subsection referred to as "*the declarer*") who holds the account in respect of which the declaration is made[...][5],

(b) is signed by the declarer,

(c) is made in such form as may be prescribed or authorised by the Revenue Commissioners,

(d) declares that at the time when the declaration is made the conditions referred to in *paragraphs (g)*, *(h)*, *(j)* and *(k)* of *subsection (1)* are satisfied in relation to the account in respect of which the declaration is made,

(e) contains the full name and address of the declarer,

(f) contains an undertaking by the declarer that, if the conditions referred to in *paragraphs (g)*, *(h)*, *(j)* and *(k)* of *subsection (1)* cease to be satisfied in respect of the account in respect of which the declaration is made, the declarer will notify the relevant deposit taker accordingly, and

(g) contains such other information as the Revenue Commissioners may reasonably require for the purposes of this Chapter.

(3) *Section 263(2)* shall apply as respects declarations of the kind mentioned in this section as it applies as respects declarations of the kind mentioned in that section.][6]

Amendments

[1] Substituted by FA02 s21(c)(i).

[2] Substituted by F(No.3)A11 sched1(51).

[3] Substituted by FA01 s57(1)(a)(v)(I). Applies as respects the year of assessment 2002 and subsequent years of assessment. With effect from 1 January 2002 per S.I. 596 of 2001.

[4] Substituted by FA01 s57(1)(a)(v)(II). Applies as respects the year of assessment 2002 and subsequent years of assessment. With effect from 1 January 2002 per S.I. 596 of 2001.

[5] Deleted by FA02 s21(c)(ii).

[6] Inserted by FA01 s57(1)(a)(iv). With effect from 1 January 2002 per S.I. 596 of 2001.

Cross References

From Section 264A

Section 256 Interpretation (Chapter 4).

Section 263 Declarations relating to deposits of non-residents.

To Section 264A

Section 256 Interpretation (Chapter 4).

Section 261A Taxation of interest on special term accounts.

264B Returns of special term accounts by relevant deposit takers

[(1) In this section "*appropriate inspector*" means—

(a) the inspector who has last given notice in writing to the relevant deposit taker that he or she is the inspector to whom the relevant deposit taker is required to deliver the return referred to in *subsection (2)*, or

(b) where there is no such inspector as is referred to in *paragraph (a)*, [the inspector of returns][1]

(2) On or before 31 March in each year of assessment, every relevant deposit taker shall prepare and deliver to the appropriate inspector a return, in such form as may be prescribed or authorised by the Revenue Commissioners specifying—

(a) the name and address of the holder or holders, as the case may be, of each special term account which was opened during the previous year of assessment,

(b) whether such account is a medium term account or a long term account, and

(c) the date of opening of such account.

(3) *Sections 1052* and *1054* shall apply to a failure by a relevant deposit taker to deliver a return required by *subsection (2)* and to each and every such failure, as they apply to a failure to deliver a return referred to in *section 1052*.][2]

Amendments

[1] Substituted by FA12 sched5(1)(l).

[2] Inserted by FA01 s57(1)(a)(iv). With effect from 1 January 2002 per S.I. 596 of 2001.

Cross References

From Section 264B

Section 950 Interpretation (Part 41).
Section 1052 Penalties for failure to make certain returns, etc.
Section 1054 Penalties in the case of a secretary of a body of persons.

To Section 264B

Schedule 29 Provisions Referred to in Sections 1052, 1053 and 1054

265 Deposits of companies and pensions schemes

[Where a return is required to be made by a relevant deposit taker under *section 891* in respect of interest on a deposit which is a deposit of a kind referred to in *paragraph (f)* of the definition of "*relevant deposit*" in *section 256*, that return shall, in addition to the matters which shall be included on the return by virtue of *section 891*, include the tax reference number (within the meaning of *section 885*) of the person beneficially entitled to the interest and where, in the case of a pension scheme, there is no such number, with the number assigned by the Revenue Commissioners to the employer to whom the pension scheme relates.][1]

Amendments

[1] Substituted by FA02 s20(1)(b). Applies as respects deposits made on or after 25 March 2002. Insofar as it relates to pension schemes, applies to interest paid or credited on or after 1 January 2003 in respect of deposits made on or after 25 March 2002.

Revenue Precedents

Whether a sporting body entitled to exemption under section 235 TCA 1997 would be entitled to receive interest without deduction of tax on the basis of a declaration under section 265 TCA 1997? No; since the sporting body would not be within the charge to corporation tax in respect of the interest, Also, the body in question could not complete a declaration to the effect that the interest will be included in the profits of the company on which it will be charged to Corporation Tax, as required by section 265. IT922034

Cross References

From Section 265

Section 256 Interpretation (Chapter 4).
Section 885 Obligation to show tax reference number on receipts.
Section 891 Returns of interest paid or credited without deduction of tax.

265A Deposits of certain persons

[Where a return is required to be made by a relevant deposit taker under *section 891* in respect of interest on a deposit which is a deposit of a kind referred to in *subsection (1A)* or *(1B)* of *section 256*, then that return shall, in addition to the matters which shall be included on the return by virtue of *section 891*, include—

(a) the PPS Number (within the meaning of *section 891B*) of the person, or

(b) where the person is not an individual, the person's tax reference number (within the meaning of *paragraphs (b)* and *(c)* of *section 885*).][1]

Amendments

[1] Inserted by FA07 s34(1)(e). Applies on and from 2 April 2007

Cross References

From Section 265A

Section 256 Interpretation (Chapter 4).
Section 885 Obligation to show tax reference number on receipts.
Section 891 Returns of interest paid or credited without deduction of tax.
Section 891B Returns of certain payments made by certain persons.

266 Deposits of charities

[Where a return is required to be made by a relevant deposit taker under *section 891* in respect of interest on a deposit which is a deposit of a kind referred to in *paragraph (h)* of the definition of "*relevant deposit*" in *section 256*, that return shall, in addition to the matters which shall be included on that return by virtue of *section 891*, include the reference number assigned to that person by the Revenue Commissioners in recognition of that person's entitlement to exemption from tax under *section 207* and known as the charity (CHY) number.][1]

Amendments

[1] Substituted by FA02 s20(1)(c). Applies as respects deposits made on or after 25 March 2002. Insofar as it relates to pension schemes, applies to interest paid or credited on or after 1 January 2003 in respect of deposits made on or after 25 March 2002

Revenue Information Notes

CHY 1 – Applying for Relief from tax on the Income and Property of Charities

Cross References

From Section 266

Section 207 Rents of properties belonging to hospitals and other charities.
Section 256 Interpretation (Chapter 4).
Section 891 Returns of interest paid or credited without deduction of tax.

266A Repayments of appropriate tax to first-time purchasers

[(1) In this section—

'completion value', in relation to a dwelling, means the price which the unencumbered fee simple of the dwelling might reasonably be expected to fetch on a sale in the open market were that dwelling to be sold on the relevant completion date in such manner and subject to such conditions as might reasonably be calculated to obtain for the vendor the best price for the dwelling and with the benefit of any easement necessary to afford the same access to the dwelling as would have existed prior to that sale;

'first-time purchaser' means a person, being an individual who, at the time of a relevant purchase or on the relevant completion date, as the case may be, has not, either individually or jointly with any other person or persons, previously purchased or

previously built directly or indirectly on his or her own behalf any other dwelling;

'relevant completion' means the completion of the construction of a new dwelling, on or after 14 October 2014 and on or before 31 December 2017, to a standard where it is suitable for immediate occupation as a dwelling and the dwelling—

(a) has been built directly or indirectly—

(i) on his or her own behalf by a first-time purchaser only, for occupation as his or her place of residence, or

(ii) on their own behalf by more than one person, where each such person is a first-time purchaser only, for occupation as their place of residence,

and

(b) is constructed on property conveyed or transferred, on or before 31 December 2017, into the name or names of the first-time purchaser or first-time purchasers only, as the case may be;

'relevant completion date', in relation to a relevant completion, means the date on which the dwelling becomes suitable for immediate occupation as a dwelling;

'relevant purchase' means the conveyance or transfer of a dwelling on or after 14 October 2014 and on or before 31 December 2017—

(a) into the name of a first-time purchaser only, for occupation as his or her place of residence, or

(b) into the names of more than one person, where each such person is a first-time purchaser only, for occupation as their place of residence;

'relevant savings' means—

(a) in the case of a relevant purchase, so much of the aggregate amount at any time of any relevant deposits held in the name of a first-time purchaser, individually or jointly with another first-time purchaser only, as does not exceed 20 per cent of the amount of the consideration paid in respect of the relevant purchase by the first- time purchaser, or

(b) in the case of a relevant completion, so much of the aggregate amount at any time of any relevant deposits held in the name of a first-time purchaser, individually or jointly with another first-time purchaser only, as does not exceed 20 per cent of the completion value of the dwelling;

'relevant savings interest' means relevant interest paid—

(a) in the case of a relevant purchase, at any time during the period of 48 months ending on the date of the relevant purchase by a first-time purchaser, to the first-time purchaser in respect of relevant savings, or

(b) in the case of a relevant completion, at any time during the period of 48 months ending on the relevant completion date, to the first-time purchaser in respect of relevant savings.

(2) Notwithstanding *section 261(b)*, appropriate tax which—

(a) has been deducted from relevant savings interest paid to a first-time purchaser, and

(b) would not otherwise fall to be repaid under this section or any other provision of the Tax Acts,

shall be repaid to the first-time purchaser on the making of a claim by that first-time purchaser to the inspector in that behalf.][1]

Amendments

[1] Inserted by FA14 s22(1). Has effect on and from 14 October 2014.

267 Repayment of appropriate tax in certain cases

[FA 86 s39]

(1) In this section, "*relevant person*" means an individual who proves to the satisfaction of the inspector or, on appeal, to the Appeal Commissioners that—

(a) at some time during the relevant year the individual or his or her [spouse or civil partner][1] was of the age of 65 years or over, or

(b) throughout the relevant year the individual or his or her [spouse or civil partner][2] was, or as on and from some time during the relevant year the individual or his or her [spouse or civil partner][3] became, permanently incapacitated by reason of mental or physical infirmity from maintaining himself or herself.

(2) Notwithstanding *section 261(b)*, repayment of appropriate tax in respect of any relevant interest shall be made to a person entitled to exemption in respect of that interest—

(a) from income tax under Schedule D by virtue of [*section 189A(2)* or][4] *section 207(1)(b)*, or

(b) from corporation tax by virtue of *section 207(1)(b)* as it applies for the purposes of corporation tax by virtue of *section 76(6)*.

(3) Where in any year of assessment (in this subsection referred to as "*the relevant year*") the total income of a relevant person includes any relevant interest[or would, but for the provisions of *section 189(2)*, [section 189A(4)][5] or *section 192(2)*, have included relevant interest,][6] and apart from *section 261(b)* the relevant person would be entitled to repayment of the whole or any part of the appropriate tax deducted from that relevant interest, then, notwithstanding *section 261(b)*, the repayment to which the relevant person would be so entitled may be made to the relevant person on the making by the relevant person to the inspector, not earlier than the end of the relevant year, of a claim in that behalf.

Amendments

1 Substituted by F(No.3)A11 sched1(52).

2, 3 Substituted by F(No.3)A11 sched1(53).

4 Inserted by FA99 s12(b)(i). Applies as respects relevant interest paid on or after the 6th day of April, 1997.

5 Substituted by FA07 s34(1)(f). Applies on and from 2 April 2007

6 Inserted by FA99 s12(b)(ii). Applies as respects relevant interest paid on or after the 6th day of April, 1997.

Revenue Information Notes

DE1 – DIRT-free Deposit Accounts for those aged 65 or over

Revenue Precedents

Whether DIRT can be repaid to a mining company where DIRT was deducted from deposit interest because the company failed to complete a declaration under section 265 TCA 1997? DIRT cannot be repaid. Section 267 TCA 1997 prevents repayment. IT952543

Whether a person suffering from depression and/or ME is considered to be permanently incapacitated for the purposes of entitlement to a repayment of DIRT? A person suffering from depression and/or ME will be considered to be permanently incapacitated for the purposes of a DIRT repayment where there is medical evidence to show the condition is permanent. IT972537

Cross References

From Section 267

Section 76 Computation of income: application of income tax principles.
Section 189 Payments in respect of personal injuries.
Section 189A Special trusts for permanently incapacitated individuals.
Section 192 Payments in respect of thalidomide children.
Section 207 Rents of properties belonging to hospitals and other charities.
Section 261 Taxation of relevant interest, etc.

To Section 267

Section 227 Certain income arising to specified non-commercial state-sponsored bodies.
Section 256 Interpretation (Chapter 4).
Section 261 Taxation of relevant interest, etc.
Section 261A Taxation of interest on special term accounts.
Section 263B Declarations to the Revenue Commissioners relating to deposits of certain persons.
Section 264 Conditions and declarations relating to special savings accounts.
Section 267F Supplementary provisions (Chapter 5).
Section 485G Miscellaneous (Chapter 2A).

CHAPTER 5

Dividend Payments by Credit Unions

267A Interpretation (Chapter 5)

[(1) In this Chapter—

"*appropriate tax*" has the same meaning as in *section 256(1)*;

"*dividend*" means a dividend on shares declared by a credit union at an annual general meeting of that credit union;

"*long term share account*" means an [account that is opened before 16 October 2013][1] by a member (being an individual) with a credit union on terms under which the member has agreed that each share subscribed for by the member to be held in the account is to be held in the account for a period of not less than 5 years;

"*medium term share account*" means an [account that is opened before 16 October 2013][2] by a member (being an individual) with a credit union on terms under which the member has agreed that each share subscribed for by the member to be held in the account is to be held in the account for a period of not less than 3 years;

["*regular share account*" means an account, other than a special share account or a special term share account, opened by a member (being an individual) with a credit union;][3]

"*relevant deposit*" has the same meaning as in *section 256(1)*;

"*relevant deposit taker*" has the same meaning as in *section 256(1)*;

"*relevant interest*" has the same meaning as in *section 256(1)*;

"*savings*" includes shares and deposits;

"*share*" has the same meaning as in *Chapter 4* of this Part—

(a) the value of the shares held in the account at any time is to be treated as an amount of a relevant deposit held by the credit union at that time, and

(b) the value of any dividend paid on those shares at any time is to be treated as an amount of relevant interest paid in respect of such relevant deposit by the credit union at that time;

"*special term share account*" means—

(a) a medium term share account, or

(b) a long term share account,

being an account in which shares subscribed for by a member are held by a credit union and in respect of which—

(i) the conditions specified in *section 267D(1)* are satisfied, and

(ii) a declaration of the kind mentioned in *section 267D(2)* has been made to the credit union.

[(2) For the purposes of this Chapter the amount of any dividend credited to a member's account shall be treated as if it were a dividend paid, and references in this Chapter to any dividend paid shall be construed accordingly.][4][5]

Amendments

[1] Substituted by F(No.2)A13 s23(1)(d)(i). Applies to interest or dividends (within the meaning of Part 8) paid on or after 1 January 2014.

[2] Substituted by F(No.2)A13 s23(1)(d)(ii). Applies to interest or dividends (within the meaning of Part 8) paid on or after 1 January 2014.

[3] Inserted by F(No.2)A13 s23(1)(d)(iii). Applies to interest or dividends (within the meaning of Part 8) paid on or after 1 January 2014.

[4] Inserted by FA02 s21(d)(ii).

[5] Inserted by FA01 s57(1)(a)(vi). With effect from 1 January 2002 per S.I. 596 of 2001.

Revenue Briefings

Tax Briefing

Tax Briefing April 2001 – Issue 43 pg 18 – Taxation of Credit Unions Dividends and Interest

eBrief

eBrief No. 71/09 – Extension of Voluntary Disclosure Initiative for Interest Reporting to include Credit Unions.

Cross References

From Section 267A

Section 256 Interpretation (Chapter 4).
Section 267D Conditions and declarations relating to special term share accounts.

To Section 267A

Section 256 Interpretation (Chapter 4).
Section 267D Conditions and declarations relating to special term share accounts.
Section 848E Payment of tax credit.

267AA Taxation of dividends on regular share accounts

[A credit union shall treat—

(a) the value of shares held in a regular share account at any time, as an amount of a relevant deposit held by it at that time, and

(b) the value of any dividend paid on those shares at any time, as an amount of relevant interest paid at that time in respect of such relevant deposit and the provisions of *Chapter 4* of this Part shall apply to such relevant interest treated as paid by the credit union as they apply to relevant interest paid by a relevant deposit taker.][1]

Amendment

[1] Inserted by F(No.2)A13 s23(1)(e). Applies to interest or dividends (within the meaning of Part 8) paid on or after 1 January 2014.

267B Election to open a special share account or a special term share account

[(1) A person, who is a member or is about to become a member of a credit union, may either or both—

(a) make an election in writing to the credit union to open an account which is a special share account, and

(b) where the person is an individual, make an election in writing to the credit union to open either a medium term share account or a long term share account.

(2) Where an election is made in accordance with *subsection (1)(a)*, the credit union shall designate the account as a special share account and shall treat—

(a) the value of the shares held in the account at any time, as an amount of a relevant deposit held by it at that time, and

(b) the value of any dividend paid on those shares at any time, as an amount of relevant interest paid at that time in respect of such relevant deposit and the provisions of *Chapter 4* of this Part shall apply to such relevant interest treated as paid by a credit union as they apply to relevant interest paid by a relevant deposit taker [...][1].

(3) Where an election is made in accordance with *subsection (1)(b)*, the credit union shall treat—

(a) the value of the shares held in the account at any time, as an amount of a relevant deposit held by it at that time, and

(b) subject to *section 267C*, the value of any dividend paid on those shares at any time, as an amount of relevant interest paid at that time in respect of such relevant deposit and the provisions of *Chapter 4* of this Part shall apply to such relevant interest treated as paid by the credit union as they apply to relevant interest paid by a relevant deposit taker [...][2].][3]

Amendments

[1] Deleted by F(No.2)A13 s23(1)(f)(i). Applies to interest or dividends (within the meaning of Part 8) paid on or after 1 January 2014.

[2] Deleted by F(No.2)A13 s23(1)(f)(ii). Applies to interest or dividends (within the meaning of Part 8) paid on or after 1 January 2014.

[3] Inserted by FA01 s57(1)(a)(vi). With effect from 1 January 2002 per S.I. 596 of 2001.

Cross References

From Section 267B

Section 256 Interpretation (Chapter 4).
Section 267C Taxation of dividends on special term share accounts.

To Section 267B

Section 267F Supplementary provisions (Chapter 5).
Section 848E Payment of tax credit.
Schedule 29 Provisions Referred to in Sections 1052, 1053 and 1054

267C Taxation of dividends on special term share accounts

[(1) The value of the dividend paid in a year of assessment on shares held in a medium term share account shall—

(a) be treated as an amount of relevant interest paid in that year of assessment only to the extent that such value exceeds €480, and

(b) as respects the first €480 of such value, be exempt from income tax and shall not be reckoned in computing total income for the purposes of the Income Tax Acts.

(2) The value of the dividend paid in a year of assessment on shares held in a long term share account shall—

(a) be treated as an amount of relevant interest paid in that year of assessment only to the extent that such value exceeds €635, and

(b) as respects the first €635 of such value, be exempt from income tax and shall not be reckoned in computing total income for the purposes of the Income Tax Acts.][1]

(3) Where an account is opened by a member as a medium term share account, the member may subsequently make an election in writing to the credit union to have the account converted to a long term share account.

[(4) Where an election is made in accordance with *subsection (3)*, the value of the dividend paid on shares in a year of assessment which commences on or after the date the election is made shall—

(a) be treated as an amount of relevant interest paid in that year of assessment only to the extent that such value exceeds €635, and

(b) as respects the first €635 of such value, be exempt from income tax and shall not be reckoned in computing total income for the purposes of the Income Tax Acts.][2]

(5) An account shall cease to be a special term share account if any of the conditions specified in *subsection (1)* of *section 267D* cease to be satisfied, and where that occurs—

(a) the account shall be treated as a special share account from the time of the occurrence, and

(b) the value of all dividends (in this paragraph referred to as "*past dividends*") paid prior to the occurrence, on shares held in the account, shall be treated by the credit union as an amount of relevant interest to the extent that the value of such dividends has not already been treated as an amount of relevant interest, and—

(i) the provisions of *section 257(1)* shall apply as if the payment of past dividends was being made on the date of the occurrence, and

(ii) where on that date the past dividends have already been withdrawn from the account—

(I) the credit union shall deduct from the value of the shares in the account on that date, an amount equal to the amount of the appropriate tax which would have been deducted from the past dividends under *subparagraph (i)*, but for the withdrawal, and such amount shall be treated as appropriate tax, and

(II) the provisions of *paragraphs (b)* and *(c)* of *section 257(1)* shall apply to such deduction as they apply to a deduction from relevant interest.][3]

[(6) An account shall cease to be a special term share account on a date which is—

(a) 3 years after the day on which the account was opened if the account is a medium term share account, or

(b) 5 years after the day on which the account was opened if the account is a long term share account, including an account which was opened as a medium term share account but which was subsequently converted into a long term share account.][4]

Amendments

[1] Substituted by FA02 s21(e)(i).

[2] Substituted by FA02 s21(e)(ii).

[3] Inserted by FA01 s57(1)(a)(vi). With effect from 1 January 2002 per S.I. 596 of 2001.

[4] Inserted by F(No.2)A13 s23(1)(g). Applies to interest or dividends (within the meaning of Part 8) paid on or after 1 January 2014.

Cross References

From Section 267C

Section 257 Deduction of tax from relevant interest.

Section 267D Conditions and declarations relating to special term share accounts.

To Section 267C

Section 267B Election to open a special share account or a special term share account.

267D Conditions and declarations relating to special term share accounts

[(1) The following are the conditions referred to in *subparagraph (i)* of the definition of "*special term share account*" in *section 267A(1)*:

(a) the account shall be opened and designated by the credit union as a medium term share account or, as the case may be, a long term share account;

(b) the account shall not be denominated in a foreign currency;

(c) the account shall not be connected with any other share account or deposit account held by the member or any other person; and for this purpose an account shall be connected with another account if—

(i) (I) either account was opened with reference to the other account, or with a view to enabling the other account to be opened on particular terms, or with a view to facilitating the opening of the other account on particular terms, and

(II) the terms on which either account was opened would have been significantly less favourable to the member if the other account had not been opened,

or

(ii) the terms on which either account is operated are altered or affected in any way whatever because of the existence of the other account;

(d) all shares held in the account shall be subject to the same terms;

(e) there shall not be any agreement, arrangement or understanding in existence, whether express or implied, which influences or determines, or could influence or determine, the rate (other than an unspecified and variable rate) of dividend which is paid or payable, in respect of the share or shares held in the account, in or in respect of any period which is more than 12 months;

(f) dividends paid or payable in respect of the share or shares held in the account shall not directly or indirectly be linked to or determined by any change in the price or value of any shares, stocks, debentures or securities listed on a stock exchange or dealt in on an unlisted securities market;

(g) the account shall not be opened by or held in the name of a member who is under 16 years of age;

(h) the account shall be opened by and held in the name of the member beneficially entitled to the dividend payable in respect of the share or shares held in the account;

(i) an account may be held jointly by not more than 2 individual members;

[(j) a member shall not simultaneously hold whether solely or jointly—

(I) a special term account, or

(II) subject to *paragraph (k)*, another special term share account;][1]

(k) where the account is held jointly by [individuals who are married to each other or who are civil partners of each other][2] they may simultaneously hold one other such account jointly;

(l) subject to *paragraphs (m)* and *(n)* the amount of a subscription or aggregate amount of subscriptions for shares which may be added to an account in any one month shall not exceed [€635][3];

(m) at the time a member opens an account with a credit union, a single subscription for shares consisting of all or part of the savings of the member which are already held by the same credit union, may be transferred to the account;

(n) otherwise than by way of a transfer under *paragraph (m)*, shares at a cost of not more than [€7,620][4] may be added by a member once and only once to an account during the period in which the account is a special term share account;

(o) any disbursement of the surplus funds of a credit union, in the form of dividends or rebate of loan interest, which is added to the account shall not be treated as a subscription for shares for the purposes of *paragraph (l)* or *(p)*, but such dividend or rebate of loan interest may not be withdrawn from the account, otherwise than in accordance with *paragraph (q)*, unless the withdrawal is made within the period of 12 months from the date it was so added;

(p) subject to *paragraph (q)*, a share may not be withdrawn from an account held by a member within—

(i) 3 years from the date the share was subscribed for, in the case of a medium term share account, and

(ii) 5 years from the date the share was subscribed for, in the case of a long term share account,

otherwise than on the death of the member or, where the account is an account held jointly by 2 members, on the death of one of them;

(q) one and only one withdrawal may be made from an account by a member who is 60 years of age or over on the date of the withdrawal, provided that the account was opened when the member was under that age;

(r) a transfer of shares from an account by a credit union to reduce a balance outstanding on a loan from the credit union to a member shall not be treated as a withdrawal from the account for the purposes of *paragraph (p)* where—

(i) such shares were pledged as security for the loan at the time the loan was granted,

(ii) a default (whether of interest or otherwise) in the terms of the repayment of the loan of not less than 6 months has occurred, and

(iii) the credit union has followed its standard procedures in seeking to recover the loan.

(2) The declaration referred to in *subparagraph (ii)* of the definition of "*special term share account*" in *section 267A(1)* shall be a declaration in writing to the credit union which—

(a) is made by the member (in this subsection referred to as "*the declarer*") who holds the account in respect of which the declaration is made[...][5],

(b) is signed by the declarer,

(c) is made in such form as may be prescribed or authorised by the Revenue Commissioners,

(d) declares that at the time when the declaration is made the conditions referred to in *paragraphs (g), (h), (j)* and *(k)* of *subsection (1)* are satisfied in relation to the account in respect of which the declaration is made,

(e) contains the full name and address of the declarer,

(f) contains an undertaking by the declarer that, if the conditions referred to in *paragraphs (g), (h), (j)* and *(k)* of *subsection (1)* cease to be satisfied in respect of the account in respect of which the declaration is made, the declarer will notify the credit union accordingly, and

(g) contains such other information as the Revenue Commissioners may reasonably require for the purposes of this Chapter.

(3) *Section 263(2)* shall apply as respects declarations of the kind mentioned in this section as it applies as respects declarations of the kind mentioned in that section.][6]

Amendments

[1] Substituted by FA02 s21(f)(i).

[2] Substituted by F(No.3)A11 sched1(54).

[3] Substituted by FA01 s57(1)(a)(viii)(I). Applies as respects the year of assessment 2002 and subsequent years of assessment. With effect from 1 January 2002 per S.I. 596 of 2001.

[4] Substituted by FA01 s57(1)(a)(viii)(II). Applies as respects the year of assessment 2002 and subsequent years of assessment. With effect from 1 January 2002 per S.I. 596 of 2001.

[5] Deleted by FA02 s21(f)(ii).

[6] Inserted by FA01 s57(1)(a)(vi). With effect from 1 January 2002 per S.I. 596 of 2001.

Cross References

From Section 267D

Section 263 Declarations relating to deposits of non-residents.

Section 267A Interpretation (Chapter 5).

To Section 267D

Section 267A Interpretation (Chapter 5).

Section 267C Taxation of dividends on special term share accounts.

267E Returns of special term share accounts by credit unions

[(1) In this section "*appropriate inspector*" means—

(a) the inspector who has last given notice in writing to the credit union that he or she is the inspector to whom the credit union is required to deliver the return required under *subsection (2)*, or

(b) where there is no such inspector as is referred to in *paragraph (a)*, [the inspector of returns][1].

(2) On or before 31 March in each year of assessment, every credit union shall prepare and deliver to the appropriate inspector a return, in such form as may be prescribed or authorised by the Revenue Commissioners specifying—

(a) the name and address of the holder or holders, as the case may be, of each special term share account which was opened during the previous year of assessment,

(b) whether the account is a medium term share account or a long term share account, and

(c) the date of opening of such account.

(3) *Sections 1052* and *1054* shall apply to a failure by a credit union to deliver a return required by *subsection (2)* and to each and every such failure, as they apply to a failure to deliver a return referred to in *section 1052*.][2]

Amendments

[1] Substituted by FA12 sched5(1)(l).

[2] Inserted by FA01 s57(1)(a)(vi). With effect from 1 January 2002 per S.I. 596 of 2001.

Cross References

From Section 267E

Section 950 Interpretation (Part 41).
Section 1052 Penalties for failure to make certain returns, etc.
Section 1054 Penalties in the case of a secretary of a body of persons.

To Section 267E

Schedule 29 Provisions Referred to in Sections 1052, 1053 and 1054

267F Supplementary provisions (Chapter 5)

[(1) The provisions of *section 904A* shall apply to a credit union, treated under this Chapter as paying relevant interest, as they apply to a relevant deposit taker paying relevant interest.

[...][1]

(3) *Section 261* shall apply in relation to any dividend paid on shares held in a special share account or a special term share account which under *section 267B* is treated in whole or in part as relevant interest paid in respect of a relevant deposit, as if the following paragraph were substituted for *paragraph (c)* of that section:

"(c) the amount of any payment of relevant interest paid in respect of a relevant deposit shall not, except for the purposes of a claim to repayment under *section 267(3)* in respect of the appropriate tax deducted from such relevant interest, be reckoned in computing total income for the purposes of the Income Tax Acts;".][2]

Amendments

[1] Deleted by FA12 s36(1)(e). Applies to any payment or crediting of relevant interest (within the meaning of Chapter 4 of Part 8) made on or after 1 January 2012.

[2] Inserted by FA01 s57(1)(a)(vi). With effect from 1 January 2002 per S.I. 596 of 2001.

Cross References

From Section 267F

Section 256 Interpretation (Chapter 4).
Section 258 Returns and collection of appropriate tax.
Section 261 Taxation of relevant interest, etc.
Section 267 Repayment of appropriate tax in certain cases.
Section 267B Election to open a special share account or a special term share account.
Section 904A Power of inspection: returns and collection of appropriate tax.

CHAPTER 6

Implementation of Council Directive 2003/49/EC of 3 June 2003 on a Common System of Taxation Applicable to Interest and Royalty Payments Made between Associated Companies of Different Member States

267G Interpretation (Chapter 6)

[(1) In this Chapter—

"*arrangements*" means arrangements having the force of law by virtue of [*section 826(1)*][1];

"*bilateral agreement*" means any arrangements, protocol or other agreement between the Government and the government of another state;

"*permanent establishment*" means a fixed place of business through which the business of a company of a Member State is wholly or partly carried on which place of business is situated in a territory other than that Member State;

"*company*" means a company of a Member State;

"*company of a Member State*" has the meaning assigned to it by Article 3(*a*) of the Directive;

["*the Directive*" means Council Directive 2003/49/EC of 3 June 2003* as amended;][2]

* OJ No. L157, 26.6.2003, p.49

"*interest*" means income from debt-claims of every kind, whether or not secured by mortgage and whether or not carrying a right to participate in the debtor's profits, and in particular, income from securities and income from bonds or debentures, including premiums and prizes attaching to such securities, bonds or debentures but does not include penalty charges for late payment;

"*Member State*" means a Member State of the European Communities;

"*royalties*" means payments of any kind as consideration for

(a) the use of, or the right to use—

(i) any copyright of literary, artistic or scientific work, including cinematograph films and software,

(ii) any patent, trade mark, design or model, plan, secret formula or process,

(b) information concerning industrial, commercial or scientific experience;

(c) the use of, or the right to use, industrial, commercial or scientific equipment;

"*tax*", in relation to a Member State other than the State, means any tax imposed in that Member State which is specified in Article 3(*a*)(iii) of the Directive.

(2) For the purposes of this Chapter—

(a) a company shall be treated as an "associated company" of another company during an uninterrupted period of at least 2 years throughout which—

(i) one of them directly controls not less than 25 per cent of the voting power of the other company, or

(ii) in respect of those companies, a third company directly controls not less than 25 per cent of the voting power of each of them,

(b) a permanent establishment of a company in a Member State shall be treated as being the beneficial owner of interest or royalties if—

(i) the debt-claim, right or asset in respect of which the interest arises, or as the case may be the royalties arise, consists of property or rights used by, or held by or for, the permanent establishment, and

(ii) the interest or royalties are taken into account in computing income of the permanent establishment which is subject to one of the taxes specified in Article 1.5(*b*) or Article 3(*a*)(iii) of the Directive,

(c) a word or expression used in this Chapter and in the Directive has, unless the contrary intention appears, the same meaning in this Chapter as in the Directive.

Amendments

[1] Substituted by FA07 sched2(1)(j). Has effect as on and from 2 April 2007

[2] Substituted by FA06 sched2(1)(c). Has effect as on and from 31 March 2006

Statements of Practice

Treatment of Certain Patent Royalties Paid to Companies Resident outside the State – SP – CT/01/10

Cross References

From Section 267G

Section 826 Agreements for relief from double taxation.

To Section 267G

Section 267K Miscellaneous.

Section 267L Application of this Chapter to certain payments made to companies in Switzerland.

267H Application (Chapter 6)

[(1) Subject to *subsection (2)*, this Chapter shall apply to a payment, being interest or royalties, made—

(a) by either—

(i) a company resident in the State, or

(ii) a company not so resident which carries on a trade in the State through a permanent establishment if, in relation to the trade the interest gives, or as the case may be the royalties give, rise to a deduction under *section 81* or *97* or relief under *Part 8*,

(b) to or for the benefit of—

(i) where *subparagraph (ii)* does not apply, a company which—

(I) is the beneficial owner of the interest, or as the case may be the royalties, and

(II) is, by virtue of the law of a Member State other than the State, resident for the purposes of tax in such a Member State,

or

(ii) a permanent establishment—

(I) which is situated in a Member State (in this subparagraph referred to as the "*first Member State*") other than the State,

(II) which is treated as the beneficial owner of the interest, or as the case may be the royalties, and

(III) through which a company, which is (by virtue of the law of a Member State other than the State) resident for the purposes of tax in such a Member State, carries on a business in the first Member State,

if the company referred to in *paragraph (a)* is an associated company of the company referred to in *paragraph (b)*.

(2) This Chapter shall not apply to—

(a) interest or royalties paid—

(i) to a company where the debt-claim, right or asset in respect of which the payment is made consists of property or rights used by, or held by or for, a permanent establishment of the company through which the company carries on a trade—

(I) in the State, or

(II) in a territory which is not a Member State,

or

(ii) by a company for the purposes of a business carried on by it through a permanent establishment in a territory which is not a Member State,

(b) interest on a debt-claim in respect of which there is no provision for repayment of the principal amount or where the repayment is due more than 50 years after the creation of the debt, or

(c) so much of any royalties paid as exceeds the amount which would have been agreed by the payer, and the beneficial owner, of the royalties if they were independent persons acting at arms' length.][1]

Amendments

[1] Inserted by FA04 sched1.

Statements of Practice

Treatment of Certain Patent Royalties Paid to Companies Resident outside the State – SP – CT/01/10

Cross References

From Section 267H

Section 81 General rule as to deductions.

Section 97 Computational rules and allowable deductions.

Section 237 Annual payments payable wholly out of taxed income.

To Section 267H

Section 267K Miscellaneous.

267I Exemptions from tax and withholding tax

[(1) Where, apart from this section, *section 238*, *246(2)* or *257* would apply to a payment of interest or royalties to which this Chapter applies, those sections shall not apply to that payment.

(2) A company which, by virtue of the law of a Member State other than the State, is resident for the purposes of tax in that Member State, shall not be chargeable to corporation tax or income tax in respect of interest or royalties to which this Chapter applies except where the interest is, or as the case may be the royalties are, paid to the company in connection with a trade which is carried on in the State by that company through a permanent establishment.][1]

Amendments

[1] Inserted by FA04 sched1.

Statements of Practice

Treatment of Certain Patent Royalties Paid to Companies Resident outside the State – SP – CT/01/10

Cross References

From Section 267I

Section 238 Annual payments not payable out of taxed income.

Section 246 Interest payments by companies and to non-residents.

Section 257 Deduction of tax from relevant interest.

To Section 267I

Section 243 Allowance of charges on income.

Section 267K Miscellaneous.

Section 267L Application of this Chapter to certain payments made to companies in Switzerland.

267J Credit for foreign tax

[(1) Where interest or royalties are received by a company resident in the State from an associated company, credit shall be allowed for—

(a) any withholding tax charged on the interest or royalties by Greece or Portugal, and

(b) any withholding tax charged on the royalties by Spain,

pursuant to the derogations provided for in Article 6 of the Directive against corporation tax in respect of the interest or royalties to the extent that credit for such withholding tax would not otherwise be allowed.

[(2) Where by virtue of *subsection (1)* a company is to be allowed credit for tax payable under the laws of a Member State other than the State, *Schedule 24* shall apply for the purposes of that subsection as if that subsection were arrangements providing that the tax so payable shall be allowed as a credit against tax payable in the State.][1]

(3) This section applies without prejudice to a provision of a bilateral agreement.][2]

Amendments

[1] Substituted by FA05 sched6(1)(d). This section is deemed to have come into force as on and from 1 January 2004.

[2] Inserted by FA04 sched1.

Statements of Practice

Treatment of Certain Patent Royalties Paid to Companies Resident outside the State – SP – CT/01/10

Cross References

From Section 267J

Schedule 24 Relief from Income Tax and Corporation Tax by Means of Credit in Respect of Foreign Tax

To Section 267J

Section 267K Miscellaneous.

267K Miscellaneous

[(1) *Sections 267G, 267H, 267I* and *267J* shall not apply to interest or royalties unless it can be shown that the payment of the interest or royalties was made for bona fide commercial reasons and does not form part of any arrangement or scheme of which the main purpose or one of the main purposes is avoidance of liability to income tax, corporation tax or capital gains tax.

(2) Where a company which—

(a) is entitled to receive a payment of interest or royalties from any person, and

(b) had received from that person a payment of interest or royalties which was exempt from tax in accordance with the Directive,

ceases to fulfil the requirements specified in the Directive for exemption to apply, the company shall without delay inform that person that it has so ceased.][1]

Amendments

[1] Inserted by FA04 sched1.

Statements of Practice

Treatment of Certain Patent Royalties Paid to Companies Resident outside the State – SP – CT/01/10

Cross References

From Section 267K

Section 267G Interpretation (Chapter 6).
Section 267H Application (Chapter 6).
Section 267I Exemptions from tax and withholding tax.
Section 267J Credit for foreign tax.

To Section 267K

Section 267L Application of this Chapter to certain payments made to companies in Switzerland.

267L Application of this Chapter to certain payments made to companies in Switzerland

[(1) This section applies to a payment, being interest or royalties, made to or for the benefit of—

(a) where *paragraph (b)* does not apply, a company which—

(i) is the beneficial owner of the interest, or as the case may be the royalties,

(ii) is, by virtue of the law of Switzerland, resident for the purposes of tax in Switzerland, and

(iii) is not treated, by virtue of any arrangements made by the government of Switzerland with the government of any territory for the purposes of tax, as resident in any territory which is not—

(I) a Member State of the European Communities, or

(II) Switzerland,

or

(b) a permanent establishment situated in Switzerland through which a company carries on business in Switzerland, being a permanent establishment which would, in accordance with the Directive, be treated as the beneficial owner of the interest, or as the case may be the royalties.

(2) *Sections 267G* to *267I* shall have effect in relation to a payment to which this section applies as if—

(a) a reference in those sections to a Member State of the European Communities included a reference to Switzerland,

(b) a reference in those sections to a company of a Member State included a company (being a company which takes one of the forms specified in Article 15 of the Agreement attached to the Council Decision (2004/911/EC) of

2 June 2004 on the signing and conclusion of the Agreement between the European Community and the Swiss Confederation providing for measures equivalent to those laid down in Council Directive 2003/48/EC of 3 June 2003 on taxation of savings income in the form of interest payments and the accompanying Memorandum of Understanding*) resident for the purposes of tax in Switzerland, and

* OJ No. L385, 29.12.2004, p. 28

(c) a reference in those sections to tax included any tax imposed in Switzerland which corresponds to income tax or corporation tax in the State.

(3) *Section 267K* applies in relation to this section as it applies in relation to *sections 267G* to *267I*.][1]

Amendments

[1] Inserted by FA05 s50(1). This section applies as respects any payment made on or after 1 July 2005.

Statements of Practice

Treatment of Certain Patent Royalties Paid to Companies Resident outside the State – SP – CT/01/10

Cross References

From Section 267L

Section 267G Interpretation (Chapter 6).
Section 267I Exemptions from tax and withholding tax.
Section 267K Miscellaneous.

CHAPTER 7

Certain Interest from Sources [Outside the State]

[Substituted by FA12 s36(1)(f). Applies to foreign deposit interest or specified interest (both within the meaning of section 267M(1) (as amended by subsection (1)(g))), as the case may be, which is received on or after 8 February 2012.]

267M Tax rate applicable to certain deposit interest received by individuals

[(1) In this section—

['*foreign deposit interest*' means interest arising in a foreign territory which would be interest payable in respect of a relevant deposit within the meaning of *section 256(1)* if—

(*a*) *paragraphs (c)*, *(d)* and *(g)* of the definition of *'relevant deposit'* in *section 256(1)* were deleted, and

(*b*) there were included in the definition of *'relevant deposit taker'* in *section 256(1)*, bodies—

(i) established in accordance with the law of a foreign territory, and

(ii) authorised under the laws of that foreign territory to accept deposits of money;

'*foreign territory*' means a territory other than a Member State of the European Communities;][1]

"*specified interest*" means interest arising in a Member State of the European Communities other than the State which would be interest payable in respect of a relevant deposit within the meaning of *section 256(1)* if—

(a) in the definition of "*relevant deposit*" in *section 256(1)*—

(i) the following were substituted for *paragraphs (c)* and *(d)*:

"(c) which, in the case of a relevant deposit taker which, by virtue of the law of a Member State of the European Communities other than the State, is resident for the purposes of tax in such a Member State, is held at a branch of the relevant deposit taker situated in a territory which is not a Member State,

(d) which, in the case of a relevant deposit taker not so resident in a Member State of the European Communities for the purposes of tax, is held otherwise than at a branch of the relevant deposit taker situated in a Member State,",

and

(ii) *paragraph (g)* were deleted,

and

(b) there were included in the definition of "*relevant deposit taker*" in *section 256(1)* bodies established in accordance with the law of any Member State of the European Communities other than the State which corresponds to—

(i) the Credit Union Act 1997,

(ii) the Trustee Savings Banks Acts 1989 and 2001, or

(iii) the Post Office Savings Bank Acts 1861 to 1958;

"*tax*" in relation to a Member State other than the State means tax which corresponds to income tax or corporation tax in the State.

[(2) (*a*) Notwithstanding *section 15* [...][2], where the taxable income of an individual includes—

(i) specified interest, the part of taxable income, equal to that specified interest, shall be chargeable to tax at the rate specified in [...][3] the definition of '*appropriate tax*' in *section 256(1)*, or

(ii) foreign deposit interest, so much of the part of taxable income, equal to that foreign deposit interest, as would otherwise be chargeable to tax at the standard rate, shall instead be chargeable to tax at the rate specified in [...][4] of the definition of '*appropriate tax*' in *section 256(1)*.

[...][5]

Amendments

[1] Inserted by FA12 s36(1)(g). Applies to foreign deposit interest or specified interest (both within the meaning of section 267M(1) (as amended by subsection (1)(g))), as the case may be, which is received on or after 8 February 2012.

[2] Deleted by FA14 s23(a). Comes into operation on 1 January 2015.

[3, 4] Deleted by F(No.2)A13 s23(1)(h). Applies to interest or dividends (within the meaning of Part 8) paid on or after 1 January 2014.

[5] Deleted by FA14 s23(b). Comes into operation on 1 January 2015.

Cross References

From Section 267M

Section 15 Rate of charge.

Section 256 Interpretation (Chapter 4).

Section 950 Interpretation (Part 41).

To Section 267M

Section 485C Interpretation (Chapter 2A).

PART 8A

Specified Financial Transactions

CHAPTER 1

Interpretation

267N Interpretation

[(1) For the purpose of this Part—

"*asset*" has the same meaning as in *section 532*;

"*charges on income*" has the same meaning as in *section 243*;

"*credit return*" means—

(a) in the case of a credit transaction within the meaning of *paragraph (a)* or *(b)* of the definition of "*credit transaction*", the excess of the consideration accruing to the finance undertaking from the borrower in respect of the asset over the consideration paid or payable by the finance undertaking for that asset, and

(b) in the case of a credit transaction within the meaning of *paragraph (c)* of the definition of "*credit transaction*", the excess of the consideration (including any consideration paid or payable for the use of the asset during the period of the arrangement) accruing to the finance undertaking from the borrower in respect of the interest of the finance undertaking in the asset over the consideration paid or payable by the finance undertaking for that asset;

"*credit transaction*" means—

(a) an arrangement whereby a finance undertaking acquires an asset for the purpose of disposing of the full interest in that asset to a borrower in circumstances where—

(i) the consideration paid or payable by the borrower exceeds the consideration paid or payable by the finance undertaking for the asset,

(ii) all or part of that consideration is not required to be paid until a date later than the date of the disposal, and

(iii) the excess of the consideration paid or payable to the finance undertaking by the borrower in respect of the asset over the consideration paid or payable by the finance undertaking for the asset is equivalent to the return on a loan of money at interest,

(b) an arrangement whereby a finance undertaking acquires an asset and—

(i) immediately disposes of its full interest in that asset to a borrower for a consideration which exceeds the consideration paid or payable by the finance undertaking for the asset,

(ii) the borrower acquires and immediately disposes of the full interest in that asset to another person for a consideration which is at least 95 per cent of the consideration paid or payable by the finance undertaking for the acquisition of that asset,

(iii) all or part of the consideration for the acquisition of the asset by the borrower is not required to be paid by the borrower until a date later than the date of the purchase of the asset, and

(iv) the excess of the consideration paid or payable to the finance undertaking by the borrower in respect of the asset over the consideration paid or payable by the finance undertaking for the asset is equivalent to the return on a loan of money at interest,

or

(c) an arrangement whereby—

(i) a finance undertaking and a borrower jointly acquire an asset, or

(ii) a finance undertaking acquires an interest in an asset from a borrower, in circumstances where the borrower retains an interest in that asset,

on terms whereby—

(I) the borrower—

(A) in the circumstances referred to in *subparagraph (i)* has exclusive use of the asset immediately and, in the circumstances referred to in *subparagraph (ii)*, retains exclusive use of the asset immediately, as the case may be,

(B) is exclusively entitled to any income, profit or gain arising from or attributable to the asset (including any increase in the value of the asset), and

(C) agrees to make payments to the finance undertaking amounting to the aggregate of the consideration paid or payable by the finance undertaking for the acquisition of its interest in the asset and any consideration paid or payable by the borrower for the use of the asset during the period of the arrangement,

(II) the excess of the consideration (including any consideration paid or payable for the use of the asset during the period of the arrangement) accruing to the finance undertaking from the borrower in respect of the interest of the finance undertaking in the asset over the consideration paid or payable by the finance undertaking for the asset is equivalent to the return on a loan of money at interest, and

(III) the finance undertaking's interest in the asset passes either immediately or by the end of a specified period of time, to the borrower for a consideration which exceeds the consideration paid by the finance undertaking for the asset;

"*deposit transaction*" means a transaction whereby—

(a) a person deposits a sum of money with a relevant deposit taker on terms under which it or any part of it may be repaid, either on demand or at a time or in circumstances agreed by or on behalf of the person making the deposit and the relevant deposit taker,

(b) the relevant deposit taker makes or credits a payment or a series of payments (in this Part referred to as the "*deposit return*") over a period of time to the person—

(i) out of any profit resulting from the use of that money, and

(ii) in proportion to the money deposited by the person;

[*finance company*' means a company whose income consists wholly or mainly of either or both of the following—

(*a*) income from the leasing of machinery or plant, and

(*b*) income from the carrying on of specified financial transactions;][1]

"*finance institution*" has the same meaning as in *section 891B*;

"*finance undertaking*" means a finance company or a financial institution;

"*investment certificate*" means a security which—

(a) is issued by a qualifying company to a person in order to establish the claim of that person over the rights and obligations represented by the certificate,

(b) entitles the owner to an amount equivalent to a share in the profits or losses derived from an asset held by the qualifying company which issued the certificate, in proportion to the number and value of the certificates owned,

[(c) is issued to a person who is not a specified person, and][2]

(d) is wholly or partly treated in accordance with generally accepted accounting practice as a financial liability of the qualifying company which issued the certificate;

"*investment return*" means—

(a) the excess (if any) of the consideration paid by the qualifying company on redemption of an investment certificate over the consideration paid in respect of that certificate by the beneficial owner to whom the certificate was first issued, and

(b) any other payments (if any) made from time to time by the qualifying company to the beneficial owner from profits or gains derived by the qualifying company from the asset and in consideration of the holding of the investment certificate;

"*investment transaction*" means a transaction whereby a person acquires investment certificates and receives an investment return;

"*loan*" means any loan or advance or any other arrangement whatever by virtue of which an amount equivalent to interest is paid or payable;

"*owner*", in relation to any security, means at any time the person who would be entitled, if the securities were redeemed at that time by the issuer, to the proceeds of the redemption, and "*owned*" shall be construed accordingly;

"*public*" means individuals generally, companies generally, or individuals and companies generally;

"*qualifying company*" means a company which—

(a) is resident in the State,

(b) issues investment certificates to investors, and

(c) redeems the investment certificates after a specified period of time;

"*relevant deposit*", "*relevant deposit taker*" and "*relevant interest*" have, respectively, the meanings assigned to them by *section 256*;

"*specified financial transaction*" means—

(a) a credit transaction,

(b) a deposit transaction, or

(c) an investment transaction,

but a transaction shall not be a specified financial transaction if the terms of the transaction are not such as would reasonably have been expected if the parties to the transaction were independent persons acting at arm's length.

["*specified person*" has the meaning assigned to it by *section 110* as if a reference in the definition of "*specified person*" in that section—

(a) to a qualifying company included a reference to a qualifying company within the meaning of this section, and

(b) to qualifying assets were a reference to assets within the meaning of this section;][3]

(2) Any reference in this Part to consideration—

(a) paid or payable by a borrower or a finance undertaking shall be construed as a reference to the aggregate of amounts paid or payable by the borrower or finance undertaking, as the case may be,

(b) shall not include any amount in respect of which a borrower or a finance undertaking may claim—

(i) a deduction under Chapter 1 of Part 8 of the Value-Added Tax Consolidation Act 2010, or

(ii) a refund of value-added tax under an order under section 103 of that Act,

and

(c) shall not include any amount chargeable by a finance undertaking in respect of fees, charges or similar payments.][4]

Amendments

[1] Substituted by FA12 s37(a). Deemed to have come into force and takes effect on and from 1 January 2012.

[2] Substituted by FA13 s24(1)(a). Applies as respects an investment certificate (within the meaning of section 267N) issued on or after 1 January 2013.

[3] Inserted by FA13 s24(1)(b). Applies as respects an investment certificate (within the meaning of section 267N) issued on or after 1 January 2013.

[4] Inserted by FA10 s39. Deemed to have come into force and takes effect as on and from 1 January 2010.

Cross References

From Section 267N

Section 243 Allowance of charges on income.
Section 256 Interpretation (Chapter 4).
Section 532 Assets.
Section 891B Returns of certain payments made by certain persons.

To Section 267N

Section 267P Treatment of credit transaction.

CHAPTER 2

Credit Return

267O Treatment of credit return

[(1) Subject to *section 130*, a credit return shall be treated for all the purposes of the Tax Acts as if it were interest paid or payable, as the case may be, on a loan made by the finance undertaking to the borrower, or a security issued by the borrower to the finance undertaking, as the case may be, and the return shall be chargeable to tax accordingly.

(2) The amount of the credit return shall not be regarded as expenditure on an asset for the purpose of an allowance under *Part 9*, *section 670*, *Part 29* or any other provision of the Tax Acts relating to the making of allowances in accordance with *Part 9*.

(3) The amount of the credit return shall not be regarded as expenditure on an asset for the purpose of *section 552*.][1]

Amendments

[1] Inserted by FA10 s39. Deemed to have come into force and takes effect as on and from 1 January 2010.

Cross References

From Section 267O

Section 130 Matters to be treated as distributions.
Section 320 Other interpretation (Part 9).
Section 552 Acquisition, enhancement and disposal costs.
Section 670 Mine development allowance.
Section 754 Interpretation (Chapter 1).

267P Treatment of credit transaction

[(1) A reference to a loan in *section 122* or in *Part 8* shall be deemed to include a reference to a credit transaction.

(2) Acquisitions and disposals of an asset by the finance undertaking for the purpose of a credit transaction, within the meaning of *paragraph (a)* or *(b)* of the definition of "*credit transaction*" in *section 267N* shall, where the finance undertaking is carrying on a trade which consists of or includes specified financial transactions, be regarded as made in the course of that trade.

(3) The borrower shall not be treated as having incurred a loss, for any purpose of the Tax Acts, on the disposal of the asset in the circumstances referred to in *paragraph (b)(ii)* of the definition of "*credit transaction*" in *section 267N*.

(4) The finance undertaking shall not be entitled to any allowance under *Part 9*, *section 670*, *Part 29* or any other provision of the Tax Acts relating to the making of allowances in accordance with *Part 9*, in respect of expenditure incurred on assets acquired for the purpose of entering into a credit transaction.

(5) Where an asset is acquired by a borrower under a credit transaction, in the circumstances referred to in *paragraph (c)(i)* of the definition of "*credit transaction*" in *section 267N*, the borrower shall be deemed to have acquired the full interest in that asset for the purpose of claiming any allowance under *Part 9*, *section 670*, *Part 29* or any other provision of the Tax Acts relating to the making of allowances in accordance with *Part 9*.

(6) The disposal of the borrower's interest in the asset to the financial undertaking, in the circumstances referred to in *paragraph (c)(ii)* of the definition of "*credit transaction*" in *section 267N*, shall not be construed as an event giving rise to an allowance or charge, as the case may be, within the meaning of *section 274* or *288*.

(7) The acquisition of an asset by the borrower, in the circumstances referred to in *paragraph (c)(III)* of the definition of "*credit transaction*" in *section 267N*, shall not be

construed as expenditure on an asset for the purpose of claiming any allowance under *Part 9*, *section 670*, *Part 29* or any other provision of the Tax Acts relating to the making of allowances in accordance with *Part 9*.

(8) Except in respect of a claim to any allowance referred to in *subsection (5)*, no part of the consideration paid or payable by the borrower to the finance undertaking, other than an amount equal to the credit return, may be treated by the borrower as an amount which may be deducted in the computation of the profits or gains to be charged to tax under Schedule D.][1]

Amendments

[1] Inserted by FA10 s39. Deemed to have come into force and takes effect as on and from 1 January 2010.

Cross References

From Section 267P

Section 122 Preferential loan arrangements.
Section 237 Annual payments payable wholly out of taxed income.
Section 267N Interpretation.
Section 274 Balancing allowances and balancing charges.
Section 288 Balancing allowances and balancing charges.
Section 320 Other interpretation (Part 9).
Section 670 Mine development allowance.
Section 754 Interpretation (Chapter 1).

CHAPTER 3

Deposit Return

267Q Treatment of deposit return

[Subject to *section 130*, a deposit return shall be treated for all the purposes of the Tax Acts as if it were relevant interest paid on a deposit of money and for this purpose—

(a) *Chapter 4* of *Part 8* shall apply to the deposit return as if it were relevant interest on a relevant deposit, and

(b) the relevant deposit taker shall not be regarded as carrying on a trade in partnership with the beneficial owner of the deposit for the purposes of *Part 43* merely by virtue of the deposit arrangement.][1]

Amendments

[1] Inserted by FA10 s39. Deemed to have come into force and takes effect as on and from 1 January 2010.

Cross References

From Section 267Q

Section 130 Matters to be treated as distributions.
Section 237 Annual payments payable wholly out of taxed income.
Section 256 Interpretation (Chapter 4).
Section 1007 Interpretation (Part 43).

CHAPTER 4

Investment Certificates and Returns

267R Treatment of investment return

[Subject to *section 130*, the Tax Acts shall apply to an investment return as if that investment return were interest on a security and the return shall be chargeable to tax accordingly.][1]

Amendments

[1] Inserted by FA10 s39. Deemed to have come into force and takes effect as on and from 1 January 2010.

Cross References

From Section 267R

Section 130 Matters to be treated as distributions.

267S Treatment of certificate owner

[(1) For the purposes of the Tax Acts, the owner of the investment certificate shall not be regarded as having a legal or beneficial interest in the assets held by the qualifying company.

(2) Income, profits, gains or losses arising from or attributable to the assets held by the qualifying company (including any increase or decrease in the value of the asset) shall be income, profits, gains or losses, as the case may be, of the qualifying company and the qualifying company shall be chargeable to corporation tax accordingly.

(3) The owner of the investment certificate shall not be entitled to an allowance under *Part 9*, *section 670*, *Part 29* or any other provision of the Tax Acts relating to the making of allowances in accordance with Part 9 in respect of expenditure on the assets held by the qualifying company.][1]

Amendments

[1] Inserted by FA10 s39. Deemed to have come into force and takes effect as on and from 1 January 2010.

Cross References

From Section 267S

Section 320 Other interpretation (Part 9).

Section 670 Mine development allowance.

Section 754 Interpretation (Chapter 1).

Chapter 5

Reporting

267T Reporting

[*Part 38* in so far as it relates to the reporting of interest payments shall apply to a deposit return, a credit return or an investment return as if that return were an interest payment.][1]

Amendments

[1] Inserted by FA10 s39. Deemed to have come into force and takes effect as on and from 1 January 2010.

Cross References

From Section 267T

Section 876 Notice of liability to income tax.

CHAPTER 6

Application

267U Application

[(1) This Part applies to a specified financial transaction where a person who is—

(*a*) a party to the transaction, and

(*b*) within the charge to tax,

makes an election in writing to [the appropriate inspector][1] that this Part applies to that transaction.

(2) An election under this section—

(*a*) shall be made in a form approved by the Revenue Commissioners and containing such particulars relating to the transaction concerned, and the parties to that transaction, as may be specified in that form, and

(*b*) may be made either in respect of an individual transaction or in respect of a series of transactions of a similar nature.

(3) Where an election is made in accordance with this section—

(*a*) this Part applies to that transaction or series of transactions, and

(*b*) the party making the election shall notify any other person who is a party to a specified financial transaction, that the transaction is a specified financial transaction.][2]

Amendments

[1] Substituted by FA12 sched5(1)(l).

[2] Substituted by FA12 s37(b). Deemed to have come into force and takes effect on and from 1 January 2012.

Cross References

From Section 267U

Section 950 Interpretation (Part 41).

267V Transactions to avoid tax

[This Part shall not apply to any transaction unless that transaction has been undertaken for *bona fide* commercial reasons and does not form part of any arrangement or scheme of which the main purpose or one of the main purposes is avoidance of liability to income tax, corporation tax, capital gains tax, value-added tax, stamp duty or capital acquisitions tax.][1]

Amendments

[1] Inserted by FA10 s39. Deemed to have come into force and takes effect as on and from 1 January 2010.

PART 9

Principal Provisions Relating to Relief for Capital Expenditure

CHAPTER 1

Industrial Buildings or Structures: Industrial Building Allowances, Writing-down Allowances, Balancing Allowances and Balancing Charges

268 Meaning of "industrial building or structure"

[ITA67 s255(1) to (5), s257 and s263(4); FA69 s64(1), (2) and (5), FA75 s34(1) and (3); FA84 s36; FA92 s27; FA96 s29]

(1) In this Part, "*industrial building or structure*" means a building or structure in use—

(a) for the purposes of a trade carried on in—

(i) a mill, factory or other similar premises, or

(ii) a laboratory the sole or main function of which is the analysis of minerals (including oil and natural gas) in connection with the exploration for, or the extraction of, such minerals,

(b) for the purposes of a dock undertaking,

(c) for the purposes of growing fruit, vegetables or other produce in the course of a trade of market gardening within the meaning of *section 654*,

(d) for the purposes of the trade of hotel-keeping,

(e) for the purposes of the intensive production of cattle, sheep, pigs, poultry or eggs in the course of a trade other than the trade of farming within the meaning of [*section 654*,][1]

(f) for the purposes of a trade which consists of the operation or management of an airport and which is an airport runway or an airport apron used solely or mainly by aircraft carrying passengers or cargo for hire or reward,

[(g) for the purposes of a trade which consists of the operation or management of a nursing home [(in this section referred to as a "registered nursing home")][2] within the meaning of section 2 of the Health (Nursing Homes) Act, 1990, being a nursing home which is registered under [section 4 of that Act,][3]][4]

[(h) for the purposes of a trade which consists of the operation or management of an airport, other than a building or structure to which [*paragraph (f)* relates, […][5]][6]][7]

[(i) for the purposes of a trade which consists of the operation or management of a convalescent home for the provision of medical and nursing care for persons recovering from treatment in a hospital, being a hospital that provides treatment for acutely ill patients, and in respect of which convalescent home [the Health Service Executive][8] is satisfied that the convalescent home satisfies the requirements of sections 4 and 6 of the Health (Nursing Homes) Act, 1990, and any regulations made under section 6 of that Act as if it were a nursing home within the meaning of section 2 of [that Act,[…][9]][10]][11]

[(j) for the purposes of a trade which consists of the operation or management of a [qualifying hospital, […][12]][13]][14]

[(k) for the purposes of a trade which consists of the operation or management of a qualifying sports injuries [clinic, [...][15]][16]][17]

[(l) for the purposes of a trade which consists of the operation or management of a qualifying mental health [centre, [...][18]][19]][20]

[(m) for the purposes of a trade which consists of the operation or management of a qualifying specialist palliative care [unit, or][21]][22]

[(n) for the purposes of a trade which consists of—

(i) the maintenance, repair or overhaul of aircraft used to carry passengers or cargo for hire or reward, or

(ii) the dismantling of aircraft of the kind referred to in *subparagraph (i)*, for the purposes of the salvaging or recycling of parts or materials,][23]

and in particular, in relation to capital expenditure incurred on or after the 6th day of April, 1969, includes any building or structure provided by the person carrying on such a trade or undertaking for the recreation or welfare of workers employed in that trade or undertaking and in use for that purpose.

[(1A) Where the relevant interest in relation to capital expenditure incurred on the construction of a building or structure in use for the purposes specified in *subsection (1)(j)* is held by—

(a) a company,

(b) the trustees of a trust,

(c) an individual who is involved in the operation or management of the qualifying hospital concerned either as an employee or director or in any other capacity, or

[(d) a property developer (within the meaning of *section 843A*) or a person who is connected with the property developer, in the case where either of such persons incurred the capital expenditure on the construction of that building or structure, or such expenditure was incurred by any other person connected with the property developer,][24]

then, notwithstanding that subsection, that building or structure [shall not, as regards a claim for any allowance under this Part by any such person, be regarded as an industrial building or structure][25] for the purposes of this Part, irrespective of whether that relevant interest is held by the person referred to in *paragraph (a), (b), (c)* or *(d)*, as the case may be, in a sole capacity or jointly or in partnership with another person or persons.][26]

[(1B) Where the relevant interest in relation to capital expenditure incurred on the construction of a building or structure in use for the purposes specified in *subsection (1)(k)* is held by—

(a) a company,

(b) the trustees of a trust,

(c) an individual who is involved in the operation or management of the qualifying sports injuries clinic concerned either as an employee or director or in any other capacity, or

(d) a property developer (within the meaning of *section 372A*), in the case where either such property developer or a person connected with such property developer incurred the capital expenditure on the construction of that building or structure, then, notwithstanding that subsection, that building or structure [shall not, as regards a claim for any allowance under this Part by any such person, be regarded as an industrial building or structure][27] for the purposes of this Part, irrespective of whether that relevant interest is held by the person referred to in *paragraph (a)*, *(b)*, *(c)* or *(d)*, as the case may be, in a sole capacity or jointly or in partnership with another person or persons.][28]

[(1C) In this section "*qualifying mental health centre*" means a centre (within the meaning of section 62 of the Mental Health Act 2001) which—

(a) is an approved centre for the purposes of the Mental Health Act 2001,

(b) has the capacity to provide day-patient and out-patient services and accommodation on an overnight basis of not less than 20 in-patient beds,

(c) provides to the Health Service Executive relevant data, for onward transmission to the Minister for Health and Children and the Minister for Finance, in relation to—

(i) the amount of the capital expenditure actually incurred on the construction or refurbishment of the centre,

(ii) the number and nature of the investors that are investing in the centre,

(iii) the amount to be invested by each investor, and

(iv) the nature of the structures which are being put in place to facilitate the investment in the centre,

together with such other information as may be specified by the Minister for Finance, in consultation with the Minister for Health and Children, as being of assistance in evaluating the costs, including but not limited to exchequer costs, and the benefits arising from the operation of tax relief under this Part for qualifying mental health centres,

(d) undertakes to the Health Service Executive—

(i) to make available annually, for the treatment of persons who have been awaiting day-patient, in-patient or out-patient services as public patients, not less than 20 per cent of its capacity, subject to service requirements to be specified by the Health Service Executive in advance and to the proviso that nothing in this subparagraph shall require the Health Service Executive to take up all or any part of the capacity made available to the Health Service Executive by the centre, and

(ii) in relation to the fees to be charged in respect of the treatment afforded to any such person, that such fees shall not be more than 90 per cent of the fees which would be charged in respect of similar treatment afforded to a person who has private medical insurance,

and

(e) in respect of which the Health Service Executive, in consultation with the Minister for Health and Children and with the consent of the Minister for Finance, gives an annual certificate in writing during the period of—

(i) 15 years beginning with the time when the centre was first used, or

(ii) where capital expenditure on the refurbishment of the centre is incurred, 15 years beginning with the time when the centre was first used subsequent to the incurring of that expenditure, stating that it is satisfied that the centre complies with the conditions mentioned in *paragraphs (a), (b), (c)* and *(d)*,

and—

(I) subject to *paragraph (II)*, includes any part of the centre which consists of rooms used exclusively for the assessment or treatment of patients, but

(II) does not include any part of the centre which consists of consultants' rooms or offices.

(1D) Where the relevant interest in relation to capital expenditure incurred on the construction of a building or structure in use for the purposes specified in *subsection (1)(l)* is held by—

(a) a company,

(b) the trustees of a trust,

(c) an individual who is involved in the operation or management of the centre concerned either as an employee or director or in any other capacity, or

[(d) a property developer (within the meaning of *section 843A*) or a person who is connected with the property developer, in the case where either of such persons incurred the capital expenditure on the construction of that building or structure, or such expenditure was incurred by any other person connected with the property developer,][29]

then, notwithstanding that subsection, that building or structure shall not, as regards a claim for any allowance under this Part by any such person, be regarded as an industrial building or structure for the purposes of this Part, irrespective of whether that relevant interest is held by the person referred to in *paragraph (a), (b), (c)* or *(d)*, as the case may be, in a sole capacity or jointly or in partnership with another person or persons.][30]

[(1E) Where the relevant interest in relation to capital expenditure incurred on the construction of a building or structure in use for the purposes specified in *subsection (1)(m)* is held by—

(a) a company,

(b) the trustees of a trust,

(c) an individual who is involved in the operation or management of the unit concerned either as an employee or director or in any other capacity, or

(d) a property developer (within the meaning of *section 843A*) or a person who is connected with the property developer, in the case where either of such persons incurred the capital expenditure on the construction of that building or structure, or such expenditure was incurred by any other person connected with the property developer,

then, notwithstanding that subsection, that building or structure shall not, as regards a claim for any allowance under this Part by any such person, be regarded as an industrial building or structure for the purposes of this Part, irrespective of whether that relevant interest is held by the person referred to in paragraph *(a)*, *(b)*, *(c)* or *(d)*, as the case may be, in a sole capacity or jointly or in partnership with another person or persons.][31]

[(1F) Where the relevant interest in relation to capital expenditure incurred on the construction of a building or structure in use for the purposes specified in *subsection (1)(n)* is held by a property developer (within the meaning of *section 843A*) or a person who is connected with the property developer, in the case where either of such persons incurred the capital expenditure on the construction of that building or structure, or such expenditure was incurred by any other person connected with the property developer, then, notwithstanding that subsection, that building or structure shall not, as regards a claim for any allowance under this Part by any such person, be regarded as an industrial building or structure for the purposes of this Part, irrespective of whether that relevant interest is held by the person in a sole capacity or jointly or in partnership with another person or persons.][32]

(2) In this section, "dock" includes any harbour, wharf, pier or jetty or other works in or at which vessels can ship or unship merchandise or passengers, not being a pier or jetty primarily used for recreation, and "dock undertaking" shall be construed accordingly.

[(2A) In this section—

[...][33]

"*qualifying hospital*" means a hospital [...][34] which—

(a) is a private hospital (within the meaning of the Health Insurance Act, 1994 (Minimum Benefits) Regulations, 1996 (S.I. No. 83 of 1996)),

[...][35]

(c) has the capacity to provide and normally provides medical and surgical services to persons every day of the year,

[(d) has the capacity to provide—

(i) out-patient services and accommodation on an overnight basis of not less than 70 in-patient beds, or

(ii) day-case and out-patient medical and surgical services and accommodation for such services of not less than 40 beds,][36]

(e) contains an operating theatre or theatres and related on-site diagnostic and therapeutic facilities,

(f) contains facilities to provide not less than 5 of the following services:

(i) accident and emergency,

(ii) cardiology and vascular,

(iii) eye, ear, nose and throat,

(iv) gastroenterology,

(v) geriatrics,

(vi) haematology,

(vii) maternity,

(viii) medical,

(ix) neurology,

(x) oncology,

(xi) orthopaedic,

(xii) respiratory,

(xiii) rheumatology, [...][37]

(xiv) paediatric, [and][38]

[(xv) mental health services (within the meaning of the Mental Health Act 2001),][39]

[(fa) in the case of a building or structure which—

(i) is first used on or after 1 February 2007, or

(ii) where capital expenditure on the refurbishment of the building or structure is incurred, is, subsequent to the incurring of that expenditure, first used on or after 1 February 2007,

provides to the Health Service Executive relevant data, for onward transmission to the Minister for Health and Children and the Minister for Finance, in relation to—

(I) the amount of the capital expenditure actually incurred on the construction or refurbishment of the building or structure,

(II) the number and nature of the investors that are investing in the building or structure,

(III) the amount to be invested by each investor, and

(IV) the nature of the structures which are being put in place to facilitate the investment in the building or structure,

together with such other information as may be specified by the Minister for Finance, in consultation with the Minister for Health and Children, as being of assistance in evaluating the costs, including but not limited to exchequer costs, and the benefits arising from the operation of tax relief under this Part for qualifying hospitals,][40]

(g) undertakes to [the Health Service Executive][41]—

(i) to make available annually, for the treatment of persons who have been awaiting in-patient or out-patient hospital services as public patients, not less than 20 per cent of its capacity, subject to service requirements to be specified by [the Health Service Executive][42] in advance and to the proviso that nothing in this subparagraph shall require [the Health Service Executive][43] to take up all or any part of the capacity made available to [the Health Service Executive][44] by the hospital, and

(ii) in relation to the fees to be charged in respect of the treatment afforded to any such person, that such fees shall not be more than 90 per cent of the fees which would be charged in respect of similar treatment afforded to a person who has private medical insurance,

and

[(h) in respect of which the Health Service Executive, in consultation with the Minister for Health and Children and with the consent of the Minister for Finance, gives an annual certificate in writing during the period of—

(i) 10 years beginning with the time referred to in *section 272(4)(ga)(i)*, or

(ii) as respects a building or structure which is first used on or after 1 February 2007, 15 years beginning with the time when the building or structure was first used, or

(iii) where capital expenditure on the refurbishment of a building or structure is incurred and, subsequent to the incurring of that expenditure, the building or structure is first used on or after 1 February 2007, 15 years beginning with the time when the building or structure was first used subsequent to the incurring of that expenditure,

stating that it is satisfied that the hospital complies with the conditions mentioned in *paragraphs (a)*, *(c)*, *(d)*, *(e)*, *(f)*, *(fa)* and *(g)*,][45] [and—][46]

[(I) [subject to paragraph (II),][47] includes any part of the hospital which consists of rooms used exclusively for the assessment or treatment of patients, but

(II) does not include any part of the hospital which consists of consultants' rooms or offices.][48]][49]

[(2B) In this section "*qualifying sports injuries clinic*" means a medical clinic—

(a) which does not (other than by virtue of *paragraph (e)*) provide health care services to a person pursuant to his or her entitlements under Chapter II of Part IV of the Health Act, 1970,

(b) in which the sole or main business carried on is the provision, by or under the control of medical or surgical specialists, of health care consisting of the diagnosis, alleviation and treatment of physical injuries sustained by persons in participating, or in training for participation, in athletic games or sports,

(c) which has the capacity to provide day-patient, in-patient and out-patient medical and surgical services and in-patient accommodation of not less than 20 beds,

(d) which contains an operating theatre or theatres and related on-site diagnostic and therapeutic facilities,

(e) which undertakes to [the Health Service Executive][50]—

(i) to make available annually, for the treatment of persons who have been awaiting day-patient, in-patient or out-patient hospital services as public patients, not less than 20 per cent of its capacity, subject to service requirements to be specified by [the Health Service Executive][51] in advance and to the condition that nothing in this subparagraph shall require [the Health Service Executive][52] to take up all or any part of the capacity made available to [the Health Service Executive][53] by the medical clinic, and

(ii) in relation to the fees to be charged in respect of the treatment afforded to any such person, that such fees shall not be more than 90 per cent of the fees which would be charged in respect of similar treatment afforded to a person who has private medical insurance,

and

(f) in respect of which [the Health Service Executive][54], in consultation with the Minister for Health and Children and with the consent of the Minister for Finance, gives, [during the period of 10 years beginning with the time referred to in *section 272(4)(h)*][55], an annual certificate in writing stating that it is satisfied that the medical clinic complies with the conditions mentioned in *paragraphs (a)* to *(e)*,

and—

(I) [subject to *paragraph (II)*][56] includes any part of the clinic which consists of rooms used exclusively for the assessment or treatment of patients, but

(II) does not include any part of the clinic which consists of consultants' rooms or offices.][57]

[(2BA) In this section—

"*palliative care*" means the active total care of patients who suffer from illnesses or diseases which are active, progressive and advanced in nature and which are no longer curable by means of the administration of existing or available medical treatments;

"*qualifying specialist palliative care unit*" means, subject to *subsection (2BB)*, a building or structure—

(a) which is a hospital, hospice (within the meaning of section 47 (as amended by section 16 of the Public Health (Tobacco) (Amendment) Act 2004) of the Public Health (Tobacco) Act 2002) or similar facility which has palliative care as its main activity,

(b) which, before entering into a legal commitment for its design, commissioning, construction or refurbishment, is approved by the Health Service Executive, with the consent of the Minister for Health and Children, as being in accordance with national development plans or national needs assessments for palliative care facilities,

(c) which has the capacity to provide—

(i) day-patient and out-patient palliative care services, and

(ii) palliative care accommodation on an overnight basis of not less than 8 in-patient beds,

(d) in respect of which relevant data is provided to the Health Service Executive, for onward transmission to the Minister for Health and Children and the Minister for Finance, in relation to—

(i) the amount of the capital expenditure actually incurred on the construction or refurbishment of the unit,

(ii) the amount, if any, of such expenditure which has been or is to be met directly or indirectly by the State or by any other person by way of grant or other financial assistance,

(iii) the number and nature of the investors that are investing in the unit,

(iv) the amount to be invested by each investor, and

(v) the nature of the structures which are being put in place to facilitate the investment in the unit,

together with such other information as may be specified by the Minister for Finance, in consultation with the Minister for Health and Children, as being of assistance in evaluating the costs, including but not limited to exchequer costs, and the benefits arising from the operation of tax relief under this Part for qualifying specialist palliative care units,

(e) in relation to which an undertaking is given to the Health Service Executive—

(i) to make available annually, for the palliative care of persons who have been awaiting day-patient, in-patient or out-patient palliative care services as public patients, not less than 20 per cent of its capacity, subject to service requirements to be specified by the Health Service Executive in advance and to the proviso that nothing in this subparagraph shall require the Health Service Executive to take up all or any part of the capacity made available to the Health Service Executive by the unit, and

(ii) in relation to the fees to be charged in respect of the palliative care afforded to any such person, that such fees shall not be more than 90 per cent of the fees which would be charged in respect of similar palliative care afforded to a person who has private medical insurance,

and

(f) in respect of which the Health Service Executive, in consultation with the Minister for Health and Children and with the consent of the Minister for Finance, gives an annual certificate in writing during the period of—

(i) 15 years beginning with the time when the unit was first used, or

(ii) where capital expenditure on the refurbishment of the unit is incurred, 15 years beginning with the time when the unit was first used subsequent to the incurring of that expenditure,

stating that it is satisfied that the unit complies with the conditions mentioned in paragraphs *(a)* to *(e)*.

(2BB) (a) Subject to paragraphs *(b)* and *(c)*, a qualifying specialist palliative care unit includes any part of the unit which consists of rooms used exclusively for the assessment, treatment or care of patients.

(b) A qualifying specialist palliative care unit does not include any part of the unit which consists of consultants' rooms or offices.

(c) A qualifying specialist palliative care unit does not include any part of the unit in which a majority of the persons being maintained are being treated for acute illnesses.][58]

[(2C) For the purposes of this Part, a building or structure (other than a building or structure which is in use for the purposes of the trade of hotel-keeping) which is in use as—

(a) a guest house and is registered in the register of guest houses kept under the Tourist Traffic Acts 1939 to 2003, or

(b) a holiday hostel and is registered in the register of holiday hostels kept under the Tourist Traffic Acts 1939 to 2003,

shall, as respects capital expenditure incurred on or after 3 February 2005 on its construction (within the meaning of *section 270*), be deemed to be a building or structure in use for the purposes of the trade of hotel-keeping.][59]

[(2D) For the purposes of this Part, a building or structure which is comprised in, and is in use as part of, premises which are registered in the register of caravan sites and camping sites kept under the Tourist Traffic Acts 1939 to 2003 shall, as respects capital expenditure incurred on or after 1 January 2008 on its construction (within the meaning of *section 270*), be deemed to be a building or structure in use for the purposes of the trade of hotel-keeping.][60]

(3) For the purpose of this Part, a building or structure in use as [a holiday camp registered in the register of holiday camps kept under the Tourist Traffic Acts 1939 to 2003][61] or, in relation to capital expenditure incurred on or after the 1st day of July, 1968, a building or structure in use as a holiday cottage and comprised in premises registered in any register of holiday cottages established by [the National Tourism Development Authority][62] under any Act of the Oireachtas passed on or after the 29th day of July, 1969, [shall, subject to *subsection (13)*, be deemed][63] to be a building or structure in use for the purposes of the trade of hotel-keeping.

[(3A) [Subject to *subsections (3B)* to *(3E)*, in this section][64] "*qualifying residential unit*" means a house which—

(a) is constructed on the site of, or on a site which is immediately adjacent to the site of, a registered nursing home,

(b) is—

(i) a single storey house, or

(ii) a house that is [comprised in a building of one or more storeys in relation to which building a fire safety certificate under Part III of the Building Control Regulations 1997 (S.I. No. 496 of 1997) (as amended from time to time) is required, and prior to the commencement of the construction works on the building, is granted by the building control authority (within the meaning of *section 2* of the Building Control Act 1990, as amended by the Local Government (Dublin) Act 1993 and the Local Government Act 2001) in whose functional area the building is situated][65],

where—

(I) the house is, or (as the case may be) the house and the building in which it is comprised are, designed and constructed to meet the needs of persons with disabilities, including in particular the needs of persons who are confined to wheelchairs, and

(II) the house consists of 1 or 2 bedrooms, a kitchen, a living room, bath or shower facilities, toilet facilities and a nurse call system linked to the registered nursing home,

(c) is comprised in a development of [not less than 10 qualifying residential units][66] where—

(i) that development also includes a day-care centre,

(ii) those units are operated or managed by the registered nursing home and an on-site caretaker is provided,

(iii) back-up medical care, including nursing care, is provided by the registered nursing home to the occupants of those units when required by those occupants,

(iv) not less than 20 per cent of those units are made available for renting to persons who are eligible for a rent subsidy from [the Health Service Executive][67], subject to service requirements to be specified by [the Health Service Executive][68] in advance and to the condition that nothing in this subparagraph shall require [the Health Service Executive][69] to take up all or any of the units so made available, and

(v) the rent to be charged in respect of any such unit made available in accordance with *subparagraph (iv)* is not more than 90 per cent of the rent which would be charged if that unit were rented to a person who is not in receipt of a subsidy referred to in that subparagraph,

and

[(d)[(i) is leased to a person and, as the case may be, the [spouse or civil partner][70] of that person—][71]

[(I) who is or, as the case may be, are not connected (within the meaning of *section 10*) with the lessor,

(II) who has or have been selected as the occupant or occupants of the house by the registered nursing home, and

(III) either the person or the [spouse or civil partner][72] of that person has been certified by a person, who is registered in the General Register of Medical Practitioners, as requiring such accommodation by reason of old age or infirmity, or][73]

(ii) is leased to the registered nursing home on condition that it will be subsequently leased to a person or persons referred to in *subparagraph (i)* and which is subsequently used for no other purpose other than use by such person or persons.][74]

[(3B) (a) For the purposes of this section "house", in relation to a qualifying residential unit, has the same meaning as in *section 372AK.*

(b) For the purposes only of the making of allowances and charges under this Part but subject to *subsection (3C)* and *sections 270* and *316* (as amended by the Finance Act 2007), as respects capital expenditure incurred in the period commencing on 25 March 2002 and ending on 30 April 2010, a house in use as a qualifying residential unit shall be deemed to be a building in use for the purposes of a trade referred to in *subsection (1)(g)*.][75]

(3C) *Subsection (3B)* shall not apply in respect of expenditure incurred on the construction of a qualifying residential unit where any part of that expenditure has been or is to be met, directly or indirectly, by grant assistance or any other assistance which is granted by or through the State, any board established by statute, any public or local authority or any other agency of the State.][76]

[(3D) Where the relevant interest in relation to capital expenditure incurred on the construction or refurbishment of all qualifying residential units in a development is held by a company (within the meaning of *section 4(1)*) then *subsection (3A)* shall apply as if *subparagraphs (iv)* and *(v)* of *paragraph (c)* of that subsection were deleted.

(3E) A house shall not be a qualifying residential unit for the purposes of this section unless—

(a) the following information has been provided to the Health Service Executive, by the person who is entitled to the relevant interest in relation to the capital expenditure incurred on the construction or refurbishment of the house, for onward transmission to the Minister for Health and Children and the Minister for Finance:

(i) the amount of the capital expenditure actually incurred on the construction or refurbishment of the house;

(ii) the number and nature of the investors that are investing in the house;

(iii) the amount to be invested by each investor; and

(iv) the nature of the structures which are being put in place to facilitate the investment in the house,

together with such other information as may be specified by the Minister for Finance, in consultation with the Minister for Health and Children, as being of assistance in evaluating the costs, including but not limited to exchequer costs, and the benefits arising from the operation of tax relief under this Part for qualifying residential units,

(b) the Health Service Executive, in consultation with the Minister for Health and Children, gives a certificate in writing after the house is first leased or, where capital expenditure is incurred on the refurbishment of a house, first leased subsequent to the incurring of that expenditure stating that it is satisfied that—

(i) the house and the development in which it is comprised complies with all the conditions mentioned in *paragraphs (a)*, *(b)*, *(c)* and *(d)* of *subsection (3A)*, and

(ii) the information required in accordance with *paragraph (a)* of this subsection has been provided,

and

(c) an annual report in writing is provided, by the person who is entitled to the relevant interest in relation to the capital expenditure incurred on the construction or refurbishment of the house, to the Health Service Executive, for onward transmission to the Minister for Health and Children and the Minister for Finance, by the end of each year in the 20 year period referred to in *section 272(4)(fa)* (inserted by the Finance Act 2007), which—

(i) confirms whether the house and the development in which it is comprised continue to comply with all the conditions mentioned in *paragraphs (a)*, *(b)*, *(c)* and *(d)* of *subsection (3A)*, and

(ii) provides details of the level of occupation of the house for the previous year including the age of and, as the case may be, the nature of the infirmity of the occupants.][77]

(4) Where capital expenditure is incurred on preparing, cutting, tunnelling or levelling land for the purposes of preparing the land as a site for the installation of machinery or plant, the machinery or plant shall, as regards that expenditure, be treated for the purposes of this Chapter as a building or structure.

(5) For the purposes of this Part, expenditure incurred by a person on or after the 23rd day of April, 1996, either on the construction of, or on the acquisition of the relevant interest in, a building or structure not situated in the State shall not be treated as expenditure on a building or structure within the meaning of this section unless, being a building or structure not situated in the State—

(a) it is a building or structure which is to be constructed or which is in the course of construction and in respect of which it can be shown that—

(i) the person has either entered into a binding contract in writing for the acquisition of the site for the building or structure or has entered into an agreement in writing in relation to an option to acquire that site on or before the 23rd day of April, 1996,

(ii) the person has entered into a binding contract in writing for the construction of the building or structure on or before the 1st day of July, 1996, and

(iii) the construction of the building or structure had commenced on or before the 1st day of July, 1996, and had been completed before the [30th day of September, 1998][78],

and

(b) it is a building or structure to be constructed or which is being constructed which will be used for the purposes of a trade the profits or gains from which are taxable in the State.

[(5A) Notwithstanding *paragraph (n)* of *subsection (1)*, expenditure incurred by a person on the construction of a building or structure to which that paragraph applies, shall not be treated as expenditure on an industrial building or structure for the purposes of this Part unless—

(a) the building or structure is situated in an area specified in the National Regional Aid Map for the State in relation to the period 1 July 2014 to 31 December 2020, approved under Commission Decision No. N3153/2014 of 21 May 2014*, and

*OJ No. C251, 1.8.2014, p.1

(b) the expenditure satisfies all of the relevant conditions set out in the European Commission Guidelines on regional state aid for 2014–2020, adopted on 19 June 2013*, and

*OJ No. C209, 23.7.2013, p.1

(c) the following information has been provided to the Revenue Commissioners before the first claim for a writing down allowance is made, in accordance with *section 272*, by the person who incurred expenditure on the construction of the building or structure:

(i) the name, address and tax reference number (within the meaning of *section 477B(1)*) of the person making the claim;

(ii) the address of the building or structure in respect of which the expenditure was incurred or deemed to have been incurred; and

(iii) details of the aggregate of the amount of all expenditure incurred or deemed to have been incurred by the person in respect of which the claim is to be made.

(5B) Notwithstanding any obligation to the contrary imposed on them by *section 851A*, the Revenue Commissioners may furnish to one or more persons such information as is referred to in *subsection (5A)(c)* where the Revenue Commissioners are satisfied that doing so is reasonably related to achieving the following objective.

(5C) The objective mentioned in *subsection (5B)* is ensuring that any claim to relief in respect of expenditure which has been incurred or deemed to have been incurred on the construction of a building or structure to which *subsection (1)(n)* applies is in compliance with the Guidelines referred to in *subsection (5A)(b)*.

(5D) The Minister for Finance shall, after consultation with the Revenue Commissioners, draw up—

(a) guidelines for determining whether, and to what extent, expenditure incurred by a person is to be treated as expenditure on the construction of a building or structure to which *subsection (1)(n)* applies, and

(b) guidelines (being guidelines that are expressed to be for the purpose, and which shall operate for the purpose, of enabling full regard to be had to the Guidelines referred in to *subsection (5A)(b)* as concerns the operation of that provision) whether the foregoing expenditure qualifies for a writing down allowance in accordance with the last-mentioned Guidelines, with particular regard (but not limited) to—

(i) any restrictions that may apply as respects aid to firms in difficulties,

(ii) the maximum level of aid intensity permitted for enterprises, and

(iii) any restrictions that may apply to aid aimed at a reduction of current expenses of an undertaking.

(5E) In determining a claim to a writing down allowance that is made in respect of expenditure on the construction of a building or structure, being expenditure claimed to be expenditure to which *subsection (1)(n)* applies, regard shall be had to whether each of the provisions that are set out in the guidelines drawn up under *subsection (5D)(a)* and *(b)* concerning the building or structure and the expenditure, respectively, has been satisfied.][79]

(6) *Subsection (1)* shall apply in relation to a part of a trade as it applies in relation to a trade but, where part only of a trade complies with the conditions set out in that subsection, a building or structure shall not by virtue of this subsection be an industrial building or structure unless it is in use for the purposes of that part of that trade.

(7) (a) In this subsection, "retail shop" includes any premises of a similar character where retail trade or business (including repair work) is carried on.

(b) Notwithstanding anything in *subsections (1)* to *(6)* but subject to *subsection (8)*, in this Part, "industrial building or structure" does not include any building or structure in use as, or as part of, a dwelling house (other than a holiday cottage referred to in *subsection (3)* [or a qualifying residential unit][80]), retail shop, showroom or office or for any purpose ancillary to the purposes of a dwelling house (other than a holiday cottage referred to in *subsection (3)* [or a qualifying residential unit][81]), retail shop, showroom or office.

(8) Where part of the whole of a building or structure is, and part of the whole of the building or structure is not, an industrial building or structure, and the capital expenditure incurred on the construction of the second-mentioned part is not more than 10 per cent of the total capital expenditure incurred on the construction of the whole building or structure, the whole building or structure and every part of the whole of the building or structure shall be treated as an industrial building or structure.

(9) *Subsection (1)* shall apply—

(a) by reference to *paragraph (a)(ii)*, as respects capital expenditure incurred on or after the 25th day of January, 1984,

(b) by reference to *paragraph (e)*, as respects capital expenditure incurred on or after the 6th day of April, 1971, […][82]

(c) by reference to *paragraph (f)*, as respects capital expenditure incurred on or after the 24th day of April, [1992,][83]

[(d) by reference to paragraph *(g)*, as respects capital expenditure incurred in the period commencing on 3 December 1997 and ending—

(i) on 31 December 2009, or

(ii) where subsection (17)*(a)* applies, on 30 June 2010, or

(iii) where *subsection (17)(b)* applies, on 30 June 2011,][84]

[(e) by reference to *paragraph (h)*, as respects capital expenditure incurred—

(i) by [Dublin Airport Authority][85] on or after the vesting day, and

[(ii) by any other person on or after the date of the passing of the Finance Act, 1998,

[…][86]][87]][88]

[(f) by reference to paragraph *(i)*, as respects capital expenditure incurred in the period commencing on 2 December 1998 and ending—

(i) on 31 December 2009, or

(ii) where *subsection (17)(a)* applies, on 30 June 2010, or

(iii) where *subsection (17)(b)* applies, on 30 June 2011,][89]

[(g) by reference to paragraph (*j*), as respects capital expenditure incurred in the period commencing—

(i) where *subsection (2A)(d)(i)* applies, on 15 May 2002, or

(ii) where *subsection (2A)(d)(ii)* applies, on 28 March 2003,

and ending—

(I) on 31 December 2009, or

(II) where *subsection (17)(a)* applies, on 30 June 2010, or

(III) where *subsection (17)(b)* applies, on 31 December 2013,][90]

[(h) by reference to paragraph (k), as respects capital expenditure incurred in the period commencing on 15 May 2002 and ending on 31 December 2006 or, where subsection (16) applies, ending on 31 July [2008, [...][91]][92]][93]

[(i) by reference to paragraph (l), as respects capital expenditure incurred in the period commencing on 23 January 2007 and ending—

(i) on 31 December 2009, or

(ii) where *subsection (17)(a)* applies, on 30 June 2010, or

(iii) where *subsection (17)(b)* applies, on 30 June 2011, [...][94]][95]

[(j) by reference to paragraph (*m*), as respects capital expenditure incurred on or after the date of the coming into operation of *section 26* of the *Finance Act* [*2008,* and][96]][97]

[(k) by reference to *paragraph (n)*, as respects capital expenditure incurred in the period commencing on the date of the coming into operation of *section 31* of the *Finance Act 2013* and ending 5 years after that date.][98]

[(10) For the purposes of this Part—

"*Dublin Airport Authority*" means the Dublin Airport Authority, public limited company, and includes—

(a) where a day has been appointed under section 5 of the State Airports Act 2004 in respect of the Cork Airport Authority, public limited company, that company, and

(b) where a day has been appointed under the said section 5 in respect of the Shannon Airport Authority, public limited company, that company;

"*vesting day*" means the day appointed by order under section 9(6) of the State Airports Act 2004 in respect of the Dublin Airport Authority and such other day or days as may be appointed by order or orders under section 5 of the State Airports Act 2004 in respect of the Cork Airport Authority, public limited company, and the Shannon Airport Authority, public limited company.][99]

[(11) Notwithstanding any other provision of this section, as respects capital expenditure incurred on or after 20 March 2001, a building or structure in use for the purposes of the trade of hotel-keeping shall not be treated as an industrial building or structure where any part of that expenditure has been or is to be met, directly or indirectly, by [grant assistance or any other assistance which is granted by or through the State, any board established by statute, any public or local authority or any other agency of the State.][100]

(12) Notwithstanding any other provision of this section, as respects capital expenditure incurred on the construction or refurbishment of a building or structure in respect of which construction or refurbishment first commences on or after [6 April 2001

(being capital expenditure in respect of which but for this subsection a writing-down allowance in excess of 4 per cent would be available under section 272 for a chargeable period),][101] a building or structure in use for the purposes of the trade of hotel-keeping shall not be treated as an industrial building or structure unless, on the making of an application by the person who incurs the capital expenditure on the construction or refurbishment of the building or structure, [the National Tourism Development Authority][102] gives a certificate in writing to that person, in relation to that expenditure, stating—

[(a) that it has received a declaration from that person as to whether or not that person is—

(i) a small or medium-sized enterprise within the meaning of Annex I to Commission Regulation (EC) No. 70/2001 of 12 January 2001 on the application of Articles 87 and 88 of the European Communities Treaty to State aid to small and medium-sized enterprises*, or

*OJ No. L10 of 13 January 2001, p.33

(ii) a micro, small or medium-sized enterprise within the meaning of the Annex to Commission Recommendation of 6 May 2003 concerning the definition of micro, small and medium-sized enterprises*,][103]

*OJ No. L124 of 20 May 2003, p.36

[(b) that the expenditure concerned falls within the meaning of "*initial investment*" contained in point 4.4 of the "Guidelines on National Regional Aid"* prepared by the Commission of the European Communities,

*OJ No. C 74 of 10 March 1998, p.9

[(c) that, in the case of expenditure incurred on or after 1 January 2003 on the construction or refurbishment of a building or structure provided for the purposes of a project which is subject to the notification requirements of—

(i) the "Multisectoral framework on regional aid for large investment projects"* prepared by the Commission of the European Communities and dated 7 April 1998, or

*OJ No. C 107, 7.4.1998, p.7

(ii) the "Multisectoral framework on regional aid for large investment projects"* prepared by the Commission of the European Communities and dated 19 March 2002,

*OJ No. C 70 of 19 March 2002, p.8

as the case may be, approval of the potential capital allowances involved [, or part thereof][104] has been received from that Commission by the Minister for Finance, or by such other Minister of the Government, agency or body as may be nominated for that purpose by the Minister for Finance, and][105]

(d) that such person has undertaken to furnish to the Minister for Finance, or to such other Minister of the Government, agency or body as may be nominated for that purpose by the Minister for Finance, upon request in writing by the Minister concerned or that agency or body, such further information as may be necessary to enable compliance with the reporting requirements of—

(i) [the Regulation or Recommendation][106] referred to in *paragraph (a)* or the Multisectoral framework referred to in *paragraph (c)*,

(ii) "Community guidelines on State aid for rescuing and restructuring firms in difficulty"* prepared by the Commission of the European

Communities [or, as the case may be, "Community guidelines on State aid for rescuing and restructuring firms in difficulty"† prepared by that Commission][107], or

* OJ No. C 288, 9.10.1999, p.2
†OJ No. C244 of 1 October 2004, p.2

(iii) any other European Communities Regulation or Directive under the European Communities Treaty governing the granting of State aid in specific sectors.][108][109]

[(12A) (a) Where the National Tourism Development Authority gives a certificate in writing to the person who has incurred the capital expenditure on the construction or refurbishment of the building or structure stating that the approval referred to in *subsection (12)(c)* has been received, the building or structure shall, for the purposes of this Part, be treated as an industrial building or structure from the date on which it was first used for the purposes of the trade of hotel-keeping, and tax shall be discharged or repaid accordingly in giving effect to the allowances to be made under this Part.

(b) Where the Commission of the European Communities has approved an amount—

(i) which is lower than the amount of capital expenditure actually incurred on the construction or refurbishment of the building or structure, then, for the purposes of this Part, that lower amount shall be substituted for the amount actually incurred, or

(ii) which is lower than the amount of the net price paid within the meaning of *section 279*, that section shall apply as if the reference to the net price paid in *subsection (2)(b)* were a reference to the lower amount so approved.][110]

[(13) (a) Notwithstanding *subsection (3)* but [subject to *paragraphs (b)* and *(c)*][111], a holiday cottage referred to in that subsection shall not, as respects capital expenditure incurred on or after 4 December 2002 on its construction (within the meaning of *section 270*), be deemed to be a building or structure in use for the purposes of the trade of hotel-keeping.

(b) This subsection shall not apply as respects expenditure incurred on or before [31 December 2006][112] on the construction or refurbishment of a holiday cottage if—

(i) (I) a planning application (not being an application for outline permission within the meaning of section 36 of the Planning and Development Act 2000)[, in so far as planning permission is required,][113] in respect of the holiday cottage is made in accordance with the Planning and Development Regulations 2001 to 2002,

(II) an acknowledgement of the application, which confirms that the application was received on or before [31 December 2004][114], is issued by the planning authority in accordance with article 26(2) of the Planning and Development Regulations 2001 (S.I. No. 600 of 2001), and

(III) the application is not an invalid application in respect of which a notice is issued by the planning authority in accordance with article 26(5) of those regulations,

[...][115]

(ii) (I) [a planning application, in so far as planning permission was required,][116] in respect of the holiday cottage was made in accordance with the Local Government (Planning and Development) Regulations 1994 (S.I. No. 86 of 1994), not being an application for outline permission within the meaning of article 3 of those regulations,

(II) an acknowledgement of the application, which confirms that the application was received on or before 10 March 2002, was issued by the planning authority in accordance with article 29(2)(a) of the regulations referred to in clause (I), and

(III) the application was not an invalid application in respect of which a notice was issued by the planning authority in accordance with article 29(2)(b)(i) of those [regulations,][117]][118]

[or

(iii) where the construction or refurbishment work on the holiday cottage represented by that expenditure is exempted development for the purposes of the Planning and Development Act 2000 by virtue of section 4 of that Act or by virtue of Part 2 of the Planning and Development Regulations 2001 (S.I. No. 600 of 2001) and—

(I) a detailed plan in relation to the development work is prepared,

(II) a binding contract in writing, under which the expenditure on the development is incurred, is in existence, and

(III) work to the value of 5 per cent of the development costs is carried out,

not later than 31 December 2004.][119]

[(c) This subsection shall not apply as respects expenditure incurred on or before 31 July 2008 on the construction or refurbishment of a holiday cottage if—

(i) the conditions of *subparagraph (i), (ii)* or *(iii)*, as the case may be, of *paragraph (b)* have been satisfied,

(ii) subject to *paragraphs (a)* and *(b)* of *section 270(7)*—

(I) the person who is constructing or refurbishing the holiday cottage has, on or before 31 December 2006, carried out work to the value of not less than 15 per cent of the actual construction or, as the case may be, refurbishment costs of the holiday cottage, and

(II) the person referred to in clause (I) or, where the holiday cottage is sold by that person, the person who is claiming a deduction under this Chapter in relation to the expenditure incurred, can show that the condition in clause (I) was satisfied,

(iii) a binding contract in writing under which expenditure on the construction or refurbishment of the holiday cottage is incurred was in existence on or before 31 July 2006, and

(iv) such other conditions, as may be specified in regulations made for the purposes of this subparagraph by the Minister for Finance, have been satisfied; but such conditions shall be limited to those necessary to ensure compliance with the laws of the European Communities governing State aid or with a decision of the Commission of the European Communities as to whether aid to which this subsection relates is compatible with the common market having regard to Article 87 of the European Communities Treaty.][120]

[(14) Subject to *subsection (15)*, a building or structure in use for the purposes of the trade of hotel-keeping (but not including a building or structure deemed to be such a building or structure) shall not, as respects capital expenditure incurred on or after 3 February 2005 on its construction (within the meaning of *section 270*), be treated as an industrial building or structure unless the building or structure is registered in the register of hotels kept under the Tourist Traffic Acts 1939 to 2003.

(15) *Subsection (14)* shall not apply as respects capital expenditure incurred on or before 31 July 2006 on the construction or refurbishment of a building or structure in use for the purposes of the trade of hotel-keeping if—

(a) (i) a planning application (not being an application for outline permission within the meaning of section 36 of the Planning and Development Act 2000), in so far as planning permission was required, in respect of the construction or refurbishment work on the building or structure represented by that expenditure, was made in accordance with the Planning and Development Regulations 2001 to 2004,

(ii) an acknowledgement of the application, which confirms that the application was received on or before 31 December 2004, was issued by the planning authority in accordance with article 26(2) of the Planning and Development Regulations 2001 (S.I. No. 600 of 2001), and

(iii) the application was not an invalid application in respect of which a notice was issued by the planning authority in accordance with article 26(5) of those regulations,

(b) (i) a planning application, in so far as planning permission was required, in respect of the construction or refurbishment work on the building or structure represented by that expenditure, was made in accordance with the Local Government (Planning and Development) Regulations 1994 (S.I. No. 86 of 1994), not being an application for outline permission within the meaning of article 3 of those regulations,

(ii) an acknowledgement of the application, which confirms that the application was received on or before 10 March 2002, was issued by the planning authority in accordance with article 29(2)(*a*) of the regulations referred to in *subparagraph (i)*, and

(iii) the application was not an invalid application in respect of which a notice was issued by the planning authority in accordance with article 29(2)(*b*)(i) of those regulations,

(c) where the construction or refurbishment work on the building or structure represented by that expenditure is exempted development for the purposes of the Planning and Development Act 2000 by virtue of section 4 of that Act or by virtue of Part 2 of the Planning and Development Regulations 2001 (S.I. No. 600 of 2001) and—

(i) a detailed plan in relation to the development work was prepared,

(ii) a binding contract in writing, under which the expenditure on the development is incurred, was in existence, and

(iii) work to the value of 5 per cent of the development costs was carried out,

not later than 31 December 2004, or

(d) (i) the construction or refurbishment of the building or structure is a development in respect of which an application for a certificate under section 25(7)(*a*)(ii) of the Dublin Docklands Development Authority Act 1997 was made to the Authority (within the meaning of that Act),

(ii) an acknowledgement of the application, which confirms that the application was received on or before 31 December 2004, was issued by that Authority, and

(iii) the application was not an invalid application.][121]

[(16) This subsection shall apply in relation to the construction or refurbishment of a qualifying sports injuries clinic where—

(a) the person who is constructing or refurbishing the clinic has, on or before 31 December 2006, carried out work to the value of not less than 15 per cent of the actual construction or, as the case may be, refurbishment costs of the clinic, and

(b) the person referred to in *paragraph (a)* or, where the clinic is sold by that person, the person who is claiming a deduction under this Chapter in relation to the expenditure incurred, can show that the condition in *paragraph (a)* was satisfied.][122]

[(17) (a) This paragraph shall apply where—

(i) capital expenditure is incurred on the construction or refurbishment of a building or structure referred to in paragraphs (*g*), (*i*), (*j*) or (*l*) of *subsection (1)*,

(ii) the construction or refurbishment work on the building or structure represented by that expenditure is exempted development for the purposes of the Planning and Development Act 2000 by virtue of section 4 of that Act or by virtue of Part 2 of the Planning and Development Regulations 2001 (S.I. No. 600 of 2001) (in this subsection referred to as the "Regulations of 2001"), and

(iii) not less than 30 per cent of the total construction or refurbishment costs has been incurred on or before 31 December 2009.

(b) This paragraph shall apply where—

(i) capital expenditure is incurred on the construction or refurbishment of a building or structure referred to in paragraphs (*g*), (*i*), (*j*) or (*l*) of *subsection (1)*,

(ii) a planning application (not being an application for outline permission within the meaning of section 36 of the Planning and Development Act 2000), in so far as planning permission is required, in respect of the construction or refurbishment work on the building or structure represented by that expenditure, is made in accordance with the Regulations of 2001,

(iii) an acknowledgement of the application, which confirms that the application was received on or before 31 December 2009, is issued by the planning authority in accordance with article 26(2) of the Regulations of 2001, and

(iv) the application is not an invalid application in respect of which a notice was issued by the planning authority in accordance with article 26(5) of the Regulations of 2001.][123]

Amendments

[1] Substituted by FA98 s22(a)(i)(I).

[2] Inserted by FA02 s33(a).

[3] Substituted by FA99 s48(a)(i)(I).

[4] Inserted by FA98 s22(a)(i)(II).

[5] Deleted by FA01 s64(1)(a)(i)(I). With effect from 15 May 2002 per S.I. 210 of 2002.

[6] Substituted by FA99 s48(a)(i)(II).

[7] Inserted by FA98 s20(a)(i).

[8] Substituted by FA05 sched6(1)(e)(i). Applies as on and from 25 March 2005

[9] Deleted by FA02 s34(1)(a)(i)(I). With effect from 15 May 2002 per S.I. 211 of 2002.

[10] Substituted by FA01 s64(1)(a)(i)(II). With effect from 15 May 2002 per S.I. 210 of 2002.

[11] Substituted by FA00 s36.

[12] Deleted by FA06 s36(1)(a)(i)(I). With effect from 23 January 2007 per S.I. 20 of 2007.

[13] Inserted by FA02 s34(1)(a)(i)(I). With effect from 15 May 2002 per S.I. 211 of 2002.

[14] Inserted by FA01 s64(1)(a)(i)(III). With effect from 15 May 2002 per S.I. 210 of 2002.

[15] Deleted by FA08 s26(1)(a)(i)(I). This section comes into operation on such day or days as the Minister for Finance may by order or orders appoint and different days may be appointed for different purposes or different provisions.

[16] Substituted by FA06 s36(1)(a)(i)(I). This section shall come into operation on such day or days as the Minister for Finance may by order appoint and different days may be appointed for different purposes or different provisions. With effect from 23 January 2007 per S.I. 20 of 2007.

[17] Inserted by FA02 s34(1)(a)(i)(II). This section comes into operation on such day as the Minister for Finance may by order appoint. With effect from 15 May 2002 per S.I. 211 of 2002.

[18, 21] Deleted by FA13 s31(1)(a). Comes into operation on such day or days as the Minister for Finance may by order or orders appoint and different days may be appointed for different purposes or for different provisions.

[19] Substituted by FA08 s26(1)(a)(i)(I). This section comes into operation on such day or days as the Minister for Finance may by order or orders appoint and different days may be appointed for different purposes or different provisions.

[20] Inserted by FA06 s36(1)(a)(i)(II). This section shall come into operation on such day or days as the Minister for Finance may by order appoint and different days may be appointed for different purposes or different provisions. With effect from 23 January 2007 per S.I. 20 of 2007.

[22] Inserted by FA08 s26(1)(a)(i)(II). This section comes into operation on such day or days as the Minister for Finance may by order or orders appoint and different days may be appointed for different purposes or different provisions.

[23] Inserted by FA13 s31(1)(b). Comes into operation on such day or days as the Minister for Finance may by order or orders appoint and different days may be appointed for different purposes or for different provisions.

[24] Substituted by FA08 s29(1)(a)(i). Applies as respects capital expenditure incurred on or after 1 January 2008.

[25] Substituted by FA04 s24(1)(a). This section applies as respects capital expenditure incurred on the construction or refurbishment of a building or structure on or after 1 May 2004.

[26] Inserted by FA02 s32(a).

[27] Substituted by FA04 s24(1)(b). This section applies as respects capital expenditure incurred on the construction or refurbishment of a building or structure on or after 1 May 2004.

[28] Inserted by FA02 s34(1)(a)(ii). With effect from 15 May 2002 per S.I. 211 of 2002.

[29] Substituted by FA08 s29(1)(a)(ii). Applies as respects capital expenditure incurred on or after 1 January 2008.

[30] Inserted by FA06 s36(1)(a)(ii). With effect from 23 January 2007 per S.I. 20 of 2007.

[31] Inserted by FA08 s26(1)(a)(ii). This section comes into operation on such day or days as the Minister for Finance may by order or orders appoint and different days may be appointed for different purposes or different provisions.

[32] Inserted by FA13 s31(1)(c). Comes into operation on such day or days as the Minister for Finance may by order or orders appoint and different days may be appointed for different purposes or for different provisions.

[33] Deleted by FA05 sched6(1)(e)(ii)(I). Applies as on and from 25 March 2005

[34] Deleted by FA06 s35(1)(a)(i). This section is deemed to have applied as on and from 29 March 2004.

[35] Deleted by FA02 s32(b)(i).

[36] Substituted by FA03 s24(1). Applies as respects capital expenditure incurred on or after 28 March 2003 on the construction of a building or structure.

[37] Deleted by FA06 s35(1)(a)(ii)(I). Applies as respects capital expenditure incurred on or after 1 January 2006.

[38] Inserted by FA06 s35(1)(a)(ii)(II). Applies as respects capital expenditure incurred on or after 1 January 2006.

[39] Inserted by FA06 s35(1)(a)(ii)(III). Applies as respects capital expenditure incurred on or after 1 January 2006.

[40] Inserted by FA06 s35(1)(a)(iii).

[41] Substituted by FA05 sched6(1)(e)(ii)(II)(A). Applies as on and from 25 March 2005

[42, 43, 44] Substituted by FA05 sched6(1)(e)(ii)(II)(B). Applies as on and from 25 March 2005

[45] Substituted by FA06 s35(1)(a)(iv).

[46, 48] Substituted by FA02 s32(b)(iv).

[47] Inserted by FA06 s35(1)(a)(v).

[49] Inserted by FA01 s64(1)(a)(ii). With effect from 15 May 2002 per S.I. 210 of 2002.

[50] Substituted by FA05 sched6(1)(e)(iii)(I)(A). Applies as on and from 25 March 2005

[51, 52, 53] Substituted by FA05 sched6(1)(e)(iii)(I)(B). Applies as on and from 25 March 2005

[54] Substituted by FA05 sched6(1)(e)(iii)(II). Applies as on and from 25 March 2005

[55] Substituted by FA06 s28(a)(i).

[56] Inserted by FA06 s28(a)(ii).

[57] Inserted by FA02 s34(1)(a)(iii). With effect from 15 May 2002 per S.I. 211 of 2002.

[58] Inserted by FA08 s26(1)(a)(iii). This section comes into operation on such day or days as the Minister for Finance may by order or orders appoint and different days may be appointed for different purposes or different provisions.

[59] Inserted by FA05 s34(a)(i).

[60] Inserted by FA08 s28(a).

[61] Substituted by FA05 s34(a)(ii).

[62] Substituted by FA06 sched2(1)(d)(i). This section is deemed to have come into force and have taken effect as on and from 28 May 2003.

[63] Substituted by FA03 s25(1)(a)(i).

[64] Substituted by FA07 s28(1)(a)(i)(I). Applies as respects capital expenditure incurred on or after 1 May

2007 under a contract or agreement for the construction, refurbishment or development of a qualifying residential unit which is entered into on or after that date.

[65] Substituted by FA04 s23(1)(a). This section applies as respects capital expenditure incurred on or after 4 February 2004.

[66] Substituted by FA04 s23(1)(b). This section applies as respects capital expenditure incurred on or after 4 February 2004.

[67] Substituted by FA05 sched6(1)(e)(iv)(I). Applies as on and from 25 March 2005

[68, 69] Substituted by FA05 sched6(1)(e)(iv)(II). Applies as on and from 25 March 2005

[70, 72] Substituted by F(No.3)A11 sched1(55). Shall have effect from 27 July 2011.

[71, 73] Substituted by FA07 s28(1)(a)(i)(II). Applies as respects capital expenditure incurred on or after 1 May 2007 under a contract or agreement for the construction, refurbishment or development of a qualifying residential unit which is entered into on or after that date.

[74] Substituted by FA06 s37(a).

[75] Substituted by FA07 s28(1)(a)(ii). Applies as respects capital expenditure incurred on or after 1 May 2007 under a contract or agreement for the construction, refurbishment or development of a qualifying residential unit which is entered into on or after that date.

[76] Inserted by FA02 s33(b).

[77] Inserted by FA07 s28(1)(a)(iii). Applies as respects capital expenditure incurred on or after 1 May 2007 under a contract or agreement for the construction, refurbishment or development of a qualifying residential unit which is entered into on or after that date.

[78] Substituted by FA98 s19.

[79] Inserted by FA14 s33(1). Comes into operation on such day as the Minister for Finance may by order appoint.

[80, 81] Inserted by FA02 s33(c).

[82] Deleted by FA98 s22(a)(ii)(I).

[83] Substituted by FA98 s22(a)(ii)(II).

[84] Substituted by FA09 s8(a). This section is deemed to have come into force and takes effect as on and from 1 January 2009.

[85] Substituted by FA08 sched8(1)(c)(i). Has effect as on and from 13 March 2008.

[86] Deleted by FA01 s64(1)(a)(iii)(I). With effect from 15 May 2002 per S.I. 210 of 2002.

[87] Substituted by FA99 s48(a)(ii)(II).

[88] Inserted by FA98 s20(a)(ii).

[89, 90] Substituted by FA09 s8(b). This section is deemed to have come into force and takes effect as on and from 1 January 2009.

[91] Deleted by FA08 s26(1)(a)(iv)(I). This section comes into operation on such day or days as the Minister for Finance may by order or orders appoint and different days may be appointed for different purposes or different provisions.

[92] Substituted by FA06 s36(1)(a)(iii)(I). With effect from 23 January 2007 per S.I. 20 of 2007.

[93] Substituted by FA06 s28(b).

[94] Deleted by FA13 s31(1)(d). Comes into operation on such day or days as the Minister for Finance may by order or orders appoint and different days may be appointed for different purposes or for different provisions.

[95] Substituted by FA09 s8(c). This section is deemed to have come into force and takes effect as on and from 1 January 2009.

[96] Substituted by FA13 s31(1)(d). Comes into operation on such day or days as the Minister for Finance may by order or orders appoint and different days may be appointed for different purposes or for different provisions.

[97] Inserted by FA08 s26(1)(a)(iv)(II). This section comes into operation on such day or days as the Minister for Finance may by order or orders appoint and different days may be appointed for different purposes or different provisions.

[98] Inserted by FA13 s31(1)(e). Comes into operation on such day or days as the Minister for Finance may by order or orders appoint and different days may be appointed for different purposes or for different provisions.

[99] Substituted by FA08 sched8(1)(c)(ii). Has effect as on and from 13 March 2008.

[100] Substituted by FA02 s22(1)(a). This section applies as respects expenditure incurred on or after 1 January 2002.

[101] Substituted by FA03 s25(1)(a)(ii)(I).

[102] Substituted by FA06 sched2(1)(d)(ii). This section is deemed to have come into force and have taken effect as on and from 28 May 2003.

[103] Substituted by FA05 s34(a)(iii)(I).

[104] Inserted by F(No.2)A08 s22(1)(a). This section is deemed to have come into force and takes effect as on and from 1 January 2009.

[105] Substituted by FA03 s25(1)(a)(ii)(II).

[106] Substituted by FA05 s34(a)(iii)(II).

[107] Inserted by FA05 s34(a)(iii)(III).

[108] Substituted by FA02 s22(1)(b)(ii). This section applies as respects expenditure incurred on or after 1 January 2002.

[109] Inserted by FA01 s81.

[110] Inserted by FA03 s25(1)(a)(iii).

[111] Substituted by FA06 s27(1)(a)(i). With effect from 26 June 2006 per S.I. No. 323 of 2006.

[112] Substituted by FA06 s27(1)(a)(ii). With effect from 26 June 2006 per S.I. No. 323 of 2006.

[113] Inserted by FA04 s25(1)(a)(ii). This section is deemed to have applied as on and from 4 December 2002.

[114] Substituted by FA04 s25(1)(a)(iii).

[115] Deleted by FA04 s25(1)(a)(iv). This section is deemed to have applied as on and from 4 December 2002.

[116] Substituted by FA04 s25(1)(a)(v).

[117] Substituted by FA04 s25(1)(a)(vi).

[118] Inserted by F(No.2)A08 s22(1)(b). This section is deemed to have come into force and takes effect as on and from 1 January 2009.

[119] Inserted by FA04 s25(1)(a)(vii).

[120] Inserted by FA06 s27(1)(a)(iii). With effect from 26 June 2006 per S.I. 323 of 2006.

[121] Inserted by FA05 s34(a)(iv).

[122] Inserted by FA06 s28(c).

[123] Inserted by FA09 s8(d). This section is deemed to have come into force and takes effect as on and from 1 January 2009.

Case Law

A warehouse used to store goods, which the taxpayer imported and exported, was not an industrial building. Maco Door & Window Hardware (UK) Ltd v Revenue and Customs Commissioners 2008 STC 2594

Capital allowances could be claimed in respect of a building which was used for the trade "hotel-keeping". Kevin McGarry (Inspector of Taxes) v Harding (Lord Edward St.) Properties Ltd 2004 IEHC 131

In Girobank plc v Clarke (HM Inspector of Taxes) 1998 STC 182 an office was held to be the place where the management or administration of an enterprise is carried on. Therefore a data processing center was not an industrial building.

Activities carried out in a wholesale building were not a significant, separate, and identifiable activity, of the trade and therefore the building did not qualify as an industrial building. Bestway (Holdings) Ltd v Luff (HM Inspector of Taxes) 1998 STC 357

A warehouse used for the purpose of storing goods exclusively for delivery did not qualify as an industrial building. Sarsfield (HM Inspector of Taxes) v Dixons Group plc and related appeals 1998 STC 938 Transit sheds, used by a company carrying on a dock undertaking, to store goods under bond while they were being cleared by customs, were held to be industrial buildings. Patrick Monahan (Drogheda)

Limited v O'Connell (Inspector of Taxes) 1987 III ITR 661
An administrative center, separate from the main factory premises, qualified as an industrial building where the center was used to store a computer integral to the manufacturing operations. O'Connaill (Inspector of Taxes) v Waterford Glass 1983 III ITR 65
Buildings used to service and repair plant were not industrial buildings. Vibroplant v Holland (H. M. Inspector of Taxes) 1981 54 TC 548

Revenue Briefings

Tax Briefing

Tax Briefing October 2002 – Issue 50 pg 5 – Registered Nursing Homes
Tax Briefing April 2005 – Issue 59 pg 24 – Nursing Homes Residential Units
Tax Briefing August 2005 – Issue 60 – Capital Allowances for Hotels and Other Holiday Accommodation
Tax Briefing November 2005 – Issue 61 – Capital Allowances in respect of Private Hospitals
Tax Briefing May 2006 – Issue 63 – Capital Allowances and Property-Based Incentive Schemes
Tax Briefing August 2006 – Issue 64 – Capital Allowances and Property-Based Incentive Schemes
Tax Briefing December 2006 – Issue 65 – Capital Allowances for Registered Holiday Cottages
Tax Briefing July 2007 – Issue 66 – Nursing Home Residential Units
Tax Briefing April 2008 – Issue 68 – Plant integral to Industrial/Commercial Buildings

eBrief

eBrief No. 26/2006 – Transitional Arrangements for Property Incentive Schemes Binding Contracts – Further Clarification (1)
eBrief No. 29/2006 – Transitional Arrangements for Property Incentive Schemes Binding Contracts – Further Clarification (2)
eBrief No. 55/2006 – Property-Based Incentive Schemes '15%' Test – Payments to Local Authorities

Revenue Precedents

Does a hotel have to be registered as a hotel with Bord Fáilte in order for it to be regarded as a building or structure in use for the purposes of the trade of hotel keeping? There is no requirement that a building be registered as a hotel with Bord Fáilte for it to be regarded as a building in use for the purposes of the trade of hotel keeping. IT973009

Can capital allowances be claimed on the office comprised in the premises which is registered by Bord Fáilte under the Registration and Renewal of Holiday Cottages regulations? Section 268(3) Taxes Consolidation Act 1997 provides that a building in use as a holiday cottage and comprised in premises registered in any register of holiday cottages established by Bord Fáilte Éireann shall be deemed to be a building in use for the purposes of the trade of hotel-keeping. Therefore only the building used as a holiday cottage qualifies for allowances and not the office. 954

In order for a holiday camp to qualify for industrial buildings allowances is it necessary for it to be registered as a holiday camp with Bord Fáilte?. There is no requirement that a holiday camp be registered as a holiday camp with Bord Fáilte. Section 37 of the Tourist Traffic Act 1939 states that: "it shall not be lawful to describe or holdout or permit any person to describe or holdout any premises as a holiday camp unless such premises are registered in the Register of Holiday camps and such proprietor is registered as the registered proprietor of the holiday camp". Thus, while it is illegal to hold out a premises as a holiday camp unless it is registered with Bord Fáilte, the fact that it is not registered does not mean that it is not a holiday camp – just that it cannot be held out as such. IT953025

An individual incurs expenditure on the construction of a holiday cottage and leases it to an operator. If the operator rather than the individual registers the cottage in the Register of Holiday Cottages maintained by Bord Fáilte will the building be regarded as an industrial building within the meaning of section 268? The section is silent on who actually registers the property. Therefore an operator may register properties owned by other parties. 951

Whether a jetty on the Shannon used for charter cruisers is an industrial building or structure? Section 268(2) of the Taxes Consolidation Act provides that a dock includes a jetty at which vessels can ship or unship passengers, not being a jetty primarily used for recreation. The occupants of bareboat charters may be regarded as passengers and boarding these vessels comes within the test to "ship or unship". The jetty itself is not used primarily for recreation it is used to gain access to the boats. It therefore comes within the meaning of industrial building or structure. 958

Whether a hostel which offers budget accommodation to tourists is a building or structure in use for the purposes of the trade of hotel-keeping? Section 268(1)(d) of the Taxes Consolidation Act, 1997 provides that an industrial building or structure means a building or structure in use for the purposes of. inter alia, the trade of hotel-keeping. Since hotel-keeping is not defined in the Act it must be construed in the ordinary sense of the word. Revenue's view is that the following factors must be considered when deciding whether a building is in use for the trade of hotel-keeping: 1. the establishment must provide sleeping accommodation, food and drink. The provision of alcoholic drink is not a requirement. 2. There is an obligation on the hotel-keeper to receive all lawful travellers. Travellers include all comers to the hotel whether they avail of sleeping accommodation or not. The hotel-keeper must therefore provide food for all reasonable times, such as breakfast lunch and evening meals, as a matter of course, to the public at large. A hotel may be contrasted with a guest house in which control may be retained over the choice of lodgers to be admitted, and in which there is no obligation to the public generally. 3. The hotel-keeper is liable for the property of the persons in his establishment without them having to prove negligence. 4. the term hotel-keeping implies a certain standard of facilities and services e.g. reception desk, adequately trained kitchen staff and hall porter. A minimum number of rooms are required in order to provide facilities and services intrinsic to hotel-keeping. It is a question of fact whether or not such facilities are provided at any given number of guest bedrooms. Generally, a building does not have to be registered with Bord Fáilte in order for it to be regarded as a building in use for the trade of hotel-keeping for capital allowances purposes. The fact that it is unlawful for a proprietor to describe or hold out a premises as a hotel is not, by any means, conclusive, as to the nature of the trade being carried out. Only where accelerated capital allowances are being claimed must a hotel be registered with Bord Fáilte. The issue has been the subject of an appeal in the Circuit Court. Based on the particular circumstance of the case a hostel offering budget accommodation to tourists was regarded as a building in use for the purposes of the trade of hotel-keeping. Revenue has appealed the decision to the High Court. GD96047B

Industrial Buildings Allowance was granted in respect of the facilities at a salmon hatchery. 10407/31/92

Industrial Buildings Allowances granted for caravan parks registered with Bord Fáilte. 10407/105/87

Is a building in which grain is subjected to a process of drying an industrial building? On the basis of the case of CIR-v-Leith Harbour and Docks Commissioners the building in this case appears to be similar to a mill. IT 963501

Cross References

From Section 268

Section 4 Interpretation of Corporation Tax Acts.
Section 10 Connected persons.
Section 270 Meaning of "expenditure on construction of building or structure".
Section 272 Writing-down allowances.
Section 279 Purchases of certain buildings or structures.
Section 316 Interpretation of certain references to expenditure and time when expenditure is incurred.
Section 372A Interpretation and application (Chapter 7).
Section 372AK Interpretation (Chapter 11).
Section 654 Interpretation (Part 23).
Section 843A Capital allowances for buildings used for certain childcare purposes.

To Section 268

Section 80A Taxation of certain short-term leases plant and machinery.
Section 85 Deduction for certain industrial premises.
Section 97 Computational rules and allowable deductions.
Section 102 Deduction by reference to premium, etc. paid in computation of profits for purposes of Schedule D, Cases I and II.
Section 103 Deduction by reference to premiums, etc. paid in computation of profits for purposes of this Chapter.
Section 250A Restriction of relief to individuals in respect of loans applied in acquiring interest in companies.
Section 270 Meaning of "expenditure on construction of building or structure".
Section 271 Industrial building allowances.
Section 272 Writing-down allowances.
Section 273 Acceleration of writing-down allowances in respect of certain expenditure on certain industrial buildings or structures.
Section 274 Balancing allowances and balancing charges.
Section 284 Wear and tear allowances.
Section 285 Acceleration of wear and tear allowances.
Section 302 Interpretation (Chapter 3).

Section 316 Interpretation of certain references to expenditure and time when expenditure is incurred.
Section 323 Capital allowances in relation to construction of certain commercial premises.
Section 324 Double rent allowance in respect of rent paid for certain business premises.
Section 331 Accelerated capital allowances in relation to construction or refurbishment of certain industrial buildings or structures.
Section 332 Capital allowances in relation to construction or refurbishment of certain commercial premises.
Section 333 Double rent allowance in respect of rent paid for certain business premises.
Section 341 Accelerated capital allowances in relation to construction or refurbishment of certain industrial buildings or structures.
Section 342 Capital allowances in relation to construction or refurbishment of certain commercial premises.
Section 343 Capital allowances in relation to construction or refurbishment of certain buildings or structures in enterprise areas.
Section 344 Capital allowances in relation to construction or refurbishment of certain multi-storey car parks.
Section 345 Double rent allowance in respect of rent paid for certain business premises.
Section 352 Accelerated capital allowances in relation to construction or refurbishment of certain industrial buildings or structures.
Section 353 Capital allowances in relation to construction or refurbishment of certain commercial premises.
Section 354 Double rent allowance in respect of rent paid for certain business premises.
Section 355 Disclaimer of capital allowances on holiday cottages, holiday apartments, etc.
Section 372A Interpretation and application (Chapter 7).
Section 372C Accelerated capital allowances in relation to construction or refurbishment of certain industrial buildings or structures.
Section 372D Capital allowances in relation to construction or refurbishment of certain commercial premises.
Section 372L Interpretation (Chapter 8).
Section 372M Accelerated capital allowances in relation to construction or refurbishment of certain industrial buildings or structures.
Section 372N Capital allowances in relation to construction or refurbishment of certain commercial buildings or structures.
Section 372U Interpretation (Chapter 9).
Section 372V Capital allowances in relation to construction or refurbishment of certain park and ride facilities.
Section 372W Capital allowances in relation to construction or refurbishment of certain commercial premises.
Section 372AA Interpretation and application (Chapter 10).
Section 372AD Capital allowances in relation to construction or refurbishment of certain commercial premises.
Section 372AX Accelerated capital allowances in relation to the construction or refurbishment of certain registered holiday camps.
Section 372AY Capital allowances in relation to the construction or refurbishment of certain tourism infrastructure facilities.
Section 372AZ Restrictions on relief, non-application of relief in certain cases and provision against double relief.
Section 373 Interpretation (Part 11).
Section 374 Capital allowances for cars costing over certain amount.
Section 378 Cars: provisions as to hire-purchase, etc.
Section 380K Interpretation and general (Part 11C).
Section 380L Emissions-based limits for certain cars.
Section 380N Cars: provisions as to hire-purchase, etc.
Section 391 Interpretation (Chapter 2).
Section 401 Change in ownership of company: disallowance of trading losses.
Section 404 Restriction on use of capital allowances for certain leased machinery or plant.
Section 405 Restriction on use of capital allowances on holiday cottages.
Section 409 Capital allowances: room ownership schemes.
Section 409A Income tax: restriction on use of capital allowances on certain industrial buildings and other premises.

Section 409B Income tax: restriction on use of capital allowances on certain hotels, etc.
Section 409E Income tax: ringfence on use of certain capital allowances on certain industrial buildings and other premises.
Section 413 Profits or assets available for distribution.
Section 428 Exclusion of double allowances, etc.
Section 485G Miscellaneous (Chapter 2A).
Section 551 Exclusion from consideration for disposals of sums chargeable to income tax.
Section 658 Farming: allowances for capital expenditure on construction of buildings and other works.
Section 659 Farming: allowances for capital expenditure on the construction of farm buildings, etc. for control of pollution.
Section 660 Farming: wear and tear allowances deemed to have been made in certain cases.
Section 669E Application of Chapter 4 of Part 9.
Section 670 Mine development allowance.
Section 678 Allowance for machinery and plant.
Section 681 Allowance for mine rehabilitation expenditure.
Section 692 Development expenditure: allowances and charges.
Section 693 Exploration expenditure: allowances and charges.
Section 695 Abandonment expenditure: allowances and loss relief.
Section 697O Capital allowances: general.
Section 699 Deduction as expenses of certain sums, etc.
Section 760 Capital sums: effect of death, winding up and partnership changes.
Section 762 Application of Chapter 4 of Part 9.
Section 765 Allowances for capital expenditure on scientific research.
Section 766 Tax credit for research and development expenditure.
Section 766A Tax credit on expenditure on buildings or structures used for research and development.
Section 769 Relief for training of local staff before commencement of trading.
Section 769E Application of Chapter 4 of Part 9.
Section 840 Business entertainment.
Section 843 Capital allowances for buildings used for third level educational purposes.
Section 843A Capital allowances for buildings used for certain childcare purposes.
Section 848V Interpretation (Part 36B).
Section 1007 Interpretation (Part 43).
Section 1013 Limited partnerships.
Schedule 18B Tonnage Tax
Schedule 25B List of Specified Reliefs and Method of Determining Amount of Specified Relief Used in a Tax Year
Schedule 25C Determination of Amount of Relief to be Treated as Referable to Specified Reliefs as Respects Relief Carried Forward from Tax Year 2006 to Tax Year 2007
Schedule 32 Transitional Provisions

269 Meaning of "the relevant interest"

[ITA67 s268]

(1) Subject to this section, in this Chapter, "*the relevant interest*", in relation to any expenditure incurred on the construction of a building or structure, means the interest in that building or structure to which the person who incurred the expenditure was entitled when the person incurred the expenditure.

(2) Where, when a person incurs expenditure on the construction of a building or structure, the person is entitled to 2 or more interests in the building or structure and one of those interests is an interest which is reversionary on all the others, that interest shall be the relevant interest for the purposes of this Chapter.

(3) An interest shall not cease to be the relevant interest for the purposes of this Chapter by reason of the creation of any lease or other interest to which that interest is subject, and where the relevant interest is a leasehold interest and is extinguished by reason of the surrender of the leasehold interest, or on the person

entitled to the leasehold interest acquiring the interest which is reversionary on the leasehold interest, the interest into which that leasehold interest merges shall thereupon become the relevant interest.

Cross References

To Section 269

Section 250A Restriction of relief to individuals in respect of loans applied in acquiring interest in companies.

Section 343 Capital allowances in relation to construction or refurbishment of certain buildings or structures in enterprise areas.

Section 345 Double rent allowance in respect of rent paid for certain business premises.

Section 355 Disclaimer of capital allowances on holiday cottages, holiday apartments, etc.

Section 372K Non-application of relief in certain cases and provision against double relief.

Section 372T Non-application of relief in certain cases and provision against double relief.

Section 372V Capital allowances in relation to construction or refurbishment of certain park and ride facilities.

Section 372W Capital allowances in relation to construction or refurbishment of certain commercial premises.

Section 372AJ Non-application of relief in certain cases and provision against double relief.

Section 372AZ Restrictions on relief, non-application of relief in certain cases and provision against double relief.

Section 409E Income tax: ringfence on use of certain capital allowances on certain industrial buildings and other premises.

Section 843A Capital allowances for buildings used for certain childcare purposes.

270 Meaning of "expenditure on construction of building or structure"

[ITA67 s256, s263(4); CTA76 s21(1) and Sch1 par18; FA94 s22(1)(b); FA97 s146(1) and Sch9 PtI par1(18)]

(1) In this section, "*refurbishment*", in relation to a building or structure, means any work of construction, reconstruction, repair or renewal, including the provision of water, sewerage or heating facilities carried out in the course of the repair or restoration, or maintenance in the nature of repair or restoration, of the building or structure.

(2) A reference in this Chapter to expenditure incurred on the construction of a building or structure includes expenditure on the refurbishment of the building or structure, but does not include—

(a) any expenditure incurred on the acquisition of, or of rights in or over, any land,

(b) any expenditure on the provision of machinery or plant or on any asset treated for any chargeable period as machinery or plant, or

(c) any expenditure in respect of which an allowance is or may be made for the same or for any other chargeable period under *section 670* or *765(1)*.

(3) Where a building or structure which is to be an industrial building or structure forms part of a building or is one of a number of buildings in a single development, or forms a part of a building which is itself one of a number of buildings in a single development, there shall be made such apportionment as is necessary of the expenditure incurred on the construction of the whole building or number of buildings, as the case may be, for the purpose of determining the expenditure incurred on the construction of the building or structure which is to be an industrial building or structure.

[(4) This subsection applies where capital expenditure on the construction or refurbishment of a building or structure (or, in the case of *section 843*, qualifying expenditure within the meaning of that section) is incurred at any time in the period from 1 January 2006 to 31 July 2008 and the building or structure—

(a) is, or by virtue of *section 268(3)* is deemed to be, an industrial building or structure within the meaning of *section 268(1)(d)*,

(b) is an industrial building or structure within the meaning of *section 268(1)(k)*,

(c) is a qualifying multi-storey car park within the meaning of *section 344*,

(d) is a building or structure to which *section 372C* applies or a qualifying premises within the meaning of *section 372D*,

(e) is a building or structure to which *section 372M* applies or a qualifying premises within the meaning of *section 372N*,

(f) is a qualifying park and ride facility within the meaning of *section 372U* or a qualifying premises within the meaning of *section 372W*,

(g) is a building or structure to which *section 372AC* applies or a qualifying premises within the meaning of *section 372AD*,

(h) is a qualifying premises within the meaning of *section 843*, or

(i) is a qualifying residential unit within the meaning of *section 268(3A)*.

(5) Where *subsection (4)* applies, then, notwithstanding any other provision of the Tax Acts but subject to *subsections (6)* and *(7)*, the amount of the capital expenditure or, as the case may be, qualifying expenditure referred to in *subsection (4)* which is to be treated as incurred for the purposes of the making of allowances and charges under this Part (including the making of balancing allowances and charges under *section 274* and the calculation of the residue of expenditure under *section 277*), whether or not those allowances or charges are to be made directly under this Part or under this Part by virtue of the application of any provision of *Part 10* or *section 843*, shall be reduced—

(a) in the case of expenditure incurred in—

(i) where *subsection (4)(i)* applies, the period from 25 March 2007 to 31 December 2007, and

(ii) in any other case, the period from 1 January 2007 to 31 December 2007,

to 75 per cent, and

(b) in the case of expenditure incurred in the period from 1 January 2008 to 31 July 2008, to 50 per cent,

of the amount which, apart from this subsection, would otherwise be so treated and, for those purposes, references in the Tax Acts, other than those in *section 279* as applied by *subsection (6)*, to expenditure incurred on the construction of a building or structure shall be construed as a reference to such expenditure as reduced in accordance with this subsection.

(6) Where *subsections (4)* and *(5)* and, as the case may be, *subsection (7)* apply in relation to capital expenditure or qualifying expenditure incurred on a building or structure, *section 279* shall apply in relation to the building or structure as if—

(a) in *subsection (1)* of that section, the following were substituted for the definition of "the net price paid":

" "*the net price paid*" means the amount represented by A in the equation—

$$A = B \times \frac{C}{D + E}$$

where—

B is the amount paid by a person on the purchase of the relevant interest in the building or structure,

C is the amount of the expenditure actually incurred on the construction of the building or structure as reduced in accordance with *section 270(5)* and, as the case may be, *section 270(7)*,

D is the amount of the expenditure actually incurred on the construction of the building or structure, and

E is the amount of any expenditure actually incurred which is expenditure for the purposes of *paragraph (a)*, *(b)* or *(c)* of *section 270(2)*.",

(b) in *subsection (2)* of that section, the following were substituted for *paragraph (b)*:

"(b) the person who buys that interest shall be deemed for those purposes to have incurred, on the date when the purchase price becomes payable, expenditure on the construction of the building or structure equal to that expenditure as reduced in accordance with *section 270(5)* and, as the case may be, *section 270(7)* or to the net price paid (within the meaning of that term as applied by *section 270(6)(a)*) by such person for that interest, whichever is the less;",

and

(c) in *subsection (3)* of that section, the reference to "that expenditure or to" were a reference to "that expenditure as reduced in accordance with *section 270(5)* and, as the case may be, *section 270(7)* or to".

(7) (a) This subsection applies to a building or structure to which *paragraph (a)*, *paragraph (d)* (other than a qualifying premises which fronts on to a qualifying street (within the meaning of *section 372A*)), *paragraph (e)* or *paragraph (g)* of *subsection (4)* applies and in relation to which building or structure a person must show that the condition in—

(i) where *subsection (4)(a)* applies, *section 268(13)(c)(ii)(I)* or, as the case may be, *sections 272(9)(b)(i)* and *274(1B)(b)(i)*,

(ii) where *subsection (4)(d)* applies, *section 372A(3)(a)*,

(iii) where *subsection (4)(e)* applies, *section 372L(3)(a)*, or

(iv) where *subsection (4)(g)* applies, *section 372AA(3)(a)*,

was satisfied on or before 31 December 2006.

(b) (i) A person shall not be treated as having satisfied the condition referred to in *paragraph (a)* in relation to a building or structure unless—

(I) where *paragraph (a)(ii)* applies, the relevant local authority (within the meaning of *section 372A*), and

(II) in any other case, the local authority (within the meaning of the Local Government Act 2001),

in whose administrative area the building or structure is situated, gives a certificate in writing on or before 30 March 2007, to the person constructing or refurbishing the building or structure stating—

(A) that it is satisfied that work to the value of not less than 15 per cent of the actual construction or refurbishment costs of the building or structure involved was carried out on or before 31 December 2006,

(B) the actual amount of the capital expenditure incurred on the construction or refurbishment of the building or structure by 31 December 2006, and

(C) the projected amount of the balance of the capital expenditure (other than that referred to in clause (B)) which is to be incurred on the construction or refurbishment of the building or structure.

(ii) An application for a certificate referred to in *subparagraph (i)* shall be made on or before 31 January 2007 by the person who is constructing or refurbishing the building or structure.

(iii) In considering whether to give a certificate referred to in *subparagraph (i)*, the relevant local authority or, as the case may be, the local authority shall have regard to guidelines in relation to the giving of such certificates issued by the Department of the Environment, Heritage and Local Government.

(c) Where this subsection applies, the amount of capital expenditure referred to in *subsection (4)* which is to be treated as incurred in the period from 1 January 2007 to 31 July 2008 for the purposes of the making of allowances and charges (as referred to in *subsection (5)*) under this Part, shall not exceed the amount which has been certified by the relevant local authority or, as the case may be, the local authority under clause (C) of *paragraph (b)(i)* in relation to that building or structure.

(d) The provisions of this subsection shall apply prior to the application of the provisions of *subsections (5)* and *(6)* and where the provisions of this subsection apply to reduce the amount of capital expenditure which is to be treated as incurred in the period from 1 January 2007 to 31 July 2008, such reduction shall be made in relation to expenditure incurred in the period from 1 January 2008 to 31 July 2008 in priority to the period from 1 January 2007 to 31 December 2007.

(e) Where a building or structure to which this subsection applies is sold by the person who constructed or refurbished the building or structure, such person shall, at the time of such sale, supply the purchaser with a copy of the certificate referred to in *paragraph (b)(i)* for the purposes of the making of a claim by the purchaser under any of the provisions of this Part.

[(8) Where capital expenditure is incurred on or after 1 May 2007 under a contract or agreement which is entered into on or after that date for the construction, refurbishment or development of a qualifying residential unit as is referred to in *subsection (4)(i)*, then—

(a) *subsection (4)* shall apply as if the reference to "31 July 2008" were a reference to "30 April 2010",

(b) *subsection (5)* shall apply as if—

(i) the reference to "subject to *subsections (6)* and *(7)*" were a reference to "subject to *subsections (6)* to *(8)*", and

(ii) the following paragraphs were substituted for *paragraphs (a)* and *(b)*:

"(a) in the case of expenditure incurred by a company (within the meaning of *section 4(1)*) in the period from 1 May 2007 to 30 April 2010, to 75 per cent, and

(b) in the case of expenditure incurred by a person other than a company (within the meaning of *section 4(1)*) in the period from 1 May 2007 to 30 April 2010, to 50 per cent,",][1]][2]

Amendments

[1] Inserted by FA07 s28(1)(b). Applies as respects capital expenditure incurred on or after 1 May 2007 under a contract or agreement for the construction, refurbishment or development of a qualifying residential unit which is entered into on or after that date.

[2] Inserted by FA06 s26(1)(a). With effect from 26 June 2006 per S.I. 322 of 2006.

Revenue Briefings

Tax Briefing

Tax Briefing May 2006 – Issue 63 – Capital Allowances and Property-Based Incentive Schemes

Tax Briefing December 2006 – Issue 65 – Capital Allowances and Property-based Incentive Schemes

Tax Briefing December 2006 – Issue 65 – Property-Based Incentive Schemes – Inducements for Purchase of Property

eBrief

eBrief No. 55/2006 – Property-Based Incentive schemes '15%' Test – Payments to Local Authorities

Cross References

From Section 270

Section 4 Interpretation of Corporation Tax Acts.

Section 268 Meaning of "industrial building or structure".

Section 270 Meaning of "expenditure on construction of building or structure".

Section 272 Writing-down allowances.

Section 274 Balancing allowances and balancing charges.

Section 277 Writing off of expenditure and meaning of "residue of expenditure".

Section 279 Purchases of certain buildings or structures.

Section 322 Interpretation (Chapter 1).

Section 344 Capital allowances in relation to construction or refurbishment of certain multi-storey car parks.

Section 372A Interpretation and application (Chapter 7).

Section 372C Accelerated capital allowances in relation to construction or refurbishment of certain industrial buildings or structures.

Section 372D Capital allowances in relation to construction or refurbishment of certain commercial premises.

Section 372L Interpretation (Chapter 8).

Section 372M Accelerated capital allowances in relation to construction or refurbishment of certain industrial buildings or structures.

Section 372N Capital allowances in relation to construction or refurbishment of certain commercial buildings or structures.

Section 372U Interpretation (Chapter 9).

Section 372W Capital allowances in relation to construction or refurbishment of certain commercial premises.

Section 372AA Interpretation and application (Chapter 10).

Section 372AC Accelerated capital allowances in relation to construction or refurbishment of certain industrial buildings or structures.

Section 372AD Capital allowances in relation to construction or refurbishment of certain commercial premises.

Section 670 Mine development allowance.

Section 765 Allowances for capital expenditure on scientific research.

Section 843 Capital allowances for buildings used for third level educational purposes.

To Section 270

Section 268 Meaning of "industrial building or structure".
Section 270 Meaning of "expenditure on construction of building or structure".
Section 272 Writing-down allowances.
Section 274 Balancing allowances and balancing charges.
Section 279 Purchases of certain buildings or structures.
Section 316 Interpretation of certain references to expenditure and time when expenditure is incurred.
Section 344 Capital allowances in relation to construction or refurbishment of certain multi-storey car parks.
Section 372A Interpretation and application (Chapter 7).
Section 372C Accelerated capital allowances in relation to construction or refurbishment of certain industrial buildings or structures.
Section 372D Capital allowances in relation to construction or refurbishment of certain commercial premises.
Section 372L Interpretation (Chapter 8).
Section 372M Accelerated capital allowances in relation to construction or refurbishment of certain industrial buildings or structures.
Section 372N Capital allowances in relation to construction or refurbishment of certain commercial buildings or structures.
Section 372V Capital allowances in relation to construction or refurbishment of certain park and ride facilities.
Section 372W Capital allowances in relation to construction or refurbishment of certain commercial premises.
Section 372AA Interpretation and application (Chapter 10).
Section 372AC Accelerated capital allowances in relation to construction or refurbishment of certain industrial buildings or structures.
Section 372AD Capital allowances in relation to construction or refurbishment of certain commercial premises.
Section 372AZ Restrictions on relief, non-application of relief in certain cases and provision against double relief.
Section 843 Capital allowances for buildings used for third level educational purposes.

271 Industrial building allowances

[ITA67 s254(1)(a), (b) and (c), (2A), (2B), (3) and (7); FA75 s34(2)(a)(i); CTA76 s 21(1) and Sch1 par17and par72; FA81 s27; FA88 s51(1)(a) and (cc), (4)(a) and (6); FA89 s14; FA90 s74, s80 and s81(1)(a) and (4); FA91 s22(1); FA93 s33(1); FA95 s26 and s27; FA96 s27 and s43]

(1) In this section—

"*industrial development agency*" means the Industrial Development Authority, the Shannon Free Airport Development Company Limited or Údarás na Gaeltachta;

"*appropriate chargeable period*", in relation to any person who has incurred expenditure on the construction of a building or structure, means the chargeable period related to the expenditure or, if it is later, the chargeable period related to the event (which shall be regarded as an event within the meaning of *section 321(2)(b)*), where such event is—

(a) the commencement of the tenancy in a case in which the first use to which the building or structure is put is a use by a person occupying it by virtue of a tenancy to which the relevant interest is reversionary, or

(b) in a case to which *subsection (2)(b)(ii)* refers, the commencement of the tenancy to which the relevant interest is reversionary;

"*relevant lease*" means a lease to which the relevant interest is reversionary.

(2) (a) Subject to the Tax Acts, where a person incurs capital expenditure on the construction of a building or structure—

(i) which is to be an industrial building or structure to which *subsection (3)* applies, and

(ii) which is to be occupied for the purposes of a trade carried on either by the person or by a lessee mentioned in *paragraph (b)*,

there shall be made to the person who incurred the expenditure, for the appropriate chargeable period, an allowance (in this Chapter referred to as an "*industrial building allowance*").

(b) The lessee referred to in *paragraph (a)* is a lessee occupying the building or structure on the construction of which the expenditure was incurred and who so occupies it—

(i) under a relevant lease, or

(ii) under a lease to which a relevant lease granted to an industrial development agency is reversionary.

(3) This subsection shall apply to—

(a) an industrial building or structure provided—

(i) before the 23rd day of April, 1996, for use for the purposes of trading operations, or

(ii) on or after the 23rd day of April, 1996, by a company for use for the purposes of trading operations carried on by the company,

which are relevant trading operations within the meaning of *section 445* or *446* but, in relation to capital expenditure incurred on the provision of an industrial building or structure on or after the 6th day of May, 1993, excluding an industrial building or structure provided by a lessor to a lessee other than in the course of the carrying on by the lessor of those relevant trading operations,

(b) an industrial building or structure provided for the purposes of a project approved by an industrial development agency on or before the 31st day of December, 1988, and in respect of the provision of which expenditure was incurred before the 31st day of December, 1995; but, as respects an industrial building or structure provided for the purposes of a project approved by an industrial development agency in the period from the 1st day of January, 1986, to the 31st day of December, 1988, this paragraph shall apply as if the reference to the 31st day of December, 1995, were a reference to the 31st day of December, 1996,

and

(c) an industrial building or structure provided for the purposes of a project approved for grant assistance by an industrial development agency in the period from the 1st day of January, 1989, to the 31st day of December, 1990, and in respect of the provision of which expenditure is incurred before the 31st day of December, 1997[, or before the 30th day of June, 1998, if such expenditure would have been incurred before the 31st day of December, 1997, but for the existence of circumstances which resulted in legal proceedings being initiated, being proceedings which were the subject of an order of the High Court made before the 1st day of January, 1998][1]; but, as respects an industrial building or structure provided for the purposes of any such project specified in the list referred to in *section 133(8)(c)(iv)*, this paragraph shall apply as if the reference to the 31st day of December, 1997, [where it first occurs,][2] were a reference to the 31st day of December, 2002.

(4) An industrial building allowance shall be of an amount equal to—

(a) where the building or structure is to be used for a purpose specified in *paragraph (a)* or *(b)* of *section 268(1)*, 50 per cent of the capital expenditure mentioned in *subsection (2)*; but, in the case of a building or structure to which *subsection (3)(a)* applies, this paragraph shall apply only if that expenditure is incurred before the 25th day of January, 1999,

(b) where the building or structure is to be used for a purpose specified in *paragraph (c)* or *(e)* of *section 268(1)*, 20 per cent of the capital expenditure mentioned in *subsection (2)*, and

(c) in any other case, 10 per cent of the capital expenditure mentioned in *subsection (2)*.

(5) Where an industrial building allowance in respect of capital expenditure incurred on the construction of a building or structure to which *subsection (3)(c)* applies is made under this section for any chargeable period—

(a) no allowance in relation to that capital expenditure shall be made under *section 272* for that chargeable period, and

(b) an allowance in relation to that capital expenditure which is to be made under *section 272* for any chargeable period subsequent to that chargeable period shall not be increased under *section 273*.

(6) Notwithstanding any other provision of this section, no industrial building allowance shall be made in respect of any expenditure on a building or structure if the building or structure, when it comes to be used, is not an industrial building or structure, and where an industrial building allowance has been granted in respect of any expenditure on any such building or structure, [any assessments may, as necessary, be amended][3] to give effect to this subsection.

Amendments

[1] Inserted by FA98 s21(a)(i).

[2] Inserted by FA98 s21(a)(ii).

[3] Substituted by FA12 sched4(part 2)(g).

Revenue Briefings

Tax Briefing

Tax Briefing April 2001 – Issue 43 pg 38 – Resort Areas Timing of Claim for Capital Allowances

Revenue Precedents

Whether IBA due where property occupied by tenant of lessee who carries on qualifying trade – lessee does not carry on such a trade? IBA not due unless the lessee is IDA, SFADCO or Udaras na Gaeilge. Otherwise, the trade to be considered is that carried on by the lessee who must occupy it for the purposes of that trade. IT962002

Cross References

From Section 271

Section 133 Limitation on meaning of "distribution" – general.

Section 268 Meaning of "industrial building or structure".

Section 272 Writing-down allowances.

Section 273 Acceleration of writing-down allowances in respect of certain expenditure on certain industrial buildings or structures.

Section 321 Provisions of general application in relation to the making of allowances and charges.
Section 445 Certain trading operations carried on in Shannon Airport.
Section 446 Certain trading operations carried on in Custom House Docks Area.

To Section 271

Section 273 Acceleration of writing-down allowances in respect of certain expenditure on certain industrial buildings or structures.
Section 279 Purchases of certain buildings or structures.
Section 283 Initial allowances.
Section 285 Acceleration of wear and tear allowances.
Section 304 Income tax: allowances and charges in taxing a trade, etc.
Section 307 Corporation tax: allowances and charges in taxing a trade.
Section 316 Interpretation of certain references to expenditure and time when expenditure is incurred.
Section 323 Capital allowances in relation to construction of certain commercial premises.
Section 331 Accelerated capital allowances in relation to construction or refurbishment of certain industrial buildings or structures.
Section 332 Capital allowances in relation to construction or refurbishment of certain commercial premises.
Section 341 Accelerated capital allowances in relation to construction or refurbishment of certain industrial buildings or structures.
Section 342 Capital allowances in relation to construction or refurbishment of certain commercial premises.
Section 343 Capital allowances in relation to construction or refurbishment of certain buildings or structures in enterprise areas.
Section 344 Capital allowances in relation to construction or refurbishment of certain multi-storey car parks.
Section 345 Double rent allowance in respect of rent paid for certain business premises.
Section 352 Accelerated capital allowances in relation to construction or refurbishment of certain industrial buildings or structures.
Section 353 Capital allowances in relation to construction or refurbishment of certain commercial premises.
Section 354 Double rent allowance in respect of rent paid for certain business premises.
Section 355 Disclaimer of capital allowances on holiday cottages, holiday apartments, etc.
Section 372C Accelerated capital allowances in relation to construction or refurbishment of certain industrial buildings or structures.
Section 372D Capital allowances in relation to construction or refurbishment of certain commercial premises.
Section 372M Accelerated capital allowances in relation to construction or refurbishment of certain industrial buildings or structures.
Section 372N Capital allowances in relation to construction or refurbishment of certain commercial buildings or structures.
Section 372V Capital allowances in relation to construction or refurbishment of certain park and ride facilities.
Section 372W Capital allowances in relation to construction or refurbishment of certain commercial premises.
Section 372AC Accelerated capital allowances in relation to construction or refurbishment of certain industrial buildings or structures.
Section 372AD Capital allowances in relation to construction or refurbishment of certain commercial premises.
Section 380U Allowances in respect of certain buildings.
Section 405 Restriction on use of capital allowances on holiday cottages.
Section 408 Restriction on tax incentives on property investment.
Section 843A Capital allowances for buildings used for certain childcare purposes.

272 Writing-down allowances

[ITA67 s264; FA75 s34(2)(a)(ii) and (iii) and (3); CTA76 s21(1) and Sch1 pars23 and 72; FA86 s52(2); FA94 s22(1)(c) and (2); FA96 s28(1)]

(1) A building or structure shall be one to which this section applies only if the capital expenditure incurred on the construction of it has been incurred on or after the 30th day of September, 1956.

(2) Subject to this Part, where—

(a) any person is, at the end of a chargeable period or its basis period, entitled to an interest in a building or structure to which this section applies,

(b) at the end of the chargeable period or its basis period, the building or structure is an industrial building or structure, and

(c) that interest is the relevant interest in relation to the capital expenditure incurred on the construction of that building or structure,

an allowance (in this Chapter referred to as a "writing-down allowance") shall be made to such person for that chargeable period.

(3) A writing-down allowance shall be of an amount equal to—

(a) in relation to a building or structure which is to be regarded as an industrial building or structure within the meaning of *paragraph (a)* or *(b)* of *section 268(1)*—

(i) 2 per cent of the expenditure referred to in *subsection (2)(c)*, if that expenditure was incurred before the 16th day of January, 1975, or

(ii) 4 per cent of the expenditure referred to in *subsection (2)(c)*, if that expenditure is incurred on or after the 16th day of January, 1975,

(b) in relation to a building or structure which is to be regarded as an industrial building or structure within the meaning of *paragraph (c)* or *(e)* of *section 268(1)*, 10 per cent of the expenditure referred to in *subsection (2)(c)*,

(c) in relation to a building or structure which is to be regarded as an industrial building or structure within the meaning of *section 268(1)(d)*, other than a building or structure to which [paragraph *(d)*, *(da)* or *(db)*][1] relates—

(i) 10 per cent of the expenditure referred to in *subsection (2)(c)*, if that expenditure was incurred before the 27th day of January, 1994, [...][2]

(ii) 15 per cent of the expenditure referred to in *subsection (2)(c)*, if that expenditure is incurred on or after the 27th day of January, 1994, [or][3]

[(iii) [subject to *subsections (8)* and *(9)*][4], 4 per cent of the expenditure referred to in *subsection (2)(c)*, if the capital expenditure on the construction (within the meaning of *section 270*) of the building or structure is incurred on or after 4 December 2002,][5]

(d) in relation to a building or structure which is to be regarded as an industrial building or structure within the meaning of *section 268(1)(d)* by reason of its use as a holiday cottage, 10 per cent of the expenditure referred to in *subsection (2)(c)*, [...][6]

[(da) in relation to a building or structure which is to be regarded as an industrial building or structure within the meaning of *section 268(1)(d)* by reason of its use as a guest house or a holiday hostel to which *section 268(2C)* applies, 4 per cent of the capital expenditure on the construction (within the meaning of *section 270*) of the building or structure which is incurred on or after 3 February 2005,][7]

[(db) in relation to a building or structure which is to be regarded as an industrial building or structure within the meaning of *section 268(1)(d)* by reason of being comprised in, and in use as part of, premises which are registered in the register of caravan sites and camping sites kept under the Tourist Traffic Acts 1939 to 2003, 4 per cent of the capital expenditure on the construction (within the meaning of *section 270*) of the building or structure which is incurred on or after 1 January 2008,][8]

(e) in relation to a building or structure which is to be regarded as an industrial building or structure within the meaning of *section 268(1)(f)*, 4 per cent of the expenditure referred to in [*subsection (2)(c)*,][9]

[(f) in relation to a building or structure which is to be regarded as an industrial building or structure within the meaning of *paragraph (g)* or *(i)* of *section 268(1)*, 15 per cent of the expenditure referred to in *subsection (2)(c)*, [...][10]][11]

[(g) in relation to a building or structure which is to be regarded as an industrial building or structure within the meaning of *section 268(1)(h)*, 4 per cent of the expenditure referred to in [*subsection (2)(c)*, [...][12]][13]][14]

[(h) in relation to a building or structure which is to be regarded as an industrial building or structure within the meaning of [*paragraph (j)* or *(k)* of *section 268(1)*][15], 15 per cent of the expenditure referred to in [*subsection (2)(c)*, [...][16]][17]][18]

[(i) in relation to a building or structure which is to be regarded as an industrial building or structure within the meaning of *paragraph (l)* of *section 268(1)*, 15 per cent of the expenditure referred to in [subsection (2)(*c*), [...][19]][20]][21]

[(j) in relation to a building or structure which is to be regarded as an industrial building or structure within the meaning of *paragraph (m)* of *section 268(1)*, 15 per cent of the expenditure referred to in [*subsection (2)(c)*, and][22]][23]

[(k) in relation to a building or structure which is to be regarded as an industrial building or structure within the meaning of *paragraph (n)* of *section 268(1)*, 15 per cent of the expenditure referred to in *subsection (2)(c)*.][24]

[(3A) (a) This subsection shall apply to a building or structure in existence on—

(i) in the case of [Dublin Airport Authority][25], the vesting day, and

(ii) in the case of any other person, the date of the passing of the Finance Act, 1998,

and in use for the purposes of a trade which consists of the operation or management of an airport, not being either machinery or plant or a building or structure to which *section 268(1)(f)* applies.

(b) For the purposes of this Part, in relation to a building or structure to which this subsection applies, expenditure shall be deemed to have been incurred on—

(i) in the case of [Dublin Airport Authority][26], the vesting day, and

(ii) in the case of any other person, the date of the passing of the Finance Act, 1998,

on the construction of the building or structure of an amount determined by the formula—

$$A - B$$

where—

A is the amount of the capital expenditure originally incurred on the construction of the building or structure, and

B is the amount of the writing-down allowances which would have been made under this section in respect of the capital expenditure referred to in A if the building or structure had at all times been an industrial building or structure within the meaning of *section 268(1)(b)* and on the assumption that that section had applied as respects capital expenditure incurred before—

(I) in the case of [Dublin Airport Authority][27], the vesting day, and

(II) in the case of any other person, the date of the passing of the Finance Act, 1998.

(3B) (a) This subsection shall apply to a building or structure to which *section 268(1)(f)* applies, being a building or structure in existence on the vesting day and vested in [Dublin Airport Authority][28] on that day.

(b) For the purposes of this Part, in the case of a building or structure to which this subsection applies, expenditure shall be deemed to have been incurred by [Dublin Airport Authority][29] on the vesting day on the construction of the building or structure of an amount determined by the formula—

$$A - B$$

where—

A is the amount of the capital expenditure originally incurred on the construction of the building or structure, and

B is the amount of the writing-down allowances which would have been made under this section in respect of the capital expenditure referred to in A for the period to the day before the vesting day if a claim for those allowances had been duly made and allowed.][30]

(4) Where the interest in a building or structure which is the relevant interest in relation to any expenditure is sold while the building or structure is an industrial building or structure, then, subject to any further adjustment under this subsection on a later sale, the writing-down allowance for any chargeable period, if that chargeable period or its basis period ends after the time of the sale, shall be the residue (within the meaning of *section 277*) of that expenditure immediately after the sale, reduced in the proportion (if it is less than one) which the length of the chargeable period bears to the part unexpired at the date of the sale of the period of—

(a) in relation to a building or structure which is to be regarded as an industrial building or structure within the meaning of *paragraph (a)* or *(b)* of *section 268(1)*—

(i) 50 years beginning with the time when the building or structure was first used, in the case where the capital expenditure on the construction of the building or structure was incurred before the 16th day of January, 1975, or

(ii) 25 years beginning with the time when the building or structure was first used, in the case where the capital expenditure on the construction of the building or structure is incurred on or after the 16th day of January, 1975,

(b) in relation to a building or structure which is to be regarded as an industrial building or structure within the meaning of *paragraph (c)* or *(e)* of *section*

268(1), 10 years beginning with the time when the building or structure was first used,

(c) in relation to a building or structure which is to be regarded as an industrial building or structure within the meaning of *section 268(1)(d)*, other than a building or structure referred to in [paragraph (*d*), (*da*) or (*db*)][31]—

(i) 10 years beginning with the time when the building or structure was first used, in the case where the capital expenditure on the construction of the building or structure was incurred before the 27th day of January, 1994, [...][32]

(ii) 7 years beginning with the time when the building or structure was first used, in the case where the capital expenditure on the construction of the building or structure is incurred on or after the 27th day of January, 1994, [and][33]

[(iii) [subject to *subsections (8)* and *(9)*][34], 25 years beginning with the time when the building or structure was first used, in the case where the capital expenditure on the construction (within the meaning of *section 270*) of the building or structure is incurred on or after 4 December 2002,][35]

(d) in relation to a building or structure which is to be regarded as an industrial building or structure within the meaning of *section 268(1)(d)* by reason of its use as a holiday cottage, 10 years beginning with the time when the building or structure was first used, [...][36]

[(da) in relation to a building or structure which is to be regarded as an industrial building or structure within the meaning of *section 268(1)(d)* by reason of its use as a guest house or a holiday hostel to which *section 268(2C)* applies, 25 years beginning with the time when the building or structure was first used, in the case where the capital expenditure on the construction (within the meaning of *section 270*) of the building or structure is incurred on or after 3 February 2005,][37]

[(db) in relation to a building or structure which is to be regarded as an industrial building or structure within the meaning of *section 268(1)(d)* by reason of being comprised in, and in use as part of, premises which are registered in the register of caravan sites and camping sites kept under the Tourist Traffic Acts 1939 to 2003—

(i) 25 years beginning with the time when the building or structure was first used, or

(ii) where capital expenditure on the refurbishment of the building or structure is incurred, 25 years beginning with the time when the building or structure was first used subsequent to the incurring of that expenditure,

in the case where the capital expenditure on the construction (within the meaning of *section 270*) of the building or structure is incurred on or after 1 January 2008,][38]

[(e) in relation to a building or structure which is to be regarded as an industrial building or structure within the meaning of *section 268(1)(f)*, 25 years beginning with—

(i) the time when the building or structure was first used, or

(ii) in the case of a building or structure to which *subsection (3B)* applies, the vesting day,][39]

[(f) [subject to *paragraph (fa)*,][40] in relation to a building or structure which is to be regarded as an industrial building or structure within the meaning of *paragraph (g)* or *(i)* of *section 268(1)*—

(i) 7 years beginning with the time when the building or structure was first used, or

(ii) as respects a building or structure which is first used on or after 1 February 2007, 15 years beginning with the time when the building or structure was first used, or

(iii) where capital expenditure on the refurbishment of the building or structure is incurred and, subsequent to the incurring of that expenditure, the building or structure is first used on or after 1 February 2007, 15 years beginning with the time when the building or structure was first used subsequent to the incurring of that expenditure,][41]

[(fa) where *subsection (8)* of *section 270* applies in relation to a qualifying residential unit as is referred to in *subsection (4)(i)* of that section—

(i) 20 years beginning with the time when the unit was first used, or

(ii) where capital expenditure on the refurbishment of the unit is incurred, 20 years beginning with the time when the unit was first used subsequent to the incurring of that expenditure,][42]

[(g) in relation to a building or structure which is to be regarded as an industrial building or structure within the meaning of *section 268(1)(h)*, 25 years beginning with—

(i) the time when the building or structure was first used, or

(ii) as respects a building or structure to which *subsection (3A)* applies—

(I) in the case of [Dublin Airport Authority][43], the vesting day, and

(II) in the case of any other person, the date of the passing of the Finance Act, [1998,][44]][45]

[...][46]

[(ga) in relation to a building or structure which is to be regarded as an industrial building or structure within the meaning of *paragraph (j)* of *section 268(1)*—

(i) 7 years beginning with the time when the building or structure was first used, or

(ii) as respects a building or structure which is first used on or after 1 February 2007, 15 years beginning with the time when the building or structure was first used, or

(iii) where capital expenditure on the refurbishment of the building or structure is incurred and, subsequent to the incurring of that expenditure, the building or structure is first used on or after 1 February 2007, 15 years beginning with the time when the building or structure was first used subsequent to the incurring of that expenditure,

[...][47]][48]

[(h) in relation to a building or structure which is to be regarded as an industrial building or structure within the meaning of [*paragraph [...]*[49] *(k)* of *section 268(1)*][50], 7 years beginning with the time when the building or structure was first [used, [...]][51]][52]][53]

[(i) in relation to a building or structure which is to be regarded as an industrial building or structure within the meaning of *paragraph (l)* of *section 268(1)*—

(I) 15 years beginning with the time when the building or structure was first used, or

(II) where capital expenditure on the refurbishment of the building or structure is incurred, 15 years beginning with the time when the building or structure was first used subsequent to the incurring of that [expenditure, [...]][54]][55]][56]

[(j) in relation to a building or structure which is to be regarded as an industrial building or structure within the meaning of *paragraph (m)* of *section 268(1)*—

(I) 15 years beginning with the time when the building or structure was first used, or

(II) where capital expenditure on the refurbishment of the building or structure is incurred, 15 years beginning with the time when the building or structure was first used subsequent to the incurring of [that expenditure, and]][57]][58]

[(k) in relation to a building or structure which is to be regarded as an industrial building or structure within the meaning of *paragraph (n)* of *section 268(1)*—

(i) 7 years beginning with the time when the building or structure was first used, or

(ii) where capital expenditure on the refurbishment of the building or structure is incurred, 7 years beginning with the time when the building or structure was first used subsequent to the incurring of that expenditure.][59]

(5) In ascertaining a writing-down allowance to be made to a person under *subsection (4)*, the residue of expenditure mentioned in that subsection shall, where it exceeds the amount of expenditure incurred by that person in respect of the sale, be taken to be the amount of the expenditure so incurred.

(6) Notwithstanding any other provision of this section, in no case shall the amount of a writing-down allowance made to a person for any chargeable period in respect of any expenditure exceed what, apart from the writing off to be made by reason of the making of that allowance, would be the residue of that expenditure at the end of that chargeable period or its basis period.

[(7) For the purposes of this section, where a writing-down allowance has been made to a person for any chargeable period in respect of capital expenditure incurred on the construction of a building or structure within the meaning of *paragraph (d)* of *section 268(1)* and at the end of a chargeable period or its basis period the building or structure is not in use for the purposes specified in that paragraph, then, in relation to that expenditure—

(a) the building or structure shall not be treated as ceasing to be an industrial building or structure if, on the cessation of its use for the purposes specified in *paragraph (d)* of *section 268(1)*, it is converted to use for the purposes specified in *paragraph (g)* of that section and at the end of the chargeable period or its basis period it is in use for those latter purposes, and

(b) as respects that chargeable period or its basis period and any subsequent chargeable period or basis period of it, the building or structure shall, notwithstanding the cessation of its use for the purposes specified in *paragraph (d)* of *section 268(1)*, be treated as if it were in use for those purposes if at the end of the chargeable period or its basis period the building or structure is in use for the purposes specified in *paragraph (g)* of that section.][60]

[(8) *Subsections (3)(c)(iii)* and *(4)(c)(iii)* (as inserted by the Finance Act 2003) shall not apply as respects capital expenditure incurred on or before [31 December 2006][61] on the construction or refurbishment of a building or structure if—

(a) (i) a planning application (not being an application for outline permission within the meaning of section 36 of the Planning and Development Act 2000)[, in so far as planning permission is required,][62] in respect of the building or structure is made in accordance with the Planning and Development Regulations 2001 to 2002,

(ii) an acknowledgement of the application, which confirms that the application was received on or before [31 December 2004][63], is issued by the planning authority in accordance with article 26(2) of the Planning and Development Regulations 2001 (S.I. No. 600 of 2001), and

(iii) the application is not an invalid application in respect of which a notice is issued by the planning authority in accordance with article 26(5) of those regulations,

(b) (i) [a planning application, in so far as planning permission was required,][64] in respect of the building or structure was made in accordance with the Local Government (Planning and Development) Regulations 1994 (S.I. No. 86 of 1994), not being an application for outline permission within the meaning of article 3 of those regulations,

(ii) an acknowledgement of the application, which confirms that the application was received on or before 10 March 2002, was issued by the planning authority in accordance with article *29(2)(a)* of the regulations referred to in *subparagraph (i)*, and

(iii) the application was not an invalid application in respect of which a notice was issued by the planning authority in accordance with article 29(2)(*b*)(i) of those regulations,

[(ba) where the construction or refurbishment work on the building or structure represented by that expenditure is exempted development for the purposes of the Planning and Development Act 2000 by virtue of section 4 of that Act or by virtue of Part 2 of the Planning and Development Regulations 2001 (S.I. No. 600 of 2001) and—

(i) a detailed plan in relation to the development work is prepared,

(ii) a binding contract in writing, under which the expenditure on the development is incurred, is in existence, and

(iii) work to the value of 5 per cent of the development costs is carried out,

not later than 31 December 2004.][65]

or

(c) (i) the construction or refurbishment of the building or structure is a development in respect of which an application for a certificate under section 25(7)(a)(ii) of the Dublin Docklands Development Authority Act 1997 is made to the Authority (within the meaning of that Act),

(ii) an acknowledgement of the application, which confirms that the application was received on or before [31 December 2004][66], is issued by that Authority, and

(iii) the application is not an invalid application.

[(9) *Subsections (3)(c)(iii)* and *(4)(c)(iii)* shall not apply as respects capital expenditure incurred on or before 31 July 2008 on the construction or refurbishment of a building or structure if—

(a) the conditions of *paragraph (a)*, *(b)*, *(ba)* or *(c)*, as the case may be, of *subsection (8)* have been satisfied,

(b) subject to *paragraphs (a)* and *(b)* of *section 270(7)*—

(i) the person who is constructing or refurbishing the building or structure has, on or before 31 December 2006, carried out work to the value of not less than 15 per cent of the actual construction or, as the case may be, refurbishment costs of the building or structure, and

(ii) the person referred to in *subparagraph (i)* or, where the building or structure is sold by that person, the person who is claiming a deduction under this Chapter in relation to the expenditure incurred, can show that the condition in *subparagraph (i)* was satisfied,

(c) a binding contract in writing under which expenditure on the construction or refurbishment of the building or structure is incurred was in existence on or before 31 July 2006, and

(d) such other conditions, as may be specified in regulations made for the purposes of this paragraph by the Minister for Finance, have been satisfied; but such conditions shall be limited to those necessary to ensure compliance with the laws of the European Communities governing State aid or with a decision of the Commission of the European Communities as to whether aid to which this subsection relates is compatible with the common market having regard to Article 87 of the European Communities Treaty.][67]][68]

Amendments

[1] Substituted by FA08 s28(b)(i)(I).

[2] Deleted by FA03 s25(1)(b)(i)(I). Applies as on and from 4 December 2002.

[3] Inserted by FA03 s25(1)(b)(i)(II). Applies as on and from 4 December 2002.

[4, 34] Substituted by FA06 s27(1)(b)(i). With effect from 26 June 2006 per S.I. 323 of 2006.

[5] Inserted by FA03 s25(1)(b)(i)(III). Applies as on and from 4 December 2002.

[6] Deleted by FA98 s22(b)(i)(I).

[7] Inserted by FA05 s34(b)(i)(II).

[8] Inserted by FA08 s28(b)(i)(II).

[9] Substituted by FA98 s22(b)(i)(II).

[10] Deleted by FA01 s64(1)(b)(i)(I). With effect from 15 May 2002 per S.I. 210 of 2002.

[11] Substituted by FA99 s48(b)(i).

[12] Deleted by FA06 s36(1)(b)(i)(I). With effect from 23 January 2007 per S.I. 20 of 2007.

[13] Substituted by FA01 s64(1)(b)(i)(II). With effect from 15 May 2002 per S.I. 210 of 2002.

[14] Inserted by FA98 s20(b)(i).

[15, 50] Substituted by FA02 s34(1)(b). With effect from 15 May 2002 per S.I. 211 of 2002.

[16] Deleted by FA08 s26(1)(b)(i)(I). This section comes into operation on such day or days as the Minister for Finance may by order or orders appoint and different days may be appointed for different purposes or different provisions.

[17] Substituted by FA06 s36(1)(b)(i)(I). With effect from 23 January 2007 per S.I. 20 of 2007.

[18] Inserted by FA01 s64(1)(b)(i)(III). With effect from 15 May 2002 per S.I. 210 of 2002.

[19] Deleted by FA13 s31(1)(f). Comes into operation on such day or days as the Minister for Finance may by order or orders appoint and different days may be appointed for different purposes or for different provisions.

[20] Substituted by FA08 s26(1)(b)(i)(I). This section comes into operation on such day or days as the Minister for Finance may by order or orders appoint and different days may be appointed for different purposes or different provisions.

[21] Inserted by FA06 s36(1)(b)(i)(II). With effect from 23 January 2007 per S.I. 20 of 2007.

[22] Substituted by FA13 s31(1)(f). Comes into operation on such day or days as the Minister for Finance may by order or orders appoint and different days may be appointed for different purposes or for different provisions.

[23] Inserted by FA08 s26(1)(b)(i)(II). This section comes into operation on such day or days as the Minister for Finance may by order or orders appoint and different days may be appointed for different purposes or different provisions.

[24] Inserted by FA13 s31(1)(g). Comes into operation on such day or days as the Minister for Finance may by order or orders appoint and different days may be appointed for different purposes or for different provisions.

[25, 26, 27] Substituted by FA08 sched8(1)(d)(i). Has effect as on and from 13 March 2008.

[28, 29] Substituted by FA08 sched8(1)(d)(ii). Has effect as on and from 13 March 2008.

[30] Inserted by FA98 s20(b)(ii).

[31] Substituted by FA08 s28(b)(ii)(I).

[32] Deleted by FA03 s25(1)(b)(ii)(I). Applies as on and from 4 December 2002.

[33] Inserted by FA03 s25(1)(b)(ii)(II). Applies as on and from 4 December 2002.

[35] Inserted by FA03 s25(1)(b)(ii)(III). Applies as on and from 4 December 2002.

[36] Deleted by FA98 s20(b)(iii)(I).

[37] Inserted by FA05 s34(b)(ii)(II).

[38] Inserted by FA08 s28(b)(ii)(II).

[39] Substituted by FA98 s20(b)(iii)(II).

[40] Inserted by FA07 s28(1)(c)(i). Applies as respects capital expenditure incurred on or after 1 May 2007 under a contract or agreement for the construction, refurbishment or development of a qualifying residential unit which is entered into on or after that date.

[41] Substituted by FA06 s37(c).

[42] Inserted by FA07 s28(1)(c)(ii). Applies as respects capital expenditure incurred on or after 1 May 2007 under a contract or agreement for the construction, refurbishment or development of a qualifying residential unit which is entered into on or after that date.

[43] Substituted by FA08 sched8(1)(d)(iii). Has effect as on and from 13 March 2008.

[44] Substituted by FA01 s64(1)(b)(ii)(II). With effect from 15 May 2002 per S.I. 210 of 2002.

[45] Inserted by FA98 s20(b)(iii)(III).

[46] Deleted by FA06 s35(1)(b)(i).

[47] Deleted by FA06 s36(1)(b)(ii)(I). With effect from 23 January 2007 per S.I. 20 of 2007.

[48] Inserted by FA06 s35(1)(b)(ii).

[49] Deleted by FA06 s35(1)(b)(iii).

[51] Deleted by FA08 s26(1)(b)(ii)(I). This section comes into operation on such day or days as the Minister for Finance may by order or orders appoint and different days may be appointed for different purposes or different provisions.

[52] Substituted by FA06 s36(1)(b)(ii)(I). With effect from 23 January 2007 per S.I. 20 of 2007.

[53] Inserted by FA01 s64(1)(b)(ii)(III). This section shall come into operation on such day as the Minister for Finance may by order appoint. With effect from 15 May 2002 per S.I. 210 of 2002.

[54] Deleted by FA13 s31(1)(h). Comes into operation on such day or days as the Minister for Finance may by order or orders appoint and different days may be appointed for different purposes or for different provisions.

[55] Substituted by FA08 s26(1)(b)(ii)(I). This section comes into operation on such day or days as the Minister for Finance may by order or orders appoint and different days may be appointed for different purposes or different provisions.

[56] Inserted by FA06 s36(1)(b)(ii)(II). This section shall come into operation on such day or days as the Minister for Finance may by order appoint and different days may be appointed for different purposes or different provisions. With effect from 23 January 2007 per S.I. 20 of 2007.

[57] Substituted by FA13 s31(1)(h). Comes into operation on such day or days as the Minister for Finance may by order or orders appoint and different days may be appointed for different purposes or for different provisions.

[58] Inserted by FA08 s26(1)(b)(ii)(II). This section comes into operation on such day or days as the Minister for Finance may by order or orders appoint and different days may be appointed for different purposes or different provisions.

[59] Inserted by FA13 s31(1)(i). Comes into operation on such day or days as the Minister for Finance may by order or orders appoint and different days may be appointed for different purposes or for different provisions.

[60] Inserted by FA98 s22(b)(iii).

[61] Substituted by FA06 s27(1)(b)(ii). This section shall come into operation on such day or days as the Minister for Finance may by order or orders appoint and different days may be appointed for different purposes or different provisions. With effect from 26 June 2006 per S.I. 323 of 2006.

[62] Inserted by FA04 s25(1)(b)(ii). This section is deemed to have applied as on and from 4 December 2002.

[63] Substituted by FA04 s25(1)(b)(iii). This section is deemed to have applied as on and from 4 December 2002.

[64] Substituted by FA04 s25(1)(b)(iv).

[65] Inserted by FA04 s25(1)(b)(v).

[66] Substituted by FA04 s25(1)(b)(vi).

[67] Inserted by FA06 s27(1)(b)(iii). This section shall come into operation on such day or days as the Minister for Finance may by order or orders appoint and different days may be appointed for different purposes or different provisions. With effect from 26 June 2006 per S.I. 323 of 2006.

[68] Inserted by FA03 s25(1)(b)(iii). Applies as on and from 4 December 2002.

Revenue Briefings

Tax Briefing

Tax Briefing August 2005 – Issue 60 – Capital Allowances for Hotels and Other Holiday Accommodation

Revenue Precedents

Abattoirs qualify as industrial buildings unless ancillary to a retail outlet. 319.10(2)

A distribution in specie does not constitute a sale for the purposes of the section. IT 96 3505

Whether industrial buildings allowances apply to sawmills? Yes, provided treatment or processing carried on in the mill and machinery is involved. 319.8

Section 22 Finance Act 1994 changed the industrial building writing down allowance from 10% to 15%. Does the new rate apply to existing hotels on or after 27/01/94?. In the event of a sale after 27 January 1994, is the residue after sale written off over 7 years. Section 22 of the Finance Act 1994 provides that the 15% allowance and 7 year life only apply where the expenditure on construction is incurred on or after 27 January 1994. Where the construction expenditure is incurred before this date, there is a 10% allowance, and the building has a 10 year life. A person who purchases a hotel second hand does not incur expenditure on the construction of the hotel. If, on or after 27 January 1994, a person purchases second hand a hotel, the construction expenditure on which was incurred before that date, the building still has a 10 year life, and the industrial buildings annual allowances will be by reference to the residue of the expenditure over the remainder of that 10 year life. IT953003

A building was used for the purpose of a trade carried on in a factory for a number of years. No industrial buildings writing down allowances were claimed. The building was subsequently sold while it was an industrial building by the I.D.A. What allowance is the purchaser entitled to? The allowance available to the purchaser is the expenditure incurred on the construction written off over the unexpired part of the tax life of the building. 949

A company received Industrial Development Authority grants in respect of an industrial building. In the event of the company ceasing to trade, these grants were repayable. The company ceased trading and sold the industrial building for a nominal sum conditional on the purchaser entering into an agreement with the IDA to assume liability for the vendors grants if the purchaser ceased to trade. Is this contingent liability regarded as expenditure incurred for the purposes of section 272(5) Taxes Consolidation Act 1997. Expenditure is incurred on the date on which it becomes payable. If the liability is contingent on some future uncertain event it cannot be regarded as payable until that event is no longer contingent but certain. It therefore follows that the current expenditure incurred is the nominal sum. IT973013

Where warehousing facilities provided to person carrying on a qualifying trade for IBA purposes is building in use for qualifying trade? Where the building is let to a person carrying on a trade carried on in a mill, factory or other similar premises, it is in use for the lessee's trade. Where the person providing the warehousing facilities does so as part of a trade, the building is in use for the purposes of the trade of that person and is not in use for the purposes of a qualifying trade. IT962002B

Cross References

From Section 272

Section 268 Meaning of "industrial building or structure".

Section 270 Meaning of "expenditure on construction of building or structure".

Section 277 Writing off of expenditure and meaning of "residue of expenditure".

To Section 272

Section 85 Deduction for certain industrial premises.

Section 268 Meaning of "industrial building or structure".

Section 270 Meaning of "expenditure on construction of building or structure".

Section 271 Industrial building allowances.

Section 273 Acceleration of writing-down allowances in respect of certain expenditure on certain industrial buildings or structures.

Section 274 Balancing allowances and balancing charges.

Section 276 Application of sections 272 and 274 in relation to capital expenditure on refurbishment.

Section 277 Writing off of expenditure and meaning of "residue of expenditure".
Section 279 Purchases of certain buildings or structures.
Section 310 Allowances in respect of certain contributions to capital expenditure of local authorities.
Section 331 Accelerated capital allowances in relation to construction or refurbishment of certain industrial buildings or structures.
Section 341 Accelerated capital allowances in relation to construction or refurbishment of certain industrial buildings or structures.
Section 343 Capital allowances in relation to construction or refurbishment of certain buildings or structures in enterprise areas.
Section 352 Accelerated capital allowances in relation to construction or refurbishment of certain industrial buildings or structures.
Section 353 Capital allowances in relation to construction or refurbishment of certain commercial premises.
Section 354 Double rent allowance in respect of rent paid for certain business premises.
Section 355 Disclaimer of capital allowances on holiday cottages, holiday apartments, etc.
Section 372D Capital allowances in relation to construction or refurbishment of certain commercial premises.
Section 372N Capital allowances in relation to construction or refurbishment of certain commercial buildings or structures.
Section 372V Capital allowances in relation to construction or refurbishment of certain park and ride facilities.
Section 372W Capital allowances in relation to construction or refurbishment of certain commercial premises.
Section 372AC Accelerated capital allowances in relation to construction or refurbishment of certain industrial buildings or structures.
Section 372AD Capital allowances in relation to construction or refurbishment of certain commercial premises.
Section 372AX Accelerated capital allowances in relation to the construction or refurbishment of certain registered holiday camps.
Section 372AY Capital allowances in relation to the construction or refurbishment of certain tourism infrastructure facilities.
Section 405 Restriction on use of capital allowances on holiday cottages.
Section 408 Restriction on tax incentives on property investment.
Section 531AM Charge to universal social charge.
Section 531AU Capital allowances and losses.
Section 843 Capital allowances for buildings used for third level educational purposes.
Section 843A Capital allowances for buildings used for certain childcare purposes.
Schedule 25B List of Specified Reliefs and Method of Determining Amount of Specified Relief Used in a Tax Year

273 Acceleration of writing-down allowances in respect of certain expenditure on certain industrial buildings or structures

[FA78 s25; FA79 s25; FA88 s48 and s51(1)(a), (c) and (cc), (4)(b) and (6); FA89 s16; FA90 s76, s80 and s81(1)(a) and (b), proviso to (1), and (5); FA93 s33; FA95 s26 and s27; FA96 s43 and s132(1) and Sch 5 PtI par11]

(1) In this section—

"*industrial development agency*" means the Industrial Development Authority, Shannon Free Airport Development Company Limited or Údarás na Gaeltachta;

"*qualifying expenditure*" means capital expenditure incurred on or after the 2nd day of February, 1978, by the person to whom the allowance under *section 272* is to be made on the construction of a building or structure which is to be an industrial building or structure occupied by that person for a purpose specified in *paragraph (a)*, *(b)* or *(d)* of *section 268(1)*, but excluding such expenditure incurred for the purposes of the trade of hotel-keeping unless it is incurred on the construction of premises which are registered in a register kept by [the National Tourism Development Authority][1] under the Tourist Traffic Acts, 1939 to 1995.

(2) (a) Subject to this section, where for any chargeable period an allowance is to be made under *section 272* in respect of qualifying expenditure, the allowance shall, subject to *subsection (6)* of that section, be increased by such amount as is specified by the person to whom the allowance is to be made and, in relation to a case in which this subsection has applied, any reference in the Tax Acts to an allowance made under *section 272* shall be construed as a reference to that allowance as increased under this section.

(b) As respects any qualifying expenditure incurred on or after the 1st day of April, 1988, any allowance made under *section 272* and increased under *paragraph (a)* in respect of that expenditure, whether claimed for one chargeable period or more than one such period, shall not in the aggregate exceed—

(i) if the qualifying expenditure was incurred before the 1st day of April, 1989, 75 per cent,

(ii) if the qualifying expenditure was incurred on or after the 1st day of April, 1989, and before the 1st day of April, 1991, 50 per cent, or

(iii) if the qualifying expenditure was incurred on or after the 1st day of April, 1991, and before the 1st day of April, 1992, 25 per cent,

of the amount of that qualifying expenditure.

(3) Notwithstanding *subsection (2)*, but subject to *subsections (4)* and *(6)*—

(a) no allowance made under *section 272* in respect of qualifying expenditure incurred on or after the 1st day of April, 1992, shall be increased under this section, and

(b) as respects chargeable periods ending on or after the 6th day of April, 1999, no allowance made under *section 272* in respect of qualifying expenditure incurred before the 1st day of April, 1992, shall be increased under this section.

(4) This section shall apply in relation to capital expenditure incurred on the construction of an industrial building or structure to which *subsection (5)* applies as if *subsections (2)(b)* and *(3)* were deleted.

(5) This subsection shall apply to—

(a) an industrial building or structure provided—

(i) before the 23rd day of April, 1996, for use for the purposes of trading operations, or

(ii) on or after the 23rd day of April, 1996, by a company for use for the purposes of trading operations carried on by the company,

which are relevant trading operations within the meaning of *section 445* or *446* but, in relation to capital expenditure incurred on the provision of an industrial building or structure on or after the 6th day of May, 1993, excluding an industrial building or structure provided by a lessor to a lessee other than in the course of the carrying on by the lessor of those relevant trading operations,

(b) an industrial building or structure the expenditure on the provision of which was incurred before the 31st day of December, 1995, under a binding contract entered into on or before the 27th day of January, 1988, and

(c) an industrial building or structure provided for the purposes of a project approved by an industrial development agency on or before the 31st day of December, 1988, and in respect of the provision of which expenditure was incurred before the 31st day of December, 1995; but, as respects an industrial building or structure provided for the purposes of a project approved by an industrial development agency in the period from the 1st day of January, 1986, to the 31st day of December, 1988, this paragraph shall apply as if the reference to the 31st day of December, 1995, were a reference to the 31st day of December, 1996.

(6) This section shall apply in relation to capital expenditure incurred on the construction of a building or structure which is to be an industrial building or structure to which *subsection (7)(a)* applies—

(a) as if in *subsection (2)(b)*—

(i) the following subparagraph were substituted for *subparagraph (ii)*:

"(ii) if the qualifying expenditure is incurred on or after the 1st day of April, 1989, 50 per cent,",

and

(ii) *subparagraph (iii)* were deleted,

and

(b) as if *subsection (3)* were deleted.

(7) (a) This subsection shall apply to—

(i) an industrial building or structure provided for the purposes of a project approved for grant assistance by an industrial development agency in the period from the 1st day of January, 1989, to the 31st day of December, 1990, and in respect of the provision of which expenditure is incurred before the 31st day of December, 1997[, or before the 30th day of June, 1998, if such expenditure would have been incurred before the 31st day of December, 1997, but for the existence of circumstances which resulted in legal proceedings being initiated, being proceedings which were the subject of an order of the High Court made before the 1st day of January, 1998][2]; but, as respects an industrial building or structure provided for the purposes of any such project specified in the list referred to in *section 133(8)(c)(iv)*, this paragraph shall apply as if the reference to the 31st day of December, 1997, [where it first occurs,][3] were a reference to the 31st day of December, 2002, and

(ii) a building or structure which is to be an industrial building or structure within the meaning of *section 268(1)(d)* and in respect of the provision of which expenditure was incurred before the 31st day of December, 1995, where a binding contract for the provision of the building or structure was entered into before the 31st day of December, 1990.

(b) *Paragraph (a)(ii)* shall not apply if the building or structure referred to in that paragraph is not registered within 6 months after the date of the completion of that building or structure in a register kept by [the National Tourism Development Authority][4] under the Tourist Traffic Acts, 1939 to 1995, and where by virtue of this section any allowance or increased allowance has been granted, any necessary additional assessments may be made to give effect to this paragraph.

(8) Where for any chargeable period an allowance under *section 272* in respect of qualifying expenditure is increased under this section, no allowance under *section 271* shall be made in respect of that qualifying expenditure for that or any subsequent chargeable period.

Amendments

[1] Substituted by FA06 sched2(1)(e)(i). This section is deemed to have come into force and have taken effect as on and from 28 May 2003.

[2] Inserted by FA98 s21(a)(i).

[3] Inserted by FA98 s21(a)(ii).

[4] Substituted by FA06 sched2(1)(e)(ii). This section is deemed to have come into force and have taken effect as on and from 28 May 2003.

Revenue Precedents

Are owners of holiday apartments, listed with Bord Fáilte, who let such premises to tourists entitled to free depreciation under the section? No. The owners are lessors and not owner-occupiers. IT963514

Cross References

From Section 273

Section 133 Limitation on meaning of "distribution" – general.
Section 268 Meaning of "industrial building or structure".
Section 271 Industrial building allowances.
Section 272 Writing-down allowances.
Section 445 Certain trading operations carried on in Shannon Airport.
Section 446 Certain trading operations carried on in Custom House Docks Area.

To Section 273

Section 271 Industrial building allowances.
Section 283 Initial allowances.
Section 285 Acceleration of wear and tear allowances.
Section 323 Capital allowances in relation to construction of certain commercial premises.
Section 331 Accelerated capital allowances in relation to construction or refurbishment of certain industrial buildings or structures.
Section 332 Capital allowances in relation to construction or refurbishment of certain commercial premises.
Section 341 Accelerated capital allowances in relation to construction or refurbishment of certain industrial buildings or structures.
Section 342 Capital allowances in relation to construction or refurbishment of certain commercial premises.
Section 343 Capital allowances in relation to construction or refurbishment of certain buildings or structures in enterprise areas.
Section 344 Capital allowances in relation to construction or refurbishment of certain multi-storey car parks.
Section 345 Double rent allowance in respect of rent paid for certain business premises.
Section 352 Accelerated capital allowances in relation to construction or refurbishment of certain industrial buildings or structures.
Section 353 Capital allowances in relation to construction or refurbishment of certain commercial premises.
Section 354 Double rent allowance in respect of rent paid for certain business premises.
Section 372C Accelerated capital allowances in relation to construction or refurbishment of certain industrial buildings or structures.
Section 372D Capital allowances in relation to construction or refurbishment of certain commercial premises.
Section 372M Accelerated capital allowances in relation to construction or refurbishment of certain industrial buildings or structures.
Section 372N Capital allowances in relation to construction or refurbishment of certain commercial buildings or structures.

Section 372V Capital allowances in relation to construction or refurbishment of certain park and ride facilities.
Section 372W Capital allowances in relation to construction or refurbishment of certain commercial premises.
Section 372AC Accelerated capital allowances in relation to construction or refurbishment of certain industrial buildings or structures.
Section 372AD Capital allowances in relation to construction or refurbishment of certain commercial premises.
Section 843A Capital allowances for buildings used for certain childcare purposes.
Schedule 25B List of Specified Reliefs and Method of Determining Amount of Specified Relief Used in a Tax Year
Schedule 32 Transitional Provisions

274 Balancing allowances and balancing charges

[ITA67 s265; FA69 s64(3) and (4); FA75 s34(2)(a)(iii); CTA76 s21(1) and Sch1 pars24 and 72; FA80 s58; FA88 s45 and s51(1)(d) and (5); FA90 s78; FA94 s22(1)(d) and (2); FA95 s24; FA96 s28(2); FA97 s23(1)(a) and (2)]

(1) (a) Where any capital expenditure has been incurred on the construction of a building or structure in respect of which an allowance has been made under this Chapter, and any of the following events occurs—

(i) the relevant interest in the building or structure is sold,

(ii) that interest, being a leasehold interest, comes to an end otherwise than on the person entitled to the leasehold interest acquiring the interest which is reversionary on the leasehold interest,

(iii) the building or structure is demolished or destroyed or, without being demolished or destroyed, ceases altogether to be used, or

(iv) subject to *subsection (2)*, where consideration (other than rent or an amount treated or, as respects consideration received on or after the 26th day of March, 1997, partly treated as rent under *section 98*) is received by the person entitled to the relevant interest in respect of an interest which is subject to that relevant interest,

an allowance or charge (in this Chapter referred to as a "balancing allowance" or a "balancing charge") shall, in the circumstances mentioned in this section, be made to or on, as the case may be, the person entitled to the relevant interest immediately before that event occurs, for the chargeable period related to that event.

(b) [Notwithstanding *paragraph (a)* and *subsection (2A)(b)*][1], no balancing allowance or balancing charge shall be made by reason of any event referred to in that paragraph occurring more than—

(i) in relation to a building or structure which is to be regarded as an industrial building or structure within the meaning of *paragraph (a)* or *(b)* of *section 268(1)*—

(I) 50 years after the building or structure was first used, in the case where the capital expenditure on the construction of the building or structure was incurred before the 16th day of January, 1975, or

(II) 25 years after the building or structure was first used, in the case where the capital expenditure on the construction of the building or structure is incurred on or after the 16th day of January, 1975, [(ii) in relation to a building or structure which is to be regarded as an industrial building or structure within the meaning of [*paragraph (c)* or *(e)*][2] of *section 268(1)*, 10 years after the building or structure was first used,][3]

[(iia) [subject to *subparagraph (iib)*,][4] in relation to a building or structure which is to be regarded as an industrial building or structure within the meaning of *paragraph (g)* or *(i)* of *section 268(1)*—

(I) 10 years after the building or structure was first used, or

(II) as respects a building or structure which is first used on or after 1 February 2007, 15 years after the building or structure was first used, or

(III) where capital expenditure on the refurbishment of the building or structure is incurred and, subsequent to the incurring of that expenditure, the building or structure is first used on or after 1 February 2007, 15 years after the building or structure was first used subsequent to the incurring of that expenditure,][5]

[(iib) where *subsection (8)* of *section 270* applies in relation to a qualifying residential unit as is referred to in *subsection (4)(i)* of that section—

(I) 20 years after the unit was first used, or

(II) where capital expenditure on the refurbishment of the unit is incurred, 20 years after the unit was first used subsequent to the incurring of that expenditure,][6]

(iii) in relation to a building or structure which is to be regarded as an industrial building or structure within the meaning of *section 268(1) (d)*, other than a building or structure to which [subparagraph (iv), (iva) or (ivb)][7] relates—

(I) 10 years after the building or structure was first used, in the case where the capital expenditure on the construction of the building or structure was incurred before the 27th day of January, 1994, […][8]

(II) 7 years after the building or structure was first used, in the case where the capital expenditure on the construction of the building or structure is incurred on or after the 27th day of January, 1994, [or][9]

[(III) subject to [subject to *subsections (1A)* and *(1B)*][10], 25 years after the building or structure was first used, in the case where the capital expenditure on the construction (within the meaning of *section 270*) of the building or structure is incurred on or after 4 December 2002,][11]

(iv) in relation to a building or structure which is to be regarded as an industrial building or structure within the meaning of *section 268(1)(d)* by reason of its use as a holiday cottage, 10 years after the building or structure was first used, […][12]

[(iva) in relation to a building or structure which is to be regarded as an industrial building or structure within the meaning of *section 268(1) (d)* by reason of its use as a guest house or a holiday hostel to which *section 268(2C)* applies, 25 years after the building or structure was first used, in the case where the capital expenditure on the construction (within the meaning of *section 270*) of the building or structure is incurred on or after 3 February 2005,][13]

[(ivb) in relation to a building or structure which is to be regarded as an industrial building or structure within the meaning of *section 268(1)(d)* by reason of being comprised in, and in use as part of, premises which are registered in the register of caravan sites and camping sites kept under the Tourist Traffic Acts 1939 to 2003—

(i) 25 years after the building or structure was first used, or

(ii) where capital expenditure on the refurbishment of the building or structure is incurred, 25 years after the building or structure was first used subsequent to the incurring of that expenditure,

in the case where the capital expenditure on the construction (within the meaning of *section 270*) of the building or structure is incurred on or after 1 January 2008,][14]

[(v) in relation to a building or structure which is to be regarded as an industrial building or structure within the meaning of *section 268(1)(f)*, 25 years after—

(I) the building or structure was first used, or

(II) in the case of a building or structure to which *section 272(3B)* applies, the vesting day, [...][15]][16]

[(vi) in relation to a building or structure which is to be regarded as an industrial building or structure within the meaning of *section 268(1)(h)*, 25 years after—

(I) the building or structure was first used, or

(II) as respects a building or structure to which *section 272(3A)* applies—

(A) in the case of [Dublin Airport Authority][17], the vesting day, and

(B) in the case of any other person, the date of the passing of the Finance Act, [1998,][18]][19]

[...][20]

[(via) in relation to a building or structure which is to be regarded as an industrial building or structure within the meaning of *paragraph (j)* of *section 268(1)*—

(I) 10 years after the building or structure was first used, or

(II) as respects a building or structure which is first used on or after 1 February 2007, 15 years after the building or structure was first used, or

(III) where capital expenditure on the refurbishment of the building or structure is incurred and, subsequent to the incurring of that expenditure, the building or structure is first used on or after 1 February 2007, 15 years after the building or structure was first used subsequent to the incurring of that expenditure,

[...][21][22]

[(vii) in relation to a building or structure which is to be regarded as an industrial building or structure within the meaning of [*paragraph [...][23] (k)* of *section 268(1)*][24], [10 years after][25] the building or structure was first [used, [...][26]][27][28]

[(viii) in relation to a building or structure which is to be regarded as an industrial building or structure within the meaning of *paragraph (l)* of *section 268(1)*—

(I) 15 years after the building or structure was first used, or

(II) where capital expenditure on the refurbishment of the building or structure is incurred, 15 years after the building or structure was first used subsequent to the incurring of that [expenditure, [...][29]][30]][31]

[(ix) in relation to a building or structure which is to be regarded as an industrial building or structure within the meaning of *paragraph (m)* of *section 268(1)*—

(I) 15 years after the building or structure was first used, or

(II) where capital expenditure on the refurbishment of the building or structure is incurred, 15 years after the building or structure was first used subsequent to the incurring of [that expenditure, and][32]][33]

[(x) in relation to a building or structure which is to be regarded as an industrial building or structure within the meaning of *paragraph (n)* of *section 268(1)*—

(I) 7 years after the building or structure was first used, or

(II) where capital expenditure on the refurbishment of the building or structure is incurred, 7 years after the building or structure was first used subsequent to the incurring of that expenditure.][34]

[(1A) *Subsection (1)(b)(iii)(III)* (as inserted by the Finance Act 2003) shall not apply as respects capital expenditure incurred on or before [31 December 2006][35] on the construction or refurbishment of a building or structure if—

(a) (i) a planning application (not being an application for outline permission within the meaning of section 36 of the Planning and Development Act 2000)[, in so far as planning permission is required,][36] in respect of the building or structure is made in accordance with the Planning and Development Regulations 2001 to 2002,

(ii) an acknowledgement of the application, which confirms that the application was received on or before [31 December 2004][37], is issued by the planning authority in accordance with article 26(2) of the Planning and Development Regulations 2001 (S.I. No. 600 of 2001), and

(iii) the application is not an invalid application in respect of which a notice is issued by the planning authority in accordance with article 26(5) of those regulations,

(b) (i) [a planning application, in so far as planning permission was required,][38] in respect of the building or structure was made in accordance with the Local Government (Planning and Development) Regulations 1994 (S.I. No. 86 of 1994), not being an application for outline permission within the meaning of article 3 of those regulations,

(ii) an acknowledgement of the application, which confirms that the application was received on or before 10 March 2002, was issued by the planning authority in accordance with article 29(2)(a) of the regulations referred to in *subparagraph (i)*, and

(iii) the application was not an invalid application in respect of which a notice was issued by the planning authority in accordance with article 29(2)(b)(i) of those regulations,

[(ba) where the construction or refurbishment work on the building or structure represented by that expenditure is exempted development for the purposes of the Planning and Development Act 2000 by virtue of section 4 of that Act or by virtue of Part 2 of the Planning and Development Regulations 2001 (S.I. No. 600 of 2001) and—

(i) a detailed plan in relation to the development work is prepared,

(ii) a binding contract in writing, under which the expenditure on the development is incurred, is in existence, and

(iii) work to the value of 5 per cent of the development costs is carried out,

not later than 31 December 2004.][39]

or

(c) (i) the construction or refurbishment of the building or structure is a development in respect of which an application for a certificate under section 25(7)(a)(ii) of the Dublin Docklands Development Authority Act 1997 is made to the Authority (within the meaning of that Act),

(ii) an acknowledgement of the application, which confirms that the application was received on or before [31 December 2004][40], is issued by that Authority, and

(iii) the application is not an invalid application.][41]

[(1B) *Subsection (1)(b)(iii)(III)* shall not apply as respects capital expenditure incurred on or before 31 July 2008 on the construction or refurbishment of a building or structure if—

(a) the conditions of *paragraph (a)*, *(b)*, *(ba)* or *(c)*, as the case may be, of *subsection (1A)* have been satisfied,

(b) subject to *paragraphs (a)* and *(b)* of *section 270(7)*—

(i) the person who is constructing or refurbishing the building or structure has, on or before 31 December 2006, carried out work to the value of not less than 15 per cent of the actual construction or, as the case may be, refurbishment costs of the building or structure, and

(ii) the person referred to in *subparagraph (i)* or, where the building or structure is sold by that person, the person who is claiming a deduction under this Chapter in relation to the expenditure incurred, can show that the condition in *subparagraph (i)* was satisfied,

(c) a binding contract in writing under which expenditure on the construction or refurbishment of the building or structure is incurred was in existence on or before 31 July 2006, and

(d) such other conditions, as may be specified in regulations made for the purposes of this paragraph by the Minister for Finance, have been satisfied; but such conditions shall be limited to those necessary to ensure compliance with the laws of the European Communities governing State aid or with a decision of the Commission of the European Communities as to whether aid to which this subsection relates is compatible with the common market having regard to Article 87 of the European Communities Treaty.][42]

(2) *Subsection (1)(a)(iv)* shall not apply as respects the relevant interest in a building or structure in use for the purposes of a trade or part of a trade of hotel-keeping where a binding contract for the provision of the building or structure was entered into after the 27th day of January, 1988, and before the 1st day of June, 1988.

[(2A) (a) In this subsection "*relevant facility*" means a building or structure which—

(i) is in use for the purposes of a trade referred to in *paragraph (g)* of *section 268(1)*,

(ii) is in use as a qualifying residential unit (within the meaning of *section 268(3A)*) which, by virtue of *section 268(3B)*, is deemed to be a building or structure referred to in *subparagraph (i)*,

(iii) is in use for the purposes of a trade referred to in *paragraph (i)* of *section 268(1)*,

(iv) is in use for the purposes of a trade referred to in *paragraph (j)* of *section 268(1)*,

(v) is in use for the purposes of a trade referred to in *paragraph (l)* (as inserted by the Finance Act 2006) of *section 268(1)*, […][43]

(vi) is a qualifying premises (within the meaning of *section 843A(1)*) which is in use for the purposes of providing the service or services referred to in *paragraph (b)* of the definition of "*qualifying premises*" in that [section, or][44]

[(vii) is in use for the purposes of a trade referred to in *paragraph (m)* of *section 268(1)*.][45]

(b) Where—

(i) a building or structure is a relevant facility to which *subparagraph (i)*, *(ii)*, *(iii)*, *(iv)*, [*(v)*, *(vi)* or *(vii)*][46] of *paragraph (a)* applies,

(ii) an allowance has been made under this Chapter in respect of capital expenditure incurred on the construction or refurbishment of the building or structure, and

(iii) the building or structure concerned ceases to be a relevant facility,

then, subject to *paragraph (c)*, such cessation shall be treated as an event which gives rise to a balancing charge under this section and that balancing charge shall be made on the person entitled to the relevant interest in the building or structure concerned immediately before that event occurs, for the chargeable period related to that event.

(c) *Paragraph (b)* shall not apply if, within 6 months of the cessation referred to in *subparagraph (iii)* of that paragraph, the building or structure concerned is again a relevant facility by virtue of the application of any subparagraph of *paragraph (a)*, other than the subparagraph by virtue of which the building or structure was previously treated as a relevant facility.][47]

(3) Where there are no sale, insurance, salvage or compensation moneys, or consideration of the type referred to in *subsection (1)(a)(iv)*, or where the residue of the expenditure immediately before the event exceeds those moneys or that consideration, a balancing allowance shall be made, and the amount of that allowance shall be the amount of that residue or, as the case may be, of the excess of that residue over those moneys [or that consideration; but this subsection shall not apply in the case of consideration of the type referred to in *subsection (1)(a)(iv)* which is received on or after 5 March 2001.][48]

(4) Where the sale, insurance, salvage or compensation moneys, or consideration of the type referred to in *subsection (1)(a)(iv)*, exceed the residue, if any, of the expenditure immediately before the event, a balancing charge shall be made, and the amount on which it is made shall be an amount equal to the excess or, where the residue is nil, to those moneys or that consideration.

(5) (a) In this subsection, "*the relevant period*" means the period beginning when the building or structure was first used for any purpose and ending—

(i) if the event giving rise to the balancing allowance or balancing charge occurs on the last day of a chargeable period or its basis period, on that day, or

(ii) in any other case, on the latest date before that event which is the last day of a chargeable period or its basis period;

but where before that event the building or structure has been sold while an industrial building or structure, the relevant period shall begin on the day following that sale or, if there has been more than one such sale, the last such sale.

(b) Where a balancing allowance or a balancing charge is to be made to or on a person, and any part of the relevant period is not comprised in a chargeable period for which a writing-down allowance has been made to such person or is not comprised in the basis period for such chargeable period, the amount of the balancing allowance or, as the case may be, the amount on which the balancing charge is to be made shall be reduced in the proportion which the part or parts so comprised bears to the whole of the relevant period.

(c) Notwithstanding *paragraph (b)*, where but for *section 272(6)* or *321(5)* a writing-down allowance would have been made to a person for any chargeable period, the part of the relevant period comprised in that chargeable period or its basis period shall be deemed for the purposes of this subsection to be comprised in a chargeable period for which a writing-down allowance was made to the person.

(6) Where a building or structure which is to be regarded as an industrial building or structure within the meaning of *section 268(1)(d)* by reason of its use as a holiday cottage ceases to be comprised in premises registered in a register referred to in *section 268* in such circumstances that apart from this subsection this section would not apply in relation to the building or structure, the relevant interest

in the building or structure shall for the purposes of this Chapter (other than *section 272(4)*) be deemed on such cesser to have been sold while the building or structure was an industrial building or structure and the net proceeds of the sale shall be deemed for those purposes to be an amount equal to the capital expenditure incurred on the construction of the building or structure.

(7) Where a balancing charge is made under this section by virtue of *subsection (6)* and the relevant interest in the building or structure is not subsequently sold by the person on whom the charge is made while the building or structure is not an industrial building or structure, such person shall, if the building or structure again becomes comprised in a premises registered in a register referred to in *section 268*, be treated for the purposes of this Chapter as if, at the time of the cesser referred to in *subsection (6)*, such person were the buyer of the relevant interest deemed under that subsection to have been sold.

(8) Notwithstanding any other provision of this section, in no case shall the amount on which a balancing charge is made on a person in respect of any expenditure on the construction of a building or structure exceed the amount of the industrial building allowance, if any, made to such person in respect of that expenditure together with the amount of any writing-down allowances made to such person in respect of that expenditure for chargeable periods which end on or before the date of the event giving rise to the charge or, as the case may be, for chargeable periods for which the basis periods end on or before that date.

Amendments

[1] Substituted by FA06 s39(1)(a)(i). Applies in relation to a building or structure which is first used on or after 1 January 2006.

[2] Substituted by FA06 s37(d)(i).

[3] Substituted by FA99 s48(c).

[4] Inserted by FA07 s28(1)(d)(i). Applies as respects capital expenditure incurred on or after 1 May 2007 under a contract or agreement for the construction, refurbishment or development of a qualifying residential unit which is entered into on or after that date.

[5] Inserted by FA06 s37(d)(ii).

[6] Inserted by FA07 s28(1)(d)(ii). Applies as respects capital expenditure incurred on or after 1 May 2007 under a contract or agreement for the construction, refurbishment or development of a qualifying residential unit which is entered into on or after that date.

[7] Substituted by FA08 s28(c)(i).

[8] Deleted by FA03 s25(1)(c)(i)(I).

[9] Inserted by FA03 s25(1)(c)(i)(II).

[10] Substituted by FA06 s27(1)(c)(i). With effect from 26 June 2006 per S.I. 323 of 2006.

[11] Inserted by FA03 s25(1)(c)(i)(III).

[12] Deleted by FA98 s20(c)(i).

[13] Inserted by FA05 s34(c)(ii).

[14] Inserted by FA08 s28(c)(ii).

[15] Deleted by FA01 s64(1)(c)(i). This section shall come into operation on such day as the Minister for Finance may by order appoint.

[16] Substituted by FA98 s20(c)(ii).

[17] Substituted by FA08 sched8(1)(e). Has effect as on and from 13 March 2008.

[18] Substituted by FA01 s64(1)(c)(ii). This section shall come into operation on such day as the Minister for Finance may by order appoint.

[19] Inserted by FA98 s20(c)(iii).

[20] Deleted by FA06 s35(1)(c)(i).

[21] Deleted by FA06 s36(1)(c)(i). This section shall come into operation on such day or days as the Minister for Finance may by order appoint and different days may be appointed for different purposes or different provisions.

[22] Inserted by FA06 s35(1)(c)(ii).

[23] Deleted by FA06 s35(1)(c)(iii)(I).

[24] Substituted by FA02 s34(1)(b). This section comes into operation on such day as the Minister for Finance may by order appoint.

[25] Substituted by FA06 s35(1)(c)(iii)(II). This section is deemed to have applied as on and from 15 May 2002.

[26] Deleted by FA08 s26(1)(c)(i)(I). This section comes into operation on such day or days as the Minister for Finance may by order or orders appoint and different days may be appointed for different purposes or different provisions.

[27] Substituted by FA06 s36(1)(c)(i). With effect from 23 January 2007 per S.I. No. 20 of 2007.

[28] Inserted by FA01 s64(1)(c)(iii). This section shall come into operation on such day as the Minister for Finance may by order appoint.

[29] Deleted by FA13 s31(1)(j). Comes into operation on such day or days as the Minister for Finance may by order or orders appoint and different days may be appointed for different purposes or for different provisions.

[30] Substituted by FA08 s26(1)(c)(i)(I). This section comes into operation on such day or days as the Minister for Finance may by order or orders appoint and different days may be appointed for different purposes or different provisions.

[31] Inserted by FA06 s36(1)(c)(ii). With effect from 23 January 2007 per S.I. No. 20 of 2007.

[32] Substituted by FA13 s31(1)(j). Comes into operation on such day or days as the Minister for Finance may by order or orders appoint and different days may be appointed for different purposes or for different provisions.

[33] Inserted by FA08 s26(1)(c)(i)(II). This section comes into operation on such day or days as the Minister for Finance may by order or orders appoint and different days may be appointed for different purposes or different provisions.

[34] Inserted by FA13 s31(1)(k). Comes into operation on such day or days as the Minister for Finance may by order or orders appoint and different days may be appointed for different purposes or for different provisions.

[35] Substituted by FA06 s27(1)(c)(ii). With effect from 26 June 2006 per S.I. 323 of 2006.

[36] Inserted by FA04 s25(1)(c)(ii). This section is deemed to have applied as on and from 4 December 2002.

[37] Substituted by FA04 s25(1)(c)(iii). This section is deemed to have applied as on and from 4 December 2002.

[38] Substituted by FA04 s25(1)(c)(iv).

[39] Inserted by FA04 s25(1)(c)(v).

[40] Substituted by FA04 s25(1)(c)(vi).

[41] Inserted by FA03 s25(1)(c)(ii).

[42] Inserted by FA06 s27(1)(c)(iii). With effect from 26 June 2006 per S.I. 323 of 2006.

[43] Deleted by FA08 s26(1)(c)(ii)(I). This section comes into operation on such day or days as the Minister for Finance may by order or orders appoint and different days may be appointed for different purposes or different provisions.

[44] Substitued by FA08 s26(1)(c)(ii)(I). This section comes into operation on such day or days as the Minister for Finance may by order or orders appoint and different days may be appointed for different purposes or different provisions.

[45] Inserted by FA08 s26(1)(c)(ii)(II). This section comes into operation on such day or days as the Minister for Finance may by order or orders appoint and different days may be appointed for different purposes or different provisions.

[46] Substituted by FA08 s26(1)(c)(iii). This section comes into operation on such day or days as the Minister for Finance may by order or orders appoint and different days may be appointed for different purposes or different provisions.

[47] Inserted by FA06 s39(1)(a)(ii). Applies in relation to a building or structure which is first used on or after 1 January 2006.

[48] Substituted by FA01 s54.

Revenue Precedents

Death of an individual is not a balancing event for the purposes of the section. IT963510

If there is a termination of a "relevant period", as defined in Section 1007 Taxes Consolidation Act 1997, in relation to a non trading partnership does a balancing charge arise?. The provisions of Part 43 Taxes Consolidation Act 1997 apply to trades and professions carried on in partnership. They do not apply to non-trading or non-professional partnerships, such as a partnership which exists solely to own and let property. The provisions of Section 274 Taxes Consolidation Act 1997 will determine if and when a balancing allowance/charge will arise in the case of such non-trading partnerships. IT913068

Cross References

From Section 274

Section 98 Treatment of premiums, etc. as rent.

Section 268 Meaning of "industrial building or structure".

Section 270 Meaning of "expenditure on construction of building or structure".

Section 272 Writing-down allowances.

Section 321 Provisions of general application in relation to the making of allowances and charges.

Section 843A Capital allowances for buildings used for certain childcare purposes.

To Section 274

Section 267P Treatment of credit transaction.

Section 270 Meaning of "expenditure on construction of building or structure".

Section 275 Restriction of balancing allowances on sale of industrial building or structure.

Section 276 Application of sections 272 and 274 in relation to capital expenditure on refurbishment.

Section 277 Writing off of expenditure and meaning of "residue of expenditure".

Section 279 Purchases of certain buildings or structures.

Section 318 Meaning of "sale, insurance, salvage or compensation moneys".

Section 323 Capital allowances in relation to construction of certain commercial premises.

Section 331 Accelerated capital allowances in relation to construction or refurbishment of certain industrial buildings or structures.

Section 332 Capital allowances in relation to construction or refurbishment of certain commercial premises.

Section 341 Accelerated capital allowances in relation to construction or refurbishment of certain industrial buildings or structures.

Section 342 Capital allowances in relation to construction or refurbishment of certain commercial premises.

Section 343 Capital allowances in relation to construction or refurbishment of certain buildings or structures in enterprise areas.

Section 344 Capital allowances in relation to construction or refurbishment of certain multi-storey car parks.

Section 345 Double rent allowance in respect of rent paid for certain business premises.

Section 353 Capital allowances in relation to construction or refurbishment of certain commercial premises.

Section 355 Disclaimer of capital allowances on holiday cottages, holiday apartments, etc.

Section 372C Accelerated capital allowances in relation to construction or refurbishment of certain industrial buildings or structures.

Section 372D Capital allowances in relation to construction or refurbishment of certain commercial premises.

Section 372M Accelerated capital allowances in relation to construction or refurbishment of certain industrial buildings or structures.

Section 372N Capital allowances in relation to construction or refurbishment of certain commercial buildings or structures.

Section 372V Capital allowances in relation to construction or refurbishment of certain park and ride facilities.
Section 372W Capital allowances in relation to construction or refurbishment of certain commercial premises.
Section 372AC Accelerated capital allowances in relation to construction or refurbishment of certain industrial buildings or structures.
Section 372AD Capital allowances in relation to construction or refurbishment of certain commercial premises.
Section 372AX Accelerated capital allowances in relation to the construction or refurbishment of certain registered holiday camps.
Section 372AY Capital allowances in relation to the construction or refurbishment of certain tourism infrastructure facilities.
Section 372AZ Restrictions on relief, non-application of relief in certain cases and provision against double relief.
Section 485G Miscellaneous (Chapter 2A).
Section 699 Deduction as expenses of certain sums, etc.
Section 843 Capital allowances for buildings used for third level educational purposes.
Section 843A Capital allowances for buildings used for certain childcare purposes.
Schedule 25B List of Specified Reliefs and Method of Determining Amount of Specified Relief Used in a Tax Year

275 Restriction of balancing allowances on sale of industrial building or structure

[FA73 s40(1) to (5)]

(1) In this section—

"*inferior interest*" means any interest in or right over the building or structure in question, whether granted by the relevant person or by someone else;

"*premium*" includes any capital consideration except so much of any sum as corresponds to any amount of rent or profits which is to be computed by reference to that sum under *section 98*;

"*capital consideration*" means consideration which consists of a capital sum or would be a capital sum if it had taken the form of a money payment;

"*rent*" includes any consideration which is not capital consideration;

"*commercial rent*" means such rent as might reasonably be expected to have been required in respect of the inferior interest in question, having regard to any premium payable for the grant of the interest, if the transaction had been at arm's length.

(2) This section shall apply where—

(a) the relevant interest in a building is sold subject to an inferior interest,

(b) by virtue of the sale a balancing allowance under *section 274* would apart from this section be made to or for the benefit of the person (in this section referred to as "*the relevant person*") who was entitled to the relevant interest immediately before the sale, and

(c) either—

(i) the relevant person, the person to whom the relevant interest is sold and the grantee of the inferior interest, or any 2 of them, are connected with each other, or

(ii) it appears with respect to the sale or the grant of the inferior interest, or with respect to transactions including the sale or grant, that the sole or main benefit which but for this section might have been expected to accrue to the parties or any of them was the obtaining of an allowance or deduction under this Chapter.

(3) For the purposes of *section 274*, the net proceeds to the relevant person of the sale—

(a) shall be taken to be increased by an amount equal to any premium receivable by the relevant person for the grant of the inferior interest, and

(b) where no rent or no commercial rent is payable in respect of the inferior interest, shall be taken to be the sum of—

(i) what those proceeds would have been if a commercial rent had been payable and the relevant interest had been sold in the open market, and

(ii) any amount to be added under *paragraph (a)*;

but the net proceeds of the sale shall not by virtue of this subsection be taken to be greater than such amount as will secure that no balancing allowance is to be made.

(4) Where *subsection (3)* operates in relation to a sale to deny or reduce a balancing allowance in respect of any expenditure, the residue of that expenditure immediately after the sale shall be calculated for the purposes of this Chapter as if that balancing allowance had been made or, as the case may be, had not been reduced.

(5) Where the terms on which the inferior interest is granted are varied before the sale of the relevant interest, any capital consideration for the variation shall be treated for the purposes of this section as a premium for the grant of the interest, and the question whether any and, if so, what rent is payable in respect of the interest shall be determined by reference to the terms as in force immediately before the sale.

Cross References

From Section 275

Section 98 Treatment of premiums, etc. as rent.

Section 274 Balancing allowances and balancing charges.

276 Application of sections 272 and 274 in relation to capital expenditure on refurbishment

[FA91 s26]

(1) In this section, "*refurbishment*" means any work of construction, reconstruction, repair or renewal, including the provision or improvement of water, sewerage or heating facilities, carried out in the course of repair or restoration, or maintenance in the nature of repair or restoration, of a building or structure.

(2) Notwithstanding any other provision of the Tax Acts, where on or after the 6th day of April, 1991, any capital expenditure has been incurred on the refurbishment of a building or structure in respect of which an allowance is to be made for the purposes of income tax or corporation tax, as the case may be, under this Chapter, *sections 272* and *274* shall apply as if "the capital expenditure on refurbishment of the building or structure was incurred" were substituted for "the building or structure was first used" in each place where it occurs in *sections 272(4)* and *274(1)(b)*.

(3) For the purposes of giving effect to this section in so far as the computation of a balancing allowance or balancing charge is concerned, all such apportionments shall be made as are in the circumstances just and reasonable.

Cross References

From Section 276

Section 272 Writing-down allowances.
Section 274 Balancing allowances and balancing charges.

To Section 276

Section 323 Capital allowances in relation to construction of certain commercial premises.
Section 331 Accelerated capital allowances in relation to construction or refurbishment of certain industrial buildings or structures.
Section 332 Capital allowances in relation to construction or refurbishment of certain commercial premises.
Section 341 Accelerated capital allowances in relation to construction or refurbishment of certain industrial buildings or structures.
Section 342 Capital allowances in relation to construction or refurbishment of certain commercial premises.
Section 343 Capital allowances in relation to construction or refurbishment of certain buildings or structures in enterprise areas.
Section 344 Capital allowances in relation to construction or refurbishment of certain multi-storey car parks.
Section 353 Capital allowances in relation to construction or refurbishment of certain commercial premises.
Section 372C Accelerated capital allowances in relation to construction or refurbishment of certain industrial buildings or structures.
Section 372D Capital allowances in relation to construction or refurbishment of certain commercial premises.
Section 372M Accelerated capital allowances in relation to construction or refurbishment of certain industrial buildings or structures.
Section 372N Capital allowances in relation to construction or refurbishment of certain commercial buildings or structures.
Section 372V Capital allowances in relation to construction or refurbishment of certain park and ride facilities.
Section 372W Capital allowances in relation to construction or refurbishment of certain commercial premises.
Section 372AC Accelerated capital allowances in relation to construction or refurbishment of certain industrial buildings or structures.
Section 372AD Capital allowances in relation to construction or refurbishment of certain commercial premises.
Section 843A Capital allowances for buildings used for certain childcare purposes.

277 Writing off of expenditure and meaning of "residue of expenditure"

[ITA67 s266; CTA76 s21(1) and Sch1 par25; FA97 s23(b)]

(1) For the purposes of this Chapter, any expenditure incurred on the construction of any building or structure shall be treated as written off to the extent and at the times specified in this section, and references in this Chapter to the residue of any such expenditure shall be construed accordingly.

(2) Where an industrial building allowance is made in respect of the expenditure, the amount of that allowance shall be written off at the time when the building or structure is first used.

(3) Where, by reason of the building or structure being at any time an industrial building or structure, a writing-down allowance is made for any chargeable period in respect of the expenditure, the amount of that allowance shall be written off at that time; but, where at that time an event occurs which gives

rise or may give rise to a balancing allowance or balancing charge, the amount directed to be written off by this subsection at that time shall be taken into account in computing the residue of that expenditure immediately before that event for the purpose of determining whether any, and if so what, balancing allowance or balancing charge is to be made.

(4) (a) Where, for any period or periods between the time when the building or structure was first used for any purpose and the time at which the residue of the expenditure is to be ascertained, the building or structure has not been in use as an industrial building or structure, there shall in ascertaining that residue be treated as having been previously written off in respect of that period or those periods amounts equal to writing-down allowances made for chargeable periods of a total length equal to the length of that period, or the aggregate length of those periods, as the case may be, at such rate or rates as would have been appropriate having regard to any sale on which *section 272(4)* operated.

(b) Where the building or structure was in use as an industrial building or structure at the end of the basis period for any year of assessment before the year 1960-61, an amount equal to 2 per cent of the expenditure shall be treated as written off at the end of the previous year of assessment.

(5) Where on the occasion of a sale a balancing allowance is made in respect of the expenditure, there shall be written off at the time of the sale the amount by which the residue of the expenditure before the sale exceeds the net proceeds of the sale.

(6) Where on the occasion of a sale a balancing charge is made in respect of the expenditure, the residue of the expenditure shall be deemed for the purposes of this Chapter to be increased at the time of the sale by the amount on which the charge is made.

(7) Where, on receipt of consideration of the type referred to in *section 274(1)(a)(iv)*, a balancing allowance is made in respect of the expenditure, there shall be written off at the time of the event giving rise to the balancing allowance or, if later, on the 26th day of March, 1997, the amount by which the residue of the expenditure before that event exceeds that consideration.

Cross References

From Section 277

Section 272 Writing-down allowances.

Section 274 Balancing allowances and balancing charges.

To Section 277

Section 250A Restriction of relief to individuals in respect of loans applied in acquiring interest in companies.

Section 270 Meaning of "expenditure on construction of building or structure".

Section 272 Writing-down allowances.

Section 279 Purchases of certain buildings or structures.

Section 312 Special provisions as to certain sales.

Section 318 Meaning of "sale, insurance, salvage or compensation moneys".

Section 345 Double rent allowance in respect of rent paid for certain business premises.

Section 353 Capital allowances in relation to construction or refurbishment of certain commercial premises.

Section 355 Disclaimer of capital allowances on holiday cottages, holiday apartments, etc.

Section 372V Capital allowances in relation to construction or refurbishment of certain park and ride facilities.

Section 372W Capital allowances in relation to construction or refurbishment of certain commercial premises.
Section 372AZ Restrictions on relief, non-application of relief in certain cases and provision against double relief.
Section 409E Income tax: ringfence on use of certain capital allowances on certain industrial buildings and other premises.
Schedule 18B Tonnage Tax

278 Manner of making allowances and charges

[ITA67 s254(1)(d) and (e) and s267; CTA76 s21(1) and Sch1 par17 and par26]

(1) Except in the cases mentioned in this section, any allowance or charge made to or on a person under the preceding provisions of this Part shall be made to or on such person in taxing such person's trade or, as the case may require, in charging such person's income under Case V of Schedule D.

(2) An industrial building allowance shall be made to a person by discharge or repayment of tax if such person's interest in the building or structure is subject to any lease when the expenditure is incurred or becomes subject to any lease before the building or structure is first used for any purpose[...][1]; but this subsection shall not apply as respects income chargeable under Case V of Schedule D.

(3) A writing-down allowance shall be made to a person for a chargeable period by means of discharge or repayment of tax if such person's interest is subject to any lease at the end of that chargeable period or its basis period; but this subsection shall not apply as respects income chargeable under Case V of Schedule D.

(4) A balancing allowance shall be made to a person by means of discharge or repayment of tax if such person's interest is subject to any lease immediately before the event giving rise to the allowance; but this subsection shall not apply as respects income chargeable under Case V of Schedule D.

(5) A balancing charge shall be made on a person under Case IV of Schedule D if such person's interest is subject to any lease immediately before the event giving rise to the charge and the corresponding income is chargeable under that Case.

(6) Any allowance which under *subsections (1)* to *(4)* is to be made otherwise than in taxing a trade shall be available primarily against the following income—

(a) where the income (whether arising by means of rent or receipts in respect of premises or easements or otherwise) from the industrial building or structure in respect of the capital expenditure on which the allowance is given is chargeable under Case V of Schedule D, against income chargeable under that Case,

(b) where the income (whether arising by means of rent or receipts in respect of premises or easements or otherwise) from the industrial building or structure in respect of the capital expenditure on which the allowance is given is chargeable under Case IV of Schedule D, against income chargeable under that Case, or

(c) income chargeable under Case IV or V of Schedule D respectively which is the subject of a balancing charge.

Amendments

[1] Deleted by FA00 s40(a).

Cross References

To Section 278

Section 372V Capital allowances in relation to construction or refurbishment of certain park and ride facilities.

Section 372W Capital allowances in relation to construction or refurbishment of certain commercial premises.

Section 409E Income tax: ringfence on use of certain capital allowances on certain industrial buildings and other premises.

Schedule 25B List of Specified Reliefs and Method of Determining Amount of Specified Relief Used in a Tax Year

279 Purchases of certain buildings or structures

FA70 s19(1), (2) and (2A); FA90 s75; FA91 s23; FA97 s146(1) and Sch9 PtI par4(2)]

(1) For the purposes of this section—

[…][1]

"*the net price paid*" means the amount represented by A in the equation—

$$A = B \times \frac{C}{C + D}$$

where—

B is the amount paid by a person on the purchase of the relevant interest in a building or structure,

C is the amount of the expenditure actually incurred on the construction of the building or structure, and

D is the amount of any expenditure actually incurred which is expenditure for the purposes of *paragraph (a)*, *(b)* or *(c)* of *section 270(2)*.

(2) Where expenditure is incurred on the construction of a building or structure and, before the building or structure is used or within a period of [2 years][2] after it commences to be used, the relevant interest in the building or structure is sold, then, if an allowance has not been claimed by any other person in respect of that building or structure under this Chapter—

(a) the expenditure actually incurred on the construction of the building or structure shall be disregarded for the purposes of *sections 271*, *272*, *274* and *277*, but

(b) the person who buys that interest shall be deemed for those purposes to have incurred, on the date when the purchase price becomes payable, expenditure on the construction of the building or structure equal to that expenditure or to the net price paid by such person for that interest, whichever is the less;

but, where the relevant interest in the building or structure is sold more than once before the building or structure is used or within the period of [2 years][3] after it commences to be used, *paragraph (b)* shall apply only in relation to the last of those sales.

(3) Where the expenditure incurred on the construction of a building or structure was incurred by a person carrying on a trade which consists, as to the whole or any part of the trade, of the construction of buildings or structures with a view to their sale and, before the building or structure is used or within a period of [2 years][4] after it commences to be used, such person sells the relevant

interest in the building or structure in the course of that trade or, as the case may be, of that part of that trade, *subsection (2)* shall apply subject to the following modifications—

(a) if that sale is the only sale of the relevant interest before the building or structure is used or within the period of [2 years][5] after it commences to be used, *subsection (2)* shall apply as if in *paragraph (b)* of that subsection "that expenditure or to" and ", whichever is the less" were deleted, and

(b) if there is more than one sale of the relevant interest before the building or structure is used or within the period of [2 years][6] after it commences to be used, *subsection (2)* shall apply as if the reference to the expenditure actually incurred on the construction of the building or structure were a reference to the price paid on that sale.

Amendments

[1] Deleted by FA98 sched9(5).

[2, 3] Substituted by F(No.2)A08 s19(a). Applies as respects a sale of the relevant interest in a building or structure which occurs on or after 14 October 2008.

[4, 5, 6] Substituted by F(No.2)A08 s19(b). Applies as respects a sale of the relevant interest in a building or structure which occurs on or after 14 October 2008.

Revenue Briefings

Tax Briefing

Tax Briefing August 2005 – Issue 60 – Industrial and Commercial Buildings

Tax Briefing August 2005 – Issue 60 – Treatment of Social and Affordable Housing Costs for Section 23 and Owner-Occupier Relief Purposes

Tax Briefing December 2006 – Issue 65 – Capital Allowances and Property-based Incentive Schemes

Tax Briefing December 2006 – Issue 65 – Property-Based Incentive Schemes – Inducements for Purchase of Property

Tax Briefing July 2007 – Issue 66 – The 'Net Price Paid' Formula and Separate Site Sales and Building Agreements

Tax Briefing September 2008 – Issue 69 – Property Developers and Capital Allowances

Cross References

From Section 279

Section 270 Meaning of "expenditure on construction of building or structure".

Section 271 Industrial building allowances.

Section 272 Writing-down allowances.

Section 274 Balancing allowances and balancing charges.

Section 277 Writing off of expenditure and meaning of "residue of expenditure".

To Section 279

Section 268 Meaning of "industrial building or structure".

Section 270 Meaning of "expenditure on construction of building or structure".

Section 324 Double rent allowance in respect of rent paid for certain business premises.

Section 333 Double rent allowance in respect of rent paid for certain business premises.

Section 345 Double rent allowance in respect of rent paid for certain business premises.

Section 354 Double rent allowance in respect of rent paid for certain business premises.

Section 355 Disclaimer of capital allowances on holiday cottages, holiday apartments, etc.

Section 372V Capital allowances in relation to construction or refurbishment of certain park and ride facilities.

Section 372W Capital allowances in relation to construction or refurbishment of certain commercial premises.

Section 372AZ Restrictions on relief, non-application of relief in certain cases and provision against double relief.

Section 409A Income tax: restriction on use of capital allowances on certain industrial buildings and other premises.

280 Temporary disuse of building or structure

[ITA67 s270; CTA76 s21(1) and Sch1 par27]

(1) For the purposes of this Chapter, a building or structure shall not be deemed to cease altogether to be used by reason that it is temporarily out of use and where, immediately before any period of temporary disuse, a building or structure is an industrial building or structure, it shall be deemed to continue to be an industrial building or structure during the period of temporary disuse.

(2) (a) Notwithstanding any other provision of this Part as to the manner of making allowances and charges but subject to *paragraph (b)*, where by virtue of *subsection (1)* a building or structure is deemed to continue to be an industrial building or structure while temporarily out of use, then, if—

(i) on the last occasion on which the building or structure was in use as an industrial building or structure, it was in use for the purposes of a trade which has since been permanently discontinued, or

(ii) on the last occasion on which the building or structure was in use as an industrial building or structure, the relevant interest in the building or structure was subject to a lease which has since come to an end,

any writing-down allowance or balancing allowance to be made to any person in respect of the building or structure during any period for which the temporary disuse continues after the discontinuance of the trade or the coming to an end of the lease shall be made by means of discharge or repayment of tax, and any balancing charge to be made on any person in respect of the building or structure during that period shall be made under Case IV of Schedule D.

(b) Where for a chargeable period the person has income chargeable to tax under Case V of Schedule D and at the end of the chargeable period or its basis period the building or structure is one to which *paragraph (a)* applies, any writing-down allowance or balancing allowance or balancing charge to be made to or on the person in respect of the building or structure shall be made in charging that person's income under Case V of Schedule D.

(3) The reference in this section to the permanent discontinuance of a trade does not include a reference to the happening of any event which by virtue of the Income Tax Acts is to be treated as equivalent to the discontinuance of the trade.

281 Special provisions in regard to leases

[ITA67 s269]

(1) Where with the consent of the lessor a lessee of any building or structure remains in possession of that building or structure after the termination of the lease without a new lease being granted to the lessee, that lease shall be deemed for the purposes of this Chapter to continue so long as the lessee remains so in possession.

(2) Where on the termination of a lease a new lease is granted to the lessee consequent on the lessee being entitled by statute to a new lease or in pursuance of an option available to the lessee under the terms of the first lease, this Chapter shall apply as if the second lease were a continuation of the first lease.

(3) Where on the termination of a lease the lessor pays any sum to the lessee in respect of a building or structure comprised in the lease, this Chapter shall apply

as if the lease had come to an end by reason of the surrender of the lease in consideration of the payment.

282 Supplementary provisions (Chapter 1)

[ITA67 s263(2) and (3)]

(1) A person who has incurred expenditure on the construction of a building or structure shall be deemed, for the purposes of any provision of this Chapter referring to such person's interest in the building or structure at the time when the expenditure was incurred, to have had the same interest in the building or structure as such person would have had if the construction of the building or structure had been completed at that time.

(2) Without prejudice to any other provision of this Part relating to the apportionment of sale, insurance, salvage or compensation moneys, the sum paid on the sale of the relevant interest in a building or structure, or any other sale, insurance, salvage or compensation moneys payable in respect of any building or structure, shall for the purposes of this Chapter be deemed to be reduced by an amount equal to so much of that sum or those moneys, as the case may be, as on a just apportionment is attributable to assets representing expenditure other than expenditure in respect of which an allowance may be made under this Chapter.

CHAPTER 2

Machinery or Plant: Initial Allowances, Wear and Tear Allowances, Balancing Allowances and Balancing Charges

283 Initial allowances

[ITA67 s251(1), (4)(bb)(ii) and (d), (6) and (7); FA73 s9(2) (apart from the proviso); CTA76 s 21(1) and Sch1 par15 and par61; FA88 s43(b), s51(1)(a) and (cc) (proviso thereto), (2)(a), (c) and (d) and (6); FA89 s13; FA90 s73(a) and (b), s80, s81(1)(a) and (2)(a) and (b); FA93 s33; FA95 s27; FA96 s43]

(1) In this section—

"*industrial development agency*" means the Industrial Development Authority, Shannon Free Airport Development Company Limited or Údarás na Gaeltachta;

"*new*" means unused and not secondhand, but a ship shall be deemed to be new even if it has been used or is secondhand.

(2) Subject to the Tax Acts, where—

(a) a person carrying on a trade, the profits or gains of which are chargeable under Case I of Schedule D, incurs capital expenditure on the provision for the purposes of the trade of new machinery or new plant, other than vehicles suitable for the conveyance by road of persons or goods or the haulage by road of other vehicles,

(b) that machinery or plant is machinery or plant to which *subsection (4)* or *(5)* applies, and

(c) that machinery or plant while used for the purposes of that trade is wholly and exclusively so used, there shall be made to such person for the chargeable period related to the expenditure an allowance (in this Chapter referred to as an "*initial allowance*").

(3) An initial allowance shall be of an amount equal to—

(a) in the case of machinery or plant to which *subsection (4)* applies, 100 per cent of the capital expenditure mentioned in *subsection (2)*, or

(b) in the case of machinery or plant to which *subsection (5)* applies, 50 per cent of the capital expenditure mentioned in *subsection (2)*.

(4) This subsection shall apply to—

(a) machinery or plant provided—

(i) before the 23rd day of April, 1996, for use for the purposes of trading operations, or

(ii) on or after the 23rd day of April, 1996, by a company for use for the purposes of trading operations carried on by the company,

which are relevant trading operations within the meaning of *section 445* or *446* but, in relation to capital expenditure incurred on the provision of machinery or plant on or after the 6th day of May, 1993, excluding machinery or plant provided by a lessor to a lessee other than in the course of the carrying on by the lessor of those relevant trading operations, and

(b) machinery or plant provided for the purposes of a project approved by an industrial development agency in the period from the 1st day of January, 1986, to the 31st day of December, 1988, and in respect of the provision of which expenditure was incurred before the 31st day of December, 1996.

(5) This subsection shall apply to machinery or plant provided for the purposes of a project approved for grant assistance by an industrial development agency in the period from the 1st day of January, 1989, to the 31st day of December, 1990, and in respect of the provision of which expenditure is incurred before the 31st day of December, 1997[, or before the 30th day of June, 1998, if its provision is solely for use in an industrial building or structure referred to in *sections 271(3)(c)* and *273(7)(a)(i)* and expenditure in respect of such provision would have been incurred before the 31st day of December, 1997, but for the existence of circumstances which resulted in legal proceedings being initiated, being proceedings which were the subject of an order of the High Court made before the 1st day of January, 1998][1]; but, as respects machinery or plant provided for the purposes of any such project specified in the list referred to in *section 133(8)(c)(iv)*, this subsection shall apply as if the reference to the 31st day of December, 1997, [where it first occurs,][2] were a reference to the 31st day of December, 2002.

(6) Where an initial allowance in respect of capital expenditure incurred on or after the 1st day of April, 1989, on the provision of machinery or plant, other than machinery or plant to which *subsection (4)* applies, is made under this section for any chargeable period—

(a) no allowance for wear and tear of that machinery or plant shall be made under *section 284* for that chargeable period, and

(b) an allowance for wear and tear of that machinery or plant which is to be made under *section 284* for any chargeable period subsequent to that chargeable period shall not be increased under *section 285*.

(7) Any initial allowance under this section made to a person for any chargeable period in respect of machinery or plant shall not exceed such sum as will, when added to—

(a) the amount of any allowance in respect of the machinery or plant made to the person under *section 284* for that chargeable period, and

(b) the aggregate amount of any allowances made to the person in respect of the machinery or plant under this section and *section 284* for earlier chargeable periods,

equal the amount of the expenditure incurred by such person on the provision of the machinery or plant.

Amendments

[1] Inserted by FA98 s21(b)(ii).

[2] Inserted by FA98 s21(b)(i).

Revenue Precedents

Are large ocean going dredgers considered as ships for the purposes of section 283(1) of the Taxes Consolidation Act 1997?. Large vessels of burden that substantially go to sea may be regarded as ships. Accordingly, large ocean going dredgers may be considered ships for the purposes of Section 283(1) Taxes Consolidation Act 1997. IT973006

New machines incorporating a limited number of recycled parts but sold as a "new build" machine would be regarded as "unused and not secondhand" i.e. "new" for the purposes of section 283. CTF190

Cross References

From Section 283

Section 133 Limitation on meaning of "distribution" – general.
Section 271 Industrial building allowances.
Section 273 Acceleration of writing-down allowances in respect of certain expenditure on certain industrial buildings or structures.
Section 284 Wear and tear allowances.
Section 285 Acceleration of wear and tear allowances.
Section 445 Certain trading operations carried on in Shannon Airport.
Section 446 Certain trading operations carried on in Custom House Docks Area.

To Section 283

Section 284 Wear and tear allowances.
Section 285 Acceleration of wear and tear allowances.
Section 298 Allowances to lessors.
Section 299 Allowances to lessees.
Section 301 Application to professions, employments and offices.
Section 304 Income tax: allowances and charges in taxing a trade, etc.
Section 307 Corporation tax: allowances and charges in taxing a trade.
Section 316 Interpretation of certain references to expenditure and time when expenditure is incurred.
Section 317 Treatment of grants.
Section 374 Capital allowances for cars costing over certain amount.
Section 378 Cars: provisions as to hire-purchase, etc.
Section 380L Emissions-based limits for certain cars.
Section 380N Cars: provisions as to hire-purchase, etc.
Section 403 Restriction on use of capital allowances for certain leased assets.
Section 404 Restriction on use of capital allowances for certain leased machinery or plant.
Section 413 Profits or assets available for distribution.
Section 425 Leasing contracts: effect on claims for losses of company reconstructions.
Section 660 Farming: wear and tear allowances deemed to have been made in certain cases.
Section 692 Development expenditure: allowances and charges.

284 Wear and tear allowances

[ITA67 s241(1)(a) and (b) and proviso to (1), (6), (6A), (10) and (11); CTA76 s21(1) and Sch1 par6; FA92 s26(4); FA96 s132(1) and Sch5 PtI par1(12)(a); FA97 s22 and s146(1) and Sch9 PtI par1(16)]

(1) Subject to the Tax Acts, where a person carrying on a trade in any chargeable period has incurred capital expenditure on the provision of machinery or plant

for the purposes of the trade, an allowance (in this Chapter referred to as a "*wear and tear allowance*") shall be made to such person for that chargeable period on account of the wear and tear of any of the machinery or plant which belongs to such person and is in use for the purposes of the trade at the end of that chargeable period or its basis period and which, while used for the purposes of the trade, is wholly and exclusively so used.

(2) (a) Subject to [[*paragraphs (aa), (ab)* and *(ad)*][1] and][2] *subsection (4)*, the amount of the wear and tear allowance to be made shall be an amount equal to—

(i) in the case of machinery or plant, other than machinery or plant of the type referred to in *subparagraph (ii)*, 15 per cent of the actual cost of the machinery or plant, including in that actual cost any expenditure in the nature of capital expenditure on the machinery or plant by means of renewal, improvement or reinstatement, or

(ii) in the case of machinery or plant which consists of a vehicle suitable for the conveyance by road of persons or goods or the haulage by road of other vehicles, 20 per cent of the value of that machinery or plant at the commencement of the chargeable period.

[(aa) Notwithstanding *paragraph (a)*, where capital expenditure is incurred on or after 1 January 2001 on the provision of—

(i) machinery or plant, other than machinery or plant to which *paragraph (a)(ii)* and *subsection (3A)* relates, or

(ii) machinery or plant to which *paragraph (a)(ii)* relates, other than a car within the meaning of *section 286* used for qualifying purposes within the meaning of that section,

the amount of the wear and tear allowance to be made shall be an amount equal to 20 per cent of the actual cost of the machinery or plant, including in that actual cost any expenditure in the nature of capital expenditure on the machinery or plant by means of renewal, improvement or reinstatement.][3]

[(ab) Where for any chargeable period ending on or after 1 January 2002 a wear and tear allowance would be due to be made to a person in respect of machinery or plant in accordance with *paragraph (a)*, the person may elect that the amount of the wear and tear allowance to be made for that chargeable period and any subsequent chargeable period in respect of each and every item of the machinery or plant concerned shall, subject to *subsection (4)*, instead of being the amount referred to in *paragraph (a)*, be an amount equal to—

(i) where, apart from this paragraph, the allowance would be made in accordance with *paragraph (a)(i)*, 20 per cent of the amount of the capital expenditure incurred on the provision of that machinery or plant which is still unallowed as at the commencement of the first-mentioned chargeable period, and

(ii) where, apart from this paragraph, the allowance would be made in accordance with *paragraph (a)(ii)*, 20 per cent of the value of that machinery or plant at the commencement of the first-mentioned chargeable period.

(ac) An election under *paragraph (ab)* shall be irrevocable, and shall be included—

(i) where such an election is made by a chargeable person within the meaning of *Part 41*, in the return required to be made by that person under *section 951* for the first chargeable period, and

(ii) where such an election is made by any other person, in the annual statement of profits or gains required to be delivered by that person under the Income Tax Acts, for the first year of assessment,

for which a wear and tear allowance in respect of machinery or plant is to be made in accordance with that paragraph.][4]

[(ad) Notwithstanding any other provision of this subsection but subject to *subsection (4)*, where capital expenditure is incurred on or after 4 December 2002 on the provision of machinery or plant, the amount of the wear and tear allowance to be made shall be an amount equal to 12.5 per cent of the actual cost of the machinery or plant, including in that actual cost any expenditure in the nature of capital expenditure on the machinery or plant by means of renewal, improvement or reinstatement; but this paragraph shall not apply in the case of—

(i) machinery or plant to which *subsection (3A)* relates,

(ii) machinery or plant which consists of a car within the meaning of *section 286*, used for qualifying purposes, within the meaning of that section, or

(iii) machinery or plant provided under the terms of a binding contract evidenced in writing before 4 December 2002 and in respect of the provision of which capital expenditure is incurred on or before 31 January 2003.][5]

(b) Where a chargeable period or its basis period consists of a period less than one year in length, the wear and tear allowance shall not exceed such portion of [the amount specified in any other provision of this subsection][6] as bears to that amount the same proportion as the length of the chargeable period or its basis period bears to a period of one year.

(3) [For the purposes of *paragraphs (a)(ii)* and *(ab)(ii)* of *subsection (2)*, the value at the commencement of a chargeable period][7] of the machinery or plant shall be taken to be the actual cost to the person of such machinery or plant reduced by the total of any wear and tear allowances made to that person in relation to the machinery or plant for previous chargeable periods.

[(3A) (a) This subsection applies to machinery or plant consisting of a sea fishing boat registered in the Register of Fishing Boats and in respect of which capital expenditure is incurred in the period of [6 years][8] commencing on the appointed day, being expenditure that is certified by Bord Iascaigh Mhara as capital expenditure incurred for the purposes of fleet renewal in the polyvalent and beam trawl segments of the fishing fleet.

(b) Notwithstanding *subsection (2)*, but subject to [*paragraph (ba)* and *subsection (4)*][9], wear and tear allowances to be made to any person in respect of machinery or plant to which this subsection applies shall be made during a writing-down period of 8 years beginning with the first chargeable period or its basis period at the end of which the machinery or plant belongs to that person and is in use for the purposes of that person's trade, and shall be of an amount equal to—

(i) as respects the first year of the writing-down period, 50 per cent of the actual cost of the machinery or plant, including in that actual cost any expenditure in the nature of capital expenditure on that machinery or plant by means of renewal, improvement or reinstatement,

(ii) as respects each of the next 6 years of the writing-down period, 15 per cent of the balance of that actual cost after the deduction of any allowance made by virtue of *subparagraph (i)*, and

(iii) as respects the last year of the writing-down period, 10 per cent of the balance of that actual cost after the deduction of any allowance made by virtue of *subparagraph (i)*.

[(ba) Notwithstanding *subsection (2)*, but subject to *subsection (4)*, wear and tear allowances to be made to any person in respect of machinery or plant to which this subsection applies, and in respect of which capital expenditure is incurred on or after the date of the coming into operation of section 52 of the Finance Act, 2001, shall be made during a writing-down period of 6 years beginning with the first chargeable period or its basis period at the end of which the machinery or plant belongs to that person and is in use for the purposes of that person's trade, and shall be of an amount equal to—

(i) as respects the first year of the writing-down period, 50 per cent of the actual cost of the machinery or plant, including in that actual cost any expenditure in the nature of capital expenditure on that machinery or plant by means of renewal, improvement or reinstatement, and

(ii) as respects the next 5 years of the writing-down period, 20 per cent of the balance of that actual cost after the deduction of any allowance made by virtue of *subparagraph (i)*.][10]

(c) Where a chargeable period or its basis period consists of a period less than one year in length, the wear and tear allowance shall not exceed such portion of the amount specified in *subparagraph (i)*, *(ii)* or *(iii)*, as may be appropriate, of *paragraph (b)*, [or in *subparagraph (i)* or *(ii)*, as may be appropriate, of *paragraph (ba)*,][11] as bears to that amount the same proportion as the length of the chargeable period or its basis period bears to a period of one year.

(d) This subsection shall come into operation on such day (in this subsection referred to as the "appointed day") as the Minister for Finance may, by order, appoint.][12]

[(3B) For the purposes of *subsections (2)(b)* and *(3A)(c)*, and notwithstanding any other provision of the Income Tax Acts, the length of the basis period for the year of assessment 2001 shall be deemed to be—

(a) the length of that period as determined in accordance with *section 306*, or

(b) 270 days,

whichever is the lesser.][13]

(4) No wear and tear allowance or repayment on account of any such allowance shall be made for any chargeable period if such allowance, when added to—

(a) the allowances on that account, and

(b) any initial allowances in relation to the machinery or plant under *section 283*,

made for any previous chargeable periods to the person by whom the trade is carried on, will make the aggregate amount of the allowances exceed the actual cost to that person of the machinery or plant, including in that actual cost any expenditure in the nature of capital expenditure on the machinery or plant by means of renewal, improvement or reinstatement.

(5) No wear and tear allowance shall be made under this section in respect of capital expenditure incurred on the construction of a building or structure which is or is deemed to be an industrial building or structure within the meaning of *section 268*.

(6) Subject to *subsection (7)*, this section shall, with any necessary modifications, apply in relation to the letting of any premises the profits or gains from which are chargeable under *Chapter 8* of *Part 4* as it applies in relation to trades.

(7) Where by virtue of *subsection (6)* this section applies to the letting of any premises, it shall apply as respects the year of assessment 1997-98 and subsequent years of assessment in respect of capital expenditure incurred on the provision of machinery or plant within the meaning of *subsection (2)(a)(i)* where—

(a) such expenditure is incurred wholly and exclusively in respect of a house used solely as a dwelling which is or is to be let as a furnished house, and

(b) that furnished house is provided for renting or letting on bona fide commercial terms in the open market.

[(8) For the purposes of this Part, [Dublin Airport Authority][14] shall be deemed to have incurred, on the vesting day, capital expenditure on the provision of machinery or plant, being the machinery or plant vested in [Dublin Airport Authority][15] on that day, and the actual cost of that machinery or plant shall be deemed to be an amount determined by the formula—

$$A - B$$

where—

A is the original actual cost of the machinery or plant, including in that cost any expenditure in the nature of capital expenditure on the machinery or plant by means of renewal, improvement or reinstatement, and

B is the amount of any wear and tear allowances which would have been made under this section in respect of the machinery or plant since the original provision of the machinery or plant if a claim for those allowances had been duly made and allowed.][16]

Amendments

[1] Substituted by FA03 s23(1)(a)(i). This section applies as on and from 4 December 2002.

[2] Inserted by FA01 s53(a). Applies as respects capital expenditure incurred on or after 1 January 2001.

[3] Inserted by FA01 s53(b). Applies as respects capital expenditure incurred on or after 1 January 2001.

[4] Inserted by FA02 s31(1)(a)(ii).

[5] Inserted by FA03 s23(1)(a)(ii). This section applies as on and from 4 December 2002.

[6] Substituted by FA03 s23(1)(a)(iii). This section applies as on and from 4 December 2002.

[7] Substituted by FA02 s31(1)(b).

[8] Substituted by FA01 s52(1)(a). With effect from 24 March 2004 per S.I. 124 of 2004.

[9] Substituted by FA01 s52(1)(b). With effect from 24 March 2004 per S.I. 124 of 2004.

[10] Inserted by FA01 s52(1)(c). With effect from 24 March 2004 per S.I. 124 of 2004.

[11] Inserted by FA01 s52(1)(d). With effect from 24 March 2004 per S.I. 124 of 2004.

[12] Inserted by FA98 s23(a).

[13] Inserted by FA01 sched2(19).

[14, 15] Substituted by FA08 sched8(1)(f). Has effect as on and from 13 March 2008.

[16] Inserted by FA98 s20(d).

Case Law

Moveable partitioning used to adjust office floor space was held to be plant. Jarrold (HM Inspector of Taxes) v John Good & Sons Limited 1962 40 TC 681

A swimming pool was held to be plant in Cooke v Beach Caravans Ltd 1974 STC 402.

In Dixon v Fitches Garage 1975 STC 480 a canopy constructed over pumps of a petrol station was not plant. However, in O'Culachain v McMullan Bros 1995 V ITR 200 it was held that the canopy provided an attractive setting for the sale of the taxpayer's product and constituted plant.

A boat wreck used as a floating restaurant was regarded as the structure in which the business was carried on rather than an apparatus used in the trade. Benson v Yard Arm Club 1979 STC 266

Electric light fittings, decor and murals in a hotel were plant as they were used to create an atmosphere. IRC v Scottish and Newcastle Breweries Limited 1982 STC 296

An inflatable cover for a tennis court was not plant in Thomas v Reynolds 1988 STC 135

A demountable suspended ceiling was not plant but was part of the premises. Dunnes Stores (Oakville) Ltd v McCronin (Inspector of Taxes) 1988 IV ITR 68

In Gray v Seymour Garden Centre 1995 STC 706, a specialised glasshouse was categorised as a 'purpose built structure' and did not qualify as plant.

A car wash facility was held to be merely a building which housed machinery in Attwood (HMIT) v Anduff Car Wash Ltd 1997 STC 1167.

An all weather racetrack functioned as part of the premises or setting of the company's business and therefore did not qualify as plant. Shove (Inspector of Taxes) v Lingfield Park 1991 Ltd 2004 STC 805

Revenue Briefings

Tax Briefing

Tax Briefing December 2008 – Issue 70 – Capital Allowances for Energy-Efficient Equipment

Revenue Precedents

Revenue does not consider tennis courts constitute plant for capital allowances purposes. IT933033

Can a taxpayer opt not to claim capital allowances on a particular asset in a particular basis period, while preserving the written down value forward for future claims? Following the decision in the UK cases of Elliss v BP Oil Northern Ireland Refinery Ltd., and Elliss v BP Tyne Tanker Co., Ltd., capital allowances are not automatically deductible in computing the profits of a company for corporation tax purposes, and a company, if it so desires, may disclaim capital allowances for a particular accounting period. It should be noted that in the case of plant and machinery, the provisions of Section 287 Taxes Consolidation Act 1997 will apply. IT953012

Is a roller shutter fire door regarded as plant? The treatment of expenditure on fire safety equipment differs here from that in the U.K., where capital allowances are available for equipment purchased to comply with a notice served under the Fire Precautions Act, 1971. There is no similar tax legislation in this country. That the doors are part of the premises cannot be disputed. It is the view of this Office that they do not function as part of the plant with which the business is carried on, and are therefore no more than the setting. IT953001

Does the cost of a taxi plate qualify for capital allowances? The cost or value of the taxi licence plate represents both the actual licence plate itself, which is plant, and the right to trade, which is not. It is only the part of the cost which is attributable to the actual licence plate that qualifies for capital allowances as expenditure on the provision of machinery or plant. This will be a nominal amount. IT913025

Is a suspended ceiling which forms one side of an air conditioning plenum regarded as plant? It is the view of this Office that the ceiling is not apparatus used by the company for the carrying on of its business but functions primarily as part of the setting in which that business is carried on. IT953001A

Vehicles used for towing aircraft, stairways for aircraft and luggage at airport – whether vehicle suitable for conveyance by road of persons or goods? Not a vehicle suitable for conveyance by road of persons or goods. IT2041

What is the amount of the wear and tear allowance to be made in the case of refuse trucks? The Revenue Commissioners are prepared to regard refuse trucks as not suitable for the conveyance by road of goods. Therefore allowances claimed under section 284 are given at the rate of 15% per annum on a straight line basis. IT923068

Cross References

From Section 284

Section 52 Persons chargeable.

Section 96 Interpretation (Chapter 8).

Section 268 Meaning of "industrial building or structure".

Section 283 Initial allowances.

Section 286 Increased wear and tear allowances for taxis and cars for short-term hire.

Section 306 Meaning of basis period.

Section 950 Interpretation (Part 41).

Section 951 Obligation to make a return.

To Section 284

Section 5 Interpretation of Capital Gains Tax Acts.

Section 80A Taxation of certain short-term leases plant and machinery.

Section 216A Rent-a-room relief.

Section 216C Childcare services relief.
Section 247 Relief to companies on loans applied in acquiring interest in other companies.
Section 283 Initial allowances.
Section 285 Acceleration of wear and tear allowances.
Section 285A Acceleration of wear and tear allowances for certain energy efficient equipment.
Section 286 Increased wear and tear allowances for taxis and cars for short-term hire.
Section 286A Wear and tear allowances for licences for public hire vehicles.
Section 287 Wear and tear allowances deemed to have been made in certain cases.
Section 291A Intangible assets.
Section 298 Allowances to lessors.
Section 299 Allowances to lessees.
Section 300 Manner of making allowances and charges.
Section 310 Allowances in respect of certain contributions to capital expenditure of local authorities.
Section 316 Interpretation of certain references to expenditure and time when expenditure is incurred.
Section 317 Treatment of grants.
Section 374 Capital allowances for cars costing over certain amount.
Section 380L Emissions-based limits for certain cars.
Section 380T Allowance for machinery or plant.
Section 403 Restriction on use of capital allowances for certain leased assets.
Section 404 Restriction on use of capital allowances for certain leased machinery or plant.
Section 406 Restriction on use of capital allowances on fixtures and fittings for furnished residential accommodation.
Section 531AM Charge to universal social charge.
Section 531AU Capital allowances and losses.
Section 660 Farming: wear and tear allowances deemed to have been made in certain cases.
Section 670 Mine development allowance.
Section 678 Allowance for machinery and plant.
Section 692 Development expenditure: allowances and charges.
Section 756 Effect of lapse of patent rights.
Section 765 Allowances for capital expenditure on scientific research.
Section 1013 Limited partnerships.
Schedule 18B Tonnage Tax

285 Acceleration of wear and tear allowances

[FA67 s11(1), (2), (2A) and (4); FA71 s26(1), (2), (2A) and (4); CTA76 s21(1) and Sch1 par53 and par60; FA78 s22; FA88 s46, s47 and s51(1)(a), (c), (cc) and the proviso thereto and (d), (3) and (6); FA90 s71, s72, s80 and s81(1)(a) and (c) and proviso to (1), and (3); FA95 s26 and s27; FA96 s43 and s132(1) and Sch5 PtI pars2 and 5]

(1) In this section—

"*designated area*" means a designated area for the purposes of the Industrial Development Act, 1969;

"*industrial development agency*" means the Industrial Development Authority, Shannon Free Airport Development Company Limited or Údarás na Gaeltachta;

"*qualifying building or structure*" means a building or structure which is to be an industrial building or structure within the meaning of *section 268(1)(d)*, and in respect of the provision of which expenditure was incurred before the 31st day of December, 1995, where a binding contract for the provision of the building or structure was entered into before the 31st day of December, 1990;

"*qualifying machinery or plant*" means machinery or plant, other than vehicles suitable for the conveyance by road of persons or goods or the haulage by road of other vehicles, provided—

(a) on or after the 1st day of April, 1967, for use in any designated area, or

(b) on or after the 1st day of April, 1971, for use in any area other than a designated area,

for the purposes of a trade and which at the time it is so provided is unused and not secondhand.

(2) (a) Subject to this section and *section 299(2)*, where for any chargeable period a wear and tear allowance is to be made under *section 284* in relation to any qualifying machinery or plant, the allowance shall, subject to *section 284(4)*, be increased by such amount as is specified by the person to whom the allowance is to be made and, in relation to a case in which this subsection has applied, any reference in the Tax Acts to an allowance made under *section 284* shall be construed as a reference to that allowance as increased under this subsection.

(b) Subject to *subsections (4)* and *(6)*, as respects any machinery or plant provided for use on or after the 1st day of April, 1988, any wear and tear allowance made under *section 284* and increased under *paragraph (a)* in respect of that machinery or plant, whether claimed for one chargeable period or more than one such period, shall not in the aggregate exceed—

(i) if the machinery or plant was provided for use before the 1st day of April, 1989, 75 per cent,

(ii) if the machinery or plant was provided for use on or after the 1st day of April, 1989, and before the 1st day of April, 1991, 50 per cent, or

(iii) if the machinery or plant was provided for use on or after the 1st day of April, 1991, and before the 1st day of April, 1992, 25 per cent,

of the capital expenditure incurred on the provision of that machinery or plant.

(3) Notwithstanding *subsection (2)* but subject to *subsections (4)* and *(6)*—

(a) no allowance made under *section 284* for wear and tear of any qualifying machinery or plant provided for use on or after the 1st day of April, 1992, shall be increased under this section, and

(b) as respects chargeable periods ending on or after the 6th day of April, 1999, no allowance made under *section 284* for wear and tear of any qualifying machinery or plant provided for use before the 1st day of April, 1992, shall be increased under this section.

(4) This section shall apply in relation to machinery or plant to which *subsection (5)* applies as if *subsections (2)(b)* and *(3)* were deleted.

(5) This subsection shall apply to—

(a) machinery or plant provided—

(i) before the 23rd day of April, 1996, for use for the purposes of trading operations, or

(ii) on or after the 23rd day of April, 1996, by a company for use for the purposes of trading operations carried on by the company,

which are relevant trading operations within the meaning of *section 445* or *446* but, in relation to capital expenditure incurred on the provision of machinery or plant on or after the 6th day of May, 1993, excluding machinery or plant provided by a lessor to a lessee other than in the course of the carrying on by the lessor of those relevant trading operations,

(b) machinery or plant the expenditure on the provision of which was incurred before the 31st day of December, 1995, under a binding contract entered into on or before the 27th day of January, 1988,

(c) machinery or plant provided for the purposes of a project approved by an industrial development agency on or before the 31st day of December, 1988, and in respect of the provision of which expenditure was incurred before the

31st day of December, 1995; but, as respects machinery or plant provided for the purposes of a project approved by an industrial development agency in the period from the 1st day of January, 1986, to the 31st day of December, 1988, this paragraph shall apply as if the reference to the 31st day of December, 1995, were a reference to the 31st day of December, 1996,

and

(d) machinery or plant provided before the 1st day of April, 1991, for the purposes of a trade or part of a trade of hotel-keeping carried on in a building or structure or part of a building or structure, including machinery or plant provided by a lessor to a lessee for use in such a trade or part of a trade, where a binding contract for the provision of that building or structure was entered into after the 27th day of January, 1988, and before the 1st day of June, 1988.

(6) This section shall apply in relation to machinery or plant to which *subsection (7)(a)* applies—

(a) as if in *subsection (2)(b)*—

(i) the following subparagraph were substituted for *subparagraph (ii)*:

"(ii) if the machinery or plant is provided for use on or after the 1st day of April, 1989, 50 per cent,",

and

(ii) *subparagraph (iii)* were deleted,

and

(b) as if *subsection (3)* were deleted.

(7) (a) This subsection shall apply to—

(i) machinery or plant provided for the purposes of a project approved for grant assistance by an industrial development agency in the period from the 1st day of January, 1989, to the 31st day of December, 1990, and in respect of the provision of which expenditure is incurred before the 31st day of December, 1997[, or before the 30th day of June, 1998, if its provision is solely for use in an industrial building or structure referred to in *sections 271(3)(c)* and *273(7)(a)(i)* and expenditure in respect of such provision would have been incurred before the 31st day of December, 1997, but for the existence of circumstances which resulted in legal proceedings being initiated, being proceedings which were the subject of an order of the High Court made before the 1st day of January, 1998][1]; but, as respects machinery or plant provided for the purposes of any such project specified in the list referred to in *section 133(8)(c)(iv)*, this subparagraph shall apply as if the reference to the 31st day of December, 1997, [where it first occurs,][2] were a reference to the 31st day of December, 2002,

and

(ii) machinery or plant provided for the purposes of a trade or part of a trade of hotel-keeping carried on in a qualifying building or structure and in respect of the provision of which expenditure was incurred before the 31st day of December, 1995.

(b) *Paragraph (a)(ii)* shall not apply if the qualifying building or structure is not registered within 6 months after the date of the completion of that building or structure in a register kept by [the National Tourism Development Authority][3] under the Tourist Traffic Acts, 1939 to 1995, and where by virtue of this section any allowance or increased allowance has been granted any necessary additional assessments may be made to give effect to this paragraph.

(8) Where for any chargeable period a wear and tear allowance under *section 284* in relation to any machinery or plant is increased under this section, no allowance under *section 283* shall be made in relation to the machinery or plant for that or any subsequent chargeable period.

Amendments

[1] Inserted by FA98 s21(b)(ii).

[2] Inserted by FA98 s21(b)(i).

[3] Substituted by FA06 sched2(1)(f). This section is deemed to have come into force and have taken effect as on and from 28 May 2003.

Cross References

From Section 285

Section 133 Limitation on meaning of "distribution" – general.
Section 268 Meaning of "industrial building or structure".
Section 271 Industrial building allowances.
Section 273 Acceleration of writing-down allowances in respect of certain expenditure on certain industrial buildings or structures.
Section 283 Initial allowances.
Section 284 Wear and tear allowances.
Section 299 Allowances to lessees.
Section 445 Certain trading operations carried on in Shannon Airport.
Section 446 Certain trading operations carried on in Custom House Docks Area.

To Section 285

Section 283 Initial allowances.
Section 287 Wear and tear allowances deemed to have been made in certain cases.
Section 299 Allowances to lessees.
Section 301 Application to professions, employments and offices.
Section 403 Restriction on use of capital allowances for certain leased assets.
Section 404 Restriction on use of capital allowances for certain leased machinery or plant.
Section 425 Leasing contracts: effect on claims for losses of company reconstructions.
Section 678 Allowance for machinery and plant.

285A Acceleration of wear and tear allowances for certain energy efficient equipment

[(1) In this section—

"*energy-efficient equipment*" means equipment, named on and complying with the criteria stated on the specified list, provided for the purposes of a trade and which at the time it is so provided is unused and not second-hand;

"*relevant period*" means the period commencing on the date on which the first order is made under *subsection (4)* and [ending on [31 December 2017][1]][2];

"*the specified list*" means the list of energy-efficient equipment which—

(a) complies with *subsections (3)* and *(4)*, and

(b) is maintained for the purposes of this section by Sustainable Energy Ireland—The Sustainable Energy Authority of Ireland;

"*Table*" means the Table in Schedule 4A.

(2) Subject to this section, where for any chargeable period a wear and tear allowance is to be made under *section 284* to a company which has incurred capital expenditure on the provision of energy-efficient equipment for the purposes of a trade carried on by that company, *section 284(2)* shall apply as if the reference in *paragraph (ad)* of that section to 12.5 per cent were a reference to 100 per cent.

(3) The specified list shall contain only such equipment that—

(a) is in a class of technology specified in column (1) of the Table, and

(b) is of a description for that class of technology specified in column (2) of the Table.

(4) For the purposes of this section, the Minister for Communications, Energy and Natural Resources, after consultation with and the approval of the Minister for Finance—

(a) shall by order make the specified list—

(i) stating the energy efficiency criteria to be met for, and

(ii) naming the eligible products in,

each class of technology specified in column (1) of the Table, and

(b) may by order amend the specified list—

(i) stating energy efficiency criteria to be met for, or

(ii) naming eligible products in,

any class of technology specified in column (1) of the Table.

(5) *Subsection (2)* shall not apply—

(a) where the person to whom the allowance is to be made in accordance with *section 284* is not a company, or

(b) where the energy-efficient equipment is leased, let or hired to any person.

(6) *Subsection (2)* shall not apply in respect of expenditure incurred in a chargeable period on the provision of energy-efficient equipment in relation to a class of technology where the amount of that expenditure is less than the minimum amount specified in column (3) of the Table in relation to that class of technology.

(7) (a) *Subsection (2)* shall not apply in respect of expenditure incurred on the provision of equipment where that expenditure is not incurred in the relevant period.

(b) Where—

(i) expenditure on equipment is incurred on or after 31 January 2008 but before the first order is made under *subsection (4)*, and

(ii) that equipment would have qualified as energy-efficient equipment under this section had such an order been made at the time the expenditure was incurred,

then this section shall apply as if the order had been made at that time.

(8) Where this section applies to capital expenditure incurred by a company on the provision of energy-efficient equipment and that equipment would not, apart from this section, be treated as machinery or plant, then that equipment shall be treated as machinery or plant for the purposes of this Chapter and *Chapter 4* of this Part.

[(8A) (a) Notwithstanding *Part 11C*, where an allowance is increased under this section in respect of expenditure incurred in a chargeable period on the provision of any vehicle (being a vehicle to which *subsection (1)* of *section*

380K relates) in relation to the class of technology described in column (1) of the Table as "Electric and Alternative Fuel Vehicles", then *subsection (2)* shall apply as if the reference in *paragraph (ad)* of *section 284(2)* to the actual cost were a reference to the lower of the actual cost of the vehicle or the specified amount referred to in *section 380K(4)*.

(b) *Subsection (2)* shall not apply where an allowance in respect of expenditure incurred on the provision of a vehicle referred to in *paragraph (a)* is made under *section 284(2)* as applied by *section 380L*.][3]

(9) Any order made by the Minister for Communications, Energy and Natural Resources for the purpose of this section shall be laid before Dáil Éireann as soon as may be after it is made and, if a resolution annulling the order is passed by Dáil Éireann within the next 21 days on which Dáil Éireann has sat after the order is laid before it, the order shall be annulled accordingly, but without prejudice to the validity of anything previously done thereunder.][4]

Amendments

[1] Substituted by FA14 s38(a). Comes into operation on 1 January 2015.

[2] Substituted by FA11 s38. Deemed to have come into force and takes effect as on and from 1 January 2011.

[3] Inserted by F(No.2)A08 s37(1)(a). With effect from 23 March 2009 per S.I. No. 91 of 2009.

[4] Inserted by FA08 s46(1)(a). This section comes into operation on such day or days as the Minister for Finance may by order or orders appoint and different days may be appointed for different purposes or different provisions.

Revenue Briefings

Tax Briefing

Tax Briefing December 2008 – Issue 70 – Capital Allowances for Energy-Efficient Equipment

Cross References

From Section 285A

Section 284 Wear and tear allowances.
Section 380K Interpretation and general (Part 11C).
Section 380L Emissions-based limits for certain cars.
Schedule 4A Class of Technology

To Section 285A

Section 380K Interpretation and general (Part 11C).

286 Increased wear and tear allowances for taxis and cars for short-term hire

[FA87 s24; FA96 s131, s132(1) and Sch5 PtI par16]

(1) (a) In this section—

"*car*" means any mechanically propelled road vehicle, being a vehicle which has been constructed or adapted to be primarily suited to the carriage of passengers and not to the conveyance of goods or burden of any description or to the haulage by road of other vehicles, and which is a vehicle of a type commonly used as a private vehicle and suitable to be so used, and includes a vehicle in use for the purpose referred to in *paragraph (ii)* of the definition of "*qualifying purposes*";

"*qualifying purposes*" means, subject to *paragraphs (c)* and *(d)*, the use in the ordinary course of trade of a car for the purposes of—

(i) short-term hire to members of the public, or

(ii) the carriage of members of the public while the car is a licensed public hire vehicle fitted with a taximeter in accordance with the Road Traffic (Public Service Vehicles) Regulations, 1963 (S.I. No. 191 of 1963);

"*short-term hire*", in relation to a car and subject to *paragraph (b)*, means the hire of the car to a person under a hire-drive agreement (within the meaning of section 3 of the Road Traffic Act, 1961) for a continuous period which does not exceed 8 weeks.

(b) Where a period of hire of a car to a person by another person is followed within 7 days of the end of that period by a further period of hire of a car (whether the same car or not) to that person by that other person, the 2 periods shall be deemed for the purposes of this section, including any subsequent application of this paragraph, to constitute together a single continuous period of hire so that, where that continuous period of hire exceeds 8 weeks, the period of hire of any car included in that continuous period of hire shall not be treated as a period of short-term hire, and for the purposes of this paragraph any reference to a person shall be treated as including a reference to any other person who is connected with that person.

(c) For the purposes of this section, a car shall be regarded as used by a person for qualifying purposes as respects a chargeable period only if not less than 75 per cent of its use (determined by reference to the periods of time in which the car is used, or available for use, for any purpose) by that person in the chargeable period or its basis period is for qualifying purposes.

(d) Notwithstanding *paragraph (c)*, where as respects a chargeable period the use of a car for qualifying purposes does not satisfy the requirements of that paragraph but would have satisfied those requirements if the reference in that paragraph to 75 per cent were a reference to 50 per cent, the car shall be deemed to be used for qualifying purposes as respects that chargeable period if the use of the car by that person for qualifying purposes satisfied the requirements of that paragraph as respects the immediately preceding chargeable period, or the car shall be deemed to be so used if that use of the car has satisfied those requirements as respects the immediately succeeding chargeable period, and the inspector shall accordingly adjust the amount of capital allowances to be made in taxing the person's trade and any amount of tax overpaid shall be repaid.

(2) In determining what capital allowances are to be made to a person for any chargeable period in taxing a trade which consists of or includes the carrying on of qualifying purposes, *section 284* shall apply to a car which as respects that period has been used by the person for qualifying purposes as if the reference in *subsection (2)(a)(ii)* of that section to 20 per cent were a reference to 40 per cent.

Cross References

From Section 286

Section 284 Wear and tear allowances.

To Section 286

Section 284 Wear and tear allowances.

Section 301 Application to professions, employments and offices.

286A Wear and tear allowances for licences for public hire vehicles

[(1) In this section—

"*licence*" means a taxi licence or a wheelchair accessible taxi licence granted in respect of a small public service vehicle by a licensing authority in accordance with the Road Traffic (Public Service Vehicles) Regulations, 1963 to 2000, made under section 82 of the Road Traffic Act, 1961, as amended by section 57 of the Road Traffic Act, 1968;

"*qualifying expenditure*" means—

(a) capital expenditure incurred on the acquisition of a licence on or before 21 November 2000 and for the purposes of this section, where capital expenditure is so incurred it shall be deemed to have been incurred on 21 November 1997 or, if later, on the day on which the trade commenced, or

(b) where a licence formed part of an inheritance taken by an individual on or before 21 November 2000 and inheritance tax or probate tax was paid in relation to that licence, an amount equal to the open market value of the licence used for the purpose of inheritance tax or probate tax if that amount is greater than the amount of the capital expenditure incurred on the acquisition of the licence and, where this paragraph applies, the first-mentioned amount shall be deemed to have been capital expenditure incurred on the acquisition of a licence on 21 November 1997 or, if later, on the date on which the trade commenced;

"*qualifying trade*", means a trade carried on by an individual which consists of the carriage of members of the public for reward in a vehicle in respect of which a licence has been granted but excluding any trade or part of a trade which consists of the letting of such a vehicle.

(2) (a) Where an individual carrying on a qualifying trade proves to have incurred qualifying expenditure, then, for the purposes of this Chapter, other than *sections 298* and *299*, and for the purposes of Chapter 4 of this Part—

(i) the licence shall, subject to *paragraph (c)*, be treated as machinery or plant,

(ii) such machinery or plant shall be treated as having been provided for the purposes of the trade, and

(iii) for so long as the individual is entitled to the licence, that machinery or plant shall be treated as belonging to that individual.

(b) Where an individual who has incurred qualifying expenditure carries on a qualifying trade and uses a vehicle, being the vehicle to which the machinery or plant referred to in *paragraph (a)* relates, partly for letting to another person and partly for the purposes of the qualifying trade, the machinery or plant shall be deemed for the purposes of *section 284(1)* to be used only for the purposes of the qualifying trade.

(c) Notwithstanding *paragraph (a)*, where an individual who has incurred qualifying expenditure in relation to more than one licence carries on a qualifying trade and lets more than one of the vehicles, which are used for the purposes of the trade, being the vehicles to which the machinery or plant referred to in *paragraph (a)* relates, to another person or persons for use also by that other person or persons, *paragraph (a)* shall apply in respect of so much of that machinery or plant as relates to one licence only (in this section referred to as "*the relevant licence*").

(3) Where an individual who is not, apart from this subsection, entitled to allowances under this Chapter by virtue of this section, becomes the beneficial owner of a licence [on the death of his or her spouse or civil partner, and that spouse or civil partner][1]—

(a) had incurred qualifying expenditure in respect of the licence, and

(b) had carried on a qualifying trade,

then, for the purposes of this section, if the individual lets the vehicle to which the licence relates, or lets the licence, for use for the purposes of a qualifying trade carried on by another person—

(i) the individual shall be deemed to have incurred the qualifying expenditure in respect of the licence,

(ii) that licence shall be treated as machinery or plant, and

(iii) the letting of that vehicle or of that licence by the individual shall be deemed to be a qualifying trade carried on by the individual which commenced on the date of the first letting of that vehicle,

but this subsection shall apply in relation to an individual as respects one licence only.

(4) In determining what capital allowances are to be made in taxing the trade of an individual to which *subsection (2)* refers for any year of assessment, *section 284(2)(aa)* (inserted by the Finance Act, 2001) shall apply—

(a) as if the machinery or plant to which *subsection (2)* refers were machinery or plant to which *section 284(2)(aa)* applies, and

(b) as if the reference to "on or after 1 January 2001" in *section 284(2)(aa)* were a reference to "on 21 November 1997".

(5) (a) This subsection shall apply to an individual to whom *paragraph (b)* or *(c)* of *subsection (2)* relates who lets a vehicle to which *subsection (2)(b)* relates or a vehicle relating to a relevant licence.

(b) Notwithstanding *section 381*, where relief is claimed under that section in respect of a loss sustained in a qualifying trade, the amount of that loss, in so far as by virtue of *section 392* it is referable to an allowance under this section, shall be treated for the purposes of *subsections (1)* and *(3)(b)* of *section 381* as reducing income only from a letting to which *paragraph (a)* refers and shall not be treated as reducing any other income.

(6) *Subsection (7)* of *section 953* shall apply to an excess, referred to in that subsection, arising by virtue of an allowance made under this section as if the reference in *paragraph (a)(ii)* of that subsection to "*section 438(4)*" were a reference to this section.

(7) This section shall be deemed to have come into operation as on and from 6 April 1997.][2]

Amendments

[1] Substituted by FA12 s134(1)(b). Has effect as if it had come into operation for the year of assessment (within the meaning of the Income Tax Acts and the Capital Gains Tax Acts) 2011 and each subsequent year of assessment.

[2] Inserted by FA01 s51.

Cross References

From Section 286A

Section 284 Wear and tear allowances.

Section 298 Allowances to lessors.

Section 299 Allowances to lessees.

Section 381 Right to repayment of tax by reference to losses.
Section 392 Option to treat capital allowances as creating or augmenting a loss.
Section 438 Loans to participators, etc.
Section 953 Notices of preliminary tax.

287 Wear and tear allowances deemed to have been made in certain cases

[FA 1970 s 14(1),(2) and (3); CTA76 s21(1) and Sch1 par56; FA97 s146(1) and Sch9 PtI par4 (1)]

(1) In this section—

"*wear and tear allowance*" means an allowance made under *section 284* otherwise than by virtue of *section 285*;

"*normal wear and tear allowance*" means such wear and tear allowance or greater wear and tear allowance, if any, as would have been made to a person in respect of any machinery or plant used by such person during any chargeable period if all the conditions specified in *subsection (3)* had been fulfilled in relation to that chargeable period.

(2) Where for any chargeable period during which any machinery or plant has been used by a person no wear and tear allowance or a wear and tear allowance less than the normal wear and tear allowance is made to such person in respect of the machinery or plant, the normal wear and tear allowance shall be deemed for the purposes of *subsections (3)* and *(4)* of *section 284* to have been made to such person in respect of the machinery or plant for that chargeable period.

(3) The conditions referred to in *subsection (1)* are—

(a) that the trade had been carried on by the person in question since the date on which such person acquired the machinery or plant and had been so carried on by such person in such circumstances that the full amount of the profits or gains of the trade was liable to be charged to tax,

(b) that the trade had at no time consisted wholly or partly of exempted trading operations within the meaning of Chapter I of Part XXV of the Income Tax Act, 1967, or Part V of the Corporation Tax Act, 1976,

(c) that the machinery or plant had been used by such person solely for the purposes of the trade since that date,

(d) that a proper claim had been duly made by such person for wear and tear allowance in respect of the machinery or plant for every relevant chargeable period, and

(e) that no question arose in connection with any chargeable period as to there being payable to such person directly or indirectly any sums in respect of, or taking account of, the wear and tear of the machinery or plant.

(4) In the case of a company, *subsection (3)(a)* shall not alter the periods which are to be taken as chargeable periods but if, during any time after the year 1975-76 and after the company acquired the machinery or plant, the company has not been within the charge to corporation tax, any year of assessment or part of a year of assessment falling within that time shall be taken as a chargeable period as if it had been an accounting period of the company.

Cross References

From Section 287

Section 284 Wear and tear allowances.
Section 285 Acceleration of wear and tear allowances.

To Section 287

Schedule 18B Tonnage Tax

288 Balancing allowances and balancing charges

[ITA67 s272(1) to (4), (5)(a) and (b) and (6) and definition of "*scientific research allowance*" in ITA67 s271; CTA76 s21(1) and Sch1 par28 and par29; FA94 s24(b); FA95 s25(1)]

(1) Subject to this section, where any of the following events occurs in the case of any machinery or plant in respect of which an initial allowance or a wear and tear allowance has been made for any chargeable period to a person carrying on a trade—

(a) any event occurring after the setting up and before the permanent discontinuance of the trade whereby the machinery or plant ceases to belong to the person carrying on the trade (whether on a sale of the machinery or plant or in any other circumstances of any description),

(b) any event occurring after the setting up and before the permanent discontinuance of the trade whereby the machinery or plant (while continuing to belong to the person carrying on the trade) permanently ceases to be used for the purposes of a trade carried on by the person,

(c) the permanent discontinuance of the trade, the machinery or plant not having previously ceased to belong to the person carrying on the trade,

(d) in the case of machinery or plant consisting of [a specified intangible asset within the meaning of *section 291A*,][1] computer software or the right to use or otherwise deal with computer software, any event whereby the person grants to another person a right to use or otherwise deal with the whole or part of the ["*that machinery or plant*"][2] in circumstances where the consideration in money for the grant constitutes (or, if there were consideration in money for the grant, would constitute) a capital sum, an allowance or charge (in this Chapter referred to as a "*balancing allowance*" or a "*balancing charge*") shall, in the circumstances mentioned in this section, be made to or, as the case may be, on that person for the chargeable period related to that event.

(2) Where there are no sale, insurance, salvage or compensation moneys or where the amount of the capital expenditure of the person in question on the provision of the machinery or plant still unallowed as at the time of the event exceeds those moneys, a balancing allowance shall be made, and the amount of the allowance shall be the amount of the expenditure still unallowed as at that time or, as the case may be, of the excess of that expenditure still unallowed as at that time over those moneys.

(3) Where the sale, insurance, salvage or compensation moneys exceed the amount, if any, of that expenditure still unallowed as at the time of the event, a balancing charge shall be made, and the amount on which it is made shall be an amount equal to—

(a) the excess, or

(b) where the amount still unallowed is nil, those moneys.

[(3A) Where, in relation to an event referred to in *subsection (1)(d)*, a balancing allowance or balancing charge is to be made to or, as the case may be, on a person for the chargeable period related to that event and following that event, the person retains an interest in the machinery or plant, then, for the purposes of this Chapter—

(a) the amount of capital expenditure still unallowed at the time of the event, which is to be taken into account in calculating the balancing allowance or balancing charge, shall be such portion of the unallowed expenditure relating to the machinery or plant in question as the sale, insurance, salvage or compensation moneys bear to the aggregate of those moneys and the market value of the machinery or plant which remains undisposed of, and the balance of the unallowed expenditure shall be attributed to the machinery or plant which remains undisposed of, and

(b) the amount of capital expenditure incurred on the machinery or plant in question shall be treated as reduced by such portion of that expenditure as the sale, insurance, salvage or compensation moneys bear to the aggregate of those moneys and the market value of the machinery or plant which remains undisposed of.][3]

[(3B) Notwithstanding *subsection (3)*, a balancing charge shall not be made where the amount of the sale, insurance, salvage or compensation moneys received by the person in question in respect of the machinery or plant is less than €2,000; but this subsection shall not apply in the case of the sale or other disposal of the machinery or plant to a connected person.][4]

[(3C) Notwithstanding *subsection (3)*, a balancing charge shall not be made by reference to a wear and tear allowance made to a company (in this subsection referred to as the 'first-mentioned company') in respect of capital expenditure incurred on the provision of a specified intangible asset (within the meaning of *section 291A*) where an event referred to in *subsection (1)* occurs more than 5 years after the beginning of the accounting period of the company in which the asset was first provided, but if—

(a) that event, or any scheme or arrangement which includes that event, results in a company which is connected (within the meaning of *section 10*) with the first-mentioned company incurring capital expenditure on the specified intangible asset, and

(b) for the purposes of this Chapter and *Chapter 4*, the amount of that expenditure would, apart from this subsection, exceed the amount still unallowed, at the time of the event, of capital expenditure incurred by the first-mentioned company on the provision of that asset,

the amount of such expenditure shall be deemed, for those purposes, to be equal to the said amount still unallowed.][5]

(4) (a) In this subsection, "*scientific research allowance*" means—

(i) in relation to any expenditure incurred before the 6th day of April, 1965, the total amount of any allowances made in respect of that expenditure under section 244(3) of the Income Tax Act, 1967, increased by the amount of any allowance made under *section 244(4)(b)* of that Act or, as the case may be, reduced by any amount treated as a trading receipt in accordance with *section 244(4)(c)* of that Act, and

(ii) in relation to any expenditure incurred on or after the 6th day of April, 1965, the amount of any allowance made in respect of that expenditure under *subsection (1)* or *(2)* of *section 765*, reduced by any amount treated as a trading receipt in accordance with *section 765(3)(a)*.

(b) Notwithstanding anything in *subsection (3)*, in no case shall the amount on which a balancing charge is made on a person exceed the aggregate of the following amounts—

(i) the amount of the initial allowance, if any, made to the person in respect of the expenditure in question,

(ii) the amount of any wear and tear allowance made to the person in respect of the machinery or plant in question,

(iii) the amount of any scientific research allowance made to the person in respect of the expenditure, and

(iv) the amount of any balancing allowance previously made to the person in respect of the expenditure.

[(c) Where *subsection (3A)* applies, the amount of any allowances referred to in *paragraph (b)* made in respect of the machinery or plant in question shall, for the purposes of this Chapter, be apportioned so that:

(i) such portion of those allowances as the sale, insurance, salvage or compensation moneys bear to the aggregate of those moneys and the market value of the machinery or plant which remains undisposed of, shall be attributed to the grant of the right to use or otherwise deal with, referred to in *subsection (1)(d)*, and

(ii) the balance of those allowances shall be attributed to the machinery or plant which remains undisposed of.][6]

(5) (a) Where the aggregate amount of initial allowances and wear and tear allowances made to any person in respect of any machinery or plant exceeds the actual amount of the expenditure incurred by that person on the provision of that machinery or plant, the amount of such excess (in this paragraph referred to as "*the excess amount*") shall, on the occurrence of an event within *paragraph (a), (b), (c)* or *(d)* of *subsection (1)*, be deemed to be a payment of an equal amount received by that person on account of sale, insurance, salvage or compensation moneys and shall be added to any other such moneys received in respect of that machinery or plant, and a balancing charge shall be made and the amount on which it is made shall be an amount equal to—

(i) where there are no sale, insurance, salvage or compensation moneys, the excess amount, or

(ii) where there are sale, insurance, salvage or compensation moneys, the aggregate of such moneys and the excess amount.

(b) Where as respects any machinery or plant an event within *paragraph (a), (b), (c)* or *(d)* of *subsection (1)* is followed by another event within any of those paragraphs, any balancing allowance or balancing charge made to or on the person by virtue of the happening of the later event shall take account of any balancing allowance or balancing charge previously made to or on that person in respect of the expenditure incurred by the person on the provision of that machinery or plant.

(6) (a) Where—

(i) the sale, insurance, salvage or compensation moneys consist of a payment or payments to a person under the scheme for compensation in respect of the decommissioning of fishing vessels implemented by the Minister for the Marine and Natural Resources in accordance with Council Regulation (EC) No. 3699/93 of 21 December 1993,* and

* O.J. No. L 346, 31.12.1993, p.1.

(ii) on account of the receipt by the person of such payment or payments, a balancing charge is to be made on the person for any chargeable period other than by virtue of *paragraph (b)*,

then, the amount on which the balancing charge is to be made for that chargeable period shall be an amount equal to one-third of the amount (in this subsection referred to as "*the original amount*") on which the balancing charge would but for this subsection have been made.

(b) Notwithstanding *paragraph (a)*, there shall be made on the person for each of the 2 immediately succeeding chargeable periods a balancing charge, and the amount on which that charge is made for each of those periods shall be an amount equal to one-third of the original amount.

[(6A) (a) Where—

(i) the sale, insurance, salvage or compensation moneys consist of a payment or payments to a person under the scheme for compensation in respect of the decommissioning of fishing vessels implemented by the Minister for Agriculture, Fisheries and Food in accordance with Council Regulation (EC) No. 1198/2006 of 27 July 2006*, and

* OJ No. L233, 15 August 2006, p.1

(ii) on account of the receipt by the person of such payment or payments, a balancing charge is to be made on the person for any chargeable period other than by virtue of paragraph (*b*),

then, the amount on which the balancing charge is to be made for that chargeable period shall be an amount equal to one-fifth of the amount (in this subsection referred to as "*the original amount*") on which the balancing charge would but for this subsection have been made.

(b) Notwithstanding paragraph (*a*), there shall be made on the person for each of the 4 immediately succeeding chargeable periods a balancing charge, and the amount on which that charge is made for each of those periods shall be an amount equal to one-fifth of the original amount.][7]

Amendments

[1] Inserted by FA09 s13(1)(b). Applies to expenditure incurred by a company after 7 May 2009.

[2] Substituted by FA00 s41(1)(a)(i). This section shall apply as on and from 29 February 2000.

[3] Inserted by FA00 s41(1)(a)(ii). This section shall apply as on and from 29 February 2000.

[4] Inserted by FA02 s31(2).

[5] Substituted by FA14 s40(1)(a). Applies as respects any event referred to in subsection (1) which occurs on or after 23 October 2014.

[6] Inserted by FA00 s41(1)(a)(iii). This section shall apply as on and from 29 February 2000.

[7] Inserted by FA08 s30(1). With effect from 17 April 2008 per S.I. 104 of 2008.

Revenue Precedents

It is acceptable to reclassify as stocks rather than fixed assets linen used by companies providing a hiring and cleaning service in respect of linen. (2) Section 288 applies to the re Classification as if it were a sale at the open market price. CTF92/1005

Prior to 1973 a person could claim initial allowances and wear and tear allowances amounting to more than the cost of the plant and machinery. Section 11 Finance Act 1973 provided for the charging of the excess of the allowances over the actual cost. The question that arises is whether the actual cost is the cost as reduced by grants. At the time grants were not deducted in arriving at the qualifying expenditure for wear and tear purposes but were deducted for the purpose of a balancing charge. A strict application of the section could have had the effect of imposing a balancing charge on the excess of the allowances made over the expenditure incurred as reduced by grants. The Revenue Commissioners are prepared to accept that the provisions of Section 11 Finance Act 1973 (now section 288(5) Taxes Consolidation Act 1997) will not apply to this excess. The provision is only applied where the capital allowances granted exceed the gross cost. 00gm120

Cross References

From Section 288

Section 10 Connected persons.

Section 244 Relief for interest paid on certain home loans.

Section 291A Intangible assets.
Section 765 Allowances for capital expenditure on scientific research.

To Section 288
Section 267P Treatment of credit transaction.
Section 290 Option in case of replacement.
Section 292 Meaning of "amount still unallowed".
Section 293 Application to partnerships.
Section 296 Balancing allowances and balancing charges: wear and tear allowances deemed to have been made in certain cases.
Section 297 Subsidies towards wear and tear.
Section 660 Farming: wear and tear allowances deemed to have been made in certain cases.
Schedule 18B Tonnage Tax

289 Calculation of balancing allowances and balancing charges in certain cases

[ITA67 s277]

(1) In this section, "*open-market price*", in relation to any machinery or plant, means the price which the machinery or plant would have fetched if sold in the open market at the time of the event in question.

(2) Where—

(a) an event occurs which gives rise or might give rise to a balancing allowance or balancing charge in respect of machinery or plant,

(b) the event is the permanent discontinuance of a trade, and

(c) at or about the time of the discontinuance there occurs in relation to the machinery or plant any event mentioned in *paragraphs (a)* to *(c)* of *section 318*, not being a sale at less than open-market price other than a sale to which *section 312* applies,

then, for the purpose of determining—

(i) whether the discontinuance gives rise to a balancing allowance or balancing charge, and, if so,

(ii) the amount of the allowance or, as the case may be, the amount on which the charge is to be made,

the amount of the net proceeds, compensation, receipts or insurance moneys mentioned in *paragraphs (a)* to *(c)* of *section 318* which arise on the last-mentioned event shall be deemed to be an amount of sale, insurance, salvage or compensation moneys arising on the permanent discontinuance of the trade.

(3) (a) Subject to *subsections (4)* and *(6)*, *paragraph (b)* shall apply where an event occurs which gives rise or might give rise to a balancing allowance or balancing charge in respect of machinery or plant, and—

(i) the event is the permanent discontinuance of the trade and immediately after the time of the discontinuance the machinery or plant continues to belong to the person by whom the trade was carried on immediately before that time and the case is not one within *subsection (2)*,

(ii) the event is the permanent discontinuance of the trade and at the time of the discontinuance the machinery or plant is either sold at less than the open-market price, the sale not being one to which *section 312* applies, or the machinery or plant is given away,

(iii) the event is the sale of the machinery or plant at less than the open-market price, not being a sale to which *section 312* applies, or is the gift of the machinery or plant, or

(iv) the event is that, after the setting up and before the permanent discontinuance of the trade, the machinery or plant permanently ceases to be used for the purposes of a trade carried on by the person by whom the first-mentioned trade is being carried on, and so ceases either by reason of that person's transferring the machinery or plant to other use or, on a transfer of the trade which is not treated as involving a discontinuance of the trade, by reason of the retention of the machinery or plant by the transferor.

(b) For the purpose of determining whether a balancing allowance or balancing charge is to be made and, if so, the amount of the allowance or, as the case may be, the amount on which the charge is to be made, the event shall be treated as if it had given rise to sale, insurance, salvage or compensation moneys of an amount equal to the open-market price of the machinery or plant.

(4) References in *subsection (3)* to the sale of machinery or plant at less than the open-market price do not include references to the sale of machinery or plant in such circumstances that there is a charge to income tax under Schedule E by virtue of *Chapter 3* of *Part 5*, and *subsection (3)(b)* shall not apply by reason of the gift of machinery or plant if the machinery or plant is given away in any such circumstances.

(5) Subject to *subsection (6)*, where *subsection (3)(b)* applies by reason of the gift or sale of machinery or plant to any person, and that person receives or purchases the machinery or plant with a view to using it for the purposes of a trade carried on by that person, then, in determining whether any, and if so what, wear and tear allowances, balancing allowances or balancing charges are to be made in connection with that trade, the like consequences shall ensue as if the recipient or purchaser had purchased the machinery or plant at the open-market price.

(6) [Subject to *subsection (6A)*, where in a case within *subsection (5)*][1] the recipient or purchaser and the donor or seller, by notice in writing to the inspector, jointly so elect, the following provisions shall apply:

(a) *subsections (3)(b)* and *(5)* shall apply as if for the references in those subsections to the open-market price there were substituted references to that price or the amount of the expenditure on the provision of the machinery or plant still unallowed immediately before the gift or sale, whichever is the lower;

(b) notwithstanding anything in this Chapter, such balancing charge, if any, shall be made on the recipient or purchaser on any event occurring after the date of the gift or sale as would have been made on the donor or seller if the donor or seller had continued to own the machinery or plant and had done all such things and been allowed all such allowances in connection with the machinery or plant as were done by or allowed to the recipient or purchaser.

[(6A) (a) *Subsection (6)* shall only apply in a case where the donor or seller is connected with the recipient or purchaser.

(b) Notwithstanding *paragraph (a)*, *subsection (6)* shall not apply in any case where the donor or seller is not a company and the recipient or purchaser is a company.][2]

Amendments

[1] Substituted by FA03 s47(1)(a). This section shall apply as respects a gift or sale of machinery or plant on or after 6 February 2003.

[2] Inserted by FA03 s47(1)(b). This section shall apply as respects a gift or sale of machinery or plant on or after 6 February 2003.

Cross References

From Section 289

Section 112 Basis of assessment, persons chargeable and extent of charge.
Section 123 General tax treatment of payments on retirement or removal from office or employment.
Section 312 Special provisions as to certain sales.
Section 318 Meaning of "sale, insurance, salvage or compensation moneys".

To Section 289

Section 374 Capital allowances for cars costing over certain amount.
Section 380L Emissions-based limits for certain cars.
Section 555 Restriction of losses by reference to capital allowances and renewals allowances.
Schedule 18B Tonnage Tax

290 Option in case of replacement

[ITA67 s273(1)]

Where machinery or plant, in the case of which any of the events mentioned in *section 288(1)* has occurred, is replaced by the owner of the machinery or plant and a balancing charge is to be made on that owner by reason of that event, or but for this section a balancing charge would have been made on that owner by reason of that event, then, if by notice in writing to the inspector that owner so elects, the following provisions shall apply:

(a) if the amount on which the charge would have been made is greater than the capital expenditure on providing the new machinery or plant—

(i) the charge shall be made only on an amount equal to the difference,

(ii) no initial allowance, no balancing allowance and no wear and tear allowance shall be made in respect of the new machinery or plant or the expenditure on the provision of the new machinery or plant, and

(iii) in considering whether any, and if so what, balancing charge is to be made in respect of the expenditure on the new machinery or plant, there shall be deemed to have been made in respect of that expenditure an initial allowance equal to the full amount of that expenditure;

(b) if the capital expenditure on providing the new machinery or plant is equal to or greater than the amount on which the charge would have been made—

(i) the charge shall not be made,

(ii) the amount of any initial allowance in respect of that expenditure and the amount of any wear and tear allowance shall be calculated as if the expenditure had been reduced by the amount on which the charge would have been made, and

(iii) in considering whether any, and if so what, balancing allowance or balancing charge is to be made in respect of the new machinery or plant, there shall be deemed to have been granted in respect of the new machinery or plant an initial allowance equal to the amount on which the charge would have been made, in addition to any initial allowance actually granted in respect of the new machinery or plant.

Revenue Precedents

Where a balancing charge arises on the disposal of a motor vehicle what amount is deducted from the replacement cost i.e. is it the amount of the charge before or after adjustment has been made for private use? The amount to be deducted is the amount of the charge after adjustment has been made for private use. IT963523

Cross References

From Section 290
Section 288 Balancing allowances and balancing charges.

To Section 290
Section 374 Capital allowances for cars costing over certain amount.
Section 380L Emissions-based limits for certain cars.
Section 555 Restriction of losses by reference to capital allowances and renewals allowances.
Schedule 18B Tonnage Tax

291 Computer software

[ITA67 s241A(1) and (2); FA94 s24(a)]

(1) [Subject to *subsection (3)*, where a person carrying on a trade has incurred][1] capital expenditure in acquiring for the purposes of the trade a right to use or otherwise deal with computer software, then, for the purposes of this Chapter and *Chapter 4* of this Part—

(a) the right and the software to which the right relates shall be treated as machinery or plant,

(b) such machinery or plant shall be treated as having been provided for the purposes of the trade, and

(c) for so long as the person is entitled to the right, that machinery or plant shall be treated as belonging to that person.

(2) [Subject to *subsection (3)*, in any case where][2]—

(a) a person carrying on a trade [has incurred][3] capital expenditure on the provision of computer software for the purposes of the trade, and

(b) in consequence of the person [having incurred][4] that expenditure, the computer software belongs to that person but does not constitute machinery or plant,

then, for the purposes of this Chapter and *Chapter 4* of this Part, the computer software shall be treated as machinery or plant.

[(3) Subject to *subsection (4)*, where the person is a company, this section shall operate as if computer software or a right to use or otherwise deal with computer software were construed as being any such software or any such right—

(a) which is provided for computer systems or processes or computer operated machinery or equipment for use in the operation of the trade carried on by the company, and

(b) (i) the provision of which does not limit or restrict the person from whom the company acquired the software or the right in—

(I) the use of that software or exercise of that right, or

(II) the provision of that software or granting of that right to other persons,

or

(ii) which is not provided for activities of managing, developing or exploiting that software or that right for the purposes of receiving a royalty or other sum in respect of the use of that software or the exercise of that right by other persons.

(4) (a) Subject to *paragraph (b)*, where a company elects in writing, *subsection (3)* shall not apply to expenditure, specified in the election, incurred by it after

4 February 2010 and before 4 February 2012 on computer software or on a right to use or otherwise deal with computer software.

(b) An election under *paragraph (a)* shall be made in the return required to be made under *section 951* for the accounting period of the company in which the expenditure is incurred and shall not be made later than 12 months from the end of the accounting period in which the capital expenditure, giving rise to the claim, is incurred.][5]

Amendments

[1] Substituted by FA10 s43(1)(b)(i). Applies to expenditure incurred by a company after 4 February 2010.

[2] Substituted by FA10 s43(1)(b)(ii)(I). Applies to expenditure incurred by a company after 4 February 2010.

[3] Substituted by FA10 s43(1)(b)(ii)(II). Applies to expenditure incurred by a company after 4 February 2010.

[4] Substituted by FA10 s43(1)(b)(ii)(III). Applies to expenditure incurred by a company after 4 February 2010.

[5] Inserted by FA10 s43(1)(c). Applies to expenditure incurred by a company after 4 February 2010.

Cross References

From Section 291

Section 951 Obligation to make a return.

To Section 291

Section 291A Intangible assets.

291A Intangible assets

[(1) In this section—

"*authorised officer*" means an officer of the Revenue Commissioners authorised by them in writing for the purposes of this section;

"*intangible asset*" shall be construed in accordance with generally accepted accounting practice;

"*specified intangible asset*" means an intangible asset, being—

(a) any patent, registered design, design right or invention,

(b) any trade mark, trade name, trade dress, brand, brand name, domain name, service mark or publishing title,

(c) any copyright or related right within the meaning of the Copyright and Related Rights Act 2000,

[(ca) computer software or a right to use or otherwise deal with computer software other than such software or such right construed in accordance with *section 291(3)*,][1]

(d) any supplementary protection certificate provided for under Council Regulation (EEC) No. 1768/92 of 18 June 1992*,

*OJ No. L182, 2.7.1992, p.1

(e) any supplementary protection certificate provided for under Regulation (EC) No. 1610/96 of the European Parliament and of the Council of 23 July 1996*,

*OJ No. L198, 8.8.1996, p.30

(f) any plant breeders' rights within the meaning of section 4 of the Plant Varieties (Proprietary Rights) Act 1980, as amended by the Plant Varieties (Proprietary Rights) (Amendment) Act 1998,

[(fa) any application for the grant or registration of anything within *paragraphs (a)* to *(f)*,][2] [(g) secret processes or formulae or other secret information concerning industrial, commercial or scientific experience, whether protected or not by patent, copyright or a related right, including know-how within the meaning of [*section 768* and, except where such asset is provided directly or indirectly in connection with the transfer of a business as a going 40 concern, customer lists][3],][4]

(h) any authorisation without which it would not be permissible for—

(i) a medicine, or

(ii) a product of any design, formula, process or invention,

to be sold for any purpose for which it was intended[, but this paragraph does not relate to a licence within the meaning of section 2 of the Intoxicating Liquor Act 2008][5],

(i) any rights derived from research, undertaken prior to any authorisation referred to in paragraph (*h*), into the effects of—

(i) a medicine, or

(ii) a product of any design, formula, process or invention,

(j) any licence in respect of an intangible asset referred to in any of paragraphs (*a*) to (*i*),

(k) any rights granted under the law of any country, territory, state or area, other than the State, or under any international treaty, convention or agreement to which the State is a party, that correspond to or are similar to those within any of paragraphs (*a*) to (*j*), or

(l) goodwill to the extent that it is directly attributable to anything within any of paragraphs (*a*) to (*k*);

"***profit and loss account***", in relation to an accounting period of a company, has the meaning assigned to it by generally accepted accounting practice and includes an income and expenditure account where a company prepares accounts in accordance with international accounting standards.

(2) Where a company carrying on a trade [has incurred][6] capital expenditure on the provision of a specified intangible asset for the purposes of the trade, then, for the purposes of this Chapter and Chapter 4 of this Part—

(a) the specified intangible asset shall be treated as machinery or plant,

(b) such machinery or plant shall be treated as having been provided for the purposes of the trade, and

(c) for so long as the company is the owner of the specified intangible asset or, where the asset consists of a right, is entitled to that right, that machinery or plant shall be treated as belonging to that company.

(3) Subject to this section, where for any accounting period a wear and tear allowance is to be made under *section 284* to a company which has incurred capital expenditure on the provision of a specified intangible asset for the purposes of a trade carried on by that company, *subsection (2)* of *section 284* shall apply as if the reference in *paragraph (ad)* of that subsection to a rate per cent of 12.5 were a reference to a rate per cent determined by the formula—

$$\frac{A}{B} \times 100$$

where—

A is—

(a) the amount, computed in accordance with generally accepted accounting practice, charged to the profit and loss account of the company, for the period of account which is the same as the accounting period, in respect of the [amortisation and any impairment][7] of the specified intangible asset, or

(b) where the period of account beginning in the accounting period is not the same as that accounting period, so much of the amount, so computed and charged in that respect to the profit and loss account of the company for any such period of account, as may be apportioned to the accounting period on a just and reasonable basis taking account of the respective lengths of the periods concerned and the duration of use and ownership of the asset in each of those periods,

and

B is the actual cost, within the meaning of *paragraph (ad)* of *section 284(2)*, of the specified intangible asset or, if greater than the actual cost, the value of that asset by reference to which [amortisation and any impairment][8] have been computed for the period of account referred to in *paragraph (a)* or *(b)*.

(4) (a) Notwithstanding *subsection (3)*, where a company makes an election under this subsection in respect of capital expenditure incurred on the provision of a specified intangible asset for the purposes of a trade carried on by the company, *subsection (2)* of *section 284* shall apply as if the reference in *paragraph (ad)* of that subsection to 12.5 per cent were a reference to 7 per cent.

(b) An election by a company under paragraph (*a*) shall—

(i) be made in the return required to be made under [*Chapter 3* of *Part 41A*][9] for the accounting period of the company in which the expenditure on the provision of the specified intangible asset is first incurred, and

(ii) apply to all capital expenditure incurred on the asset.

(5)

[(a) In relation to the activities of a company carried on as part of a trade—

(i) the whole of such activities, if any, that—

(I) comprise the sale of goods or services which are goods or services that derive the greater part of their value from, or

(II) consist of managing, developing or exploiting,

a specified intangible asset or specified intangible assets in respect of which allowances under this Chapter have been made to the company, and

(ii) such parts of other such activities, if any, being parts that—

(I) consist of managing, developing or exploiting such assets, or

(II) contribute to the value of goods or services by using such assets,

are referred to in *paragraph (b)* as "*relevant activities*" and shall be treated for the purposes of the Tax Acts, other than any provisions of those Acts relating to the commencement or cessation of a trade, as a separate trade (in *paragraph (b)* and *subsection (6)* referred to as a "*relevant trade*") which is distinct from any other trade or part of a trade carried on by the company.][10]

(b) For the purposes of treating relevant activities as a separate trade in accordance with *paragraph (a)*, any necessary apportionment shall be made so that income shall be attributed to the relevant trade on a just and reasonable basis and the amount of that income shall not exceed the amount which would be attributed to a distinct and separate company, engaged in the relevant activities, if it were independent of, and dealing at arm's length with, the company mentioned in *paragraph (a)*.

(6) (a) Subject to *paragraphs (b)* and *(c)*, the aggregate amount for an accounting period of—

(i) any allowances to be made to a company under *section 284* as applied by this section, and

(ii) any interest incurred in connection with the provision of a specified intangible asset by reference to which allowances referred to in *subparagraph (i)* are made,

shall not exceed [...][11] of the amount which would be the amount of the trading income from the relevant trade carried on by the company for that accounting period if no such allowances were to be made to the company and no such interest were to be deducted in computing that income for that accounting period and, for the purposes of this paragraph, the whole or part of any such allowances shall not be allowed for that accounting period and, only if it is then necessary for the purposes of this paragraph, the whole or part of any such interest shall not be deducted for that accounting period.

(b) (i) The amount of any allowances which, by virtue of *paragraph (a)*, remains unallowed for an accounting period (in this subparagraph referred to as the "*excess amount*") shall be carried forward and treated as an allowance within the meaning of *paragraph (a)(i)* for the succeeding accounting period to be added to the amount of any allowances within that meaning which, subject to *paragraph (a)*, are available for offset against trading income of the relevant trade for that succeeding accounting period and any excess amount in that succeeding accounting period shall, in turn, be carried forward and treated as an allowance within the meaning of *paragraph (a)(i)* for the next succeeding accounting period to be added to the amount of any allowances within that meaning which, subject to *paragraph (a)*, are available for offset against trading income of the relevant trade for that accounting period and so on for each succeeding accounting period.

(ii) The amount of any interest for which relief cannot be given, by virtue of *paragraph (a)*, for an accounting period (in this subparagraph referred to as "*excess interest*") shall be carried forward and treated as interest within the meaning of *paragraph (a)(ii)* for the succeeding accounting period to be added to the amount of any interest within that meaning for which relief, subject to *paragraph (a)*, can be given for that succeeding accounting period and any excess interest in that succeeding accounting period shall, in turn, be carried forward and treated as interest within the meaning of *paragraph (a)(ii)* for the next succeeding accounting period to be added to the amount of any interest within that meaning, for which relief, subject to *paragraph (a)*, can be given for that accounting period and so on for each succeeding accounting period.

(c) In computing, for the purposes of this subsection, the trading income from a relevant trade for an accounting period of a company, no account shall be taken of any income which is disregarded for the purposes of the Tax Acts.

(7) This section shall not apply to capital expenditure incurred by a company—

(a) for which any relief or deduction under the Tax Acts may be given or allowed other than by virtue of this section,

(b) to the extent that the expenditure incurred on the provision of a specified intangible asset exceeds the amount which would have been paid or payable for the asset in a transaction between independent persons acting at arm's length, or

(c) that is not made wholly and exclusively for bona fide commercial reasons and that was incurred as part of a scheme or arrangement of which the main purpose or one of the main purposes is the avoidance of, or reduction in, liability to tax.

(8) (a) The Revenue Commissioners or an authorised officer may, in relation to an allowance made or to be made to a company under *section 284* as applied by this section in respect of capital expenditure incurred on a specified intangible asset—

(i) consult with any person (in this subsection referred to as an "*expert*") who in their opinion may be of assistance in ascertaining the extent to which such expenditure is incurred on the specified intangible asset and, where such an asset is acquired from a connected person (within the meaning of section 10), the amount which would have been payable for the asset in a transaction between independent persons acting at arm's length, and

(ii) notwithstanding any obligation as to secrecy or other restriction on the disclosure of information imposed by, or under, the Tax Acts or any other statute or otherwise, but subject to *paragraph (b)*, disclose to the expert any detail in relation to the allowance claimed under this section which they consider necessary for such consultation.

(b) (i) Before disclosing information to any expert under *paragraph (a)*, the Revenue Commissioners or authorised officer shall make known to the company—

(I) the identity of the expert who they intend to consult, and

(II) the information they intend to disclose to the expert.

(ii) Where the company shows to the satisfaction of the Revenue Commissioners or authorised officer (or on appeal to the Appeal Commissioners) that disclosure of such information to that expert could prejudice the company's trade, then the Revenue Commissioners or authorised officer shall not make such disclosure.

(9) (a) This section shall not apply to the acquisition by a company (in this subsection referred to as "*the transferee*") of a specified intangible asset where the acquisition is from another company (in this subsection referred to as "*the transferor*") and, by virtue of *section 615(2)* or *617(1)*, the transferee is treated as having acquired the asset for a consideration of such amount as would secure that neither a gain nor a loss would accrue on the transferor's disposal of the asset to the transferee.

(b) Notwithstanding *paragraph (a)*, where the transferor and transferee make a joint election under *section 615(4)* or *617(4)*, the transferee shall be entitled to claim an allowance under *section 284* as applied by this section in respect of capital expenditure incurred by it on acquiring the specified intangible asset from the transferor.

(10) Any claim made by reference to this section shall be made within 12 months from the end of the accounting period in which the capital expenditure, giving rise to the claim, is incurred.][12]

Amendments

[1] Inserted by FA10 s43(1)(d). Applies to expenditure incurred by a company after 4 February 2010.

[2] Inserted by FA10 s43(1)(e). Applies to expenditure incurred by a company after 4 February 2010.

[3] Substituted by FA14 s40(1)(b)(i). Has effect for accounting periods commencing on or after 1 January 2015.

[4] Substituted by FA10 s43(1)(f). Applies to expenditure incurred by a company after 4 February 2010.

[5] Inserted by FA10 s43(1)(g). Has effect as respects any allowance to be made for an accounting period commencing on or after 1 January 2010.

[6] Substituted by FA10 s43(1)(h). Applies to expenditure incurred by a company after 4 February 2010.

[7] Substituted by FA10 s43(1)(i)(i). Applies to expenditure incurred by a company after 4 February 2010.

[8] Substituted by FA10 s43(1)(i)(ii). Applies to expenditure incurred by a company after 4 February 2010.

[9] Substituted by FA12 sched4(part 2)(g).

[10] Substituted by FA10 s43(1)(j). Applies to expenditure incurred by a company after 4 February 2010.

[11] Deleted by FA14 s40(1)(b)(ii). Has effect for accounting periods commencing on or after 1 January 2015.

[12] Inserted by FA09 s13(1)(d). Applies to expenditure incurred by a company after 7 May 2009.

Cross References

From Section 291A

Section 284 Wear and tear allowances.
Section 291 Computer software.
Section 615 Company reconstruction or amalgamation: transfer of assets.
Section 617 Transfers of assets, other than trading stock, within group.
Section 768 Allowance for know-how.
Section 951 Obligation to make a return.

To Section 291A

Section 247 Relief to companies on loans applied in acquiring interest in other companies.
Section 288 Balancing allowances and balancing charges.
Section 494 Qualifying companies.
Section 590 Attribution to participators of chargeable gains accruing to non-resident company.
Section 615 Company reconstruction or amalgamation: transfer of assets.
Section 617 Transfers of assets, other than trading stock, within group.
Section 756 Effect of lapse of patent rights.
Section 766 Tax credit for research and development expenditure.
Section 840A Interest on loans to defray money applied for certain purposes.

292 Meaning of "amount still unallowed"

[ITA67 s274; CTA76 s21(1) and Sch1 par30]

References in this Chapter to the amount still unallowed as at any time of any expenditure on the provision of machinery or plant shall be construed as references to the amount of that expenditure less—

(a) any initial allowance made or deemed under this Chapter to have been made in respect of that expenditure to the person who incurred the expenditure,

(b) any wear and tear allowances made or deemed under this Chapter to have been made to that person in respect of the machinery or plant on the provision of which the expenditure was incurred, being allowances made for any chargeable period such that the chargeable period or its basis period ended before the time in question,

(c) any scientific research allowance (within the meaning of *section 288(4)(a)*) made to that person in respect of the expenditure, and

(d) any balancing allowance made to that person in respect of the expenditure.

Cross References

From Section 292

Section 288 Balancing allowances and balancing charges.

To Section 292

Section 312 Special provisions as to certain sales.

Section 485G Miscellaneous (Chapter 2A).

293 Application to partnerships

[ITA67 s275; CTA76 s21(1) and Sch1 par31]

(1) (a) Where, after the setting up and on or before the permanent discontinuance of a trade which at any time is carried on in partnership, any event occurs which gives rise or may give rise to a balancing allowance or balancing charge in respect of machinery or plant—

(i) any balancing allowance or balancing charge which, if the trade had at all times been carried on by one and the same person, would have been made to or on that person in respect of that machinery or plant by reason of that event shall, subject to *section 1010*, be made to or on the person or persons carrying on the trade in the chargeable period related to that event (in this paragraph referred to as "*the relevant person or persons*"), and

(ii) the amount of any such allowance or charge shall be computed as if the relevant person or persons had at all times been carrying on the trade and as if everything done to or by the predecessors of the relevant person or persons in the carrying on of the trade had been done to or by the relevant person or persons.

(b) Notwithstanding *paragraph (a)*, in applying *section 288(4)* to any balancing charge to be made in accordance with that paragraph, the allowances made in respect of the machinery or plant for the year beginning on the 6th day of April, 1959, or for any earlier year of assessment shall not be taken to include allowances made to, or attributable to the shares of, persons who were not, either alone or in partnership with other persons, carrying on the trade at the beginning of the year beginning on the 6th day of April, 1959.

(2) (a) In this subsection, "*several trade*" has the meaning assigned to it by *section 1008*.

(b) In taxing the several trade of any partner in a partnership, the same allowances and charges shall be made in respect of machinery or plant used for the purposes of that trade, and belonging to one or more of the partners but not being partnership property, as would be made if the machinery or plant had at all material times belonged to all the partners and been partnership property and everything done by or to any of the partners in relation to the machinery or plant had been done by or to all the partners.

(3) Notwithstanding *section 288*, a sale or gift of machinery or plant used for the purposes of a trade carried on in partnership, being a sale or gift by one or more of the partners to one or more of the partners, shall not be treated as an event

giving rise to a balancing allowance or balancing charge if the machinery or plant continues to be used after the sale or gift for the purposes of that trade.

(4) References in *subsections (2)* and *(3)* to use for the purposes of a trade do not include references to use in pursuance of a letting by the partner or partners in question to the partnership or to use in consideration of the making to the partner or partners in question of any payment which may be deducted in computing under *section 1008(3)* the profits or gains of the trade.

Cross References

From Section 293

Section 288 Balancing allowances and balancing charges.

Section 1008 Separate assessment of partners.

Section 1010 Capital allowances and balancing charges in partnership cases.

294 Machinery or plant used partly for non-trading purposes

[ITA67 s276; FA90 s79]

Where an event occurs which gives rise or might give rise to a balancing allowance or balancing charge to or on any person and the machinery or plant concerned is machinery or plant which—

(a) has been used by that person for the purposes of a trade carried on by that person and, in relation to machinery or plant provided for use for the purposes of a trade on or after the 1st day of April, 1990, while so used, was used wholly and exclusively for those purposes, and

(b) has also been used for other purposes,

then, in determining the amount of the allowance or, as the case may be, the amount on which the charge is to be made, regard shall be had to all the relevant circumstances and in particular to the extent of the use for those other purposes, and there shall be made to or on that person an allowance of such an amount or a charge on such an amount, as the case may be, as may be just and reasonable.

295 Option in case of succession under will or intestacy

[ITA67 s278]

Where a person succeeds to a trade as a beneficiary under the will or on the intestacy of a deceased person who carried on that trade, the following provisions shall, if the beneficiary by notice in writing to the inspector so elects, apply in relation to any machinery or plant previously owned by the deceased person and used by the deceased person for the purposes of that trade:

(a) the reference in *section 313* to the price which the machinery or plant would have fetched if sold in the open market shall, in relation to the succession and any previous succession occurring on or after the death of the deceased, be deemed to be a reference to that price or the amount of the expenditure on the provision of the machinery or plant still unallowed immediately before the succession in question, whichever is the lower, and

(b) notwithstanding anything in that section, such balancing charge, if any, shall be made on the beneficiary on any event occurring after the succession as would have been made on the deceased if he or she had not died and had continued to own the machinery or plant and had done all such things and been allowed all such allowances in connection with the machinery or plant as were done by or allowed to the beneficiary or the successor on any previous succession mentioned in *paragraph (a)*.

Cross References

From Section 295

Section 313 Effect, in certain cases, of succession to trade, etc.

To Section 295

Section 555 Restriction of losses by reference to capital allowances and renewals allowances.

296 Balancing allowances and balancing charges: wear and tear allowances deemed to have been made in certain cases

[ITA67 s279; CTA76 s21(1) and Sch1 par32]

(1) In determining whether any, and if so what, balancing allowance or balancing charge is to be made to or on any person for any chargeable period in taxing a trade, there shall be deemed to have been made to that person, for every previous chargeable period in which the machinery or plant belonged to that person and which is a chargeable period to be taken into account for the purpose of this section, such wear and tear allowance or greater wear and tear allowance, if any, in respect of the machinery or plant as would have been made to that person if all the conditions specified in *subsection (3)* had been fulfilled in relation to every such previous chargeable period.

(2) There shall be taken into account for the purposes of this section every previous chargeable period in which the machinery or plant belonged to the person and—

(a) during which the machinery or plant was not used by the person for the purposes of the trade,

(b) during which the trade was not carried on by the person,

(c) during which the trade was carried on by the person in such circumstances that, otherwise than by virtue of Chapter I of Part XXV of the Income Tax Act, 1967, or Part V of the Corporation Tax Act, 1976, the full amount of the profits or gains of the trade was not liable to be charged to tax,

(d) for which the whole or a part of the tax chargeable in respect of the profits of the trade was not payable by virtue of Chapter II of Part XXV of the Income Tax Act, 1967, or

(e) for which the tax payable in respect of the profits of the trade was reduced by virtue of Chapter III or IV of Part XXV of the Income Tax Act, 1967, or Part IV of the Corporation Tax Act, 1976.

(3) The conditions referred to in *subsection (1)* are—

(a) that the trade had been carried on by the person in question since the date on which that person acquired the machinery or plant and had been so carried on by that person in such circumstances that the full amount of the profits or gains of the trade was liable to be charged to tax,

(b) that the trade had at no time consisted wholly or partly of exempted trading operations within the meaning of Chapter I of Part XXV of the Income Tax Act, 1967, or Part V of the Corporation Tax Act, 1976,

(c) that the machinery or plant had been used by that person solely for the purposes of the trade since that date, and

(d) that a proper claim had been duly made by that person for wear and tear allowance in respect of the machinery or plant for every relevant chargeable period.

(4) In the case of a company (within the meaning of *section 4(1)*), *subsection (3)(a)* shall not alter the periods which are to be taken as chargeable periods but, if during any time after the 5th day of April, 1976, and after the company acquired the machinery or

plant, the company has not been within the charge to corporation tax, any year of assessment or part of a year of assessment falling within that time shall be taken as a chargeable period as if it had been an accounting period of the company.

(5) Nothing in this section shall affect *section 288(4)*.

Cross References

From Section 296

Section 4 Interpretation of Corporation Tax Acts.

Section 288 Balancing allowances and balancing charges.

To Section 296

Schedule 18B Tonnage Tax

297 Subsidies towards wear and tear

[ITA67 s280; CTA76 s21(1) and Sch1 par33]

(1) Where—

(a) an event occurs which gives rise or might give rise to a balancing allowance or balancing charge to or on any person in respect of any machinery or plant provided or used by that person for the purposes of a trade, and

(b) any sums which—

(i) are in respect of, or take account of, the wear and tear to the machinery or plant occasioned by its use for the purposes of the trade, and

(ii) do not fall to be taken into account as that person's income or in computing the profits or gains of any trade carried on by that person,

have been paid, or are to be payable, to that person directly or indirectly,

then, in determining whether any and, if so, what balancing allowance or balancing charge is to be made to or on that person, there shall be deemed to have been made to that person for the chargeable period related to the event a wear and tear allowance in respect of the machinery or plant of an amount equal to the total amount of those sums.

(2) Nothing in this section shall affect *section 288(4)*.

Cross References

From Section 297

Section 288 Balancing allowances and balancing charges.

298 Allowances to lessors

[ITA67 s241(5), s252 and s281; CTA76 s21(1) and Sch1 par6 and par16; FA80 s17(3)]

(1) Where machinery or plant is let on such terms that the burden of the wear and tear of the machinery or plant falls directly on the lessor, the lessor shall be entitled, on making a claim to the inspector within 24 months after the end of the chargeable period, to—

(a) an initial allowance under *section 283*, and

(b) a wear and tear allowance under *section 284*,

in relation to the machinery or plant, equal to the amount which might have been allowed if during the period of the letting the machinery or plant were in use for the purposes of a trade carried on by the lessor.

(2) Where machinery or plant is let on such terms as are referred to in *subsection (1)*, the preceding provisions of this Chapter, in so far as they relate to balancing

allowances and balancing charges, shall apply in relation to the lessor as if the machinery or plant were, during the term of the letting, in use for the purposes of a trade carried on by the lessor.

Cross References

From Section 298

Section 283 Initial allowances.
Section 284 Wear and tear allowances.

To Section 298

Section 286A Wear and tear allowances for licences for public hire vehicles.
Section 300 Manner of making allowances and charges.
Section 692 Development expenditure: allowances and charges.

299 Allowances to lessees

[ITA67 s241(2) and s252; FA67 s11(3); FA71 s26(3); CTA76 s21(1) and Sch1 par6, par16, par53 and par60]

[(1) Subject to *subsection (3)*, where machinery or plant is let by means of a finance lease (within the meaning of *section 76D*) to a person, by whom a trade is carried on, on the terms of that person being bound to maintain the machinery or plant and deliver it over in good condition at the end of the lease, and if the burden of the wear and tear of the machinery or plant in fact falls directly on that person, then, for the purposes of *sections 283* and *284*, the capital expenditure on the provision of the machinery or plant shall be deemed to have been incurred by that person and not by any other person and the machinery or plant shall be deemed to belong to that person and not to any other person.][1]

(2) *Subsection (2)* of *section 285* shall not apply to qualifying machinery or plant (within the meaning of that section) which is let to a person on the terms mentioned in *subsection (1)*, unless the contract of letting provides that the person shall or may become the owner of the machinery or plant on the performance of the contract, and, where the contract so provides but without becoming the owner of the machinery or plant the person ceases to be entitled (otherwise than on his or her death) to the benefit of the contract in so far as it relates to the machinery or plant, *subsection (2)* of *section 285* shall be deemed not to have applied in relation to the machinery or plant and accordingly there shall be made [all such assessments or amendments of assessments][2] as may be appropriate.

[(3) (a) In this subsection "*lease payments*", "*lessee*" and "*lessor*" have, respectively, the same meanings as in *section 80A*.

(b) *Subsection (1)* shall only apply where—

(i) the lessor and lessee jointly elect, or

(ii) where the lessor is not a person within the charge to tax under Schedule D, the lessee elects,

that this section shall apply for the purposes of *sections 283* and *284* by giving notice in writing to the inspector on or before the specified return date for the chargeable period (within the meaning of [*section 959A*][3]) in a form approved by the Revenue Commissioners and containing such particulars relating to the lessor and lessee and in connection with the lease as may be specified in the approved form.

(c) Where this section applies—

(i) the amount to be deducted in computing the profits or gains to be charged to tax under Case 1 of Schedule D for any chargeable period of the lessee in relation to lease payments to be paid in respect of the finance lease, shall be the amount in respect of those lease payments which in accordance with generally accepted accounting practice would be deducted in a profit and loss account for that period, and accordingly, the aggregate amount (referred to in *subparagraph (ii)* as the "*aggregate deductible amount*") to be deducted in computing the profits or gains to be charged to tax under Case 1 of Schedule D for any chargeable period of the lessee in relation to lease payments to be paid in respect of and over the term of the lease, shall be the amount in relation to those lease payments which in accordance with generally accepted accounting practice would be deducted in the profit and loss account over the term of the lease, and

(ii) where capital expenditure deemed to have been incurred by the lessee would otherwise exceed the amount by which the aggregate amount of lease payments to be paid in respect of the lease exceeds the aggregate deductible amount, then the amount of capital expenditure on the provision of plant and machinery for the purposes of *subsection (1)* shall be deemed to be the amount by which the aggregate amount of the lease payments made in respect of and over the term of the lease exceeds the aggregate deductible amount.][4]

Amendments

[1] Substituted by FA10 s36(1)(a). Applies to chargeable periods (within the meaning of Part 9) commencing on, or after, 3 April 2010.

[2, 3] Substituted by FA12 sched4(part 2)(g).

[4] Inserted by FA10 s36(1)(b). Applies to chargeable periods (within the meaning of Part 9) commencing on, or after, 3 April 2010.

Cross References

From Section 299

Section 76D Computation of income from finance leases.
Section 80A Taxation of certain short-term leases plant and machinery.
Section 283 Initial allowances.
Section 284 Wear and tear allowances.
Section 285 Acceleration of wear and tear allowances.
Section 950 Interpretation (Part 41).

To Section 299

Section 285 Acceleration of wear and tear allowances.
Section 286A Wear and tear allowances for licences for public hire vehicles.
Section 317 Treatment of grants.

300 Manner of making allowances and charges

[ITA67 s241(1)(c), s251(1) and s282; CTA76 s21(1) and Sch1 par15, par34; FA96 s132(1) and Sch5 PtI par1(12)]

(1) Any allowance or charge made to or on any person under the preceding provisions of this Chapter shall, unless it is made under or by virtue of [*section 284(6)* or *298*][1], be made to or on that person in taxing such person's trade.

(2) Any initial allowance or wear and tear allowance made under or by virtue of *section 298(1)* or any balancing allowance made under or by virtue of *section 298(2)* shall be made by means of discharge or repayment of tax, and shall be available primarily against income from the letting of machinery or plant.

(3) Any balancing charge made under or by virtue of *section 298(2)* shall be made under Case IV of Schedule D.

[(4) Any wear and tear allowance made to any person under or by virtue of *section 284(6)* shall be made in charging that person's income under Case V of Schedule D.][2]

Amendments

[1] Substituted by FA00 s40(b)(i).

[2] Inserted by FA00 s40(b)(ii).

Cross References

From Section 300

Section 284 Wear and tear allowances.
Section 298 Allowances to lessors.

301 Application to professions, employments and offices

[ITA67 s241(10), s241A(3), s253 and s283(1); FA70 s14(4); CTA76 s21(1) and Sch1 par6; FA97 s22, s146(1) and Sch9 PtI par1(17)]

(1) The preceding provisions of this Chapter (other than *sections 283*, *285* and *286*) shall, with any necessary modifications, apply in relation to professions, employments and offices as they apply in relation to trades.

(2) *Sections 283* and *285* shall, with any necessary modifications, apply in relation to professions as they apply in relation to trades.

Cross References

From Section 301

Section 283 Initial allowances.
Section 285 Acceleration of wear and tear allowances.
Section 286 Increased wear and tear allowances for taxis and cars for short-term hire.

CHAPTER 3

Dredging: Initial Allowances and Annual Allowances

302 Interpretation (Chapter 3)

[ITA67 s294(6), (8) and (10); CTA76 s21(1) and Sch1 par43]

(1) In this Chapter—

"*dredging*" does not include things done otherwise than in the interests of navigation, but (subject to that) includes the removal of anything forming part of or projecting from the bed of the sea or of any inland water, by whatever means it is removed and whether or not at the time of removal it is wholly or partly above water, and also includes the widening of an inland waterway in the interests of navigation;

"*qualifying trade*" means any trade or undertaking which, or a part of which, complies with either of the following conditions—

(a) that it consists of the maintenance or improvement of the navigation of a harbour, estuary or waterway, or

(b) that it is for a purpose set out in *section 268(1)*,

but, where part only of a trade or undertaking complies with *paragraph (a)* or *(b)*, *section 303(5)* shall apply as if the part which does and the part which does not so comply were separate trades.

(2) For the purposes of this Chapter, the first relevant chargeable period, in relation to expenditure incurred by any person, shall be the chargeable period related to the following event or occasion—

(a) the incurring of the expenditure, or

(b) in the case of expenditure for which allowances are to be made by virtue of *section 303(6)*, the occasion when that person first both carries on the trade or part of the trade for the purposes of which the expenditure was incurred, and occupies for the purposes of that trade or part of the trade the dock or other premises in connection with which the expenditure was incurred.

Cross References

From Section 302

Section 268 Meaning of "industrial building or structure".
Section 303 Allowances for expenditure on dredging.

To Section 302

Section 692 Development expenditure: allowances and charges.

303 Allowances for expenditure on dredging

[ITA67 s294(1) to (5), (7), (9), (11) and (12); CTA76 s21(1) and Sch1 par43]

(1) (a) Subject to this section, where for the purposes of any qualifying trade carried on by a person the person incurs capital expenditure on dredging, and either the trade consists of the maintenance or improvement of the navigation of a harbour, estuary or waterway or the dredging is for the benefit of vessels coming to, leaving or using any dock or other premises occupied by the person for the purposes of the trade, then—

(i) an initial allowance equal to 10 per cent of the expenditure shall be made for the first relevant chargeable period to the person incurring the expenditure, and

(ii) writing-down allowances shall be made in respect of that expenditure to the person for the time being carrying on the trade during a writing-down period of 50 years beginning with the first relevant chargeable period; but, where a writing-down allowance is to be made for a year of assessment to such a person and such person is within the charge to income tax in respect of the trade for part only of that year, that part shall be treated as a separate chargeable period for the purposes of computing allowances under this section.

(b) This subsection shall not apply to any expenditure incurred before the 30th day of September, 1956.

(2) Where the trade is permanently discontinued in any chargeable period, then, for that chargeable period there shall be made to the person last carrying on the trade, in addition to any other allowance made to that person, an allowance equal to the amount of the expenditure less the allowances made in respect of the expenditure under *subsection (1)* for that and previous chargeable periods.

(3) For the purposes of this section, a trade shall not be treated by virtue of the Income Tax Acts as discontinued on a change in the persons engaged in carrying it on.

(4) Any allowance under this section shall be made in taxing the trade.

(5) Where expenditure is incurred partly for the purposes of a qualifying trade and partly for other purposes, *subsection (1)* shall apply to so much only of that expenditure as on a just apportionment ought fairly to be treated as incurred for the purposes of that trade.

(6) Where a person incurs capital expenditure for the purposes of a trade or part of a trade not yet carried on by the person but with a view to carrying it on, or incurs capital expenditure in connection with a dock or other premises not yet occupied by the person for the purposes of a qualifying trade but with a view to so occupying the dock or premises, *subsections (1)* to *(5)* shall apply as if the person had been carrying on the trade or part of the trade or occupying the dock or premises for the purposes of the qualifying trade, as the case may be, at the time when the expenditure was incurred.

(7) Where a person contributes a capital sum to expenditure on dredging incurred by another person, the person shall for the purposes of this section be treated as incurring capital expenditure on that dredging equal to the amount of the contribution, and the capital expenditure incurred by the other person on that dredging shall for those purposes be deemed to be reduced by the amount of the contribution.

(8) No allowance shall be made by virtue of this section in respect of any expenditure if for the same or any other chargeable period an allowance is or can be made in respect of that expenditure under *Chapter 1* of this Part.

(9) Notwithstanding any other provision of this section, in determining the allowances to be made under this section in any particular case, there shall be deemed to have been made in that case all such allowances (other than initial allowances) as could have been made if this section had always applied.

Cross References

To Section 303

Section 302 Interpretation (Chapter 3).

Section 307 Corporation tax: allowances and charges in taxing a trade.

CHAPTER 4

Miscellaneous and General

304 Income tax: allowances and charges in taxing a trade, etc

[ITA67 s241(3) and (4), s251(5), s252, s253, s254(5) and (6), s295, CTA76 s21(1) and Sch1 par6, par15, par16, par17 and par44]

(1) This section and *section 305* shall apply as respects allowances and charges which are to be made under this Part[…][1] for the purposes of income tax.

(2) Any claim by a person for an allowance under this Part in charging profits or gains of any description shall be included in the annual statement required to be delivered under the Income Tax Acts of those profits or gains, and the allowance shall be made as a deduction in charging those profits or gains.

(3) (a) A claim for an industrial building allowance under *section 271* shall be accompanied by a certificate signed by the claimant (which shall be deemed

to form part of the claim) stating that the expenditure was incurred on the construction of an industrial building or structure and giving such particulars as show that the allowance is to be made.

(b) A claim for an initial allowance under *section 283* shall be accompanied by a certificate signed by the claimant (which shall be deemed to form part of the claim) stating that the expenditure was incurred on new machinery or new plant and giving such particulars as show that the allowance is to be made.

(4) […][2] where full effect cannot be given in any year to any allowance to be made under this Part in taxing a trade[, or in charging profits or gains of any description, as the case may be,][3] owing to there being no profits or gains chargeable for that year, or owing to the profits or gains chargeable being less than the allowance, then, the allowance or part of the allowance to which effect has not been given, as the case may be, shall, for the purpose of making the assessment to income tax for the following year, be added to the amount of the allowances to be made under this Part in taxing the trade [or in charging the profits or gains, as the case may be,][4] for that following year, and be deemed to be part of those allowances, or, if there is no such allowance for that following year, be deemed to be the allowance for that following year, and so on for succeeding years.

(5) Any charge to be made under this Part on a person for any chargeable period in taxing the person's trade or in charging the person's income under Case V of Schedule D shall be made [by means of an assessment or, as the case may be, an amendment of an assessment on or in relation to the person for that period][5].

(6) (a) The preceding provisions of this section (other than *subsection (3)*) shall apply in relation to professions, employments and offices as they apply in relation to trades.

(b) *Subsection (3)(b)* shall, with any necessary modifications, apply in relation to professions as it applies in relation to trades.

[(c) *Subsection (4)* shall not apply as respects an allowance given by means of discharge or repayment of tax or in charging income under Case V of Schedule D.][6]

Amendments

[1] Deleted by FA00 s40(c)(i).

[2] Deleted by FA00 s40(c)(ii)(I).

[3] Inserted by FA00 s40(c)(ii)(II).

[4] Inserted by FA00 s40(c)(ii)(III).

[5] Substituted by FA13 s92 and sched1(part 2)(c).

[6] Inserted by FA00 s40(c)(iii).

Note:

FA13 s92 applies—

(a) in the case of a chargeable period (within the meaning of section 321(2)) which is an accounting period of a company, as respects chargeable periods that start on or after 1 January 2013, and

(b) in a case other than that referred to in paragraph (a), as respects the year of assessment (within the meaning of section 2(1)) 2013 and subsequent years of assessment.

Cross References

From Section 304

Section 271 Industrial building allowances.

Section 283 Initial allowances.

Section 305 Income tax: manner of granting, and effect of, allowances made by means of discharge or repayment of tax.

To Section 304

Section 531AU Capital allowances and losses.
Section 658 Farming: allowances for capital expenditure on construction of buildings and other works.
Section 659 Farming: allowances for capital expenditure on the construction of farm buildings, etc. for control of pollution.
Section 666 Deduction for increase in stock values.
Section 669E Application of Chapter 4 of Part 9.
Section 670 Mine development allowance.
Section 678 Allowance for machinery and plant.
Section 681 Allowance for mine rehabilitation expenditure.
Section 693 Exploration expenditure: allowances and charges.
Section 760 Capital sums: effect of death, winding up and partnership changes.
Section 762 Application of Chapter 4 of Part 9.
Section 765 Allowances for capital expenditure on scientific research.
Section 769 Relief for training of local staff before commencement of trading.
Section 769E Application of Chapter 4 of Part 9.
Schedule 17 Reorganisation into Companies of Trustee Savings Banks
Schedule 25B List of Specified Reliefs and Method of Determining Amount of Specified Relief Used in a Tax Year
Schedule 25C Determination of Amount of Relief to be Treated as Referable to Specified Reliefs as Respects Relief Carried Forward from Tax Year 2006 to Tax Year 2007

305 Income tax: manner of granting, and effect of, allowances made by means of discharge or repayment of tax

[ITA67 s254(1)(e), s296(1), (3), (4) and (5), F(MP)A68 s3(2) and Sch1; CTA76 s21(1) and Sch1 par17; FA80 s17(1)]

(1) (a) Where under this Part an allowance is to be made to a person for any year of assessment which is to be given by means of discharge or repayment of tax, [or in charging income under Case V of Schedule D][1] and is to be available or available primarily against a specified class of income, the amount of the allowance shall be deducted from or set off against the person's income of that class for that year of assessment and, if the amount to be allowed is greater than the amount of the person's income of that class for that year of assessment, the balance shall be deducted from or set off against the person's income of that class for the next year of assessment, and so on for subsequent years of assessment, and tax shall be discharged or repaid accordingly.

[(b) (i) Notwithstanding *paragraph (a)*, where an allowance referred to in that paragraph is available primarily against income of the specified class and the amount of the allowance is greater than the amount of the person's income of that class for the first-mentioned year of assessment (after deducting or setting off any allowances for earlier years), then the person may, by notice in writing given to the inspector not later than 2 years after the end of the year of assessment, elect that the excess shall be deducted from or set off—

(I) in the case of an individual—

(A) against the individual's other income for that year of [assessment,][2]

[(B) where the individual, or, being a husband or wife, the individual's spouse, is assessed to tax in accordance with *section 1017*, firstly, against the individual's other income for that year of assessment and, subsequently, against the income of the individual's husband or wife, as the case may be, for that year of assessment, or

(C) where the individual, or, the individual's civil partner, is assessed to tax in accordance with *section 1031C*, firstly, against the individual's other income for that year of assessment and, subsequently, against the income of the individual's civil partner, for that year of assessment,][3]

(II) in the case of a person other than an individual, against the person's other income for that year of assessment.

(ii) Where an election is made in accordance with *subparagraph (i)*, the excess shall be deducted from or set off against the income referred to in subclause (A) or (B) of clause (I) or in clause (II), as the case may be, and tax shall be discharged or repaid accordingly and only the balance, if any, of the amount of the excess over all the income referred to in subclause (A) or (B) of clause (I) or in clause (II), as the case may be, for that year of assessment shall be deducted from or set off against the person's income of the specified class for succeeding years.][4]

[(c) Notwithstanding any other provision of this subsection, where under this Part an allowance, the amount of which has been determined in accordance with *section 409E(3)(a)(i)*, is to be made to an individual for any year of assessment and the allowance is to be—

(a) made in charging the specified amount of rent (within the meaning of *section 409E*) under Case V of Schedule D for that year of assessment, and

(b) is to be available only in charging that specified amount of rent,

then—

(i) in charging income under Case V of Schedule D the amount of that allowance shall be deducted from or set off against that specified amount of rent, and

(ii) if the amount of the allowance which would have been made in charging income under Case V of Schedule D if *section 409E* had not been enacted is greater than that specified amount of rent, the excess shall—

(I) be added to the amount of the allowance to be made to the individual for the next year of assessment under *Chapter 1* of this Part in respect of the capital expenditure incurred on the construction or refurbishment of the specified building (within the meaning of *section 409E*) or the residue of that expenditure (within the meaning of *section 409E*), and be deemed to be part of the allowance to be so made for that next year, or

(II) if there is no such allowance for that next year, be deemed to be the allowance for that next year, and so on for subsequent years of assessment, and *section 409E(3)* shall apply in relation to the resulting allowance to be made for that next year or, as the case may be, for any subsequent year of assessment.][5]

(2) Any claim for an allowance mentioned in *subsection (1)* shall be made to and determined by the inspector, but any person aggrieved by any decision of the inspector on any such claim may, on giving notice in writing to the inspector within 21 days after the notification to that person of the decision, appeal to the Appeal Commissioners.

(3) The Appeal Commissioners shall hear and determine an appeal to them under *subsection (2)* as if it were an appeal against an assessment to income tax, and the provisions of the Income Tax Acts relating to the rehearing of an appeal and to the statement of a case for the opinion of the High Court on a point of law shall, with the necessary modifications, apply accordingly.

(4) Where any person, for the purpose of obtaining for that person or any other person any relief from or repayment of tax in respect of an allowance mentioned in *subsection (1)*, [...][6] makes any false statement or false representation, that person shall be liable to a penalty of [€3,000][7].

Amendments

[1] Inserted by FA00 s40(d)(i).

[2] Substituted by F(No.3)A11 sched1(56).

[3] Substituted by F(No.3)A11 sched1(57).

[4] Substituted by FA00 s40(d)(ii).

[5] Inserted by FA03 s13(2).

[6] Deleted by F(No.2)A08 sched5(part2)(1)(b)(i). The enactments specified in Schedule 5 are amended or repealed to the extent and manner specified in that Schedule and, unless the contrary is stated, shall come into effect after 24 December 2008.

[7] Substituted by F(No.2)A08 sched5(part2)(1)(b)(ii). The enactments specified in Schedule 5 are amended or repealed to the extent and manner specified in that Schedule and, unless the contrary is stated, shall come into effect after 24 December 2008.

Revenue Precedents

Where a claim is made to have excess capital allowances set off against other income in a year and there are still excess capital allowances remaining and they are carried forward can they go against other income? No, the excess carried forward can be set against income from that specified class only. IT953505

What is the order of set off if you have excess Case V capital allowances carried forward and also current year Case V capital allowances? Firstly use current year Case V capital allowances against Case V income and then Case V capital allowances coming forward. IT943516

What is the order of set off if you have losses carried forward and also current year Case V capital allowances? Firstly use current year Case V capital allowances against Case V income and then losses coming forward. GD97082

Cross References

From Section 305

Section 381 Right to repayment of tax by reference to losses.

Section 409E Income tax: ringfence on use of certain capital allowances on certain industrial buildings and other premises.

Section 1017 Assessment of husband in respect of income of both spouses.

To Section 305

Section 304 Income tax: allowances and charges in taxing a trade, etc.

Section 355 Disclaimer of capital allowances on holiday cottages, holiday apartments, etc.

Section 384 Relief under Case V for losses.
Section 403 Restriction on use of capital allowances for certain leased assets.
Section 404 Restriction on use of capital allowances for certain leased machinery or plant.
Section 405 Restriction on use of capital allowances on holiday cottages.
Section 406 Restriction on use of capital allowances on fixtures and fittings for furnished residential accommodation.
Section 408 Restriction on tax incentives on property investment.
Section 409A Income tax: restriction on use of capital allowances on certain industrial buildings and other premises.
Section 409B Income tax: restriction on use of capital allowances on certain hotels, etc.
Section 409D Restriction of reliefs where individual is not actively participating in certain trades.
Section 409E Income tax: ringfence on use of certain capital allowances on certain industrial buildings and other premises.
Section 687 Treatment of losses.
Section 1013 Limited partnerships.
Section 1061 Recovery of penalties.
Schedule 25B List of Specified Reliefs and Method of Determining Amount of Specified Relief Used in a Tax Year
Schedule 25C Determination of Amount of Relief to be Treated as Referable to Specified Reliefs as Respects Relief Carried Forward from Tax Year 2006 to Tax Year 2007

306 Meaning of basis period

[ITA67 s297; CTA76 s21(1) and Sch1 par45; FA90 s22(1)(b); FA96 s132(1) and Sch5 PtI par1(13)]

(1) In this Part, as it applies for income tax purposes, "*basis period*" has the meaning assigned to it by this section.

(2) (a) Subject to *paragraph (b)*, in the case of a person to whom an allowance or on whom a charge is to be made under Case I of Schedule D in charging the profits or gains of the person's trade or under Case V of Schedule D in charging income arising from rents or receipts in respect of premises or easements, the person's basis period for any year of assessment shall be the period on the profits or gains of which income tax for that year is to be finally computed under Case I of Schedule D in respect of the trade in question or, as the case may be, under Case V of Schedule D in respect of the income arising from rents or receipts in respect of premises or easements or, where by virtue of the Income Tax Acts the profits or gains or income of any other period are to be taken to be the profits or gains or income of that period, that other period.

(b) In the case of any trade—

(i) where 2 basis periods overlap, the period common to both shall be deemed for the purpose of this subsection to fall in the first basis period only,

(ii) where there is an interval between the end of the basis period for one year of assessment and the basis period for the next year of assessment, then, unless the second-mentioned year of assessment is the year of the permanent discontinuance of the trade, the interval shall be deemed to be part of the second basis period, and

(iii) where there is an interval between the end of the basis period for the year of assessment preceding that in which the trade is permanently discontinued and the basis period for the year in which the permanent discontinuance occurs, the interval shall be deemed to form part of the first basis period.

(3) (a) Any reference in *subsection (2)(b)* to the overlapping of 2 periods shall be construed as including a reference to the coincidence of 2 periods or to the inclusion of one period in another, and references to the period common to both of 2 periods shall be construed accordingly.

(b) Any reference in *subsection (2)(b)* to the permanent discontinuance of a trade shall be construed as including a reference to the occurring of any event which under the Income Tax Acts is to be treated as equivalent to the permanent discontinuance of a trade.

(4) Where an allowance or charge is to be made under *Chapter* 2 of this Part to or on a person carrying on or holding a profession, employment or office, *subsections (1)* to *(3)* shall apply as if the references to a trade included references to a profession, employment or office and as if the references to Case I of Schedule D included references to Case II of Schedule D and Schedule E.

(5) In the case of any other person to whom an allowance or on whom a charge is to be made under this Part, that other person's basis period for any year of assessment shall be the year of assessment itself.

Cross References

To Section 306

Section 284 Wear and tear allowances.
Section 658 Farming: allowances for capital expenditure on construction of buildings and other works.
Section 659 Farming: allowances for capital expenditure on the construction of farm buildings, etc. for control of pollution.
Section 678 Allowance for machinery and plant.
Section 681 Allowance for mine rehabilitation expenditure.
Section 693 Exploration expenditure: allowances and charges.

307 Corporation tax: allowances and charges in taxing a trade

[CTA76 s14(1) and (2)]

(1) In computing for the purposes of corporation tax a company's profits for any accounting period, there shall be made in accordance with this section and *section 308* all such deductions and additions as are required to give effect to the provisions of the Tax Acts which relate to allowances (including investment allowances) and charges in respect of capital expenditure, and *subsection (2)* and *section 308* shall apply as respects allowances and charges which are to be made under those provisions as they apply for the purposes of corporation tax.

(2) (a) Allowances and charges to be made for any accounting period in taxing a trade shall be given effect by treating the amount of any allowance as a trading expense of the trade in that period and by treating the amount on which any such charge is to be made as a trading receipt of the trade in that period.

(b) (i) A company to which an industrial building allowance under *section 271*, an initial allowance under *section 283* or an initial allowance under *section 303(1)(a)* is to be made in taxing a trade for any accounting period may disclaim the allowance by notice in writing given to the inspector not later than 2 years after the end of that period.

(ii) Any such notice shall be accompanied by a certificate signed by the person by whom the notice is given giving such particulars as show that the allowance would be made if no such notice were given and the amount which would be so made.

(iii) Where notice is given under *subparagraph (i)* for any accounting period, the inspector may make an assessment to corporation tax on the company for that accounting period on the amount or the further amount which in the inspector's opinion ought to be charged.

Case Law

Section 307(1) provides that in computing a company's profits for any period "there should be made" all deductions and additions as are required to give effect to the provisions of the Tax Acts which relate to allowances and charges for capital expenditure. The reference to "shall be made" is not mandatory in relation to allowances but is directive in that it requires the relevant allowances to be made on due claim by the company concerned. Elliss v BP Northern Ireland Refinery Ltd; Elliss v BP Tyne Tanker Co Ltd) 1987 STC 52

Cross References

From Section 307

Section 271 Industrial building allowances.
Section 283 Initial allowances.
Section 303 Allowances for expenditure on dredging.
Section 308 Corporation tax: manner of granting, and effect of, allowances made by means of discharge or repayment of tax.

To Section 307

Section 308A Assets transferred in course of scheme of reconstruction or amalgamation.
Section 400 Company reconstructions without change of ownership.
Section 402 Foreign currency: tax treatment of capital allowances and trading losses of a company.
Section 403 Restriction on use of capital allowances for certain leased assets.
Section 404 Restriction on use of capital allowances for certain leased machinery or plant.
Section 517 Payments to trustees of approved profit sharing scheme.
Section 631 Transfer of assets generally.
Section 633A Formation of SE or SCE by merger — leaving assets in the State.
Section 663 Corporation tax: restriction of relief for losses in farming or market gardening.
Section 666 Deduction for increase in stock values.
Section 693 Exploration expenditure: allowances and charges.
Section 766 Tax credit for research and development expenditure.
Schedule 16 Building Societies: Change of Status
Schedule 17 Reorganisation into Companies of Trustee Savings Banks
Schedule 18B Tonnage Tax
Schedule 22 Dividends Regarded as Paid Out of Profits Accumulated Before Given Date
Schedule 26 Replacement of Harbour Authorities by Port Companies

308 Corporation tax: manner of granting, and effect of, allowances made by means of discharge or repayment of tax

[CTA76 s14(3) to (8)]

(1) Where an allowance is to be made to a company for any accounting period which is to be given by discharge or repayment of tax or in charging its income under Case V of Schedule D, and is to be available primarily against a specified class of income, it shall, as far as may be, be given effect by deducting the amount of the allowance from any income of the period, being income of the specified class.

(2) Balancing charges for any accounting period which are not to be made in taxing a trade shall, notwithstanding any provision for them to be made under Case IV or V of Schedule D, as the case may be, be given effect by treating the amount on

which the charge is to be made as income of the same class as that against which the corresponding allowances are available or primarily available.

(3) Where an allowance which is to be made for any accounting period by means of discharge or repayment of tax, or in charging income under Case V of Schedule D, as the case may be, cannot be given full effect under *subsection (1)* in that period by reason of a want or deficiency of income of the relevant class, then, so long as the company remains within the charge to corporation tax, the amount unallowed shall be carried forward to the succeeding accounting period, except in so far as effect is given to it under *subsection (4)*, and the amount so carried forward shall be treated for the purposes of this section, including any further application of this subsection, as the amount of a corresponding allowance for that period.

(4) Where an allowance (other than an allowance carried forward from an earlier accounting period) which is to be made for any accounting period by means of discharge or repayment of tax, or in charging income under Case V of Schedule D, as the case may be, and which is available primarily against income of a specified class cannot be given full effect under *subsection (1)* in that period by reason of a want or deficiency of income of that class, the company may claim that effect shall be given to the allowance against the profits (of whatever description) of that accounting period and, if the company was then within the charge to corporation tax, of preceding accounting periods ending within the time specified in *subsection (5)*, and, subject to that subsection and to any relief for earlier allowances or for losses, the profits of any of those accounting periods shall then be treated as reduced by the amount unallowed under *subsection (1)*, or by so much of that amount as cannot be given effect under this subsection against profits of a later accounting period.

(5) The time referred to in *subsection (4)* is a time immediately preceding the accounting period first mentioned in *subsection (4)* equal in length to the accounting period for which the allowance is to be made; but the amount or aggregate amount of the reduction which may be made under that subsection in the profits of an accounting period falling partly before that time shall not, with the amount of any reduction to be made in those profits under any corresponding provision of the Corporation Tax Acts relating to losses, exceed a part of those profits proportionate to the part of the period falling within that time.

(6) A claim under *subsection (4)* shall be made by notice in writing given to the inspector not later that 2 years from the end of the accounting period in which an allowance cannot be given full effect under *subsection (1)*.

Cross References

To Section 308

Section 307 Corporation tax: allowances and charges in taxing a trade.
Section 308A Assets transferred in course of scheme of reconstruction or amalgamation.
Section 355 Disclaimer of capital allowances on holiday cottages, holiday apartments, etc.
Section 396B Relief for certain trading losses on a value basis.
Section 400 Company reconstructions without change of ownership.
Section 403 Restriction on use of capital allowances for certain leased assets.
Section 404 Restriction on use of capital allowances for certain leased machinery or plant.
Section 405 Restriction on use of capital allowances on holiday cottages.
Section 406 Restriction on use of capital allowances on fixtures and fittings for furnished residential accommodation.

Section 408 Restriction on tax incentives on property investment.
Section 421 Relation of group relief to other relief.
Section 517 Payments to trustees of approved profit sharing scheme.
Section 631 Transfer of assets generally.
Section 633A Formation of SE or SCE by merger – leaving assets in the State.
Section 644C Relief from corporation tax for losses from dealing in residential development land.
Section 663 Corporation tax: restriction of relief for losses in farming or market gardening.
Section 666 Deduction for increase in stock values.
Section 687 Treatment of losses.
Section 1013 Limited partnerships.
Section 1085 Corporation tax – late returns: restriction of certain claims for relief.
Schedule 16 Building Societies: Change of Status
Schedule 17 Reorganisation into Companies of Trustee Savings Banks
Schedule 18B Tonnage Tax
Schedule 26 Replacement of Harbour Authorities by Port Companies

308A Assets transferred in course of scheme of reconstruction or amalgamation

[(1) In this section "*scheme of reconstruction or amalgamation*" means a scheme for the reconstruction of any company or companies or the amalgamation of any 2 or more companies.

(2) Where—

(a) any scheme of reconstruction or amalgamation involves the transfer of the whole or part of the trade of a company (in this section referred to as the "*transferring company*") to another company (in this section referred to as the "*acquiring company*"),

(b) (i) the acquiring company is resident in the State at the time of the transfer, or the acquiring company uses the assets of the transferred trade for the purposes of a trade carried on by it in the State through a branch or agency immediately after that time, and

(ii) the transferring company is resident in the State at the time of the transfer, or the trade was carried on by it in the State through a branch or agency immediately before that time,

and

(c) the transferring company receives no part of the consideration for the transfer (otherwise than by the acquiring company taking over the whole or part of the liabilities of the trade),

then, subject to *subsection (4)*, *subsection (3)* shall apply in relation to the assets of the trade transferred by the transferring company.

(3) Where this subsection applies—

(a) the transfer shall not be treated as giving rise to any allowance or charge provided for by *section 307* or *308*, and

(b) there shall be made to or on the acquiring company in accordance with *sections 307* and *308* all such allowances and charges as would, if the transferring company had continued to carry on the trade and had continued to use the transferred assets for the purposes of the trade, have been made to or on the transferring company in respect of any assets transferred in the course of the transfer, and the amount of any such allowance or charge shall be computed as if the acquiring company had been carrying on the trade since the transferring company began to do so and as if everything done to or by the transferring company had been done to or by the acquiring company.

(4) *Subsection (3)* shall not apply as respects assets transferred in the course of a transfer if in consequence of the transfer, or a transaction of which the transfer is a part, the Corporation Tax Acts are to apply subject to *subsections (6)* to *(9)* of *section 400*.][1]

Amendments

[1] Inserted by FA10 s51(1). This section shall have effect in relation to assets transferred on or after 1 January 2010.

Cross References

From Section 308A

Section 307 Corporation tax: allowances and charges in taxing a trade.
Section 308 Corporation tax: manner of granting, and effect of, allowances made by means of discharge or repayment of tax.
Section 400 Company reconstructions without change of ownership.

309 Companies not resident in the State

[CTA76 s21(4)]

Where a company not resident in the State is within the charge to corporation tax in respect of one source of income and to income tax in respect of another source, then, in applying—

(a) this Part,
(b) *section 374*,
(c) *sections 658* and *660*,
(d) *sections 670* and *672* to *678*,
(e) *sections 764* and *765*,
(f) *section 769*, and
(g) any other provision of the Tax Acts relating to the making of allowances or charges under or in accordance with the provisions referred to in *paragraphs (a)* to *(f)*,

allowances relating to any source of income shall be given effect against income chargeable to the same tax as is chargeable on income from that source.

Cross References

From Section 309

Section 374 Capital allowances for cars costing over certain amount.
Section 658 Farming: allowances for capital expenditure on construction of buildings and other works.
Section 660 Farming: wear and tear allowances deemed to have been made in certain cases.
Section 670 Mine development allowance.
Section 672 Interpretation (sections 672 to 683).
Section 678 Allowance for machinery and plant.
Section 764 Deduction for revenue expenditure on scientific research.
Section 765 Allowances for capital expenditure on scientific research.
Section 769 Relief for training of local staff before commencement of trading.

310 Allowances in respect of certain contributions to capital expenditure of local authorities

[FA78 s26]

(1) In this section—

"*approved scheme*" means a scheme undertaken by a local authority with the approval of the Minister for the Environment and Local Government which has as its object or among its objects the treatment of trade effluents;

['*local authority*' means a local authority for the purposes of the Local Government Act 2001 (as amended by the *Local Government Reform Act 2014*);][1]

"*trade effluents*" means liquid or other matter discharged into public sewers from premises occupied for the purposes of a trade.

[(2) Where a person, for the purposes of a trade carried on or to be carried on by the person, contributes a capital sum to capital expenditure incurred by a local authority on or after 15 February 2001 on the provision of an asset to be used for the purposes of—

(a) an approved scheme, in so far as the scheme relates to the treatment of trade effluents, or

(b) the supply of water under an agreement in writing between the person and the local authority,

then, such allowances, if any, shall be made to the person under *section 272* or *284* as would have been made to the person if the capital sum contributed in the chargeable period or its basis period had been expenditure on the provision for the purposes of that trade of a similar asset and that asset had continued at all material times to be in use for the purposes of the trade.][2]

[(2A) Where, by virtue of *subsection (2)*, a person is entitled to an allowance under *section 284* then, for the purposes of determining the amount of wear and tear allowances to be made for any chargeable period or its basis period for the purposes of this section, *section 284* shall apply—

(a) as if the reference in *paragraph (aa)* of *subsection (2)* of that section to "20 per cent of the actual cost of the machinery or plant, including in that actual cost any expenditure in the nature of capital expenditure on the machinery or plant by means of renewal, improvement or reinstatement" were a reference to "20 per cent of the capital sum contributed in the chargeable period or its basis period", and

(b) as if the reference in *paragraph (ad)* of *subsection (2)* of that section to "12.5 per cent of the actual cost of the machinery or plant, including in that actual cost any expenditure in the nature of capital expenditure on the machinery or plant by means of renewal, improvement or reinstatement" were a reference to "12.5 per cent of the capital sum contributed in the chargeable period or its basis period".][3]

(3) The following provisions shall apply in relation to a transfer of a trade or part of a trade for the purposes of which a contribution referred to in *subsection (2)* was made:

(a) where the transfer is of the whole trade, allowances which, if the transfer had not taken place, would have been made to the transferor under *section 272* or *284* for chargeable periods ending after the date of the transfer shall be made to the transferee and shall not be made to the transferor;

(b) where the transfer is of part only of the trade, *paragraph (a)* shall apply in relation to so much of the allowance as is properly referable to the part of the trade transferred.

Amendments

[1] Substituted by LGRA14 sched2(part5).

[2] Substituted by FA01 s50(1)(b). With effect from 22 October 2001 per S.I. No. 471 of 2001.

[3] Substituted by FA03 s23(1)(b). This section applies as on and from 4 December 2002.

Cross References

From Section 310

Section 272 Writing-down allowances.

Section 284 Wear and tear allowances.

311 Apportionment of consideration and exchanges and surrenders of leasehold interests

[ITA67 s298; FA96 s132(1) and Sch5 PtI par1(14)]

(1) (a) Any reference in this Part to the sale of any property includes a reference to the sale of that property together with any other property and, where property is sold together with other property, so much of the net proceeds of the sale of the whole property as on a just apportionment is properly attributable to the first-mentioned property shall for the purposes of this Part be deemed to be the net proceeds of the sale of the first-mentioned property, and references to expenditure incurred on the provision or the purchase of property shall be construed accordingly.

(b) For the purposes of this subsection, all the property which is sold in pursuance of one bargain shall be deemed to be sold together, notwithstanding that separate prices are, or purport to be, agreed for separate items of that property or that there are, or purport to be, separate sales of separate items of that property.

(2) *Subsection (1)* shall, with the necessary modifications, apply in relation to other sale, insurance, salvage or compensation moneys as it applies in relation to the net proceeds of sales.

(3) This Part shall apply as if any reference in this Part to the sale of any property included a reference to the exchange of any property and, in the case of a leasehold interest, also included a reference to the surrender of that interest for valuable consideration, and any provisions of this Part referring to the sales shall apply accordingly with the necessary modifications and in particular with the modifications that references to the net proceeds of sale and to the price shall be taken to include references to the consideration for the exchange or surrender, and references to capital sums included in the price shall be taken to include references to so much of the consideration as would have been a capital sum if the consideration had taken the form of a money payment.

[(3A) For the purposes of *subsection (3)*, any transfer of property by a person to another person, pursuant to a Debt Settlement Arrangement or a Personal Insolvency Arrangement entered into under the Personal Insolvency Act 2012, whereby such property is held in trust for the creditors of the person making the transfer shall not, where that property is an industrial building or structure (within the meaning of *section 268*), be treated as an exchange of property.][1]

(4) This section shall, with the necessary modifications, apply in relation to *Chapter 1* of *Part 24* and *sections 764* and *765* as if that Chapter and those sections were contained in this Part.

Amendments

[1] Inserted by FA13 s100(1)(c). Applies on and from 27 March 2013.

Revenue Precedents

Where the contract for the purchase price of a property does not distinguish between the building element and the plant and machinery element can you apportion the purchase price? Yes, provide a professional valuation. IT963520

Cross References

From Section 311

Section 670 Mine development allowance.
Section 764 Deduction for revenue expenditure on scientific research.
Section 765 Allowances for capital expenditure on scientific research.

312 Special provisions as to certain sales

[ITA67 s299 other than subsection (4)(b)(iii); CTA76 s21(1) Sch1 par46; FA96 s132(1) and Sch5 PtI par1(15)]

(1) In this section, "*control*", in relation to a body corporate, means the power of a person to secure—

(a) by means of the holding of shares or the possession of voting power in or in relation to that or any other body corporate, or

(b) by virtue of any powers conferred by the articles of association or other document regulating that or any other body corporate,

that the affairs of the first-mentioned body corporate are conducted in accordance with the wishes of that person and, in relation to a partnership, means the right to a share of more than 50 per cent of the assets, or of more than 50 per cent of the income, of the partnership.

(2) (a) This section shall apply in relation to sales of any property where either—

(i) the buyer is a body of persons over whom the seller has control, or the seller is a body of persons over whom the buyer has control, or both the seller and the buyer are bodies of persons and some other person has control over both of them, or

(ii) it appears with respect to the sale, or with respect to transactions of which the sale is one, that the sole or main benefit which apart from this section might have been expected to accrue to the parties or any of them was the obtaining of an allowance under this Part or under *Chapter 1* of *Part 24* or *section 764* or *765*.

(b) References in this subsection to a body of persons include references to a partnership.

(3) Where the property is sold at a price other than the price it would have fetched if sold in the open market, then, subject to *subsections (4)* and *(5)*, the like consequences shall ensue for the purposes of the enactments mentioned in *subsection (2)*, in their application to the tax of all persons concerned, as would have ensued if the property had been sold for the price it would have fetched if sold in the open market.

(4) (a) Subject to *paragraph (b)*, where the sale is a sale of machinery or plant—

(i) no initial allowance shall be made to the buyer, and

(ii) subject to *subsection (5)*, if the price which the property would have fetched if sold in the open market is greater than the amount which, for the purpose of determining whether any, and if so, what, balancing charge should be made on the seller in respect of the property under *Chapter 2* of this Part, would be taken to be the amount of the capital expenditure incurred by the seller on the provision of the property, *subsection (3)* shall apply as if for each of the references to the price which the property would have fetched if sold in the open market there were substituted a reference to that amount.

(b) This subsection shall not apply in relation to a sale of machinery or plant which was never used if the business or part of the business of the seller was the manufacture or supply of machinery or plant of that class and the sale was effected in the ordinary course of the seller's business.

(5) (a) Subject to *subsection (6)*, where the sale is one to which *subsection (2)(a)(i)* applies and *subsection (2)(a)(ii)* does not apply, and the parties to the sale by notice in writing to the inspector so elect, the following provisions shall apply:

(i) *subsection (3)* shall apply as if for each of the references to the price which the property would have fetched if sold in the open market there were substituted a reference to that price or to the sum mentioned in *paragraph (b)*, whichever is the lower;

(ii) *subsection (4)(a)(ii)* shall not apply;

(iii) notwithstanding anything in the preceding provisions of this section, such balancing charge, if any, shall be made on the buyer on any event occurring after the date of the sale as would have been made on the seller if the seller had continued to own the property and had done all such things and been allowed all such allowances or deductions in connection with the property as were done by or allowed to the buyer.

(b) The sum referred to in *paragraph (a)(i)* is—

(i) in the case of an industrial building or structure, the residue of the expenditure on the construction of that building or structure immediately before the sale, computed in accordance with *section 277*, and

(ii) in the case of machinery or plant, the amount of the expenditure on the provision of the machinery or plant still unallowed immediately before the sale, computed in accordance with *section 292*.

(6) (a) An election under *subsection (5)(a)* may not be made if—

(i) any of the parties to the sale is not resident in the State at the time of the sale, and

(ii) the circumstances are not at that time such that an allowance or charge under this Part is to be or might be made to or on that party in consequence of the sale.

(b) Except where referred to in *paragraph (a)*, this section shall apply in relation to a sale notwithstanding that it is not fully applicable by reason of the non-residence of a party to the sale or otherwise.

Case Law

Section 312 applies open market value treatment in cases where it appears in relation to the sale of property the arrangement was designed to result in an amount of capital allowances that was greater than would normally be available. Barclays Mercantile Industrial v Melluish 1990 STC 314

Cross References

From Section 312

Section 277 Writing off of expenditure and meaning of "residue of expenditure".
Section 292 Meaning of "amount still unallowed".
Section 670 Mine development allowance.
Section 764 Deduction for revenue expenditure on scientific research.
Section 765 Allowances for capital expenditure on scientific research.

To Section 312

Section 289 Calculation of balancing allowances and balancing charges in certain cases.
Section 374 Capital allowances for cars costing over certain amount.
Section 380L Emissions-based limits for certain cars.
Section 555 Restriction of losses by reference to capital allowances and renewals allowances.
Section 669E Application of Chapter 4 of Part 9.
Section 693 Exploration expenditure: allowances and charges.
Section 762 Application of Chapter 4 of Part 9.
Section 768 Allowance for know-how.
Section 769E Application of Chapter 4 of Part 9.

313 Effect, in certain cases, of succession to trade, etc

[ITA67 s300; FA96 s132(2) and Sch5 PtII]

(1) Where a person succeeds to any trade or profession which until that time was carried on by another person and by virtue of *section 69* the trade or profession is to be treated as discontinued, any property which, immediately before the succession takes place, was in use for the purposes of the discontinued trade or profession and without being sold is, immediately after the succession takes place, in use for the purposes of the new trade or profession shall for the purposes of this Part be treated as if it had been sold to the successor when the succession takes place and as if the net proceeds of that sale had been the price which that property would have fetched if sold in the open market.

(2) Where, after the setting up and before the permanent discontinuance of a trade or profession which at any time is carried on in partnership anything is done for the purposes of that trade or profession, any allowance or charge which, if the trade or profession had at all times been carried on by one and the same person, would have been made to or on that person under this Part shall, subject to *section 1010*, be made to or on the person or persons from time to time carrying on that trade or profession (in this subsection referred to as "*the relevant person or persons*"), and the amount of any such allowance or charge shall be computed as if the relevant person or persons had at all times been carrying on the trade or profession and as if everything done to or by the predecessors of the relevant person or persons in the carrying on of that trade or profession had been done to or by the relevant person or persons.

(3) In relation to machinery or plant, this section shall apply subject to *Chapter 2* of this Part in so far as that Chapter relates to balancing allowances and balancing charges.

Cross References

From Section 313

Section 69 Changes of proprietorship.
Section 1010 Capital allowances and balancing charges in partnership cases.

To Section 313

Section 295 Option in case of succession under will or intestacy.
Section 374 Capital allowances for cars costing over certain amount.
Section 380L Emissions-based limits for certain cars.
Section 1010 Capital allowances and balancing charges in partnership cases.

314 Procedure on apportionment

[ITA67 s301; CTA76 s21(1) and Sch1 par47]

(1) Where under or by virtue of this Part any sum is to be apportioned and at the time of the apportionment it appears that it is material as respects the liability to tax (for whatever chargeable period) of 2 or more persons, any question which arises as to the manner in which the sum is to be apportioned shall be determined, for the purposes of the tax of all those persons, by the Appeal Commissioners in the like manner as if it were an appeal against an assessment to income tax under Schedule D, and the provisions of the Income Tax Acts relating to such an appeal shall apply accordingly with any necessary modifications, and all those persons shall be entitled to appear and be heard by the Appeal Commissioners or to make representations to them in writing.

(2) This section shall apply in relation to any determination for the purposes of this Part of the price which property would have fetched if sold in the open market as it applies in relation to apportionments.

315 Property used for purposes of "exempted trading operations"

[ITA67 s302; CTA76 s21(1) and Sch1 par48]

(1) Where an event occurs which gives rise, or would but for this section give rise, to a balancing allowance or balancing charge in respect of any property to or on a company in relation to which a certificate under section 374(2) of the Income Tax Act, 1967, or section 70(2) of the Corporation Tax Act, 1976, has been given, then, whether the certificate is still in force or not, this section shall apply.

(2) Where the property has been used by the company exclusively for the purposes of its exempted trading operations within the meaning of Chapter I of Part XXV of the Income Tax Act, 1967, or Part V of the Corporation Tax Act, 1976, no balancing allowance or balancing charge shall be made.

(3) Where the property has been used partly for the purposes of the company's exempted trading operations and partly for the purposes of its other trading operations, regard shall be had to all the relevant circumstances of the case and there shall be made to or on the company an allowance of such an amount, or, as the case may be, a charge on such an amount, as may be just and reasonable.

316 Interpretation of certain references to expenditure and time when expenditure is incurred

[ITA67 s241(9A), s251(2), s254(4)(a), s260, s261, s303(1), (2); CTA76 s21(1) and Sch1 par15, par17, par21 and par49; FA96 s132(1) and Sch5 PtI par1(12)(b)]

(1) References in this Part to capital expenditure and capital sums—

(a) in relation to the person incurring the expenditure or paying the sums, do not include any expenditure or sum allowed to be deducted in computing for the purposes of tax the profits or gains of a trade, profession, office or employment carried on or held by that person, and

(b) in relation to the person receiving the amounts expended or the sums in question, do not include references to any amounts or sums which are to be taken into account as receipts in computing the profits or gains of any trade, profession, office or employment carried on or held by that person, and do not include, in relation to any person referred to in *paragraphs (a)* and *(b)*, any expenditure or sum in the case of which a deduction of tax is to be or may be made under *section 237* or *238*.

(2) Any reference in this Part to the date on which expenditure is incurred shall be construed as a reference to the date when the sums in question become payable; but, for the purposes of *section 284*, this subsection shall apply only in respect of machinery and plant provided for use for the purposes of a trade on or after the 6th day of April 1996.

[(2A) For the purposes only of determining, in relation to a claim for an allowance under *Chapter 1* of this Part, whether and to what extent capital expenditure incurred on the construction (within the meaning of *section 270*) of:

(a) a building or structure in use for the purposes of the trade of hotel keeping, or

(b) a building or structure deemed to be a building or structure in use for such purposes by virtue of *section 268(3)*,

is incurred or not incurred on or before [31 July 2008][1], only such an amount of that capital expenditure as is properly attributable to work on the construction or refurbishment of the building or structure actually carried out on or before [31 July 2008][2] shall (notwithstanding *subsection (2)* and any other provision of the Tax Acts as to the time when any capital expenditure is or is to be treated as incurred) be treated as having been incurred on or before that date.][3]

[(2B) For the purposes only of determining, in relation to a claim for an allowance under this Part, whether and to what extent capital expenditure incurred on the construction or refurbishment of a building or structure referred to in *paragraph (a), (b), (c), (d), (e), (f), (g), (h)* or *(i)* of *section 270(4)* (as inserted by the Finance Act 2006) is incurred or not incurred in—

(a) (i) where *section 270(4)(i)* applies, the period from 1 January 2006 to 24 March 2007, and

(ii) in any other case, the period from 1 January 2006 to 31 December 2006,

(b) (i) where *section 270(4)(i)* applies, the period from 25 March 2007 to 31 December 2007, and

(ii) in any other case, the period from 1 January 2007 to 31 December 2007,

[…][4]

(c) the period from 1 January 2008 to [31 July 2008, or][5]

[(d) where *subsection (8)* of *section 270* applies in relation to a qualifying residential unit as is referred to in *subsection (4)(i)* of that section, the period from 1 May 2007 to 30 April 2010,][6]

only such an amount of that capital expenditure as is properly attributable to work on the construction or refurbishment of the building or structure actually carried out in such a period shall (notwithstanding *subsection (2)* and any other provision of the Tax Acts as to the time when any capital expenditure is or is to be treated as incurred) be treated as having been incurred in that period.][7]

[(2C) For the purposes only of determining, in relation to a claim for an allowance under this Part, whether and to what extent capital expenditure incurred on the construction or refurbishment of a building or structure referred to in [*paragraph (g), (i), (j), (l)* or *(n)* of *section 268(1)* is incurred or not incurred in any of the periods referred to in *paragraph (d)*, *(f)*, *(g)*, *(i)* or *(k)* of *section 268(9)*,][8] only such an amount of that capital expenditure as is properly attributable to work on the construction or refurbishment of the building or structure actually carried out in any such period shall (notwithstanding *subsection (2)* and any other provision of the Tax Acts as to the time when any capital expenditure is or is to be treated as incurred) be treated as having been incurred within that period.][9]

(3) For the purposes of *sections 271* and *283*, any expenditure incurred for the purposes of a trade by a person about to carry on the trade shall be treated as if it had been incurred by that person on the first day on which that person carries on the trade.

Amendments

[1, 2] Substituted by FA06 s26(1)(b)(i). With effect from 26 June 2006 as per S.I. No 322 of 2006.

[3] Inserted by FA04 s25(1)(d).

[4] Deleted by FA07 s28(1)(e)(i). Applies as respects capital expenditure incurred on or after 1 May 2007 under a contract or agreement for the construction, refurbishment or development of a qualifying residential unit which is entered into on or after that date.

[5] Substituted by FA07 s28(1)(e)(i). Applies as respects capital expenditure incurred on or after 1 May 2007 under a contract or agreement for the construction, refurbishment or development of a qualifying residential unit which is entered into on or after that date.

[6] Inserted by FA07 s28(1)(e)(ii). Applies as respects capital expenditure incurred on or after 1 May 2007 under a contract or agreement for the construction, refurbishment or development of a qualifying residential unit which is entered into on or after that date.

[7] Inserted by FA06 s26(1)(b)(ii). With effect from 26 June 2006 per S.I. No. 322 of 2006.

[8] Substituted by FA13 s31(1)(l). Comes into operation on such day or days as the Minister for Finance may by order or orders appoint and different days may be appointed for different purposes or for different provisions.

[9] Inserted by FA09 s8(e). This section is deemed to have come into force and takes effect as on and from 1 January 2009.

Cross References

From Section 316

Section 237 Annual payments payable wholly out of taxed income.
Section 238 Annual payments not payable out of taxed income.
Section 268 Meaning of "industrial building or structure".
Section 270 Meaning of "expenditure on construction of building or structure".
Section 271 Industrial building allowances.
Section 283 Initial allowances.
Section 284 Wear and tear allowances.

To Section 316

Section 268 Meaning of "industrial building or structure".
Section 321 Provisions of general application in relation to the making of allowances and charges.
Section 344 Capital allowances in relation to construction or refurbishment of certain multi-storey car parks.
Section 372C Accelerated capital allowances in relation to construction or refurbishment of certain industrial buildings or structures.
Section 372D Capital allowances in relation to construction or refurbishment of certain commercial premises.
Section 372M Accelerated capital allowances in relation to construction or refurbishment of certain industrial buildings or structures.
Section 372N Capital allowances in relation to construction or refurbishment of certain commercial buildings or structures.
Section 372V Capital allowances in relation to construction or refurbishment of certain park and ride facilities.
Section 372W Capital allowances in relation to construction or refurbishment of certain commercial premises.
Section 372AC Accelerated capital allowances in relation to construction or refurbishment of certain industrial buildings or structures.
Section 372AD Capital allowances in relation to construction or refurbishment of certain commercial premises.

Section 373 Interpretation (Part 11).
Section 693 Exploration expenditure: allowances and charges.
Section 695 Abandonment expenditure: allowances and loss relief.
Section 762 Application of Chapter 4 of Part 9.
Section 843 Capital allowances for buildings used for third level educational purposes.

317 Treatment of grants

[ITA67 s254(4)(b), s303(3), FA86 s52(1), FA87 s25; CTA76 s 21(1) and Sch1 par1, par17 and par49; FA93 s34(1)(a) and (b) and (3)]

(1) In this section—

"*food processing trade*" means a trade which consists of or includes the manufacture of processed food;

"*processed food*" means goods manufactured in the State in the course of a trade by a company, being goods which—

(a) are intended for human consumption as a food, and

(b) have been manufactured by a process involving the use of machinery or plant whereby the goods produced by the application of that process differ substantially in form and value from the materials to which the process has been applied and whereby, without prejudice to the generality of the foregoing, the process does not consist primarily of—

(i) the acceleration, retardation, alteration or application of a natural process, or

(ii) the application of methods of preservation, pasteurisation or any similar treatment;

"*qualifying machinery or plant*" means machinery or plant used solely in the course of a process of manufacture whereby processed food is produced.

(2) Subject to *subsection (3)*, expenditure shall not be regarded for any of the purposes of this Part, other than *sections 283* and *284*, as having been incurred by a person in so far as the expenditure has been or is to be met directly or indirectly—

(a) in relation to expenditure incurred before the 6th day of May, 1993, by the State, by any board established by statute or by any public or local authority, and

(b) in relation to expenditure incurred on or after the 6th day of May, 1993, by the State or by any person other than the first-mentioned person.

(3) (a) Subject to *paragraph (b)* and *subsection (4)*, where an allowance is to be made for the purposes of income tax or corporation tax, as the case may be, under *section 283* or *284* and the capital expenditure incurred on the provision of the machinery or plant in respect of which the allowance is to be made was incurred on or after the 29th day of January, 1986, the following provisions shall apply:

(i) expenditure shall not be regarded as having been incurred by a person in so far as the expenditure has been or is to be met directly or indirectly—

(I) in relation to expenditure incurred before the 6th day of May, 1993, by the State, by any board established by statute or by any public or local authority, and

(II) in relation to expenditure incurred on or after the 6th day of May, 1993, by the State or by any person other than the first-mentioned person, and

(ii) the actual cost of any machinery or plant to any person shall for the purposes of *section 284* be taken to be the amount of capital expenditure incurred on the provision of such machinery or plant less any expenditure referred to in *subparagraph (i)*.

(b) *Paragraph (a)* shall not apply in relation to any capital expenditure which is met or is to be met in the manner mentioned in *paragraph (a)(i)*—

(i) under the terms of an agreement finally approved on or before the 29th day of January, 1986, by a Department of State, any board established by statute or any public or local authority, or

(ii) under the terms of an agreement which—

(I) was the subject of negotiations which were in progress on the 29th day of January, 1986, with a Department of State, any board established by statute or any public or local authority, and

(II) was finally approved by such Department, board or authority not later than the 31st day of December, 1986.

(4) (a) *Subsection (3)* shall not apply where an allowance is to be made under *section 283* or *284* in taxing a food processing trade carried on by a company and the capital expenditure in respect of which the allowance is to be made was incurred by that company and was so incurred in respect of qualifying machinery or plant.

(b) The reference in *paragraph (a)* to expenditure incurred by a company shall not include any expenditure which it is deemed to have incurred in accordance with *section 299*.

Case Law

In McKinney (HMIT) v Hagan Caravans Manufacturing Ltd 1997 STC 1023 grants paid to a caravan site by the International Fund for Ireland did not qualify for capital allowances as they were met by "government or public or local authority"

In Cyril Lord Carpets v Schofiled 42 TC 637 capital expenditure which has been incurred and which was subsequently reimbursed by way of grant was held to have been met directly or indirectly by the person providing the grant.

In Stokes v Costain Property Investments Ltd 1984 STC 204 it was held that land development expenditure financed by a loan which was to be repaid on the satisfactory completion of the development agreement had been incurred by the developer and that the expenditure should not be regarded as having been met by a third party.

Revenue Precedents

Capital allowances for Industrial Buildings and Plant and Machinery are computed on a net of grant basis. In the event of a grant being repaid, may the grant be treated as expenditure incurred and qualifying for capital allowances? The grant repaid may be treated as expenditure incurred for the purposes of claiming capital allowances on industrial buildings, machinery and plant. The date on which the expenditure is incurred may be taken as the date when the grants are repaid. IT973003

Where a company is engaged in a food processing trade, as defined, and receives grants in respect of machinery and plant which it uses in that trade, the grants may only be excluded in respect of machinery and plant which is used solely in the course of manufacturing processed food and which is not used in any other process. IT943040

Cross References

From Section 317

Section 283 Initial allowances.

Section 284 Wear and tear allowances.

Section 299 Allowances to lessees.

To Section 317

Section 374 Capital allowances for cars costing over certain amount.
Section 693 Exploration expenditure: allowances and charges.
Section 695 Abandonment expenditure: allowances and loss relief.
Section 843 Capital allowances for buildings used for third level educational purposes.

318 Meaning of "sale, insurance, salvage or compensation moneys"

[ITA67 s304(1); CTA76 s21(1) and Sch1 par50; FA94 s24(c)]

In this Part, except where the context otherwise requires, "*sale, insurance, salvage or compensation moneys*", in relation to an event which gives rise or might give rise to a balancing allowance or a balancing charge to or on any person, means—

(a) where the event is a sale of any property, including the sale of a right to use or otherwise deal in machinery or plant consisting of computer software, the net proceeds to that person of the sale,

[(aa) as respects machinery or plant consisting of computer software or the right to use or otherwise deal with computer software, where the event is the grant of a right to use or otherwise deal with the whole or part of that machinery or plant, the consideration in money or money's worth received by that person for the grant of the right,][1]

(b) where the event is the demolition or destruction of any property, the net amount received by that person for the remains of the property, together with any insurance moneys received by that person in respect of the demolition or destruction and any other compensation of any description received by that person in respect of the demolition or destruction, in so far as that compensation consists of capital sums,

(c) as respects machinery or plant, where the event is the permanent loss of the machinery or plant otherwise than in consequence of its demolition or destruction, any insurance moneys received by that person in respect of any loss and any other compensation of any description received by that person in respect of that loss, in so far as that compensation consists of capital sums,[…][2]

(d) where the event is that a building or structure ceases altogether to be used, any compensation of any description received by that person in respect of that event, in so far as that compensation consists of capital [sums, and][3]

[(e) where the event is a cessation referred to in *section 274(2A)(b)*, the aggregate of—

(i) the residue of expenditure (within the meaning of *section 277*) incurred on the construction or refurbishment of the building or structure immediately before that event, and

(ii) the allowances made under Chapter 1 of this Part in respect of the capital expenditure incurred on the construction or refurbishment of the building or structure.][4]

Amendments

[1] Inserted by FA00 s41(1)(b). This section shall apply as on and from 29 February 2000.

[2] Deleted by FA06 s39(1)(b)(i). Applies in relation to a building or structure which is first used on or after 1 January 2006.

[3] Substituted by FA06 s39(1)(b)(ii). Applies in relation to a building or structure which is first used on or after 1 January 2006.

[4] Inserted by FA06 s39(1)(b)(iii). Applies in relation to a building or structure which – (a) is first used on or after 1 January 2006, or (b) where capital expenditure on the refurbishment of the building or structure is incurred, is, subsequent to the incurring of that expenditure, first used on or after 1 January 2006.

Cross References

From Section 318

Section 274 Balancing allowances and balancing charges.

Section 277 Writing off of expenditure and meaning of "residue of expenditure".

To Section 318

Section 289 Calculation of balancing allowances and balancing charges in certain cases.

Section 353 Capital allowances in relation to construction or refurbishment of certain commercial premises.

Section 693 Exploration expenditure: allowances and charges.

319 Adjustment of allowances by reference to value-added tax

[FA75 s29; FA97 s20(14)]

(1) In computing any deduction, allowance or relief for the purposes of—

(a) this Part,

(b) *sections 658* and *659*,

(c) *Chapter 1* of *Part 24*, or

(d) *sections 764*, *765* and *769*,

the cost to a person of any machinery or plant, or the amount of any expenditure incurred by a person, shall not take account of any amount included in such cost or expenditure for value-added tax in respect of which the person may claim—

(i) a deduction under Chapter 1 of Part 8 of the Value-Added Tax Consolidation Act 2010, or

(ii) a refund of value-added tax under an order under section 103 of that Act.

(2) In calculating for the purposes of this Part the amount of sale, insurance, salvage or compensation moneys to be taken into account in computing a balancing allowance or balancing charge to be made to or on a person, no account shall be taken of the amount of value-added tax (if any) chargeable to the person in respect of those moneys.

Cross References

From Section 319

Section 658 Farming: allowances for capital expenditure on construction of buildings and other works.

Section 659 Farming: allowances for capital expenditure on the construction of farm buildings, etc. for control of pollution.

Section 670 Mine development allowance.

Section 764 Deduction for revenue expenditure on scientific research.

Section 765 Allowances for capital expenditure on scientific research.

Section 769 Relief for training of local staff before commencement of trading.

To Section 319

Section 693 Exploration expenditure: allowances and charges.

320 Other interpretation (Part 9)

[ITA67 s254(1)(c), s255(6) and s304(1) to (6); CTA76 s21(1) and Sch1 par17 and par50; FA97 s146(1) and Sch9 PtI par1(20)]

(1) In this Part, except where the context otherwise requires—

"*income*" includes any amount on which a charge to tax is authorised to be made under this Part;

"*lease*" includes an agreement for a lease where the term to be covered by the lease has begun, and any tenancy, but does not include a mortgage, and "*lessee*", "*lessor*" and "*leasehold interest*" shall be construed accordingly.

(2) Any reference in this Part to any building, structure, machinery or plant shall be construed as including a reference to a part of any building, structure, machinery or plant except, in relation to a building or structure, where the reference is comprised in a reference to the whole of a building or structure.

(3) This Part shall apply in relation to a share in machinery or plant as it applies in relation to a part of machinery or plant and, for the purposes of this Part, a share in machinery or plant shall be deemed to be used for the purposes of a trade only so long as the machinery or plant is used for the purposes of the trade.

(4) Any reference in this Part to the time of any sale shall be construed as a reference to the time of completion or the time when possession is given, whichever is the earlier.

(5) Any reference in this Part to the setting up or permanent discontinuance of a trade includes, except where the contrary is expressly provided, a reference to the occurring of any event which under any provision of the Income Tax Acts is to be treated as equivalent to the setting up or permanent discontinuance of a trade.

(6) Any reference in this Part to an allowance made includes a reference to an allowance which would be made but for an insufficiency of profits or gains, or other income, against which to make the allowance.

Cross References

From Section 320

Section 320 Other interpretation (Part 9).

To Section 320

Section 80A Taxation of certain short-term leases plant and machinery.
Section 267O Treatment of credit return.
Section 267P Treatment of credit transaction.
Section 267S Treatment of certificate owner.
Section 320 Other interpretation (Part 9).
Section 401 Change in ownership of company: disallowance of trading losses.
Section 428 Exclusion of double allowances, etc.
Section 693 Exploration expenditure: allowances and charges.
Section 695 Abandonment expenditure: allowances and loss relief.
Schedule 17 Reorganisation into Companies of Trustee Savings Banks
Schedule 22 Dividends Regarded as Paid Out of Profits Accumulated Before Given Date
Schedule 26 Replacement of Harbour Authorities by Port Companies
Schedule 32 Transitional Provisions

321 Provisions of general application in relation to the making of allowances and charges

[CTA76 Sch1 par1, 2, 3; FA97 s20(4)]

(1) *Subsections (2)* to *(7)* shall apply for the interpretation of—

(a) this Part,

(b) *section 374*,

(c) *sections 658* to *660*,

(d) *Chapter 1* of *Part 24*,

(e) *sections 764* and *765*,

(f) *section 769*, and

(g) any other provision of the Tax Acts relating to the making of allowances or charges under or in accordance with the provisions referred to in *paragraphs (a)* to *(f)*.

(2) "*Chargeable period*" means an accounting period of a company or a year of assessment, and—

(a) a reference to a chargeable period or its basis period is a reference to the chargeable period if it is an accounting period and to the basis period for it if it is a year of assessment;

(b) a reference to a chargeable period related to expenditure, or a sale or other event, is a reference to the chargeable period in which, or to that in the basis period for which, the expenditure is incurred or the sale or other event takes place, and means the latter only if the chargeable period is a year of assessment.

[(2A) Subject to *section 316*, references to expenditure in relation to an asset—

(a) include expenditure on labour costs including emoluments paid to employees of the company, and

(b) do not include interest payable,

which for accounting purposes is taken into account by the company in determining the value of the asset.][1]

(3) References to tax for a chargeable period shall be construed in relation to corporation tax as referring to the tax for any financial year which is chargeable in respect of that period.

(4) A reference to allowances or charges being made in taxing a trade is a reference to their being made in computing the trading income for corporation tax or in charging the profits or gains of the trade to income tax.

(5) (a) Where it is provided that writing-down allowances shall be made in respect of any expenditure during a writing-down period of a specified length, there shall for any chargeable period wholly or partly comprised in the writing-down period be made an allowance equal to the appropriate fraction of the expenditure and, subject to any provision to the contrary, the appropriate fraction shall be such fraction of the writing-down period as falls within the chargeable period.

(b) Notwithstanding *paragraph (a)*, the aggregate amount of the writing-down allowances made, whether to the same or to different persons, together with the amount of any initial allowance (but not of any investment allowance), shall not exceed the amount of the expenditure.

(6) Where the reference is partly to years of assessment before the year 1976–77—

(a) a writing-down allowance includes an annual allowance, and

(b) an allowance on account of wear and tear of machinery or plant includes a deduction on account of wear and tear of machinery or plant,

in the sense which in the context those expressions had immediately before the commencement of the Corporation Tax Act, 1976.

(7) Where any enactment referred to in *subsection (1)* provides for an amount of a writing-down allowance or an allowance on account of wear and tear of machinery or plant to be determined by a fraction or percentage, specified numerically, of any expenditure or other sum, or by reference to a percentage determined or deemed to be determined for a chargeable period of one year, then for a chargeable period of less than a year the fraction or percentage shall be proportionately reduced.

(8) Except where the context otherwise requires, in any provision of the Income Tax Acts not referred to in *subsection (1)* any reference to an allowance or charge for a year of assessment under a provision referred to in that subsection shall include the like allowance or charge for an accounting period of a company, and any reference to the making of an allowance or charge in charging profits or gains of a trade shall be construed as a reference to making the allowance in taxing a trade.

(9) Any provision of the Income Tax Acts whereby, for the purposes of—

(a) this Part,

(b) *section 670*,

(c) *section 764* or *765*,

(d) *section 769*, or

(e) any provision of the Income Tax Acts relating to the making of allowances or charges under or in accordance with the provisions referred to in *paragraphs (a)* to *(d)*,

a trade is or is not to be treated as permanently discontinued or a new trade as set up and commenced shall apply in the like manner in the case of a trade so treated by virtue of the Corporation Tax Acts.

[(10) Where but for the deletion of *sections 445* and *446*, an allowance or charge would be made to or on a company for any chargeable period under this Part then, notwithstanding that those sections have been deleted, that allowance or charge shall be made to or on the company and, accordingly this Part shall apply with any modifications necessary to give effect to this subsection.][2]

Amendments

[1] Inserted by FA05 s48(1)(e). This section applies as respects any period of account beginning on or after 1 January 2005.

[2] Inserted by FA12 sched1(12).

Cross References

From Section 321

Section 316 Interpretation of certain references to expenditure and time when expenditure is incurred.
Section 374 Capital allowances for cars costing over certain amount.
Section 658 Farming: allowances for capital expenditure on construction of buildings and other works.
Section 660 Farming: wear and tear allowances deemed to have been made in certain cases.
Section 670 Mine development allowance.
Section 764 Deduction for revenue expenditure on scientific research.
Section 765 Allowances for capital expenditure on scientific research.
Section 769 Relief for training of local staff before commencement of trading.

To Section 321

Section 55 Taxation of strips of securities.
Section 81A Restriction of deductions for employee benefit contributions.
Section 88A Double deduction in respect of certain emoluments.
Section 95A Change of basis of computation of profits or gains of a trade or profession.
Section 97 Computational rules and allowable deductions.
Section 130 Matters to be treated as distributions.
Section 231 Profits or gains from stallion fees.
Section 232 Profits from occupation of certain woodlands.
Section 233 Stud greyhound service fees.
Section 234 Certain income derived from patent royalties.
Section 246A Interest in respect of wholesale debt instruments.
Section 248A Restriction of relief in respect of loans applied in acquiring interest in companies and partnerships.
Section 271 Industrial building allowances.

Section 274 Balancing allowances and balancing charges.
Section 372AM Grant of certain certificates and guidelines, qualifying and special qualifying premises.
Section 403 Restriction on use of capital allowances for certain leased assets.
Section 404 Restriction on use of capital allowances for certain leased machinery or plant.
Section 482 Relief for expenditure on significant buildings and gardens.
Section 530 Interpretation (Chapter 2).
Section 531 Payments to subcontractors in certain industries.
Section 539 Disposals in cases of hire purchase and similar transactions.
Section 562 Contingent liabilities.
Section 658 Farming: allowances for capital expenditure on construction of buildings and other works.
Section 659 Farming: allowances for capital expenditure on the construction of farm buildings, etc. for control of pollution.
Section 665 Interpretation (Chapter 2).
Section 693 Exploration expenditure: allowances and charges.
Section 730H Interpretation and application.
Section 734 Taxation of collective investment undertakings.
Section 745 Charge to income tax or corporation tax of offshore income gain.
Section 747B Interpretation and application.
Section 751B Exchange of Irish Government bonds.
Section 774 Certain approved schemes: exemptions and reliefs.
Section 787J Allowance to employer.
Section 835A Interpretation.
Section 865 Repayment of tax.
Section 891A Returns of interest paid to non-residents.
Section 894 Returns of certain information by third parties.
Section 895 Returns in relation to foreign accounts.
Section 896 Returns in relation to certain offshore products.
Section 950 Interpretation (Part 41).
Section 1080 Interest on overdue income tax, corporation tax and capital gains tax.
Section 1084 Surcharge for late returns.
Schedule 32 Transitional Provisions

PART 10

Income Tax and Corporation Tax: Reliefs for Renewal and Improvement of Certain Urban Areas, Certain Resort Areas and Certain Islands

CHAPTER 1

Custom House Docks Area

322 Interpretation (Chapter 1)

[FA86 s41; FA87 s27(1)(b) and (2); FA94 s36(c) and (d); FA95 s32(1)(a) and s33]

(1) In this Chapter, but subject to *subsection (2)*—

"*the Custom House Docks Area*" means the area described in *paragraph 2* of *Schedule 5*;

["'*the specified period*' means the period commencing on the 25th day of January, 1988, and ending on—

(a) the 24th day of January, 1999, for the purposes of section 324,

(b) the 31st day of December, 1999, for the purposes of sections 325 to 328, and

(c) the 31st day of December, 1999, for the purposes of section 323; but where, in relation to the construction of a qualifying premises within the meaning of that section, at least 51 per cent of the total capital expenditure which is incurred on the construction of the premises is incurred before the 1st day of January, 2000, the reference in this paragraph to the 31st day of December, 1999, shall be construed as a reference to the 30th day of June, 2000."][1]

(2) For the purposes of this Chapter, the Minister for Finance, after consultation with the Minister for the Environment and Local Government, may by order direct that—

(a) the definition of "*the Custom House Docks Area*" shall include such area or areas described in the order which but for the order would not be included in that definition, and

[(b) as respects any such area so described, the definition of "*the specified period*" shall be construed as a reference to such period as shall be specified in the order in relation to that area; but no such period specified in the order shall commence before the 26th day of January, 1994, or end after—

(i) the 24th day of January, 1999, for the purposes of *section 324*,

(ii) the 31st day of December, 1999, for the purposes of *sections 325* to *328*, and

(iii) the 31st day of December, 1999, for the purposes of *section 323*; but where, in relation to the construction of a qualifying premises within the meaning of that section, at least 51 per cent of the total capital expenditure which is incurred on the construction of the premises is incurred before the 1st day of January, 2000, the reference in this subparagraph to the 31st day of December, 1999, shall be construed as a reference to the 30th day of June, 2000,][2]

and, where the Minister for Finance so orders, the definition of "*the Custom House Docks Area*" shall be deemed to include that area or those areas and the definition of "*the specified period*" shall be construed as a reference to the period specified in the order.

(3) The Minister for Finance may make orders for the purpose of this section and any order made under this section shall be laid before Dáil Éireann as soon as may be after it is made and, if a resolution annulling the order is passed by Dáil Éireann within the next 21 days on which Dáil Éireann has sat after the order is laid before it, the order shall be annulled accordingly, but without prejudice to the validity of anything previously done thereunder.

(4) *Schedule 5* shall apply for the purposes of supplementing this Chapter.

Amendments

[1] Substituted by URA98 s20(1)(a)(i). With effect from 5 January 2000 per S.I. 465 of 1999.

[2] Substituted by URA98 s20(1)(a)(ii). With effect from 5 January 2000 per S.I. 465 of 1999.

Cross References

From Section 322

Section 323 Capital allowances in relation to construction of certain commercial premises.
Section 324 Double rent allowance in respect of rent paid for certain business premises.
Section 325 Rented residential accommodation: deduction for certain expenditure on construction.
Section 328 Residential accommodation: allowance to owner-occupiers in respect of certain expenditure on construction or refurbishment.
Schedule 5 Description of Custom House Docks Area

To Section 322

Section 250A Restriction of relief to individuals in respect of loans applied in acquiring interest in companies.
Section 270 Meaning of "expenditure on construction of building or structure".
Section 324 Double rent allowance in respect of rent paid for certain business premises.
Section 409A Income tax: restriction on use of capital allowances on certain industrial buildings and other premises.
Section 409B Income tax: restriction on use of capital allowances on certain hotels, etc.
Section 409E Income tax: ringfence on use of certain capital allowances on certain industrial buildings and other premises.
Section 446 Certain trading operations carried on in Custom House Docks Area.
Schedule 5 Description of Custom House Docks Area

323 Capital allowances in relation to construction of certain commercial premises

[FA86 s42(1), (2), proviso to (4), and (7); FA92 s29(b)(ii); FA93 s30(1)(a)(ii); FA95 s32(1)(b)]

(1) In this section, "*qualifying premises*" means a building or structure the site of which is wholly within the Custom House Docks Area and which—

(a) apart from this section is not an industrial building or structure within the meaning of *section 268(1)*, and

(b) (i) is in use for the purposes of a trade or profession, or

(ii) whether or not it is so used, is let on bona fide commercial terms for such consideration as might be expected to be paid in a letting of the building or structure negotiated on an arm's length basis,

but does not include any building or structure in use as or as part of a dwelling house.

(2) (a) Subject to *subsections (3)* to *(5)*, the provisions of the Tax Acts relating to the making of allowances or charges in respect of capital expenditure incurred on the construction of an industrial building or structure shall, notwithstanding anything to the contrary in those provisions, apply—

(i) as if a qualifying premises were, at all times at which it is a qualifying premises, a building or structure in respect of which an allowance is to be made for the purposes of income tax or corporation tax, as the case may be, under *Chapter 1* of *Part 9* by reason of its use for a purpose specified in *section 268(1)(a)*, and

(ii) where any activity carried on in the qualifying premises is not a trade, as if it were a trade.

(b) An allowance shall be given by virtue of this subsection in respect of any capital expenditure incurred on the construction of a qualifying premises only in so far as that expenditure is incurred in the specified period.

(3) (a) For the purposes of the application, by *subsection (2)*, of *sections 271* and *273* in relation to capital expenditure incurred in the specified period on the construction of a qualifying premises—

(i) *section 271* shall apply as if—

(I) in *subsection (1)* of that section the definition of "*industrial development agency*" were deleted,

(II) in *subsection (2)(a)(i)* of that section "to which *subsection (3)* applies" were deleted,

(III) *subsections (3)* and *(5)* of that section were deleted, and

(IV) the following subsection were substituted for *subsection (4)* of that section:

"(4) An industrial building allowance shall be of an amount equal to 50 per cent of the capital expenditure mentioned in *subsection (2)*.",

and

(ii) *section 273* shall apply as if—

(I) in *subsection (1)* of that section the definition of "*industrial development agency*" were deleted, and

(II) *subsections (2)(b)* and *(3)* to *(7)* of that section were deleted.

[…][1]

(4) Notwithstanding *section 274(1)*, no balancing charge shall be made in relation to a qualifying premises by reason of any of the events specified in that section which occurs—

(a) more than 13 years after the qualifying premises was first used, or

(b) in a case where *section 276* applies, more than 13 years after the capital expenditure on refurbishment of the qualifying premises was incurred.

(5) For the purposes only of determining, in relation to a claim for an allowance by virtue of *subsection (2)*, whether and to what extent capital expenditure incurred on the construction of a qualifying premises is incurred in the specified period, only such an amount of that capital expenditure as is determined by the inspector, according to the best of the inspector's knowledge and judgment, to be properly attributable to work on the construction of the premises actually carried out during the specified period shall (notwithstanding any other provision of the Tax Acts as to the time when any capital expenditure is or is to be treated as incurred) be treated as having been incurred in that period, and any amount which by virtue of this subsection is determined by the inspector may be amended by the Appeal Commissioners or by the Circuit Court on the hearing or the rehearing of an appeal against that determination.

Amendments

[1] Deleted by URA98 s20(1)(b). With effect from 5 January 2000 per S.I. 465 of 1999.

Cross References

From Section 323

Section 268 Meaning of "industrial building or structure".
Section 271 Industrial building allowances.
Section 273 Acceleration of writing-down allowances in respect of certain expenditure on certain industrial buildings or structures.
Section 274 Balancing allowances and balancing charges.
Section 276 Application of sections 272 and 274 in relation to capital expenditure on refurbishment.

To Section 323

Section 322 Interpretation (Chapter 1).
Section 324 Double rent allowance in respect of rent paid for certain business premises.
Schedule 25B List of Specified Reliefs and Method of Determining Amount of Specified Relief Used in a Tax Year

324 Double rent allowance in respect of rent paid for certain business premises

[FA86 s45(1)(a) and (c) and (2) (apart from paragraph (a) of 1st proviso, and 2nd proviso thereto); FA90 s32 and s33(1) and (2)(a); FA91 s21; FA92 s29(d)(ii); FA93 s30(1)(c) and (2)(b); FA94 s35(1)(d) and (2)(c); FA96 s131; FA97 s27]

(1) (a) In this section—

"*lease*", "*lessee*", "*lessor*" and "*rent*" have the same meanings respectively as in *Chapter 8* of *Part 4*;

"*market value*", in relation to a building or structure, means the price which the unencumbered fee simple of the building or structure would fetch if sold in the open market in such manner and subject to such conditions as might reasonably be calculated to obtain for the vendor the best price for the building or structure, less the part of that price which would be attributable to the acquisition of, or of rights in or over, the land on which the building or structure is constructed;

"*qualifying lease*" means, subject to *subsection (4)*, a lease in respect of a qualifying premises granted in the specified period, or within the period of 2 years from the day next after the end of the specified period, on bona fide commercial terms by a lessor to a lessee not connected with the lessor, or with any other person entitled to a rent in respect of the qualifying premises, whether under that lease or any other lease;

"*qualifying premises*" means a building or structure the site of which is wholly within the Custom House Docks Area and—

(i) (I) which is an industrial building or structure within the meaning of *section 268(1)*, and in respect of which capital expenditure is incurred in the specified period for which an allowance is to be made for the purposes of income tax or corporation tax, as the case may be, under *Chapter 1* of *Part 9*, or

(II) in respect of which an allowance is to be made, or, as respects rent payable under a qualifying lease entered into on or after the 18th day of April, 1991, will by virtue of *section 279* be made, for the purposes of income tax or corporation tax, as the case may be, under *Chapter 1* of *Part 9* by virtue of *section 323*, and

(ii) which is let on bona fide commercial terms for such consideration as might be expected to be paid on a letting of the building or structure negotiated on an arm's length basis, but, as respects rent payable under a qualifying lease entered into on or after the 6th day of May, 1993, where capital expenditure is incurred in the specified period on the refurbishment of a building or structure in respect of which an allowance is to be made for the purposes of income tax or corporation tax, as the case may be, under *Chapter 1* of *Part 9*, the building or structure shall not be regarded as a qualifying premises unless the total amount of the expenditure so incurred is not less than an amount equal to 10 per cent of the market value of the building or structure immediately before that expenditure is incurred;

"*refurbishment*", in relation to a building or structure, means any work of construction, reconstruction, repair or renewal, including the provision or improvement of water, sewerage or heating facilities, carried out in the course of repair or restoration, or maintenance in the nature of repair or restoration, of the building or structure.

(b) For the purposes of this section but subject to *paragraph (c)*, so much of a period, being a period when rent is payable by a person in relation to a qualifying premises under a qualifying lease, shall be a relevant rental period as does not exceed—

(i) 10 years, or

(ii) the period by which 10 years exceeds—

(I) any preceding period, or

(II) if there is more than one preceding period, the aggregate of those periods,

for which rent was payable—

(A) by that person or any other person, or

(B) as respects rent payable in relation to any qualifying premises under a qualifying lease entered into before the 11th day of April, 1994, by that person or any person connected with that person,

in relation to that premises under a qualifying lease.

(c) As respects rent payable in relation to any qualifying premises under a qualifying lease entered into before the 18th day of April, 1991, "*relevant rental period*", in relation to a qualifying premises, means the period of 10 years commencing on the day on which rent in respect of that premises is first payable under any qualifying lease.

(2) Subject to *subsection (3)*, where in the computation of the amount of the profits or gains of a trade or profession a person is apart from this section entitled to any deduction (in this subsection referred to as "*the first-mentioned deduction*") on account of rent in respect of a qualifying premises occupied by such person for the purposes of that trade or profession which is payable by such person—

(a) for a relevant rental period, or

(b) as respects rent payable in relation to any qualifying premises under a qualifying lease entered into before the 18th day of April, 1991, in the relevant rental period,

in relation to that qualifying premises under a qualifying lease, such person shall be entitled in that computation to a further deduction (in this subsection referred to as "*the second-mentioned deduction*") equal to the amount of the first-mentioned deduction but, as respects a qualifying lease granted on or after the 21st day of April, 1997, where the first-mentioned deduction is on account of rent payable by such person to a connected person, such person shall not be entitled in that computation to the second-mentioned deduction.

(3) Where a person holds an interest in a qualifying premises out of which interest a qualifying lease is created directly or indirectly in respect of the qualifying premises and in respect of rent payable under the qualifying lease a claim for a further deduction under this section is made, and such person or, as respects rent payable in relation to any qualifying premises under a qualifying lease entered into on or after the 6th day of May, 1993, either such person or another person connected with such person—

(a) takes under a qualifying lease a qualifying premises (in this subsection referred to as "*the second-mentioned premises*") occupied by such person or such other person, as the case may be, for the purposes of a trade or profession, and

(b) is apart from this section entitled, in the computation of the amount of the profits or gains of that trade or profession, to a deduction on account of rent in respect of the second-mentioned premises,

then, unless such person or such other person, as the case may be, shows that the taking on lease of the second-mentioned premises was not undertaken for the sole or main benefit of obtaining a further deduction on account of rent under this section, such person or such other person, as the case may be, shall not be entitled in the computation of the amount of the profits or gains of that trade or profession to any further deduction on account of rent in respect of the second-mentioned premises.

(4) (a) In this subsection—

"*current value*", in relation to minimum lease payments, means the value of those payments discounted to their present value at a rate which, when applied at the inception of the lease to—

(i) those payments, including any initial payment but excluding any payment or part of any payment for which the lessor will be accountable to the lessee, and

(ii) any unguaranteed residual value of the qualifying premises, excluding any part of such value for which the lessor will be accountable to the lessee,

produces discounted present values the aggregate amount of which equals the amount of the fair value of the qualifying premises;

"*fair value*", in relation to a qualifying premises, means an amount equal to such consideration as might be expected to be paid for the premises on a sale negotiated on an arm's length basis less any grants receivable towards the purchase of the qualifying premises;

"*inception of the lease*" means the earlier of the time the qualifying premises is brought into use or the date from which rentals under the lease first accrue;

"*minimum lease payments*" means the minimum payments over the remaining part of the term of the lease to be paid to the lessor, and includes any residual amount to be paid to the lessor at the end of the term of the lease and guaranteed by the lessee or by a person connected with the lessee;

"*unguaranteed residual value*", in relation to a qualifying premises, means that part of the residual value of that premises at the end of a term of a lease, as estimated at the inception of the lease, the realisation of which by the lessor is not assured or is guaranteed solely by a person connected with the lessor.

(b) A finance lease, that is—

(i) a lease in respect of a qualifying premises where, at the inception of the lease, the aggregate of the current value of the minimum lease payments (including any initial payment but excluding any payment or part of any payment for which the lessor will be accountable to the lessee) payable by the lessee in relation to the lease amounts to 90 per cent or more of the fair value of the qualifying premises, or

(ii) a lease which in all the circumstances is considered to provide in substance for the lessee the risks and benefits associated with ownership of the qualifying premises other than legal title to that premises,

shall not be a qualifying lease for the purposes of this section.

[(5) Notwithstanding any other provision of this section, *subsection (2)* shall not apply—

(a) in respect of rent payable, under a qualifying lease, for any part of a relevant rental period between 3 December 1998 and 31 December 2003 unless—

(i) in the case of a qualifying premises within an area or areas included in the definition of "*the Custom House Docks Area*" by virtue of being described in an order of the Minister for Finance made under *section 322(2)*, an agreement in writing or a contract in writing to secure the development of the building or structure, which comprises the qualifying premises or in which the qualifying premises is located, was entered into in the specified period, but by 2 December 1998, with the Dublin Docklands Development Authority (within the meaning of *section 14* of the *Dublin Docklands Development Authority Act, 1997*), or

(ii) in the case of any other qualifying premises, an agreement in writing or a contract in writing to secure the development of the building or structure, which comprises the qualifying premises or in which the qualifying premises is located, was entered into in the specified period, but by 2 December 1998, and such development was wholly or mainly completed before 1 January 2000,

(b) in respect of rent payable, under a qualifying lease, for any part of a relevant rental period between 1 January 2004 and 31 December 2008, in the case of a qualifying premises to which *subsection (2)* applies by virtue of *paragraph (a)(i)*,

(c) in respect of rent payable, under a qualifying lease, for any part of a relevant rental period between 1 January 2004 and 31 December 2008, in the case of a qualifying premises to which *subsection (2)* applies by virtue of *paragraph (a)(ii)*, unless—

(i) the construction or refurbishment of the qualifying premises, which is the subject of the qualifying lease, was completed prior to 1 April 1998, or

(ii) (I) the construction or refurbishment of the qualifying premises, which is the subject of the qualifying lease, commenced prior to 1 April 1998, and

(II) such premises was occupied by a lessee, under a qualifying lease, prior to 9 February 1999,

or

(d) in respect of rent payable, under a qualifying lease, for any part of a relevant rental period after 31 December 2008.][1]

Amendments

[1] Inserted by FA00 s39(1). This section shall be deemed to have applied as on and from 3 December 1998.

Revenue Precedents

Do payments for certain service charges made in accordance with the terms of a qualifying lease qualify for a double rent deduction? In order to qualify the payments must be in the nature of rent as defined by section 96 TCA 1997. If the payments do not arise from the holding of the premises but from the use to which the premises are put they are less likely to be in the nature of rent. If the payments would arise irrespective of the nature of the occupier's interest in the premises , they are not in the nature of rent. IT962013

Payment of irrecoverable VAT under section 4 VAT Act 1972 does not qualify for double rent deduction since the payment is not rent. The deduction is not given on account of rent. If given, it is on account of the VAT payable by the lessee. IT982001

Cross References

From Section 324

Section 52 Persons chargeable.
Section 96 Interpretation (Chapter 8).
Section 268 Meaning of "industrial building or structure".
Section 279 Purchases of certain buildings or structures.
Section 322 Interpretation (Chapter 1).
Section 323 Capital allowances in relation to construction of certain commercial premises.

To Section 324

Section 322 Interpretation (Chapter 1).
Section 485C Interpretation (Chapter 2A).
Section 531B Charge to income levy.
Section 531AA Interpretation (Part 18C).
Section 531AM Charge to universal social charge.
Section 708 Acquisition expenses.
Section 1013 Limited partnerships.
Schedule 25B List of Specified Reliefs and Method of Determining Amount of Specified Relief Used in a Tax Year
Schedule 25C Determination of Amount of Relief to be Treated as Referable to Specified Reliefs as Respects Relief Carried Forward from Tax Year 2006 to Tax Year 2007

325 Rented residential accommodation: deduction for certain expenditure on construction [Repealed]

Repealed by FA02 s24(3)(a).

Cross References

To Section 325

Section 322 Interpretation (Chapter 1).
Section 372AU Saver for relief due, and for clawback of relief given under, old schemes.

326 Rented residential accommodation: deduction for certain expenditure on conversion [Repealed]

Repealed by FA02 s24(3)(a).

Cross References

To Section 326

Section 372AU Saver for relief due, and for clawback of relief given under, old schemes.

327 Rented residential accommodation: deduction for certain expenditure on refurbishment [Repealed]

Repealed by FA02 s24(3)(a).

Cross References

To Section 327

Section 372AU Saver for relief due, and for clawback of relief given under, old schemes.

328 Residential accommodation: allowance to owner-occupiers in respect of certain expenditure on construction or refurbishment [Repealed]

Repealed by FA02 s24(3)(a).

Cross References

To Section 328

Section 322 Interpretation (Chapter 1).

Section 372AU Saver for relief due, and for clawback of relief given under, old schemes.

329 Provisions supplementary to sections 325 to 328. [Repealed]

Repealed by FA02 s24(3)(a).

CHAPTER 2

Temple Bar Area

330 Interpretation. (Chapter 2)

[FA97 s147]

(1) In this Chapter—

["*qualifying period*" means the period commencing—

(a) for the purposes of any provision of this Chapter other than *section 334, 335* or *336*, the 6th day of April, 1991, or

(b) for the purposes of *sections 334* to *336*, the 30th day of January, 1991,

and ending on—

(i) the 5th day of April, 1999, or

(ii) the 31st day of December, 1999, where, in relation to the construction of, conversion into, refurbishment of, or, as the case may be, construction or refurbishment of a house which is a qualifying premises within the meaning of *section 334, 335, 336* or *337*, the corporation of the county borough of Dublin gives a certificate in writing, on or before the 31st day of July, 1999, to the person constructing, converting or refurbishing, as the case may be, the house stating that it is satisfied that not less than 50 per cent of the total cost of the house and the site thereof had been incurred on or before the 5th day of April, 1999;][1]

"*refurbishment*" means any work of construction, reconstruction, repair or renewal, including the provision or improvement of water, sewerage or heating facilities, carried out in the course of repair or restoration, or maintenance in the nature of repair or restoration, of a building or structure, which is consistent with the original character or fabric of the building or structure;

"*the Temple Bar Area*" means the area described in *paragraph 2* of *Schedule 6*.

(2) The provisions specified in this Chapter as applying in relation to capital or other expenditure incurred or rent payable in relation to any building or premises (however described in this Chapter) in the Temple Bar Area shall apply only

if the relevant building or premises, in relation to which that capital or other expenditure was incurred or rent is so payable, is approved for the purposes of this Chapter by the company known as Temple Bar Renewal Limited.

(3) Notwithstanding any other provision of the Tax Acts, where part of a building or structure is used for commercial purposes and part is used for residential purposes, the total amount of the expenditure incurred on the construction or refurbishment of the building or structure shall be apportioned as between the respective parts of the building or structure in such manner as is just and reasonable for the purpose of giving effect to this Chapter.

(4) *Schedule 6* shall apply for the purposes of supplementing this Chapter.

Amendments

[1] Substituted by FA99 s43.

Revenue Precedents

If in the course of 'refurbishment' of a building in Temple Bar an extention is built on to part of the building will the expenditure on the addition qualify as 'refurbishment'?. No. Such expenditure is not considered to be carried on the repair or restoration of the building, rather it is considered to be new construction. IT943030

Cross References

From Section 330

Section 334 Rented residential accommodation: deduction for certain expenditure on construction.
Section 335 Rented residential accommodation: deduction for certain expenditure on conversion.
Section 336 Rented residential accommodation: deduction for certain expenditure on refurbishment.
Section 337 Residential accommodation: allowance to owner-occupiers in respect of certain expenditure on construction or refurbishment.
Schedule 6 Description of Temple Bar Area

To Section 330

Schedule 6 Description of Temple Bar Area

331 Accelerated capital allowances in relation to construction or refurbishment of certain industrial buildings or structures

[FA97 s148]

(1) This section shall apply to a building or structure—

(a) which is—

(i) constructed in the Temple Bar Area in the qualifying period, or

(ii) an existing building or structure in the Temple Bar Area as on the 1st day of January, 1991, and is the subject of refurbishment in the qualifying period,

and

(b) which is to be an industrial building or structure by reason of its use for a purpose specified in *paragraph (a)* or *(d)* of *section 268(1)*.

(2) *Section 271* shall apply in relation to capital expenditure incurred in the qualifying period on the construction or refurbishment of a building or structure to which this section applies as if—

(a) in *subsection (1)* of that section the definition of "*industrial development agency*" were deleted,

(b) in *subsection (2)(a)(i)* of that section "to which *subsection (3)* applies" were deleted,

(c) *subsections (3)* and *(5)* of that section were deleted, and

(d) (i) in the case where the capital expenditure is incurred on the construction of the building or structure, the following subsection were substituted for *subsection (4)* of that section:

"(4) An industrial building allowance shall be of an amount equal to 25 per cent of the capital expenditure mentioned in *subsection (2)*.",

and

(ii) in the case where the capital expenditure is incurred on the refurbishment of the building or structure, the following subsection were substituted for *subsection (4)* of that section:

"(4) An industrial building allowance shall be of an amount equal to 50 per cent of the capital expenditure mentioned in *subsection (2)*.".

(3) *Section 273* shall apply in relation to capital expenditure incurred in the qualifying period on the construction or refurbishment of a building or structure to which this section applies—

(a) in the case where the capital expenditure is incurred on the construction of the building or structure as if—

(i) in *subsection (1)* of that section the definition of "*industrial development agency*" were deleted,

(ii) the following paragraph were substituted for *paragraph (b)* of *subsection (2)* of that section:

"(b) As respects any qualifying expenditure, any allowance made under *section 272* and increased under *paragraph (a)* in respect of that expenditure, whether claimed for one chargeable period or more than one such period, shall not in the aggregate exceed 50 per cent of the amount of that qualifying expenditure.",

and

(iii) *subsections (3)* to *(7)* of that section were deleted,

and

(b) in the case where the capital expenditure is incurred on the refurbishment of the building or structure as if—

(i) in *subsection (1)* of that section the definition of "*industrial development agency*" were deleted, and

(ii) *subsections (2)(b)* and *(3)* to *(7)* of that section were deleted.

(4) For the purposes of this section, where capital expenditure is incurred in the qualifying period on the refurbishment of a building or structure to which this section applies, such expenditure shall be deemed to include the lesser of—

(a) any expenditure incurred on the purchase of the building or structure, other than expenditure incurred on the acquisition of, or of rights in or over, any land, and

(b) an amount which is equal to the value of the building or structure on the 1st day of January, 1991, other than any amount of such value as is attributable to, or to rights in or over, any land,

if the expenditure referred to in *paragraph (a)* or the amount referred to in *paragraph (b)*, as the case may be, is not greater than the amount of the capital expenditure actually incurred in the qualifying period on the refurbishment of the building or structure.

(5) Notwithstanding *section 274(1)*, in the case of a building or structure to which this section applies by reason of its use for a purpose specified in *section 268(1)(a)*, no balancing charge shall be made by reason of any of the events specified in *section 274(1)* which occurs—

(a) more than 13 years after the building or structure was first used, or

(b) in a case where *section 276* applies, more than 13 years after the capital expenditure on refurbishment of the building or structure was incurred.

(6) For the purposes only of determining, in relation to a claim for an allowance under *section 271* or *273* as applied by this section, whether and to what extent capital expenditure incurred on the construction or refurbishment of an industrial building or structure is incurred or not incurred in the qualifying period, only such an amount of that capital expenditure as is properly attributable to work on the construction or, as the case may be, refurbishment of the building or structure actually carried out during the qualifying period shall (notwithstanding any other provision of the Tax Acts as to the time when any capital expenditure is or is to be treated as incurred) be treated as having been incurred in that period; but nothing in this subsection shall affect the operation of *subsection (4)*.

(7) Where, in relation to capital expenditure incurred in the qualifying period on the construction or refurbishment of a building or structure to which this section applies, any allowance or charge has been made under the provisions of the Tax Acts relating to the making of allowances and charges in respect of capital expenditure incurred on the construction or refurbishment of an industrial building or structure by virtue of section 42 of the Finance Act, 1986, as applied by section 55 of the Finance Act, 1991, that allowance or charge shall be deemed to have been made under those provisions by virtue of this section.

Cross References

From Section 331

Section 268 Meaning of "industrial building or structure".
Section 271 Industrial building allowances.
Section 272 Writing-down allowances.
Section 273 Acceleration of writing-down allowances in respect of certain expenditure on certain industrial buildings or structures.
Section 274 Balancing allowances and balancing charges.
Section 276 Application of sections 272 and 274 in relation to capital expenditure on refurbishment.

To Section 331

Schedule 25B List of Specified Reliefs and Method of Determining Amount of Specified Relief Used in a Tax Year

332 Capital allowances in relation to construction or refurbishment of certain commercial premises

[FA97 s149]

(1) In this section—

"*multi-storey car park*" means a building or structure consisting of 3 or more storeys wholly or mainly in use for the purpose of providing, for members of the public generally without preference for any particular class of person, on payment of an appropriate charge, parking space for mechanically propelled vehicles;

"*qualifying premises*" means a building or structure which—

(a) (i) is constructed in the Temple Bar Area in the qualifying period, or

(ii) is an existing building or structure in the Temple Bar Area as on the 1st day of January, 1991, and is the subject of refurbishment in the qualifying period,

(b) apart from this section is not an industrial building or structure within the meaning of *section 268*, and

(c) (i) is in use for the purposes of a trade or profession, or

(ii) whether or not it is so used, is let on bona fide commercial terms for such consideration as might be expected to be paid in a letting of the building or structure negotiated on an arm's length basis,

but does not include any part of a building or structure in use as or as part of a dwelling house.

(2) (a) Subject to *subsections (3)* to *(8)*, the provisions of the Tax Acts relating to the making of allowances or charges in respect of capital expenditure incurred on the construction or refurbishment of an industrial building or structure shall, notwithstanding anything to the contrary in those provisions, apply—

(i) as if a qualifying premises were, at all times at which it is a qualifying premises, a building or structure in respect of which an allowance is to be made for the purposes of income tax or corporation tax, as the case may be, under *Chapter 1* of *Part 9* by reason of its use for a purpose specified in *section 268(1)(a)*, and

(ii) where any activity carried on in the qualifying premises is not a trade, as if it were a trade.

(b) An allowance shall be given by virtue of this subsection in respect of any capital expenditure incurred on the construction or refurbishment of a qualifying premises only in so far as that expenditure is incurred in the qualifying period.

(3) *Section 271* shall apply in relation to capital expenditure incurred in the qualifying period on the construction or refurbishment of a qualifying premises as if—

(a) in *subsection (1)* of that section the definition of "*industrial development agency*" were deleted,

(b) in *subsection (2)(a)(i)* of that section "to which *subsection (3)* applies" were deleted,

(c) *subsections (3)* and *(5)* of that section were deleted, and

(d) the following subsection were substituted for *subsection (4)* of that section:

"(4) An industrial building allowance shall be of an amount equal to 50 per cent of the capital expenditure mentioned in *subsection (2)*.".

(4) *Section 273* shall apply in relation to capital expenditure incurred in the qualifying period on the construction or refurbishment of a qualifying premises as if—

(a) in *subsection (1)* of that section the definition of "*industrial development agency*" were deleted, and

(b) *subsections (2)(b)* and *(3)* to *(7)* of that section were deleted.

(5) For the purposes of this section, where capital expenditure is incurred in the qualifying period on the refurbishment of a qualifying premises, such expenditure shall be deemed to include the lesser of—

(a) any expenditure incurred on the purchase of the building or structure, other than expenditure incurred on the acquisition of, or of rights in or over, any land, and

(b) an amount which is equal to the value of the building or structure as on the 1st day of January, 1991, other than any amount of such value as is attributable to, or to rights in or over, any land,

if the expenditure referred to in *paragraph (a)* or the amount referred to in *paragraph (b)*, as the case may be, is not greater than the amount of the capital expenditure actually incurred in the qualifying period on the refurbishment of the qualifying premises.

(6) Notwithstanding *section 274(1)*, no balancing charge shall be made in relation to a qualifying premises by reason of any of the events specified in that section which occurs—

(a) more than 13 years after the qualifying premises was first used, or

(b) in a case where *section 276* applies, more than 13 years after the capital expenditure on refurbishment of the qualifying premises was incurred.

(7) (a) Notwithstanding *subsections (2)* to *(4)*, any allowance or charge which apart from this subsection would be made by virtue of *subsection (2)* in respect of capital expenditure incurred on the construction of a qualifying premises, other than a qualifying premises which is a multi-storey car park, shall be reduced to one-half of the amount which apart from this subsection would be the amount of that allowance or charge.

(b) For the purposes of *paragraph (a)*, the amount of an allowance or charge to be reduced to one-half shall be computed as if—

(i) this subsection had not been enacted, and

(ii) effect had been given to all allowances taken into account in so computing that amount.

(c) Nothing in this subsection shall affect the operation of *section 274(8)*.

(8) For the purposes only of determining, in relation to a claim for an allowance by virtue of *subsection (2)*, whether and to what extent capital expenditure incurred on the construction or refurbishment of a qualifying premises is incurred or not incurred in the qualifying period, only such an amount of that capital expenditure as is properly attributable to work on the construction or, as the case may be, refurbishment of the premises actually carried out during the qualifying period shall (notwithstanding any other provision of the Tax Acts as to the time when any capital expenditure is or is to be treated as incurred) be treated as having been incurred in that period; but nothing in this subsection shall affect the operation of *subsection (5)*.

(9) Where, in relation to capital expenditure incurred in the qualifying period on the construction or refurbishment of a qualifying premises, any allowance or charge has been made under the provisions of the Tax Acts relating to the making of allowances and charges in respect of capital expenditure incurred on the construction or refurbishment of an industrial building or structure by virtue of section 42 of the Finance Act, 1986, as applied by section 55 of the Finance Act, 1991, that allowance or charge shall be deemed to have been made under those provisions by virtue of this section.

Revenue Precedents

Where retail units are contained in a development which incorporates a multi-storey car-park, are the retail units treated as part of the multi-storey car-park and accordingly do they qualify for capital allowances at the same rate as the car-park? No. The retail units must be looked at in their own right and will qualify at the rate appropriate to them. IT933038

Cross References

From Section 332

Section 268 Meaning of "industrial building or structure".
Section 271 Industrial building allowances.
Section 273 Acceleration of writing-down allowances in respect of certain expenditure on certain industrial buildings or structures.
Section 274 Balancing allowances and balancing charges.
Section 276 Application of sections 272 and 274 in relation to capital expenditure on refurbishment.

To Section 332

Section 333 Double rent allowance in respect of rent paid for certain business premises.
Schedule 25B List of Specified Reliefs and Method of Determining Amount of Specified Relief Used in a Tax Year

333 Double rent allowance in respect of rent paid for certain business premises

[FA90 s33(1) and (2)(a); FA97 s150]

(1) (a) In this section—

"*lease*", "*lessee*", "*lessor*" and "*rent*" have the same meanings respectively as in *Chapter 8* of *Part 4*;

"*market value*", in relation to a building or structure, means the price which the unencumbered fee simple of the building or structure would fetch if sold in the open market in such manner and subject to such conditions as might reasonably be calculated to obtain for the vendor the best price for the building or structure, less the part of that price which would be attributable to the acquisition of, or of rights in or over, the land on which the building or structure is constructed;

["*qualifying lease*" means, subject to *subsection (4)*, a lease in respect of a qualifying premises granted in the qualifying period, or granted in any subsequent period ending on or before 31 December 1999, on bona fide commercial terms by a lessor to a lessee not connected with the lessor, or with any other person entitled to a rent in respect of the qualifying premises, whether under that lease or any other lease;][1]

"*qualifying premises*" means a building or structure in the Temple Bar Area—

(i) (I) which is an industrial building or structure within the meaning of *section 268(1)*, and in respect of which capital expenditure is incurred in the qualifying period for which an allowance is to be made for the purposes of income tax or corporation tax, as the case may be, under *Chapter 1* of *Part 9*, or

(II) in respect of which an allowance is to be made, or, as respects rent payable under a qualifying lease entered into on or after the 18th day of April, 1991, will by virtue of *section 279* be made, for the purposes of income tax or corporation tax, as the case may be, under *Chapter 1* of *Part 9* by virtue of *section 332*, and

(ii) which is let on bona fide commercial terms for such consideration as might be expected to be paid in a letting of the building or structure negotiated on an arm's length basis,

but, as respects rent payable under a qualifying lease entered into on or after the 6th day of May, 1993, where capital expenditure is incurred in the qualifying period on the refurbishment of a building or structure in respect of which an allowance is to be made for the purposes of income tax or corporation tax, as the case may be, under *Chapter 1* of *Part 9*, the building or structure shall not be regarded as a qualifying premises unless the total amount of the expenditure so incurred is not less than an amount equal to 10 per cent of the market value of the building or structure immediately before that expenditure is incurred.

(b) For the purposes of this section but subject to *paragraph (c)*, so much of a period, being a period when rent is payable by a person in relation to a qualifying premises under a qualifying lease, shall be a relevant rental period as does not exceed—

(i) 10 years, or

(ii) the period by which 10 years exceeds—

(I) any preceding period, or

(II) if there is more than one preceding period, the aggregate of those periods,

for which rent was payable—

(A) by that person or any other person, or

(B) as respects rent payable in relation to any qualifying premises under a qualifying lease entered into before the 11th day of April, 1994, by that person or any person connected with that person,

in relation to that premises under a qualifying lease.

(c) As respects rent payable in relation to any qualifying premises under a qualifying lease entered into before the 18th day of April, 1991, "*relevant rental period*", in relation to a qualifying premises, means the period of 10 years commencing on the day on which rent in respect of that premises is first payable under any qualifying lease.

(2) Subject to *subsection (3)*, where in the computation of the amount of the profits or gains of a trade or profession a person is apart from this section entitled to any deduction (in this subsection referred to as "the first-mentioned deduction") on account of rent in respect of a qualifying premises occupied by such person for the purposes of that trade or profession which is payable by such person—

(a) for a relevant rental period, or

(b) as respects rent payable in relation to any qualifying premises under a qualifying lease entered into before the 18th day of April, 1991, in the relevant rental period,

in relation to that qualifying premises under a qualifying lease, such person shall be entitled in that computation to a further deduction (in this subsection referred to as "the second-mentioned deduction") equal to the amount of the first-mentioned deduction but, as respects a qualifying lease granted on or after the 21st day of April, 1997, where the first-mentioned deduction is on account of rent payable by such person to a connected person, such person shall not be entitled in that computation to the second-mentioned deduction.

(3) Where a person holds an interest in a qualifying premises out of which interest a qualifying lease is created directly or indirectly in respect of that qualifying premises and in respect of rent payable under the qualifying lease a claim for a further deduction under this section is made, and such person or, as respects rent payable in relation to any qualifying premises under a qualifying lease entered into on or after the 6th day of May, 1993, either such person or another person connected with such person—

(a) takes under a qualifying lease a qualifying premises (in this subsection referred to as "the second-mentioned premises") occupied by such person or such other person, as the case may be, for the purposes of a trade or profession, and

(b) is apart from this section entitled, in the computation of the amount of the profits or gains of that trade or profession, to a deduction on account of rent in respect of the second-mentioned premises,

then, unless such person or such other person, as the case may be, shows that the taking on lease of the second-mentioned premises was not undertaken for the sole or main benefit of obtaining a further deduction on account of rent under this section, such person or such other person, as the case may be, shall not be entitled in the computation of the amount of the profits or gains of that trade or profession to any further deduction on account of rent in respect of the second-mentioned premises.

(4) (a) In this subsection—

"*current value*", in relation to minimum lease payments, means the value of those payments discounted to their present value at a rate which, when applied at the inception of the lease to—

(i) those payments, including any initial payment but excluding any payment or part of any payment for which the lessor will be accountable to the lessee, and

(ii) any unguaranteed residual value of the qualifying premises, excluding any part of such value for which the lessor will be accountable to the lessee,

produces discounted present values the aggregate amount of which equals the amount of the fair value of the qualifying premises;

"*fair value*", in relation to a qualifying premises, means an amount equal to such consideration as might be expected to be paid for the premises on a sale negotiated on an arm's length basis less any grants receivable towards the purchase of the qualifying premises;

"*inception of the lease*" means the earlier of the time the qualifying premises is brought into use or the date from which rentals under the lease first accrue;

"*minimum lease payments*" means the minimum payments over the remaining part of the term of the lease to be paid to the lessor, and includes any residual amount to be paid to the lessor at the end of the term of the lease and guaranteed by the lessee or by a person connected with the lessee;

"*unguaranteed residual value*", in relation to a qualifying premises, means that part of the residual value of that premises at the end of a term of a lease, as estimated at the inception of the lease, the realisation of which by the lessor is not assured or is guaranteed solely by a person connected with the lessor.

(b) A finance lease, that is—

(i) a lease in respect of a qualifying premises where, at the inception of the lease, the aggregate of the current value of the minimum lease payments (including any initial payment but excluding any payment or part of any payment for which the lessor will be accountable to the lessee) payable by the lessee in relation to the lease amounts to 90 per cent or more of the fair value of the qualifying premises, or

(ii) a lease which in all the circumstances is considered to provide in substance for the lessee the risks and benefits associated with ownership of the qualifying premises other than legal title to that premises,

shall not be a qualifying lease for the purposes of this section.

(5) In determining whether a period is a relevant rental period for the purposes of this section, rent payable by any person in relation to a premises in respect of which a further deduction was given under section 45 of the Finance Act, 1986, as applied by section 55 of the Finance Act, 1991 (or would have been so given but for the operation of *paragraph (b)* of the proviso to *subsection (2)* of section 45 of the Finance Act, 1986), shall be treated as having been payable by that person in relation to the premises under a qualifying lease.

Amendments

[1] Substituted by FA00 s37.

Revenue Precedents

The total amount of expenditure incurred on refurbishment may not be less than an amount equal to 10% of the market value of the building immediately before that expenditure is incurred. The issue arises as to whether in computing that total amount, the expenditure incurred by the lessee as well as the lessor may be taken in? The total amount of the expenditure incurred on refurbishment includes the expenditure incurred by the vendor as well as the purchaser. In such a case, the market value to be used is the market value immediately before the expenditure incurred by the vendor. IT973005

Cross References

From Section 333

Section 52 Persons chargeable.

Section 96 Interpretation (Chapter 8).

Section 268 Meaning of "industrial building or structure".

Section 279 Purchases of certain buildings or structures.

Section 332 Capital allowances in relation to construction or refurbishment of certain commercial premises.

To Section 333

Section 485C Interpretation (Chapter 2A).

Section 531B Charge to income levy.

Section 531AA Interpretation (Part 18C).

Section 531AM Charge to universal social charge.

Section 708 Acquisition expenses.

Section 1013 Limited partnerships.

Schedule 25B List of Specified Reliefs and Method of Determining Amount of Specified Relief Used in a Tax Year

Schedule 25C Determination of Amount of Relief to be Treated as Referable to Specified Reliefs as Respects Relief Carried Forward from Tax Year 2006 to Tax Year 2007

334 Rented residential accommodation: deduction for certain expenditure on construction [Repealed]

Repealed by FA02 s24(3)(b).

Cross References

To Section 334

Section 330 Interpretation. (Chapter 2).

Section 372AU Saver for relief due, and for clawback of relief given under, old schemes.

335 Rented residential accommodation: deduction for certain expenditure on conversion [Repealed]

Repealed by FA02 s24(3)(b).

Cross References

To Section 335

Section 330 Interpretation. (Chapter 2).

Section 372AU Saver for relief due, and for clawback of relief given under, old schemes.

336 Rented residential accommodation: deduction for certain expenditure on refurbishment [Repealed]

Repealed by FA02 s24(3)(b).

Cross References

To Section 336

Section 330 Interpretation. (Chapter 2).

Section 372AU Saver for relief due, and for clawback of relief given under, old schemes.

337 Residential accommodation: allowance to owner-occupiers in respect of certain expenditure on construction or refurbishment [Repealed]

Repealed by FA02 s24(3)(b).

Cross References

To Section 337

Section 330 Interpretation. (Chapter 2).

Section 372AU Saver for relief due, and for clawback of relief given under, old schemes.

338 Provisions supplementary to sections 334 to 337. [Repealed]

Repealed by FA02 s24(3)(b).

CHAPTER 3

Designated Areas, Designated Streets, Enterprise Areas and Multi-Storey Car Parks in Certain Urban Areas

339 Interpretation (Chapter 3)

[FA94 s38(1), (3) and (4); FA95 s35(1)(a); FA97 s26(a)]

(1) In this Chapter—

"*designated area*" and "*designated street*" mean respectively an area or areas or a street or streets specified as a designated area or a designated street, as the case may be, by order under *section 340*;

"*enterprise area*" means—

(a) an area or areas specified as an enterprise area by order under *section 340*, or

(b) an area or areas described in *Schedule 7*;

"*lease*", "*lessee*", "*lessor*", "*premium*" and "*rent*" have the same meanings respectively as in *Chapter 8* of *Part 4*;

"*market value*", in relation to a building, structure or house, means the price which the unencumbered fee simple of the building, structure or house would fetch if sold in the open market in such manner and subject to such conditions as might reasonably be calculated to obtain for the vendor the best price for the building, structure or house, less the part of that price which would be attributable to the acquisition of, or of rights in or over, the land on which the building, structure or house is constructed;

"*qualifying period*" means—

(a) subject to *subsection (2)* and *section 340* and other than for the purposes of *section 344*, the period commencing on the 1st day of August, 1994, and ending on the 31st day of July, 1997, or

(b) in respect of an area or areas described in *Schedule 7*, the period commencing on the 1st day of July, 1997, and ending on the [31st day of December, 1999][1];

"*refurbishment*", in relation to a building or structure and other than for the purposes of *sections 348* and *349*, means any work of construction, reconstruction, repair or renewal, including the provision or improvement of water, sewerage or heating facilities, carried out in the course of the repair or restoration, or maintenance in the nature of repair or restoration, of the building or structure;

"*the relevant local authority*", in relation to the construction of, conversion into, refurbishment of, or, as the case may be, construction or refurbishment of a building or structure to which [*paragraph (a)* or *(e)* of *subsection (2)*][2] applies, means [the local authority for the purposes of the Local Government Act 2001 (as amended by the *Local Government Reform Act 2014*)][3] in whose functional area the qualifying premises is situated;

"*street*" includes part of a street and the whole or part of any road, square, quay or lane.

(2) (a) Where in relation to the construction of, conversion into, refurbishment of, or, as the case may be, construction or refurbishment of a building or structure which is—

(i) to be an industrial building or structure to which *section 341* applies,

(ii) a qualifying premises within the respective meanings assigned in *sections 342*, *345* (other than a building or structure to which *paragraph (a)(v)* of that meaning in that section applies), *346*, *347*, *348* and *349*, or

(iii) a qualifying building within the meaning of *section 343*,

the relevant local authority gives a certificate in writing, on or before the 30th day of September, 1997, to the person constructing, converting or refurbishing, as the case may be, such a building or structure stating that it is satisfied that not less than 15 per cent of the total cost of the building or structure had been incurred before the 31st day of July, 1997, then, [the reference in *paragraph (a)* of the definition of "*qualifying period*" in *subsection (1)* to the period ending on the 31st day of July, 1997, shall be construed as a reference to the period ending on the 31st day of July, 1998.][4]

(b) In considering whether to give a certificate referred to in *paragraph (a)*, the relevant local authority shall have regard only to the guidelines in relation to the giving of such certificates entitled "*Extension from 31 July, 1997, to 31 July, 1998, of the time limit for qualifying expenditure on developments*" issued by the Department of the Environment on the 28th day of January, 1997.

[(c) Where in relation to the construction of, conversion into, refurbishment of, or, as the case may be, construction or refurbishment of a building or structure to which *paragraph (a)* relates—

(i) the relevant local authority has given to the person constructing, converting or refurbishing, as the case may be, that building or structure, a certificate in writing to which that paragraph refers certifying that not less than 15 per cent of the total cost of the building or structure had been incurred before the 31st day of July, 1997, and

(ii) an application for planning permission for the work represented by the expenditure incurred or to be incurred on the building or structure had (in so far as such permission is required) been received by a planning authority not later than the 1st day of March, 1998, and

(iii) where the expenditure to be incurred on a building or structure has not been fully incurred by the 31st day of July, 1998, the relevant local authority gives a certificate in writing to the person referred to in *subparagraph (i)* stating that in its opinion—

(I) that person had, on the 31st day of July, 1997, a reasonable expectation that the expenditure to be incurred on the building or structure would have been incurred in full on or before the 31st day of July, 1998, and

(II) the failure to incur that expenditure in full on or before the 31st day of July, 1998, was, on the basis of reasons of a bona fide character stated to it, due, to a significant extent, to a delay outside the direct control of that person, including an unanticipated delay in obtaining the grant of planning permission or a fire certificate, an unanticipated delay due to legal proceedings or unanticipated difficulties in completing the acquisition of a site or involving the failure of a building contractor to fulfil his or her obligations or the need to respect any archaeological site or remains,

then, the reference in *paragraph (a)* of the definition of "*qualifying period*" to the period ending on the 31st day of July, 1997, shall be construed as a reference to the period ending on the 31st day of December, 1998.][5]

[(d) Where, in relation to the construction of, conversion into, refurbishment of, or, as the case may be, construction or refurbishment of a building or structure which complies with the requirements of *subparagraphs (i)*, *(ii)* and *(iii)* of *paragraph (c)*, being a qualifying premises within the meaning of *section 346*, *347*, *348* or *349*, where—

(i) the expenditure to be incurred on the house has not been fully incurred by the 31st day of December, 1998, and

(ii) the relevant local authority gives a certificate in writing on or before the 28th day of February, 1999, to the person constructing, converting or refurbishing, as the case may be, the house stating that it is satisfied that not less than 50 per cent of the total cost of the house and the site thereof had been incurred on or before the 31st day of December, 1998,

then, the reference in *paragraph (a)* of the definition of "*qualifying period*" in *subsection (1)* to the period ending on the 31st day of July, 1997, shall be construed as a reference to the period ending on the 30th day of April, 1999.][6]

[(e) (i) Where, in relation to the construction or refurbishment of a qualifying building within the meaning of *section 343*, the relevant local authority gives a certificate in writing on or before 31 May 2000 to the person constructing or refurbishing the qualifying building stating that it is satisfied that not less than 50 per cent of the total cost of the qualifying building and the site thereof had been incurred on or before 31 December 1999, then the reference in *paragraph (b)* of the definition of "*qualifying period*" in *subsection (1)* to the period ending on the 31st day of December, 1999, shall be construed as a reference to the period ending on 31 December 2000.

(ii) In considering whether to give such a certificate, the relevant local authority shall have regard only to guidelines in relation to the giving of such certificates issued by the Department of the Environment and Local Government.][7]

(3) *Schedule 7* shall apply for the purposes of supplementing this Chapter.

Amendments

[1] Substituted by FA98 s24(1)(a)(i).

[2] Substituted by FA00 s42(1)(a)(i). This section shall apply as on and from 1 July 1999.

[3] Substituted by LGRA14 sched2(part5).

[4] Substituted by FA98 s24(1)(a)(ii)(I).

[5] Inserted by FA98 s24(1)(a)(ii)(II).

[6] Inserted by FA99 s44(a).

[7] Inserted by FA00 s42(1)(a)(ii). This section shall apply as on and from 1 July 1999.

Revenue Briefings

Tax Briefing

Tax Briefing August 2005 – Issue 60 – Property Based Incentive Schemes

Tax Briefing May 2006 – Issue 63 – Capital Allowances and Property Based Incentive Schemes

Tax Briefing August 2006 – Issue 64 – Capital Allowances and Property Based Incentive Schemes

Tax Briefing December 2006 – Issue 65 – Capital Allowances and Property Based Incentive Schemes

Tax Briefing December 2006 – Issue 65 – Property-based Incentive Schemes – 15% test

Revenue Information Notes

Transitional Arrangements for Property-Based Incentive Schemes

Revenue Precedents

A developer receives a certificate from a local authority certifying that not less than 15% of the total project costs have been incurred before 31 July 1997 and the developer sells the site. Can the vendor be regarded as the person constructing the building for section 339(2a) TCA 1997? Yes, if no change has occurred in the project as submitted by the vendors. IT983001

Is it Revenue practice to accept that site costs may be included in the computation of the cost of construction of a building for the purpose of section 339 (2a) TCA 1997? 15% means 15% of the total project costs including site costs.

Cross References

From Section 339

Section 52 Persons chargeable.

Section 96 Interpretation (Chapter 8).

Section 340 Designated areas, designated streets and enterprise areas.

Section 341 Accelerated capital allowances in relation to construction or refurbishment of certain industrial buildings or structures.

Section 342 Capital allowances in relation to construction or refurbishment of certain commercial premises.

Section 343 Capital allowances in relation to construction or refurbishment of certain buildings or structures in enterprise areas.

Section 344 Capital allowances in relation to construction or refurbishment of certain multi-storey car parks.

Section 345 Double rent allowance in respect of rent paid for certain business premises.

Section 346 Rented residential accommodation: deduction for certain expenditure on construction.

Section 347 Rented residential accommodation: deduction for certain expenditure on conversion.

Section 348 Rented residential accommodation: deduction for certain expenditure on refurbishment.

Section 349 Residential accommodation: allowance to owner-occupiers in respect of certain expenditure on construction or refurbishment.
Schedule 7 Description of Certain Enterprise Areas

To Section 339
Section 340 Designated areas, designated streets and enterprise areas.
Schedule 7 Description of Certain Enterprise Areas

340 Designated areas, designated streets and enterprise areas

[FA94 s39; FA95 s35(1)(b); FA97 s26(b)]

(1) The Minister for Finance may, after consultation with the Minister for the Environment and Local Government, by order direct that—

(a) the area or areas, or street or streets, described in the order shall be a designated area, a designated street or, as the case may be, an enterprise area for the purposes of this Chapter, and

(b) as respects any such area or any such street so described, the definition of "*qualifying period*" in *section 339* shall be construed as a reference to such period as shall be specified in the order in relation to that area or, as the case may be, that street; but no such period specified in the order shall commence before the 1st day of August, 1994, or end after the 31st day of July, 1997[, or, as the case may be, after the day to which the reference to the 31st day of July, 1997, is, by virtue of *section 339(2)*, to be construed][1].

(2) The Minister for Finance may, after consultation with the Minister for Public Enterprise and following receipt of a proposal from or on behalf of a company intending to carry on qualifying trading operations (within the meaning of *section 343*) in an area or areas immediately adjacent to any of the airports commonly known as—

(a) Cork Airport,

(b) Donegal Airport,

(c) Galway Airport,

(d) Kerry Airport,

(e) Knock International Airport,

(f) Sligo Airport, or

(g) Waterford Airport,

being a company which, if those trading operations were to be carried on in an area which apart from this subsection would be an enterprise area, would be a qualifying company (within the meaning of *section 343*), by order direct that—

(i) the area or areas described in the order shall be an enterprise area for the purposes of this Chapter, and

[(ii) as respects any such area so described in the order, the reference in *paragraph (a)* of the definition of "*qualifying period*" in *section 339(1)* to the period commencing on the 1st day of August, 1994, and ending on the 31st day of July, 1997, shall be construed as a reference to such period as shall be specified in the order in relation to that area, but no such period specified in the order shall commence before 1 August 1994 or end after—

(I) 31 December 1999, or

(II) 31 December 2000, where in relation to the construction or refurbishment of a qualifying building within the meaning of *section 343*, the relevant local authority gives a certificate in writing on or before 31 May 2000 to the person constructing or refurbishing the qualifying building stating that it is satisfied that not less than 50 per cent of the total cost of the qualifying building and the site thereof had been incurred on or before 31 December 1999 and, in considering whether to give such a certificate, the relevant local authority shall have regard only to guidelines in relation to the giving of such certificates issued by the Department of the Environment and Local Government.][2]

(3) Every order made by the Minister for Finance under *subsection (1)* or *(2)* shall be laid before Dáil Éireann as soon as may be after it is made and, if a resolution annulling the order is passed by Dáil Éireann within the next 21 days on which Dáil Éireann has sat after the order is laid before it, the order shall be annulled accordingly, but without prejudice to the validity of anything previously done thereunder.

Amendments

[1] Inserted by FA99 s44(b).

[2] Substituted by FA00 s42(1)(b). This section shall apply as on and from 1 July 1999.

Cross References

From Section 340

Section 339 Interpretation (Chapter 3).

Section 343 Capital allowances in relation to construction or refurbishment of certain buildings or structures in enterprise areas.

To Section 340

Section 339 Interpretation (Chapter 3).

Section 343 Capital allowances in relation to construction or refurbishment of certain buildings or structures in enterprise areas.

Section 345 Double rent allowance in respect of rent paid for certain business premises.

341 Accelerated capital allowances in relation to construction or refurbishment of certain industrial buildings or structures

[FA94 s40; FA95 s35(1)(c)]

(1) This section shall apply to a building or structure the site of which is wholly within a designated area, or which fronts on to a designated street, and which is to be an industrial building or structure by reason of its use for a purpose specified in *section 268(1)(a)*.

(2) Subject to *subsection (4)*, *section 271* shall apply in relation to capital expenditure incurred in the qualifying period on the construction or refurbishment of a building or structure to which this section applies as if—

(a) in *subsection (1)* of that section the definition of "*industrial development agency*" were deleted,

(b) in *subsection (2)(a)(i)* of that section "to which *subsection (3)* applies" were deleted,

(c) *subsection (3)* of that section were deleted,

(d) the following subsection were substituted for *subsection (4)* of that section:

"(4) An industrial building allowance shall be of an amount equal to 25 per cent of the capital expenditure mentioned in *subsection (2)*.",

and

(e) in *subsection (5)* of that section "to which *subsection (3)(c)* applies" were deleted.

(3) Subject to *subsection (4)*, *section 273* shall apply in relation to capital expenditure incurred in the qualifying period on the construction or refurbishment of a building or structure to which this section applies as if—

(a) in *subsection (1)* of that section the definition of "*industrial development agency*" were deleted,

(b) the following paragraph were substituted for *paragraph (b)* of *subsection (2)* of that section:

"(b) As respects any qualifying expenditure, any allowance made under *section 272* and increased under *paragraph (a)* in respect of that expenditure, whether claimed for one chargeable period or more than one such period, shall not in the aggregate exceed 50 per cent of the amount of that qualifying expenditure.",

and

(c) *subsections (3)* to *(7)* of that section were deleted.

(4) (a) In the case of an industrial building or structure which fronts on to a designated street, *subsections (2)* and *(3)* shall apply only in relation to capital expenditure incurred in the qualifying period on the refurbishment of the industrial building or structure and only if the following conditions are satisfied—

(i) that the industrial building or structure was comprised in an existing building or structure (in this subsection referred to as "the existing building") on the 1st day of August, 1994, which fronts on to the designated street, and

(ii) that, apart from the capital expenditure incurred in the qualifying period on the refurbishment of the industrial building or structure, expenditure is incurred on the existing building which is—

(I) conversion expenditure within the meaning of *section 347*,

(II) relevant expenditure within the meaning of *section 348*, or

(III) qualifying expenditure within the meaning of *section 349* (being qualifying expenditure on refurbishment within the meaning of that section),

and in respect of which a deduction has been given, or would on due claim being made be given, under *section 347*, *348* or *349*, as the case may be.

(b) Notwithstanding *paragraph (a)*, *subsections (2)* and *(3)* shall not apply in relation to so much (if any) of the capital expenditure incurred in the qualifying period on the refurbishment of the industrial building or structure as exceeds the amount of the deduction, or the aggregate amount of the deductions, which has been given, or which would on due claim being made be given, under *section 347*, *348* or *349*, as the case may be, in respect of the conversion expenditure, the relevant expenditure or, as the case may be, the qualifying expenditure.

(5) Notwithstanding *section 274(1)*, no balancing charge shall be made in relation to a building or structure to which this section applies by reason of any of the events specified in that section which occurs—

(a) more than 13 years after the building or structure was first used, or

(b) in a case where *section 276* applies, more than 13 years after the capital expenditure on refurbishment of the building or structure was incurred.

(6) For the purposes only of determining, in relation to a claim for an allowance under *section 271* or *273* as applied by this section, whether and to what extent capital expenditure incurred on the construction or refurbishment of an industrial building or structure is incurred or not incurred in the qualifying period, only such an amount of that capital expenditure as is properly attributable to work on the construction or, as the case may be, the refurbishment of the building or structure actually carried out during the qualifying period shall (notwithstanding any other provision of the Tax Acts as to the time when any capital expenditure is or is to be treated as incurred) be treated as having been incurred in that period.

Cross References

From Section 341

Section 268 Meaning of "industrial building or structure".
Section 271 Industrial building allowances.
Section 272 Writing-down allowances.
Section 273 Acceleration of writing-down allowances in respect of certain expenditure on certain industrial buildings or structures.
Section 274 Balancing allowances and balancing charges.
Section 276 Application of sections 272 and 274 in relation to capital expenditure on refurbishment.
Section 347 Rented residential accommodation: deduction for certain expenditure on conversion.
Section 348 Rented residential accommodation: deduction for certain expenditure on refurbishment.
Section 349 Residential accommodation: allowance to owner-occupiers in respect of certain expenditure on construction or refurbishment.

To Section 341

Section 339 Interpretation (Chapter 3).
Section 342 Capital allowances in relation to construction or refurbishment of certain commercial premises.
Section 343 Capital allowances in relation to construction or refurbishment of certain buildings or structures in enterprise areas.
Section 344 Capital allowances in relation to construction or refurbishment of certain multi-storey car parks.
Section 345 Double rent allowance in respect of rent paid for certain business premises.
Schedule 25B List of Specified Reliefs and Method of Determining Amount of Specified Relief Used in a Tax Year

342 Capital allowances in relation to construction or refurbishment of certain commercial premises

[FA94 s41; FA95 s35(1)(d)]

(1) (a) In this section, "*qualifying premises*" means a building or structure the site of which is wholly within a designated area, or which fronts on to a designated street, and which—

(i) apart from this section is not an industrial building or structure within the meaning of *section 268*, and

(ii) (I) is in use for the purposes of a trade or profession, or

(II) whether or not it is so used, is let on bona fide commercial terms for such consideration as might be expected to be paid in a letting of the building or structure negotiated on an arm's length basis,

but does not include any part of a building or structure in use as or as part of a dwelling house or an office.

(b) Notwithstanding *paragraph (a)*—

(i) in relation to a building or structure no part of the site of which is within any one of the county boroughs of Dublin, Cork, Limerick,

Galway or Waterford, *paragraph (a)* shall be construed as if "or an office" were deleted;

(ii) where, in relation to a building or structure any part of the site of which is within any one of the county boroughs of Dublin, Cork, Limerick, Galway or Waterford, any part (in this paragraph referred to as "the specified part") of the building or structure is not a qualifying premises and—

(I) the specified part is in use as, or as part of, an office, and

(II) the capital expenditure incurred in the qualifying period on the construction or refurbishment of the specified part is not more than 10 per cent of the total capital expenditure incurred in that period on the construction or refurbishment of the building or structure,

then, the specified part shall be treated as a qualifying premises.

(2) (a) Subject to *subsections (3)* to *(6)*, the provisions of the Tax Acts (other than *section 341*) relating to the making of allowances or charges in respect of capital expenditure incurred on the construction or refurbishment of an industrial building or structure shall, notwithstanding anything to the contrary in those provisions, apply—

(i) as if a qualifying premises were, at all times at which it is a qualifying premises, a building or structure in respect of which an allowance is to be made for the purposes of income tax or corporation tax, as the case may be, under *Chapter 1* of *Part 9* by reason of its use for a purpose specified in *section 268(1)(a)*, and

(ii) where any activity carried on in the qualifying premises is not a trade, as if it were a trade.

(b) An allowance shall be given by virtue of this subsection in respect of any capital expenditure incurred on the construction or refurbishment of a qualifying premises only in so far as that expenditure is incurred in the qualifying period.

(3) (a) In the case of a qualifying premises which fronts on to a designated street, *subsection (2)* shall apply only in relation to capital expenditure incurred in the qualifying period on the refurbishment of the qualifying premises and only if the following conditions are satisfied—

(i) that the qualifying premises were comprised in an existing building or structure (in this subsection referred to as "the existing building") on the 1st day of August, 1994, which fronts on to the designated street, and

(ii) that, apart from the capital expenditure incurred in the qualifying period on the refurbishment of the qualifying premises, expenditure is incurred on the existing building which is—

(I) conversion expenditure within the meaning of *section 347*,

(II) relevant expenditure within the meaning of *section 348*, or

(III) qualifying expenditure within the meaning of *section 349* (being qualifying expenditure on refurbishment within the meaning of that section),

and in respect of which a deduction has been given, or would on due claim being made be given, under *section 347*, *348* or *349*, as the case may be.

(b) Notwithstanding *paragraph (a)*, *subsection (2)* shall not apply in relation to so much (if any) of the capital expenditure incurred in the qualifying period on the refurbishment of the qualifying premises as exceeds the amount of the deduction, or the aggregate amount of the deductions, which has been given, or which would on due claim being made be given, under *section 347*, *348* or *349*, as the case may be, in respect of the conversion expenditure, the relevant expenditure or, as the case may be, the qualifying expenditure.

(4) For the purposes of the application, by *subsection (2)*, of *sections 271* and *273* in relation to capital expenditure incurred in the qualifying period on the construction or refurbishment of a qualifying premises—

(a) *section 271* shall apply as if—

(i) in *subsection (1)* of that section the definition of "*industrial development agency*" were deleted,

(ii) in *subsection (2)(a)(i)* of that section "to which *subsection (3)* applies" were deleted,

(iii) *subsection (3)* of that section were deleted,

(iv) the following subsection were substituted for *subsection (4)* of that section:

"(4) An industrial building allowance shall be of an amount equal to 50 per cent of the capital expenditure mentioned in *subsection (2)*.",

and

(v) in *subsection (5)* of that section "to which *subsection (3)(c)* applies" were deleted,

and

(b) *section 273* shall apply as if—

(i) in *subsection (1)* of that section the definition of "*industrial development agency*" were deleted, and

(ii) *subsections (2)(b)* and *(3)* to *(7)* of that section were deleted.

(5) Notwithstanding *section 274(1)*, no balancing charge shall be made in relation to a qualifying premises by reason of any of the events specified in that section which occurs—

(a) more than 13 years after the qualifying premises was first used, or

(b) in a case where *section 276* applies, more than 13 years after the capital expenditure on refurbishment of the qualifying premises was incurred.

(6) (a) Notwithstanding *subsections (2)* to *(5)*, any allowance or charge which apart from this subsection would be made by virtue of *subsection (2)* in respect of capital expenditure incurred on the construction or refurbishment of a qualifying premises shall be reduced to one-half of the amount which apart from this subsection would be the amount of that allowance or charge.

(b) For the purposes of *paragraph (a)*, the amount of an allowance or charge to be reduced to one-half shall be computed as if—

(i) this subsection had not been enacted, and

(ii) effect had been given to all allowances taken into account in so computing that amount.

(c) Nothing in this subsection shall affect the operation of *section 274(8)*.

(7) For the purposes only of determining, in relation to a claim for an allowance by virtue of *subsection (2)*, whether and to what extent capital expenditure incurred

on the construction or refurbishment of a qualifying premises is incurred or not incurred in the qualifying period, only such an amount of that capital expenditure as is properly attributable to work on the construction or refurbishment of the premises actually carried out during the qualifying period shall (notwithstanding any other provision of the Tax Acts as to the time when any capital expenditure is or is to be treated as incurred) be treated as having been incurred in that period.

Revenue Precedents

If there is a mixture of residential and commercial units in a building in an Urban Renewal Area what does the 10% rule apply to? Where the capital expenditure incurred on the provision of the office accommodation in the qualifying period is not more than 10% of the capital expenditure incurred in that period on the entirety of the building or structure housing the office accommodation, the office is regarded as a qualifying premises for the purposes of section 342(1) TCA 1997. IT983002

Can the beneficiary of a settlement trust claim capital allowances on a property situated in an Urban Renewal Area if the expenditure is incurred by the Trust? Expenditure incurred by the trustees is not expenditure incurred by the beneficiaries for the purpose of TCA 1997 Part 10 Chapter 3.

Cross References

From Section 342

Section 268 Meaning of "industrial building or structure".

Section 271 Industrial building allowances.

Section 273 Acceleration of writing-down allowances in respect of certain expenditure on certain industrial buildings or structures.

Section 274 Balancing allowances and balancing charges.

Section 276 Application of sections 272 and 274 in relation to capital expenditure on refurbishment.

Section 341 Accelerated capital allowances in relation to construction or refurbishment of certain industrial buildings or structures.

Section 347 Rented residential accommodation: deduction for certain expenditure on conversion.

Section 348 Rented residential accommodation: deduction for certain expenditure on refurbishment.

Section 349 Residential accommodation: allowance to owner-occupiers in respect of certain expenditure on construction or refurbishment.

To Section 342

Section 339 Interpretation (Chapter 3).

Section 345 Double rent allowance in respect of rent paid for certain business premises.

Schedule 25B List of Specified Reliefs and Method of Determining Amount of Specified Relief Used in a Tax Year

343 Capital allowances in relation to construction or refurbishment of certain buildings or structures in enterprise areas

[FA94 s41A; FA95 s35(1)(e)]

(1) In this section—

["*property developer*" means a person carrying on a trade which consists wholly or mainly of the construction or refurbishment of buildings or structures with a view to their sale;][1]

"*the Minister*", except where the context otherwise requires, means the Minister for Enterprise, Trade and Employment;

"*qualifying building*" means a building or structure the site of which is wholly within an enterprise area and which is in use for the purposes of the carrying on of qualifying trading operations by a qualifying company, but does not include any part of a building or structure in use as or as part of a dwelling house;

["*qualifying company*" means a company—

(a) (i) which has been approved for financial assistance under a scheme administered by Forfás, Enterprise Ireland, the Industrial Development Agency (Ireland) or Údarás na Gaeltachta, or

(ii) which is engaged in a qualifying trading operation within the meaning of *paragraph (c)* of the definition of "*qualifying trading operations*",

and

(b) to which the Minister has given a certificate under *subsection (2)* which has not been withdrawn in accordance with *subsection (5)* or *(6)*;][2]

"*qualifying trading operations*" means—

[(a) the manufacture of goods within the meaning of *Part 14*,

(b) the rendering of services in the course of a service industry (within the meaning of the Industrial Development Act, 1986), or

(c) the rendering of services in the course or furtherance of a business of freight forwarding or the provision of logistical services in relation to such business where the rendering or provision of those services is carried on in an area or areas immediately adjacent to any of the airports to which *section 340(2)* refers.][3]

(2) Subject to *subsection (4)*, the Minister may—

[(a) on the recommendation of Forfás (in conjunction with Enterprise Ireland, the Industrial Development Agency (Ireland) or Údarás na Gaeltachta, as may be appropriate, or the Minister for Public Enterprise in the case of a company to which *paragraph (a)(ii)* of the definition of "*qualifying company*" refers) in accordance with guidelines laid down by the Minister, and][4]

(b) following consultation with the Minister for Finance,

give a certificate to a company certifying that the company is, with effect from a date to be specified in the certificate, to be treated as a qualifying company for the purposes of this section.

(3) A certificate under *subsection (2)* may be given either without conditions or subject to such conditions as the Minister considers proper and specifies in the certificate.

(4) The Minister shall not certify under *subsection (2)* that a company is a qualifying company for the purposes of this section unless—

(a) the company is carrying on or intends to carry on qualifying trading operations in an enterprise area, and

(b) the Minister is satisfied that the carrying on by the company of such trading operations will contribute to the balanced development of the enterprise area.

(5) Where, in the case of a company in relation to which a certificate under *subsection (2)* has been given—

(a) the company ceases to carry on or, as the case may be, fails to commence to carry on qualifying trading operations in the enterprise area, or

(b) the Minister is satisfied that the company has failed to comply with any condition subject to which the certificate was given,

the Minister may, by notice in writing served by registered post on the company, revoke the certificate with effect from such date as may be specified in the notice.

(6) Where, in the case of a company in relation to which a certificate under *subsection (2)* has been given, the Minister is of the opinion that any activity of the company has had or may have an adverse effect on the use or development of the enterprise area or is otherwise inimical to the balanced development of the enterprise area, then—

(a) the Minister may, by notice in writing served by registered post on the company, require the company to desist from such activity with effect from such date as may be specified in the notice, and

(b) if the Minister is not satisfied that the company has complied with the requirements of the notice, the Minister may, by a further notice in writing served by registered post on the company, revoke the certificate with effect from such date as may be specified in the further notice.

(7) (a) Subject to [*subsections (8), (9)* and *(11)*][5], the provisions of the Tax Acts (other than *section 341*) relating to the making of allowances or charges in respect of capital expenditure incurred on the construction or refurbishment of an industrial building or structure shall, notwithstanding anything to the contrary in those provisions, apply as if a qualifying building were, at all times at which it is a qualifying building, a building or structure in respect of which an allowance is to be made for the purposes of income tax or corporation tax, as the case may be, under *Chapter 1* of *Part 9* by reason of its use for a purpose specified in *section 268(1)(a).*

(b) An allowance shall be given by virtue of this subsection in respect of any capital expenditure incurred on the construction or refurbishment of a qualifying building only in so far as that expenditure is incurred in the qualifying period.

(8) For the purposes of the application, by *subsection (7)*, of *sections 271* and *273* in relation to capital expenditure incurred in the qualifying period on the construction or refurbishment of a qualifying building—

(a) *section 271* shall apply as if—

(i) in *subsection (1)* of that section the definition of "*industrial development agency*" were deleted,

(ii) in *subsection (2)(a)(i)* of that section "to which *subsection (3)* applies" were deleted,

(iii) *subsection (3)* of that section were deleted,

[(iv) the following subsection were substituted for *subsection (4)* of that section:

"(4) An industrial building allowance, in the case of a qualifying building (within the meaning of *section 343(1)*), shall be of an amount equal to—

(a) 25 per cent, or

(b) in the case of such a building the site of which is wholly within an area described in an order referred to in *section 340(2)(i)*, 50 per cent,

of the capital expenditure mentioned in *subsection (2)*.",][6]

(v) in *subsection (5)* of that section "to which *subsection (3)(c)* applies" were deleted,

and

(b) *section 273* shall apply as if—

(i) in *subsection (1)* of that section the definition of "*industrial development agency*" were deleted,

(ii) the following paragraph were substituted for *paragraph (b)* of *subsection (2)* of that section:

"(b) As respects any qualifying expenditure, any allowance made under *section 272* and increased under *paragraph (a)* in respect of that expenditure, whether claimed for one chargeable period or more than one such period, shall not in the aggregate exceed 50 per cent of the amount of that qualifying expenditure.",

and

(iii) *subsections (3)* to *(7)* of that section were deleted.

(9) Notwithstanding *section 274(1)*, no balancing charge shall be made in relation to a qualifying building by reason of any of the events specified in that section which occurs—

(a) more than 13 years after the qualifying building was first used, or

(b) in a case where *section 276* applies, more than 13 years after the capital expenditure on refurbishment of the qualifying building was incurred.

(10) For the purposes only of determining, in relation to a claim for an allowance by virtue of *subsection (7)*, whether and to what extent capital expenditure incurred on the construction or refurbishment of a qualifying building is incurred or not incurred in the qualifying period, only such an amount of that capital expenditure as is properly attributable to work on the construction or refurbishment of the building actually carried out during the qualifying period shall (notwithstanding any other provision of the Tax Acts as to the time when any capital expenditure is or is to be treated as incurred) be treated as having been incurred in that period.

[(11) Notwithstanding the preceding provisions of this section, this section shall not apply in respect of expenditure incurred on the construction or refurbishment of a qualifying building, the site of which is wholly within an area described in an order referred to in *section 340(2)(i)*—

(a) where a property developer is entitled to the relevant interest, within the meaning of *section 269*, in relation to that expenditure, and

(b) either the person referred to in *paragraph (a)* or a person connected (within the meaning of *section 10*) with that person incurred the expenditure on the construction or refurbishment of the qualifying building concerned.][7]

Amendments

[1] Inserted by FA00 s42(1)(c)(i). This section shall apply as on and from 1 July 1999.

[2] Substituted by FA99 s44(c)(i).

[3] Substituted by FA98 s24(1)(c)(ii). This section shall come into operation on such day as the Minister for Finance may, by order, appoint.

[4] Substituted by FA99 s44(c)(ii).

[5] Substituted by FA00 s42(1)(c)(ii). This section shall apply as on and from 1 July 1999.

[6] Substituted by FA99 s44(c)(iii). This section shall apply with effect as on and from the 1st day of January, 1998.

[7] Inserted by FA00 s42(1)(c)(iii). This section shall apply as on and from 1 July 1999.

Revenue Briefings

Tax Briefing

Tax Briefing September 2000 – Issue 41 pg 16 – Industrial & Commercial Buildings Capital Allowances

Cross References

From Section 343

Section 10 Connected persons.

Section 268 Meaning of "industrial building or structure".

Section 269 Meaning of "the relevant interest".

Section 271 Industrial building allowances.

Section 272 Writing-down allowances.
Section 273 Acceleration of writing-down allowances in respect of certain expenditure on certain industrial buildings or structures.
Section 274 Balancing allowances and balancing charges.
Section 276 Application of sections 272 and 274 in relation to capital expenditure on refurbishment.
Section 340 Designated areas, designated streets and enterprise areas.
Section 341 Accelerated capital allowances in relation to construction or refurbishment of certain industrial buildings or structures.
Section 343 Capital allowances in relation to construction or refurbishment of certain buildings or structures in enterprise areas.
Section 442 Interpretation (Part 14).

To Section 343

Section 339 Interpretation (Chapter 3).
Section 340 Designated areas, designated streets and enterprise areas.
Section 343 Capital allowances in relation to construction or refurbishment of certain buildings or structures in enterprise areas.
Section 345 Double rent allowance in respect of rent paid for certain business premises.
Schedule 25B List of Specified Reliefs and Method of Determining Amount of Specified Relief Used in a Tax Year

344 Capital allowances in relation to construction or refurbishment of certain multi-storey car parks

[FA94 s41B; FA95 s35(1)(f); FA96 s26(1)]

(1) In this section—

"*multi-storey car park*" means a building or structure consisting of 2 or more storeys wholly in use for the purpose of providing, for members of the public generally without preference for any particular class of person, on payment of an appropriate charge, parking space for mechanically propelled vehicles;

"*qualifying multi-storey car park*" means a multi-storey car park in respect of which the relevant local authority gives a certificate in writing to the person providing the multi-storey car park stating that it is satisfied that the multi-storey car park has been developed in accordance with criteria laid down by the Minister for the Environment and Local Government following consultation with the Minister for Finance;

["*qualifying period*" means the period commencing on the 1st day of July, 1995, and ending on—

(a) the 30th day of June, 1998, or

(b) [30 September 1999][1], where, in relation to the construction or refurbishment of the qualifying multi-storey car park concerned, the relevant local authority gives a certificate in writing on or before the 30th day of September, 1998, to the person constructing or refurbishing the qualifying multi-storey car park stating that it is satisfied that not less than 15 per cent of the total cost of the qualifying multi-storey car park and the site thereof had been incurred prior to the 1st day of July, 1998, and, in considering whether to give such a certificate, the relevant local authority shall have regard only to guidelines in relation to the giving of such certificates issued by the Department of the Environment and Local Government for the purposes [of this definition, or][2

[(c) [31 December 2006][3], where, in relation to the construction or refurbishment of the qualifying multi-storey car park concerned (not being a qualifying multi-storey car park any part of the site of which is within either of the county boroughs of Cork or Dublin), the relevant local authority gives a certificate in writing on or before [31 December 2003][4] to the person constructing or refurbishing the qualifying multi-storey car park stating that it is satisfied that not less than 15 per cent of the total cost of the qualifying multi-storey car park and the site thereof had been incurred on or before [30 September 2003][5] and, in considering whether to give such a certificate, the relevant local authority shall have regard only to guidelines in relation to the giving of such certificates issued by the Department of the Environment and Local Government for [the purposes of this definition, or][6]][7]][8]

[(d) 31 July 2008, where in relation to the construction or refurbishment of the qualifying multi-storey car park—

(i) the relevant local authority has issued the certificate referred to in *paragraph (c)* on or before 31 December 2003, and

(ii) (I) the person who is constructing or refurbishing the qualifying multi-storey car park has, on or before 31 December 2006, carried out work to the value of not less than 15 per cent of the actual construction or, as the case may be, refurbishment costs of the qualifying multi-storey car park, and

(II) the person referred to in clause (I) or, where the qualifying multi-storey car park is sold by that person, the person who is claiming a deduction under *Chapter 1* of *Part 9* in relation to the expenditure incurred, can show that the condition in clause (I) was satisfied;][9]

['*the relevant local authority*', in relation to the construction or replacement of a multi-storey car park, means the local authority for the purposes of the Local Government Act 2001 (as amended by the *Local Government Reform Act 2014*) in whose functional area the multi-storey car park is situated.][10]

(2) (a) [Subject to *subsections (3)* to *(6A)* and (as inserted by the Finance Act 2006) *sections 270(4)*, *270(5)*, *270(6)* and *316(2B)*][11], the provisions of the Tax Acts (other than *section 341*) relating to the making of allowances or charges in respect of capital expenditure incurred on the construction or refurbishment of an industrial building or structure shall, notwithstanding anything to the contrary in those provisions, apply as if a qualifying multi-storey car park were, at all times at which it is a qualifying multi-storey car park, a building or structure in respect of which an allowance is to be made for the purposes of income tax or corporation tax, as the case may be, under *Chapter 1* of *Part 9* by reason of its use for a purpose specified in *section 268(1)(a)*.

(b) An allowance shall be given by virtue of this subsection in respect of any capital expenditure incurred on the construction or refurbishment of a qualifying multi-storey car park only in so far as that expenditure is incurred in the qualifying period.

(3) In a case where capital expenditure is incurred in the qualifying period on the refurbishment of a qualifying multi-storey car park, *subsection (2)* shall apply only if the total amount of the capital expenditure so incurred is not less than an amount equal to 20 per cent of the market value of the qualifying multi-storey car park immediately before that expenditure is incurred.

(4) For the purposes of the application, by *subsection (2)*, of *sections 271* and *273* in relation to capital expenditure incurred in the qualifying period on the construction or refurbishment of a qualifying multi-storey car park—

(a) *section 271* shall apply as if—

(i) in *subsection (1)* of that section the definition of "*industrial development agency*" were deleted,

(ii) in *subsection (2)(a)(i)* of that section "to which *subsection (3)* applies" were deleted,

(iii) *subsection (3)* of that section were deleted,

(iv) the following subsection were substituted for *subsection (4)* of that section:

"(4) An industrial building allowance shall be of an amount equal to 50 per cent of the capital expenditure mentioned in *subsection (2)*.",

and

(v) in *subsection (5)* of that section "to which *subsection (3)(c)* applies" were deleted,

and

(b) *section 273* shall apply as if—

(i) in *subsection (1)* of that section, the definition of "*industrial development agency*" were deleted, and

(ii) *subsections (2)(b)* and *(3)* to *(7)* of that section were deleted.

(5) Notwithstanding *section 274(1)*, no balancing charge shall be made in relation to a qualifying multi-storey car park by reason of any of the events specified in that section which occurs—

(a) more than 13 years after the qualifying multi-storey car park was first used, or

(b) in a case where *section 276* applies, more than 13 years after the capital expenditure on refurbishment of the multi-storey car park was incurred.

(6) (a) Notwithstanding *subsections (2)* to *(5)*, any allowance or charge which apart from this subsection would be made by virtue of *subsection (2)* in respect of capital expenditure incurred on the construction or refurbishment of a qualifying multi-storey car park shall be reduced to one-half of the amount which apart from this subsection would be the amount of that allowance or charge.

(b) For the purposes of *paragraph (a)*, the amount of an allowance or charge to be reduced to one-half shall be computed as if—

(i) this subsection had not been enacted, and

(ii) effect had been given to all allowances taken into account in so computing that amount.

(c) Nothing in this subsection shall affect the operation of *section 274(8)*.

[(6A) *Subsection (6)* shall apply and have effect as respects capital expenditure referred to in *subsection (2)(b)*, which is incurred after the 31st day of July, 1998, only if a qualifying lease, within the meaning of *section 345*, is granted in respect of the qualifying multi-storey car park in respect of which that expenditure is incurred.][12]

(7) For the purposes only of determining, in relation to a claim for an allowance by virtue of *subsection (2)*, whether and to what extent capital expenditure incurred on the construction or refurbishment of a qualifying multi-storey car park is incurred or not incurred in the qualifying period, only such an amount of that capital expenditure as is properly attributable to work on the construction or refurbishment of the qualifying multi-storey car park actually carried out during the qualifying period shall (notwithstanding any other provision of the Tax Acts as to the time when any capital expenditure is or is to be treated as incurred) be treated as having been incurred in that period.

(8) Where by virtue of *subsection (2)* an allowance is given under *Chapter 1* of *Part 9* in respect of capital expenditure incurred on the construction or refurbishment of a qualifying multi-storey car park, no allowance shall be given in respect of that expenditure under that Chapter by virtue of any other provision of the Tax Acts.

Amendments

[1] Substituted by FA00 s42(1)(d)(i)(I). This section shall apply as on and from 1 July 1999.

[2] Substituted by FA99 s44(d)(i)(I).

[3, 6] Substituted by FA06 s29(1)(a)(i). This section shall come into operation on such day or days as the Minister for Finance may by order or orders appoint and different days may be appointed for different purposes or different provisions.

[4] Substituted by FA02 s23(1)(a)(ii).

[5] Substituted by FA02 s23(1)(a)(iii).

[7] Substituted by FA00 s42(1)(d)(i)(II). This section shall apply as on and from 1 July 1999.

[8] Substituted by FA98 s26.

[9] Inserted by FA06 s29(1)(a)(ii). With effect from 26 June 2006 per S.I. No. 324 of 2006.

[10] Substituted by LGRA14 sched2(part5).

[11] Substituted by FA06 s29(1)(b). With effect from 26 June 2006 per S.I. No. 324 of 2006.

[12] Inserted by FA99 s44(d)(iii).

Revenue Briefings

Tax Briefing

Tax Briefing November 1995 – Issue 18 pg 17 – Capital Allowances for Multi-storey Car Parks

Tax Briefing March 1996 – Issue 21 pg 9 – Urban Renewal Relief – Multi-storey Car Parks

Cross References

From Section 344

Section 268 Meaning of "industrial building or structure".

Section 270 Meaning of "expenditure on construction of building or structure".

Section 271 Industrial building allowances.

Section 273 Acceleration of writing-down allowances in respect of certain expenditure on certain industrial buildings or structures.

Section 274 Balancing allowances and balancing charges.

Section 276 Application of sections 272 and 274 in relation to capital expenditure on refurbishment.

Section 316 Interpretation of certain references to expenditure and time when expenditure is incurred.

Section 341 Accelerated capital allowances in relation to construction or refurbishment of certain industrial buildings or structures.

Section 345 Double rent allowance in respect of rent paid for certain business premises.

To Section 344

Section 270 Meaning of "expenditure on construction of building or structure".

Section 339 Interpretation (Chapter 3).

Section 345 Double rent allowance in respect of rent paid for certain business premises.

Schedule 25B List of Specified Reliefs and Method of Determining Amount of Specified Relief Used in a Tax Year

345 Double rent allowance in respect of rent paid for certain business premises

[FA90 s33(1) and (2)(a); FA94 s42; FA95 s35(1)(g); FA97 s26(c) and s27]

(1) In this section—

["*qualifying lease*" means, subject to *subsections (1A)* and *(8)*, a lease in respect of a qualifying premises granted in the qualifying period, or within the period of one year from the day next after the end of the qualifying period, on bona fide commercial terms by a lessor to a lessee not connected with the lessor, or with any other person entitled to a rent in respect of the qualifying premises, whether under that lease or any other lease but, notwithstanding the foregoing, a lease which would otherwise be a qualifying lease shall not be such a lease if granted in respect of a building or structure within the meaning of *paragraph (a)(iii)* of the definition of "*qualifying premises*" the site of which is wholly within an area—

(a) described in an order referred to in *section 340(1)(a)*, if the lease is granted on or after the 31st day of July, 1999, or

(b) described in *Schedule 7*, if the lease is granted on or after the 31st day of December, 1999, or

(c) described in an order referred to in *section 340(2)(i)*, irrespective of the date of the granting of the lease;][1]

"*qualifying premises*" means, subject to *subsection (5)(a)*, a building or structure—

(a) (i) the site of which is wholly within a designated area and which is a building or structure in use for a purpose specified in *section 268(1)(a)*, and in respect of which capital expenditure is incurred in the qualifying period for which an allowance is to be made, or will by virtue of *section 279* be made, for the purposes of income tax or corporation tax, as the case may be, under *section 271* or *273*, as applied by *section 341*,

(ii) the site of which is wholly within a designated area and in respect of which an allowance is to be made, or will by virtue of *section 279* be made, for the purposes of income tax or corporation tax, as the case may be, under *Chapter 1* of *Part 9* by virtue of *section 342*,

(iii) the site of which is wholly within an enterprise area and in respect of which an allowance is to be made, or will by virtue of *section 279* be made, for the purposes of income tax or corporation tax, as the case may be, under *Chapter 1* of *Part 9* by virtue of *section 343*,

(iv) the site of which is wholly within a designated area and which is a building or structure in use for the purposes specified in *section 268(1)(d)*, and in respect of the construction or refurbishment of which capital expenditure is incurred in the qualifying period for which an allowance would but for *subsection (6)* be made for the purposes of income tax or corporation tax, as the case may be, under *Chapter 1* of *Part 9*, or

(v) in respect of which an allowance is to be made, or will by virtue of *section 279* be made, for the purposes of income tax or corporation tax, as the case may be, under *Chapter 1* of *Part 9* by virtue of *section 344*,

and

(b) which is let on bona fide commercial terms for such consideration as might be expected to be paid in a letting of the building or structure negotiated on an arm's length basis, but, where capital expenditure is incurred in the qualifying period on the refurbishment of a building or structure in respect of which an allowance is to be made, or will by virtue of *section 279* be made, or in respect of which an allowance would but for *subsection (6)* be made, for the purposes of income tax or corporation tax, as the case may be, under any of the provisions referred to in *paragraph (a)*, the building or structure shall not be regarded as a qualifying premises unless the total amount of the expenditure so incurred is not less than an amount equal to 10 per cent of the market value of the building or structure immediately before that expenditure is incurred.

[(1A) Notwithstanding any other provision of this Chapter, including this section, "*qualifying period*" for the purposes of this section in the case of a building or structure within the meaning of *paragraph (a)(v)* of the definition of "*qualifying premises*" in *subsection (1)* means the period commencing on the 1st day of August, 1994, and ending on—

(a) the 31st day of July, 1997, or

(b) [30 September 1998][2], where, in relation to the construction or refurbishment of the qualifying multi-storey car park concerned, the relevant local authority has certified in accordance with the requirements of *paragraph (b)* of the definition of "*qualifying period*" in *section 344(1)*.][3]

(2) For the purposes of this section, so much of a period, being a period when rent is payable by a person in relation to a qualifying premises under a qualifying lease, shall be a relevant rental period as does not exceed—

(a) 10 years, or

(b) the period by which 10 years exceeds—

(i) any preceding period, or

(ii) if there is more than one preceding period, the aggregate of those periods,

for which rent was payable by that person or any other person in relation to that premises under a qualifying lease.

(3) Subject to *subsection (4)*, where in the computation of the amount of the profits or gains of a trade or profession a person is apart from this section entitled to any deduction (in this subsection referred to as "the first-mentioned deduction") on account of rent in respect of a qualifying premises occupied by such person for the purposes of that trade or profession which is payable by such person for a relevant rental period in relation to that qualifying premises under a qualifying lease, such person shall be entitled in that computation to a further deduction (in this subsection referred to as "the second-mentioned deduction") equal to the amount of the first-mentioned deduction but, as respects a qualifying lease granted on or after the 21st day of April, 1997, where the first-mentioned deduction is on account of rent payable by such person to a connected person, such person shall not be entitled in that computation to the second-mentioned deduction.

(4) Where a person holds an interest in a qualifying premises out of which interest a qualifying lease is created directly or indirectly in respect of the qualifying premises and in respect of rent payable under the qualifying lease a claim for a further deduction under this section is made, and either such person or another person connected with such person—

(a) takes under a qualifying lease a qualifying premises (in this subsection referred to as "the second-mentioned premises") occupied by such person or such other person, as the case may be, for the purposes of a trade or profession, and

(b) is apart from this section entitled, in the computation of the amount of the profits or gains of that trade or profession, to a deduction on account of rent in respect of the second-mentioned premises,

then, unless such person or such other person, as the case may be, shows that the taking on lease of the second-mentioned premises was not undertaken for the sole or main benefit of obtaining a further deduction on account of rent under this section, such person or such other person, as the case may be, shall not be entitled in the computation of the amount of the profits or gains of that trade or profession to any further deduction on account of rent in respect of the second-mentioned premises.

(5) (a) A building or structure in use for the purposes specified in *section 268(1)(d)* shall not be a qualifying premises for the purposes of this section unless the person to whom an allowance under *Chapter 1* of *Part 9* would but for *subsection (6)* be made for the purposes of income tax or corporation tax, as the case may be, in respect of the capital expenditure incurred in the qualifying period on the construction or refurbishment of the building or structure elects by notice in writing to the appropriate inspector (within the meaning of *section 950*) to disclaim all allowances under that Chapter in respect of that capital expenditure.

(b) An election under *paragraph (a)* shall be included in the return required to be made by the person concerned under *section 951* for the first year of assessment or the first accounting period, as the case may be, for which an allowance would but for *subsection (6)* have been made to that person under *Chapter 1* of *Part 9* in respect of that capital expenditure.

(c) An election under *paragraph (a)* shall be irrevocable.

(d) A person who has made an election under *paragraph (a)* shall furnish a copy of that election to any person (in this paragraph referred to as "the second-mentioned person") to whom the person grants a qualifying lease in respect of the qualifying premises, and the second-mentioned person shall include the copy in the return required to be made by the second-mentioned person under *section 951* for the year of assessment or accounting period, as the case may be, in which rent is first payable by the second-mentioned person under the qualifying lease in respect of the qualifying premises.

(6) Where a person who has incurred capital expenditure in the qualifying period on the construction or refurbishment of a building or structure in use for the purposes specified in *section 268(1)(d)* makes an election under *subsection (5)(a)*, then, notwithstanding any other provision of the Tax Acts—

(a) no allowance under *Chapter 1* of *Part 9* shall be made to the person in respect of that capital expenditure,

(b) on the occurrence, in relation to the building or structure, of any of the events referred to in *section 274(1)*, the residue of expenditure (within the meaning of *section 277*) in relation to that capital expenditure shall be deemed to be nil, and

(c) *section 279* shall not apply in the case of any person who buys the relevant interest (within the meaning of *section 269*) in the building or structure.

(7) For the purposes of determining, in relation to *paragraph (a)(iv)* of the definition of "*qualifying premises*" and *subsections (5)* and *(6)*, whether and to what extent capital expenditure incurred on the construction or refurbishment of a building or structure is incurred or not incurred in the qualifying period, only such an amount of that capital expenditure as is properly attributable to work on the construction or refurbishment of the building or structure actually carried out in the qualifying period shall (notwithstanding any other provision of the Tax Acts as to the time when any capital expenditure is or is to be treated as incurred) be treated as having been incurred in that period.

(8) (a) In this subsection—

"*current value*", in relation to minimum lease payments, means the value of those payments discounted to their present value at a rate which, when applied at the inception of the lease to—

(i) those payments, including any initial payment but excluding any payment or part of any payment for which the lessor will be accountable to the lessee, and

(ii) any unguaranteed residual value of the qualifying premises, excluding any part of such value for which the lessor will be accountable to the lessee,

produces discounted present values the aggregate amount of which equals the amount of the fair value of the qualifying premises;

"*fair value*", in relation to a qualifying premises, means an amount equal to such consideration as might be expected to be paid for the premises on a sale negotiated on an arm's length basis less any grants receivable towards the purchase of the qualifying premises;

"*inception of the lease*" means the earlier of the time the qualifying premises is brought into use or the date from which rentals under the lease first accrue;

"*minimum lease payments*" means the minimum payments over the remaining part of the term of the lease to be paid to the lessor, and includes any residual amount to be paid to the lessor at the end of the term of the lease and guaranteed by the lessee or by a person connected with the lessee;

"*unguaranteed residual value*", in relation to a qualifying premises, means that part of the residual value of that premises at the end of a term of a lease, as estimated at the inception of the lease, the realisation of which by the lessor is not assured or is guaranteed solely by a person connected with the lessor.

(b) A finance lease, that is—

(i) a lease in respect of a qualifying premises where, at the inception of the lease, the aggregate of the current value of the minimum lease payments (including any initial payment but excluding any payment or part of any payment for which the lessor will be accountable to the lessee) payable by the lessee in relation to the lease amounts to 90 per cent or more of the fair value of the qualifying premises, or

(ii) a lease which in all the circumstances is considered to provide in substance for the lessee the risks and benefits associated with ownership of the qualifying premises other than legal title to that premises,

shall not be a qualifying lease for the purposes of this section.

Amendments

[1] Substituted by FA99 s44(e)(i).

[2] Substituted by FA00 s42(1)(e). This section shall apply as on and from 1 July 1999.

[3] Inserted by FA99 s44(e)(ii).

Revenue Briefings

Tax Briefing

Tax Briefing February 1997 – Issue 25 pg 16 – Urban Renewal Relief
Tax Briefing December 2000 – Issue 42 pg 11 – Town Renewal Scheme

Revenue Information Notes

A Guide to Section 23 relief – Rented Residential Relief in a Tax Incentive Area

Revenue Precedents

If part of the capital expenditure incurred on a building in a designated area qualifies for capital allowances and part does not due to the expenditure falling outside the qualifying period, is there an apportionment of the double rent allowance?. The double rent deduction which is available by virtue of section 345 Taxes Consolidation Act 1997 is given where an allowance falls to be made by reason of section 342 of that Act. Once an allowance is given, and all the other conditions of the section are met, double rent deduction will be given, even where part of the capital expenditure does not qualify for capital allowances because it was incurred prior to designation. IT903014

Is a double rent allowance available in Urban Renewal areas for car spaces let on long lease to traders and professionals? Section 345 Taxes Consolidation Act 1997 , provides that a Double Rent Allowance will be available to a person who is entitled to a deduction on account of rent in respect of a qualifying premises (as defined) occupied by him for the purposes of that trade or profession, and who otherwise meets the conditions laid down in that section. Provided therefore that the car park spaces are in use for the purposes of the trade or profession of the lessee, and subject to all other conditions being met, the provisions of the aforesaid section 345 would apply. IT923069

Can a person claim the double deduction in circumstances where the property is owned and developed by charitable or religious institutions which are exempt from tax and as a result do not claim the capital allowances? Yes, provided all other aspects of the legislation are complied with. IT943506

The taxpayer paid rent under a qualifying lease and was entitled to the double deduction. A connected company was to purchase the property. Would the taxpayer still be entitled to the double decuction even though it would be connected with the new owner? Yes, provided that the rent was still payable under the original lease. (this does not apply to leases granted on or after 21 April 1997). IT953556

A lessee enters into a qualifying lease with effect from the date the main contractor completes the landlords work. Rent commences to be payable one month after the grant of the lease Would the lessee be regarded as occupying the qualifying premises during a fit out period which could take several months? Yes, the lessee would be regarded as occupying the premises for the purposes of the trade or profession during the fit out period provided that during the period they hold a qualifying lease on the premises. IT903121

Is it possible for a lessee to claim the double deduction in circumstances where the refurbishment expenditure on the premises is incurred by the lessee rather than the lessor? In order for the double deduction to be due the rent in respect of which the double deduction is claimed would need to be paid under a lease which is granted after the necessary amount of refurbishment expenditure has been incurred. IT953522

A lease is granted in respect of a premises in a designated area in the qualifying period. The lessor subsequently incurs capital expenditure and qualifies for capital allowances under section 443 TCA 1997. Is the lease qualifying under section 345 TCA 1997? The double rent allowance is granted under section 345 Taxes Consolidation Act 1997 in respect of a letting under a qualifying lease which is defined as "a lease in respect of a qualifying premises granted in the qualifying period on bona fide commercial terms ...". The Commissioners interpret this to mean that a lease must be granted in respect of a qualifying premises before it can be a "qualifying lease" within the meaning of the section. A lease granted in respect of a premises in a designated area which is not a qualifying premises is not a qualifying lease. The subsequent incurring by the lessor of capital expenditure in respect of the premises will not alter the position. IT903023

A company and its wholly owned subsidiary, as joint tenants, will enter into a 35 year lease agreement in respect of a premises situated in a designated area. Part of the building will be used as an industrial building by the parent. The other part used by the subsidiary will also be a qualifying premises. The lease payments will be apportioned between both companies and each company will make its own lease payments to the landlord. Is a double rent allowance is available? Provided that both companies enter into a "qualifying lease" in respect of a "qualifying premises" (both terms within the meaning of section

345 Taxes Consolidation Act 1997) the fact that both companies will have equal tenancy rights in respect of the entire premises will not prevent them from claiming the double rent allowance under the said section 345. IT923071

Where an assignment of a qualifying lease takes place can the person to whom the lease is assigned claim the double deduction, regardless of whether the assignment takes place within the qualifying period? Yes, provided the normal conditions to qualify are satisfied. IT953527

The lessee of a premises which is owned by a local authority can claim the double deduction in circumstances where the local authority is exempt from tax and does not claim capital allowances in respect of the premises, provided all other conditions are satisfied. IT953521

This case involves a company group. Trading is conducted through numerous retail outlets. All property is managed through one property investment company. If this company takes a lease of four qualifying units and sub-lets them to connected trading entities on the same terms and conditions as the head lease can the trading entities claim the double deduction? Yes, in the circulstances of this case the trading entities may claim the double deduction. The intermediary lease appears to be for practial purposes only. IT953532

Payments for off-site storage of documents do not qualify for a double deduction in computing trading profits unless rent is paid under a qualifying lease. Rent must be paid and a leasehold interest must be held by the claimant. IT963502

Pension schemes are exempt from income tax on investment income, by virtue of section 774 Taxes Consolidation Act 1997. Please confirm that a premises in a designated area which is owned by a pension scheme will be a qualifying premises for the purposes of a double rent allowance.? It is accepted that for the purposes of section 45, Finance Act 1986, a building which is owned by a pension scheme which is exempt by virtue of section 16, Finance Act 1972, will be regarded as a qualifying premises. A lessee of such a building will not be denied the double rent allowance on the grounds that a capital allowance has not fallen to be made to the lessor where the lessor is such a pension scheme. IT913053

A person who obtains a property by way of a distribution in specie can qualify for rented residentiial relief if the ownership of a lessor's interest passes by way of a distribution in specie the person to whom that interest passes will subject to meeting all other conditions of section 345 TCA 1997 be entitled to rented residential relief.

Cross References

From Section 345

Section 268 Meaning of "industrial building or structure".
Section 269 Meaning of "the relevant interest".
Section 271 Industrial building allowances.
Section 273 Acceleration of writing-down allowances in respect of certain expenditure on certain industrial buildings or structures.
Section 274 Balancing allowances and balancing charges.
Section 277 Writing off of expenditure and meaning of "residue of expenditure".
Section 279 Purchases of certain buildings or structures.
Section 340 Designated areas, designated streets and enterprise areas.
Section 341 Accelerated capital allowances in relation to construction or refurbishment of certain industrial buildings or structures.
Section 342 Capital allowances in relation to construction or refurbishment of certain commercial premises.
Section 343 Capital allowances in relation to construction or refurbishment of certain buildings or structures in enterprise areas.
Section 344 Capital allowances in relation to construction or refurbishment of certain multi-storey car parks.
Section 950 Interpretation (Part 41).
Section 951 Obligation to make a return.
Schedule 7 Description of Certain Enterprise Areas

To Section 345

Section 339 Interpretation (Chapter 3).
Section 344 Capital allowances in relation to construction or refurbishment of certain multi-storey car parks.
Section 485C Interpretation (Chapter 2A).
Section 531B Charge to income levy.
Section 531AA Interpretation (Part 18C).
Section 531AM Charge to universal social charge.

Section 708 Acquisition expenses.
Section 1013 Limited partnerships.
Schedule 25B List of Specified Reliefs and Method of Determining Amount of Specified Relief Used in a Tax Year
Schedule 25C Determination of Amount of Relief to be Treated as Referable to Specified Reliefs as Respects Relief Carried Forward from Tax Year 2006 to Tax Year 2007

346 Rented residential accommodation: deduction for certain expenditure on construction [Repealed]

Repealed by FA02 s24(3)(c).

Cross References

To Section 346

Section 339 Interpretation (Chapter 3).
Section 372AU Saver for relief due, and for clawback of relief given under, old schemes.

347 Rented residential accommodation: deduction for certain expenditure on conversion [Repealed]

Repealed by FA02 s24(3)(c).

Cross References

To Section 347

Section 339 Interpretation (Chapter 3).
Section 341 Accelerated capital allowances in relation to construction or refurbishment of certain industrial buildings or structures.
Section 342 Capital allowances in relation to construction or refurbishment of certain commercial premises.
Section 372AU Saver for relief due, and for clawback of relief given under, old schemes.

348 Rented residential accommodation: deduction for certain expenditure on refurbishment [Repealed]

Repealed by FA02 s24(3)(c).

Cross References

To Section 348

Section 339 Interpretation (Chapter 3).
Section 341 Accelerated capital allowances in relation to construction or refurbishment of certain industrial buildings or structures.
Section 342 Capital allowances in relation to construction or refurbishment of certain commercial premises.
Section 372AU Saver for relief due, and for clawback of relief given under, old schemes.

349 Residential accommodation: allowance to owner-occupiers in respect of certain expenditure on construction or refurbishment [Repealed]

Repealed by FA02 s24(3)(c).

Cross References

To Section 349

Section 339 Interpretation (Chapter 3).
Section 341 Accelerated capital allowances in relation to construction or refurbishment of certain industrial buildings or structures.
Section 342 Capital allowances in relation to construction or refurbishment of certain commercial premises.
Section 372AU Saver for relief due, and for clawback of relief given under, old schemes.

350 Provisions supplementary to sections 346 to 349. [Repealed]

Repealed by FA02 s24(3)(c).

Cross References

To Section 350

Section 403 Restriction on use of capital allowances for certain leased assets.

350A Provision against double relief

[Where relief is given by virtue of any provision of this Chapter in relation to capital expenditure or other expenditure incurred on, or rent payable in respect of, any building or structure, premises or multi-storey car park, relief shall not be given in respect of that expenditure or that rent under any other provision of the Tax Acts.][1]

Amendments

[1] Inserted by FA98 s24(1)(e).

CHAPTER 4

Qualifying Resort Areas

351 Interpretation (Chapter 4)

[FA95 s46(1)]

In this Chapter—

"*lease*", "*lessee*", "*lessor*" and "*rent*" have the same meanings respectively as in *Chapter 8* of *Part 4*;

"*market value*", in relation to a building or structure, means the price which the unencumbered fee simple of the building or structure would fetch if sold in the open market in such manner and subject to such conditions as might reasonably be calculated to obtain for the vendor the best price for the building or structure, less the part of that price which would be attributable to the acquisition of, or of rights in or over, the land on which the building or structure is constructed;

["*qualifying period*" means the period commencing on the 1st day of July, 1995, and ending on—

(a) the 30th day of June, 1998, or

(b) the 31st day of December, 1999, where, in relation to the construction of, conversion into, refurbishment of, or, as the case may be, construction or refurbishment of the building or structure concerned, being—

(i) a building or structure to which *section 352* applies, or

(ii) a qualifying premises within the meaning of *section 353, 354, 356, 357* or *358*,

the relevant local authority gives a certificate in writing, on or before the 30th day of September, 1999, to the person constructing, converting or refurbishing, as the case may be, the building or structure stating that it is satisfied that not less than 50 per cent of the total cost of the building or structure and the site thereof had been incurred on or before the 30th day of June, 1999, and, in considering whether to give such a certificate, the relevant local authority shall have regard only to guidelines in relation to the giving of such certificates issued by the Department of the Environment and Local Government for the purposes of this definition;][1]

"*qualifying resort area*" means any area described in *Schedule 8*;

"*refurbishment*", in relation to a building or structure and other than for the purposes of *section 358*, means any work of construction, reconstruction, repair or renewal, including the provision or improvement of water, sewerage or heating facilities, carried out in the course of the repair or restoration, or maintenance in the nature of repair or restoration, of the building or structure.

["the relevant local authority", in relation to the construction of, conversion into, refurbishment of, or, as the case may be, construction or refurbishment of a building or structure of the kind referred to in *paragraph (b)* of the definition of "*qualifying period*", means the council of a county or the corporation of a county or other borough or, where appropriate, the urban district council, in whose functional area the building or structure is situated.][2]

Amendments

[1] Substituted by FA99 s45.

[2] Inserted by FA98 s27(b).

Revenue Briefings

Tax Briefing

Tax Briefing April 1997 – Issue 26 pg 24 – Resort Areas – Capital Allowances
Tax Briefing April 2002 – Issue 47 pg 20 – Qualifying Resort Areas
Tax Briefing September 2008 – Issue 69 – Qualifying Resort Areas – listed self-catering accommodation

Revenue Information Notes

Tax relief for renewal and improvement of certain resort areas

Cross References

From Section 351

Section 52 Persons chargeable.
Section 96 Interpretation (Chapter 8).
Section 352 Accelerated capital allowances in relation to construction or refurbishment of certain industrial buildings or structures.
Section 353 Capital allowances in relation to construction or refurbishment of certain commercial premises.
Section 354 Double rent allowance in respect of rent paid for certain business premises.
Section 356 Rented residential accommodation: deduction for certain expenditure on construction.
Section 357 Rented residential accommodation: deduction for certain expenditure on conversion.
Section 358 Rented residential accommodation: deduction for certain expenditure on refurbishment.
Schedule 8 Description of Qualifying Resort Areas

To Section 351

Section 409B Income tax: restriction on use of capital allowances on certain hotels, etc.
Schedule 8 Description of Qualifying Resort Areas

352 Accelerated capital allowances in relation to construction or refurbishment of certain industrial buildings or structures

[FA95 s47]

(1) This section shall apply to a building or structure the site of which is wholly within a qualifying resort area and which is to be an industrial building or structure by reason of its use for the purposes specified in *section 268(1)(d)*.

(2) Subject to *subsection (5)*, *section 271* shall apply in relation to capital expenditure incurred in the qualifying period on the construction or refurbishment of a building or structure to which this section applies as if—

(a) in *subsection (1)* of that section the definition of "*industrial development agency*" were deleted,

(b) in *subsection (2)(a)(i)* of that section "to which *subsection (3)* applies" were deleted,

(c) *subsection (3)* of that section were deleted,

(d) the following subsection were substituted for *subsection (4)* of that section:

"(4) An industrial building allowance shall be of an amount equal to 50 per cent of the capital expenditure mentioned in *subsection (2)*.",

and

(e) in *subsection (5)* of that section "to which *subsection (3)(c)* applies" were deleted.

(3) Subject to *subsection (5)*, *section 272* shall apply in relation to capital expenditure incurred in the qualifying period on the construction or refurbishment of a building or structure to which this section applies as if the following subsection were substituted for *subsection (3)* of that section:

"(3) A writing down allowance shall be of an amount equal to 5 per cent of the expenditure referred to in *subsection (2)(c)*.".

(4) Subject to *subsection (5)*, *section 273* shall apply in relation to capital expenditure incurred in the qualifying period on the construction or refurbishment of a building or structure to which this section applies as if—

(a) in *subsection (1)* of that section the definition of "*industrial development agency*" were deleted,

(b) the following paragraph were substituted for *paragraph (b)* of *subsection (2)* of that section:

"(b) As respects any qualifying expenditure, any allowance made under *section 272* and increased under *paragraph (a)* in respect of that expenditure, whether claimed for one chargeable period or more than one such period, shall not in the aggregate exceed 75 per cent of the amount of that qualifying expenditure.",

and

(c) *subsections (3)* to *(7)* of that section were deleted.

(5) In the case where capital expenditure is incurred in the qualifying period on the refurbishment of a building or structure to which this section applies, *subsections (2)* to *(4)* shall apply only if the total amount of the capital expenditure so incurred is not less than an amount which is equal to 20 per cent of the market value of the building or structure immediately before that expenditure is incurred.

(6) For the purposes only of determining, in relation to a claim for an allowance under *section 271*, *272* or *273*, as applied by this section, whether and to what extent capital expenditure incurred on the construction or refurbishment of an industrial building or structure is incurred or not incurred in the qualifying period, only such an amount of that capital expenditure as is properly attributable to work on the construction or, as the case may be, the refurbishment of the building or structure actually carried out during the qualifying period shall (notwithstanding any other provision of the Tax Acts as to the time when any capital expenditure is or is to be treated as incurred) be treated as having been incurred in that period.

Revenue Briefings

Tax Briefing

Tax Briefing April 2002 – Issue 47 pg 20 – Qualifying Resort Areas

Cross References

From Section 352

Section 268 Meaning of "industrial building or structure".
Section 271 Industrial building allowances.
Section 272 Writing-down allowances.
Section 273 Acceleration of writing-down allowances in respect of certain expenditure on certain industrial buildings or structures.

To Section 352

Section 97 Computational rules and allowable deductions.
Section 351 Interpretation (Chapter 4).
Section 354 Double rent allowance in respect of rent paid for certain business premises.
Section 355 Disclaimer of capital allowances on holiday cottages, holiday apartments, etc.
Schedule 25B List of Specified Reliefs and Method of Determining Amount of Specified Relief Used in a Tax Year

353 Capital allowances in relation to construction or refurbishment of certain commercial premises

[FA95 s48; FA97 s146(1) and Sch9 PtI par19]

(1) In this section—

"*qualifying premises*" means a building or structure the site of which is wholly within a qualifying resort area and which—

(a) apart from this section is not an industrial building or structure within the meaning of *section 268*, and

(b) is in use for the purposes of the operation of one or more qualifying tourism facilities,

but does not include any part of a building or structure in use as or as part of a dwelling house, other than a tourist accommodation facility of the type referred to in the definition of "*qualifying tourism facilities*";

"*qualifying tourism facilities*" means—

(a) tourist accommodation facilities registered by [the National Tourism Development Authority][1] under Part III of the Tourist Traffic Act, 1939, or specified in a list published under section 9 of the Tourist Traffic Act, 1957, and

(b) such other classes of facilities as may be approved of for the purposes of this section by the Minister for Tourism, Sport and Recreation in consultation with the Minister for Finance.

(2) (a) Subject to *subsection (3)* to *(6)*, the provisions of the Tax Acts relating to the making of allowances or charges in respect of capital expenditure incurred on the construction or refurbishment of an industrial building or structure shall, notwithstanding anything to the contrary in those provisions, apply—

(i) as if a qualifying premises were, at all times at which it is a qualifying premises, a building or structure in respect of which an allowance is to be made for the purposes of income tax or corporation tax, as the case may be, under *Chapter 1* of *Part 9* by reason of its use for a purpose specified in *section 268(1)(a)*, and

(ii) where any activity carried on in the qualifying premises is not a trade, as if it were a trade.

(b) An allowance shall be given by virtue of this subsection in respect of any capital expenditure incurred on the construction or refurbishment of a qualifying premises only in so far as that expenditure is incurred in the qualifying period.

(3) In the case where capital expenditure is incurred in the qualifying period on the refurbishment of a qualifying premises, *subsection (2)* shall apply only if the total amount of the capital expenditure so incurred is not less than an amount which is equal to 20 per cent of the market value of the qualifying premises immediately before that expenditure is incurred.

(4) For the purposes of the application, by *subsection (2)*, of *sections 271*, *272* and *273* in relation to capital expenditure incurred in the qualifying period on the construction or refurbishment of a qualifying premises—

(a) *section 271* shall apply as if—

(i) in *subsection (1)* of that section the definition of "*industrial development agency*" were deleted,

(ii) in *subsection (2)(a)(i)* of that section "to which *subsection (3)* applies" were deleted,

(iii) *subsection (3)* of that section were deleted,

(iv) the following subsection were substituted for *subsection (4)* of that section:

"(4) An industrial building allowance shall be of an amount equal to 50 per cent of the capital expenditure mentioned in *subsection (2)*.",

and

(v) in *subsection (5)* of that section "to which *subsection (3)(c)* applies" were deleted,

(b) *section 272* shall apply as if the following subsection were substituted for *subsection (3)* of that section:

"(3) A writing down allowance shall be of an amount equal to 5 per cent of the expenditure referred to in *subsection (2)(c)*.",

and

(c) *section 273* shall apply as if—

(i) in *subsection (1)* of that section the definition of "*industrial development agency*" were deleted,

(ii) the following paragraph were substituted for *paragraph (b)* of *subsection (2)* of that subsection:

"(b) As respects any qualifying expenditure, any allowance made under *section 272* and increased under *paragraph (a)* in respect of that expenditure, whether claimed in one chargeable period or more than one such period, shall not in the aggregate exceed 75 per cent of the amount of that qualifying expenditure.",

and

(iii) *subsections (3)* to *(7)* of that section were deleted.

(5) In the case of a qualifying premises which is such a premises by virtue of being a tourist accommodation facility of a type referred to in *paragraph (a)* of the definition of "*qualifying tourism facilities*"—

(a) the event of the premises ceasing to be registered or specified in the manner referred to in that paragraph of that definition shall be treated as if it were an event specified in *section 274(1)*, and

(b) for the purposes of the application of *section 274* on the occurrence of any such event, there shall, notwithstanding anything to the contrary in *section 318*, be treated as arising in relation to that event sale, insurance, salvage or compensation moneys in an amount equal to the aggregate of—

(i) the residue of the expenditure (within the meaning of *section 277*) incurred on the construction or refurbishment of the premises immediately before that event, and

(ii) the allowances made under *Chapter 1* of *Part 9* by virtue of *subsection (2)* in respect of the expenditure incurred on the construction or refurbishment of the premises.

(6) Notwithstanding *section 274(1)*, no balancing charge shall be made in relation to any qualifying premises by reason of any of the events specified, or by virtue of *subsection (5)* treated as specified, in *section 274(1)* which occurs—

(a) more than 11 years after the qualifying premises was first used, or

(b) in a case where *section 276* applies, more than 11 years after the capital expenditure on refurbishment of the qualifying premises was incurred.

(7) For the purposes only of determining, in relation to a claim for an allowance by virtue of *subsection (2)*, whether and to what extent capital expenditure incurred on the construction or refurbishment of a qualifying premises is incurred or not incurred in the qualifying period, only such an amount of that capital expenditure as is properly attributable to work on the construction or refurbishment of the premises actually carried out during the qualifying period shall (notwithstanding any other provision of the Tax Acts as to the time when any capital expenditure is or is to be treated as incurred) be treated as having been incurred in that period.

(8) Where by virtue of *subsection (2)* an allowance is given under *Chapter 1* of *Part 9* in respect of any capital expenditure incurred on the construction or refurbishment of a qualifying premises, relief shall not be given in respect of that expenditure under any provision of the Tax Acts other than that Chapter.

Amendments

[1] Substituted by FA06 sched2(1)(g). This section is deemed to have come into force and have taken effect as on and from 28 May 2003.

Revenue Briefings

Tax Briefing

Tax Briefing April 2002 – Issue 47 pg 20 – Qualifying Resort Areas

Revenue Precedents

Is it possible to claim capital allowances in respect of listed holiday homes whether these are single holiday homes or a group of holiday homes even where the holiday homes are not registered as a holiday cottage scheme with Bord Failte? Tourist accommodation facilities listed under Section 9, Tourist Traffic Act 1957 come within the definition of qualifying tourism facilities in section 353 Taxes Consolidation Act 1997. Single homes or groups of houses which are not registered under Part III of the Tourist Traffic Act 1939 are capable of being listed, provided that they meet with the neccessary standards and criteria laid down by the Bord Failte. The question of what is, or is not, listed is of course a matter for Bord Failte. IT953021

The Department of Environment and Local Government has issued guidelines on residential development in urban renewal designated areas requiring a certain floor area . Bord Failte have their own separate requirements for floor area for tourist accommodation facilities. Which of the above guidelines should be followed in deciding floor area for residential properties in the Scheme for Renewal and Improvement of Certain Resort Areas? The question of the floor area of a particular unit is dependent on the nature of the claim in respect of that unit. If capital allowances are being claimed by virtue of section 353 Taxes Consolidation Act 1997, it is the floor area requirement of Bord Failte for listing which must be complied with. If rented residential accommodation reliefs under section 356, 357 or 358 Taxes Consolidation Act 1997 (whichever section is appropriate) are being claimed, it is the floor area requirements of those sections which must be complied with. T953024

Qualifying premises for the purposes of section 353 Taxes Consolidation Act 1997 means, inter alia, a building in use for the purposes of the operation of one or more qualifying tourism facilities. Qualifying tourism facilities means tourist accommodation facilities ...specified in a list published under section 9 of the Tourist Traffic Act, 1957. Where the premises are only partly in use for letting to tourists or where they are let to persons other than tourists will the amount of the allowances be restricted? Once the conditions for listing continue to be satisfied and the premises continues to be listed, the allowances will continue to be available. Non-tourist lettings during the months not advertised in the Self-Catering Guide will not debar the premises once none of the lettings are for more than two consecutive calendar months at any one time or for more than six months in any calendar year. The quantum of the available allowance are not restricted where there are any such non-tourist lettings. IT953028

In the case of qualifying tourism facilities which are Bed and Breakfasts, is expenditure incurred on the private element disallowed? No. IT963513

Retail outlets located in the same building as a holiday complex and with access only from within the complex (i.e. no street access) are considered eligible. In other words, a shop which is only accessible from within the holiday complex and presumably frequented predominately by the users of the holiday complex will qualify. GD95.022

Cross References

From Section 353

Section 268 Meaning of "industrial building or structure".
Section 271 Industrial building allowances.
Section 272 Writing-down allowances.
Section 273 Acceleration of writing-down allowances in respect of certain expenditure on certain industrial buildings or structures.
Section 274 Balancing allowances and balancing charges.
Section 276 Application of sections 272 and 274 in relation to capital expenditure on refurbishment.
Section 277 Writing off of expenditure and meaning of "residue of expenditure".
Section 318 Meaning of "sale, insurance, salvage or compensation moneys".

To Section 353

Section 97 Computational rules and allowable deductions.
Section 351 Interpretation (Chapter 4).
Section 354 Double rent allowance in respect of rent paid for certain business premises.
Section 355 Disclaimer of capital allowances on holiday cottages, holiday apartments, etc.
Section 405 Restriction on use of capital allowances on holiday cottages.
Schedule 25B List of Specified Reliefs and Method of Determining Amount of Specified Relief Used in a Tax Year

354 Double rent allowance in respect of rent paid for certain business premises

[FA90 s33(1) and (2)(a); FA95 s49; FA97 s27]

(1) In this section—

"*qualifying lease*" means, subject to *subsection (5)*, a lease in respect of a qualifying premises granted in the qualifying period on bona fide commercial terms by a lessor to a lessee not connected with the lessor, or with any other person who is entitled to a rent in respect of the qualifying premises, whether under that lease or any other lease;

"*qualifying premises*" means, subject to *section 355(2)*, a building or structure the site of which is wholly within a qualifying resort area and—

(a) (i) which is a building or structure in use for the purposes specified in *section 268(1)(d)*, and in respect of which capital expenditure is incurred in the qualifying period for which an allowance is to be made, or will by virtue of *section 279* be made, for the purposes of income tax or corporation tax, as the case may be, under *section 271*, *272* or *273*, as applied by *section 352*, or

(ii) in respect of which an allowance is to be made, or will by virtue of *section 279* be made, for the purposes of income tax or corporation tax, as the case may be, under *Chapter 1* of *Part 9* by virtue of *section 353*,

and

(b) which is let on bona fide commercial terms for such consideration as might be expected to be paid in a letting of the building or structure negotiated on an arm's length basis,

but, where capital expenditure is incurred in the qualifying period on the refurbishment of a building or structure in respect of which an allowance is to be made, or will by virtue of *section 279* be made, for the purposes of income tax or corporation tax, as the case may be, under any of the provisions referred to in *paragraph (a)*, the building or structure shall not be regarded as a qualifying premises unless the total amount of the expenditure so incurred is not less than an amount equal to 20 per cent of the market value of the building or structure immediately before that expenditure is incurred.

(2) For the purposes of this section, so much of a period, being a period when rent is payable by a person in relation to a qualifying premises under a qualifying lease, shall be a relevant rental period as does not exceed—

(a) 10 years, or

(b) the period by which 10 years exceeds—

(i) any preceding period, or

(ii) if there is more than one preceding period, the aggregate of those periods,

for which rent was payable by that person or any other person in relation to that premises under a qualifying lease.

(3) Subject to *subsection (4)*, where in the computation of the amount of the profits or gains of a trade or profession a person is apart from this section entitled to any deduction (in this subsection referred to as "*the first-mentioned deduction*") on account of rent in respect of a qualifying premises occupied by such person for the purposes of that trade or profession which is payable by such person for a relevant rental period in relation to that qualifying premises under a qualifying lease, such person shall be entitled in that computation to a further deduction (in this subsection referred to as "*the second-mentioned deduction*") equal to the amount of the first-mentioned deduction but, as respects a qualifying lease granted on or after the 21st day of April, 1997, where the first-mentioned deduction is on account of rent payable by such person to a connected person, such person shall not be entitled in that computation to the second-mentioned deduction.

(4) Where a person holds an interest in a qualifying premises out of which interest a qualifying lease is created directly or indirectly in respect of the qualifying premises and in respect of rent payable under the qualifying lease a claim for a

further deduction under this section is made, and either such person or another person connected with such person—

(a) takes under a qualifying lease a qualifying premises (in this subsection referred to as "*the second-mentioned premises*") occupied by such person or such other person, as the case may be, for the purposes of a trade or profession, and

(b) is apart from this section entitled, in the computation of the amount of the profits or gains of that trade or profession, to a deduction on account of rent in respect of the second-mentioned premises,

then, unless such person or such other person, as the case may be, shows that the taking on lease of the second-mentioned premises was not undertaken for the sole or main benefit of obtaining a further deduction on account of rent under this section, such person or such other person, as the case may be, shall not be entitled in the computation of the amount of the profits or gains of that trade or profession to any further deduction on account of rent in respect of the second-mentioned premises.

(5) (a) In this subsection—

"*current value*", in relation to minimum lease payments, means the value of those payments discounted to their present value at a rate which, when applied at the inception of the lease to—

(i) those payments, including any initial payment but excluding any payment or part of any payment for which the lessor will be accountable to the lessee, and

(ii) any unguaranteed residual value of the qualifying premises, excluding any part of such value for which the lessor will be accountable to the lessee,

produces discounted present values the aggregate amount of which equals the amount of the fair value of the qualifying premises;

"*fair value*", in relation to a qualifying premises, means an amount equal to such consideration as might be expected to be paid for the premises on a sale negotiated on an arm's length basis less any grants receivable towards the purchase of the qualifying premises;

"*inception of the lease*" means the earlier of the time the qualifying premises is brought into use or the date from which rentals under the lease first accrue;

"*minimum lease payments*" means the minimum payments over the remaining part of the term of the lease to be paid to the lessor, and includes any residual amount to be paid to the lessor at the end of the term of the lease and guaranteed by the lessee or by a person connected with the lessee;

"*unguaranteed residual value*", in relation to a qualifying premises, means that part of the residual value of that premises at the end of a term of a lease, as estimated at the inception of the lease, the realisation of which by the lessor is not assured or is guaranteed solely by a person connected with the lessor.

(b) A finance lease, that is—

(i) a lease in respect of a qualifying premises where, at the inception of the lease, the aggregate of the current value of the minimum lease payments (including any initial payment but excluding any payment or part of any payment for which the lessor will be accountable to the lessee) payable by the lessee in relation to the lease amounts to 90 per cent or more of the fair value of the qualifying premises, or

(ii) a lease which in all the circumstances is considered to provide in substance for the lessee the risks and benefits associated with ownership of the qualifying premises other than legal title to that premises,

shall not be a qualifying lease for the purposes of this section.

Revenue Briefings

Tax Briefing

Tax Briefing April 2002 – Issue 47 pg 20 – Qualifying Resort Areas

Revenue Information Notes

Tax relief for renewal and improvement of certain resort areas.

Revenue Precedents

Where a partnership takes a lease of a scheme of registered holiday cottages and lets them to tourists will the partnership be entitled to a double deduction for the rent which it pays under the lease? If the partnership is occupying qualifying premises for the purposes of a trade and there is no connection between the lessor and the lessee it will be entitled to the double deduction. However it will be a question of fact whether the income arising from the cottages is chargeable Case I or Case V and whether the cottages will be occupied by the partnership. Prima facie, property which is let would appear not to be occupied by the lessor. IT953544

Cross References

From Section 354

Section 268 Meaning of "industrial building or structure".
Section 271 Industrial building allowances.
Section 272 Writing-down allowances.
Section 273 Acceleration of writing-down allowances in respect of certain expenditure on certain industrial buildings or structures.
Section 279 Purchases of certain buildings or structures.
Section 352 Accelerated capital allowances in relation to construction or refurbishment of certain industrial buildings or structures.
Section 353 Capital allowances in relation to construction or refurbishment of certain commercial premises.
Section 355 Disclaimer of capital allowances on holiday cottages, holiday apartments, etc.

To Section 354

Section 351 Interpretation (Chapter 4).
Section 355 Disclaimer of capital allowances on holiday cottages, holiday apartments, etc.
Section 485C Interpretation (Chapter 2A).
Section 531B Charge to income levy.
Section 531AA Interpretation (Part 18C).
Section 531AM Charge to universal social charge.
Section 1013 Limited partnerships.
Schedule 25B List of Specified Reliefs and Method of Determining Amount of Specified Relief Used in a Tax Year
Schedule 25C Determination of Amount of Relief to be Treated as Referable to Specified Reliefs as Respects Relief Carried Forward from Tax Year 2006 to Tax Year 2007

355 Disclaimer of capital allowances on holiday cottages, holiday apartments, etc

[FA95 s49A; FA96 s30]

(1) This section shall apply to—

(a) a building or structure to which *section 352* applies by virtue of the building or structure being a holiday cottage of the type referred to in *section 268(3)*, and

(b) a building or structure which is a qualifying premises within the meaning of *section 353* by virtue of the building or structure being—

(i) a holiday apartment registered under Part III of the Tourist Traffic Act, 1939, or

(ii) other self-catering accommodation specified in a list published under section 9 of the Tourist Traffic Act, 1957.

(2) (a) Subject to *subsection (5)*, a building or structure to which this section applies shall not be a qualifying premises for the purposes of *section 354* unless the person to whom an allowance under *Chapter 1* of *Part 9* would but for *subsection (3)* be made for the purposes of income tax or corporation tax, as the case may be, in respect of the capital expenditure incurred in the qualifying period on the construction or refurbishment of the building or structure elects by notice in writing to the appropriate inspector (within the meaning of *section 950*) to disclaim all allowances under that Chapter in respect of that capital expenditure.

(b) An election under *paragraph (a)* shall be included in the return required to be made by the person concerned under *section 951* for the first year of assessment or the first accounting period, as the case may be, for which an allowance would but for *subsection (3)* have been made to that person under *Chapter 1* of *Part 9* in respect of that capital expenditure.

(c) An election under *paragraph (a)* shall be irrevocable.

(d) A person who has made an election under *paragraph (a)* shall furnish a copy of that election to any person (in this paragraph referred to as "*the second-mentioned person*") to whom the person grants a qualifying lease (within the meaning of *section 354*) in respect of a building or structure to which this section applies, and the second-mentioned person shall include the copy in the return required to be made by the second-mentioned person under *section 951* for the year of assessment or accounting period, as the case may be, in which rent is first payable by the second-mentioned person under the qualifying lease in respect of such a building or structure.

(3) Subject to *subsection (5)*, where a person who has incurred capital expenditure in the qualifying period on the construction or refurbishment of a building or structure to which this section applies makes an election under *subsection (2)(a)*, then, notwithstanding any other provision of the Tax Acts—

(a) no allowance under *Chapter 1* of *Part 9* shall be made to the person in respect of that capital expenditure,

(b) on the occurrence, in relation to the building or structure, of any of the events referred to in *section 274(1)*, the residue of expenditure (within the meaning of *section 277*) in relation to that capital expenditure shall be deemed to be nil, and

(c) *section 279* shall not apply in the case of any person who buys the relevant interest (within the meaning of *section 269*) in the building or structure.

(4) Subject to *subsection (5)*, where in the qualifying period a person incurs capital expenditure on the acquisition, construction or refurbishment of a building or structure which is or is to be a building or structure to which *subsection (1)(b)* applies and an allowance is to be made in respect of that expenditure under *section 271* or *272*, then—

(a) neither *section 305(1)(b)* nor *section 308(4)* shall apply as respects that allowance, and

(b) neither *section 381* nor *section 396(2)* shall apply as respects the whole or part, as the case may be, of any loss which would not have arisen but for the making of that allowance.

(5) This section shall not apply—

(a) to expenditure incurred in the qualifying period on the acquisition, construction or refurbishment of a building or structure (in this subsection referred to as "the holiday cottage or apartment") which is or is to be a building or structure to which this section applies where before the 5th day of April, 1996—

(i) a binding contract in writing was entered into for the acquisition or construction of the holiday cottage or apartment,

(ii) an application for planning permission for the construction of the holiday cottage or apartment was received by a planning authority, or

(iii) in relation to the holiday cottage or apartment, an opinion in writing was issued by the Revenue Commissioners to the effect that an allowance to be made in respect of expenditure on the holiday cottage or apartment would not be restricted by virtue of *section 408*,

or

(b) where before the 5th day of April, 1996—

(i) expenditure was incurred on the acquisition of land on which the holiday cottage or apartment is to be constructed or refurbished, by the person who incurred the expenditure on that construction or refurbishment, or

(ii) a binding contract in writing was entered into for the acquisition of that land by that person,

and that person can prove to the satisfaction of the Revenue Commissioners that a detailed plan had been prepared and that detailed discussions had taken place with a planning authority in relation to the holiday cottage or apartment on or after the 8th day of February, 1995, but before the 5th day of April, 1996, and that this can be supported by means of an affidavit from the planning authority.

Revenue Briefings

Tax Briefing

Tax Briefing April 1998 – Issue 31 pg 16 – Seaside Resort Scheme

Tax Briefing April 2002 – Issue 47 pg 20 – Qualifying Resort Areas

Cross References

From Section 355

Section 268 Meaning of "industrial building or structure".

Section 269 Meaning of "the relevant interest".

Section 271 Industrial building allowances.

Section 272 Writing-down allowances.

Section 274 Balancing allowances and balancing charges.

Section 277 Writing off of expenditure and meaning of "residue of expenditure".

Section 279 Purchases of certain buildings or structures.

Section 305 Income tax: manner of granting, and effect of, allowances made by means of discharge or repayment of tax.

Section 308 Corporation tax: manner of granting, and effect of, allowances made by means of discharge or repayment of tax.

Section 352 Accelerated capital allowances in relation to construction or refurbishment of certain industrial buildings or structures.

Section 353 Capital allowances in relation to construction or refurbishment of certain commercial premises.
Section 354 Double rent allowance in respect of rent paid for certain business premises.
Section 381 Right to repayment of tax by reference to losses.
Section 396 Relief for trading losses other than terminal losses.
Section 408 Restriction on tax incentives on property investment.
Section 950 Interpretation (Part 41).
Section 951 Obligation to make a return.

To Section 355

Section 354 Double rent allowance in respect of rent paid for certain business premises.
Section 405 Restriction on use of capital allowances on holiday cottages.
Section 409A Income tax: restriction on use of capital allowances on certain industrial buildings and other premises.

356 Rented residential accommodation: deduction for certain expenditure on construction [Repealed]

Repealed by FA02 s24(3)(d).

Cross References

To Section 356

Section 97 Computational rules and allowable deductions.
Section 351 Interpretation (Chapter 4).
Section 372AU Saver for relief due, and for clawback of relief given under, old schemes.

357 Rented residential accommodation: deduction for certain expenditure on conversion [Repealed]

Repealed by FA02 s24(3)(d).

Cross References

To Section 357

Section 97 Computational rules and allowable deductions.
Section 351 Interpretation (Chapter 4).
Section 372AU Saver for relief due, and for clawback of relief given under, old schemes.

358 Rented residential accommodation: deduction for certain expenditure on refurbishment [Repealed]

Repealed by FA02 s24(3)(d).

Cross References

To Section 358

Section 97 Computational rules and allowable deductions.
Section 351 Interpretation (Chapter 4).
Section 372AU Saver for relief due, and for clawback of relief given under, old schemes.

359 Provisions supplementary to sections 356 to 358. [Repealed]

Repealed by FA02 s24(3)(d).

CHAPTER 5

Designated Islands

360 Interpretation (Chapter 5) [Repealed]

Repealed by FA02 s24(3)(e).

361 Rented residential accommodation: deduction for certain expenditure on construction [Repealed]

Repealed by FA02 s24(3)(e).

Cross References

To Section 361

Section 372AU Saver for relief due, and for clawback of relief given under, old schemes.

362 Rented residential accommodation: deduction for certain expenditure on conversion [Repealed]

Repealed by FA02 s24(3)(e).

Cross References

To Section 362

Section 372AU Saver for relief due, and for clawback of relief given under, old schemes.

363 Rented residential accommodation: deduction for certain expenditure on refurbishment [Repealed]

Repealed by FA02 s24(3)(e).

Cross References

To Section 363

Section 372AU Saver for relief due, and for clawback of relief given under, old schemes.

364 Residential accommodation: allowance to owner-occupiers in respect of certain expenditure on construction or refurbishment [Repealed]

Repealed by FA02 s24(3)(e).

Cross References

To Section 364

Section 372AU Saver for relief due, and for clawback of relief given under, old schemes.

365 Provisions supplementary to sections 360 to 364. [Repealed]

Repealed by FA02 s24(3)(e).

Chapter 6

Dublin Docklands Area

366 Interpretation. (Chapter 6) [Repealed]
Repealed by FA02 s24(3)(e).

367 Qualifying areas [Repealed]
Repealed by FA02 s24(3)(e).

368 Accelerated capital allowances in relation to construction or refurbishment of certain industrial buildings or structures [Repealed]
Repealed by FA02 s24(3)(e).

369 Capital allowances in relation to construction or refurbishment of certain commercial premises [Repealed]
Repealed by FA02 s24(3)(e).

370 Double rent allowance in respect of rent paid for certain business premises [Repealed]
Repealed by FA02 s24(3)(e).

Cross References

To Section 370
Section 1013 Limited partnerships.

371 Residential accommodation: allowance to owner-occupiers in respect of certain expenditure on construction or refurbishment [Repealed]
Repealed by FA02 s24(3)(e).

372 Provisions supplementary to section 371 [Repealed]
Repealed by FA02 s24(3)(e).

CHAPTER 7

Qualifying Areas

372A Interpretation and application (Chapter 7)

[(1) In this Chapter—

["*existing building*" means a building or structure which—

(a) fronts on to a qualifying street, and

(b) existed on 13 September 2000;][1]

["*facade*", in relation to a building or structure or part of a building or structure, means the exterior wall of the building or structure or, as the case may be, the part of the building or structure which fronts on to a street;][2]

"*lease*", "*lessee*", "*lessor*", "*premium*" and "*rent*" have the same meanings respectively as in *Chapter 8* of *Part 4*;

"*market value*", in relation to a building, structure or house, means the price which the unencumbered fee simple of the building, structure or house would fetch if sold in the open market in such manner and subject to such conditions as might reasonably be calculated to obtain for the vendor the best price for the building, structure or house, less the part of that price which would be attributable to the acquisition of, or of rights in or over, the land on which the building, structure or house is constructed;

"*multi-storey car park*" means a building or structure consisting of 2 or more storeys wholly or mainly in use for the purpose of providing, for members of the public generally without preference for any particular class of person, on payment of an appropriate charge, parking space for mechanically propelled vehicles;

["*necessary construction*", in relation to an existing building, means one or more of the following:

(a) construction of an extension to the building which does not exceed 30 per cent of the floor area of the building immediately before expenditure on the construction, conversion or refurbishment of the building was incurred, where such extension is necessary for the purposes of facilitating access to, or providing essential facilities in, one or more qualifying premises within the meaning of [Chapter 11 of this Part][3],

(b) construction of an additional storey or additional storeys to the building which was or were, as the case may be, necessary for the restoration or enhancement of the streetscape, or

(c) construction of a replacement building;][4]

["*property developer*" means a person carrying on a trade which consists wholly or mainly of the construction or refurbishment of buildings or structures with a view to their sale;][5]

"*qualifying area*" means an area or areas specified as a qualifying area under *section 372B*;

["*qualifying period*" means—

[(a) subject to *section 372B* and in relation to a qualifying area, the period commencing on 1 August 1998 and ending on—

(i) 31 December 2002, or

(ii) where *subsection (1A)* applies, [31 December 2006, or][6]

[(iii) where *subsections (1A)* and *(3)* apply, 31 July 2008,][7]

and][8]][9]

[(b) subject to *section 372BA* and in relation to a qualifying street, the period commencing on 6 April 2001 and ending on—

(i) 31 December 2004, or

(ii) where *subsection (1B)* applies, [31 December 2006, or][10]][11]

[(iii) where *subsections (1B)* and *(3)* apply, 31 July 2008;][12]

["*qualifying street*" means a street specified as a qualifying street under *section 372BA*;][13]

"*refurbishment*", in relation to a building or structure [...][14], means any work of construction, reconstruction, repair or renewal, including the provision or improvement of water, sewerage or heating facilities, carried out in the course of the repair or restoration, or maintenance in the nature of repair or restoration, of [the building or structure;][15]

[“*replacement building*”, in relation to a building or structure which fronts on to a qualifying street, means a building or structure or part of a building or structure, as the case may be, which is constructed to replace an existing building, where—

(a) (i) a notice under *subsection (1)* of section 3 or an order under *subsection (5)* of that section, of the Local Government (Sanitary Services) Act, 1964, which required the demolition of the existing building or part of that building, was given or made, as the case may be, on or after 13 September 2000 and before 31 March 2001, and

(ii) the replacement building is consistent with the character and size of the existing building,

or

(b) the demolition of the existing building (being a single storey building) was required for structural reasons, in order to facilitate the construction of an additional storey or additional storeys to the building which was or were, as the case may be, necessary for the restoration or enhancement of the streetscape;

[“*relevant local authority*” means—

[(a) in relation to a qualifying area—

(i) the county council or the city council or the borough council or, where appropriate, the town council, within the meaning of the Local Government Act 2001, in whose functional area the area is situated, or

(ii) the authorised company (within the meaning of section 3(1) of the Urban Renewal Act 1998) which prepared the integrated area plan (within the meaning of that section) in respect of the area,

and][16]

(b) in relation to a qualifying street, in respect of the cities of Cork, Dublin, Galway, Limerick or Waterford, the city council of the city in whose functional area the street is situated;][17]

“*street*” includes part of a street and the whole or part of any road, square, quay or lane.][18]

[(1A) (a) This subsection shall apply where—

(i) the relevant local authority gives a certificate in writing on or before 30 September 2003, to the person constructing or refurbishing a building or structure or part of a building or structure, the site of which is wholly within a qualifying area, stating that it is satisfied that not less than 15 per cent of the total cost of constructing or refurbishing the building or structure or the part of the building or structure, as the case may be, and the acquisition of the site thereof had been incurred on or before 30 June 2003, and

(ii) the application for such a certificate is received by the relevant local authority on or before 31 July 2003.][19]

(b) In considering whether to give a certificate referred to in *paragraph (a)*, the relevant local authority shall have regard only to guidelines issued by the Department of the Environment and Local Government in relation to the giving of such certificates.][20]

[(1B) This subsection shall apply in relation to a qualifying street, as respects capital expenditure incurred on the construction or refurbishment of a building or structure, if—

(a) (i) a planning application (not being an application for outline permission within the meaning of section 36 of the Planning and Development Act 2000), in so far as planning permission is required, in respect of the construction or refurbishment work on the building or structure represented by that expenditure, is made in accordance with the Planning and Development Regulations 2001 to 2003,

(ii) an acknowledgement of the application, which confirms that the application was received on or before 31 December 2004, is issued by the planning authority in accordance with article 26(2) of the Planning and Development Regulations 2001 (S.I. No. 600 of 2001), and

(iii) the application is not an invalid application in respect of which a notice is issued by the planning authority in accordance with article 26(5) of those regulations,

(b) (i) a planning application, in so far as planning permission was required, in respect of the construction or refurbishment work on the building or structure represented by that expenditure, was made in accordance with the Local Government (Planning and Development) Regulations 1994 (S.I. No. 86 of 1994), not being an application for outline permission within the meaning of article 3 of those regulations,

(ii) an acknowledgement of the application, which confirms that the application was received on or before 10 March 2002, was issued by the planning authority in accordance with article 29(2)(*a*) of the regulations referred to in *subparagraph (i)*, and

(iii) the application was not an invalid application in respect of which a notice was issued by the planning authority in accordance with article 29(2)(*b*)(i) of those regulations,

or

(c) where the construction or refurbishment work on the building or structure represented by that expenditure is exempted development for the purposes of the Planning and Development Act 2000 by virtue of section 4 of that Act or by virtue of Part 2 of the Planning and Development Regulations 2001 (S.I. No. 600 of 2001) and—

(i) a detailed plan in relation to the development work is prepared,

(ii) a binding contract in writing, under which the expenditure on the development is incurred, is in existence, and

(iii) work to the value of 5 per cent of the development costs is carried out,

not later than 31 December 2004.][21]

(2) [This Chapter and Chapter 11 of this Part][22] shall apply [in relation to qualifying areas][23] if the Oireachtas passes an Act which refers to this Chapter and provides for the renewal of certain urban areas and the submission of plans (to be known as "Integrated Area Plans") to the Minister for the Environment and Local Government which have been drawn up by local authorities or companies established by local authorities (being local authorities as referred to in such Act) in respect of an area or areas identified by such an authority or company on the

basis of criteria prepared by that Minister, including physical and socioeconomic renewal of such an area or areas.

[(3) Subject to *paragraphs (a)* and *(b)* of *section 270(7)*, this subsection shall apply in relation to the construction or refurbishment of a building or structure or a part of a building or structure which fronts on to a qualifying street or the site of which is wholly within a qualifying area where—

(a) the person who is constructing or refurbishing the building or structure or the part of the building or structure has, on or before 31 December 2006, carried out work to the value of not less than 15 per cent of the actual construction or, as the case may be, refurbishment costs of the building or structure or the part of the building or structure, and

(b) the person referred to in *paragraph (a)* or, where the building or structure or the part of the building or structure is sold by that person, the person who is claiming a deduction under *Chapter 1* of *Part 9* in relation to the expenditure incurred, can show that the condition in *paragraph (a)* was satisfied, and

(c) in the case of a building or structure or a part of a building or structure the site of which is wholly within a qualifying area where—

(i) a binding contract in writing under which expenditure on the construction or refurbishment of the building or structure or the part of a building or structure is incurred was in existence on or before 31 July 2006, and

(ii) such other conditions, as may be specified in regulations made for the purposes of this subparagraph by the Minister for Finance, have been satisfied; but such conditions shall be limited to those necessary to ensure compliance with the laws of the European Communities governing State aid or with a decision of the Commission of the European Communities as to whether aid to which this subsection relates is compatible with the common market having regard to Article 87 of the European Communities Treaty.][24][25]

Amendments

[1] Inserted by FA01 s60(a)(i)(I).

[2] Inserted by FA03 s27(1)(a).

[3] Substituted by FA02 sched2(2)(a)(i)(I).

[4] Inserted by FA01 s60(a)(i)(II).

[5] Inserted by FA00 s44(1)(a)(i). This section shall apply as on and from 1 July 1999.

[6] Substituted by FA06 s30(1)(a)(i)(I)(A). With effect from 26 June 2006 per S.I. 327 of 2006.

[7] Inserted by FA06 s30(1)(a)(i)(I)(B). With effect from 26 June 2006 per S.I. 327 of 2006.

[8] Substituted by FA02 s23(1)(b)(i)(I). With effect from 10 September 2002 per S.I. 459 of 2002.

[9] Substituted by FA01 s60(a)(i)(III).

[10] Substituted by FA06 s30(1)(a)(i)(II)(A). With effect from 26 June 2006 per S.I. 327 of 2006.

[11] Substituted by FA04 s26(1)(b)(i)(II). Shall come into operation on the making of an order to that effect by the Minister for Finance. With effect from 24 September 2004 per S.I. 642 of 2004.

[12] Inserted by FA06 s30(1)(a)(i)(II)(B). With effect from 26 June 2006 per S.I. 327 of 2006.

[13] Inserted by FA01 s60(a)(i)(IV).

[14] Deleted by FA02 sched2(2)(a)(i)(II).
[15] Substituted by FA01 s60(a)(i)(V).
[16] Substituted by FA03 s26(a)(i).
[17] Substituted by FA02 s23(1)(b)(i)(II). With effect from 10 September 2002 per S.I. 459 of 2002.
[18] Inserted by FA01 s60(a)(i)(VI).
[19] Substituted by FA03 s26(a)(ii).
[20] Inserted by FA02 s23(1)(b)(ii). With effect from 10 September 2002 per S.I. 459 of 2002.
[21] Inserted by FA04 s26(1)(b)(ii). Shall come into operation on the making of an order to that effect by the Minister for Finance. With effect from 24 September 2004 per S.I. 642 of 2004.
[22] Substituted by FA02 sched2(2)(a)(ii).
[23] Inserted by FA01 s60(a)(ii).
[24] Inserted by FA06 s30(1)(a)(ii). With effect from 26 June 2006 per S.I. 327 of 2006.
[25] Inserted by FA98 s76.

Revenue Briefings

Tax Briefing

Tax Briefing August 2005 – Issue 60 – Property Based Incentive Schemes

Revenue Information Notes

Tax relief for renewal and improvement of certain resort areas
Countrywide refurbishment scheme

Cross References

From Section 372A

Section 52 Persons chargeable.
Section 96 Interpretation (Chapter 8).
Section 268 Meaning of "industrial building or structure".
Section 270 Meaning of "expenditure on construction of building or structure".

To Section 372A

Section 268 Meaning of "industrial building or structure".
Section 270 Meaning of "expenditure on construction of building or structure".
Section 372AK Interpretation (Chapter 11).

372B Qualifying areas

[(1) The Minister for Finance may, on the recommendation of the Minister for the Environment and Local Government (which recommendation shall take into consideration an Integrated Area Plan submitted by a local authority or a company established by a local authority to that Minister in respect of an area identified by it), by order direct that—

(a) the area or areas described (being wholly located within the boundaries of the area to which the Integrated Area Plan relates) in the order shall be a qualifying area for the purposes of one or more sections of [this Chapter or Chapter 11 of this Part][1],

[(b) where such an area or areas is or are to be a qualifying area—

(i) for the purposes of *section 372D*—

(I) one or more of the categories of building or structure mentioned in *subsection (2)* shall or shall not be a qualifying premises within the meaning of that section, and

(II) that area or those areas shall be a qualifying area for the purposes of either or both the construction of, and the refurbishment of, a qualifying premises within the meaning of that section;

(ii) for the purposes of *section 372AR*, that area or those areas shall be a qualifying area for the purposes of one or more of the following:

(I) the construction of,

(II) the conversion into, and

(III) the refurbishment (within the meaning of Chapter 11 of this Part) of,

a qualifying premises (within the meaning of that Chapter),][2]

[(ba) where such an area or areas is or are to be a qualifying area for the purposes of *section 372AP*, that section shall apply in relation to that area or those areas in so far as that section relates to one or more of the following:

(i) expenditure incurred on the construction of a house,

(ii) conversion expenditure incurred in relation to a house, and

(iii) refurbishment expenditure incurred in relation to a house,][3]

[(c) as respects any such area so described in the order and in so far as this Chapter is concerned, the definition of "*qualifying period*" in *section 372A* shall be construed as a reference to such period as shall be specified in the order in relation to that area; but no such period specified in the order shall commence before 1 August 1998 or end after—

(i) 31 December 2002, or

(ii) where *section 372A(1A)* applies, [31 December 2006, or][4]][5]

[(iii) where *subsections (1A)* and *(3)* of *section 372A* apply, 31 July 2008,][6]

[(d) as respects any such area so described in the order and in so far as *Chapter 11* of this Part is concerned, the definition of "*qualifying period*" in *section 372AL* shall be construed as a reference to such period as shall be specified in the order in relation to that area; but no such period specified in the order shall commence before 1 August 1998 or end after—

(i) 31 December 2002, or

(ii) where *section 372AL(2)* applies, [31 December 2006, or][7]][8]

[(iii) where *subsections (2)* and *(3)* of *section 372AL* apply, 31 July 2008.][9]

[(2) The categories of building or structure referred to in *subsection (1)(b)(i)(I)* shall be—

(a) buildings or structures which consist of office accommodation,

(b) multi-storey car parks,

(c) any other buildings or structures and in respect of which not more than 10 per cent of the capital expenditure incurred in the qualifying period on their construction or refurbishment relates to the construction or refurbishment of office accommodation,

(d) the facade of a building or structure or part of a building or structure referred to in *paragraph (a)*,

(e) the facade of a building or structure or part of a building or structure referred to in *paragraph (c)*.][10]

[(2A) The power to make an order under *subsection (1)* includes the power to amend or revoke the order.][11]

(3) Every order made by the Minister for Finance under *subsection (1)* shall be laid before Dáil Éireann as soon as may be after it is made and, if a resolution annulling the order is passed by Dáil Éireann within the next 21 days on which Dáil Éireann

has sat after the order is laid before it, the order shall be annulled accordingly, but without prejudice to the validity of anything previously done thereunder.

(4) Notwithstanding an order under *subsection (1)*, the granting of relief by virtue of any provision of [this Chapter or Chapter 11 of this Part][12] [in respect of the construction, refurbishment or conversion of a building, structure or house, the site of which is wholly within a qualifying area,][13] shall be subject to such other requirements as may be specified in or under the Act referred to in *section 372A(2)*.][14]

Amendments

[1] Substituted by FA02 sched2(2)(b)(i)(I).

[2] Substituted by FA03 s27(1)(b)(i). Applies as on and from 1 March 1999.

[3] Inserted by FA02 sched2(2)(b)(i)(II).

[4] Substituted by FA06 s30(1)(b)(i)(I). With effect from 26 June 2006 per S.I. No. 327 of 2006.

[5] Substituted by FA02 s23(1)(c)(i). With effect from 10 September 2002 per S.I. 459 of 2002.

[6] Inserted by FA06 s30(1)(b)(i)(II). With effect from 26 June 2006 per S.I. 327 of 2006.

[7] Substituted by FA06 s30(1)(b)(ii)(I). Applies as on and from 1 January 2006.

[8] Inserted by FA02 s23(1)(c)(ii). With effect from 10 September 2002 per S.I. 459 of 2002.

[9] Inserted by FA06 s30(1)(b)(ii)(II). Applies as on and from 1 January 2006.

[10] Substituted by FA03 s27(1)(b)(ii). Applies as on and from 1 March 1999.

[11] Inserted by FA03 s27(1)(b)(iii). Applies as on and from 1 March 1999.

[12] Substituted by FA02 sched2(2)(b)(ii).

[13] Inserted by FA01 s60(b).

[14] Inserted by FA98 s76.

Cross References

To Section 372B

Section 372AK Interpretation (Chapter 11).

372BA Qualifying streets

[(1) The Minister for Finance may, on the recommendation of the Minister for the Environment and Local Government (which recommendation shall take into consideration proposals submitted by a relevant local authority to that Minister in respect of a street identified by it), by order direct that—

(a) a street described (being a street situated in the functional area of the relevant local authority) in the order shall be a qualifying street for the purposes of one or more sections of [this Chapter or Chapter 11 of this Part][1],

(b) where such a street is to be a qualifying street for the purposes of *section 372D*, the categories of building or structure mentioned in *subsection (2)* shall not be a qualifying premises within the meaning of that section, and

[(ba) [where such a street is to be a qualifying street for the purposes of *section 372AP*, that section shall apply in relation to that street][2] in so far as that section relates to one or more of the following:

(i) expenditure incurred on the construction of a house,

(ii) conversion expenditure incurred in relation to a house, and

(iii) refurbishment expenditure incurred in relation to a house,][3]

[(bb) as respects any such street so described in the order and in so far as this Chapter is concerned, the definition of qualifying period in *section 372A* shall be construed as a reference to such period as shall be specified in the order in relation to that street; but no such period specified in the order shall commence before 6 April 2001 or end after—

(i) 31 December 2004, or

(ii) where *section 372A(1B)* applies, [31 December 2006, or][4][5]

[(iii) where *subsections (1B)* and *(3)* of *section 372A* apply, 31 July 2008,][6]

[(c) as respects any such street so described in the order and in so far as Chapter 11 of this Part is concerned, the definition of qualifying period [in *section 372AL*][7] shall be construed as a reference to such period as shall be specified in the order in relation to that street; but no such period specified in the order shall commence before 6 April 2001 or end after—

(i) 31 December 2004, or

(ii) where *section 372AL(1A)* applies, [31 December 2006, or][8]][9]

[(iii) where *subsections (1A)* and *(3)* of *section 372AL* apply, 31 July 2008.][10]

(2) The categories of building or structure referred to in *subsection (1)(b)* shall be buildings or structures—

(a) other than those in use for the purposes of the retailing of goods or the provision of services only within the State,

(b) in use as offices, and

(c) in use for the provision of mail order or financial services.

[(2A) The power to make an order under *subsection (1)* includes the power to amend or revoke the order.][11]

(3) Every order made by the Minister for Finance under *subsection (1)* shall be laid before Dáil Éireann as soon as may be after it is made and, if a resolution annulling the order is passed by Dáil Éireann within the next 21 days on which Dáil Éireann has sat after the order is laid before it, the order shall be annulled accordingly, but without prejudice to the validity of anything previously done thereunder.

(4) Notwithstanding an order under *subsection (1)*, no relief from income tax or corporation tax, as the case may be, may be granted [under this Chapter or Chapter 11 of this Part][12] in respect of the construction, refurbishment or conversion of a building, structure or house which fronts on to a qualifying street unless the relevant local authority has certified in writing that such construction, refurbishment or conversion is consistent with the aims, objectives and criteria for the Living over the Shop Scheme, as outlined in a circular of the Department of the Environment and Local Government entitled "Living Over The Shop Scheme", reference numbered UR 43A and dated 13 September 2000, or in any further circular of that Department amending *paragraph 6* of the first-mentioned circular for the purposes of increasing the aggregate length of street allowable, to the manager of the relevant local authority concerned.][13]

Amendments

[1] Substituted by FA02 sched2(2)(c)(i)(I).

[2] Substituted by FA04 s26(1)(d)(i). This section is deemed to have applied as on and from 1 January 2002.

[3] Inserted by FA02 sched2(2)(c)(i)(II).

[4] Substituted by FA06 s30(1)(c)(i)(I). With effect from 26 June 2006 per S.I. 327 of 2006.

[5] Inserted by FA04 s26(1)(d)(ii). With effect from 24 September 2004 as per S.I. No. 642 of 2004.
[6] Inserted by FA06 s30(1)(c)(i)(II). With effect from 26 June 2006 per S.I. 327 of 2006.
[7] Substituted by FA06 s30(1)(c)(ii)(I). With effect from 26 June 2006 per S.I. 327 of 2006.
[8] Substituted by FA06 s30(1)(c)(ii)(II). With effect from 26 June 2006 per S.I. 327 of 2006.
[9] Substituted by FA04 s26(1)(d)(iii).
[10] Inserted by FA06 s30(1)(c)(ii)(III). With effect from 26 June 2006 per S.I. 327 of 2006.
[11] Inserted by FA03 s27(1)(c). Applies as on and from 6 April 2001.
[12] Inserted by FA02 sched2(2)(c)(ii).
[13] Inserted by FA01 s60(c).

Cross References

To Section 372BA

Section 372AK Interpretation (Chapter 11).

372C Accelerated capital allowances in relation to construction or refurbishment of certain industrial buildings or structures

[(1) In this section "building or structure to which this section applies" means a building or structure or part of a building or structure the site of which is wholly within a qualifying area and which is to be an industrial building or structure by reason of its use for a purpose specified in *section 268(1)(a)*.][1]

(2) [Subject to *subsection (4)* and (as inserted by the Finance Act 2006) *sections 270(4), 270(5), 270(6), 270(7)* and *316(2B)*][2], *section 271* shall apply in relation to capital expenditure incurred in the qualifying period on the construction or refurbishment of a building or structure to which this section applies as if—

(a) in *subsection (1)* of that section the definition of "*industrial development agency*" were deleted,

(b) in *subsection (2) (a) (i)* of that section "to which *subsection (3)* applies" were deleted,

(c) *subsection (3)* of that section were deleted,

(d) the following subsection were substituted for *subsection (4)* of that section:

"(4) An industrial building allowance shall be of an amount equal to [50 per cent][3] of the capital expenditure mentioned in *subsection (2)*.",

and

(e) in *subsection (5)* of that section "to which *subsection (3)(c)* applies" were deleted.

(3) [Subject to *subsection (4)* and (as inserted by the Finance Act 2006) *sections 270(4), 270(5), 270(6), 270(7)* and *316(2B)*][4], *section 273* shall apply in relation to capital expenditure incurred in the qualifying period on the construction or refurbishment of a building or structure to which this section applies as if—

(a) in *subsection (1)* of that section the definition of "*industrial development agency*" were deleted,

(b) the following paragraph were substituted for *paragraph (b)* of *subsection (2)* of that section:

"(b) As respects any qualifying expenditure, any allowance made under *section 272* and increased under *paragraph (a)* in respect of that expenditure, whether claimed for one chargeable period or more than one such period, shall not in the aggregate exceed 50 per cent of the amount of that qualifying expenditure.",

and

(c) *subsections (3)* to *(7)* of that section were deleted.

(4) In the case where capital expenditure is incurred in the qualifying period on the refurbishment of a building or structure to which this section applies, *subsections (2)* and *(3)* shall apply only if the total amount of the capital expenditure so incurred is not less than an amount equal to 10 per cent of the market value of the building or structure immediately before that expenditure was incurred.

(5) Notwithstanding *section 274(1)*, no balancing charge shall be made in relation to a building or structure to which this section applies by reason of any of the events specified in that section which occurs—

(a) more than 13 years after the building or structure was first used, or

(b) in a case where *section 276* applies, more than 13 years after the capital expenditure on refurbishment of the building or structure was incurred.

(6) For the purposes only of determining, in relation to a claim for an allowance under *section 271* or *273* as applied by this section, whether and to what extent capital expenditure incurred on the construction or refurbishment of an industrial building or structure is incurred or not incurred in the qualifying period, only such an amount of that capital expenditure as is properly attributable to work on the construction or, as the case may be, the refurbishment of the building or structure actually carried out during the qualifying period shall (notwithstanding any other provision of the Tax Acts as to the time when any capital expenditure is or is to be treated as incurred) be treated as having been incurred in that period.][5]

Amendments

[1] Substituted by FA00 s44(1)(c)(i). This section shall apply as on and from 1 July 1999.

[2, 4] Substituted by FA06 s30(1)(d). With effect from 26 June 2006 per S.I. 327 of 2006.

[3] Substituted by FA00 s44(1)(c)(ii). This section shall apply as on and from 1 July 1999.

[5] Inserted by FA98 s76.

Cross References

From Section 372C

Section 268 Meaning of "industrial building or structure".

Section 270 Meaning of "expenditure on construction of building or structure".

Section 271 Industrial building allowances.

Section 273 Acceleration of writing-down allowances in respect of certain expenditure on certain industrial buildings or structures.

Section 274 Balancing allowances and balancing charges.

Section 276 Application of sections 272 and 274 in relation to capital expenditure on refurbishment.

Section 316 Interpretation of certain references to expenditure and time when expenditure is incurred.

To Section 372C

Section 270 Meaning of "expenditure on construction of building or structure".

Schedule 25B List of Specified Reliefs and Method of Determining Amount of Specified Relief Used in a Tax Year

372D Capital allowances in relation to construction or refurbishment of certain commercial premises

[(1) In this section, "*qualifying premises*" means a building or structure [or part of a building or structure][1] the site of which is wholly within a qualifying area[, or which fronts on to a qualifying street,][2] and which—

(a) apart from this section is not an industrial building or structure within the meaning of *section 268*, and

(b) (i) is in use for the purposes of a trade or profession, or

(ii) whether or not it is so used, is let on bona fide commercial terms for such consideration as might be expected to be paid in a letting of the building or structure negotiated on an arm's length basis,

but does not include any part of a building or structure in use as or as part of a dwelling house.

(2) (a) [Subject to *paragraph (b)*, *subsections (3)* to *(5)* and (as inserted by the *Finance Act 2006*) *sections 270(4)*, *270(5)*, *270(6)*, *270(7)* and *316(2B)*][3], the provisions of the Tax Acts (other than *section 372C*) relating to the making of allowances or charges in respect of capital expenditure incurred on the construction or refurbishment of an industrial building or structure shall, notwithstanding anything to the contrary in those provisions, apply—

(i) as if a qualifying premises were, at all times at which it is a qualifying premises, a building or structure in respect of which an allowance is to be made for the purposes of income tax or corporation tax, as the case may be, under *Chapter 1* of *Part 9* by reason of its use for a purpose specified in *section 268(1)(a)*, and

[(ii) where any activity—

(I) carried on in the qualifying premises, or

(II) in a case where the facade of a building or structure or part of a building or structure is a qualifying premises, carried on in the building or structure or the part of the building or structure,

is not a trade, as if it were a trade.][4]

(b) An allowance shall be given by virtue of this subsection in respect of any capital expenditure incurred on the construction or refurbishment of a qualifying premises only in so far as that expenditure is incurred in the qualifying period.

(3) In the case where capital expenditure is incurred in the qualifying period on the refurbishment of a qualifying premises, *subsection (2)* shall apply only if the total amount of the capital expenditure so incurred is not less than an amount equal to 10 per cent of the market value of the qualifying premises immediately before that expenditure was incurred.

[(3A) (a) In the case of a qualifying premises which fronts on to a [qualifying street][5], *subsection (2)* shall apply in relation to capital expenditure incurred in the qualifying period on the construction or refurbishment of the qualifying premises, only if—

(i) the qualifying premises are comprised in the ground floor of—

(I) an existing building, or

(II) a replacement building,

and

[(ii) apart from the capital expenditure incurred in the qualifying period on the construction or refurbishment of the qualifying premises, expenditure is incurred on the upper floor or floors of the existing building or the replacement building, as the case may be, which is—

(I) eligible expenditure within the meaning of Chapter 11 of this Part (being eligible expenditure on necessary construction, or conversion expenditure or refurbishment expenditure within the meaning of that Chapter), or

(II) qualifying expenditure within the meaning of Chapter 11 of this Part (being qualifying expenditure on necessary construction, on conversion or on refurbishment within the meaning of that Chapter),

and in respect of which a deduction has been given, or would on due claim being made be given, under *section 372AP* or *372AR*.][6][7]

[(b) Notwithstanding *paragraph (a)*, *subsection (2)* shall not apply in relation to so much (if any) of the capital expenditure incurred in the qualifying period on the construction or refurbishment of the qualifying premises as exceeds the amount of the deduction, or the aggregate amount of the deductions, which has been given, or which would on due claim being made be given, under *section 372AP* or *372AR* in respect of the eligible expenditure referred to in *paragraph (a)(ii)(I)* or the qualifying expenditure referred to in *paragraph (a)(ii)(II)*.][8]

(4) For the purposes of the application, by *subsection (2)*, of *sections 271* and *273* in relation to capital expenditure incurred in the qualifying period on the construction or refurbishment of a qualifying premises—

(a) *section 271* shall apply as if—

(i) in *subsection (1)* of that section the definition of "*industrial development agency*" were deleted,

(ii) in *subsection (2)(a)(i)* of that section "to which *subsection (3)* applies" were deleted,

(iii) *subsection (3)* of that section were deleted,

(iv) the following subsection were substituted for *subsection (4)* of that section:

"(4) An industrial building allowance shall be of an amount equal to 50 per cent of the capital expenditure mentioned in *subsection (2)*.",

and

(v) in *subsection (5)* of that section "to which *subsection (3)(c)* applies" were deleted,

and

(b) *section 273* shall apply as if—

(i) in *subsection (1)* of that section the definition of "*industrial development agency*" were deleted, […][9]

[(ii) the following paragraph were substituted for *paragraph (b)* of *subsection (2)* of that section:

"(b) As respects any qualifying expenditure, any allowance made under *section 272* and increased under *paragraph (a)* in respect of that expenditure, whether claimed for one chargeable period or more than one such period, shall not in the aggregate exceed 50 per cent of the amount of that qualifying expenditure.",

and

(iii) *subsections (3)* to *(7)* of that section were deleted.][10]

(5) Notwithstanding *section 274(1)*, no balancing charge shall be made in relation to a qualifying premises by reason of any of the events specified in that section which occur—

(a) more than 13 years after the qualifying premises was first used, or

(b) in a case where *section 276* applies, more than 13 years after the capital expenditure on refurbishment of the qualifying premises was incurred.

[...][11]

(7) For the purposes only of determining, in relation to a claim for an allowance by virtue of *subsection (2)*, whether and to what extent capital expenditure incurred on the construction or refurbishment of a qualifying premises is incurred or not incurred in the qualifying period, only such an amount of that capital expenditure as is properly attributable to work on the construction or refurbishment of the premises actually carried out during the qualifying period shall (notwithstanding any other provision of the Tax Acts as to the time when any capital expenditure is or is to be treated as incurred) be treated as having been incurred in that period.][12]

Amendments

[1] Inserted by FA00 s44(1)(d)(i). This section shall apply as on and from 1 July 1999.

[2] Inserted by FA01 s60(d)(i).

[3] Substituted by FA06 s30(1)(e). With effect from 26 June 2006 per S.I. 327 of 2006.

[4] Substituted by FA03 s27(1)(d)(i). Applies as on and from 1 March 1999.

[5] Substituted by FA02 sched6(3)(f). Shall be deemed to have come into force and take effect as on and from 6 April 2001.

[6] Substituted by FA03 s27(1)(d)(ii)(I). Applies as on and from 1 January 2002.

[7] Inserted by FA01 s60(d)(ii).

[8] Substituted by FA03 s27(1)(d)(ii)(II). Applies as on and from 1 January 2002.

[9] Deleted by FA00 s44(1)(d)(iii)(I). This section shall apply as on and from 1 July 1999.

[10] Substituted by FA00 s44(1)(d)(iii)(II). This section shall apply as on and from 1 July 1999.

[11] Deleted by FA00 s44(1)(d)(iv). This section shall apply as on and from 1 July 1999.

[12] Inserted by FA98 s76.

Cross References

From Section 372D

Section 268 Meaning of "industrial building or structure".

Section 270 Meaning of "expenditure on construction of building or structure".

Section 271 Industrial building allowances.

Section 272 Writing-down allowances.

Section 273 Acceleration of writing-down allowances in respect of certain expenditure on certain industrial buildings or structures.

Section 274 Balancing allowances and balancing charges.

Section 276 Application of sections 272 and 274 in relation to capital expenditure on refurbishment.

Section 316 Interpretation of certain references to expenditure and time when expenditure is incurred.

To Section 372D

Section 270 Meaning of "expenditure on construction of building or structure".

Schedule 25B List of Specified Reliefs and Method of Determining Amount of Specified Relief Used in a Tax Year

372E Double rent allowance in respect of rent paid for certain business premises [Repealed]

Repealed by FA02 s24(3)(f).

Cross References

To Section 372E

Section 1013 Limited partnerships.

372F Rented residential accommodation: deduction for certain expenditure on construction [Repealed]

Repealed by FA02 s24(3)(f).

372G Rented residential accommodation: deduction for certain expenditure on conversion [Repealed]

Repealed by FA02 s24(3)(f).

372H Rented residential accommodation: deduction for certain expenditure on refurbishment [Repealed]

Repealed by FA02 s24(3)(f).

372I Residential accommodation: allowance to owner-occupiers in respect of certain expenditure on construction or refurbishment [Repealed]

Repealed by FA02 s24(3)(f).

372J Provisions supplementary to sections 372F to 372I [Repealed]

Repealed by FA02 s24(3)(f).

372K Non-application of relief in certain cases and provision against double relief

[(1) Notwithstanding any other provision of this Chapter, *sections 372C* and *372D* shall not apply—

(a) in respect of expenditure incurred on the construction or refurbishment of a building or structure or a qualifying premises—

[(aa) in respect of expenditure incurred on or after 6 April 2001 on the construction or refurbishment of a building or structure or a qualifying premises the site of which is wholly within a qualifying area where any part of such expenditure has been or is to be met, directly or indirectly, by [grant assistance or any other assistance which is granted by or through the State, any board established by statute, any public or local authority or any other agency of the State][1],][2]

(i) where a property developer is entitled to the relevant interest, within the meaning of *section 269*, in relation to that expenditure, and

(ii) either the person referred to in *subparagraph (i)* or a person connected (within the meaning of *section 10*) with that person incurred the expenditure on the construction or refurbishment of the building, structure or premises concerned,

(b) in respect of expenditure incurred on the construction or refurbishment of a building or structure or a qualifying premises where such building or structure or premises is in use for the purposes of a trade, or any activity treated as a trade, carried on by the person who is entitled to the relevant interest, within the meaning of *section 269*, in relation to that expenditure and such trade or activity is carried on wholly or mainly—

(i) in the sector of agriculture, including the production, processing and marketing of agricultural products,

(ii) in the coal industry, fishing industry or motor vehicle industry, or

(iii) in the transport, steel, shipbuilding, synthetic fibres or financial services sectors,

or

[(c) in respect of expenditure incurred on or after 1 January 2003 on the construction or refurbishment of any building or structure or qualifying premises provided for the purposes of a project which is subject to the notification requirements of—

(i) the "Multisectoral framework on regional aid for large investment projects"* prepared by the Commission of the European Communities and dated 7 April 1998, or

* OJ No. C 107, 7.4.1998, p.7

(ii) the "Multisectoral framework on regional aid for large investment projects"* prepared by the Commission of the European Communities and dated 19 March 2002,

* OJ No. C 70, 19.3.2002, p.8

as the case may be, unless approval of the potential capital allowances involved has been received from that Commission by the Minister for Finance, or by such other Minister of the Government, agency or body as may be nominated for that purpose by the Minister for Finance.][3]

(2) For the purposes of [*sections 372C* and *372D*][4], where the site of any part of a building or structure is situate outside the boundary of a qualifying area and where expenditure incurred or treated as having been incurred in the qualifying period is attributable to the building or structure in general, such an amount of that expenditure shall be deemed to be attributable to the part which is situate outside the boundary of the qualifying area as bears to the whole of that expenditure the same proportion as the floor area of the part situate outside the boundary of the qualifying area bears to the total floor area of the building or structure.

(3) Where relief is given by virtue of any provision of this Chapter in relation to capital expenditure or other expenditure incurred on, or rent payable in respect of, any building, structure or premises, relief shall not be given in respect of that expenditure or that rent under any other provision of the Tax Acts.][5]

Amendments

[1] Substituted by FA02 s26(1)(a). This section applies as respects expenditure incurred on or after 7 February 2002.

[2] Inserted by FA01 s60(j).

[3] Substituted by FA03 s27(1)(e)(i). Applies as on and from 1 January 2003.

[4] Substituted by FA03 s27(1)(e)(ii). Applies as on and from 1 January 2002.

[5] Substituted by FA00 s44(1)(h). This section shall apply as on and from 1 July 1999.

Revenue Briefings

Tax Briefing

Tax Briefing September 2000 – Issue 41 pg 16 – Industrial & Commercial Buildings Capital Allowances

Cross References

From Section 372K

Section 10 Connected persons.

Section 269 Meaning of "the relevant interest".

Chapter 8

Qualifying Rural Areas

372L Interpretation (Chapter 8)

[(1) In this Chapter—][1]

"*lease*", "*lessee*", "*lessor*", "*premium*" and "*rent*" have the same meanings respectively as in *Chapter 8* of *Part 4*;

"*market value*", in relation to a building, structure or house, means the price which the unencumbered fee simple of the building, structure or house would fetch if sold in the open market in such manner and subject to such conditions as might reasonably be calculated to obtain for the vendor the best price for the building, structure or house, less the part of that price which would be attributable to the acquisition of, or of rights in or over, the land on which the building, structure or house is constructed;

["*property developer*" means a person carrying on a trade which consists wholly or mainly of the construction or refurbishment of buildings or structures with a view to their sale;][2]

["*qualifying period*" means—

(a) for the purposes of *sections 372M*, *372N* and *372O*, the period commencing on such day as the Minister for Finance may by order appoint [and ending on—][3]

[(i) 31 December 2004, or

(ii) where *subsection (2)* applies, [31 December 2006, or][4]][5]

[(iii) where *subsections (2)* and *(3)* apply, 31 July 2008;][6]][7]

[...][8]

"*qualifying rural area*" means any area described in Schedule 8A;

"*refurbishment*", in relation to a building or structure [...][9] [...][10], means any work of construction, reconstruction, repair or renewal, including the provision or improvement of water, sewerage or heating facilities, carried out in the course of the repair or restoration, or maintenance in the nature of repair or restoration, of the building or structure.

[(2) This subsection shall apply, as respects capital expenditure incurred on the construction or refurbishment of a building or structure, if—

(a) (i) a planning application (not being an application for outline permission within the meaning of section 36 of the Planning and Development Act 2000), in so far as planning permission is required, in respect of the construction or refurbishment work on the building or structure represented by that expenditure, is made in accordance with the Planning and Development Regulations 2001 to 2003,

(ii) an acknowledgement of the application, which confirms that the application was received on or before 31 December 2004, is issued by the planning authority in accordance with article 26(2) of the Planning and Development Regulations 2001 (S.I. No. 600 of 2001), and

(iii) the application is not an invalid application in respect of which a notice is issued by the planning authority in accordance with article 26(5) of those regulations,

(b) (i) a planning application, in so far as planning permission was required, in respect of the construction or refurbishment work on the building or structure represented by that expenditure, was made in accordance with the Local Government (Planning and Development) Regulations 1994 (S.I. No. 86 of 1994), not being an application for outline permission within the meaning of article 3 of those regulations,

(ii) an acknowledgement of the application, which confirms that the application was received on or before 10 March 2002, was issued by the planning authority in accordance with article 29(2)(*a*) of the regulations referred to in *subparagraph (i)*, and

(iii) the application was not an invalid application in respect of which a notice was issued by the planning authority in accordance with article 29(2)(*b*)(i) of those regulations,

or

(c) where the construction or refurbishment work on the building or structure represented by that expenditure is exempted development for the purposes of the Planning and Development Act 2000 by virtue of section 4 of that Act or by virtue of Part 2 of the Planning and Development Regulations 2001 (S.I. No. 600 of 2001) and—

(i) a detailed plan in relation to the development work is prepared,

(ii) a binding contract in writing, under which the expenditure on the development is incurred, is in existence, and

(iii) work to the value of 5 per cent of the development costs is carried out,

not later than 31 December 2004.

[(3) Subject to *paragraphs (a)* and *(b)* of *section 270(7)*, this subsection shall apply in relation to the construction or refurbishment of a building or structure the site of which is wholly within a qualifying rural area where—

(a) the person who is constructing or refurbishing the building or structure has, on or before 31 December 2006, carried out work to the value of not less than 15 per cent of the actual construction or, as the case may be, refurbishment costs of the building or structure,

(b) the person referred to in *paragraph (a)* or, where the building or structure is sold by that person, the person who is claiming a deduction under *Chapter 1* of *Part 9* in relation to the expenditure incurred, can show that the condition in *paragraph (a)* was satisfied,

(c) a binding contract in writing, under which expenditure on the construction or refurbishment of the building or structure is incurred, was in existence on or before 31 July 2006, and

(d) such other conditions, as may be specified in regulations made for the purposes of this paragraph by the Minister for Finance, have been satisfied; but such conditions shall be limited to those necessary to ensure compliance with the laws of the European Communities governing State aid or with a decision of the Commission of the European Communities as to whether aid to which this subsection relates is compatible with the common market having regard to Article 87 of the European Communities Treaty.][11]][12]][13]

Amendments

[1] Renumbered by FA04 s26(1)(e)(i). Shall come into operation on the making of an order to that effect by the Minister for Finance. With effect from 24 September 2004 per S.I. No. 642 of 2004.

[2] Inserted by FA00 s45(1)(a)(i). This section shall apply as on and from 1 July 1999.

[3, 5] Substituted by FA04 s26(1)(e)(ii). Shall come into operation on the making of an order to that effect by the Minister for Finance. With effect from 24 September 2004 per S.I. No. 642 of 2004.

[4] Substituted by FA06 s31(1)(a)(i)(I). With effect from 26 June 2006 per S.I. 325 of 2006.

[6] Inserted by FA06 s31(1)(a)(i)(II). With effect from 26 June 2006 per S.I. 325 of 2006.

[7] Substituted by FA98No2 s4.

[8] Deleted by FA02 sched2(2)(d)(i).

[9, 10] Deleted by FA02 sched2(2)(d)(ii).

[11] Inserted by FA06 s31(1)(a)(ii). With effect from 26 June 2006 per S.I. 325 of 2006.

[12] Inserted by FA04 s26(1)(e)(iii). With effect from 24 September 2004 per S.I. No. 642 of 2004.

[13] Inserted by FA98 s77(a).

Cross References

From Section 372L

Section 52 Persons chargeable.

Section 96 Interpretation (Chapter 8).

Section 268 Meaning of "industrial building or structure".

Section 270 Meaning of "expenditure on construction of building or structure".

Section 372M Accelerated capital allowances in relation to construction or refurbishment of certain industrial buildings or structures.

Section 372N Capital allowances in relation to construction or refurbishment of certain commercial buildings or structures.

Section 372O Double rent allowance in respect of rent paid for certain business premises.

To Section 372L

Section 270 Meaning of "expenditure on construction of building or structure".

372M Accelerated capital allowances in relation to construction or refurbishment of certain industrial buildings or structures

[(1) This section shall apply to a building or structure the site of which is wholly within a qualifying rural area and which is to be an industrial building or structure by reason of its use for a purpose specified in [*paragraph (a)* or *(b)* of *section 268(1)*][1].

(2) [Subject to *subsection (4)* and (as inserted by the Finance Act 2006) *sections 270(4)*, *270(5)*, *270(6)*, *270(7)* and *316(2B)*][2], *section 271* shall apply in relation to capital expenditure incurred in the qualifying period on the construction or refurbishment of a building or structure to which this section applies as if—

(a) in *subsection (1)* of that section the definition of "*industrial development agency*" were deleted,

(b) in *subsection (2)(a)(i)* of that section "to which *subsection (3)* applies" were deleted,

(c) *subsection (3)* of that section were deleted,

(d) the following subsection were substituted for *subsection (4)* of that section:

"(4) An industrial building allowance shall be of an amount equal to [50 per cent][3] of the capital expenditure mentioned in *subsection (2)*.",

and

(e) in *subsection (5)* of that section "to which *subsection (3)(c)* applies" were deleted.

(3) [Subject to *subsection (4)* and (as inserted by the Finance Act 2006) *sections 270(4), 270(5), 270(6), 270(7)* and *316(2B)*][4], *section 273* shall apply in relation to capital expenditure incurred in the qualifying period on the construction or refurbishment of a building or structure to which this section applies as if—

(a) in *subsection (1)* of that section the definition of "*industrial development agency*" were deleted,

(b) the following paragraph were substituted for [*paragraph (b)*][5] of *subsection (2)* of that section:

"(b) As respects any qualifying expenditure, any allowance made under *section 272* and increased under *paragraph (a)* in respect of that expenditure, whether claimed for one chargeable period or more than one such period, shall not in the aggregate exceed 50 per cent of the amount of that qualifying expenditure.",

and

(c) *subsections (3)* to *(7)* of that section were deleted.

(4) In the case where capital expenditure is incurred in the qualifying period on the refurbishment of a building or structure to which this section applies, *subsections (2)* and *(3)* shall apply only if the total amount of the capital expenditure so incurred is not less than an amount equal to 10 per cent of the market value of the building or structure immediately before that expenditure was incurred.

(5) Notwithstanding *section 274(1)*, no balancing charge shall be made in relation to a building or structure to which this section applies by reason of any of the events specified in that section which occurs—

(a) more than 13 years after the building or structure was first used, or

(b) in a case where *section 276* applies, more than 13 years after the capital expenditure on refurbishment of the building or structure was incurred.

(6) For the purposes only of determining, in relation to a claim for an allowance under *section 271* or *273* as applied by this section, whether and to what extent capital expenditure incurred on the construction or refurbishment of an industrial building or structure is incurred or not incurred in the qualifying period, only such an amount of that capital expenditure as is properly attributable to work on the construction or, as the case may be, the refurbishment of the building or structure actually carried out during the qualifying period shall (notwithstanding any other provision of the Tax Acts as to the time when any capital expenditure is or is to be treated as incurred) be treated as having been incurred in that period.][6]

Amendments

[1] Substituted by FA99 s47(1)(b).

[2, 4] Substituted by FA06 s31(1)(b). With effect from 26 June 2006 per S.I. 325 of 2006.

[3] Substituted by FA00 s45(1)(b). This section shall apply as on and from 1 July 1999.

[5] Substituted by FA01 s59(1)(b)(i).

[6] Inserted by FA98 s77(a).

Cross References

From Section 372M

Section 268 Meaning of "industrial building or structure".
Section 270 Meaning of "expenditure on construction of building or structure".
Section 271 Industrial building allowances.
Section 273 Acceleration of writing-down allowances in respect of certain expenditure on certain industrial buildings or structures.
Section 274 Balancing allowances and balancing charges.
Section 276 Application of sections 272 and 274 in relation to capital expenditure on refurbishment.
Section 316 Interpretation of certain references to expenditure and time when expenditure is incurred.

To Section 372M

Section 270 Meaning of "expenditure on construction of building or structure".
Section 372L Interpretation (Chapter 8).
Schedule 25B List of Specified Reliefs and Method of Determining Amount of Specified Relief Used in a Tax Year

372N Capital allowances in relation to construction or refurbishment of certain commercial buildings or structures

[(1) In this section—

"*approved scheme*" means a scheme undertaken with the approval of a local authority which has as its object, or amongst its objects, the provision of sewerage facilities, water supplies or roads for public purposes;

"*qualifying premises*" means a building or structure the site of which is wholly within a qualifying rural area, and which—

(a) apart from this section is not an industrial building or structure within the meaning of *section 268*, and

(b) (i) is in use for the purposes of a trade or profession or for the purposes of an approved scheme, or

(ii) whether or not it is so used, is let on bona fide commercial terms for such consideration as might be expected to be paid in a letting of the building or structure negotiated on an arm's length basis,

but does not include any part of a building or structure in use as or as part of a dwelling house.

(2) (a) [Subject to *paragraph (b)*, *subsections (3)* to *(5)* and (as inserted by the *Finance Act 2006*) *sections 270(4)*, *270(5)*, *270(6)*, *270(7)* and *316(2B)*][1], the provisions of the Tax Acts (other than *section 372M*) relating to the making of allowances or charges in respect of capital expenditure incurred on the construction or refurbishment of an industrial building or structure shall, notwithstanding anything to the contrary in those provisions, apply—

(i) as if a qualifying premises were, at all times at which it is a qualifying premises, a building or structure in respect of which an allowance is to be made for the purposes of income tax or corporation tax, as the case may be, under *Chapter 1* of *Part 9* by reason of its use for a purpose specified in *section 268(1)(a)*, and

(ii) where any activity carried on in the qualifying premises is not a trade, as if it were a trade.

(b) An allowance shall be given by virtue of this subsection in respect of any capital expenditure incurred on the construction or refurbishment of a qualifying premises only in so far as that expenditure is incurred in the qualifying period.

(3) In the case where capital expenditure is incurred in the qualifying period on the refurbishment of a qualifying premises, *subsection (2)* shall apply only if the total amount of the capital expenditure so incurred is not less than an amount equal to 10 per cent of the market value of the qualifying premises immediately before that expenditure was incurred.

(4) For the purposes of the application, by *subsection (2)*, of *sections 271* and *273* in relation to capital expenditure incurred in the qualifying period on the construction or refurbishment of a qualifying premises—

(a) *Section 271* shall apply as if—

(i) in *subsection (1)* of that section the definition of "*industrial development agency*" were deleted,

(ii) in *subsection (2)(a)(i)* of that section "to which *subsection (3)* applies" were deleted,

(iii) *subsection (3)* of that section were deleted,

(iv) the following subsection were substituted for *subsection (4)* of that section:

"(4) An industrial building allowance shall be of an amount equal to 50 per cent of the capital expenditure mentioned in *subsection (2)*.",

and

(v) in *subsection (5)* of that section "to which *subsection (3)(c)* applies" were deleted,

and

(b) *section 273* shall apply as if—

(i) in *subsection (1)* of that section the definition of "*industrial development agency*" were deleted, [...][2]

[(ii) the following paragraph were substituted for *paragraph (b)* of *subsection (2)* of that section:

"(b) As respects any qualifying expenditure, any allowance made under *section 272* and increased under *paragraph (a)* in respect of that expenditure, whether claimed for one chargeable period or more than one such period, shall not in the aggregate exceed 50 per cent of the amount of that qualifying expenditure.",

and

(iii) *subsections (3)* to *(7)* of that section were deleted.][3]

(5) Notwithstanding *section 274(1)*, no balancing charge shall be made in relation to a qualifying premises by reason of any of the events specified in that section which occurs—

(a) more than 13 years after the qualifying premises was first used, or

(b) in a case where *section 276* applies, more than 13 years after the capital expenditure on refurbishment of the qualifying premises was incurred.

[...][4]

(7) For the purposes only of determining, in relation to a claim for an allowance by virtue of *subsection (2)*, whether and to what extent capital expenditure incurred on the construction or refurbishment of a qualifying premises is incurred or not incurred in the qualifying period, only such an amount of that capital expenditure

as is properly attributable to work on the construction or refurbishment of the premises actually carried out during the qualifying period shall (notwithstanding any other provision of the Tax Acts as to the time when any capital expenditure is or is to be treated as incurred) be treated as having been incurred in that period.][5]

Amendments

[1] Substituted by FA06 s31(1)(c). With effect from 26 June 2006 per S.I. 325 of 2006.

[2] Deleted by FA00 s45(1)(c)(ii)(I). This section shall apply as on and from 1 July 1999.

[3] Substituted by FA00 s45(1)(c)(ii)(II). This section shall apply as on and from 1 July 1999.

[4] Deleted by FA00 s45(1)(c)(iii). This section shall apply as on and from 1 July 1999.

[5] Inserted by FA98 s77(a).

Cross References

From Section 372N

Section 268 Meaning of "industrial building or structure".
Section 270 Meaning of "expenditure on construction of building or structure".
Section 271 Industrial building allowances.
Section 272 Writing-down allowances.
Section 273 Acceleration of writing-down allowances in respect of certain expenditure on certain industrial buildings or structures.
Section 274 Balancing allowances and balancing charges.
Section 276 Application of sections 272 and 274 in relation to capital expenditure on refurbishment.
Section 316 Interpretation of certain references to expenditure and time when expenditure is incurred.

To Section 372N

Section 270 Meaning of "expenditure on construction of building or structure".
Section 372L Interpretation (Chapter 8).
Schedule 25B List of Specified Reliefs and Method of Determining Amount of Specified Relief Used in a Tax Year

372O Double rent allowance in respect of rent paid for certain business premises [Repealed]

Repealed by FA02 s24(3)(g).

Cross References

To Section 372O

Section 372L Interpretation (Chapter 8).
Section 1013 Limited partnerships.

372P Rented residential accommodation: deduction for certain expenditure on construction [Repealed]

Repealed by FA02 s24(3)(g).

372Q Rented residential accommodation: deduction for certain expenditure on conversion [Repealed]

Repealed by FA02 s24(3)(g).

372R Rented residential accommodation: deduction for certain expenditure on refurbishment [Repealed]

Repealed by FA02 s24(3)(g).

372RA Residential accommodation: allowance to owner-occupiers in respect of certain expenditure on construction or refurbishment [Repealed]

Repealed by FA02 s24(3)(g).

372S Provisions supplementary to sections 372P to 372R [Repealed]

Repealed by FA02 s24(3)(g).

372T Non-application of relief in certain cases and provision against double relief

[(1) Notwithstanding any other provision of this Chapter *sections 372M* and *372N* shall not apply—

(a) in respect of expenditure incurred on the construction or refurbishment of a building or structure or a qualifying premises—

[(aa) in respect of expenditure incurred on or after 6 April 2001 on the construction or refurbishment of a building or structure or a qualifying premises where any part of such expenditure has been or is to be met, directly or indirectly, by [grant assistance or any other assistance which is granted by or through the State, any board established by statute, any public or local authority or any other agency of the State][1],][2]

[(ab) in respect of expenditure incurred on or after 1 January 2003 on the construction or refurbishment of any building or structure or qualifying premises provided for the purposes of a project which is subject to the notification requirements of—

(i) the "Multisectoral framework on regional aid for large investment projects"* prepared by the Commission of the European Communities and dated 7 April 1998, or

* OJ No. C 107, 7.4.1998, p.7

(ii) the "Multisectoral framework on regional aid for large investment projects"* prepared by the Commission of the European Communities and dated 19 March 2002,

* OJ No. C 70, 19.3.2002, p.8

as the case may be, unless approval of the potential capital allowances involved has been received from that Commission by the Minister for Finance, or by such other Minister of the Government, agency or body as may be nominated for that purpose by the Minister for Finance,][3]

(i) where a property developer is entitled to the relevant interest, within the meaning of *section 269*, in relation to that expenditure, and

(ii) either the person referred to in *subparagraph (i)* or a person connected (within the meaning of *section 10*) with that person incurred the expenditure on the construction or refurbishment of the building, structure or premises concerned,

(b) in respect of expenditure incurred on the construction or refurbishment of a building or structure or qualifying premises where such building or structure or premises is in use for the purposes of a trade, or any activity treated as a trade, carried on by the person who is entitled to the relevant interest, within the meaning of *section 269*, in relation to that expenditure and such trade or activity is carried on wholly or mainly—

(i) in the sector of agriculture, including the production, processing and marketing of agricultural products,

(ii) in the coal industry, fishing industry or motor vehicle industry, or

(iii) in the transport, steel, shipbuilding, synthetic fibres or financial services sectors,

or

(c) in relation to any building or structure or qualifying premises which is in use for the purposes of a trade, or any activity treated as a trade, where the number of individuals employed or engaged in the carrying on of the trade or activity amounts to or exceeds 250.

(2) Where relief is given by virtue of any provision of this Chapter in relation to capital expenditure or other expenditure incurred on, or rent payable in respect of, any building, structure or premises, relief shall not be given in respect of that expenditure or that rent under any other provision of the Tax Acts.][4]

Amendments

[1] Substituted by FA02 s26(1)(b). This section applies as respects expenditure incurred on or after 7 February 2002.

[2] Inserted by FA01 s59(1)(b)(v).

[3] Inserted by FA03 s28.

[4] Substituted by FA00 s45(1)(e). This section shall apply as on and from 1 July 1999.

Revenue Briefings

Tax Briefing

Tax Briefing September 2000 – Issue 41 pg 16 – Industrial & Commercial Buildings Capital Allowances

Cross References

From Section 372T

Section 10 Connected persons.

Section 269 Meaning of "the relevant interest".

CHAPTER 9

Park and Ride Facilities and Certain Related Developments

372U Interpretation (Chapter 9)

[(1) In this Chapter—

"*guidelines*" means, subject to *subsection (2)*, guidelines in relation to—

(a) the location, development and operation of park and ride facilities,

(b) the development of commercial activities located at qualifying park and ride facilities, and

(c) the development of certain residential accommodation located at certain qualifying park and ride facilities,

issued by the Minister for the Environment and Local Government following consultation with the Minister for Public Enterprise and with the consent of the Minister for Finance;

"*park and ride facility*" means—

(a) a building or structure served by a bus or train service, in use for the purpose of providing, for members of the public generally, intending to continue a journey by bus or train and without preference for any particular class of person and on payment of an appropriate charge, parking space for mechanically propelled vehicles, and

(b) any area under, over or immediately adjoining the building or structure to which *paragraph (a)* refers on which a qualifying premises (within the meaning of [*section 372W* or *372AK*][1]) is or is to be situated;

["*property developer*" means a person carrying on a trade which consists wholly or mainly of the construction or refurbishment of buildings or structures with a view to their sale;][2]

"*qualifying park and ride facility*" means a park and ride facility in respect of which the relevant local authority, in consultation with such other agencies as may be specified in the guidelines, gives a certificate in writing to the person constructing or refurbishing such a facility stating that it is satisfied that the facility complies with the criteria and requirements laid down in the guidelines;

["*qualifying period*" means the period commencing on 1 July 1999 and ending on—

(a) 31 December 2004, or

(b) where *subsection (1A)* applies, [31 December 2006, or][3]][4]

[(c) where *subsections (1A)* and *(3)* apply, 31 July 2008;][5]

"*the relevant local authority*", in relation to the construction or refurbishment of a park and ride facility or a qualifying premises within the meaning of *section 372W* [...][6], means—

(a) in respect of the county boroughs of Cork, Dublin, Galway, Limerick and Waterford, the corporation of the borough concerned,

(b) in respect of the administrative counties of Clare, Cork, Dún Laoghaire-Rathdown, Fingal, Galway, Kildare, Kilkenny, Limerick, Meath, South Dublin, Waterford and Wicklow, the council of the county concerned,

(c) an urban district council situated in the administrative county of Kildare, Meath or Wicklow,

in whose functional area the park and ride facility is situated.

[(1A) This subsection shall apply, as respects capital expenditure incurred on the construction or refurbishment of a building or structure, if—

(a) (i) a planning application (not being an application for outline permission within the meaning of section 36 of the Planning and Development Act 2000), in so far as planning permission is required, in respect of the construction or refurbishment work on the building or structure represented by that expenditure, is made in accordance with the Planning and Development Regulations 2001 to 2003,

(ii) an acknowledgement of the application, which confirms that the application was received on or before 31 December 2004, is issued by the planning authority in accordance with article 26(2) of the Planning and Development Regulations 2001 (S.I. No. 600 of 2001), and

(iii) the application is not an invalid application in respect of which a notice is issued by the planning authority in accordance with article 26(5) of those regulations,

(b) (i) a planning application, in so far as planning permission was required, in respect of the construction or refurbishment work on the building or structure represented by that expenditure, was made in accordance with the Local Government (Planning and Development) Regulations 1994 (S.I. No. 86 of 1994), not being an application for outline permission within the meaning of article 3 of those regulations,

(ii) an acknowledgement of the application, which confirms that the application was received on or before 10 March 2002, was issued by the planning authority in accordance with article 29(2)(*a*) of the regulations referred to in *subparagraph (i)*, and

(iii) the application was not an invalid application in respect of which a notice was issued by the planning authority in accordance with article 29(2)(*b*)(i) of those regulations,

or

(c) where the construction or refurbishment work on the building or structure represented by that expenditure is exempted development for the purposes of the Planning and Development Act 2000 by virtue of section 4 of that Act or by virtue of Part 2 of the Planning and Development Regulations 2001 (S.I. No. 600 of 2001) and—

(i) a detailed plan in relation to the development work is prepared,

(ii) a binding contract in writing, under which the expenditure on the development is incurred, is in existence, and

(iii) work to the value of 5 per cent of the development costs is carried out,

not later than 31 December 2004.][7]

(2) For the purposes of this Chapter, and without prejudice to the generality of the meaning of the guidelines referred to in *subsection (1)*, the guidelines may include provisions in relation to all or any one or more of the following:

(a) the criteria for determining the suitability of a site as a location for a park and ride facility,

(b) the conditions to apply in relation to the provision of transport services to and from a park and ride facility, including provision for a formal agreement between a transport service provider and a park and ride facility operator where these functions are discharged by separate persons,

(c) the hours of operation of a park and ride facility and the level and structure of charges to be borne by members of the public in respect of parking and the use of transport services to or from a park and ride facility,

(d) the minimum number of vehicle parking spaces to be provided in a park and ride facility,

(e) the proportion of parking space, if any, in a park and ride facility which may, subject to any necessary conditions, be allocated for purposes connected with any commercial or residential development at a park and ride facility,

(f) the requirements to apply in relation to the development and operation of commercial activities, if any, at a park and ride facility, including requirements necessary to ensure that those activities do not have an adverse effect on the development and operation of the park and ride facility, and

(g) the requirements to apply in relation to the provision of residential accommodation, if any, at a park and ride facility, including requirements necessary to ensure that such accommodation does not have an adverse effect on the development and operation of the park and ride facility.

[(3) This subsection shall apply in relation to the construction or refurbishment of a building or structure which is a qualifying park and ride facility or a qualifying premises (within the meaning of *section 372W(1)*) where—

(a) the person who is constructing or refurbishing the building or structure has, on or before 31 December 2006, carried out work to the value of not less than 15 per cent of the actual construction or, as the case may be, refurbishment costs of the building or structure, and

(b) the person referred to in *paragraph (a)* or, where the building or structure is sold by that person, the person who is claiming a deduction under *Chapter 1* of *Part 9* in relation to the expenditure incurred, can show that the condition in *paragraph (a)* was satisfied.][8]][9]

Amendments

[1] Substituted by FA02 sched2(2)(e)(i).

[2] Inserted by FA02 s23(1)(e)(i)(I). Shall apply as respects expenditure incurred on or after 7 February 2002.

[3] Substituted by FA06 s32(1)(a)(i)(I). With effect from 26 June 2006 per S.I. 326 of 2006.

[4] Substituted by FA04 s26(1)(f)(i).

[5] Inserted by FA06 s32(1)(a)(i)(II). With effect from 26 June 2006 per S.I. 326 of 2006.

[6] Deleted by FA02 sched2(2)(e)(ii).

[7] Inserted by FA04 s26(1)(f)(ii).

[8] Inserted by FA06 s32(1)(a)(ii). With effect from 26 June 2006 per S.I. 326 of 2006.

[9] Inserted by FA99 s70(1).

Revenue Briefings

Tax Briefing

Tax Briefing August 2005 – Issue 60 – Transitional Arrangements for Property-Based Incentive Schemes

Cross References

From Section 372U

Section 268 Meaning of "industrial building or structure".

To Section 372U

Section 270 Meaning of "expenditure on construction of building or structure".

Section 372AK Interpretation (Chapter 11).

372V Capital allowances in relation to construction or refurbishment of certain park and ride facilities

[(1) (a) [Subject to *subsections (2)* to *(4A)* and (as inserted by the Finance Act 2006) *section 270(4)*, *270(5)*, *270(6)* and *316(2B)*][1], the provisions of the Tax Acts relating to the making of allowances or charges in respect of capital expenditure incurred on the construction or refurbishment of an industrial building or structure shall, notwithstanding anything to the contrary in those provisions, apply as if a qualifying park and ride facility were, at all times at which it is a qualifying park and ride facility, a building or structure in respect of which an allowance is to be made for the purposes of income tax or corporation tax, as the case may be, under *Chapter 1* of *Part 9* by reason of its use for a purpose specified in *section 268(1)(a)*.

(b) An allowance shall be given by virtue of this subsection in respect of any capital expenditure incurred on the construction or refurbishment of a qualifying park and ride facility only in so far as that expenditure is incurred in the qualifying period.

(2) In a case where capital expenditure is incurred in the qualifying period on the refurbishment of a qualifying park and ride facility, *subsection (1)* shall apply only if the total amount of the capital expenditure so incurred is not less than an amount equal to 10 per cent of the market value of the qualifying park and ride facility immediately before that expenditure is incurred.

[(2A) This section shall not apply in respect of expenditure incurred on the construction or refurbishment of a qualifying park and ride facility—

(a) where a property developer is entitled to the relevant interest, within the meaning of *section 269*, in relation to that expenditure, and

(b) either the person referred to in *paragraph (a)* or a person connected (within the meaning of *section 10*) with that person incurred the expenditure on the construction or refurbishment of the qualifying park and ride facility concerned.][2]

(3) For the purposes of the application, by *subsection (1)*, of *sections 271* and *273* in relation to capital expenditure incurred in the qualifying period on the construction or refurbishment of a qualifying park and ride facility—

(a) *section 271* shall apply—

(i) as if in *subsection (1)* of that section the definition of "*industrial development agency*" were deleted,

(ii) as if in *subsection (2)(a)(i)* of that section "to which *subsection (3)* applies" were deleted,

(iii) as if *subsection (3)* of that section were deleted,

(iv) as if the following subsection were substituted for *subsection (4)* of that section:

"(4) An industrial building allowance shall be of an amount equal to 50 per cent of the capital expenditure mentioned in *subsection (2)*.",

and

(v) as if in *subsection (5)* of that section "to which *subsection (3)(c)* applies" were deleted,

and

(b) *section 273* shall apply—

(i) as if in *subsection (1)* of that section, the definition of "*industrial development agency*" were deleted, and

(ii) as if *subsections (2)(b)* and *(3)* to *(7)* of that section were deleted.

(4) Notwithstanding *section 274(1)*, no balancing charge shall be made in relation to a qualifying park and ride facility by reason of any of the events specified in that section which occurs—

(a) more than 13 years after the qualifying park and ride facility was first used [or, where *subsection (4A)* applies, first used as a qualifying park and ride facility][3], or

(b) in a case where *section 276* applies, more than 13 years after the capital expenditure on refurbishment of the [qualifying park and ride facility][4] was incurred.

[(4A) Notwithstanding *subsections (1)*, *(3)(a)* and *(4)*, where it is shown in respect of a building or structure which is to be a qualifying park and ride facility that the relevant local authority is unable to give the certificate in writing referred to in the definition of "*qualifying park and ride facility*" in *section 372U(1)* due to a delay in the provision of a train service to serve the building or structure, then, in relation to capital expenditure incurred in the qualifying period on the construction or refurbishment of that building or structure—

(a) *section 271* shall apply—

(i) as if in the definition of "*appropriate chargeable period*" in *subsection (1)* of that section "the chargeable period in which the building or structure becomes an industrial building or structure" were substituted for "the chargeable period related to the expenditure", and

(ii) as if in *subsection (6)* of that section "if, within 5 years of the building or structure coming to be used, it is not an industrial building or structure" were substituted for "if the building or structure, when it comes to be used, is not an industrial building or structure",

(b) *section 272* shall apply as if in *subsection (4)(a)(ii)* of that section "beginning with the time when the building or structure was first used as an industrial building or structure" were substituted for "beginning with the time when the building or structure was first used",

(c) *section 274* shall apply—

(i) as if in *subsection (1)(b)(i)(II)* of that section "after the building or structure was first used as an industrial building or structure" were substituted for "after the building or structure was first used", and

(ii) as if in *subsection (5)(a)* of that section "when the building or structure was first used as an industrial building or structure" were substituted for "when the building or structure was first used for any purpose",

(d) *section 277* shall apply—

(i) as if in *subsection (2)* of that section "when the building or structure is first used as an industrial building or structure" were substituted for "when the building or structure is first used", and

(ii) as if in *subsection (4)(a)* of that section "when the building or structure was first used as an industrial building or structure" were substituted for "when the building or structure was first used for any purpose",

(e) *section 278* shall apply as if in *subsection (2)* of that section "before the building or structure is first used as an industrial building or structure" were substituted for "before the building or structure is first used for any purpose", and

(f) *section 279* shall apply as if in *subsections (2)* and *(3)* of that section "before the building or structure is used as an industrial building or structure or within the period of one year after it commences to be so used" were substituted for "before the building or structure is used or within the period of one year after it commences to be used" (in each place where it occurs in those subsections).][5]

(5) For the purposes only of determining, in relation to a claim for an allowance by virtue of *subsection (1)*, whether and to what extent capital expenditure incurred on the construction or refurbishment of a qualifying park and ride facility is

incurred or not incurred in the qualifying period, only such an amount of that capital expenditure as is properly attributable to work on the construction or refurbishment of the qualifying park and ride facility actually carried out during the qualifying period shall (notwithstanding any other provision of the Tax Acts as to the time when any capital expenditure is or is to be treated as incurred) be treated as having been incurred in that period.

(6) Where an allowance is given under this section in respect of capital expenditure incurred on the construction or refurbishment of a qualifying park and ride facility, no allowance shall be given in respect of that expenditure by virtue of any other provision of the Tax Acts.][6]

Amendments

[1] Substituted by FA06 s32(1)(b). With effect from 26 June 2006 per S.I. 326 of 2006.

[2] Inserted by FA02 s23(1)(e)(ii). Shall apply as respects expenditure incurred on or after 7 February 2002.

[3] Inserted by FA01 s58(a)(ii)(I).

[4] Substituted by FA01 s58(a)(ii)(II).

[5] Inserted by FA01 s58(a)(iii).

[6] Inserted by FA99 s70(1).

Cross References

From Section 372V

Section 10 Connected persons.
Section 268 Meaning of "industrial building or structure".
Section 269 Meaning of "the relevant interest".
Section 270 Meaning of "expenditure on construction of building or structure".
Section 271 Industrial building allowances.
Section 272 Writing-down allowances.
Section 273 Acceleration of writing-down allowances in respect of certain expenditure on certain industrial buildings or structures.
Section 274 Balancing allowances and balancing charges.
Section 276 Application of sections 272 and 274 in relation to capital expenditure on refurbishment.
Section 277 Writing off of expenditure and meaning of "residue of expenditure".
Section 278 Manner of making allowances and charges.
Section 279 Purchases of certain buildings or structures.
Section 316 Interpretation of certain references to expenditure and time when expenditure is incurred.

To Section 372V

Schedule 25B List of Specified Reliefs and Method of Determining Amount of Specified Relief Used in a Tax Year

372W Capital allowances in relation to construction or refurbishment of certain commercial premises

[(1) In this section "*qualifying premises*" means a building or structure the site of which is wholly within the site of a qualifying park and ride facility and—

(a) in respect of which the relevant local authority gives to the person constructing or refurbishing the premises a certificate in writing stating that it is satisfied that the premises and the activity to be carried on in the premises complies with the requirements laid down in the guidelines in relation to the development of commercial activity at a qualifying park and ride facility, [...][1]

(b) which apart from this section is not an industrial building or structure within the meaning of *section 268(1)*, and [(c) (i) is in use for the purposes of the retailing of goods or the provision of services only within the State but excluding any building or structure in use—

(I) as offices, or

(II) for the provision of mail order or financial services,

or

(ii) is let on bona fide commercial terms for such use as is referred to in *subparagraph (i)* and for such consideration as might be expected to be paid in a letting of the building or structure negotiated on an arm's length basis,][2]

but does not include any part of a building or structure in use as or as part of a dwelling house.

(2) (a) [Subject to *paragraphs (b)* and *(c)*, *subsections (3)* to *(5A)* and (as inserted by the Finance Act 2006) *sections 270(4)*, *270(5)*, *270(6)* and *316(2B)*][3], the provisions of the Tax Acts relating to the making of allowances or charges in respect of capital expenditure incurred on the construction or refurbishment of an industrial building or structure shall, notwithstanding anything to the contrary in those provisions, apply—

(i) as if a qualifying premises were, at all times at which it is a qualifying premises, a building or structure in respect of which an allowance is to be made for the purposes of income tax or corporation tax, as the case may be, under *Chapter 1* of *Part 9* by reason of its use for a purpose specified in *section 268(1)(a)*, and

(ii) where any activity carried on in the qualifying premises is not a trade, as if it were a trade.

(b) An allowance shall be given by virtue of this subsection in respect of any capital expenditure incurred on the construction or refurbishment of a qualifying premises only in so far as that expenditure is incurred in the qualifying period.

(c) (i) An allowance shall be given by virtue of this subsection in respect of any capital expenditure incurred on the construction or refurbishment of a qualifying premises at a park and ride facility only in so far as that expenditure when aggregated with—

(I) other capital expenditure, if any, incurred on the construction or refurbishment of other qualifying premises and in respect of which an allowance would or would but for this paragraph be given, and

(II) other expenditure, if any, in respect of which there is provision for a deduction to be made by virtue of [section 372AP or 372AR][4],

incurred at that park and ride facility, does not exceed one-half of the total capital expenditure incurred at that park and ride facility in respect of which an allowance or deduction is to be made or would, but for this paragraph or [372AP(5) or 372AR(5)][5], be made by virtue of any provision of [this Chapter or Chapter 11][6].

(ii) A person who has incurred capital expenditure on the construction or refurbishment of a qualifying premises at a park and ride facility and who claims to have complied with the requirements of *subparagraph (i)* in relation to that expenditure, shall be deemed not to have so complied unless the person has received from the relevant local authority a certificate in writing issued by it stating that it is satisfied that those requirements have been met.

(3) In the case where capital expenditure is incurred in the qualifying period on the refurbishment of a qualifying premises, *subsection (2)* shall apply only if the total amount of the capital expenditure so incurred is not less than an amount equal to 10 per cent of the market value of the qualifying premises immediately before that expenditure was incurred.

[(3A) This section shall not apply in respect of expenditure incurred on the construction or refurbishment of a qualifying premises—

(a) where a property developer is entitled to the relevant interest, within the meaning of *section 269*, in relation to that expenditure, and

(b) either the person referred to in *paragraph (a)* or a person connected (within the meaning of *section 10*) with that person incurred the expenditure on the construction or refurbishment of the qualifying premises concerned.][7]

(4) For the purposes of the application, by *subsection (2)*, of *sections 271* and *273* in relation to capital expenditure incurred in the qualifying period on the construction or refurbishment of a qualifying premises—

(a) *section 271* shall apply—

(i) as if in *subsection (1)* of that section the definition of "*industrial development agency*" were deleted,

(ii) as if in *subsection (2)(a)(i)* of that section "to which *subsection (3)* applies" were deleted,

(iii) as if *subsection (3)* of that section were deleted,

(iv) as if the following subsection were substituted for *subsection (4)* of that section:

"(4) An industrial building allowance shall be of an amount equal to 50 per cent of the capital expenditure mentioned in *subsection (2)*.",

and

(v) as if in *subsection (5)* of that section "to which *subsection (3)(c)* applies" were deleted,

and

(b) *section 273* shall apply—

(i) as if in *subsection (1)* of that section the definition of "*industrial development agency*" were deleted, and

(ii) as if *subsections (2)(b)* and *(3)* to *(7)* of that section were deleted.

(5) Notwithstanding *section 274(1)*, no balancing charge shall be made in relation to a qualifying premises by reason of any of the events specified in that section which occur—

(a) more than 13 years after the qualifying premises was first used [or, where *subsection (5A)* applies, first used as a qualifying premises][8], or

(b) in a case where *section 276* applies, more than 13 years after the capital expenditure on refurbishment of the qualifying premises was incurred.

[(5A) Notwithstanding *subsections (2)(a)*, *(4)(a)* and *(5)*, where it is shown in respect of a building or structure which is to be a qualifying premises that the relevant local authority is unable to give the certificate in writing referred to in *subsection (1)(a)* relating to compliance with certain requirements at a park and ride facility which would be a qualifying park and ride facility but for the delay referred to in *section 372V(4A)*, then, in relation to capital expenditure incurred in the qualifying period on the construction or refurbishment of the building or structure—

(a) *section 271* shall apply—

(i) as if in the definition of "*appropriate chargeable period*" in *subsection (1)* of that section "the chargeable period in which the building or structure becomes an industrial building or structure" were substituted for "the chargeable period related to the expenditure", and

(ii) as if in *subsection (6)* of that section "if, within 5 years of the building or structure coming to be used, it is not an industrial building or structure" were substituted for "if the building or structure, when it comes to be used, is not an industrial building or structure",

(b) *section 272* shall apply as if in *subsection (4)(a)(ii)* of that section "beginning with the time when the building or structure was first used as an industrial building or structure" were substituted for "beginning with the time when the building or structure was first used",

(c) *section 274* shall apply—

(i) as if in *subsection (1)(b)(i)(II)* of that section "after the building or structure was first used as an industrial building or structure" were substituted for "after the building or structure was first used", and

(ii) as if in *subsection (5)(a)* of that section "when the building or structure was first used as an industrial building or structure" were substituted for "when the building or structure was first used for any purpose",

(d) *section 277* shall apply—

(i) as if in *subsection (2)* of that section "when the building or structure is first used as an industrial building or structure" were substituted for "when the building or structure is first used", and

(ii) as if in *subsection (4)(a)* of that section "when the building or structure was first used as an industrial building or structure" were substituted for "when the building or structure was first used for any purpose",

(e) *section 278* shall apply as if in *subsection (2)* of that section "before the building or structure is first used as an industrial building or structure" were substituted for "before the building or structure is first used for any purpose", and

(f) *section 279* shall apply as if in *subsections (2)* and *(3)* of that section "before the building or structure is used as an industrial building or structure or within the period of one year after it commences to be so used" were substituted for "before the building or structure is used or within the period of one year after it commences to be used" (in each place where it occurs in those subsections).][9]

(6) For the purposes only of determining, in relation to a claim for an allowance by virtue of *subsection (2)*, whether and to what extent capital expenditure incurred on the construction or refurbishment of a qualifying premises is incurred or not incurred in the qualifying period, only such an amount of that capital expenditure as is properly attributable to work on the construction or refurbishment of the premises actually carried out during the qualifying period shall (notwithstanding any other provision of the Tax Acts as to the time when any capital expenditure is or is to be treated as incurred) be treated as having been incurred in that period.

(7) Where an allowance is given under this section in respect of capital expenditure incurred on the construction or refurbishment of a qualifying premises, no allowance shall be given in respect of that expenditure by virtue of any other provision of the Tax Acts.][10]

Amendments

[1] Deleted by FA01 s58(b)(i)(I).

[2] Substituted by FA01 s58(b)(i)(II).

[3] Substituted by FA06 s32(1)(c). With effect from 26 June 2006 per S.I. 326 of 2006.

[4, 5] Substituted by FA02 sched2(2)(f).

[6] Substituted by FA04 s26(1)(g). This section is deemed to have applied as on and from 1 January 2002.

[7] Inserted by FA02 s23(1)(e)(iii). Shall apply as respects expenditure incurred on or after 7 February 2002.

[8] Inserted by FA01 s58(b)(iii).

[9] Inserted by FA01 s58(b)(iv).

[10] Inserted by FA99 s70(1).

Cross References

From Section 372W

Section 10 Connected persons.
Section 268 Meaning of "industrial building or structure".
Section 269 Meaning of "the relevant interest".
Section 270 Meaning of "expenditure on construction of building or structure".
Section 271 Industrial building allowances.
Section 272 Writing-down allowances.
Section 273 Acceleration of writing-down allowances in respect of certain expenditure on certain industrial buildings or structures.
Section 274 Balancing allowances and balancing charges.
Section 276 Application of sections 272 and 274 in relation to capital expenditure on refurbishment.
Section 277 Writing off of expenditure and meaning of "residue of expenditure".
Section 278 Manner of making allowances and charges.
Section 279 Purchases of certain buildings or structures.
Section 316 Interpretation of certain references to expenditure and time when expenditure is incurred.

To Section 372W

Section 270 Meaning of "expenditure on construction of building or structure".
Section 372AK Interpretation (Chapter 11).
Schedule 25B List of Specified Reliefs and Method of Determining Amount of Specified Relief Used in a Tax Year

372X Rented residential accommodation: deduction for certain expenditure on construction [Repealed]

Repealed by FA02 s24(3)(h).

372Y Residential accommodation: allowance to owner-occupiers in respect of certain expenditure on construction [Repealed]

Repealed by FA02 s24(3)(h).

372Z Provisions supplementary to sections 372X and 372Y [Repealed]

Repealed by FA02 s24(3)(h).

CHAPTER 10

Designated Areas of Certain Towns

372AA Interpretation and application (Chapter 10)

[(1) In this Chapter—

["*facade*", in relation to a building or structure, part of a building or structure, or a house, means the exterior wall of the building or structure, the part of the building or structure or, as the case may be, the house which fronts on to a street;][1]

"*lease*", "*lessee*", "*lessor*", "*premium*" and "*rent*" have the same meanings respectively as in *Chapter 8* of *Part 4*;

"*market value*", in relation to a building, structure or house, means the price which the unencumbered fee simple of the building, structure or house would fetch if sold in the open market in such manner and subject to such conditions as might reasonably be calculated to obtain for the vendor the best price for the building, structure or house, less the part of that price which would be attributable to the acquisition of, or of rights in or over, the land on which the building, structure or house is constructed;

"*property developer*" means a person carrying on a trade which consists wholly or mainly of the construction or refurbishment of buildings or structures with a view to their sale;

"*qualifying area*" means an area or areas specified as a qualifying area under *section 372AB*;

["*qualifying period*" means, subject to *section 372AB*, the period commencing on 6 April 2001 and ending on—

(a) 31 December 2004, or

(b) where *subsection (1A)* applies, [31 December 2006, or][2]][3]

[(c) where *subsections (1A)* and *(3)* apply, 31 July 2008;][4]

"*refurbishment*", in relation to a building or structure [...][5], means any work of construction, reconstruction, repair or renewal, including the provision or improvement of water, sewerage or heating facilities, carried out in the course of the repair or restoration, or maintenance in the nature of repair or restoration, of the building or [structure;]6

["*street*", includes part of a street and the whole or part of any road, square, quay or lane.][7]

[(1A) This subsection shall apply, as respects capital expenditure incurred on the construction or refurbishment of a building or structure, if—

(a) (i) a planning application (not being an application for outline permission within the meaning of section 36 of the Planning and Development Act 2000), in so far as planning permission is required, in respect of the construction or refurbishment work on the building or structure represented by that expenditure, is made in accordance with the Planning and Development Regulations 2001 to 2003,

(ii) an acknowledgement of the application, which confirms that the application was received on or before 31 December 2004, is issued by the planning authority in accordance with article 26(2) of the Planning and Development Regulations 2001 (S.I. No. 600 of 2001), and

(iii) the application is not an invalid application in respect of which a notice is issued by the planning authority in accordance with article 26(5) of those regulations,

(b) (i) a planning application, in so far as planning permission was required, in respect of the construction or refurbishment work on the building or structure represented by that expenditure, was made in accordance with the Local Government (Planning and Development) Regulations 1994 (S.I. No. 86 of 1994), not being an application for outline permission within the meaning of article 3 of those regulations,

(ii) an acknowledgement of the application, which confirms that the application was received on or before 10 March 2002, was issued by the planning authority in accordance with article 29(2)(*a*) of the regulations referred to in *subparagraph (i)*, and

(iii) the application was not an invalid application in respect of which a notice was issued by the planning authority in accordance with article 29(2)(*b*)(i) of those regulations,

or

(c) where the construction or refurbishment work on the building or structure represented by that expenditure is exempted development for the purposes of the Planning and Development Act 2000 by virtue of section 4 of that Act or by virtue of Part 2 of the Planning and Development Regulations 2001 (S.I. No. 600 of 2001) and—

(i) a detailed plan in relation to the development work is prepared,

(ii) a binding contract in writing, under which the expenditure on the development is incurred, is in existence, and

(iii) work to the value of 5 per cent of the development costs is carried out,

not later than 31 December 2004.][8]

(2) [This Chapter and Chapter 11 of this Part][9] shall apply if the Oireachtas passes an Act which refers to this Chapter and provides for the renewal of certain urban areas and the submission of plans (to be known as "*Town Renewal Plans*") to the Minister for the Environment and Local Government which have been drawn up by county councils (being county councils as referred to in such Act) in respect of an area or areas identified by such an authority on the basis of criteria prepared by that Minister, including physical and socio-economic renewal of such an area or areas.

[(3) Subject to *paragraphs (a)* and *(b)* of *section 270(7)*, this subsection shall apply in relation to the construction or refurbishment of a building or structure or part of a building or structure the site of which is wholly within a qualifying area where—

(a) the person who is constructing or refurbishing the building or structure or the part of the building or structure has, on or before 31 December 2006, carried out work to the value of not less than 15 per cent of the actual construction or, as the case may be, refurbishment costs of the building or structure or the part of the building or structure,

(b) the person referred to in *paragraph (a)* or, where the building or structure or the part of the building or structure is sold by that person, the person who is claiming a deduction under *Chapter 1* of *Part 9* in relation to the expenditure incurred, can show that the condition in *paragraph (a)* was satisfied,

(c) a binding contract in writing under which expenditure on the construction or refurbishment of the building or structure or the part of a building or structure is incurred was in existence on or before 31 July 2006, and

(d) such other conditions, as may be specified in regulations made for the purposes of this paragraph by the Minister for Finance, have been satisfied; but such conditions shall be limited to those necessary to ensure compliance with the laws of the European Communities governing State aid or with a decision of the Commission of the European Communities as to whether aid to which this subsection relates is compatible with the common market having regard to Article 87 of the European Communities Treaty.][10]][11]

Amendments

[1] Inserted by FA03 s29(1)(a)(i).

[2] Substituted by FA06 s33(1)(a)(i)(I). With effect from 26 June 2006 per S.I. 328 of 2006.

[3] Substituted by FA04 s26(1)(h)(i).

[4] Inserted by FA06 s33(1)(a)(i)(II). With effect from 26 June 2006 per S.I. 328 of 2006.

[5] Deleted by FA02 sched2(2)(g)(i)(II).

[6] Substituted by FA03 s29(1)(a)(ii).

[7] Inserted by FA03 s29(1)(a)(iii).

[8] Inserted by FA04 s26(1)(h)(ii).

[9] Substituted by FA02 sched2(2)(g)(ii).

[10] Inserted by FA06 s33(1)(a)(ii). With effect from 26 June 2006 per S.I. 328 of 2006.

[11] Inserted by FA00 s89(a).

Revenue Briefings

Tax Briefing

Tax Briefing December 2000 – Issue 42 pg 24 – Town Renewal Scheme – tax incentives
Tax Briefing August 2005 – Issue 60 – Transitional Arrangements for Property-Based Incentive Schemes

Cross References

From Section 372AA

Section 52 Persons chargeable.
Section 96 Interpretation (Chapter 8).
Section 268 Meaning of "industrial building or structure".
Section 270 Meaning of "expenditure on construction of building or structure".

To Section 372AA

Section 270 Meaning of "expenditure on construction of building or structure".

372AB Qualifying areas

[(1) The Minister for Finance may, on the recommendation of the Minister for the Environment and Local Government (which recommendation shall take into consideration a Town Renewal Plan submitted by a local authority to that Minister in respect of an area identified by it), by order direct that—

(a) the area or areas described (being wholly located within the boundaries of the area to which the Town Renewal Plan relates) in the order shall be a qualifying area for the purposes of one or more sections of [this Chapter or Chapter 11 of this Part][1],

[(b) where such an area or areas is or are to be a qualifying area—

(i) for the purposes of *section 372AC*, that area or those areas shall be a qualifying area for the purposes of one or more of the following—

(I) the construction,

(II) the refurbishment, and

(III) the refurbishment of the facade,

of a building or structure to which that section applies,

(ii) for the purposes of *section 372AD*—

(I) one or more of the categories of building or structure mentioned in *subsection (2)* shall or shall not be a qualifying premises within the meaning of that section, and

(II) that area or those areas shall be a qualifying area for the purposes of either or both the construction of, and the refurbishment of, a qualifying premises within the meaning of that section,

and

(iii) for the purposes of *section 372AR*, that area or those areas may be a qualifying area for the purposes of one or more of the following—

(I) the construction of,

(II) the conversion into,

(III) the refurbishment (within the meaning of Chapter 11 of this Part) of, and

(IV) the refurbishment (within the meaning of Chapter 11 of this Part) of the facade of,

a qualifying premises (within the meaning of that Chapter),][2]

[(ba) where such an area or areas is or are to be a qualifying area for the purposes of *section 372AP*, that section shall apply in relation to that area or those areas in so far as that section relates to one or more of the following:

(i) expenditure incurred on the construction of a house,][3]

[(ii) conversion expenditure incurred in relation to a house,

(iii) refurbishment expenditure incurred in relation to a house, and

(iv) refurbishment expenditure incurred in relation to the facade of a house,][4]

(c) as respects any such area so described in the order, the definition of "*qualifying period*" in *section 372AA* [and *section 372AL*][5] shall be construed as a reference to such period as shall be specified in the order in relation to that area; but no such period specified in the order shall commence before—

(i) in the case of *sections 372AC* and *372AD*, [6 April 2001][6], and

(ii) in the case of [any provision of Chapter 11 of this Part][7], 1 April 2000,

[or end after 31 December 2004, or—

[(I) in the case of *sections 372AC* and *372AD*—

(A) where *subsection (1A)* of *section 372AA* applies, end after 31 December 2006, or

(B) where *subsections (1A)* and *(3)* of *section 372AA* apply, end after 31 July 2008,

and][8]

[(II) in the case of any provision of Chapter 11 of this Part—

(A) where *subsection (1A)* of *section 372AL* applies, end after 31 December 2006, or

(B) where *subsections (1A)* and *(3)* of *section 372AL* apply, end after 31 July 2008.][9]][10]

[(2) The categories of building or structure referred to in *subsection (1)(b)(ii)(I)* shall be—

(a) buildings or structures in use as offices,

(b) any other buildings or structures and in respect of which not more than 10 per cent of the capital expenditure incurred in the qualifying period on their construction or refurbishment relates to the construction or refurbishment of buildings or structures in use as offices,

(c) the facade of a building or structure or part of a building or structure referred to in *paragraph (a)*, and

(d) the facade of a building or structure or part of a building or structure referred to in *paragraph (b)*.][11]

[(2A) The power to make an order under *subsection (1)* includes the power to amend or revoke the order.][12]

(3) Every order made by the Minister for Finance under *subsection (1)* shall be laid before Dáil Éireann as soon as may be after it is made and, if a resolution annulling the order is passed by Dáil Éireann within the next 21 days on which Dáil Éireann has sat after the order is laid before it, the order shall be annulled accordingly, but without prejudice to the validity of anything previously done thereunder.

(4) Notwithstanding an order under *subsection (1)*, the granting of relief by virtue of any provision of [this Chapter or Chapter 11 of this Part][13] shall be subject to such other requirements as may be specified in or under the Act referred to in *section 372AA(2)*.][14]

Amendments

[1] Substituted by FA02 sched2(2)(h)(i)(I).

[2] Substituted by FA03 s29(1)(b)(i). Applies as on and from 6 April 2000.

[3] Inserted by FA02 sched2(2)(h)(i)(III).

[4] Substituted by FA03 s29(1)(b)(ii). Applies as on and from 6 April 2000.

[5] Inserted by FA02 sched2(2)(h)(i)(IV)(A).

[6] Substituted by FA04 s26(1)(i)(i). This section is deemed to have applied as on and from 1 January 2002.

[7] Substituted by FA02 sched2(2)(h)(i)(IV)(B).

[8] Substituted by FA06 s33(1)(b)(i). With effect from 26 June 2006 per S.I. 328 of 2006.

[9] Substituted by FA06 s33(1)(b)(ii). With effect from 26 June 2006 per S.I. 328 of 2006.

[10] Substituted by FA04 s26(1)(i)(ii).

[11] Substituted by FA03 s29(1)(b)(iii). Applies as on and from 6 April 2000.

[12] Inserted by FA03 s29(1)(b)(iv). Applies as on and from 6 April 2000.

[13] Substituted by FA02 sched2(2)(h)(ii).

[14] Inserted by FA00 s89(a).

Cross References

To Section 372AB

Section 372AK Interpretation (Chapter 11).

372AC Accelerated capital allowances in relation to construction or refurbishment of certain industrial buildings or structures

[(1) In this section, "*building or structure to which this section applies*" means a building or structure or part of a building or structure the site of which is wholly within a qualifying area and which is to be an industrial building or structure by reason of its use for a purpose specified in *section 268(1)(a)*.

(2) [Subject to *section 372AJ* and (as inserted by the Finance Act 2006) *sections 270(4)*, *270(5)*, *270(6)*, *270(7)* and *316(2B)*][1], *section 271* shall apply in relation to capital expenditure incurred in the qualifying period on the construction or refurbishment of a building or structure to which this section applies as if—

(a) in *subsection (1)* of that section the definition of "*industrial development agency*" were deleted,

(b) in *subsection (2)(a)(i)* of that section "to which *subsection (3)* applies" were deleted,

(c) *subsection (3)* of that section were deleted,

(d) the following subsection were substituted for *subsection (4)* of that section:

"(4) An industrial building allowance shall be of an amount equal to 50 per cent of the capital expenditure mentioned in *subsection (2)*.",

and

(e) in *subsection (5)* of that section "to which *subsection (3)(c)* applies" were deleted.

(3) [Subject to *section 372AJ* and (as inserted by the Finance Act 2006) *sections 270(4)*, *270(5)*, *270(6)*, *270(7)* and *316(2B)*][2], *section 273* shall apply in relation to capital expenditure incurred in the qualifying period on the construction or refurbishment of a building or structure to which this section applies as if—

(a) in *subsection (1)* of that section the definition of "*industrial development agency*" were deleted,

(b) the following paragraph were substituted for *paragraph (b)* of *subsection (2)* of that section:

"(b) As respects any qualifying expenditure, any allowance made under *section 272* and increased under *paragraph (a)* in respect of that expenditure, whether claimed for one chargeable period or more than one such period, shall not in the aggregate exceed 50 per cent of the amount of that qualifying expenditure.",

and

(c) *subsections (3)* to *(7)* of that section were deleted.

(4) Notwithstanding *section 274(1)*, no balancing charge shall be made in relation to a building or structure to which this section applies by reason of any of the events specified in that section which occurs—

(a) more than 13 years after the building or structure was first used, or

(b) in a case where *section 276* applies, more than 13 years after the capital expenditure on refurbishment of the building or structure was incurred.

(5) For the purposes only of determining, in relation to a claim for an allowance under *section 271* or *273* as applied by this section, whether and to what extent capital expenditure incurred on the construction or refurbishment of an industrial building or structure is incurred or not incurred in the qualifying period, only such an amount of that capital expenditure as is properly attributable to work on the construction or, as the case may be, the refurbishment of the building or structure actually carried out during the qualifying period shall (notwithstanding any other provision of the Tax Acts as to the time when any capital expenditure is or is to be treated as incurred) be treated as having been incurred in that period.][3]

Amendments

[1, 2] Substituted by FA06 s33(1)(c). With effect from 26 June 2006 per S.I. 328 of 2006.

[3] Inserted by FA00 s89(a).

Cross References

From Section 372AC

Section 270 Meaning of "expenditure on construction of building or structure".
Section 271 Industrial building allowances.
Section 272 Writing-down allowances.
Section 273 Acceleration of writing-down allowances in respect of certain expenditure on certain industrial buildings or structures.
Section 274 Balancing allowances and balancing charges.
Section 276 Application of sections 272 and 274 in relation to capital expenditure on refurbishment.
Section 316 Interpretation of certain references to expenditure and time when expenditure is incurred.

To Section 372AC

Section 270 Meaning of "expenditure on construction of building or structure".
Section 372AD Capital allowances in relation to construction or refurbishment of certain commercial premises.
Schedule 25B List of Specified Reliefs and Method of Determining Amount of Specified Relief Used in a Tax Year

372AD Capital allowances in relation to construction or refurbishment of certain commercial premises

[(1) In this section, "*qualifying premises*" means a building or structure or part of a building or structure the site of which is wholly within a qualifying area and which—

(a) apart from this section is not an industrial building or structure within the meaning of *section 268*, and

(b) (i) is in use for the purposes of a trade or profession, or

(ii) whether or not it is so used, is let on bona fide commercial terms for such consideration as might be expected to be paid in a letting of the building or structure negotiated on an arm's length basis,

but does not include any part of a building or structure in use as or as part of a dwelling house.

(2) (a) [Subject to *paragraph (b)*, *subsections (3)* and *(4)*, *section 372AJ* and (as inserted by the Finance Act 2006) *sections 270(4)*, *270(5)*, *270(6)*, *270(7)* and *316(2B)*][1], the provisions of the Tax Acts (other than *section 372AC*) relating to the making of allowances or charges in respect of capital expenditure incurred on the construction or refurbishment of an industrial building or structure shall, notwithstanding anything to the contrary in those provisions, apply—

(i) as if a qualifying premises were, at all times at which it is a qualifying premises, a building or structure in respect of which an allowance is to be made for the purposes of income tax or corporation tax, as the case may be, under *Chapter 1* of *Part 9* by reason of its use for a purpose specified in *section 268(1)(a)*, and

[(ii) where any activity—

(I) carried on in the qualifying premises, or

(II) in a case where the facade of a building or structure or part of a building or structure is a qualifying premises, carried on in the building or structure or the part of the building or structure,

is not a trade, as if it were a trade.][2]

(b) An allowance shall be given by virtue of this subsection in respect of any capital expenditure incurred on the construction or refurbishment of a qualifying premises only in so far as that expenditure is incurred in the qualifying period.

(3) For the purposes of the application, by *subsection (2)*, of *sections 271* and *273* in relation to capital expenditure incurred in the qualifying period on the construction or refurbishment of a qualifying premises—

(a) *section 271* shall apply as if—

(i) in *subsection (1)* of that section the definition of "*industrial development agency*" were deleted,

(ii) in *subsection (2)(a)(i)* of that section "to which *subsection (3)* applies" were deleted,

(iii) *subsection (3)* of that section were deleted,

(iv) the following subsection were substituted for *subsection (4)* of that section:

"(4) An industrial building allowance shall be of an amount equal to 50 per cent of the capital expenditure mentioned in *subsection (2)*.",

and

(v) in *subsection (5)* of that section "to which *subsection (3)(c)* applies" were deleted,

and

(b) *section 273* shall apply as if—

(i) in *subsection (1)* of that section the definition of "*industrial development agency*" were deleted,

(ii) the following paragraph were substituted for *paragraph (b)* of *subsection (2)* of that section:

"(b) As respects any qualifying expenditure, any allowance made under *section 272* and increased under *paragraph (a)* in respect of that expenditure, whether claimed for one chargeable period or more than one such period, shall not in the aggregate exceed 50 per cent of the amount of that qualifying expenditure.",

and

(iii) *subsections (3)* to *(7)* of that section were deleted.

(4) Notwithstanding *section 274(1)*, no balancing charge shall be made in relation to a qualifying premises by reason of any of the events specified in that section which occur—

(a) more than 13 years after the qualifying premises was first used, or

(b) in a case where *section 276* applies, more than 13 years after the capital expenditure on refurbishment of the qualifying premises was incurred.

(5) For the purposes only of determining, in relation to a claim for an allowance by virtue of *subsection (2)*, whether and to what extent capital expenditure incurred on the construction or refurbishment of a qualifying premises is incurred or not incurred in the qualifying period, only such an amount of that capital expenditure as is properly attributable to work on the construction or refurbishment of the premises actually carried out during the qualifying period shall (notwithstanding any other provision of the Tax Acts as to the time when any capital expenditure is or is to be treated as incurred) be treated as having been incurred in that period.][3]

Amendments

[1] Substituted by FA06 s33(1)(d). With effect from 26 June 2006 per S.I. 328 of 2006.

[2] Substituted by FA03 s29(1)(c). Applies as on and from 6 April 2000.

[3] Inserted by FA00 s89(a).

Cross References

From Section 372AD

Section 268 Meaning of "industrial building or structure".

Section 270 Meaning of "expenditure on construction of building or structure".

Section 271 Industrial building allowances.

Section 272 Writing-down allowances.

Section 273 Acceleration of writing-down allowances in respect of certain expenditure on certain industrial buildings or structures.

Section 274 Balancing allowances and balancing charges.

Section 276 Application of sections 272 and 274 in relation to capital expenditure on refurbishment.

Section 316 Interpretation of certain references to expenditure and time when expenditure is incurred.

Section 372AC Accelerated capital allowances in relation to construction or refurbishment of certain industrial buildings or structures.

Section 372AJ Non-application of relief in certain cases and provision against double relief.

To Section 372AD

Section 270 Meaning of "expenditure on construction of building or structure".

Schedule 25B List of Specified Reliefs and Method of Determining Amount of Specified Relief Used in a Tax Year

372AE Rented residential accommodation: deduction for certain expenditure on construction [Repealed]

Repealed by FA02 s24(3)(i).

372AF Rented residential accommodation: deduction for certain expenditure on conversion [Repealed]

Repealed by FA02 s24(3)(i).

372AG Rented residential accommodation: deduction for certain expenditure on refurbishment [Repealed]

Repealed by FA02 s24(3)(i).

372AH Residential accommodation: allowance to owner-occupiers in respect of certain expenditure on construction or refurbishment [Repealed]

Repealed by FA02 s24(3)(i).

372AI Provisions supplementary to sections 372AE to 372AH [Repealed]

Repealed by FA02 s24(3)(i).

372AJ Non-application of relief in certain cases and provision against double relief

[(1) Notwithstanding any other provision of this Chapter, *sections 372AC* and *372AD* shall not apply—

(a) in respect of expenditure incurred on the construction or refurbishment of a building or structure or a qualifying premises—

(i) where a property developer is entitled to the relevant interest, within the meaning of *section 269*, in relation to that expenditure, and

(ii) either the person referred to in *subparagraph (i)* or a person connected (within the meaning of *section 10*) with that person incurred the expenditure on the construction or refurbishment of the building, structure or premises concerned,

[(aa) in respect of expenditure incurred on or after 6 April 2001 on the construction or refurbishment of a building or structure or a qualifying premises where any part of such expenditure has been or is to be met, directly or indirectly, by [grant assistance or any other assistance which is granted by or through the State, any board established by statute, any public or local authority or any other agency of the State][1],

(ab) in respect of expenditure incurred on or after 6 April 2001 on the construction or refurbishment of a building or structure or a qualifying premises unless the relevant interest, within the meaning of *section 269*, in such expenditure is held by a small or mediumsized enterprise within the meaning of Annex I to Commission Regulation (EC) No. 70/2001 of 12 January 2001*, [or, as the case may be, by a micro, small or medium-sized enterprise within the meaning of the Annex to Commission Recommendation of 6 May 2003 concerning the definition of micro, small and medium-sized enterprises†][2]

* OJ No. L10 of 13 January 2001, p.33

† OJ No. L124 of 20 May 2003, p.36

[…][3]][4]

(b) in respect of expenditure incurred on the construction or refurbishment of a building or structure or a qualifying premises where such building or structure or premises is in use for the purposes of a trade, or any activity treated as a trade, carried on by the person who is entitled to the relevant interest, within the meaning of *section 269*, in relation to that expenditure and such trade or activity is carried on wholly or mainly—

(i) in the sector of agriculture, including the production, processing and marketing of agricultural products,

(ii) in the coal industry, fishing industry or motor vehicle industry, or

(iii) in the transport, steel, shipbuilding, synthetic fibres or financial services sectors,

or

[(c) in respect of expenditure incurred on or after 1 January 2003 on the construction or refurbishment of any building or structure or qualifying premises provided for the purposes of a project which is subject to the notification requirements of—

(i) the "Multisectoral framework on regional aid for large investment projects"* prepared by the Commission of the European Communities and dated 7 April 1998, or

* OJ No. C 107, 7.4.1998, p.7

(ii) the "Multisectoral framework on regional aid for large investment projects"* prepared by the Commission of the European Communities and dated 19 March 2002,

* OJ No. C 70, 19.3.2002, p.8

as the case may be, unless approval of the potential capital allowances involved has been received from that Commission by the Minister for Finance, or by such other Minister of the Government, agency or body as may be nominated for that purpose by the Minister for Finance.][5]

(2) For the purposes of [*sections 372AC* and *372AD*][6], where the site of any part of a building or structure is situated outside the boundary of a qualifying area and where expenditure incurred or treated as having been incurred in the qualifying period is attributable to the building or structure in general, such an amount of that expenditure shall be deemed to be attributable to the part which is situated outside the boundary of the qualifying area as bears to the whole of that expenditure the same proportion as the floor area of the part situated outside the boundary of the qualifying area bears to the total floor area of the building or structure.

(3) Where relief is given by virtue of any provision of this Chapter in relation to capital expenditure or other expenditure incurred on any building, structure or premises, relief shall not be given in respect of that expenditure under any other provision of the Tax Acts.][7]

Amendments

[1] Substituted by FA02 s26(1)(c). This section applies as respects expenditure incurred on or after 7 February 2002.

[2] Inserted by FA05 s35.

[3] Deleted by FA02 s27(1). This section shall be deemed to have applied as on and from 6 April 2001.

[4] Inserted by FA01 s80(1)(f).

[5] Substituted by FA03 s29(1)(d)(i). applies as on and from 1 January 2003.

[6] Substituted by FA03 s29(1)(d)(ii). Applied as on and from 1 January 2002.

[7] Inserted by FA00 s89(a).

Revenue Briefings

Tax Briefing

Tax Briefing September 2000 – Issue 41 pg 16 – Industrial & Commercial Buildings Capital Allowances

Cross References

From Section 372AJ

Section 10 Connected persons.

Section 269 Meaning of "the relevant interest".

To Section 372AJ

Section 372AD Capital allowances in relation to construction or refurbishment of certain commercial premises.

CHAPTER 11

Reliefs for Lessors and Owner-Occupiers in Respect of Expenditure Incurred on the Provision of Certain Residential Accommodation

372AK Interpretation (Chapter 11)

[In this Chapter—

"*certificate of compliance*" and "*certificate of reasonable cost*" shall be construed, respectively, in accordance with *section 372AM*;

"*conversion expenditure*" shall be construed in accordance with *section 372AN*;

"*eligible expenditure*" shall be construed in accordance with *section 372AN*;

"*existing building*" has the same meaning as in *section 372A*;

"*facade*", in relation to a house, means the exterior wall of the house which fronts on to a street;

"*guidelines*", in relation to a house the site of which is wholly within the site of a qualifying park and ride facility, has the same meaning as in *section 372U*;

"*house*" includes any building or part of a building used or suitable for use as a dwelling and any out-office, yard, garden or other land appurtenant to or usually enjoyed with that building or part of a building;

"*lease*", "*lessee*" and "*lessor*" have the same meanings, respectively, as in *Chapter 8* of *Part 4*;

"*Minister*", except where the context otherwise requires, means the Minister for the Environment and Local Government;

"*necessary construction*" has the same meaning as in *section 372A* and any reference in this Chapter (other than in *section 372AR(1)(a)*) to construction shall, in the case of a house which fronts on to a qualifying street or is comprised in a building or part of a building which fronts on to a qualifying street, apply as if it were a reference to necessary construction, unless the context requires otherwise;

"*premium*" has the same meaning as in *Chapter 8* of *Part 4*;

"*qualifying expenditure*" shall be construed in accordance with *section 372AQ*;

"*qualifying lease*" shall be construed in accordance with *section 372AO*;

"*qualifying period*" shall be construed in accordance with *section 372AL*;

"*qualifying park and ride facility*" has the same meaning as in *section 372U(1)*;

"*qualifying premises*" shall be construed in accordance with *section 372AM*;

"*qualifying rural area*" means any area described in *Schedule 8A*;

"*qualifying street*" means a street specified as a qualifying street under *section 372BA*;

"*qualifying student accommodation area*" means an area or areas specified as a qualifying area in the relevant guidelines;

"*qualifying town area*" means an area or areas specified as a qualifying area under *section 372AB*;

"*qualifying urban area*" means an area or areas specified as a qualifying area under *section 372B*;

"*refurbishment*" means—

(a) in relation to a building or a part of a building other than a special specified building, either or both of the following—

(i) the carrying out of any works of construction, reconstruction, repair or renewal, and

(ii) the provision or improvement of water, sewerage or heating facilities,

where the carrying out of such works or the provision of such facilities is certified by the Minister, in any certificate of reasonable cost or certificate of compliance, as the case may be, granted by the Minister under *section 372AM*,

(b) in relation to a facade, any works of construction, reconstruction, repair or renewal [carried out][1] in the course of the repair or restoration, or maintenance in the nature of repair or restoration, of a facade, and

(c) in relation to a special specified building, any works of construction, reconstruction, repair or renewal, including the provision or improvement of water, sewerage or heating facilities, carried out in the course of the repair or restoration, or maintenance in the nature of repair or restoration, of the building or for the purposes of compliance with the requirements of the Housing (Standards for Rented Houses) Regulations 1993 (S.I. No. 147 of 1993),

but *paragraph (c)* shall not apply for the purposes of *section 372AQ* and *372AR*;

"*refurbishment expenditure*" shall be construed in accordance with *section 372AN*;

"*relevant cost*" has the same meaning as in *section 372AP*;

"*relevant guidelines*", in relation to a house or building the site of which is wholly within a qualifying student accommodation area, means guidelines entitled "*Guidelines on Residential Developments for 32Level Students*" issued by the Minister for Education and Science in consultation with the Minister and with the consent of the Minister for Finance, or such other guidelines amending or replacing those guidelines issued in accordance with *section 372AM(1)(c)*;

["*relevant local authority*",—

[(a) a qualifying urban area means the local authority for the purposes of the Local Government Act 2001 (as amended by the *Local Government Reform Act 2014*) in whose functional area the area is situated, and][2]

(b) in relation to the construction of a house the site of which is wholly within the site of a qualifying park and ride facility and which is a qualifying premises for the purposes of this Chapter, has the same meaning as it has in *section 372U(1)* in relation to the construction or refurbishment of a park and ride facility or a qualifying premises within the meaning of *section 372W*;][3]

"*relevant period*" has the meaning assigned to it in *section 372AP*;

"*rent*" has the same meaning as in *Chapter 8* of *Part 4*;

"*replacement building*" has the same meaning as in *section 372A*;

"*special qualifying premises*" shall be construed in accordance with *section 372AM*;

"*special specified building*" and "*specified building*" have the same meanings, respectively, as in *section 372AN(6)*;

"*street*" includes part of a street and the whole or part of any road, square, quay or lane;

"*tax incentive area*" means—

(a) a qualifying urban area,

(b) a qualifying rural area,

(c) the site of a qualifying park and ride facility,

(d) a qualifying town area, or

(e) a qualifying student accommodation area;

"*total floor area*" means the total floor area of a house measured in the manner referred to in section 4(2)(*b*) of the Housing (Miscellaneous Provisions) act, 1979.][4]

Amendments

[1] Inserted by FA03 s30(1)(a). Applies as on and from 1 January 2002.

[2] Substituted by LGRA14 sched2(part5).

[3] Substituted by FA03 s26(d).

[4] Inserted by FA02 sched2(1).

Revenue Briefings

Tax Briefing

Tax Briefing September 1996 – Issue 23 pg 15 – Transfer of Section 23/43 properties
Tax Briefing December 1997 – Issue 29 pg 10 – Owner-Occupiers of Residential Property
Tax Briefing September 1998 – Issue 33 pg 22 – Urban Renewal – Residential Properties Update
Tax Briefing October 1999 – Issue 37 pg 9 – Capital Allowances/Owner-Occupier Relief
Tax Briefing August 2005 – Issue 60 – Transitional Arrangements for Property-Based Incentive Schemes
Tax Briefing August 2005 – Issue 60 – Section 23 and Owner-Occupier Relief
Tax Briefing August 2005 – Issue 60 – Student Accommodation Scheme
Tax Briefing May 2006 – Issue 63 – Capital Allowances and Property-Based Incentive Schemes
Tax Briefing August 2006 – Issue 64 – Capital Allowances and Property-Based Incentive Schemes
Tax Briefing December 2006 – Issue 65 – Property-Based Incentive Schemes – 15% test
Tax Briefing December 2006 – Issue 65 – Property-Based Incentive Schemes – Inducements for purchase of property
Tax Briefing December 2006 – Issue 65 – Registration of Tenancies and Property-Based Incentive Schemes
Tax Briefing December 2006 – Issue 65 – Capital Allowances and Property-Based Incentive Schemes

Tax Briefing July 2007 – Issue 66 – The 'Net Price Paid' Formula and Separate Site Sales and Building Agreements
Tax Briefing April 2009 – Issue 71 – Rent Pooling
Tax Briefing June 2010 – Issue 6 – Clawback of "section 23 type" relief in death cases

eBrief

eBrief No. 55/2006 – Property-Based Incentive Schemes '15%' test – payments to local authorities

Revenue Information Notes

A Guide to Section 23 Relief – Rented Residential Relief in a Tax Incentive Area
A Guide to Residential Owner-Occupier Relief

Revenue Precedents

The allowance is available outside the 10 year period if it is not used up within that time. The allowance can be set against rental income from other investment properties. IT 96 3503

A bona fides company reconstruction takes place whereby a new company is formed and the assets of an existing company are transferred to it. The shareholders and the number of shares held are the same in both companies. One of the assets transferred is a property on which rented residential relief has been claimed. Will a clawback arise in such circumstances?

It has been decided not to allow the concessional treatment sought. This is on the basis that 1) there is no hardship involved, 2) the properties are to be transferred between two separate legal entities. IT983006

The use of a house by a builder as a show house does not prevent it from being a qualifying premises for the purposes of section 23 relief. IT923032

Where two or more units of two or more storeys have a common or shared external entrance, such units are regarded as a maisonette. IT903009

A deduction allowable under section 23 can be carried forward for more than 10 years if it exceeds the Case V profits in those 10 years. IT913051

Where a qualifying premises is purchased by a bare trust on behalf of more than one partner, each partner is entitled to his/her proportionate share of the relief under section 23. IT913006

Where a property is purchased in joint names, how is relief apportioned? Each party is entitled to treat his/her share of the expenditure as a deduction under section 97. Where a party has a life interest in the income from the property, that person's deduction is still confined to his/her share of the qualifying expenditure. IT913015

The taxpayer paid a sum of money to a member of the public who was injured on a site where the taxpayer was constructing a rented residential premises. The taxpayer also incurred legal fees in connection with the claim. These amounts cannot be claimed as part of the costs of the construction of the premises. These are not direct costs associated with the construction of the premises in question. IT963519

Three artisan dwellings stand side by side and front onto a designated street. The developer wishes to demolish two and retain the facade of the remaining house. On completion of the development two or more houses will exist. Having regard to the fact that the meaning of refurbishment includes the carrying out of any works of construction would the development qualify for rented residential relief under section 348(1) Taxes Consolidation Act 1997? With regard to the first two buildings, refurbishment in Section 348(1) Taxes Consolidation Act 1997 is defined in relation to a building, not in relation to a proposed building. If the two buildings are demolished refurbishment cannot be regarded as being carried out in relation to those buildings as they no longer exist. The building referred to in the definition of a specified building in Section 348 is either of the three buildings and not the aggregate of those buildings. In order for either of the buildings to be regarded as a specified building it must contain two or more residential units prior to refurbishment. As the dwellings did not contain two or more such units rented residential relief is not available. IT973012

Should the grant received by an owner occupier be deducted from the purchase price of the property or from the amount of construction expenditure which the purchaser is deemed to have incurred? From the latter. IT943504

Is Urban Renewal Relief available in respect of car park spaces in a multi-storey car park which are sold with and apportioned to residential units which are part of the same development? Where a car space belongs to or is necessarily or usually enjoyed with a residential unit the car space will be regarded as included in the definition of a house in Section 350(1) Taxes Consolidation Act 1997. GD95.003

If a deduction is available under either Section 356, 357 or 358 Taxes Consolidation Act 1997 can it be set against all rental income of the claimant in computing liability to tax under Case V of Schedule D.

The Explanatory Memorandum accompanying the Finance Act 1995 appears to distinguish the way the deduction in respect of expenditure incurred can be used.
Subsections (2) of Section 356, (4) of 357 and (2) of 358 Taxes Consolidation Act 1997 all regard the qualifying expenditure as if it were a deduction authorised by the provisions of section 97(2) Taxes Consolidation Act 1997. Section 75(2) of that act states: "Profits or gains chargeable under Case V of Schedule D shall, for all the .purposes of ascertaining liability to income tax, be deemed to issue from a .single source....". The effect of all Case V income being deemed to issue from a single source is that only one Case V figure is chargeable, this being the sum of all Case V income less the deductions authorised by section 97(2) Taxes Consolidation Act 1997, including any amounts regarded as a Case V deduction by virtue of sections 356, 357 or 358. IT953014

Cross References

From Section 372AK

Section 52 Persons chargeable.
Section 96 Interpretation (Chapter 8).
Section 372A Interpretation and application (Chapter 7).
Section 372B Qualifying areas.
Section 372BA Qualifying streets.
Section 372U Interpretation (Chapter 9).
Section 372W Capital allowances in relation to construction or refurbishment of certain commercial premises.
Section 372AB Qualifying areas.
Section 372AL Qualifying period.
Section 372AM Grant of certain certificates and guidelines, qualifying and special qualifying premises.
Section 372AN Eligible expenditure: lessors.
Section 372AO Qualifying lease.
Section 372AP Relief for lessors.
Section 372AQ Qualifying expenditure: owner-occupiers.
Section 372AR Relief for owner-occupiers.
Schedule 8A Description of Qualifying Rural Areas

To Section 372AK

Section 268 Meaning of "industrial building or structure".
Section 980 Deduction from consideration on disposal of certain assets.

372AL Qualifying period

[(1) For the purposes of this Chapter, "*qualifying period*", in relation to—

(a) a qualifying urban area, means, subject to *section 372B*, the period commencing on 1 August 1998 and ending on—

(i) 31 December 2002, or

(ii) where *subsection (2)* applies, [31 December 2006][1],

[(iii) where *subsections (2)* and *(3)* apply, 31 July 2008,][2]

(b) a qualifying street, means, subject to *section 372BA*, the period commencing on 6 April 2001 [and ending on 31 December 2004 or, where *subsection (1A)* applies,][3][ending on 31 December 2006 or, where *subsections (1A)* and *(3)* apply, ending on 31 July 2008][4],

(c) a qualifying rural area, means—

(i) for the purposes of *sections 372AP* and (in so far as it relates to that section) *section 372AS*, the period commencing on 1 June 1998 [and ending on 31 December 2004 or, where *subsection (1A)* applies,][5] [ending on 31 December 2006 or, where *subsections (1A)* and *(3)* apply, ending on 31 July 2008][6], and

(ii) for the purposes of *section 372AR* and (in so far as it relates to that section) *section 372AS*, the period commencing on 6 April 1999 [and ending on 31 December 2004 or, where *subsection (1A)* applies,][7][ending on 31 December 2006 or, where *subsections (1A)* and *(3)* apply, ending on 31 July 2008][8],

(d) the site of a qualifying park and ride facility, means the period commencing on 1 July 1999 [and ending on 31 December 2004 or, where *subsection (1A)* applies,][9][ending on 31 December 2006 or, where *subsections (1A)* and *(3)* apply, ending on 31 July 2008][10],

(e) a qualifying town area, means, subject to *section 372AB*, the period commencing on 1 April 2000 [and ending on 31 December 2004 or, where *subsection (1A)* applies,][11][ending on 31 December 2006 or, where *subsections (1A)* and *(3)* apply, ending on 31 July 2008][12],

(f) a qualifying student accommodation area, means the period commencing on 1 April 1999 and ending on—

(i) 31 March 2003, or

[(ii) where *subsection (1A)* applies, [31 December 2006, or][13]][14]

[(iii) where *subsections (1A)* and *(3)* apply, 31 July 2008,][15]

and

(g) a special specified building, means the period [commencing on 6 April 2001 and ending on 31 July 2008][16].

[(1A) This subsection shall apply, as respects expenditure incurred on the construction, conversion or, as the case may be, refurbishment of a building or structure, if—

(a) (i) a planning application (not being an application for outline permission within the meaning of section 36 of the Planning and Development Act 2000), in so far as planning permission is required, in respect of the construction, conversion or refurbishment work on the building or structure represented by that expenditure, is made in accordance with the Planning and Development Regulations 2001 to 2003,

(ii) an acknowledgement of the application, which confirms that the application was received on or before 31 December 2004, is issued by the planning authority in accordance with article 26(2) of the Planning and Development Regulations 2001 (S.I. No. 600 of 2001), and

(iii) the application is not an invalid application in respect of which a notice is issued by the planning authority in accordance with article 26(5) of those regulations,

(b) (i) a planning application, in so far as planning permission was required, in respect of the construction, conversion or refurbishment work on the building or structure represented by that expenditure, was made in accordance with the Local Government (Planning and Development) Regulations 1994 (S.I. No. 86 of 1994), not being an application for outline permission within the meaning of article 3 of those regulations,

(ii) an acknowledgement of the application, which confirms that the application was received on or before 10 March 2002, was issued by the planning authority in accordance with article 29(2)(*a*) of the regulations referred to in *subparagraph (i)*, and

(iii) the application was not an invalid application in respect of which a notice was issued by the planning authority in accordance with article 29(2)(*b*)(i) of those regulations,

or

(c) where the construction, conversion or refurbishment work on the building or structure represented by that expenditure is exempted development for the purposes of the Planning and Development Act 2000 by virtue of section 4 of that Act or by virtue of Part 2 of the Planning and Development Regulations 2001 (S.I. No. 600 of 2001) and—

(i) a detailed plan in relation to the development work is prepared,

(ii) a binding contract in writing, under which the expenditure on the development is incurred, is in existence, and

(iii) work to the value of 5 per cent of the development costs is carried out,

not later than 31 December 2004.][17]

(2)[(a) This subsection shall apply where—][18]

[(i) the relevant local authority gives a certificate in writing on or before 30 September 2003, to the person constructing, converting or, as the case may be, refurbishing a building or part of a building, the site of which is wholly within a qualifying urban area, stating that it is satisfied that not less than 15 per cent of the total cost of constructing, converting or refurbishing the building or the part of the building, as the case may be, and the acquisition of the site thereof had been incurred on or before 30 June 2003, and

(ii) the application for such a certificate is received by the relevant local authority on or before 31 July 2003.][19]

(b) In considering whether to give a certificate referred to in *paragraph (a)*, the relevant local authority shall have regard only to guidelines issued by the Department of the Environment and Local Government in relation to the giving of such certificates.

[(3) This subsection shall apply in relation to the construction, conversion or refurbishment of a building or part of a building which fronts on to a qualifying street or the site of which is wholly within a tax incentive area where—

(a) the person who is constructing, converting or, as the case may be, refurbishing the building or the part of the building has, on or before 31 December 2006, carried out work to the value of not less than 15 per cent of the actual construction, conversion or, as the case may be, refurbishment costs of the building or the part of the building, and

(b) the person referred to in *paragraph (a)* or, where the building or the part of the building is sold by that person, the person who is claiming a deduction under *section 372AP* or under *section 372AR*, as the case may be, can show that the condition in *paragraph (a)* was satisfied.][20]][21]

Amendments

[1] Substituted by FA06 s25(a)(i)(I)(A).

[2] Inserted by FA06 s25(a)(i)(I)(B).

[3] Substituted by FA04 s26(1)(j)(i)(II).

[4] Substituted by FA06 s25(a)(i)(II).

[5, 7] Substituted by FA04 s26(1)(j)(i)(III).

[6, 8] Substituted by FA06 s25(a)(i)(III).

[9] Substituted by FA04 s26(1)(j)(i)(IV).

[10] Substituted by FA06 s25(a)(i)(IV).

[11] Substituted by FA04 s26(1)(j)(i)(V).

[12] Substituted by FA06 s25(a)(i)(V).

[13] Substituted by FA06 s25(a)(i)(VI)(A).

[14] Substituted by FA04 s26(1)(j)(i)(VI).

[15] Inserted by FA06 s25(a)(i)(VI)(B).

[16] Substituted by FA06 s25(a)(i)(VII).

[17] Inserted by FA04 s26(1)(j)(ii).

[18, 19] Substituted by FA03 s26(e)(ii).

[20] Inserted by FA06 s25(a)(ii).

[21] Inserted by FA02 sched2(1).

Cross References

To Section 372AL

Section 372AK Interpretation (Chapter 11).

372AM Grant of certain certificates and guidelines, qualifying and special qualifying premises

[(1) (a) The Minister may grant a certificate (in this Chapter referred to as a "*certificate of compliance*") for the purposes of *section 372AP* or *372AR*, as the case may be, certifying that, at the time of granting the certificate and on the basis of the information available to the Minister at that time—

(i) the house to which the certificate relates complies—

(I) in the case of construction, with such conditions, if any, as may be determined by the Minister from time to time for the purposes of section 4 of the Housing (Miscellaneous Provisions) act, 1979, in relation to standards of construction of houses and the provision of water, sewerage and other services in houses,

(II) in the case of conversion or refurbishment, with such conditions, if any, as may be determined by the Minister from time to time for the purposes of section 5 of the Housing (Miscellaneous Provisions) act, 1979, in relation to standards for improvement of houses and the provision of water, sewerage and other services in houses,

(ii) the total floor area of that house is within the relevant floor area limits as specified in *subsection (4)*, and

(iii) in the case of refurbishment, the refurbishment work was necessary for the purposes of ensuring the suitability as a dwelling of any house in the building or the part of the building and whether or not the number of houses in the building or the part of the building, or the shape or size of any such house, is altered in the course of such refurbishment, but—

(A) in the case of a house the site of which is wholly within a qualifying town area, such certificate shall be granted only where an application has been received by the Minister within a period of one year from the day next after the end of the qualifying period, and

(B) in the case of a house, the site of which is wholly within a qualifying student accommodation area, such certificate shall be granted having regard to the relevant guidelines.

(b) (i) The Minister may grant a certificate (in this Chapter referred to as a "*certificate of reasonable cost*") for the purposes of *section 372AP* or *372AR*, as the case may be, certifying that, at the time of granting the certificate and on the basis of the information available to the Minister at that time—

(I) the house to which the certificate relates complies—

(A) in the case of construction, with such conditions, if any, as may be determined by the Minister from time to time for the purposes of section 4 of the Housing (Miscellaneous Provisions) act, 1979, in relation to standards of construction of houses and the provision of water, sewerage and other services in houses,

(B) in the case of conversion or refurbishment, with such conditions, if any, as may be determined by the Minister from time to time for the purposes of section 5 of the Housing (Miscellaneous Provisions) act, 1979, in relation to standards for improvement of houses and the provision of water, sewerage and other services in houses,

(II) the amount specified in the certificate in relation to the cost of construction of, conversion into, or, as the case may be, refurbishment of, the house to which the certificate relates appears to the Minister to be reasonable,

(III) the total floor area of that house is within the relevant floor area limits as specified in *subsection (4)*, and

(IV) in the case of refurbishment, the refurbishment work was necessary for the purposes of ensuring the suitability as a dwelling of any house in the building or the part of the building and whether or not the number of houses in the building or the part of the building, or the shape or size of any such house, is altered in the course of such refurbishment,

but—

(A) in the case of a house, the site of which is wholly within a qualifying town area, such certificate shall be granted only where an application has been received by the Minister within a period of one year from the day next after the end of the qualifying period, and

(B) in the case of a house, the site of which is wholly within a qualifying student accommodation area, such certificate shall be granted having regard to the relevant guidelines.

(ii) Section 18 of the Housing (Miscellaneous Provisions) act, 1979, applies, with any necessary modifications, to a certificate of reasonable cost as if it were a certificate of reasonable value within the meaning of that section.

(c) The Minister for Education and Science may, in relation to a house or building the site of which is wholly within a qualifying student accommodation area, in consultation with the Minister and with the consent of the Minister for Finance—

(i) issue guidelines for the purposes of this Chapter and, without prejudice to the generality of the foregoing, such guidelines may include provisions in relation to all or any one or more of the following—

(I) the design and the construction of, conversion into, or refurbishment of, houses,

(II) the total floor area and dimensions of rooms within houses, measured in such manner as may be determined by the Minister,

(III) the provision of ancillary facilities and amenities in relation to houses,

(IV) the granting of certificates of reasonable cost and of certificates of compliance,

(V) the designation of qualifying areas,

(VI) the terms and conditions relating to qualifying leases, and

(VII) the educational institutions and the students attending those institutions for whom the accommodation is provided,

and

(ii) amend or replace relevant guidelines in like manner.

(2) Subject to this section, a house is a qualifying premises for the purposes of *section 372AP* or *372AR*, as the case may be, where—

(a) the house fronts on to a qualifying street or is comprised in a building or part of a building which fronts on to a qualifying street, or the site of the house is wholly within a tax incentive area,

(b) the house is used solely as a dwelling,

(c) the house complies with the requirements of *subsection (4)* in respect of its total floor area,

(d) there is in force in respect of the house—

(i) a certificate of compliance or,

(ii) if it is not a house provided for sale, a certificate of reasonable cost the amount specified in which in respect of the cost of construction of the house, the cost of conversion in relation to the house or the cost of the refurbishment in relation to the house is not less than the expenditure actually incurred on such construction, conversion, or, as the case may be, refurbishment,

but where, in the case of *section 372AP*, the refurbishment expenditure or, in the case of *section 372AR*, the qualifying expenditure relates solely to the refurbishment of a facade, this paragraph shall not apply,

(e) in the case of a house the site of which is wholly within the site of a qualifying park and ride facility, the relevant local authority gives to the person constructing the house a certificate in writing stating that it is satisfied that the house or, in a case where the house is one of a number of houses in a single development, the development of which it is part complies with the requirements laid down in the guidelines in relation to the development of certain residential accommodation at a park and ride facility, and

(f) in so far as *section 372AP* is concerned, the house—

(i) where the eligible expenditure has been incurred on the construction of the house, without having been used is first let in its entirety under a qualifying lease,

(ii) where the eligible expenditure incurred is conversion expenditure in relation to the house, without having been used subsequent to the incurring of the expenditure on the conversion is first let in its entirety under a qualifying lease, and

(iii) where the eligible expenditure incurred is refurbishment expenditure in relation to the house, on the date of completion of the refurbishment to which the expenditure relates is let (or, if not let on that date, is, without having been used after that date, first let) in its entirety under a qualifying lease,

and thereafter throughout the remainder of the relevant period (except for reasonable periods of temporary disuse between the ending of one qualifying lease and the commencement of another such lease) continues to be let under such a lease.

(3) Subject to this section, a house is a special qualifying premises for the purposes of *section 372AP* where—

(a) the house is comprised in a special specified building,

(b) the house is used solely as a dwelling,

(c) on the date of completion of the refurbishment to which the refurbishment expenditure in relation to the house relates, the house is let (or, if not let on that date, the house is, without having been used after that date, first let) in its entirety under a qualifying lease and thereafter throughout the remainder of the relevant period (except for reasonable periods of temporary disuse between the ending of one qualifying lease and the commencement of another such lease) continues to be let under such a lease, and

(d) the house is not a house on which expenditure has been incurred which qualified, or on due claim being made would qualify, for relief under—

(i) *section 372AP* on the basis that the house is a qualifying premises, or

(ii) any other provision of this Part.

(4) A house is not a qualifying premises for the purposes of *section 372AP* or *372AR* unless—

(a) where the house fronts on to a qualifying street or is comprised in a building or part of a building which fronts on to a qualifying street, or where its site is wholly within—

(i) a qualifying urban area, or

(ii) the site of a qualifying park and ride facility,

the total floor area of the house is not less than 38 square metres and not more than 125 square metres,

(b) where the site of the house is wholly within a qualifying rural area, the total floor area of the house is not less than 38 square metres and—

(i) in the case of *section 372AP*—

(I) not more than 140 square metres, if the eligible expenditure incurred was incurred on the construction of the house before 6 December 2000,

(II) not more than 150 square metres, if the eligible expenditure incurred on or in relation to the house was conversion expenditure or refurbishment expenditure incurred before 6 December 2000, or

(III) not more than 175 square metres if the eligible expenditure incurred on or in relation to that house was or is incurred on or after 6 December 2000,

and

(ii) in the case of *section 372AR*, not more than 210 square metres,

(c) where the site of the house is wholly within a qualifying town area, the total floor area of the house is not less than 38 square metres and—

(i) in the case of *section 372AP*—

(I) not more than 125 square metres, or

(II) not more than 150 square metres, if the eligible expenditure incurred on or in relation to the house is conversion expenditure or refurbishment expenditure incurred on or after 6 April 2001,

and

(ii) in the case of *section 372AR*—

(I) not more than 125 square metres, or

(II) not more than 210 square metres, if the qualifying expenditure incurred on or in relation to the house is incurred on or after 6 April 2001 on [the conversion or the refurbishment of the house][1],

and

(d) where the site of the house is wholly within a qualifying student accommodation area, the total floor area of the house complies with the requirements of the relevant guidelines.

(5) A house is not a qualifying premises or a special qualifying premises for the purposes of *section 372AP* if—

(a) it is occupied as a dwelling by any person connected with the person entitled to a deduction under that section in respect of the eligible expenditure incurred on or in relation to the house, and

(b) the terms of the qualifying lease in relation to the house are not such as might have been expected to be included in the lease if the negotiations for the lease had been at arm's length.

(6) (a) A house—

(i) which fronts on to a qualifying street or is comprised in a building or part of a building which fronts on to a qualifying street, or

(ii) the site of which is wholly within a qualifying urban area or a qualifying town area, is not a qualifying premises for the purposes of *section 372AP* or *372AR* unless the house or, in a case where the house is one of a number of houses in a single development, the development of which it is a part complies with such guidelines as may from time to time be issued by the Minister, with the consent of the Minister for Finance, for the purposes of furthering the objectives of urban renewal.

(b) Without prejudice to the generality of *paragraph (a)*, guidelines issued for the purposes of that paragraph may include provisions in relation to all or any one or more of the following—

(i) the design and the construction of, conversion into, or, as the case may be, refurbishment of, houses,

(ii) the total floor area and dimensions of rooms within houses, measured in such manner as may be determined by the Minister,

(iii) the provision of ancillary facilities and amenities in relation to houses, and

(iv) the balance to be achieved between houses of different types and sizes within a single development of 2 or more houses or within such a development and its general vicinity having regard to the housing existing or proposed in that vicinity.

(7) A house, the site of which is wholly within a qualifying rural area, is not a qualifying premises for the purposes of *section 372AP* unless throughout the period of any qualifying lease related to that house, the house is used as the sole or main residence of the lessee in relation to that qualifying lease.

(8) A house which fronts on to a qualifying street or is comprised in a building or part of a building which fronts on to a qualifying street is not a qualifying premises for the purposes of *section 372AP* or *372AR* unless—

(a) the house is comprised in the upper floor or floors of an existing building or a replacement building, and

(b) the ground floor of such building is in use for commercial purposes or, where it is temporarily vacant, it is subsequently so used.

(9) A house, the site of which is wholly within a qualifying student accommodation area, is not a qualifying premises for the purposes of *section 372AP* unless throughout the relevant period it is used for letting to and occupation by students in accordance with the relevant guidelines.

[(9A) A house, the site of which is wholly within a qualifying student accommodation area, is not a qualifying premises or a special qualifying premises for the purposes of *section 372AP*—

(a) (i) if any person, other than the person (in this subsection referred to as the "*investor*") who incurred or, by virtue of *subsection (8)*, *(9)* or *(10)* of that section, is treated as having incurred eligible expenditure on or in relation to the house, receives or is entitled to receive the rent, or any part of the rent, from the letting of the house during the relevant period in relation to the house, or

(ii) where two or more investors have incurred or, by virtue of *subsection (8)*, *(9)* or *(10)* of that section, are treated as having incurred eligible expenditure on or in relation to the house, unless that part of the gross rent received or receivable from the letting of the house during the relevant period in relation to the house which is received or receivable by each investor bears the same proportion to that gross rent as the amount of the eligible expenditure which is incurred, or is so treated as having been incurred, on or in relation to the house by that investor bears to the total amount of the eligible expenditure which is incurred, or is so treated as having been incurred, on or in relation to the house by all such investors;

(b) where borrowed money is employed by an investor in the construction of, conversion into, refurbishment of, or, as the case may be, purchase of, the house, unless—

(i) that borrowed money is borrowed directly by the investor from a financial institution (within the meaning of *section 906A*),

(ii) the investor is personally responsible for the repayment of, the payment of interest on, and the provision of any security required in relation to, that borrowed money, and

(iii) there is no arrangement or agreement, whether in writing or otherwise and whether or not the person providing that borrowed money is aware of such agreement or arrangement, whereby any other person agrees to be responsible for any of the investor's obligations referred to in *subparagraph (ii)*;

(c) where management or letting fees payable to a person in relation to the letting of the house are claimed by the investor as a deduction under *section 97(2)* for any chargeable period (within the meaning of *section 321*) ending in the relevant period in relation to the house, unless—

(i) such fees are shown by the claimant to be bona fide fees which reflect the level and extent of the services rendered by the person, and

(ii) the aggregate amount of such fees for that chargeable period is not more than an amount which is equal to 15 per cent of the gross amount of the rent received or receivable by the investor from the letting of the house for that chargeable period.

(9B) Subject to *subsection (9C)*, *subsection (9A)* applies—

(a) as respects eligible expenditure incurred on or in relation to a house on or after 18 July 2002, unless a binding contract for the construction of, conversion into or, as the case may be, refurbishment of the house was evidenced in writing before that date, and

(b) where *subsection (9)* or *(10)* of *section 372AP* applies, as respects expenditure incurred on the purchase of a house on or after 18 July 2002, unless a binding contract for the purchase of the house was evidenced in writing before that date.

(9C) *Paragraphs (a)* and *(c)* of *subsection (9A)* shall not apply as respects eligible expenditure incurred on or in relation to a house or, where *subsection (9)* or *(10)* of *section 372AP* applies, as respects expenditure incurred on the purchase of a house where, before 6 February 2003, the Revenue Commissioners have given an opinion in writing to the effect that the lease of the house between an investor and an educational institution referred to in the relevant guidelines, or a subsidiary (within the meaning of section 155 of the Companies Act 1963) of such an institution, would be a qualifying lease.][2]

(10) (a) A house is not a special qualifying premises for the purposes of *section 372AP* if the lessor has not complied with all the requirements of—

(i) the Housing (Standards for Rented Houses) Regulations 1993 (S.I. No. 147 of 1993),

(ii) the Housing (Rent Books) Regulations 1993 (S.I. No. 146 of 1993), and

[(iii) Part 7 of the Residential Tenancies Act 2004 in respect of all tenancies relating to that premises.][3]

[(aa) For the purposes of *paragraph (a)(iii)* a written communication from the Private Residential Tenancies Board to the chargeable person confirming the registration of a tenancy relating to a special qualifying premises shall be accepted as evidence that the registration requirement in respect of that tenancy (and that tenancy only) has been complied with.][4]

(b) A house is not a special qualifying premises for the purposes of *section 372AP* unless the house or, in a case where the house is one of a number of houses in a single development, the development of which it is a part complies with such guidelines as may from time to time be issued by the Minister, with the consent of the Minister for Finance, in relation to the refurbishment of houses as special qualifying premises.

(c) Without prejudice to the generality of *paragraph (b)*, guidelines issued for the purposes of that paragraph may include provisions in relation to refurbishment of houses and the provision of ancillary facilities and amenities in relation to houses.

(11) A house is not a qualifying premises for the purposes of *section 372AP* or *372AR*, or a special qualifying premises for the purposes of *section 372AP*, unless any person authorised in writing by the Minister for the purposes of those sections is permitted to inspect the house at all reasonable times on production, if so requested by a person affected, of his or her authorisation.][5]

Amendments

[1] Substituted by FA03 s30(1)(b). Applies as on and from 1 January 2002.

[2] Inserted by FA03 s32(1). Has come into operation as on and from 18 July 2002.

[3] Substituted by FA06 s11(1)(b)(i).

[4] Inserted by FA06 s11(1)(b)(ii).

[5] Inserted by FA02 sched2(1).

Cross References

From Section 372AM

Section 97 Computational rules and allowable deductions.

Section 321 Provisions of general application in relation to the making of allowances and charges.

To Section 372AM

Section 372AK Interpretation (Chapter 11).

Schedule 25B List of Specified Reliefs and Method of Determining Amount of Specified Relief Used in a Tax Year

372AN Eligible expenditure: lessors

[(1) Expenditure is eligible expenditure for the purposes of this Chapter where it is—

(a) expenditure incurred on—

(i) the construction of a house, other than a house referred to in *subparagraph (ii)*, or

(ii) the necessary construction of a house which fronts on to a qualifying street or is comprised in a building or part of a building which fronts on to a qualifying street,

(b) conversion expenditure, or

(c) refurbishment expenditure.

(2) In this Chapter "*conversion expenditure*" means, subject to *subsection (3)*, expenditure incurred on—

(a) the conversion into a house of—

(i) a building which fronts on to a qualifying street or the site of which is wholly within a tax incentive area other than the site of a qualifying park and ride facility, or

(ii) a part of a building which fronts on to a qualifying street or the site of which is wholly within a qualifying urban area or a qualifying town area,

where the building or, as the case may be, the part of the building has not been previously in use as a dwelling, and

(b) the conversion into 2 or more houses of—

(i) a building which fronts on to a qualifying street or the site of which is wholly within a tax incentive area other than the site of a qualifying park and ride facility, or

(ii) a part of a building which fronts on to a qualifying street or the site of which is wholly within a qualifying urban area or a qualifying town area,

where before the conversion the building or, as the case may be, the part of the building had not been in use as a dwelling or had been in use as a single dwelling,

and references in this Chapter to "*conversion*", "*conversion into a house*" and "*expenditure incurred on conversion*" shall be construed accordingly.

(3) For the purposes of *subsection (2)*, expenditure incurred on the conversion of a building or a part of a building includes expenditure incurred in the course of the conversion on either or both of the following—

(a) the carrying out of any works of construction, reconstruction, repair or renewal, and

(b) the provision or improvement of water, sewerage or heating facilities,

in relation to the building or the part of the building, as the case may be, or any outoffice appurtenant to or usually enjoyed with that building or part, but does not include—

(i) any expenditure in respect of which any person is entitled to a deduction, relief or allowance under any other provision of the Tax acts, or

(ii) any expenditure attributable to any part (in this subsection referred to as a "*non-residential unit*") of the building or, as the case may be, the part of the building which on completion of the conversion is not a house.

(4) For the purposes of *subsection (3)(ii)*, where expenditure is attributable to a building or a part of a building in general and not directly to any particular house or non-residential unit (within the meaning given by that subsection) comprised in the building or the part of the building on completion of the conversion, then such an amount of that expenditure shall be deemed to be attributable to a non-residential unit as bears to the whole of that expenditure the same proportion as the total floor area of the non-residential unit bears to the total floor area of the building or the part of the building, as the case may be.

(5) (a) For the purposes of this Chapter "*refurbishment expenditure*" means expenditure incurred on—

(i) (I) the refurbishment of a specified building, and

(II) in the case of a specified building the site of which is wholly within a qualifying town area, the refurbishment of a facade,

or

(ii) the refurbishment of a special specified building,

other than expenditure attributable to any part (in this subsection and in *subsection (6)* referred to as a "*non-residential unit*") of the building which on completion of the refurbishment is not a house.

(b) For the purposes of *paragraph (a)*, where expenditure is attributable to—

(i) the specified building, or

(ii) the special specified building,

as the case may be, in general and not directly to any particular house or non-residential unit comprised in the building on completion of the refurbishment, then such an amount of that expenditure shall be deemed to be attributable to a non-residential unit as bears to the whole of that expenditure the same proportion as the total floor area of the non-residential unit bears to the total floor area of the building.

(6) For the purposes of *subsection (5)*—

"*special specified building*" means a building or part of a building—

(a) in which before the refurbishment to which the refurbishment expenditure relates there is one or more than one house, and

(b) which on completion of that refurbishment contains, whether in addition to any non-residential unit or not, one or more than one house;

"*specified building*" means—

(a) a building which fronts on to a qualifying street or the site of which is wholly within a tax incentive area other than the site of a qualifying park and ride facility, or

(b) a part of a building which fronts on to a qualifying street or the site of which is wholly within a qualifying urban area or a qualifying town area,

and in which before the refurbishment to which the refurbishment expenditure relates—

(i) there is one or more than one house—

(I) in the case of a building, the site of which is wholly within a qualifying rural area, or

(II) in the case of a building or part of a building, the site of which is wholly within a qualifying town area,

and

(ii) there are 2 or more houses—

(I) in the case of a building or part of a building which fronts on to a qualifying street or the site of which is wholly within a qualifying urban area, or

(II) in the case of a building the site of which is wholly within a qualifying student accommodation area,

and which on completion of that refurbishment contains, whether in addition to any non-residential unit or not—

(A) in the case of a building or part of a building to which *paragraph (i)* applies, one or more than one house,

(B) in the case of a building or part of a building to which *paragraph (ii)* applies, 2 or more houses.

(7) Other than in relation to a special qualifying premises, references in this section to the construction of, conversion into, or, as the case may be, refurbishment of, any premises shall be construed as including references to the development of the land on which the premises is situated or which is used in the provision of gardens, grounds, access or amenities in relation to the premises and, without prejudice to the generality of the foregoing, as including in particular—

(a) demolition or dismantling of any building on the land,

(b) site clearance, earth moving, excavation, tunnelling and boring, laying of foundations, erection of scaffolding, site restoration, landscaping and the provision of roadways and other access works,

(c) walls, power supply, drainage, sanitation and water supply, and

(d) the construction of any outhouses or other buildings or structures for use by the occupants of the premises or for use in the provision of amenities for the occupants.][1]

Amendments

[1] Inserted by FA02 sched2(1).

Cross References

To Section 372AN

Section 372AK Interpretation (Chapter 11).

372AO Qualifying lease

[(1) In this section "*market value*", in relation to a building, structure or house, means the price which the unencumbered fee simple of the building, structure or house would fetch if sold in the open market in such manner and subject to such conditions as might reasonably be calculated to obtain for the vendor the best price for the building, structure or house, less the part of that price which would be attributable to the acquisition of, or of rights in or over, the land on which the building, structure or house is constructed.

(2) Subject to *subsection (4)*, a lease of a house is a qualifying lease for the purposes of this Chapter where the consideration for the grant of the lease consists—

(a) solely of periodic payments all of which are or are to be treated as rent for the purposes of *Chapter 8* of *Part 4*, or

(b) of payments of the kind mentioned in *paragraph (a)*, together with a payment by means of a premium which—

(i) in the case of the construction of a house, does not exceed 10 per cent of the relevant cost of the house,

(ii) in the case of the conversion of a building into a house, does not exceed 10 per cent of the market value of the house at the time the conversion is completed, and

(iii) in the case of the refurbishment of a house—

(I) is payable on or subsequent to the date of the completion of the refurbishment to which the refurbishment expenditure relates or which, if payable before that date, is so payable by reason of or otherwise in connection with the carrying out of the refurbishment, and

(II) does not exceed 10 per cent of the market value of the house at the time of the completion of the refurbishment to which the refurbishment expenditure relates.

(3) For the purposes of *subparagraph (ii)* or *(iii)* of *subsection (2)(b)*, as the case may be, where a house is a part of a building and is not saleable apart from the building of which it is a part, the market value of the house at the time the conversion is completed or, as the case may be, at the time of the completion of the refurbishment to which the refurbishment expenditure relates shall be taken to be an amount which bears to the market value of the building at that time the same proportion as the total floor area of the house bears to the total floor area of the building.

(4) A lease is not a qualifying lease for the purposes of this Chapter—

(a) if the terms of the lease contain any provision enabling the lessee or any other person, directly or indirectly, at any time to acquire any interest in the house to which the lease relates for a consideration less than that which might be expected to be given at that time for the acquisition of the interest if the negotiations for that acquisition were conducted in the open market at arm's length,

(b) where the lease relates to a qualifying rural area, if the duration of the lease is for a period of less than 3 months, or

(c) where the lease relates to a qualifying student accommodation area, if the lease does not comply with the requirements of the relevant guidelines.][1]

Amendments

[1] Inserted by FA02 sched2(1).

Cross References

From Section 372AO

Section 52 Persons chargeable.

Section 96 Interpretation (Chapter 8).

To Section 372AO

Section 372AK Interpretation (Chapter 11).

372AP Relief for lessors

[(1) In this section—

"*chargeable period*" means an accounting period of a company or a year of assessment;

"*relevant cost*", in relation to a house, means, subject to *subsection (6)*, an amount equal to the aggregate of—

(a) (i) where the eligible expenditure is on the construction of the house, the expenditure incurred on the acquisition of, or of rights in or over, any land on which the house is situated, or

(ii) where the eligible expenditure is conversion expenditure or refurbishment expenditure, the expenditure incurred on the acquisition of, or of rights in or over—

(I) any land on which the house is situated, and

(II) any building in which the house is comprised,

and

(b) the expenditure actually incurred on the construction of, conversion into, or, as the case may be, refurbishment of the house;

[…][1]

"*relevant period*", in relation to the incurring of eligible expenditure on or in relation to a qualifying premises or a special qualifying premises, means—

(a) where the eligible expenditure is incurred on the construction of, or in relation to the conversion of a building into, a qualifying premises, the period of 10 years beginning on the date of the first letting of the qualifying premises under a qualifying lease, and

(b) where—

(i) the eligible expenditure incurred is refurbishment expenditure in relation to a qualifying premises or a special qualifying premises, the period of 10 years beginning on the date of the completion of the refurbishment to which the refurbishment expenditure relates, or

(ii) where the qualifying premises or, as the case may be, the special qualifying premises was not let under a qualifying lease on the date referred to in *subparagraph (i)*, the period of 10 years beginning on the date of the first such letting [after the date of such completion;][2]

[…][3]

"*relevant price paid*", in relation to the purchase by a person of a house, means the amount which bears to the net price paid by such person on that purchase the same proportion as the amount of the eligible expenditure actually incurred on or in relation to the house, which is to be treated under *section 372AS(1)* as having been incurred in the qualifying period, bears to the relevant cost in relation to that house.

(2) [Subject to *subsections (3), (4)* and *(5)*,][4] where a person, having made a claim in that behalf, proves to have incurred eligible expenditure on or in relation to a house which is a qualifying premises or a special qualifying premises—

(a) such person is entitled, in computing for the purposes of *section 97(1)* the amount of a surplus or deficiency in respect of the rent from the qualifying premises or, as the case may be, the special qualifying premises, to a deduction of so much (if any) of that expenditure as is to be treated under *section 372AS(1)* or under this section as having been incurred by such person in the qualifying period, and

(b) *Chapter 8* of *Part 4* shall apply as if that deduction were a deduction authorised by *section 97(2)*.

(3) (a) Where the eligible expenditure incurred is refurbishment expenditure in relation to a house which is a special qualifying premises—

(i) the deduction to be given under *subsection (2)(a)* shall be given—

(I) for the chargeable period in which the expenditure is incurred or, if the special qualifying premises was not let under a qualifying lease during that chargeable period, the chargeable period in which occurs the date of the first such letting after the expenditure is incurred, and

(II) for any subsequent chargeable period in which that premises continues to be a special qualifying premises,

and

(ii) the deduction for each such chargeable period shall be of an amount equal to 15 per cent of the expenditure to which *subsection (2)(a)* refers.

(b) For the purposes of *paragraph (a)*—

(i) the aggregate amount to be deducted by virtue of that paragraph shall not exceed 100 per cent of the expenditure to which *subsection (2)(a)* refers, and

(ii) where a chargeable period consists of a period less than one year in length, the amount of the deduction to be given for the chargeable period shall be proportionately reduced.

[...][5]

(4) (a) This subsection applies to any premium or other sum which—

(i) is payable, directly or indirectly, under a qualifying lease or otherwise under the terms subject to which the lease is granted, to or for the benefit of the lessor or to or for the benefit of any person connected with the lessor, and

(ii) where the eligible expenditure incurred is refurbishment expenditure in relation to a qualifying premises or a special qualifying premises—

(I) is payable on or subsequent to the date of completion of the refurbishment to which the refurbishment expenditure relates, or

(II) if payable before that date, is so payable by reason of or otherwise in connection with the carrying out of the refurbishment.

(b) Where any premium or other sum to which this subsection applies, or any part of such premium or such other sum, is not or is not treated as rent for the purposes of *section 97*, the eligible expenditure to be treated as having been incurred in the qualifying period on or in relation to the qualifying premises or the special qualifying premises to which the qualifying lease relates shall be deemed for the purposes of *subsection (2)* to be reduced by the lesser of—

(i) the amount of such premium or such other sum or, as the case may be, that part of such premium or such other sum, and

(ii) the amount which bears to the amount mentioned in *subparagraph (i)* the same proportion as the amount of the eligible expenditure actually incurred on or in relation to the qualifying premises or, as the case may be, the special qualifying premises and which is to be treated under *section 372AS(1)* as having been incurred in the qualifying period bears to the whole of the eligible expenditure incurred on or in relation to the qualifying premises or the special qualifying premises, as the case may be.

(5) (a) A person is entitled to a deduction by virtue of *subsection (2)* in respect of eligible expenditure incurred on a qualifying premises at a park and ride facility only in so far as that expenditure when aggregated with—

(i) other eligible expenditure, if any, incurred on other qualifying premises at the park and ride facility and in respect of which a deduction is to be made or would, but for this subsection, be made, and

(ii) other expenditure, if any, incurred at the park and ride facility, in respect of which there is provision for a deduction under *section 372AR*,

does not exceed 25 per cent of the total expenditure incurred at the park and ride facility in respect of which an allowance or deduction is to be made or would, but for this subsection or *section 372W(2)(c)* or 372AR(5), be made by virtue of any provision of this Chapter or *Chapter 9*.

(b) A person who has incurred eligible expenditure on a qualifying premises at a park and ride facility and who claims to have complied with the requirements of *paragraph (a)* in relation to that expenditure, shall be deemed not to have so complied unless the person has received from the relevant local authority a certificate in writing issued by that authority stating that it is satisfied that those requirements have been met.

(6) Where a qualifying premises or a special qualifying premises forms a part of a building or is one of a number of buildings in a single development, or forms a part of a building which is itself one of a number of buildings in a single development, there shall be made such apportionment as is necessary—

(a) of the eligible expenditure incurred on the construction, conversion or, as the case may be, refurbishment of that building or those buildings, and

(b) of the amount which would be the relevant cost in relation to that building or those buildings if the building or buildings, as the case may be, were a single qualifying premises,

for the purposes of determining the eligible expenditure incurred on or in relation to the qualifying premises or the special qualifying premises, as the case may be, and the relevant cost in relation to the qualifying premises or the special qualifying premises, as the case may be.

(7) Where a house is a qualifying premises or a special qualifying premises and at any time during the relevant period in relation to the premises either of the following events occurs—

(a) the house ceases to be a qualifying premises or a special qualifying premises, as the case may be, or

(b) the ownership of the lessor's interest in the house passes to any other person but the house does not cease to be a qualifying premises or a special qualifying premises, as the case may be,

then, the person who before the occurrence of the event received or was entitled to receive a deduction or, as the case may be, deductions under *subsection (2)* in respect of eligible expenditure incurred on or in relation to that premises shall be deemed to have received on the day before the day of the occurrence of the event [an amount as rent from that premises equal to the amount determined by the formula—

$$A - B$$

where—

A is the amount of the deduction or, as the case may be, the aggregate amount of the deductions under *subsection (2)* in respect of eligible expenditure incurred on or in relation to the premises, and

B is that part of the amount of any excess (within the meaning of *section 384*) that is attributable to the deduction or, as the case may be, the aggregate amount of the deductions under *subsection (2)* in respect of eligible expenditure incurred on or in relation to the premises and which has been carried forward under *section 384* to the year of assessment in which either of the events, referred to in *paragraphs (a)* and *(b)*, occurs][6].

[(7A) For the purposes of *subsection (7)*, any transfer of property by a person to another person, pursuant to a Debt Settlement Arrangement or a Personal Insolvency Arrangement entered into under the Personal Insolvency Act 2012, whereby such property is held in trust for the creditors of the person making the transfer shall not, where that property is a house which is a qualifying premises or a special qualifying premises, be treated as the passing of the ownership of the lessor's interest in that property to another person.][7]

(8) (a) Where the event mentioned in *subsection (7)(b)* occurs in the relevant period in relation to a house which is a qualifying premises or a special qualifying premises, the person to whom the ownership of the lessor's interest in the house passes shall be treated for the purposes of this section as having incurred in the qualifying period an amount of eligible expenditure on or in relation to the house equal to the amount which under *section 372AS(1)* or under this section (apart from *subsection (4)(b)*) the lessor was treated as having incurred in the qualifying period on or in relation to the house.

(b) Where a person purchases a house to which *paragraph (a)* applies, the amount treated under that paragraph as having been incurred by such person shall not exceed the relevant price paid by such person on the purchase.

[...][8, 9]

(9) Subject to *subsection (10)*, where eligible expenditure is incurred on or in relation to a house and—

(a) where the eligible expenditure was expenditure on the construction of the house, before the house is used it is sold, or

(b) where the eligible expenditure was conversion expenditure or refurbishment expenditure, before the house is used subsequent to the incurring of that expenditure it is sold,

then, the person who purchases the house shall be treated for the purposes of this section as having incurred in the qualifying period eligible expenditure on or in relation to the house equal to the lesser of—

(i) the amount of such expenditure which is to be treated under *section 372AS(1)* as having been incurred in the qualifying period, and

(ii) the relevant price paid by such person on the purchase,

but, where the house is sold more than once before it is used, or, as the case may be, before the house is used subsequent to the incurring of the expenditure, this subsection shall apply only in relation to the last of those sales.

(10) Where eligible expenditure is incurred on or in relation to a house by a person carrying on a trade or part of a trade which consists, as to the whole or any part of that trade, of the construction, conversion or refurbishment of buildings with a view to their sale and the house is sold in the course of that trade or, as the case may be, that part of that trade—

(a) where the eligible expenditure was expenditure on the construction of the house—

(i) before the house is used, or

(ii) where a house, the site of which is wholly within a qualifying student accommodation area, is sold on or after 5 December 2001, within a period of one year after it commences to be used,

and

(b) where the eligible expenditure was conversion expenditure or refurbishment expenditure—

(i) before the house is used subsequent to the incurring of that expenditure, or

(ii) where a house, the site of which is wholly within a qualifying student accommodation area, is sold on or after 5 December 2001, within a period of one year after it commences to be used subsequent to the incurring of that expenditure,

then—

(I) the person (in this subsection referred to as the "*purchaser*") who purchases the house shall be treated for the purposes of this section as having incurred in the qualifying period eligible expenditure on or in relation to the house equal to the relevant price paid by the purchaser on the purchase (in this subsection referred to as the "*first purchase*"), and

(II) in relation to any subsequent sale or sales of the house before the house is used, or, as the case may be, before the house is used subsequent to the incurring of the expenditure, *subsection (9)* shall apply as if the reference to the amount of eligible expenditure which is to be treated as having been incurred in the qualifying period were a reference to the relevant price paid on the first purchase.

(11) Expenditure in respect of which a person is entitled to relief under this section shall not include any expenditure in respect of which any person is entitled to a deduction, relief or allowance under any other provision of the Tax acts.

(12) For the purposes of this section, expenditure shall not be regarded as incurred by a person in so far as it has been or is to be met, directly or indirectly, by the State, by any board established by statute or by any public or local authority.

(13) *Section 555* shall apply as if a deduction under this section were a capital allowance and as if any rent deemed to have been received by a person under this section were a balancing charge.

(14) This section shall not apply in the case of any conversion or refurbishment unless planning permission, in so far as it is required, in respect of the conversion or,

as the case may be, the work carried out in the course of the refurbishment has been granted under the Local Government (Planning and Development) acts, 1963 to 1999, or the Planning and Development act, 2000.

(15) *Section 372AS* shall apply for the purposes of supplementing this section.][10]

Amendments

[1] Deleted by FA12 s16(1)(a). Deemed to have come into force and takes effect on and from 1 January 2012.

[2] Deleted by FA12 s16(1)(a). Deemed to have come into force and takes effect on and from 1 January 2012.

[3] Deleted by FA12 s16(1)(c). Deemed to have come into force and takes effect on and from 1 January 2012.

[4] Substituted by FA12 s16(1)(d). Deemed to have come into force and takes effect on and from 1 January 2012.

[5] Deleted by FA12 s16(1)(e). Deemed to have come into force and takes effect on and from 1 January 2012.

[6] Substituted by FA12 s16(1)(f). Applies to an event referred to in paragraph (a) or (b) of section 372AP(7) that occurs on or after 1 January 2012.

[7] Inserted by FA13 s100(1)(d). Applies on and from 27 March 2013.

[8] Deleted by FA12 s16(1)(g). Deemed to have come into force and takes effect on and from 1 January 2012.

[9] Deleted by FA12 s16(1)(h). Deemed to have come into force and takes effect on and from 1 January 2012.

[10] Inserted by FA02 sched2(1).

Cross References

From Section 372AP

Section 52 Persons chargeable.

Section 96 Interpretation (Chapter 8).

Section 97 Computational rules and allowable deductions.

Section 372AS Determination of expenditure incurred in qualifying period, and date expenditure treated as incurred for relief purposes.

Section 384 Relief under Case V for losses.

Section 485C Interpretation (Chapter 2A).

Section 555 Restriction of losses by reference to capital allowances and renewals allowances.

To Section 372AP

Section 372AK Interpretation (Chapter 11).

Section 531B Charge to income levy.

Section 531AA Interpretation (Part 18C).

Section 531AM Charge to universal social charge.

Section 848V Interpretation (Part 36B).

Schedule 25B List of Specified Reliefs and Method of Determining Amount of Specified Relief Used in a Tax Year

Schedule 25C Determination of Amount of Relief to be Treated as Referable to Specified Reliefs as Respects Relief Carried Forward from Tax Year 2006 to Tax Year 2007

372AQ Qualifying expenditure: owner-occupiers

[(1) For the purposes of this Chapter, but subject to *subsection (3)*, "*qualifying expenditure*" means expenditure incurred by an individual on—

(a) the construction of, conversion into, or, as the case may be, refurbishment of a qualifying premises, and

(b) in the case of a qualifying premises the site of which is wholly within a qualifying town area, the refurbishment of a facade,

where the qualifying premises is a qualifying owner-occupied dwelling in relation to the individual, after deducting from that amount of expenditure any sum in respect of or by reference to—

(i) that expenditure,

(ii) the qualifying premises, or

(iii) the construction, conversion or, as the case may be, refurbishment work in respect of which that expenditure was incurred,

which the individual has received or is entitled to receive, directly or indirectly, from the State, any board established by statute or any public or local authority.

(2) For the purposes of this section, "*qualifying owner-occupied dwelling*", in relation to an individual, means a qualifying premises which is first used, after the qualifying expenditure has been incurred, by the individual as his or her only or main residence.

(3) *Subsection (1)* applies—

(a) in the case of a qualifying premises which fronts on to a qualifying street or is comprised in a building or part of a building which fronts on to a qualifying street, as if the reference in that subsection to "*construction*" were a reference to "*necessary construction*", and

(b) in the case of a qualifying premises the site of which is wholly within the site of a qualifying park and ride facility, as if the reference in that subsection to "construction of, conversion into, or, as the case may be, refurbishment of" were a reference to "construction of".

(4) *Subsection (7)* of *section 372AN*, which relates to the construing of references in that section to the construction of, conversion into, or, as the case may be, refurbishment of, any premises, shall apply with any necessary modifications in construing references in this section to the construction of, conversion into, or, as the case may be, refurbishment of any premises.][1]

Amendments

[1] Inserted by FA02 sched2(1).

Cross References

To Section 372AQ

Section 372AK Interpretation (Chapter 11).

372AR Relief for owner-occupiers

[(1) Subject to this section, where an individual, having duly made a claim, proves to have incurred qualifying expenditure in a year of assessment, the individual is entitled, for that year of assessment and for any of the 9 subsequent years of assessment in which the qualifying premises in respect of which the individual incurred the qualifying expenditure is the only or main residence of the individual, to have a deduction made from his or her total income of an amount equal to—

(a) 5 per cent of the amount of that expenditure, where the qualifying expenditure has been incurred on the construction of the qualifying premises,

(b) 10 per cent of the amount of that expenditure, where the qualifying expenditure has been incurred on the necessary construction of a qualifying premises which fronts on to a qualifying street or is comprised in a building or part of a building which fronts on to a qualifying street, or

(c) 10 per cent of the amount of that expenditure, where the qualifying expenditure has been incurred on the conversion into or the refurbishment of the qualifying premises.

(2) Where the year of assessment first mentioned in *subsection (1)* or any of the 9 subsequent years of assessment is the year of assessment 2001, that subsection applies—

(a) as if for "any of the 9 subsequent years of assessment" there were substituted "any of the 10 subsequent years of assessment",

(b) as respects the year of assessment 2001, as if "3.7 per cent" and "7.4 per cent" were substituted for "5 per cent" and "10 per cent", respectively, and

(c) as respects the year of assessment which is the 10th year of assessment subsequent to the year of assessment first mentioned in that subsection, as if "1.3 per cent" and "2.6 per cent" were substituted for "5 per cent" and "10 per cent", respectively.

[(3) Notwithstanding *subsection (1)*—

(a) where the individual or, being a husband or wife, the individual's spouse, is assessed to tax in accordance with *section 1017*, then, except where *section 1023* applies, the individual shall be entitled to have the deduction, to which he or she is entitled under that subsection, made from his or her total income and the total income of his or her spouse, if any, and

(b) where the individual or the individual's civil partner is assessed to tax in accordance with *section 1031C*, then, except where *section 1031H* applies, the individual shall be entitled to have the deduction, to which he or she is entitled under that subsection, made from his or her total income and the total income of his or her civil partner, if any.][1]

(4) A deduction shall be given under this section in respect of qualifying expenditure only in so far as that expenditure is to be treated under *section 372AS(1)* as having been incurred in the qualifying period.

(5) (a) A person is entitled to a deduction by virtue of *subsection (1)* in respect of qualifying expenditure incurred at a park and ride facility only in so far as that expenditure when aggregated with—

(i) other qualifying expenditure, if any, incurred at that park and ride facility in respect of which a deduction is to be made or would, but for this subsection, be made, and

(ii) other expenditure, if any, incurred at that park and ride facility in respect of which there is provision for a deduction under *section 372AP*,

does not exceed 25 per cent of the total expenditure incurred at that park and ride facility in respect of which an allowance or deduction is to be made or would, but for this subsection or *section 372W(2)(c)* or 372AP(5), be made by virtue of any provision of this Chapter or Chapter 9.

(b) A person who has incurred qualifying expenditure at a park and ride facility and who claims to have complied with the requirements of *paragraph (a)* in relation to that expenditure, shall be deemed not to have so complied unless the person has received from the relevant local authority a certificate in writing issued by that authority stating that it is satisfied that those requirements have been met.

(6) Where qualifying expenditure in relation to a qualifying premises is incurred by 2 or more persons, each of those persons shall be treated as having incurred the expenditure in the proportions in which they actually bore the expenditure, and the expenditure shall be apportioned accordingly.

(7) *Subsections (6), (9)* and *(10)* of *section 372AP*, in relation to—

(a) the apportionment of eligible expenditure incurred on or in relation to a qualifying premises and of the relevant cost in relation to that premises, and

(b) the amount of eligible expenditure to be treated as incurred in the qualifying period,

apply, with any necessary modifications, for the purposes of this section, in determining—

(i) the amount of qualifying expenditure incurred on or in relation to a qualifying premises, and

(ii) the amount of qualifying expenditure to be treated as incurred in the qualifying period,

as they apply for the purposes of *section 372AP*.

(8) Expenditure in respect of which an individual is entitled to relief under this section shall not include any expenditure in respect of which any person is entitled to a deduction, relief or allowance under any other provision of the Tax acts.

(9) This section shall not apply in the case of any conversion or refurbishment unless planning permission, in so far as it is required, in respect of the conversion or, as the case may be, the work carried out in the course of the refurbishment has been granted under the Local Government (Planning and Development) acts, 1963 to 1999 or the Planning and Development act, 2000.

(10) *Section 372AS* applies for the purposes of supplementing this section.][2]

Amendments

[1] Substituted by F(No.3)A11 sched1(58).

[2] Inserted by FA02 sched2(1).

Cross References

From Section 372AR

Section 1017 Assessment of husband in respect of income of both spouses.

Section 1023 Application for separate assessments.

To Section 372AR

Section 372AK Interpretation (Chapter 11).

Section 458 Deductions allowed in ascertaining taxable income and provisions relating to reductions in tax.

Section 848V Interpretation (Part 36B).

Section 1024 Method of apportioning reliefs and charging tax in cases of separate assessments.

372AS Determination of expenditure incurred in qualifying period, and date expenditure treated as incurred for relief purposes

[(1) For the purposes of determining whether and to what extent—

(a) in relation to any claim under *section 372AP(2)*, eligible expenditure incurred on or in relation to a qualifying premises or a special qualifying premises, and

(b) in relation to any claim under *section 372AR(1)*, qualifying expenditure incurred on or in relation to a qualifying premises,

is incurred or not incurred during the qualifying period, only such an amount of that expenditure as is properly attributable to work on—

(i) in the case of a claim under *section 372AP(2)*, the construction of, conversion into, or refurbishment of, the qualifying premises or, as the case may be, the refurbishment of the special qualifying premises, and

(ii) in the case of a claim under *section 372AR(1)*, the construction of, conversion into, or refurbishment of the qualifying premises, actually carried out during the qualifying period shall be treated as having been incurred during that period.

[(1A) (a) Where a person incurs eligible expenditure or qualifying expenditure at any time in the period 1 January 2006 to 31 July 2008 on or in relation to a qualifying premises or a special qualifying premises the amount of eligible expenditure or qualifying expenditure which is to be treated under *subsection (1)* as having been incurred in the qualifying period for the purposes of granting a deduction under *section 372AP* or under *section 372AR*, as the case may be, shall be reduced—

(i) in the case of expenditure incurred in the period 1 January 2007 to 31 December 2007, to 75 per cent, and

(ii) in the case of expenditure incurred in the period 1 January 2008 to 31 July 2008, to 50 per cent,

of the amount which, apart from this subsection, would otherwise be so treated and, for those purposes, references in this Chapter to expenditure which is to be treated under *section 372AS(1)* as having been incurred in the qualifying period shall be construed accordingly.

(b) For the purposes of *paragraph (a)* and in determining whether and to what extent eligible expenditure or qualifying expenditure is incurred or not incurred on or in relation to a qualifying premises or a special qualifying premises in—

(i) the period from 1 January 2006 to 31 December 2006,

(ii) the period from 1 January 2007 to 31 December 2007, or

(iii) the period from 1 January 2008 to 31 July 2008,

only such an amount of that expenditure as is properly attributable to work on the construction of, conversion into, or refurbishment of, the qualifying premises or, as the case may be, the refurbishment of the special qualifying premises actually carried out in such a period shall be treated as having been incurred in that period.][1]

(2) Where, by virtue of *section 372AN(7)* or *372AQ(4)*, expenditure on the construction of, conversion into, or, as the case may be, refurbishment of, a qualifying premises includes expenditure on the development of any land, *subsection (1)* applies with any necessary modifications as if the references in that subsection to the construction of, conversion into, or, as the case may be, refurbishment of, the qualifying premises were references to the development of such land.

[(2A) For the purposes of determining the amount of eligible expenditure or qualifying expenditure incurred on or in relation to a building, the site of which—

(a) is situated partly inside and partly outside the boundary of a qualifying urban area, or

(b) is situated partly inside and partly outside the boundary of a qualifying town area,

and where expenditure incurred or treated as having been incurred in the qualifying period is attributable to the building in general, such an amount of that expenditure shall be deemed to be attributable to the part which is situated outside the boundary of the qualifying area as bears to the whole of that expenditure the same proportion as the floor area of the part situated outside the boundary of the qualifying area bears to the total floor area of the building.][2]

(3) (a) For the purposes of *section 372AP* other than those to which *subsection (1)* relates, expenditure incurred on the construction of, or, as the case may be,

conversion into, a qualifying premises shall be deemed to have been incurred on the date of the first letting of the premises under a qualifying lease.

(b) For the purposes of *section 372AP* other than those to which *subsection (1)* relates, refurbishment expenditure incurred in relation to the refurbishment of a qualifying premises or a special qualifying premises shall be deemed to have been incurred on the date of the commencement of the relevant period, in relation to the premises, determined as respects the refurbishment to which the refurbishment expenditure relates.

(c) For the purposes of *section 372AR* other than those to which *subsection (1)* relates, expenditure incurred on the construction of, conversion into, or, as the case may be, refurbishment of a qualifying premises shall be deemed to have been incurred on the earliest date after the expenditure was actually incurred on which the premises is in use as a dwelling.][3]

Amendments

[1] Inserted by FA06 s25(b).

[2] Inserted by FA03 s30(1)(c). Applies as on and from 1 January 2002.

[3] Inserted by FA02 sched2(1).

Cross References

To Section 372AS

Section 372AP Relief for lessors.

372AT Appeals

[An appeal to the Appeal Commissioners lies on any question arising under this Chapter (other than a question on which an appeal lies under section 18 of the Housing (Miscellaneous Provisions) act, 1979) in the like manner as an appeal would lie against an assessment to income tax or corporation tax, and the provisions of the Tax acts relating to appeals apply accordingly.][1]

Amendments

[1] Inserted by FA02 sched2(1).

372AU Saver for relief due, and for clawback of relief given under, old schemes

[(1) Where, but for the repeal by *section 24(3)* of the Finance act, 2002, of the provision concerned, a person would, in computing the amount of a surplus or deficiency in respect of rent from any premises—

(a) be entitled to a deduction, or

(b) be deemed to have received an amount as rent,

under—

(i) *section 325*, *326* or *327*,

(ii) *section 334*, *335* or *336*,

(iii) *section 346*, *347* or *348*,

(iv) *section 356*, *357* or *358*, or

(v) *section 361*, *362*, or *363*,

then, notwithstanding that repeal, the person is entitled to that deduction or is deemed to have received that amount as rent, as the case may be, under this Chapter, and accordingly this Chapter applies with any modifications necessary to give effect to this subsection.

(2) Where, but for the repeal by *section 24(3)* of the Finance act, 2002, of the provision concerned, a person would, in the computation of his or her total income for any year of assessment, be entitled to a deduction under—

(a) *section 328*,

(b) *section 337*,

(c) *section 349*, or

(d) *section 364*,

then, notwithstanding that repeal, the person is entitled to that deduction for that year of assessment under this Chapter, and accordingly this Chapter applies with any modifications necessary to give effect to this subsection.][1]

Amendments

[1] Inserted by FA02 sched2(1).

Cross References

From Section 372AU

Section 24 Companies resident in the State: income tax on payments made or received.
Section 325 Rented residential accommodation: deduction for certain expenditure on construction.
Section 326 Rented residential accommodation: deduction for certain expenditure on conversion.
Section 327 Rented residential accommodation: deduction for certain expenditure on refurbishment.
Section 328 Residential accommodation: allowance to owner-occupiers in respect of certain expenditure on construction or refurbishment.
Section 334 Rented residential accommodation: deduction for certain expenditure on construction.
Section 335 Rented residential accommodation: deduction for certain expenditure on conversion.
Section 336 Rented residential accommodation: deduction for certain expenditure on refurbishment.
Section 337 Residential accommodation: allowance to owner-occupiers in respect of certain expenditure on construction or refurbishment.
Section 346 Rented residential accommodation: deduction for certain expenditure on construction.
Section 347 Rented residential accommodation: deduction for certain expenditure on conversion.
Section 348 Rented residential accommodation: deduction for certain expenditure on refurbishment.
Section 349 Residential accommodation: allowance to owner-occupiers in respect of certain expenditure on construction or refurbishment.
Section 356 Rented residential accommodation: deduction for certain expenditure on construction.
Section 357 Rented residential accommodation: deduction for certain expenditure on conversion.
Section 358 Rented residential accommodation: deduction for certain expenditure on refurbishment.
Section 361 Rented residential accommodation: deduction for certain expenditure on construction.
Section 362 Rented residential accommodation: deduction for certain expenditure on conversion.
Section 363 Rented residential accommodation: deduction for certain expenditure on refurbishment.
Section 364 Residential accommodation: allowance to owner-occupiers in respect of certain expenditure on construction or refurbishment.

To Section 372AU

Section 531B Charge to income levy.
Section 531AA Interpretation (Part 18C).
Section 531AM Charge to universal social charge.
Section 848V Interpretation (Part 36B).
Schedule 25B List of Specified Reliefs and Method of Determining Amount of Specified Relief Used in a Tax Year
Schedule 25C Determination of Amount of Relief to be Treated as Referable to Specified Reliefs as Respects Relief Carried Forward from Tax Year 2006 to Tax Year 2007

372AV Continuity

[(1) In this section, the "*old enactments*" means *sections 372F, 372G, 372H, 372I, 372J, 372P, 372Q, 372R, 372RA, 372S, 372X, 372Y, 372Z, 372AE, 372AF, 372AG, 372AH* and *372AI*, and *Parts 11A* and *11B*, being enactments repealed under *section 24(3)* of the Finance act, 2002.

(2) The continuity of the operation of the law relating to income tax, corporation tax and capital gains tax is not affected by the substitution of this Chapter for the old enactments.

(3) Any reference, whether express or implied, in any enactment or document, including this Chapter—

(a) to any provision of this Chapter, or

(b) to things done or to be done under or for the purposes of any provision of this Chapter,

shall, if and in so far as the nature of the reference permits, be construed as including, in relation to the times, years or periods, circumstances or purposes in relation to which the corresponding provision in the old enactments applied or had applied, a reference to, or, as the case may be, to things done or to be done under or for the purposes of, that corresponding provision.

(4) Any reference, whether express or implied, in any enactment or document, including the old enactments—

(a) to any provision of the old enactments, or

(b) to things done or to be done under or for the purposes of any provision of the old enactments,

shall, if and in so far as the nature of the reference permits, be construed as including, in relation to the times, years or periods, circumstances or purposes in relation to which the corresponding provision of this Chapter applies, a reference to, or as the case may be, to things done or deemed to be done or to be done under or for the purposes of, that corresponding provision.

(5) If and in so far as a provision of this Chapter operates, as on and from the date of the passing of the Finance act, 2002, in substitution for a provision of the old enactments, anything done or having effect as if done under the provision of the old enactments before that date shall be treated on and from that date as if it were a thing done under the provision of this Chapter which so operates.

(6) Without prejudice to the generality of *subsections (2)* to *(5)*, this Chapter applies as if a deduction given to a person under the old enactments were a deduction given to such person under this Chapter in respect of, as may be appropriate—

(a) eligible expenditure incurred in the qualifying period, on or in relation to a qualifying premises or a special qualifying premises, as the case may be, or

(b) qualifying expenditure incurred in the qualifying period on or in relation to a qualifying premises.

(7) Without prejudice to the generality of *subsections (2)* to *(5)*, any reference in an order made under *section 372B(1)* or *372BA(1)* to *section 372F*, *372G*, *372H* or *372I* shall, as on and from the date of the passing of the Finance act, 2002, be construed respectively as if it were a reference to—

(a) *section 372AP*, in so far as it relates to expenditure on construction,

(b) *section 372AP*, in so far as it relates to conversion expenditure,

(c) *section 372AP*, in so far as it relates to refurbishment expenditure, and

(d) *section 372AR*.

(8) Without prejudice to the generality of *subsections (2)* to *(5)*, any reference in an order made under *section 372AB(1)* to *section 372AE*, *372AF*, *372AG* or *372AH* shall, as on and from the date of the passing of the Finance act, 2002, be construed respectively as if it were a reference to—

(a) *section 372AP*, in so far as it relates to expenditure on construction,

(b) *section 372AP*, in so far as it relates to conversion expenditure,

(c) *section 372AP*, in so far as it relates to refurbishment expenditure, and

(d) *section 372AR*.

(9) All officers who immediately before the date of the passing of the Finance act, 2002, stood authorised or nominated for the purposes of any provision of the old enactments shall be deemed to be authorised or nominated, as the case may be, for the purposes of the corresponding provision of this Chapter.

(10) All instruments, documents, authorisations and letters or notices of appointment made or issued under the old enactments and in force immediately before the date of the passing of the Finance act, 2002, shall continue in force as if made or issued under this Chapter.][1]

Amendments

[1] Inserted by FA02 sched2(1).

Cross References

From Section 372AV

Section 24 Companies resident in the State: income tax on payments made or received.

CHAPTER 12

Mid-Shannon Corridor Tourism Infrastructure Investment Scheme

372AW Interpretation, applications for approval and certification

[(1) In this Chapter—

"*accommodation building*", in relation to a project, means a building or structure or part of a building or structure which consists of accommodation facilities or which is to be used or is suitable for use for the provision of such facilities;

"*market value*", in relation to a building or structure, means the price which the unencumbered fee simple of the building or structure would fetch if sold in the open market in such manner and subject to such conditions as might reasonably be calculated to obtain for the vendor the best price for the building or structure, less the part of that price which would be attributable to the acquisition of, or of rights in or over, the land on which the building or structure is constructed;

"*mid-Shannon corridor*" means the corridor of land comprising all qualifying mid-Shannon areas;

"*mid-Shannon Tourism Infrastructure Board*" means a board consisting of not more than 5 persons selected for the purposes of this Chapter by the Minister in consultation with the Minister for Finance;

"*Minister*" means the Minister for Arts, Sport and Tourism;

"*project*" means the construction or refurbishment of buildings and structures comprising—

(a) a holiday camp of the type referred to in *section 372AX(1)(b)*, or

(b) one or more qualifying tourism infrastructure facilities,

the site or sites of which is or are wholly within a qualifying mid-Shannon area;

"*property developer*" means a person carrying on a trade which consists wholly or mainly of the construction or refurbishment of buildings or structures with a view to their sale;

"*qualifying mid-Shannon area*" means any area described in Schedule 8B;

["*qualifying period*" means the period commencing on 1 June 2008 and ending on [31 May 2015][1];][2]

"*qualifying tourism infrastructure facilities*" means such class or classes of facilities, comprising of buildings and structures only, as may be approved for the purposes of this Chapter by the Minister, in consultation with the Minister for Finance, and published in the relevant guidelines;

"*refurbishment*", in relation to a building or structure, means any work of construction, reconstruction, repair or renewal, including the provision or improvement of water, sewerage or heating facilities, carried out in the course of—

(a) the repair or restoration, or

(b) maintenance in the nature of repair or restoration,

of the building or structure;

"*relevant guidelines*" mean guidelines issued in accordance with *subsection (3)* of this section or any guidelines issued in accordance with that subsection which amend or replace those guidelines.

(2) (a) Notwithstanding *sections 372AX* and *372AY*, but subject to the subsequent provisions of this section and to *section 372AZ*, no relief from income tax or corporation tax, as the case may be, may be granted by virtue of this Chapter in respect of capital expenditure incurred in the qualifying period on the construction or refurbishment of a building or structure unless the mid-Shannon Tourism Infrastructure Board has—

(i) prior to such expenditure being incurred, but subject to *paragraph (b)*, granted approval in principle in relation to the construction or refurbishment of the building or structure, and

(ii) after the expenditure is incurred, certified in writing that the construction or refurbishment which was carried out is in accordance with the criteria specified in the relevant guidelines, having regard to any relevant conditions and requirements imposed by the Board in the approval granted under *subparagraph (i)*.

(b) Approval in principle shall not be granted in accordance with *paragraph (a)(i)* unless an application for such approval, in which the information and details as may be required in accordance with *subsection (3)(b)* are included, is received by the mid-Shannon Tourism Infrastructure Board within a period of [4 years][3] commencing on the date on which this Chapter comes into effect.

(3) Subject to *subsection (4)*, for the purposes of approval and certification in accordance with *subsection (2)* and, as the case may be, certification in accordance with *section 372AX(1)(d)* or *372AY(1)(g)* the Minister shall, in consultation with the Minister for Finance, issue guidelines to which the mid-Shannon Tourism Infrastructure Board shall have regard in deciding whether to grant approval in principle or to issue certification in relation to any building or structure and which guidelines may include criteria in relation to all or any one or more of the following:

(a) the nature and extent of the contribution which the project, in which the building or structure is comprised, makes to tourism development in the mid-Shannon corridor or the qualifying mid-Shannon area;

(b) coherence with national tourism strategy;

(c) environmental sensitivity, having particular regard to any area which is—

(i) a European site within the meaning of the European Communities (Natural Habitats) Regulations 1997 (S.I. No. 94 of 1997), or

(ii) a natural heritage area, a nature reserve or a refuge for fauna for the purposes of the Wildlife Acts 1976 and 2000;

(d) the amenities and facilities required to be provided in each type of project;

(e) the nature of and maximum extent to which accommodation buildings (if any) are allowable in each type of project;

(f) specific standards of design and construction in relation to buildings and structures which may qualify for relief under this Chapter;

(g) relevant planning matters, including the need for consistency with the requirements of a development plan or a local area plan within the meaning of those terms in the Planning and Development Act 2000;

(h) the details and information required to be provided in an application for approval or certification in accordance with *section 372AW(2)* and, as the case may be, an application for certification in accordance with *section 372AX(1)(d)* or *372AY(1)(g)*; and

(i) matters relating to the provision of information in accordance with *sections 372AX(1)(c)* and *372AY(1)(f)*,

together with such other matters as the Minister, in consultation with the Minister for Finance, may consider are required to be included.

(4) (a) Subject to *paragraphs (b)* and *(c)*, approval and certification in accordance with *subsection (2)* shall not be granted or issued by the mid-Shannon Tourism Infrastructure Board in relation to capital expenditure incurred in the qualifying period on the construction or refurbishment of one or more than one accommodation building comprised in a project to the extent that such expenditure exceeds (or, where an application for approval is involved, is projected to exceed) an amount (referred to in this subsection as the "*limit amount*") which is equal to the lesser of—

(i) 50 per cent, or such lower percentage as may be specified (in accordance with *subsection (3)(e)*) in the relevant guidelines for the type of project involved, of the total amount of the capital expenditure incurred in the qualifying period on the construction or refurbishment of all the buildings or structures comprised in the project, and

(ii) the amount of the capital expenditure incurred in the qualifying period on the construction or refurbishment of buildings and structures comprised in the project which are other than accommodation buildings.

(b) In any case where—

(i) there is more than one accommodation building comprised in a project, and

(ii) the aggregate of the amounts of capital expenditure incurred in the qualifying period on the construction or refurbishment of each accommodation building exceeds the limit amount,

then that aggregate shall, for the purposes of an application for approval or for certification in accordance with *subsection (2)*, be reduced to an amount equivalent to the limit amount and that equivalent amount shall be apportioned on a just and reasonable basis between all the accommodation buildings comprised in the project.

(c) Subject to the criteria in the relevant guidelines being satisfied, the mid-Shannon Tourism Infrastructure Board may grant approval or issue certification in accordance with *subsection (2)* in relation to an accommodation building—

(i) where there is one accommodation building comprised in a project, only in relation to the amount of the capital expenditure incurred on the construction or refurbishment of the building in the qualifying period as does not exceed the limit amount, and

(ii) where *paragraph (b)* applies, provided that it is satisfied with the basis on which the apportionment has been made, only in relation to that part of the equivalent amount (as referred to in *paragraph (b)*) which is attributable to the building following the apportionment made in accordance with that paragraph.][4]

Amendments

[1] Substituted by FA10 s(27)(1)(a). This section comes into operation on the making of an order to that effect by the Minister for Finance.

[2] Substituted by FA09 s7(a). This section is deemed to have come into force and takes effect as on and from 1 January 2009.

[3] Substituted by FA10 s(27)(1)(b). This section comes into operation on the making of an order to that effect by the Minister for Finance.

[4] Inserted by FA07 s29(1)(a). With effect from 1 June 2008 per S.I. No. 159 of 2008.

Revenue Briefings

Tax Briefing

Tax Briefing July 2007 – Issue 66 – Mid Shannon Scheme

Cross References

From Section 372AW

Section 372AW Interpretation, applications for approval and certification.

Section 372AX Accelerated capital allowances in relation to the construction or refurbishment of certain registered holiday camps.

Section 372AY Capital allowances in relation to the construction or refurbishment of certain tourism infrastructure facilities.

Section 372AZ Restrictions on relief, non-application of relief in certain cases and provision against double relief.

To Section 372AW

Section 372AW Interpretation, applications for approval and certification.

372AX Accelerated capital allowances in relation to the construction or refurbishment of certain registered holiday camps

[(1) In this section "building or structure to which this section applies" means a building or structure—

(a) the site of which is wholly within a qualifying mid-Shannon area,

(b) which is in use as a holiday camp—

(i) registered in the register of holiday camps kept under the Tourist Traffic Acts 1939 to 2003, and

(ii) which meets the requirements of the relevant guidelines in relation to the types of amenities and facilities that need to be provided in a holiday camp for the purposes of this Chapter,

(c) in relation to which the following data has been provided to the mid-Shannon Tourism Infrastructure Board for onward transmission to the Minister and the Minister for Finance:

(i) (I) the amount of the capital expenditure actually incurred in the qualifying period on the construction or refurbishment of the building or structure, and

(II) where *subsection (4)* of *section 372AW* applies in relation to an accommodation building, the amount of such expenditure which is eligible for certification in accordance with that section;

(ii) the number and nature of the investors that are investing in the building or structure;

(iii) the amount to be invested by each investor; and

(iv) the nature of the structures which are being put in place to facilitate the investment in the building or structure;

together with such other information as may be specified in the relevant guidelines as being of assistance to the Minister for Finance in evaluating the costs, including but not limited to exchequer costs, and the benefits arising from the operation of tax relief for buildings and structures under this Chapter, and

(d) in respect of which the mid-Shannon Tourism Infrastructure Board gives a certificate in writing after the building or structure is first used or, where capital expenditure is incurred on the refurbishment of a building or structure, first used subsequent to the incurring of that expenditure—

(i) stating that it is satisfied that the conditions in *paragraphs (a)*, *(b)* and *(c)* have been met,

(ii) confirming the date of first use or, as the case may be, first use after refurbishment, and

(iii) which includes certification in accordance with *section 372AW(2)(a)(ii)* or a copy of such certification (if previously issued).

(2) Subject to *subsections (3)* and *(4)* and to *section 372AZ*, *Chapter 1* of *Part 9* applies in relation to capital expenditure incurred in the qualifying period on the construction or refurbishment of a building or structure to which this section applies as if—

(a) in *section 272*—

(i) in *subsection (3)*, the following were substituted for *paragraph (c)*:

"(c) in relation to a building or structure to which *section 372AX* applies, 15 per cent of the capital expenditure referred to in *subsection (2)* of that section,",

and

(ii) in *subsection (4)*, the following were substituted for *paragraph (c)*:

"(c) in relation to a building or structure to which *section 372AX* applies, 15 years beginning with the time when the building or structure was first used or, where capital expenditure on the refurbishment of the building or structure is incurred, 15 years beginning with the time when the building or structure was first used subsequent to the incurring of that expenditure,",

and

(b) in *section 274(1)(b)*, the following were substituted for *subparagraph (iii)*:

"(iii) in relation to a building or structure to which *section 372AX* applies, 15 years after the building or structure was first used or, where capital expenditure on the refurbishment of the building or structure is incurred, 15 years after the building or structure was first used subsequent to the incurring of that expenditure,".

(3) In the case where capital expenditure is incurred in the qualifying period on the refurbishment of a building or structure to which this section applies, *subsection (2)* shall apply only if the total amount of the capital expenditure so incurred is not less than an amount equal to 20 per cent of the market value of the building or structure immediately before that expenditure was incurred.

(4) In determining for the purposes of this Chapter whether and to what extent capital expenditure incurred on the construction or refurbishment of a building or structure to which this section applies is incurred or not incurred in the qualifying period, such an amount of that capital expenditure as is properly attributable to work on the construction or, as the case may be, refurbishment of the building or structure actually carried out during the qualifying period shall (notwithstanding any other provision of the Tax Acts as to the time when any capital expenditure is or is to be treated as incurred) be treated as having been incurred in that period.][1]

Amendments

[1] Inserted by FA07 s29(1)(a). With effect from 1 June 2008 per S.I. No. 159 of 2008.

Cross References

From Section 372AX

Section 268 Meaning of "industrial building or structure".
Section 272 Writing-down allowances.
Section 274 Balancing allowances and balancing charges.

To Section 372AX

Section 372AW Interpretation, applications for approval and certification.
Schedule 25B List of Specified Reliefs and Method of Determining Amount of Specified Relief Used in a Tax Year

372AY Capital allowances in relation to the construction or refurbishment of certain tourism infrastructure facilities

[(1) In this section "*qualifying premises*" means a building or structure—

(a) the site of which is wholly within a qualifying mid-Shannon area,

(b) which apart from this section is not an industrial building or structure within the meaning of *section 268* or deemed to be such a building or structure,

(c) which is in use for the purposes of the operation of one or more qualifying tourism infrastructure facilities,

(d) (i) subject to *subparagraph (ii)*, which does not include a building or structure or part of a building or structure which is a licensed premises (as defined in section 2 of the Intoxicating Liquor Act 1988), but

(ii) which may include a building or structure or part of a building or structure which is a restaurant (as defined in section 6 of the Intoxicating Liquor Act 1988) in relation to which—

(I) a wine retailer's onlicence, within the meaning of the Finance (1909-10) Act 1910, is currently in force, or

(II) a special restaurant licence, within the meaning of the Intoxicating Liquor Act 1988, has been granted under section 9 of that Act,

(e) which does not include a building or structure or part of a building or structure in use as a facility in which gambling, gaming or wagering of any sort is carried on for valuable consideration or which supports the carrying on of such activities,

(f) in relation to which the following data has been provided to the mid-Shannon Tourism Infrastructure Board for onward transmission to the Minister and the Minister for Finance:

(i) (I) the amount of the capital expenditure actually incurred in the qualifying period on the construction or refurbishment of the building or structure; and

(II) where *subsection (4)* of *section 372AW* applies in relation to an accommodation building, the amount of such expenditure which is eligible for certification in accordance with that section;

(ii) the number and nature of the investors that are investing in the building or structure;

(iii) the amount to be invested by each investor; and

(iv) the nature of the structures which are being put in place to facilitate the investment in the building or structure;

together with such other information as may be specified in the relevant guidelines as being of assistance to the Minister for Finance in evaluating the costs, including but not limited to exchequer costs, and the benefits arising from the operation of tax relief for buildings and structures under this Chapter, and

(g) in respect of which the mid-Shannon Tourism Infrastructure Board gives a certificate in writing after the building or structure is first used or, where capital expenditure is incurred on the refurbishment of the building or structure, first used subsequent to the incurring of that expenditure—

(i) stating that it is satisfied that the conditions in *paragraphs (a)*, *(b)*, *(c)*, *(d)*, *(e)* and *(f)* have been met,

(ii) confirming the date of first use or, as the case may be, first use after refurbishment, and

(iii) which includes certification in accordance with *section 372AW(2)(a)(ii)* or a copy of such certification (if previously issued).

(2) (a) Subject to *paragraph (b)*, *subsections (3)* to *(5)* and *section 372AZ*, the provisions of the Tax Acts relating to the making of allowances and charges in respect of capital expenditure incurred on the construction or refurbishment of an industrial building or structure shall, notwithstanding anything to the contrary in those provisions, apply—

(i) as if the qualifying premises were, at all times at which it is a qualifying premises, a building or structure in respect of which an allowance is to be made for the purposes of income tax or corporation tax, as the case may be, under *Chapter 1* of *Part 9* by reason of its use for a purpose specified in *section 268(1)(a)*, and

(ii) where any activity carried on in the qualifying premises is not a trade, as if (for the purposes only of the making of allowances and charges by virtue of *subparagraph (i)*), it were a trade.

(b) An allowance shall be given by virtue of this subsection in respect of any capital expenditure incurred on the construction or refurbishment of a qualifying premises only in so far as that expenditure is incurred in the qualifying period.

(3) In the case where capital expenditure is incurred in the qualifying period on the refurbishment of a qualifying premises, *subsection (2)* shall apply only if the total amount of the capital expenditure so incurred is not less than an amount equal to 20 per cent of the market value of the building or structure immediately before that expenditure was incurred.

(4) For the purposes of the application, by *subsection (2)*, of *Chapter 1* of *Part 9* in relation to capital expenditure incurred in the qualifying period on the construction or refurbishment of a qualifying premises—

(a) *section 272* shall apply as if—

(i) in *subsection (3)*, the following were substituted for *paragraph (a)*:

"(a) in relation to a building or structure to which *section 372AY* applies, 15 per cent of the capital expenditure referred to in *subsection (2)(b)* of that section,",

and

(ii) in *subsection (4)*, the following were substituted for *paragraph (a)*:

"(a) in relation to a building or structure to which *section 372AY* applies, 15 years beginning with the time when the building or structure was first used or, where capital expenditure on the refurbishment of the building or structure is incurred, 15 years beginning with the time when the building or structure was first used subsequent to the incurring of that expenditure,",

and

(b) *section 274(1)(b)* shall apply as if the following were substituted for *subparagraph (i)*:

"(i) in relation to a building or structure to which *section 372AY* applies, 15 years after the building or structure was first used or, where capital expenditure on the refurbishment of the building or structure is incurred, 15 years after the building or structure was first used subsequent to the incurring of that expenditure,".

(5) In determining for the purposes of this Chapter whether and to what extent capital expenditure incurred on the construction or refurbishment of a qualifying premises is incurred or not incurred in the qualifying period, such an amount of that capital expenditure as is properly attributable to work on the construction or, as the case may be, refurbishment of the premises actually carried out during the qualifying period shall (notwithstanding any other provision of the Tax Acts as to the time when any capital expenditure is or is to be treated as incurred) be treated as having been incurred in that period.][1]

Amendments

[1] Inserted by FA07 s29(1)(a). With effect from 1 June 2008 per S.I. No. 159 of 2008.

Cross References

From Section 372AY

Section 268 Meaning of "industrial building or structure".
Section 272 Writing-down allowances.
Section 274 Balancing allowances and balancing charges.

To Section 372AY

Section 372AW Interpretation, applications for approval and certification.
Schedule 25B List of Specified Reliefs and Method of Determining Amount of Specified Relief Used in a Tax Year

372AZ Restrictions on relief, non-application of relief in certain cases and provision against double relief

[(1) Notwithstanding any other provision of this Chapter, *sections 372AX* and *372AY* shall not apply in respect of expenditure incurred on the construction or refurbishment of a building or structure—

(a) (i) where a property developer [or a person who is connected (within the meaning of *section 10*) with the property developer][1] is entitled to the relevant interest, within the meaning of *section 269*, in relation to that expenditure, and

[(ii) either of the persons referred to in *subparagraph (i)* incurred the capital expenditure on the construction or refurbishment of the building or structure concerned, or such expenditure was incurred by any other person connected (within the meaning of *section 10*) with the property developer,][2]

(b) where any part of such expenditure has been or is to be met, directly or indirectly, by grant assistance or any other assistance which is granted by or through the State, any board established by statute, any public or local authority or any other agency of the State,

[(c) unless the potential capital allowances in relation to the building or structure concerned and the project in which it is comprised comply with—

(i) the requirements of the Guidelines on National Regional Aid for 2007-2013 prepared by the Commission of the European Communities and issued on 4 March 2006*, and

* OJ No. C54 of 4 March 2006, p.13

(ii) the National Regional Aid Map for Ireland for the period 1 January 2007 to 31 December 2013 which was approved by the said Commission on 24 October 2006*,

* OJ No. C292 of 1 December 2006, p.11

or

(d) where the person who is entitled to the relevant interest, within the meaning of *section 269*, in relation to that expenditure is subject to an outstanding recovery order following a previous decision of the Commission of the European Communities declaring aid in favour of that person to be illegal and incompatible with the common market.][3]

(2) Where relief is given by virtue of *section 372AX* or *372AY* in relation to capital expenditure incurred on the construction or refurbishment of a building or structure, relief shall not be given in respect of that expenditure under any other provision of the Tax Acts.

(3) Where—

(a) capital expenditure is incurred in the qualifying period on the construction or refurbishment of an accommodation building, and

(b) *subsection (4)* of *section 372AW* applies so as to reduce the amount of such expenditure which is eligible for certification in accordance with that section by the mid-Shannon Tourism Infrastructure Board,

then the amount of the capital expenditure actually incurred in the qualifying period on the construction or refurbishment of the accommodation building which is to be treated as incurred—

(i) for the purposes of the making of allowances and charges under *Chapter 1* of *Part 9*, by virtue of *section 372AX* or *372AY*, (including the making of balancing allowances and charges under *section 274* and the calculation of the residue of expenditure under *section 277*), but

(ii) prior to the operation of *subsection (4)*,

shall be reduced to the amount of the capital expenditure which was eligible for certification by the mid-Shannon Tourism Infrastructure Board in relation to that building.

(4) Where relief under *Chapter 1* of *Part 9* is, by virtue of *section 372AX* or *372AY*, to apply in relation to capital expenditure incurred in the qualifying period on the construction or refurbishment of a building or structure the site of which is wholly within a qualifying mid-Shannon area described in either Part 1 or Part 5 of Schedule 8B (as inserted by the Finance Act 2007), then the amount of that capital expenditure which is to be treated as incurred for the purposes of the making of allowances and charges under that Chapter (including the making of balancing allowances and charges under *section 274* and the calculation of the residue of expenditure under *section 277*) shall be reduced to 80 per cent of the amount which, apart from this subsection, would otherwise be so treated.

(5) (a) For the purposes of the making of allowances and charges under *Chapter 1* of *Part 9* as is referred to in *subsections (3)* and *(4)*, references in the Tax Acts, other than those in *section 279* as applied by *paragraph (b)*, to expenditure incurred on the construction or, as the case may be, refurbishment of a building or structure shall be construed as a reference to such expenditure as reduced in accordance with either or both of those subsections.

(b) *Section 279* shall apply in relation to a building or structure to which either or both *subsections (3)* and *(4)* apply as if—

(i) in *subsection (1)* of that section, the following were substituted for the definition of "*the net price paid*":

" "*the net price paid*" means the amount represented by A in the equation—

$$A = B \times \frac{C}{D + E}$$

where—

B is the amount paid by a person on the purchase of the relevant interest in the building or structure,

C is the amount of the expenditure actually incurred on the construction of the building or structure as reduced in accordance with either or both *subsections (3)* and *(4)* of *section 372AZ*,

D is the amount of the expenditure actually incurred on the construction of the building or structure, and

E is the amount of any expenditure actually incurred which is expenditure for the purposes of *paragraph (a), (b)* or *(c)* of *section 270(2)*.",

(ii) in *subsection (2)* of that section, the following were substituted for *paragraph (b)*:

"(b) the person who buys that interest shall be deemed for those purposes to have incurred, on the date when the purchase price becomes payable, expenditure on the construction of the building or structure equal to that expenditure as reduced in accordance with either or both *subsections (3)* and *(4)* of *section 372AZ* or to the net price paid (within the meaning of that term as applied by *section 372AZ(5)*) by such person for that interest, whichever is the less;",

and

(iii) in *subsection (3)* of that section, the reference to "that expenditure or to" were a reference to "that expenditure as reduced in accordance with either or both *subsections (3)* and *(4)* of *section 372AZ* or to".][4]

Amendments

[1] Inserted by FA08 s29(1)(b)(i). Applies from 1 January 2008.

[2] Substituted by FA08 s29(1)(b)(ii). Applies from 1 January 2008.

[3] Substituted by FA08 s27.

[4] Inserted by FA07 s29(1)(a). With effect from 1 June 2008 per S.I. No. 159 of 2008.

Cross References

From Section 372AZ

Section 10 Connected persons.
Section 268 Meaning of "industrial building or structure".
Section 269 Meaning of "the relevant interest".
Section 270 Meaning of "expenditure on construction of building or structure".
Section 274 Balancing allowances and balancing charges.
Section 277 Writing off of expenditure and meaning of "residue of expenditure".
Section 279 Purchases of certain buildings or structures.

To Section 372AZ

Section 372AW Interpretation, applications for approval and certification.

CHAPTER 13

Living City Initiative

372AAA Interpretation

[In this Chapter—

[...][1]

"*market value*", in relation to a building, structure or house, means the price which the unencumbered fee simple of the building, structure or house would fetch if sold in the open market in such manner and subject to such conditions as might reasonably be calculated to obtain for the vendor the best price for the building, structure or house, less the part of that price which would be attributable to the acquisition of, or of rights in or over, the land on which the building, structure or house is constructed;

['*PPS number*' and '*tax reference number*' have the same meanings respectively as in *section 477B(1)*;][2]

"*qualifying period*" means the period commencing on the date of the coming into operation of *section 30* of the *Finance Act 2013* and ending 5 years after that date;

"*refurbishment*", in relation to a building, structure or house, means any work of construction, reconstruction, repair or renewal, including the provision or improvement of water, sewerage or heating facilities, carried out in the course of the repair or restoration, or maintenance in the nature of repair or restoration, of the building, structure or house;

['*relevant house*' means a building constructed before 1915 for use as a dwelling;][3]

"*special regeneration area*" means an area or areas specified as a special regeneration area by order of the Minister for Finance.][4]

Amendments

[1] Deleted by F(No.2)A13 s31(1)(a)(i).

[2] Inserted by FA14 s32(a)(ii).

[3] Substituted by FA14 s32(a)(i).

[4] Inserted by FA13 s30(1)(a). Comes into operation on such day as the Minister for Finance may by order appoint.

372AAB Residential accommodation: allowance to owner-occupiers in respect of qualifying expenditure incurred on the conversion and refurbishment of Georgian houses

[(1) In this section—

"*conversion*" in relation to a building, structure or house, means any work of—

(a) conversion into a house of a building or part of a building where the building or, as the case may be, the part of the building has not, immediately prior to the conversion, been in use as a dwelling, and

(b) conversion into 2 or more houses of a building or part of a building where before the conversion the building or, as the case may be, the part of the building has not, immediately prior to the conversion, been in use as a dwelling or had been in use as a single dwelling,

including the carrying out of any necessary works of construction, reconstruction, repair or renewal, and the provision or improvement of water, sewerage or heating facilities in relation to the building or the part of the building, as the case may be;

"*house*" includes any building or part of a building used or suitable for use as a dwelling and any out office, yard, garden or other land appurtenant to or usually enjoyed with that building or part of a building;

"*letter of certification*" means a letter from the relevant local authority stating that—

(a) planning permission, in so far as it is required, in respect of the work carried out in the course of the refurbishment or conversion has been granted under the Planning and Development Acts 2000 to 2010,

(b) the total floor area of the house is not less than 38 square metres and not more than 210 square metres,

(c) the house to which the letter relates complies with such conditions, if any, as may be determined by the Minister for the Environment, Community and Local Government from time to time for the purposes of *section 5* of the Housing (Miscellaneous Provisions) Act 1979, in relation to standards for improvement of houses and the provision of water, sewerage and other services in houses, and

(d) that at the time of issuing of the letter and on the basis of the information available at that time the cost of conversion into, or as the case may be, refurbishment of, the house appears to be reasonable;

"*qualifying expenditure*" means expenditure incurred by an individual, in the qualifying period, on the conversion into, or, as the case may be, the refurbishment of a qualifying premises, after deducting from that amount of expenditure any sum in respect of or by reference to—

(a) that expenditure,

(b) the qualifying premises, or

(c) the conversion or, as the case may be, the refurbishment work in respect of which that expenditure was incurred;

which the individual has received or is entitled to receive, directly or indirectly, from the State, any board established by statute or any public or local authority;

"*qualifying premises*" means a [relevant][1] house—

(a) the site of which is wholly within a special regeneration area,

(b) which is used solely as a dwelling,

(c) in respect of which a letter of certification has issued, and

(d) which is first used, after the qualifying expenditure has been incurred, by the individual as his or her only or main residence;

['*relevant local authority*' means the local authority, within the meaning of the Local Government Act 2001 (as amended by the *Local Government Reform* Act 2014), in whose functional area the special regeneration area is situated;][2]

"*total floor area*" means the total floor area of a house, measured in the manner referred to in *section 4(2)(b)* of the Housing (Miscellaneous Provisions) Act 1979.

(2) Where an individual, having duly made a claim, proves to have incurred qualifying expenditure on a qualifying premises in a year of assessment, the individual is entitled, for the year of assessment and for any of the 9 subsequent years of assessment in which the qualifying premises is his or her only or main residence, to have a deduction made from his or her total income of an amount equal to 10 per cent of the amount of that expenditure.

[(2A) Relief under this section shall not be given unless the following information is provided to the Revenue Commissioners as part of the claim, referred to in *subsection (2)*, made by the individual:

(a) the name and PPS number of the individual making the claim;

(b) the address of the qualifying premises in respect of which the qualifying expenditure was incurred;

(c) the unique identification number (if any) assigned to the qualifying premises under *section 27* of the Finance (Local Property Tax) Act 2012; and

(d) details of the aggregate of all qualifying expenditure incurred by the individual in respect of the qualifying premises.

(2B) Any claim made, or information required to be provided, to the Revenue Commissioners under this section, shall be made or provided by electronic means and through such electronic systems as the Revenue Commissioners may make available for the time being for any such purpose.][3]

(3) Where the individual or—

(a) the individual's spouse, is assessed to tax in accordance with *section 1017*, or

(b) the individual's civil partner is assessed to tax in accordance with *section 1031C*,

then, except where *section 1023* or *1031H*, as the case may be, applies, the individual shall be entitled to have the deduction, to which he or she is entitled under s*ubsection (2)*, made from his or her total income and the total income of his or her spouse or civil partner, as the case may be, if any.

(4) For the purposes of determining whether and to what extent qualifying expenditure incurred on or in relation to a qualifying premises is incurred or not incurred during the qualifying period, only such an amount of that expenditure as is properly attributable to work on the conversion into or refurbishment of the qualifying premises actually carried out during the qualifying period shall be treated as having been incurred in that period.

(5) Where qualifying expenditure, in relation to a qualifying premises, is incurred by 2 or more persons, each of those persons shall be treated as having incurred the expenditure in the proportions in which they actually bore the expenditure, and the expenditure shall be apportioned accordingly.

(6) *Subsections (6), (9)* and *(10)* of *section 372AP* shall, with any necessary modifications, apply in relation to—

(a) the apportionment of eligible expenditure (within the meaning of *section 372AN*) incurred on or in relation to a qualifying premises and of the relevant cost (within the meaning of *section 372AP*) in relation to that premises, and

(b) the amount of eligible expenditure (within the meaning aforesaid) to be treated as incurred in the qualifying period,

for the purposes of this section, in determining—

(i) the amount of qualifying expenditure incurred on or in relation to a qualifying premises, and

(ii) the amount of qualifying expenditure to be treated as incurred in the qualifying period,

as they apply for the purposes of *section 372AP*.

(7) Expenditure in respect of which an individual is entitled to relief under this section shall not include any expenditure in respect of which any person is entitled to a deduction, relief or allowance under any other provision of the Tax Acts.

(8) For the purposes of this section, expenditure incurred on the conversion into, or, as the case may be, refurbishment of a qualifying premises shall be deemed to have been incurred on the earliest date after the expenditure was actually incurred on which the premises is in use as a dwelling.

(9) This section shall not apply where qualifying expenditure incurred does not exceed 10 per cent of the market value of the building, structure or house immediately before that expenditure was incurred.

(10) An appeal to the Appeal Commissioners shall lie on any question arising under this section in like manner as an appeal would lie against an assessment to income tax and the provisions of the Tax Acts relating to appeals shall apply accordingly.][4]

Amendments

[1] Substituted by F(No.2)A13 s31(1)(b).

[2] Substituted by LGRA14 sched2(part5).

[3] Inserted by FA14 s32(b).

[4] Inserted by FA13 s30(1)(a). Comes into operation on such day as the Minister for Finance may by order appoint.

372AAC Capital allowances in relation to conversion or refurbishment of certain commercial premises

[(1) In this section—

"*conversion*", in relation to a building or structure, means any work of conversion, reconstruction or renewal, into a building suitable for use for the purposes of the retailing of goods or the provision of services only within the State and includes the provision or improvement of water, sewerage or heating facilities carried out, or maintenance in the nature of repair;

"*property developer*" means a person carrying on a trade which consists wholly or mainly of the construction or refurbishment of buildings or structures with a view to their sale;

['*qualifying expenditure*', in relation to capital expenditure incurred in the qualifying period on the conversion or the refurbishment of a qualifying premises and subject to *subsection (1A)*, means, notwithstanding *section 279*, the lesser of—

(a) the aggregate of all such capital expenditure, and

(b) (i) where the person who incurred the capital expenditure is a company, €1,600,000, or

(ii) where the person who incurred the capital expenditure is an individual, €400,000,

and, for the purposes of giving relief under this section, any reference to expenditure being incurred shall include a reference to expenditure deemed under any provision of *Part 9* to be incurred.][1]

"*qualifying premises*" means a building or structure (or part of a building or structure) the site of which is wholly within a special regeneration area, and which—

(a) apart from this section is not an industrial building or structure within the meaning of *section 268*, and

[(b) is—

(i) in use for the purposes of the retailing of goods or the provision, only within the State, of services, or

(ii) let on *bona fide* commercial terms for such use as is referred to in *subparagraph (i)* and for such consideration as might be expected to be paid in a letting of the building or structure negotiated on an arm's length basis,

but does not include any part of a building or structure in use as or as part of a dwelling house.][2]

[(1A) Notwithstanding the definition of qualifying expenditure in *subsection (1)*, where capital expenditure is incurred in the qualifying period on a qualifying premises by 2 or more persons, being either individuals or companies or individuals and companies, the amount of expenditure which is to be treated as qualifying expenditure incurred by each person for the purposes of this section, shall, if necessary and notwithstanding *section 279*, be reduced, such that the amount determined by the formula—

(A × 50 per cent) + (B × 12½ per cent)

does not exceed €200,000,

where—

A is the aggregate of all qualifying expenditure incurred by the individual or individuals, and

B is the aggregate of all qualifying expenditure incurred by the company or companies.][3]

(2) (a) [Subject to *paragraph (b)* and *subsections (4)* to *(8)*][4], the provisions of the Tax Acts relating to the making of allowances or charges in respect of capital expenditure incurred on the construction or refurbishment of an industrial building or structure shall, notwithstanding anything to the contrary in those provisions, apply in relation to qualifying expenditure on a qualifying premises—

(i) as if the qualifying premises were, at all times at which it is a qualifying premises, a building or structure in respect of which an allowance is to be made for the purposes of income tax or corporation tax, as the case may be, under Chapter 1 of Part 9 by reason of its use for the purpose specified in *section 268(1)(a)*, and

(ii) where any activity carried on in the qualifying premises is not a trade, as if (for the purposes only of the making of allowances and charges by virtue of *subparagraph (i)*), it were a trade.

(b) An allowance shall be given by virtue of this subsection in relation to any qualifying expenditure on a qualifying premises only in so far as that expenditure is incurred in the qualifying period.

[...][5]

(4) In relation to qualifying expenditure incurred in the qualifying period on a qualifying premises, *section 272* shall apply as if—

(a) in *subsection (3)(a)(ii)* of that section the reference to 4 per cent were a reference to 15 per cent, and

(b) in *subsection (4)(a)* of that section the following were substituted for *subparagraph (ii)*:

"(ii) where capital expenditure on the conversion or refurbishment of the building or structure is incurred, 7 years beginning with the time when the building or structure was first used subsequent to the incurring of that expenditure."

(5) Notwithstanding *section 274(1)*, no balancing allowance or balancing charge shall be made in relation to a qualifying premises by reason of any event referred to in that section which occurs more than 7 years after the qualifying premises was first used subsequent to the incurring of the qualifying expenditure on the conversion or refurbishment of the qualifying premises.

(6) This section shall not apply where qualifying expenditure incurred does not exceed 10 per cent of the market value of the building, structure or house immediately before that expenditure was incurred.

[(6A) Relief under this section shall not be given unless the following information is provided to the Revenue Commissioners before the first claim is made by the person in accordance with *subsection (2)*:

(a) the name, address and tax reference number of the person making the claim;

(b) the address of the qualifying premises in respect of which the qualifying expenditure was incurred;

(c) details of the aggregate of all qualifying expenditure incurred by the person in respect of the qualifying premises; and

(d) a brief description of the nature of the retail or other service which is provided or is to be provided in the qualifying premises.

(6B) Any information required to be provided to the Revenue Commissioners under this section shall be provided by electronic means and through such electronic systems as the Revenue Commissioners may make available for the time being for such purpose.][6]

(7) For the purposes only of determining, in relation to a claim for an allowance by virtue of *subsection (2)*, whether and to what extent capital expenditure incurred on the conversion or refurbishment of a qualifying premises is incurred or not incurred in the qualifying period, only such an amount of that capital expenditure as is properly attributable to work on the conversion or refurbishment of the premises actually carried out during the qualifying period shall (notwithstanding any other provision of the Tax Acts as to the time when any capital expenditure is or is to be treated as incurred) be treated as having been incurred in that period.

(8) Notwithstanding any other provision of this section, this section shall not apply in respect of qualifying expenditure incurred on a qualifying premises where—

(a) (i) a property developer, or a person who is connected (within the meaning of *section 10*) with the property developer is entitled to the relevant interest, within the meaning of *section 269*, in relation to that expenditure, and

(ii) either of the persons referred to in *subparagraph (i)* incurred the qualifying expenditure on that qualifying premises, or such expenditure was incurred by any other person connected (within the meaning of *section 10*) with the property developer,

or

(b) any part of such expenditure has been or is to be met, directly or indirectly, by grant assistance or any other assistance which is granted by or through the State, any board established by statute, [any public or local authority][7] or any other agency of the State.

(9) Where relief is given by virtue of this section in relation to capital expenditure incurred on the conversion or refurbishment of a building or structure, relief shall not be given in respect of that expenditure under any other provision of the Tax Acts.][8]

Amendments

[1] Substituted by FA14 s32(c)(i)(I).

[2] Substituted by FA14 s32(c)(i)(II).

[3] Inserted by FA14 s32(c)(ii).

[4] Substituted by FA14 s32(c)(iii).

[5] Deleted by FA14 s32(c)(iv).

[6] Inserted by FA14 s32(c)(v).

[7] Substituted by F(No.2)A13 s31(1)(c)(ii).

[8] Inserted by FA13 s30(1)(a). Comes into operation on such day as the Minister for Finance may by order appoint.

PART 11

Capital Allowances and Expenses for Certain Road Vehicles

373 Interpretation (Part 11)

[FA73 s30(1), (5) and (6); FA76 s31, FA86 s50(1); FA88 s24(1); FA89 s12(1); FA92 s21(1); FA94 s21(1); FA95 s23(1); FA97 s21(1)]

(1) Subject to *section 380(1)*, this Part shall apply to a vehicle which is a mechanically propelled road vehicle constructed or adapted for the carriage of passengers, other than a vehicle of a type not commonly used as a private vehicle and unsuitable to be so used.

(2) In this Part, "*the specified amount*", in relation to expenditure incurred on the provision or hiring of a vehicle to which this Part applies, means—

(a) [€3,174.35][1], where the expenditure was incurred on or after the 16th day of May, 1973, but such expenditure does not include—

(i) as respects *sections 374*, *375* and *377*, expenditure incurred under a contract entered into before that day where either—

(I) the expenditure was incurred within 12 months after that day, or

(II) the contract was one of hire-purchase or for purchase by instalments,

and

(ii) as respects *subsections (2)* and *(3)* of *section 378* and *section 379*, expenditure where the contract of hire-purchase or for purchase by instalments was entered into before that day;

(b) [€4,444.08][2], where the expenditure was incurred after the 28th day of January, 1976, but such expenditure does not include—

(i) as respects *sections 374*, *375* and *377*, expenditure incurred within 12 months after that day under a contract entered into before that day, and

(ii) as respects *subsections (2)* and *(3)* of *section 378* and *section 379*, expenditure under a contract entered into on or before that day;

(c) [€5,078.95][3], where the expenditure was incurred on or after the 6th day of April, 1986, but such expenditure does not include—

(i) as respects *sections 374*, *375* and *377*, expenditure incurred within 12 months after that day under a contract entered into before that day, and

(ii) as respects *subsections (2)* and *(3)* of *section 378* and *section 379*, expenditure under a contract entered into before that day;

(d) [€7,618.43][4], where the expenditure was incurred on or after the 28th day of January, 1988, but such expenditure does not include—

(i) as respects *sections 374*, *375* and *377*, expenditure incurred within 12 months after that day under a contract entered into before that day, and

(ii) as respects *subsections (2)* and *(3)* of *section 378* and *section 379*, expenditure under a contract entered into before that day;

(e) [€8,888.17][5], where the expenditure was incurred on or after the 26th day of January, 1989, but such expenditure does not include—

(i) as respects *sections 374*, *375* and *377*, expenditure incurred within 12 months after that day under a contract entered into before that day, and

(ii) as respects *subsections (2)* and *(3)* of *section 378* and *section 379*, expenditure under a contract entered into before that day;

(f) [€12,697.38][6], where the expenditure was incurred on or after the 30th day of January, 1992, but such expenditure does not include—

(i) as respects *sections 374*, *375* and *377*, expenditure incurred within 12 months after that day under a contract entered into before that day, and

(ii) as respects *subsections (2)* and *(3)* of *section 378* and *section 379*, expenditure under a contract entered into before that day;

(g) [€16,506.60][7], where the expenditure was incurred on or after the 27th day of January, 1994, on the provision or hiring of a vehicle which on or after that day was first registered in the State under section 131 of the Finance Act, 1992, without having been previously registered in any other State which provides for the registration of a mechanically propelled vehicle, but such expenditure does not include—

(i) as respects *sections 374*, *375* and *377*, expenditure incurred within 12 months after that day under a contract entered into before that day, and

(ii) as respects *subsections (2)* and *(3)* of *section 378* and *section 379*, expenditure incurred under a contract entered into before that day;

(h) [€17,776.33][8], where the expenditure was incurred on or after the 9th day of February, 1995, on the provision or hiring of a vehicle which on or after that day was not a used or secondhand vehicle and was first registered in the State under section 131 of the Finance Act, 1992, without having been previously registered in any other State which provides for the registration of a mechanically propelled vehicle, but such expenditure does not include—

(i) as respects *sections 374*, *375* and *377*, expenditure incurred within 12 months after that day under a contract entered into before that day, and

(ii) as respects *subsections (2)* and *(3)* of *section 378* and *section 379*, expenditure incurred under a contract entered into before that day;

(i) [€19,046.07][9], where the expenditure was incurred on or after the 23rd day of January, 1997, on the provision or hiring of a vehicle which, on or after that date was not a used or secondhand vehicle and was first registered in the State under section 131 of the Finance Act, 1992, without having been previously registered in any other State which duly provides for the registration of a [mechanically propelled vehicle][10].

[(j) [€19,680.94][11], where the expenditure was incurred on or after the 3rd day of December, 1997, on the provision or hiring of a vehicle which, on or after that date was not a used or secondhand vehicle and was first registered in the State under section 131 of the Finance Act, 1992, without having been previously registered in any other state which duly provides for the registration of a [mechanically propelled vehicle;][12][13]

[(k) [€20,315.81][14], where the expenditure was incurred on or after the 2nd day of December, 1998, on the provision or hiring of a vehicle which, on or after that date was not a used or secondhand vehicle and was first registered in the State under section 131 of the Finance Act, 1992, without having been previously registered in any other state which duly provides for the registration of a [mechanically propelled vehicle;][15][16]

[(l) [€20,950.68][17], where the expenditure was incurred on or after 1 December 1999 on the provision or hiring of a vehicle which, on or after that date was not a used or secondhand vehicle and was first registered in the State under section 131 of the Finance Act, 1992, without having been previously registered in any other state which duly provides for the registration of a [mechanically propelled vehicle;][18][19]

[(m) [€21,585.55][20], where the expenditure was incurred—

(i) in an accounting period ending on or after 1 January 2001, or

(ii) in a basis period for the year of assessment 2000-2001 or for a subsequent year of assessment, where that basis period ends on or after 1 [January 2001;][21][22]

[(n) €22,000, where the expenditure was incurred—

(i) in an accounting period ending on or after 1 January 2002, or

(ii) in a basis period for a year of assessment, where that basis period ends on or after [1 January 2002;][23][24]

[(o) €23,000, where the expenditure was incurred—

(i) in an accounting period ending on or after 1 January 2006, or

(ii) in a basis period for a year of assessment, where that basis period ends on or after [January 2006;][25][26]

[(p) €24,000, where the expenditure was incurred—

(i) in an accounting period ending on or after 1 January 2007, or

(ii) in a basis period for a year of assessment, where that basis period ends on or after 1 January 2007.][27]

(3) This Part (other than *section 376*) shall be construed as one with *Part 9*, except that in *section 375* "*capital expenditure*" shall be construed without regard to *section 316(1)*.

Amendments

1, 2, 3, 4, 5, 6, 7, 8, 9, 11, 14, 17 Substituted by FA01 s240 and sched5 part1.

10 Substituted by FA98 s29(a)(i).

12 Substituted by FA99 s53(a)(i).

13 Inserted by FA98 s29(a)(ii).

15 Substituted by FA00 s35(a)(i).

16 Inserted by FA99 s53(a)(ii).

18 Substituted by FA01 s61(1)(a)(i).

19 Inserted by FA00 s35(a)(ii).

20 Substituted by FA01 s61(1)(a)(iii). Applies as respects the year of assessment 2002 and subsequent years of assessment.

[21] Substituted by FA02 s28(1)(a)(i).

[22] Inserted by FA01 s61(1)(a)(ii).

[23] Substituted by FA06 s21(a).

[24] Inserted by FA02 s28(1)(a)(ii).

[25] Substituted by FA07 s21(a).

[26] Inserted by FA06 s21(b).

[27] Inserted by FA07 s21(b).

Case Law

In Tapper v Eyre 43 TC 720 it was held that a mini van used solely for business purposes was nevertheless a vehicle commonly used as a private vehicle. A similar judgement was given in Laing v IRC 44 TC 7682. However, in Roberts v Granad TV Rental 46 TC 295 a different view was taken. In this case it was held that even if a majority of vehicles were registered for private use, this did not mean that they were necessarily suitable for such use. Similarly, in S&U Stores v Gordon 1970 WLR 889 the test was one of suitability and not usability.

A family car fitted with dual controls (which could have been removed within two hours) were of a type not commonly used on a private vehicle and unsuitable to be so used. Bourne v Auto School of motoring (Norwich) 42 TC 217

A salon car fitted with a flashing light for use by a fireman was not commonly used as a private vehicle and was unsuitable for such use. The court relied on the fact that it would be illegal for anyone other than the emergency services to drive a vehicle adapted in this way. Gurney v Richards 1989 STC 682

Revenue Precedent

Where a rebate of rentals arises in respect of leasing charges which have been restricted under section 373 TCA 1997, whether Revenue assesses the full amount of the rebate. The amount of a rebate of rentals represents a return of leasing charges already allowed for tax purposes. Where a rebate of rentals arises in respect of leasing charges which have been restricted under section 373, Revenue will seek to assess only the proportion of the rebate which has been allowed for tax purposes to the lessee. IT962518

Cross References

From Section 373

Section 268 Meaning of "industrial building or structure".
Section 316 Interpretation of certain references to expenditure and time when expenditure is incurred.
Section 373 Interpretation (Part 11).
Section 374 Capital allowances for cars costing over certain amount.
Section 375 Limit on renewals allowance for cars.
Section 376 Restriction of deduction in respect of running expenses of cars.
Section 377 Limit on deductions, etc. for hiring cars.
Section 378 Cars: provisions as to hire-purchase, etc.
Section 379 Cars: provisions where hirer becomes owner.
Section 380 Provisions supplementary to sections 374 to 379.

To Section 373

Section 373 Interpretation (Part 11).
Section 380K Interpretation and general (Part 11C).
Section 380L Emissions-based limits for certain cars.

374 Capital allowances for cars costing over certain amount

[FA73 s25; CTA76 s21(1) and Sch1 par62; FA97 s146(1) and Sch9 PtI par6(1)]

(1) In relation to a vehicle to which this Part applies, *section 284* shall apply as if, for [the purposes of that section][1], the actual cost of the vehicle were taken to be the specified amount where the expenditure incurred on the provision of the vehicle exceeded that amount and, where an allowance which apart from this subsection would be made under *section 284* is to be reduced by virtue of this subsection, any reference in the Tax Acts to an allowance made under *section 284* shall be construed as a reference to that allowance as reduced under this subsection.

(2) In relation to a vehicle to which this Part applies, the allowances under *section 284* to be taken into account for the purposes of *Chapter 2* of *Part 9* in computing the amount of expenditure still unallowed at any time shall be limited to those computed in accordance with *subsection (1)*, and the expenditure incurred on the provision of the vehicle to be taken into account for the purposes of that Chapter shall be limited to the specified amount.

(3) Where the expenditure incurred on the provision of a vehicle to which this Part applies exceeds the specified amount, any balancing allowance or balancing charge shall be computed, in a case where there are sale, insurance, salvage or compensation moneys, as if the amount of those moneys (or, where in consequence of any provision of the Tax Acts other than this subsection some other amount is to be treated as the amount of those moneys, that other amount) were reduced in the proportion which the specified amount bears to the actual amount of that expenditure.

(4) (a) Where the expenditure incurred on the provision of a vehicle to which this Part applies exceeds the specified amount and—

(i) the person providing the vehicle (in this section referred to as "*the prior owner*") sells the vehicle or gives it away so that *subsection (5)* of *section 289*, or that subsection as applied by *subsection (6)* of that section, applies in relation to the purchaser or donee,

(ii) the prior owner sells the vehicle and the sale is a sale to which *section 312* applies, or

(iii) in consequence of a succession to the trade or profession of the prior owner, *section 313(1)* applies, then, in relation to the purchaser, donee or successor, the price which the vehicle would have fetched if sold in the open market or the expenditure incurred by the prior owner on the provision of the vehicle shall be treated for the purposes of *section 289, 312* or *313* as reduced in the proportion which the specified amount bears to the actual amount of that expenditure, and, in the application of *subsection (3)* to the purchaser, donee or successor, references to the expenditure incurred on the provision of the vehicle shall be construed as references to the expenditure so incurred by the prior owner.

(b) Where *paragraph (a)* has applied on any occasion in relation to a vehicle, and no sale or gift of the vehicle has since occurred other than one to which either *section 289* or *312* applies, then, in relation to all persons concerned, the like consequences under *paragraph (a)* shall ensue as respects a gift, sale or succession within *subparagraphs (i)* to *(iii)* of that paragraph which occurs on any subsequent occasion as would ensue if the person who in relation to that sale, gift or succession is the prior owner had incurred expenditure on the provision of the vehicle of an amount equal to the expenditure so incurred by the person who was the prior owner on the first-mentioned occasion.

(5) In the application of *section 290* to a case where the vehicle is the new machinery or plant referred to in that subsection, the expenditure shall be disregarded in so far as it exceeds the specified amount, but without prejudice to the application of *subsections (1)* to *(4)* to the vehicle.

(6) Where the capital expenditure incurred on the provision of a vehicle exceeds the specified amount but under *section 317(2)* any part of that expenditure is to

be treated as not having been incurred by a person, the amount which (subject to *subsections (1)* to *(5)*) is to be treated for the purposes of *Part 9* as having been incurred by that person shall be reduced in the proportion which the specified amount bears to the capital expenditure incurred on the provision of the vehicle.

Amendments

[1] Substituted by FA02 s28(1)(b). Applies as respects capital expenditure incurred on or after 1 January 2001.

Cross References

From Section 374

Section 268 Meaning of "industrial building or structure".
Section 283 Initial allowances.
Section 284 Wear and tear allowances.
Section 289 Calculation of balancing allowances and balancing charges in certain cases.
Section 290 Option in case of replacement.
Section 312 Special provisions as to certain sales.
Section 313 Effect, in certain cases, of succession to trade, etc.
Section 317 Treatment of grants.

To Section 374

Section 309 Companies not resident in the State.
Section 321 Provisions of general application in relation to the making of allowances and charges.
Section 373 Interpretation (Part 11).
Section 379 Cars: provisions where hirer becomes owner.
Section 380 Provisions supplementary to sections 374 to 379.

375 Limit on renewals allowance for cars

[FA73 s26; CTA76 s140(1) and Sch2 PtI par33 and s164 and Sch3 PtI]

In determining what amount (if any) is allowable—

(a) to be deducted in computing profits or gains chargeable to tax under Schedule D,

(b) to be deducted from emoluments chargeable to tax under Schedule E, or

(c) to be taken into account for the purposes of a management expenses claim under *section 83* or under that section as applied by *section 707*,

in respect of capital expenditure incurred on the provision of a vehicle to which this Part applies, being expenditure exceeding the specified amount, the excess over the specified amount shall be disregarded; but, if on the replacement of the vehicle any amount becomes so allowable in respect of capital expenditure on any other vehicle, any deduction to be made, in determining the last-mentioned amount, for the value or proceeds of sale of the replaced vehicle or otherwise in respect of the replaced vehicle shall be reduced in the proportion which the specified amount bears to the cost of the replaced vehicle.

Cross References

From Section 375

Section 83 Expenses of management of investment companies.
Section 707 Management expenses.

To Section 375

Section 373 Interpretation (Part 11).
Section 377 Limit on deductions, etc. for hiring cars.
Section 378 Cars: provisions as to hire-purchase, etc.
Section 380 Provisions supplementary to sections 374 to 379.
Section 380M Limit on deductions, etc. for hiring cars.
Section 380N Cars: provisions as to hire-purchase, etc.

376 Restriction of deduction in respect of running expenses of cars

[Deleted]

Deleted by FA02 s28(1)(c). Applies as respects expenditure incurred in an accounting period ending on or after 1 January 2002, or in a basis period for a year of assessment, where that basis period ends on or after 1 January 2002.

Cross References

To Section 376

Section 373 Interpretation (Part 11).

377 Limit on deductions, etc. for hiring cars

[FA73 s27]

Where apart from this section the amount of any expenditure on the hiring (otherwise than by means of hire-purchase) of a vehicle to which this Part applies would be allowed to be deducted or taken into account as mentioned in *section 375*, and the retail price of the vehicle at the time it was made exceeded the specified amount, the amount of that expenditure shall be reduced in the proportion which the specified amount bears to that price.

Case Law

Lloyds UDT Finance Ltd v Chartered Finance Trust Holdings plc and Others 2002 STC 956 analysed what constituted the hire of a car for the purpose of the restriction. The case related to a Finance Company, which hired in cars for onward rental. It also considered the use of accountancy principles in the computation of profits.

Cross References

From Section 377

Section 375 Limit on renewals allowance for cars.

To Section 377

Section 373 Interpretation (Part 11).
Section 378 Cars: provisions as to hire-purchase, etc.
Section 379 Cars: provisions where hirer becomes owner.
Section 380 Provisions supplementary to sections 374 to 379.

378 Cars: provisions as to hire-purchase, etc

[FA73 s28]

(1) In the case of a vehicle to which this Part applies, being a vehicle the retail price of which at the time of the contract in question exceeds the specified amount, *subsections (2)* to *(4)* shall apply.

(2) Where a person, having incurred capital expenditure on the provision of a vehicle to which this Part applies under a contract providing that such person shall or may become the owner of the vehicle on the performance of the contract, ceases to be entitled to the benefit of the contract without becoming the owner of the vehicle, that expenditure shall, in so far as it relates to the vehicle, be disregarded for the purposes of *Chapter 2* of *Part 9* and in determining what amount (if any) is allowable as mentioned in *section 375*.

(3) Where *subsection (2)* applies, all payments made under the contract shall be treated for tax purposes (including in particular for the purposes of *section 377*) as expenditure incurred on the hiring of the vehicle otherwise than by means of hire-purchase.

(4) Where the person providing the vehicle takes it under a hire-purchase contract, then, in apportioning the payments under the contract between capital expenditure incurred on the provision of the vehicle and other expenditure, so much of those

payments shall be treated as such capital expenditure as is equal to the price which would be chargeable, at the time the contract is entered into, to the person providing the vehicle if that person were acquiring it on a sale outright.

Cross References

From Section 378

Section 268 Meaning of "industrial building or structure".
Section 283 Initial allowances.
Section 375 Limit on renewals allowance for cars.
Section 377 Limit on deductions, etc. for hiring cars.

To Section 378

Section 373 Interpretation (Part 11).
Section 380 Provisions supplementary to sections 374 to 379.

379 Cars: provisions where hirer becomes owner

[FA73 s29]

Where, having hired (otherwise than by means of hire-purchase) a vehicle to which this Part applies, a person subsequently becomes the owner of the vehicle and the retail price of the vehicle at the time it was made exceeded the specified amount, then, for the purposes of the Tax Acts (and in particular *sections 374* and *377*)—

(a) so much of the aggregate of the payments for the hire of the vehicle and of any payment for the acquisition of the vehicle as does not exceed the retail price of the vehicle at the time it was made shall be treated as capital expenditure incurred on the provision of the vehicle, and as having been incurred when the hiring began, and

(b) the payments to be treated as expenditure on the hiring of the vehicle shall be rateably reduced so as to amount in the aggregate to the balance.

Cross References

From Section 379

Section 374 Capital allowances for cars costing over certain amount.
Section 377 Limit on deductions, etc. for hiring cars.

To Section 379

Section 373 Interpretation (Part 11).
Section 380 Provisions supplementary to sections 374 to 379.

380 Provisions supplementary to sections 374 to 379.

[FA73 s30(2) to (4); CTA76 s164 and Sch3 PtII]

(1) *Sections 374*, *375* and *377*, *subsections (2)* and *(3)* of *section 378* and *section 379* shall not apply where a vehicle is provided or hired, wholly or mainly, for the purpose of hire to or the carriage of members of the public in the ordinary course of trade.

(2) *Sections 374* and *375*, *subsections (2)* and *(3)* of *section 378* and *section 379* shall not apply in relation to a vehicle provided by a person who is a manufacturer of a vehicle to which this Part applies, or of parts or accessories for such a vehicle, if the person shows that the vehicle was provided solely for the purpose of testing the vehicle or parts or accessories for such vehicle; but, if during the period of 5 years beginning with the time when the vehicle was provided, such person puts it to any substantial extent to a use which

does not serve that purpose only, this subsection shall be deemed not to have applied in relation to the vehicle.

(3) [(a) Subject to *Chapter 5* of *Part 41A*, assessments may, as necessary, be made or amended at any time for the purpose of applying *subsections (2)* and *(3)* of *section 378*, *section 379* and *subsection (2)*.][1]

(b) In the case of the death of a person who, if he or she had not died, would under *subsections (2)* and *(3)* of *section 378*, *section 379* and *subsection (2)* have become chargeable to tax for any year, the tax which would have been so chargeable shall be assessed and charged on his or her executors or administrators and shall be a debt due from and payable out of his or her estate.

Amendments

[1] Substituted by FA12 sched4(part 2)(b).

Cross References

From Section 380

Section 374 Capital allowances for cars costing over certain amount.
Section 375 Limit on renewals allowance for cars.
Section 377 Limit on deductions, etc. for hiring cars.
Section 378 Cars: provisions as to hire-purchase, etc.
Section 379 Cars: provisions where hirer becomes owner.

To Section 380

Section 373 Interpretation (Part 11).

PART 11A

Income Tax and Corporation Tax: Deduction for Expenditure on Construction, Conversion and Refurbishment of Certain Residential Accommodation for Certain Students

380A Interpretation (Part 11A) [Repealed]

Repealed by FA02 s24(3)(j).

380B Rented residential accommodation: deduction for certain expenditure on construction [Repealed]

Repealed by FA02 s24(3)(j).

380C Rented residential accommodation: deduction for certain expenditure on conversion [Repealed]

Repealed by FA02 s24(3)(j).

380D Rented residential accommodation: deduction for certain expenditure on refurbishment [Repealed]

Repealed by FA02 s24(3)(j).

380E Provisions supplementary to sections 380B to 380D [Repealed]

Repealed by FA02 s24(3)(j).

380F Provision against double relief [Repealed]

Repealed by FA02 s24(3)(j).

PART 11B

Income Tax and Corporation Tax: Deduction for Expenditure on Refurbishment of Certain Residential Accomodation

380G Interpretation (Part 11B) [Repealed]

Repealed by FA02 s24(3)(k).

380H Rented residential accommodation: deduction for certain expenditure on refurbishment [Repealed]

Repealed by FA02 s24(3)(k).

380I Provisions supplementary to section 380H [Repealed]

Repealed by FA02 s24(3)(k).

380J Provision against double relief [Repealed]

Repealed by FA02 s24(3)(k).

PART 11C

Emissions-based Limits on Capital Allowances and Expenses for Certain Road Vehicles

380K Interpretation and general (Part 11C)

[(1) Subject to *section 380P(1)*, this Part and not Part 11 shall apply to a vehicle which is a mechanically propelled road vehicle constructed or adapted for the carriage of passengers, other than a vehicle of a type not commonly used as a private vehicle and unsuitable to be so used[, but this Part shall not apply where an allowance for a vehicle is increased under *section 285A*][1].

(2) Any reference in this Part to a vehicle in any of the vehicle Categories A to G as set out in the first column of the Table to this subsection is a reference to a vehicle whose CO_2emissions, confirmed by reference to the relevant EC type approval certificate or EC certificate of conformity, are set out in the corresponding entry in the second column of the Table to this subsection.

TABLE

Vehicle Category	CO_2Emissions (CO_2g/km)
A	0g/km up to and including 120g/km
B	More than 120g/km up to and including 140g/km
C	More than 140g/km up to and including 155g/km
D	More than 155g/km up to and including 170g/km
E	More than 170g/km up to and including 190g/km
F	More than 190g/km up to and including 225g/km
G	More than 225g/km

(3) Where the Revenue Commissioners are not satisfied of the level of CO_2emissions relating to a vehicle by reference to any document other than either of the certificates referred to in subsection (2), or where no document has been provided, the vehicle shall, for the purposes of this Part, be treated as if it were a vehicle in Category G.

(4) In this Part—

"*CO_2 emissions*" means the level of carbon dioxide (CO_2) emissions for a vehicle measured in accordance with the provisions of Council Directive 80/1268/EEC of 16 December 1980* (as amended) and listed in Annex VIII of Council Directive 70/156/EEC of 6 February 1970† (as amended) and contained in the relevant EC type approval certificate or EC certificate of conformity or any other appropriate documentation which confirms compliance with any measures taken to give effect in the State to any act of the European Communities relating to the approximation of the laws of Member States in respect of type approval for the type of vehicle concerned;

* OJ No. L375 of 31 December 1980, p.36

† OJ No. L42 of 23 February 1970, p.1

"*specified amount*", in relation to expenditure incurred on the provision or hiring of a vehicle to which this Part applies, means €24,000, where the expenditure was incurred—

(a) in an accounting period ending on or after 1 January 2007, or

(b) in a basis period for a year of assessment where that basis period ends on or after 1 January 2007.

(5) This Part shall be construed as one with Part 9.][2]

Amendments

[1] Inserted by F(No.2)A08 s37(1)(b). With effect from 23 March 2009 per S.I. No. 91 of 2009.

[2] Inserted by FA08 s31(1). Applies to expenditure incurred on the provision or hiring of a vehicle on or after 1 July 2008.

Cross References

From Section 380K

Section 268 Meaning of "industrial building or structure".
Section 285A Acceleration of wear and tear allowances for certain energy efficient equipment.
Section 373 Interpretation (Part 11).
Section 380P Provisions supplementary to sections 380L to 380O.

To Section 380K

Section 285A Acceleration of wear and tear allowances for certain energy efficient equipment.

380L Emissions-based limits for certain cars

[(1) In relation to a vehicle to which this Part applies, where an allowance which, apart from this section, would be made under *section 284* is to be increased or reduced, as the case may be, by virtue of this section, any reference in the Tax Acts to an allowance made under *section 284* shall be construed as a reference to that allowance as increased or reduced under this section.

(2) In relation to a vehicle to which this Part applies, the allowances under *section 284* to be taken into account for the purposes of Chapter 2 of Part 9 in computing the amount of expenditure still unallowed at any time shall be determined by reference to the allowances computed in accordance with this section, and the expenditure incurred on the provision of the vehicle to be taken into account for the purposes of that Chapter shall be determined accordingly.

(3) *Section 284* shall apply as if, for the purposes of that section, the actual cost of the vehicle were taken to be—

(a) in the case of a vehicle in Category A, B or C, an amount equal to the specified amount,

(b) in the case of a vehicle in Category D or E, where the retail price of the vehicle at the time it was made was—

(i) less than or equal to the specified amount, 50 per cent of that price, and

(ii) greater than the specified amount, 50 per cent of the specified amount,

and

(c) in the case of a vehicle in Category F or G, nil.

(4) Where expenditure has been incurred on the provision of a vehicle to which this Part applies, then any balancing allowance or balancing charge shall be computed, in a case where there are sale, insurance, salvage or compensation moneys, as if the amount of those moneys (or, where in consequence of any provision of the Taxes Acts, other than Part 11 or this section, some other amount is to be treated as the amount of those moneys, that other amount) were—

(a) in the case of a vehicle in Category A, B or C, increased or reduced, as the case may be, in the proportion which the specified amount bears to the actual amount of that expenditure,

(b) in the case of a vehicle in Category D or E where the expenditure incurred was—

(i) less than or equal to the specified amount, reduced by 50 per cent, and

(ii) greater than the specified amount, reduced in the proportion which 50 per cent of the specified amount bears to that actual amount of that expenditure,

and

(c) in the case of a vehicle in Category F or G, nil.

(5) (a) Where expenditure is incurred on the provision of a vehicle to which this Part applies and—

(i) the person providing the vehicle (in this section referred to as the "*prior owner*") sells the vehicle or gives it away so that *subsection (5)* of *section 289*, or that subsection as applied by subsection (6) of that section, applies in relation to the purchaser or donee,

(ii) the prior owner sells the vehicle and the sale is a sale to which *section 312* applies, or (iii) in consequence of a succession to the trade or profession of the prior owner, *section 313(1)* applies,

then, in relation to the purchaser, donee or successor, the price which the vehicle would have fetched if sold in the open market or the expenditure incurred by the prior owner on the provision of the vehicle shall be treated for the purposes of *section 289, 312* or *313* as—

(I) in the case of a vehicle in Category A, B or C, an amount equal to the specified amount,

(II) in the case of a vehicle in Category D or E where the retail price of the vehicle at the time it was made was—

(A) less than or equal to the specified amount, 50 per cent of that price, and

(B) greater than the specified amount, 50 per cent of the specified amount,

and

(III) in the case of a vehicle in Category F or G, nil,

and, in the application of subsection (4) to the purchaser, donee or successor, references to the expenditure incurred on the provision of the vehicle shall be construed as references to the expenditure so incurred by the prior owner.

(b) Where *paragraph (a)* has applied on any occasion in relation to a vehicle, and no sale or gift of the vehicle has since occurred other than one to which either *section 289* or *312* applies, then, in relation to all persons concerned, the like consequences under *paragraph (a)* shall ensue as respects a gift, sale or succession within *subparagraphs (i)* to *(iii)* of that paragraph which occurs on any subsequent occasion as would ensue if the person who in relation to that sale, gift or succession is the prior owner had incurred expenditure on the provision of the vehicle of an amount equal to the expenditure so incurred by the person who was the prior owner on the first-mentioned occasion.

(6) In the application of *section 290* to a case where the vehicle is the new machinery referred to in that section, the expenditure shall be disregarded in so far as it exceeds—

(a) in the case of a vehicle in Category A, B or C, the specified amount,

(b) in the case of a vehicle in Category D or E, where the retail price of the vehicle at the time it was made was—

(i) less than or equal to the specified amount, 50 per cent of that price, and

(ii) greater than the specified amount, 50 per cent of the specified amount,

and

(c) in the case of a vehicle in Category F or G, nil,

but without prejudice to the application of subsections (1) to (5) to the vehicle.

(7) Expenditure shall not be regarded for the purposes of this Part as having been incurred by a person in so far as the expenditure has been or is to be met directly or indirectly by the State or by any person other than the first-mentioned person.][1]

Amendments

[1] Inserted by FA08 s31(1). Applies to expenditure incurred on the provision or hiring of a vehicle on or after 1 July 2008.

Cross References

From Section 380L

Section 268 Meaning of "industrial building or structure".
Section 283 Initial allowances.
Section 284 Wear and tear allowances.
Section 289 Calculation of balancing allowances and balancing charges in certain cases.
Section 290 Option in case of replacement.
Section 312 Special provisions as to certain sales.
Section 313 Effect, in certain cases, of succession to trade, etc.
Section 373 Interpretation (Part 11).

To Section 380L

Section 285A Acceleration of wear and tear allowances for certain energy efficient equipment.
Section 380O Cars: provisions where hirer becomes owner.
Section 380P Provisions supplementary to sections 380L to 380O.

380M Limit on deductions, etc. for hiring cars

[Where apart from this section the amount of any expenditure on the hiring (otherwise than by means of hire-purchase) of a vehicle to which this Part applies would be allowed to be deducted or taken into account as mentioned in *section 375*, then the amount of that expenditure shall—

(a) in the case of a vehicle in Category A, B or C, be increased or reduced, as the case may be, in the proportion which the specified amount bears to the retail price of the vehicle at the time it was made,

(b) in the case of a vehicle in category D or E where the retail price of the vehicle at the time it was made was—

(i) less than or equal to the specified amount, be reduced by 50 per cent, and

(ii) greater than the specified amount, be reduced in the proportion which 50 per cent of the specified amount bears to that price,

and

(c) in the case of a vehicle in category F or G, be nil.][1]

Amendments

[1] Inserted by FA08 s31(1). Applies to expenditure incurred on the provision or hiring of a vehicle on or after 1 July 2008.

Cross References

From Section 380M

Section 375 Limit on renewals allowance for cars.

To Section 380M

Section 380N Cars: provisions as to hire-purchase, etc.
Section 380O Cars: provisions where hirer becomes owner.
Section 380P Provisions supplementary to sections 380L to 380O.

380N Cars: provisions as to hire-purchase, etc

[(1) In the case of a vehicle to which this Part applies, subsections (2) to (4) shall apply.

(2) Where a person, having incurred capital expenditure on the provision of a vehicle to which this Part applies under a contract providing that such person shall or may become the owner of the vehicle on the performance of the contract, ceases to be entitled to the benefit of the contract without becoming the owner of the vehicle, then that expenditure shall, in so far as it relates to the vehicle, be disregarded for the purposes of Chapter 2 of Part 9 and in determining what amount (if any) is allowable as mentioned in *section 375*.

(3) Where subsection (2) applies, all payments made under the contract shall be treated for tax purposes (including in particular for the purposes of *section 380M*) as expenditure incurred on the hiring of the vehicle otherwise than by means of hire-purchase.

(4) Where the person providing the vehicle takes it under a hire-purchase contract, then, in apportioning the payments under the contract between capital expenditure incurred on the provision of the vehicle and other expenditure, so much of those payments shall be treated as such capital expenditure as is equal to the price which would be chargeable, at the time the contract is entered into, to the person providing the vehicle if that person were acquiring it on a sale outright.][1]

Amendments

[1] Inserted by FA08 s31(1). Applies to expenditure incurred on the provision or hiring of a vehicle on or after 1 July 2008.

Cross References

From Section 380N

Section 268 Meaning of "industrial building or structure".
Section 283 Initial allowances.
Section 375 Limit on renewals allowance for cars.
Section 380M Limit on deductions, etc. for hiring cars.

To Section 380N

Section 380P Provisions supplementary to sections 380L to 380O.

380O Cars: provisions where hirer becomes owner

[Where, having hired (otherwise than by means of hire-purchase) a vehicle to which this Part applies, a person subsequently becomes the owner of the vehicle, then, for the purposes of the Tax Acts (and in particular *sections 380L* and *380M*)—

(a) so much of the aggregate of the payments for the hire of the vehicle and of any payment for the acquisition of the vehicle as does not exceed the retail price of the vehicle at the time it was made shall be treated as capital expenditure incurred on the provision of the vehicle, and as having been incurred when the hiring began, and

(b) the payments to be treated as expenditure on the hiring of the vehicle shall be rateably reduced so as to amount in the aggregate to the balance.][1]

Amendments

[1] Inserted by FA08 s31(1). Applies to expenditure incurred on the provision or hiring of a vehicle on or after 1 July 2008.

Cross References

From Section 380O

Section 380L Emissions-based limits for certain cars.
Section 380M Limit on deductions, etc. for hiring cars.

To Section 380O

Section 380P Provisions supplementary to sections 380L to 380O.

380P Provisions supplementary to sections 380L to 380O

[(1) *Sections 380L* and *380M*, *subsections (2)* and *(3)* of *section 380N* and *section 380O* shall not apply where a vehicle is provided or hired, wholly or mainly, for the purpose of hire to or the carriage of members of the public in the ordinary course of trade.

(2) *Section 380L*, *subsections (2)* and *(3)* of *section 380N* and *section 380O* shall not apply in relation to a vehicle provided by a person who is a manufacturer of a vehicle to which this Part applies, or of parts or accessories for such a vehicle, if the person shows that the vehicle was provided solely for the purpose of testing the vehicle or parts or accessories for such vehicle; but, if during the period of 5 years beginning with the time when the vehicle was provided, such person puts it to any substantial extent to a use which does not serve that purpose only, this subsection shall be deemed not to have applied in relation to the vehicle.

(3) [(a) Subject to *Chapter 5* of *Part 41A*, assessments may, as necessary, be made or amended at any time for the purpose of applying *subsections (2)* and *(3)* of *section 380N*, *section 380O* and *subsection (2)*.][1]

(b) In the case of the death of a person who, if he or she had not died, would under *subsections (2)* and *(3)* of *section 380N*, *section 380O* and *subsection (2)* have become chargeable to tax for any year, the tax which would have been so chargeable shall be assessed and charged on his or her executors or administrators and shall be a debt due from and payable out of his or her estate.][2]

Amendments

[1] Substituted by FA12 sched4(part 2)(c).

[2] Inserted by FA08 s31(1). Applies to expenditure incurred on the provision or hiring of a vehicle on or after 1 July 2008.

Cross References

From Section 380P

Section 380L Emissions-based limits for certain cars.
Section 380M Limit on deductions, etc. for hiring cars.
Section 380N Cars: provisions as to hire-purchase, etc.
Section 380O Cars: provisions where hirer becomes owner.

To Section 380P

Section 380K Interpretation and general (Part 11C).

PART 11D

Income Tax and Corporation Tax: Reliefs for the Removal and Relocation of Certain Industrial Facilities

380Q Interpretation (Part 11D)

[(1) In this Part—

"*dangerous substance*" has the meaning assigned to it by [Regulation 3][1] of the European Communities (Control of Major Accident Hazards Involving Dangerous Substances) Regulations 2000 (S.I. No. 476 of 2000);

"*enhancement expenditure*", in relation to establishment land, means the amount of any capital expenditure wholly and exclusively incurred on the land for the purpose of enhancing the value of the land, being expenditure reflected in the state or nature of the land at the time of the disposal but does not include expenditure for which relief may be claimed under this Part;

"*establishment*", in relation to a person who carries on a relevant trade, means the whole area under that person's control where dangerous substances are present in one or more installations, including common or related infrastructure or activities;

"*establishment land*", in relation to a relevant trade, means the area of land of the establishment of which the old installation is a unit;

['*local authority*' means a local authority for the purposes of the Local Government Act 2001 (as amended by the *Local Government Reform Act 2014*);][2]

"*installation*" means a unit within an establishment in which dangerous substances are produced, used, handled or stored, and includes—

(a) equipment, structures, pipework, machinery and tools,

(b) docks and unloading quays serving the installation, and

(c) jetties, warehouses or similar structures, whether floating or not,

which are necessary for the operation of the installation;

"*land*" includes any interest in land and references to establishment land include references to any interest in that land;

"*market value*", in relation to the whole or part of establishment land, means the price that whole or part might reasonably be expected to fetch on a sale in the open market if the old installation was removed;

"*new installation*" means an installation which replaces an old installation;

"*old installation*" means an installation located in an urban dockland area which, by agreement with the relevant local authority, an operator relocates to facilitate the regeneration of that area;

"*operator*" means any person who in the course of a trade operates an establishment or installation;

"*relocation expenditure*" means relevant expenses incurred by a person who carries on a relevant trade in an establishment situated within an urban dockland area in relocating that trade to an establishment in a new location;

"*relevant expenses*" means capital expenditure, incurred in connection with the removal of an old installation and the set up of a replacement installation including the cost of acquiring such land as is necessary for the operation of the new installation but not including expenditure relating to—

(a) any building or structure on that land other than a building or structure which is demolished in the course of the set-up,

(b) the construction of any building or structure, or

(c) machinery or plant;

"*relevant trade*" means a trade of operating an establishment or installation;

"*urban dockland area*" means a dockland area which is the subject of either a local area plan adopted by the relevant local authority under the Planning and Development Acts 2000 to 2006 or a planning scheme approved by the Minister for the Environment, Heritage and Local Government under section 25 of the Dublin Docklands Development Authority Act 1997 and comprises an area designated by that Minister, with the approval of the Minister for Finance, to be regenerated for the purposes set out in the local area plan or planning scheme.

[(2) This Part shall apply to any expenditure incurred on or after 1 January 2009 and before 1 January 2014.][3]][4]

Amendments

[1] Substituted by FA09 s30(1)(a). This section comes into operation on the making of an order to that effect by the Minister for Finance.

[2] Substituted by LGRA14 sched2(part5).

[3] Substituted by FA09 s30(1)(b). This section comes into operation on the making of an order to that effect by the Minister for Finance.

[4] Inserted by F(No.2)A08 s21(1). This section comes into operation on the making of an order to that effect by the Minister for Finance.

Cross References

To Section 380Q

Section 380R Relocation allowance.

380R Relocation allowance

[(1) A person carrying on a relevant trade, who incurs relocation expenditure in relation to that trade, may claim an allowance (in this section referred to as a "relocation allowance") under this section in respect of that expenditure.

(2) A relocation allowance made to a person carrying on a relevant trade shall be made in taxing the trade.

(3) Where a person carrying on a relevant trade owns or owned establishment land and the whole of that land has not been disposed of at the end of the chargeable period, then the following provisions shall apply:

(a) no amount incurred in the chargeable period in respect of the cost of acquiring land may be included as relevant expenses unless the aggregate of the expenditure incurred in acquiring land necessary for the operation of the new installation in that and previous chargeable periods exceeds the market value of the establishment land at the date relevant expenses were first incurred, and

(b) for the first chargeable period in which the aggregate of the expenditure incurred in acquiring land necessary for the operation of the new installation exceeds the market value mentioned in paragraph (*a*), the amount to be included is the excess.

(4) Where a person carrying on a relevant trade owned establishment land in relation to that trade and is entitled to a relocation allowance for a chargeable period, which is or is subsequent to the first chargeable period at or before the end of which the whole of that land is disposed of, then the following provisions shall apply:

(a) no expenditure incurred in the chargeable period in respect of the cost of acquiring land may be included as relevant expenses unless the aggregate of the expenditure incurred on acquiring land necessary for the operation of the new installation in that and previous chargeable periods exceeds the total consideration received on the disposal of the establishment land reduced by any enhancement expenditure in relation to that establishment land incurred by that person at a time after all the old installations have been removed from that land, and

(b) the amount of expenditure which is included in relevant expenditure in respect of the cost of acquisition of land shall not exceed that excess.

(5) Notwithstanding *section 380Q(2)*, where, in a chargeable period, a person carrying on a relevant trade in respect of which a relocation allowance has been granted under *subsection (2)* for previous chargeable periods, disposes of the whole or part of the establishment land in relation to that trade and as a consequence the whole of the establishment land in relation to that trade is disposed of at the end of that period, then the following provisions shall apply:

(a) if the aggregate of all consideration received on disposals of all establishment land reduced by any enhancement expenditure in relation to that establishment land incurred by that person at a time after all the old installations have been removed from that land—

(i) is less than the market value mentioned in *subsection (3)(a)*, then a relocation allowance under subsection (2) shall be made in respect of the difference, in addition to a relocation allowance (if any) which may be due in respect of expenditure incurred in the chargeable period,

(ii) is greater than the market value mentioned in *subsection (3)(a)*, then the difference shall, subject to *paragraph (b)*, be treated as a trading receipt of that trade,

and

(b) the amount treated as a trading receipt of the trade under *paragraph (a)(ii)* shall not exceed the aggregate of relocation allowances in respect of establishment land allowed in previous chargeable periods.

(6) Where a person carrying on a relevant trade does not dispose of the whole of the establishment land in relation to the relevant trade within a period of 2 years beginning on the date on which that person ceases to use the old installation for the purposes of a relevant trade, then the person shall be deemed to have disposed of the establishment land in relation to that trade on the last day of the chargeable period in which that period ends for consideration equal to the aggregate of all consideration (if any) received in respect of parts of establishment land which have been disposed of and the market value of the whole or part of such land which the person owns at that date reduced by any enhancement expenditure in relation to that establishment land incurred by that person at a time after all the old installations have been removed from that land.

(7) Where land is appropriated as trading stock, *section 596(1)* shall apply for the purposes of this section, as it applies for the purposes of the Capital Gains Tax Acts.

(8) Where the relevant trade ceases before all establishment land in relation to that trade is disposed of, then the remaining land shall be deemed, for the purposes of this section, to have been disposed of on the date of cessation of the trade for its market value at that date.

(9) Where the whole or part of the establishment land is owned by a person (in this subsection referred to as the "first mentioned person") connected with the person claiming relief under this Part, then that whole or part, as the case may be, shall be treated for the purposes of this Part as owned by the person claiming relief and this Part shall apply as if all actions of the first mentioned person in relation to the whole or part were actions of the person claiming relief.][1]

Amendments

[1] Inserted by F(No.2)A08 s21(1). This section comes into operation on the making of an order to that effect by the Minister for Finance.

Cross References

From Section 380R

Section 380Q Interpretation (Part 11D).

Section 596 Appropriations to and from stock in trade.

To Section 380R

Section 380S Additional allowance for relocation expenditure.

Section 380X Restrictions on relief — non-application of relief in certain cases.

380S Additional allowance for relocation expenditure

[(1) Where a person carrying on a relevant trade incurs relocation expenditure in relation to which *section 380R* applies, there shall, in addition to any relocation allowance made in respect of such expenditure, be made to the person in taxing the trade for the chargeable period for which such relocation allowance is made, an additional relocation allowance (which shall be known as an "additional relocation allowance") equal to 50 per cent of the expenditure and *section 380R(2)* shall apply to such additional relocation allowance as if it were an allowance under that subsection.

(2) Where, in a chargeable period, an amount is treated as a trading receipt of a trade under [*section 380R(5)(a)(ii)*][1], an additional amount equal to 50 per cent of that amount shall also be treated as a trading receipt of the trade for that chargeable period.][2]

Amendments

[1] Substituted by FA09 s30(1)(c). This section comes into operation on the making of an order to that effect by the Minister for Finance.

[2] Inserted by F(No.2)A08 s21(1). This section comes into operation on the making of an order to that effect by the Minister for Finance.

Cross References

From Section 380S

Section 380R Relocation allowance.

To Section 380S

Section 380X Restrictions on relief — non-application of relief in certain cases.

380T Allowance for machinery or plant

[(1) Where, for any chargeable period, expenditure incurred by a person on a new installation includes expenditure (in this section referred to as "qualifying expenditure') on the provision of new machinery or new plant (other than vehicles suitable for the conveyance by road of persons or goods or the haulage by road of other vehicles) provided for use in the relevant trade, then the following provisions shall apply:

(a) that person may claim that the wear and tear allowance to be made under *section 284* to the person in respect of that expenditure is to be determined as if the reference to 12.5 per cent in *section 284(2)(ad)* were a reference to 100 per cent, and

(b) there shall be made to the person for the chargeable period related to the expenditure an allowance equal to 50 per cent of the qualifying expenditure in relation to that plant or machinery, and such allowance shall be made in taxing the relevant trade.

(2) For the purposes of ascertaining the amount of any allowance to be made to any person under *section 284* in respect of expenditure incurred during a chargeable period on any qualifying machinery or plant, no account shall be taken of an allowance under *subsection (1)(b)* in respect of that expenditure, and in *section 284(4)* "the allowances on that account" and "the allowances" where it occurs before "exceed" shall each be construed as not including a reference to any allowance made under *subsection (1)(b)* to the person by whom the relevant trade is carried on.][1]

Amendments

[1] Inserted by F(No.2)A08 s21(1). This section comes into operation on the making of an order to that effect by the Minister for Finance.

Cross References

From Section 380T

Section 284 Wear and tear allowances.

To Section 380T

Section 380V Improvement.

Section 380W Supplementary provisions.

Section 380X Restrictions on relief — non-application of relief in certain cases.

380U Allowances in respect of certain buildings

[Where a person carrying on a relevant trade incurs expenditure (in this section referred to as "qualifying expenditure') on a new installation which includes capital expenditure on the construction of a new building or structure which is to be an industrial building or structure to be occupied for the purposes of that trade, then the following provisions shall apply:

(a) section 271 shall apply as if—

(i) in subsection (1) of that section the definition of "industrial development agency' were deleted,

(ii) in subsection (2)(*a*)(i) of that section "to which subsection (3) applies' were deleted,

(iii) subsection (3) of that section were deleted,

(iv) the following subsection were substituted for subsection (4) of that section:

"(4) An industrial building allowance shall be of an amount equal to 100 per cent of the capital expenditure mentioned in subsection (2).',

and

(v) in subsection (5) of that section "to which subsection (3)(*c*) applies' were deleted,

and

(b) there shall be made to that person for the chargeable period related to the expenditure an allowance equal to 50 per cent of the qualifying expenditure in relation to that building or structure, and such allowance shall be made in taxing the relevant trade.][1]

Amendments

[1] Inserted by F(No.2)A08 s21(1). This section comes into operation on the making of an order to that effect by the Minister for Finance.

Cross References

From Section 380U

Section 271 Industrial building allowances.

To Section 380U

Section 380V Improvement.

Section 380W Supplementary provisions.

Section 380X Restrictions on relief — non-application of relief in certain cases.

380V Improvement

[(1) A new installation is an improved installation where its capacity is greater or it has improved efficiency or productivity beyond normal modernisation or upgrading than the old installation which it replaced.

(2) Where expenditure incurred on the provision of an improved installation includes expenditure on new machinery or new plant or on the construction of a new building or structure which is to be an industrial building or structure to be occupied for the purposes of [a relevant trade][1], then the amount of that expenditure qualifying for relief under *section 380T(1)(b)* or [*380U(b)*][2] shall be the expenditure on the new machinery or the new plant or on the construction of a new building or structure, as the case may be, reduced by an amount representing improvement and the amount of expenditure representing improvement shall be such proportion of the expenditure in relation to the new machinery or new plant or in relation to the construction of a new building or structure, as the case may be, as appears to the inspector (or on appeal, the Appeal Commissioners) to be just and reasonable as representing costs relating to providing increased capacity or improved efficiency or productivity.][3]

Amendments

[1] Substituted by FA09 s30(1)(d)(i). This section comes into operation on the making of an order to that effect by the Minister for Finance.

[2] Substituted by FA09 s30(1)(d)(ii). This section comes into operation on the making of an order to that effect by the Minister for Finance.

[3] Inserted by F(No.2)A08 s21(1). This section comes into operation on the making of an order to that effect by the Minister for Finance.

Cross References

From Section 380V

Section 380T Allowance for machinery or plant.

Section 380U Allowances in respect of certain buildings.

380W Supplementary provisions

[(1) Where an allowance under *section 380T(1)(b)* or [*380U(b)*][1] has been made to any person in respect of expenditure incurred on the provision of machinery or plant or on the construction of a building or structure and the machinery or plant or building or structure is sold by that person without the machinery or plant or building or structure having been used by that person for the purposes of a relevant trade or before the expiration of the period of 2 years from the day on which the machinery or plant or, as the case may be, the building or structure, began to be so used, then the allowance under those sections shall be withdrawn and [all such assessments and amendments of assessments][2] shall be made as may be necessary for or in consequence of the withdrawal of the allowance.

(2) For the purposes of this Part, capital expenditure does not include any expenditure which is allowed to be deducted in computing for the purposes of tax the profits or gains of a trade carried on by the person incurring the expenditure.

(3) Where relief is given by any provision of this Part in relation to relocation expenditure, then relief shall not be given in respect of that expenditure under any other provision of the [Tax][3] Acts.

(4) Chapter 4 of Part 9 shall apply as if this Part were contained in that Part.][4]

Amendments

[1] Substituted by FA09 s30(1)(e)(i). This section comes into operation on the making of an order to that effect by the Minister for Finance.

[2] Substituted by FA12 sched4(part 2)(g).

[3] Substituted by FA09 s30(1)(e)(ii). This section comes into operation on the making of an order to that effect by the Minister for Finance.

[4] Inserted by F(No.2)A08 s21(1). This section comes into operation on the making of an order to that effect by the Minister for Finance.

Cross References

From Section 380W

Section 380T Allowance for machinery or plant.

Section 380U Allowances in respect of certain buildings.

380X Restrictions on relief—non-application of relief in certain cases

[Notwithstanding any other provision of this Part, no allowances under *sections 380R*, *380S*, *380T* and *380U* shall be made in relation to expenditure—

(a) where any part of such expenditure has been or is to be met, directly or indirectly, by grant assistance or any other assistance which is granted by or through the State, any board established by statute, any public or local authority or any other agency of the State,

(b) unless the potential allowances in relation to that expenditure comply with—

(i) the requirements of the Guidelines on National Regional Aid for 2007-2013 prepared by the Commission of the European Communities and issued on 4 March 2006*,

*OJ No. C54 of 4 March 2006, p.13.

(ii) the National Regional Aid Map for Ireland for the period 1 January 2007 to 31 December 2013 which was approved by the Commission of the European Communities on 24 October 2006*, and

*OJ No. C292 of 1 December 2006, p. 11.

(iii) the requirements of the Community Guidelines on State Aid for Environmental Protection prepared by the Commission of the European Communities and issued on 1 April 2008*,

*OJ No. C 82 of 1 April 2008, p. 1.

(c) where the person who is entitled to the allowances in relation to that expenditure is subject to an outstanding recovery order following a previous decision of the Commission of the European Communities declaring aid in favour of that person to be illegal and incompatible with the common market,

or

(d) where the person who is entitled to the allowances is a person in difficulty under the Community Guidelines on State Aid for Rescuing and Restructuring Firms in Difficulty*.][1]

*OJ No. C288 of 9 October 1999, p. 2, and OJ No. C244 of 1 October 2004, p. 2.

Amendments

[1] Inserted by F(No.2)A08 s21(1). This section comes into operation on the making of an order to that effect by the Minister for Finance.

Cross References

From Section 380X

Section 380R Relocation allowance.
Section 380S Additional allowance for relocation expenditure.
Section 380T Allowance for machinery or plant.
Section 380U Allowances in respect of certain buildings.

PART 12

Principal Provisions Relating to Loss Relief, Treatment of Certain Losses and Capital Allowances, and Group Relief

CHAPTER 1

Income Tax: Loss Relief

381 Right to repayment of tax by reference to losses

[ITA67 s307(1), (1AAA) and (2) to (6); F(MP)A68 s3(2) and Sch PtI; FA74 s26; FA79 s17; FA80 s19 and Sch1 PtIII; FA97 s146(2) and Sch9 PtII]

(1) Subject to [this section and *sections 381A, 381B* and *381C*][1], where in any year of assessment any person has sustained a loss in any trade, profession or employment carried on by that person either solely or in partnership, that person shall be entitled, on making a claim in that behalf, to such repayment of income tax as is necessary to secure that the aggregate amount of income tax for the year ultimately borne by that person will not exceed the amount which would have been borne by that person if the income of that person had been reduced by the amount of the loss.

(2) This section shall not apply to any loss sustained in any year of assessment by the owner of a stallion from the sale of services of mares by the stallion or of rights to such services or by the part-owner of a stallion from the sale of such services or such rights.

[(2A) *Subsection (2)* shall cease to have effect as respects losses arising on or after 1 August 2008 and, as respects the chargeable period in which 1 August 2008 occurs, the amount of such losses will be determined by the formula—

$$A \times \frac{B}{C}$$

where—

A is the total amount of losses arising in the chargeable period,

B is the length, in days, of the period beginning on 1 August 2008 and ending on the last day of the chargeable period in which 1 August 2008 occurs, and

C is the length, in days, of the chargeable period.][2]

(3) (a) In this subsection, "*appropriate income*" means either earned or unearned income according as income arising during the same period as the loss to the person sustaining the loss from the same activity would have been that person's earned or unearned income.

(b) For the purposes of *subsection (1)*, the amount of income tax which would have been borne if income had been reduced by the amount of a loss shall be computed—

(i) where the loss has been sustained by an individual, on the basis of treating the loss as reducing—

(I) firstly, the appropriate income of the individual,

(II) secondly, the other income of the individual,

[(III) thirdly, in a case—

(A) where the individual, or, being a husband or wife, the individual's spouse, is assessed to tax in accordance with *section 1017*, the appropriate income of the individual's wife or husband, as the case may be, or

(B) where the individual, or the individual's civil partner, is assessed to tax in accordance with *section 1031C*, the appropriate income of the individual's civil partner,

and][3]

(IV) finally, the other income of the [individual's wife, husband or civil partner,][4] as the case may be, and

(ii) where the loss has been sustained in a trade carried on by a body corporate, on the basis of treating the loss as reducing—

(I) firstly, the income of the body corporate from profits or gains of the trade in which the loss was sustained, and

(II) then, the other income of the body corporate.

(4) The amount of a loss sustained in an activity shall for the purposes of this section be computed in the like manner as profits or gains arising or accruing from the activity would be computed under the relevant provisions of the Income Tax Acts.

(5) Where repayment has been made to a person for any year under this section—

(a) no portion of the loss which in the computation of the repayment was treated as reducing the person's income shall be taken into account in computing the amount of an assessment for any subsequent year, and

(b) so much of the loss as was required by *subsection (3)* to be treated as reducing income of a particular class or income from a particular source shall for the purposes of the Income Tax Acts be regarded as a deduction to be made from income of that class or from income from that source, as the case may be, in computing the person's total income for the year.

(6) Any claim to repayment under this section shall be made, in a form prescribed by the Revenue Commissioners, not later than 2 years after the end of the year of assessment and shall be made to and determined by the inspector; but any person aggrieved by any determination of the inspector on any such claim may, on giving notice in writing to the inspector within 21 days after notification to that person of the determination, appeal to the Appeal Commissioners.

(7) The Appeal Commissioners shall hear and determine an appeal to them under *subsection (6)* as if it were an appeal to them against an assessment to income tax, and the provisions of the Income Tax Acts relating to the rehearing of an appeal and to the statement of a case for the opinion of the High Court on a point of law shall, with the necessary modifications, apply accordingly.

Amendments

[1] Substituted by FA14 s11(1)(a). Applies as respects a basis period for a year of assessment which commences after 23 October 2014.

[2] Inserted by FA07 s26(1)(a). With effect from 1 August 2008 per S.I. No. 160 of 2008.

[3] Substituted by F(No.3)A11 sched1(59).

[4] Substituted by F(No.3)A11 sched1(60).

Revenue Briefings

Tax Briefing

Tax Briefing April 2002 – Issue 47 pg 26 – Income Tax Losses

Cross References

From Section 381

Section 1017 Assessment of husband in respect of income of both spouses.

To Section 381

Section 21B Tax treatment of certain dividends.
Section 23A Company residence.
Section 80A Taxation of certain short-term leases plant and machinery.
Section 82 Pre-trading expenditure.
Section 110 Securitisation.
Section 141 Distributions out of income from patent royalties.
Section 153 Distributions to certain nonresidents.
Section 172D Exemption from dividend withholding tax for certain non-resident persons.
Section 247 Relief to companies on loans applied in acquiring interest in other companies.
Section 286A Wear and tear allowances for licences for public hire vehicles.
Section 305 Income tax: manner of granting, and effect of, allowances made by means of discharge or repayment of tax.
Section 355 Disclaimer of capital allowances on holiday cottages, holiday apartments, etc.
Section 382 Right to carry forward losses to future years.
Section 391 Interpretation (Chapter 2).
Section 392 Option to treat capital allowances as creating or augmenting a loss.
Section 394 Effect of giving relief under section 381 by reference to capital allowances.
Section 403 Restriction on use of capital allowances for certain leased assets.
Section 404 Restriction on use of capital allowances for certain leased machinery or plant.
Section 405 Restriction on use of capital allowances on holiday cottages.
Section 409C Income tax: restriction on use of losses on approved buildings.
Section 409D Restriction of reliefs where individual is not actively participating in certain trades.
Section 443 Meaning of "goods".
Section 450 Double taxation relief.
Section 480A Relief on retirement for certain income of certain sportspersons.
Section 487 Corporation tax: credit for bank levy.
Section 531AU Capital allowances and losses.
Section 616 Groups of companies: interpretation.
Section 626B Exemption from tax in the case of gains on disposals of shares.
Section 644AA Treatment of losses from dealing in residential development land.
Section 657 Averaging of farm profits.
Section 662 Income tax: restriction of relief for losses in farming or market gardening.
Section 687 Treatment of losses.
Section 695 Abandonment expenditure: allowances and loss relief.
Section 697LA Transactions between associated persons and between tonnage tax trade and other activities of same company.
Section 730A Profits of life business: new basis.
Section 730K Disposal of foreign life policy.
Section 747E Disposal of an interest in offshore funds.
Section 751 Traders other than dealers in securities.
Section 753 Restriction on relief for losses by repayment of tax in case of dividends paid out of accumulated profits.
Section 766 Tax credit for research and development expenditure.
Section 817 Schemes to avoid liability to tax under Schedule F.
Section 847 Tax relief for certain branch profits.
Section 1012 Modification of provisions as to appeals.
Section 1013 Limited partnerships.
Section 1085 Corporation tax — late returns: restriction of certain claims for relief.
Schedule 22 Dividends Regarded as Paid Out of Profits Accumulated Before Given Date
Schedule 24 Relief from Income Tax and Corporation Tax by Means of Credit in Respect of Foreign Tax

381A Restriction of loss relief in certain cases

[(1) In this section—

"*aggregate income for the tax year*" has the same meaning as in *section 531AL*;

"*specified loss*", in relation to a tax year and a specified trade, means any loss sustained in the course of the specified trade, which is referable to a deduction allowed in computing the profits or gains of the trade, in respect of either or both—

(a) interest on borrowed money employed in the purchase or development of land which is held as trading stock (within the meaning of *section 89*) of the trade, and

(b) any reduction in the value of land held as trading stock (within the meaning of *section 89*) of the trade;

"*specified trade*" means a trade, or a business which is deemed to be a trade by virtue of *section 640(2)(a)*, consisting of or including dealing in or developing land to which *Chapter 1* of *Part 22* applies;

"*specified trader*", in relation to a specified trade and a tax year, means an individual in respect of whom that part of the total of the individual's aggregate income for the tax year and the 2 immediately preceding tax years deriving from the specified trade is less than 50 per cent of the total for those 3 tax years of the individual's aggregate income for the tax year;

"*tax year*" means a year of assessment.

(2) Subject to *subsection (3)*, a claim to repayment of income tax under *section 381* may not be made as respects a specified loss sustained by a specified trader in a tax year where the specified loss—

(a) is in respect of interest, unless the interest has been paid, or

(b) is in respect of a reduction in the value of land, unless the loss has been realised by way of a disposal of the land,

prior to the claim being made.

(3) *Section 381* shall not apply as respects any specified loss where the disposal of the land to which *subsection (2)(b)* refers is to a connected person (within the meaning of *section 10*).

(4) For the purposes of determining the amount of any interest which has been paid, and which is referable to a specified loss sustained in any particular tax year, interest is treated as having been paid in respect of an earlier tax year in preference to a later tax year.

(5) For the purposes of determining the amount of a specified loss sustained in any particular tax year which is referable to a deduction allowed in respect of either interest or a reduction in the value of land—

(a) the deduction allowed in respect of interest is treated as being deducted after all other deductions, and

(b) the deduction allowed in respect of a reduction in the value of land is treated as being deducted immediately prior to the deduction allowed in respect of interest.][1]

Amendments

[1] Inserted by FA13 s18(1)(d). Comes into operation in respect of interest becoming payable or a reduction in the value of land held as trading stock (within the meaning of section 89) occurring on or after 13 February 2013.

381B Restriction of loss relief — passive trades

[(1) (a) In this section 'relevant loss' means a loss in a trade or profession (including any amount in respect of allowances which, pursuant to *section 392*, is to be treated as a loss for the purposes of *section 381*) but does not include a loss which arises from—

(i) farming, within the meaning of *Part 23*,

(ii) market gardening,

(iii) a trade which consists of the underwriting business of a member of Lloyd's,

(iv) any amount in respect of qualifying expenditure which by virtue of *section 482(2)* is to be treated as a loss, or

(v) any amount in respect of specified capital allowances, within the meaning of *section 531AAE*, which pursuant to *section 392* is to be treated as a loss.

(b) For the purposes of this section—

(i) an individual carries on a trade in a non-active capacity during a period if the individual does not work for the greater part of his or her time on the day to day management or conduct of the trade or profession during that period, and

(ii) an individual does not work for the greater part of his or her time on the day to day management or conduct of the trade or profession during a period unless, over the course of that period, he or she spends an average of at least 10 hours a week personally engaged in the activities of the trade or profession and those activities are carried on on a commercial basis and in such a way that profits of the trade or profession could reasonably be expected to be made in that period or within a reasonable time afterwards.

(2) (a) Subject to *paragraphs (b)* and *(c)*, where a person carries on a trade or profession in a non-active capacity during a year of assessment then for the purposes of *section 381*, the amount of any relevant loss sustained by that person in that trade or profession in that year of assessment shall be the actual amount of the loss so sustained, or €31,750, whichever is the lower.

(b) Where the basis period for a year of assessment is shorter than 12 months, then the reference to €31,750 in *paragraph (a)* shall be construed as €31,750 reduced in the proportion that the length of the basis period bears to 12 months.

(c) Where a person carries on 2 or more trades or professions to which this subsection applies, then for the purposes of *section 381*, the aggregate of the amount of the losses sustained by that person in those trades or professions in any year of assessment shall be the aggregate of the actual amount of the losses so sustained, or €31,750, whichever is the lower.][1]

Amendments

[1] Inserted by FA14 s11(1)(b). Applies as respects the year of assessment 2015 and subsequent years of assessment.

381C Restriction of loss relief — anti-avoidance

[(1) (a) In this section—

'arrangements' includes any agreement, understanding, scheme, transaction or series of transactions (whether or not legally enforceable);

'relevant loss' means a loss in a trade or profession (including any amount in respect of allowances which, pursuant to *section 392*, is to be treated as a loss for the purposes of *section 381*) but does not include a loss which arises from—

(i) any amount in respect of qualifying expenditure which by virtue of *section 482(2)* is to be treated as a loss, or

(ii) any amount in respect of specified capital allowances, within the meaning of *section 531AAE*, which by virtue of *section 392* is to be treated as a loss;

'relevant period for a year of assessment' means the basis period for the year of assessment, or where that basis period is shorter than 6 months—

(i) where the basis period is determined in accordance with *section 67(1)(a)*, a period of 6 months ending on the last day of that basis period, or

(ii) in all other cases, a period of 6 months starting on the first day of the basis period;

'relevant tax avoidance arrangements' means arrangements the main purpose, or one of the main purposes of which, is to give rise to a claim under *section 381*.

(b) For the purposes of this section—

(i) an individual carries on a trade in a non-active capacity during the relevant period for a year of assessment if the individual does not work for the greater part of his or her time on the day to day management or conduct of the trade or profession during that period, and

(ii) an individual does not work for the greater part of his or her time on the day to day management or conduct of the trade or profession during the relevant period for a year of assessment unless, over the course of that period, he or she spends an average of at least 10 hours a week personally engaged in the activities of the trade or profession and those activities are carried on on a commercial basis and in such a way that profits of the trade or profession could reasonably be expected to be made in that relevant period for a year of assessment or within a reasonable time afterwards.

(2) Where a person carries on a trade or profession in a non-active capacity in the relevant period for a year of assessment and sustains a relevant loss in that trade or profession for that year of assessment and that loss arises in whole or in part, directly or indirectly, in consequence of or otherwise in connection with relevant tax avoidance arrangements, then for the purposes of *section 381* that person shall be deemed not to have sustained a loss in that trade or profession for that year of assessment.][1]

Amendments

[1] Inserted by FA14 s11(1)(c). Applies as respects a basis period for a year of assessment which commences after 23 October 2014.

382 Right to carry forward losses to future years

[ITA67 s309(1) and (2); FA96 s132(2) and Sch5 PtII; FA97 s146(1) and Sch9 PtI par1(21)]

(1) Where, in any trade or profession carried on by a person, either solely or in partnership, such person has sustained a loss (to be computed in the like manner as profits or gains under the provisions of the Income Tax Acts applicable to Cases I and II of Schedule D) in respect of which relief has not been wholly given under *section 381* or under any other provision of the Income Tax Acts, such person may claim that any portion of the loss for which relief has not been so given shall be carried forward and, in so far as may be, deducted from or set off against the amount of profits or gains on which such person is assessed under Schedule D in respect of that trade or profession for any subsequent year of assessment, except that, if and in so far as relief in respect of any loss has been given to any person under this section, that person shall not be entitled to claim relief in respect of that loss under any other provision of the Income Tax Acts.

(2) Any relief under this section shall be given as far as possible from the assessment for the first subsequent year of assessment and, in so far as it cannot be so given, from the assessment for the next year of assessment and so on.

Case Law

Trading losses forward are not available for offset against personal investment income. Rigby v Samson (HM Inspector of Taxes) 1997 STC 524

Section 381 loss must be set off in priority to annual payment. Navan Carpets Ltd v O'Culachain III ITR 403

If the tax loss of one period of account is used to produce losses in the basis period for more than one year of assessment, the relief claimed for such losses by carry forward under section 382 TCA 1997 cannot exceed the actual tax loss sustained in the period of account. IRC v Scott Adamson 17 TC 679

Revenue Briefings

Tax Briefing

Tax Briefing April 2002 – Issue 47 pg 26 – Income Tax Losses

Revenue Precedents

Losses of farming partnership trade are not available for carry forward against profits of farming sole trade which farmer commences subsequently. IT892034

Cross References

From Section 382

Section 381 Right to repayment of tax by reference to losses.

To Section 382

Section 66 Special basis at commencement of trade or profession.

Section 67 Special basis on discontinuance of trade or profession.

Section 390 Amount of assessment made under section 238 to be allowed as a loss for certain purposes.

Section 531AM Charge to universal social charge.

Section 531AU Capital allowances and losses.

Section 644AA Treatment of losses from dealing in residential development land.

Section 657 Averaging of farm profits.

Section 661 Farming: restriction of relief in respect of certain losses.

Section 666 Deduction for increase in stock values.

Schedule 25B List of Specified Reliefs and Method of Determining Amount of Specified Relief Used in a Tax Year

Schedule 25C Determination of Amount of Relief to be Treated as Referable to Specified Reliefs as Respects Relief Carried Forward from Tax Year 2006 to Tax Year 2007

383 Relief under Case IV for losses

[ITA67 s310; FA97 s146(1) and Sch9 PtI par1(22)]

(1) Where in any year of assessment a person sustains a loss in any transaction (being a transaction of such kind that, if any profits had arisen from the transaction, such person would have been liable to be assessed in respect of those profits under Case IV of Schedule D) in which such person engages, whether solely or in partnership, such person may claim for the purposes of the Income Tax Acts that the amount of that loss shall, as far as may be, be deducted from or set off against the amount of profits or gains on which such person is assessed under Case IV of Schedule D for that year and that any portion of the loss for which relief is not so given shall be carried forward and, in so far as may be, deducted from or set off against the amount of profits or gains on which such person is assessed under that Case for any subsequent year of assessment.

(2) In the application of this section to a loss sustained by a partner in a partnership, "the amount of profits or gains on which such person is assessed" shall, in respect of any year, be taken to mean such portion of the amount on which the partnership is assessed under Case IV of Schedule D as the partner would be required under the Income Tax Acts to include in a return of the partner's total income for that year.

(3) Any relief under this section by means of carrying forward any portion of a loss shall be given as far as possible from the assessment for the first subsequent year of assessment and, in so far as it cannot be so given, from the assessment for the next year of assessment and so on.

Cross References

To Section 383

Section 669K Miscellaneous (Chapter 4).

Section 687 Treatment of losses.

Section 730K Disposal of foreign life policy.

Section 747E Disposal of an interest in offshore funds.

Section 814 Taxation of income deemed to arise from transactions in certificates of deposit and assignable deposits.

Schedule 25B List of Specified Reliefs and Method of Determining Amount of Specified Relief Used in a Tax Year

384 Relief under Case V for losses

[ITA67 s89; FA69 s24; FA90 s18(1)(b) and (c); FA97 s146(1) and Sch9 PtI par1(7)]

(1) In this section, "*the person chargeable*" has the same meaning as in *Chapter 8* of *Part 4*.

(2) Where in any year of assessment the aggregate amount of the deficiencies computed in accordance with *section 97(1)* exceeds the aggregate of the surpluses as so computed, the excess shall be carried forward and, in so far as may be, deducted from or set off against the amount of profits or gains on which the person chargeable is assessed under Case V of Schedule D for any subsequent year of assessment, and if income tax has been overpaid the amount overpaid shall be repaid.

[(2A) Where *section 372AP(7)* applies, the amount of the excess, which by virtue of *subsection (2)* has been carried forward to a year of assessment in which either of the events referred to in *section 372AP(7)* occurs, shall be reduced by the amount represented by B in the formula in that section and this section shall not apply in that year of assessment or in any subsequent year of assessment to the amount of that reduction.][1]

(3) [Subject to *subsection (4)*, any][2] relief under this section shall be given as far as possible from the assessment for the first subsequent year of assessment and, in so far as it cannot be so given, from the assessment for the next year of assessment and so on.

[(4) Any allowance to be made in charging income under Case V of Schedule D in accordance with *section 305(1)(a)* shall be made in priority to any relief to be given under this section.][3]

Amendments

[1] Inserted by FA12 s16(2). Applies to an event referred to in paragraph (a) or (b) of section 372AP(7) that occurs on or after 1 January 2012.

[2] Substituted by FA10 s(15)(a). Deemed to have come into force and takes effect as on and from 1 January 2010.

[3] Inserted by FA10 s(15)(b). Deemed to have come into force and takes effect as on and from 1 January 2010.

Revenue Briefings

eBrief

eBrief No. 65/2011 – Recording of Losses Forward on Form CT1

Cross References

From Section 384

Section 52 Persons chargeable.

Section 96 Interpretation (Chapter 8).

Section 97 Computational rules and allowable deductions.

Section 305 Income tax: manner of granting, and effect of, allowances made by means of discharge or repayment of tax.

To Section 384

Section 75 Case V: basis of assessment.

Section 372AP Relief for lessors.

Schedule 25B List of Specified Reliefs and Method of Determining Amount of Specified Relief Used in a Tax Year

Schedule 25C Determination of Amount of Relief to be Treated as Referable to Specified Reliefs as Respects Relief Carried Forward from Tax Year 2006 to Tax Year 2007

385 Terminal loss

[ITA67 s311]

(1) Where a trade or profession is permanently discontinued, and any person carrying on the trade or profession either solely or in partnership immediately before the time of the discontinuance has sustained in the trade or profession a loss to which this section applies (in this Chapter referred to as a "*terminal loss*"), then, subject to *sections 386* to *389*, that person may claim for the purposes of the Income Tax Acts that the amount of the terminal loss shall, as far as may be, be deducted from or set off against the amount of profits or gains on which that person has been charged to income tax under Schedule D in respect of the trade or profession for the 3 years of assessment last preceding that in which the discontinuance occurs, and there shall be made all such amendments of assessments or repayments of tax as may be necessary to give effect to the claim.

(2) Relief shall not be given in respect of the same matter both under this section and under any other provision of the Income Tax Acts.

(3) Any relief under this section shall be given as far as possible from the assessment for a later rather than an earlier year.

Cross References

From Section 385

Section 386 Determination of terminal loss.

Section 389 Determination of claim for terminal loss.

To Section 385

Section 386 Determination of terminal loss.

Section 387 Calculation of amount of profits or gains for purposes of terminal loss.

Section 388 Meaning of "permanently discontinued" for purposes of terminal loss.

Section 389 Determination of claim for terminal loss.

Section 390 Amount of assessment made under section 238 to be allowed as a loss for certain purposes.

Section 644AA Treatment of losses from dealing in residential development land.

Section 666 Deduction for increase in stock values.

Schedule 25B List of Specified Reliefs and Method of Determining Amount of Specified Relief Used in a Tax Year

386 Determination of terminal loss

[ITA67 s312; FA96 s131(2) and Sch5 PtI par1(16)]

(1) In this section, "*the relevant capital allowances*", in relation to any year of assessment, means the capital allowances to be made in charging the profits or gains of the trade or profession for that year, excluding amounts carried forward from an earlier year, and for the purposes of *paragraphs (a)* and *(c)* of *subsection (2)* the amount of a loss shall be computed in the like manner as profits or gains are computed under the provisions of the Income Tax Acts applicable to Cases I and II of Schedule D.

(2) The question whether a person has sustained any, and if so what, terminal loss in a trade or profession shall for the purposes of *section 385* be determined by taking the amounts, if any, of the following (in so far as they have not been otherwise taken into account so as to reduce or relieve any charge to income tax)—

(a) the loss sustained by the person in the trade or profession in the year of assessment in which it is permanently discontinued;

(b) the relevant capital allowances for that year of assessment;

(c) the loss sustained by the person in the trade or profession in the part of the preceding year of assessment beginning 12 months before the date of the discontinuance;

(d) the same fraction of the relevant capital allowances for that preceding year of assessment as the part beginning 12 months before the date of the discontinuance is of a year.

Cross References

From Section 386

Section 385 Terminal loss.

To Section 386

Section 385 Terminal loss.

Section 388 Meaning of "permanently discontinued" for purposes of terminal loss.

Section 644AA Treatment of losses from dealing in residential development land.

387 Calculation of amount of profits or gains for purposes of terminal loss

[ITA67 s313(1) and (2)]

(1) The amount of the profits or gains on which a person has been charged to income tax for any year of assessment in respect of the profits or gains of a trade or profession shall, for the purposes of relief under *section 385* from the

assessment for that year, be taken to be the full amount of the profits or gains on which the person was assessable for that year reduced by—

(a) a sum equal to the total amount of the deductions, if any, in respect of capital allowances made in charging the profits or gains,

(b) a sum equal to the amount of the deductions, if any, in respect of payments made or losses sustained, which were to be made from the profits or gains in computing for income tax purposes the person's total income for the year, or would have been so made if the person were an individual, and

(c) in the case of a body of persons, a sum equal to so much of the profits or gains as was applied in payment of dividends;

but, where any deduction mentioned in *paragraph (b)* may be treated in whole or in part either as having been made from the profits or gains or as having been made from other income, the deduction shall, as far as may be, be treated for the purposes of this subsection as made from the other income.

(2) Where under *subsection (1)(b)* the amount of the profits or gains on which a person was assessable for any year is reduced by reference to a payment made by the person, a like reduction shall be made in the amount of the terminal loss for which relief may be given under *section 385* for earlier years unless the payment was made wholly and exclusively for the purposes of the trade or profession.

Cross References

From Section 387

Section 385 Terminal loss.

388 Meaning of "*permanently discontinued*" for purposes of terminal loss

[ITA67 s314(1)]

For the purposes of *sections 385* to *389*, a trade or profession shall be treated as permanently discontinued and a new trade or profession set up or commenced when it is so treated for the purposes of *section 69*, or where by reference to *section 1008(1)(a)(ii)* a several trade of a partner has been deemed to have been permanently discontinued; but—

(a) a person who continues to be engaged in carrying on the trade or profession immediately after such a discontinuance shall not be entitled to relief in respect of any terminal loss on that discontinuance, and

(b) on any discontinuance, a person not continuing to be so engaged may be given relief in respect of a terminal loss against profits or gains on which the person was charged in respect of the same trade or profession for a period before a previous discontinuance, if the person has been continuously engaged in carrying on the trade or profession between the 2 discontinuances, and, in the person's case, if the previous discontinuance occurred within 12 months before the others, it shall be disregarded for the purposes of *section 386(2)*.

Cross References

From Section 388

Section 69 Changes of proprietorship.
Section 385 Terminal loss.
Section 386 Determination of terminal loss.
Section 389 Determination of claim for terminal loss.
Section 1008 Separate assessment of partners.

389 Determination of claim for terminal loss

[ITA67 s315; F(MP)A68 s3(2) and Sch PtI]

(1) Any claim under *section 385* shall be made to and determined by the inspector, but any person aggrieved by any decision of the inspector on any such claim may, on giving notice in writing to the inspector within 21 days after the notification to that person of the decision, appeal to the Appeal Commissioners.

(2) The Appeal Commissioners shall hear and determine an appeal to them under *subsection (1)* as if it were an appeal against an assessment to income tax, and the provisions of the Income Tax Acts relating to the rehearing of an appeal and to the statement of a case for the opinion of the High Court on a point of law shall, with the necessary modifications, apply accordingly.

Cross References

From Section 389

Section 385 Terminal loss.

To Section 389

Section 385 Terminal loss.
Section 388 Meaning of "permanently discontinued" for purposes of terminal loss.
Section 390 Amount of assessment made under section 238 to be allowed as a loss for certain purposes.
Section 644AA Treatment of losses from dealing in residential development land.

390 Amount of assessment made under section 238 to be allowed as a loss for certain purposes

[ITA67 s316; FA96 s132(1) and Sch5 PtI par 1(17); FA97 s29(3), (5) and (6)]

(1) Subject to this section, where a person has been assessed to income tax for a year of assessment under *section 238* in respect of a payment made wholly and exclusively for the purposes of a trade or profession, the amount on which income tax has been paid under that assessment shall for the purposes of *sections 382* and *385* to *389* be treated as if it were a loss sustained in that trade or profession and relief in respect of such loss shall be allowed accordingly; but no relief shall be allowed under this section in respect of any such payment or any part of such payment which is not ultimately borne by the person assessed or which is charged to capital.

(2) (a) This subsection shall apply to expenditure incurred for the purposes of a trade or profession which is set up and commenced on or after the 22nd day of January, 1997.

(b) Where an individual who has set up and commenced a trade or profession has been assessed to tax for any year of assessment under *section 238* in respect of a payment made—

(i) before the time the trade or profession has been set up and commenced, and

(ii) wholly and exclusively for the purposes of the trade or profession,

then, this section shall apply in relation to the payment as it would apply if the payment were made at that time.

(c) An allowance or deduction shall not be made under any provision of the Tax Acts, other than this section, in respect of any expenditure or payment which is treated under this section as incurred on the day on which a trade or profession is set up and commenced.

(3) This section shall not apply to any sum assessed under *section 238* by virtue of *section 246(2)*, *757* or *1041(1)*.

Cross References

From Section 390

Section 238 Annual payments not payable out of taxed income.
Section 246 Interest payments by companies and to non-residents.
Section 382 Right to carry forward losses to future years.
Section 385 Terminal loss.
Section 389 Determination of claim for terminal loss.
Section 757 Charges on capital sums received for sale of patent rights.
Section 1041 Rents payable to non-residents.

To Section 390

Section 690 Interest and charges on income.

CHAPTER 2

Income Tax: Loss Relief—Treatment of Capital Allowances

391 Interpretation (Chapter 2)

[ITA67 s317(1), (2)(b), (c) and (d) and s322; FA69 s65(1) and Sch5 PtI; FA75 s33(2) and Sch1 PtII; FA97 s146(2) and Sch9 PtII]

(1) In this Chapter—

"*balancing charges*" means balancing charges under *Part 9* or *Chapter 1* of *Part 29*;

"*year of claim*", in relation to any claim under *section 381*, means the year of assessment for which the claim is made.

(2) For the purposes of this Chapter—

(a) any reference to capital allowances or balancing charges for a year of assessment shall be construed as a reference to those to be made in charging the profits or gains of the trade for that year, excluding, in the case of allowances, amounts carried forward from an earlier year,

(b) effect shall be deemed to be given in charging the profits or gains of the trade for a year of assessment to allowances carried forward from an earlier year before it is given to allowances for the year of assessment, and

(c) any reference to an amount of capital allowances non-effective in a year of assessment shall be construed as referring to the amount to which effect cannot be given in charging the profits or gains of the trade for that year by reason of an insufficiency of profits or gains.

(3) This Chapter shall apply, with any necessary modifications, in relation to a profession or employment as it applies in relation to a trade.

Cross References

From Section 391

Section 268 Meaning of "industrial building or structure".
Section 381 Right to repayment of tax by reference to losses.
Section 754 Interpretation (Chapter 1).

To Section 391

Schedule 25C Determination of Amount of Relief to be Treated as Referable to Specified Reliefs as Respects Relief Carried Forward from Tax Year 2006 to Tax Year 2007

392 Option to treat capital allowances as creating or augmenting a loss

[ITA67 s318; FA97 s146(1) and Sch9 PtI par1(23)]

(1) Subject to this Chapter, any claim made under *section 381* for relief in respect of a loss sustained in any trade in any year of assessment (in this Chapter referred to as "*the year of the loss*") may require the amount of the loss to be determined as if an amount equal to the capital allowances for the year of the loss were to be deducted in computing the profits or gains or losses of the trade in the year of the loss, and a claim may be so made notwithstanding that apart from those allowances a loss had not been sustained in the trade in the year of the loss.

(2) Where on any claim made by virtue of this Chapter relief is not given under *section 381* for the full amount of the loss determined under *subsection (1)*, the relief shall be referred, as far as may be, to the loss sustained in the trade rather than to the capital allowances in respect of the trade.

Cross References

From Section 392

Section 381 Right to repayment of tax by reference to losses.

To Section 392

Section 286A Wear and tear allowances for licences for public hire vehicles.
Section 393 Extent to which capital allowances to be taken into account for purposes of section 392.
Section 395 Relief affected by subsequent changes of law, etc.
Section 403 Restriction on use of capital allowances for certain leased assets.
Section 409A Income tax: restriction on use of capital allowances on certain industrial buildings and other premises.
Section 409B Income tax: restriction on use of capital allowances on certain hotels, etc.
Section 531AU Capital allowances and losses.
Section 662 Income tax: restriction of relief for losses in farming or market gardening.
Section 666 Deduction for increase in stock values.
Section 695 Abandonment expenditure: allowances and loss relief.
Section 1013 Limited partnerships.
Schedule 25B List of Specified Reliefs and Method of Determining Amount of Specified Relief Used in a Tax Year

393 Extent to which capital allowances to be taken into account for purposes of section 392

[ITA67 s319; FA97 s146(1) and Sch9 PtI par1(24)]

(1) The capital allowances for any year of assessment shall be taken into account under *section 392(1)* only if and in so far as such capital allowances are not required to offset balancing charges for the year, and relief shall not be given by reference to the capital allowances so taken into account in respect of an amount greater than the amount non-effective in the year of assessment for which the claim is made.

(2) For the purposes of *subsection (1)*, the capital allowances for any year of assessment shall be treated as required to offset balancing charges for the year up to the amount on which the balancing charges are to be made after deducting from that amount the amount, if any, of capital allowances for earlier years which is carried forward to that year and would, without the balancing charges, be non-effective in that year.

Cross References

From Section 393

Section 392 Option to treat capital allowances as creating or augmenting a loss.

To Section 393

Section 403 Restriction on use of capital allowances for certain leased assets.

394 Effect of giving relief under section 381 by reference to capital allowances

[ITA67 s320]

Where for any year of claim relief is given under *section 381* by reference to any capital allowances, then, for the purposes of the Income Tax Acts, effect shall be deemed to have been given to those allowances up to the amount in respect of which relief is so given, and any relief previously given for a subsequent year on the basis that effect had not been so given to those allowances shall be adjusted, where necessary, [by amended assessment][1].

Amendments

[1] Substituted by FA12 sched4(part 2)(g).

Cross References

From Section 394

Section 381 Right to repayment of tax by reference to losses.

To Section 394

Section 403 Restriction on use of capital allowances for certain leased assets.

395 Relief affected by subsequent changes of law, etc

[ITA67 s321; FA96 s132(1) and Sch5 PtI par1(18)]

(1) Where relief given to a person by virtue of *section 392(1)* for any year of claim is affected by a subsequent alteration of the law, or by any discontinuance of the trade or other event occurring after the end of the year, any necessary adjustment may be made, and so much of any repayment of tax as exceeded the amount repayable in the events that happened shall, if not otherwise made good, be recovered from the person by assessment under Case IV of Schedule D.

(2) For the purpose of an assessment mentioned in *subsection (1)*, the amount of capital allowances by reference to which the repayment was made, or an appropriate part of that amount, shall be deemed to be income chargeable under Case IV of Schedule D for the year of claim and shall be included in the return of income which the person is required to make under the Income Tax Acts for that year.

Cross References

From Section 395

Section 392 Option to treat capital allowances as creating or augmenting a loss.

CHAPTER 3

Corporation Tax: Loss Relief

396 Relief for trading losses other than terminal losses

[CTA76 s16(1) to (8) and (10); FA92 s46(1)(b); FA93 s22]

(1) [Subject to *section 396C*, where in any accounting period][1] a company carrying on a trade incurs a loss in the trade, the company may make a claim requiring that the loss be set off for the purposes of corporation tax against any trading income from the trade in succeeding accounting periods, and (so long as the company continues to carry on the trade) its trading income from the trade in any succeeding accounting period shall then be treated as reduced by the amount of the loss, or by so much of that amount as cannot, on that claim or on a claim (if made) under [*subsection (2)*, *section 396A(3)*, or *396B(2)*][2], be relieved against income or profits of an earlier accounting period.

(2) Where in any accounting period a company carrying on a trade incurs a loss in the trade, then, subject to *subsection (4)*, the company may make a claim requiring that the loss be set off for the purposes of corporation tax against profits (of whatever description) of that accounting period and, if the company was then carrying on the trade and the claim so requires, of preceding accounting periods ending within the time specified in *subsection (3)*, and, subject to that subsection and to any relief for an earlier loss, the profits of any of those periods shall then be treated as reduced by the amount of the loss, or by so much of that amount as cannot be relieved under this subsection against profits of a later accounting period.

(3) The time referred to in *subsection (2)* shall be a time immediately preceding the accounting period first mentioned in *subsection (2)* equal in length to the accounting period in which the loss is incurred; but the amount of the reduction which may be made under that subsection in the profits of an accounting period falling partly before that time shall not exceed a part of those profits proportionate to the part of the period falling within that time.

(4) *Subsection (2)* shall not apply to trades within Case III of Schedule D.

(5) (a) Subject to *paragraph (b)*, the amount of a loss incurred in a trade in an accounting period shall be computed for the purposes of this section in the like manner as trading income from the trade in that period would have been computed.

(b) Where expenses of management of an assurance company (within the meaning of *section 706*) are deductible under *section 83* from the profits of the accounting period in which they were incurred, or of any accounting period subsequent to that period, those expenses shall not be taken into account in computing a loss incurred in a trade of the company.

(6) For the purposes of this section, "*trading income*", in relation to any trade, means the income which is to be, or would be, included in respect of the trade in the total profits of the company; but where in an accounting period a company incurs a loss in a trade in respect of which it is within the charge to corporation tax under Case I or III of Schedule D, and in any later accounting period to which the loss or any part of the loss is carried forward under *subsection (1)* relief in respect of the loss or that part of the loss cannot be given, or cannot wholly be given, because the amount of the trading income of the trade is insufficient, any interest or dividends on investments which would be taken into account as trading receipts in computing that trading income but for the fact that they have been subjected to tax under other provisions shall be treated for the purposes of *subsection (1)* as if they were trading income of the trade.

(7) Where in an accounting period the charges on income paid by a company [net of any part of those charges relieved under *section 243B*][3]—

(a) exceed the amount of the profits against which they are deductible, and

(b) include payments made wholly and exclusively for the purposes of a trade carried on by the company,

then, up to the amount of that excess or of those payments, whichever is the less, the charges on income so paid shall in computing a loss for the purposes of *subsection (1)* be deductible as if they were trading expenses of the trade.

(8) In this section, references to a company carrying on a trade are references to the company carrying on the trade so as to be within the charge to corporation tax in respect of the trade.

(9) A claim under *subsection (2)* shall be made within 2 years from the end of the accounting period in which the loss is incurred.

Amendments

[1] Substituted by the National Asset Management Agency Act 2009 Sched 3 part 10.

[2] Substituted by FA12 sched1(13).

[3] Inserted by FA02 s54(1)(b)(i)(II). This section applies as respects an accounting period ending on or after 6 March 2001.

Case Law

In Commercial Union Assurance Co plc v Shaw (HM Inspector of Taxes) 1999 STC 109 it was held that charges on income must be used before double tax relief is taken.

Whether a company is or is not carrying on the same trade at different times is a question of fact. In the case of Bolands Ltd v Davis 1 ITC 91 a flour milling and bread making company closed down its two mills after incurring losses. About half of the flour it milled had been used to supply the bakeries. After about eight months the mills were reopened, mainly to supply the bakeries. It was held that the same trade had been carried on throughout.

A brewing company ceased brewing but continued to sell beer which was supplied to its specification by another company. It was held that the company had ceased one trade, the trade of brewing and had commenced another trade, the trade of selling beer. Gordon & Blair Ltd v CIR 1962 40 TC 358

In R v IRC, ex parte Unilever plc 1996 STC 681 it was held that where the Revenue had accepted informal claims for loss relief over a period of 20 years, it would be unfair and an abuse of power to insist on a formal claim being made within the time limit.

Revenue Briefings

eBrief

eBrief No. 65/2011 – Recording of Losses Forward on Form CT1

Cross References

From Section 396

Section 83 Expenses of management of investment companies.
Section 455 Restriction of certain losses.
Section 706 Interpretation and general (Part 26).

To Section 396

Section 22A Reduction of corporation tax liability in respect of certain trading income.
Section 82 Pre-trading expenditure.
Section 247 Relief to companies on loans applied in acquiring interest in other companies.
Section 355 Disclaimer of capital allowances on holiday cottages, holiday apartments, etc.
Section 396A Relief for relevant trading losses.
Section 396B Relief for certain trading losses on a value basis.
Section 397 Relief for terminal loss in a trade.
Section 398 Computation of losses attributable to exemption of income from certain securities.
Section 400 Company reconstructions without change of ownership.
Section 401 Change in ownership of company: disallowance of trading losses.
Section 402 Foreign currency: tax treatment of capital allowances and trading losses of a company.
Section 403 Restriction on use of capital allowances for certain leased assets.
Section 404 Restriction on use of capital allowances for certain leased machinery or plant.
Section 405 Restriction on use of capital allowances on holiday cottages.
Section 407 Restriction on use of losses and capital allowances for qualifying shipping trade.
Section 420 Losses, etc. which may be surrendered by means of group relief.
Section 420A Group relief: relevant losses and charges.
Section 420B Group relief: Relief for certain losses on a value basis.
Section 421 Relation of group relief to other relief.
Section 425 Leasing contracts: effect on claims for losses of company reconstructions.
Section 448 Relief from corporation tax.
Section 517 Payments to trustees of approved profit sharing scheme.
Section 644C Relief from corporation tax for losses from dealing in residential development land.
Section 663 Corporation tax: restriction of relief for losses in farming or market gardening.

Section 666 Deduction for increase in stock values.
Section 679 Exploration expenditure.
Section 687 Treatment of losses.
Section 690 Interest and charges on income.
Section 695 Abandonment expenditure: allowances and loss relief.
Section 707 Management expenses.
Section 709 Companies carrying on life business.
Section 730A Profits of life business: new basis.
Section 730K Disposal of foreign life policy.
Section 747E Disposal of an interest in offshore funds.
Section 751 Traders other than dealers in securities.
Section 753 Restriction on relief for losses by repayment of tax in case of dividends paid out of accumulated profits.
Section 841 Voluntary Health Insurance Board: restriction of certain losses and deemed disposal of certain assets.
Section 847 Tax relief for certain branch profits.
Section 1013 Limited partnerships.
Section 1085 Corporation tax — late returns: restriction of certain claims for relief.
Schedule 17 Reorganisation into Companies of Trustee Savings Banks

396A Relief for relevant trading losses

[(1) In this section—

["*relevant trading loss*", in relation to an accounting period of a company, means a loss incurred in the accounting period in a trade carried on by the company, other than—

(a) so much of the loss as is a loss incurred in an excepted trade within the meaning of *section 21A*, and

(b) any amount which is or would, if *subsection (8)* of *section 403* had not been enacted, be the relevant amount of the loss for the purposes of *subsection (4)* of that section.][1]

(2) Notwithstanding *subsection (2)* of *section 396*, for the purposes of that subsection the amount of a loss in a trade incurred by a company in an accounting period shall be deemed to be reduced by the amount of a relevant trading loss incurred by the company in the accounting period.

(3) [Where][2] in an accounting period a company carrying on a trade incurs a relevant trading loss, the company may make a claim requiring that the loss be set off for the purposes of corporation tax against income of the company, being—

(a) income specified in [*section 21A(4)*][3] […][4]

(b) relevant trading [income, and][5]

[(c) income to which *section 21A(3)* does not apply by virtue of *section 21B*,][6]

of that accounting period and, if the company was then carrying on the trade and if the claim so requires, of preceding accounting periods ending within the time specified in *subsection (4)*, and subject to that subsection and any relief for an earlier relevant trading loss, to the extent that the income of any of those accounting periods consists of or includes income specified in [*section 21A(4)*][7] or relevant trading income, that income shall then be reduced by the amount of the relevant trading loss or by so much of that amount as cannot be relieved against income of a later accounting period.

(4) For the purposes of *subsection (3)*, the time referred to in *paragraph (b)* of that subsection shall be the time immediately preceding the accounting period first mentioned in *subsection (3)* equal in length to that accounting period; but the

amount of the reduction which may be made under *subsection (3)* in the relevant trading income of an accounting period falling partly before that time shall not exceed such part of that relevant trading income as bears to the whole of the relevant trading income the same proportion as the part of the accounting period falling within that time bears to the whole of that accounting period.

[(5) A claim under *subsection (3)* shall be made within 2 years from the end of the accounting period in which the loss is incurred.][8]][9]

Amendments

[1] Substituted by FA05 s45(1)(a). Applies as respects any claim made by a company on or after 3 February 2005 for relief for a loss.

[2] Substituted by FA12 sched1(14)(a).

[3,7] Substituted by FA12 sched1(14)(b).

[4] Deleted by FA08 s43(1)(d)(i). This section shall be deemed to have applied as respects a dividend received on or after 1 January 2007.

[5] Substituted by FA08 s43(1)(d)(i). This section shall be deemed to have applied as respects a dividend received on or after 1 January 2007.

[6] Inserted by FA08 s43(1)(d)(ii). This section shall be deemed to have applied as respects a dividend received on or after 1 January 2007.

[8] Inserted by FA03 s59(1)(b). Applies as respects accounting periods ending on or after 6 February 2003.

[9] Inserted by FA01 s90(1)(b)(i). Applies as respects an accounting period ending on or after 6 March 2001.

Revenue Briefings

Tax Briefing

Tax Briefing July 2001 – Issue 44 pg 39 – Losses, charges and group relief offset

eBrief

eBrief No. 94/2014 – CT 1 2014 and claims for the set back of excess Trading Losses and excess Research & Development Credit

Cross References

From Section 396A

Section 21A Higher rate of corporation tax.
Section 21B Tax treatment of certain dividends.
Section 396 Relief for trading losses other than terminal losses.
Section 403 Restriction on use of capital allowances for certain leased assets.
Section 455 Restriction of certain losses.

To Section 396A

Section 243A Restriction of relevant charges on income.
Section 420A Group relief: relevant losses and charges.
Section 448 Relief from corporation tax.
Section 644C Relief from corporation tax for losses from dealing in residential development land.
Section 713 Investment income reserved for policyholders.
Section 1085 Corporation tax — late returns: restriction of certain claims for relief.

396B Relief for certain trading losses on a value basis

[(1) In this section—

[...][1]

["*relevant corporation tax*", in relation to an accounting period of a company, means the corporation tax which would be chargeable on the company for the accounting period apart from—

(a) this section and *sections 239, 241, 420B, 440* and *441*, and

(b) where the company carries on a life business (within the meaning of *section 706* [...][2]), any corporation tax which would be attributable to policyholders' profits;][3]

"*relevant trading loss*" has the same meaning as in *section 396A* [...][4]

[(2) Where in any accounting period a company carrying on a trade incurs a relevant trading loss and the amount of the loss exceeds an amount equal to the aggregate of the amounts which could, if a timely claim for such set off had been made by the company, have been set off in respect of that loss for the purposes of corporation tax against income of the company of that accounting period and any preceding accounting period in accordance with *section 396A(3)*, then the company may claim relief under this section in respect of the excess.][5]

[(3) Where for any accounting period a company claims relief under this section in respect of the excess, the relevant corporation tax of the company for that accounting period and, if the company was then carrying on the trade and the claim so requires, for preceding accounting periods ending within the time specified in *subsection (4)*, shall be reduced, in so far as the excess consists of a relevant trading loss, by an amount determined by the formula—

$$L \times \frac{R}{100}$$

where—

L is the amount of the excess, and

R is the rate per cent of corporation tax which, by virtue of *section 21*, applies in relation to the accounting period.][6]

and

(4) For the purposes of *subsection (3)*, the time referred to in that subsection shall be the time immediately preceding the accounting period first mentioned in *subsection (3)* equal in length to that accounting period; but the amount of the reduction which may be made under *subsection (3)* in the relevant corporation tax for an accounting period falling partly before that time shall not exceed such part of that relevant corporation tax as bears to the whole of that relevant corporation tax the same proportion as the part of the accounting period falling within that time bears to the whole of that accounting period.

[(5) [(a) Subject to *paragraph (b)*, where a company][7] makes a claim for relief for any accounting period under this section in respect of any relevant trading loss incurred in a trade in an accounting period, an amount (which shall not exceed the amount of the excess in respect of which a claim under this section may be made), determined by the formula—

$$T \times \frac{100}{R}$$

where —

T is the amount by which the relevant corporation tax for the accounting period is reduced by virtue of *subsection (3)*, and

R is the rate per cent of corporation tax which, by virtue of *section 21*, applies in relation to the accounting period,

shall be treated for the purposes of the Tax Acts as an amount of loss relieved against profits of that accounting period.][8]][9]

[(b) (i) In this paragraph "*relevant amount*" means an amount (not being an amount incurred by a company for the purposes of a trade carried on by it) of charges on income, expenses of management or other amount (not being an allowance to which effect is given under *section 308(4)*) which is deductible from, or may be treated as reducing, profits of more than one description.

(ii) For the purposes of *paragraph (a)*, where as respects an accounting period of a company a relevant amount is deductible from, or may be treated as reducing, profits of more than one description, the amount by which corporation tax is reduced by virtue of *subsection (3)* shall be deemed to be the amount by which it would have been reduced if no relevant amount were so deductible or so treated.][10]

[(6) A claim under *subsection (2)* shall be made within 2 years from the end of the accounting period in which the loss is incurred.][11]][12]

Amendments

[1] Deleted by FA12 sched1(15)(a).

[2] Deleted by FA07 sched4(1)(g). Apply to accounting periods ending on or after 1 January 2007.

[3] Substituted by FA04 s37(1). This section shall apply as respects any claim for relief made on or after 4 February 2004.

[4] Deleted by FA05 s45(1)(b). Applies as respects any claim made by a company on or after 3 February 2005 for relief for a loss.

[5] Substituted by FA06 sched2(1)(h)(ii). Applies to accounting periods ending on or after 2 February 2006.

[6] Substituted by FA12 sched1(15)(b).

[7] Substituted by FA13 s37(1)(a). Applies as respects accounting periods commencing on or after 1 January 2013.

[8] Renumbered by FA13 s37(1)(b). Applies as respects accounting periods commencing on or after 1 January 2013.

[9] Substituted by FA12 sched1(15)(c).

[10] Inserted by FA13 s37(1)(c). Applies as respects accounting periods commencing on or after 1 January 2013.

[11] Inserted by FA03 s59(1)(c)(ii).

[12] Inserted by FA02 s54(1)(b)(ii). For the purposes of computing the amount of— (a) charges on income paid for the purposes of the sale of goods (within the meaning of section 454), (b) a loss from the sale of goods (within the meaning of section 455), (c) relevant trading charges on income (within the meaning of section 243A), and (d) relevant trading losses (within the meaning of section 396A), in respect of which relief may be claimed by virtue of this section, where an accounting period of a company begins before 6 March 2001 and ends on or after that date, it shall be divided into 2 parts, one beginning on the date on which the accounting period begins and ending on 5 March 2001 and the other beginning on 6 March 2001 and ending on the date on which the accounting period ends, and both parts shall be treated as if they were separate accounting periods of the company.

Revenue Briefings

Tax Briefing

Tax Briefing January 2003 – Issue 51 pg 14 – Losses, charges and group relief offset

eBrief

eBrief No. 94/2014 – CT 1 2014 and claims for the set back of excess Trading Losses and excess Research & Development Credit

Cross References

From Section 396B

Section 21 The charge to corporation tax and exclusion of income tax and capital gains tax.
Section 239 Income tax on payments by resident companies.
Section 241 Income tax on payments by non-resident companies.
Section 308 Corporation tax: manner of granting, and effect of, allowances made by means of discharge or repayment of tax.

Section 396 Relief for trading losses other than terminal losses.
Section 407 Restriction on use of losses and capital allowances for qualifying shipping trade.
Section 440 Surcharge on undistributed investment and estate income.
Section 441 Surcharge on undistributed income of service companies.
Section 448 Relief from corporation tax.
Section 706 Interpretation and general (Part 26).

To Section 396B

Section 243B Relief for certain charges on income on a value basis.
Section 747E Disposal of an interest in offshore funds.
Section 1085 Corporation tax — late returns: restriction of certain claims for relief.

396C Relief from Corporation Tax for losses of participating institutions

[(1) (a) In this section—

"*available losses*", in relation to an accounting period of a participating institution, means losses, carried forward from preceding accounting periods, for which relief is available under section 396(1) in that accounting period or succeeding accounting periods;

"*group company*", for an accounting period in relation to a participating institution (in this definition referred to as the "*first-mentioned institution*"), means a company which is a participating institution that has an accounting period that coincides with the accounting period of the first-mentioned institution where, throughout the accounting period of the first-mentioned institution—

(a) the company is a subsidiary of the first-mentioned institution,

(b) the first-mentioned institution is a subsidiary of the company, or

(c) both the company and the first-mentioned institution are subsidiaries of a third company;

"*participating institution*" and "*subsidiary*" have the same meanings respectively as in section 4 of the National Asset Management Agency Act 2009;

"*relevant amount*" for an accounting period in relation to a participating institution means 50 per cent of the amount, if any, by which the aggregate of the trading income, if any, of the participating institution and its group companies for the accounting period exceeds the aggregate of the trading losses, if any, incurred by the participating institution and its group companies in that accounting period;

"*relevant limit*" in relation to an accounting period of a participating institution means an amount determined by the formula—

$$A \times \frac{B}{C}$$

where—

A is the relevant amount for the accounting period in relation to the participating institution,

B is the aggregate amount of the trading income, if any, of the participating institution for the accounting period before any relief for available losses, and

C is the aggregate amount of the trading income, if any, of the participating institution and its group companies for the accounting period before any relief for available losses.

(b) For the purposes of this section—

(i) an accounting period of a company coincides with an accounting period of another company if the first-mentioned accounting period begins on the same day and ends on the same day as the second-mentioned accounting period, and

(ii) references to trading income or trading losses are references to trading income or trading losses, as the case may be, arising—

(I) to a company resident in the State, or

(II) through or from a branch or agency in the State of a company that is not so resident.

(2) Where for any accounting period a participating institution makes a claim under subsection 396(1) for relief in respect of available losses incurred, or deemed under *subsection (3)* to have been incurred, in a trade carried on by that institution, the amount of the losses which may be set off against trading income of the trade in that accounting period shall not exceed the relevant limit of the participating institution for that period.

(3) (a) Subject to *subsection (2)* and *paragraphs (b)* and (*c*), where in relation to an accounting period—

(i) a participating institution has an amount of available losses (referred to in this subsection as the "excess available losses") in respect of which it cannot obtain relief for that period, and

(ii) a group company in relation to that institution, having claimed all relief under section 396(1), if any, to which it would otherwise be entitled (including by reference to other claims made under this subsection), could obtain relief, or more relief, under section 396(1) for that accounting period if some or all of the excess available losses of the participating institution were deemed to have been incurred by the group company,

then, on the making of a claim in that regard by the group company, the participating institution may surrender to the group company an amount of those excess available losses that does not exceed the amount for which the group company could obtain relief for that accounting period, having claimed all other relief under section 396(1) to which it is entitled, and—

(I) that group company shall be deemed for the purposes of section 396(1) to have incurred those losses and shall set off the amount so surrendered against its trading income for the accounting period, which income shall be treated as reduced by that amount, and

(II) the available losses of the surrendering company shall be deemed for all purposes of the Corporation Tax Acts to be reduced by the amount surrendered.

(b) More than one group company may make a claim under this subsection relating to the same participating institution and to the same accounting period of that institution but, whether by reference to this section or any other section of the Corporation Tax Acts or any combination thereof, relief shall not be given more than once in respect of an amount of available losses.

(c) A claim for relief under this subsection—

(i) shall be made in the return required to be made under [*Chapter 3* of *Part 41A*][1] for the accounting period of the group company which is claiming the relief,

(ii) shall require the consent of the participating institution notified to the inspector in such form as the Revenue Commissioners may require, and

(iii) shall be made within 2 years from the end of the accounting period to which the claim relates.

(4) (a) Subject to [*paragraph (b)*][2], where the inspector ascertains that any relief claimed in accordance with this section is or has become excessive, he or she may make an assessment to corporation tax under Case I of Schedule D in the amount which in his or her opinion ought to be charged.

(b) [*paragraph (a)*][3] is without prejudice to the making of an assessment under section 919(5)(*b*)(iii) and to the making of all such other adjustments by means of discharge or repayment of tax or otherwise as may be required where a company has obtained too much relief.

(5) This section has effect for accounting periods commencing on or after the passing of the National Asset Management Agency Act 2009 [and before 1 January 2014][4].][5]

Amendments

[1] Substituted by FA12 sched4(part 2)(g).

[2] Substituted by FA12 sched6(1)(c)(i). Has effect as on and from 31 March 2012.

[3] Substituted by FA12 sched6(1)(c)(ii). Has effect as on and from 31 March 2012.

[4] Inserted by F(No.2)A13 s33. Comes into operation on 1 January 2014.

[5] Inserted by the National Asset Management Agency Act 2009 Sched 3 part 10. This section has effect for accounting periods commencing on or after the passing of the National Asset Management Agency Act 2009

397 Relief for terminal loss in a trade

[CTA76 s18(1) to (3)]

(1) (a) Where a company ceasing to carry on a trade has, in any accounting period falling wholly or partly within the previous 12 months, incurred a loss in the trade, the company may claim to set the loss off for the purposes of corporation tax against trading income from the trade in accounting periods falling wholly or partly within the 3 years preceding those 12 months (or within any shorter period throughout which the company has carried on the trade) and, subject to *subsections (2)* and *(3)* and to any relief for earlier losses, the trading income of any of those accounting periods shall then be treated as reduced by the amount of the loss, or by so much of that amount as cannot be relieved under this subsection against income of a later accounting period.

(b) Relief shall not be given under this subsection in respect of any loss in so far as the loss has been or can be otherwise taken into account so as to reduce or relieve any charge to tax.

(2) Where a loss is incurred in an accounting period falling partly outside the 12 months mentioned in *subsection (1)*, relief shall be given under that subsection in respect of a part only of that loss proportionate to the part of the period falling within those 12 months, and the amount of the reduction which may be made under that

subsection in the trading income of an accounting period falling partly outside the 3 years mentioned in that subsection shall not exceed a part of that income proportionate to the part of the period falling within those 3 years.

(3) *Subsections (5)* to *(8)* of *section 396* shall apply for the purposes of this section as they apply for the purposes of *section 396(1)*, and relief shall not be given under this section in respect of a loss incurred in a trade so as to interfere with any relief under [*section 243* or *243A*][1] in respect of payments made wholly and exclusively for the purposes of that trade.

Amendments

[1] Substituted by FA05 sched6(1)(f). Applies as respects accounting periods ending on or after 3 February 2005.

Cross References

From Section 397

Section 243 Allowance of charges on income.
Section 396 Relief for trading losses other than terminal losses.

To Section 397

Section 398 Computation of losses attributable to exemption of income from certain securities.
Section 400 Company reconstructions without change of ownership.
Section 402 Foreign currency: tax treatment of capital allowances and trading losses of a company.
Section 420A Group relief: relevant losses and charges.
Section 420C Group relief: relief for certain losses of non-resident companies.
Section 421 Relation of group relief to other relief.
Section 517 Payments to trustees of approved profit sharing scheme.
Section 644C Relief from corporation tax for losses from dealing in residential development land.
Section 666 Deduction for increase in stock values.
Section 679 Exploration expenditure.
Section 709 Companies carrying on life business.

398 Computation of losses attributable to exemption of income from certain securities

[FA92 s42(2) and (3)(b) (apart from proviso thereto)]

(1) Notwithstanding *subsection (5)* of *section 396* or *subsection (3)* of *section 397*, in ascertaining for the purposes of those sections whether and to what extent a company has incurred a loss in carrying on a trade in the State through a branch or agency, the interest on, and other profits or gains from, a security held by or for the branch or agency shall be treated as a trading receipt of the trade if such interest or other profits or gains would, if *sections 43*, *49* and *50* had not been enacted, have been so treated, or have been included in an amount so treated.

(2) *Subsection (1)* shall apply for the purposes of ascertaining whether and to what extent a company has incurred a loss where apart from that subsection the company would be treated as having incurred a loss and that loss would be—

(a) set-off against the trading income or profits (whether of that company or any other company) of, or

(b) incurred in,

an accounting period.

Cross References

From Section 398

Section 43 Certain securities issued by Minister for Finance.
Section 49 Exemption of certain securities.
Section 50 Securities of Irish local authorities issued abroad.

Section 396 Relief for trading losses other than terminal losses.
Section 397 Relief for terminal loss in a trade.

399 Losses in transactions from which income would be chargeable under Case IV or V of Schedule D

[CTA76 s19]

(1) (a) Where in any accounting period a company incurs a loss in a transaction in respect of which the company is within the charge to corporation tax under Case IV of Schedule D, the company may claim to set the loss off against the amount of any income arising from such transactions in respect of which the company is assessed to corporation tax under that Case for the same or any subsequent accounting period, and the company's income in any accounting period from such transactions shall then be treated as reduced by the amount of the loss, or by so much of that amount as cannot be relieved under this section against income of an earlier accounting period.

(b) Where a company sustains a loss in a transaction which, if profit had arisen from it, would be chargeable to tax by virtue of *subsection (3)* or *(4)* of *section 814*, then, if the company is chargeable to tax in respect of the interest payable on the amount of money the right to which has been disposed of, the amount of that interest shall be included in the amounts against which the company may claim to set off the amount of its loss under this subsection.

(2) (a) Where in any accounting period a company is within the charge to corporation tax under Case V of Schedule D and the aggregate of the deficiencies, computed in accordance with *section 97(1)*, exceeds the aggregate of the surpluses as so computed, the excess may, on a claim being made in that behalf, be deducted from or set off, as far as may be, against the amount of any income in respect of which the company is assessed to corporation tax under Case V of Schedule D for previous accounting periods ending within the time specified in *subsection (3)*, and, subject to that subsection and to any relief for an earlier excess of deficiencies, that income of any of those periods shall then be treated as reduced, as far as may be, by the amount of the excess, and any portion of the excess for which relief is not so given shall be set off against the income in respect of which the company is assessed to corporation tax under Case V of Schedule D for any subsequent accounting period.

(b) Any relief under this subsection by means of carrying forward any portion of the excess referred to in *paragraph (a)* shall be given as far as possible from the first subsequent assessment and, in so far as it cannot be so given, then from the next assessment and so on.

(3) The time referred to in *subsection (2)* shall be a time immediately preceding the accounting period first mentioned in *subsection (2)* equal in length to the accounting period in which the excess of deficiencies occurred; but the amount of the reduction which may be made under that subsection in the income of an accounting period falling partly before that time shall not exceed a part of that income proportionate to the part of the period falling within that time.

(4) A claim under *subsection (2)* shall be made within 2 years from the end of the accounting period in which the excess of deficiencies was incurred.

Cross References

From Section 399

Section 97 Computational rules and allowable deductions.
Section 814 Taxation of income deemed to arise from transactions in certificates of deposit and assignable deposits.

To Section 399

Section 402 Foreign currency: tax treatment of capital allowances and trading losses of a company.
Section 687 Treatment of losses.
Section 715 Annuity business: separate charge on profits.
Section 730K Disposal of foreign life policy.
Section 747E Disposal of an interest in offshore funds.
Section 814 Taxation of income deemed to arise from transactions in certificates of deposit and assignable deposits.
Section 1085 Corporation tax — late returns: restriction of certain claims for relief.

400 Company reconstructions without change of ownership

[CTA76 s20]

(1) For the purposes of this section—

(a) a trade carried on by 2 or more persons shall be treated as belonging to them in the shares in which they are entitled to the profits of the trade;

(b) a trade or interest in a trade belonging to any person as trustee (otherwise than for charitable or public purposes) shall be treated as belonging to the persons for the time being entitled to the income under the trust;

(c) a trade or interest in a trade belonging to a company shall, where the result of so doing is that *subsection (5)* or *(10)* applies in relation to an event, be treated in any of the ways permitted by *subsection (2)*.

(2) For the purposes of this section, a trade or interest in a trade which belongs to a company engaged in carrying on the trade may be regarded—

(a) as belonging to the persons owning the ordinary share capital of the company and as belonging to those persons in proportion to the amount of their holdings of that capital, or

(b) in the case of a company which is a subsidiary company, as belonging to a company which is its parent company, or as belonging to the persons owning the ordinary share capital of that parent company, and as belonging to those persons in proportion to the amount of their holdings of that capital,

and any ordinary share capital owned by a company may, if any person or body of persons has the power to secure by means of the holding of shares or the possession of voting power in or in relation to any company, or by virtue of any power conferred by the articles of association or other document regulating any company, that the affairs of the company owning the share capital are conducted in accordance with that person's or that body of persons' wishes, be regarded as owned by that person or body of persons having that power.

(3) For the purposes of *subsection (2)*—

(a) references to ownership shall be construed as references to beneficial ownership;

(b) a company shall be deemed to be a subsidiary of another company if and so long as not less than 75 per cent of its ordinary share capital is owned by that other company, whether directly or through another company or other companies, or partly directly and partly through another company or other companies;

(c) the amount of ordinary share capital of one company owned by a second company through another company or other companies, or partly directly and partly through another company or other companies, shall be determined in accordance with *subsections (5)* to *(10)* of *section 9*;

(d) where any company is a subsidiary of another company, that other company shall be considered as its parent company unless both are subsidiaries of a third company.

(4) In determining for the purposes of this section whether or to what extent a trade belongs at different times to the same persons, persons who are relatives of one another and the persons from time to time entitled to the income under any trust shall respectively be treated as a single person, and for this purpose "*relative*" means [husband, wife, civil partner,][1] ancestor, lineal descendant, brother or sister.

(5) (a) Where, on a company (in this section referred to as "*the predecessor*") ceasing to carry on a trade, another company (in this section referred to as "*the successor*") begins to carry on the trade and—

(i) on or at any time within 2 years after that event, the trade or an interest amounting to not less than a 75 per cent share in the trade belongs to the same persons as the trade or such an interest belonged to at some time within a year before that event, and

(ii) the trade is not, within the period taken for the comparison under *subparagraph (i)*, carried on otherwise than by a company within the charge to tax in respect of the trade,

then, the Corporation Tax Acts shall apply subject to *subsections (6)* to *(9)*.

(b) In *subparagraphs (i)* and *(ii)* of *paragraph (a)*, references to the trade shall apply also to any other trade of which the activities comprise the activities of the first-mentioned trade.

(6) The trade shall not be treated as permanently discontinued nor a new trade as set up and commenced for the purpose of the allowances and charges provided for by *sections 307* and *308*; but there shall be made to or on the successor in accordance with those sections all such allowances and charges as would, if the predecessor had continued to carry on the trade, have been made to or on the predecessor, and the amount of any such allowance or charge shall be computed as if the successor had been carrying on the trade since the predecessor began to do so and as if everything done to or by the predecessor had been done to or by the successor (but so that no sale or transfer which on the transfer of the trade is made to the successor by the predecessor of any assets in use for the purpose of the trade shall be treated as giving rise to any such allowance or charge).

(7) The predecessor shall not be entitled to relief under *section 397* except as provided by *subsection (9)* and, subject to any claim made by the predecessor under *section 396(2)*, the successor shall be entitled to relief under *section 396(1)*, as for a loss sustained by the successor in carrying on the trade, for any amount for which the predecessor would have been entitled to claim relief if the predecessor had continued to carry on the trade.

(8) Any securities within the meaning of *section 748* which, at the time when the predecessor ceases to carry on the trade, form part of the trading stock belonging

to the trade shall be treated for the purposes of that section as having been sold at that time in the open market by the predecessor and as having been purchased at that time in the open market by the successor.

(9) On the successor ceasing to carry on the trade—

(a) if the successor does so within 4 years of succeeding to the trade, any relief which might be given to the successor under *section 397* on the successor ceasing to carry on the trade may, in so far as that relief cannot be given to the successor, be given to the predecessor as if the predecessor had incurred the loss (including any amount treated as a loss under *section 397(3)*), and

(b) if the successor ceases to carry on the trade within one year of succeeding to the trade, relief may be given to the predecessor under *section 397* in respect of any loss incurred by the predesessor (or any amount treated as such a loss under *section 397(3)*);

but, for the purposes of *section 397* as it applies by virtue of this subsection to the giving of relief to the predecessor, the predecessor shall be treated as ceasing to carry on the trade when the successor does so.

(10) Where the successor ceases to carry on the trade within the period taken for the comparison under *subsection (5)(a)(i)* and, on its doing so, a third company begins to carry on the trade, then, no relief shall be given to the predecessor by virtue of *subsection (9)* by reference to that event; but, subject to that, *subsections (6)* to *(9)* shall apply both in relation to that event (together with the new predecessor and successor) and to the earlier event (together with the original predecessor and successor), but so that—

(a) in relation to the earlier event, "*successor*" shall include the successor at either event, and

(b) in relation to the later event, "*predecessor*" shall include the predecessor at either event,

and, if the conditions of this subsection are thereafter again satisfied, this subsection shall apply again in the like manner.

(11) Where, on a company ceasing to carry on a trade, another company begins to carry on the activities of the trade as part of its trade, that part of the trade carried on by the successor shall for the purposes of this subsection be treated as a separate trade, if the effect of so treating it is that *subsection (5)* or *(10)* applies to that event in relation to that separate trade, and where, on a company ceasing to carry on part of a trade, another company begins to carry on the activities of that part as its trade or part of its trade, the predecessor shall for the purposes of this section be treated as having carried on that part of its trade as a separate trade, if the effect of so treating it is that *subsection (5)* or *(10)* applies to that event in relation to that separate trade.

(12) Where under *subsection (11)* any activities of a company's trade are to be treated as a separate trade on the company ceasing or beginning to carry them on, any necessary apportionment shall be made of receipts or expenses.

(13) Where by virtue of *subsection (12)* any sum is to be apportioned and, at the time of the apportionment, it appears that it is material as respects the liability to tax (for whatever period) of 2 or more companies, any question which arises as to the manner in which the sum is to be apportioned shall, for the purposes of the tax of all those companies,

be determined by the Appeal Commissioners who shall determine the question in the like manner as if it were an appeal against an assessment, and the provisions of the Income Tax Acts relating to the rehearing of an appeal and to the statement of a case for the opinion of the High Court on a point of law shall apply accordingly with any necessary modifications, and all those companies shall be entitled to appear before and be heard by the Appeal Commissioners or to make representations to them in writing.

(14) Any relief to be given under this section by means of discharge or repayment of tax shall be given on the making of a claim.

Amendments

[1] Substituted by F(No.3)A11 sched1(61). Shall have effect from 27 July 2011.

Case Law

Rolls Royce Motors Ltd v Bamford 1976 STC 162 considered the status of the trading activities that remained following the transfer of part of a trade. There were three trades and then one (80% of company's business) was transferred to a State owned company following the appointment of a receiver. The question arose if the two remaining trades were a continuation of the company's trade or a new trade? It was held the fact that 80% of company's business had been transferred there was a discontinuance of the company's trade at the time of the transfer.

Where a transferee company merges certain trading activities into its existing trade, that may result in the commencement of a new single trade where the merged and the preexisting activities of the company are of a similar scale. George Humphries & Co v Cook 19 TC 191

A company selling shoes retail was denied relief for losses of shoe manufacturing trades carried on by two of its subsidiaries after acquiring the assets of those companies and commencing to manufacture the shoes itself. It was held that the company had not succeeded to the trades of the subsidiaries as those trades consisted of the manufacture of shoes and their sale wholesale whereas after the transfer the trade was the manufacture and their sale retail. Laylock v Freeman Hardy & Wlillis Ltd 22 TC 288

Where a company took over the trade of its supplier, even though the profits of that trade were no longer being separately realised, the claim for losses was allowed. Falmer Jeans Ltd v Rodin 1990 STC 270

Revenue Precedents

A transfer of plant is not necessary in a company reconstruction in order for S400(6) TCA 1997 to apply. IT962003

Cross References

From Section 400

Section 9 Subsidiaries.
Section 307 Corporation tax: allowances and charges in taxing a trade.
Section 308 Corporation tax: manner of granting, and effect of, allowances made by means of discharge or repayment of tax.
Section 396 Relief for trading losses other than terminal losses.
Section 397 Relief for terminal loss in a trade.
Section 748 Interpretation and application (Chapter 1).

To Section 400

Section 308A Assets transferred in course of scheme of reconstruction or amalgamation.
Section 401 Change in ownership of company: disallowance of trading losses.
Section 424 Effect of arrangements for transfer of company to another group, etc.
Section 425 Leasing contracts: effect on claims for losses of company reconstructions.
Section 494 Qualifying companies.
Section 498 Replacement capital.
Section 615 Company reconstruction or amalgamation: transfer of assets.
Section 631 Transfer of assets generally.
Section 663 Corporation tax: restriction of relief for losses in farming or market gardening.

401 Change in ownership of company: disallowance of trading losses

[CTA76 s27(1) to (7)]

(1) In this section, "major change in the nature or conduct of a trade" includes—

(a) a major change in the type of property dealt in, or services or facilities provided, in the trade, or

(b) a major change in customers, outlets or markets of the trade,

and this section shall apply even if the change is the result of a gradual process which began outside the period of 3 years mentioned in *subsection (2)(a).*

(2) Where—

(a) within any period of 3 years, there is both a change in the ownership of a company and (whether earlier or later in that period or at the same time) a major change in the nature or conduct of a trade carried on by the company, or

(b) at any time after the scale of the activities in a trade carried on by a company has become small or negligible and before any considerable revival of the trade, there is a change in the ownership of the company,

relief shall not be given—

(i) under *section 396* by setting a loss incurred by the company in an accounting period beginning before the change of ownership against any income or other profits of an accounting period ending after the change of ownership, or

(ii) under *paragraph 16* or *18* of *Schedule 32* against corporation tax payable for any accounting period ending after the change of ownership.

(3) (a) In applying this section to the accounting period in which the change of ownership occurs, the part ending with the change of ownership and the part after that change shall be treated as 2 separate accounting periods, and the profits or losses of the accounting period shall be apportioned to the 2 parts.

(b) The apportionment under *paragraph (a)* shall be on a time basis according to the respective lengths of the 2 parts except that, if it appears that that method would operate unreasonably or unjustly, such other method shall be used as appears just and reasonable.

(4) In relation to any relief available under *section 400*, *subsection (2)* shall apply as if any loss sustained by a predecessor company had been sustained by a successor company and as if the references to a trade included references to the trade as carried on by a predecessor company.

(5) (a) Where relief in respect of a company's losses has been restricted under this section, then, notwithstanding *section 320(6)*, in applying the provisions of *Part 9* and of *Chapter 1* of *Part 29* relating to balancing charges to the company by reference to any event after the change of ownership of the company, any allowance or deduction to be made in taxing the company's trade for any chargeable period before the change of ownership shall be disregarded unless the profits or gains of that chargeable period, or of any subsequent chargeable period before the change of ownership, were sufficient to give effect to the allowance or deduction.

(b) In applying this subsection, it shall be assumed that any profits or gains are applied in giving effect to any such allowance or deduction in preference to being set off against any loss which is not attributable to such an allowance or deduction.

(6) Where the operation of this section depends on circumstances or events at a time after the change of ownership (but not more than 3 years after that change), an assessment to give effect to this section shall not be out of time if made within [4 years][1] from that time or the latest of those times.

(7) *Schedule 9* shall apply for the purpose of supplementing this section.

Amendments

[1] Substituted by FA03 s17(1)(f). Applies with effect from the day appointed by the Minister for Finance in accordance with different provisions. With effect from 1 January 2005 per S.I. 508 of 2003.

Case Law

The cessation of one activity of a company does not necessarily denote the cessation of the trade as a whole. M Cronin (Inspector of Taxes) v Lunham Brothers Ltd 1985 III ITR 363

In Willis v Peeters Picture Frames Ltd 1983 STC 453 it was found that a company that had sold its products directly to customers, mainly wholesalers, and which later sold them through distribution companies had not effected a major change in the conduct of its trades.

In Purchase v Tesco Stores Ltd 1984 STC 304 the company achieved a major increase in turnover as a result of discontinuing the issue of stamps and reducing prices. It was held that a major change in the company's trade had occurred.

In Pobjoy Mint Ltd v Lane 1984 STC 327 a company was in the business of minting coins and medallions. It purchased its main supplier's stock of gold and purchased gold directly from wholesalers, resulting in a large increase in stock levels. It was held that there was a major change in the conduct of the trade where stock levels had substantially increased.

Cross References

From Section 401

Section 268 Meaning of "industrial building or structure".
Section 320 Other interpretation (Part 9).
Section 396 Relief for trading losses other than terminal losses.
Section 400 Company reconstructions without change of ownership.
Section 754 Interpretation (Chapter 1).
Schedule 9 Change in Ownership of Company: Disallowance of Trading Losses
Schedule 32 Transitional Provisions

To Section 401

Section 1075 Penalties for failure to furnish certain information and for incorrect information.
Schedule 9 Change in Ownership of Company: Disallowance of Trading Losses

CHAPTER 4

Income Tax and Corporation Tax: Treatment of Certain Losses and Certain Capital Allowances

402 Foreign currency: tax treatment of capital allowances and trading losses of a company

[CTA76 s14A; FA94 s56(b)]

(1) (a) In this section—

"*functional currency*" means—

(i) in relation to a company resident in the State, the currency of the primary economic environment in which the company operates, and

(ii) in relation to a company not resident in the State, the currency of the primary economic environment in which the company carries on trading activities in the State, but, where the profit and loss account of a company for any period of account has been prepared in terms of the currency of the State, that currency shall be the functional currency of the company for that period;

"*profit and loss account*" and "*rate of exchange*" have the same meanings respectively as in *section 79*;

"*representative rate of exchange*" means a rate of exchange of a currency for another currency equal to the mid-market rate at close of business recorded by the Central Bank of Ireland, or by a similar institution of another State, for those 2 currencies.

(b) For the purposes of this section, the currency of the primary economic environment of a company shall be determined—

(i) in the case of a company resident in the State, with reference to the currency in which—

(I) revenues and expenses of the company are primarily generated, and

(II) the company primarily borrows and lends, and

(ii) in the case of a company not so resident which carries on trading activities in the State, with reference to the currency in which—

(I) revenues and expenses of those activities are primarily generated, and

(II) the company primarily borrows and lends for the purposes of those activities.

(c) For the purposes of this section, the day on which any expenditure is incurred shall be taken to be the day on which the sum in question becomes payable.

[(d) In this section references to an amount having been incurred in, or computed in terms of, a currency other than the functional currency of a company shall not include a reference to an amount having been incurred in, or computed in terms of, the currency of a state, which currency has been substituted by another currency of that state, where that other currency is the functional currency of the company.

(e) For the purposes of this section where at any time, in relation to a state, the currency (hereafter in this paragraph referred to as "the old currency") is substituted by another currency, the representative rate of exchange of the currency of that state for the currency of another state at any previous time shall mean the representative rate of exchange of the old currency of that state for the currency of that other state.][1]

(2) (a) Subject to *paragraph (b)*, the amount (which may be nil) of any allowance or charge to be made for any accounting period—

(i) in taxing a trade of a company, and

(ii) by reference to capital expenditure incurred by the company on or after the 1st day of January, 1994,

shall be—

(I) computed in terms of the functional currency of the company by reference to amounts expressed in that currency, and

(II) given effect, in accordance with *section 307(2)(a)*, by being treated as a trading expense or receipt, as the case may be, of the trade in computing the trading income or loss, expressed in that functional currency, of the trade for that accounting period.

(b) (i) For the purposes of the computation of an allowance or charge to be made for an accounting period (in this paragraph referred to as "*the first-mentioned period*") by reference to capital expenditure incurred by a company on or after the 1st day of January, 1994, and

(ii) without prejudice to any allowance made by reference to that expenditure for an accounting period earlier than the first-mentioned period,

where that expenditure was incurred, or an allowance referable to that expenditure was computed, in terms of a currency other than the functional currency of the company for the first-mentioned period, then, that expenditure or allowance, as the case may be, shall be expressed in terms of that functional currency by reference to a representative rate of exchange of that functional currency for the other currency for the day on which that expenditure was incurred.

[(c) For the purposes of this subsection, references to an amount of any allowance or charge to be made in taxing a trade shall include a reference to an amount of any allowance or charge to be made by means of discharge or repayment of tax in taxing the leasing activities of a company, where those activities are charged to tax under Case IV of Schedule D and references to a trading expense or receipt shall be construed accordingly.][2]

(3) (a) Subject to *paragraph (b)*, for the purposes of [*sections 396, 396A* and *397*][3], the amount (which may be nil) of any set-off due to a company against income or profits of an accounting period in respect of a loss from a trade incurred by the company in an accounting period shall—

(i) be computed in terms of the company's functional currency by reference to amounts expressed in that currency, and

(ii) then be expressed in terms of the currency of the State by reference to the rate of exchange which—

(I) is used to express in terms of the currency of the State the amount of the income from the trade for the accounting period in which the loss is to be set off, or

(II) would be so used if there were such income.

(b) (i) For the purposes of the computation of any set-off due to a company against income or profits of an accounting period (in this paragraph referred to as "*the first-mentioned period*") in respect of a loss from a trade incurred by the company in an accounting period, and

(ii) without prejudice to any set-off made against the income or profits of an accounting period earlier than the first-mentioned period by reference to that loss,

where that loss, or any set-off referable to that loss, was computed in terms of a currency other than the functional currency of the company for the first-mentioned period, then, that loss or set-off, as the case may be, shall be expressed in terms of that functional currency by reference to a rate of exchange of that functional currency for the other currency, being an average of representative rates of exchange of that functional currency for the other currency during the accounting period in which the loss was incurred.

[(4) (a) Subject to *paragraph (b)*, where a company incurs a loss in an accounting period arising from a leasing activity in respect of which the company is within the charge to corporation tax under Case IV of Schedule D and makes a claim under *section 399(1)* to set that loss off against the amount of any income arising from such activities in respect of which the company is assessed to corporation tax under that Case for the same or any subsequent accounting period, the amount (which may be nil) of any set-off due to the company against that income in an accounting period shall—

(i) be computed in terms of the company's functional currency by reference to amounts expressed in that currency, and

(ii) then be expressed in terms of the currency of the State by reference to the rate of exchange which—

(I) is used to express in terms of the currency of the State the amount of the income assessed to corporation tax under Case IV for the accounting period in which the loss is to be set off, or

(II) would be so used if there were such income.

(b) For the purposes of the computation of any setoff due to a company in accordance with *paragraph (a)* against income of an accounting period, in respect of a loss arising from a leasing activity in such period, where that loss or any set-off referable to that loss was computed in terms of a currency other than the functional currency of the company for the first-mentioned period, then that loss or set-off, as the case may be, shall be expressed in terms of that functional currency by reference to a rate of exchange of that functional currency for the other currency, being an average of representative rates of exchange of that functional currency for the other currency during the accounting period in which the loss was incurred.][4]

Amendments

[1] Inserted by FA98 sched2(5). With effect from 31 December 1998 per S.I. 502 of 1998.

[2] Inserted by FA10 s53(a). Deemed to have come into force and takes effect as on and from 1 January 2010.

[3] Substituted by FA07 sched4(1)(h). Apply to accounting periods ending on or after 1 January 2007.

[4] Inserted by FA10 s53(b). Deemed to have come into force and takes effect as on and from 1 January 2010.

Revenue Briefings

Tax Briefing

Tax Briefing April 1998 – Issue 31 pg 5 – The Euro and Tax

Cross References

From Section 402

Section 79 Foreign currency: computation of income and chargeable gains.

Section 307 Corporation tax: allowances and charges in taxing a trade.

Section 396 Relief for trading losses other than terminal losses.

Section 397 Relief for terminal loss in a trade.

Section 399 Losses in transactions from which income would be chargeable under Case IV or V of Schedule D.

To Section 402

Section 79 Foreign currency: computation of income and chargeable gains.

Section 79B Matching of foreign currency assets with certain foreign currency share capital.

403 Restriction on use of capital allowances for certain leased assets

[FA84 s40(1) to (10); FA86s53; FA87 s26; FA90 s41(5)(a) and (c); FA94 s61(1)]

(1) (a) In this section—

"*chargeable period or its basis period*" has the same meaning as in *section 321(2)*;

"*lessee*" and "*lessor*", in relation to machinery or plant provided for leasing, mean respectively the person to whom the machinery or plant is or is to be leased and the person providing the machinery or plant for leasing, and "*lessee*" and "*lessor*" include respectively the successors in title of a lessee or a lessor;

"*the relevant period*" has the meaning assigned to it by *subsection (9)(b)*;

"*the specified capital allowances*" means capital allowances in respect of—

(i) expenditure incurred on machinery or plant provided on or after the 25th day of January, 1984, for leasing in the course of a trade of leasing, or

(ii) the diminished value of such machinery or plant by reason of wear and tear,

other than capital allowances in respect of machinery or plant to which *subsection (6)*, *(7)*, *(8)* or *(9)* applies;

"*trade of leasing*" means—

(i) a trade which consists wholly of the leasing of machinery or plant, or

(ii) any part of a trade treated as a separate trade by virtue of *subsection (2)*.

(b) For the purposes of this section—

(i) letting on charter a ship or aircraft which has been provided for such letting, and

(ii) letting any item of machinery or plant on hire,

shall be regarded as leasing of machinery or plant if apart from this paragraph it would not be so regarded.

(c) Where a company carries on a trade of operating ships in the course of which a ship is let on charter, *paragraph (b)* shall not apply so as to treat the letting on charter as the leasing of machinery or plant if apart from this section the letting would be regarded for the purposes of Case I of Schedule D as part of the activities of the trade.

[(d) For the purposes of this section, where, in relation to a company which carries on a business—

(i) the activities—

(I) of the company,

(II) of the company and all companies of which it is a 75 per cent subsidiary (within the meaning of *section 9*) and all companies which are its 75 per cent subsidiaries (within the same meaning), or

(III) of the company and all companies (being companies which, by virtue of the law of the territory in which the company is resident for the purposes of tax, are so resident in that territory; and for this purpose, "*tax*", in relation to such a territory, means any tax imposed in the territory which corresponds to corporation tax in the State) of which it is a 75 per cent subsidiary (within the meaning of *section 9*) or which are its 75 per cent subsidiaries (within the same meaning),

consist wholly or mainly of the leasing of machinery or plant, and

(ii) not less than 90 per cent of the activities of the company consist of one or more of the following:

(I) the leasing of machinery or plant;

(II) the provision of finance and guarantees to fund the purchase of machinery or plant of a type which is similar to the type of machinery or plant leased by the companies referred to in *subparagraph (i)*;

(III) the provision of leasing expertise in connection with machinery or plant of a type which is similar to the type of machinery or plant leased by the companies referred to in *subparagraph (i)*;

(IV) the disposal of machinery or plant acquired by the company in the course of its leasing trade;

(V) activities which are ancillary to the activities referred to in clauses (I) to (IV):

[...][1]][2]

[then, subject to *section 80A(2)(c)*, income from the company's trade of leasing shall be treated as including—

(A) income from the activities referred to in *subparagraph (ii)*, and

(B) chargeable gains on the disposal of machinery or plant acquired by the company in the course of its leasing trade; and for this purpose the amount of such a gain shall be computed without regard to any adjustment made under *section 556(2)*.][3]

(2) Where in any chargeable period or its basis period a person carries on as part of a trade any leasing of machinery or plant, that leasing shall be treated for the purposes of the Tax Acts, other than any provision of those Acts relating to the commencement or cessation of a trade, as a separate trade distinct from all other activities carried on by such person as part of the trade, and any necessary apportionment shall be made of receipts or expenses.

(3) (a) Notwithstanding *section 381*, where relief is claimed under that section in respect of a loss sustained in a trade of leasing, the amount of that loss, in so far as by virtue of *section 392* it is referable to the specified capital allowances, shall be treated for the purposes of *subsections (1)* and *(3)(b)* of *section 381* as reducing profits or gains of that trade of leasing only and shall not be treated as reducing any other income.

(b) Where *paragraph (a)* applies in the case of any claimant to relief under *section 381*—

(i) any limitation imposed by *section 393* on the amount of capital allowances which may be taken into account under *section 392* shall be referred, as far as may be, to the specified capital allowances rather than to any other capital allowances, and

(ii) notwithstanding *section 392(2)* (but without prejudice to *paragraph (a)* and to the order in which income is to be treated as reduced under *section 381(3)(b)*), the claimant may specify the extent to which any reduction of income treated as occurring by virtue of *section 381* is to be referred to so much of the loss as is attributable to the loss, if any, actually sustained in the trade of leasing, the specified capital allowances or any other capital allowances, and, where the claimant so specifies, *section 394* shall apply in accordance with the claimant's specification and not in accordance with *section 392(2)*.

(4) (a) Where in an accounting period a company carrying on a trade of leasing incurs a loss in that trade and any specified capital allowances have been treated by virtue of *section 307* or *308* as trading expenses in arriving at the amount of the loss, the relevant amount of the loss shall not be available—

(i) for relief under *section 396(2)*, except to the extent that it can be set off under that section against the company's income from the trade of leasing only, or

(ii) to be surrendered by means of [group relief except to the extent that it could be set off under *section 420A* against income of a trade of leasing carried on by the claimant company if *paragraph (b)* of the definition of relevant trading loss in *section 420A* were deleted][4].

(b) For the purposes of *paragraph (a)*, the relevant amount of the loss shall be the full amount of the loss or, if it is less, an amount equal to—

(i) where no capital allowances, other than the specified capital allowances, have been treated by virtue of *section 307* or *308* as trading expenses in arriving at the amount of the loss, the amount of the specified capital allowances, or

(ii) where, in addition to the specified capital allowances, other capital allowances have been so treated by virtue of *section 307* or *308*, the lesser of—

(I) the amount of the specified capital allowances, and

(II) the amount by which the loss exceeds the amount of the other capital allowances;

but, where the amount of the loss does not exceed the amount of the other capital allowances, the relevant amount of the loss shall be nil.

(5) *Sections 305(1)(b)*, *308(4)* and *420(2)* shall not apply in relation to capital allowances—

(a) in respect of expenditure incurred on or after the 25th day of January, 1984, on the provision of machinery or plant, or

(b) in respect of the diminished value of machinery or plant by reason of wear and tear, if that machinery or plant was first acquired on or after the 25th day of January, 1984, by the person to whom the capital allowances are to be or have been made,

other than capital allowances in respect of machinery or plant to which *subsection (6)* or *(7)* applies.

[(5A) (a) In this subsection "*appointed day*" has the same meaning as in *section 284(3A)*.

(b) In relation to capital allowances in respect of machinery or plant to which *section 284(3A)* applies—

(i) notwithstanding *subsections (3)* and *(5)*—

(I) *subsection (3)* shall not apply, and

(II) *section 305(1)(b)* shall apply,

where the capital expenditure on that machinery or plant is incurred in the period of 2 years commencing on the appointed day, and

(ii) notwithstanding *subsections (4)* and *(5)*—

(I) *subsection (4)* shall not apply, and

(II) *sections 308(4)* and *420(2)* shall apply,

where the capital expenditure on that machinery or plant is incurred in the period of [6 years][5] commencing on the appointed day.

(c) This subsection shall come into operation on the appointed day.][6]

(6) References in this section to machinery or plant to which this subsection applies are references to machinery or plant provided on or after the 25th day of January, 1984, for leasing where the expenditure incurred on the provision of the machinery or plant was incurred under an obligation entered into by the lessor and the lessee before—

(a) the 25th day of January, 1984, or

(b) the 1st day of March, 1984, pursuant to negotiations which were in progress between the lessor and the lessee before the 25th day of January, 1984.

(7) References in this section to machinery or plant to which this subsection applies are references to machinery or plant [(not being either or both a film negative and its associated soundtrack, or a film tape or a film disc)][7] provided on or after the 25th day of January, 1984, for leasing where the expenditure incurred on the provision of the machinery or plant (or, in the case of a film to which section 6 or 7 of the Irish Film Board Act, 1980, applies, the cost of the making of the film) has been or is to be met directly or indirectly, wholly or partly, by the Industrial Development Authority, the Irish Film Board, the Shannon Free Airport Development Company Limited, or Údarás na Gaeltachta; but this subsection shall not apply to machinery or plant provided for leasing on or after the 13th day of May, 1986, unless—

(a) the machinery or plant is a film to which section 6 or 7 of the Irish Film Board Act, 1980, applies, or

(b) the expenditure incurred on the provision of the machinery or plant (not being a film of the kind mentioned in *paragraph (a)*) was incurred under an obligation entered into by the lessor and the lessee before—

(i) the 13th day of May, 1986, or

(ii) the 1st day of September, 1986, pursuant to negotiations which were in progress between the lessor and the lessee before the 13th day of May, 1986.

(8) The reference in the definition of "*the specified capital allowances*" to machinery or plant to which this subsection applies is a reference to machinery or plant provided for leasing by a lessor to a lessee in the course of the carrying on by the lessor of relevant trading operations within the meaning of *section 445* or *446*, and—

(a) in respect of the expenditure on which no allowance has been or will be made under *section 283*, or

(b) in respect of which no allowance on account of wear and tear to be made under *section 284* has been or will be increased under *section 285*.

[(8A) Where, but for the deletion of *sections 445* and *446*, any machinery or plant would, for the purposes of the definition of 'the specified capital allowances', be machinery or plant to which *subsection (8)* applies, then, notwithstanding the deletion of those sections, the machinery or plant shall be machinery or plant to which *subsection (8)* applies for those purposes and this section shall apply with any modifications necessary to give effect to this subsection.][8]

(9) (a) (i) In this subsection, "*specified trade*", in relation to a [lessee or lessor][9], means a trade which throughout the relevant period consists wholly or mainly of the manufacture of goods (including activities which, if the [lessee or lessor][10] were to make a claim for relief in respect of the trade under *Part 14*, would be regarded for the purposes of that Part as the manufacture of goods).

(ii) For the purposes of *subparagraph (i)*, a trade shall be regarded, as respects the relevant period, as consisting wholly or mainly of particular activities only if the total amount receivable by the [lessee or lessor][11] from sales made or, as the case may be, in payment for services rendered in the course of those activities in the relevant period is not less than 75 per cent of the total amount receivable by the [lessee or lessor][12] from all sales made or, as the case may be, in payment for all services rendered in the course of the trade in the relevant period.

(iii) As respects a person who carries on a trade of leasing and who incurred expenditure on the provision before the 20th day of April, 1990, of machinery or plant for leasing under an obligation entered into before that date by the lessor and a lessee who carries on a trade which but for *section 443(6)* would be a specified trade, this subsection shall apply as if the trade carried on by the lessee were a specified trade.

(iv) For the purposes of *subparagraph (iii)*, an obligation shall be treated as entered into before the 20th day of April, 1990, only if before that date there were in existence a binding contract in writing under which that obligation arose.

[(b) The reference in the definition of "*the specified capital allowances*" to machinery or plant to which this subsection applies is a reference to machinery or plant (not being a film of the kind mentioned in *subsection (7)(a)*) provided on or after the 13th day of May, 1986, for leasing by a lessor to a lessee (who is not a person connected with the lessor) under a lease the terms of which include an undertaking given by the lessee that, during a period (in this section referred to as "the relevant period") which is not less than 3 years and which commences on the day on which the machinery or plant is first brought into use by the lessee, the machinery or plant so provided will—

(i) where it is so provided before the 4th day of March, 1998, be used by the lessee for the purposes only of a specified trade carried on in the State by the lessee, and][13] [(ii) where it is so provided on or after that day, be used by the lessee for the purposes only of a specified trade carrried on in the State by the lessee and, except where the lessor provides the machinery or plant for leasing in the course of a specified trade carried on by the lessor, that it will not be used for the purposes of any other trade, or business or activity other than the lessor's trade.][14]

(c) Any machinery or plant in respect of which an undertaking mentioned in *paragraph (b)* has been given by a lessee, and which at any time has been treated as machinery or plant to which this subsection applies, shall at any later time cease to be machinery or plant to which this subsection applies if at that later time it appears to the inspector (or on appeal to the Appeal Commissioners) that the undertaking has not been fulfilled by the lessee.

(d) Where any machinery or plant ceases in accordance with *paragraph (c)* to be machinery or plant to which this subsection applies, such assessments or adjustments of assessments shall be made to recover from the lessor any relief from tax given to the lessor because the machinery or plant was treated as machinery or plant to which this subsection applies.

(e) This subsection shall not apply to machinery or plant provided for leasing on or after the 13th day of May, 1986, if the expenditure incurred on the provision of the machinery or plant was incurred under an obligation entered into by the lessor and the lessee before—

(i) the 13th day of May, 1986, or

(ii) the 1st day of September, 1986, pursuant to negotiations which were in progress between the lessor and the lessee before the 13th day of May, 1986.

(10) For the purposes of *subsections (6)*, *(7)* and *(9)*—

(a) an obligation shall be treated as having been entered into before a particular date only if before that date there was in existence a binding contract in writing under which that obligation arose, and

(b) negotiations pursuant to which an obligation was entered into shall not be regarded as having been in progress between a lessor and a lessee before a particular date unless on or before that date preliminary commitments or agreements in relation to that obligation had been entered into between the lessor and the lessee.

Amendments

[1] Deleted by FA07 sched4(1)(i). Apply to accounting periods ending on or after 1 January 2007.

[2] Inserted by FA06 s68(1)(a)(i).

[3] Inserted by FA07 sched4(1)(i). Apply to accounting periods ending on or after 1 January 2007.

[4] Substituted by FA05 s45(1)(c). Applies as respects an accounting period ending on or after 3 February 2005.

[5] Substituted by FA01 s52(2). With effect from 24 March 2004 per S.I. 124 of 2004.

[6] Inserted by FA98 s23(b).

[7] Inserted by FA06 s68(1)(a)(ii). Applies from 2 February 2006.

[8] Inserted by FA12 sched1(16).

[9, 10, 11, 12] Substituted by FA99 s52(1)(a). This section shall apply as on and from the 4th day of March, 1998.

[13] Substituted by FA98 s31.

[14] Substituted by FA99 s52(1)(b). This section shall apply as on and from the 4th day of March, 1998.

Revenue Information Notes

Income Tax, Corporation Tax and CGT Manuals: Section 403 ringfences wear and tear allowances relating to leased assets to the income from those leased assets. Subsection (5) disapplies section 305 (1) (b) and the sideways set off of excess allowances against other income where the relevant expenditure has been incurred on the provision of plant.

Revenue Precedents

If a racecourse stand, which qualifies for capital allowances as plant, is leased can excess allowances be set against other income? No, such allowances are restricted by section 403 (5) TCA 1997. GD95062

Where some unexpected event occurs so that plant and equipment provided for use in a specified trade is destroyed or otherwise cannot be used necessitating its replacement before the 3 year period required by section 403(9) has expired ,will this be regarded as a breach of the undertaking given for the purposes of that section? In the circumstances it is agreed that such an occurance will not be treated as a breach of this undertaking. The key issue is that the machinery is not used for any non-qualifying purpose. DTX 5063/94

Cross References

From Section 403

Section 9 Subsidiaries.
Section 283 Initial allowances.
Section 284 Wear and tear allowances.
Section 285 Acceleration of wear and tear allowances.
Section 305 Income tax: manner of granting, and effect of, allowances made by means of discharge or repayment of tax.
Section 307 Corporation tax: allowances and charges in taxing a trade.
Section 308 Corporation tax: manner of granting, and effect of, allowances made by means of discharge or repayment of tax.
Section 321 Provisions of general application in relation to the making of allowances and charges.
Section 350 Provisions supplementary to sections 346 to 349.
Section 381 Right to repayment of tax by reference to losses.
Section 392 Option to treat capital allowances as creating or augmenting a loss.
Section 393 Extent to which capital allowances to be taken into account for purposes of section 392.
Section 394 Effect of giving relief under section 381 by reference to capital allowances.
Section 396 Relief for trading losses other than terminal losses.
Section 420 Losses, etc. which may be surrendered by means of group relief.
Section 442 Interpretation (Part 14).
Section 443 Meaning of "goods".
Section 445 Certain trading operations carried on in Shannon Airport.
Section 446 Certain trading operations carried on in Custom House Docks Area.
Section 556 Adjustment of allowable expenditure by reference to consumer price index.

To Section 403

Section 80A Taxation of certain short-term leases plant and machinery.
Section 396A Relief for relevant trading losses.
Section 404 Restriction on use of capital allowances for certain leased machinery or plant.
Section 407 Restriction on use of losses and capital allowances for qualifying shipping trade.
Section 420A Group relief: relevant losses and charges.
Section 692 Development expenditure: allowances and charges.
Section 697O Capital allowances: general.
Section 1013 Limited partnerships.

404 Restriction on use of capital allowances for certain leased machinery or plant

[FA94 s30(1) to (5) and (7)]

(1) (a) In this section—

"*agricultural machinery*" means machinery or plant used or intended to be used for the purposes of a trade of farming (within the meaning of *section 654*) or machinery or plant of a type commonly used for such a trade which is used or intended to be used for the purposes of a trade which consists of supplying services which normally play a part in agricultural production;

"*asset*" means machinery or plant;

"*chargeable period*", "*chargeable period related to*", and "*chargeable period or its basis period*" have the same meanings respectively as in *section 321(2)*;

"*fair value*", in relation to a leased asset, means an amount equal to such consideration as might be expected to be paid for the asset at the inception of the lease on a sale negotiated on an arm's length basis, less any grants receivable by the lessor towards the purchase of the asset;

"*inception of the lease*" means the date on which the leased asset is brought into use by the lessee or the date from which lease payments under the lease first accrue, whichever is the earlier;

"*lease payments*" means the lease payments over the term of the lease to be paid to the lessor in relation to the leased asset, and includes any residual amount to be paid to the lessor at or after the end of the term of the lease and guaranteed by the lessee or by a person connected with the lessee or under the terms of any scheme or arrangement between the lessee and any other person;

"*lessee*" and "*lessor*" have the same meanings respectively as in *section 403*;

"*predictable useful life*", in relation to an asset, means the useful life of the asset estimated at the inception of the lease, having regard to the purpose for which the asset was acquired and on the assumption that—

(i) its life will end when it ceases to be useful for the purpose for which it was acquired, and

(ii) it will be used in the normal manner and to the normal extent throughout its life;

"*relevant lease payment*" means—

(i) the amount of any lease payment as provided under the terms of the lease, or

(ii) where the lease provides for the amount of any lease payment to be determined by reference to [a rate known as the European Interbank Offered Rate][1], or a similar rate, the amount calculated by reference to that rate if the rate per cent at the inception of the lease were the rate per cent at the time of the payment;

"relevant lease payments related to a chargeable period or its basis period" means relevant lease payments under the lease or the amounts which are treated as the relevant lease payments and which, if they were the actual amounts payable under the lease, would be taken into account in computing the income of the lessor for that chargeable period or its basis period or any earlier such period;

"*relevant period*" means the period—

(i) beginning at the inception of the lease, and

(ii) ending at—

(I) the earliest time at which the aggregate of amounts of the discounted present value at the inception of the lease of relevant lease payments which are payable at or before that time amounts to 90 per cent or more of the fair value of the leased asset, or

(II) if it is earlier, at the end of the predictable useful life of the asset,

and, for the purposes of this definition, relevant lease payments shall be discounted at a rate which, when applied at the inception of the lease to the amount of the relevant lease payments, produces discounted present values the aggregate of which equals the amount of the fair value of the leased asset at the inception of the lease, but where the duration of the relevant period determined in accordance with the preceding provisions of this definition is more than 7 years, the relevant period shall not be the period so determined but shall be the period which would be determined in accordance with this definition if for "90 per cent" there were substituted "95 per cent".

(b) For the purposes of this section—

(i) a lease of an asset shall be a relevant lease unless—

(I) as respects any chargeable period or its basis period of the lessor which falls wholly or partly in the relevant period, the aggregate of the amounts of relevant lease payments related to the chargeable period or its basis period and the amounts of relevant lease payments related to any earlier chargeable period or its basis period is not less than an amount determined by the formula—

$$W \times P \times \frac{90 + (10 \times W)}{100}$$

where—

P is the aggregate of the amounts of relevant lease payments payable by the lessee in relation to the leased asset in the relevant period, and

W is an amount determined by the formula—

$$\frac{E}{R}$$

where—

E is the length of the part of the relevant period which has expired at the end of the chargeable period or its basis period, and

R is the length of the relevant period, and

(II) except for an amount of relevant lease payments which is inconsequential, the excess of the total relevant lease payments under the lease over the aggregate of the relevant lease payments in the relevant period is payable to the lessor, or would be so payable if the relevant lease payments were the actual amounts payable under the lease, within a period the duration of which does not exceed—

(A) where the exception to the definition of "*relevant period*" does not apply, one-seventh of the duration of the relevant period, and

(B) where that exception does apply, one-ninth of the duration of the relevant period,

or one year, whichever is the greater, and which commences immediately after the end of the relevant period,

(ii) a lease, the duration of the relevant period in respect of which exceeds 10 years and which apart from this subparagraph would be a relevant lease, shall not be a relevant lease if it is a lease of an asset, being an asset—

(I) provided for the purposes of a project, specified in the list referred to in *section 133(8)(c)(iv)*, which has been approved for grant aid by the Industrial Development Authority, the Shannon Free Airport Development Company Limited or Udarás na Gaeltachta, and

(II) to which *section 283(5)* or *285(7)(a)(i)* applies,

and it would not be a relevant lease if for *clauses (I)* and *(II)* of *subparagraph (i)* there were substituted the following:

"(I) the aggregate of the relevant lease payments related to a chargeable period or its basis period of the lessor which falls wholly or partly in the period (in this subsection referred to as the "first period") of 3 years beginning at the inception of the lease is not less than an amount determined by the formula—

$$V \times \frac{D}{100} \times \frac{80}{100} \times \frac{M}{12}$$

where—

D is the rate per cent at the inception of the lease of [the rate known as the 6 month European Interbank Offered Rate][2], expressed as a rate per annum,

M is the number of months in the chargeable period or its basis period, and

V is the fair value of the asset at the inception of the lease,

(II) as respects any chargeable period or its basis period of the lessor which falls wholly or partly in the period (in this subsection referred to as "the second period") commencing immediately after the first period and ending at the end of the relevant period, the aggregate of the amounts of relevant lease payments related to the chargeable period or its basis period and the amounts of relevant lease payments related to any earlier chargeable period or its basis period falling wholly or partly in the second period is not less than an amount determined by the formula—

$$\frac{E}{R} \times P$$

where—

E is the length of the part of the second period which has expired at the end of the chargeable period or its basis period,

P is the aggregate of the amounts of relevant lease payments payable by the lessee in relation to the leased asset in the second period, and

R is the length of the second period, and

(III) except for an amount of relevant lease payments which is inconsequential, the excess of the total relevant lease payments under the lease over the aggregate of the relevant lease payments in the relevant period is payable to the lessor, or would be so payable if the relevant lease payments were the actual amounts payable under the lease, within a period of one year after the end of the relevant period.",

(iii) an amount of relevant lease payments shall be treated as inconsequential if the aggregate of amounts, estimated at the inception of the lease, of discounted value, at the end of the period specified in *clause (II)* of *subparagraph (i)* or *clause (III)* of that subparagraph (construed in accordance with *subparagraph (ii)*), as the case may be, of the relevant lease payments after that time does not exceed 5 per cent of the fair value of the leased asset or [€2,540][3], whichever is the lesser, and, for the purposes of this subparagraph, relevant lease payments shall be discounted at the rate specified in the definition of "*relevant period*", […][4]

(iv) where a chargeable period or its basis period, being an accounting period of a company, begins before and ends after a date, being the commencement of the relevant period, the first period or the second period or the end of such a period, as the case may be, it shall be divided into one part beginning on the day on which the accounting period begins and ending at the beginning or the end, as the case may be, of the relevant period, the first period or the second period, and another part beginning immediately after that time and ending on the day on which the accounting period ends, and both parts shall be treated as if they were separate accounting periods.

[(v) where a lease the relevant lease payments in relation to which are denominated in a currency (in this subparagraph referred to as the "*relevant currency*") other than the currency of the State—

(I) is a relevant lease, and

(II) would not be a relevant lease if *subparagraphs (i)* to *(iv)* were applied by reference to the value of those relevant lease payments in the relevant currency,

the lease shall not be treated as a relevant lease.][5]

(2) (a) [Subject to *subsection (2A)*, where][6] in the course of a trade an asset is provided by a person for leasing under a relevant lease, the letting of the asset under that relevant lease shall be treated as a separate trade of leasing (in this subsection referred to as a "*specified leasing trade*") distinct

from all other activities, including other leasing activities, of the person, and *section 403*, apart from *subsections (5)* to *(9)* of that section, shall apply in relation to a specified leasing trade as it applies in relation to a trade of leasing within the meaning of that section.

(b) *Sections 305(1)(b)*, *308(4)* and *420(2)* shall not apply in relation to capital allowances—

(i) in respect of expenditure incurred on the provision of an asset, or

(ii) on account of the wear and tear of an asset,

which is provided by a person for leasing under a relevant lease.

[(2A) (a) In this subsection—

"*relevant long-term lease*" means a lease of an asset the predictable useful life of which exceeds 8 years;

"*predictable useful life*" and "*relevant period*" have, respectively, the same meanings as they have in *section 80A*.

(b) Where—

(i) in the course of a trade an asset is provided by a person for leasing under a relevant lease, and

(ii) the lease is a relevant long-term lease,

then this section shall apply as if—

(I) in *subsection (2)(a)* "and the letting of any other asset under a relevant long-term lease" were inserted after "under that relevant lease", and

(II) the following were substituted for *subparagraphs (i)* and *(ii)* of *section 403(4)(a)*:

"(i) for relief under *section 396(2)*, except to the extent that it can be set off under that section against—

(I) the company's income from the trade of leasing,

(II) in the case of a company referred to in *paragraph (d)* of *section 403(1)*, income specified in *subparagraph (A)* and *(B)* of that paragraph, or

(III) income from the leasing by the company of any other asset under a relevant long-term lease,

or

(ii) to be surrendered by means of group relief except to the extent that it—

(I) could be set off under *section 420A* against income of a trade of leasing carried on by the claimant company if *paragraph (b)* of the definition of relevant trading loss in *section 420A* were deleted, or

(II) where the surrendering company and the claimant company are companies referred to in *paragraph (d)* of *section 403(1)*, can be set off—

(A) under *section 420A* against income specified in *subparagraphs (A)* and *(B)* of that paragraph, or

(B) under *section 420A* against income from the leasing by the company of any other asset under a relevant long-term lease.",][7]

(3) Notwithstanding *subsection (1)(b)*, a lease of an asset which consists of agricultural machinery or plant shall not be a relevant lease unless it would be such a lease if the amounts of relevant lease payments related to any chargeable period or its basis period were taken to be an amount equal to 50 per cent of the aggregate of the amounts of relevant lease payments related to that chargeable period or its basis period and the amounts of relevant lease payments related to a period equal in length to, and ending immediately before the commencement of, that period.

(4) (a) [Subject to *subsection (4A)*, where at any time][8] after the 11th day of April, 1994, either of the following events occurs—

(i) the terms of a lease of an asset entered into before that day are altered, or

(ii) a lessor and a lessee agree to terminate a lease of an asset and, at or about that time, a further agreement to lease the asset is entered into by the lessor and the lessee or an agreement is entered into by the lessor and a person connected with the lessee, by the lessee and a person connected with the lessor or by a person connected with the lessor and a person connected with the lessee,

such that the aggregate of the amounts of the lease payments which are payable, or which would be payable if the relevant lease payments were the actual amounts payable under the lease, after any time exceeds the aggregate of the amounts of such relevant lease payments which would have been payable after that time if the events in *subparagraph (i)* or *(ii)* had not taken place, then, notwithstanding *subsection (6)(a)*, unless it is shown that the change or the termination was effected for bona fide commercial reasons, the lease (including the terminated lease) shall be treated as if it were at all times a relevant lease, and relief given under *Part 9*, *Chapter 1* or *2* of this Part, or *section 396* or *420*, which would not have been given if the lease was a relevant lease, shall be withdrawn.

(b) The withdrawal of an allowance or relief under *paragraph (a)* shall be made—

(i) for the chargeable period related to the event giving rise to the withdrawal of the relief, and

(ii) in accordance with *paragraph (c)*,

and both—

(I) details of the event giving rise to the withdrawal of the allowance or relief, and

(II) the amount to be treated as income under *paragraph (c)*,

shall be included in the return required to be made by the lessor under [*Chapter 3* of *Part 41A*][9] for that chargeable period.

(c) (i) Notwithstanding any other provision of the Tax Acts, where relief is to be withdrawn under *paragraph (a)* in respect of—

(I) any amount which was set off against income under *section 305*,

(II) the amount of any loss which was set off under *section 307, 308, 396* or *420* against profits, or

(III) the amount of any loss which was treated by virtue of a claim under *section 381* as reducing income,

and which would not have been so set off or treated if the lease were a relevant lease, such amount (in this subsection referred to as "*the relevant amount*") as would not have been so set off or treated, increased in accordance with *subparagraph (ii)*, shall be treated as income arising in the chargeable period specified in *paragraph (b)(i)*.

(ii) The amount by which the relevant amount is to be increased under *subparagraph (i)* shall be an amount determined by the formula—

$$A \times \frac{R}{100} \times M$$

where—

A is the relevant amount,

M is the number of [days][10] in the period beginning on the date on which tax for the chargeable period in which the losses were treated as reducing income, or set off against profits, as the case may be, was due and payable and ending on the date on which tax for the chargeable period for which the withdrawal of relief is to be made is due and payable, and

R [is 0.0273.][11]

[(4A) (a) Where the terms of a lease entered into before 2 February 2006, being a lease which would, apart from *subsection (1)(b)(ii)* or *subsection (6)(a)*, have been a relevant lease, are altered after that day, then—

(i) such a lease shall not be treated as a relevant lease by virtue of that alteration, and

(ii) unless the alteration involves a reduction in the value of any payment (or a part of a payment) under the lease, not being a payment (or a part of a payment) the amount of which is computed under the lease by reference to any rate of interest, the alteration shall be disregarded as respects the treatment for tax purposes of any defeasance payment made in connection with the lease.

(b) *Paragraph (a)* shall not apply as respects a lease if any amount payable under the lease is, by virtue of the alteration of the terms of the lease, to be paid under the lease more than 20 years after the time at which it would otherwise have been payable.][12]

(5) Notwithstanding *subsection (1)(b)*, where at any time on or after the 11th day of April, 1994, a person (in this subsection referred to as "*the lessor*") acquires an asset from another person who before that date was the owner of the asset and at or about that time the lessor or a person connected with the lessor leases the asset to the other person or a person connected with the other person, then, unless—

(a) the asset is new and unused, or

(b) the lease would not be a relevant lease if—

(i) for the first formula in *subsection (1)(b)(i)(I)* there were substituted "W × P", and

(ii) *subsection (1)(b)(ii)* had not been enacted,

the lease shall be a relevant lease for the purposes of this section.

[(6) (a) This section shall apply as on and from 23 December 1993; but a lease of an asset shall not be a relevant lease if—

(i) a binding contract in writing for the letting of the asset was concluded before that day, or

(ii) (I) the relevant period does not exceed 5 years,

(II) the predictable useful life of the asset does not exceed 8 years,

(III) the lease provides for lease payments to be made at annual or more frequent regular intervals throughout the relevant period such that, in relation to any chargeable period (in this subsection referred to as the "*current chargeable period*") falling wholly or partly into the relevant period (other than the earliest such chargeable period), the aggregate of the amounts of lease payments payable under the lease before the end of the current chargeable period is not less than an amount determined by the formula—

$$\frac{V \times T}{2920}$$

where—

V is an amount equal to the fair value of the asset at the inception of the lease, and

T is the number of days in the period commencing at the inception of the lease and ending at the end of the current chargeable period,

and

(IV) the lessor has made an election in relation to the lease for the treatment referred to in *paragraph (b)*.

(b) Where a lessor has made an election under *paragraph (a)(ii)(IV)* in relation to a lease, the Tax Acts shall apply as respects assets leased under that lease as they would if the following were inserted in *section 284(2)*:

'(c) Where machinery or plant which is used in a chargeable period or its basis period is not used throughout that period, the amount of the wear and tear allowance for the chargeable period in respect of the machinery or plant, computed by reference to *paragraph (b)*, shall be reduced to so much as bears to that amount the same proportion as the part of the chargeable period or its basis period throughout which the machinery or plant is used bears to the length of the chargeable period or its basis period.'.][13]

Amendments

[1] Substituted by FA98 sched2(6)(a). With effect from 1 January 1999 per S.I. 502 of 1998.

[2] Substituted by FA98 sched2(6)(b). With effect from 1 January 1999 per S.I. 502 of 1998.

[3] Substituted by FA01 sched5.

[4] Deleted by FA06 s68(1)(b)(i)(I). This section applies to accounting periods ending on or after 1 January 2006.

[5] Inserted by FA06 s68(1)(b)(i)(III). This section applies to accounting periods ending on or after 1 January 2006.

[6] Substituted by FA06 s68(1)(b)(ii). This section applies to accounting periods ending on or after 1 January 2006.

[7] Inserted by FA06 s68(1)(b)(iii). This section applies to accounting periods ending on or after 1 January 2006.

[8] Substituted by FA06 s68(1)(b)(iv). This section applies to accounting periods ending on or after 1 January 2006.

[9] Substituted by FA12 sched4(part 2)(g).

[10] Substituted by FA05 sched6(1)(g)(i). Applies and comes into effect as on and from 3 February 2005.

[11] Substituted by FA05 sched6(1)(g)(ii). Applies and comes into effect as on and from 3 February 2005.

[12] Inserted by FA06 s68(1)(b)(v). This section applies to accounting periods ending on or after 1 January 2006.

[13] Substituted by FA06 s68(1)(b)(vi). This section applies to accounting periods ending on or after 1 January 2006.

Cross References

From Section 404

Section 133 Limitation on meaning of "distribution" — general.
Section 268 Meaning of "industrial building or structure".
Section 283 Initial allowances.
Section 284 Wear and tear allowances.
Section 285 Acceleration of wear and tear allowances.
Section 305 Income tax: manner of granting, and effect of, allowances made by means of discharge or repayment of tax.
Section 307 Corporation tax: allowances and charges in taxing a trade.
Section 308 Corporation tax: manner of granting, and effect of, allowances made by means of discharge or repayment of tax.
Section 321 Provisions of general application in relation to the making of allowances and charges.
Section 381 Right to repayment of tax by reference to losses.
Section 396 Relief for trading losses other than terminal losses.
Section 403 Restriction on use of capital allowances for certain leased assets.
Section 420 Losses, etc. which may be surrendered by means of group relief.
Section 654 Interpretation (Part 23).
Section 951 Obligation to make a return.

To Section 404

Section 407 Restriction on use of losses and capital allowances for qualifying shipping trade.

405 Restriction on use of capital allowances on holiday cottages

[FA92 s25]

(1) [Subject to *subsections (2)* and *(3)*][1], where on or after the 24th day of April, 1992, a person incurs capital expenditure on the acquisition or construction of a building or structure which is or is to be an industrial building or structure by virtue of being a holiday cottage within the meaning of *section 268*, and an allowance is to be made in respect of that expenditure under *section 271* or *272*—

[(a) *sections 305(1)(b)*, *308(4)* and *420(2)* shall not apply as respects that allowance, and][2]

(b) neither *section 381* nor *section 396(2)* shall apply as respects the whole or part (as the case may be) of any loss which would not have arisen but for the making of that allowance.

(2) This section shall not apply to expenditure incurred before the 6th day of April, 1993, on the acquisition or construction of a building or structure (in this subsection referred to as "*the holiday cottage*") which is or is to be an industrial building or structure by virtue of being a holiday cottage within the meaning of *section 268* if before the 24th day of April, 1992—

(a) a binding contract in writing for the construction of the holiday cottage was entered into, or

(b) (i) a binding contract in writing for the purchase or lease of land for the construction of the holiday cottage was entered into, and

(ii) an application for planning permission for the construction of the holiday cottage was received by a planning authority.

[(3) This section shall not apply to a building or structure which is in use as a holiday cottage and comprised in premises first registered on or after 6 April 2001 in a register of approved holiday cottages established by [the National Tourism Development Authority][3] under Part III of the Tourist Traffic Act, 1939, where, prior to such premises becoming so registered—

(a) the building or structure was a qualifying premises within the meaning of *section 353*, by virtue of being in use for the purposes of the operation of a tourist accommodation facility specified in a list published under section 9 of the Tourist Traffic Act, 1957, and

(b) the provisions of *section 355(4)* did not apply to expenditure incurred on the acquisition, construction or refurbishment of that building or structure, by virtue of the provisions of *section 355(5)*.][4]

Amendments

[1] Substituted by FA01 s62(1)(a)(i)(I).

[2] Substituted by FA01 s62(1)(a)(i)(II).

[3] Substituted by FA06 sched2(1)(i). This section is deemed to have come into force and have taken effect as on and from 28 May 2003.

[4] Inserted by FA01 s62(1)(a)(ii).

Revenue Precedents

An application for outline planning permission satisfies the requirement of section 405(2)(b)(ii). IT923066

Do the ring-fence provisions in the section apply to the purchaser of a holiday cottage, in respect of which allowances have been claimed, where the original construction expenditure was incurred before the cut-off date? No. – the purchaser is claiming in respect of the residue of the original expenditure – not in respect of the expenditure incurred on the purchase of the property. IT963505

Cross References

From Section 405

Section 268 Meaning of “industrial building or structure”.

Section 271 Industrial building allowances.

Section 272 Writing-down allowances.

Section 305 Income tax: manner of granting, and effect of, allowances made by means of discharge or repayment of tax.

Section 308 Corporation tax: manner of granting, and effect of, allowances made by means of discharge or repayment of tax.

Section 353 Capital allowances in relation to construction or refurbishment of certain commercial premises.

Section 355 Disclaimer of capital allowances on holiday cottages, holiday apartments, etc.

Section 381 Right to repayment of tax by reference to losses.

Section 396 Relief for trading losses other than terminal losses.

Section 420 Losses, etc. which may be surrendered by means of group relief.

406 Restriction on use of capital allowances on fixtures and fittings for furnished residential accommodation

[Where a person incurs capital expenditure of the type to which *subsection (7)* of *section 284* applies and an allowance is to be made in respect of that expenditure under that section, *sections 305(1)(b)*, *308(4)* and *420(2)* shall not apply as respects that allowance.][1]

Amendments

[1] Substituted by FA01 s62(1)(b).

Cross References

From Section 406

Section 284 Wear and tear allowances.

Section 305 Income tax: manner of granting, and effect of, allowances made by means of discharge or repayment of tax.

Section 308 Corporation tax: manner of granting, and effect of, allowances made by means of discharge or repayment of tax.

Section 420 Losses, etc. which may be surrendered by means of group relief.

407 Restriction on use of losses and capital allowances for qualifying shipping trade

[FA87 s28(1), (2), (4) and (5)(a); FA88 s40(1) and (3); FA90 s42(1); FA94 s62; FA96 s54]

(1) In this section—

"*lessee*", in relation to a ship provided for leasing, means the person to whom the ship is or is to be leased and includes the successors in title of a lessee;

"*qualifying ship*" means a seagoing vessel which—

(a) (i) is owned to the extent of not less than 51 per cent by a person or persons resident in the State, or

(ii) is the subject of a letting on charter without crew by a lessor not resident in the State,

(b) in the case of a vessel to which *paragraph (a)(i)* applies, is registered in the State under Part II of the Mercantile Marine Act, 1955, and, in the case of a vessel to which *paragraph (a)(ii)* applies, is a vessel in respect of which it can be shown that the requirements of the Merchant Shipping Acts, 1894 to 1993, have been complied with as if it had been a vessel registered under that Part,

(c) is of not less than 100 tons gross tonnage, and

(d) is self-propelled,

but, notwithstanding anything in *paragraph (a)*, *(b)*, *(c)* or *(d)*, does not include—

(i) a fishing vessel, other than a vessel normally used for the purposes of an activity mentioned in *paragraph (d)* of the definition of "*qualifying shipping activities*",

(ii) a tug, other than a tug in respect of which a certificate has been given by the Minister for the Marine and Natural Resources certifying that in the opinion of the Minister the tug is capable of operating in seas outside the portion of the seas which are, for the purposes of the Maritime Jurisdiction Act, 1959 (as amended by the Maritime Jurisdiction (Amendment) Act, 1988), the territorial seas of the State,

(iii) a vessel (including a dredger) used primarily as a floating platform for working machinery or as a diving platform, and

(iv) any other vessel of a type not normally used for the purposes of qualifying shipping activities;

"*qualifying shipping activities*" means activities carried on by a company in the course of a trade and which consist of—

(a) the use of a qualifying ship for the purpose of carrying by sea passengers or cargo for reward,

(b) the provision on board the qualifying ship of services ancillary to that use of the qualifying ship,

(c) the granting of rights by virtue of which another person provides or will provide those services on board that qualifying ship,

(d) the subjecting of fish to a manufacturing process on board a qualifying ship,

(e) the letting on charter of a qualifying ship for use for those purposes where the operation of the ship and the crew of the ship remain under the direction and control of the company, or

(f) the use of a qualifying ship for the purposes of transporting supplies or personnel to, or providing services in respect of, a mobile or fixed rig, platform, vessel or installation of any kind at sea;

"*qualifying shipping trade*" means a trade, the income from which is within the charge to corporation tax, carried on in the relevant period, which consists solely of the carrying on of qualifying shipping activities or, in the case of a trade consisting partly of the carrying on of such activities and partly of the carrying on of other activities, that part of the trade consisting solely of the carrying on of qualifying shipping activities and which is treated by virtue of *subsection (3)* as a separate trade;

"*relevant certificate*" means a certificate issued with the consent of the Minister for Finance by the Minister for the Marine and Natural Resources in relation to the letting on charter of a ship certifying, on the basis of a business plan and any other information supplied by the lessee to the Minister for the Marine and Natural Resources, that that Minister is satisfied that the lease is in respect of a ship which—

(a) will result in an upgrading and enhancement of the lessee's fleet leading to improved efficiency and the maintenance of competitiveness,

(b) (i) has the potential to create a reasonable level of additional sustainable employment and other socioeconomic benefits in the State, or

(ii) will assist in maintaining or promoting the lessee's trade in the carrying on of a qualifying shipping activity and the maintenance of a reasonable level of sustainable employment and other socio-economic benefits in the State,

and

(c) will result in the leasing of a ship which complies with current environmental and safety standards;

"*the relevant period*" means the period from the [1 January 1987 to][1][31 December 2010][2];

"*specified capital allowances*" means capital allowances in respect of—

(a) expenditure incurred by any person in the relevant period on the provision of a qualifying ship which is in use in or is intended to be used in a qualifying shipping trade, or

(b) the diminished value by reason of wear and tear during the relevant period of a qualifying ship in use for the purposes of a qualifying shipping trade,

notwithstanding that any such capital allowances are not treated as trading expenses of the qualifying shipping trade.

(2) Before issuing a relevant certificate, the Minister for the Marine and Natural Resources shall be satisfied that the lease concerned is for bona fide commercial purposes and not part of a scheme or arrangement the main purpose or one of the main purposes of which is the avoidance of tax.

(3) (a) Subject to *paragraph (b)*, where during the relevant period a company carries on qualifying shipping activities as part of a trade, those activities shall be treated for the purposes of the Tax Acts, other than any provision of those Acts relating to the commencement or cessation of a trade, as a separate trade distinct from all other activities carried on by the company as part of the trade, and any necessary apportionment shall be made of receipts or expenses.

(b) This subsection shall not apply in relation to a claim by the company for the set-off under *section 396(1)*—

(i) against income arising during the relevant period, of a loss incurred before the commencement of the relevant period, and

(ii) against income arising after the end of the relevant period, of a loss incurred during the relevant period.

(4) Notwithstanding any other provision of the Tax Acts apart from *subsection (5)*, for the purposes of granting relief from tax in respect of any income or profits arising in the relevant period or for the purposes of determining the amount of such income or profits which is chargeable to tax—

(a) specified capital allowances shall be allowed only—

(i) in computing the income from a qualifying shipping trade, or

(ii) in computing or charging to tax any income arising from the letting on charter of the qualifying ship to which the specified capital allowances refer, other than letting on charter which is a qualifying shipping activity,

and shall not be allowed in computing any other income or profits or in taxing any other trade or in charging any other income to tax,

(b) a loss incurred in the relevant period in a qualifying shipping trade shall not be set off—

(i) against any profits under *section 396(2)*, except to the extent of the amount of income from a qualifying shipping trade included in those profits, or

(ii) against the total profits of a claimant company under *section 420(1)*, except to the extent of the amount of income from a qualifying shipping trade included in those total profits,

and

(c) the letting on charter of a ship referred to in *paragraph(a)(ii)* in the course of a trade shall be deemed, notwithstanding *subsection (1)(c)* of *section 403*, to be a trade of leasing for the purposes of that section and to be a separate trade as provided for in *subsection (2)* of that section.

(5) As respects a ship a binding contract in writing for the acquisition or construction of which was concluded on or after the 1st day of July, 1996, *subsection (4)(c)* shall not apply in the case of a letting on charter of a ship referred to in that subsection where the lease in respect of the ship is a lease the terms of which comply with *clauses (I)* and *(II)* of *section 404(1)(b)(i)*, and where the lessee produces to the Revenue Commissioners a relevant certificate.

(6) A qualifying shipping trade shall not be regarded as a specified trade for the purposes of *section 403*.

Amendments

[1] Substituted by FA01 s82(1)(b). This section applies as on and from 1 January 2001.

[2] Substituted by FA06 s58.

Cross References

From Section 407

Section 396 Relief for trading losses other than terminal losses.
Section 403 Restriction on use of capital allowances for certain leased assets.
Section 404 Restriction on use of capital allowances for certain leased machinery or plant.
Section 420 Losses, etc. which may be surrendered by means of group relief.

To Section 407

Section 21 The charge to corporation tax and exclusion of income tax and capital gains tax.
Section 133 Limitation on meaning of "distribution" — general.
Section 134 Limitation on meaning of "distribution" in relation to certain payments made in respect of "foreign source" finance.
Section 396B Relief for certain trading losses on a value basis.
Section 420B Group relief: Relief for certain losses on a value basis.
Section 443 Meaning of "goods".
Section 448 Relief from corporation tax.

408 Restriction on tax incentives on property investment

[FA91 s24]

(1) In this section—

"*property investment scheme*" means any scheme or arrangement made for the purpose, or having the effect, of providing facilities, whether promoted by means of public advertisement or otherwise, for the public or a section of the public to share, either directly or indirectly and whether as beneficiaries under a trust or by any other means, in income or gains arising or deriving from the acquisition, holding or disposal of, or of an interest in, a building or structure or a part of a building or structure, but does not include a scheme or arrangement as respects which the Revenue Commissioners or, on appeal, the Appeal Commissioners, having regard to such information as may be produced to them, are of the opinion that—

(a) the manner in which persons share in the income or gains, and

(b) the number of persons who so share,

are in accordance with a practice which commonly prevailed in the State during the period of 5 years ending immediately before the 30th day of January, 1991, for the sharing of such income or gains by persons resident in the State and such that the persons so sharing qualified for relief under *section 305(1)(b)* or *308(4)*;

"*specified interest*" means an interest in or deriving from a building or structure held by a person pursuant to a property investment scheme.

(2) Where a person holds a specified interest, then, as respects expenditure incurred or deemed to be incurred on or after the 30th day of January, 1991, *sections 305(1)(b)* and *308(4)* shall not apply as respects an allowance under *section 271* or *272* which is to be made to the person by reason of the holding by the person of the specified interest.

(3) The Appeal Commissioners shall hear and determine an appeal made to them under this section as if it were an appeal against an assessment to income tax, and the provisions of the Income Tax Acts relating to the rehearing of an appeal and to the statement of a case for the opinion of the High Court on a point of law shall apply accordingly with any necessary modifications.

Revenue Briefings

Tax Briefing

Tax Briefing November 2005 – Issue 61 – Capital Allowances in respect of Private Hospitals

Revenue Precedents

Two groups of investors purpose to buy one floor each of a two storey building in an Enterprise Area. The building as a whole is to be let to the same tenant. The two groups have engaged separate tax agents. Does the number of persons referred to under section 408(1) relate to the whole building or each floor? The number 13 relates to the whole building. Oogm10

Cross References

From Section 408

Section 271 Industrial building allowances.

Section 272 Writing-down allowances.

Section 305 Income tax: manner of granting, and effect of, allowances made by means of discharge or repayment of tax.

Section 308 Corporation tax: manner of granting, and effect of, allowances made by means of discharge or repayment of tax.

To Section 408

Section 355 Disclaimer of capital allowances on holiday cottages, holiday apartments, etc.

409 Capital allowances: room ownership schemes

[FA97 s24(1) to (3), (4)(a) and (b) and (5)]

(1) In this section—

"*hotel investment*" means capital expenditure incurred either on the construction of, or the acquisition of a relevant interest in, a building or structure which is to be regarded as an industrial building or structure within the meaning of *subsection (1)(d)* of *section 268*, other than a building or structure to which *subsection (3)* of that section relates;

"*hotel partnership*" includes any syndicate, group or pool of persons, whether or not a partnership, through or by means of which a hotel investment is made;

"*market value*" shall be construed in accordance with *section 548*;

"*member*", in relation to a hotel partnership, includes every person who participates in that partnership or who has contributed capital, directly or indirectly, to that partnership;

"*preferential terms*", in relation to the acquisition of an interest referred to in *subsection (3)(a)(i)*, means terms under which such interest is acquired for a consideration which, at the time of the acquisition, is or may be other than its market value.

(2) This section is for the purpose of counteracting any room ownership scheme entered into in connection with a hotel investment by a hotel partnership.

(3) For the purposes of this section—

(a) a scheme shall be a room ownership scheme in connection with a hotel investment if, at the time a hotel investment is made by a hotel partnership, there exists any agreement, arrangement, understanding, promise or undertaking (whether express or implied and whether or not enforceable or intended to be enforceable by legal proceedings) under or by virtue of which any member of that hotel partnership, or a person connected with such member, may—

(i) acquire on preferential terms an interest in, or

(ii) retain for use other than for the purposes of the trade of hotel-keeping,

any room or rooms in, or any particular part of, the building or structure which is the subject of the hotel investment, and

(b) where a hotel investment is made by one or more than one member of a hotel partnership, it shall be deemed to be made by the hotel partnership.

(4) Subject to *subsection (5)*, no allowance shall be made under *Chapter 1* of *Part 9* in respect of a hotel investment by a hotel partnership where, in connection with any such investment, there exists a room ownership scheme.

(5) (a) Except where provided for in *paragraph (b)*, this section shall apply to a hotel investment the capital expenditure in respect of which is incurred on or after the 26th day of March, 1997.

(b) This section shall not apply to a hotel investment if, before the 26th day of March, 1997, in respect of a building or structure which is the subject of such investment—

(i) a binding contract in writing was entered into for the construction of, or the acquisition of a relevant interest in, the building or structure, or

(ii) an application for planning permission for the construction of the building or structure was received by a planning authority.

Cross References

From Section 409

Section 268 Meaning of "industrial building or structure".

Section 548 Valuation of assets.

409A Income tax: restriction on use of capital allowances on certain industrial buildings and other premises

[(1) In this section—

"*active partner*", in relation to a partnership trade, means a partner who works for the greater part of his or her time on the day-to-day management or conduct of the partnership trade;

"*industrial development agency*" means the Industrial Development Agency (Ireland);

"*partnership trade*" and "*several trade*" have the same meanings, respectively, as in *Part 43*;

"*specified building*" means—

(a) a building or structure which is or is to be an industrial building or structure by reason of its use or its deemed use for a purpose specified in *section 268(1)*, and

(b) any other building or structure in respect of which an allowance is to be made, or will by virtue of *section 279* be made, for the purposes of income tax under *Chapter 1* of *Part 9* by virtue of *Part 10* or *section 843* [or *843A*][1],

but does not include a building or structure—

(i) which is or is deemed to be an industrial building or structure by reason of its use for the purposes specified in *section 268(1)(d)*, or

(ii) to which *section 355(1)(b)* applies.

[(2) Subject to *subsection (5)*, in relation to any allowance to be made to an individual under *Chapter 1* of *Part 9* for any year of assessment in respect of capital expenditure incurred on or after 3 December 1997, on a specified building, *section 305* shall apply as if the following were substituted for *subsection (1)(b)* of that section:

(b) (i) Notwithstanding *paragraph (a)*, where an allowance referred to in that paragraph is available primarily against income of the specified class and the amount of the allowance is greater than the amount of the person's income of that class for the first-mentioned year of assessment (after deducting or setting off any allowances for earlier years), then the person may, by notice in writing given to the inspector not later than 2 years after the end of the year of assessment, elect that the excess or [€31,750][2], whichever is the lower, shall be deducted from or set off—

[(I) against the individual's other income for that year of assessment,

(II) where the individual, or, being a husband or wife, the individual's spouse, is assessed to tax in accordance with *section 1017*, firstly, against the individual's other income for that year of assessment and, subsequently, against the income of the individual's husband or wife, as the case may be, for that year of assessment, or

(III) where the individual, or the individual's civil partner, is assessed to tax in accordance with *section 1031C*, firstly, against the individual's other income for that year of assessment and, subsequently, against the income of the individual's civil partner for that year of assessment.][3]

(ii) Where an election is made in accordance with *subparagraph (i)*, the excess or [€31,750][4], whichever is the lower, shall be deducted from or set off against the income referred to in clause (I) or (II) of that subparagraph, as the case may be, and tax shall be discharged or repaid accordingly and only the balance, if any, of the amount of the allowance referred to in *paragraph (a)* over all the income referred to in the said clause (I) or (II), as the case may be, for that year of assessment shall be deducted from or set off against the person's income of the specified class for succeeding years.'.][5]

(3) Subject to *subsection (5)*, where—

(a) any allowance or allowances under *Chapter 1* of *Part 9* is or are to be made for a year of assessment to an individual, being an individual who is a partner in a partnership trade, in respect of capital expenditure incurred on or after the 3rd day of December, 1997, on a specified building, and

(b) that allowance or those allowances is or are to be made in taxing the individual's several trade,

then, unless in the basis period for the year of assessment in respect of which that allowance or those allowances is or are to be made the individual is an active partner in relation to the partnership trade, the amount of any such allowance or allowances which is to be taken into account for the purposes of *section 392(1)* shall not exceed an amount determined by the formula—

A + [€31,750][6]

where A is the amount of the profits or gains of the individual's several trade in the year of loss before *section 392(1)* is applied.

(4) Where an individual is a partner in 2 or more partnership trades, then, for the purposes of *subsection (3)*, those partnership trades in relation to which the individual is not an active partner shall, in relation to that individual, be deemed to be a single partnership trade and the individual's several trades in relation to those partnership trades shall be deemed to be a single several trade.

(5) This section shall not apply to an allowance to be made to an individual under *Chapter 1* of *Part 9* in respect of capital expenditure incurred on or after the 3rd day of December, 1997, on a specified building where before that date—

(a) (i) in the case of construction, the foundation for the specified building was laid in its entirety,

(ii) in the case of a refurbishment project, work to the value of 5 per cent of the total cost of that refurbishment project was carried out, or

(iii) a project for which the specified building is to be provided had been approved for grant assistance by an industrial development agency but only where that approval was given within a period of 2 years preceding that date,

or.

(b) (i) an application for planning permission for the work represented by that expenditure on the specified building had (in so far as such permission is required) been received by a planning authority before the 3rd day of December, 1997, or

(ii) the individual can prove, to the satisfaction of the Revenue Commissioners, that a detailed plan had been prepared for the work represented by that expenditure and that detailed discussions had taken place with a planning authority in relation to the specified building before the 3rd day of December, 1997, and that this can be supported by means of an affidavit or statutory declaration duly made on behalf of the planning authority concerned,

and that expenditure is incurred under an obligation entered into by the individual in relation to the specified building before—

(i) the 3rd day of December, 1997, or

(ii) [the 1st day of May, 1998, pursuant to negotiations which were in progress before the 3rd day of December, 1977.][7]

(6) For the purposes of *subsection (5)*—

(a) an obligation shall be treated as having been entered into before a particular date only if, before that date, there was in existence a binding contract in writing under which that obligation arose, and

(b) negotiations pursuant to which an obligation was entered into shall not be regarded as having been in progress before a particular date unless preliminary commitments or agreements in writing in relation to that obligation had been entered into before that date.

(7) Where an individual has entered into an obligation to which *subsection (5)* relates to incur capital expenditure on a specified building on or after the 3rd day of December, 1997, and that individual dies before any part of that expenditure has been incurred, another individual who—

(a) undertakes in writing to honour the obligation entered into by the deceased individual, and

(b) incurs that part of the capital expenditure on the specified building which would otherwise have been incurred by the deceased individual,

shall be deemed to have complied with the requirements of *subsection (5)* in relation to that expenditure.

(8) This section shall, with any necessary modifications, apply in relation to a profession as it applies in relation to a trade.][8]

Amendments

[1] Inserted by FA99 s49(a).

[2, 4] Substituted by FA01 s62(1)(c)(i)(II). Applies as respects an allowance to be made for the year of assessment 2002 and subsequent years of assessment.

[3] Substituted by F(No.3)A11 sched1(62).

[5] Substituted by FA01 s62(1)(c)(i)(I). Applies as respects an allowance to be made for the year of assessment 2001 and subsequent years of assessment.

[6] Substituted by FA01 s62(1)(c)(ii)(II). Applies as respects an allowance to be made for the year of assessment 2002 and subsequent years of assessment.

[7] Amended by FA00 s38 (Repeal of earlier amendment URU 98 s20)

[8] Inserted by FA98 s30.

Revenue Briefings

Tax Briefing

Tax Briefing April 1998 – Issue 31 pg 23 – Capital Allowances Restrictions

Cross References

From Section 409A

Section 268 Meaning of "industrial building or structure".

Section 279 Purchases of certain buildings or structures.

Section 305 Income tax: manner of granting, and effect of, allowances made by means of discharge or repayment of tax.

Section 322 Interpretation (Chapter 1).

Section 355 Disclaimer of capital allowances on holiday cottages, holiday apartments, etc.

Section 392 Option to treat capital allowances as creating or augmenting a loss.

Section 843 Capital allowances for buildings used for third level educational purposes.

Section 1007 Interpretation (Part 43).

Section 1017 Assessment of husband in respect of income of both spouses.

To Section 409A

Section 531AU Capital allowances and losses.

Section 1013 Limited partnerships.

409B Income tax: restriction on use of capital allowances on certain hotels, etc

[(1) In this section—

"*active partner*", in relation to a partnership trade, has the same meaning as in *section 409A*;

"*partnership trade*" and "*several trade*" have the same meanings, respectively, as in *Part 43*;

"*specified building*" means a building or structure which is or is deemed to be an industrial building or structure by reason of its use for a purpose specified in *section 268(1)(d)* but does not include—

(a) any such building or structure (not being a building or structure in use as a holiday camp referred to in *section 268(3)*)—

(i) the site of which is wholly within any of the administrative counties of Cavan, Donegal, Leitrim, Mayo, Monaghan, Roscommon and Sligo but not within a qualifying resort area within the meaning of *Chapter 4* of *Part 10*, and

(ii) in which the accommodation and other facilities provided meet a standard specified in guidelines issued by the Minister for Tourism, Sport and Recreation with the consent of the Minister for Finance,

and

(b) a building or structure which is deemed to be such a building or structure by reason of its use as a holiday cottage of the type referred to in *section 268(3)*.

(2) Subject to *subsection (4)*, *section 305(1)(b)* shall not apply in relation to any allowance to be made to an individual for a year of assessment under *Chapter 1* of *Part 9* in respect of capital expenditure incurred on or after the 3rd day of December, 1997, on a specified building.

(3) Subject to *subsection (4)*, where—

(a) any allowance or allowances under *Chapter 1* of *Part 9* is or are to be made for a year of assessment to an individual, being an individual who is a partner in a partnership trade, in respect of capital expenditure incurred on or after the 3rd day of December, 1997, on a specified building, and

(b) that allowance or those allowances is or are to be made in taxing the individual's several trade,

then, unless in the basis period for the year of assessment in respect of which that allowance or those allowances is or are to be made the individual is an active partner in relation to the partnership trade, the amount of any such allowance or allowances which is to be taken into account for the purposes of *section 392(1)* shall not exceed the amount of the profits or gains of the individual's several trade in the year of loss before that section is applied.

(4) This section shall not apply to an allowance to be made to an individual under *Chapter 1* of *Part 9* in respect of capital expenditure incurred on or after the 3rd day of December, 1997, on a specified building where before that date—

(a) (i) in the case of construction, the foundation for the specified building was laid in its entirety, or

(ii) in the case of a refurbishment project, work to the value of 5 per cent of the total cost of that refurbishment project was carried out,

or

(b) (i) an application for planning permission for the work represented by that expenditure on the specified building had (in so far as such permission is required) been received by a planning authority before the 3rd day of December, 1997, or

(ii) the individual can prove, to the satisfaction of the Revenue Commissioners, that a detailed plan had been prepared for the work represented by that expenditure and that detailed discussions had taken place with a planning authority in relation to the specified building before the 3rd day of December, 1997, and that this can be supported by means of an affidavit or statutory declaration duly made on behalf of the planning authority concerned,

and that expenditure is incurred under an obligation entered into by the individual in relation to the specified building before—

(i) the 3rd day of December, 1997, or

(ii) the 1st day of May, 1998, pursuant to negotiations which were in progress before the 3rd day of December, 1997.

(5) For the purposes of *subsection (4)*—

(a) an obligation shall be treated as having been entered into before a particular date only if, before that date, there was in existence a binding contract in writing under which that obligation arose, and

(b) negotiations pursuant to which an obligation was entered into shall not be regarded as having been in progress before a particular date unless preliminary commitments or agreements in writing in relation to that obligation had been entered into before that date.

(6) Where an individual has entered into an obligation to which *subsection (4)* relates to incur capital expenditure on a specified building on or after the 3rd day of December, 1997, and that individual dies before any part of that expenditure has been incurred, another individual who—

(a) undertakes in writing to honour the obligation entered into by the deceased individual, and

(b) incurs that part of the capital expenditure on the specified building which would otherwise have been incurred by the deceased individual,

shall be deemed to have complied with the requirements of *subsection (4)* in relation to that expenditure.

(7) This section shall, with any necessary modifications, apply in relation to a profession as it applies in relation to a trade.][1]

Amendments

[1] Inserted by FA98 s30.

Revenue Briefings

Tax Briefing

Tax Briefing April 1998 – Issue 31 pg 23 – Capital Allowances Restrictions

Cross References

From Section 409B

Section 268 Meaning of "industrial building or structure".

Section 305 Income tax: manner of granting, and effect of, allowances made by means of discharge or repayment of tax.

Section 322 Interpretation (Chapter 1).

Section 351 Interpretation (Chapter 4).

Section 392 Option to treat capital allowances as creating or augmenting a loss.

Section 1007 Interpretation (Part 43).

To Section 409B

Section 1013 Limited partnerships.

409C Income tax: restriction on use of losses on approved buildings

[(1) In this section—

"*approved building*", "*the Minister*" and "*qualifying expenditure*" have, respectively, the meaning assigned to each of them by *section 482(1)(a)*;

"*the claimant*" has the meaning assigned to it by *section 482(2)(a)*;

"*eligible charity*" has the meaning assigned to it by *paragraph 1* of Part 3 of Schedule 26A;

"*ownership interest*", in relation to a building, means an estate or interest in a building which would entitle the person who holds it, to make a claim under *section 482* as owner of the building;

"*relevant determinations*", in relation to a building, means the determinations made by the Minister and the Revenue Commissioners, respectively, in accordance with *section 482(5)(a)*.

(2) For purposes of this section, a scheme shall be a passive investment scheme, in relation to a building, in any case where—

(a) an ownership interest, in relation to the building, is transferred by one person (in this section referred to as the "*transferor*") to another person (in this section referred to as the "*transferee*"),

(b) at the time of the transfer, or at any time in the period of 5 years commencing at that time, the building is an approved building, and

(c) (i) at the time of the transfer, arrangements subsist (whether express or implied and whether or not enforceable by legal proceedings) under or by virtue of which the transferor, or any person connected with the transferor (within the meaning of *section 10*)—

(I) may retain the right to determine how any qualifying expenditure in relation to the building is to be incurred,

(II) may obtain, whether directly or indirectly, a payment or other benefit representing any part of the value to the transferee of relief under the Tax Acts by virtue of a claim under *section 482(2)* in respect of qualifying expenditure in relation to the building, or

(III) may re-acquire the transferee's ownership interest (referred to in *paragraph (a)*),

or

(ii) the transfer is made for the sole or main purpose of facilitating a claim by the transferee under *section 482(2)*.

(3) This section applies where—

(a) by virtue of *subsection (2)* of *section 482*, qualifying expenditure in relation to an approved building is treated as a loss sustained in a trade carried on by a claimant, as owner of the building, in a chargeable period (referred to in *paragraph (b)(i)* of that subsection),

(b) the claimant is an individual who is a transferee [under a passive investment scheme][1], and

(c) relief is claimed under *section 381* in respect of the loss referred to in *paragraph (a)*.

(4) Where this section applies, the amount of the loss referred to in *subsection (3)(a)* which can be treated as reducing income for a year of assessment under *section 381(1)* shall be—

(a) the full amount of the loss, or

(b) €31,750,

whichever is the lesser.

[(4A) (a) Notwithstanding *subsection (4)*, where this section applies for the year of assessment 2010 or a later year of assessment, the amount of the loss referred to in *subsection (3)(a)* which can be treated as reducing income for each such year of assessment under *section 381(1)* shall be nil.

(b) This subsection shall not apply for the years of assessment 2010 or 2011 in relation to—

(i) work which was completed before 4 February 2010,

(ii) work which was underway on 4 February 2010, or

(iii) work carried out under a contractual commitment entered into before 4 February 2010 and evidenced in writing before that date where the work begins after that date.][2]

(5) Where by virtue of *subsection (4)* relief cannot be given for a year of assessment for part of the loss referred to in *subsection (3)(a)*, then for the purposes of *section 482(3)* such relief shall be treated as not being given owing to an insufficiency of income.

(6) This section shall not apply—

(a) to qualifying expenditure, in relation to an approved building, incurred before 5 December 2001,

(b) to qualifying expenditure, in relation to an approved building, incurred on or after 5 December 2001 and before 31 December 2003, where the relevant determinations have been made in relation to that building before 5 December 2001,

(c) to qualifying expenditure, incurred before 31 December 2003, in relation to a building, in respect of which—

(i) the Revenue Commissioners have, before 5 December 2001, indicated in writing, that proposals made to them are broadly acceptable, so as to enable them to make a determination under *section 482(5)(a)*, and

(ii) an officer of the Department of Arts, Heritage, Gaeltacht and the Islands has, before 5 December 2001, indicated in writing that, having inspected the building, the officer is satisfied that, if required, the officer would recommend to the Minister that a determination under *section 482(5)(a)* be made by the Minister, or

(d) to qualifying expenditure, incurred before 31 December 2003, in relation to a building where—

(i) the Minister has made a determination under *section 482(5)(a)* before 5 December 2001, in relation to the building, and

(ii) the claimant has undertaken to gift, whether directly or indirectly, to the transferor, who is an eligible charity, the full value of the relief to which the individual is entitled under the Tax Acts by virtue of making a claim under *section 482(2)*, and the individual does so.][3]

Amendments

[1] Inserted by FA03 sched6(1)(a). This section shall be deemed to have come into force and take effect as on and from 1 January 2002.

[2] Inserted by FA10 s21. Deemed to have come into force and takes effect as on and from 1 January 2010.

[3] Inserted by FA02 s14.

Cross References

From Section 409C

Section 10 Connected persons.

Section 381 Right to repayment of tax by reference to losses.

Section 482 Relief for expenditure on significant buildings and gardens.

409D Restriction of reliefs where individual is not actively participating in certain trades

[(1) In this section—

"*active trader*", in relation to a trade, means an individual who works for the greater part of his or her time on the day-to-day management or conduct of the trade;

"*electronic*" includes electrical, digital, magnetic, optical, electromagnetic, biometric, photonic and any other form of related technology;

"*specified provisions*" means *sections 305* and *381*;

"*specified trade*" means a trade consisting of or including—

(a) the generation of electricity,

(b) trading operations which are petroleum activities (within the meaning of *section 21A*),

(c) the development or production of—

(i) films,

(ii) film projects,

(iii) film properties, or

(iv) music properties,

(d) the acquisition of rights to participate in the revenues of—

(i) film properties, or

(ii) music properties,

or

(e) the production of, the distribution of, or the holding of an interest in—

(i) either or both a film negative and its associated soundtrack, a film tape or a film disc,

(ii) an audio tape or audio disc, or

(iii) a film property produced by electronic means or a music property produced by electronic means;

"*relevant year of assessment*" means—

(a) in relation to a trade consisting of or including the generation of electricity, the year of assessment 2002 or any subsequent year during which the individual carried on such trade otherwise than as an active trader, and

(b) in relation to any other specified trade, the year of assessment 2003 or any subsequent year during which the individual carried on that trade otherwise than as an active trader.

(2) Where, in the case of an individual who carries on a specified trade otherwise than as an active trader, an amount may apart from this section be given or allowed under any of the specified provisions—

(a) in respect of a loss sustained by the individual in the specified trade in a relevant year of assessment, including a loss which is computed taking account of interest laid out or expended by the individual in respect of a loan where the proceeds of the loan were used to incur expenditure on machinery or plant used for the purposes of the specified trade concerned, or

(b) as an allowance to be made to the individual for a relevant year of assessment either in taxing the specified trade or by means of discharge or repayment of tax to which he or she is entitled by reason of the individual carrying on the specified trade concerned,

then, notwithstanding any other provision of the Tax Acts, such an amount may be given or allowed only against income from the specified trade concerned and shall not be allowed in computing any other income or profits or in taxing any other trade or in charging any other income to tax.][1]

Amendments

[1] Inserted by FA03 s12(1). Applies as respects— (a) an allowance under Part 9 in respect of machinery or plant to be made— (i) for the year of assessment 2002 or any subsequent year in relation to a trade consisting of or including the generation of electricity, and (ii) for the year of assessment 2003 or any subsequent year in relation to any other trade, and (b) any loss sustained in— (i) a trade consisting of or including the generation of electricity in the year of assessment 2002 or any subsequent year, and (ii) any other trade in the year of assessment 2003 or any subsequent year.

Cross References

From Section 409D

Section 305 Income tax: manner of granting, and effect of, allowances made by means of discharge or repayment of tax.

Section 381 Right to repayment of tax by reference to losses.

409E Income tax: ringfence on use of certain capital allowances on certain industrial buildings and other premises

[(1) In this section—

"*company*" has the same meaning as in *section 4*;

"*rent*" has the same meaning as in *Chapter 8* of *Part 4*;

"*relevant interest*" has the same meaning as in *section 269*;

"residue of expenditure" shall be construed in accordance with *section 277*;

"*specified amount of rent*", in relation to a specified building and an individual for a year of assessment, means the amount of the surplus in respect of the rent from the specified building to which the individual becomes entitled for the year of assessment, as computed in accordance with *section 97(1)*;

"*specified building*" means—

(a) a building or structure, or a part of a building or structure, which is or is to be an industrial building or structure by reason of its use or deemed use for a purpose specified in *section 268(1)* and in relation to which an allowance has been, or is to be, made to a company under *Chapter 1* of *Part 9*, or

(b) any other building or structure, or a part of any other building or structure, in relation to which an allowance has been, or is to be, so made to a company by virtue of *Part 10* or *section 843* or *843A*,

in respect of—

(i) the capital expenditure incurred or deemed to be incurred on the construction or refurbishment of the building or structure or, as the case may be, the part of the building or structure, or

(ii) the residue of that expenditure.

(2) This section applies where—

(a) at any time beginning on or after 1 January 2003 a company is entitled to the relevant interest in relation to any capital expenditure incurred or deemed to be incurred on the construction or refurbishment of a specified building,

(b) subsequent to the time referred to in *paragraph (a)* an individual becomes entitled to that relevant interest or any part of that relevant interest, whether or not subsequent to that time any other person or persons had previously become so entitled, and

(c) the individual is entitled, in charging income under Case V of Schedule D, to an allowance under *Chapter 1* of *Part 9* in respect of the capital expenditure referred to in *paragraph (a)* or the residue of that expenditure.

(3) Where this section applies, then, notwithstanding any other provision of the Income Tax Acts—

(a) any allowance to be made to the individual for any year of assessment (being the year of assessment 2003 or any subsequent year of assessment) under *Chapter 1* of *Part 9*, in respect of the capital expenditure referred to in *subsection (2)(a)* or the residue of that expenditure, shall—

(i) not exceed the specified amount of rent for that year of assessment,

(ii) be made in charging the specified amount of rent under Case V of Schedule D for that year of assessment, and

(iii) be available only in charging the specified amount of rent,

(b) *section 278* shall apply with any modifications necessary to give effect to *paragraph (a)*, and

(c) *section 305(1)(c)* shall apply in relation to an allowance to be made in accordance with *paragraph (a)*.][1]

Amendments

[1] Inserted by FA03 s13(1).

Cross References

From Section 409E

Section 4 Interpretation of Corporation Tax Acts.

Section 97 Computational rules and allowable deductions.

Section 256 Interpretation (Chapter 4).

Section 268 Meaning of "industrial building or structure".
Section 269 Meaning of "the relevant interest".
Section 277 Writing off of expenditure and meaning of "residue of expenditure".
Section 278 Manner of making allowances and charges.
Section 305 Income tax: manner of granting, and effect of, allowances made by means of discharge or repayment of tax.
Section 322 Interpretation (Chapter 1).
Section 843 Capital allowances for buildings used for third level educational purposes.

To Section 409E

Section 305 Income tax: manner of granting, and effect of, allowances made by means of discharge or repayment of tax.

CHAPTER 4A

Termination of Carry Forward of Certain Losses

409F Interpretation and general (Chapter 4A)

[(1) This Chapter applies notwithstanding any other provision of the Tax Acts.

(2) In this Chapter—

'*active partner*' has the same meaning as in *section 409A*;

'*active trader*' has the same meaning as in *section 409D*;

'*area-based capital allowance*' means any allowance, or part of such allowance, made under *Chapter 1* of *Part 9* as that Chapter is applied—

(a) by *section 323, 331, 332, 341, 342, 343, 344, 352, 353, 372C, 372D, 372M, 372N, 372V, 372W*, [*372AC, 372AD or 372AAC*][1] for a chargeable period, or

(b) by virtue of *paragraph 11* of *Schedule 32* for a chargeable period,

including any such allowance, or part of any such allowance, made for a previous chargeable period and carried forward from that previous chargeable period in accordance with *Part 9*;

'*balancing allowance*' and '*balancing charge*' mean any allowance or charge, as the case may be, made under *section 274*;

'*capital allowance*' means any allowance, or part of such allowance, specified in the definition of '*area-based capital allowance*' or '*specified capital allowance*';

'*chargeable period*' has the same meaning as in *section 321* and a reference to a chargeable period or its basis period shall be construed in accordance with *subsection (2)* of that section;

'*relevant accounting period*' means the later of—

(a) the accounting period which begins immediately after the accounting period in which the tax life of the building or structure has ended, or

(b) the accounting period, or the first accounting period if there are more than one, ending in 2015;

'*relevant chargeable period*' means the later of—

(a) the chargeable period which begins immediately after the chargeable period in which the tax life of the building or structure has ended, or

(b) the chargeable period, or the first chargeable period if there are more than one, ending in 2015;

'*relevant tax year*' means the later of—

(a) the tax year which begins immediately after the tax year in which the tax life of the building or structure has ended, or

(b) the tax year 2015;

'*specified capital allowance*' means any specified relief that is—

(a) a writing down allowance or a balancing allowance made for a chargeable period, or

(b) an allowance, or part of such allowance, made under *Chapter 1* of *Part 9* as that Chapter is applied by *section 372AX*, *372AY*, *843* or *843A* for a chargeable period,

including any such allowance or part of such allowance made for a previous chargeable period and carried forward from that previous chargeable period in accordance with *Part 9*;

'*specified relief*' has the same meaning as in *section 485C*;

'*tax life*', in relation to a building or structure, means the appropriate period referred to in *section 272(4)* in respect of that building or structure, after the end of which period no capital allowance may be made following the disposal of the relevant interest (within the meaning of *section 269*) in that building or structure;

'*tax year*' means a year of assessment;

'*writing down allowance*' means any allowance made under *section 272* and includes any such allowance as increased under *section 273*.][2]

Amendments

[1] Substituted by FA13 s30(1)(b). Comes into operation on such day as the Minister for Finance may by order appoint.

[2] Substituted by FA12 s17.

409G Termination of capital allowances

[(1) As respects any tax year, the amount of any specified capital allowance, in relation to a building or structure, that is available to be carried forward, in accordance with *section 304* or *305*, to a relevant tax year or to any subsequent tax year, shall, subject to *subsections (5)* and *(6)*, be zero for all the purposes of the Tax Acts.

(2) As respects any accounting period, the amount of any specified capital allowance, in relation to a building or structure, that—

(a) is available to be carried forward to a relevant accounting period, or to any subsequent accounting period, in accordance with *section 308(3)*, or

(b) may be set, in accordance with *section 308(4)*, against the profits of an accounting period preceding the relevant accounting period to which *paragraph (a)* applies,

shall, subject to *subsection (6)*, be zero for all the purposes of the Tax Acts.

(3) As respects any tax year, the amount of any area-based capital allowance, in relation to a building or structure, that is available to be carried forward to a relevant tax year or to any sub sequent tax year, in accordance with *section 304* or *305*, as those provisions are applied or modified by any other provision of the Tax Acts shall, subject to *subsections (5)* and *(6)*, be zero for all the purposes of those Acts.

(4) As respects any accounting period, the amount of any area-based capital allowance, in relation to a building or structure, that—

(a) is available to be carried forward to a relevant accounting period or to any subsequent accounting period, in accordance with *section 308(3)*, or

(b) may be set, in accordance with *section 308(4)*, against the profits of an accounting period preceding the relevant accounting period to which *paragraph (a)* applies,

shall, subject to *subsection (6)*, be zero for all the purposes of the Tax Acts.

(5) *Subsections (1)* and *(3)* shall not apply to an individual where any capital allowance is made in taxing a trade in relation to which trade the individual is an active partner or an active trader.

(6) Notwithstanding *subsections (1)* to *(4)*, where in a relevant chargeable period or a subsequent chargeable period a balancing charge falls due to be made on a person in relation to any building or structure, any capital allowance in relation to that building or structure which would, but for those subsections, have been carried forward to that chargeable period may be set against that balancing charge and against no other income, profits or gains in that or any subsequent or preceding chargeable period.][1]

Amendments

[1] Substituted by FA12 s17.

409H Restriction on use of capital allowances [Repealed]

Repealed by FA12 s17.

CHAPTER 5

Group Relief

410 Group payments

[CTA76 s105; FA92 s50(1)]

(1) (a) In this section—

["*EEA Agreement*" means the Agreement on the European Economic Area signed at Oporto on 2 May 1992, as adjusted by the Protocol signed at Brussels on 17 March 1993;

"*EEA State*" means a state which is a contracting party to the EEA Agreement;

"*relevant Member State*" means—

(i) a Member State of the European Communities, or

(ii) not being such a Member State, an EEA State which is a territory with the government of which arrangements having the force of law by virtue of [*section 826(1)*][1] have been made;][2]

["*tax*", in relation to a [relevant Member State][3] other than the State, means any tax imposed in the Member State which corresponds to corporation tax in the State;][4]

"*trading or holding company*" means a trading company or a company whose business consists wholly or mainly in the holding of shares or securities of trading companies which are its 90 per cent subsidiaries;

"*trading company*" means a company whose business consists wholly or mainly of the carrying on of a trade or trades.

[(b) For the purposes of this section—

(i) a company shall be owned by a consortium if 75 per cent or more of the ordinary share capital of the company is beneficially owned between them by 5 or fewer companies resident in one or more than one [relevant Member State][5] of which none of these companies beneficially owns less than 5 per cent of that capital, and those companies shall be called the members of the consortium, and][6]

[(ii) references to a company resident in a relevant Member State shall be construed as references to a company which, by virtue of the law of a relevant Member State, is resident for the purposes of tax in such a relevant Member State.][7]

(2) References in this section to payments received by a company shall apply to any payments received by another person on behalf of or in trust for the company, but shall not apply to any payments received by the company on behalf of or in trust for another person.

(3) In determining for the purposes of this section whether one company is a 51 per cent subsidiary of another company, that other company shall be treated as not being the owner of—

(a) any share capital which it owns directly or indirectly in a company not resident [relevant Member State][8], or

(b) any share capital which it owns indirectly and which is owned directly by a company for which a profit on the sale of the shares would be a trading receipt.

(4) Where a company receives from another company (both being companies resident in [a relevant Member State][9]) any payments to which this section applies, and either—

(a) the company making the payment is—

(i) a 51 per cent subsidiary of the other company or of a company so resident of which the other company is a 51 per cent subsidiary, or

(ii) a trading or holding company owned by a consortium the members of which include the company receiving the payment, or

(b) the company receiving the payment is a 51 per cent subsidiary of the company making the payment,

then, subject to *subsections (5)* to *(7)*, the payment shall be made without deduction of income tax and neither *section 238* nor *section 246* shall apply to the payment.

[(5) This section shall apply to any payments which—

(a) for the purposes of corporation tax, are charges on income of the company making them or would be so if they were not deductible in computing profits or any description of profits or if *section 243(7)* did not apply to them, and

(b) where the company receiving the payments is not resident in the State, are taken into account in computing income of that company chargeable to tax in a relevant Member State,

but shall not apply to payments received by a company on any investments if a profit on the sale of those investments would be treated as a trading receipt of that company.][10]

(6) Where a company purports by virtue of *subsection (4)* to make any payment without deduction of income tax and income tax ought to have been deducted, the inspector

may make such assessments, adjustments or set-offs as may be required for securing that the resulting liabilities to tax (including interest on unpaid tax) of the company making and the company receiving the payment are, in so far as possible, the same as they would have been if the income tax had been duly deducted.

(7) Where tax assessed under *subsection (6)* on the company which made the payment is not paid by that company before the expiry of 3 months from the date on which that tax is payable, that tax shall, without prejudice to the right to recover it from that company, be recoverable from the company which received the payment.

Amendments

[1] Substituted by FA07 sched2(1)(k). Has effect as on and from 2 April 2007

[2] Inserted by FA02 s37(a)(i)(I).

[3] Substituted by FA02 s37(a)(i)(II).

[4] Inserted by FA99 s78(1)(a)(i). This section shall apply as respects accounting periods ending on or after the 1st day of July, 1998.

[5] Substituted by FA02 s37(a)(ii)(I).

[6] Substituted by FA99 s78(1)(a)(ii). This section shall apply as respects accounting periods ending on or after the 1st day of July, 1998.

[7] Substituted by FA02 s37(a)(ii)(II).

[8] Substituted by FA02 s37(a)(iii).

[9] Substituted by FA05 s52(1)(a). This section applies as respects accounting periods ending on or after 1 March 2005.

[10] Substituted by FA05 s52(1)(b). This section applies as respects accounting periods ending on or after 1 March 2005.

Revenue Briefings

Tax Briefing

Tax Briefing July 2007 – Issue 66 pg 22 – Group Relief – Section 48 Finance Act 2007

Cross References

From Section 410

Section 238 Annual payments not payable out of taxed income.
Section 243 Allowance of charges on income.
Section 246 Interest payments by companies and to non-residents.
Section 826 Agreements for relief from double taxation.

To Section 410

Section 21B Tax treatment of certain dividends.
Section 23A Company residence.
Section 80A Taxation of certain short-term leases plant and machinery.
Section 110 Securitisation.
Section 153 Distributions to certain nonresidents.
Section 172D Exemption from dividend withholding tax for certain non-resident persons.
Section 247 Relief to companies on loans applied in acquiring interest in other companies.
Section 443 Meaning of "goods".
Section 450 Double taxation relief.
Section 487 Corporation tax: credit for bank levy.
Section 616 Groups of companies: interpretation.
Section 626B Exemption from tax in the case of gains on disposals of shares.
Section 766 Tax credit for research and development expenditure.
Section 817 Schemes to avoid liability to tax under Schedule F.
Section 847 Tax relief for certain branch profits.
Section 1085 Corporation tax — late returns: restriction of certain claims for relief.
Schedule 22 Dividends Regarded as Paid Out of Profits Accumulated Before Given Date
Schedule 24 Relief from Income Tax and Corporation Tax by Means of Credit in Respect of Foreign Tax

411 Surrender of relief between members of groups and consortia

[CTA76 s107]

(1) (a) For the purposes of this section and the following sections of this Chapter—

["*EEA Agreement*" means the Agreement on the European Economic Area signed at Oporto on 2 May 1992, as adjusted by the Protocol signed at Brussels on 17 March 1993;

"*EEA State*" means a state which is a contracting party to the EEA Agreement;][1]

"*holding company*" means a company whose business consists wholly or mainly in the holding of shares or securities of companies which are its 90 per cent subsidiaries and are trading companies;

["*relevant Member State*" means—

(i) a Member State of the European Communities, or

(ii) not being such a Member State, an EEA State which is a territory with the government of which arrangements having the force of law by virtue of [*section 826(1)*][2] have been [made;][3]][4]

['*relevant territory*' means—

(i) a relevant Member State,

(ii) not being such a Member State, a territory with the government of which arrangements having the force of law by virtue of *section 826(1)* have been made, or

(iii) not being a territory referred to in *subparagraph (i)* or *(ii)*, a territory with the government of which arrangements have been made which on completion of the procedures set out in *section 826(1)* will have the force of law;][5]

["*tax*", in relation to a [relevant Member State][6] other than the State, means any tax imposed in the Member State which corresponds to corporation tax in the State;][7]

"*trading company*" means a company whose business consists wholly or mainly of the carrying on of a trade or trades;

[a company shall be owned by a consortium if 75 per cent or more of the ordinary share capital][8] of the company is directly and beneficially owned between them by 5 or fewer companies, and those companies shall be called the members of the consortium;

2 companies shall be deemed to be members of a group of companies if one company is the 75 per cent subsidiary of the other company or both companies are 75 per cent subsidiaries of a third company.

(b) In applying for the purposes of this section and the following sections of this Chapter the definition of "75 per cent subsidiary" in *section 9*, any share capital of a registered industrial and provident society shall be treated as ordinary share capital.

[[(c) In determining for the purposes of this section and the following provisions of this Chapter whether one company (in this paragraph referred to as the "*first-mentioned company*") is a 75 per cent subsidiary of another company—

(i) the other company shall be treated as not being the owner of—

(I) any share capital which it owns directly in a company if a profit on a sale of the shares would be treated as a trading receipt of its trade,

(II) any share capital which it owns indirectly and which is owned directly by a company for which a profit on the sale of the shares would be a trading receipt, or

(III) any share capital which it owns directly or indirectly in a company that is not a company which, by virtue of the law of a relevant territory, is resident for the purposes of tax in such a relevant territory,

and

(ii) the first-mentioned company shall not be treated as a 75 per cent subsidiary of the other company unless—

(I) that other company, by virtue of the law of a relevant territory, is resident for the purposes of tax in such a relevant territory, or

(II) the principal class of shares of that other company [...][9] is substantially and regularly traded on a stock exchange in the State, on one or more than one recognised stock exchange in a relevant territory or territories or on such other stock exchange as may be approved of by the Minister for Finance for the purposes of *Chapter 8A* of *Part 6*.][10]

(d) References in this Chapter to a company which is a surrendering company or a claimant company shall apply only to a company which, by virtue of the law of a relevant Member State, is resident for the purposes of tax in such a Member State.][11]

[(2) Subject to *subsection (2A)*, relief for—

(a) trading losses and other amounts eligible for relief from corporation tax, and

(b) trading losses incurred by non-resident companies and other amounts not otherwise eligible for relief from corporation tax,

may in accordance with this Chapter be surrendered by a company (in this Chapter referred to as the "*surrendering company*") which is a member of a group of companies and, on the making of a claim by another company (in this Chapter referred to as the "*claimant company*") which is a member of the same group, may be allowed to the claimant company by means of a relief from corporation tax (in this Chapter referred to as "*group relief*").][12]

[(2A) Where the trading losses or other amounts are of the type referred to in *paragraph (b)* of *subsection (2)*, group relief shall only be available in accordance with this Chapter where—

(a) the surrendering company is—

(i) resident in a relevant Member State, other than the State, and

(ii) a 75 per cent subsidiary of the claimant company,

and

(b) the claimant company is resident in the State.][13]

(3) Group relief shall also be available in accordance with the following provisions of this Chapter—

(a) where the surrendering company is a trading company owned by a consortium and is not a 75 per cent subsidiary of any company, and the claimant company is a member of the consortium,

(b) where the surrendering company is a trading company which—

(i) is a 90 per cent subsidiary of a holding company owned by a consortium, and

(ii) is not a 75 per cent subsidiary of a company other than the holding company,

and the claimant company is a member of the consortium, or

(c) where the surrendering company is a holding company owned by a consortium and is not a 75 per cent subsidiary of any company, and the claimant company is a member of the consortium;

but no claim may be made by a member of a consortium if a profit on a sale of the share capital of the surrendering company or holding company which that member owns would be treated as a trading receipt of that member nor if the member's share in the consortium in the relevant accounting period of the surrendering company or holding company is nil.

(4) Subject to the following provisions of this Chapter, 2 or more claimant companies may make claims relating to the same surrendering company and to the same accounting period of that surrendering company.

(5) A payment for group relief shall not—

(a) be taken into account in computing profits or losses of either company for corporation tax purposes, and

(b) be regarded as a distribution or a charge on income for any of the purposes of the Corporation Tax Acts,

and, in this subsection, "*payment for group relief*" means a payment made by the claimant company to the surrendering company in pursuance of an agreement between them as respects an amount surrendered by means of group relief, being a payment not exceeding that amount.

Amendments

[1] Inserted by FA02 s37(b)(i)(I).

[2] Substituted by FA07 sched2(1)(l). Has effect as on and from 2 April 2007

[3] Substituted by FA12 s47(1)(a). Applies as respects accounting periods ending on or after 1 January 2012.

[4] Inserted by FA02 s37(b)(i)(II).

[5] Inserted by FA12 s47(1)(b). Applies as respects accounting periods ending on or after 1 January 2012.

[6] Substituted by FA02 s37(b)(i)(III).

[7] Inserted by FA99 s78(1)(b)(i). This section shall apply as respects accounting periods ending on or after the 1st day of July, 1998.

[8] Substituted by FA00 s79.

[9] Deleted by F(No.2)A13 s34(1). Applies as respects accounting periods commencing on or after 18 December 2013.

[10] Substituted by FA13 s38(1). Applies as respects accounting periods ending on or after 1 January 2013.

[11] Substituted by FA12 s47(1)(c). Applies as respects accounting periods ending on or after 1 January 2012.

[12] Substituted by FA07 s48(1)(a)(i). This section is deemed to have applied as respects an accounting period ending on or after 1 January 2006.

[13] Inserted by FA07 s48(1)(a)(ii). This section is deemed to have applied as respects an accounting period ending on or after 1 January 2006.

Note

FA12 s47

(a) This section applies as respects accounting periods ending on or after 1 January 2012.

(b) This section shall not have effect in relation to the determination of the amount of loss or other amount available for surrender under section 411(2) available for surrender for an accounting period beginning before 1 January 2012 and ending after that date to the extent that the loss or other amount is attributable to the part of the accounting period falling before that date.

(c) Any apportionment necessary for the purposes of giving effect to *paragraph (b)* shall be made in accordance with section 4(6).

Case Law

Imperial Chemical Industries plc v Colmer (Inspector of Taxes) 1999 STC 1089 concerned a claim for group relief by a consortium member, although it was relevant for the wider purpose of group relief.

Total income for the purposes of export sales relief was to be calculated after allowing for group relief. Cronin (Inspector of Taxes) v Youghal Carpets (Yarns) Limited 1985 III ITR 229

In Wood Preservation Ltd v Prior 45 TC 112 the owner of certain shares entered into a contract of sale for the shares conditional on the consent of a third party. It was held that the owner ceased to be the beneficial owner of the shares from the contract date although the purchaser could not be regarded as having become the beneficial owner at that time.

There was no justification for denying a repayment supplement on tax refunded to a German company on grounds of its non residence in the UK. R v Inland Revenue Commissioners, ex parte Commerzbank AG 1993 STC 605

Marks & Spencer plc v Halsey Case C-446/03 considered if the UK group relief provisions which prohibited an offset of foreign losses against UK group members contravened the Freedom of Establishment in the European Treaty. The case related to whether a UK parent company could offset losses that had arisen in its foreign subsidiaries against the group's UK profits under the UK group relief rules. The ECJ held that the exclusion from the UK loss relief regime of losses incurred by an EU subsidiary did constitute a restriction on the freedom of establishment provisions but in some cases the restrictions were justified. The ECJ felt the occasion that foreign losses could be set against UK profits were when; the EU subsidiary had exhausted the possibilities available in the home territory for offsetting the losses in the current accounting period, and also the previous accounting periods and there is no possibility for the EU subsidiary's losses to be taken into account in its country of residence for future periods, either by the subsidiary itself or a third party.

Cross References

From Section 411

Section 9 Subsidiaries.
Section 826 Agreements for relief from double taxation.

To Section 411

Section 4 Interpretation of Corporation Tax Acts.
Section 21B Tax treatment of certain dividends.
Section 23A Company residence.
Section 80A Taxation of certain short-term leases plant and machinery.
Section 153 Distributions to certain nonresidents.
Section 172D Exemption from dividend withholding tax for certain non-resident persons.
Section 250 Extension of relief under section 248 to certain individuals in relation to loans applied in acquiring interest in certain companies.
Section 420C Group relief: relief for certain losses of non-resident companies.
Section 424 Effect of arrangements for transfer of company to another group, etc.
Section 427 Information as to arrangements for transferring relief, etc.
Section 450 Double taxation relief.
Section 479 Relief for new shares purchased on issue by employees.
Section 492 Individuals qualifying for relief.
Section 626B Exemption from tax in the case of gains on disposals of shares.
Section 688 Treatment of group relief.
Section 766 Tax credit for research and development expenditure.
Section 817 Schemes to avoid liability to tax under Schedule F.
Section 817A Restriction of relief for payments of interest.

Section 847 Tax relief for certain branch profits.
Section 958 Date for payment of tax.
Section 1085 Corporation tax — late returns: restriction of certain claims for relief.
Schedule 24 Relief from Income Tax and Corporation Tax by Means of Credit in Respect of Foreign Tax

412 Qualification for entitlement to group relief

[CTA76 s108]

(1) Notwithstanding that at any time a company (in this subsection referred to as "*the subsidiary company*") is a 75 per cent subsidiary or a 90 per cent subsidiary, within the meaning of *section 9*, of another company (in this section referred to as "*the parent company*"), it shall not be treated at that time as such a subsidiary for the purposes of group relief unless additionally at that time—

(a) the parent company is beneficially entitled to not less than 75 per cent or, as the case may be, 90 per cent of any profits available for distribution to equity holders of the subsidiary company, and

(b) the parent company would be beneficially entitled to not less than 75 per cent or, as the case may be, 90 per cent of any assets of the subsidiary company available for distribution to its equity holders on a winding up.

(2) Subject to *subsection (3)*, for the purposes of group relief a member's share in a consortium, in relation to an accounting period of the surrendering company, shall be whichever is the lowest in that period of the following percentages—

(a) the percentage of the ordinary share capital of the surrendering company beneficially owned by that member,

(b) the percentage to which that member is beneficially entitled of any profits available for distribution to equity holders of the surrendering company, and

(c) the percentage to which that member would be beneficially entitled of any assets of the surrendering company available for distribution to its equity holders on a winding up,

and, if any of those percentages have fluctuated in that accounting period, the average percentage over the period shall be taken for the purposes of this subsection.

(3) In any case where the surrendering company is a subsidiary of a holding company owned by a consortium, for references in *subsection (2)* to the surrendering company there shall be substituted references to the holding company.

Case Law

Sainsbury plc v O'Connor (Inspector of Taxes) 1991 STC 318 considered the nature of beneficial ownership. The grant of a call option did not result in the loss of beneficial ownership, as long as the registered owner of the shares retained all the normal benefits associated with share ownership, in particular the right to receive dividends during the option period.

In Algemene Maatschappij voor Investering en Dienstverlening NV v Belgian State 2003 STC 356 the ECJ ruled that it was in contravention of the Freedom of Establishment principle of the EC Treaty to apply a different loss treatment to Belgian residents with a foreign permanent establishment to that afforded to a Belgian company operating solely in Belgium.

Cross References

From Section 412

Section 9 Subsidiaries.

To Section 412

Section 21B Tax treatment of certain dividends.

Section 23A Company residence.
Section 80A Taxation of certain short-term leases plant and machinery.
Section 141 Distributions out of income from patent royalties.
Section 153 Distributions to certain nonresidents.
Section 172D Exemption from dividend withholding tax for certain non-resident persons.
Section 414 Meaning of "the profit distribution".
Section 415 Meaning of "the notional winding up".
Section 416 Limited right to profits or assets.
Section 418 Beneficial percentage.
Section 419 The relevant accounting period, etc.
Section 443 Meaning of "goods".
Section 487 Corporation tax: credit for bank levy.
Section 766 Tax credit for research and development expenditure.
Section 847 Tax relief for certain branch profits.

413 Profits or assets available for distribution

[CTA76 s109; FA77 s42 and Sch1 PtIV par1(b)]

(1) In this Chapter, "*fixed-rate preference shares*" means shares which—

(a) are issued for consideration which is or includes new consideration,

(b) do not carry any right either to conversion into shares or securities of any other description or to the acquisition of any additional shares or securities,

(c) do not carry any right to dividends other than dividends which—

(i) are of a fixed amount or at a fixed rate per cent of the nominal value of the shares, and

(ii) represent no more than a reasonable commercial return on the new consideration received by the company in respect of the issue of the shares,

and

(d) on repayment do not carry any rights to an amount exceeding that new consideration except in so far as those rights are reasonably comparable with those general for fixed dividend shares quoted on a stock exchange in the State.

(2) In this section, "*new consideration*" has the same meaning as in *section 135*.

(3) (a) In this subsection—

"*normal commercial loan*" means a loan of or including new consideration and—

(i) which does not carry any right either to conversion into shares or securities of any other description or to the acquisition of additional shares or securities,

(ii) which does not entitle the loan creditor to any amount by means of interest which depends to any extent on the results of the company's business or any part of it or on the value of any of the company's assets or which exceeds a reasonable commercial return on the new consideration loaned, and

(iii) in respect of which the loan creditor is entitled on repayment to an amount which either does not exceed the new consideration loaned or is reasonably comparable with the amount generally repayable (in respect of an equal amount of new consideration) under the terms of issue of securities quoted on a stock exchange in the State;

"*ordinary shares*" means all shares other than fixed-rate preference shares.

(b) For the purposes of this Chapter, an equity holder of a company shall be any person who—

(i) holds ordinary shares in the company, or

(ii) is a loan creditor of the company in respect of a loan which is not a normal commercial loan,

and any reference in this Chapter to profits or assets available for distribution to a company's equity holders shall not include a reference to any profits or assets available for distribution to any equity holder otherwise than as an equity holder.

(4) *Subsection (6)* of *section 433* apart from *paragraph (b)* of that subsection shall apply for the purposes of *subsection (3)(b)(ii)* as it applies for the purposes of *Part 13*.

(5) Notwithstanding anything in *subsections (1)* to *(4)* but subject to *subsection (6)*, where—

(a) any person has directly or indirectly provided new consideration for any shares or securities in the company, and

(b) that person or any person connected with that person uses for the purposes of such person's trade assets which belong to the company and in respect of which there is made to the company any of the allowances specified in *Chapter 2* of *Part 9* or *section 670, 673, 674, 677, 680* or *765*,

then, for the purposes of this Chapter, that person and no other person shall be treated as being an equity holder in respect of those shares or securities and as being beneficially entitled to any distribution of profits or assets attributable to those shares or securities.

(6) In any case where *subsection (5)* applies in relation to a bank in such circumstances that—

(a) the only new consideration provided by the bank as mentioned in *subsection (5)(a)* is provided in the normal course of its banking business by means of a normal commercial loan within the meaning of *subsection (3)*, and

(b) the cost to the company concerned of the assets within *subsection (5)(b)* which are used as mentioned in that subsection by the bank or a person connected with the bank is less than the amount of that new consideration,

references in *subsection (5)*, other than the reference in *subsection (5)(a)*, to shares or securities in the company shall be construed as a reference to so much only of the loan referred to in *paragraph (a)* as is equal to the cost referred to in *paragraph (b)*.

Cross References

From Section 413

Section 135 Distributions: supplemental.
Section 268 Meaning of "industrial building or structure".
Section 283 Initial allowances.
Section 430 Meaning of "close company".
Section 433 Meaning of "participator", "associate", "director" and "loan creditor".
Section 670 Mine development allowance.
Section 673 Allowance in respect of development expenditure and exploration expenditure.
Section 674 Expenditure on abortive exploration.
Section 677 Investment allowance in respect of exploration expenditure.
Section 680 Annual allowance for mineral depletion.
Section 765 Allowances for capital expenditure on scientific research.

To Section 413

Section 186 Connected persons.
Section 419 The relevant accounting period, etc.
Section 450 Double taxation relief.
Section 492 Individuals qualifying for relief.
Section 616 Groups of companies: interpretation.
Section 626B Exemption from tax in the case of gains on disposals of shares.
Section 817 Schemes to avoid liability to tax under Schedule F.
Schedule 24 Relief from Income Tax and Corporation Tax by Means of Credit in Respect of Foreign Tax

414 Meaning of "*the profit distribution*"

[CTA76 s110]

(1) Subject to the following provisions of this Chapter, for the purposes of *section 412* the percentage to which one company is beneficially entitled of any profits available for distribution to the equity holders of another company means the percentage to which the first company would be so entitled in the relevant accounting period on a distribution in money to those equity holders of—

(a) an amount of profits equal to the total profits of the other company which arise in that accounting period (whether or not any of those profits are in fact distributed), or

(b) if there are no profits of the other company in that accounting period, profits of [€100][1],

and in the following provisions of this Chapter that distribution is referred to as "*the profit distribution*".

(2) For the purposes of the profit distribution, it shall be assumed that no payment is made by means of repayment of share capital or of the principal secured by any loan unless that payment is a distribution.

(3) Subject to *subsection (2)*, where an equity holder is entitled as such to a payment of any description which apart from this subsection would not be treated as a distribution, it shall nevertheless be treated as an amount to which the equity holder is entitled on the profit distribution.

Amendments

[1] Substituted by FA01 s240 and sched5 part1.

Cross References

From Section 414

Section 412 Qualification for entitlement to group relief.

To Section 414

Section 416 Limited right to profits or assets.
Section 417 Diminished share of profits or assets.
Section 418 Beneficial percentage.
Section 450 Double taxation relief.
Schedule 24 Relief from Income Tax and Corporation Tax by Means of Credit in Respect of Foreign Tax

415 Meaning of "*the notional winding up*"

[CTA76 s111]

(1) Subject to the following provisions of this Chapter, for the purposes of *section 412* the percentage to which one company would be beneficially entitled of any assets of another company available for distribution to its equity holders on

a winding up means the percentage to which the first company would be so entitled if the other company were to be wound up and on that winding up the value of the assets available for distribution to its equity holders (after deducting any liabilities to other persons) were equal to—

(a) the excess, if any, of the total amount of the assets of the company, as shown in the balance sheet relating to its affairs as at the end of the relevant accounting period, over the total amount of those of its liabilities as so shown which are not liabilities to equity holders as such, or

(b) if there is no such excess or if the company's balance sheet is prepared to a date other than the end of the relevant accounting period, [€100][1].

(2) In the following provisions of this Chapter, a winding up on the basis specified in *subsection (1)* is referred to as "*the notional winding up*".

(3) If on the notional winding up an equity holder would be entitled as such to an amount of assets of any description which apart from this subsection would not be treated as a distribution of assets, it shall nevertheless be treated, subject to *subsection (4)*, as an amount to which the equity holder is entitled on the distribution of assets on the notional winding up.

(4) (a) In this subsection, "*new consideration*" has the same meaning as in *section 135*.

(b) Where an amount (in this subsection referred to as "*the returned amount*"), which corresponds to the whole or any part of the new consideration provided by a person who is an equity holder of a company for any shares or securities in respect of which such person is an equity holder, is applied by the company directly or indirectly in the making of a loan to, or in the acquisition of any shares or securities in, the equity holder or any person connected with the equity holder, then, for the purposes of this Chapter—

(i) the total amount of the assets referred to in *subsection (1)(a)* shall be taken to be reduced by a sum equal to the returned amount, and

(ii) the amount of assets to which the equity holder is beneficially entitled on the notional winding up shall be taken to be reduced by a sum equal to the returned amount.

Amendments

[1] Substituted by FA01 s240 and sched5 part1.

Cross References

From Section 415

Section 135 Distributions: supplemental.
Section 412 Qualification for entitlement to group relief.

To Section 415

Section 186 Connected persons.
Section 416 Limited right to profits or assets.
Section 417 Diminished share of profits or assets.
Section 450 Double taxation relief.
Section 492 Individuals qualifying for relief.
Section 817 Schemes to avoid liability to tax under Schedule F.
Schedule 24 Relief from Income Tax and Corporation Tax by Means of Credit in Respect of Foreign Tax

416 Limited right to profits or assets

[CTA76 s112]

(1) This section shall apply if any of the equity holders—

(a) to whom the profit distribution is made, or

(b) who is entitled to participate in the notional winding up,

holds as such equity holder any shares or securities which carry rights in respect of dividend or interest or assets on a winding up which are wholly or partly limited by reference to a specified amount or amounts (whether the limitation takes the form of the capital by reference to which a distribution is calculated or operates by reference to an amount of profits or assets or otherwise).

(2) Where this section applies, there shall be determined—

(a) the percentage of profits to which on the profit distribution the first company referred to in *section 414(1)* would be entitled, and

(b) the percentage of assets to which on the notional winding up the first company referred to in *section 415(1)* would be entitled,

if, to the extent that they are limited as mentioned in *subsection (1)*, the rights of every equity holder within that subsection (including the first company concerned if it is such an equity holder) had been waived.

(3) Where on the profit distribution the percentage of profits determined as mentioned in *subsection (2)(a)* is less than the percentage of profits determined under *section 414(1)* without regard to *subsection (2)(a)*, the lesser percentage shall be taken for the purposes of *section 412* to be the percentage of profits to which on the profit distribution the first company referred to in *section 414(1)* would be entitled as mentioned in that section.

(4) Where on the notional winding up the percentage of assets determined as mentioned in *subsection (2)(b)* is less than the percentage of assets determined under *section 415(1)* without regard to *subsection (2)(b)*, the lesser percentage shall be taken for the purposes of *section 412* to be the percentage to which on the notional winding up the first company referred to in *section 415(1)* would be entitled of any assets of the other company available for distribution to its equity holders on a winding up.

Cross References

From Section 416

Section 412 Qualification for entitlement to group relief.
Section 414 Meaning of "the profit distribution".
Section 415 Meaning of "the notional winding up".

To Section 416

Section 417 Diminished share of profits or assets.

417 Diminished share of profits or assets

[CTA76 s113]

(1) This section shall apply if at any time in the relevant accounting period any of the equity holders—

(a) to whom the profit distribution is made, or

(b) who is entitled to participate in the notional winding up,

holds as such an equity holder any shares or securities which carry rights in respect of dividend or interest or assets on a winding up which are of such a nature (as, for example, if any shares will cease to carry a right to a dividend at a future time) that, if the profit distribution or the notional winding up were to take place in a different accounting period, the percentage to which, in accordance with the preceding provisions of this Chapter, that equity holder would be entitled of profits on the profit distribution or of assets on the notional winding up would be different from the percentage determined in the relevant accounting period.

(2) Where this section applies, there shall be determined—

(a) the percentage of profits to which on the profit distribution the first company referred to in *section 414(1)* would be entitled, and

(b) the percentage of assets to which on the notional winding up the first company referred to in *section 415(1)* would be entitled,

if the rights of the equity holders in the relevant accounting period were the same as they would be in the different accounting period referred to in *subsection (1)*.

(3) Where in the relevant accounting period an equity holder holds as such any shares or securities in respect of which arrangements exist by virtue of which, in that or any subsequent accounting period, the equity holder's entitlement to profits on the profit distribution or to assets on the notional winding up could be different as compared with the equity holder's entitlement if effect were not given to the arrangements, then, for the purposes of this section—

(a) it shall be assumed that effect would be given to those arrangements in a later accounting period, and

(b) those shares or securities shall be treated as though any variation in the equity holder's entitlement to profits or assets resulting from giving effect to the arrangements were the result of the operation of such rights attaching to the shares or securities as are referred to in *subsection (1)*.

(4) *Subsections (3)* and *(4)* of *section 416* shall apply for the purposes of this section as they apply for the purposes of that section, and accordingly references in those subsections to *subsection (2)(a)* and *subsection (2)(b)* of that section shall be construed respectively as references to *subsection (2)(a)* and *subsection (2)(b)* of this section.

(5) In any case where *section 416* applies as well as this section, *section 416* shall be applied separately (in relation to the profit distribution and the notional winding up)—

(a) on the basis specified in *subsection (2)*, and

(b) without regard to that subsection,

and *subsections (3)* and *(4)* of *section 416* shall apply accordingly in relation to the percentages so determined as if for "*lesser*" there were substituted "*lowest*".

Case Law

Sainsbury plc v O'Connor (Inspector of Taxes) 1991 STC 318 considered the nature of beneficial ownership. The grant of a call option did not result in the loss of beneficial ownership, as long as the registered owner of the shares retained all the normal benefits associated with share ownership, in particular the right to receive dividends during the option period.

Cross References

From Section 417

Section 414 Meaning of "the profit distribution".
Section 415 Meaning of "the notional winding up".
Section 416 Limited right to profits or assets.

To Section 417

Section 418 Beneficial percentage.
Section 427 Information as to arrangements for transferring relief, etc.
Section 443 Meaning of "goods".

418 Beneficial percentage

[CTA76 s114]

For the purposes of *section 412* and *sections 414* to *417*—

(a) the percentage to which one company is beneficially entitled of any profits available for distribution to the equity holders of another company, and

(b) the percentage to which one company would be beneficially entitled of any assets of another company on a winding up,

means the percentage to which the first company is or would be so entitled either directly or through another company or other companies or partly directly and partly through another company or other companies.

Cross References

From Section 418

Section 412 Qualification for entitlement to group relief.
Section 414 Meaning of "the profit distribution".
Section 417 Diminished share of profits or assets.

To Section 418

Section 21B Tax treatment of certain dividends.
Section 23A Company residence.
Section 80A Taxation of certain short-term leases plant and machinery.
Section 141 Distributions out of income from patent royalties.
Section 153 Distributions to certain nonresidents.
Section 172D Exemption from dividend withholding tax for certain non-resident persons.
Section 419 The relevant accounting period, etc.
Section 450 Double taxation relief.
Section 487 Corporation tax: credit for bank levy.
Section 766 Tax credit for research and development expenditure.
Section 817 Schemes to avoid liability to tax under Schedule F.
Section 847 Tax relief for certain branch profits.
Schedule 24 Relief from Income Tax and Corporation Tax by Means of Credit in Respect of Foreign Tax

419 The relevant accounting period, etc

[CTA76 s115]

(1) In this Chapter, "*the relevant accounting period*" means—

(a) in a case within *section 412(1)*, the accounting period current at the time in question, and

(b) in a case within *section 412(2)*, the accounting period in relation to which the share in the consortium is to be determined.

(2) For the purposes of *sections 413* to *418*, a loan to a company shall be treated as a security whether or not it is a secured loan and, if it is a secured loan, regardless of the nature of the security.

Cross References

From Section 419

Section 412 Qualification for entitlement to group relief.
Section 413 Profits or assets available for distribution.
Section 418 Beneficial percentage.

To Section 419
Section 616 Groups of companies: interpretation.
Section 626B Exemption from tax in the case of gains on disposals of shares.

420 Losses, etc. which may be surrendered by means of group relief

[CTA76 s116(1) to (8) and (10)]

[(1) Where in any accounting period the surrendering company has incurred a loss, computed as for the purposes of *section 396(2)*, in carrying on a trade in respect of which the company is within the charge to corporation tax, the amount of the loss may be set off for the purposes of corporation tax against the total profits of the claimant company for its corresponding accounting period; but this subsection shall not apply—

(a) to so much of a loss as is excluded from *section 396(2)* by *section 396(4)* or *663*, or

(b) so as to reduce the profits of a claimant company which carries on life business (within the meaning of *section 706*) by an amount greater than the amount of such profits (before a set off under this subsection) computed in accordance with Case I of Schedule D and *section 710(1)*.][1]

(2) Where for any accounting period any capital allowances are to be made to the surrendering company which are to be given by discharge or repayment of tax or in charging its income under Case V of Schedule D and are to be available primarily against a specified class of income, so much of the amount of those capital allowances (exclusive of any carried forward from an earlier period) as exceeds its income of the relevant class arising in that accounting period (before deduction of any losses of any other period or of any capital allowances) may be set off for the purposes of corporation tax against the total profits of the claimant company for its corresponding accounting period.

(3) Where for any accounting period the surrendering company (being an investment company) may under *section 83(2)* deduct any amount as expenses of management disbursed for that accounting period, so much of that amount (exclusive of any amount deductible only by virtue of *section 83(3)*) as exceeds the company's profits of that accounting period may be set off for the purposes of corporation tax against the total profits of the claimant company (whether an investment company or not) for its corresponding accounting period.

(4) The surrendering company's profits of the period shall be determined for the purposes of *subsection (3)* without any deduction under *section 83* and without regard to any deduction to be made in respect of losses or allowances of any other period.

(5) References in *subsections (3)* and *(4)* to *section 83* shall not include references to that section as applied by *section 707* to companies carrying on life business.

(6) Where in any accounting period the surrendering company has paid any amount by means of charges on income, so much of that amount as exceeds its profits of the period may be set off for the purposes of corporation tax against the total profits of the claimant company for its corresponding accounting period.

(7) The surrendering company's profits of the period shall be determined for the purposes of *subsection (6)* without regard to any deduction to be made in respect of losses or allowances of any other period or to expenses of management deductible only by virtue of *section 83(3)*.

(8) In applying any of the preceding subsections in the case of a claim made by a company as a member of a consortium, only a fraction of the loss referred to in

subsection (1), or of the excess referred to in *subsection (2)*, *(3)* or *(6)*, as the case may be, may be set off under the subsection in question, and that fraction shall be equal to that member's share in the consortium, subject to any further reduction under *section 422(2)*.

[(9) (a) References in the preceding subsections to a surrendering company shall not include references to a company carrying on life business except to the extent that such life business is new basis business within the meaning of *section 730A* (inserted by the Finance Act, 2000).

(b) For the purposes of this section "life business" shall be construed in accordance with *section 706(1)*.][2]

Amendments

[1] Substituted by FA01 s65(1). This section shall be deemed to have applied as respects accounting periods commencing on or after 1 January 1999.

[2] Substituted by FA00 s54.

Case Law

The ECJ held that the occasion that foreign losses could be set against UK profits were when EU subsidiary had exhausted the possibilities available in the home territory for offsetting the losses in the current accounting period and also the previous accounting periods and there is no possibility for the EU subsidiary's losses to be taken into account in its country of residence for future periods either by the subsidiary itself or a third party. Marks & Spencer plc v Halsey Case C-446/03

Revenue Briefings

Tax Briefing

Tax Briefing September 2000 – Issue 41 pg 21 – Life Assurance Companies and Group Relief
Tax Briefing June 2001 – Issue 44 pg 39 – Losses, Charges and Group Relief Offset

Revenue Precedents

Section 342(2)(a) Taxes Consolidation Act 1997 states that all the provisions of the Tax Acts relating to the making of allowances or charges in respect of capital expenditure incurred shall apply. Does section 420(2) Taxes Consolidation Act 1997 relate to the making of allowances and thereby permitting the set off of allowances against the profits of a group company? If capital allowances are available to the lessor, the provisions of Section 420(2) Taxes Consolidation Act 1997 will apply. IT902035

Cross References

From Section 420

Section 83 Expenses of management of investment companies.
Section 396 Relief for trading losses other than terminal losses.
Section 422 Corresponding accounting periods.
Section 663 Corporation tax: restriction of relief for losses in farming or market gardening.
Section 706 Interpretation and general (Part 26).
Section 707 Management expenses.
Section 710 Profits of life business.

To Section 420

Section 82 Pre-trading expenditure.
Section 243 Allowance of charges on income.
Section 403 Restriction on use of capital allowances for certain leased assets.
Section 404 Restriction on use of capital allowances for certain leased machinery or plant.
Section 405 Restriction on use of capital allowances on holiday cottages.
Section 406 Restriction on use of capital allowances on fixtures and fittings for furnished residential accommodation.
Section 407 Restriction on use of losses and capital allowances for qualifying shipping trade.
Section 420A Group relief: relevant losses and charges.
Section 420C Group relief: relief for certain losses of non-resident companies.
Section 421 Relation of group relief to other relief.

Section 423 Company joining or leaving group or consortium.
Section 448 Relief from corporation tax.
Section 644C Relief from corporation tax for losses from dealing in residential development land.
Section 679 Exploration expenditure.
Section 690 Interest and charges on income.
Section 817A Restriction of relief for payments of interest.
Section 1013 Limited partnerships.
Section 1085 Corporation tax — late returns: restriction of certain claims for relief.

420A Group relief: relevant losses and charges

[(1) In this section—

"*relevant trading charges on income*" and "*relevant trading income*" have the same meanings, respectively, as in *section 243A*;

["*relevant trading loss*", in relation to an accounting period of a company, means a loss incurred in the accounting period in a trade carried on by the company, other than—

(a) so much of the loss as is a loss incurred in an excepted trade within the meaning of *section 21A*, and

(b) any amount which is or would, if *subsection (8)* of *section 403* had not been enacted, be the relevant amount of the loss for the purposes of *subsection (4)* of that section.][1]

(2) Notwithstanding *subsections (1)* and *(6)* of *section 420* and *section 421*, where in any accounting period the surrendering company incurs a relevant trading loss or an excess of relevant trading charges on income, that loss or excess may not be set off for the purposes of corporation tax against the total profits of the claimant company for its corresponding accounting period.

(3) (a) [Where][2] in any accounting period the surrendering company incurs a relevant trading loss, computed as for the purposes of *section 396(2)*, or an excess of relevant trading charges on income in carrying on a trade in respect of which the company is within the charge to corporation tax, that loss or excess may be set off for the purposes of corporation tax against—

(i) income specified in [*section 21A(4)*][3], […][4]

(ii) relevant trading [income, and][5]

[(iii) income to which *section 21A(3)* does not apply by virtue of *section 21B*,][6]

of the claimant company for its corresponding accounting period as reduced by any amounts allowed as deductions against that income under *section 243A* or set off against that income under *section 396A*.

(b) *Paragraph (a)* shall not apply—

(i) to so much of a loss as is excluded from *section 396(2)* by *section 396(4)* or *663*, or

(ii) so as to reduce the profits of a claimant company which carries on life business (within the meaning of *section 706*) by an amount greater than the amount of such profits (before a set off under this subsection) computed in accordance with Case 1 of Schedule D and *section 710(1)*.

(4) Group relief allowed under *subsection (3)* shall reduce the income from a trade of the claimant company for an accounting period—

(a) before relief granted under *section 397* in respect of a loss incurred in a succeeding accounting period or periods, and

(b) after the relief granted under *section 396* in respect of a loss incurred in a preceding accounting period or periods.

(5) For the purposes of this section in the case of a claim made by a company as a member of a consortium, only a fraction of a relevant trading loss or an excess of relevant trading charges on income may be set off, and that fraction shall be equal to that member's share in the consortium, subject to any further reduction under *section 422(2)*.][7]

Amendments

[1] Substituted by FA05 s45(1)(d). Applies as respects any claim made by a company on or after 3 February 2005 for relief for a loss.

[2] Substituted by FA12 sched1(17)(a).

[3] Substituted by FA12 sched1(17)(b).

[4] Deleted by FA08 s43(1)(e)(i). This section shall be deemed to have applied as respects a dividend received on or after 1 January 2007.

[5] Substituted by FA08 s43(1)(e)(i). This section shall be deemed to have applied as respects a dividend received on or after 1 January 2007.

[6] Inserted by FA08 s43(1)(e)(ii). This section shall be deemed to have applied as respects a dividend received on or after 1 January 2007.

[7] Inserted by FA01 s90(1)(b)(ii). Applies as respects an accounting period ending on or after 6 March 2001.

Revenue Briefings

Tax Briefing

Tax Briefing July 2001 – Issue 44 pg 39 – Losses, Charges and Group Relief Offset

Revenue Information Notes

Application of Section 54 of the Finance Act 2002 to IFSC/Shannon certified companies

Cross References

From Section 420A

Section 21A Higher rate of corporation tax.
Section 21B Tax treatment of certain dividends.
Section 243A Restriction of relevant charges on income.
Section 396 Relief for trading losses other than terminal losses.
Section 396A Relief for relevant trading losses.
Section 397 Relief for terminal loss in a trade.
Section 403 Restriction on use of capital allowances for certain leased assets.
Section 420 Losses, etc. which may be surrendered by means of group relief.
Section 421 Relation of group relief to other relief.
Section 422 Corresponding accounting periods.
Section 456 Restriction of group relief.
Section 663 Corporation tax: restriction of relief for losses in farming or market gardening.
Section 706 Interpretation and general (Part 26).
Section 710 Profits of life business.

To Section 420A

Section 448 Relief from corporation tax.
Section 713 Investment income reserved for policyholders.
Section 1085 Corporation tax — late returns: restriction of certain claims for relief.

420B Group relief: Relief for certain losses on a value basis

[(1) In this section—

[...][1]

["*relevant corporation tax*", in relation to an accounting period of a company, means the corporation tax which would be chargeable on the company for the accounting period apart from—

(a) this section and *sections 239*, *241*, *440* and *441*, and

(b) where the company carries on a life business (within the meaning of *section 706* [...][2]), any corporation tax which would be attributable to policyholders' profits;][3]

"*relevant trading charges on income*" has the same meaning as in *section 243A*;

"*relevant trading loss*" has the same meaning as in *section 396A* [...][4]

[(2) Where in any accounting period the surrendering company has incurred a relevant trading loss, computed as for the purposes of *section 396(2)*, or an excess of relevant trading charges on income, in carrying on a trade in respect of which the company is within the charge to corporation tax, and the amount of the loss or excess is greater than an amount equal to the aggregate of the amounts which could, if timely claims had been made for such set off, have been set off in respect of that loss or excess for the purposes of corporation tax against—

(a) the income of the company in accordance with *section 243A* or *section 396A*,

[...][5]

(c) income of any other company in accordance with *section 420A* [...][6],

the claimant company may claim relief under this section for its corresponding accounting period in respect of the amount (in this section referred to as the "*relievable loss*") by which the loss or excess is greater than that aggregate.][7]

[(3) Where for any accounting period a company claims relief under this section in respect of a relievable loss, the relevant corporation tax of the company for the accounting period shall be reduced in so far as the relievable loss consists of a loss or charges on income by an amount determined by the formula—

$$L \times \frac{R}{100}$$

where—

L is an amount equal to the amount of the relievable loss, and

R is the rate per cent specified in *section 21* in relation to the accounting period.][8]

(4) Where for any accounting period a company claims relief under this section in respect of any relevant trading loss or excess of relevant trading charges on income, the surrendering company shall be treated as having surrendered, and the claimant company shall be treated as having claimed relief for, trading losses and charges on income of an amount determined by the formula—

$$T \times \frac{100}{R}$$

where—

T is the amount by which the relevant corporation tax payable for the accounting period is reduced by virtue of *subsection (3)*, and

R is the rate per cent of corporation tax which, by virtue of *section 21*, applies in relation to the accounting period.][9]

Amendments

[1] Deleted by FA12 sched1(18)(a).

[2] Deleted by FA07 sched4(1)(k). Apply to accounting periods ending on or after 1 January 2007.

[3] Substituted by FA04 s38(1). This section shall apply as respects any claim for relief made on or after 4 February 2004.

[4] Deleted by FA05 s45(1)(e).

[5] Deleted by FA06 sched2(1)(j)(ii)(I). Applies to accounting periods ending on or after 2 February 2006.

[6] Deleted by FA06 sched2(1)(j)(ii)(II). Applies to accounting periods ending on or after 2 February 2006.

[7] Substituted by FA03 s59(1)(d). Applies as on or after 6 February 2003.

[8] Substituted by FA12 sched1(18)(b).

[9] Substituted by FA12 sched1(18)(c).

Revenue Briefings

Tax Briefing

Tax Briefing January 2003 – Issue 51 pg 15 – Losses, Charges and Group Relief

Cross References

From Section 420B

Section 21 The charge to corporation tax and exclusion of income tax and capital gains tax.
Section 239 Income tax on payments by resident companies.
Section 241 Income tax on payments by non-resident companies.
Section 396 Relief for trading losses other than terminal losses.
Section 407 Restriction on use of losses and capital allowances for qualifying shipping trade.
Section 440 Surcharge on undistributed investment and estate income.
Section 441 Surcharge on undistributed income of service companies.
Section 448 Relief from corporation tax.
Section 706 Interpretation and general (Part 26).

To Section 420B

Section 243B Relief for certain charges on income on a value basis.
Section 644C Relief from corporation tax for losses from dealing in residential development land.
Section 1085 Corporation tax — late returns: restriction of certain claims for relief.

420C Group relief: relief for certain losses of non-resident companies

[(1) In this section—

"*foreign loss*" means a loss or other amount eligible for group relief in accordance with *section 411(2A)*;

"*relevant foreign loss*" means the amount of a foreign loss that—

(a) corresponds to an amount of a kind that, for the purposes of *section 420* or *420A*, could be available for surrender by means of group relief by a company resident in the State,

(b) is calculated in accordance with the applicable rules under the law of the surrendering state for determining the amount of loss or other amount eligible for relief from tax in that state,

(c) is not attributable to a trade carried on in the State through a branch or agency,

(d) is not otherwise available for surrender, relief or offset in accordance with any provisions of the Tax Acts,

(e) is a trapped loss within the meaning of *subsection (2)*, and

(f) is not available for surrender, relief or offset under the law of any relevant Member State, other than the State or the surrendering state;

"*surrendering state*" means the relevant Member State in which the surrendering company referred to in *section 411(2A)* is resident for the purposes of tax.

(2) For the purposes of this section a "*trapped loss*", in relation to an accounting period of a company, means a foreign loss that under the law of the surrendering state cannot be (or, if a timely claim for such set off or relief had been made, could not have been) set off or otherwise relieved for the purposes of tax against profits (of whatever description) of—

(a) that accounting period of the company,

(b) any preceding accounting period of the company,

(c) any later accounting period of the company, and

(d) any period of any other company resident in the surrendering state.

(3) (a) Subject to *subsection (4)*, where in any accounting period the surrendering company has incurred a relevant foreign loss, then the amount of the loss shall be treated (with any necessary modifications) for the purposes of *sections 420A* and *420B* as a relevant trading loss incurred by the surrendering company in the accounting period.

(b) Relief for a relevant foreign loss shall be given after relief for any losses (including relief for losses under *section 397*) which are not relevant foreign losses.

(4) This section does not apply where the relevant foreign loss arose as the result of any arrangements whatsoever the main purpose, or one of the main purposes, of which was to secure that the loss would qualify for group relief.

(5) Subject to *subsection (6)*, a claim under *subsection (3)* shall be made within 2 years from the end of the accounting period in which the loss is incurred.

(6) Where—

(a) at any time relief under *subsection (3)* may not be given in respect of a loss by virtue only of *paragraph (c)* of *subsection (2)*, and

(b) at any later time the claimant company proves to the satisfaction of the Revenue Commissioners that the condition in *subsection (2)(c)* is satisfied in relation to the loss at that time,

the claimant company may make a claim for relief under *subsection (3)* in respect of the loss and any such claim shall be made within 2 years from the time at which the condition in *subsection (2)(c)* is first met.

(7) For the purpose of giving effect to this section "*accounting period*", in relation to a surrendering company, means a period which would be an accounting period of the company if the company became resident in the State, and accordingly within the charge to corporation tax, at the time when it became a 75 per cent subsidiary referred to in *section 411(2A)(a)(ii)*.

(8) The inspector may by notice in writing require a company claiming relief from tax by virtue of this section to furnish him or her with such information or particulars as may be necessary for the purpose of giving effect to this section.][1]

Amendments

[1] Inserted by FA07 s48(1)(b). This section is deemed to have applied as respects an accounting period ending on or after 1 January 2006.

Cross References

From Section 420C

Section 397 Relief for terminal loss in a trade.
Section 411 Surrender of relief between members of groups and consortia.
Section 420 Losses, etc. which may be surrendered by means of group relief.

421 Relation of group relief to other relief

[CTA76 s117(1), (2), (3)(a), (b) and (d) and (4)]

(1) In this section, "*relief derived from a subsequent accounting period*" means—

(a) relief under *section 308(4)* in respect of capital allowances to be made for an accounting period after the accounting period the profits of which are being computed,

(b) relief under *section 396(2)* in respect of a loss incurred in an accounting period after the accounting period the profits of which are being computed, and

(c) relief under *section 397* in respect of a loss incurred in an accounting period after the end of the accounting period the profits of which are being computed.

(2) Group relief [in accordance with *section 420*][1] for an accounting period shall be allowed as a deduction against the claimant company's total profits for the period before reduction by any relief derived from a subsequent accounting period, but as reduced by any other relief from tax (including relief in respect of charges on income under *section 243(2)*).

(3) That other relief shall be determined on the assumption that the company makes all relevant claims under *section 308(4)* or *396(2)*.

(4) The reductions to be made in total profits of an accounting period against which any relief derived from a subsequent accounting period is to be set off shall include any group relief for the first-mentioned accounting period.

Amendments

[1] Inserted by FA06 sched2(1)(k). Applies to accounting periods ending on or after 2 February 2006.

Cross References

From Section 421

Section 243 Allowance of charges on income.
Section 308 Corporation tax: manner of granting, and effect of, allowances made by means of discharge or repayment of tax.
Section 396 Relief for trading losses other than terminal losses.
Section 397 Relief for terminal loss in a trade.
Section 420 Losses, etc. which may be surrendered by means of group relief.

To Section 421

Section 420A Group relief: relevant losses and charges.
Section 423 Company joining or leaving group or consortium.
Section 644C Relief from corporation tax for losses from dealing in residential development land.

422 Corresponding accounting periods

[CTA76 s118]

(1) For the purposes of group relief, any accounting period of the claimant company which falls wholly or partly within an accounting period of the surrendering company shall correspond to that accounting period.

(2) Where an accounting period of the surrendering company and a corresponding accounting period of the claimant company do not coincide—

(a) the amount which may be set off against the total profits of the claimant company for the corresponding accounting period shall be reduced by applying the fraction—

$$\frac{A}{B}$$

(if that fraction is less than unity), and

(b) those profits against which the amount mentioned in *paragraph (a)* (as reduced where so required) may be set off shall be reduced by applying the fraction—

$$\frac{A}{C}$$

(if that fraction is less than unity),

where—

A is the length of the period common to the 2 accounting periods,

B is the length of the accounting period of the surrendering company, and

C is the length of the corresponding accounting period of the claimant company.

Cross References

To Section 422

Section 420 Losses, etc. which may be surrendered by means of group relief.

Section 420A Group relief: relevant losses and charges.

Section 423 Company joining or leaving group or consortium.

Section 644C Relief from corporation tax for losses from dealing in residential development land.

423 Company joining or leaving group or consortium

[CTA76 s119]

(1) Subject to this section, group relief shall be given only if the surrendering company and the claimant company are members of the same group, or fulfil the conditions for relief for a consortium, throughout the whole of the surrendering company's accounting period to which the claim relates and throughout the whole of the corresponding accounting period of the claimant company.

(2) Where on any occasion 2 companies become or cease to be members of the same group, then, for the purposes specified in *subsection (3)*, it shall be assumed as respects each company that on that occasion (unless a true accounting period of the company begins or ends then) an accounting period of the company ends and a new one begins, the new accounting period to end with the end of the true accounting period (unless before then there is a further break under this subsection) and—

(a) that the losses or other amounts of the true accounting period are apportioned to the component accounting periods on a time basis according to their lengths, and

(b) that the amount of total profits for the true accounting period of the company against which group relief may be allowed in accordance with *section 421(2)* is also so apportioned to the component accounting periods.

(3) Where the one company is the surrendering company and the other company is the claimant company—

(a) references in *section 420* to accounting periods, to profits, and to losses, allowances, expenses of management or charges on income of the surrendering company, shall be construed in accordance with *subsection (2)*;

(b) references in *subsection (1)* and in *section 422* to accounting periods shall be so construed that if the 2 companies are members of the same group in the surrendering company's accounting period they shall under *section 422* also be members of the same group in any corresponding accounting period of the claimant company;

(c) references in *section 422* to profits, and amounts to be set off against the profits, shall be so construed that an amount apportioned under *subsection (2)* to a component accounting period may fall to be reduced under *section 422(2)*.

(4) *Subsections (2)* and *(3)* shall apply with the necessary modifications where a company begins or ceases to fulfil the conditions for relief for a consortium, either as a surrendering company or as a claimant company, as they apply where 2 companies become or cease to be members of the same group.

Cross References

From Section 423

Section 420 Losses, etc. which may be surrendered by means of group relief.
Section 421 Relation of group relief to other relief.
Section 422 Corresponding accounting periods.

To Section 423

Section 428 Exclusion of double allowances, etc.

424 Effect of arrangements for transfer of company to another group, etc

[CTA76 s120]

(1) In this section—

"*control*" has the meaning assigned to it by *section 11*;

"*third company*" means a company which, apart from any provision made by or under any arrangements specified in *subsection (3)(b)* or *(4)(b)*, is not a member of the same group of companies as the first company (within the meaning of *subsection (3)*) or, as the case may be, the trading company or holding company to which *subsection (4)* applies.

(2) For the purposes of this section, a company shall be a successor of another company if it carries on a trade which in whole or in part the other company has ceased to carry on and the circumstances are such that—

(a) *section 400* applies in relation to the 2 companies as the predecessor and the successor within the meaning of that section, or

(b) the 2 companies are connected with each other.

(3) Where apart from this section 2 companies (in this subsection referred to as respectively as "*the first company*" and "*the second company*") would be treated as members of the same group of companies and—

(a) in an accounting period one of the 2 companies has trading losses or other amounts eligible for relief from corporation tax which apart from this section it would be entitled to surrender as mentioned in *section 411(2)*, and

(b) arrangements are in existence by virtue of which, at some time during or after the expiry of that accounting period—

(i) the first company or any successor of the first company could cease to be a member of the same group of companies as the second company and could become a member of the same group of companies as a third company,

(ii) any person has or could obtain, or any persons together have or could obtain, control of the first company but not of the second company, or

(iii) a third company could begin to carry on the whole or any part of a trade which at any time in that accounting period is carried on by the first company, and could do so either as a successor of the first company or as a successor of another company which is not a third company but which, at some time during or after the expiry of that accounting period, has begun to carry on the whole or any part of that trade,

then, for the purposes of this Chapter, the first company shall be treated as not being a member of the same group of companies as the second company.

(4) Where a trading company is owned by a consortium or is a 90 per cent subsidiary of a holding company owned by a consortium and—

(a) in any accounting period the trading company had trading losses or other amounts eligible for relief from corporation tax which apart from this section it would be entitled to surrender as mentioned in *section 411(2)*, and

(b) arrangements are in existence by virtue of which—

(i) the trading company or any successor of the trading company could, at some time during or after the expiry of that accounting period, become a 75 per cent subsidiary of a third company,

(ii) any person who owns, or any persons who together own, less than 50 per cent of the ordinary share capital of the trading company has or together have, or could at some time during or after the expiry of that accounting period obtain, control of the trading company,

(iii) any person, other than a holding company of which the trading company is a 90 per cent subsidiary, either alone or together with connected persons, holds or could obtain, or controls or could control, the exercise of not less than 75 per cent of the votes which may be cast on a poll taken at a general meeting of the trading company in that accounting period or in any subsequent accounting period, or

(iv) a third company could begin to carry on, at some time during or after the expiry of that accounting period, the whole or any part of a trade which at any time in that accounting period is carried on by the trading company, and could do so either as a successor of the trading company or as a successor of another company which is not a third company but which, at some time during or after the expiry of that accounting period, has begun to carry on the whole or any part of that trade,

then, for the purposes of this Chapter, the trading company shall be treated as though it were not (as the surrendering company) within *paragraph (a), (b)* or *(c)* of *section 411(3)*.

(5) In any case where a trading company is a 90 per cent subsidiary of a holding company owned by a consortium, any reference in *subsection (4)* to the trading company, other than a reference in *paragraph (b)(iv)* of that subsection, shall be construed as including a reference to the holding company.

Case Law

In Pilkington v IRC 1982 STC 103 a company (ML) entered into an arrangement with another company (P) to enable capital allowances in respect of a ship which ML was about to purchase to be surrendered to P by way of group relief. A reorganisation took place. It was held the companies were not members of the same group for the duration of the arrangement in question, so the claim for group relief failed. Where either the profit distribution or asset distribution test cease to be satisfied during an accounting period, group relief as between the two companies concerned may not be availed of from the relevant time. It was held in Shepherd v Law Land plc 1990 STC 795 that the provision has effect only in so long as the "arrangements" in questions subsist, as soon as the arrangements no longer exist, the group relationship which has been treated as broken will be restored.

Cross References

From Section 424

Section 11 Meaning of "control" in certain contexts.
Section 400 Company reconstructions without change of ownership.
Section 411 Surrender of relief between members of groups and consortia.

To Section 424

Section 427 Information as to arrangements for transferring relief, etc.

425 Leasing contracts: effect on claims for losses of company reconstructions

[CTA76 s121]

(1) Subject to this section, where—

(a) under a contract entered into after the 27th day of November, 1975, a company (in this section referred to as "*the first company*") incurs capital expenditure on the provision of machinery or plant which the first company lets to another person by another contract (in this section referred to as a "*leasing contract*"),

(b) apart from this subsection the first company would be entitled to claim relief under *subsection (1)* or *(2)* of *section 396* in respect of losses incurred on the leasing contract, and

(c) in the accounting period for which an allowance under *section 283* or *285* in respect of the expenditure referred to in *paragraph (a)* is made to the first company, arrangements are in existence by virtue of which, at some time during or after the expiry of that accounting period, a successor company will be able to carry on any part of the first company's trade which consists of or includes the performance of all or any of the obligations which apart from the arrangements would be the first company's obligations under the leasing contract,

then, in the accounting period specified in *paragraph (c)* and in any subsequent accounting period, the first company shall not be entitled to claim relief as mentioned in *paragraph (b)* except in computing its profits (if any) arising under the leasing contract.

(2) For the purposes of this section, a company shall be a successor of the first company if the circumstances are such that—

(a) *section 400* applies in relation to the first company and the other company as the predecessor and the successor respectively within the meaning of that section, or

(b) the 2 companies are connected with each other.

(3) For the purposes of this section, losses incurred on a leasing contract and profits arising under such a contract shall be computed as if the performance of the leasing contract were a trade begun to be carried on by the first company, separately from any other trade which it may carry on, at the commencement of the letting under the leasing contract.

(4) In determining whether the first company would be entitled to claim relief as mentioned in *subsection (1)(b)*, any losses incurred on the leasing contract shall be treated as incurred in a trade carried on by that company separately from any other trade which it may carry on.

Cross References

From Section 425

Section 283 Initial allowances.
Section 285 Acceleration of wear and tear allowances.
Section 396 Relief for trading losses other than terminal losses.
Section 400 Company reconstructions without change of ownership.

To Section 425

Section 427 Information as to arrangements for transferring relief, etc.

426 Partnerships involving companies: effect of arrangements for transferring relief

[CTA76 s122(1) to (5)]

(1) For the purposes of this section, the amount of a company's share in the profits or loss of any accounting period of a partnership shall be such amount as is determined in accordance with *section 1009*.

(2) *Subsection (3)* shall apply in relation to a company (in this section referred to as "*the partner company*") which is a member of a partnership carrying on a trade if arrangements are in existence (whether as part of the terms of the partnership or otherwise) whereby—

(a) in respect of the whole or any part of the value of, or of any portion of, the partner company's share in the profits or loss of any accounting period of the partnership, another member of the partnership or any person connected with another member of the partnership receives any payment or acquires or enjoys, directly or indirectly, any other benefit in money's worth, or

(b) in respect of the whole or any part of the cost of, or any portion of, the partner company's share in the loss of any accounting period of the partnership, the partner company, or any person connected with that company, receives any payment or acquires or enjoys, directly or indirectly, any other benefit in money's worth, other than a payment in respect of group relief to the partner company by a company which is a member of the same group as the partner company for the purposes of group relief.

(3) (a) In this subsection, "*relevant accounting period of the partnership*" means any accounting period of the partnership in which any arrangements specified in *subsection (2)* are in existence or to which any such arrangements apply.

(b) In any case where this subsection applies in relation to the partner company—

(i) the company's share in the loss of the relevant accounting period of the partnership and its share in any charges on income (within the meaning of *section 243*) paid by the partnership in that accounting period shall not be available for set-off for the purposes of corporation tax except against its profits of the several trade,

(ii) except in accordance with *subparagraph (i)*, no trading losses shall be available for set-off for the purposes of corporation tax against the profits of the company's several trade for the relevant accounting period of the partnership, and

(iii) except in accordance with *subparagraphs (i)* and *(ii)*, no amount which apart from this subsection would be available for relief against profits shall be available for set-off for the purposes of corporation tax against so much of the company's total profits as consists of profits of its several trade for the relevant accounting period of the partnership.

(4) Where a company is a member of a partnership and tax in respect of any profits of the partnership is chargeable under Case IV or V of Schedule D, this section shall apply in relation to the company's share in the profits or loss of the partnership as if—

(a) the profits or loss to which the company's share is attributable were the profits of, or the loss incurred in, a several trade carried on by the company, and

(b) any allowance to be made by discharge or repayment of tax or in charging income under Case V of Schedule D were an allowance made in taxing that trade.

Cross References

From Section 426

Section 243 Allowance of charges on income.

Section 1009 Partnerships involving companies.

To Section 426

Section 427 Information as to arrangements for transferring relief, etc.

427 Information as to arrangements for transferring relief, etc

[CTA76 s123]

(1) In this section, *section 417(3)* and *sections 424* to *426*, "*arrangements*" means arrangements of any kind, whether in writing or not.

(2) Where a company—

(a) makes a claim for group relief,

(b) being a party to a leasing contract (within the meaning of *section 425*) claims relief as mentioned in *subsection (1)(b)* of that section, or

(c) being a member of a partnership, claims any relief which, if *section 426(3)* applied in relation to it, it would not be entitled to claim,

and the inspector has reason to believe that any relevant arrangements may exist, or may have existed at any time material to the claim, then, at any time after the claim is made, the inspector may serve notice in writing on the company requiring it to furnish the inspector, within such time, being not less than 30 days, from the giving of the notice as the inspector may direct, with—

(i) a declaration in writing stating whether or not any such arrangements exist or existed at any material time,

(ii) such information as the inspector may reasonably require for the purpose of satisfying the inspector whether or not any such arrangements exist or existed at any material time, or

(iii) both such a declaration and such information.

(3) In this section, "*relevant arrangements*", in relation to a claim within any of *paragraphs (a)* to *(c)* of *subsection (2)*, means arrangements referred to in the provision specified in the corresponding paragraph below—

(a) *section 417(3)* or *subsection (3)* or *(4)* of *section 424*,

(b) *section 425(1)(c)*, or

(c) *section 426(2)*.

(4) In a case within *paragraph (a)* of *subsection (2)*, a notice under that subsection may be served on the surrendering company (within the meaning of *section 411*) instead of or as well as on the company claiming relief.

(5) In a case within *paragraph (c)* of *subsection (2)*, a notice under that subsection may be served on the partners instead of or as well as on the company, and accordingly may require the partners, instead of or as well as the company, to furnish the declaration, information or declaration and information concerned.

Case Law

Arrangements in relation to restrictive trade practices held to include "the mutual arousal of expectations". British Basic Slag Ltd's Application 1963 WLR 727

Cross References

From Section 427

Section 411 Surrender of relief between members of groups and consortia.

Section 417 Diminished share of profits or assets.

Section 424 Effect of arrangements for transfer of company to another group, etc.

Section 425 Leasing contracts: effect on claims for losses of company reconstructions.

Section 426 Partnerships involving companies: effect of arrangements for transferring relief.

To Section 427

Section 1075 Penalties for failure to furnish certain information and for incorrect information.

428 Exclusion of double allowances, etc

[CTA76 s124; FA97 s146(1) and Sch9 PtI par10(6)]

(1) Relief shall not be given more than once in respect of the same amount, whether by giving group relief and by giving some other relief (in any accounting period) to the surrendering company or by giving group relief more than once.

(2) In accordance with *subsection (1)*, 2 or more claimant companies shall not, in respect of any one loss or other amount for which group relief may be given, and whatever their accounting periods corresponding to that of the surrendering company, obtain in aggregate more relief than could be obtained by a single claimant company whose corresponding accounting period coincided with the accounting period of the surrendering company.

(3) Where claims for group relief are made by more than one claimant company which relate to the same accounting period of the same surrendering company, and—

(a) all the claims so made are admissible only by virtue of *subsection (2)* or *(3)* of *section 423*, and

(b) there is a part of the surrendering company's accounting period during which none of those claimant companies is a member of the same group as the surrendering company,

then, those claimant companies shall not obtain in all more relief than could be obtained by a single claimant company which was not a member of the same group as the surrendering company during that part of the surrendering company's accounting period (but was a member during the remainder of that accounting period).

(4) Where claims for group relief are made by a claimant company as respects more than one surrendering company for group relief to be set off against its total profits for any one accounting period, and—

(a) all the claims so made are admissible only by virtue of *subsection (2)* or *(3)* of *section 423*, and

(b) there is a part of the claimant company's accounting period during which none of the surrendering companies by reference to which the claims are made is a member of the same group as the claimant company,

then, the claimant company shall not obtain in all more relief to be set off against its profits for the accounting period than it could obtain on a claim as respects a single surrendering company (with unlimited losses and other amounts eligible for relief) which was not a member of the same group as the claimant company during that part of the claimant company's accounting period (but was a member during the remainder of that accounting period).

(5) The following provisions shall apply as respects a claim (in this subsection referred to as a "*consortium claim*") for group relief made by a company as a member of a consortium:

(a) a consortium claim, and a claim other than a consortium claim, shall not both have effect as respects the loss or other amount of the same accounting period of the same surrendering company unless each of the 2 claims is as respects a loss or other amount apportioned under *section 423(2)(a)* to a component of that accounting period, and the 2 components do not overlap;

(b) in *subsections (3)* and *(4)* consortium claims shall be disregarded;

(c) *paragraph (a)* shall apply according to the order in which claims are made.

(6) Without prejudice to *section 320(6)*, any reference in *Part 9*, *Chapter 1* of *Part 24*, *Chapter 1* of *Part 29* and *section 765* to an allowance made shall include a reference to an allowance which would be made but for the granting of group relief or but for that and but for an insufficiency of profits or other income against which to make it.

Cross References

From Section 428

Section 268 Meaning of "industrial building or structure".
Section 320 Other interpretation (Part 9).
Section 423 Company joining or leaving group or consortium.
Section 670 Mine development allowance.
Section 754 Interpretation (Chapter 1).
Section 765 Allowances for capital expenditure on scientific research.

429 Claims and adjustments

[CTA76 s125]

(1) A claim for group relief—

(a) need not be for the full amount available,

(b) shall require the consent of the surrendering company notified to the inspector in such form as the Revenue Commissioners may require, and

(c) shall be made within 2 years from the end of the surrendering company's accounting period to which the claim relates.

(2) A claim for group relief by a company as a member of a consortium shall require the consent of each other member of the consortium, notified to the inspector in such form as the Revenue Commissioners may require, in addition to the consent of the surrendering company.

(3) Where the inspector ascertains that any group relief which has been given is or has become excessive, he or she may make an assessment to corporation tax under Case IV of Schedule D in the amount which in his or her opinion ought to be charged.

(4) *Subsection (3)* is without prejudice to the making of an assessment under [*Chapter 5 Part 41A*][1] and to the making of all such other adjustments by means of discharge or repayment of tax or otherwise as may be required where a claimant company has obtained too much relief, or a surrendering company has foregone relief in respect of a corresponding amount.

Amendments

[1] Substituted by FA12 sched4(part 2)(g).

Case Law

In Farmer v Bankers Trust International Ltd 1990 STC 564 the taxpayer lost its claim to modify a claim to group relief, which it had made within the two year limit, subsequent to the expiry of that limit. However, in Gallic Leasing Ltd v Coburn 1991 STC 699 it was held that the claim for group relief was valid even though the amount of the relief was not made available within the two year period. There is no time limit within which the surrendering company had to inform the Revenue of its consent.

A claim for group relief could be made after a company has left the group. AW Chapman Ltd v Hennessy 1982 STC 214

Cross References

From Section 429

Section 919 Assessments to corporation tax.

PART 13

Close Companies

CHAPTER 1

Interpretation and General

430 Meaning of "close company"

[CTA76 s94]

(1) For the purposes of the Corporation Tax Acts, "*close company*" means a company under the control of 5 or fewer participators, or of participators who are directors, but does not include—

(a) a company not resident in the State,

(b) a registered industrial and provident society, being a society within the meaning of *section 698*,

(c) a building society within the meaning of *section 702*,

(d) a company controlled by or on behalf of the State and not otherwise a close company, […][1]

[(da) a company controlled by or on behalf of—

(i) a Member State of the European Communities (other than the State) or,

(ii) the government of a territory, with which government, arrangements having the force of law by virtue of [*section 826(1)*][2] have been made,

and which company is not otherwise a close company, or][3]

(e) a company within *subsection (4)* or *section 431*.

(2) For the purposes of this section—

(a) a company shall be treated as controlled by or on behalf of the State only if it is under the control of the State, or of persons acting on behalf of the State, independently of any other person, and

(b) where a company is so controlled, it shall not be treated as being otherwise a close company unless it can be treated as a close company by virtue of being under the control of persons acting independently of the State.

[(2A) For the purposes of this section—

(a) a company shall be treated as controlled by or on behalf of a Member State of the European Communities (other than the State) or the government of a territory with which arrangements having the force of law by virtue of [*section 826(1)*][4] have been made only if it is under the control of that Member State or the government of that territory, or of persons acting on behalf of that Member State or the government of that territory, independently of any other person, and

(b) where a company is so controlled, it shall not be treated as being otherwise a close company unless it can be treated as a close company by virtue of being under the control of persons acting independently of that Member State or the government of that territory.][5]

(3) A company resident in the State (but not within *paragraph (b)* or *(c)* of *subsection (1)*) shall also be a close company if, on a full distribution of its distributable income, more than 50 per cent of that income would be paid directly or indirectly to 5 or fewer participators, or to participators who are directors.

(4) A company shall not be treated as a close company—

(a) if—

(i) it is controlled by a company which is not a close company, or by 2 or more companies none of which is a close company, and

(ii) it cannot be treated as a close company except by taking as one of the 5 or fewer participators requisite for its being so treated a company which is not a close company,

or

(b) if it cannot be treated as a close company except by virtue of *paragraph (c)* of *section 432(2)* and would not be a close company if the reference in that paragraph to participators did not include loan creditors who are companies other than close companies.

(5) References in *subsection (4)* to a close company shall be treated as including a company which if resident in the State would be a close company.

(6) Where shares in any company (in this subsection referred to as "*the first company*") are at any time after the 5th day of April, 1976, held on trust for an exempt approved scheme (within the meaning of *Chapter 1* of *Part 30*), then, unless the scheme is established wholly or mainly for the benefit of persons who are, or are dependants of, employees or directors or past employees or directors of—

(a) the first company,

(b) an associated company of the first company,

(c) a company under the control of any director, or associate of a director, of the first company or of 2 or more persons each of whom is such a director or associate, or

(d) a close company,

the persons holding the shares shall for the purposes of *subsection (4)* be deemed to be the beneficial owners of the shares and in that capacity to be a company which is not a close company.

Amendments

[1] Deleted by FA03 s63(a)(i).

[2] Substituted by FA07 sched2(1)(m)(i). Has effect as on and from 2 April 2007

[3] Inserted by FA03 s63(a)(ii).

[4] Substituted by FA07 sched2(1)(m)(ii). Has effect as on and from 2 April 2007

[5] Inserted by FA03 s63(b).

Revenue Information Notes

IT, CGT and CT – Part 13 Close Companies

Cross References

From Section 430

Section 431 Certain companies with quoted shares not to be close companies.

Section 432 Meaning of "associated company" and "control".

Section 698 Interpretation (Chapter 1).
Section 702 Union or amalgamation of, transfer of engagement between, societies.
Section 770 Interpretation and supplemental (Chapter 1).
Section 826 Agreements for relief from double taxation.

To Section 430

Section 4 Interpretation of Corporation Tax Acts.
Section 5 Interpretation of Capital Gains Tax Acts.
Section 10 Connected persons.
Section 131 Bonus issues following repayment of share capital.
Section 132 Matters to be treated or not treated as repayments of share capital.
Section 413 Profits or assets available for distribution.
Section 438 Loans to participators, etc.
Section 488 Interpretation (Part 16).
Section 531AA Interpretation (Part 18C).
Section 783 Interpretation and general (Chapter 2).
Section 808 Power to obtain information.
Section 817 Schemes to avoid liability to tax under Schedule F.
Schedule 11 Profit Sharing Schemes
Schedule 12A Approved Savings-Related Share Option Schemes
Schedule 12C Approved Share Option Schemes

431 Certain companies with quoted shares not to be close companies

[CTA76 s95]

(1) In this section, "*share*" includes "*stock*".

(2) For the purposes of this section—

(a) a person shall be a principal member of a company—

(i) if such person possesses a percentage of the voting power in the company of more than 5 per cent and, where there are more than 5 such persons, if such person is one of the 5 persons who possess the greatest percentages, or

(ii) if (because 2 or more persons possess equal percentages of the voting power in the company) there are no such 5 persons, such person is one of the 6 or more persons (so as to include those 2 or more who possess equal percentages) who possess the greatest percentages,

(b) a principal member's holding shall consist of the shares which carry the voting power possessed by the principal member, and

(c) in determining the voting power which a person possesses, there shall be attributed to such person any voting power which for the purposes of *section 432* would be attributed to such person under *subsection (5)* or *(6)* of that section.

(3) Subject to this section, a company shall not be treated as being at any time a close company if—

(a) shares in the company carrying not less than 35 per cent of the voting power in the company (not being shares entitled to a fixed rate of dividend, whether with or without a further right to participate in profits) have been allotted unconditionally to, or acquired unconditionally by, and are at that time beneficially held by, the public, and

(b) any such shares have within the preceding 12 months been the subject of dealings on a recognised stock exchange, and the shares have within those 12 months been quoted in the official list of a recognised stock exchange.

(4) *Subsection (3)* shall not apply to a company at any time when the total percentage of the voting power in the company possessed by all of the company's principal members exceeds 85 per cent.

(5) For the purposes of *subsection (3)*, shares in a company shall be deemed to be beneficially held by the public only if the shares—

(a) are within *subsection (6)*, and

(b) are not within the exceptions in *subsection (7)*,

and the reference to shares which have been allotted unconditionally to, or acquired unconditionally by, the public shall be construed accordingly.

(6) Shares are within this subsection (as being beneficially held by the public) if the shares—

(a) are beneficially held by a company resident in the State which is not a close company, or by a company not so resident which would not be a close company if it were so resident,

(b) are held on trust for an exempt approved scheme (within the meaning of *Chapter 1* of *Part 30*), or

(c) are not comprised in a principal member's holding.

(7) (a) Shares shall be deemed not to be held by the public if the shares are held—

(i) by any director, or associate of a director, of the company,

(ii) by any company under the control of any such director or associate, or of 2 or more persons each of whom is such a director or associate,

(iii) by an associated company of the company, or

(iv) as part of any fund the capital or income of which is applicable or applied wholly or mainly for the benefit of, or of the dependants of, the employees or directors, or past employees or directors, of the company, or of any company within *subparagraph (ii)* or *(iii)*.

(b) References in this subsection to shares held by any person include references to any shares the rights or powers attached to which could for the purposes of *section 432* be attributed to that person under *subsection (5)* of that section.

Cross References

From Section 431

Section 432 Meaning of "associated company" and "control".
Section 770 Interpretation and supplemental (Chapter 1).

To Section 431

Section 4 Interpretation of Corporation Tax Acts.
Section 10 Connected persons.
Section 430 Meaning of "close company".
Section 808 Power to obtain information.
Section 817 Schemes to avoid liability to tax under Schedule F.
Schedule 11 Profit Sharing Schemes
Schedule 12A Approved Savings-Related Share Option Schemes
Schedule 12C Approved Share Option Schemes
Schedule 31 Consequential Amendments

432 Meaning of "*associated company*" and "*control*"

[CTA76 s102; FA96 s132(1) and Sch5 Pt1 par10(4)]

(1) For the purposes of this Part, a company shall be treated as another company's associated company at a particular time if, at that time or at any time within one year previously, one of the 2 companies has control of the other company, or both companies are under the control of the same person or persons.

(2) For the purposes of this Part, a person shall be taken to have control of a company if such person exercises, or is able to exercise or is entitled to acquire, control, whether direct or indirect, over the company's affairs, and in particular, but without prejudice to the generality of the foregoing, if such person possesses or is entitled to acquire—

(a) the greater part of the share capital or issued share capital of the company or of the voting power in the company,

(b) such part of the issued share capital of the company as would, if the whole of the income of the company were distributed among the participators (without regard to any rights which such person or any other person has as a loan creditor), entitle such person to receive the greater part of the amount so distributed, or

(c) such rights as would, in the event of the winding up of the company or in any other circumstances, entitle such person to receive the greater part of the assets of the company which would then be available for distribution among the participators.

(3) Where 2 or more persons together satisfy any of the conditions of *subsection (2)*, they shall be taken to have control of the company.

(4) For the purposes of *subsection (2)*, a person shall be treated as entitled to acquire anything which such person is entitled to acquire at a future date or will at a future date be entitled to acquire.

(5) For the purposes of *subsections (2)* and *(3)*, there shall be attributed to any person any rights or powers of a nominee for such person, that is, any rights or powers which another person possesses on such person's behalf or may be required to exercise on such person's direction or behalf.

(6) For the purposes of *subsections (2)* and *(3)*, there may also be attributed to any person all the rights and powers of—

(a) any company of which such person has, or such person and associates of such person have, control,

(b) any 2 or more companies of which such person has, or such person and associates of such person have, control,

(c) any associate of such person, or

(d) any 2 or more associates of such person,

including the rights and powers attributed to a company or associate under *subsection (5)*, but excluding those attributed to an associate under this subsection, and such attributions shall be made under this subsection as will result in the company being treated as under the control of 5 or fewer participators if it can be so treated.

Case Law

A settlor of a trust was taken to have control of the trust property by way of his "association" with the trustees. Gascoines Group Ltd v Inspector of Taxes 2004 STC 844

The rights and powers of certain associates and companies may be attributed to a person. R v IR Commissioners ex parte Newfields Developments Ltd 2000 STC 52

Cross References

To Section 432

Section 5 Interpretation of Capital Gains Tax Acts.
Section 10 Connected persons.
Section 22A Reduction of corporation tax liability in respect of certain trading income.
Section 23A Company residence.
Section 44 Exemption from corporation tax of certain securities issued by Minister for Finance.
Section 76C Use of different accounting policies within a group of companies.
Section 128D Tax treatment of directors of companies and employees who acquire restricted shares.
Section 129A Dividends paid out of foreign profits.
Section 153 Distributions to certain nonresidents.
Section 172D Exemption from dividend withholding tax for certain non-resident persons.
Section 247 Relief to companies on loans applied in acquiring interest in other companies.
Section 430 Meaning of "close company".
Section 431 Certain companies with quoted shares not to be close companies.
Section 486C Relief from tax for certain start-up companies.
Section 488 Interpretation (Part 16).
Section 519 Employee share ownership trusts.
Section 531 Payments to subcontractors in certain industries.
Section 579A Attribution of gains to beneficiaries.
Section 627 Deemed disposal of assets.
Section 629 Tax on non-resident company recoverable from another member of group or from controlling director.
Section 697A Interpretation (Part 24A).
Section 701 Transfer of shares held by certain societies to members of society.
Section 743 Material interest in offshore funds.
Section 769A Interpretation (Chapter 4).
Section 817 Schemes to avoid liability to tax under Schedule F.
Section 817C Restriction on deductibility of certain interest.
Section 825B Repayment of tax where earnings not remitted.
Section 882 Particulars to be supplied by new companies.
Section 898N Audit.
Section 904A Power of inspection: returns and collection of appropriate tax.
Section 908B Application to High Court seeking order requiring information: associated institutions.
Section 985A Application of section 985 to certain perquisites, etc.
Section 997A Credit in respect of tax deducted from emoluments of certain directors.
Schedule 11 Profit Sharing Schemes
Schedule 12 Employee Share Ownership Trusts
Schedule 12A Approved Savings-Related Share Option Schemes
Schedule 12C Approved Share Option Schemes

433 Meaning of "*participator*", "*associate*", "*director*" and "*loan creditor*"

[CTA76 s103; FA97 s146(1) and Sch9 PtI par10(5)]

(1) For the purposes of this Part, "*participator*", in relation to any company, means a person having a share or interest in the capital or income of the company and, without prejudice to the generality of the foregoing, includes—

(a) any person who possesses, or is entitled to acquire, share capital or voting rights in the company,

(b) any loan creditor of the company,

(c) any person who possesses, or is entitled to acquire, a right to receive or participate in distributions of the company (construing "*distributions*" without regard to *section 436* or *437*) or any amounts payable by the company (in cash or in kind) to loan creditors by means of premium on redemption, and

(d) any person who is entitled to secure that income or assets (whether present or future) of the company will be applied directly or indirectly for such person's benefit.

(2) (a) References in *subsection (1)* to being entitled to do anything apply where a person is entitled to do it at a future date or will at a future date be entitled to do it.

(b) *Subsection (1)* is without prejudice to any particular provision of this Part requiring a participator in one company to be treated as being also a participator in another company.

(3) (a) In this subsection, "*relative*" means [husband, wife, civil partner,][1] ancestor, lineal descendant, brother or sister.

(b) For the purposes of this Part but subject to *paragraph (c)*, "*associate*", in relation to a participator, means—

(i) any relative or partner of the participator,

(ii) the trustee or trustees of any settlement in relation to which the participator is, or any relative (living or dead) of the participator is or was, a settlor ("*settlement*" and "*settlor*" having the same meanings respectively as in *section 10*), and

(iii) where the participator is interested in any shares or obligations of the company which are subject to any trust or are part of the estate of a deceased person, any other person interested in those shares or obligations,

and has a corresponding meaning in relation to a person other than a participator.

(c) *Paragraph (b)(iii)* shall not apply so as to make an individual an associate as being entitled or eligible to benefit under a trust—

(i) if the trust relates exclusively to an exempt approved scheme (within the meaning of *Chapter 1* of *Part 30*), or

(ii) if the trust is exclusively for the benefit of the employees, or the employees and directors, of the company or their dependants (and not wholly or mainly for the benefit of the directors or their relatives) and the individual in question is not (and could not as a result of the operation of the trust become), either on his or her own or with his or her relatives, the beneficial owner of more than 5 per cent of the ordinary share capital of the company,

and, in applying *subparagraph (ii)*, any charitable trusts which may arise on the failure or determination of other trusts shall be disregarded.

[(4) For the purposes of this Part "*director*" includes—

(a) any person occupying the position of director by whatever name called,

(b) any person in accordance with whose directions or instructions the directors are accustomed to act, and

(c) any person—

(i) who is a manager of the company or otherwise concerned in the management of the company's trade or business, and

(ii) who is, either on his or her own or with one or more associates, the beneficial owner of, or able, directly or through the medium of other companies or by any other indirect means, to control, 20 per cent or more of the ordinary share capital of the company.][2]

(5) In [*subsection (4)(c)(ii)*][3], "either on his or her own or with one or more associates" requires a person to be treated as owning or, as the case may be, controlling what any associate owns or controls, even if he or she does not own or control share capital on his or her own and, in *subsection (3)(c)(ii)*, "either on his or her own or with his or her relatives" has a corresponding meaning.

(6) (a) For the purposes of this Part but subject to *paragraph (b)*, "*loan creditor*", in relation to a company, means a creditor in respect of—

(i) any debt incurred by the company for—

(I) any money borrowed or capital assets acquired by the company,

(II) any right to receive income created in favour of the company, or

(III) consideration the value of which to the company was (at the time when the debt was incurred) substantially less than the amount of the debt (including any premium on the debt),

or

(ii) any redeemable loan capital issued by the company.

(b) A person carrying on a business of banking shall not be deemed to be a loan creditor in respect of any loan capital issued or debt incurred by the company for money loaned by such person to the company in the ordinary course of that business.

(7) A person who is not the creditor in respect of any debt or loan capital to which *subsection (6)* applies but nevertheless has a beneficial interest in that debt or loan capital shall to the extent of that interest be treated for the purposes of this Part as a loan creditor in respect of that debt or loan capital.

Amendments

[1] Substituted by F(No.3)A11 sched1(63). Shall have effect from 27 July 2011.

[2] Substituted by FA10 sched4(1)(c). Has effect as on and from 3 April 2010.

[3] Substituted by FA11 sched3(1)(c). Has effect as on and from 6 February 2011.

Case Law

In IRC v Buchanan 37 TC 365 it was held that a trust created by will is not a disposition and therefore not a settlement. It follows that a testator of a will is not a settlor.

Willingale v Islington Green Investment Co 48 TC 547 discussed the meaning of associate.

J Bibby & Sons Ltd v CIR 29 TC 167 outlines the distinction between legal and beneficial interest.

Cross References

From Section 433

Section 10 Connected persons.

Section 436 Certain expenses for participators and associates.

Section 437 Interest paid to directors and directors' associates.

Section 770 Interpretation and supplemental (Chapter 1).

To Section 433

Section 413 Profits or assets available for distribution.

Section 488 Interpretation (Part 16).

Section 590 Attribution to participators of chargeable gains accruing to non-resident company.

Section 783 Interpretation and general (Chapter 2).

Section 835B Meaning of associated.

Section 892 Returns by nominee holders of securities.

Schedule 11 Profit Sharing Schemes
Schedule 12 Employee Share Ownership Trusts
Schedule 12A Approved Savings-Related Share Option Schemes
Schedule 12C Approved Share Option Schemes

434 Distributions to be taken into account and meaning of "*distributable income*", "*investment income*", "*estate income*", etc

[CTA76 s100; FA89 s27(1)]

(1) In this section—

[...][1]

"*estate income*" means income (other than yearly or other interest) chargeable to tax under Case III, IV or V of Schedule D, and arising from the ownership of land (including any interest in or right over land) or from the letting furnished of any building or part of a building;

["*franked investment income*" excludes—

(a) a distribution made out of exempt profits within the meaning of *section 140*,

(b) a distribution made out of disregarded income within the meaning of *section 141* and to which *subsection (3)(a)* of that section applies, and

(c) a distribution made out of exempted income within the meaning of *section 142*;

"*income*" of a company for an accounting period means the income as computed in accordance with *subsection (4)*;][2]

["*investment income*" of a company means income other than estate income which, if the company were an individual, would not be earned income within the meaning of *section 3*, but, without prejudice to the meaning of "*franked investment income*" in this section, does not include—

(a) any interest or dividends on investments which, having regard to the nature of the company's trade, would be taken into account as trading receipts in computing trading income but for the fact that they have been subjected to tax otherwise than as trading receipts, or but for the fact that by virtue of *section 129* they are not to be taken into account in computing income for corporation tax, and

(b) any dividends or other distributions received by the company in respect of shares at a time when any gain on a disposal of the shares would not have been a chargeable gain by virtue of *section 626B* or would not have been a chargeable gain by virtue of *section 626B* if *paragraphs (a)* and *(b)* of *subsection (3)* of that section were deleted.][3]

["*relevant charges*", in relation to an accounting period of a company, means charges on income paid in the accounting period by the company and which are allowed as deductions under *section 243*, other than so much of those charges as is paid for the purposes of an excepted trade within the meaning of *section 21A*;][4]

[...][5]

"*trading company*" means any company which exists wholly or mainly for the purpose of carrying on a trade and any other company whose income does not consist wholly or mainly of investment or estate income.

(2) For the purposes of *section 440*[and subject to subsection (3A) the distributions of a company][6] for an accounting period shall be taken to be the aggregate of—

(a) any dividends which are declared for or in respect of the accounting period and are paid or payable during the accounting period or within 18 months after the end of the accounting period, and

(b) all distributions, other than dividends, made in the accounting period.

(3) Where—

(a) a period of account for or in respect of which a company declares a dividend is not an accounting period,

(b) the dividend is paid or payable during the period of account or within 18 months after the end of the period of account, and

(c) part of the period of account falls within an accounting period,

then, the proportion of the amount of the dividend to be treated for the purposes of *subsection (2)* as being for or in respect of the accounting period shall be the same as the proportion which that part of the period of account bears to the whole of that period.

[(3A) (a) Where a close company pays a dividend, or makes a distribution, to another close company, the companies may jointly elect, by giving notice to the Collector-General in such manner as the Revenue Commissioners may require, that the dividend, or as the case may be the distribution, is to be treated for the purposes of *section 440* as not being a distribution.

(b) Where notice is given in accordance with *paragraph (a)*, the dividend, or as the case may be the distribution, shall be treated—

(i) for the purposes of *section 440* as not being a distribution, and

(ii) for the purposes of *subsection (5)* as not being franked investment income.

(c) An election by a company under *paragraph (a)* as respects an accounting period shall be included with the return under [chapter 3 of Part 41A][7] which falls to be made by the company for the accounting period.][8]

(4) [The income][9] of a company for an accounting period shall be the income for the accounting period, computed in accordance with the Corporation Tax Acts, exclusive of franked investment income, before deducting—

(a) any loss incurred in any trade or profession carried on by the company which is carried forward from an earlier, or carried back from a later, accounting period,

(b) any loss which if it were a profit would be chargeable to corporation tax on the company under Case III or IV of Schedule D and which is carried forward from an earlier accounting period or any expenses of management or any charges on income which are so carried forward, and

(c) any excess of deficiencies over surpluses which if such excess were an excess of surpluses over deficiencies would be chargeable to corporation tax on the company under Case V of Schedule D and which is carried forward from an earlier, or carried back from a later, accounting period,

and after deducting—

(d) any loss incurred in the accounting period in any trade or profession carried on by the company,

(e) any loss incurred in the accounting period which if it were a profit would be chargeable to corporation tax on the company under Case III or IV of Schedule D,

(f) any excess of deficiencies over surpluses which if such excess were an excess of surpluses over deficiencies would be chargeable to corporation tax on the company for the accounting period under Case V of Schedule D, [(g) any amount which is an allowable deduction against relevant trading income by virtue of *section 243A*.][10]

[(5) (a) The estate and investment income of a company for an accounting period shall be the amount by which the sum of—

(i) the amount of franked investment income for the accounting period, and

[(ii) an amount determined by applying to the amount of the income of the company for the accounting period the fraction—

$$\frac{A}{B}$$

where—

A is the aggregate of the amounts of estate income and investment income taken into account in computing the income of the company for the accounting period, and

B is the amount of the company's income before taking account of any amount specified in *paragraphs (d)* to *(g)* of *subsection (4)*,][11]

exceeds the aggregate of—

(I) the amount of relevant charges, and

(II) the amount which is an allowable deduction in computing the total profits for the accounting period in respect of expenses of management by virtue of *section 83(2)*.

(b) The trading income of a company for an accounting period shall be the income of the company for the accounting period after deducting—

[(i) an amount equal to the amount specified in *subparagraph (ii)* of *paragraph (a)*,][12]

(ii) where the aggregate of the amounts specified in clauses (I) and (II) of *paragraph (a)* exceeds the sum of the amounts specified in *subparagraphs (i)* and *(ii)* of that paragraph, the amount of the excess, and

(iii) charges on income paid for the purposes of an excepted trade within the meaning of *section 21A*.

(5A) (a) For the purposes of *sections 440* and *441*, but subject to *paragraph (b)*—

"*distributable estate and investment income*" of a company for an accounting period means the estate and investment income of the company for the accounting period after deducting the amount of corporation tax which would be payable by the company for the accounting period if the tax were computed on the basis of that income;

['*distributable trading income*' of a company for an accounting period means the trading income of the company for the accounting period after deducting the amount of corporation tax which would be payable by the company for the accounting period if the tax were computed on the basis of that income;][13]

(b) In the case of a trading company, the distributable estate and investment income for an accounting period shall be the amount determined in accordance with *paragraph (a)* reduced by 7.5 per cent.][14]

(6) The amount for part of an accounting period of any description of income referred to in this section shall be a proportionate part of the amount for the whole period.

(7) Where a company is subject to any restriction imposed by law as regards the making of distributions, regard shall be had to this restriction in determining the amount of income on which a surcharge shall be imposed under *section 440*.

Amendments

[1, 5] Deleted by FA03 sched6(1)(b)(i). This section shall be deemed to apply to accounting periods ending on or after 14 March 2001.

[2] Inserted by FA01 s91(1)(a)(ii). Applies as respects an accounting period ending on or after 14 March 2001.

[3] Substituted by FA04 s36.

[4] Inserted by FA01 s91(1)(a)(iii). Applies as respects an accounting period ending on or after 14 March 2001.

[6] Substituted by FA08 s44(1)(a)(i). Applies as respects a dividend paid, or distribution made, on or after 31 January 2008.

[7] Substituted by FA12 sched4(part 2)(g).

[8] Inserted by FA08 s44(1)(a)(ii). Applies as respects a dividend paid, or distribution made, on or after 31 January 2008.

[9] Substituted by FA01 s91(1)(b)(i). Applies as respects an accounting period ending on or after 14 March 2001.

[10] Substituted by FA01 s91(1)(b)(ii). Applies as respects an accounting period ending on or after 14 March 2001.

[11] Substituted by FA03 sched6(1)(b)(ii). This section shall be deemed to apply to accounting periods ending on or after 14 March 2001.

[12] Substituted by FA06 sched2(1)(l). Applies to accounting periods ending on or after 2 February 2006.

[13] Substituted by FA12 sched1(19).

[14] Substituted by FA01 s91(1)(c). Applies as respects an accounting period ending on or after 14 March 2001.

Cross References

From Section 434

Section 3 Interpretation of Income Tax Acts.
Section 129 Irish resident company distributions not generally chargeable to corporation tax.
Section 140 Distributions out of profits or gains from stallion fees, stud greyhound services fees and occupation of certain woodlands.
Section 141 Distributions out of income from patent royalties.
Section 142 Distributions out of profits of certain mines.
Section 243 Allowance of charges on income.
Section 440 Surcharge on undistributed investment and estate income.
Section 441 Surcharge on undistributed income of service companies.
Section 448 Relief from corporation tax.
Section 951 Obligation to make a return.

To Section 434

Section 441 Surcharge on undistributed income of service companies.

435 Information

[CTA76 s104]

(1) The inspector may by notice in writing require any company which is, or appears to the inspector to be, a close company to furnish him or her within such time (not being less than 30 days) as may be specified in the notice with such particulars as he or she thinks necessary for the purposes of this Part.

(2) Where for the purposes of this Part any person in whose name any shares are registered is so required by notice in writing by the inspector, such person—

(a) shall state whether or not such person is the beneficial owner of the shares, and

(b) if not the beneficial owner of the shares or any of them, shall furnish the name and address of the person or persons on whose behalf the shares are registered in such person's name.

(3) *Subsection (2)* shall apply in relation to loan capital as it applies in relation to shares.

(4) (a) In this subsection, "*securities*" includes shares, stocks, bonds, debentures and debenture stock and any promissory note or other instrument evidencing indebtedness issued to a loan creditor of the company.

(b) For the purposes of this Part, the inspector may by notice in writing require—

(i) any company which appears to the inspector to be a close company to furnish him or her with particulars of any bearer securities issued by the company and the names and addresses of the persons to whom the securities were issued and the respective amounts issued to each person, and

(ii) any person to whom securities were so issued, or any person to whom or through whom such securities were subsequently sold or transferred, to furnish the inspector with such further information as he or she may require with a view to enabling him or her to ascertain the names and addresses of the persons beneficially interested in the securities.

CHAPTER 2

Additional Matters to be Treated as Distributions, Charges to tax in Respect of Certain Loans and Surcharges on Certain Undistributed Income

436 Certain expenses for participators and associates

[CTA76 s96]

(1) Subject to the exceptions mentioned in *section 130*, "*distribution*", in relation to a close company, includes, unless otherwise stated, any such amount as is required to be treated as a distribution by *subsection (3)*.

(2) For the purposes of this section, any reference to a participator includes an associate of a participator, and any participator in a company which controls another company shall be treated as being also a participator in that other company.

(3) (a) Subject to *paragraph (b)*, where a close company incurs expense in or in connection with the provision for any participator of living or other accommodation, entertainment, domestic or other services, or other benefits or facilities of whatever nature, the company shall be treated as making a distribution to such participator of an amount equal to so much of that expense as is not made good to the company by such participator.

(b) *Paragraph (a)* shall not apply to expense incurred in or in connection with the provision of benefits or facilities for a person to whom *section 118* applies as a director or employee of the company, or the provision for the [spouse, civil partner, children, dependants or children of the civil partner][1] of any such person of any pension, annuity, lump sum, gratuity or other like benefit to be given on his or her death or retirement.

(4) Any reference in *subsection (3)* to expense incurred in or in connection with any matter shall include a reference to a proper proportion of any expense incurred partly in or in connection with that matter, and *section 119* shall apply for the purposes of *subsection (3)* as it applies for the purposes of *section 118*, references to *subsection (3)* being substituted for references to *section 118(1)*.

(5) *Subsection (3)* shall not apply if the company and the participator are both resident in the State and—

(a) one is a subsidiary of the other or both are subsidiaries of a third company also so resident, and

(b) the benefit to the participator arises on or in connection with the transfer of assets or liabilities by the company to the participator, or to the company by the participator.

(6) The question whether one company is a subsidiary of another company for the purpose of *subsection (5)* shall be determined as if it were a question whether it is a 51 per cent subsidiary of the other company, except that the other company shall be treated as not being the owner of—

(a) any share capital which it owns directly in a company if a profit on a sale of the shares would be treated as a trading receipt of its trade,

(b) any share capital which it owns indirectly and which is owned directly by a company for which a profit on the sale of the shares would be a trading receipt, or

(c) any share capital which it owns directly or indirectly in a company not resident in the State.

(7) (a) Where each of 2 or more close companies makes a payment to a person (in this paragraph referred to as "*the first-mentioned person*") who is not a participator in that company, but is a participator in another of those companies, and the companies are acting in concert or under arrangements made by any person, then, each of those companies and any participator in it shall be treated as if the payment made to the first-mentioned person had been made by that company.

(b) This subsection shall apply with any necessary modifications in relation to the giving of any consideration and to the provision of any facilities as it applies in relation to the making of a payment.

Amendments

[1] Substituted by F(No.3)A11 sched1(64).

Cross References

From Section 436

Section 118 Benefits in kind: general charging provision.
Section 119 Valuation of benefits in kind.
Section 130 Matters to be treated as distributions.

To Section 436

Section 4 Interpretation of Corporation Tax Acts.
Section 20 Schedule F.
Section 130 Matters to be treated as distributions.
Section 236 Loan of certain art objects.
Section 433 Meaning of "participator", "associate", "director" and "loan creditor".
Section 437 Interest paid to directors and directors' associates.

436A Certain settlements made by close companies

[(1) (a) In this section—

"*member*", in relation to a company, includes a participator in the company other than a loan creditor of the company;

"*relative*" has the same meaning as in section 433(3)(*a*);

"*relevant settlement*", in relation to a close company, means a settlement made by, or on behalf of, the close company other than a settlement which—

(i) is made expressly for the exclusive benefit of one or more than one person, who is neither a member of the company nor a relative of such a member, and

(ii) does not allow at any time for the possibility of providing any benefit to such member or relative;

"*settlement*" has the same meaning as in section 10 and "*settled*" shall be read accordingly.

(b) For the purposes of this section, any participator in a company which controls another company shall be treated as being also a participator in that other company.

(2) Where any amount, in money or money's worth, is settled by, or on behalf of, a close company on or after 21 January 2011 in connection with a relevant settlement, that amount shall, for the purposes of the Tax Acts, be deemed to be a distribution by the company to the trustees of the settlement.

(3) Where, on or after 21 January 2011, an individual who is or was a member of a close company, or a relative of such an individual, receives directly or indirectly an amount in money or money's worth out of, or indirectly attributable to, assets comprised in a relevant settlement (whenever made) in relation to the close company, then so much of that amount as exceeds any consideration given by the individual or relative of the individual, as the case may be, to the extent that the individual or relative is not otherwise chargeable to income tax in respect of so much of that amount, shall be deemed for the purposes of the Income Tax Acts to be annual profits or gains of that individual or relative, as the case may be, chargeable to tax under Case IV of Schedule D for the year of assessment in which the amount is received.

(4) This section shall not apply as respects a relevant settlement where it is shown to the satisfaction of the inspector or, on the hearing or the rehearing of an appeal, to the satisfaction of the Appeal Commissioners or a judge of the Circuit Court, as the case may be, that the settlement was not made as part of a scheme or arrangement the purpose or one of the purposes of which was the avoidance of tax.][1]

Amendments

[1] Inserted by FA11 s29(c).

Cross References

To Section 436A

Section 20 Schedule F.

Section 130 Matters to be treated as distributions.

437 Interest paid to directors and directors' associates

[CTA76 s97]

(1) In this section, "*interest*" includes any other consideration paid or given by the close company for the use of money advanced, or credit given, by any person, and references to interest paid shall be construed accordingly.

(2) For the purposes of this section, a person shall have a material interest in a company if the person, either on the person's own or with any one or more of the person's associates, or if any associate of the person with or without any such other associates, is the beneficial owner of, or is able, directly or through the medium of other companies or by any other indirect means, to control, more than 5 per cent of the ordinary share capital of the company.

(3) Subject to the exceptions mentioned in *section 130(1)*, this section shall apply where in any accounting period any interest is paid by a close company to, or to an associate of, a person—

(a) who is a director of the close company, or of any company which controls or is controlled by the close company, and

(b) who has a material interest—

(i) in the close company, or

(ii) where the close company is controlled by another company, in that other company.

(4) Where the total amount so paid to any person in the accounting period exceeds the limit imposed in that person's case, the excess shall be deemed to be a distribution made by the close company to that person.

(5) The limit shall be calculated in the first instance as an overall limit applying to the aggregate of all interest which is within *subsection (3)* and which was paid by the close company in the accounting period and, where there are 2 or more different recipients, that overall limit shall be apportioned between them according to the amounts of interest paid to them respectively.

(6) The overall limit shall be a sum equal to interest at 13 per cent per annum or such other rate of interest as the Minister for Finance may from time to time prescribe on whichever is the lesser of—

(a) the total of the loans, advances and credits on which the interest within *subsection (3)* was paid by the close company in the accounting period or, if the total was different at different times in the accounting period, the average total over the accounting period, and

(b) the nominal amount of the issued share capital of the close company plus the amount of any share premium account (or other comparable account by whatever name called) of the company, taking both amounts as at the beginning of the accounting period.

(7) This section shall apply subject to *section 436(7)*.

Cross References

From Section 437

Section 130 Matters to be treated as distributions.

Section 436 Certain expenses for participators and associates.

To Section 437

Section 4 Interpretation of Corporation Tax Acts.

Section 20 Schedule F.

Section 130 Matters to be treated as distributions.

Section 246 Interest payments by companies and to non-residents.
Section 433 Meaning of "participator", "associate", "director" and "loan creditor".
Section 438 Loans to participators, etc.
Schedule 11 Profit Sharing Schemes
Schedule 12A Approved Savings-Related Share Option Schemes
Schedule 12C Approved Share Option Schemes

438 Loans to participators, etc

[CTA76 s98(1) to (7) and (9); FA83 s35]

(1) (a) Subject to this section, where a close company, otherwise than in the ordinary course of a business carried on by it which includes the lending of money, makes any loan or advances any money to an individual who is a participator in the company or an associate of a participator, the company shall be deemed for the purposes of this section to have paid in the year of assessment in which the loan or advance is made an annual payment of an amount which, after deduction of income tax at the standard rate for the year of assessment in which the loan or advance is made, is equal to the amount of the loan or advance.

(b) *Section 239* shall apply for the purposes of the charge, assessment and recovery of the tax referred to in *paragraph (a)*.

(c) The annual payment referred to in *paragraph (a)* shall not be a charge on the company's income within the meaning of *section 243*.

(2) For the purposes of this section, the cases in which a close company is to be regarded as making a loan to any person shall include a case where—

(a) that person incurs a debt to the close company, or

(b) a debt due from that person to a third person is assigned to the close company,

and in such a case the close company shall be regarded as making a loan of an amount equal to the debt; but *paragraph (a)* shall not apply to a debt incurred for the supply by the close company of goods or services in the ordinary course of its trade or business unless the period of credit given exceeds 6 months or is longer than that normally given to the company's customers.

(3) *Subsection (1)* shall not apply to a loan made to a director or employee of a close company, or of an associated company of the close company, if—

(a) the amount of the loan, or that amount when taken together with any other outstanding loans which were made by the close company or any of its associated companies to the borrower, or to the [spouse or civil partner][1] of the borrower, does not exceed [€19,050][2],

(b) the borrower works full-time for the close company or any of its associated companies, and

(c) the borrower does not have a material interest in the close company or in any associated company of the close company but, if the borrower acquires such a material interest at a time when the whole or part of any such loan remains outstanding, the close company shall be regarded as making to the borrower at that time a loan of an amount equal to the sum outstanding.

(4) (a) Where, after a company has been assessed to tax under this section in respect of any loan or advance, the loan or advance or any part of it is repaid to the company, relief shall be given from that tax or a proportionate part of that tax by discharge or repayment.

[(b) Notwithstanding any limitation in *section 865(4)* on the time within which a claim for a repayment of tax is required to be made, relief under this subsection shall be given on a claim which shall be made within 4 years from the end of the year of assessment in which the loan or advance, or any part of it, as the case may be, is repaid to the company.][3]

(5) Where under arrangements made by any person otherwise than in the ordinary course of a business carried on by that person—

(a) a close company makes a loan or advance which apart from this subsection does not give rise to any charge on the company under *subsection (1)*, and

(b) some person other than the close company makes a payment or transfers property to, or releases or satisfies (in whole or in part) a liability of, an individual who is a participator in the company or an associate of a participator,

then, unless in respect of the matter referred to in *paragraph (b)* there is to be included in the total income of the participator or associate an amount not less than the loan or advance, this section shall apply as if the loan or advance had been made to the participator or associate.

(6) In *subsections (1)* and *(5)(b)*, the references to an individual shall apply also to a company receiving the loan or advance in a fiduciary or representative capacity and [to a company not resident in a Member State of the European Communities and, for the purposes of this subsection, a company is a resident of a Member State of the European Communities if the company is by virtue of the law of that Member State resident for the purposes of tax (being, in the case of the State, corporation tax and, in any other case, being any tax imposed in the Member State which corresponds to corporation tax in the State) in such Member State][4].

(7) For the purposes of this section, any participator in a company which controls another company shall be treated as being also a participator in that other company, and *section 437(2)* shall apply for the purpose of determining whether a person has for the purpose of *subsection (3)* a material interest in a company.

(8) For the purposes of this section and in relation to any loan or advance made on or after the 23rd day of May, 1983, *section 430(1)* shall apply as if *paragraph (b)* of that section were deleted.

Amendments

[1] Substituted by F(No.3)A11 sched1(65). Shall have effect from 27 July 2011.

[2] Substituted by FA01 sched5.

[3] Substituted by FA08 sched6(1)(c). Applies as on and from 31 January 2008.

[4] Substituted by FA03 s45(1)(a). (2) This section applies as respects— (a) the making of a loan, (b) the advance of any money, (c) the incurring of any debt, or (d) the assignment of any debt, on or after 6 February 2003.

Case Law

Legal advice used by both the company and also the director/shareholder was accessible as a benefit in kind on the director. Xi Software Ltd v Laing (Inspector of Taxes) 2004 SpC 450

In Stephens v T Pittas Ltd 1983 STC 576 it was held that a sum of money misappropriated by a participator was not considered a loan.

A UK close company lent money to its chairman and the Inland Revenue issued an assessment for income tax. The company argued that the loan was made in the normal course of businesses. The Special Commissioners agreed and held that the taxpayer made loans in the ordinary course of business and no liability arose under the UK equivalent of section 438 TCA 1997. Brennan v Deanby Investment Co 2001 STC 536

In Greenfields v Bains 1992 STC 746 the taxpayer unsuccessfully argued that their liability had been satisfied by arranging for a third party to assume it.

The participator incurred a debt when the company provided services and for which payment was made at year end. Grant v Watton 1999 STC 330

An overdrawn director's account was held to constitute a loan to a participator. Joint v Bracken Developments Ltd 1994 STC 300

In Earlspring Properties v Guest 1995 STC 479 a company was obliged to give notice under this section and failure to do so constituted neglect.

Revenue Briefings

eBrief

eBrief No. 56/2007 – Loans to participators and preliminary tax

Cross References

From Section 438

Section 239 Income tax on payments by resident companies.
Section 243 Allowance of charges on income.
Section 430 Meaning of "close company".
Section 437 Interest paid to directors and directors' associates.
Section 865 Repayment of tax.

To Section 438

Section 239 Income tax on payments by resident companies.
Section 240 Provisions as to tax under section 239.
Section 286A Wear and tear allowances for licences for public hire vehicles.
Section 438A Extension of section 438 to loans by companies controlled by close companies.
Section 439 Effect of release, etc. of debt in respect of loan under section 438.
Section 884 Returns of profits.

438A Extension of section 438 to loans by companies controlled by close companies

[(1) In this section "*loan*" includes advance.

(2) Subject to *subsection (5)*, where a company which is controlled by a close company makes a loan which, apart from this section, does not give rise to a charge under *subsection (1)* of *section 438*, that section applies as if the loan had been made by the close company.

(3) Subject to *subsection (5)*, where a company which is not controlled by a close company makes a loan which, apart from this section, does not give rise to a charge under *subsection (1)* of *section 438* and a close company subsequently acquires control of it, that section applies as if the loan had been made by the close company immediately after the time when it acquired control.

(4) Where 2 or more close companies together control the company that makes or has made the loan, *subsections (2)* and *(3)* apply—

(a) as if each of them controlled that company, and

(b) as if the loan had been made by each of those close companies,

but the loan shall be apportioned between those close companies in such proportion as may be appropriate having regard to the nature and amount of their respective interests in the company that makes or has made the loan.

(5) *Subsections (2)* and *(3)* do not apply if it is shown that no person has made any arrangements (otherwise than in the ordinary course of a business carried on by that person) as a result of which there is a connection—

(a) between the making of the loan and the acquisition of control, or

(b) between the making of the loan and the provision by the close company of funds for the company making the loan,

and the close company shall be regarded as providing funds for the company making the loan if it directly or indirectly makes any payment or transfers any property to, or releases or satisfies (in whole or in part) a liability of, the company making the loan.

(6) Where, by virtue of this section, *section 438* applies as if a loan made by one company had been made by another company, any question under that section whether—

(a) the company making the loan did so otherwise than in the ordinary course of a business carried on by it which includes the lending of money,

(b) the loan or any part of it has been repaid to the company,

(c) the company has released or written off the whole or part of the debt in respect of the loan,

shall be determined by reference to the company that makes the loan.

(7) References to a company making a loan include references to cases in which the company is, or if it were a close company would be, regarded as making a loan by virtue of *section 438(2)*.

(8) This section shall be construed together with *section 438*.][1]

Amendments

[1] Inserted by FA03 s45(1)(b). (2) This section applies as respects—(a) the making of a loan, (b) the advance of any money, (c) the incurring of any debt, or (d) the assignment of any debt, on or after 6 February 2003.

Cross References

From Section 438A

Section 438 Loans to participators, etc.

439 Effect of release, etc. of debt in respect of loan under section 438.

[CTA76 s99(1), (2) and (4)]

(1) Subject to this section, where a company is assessed or liable to be assessed under *section 438* in respect of a loan or advance and releases or writes off the whole or part of the debt in respect of the loan or advance, then—

(a) for the purpose of computing the total income of the person to whom the loan or advance was made, a sum equal to the amount so released or written off shall be treated as income received by such person after deduction of income tax by virtue of *section 238* (at the standard rate for the year of assessment in which the whole or part of the debt was released or written off) from a corresponding gross amount,

(b) no repayment of income tax shall be made in respect of that income,

(c) notwithstanding *paragraph (a)*, the income included by virtue of that paragraph in the total income of that person shall be treated for the purposes of *sections 237* and *238* as not brought into charge to income tax, and

(d) for the purposes of *section 59(ii)*, any amount to be treated as income by virtue of *paragraph (a)* shall be treated as if income tax had been deducted from that amount at the standard rate for the year of assessment in which the whole or part of the debt was released or written off; but, where such amount (or the aggregate of such amounts if more than one) exceeds the amount of the individual's taxable income charged at the standard rate or the higher rate, the amount of the credit under *section 59(ii)* in respect of the excess shall not, notwithstanding anything in *section 59*, exceed the amount of the income tax, if any, charged on that excess.

(2) If the loan or advance referred to in *subsection (1)* was made to a person who has since died, or to trustees of a trust which has come to an end, this section, instead of applying to the person to whom it was made, shall apply to the person from whom

the debt is due at the time of release or writing off (and accordingly, if it is due from such person as personal representative within the meaning of *Chapter 1* of *Part 32*, the amount treated as received by such person shall be, as regards the higher rate of tax, included for the purposes of that Chapter in the aggregate income of the estate), and *subsection (1)* shall apply accordingly with the necessary modifications.

(3) This section shall be construed together with *section 438*.

Cross References

From Section 439

Section 59 Charge to tax of income from which tax has been deducted.
Section 237 Annual payments payable wholly out of taxed income.
Section 238 Annual payments not payable out of taxed income.
Section 438 Loans to participators, etc.
Section 779 Charge to income tax of pensions under Schedule E.

To Section 439

Section 799 Interpretation (Chapter 1).

440 Surcharge on undistributed investment and estate income

[CTA76 s101; FA90 s47; FA97 s146(1) and Sch9 PtI par10(4)]

(1) (a) Where for an accounting period of a close company the [distributable estate and investment income][1] exceeds the distributions of the company for the accounting period, there shall be charged on the company an additional duty of corporation tax (in this section referred to as a "*surcharge*") amounting to 20 per cent of the excess.

(b) Notwithstanding *paragraph (a)*—

(i) a surcharge shall not be made on a company where the excess is equal to or less than the lesser of the following amounts—

(I) [€2,000][2] or, if the accounting period is less than 12 months, £500 proportionately reduced, and

(II) where the company has one or more associated companies, [€2,000][3] divided by one plus the number of those associated companies or, if the accounting period is less than 12 months, [€2,000][4] proportionately reduced divided by one plus the number of those associated companies;

(ii) where the excess is greater than the lesser amount on which by virtue of *subparagraph (i)* a surcharge would not be made, the amount of the surcharge shall not be greater than a sum equal to 80 per cent of the amount by which the excess is greater than that lesser amount.

(2) Where the aggregate of—

(a) the accumulated undistributed income of the company at the end of the accounting period, and

(b) any amount which, on or after the 27th day of November, 1975, was transferred to capital reserves or was used to issue shares, stock or securities as paid up otherwise than for new consideration (within the meaning of *section 135*) or was otherwise used so as to reduce the amount referred to in *paragraph (a)*,

is less than the excess referred to in *subsection (1)*, that subsection shall apply as if the amount of that aggregate were substituted for the excess.

[...][5]

(3) In applying *subsection (1)* to any accounting period of a company, an associated company which has not carried on any trade or business at any time in that accounting period (or, if an associated company during part only of that accounting period, at any time in that part of that accounting period) shall be disregarded.

(4) In determining how many associated companies a company has in an accounting period or whether a company has an associated company in an accounting period, an associated company shall be counted even if it was an associated company for part only of the accounting period, and 2 or more associated companies shall be counted even if they were associated companies for different parts of the accounting period.

[…][6]

(6) A surcharge made under this section on a company in respect of an accounting period (in this subsection referred to as "*the first-mentioned accounting period*")—

(a) shall be charged on the company for the earliest accounting period which ends on or after a day which is 12 months after the end of the first-mentioned accounting period, and

(b) shall be treated as corporation tax chargeable for that accounting period;

but where there is no such accounting period so ending, the surcharge shall be charged for, and treated as corporation tax of, the accounting period in respect of which it is made.

(7) The provisions of the Corporation Tax Acts relating to—

(a) assessments to corporation tax,

(b) appeals against such assessments (including the rehearing of appeals and the statement of a case for the opinion of the High Court), and

(c) the collection and recovery of corporation tax,

shall apply in relation to a surcharge made under this section as they apply to corporation tax charged otherwise than under this section.

Amendments

[1] Substituted by FA01 s91(2)(a). Applies as respects an accounting period ending on or after 14 March 2001.

[2, 3, 4] Substituted by FA13 s33(1). Has effect in relation to accounting periods ending on or after 1 January 2013.

[5] Deleted by FA03 sched6(1)(c). This section shall be deemed to apply to accounting periods ending on or after 14 March 2001.

[6] Deleted by FA00 sched2(i)(i)(II).

Cross References

From Section 440

Section 135 Distributions: supplemental.

To Section 440

Section 176 Purchase of unquoted shares by issuing company or its subsidiary.
Section 243B Relief for certain charges on income on a value basis.
Section 396B Relief for certain trading losses on a value basis.
Section 420B Group relief: Relief for certain losses on a value basis.
Section 434 Distributions to be taken into account and meaning of "distributable income", "investment income", "estate income", etc.
Section 441 Surcharge on undistributed income of service companies.
Section 448 Relief from corporation tax.
Section 486C Relief from tax for certain start-up companies.
Section 644C Relief from corporation tax for losses from dealing in residential development land.
Section 697H Relevant shipping income: distributions of overseas shipping companies.
Section 734 Taxation of collective investment undertakings.
Schedule 22 Dividends Regarded as Paid Out of Profits Accumulated Before Given Date
Schedule 32 Transitional Provisions

441 Surcharge on undistributed income of service companies

[CTA76 s162(1) to (6); FA90 s48; FA95 s55(1); FA96 s52(1); FA97 s146(1) and Sch9 PtI par10(9)]

(1) In this section, "*service company*" means, subject to *subsection (2)*—

(a) a close company whose business consists of or includes the carrying on of a profession or the provision of professional services,

(b) a close company having or exercising an office or employment, or

(c) a close company whose business consists of or includes the provision of services or facilities of whatever nature to or for—

(i) a company within either of the categories referred to in *paragraphs (a)* and *(b)*,

(ii) an individual who carries on a profession,

(iii) a partnership which carries on a profession,

(iv) a person who has or exercises an office or employment, or

(v) a person or partnership connected with any person or partnership referred to in *subparagraphs (i)* to *(iv)*;

but the provision by a close company of services or facilities to or for a person or partnership not connected with the company shall be disregarded for the purposes of this paragraph.

(2) Where the principal part of a company's income which is chargeable to corporation tax under Cases I and II of Schedule D and Schedule E is not derived from—

(a) carrying on a profession,

(b) providing professional services,

(c) having or exercising an office or employment,

(d) providing services or facilities (other than providing services or facilities to or for a person or partnership not connected with the company) to or for any person or partnership referred to in *subparagraphs (i)* to *(v)* of *subsection (1)(c)*, or

(e) any 2 or more of the activities specified in *paragraphs (a)* to *(d)*,

the company shall be deemed not to be a service company.

(3) For the purposes of this section—

(a) a partnership shall be treated as connected with a company or individual (and a company or individual shall be treated as connected with a partnership) if any one of the partners in the partnership is connected with the company or individual, and

(b) a partnership shall be treated as connected with another partnership if any one of the partners in the partnership is connected with any one of the partners in the other partnership.

(4) (a) Where for an accounting period of a service company the aggregate of—

[(i) the distributable estate and investment income, and

(ii) 50 per cent of the distributable trading income,][1]

exceeds the distributions of the company for the accounting period, there shall be charged on the company an additional duty of corporation tax (in this section referred to as a "*surcharge*") amounting to 15 per cent of the excess.

(b) Notwithstanding *paragraph (a)*—

(i) a surcharge shall not be made on a company where the excess is equal to or less than the lesser of the following amounts—

(I) [€2,000][2] or, if the accounting period is less than 12 months, £500 proportionately reduced, and

(II) where the company has one or more associated companies, [€2,000][3] divided by one plus the number of those associated companies or, if the accounting period is less than 12 months, [€2,000][4] proportionately reduced divided by one plus the number of those associated companies;

(ii) where the excess is greater than the lesser amount on which by virtue of *subparagraph (i)* a surcharge would not be made, the amount of the surcharge shall not be greater than a sum equal to 80 per cent of the amount by which the excess is greater than that lesser amount;

(iii) the surcharge shall apply to so much of the excess calculated under this subsection in respect of an accounting period of a company as is not greater than the excess of the [distributable estate and investment income][5] of the accounting period over the distributions of the company for the accounting period as if the reference in this subsection apart from this subparagraph to 15 per cent were a reference to 20 per cent.

(5) *Section 440(1)* shall not apply in relation to a service company, but *subsections (2)* to *(7)* of *section 440* shall apply in relation to a surcharge made under this section as they apply in relation to a surcharge made under *section 440* with the substitution in *subsections (2)* and *(3)* of *section 440* of a reference to *subsection (4)* of this section for the reference to *subsection (1)* of that section.

(6) (a) [Subsections (2), (3), (3A), (6) and (7)][6] of *section 434* shall apply for the purposes of this section as they apply for the purposes of *section 434* or *440*, as the case may be.

(b) For the purposes of this section—

(i) the income of a company for an accounting period shall be its income computed for that period in accordance with *section 434(4)*;

(ii) ["*distributable estate and investment income*" and "*distributable trading income*"][7] of a company for an accounting period have the same meanings respectively as in *subsections (1)* and [*(5A)*][8] of *section 434* with the substitution for the reference to a trading company in each place where it occurs in *subsection* [*(5A)*][9] of that section of a reference to a service company.

Amendments

[1] Substituted by FA01 s91(3)(a)(i). Applies as respects an accounting period ending on or after 14 March 2001.

[2, 3, 4] Substituted by FA13 s33(2)(a). Has effect in relation to accounting periods ending on or after 1 January 2013.

[5] Substituted by FA01 s91(3)(a)(ii). Applies as respects an accounting period ending on or after 14 March 2001.

[6] Substituted by FA08 s44(1)(b). Applies as respects a dividend paid, or distribution made, on or after 31 January 2008.

[7] Substituted by FA01 s91(3)(b). Applies as respects an accounting period ending on or after 14 March 2001.

[8, 9] Substituted by FA13 s33(2)(b). Deemed to have come into force and takes effect on and from 1 January 2013.

Case Law

In Mac Giolla Mhaith (Inspector of Taxes) v Cronin & Associates Ltd 1984 III ITR 211 the company carried on an advertising business. The High Court held that the company was not carrying on a profession so no surcharge was payable on the company's trading income.

In Rahinstown Estates Co v M Hughes (Inspector of Taxes) 1976 III ITR 517 a close company went into voluntary liquidation and Revenue sought to impose a surcharge on undistributed investment income. Distributions made in the course of a winding up were treated as distributions for surcharge purposes, therefore it was held that the surcharge applied.

The surcharge position of a company for any accounting period should be decided by reference to the company's status at the balance sheet date. CHW (Huddersfield) Ltd v CIR 41 TC 92

Emerging from the case of CIR v Maxse 1919 12 TC 41, the factors indicative of a profession would be a requirement for either a purely intellectual skill or for a manual skill controlled by an intellectual skill of the operation, such as painting, sculptor or surgery.

Held to be Carrying on a Profession

Actress – Davies v Braithwaite 1931 18 TC 198
Barrister – Seldon v Croom-Johnson 1932 TC 740
Journalist – CIR v Maxse 1919 12 TC 41
Optician – CIR v North and Ingram 1918 KB 705

Held Not to be Carrying on a Profession

Dance band leader – Loss v CIR 1945 ER 683
Insurance broker – Durant v CIR 1921 TC 245
Chartered secretary – Burt & Co v CIR 1919 KB 650
Photographer – Cecil v CIR 1919 TLR 164
Stockbroker – Christopher Barker & Sons v CIR 1919 KB 222
Tax agent – Currie v CIR 1921 TC 245
Professional gambler – Graham v Green 1925 TC 309

Revenue Briefings

Tax Briefing

Tax Briefing February 1997 – Issue 25 pg 13 – Surcharge on Undistributed Income of Service Companies
Tax Briefing December 1998 – Issue 34 pg 18 – Corporation Tax – ACT & Surcharge
Tax Briefing June 2002 – Issue 48 pg 19 – Professional Service Company Surcharge

Revenue Precedents

The following activities were not considered to be carrying on a profession, a public relations company, an insurance broker and a livestock auctioneering in a cattle mart. Both auctioneers/estate agents and quantity surveyors were carrying on a profession. CTF 101.1

Cross References

From Section 441

Section 434 Distributions to be taken into account and meaning of "distributable income", "investment income", "estate income", etc.
Section 440 Surcharge on undistributed investment and estate income.

To Section 441

Section 176 Purchase of unquoted shares by issuing company or its subsidiary.
Section 243B Relief for certain charges on income on a value basis.
Section 396B Relief for certain trading losses on a value basis.
Section 420B Group relief: Relief for certain losses on a value basis.
Section 434 Distributions to be taken into account and meaning of "distributable income", "investment income", "estate income", etc.
Section 448 Relief from corporation tax.
Section 486C Relief from tax for certain start-up companies.
Section 488 Interpretation (Part 16).
Section 644C Relief from corporation tax for losses from dealing in residential development land.
Schedule 22 Dividends Regarded as Paid Out of Profits Accumulated Before Given Date
Schedule 32 Transitional Provisions

PART 14

Taxation of Companies Engaged in Manufacturing Trades, Certain Trading Operations Carried on in Shannon Airport and Certain Trading Operations Carried on in the Custom House Docks Area

CHAPTER 1

Interpretation and General

442 Interpretation (Part 14) [Deleted]

Deleted by FA12 sched1(20).

443 Meaning of "*goods*" [Deleted]

Deleted by FA12 sched1(20).

444 Exclusion of mining and construction operations [Deleted]

Deleted by FA12 sched1(20).

445 Certain trading operations carried on in Shannon Airport [Deleted]

Deleted by FA12 sched1(20).

446 Certain trading operations carried on in Custom House Docks Area [Deleted]

Deleted by FA12 sched1(20).

447 Appeals [Deleted]

Deleted by FA12 sched1(20).

CHAPTER 2

Principal Provisions

448 Relief from corporation tax [Deleted]

Deleted by FA12 sched1(20).

449 Credit for foreign tax not otherwise credited [Deleted]

Deleted by FA12 sched1(20).

450 Double taxation relief [Deleted]

Deleted by FA12 sched1(20).

451 Treatment of income and gains of certain trading operations carried on in Custom House Docks Area from investments held outside the State [Deleted]

Deleted by FA12 sched1(20).

452 Application of section 130 to certain interest

[(1) (a) In this section—

"*arrangements*" means arrangements having the force of law by virtue of [*section 826(1)*][1] [or arrangements made with the government of a territory which on completion of the procedures set out in *section 826(1)* will have the force of law;][2]

"*relevant territory*" means—

(i) a Member State of the European Communities other than the State, or

(ii) not being such a Member State, a territory with the government of which arrangements have been made;

[…][3]

"*tax*", in relation to a relevant territory, means any tax imposed in that territory which corresponds to corporation tax in the State.

(b) For the purposes of this section, a company shall be regarded as being a resident of a relevant territory if—

(i) in a case where the relevant territory is a territory with the government of which arrangements have been made [and have effect in accordance with the provisions of those arrangements][4], the company is regarded as being a resident of that territory under those arrangements, and

(ii) in any other case, the company is by virtue of the law of the relevant territory resident for the purposes of tax in that territory.

(2) (a) This paragraph shall apply to so much of any interest as—

(i) is a distribution by virtue only of *section 130(2)(d)(iv)*,

(ii) is payable by a company in the ordinary course of a trade carried on by that company and would, but for *section 130(2)(d)(iv)*, be deductible as a trading expense in computing the amount of the company's income from the trade, and

(iii) is interest payable to a company which is a resident of a relevant territory.

(b) Where a company proves that *paragraph (a)* applies to any interest payable by it for an accounting period and elects to have that interest treated as not being a distribution for the purposes of *section 130(2)(d)(iv)*, then, *section 130(2)(d)(iv)* shall not apply to that interest.

[…][5]

[(3A) (a) This paragraph shall apply to so much of any yearly interest as—

(i) is a distribution by virtue only of *section 130(2)(d)(iv)*,

(ii) is payable by a company in the ordinary course of a trade carried on by that company and would, but for *section 130(2)(d)(iv)*, be deductible as a trading expense in computing the amount of the company's income from the trade, and

(iii) is not interest to which *subsection (2)(a)* applies.

(b) Where a company proves that *paragraph (a)* applies to any interest payable by it for an accounting period and elects to have that interest treated as not being a distribution for the purposes of *section 130(2)(d)(iv)*, then *section 130(2)(d)(iv)* shall not apply to that interest.][6]

(4) An election under [*subsection (2)(b)*, [...][7] or *(3A)(b)*][8] in relation to interest payable by a company for an accounting period shall be made in writing to the inspector and furnished together with the company's return of its profits for the period.][9]

Amendments

[1] Substituted by FA07 sched2(1)(n). Has effect as on and from 2 April 2007

[2] Inserted by F(No.2)A08 s33(f)(i). This section is deemed to have come into force and takes effect as on and from 1 January 2009.

[3] Deleted by FA12 sched1(21)(a).

[4] Inserted by F(No.2)A08 s33(f)(ii). This section is deemed to have come into force and takes effect as on and from 1 January 2009.

[5] Deleted by FA12 sched1(21)(b).

[6] Inserted by FA07 s50(1)(a). Applies as respects interest paid on or after 1 February 2007.

[7] Deleted by FA12 sched1(21)(c).

[8] Substituted by FA07 s50(1)(b). Applies as respects interest paid on or after 1 February 2007.

[9] Substituted by FA01 s87.

Cross References

From Section 452

Section 130 Matters to be treated as distributions.
Section 445 Certain trading operations carried on in Shannon Airport.
Section 446 Certain trading operations carried on in Custom House Docks Area.
Section 826 Agreements for relief from double taxation.

To Section 452

Section 130 Matters to be treated as distributions.

452A Application of section 130 of Principal Act to certain non-yearly interest

[(1) In this section—

'*additional tax*', in relation to a territory in respect of a qualifying company for an accounting period, means the amount determined by the formula—

$$A \times B/100$$

where—

A is the specified amount for that territory in respect of the qualifying company for the accounting period, and

B is the rate per cent specified in *section 21(1)(f)*;

'*deductible amount*', in relation to a territory in respect of a qualifying company for an accounting period, means the amount determined by the formula—

$$C \times D/E$$

where—

C is the specified amount for that territory in respect of the qualifying company for the accounting period,

D is the specified tax in relation to such specified amount, and

E is the additional tax in relation to that specified amount;

'*foreign tax in respect of a qualifying company for an accounting period*' means, in relation to a company carrying on business in a territory, the amount determined by the formula—

$$F \times G/100$$

where—

F is so much of the specified amount for the territory in respect of the qualifying company for the accounting period as is payable to the company carrying on business, and

G is the rate per cent of tax in the territory which is chargeable on—

(a) interest received in the territory by a company from sources outside the territory, or

(b) where the amount of interest payable to the company carrying on business is taken into account in computing business profits of that company, business profits;

'*interest*' means interest other than—

(a) yearly interest, and

(b) interest to which *subsection (2B)* of *section 130*, *subsection (2)(a)* […][1] or *(3A)(a)* of *section 452* or *subsection (2)* of *section 845A* applies;

'*qualifying company*' means a company—

(a) which advances money in the ordinary course of a trade carried on in the State which includes the lending of money, and

(b) for which any interest payable in respect of money so advanced is taken into account in computing the income of that trade of the company;

'*specified amount*', in relation to a territory in respect of a qualifying company for an accounting period, means the amount of specified interest that is payable for that accounting period by the qualifying company to a company or more than one company carrying on a business in the territory where the interest is taken into account in that territory in computing the income, profits or gains of that business;

'*specified interest*', in relation to a qualifying company, means interest, payable by the company in the course of a trade referred to in the definition of '*qualifying company*', which apart from this section, would be treated as a distribution by virtue only of *section 130(2)(d)(iv)*;

'*specified tax*', in relation to a specified amount in respect of a qualifying company for an accounting period, means the lesser of—

(a) the additional tax in relation to that specified amount, and

(b) the aggregate amount of foreign tax in respect of the qualifying company for the accounting period, in relation to companies carrying on business in the territory to which the specified amount relates;

'*territory*' means a territory other than a relevant territory within the meaning of *section 246*.

(2) *Section 130(2)(d)(iv)* shall not apply to the deductible amount for a territory in respect of a qualifying company for an accounting period.][2]

Amendments

[1] Deleted by FA13 sched2(1)(e). Has effect on and from 27 March 2013.

[2] Inserted by FA12 s42(1). Applies in respect of accounting periods commencing on or after 1 January 2012.

453 Transactions between associated persons [Deleted]

Deleted by FA12 sched1(20).

454 Restriction of certain charges on income [Deleted]

Deleted by FA01 s90(3). shall cease to have effect as on and from 1 January 2003.

Cross References

To Section 454

Section 22A Reduction of corporation tax liability in respect of certain trading income.
Section 243A Restriction of relevant charges on income.

455 Restriction of certain losses [Deleted]

Deleted by FA01 s90(3). shall cease to have effect as on and from 1 January 2003.

Cross References

To Section 455

Section 22A Reduction of corporation tax liability in respect of certain trading income.
Section 82 Pre-trading expenditure.
Section 396 Relief for trading losses other than terminal losses.
Section 396A Relief for relevant trading losses.

456 Restriction of group relief [Deleted]

Deleted by FA01 s90(3). shall cease to have effect as on and from 1 January 2003.

Cross References

To Section 456

Section 82 Pre-trading expenditure.
Section 420A Group relief: relevant losses and charges.

457 Application of section 448 where profits are charged to corporation tax at the reduced rate [Deleted]

Deleted by FA01 s90(1)(c)(v). Applies as respects an accounting period ending on or after 6 March 2001.

PART 15

Personal Allowances and Reliefs and Certain Other Income Tax and Corporation Tax Reliefs

CHAPTER 1

Personal Allowances and Reliefs

458 Deductions allowed in ascertaining taxable income and provisions relating to reductions in tax

[ITA67 s137; FA96 s132(1) and Sch5 par1(3); FA97 s8(8), s57(4) and s146(1) and Sch9 PtI par1(8)]

(1) An individual who, in the manner prescribed by the Income Tax Acts, makes a claim in that behalf and[, subject to *subsection (1B)*,][1] makes a return in the prescribed form of the individual's total income shall be entitled—

(a) for the purpose of ascertaining the amount of the income on which he or she is to be charged to income tax (in the Income Tax Acts referred to as "*the taxable income*") to have such deductions as are specified in the provisions referred to in *Part 1* of the Table to this section, but subject to those provisions, made from the individual's total income, and

[(b) to have the income tax to be charged on the individual reduced by such tax credits and other reductions as are specified in the provisions referred to in *Part 2* of that Table, but subject to *subsection (1A)* and those provisions.][2]

[(1A) Where an individual is entitled to a tax credit specified in a provision referred to in *Part 2* of the Table to this section, the income tax to be charged on the individual for the year of assessment, other than in accordance with *section 16(2)*, shall be reduced by the lesser of—

(a) the amount of the tax credit, or

(b) the amount which reduces that income tax to nil.][3]

[(1B) The requirement in *subsection (1)* to make a return in the prescribed form of the individual's total income shall not apply, except where the Revenue Commissioners otherwise direct, where the claim falls to be taken into account—

(a) in the making of deductions or repayments of tax under *Chapter 4* of *Part 42* and the regulations made under that Chapter, or

(b) except in the case of a chargeable person (within the meaning of [*Part 41A*][4]), in relation to a repayment of tax deducted under that Chapter and those regulations.][5]

(2) *Subsections (3)* and *(4)* of *section 459* and *paragraph 8* of *Schedule 28* shall apply for the purposes of claims for—

(a) any such deductions from total income as are specified in the provisions referred to in *Part 1* of the Table to this section, and

[(b) any such tax credits or reductions in tax as are specified in the provisions referred to in *Part 2* of the Table to this section.][6]

TABLE

Part 1

[*Section 372AR*][7]

[*Section 372AAB*][8]

[…][9]

[…][10]

[…][11]

[…][12]

[…][13]

[…][14]

Section 467

[…][15]

Section 469

Section 471

[…][16]

[*Section 472A*][17]

[*Section 472B*][18]

[…][19]

Section 479

Section 481

[*Section 485F*][20]

Section 489

[*Section 493*][21]

[…][22]

Paragraphs 12 and *20* of *Schedule 32*

Part 2

Section 244

[*Section 461*][23]

[*Section 461A*][24]

[*Section 462B*][25]

[*Section 463*][26]

[*Section 464*][27]

[*Section 465*][28]

[*Section 466*][29]

[*Section 466A*][30]

[*Section 468*][31]

[*Section 470B*][32]

[*Section 472*][33]

[*Section 472C*][34]

Section 470

[*Section 470A*][35]

[*Section 473*][36]

[*Section 473A*][37]

Section 476

Section 477

Section 478

[…][38]

Amendments

[1] Inserted by FA05 s24(1)(a)(i). Applies with effect from 25 March 2005

[2, 23] Substituted by FA01 sched1(1)(e)(i). Applies as respects the year of assessment 2001 and subsequent years of assessment.

[3] Inserted by FA01 sched1(1)(e)(ii). Applies as respects the year of assessment 2001 and subsequent years of assessment.

[4] Substituted by FA12 sched4(part 2)(g).

[5] Inserted by FA05 s24(1)(a)(ii). Applies with effect from 25 March 2005

[6] Substituted by FA01 sched1(1)(e)(iii). Applies as respects the year of assessment 2001 and subsequent years of assessment.

[7] Substituted by FA02 sched2(2)(i).

[8] Inserted by F(No.2)A13 s31(2)(a). Comes into operation on such date as the Minister for Finance may appoint by order.

[9, 13] Deleted by FA00 s5(b)(i). Applies as respects the year of assessment 2000-2001 and subsequent years of assessment.

[10] Deleted by FA00 s6(c). Applies as respects the year of assessment 2000-2001 and subsequent years of assessment.

[11] Deleted by FA00 s7(b)(i). Applies as respects the year of assessment 2000-2001 and subsequent years of assessment.

[12] Deleted by FA00 s8(b)(i). Applies as respects the year of assessment 2000-2001 and subsequent years of assessment.

[14] Deleted by FA00 s10(b)(i). Applies as respects the year of assessment 2000-2001 and subsequent years of assessment.

[15] Deleted by FA00 s11(b)(i). Applies as respects the year of assessment 2000-2001 and subsequent years of assessment.

[16, 33] Substituted by FA99 s4(b)(i). Applies as respects the year of assessment 1999-2000 and subsequent years of assessment.

[17] Inserted by FA98 s16(b)(i).

[18] Inserted by FA98 s14(1)(a).

[19] Deleted by FA00 s13(e)(i). Applies as respects the year of assessment 2000-2001 and subsequent years of assessment.

[20] Inserted by FA14 sched3(1)(b). Has effect on and from 23 December 2014.

[21] Inserted by F(No.2)A13 sched(1)(e). Has effect on and from 18 December 2013.

[22] Deleted by FA11 sched3(1)(d). Deemed to have come into force and have taken effect as on and from 6 April 2001.

[24, 28] Inserted by FA00 s5(b)(ii). Applies as respects the year of assessment 2000-2001 and subsequent years of assessment.

[25] Substituted by F(No.2)A13 s7(1)(e). Applies for the year of assessment 2014 and subsequent years of assessment.

[26] Inserted by FA00 s7(b)(ii). Applies as respects the year of assessment 2000-2001 and subsequent years of assessment.

[27] Inserted by FA00 s8(b)(ii). Applies as respects the year of assessment 2000-2001 and subsequent years of assessment.

[29] Inserted by FA00 s10(b)(ii). Applies as respects the year of assessment 2000-2001 and subsequent years of assessment.

[30] Inserted by FA00 s12(b). Applies as respects the year of assessment 2000-2001 and subsequent years of assessment.

[31] Inserted by FA00 s11(b)(ii). Applies as respects the year of assessment 2000-2001 and subsequent years of assessment.

[32] Inserted by the Health Insurance (Miscellaneous Provisions) Act 2009 sec 20.

[34] Inserted by FA01 s11(1)(a). Applies as respects the year of assessment 2001 and subsequent years of assessment.

[35] Inserted by FA01 s20(a)(i).

[36] Substituted by FA00 s13(e)(ii). Applies as respects the year of assessment 2000-2001 and subsequent years of assessment.

[37] Deleted by FA01 s29(2).

[38] Deleted by FA10 sched4(1)(d)(ii). Deemed to have come into force and have taken effect as on and from 6 April 2001.

Revenue Briefings

Tax Briefing

Tax Briefing March 1999 – Issue 35 pg 1 – Standard Rating 1999/00
Tax Briefing September 2000 – Issue 41 pg 5 – Tax Credit System from 6 April 2001
Tax Briefing December 2000 – Issue 42 pg 1 – Tax Credit System
Tax Briefing August 2006 – Issue 64 pg 11 – New Electronic Services for Employees – ROS

Revenue Information Notes

IT1 – Tax Credits, Relief and Rates
IT10 – A Guide to Self Assessment
IT45 – Tax Credits and Relief for Over 65's

Cross References

From Section 458

Section 16 Income tax charged by deduction.
Section 244 Relief for interest paid on certain home loans.
Section 372AR Relief for owner-occupiers.
Section 459 General provisions relating to allowances, deductions and reliefs.
Section 461 Basic personal tax credit.
Section 461A Additional tax credit for certain widowed persons.
Section 462 One-parent family tax credit.
Section 463 Widowed parent tax credit.
Section 464 Age tax credit.
Section 465 Incapacitated child tax credit.
Section 466 Dependent relative tax credit.
Section 466A Home carer tax credit.
Section 467 Employed person taking care of incapacitated individual.
Section 468 Blind person's tax credit.
Section 469 Relief for health expenses.
Section 470 Relief for insurance against expenses of illness.
Section 470A Relief for premiums under qualifying long-term care policies.
Section 470B Age-related relief for health insurance premiums.
Section 471 Relief for contributions to permanent health benefit schemes.
Section 472 Employee tax credit.
Section 472A Relief for the long-term unemployed.
Section 472B Seafarer allowance, etc.
Section 472C Relief for trade union subscriptions.
Section 473 Allowance for rent paid by certain tenants.
Section 473A Relief for fees paid for third level education, etc.
Section 476 Relief for fees paid for training courses.
Section 477 Relief for service charges.
Section 478 Relief for payments made by certain persons in respect of alarm systems.
Section 479 Relief for new shares purchased on issue by employees.
Section 481 Relief for investment in films.
Section 489 The relief.
Section 950 Interpretation (Part 41).
Section 960 Date for payment of income tax other than under self assessment.
Section 983 Interpretation (Chapter 4).
Schedule 28 Statements, Lists and Declarations
Schedule 32 Transitional Provisions

To Section 458

Section 3 Interpretation of Income Tax Acts.
Section 188 Age exemption and associated marginal relief.
Section 459 General provisions relating to allowances, deductions and reliefs.
Section 460 Rate of tax at which repayments are to be made.
Section 469 Relief for health expenses.
Section 472C Relief for trade union subscriptions.
Section 485FA Adaptation of provisions relating to taxation of married persons.
Section 644A Relief from income tax in respect of income from dealing in residential development land.
Section 664 Relief for certain income from leasing of farm land.
Section 669J Credit for tax paid.
Section 739G Taxation of unit holders in investment undertakings.Taxation of unit holders in investment undertakings.
Section 787R Liability to tax and rate of tax on chargeable excess.
Section 790AA Taxation of lump sums in excess of the tax free amount.
Section 825A Reduction in income tax for certain income earned outside the State.
Section 894A Returns by third parties in relation to personal reliefs.
Section 921 Aggregation of assessments.
Section 1020 Special provisions relating to year of marriage.
Section 1023 Application for separate assessments.
Section 1025 Maintenance in case of separated spouses.
Section 1032 Restrictions on certain reliefs.
Schedule 28 Statements, Lists and Declarations

459 General provisions relating to allowances, deductions and reliefs

[ITA67 s146, s149 and Sch4 par1(1) and par2(1) and (3) to (5); F(MP)A68 s3(4) and (5) and Sch PtIII and PtIV; FA96 s132(1) and Sch5 PtI par1(5) and (6)]

(1) A claimant shall not be entitled to an allowance, deduction or relief under the provisions specified in the Table to *section 458* in respect of any income the tax on which the claimant is entitled to charge against any other person, or to deduct, retain or satisfy out of any payment which the claimant is liable to make to any other person.

(2) Except where otherwise provided, any allowance, deduction or relief under the provisions specified in the Table to *section 458* shall be given either by discharge or reduction of the assessment, or by repayment of the excess which has been paid, or by all of those means, as the case may require.

(3) Any claim shall be accompanied by a declaration and statement in the prescribed form signed by the claimant setting out—

(a) all the particular sources from which the claimant's income arises and the particular amount arising from each source,

(b) all particulars of any yearly interest or other annual payments reserved or charged on the claimant's income, whereby the claimant's income is or may be diminished, and

(c) all particulars of sums which the claimant has charged or may be entitled to charge on account of tax against any other person, or which the claimant has deducted, or may be entitled to deduct, out of any payment to which the claimant is or may be liable.

(4) (a) The claim shall be made and proved in accordance with the powers and provisions under which tax under Schedule D is ascertained and charged.

(b) Where a claimant is not in the State, an affidavit stating the particulars required by the Income Tax Acts, and taken before any person who has authority to administer in the place where the claimant resides an oath with regard to any matter relating to the public revenue of the State, may be received by the Revenue Commissioners.

(c) Where satisfactory proof is given that a claimant is unable to attend in person, a claim on the claimant's behalf may be made by any guardian, trustee, attorney, agent or factor acting for the claimant.

(d) Where a person is assessable on behalf of any other person, such person may make a claim on behalf of that other person.

[(5) *Subsections (3)* and *(4)* shall not apply, except where the Revenue Commissioners otherwise direct, in relation to a claim which falls to be taken into account—

(a) in the making of deductions or repayments of tax under *Chapter 4* of *Part 42* and the regulations made under that Chapter, or

(b) except in the case of a chargeable person (within the meaning of [*Part 41A*][1]), in relation to a repayment of tax deducted under that Chapter and those regulations.][2]

[(6) Where, on the basis of the information furnished to them under *section 894A(2)* or any other information in their possession, the Revenue Commissioners are satisfied as to the title of an individual to relief under any of the provisions specified in the Table to *section 458* or under [section 188][3] then, notwithstanding any other provision of the Income Tax Acts to the contrary, if the Revenue Commissioners consider it appropriate in the circumstances, the relief due may be given to the individual without the making of and proving of a claim for that relief.][4]

Amendments

[1] Substituted by FA12 sched4(part 2)(g).

[2] Inserted by FA05 s24(1)(b). Applies with effect from 25 March 2005

[3] Substituted by FA08 s5(e).

[4] Inserted by FA07 s9(1)(a). Applies with effect from 2 April 2007

Case Law

M. Deighan v E. Hearne and others 1986 III ITR 533 referred to the fact that section 459 TCA 1997 allows a notice of assessment to become final if it is not appealed. It was held that this was not unconstitutional.

Cross References

From Section 459

Section 188 Age exemption and associated marginal relief.

Section 458 Deductions allowed in ascertaining taxable income and provisions relating to reductions in tax.

Section 894 Returns of certain information by third parties.

Section 950 Interpretation (Part 41).

Section 983 Interpretation (Chapter 4).

To Section 459

Section 188 Age exemption and associated marginal relief.

Section 234 Certain income derived from patent royalties.

Section 458 Deductions allowed in ascertaining taxable income and provisions relating to reductions in tax.

Section 469 Relief for health expenses.

Section 664 Relief for certain income from leasing of farm land.

Section 1020 Special provisions relating to year of marriage.

Section 1025 Maintenance in case of separated spouses.

Schedule 32 Transitional Provisions

460 Rate of tax at which repayments are to be made

[ITA67 s497; FA76 s7; FA96 s132(2) and Sch5 par1(23)]

(1) Subject to *subsections (2)* and *(3)*, any repayment of income tax for any year of assessment to which any person may be entitled in respect of any allowance, deduction, relief or reduction under the provisions specified in the Table to *section 458* shall, except where otherwise provided by the Income Tax Acts, be made at the standard rate of tax or at the higher rate, as the case may be.

(2) In the case of any person who proves as regards any year that, by reason of the allowances, deductions or reliefs to which that person is entitled, he or she has no taxable income for that year, any repayment to be made shall be a repayment of the whole amount of the tax paid by him or her, whether by deduction or otherwise, in respect of his or her income for that year.

(3) In relation to repayments of tax, the amount of tax to be repaid under this section to any person for any year shall not exceed a sum equal to the difference between the amount of tax paid by that person, whether by deduction or otherwise, in respect of his or her income for that year and the amount of tax which would be payable by him or her for that year if his or her total income had been charged to tax in accordance with the Income Tax Acts.

Cross References

From Section 460

Section 458 Deductions allowed in ascertaining taxable income and provisions relating to reductions in tax.

To Section 460

Section 188 Age exemption and associated marginal relief.
Section 664 Relief for certain income from leasing of farm land.
Section 1020 Special provisions relating to year of marriage.
Section 1025 Maintenance in case of separated spouses.

461 Basic personal tax credit

[In relation to any year of assessment, an individual shall be entitled to a tax credit (to be known as the "basic personal tax credit") of—

(a) [€3,300][1], in a case in which the claimant is [a married person or a civil partner][2] who—

(i) is assessed to tax for the year of assessment in accordance with [*section 1017* or *1031C*, as the case may be][3], or

(ii) proves that [his or her spouse or civil partner][4] is not living with him or her but is wholly or mainly maintained by him or her for the year of assessment and that the claimant is not entitled, in computing his or her income for tax purposes for that year, to make any deduction in respect of the sums paid by him or her for the maintenance of [his or her spouse or civil partner][5],

(b) [€3,300][6], in a case in which the claimant in the year of assessment is a [widowed person or surviving civil partner,][7] other than a person to whom *paragraph (a)* applies, whose [spouse or civil partner][8] has died in the year of assessment, and

(c) [€1,650][9], in the case of any other claimant.][10]

Amendments

[1] Substituted by FA11 sched1(1)(a)(i). Has effect as on and from 1 January 2011.

[2] Substituted by F(No.3)A11 sched1(66).

[3] Substituted by F(No.3)A11 sched1(67).

[4, 5] Substituted by F(No.3)A11 sched1(68).

[6] Substituted by FA11 sched1(1)(a)(ii). Has effect as on and from 1 January 2011.

[7] Substituted by F(No.3)A11 sched1(69).

[8] Substituted by F(No.3)A11 sched1(70).

[9] Substituted by FA11 sched1(1)(a)(iii). Has effect as on and from 1 January 2011.

[10] Substituted by FA01 sched1(1)(f). Applies as respects the year of assessment 2001 and subsequent years of assessment.

Case Law

If the taxpayer's wife is not resident in Ireland the taxpayer is not entitled to claim the married allowance. Fennessy (Inspector of Taxes) v John McConellogue 1995 V ITR 129

D Ua Clothasaignh (Inspector of Taxes) v Patrick McCann 1947 II ITR 75 referred to the phrase "living with her husband".

In Donovan (Inspector of Taxes) v CG Crofts 1926 I ITR 115 the taxpayer was not taxed on his wife's earnings where they were not deemed to be living as man and wife.

The difference in treatment of different categories of person was not in itself unconstitutional. Mac Mathuna v Ireland and the Attorney General 1994 SC

Cross References

From Section 461

Section 1017 Assessment of husband in respect of income of both spouses.

To Section 461

Section 3 Interpretation of Income Tax Acts.

Section 187 Exemption from income tax and associated marginal relief.

Section 188 Age exemption and associated marginal relief.

Section 458 Deductions allowed in ascertaining taxable income and provisions relating to reductions in tax.

Section 461A Additional tax credit for certain widowed persons.

Section 462 One-parent family tax credit.

Section 464 Age tax credit.

Section 1024 Method of apportioning reliefs and charging tax in cases of separate assessments.

461A Additional tax credit for certain widowed persons

[A [widowed person or surviving civil partner][1], other than a person to whom *paragraph (a)* or *(b)* of *section 461*, or to whom [*section 462B*][2], applies, shall, in addition to the basic personal tax credit referred to in *section 461(c)*, be entitled to a tax credit (to be known as the "widowed person tax credit") of [€540][3].][4]

Amendments

[1] Substituted by F(No.3)A11 sched1(71).

[2] Substituted by F(No.2)A13 s7(1)(f). Applies for the year of assessment 2014 and subsequent years of assessment.

[3] Substituted by FA11 sched1(1)(b). Has effect as on and from 1 January 2011.

[4] Substituted by FA01 sched1(1)(g). Applies as respects the year of assessment 2001 and subsequent years of assessment.

Cross References

From Section 461A

Section 461 Basic personal tax credit.

Section 462 One-parent family tax credit.

To Section 461A

Section 3 Interpretation of Income Tax Acts.

Section 458 Deductions allowed in ascertaining taxable income and provisions relating to reductions in tax.

Section 1023 Application for separate assessments.

462 One-parent family tax credit

[(1) (a) In this section, "*qualifying child*", in relation to any claimant and year of assessment, means—

(i) a child—

(I) born in the year of assessment,

(II) who, at the commencement of the year of assessment, is under the age of 18 years, or

(III) who, if over the age of 18 years at the commencement of the year of assessment—

(A) is receiving full-time instruction at any university, college, school or other educational establishment, or

(B) is permanently incapacitated by reason of mental or physical infirmity from maintaining himself or herself and had become so permanently incapacitated before he or she had attained the age of 21 years or had become so permanently incapacitated after attaining the age of 21 years but while he or she had been in receipt of such full-time instruction,

and

(ii) a child who is a child of the claimant or, not being such a child, is in the custody of the claimant and is maintained by the claimant at the claimant's own expense for the whole or part of the year of assessment.

(b) This section shall apply to an individual who is not entitled to a basic personal tax credit mentioned in *paragraph (a)* or *paragraph (b)* of *section 461*.

[(2) Subject to *subsection (3)*, where a claimant, being an individual to whom this section applies, proves for a year of assessment that a qualifying child is resident with the claimant for the whole or part of the year, the claimant shall be entitled to a tax credit (to be known as the "*one-parent family tax credit*") of €1,650, but this section shall not apply for any year of assessment—

(a) in the case of a husband or a wife where the wife is living with her husband,

(b) [in the case of civil partners who are not living separately][1] in circumstances where reconciliation is unlikely, or

(c) in the case of cohabitants.][2]

(3) A claimant shall be entitled to only one tax credit under *subsection (2)* for any year of assessment irrespective of the number of qualifying children resident with the claimant in that year.

(4) (a) The references in *subsection (1)(a)* to a child receiving full-time instruction at an educational establishment shall include references to a child undergoing training by any person (in this subsection referred to as "*the employer*") for any trade or profession in such circumstances that the child is required to devote the whole of his or her time to the training for a period of not less than 2 years.

(b) For the purpose of a claim in respect of a child undergoing training, the inspector may require the employer to furnish particulars with respect to the training of the child in such form as may be prescribed by the Revenue Commissioners.

(5) Where any question arises as to whether any person is entitled to a tax credit under this section in respect of a child over the age of 18 years as being a child who is receiving full-time instruction referred to in this section, the Revenue Commissioners may consult the Minister for Education and Science.][3]

[(6) This section shall cease to apply for the year of assessment 2014 and subsequent years of assessment.][4]

Amendments

[1] Substituted by FA12 s134(1)(c). Has effect as if it had come into operation for the year of assessment (within the meaning of the Income Tax Acts and the Capital Gains Tax Acts) 2011 and each subsequent year of assessment.

[2] Substituted by F(No.3)A11 sched1(72). Shall have effect from 27 July 2011.

[3] Substituted by FA01 sched1(1)(h). Applies as respects the year of assessment 2001 and subsequent years of assessment.

[4] Inserted by F(No.2)A13 s7(1)(g). Comes into operation on 1 January 2014.

Case Law

In Mhic Mhathuna v Ireland 1995 ILRM 69 a challenge to the constitutionality of this provision by married parents with dependent children was defeated.

Revenue Information Notes

IT9 – One Parent Family Tax Credit

Cross References

From Section 462

Section 461 Basic personal tax credit.

To Section 462

Section 3 Interpretation of Income Tax Acts.
Section 7 Application to certain taxing statutes of Age of Majority Act, 1985.
Section 15 Rate of charge.
Section 187 Exemption from income tax and associated marginal relief.
Section 188 Age exemption and associated marginal relief.
Section 458 Deductions allowed in ascertaining taxable income and provisions relating to reductions in tax.
Section 461A Additional tax credit for certain widowed persons.
Section 463 Widowed parent tax credit.
Section 472A Relief for the long-term unemployed.
Section 1023 Application for separate assessments.

462A Additional allowance for widowed parents and other single parents.

[Deleted]

Deleted by FA00 s6(b). Applies as respects the year of assessment 2000-2001 and subsequent years of assessment.

462B Single person child carer credit

[(1) (a) In this section—

"*order*", in relation to a child, means an order made by the court under *section 11* of the Guardianship of Infants Act 1964 granting custody of the child to the child's father and mother jointly;

"*qualifying child*" in relation to any primary claimant and year of assessment means a child—

(i) who is born in the year of assessment,

(ii) who, at the commencement of the year of assessment, is under the age of 18 years, or

(iii) who, if over the age of 18 years at the commencement of the year of assessment—

(I) is receiving full-time instruction at any university, college, school or other educational establishment, or

(II) is permanently incapacitated by reason of mental or physical infirmity from maintaining himself or herself and had become so permanently incapacitated before he or she had attained the age of 21 years or had become so permanently incapacitated after attaining the age of 21 years but while he or she had been in receipt of such full-time instruction,

and who—

(A) is a child of the primary claimant, or

(B) not being such a child is in the custody of the primary claimant, and is maintained by the primary claimant at the primary claimant's own expense for the whole or the greater part of the year of assessment or, in respect of a child born in the year of assessment, for the greater part of the period remaining in that year of assessment from the date of birth of that child.

(b) This section shall apply to an individual who is not entitled to a basic personal credit referred to in *paragraph (a)* or *(b)* of *section 461*.

(c) This section shall not apply for any year of assessment—

(i) in the case of either party to a marriage unless—

(I) the parties are separated under an order of a court of competent jurisdiction or by deed of separation, or

(II) they are in fact separated in such circumstances that the separation is likely to be permanent,

(ii) in the case of either civil partner in a civil partnership unless the civil partners are living separately in circumstances where reconciliation is unlikely, or

(iii) in the case of cohabitants.

(2) (a) This paragraph applies to an individual (in this section referred to as the 'primary claimant'), being an individual to whom this section applies, who proves for a year of assessment that a qualifying child is resident with him or her for the whole or the greater part of that year of assessment or, in respect of a child born in that year of assessment, for the greater part of the period remaining in that year of assessment from the date of birth of that child, provided that where a child is the subject of an order and the child resides with each parent for an equal part of the year of assessment, this paragraph shall apply to whichever of the parents referred to in that order is the recipient of the child benefit payment made under Part 4 of the Social Welfare Consolidation Act 2005.

(b) This paragraph applies to an individual (in this section referred to as the 'secondary claimant'), being an individual to whom this section applies, who proves for a year of assessment that a qualifying child of a primary claimant is resident with him or her for a period of, or periods that in aggregate amount to, not less than 100 days.

(3) Subject to *subsection (5)*, an individual to whom *subsection (2)(a)* applies, shall be entitled to a tax credit (in this section referred to as a 'single person child carer credit') of €1,650.

(4) Subject to *subsection (5)*, and notwithstanding *subsection (3)*, where for any year of assessment a primary claimant would be entitled to a single person child carer credit but for the fact that he or she has, in the form specified by the Revenue Commissioners, relinquished his or her claim to that credit, a secondary claimant shall be entitled to claim a single person child carer credit in respect of the qualifying child concerned.

(5) A claimant under this section shall be entitled to only one single person child carer credit for any year of assessment irrespective of the number of qualifying children resident with the claimant in that year.

(6) (a) The references in *subsection (1)(a)* to a child receiving full-time instruction at an educational establishment shall include references to a child undergoing training by any person (in this subsection referred to as 'the employer') for any trade or profession in such circumstances that the child is required to devote the whole of his or her time to the training for a period of not less than 2 years.

(b) For the purpose of a claim in respect of a child undergoing training, the inspector may require the employer to furnish particulars with respect to the training of the child in such form as may be prescribed by the Revenue Commissioners.

(7) Where any question arises as to whether any person is entitled to a single person child carer credit in respect of a child over the age of 18 years as being a child who is receiving full-time instruction referred to in this section, the Revenue Commissioners may consult the Minister for Education and Skills.

(8) For the purposes of this section a child shall be treated as resident with an individual for any day where the child so resides for the greater part of that day.][1]

Amendments

[1] Inserted by F(No.2)A13 s7(1)(h). Applies for the year of assessment 2014 and subsequent years of assessment.

Revenue Briefings

eBrief

eBrief No. 21/2014 – Single Person Child Carer Credit

eBrief No. 81/2014 – Updates to the Tax credits for Widowed Persons or Surviving Civil Partners Manual and to the Single Person Child Carer Credit Manual

463 Widowed parent tax credit

[(1) In this section—

"*claimant*" means an individual whose [spouse or civil partner][1] dies in a year of assessment;

["*qualifying child*", in relation to a claimant and a year of assessment, has the same meaning as in *section 462B*, and the question of whether a child is a qualifying child shall be determined on the same basis as it would be for the purposes of *section 462B*, and *subsections (5), (6)* and *(7)* of that section shall apply accordingly.][2]

(2) Where a claimant proves, in relation to any of the 5 years of assessment immediately following the year of assessment in which the claimant's [spouse or civil partner][3] dies, that—

(a) [he or she has not married, remarried, or entered into a civil partnership or a new civil partnership,][4] before the commencement of the year, and

(b) a qualifying child is resident with him or her for the whole or part of the year,

the claimant shall, in respect of each of the years in relation to which the claimant so proves, be entitled to a tax credit (to be known as "the [widowed person, or surviving civil partner, with dependent child tax credit][5]") as follows—

(i) for the first of those 5 years, [€3,600][6],

(ii) for the second of those 5 years, [€3,150][7],

(iii) for the third of those 5 years, [€2,700][8],

(iv) for the fourth of those 5 years, [€2,250][9], and

(v) for the fifth of those 5 years, [€1,800][10],

but this section shall not apply for any year of assessment in the case of [cohabitants.][11]][12]

Amendments

[1, 3] Substituted by F(No.3)A11 sched1(73).

[2] Substituted by F(No.2)A13 s7(1)(i). Applies for the year of assessment 2014 and subsequent years of assessment.

[4] Substituted by F(No.3)A11 sched1(74).

[5] Substituted by F(No.3)A11 sched1(75).

[6] Substituted by FA11 sched1(1)(d)(i). Has effect as on and from 1 January 2011.

[7] Substituted by FA11 sched1(1)(d)(ii). Has effect as on and from 1 January 2011.

[8] Substituted by FA11 sched1(1)(d)(iii). Has effect as on and from 1 January 2011.

[9] Substituted by FA11 sched1(1)(d)(iv). Has effect as on and from 1 January 2011.

[10] Substituted by FA11 sched1(1)(d)(v). Has effect as on and from 1 January 2011.

[11] Substituted by F(No.3)A11 sched1(76).

[12] Substituted by FA01 sched1(1)(i). Applies as respects the year of assessment 2001 and subsequent years of assessment.

Revenue Briefings

eBrief

eBrief No. 21/2014 – Single Person Child Carer Credit

eBrief No. 81/2014 – Updates to the Tax credits for Widowed Persons or Surviving Civil Partners Manual and to the Single Person Child Carer Credit Manual

Cross References

From Section 463

Section 462 One-parent family tax credit.

To Section 463

Section 3 Interpretation of Income Tax Acts.

Section 458 Deductions allowed in ascertaining taxable income and provisions relating to reductions in tax.

Section 1023 Application for separate assessments.

464 Age tax credit

[Where for any year of assessment an individual is entitled to a basic personal tax credit under *section 461* and proves that at any time during that year of assessment—

[(a) the individual,

(b) in the case of a married person whose spouse is living with him or her and who is assessed to tax in accordance with *section 1017*, either the individual or the individual's spouse, or

(c) in the case of a civil partner whose civil partner is living with him or her and who is assessed to tax in accordance with *section 1031C*, either the individual or the individual's civil partner,][1]

was of the age of 65 years or over, the individual shall, in addition to the tax credit to which the individual is entitled under *section 461* for that year of assessment, be entitled to an additional tax credit (to be known as the "age tax credit") of—

(i) in a case where the individual is [a married person whose spouse is living with him or her and who is assessed to tax in accordance with *section 1017*, or a civil partner whose civil partner is living with him or her and who is assessed to tax in accordance with *section 1031C*,][2] [€490][3], and

(ii) in any other case, [€245][4].][5]

Amendments

[1] Substituted by F(No.3)A11 sched1(77).

[2] Substituted by F(No.3)A11 sched1(78).

[3, 4] Substituted by FA11 sched1(1)(e). Has effect as on and from 1 January 2011.

[5] Substituted by FA01 sched1(1)(j). Applies as respects the year of assessment 2001 and subsequent years of assessment.

Revenue Information Notes

IT45 – Tax Credits and Relief for Over 65's

Cross References

From Section 464

Section 461 Basic personal tax credit.

Section 1017 Assessment of husband in respect of income of both spouses.

To Section 464

Section 3 Interpretation of Income Tax Acts.

Section 458 Deductions allowed in ascertaining taxable income and provisions relating to reductions in tax.

Section 1024 Method of apportioning reliefs and charging tax in cases of separate assessments.

465 Incapacitated child tax credit

[(1) Where a claimant proves that he or she has living at any time during a year of assessment any child who—

(a) is under the age of 18 years and is permanently incapacitated by reason of mental or physical infirmity, or

(b) if over the age of 18 years at the commencement of the year, is permanently incapacitated by reason of mental or physical infirmity from maintaining himself or herself and had become so permanently incapacitated before he or she had attained the age of 21 years or had become so permanently incapacitated after attaining the age of 21 years but while he or she had been in receipt of full-time instruction at any university, college, school or other educational establishment,

the claimant shall, subject to this section, be entitled in respect of each such child to a tax credit (to be known as the "incapacitated child tax credit") of [€3,300][1].

(2) (a) A child under the age of 18 years shall be regarded as permanently incapacitated by reason of mental or physical infirmity only if the infirmity

is such that there would be a reasonable expectation that if the child were over the age of 18 years the child would be incapacitated from maintaining himself or herself.

(b) A tax credit under this section shall be in substitution for and not in addition to any tax credit to which the individual might be entitled in respect of the same child under *section 466*.

(3) Where the claimant proves for the year of assessment—

(a) that the claimant has the custody of and maintains at his or her own expense any child who, but for the fact that that child is not a child of the claimant, would be a child referred to in *subsection (1)*, and

(b) that neither the claimant nor any other individual is entitled to a tax credit in respect of the same child under *subsection (1)* or under any other provision of this Part (other than *section 466A*), or, if any other individual is entitled to such a tax credit, that such other individual has relinquished his or her claim to that tax credit, the claimant shall be entitled to the same tax credit in respect of the child as if the child were a child of the claimant.

(4) (a) The reference in *subsection (1)* to a child receiving full-time instruction at an educational establishment shall include a reference to a child undergoing training by any person (in this subsection referred to as "*the employer*") for any trade or profession in such circumstances that the child is required to devote the whole of his or her time to the training for a period of not less than 2 years.

(b) For the purpose of a claim in respect of a child undergoing training, the inspector may require the employer to furnish particulars with respect to the training of the child in such form as may be prescribed by the Revenue Commissioners.

(5) Where any question arises as to whether any person is entitled to a tax credit under this section in respect of a child over the age of 21 years as being a child who had become permanently incapacitated by reason of mental or physical infirmity from maintaining himself or herself after attaining that age but while in receipt of full-time instruction referred to in this section, the Revenue Commissioners may consult the Minister for Education and Science.

(6) Where for any year of assessment 2 or more individuals are or would but for this subsection be entitled under this section to relief in respect of the same child, the following provisions shall apply:

(a) only one tax credit under this section shall be allowed in respect of the child;

(b) where the child is maintained by one individual only, that individual only shall be entitled to claim such tax credit;

(c) where the child is maintained jointly by two or more individuals, each of those individuals shall be entitled to claim such part of such tax credit as is proportionate to the amount expended by him or her on the maintenance of the child;

(d) in ascertaining for the purposes of this subsection whether an individual maintains a child and, if so, to what extent, any payment made by the individual for or towards the maintenance of the child which the individual is entitled to deduct in computing his or her total income for the purposes of the Income Tax Acts shall be deemed not to be a payment for or towards the maintenance of the child.][2]

Amendments

[1] Substituted by FA11 sched1(1)(f). Has effect as on and from 1 January 2011.

[2] Substituted by FA01 sched1(1)(k). Applies as respects the year of assessment 2001 and subsequent years of assessment.

Case Law

The restriction of allowance for dependent children to incapacitated children was held not to be unconstitutional. Mhic Mhathuna v Ireland 1995 ILRM 69

Revenue Information Notes

IT 18 – Incapacitated Child Allowance

Revenue Precedents

Is a child suffering from Dyslexia regarded as permanently incapacitated from maintaining him/herself? Generally, it is taken that there is a reasonable expectation that, if the child was over the age of 16 years, it would not prevent him/her from maintaining him/herself. IT 96 1563

Cross References

From Section 465

Schedule
Section 466 Dependent relative tax credit.

To Section 465

Section 3 Interpretation of Income Tax Acts.
Section 7 Application to certain taxing statutes of Age of Majority Act, 1985.
Section 458 Deductions allowed in ascertaining taxable income and provisions relating to reductions in tax.
Section 467 Employed person taking care of incapacitated individual.
Section 1024 Method of apportioning reliefs and charging tax in cases of separate assessments.
Section 1025 Maintenance in case of separated spouses.

466 Dependent relative tax credit

[(1) In this section "*specified amount*" means an amount which does not exceed by more than [€280][1] the aggregate of the payments to which an individual is entitled in a year of assessment in respect of an old age (contributory) pension at the maximum rate under the [Social Welfare Consolidation Act 2005,][2] if throughout that year of assessment such individual were entitled to such a pension and—

(a) has no adult dependant or qualified children (within the meaning, in each case, of that Act),

(b) is over the age of 80 years (or such other age as may be specified in that Act for the time being in place of 80 years),

(c) is living alone, and

(d) is ordinarily resident on an island.

(2) Where for any year of assessment a claimant proves that he or she maintains at his or her own expense any person, being—

(a) a relative of the claimant, or of the claimant's spouse, incapacitated by old age or infirmity from maintaining himself or herself,

(b) the widowed father or widowed mother of the claimant or of the claimant's spouse, whether incapacitated or not, or

(c) [a child of the claimant][3] who resides with the claimant and on whose services the claimant, by reason of old age or infirmity, is compelled to depend,

and being an individual whose total income from all sources for that year of assessment does not exceed a sum equal to the specified amount, the claimant shall be entitled in respect of each individual whom the claimant so maintains to a tax credit (to be known as the "dependent relative tax credit") of [€70][4] for the year of assessment.

[(2A) A tax credit under this section may also be claimed by a claimant where all other conditions of this section have been met but the person being maintained is—

(a) a relative of the claimant's civil partner,

(b) the widowed father or widowed mother of the claimant's civil partner or a parent of the claimant's civil partner who is a surviving civil partner, or

(c) a child of the civil partner of the claimant who resides with the claimant and on whose services the claimant, by reason of old age or infirmity, is compelled to depend.][5]

(3) Where 2 or more individuals jointly maintain [any individual referred to in *subsection (2)* or *(2A)*][6], the tax credit to be granted under this section in respect of that individual shall be apportioned between them in proportion to the amount or value of their respective contributions towards the maintenance of that individual.][7]

Amendments

[1] Substituted by FA01 sched1(2)(h)(i). Applies as respects the year of assessment 2002 and subsequent years of assessment.

[2] Substituted by FA07 sched4(1)(l). Shall have effect as on and from 2 April 2007

[3] Substituted by F(No.3)A11 sched1(79).

[4] Substituted by FA11 sched1(1)(g). Has effect as on and from 1 January 2011.

[5] Inserted by F(No.3)A11 sched1(80).

[6] Substituted by F(No.3)A11 sched1(81).

[7] Substituted by FA01 sched1(1)(l). Applies as respects the year of assessment 2001 and subsequent years of assessment.

Revenue Information Notes

IT46 – Dependent Relative Tax Credit

Revenue Precedents

Any claim for the dependent relative tax credit that is supported by a certificate signed by a medical practitioner to the effect that the relative was incapacitated by infirmity from maintaining himself/herself during the tax year will be allowed. PTU 4043

Cross References

To Section 466

Section 3 Interpretation of Income Tax Acts.
Section 458 Deductions allowed in ascertaining taxable income and provisions relating to reductions in tax.
Section 465 Incapacitated child tax credit.
Section 467 Employed person taking care of incapacitated individual.
Section 1024 Method of apportioning reliefs and charging tax in cases of separate assessments.
Schedule 31 Consequential Amendments

466A Home carer tax credit

[(1) In this section—

"*dependent person*", in relation to a qualifying claimant, means a person (other than the [spouse or civil partner][1] of the qualifying claimant) who, subject to subsection (3), resides with that qualifying claimant and who is—

(a) a child in respect of whom either the qualifying claimant or his or her [spouse or civil partner][2] is, at any time in a year of assessment, in receipt of child benefit under [Part 4 of the Social Welfare Consolidation Act 2005,][3] or

(b) an individual who, at any time during a year of assessment, is of the age of 65 years or over, or

(c) an individual who is permanently incapacitated by reason of mental or physical infirmity;

"*qualifying claimant*", in relation to a year of assessment, means an individual—

(a) who is assessed to tax for that year in accordance with [*section 1017* or *1031C*][4], and

(b) who, or whose [spouse or civil partner][5] (in this section referred to as the ["*carer spouse*" or "*carer civil partner*"][6]) is engaged during that year in caring for one or more dependent persons;

"*relative*", in relation to a qualifying claimant, includes a relation by marriage and a person in respect of whom the qualifying claimant is or was the legal guardian.

(2) Where for any year of assessment an individual proves that he or she is a qualifying claimant he or she shall be entitled to a tax credit (to be known as the "home carer tax credit") of [€810][7].

(3) For the purposes of this section—

(a) a dependent person in relation to a qualifying claimant who is a relative of that claimant or the claimant's spouse shall be regarded as residing with the qualifying claimant if—

(i) the relative lives in close proximity to the qualifying claimant, and

(ii) a direct system of communication exists between the qualifying claimant's residence and the residence of the relative,

[(aa) a dependent person in relation to a qualifying claimant who is a relative of that claimant or the claimant's civil partner shall be regarded as residing with the qualifying claimant if—

(i) the relative lives in close proximity to the qualifying claimant, and

(ii) a direct system of communication exists between the qualifying claimant's residence and the residence of the relative,][8]

and

(b) a qualifying claimant and a relative shall be regarded as living in close proximity if they reside—

(i) next door in adjacent residences, or

(ii) on the same property, or

(iii) within 2 kilometres of each other.

(4) A qualifying claimant shall be entitled to only one tax credit under *subsection (2)* for any year of assessment irrespective of the number of dependent persons resident with the qualifying claimant in that year.

(5) A tax credit under this section in respect of a dependent person shall be granted to one and only one qualifying claimant being the person with whom that dependent person normally resides or, where *subsection (3)* applies, the person who, or whose [spouse or civil partner][9], normally cares for the dependent person.

(6) (a) Where in any year of assessment the [carer spouse or carer civil partner][10] is entitled in his or her own right to [total income][11] exceeding [€5,080][12] in that year, the tax credit shall be reduced by one-half of the amount of that excess.

(b) For the purposes of *paragraph (a)*, no account shall be taken of—

(i) any Carer's Benefit payable under [Chapter 14 of Part 2 of the Social Welfare Consolidation Act 2005,][13] or

(ii) any Carer's Allowance payable under [Chapter 8 of Part 3 of that Act.][14]

(7) (a) Notwithstanding *subsection (6)* but subject to the other provisions of this section including this subsection, a tax credit may be granted for a year of assessment where the claimant was entitled to a tax credit under this section for the immediately preceding year of assessment.

(b) Where a tax credit is to be granted for a year of assessment by virtue of *paragraph (a)*, it shall not exceed the amount of the tax credit granted in the immediately preceding year of assessment.

(c) A tax credit shall not be granted for a year of assessment by virtue of *paragraph (a)* if it was so granted for the immediately preceding year of assessment.

(8) Where for any year of assessment a tax credit is granted to an individual under this section, the individual shall not also be entitled to the benefit of the provision contained in *section 15(3)* but the individual may elect by notice in writing to the inspector to have the benefit under the said section granted instead of the tax credit granted under this section.][15]

Amendments

[1, 2, 5] Substituted by F(No.3)A11 sched1(82).

[3] Substituted by FA07 sched4(1)(m)(i). Shall have effect as on and from 2 April 2007

[4] Substituted by F(No.3)A11 sched1(83).

[6] Substituted by F(No.3)A11 sched1(84).

[7] Substituted by FA11 sched1(1)(h). Has effect as on and from 1 January 2011.

[8] Inserted by F(No.3)A11 sched1(85).

[9] Substituted by F(No.3)A11 sched1(86).

[10] Substituted by F(No.3)A11 sched1(87).

[11] Substituted by FA02 sched1(h)(ii). Applies as respects the year of assessment 2002 and subsequent years of assessment.

[12] Substituted by FA01 sched1(2)(i)(ii). Applies as respects the year of assessment 2002 and subsequent years of assessment.

[13] Substituted by FA07 sched4(1)(m)(ii)(I). Shall have effect as on and from 2 April 2007

[14] Substituted by FA07 sched4(1)(m)(ii)(II). Shall have effect as on and from 2 April 2007

[15] Substituted by FA01 sched1(1)(m). Applies as respects the year of assessment 2001 and subsequent years of assessment.

Revenue Briefings

Tax Briefing

Tax Briefing March 2000 – Issue 39 pg 10 – Home Carer's Allowance from 6 April 2000

Tax Briefing January 2003 – Issue 51 pg 20 – Topical Questions, Home Carer Tax Credit

Revenue Information Notes

IT66 – Home Carer's Tax Credit

Cross References

From Section 466A

Section 15 Rate of charge.

Section 1017 Assessment of husband in respect of income of both spouses.

To Section 466A

Section 3 Interpretation of Income Tax Acts.

Section 458 Deductions allowed in ascertaining taxable income and provisions relating to reductions in tax.

467 Employed person taking care of incapacitated individual

[(1) In this section—

"*qualifying individual*", in relation to an individual, means—

(a) a relative of the individual,

(b) the individual's civil partner, or

(c) a relative of the individual's spouse or civil partner;

"*relative*", in relation to an individual, includes a relation by marriage and a person in respect of whom the individual is or was the legal guardian.][1]

[(2) Subject to this section, where an individual for a year of assessment proves—

(a) that throughout the year of assessment either he or she or a qualifying individual in relation to the individual was totally incapacitated by physical or mental infirmity, and

(b) that for the year of assessment the individual, or in a case to which *section 1017* or *1031C* applies, the individual's spouse or civil partner, has employed a person (including a person whose services are provided by or through an agency) for the purpose of having care of the individual (being the individual or qualifying individual) who is so incapacitated,

the individual shall, in computing the amount of his or her taxable income, be entitled to a deduction from his or her total income of the lesser of—

(i) the amount ultimately borne by him or her or the individual's spouse or civil partner in the year of assessment in employing the employed person, and

(ii) [€75,000][2] in respect of each such incapacitated individual.][3]

[(2A) Notwithstanding *subsection (2)(a)* but subject to all other provisions of this section, relief may be granted under this section in the first year in which the individual proves that either he or she or the qualifying individual concerned was totally incapacitated by physical or mental infirmity.][4]

(3) Where 2 or more individuals are entitled for a year of assessment to a deduction under this section in respect of the same incapacitated individual, the following provisions shall apply:

(a) the aggregate of the deductions to be granted to those individuals shall not exceed [€75,000][5], and

(b) the relief to be granted under this section in relation to the incapacitated individual shall be apportioned between them in proportion to the amount ultimately borne by each of them in employing the employed person.

(4) Where for any year of assessment a deduction is allowed to an individual under this section, the individual shall not be [entitled to relief][6] in respect of the employed person (including a person whose services are provided by or through an agency) under *section 465* or *section 466*.][7]

Amendments

[1] Substituted by F(No.3)A11 sched1(88).

[2, 5] Substituted by FA14 s12. Comes into operation on 1 January 2015.

[3] Substituted by F(No.3)A11 sched1(89).

[4] Substituted by F(No.3)A11 sched1(90).

[6] Substituted by FA00 sched1(4).

[7] Substituted by FA99 s9. Applies as respects the year of assessment 1999-2000 and subsequent years of assessment.

Revenue Briefings

Tax Briefing

Tax Briefing April 2005 – Issue 59 pg 19 – Incapacitated Individual Deduction

Tax Briefing December 2006 – Issue 65 – Employed Person Taking Care of an Incapacitated Person

Revenue Information Notes

IT12 – People with Disabilities and Income Tax

IT47 – Employed Person taking Care of an Incapacitated Person

Cross References

From Section 467

Section 465 Incapacitated child tax credit.

Section 466 Dependent relative tax credit.

Section 1017 Assessment of husband in respect of income of both spouses.

To Section 467

Section 458 Deductions allowed in ascertaining taxable income and provisions relating to reductions in tax.

Section 1024 Method of apportioning reliefs and charging tax in cases of separate assessments.

468 Blind person's tax credit

[(1) In this section, "*blind person*" means a person whose central visual acuity does not exceed 6/60 in the better eye with correcting lenses, or whose central visual acuity exceeds 6/60 in the better eye or in both eyes but is accompanied by a limitation in the fields of vision that is such that the widest diameter of the visual field subtends an angle no greater than 20 degrees.

(2) Where an individual proves for a year of assessment that—

(a) he or she was for the whole or any part of the year of assessment a blind person, or

(b) where he or she is assessed to tax in accordance with [*section 1017* or *1031C*][1], either or both he or she and his or her [spouse or civil partner][2] was for the whole or any part of the year of assessment a blind person,

the individual shall be entitled to a tax credit (to be known as the "blind person's tax credit") of [€1,650][3], or where the individual and his or her [spouse or civil partner][4] are both blind, [€3,300][5].][6]

Amendments

[1] Substituted by F(No.3)A11 sched1(91).

[2, 4] Substituted by F(No.3)A11 sched1(92).

[3, 5] Substituted by FA11 sched1(1)(i). Has effect as on and from 1 January 2011.

[6] Substituted by FA01 sched1(1)(n). Applies as respects the year of assessment 2001 and subsequent years of assessment.

Revenue Information Notes

IT35 – Blind Person Tax Credits and Reliefs

Cross References

From Section 468

Section 1017 Assessment of husband in respect of income of both spouses.

To Section 468

Section 3 Interpretation of Income Tax Acts.

Section 458 Deductions allowed in ascertaining taxable income and provisions relating to reductions in tax.

Section 1024 Method of apportioning reliefs and charging tax in cases of separate assessments.

469 Relief for health expenses

[ITA67 s195B(3) and (6); FA67 s12(1), (2)(a) and (c), (3), (4) and (5)(a) and (b); FA69 s7; FA72 s9; FA80 s19 and Sch1 PtIII par2; FA86 s5; FA93 s10(1); FA94 s8; FA97 s146(1) and Sch9 PtI par2]

(1) In this section—

[…][1]

["*appropriate percentage*", in relation to a year of assessment, means a percentage equal to the standard rate of tax for that year;][2]

["*educational psychologist*" means a psychologist who has expertise in the education of students;][3]

["*health care*" means prevention, diagnosis, alleviation or treatment of an ailment, injury, infirmity, defect or disability, and includes care received by a woman in respect of a pregnancy, but does not include—

(a) routine ophthalmic treatment,

(b) routine dental treatment, or

(c) cosmetic surgery or similar procedures, unless the surgery or procedure is necessary to ameliorate a physical deformity arising from, or directly related to, a congenital abnormality, a personal injury or a disfiguring disease;][4]

"*health expenses*" means expenses in respect of the provision of health care, being expenses representing the cost of—

(a) the services of a practitioner,

(b) diagnostic procedures carried out on the advice of a practitioner,

[(c) maintenance or treatment necessarily incurred in connection with the services or procedures referred to in *paragraph (a)* or *(b)*,][5]

(d) drugs or medicines supplied on the prescription of a practitioner,

(e) the supply, maintenance or repair of any medical, surgical, dental or nursing appliance used on the advice of a practitioner,

(f) physiotherapy or similar treatment prescribed by a practitioner,

(g) orthoptic or similar treatment prescribed by a practitioner, […][6]

(h) transport by [ambulance, or][7]

[(i) as respects a [person][8] who for the year of assessment—

(a) is under the age of 18 years, or

(b) if over the age of 18 years, at the commencement of the year of assessment, is receiving full-time instruction at any university, college, school or other educational establishment,

either or both—

(i) educational psychological assessment carried out by an educational psychologist, and

(ii) speech and language therapy carried out by a speech and language therapist;][9]

[…][10]

"*practitioner*" means any person who is—

(a) registered in the register established under [section 43 of the Medical Practitioners Act 2007][11],

(b) registered in the register established under section 26 of the Dentists Act, 1985, or,

(c) in relation to health care provided outside the State, entitled under the laws of the country in which the care is provided to [practice][12] medicine or dentistry there;

[...][13]

"*routine dental treatment*" means the extraction, scaling and filling of teeth and the provision and repairing of artificial teeth or dentures;

[...][14]

"*routine ophthalmic treatment*" means sight testing and advice as to the use of spectacles or contact lenses and the provision and repairing of spectacles or [contact lenses;][15]

["*specified amount*", in relation to a year of assessment, means the amount of expenditure which qualifies for income tax relief in accordance with this section;][16]

[...][17]

[(2) (a) Subject to this section, where an individual for a year of assessment proves that in the year of assessment he or she defrayed health expenses incurred for the provision of health care, the income tax to be charged on the individual, other than in accordance with *section 16(2)*, for that year of assessment shall be reduced by the lesser of—

(i) the amount equal to the appropriate percentage of the specified amount, and

(ii) the amount which reduces that income tax to nil,

but, where an individual proves that he or she defrayed health expenses incurred for the provision of health care in the nature of maintenance or treatment in a nursing home, other than a nursing home which does not provide access to 24 hour nursing care on-site, the individual shall be entitled for the purpose of ascertaining the amount of the income on which he or she is to be charged to income tax, to have a deduction made from his or her total income of the amount proved to have been so defrayed.

(b) For the purposes of this section any contribution made by an individual in defraying expenses incurred in respect of nursing home fees where such an individual is entitled to or has received State support (within the meaning of section 3(1) of the Nursing Homes Support Scheme Act 2009) shall be treated as health expenses qualifying for relief under this section.

(c) Financial support (within the meaning of the Nursing Homes Support Scheme Act 2009) shall not be treated as health expenses for the purposes of this section.][18]

(3) For the purposes of this section—

(a) [(i) any expenses defrayed by a married man in a year of assessment shall be deemed to have been defrayed by his wife if for the year of assessment she is to be treated under the Income Tax Acts as living with him and she is assessed to tax in accordance with *section 1017*,][19]

[(ii) any expenses defrayed by a married woman in a year of assessment shall be deemed to have been defrayed by her husband if for the year of assessment she is to be treated under the Income Tax Acts as living with him and he is assessed to tax in accordance with *section 1017*, or

(iii) any expenses defrayed by a civil partner in a year of assessment shall be deemed to have been defrayed by his or her civil partner if for the year of assessment the first-mentioned civil partner is to be treated under the Income Tax Acts as living with his or her civil partner and is assessed to tax in accordance with *section 1031C*,][20]

(b) any expenses defrayed out of the estate of a deceased person by his or her executor or administrator shall be deemed to have been defrayed by the deceased person immediately before his or her death, and

(c) expenses shall be regarded as not having been defrayed in so far as any sum in respect of, or by reference to, the health care to which they relate has been, or is to be, received, directly or indirectly, by the individual or the individual's estate, or by any dependant of the individual or such dependant's estate, from any public or local authority or under any contract of insurance or by means of compensation or otherwise.

[…][21]

(5) In making a claim for a deduction under this section, an individual who, after the end of the year of assessment for which the claim is made, has defrayed or is deemed to have defrayed any expenses relating to health care provided in that year may elect that all deductions to be allowed to him or her under this section for that year and for subsequent years of assessment shall be determined as if those expenses had been defrayed at the time when the health care to which they relate was provided.

(6) Notwithstanding *sections 458(2)* and *459(2)*—

(a) any claim for a deduction under this section—

(i) shall be made in such form as the Revenue Commissioners may from time to time prescribe, and

(ii) shall be accompanied by such statements in writing as regards any class of expenses by reference to which the deduction is claimed, including statements by persons to whom payments were made, as may be indicated by the prescribed form as being required as regard expenses of that class, and

(b) in all cases relief from tax consequent on the allowance of a deduction under this section shall be given by means of repayment.

[(7) Where relief is given under this section to any individual in respect of an amount used to defray health expenses, relief shall not be given under any other provision of the Income Tax Acts to that individual in respect of that amount.][22]

[(8) (a) Where the Minister for Finance determines that expenses, or a class of expenses, representing the cost of anything referred to in *paragraphs (a)* to *(i)* in the definition of "*health expenses*" in *subsection (1)* has been or may be incurred in the provision of health care which in the opinion of the Minister for Finance is inappropriate having regard to public policy, then the Minister may by order prescribe those expenses, or class of expenses, as not being eligible for relief under this section.

(b) The Minister for Finance shall not make an order under *paragraph (a)* unless he or she has consulted with the Minister for Health and Children and such appropriately qualified persons, bodies or institutions (if any), which in the opinion of the Minister for Finance or the Minister for Health and Children should be consulted.

(c) Every order made by the Minister for Finance under *paragraph (a)* shall be laid before Dáil Éireann as soon as may be after it is made and, if a resolution annulling the order is passed by Dáil Éireann within the next 21 days on which Dáil Éireann has sat after the order is laid before it, the order shall be annulled accordingly, but without prejudice to the validity of anything previously done thereunder.][23]

Amendments

[1, 13] Deleted by FA07 s9(1)(b)(i)(II). Applies as respects the year of assessment 2007 and subsequent years of assessment.

[2] Inserted by F(No.2)A08 s8(a)(i). Applies as respects the year of assessment 2009 and subsequent years of assessment.

[3] Substituted by F(No.2)A13 s9(a). Comes into operation on 1 January 2014.

[4] Substituted by FA10 s6(1)(a). This section shall have effect for the year of assessment 2010 and subsequent years.

[5] Substituted by FA10 s6(1)(b). This section shall have effect for the year of assessment 2010 and subsequent years.

[6] Deleted by FA02 s9(a)(ii)(I). Applies as respects the year of assessment 2002 and subsequent years of assessment.

[7] Substituted by FA02 s9(a)(ii)(II). Applies as respects the year of assessment 2002 and subsequent years of assessment.

[8] Substituted by FA07 s9(1)(b)(i)(I). Applies as respects the year of assessment 2007 and subsequent years of assessment.

[9] Substituted by FA03 sched6(1)(d). Has effect as on and from 28 March 2003

[10] Deleted by FA10 s6(1)(c). This section shall have effect for the year of assessment 2010 and subsequent years.

[11] Substituted by FA10 s6(1)(d). This section shall have effect for the year of assessment 2010 and subsequent years.

[12] Substituted by FA05 sched6(1)(h)(ii). Applies as on and from 25 March 2005

[14] Deleted by FA01 s8(e). Applies as respects the year of assessment 2001 and subsequent years of assessment.

[15] Substituted by FA02 s9(a)(iii). Applies as respects the year of assessment 2002 and subsequent years of assessment.

[16] Inserted by F(No.2)A08 s8(a)(ii). Applies as respects the year of assessment 2009 and subsequent years of assessment.

[17] Deleted by F(No.2)A13 s9(b). Comes into operation on 1 January 2014.

[18] Substituted by FA10 s6(1)(e). This section shall have effect for the year of assessment 2010 and subsequent years.

[19, 20] Substituted by F(No.3)A11 sched1(93).

[21] Deleted by FA02 s9(b). Applies as respects the year of assessment 2002 and subsequent years of assessment.

[22] Inserted by FA07 s9(1)(b)(iii). Applies as respects the year of assessment 2007 and subsequent years of assessment.

[23] Inserted by FA10 s6(1)(f). This section shall have effect for the year of assessment 2010 and subsequent years.

Revenue Briefings

Tax Briefing

Tax Briefing January 1995 – Issue 17 pg 5 – Income tax; health expenses dependent relative

Tax Briefing August 1997 – Issue 27 pg 4 – Health expenses: kidney patients and children with cancer

Tax Briefing September 1998 – Issue 33 pg 7 – Health expenses: Guidelines and procedures on claims
Tax Briefing October 1999 – Issue 37 pg 13 – Revenue News Update, Health expenses
Tax Briefing September 2000 Issue 41 pg 30 – Health expenses: Kidney patients
Tax Briefing April 2001 Issue 43 pg 15 – Finance Act 2001: Health expenses relief
Tax Briefing October 2002 – Issue 50 pg 15 – Health expenses, dental treatment
Tax Briefing April 2004 – Issue 55 pg 12 – Health expenses: kidney patients, child oncology patients and children with permanent disabilities
Tax Briefing May 2006 – Issue 63 – Health expenses: kidney patients, child oncology patients and children with permanent disabilities
Tax Briefing April 2008 – Issue 68 – Health expenses: Guidelines and procedures on claims

Revenue Information Notes

IT6 – A Guide to Claiming Health/Medical Expenses Relief
List of approved hospitals and nursing homes

Revenue Precedents

If a stair lift or personal pendant monitoring alarm are supplied on the advice of a medical practitioner as registered under section 25 of the Medical Practitioners Act 1978, tax relief may be claimed under health expenses on the cost of the annula maintenance charge of the appliance. 4905

Relief is allowed where medical expenses were incurred on a caesarean section operation prior to 2001 and the expenses were not reimbursed by private medical insurance schemes. PTU 5060

Cross References

From Section 469

Section 16 Income tax charged by deduction.
Section 458 Deductions allowed in ascertaining taxable income and provisions relating to reductions in tax.
Section 459 General provisions relating to allowances, deductions and reliefs.
Section 1017 Assessment of husband in respect of income of both spouses.

To Section 469

Section 458 Deductions allowed in ascertaining taxable income and provisions relating to reductions in tax.
Section 470 Relief for insurance against expenses of illness.
Section 470B Age-related relief for health insurance premiums.
Section 520 Interpretation (Chapter 1).
Section 1024 Method of apportioning reliefs and charging tax in cases of separate assessments.

470 Relief for insurance against expenses of illness

[ITA67 s145(1), (2), (3) and (4); FA80 s19 and Sch1 PtIII par1; FA96 s7 and s132(1) and Sch5 PtI par1(4)]

(1) In this section—

"*appropriate percentage*", in relation to a year of assessment, means a percentage equal to the standard rate of tax for that year;

["*authorised insurer*" means—

(a) any undertaking entered in the Register of Health Benefits Undertakings, lawfully carrying on such business of medical insurance referred to in *paragraph (a)* of the definition of "*relevant contract*" but, in relation to an individual, also means any undertaking authorised pursuant to Council Directive No. 73/239/EEC of 24 July 1973*, Council Directive No. 88/357/EEC of 22 June 1988†, and Council Directive No. 92/49/EEC of 18 June 1992‡, where such a contract was effected with the individual when the individual was not resident in the State but was resident in another Member State of the European Communities, or

* OJ No. L228, 16.8.1973, p.3
† OJ No. L172, 4.7.1988, p.1
‡ OJ No. L228, 11.8.1992, p.1

(b) (i) any undertaking standing authorised under—

(I) the European Communities (Non-Life Insurance) Framework Regulations 1994 (S.I. No. 359 of 1994),

(II) the European Communities (Non-Life Insurance) Regulations 1976 (S.I. No. 115 of 1976), or

(III) the European Communities (Non-Life Insurance) (Amendment) (No. 2) Regulations 1991 (S.I. No. 142 of 1991),

or

(ii) any undertaking authorised by the authority charged by law with the duty of supervising the activities of insurance undertakings in a Member State of the European Communities other than the State in accordance with Article 6 of Council Directive No. 73/239/EEC of 24 July 1973 as inserted by Article 4 of Council Directive No. 92/49/EEC of 18 June 1992,

lawfully carrying on such business of dental insurance referred to in *paragraph (b)* of the definition of "*relevant contract*";][1]

["*child*" means an individual under the age of 18 years or, if over the age of 18 years and under the age of 23 years, who is receiving full-time education and in respect of whom the payment under a relevant contract has been reduced in accordance with *paragraph (a)(ii)* or *(b)(i)* of *section 7(5)* of the Health Insurance Act 1994;][2]

["*relevant contract*" means a contract of insurance which provides specifically, whether in conjunction with other benefits or not, for the reimbursement or discharge, in whole or in part, of—

(a) actual health expenses (within the meaning of *section 469*), being a contract of medical insurance, or

(b) dental expenses other than expenses in respect of routine dental treatment (within the meaning of *section 469*), being a contract of dental insurance;][3]

["*relievable amount*", in relation to a payment to an authorised insurer under a relevant contract, means—

(a) where the payment covers no benefits other than such reimbursement or discharge as is referred to in the definition of 'relevant contract', an amount equal to the full amount of the payment reduced by the amount of credit due (if any) under *section 470B(4)* and credit due (if any) under a risk equalisation scheme (within the meaning of the Health Insurance Act 1994), or

(b) where the payment covers benefits other than such reimbursement or discharge as is referred to in that definition, an amount equal to so much of the payment as is referable to such reimbursement or discharge reduced by the amount of credit due (if any) under *section 470B(4)* and credit due (if any) under a risk equalisation scheme (within the meaning of the Health Insurance Act 1994),

provided that in respect of a relevant contract renewed or entered into on or after 16 October 2013 the relievable amount in respect of any payment made under a relevant contract, in respect of any 12 month period covered by that contract, shall not exceed the aggregate of—

(i) the lesser of the relievable amount attributable to each individual, other than a child, to whom the relevant contract relates, or €1,000 in respect of each individual, and

(ii) the lesser of the relievable amount attributable to each child to whom the relevant contract relates, or €500 in respect of each child,

and where the contract is for a period of less than 12 months or being for a period of 12 months is terminated before the end of that period, the relievable amount shall be reduced proportionately.][4]

[(2) Subject to subsection (3), where for a year of assessment—

(a) an individual, or

(b) if the individual is [a married person assessed to tax in accordance with *section 1017*, or a civil partner assessed to tax in accordance with *section 1031C*, the individual's spouse or civil partner, as the case may be,][5]

has made a payment to an authorised insurer under a relevant contract, then, the income tax to be charged on the individual for the year of assessment, other than in accordance with *section 16(2)*, shall be reduced by an amount which is the lesser of—

(i) an amount equal to the appropriate percentage of the relievable amount in relation to the payment, and

(ii) the amount which reduces that income tax to nil.

(3) (a) Where, on or after 6 April 2001, an individual makes a payment to an authorised insurer in respect of a premium due on or after that date under a relevant contract for which relief is due under subsection (2), the individual shall be entitled to deduct and retain out of it an amount equal to the appropriate percentage, for the year of assessment in which the payment is due, of the relievable amount in relation to the payment.

(b) An authorised insurer to which a payment referred to in *paragraph (a)* is made—

(i) shall accept the amount paid after deduction in discharge of the individual's liability to the same extent as if the deduction had not been made, and

(ii) may, on making a claim in accordance with regulations, recover from the Revenue Commissioners an amount equal to the amount deducted.][6]

(4) Where relief is given under this section, no relief or deduction under any other provision of the Income Tax Acts shall be given or allowed in respect of the payment or part of a payment, as the case may be.

[(5) (a) The Revenue Commissioners shall make regulations providing generally as to administration of this section and those regulations may, in particular and without prejudice to the generality of the foregoing, include provision—

(i) that a claim under *subsection (3)(b)(ii)* by an authorised insurer, which has registered with the Revenue Commissioners for the purposes of making such a claim, shall—

(I) be made in such form and manner,

(II) be made at such time, and

(III) be accompanied by such documents,

as provided for in the regulations;

(ii) for the making of annual information returns by authorised insurers, in such form (including electronic form) and manner as may be prescribed, and containing specified details in relation to—

(I) each individual making payments to such insurers under relevant contracts in a year of assessment,

(II) the total amount of premiums paid under a relevant contract by that individual in the year of assessment, and

(III) the total amount deducted by that individual under *subsection (3)(a)*;

and

(iii) for the furnishing of information to the Revenue Commissioners for the purposes of the regulations.

(b) Every regulation made under this section shall be laid before Dáil Éireann as soon as may be after it is made and, if a resolution annulling the regulation is passed by Dáil Éireann within the next 21 days on which Dáil Éireann has sat after the regulation is laid before it, the regulation shall be annulled accordingly, but without prejudice to the validity of anything previously done thereunder.

(6) (a) Where any amount is paid to an authorised insurer by the Revenue Commissioners as an amount recoverable by virtue of *subsection (3)(b)(ii)* but is an amount to which that authorised insurer is not entitled, that amount shall be repaid by the authorised insurer.

(b) There shall be made such assessments, adjustments or set-offs as may be required for securing repayment of the amount referred to in *paragraph (a)* and the provisions of this Act relating to the assessment, collection and recovery of income tax shall, in so far as they are applicable and with necessary modification, apply in relation to the recovery of such amount.][7]

Amendments

[1] Substituted by FA04 s11(a). Applies as on and from 25 March 2004

[2] Inserted by F(No.2)A13 s8(1)(a). Applies in respect of relevant contracts (within the meaning of section 470) entered into or renewed on or after 16 October 2013.

[3] Substituted by F(No.2)A13 s8(1)(b). Applies in respect of relevant contracts (within the meaning of section 470) entered into or renewed on or after 16 October 2013.

[4] Substituted by F(No.2)A13 s8(1)(c). Applies in respect of relevant contracts (within the meaning of section 470) entered into or renewed on or after 16 October 2013.

[5] Substituted by F(No.3)A11 sched1(95).

[6] Substituted by FA01 s19(1)(b). Applies as respects the year of assessment 2001 and subsequent years of assessment.

[7] Inserted by FA01 s19(1)(c). Applies as respects the year of assessment 2001 and subsequent years of assessment.

Revenue Briefings

Tax Briefing

Tax Briefing February 1997 – Issue 25 pg 17 – Medical Insurance Relief – BUPA

Tax Briefing April 1997 – Issue 26 pg 12 – Medical Insurance Relief

Tax Briefing February 1998 – Issue 30 pg 18 – Revenue News – Latest List of Authorised Medical Insurers in the State

Tax Briefing April 2001 – Issue 43 pg 23 – Medical Insurance Relief
Tax Briefing Supplement May 2004 pg 30 – List of Authorised Medical Insurers

eBrief

eBrief No. 58/2013 – Changes to P35 and P60 forms for 2014
eBrief No. 47/2014 – Income tax relief for insurance against expenses of illness (Medical/Dental Insurance) operations

Revenue Information Notes

List of Approved Hospitals and Nursing Homes
List of Authorised Insurers

Cross References

From Section 470

Section 16 Income tax charged by deduction.
Section 469 Relief for health expenses.
Section 470B Age-related relief for health insurance premiums.
Section 1017 Assessment of husband in respect of income of both spouses.

To Section 470

Section 112A Taxation of certain perquisites.
Section 458 Deductions allowed in ascertaining taxable income and provisions relating to reductions in tax.
Section 470B Age-related relief for health insurance premiums.
Section 520 Interpretation (Chapter 1).
Section 904E Power of inspection: claims by authorised insurers.
Section 1024 Method of apportioning reliefs and charging tax in cases of separate assessments.
Schedule 13 Accountable Persons for Purposes of Chapter 1 of Part 18
Schedule 29 Provisions Referred to in Sections 1052, 1053 and 1054

470A Relief for premiums under qualifying long-term care policies

[(1) In this section—

"*activities of daily living*" means one or more of the following, that is to say, washing, dressing, feeding, toileting, mobility and transferring;

"*appropriate percentage*", in relation to a year of assessment, means a percentage equal to the standard rate of tax for that year;

"*long-term care services*" means necessary diagnostic, preventive, therapeutic, curing, treating, mitigating and rehabilitative services and maintenance or personal care services carried out by or on the advice of a practitioner;

"*maintenance or personal care services*" means any care the primary purpose of which is the provision of needed assistance with any of the disabilities as a result of which an individual is a relevant individual (including protection from threats to health and safety due to severe cognitive impairment);

"*mobility*" means the ability to move indoors from room to room on level surfaces;

"*policy*" means a policy of insurance;

"*PPS Number*", in relation to an individual, means that individual's Personal Public Service Number within the meaning of [section 262 of the Social Welfare Consolidation Act 2005;][1]

"*practitioner*" means any person who is registered in the register established under section 26 of the Medical Practitioners Act, 1978, or, in relation to long-term care services provided outside the State, is entitled under the laws of the territory in which such services are provided to practice medicine there;

"*qualifying individual*" in relation to an individual and a qualifying long-term care policy, means—

(a) the individual,

(b) the spouse or a child of the individual, or

(c) a relative of the individual or of the spouse of the individual;

"*qualifying insurer*" means, subject to subsection (2), the holder of—

(i) an authorisation issued by the Minister for Enterprise, Trade and Employment under the European Communities (Life Assurance) Regulations of 1984 (S.I. No. 57 of 1984) as amended, or

(ii) an authorisation granted by the authority charged by law with the duty of supervising the activities of insurance undertakings in a Member State of the European Communities, other than the State, in accordance with Article 6 of Directive No. 79/267/EEC*, who is carrying on the business of life assurance in the State, or

* O.J. No. L63 of 13 March, 1979, P.1.

(iii) an official authorisation to undertake insurance in Iceland, Liechtenstein and Norway pursuant to the EEA Agreement within the meaning of the European Communities (Amendment) Act, 1993, and who is carrying on the business of life assurance in the State;

"*qualifying long-term care policy*" means a policy which provides for the discharge or reimbursement of expenses of long-term care services for a relevant individual and which, in accordance with the provisions of this section, is approved of by the Revenue Commissioners for the purposes of this section;

"*relative*", in relation to an individual or the spouse of the individual, includes a relation by marriage and a person in respect of whom the individual is or was the legal guardian;

"*relevant individual*", in relation to a qualifying long-term care policy, means a qualifying individual in relation to that policy in respect of whom a practitioner has certified that the individual is—

(a) unable to perform (without substantial assistance from another individual) at least 2 of the activities of daily living for a period of at least 90 days due to a loss of functional capacity, or

(b) requires substantial supervision to protect such individual from threats to health and safety due to severe cognitive impairment;

"*transferring*" means the ability to move from a bed to an upright chair or a wheelchair and *vice versa*.

(2) (a) A person shall not be a qualifying insurer until such time as the person has been entered in a register maintained by the Revenue Commissioners for the purposes of this section and any regulations made thereunder.

(b) Where at any time a qualifying insurer—

(i) is not resident in the State, or

(ii) is not carrying on business in the State through a fixed place of business,

the qualifying insurer shall ensure that there is a person resident in the State and appointed by the qualifying insurer to be responsible for the discharge of all the duties and obligations imposed on the qualifying insurer by this section and any regulations made thereunder.

(c) Where a qualifying insurer appoints a person in accordance with *paragraph (b)*, that insurer shall advise the Revenue Commissioners of the identity of that person and the fact of the person's appointment.

(3) (a) The Revenue Commissioners shall not approve a policy for the purposes of this section unless they are satisfied that—

(i) the only benefits provided under the policy are the discharge or reimbursement of expenses of long-term care services in respect of an individual who is a relevant individual in relation to the policy,

(ii) the policy is either not expressed to be terminable by the insurer under the terms of the policy, or is expressed to be so terminable only in special circumstances mentioned in the policy,

(iii) the policy secures that for the purposes of the policy the question of whether an individual is a relevant individual shall be determined by reference to at least 5 activities of daily living,

(iv) subject to *paragraph (b)*, the policy does not provide for—

(I) a lump sum payment on termination,

(II) a cash surrender value, or

(III) any other money,

that can be paid or assigned to any person, borrowed, or pledged as collateral for a loan, and

(v) the policy is not connected with any other policy.

(b) A policy shall not fail to meet the requirements of *paragraph (a)(iv)* merely because it provides for the payment of periodic amounts of money without regard to the expenses incurred on the services provided during the period to which the payments relate.

(c) A policy is connected with another policy, whether held by the same person or another person, if—

(i) either policy was issued in respect of an assurance made with reference to the other, or with a view to enabling the other to be made on particular terms, or with a view to facilitating the making of the other on particular terms, and

(ii) the terms on which either policy was issued would have been different if the other policy had not been issued.

(4) (a) A long-term care policy shall be a qualifying long-term care policy within the meaning of this section if it conforms with a form which at the time it is issued is either—

(i) a standard form approved by the Revenue Commissioners as a standard form of qualifying long-term care policy, or

(ii) a form varying from a standard form so approved in no other respects than by making such alterations to that standard form as are, at the time the policy is issued, approved by the Revenue Commissioners as being compatible with a qualifying long-term care policy when made to that standard form and satisfying any conditions subject to which the alterations are so approved.

(b) In approving a policy, or a standard form of a policy, as a qualifying long-term care policy for the purposes of this section, the Revenue Commissioners may disregard any provision of the policy which appears to them insignificant.

(5) Where, for any year of assessment, an individual, who is resident in the State, makes a payment to a qualifying insurer in respect of a premium under a qualifying

long-term care policy, the beneficiary of which is a qualifying individual in relation to the individual, the individual making the payment shall, subject to the condition specified in *subsection (6)*, be entitled to relief under this section in accordance with *subsection (8)*.

(6) The condition specified in this subsection is that, at the time the long-term care policy is entered into, the individual (in this subsection referred to as the "*declarer*") furnishes to the qualifying insurer a declaration in writing which—

(a) is made and signed by the declarer,

(b) is made in such form as may be prescribed or authorised by the Revenue Commissioners,

(c) contains the declarer's full name, the address of his or her permanent residence and his or her PPS Number,

(d) declares that—

(i) at the time the declaration is made that he or she is resident in the State, and

(ii) the beneficiary under the policy is a qualifying individual in relation to the declarer,

and

(e) contains an undertaking that if, at any time while the long-term care policy is in force, the declarer ceases to be resident in the State he or she will notify the qualifying insurer accordingly.

(7) (a) A qualifying insurer shall—

(i) keep and retain for the longer of the following periods—

(I) a period of 6 years, and

(II) a period which, in relation to the long-term care policy in respect of which the declaration is made, ends not [earlier][2] than 3 years after the date on which premiums have ceased to be paid or payable in respect of the policy,

all declarations of the kind mentioned in *subsection (6)* which have been made in respect of qualifying long-term care policies issued by the qualifying insurer, and

(ii) on being so required by notice given to that insurer in writing by an inspector, make available within the State to the inspector, within the time specified in the notice, all or any of the declarations of the kind mentioned in *subsection (6)*.

(b) The inspector may examine or take extracts from or copies of any declarations made available to him or her under *paragraph (a)*.

(8) (a) Where an individual makes a payment to a qualifying insurer in respect of which he or she is entitled to relief under this section, the individual shall be entitled to deduct and retain out of the payment an amount equal to the appropriate percentage for the year of assessment in which payment of the premium falls due.

(b) The qualifying insurer to whom a payment referred to in *paragraph (a)* is made—

(i) shall accept the amount paid after deduction in discharge of the individual's liability to the same extent as if the deduction had not been made, and

(ii) may, on making a claim in accordance with regulations, recover from the Revenue Commissioners an amount equal to the amount deducted.

(9) (a) The Revenue Commissioners shall make regulations providing generally as to administration of this section and those regulations may, in particular and without prejudice to the generality of the foregoing, include provision—

(i) for the registration of persons as qualifying insurers for the purposes of this section and those regulations,

(ii) that a claim under *subsection (8)(b)(ii)* by a qualifying insurer shall—

(I) be made in such form and manner,

(II) be made at such time, and

(III) be accompanied by such documents,

as provided for in the regulations,

(iii) for the making of annual information returns by qualifying insurers, in such form (including electronic form) and manner as may be prescribed, and containing specified details in relation to—

(I) each individual making payments to such insurers under qualifying long-term care policies in a year of assessment,

(II) the total amount of premiums paid under a qualifying long-term care policy by that individual in the year of assessment, and

(III) the total amount deducted by that individual under *subsection (8)(a)*,

and

(iv) for the furnishing of information to the Revenue Commissioners for the purposes of the regulations.

(b) Every regulation made under this section shall be laid before Dáil Éireann as soon as may be after it is made and, if a resolution annulling the regulation is passed by Dáil Éireann within the next 21 days on which Dáil Éireann has sat after the regulation is laid before it, the regulation shall be annulled accordingly, but without prejudice to the validity of anything previously done thereunder.

(10) (a) Where any amount is paid to a qualifying insurer by the Revenue Commissioners as an amount recoverable by virtue of *subsection (8)(b)(ii)* but is an amount to which that qualifying insurer is not entitled, that amount shall be repaid by the qualifying insurer.

(b) There shall be made such assessments, adjustments or set-offs as may be required for securing repayment of the amount referred to in *paragraph (a)* and the provisions of this Act relating to the assessment, collection and recovery of income tax shall, in so far as they are applicable and with necessary modification, apply in relation to the recovery of such amount.

(11) Where relief is given under this section in respect of a payment, relief shall not be given under any other provision of the Income Tax Acts in respect of that payment.

(12) The Revenue Commissioners may nominate any of their officers, including an inspector, to perform any acts and discharge any functions authorised by this section, other than those specified in *subsection (9)*, to be performed or discharged by them.

[(13) This section ceases to have effect for the year of assessment 2010 and subsequent years of assessment.][3]][4]

Amendments

[1] Substituted by FA07 sched4(1)(n). Shall have effect as on and from 2 April 2007

[2] Substituted by FA02 sched6(3)(h). Shall be deemed to have come into force and take effect as on and from 6 April 2001.

[3] Inserted by FA10 s5(b). Deemed to have come into force and takes effect as on and from 1 January 2010.

[4] Inserted by FA01 s20(a)(ii).

Revenue Briefings

Tax Briefing

Tax Briefing April 2001 – Issue 43 pg 16 – Finance Act 2001

Cross References

To Section 470A

Section 112A Taxation of certain perquisites.

Section 458 Deductions allowed in ascertaining taxable income and provisions relating to reductions in tax.

Section 904G Power of inspection: claims by qualifying insurers.

Section 1024 Method of apportioning reliefs and charging tax in cases of separate assessments.

Schedule 29 Provisions Referred to in Sections 1052, 1053 and 1054

470B Age-related relief for health insurance premiums

[(1) In this section—

"*age-related tax credit*" has the same meaning as in *subsection (4)*;

"*authorised insurer*" means any undertaking (not being a restricted membership undertaking) entered in The Register of Health Benefits Undertakings, lawfully carrying on such business of medical insurance referred to in the definition of "*relevant contract*" but, in relation to an individual, also means any undertaking (not being a restricted membership undertaking) authorised pursuant to Council Directive No. 73/239/EEC of 24 July 1973*, Council Directive No. 88/357/EEC of 22 June 1988†, and Council Directive No. 92/49/EEC of 18 June 1992‡, where such a contract was effected with the individual when the individual was not resident in the State but was resident in another Member State of the European Communities;

*OJ No. L228 of 16 August 1973, p.3
†OJ No. L172 of 4 July 1988, p.1
‡OJ No. L228 of 11 August 1992, p.1

"*employee*" and "*employer*" have the same meanings, respectively, as in *section 983*;

"*excluded contract of insurance*" means—

(a) a contract of insurance which comes within the meaning of *paragraph (d)* of the definition of "*health insurance contract*" in section 2(1) of the Health Insurance Act 1994, or

(b) a contract of insurance relating solely to charges for public hospital in-patient services made under the Health (In-Patient Charges) Regulations 1987 (S.I. No. 116 of 1987);

"*in-patient indemnity payment*" has the same meaning as in section 2(1) of the Health Insurance Act 1994;

"*insured person*", in relation to a relevant contract, means an individual, the [spouse or civil partner][1] of the individual, or the children or other dependents of the individual or of the [spouse or civil partner][2] of the individual, in respect of whom the relevant contract provides specifically, whether in conjunction with other benefits or not, for the reimbursement or discharge, in whole or in part, of actual health expenses (within the meaning of *section 469*);

"*PPS Number*", in relation to an individual, means that individual's Personal Public Service Number within the meaning of section 262 of the Social Welfare Consolidation Act 2005;

"*relevant contract*" means a contract of insurance (not being an excluded contract of insurance) which provides for the making of in-patient indemnity payments under the contract and which, in relation to an individual, the [spouse or civil partner][3] of the individual, or the children or other dependents of the individual or of the [spouse or civil partner][4] of the individual, provides specifically, whether in conjunction with other benefits or not, for the reimbursement or discharge, in whole or in part, of actual health expenses (within the meaning of *section 469*), being a contract of medical insurance;

"*relevant year of assessment*" means—

(a) subject to *paragraph (b)*, the year of assessment 2009, 2010, [2011 or 2012][5],

(b) where a payment made to an authorised insurer is a monthly or other instalment towards the payment of the total annual premium due under a relevant contract, and the payment of such an instalment becomes due and is made in the year of assessment [2013, the year of assessment 2013][6];

"*relievable amount*", in relation to a payment to an authorised insurer under a relevant contract, means—

(a) where the payment covers no benefits other than such reimbursement or discharge as is referred to in the definition of "*relevant contract*", an amount equal to the full amount of the payment, or

(b) where the payment covers benefits other than such reimbursement or discharge as is referred to in that definition, an amount equal to so much of the payment as is referable to such reimbursement or discharge;

"*restricted membership undertaking*" has the same meaning as in section 2(1) of the Health Insurance Act 1994.

(2) This section applies to a payment made to an authorised insurer under a relevant contract renewed or entered into on or after 1 January 2009 but before [1 January 2013][7] where the payment qualifies for relief under *section 470(2)*.

(3) Notwithstanding *section 470(4)*, relief due under this section shall be given in addition to relief given under *section 470*.

[(4) Subject to *subsections (5)* and *(6)*, where, for a relevant year of assessment, an individual, or—

(a) if the individual is a married person assessed to tax in accordance with *section 1017*, the individual's spouse, or

(b) if the individual is a civil partner assessed to tax in accordance with *section 1031C*, the individual's civil partner,

makes a payment to an authorised insurer under a relevant contract and—

(i) the payment is in respect of a premium due under the relevant contract and the relevant contract was renewed or entered into on or after 1 January 2009 but before [1 January 2013][8], and

(ii) the payment or part of the payment, as the case may be, is attributable to an insured person, and only to an insured person, who is aged 50 years or over on the date the relevant contract is renewed or entered into, as the case may be,

then the individual shall, for the relevant year of assessment, in respect of so much of the relievable amount of the payment or part of the payment, as the case may be, as is attributable to an insured person referred to in *paragraph (b)*, be entitled to a credit (referred to in this section as "*age-related tax credit*") equal to the lower of—

(I) as respects a relevant contract renewed or entered into on or after 1 January 2009 but before 1 January 2010, the amount specified in column (2) of the Table to this subsection corresponding to the class of insured person mentioned in column (1) of that Table or, where the payment made to the authorised insurer is a monthly or other instalment towards the payment of the total annual premium due under the relevant contract, an amount equal to the amount so specified divided by the total number of instalments to be made to pay such total annual premium,

(II) as respects a relevant contract renewed or entered into on or after 1 January 2010 [but before 1 January 2011][9], the amount specified in column (3) of the Table to this subsection corresponding to the class of insured person mentioned in column (1) of that Table or, where the payment made to the authorised insurer is a monthly or other instalment towards the payment of the total annual premium due under the relevant contract, an amount equal to the amount so specified divided by the total number of instalments to be made to pay such total annual premium,

(III) as respects a relevant contract renewed or entered into on or after 1 January 2011 [but before 1 January 2012][10], the amount specified in column (4) of the Table to this subsection corresponding to the class of insured person mentioned in column (1) of that Table or, where the payment made to the authorised insurer is a monthly or other instalment towards the payment of the total annual premium due under the relevant contract, an amount equal to the amount so specified divided by the total number of instalments to be made to pay [such total annual premium,][11]

[(IIIa) as respects a relevant contract renewed or entered into on or after 1 January 2012, the amount specified in *column (5)* of the Table to this subsection corresponding to the class of insured person mentioned in *column (1)* of that Table or, where the payment made to the authorised insurer is a monthly or other instalment towards the payment of the total annual premium due under the relevant contract, an amount equal to the amount so specified divided by the total number of instalments to be made to pay such total annual premium, and][12]

(IV) an amount which reduces the income tax to be charged on the individual for the relevant year of assessment, other than in accordance with section 16(2), to nil.][13]

[TABLE

Class of insured person (1)	Amount of age-related tax credit (2)	Amount of age-related tax credit (3)	Amount of age-related tax credit (4)	Amount of age-related tax credit (5)
Aged 50 years and over but less than 55 years on the date the relevant contract is renewed or entered into, as the case may be.	€200.00	€200.00	Nil	Nil
Aged 55 years and over but less than 60 years on the date the relevant contract is renewed or entered into, as the case may be.	€200.00	€200.00	Nil	Nil
Aged 60 years and over but less than 65 years on the date the relevant contract is renewed or entered into, as the case may be.	€500.00	€525.00	€625.00	€600.00
Aged 65 years and over but less than 70 years on the date the relevant contract is renewed or entered into, as the case may be.	€500.00	€525.00	€625.00	€975.00
Aged 70 years and over but less than 75 years on the date the relevant contract is renewed or entered into, as the case may be.	€950.00	€975.00	€1,275.00	€1,400.00
Aged 75 years and over but less than 80 years on the date the relevant contract is renewed or entered into, as the case may be.	€950.00	€975.00	€1,275.00	€2,025.00
Aged 80 years and over but less than 85 years on the date the relevant contract is renewed or entered into, as the case may be.	€1,175.00	€1,250.00	€1,725.00	€2,400.00
Aged 85 years and over on the date the relevant contract is renewed or entered into, as the case may be.	€1,175.00	€1,250.00	€1,725.00	€2,700.00][14]

(5) (a) The amount of age-related tax credit given for a relevant year of assessment in respect of an insured person shall not exceed the amount of the payment made to an authorised insurer under a relevant contract in respect of the insured person for the relevant year of assessment.

(b) Where an individual makes a payment to an authorised insurer that entitles the individual to an age-related tax credit or age-related tax credits, as the case may be, for the year of assessment [2013][15], the aggregate amount of the age-related tax credit given to the individual in respect of an insured person or insured persons, as the case may be, for that year and the year of assessment [2012][16] shall not exceed the age-related tax credit or age-related tax credits, as the case may be, that the individual would have been entitled to if the total annual premium due under the relevant contract in respect of the insured person or insured persons, as the case may be, had been paid in the year of assessment [2012][17].

(c) Where, for any relevant year of assessment, an employer makes a payment of emoluments to an employee consisting of a perquisite in the form of a payment to an authorised insurer under a relevant contract, and—

(i) the payment qualifies for relief under this section for that relevant year of assessment, and

(ii) the aggregate of the age-related tax credit or age-related tax credits, as the case may be, and relief under *section 470* due in respect of the payment exceeds the amount of the income tax chargeable, in accordance with *sections 112* and *112A*, in respect of the perquisite (in this paragraph referred to as "*the excess*"),

[the excess may not reduce the income tax chargeable on any other income of the employee for that year of assessment, or—

(I) if the employee is a married person assessed to tax in accordance with *section 1017*, the income tax chargeable on any income of the employee's spouse for that year of assessment, or

(II) if the employee is a civil partner assessed to tax in accordance with *section 1031C*, the income tax chargeable on any income of the employee's civil partner for that year of assessment.][18]

(6) (a) Where an individual makes a payment to an authorised insurer that entitles the individual to an age-related tax credit or age-related tax credits, as the case may be, for a relevant year of assessment, the individual shall be entitled to deduct and retain out of it—

(i) if the payment made is the total annual premium due under the relevant contract concerned for the relevant year of assessment, an amount equal to the total amount of the age-related tax credit or age-related tax credits, as the case may be,

(ii) if the payment made is a monthly or other instalment towards the payment of the total annual premium due under the relevant contract concerned for the relevant year of assessment, an amount equal to the total amount of the age-related tax credit or age-related tax credits, as the case may be, to which the individual would be entitled if all of that total annual premium were paid divided by the total number of such instalments to be made to pay that total annual premium.

(b) An authorised insurer to which a payment referred to in *paragraph (a)* is made—

(i) shall accept the amount paid, after the deduction of the age-related tax credit or age-related tax credits, as the case may be, in discharge of the individual's liability to the same extent as if the deduction had not been made, and

(ii) may, on making a claim in accordance with regulations, recover from the Revenue Commissioners an amount equal to the amount deducted.

(c) Where an individual makes a payment referred to in *paragraph (a)* in respect of a premium due under a contract renewed or entered into on or after 1 January 2009 but before the passing of the Health Insurance (Miscellaneous Provisions) Act 2009, the individual shall be deemed to have deducted and retained out of the payment an amount equal to the amount of the age-related tax credit or age-related tax credits, as the case may be, that the individual is entitled to under this section in respect of that payment.

(d) An amount that an individual is entitled to deduct and retain out of a payment referred to in *paragraph (a)* shall be in addition to the amount that the individual is entitled to deduct and retain out of the payment in accordance with *section 470(3)*.

(7) (a) The Revenue Commissioners shall make regulations providing generally for the administration of this section and those regulations may, in particular and without prejudice to the generality of the foregoing, include provision—

(i) that a claim under *subsection (6)(b)(ii)* by an authorised insurer, which has registered with the Revenue Commissioners for the purposes of making such a claim, shall—

(I) be made in such form and manner,

(II) be made at such time,

(III) be accompanied by such documents, and

(IV) be accompanied by such information as respects the amount of premiums paid under relevant contracts in respect of insured persons aged 50 years or over in a relevant year of assessment and the number of such individuals within each class, as provided for in the regulations,

(ii) for the making of annual information returns by authorised insurers, in such form (including electronic form) and manner as may be provided for in the regulations, and containing specified details in relation to—

(I) each individual making payments, to which this section applies, to such insurers under relevant contracts in a relevant year of assessment,

(II) each insured person aged 50 years or over, in respect of whom such payments were made in the relevant year of assessment, including—

(A) the name of the insured person,

(B) the date of birth of the insured person, and

(C) the PPS Number of the insured person,

(III) the total amount of premiums paid by the individual under a relevant contract in respect of an insured person aged 50 years or over in a relevant year of assessment, and

(IV) the total amount deducted under *subsection (6)(a)* by the individual making the payments in the relevant year of assessment concerned,

and

(iii) for the furnishing of any other information that the Revenue Commissioners may reasonably require for the purposes of the regulations.

(b) Every regulation made under this section shall be laid before Dáil Éireann as soon as may be after it is made and, if a resolution annulling the regulation is passed by Dáil Éireann within the next 21 days on which Dáil Éireann has sat after the regulation is laid before it, the regulation shall be annulled accordingly, but without prejudice to the validity of anything previously done thereunder.

(8) (a) Where any amount is paid to an authorised insurer by the Revenue Commissioners as an amount recoverable by virtue of *subsection (6)(b)* but is an amount to which the authorised insurer is not entitled, that amount shall be repaid by the authorised insurer.

(b) There shall be made such assessments, adjustments or set-offs as may be required for securing repayment of the amount referred to in *paragraph (a)* and the provisions of the Income Tax Acts relating to the assessment, collection and recovery of income tax shall, in so far as they are applicable and with necessary modification, apply in relation to the recovery of such amount.][19]

Amendments

1, 2, 3, 4 Substituted by F(No.3)A11 sched1(96).

5 Substituted by HI(MP)A11 s5(a)(i).

6 Substituted by HI(MP)A11 s5(a)(ii).

7 Substituted by HI(MP)A11 s5(b).

8 Substituted by FA12 s6(1)(a). Deemed to have come into force and takes effect on and from 1 January 2012.

9 Inserted by FA12 s6(1)(b). Deemed to have come into force and takes effect on and from 1 January 2012.

10 Inserted by FA12 s6(1)(c). Deemed to have come into force and takes effect on and from 1 January 2012.

11 Substituted by FA12 s6(1)(d). Deemed to have come into force and takes effect on and from 1 January 2012.

12 Inserted by FA12 s6(1)(e). Deemed to have come into force and takes effect on and from 1 January 2012.

13 Substituted by F(No.3)A11 sched1(97).

14 Substituted by FA12 s6(1)(f). Deemed to have come into force and takes effect on and from 1 January 2012.

15 Substituted by HI(MP)A11 s5(d)(i).

16, 17 Substituted by HI(MP)A11 s5(d)(ii).

18 Substituted by F(No.3)A11 sched1(98).

19 Inserted by the Health Insurance (Miscellaneous Provisions) Act 2009 s22.

Cross References

From Section 470B

Section 12A
Section 16 Income tax charged by deduction.
Section 112 Basis of assessment, persons chargeable and extent of charge.
Section 469 Relief for health expenses.
Section 470 Relief for insurance against expenses of illness.
Section 983 Interpretation (Chapter 4).
Section 1017 Assessment of husband in respect of income of both spouses.

To Section 470B

Section 112A Taxation of certain perquisites.
Section 458 Deductions allowed in ascertaining taxable income and provisions relating to reductions in tax.
Section 470 Relief for insurance against expenses of illness.
Section 904E Power of inspection: claims by authorised insurers.

Section 1024 Method of apportioning reliefs and charging tax in cases of separate assessments.
Schedule 29 Provisions Referred to in Sections 1052, 1053 and 1054

471 Relief for contributions to permanent health benefit schemes

[FA79 s8(1), (2)(a) and (3)]

(1) In this section—

"*benefit*" and "*permanent health benefit scheme*" have the same meanings respectively as in *section 125*;

"*contribution*", in relation to a permanent health benefit scheme, means any premium paid or other periodic payment made to the scheme in consideration of the right to benefit under it, being a premium or payment which bears a reasonable relationship to the benefits secured by it.

(2) Where an individual for a year of assessment proves that in that year of assessment he or she made a contribution or contributions to a bona fide permanent health benefit scheme or schemes, the individual shall be entitled, for the purpose of ascertaining the amount of the income on which he or she is to be charged to income tax, to have a deduction of so much of the contributions as does not exceed 10 per cent of his or her total income for that year of assessment made from his or her total income.

(3) In a case where the amount of a contribution made by an employer to a permanent health benefit scheme is charged to income tax under *Chapter 3* of *Part 5* as a perquisite of the office or employment of a director or employee, that amount shall be deemed for the purposes of *subsection (2)* to be a contribution made by the director or employee to the scheme in the year in respect of which it is so charged to income tax.

Cross References

From Section 471

Section 112 Basis of assessment, persons chargeable and extent of charge.
Section 123 General tax treatment of payments on retirement or removal from office or employment.
Section 125 Tax treatment of benefits received under permanent health benefit schemes.

To Section 471

Section 458 Deductions allowed in ascertaining taxable income and provisions relating to reductions in tax.
Section 986 Regulations.
Section 1024 Method of apportioning reliefs and charging tax in cases of separate assessments.

472 Employee tax credit

[(1) (a) In this section—

"*appropriate percentage*", in relation to a year of assessment, means a percentage equal to the standard rate of tax for that year; "*emoluments*" means emoluments to which *Chapter 4* of *Part 42* applies or is applied, but does not include—

(i) emoluments paid directly or indirectly by a body corporate (or by any person who would be regarded as connected with the body corporate) to a proprietary director of the body corporate or to the [spouse, civil partner, child or child of the civil partner][1] of such a proprietary director, and

(ii) emoluments paid directly or indirectly by an individual (or by a partnership in which the individual is a partner) to the [spouse, civil partner, child or child of the civil partner][2] of the individual;

"*director*" means—

(i) in relation to a body corporate the affairs of which are managed by a board of directors or similar body, a member of that board or body,

(ii) in relation to a body corporate the affairs of which are managed by a single director or similar person, that director or person, and

(iii) in relation to a body corporate the affairs of which are managed by the members themselves, a member of the body corporate,

and includes any person who is or has been a director;

"*proprietary director*" means a director of a company who is either the beneficial owner of, or able, either directly or through the medium of other companies or by any other indirect means, to control, more than 15 per cent of the ordinary share capital of the company;

"*specified employed contributor*" means a person who is an employed contributor for the purposes of the [Social Welfare Consolidation Act 2005,][3] but does not include a person—

(i) who is an employed contributor for those purposes by reason only of [*section 12(1)(b)* of that Act,][4] or

(ii) to whom Article 81, 82 or 83 of the Social Welfare (Consolidated Contributions and Insurability) Regulations, 1996 (S.I. No. 312 of 1996), applies.

(b) For the purposes of the definition of "*proprietary director*", ordinary share capital which is owned or controlled as referred to in that definition by a person, being [a spouse, a civil partner, a minor child, or a minor child of the civil partner, of a director][5], or by a trustee of a trust for the benefit of a person or persons, being or including any such person or such director, shall be deemed to be owned or controlled by such director and not by any other person.

(2) The exclusion from the definition of "*emoluments*" of the emoluments referred to in *subparagraphs (i)* and *(ii)* of that definition shall not apply for any year of assessment to any such emoluments paid to an individual, being a child (other than a child who is a proprietary director) to whom *subparagraph (i)* or *(ii)* of that definition relates, if for that year—

(a) (i) the individual is a specified employed contributor, or

(ii) the [Income Tax (Employments) (Consolidated) Regulations 2001 (S.I. No. 559 of 2001)][6], in so far as they apply, have, in relation to any such emoluments paid to the individual in the year of assessment, been complied with by the person by whom the emoluments are paid,

(b) the conditions of the office or employment, in respect of which any such emoluments are paid, are such that the individual is required to devote, throughout the year of assessment, substantially the whole of the individual's time to the duties of the office or employment and the individual does in fact do so, and

(c) the amount of any such emoluments paid to the individual in the year of assessment are not less than [€4,572][7].

(3) Where an individual is in receipt of profits or gains from an office or employment held or exercised outside the State, such profits or gains shall be deemed to be emoluments within the meaning of *subsection (1)* if such profits or gains—

(a) are chargeable to tax in the country in which they arise,

(b) on payment by the person making such payment, are subject to a system of tax deduction similar in form to that provided for in *Chapter 4* of *Part 42*,

(c) are chargeable to tax in the State on the full amount of such profits or gains under Schedule D, and

(d) if the office or employment was held or exercised in the State and the person was resident in the State, would be emoluments within the meaning of that subsection.

(4) Where, for any year of assessment, a claimant proves that his or her total income for the year consists in whole or in part of emoluments (including, in a case where the claimant is [a married person assessed to tax in accordance with *section 1017*, or a civil partner assessed to tax in accordance with *section 1031C*,][8] any emoluments of the claimant's [spouse or civil partner][9] deemed to be income of the claimant by that section for the purposes referred to in that section) the claimant shall be entitled to a tax credit (to be known as the "*employee tax credit*") of—

(a) where the emoluments (but not including, in the case where the claimant is a [married person or a civil partner][10] so assessed, the emoluments, if any, of the claimant's [spouse or civil partner][11]) arise to the claimant, the lesser of an amount equal to the appropriate percentage of the emoluments and [€1,650][12], and

(b) where, in a case where the claimant is a [married person or a civil partner][13] so assessed, the emoluments arise to the claimant's [spouse or civil partner][14], the lesser of an amount equal to the appropriate percentage of the emoluments and [€1,650][15].

(5) Where a tax credit is due under this section by virtue of *subsection (2)*, it shall be given by means of repayment of tax.][16]

Amendments

[1, 2] Substituted by F(No.3)A11 sched1(99).

[3] Substituted by FA07 sched4(1)(o)(i). Shall have effect as on and from 2 April 2007

[4] Substituted by FA07 sched4(1)(o)(ii). Shall have effect as on and from 2 April 2007

[5] Substituted by F(No.3)A11 sched1(100).

[6] Substituted by FA02 sched6(3)(i). Shall be deemed to have come into force and take effect as on and from 1 January 2002.

[7] Substituted by FA01 sched1(2)(k)(i). Applies as respects the year of assessment 2002 and subsequent years of assessment.

[8] Substituted by F(No.3)A11 sched1(101).

[9, 11, 14] Substituted by F(No.3)A11 sched1(102).

[10, 13] Substituted by F(No.3)A11 sched1(103).

[12, 15] Substituted by FA11 sched1(1)(j). Has effect as on and from 1 January 2011.

[16] Substituted by FA01 sched1(1)(o). Applies as respects the year of assessment 2001 and subsequent years of assessment.

Revenue Briefings

Tax Briefing

Tax Briefing April 2008 – Issue 68 – Employee (PAYE) credit

Cross References

From Section 472

Section 12 The charge to income tax.

Section 960 Date for payment of income tax other than under self assessment.

Section 983 Interpretation (Chapter 4).

Section 1017 Assessment of husband in respect of income of both spouses.

To Section 472

Section 3 Interpretation of Income Tax Acts.

Section 122 Preferential loan arrangements.

Section 202 Relief for agreed pay restructuring.

Section 458 Deductions allowed in ascertaining taxable income and provisions relating to reductions in tax.

Section 472A Relief for the long-term unemployed.

Section 480 Relief for certain sums chargeable under Schedule E.

Section 825A Reduction in income tax for certain income earned outside the State.

Section 1024 Method of apportioning reliefs and charging tax in cases of separate assessments.

472A Relief for the long-term unemployed

[(1) (a) In this section—

[["*the Act of 2005*" means the Social Welfare Consolidation Act 2005;][1]

"*continuous period of unemployment*" has the meaning assigned in [section 141(3) of the Act of 2005;][2]][3]

"*director*" and "*proprietary director*" have the same meanings, respectively, as in *section 472*;

"*emoluments*" has the same meaning as in *subsection (1)(a)* of *section 472* and, in relation to the exclusions from that definition, *subsection (2)* of that section shall apply accordingly;

"*employment*" means an office or employment of profit such that any emoluments of the office or employment of profit are to be charged to tax under Schedule E;

"*employment scheme*" means a scheme or programme which provides for the payment in respect of an employment to an employer or an employee of a grant, subsidy or other such payment funded wholly or mainly, directly or indirectly, by the State or by any board established by statute or by any public or local authority;

"*qualifying child*", in relation to a claimant and a year of assessment, has the same meaning as in *section 462*, and the question of whether a child is a qualifying child shall be determined on the same basis as it would be for the purposes of *section 462*, and [*subsections (4) and (5)*][4] of that section shall apply accordingly;

"*qualifying employment*" means an employment which—

[(i) commences on or after 6 April 1998 and before such day as the Minister for Finance may by order appoint,][5]

(i) commences on or after the 6th day of April, 1998,

(ii) is of at least 30 hours duration per week, and

(iii) is capable of lasting at least 12 months,

but does not include—

(I) an employment from which the previous holder was unfairly dismissed,

(II) an employment with a person who, in the 26 weeks immediately prior to the commencement of an employment by a qualifying individual, has reduced, by way of redundancy, the number of employees in such person's trade or profession, or

(III) an employment in respect of which more than 75 per cent of the emoluments therefrom arise from commissions;

["*qualifying individual*" means an individual who commences a qualifying employment and who—

(i) (I) immediately prior to the commencement of that qualifying employment has been unemployed throughout the period of 12 months immediately preceding the commencement of the employment [and, in respect of that period of unemployment, is entitled to credited contributions in accordance with *section 33* of the Act of 2005 and regulations made under that section or has been in receipt of][6]

(A) unemployment benefit under [Chapter 12 of Part 2 of the Act of 2005,][7] in respect of a continuous period of unemployment of not less than 312 days, or

(B) unemployment assistance under [Chapter 2 of Part 3 of the Act of 2005,][8] in respect of a continuous period of unemployment of not less than 312 days, or

(C) one-parent family payment under [Chapter 7 of Part 3 of the Act of 2005,][9] in respect of a continuous period of unemployment of not less than 312 days, or

(II) is in any other separate category of persons approved of for the purposes of this section by the Minister for Social, Community and Family Affairs with the consent of the Minister for Finance,

and

(ii) was not previously a qualifying individual for the purposes of this section;][10]

"*unemployment payment*" means a payment of unemployment benefit or unemployment assistance payable under the Social Welfare Acts.

(b) For the purposes of the definition of "*qualifying individual*"—

(i) any period of—

(I) attendance at a non-craft training course provided or approved of by An Foras Áiseanna Saothair,

(II) participation in a programme administered by An Foras Áiseanna Saothair and known as the Community Employment Scheme,

(III) participation in a programme administered by An Foras Áiseanna Saothair and known as the Job Initiative,

(IV) participation in, or participation in or attendance at, an activity to which [*paragraph (b)* or *(i)*, respectively, of *section 141(6)* of the Social Welfare Consolidation Act 2005,][11] relates,

shall be deemed to be a period of unemployment for the purposes of this section, and

(ii) any payment in respect of a period of attendance at, or participation in, an activity, programme or scheme mentioned in subparagraph (i) shall be deemed to be an unemployment payment for the purposes of this section if the qualifying individual concerned was in receipt of an unemployment payment immediately prior to the commencement [of such period, and][12]

[(iii) every Sunday in any period of consecutive days shall not be treated as a day of unemployment and shall be disregarded in computing any such period.][13]

(2) Subject to the provisions of this section, where an individual proves that he or she is a qualifying individual, he or she shall, in relation to the 3 years of assessment commencing with either—

(a) the year of assessment in which a qualifying employment commences, or

(b) by election made by him or her in writing to the inspector, the year of assessment following the year of assessment in which the qualifying employment commences,

be entitled, in computing the amount of his or her taxable income, to have a deduction made from so much of his or her total income as is attributable to emoluments from that qualifying employment as follows:

(i) for the first of those 3 years, [€3,810][14],

(ii) for the second of those 3 years, [€2,540][15], and

(iii) for the third of those 3 years, [€1,270][16].

(3) (a) Subject to the provisions of *paragraphs (b)* and *(c)*, where a qualifying individual who is entitled to a deduction under *subsection (2)* for one or more of the 3 years of assessment referred to in that subsection proves that, for one or more of those years, a qualifying child is resident with him or her for the whole or part of the year, he or she shall, in respect of each of the 3 years referred to in *subsection (2)* in relation to which he or she so proves, be entitled, in computing the amount of his or her taxable income, to have a deduction made from so much of his or her total income as is attributable to emoluments from the qualifying employment as follows:

(i) for the first of those 3 years, [€1,270][17] in respect of each qualifying child,

(ii) for the second of those 3 years, [€850][18] in respect of each qualifying child, and

(iii) for the third of those 3 years, [€425][19] in respect of each qualifying child.

(b) Only one deduction of [€1,270][20], [€850][21] and [€425][22] shall be allowed in respect of each qualifying child.

(c) Where for a year of assessment, 2 or more qualifying individuals would but for this paragraph be entitled under this section to relief in respect of the same qualifying child, the following provisions shall apply:

(i) the amount of the deduction to be granted for that year in respect of the qualifying child will be the amount due under *paragraph (a)* subject to the provisions of *paragraph (b)*,

(ii) where the qualifying child is maintained by only one of the qualifying individuals concerned, that individual shall be entitled to claim the deduction,

(iii) where the qualifying child is maintained jointly by one or more qualifying individuals, the deduction due for the year of assessment in respect of the child shall be apportioned between the qualifying individuals who contribute to the maintenance of the child—

(I) in the same proportion as each maintains the child, or

(II) in such manner as they jointly notify in writing to the inspector;

(iv) in ascertaining for the purposes of this subsection whether a qualifying individual maintains a qualifying child, any payment made by that individual for or towards the maintenance of the child which the individual is entitled to deduct in computing his or her total income for the purposes of the Income Tax Acts shall be deemed not to be a payment for or towards the maintenance of the child.

(4) Where, within the 3 years mentioned in *subsection (3)*, the qualifying employment (in this subsection referred to as "the first-mentioned employment") in respect of which the qualifying individual is entitled to a deduction under *subsection (2)* ceases, the qualifying individual shall be entitled to have so much of the deductions mentioned in *subsections (2)* and *(3)* as cannot be set against his or her emoluments from the first-mentioned employment carried forward and set against the emoluments from his or her next, and only next, qualifying employment, but the deduction for any year of assessment to be set against the emoluments from either or both qualifying employments shall not exceed the deductions due under *subsections (2)* and *(3)* for that year.

(5) (a) The deductions mentioned in subsections (2) and (3) shall not be due if the qualifying individual, or his or her employer, is benefiting, or has benefited, in respect of the qualifying employment in respect of which a claim under this section is made, under an employment scheme, whether statutory or otherwise.

(b) For the purposes of the definition of an employment scheme, an activity, programme or course mentioned in [subsection (1)*(b)*(i)][23] shall be deemed not to be an employment scheme.

(6) Any claim for relief under this section—

(a) shall be made in such form as the Revenue Commissioners may from time to time provide, and

(b) shall contain such information and be accompanied by such statement in writing as may be indicated in the said form as the Revenue Commissioners may reasonably require for the purposes of the section.][24]

[(7) This section shall cease to have effect in respect of all claims relating to emoluments from an employment commencing on or after such day as the Minister for Finance may by order appoint.][25]

Amendments

[1] Substituted by FA07 sched4(1)(p)(i)(I). Shall have effect as on and from 2 April 2007

[2] Substituted by FA07 sched4(1)(p)(i)(II). Shall have effect as on and from 2 April 2007

[3, 10] Inserted by FA99 s35(a)(i).

[4] Substituted by FA02 sched6(3)(j). Shall be deemed to have come into force and take effect as on and from 6 April 2001.

[5] Substituted by FA13 s7(2)(a). Deemed to have come into force and takes effect on and from 1 January 2013.

[6] Substituted by FA12 s10. Applies as respects the year of assessment 2012 and each subsequent year of assessment.

[7] Substituted by FA07 sched4(1)(p)(i)(III)(A). Shall have effect as on and from 2 April 2007

[8] Substituted by FA07 sched4(1)(p)(i)(III)(B). Shall have effect as on and from 2 April 2007

[9] Substituted by FA07 sched4(1)(p)(i)(III)(C). Shall have effect as on and from 2 April 2007

[11] Substituted by FA07 sched4(1)(p)(ii). Shall have effect as on and from 2 April 2007

[12] Substituted by FA99 s35(b)(i).

[13] Inserted by FA99 s35(b)(ii).

[14, 15, 16, 17, 18, 19, 20, 21, 22] Substituted by FA01 sched5.

[23] Substituted by FA99 s35(c).

[24] Inserted by FA98 s16(b)(ii).

[25] Inserted by FA13 s7(2)(b). With effect from 1 July 2013 as per S.I. No. 227 of 2013.

Revenue Briefings

Tax Briefing

Tax Briefing April 1998 – Issue 31 pg 19 – Revenue Job Assist – New tax incentives
Tax Briefing March 1999 – Issue 35 pg 21 – Revenue Job Assist – Special categories
Tax Briefing May 2006 – Issue 63 – Revenue Job Assist – Special categories

Revenue Information Notes

Job Assist (long term unemployed taking up a job)
IT58 – Revenue Job Assist Information for Employees

Cross References

From Section 472A

Section 141 Distributions out of income from patent royalties.
Section 462 One-parent family tax credit.
Section 472 Employee tax credit.

To Section 472A

Section 88A Double deduction in respect of certain emoluments.
Section 458 Deductions allowed in ascertaining taxable income and provisions relating to reductions in tax.
Section 531A Definitions (Part 18A).
Section 531AL Definitions (Part 18D).
Section 1024 Method of apportioning reliefs and charging tax in cases of separate assessments.

472AA Relief for long-term unemployed starting a business

[(1) In this section—

"*Act of 2005*" means the Social Welfare Consolidation Act 2005;

"*basis period*", in relation to a year of assessment, means the period on the profit or gains of which income tax for the year of assessment is to be finally computed under the Income Tax Acts;

"*continuous period of unemployment*" has the meaning assigned to it in *section 141(3)* of the Act of 2005;

"*crediting contribution*" means a crediting contribution provided for by regulations made under *section 33* of the Act of 2005;

"*new business*" means a trade or profession which is set up and commenced by a qualifying individual during the period beginning on 25 October 2013 and ending on 31 December 2016, other than a trade or profession—

(a) which was previously carried on by another person and to which the qualifying individual has succeeded, or

(b) the activities of which were previously carried on as part of another person's trade or profession;

"*qualifying individual*" means an individual who commences a new business and—

(a) who—

(i) has been continuously unemployed for the period of 12 months immediately preceding the commencement of that business, and in respect of that period of unemployment, was entitled to crediting contributions, or

(ii) in respect of a continuous period of unemployment of not less than 312 days immediately preceding the commencement of that business, has been in receipt of—

(I) jobseeker's benefit under *Chapter 12* of *Part 2* of the Act of 2005,

(II) jobseeker's allowance under *Chapter 2* of *Part 3* of the Act of 2005,

(III) one-parent family payment under *Chapter 7* of *Part 3* of the Act of 2005, or

(IV) partial capacity payment under *Chapter 8A* of *Part 2* of the Act of 2005,

and

(b) who was not previously a qualifying individual for the purposes of this section;

"*qualifying period*" means a period of 24 months beginning on the date the qualifying individual commenced a new business;

"*unemployment payment*" means a payment of jobseeker's benefit or jobseeker's allowance payable under the Social Welfare Acts.

(2) For the purposes of the definition of "*qualifying individual*" in *subsection (1)*—

(a) any period where an individual is in attendance at, or participating in, a scheme or programme of employment or work experience, or a course of education, training or development, where such a scheme, programme or course is approved for the purposes of this paragraph by the Minister for Social Protection or the Minister for Education and Skills, with the consent of the Minister for Finance, shall be deemed to be part of a continuous period of unemployment for the purposes of this section,

(b) any payment in respect of a period of attendance at, or participation in, a scheme, programme or course mentioned in *paragraph (a)* shall be deemed to be an unemployment payment for the purposes of this section if the qualifying individual concerned was in receipt of an unemployment payment immediately prior to the commencement of such period, and

(c) any Sunday in any period of consecutive days shall not be treated as a day of unemployment and shall be disregarded in computing any such period.

(3) Subject to this section, where, on making a claim, an individual proves that he or she is a qualifying individual, he or she shall be entitled in any year of assessment falling wholly or partly within the qualifying period to deduct from or set off against the profits or gains of the new business, on which that individual is assessed under Case I or Case II of *Schedule D*, an amount equal to the amount referred to in *subsection (4)*.

(4) The amount to which *subsection (3)* refers is an amount equal to the lesser of—

$$A \times \frac{B}{C}$$

or

$$€40{,}000 \times \frac{B}{12}$$

where—

A is the profit or gains of the new business which would, but for this section, be charged to tax in the year of assessment,

B is the number of months or fractions of months within the year of assessment which fall within the qualifying period, and

C is the number of months or fractions of months in the basis period for the year of assessment.

(5) Notwithstanding any other provision of the Tax Acts, effect shall be given to a deduction or set-off under *subsection (4)* in priority to any relief under *section 382* and any allowance made in respect of the new business in accordance with *Part 9*.

(6) Where a qualifying individual commences 2 or more new businesses, the total deduction available under this section shall not exceed €40,000 for a year of assessment.

(7) Notwithstanding any other provision of the Tax Acts, an individual who makes a claim under this section shall be a chargeable person within the meaning of *section 959A*.][1]

Amendments

[1] Inserted by F(No.2)A13 s6. Comes into operation on 25 October 2013.

Revenue Briefings

eBrief

eBrief No. 03/2014 – Start Your Own Business Relief

472B Seafarer allowance, etc

[(1) In this section—

"*authorised officer*" has the same meaning as in *section 818*;

"*employment*" means an office or employment of profit such that any emoluments of the office or employment of profit are to be charged to tax under Schedule D or Schedule E;

"*international voyage*" means a voyage beginning or ending in a port outside the State;

"*Member State*" means a member state of the European Communities;

"*Member State's Register*" shall be construed in accordance with the Annex to the Official Journal of the European Communities (No. C205) of the 5th day of July, 1997;

"*qualifying employment*" means an employment, being an employment to which this section applies, the duties of which are performed wholly on board a sea–going ship on an international voyage;

"*qualifying individual*" means an individual who—

(a) holds a qualifying employment, and

(b) has entered into an agreement (known as "*articles of agreement*") with the master of that ship;

"*sea-going ship*" means a ship which—

(a) is registered in a Member State's Register, and

(b) is used solely for the trade of carrying by sea passengers or cargo for reward,

but does not include a fishing vessel.

(2) For the purposes of this section—

(a) an individual shall be deemed to be absent from the State for a day if the individual is absent from the State at the end of the day, and

[(b) a port outside the State shall be deemed to include a mobile or fixed rig, platform or installation of any kind in any maritime area.][1]

(3) (a) Subject to *paragraph (b)*, this section shall apply to an employment other than—

(i) an employment the emoluments of which are paid out of the revenue of the State, or

(ii) an employment with any board, authority or other similar body established in the State by or under statute.

(b) This section shall not apply in any case where the income from an employment—

(i) is chargeable to tax in accordance with *section 71(3)*, or

(ii) is income to which *section 822* applies.

(4) Where for any year of assessment an individual resident in the State makes a claim in that behalf to an authorised officer and satisfies that officer that he or she is a qualifying individual and that he or she was absent from the State for at least [125 days][2], or such greater number of days as the Minister for Finance, after consultation with the Minister for the Marine and Natural Resources, may from time to time, by order made for the purposes of this subsection, substitute for that number of days (or, as the case may be, for the number of days substituted by the last previous order under this subsection), in that year for the purposes of performing the duties of a qualifying employment, he or she shall be entitled, in computing the amount of his or her taxable income, to have a deduction of [€6,350][3] made from so much, if any, of his or her total income as is attributable to the income, profits or gains from the qualifying employment.

[(4A) (a) Notwithstanding *subsection (4)*, but subject to *paragraph (b)*—

(i) as respects the year of assessment 2001, the reference in that subsection to "125 days" shall be construed as a reference to "119 days", and

(ii) as respects the year of assessment 2002 and subsequent years of assessment, the reference in that subsection to "169 days" shall be construed as a reference to "161 days".

(b) *Paragraph (a)* shall come into operation on such day as the Minister for Finance may by order appoint.][4]

(5) Where, for a year of assessment, an individual claims a deduction under this section, he or she shall not be entitled to a deduction under *section 823*.

(6) For the purposes of the definition of "*qualifying employment*" in this section, any duties of the employment not performed on board a sea-going ship on an international voyage, the performance of which is merely incidental to the performance of the duties of the employment on board a sea-going ship on an international voyage, shall be treated for the purposes of that definition as having been performed on board the sea-going ship.][5]

Amendments

[1] Substituted by FA99 s15.

[2] Substituted by FA01 s30(a)(i). Applies as respects the year of assessment 2001.

[3] Substituted by FA01 s30(a)(ii). Applies as respects the year of assessment 2002 and subsequent years of assessment.

[4] Inserted by FA01 s30(b). With effect from 6 April 2001 per S.I. 126 of 2003.

[5] Inserted by FA98 s14(1)(b). With effect from 17 February 1999 per S.I. No. 48 of 1999.

Revenue Briefings

Tax Briefing

Tax Briefing June 1999 – Issue 36 pg 18 – Seafarer's allowance update
Tax Briefing April 2001 – Issue 41 pg 16 – Finance Act 2001 Seafarer's allowance

Cross References

From Section 472B

Section 71 Foreign securities and possessions.
Section 818 Interpretation (Part 34).
Section 822 Split year residence.
Section 823 Deduction for income earned outside the State.

To Section 472B

Section 458 Deductions allowed in ascertaining taxable income and provisions relating to reductions in tax.
Section 823 Deduction for income earned outside the State.
Section 825A Reduction in income tax for certain income earned outside the State.
Section 1024 Method of apportioning reliefs and charging tax in cases of separate assessments.

472C Relief for trade union subscriptions

[(1) In this section—

"*appropriate percentage*", in relation to a year of assessment, means a percentage equal to the standard rate of tax for that year;

"*specified amount*", in relation to an individual for a year of assessment, means [€350][1];

"*trade union*" means a body which is either—

(a) the holder of a negotiation licence under the Trade Union Act, 1941,

(b) an excepted body within the meaning of section 6 of that Act as amended by the Trade Union Act, 1942,

(c) a garda representative body established under the Garda Síochána Act, 1977, namely—

(i) the association known as the Association of Garda Sergeants and Inspectors established under regulation 5(1) of the Garda Síochána (Associations) Regulations, 1978 (S.I. No. 135 of 1978),

(ii) the association known as the Garda Representative Association established under regulation 4(1) of the Garda Síochána (Associations) Regulations, 1978,

(iii) the association known as the Association of Garda Superintendents established under regulation 4(1) of the Garda Síochána (Associations) (Superintendents and Chief Superintendents) Regulations, 1987 (S.I. No. 200 of 1987),

or

(d) a Defence Forces representative body established under section 2 of the Defence (Amendment) Act, 1990, and regulations pursuant to that Act.

(2) Where an individual is a member of a trade union at any time in a year of assessment (being the year of assessment 2001 or a subsequent year of assessment), the income tax to be charged on the individual or, in the case of an individual whose spouse is assessed to tax in accordance with the provisions of *section 1017*, the individual's spouse, for the year of assessment, other than in accordance with *section 16(2)*, shall, subject to the following provisions of this section, be reduced by the lesser of—

(a) the appropriate percentage of the specified amount, or

(b) the amount which reduces that income tax to nil.

(3) Notwithstanding *subsection (2)*, the relief (if any) to which an individual is entitled under this section for the year of assessment 2001 shall, in addition to the relief (if any) to which the individual is entitled for the year of assessment 2002, be allowed to the individual in accordance with the provisions of *subsection (2)*, in respect of the income tax to be charged on the individual for the year of assessment 2002.

(4) Relief under this section shall be allowed in priority to relief under any of the other provisions mentioned in the Table to *section 458*.

(5) Where the relief (if any) to which an individual is entitled under this section in respect of income tax to be charged on the individual for the year of assessment 2001 is not wholly allowed to the individual in respect of the income tax to be charged on the individual for the year of assessment 2002 owing to an insufficiency of total income of the individual in that year of assessment, the portion of the relief not so allowed shall be allowed to the individual in respect of the income tax to be charged on the individual for the year of assessment 2001 such relief being limited to the lesser of—

(a) the portion of the relief not so allowed, and

(b) the relief which reduces that income tax to nil.

(6) If an individual is a member of more than one trade union, either at the same time or at different times in a year of assessment, the individual shall be treated, for the purposes of the relief under this section, as if the individual were a member of one trade union only in that year of assessment.

(7) (a) Notwithstanding the provisions of any other enactment—

(i) an employer of individuals entitled to relief under this section, or

(ii) a trade union of which such individuals are or were members,

[may on receipt of a request][2] from the Revenue Commissioners furnish to them either directly or indirectly the following information, to the extent that such information is in their possession, in relation to any such individual—

(I) the name and address of the individual,

(II) the name of the trade union of which the individual is a member,

(III) the Personal Public Service Number of the individual, and

(IV) the name and address of the employer of the individual.

(b) A return by an employer or a trade union under *paragraph (a)* shall, unless the Revenue Commissioners otherwise direct, be in an electronic format approved by the Revenue Commissioners.

[(7A) Notwithstanding the provisions of any other enactment, where trade union subscriptions of employees of an employer are deducted by the employer from the emoluments of those employees and remitted to the trade union concerned, the employer may, for the purposes of enabling that trade union to make a return under the provisions of *subsection (7)* and for that purpose only, on receipt of a request in that behalf from the trade union furnish to the trade union the names and the Personal Public Service Numbers of the employees who are members of that trade union, and only those employees, from whose emoluments those deductions have been made.][3]

(8) (a) The information referred to in *subsection (7)(a)* shall be used by the Revenue Commissioners for the purposes of facilitating the granting of relief under this section and shall be used for no other purpose.

(b) The provisions of *section 872* shall not apply or have effect in relation to such information.

[(9) This section ceases to have effect for the year of assessment 2011 and each subsequent year of assessment.][4]][5]

Amendments

[1] Substituted by FA08 s10. As respects the year of assessment 2008 and subsequent years of assessment.

[2] Substituted by FA07 s9(1)(c)(i). Applies with effect from 2 April 2007

[3] Inserted by FA07 s9(1)(c)(ii). Applies with effect from 2 April 2007

[4] Inserted by FA11 s12. Deemed to have come into force and takes effect as on and from 1 January 2011.

[5] Inserted by FA01 s11(1)(b). Applies as respects the year of assessment 2001 and subsequent years of assessment.

Cross References

From Section 472C

Section 16 Income tax charged by deduction.

Section 458 Deductions allowed in ascertaining taxable income and provisions relating to reductions in tax.

Section 872 Use of information relating to other taxes and duties.

Section 1017 Assessment of husband in respect of income of both spouses.

To Section 472C

Section 458 Deductions allowed in ascertaining taxable income and provisions relating to reductions in tax.

Section 1024 Method of apportioning reliefs and charging tax in cases of separate assessments.

472D Relief for key employees engaged in research and development activities

[(1) In this section—

'*associated company*', in relation to a relevant employer, means a company which is that employer's associated company within the meaning of *section 432*;

'*control*' has the same meaning as in *section 432*;

'*emoluments*' has the same meaning as in *Chapter 4* of *Part 42*;

'*key employee*' means an individual—

(a) who—

(i) is not, and has not been, a director of his or her employer or an associated company and is not connected to such a director,

(ii) does not, and did not, have a material interest in his or her employer or an associated company and is not connected to a person who has such a material interest, and

(iii) in the accounting period for which his or her employer was entitled to claim relief under *section 766(2)*, performed [50 per cent][1] or more of the duties of his or her employment in the conception or creation of new knowledge, products, processes, methods or systems,

and

(b) [50 per cent][2] or more of the cost of [whose emoluments][3] that arise from his or her employment with that relevant employer qualify as expenditure on research and development under *section 766(1)(a)* in the accounting period referred to in *paragraph (a)(iii)*;

'*material interest*', in relation to a company, means the beneficial ownership of or ability to control, directly or through the medium of a connected company or connected companies or by any other indirect means, more than 5 percent of the ordinary share capital of the company;

'*ordinary share capital*', in relation to a company, means all the issued share capital (by whatever name called) of the company;

'*relevant emoluments*' means emoluments paid by a relevant employer to a key employee;

'*relevant employer*' means a company that is entitled to relief under *section 766(2)* and that employs a key employee;

'*tax year*' means a year of assessment for income tax purposes.

[(2) (a) Where, as respects an accounting period, a relevant employer surrenders an amount under *section 766(2A)* for the benefit of a key employee, then subject to *subsection (3)*, on the making of a claim, that employee shall be entitled for a tax year to have the income tax charged on his or her relevant emoluments for that tax year reduced by the amount surrendered.

(b) The tax year referred to in *paragraph (a)* is the tax year following the tax year during which the accounting period, referred to in that paragraph, of the relevant employer ends.

(c) Notwithstanding that, for the tax year for which a claim is made under this section, an employee is no longer a key employee of the company that surrendered an amount referred to in *paragraph (a)* but is an employee of that company, then he or she shall be entitled to have the income tax charged on emoluments from that company for that tax year reduced by the amount so referred to.][4]

(3) (a) Notwithstanding *subsection (2)*, the amount surrendered under *section 766(2A)* shall not for any tax year reduce the amount of income tax payable on the total income of [the employee concerned or][5], where *section 1017* or *1019* [applies][6], on the total income of his or her spouse or his or her civil partner to not less than the income tax that would be charged if such total income were charged to income tax at a rate of 23 per cent.

[(b) *Paragraph (a)* also applies where—

(i) *paragraph (a)* or *(b)* of *subsection (4)* applies, or

(ii) *subsection (2)* and *paragraph (a)* or *(b)* of *subsection (4)* apply for the same tax year.][7]

(4) (a) Where, by virtue of *subsection (3)*, part of the amount surrendered under *section 766(2A)* by a relevant employer to a key employee cannot be used by that employee to reduce the income tax charged on his or her [emoluments from that employer][8] for the tax year referred to in *subsection (2)(b)*, that employee shall be entitled to have the income tax charged on his or her [emoluments from that employer][9] for the next tax year reduced by that part.

(b) If and so far as any part of the amount surrendered by a relevant employer under *section 766(2A)* to a key employee carried forward under *paragraph (a)* to the next tax year cannot be used in that next tax year, then it may be used in the next following tax year and so on for each succeeding tax year until the full amount of that part has been used or until the key employee referred to in *paragraph (a)* ceases to be an employee of the relevant employer that surrendered the amount under *section 766(2A)*.

(5) The amount that a relevant employer is entitled to surrender, and so surrenders, under *section 766(2A)* to a key employee is exempt from income tax and shall not be reckoned in computing income for the purposes of the Income Tax Acts.

[(6) No reduction in income tax shall be given under this section for any tax year unless all tax deductible for that tax year from emoluments paid by the employer to the employee to whom the amount was surrendered has been remitted by that employer to the Collector-General in accordance with regulations made under *Chapter 4* of *Part 42*.][10]

[...][11]

(9) Where for a tax year, [an individual makes a claim for relief under this section or has the income tax charged on his or her emoluments reduced as a consequence of a claim under this section][12], the individual shall, notwithstanding anything to the contrary in [*Part 41A* or *section 1084*][13], be deemed for that tax year to be a chargeable person for the purposes of [*Part 41A*][14].][15]

Amendments

[1,2] Substituted by FA13 s5(a). Deemed to have come into force and takes effect on and from 1 January 2013.

[3] Substituted by F(No.2)A13 s13(a). Comes into operation on 1 January 2014.

[4] Substituted by F(No.2)A13 s13(b). Comes into operation on 1 January 2014.

[5] Substituted by F(No.2)A13 s13(c)(i)(I). Comes into operation on 1 January 2014.

[6] Substituted by F(No.2)A13 s13(c)(i)(II). Comes into operation on 1 January 2014.

[7] Substituted by F(No.2)A13 s13(c)(ii). Comes into operation on 1 January 2014.

[8,9] Substituted by F(No.2)A13 s13(d). Comes into operation on 1 January 2014.

[10] Substituted by F(No.2)A13 s13(e). Comes into operation on 1 January 2014.

[11] Deleted by F(No.2)A13 s13(f). Comes into operation on 1 January 2014.

[12] Substituted by F(No.2)A13 s13(g). Comes into operation on 1 January 2014.

[13] Substituted by FA13 s92 and sched1(part 2)(d)(i).

[14] Substituted by FA13 s92 and sched1(part 2)(d)(ii).

[15] Inserted by FA12 s8. Deemed to have come into force and takes effect on and from 1 January 2012.

Note:

FA13 s92 applies—

(a) in the case of a chargeable period (within the meaning of section 321(2)) which is an accounting period of a company, as respects chargeable periods that start on or after 1 January 2013, and

(b) in a case other than that referred to in paragraph (a), as respects the year of assessment (within the meaning of section 2(1)) 2013 and subsequent years of assessment.

473 Allowance for rent paid by certain tenants

[ITA67 s142A and 195B(3) and (6); FA82 s5(1); FA85 s7(a); FA91 s8; FA93 s10(1); FA95 s5]

(1) In this section—

["*appropriate percentage*", in relation to a year of assessment, means a percentage equal to the standard rate of tax for that year;][1]

"*residential premises*" means property held under a tenancy, being—

(a) a building or part of a building used or suitable for use as a dwelling, and

(b) land which the occupier of a building or part of a building used as a dwelling has for his or her own occupation and enjoyment with the building or part of a building as its garden or grounds of an ornamental nature;

"*rent*" includes any periodical payment in the nature of rent made in return for a special possession of residential premises or for the use, occupation or enjoyment of residential premises, but does not include so much of any rent or payment as—

(a) is paid or made to defray the cost of maintenance of or repairs to residential premises for which in the absence of agreement to the contrary the tenant would be liable,

(b) relates to the provision of goods or services,

(c) relates to any right or benefit other than the bare right to use, occupy and enjoy residential premises, or

(d) is the subject of a right of reimbursement or a subsidy from any source enjoyed by the person making the payment, unless such reimbursement or subsidy cannot be obtained;

["*specified limit*", in relation to an individual for a year of assessment specified in column (1) of the Table to this definition, means—

(a) in the case of—

(i) [a married person assessed to tax in accordance with *section 1017*, or a civil partner assessed to tax in accordance with *section 1031C*,][2] or

(ii) [a widowed person or a surviving civil partner][3],

the corresponding amount specified in column (2) of the Table to this definition; but, if at any time during the year of assessment the individual was of the age of 55 years or over, "*specified limit*" means the corresponding amount specified in column (3) of the Table to this definition, and

(b) in any other case, the corresponding amount specified in column (3) of the Table to this definition; but, if at any time during the year of assessment the individual was of the age of 55 years or over, "*specified limit*" means the corresponding amount specified in column (5) of the Table to this definition;

TABLE

(1)	(2)	(3)	(4)	(5)
	€	€	€	€
2011	3,200	6,400	1,600	3,200
2012	2,400	4,800	1,200	2,400
2013	2,000	[4,000][4]	1,000	2,000
2014	1,600	3,200	800	1,600
2015	1,200	2,400	600	1,200
2016	800	1,600	400	800
2017	400	800	200	400
2018	0	0	0	0
				][5]

"*tenancy*" includes any contract, agreement or licence under or in respect of which rent is paid, but does not include—

(a) a tenancy which apart from any statutory extension is a tenancy for a freehold estate or interest or for a definite period of 50 years or more,

(b) a tenancy in relation to which the person beneficially entitled to the rent is a Minister of the Government, the Commissioners of Public Works in Ireland or a housing authority for the purposes of the Housing Act, 1966, or

(c) a tenancy in relation to which an agreement or provision exists under which the rent paid or part of it is or may be treated as consideration or part consideration, in whatever form, for the creation of a further or greater estate, tenancy or interest in the residential premises concerned or in any other property.

[(1A) (a) This section shall not apply as respects rent paid on or after 8 December 2010.

(b) Notwithstanding *paragraph (a)*, this section shall continue to apply for the year of assessment 2010 and each subsequent year of assessment up to and including the year of assessment 2017 in respect of rent paid by a tenant who on 7 December 2010 is paying rent under a tenancy.][6]

[(2) Where an individual (in this section referred to as the "*claimant*") proves that in the year of assessment he or she has made a payment on account of rent in respect of residential premises which, during the period in respect of which the payment was made, was his or her main residence, the income tax to be charged on the claimant, other than in accordance with *section 16(2)*, for that year of assessment shall be reduced by an amount which is the least of—

(a) the amount equal to the appropriate percentage of the aggregate of such payments proved to be so made,

(b) the appropriate percentage of the specified limit in relation to the claimant for the year of assessment, and

(c) the amount that reduces that income tax to nil.][7]

[(3) For the purposes of this section, where a claimant is [a married person assessed to tax for the year of assessment in accordance with *section 1017*, or a civil partner assessed to tax for the year of assessment in accordance with *section 1031C*,][8] any payments made by the claimant's [spouse or civil partner][9], in respect of which that [spouse or civil partner][10] would have been entitled to relief under this section if he or she were assessed to tax for the year of assessment in accordance with [*section 1016* (apart from *subsection (2)* of that section) or *section 1031B* (apart from *subsection (2)* of that section)][11], shall be deemed to have been made by the claimant.][12]

(4) (a) Where a payment is made partly on account of rent and partly on account of anything which is not rent, such apportionment of the payment shall be made as is necessary in order to determine for the purposes of this section the amount paid on account of rent.

(b) Any apportionment required by this subsection shall be made by the inspector according to the best of his or her knowledge and judgment.

(5) Where a payment on account of rent is made in respect of any period, that payment shall be deemed for the purposes of this section to be made in the year in which the period falls; but, if the period falls partly in one year and partly in another year, the amount of the payment made in respect of that period shall be apportioned to each year in the proportion which the part of the period falling in that year bears to the whole of the period, and the amount so apportioned to a year shall be deemed for the purposes of this section to be paid in that year.

(6) (a) Any claim for relief under this section in respect of rent paid in a year of assessment shall be accompanied by—

(i) a certificate and statement, in a form prescribed by the Revenue Commissioners, signed by the claimant setting out—

(I) the name, address and income tax reference number of the claimant,

(II) the name, address and, as may be appropriate, the income tax or corporation tax reference number of the person or body of persons beneficially entitled to the rent under the tenancy under which the rent was paid,

(III) the postal address of the premises in respect of which the rent was paid, and

(IV) full particulars of the tenancy under which the rent was paid,

and

(ii) a receipt or acknowledgement in respect of such rent given in accordance with *subsection (8)*.

(b) Failure to furnish any of the particulars mentioned in *paragraph (a)(i)* or failure to furnish a receipt or acknowledgement mentioned in *paragraph (a)(ii)* shall be grounds for refusal of the claim; but—

(i) the inspector may waive the requirement at *paragraph (a)(i)(II)* on receipt of satisfactory proof that the claimant's inability to comply with that requirement is bona fide, and

(ii) the inspector may waive the requirements at *paragraph (a)(ii)* on receipt of satisfactory proof of the total rent paid in the relevant period and on being furnished with the name and address of the person or body of persons to whom it was paid.

(7) (a) Any person aggrieved by a decision of the inspector on any question arising under *subsection (4)* or *(6)* may, by notice in writing to that effect given to the inspector within 30 days from the date on which notice of the decision is given to that person, make an application to have his or her claim for relief heard and determined by the Appeal Commissioners.

(b) Where an application is made under *paragraph (a)*, the Appeal Commissioners shall hear and determine the claim in the like manner as an appeal made to them against an assessment to income tax, and the provisions of the Income Tax Acts relating to such an appeal (including the provisions relating to the rehearing of an appeal and to the statement of a case for the opinion of the High Court on a point of law) shall apply accordingly with any necessary modifications.

(8) (a) Where a person (in this subsection referred to as "*the tenant*") who is entitled to relief under this section for a year of assessment, or who has reason to believe that he or she may be so entitled, requests a receipt or acknowledgement of the rent paid by him or her in that year, the person or body of persons beneficially entitled to the rent shall, within 7 days from the date of the request, give to the tenant a receipt or acknowledgement of the rent paid by the tenant in that year of assessment.

(b) Any receipt or acknowledgement given in accordance with this subsection shall be in writing and shall contain—

(i) the name and address of the tenant,

(ii) the name, address and, as may be appropriate, the income tax or corporation tax reference number of the person or body of persons giving the receipt or acknowledgement, and

(iii) the amount of the rent paid in the year of assessment and the period within that year in respect of which it is paid.

(9) (a) The Revenue Commissioners may make regulations, for the purpose of giving effect to this section, with respect to the allowance granted by this section, or to any matter ancillary or incidental thereto, or, in particular and without prejudice to the generality of the foregoing, to provide for—

(i) the proof by a claimant of a payment on account of rent,

(ii) the disclosure of information by a person in receipt of a payment on account of rent,

(iii) the maintenance of records and the production to and inspection by persons authorised by the Revenue Commissioners of such records and the taking by such persons of copies of or of extracts from such records, and

(iv) appeals with respect to matters arising under the regulations which would not otherwise be the subject of an appeal.

(b) Every regulation made under this section shall be laid before Dáil Éireann as soon as may be after it is made and, if a resolution annulling the regulation is passed by Dáil Éireann within the next 21 days on which Dáil Éireann has sat after the regulation is laid before it, the regulation shall be annulled accordingly, but without prejudice to the validity of anything previously done thereunder.

[(10) Any relief under this section shall be in substitution for and not in addition to any relief to which the claimant might be entitled in respect of the same payment under any other provision of the Income Tax Acts.][13]

Amendments

[1] Inserted by FA00 s13(a)(i). Applies as respects the year of assessment 2000-2001 and subsequent years of assessment.

[2] Substituted by F(No.3)A11 sched1(104).

[3] Substituted by F(No.3)A11 sched1(105).

[4] Substituted by FA12 sched6(1)(d). Has effect as on and from 31 March 2012.

[5] Substituted by FA11 s14(a).

[6] Inserted by FA11 s14(b).

[7] Substituted by FA00 s13(b). Applies as respects the year of assessment 2000-2001 and subsequent years of assessment.

[8] Substituted by F(No.3)A11 sched1(106).

[9, 10] Substituted by F(No.3)A11 sched1(107).

[11] Substituted by F(No.3)A11 sched1(108).

[12] Substituted by FA00 s13(c). Applies as respects the year of assessment 2000-2001 and subsequent years of assessment.

[13] Substituted by FA00 s13(d). Applies as respects the year of assessment 2000-2001 and subsequent years of assessment.

Revenue Briefings

Tax Briefing

Tax Briefing September 2009 – Issue 73 – Rent to buy and similar schemes

Revenue Precedents

Whether property for which rent paid must be situated in the State; whether land lord must be resident in the State? No requirement that property must be in the State or that landlord must be resident in the State. IT902028

A housing authority for the purposes of the Housing act, 1966? A county council, A county borough corporation, A borough corporation, An urban district council or Town commissioners. IT 95 1622

Cross References

From Section 473

Section 16 Income tax charged by deduction.
Section 1016 Assessment as single persons.
Section 1017 Assessment of husband in respect of income of both spouses.

To Section 473

Section 458 Deductions allowed in ascertaining taxable income and provisions relating to reductions in tax.
Section 1024 Method of apportioning reliefs and charging tax in cases of separate assessments.
Schedule 29 Provisions Referred to in Sections 1052, 1053 and 1054
Schedule 31 Consequential Amendments

473A Relief for fees paid for third level education, etc

[(1) In this section—

"*academic year*", in relation to an approved course, means a year of study commencing on a date not earlier than the 1st day of August in a year of assessment;

"*appropriate percentage*", in relation to a year of assessment, means a percentage equal to the standard rate of tax for that year;

"*approved college*", in relation to a year of assessment, means—

(a) a college or institution of higher education in the State which—

(i) provides courses to which [a scheme or schemes of grants approved by the Minister under the Student Support Act 2011][1], applies, or

(ii) operates in accordance with a code of standards which from time to time may, with the consent of the Minister for Finance, be laid down by the Minister, and which the Minister approves for the purposes of this section;

(b) any university or similar institution of higher education in a Member State of the European Union (other than the State) which—

(i) is maintained or assisted by recurrent grants from public funds of that or any other Member State of the European Union (including the State), or

(ii) is a duly accredited university or institution of higher education in the Member State in which it is situated;

(c) a college or institution in another Member State of the European Union providing distance education in the State, which—

(i) provides courses to which [a scheme or schemes of grants approved by the Minister under the Student Support Act 2011][2], applies, or

(ii) operates in accordance with a code of standards which from time to time may, with the consent of the Minister for Finance, be laid down by the Minister, and which the Minister approves for the purposes of this section;

(d) any university or similar institution of higher education in any country, other than the State or a Member State of the European Union which—

(i) is maintained or assisted by recurrent grants from public funds of that country, or

(ii) is a duly accredited university or institution of higher education in the country in which it is situated;

"*approved course*" means—

(a) a full-time or part-time undergraduate course of study provided by a college to which *paragraph (a)*, *(b)* or *(c)* of the definition of "*approved college*" relates which—

(i) is of at least 2 academic years' duration, and

(ii) in the case of a course provided by a college to which *paragraph (a)(ii)* or *(c)(ii)* of the definition of "*approved college*" relates, the Minister, having regard to a code of standards which from time to time may, with the consent of the Minister for Finance, be laid down by the Minister in relation to the quality of education to be offered on such approved course, approves of for the purposes of this section;

(b) a postgraduate course of study leading to a postgraduate award, based on a thesis or on the results of an examination or both, in an approved college—

(i) of not less than one academic year, but not more than 4 academic years, in duration,

(ii) that requires an individual, undertaking the course, to have been conferred with a degree or an equivalent qualification, and

(iii) that, in the case of a course provided by a college to which *paragraph (a)(ii)* of the definition of "*approved college*" relates, the Minister, having regard to any code of standards which from time to time may, with the consent of the Minister for Finance, be laid down by the Minister in relation to the quality of education to be offered on such approved course, approves for the purposes of this section;

[...][3]

"*the Minister*" means the Minister for Education and Science;

"*qualifying fees*", in relation to an approved course and an academic year, means the amount of fees chargeable in respect of tuition to be provided in relation to that course in that year which, with the consent of the Minister for Finance, the Minister approves of for the purposes of this section.

(2) Subject to this section, where an individual for a year of assessment proves that he or she has, [...][4] made a payment in respect of qualifying fees in respect of an approved course for the academic year in relation to that course commencing in that year of assessment, the income tax to be charged on the individual for that year of assessment, other than in accordance with *section 16(2)*, shall be reduced by an amount which is the lesser of—

(a) the amount equal to the appropriate percentage of the aggregate of all such payments proved to be so made, and

(b) the amount which reduces that income tax to nil.

(3) In the case of an individual who is [a married person assessed to tax for the year of assessment in accordance with *section 1017*, or a civil partner assessed to tax for the year of assessment in accordance with *section 1031C*,][5] any payment in respect of qualifying fees made by the individual's [spouse or civil partner][6] shall, except where [*section 1023* or *1031H*][7] applies, be deemed to have been made by the individual.

[(4) For the purposes of this section, a payment in respect of qualifying fees shall be regarded as not having been made in so far as any sum in respect of, or by reference to, such fees—

(a) has been or is to be received, directly or indirectly, by the individual or, as the case may be, the person by whom the course is being, or was, undertaken, from any source whatever by means of grant, scholarship or otherwise, or

(b) is refunded or partly refunded by an approved college.][8]

[(4A) In any claim or claims for relief under this section made by an individual in respect of qualifying fees—

(a) where the qualifying fees, or part of the qualifying fees, the subject of the claim or claims concerned relate to a full-time course or full-time courses—

(i) for the year of assessment 2013 there shall be disregarded the first €2,500 or the full amount of those fees, whichever is the lesser,

(ii) for the year of assessment 2014 there shall be disregarded the first €2,750 or the full amount of those fees, whichever is the lesser, and

(iii) for the year of assessment 2015 and each subsequent year of assessment there shall be disregarded the first €3,000 or the full amount of those fees, whichever is the lesser,

(b) where all the qualifying fees the subject of the claim or claims concerned relate only to a part-time course or part-time courses—

(i) for the year of assessment 2013 there shall be disregarded the first €1,250 or the full amount of those fees, whichever is the lesser,

(ii) for the year of assessment 2014 there shall be disregarded the first €1,375 or the full amount of those fees, whichever is the lesser, and

(iii) for the year of assessment 2015 and each subsequent year of assessment there shall be disregarded the first €1,500 or the full amount of those fees, whichever is the lesser.][9]

(5) (a) Where the Minister is satisfied that an approved college, within the meaning of *paragraph (a)(ii)* or *(c)(ii)* of the definition of "*approved college*", or an approved course in that college, no longer meets the appropriate code of standards laid down, the Minister may by notice in writing given to the approved college withdraw, with effect from the year of assessment following the year of assessment in which the notice is given, the approval of that college or course, as the case may be, for the purposes of this section.

(b) Where the Minister withdraws the approval of any college or course for the purposes of this section, notice of its withdrawal shall be published as soon as may be in *Iris Oifigiúil*.

(6) Any claim for relief under this section made by an individual in respect of fees paid to an approved college shall be accompanied by a statement in writing made by the approved college concerned stating each of the following, namely—

(a) that the college is an approved college for the purposes of this section,

(b) the details of the course undertaken [...][10]

(c) the duration of the course, and

(d) the amount of the fees paid in respect of the course.

(7) Where for the purposes of this section any question arises as to whether—

(a) a college is an approved college, or

(b) a course of study is an approved course, the Revenue Commissioners may consult with the Minister.

(8) On or before 1 July in each year of assessment, the Minister shall furnish the Revenue Commissioners with full details of—

(a) all colleges and courses in respect of which approval has been granted and not withdrawn for the purposes of this section, and

(b) the amount of the qualifying fees in respect of each such course for the academic year commencing in that year of assessment.

[(9) Where relief is given under this section to any individual in respect of a payment of qualifying fees, relief shall not be given under any other provision of the Income Tax Acts to that individual in respect of that payment.][11]][12]

[(10) Where any fees that are the subject of a claim for relief under this section are refunded or partly refunded by an approved college, it shall be the duty of the individual by whom the claim is made to notify the Revenue Commissioners within 21 days of receipt of such refund that the refund has been received.][13]

Amendments

[1] Substituted by FA14 sched3(1)(c)(i). Has effect on and from 23 December 2014.

[2] Substituted by FA14 sched3(1)(c)(ii). Has effect on and from 23 December 2014.

[3] Deleted by FA07 s9(1)(d)(i). Applies as respects the year of assessment 2007 and subsequent years of assessment.

[4] Deleted by FA07 s9(1)(d)(ii). Applies as respects the year of assessment 2007 and subsequent years of assessment.

[5] Substituted by F(No.3)A11 sched1(109).

[6] Substituted by F(No.3)A11 sched1(110).

[7] Substituted by F(No.3)A11 sched1(111).

[8] Substituted by F(No.2)A13 s14(a)(i). Comes into operation on 1 January 2014.

[9] Substituted by FA13 s11. Deemed to have come into force and takes effect on and from 1 January 2013.

[10] Deleted by FA07 s9(1)(d)(iv). Applies as respects the year of assessment 2007 and subsequent years of assessment.

[11] Inserted by FA07 s9(1)(d)(v). Applies as respects the year of assessment 2007 and subsequent years of assessment.

[12] Inserted by FA01 s29(1).

[13] Inserted by F(No.2)A13 s14(a)(ii). Comes into operation on 1 January 2014.

Cross References

From Section 473A

Section 16 Income tax charged by deduction.
Section 1017 Assessment of husband in respect of income of both spouses.
Section 1023 Application for separate assessments.

To Section 473A

Section 458 Deductions allowed in ascertaining taxable income and provisions relating to reductions in tax.
Section 766 Tax credit for research and development expenditure.
Section 1024 Method of apportioning reliefs and charging tax in cases of separate assessments.

474 Relief for fees paid to private colleges for full-time third level education [Repealed]

Repealed by FA01 s29(3).

474A Relief for fees paid to publicly funded colleges in the European Union for full-time third level education [Repealed]

Repealed by FA01 s29(3).

475 Relief for fees paid for part-time third level education [Repealed]

Repealed by FA01 s29(3).

475A Relief for postgraduate fees [Repealed]

Repealed by FA01 s29(3).

476 Relief for fees paid for training courses

[FA97 s8(1) to (7) and (10) and (11)]

(1) In this section—

"*An Foras*" means An Foras Áiseanna Saothair;

["*appropriate percentage*" means, in relation to a year of assessment, a percentage equal to the standard rate of tax for that year;][1]

"*approved course provider*" means a person providing approved courses who—

(a) operates in accordance with a code of standards which from time to time may, with the consent of the Minister for Finance, be agreed between An Foras and the Minister, and

(b) is approved of by An Foras for the purposes of this section;

"*approved course*" means a course of study or training, other than a postgraduate course, provided by an approved course provider which—

(a) is confined to—

(i) such aspects of information technology, or

(ii) such foreign languages,

as are approved of by the Minister, with the consent of the Minister for Finance, for the purposes of this section,

(b) is of less than 2 years' duration,

(c) results in the awarding of a certificate of competence, and

(d) having regard to a code of standards which from time to time may, with the consent of the Minister for Finance, be agreed between An Foras and the Minister in relation to—

(i) the quality and standard of training to be provided on the approved course, and

(ii) the methods and facilities to be used by the course provider in delivering the course and in assessing competence,

is approved of by An Foras for the purposes of this section;

"*certificate of competence*", in relation to an approved course, means a certificate awarded in accordance with the standards set out in the code of standards referred to in *paragraph (d)* of the definition of "*approved course*" and certifying that a minimum level of competence has been achieved by the individual to whom the certificate is awarded;

[…][2]

"*foreign language*" means a language other than an official language of the State;

"*the Minister*" means the Minister for Enterprise, Trade and Employment;

"*qualifying fees*", in relation to an approved course, means the amount of fees chargeable in respect of tuition to be provided in relation to such course where the net amount of such fees are not less than [€315][3] and to the extent that they do not exceed [€1,270][4].

[(2) Subject to this section, where an individual proves that—

(a) he or she has, […][5] made a payment in respect of qualifying fees in respect of an approved course, and

(b) the individual in respect of whom the fees are paid has been awarded a certificate of competence in respect of that course,

the income tax to be charged on the individual, other than in accordance with *section 16(2)*, for the year of assessment in which that certificate of competence is awarded shall be reduced by an amount which is the lesser of—

(i) the amount equal to the appropriate percentage of the aggregate of all such payments proved to be so made, and

(ii) the amount which reduces that income tax to nil.

(3) In the case of an individual who is [a married person assessed to tax for the year of assessment in accordance with *section 1017*, or a civil partner assessed to tax for the year of assessment in accordance with *section 1031C*,][6] any payment in respect of qualifying fees made by the individual's [spouse or civil partner][7] shall, except where [*section 1023* or *1031H*][8] applies, be deemed to have been made by the individual.][9]

(4) Relief under this section shall not be given in respect of an individual for a year of assessment in respect of more than one approved course.

(5) For the purposes of this section, a payment in respect of qualifying fees shall be regarded as not having been made in so far as any sum, in respect of or by reference to such fees, has been or is to be received either directly or indirectly by an individual from any source whatever by means of grant, scholarship or otherwise.

(6) An Foras, where it is satisfied that an approved course provider, or an approved course provided by an approved course provider, no longer meets the appropriate code of standards laid down, may by notice in writing given to the approved course provider withdraw the approval of that course provider or approved course, as the case may be, from such date as it considers appropriate, and this section shall cease to apply to that course provider or that course, as the case may be, with effect from that date.

(7) (a) As soon as may be practicable after An Foras has—

(i) approved a course provider or a course for the purposes of this section, or

(ii) withdrawn such approval,

An Foras shall notify the Revenue Commissioners in writing of such approval or withdrawal of approval.

(b) Where any question arises as to whether for the purposes of this section—

(i) a course provider is an approved course provider, or

(ii) a training course is an approved course,

the Revenue Commissioners may consult with An Foras.

(8) Any relief under this section shall be in substitution for and not in addition to any relief to which the individual might be entitled to in respect of the same payment under any other provision of the Income Tax Acts.

(9) This section shall come into operation on such date as may be fixed by order of the Minister for Finance.[][10]

Amendments

[1] Inserted by FA00 s21(1)(e)(i)(I). Applies as respects the year of assessment 2000-2001 and subsequent years of assessment.

[2] Deleted by FA08 sched8(1)(g)(i). Deemed to have come into force and have taken effect as respects the year of assessment 2007 and subsequent years of assessment.

[3, 4] Substituted by FA01 sched5.

[5] Deleted by FA08 sched8(1)(g)(ii). Deemed to have come into force and have taken effect as respects the year of assessment 2007 and subsequent years of assessment.

[6] Substituted by F(No.3)A11 sched1(112).

[7] Substituted by F(No.3)A11 sched1(113).

[8] Substituted by F(No.3)A11 sched1(114).

[9] Substituted by FA00 s21(1)(e)(ii). Applies as respects the year of assessment 2000-2001 and subsequent years of assessment.

[10] With effect from 31 March 1998 per S.I. 87 of 1998.

Revenue Briefings

Tax Briefing

Tax Briefing December 1998 – Issue 34 pg 7 – Training Courses, IT and Foreign Languages
Tax Briefing May 2003 – Issue 52 pg 16 – Relief for Tuition Fees

Revenue Information Notes

Lists of approved courses and approved course providers are available on the Revenue website

Cross References

From Section 476

Section 16 Income tax charged by deduction.

Section 1017 Assessment of husband in respect of income of both spouses.

Section 1023 Application for separate assessments.

To Section 476

Section 458 Deductions allowed in ascertaining taxable income and provisions relating to reductions in tax.

Section 1024 Method of apportioning reliefs and charging tax in cases of separate assessments.

477 Relief for service charges

[(1) In this section—

"*appropriate percentage*", in relation to a year of assessment, means a percentage equal to the standard rate of tax for that year;

"*claimant*" has the meaning assigned to it by *subsection (2)*;

"*financial year*", in relation to any year, means the period of 12 months ending on 31 December in that year;

"*group water supply scheme*" means a scheme referred to in the Housing (Improvement Grants) Regulations 1983 (S.I. No. 330 of 1983);

"*service*" means the provision by or on behalf of a local authority of—

(a) a supply of water for domestic purposes,

(b) domestic refuse collection or disposal, or

(c) domestic sewage disposal facilities;

"*service charge*" means a charge imposed under—

(a) the Local Government (Financial Provisions) (No. 2) Act 1983, or

(b) section 65A (inserted by the Local Government (Sanitary Services) Act 1962, and amended by the Local Government (Financial Provisions) (No. 2) Act 1983) of the Public Health (Ireland) Act 1878,

in respect of the provision by a local authority of any service or services;

"*specified amount*", in relation to a claimant, means the lesser of—

(a) the amount proved to have been paid in the financial year immediately before the year of assessment in respect of service charges, or

(b) €400,

but if, in respect of the financial year ended on 31 December 2005 a claimant proves that he or she paid an amount greater than €400 by way of a fixed annual charge, then, in relation to that claimant, the specified amount for the year of assessment 2006 shall mean the amount proved to have been so paid.

(2) Where in relation to income tax for a year of assessment an individual (in this section referred to as a "*claimant*") proves that in the financial year immediately before the year of assessment he or she has paid service charges for that financial year, the income tax to be charged on the claimant for that year of assessment, other than in accordance with *section 16(2)*, shall, subject to *subsection (3)*, be reduced by an amount which is the lesser of—

(a) the amount equal to the appropriate percentage of the specified amount, and

(b) the amount which reduces that income tax to nil.

(3) (a) In the case of a claimant assessed to tax for the year of assessment in accordance with *section 1017*, any payments made by the spouse of the claimant, in respect of which that spouse would have been entitled to relief under this section if the spouse were assessed to tax for the year of assessment in accordance with *section 1016* (apart from *subsection (2)* of that section), shall be deemed to have been made by the claimant.

[(aa) In the case of a claimant assessed to tax for the year of assessment in accordance with *section 1031C*, any payments made by the civil partner of the claimant, in respect of which that civil partner would have been entitled to relief under this section if the civil partner were assessed to tax for the year of assessment in accordance with *section 1031B* (apart from *subsection (2)* of that section), shall be deemed to have been made by the claimant.][1]

(b) In the case of an individual who resides on a full-time basis in the premises to which the service charges relate and pays such service charges on behalf of the claimant, that claimant may disclaim the relief provided by this section in favour of the individual, and such disclaimer shall be in such form as the Revenue Commissioners may require.

(4) Where the service consists of the provision of domestic refuse collection or disposal, is provided and charged for by a person or body of persons other than a local authority, and where such person or body of persons has—

(a) notified its provision to the local authority in whose functional area such service is provided, and

(b) furnished to that local authority such information as the local authority may from time to time request concerning that person or body of persons or the service provided by that person or body of persons,

the service provided shall be deemed for the purposes of this section as having been provided on behalf of the local authority and a payment in respect of such service shall be deemed a payment in respect of service charges.

(5) The provision of a supply of water for domestic purposes effected by a group water supply scheme shall be treated for the purposes of this section as if it were provided on behalf of a local authority, and a payment by an individual member of such a scheme in respect of such provision shall be deemed to be a payment in respect of service charges.

(6) Where a person makes a claim for relief under this section they shall, when requested by the Revenue Commissioners, indicate the name of the local authority, or person referred to in *subsection (4)* who provides the service on behalf of a local authority, and whether the charge consists of either or both of—

(a) a charge which is a fixed annual charge, or

(b) a charge determined by other means.

(7) Any deduction made under this section shall be in substitution for and not in addition to any deduction to which the individual might be entitled in respect of the same payment under any other provision of the Income Tax Acts.][2]

[(8) This section ceases to have effect as respects service charges paid in the financial year 2011 for that financial year and subsequent financial years for those financial years.][3]

Amendments

[1] Inserted by F(No.3)A11 sched1(115).

[2] Substituted by FA06 s8. Applies as respects the year of assessment 2006 and subsequent years of assessment.

[3] Inserted by FA10 s12. Deemed to have come into force and takes effect as on and from 1 January 2010.

Revenue Briefings

Tax Briefing

Tax Briefing March 1996 – Issue 21 pg 4 – Relief for Service Charges

Revenue Information Notes

IT27 – Tax Relief for Service Charges

Cross References

From Section 477

Section 16 Income tax charged by deduction.

Section 1016 Assessment as single persons.

Section 1017 Assessment of husband in respect of income of both spouses.

To Section 477

Section 458 Deductions allowed in ascertaining taxable income and provisions relating to reductions in tax.

Section 1024 Method of apportioning reliefs and charging tax in cases of separate assessments.

Schedule 29 Provisions Referred to in Sections 1052, 1053 and 1054

477A Relief for energy efficient works [Repealed]

Repealed by F(No.2)A13 s5(a)(i).

477B Home renovation incentive

[(1) In this section—

"*contractor'* means a person engaged by an individual to carry out qualifying work, and who is an accountable person under *section 5* of the Value-Added Tax Consolidation Act 2010 and has been assigned a registration number under *section 65* of that Act;

"*PPS number*", in relation to an individual, means the individual's personal public service number within the meaning of *section 262* of the Social Welfare Consolidation Act 2005;

"*qualifying contractor*" means a contractor who—

(a) complies with the obligations referred to in *section 530G* or *530H*, as the case may be, or

(b) in the case of a contractor who is not a subcontractor to whom *Chapter 2* of *Part 18* applies, complies with the obligations referred to in *paragraph (a)*, other than the obligations referred to in *paragraphs (a)* and *(b)* of *subsection (1)* of *section 530G* or *530H*, as the case may be;

"*qualifying expenditure*", in relation to an individual, means expenditure incurred by the individual on qualifying work carried out by a qualifying contractor on a qualifying residence;

'*qualifying residence*', in relation to an individual, means a residential premises situate in the State—

(a) which is owned by the individual and which is occupied by the individual as his or her only or main residence,

(b) which has previously been occupied as a residence and has been acquired by the individual for the purposes of occupation by the individual as his or her only or main residence on completion of the qualifying work and which is so occupied upon completion,

(c) which is owned by an individual and occupied by a tenant under a tenancy for which registration is required under *Part 7* of the Residential Tenancies Act 2004, and where such registration requirements have been complied with by the individual, or

(d) which is owned by an individual and which is intended by the individual to be occupied by a tenant under a tenancy for which registration is required under *Part 7* of the Residential Tenancies Act 2004, and where such registration requirements have been complied with by the individual and which is occupied by a tenant within 6 months of completion of the qualifying work;][1]

"*qualifying work*" means any work of repair, renovation or improvement to which the rate of tax specified in *section 46(1)(c)* of the Value-Added Tax Consolidation Act 2010 applies, and which is carried out on a qualifying residence;

['*rental unit*' means—

(a) part of a building used, or suitable for use, as a dwelling which is occupied by a tenant under a tenancy for which registration is required under *Part 7* of the Residential Tenancies Act 2004, and where such registration requirements have been complied with, or

(b) part of a building used, or suitable for use, as a dwelling which is owned by an individual and which is intended by the individual to be occupied by a tenant under a tenancy for which registration is required under *Part 7* of the Residential Tenancies Act 2004, and where such registration requirements have been complied with by the individual and which is occupied by a tenant within 6 months of completion of the qualifying work;][2]

"*residential premises*" means—

(a) a building or part of a building used, or suitable for use, as a dwelling, and

(b) land which the occupier of a building or part of a building used as a dwelling has for the occupier's own occupation and enjoyment with that building or that part of a building as its garden or grounds of an ornamental nature;

"*specified amount*", in relation to a payment in respect of qualifying expenditure, means 13.5 per cent of the amount of the payment on which value-added tax is charged, subject to a maximum amount of €4,050, provided that, where more than one payment is made in respect of qualifying expenditure, the aggregate of the specified amounts in respect of those payments shall not exceed €4,050;

"*tax reference number*", means in the case of an individual, the individual's PPS number or in the case of a company, the reference number stated on any return of income form or notice of assessment issued to that company by the Revenue Commissioners;

['*tenancy*' has the same meaning as it has in the Residential Tenancies Act 2004;

'*tenant*' has the same meaning as it has in the Residential Tenancies Act 2004;][3]

"*unique reference number*" has the meaning given to it by *subsection (4)(b)*;

"*VAT registration number*", in relation to a person, means the registration number assigned to the person under *section 65* of the Value-Added Tax Consolidation Act 2010.

[(1A) Where, as a result of the carrying out of qualifying work, a residential premises referred to in *paragraph (c)* or *(d)* of the definition of 'qualifying residence' in *subsection (1)* is converted into more than one rental unit, each such rental unit shall be a qualifying residence.][4]

[(2) (a) This section applies to qualifying expenditure incurred on qualifying work carried out—

(i) during the period from 25 October 2013 to 31 December 2015 in the case of a qualifying residence to which *paragraph (a)* or *(b)* of the definition of 'qualifying residence' in *subsection (1)* refers, and

(ii) during the period from 15 October 2014 to 31 December 2015 in the case of a qualifying residence to which *paragraph (c)* or *(d)* of the definition of 'qualifying residence' in *subsection (1)* refers.

(b) Where, during the period from 25 October 2013 to 31 December 2013, qualifying work is carried out on a qualifying residence to which *paragraph (a)* or *(b)* of the definition of 'qualifying residence' in *subsection (1)* refers, and where payments in respect of such work are made during that period, any such payments shall be deemed to have been made in the year of assessment 2014.

(c) Where, during the period from 15 October 2014 to 31 December 2014, qualifying work is carried out on a qualifying residence to which *paragraph (c)* or *(d)* of the definition of 'qualifying residence' in *subsection (1)* refers, and where payments in respect of such work are made during that period, any such payments shall be deemed to have been made in the year of assessment 2015.

(d) Notwithstanding *paragraph (a)*, where qualifying work, for which permission is required under the Planning and Development Act 2000, is carried out during the period from 1 January 2016 to 31 March 2016, then provided such permission is granted on or before 31 December 2015, that work shall be deemed to be carried out in the year of assessment 2015.][5]

(3) (a) Subject to the provisions of this section, where an individual (in this section referred to as 'the claimant'), on making a claim in that behalf, proves that in a year of assessment he or she has made a payment or payments to a qualifying contractor in respect of qualifying expenditure to which this section applies, the income tax to be charged on the claimant, other than in accordance with *section 16(2)*, shall be reduced—

(i) in the case of the first subsequent year of assessment, by an amount which is the lesser of—

(I) 50 per cent of the specified amount of the payment or payments, and

(II) the amount which reduces the income tax of that year of assessment to nil,

and

(ii) in the case of the next subsequent year of assessment, by an amount which is the lesser of—

(I) that part of the specified amount not used in the year of assessment referred to in *subparagraph (i)*, and

(II) the amount which reduces the income tax of that year of assessment to nil.

(b) Insofar as any part of the specified amount cannot be used under *paragraph (a)* (in this paragraph referred to as 'excess relief') due to the insufficiency of income tax charged on the claimant in the two years of assessment following the year of assessment in which the payment or payments referred to in *paragraph (a)* were made, the income tax for the year of assessment following those two years of assessment and so on for each succeeding year of assessment shall be reduced by the excess relief until the full amount of the excess relief has been used, provided that the amount of the excess relief used in any year of assessment shall not be greater than the amount which reduces the income tax charged on the claimant in that year of assessment to nil.

(c) The maximum amount of relief available under this section in respect of a qualifying residence shall not exceed €4,050.

[(ca) Where the qualifying work involves the conversion of a residential premises referred to in *paragraph (c)* or *(d)* of the definition of 'qualifying residence' in *subsection (1)* into more than one rental unit, *paragraph (c)* shall be read as if it applies to each of those units.][6]

(d) No claim shall be made under this section unless the payment, or where there is more than one payment the aggregate of those payments, in respect of qualifying expenditure made to a qualifying contractor or qualifying contractors is equal to or greater than €5,000.

(e) Where an individual engages a contractor to carry out qualifying work, it shall be the responsibility of that individual to be satisfied that the contractor is a qualifying contractor.

(4) (a) Subject to *paragraph (c)*, a contractor shall, before commencing qualifying work under this section, provide to the Revenue Commissioners—

(i) the contractor's name,

(ii) the contractor's tax reference number and VAT registration number,

(iii) the unique identification number assigned in accordance with *section 27* of the Finance (Local Property Tax) Act 2012 to the property on which the qualifying work is to be carried out,

(iv) the name of the claimant,

(v) the address of the property at which the work will be carried out,

(vi) a description of the work to be carried out,

(vii) the estimated cost of the work to be carried out, separately identifying the amount of value-added tax, [...][7]

(viii) the estimated duration of the work, including the estimated start date and [estimated end date,][8]

[(ix) confirmation as to whether or not the property referred to in *subparagraph (iii)* is a residential premises to which *paragraph (c)* or *(d)* of the definition of 'qualifying residence' in *subsection (1)* refers, and

(x) in the case of a property to which *paragraph (c)* or *(d)* of the definition of '*qualifying residence*' in *subsection (1)* refers, where such property is, as a result of the carrying out of the qualifying work, to be converted into more than one rental unit, the number of such rental units.][9]

(b) On receipt of the informationreferred to in *paragraph (a)*, the Revenue Commissioners shall—

(i) notify the contractor, as the case may be, that—

(I) the contractor is a qualifying contractor for the purposes of this section and such notification shall contain a number for the work (in this section referred to as the "*unique reference number*"), or

(II) that the contractor isnot a qualifying contractor for the purposes of this section,

and

(ii) where the contractor is a qualifying contractor, notify the individual concerned accordingly and the notification shall stipulate the unique reference number for the work.

(c) Where a qualifying contractor has commenced qualifying work on or after 25 October 2013 but before the electronic systems referred to in *subsection (10)* are made available by the Revenue Commissioners, the contractor shall provide to the Revenue Commissioners the information specified in *paragraph (a)* within 28 days of such electronic systems being made available.

(5) (a) Upon receipt of payment from the individual concerned in respect of qualifying work, but not later than 10 working days following receipt of such payment, the contractor shall—

(i) provide to the Revenue Commissioners the following information:

(I) the contractor's name;

(II) the contractor's tax registration number; registration number and VAT

(III) the unique reference number for the work;

(IV) details of the amount of the payment, separately identifying the amount of value-added tax;

(V) the name of the individual from whom the payment was received;

(VI) the date of the payment,

and

(ii) provide to the individual a statement showing the amount of the payment separately identifying the amount of value-added tax.

(b) Where a qualifying contractor receives payment from the individual in respect of qualifying work to which this section applies on or after 25 October 2013 and before the electronic systems referred to in *subsection (10)* are made available by the Revenue Commissioners, that contractor shall provide to the Revenue Commissioners the information specified in *paragraph (a)* within 28 days of such electronic systems being made available.

(6) On making a claim under this section, the claimant shall provide to the Revenue Commissioners—

(a) the following information:

(i) his or her name and tax reference number;

(ii) the unique reference number for the work;

(iii) the unique identification number assigned in accordance with *section 27* of the Finance (Local Property Tax) Act 2012 to the property on which the qualifying work was carried out;

(iv) details of any sum referred to in *paragraph (a)* or *(b)* [of *subsection (7)*;][10]

[(v) confirmation as to whether or not the property referred to in *subparagraph (iii)* is a residential premises to which *paragraph (c)* or *(d)* of the definition of 'qualifying residence' in *subsection (1)* refers;

(vi) in the case of a property to which *paragraph (c)* or *(d)* of the definition of '*qualifying residence*' in *subsection (1)* refers, where such property as a result of the carrying out of the qualifying work, was converted into more than one rental unit, the number of such rental units and the address of each rental unit,][11]

and

(b) a declaration (unless the contrary is the case) in respect of each such payment that—

(i) the amount of the payment advised to the Revenue Commissioners by the qualifying contractor under *subsection (5)(a)(i)(IV)* accords with the amount of the payment made by the claimant to that contractor,

(ii) the date of the payment advised to the Revenue Commissioners by the qualifying contractor under *subsection (5)(a)(i)(V)* is correct,

(iii) the work in respect of which payment was made to the qualifying contractor was qualifying work [carried out on a qualifying residence of the claimant,][12]

(iv) the work in respect of which payment was made to the qualifying contractor has been completed,

(v) the contractor has received full payment from the claimant in respect of the work, and

[(vi) the property on which the qualifying work was carried out was—

(I) in the case of a residential premises referred to in *paragraph (a)* or *(b)* of the definition of 'qualifying residence' in *subsection (1)*, occupied by the individual as his or her only or main residence on completion of the work, or

(II) in the case of a residential premises referred to in *paragraph (c)* or *(d)* of the definition of 'qualifying residence' in *subsection (1)*, occupied, within 6 months of completion of the qualifying work, by a tenant under a tenancy for which registration is required under *Part 7* of the Residential Tenancies Act 2004 and such registration requirements were complied with, and

(III) in the case of each rental unit referred to in *paragraph (a) (vi)*, occupied, within 6 months of completion of the qualifying work, by a tenant under a tenancy for which registration is required under *Part 7* of the Residential Tenancies Act 2004 and such registration requirements have been complied with.][13]

(7) Where a claimant has received or will receive, in respect of, or by reference to, qualifying work, a sum directly or indirectly—

(a) from the State or any public body or local authority, or

(b) under any contract of insurance or by way of compensation or otherwise,

then, for the purposes of *subsection (3)(a)*, the amount of any payment or payments, as specified in the information provided to the Revenue Commissioners under *subsection (5)*, made in respect of qualifying expenditure on that qualifying work shall be reduced—

(i) in the case of *paragraph (a)*, by an amount equal to 3 times the sum received or receivable, and

(ii) in the case of *paragraph (b)*, by an amount equal to the sum received or receivable.

(8) (a) Relief shall not be given under this section where the requirements of the Finance (Local Property Tax) Act 2012, in relation to the making of returns and the payment of local property tax—

(i) have not been complied with in respect of the qualifying residence, or

(ii) have not been complied with by a claimant in respect of any relevant residential property (other than the qualifying residence) in relation to which the claimant is a liable person.

(b) In this subsection 'relevant residential property' and 'liable person' have the same meanings respectively as in the Finance (Local Property Tax) Act 2012.

(9) For the purposes of this section—

(a) in the case of a claimant assessed to tax for a year of assessment in accordance with *section 1017*, any payment in respect of qualifying expenditure to a qualifying contractor made by the claimant's spouse, in respect of which the claimant's spouse would have been entitled to relief under this section if that spouse were assessed to tax for the year of assessment in accordance with *section 1016* (apart from *subsection (2)* of that section), shall be deemed to have been made by the claimant, and

(b) in the case of a nominated civil partner assessed to tax for a year of assessment in accordance with *section 1031C*, any payment in respect of qualifying expenditure to a qualifying contractor made by the other civil partner, in respect of which the other civil partner would have been entitled to relief under this section if the other civil partner were assessed to tax for the year of assessment in accordance with *section 1031B* (apart from *subsection (2)* of that section), shall be deemed to have been made by the nominated civil partner.

(10) Any claim, notification, information or declaration required by this section shall be given by electronic means and through such electronic systems as the Revenue Commissioners may make available for the time being for any such purpose, and the relevant provisions of *Chapter 6* of *Part 38* shall apply.

(11) Where qualifying expenditure, in relation to qualifying work on a qualifying residence, is incurred by 2 or more claimants, then, except where *subsection (9)* applies, for the purposes of apportioning the specified amount, each claimant shall be entitled to an amount which bears the same proportion to

the specified amount as the qualifying expenditure incurred by that claimant on the qualifying residence bears to the total qualifying expenditure incurred on that residence.

[(12) In the case of a qualifying residence to which *paragraph (a)* or *(b)* of the definition of 'qualifying residence' in *subsection (1)* refers, expenditure in respect of which a claimant is entitled to relief under this section shall not include any expenditure in respect of which that claimant is entitled to a deduction, relief or allowance under any other provision of the Tax Acts or the Value-Added Tax Consolidation Act 2010.][14]

(13) Anything required to be done by or under this section by the Revenue Commissioners, other than the making of regulations, may be done by any Revenue officer.

(14) (a) The Revenue Commissioners may make regulations for the purposes of this section and those regulations may—

(i) specify the manner in which contractors shall provide to the Revenue Commissioners the information required under *subsections (4)* and *(5)*,

(ii) specify the manner in which a claimant shall provide to the Revenue Commissioners the information and declaration required under *subsection (6)*,

(iii) specify the manner in which the Revenue Commissioners shall issue notifications under *subsection (4)(b)(ii)*, and

(iv) provide for such other matters relating to the information required under *subsections (4)(a)* and *(5)(a)* and to the information and declaration required under *subsection (6)* as are considered necessary and appropriate by the Revenue Commissioners for the purposes of this section and as may be specified in the regulations.

(b) Regulations made under this section may contain such incidental, supplemental or consequential provisions as appear to the Revenue Commissioners to be necessary or expedient—

(i) to enable persons to fulfil their obligations under this section or under regulations made under this section, or

(ii) to give effect to the proper implementation and efficient operation of the provisions of this section or regulations made under this section.

(c) Regulations made under this section shall be laid before Dáil Éireann as soon as may be after they are made and, if a resolution annulling those regulations is passed by Dáil Éireann within the 5 next 21 days on which Dáil Éireann has sat after the regulations are laid before it, the regulations shall be annulled accordingly, but without prejudice to the validity of anything previously done under them.][15]

Amendments

[1] Substituted by FA14 s13(a)(i). Comes into operation on 1 January 2015.

[2, 3] Inserted by FA14 s13(a)(ii). Comes into operation on 1 January 2015.

[4] Inserted by FA14 s13(b). Comes into operation on 1 January 2015.

[5] Substituted by FA14 s13(c). Comes into operation on 1 January 2015.

[6] Inserted by FA14 s13(d). Comes into operation on 1 January 2015.

[7] Deleted by FA14 s13(e)(i). Comes into operation on 1 January 2015.

[8] Substituted by FA14 s13(e)(ii). Comes into operation on 1 January 2015.

[9] Inserted by FA14 s13(e)(iii). Comes into operation on 1 January 2015.

[10] Substituted by FA14 s13(f)(i). Comes into operation on 1 January 2015.

[11] Inserted by FA14 s13(f)(ii). Comes into operation on 1 January 2015.

[12] Substituted by FA14 s13(f)(iii). Comes into operation on 1 January 2015.

[13] Substituted by FA14 s13(f)(iv). Comes into operation on 1 January 2015.

[14] Substituted by FA14 s13(g). Comes into operation on 1 January 2015.

[15] Inserted by F(No.2)A13 s5(a)(ii). Comes into operation on 1 January 2014. However, payments in respect of qualifying work made during the period from 25 October 2013 to 31 December 2013 are deemed to have been made in the year of assessment 2014.

Revenue Briefings

eBrief

eBrief No. 29/2014 – Home Renovation Incentive (HRI)

478 Relief for payments made by certain persons in respect of alarm systems

[FA96 s5]

(1) In this section—

"*appropriate percentage*", in relation to a year of assessment, means a percentage equal to the standard rate of tax for that year;

"*installation*" means the placing in position, including any necessary wiring, drilling, plastering or similar work, of a relevant alarm system;

"*qualifying expenditure*", in relation to a qualifying individual, means expenditure incurred in the qualifying period in connection with either or both the provision and installation of a relevant alarm system in a premises which is the qualifying individual's sole or main residence, but does not include any expenditure in so far as it is in respect of the repair, maintenance or monitoring of such an alarm system;

"*qualifying individual*", in relation to qualifying expenditure, means an individual who at the time the expenditure is incurred has attained the age of 65 years and who for the greater part of the year of assessment in which the expenditure is incurred lives alone;

"*qualifying period*" means the period beginning on the 23rd day of January, 1996, and ending on the 5th day of April, 1998;

"*relative*", in relation to a qualifying individual, includes a relation by marriage and a person in respect of whom the individual is or was the legal guardian;

"*relevant alarm system*" means an electrical apparatus which when activated is designed to give notice to the effect that there is an intruder present or attempting to enter the premises in which it is installed.

(2) Where a claimant, being a qualifying individual or a relative of that individual, having made a claim in that behalf, proves that he or she has incurred qualifying expenditure in relation to the qualifying individual, the income tax to be charged on the claimant, other than in accordance with *section 16(2)*, for the year of assessment in which the expenditure is incurred shall be reduced by an amount which is the least of—

(a) the appropriate percentage of the qualifying expenditure,

(b) the appropriate percentage of [€1,015.79][1], and

(c) the amount which reduces that income tax to nil.

(3) Any claim for relief under this section shall be in such form as may be prescribed by the Revenue Commissioners for the purpose and shall be accompanied by a receipt or receipts, as may be appropriate, for the amount of qualifying expenditure incurred; but, where the qualifying expenditure includes expenditure in respect of installation, the receipt in respect of such expenditure shall contain the installer's name and address and the installer's value-added tax registration number or income tax reference number.

(4) Any deduction made under this section shall be in substitution for and not in addition to any deduction to which the individual might be entitled in respect of the same payment under any other provision of the Income Tax Acts.

Amendments

[1] Substituted by FA01 sched5.

Revenue Precedents

Whether the provisions in section 478 TCA 1997 could be extended, by concession, to an elderly married couple, living together? Relief may only be allowed to individuals aged 65 and up, who live alone. IT 96 1557

Cross References

From Section 478

Section 16 Income tax charged by deduction.

To Section 478

Section 458 Deductions allowed in ascertaining taxable income and provisions relating to reductions in tax.

Section 1024 Method of apportioning reliefs and charging tax in cases of separate assessments.

479 Relief for new shares purchased on issue by employees

[FA86 s12(1) to (8); FA96 s12 and s132(1) and Sch5 PtI par15]

(1) (a) In this section—

"*director*" has the same meaning as in *Chapter 3* of *Part 5*;

"*eligible employee*", in relation to a qualifying company, means—

(i) where the company is a trading company, a director or an employee of the company, or

(ii) where the company is a holding company, a director or an employee of the company or of a company which is its 75 per cent subsidiary;

"*eligible shares*", in relation to a qualifying company, means new shares forming part of the ordinary share capital of the company which—

(i) are fully paid up,

(ii) throughout [the period of 3 years][1] beginning with the date on which they are issued, carry no present or future preferential right to dividends or to the company's assets on its winding up and no present or future preferential right to be redeemed,

(iii) are not subject to any restrictions other than restrictions which attach to all shares of the same class, and

(iv) are issued to and acquired by an eligible employee in relation to the company at not less than their market value at the time of issue;

"*holding company*" means a company whose business consists wholly or mainly of the holding of shares or securities of trading companies which are its 75 per cent subsidiaries;

"*market value*" shall be construed in accordance with *section 548*;

"*qualifying company*" means a company which at the time the eligible shares are issued is—

(i) incorporated in the State,

(ii) resident in the State and not resident elsewhere, and

(iii) (I) a trading company, or

(II) a holding company;

"*trading company*" means a company whose business consists wholly or mainly of the carrying on wholly or mainly in the State of a trade or trades;

"*75 per cent subsidiary*", in relation to a company, has the meaning assigned to it for the purposes of the Corporation Tax Acts by *section 9*, as applied for the purposes of *section 411* by *paragraphs (b)* and *(c)* of *subsection (1)* of that section.

(b) References in this section to a disposal of shares include references to a disposal of an interest or right in or over the shares, and an individual shall be treated for the purposes of this section as disposing of any shares which he or she is treated by virtue of *section 587* as exchanging for other shares.

(c) Shares in a company shall not be treated for the purposes of this section as being of the same class unless they would be so treated if dealt in on a stock exchange in the State.

(2) Subject to this section, where an eligible employee in relation to a qualifying company subscribes for eligible shares in the qualifying company, the eligible employee shall be entitled to have a deduction made from his or her total income for the year of assessment in which the shares are issued of an amount equal to the amount of the subscription; but a deduction shall not be given to the extent to which the amount subscribed by an eligible employee for eligible shares issued to him or her in all years of assessment exceeds [€6,350][2].

(3) *Subsection (2)* shall not apply as respects any amount subscribed for eligible shares if within [the period of 3 years][3] from the date of their acquisition—

(a) those shares are disposed of, or

(b) the eligible employee who made the subscription receives in respect of those shares any money or money's worth which does not constitute income in his or her hands for the purpose of income tax,

and there shall be made all such assessments, additional assessments or adjustments of assessments as are necessary to withdraw any relief from income tax already given under *subsection (2)* in respect of the amount subscribed[...][4].

(4) Except where the shares are in a company whose ordinary share capital, at the time of acquisition of the shares by the eligible employee, consists of shares of one class only, the majority of the issued shares of the same class as the eligible shares shall be shares other than—

(a) eligible shares, and

(b) shares held by persons who acquired their shares in pursuance of a right conferred on them or an opportunity afforded to them as a director or employee of the qualifying company or any of its 75 per cent subsidiaries.

[(5) In relation to shares in respect of which relief has been given under subsection (2) and not withdrawn, any question—

(a) as to which (if any) such shares issued to an eligible employee at different times a disposal relates, or

(b) as to whether a disposal relates to such shares or to other shares,

shall for the purposes of this section be determined as it would be determined for the purposes of *section 498* but without regard to the reference in subsection (4) (as amended by the Finance Act, 1998) of that section to subsection (3) of this section.][5]

(6) Where there occurs in relation to any of the eligible shares of an eligible employee (in this subsection referred to as "*the original holding*") a transaction which results in a new holding (within the meaning of *section 584*) being equated with the original holding for the purposes of capital gains tax, then, for the purposes of *subsection (3)*—

(a) the new holding shall be treated as shares in respect of which relief under this section has been given,

(b) the transaction shall not be treated as involving a disposal of the original holding,

(c) the consideration for the disposal of the original holding to the extent that it consists of the new holding shall not be treated as money or money's worth, and

(d) a disposal of the whole or a part of the new holding shall be treated as a disposal of the whole or a corresponding part of the shares in respect of which relief has been given under this section.

(7) Any amount in respect of which relief is allowed under *subsection (2)* and not withdrawn shall be treated as a sum which by virtue of *section 554* is to be excluded from the sums allowable under *section 552*.

(8) An eligible employee shall not be entitled to relief under *subsection (2)* in respect of any shares unless the shares are subscribed for and issued for bona fide commercial reasons and not as part of a scheme or arrangement the main purpose or one of the main purposes of which is the avoidance of tax.

[(9) The deduction authorised by subsection (2) shall not be made in respect of eligible shares where those shares are subscribed for on or after 8 December 2010.][6]

Amendments

[1] Substituted by FA98 s11(1)(a). This section shall come into operation on the 12th day of February, 1998.

[2] Substituted by FA01 sched5.

[3] Substituted by FA98 s11(1)(b)(i). This section shall come into operation on the 12th day of February, 1998.

[4] Deleted by FA98 s11(1)(b)(ii). This section shall come into operation on the 12th day of February, 1998.

[5] Substituted by FA98 s11(1)(c). This section shall come into operation on the 12th day of February, 1998.

[6] Inserted by FA11 s10(a).

Cross References

From Section 479

Section 9 Subsidiaries.

Section 112 Basis of assessment, persons chargeable and extent of charge.

Section 123 General tax treatment of payments on retirement or removal from office or employment.

Section 411 Surrender of relief between members of groups and consortia.
Section 498 Replacement capital.
Section 548 Valuation of assets.
Section 552 Acquisition, enhancement and disposal costs.
Section 554 Exclusion of expenditure by reference to income tax.
Section 584 Reorganisation or reduction of share capital.
Section 587 Company reconstructions and amalgamations.

To Section 479

Section 458 Deductions allowed in ascertaining taxable income and provisions relating to reductions in tax.
Section 1024 Method of apportioning reliefs and charging tax in cases of separate assessments.

480 Relief for certain sums chargeable under Schedule E

[FA68 s3; FA72 Sch PtIII par4; FA74 s11 and s64(2) and SchI PtII; FA97 s146(1) and Sch9 PtI par5(3)]

(1) (a) In this section—

"*director*" and "*proprietary director*" have the same meanings respectively as in *section 472*;

"*employee*", in relation to a body corporate, includes any person taking part in the management of the affairs of the body corporate who is not a director, and includes a person who is to be or has been an employee;

"*part-time director*", in relation to a body corporate, means a director who is not required to devote substantially the whole of his or her time to the service of the body corporate;

"*proprietary employee*", in relation to a company, means an employee who is the beneficial owner of, or able, either directly or through the medium of other companies or by any other indirect means, to control, more than 15 per cent of the ordinary share capital of the company.

(b) For the purposes of the definitions of "*proprietary director*" and "*proprietary employee*", ordinary share capital which is owned or controlled as referred to in those definitions by a person, being [a spouse, a civil partner, a minor child or a minor child of the civil partner,][1] of a director or employee, or by a trustee of a trust for the benefit of a person or persons, being or including any such person or such director or employee, shall be deemed to be owned or controlled by such director or employee and not by any other person.

(2) (a) Subject to *paragraph (b)*, this section shall apply to any payment which is chargeable to tax under Schedule E and made to the holder of an office or employment to compensate for—

(i) a reduction or a possible reduction of future remuneration arising from a reorganisation of the business of the employer under whom the office or employment is held or a change in the working procedures, working methods, duties or rates of remuneration of such office or employment, or

(ii) a change in the place where the duties of the office or employment are performed.

(b) This section shall not apply to—

(i) a payment to which *section 123* applies, or

(ii) a payment to—

(I) a proprietary director,

(II) a part-time director,

(III) a proprietary employee, or

(IV) a person who is a part-time employee by reason of not being required to devote substantially the whole of his or her time to the service of his or her employer.

(3) Where an individual has received a payment to which this section applies, the individual shall be entitled, on making a claim in that behalf and on proof of the relevant facts to the satisfaction of the inspector, to have the total amount of income tax payable by the individual for the year of assessment for which the payment is chargeable reduced to the total of the following amounts—

(a) the amount of income tax which would have been payable by him or her for that year if he or she had not received the payment, and

(b) income tax on the whole of the payment at the rate ascertained in the manner specified in *subsection (4)*.

(4) There shall be ascertained the additional income tax, over and above the amount referred to in *subsection (3)(a)*, which would have been payable by the holder of the office or employment if his or her total income for the year of assessment referred to in *subsection (3)* had included one-third only of the payment, and the rate of income tax for the purposes of *subsection (3)(b)* shall then be ascertained by dividing the additional income tax computed in accordance with this subsection by an amount equal to one-third of the payment.

(5) (a) Relief from tax under this section shall in all cases be given by means of repayment.

(b) A claimant shall not be entitled to relief under this section in respect of any income the tax on which he or she is entitled to charge against any other person, or to deduct, retain or satisfy out of any payment which he or she is liable to make to any other person.

Amendments

[1] Substituted by F(No.3)A11 sched1(119). Shall have effect from 27 July 2011.

Cross References

From Section 480

Section 123 General tax treatment of payments on retirement or removal from office or employment.

Section 472 Employee tax credit.

To Section 480

Section 192A Exemption in respect of certain payments under employment law.

Section 202 Relief for agreed pay restructuring.

480A Relief on retirement for certain income of certain sportspersons

[(1) In this section—

'*basis period*', in relation to a year of assessment, means the period on the profits or gains of which income tax for the year of assessment is to be finally computed under the Income Tax Acts;

"*EEA Agreement*" means the Agreement on the European Economic Area signed at Oporto on 2 May 1992, as adjusted by all subsequent amendments to that Agreement;

"*EEA state*" means a state, other than the State, which is a contracting party to the EEA Agreement;

"*EFTA state*" means a state, other than an EEA state, which is a member of the European Free Trade Association;

"*relevant individual*" means an individual who—

(a) engaged in a specified occupation or carried on a specified profession,

(b) complied with the Income Tax Acts, and

(c) is resident in the State, an EEA state or an EFTA state in the retirement year;

"*relevant period*" means the retirement year and the 14 years of assessment immediately preceding the retirement year;

"*relevant years*" means the years of assessment as specified by the relevant individual, not exceeding 10 years of assessment, in the relevant period;

"*retirement year*" means the year of assessment in respect of which the relevant individual proves to the satisfaction of the Revenue Commissioners that he or she has, in that year of assessment, ceased permanently to be engaged in a specified occupation or to carry on a specified profession;

"*specified occupation*" and "*specified profession*" mean an occupation or profession, as the case may be, specified in *Schedule 23A*.

(2) Notwithstanding any other provision of the Income Tax Acts other than *section 960H*, this section applies to a relevant individual who ceased permanently to be engaged in a specified occupation or to carry on a specified profession.

(3) Where this section applies, the relevant individual shall, on the making of a claim in that behalf, within 4 years from the end of the retirement year, be entitled to have deductions made from his or her total income for the relevant years.

(4) (a) *Subsection (3)* shall apply notwithstanding any limitation in *section 865(4)* on the time within which a claim for a repayment of tax is required to be made.

(b) *Section 865(6)* shall not prevent the Revenue Commissioners from repaying an amount of tax as a consequence of a timely claim for relief under this section where a valid claim for a repayment of tax (within the meaning of *section 865(1)(b)*) has been made.][1]

(5) The amount of the deduction to be made under *subsection (3)* for any year of assessment shall be an amount equal to 40 per cent of the receipts, before deducting expenses, of the relevant individual for the basis period for that year of assessment which arose wholly and exclusively from the engagement of the relevant individual in the specified occupation or from the carrying on by the relevant individual of the specified profession, as the case may be.

(6) For the purposes of *subsection (5)*, receipts shall be regarded as deriving wholly and exclusively from the engagement of the relevant individual in the specified occupation or from the carrying on by the relevant individual of the specified profession, as the case may be, only to the extent that such receipts derive directly from the actual participation by the relevant individual in the sport associated with the specified occupation or the specified profession, and accordingly—

(a) include—

(i) where the relevant individual is an employee, so much of all salaries, fees, wages, bonuses or perquisites paid to the relevant individual by his or her employer as a direct consequence of the participation by the relevant individual in the sport associated with the specified occupation, and

(ii) where the relevant individual carries on the specified profession, all match or performance fees, prize moneys and appearance moneys paid to the relevant individual by any other person as a direct consequence of the participation of the relevant individual in the sport associated with the specified profession,

but

(b) do not include—

(i) sponsorship moneys received by the relevant individual, or

(ii) receipts received by the relevant individual for participation in advertisements, promotions, videos or television or radio programmes, or for personal appearances or interviews, newspaper or magazine articles, or for the right to use the individual's image or name to promote or endorse products or services or in any other manner.

[(7) A claim under this section shall be made—

(a) where the relevant individual is required to submit a return of income [for the retirement year][2], by including a claim in the return of income, or

(b) where the relevant individual is not required to submit a return of income [for the retirement year][3], by submitting a claim to the Revenue Commissioners.][4]

(8) (a) Relief from income tax under this section shall in all cases be given by means of repayment.

(b) Any repayment of income tax due under this section shall not carry interest.

(c) Relief under this section for any year of assessment shall not create or augment a loss for that year of assessment for the purposes of *Chapter 1* of *Part 12*.

(9) A deduction given under this section for any year of assessment shall not be taken into account in determining the net relevant earnings (within the meaning of *section 787*) of the relevant individual for that year of assessment.

(10) Where any relief has been given to a relevant individual under this section and the relevant individual subsequently recommences to be engaged in the specified occupation or to carry on the specified profession, as the case may be, that relief shall be withdrawn by making an assessment to income tax under Case IV of Schedule D for the year of assessment for which that relief was given and, notwithstanding anything in the Income Tax Acts, such an assessment may be made at any time.][5]

Amendments

[1] Substituted by F(No.2)A13 s15(1)(a). Applies in respect of retirements on or after 1 January 2014 from occupations or professions, as the case may be, specified in Schedule 23A.

[2, 3] Substituted by FA14 sched3(1)(d). Has effect on and from 23 December 2014.

[4] Substituted by F(No.2)A13 s15(1)(b). Applies in respect of retirements on or after 1 January 2014 from occupations or professions, as the case may be, specified in Schedule 23A.

[5] Inserted by FA02 s12.

Revenue Briefings

Tax Briefing

Tax Briefing April 2002 – Issue 47 pg 9 – Finance Act 2002 – Relief from Income Tax in Respect of Certain Earnings of Sportspersons

eBrief

eBrief No. 54/2013 – Relief on Retirement for Sportspersons

Cross References

From Section 480A

Section 381 Right to repayment of tax by reference to losses.
Section 787 Nature and amount of relief for qualifying premiums.
Section 865 Repayment of tax.
Section 1006A Offset between taxes.
Schedule 23A Specified Occupations and Professions

CHAPTER 2

Income Tax and Corporation Tax: Reliefs Applicable to Both

481 Relief for investment in films

[FA87 s35(1) to (20); FA96 s31(1); FA97 s30]

(1) In this section—

[…][1]

"*authorised officer*" means an officer of the Revenue Commissioners authorised by them in writing for the purposes of this section;

["*broadcast*" and "*broadcaster*" have the meanings assigned to them by *section 2* of the Broadcasting Act 2009][2]

['*director*' shall be construed in accordance with *section 433(4)*;][3]

["*eligible individual*" means an individual employed by a qualifying company for the purposes of the production of a qualifying film;][4]

["*film*" means—

(a) a film of a kind which is included within the categories of films eligible for certification by the Revenue Commissioners under *subsection (2A)*, as specified in regulations made under *subsection (2E)*, and

(b) as respects every film, a film which is produced—

(i) on a commercial basis with a view to the realisation of profit, and

(ii) wholly or mainly for exhibition to the public in cinemas or by means of broadcast,

but does not include a film made for exhibition as an advertising programme or as a commercial;][5]

["*film corporation tax credit*", in relation to a qualifying film, means an amount equal to 32 per cent of the lowest of—

(a) the eligible expenditure amount,

(b) 80 per cent of the total cost of production of the film, and

(c) €50,000,000;][6]

["*the Minister*" means the Minister for Arts, Heritage and the Gaeltacht;][7]

["*producer company*", in relation to a film corporation tax credit specified in a film certificate, means a company that—

(a) is resident in the State, or is resident in an EEA State other than the State and carries on business in the State through a branch or agency,

(b) commencing not later than the time the qualifying period commences, carries on a trade of producing films—

(i) on a commercial basis with a view to the realisation of profit, and

(ii) that are wholly or principally for exhibition to the public in cinemas or by means of broadcast,

(c) is not a company, or a company connected to a company—

(i) that is a broadcaster, or

(ii) in the case of—

(I) a company, whose business consists wholly or mainly, or

(II) a company connected to another company, where the aggregate of the activities carried on by the company and every company to which it is connected, consists wholly or mainly,

of transmitting films on the internet,

(d) holds all of the shares in the qualifying company, and

(e) has delivered to the Collector-General, on or before the specified return date, a return, in accordance with *section 959I*, in respect of—

(i) the accounting period referred to in *paragraph (a)* of the definition of "*qualifying period*", or

(ii) each accounting period ending in the qualifying period, referred to in *paragraph (b)* of that definition,

as the case may be;][8]

["*qualifying company*" means a company which—

(a) (i) is incorporated and resident in the State, or

(ii) is carrying on a trade in the State through a branch or agency,

(b) exists solely for the purposes of the production […][9] of only one qualifying film, and

(c) does not contain in its name—

(i) registered under either or both the Companies Acts, 1963 to 1999, and the Registration of Business Names Act, 1963, or

(ii) registered under the law of the territory in which it is incorporated,

the words "*Ireland*", "*Irish*", "*Éireann*", "*Éire*" or "*National*";][10]

["*qualifying film*" means a film in respect of which the Revenue Commissioners have issued a certificate under *subsection (2A)*, which has not been revoked under *subsection (2D)*;][11]

[…][12]

["*qualifying period*", in relation to a film corporation tax credit specified in a film certificate, means—

(a) the accounting period of the producer company, in respect of whic the specified return date for the chargeable period, within the meaning of *section 959A*, immediately precedes the date the application referred to in *subsection (2A)(a)* was made, or

(b) where the accounting period referred to in *paragraph (a)* is a period of less than 12 months, the period—

(i) commencing on the date on which the most recently commenced accounting period, which commences on or before the date which is 12 months before the end of the accounting period referred to in *paragraph (a)* commences, and

(ii) ending on the date the accounting period referred to in *paragraph (a)* ends, and references in *subsection (3)* to corporation tax and corporation tax paid shall be construed accordingly;][13]

[...][14]

[...][15]

[...][16]

["*specified amount*" has the meaning given to it by *subsection (3)(b)*;

"*specified relevant person*" means a person who is a director or secretary of the producer company at any time during the period commencing when the qualifying period commences and ending 12 months after the date the compliance report referred to in *subparagraph (iii)* of *subsection (2C)(d)(iii)* is provided to the Revenue Commissioners;][17]

(2)

[(a) The Minister, on request from the Revenue Commissioners following an application to them by a [producer company][18] for a certificate under *subsection (2A)* in relation to a film to be produced by the company, may subject to *paragraph (b)* and in accordance with regulations made under *subsection (2E)*, give authorisation to the Revenue Commissioners that they may, subject to *subsection (2A)*, issue a certificate under that subsection to the [producer company][19] in relation to that film.

(b) In considering whether to give the authorisation referred to in *paragraph (a)*, the Minister, in accordance with regulations made under *subsection (2E)*, shall have regard to—

(i) the categories of films eligible for certification by the Revenue Commissioners under *subsection (2A)*, as specified in those regulations, and

(ii) any contribution which the production of the film is expected to make to either or both the development of the film industry in the State and the promotion and expression of Irish culture,

and where such authorisation is given, the Minister, having regard to those matters, shall specify in the authorisation such conditions, as the Minister may consider proper, including a condition—

[...][20]

(II) in relation to—

(A) the employment and responsibilities of the producer, and the producer company, of a film for the production of that film, and

(B) the employment of personnel, including trainees, (other than the producer) for the production of that film.][21]

[...][22]

[...][23]

[(2A) (a) Subject to the provisions of this subsection, the Revenue Commissioners, on the making of an application by a [producer company][24], may, in accordance with regulations made under *subsection (2E)*, issue a certificate to a [producercompany][25] stating, in relation to a film to be produced by the company, that the film may be treated as a qualifying film for the purpose of this section.

[(b) The Revenue Commissioners shall not issue a certificate under *paragraph (a)*if—

(i) they have not been given authorisation to do so by the Minister under *subsection (2)(a)*,

(ii) the producer company, the qualifying company[, any company controlled by the producer company][26] and each person who is either the beneficial owner of, or able directly or indirectly to control, more than 15 per cent of the ordinary share capital of the producer company or the qualifying company, as the case may be, is not in compliance with all the obligations imposed by the Tax Acts, the Capital Gains Tax Acts or the Value-Added Tax Consolidation Act 2010 in relation to—

(I) the payments or remittances of taxes, interest or penalties required to be paid or remitted under those Acts,

(II) the delivery of returns, and

(III) requests to supply to an inspector accounts of, or other information about, any business carried on, by the producer company, the qualifying company or person, as the case may be,

[…][27]

(iii) the eligible expenditure amount is less than [€125,000, or][28][29]

[(iv) the total cost of the production of the film is less than €250,000.][30]

[(c) Nothing in this section shall be construed as obliging the Revenue Commissioners to issue a certificate under *paragraph (a)*.][31]

(d) An application for a certificate under *paragraph (a)* shall be in the form prescribed by the Revenue Commissioners and shall contain such information as may be specified in regulations made under *subsection (2E)*.

(e) In considering whether to issue a certificate under *paragraph (a)* the Revenue Commissioners shall, in respect of the proposed production of the film, examine all aspects of the [producer company][32]'s proposal.

(f) The Revenue Commissioners may refuse to issue a certificate under *paragraph (a)* if they are not satisfied with any aspect of the [producer company][33]'s application and, in particular, the Revenue Commissioners may refuse to issue a certificate—

(i) if they have reason to believe that the budget or any particular item of proposed expenditure in the budget is inflated, or

(ii) where—

(I) they are not satisfied that there is a commercial rationale for the corporate structure proposed—

(A) for the production, financing, distribution or sale of the film, or

(B) for all of those purposes,

or

(II) they are of the opinion that the corporate structure proposed would hinder the Revenue Commissioners in verifying compliance with any of the provisions governing the relief.

(g) A certificate issued by the Revenue Commissioners under *paragraph (a)* shall be subject to such conditions specified in the certificate as the Revenue Commissioners may consider proper, having regard, in particular, to the examination referred to in *paragraph (e)* and any conditions specified in the authorisation given by the Minister under *subsection (2)(a)*, and in particular the Revenue Commissioners shall specify in the certificate a condition—

[…][34]

[(i) in relation to the quantum of the specified amount, and the timing and manner of a payment of the specified amount,][35]

(ii) in relation to the matters specified by the Minister in the authorisation by virtue of *subsection (2)(b)(II)*,

[(iii) in relation to the amount of the film corporation tax credit by which the producer company's corporation tax is to be reduced,][36]

[(iv) in relation to the minimum amount of money to be expended on the production of the qualifying film [(in this section referred to as the eligible expenditure amount)][37]—

(I) directly by the qualifying company on the employment, by the company, of eligible individuals, in so far as those individuals exercise their employment in the State in the production of the qualifying film, and

(II) directly or indirectly by the qualifying company, on the provision of certain goods, services and facilities, as set out in regulations made under *subsection (2E)*,][38]

[(v) where financial arrangements have been approved by the Revenue Commissioners in accordance with [*subsection (2CA)*,][39] in relation to any matter pertaining to those arrangements.][40]

(h) The Revenue Commissioners, having consulted with the Minister as appropriate, may amend or revoke any condition (including a condition added by virtue of this paragraph) specified in the certificate, or add to such conditions, by giving notice in writing to the [producer company][41] concerned of the amendment, revocation or addition, and this section shall apply as if—

(i) a condition so amended or added by the notice was specified in the certificate, and

(ii) a condition so revoked was not specified in the certificate.

(2B) In carrying out their functions under this section the Revenue Commissioners may—

(a) consult with any person, agency or body of persons, as in their opinion may be of assistance to them, and

(b) notwithstanding any obligation as to secrecy or other restriction on the disclosure of information imposed by, or under, the Tax Acts or any other statute or otherwise, disclose any detail in a [producer company][42]'s application which they consider necessary for the purposes of such consultation.

(2C) A company shall not be regarded as a [producer company][43] for the purposes of this section—

[(a) unless the company, in relation to a qualifying film, following the date on which an application has been made under *subsection (2A)(d)*, notifies the

Revenue Commissioners in writing within 7 days of the first incurring of expenditure to which *subsection (2A)(g)(iv)* refers.][44]

(b) [subject to *subsection (2CA),*][45] if the financial arrangements which the company [or the qualifying company][46] enters into in relation to the qualifying film are—

(i) financial arrangements of any type with a person resident, registered or operating in a territory other than—

(I) a Member State of the European Communities, or

(II) a territory with the government of which, arrangements having the force of law by virtue of [*section 826(1)*][47], have been made,

or

(ii) financial arrangements under which funds are channelled, directly or indirectly, to, or through, a territory other than a territory referred to in clause (I) or (II) of *subparagraph (i),*

[…][48]

(c) unless the company provides, when requested to do so by the Revenue Commissioners, for the purposes of verifying compliance with the provisions governing the relief or with any condition specified in a certificate issued by them under *subsection (2A)(a),* evidence to vouch each item of expenditure in the State or elsewhere on the production and distribution of the qualifying film, whether expended by [the producer company,][49] the qualifying company or by any other person engaged, directly or indirectly, by the [the producer company or][50] qualifying company to provide goods, services or facilities in relation to such production or distribution and, in particular, such evidence shall include—

(i) records required to be kept or retained by the [producer company or the qualifying company][51] by virtue of *section 886,* and

(ii) records, in relation to the production and distribution of the qualifying film, required to be kept or retained by that other person by virtue of *section 886,* or which would be so required if that other person were subject to the provisions of that section,

[…][52]

(d) unless the company, within such time as is specified in the regulations made under *subsection (2E)*—

(i) notifies the Revenue Commissioners in writing of the date of completion of the production of the qualifying film,

(ii) provides to the Revenue Commissioners and to the Minister, such number of copies of the film in such format and manner as may be specified in those regulations, and

(iii) provides to the Revenue Commissioners, a compliance report, in such format and manner specified in those regulations, which proves to the satisfaction of the Revenue Commissioners that—

(I) the provisions of this section in so far as they apply in relation to the company and a qualifying film have been met, and

(II) any conditions attaching to a certificate issued to the company in relation to a qualifying film under *subsection (2A) (a)* have been [fulfilled,][53]

[…][54]

[(e) if the company ceases to carry on the trade referred to in *paragraph (b)* of the definition of "*producer company*", before a time which is 12 months after the date the compliance report referred to in *subsection (2C)(d)(iii)* is provided to the Revenue Commissioners,][55]

[(f) if the company disposes of its shares in the qualifying company before a time which is 12 months after the date the compliance report referred to in *subsection (2C)(d)(iii)* is provided to the Revenue Commissioners,

(g) unless the company—

(i) enters into a contract with the qualifying company in relation to the production [...][56] of the qualifying film, and

(ii) provides an amount not less than the specified amount to the qualifying company,

and

(h) unless an amount not less than the eligible expenditure amount is expended by the qualifying company wholly and exclusively on the production of the qualifying film as specified in a condition in a film certificate, in accordance with *subsection (2A)(g)(iv)*.][57]

[(2CA) (a) *Paragraph (b)* of *subsection (2C)* shall not apply to financial arrangements in relation to a transaction, or series of transactions, where such arrangements have been approved by the Revenue Commissioners.

(b) The Revenue Commissioners shall not approve financial arrangements, to which *paragraph (b)* of *subsection (2C)* would, but for this subsection, apply unless:

[(i) the arrangements relate to the filming of part of a film in a territory other than a territory referred to in clause (I) or (II) of *subsection (2C)(b)(i)*,][58]

(ii) a request for approval is made by [the producer company][59] to the Revenue Commissioners before such arrangements are effected,

[(iii) the producer company demonstrates to the satisfaction of the Revenue Commissioners that it can provide, if requested, sufficient records to enable the Revenue Commissioners to verify, in the case of filming in a territory, the amount of each item of expenditure on the production of the qualifying film expended in the territory, whether expended by the producer company or by any other person,][60] and

(iv) they are satisfied that it is appropriate to grant such approval.

(c) In considering whether to grant an approval under this subsection in relation to financial arrangements, the Revenue Commissioners may seek any information they consider appropriate in relation to the arrangements or in relation to any person who is, directly or indirectly, a party to the arrangements.

(d) Where the Revenue Commissioners have approved financial arrangements in accordance with this subsection, no amount of money expended, either directly or indirectly, as part of the arrangements maybe regarded, for the purposes of *subsection (2A)(g)(iv)*, as an amount of money expended on either the employment of eligible individuals or on the provision of goods, services and facilities as referred to in that subsection.][61]

[(2D) Where the producer company or the qualifying company fails to comply with any of the provisions of this section or fails to fulfil any condition specified in a certificate issued to the producer company under *paragraph (a)* of *subsection (2A)*, the Revenue Commissioners may, by notice in writing, revoke the certificate.][62]

(2E) The Revenue Commissioners with the consent of the Minister for Finance, and with the consent of the Minister in relation to the matters to be considered regarding the issue of an authorisation under *subsection (2)*, shall make regulations with respect to the administration by them of the relief under this section and with respect to the matters to be considered by the Minister for the purposes of that subsection and, without prejudice to the generality of the foregoing, regulations under this subsection may include provision—

(a) governing the application for certification pursuant to *subsection (2A)* and the information and documents to be provided in or with such application,

(b) specifying the categories of films eligible for certification by the Revenue Commissioners under *subsection (2A)*,

(c) prescribing the form of such application,

(d) governing the records that [a producer company and a qualifying company][63] shall maintain or provide to the Revenue Commissioners,

(e) governing the period for which, and the place at which, such records shall be maintained,

(f) specifying the time within which a [producer company][64] shall notify the Revenue Commissioners of the completion of the production of a qualifying film,

(g) specifying the time within which, and the format, number and manner in which, copies of a qualifying film shall be provided to the Revenue Commissioners and to the Minister,

(h) specifying the form and content of the compliance report to be provided to the Revenue Commissioners, the manner in which such report shall be made and verified, the documents to accompany the report and the time within which such report shall be provided,

(i) governing the type of expenditure which may be accepted by the Revenue Commissioners as expenditure on the production of a qualifying film,

(j) governing the provision of the goods, services and facilities referred to in *subsection (2A)(g)(iv)(II)*, including the place of origin of those goods, services and facilities, the place in which they are provided and the location of the supplier,

(k) specifying the currency exchange rate to be applied to expenditure on the production of a qualifying film, [...][65]

(l) specifying the criteria to be considered by the Minister, in relation to the matters referred to in *subsections (2)(b)(i)* and *(ii)*—

(i) in deciding whether to give authorisation to the Revenue Commissioners under *subsection (2)(a)*, and

(ii) in specifying conditions in such authorisation, as provided for in *subsection (2)(b)*,

and the information required for those purposes to be included in the application made to the Revenue Commissioners under *subsection (2A)* by a [producer company][66].][67]

[(m) governing the approval of financial arrangements in accordance with [*subsection (2CA)*][68], [...][69]

(n) governing the employment of eligible individuals, as referred to in *subsection (2A)(g)(iv)*, and the circumstances in which expenditure by a qualifying company would be regarded as expenditure on the employment of those individuals in the production of a qualifying [film, and][70]][71]

[(o) governing when the specified amount may be paid by the Revenue Commissioners to the producer company.][72]

[(2F) Where a [producer company][73] fails to provide to the Revenue Commissioners a compliance report as referred to in *subsection (2C)(d)(iii)*, within the time provided for in regulations made under *subsection (2E)(h)*, the specified relevant person shall provide such compliance report to the Revenue Commissioners within 2 months after that time.][74]

[(3) (a) Where the Revenue Commissioners have—

(i) issued a film certificate to a producer company, in accordance with *subsection (2A)(a)*, and

(ii) specified an amount of a film corporation tax credit in the certificate,

the corporation tax of the company for the qualifying period, shall, subject to *subsection (2A)(g)(iii)*, be reduced by so much of an amount equal to the film corporation tax credit specified in the film certificate as does not exceed that corporation tax and where the qualifying period is a period referred to in *paragraph (b)* of the definition of "*qualifying period*", the corporation tax of an earlier accounting period shall be reduced in priority to the corporation tax of a later accounting period.

(b) Subject to *subsection (3C)*, where the Revenue Commissioners have specified a film corporation tax credit in a film certificate and the amount of the credit exceeds the corporation tax of the qualifying period, as reduced by the corporation tax paid by the company in respect of that period but before any reduction under *paragraph (a)*, the excess (in this section referred to as the "*specified amount*") shall be paid to the producer company by the Revenue Commissioners.

(c) The specified amount shall be paid by the Revenue Commissioners to the film producer company not later than the date specified in the film certificate issued to the company, which shall not be earlier than the date set out in the regulations made under *subsection (2E)*.][75]

[(3A) (a) Any amount payable by the Revenue Commissioners to the company by virtue of *subsection (3)(b)* shall be deemed to be an overpayment of corporation tax, for the purposes only of *section 960H(2)*.

(b) Any claim in respect of a specified amount shall be deemed for the purposes of *section 1077E* to be a claim in connection with a credit and, for the purposes of determining an amount in accordance with *section 1077E(11)* or *1077E(12)*, a reference to an amount of tax that would have been payable for the relevant periods by the person concerned shall be read as if it were a reference to a specified amount.

(c) Where the Revenue Commissioners have paid a specified amount to a producer company and it is subsequently found that all or part of the amount is not as authorised by this section (in this section referred to as the "*unauthorised amount*"), then—

(i) the company,

(ii) any director of the company, or

(iii) any person referred to in *subparagraph (ii)* of *paragraph (b)* of *subsection (2A)*, may be charged to tax under Case IV of Schedule D for the accounting period, or year of assessment, as the case may be, in respect of which the payment was made, in an amount equal to—

(I) in the case of a company, 4 times, and

(II) in the case of an individual, one hundred forty-firsts,

of so much of the specified amount as is not so authorised.

(d) The circumstances in which an unauthorised amount arises shall include any circumstances where the amount was paid in accordance with *paragraph (b)* of *subsection (3)* and—

(i) the Revenue Commissioners revoke a certificate issued under *subsection (2A)(a)*, or

(ii) the producer company or the qualifying company—

(I) fails to satisfy or comply with any condition or obligation required by this section or regulations made under this section,

(II) fails to satisfy or comply with any condition or obligation specified in a film certificate, including a condition to complete, deliver, exhibit or make available for exhibition the qualifying film by a time specified in a film certificate, or

(III) at any time on or before the time referred to in *subsection (2C)(e)* fails to comply with any of the obligations referred to in *subsection (2A)(b)(ii)*.

(e) Where in accordance with *paragraph (c)* an inspector makes an assessment in respect of a specified amount, the amount so charged shall for the purposes of section 1080 be deemed to be tax due and payable and shall carry interest as determined in accordance with *subsection (2)(c)* of *section 1080* as if a reference to the date when the tax became due and payable were a reference to the date the amount was paid by the Revenue Commissioners.

(3B) (a) The amount which is provided by the producer company to the qualifying company in accordance with *subparagraph (ii)* of *subsection (2C)(g)* shall not—

(i) be a sum which may be deducted in computing the profits or gains to be charged to tax under Case I of Schedule D and shall not otherwise reduce the income of the producer company,

(ii) subject to *subsection (3)*, reduce the corporation tax of the producer company,

(iii) be provided in a manner which is wholly or partly for the purpose of, or in connection with, securing a tax advantage, or

(iv) be income of the qualifying company for any tax purpose.

(b) A failure by the qualifying company to repay any part of the amount referred to in *paragraph (a)* to the producer company shall not be a sum which may be deducted in computing the profits or gains of the producer company to be charged to tax under Case I of Schedule D and shall not otherwise reduce the income of the producer company.

(c) Notwithstanding *sections 411* and *616*, the producer and the qualifying company shall be deemed not to be members of the same group of companies for the purposes of—

(i) *section 411*, or

(ii) except for the purposes of *section 626, section 616*.

(d) A loss, for the purposes of *section 546*, shall not be treated as arising on the disposal by the producer company of shares in the qualifying company.

(e) *Section 626B* shall be deemed not to apply to the disposal by the producer company of shares in the qualifying company.

(f) For the purposes of *section 538(2)*, the value of the shares held by the producer company in the qualifying company, shall not, at any time, be negligible.

(3C) The Revenue Commissioners shall not pay a specified amount to a producer company in respect of a film certificate issued after 31 December 2020.][76]

[…][77]

[(22A) Any functions which are authorised by this section to be performed or discharged by the Revenue Commissioners may be performed or discharged by an authorised officer and any references in this section to the Revenue Commissioners shall, with any necessary modifications, be construed as including references to the authorised officer.][78]

(23) Every regulation made under this section shall be laid before Dáil Éireann as soon as may be after it is made and, if a resolution annulling the regulation is passed by Dáil Éireann within the next 21 days on which Dáil Éireann has sat after the regulation is laid before it, the regulation shall be annulled accordingly, but without prejudice to the validity of anything previously done thereunder.][79]

Amendments

[1] Deleted by FA13 s21(1)(a).

[2, 6, 8, 17] Inserted by FA13 s21(1)(i).

[3] Inserted by FA12 s24(a). Deemed to have come into force and takes effect on and from 1 January 2012.

[4] Substituted by F(No.2)A13 s24(1). Comes into operation on such day as the Minister for Finance may by order appoint.

[5] Substituted by FA13 s21(1)(b).

[7] Substituted by FA13 s21(1)(c).

[9] Deleted by FA14 s24(1)(a). Comes into operation on such day as the Minister for Finance may appoint by order.

[10] Substituted by FA00 s48(1)(a)(i). With effect from 20 July 2000 per S.I. 258 of 2000.

[11] Substituted by FA04 s28(1)(a)(iv). With effect from 1 January 2005 per S.I. 814 of 2004.

[12] Deleted by FA13 s21(1)(d).

[13] Substituted by FA13 s21(1)(e).

[14] Deleted by FA13 s21(1)(f).

[15] Deleted by FA13 s21(1)(g).

[16] Deleted by FA13 s21(1)(h).

[18, 19] Substituted by FA13 s21(1)(j)(i).

[20] Deleted by FA05 s36(a).

[21] Substituted by FA04 s28(1)(b)(i). With effect from 1 January 2005 per S.I. 814 of 2004.

[22] Deleted by FA13 s21(1)(j)(ii).

[23] Deleted by FA04 s28(1)(b)(iii). With effect from 1 January 2005 per S.I. 814 of 2004.

[24, 25] Substituted by FA13 s21(1)(k).

[26] Inserted by FA14 s24(1)(b)(i)(I). Comes into operation on such day as the Minister for Finance may appoint by order.

[27] Deleted by FA14 s24(1)(b)(i)(II). Comes into operation on such day as the Minister for Finance may appoint by order.

[28] Substituted by FA14 s24(1)(b)(i)(III). Comes into operation on such day as the Minister for Finance may appoint by order.

[29] Substituted by FA13 s21(1)(l).

[30] Inserted by FA14 s24(1)(b)(i)(IV). Comes into operation on such day as the Minister for Finance may appoint by order.

[31] Substituted by FA14 s24(1)(b)(ii). Comes into operation on such day as the Minister for Finance may appoint by order.

[32, 33] Substituted by FA13 s21(1)(m).

[34] Deleted by FA05 s36(b)(i).

[35] Inserted by FA13 s21(1)(n).

[36] Substituted by FA13 s21(1)(o).

[37] Inserted by FA13 s21(1)(p).

[38] Substituted by FA05 s36(b)(iii).

[39] Substituted by FA12 s24(d). Deemed to have come into force and takes effect on and from 1 January 2012.

[40] Inserted by FA05 s36(b)(iv).

[41] Substituted by FA13 s21(1)(q).

[42] Substituted by FA13 s21(1)(r).

[43] Substituted by FA13 s21(1)(s).

[44] Substituted by FA14 s24(1)(c)(i). Comes into operation on such day as the Minister for Finance may appoint by order.

[45] Substituted by FA12 s24(e). Deemed to have come into force and takes effect on and from 1 January 2012.

[46] Substituted by FA13 s21(1)(t).

[47] Substituted by FA07 sched2(1)(o). Has effect as on and from 2 April 2007.

[48] Deleted by FA12 s24(f). Deemed to have come into force and takes effect on and from 1 January 2012.

[49] Inserted by FA13 s21(1)(u)(i).

[50] Inserted by FA13 s21(1)(u)(ii).

[51] Substituted by FA13 s21(1)(u)(iii).

[52] Deleted by FA12 s24(g). Deemed to have come into force and takes effect on and from 1 January 2012.

[53] Substituted by FA12 s24(h). Deemed to have come into force and takes effect on and from 1 January 2012.

[54] Deleted by FA13 s21(1)(v).

[55] Substituted by FA13 s21(1)(w).

[56] Deleted by FA14 s24(1)(c)(ii). Comes into operation on such day as the Minister for Finance may appoint by order.

[57] Inserted by FA13 s21(1)(x).

[58] Substituted by FA13 s21(1)(y).

[59] Substituted by FA13 s21(1)(z).

[60] Substituted by FA13 s21(1)(aa).

[61] Inserted by FA12 s24(j). Deemed to have come into force and takes effect on and from 1 January 2012.

[62] Substituted by FA13 s21(1)(ab).

[63] Substituted by FA13 s21(1)(ac)(i).

[64, 66] Substituted by FA13 s21(1)(ac)(ii).

[65] Deleted by FA05 s36(d)(i).

[67] Inserted by FA04 s28(1)(c). With effect from 1 January 2005 per S.I. 814 of 2004.

[68] Substituted by FA12 s24(k). Deemed to have come into force and takes effect on and from 1 January 2012.

[69] Deleted by FA13 s21(1)(ac)(iii).

[70] Substituted by FA13 s21(1)(ac)(iv).

[71] Inserted by FA05 s36(d)(ii).

[72] Inserted by FA13 s21(1)(ad).

[73] Substituted by FA13 s21(1)(ae).

[74] Inserted by FA12 s24(l). Deemed to have come into force and takes effect on and from 1 January 2012.

[75] Substituted by FA13 s21(1)(af).

[76] Inserted by FA13 s21(1)(ag).

[77] Deleted by FA13 s21(1)(ah).

[78] Inserted by FA06 s18(1)(b). With effect from 18 May 2006 per S.I. 256 of 2006.

[79] Inserted by FA04 s28(1)(h). With effect from 1 January 2005 per S.I. 814 of 2004.

Note

FA13 s21 comes into operation on such day or days as the Minister for Finance may by order or orders appoint and different days may be appointed for different purposes or for different provisions.

Revenue Briefings

Tax Briefing

Tax Briefing August 2003 – Issue 53 pg 14 – Investments under section 481

eBrief

eBrief No. 46/2008 – Film Relief – New regulations made

Revenue Information Notes

IT57 – Film Relief
Film 1 – Tax relief for investment in films
Guidance notes for film producers and promoters
Proposals for Investments under section 481, Advance opinions
Guidelines on the administration of the scheme

Cross References

From Section 481

Section 554 Exclusion of expenditure by reference to income tax.
Section 826 Agreements for relief from double taxation.
Section 864 Making of claims, etc.
Section 886 Obligation to keep certain records.
Section 949 Appeals against determinations of certain claims, etc.
Section 986 Regulations.
Section 1017 Assessment of husband in respect of income of both spouses.
Section 1028 Married persons.
Schedule 32 Transitional Provisions

To Section 481

Section 251 Restriction of relief to individuals on loans applied in acquiring shares in companies where a claim for "BES relief" or "film relief" is made in respect of amount subscribed for shares.
Section 458 Deductions allowed in ascertaining taxable income and provisions relating to reductions in tax.
Section 488 Interpretation (Part 16).
Section 958 Date for payment of tax.
Section 1024 Method of apportioning reliefs and charging tax in cases of separate assessments.
Schedule 25B List of Specified Reliefs and Method of Determining Amount of Specified Relief Used in a Tax Year
Schedule 32 Transitional Provisions

482 Relief for expenditure on significant buildings and gardens

[FA82 s19; FA93 s29; FA94 s18; FA95 s20; FA97 s17]

(1) (a) In this section—

"*approved building*" means a building to which *subsection (5)* applies;

"*approved garden*" means a garden (other than a garden, being land occupied or enjoyed with an approved building as part of its garden or grounds of an ornamental nature) which, on application to the Minister and the

Revenue Commissioners in that behalf by a person who owns or occupies the garden, is determined—

(i) by the Minister to be a garden which is intrinsically of significant horticultural, scientific, historical, architectural or aesthetic interest, and

(ii) by the Revenue Commissioners to be a garden to which reasonable access is afforded to the public;

"*approved object*", in relation to an approved building, has the meaning assigned to it by *subsection (6)*;

"*authorised person*" means—

(i) an inspector or other officer of the Revenue Commissioners authorised by them in writing for the purposes of this section, or

(ii) a person authorised by the Minister in writing for the purposes of this section;

"*chargeable period*" has the same meaning as in *section 321(2)*;

"*the Minister*" means the Minister for Arts, Heritage, Gaeltacht and the Islands;

"*public place*", in relation to an approved building in use as a tourist accommodation facility, means a part of the building to which all patrons of the facility have access;

"*qualifying expenditure*", in relation to an approved building, means expenditure incurred by the person who owns or occupies the approved building on one or more of the following—

(i) the repair, maintenance or restoration of the approved building or the maintenance or restoration of any land occupied or enjoyed with the approved building as part of its garden or grounds of an ornamental nature, and

(ii) to the extent that the aggregate expenditure in a chargeable period, being the year 1997–98 and any subsequent year of assessment, or an accounting period of a company beginning on or after the 6th day of April, 1997, does not exceed [€6,350][1] [or, where the chargeable period is the year of assessment 2001, £3,700][2]—

(I) the repair, maintenance or restoration of an approved object in the approved building,

(II) the installation, maintenance or replacement of a security alarm system in the approved building, and

(III) public liability insurance for the approved building;

"*relevant expenditure*", in relation to an approved garden, means—

(i) in the case of expenditure incurrred in a chargeable period, being the year 1997–98 and any subsequent year of assessment, or an accounting period of a company beginning on or after the 6th day of April, 1997, expenditure incurred by the person who owns or occupies the approved garden on one or more of the following—

(I) the maintenance or restoration of the approved garden, and

(II) to the extent that the aggregate expenditure in a chargeable period does not exceed [€6,350][3] [or, where the chargeable period is the year of assessment 2001, £3,700][4]—

(A) the repair, maintenance or restoration of an approved object in the approved garden,

(B) the installation, maintenance or replacement of a security alarm system in the approved garden, and

(C) public liability insurance for the approved garden, and

[(ii) in the case of expenditure incurred in a chargeable period earlier than that referred to in subparagraph (i), expenditure incurred by the person who owned or occupied the approved garden on the maintenance or restoration of the garden;][5]

"*security alarm system*" means an electrical apparatus installed as a fixture in the approved building or in the approved garden which when activated is designed to give notice to the effect that there is an intruder present or attempting to enter the approved building or the approved garden, as the case may be, in which it is installed;

"*tourist accommodation facility*" means an accommodation facility—

(i) registered in the register of guest houses maintained and kept by [the National Tourism Development Authority][6] under Part III of the Tourist Traffic Act, 1939, or

(ii) listed in the list published or caused to be published by [the National Tourism Development Authority][7] under section 9 of the Tourist Traffic Act, [1957;][8]

["*weekend day*" means a Saturday or a Sunday.][9]

(b) For the purposes of this section, expenditure shall not be regarded as having been incurred in so far as any sum in respect of or by reference to the work to which the expenditure relates has been or is to be received directly or indirectly by the person making a claim in respect of the expenditure under *subsection (2)* from the State, from any public or local authority, from any other person or under any contract of insurance or by means of compensation or otherwise.

(c) For the purposes of this section, references to an approved building, unless the contrary intention is expressed, shall be construed as including a reference to any land occupied or enjoyed with an approved building as part of its garden or grounds of an ornamental nature.

(2) [(a) Subject to this section, and notwithstanding any limitation in *section 865(4)* on the time within which a claim for a repayment of tax is required to be made, where a person (in this section referred to as "the claimant"), having made a claim in that behalf, proves that the conditions specified in *paragraph (b)* have been met, then, the Tax Acts shall apply as if the amount of the qualifying expenditure referred to in *subparagraph (i)* of *paragraph (b)* were a loss sustained in the chargeable period referred to in that subparagraph in a trade carried on by the claimant separate from any trade actually carried on by the claimant. *Section 865(6)* shall not prevent the Revenue Commissioners from repaying an amount of tax

as a consequence of a claim made under this section, where a valid claim for a repayment of tax (within the meaning of *section 865(1)(b)*) has been made.][10]

(b) The conditions referred to in *paragraph (a)* are—

(i) that the claimant has incurred in a chargeable period qualifying expenditure in relation to an approved building,

(ii) that the claimant has [on or before the 1st day of November][11] in the chargeable period in respect of which the claim is made and in each of the chargeable periods comprising whichever is the shortest of the following periods—

(I) the period consisting of the chargeable periods since the 23rd day of May, 1994,

(II) the period consisting of the chargeable periods since a determination under *subsection (5)(a)(ii)* was made in relation to the building,

(III) the period consisting of the chargeable periods since the approved building was purchased or occupied by the claimant,

(IV) the period consisting of the 5 chargeable periods immediately preceding the chargeable period for which the claim is made,

provided [the National Tourism Development Authority][12] (in this paragraph referred to as "*[the Authority]*[13]") with particulars of—

(A) the name, if any, and address of the approved building, and

(B) the days and times during the year when access to the approved building is afforded to the public or the period or periods during the year when the approved building is in use as a tourist accommodation facility, as the case may be,

such particulars being provided to [the Authority][14] on the understanding by the person and [the Authority][15] that they may be published by [the Authority][16] or by another body concerned with the promotion of tourism, and

(iii) where the approved building was in use as a tourist accommodation facility in any of the chargeable periods applicable for the purposes of *subparagraph (ii)*, that the approved building was registered in the register of guest houses maintained and kept by [the Authority][17] under Part III of the Tourist Traffic Act, 1939, or listed in the list published or caused to be published by the Board under section 9 of the Tourist Traffic Act, 1957, in those chargeable periods.

(c) Relief authorised by this subsection shall not apply for any chargeable period before the chargeable period in which the application concerned is made to the Revenue Commissioners under *subsection (5)(a)*.

[(d) For the purpose only of determining, in relation to a claim referred to in *paragraph (a)*, whether and to what extent qualifying expenditure incurred in relation to an approved building is incurred or not incurred in a chargeable period, only such an amount of that qualifying expenditure as is properly attributable to work which was actually carried out during the chargeable period shall (notwithstanding any other provision of the Tax Acts as to the time when any expenditure is or is to be treated as incurred) be treated as having been incurred in that period.][18]

(3) (a) Where—

(i) by virtue of *subsection (2)*, qualifying expenditure in a chargeable period is treated as if it were a loss sustained in the chargeable period in a trade carried on by the person separate from any trade actually carried on by that person, and

(ii) owing to an insufficiency of income, relief under the Tax Acts cannot be given for any part of the qualifying expenditure so treated (in this subsection referred to as "*the unrelieved amount*"),

then, the Tax Acts shall apply as if the unrelieved amount were a loss sustained in the following chargeable period in a trade carried on by the person separate from any trade actually carried on by that person.

(b) Where owing to an insufficiency of income relief under the Tax Acts cannot be given by virtue of *paragraph (a)* for any part of the unrelieved amount, then, the Tax Acts shall apply as if that part of the unrelieved amount were a loss sustained in the chargeable period following the period referred to in *paragraph (a)* in a trade carried on by the person separate from any trade actually carried on by that person.

(c) Where in any chargeable period relief under the Tax Acts is due by virtue of 2 or more of the following provisions, that is, *subsection (2)* and *paragraphs (a)* and *(b)*, then, the following provisions shall apply:

(i) any relief due under those Acts by virtue of *paragraph (b)* shall be given in priority to any relief due under those Acts by virtue of *subsection (2)* or *paragraph (a)*, and

(ii) where relief has been given in accordance with *subparagraph (i)* or where no such relief is due, any relief due under those Acts by virtue of *paragraph (a)* shall be given in priority to relief due under those Acts by virtue of *subsection (2)*.

(4) No relief shall be allowed under this section for expenditure in respect of which relief may be claimed under any other provision of the Tax Acts.

(5) (a) This subsection shall apply to a building in the State which, on application to the Minister and the Revenue Commissioners in that behalf by a person who owns or occupies the building, is determined—

(i) by the Minister to be a building which is intrinsically of significant scientific, historical, architectural or aesthetic interest, and

(ii) by the Revenue Commissioners to be a building either—

(I) to which reasonable access is afforded to the public, or

(II) which is in use as a tourist accommodation facility for at least 6 months in any calendar year (in this subsection referred to as "*the required period*") including not less than 4 months in the period commencing on the 1st day of May and ending on the 30th day of September in any such year.

(b) Without prejudice to the generality of the requirement that reasonable access be afforded to the public, access to a building shall not be regarded as being reasonable access afforded to the public unless—

(i) access to the whole or a substantial part of the building is afforded at the same time,

[(ii) subject to temporary closure necessary for the purposes of the repair, maintenance or restoration of the building, access is so afforded for a period of not less than 60 days in any year, and—

(I) such period shall include, as respects determinations made by the Revenue Commissioners in accordance with *paragraph (a)*(ii)—

(A) before the passing of the Finance Act, 2000, not less than 40 days, and

(B) on or after the passing of the Finance Act, 2000, not less than 40 days, of which not less than 10 are weekend days,

during the period commencing on 1 May and ending on 30 September, and

(II) in respect of each such period, on each day concerned access is afforded in a reasonable manner and at reasonable times for a period, or periods in the aggregate, of not less than [4 hours,][19]][20]

(iii) the price, if any, paid by the public in return for that access is in the opinion of the Revenue Commissioners reasonable in amount and does not operate to preclude the public from seeking [access to the building, and][21]

[(iv) the Revenue Commissioners are satisfied that—

(I) details relating to that access are publicised or drawn to the attention of the public by way of advertisement, leaflet, press notice or similar means annually,

(II) a notice containing the details of the dates and times at which access is afforded to the public—

(A) is displayed on the days on which such access is so afforded and in a conspicuous location at or near the place where the public can gain entrance to the building concerned, and

(B) is so displayed so as to be easily visible and legible by the public,

and

(III) conditions, if any, in regard to that access are such that they would not act as a disincentive to the public from seeking such access.][22]

[(ba) Where qualifying expenditure is incurred after 8 February 2012, the 40 days referred to in *paragraph (b)(ii)(I)(B)* shall, in relation to the chargeable period in which expenditure is incurred, include the days which comprise National Heritage Week, as designated for each year by the Heritage Council, to the extent that it falls within the period referred to in *paragraph (b)(ii)(I)*.][23]

(c) Where under *paragraph (a)* the Minister makes a determination in relation to a building and, by reason of any alteration made to the building or any deterioration of the building subsequent to the determination being made, the Minister considers that the building is no longer a building which is intrinsically of significant scientific, historical, architectural or aesthetic interest, the Minister may, by notice in writing given to the owner or occupier of the building, revoke the determination with effect from the date on which the Minister considers that the building ceased to be a building which is intrinsically of significant scientific, historical, architectural or aesthetic interest, and this subsection shall cease to apply to the building from that date.

(d) Where under *paragraph (a)* the Revenue Commissioners make a determination in relation to a building, and reasonable access to the building ceases to be afforded to the public or the building ceases to be used as a tourist accommodation facility for the required period, as the case may be, the Revenue Commissioners may, by notice in writing given to the owner or occupier of the building, revoke the determination with effect from the date on which they consider that such access or such use, as the case may be, so ceased, and—

(i) this subsection shall cease to apply to the building from that date, and

(ii) if relief has been given under this section in respect of qualifying expenditure incurred in relation to that building in the period of 5 years ending on the date from which the revocation has effect, that relief shall be withdrawn [and assessments shall, as necessary, be made or amended][24] to give effect to this subsection.

(e) Where—

(i) the Revenue Commissioners make a determination (in this paragraph referred to as the "*first-mentioned determination*") that a building is either a building to which reasonable access is afforded to the public or a building which is in use as a tourist accommodation facility for the required period,

(ii) such access ceases to be so afforded or such building ceases to be so used, as the case may be, in a chargeable period subsequent to the chargeable period in which the first-mentioned determination was made, and

(iii) on application to them in that chargeable period in that behalf by the person who owns or occupies the building, the Revenue Commissioners revoke the first-mentioned determination and make a further determination (in this paragraph referred to as the "*second-mentioned determination*") with effect from the date of revocation of the first-mentioned determination—

(I) in the case of a building in respect of which a determination was made that it is a building to which reasonable access is afforded to the public, that the building is a building which is in use as a tourist accommodation facility for the required period, or

(II) in the case of a building in respect of which a determination was made that it is a building which is in use as a tourist accommodation facility for the required period, that the building is a building to which reasonable access is afforded to the public, then, *paragraph (d)* shall not apply on the revocation of the first-mentioned determination and for the purposes of that paragraph the second-mentioned determination shall be treated as having been made at the time of the making of the first-mentioned determination.

(6) (a) In this subsection, "*approved object*", in relation to an approved building, means an object (including a picture, sculpture, print, book, manuscript, piece of jewellery, furniture, or other similar object) or a scientific collection which is owned by the owner or occupier of the approved building and which, on application to them in that behalf by that person, is determined—

(i) by the Minister, after consideration of any evidence in relation to the matter which such owner or occupier submits to the Minister and after such consultation (if any) as may seem to the Minister to be necessary with such person or body of persons as in the opinion of the Minister may be of assistance to the Minister, to be an object which is intrinsically of significant national, scientific, historical or aesthetic interest, and

(ii) by the Revenue Commissioners, to be an object reasonable access to which is afforded, and in respect of which reasonable facilities for viewing are provided, in the building to the public.

(b) Without prejudice to the generality of the requirement that reasonable access be afforded, and that reasonable facilities for viewing be provided, to the public, access to and facilities for the viewing of an object shall not be regarded as being reasonable access afforded, or the provision of reasonable facilities for viewing, to the public unless, subject to such temporary removal as is necessary for the purposes of the repair, maintenance or restoration of the object as is reasonable—

(i) in a case where the approved building is a tourist accommodation facility, the object is displayed in a public place in the building, or

(ii) in the case of any other approved building—

(I) access to the object is afforded and such facilities for viewing the object are provided to the public on the same days and at the same times as access is afforded to the public to the approved building in which the object is kept, and

(II) the price, if any, paid by the public in return for such access is in the opinion of the Revenue Commissioners reasonable in amount and does not operate to preclude the public from seeking access to the object.

(c) Where under *paragraph (a)* the Minister makes a determination in relation to an object and, by reason of any alteration made to the object, or any deterioration of the object, subsequent to the determination being made, the Minister considers that the object is no longer an object which is intrinsically of significant national, scientific, historical or aesthetic interest, the Minister may, by notice in writing given to the owner or occupier of the building, revoke the determination with effect from the date on which the Minister considers that the object ceased to be an object which is intrinsically of significant national, scientific, historical or aesthetic interest, and this subsection shall cease to apply to the object from that date.

(d) Where under *paragraph (a)* the Revenue Commissioners make a determination in relation to an object and—

(i) reasonable access to the object ceases to be afforded, or reasonable facilities for the viewing of the object cease to be provided, to the public, or

(ii) the object ceases to be owned by the person to whom relief in respect of that qualifying expenditure has been granted under this section,

the Revenue Commissioners may, by notice in writing given to the owner or occupier of the approved building in which the object is or was kept, revoke that determination with effect from the date on which they consider that such access, such facilities for viewing or such ownership, as the case may be, so ceased, and—

(I) this subsection shall cease to apply to the object from that date, and

(II) if relief has been given under this section in respect of qualifying expenditure incurred in relation to that object in the period of 2 years ending on the date from which the revocation has effect, that relief shall be withdrawn [and assessments shall, as necessary, be made or amended][25] to give effect to this subsection.

[(a) Where a person makes a claim under *subsection (2)*, an authorised person may at any reasonable time enter the building in respect of which the qualifying expenditure has been incurred for the purpose of—

(i) inspecting, as the case may be, the building or an object or of examining any work in respect of which the expenditure to which the claim relates was incurred, or

(ii) ensuring that the requirements in relation to reasonable access set out in *subsection (5)* are being complied with.][26]

(b) Whenever an authorised person exercises any power conferred on him or her by this subsection, the authorised person shall on request produce his or her authorisation for the purposes of this section to any person concerned.

(c) Any person who obstructs or interferes with an authorised person in the course of exercising a power conferred on the authorised person by this subsection shall be guilty of an offence and shall be liable on summary conviction to a fine not exceeding [€630][27].

[(8) Notwithstanding that the Revenue Commissioners have before the passing of the Finance Act, 2000, made a determination in accordance with *subsection (5)(a)(ii)* that a building is a building to which reasonable access is afforded to the public, relief under *subsection (2)*, in relation to qualifying expenditure incurred in a chargeable period beginning on or after 1 January 1995, in respect of the building shall not be given unless the person who owns or occupies the building satisfies the Revenue Commissioners [on or before 1 November][28] in the chargeable period that it is a building to which reasonable access is afforded to the public having regard to—

(a) in a case where the qualifying expenditure is incurred in a chargeable period beginning before 1 October 2000, *subsection (5)(b)(ii) (I)(A)*, and

(b) in a case where the qualifying expenditure is incurred in a chargeable period beginning on or after 1 October 2000, *subsection (5)(b)(ii) (I)(B)*.][29]

(9) In respect of relevant expenditure incurred on or after the 6th day of April, 1993, this section shall, with any necessary modifications, apply in relation to an approved garden as it applies in relation to qualifying expenditure incurred in relation to an approved building.

(10) Any claim for relief under this section—

(a) shall be made in such form as the Revenue Commissioners may from time to time prescribe, and

(b) shall be accompanied by such statements in writing as regards the expenditure for which relief is claimed, including statements by persons to whom payments were made, as may be indicated by the prescribed form.

[(11) The Tax Acts shall apply to a loss referred to in *subsection (2)* as they would apply if *sections 396A* and *420A* had not been enacted.][30]

Amendments

[1, 3, 27] Substituted by FA01 sched5.

[2] Inserted by FA01 sched2(24)(a). Shall apply only as respects the year of assessment 2001.

[4] Inserted by FA01 sched2(24)(b). Shall apply only as respects the year of assessment 2001.

[5] Substituted by FA02 s42(1)(a). Applies as on and from 30 November 1997.

[6, 7] Substituted by FA06 sched2(1)(m)(i). This section is deemed to have come into force and have taken effect as on and from 28 May 2003.

[8] Substituted by FA00 s49(a). This section shall have effect from 23 March 2000

[9] Inserted by FA00 s49(a). This section shall have effect from 23 March 2000

[10] Substituted by FA08 sched6(1)(e). Applies as on and from 31 January 2008.

[11] Substituted by FA02 s42(1)(b). Apply as respects a chargeable period, being the year of assessment 2002 and any subsequent year of assessment or an accounting period of a company beginning on or after 1 January 2002.

[12] Substituted by FA06 sched2(1)(m)(ii)(I). This section is deemed to have come into force and have taken effect as on and from 28 May 2003.

[13, 14, 15, 16, 17] Substituted by FA06 sched2(1)(m)(ii)(II). This section is deemed to have come into force and have taken effect as on and from 28 May 2003.

[18] Inserted by FA98 s33. Applies as respects qualifying expenditure incurred on or after the 12th day of February, 1998.

[19] Substituted by FA05 s28(a)(i).

[20] Substituted by FA00 s49(b). This section shall have effect from 23 March 2000

[21] Substituted by FA05 s28(a)(ii).

[22] Inserted by FA05 s28(a)(iii).

[23] Inserted by FA12 s23. Deemed to have come into force and takes effect on and from 1 January 2012.

[24] Substituted by FA12 sched4(part 2)(g).

[25] Substituted by FA12 sched4(part 2)(g).

[26] Substituted by FA05 s28(b).

[28] Substituted by FA02 s42(1)(c). Apply as respects a chargeable period, being the year of assessment 2002 and any subsequent year of assessment or an accounting period of a company beginning on or after 1 January 2002.

[29] Substituted by FA00 s49(c). This section shall have effect from 23 March 2000

[30] Inserted by FA02 s42(1)(d). Applies as on and from 6 March 2001.

Revenue Briefings

Tax Briefing

Tax Briefing January 1995 – Issue 17 – Income Tax/Corporation Tax: Relief for expenditure on approved buildings and gardens

Revenue Information Notes

IT56 – Relief for expenditure on approved objects on display in an approved building or garden.
IT30 – Relief for expenditure on approved buildings or gardens in the State.

Cross References

From Section 482

Section 321 Provisions of general application in relation to the making of allowances and charges.
Section 865 Repayment of tax.

To Section 482

Section 236 Loan of certain art objects.
Section 409C Income tax: restriction on use of losses on approved buildings.
Schedule 25B List of Specified Reliefs and Method of Determining Amount of Specified Relief Used in a Tax Year

483 Relief for certain gifts

[ITA67 s195B(3) and (6) and s547(1) to (3); CTA76 s140(1), s147(1) and (2) and Sch2 PtI par27; FA93 s10(1)]

(1) (a) In this subsection, "*public moneys*" means moneys charged on or issued out of the Central Fund or provided by the Oireachtas.

(b) This section shall apply to a gift of money made to the Minister for Finance for use for any purpose for or towards the cost of which public moneys are provided and which is accepted by that Minister.

(2) Where a person who has made a gift to which this section applies claims relief from income tax or corporation tax by reference to the gift, *subsection (3)* or, as the case may be, *subsection (4)* shall apply.

(3) For the purposes of income tax for the year of assessment in which the person makes the gift, the amount of the gift shall be deducted from or set off against any income of the person chargeable to income tax for that year and income tax shall, where necessary, be discharged or repaid accordingly, and the total income of the person or, where the person is [a married person or a civil partner][1] whose income is deemed to be the income of his or her [spouse or civil partner][2], the total income of his or her [spouse or civil partner][3] shall be calculated accordingly.

(4) For the purposes of corporation tax, where the person making the gift is a company, the amount of the gift shall be deemed to be a loss incurred by the company in a separate trade in the accounting period in which the gift is made.

[(5) The Tax Acts shall apply to a loss referred to in *subsection (4)* as they would apply if *sections 396A* and *420A* had not been enacted.][4]

Amendments

[1] Substituted by F(No.3)A11 sched1(122).

[2, 3] Substituted by F(No.3)A11 sched1(123).

[4] Inserted by FA02 s56(1). This section applies from 6 March 2001.

Cross References

To Section 483

Section 531A Definitions (Part 18A).

Section 531AL Definitions (Part 18D).

484 Relief for gifts for education in the arts [Repealed]

Repealed by TCA97 s848A, as inserted by FA01 s45.

Cross References

To Section 484

Section 848A Donations to approved bodies.

485 Relief for gifts to third-level institutions [Repealed]

Repealed by TCA97 s848A, as inserted by FA01 s45.

Cross References

To Section 485

Section 848A Donations to approved bodies.

485A Relief for gifts made to designated schools [Repealed]

Repealed by TCA97 s848A, as inserted by FA01 s45.

Cross References

To Section 485A

Section 848A Donations to approved bodies.

485B Relief for gifts to the Scientific and Technological Education (Investment) Fund [Repealed]

Repealed by TCA97 s848A, as inserted by FA01 s45.

Cross References

To Section 485B

Section 848A Donations to approved bodies.

CHAPTER 2A

Limitation on Amount of Certain Reliefs Used by Certain High Income Individuals

485C Interpretation (Chapter 2A)

[(1) [In this Chapter and in *Schedules 25B* and *25C*,][1] except where the context otherwise requires—

"*adjusted income*", in relation to a tax year and an individual, means the amount determined by the formula—

$$(T + S) - R$$

where—

[T is the amount of the individual's taxable income for the tax year determined on the basis that—

(a) this Chapter, other than *section 485F*, does not apply to the individual for the tax year, and][2] [(b) (i) if the individual, being a married person, is assessable to tax for the tax year otherwise than under *section 1016*, the provisions under which the individual is assessable are modified in accordance with *paragraphs (i)* to *(vi)*, but excluding *paragraph (iia)* of section 485FA,

(ii) if the individual, being a civil partner, is assessable to tax for the tax year otherwise than under *section 1031B*, the provisions under which the individual is assessable are modified in accordance with *paragraphs (i), (iia)* and *(vi)* of section 485FA,][3]

S is the aggregate of the specified reliefs for the tax year, and

R is the amount of the individual's ring-fenced income, if any, for the tax year;

"aggregate of the specified reliefs", in relation to a tax year and an individual, means the aggregate of the amounts of specified reliefs used by the individual in respect of the tax year;

"*amount of specified relief*", in relation to a specified relief used by an individual in respect of a tax year, [but subject to *subsection (1A)*],[4] means the amount of the specified relief used by the individual in respect of the tax year determined by reference to the entry in *column (3)* of *Schedule 25B* opposite the reference to the specified relief concerned in *column (2)* of that Schedule;

"*excess relief*", in relation to a tax year and an individual, means the amount by which the individual's taxable income for the tax year determined in accordance with section 485E exceeds the amount that the individual's taxable income for the tax year would have been had this Chapter, other than *section 485F*, not applied to that individual for that year;

["*income threshold amount*", in relation to a tax year and an individual, means—

(a) €125,000, or

(b) in a case where the individual's income for the tax year includes ring-fenced income and his or her adjusted income for the tax year is less than €400,000, the amount determined by the formula—

$$€125,000 \times \frac{A}{B}$$

where—

A is the individual's adjusted income for the year, and

B is an amount determined by the formula—

$$T + S$$

where T and S have the same meanings respectively as they have in the definition of "*adjusted income*";

"*relief threshold amount*", in relation to a tax year and an individual, means €80,000;][5]

["*Revenue officer*" means an officer of the Revenue Commissioners;][6]

"*ring-fenced income*", in relation to a tax year and an individual, means the aggregate of the following amounts, if any, charged to tax on the individual for the tax year—

(a) income chargeable to tax in accordance with *subparagraph (i)* of *paragraph (c)* of *section 261* where clause (II) of that subparagraph applies to the income concerned,

[(b) income referred to in *section 261B* or *267M*,

(c) income charged to tax in accordance with clause (I) or (II)(B) of *section 730J(1)(a)(i)* or *section 730K(1)(b)*, and

(d) income charged to tax in accordance with *section 747D(a)(i)* or *section 747E(1)(b)*;][7]

"*specified relief*", in relation to a tax year and an individual, means [any relief arising under, or by virtue of, any of the provisions][8] set out in *column (2)* of *Schedule 25B*;

"*tax year*" means a year of assessment;

[...][9]

[(1A) Where a balancing charge is made under *section 274*, in relation to a building or structure, on an individual for a tax year, then—

(a) to the extent that any unused capital allowances attributable to capital expenditure incurred on the construction or refurbishment of that building or structure, have been carried forward in accordance with *section 304* or *305* to the tax year, and are used in that tax year to reduce the amount of the balancing charge, those allowances so used shall not be treated as an amount of specified relief under this Chapter, and

(b) any amount by which the balancing charge has been reduced in the manner referred to in *paragraph (a)*, shall not be taken into account for the purposes of determining the adjusted income of the individual for the tax year.][10]

[(1B) (a) For the purposes of this subsection and *Schedule 25B* "*specified plant and machinery*" means plant and machinery on which a wear and tear allowance may be granted under *section 284*, whether by virtue of *section 298* or otherwise, which would be restricted by *section 403(3)* save for the provisions of *section 403(9)*.

(b) Subject to *paragraph (d)*, a wear and tear allowance granted under *section 284*, or deemed to have been made to an individual under *section 287*, whether by virtue of *section 298* or otherwise, shall only be a specified relief to the extent it relates to specified plant and machinery.

(c) Subject to *paragraph (d)*, a balancing allowance arising under *section 288* shall only be a specified relief to the extent it relates to specified plant and machinery.

(d) This subsection and the matters set out opposite reference numbers 15C and 15D in *Schedule 25B* shall not apply to allowances granted to an individual who in respect of the trade to which the allowances relate is an active trader, within the meaning of *section 409D*, or an active partner, within the meaning of *section 409A*.][11]

(2) (a) For the purposes of this Chapter, references in this Chapter to specified reliefs used by the individual in respect of the tax year include references in the Tax Acts to—

(i) an allowance having been made to the individual for the year, in respect of which allowance, effect has been given, in full or in part, for that year,

(ii) a deduction having been given or allowed to the individual for the year, in respect of which deduction, effect has been given, in full or in part, for that year,

(iii) a deduction from or set off against income of whatever description being allowed to the individual for the year, in respect of which deduction or set off, effect has been given, in full or in part, for that year,

(iv) relief given to the individual for the year by way of repayment or discharge of tax in respect of which repayment or discharge effect has been given, in full or in part, for that year,

(v) income, profits or gains arising to the individual in the year being exempt from income tax for the year,

(vi) income, profits or gains arising to the individual in the year being disregarded or not reckoned for the purposes of the Income Tax Acts or, as the case may be, for the purposes of income tax for the year,

and other references in the Tax Acts to methods of affording relief from tax, however expressed, and in respect of which effect, in full or in part, has been given in the tax year shall likewise be construed as included in any reference in this Chapter to specified reliefs used by the individual in respect of the tax year.

(b) For the purposes of the definition of the "*amount of specified relief*", in relation to a specified relief which is of a kind referred to in subparagraph (v) or (vi) of *paragraph (a)*, the amount of any income, profits or gains, as the case may be, shall be computed in accordance with the Tax Acts as if the specified relief concerned had not been enacted.

(3) Notwithstanding any other provision of the Tax Acts, the following provisions shall apply for the purposes of those Acts—

[(a) where, in relation to any tax year and the capital allowances to be given effect to in that year, any provision of the Tax Acts requires allowances (in this paragraph referred to as the "*first-mentioned allowances*") for one period to be given effect to, or to be deemed to be given effect to, in priority to allowances for another period (in this paragraph referred to as the "*second-mentioned allowances*"), then—

(i) as respects the first-mentioned allowances, effect shall be given, or be deemed to be given, as the case may be, for an allowance which is not a specified relief in priority to any such allowance which is a specified relief and in priority to the second-mentioned allowances, and

(ii) as respects the second-mentioned allowances, effect shall be given, or be deemed to be given, as the case may be, for an allowance which is not a specified relief in priority to any such allowance which is a specified relief,

(ab) a deduction authorised by *subsection (2)* of *section 97* shall be allowed in respect of a matter which is specifically referred to in that subsection in priority to a deduction authorised to be made under that subsection by virtue of a specified relief,

(ac) a deduction from total income shall be made in respect of a relief due for a tax year which is not a specified relief in priority to any such deduction due for the tax year which is a specified relief,][12]

(b) loss relief for any tax year shall be given in respect of a loss which is not referable to a specified relief in priority to relief being given for a loss which is referable to a specified relief,

(c) a further deduction due under *section 324*, *333*, *345*, *354* or paragraph 13 of *Schedule 32* for a tax year shall only be given effect for that year after effect is given to any other deduction the individual is entitled to for that year in computing the amount of the individual's profits or gains to be charged to tax for that year under Case I or II of *Schedule D*.

[(4) *Schedules 25B* and *25C* shall have effect for the purposes of this Chapter.][13][14]

Amendments

[1] Substituted by FA07 s18(1)(a)(i)(I). Applies for the year of assessment 2007 and subsequent years of assessment.

[2] Substituted by FA07 s18(1)(a)(i)(II). Applies for the year of assessment 2007 and subsequent years of assessment.

[3] Substituted by F(No.3)A11 sched1(124).

[4] Inserted by FA12 s16(3)(a). Applies to a balancing charge (within the meaning of *section 274*) that is made on or after 1 January 2012.

[5] Inserted by FA10 s23(1)(a). Applies as respects the year of assessment 2010 and subsequent years of assessment.

[6] Inserted by FA07 s18(1)(a)(i)(III). Applies for the year of assessment 2007 and subsequent years of assessment.

[7] Substituted by FA07 s18(1)(a)(i)(IV). Applies for the year of assessment 2007 and subsequent years of assessment.

[8] Substituted by FA07 s18(1)(a)(i)(V). Applies for the year of assessment 2007 and subsequent years of assessment.

[9] Deleted by FA10 s23(1)(b). Applies as respects the year of assessment 2010 and subsequent years of assessment.

[10] Inserted by FA12 s16(3)(b). Applies to a balancing charge (within the meaning of section 274) that is made on or after 1 January 2012.

[11] Inserted by F(No.2)A13 s16(b). Comes into operation on 1 January 2014.

[12] Substituted by FA07 s18(1)(a)(ii). Applies for the year of assessment 2007 and subsequent years of assessment.

[13] Substituted by FA07 s18(1)(a)(iii). Applies for the year of assessment 2007 and subsequent years of assessment.

[14] Inserted by FA06 s17(1). Applies for the year of assessment 2007 and subsequent years of assessment.

Revenue Briefings

Tax Briefing

Tax Briefing July 2007 – Issue 66 – Finance Act 2007 Changes to this Chapter
Tax Briefing September 2009 – Issue 75 – High Income Individuals' Restriction
Tax Briefing June 2010 – Issue 08 – Clawback of "section 23 type" relief in death cases

eBrief

eBrief No. 75/2014 – Double Taxation Relief for individuals subject to the High Earners Restriction

Cross References

From Section 485C

Section 97 Computational rules and allowable deductions.
Section 261 Taxation of relevant interest, etc.
Section 261B Taxation of specified interest.
Section 267M Tax rate applicable to certain deposit interest received by individuals.
Section 324 Double rent allowance in respect of rent paid for certain business premises.
Section 333 Double rent allowance in respect of rent paid for certain business premises.
Section 345 Double rent allowance in respect of rent paid for certain business premises.
Section 354 Double rent allowance in respect of rent paid for certain business premises.
Section 485F Carry forward of excess relief.
Section 485FA Adaptation of provisions relating to taxation of married persons.
Section 730J Payment in respect of foreign life policy.

Section 730K Disposal of foreign life policy.
Section 747D Payment in respect of offshore funds.
Section 747E Disposal of an interest in offshore funds.
Section 1016 Assessment as single persons.
Schedule 25B List of Specified Reliefs and Method of Determining Amount of Specified Relief Used in a Tax Year
Schedule 25C Determination of Amount of Relief to be Treated as Referable to Specified Reliefs as Respects Relief Carried Forward from Tax Year 2006 to Tax Year 2007
Schedule 32 Transitional Provisions

To Section 485C
Section 372AP Relief for lessors.
Section 669G Interpretation (Chapter 4).

485D Application (Chapter 2A)

[This Chapter shall apply to an individual for a tax year where—

(a) the individual's adjusted income for the tax year is equal to or greater than [the income threshold amount][1], and

(b) the aggregate of [[the specified reliefs used by the individual in respect of the tax year][2]][3] is equal to or greater than [the relief threshold amount][4],

but this Chapter, other than section 485F, shall not apply for the tax year where [20 per cent of the individual's adjusted income][5] for the tax year is equal to or greater than the aggregate of the specified reliefs used by the individual in respect of the tax year.][6]

Amendments

[1] Substituted by FA10 s23(1)(c)(i). Applies as respects the year of assessment 2010 and subsequent years of assessment.

[2, 3] Substituted by FA07 s18(1)(b). Applies for the year of assessment 2007 and subsequent years of assessment.

[4] Substituted by FA10 s23(1)(c)(ii). Applies as respects the year of assessment 2010 and subsequent years of assessment.

[5] Substituted by FA10 s23(1)(c)(iii). Applies as respects the year of assessment 2010 and subsequent years of assessment.

[6] Inserted by FA06 s17(1). Applies for the year of assessment 2007 and subsequent years of assessment.

485E Recalculation of taxable income for purposes of limiting reliefs

[Where this Chapter applies to an individual for a tax year, notwithstanding anything in any provision of the Tax Acts other than this Chapter, the individual's taxable income for the tax year shall, instead of being the amount it would have been had this Chapter not applied to the individual for the tax year, be the amount determined by the formula—

$$T + (S - Y)$$

where—

T is the amount of the individual's taxable income for the tax year determined on the basis that this Chapter, other than [sections 485F and 485FA][1], does not apply to the individual for the tax year,

S is the aggregate of the specified reliefs for the tax year, and

[Y is the greater of—

(i) the relief threshold amount, and

(ii) 20 per cent of the individual's adjusted income for the tax year.][2]][3]

Amendments

[1] Substituted by FA07 s18(1)(c). Applies for the year of assessment 2007 and subsequent years of assessment.

[2] Substituted by FA10 s23(1)(d). Applies as respects the year of assessment 2010 and subsequent years of assessment.

[3] Inserted by FA06 s17(1). Applies for the year of assessment 2007 and subsequent years of assessment.

Cross References

To Section 485E

Section 485G Miscellaneous (Chapter 2A).

Section 669J Credit for tax paid.

485F Carry forward of excess relief

[(1) Where in any tax year section 485E applies to an individual, the excess relief shall be carried forward to the next tax year and, subject to sections 485E and 485G(2)*(a)*(iii), the individual shall, in computing the amount of his or her taxable income before the application of section 485E in that next tax year, be entitled to a deduction from his or her total income of an amount equal to the amount of the excess relief.

(2) If and so far as an amount equal to the excess relief once carried forward to a tax year under subsection (1) is not deducted or is not fully deducted from the individual's total income for that year, the amount or the balance of the amount not deducted under subsection (1) shall be carried forward again to the next following tax year and, subject to section 485E, the individual shall, in that next following tax year, in computing the amount of his or her taxable income before the application of section 485E in that next following year, be entitled to a deduction from his or her total income of an amount equal to the amount so carried forward and so on for each succeeding tax year until the full amount of the excess relief has been deducted from the individual's total income for the tax years concerned.

(3) Where subsection (1) or (2) applies for any tax year, relief shall be given to the individual for the tax year in the following order—

(a) in the first instance, in respect of any other tax relief apart from the relief provided for by this section,

(b) only thereafter, in respect of an amount carried forward from an earlier year in accordance with subsection (1) or (2), and in respect of such an amount carried forward from an earlier tax year in priority to a later tax year.][1]

Amendments

[1] Inserted by FA06 s17(1). Applies for the year of assessment 2007 and subsequent years of assessment.

Cross References

To Section 485F

Section 485C Interpretation (Chapter 2A).

Section 485G Miscellaneous (Chapter 2A).

Section 669J Credit for tax paid.

Schedule 25B List of Specified Reliefs and Method of Determining Amount of Specified Relief Used in a Tax Year

485FA Adaptation of provisions relating to taxation of married persons

[Where this Chapter applies to an individual or his or her [spouse or civil partner][1] for a tax year, and—

(a) an election under [*section 1018* or *1031D* (including a deemed election under either of those sections)][2] to be assessed to tax in accordance with [*section 1017* or, as the case may be, *section 1031C*][3] has effect for the tax year,

(b) an application under [*section 1023* or, as the case may be, *section 1031H*][4] has effect for that year, or

(c) the provisions of *section 1019(3)* apply for that year,

in respect of the individual and his or her [spouse or civil partner][5], then the following provisions shall apply:

(i) the definition of "*chargeable tax*" in *section 3(1)* shall apply as if the references to total income were references to taxable income;

(ii) subsection (1) of *section 1017* shall apply as if the following paragraph was substituted for *paragraph (a)* of that subsection:

"(a) the husband shall be assessed and charged to income tax, not only in respect of his taxable income (if any) for that year, but also in respect of his wife's taxable income (if any) for any part of that year of assessment during which she is living with him and, for this purpose and for the purposes of the Income Tax Acts, the last-mentioned income shall be deemed to be his income,";

[(iia) *subsection (1)* of *section 1031C* shall apply as if the following paragraph was substituted for *paragraph (a)* of that subsection:

'(a) the nominated civil partner shall be assessed and charged to income tax, not only in respect of his or her taxable income (if any) for that year, but also in respect of his or her civil partner's taxable income (if any) for any part of that year of assessment during which he or she is living with the nominated civil partner and, for this purpose and for the purposes of the Income Tax Acts, the last-mentioned income shall be deemed to be the income of the nominated civil partner,';][6]

(iii) the references to total income in—

(I) subsection (3),

(II) *paragraph (a)* of *subsection (4)* other than the references in subparagraph (ii) of that paragraph, and

(III) subsection (4)*(b)*,

of *section 1019* shall be construed as references to taxable income;

(iv) the reference to so assessed and charged for each subsequent year of assessment in *section 1019(4)(a)* shall be construed as a reference to—

(I) assessed and charged in respect of her taxable income (if any) and the taxable income (if any) of her husband for each subsequent year of assessment, where this Chapter applies for a tax year to either or both spouses, and

(II) assessed and charged in respect of her total income (if any) and the total income (if any) of her husband for each subsequent year of assessment, in any other case;

(v) the reference to so assessed to income tax for the year of assessment in which that notice or application is withdrawn and for each subsequent year of assessment in *section 1019(4)(b)* shall be construed as a reference to—

(I) assessed to income tax in respect of her own taxable income (if any) and the taxable income (if any) of her husband for the year of assessment in which that notice or application is withdrawn and for each subsequent year of assessment, where this Chapter applies for a tax year to either or both spouses, and

(II) assessed to income tax in respect of her own total income (if any) and the total income (if any) of her husband for the year of assessment in which that notice or application is withdrawn and for each subsequent year of assessment, in any other case;

and

(vi) where *paragraph (a)* or *(c)* apply to an individual and his or her [spouse or civil partner][7] for a tax year, then to the extent that—

(I) the benefit flowing from such deductions as are specified in the provisions referred to in Part 1 of the Table to *section 458* for the tax year exceeds the income tax chargeable on the individual's income for the tax year, the balance shall be applied to reduce the income tax chargeable on the income of the individual's [spouse or civil partner][8] for that year, and

(II) the benefit flowing from such deductions exceed the income tax chargeable on the [spouse's or civil partner's][9] income for that year, the balance shall be applied to reduce the income tax chargeable on the income of the individual for that year.][10]

Amendments

[1, 5] Substituted by F(No.3)A11 sched1(125).

[2] Substituted by F(No.3)A11 sched1(126).

[3] Substituted by F(No.3)A11 sched1(127).

[4] Substituted by F(No.3)A11 sched1(128).

[6] Inserted by F(No.3)A11 sched1(129).

[7, 8] Substituted by F(No.3)A11 sched1(130).

[9] Substituted by F(No.3)A11 sched1(131).

[10] Inserted by FA07 s18(1)(d). Applies for the year of assessment 2007 and subsequent years of assessment.

Cross References

From Section 485FA

Section 3 Interpretation of Income Tax Acts.

Section 458 Deductions allowed in ascertaining taxable income and provisions relating to reductions in tax.

Section 1017 Assessment of husband in respect of income of both spouses.

Section 1018 Election for assessment under section 1017.

Section 1019 Assessment of wife in respect of income of both spouses.
Section 1023 Application for separate assessments.

To Section 485FA
Section 485C Interpretation (Chapter 2A).

485FB Requirement to provide estimates and information

[(1) In this section—

"*chargeable person*" and "*specified return date for the chargeable period*" have the same meanings as in [*Part 41A*][1];

"*prescribed form*" means a form prescribed by the Revenue Commissioners or a form used under the authority of the Revenue Commissioners, and includes a form which involves the delivery of a statement by any electronic, photographic or other process approved of by the Revenue Commissioners.

(2) Where this Chapter applies to an individual for a tax year that individual shall, if not otherwise a chargeable person, be deemed to be a chargeable person for such year for the purposes of [*Part 41A*][2].

(3) Where this Chapter applies to an individual for a tax year that individual shall, in addition to the return required to be delivered [under *Chapter 3* of *Part 41A*, prepare][3] and deliver to the Collector-General at the same time as, and together with, the return required under [*Chapter 3* of *Part 41* on or before][4] the specified return date for the chargeable period a full and true statement in a prescribed form of the details required by the form in respect of—

(a) the amounts constituting the aggregate of the specified reliefs,

(b) the determination of those amounts, and

(c) the estimates required by *subsection (4)*,

and of such further particulars in relation to this Chapter as may be required by the prescribed form.

(4) The estimates required by this subsection are estimates of—

(a) the individual's taxable income for the year determined as if this Chapter, other than section 485F, did not apply to the individual for that year,

(b) the individual's taxable income determined in accordance with section 485E, and

(c) the amount of tax that should be assessed on the individual as a consequence of the application of this Chapter,

which estimates shall be made to the best of the individual's knowledge and belief.

(5) Where this Chapter applies [to both a husband and a wife, not being persons to whom [*section 1016* or *1023*][5] applies, or to both civil partners, not being persons to whom [*section 1031B* or *1031H*][6] applies, then separate statements under this section shall be required from both the husband and the wife or, as the case may be, both civil partners][7] and both statements shall be made on the same prescribed form (in this subsection referred to as a "*combined statement*") and references in this section, other than in this subsection, to a statement required to be delivered under this section shall include references to a combined statement.

(6) (a) For the purposes of determining—

(i) the accuracy or otherwise of any details, particulars or estimates contained in the statement referred to in *subsection (3)*, or

(ii) whether or not an individual who has not provided a statement under this section is an individual to whom this Chapter applies, a Revenue officer may make such enquiries or take such actions within his or her powers as he or she considers necessary for the purposes of determining the matters set out in *subparagraph (i)* or *(ii)*, including, in the case of *subparagraph (ii)*, requiring by notice in writing the individual to furnish in writing to the officer within such time, not being less than 14 days, as may be provided by the notice, details of each provision in respect of which the individual is claiming tax relief for a tax year together with the amount of each separate claim and the particulars of each separate claim under that provision.

(b) *Subparagraph (ii)* of *paragraph (a)* shall only apply to an individual who has made a return under *section 951* for a tax year and whose income, including income exempt from tax, from all sources and disregarding all deductions, allowances and other tax reliefs is equal to or greater than [the income threshold amount][8].

(7) *Subsections (9)* and *(10)* of *section 951* shall apply to a statement required to be delivered under this section in the same way as they apply to a return required to be delivered under that section, and for this purpose a reference in those subsections to a return, other than a reference to the specified return date for the chargeable period, shall be construed as a reference to a statement under this section.

(8) *Section 1052* shall apply to a failure by an individual to deliver a statement under this section or the details, amounts and particulars referred to in *subsection (6)* as it applies to a failure to deliver a return referred to in *section 1052*.][9]

Amendments

[1, 2, 3, 4] Substituted by FA12 sched4(part 2)(g).

[5] Substituted by F(No.2)A13 s16(c)(i). Comes into operation on 1 January 2014.

[6] Substituted by F(No.2)A13 s16(c)(ii). Comes into operation on 1 January 2014.

[7] Substituted by F(No.3)A11 sched1(132). Shall have effect from 27 July 2011.

[8] Substituted by FA10 s23(1)(e). Applies as respects the year of assessment 2010 and subsequent years of assessment.

[9] Inserted by FA07 s18(1)(d). Applies for the year of assessment 2007 and subsequent years of assessment.

Cross References

From Section 485FB

Section 950 Interpretation (Part 41).

Section 951 Obligation to make a return.

Section 1016 Assessment as single persons.

Section 1052 Penalties for failure to make certain returns, etc.

485G Miscellaneous (Chapter 2A)

[(1) Nothing in this Chapter shall prevent an individual referred to in *paragraph (b)* of *section 267(1)* who is entitled to a repayment of the whole or any part of the appropriate tax (within the meaning of *section 256*) by virtue of *subsection (3)* of *section 267* from obtaining any such repayment in accordance with that subsection.

(2) (a) Where this Chapter applies to an individual for a tax year, the following provisions shall apply as respects the individual and any specified relief used by the individual in the tax year—

[(i) for the purposes of *Part 9* and that Part as applied for the purposes of any other provision of the Tax Acts, the amount of any specified relief used by the individual in the tax year shall be determined without regard to the application to the individual for that year of section 485E,][1]

(ii) the calculation of the amount unallowed under *section 292* in the case of a specified relief shall take no account of the application of this Chapter to the relief for any tax year,

(iii) the application of this Chapter to a specified relief for any tax year shall not affect the determination of the amount of a balancing charge (within the meaning of *section 274* and that section as applied for the purposes of any other provision of the Tax Acts) to be made on, or a balancing allowance (within the same meanings) to be made to, any individual in respect of that relief, but the amount of any such balancing charge to be made on that individual shall be reduced by the amount determined under *paragraph (b)* and where any such reduction applies [the sum of—][2]

[(I) the amount of the individual's excess relief for the year in which the balancing charge arises, and

(II) the amount of any excess relief carried forward to that year that is not deducted for that year,][3]

shall be reduced by an amount equal to the amount by which the balancing charge is reduced, and

(iv) the application of this Chapter to the individual for that year in respect of a specified relief shall be ignored for the purposes of determining whether any amount of the specified relief is available for carry-forward to a subsequent tax year.

(b) (i) The amount referred to in *paragraph (a)(iii)* is an amount equal to the lesser of—

[(I) the amount of the individual's excess relief carried forward to the year in which the balancing charge arises and not deducted or not fully deducted for that year, before any reduction by reference to *paragraph (a)(iii)*, and][4]

(II) an amount equal to the sum of the amounts determined in accordance with subparagraph (ii) in respect of each tax year for which—

(A) section 485E applied to the individual, and

(B) an allowance was made to the individual,

in respect of the building or structure in respect of which the balancing charge arises.

(ii) The amount referred to in subparagraph (i)(II) is an amount determined by the formula—

$$A \times \frac{E}{S}$$

where—

A is the amount of the allowance made to the individual for a year,

E is the amount of the individual's excess relief for that year, and

S is the individual's aggregate of the specified reliefs for that year.

[(3) (a) Where this Chapter applies to an individual for a tax year, then, to the extent that the individual's taxable income determined in accordance with section 485E exceeds the amount of the profits, gains or income in respect of which the individual is chargeable under Schedules C, D, E and F the amount of the excess shall, notwithstanding any other provision of the Tax Acts, be deemed to be an amount of income chargeable to income tax under Case IV of Schedule D, but—

(i) the amount so chargeable shall not be reckoned in computing the individual's total income for that year, and

(ii) this paragraph shall be disregarded for the purpose of determining—

(I) whether this Chapter should apply to an individual for a tax year, and

(II) the amount of "T" in the formula in the definition of "*adjusted income*" in section 485C(1) and in the formula in section 485E.

(b) Any assessment to income tax to be made on an individual for a tax year shall, notwithstanding any other provision of the Tax Acts, include, in addition to any income, profits or gains of the individual otherwise chargeable to income tax, any amount chargeable to income tax on the individual by virtue of *paragraph (a)*, and the provisions of the Tax Acts, including in particular those provisions relating to the assessment, collection and recovery of tax and the payment of interest on unpaid tax, shall apply as respects any amount chargeable to income tax by virtue of *paragraph (a)*.

(c) Where, but for this Chapter, no assessment to income tax would be made on an individual for a tax year, then a Revenue officer shall, notwithstanding any other provision of the Tax Acts, make an assessment to income tax on the individual to the best of the officer's judgement of the amounts chargeable to income tax, including any amount chargeable by virtue of *paragraph (a)*, and the provisions of the Tax Acts, including in particular those provisions relating to the assessment, collection and recovery of tax and the payment of interest on unpaid tax, shall apply as respects—

(i) any amount chargeable to income tax by virtue of *paragraph (a)*, and

(ii) any assessment to income tax made on the individual by virtue of this paragraph.][5]

[(4) (a) Subject to [*paragraph (b), subsection (5)* and *paragraph 5* of *Schedule 24*][6], where under any provision of the Tax Acts (other than any provision of this Chapter) the calculation of a relief, deduction, credit in relation to tax or, as the case may be, a reduction in the amount of tax payable arises for a tax year which requires total income, taxable income, tax payable or tax chargeable for the year to be taken into account as part of the calculation—

(i) that calculation shall be carried out as if this Chapter, other than *section 485F*, does not apply, and

(ii) (I) in the case of a relief or deduction, effect shall be given to such relief or deduction before the application of this Chapter but after the application of *section 485F*, or

(II) in the case of a credit in relation to tax or, as the case may be, a reduction in the amount of tax payable, the benefit of that credit or reduction (as calculated in accordance with *subparagraph (i)*) shall be given against the amount of tax to be charged on the individual for the year involved in relation to his or her taxable income as determined in accordance with *section 485E*.

(b) Where this Chapter applies to an individual for a tax year nothing in *paragraph (a)* shall affect the calculation of the amount of tax which is to be charged on the individual for the year involved in relation to his or her taxable income as determined in accordance with *section 485E*.

(5) Where this Chapter applies to an individual for a tax year, the provisions of *section 187* (as amended by the *Finance Act 2008*) or *section 188* shall not apply to the individual for that year.][7]][8]

Amendments

[1] Substituted by FA07 s18(1)(e)(i). Applies for the year of assessment 2007 and subsequent years of assessment.

[2, 3] Substituted by FA07 s18(1)(e)(ii). Applies for the year of assessment 2007 and subsequent years of assessment.

[4] Substituted by FA07 s18(1)(e)(iii). Applies for the year of assessment 2007 and subsequent years of assessment.

[5] Substituted by FA07 s18(1)(e)(iv). Applies for the year of assessment 2007 and subsequent years of assessment.

[6] Substituted by F(No.2)A13 s16(d). Comes into operation on 1 January 2014.

[7] Inserted by FA08 s23(1). Applies as respects any relief, deduction, credit in relation to tax or, as the case may be, a reduction in the amount of tax payable, details of which fall to be included in particulars on a return, required to be delivered under section 951, which is delivered on or after 31 January 2008.

[8] Inserted by FA06 s17(1). Applies for the year of assessment 2007 and subsequent years of assessment.

Cross References

From Section 485G

Section 17 Schedule C.
Section 20 Schedule F.
Section 187 Exemption from income tax and associated marginal relief.
Section 188 Age exemption and associated marginal relief.
Section 256 Interpretation (Chapter 4).
Section 267 Repayment of appropriate tax in certain cases.
Section 268 Meaning of "industrial building or structure".
Section 274 Balancing allowances and balancing charges.
Section 292 Meaning of "amount still unallowed".
Section 485E Recalculation of taxable income for purposes of limiting reliefs.
Section 485F Carry forward of excess relief.

CHAPTER 3

Corporation Tax Reliefs

486 Corporation tax: relief for gifts to First Step [Repealed]

Repealed by TCA97 s848A, as inserted by FA01 s45.

Cross References

To Section 486

Section 848A Donations to approved bodies.

486A Corporate donations to eligible charities [Repealed]

Repealed by TCA97 s848A, as inserted by FA01 s45.

Cross References

To Section 486A

Section 848A Donations to approved bodies.

486B Relief for investment in renewable energy generation

[(1) In this section—

"*authorised officer*" means an officer of the Revenue Commissioners authorised by them in writing for the purposes of this section;

"*commencement date*" means the day on which *section 62* of the Finance Act, 1998, comes into operation;

"*the Minister*" means the Minister for [Communications, Energy and Natural Resources][1];

"*new ordinary shares*" means new ordinary shares forming part of the ordinary share capital of a qualifying company which, throughout the period of five years commencing on the date such shares are issued, carry no present or future preferential right to dividends, or to a company's assets on its winding up, and no present or future preferential right to be redeemed;

"*qualifying company*" means a company which—

(a) is incorporated in the State,

(b) is resident in the State and not resident elsewhere, and

(c) exists solely for the purposes of undertaking a qualifying energy project;

"*qualifying energy project*" means a renewable energy project in respect of which the Minister has given a certificate under *subsection (2)* which has not been revoked under that subsection;

["*qualifying period*" means the period commencing on the commencement date and ending on [31 December 2014][2];][3]

"*relevant cost*" in relation to a qualifying energy project means the amount of the capital expenditure incurred or to be incurred by the qualifying company for the purposes of undertaking the qualifying energy project reduced by an amount equal to such part of that expenditure as—

(a) is attributable to the acquisition of, or of rights in or over, land, and

(b) has been or is to be met directly or indirectly by the State or by any person other than the qualifying company;

"*relevant deduction*" means, subject to subsections (4) and (5), a deduction of an amount equal to a relevant investment;

"*relevant investment*" means a sum of money which is—

(a) paid in the qualifying period by a company on its own behalf to a qualifying company in respect of new ordinary shares in the qualifying company and is paid by the company directly to the qualifying company,

(b) paid by the company for the purposes of enabling the qualifying company to undertake a qualifying energy project, and

(c) used by the qualifying company within 2 years of the receipt of that sum for those purposes,

but does not include a sum of money paid to the qualifying company on terms which provide that it will be repaid, and a reference to the making of a relevant investment shall be construed as a reference to the payment of such a sum to a qualifying company;

"*renewable energy project*" means a renewable energy project (including a project successful in the Third Alternative Energy Requirement Competition (AER III — 1997) initiated by the Minister) in one or more of the following categories of technology—

(a) solar power,

(b) windpower,

(c) hydropower, and

(d) biomass.

(2) (a) (i) The Minister, on the making of an application by a qualifying company, may give a certificate to the qualifying company stating, in relation to a renewable energy project to be undertaken by the company, that the renewable energy project is a qualifying energy project for the purposes of this section.

(ii) An application under this section shall be in such form, and shall contain such information, as the Minister may direct.

(b) A certificate given by the Minister under *paragraph (a)* shall be subject to such conditions as the Minister may consider proper and specifies in the certificate.

(c) The Minister may amend or revoke any condition (including a condition amended by virtue of this paragraph) specified in such a certificate; the Minister shall give notice in writing to the qualifying company concerned of the amendment or revocation and, on such notice being given, this section shall apply as if—

(i) a condition so amended and the amendment of which is specified in the notice was specified in the certificate, and

(ii) a condition so revoked and the revocation of which is specified in the notice was not specified in the certificate.

(d) A reference in *paragraph (c)* to the amendment of a condition specified in a certificate includes a reference to the addition of any matter, by way of a further condition, to the terms of the certificate.

(e) Where a company fails to comply with any of the conditions specified in a certificate issued to it under *paragraph (a)*—

(i) that failure shall constitute the failure of an event to happen by reason of which relief is to be withdrawn under *subsection (6)*, and

(ii) the Minister may, by notice in writing served by registered post on the company, revoke the certificate.

(3) Subject to this section, where in an accounting period a company makes a relevant investment, it shall, on making a claim in that behalf, be given a relevant deduction from its total profits for the accounting period; but, where the amount of the relevant deduction to which the company is entitled under this section in an accounting period exceeds its profits for that accounting period, an amount equal to that excess shall be carried forward to the succeeding accounting period and the amount so carried forward shall be treated for the purposes of this section as if it were a relevant investment made in that succeeding accounting period.

(4) Where in any period of 12 months ending on the day before an anniversary of the commencement date, the amount or the aggregate amount of the relevant investments made, or treated as made, by a company, or by the company and all companies which at any time in that period would be regarded as connected with the company, exceeds [€12,700,000][4]—

(a) no relief shall be given under this section in respect of the amount of the excess, and

(b) where there is more than one relevant investment, the inspector or, on appeal, the Appeal Commissioners shall make such apportionment of the relief available as shall be just and reasonable to allocate to each relevant investment a due proportion of the relief available and, where necessary, to grant to each company concerned an amount of relief proportionate to the amount of the relevant investment or the aggregate amount of the relevant investments made by it in the period.

(5) Relief under this section shall not be given in respect of a relevant investment which is made at any time in a qualifying company if, at that time, the aggregate of the amounts of that relevant investment and all other relevant investments made in the qualifying company at or before that time exceeds an amount equal to—

(a) 50 per cent of the relevant cost of the project, or

(b) [€9,525,000][5],

whichever is the lesser.

(6) (a) A claim to relief under this section may be allowed at any time after the time specified in *paragraph (c)* in respect of the payment of a sum to a qualifying company if—

(i) that payment, if it is used, within 2 years of its being paid, by the qualifying company for the purposes of a qualifying energy project, will be a relevant investment, and

(ii) all the conditions specified in this section for the giving of the relief are or will be satisfied,

but the relief shall be withdrawn if, by reason of the happening of any subsequent event including the revocation by the Minister of a certificate under *subsection (2)* or the failure of an event to happen which at the time the relief was given was expected to happen, the company making the claim was not entitled to the relief allowed.

(b) Where a company has made a relevant investment by means of a subscription for new ordinary shares of a qualifying company and any of those shares are disposed of at any time within 5 years after the time specified in *paragraph (c)*, a claim to relief under this section shall not be allowed in respect of the amount subscribed for those shares, and if any such relief has been given, it shall be withdrawn.

(c) The time referred to in *paragraph (a)* and *paragraph (b)* is the time when the payment in respect of which relief is claimed has been made.

(7) A claim for relief in respect of a relevant investment in a company shall not be allowed unless it is accompanied by a certificate issued by the company in such form as the Revenue Commissioners may direct and certifying that the conditions for the relief, in so far as they apply to the company and the qualifying energy project, are or will be satisfied in relation to that relevant investment.

(8) Before issuing a certificate for the purposes of *subsection (7)*, a qualifying company shall furnish the authorised officer with—

(a) a statement to the effect that it satisfies or will satisfy the conditions for the relief in so far as they apply in relation to the company and the qualifying energy project,

(b) a copy of the certificate, including a copy of any notice given by the Minister specifying the amendment or revocation of a condition specified in that certificate, under *subsection (2)* in respect of the qualifying energy project, and

(c) such other information as the Revenue Commissioners may reasonably require.

(9) A certificate to which *subsection (7)* relates shall not be issued—

(a) without the authority of the authorised officer, or

(b) in relation to a relevant investment in respect of which relief may not be given by virtue of *subsection (5)*.

(10) Any statement under *subsection (8)* shall—

(a) contain such information as the Revenue Commissioners may reasonably require,

(b) be in such form as the Revenue Commissioners may direct, and

(c) contain a declaration that it is correct to the best of the company's knowledge and belief.

[(11) Where a qualifying company has issued a certificate for the purposes of subsection (7) or furnished a statement under subsection (8) and either—

(a) the certificate or statement is false or misleading in a material respect, or

(b) the certificate was issued in contravention of subsection (9),

then—

(i) the company shall be liable to a penalty of €4,000, and

(ii) no relief shall be given under this section in respect of the matter to which the certificate or statement relates and, if any such relief has been given, it shall be withdrawn.][6]

(12) A company shall not be entitled to relief in respect of a relevant investment unless the relevant investment—

(a) has been made for bona fide commercial reasons and not as part of a scheme or arrangement the main purpose or one of the main purposes of which is the avoidance of tax,

(b) has been or will be used for the purposes of undertaking a qualifying energy project, and

(c) is made at the risk of the company and neither the company nor any person who would be regarded as connected with the company is entitled to receive any payment in money or money's worth or other benefit directly or indirectly borne by or attributable to the qualifying company, other than a payment made on an arm's length basis for goods or services supplied or a payment out of the proceeds of exploiting the qualifying energy project to which the company is entitled under the terms subject to which the relevant investment is made.

(13) Where any relief has been given under this section which is subsequently found not to have been due or is to be withdrawn by virtue of *subsection (6)* or *(11)*, that relief shall be withdrawn by making an assessment to corporation tax, under Case IV of Schedule D, for the accounting period or accounting periods in which relief was given and, notwithstanding anything in the Tax Acts, such an assessment may be made at any time.

(14) (a) Subject to *paragraph (b)*, where a company is entitled to relief under this section in respect of any sum or any part of a sum, or would be so entitled on duly making a claim in that behalf, as a relevant deduction from its total profits for any accounting period, it shall not be entitled to any relief for that sum or that part of a sum, in computing its income or profits, or as a deduction from its income or profits, for any accounting period under any other provision of the Tax Acts or the Capital Gains Tax Acts.

(b) Where a company has made a relevant investment by means of a subscription for new ordinary shares of a qualifying company and none of those shares is disposed of by the company within five years of their acquisition by that company, then, the sums allowable as deductions from the consideration ("the consideration concerned") in the computation for the purpose of capital gains tax of the gain or loss accruing to the company on the disposal of those shares shall be determined without regard to any relief under this section which the company has obtained, or would be entitled, on duly making a claim in that behalf, to obtain, except that, where those sums exceed the consideration concerned, they shall be reduced by an amount equal to the lesser of—

(i) the amount of the relevant deduction allowed to the company under this section in respect of the subscription for those shares, and

(ii) the amount of the excess.][7]

Amendments

[1] Substituted by FA11 sched3(1)(f). Has effect as on and from 6 February 2011.

[2] Substituted by FA12 s25. Deemed to have come into force and takes effect on and from 1 January 2012.

[3] Substituted by FA02 s43(1). This section comes into operation on such day as the Minister for Finance appoints by order. With effect from 24 September 2004 per S.I. 646 of 2004.

[4, 5] Substituted by FA01 sched5.

[6] Substituted by F(No.2)A08 sched5(part2)(1)(d). The enactments specified in Schedule 5 are amended or repealed to the extent and manner specified in that Schedule and, unless the contrary is stated, shall come into effect after 24 December 2008.

[7] Inserted by FA98 s62(1). This section shall come into operation on such day as the Minister for Finance appoints by order. With effect from 18 March 1999 per S.I. 65 of 1999.

Cross References

From Section 486B

Section 62 Dividends paid outside the State and proceeds of sale of dividend coupons.

486C Relief from tax for certain start-up companies

[(1) (a) In this section—

["*associated company*" shall be construed in accordance with *section 432*;][1]

["Commission Regulation (EC) No. 1998/2006" means Commission Regulation (EC) No. 1998/2006 of 15 December 2006* on the application of Articles 86 and 87 of the Treaty to *de minimis* aid;][2]

* OJ No. L 379 of 28.12.2006, p.5

"*EEA Agreement*" means the Agreement on the European Economic Area signed at Oporto on 2 May 1992, as adjusted by the Protocol signed at Brussels on 17 March 1993;

"*EEA state*" means a State, other than the State, which is a Contracting Party to the EEA Agreement;

["*Employer Job (PRSI) Incentive Scheme*" means the scheme provided for in the Social Welfare (Employers' Pay-Related Social Insurance Exemption Scheme) Regulations 2010 (S.I. No. 294 of 2010);

"*Employers*" Pay-Related Social Insurance' means the contribution specified in section 13(2)(*d*) of the Social Welfare Consolidation Act 2005;][3]

"*excepted trade*" has the same meaning as in *section 21A*;

"*net chargeable gains*" means chargeable gains less allowable losses;

"*new company*" means a company incorporated in the State or in an EEA State other than the State on or after 14 October 2008;

"*qualifying assets*", in relation to a qualifying trade, means relevant assets of the qualifying trade which are disposed of in the relevant period in relation to that trade;

"*qualifying trade*" has the meaning assigned to it in *subsection (2)*;

"*relevant asset*", in relation to a qualifying trade means, an asset (including goodwill but not including shares or securities or other assets held as investments) which is, or is an interest in, an asset used for the purposes of that trade other than an asset on the disposal of which no gain accruing would be a chargeable gain or an asset the consideration for the acquisition of which is determined by *section 617* or *section 631*;

"*relevant corporation tax*", in relation to an accounting period, means the corporation tax which, apart from this section, *sections 239, 241, 440, 441, 644B* and *827* and *paragraph 18* of *Schedule 32*, would be chargeable for the accounting period exclusive of—

(i) the corporation tax chargeable on the profits of the company attributable to chargeable gains for that period, and

(ii) the corporation tax chargeable on the part of the companies profits which are charged to tax at the rate specified in *section 21A*;

["*relevant limit*" means, subject to subsection (6), €5,000;][4]

"*relevant period*", in relation to a qualifying trade, means the period beginning on the day the company commences to carry on the qualifying trade and ending 3 years after that date;

["*specified contribution*", in relation to an employee or director of a company, means, subject to paragraph (*c*), the lesser of—

(i) the amount of Employers' Pay-Related Social Insurance paid by the company in an accounting period in respect of that employee or director, or which would have been so paid if relief under the Employer Job (PRSI) Incentive Scheme did not apply, and

(ii) the relevant limit;

"*total contribution*" means the lesser of—

(i) the aggregate amount of specified contributions of a company for an accounting period, and

(ii) the lower relevant maximum amount specified in subsection (5);][5]

"*total corporation tax*", in relation to an accounting period, means the corporation tax which, apart from this section, *sections 239* and *241* would be chargeable for the accounting period;

"*trade*" means a trade the profits or gains of which are charged to tax under Case I of Schedule D.

(b) For the purposes of this section, the profits of a company attributable to chargeable gains for an accounting period shall be taken to be the amount of its profits for that period on which corporation tax falls finally to be borne exclusive of the part of the profits attributable to income. That part shall be taken to be the amount brought into the company's profits for that period for the purposes of corporation tax in respect of income after any deduction for charges on income, expenses of management or other amounts which can be deducted from or set against or treated as reducing profits of more than one description.

[(c) In computing a specified contribution for an accounting period of a company which sets up and commences a qualifying trade in 2011, an amount of Employers' Pay-Related Social Insurance paid by the company, or which would have been so paid if relief under the Employer Job (PRSI) Incentive Scheme did not apply, within one month after the end of the accounting period may be treated as Employers' Pay-Related Social Insurance paid by the company in that accounting period and, where such an amount is so treated, it shall not be taken into account in computing a specified contribution for any subsequent accounting period.][6]

(2) (a) In this section "*qualifying trade*" means a trade which is set up and commenced by a new company [[at any time][7] in the period beginning on 1 January 2009 and ending on [31 December 2015][8]][9] other than a trade—

(i) which was previously carried on by another person and to which the company has succeeded,

(ii) the activities of which were previously carried on as part of another person's trade or profession,

(iii) which is an excepted trade, […][10]

(iv) the activities of which if carried on by a close company with no other source of income, would result in that company being a service company for the purposes of [*section 441*,[…][11]][12]

[(v) the activities of which form part of an undertaking to which *subparagraphs (a)* to *(h)* of Article 1 of Commission Regulation (EC) No. 1998/2006 [apply, or][13]][14]

[(vi) the activities of which, if carried on by an associated company of the new company, would form part of a trade carried on by that associated company.][15]

(b) Where a trade consists partly of excepted operations and partly of other operations or activities, then *section 21A(2)* shall apply for the purposes of this section as it applies for the purposes of *section 21A*.

[(3) Where a company carries on a qualifying trade in an accounting period falling partly within the relevant period in relation to that qualifying trade, then, for the purposes of this section, the income from the qualifying trade for that accounting period shall be the amount of the income of the qualifying trade for that part of the accounting period and that part of the accounting period shall be treated as a separate accounting period.][16]

(4) (a) Where an accounting period of a company falls [...][17] within a relevant period in relation to a qualifying trade and the total corporation tax payable by the company for that accounting period does not exceed the lower relevant maximum amount, then[the aggregate of][18]—

(i) corporation tax payable by the company for that accounting period, so far as it is referable to income from the qualifying trade for that accounting period, and

(ii) corporation tax payable by the company so far as it is referable to chargeable gains on the disposal of qualifying assets in relation to the trade,

[shall be reduced by the lesser of—

(I) that aggregate, and

(II) the total contribution for the accounting period][19]

(b) Where an accounting period of a company falls [...][20] within a relevant period in relation to a qualifying trade and the total corporation tax payable by the company for that accounting period exceeds the lower relevant maximum amount but does not exceed the upper relevant maximum amount, then the aggregate of corporation tax payable by the company for that accounting period so far as it is referable to income from the qualifying trade for that accounting period and corporation tax payable by the company for that accounting period so far as it is referable to chargeable gains on the disposal of qualifying assets in relation to the trade, [shall be reduced to the greater of—][21]

[(i) that aggregate as reduced by the total contribution for the accounting period, and

(ii) an amount determined by the following formula:][22]

$$3 \times (T - M) \times \frac{A + B}{T}$$

where—

T is the total corporation tax payable by the company for that accounting period,

M is the lower relevant maximum amount,

A is the corporation tax payable by the company for the accounting period so far as is referable to income from the qualifying trade for that accounting period, and

B is the corporation tax payable by the company for that accounting period so far as is referable to chargeable gains on the disposal of qualifying assets of the qualifying trade.

(c) [For the purposes of this subsection and *subsection (4A)*][23], the corporation tax referable to income from a qualifying trade in an accounting period is such an amount as bears to the relevant corporation tax the same proportion as the income from the qualifying trade bears to the total income brought into charge to corporation tax for that accounting period.

(d) [For the purposes of this subsection and *subsection (4A)*][24], the corporation tax referable to chargeable gains on the disposal of qualifying assets is such amount as bears to the corporation tax payable on the profits of the company attributable to the chargeable gains for the accounting period the same proportion as the net chargeable gains on qualifying assets disposed of in the accounting period bears to net chargeable gains on all chargeable assets disposed of in the accounting period.

[(4A) (a) In this subsection—

"*accounting period following the relevant period*", in relation to a company carrying on a qualifying trade, means an accounting period commencing on a date which occurs after the expiry of the relevant period in relation to the qualifying trade;

"*corporation tax referable to the qualifying trade*", in relation to an accounting period of a company, means the corporation tax payable by the company for the accounting period, so far as it is referable to—

(i) income from the qualifying trade for that accounting period, and

(ii) chargeable gains on the disposal of relevant assets in relation to the trade in that accounting period.

(b) (i) Where for an accounting period of a company falling within the relevant period in relation to a qualifying trade carried on by the company—

(I) the total corporation tax payable by the company for the accounting period does not exceed the lower relevant maximum amount, and

(II) the total contribution for the accounting period exceeds the corporation tax referable to the qualifying trade for that accounting period,

the amount (in *paragraph (c)* referred to as a "*first relevant amount*") of the excess referred to in *clause (II)* shall be available to reduce, in accordance with this subsection, the corporation tax referable to the qualifying trade for an accounting period following the relevant period.

(ii) Where for an accounting period of a company falling within the relevant period in relation to a qualifying trade carried on by a company—

(I) the total corporation tax payable by the company for the accounting period exceeds the lower relevant maximum amount but does not exceed the upper relevant maximum amount, and

(II) the total contribution for the accounting period exceeds the corporation tax referable to the qualifying trade for that accounting period, an amount (in paragraph (c) referred to as a "*second relevant amount*") determined by the following formula:

$$[C - (3 \times (T - M) \times \frac{C}{T}) - R]$$

where—

C is the total contribution for the accounting period,

T is the total corporation tax payable by the company for the accounting period,

M is the lower relevant maximum amount, and

R is the amount of relief to which the company is entitled under *subsection (4)(b)* for the accounting period,

shall be available to reduce, in accordance with this subsection, the corporation tax referable to the qualifying trade for an accounting period following the relevant period.

(c) For the purposes of this subsection, the aggregate of all amounts which are—

(i) the first relevant amount, or

(ii) the second relevant amount,

if any, for each accounting period falling within the relevant period, shall be referred to as a "*specified aggregate*".

(d) (i) Subject to *paragraphs (e)* and *(f)*, where a company carries on a qualifying trade in an accounting period following the relevant period, the corporation tax referable to the qualifying trade for that accounting period shall be reduced by the specified aggregate.

(ii) Subject to *paragraphs (e)* and *(f)*, where there is a reduction in the corporation tax for an accounting period following the relevant period by virtue of *subparagraph (i)*

and the specified aggregate exceeds the amount of that reduction, the corporation tax referable to the qualifying trade for the next accounting period shall be reduced by the amount of that excess and so much of that excess as is not applied to reduce that corporation tax shall, in turn, be applied by the company to reduce the corporation tax referable to the qualifying trade for the succeeding accounting period and so on for each succeeding accounting period.

(e) As respects a qualifying trade carried on by a company, the amount by which the corporation tax referable to the qualifying trade for an accounting period following the relevant period may be reduced under this subsection shall not exceed the lesser of—

(i) such corporation tax, and

(ii) the total contribution,

for that accounting period.

(f) So much of a specified aggregate as is applied by a company to reduce corporation tax under this subsection shall be so applied only once.][25]

(5) Subject to subsection (6), the lower relevant maximum amount and the upper relevant maximum amount mentioned in [*subsections (4)* and *(4A)*][26] are €40,000 and €60,000 respectively.

[(6) For an accounting period of less than 12 months—

(a) the relevant limit, and

(b) the relevant maximum amounts specified in subsection (5),

shall be proportionately reduced.][27]

(7) The aggregate of all reductions in corporation tax to which a company is entitled under [*subsections (4)* and *(4A)*][28] in respect of a qualifying trade, the activities of which consist wholly or mainly of the conveyance by road of persons or goods or the haulage by road of other vehicles, shall not exceed €100,000.

(8) (a) Where, on a person ceasing to carry on a trade or part of a trade, a company (in this subsection referred to as the "*successor*") begins—

(i) to carry on the activities of the trade as part of its trade, or

(ii) to carry on the activities of that part as part of its trade,

then that part of the trade carried on by the successor shall for the purposes of this section be treated as a separate trade.

(b) Where under paragraph (*a*) any activities of a company's trade are to be treated as a separate trade, then any necessary apportionment shall be made of receipts or expenses.

(9) Notwithstanding *section 4(4)(b)*, the income of a company, referred to in the expression "total income brought into charge to corporation tax", for the accounting period for the purposes of *subsection (2)* is the sum determined by *section 4(4)(b)* for that period reduced by an amount equal to so much of the profits of the company for the accounting period as are charged to tax in accordance with *section 21A*.

(10) Where in an accounting period a company transfers to a connected person part of a qualifying trade, then the company shall not be entitled to relief under this section in respect of that trade for that or any subsequent accounting periods.

(11) Where a company is entitled to relief under this section in respect of any accounting period, then it shall specify the amount of relief due in its return required under [*Chapter 3* of *Part 41A*][29] *section 951* for that accounting period.

[(12) Notwithstanding any obligation to maintain secrecy or any other restriction on the disclosure of information imposed by or under statute or otherwise, the Revenue Commissioners or any officer authorised by them for the purposes of this subsection may—

(a) disclose to any board established by statute, any public or local authority or any other agency of the State (in this paragraph referred to as a "*relevant body*") information relating to the amount of relief granted to a company under this section, being information which is required by the relevant body concerned for the purpose of ensuring that the ceilings on aid set out in Commission Regulation (EC) No. 1998/2006 are not exceeded, and

(b) provide to the European Commission such information as may be requested by the European Commission in accordance with Article 3 of Commission Regulation (EC) No. 1998/2006.][30][31]

Amendments

[1] Inserted by FA11 s34(1)(a). Has effect in relation to accounting periods beginning on or after 1 January 2011.

[2] Inserted by FA10 s45(1)(a). This section has effect in relation to accounting periods beginning on and from 1 January 2009.

[3] Inserted by FA11 s34(1)(b). Has effect in relation to accounting periods beginning on or after 1 January 2011.

[4] Inserted by FA11 s34(1)(c). Has effect in relation to accounting periods beginning on or after 1 January 2011.

[5] Inserted by FA11 s34(1)(d). Has effect in relation to accounting periods beginning on or after 1 January 2011.

[6] Inserted by FA11 s34(1)(e). Has effect in relation to accounting periods beginning on or after 1 January 2011.

[7] Substituted by FA13 s34(1)(a). Deemed to have come into force and takes effect on and from 1 January 2013.

[8] Substituted by FA14 s39. Comes into operation on 1 January 2015.

[9] Substituted by FA12 s45. Deemed to have come into force and takes effect on and from 1 January 2012.

[10] Deleted by FA10 s45(1)(b)(ii). This section has effect in relation to accounting periods beginning on and from 1 January 2009.

[11] Deleted by FA11 s34(1)(f)(ii). Has effect in relation to accounting periods beginning on or after 1 January 2011.

[12] Substituted by FA10 s45(1)(b)(iii). This section has effect in relation to accounting periods beginning on and from 1 January 2009.

[13] Substituted by FA11 s34(1)(f)(iii). Has effect in relation to accounting periods beginning on or after 1 January 2011.

[14] Inserted by FA10 s45(1)(c). This section has effect in relation to accounting periods beginning on and from 1 January 2009.

[15] Inserted by FA11 s34(1)(g). Has effect in relation to accounting periods beginning on or after 1 January 2011.

[16] Substituted by FA13 s34(1)(b). Deemed to have come into force and takes effect on and from 1 January 2013.

[17] Deleted by FA13 s34(1)(c). Deemed to have come into force and takes effect on and from 1 January 2013.

[18] Inserted by FA11 s34(1)(h)(i). Has effect in relation to accounting periods beginning on or after 1 January 2011.

[19] Substituted by FA11 s34(1)(h)(ii). Has effect in relation to accounting periods beginning on or after 1 January 2011.

[20] Deleted by FA13 s34(1)(d). Deemed to have come into force and takes effect on and from 1 January 2013.

[21, 22] Substituted by FA11 s34(1)(i). Has effect in relation to accounting periods beginning on or after 1 January 2011.

[23] Substituted by FA13 s34(1)(e). Has effect as respects any first relevant amount or second relevant amount (both within the meaning of section 486C) for accounting periods ending on or after 1 January 2013.

[24] Substituted by FA13 s34(1)(f). Has effect as respects any first relevant amount or second relevant amount (both within the meaning of section 486C) for accounting periods ending on or after 1 January 2013.

[25] Inserted by FA13 s34(1)(g). Has effect as respects any first relevant amount or second relevant amount (both within the meaning of section 486C) for accounting periods ending on or after 1 January 2013.

[26] Substituted by FA13 s34(1)(h). Has effect as respects any first relevant amount or second relevant amount (both within the meaning of section 486C) for accounting periods ending on or after 1 January 2013.

[27] Substituted by FA11 s34(1)(j). Has effect in relation to accounting periods beginning on or after 1 January 2011.

[28] Substituted by FA13 s34(1)(i). Has effect as respects any first relevant amount or second relevant amount (both within the meaning of section 486C) for accounting periods ending on or after 1 January 2013.

[29] Substituted by FA12 sched4(part 2)(g).

[30] Inserted by FA10 s45(1)(d). This section has effect in relation to accounting periods beginning on and from 1 January 2009.
[31] Inserted by F(No.2)A08 s31(1). This section comes into operation on such day as the Minister for Finance may appoint by order.

Revenue Briefings

Tax Briefing

Tax Briefing June 2010 – Issue 06 – Tax Exemption for New Start-Up Companies
Tax Briefing March 2011 – Issue 01 – Tax Exemption for New Start-up Companies
Tax Briefing June 2013 – Issue 02 of 2013 – Finance Act 2013 Changes to the 3-Year Tax Relief for Start-up Companies

eBrief

eBrief No. 18/2011 – Tax Exemption for New Start-up Companies

Cross References

From Section 486C

Section 4 Interpretation of Corporation Tax Acts.
Section 21A Higher rate of corporation tax.
Section 239 Income tax on payments by resident companies.
Section 241 Income tax on payments by non-resident companies.
Section 432 Meaning of "associated company" and "control".
Section 440 Surcharge on undistributed investment and estate income.
Section 441 Surcharge on undistributed income of service companies.
Section 617 Transfers of assets, other than trading stock, within group.
Section 631 Transfer of assets generally.
Section 644B Relief from corporation tax in respect of income from dealing in residential development land.
Section 827 Application to corporation tax of arrangements made in relation to corporation profits tax under old law.
Section 951 Obligation to make a return.

487 Corporation tax: credit for bank levy

[FA92 s45; FA95 s56; FA97 s146(1) and Sch9 PtI par16(1)]

(1) (a) In this section—

"*accounting profit*" means the amount of profit, after taxation and before extraordinary items—

(i) shown in the profit and loss account—

(I) in the case of a company resident in the State, which is required under section 148 of the Companies Act, 1963, to be laid before the annual general meeting of the company, or which would be so shown but for subsection (4) of section 149 of that Act, and

(II) in the case of a company not resident in the State and carrying on a trade in the State through a branch or agency, of that branch or agency and which is certified by the auditor appointed under section 160 of the Companies Act, 1963, or under the law of the state in which the company is incorporated and which corresponds to that section, as presenting a true and fair view of the profit or loss attributable to that branch or agency,

(ii) reduced by the amount of such profit as is attributable to—

(I) dividends received from companies resident in the State which are members of the group of which that company is a member,

(II) gains on disposal of capital assets,

[...][1]

(IV) trading operations carried on outside of the State and in respect of which the company is chargeable to corporation tax in the State and to tax on income in another state, and

(V) dividends received from companies not resident in the State,

and

(iii) increased—

(I) as respects income from sources specified in [*subparagraphs (IV)* and *(V)*][2] of *paragraph (ii)*, by an amount determined by the formula—

$$\frac{100}{R} \times T$$

where—

T is the corporation tax chargeable in respect of that income computed in accordance with the provisions of the Corporation Tax Acts and after allowing relief under [*Parts 35*][3], and

R is the rate of corporation tax for the accounting period concerned and to which *section 21* relates, but where part of the accounting period falls in one financial year and the other part falls in the financial year succeeding the first-mentioned financial year, R shall be determined by applying the formula specified in *section 78(3)(b)*, and

(II) by the amount of stamp duty charged under section 64 of the Finance Act, 1989, section 108 of the Finance Act, 1990, section 200 of the Finance Act, 1992, or section 142 of the Finance Act, 1995, and under [section 126 of the Stamp Duties Consolidation Act, 1999][4], as has been taken into account in computing that amount of profit, after taxation and before extraordinary items;

"*adjusted group base tax*", in relation to a relevant period, means—

(i) an amount determined by the formula—

$$\frac{(T \times P)}{B}$$

where—

T is the group base tax,

P is the group profit of the relevant period, and

B is the group base profit,

or

(ii) if it is greater, the group advance corporation tax of the relevant period;

"*advance corporation tax*", in relation to a relevant period, means the aggregate of the amounts of advance corporation tax paid or treated as paid by a company, and not repaid, under *Chapter 8* of *Part 6*, in respect of distributions made in accounting periods falling wholly or partly within the relevant period and, where an accounting period falls partly within a relevant period, the aggregate shall include a part of the advance corporation tax so paid proportionate to the part of the accounting period falling within the relevant period;

"*base profit*", in relation to a company, means 50 per cent of the aggregate of the amounts of accounting profit of a company for accounting periods falling wholly or partly in the period beginning on the 1st day of April, 1989, and ending on the 31st day of March, 1991, and, where an accounting period falls partly within that period, the aggregate shall include a part of the accounting profit of the accounting period proportionate to the part of the accounting period falling within that period;

"*base tax*" means 50 per cent of the aggregate of the corporation tax chargeable on a company, exclusive of the corporation tax on the part of the company's profits attributable to chargeable gains and before the set-off of advance corporation tax under *Chapter 8* of *Part 6*, for accounting periods falling wholly or partly in the period beginning on the 1st day of April, 1989, and ending on the 31st day of March, 1991, and, where an accounting period falls partly within that period, the aggregate shall include a part of the corporation tax so chargeable for the accounting period proportionate to the part of the accounting period falling within that period;

"*group advance corporation tax*", in relation to a relevant period, means the aggregate of the amounts of advance corporation tax in relation to the relevant period of companies which throughout the relevant period are members of the group;

"*group base profit*" means the aggregate of the amounts of base profit of companies which throughout the relevant period are members of the group;

"*group base tax*" means the aggregate of the amounts of base tax of companies which throughout the relevant period are members of the group, but where the amount of the group base tax is an amount which is—

(i) greater than 43 per cent, or

(ii) lower than 10 per cent,

of the group base profit, computed in accordance with this section but without regard to [*subparagraphs (IV)*][5] and *(V)* of *paragraph (ii)*, or *subparagraph (I)* of *paragraph (iii)*, of the definition of "*accounting profit*", the group base tax shall be deemed to be an amount equal to 25 per cent of the group base profit as so computed;

"*group profit*", in relation to a relevant period, means the aggregate of the amounts of profit of the relevant period of companies which throughout that period are members of the group;

"*group tax liability*", in relation to a relevant period, means the aggregate of the amounts of tax liability of the relevant period of companies which throughout that period are members of the group;

"*levy payment*" means the aggregate of the amounts charged in the year 1992 or in any later year under section 200 of the Finance Act, 1992, or section 142 of the Finance Act, 1995, and which have been paid, on or before the date by which the amounts are payable, by companies which are members of a group;

"*profit*", in relation to a relevant period, means the aggregate of the accounting profit, computed on the same basis as that on which the base profit of the company is computed, of a company for accounting periods falling wholly or partly within the relevant period, and, where an accounting period falls partly within a relevant period, the aggregate shall include a part of the accounting profit of the accounting period proportionate to the part of the accounting period falling within that relevant period;

"*relevant period*", in relation to a levy payment, means a period beginning on the 1st day of April preceding the date on or before which the levy payment is to be made and ending on the 31st day of March next after that date;

"*tax liability*", in relation to a relevant period, means the aggregate of the corporation tax which apart from this section would be chargeable on a company, exclusive of the corporation tax on the part of the company's profits attributable to chargeable gains and before the set-off of advance corporation tax under *Chapter 8* of *Part 6*, for accounting periods falling wholly or partly within the relevant period and, where an accounting period falls partly within that period, the aggregate shall include a part of the corporation tax so chargeable for the accounting period proportionate to the part of the accounting period falling within that period.

(b) For the purposes of this section—

(i) 2 companies shall be deemed to be members of a group if one company is a 75 per cent subsidiary of the other company or both companies are 75 per cent subsidiaries of a third company; but—

(I) in determining whether one company is a 75 per cent subsidiary of another company, the other company shall be treated as not being the owner of—

(A) any share capital which it owns directly in a company if a profit on a sale of the shares would be treated as a trading receipt of its trade, or

(B) any share capital which it owns indirectly, and which is owned directly by a company for which a profit on a sale of the shares would be a trading receipt,

and

(II) a company which is an assurance company within the meaning of *section 706* shall not be a member of a group,

(ii) *sections 412* to *418* shall apply for the purposes of this paragraph as they apply for the purposes of *Chapter 5* of *Part 12*,

(iii) a company and all its 75 per cent subsidiaries shall form a group and, where that company is a member of a group as being itself a 75 per cent subsidiary, that group shall comprise all its 75 per cent subsidiaries and the first-mentioned group shall be deemed not to be a group; but a company which is not a member of a group shall be treated as if it were a member of a group which consists of that company, and accordingly references to group advance corporation tax, group base profit, group base tax, group profit and group tax liability shall be construed as if they were respectively references to advance corporation tax, base profit, base tax, profit and tax liability of that company,

(iv) the part of a company's profits attributable to chargeable gains for an accounting period shall be taken to be the amount brought into the company's profits for that period for the purposes of corporation tax in respect of chargeable gains before any deduction for charges on income, expenses of management or other amounts which can be deducted from or set against or treated as reducing profits of more than one description,

(v) the income or profit attributable to any trading operations or dividends shall be such amount of the income or profit as appears to the inspector or on appeal to the Appeal Commissioners to be just and reasonable, and

(vi) corporation tax chargeable in respect of any income shall be the corporation tax which would not have been chargeable but for that income.

(2) Where for a relevant period in relation to a levy payment the group tax liability exceeds the adjusted group base tax of that relevant period, all or part of the levy payment, not being greater than the excess of the group tax liability over the adjusted group base tax, may be set against the group tax liability of the relevant period in accordance with this section.

(3) (a) In this subsection, "*appropriate inspector*" has the same meaning as in *section 950*.

(b) Where under *subsection (2)* an amount of levy payment may be set against the group tax liability of a relevant period, so much (in this paragraph referred to as "*the apportionable part*") of the amount as bears to that amount the same proportion as the tax liability of the relevant period of a company which is a member of the group bears to the group tax liability of the relevant period shall be apportioned to the company, and the companies which are members of the group may, by giving notice in writing to the appropriate inspector within a period of 9 months after the end of the relevant period, elect to have the apportionable part apportioned in such manner as is specified in the notice.

(4) Where an amount is apportioned to a company under *subsection (3)*, that amount shall be set against the tax liability of the relevant period of the company and, to the extent that an amount is so set off, it shall be treated for the purposes of the Corporation Tax Acts as if it were a payment of corporation tax made on the day on which that corporation tax is to be paid; but an amount or part of an amount which is to be treated as if it were a payment of corporation tax may not be repaid to a company by virtue of a claim to relief under the Corporation Tax Acts or for any other reason.

(5) Where under *subsection (4)* an amount is to be set against the tax liability of a relevant period of a company and the tax liability of the relevant period consists of the aggregate of corporation tax chargeable for more accounting periods than one, the amount shall be set against the corporation tax of each of those accounting periods in the proportion which the corporation tax of the accounting period or the part of the accounting period, as the case may be, and which is included

in the tax liability of the relevant period bears to the tax liability of the relevant period.

(6) Where—

(a) the end of an accounting period (in this subsection referred to as "*the first-mentioned accounting period*") of a company which is a member of a group does not coincide with the end of the relevant period,

(b) the tax liability of—

(i) one or more accounting periods of the company ending after the end of the first-mentioned accounting period, or

(ii) one or more accounting periods of any other member of the group ending after the end of the first-mentioned accounting period,

is to be taken into account in determining the amount of the levy payment which may be set off under this section against the corporation tax of—

(I) the first-mentioned accounting period, or one or more accounting periods ending before the end of that period, of the company, or

(II) one or more accounting periods of any other member of the group ending on or before the end of the first-mentioned accounting period,

and

(c) on the specified return date (within the meaning of *section 950*) it is not possible—

(i) for the first-mentioned accounting period, or any other accounting period ending before the end of that period, of the company, or

(ii) for one or more accounting periods of any other member of the group ending on or before the end of the first-mentioned accounting period,

to determine the amount of the levy payment which may be so set off,

then, the amount of levy payment which may be set off under this section against the corporation tax of an accounting period shall be taken to be the amount which would have been so set off if a period of 12 months ending on the last day of the most recent accounting period of the parent company (being a member of the group which is not a subsidiary of any other member of the group) which ends in the relevant period were the relevant period; but, where a part only of that period of 12 months falls after the 31st day of March, 1992, the amount to be set off under this subsection shall be reduced to an amount proportionate to the part of that period of 12 months falling after that day.

(7) (a) A company shall deliver, as soon as they become available, such particulars as are required to determine the amount of levy payment which apart from *subsection (6)* is to be set off against the corporation tax of an accounting period.

(b) Where an amount of levy payment has been set off against corporation tax of an accounting period under *subsection (6)* and the company delivers such particulars as are required to be delivered in accordance with *paragraph (a)*, the inspector shall adjust any computation or assessment by reference to the difference between these amounts and any amount of corporation tax overpaid shall be repaid and any amount of corporation tax under-paid shall be paid.

(8) (a) An amount of tax to be repaid under *subsection (7)* shall be repaid with interest in all respects as if it were a repayment of preliminary tax under *section 953(7)*.

(b) Interest shall not be charged under *section 1080* on any amount of tax underpaid under this subsection unless the amount is not paid within one month of the date on which the amount of the underpayment is notified to the chargeable person by the inspector, and the amount of tax so unpaid shall not be treated as part of the tax payable for the chargeable period for the purposes of *section 958(4)(b)*.

Amendments

[1] Deleted by FA12 sched1(22)(a)(i).

[2, 3] Substituted by FA12 sched1(22)(a)(ii).

[4] Substituted by SDCA99 sched4 with effect from 15 December 1999.

[5] Substituted by FA13 sched2(1)(f). Has effect on and from 27 March 2013.

Cross References

From Section 487

Section 21 The charge to corporation tax and exclusion of income tax and capital gains tax.
Section 78 Computation of companies' chargeable gains.
Section 129 Irish resident company distributions not generally chargeable to corporation tax.
Section 159 Liability for advance corporation tax.
Section 381 Right to repayment of tax by reference to losses.
Section 410 Group payments.
Section 412 Qualification for entitlement to group relief.
Section 418 Beneficial percentage.
Section 442 Interpretation (Part 14).
Section 446 Certain trading operations carried on in Custom House Docks Area.
Section 706 Interpretation and general (Part 26).
Section 826 Agreements for relief from double taxation.
Section 950 Interpretation (Part 41).
Section 953 Notices of preliminary tax.
Section 958 Date for payment of tax.
Section 1080 Interest on overdue income tax, corporation tax and capital gains tax.

PART 16

Income Tax Relief for Investment in Corporate Trades — Employment and Investment Incentive and Seed Capital Scheme

488 Interpretation (Part 16)

[(1) In this Part—

"*associate*" has the same meaning in relation to a person as it has by virtue of *subsection (3)* of *section 433* in relation to a participator, except that the reference in *paragraph* (*b*) of that subsection to any relative of a participator shall be excluded from such meaning;

"*average relevant amount*" means the total of the emoluments (other than non-pecuniary emoluments) paid by a qualifying company to the qualifying employees referred to in the definition of employment relevant number, in the year of assessment in which, in relation to a subscription for eligible shares, a relevant period ends, divided by the employment relevant number;

"*average threshold amount*" means the total of the emoluments (other than non-pecuniary emoluments) paid by the qualifying company to the qualifying employees referred to in the definition of employment threshold number, in the year of assessment preceding the year of assessment in which the subscription for eligible shares was made, divided by the employment threshold number;

"*basic pay rate*", in relation to a qualifying employee of a qualifying company, means the employee's emoluments (other than non-pecuniary emoluments) per hour from the company in respect of an employment held with the company;

"*control*", except in *sections 492(7)* and *505(2)(b)*, shall be construed in accordance with *subsections (2)* to *(6)* of *section 432*;

"*debenture*" has the same meaning as in section 2 of the Companies Act 1963;

"*director*" shall be construed in accordance with *section 433(4)*;

"*distribution system operator*" has the same meaning as in the Electricity Regulation Act 1999;

"*eligible shares*" means new ordinary shares which, throughout the period of 3 years beginning on the date on which they are issued, carry no present or future preferential right to dividends or to a company's assets on its winding up and no present or future preferential right to be redeemed;

"*emoluments*" has the same meaning as in *section 983*;

"*employment relevant number*" means the total number of qualifying employees in receipt of emoluments from the qualifying company in the year of assessment in which, in relation to a subscription for eligible shares, a relevant period ends;

"*employment threshold number*" means the total number of qualifying employees in receipt of emoluments from the qualifying company in the year of assessment preceding the year of assessment in which the subscription for eligible shares was made;

"*energy from renewable sources*" means energy from renewable non-fossil sources, that is to say wind, solar, aerothermal, geothermal, hydrothermal and ocean energy, hydropower, biomass, landfill gas, sewage treatment plant gas and biogases and includes the development of any facilities for the storage of energy from renewable sources;

"*expenditure on research and development*" has the same meaning as in *section 766*;

"*financial activities*" means the provision of, and all matters relating to the provision of, financing or refinancing facilities by any means which involves, or has an effect equivalent to, the extension of credit;

"*financing or refinancing facilities*" includes—

(a) loans, mortgages, leasing, lease rental and hire-purchase, and all similar arrangements,

(b) equity or other investment,

(c) the factoring of debts and the discounting of bills, invoices and promissory notes, and all similar instruments, and

(d) the underwriting of debt instruments and all other kinds of financial securities;

"*financial assets*" includes shares, gilts, bonds, foreign currencies and all kinds of futures, options and currency and interest rate swaps, and similar instruments, including commodity futures and commodity options, invoices and all types of receivables, obligations evidencing debt (including loans and deposits), leases and loan and lease portfolios, bills of exchange, acceptance credits and all other documents of title relating to the movement of goods, commercial paper, promissory notes and all other kinds of negotiable or transferable instruments;

"*full-time employee*" and "*full-time director*" have the same meanings respectively as in *section 250*;

"*green energy activities*" means activities undertaken with a view to producing energy from renewable sources;

"*grid connection agreement*" means an agreement with the transmission system operator or distribution system operator, or an offer from the transmission system operator or distribution system operator to enter into an agreement for connection to, or use of, the transmission or distribution system;

['*internationally traded financial services*' means the services specified in the schedule to the Industrial Development (Service Industries) Order 2010 (S.I. No. 81 of 2010) other than those falling within the meaning of *subparagraph (b)* or *(c)* of the definition of 'relevant trading activities';][1]

"*market value*" shall be construed in accordance with *section 548*;

"*ordinary shares*" means shares forming part of a company's ordinary share capital;

"*planning consent*" means any consent, permission or approval required under the Planning and Development Acts 2000 to 2010 before development can be lawfully carried out;

"*qualifying company*" has the meaning assigned to it by *section 494*;

"*qualifying employee*", in relation to a qualifying company, means an employee (within the meaning of *section 983*), other than a director, of that company who, throughout his or her period of employment with that company is employed by that company for not less than 4 week days, of each week;

"*qualifying new venture*" means a venture consisting of relevant trading activities which are set up and commenced by a new company other than—

(a) activities which were previously carried on by another person and to which the company has succeeded, or

(b) a venture, the activities of which were previously carried on as part of another person's trade or profession;

"*relevant employment*", in relation to a specified individual, means employment throughout the relevant period by the company in which the specified individual makes a relevant investment (being that individual's first such investment in that company) and where the specified individual is a full-time employee or full-time director of the company;

"*relevant investment*", in relation to a specified individual, means the amount or the aggregate of the amounts subscribed in a year of assessment by the specified individual for eligible shares in a qualifying company which carries on or intends to carry on relevant trading activities;

['*relevant period*', in relation to relief in respect of any eligible shares issued by a company, means—

(a) subject to *paragraphs (b), (c)* and *(d)*, the period beginning on the date on which the shares were issued and ending 4 years after that date or, where the company was not at that date carrying on relevant trading activities, 4 years after the date on which it subsequently began to carry on such activities,

(b) as respects a relevant employment, the period beginning on the date on which the shares are issued or, if later, the date on which the employment commences and ending 12 months after that date,

(c) as respects a specified individual, the period beginning on the date on which the shares are issued and ending either one year after that date or, where the company was not at that date carrying on relevant trading activities, one year after the date on which it subsequently began to carry on such activities, and

(d) as respects *sections 489(2)(b)* and *501(1)(a)(iii)* and the definitions of 'average relevant amount' and 'employment relevant number' in this subsection, the period beginning on the date on which the shares were issued and ending 3 years after that date or, where the company was not at that date carrying on relevant trading activities, 3 years after the date on which it subsequently began to carry on such activities;][2]

"*relevant trading activities*" means activities carried on in the course of a trade the profits or gains of which are charged to tax under Case I of Schedule D, excluding activities related to—

(a) adventures or concerns in the nature of trade,

(b) dealing in commodities or futures or in shares, securities or other financial assets,

(c) financing activities,

(d) the provision of services, which would result in a close company (within the meaning of *section 430*) that provides those services being treated as a service company for the purposes of *section 441* if that close company had no other source of income,

(e) dealing in or developing land,

(f) the occupation of woodlands within the meaning of *section 232*,

(g) operating or managing hotels, guest houses, self catering accommodation or comparable establishments or managing property used as an hotel, guest house, self catering accommodation or comparable establishment [except where the operating or managing of such hotels, guest houses, self catering accommodation or comparable establishments, or the managing of property used as a hotel, guest house, self catering accommodation or comparable establishment, is a tourist traffic undertaking,][3]

[...][4]

(i) operations carried on in the coal industry or in the steel and shipbuilding sectors, and

(j) the production of a film (within the meaning of *section 481*),

but including tourist traffic undertakings;

"*research and development activities*" has the same meaning as in *section 766*;

"*specified individual*" has the meaning assigned to it by *section 495*;

"*specified period*" means the period beginning on the incorporation of the company (or, if the company was incorporated more than 2 years before the date on which the shares were issued, beginning 2 years before that date) and ending [4 years][5] after the issue of the shares;

"*specified relevant period*" has the meaning assigned in *section 766* to relevant period;

"*relief*" means relief under *section 489* and *493*, as the case may be, and references to the amount of the relief shall be construed in accordance with subsection (2) of *section 489* and *subsection (2)* and *(3)* of *section 493*, as the case may be;

"*tourist traffic undertakings*" means—

(a) the operation of tourist accommodation facilities for which the National Tourism Development Authority maintains a register in accordance with the Tourist Traffic Acts 1939 to 2003, [...][6]

(b) the operation of such other classes of facilities as may be approved of for the purpose of the relief by the Minister for Finance, in consultation with the Minister for Tourism, Culture and Sport, on the recommendation of the National Tourism Development Authority in accordance with specific codes of standards laid down by it, or

(c) the promotion outside the State of—

(i) one or more tourist accommodation facilities for which the National Tourism Development Authority maintains a register in accordance with the Tourist Traffic Acts 1939 to 2003, or

(ii) any of the facilities mentioned in *paragraph (b)*;

"*transmission system operator*" has the same meaning as in the Electricity Regulation Act 1999;

"*unquoted company*" means a company none of whose shares, stocks or debentures are—

(a) listed in the official list of a stock exchange, or

(b) quoted on an unlisted securities market of a stock exchange other than—

(i) on the market known, and referred to in this definition, as the Enterprise Securities Market of the Irish Stock Exchange, or

(ii) on the Enterprise Securities Market of the Irish Stock Exchange and on any similar or corresponding market of the stock exchange of one or more Member States of the European Union; but this subparagraph shall not apply unless the shares, stocks or debentures are quoted on the Enterprise Securities Market of the Irish Stock Exchange before or at the same time as they are initially quoted on an unlisted securities market of a stock exchange of another Member State of the European Union.

(2) References in this Part to a disposal of shares include references to a disposal of an interest or right in or over the shares, and an individual shall be treated for the

purposes of this Part as disposing of any shares which the individual is treated by virtue of *section 587* as exchanging for other shares.

(3) References in this Part to the reduction of any amount include references to its reduction to nil.][7]

Amendments

[1] Inserted by FA14 s27(1)(a)(i). Comes into operation on such day or days as the Minister for Finance may by order or orders appoint and different days may be appointed for different purposes or different provisions.

[2] Substituted by FA14 s27(1)(a)(ii). Comes into operation on such day or days as the Minister for Finance may by order or orders appoint and different days may be appointed for different purposes or different provisions.

[3] Inserted by FA13 s22(1)(a)(i). Has effect in respect of shares issued on or after 1 January 2013.

[4] Deleted by FA14 s27(1)(a)(iii). Comes into operation on such day or days as the Minister for Finance may by order or orders appoint and different days may be appointed for different purposes or different provisions.

[5] Substituted by FA14 s27(1)(a)(iv). Comes into operation on such day or days as the Minister for Finance may by order or orders appoint and different days may be appointed for different purposes or different provisions.

[6] Deleted by FA13 s22(1)(a)(ii). Has effect in respect of shares issued on or after 1 January 2013.

[7] Substituted by FA11 s33(1)(a). Has effect in respect of shares issued on or after 25 November 2011.

Note

FA12 s26(2) amends FA11 s33 and provides:

(b) This section does not have effect in respect of shares issued before 25 November 2011 and, for all the purposes of Part 16 in connection with those shares, the Principal Act has effect as if this section had not been enacted.

(c) This section does not have effect in respect of shares issued on or after 25 November 2011 and on or before 31 December 2011 where—

(i) the company issuing the shares, or

(ii) where the shares are acquired by an investment fund, the fund acquiring the shares,

elects by notice in writing to the Revenue Commissioners on or before 31 December 2011 that, for all the purposes of Part 16 of the Principal Act in connection with those shares, the Principal Act has effect as if this section had not been enacted.

Revenue Briefings

eBrief

eBrief No. 74/2011 – Income Tax Relief for investment in Corporate Trades – Business Expansion (BES), Seed Capital (SC), and Employment and Investment Incentive (EII) Schemes

Revenue Information Notes

IT 15(A) – Guidelines on definitions used in the Employment and Investment Incentive (EII) and Seed Capital Scheme (with effect from 25 November 2011)

Cross References

From Section 488

Section 232 Profits from occupation of certain woodlands.

Section 250 Extension of relief under section 248 to certain individuals in relation to loans applied in acquiring interest in certain companies.

Section 430 Meaning of "close company".

Section 432 Meaning of "associated company" and "control".

Section 433 Meaning of "participator", "associate", "director" and "loan creditor".

Section 441 Surcharge on undistributed income of service companies.

Section 481 Relief for investment in films.

Section 489 The relief.

Section 492 Individuals qualifying for relief.

Section 493 Seed capital relief.

Section 494 Qualifying companies.

Section 495 Specified individuals.

Section 505 Application to subsidiaries.

Section 548 Valuation of assets.

Section 587 Company reconstructions and amalgamations.
Section 766 Tax credit for research and development expenditure.
Section 983 Interpretation (Chapter 4).

To Section 488

Section 251 Restriction of relief to individuals on loans applied in acquiring shares in companies where a claim for "BES relief" or "film relief" is made in respect of amount subscribed for shares.
Section 591 Relief for individuals on certain reinvestment.
Section 737 Special investment schemes.
Section 838 Special portfolio investment accounts.
Section 958 Date for payment of tax.
Section 1024 Method of apportioning reliefs and charging tax in cases of separate assessments.
Schedule 10 Relief for Investment in Corporate Trades: Subsidiaries

489 The relief

[(1) This section applies for affording relief from income tax where—

(a) an individual who qualifies for the relief subscribes for eligible shares in a qualifying company,

(b) those shares are issued to the individual for the purpose of raising money by a qualifying company where that money was used, is being used or is intended to be used by the qualifying company—

(i) for the purposes of carrying on relevant trading activities, or

(ii) in the case of a company which has not commenced to trade, in incurring expenditure on research and development within the meaning of *section 766*,

and

(c) the use of the money as set out in *paragraph (b)* will contribute directly to the creation or maintenance of employment in the company.

(2) Subject to *subsection (3)*, relief in respect of—

(a) [thirty fortieths][1] of the amount subscribed by an individual for any eligible shares shall be given as a deduction from his or her total income for the year of assessment in which the shares are issued, and

(b) subject to *subsection (10)*, [ten fortieths][2] of the amount subscribed by an individual for any eligible shares shall be given as a deduction from his or her total income for the year of assessment following the date on which the relevant period ends.

(3) Where—

(a) in accordance with *section 506*, relief is due in respect of an amount subscribed as nominee for a qualifying individual by the managers of a designated fund, and

(b) the eligible shares in respect of which the amount is subscribed are issued in the year of assessment following the year of assessment in which that amount was subscribed to the designated fund,

then the individual may elect by notice in writing to the inspector to have the relief due under *subsection (2)(a)* given as a deduction from his or her total income for the year of assessment in which the amount was subscribed to the designated fund, instead of (as provided for in *subsection (2)(a)*) as a deduction from his or her total income for the year of assessment in which the shares are issued.

(4) The relief under *subsection (2)(a)* shall be given on a claim and shall not be allowed—

(a) in the case of a company which had commenced relevant trading activities at the time the eligible shares were issued, unless and until the company has carried on those activities for 4 months, or

(b) in the case of a company which had not commenced relevant trading activities at the time the eligible shares were issued, unless the company—

(i) begins to carry on relevant trading activities within 2 years after that time, or

(ii) expends not less than 30 per cent of the money subscribed for the shares on research and development activities which are connected with and undertaken with a view to the carrying on of the relevant trading activities.

(5) Subject to *subsections (4)* and *(10)* a claim for relief may be allowed at any time if the conditions for the relief are then satisfied.

(6) In the case of a claim allowed before the end of the relevant period, the relief shall be withdrawn if by reason of any subsequent event it appears that the claimant was not entitled to the relief allowed.

(7) Where by reason of its being wound up, or dissolved without winding up, the company carries on relevant trading activities for a period shorter than 4 months, then *subsection (4)(a)* shall apply as if it referred to that shorter period but only if it is shown that the winding up or dissolution was for bona fide commercial reasons and not as part of a scheme or arrangement the main purpose or one of the main purposes of which was the avoidance of tax.

(8) Subject to *section 504*, no account shall be taken of the relief, in so far as it is not withdrawn, in determining whether any sums are excluded by virtue of *section 554* from the sums allowable as a deduction in the computation of gains and losses for the purposes of the Capital Gains Tax Acts.

(9) (a) In this subsection "*distribution*" has the same meaning as in the Corporation Tax Acts.

(b) For the purposes of this subsection, an amount specified or implied shall include an amount specified or implied in a foreign currency.

(c) This subsection applies to shares in a company where any agreement, arrangement or understanding exists which could reasonably be considered to eliminate the risk that the person beneficially owning those shares—

(i) might, at or after a time specified in or implied by that agreement, arrangement or understanding, be unable to realise directly or indirectly in money or money's worth an amount so specified or implied, other than a distribution, in respect of those shares, or

(ii) might not receive an amount so specified or implied of distributions in respect of those shares.

(d) The reference in this subsection to the person beneficially owning shares shall be deemed to be a reference to both that person and any person connected with that person.

(e) Relief from income tax shall not be allowed under this Part in respect of the amount subscribed for any shares to which this subsection applies.

(10) An amount shall not be given as a deduction by virtue of *subsection (2)(b)* unless in relation to a qualifying company—

(a) (i) the employment relevant number exceeds the employment threshold number, and

(ii) the average relevant amount is not less than the average threshold amount except to the extent that such difference corresponds with a general reduction in the basic pay rate of qualifying employees in the same period,

or

(b) the amount of expenditure on research and development incurred by the qualifying company in the specified relevant period ending in the year of assessment preceding the year of assessment in which, in relation to the subscription for eligible shares, a relevant period ends, exceeds the amount of expenditure on research and development incurred by the qualifying company in the specified relevant period ending in the year of assessment preceding the year of assessment in which the subscription for eligible shares was made.

(11) A company carrying on green energy activities shall be deemed to have commenced relevant trading activities when it has made an application for a grid connection agreement.

(12) The Revenue Commissioners may require the qualifying company to provide to them such evidence as they consider necessary and may consult with such persons or body of persons as in their opinion may be of assistance to them, to enable them to verify that the conditions necessary for the claiming and granting of the relief have been satisfied.

(13) This section shall apply only where the eligible shares are issued on or before [31 December 2020][3].][4]

Amendments

[1] Substituted by FA14 s27(1)(b)(i). Applies for the year of assessment 2015 and subsequent years.

[2] Substituted by FA14 s27(1)(b)(ii). Applies for the year of assessment 2015 and subsequent years.

[3] Substituted by FA13 s22(1)(b). Comes into operation on such day or days as the Minister for Finance may by order or orders appoint and different days may be appointed for different purposes or different provisions.

[4] Substituted by FA11 s33(1)(a). Has effect in respect of shares issued on or after 25 November 2011.

Note

FA12 s26(2) amends FA11 s33 and provides:

(b) This section does not have effect in respect of shares issued before 25 November 2011 and, for all the purposes of Part 16 in connection with those shares, the Principal Act has effect as if this section had not been enacted.

(c) This section does not have effect in respect of shares issued on or after 25 November 2011 and on or before 31 December 2011 where—

(i) the company issuing the shares, or

(ii) where the shares are acquired by an investment fund, the fund acquiring the shares,

elects by notice in writing to the Revenue Commissioners on or before 31 December 2011 that, for all the purposes of Part 16 in connection with those shares, the Principal Act has effect as if this section had not been enacted.

Case Law

In Thompson (HMIT) v Hart 2000 STC 381 the taxpayer received shares in return for properties transferred to a company as part of a BES scheme. He claimed BES relief in relation to a subscription for these shares. Relief was denied as he had transferred property in return for the shares and had not subscribed cash. The Judge ruled that "money" could not be extended to include money's worth and accordingly did not extend to include property.

In National Westminister Bank plc v IRC 1994 STC 580 it was held shares were not issued until they had been finally registered, following application and allotment.

Revenue Information Notes

IT 55 – The Business Expansion Scheme (with effect from 1 January 2007 to 31 December 2011)
IT 55 (EII) – Employment and Investment Incentive (with effect from 25 November 2011)
IT15 – Seed Capital Scheme
IT 15(A) – Guidelines on definitions used in the Employment and Investment Incentive (EII) and Seed Capital Scheme (with effect from 25 November 2011)

Revenue Precedents

Whether relief should be allowed for part shares if and when bonus share issue takes place that will eliminate any part shares being held by investors? Relief allowed as the bonus issue would ensure that each investor would be registered as the owner of full shares. 2476/87

When did shares actually issue? Would Revenue accept that the share "issued" when a mutual obligation arose whereby the applicant was obliged to take the shares and the company was obliged to cause those shares to be registered in the applicants name? The issue of shares occurred when the legal title was completed by way of registration. BES and share capital relief can be claimed only when the applicants have been issued with the relevant share certificates. 2014/93

Would the existence of a Patent Royalty Company which resulted in a return of patent income to the BES investor, offend this section? No, if the patent company is engaged in licensing arrangements with the manufacturing company and if distributable reserves are eliminated prior to BES investment. 5891/90

Whether a promise to investors of an asset in lieu of investment after the five year relevant investment period contravenes section 489(14)? Section 489(14) was contravened. 76/92

(1) Whether promoters be allowed by way of agreement with fund, to withhold some of their money until it was required by the company, and they would then subscribe for the agreed number of shares, & (2) Would an agreed investment by promoters (which is required by a designated fund) offend the risk provisions? (1) Agreed this would not eliminate risk. (2) No. It just demonstrates the commitment of the promoters to the project. 6313/95

Would an individual working 37 hours with the seed capital company and 37 hours with another company satisfy the requirement that full time employment must be taken up in the seed capital company? No 6308/96

BES money can be used to repay bank borrowings which are financing a company's trade. 3584/87A

BES relief does not apply where assets are used for the payment of shares. The shares must be issued for the purpose of raising money for the qualifying trade. 944

Cross References

From Section 489

Section 504 Capital gains tax.
Section 506 Nominees and designated funds.
Section 554 Exclusion of expenditure by reference to income tax.
Section 766 Tax credit for research and development expenditure.

To Section 489

Section 458 Deductions allowed in ascertaining taxable income and provisions relating to reductions in tax.
Section 488 Interpretation (Part 16).
Section 490 Limits on the relief.
Section 493 Seed capital relief.
Section 494 Qualifying companies.
Section 501 Claims.
Schedule 10 Relief for Investment in Corporate Trades: Subsidiaries
Schedule 25B List of Specified Reliefs and Method of Determining Amount of Specified Relief Used in a Tax Year

490 Limits on the relief

[(1) (a) Subject to *section 506* and *paragraph (b)*, the relief shall not be given in respect of any amount subscribed by an individual for eligible shares issued to the individual by a qualifying company in any year of assessment unless the amount or total amount subscribed by the individual for the eligible shares issued to the individual by the company in that year is €250 or more.

(b) In the case of an individual who is [a married person assessed to tax for a year of assessment in accordance with *section 1017*, or a nominated civil partner assessed to tax for a year of assessment in accordance with *section 1031C*,][1] any amount subscribed by the individual's [spouse or civil partner][2] for eligible shares issued to that [spouse or civil partner][3] in that year of assessment by the company shall be deemed to have been subscribed by the individual for eligible shares issued to the individual by the company.

(2) The relief shall not be given to the extent to which the amount or total amount subscribed by an individual for eligible shares issued to the individual in any year of assessment (whether or not by the same company) exceeds €100,000 in the case of a relevant investment, or €150,000 in any other case.

(3) (a) Where in any year of assessment a greater amount of relief would be given to an individual in respect of the amount or the total amount subscribed by the individual for eligible shares (in this subsection referred to as the "*relevant subscription*") issued to the individual in that year or, where *subsection (3)* of *section 489* applies, in the following year of assessment but for either or both of the following reasons—

(i) an insufficiency of total income, or

(ii) the operation of *subsection (2)*,

then the amount of the relief which would be given but for those reasons less the amount or the aggregate amount of any relief in respect of the relevant subscription which is given in that year of assessment shall be carried forward to the next year of assessment, and shall be treated for the purposes of the relief as an amount of relief under *section 489(2)(a)* in respect of an amount subscribed directly by the individual for eligible shares issued to the individual in that next year.

(b) This subsection and *subsection (4)* shall not apply for any year of assessment subsequent to the year of assessment [2020][4].

(4) If and in so far as an amount once carried forward to a year of assessment under *subsection (3)* (and treated as an amount of relief under *section 489(2)(a)* in respect of an amount subscribed directly by an individual for eligible shares issued to the individual in that year of assessment) is not deducted from his or her total income for that year of assessment, it shall be carried forward again to the next year of assessment (and treated as an amount of relief under *section 489(2)(a)* in respect of an amount subscribed directly by the individual for eligible shares issued to the individual in that next year), and so on for succeeding years of assessment.

(5) The relief shall be given to an individual for any year of assessment in the following order—

(a) in the first instance, in respect of an amount carried forward from an earlier year of assessment in accordance with *subsection (3)* or *(4)* and, in respect of such an amount so carried forward, for an earlier year of assessment in priority to a later year of assessment, and

(b) only thereafter, in respect of any other amount for which relief is to be given in that year of assessment.][5]

Amendments

[1] Substituted by F(No.3)A11 sched1(135). Shall have effect from 27 July 2011.

[2, 3] Substituted by F(No.3)A11 sched1(136). Shall have effect from 27 July 2011.

[4] Substituted by FA13 s22(1)(c). Comes into operation on such day or days as the Minister for Finance may by order or orders appoint and different days may be appointed for different purposes or different provisions.

[5] Substituted by FA11 s33(1)(a). Has effect in respect of shares issued on or after 25 November 2011.

Note

FA12 s26(2) amends FA11 s33 and provides:

(b) This section does not have effect in respect of shares issued before 25 November 2011 and, for all the purposes of Part 16 in connection with those shares, the Principal Act has effect as if this section had not been enacted.

(c) This section does not have effect in respect of shares issued on or after 25 November 2011 and on or before 31 December 2011 where—

(i) the company issuing the shares, or

(ii) where the shares are acquired by an investment fund, the fund acquiring the shares,

elects by notice in writing to the Revenue Commissioners on or before 31 December 2011 that, for all the purposes of Part 16 in connection with those shares, the Principal Act has effect as if this section had not been enacted.

Revenue Information Notes

IT 55 – The Business Expansion Scheme (with effect from 1 January 2007 to 31 December 2011)
IT 55 (EII) – Employment and Investment Incentive (with effect from 25 November 2011)
IT15 – Seed Capital Scheme
IT 15A – Guidelines on definitions used in the Employment and Investment Incentive (EII) and Seed Capital Scheme (with effect from 25 November 2011)

Revenue Precedents

Whether section 490(1)(b) TCA 1997 means that a subscrption for shares by a non-assessable spouse is regarded for all purposes as a subscription by the assessable spouse? No; the paragraphs applies only as regards the minimum subscription required for a husband and wife. A subscription of 200 by either or both will fulfill the minimum subscription rule. IT932024

Whether relief is transferable in the case of a married couple jointly assessed for tax? No. The maximum allowable subscription of €25,000 applies to each spouse seperately. 4297/86

Cross References

From Section 490

Section 489 The relief.
Section 506 Nominees and designated funds.
Section 1017 Assessment of husband in respect of income of both spouses.

To Section 490

Section 491 Restriction on relief where amounts raised exceed permitted maximum.
Section 493 Seed capital relief.
Section 506 Nominees and designated funds.
Schedule 25B List of Specified Reliefs and Method of Determining Amount of Specified Relief Used in a Tax Year

491 Restriction on relief where amounts raised exceed permitted maximum

[(1) In this section *"qualifying subsidiary"*, in relation to a company, means a subsidiary of that company of a kind which a company may have by virtue of *section 505*.

(2) Subject to this section, where a company raises any amount through the issue of eligible shares (in this section referred to as the *"relevant issue"*), relief shall not be given in respect of the excess of the amount so raised over the amount determined by the formula—

$$A - B$$

where—

A is [€15,000,000][1],

and

B is the lesser of—

(a) the amount represented by A in the formula, and

(b) an amount equal to the aggregate of all amounts raised by the company through the issue of eligible shares at any time on or after 6 April 1984 and before the relevant issue.

(3) Where, a company raises any amount through a relevant issue and that company is associated (within the meaning of this section) with one or more other companies, then, as respects that company, relief shall not be given in respect of the excess of the amount so raised over the amount determined by the formula—

$$A - B$$

where—

A is [€15,000,000][2],

and

B is the lesser of—

(a) the amount represented by A in the formula, and

(b) the aggregate of all amounts raised through the issue of eligible shares, at any time before or on the date of the relevant issue, by all of the companies (including that company) which are associated within the meaning of this section.

(4) Notwithstanding anything in *subsections (2)* and *(3)*, relief shall not be given in respect of a relevant issue to the extent that—

(a) the amount raised by the relevant issue, or

(b) the aggregate of—

(i) the amount to be raised through the relevant issue, and

(ii) the amount or amounts, if any, raised through the issue of eligible shares other than the relevant issue, within the period of 12 months ending with the date of that relevant issue, by the company or by all of the companies (including the company making the relevant issue) which are associated within the meaning of this section, as the case may be,

exceeds [€5,000,000][3].

(5) For the purposes of this section, a company shall be associated with another company where—

(a) in the case of that company, or a company which is, or was at any time, its qualifying subsidiary, and

(b) that other company, or a company which is, or was at any time, its qualifying subsidiary,

it could reasonably be considered that—

(i) both companies act in pursuit of a common purpose,

(ii) any person or any group of persons or groups of persons having a reasonable commonality of identity have or had the means or power, either directly or indirectly, to determine the trading activities carried on or to be carried on by both companies, or

(iii) both companies are under the control of any person or group of persons or groups of persons having a reasonable commonality of identity;

but for the purposes of this section a company shall not be considered as associated with another company by reason only of the fact that a subscription for eligible shares in both companies is made by a person or persons having the management of an investment fund designated under *section 506* as nominee for any person or group or groups of persons.

(6) In determining for the purposes of the formula in *subsection (2)* or *(3)*, as the case may be, the amount to which *paragraph* (*b*) of the definition of "B" in those formulas relates, account shall not be taken of any amount—

(a) which is subscribed by a person other than an individual who qualifies for relief, or

(b) in respect of which relief is precluded by virtue of *section 490*.

(7) Where as a consequence of *subsection (2)* or *(3)* the giving of relief would be precluded on claims in respect of shares issued to 2 or more individuals, the available relief shall be divided between them respectively in proportion to the amounts which have been subscribed by them for the shares to which their claims relate and which apart from this section would be eligible for relief.][4]

Amendments

[1] Substituted by FA14 s27(1)(c)(i). Comes into operation on such day or days as the Minister for Finance may by order or orders appoint and different days may be appointed for different purposes or different provisions.

[2] Substituted by FA14 s27(1)(c)(ii). Comes into operation on such day or days as the Minister for Finance may by order or orders appoint and different days may be appointed for different purposes or different provisions.

[3] Substituted by FA14 s27(1)(c)(iii). Comes into operation on such day or days as the Minister for Finance may by order or orders appoint and different days may be appointed for different purposes or different provisions.

[1] Substituted by FA11 s33(1)(a). Has effect in respect of shares issued on or after 25 November 2011.

Note

FA12 s26(2) amends FA11 s33 and provides:

(b) This section does not have effect in respect of shares issued before 25 November 2011 and, for all the purposes of Part 16 in connection with those shares, the Principal Act has effect as if this section had not been enacted.

(c) This section does not have effect in respect of shares issued on or after 25 November 2011 and on or before 31 December 2011 where—

(i) the company issuing the shares, or

(ii) where the shares are acquired by an investment fund, the fund acquiring the shares,

elects by notice in writing to the Revenue Commissioners on or before 31 December 2011 that, for all the purposes of Part 16 in connection with those shares, the Principal Act has effect as if this section had not been enacted.

Revenue Information Notes

IT55 – The Business Expansion Scheme (with effect from 1 January 2007 until 31 December 2011)

IT55 (EII) – Employment and Investment Incentive (with effect from 25 November 2011)

IT15 – The Seed Capital Scheme

IT15A – Guidelines on definitions used in the Employment and Investment Incentive (EII) and Seed Capital Scheme (with effect from 25 November 2011)

Revenue Precedents

A company had raised up to its limit in respect of its trade. The daughter of the family controlling the original company proposed to raise money for a complimentary trade. Were the companies associated for the purposes of this section? Yes. The companies were pursuing a common purpose and a group of persons with a reasonable commonality of identity had determined the trading operations to be carried on. 6576/95

An individual set up a number of companies and raised BES funds to the limit. His daughter set up a new venture to produce a completely different product. She was qualified in her own right. Were the companies associated for the purposes of this section? No, because there were no business or financial transactions between the companies, nor agreements, arrangements or understandings under which the person with the existing companies or an associated person would take over the venture at a future date. 6200/96

A manufacturer was having difficulty obtaining raw materials. The company organised a BES scheme for an entirely independent raw materials supplier. There were certain agreements between the companies including the sharing of manufacturing facilities and obligations in relation to the sale of outputs. The supplier raised BES funds up to the limit. A BES scheme was proposed for a second supplier controlled by entirely different parties. Were the companies associated for the purposes of this section? Yes. The company shared a common purpose with the first supplier. 6089/95

Cross References

From Section 491

Section 490 Limits on the relief.
Section 505 Application to subsidiaries.
Section 506 Nominees and designated funds.

492 Individuals qualifying for relief

[(1) (a) An individual shall qualify for relief if he or she subscribes on his or her own behalf for eligible shares in a qualifying company and is not at any time in the specified period connected with the company.

(b) For the purposes of this section and *paragraph 2* of *Schedule 10*, any question whether an individual is connected with a company shall be determined in accordance with this section.

(2) An individual shall be connected with a company if the individual or an associate of the individual is—

(a) a partner of the company, or

(b) subject to *subsection (3)*, a director or employee of the company or of another company which is a partner of that company.

(3) An individual shall not be connected with a company by reason only that the individual or an associate of the individual is a director or employee of the company or of another company which is a partner of that company unless the individual or the individual's associate (or a partnership of which the individual or the individual's associate is a member) receives a payment from either company during the period of [4 years][1] beginning on the date on which the shares are issued or is entitled to receive such a payment in respect of that period or any part of it; but for that purpose there shall be disregarded—

(a) any payment or reimbursement of travelling or other expenses wholly, exclusively and necessarily incurred by the individual or the individual's associate in the performance of the duties of the individual or of the associate, as the case may be, as such director or employee,

(b) any interest which represents no more than a reasonable commercial return on money lent to either company,

(c) any dividend or other distribution paid or made by either company which does not exceed a normal return on the investment,

(d) any payment for the supply of goods to either company in the course of a trade or business, which does not exceed their market value, and

(e) any reasonable and necessary remuneration which—

(i) (I) is paid for services rendered to either company in the course of a trade or profession, not being secretarial or managerial services or services of a kind provided by the company itself, and

(II) is taken into account in computing the profits or gains of the trade or profession under Case I or II of Schedule D or would be so taken into account if it fell in a period on the basis of which those profits or gains are assessed under that Schedule,

or

(ii) in a case where the individual is a director or an employee of either company and is not otherwise connected with either company, is paid for service, rendered to the company of which the individual is a director or an employee, in the course of the directorship or the employment.

(4) An individual shall be connected with a company if he or she directly or indirectly possesses or is entitled to acquire more than 30 per cent of—

(a) the issued ordinary share capital of the company,

(b) the loan capital and issued share capital of the company, or

(c) the voting power in the company.

(5) For the purposes of *subsection (4)(b)*, the loan capital of a company shall be treated as including any debt incurred by the company—

(a) for any money borrowed or capital assets acquired by the company,

(b) for any right to receive income created in favour of the company, or

(c) for consideration the value of which to the company was (at the time when the debt was incurred) substantially less than the amount of the debt (including any premium on the debt).

(6) (a) Subject to *paragraph (b)* an individual is connected with a company if he or she directly or indirectly possesses or is entitled to acquire such rights as would, in the event of the winding up of the company or in other circumstances, entitle the individual to receive more than 30 per cent of the assets of the company which would at that time be available for distribution to equity holders of the company, and for the purposes of this subsection—

(i) the persons who are equity holders of the company, and

(ii) the percentage of the assets of the company to which the individual would be entitled,

shall be determined in accordance with *sections 413* and *415*, with references in *section 415* to the first company being construed as references to an equity holder and references to a winding up being construed as including references to any other circumstances in which assets of the company are available for distribution to its equity holders.

(b) A determination in accordance with *paragraph (a)* shall be made without regard to *section 411(1)(c)* in so far as it relates to *sections 413* and *415*, with any necessary modifications, to such determination of the percentage of share capital or other amount which a shareholder beneficially owns or is beneficially entitled to, as they apply to the determination for the purposes of Chapter 5 of Part 12 of the percentage of any such amount which a company so owns or is so entitled to.

(7) An individual is connected with a company if he or she has control of it within the meaning of *section 11*.

(8) (a) An individual is not connected with a company by reason only of *subsection (4), (6)* or *(7)*—

(i) if throughout the specified period the aggregate of all amounts subscribed for the issued share capital and the loan capital (within the meaning of *subsection (5)*) of the company does not exceed €500,000, or

(ii) in the case of a specified individual, by virtue only of a relevant investment in respect of which he or she has been given relief in accordance with *section 493(2)* or (3).

(b) Notwithstanding *paragraph (a)*, relief granted to an individual in respect of a subscription for eligible shares at a time when by virtue of this subsection the individual was not connected with the company shall not be withdrawn by reason only that the individual subsequently becomes connected with the company by virtue of *subsection (4), (6)* or *(7)*.

(9) For the purposes of this section, an individual shall be treated as entitled to acquire anything which he or she is entitled to acquire at a future date or will at a future date be entitled to acquire, and there shall be attributed to any person any rights or powers of any other person who is an associate of that person.

(10) In determining for the purposes of this section whether an individual is connected with a company, a debt incurred by the company by overdrawing an account with a person carrying on a business of banking shall not be treated as loan capital of the company if the debt arose in the ordinary course of that business.

(11) Where an individual subscribes for shares in a company with which the individual is not connected (either within the meaning of this section or by virtue of *paragraph 2(2)(b)* of Schedule 10), then he or she shall nevertheless be treated as connected with it if he or she subscribes for the shares as part of any arrangement which provides for another person to subscribe for shares in another company with which the individual or any other individual who is a party to the arrangement is connected (within the meaning of this section or by virtue of that paragraph).][2]

Amendments

[1] Substituted by FA14 s27(1)(d). Comes into operation on such day or days as the Minister for Finance may by order or orders appoint and different days may be appointed for different purposes or different provisions.

[2] Substituted by FA11 s33(1)(a). Has effect in respect of shares issued on or after 25 November 2011.

Note

FA12 s26(2) amends FA11 s33 and provides:

(b) This section does not have effect in respect of shares issued before 25 November 2011 and, for all the purposes of Part 16 in connection with those shares, the Principal Act has effect as if this section had not been enacted.

(c) This section does not have effect in respect of shares issued on or after 25 November 2011 and on or before 31 December 2011 where—

(i) the company issuing the shares, or

(ii) where the shares are acquired by an investment fund, the fund acquiring the shares,

elects by notice in writing to the Revenue Commissioners on or before 31 December 2011 that, for all the purposes of Part 16 in connection with those shares, the Principal Act has effect as if this section had not been enacted.

Cross References

From Section 492

Section 11 Meaning of "control" in certain contexts.

Section 411 Surrender of relief between members of groups and consortia.

Section 413 Profits or assets available for distribution.

Section 415 Meaning of "the notional winding up".

Section 493 Seed capital relief.

To Section 492

Section 488 Interpretation (Part 16).

Section 495 Specified individuals.

Section 497 Value received from company.

Section 499 Value received by persons other than claimants.
Section 502 Assessments for withdrawing relief.
Section 503 Information.
Schedule 10 Relief for Investment in Corporate Trades: Subsidiaries

493 Seed capital relief

[(1) Notwithstanding *section 489*, this section shall apply for affording relief from income tax where—

(a) a specified individual makes a relevant investment,

(b) the shares issued to the specified individual are issued for the purposes of raising money by a qualifying company for the benefit of its activities referred to in *paragraph (d)*,

(c) the activities carried on by the qualifying company constitute a qualifying new venture,

(d) the money was used, is being used or is intended to be used for the benefit of a qualifying new venture for the purposes of—

(i) carrying on of relevant trading activities, or

(ii) in the case of a company which has not commenced the carrying on of relevant trading activities, incurring expenditure on research and development within the meaning of *section 766*,

and

(e) the use of the money as set out in *paragraph (d)* will contribute directly to the creation or maintenance of employment in the company.

(2) Subject to *subsection (3)*, relief in respect of a relevant investment made by a specified individual shall be given as a deduction of that amount from his or her total income for the year of assessment in which the shares are issued.

(3) (a) Subject to this subsection, a specified individual may, in relation to a relevant investment made by such individual (being that individual's first such investment), elect by notice in writing to the inspector to have the relief due given as a deduction from such individual's total income for any one of the 6 years of assessment immediately before the year of assessment in which the eligible shares in respect of that investment are issued which such individual nominates for the purpose, instead of (as provided for in *subsection (2)*) as a deduction from the specified individual's total income for the year of assessment in which the shares are issued, and accordingly, subject to *section 490* and *paragraphs (c)* and *(d)*, for the purpose of granting such relief (but for no other purpose of this Part) the shares shall be deemed to have been issued in the year of assessment so nominated.

(b) Where the specified individual makes a subsequent relevant investment (being that individual's second such investment)—

(i) in the same company as such individual's first such investment, and

(ii) within either the year of assessment following the end of the year of assessment in which such individual's first such investment was made or the year of assessment subsequent to that year,

then, the specified individual may, in relation to such individual's second such investment, elect by notice in writing to the inspector to have the relief due given as a deduction from such individual's total income for any one of the 6 years of assessment immediately before the year of assessment in which the eligible shares in respect of such individual's first such investment were issued which such individual nominates for the purpose, instead of (as provided for in *subsection (2)*) as a deduction from such individual's total income for the year of assessment in which the eligible shares in respect of such individual's second such investment are issued and, accordingly, subject to *section 490* and *paragraphs* (*c*) and (*d*), for the purpose of granting such relief (but for no other purpose of this Part) the shares issued in respect of the second such investment shall be deemed to have been issued in the year of assessment so nominated.

(c) Where any of the years of assessment following the year of assessment nominated under *paragraph* (*a*) or (*b*), as the case may be, precede the year of assessment in which the eligible shares in respect of the specified individual's first relevant investment are in fact issued, *subsections (3)* to *(5)* of *section 490* shall operate to give relief in such years of assessment as may be nominated by such individual for that purpose.

(d) To the extent that the amount of the relief which would be due in respect of the specified individual's first relevant investment or second relevant investment, as the case may be, has not been given in accordance with *paragraphs* (*a*) to (*c*) it shall, subject to *subsections (3)* to *(5)* of *section 490*, be given for the year of assessment in which the eligible shares in respect of the first such investment or the second such investment, as the case may be, are in fact issued or, if appropriate, a subsequent year of assessment.

(e) This subsection applies in respect of not more than 2 relevant investments made by a specified individual on or after 2 June 1995.

(f) This subsection applies notwithstanding any limitation in *section 865(4)* on the time within which a claim for a repayment of tax is required to be made. *Section 865(6)* shall not prevent the Revenue Commissioners from repaying an amount of tax as a consequence of an election made under *paragraph* (*a*) or (*b*) where the specified individual has made a timely claim for relief in accordance with *section 501* and a valid claim for a repayment of tax within the meaning of *section 865(1)*(*b*).

(4) Reference in this section to the amount of the relief are references to the amount of the deduction given under *subsection (2)* or *(3)*, as may be appropriate.

(5) Relief shall be given on a claim and shall not be allowed in the case of a relevant investment unless and until the qualifying new venture commences to carry on relevant trading activities or in the case of a company referred to in *section 493(1)*(*d*)*(ii)*, has expended not less than 30 per cent of the relevant investment on research and development activities which are connected with and undertaken with a view to the carrying on of the relevant trading activities.

(6) In the case of a claim allowed before the end of the relevant period, the relief shall be withdrawn if by reason of any subsequent event it appears that the claimant was not entitled to the relief allowed.

(7) In the case of a claim allowed before a specified individual commences a relevant employment with the company in which that individual has made a relevant investment (being that individual's first such investment), the relief shall be withdrawn if the specified individual fails to commence such employment—

(a) within the year of assessment in which the investment is made, or

(b) if later, within 6 months of the date of—

(i) where the investment consists of the subscription of only one amount for eligible shares, that subscription, or

(ii) where the investment consists of the subscription of more than one amount for eligible shares, the last such subscription.

(8) Subject to *section 504*, no account shall be taken of the relief, in so far as it is not withdrawn, in determining whether any sums are excluded by virtue of *section 554* from the sums allowable as a deduction in the computation of gains and losses for the purposes of the Capital Gains Tax Acts.

(9) (a) In this subsection "*distribution*" has the same meaning as in the Corporation Tax Acts.

(b) For the purposes of this subsection, an amount specified or implied shall include an amount specified or implied in a foreign currency.

(c) This subsection applies to shares in a company where any agreement, arrangement or understanding exists which could reasonably be considered to eliminate the risk that the person beneficially owning those shares—

(i) might, at or after a time specified in or implied by that agreement, arrangement or understanding, be unable to realise directly or indirectly in money or money's worth an amount so specified or implied, other than a distribution, in respect of those shares, or

(ii) might not receive an amount so specified or implied of distributions in respect of those shares.

(d) The reference in this subsection to the person beneficially owning shares shall be deemed to be a reference to both that person and any person connected with that person.

(e) Relief from income tax shall not be allowed under this Part in respect of the amount subscribed for any shares to which this subsection applies.

(10) Where a specified individual claims relief under this section, no relief shall be granted to that individual under *section 489* in respect of the same qualifying company.

(11) The Revenue Commissioners may require the qualifying company to provide to them such evidence as they consider necessary and may consult with such persons or body of persons as in their opinion may be of assistance to them, to enable them to verify that the conditions necessary for the claiming and granting of the relief have been satisfied.][1]

Amendments

[1] Substituted by FA11 s33(1)(a). Has effect in respect of shares issued on or after 25 November 2011.

Note

FA12 s26(2) amends FA11 s33 and provides:

(b) This section does not have effect in respect of shares issued before 25 November 2011 and, for all the purposes of Part 16 in connection with those shares, the Principal Act has effect as if this section had not been enacted.

(c) This section does not have effect in respect of shares issued on or after 25 November 2011 and on or before 31 December 2011 where—

(i) the company issuing the shares, or

(ii) where the shares are acquired by an investment fund, the fund acquiring the shares,

elects by notice in writing to the Revenue Commissioners on or before 31 December 2011 that, for all the purposes of Part 16 in connection with those shares, the Principal Act has effect as if this section had not been enacted.

Case Law

In Cook (HM Inspector of Taxes) v Billings & Ors 2001 STC 61 a claim for BES relief in the UK was denied on the basis that the seven shareholders, whom each held just under 15% of the share capital in the company were associated with each other for the purposes of this relief. Therefore, they breached the 30% limit. The taxpayer acquired over 99% of the issued share capital in April 1987. and in October 1987. In January 1988 the company issued further shares thus reducing the shareholder's % to below 30%. He claimed BES relief. This relief was not available as he was connected with the company given that he owned more than 30% of the company during the relevant period. Wild v Cannavan (HMIT) 1997 STC 966

Revenue Precedents

Would the holding of more than 30% of the shareholdings, on a temporary basis, in a new company, by promoters, disqualify them from BES relief? No. Provided their shareholding was reduced below 30% when the BES shares are issued. 3838/86

Whether section 493(1) precludes the shares of a married couple being registered in joint names? No, provided the shares are subscribed for by one spouse and the Inspector of Taxes is issued with a letter signed by both parties confirming the amount invested by each spouse. 6223/95

Cross References

From Section 493

Section 489 The relief.
Section 490 Limits on the relief.
Section 493 Seed capital relief.
Section 501 Claims.
Section 504 Capital gains tax.
Section 554 Exclusion of expenditure by reference to income tax.
Section 766 Tax credit for research and development expenditure.
Section 865 Repayment of tax.

To Section 493

Section 488 Interpretation (Part 16).
Section 492 Individuals qualifying for relief.
Section 493 Seed capital relief.
Section 497 Value received from company.
Section 501 Claims.

494 Qualifying companies

[(1) In this section—

[…][1]

"*EEA Agreement*" means the Agreement on the European Economic Area signed at Oporto on 2 May 1992, as adjusted by all subsequent amendments to that Agreement;

"*EEA State*" means a state which is a contracting party to the EEA Agreement;

"*qualifying subsidiary*", in relation to a company, means a subsidiary of that company of a kind which a company may have by virtue of *section 505*.

(2) A company shall be a qualifying company if it is incorporated in the State or in an EEA State other than the State and complies with this section.

(3) (a) The company shall throughout the relevant period be an unquoted company which is resident in the State, or is resident in an EEA State other than the State and carries on business in the State through a branch or agency, and be—

(i) a company which exists wholly for the purpose of carrying on relevant trading activities where those activities [and which carries on relevant trading activities from a fixed place of business in the State, or][2]

(ii) a company whose business consists wholly of—

(I) the holding of shares or securities of, or the making of loans to, one or more qualifying subsidiaries of the company, or

[(II) both the holding of such shares or securities or the making of such loans and the carrying on of relevant trading activities where relevant trading activities are carried on from a fixed place of business in the State.][3]

(b) Where a company raises any amount through the issue of eligible shares for the purposes of raising money for relevant trading activities which are being carried on by a qualifying subsidiary or which such a qualifying subsidiary intends to carry on, the amount so raised shall be used for the purpose of acquiring eligible shares in the qualifying subsidiary and for no other purpose.

[…][4]

[(4) The company shall be a micro, small or medium-sized enterprise within the meaning of Annex 1 to Commission Regulation (EU) No. 651/2014 of 17 June 2014 OJ No. 4187, 26.6.2014, p.1.][5]

[(5) A company whose relevant trading activities includes internationally traded financial services shall not be a qualifying company unless it is in receipt of a certificate from Enterprise Ireland to the effect that its activities are of a kind specified in the schedule to the Industrial Development (Service Industries) Order 2010 (S.I. No. 81 of 2010).][6]

(6) (a) A company whose relevant trading activities includes one or more tourist traffic undertakings shall not be a qualifying company unless and until it has shown to the satisfaction of the Revenue Commissioners that it has submitted to, and has had approved of by, the National Tourism Development Authority a 3 year development and marketing plan in respect of that undertaking or those undertakings, as the case may be, being a plan primarily designed and formulated to increase tourist traffic and revenue from outside the State.

(b) In considering whether to approve of such a plan, the National Tourism Development Authority shall have regard only to such guidelines in relation to such approval as may from time to time be agreed, with the consent of the Minister for Finance, between it and the Minister for Tourism, Culture and Sport, and those guidelines may, without prejudice to the generality of the foregoing, set out—

(i) the extent to which the company's interests in land and buildings may form part of its total assets,

(ii) specific requirements which have to be met in order to comply with the objective mentioned in *paragraph* (*a*), and

(iii) the extent to which the money raised through the issue of eligible shares should be used in promoting outside the State the undertaking or undertakings, as the case may be.

(7) A company whose relevant trading activities includes green energy activities shall cease to be a qualifying company unless it has expended all of the money subscribed for eligible shares on such activities, within a period ending 1 month before the end of the relevant period.

(8) A company referred to in *section 489(1)(b)(ii)* ceases to be a qualifying company unless it has—

(a) expended all of the money subscribed for eligible shares on research and development activities, within a period ending 1 month before the end of the relevant period and disposed of a specified intangible asset within the meaning of *section 291A*, which is connected with and arises directly from those research and development activities, to a person for the purposes of a trade carried on by that person, or

(b) commenced relevant trading activities within 2 years after the eligible shares were issued and expended all of the money subscribed for eligible shares on either of those activities or research and development activities before the end of the relevant period.

(9) Without prejudice to the generality of *subsection (3)* but subject to *subsection (10)*, a company ceases to comply with *subsection (3)* if before the end of the relevant period a resolution is passed, or an order is made, for the winding up of the company (or, in the case of a winding up otherwise than under the Companies Act 1963, any other act is done for the like purpose) or the company is dissolved without winding up.

(10) A company shall not be regarded as ceasing to comply with *subsection (3)* by reason only of the fact that it is wound up or dissolved without winding up if—

(a) it is shown that the winding up or dissolution is for bona fide commercial reasons and not part of a scheme or arrangement the main purpose or one of the main purposes of which is the avoidance of tax, and

(b) the company's net assets, if any, are distributed to its members before the end of the relevant period or, in the case of a winding up, the end (if later) of 3 years from the commencement of the winding up.

(11) The company's share capital shall not at any time in the relevant period include any issued shares not fully paid up.

(12) Subject to *section 505*, the company shall not at any time in the relevant period—

(a) control (or together with any person connected with it control) another company or be under the control of another company (or of another company and any person connected with that other company), unless such control is exercised by the National Asset Management Agency, or by a company referred to in *section 616(1)(g)*, or

(b) be a 51 per cent subsidiary of any company other than the National Asset Management Agency or a company referred to in *section 616(1)(g)*, or itself have a 51 per cent subsidiary,

and no arrangements shall be in existence at any time in that period by virtue of which the company could fall within *paragraph (a)* or *(b)*.

(13) A company shall not be a qualifying company if, in the case of a company in which a relevant investment is made by a specified individual (being that individual's first such investment in that company), any transaction in the relevant period between the company and another company (being the immediate former employer of the individual), or a company which controls or is under the control of that other company, is otherwise than by means of a transaction at arm's length, or if—

(a) (i) an individual has acquired a controlling interest in the company's trade after 5 April 1984, and

(ii) at any time in the period mentioned in *subsection (16)* the individual has or has had a controlling interest in another trade,

and

(b) the trade carried on by the company or a substantial part of that trade—

(i) is concerned with the same or similar types of property or parts of property or provides the same or similar services or facilities as the other trade, or

(ii) serves substantially the same or similar outlets or markets as the other trade.

(14) For the purposes of this section, a person has a controlling interest in a trade—

(a) in the case of a trade carried on by a company, if—

(i) such person controls the company,

(ii) the company is a close company for the purposes of the Corporation Tax Acts and such person or an associate of such person is a director of the company and the beneficial owner of, or able directly or through the medium of other companies or by any other indirect means to control, more than 30 per cent of the ordinary share capital of the company, or

(iii) not less than 50 per cent of the trade could, in accordance with *section 400(2)*, be regarded as belonging to such person,

or

(b) in any other case, if such person is entitled to not less than 50 per cent of the assets used for, or the income arising from, the trade.

(15) For the purposes of *subsection (14)*, there shall be attributed to any person any rights or powers of any other person who is an associate of that person.

(16) The period referred to in *subsection (13)(a)(ii)* is the period beginning 2 years before and ending 3 years after—

(a) the date on which the shares were issued, or

(b) if later, the date on which the company began to carry on the trade.

(17) In *subsections (13)* and *(16)*, references to a company's trade includes references to the trade of any of its subsidiaries.

(18) Notwithstanding *subsections (1)* to *(17)*, a company shall not be a qualifying company while the company is regarded as a firm in difficulty for the purposes of the Community Guidelines on State Aid for rescuing and restructuring firms in difficulty*.][7]

* OJ No. C288 of 9.10.1999, p. 2, and OJ No. C244 of 1.10.2004, p. 2

Amendments

[1] Deleted by FA14 s27(1)(e)(i). Comes into operation on such day or days as the Minister for Finance may by order or orders appoint and different days may be appointed for different purposes or different provisions.

[2] Substituted by FA12 s26(1)(a). Deemed to have come into force and takes effect on and from 1 January 2012.

[3] Substituted by FA12 s26(1)(b). Deemed to have come into force and takes effect on and from 1 January 2012.

[4] Deleted by FA12 s26(1)(c). Deemed to have come into force and takes effect on and from 1 January 2012.

[5] Substituted by FA14 s27(1)(e)(ii). Comes into operation on such day or days as the Minister for Finance may by order or orders appoint and different days may be appointed for different purposes or different provisions.

[6] Substituted by FA14 s27(1)(e)(iii). Comes into operation on such day or days as the Minister for Finance may by order or orders appoint and different days may be appointed for different purposes or different provisions.

[7] Substituted by FA11 s33(1)(a). Has effect in respect of shares issued on or after 25 November 2011.

Note

FA12 s26(2) amends FA11 s33 and provides:

(b) This section does not have effect in respect of shares issued before 25 November 2011 and, for all the purposes of Part 16 in connection with those shares, the Principal Act has effect as if this section had not been enacted.

(c) This section does not have effect in respect of shares issued on or after 25 November 2011 and on or before 31 December 2011 where—

(i) the company issuing the shares, or

(ii) where the shares are acquired by an investment fund, the fund acquiring the shares,

elects by notice in writing to the Revenue Commissioners on or before 31 December 2011 that, for all the purposes of Part 16 in connection with those shares, the Principal Act has effect as if this section had not been enacted.

Revenue Precedents

A period spent on a contract basis during which witholding tax was deducted and the same conditions as other workers applied, satisfies the requirements in relation to PAYE type employment. 6348/95

PAYE type employment in the U.S. satisfies the PAYE type employment requirement to qualify for the scheme. 6346/96

Would a 9 month period at a course abroad, during which the individual was not employed, disqualify the individual from Seed Capital Relief. The period abroad was within the three year period during which the individual was required to be in PAYE type employment? No. 6538/96

Cross References

From Section 494

Section 291A Intangible assets.
Section 400 Company reconstructions without change of ownership.
Section 489 The relief.
Section 505 Application to subsidiaries.
Section 616 Groups of companies: interpretation.

To Section 494

Section 488 Interpretation (Part 16).
Section 497 Value received from company.
Section 502 Assessments for withdrawing relief.
Section 503 Information.
Section 505 Application to subsidiaries.

495 Specified individuals

[(1) An individual shall be a specified individual if he or she qualifies for relief in respect of a relevant investment and complies with this section.

(2) The individual, in each of the 3 years of assessment preceding the year of assessment which precedes the year of assessment in which that individual makes a relevant investment (being that individual's first such investment), shall not have been in receipt of income chargeable to tax otherwise than under—

(a) Schedule E, or

(b) Case III of Schedule D in respect of profits or gains from an office or employment held or exercised outside the State,

in excess of the lesser of—

(i) the aggregate of the amounts, if any, of that individual's income chargeable to tax under Schedule E and under Case III of Schedule D in respect of the profits or gains referred to in *subparagraph (ii)*, and

(ii) €50,000.

(3) The individual shall throughout the relevant period possess at least 15 per cent of the issued ordinary share capital of the company in which that individual makes a relevant investment.

(4) (a) For the purposes of *paragraph (b)* and *subsections (5)* and *(6)*, "*specified date*", in relation to a relevant investment in a company, means—

(i) where the investment consists of the subscription of only one amount for eligible shares, the date of that subscription, or

(ii) where that investment consists of the subscription of more than one amount for eligible shares, the date of the last such subscription.

(b) Subject to *subsections (5)* and *(6)*, the individual at the specified date, in relation to that individual's first relevant investment in a company, or within the period of 12 months immediately preceding that date, either directly or indirectly, shall not possess or have possessed, or shall not be or have been entitled to acquire, more than 15 per cent of—

(i) the issued ordinary share capital,

(ii) the loan capital (within the meaning of *section 492(5)*) and the issued share capital, or

(iii) the voting power,

of any company other than—

(I) the company in which that individual makes that relevant investment, or

(II) a company to which *subsection (5)* applies.

(5) This subsection applies to a company which during a period of 3 years ending on the specified date in relation to an individual's first relevant investment in a company—

(a) was not entitled to any assets, other than cash on hands or a sum of money on deposit (within the meaning of *section 895*) not exceeding €130,

(b) did not carry on a trade, profession, business or other activity including the making of investments, and

(c) did not pay charges on income within the meaning of *section 243*.

(6) (a) For the purposes of *paragraph (b)* "*accounting period*" means an accounting period determined in accordance with *section 27*.

(b) A company shall be regarded as a company which carries on wholly or mainly relevant trading activities referred to in *paragraph (c)(i)* only if in each of the 3 accounting periods referred to in *paragraph (c)(ii)* the total amount receivable from sales made or services rendered in the course of such activities is not less than 75 per cent of the total amount receivable by the company from all sales made and services rendered in the course of tourist traffic undertakings and 90 per cent of the total amount receivable by the company from all sales made and services rendered in the course of other relevant trading activities.

(c) An individual shall not be regarded as failing to satisfy the requirements of *subsection (4)* merely by reason of the fact that the individual does not satisfy those requirements in relation to only one company (other than the company in which the individual makes his or her first relevant investment or a company to which *subsection (5)* applies)—

(i) which exists wholly or mainly for the purpose of carrying on relevant trading activities, and

(ii) where the total amount receivable by that company from sales made and services rendered in the course of that company's relevant trading activities did not exceed €127,000 in each of that company's 3 accounting periods immediately preceding the accounting period of that company in which the specified date occurs in relation to that individual's first relevant investment.

(7) An individual shall not be regarded as ceasing to comply with *subsection (3)* merely by reason of the fact that the company in which the individual makes a relevant investment is wound up, or dissolved without winding up, before the end of the relevant period but only if it is shown that the winding up or dissolution is for bona fide commercial reasons and is not part of a scheme or arrangement the main purpose or one of the main purposes of which was the avoidance of tax.][1]

Amendments

[1] Substituted by FA11 s33(1)(a). Has effect in respect of shares issued on or after 25 November 2011.

Note

FA12 s26(2) amends FA11 s33 and provides:

(b) This section does not have effect in respect of shares issued before 25 November 2011 and, for all the purposes of Part 16 in connection with those shares, the Principal Act has effect as if this section had not been enacted.

(c) This section does not have effect in respect of shares issued on or after 25 November 2011 and on or before 31 December 2011 where—

(i) the company issuing the shares, or

(ii) where the shares are acquired by an investment fund, the fund acquiring the shares,

elects by notice in writing to the Revenue Commissioners on or before 31 December 2011 that, for all the purposes of Part 16 in connection with those shares, the Principal Act has effect as if this section had not been enacted.

Case Law

A domestic tax relief which only applied to investments in local securities was held to be an unlawful interference with the free movement of capital. Ministere des Finances v Weidert and Paulas 2004 C-242/03

Revenue Precedents

Control

If two relatives have 25% each of the shares in the BES company and they also hold 60% and 20% respectively in a company carrying on a similar trade, would this offend the provisions of this rule? No. As "associate" for the purposes of Section 495(11) excludes relatives, no individual has control. 1300/91

Would a sound recording company controlled by individuals who had control of other sound recording companies breach this section? No – it is necessary for the purposes of the law to set up a separate company and this is acceptable provided that there is no attempt to breach Section 491.

Would companies serving different markets although the same industry, offend this section? No. If there was a good commercial reason for establishing the second company and if there would be no transfer of business from one to the other or winding down of one business. 6432/5/98

Where part of a trade is transferred from an existing company to a new company, can the original company retain control of the second company until a BES investment is made? No 3584/97B

A qualifying company can only have qualifying subsidiaries. Would the existence of non-qualifying subsidiaries, which are now dormant, disqualify the company? No, provided the subsidiaries remained dormant. 8085/84

If Udaras na Gaeltachta owns a majority of the shares in the company, mainly for the purpose of injecting capital into the company, would this offend this rule? No. Udaras shares are akin to a loan. 860/87A

Where it is not technically possible to organise a BES scheme because a company is a member of a group, would a hive-down of certain activities be allowed? Yes, provided the Revenue Commissioners are satisfied that the hive-down is necessary because of technical difficulties with the BES and for no other reason and the company is a stand alone company after the BES share issue, and also provided there is no attempt to breach Section 491. File not available – issue included for completion of data base.

Qualifying company

(1) Whether non-trading activities or income which arises as an incidental to the carrying on of the trade e.g. interest on cash flow, rents from letting part of the conpany's trading premises etc..., or (2) Whether incidental shareholdings in other companies, be they subsidiaries, suppliers, or customers; would be regarded as diluting the companies 100% existence for trading purposes. or (3) Whether the holding of lands and buildings by a holding company, which are used by its subsidiary companies, would be regarded as affecting the "wholly" provision of this section? (1) No; (2) No, provided such holdings are part of the natural trading environment in which the company operates and provided the holdings are for the purposes related to the trade. (3) No, so long as the holding company retains ownership and the land and buildings were used by the subsidiary companies throughout the relevant period. 991/87

Partnership

Would a company carrying on a qualifying trade in partnership be precluded per se from being considered to be a qualifying company? No, provided that the company carrying on a trade in partnership invests the monies raised in itself, then that company can be regarded as a qualifying company (provided the other conditions are met). If however, the BES monies raised are used to invest in a partnership trade then the company would not qualify. i.e. the BES money must be used for the BES company's trade. 322/92

Fully paid up share capital

Can assets be used as payment of shares? Yes, provided there is no transfer of trade. However, no BES relief is due (see Section 489 I (b) TCA 1997). 4455/88

Cross References

From Section 495

Section 27 Basis of, and periods for, assessment.
Section 243 Allowance of charges on income.
Section 492 Individuals qualifying for relief.
Section 895 Returns in relation to foreign accounts.

To Section 495

Section 488 Interpretation (Part 16).
Section 502 Assessments for withdrawing relief.
Section 503 Information.
Section 838 Special portfolio investment accounts.

496 Disposals of shares

[(1) Where an individual disposes of any eligible shares before the end of the specified period, then—

(a) in a case where the disposal is otherwise than by means of a bargain made at arm's length, the individual shall not be entitled to any relief in respect of those shares, and

(b) in any other case, the amount of relief to which the individual is entitled in respect of those shares shall be reduced by the amount or value of the consideration which the individual receives for those shares.

[(2) *Subsection (1)* shall not apply—

(a) to a disposal made by a married person to his or her spouse at a time when he or she is treated as living with his or her spouse for income tax purposes in accordance with *section 1015*, or

(b) to a disposal by a civil partner to the other civil partner at a time when he or she is treated as living with his or her civil partner for income tax purposes in accordance with *section 1031A*,

but where shares issued to one of them have been transferred to the other by a transaction *inter vivos*—

(i) that subsection shall apply on the disposal of the shares by the transferee to a third person, and

(ii) if at any time the married person ceases to be treated as living with his or her spouse for income tax purposes in accordance with *section 1015*, or the civil partner ceases to be treated as living with his or her civil partner for income tax purposes in accordance with *section 1031A*, and any of those shares have not been disposed of by the transferee before that time, any assessment for withdrawing relief in respect of those shares shall be made on the transferee.][1]

(3) (a) For the purposes of this subsection, references to an option or an agreement includes references to a right or obligation to acquire or grant an option or enter into an agreement, and references to the exercise of an option includes references to the exercise of an option which may be acquired or granted by the exercise of such a right or under such an obligation.

(b) Where in the specified period an individual, either directly or indirectly—

(i) (I) acquires an option where the exercise of the option, either under the terms of the option or under the terms of any arrangement or undertaking subject to which or otherwise in connection with which the option is acquired, would—

(A) bind the person from whom the option was acquired or any other person, or

(B) cause that person or such other person,

to purchase or otherwise acquire any eligible shares for a price which, having regard to the terms of the option or the terms of such arrangement or undertaking and the net effect of those terms considered as a whole, is other than the market value of the eligible shares at the time the purchase or acquisition is made, or

(II) enters into an agreement where, either under the terms of the agreement or under the terms of any arrangement or understanding subject to which or otherwise in connection with which the agreement is made, it would—

(A) bind the person with whom the agreement is made or any other person, or

(B) cause that person or such other person,

to purchase or otherwise acquire any eligible shares in the manner described in clause (I),

or

(ii) (I) grants to any person an option where the exercise of the option, either under the terms of the option or under the terms of any arrangement or understanding subject to which or otherwise in connection with which the option is granted, would bind the individual to dispose, or cause the individual to dispose, of any eligible shares to the person to whom the individual granted the option or any other person for a price which, having regard to the terms of the option or the terms of such arrangement or understanding and the net effect of those terms considered as a whole, is other than the market value of the eligible shares at the time the disposal is made, or

(II) enters into an agreement where, either under the terms of the agreement or under the terms of any arrangement or understanding subject to which or otherwise in connection with which the agreement is made, it would bind the individual to dispose, or cause the individual to dispose, of any eligible shares to the person with whom the agreement is made or any other person in the manner described in clause (I), then the individual is not entitled to any relief in respect of the shares to which the option or the agreement relates.

(4) Where an individual holds ordinary shares of any class in a company and the relief has been given in respect of some shares of that class but not others, then any disposal by the individual of ordinary shares of that class in the company, not being a disposal to which *section 512(2)* applies, shall be treated for the purposes of this section as relating to those in respect of which relief has been given under this Part rather than to others.

(5) Where the relief has been given to an individual in respect of shares of any class in a company which have been issued to the individual at different times, then any disposal by the individual of shares of that class shall be treated for the purposes of this section as relating to those issued earlier rather than to those issued later.

(6) Where shares in respect of which the relief was given have by virtue of any such allotment mentioned in *subsection (1)* of *section 584* (not being an allotment for payment) been treated under *subsection (3)* of that section as the same asset as a new holding, then—

(a) the new holding shall be treated for the purposes of *subsection (4)* as shares in respect of which the relief has been given, and

(b) a disposal of the whole or part of the new holding shall be treated for the purposes of this section as a disposal of the whole or a corresponding part of those shares.

(7) Shares in a company shall not be treated for the purposes of this section as being of the same class unless they would be so treated if dealt in on a stock exchange in the State.][2]

Amendments

[1] Substituted by F(No.3)A11 sched1(137). Shall have effect from 27 July 2011.

[2] Substituted by FA11 s33(1)(a). Has effect in respect of shares issued on or after 25 November 2011.

Note

FA12 s26(2) amends FA11 s33 and provides:

(b) This section does not have effect in respect of shares issued before 25 November 2011 and, for all the purposes of Part 16 in connection with those shares, the Principal Act has effect as if this section had not been enacted.

(c) This section does not have effect in respect of shares issued on or after 25 November 2011 and on or before 31 December 2011 where—

(i) the company issuing the shares, or

(ii) where the shares are acquired by an investment fund, the fund acquiring the shares,

elects by notice in writing to the Revenue Commissioners on or before 31 December 2011 that, for all the purposes of Part 16 in connection with those shares, the Principal Act has effect as if this section had not been enacted.

Revenue Precedents

Where IDA employment grant given to Co.A re: certain services, such services subsequently taken over by Co. B – would this be regarded as a"qualifying trade" within meaning of Sect. 496? It would be regarded as a "qualifying trade" within meaning of section 496. 7148/88

Cross References

From Section 496

Section 512 Disposals of scheme shares.

Section 584 Reorganisation or reduction of share capital.

Section 1015 Interpretation (Chapter 1).

To Section 496

Section 502 Assessments for withdrawing relief.

Section 503 Information.

Section 504 Capital gains tax.

497 Value received from company

[(1) In this section "*ordinary trade debt*" means any debt for goods or services supplied in the ordinary course of a trade or business where the credit period given does not exceed 6 months and is not longer than that normally given to the customers of the person carrying on the trade or business.

(2) In this section—

(a) any reference to a payment or transfer to an individual includes a reference to a payment or transfer made to the individual indirectly or to his or her order or for his or her benefit, and

(b) any reference to an individual includes a reference to an associate of the individual and any reference to the company includes a reference to any person connected with the company.

(3) For the purposes of this section, an individual receives value from a company where the company—

(a) repays, redeems or repurchases any of its share capital or securities which belong to the individual or makes any payment to the individual for giving up his or her right to any of the company's share capital or any security on its cancellation or extinguishment,

(b) repays any debt owed to the individual other than—

(i) an ordinary trade debt incurred by the company, or

(ii) any other debt incurred by the company—

(I) on or after the earliest date on which the individual subscribed for the shares in respect of which the relief is claimed, and

(II) otherwise than in consideration of the extinguishment of a debt incurred before that date,

(c) makes to the individual any payment for giving up his or her right to any debt on its extinguishment other than—

(i) a debt in respect of a payment of the kind mentioned in *paragraph (d)* or *(e)* of *section 492(3)*, or

(ii) a debt of the kind mentioned in *subparagraph (i)* or *(ii)* of *paragraph (b)*,

(d) releases or waives any liability of the individual to the company or discharges, or undertakes to 10 discharge, any liability of the individual to a third person,

(e) makes a loan or advance to the individual,

(f) provides a benefit or facility for 15 the individual,

(g) transfers an asset to the individual for no consideration or for consideration less than its market value or acquires an asset from the individual for consideration exceeding its market value, or

(h) makes to the individual any other payment except a payment of the kind mentioned in *paragraph (a)*, *(b)*, *(c)*, *(d)* or *(e)* of *section 492(3)* or a payment in discharge of an ordinary trade debt.

(4) (a) A specified individual shall not 30 have received value from a company by virtue of *subsection (3)(b)* where—

(i) the specified individual has made an investment in the 35 company by way of a loan,

(ii) the loan is converted into eligible shares within one year of the making of the loan, and

(iii) the specified individual provides a statement by the auditor of the company certifying that, in his or her opinion, the money raised by the company by way of the loan was used, and only used, by it in accordance with the provisions of *section 493(1)(d)*.

(b) Where *paragraph (a)* applies, conversion of the loan into eligible shares shall, notwithstanding any other provision of this Part, be treated as the making of a relevant investment by the specified individual on the date of the making of the loan.

(c) For the purposes of this subsection "*auditor*", in relation to a company, means the person or persons appointed as auditor of the company for all the purposes of the Companies Acts.

(5) For the purposes of this section, an individual shall also receive value from the company where the individual receives in respect of ordinary shares held by the individual any payment or asset in a winding up or in connection with a dissolution of the company, being a winding up or dissolution within *section 494(10)*.

(6) For the purposes of this section, an individual shall also receive value from the company where any person who for the purposes of *section 492* would be treated as connected with the company—

(a) purchases any of its share capital or securities which belong to the individual, or

(b) makes any payment to the individual for giving up any right in relation to any of the company's share capital or securities.

(7) The value received by an individual shall be—

(a) in a case within *paragraph (a)*, *(b)* or *(c)* of *subsection (3)*, the amount receivable by the individual or, if greater, the market value of the shares, securities or debt in question,

(b) in a case within *subsection (3)(d)*, the amount of the liability,

(c) in a case within *subsection (3)(e)*, the amount of the loan or advance,

(d) in a case within *subsection (3)(f)*, the cost to the company of providing the benefit or facility less any consideration given for it by the individual,

(e) in a case within *subsection (3)(g)*, the difference between the market value of the asset and the consideration (if any) given for it,

(f) in a case within *subsection (3)(h)*, the amount of the payment,

(g) in a case within *subsection (4)*, the amount of the payment or, as the case may be, the market value of the asset, and

(h) in a case within *subsection (5)*, the amount receivable by the individual or, if greater, the market value of the shares or securities in question.

(8) For the purposes of *subsection (3)(d)*, a company shall be treated as having released or waived a liability where the liability is not discharged by payment within 12 months of the time when it ought to have been discharged by payment.

(9) For the purposes of *subsection (3)(e)*, there shall be treated as if it were a loan made by the company to the individual—

(a) the amount of any debt (other than an ordinary trade debt) incurred by the individual to the company, and

(b) the amount of any debt due from the individual to a third person which has been assigned to the company.

(10) Where an individual who subscribes for eligible shares in a company—

(a) has, before the issue of the shares but within the specified period, received any value from the company, or

(b) on or after their issue but before the end of the specified period, receives any such value,

then, the amount of the relief to which the individual is entitled in respect of the shares shall be reduced by the value so received.

(11) Where by virtue of this section any relief is withheld or withdrawn in the case of an individual to whom ordinary shares in a company have been issued at different times, the relief shall be withheld or withdrawn in respect of shares issued earlier rather than in respect of shares issued later.][1]

Amendments

[1] Substituted by FA11 s33(1)(a). Has effect in respect of shares issued on or after 25 November 2011.

Note

FA12 s26(2) amends FA11 s33 and provides:

(b) This section does not have effect in respect of shares issued before 25 November 2011 and, for all the purposes of Part 16 in connection with those shares, the Principal Act has effect as if this section had not been enacted.

(c) This section does not have effect in respect of shares issued on or after 25 November 2011 and on or before 31 December 2011 where—

(i) the company issuing the shares, or

(ii) where the shares are acquired by an investment fund, the fund acquiring the shares,

elects by notice in writing to the Revenue Commissioners on or before 31 December 2011 that, for all the purposes of Part 16 in connection with those shares, the Principal Act has effect as if this section had not been enacted.

Cross References

From Section 497

Section 492 Individuals qualifying for relief.
Section 493 Seed capital relief.
Section 494 Qualifying companies.

To Section 497

Section 499 Value received by persons other than claimants.
Section 502 Assessments for withdrawing relief.
Section 503 Information.
Schedule 10 Relief for Investment in Corporate Trades: Subsidiaries

498 Replacement capital

[(1) In this section—

"*subsidiary*" means a subsidiary of a kind which a qualifying company may have by virtue of *section 505*;

"*trade*" includes any business, profession or vocation, and references to a trade previously carried on include references to part of such a trade.

(2) An individual to whom *subsection (3)* applies is not entitled to relief in respect of any shares in a company where at any time in the specified period the company or any of its subsidiaries—

(a) begins to carry on, as its trade or as a part of its trade, a trade previously carried on at any time in that period otherwise than by the company or any of its subsidiaries, or

(b) acquires the whole or greater part of the assets used for the purposes of a trade previously so carried on.

(3) This subsection applies to an individual where—

(a) any person or group of persons to whom an interest amounting in the aggregate to more than a 50 per cent share in the trade (as previously carried on) belonged at any time in the specified period is a person or a group of persons to whom such an interest in the trade carried on by the company, or any of its subsidiaries, belongs or has at any such time belonged, or

(b) any person or group of persons who controls or at any such time has controlled the company is a person or a group of persons who at any such time controlled another company which previously carried on the trade,

and the individual is that person or one of those persons.

(4) An individual is not entitled to relief in respect of any shares in a company where—

(a) the company comes to acquire all of the issued share capital of another company at any time in the specified period, and

(b) any person or group of persons who controls or has at any such time controlled the company is a person or a group of persons who at any such time controlled that other company,

and the individual is that person or one of those persons.

(5) For the purposes of *subsection (3)*—

(a) the person or persons to whom a trade belongs and, where a trade belongs to 2 or more persons, their respective shares in that trade shall be determined in accordance with *paragraphs (a)* and *(b)* of *subsection (1)*, and *subsections (2)* and *(3)*, of *section 400*, and

(b) any interest, rights or powers of a person who is an associate of another person shall be treated as those of that other person.][1]

Amendments

[1] Substituted by FA11 s33(1)(a). Has effect in respect of shares issued on or after 25 November 2011.

Note

FA12 s26(2) amends FA11 s33 and provides:

(b) This section does not have effect in respect of shares issued before 25 November 2011 and, for all the purposes of Part 16 in connection with those shares, the Principal Act has effect as if this section had not been enacted.

(c) This section does not have effect in respect of shares issued on or after 25 November 2011 and on or before 31 December 2011 where—

(i) the company issuing the shares, or

(ii) where the shares are acquired by an investment fund, the fund acquiring the shares,

elects by notice in writing to the Revenue Commissioners on or before 31 December 2011 that, for all the purposes of Part 16 in connection with those shares, the Principal Act has effect as if this section had not been enacted.

Revenue Precedents

Does the death of an individual constitute a disposal of shares for the purposes of this section? No IT943510

Would the exchange of shares in a RICT company for equal shares in a new holding company (also a qualifying company) lead to a loss of RICT relief? No – where the restructuring is essential to ensure that the existing employment is safeguarded and future job creation is facilitated. 191/85

If investors swap their shares in a subsidiary for shares in a holding company, it would normally be referred to as disposal. However, because Section 498(1)(b) [previously 17(1)(b)] applies, there is no clawback of the relief because no consideration was received by the shareholders. Is this true? No. Revenue would not accept this interpretation of the section. However, they would be prepared to consider allowing investors to retain relief if the existing investors in the qualifying subsidiary were given shares in the qualifying company on a share for share basis. 4395/88

Where an individual disposes of shares in a company on the take-over of that company within the three year "relevant period", would the relief be withdrawn by virtue of this section? Yes 3584/87C

Would the existance of a CAP on dividends and assets on a winding up, and a put-call option offend this rule? No. The existence of a CAP would not necessarily preclude the granting of approval but its bearing on other aspects of the case would need to be examined. 1034/92

Cross References

From Section 498

Section 400 Company reconstructions without change of ownership.

Section 505 Application to subsidiaries.

To Section 498

Section 479 Relief for new shares purchased on issue by employees.

Section 502 Assessments for withdrawing relief.

Section 503 Information.

499 Value received by persons other than claimants

[(1) The relief to which an individual is entitled in respect of any shares in a company shall be reduced in accordance with *subsection (4)* if at any time in the specified period the company repays, redeems or repurchases any of its share capital which belongs to any member other than—

(a) that individual, or

(b) another individual whose relief is thereby reduced by virtue of *section 497(3)*,

or makes any payment to any such member for giving up such member's right to any of the company's share capital on its cancellation or extinguishment.

(2) *Subsection (1)* does not apply in relation to the redemption of any share capital for which the redemption date was fixed before 26 January 1984.

(3) Where—

(a) after 5 April 1984, a company issues share capital (in this subsection referred to as the "*original shares*") of nominal value equal to the authorised minimum (within the meaning of the Companies (Amendment) Act 1983) for the purposes of complying with the requirements of *section 6* of that Act, and

(b) after the registrar of companies has issued the company with a certificate under *section 6* of that Act the company issues eligible shares,

then *subsection (1)* does not apply in relation to any redemption of any of the original shares within 12 months of the date on which those shares were issued.

(4) Where *subsection (1)* applies, the amount of relief to which an individual is entitled shall be reduced by the amount receivable by the member or, if greater, the nominal value of the share capital in question and, where apart from this subsection, 2 or more individuals would be entitled to relief, the reduction shall be made in proportion to the amounts of relief to which those individuals would have been entitled apart from this subsection.

(5) Where at any time in the specified period a member of a company receives or is entitled to receive any value from the company within the meaning of this subsection, then, for the purposes of *section 492(4)* in its application to any subsequent time—

(a) the amount of the company's issued ordinary share capital, and

(b) the amount of the part of that capital which consists of the shares relevant to *section 492(4)* and the amount of the part consisting of the remainder,

shall each be treated as reduced in accordance with *subsection (6)*.

(6) The amount of each of the parts mentioned in *subsection (5)(b)* shall be treated as equal to such proportion of that amount as the amount subscribed for that part less the relevant value bears to the amount subscribed, and the amount of the issued share capital shall be treated as equal to the sum of the amounts treated under this subsection as the amount of those parts respectively.

(7) In *subsection (5)(b)*, the reference to the part of the capital which consists of the shares relevant to *section 492(4)* is a reference to the part consisting of shares which (within the meaning of that section) the individual directly or indirectly possesses or is entitled to acquire, and in *subsection (6)* the "*relevant value*", in relation to each of the parts mentioned in that subsection, means the value received by the member or members entitled to the shares of which that part consists.

(8) For the purposes of *subsection (5)*, a member of a company receives or is entitled to receive value from the company within the meaning of that subsection in any case in which an individual would receive value from the company by virtue of *paragraph* (*d*), (*e*), (*f*), (*g*) or (*h*) of *section 497(3)* (but treating as excepted from *paragraph* (*h*) all payments made for full consideration), and the value received shall be determined as for the purposes of that section.

(9) For the purposes of *subsection (8)*, a person shall be treated as entitled to receive anything which the person is entitled to receive at a future date or will at a future date be entitled to receive.

(10) Where by virtue of this section any relief is withheld or withdrawn in the case of an individual to whom ordinary shares in the company have been issued at different times, the relief shall be withheld or withdrawn in respect of shares issued earlier rather than in respect of shares issued later.][1]

Amendments

[1] Substituted by FA11 s33(1)(a). Has effect in respect of shares issued on or after 25 November 2011.

Note

FA12 s26(2) amends FA11 s33 and provides:

(b) This section does not have effect in respect of shares issued before 25 November 2011 and, for all the purposes of Part 16 in connection with those shares, the Principal Act has effect as if this section had not been enacted.

(c) This section does not have effect in respect of shares issued on or after 25 November 2011 and on or before 31 December 2011 where—

(i) the company issuing the shares, or

(ii) where the shares are acquired by an investment fund, the fund acquiring the shares,

elects by notice in writing to the Revenue Commissioners on or before 31 December 2011 that, for all the purposes of Part 16 in connection with those shares, the Principal Act has effect as if this section had not been enacted.

Case Law

Fletcher (Inspector of Taxes) v Thompson and anor 2002 STC 1149 considered a clawback of BES relief.

Revenue Precedents

Whether value received for the purposes of subsection 3(b) where a director's loan is repaid? Yes. 319.21(4)

Does the provision of company cars for directors as part of the remuneration package, where the directors are assessable to tax under Schedule E in respect of the benefit, constitute value received from the company? No, provided the level of benefit does not exceed the generally accepted levels. 2273/87

Would a payment of "hello money" which is not outside of the industry norm, be regarded as value received as provided for in this section? No 6151/94

Would the issue of bonus shares be regarded as value received? No, where the overall value of the individual shareholding is not increased. 6081/96

Cross References

From Section 499

Section 6 Construction of references to child in Tax Acts and Capital Gains Tax Acts.

Section 492 Individuals qualifying for relief.

Section 497 Value received from company.

To Section 499

Section 502 Assessments for withdrawing relief.

Section 503 Information.

Schedule 10 Relief for Investment in Corporate Trades: Subsidiaries

500 Prevention of misuse

[An individual shall not be entitled to relief in respect of any shares unless the shares are subscribed and issued for bona fide commercial purposes and not as part of a scheme or arrangement the main purpose or one of the main purposes of which is the avoidance of tax.][1]

Amendments

[1] Substituted by FA11 s33(1)(a). Has effect in respect of shares issued on or after 25 November 2011.

Note

FA12 s26(2) amends FA11 s33 and provides:

(b) This section does not have effect in respect of shares issued before 25 November 2011 and, for all the purposes of Part 16 in connection with those shares, the Principal Act has effect as if this section had not been enacted.

(c) This section does not have effect in respect of shares issued on or after 25 November 2011 and on or before 31 December 2011 where—

(i) the company issuing the shares, or

(ii) where the shares are acquired by an investment fund, the fund acquiring the shares,

elects by notice in writing to the Revenue Commissioners on or before 31 December 2011 that, for all the purposes of Part 16 in connection with those shares, the Principal Act has effect as if this section had not been enacted.

Cross References

To Section 500

Section 502 Assessments for withdrawing relief.

Section 503 Information.

Schedule 10 Relief for Investment in Corporate Trades: Subsidiaries

501 Claims

[(1) A claim for the relief in respect of eligible shares issued by a company in any year of assessment shall be made—

(a) not earlier than—

(i) in the case of a claim under *section 493*, the date on which the company commences to carry on the relevant trading activities or in the case of a company referred to in *section 493(1)(d)*(ii), has expended not less than 30 per cent of the relevant investment on research and development activities which are connected with and undertaken with a view to the carrying on of the relevant trading activities,

(ii) in the case of a relief under *section 489(2)(a)*—

(I) where the company is a company referred to in *section 489(4)(b)*, which does not begin to carry on relevant trading activities, the time of the disposal, and

(II) in any other case, the end of the period of 4 months mentioned in *section 489(4)(a)*,

and

(iii) in the case of a relief under *section 489(2)(b)*, the date on which the relevant period ends,

and

(b) not later than—

(i) the period of 2 years after the end of that year of assessment or, if the period of 4 months mentioned in *section 489(4)(a)* ended after the end of that year, the period of 2 years after the end of that 4 month period, whichever last occurs, or

(ii) the period of 3 months after the date the statement referred to in *subsection (3)* is furnished, where such statement is furnished within the 3 months prior to the expiry of the time specified in *subparagraph (i)*.

(2) A claim for relief in respect of eligible shares in a company shall not be allowed unless it is accompanied by a certificate issued by the company in such form as the Revenue Commissioners may direct and certifying that the conditions for the relief, in so far as they apply to the company and the trade, are satisfied in relation to those shares.

(3) Before issuing a certificate under *subsection (2)*, a company shall furnish the inspector with a statement to the effect that it satisfies the conditions for the relief, in so far as they apply in relation to the company and the trade, and has done so at all times since the beginning of the relevant period.

(4) No certificate to which *subsection (3)* relates shall be issued without the authority of the inspector or where the company or a person connected with the company has given notice to the inspector under *section 503(2)*.

(5) Any statement under *subsection (3)* shall—

(a) contain such information as the Revenue Commissioners may reasonably require,

(b) be in such form as the Revenue Commissioners may direct, and

(c) contain a declaration that it is correct to the best of the company's knowledge and belief.

(6) Where a company has issued a certificate under *subsection (2)* or furnished a statement under *subsection (3)*, and—

(a) the certificate or statement is false or misleading, or

(b) the certificate was issued in contravention of *subsection (4)*,

then the company shall be liable to a penalty of €4,000.

(7) For the purpose of regulations made under *section 986*, no regard shall be had to the relief unless a claim for it has been duly made and admitted.

(8) For the purposes of *section 1080*, income tax—

(a) shall be regarded as due and payable notwithstanding that relief from the tax (whether by discharge or repayment) is subsequently given on a claim for the relief, but

(b) shall, unless paid earlier or due and payable later, be regarded as paid, to the extent that relief from tax is due under this Part, on the date of the making of the claim on which the relief is given,

and *section 1081* shall not apply in consequence of any discharge or repayment for giving effect to the relief.][1]

[(9) A claim for relief under *section 489(2)* or 493 in respect of eligible shares in a company shall not be allowed unless, at the time the claim is made, the company qualifies for a tax clearance certificate within the meaning of *section 1095*.][2]

Amendments

[1] Substituted by FA11 s33(1)(a). Has effect in respect of shares issued on or after 25 November 2011.

[2] Inserted by FA14 s27(1)(f). Comes into operation on such day or days as the Minister for Finance may by order or orders appoint and different days may be appointed for different purposes or different provisions.

Note

FA12 s26(2) amends FA11 s33 and provides:

(b) This section does not have effect in respect of shares issued before 25 November 2011 and, for all the purposes of Part 16 in connection with those shares, the Principal Act has effect as if this section had not been enacted.

(c) This section does not have effect in respect of shares issued on or after 25 November 2011 and on or before 31 December 2011 where—

(i) the company issuing the shares, or

(ii) where the shares are acquired by an investment fund, the fund acquiring the shares,

elects by notice in writing to the Revenue Commissioners on or before 31 December 2011 that, for all the purposes of Part 16 in connection with those shares, the Principal Act has effect as if this section had not been enacted.

Revenue Precedents

The repurchase by a company of shares held by Foir Teo would not disqualify the BES shareholders provided the shares are temporary redeemable shares. 860/87B

A bank backed management buy-out (after the three years relevant period), where the bank insists on being given security over the assets of the company, would not constitute a receipt of value received by non-BES members, where the BES money has long since been dissipated. 922/87

Would capitalisation of reserves effect BES applications? No, as long as the market value of the shareholders capital remains the same and the company does not repay, redeem, or repurchase any of the share capital. 6264/96

Cross References

From Section 501

Section 489 The relief.

Section 493 Seed capital relief.

Section 503 Information.

Section 986 Regulations.

Section 1080 Interest on overdue income tax, corporation tax and capital gains tax.

Section 1081 Effect on interest of reliefs given by discharge or repayment.

To Section 501

Section 493 Seed capital relief.

Section 506 Nominees and designated funds.

502 Assessments for withdrawing relief

[(1) Where any relief has been given which is subsequently found not to have been due, that relief shall be withdrawn by the making of an assessment to income tax under Case IV of Schedule D for the year of assessment for which the relief was given.

[(2) (a) Where any relief given in respect of shares for which either a married person or his or her spouse has subscribed, and which were issued while the married person was assessed in accordance with *section 1017*, is to be withdrawn by virtue of a subsequent disposal of those shares by the person who subscribed for them and at the time of the disposal the married person is not so assessable, any assessment for withdrawing that relief shall be made on the person making the disposal and shall be made by reference to the reduction of tax flowing from the amount of the relief regardless of any allocation of that reduction under *subsections (2)* and *(3)* of *section 1024* or of any allocation of a repayment of income tax under *section 1020*.

(b) Where any relief given in respect of shares for which either a nominated civil partner or the other civil partner has subscribed, and which were issued while the nominated civil partner was assessed in accordance with *section 1031C*, is to be withdrawn by virtue of a subsequent disposal of those shares by the person who subscribed for them and at the time of the disposal the nominated civil partner is not so assessable, any assessment for withdrawing that relief shall be made on the person making the disposal and shall be made by reference to the reduction of tax flowing from the amount of the relief regardless of any allocation of that reduction under *subsections (2)* and *(3)* of *section 1031I* or of any allocation of a repayment of income tax under *section 1031E*.][1]

(3) Subject to this section, any assessment for withdrawing relief which is made by reason of an event occurring after the date of the claim may be made within 4 years after the end of the year of assessment in which that event occurs.

(4) No assessment for withdrawing relief in respect of shares issued to any person shall be made by reason of any event occurring after his or her death.

(5) Where a person has, by a disposal or disposals to which *section 496(1)(b)* applies, disposed of all the ordinary shares issued to the person by a company, no assessment for withdrawing relief in respect of any of those shares shall be made by reason of any subsequent event unless it occurs at a time when the person is connected with the company within the meaning of *section 492*.

(6) *Subsection (3)* is without prejudice to [*section 959AD*][2].

(7) In its application to an assessment made by virtue of this section, *section 1080* applies as if the date on which the income tax charged by the assessment becomes due and payable were—

(a) in the case of relief withdrawn by virtue of *section 492, 494, 495, 498(2)* or *499(1)* in consequence of any event after the grant of the relief, the date of that event;

(b) in the case of relief withdrawn by virtue of *section 496(1)* in consequence of a disposal after the grant of the relief, the date of the disposal;

(c) in the case of relief withdrawn by virtue of *section 497* in consequence of a receipt of value after the grant of the relief, the date of the receipt;

(d) in the case of relief withdrawn by virtue of *section 500*—

(i) in so far as effect has been given to the relief in accordance with regulations under *section 986*, the 5th day of April in the year of assessment in which effect was so given, and

(ii) in so far as effect has not been so given, the date on which the relief was granted;

(e) in the case of relief withdrawn by virtue of—

(i) a specified individual failing or ceasing to hold a relevant employment, or

(ii) an individual ceasing to be a specified individual,

the date of the failure or the cessation, as the case may be.

(8) For the purposes of *subsection (7)*, the date on which the relief shall be granted is the date on which a repayment of tax for giving effect to the relief was made or, if there was no such repayment, the date on which the inspector issued a notice to the claimant showing the amount of tax payable after giving effect to the relief.][3]

Amendments

[1] Substituted by F(No.3)A11 sched1(139). Shall have effect from 27 July 2011.

[2] Substituted by FA12 sched4(part 2)(g).

[3] Substituted by FA11 s33(1)(a). Has effect in respect of shares issued on or after 25 November 2011.

Note

FA12 s26(2) amends FA11 s33 and provides:

(b) This section does not have effect in respect of shares issued before 25 November 2011 and, for all the purposes of Part 16 in connection with those shares, the Principal Act has effect as if this section had not been enacted.

(c) This section does not have effect in respect of shares issued on or after 25 November 2011 and on or before 31 December 2011 where—

(i) the company issuing the shares, or

(ii) where the shares are acquired by an investment fund, the fund acquiring the shares,

elects by notice in writing to the Revenue Commissioners on or before 31 December 2011 that, for all the purposes of Part 16 in connection with those shares, the Principal Act has effect as if this section had not been enacted.

Cross References

From Section 502

Section 492 Individuals qualifying for relief.
Section 494 Qualifying companies.
Section 495 Specified individuals.
Section 496 Disposals of shares.
Section 497 Value received from company.
Section 498 Replacement capital.
Section 499 Value received by persons other than claimants.
Section 500 Prevention of misuse.
Section 924 Additional assessments.
Section 986 Regulations.
Section 1017 Assessment of husband in respect of income of both spouses.
Section 1020 Special provisions relating to year of marriage.
Section 1024 Method of apportioning reliefs and charging tax in cases of separate assessments.
Section 1080 Interest on overdue income tax, corporation tax and capital gains tax.

503 Information

[(1) Where an event occurs by reason of which any relief given to an individual is to be withdrawn by virtue of *section 492*, *496* or *497*, the individual shall within 60 days of coming to know of the event give a notice in writing to the inspector containing particulars of the event.

(2) Where an event occurs by reason of which any relief in respect of any shares in a company is to be withdrawn by virtue of *section 494*, *495*, *497*, *498*, *499* or *500*—

(a) the company, and

(b) any person connected with the company who has knowledge of that matter, shall within 60 days of the event or, in the case of a person within *paragraph (b)*, of that person coming to know of it, give a notice in writing to the inspector containing particulars of the event.

(3) Where the inspector has reason to believe that a person has not given a notice which the person is required to give under *subsection (1)* or *(2)* in respect of any event, the inspector may by notice in writing require that person to furnish him or her within such time (not being less than 60 days) as may be specified in the notice with such information relating to the event as the inspector may reasonably require for the purposes of this Part.

(4) Where relief is claimed in respect of shares in a company and the inspector has reason to believe that it may not be due by reason of any arrangement or scheme mentioned in *section 492(11)*, *494(9)* or *500*, the inspector may by notice in writing require any person concerned to furnish him or her within such time (not being less than 60 days) as may be specified in the notice with—

(a) a declaration in writing stating whether or not, according to the information which that person has or can reasonably obtain, any such arrangement or scheme exists or has existed, and

(b) such other information as the inspector may reasonably require for the purposes of the provision in question and as that person has or can reasonably obtain.

(5) References in *subsection (4)* to the person concerned are, in relation to *sections 492(11)* and *500*, references to the claimant and, in relation to *sections 494(9)* and *500*, references to the company and any person controlling the company.

(6) Where relief has been given in respect of shares in a company—

(a) any person who receives from the company any payment or asset which may constitute value received (by that person or another) for the purposes of *section 497* or *499(5)*, and

(b) any person on whose behalf such a payment or asset is received,

shall, if so required by the inspector, state whether the payment or asset received by that person or on that person's behalf is received on behalf of any person other than that person and, if so, the name and address of that other person.

(7) Where relief has been claimed in respect of shares in a company, any person who holds or has held shares in the company and any person on whose behalf any such shares are or were held shall, if so required by the inspector, state whether the shares which are or were held by that person or on that person's behalf are or were held on behalf of any person other than that person and, if so, the name and address of that other person.

(8) No obligation as to secrecy imposed by statute or otherwise shall preclude the inspector from disclosing to a company that relief has been given or claimed in respect of a particular number or proportion of its shares.][1]

Amendments

[1] Substituted by FA11 s33(1)(a). Has effect in respect of shares issued on or after 25 November 2011.

Note

FA12 s26(2) amends FA11 s33 and provides:

(b) This section does not have effect in respect of shares issued before 25 November 2011 and, for all the purposes of Part 16 in connection with those shares, the Principal Act has effect as if this section had not been enacted.

(c) This section does not have effect in respect of shares issued on or after 25 November 2011 and on or before 31 December 2011 where—
(i) the company issuing the shares, or
(ii) where the shares are acquired by an investment fund, the fund acquiring the shares,
elects by notice in writing to the Revenue Commissioners on or before 31 December 2011 that, for all the purposes of Part 16 in connection with those shares, the Principal Act has effect as if this section had not been enacted.

Cross References

From Section 503

Section 492 Individuals qualifying for relief.
Section 494 Qualifying companies.
Section 495 Specified individuals.
Section 496 Disposals of shares.
Section 497 Value received from company.
Section 498 Replacement capital.
Section 499 Value received by persons other than claimants.
Section 500 Prevention of misuse.

To Section 503

Section 501 Claims.
Schedule 10 Relief for Investment in Corporate Trades: Subsidiaries

504 Capital gains tax

[(1) The sums allowable as deductions from the consideration in the computation for the purposes of capital gains tax of the gain or loss accruing to an individual on the disposal of shares in respect of which any relief has been given and not withdrawn shall be determined without regard to that relief, except that where those sums exceed the consideration they shall be reduced by an amount equal to the lesser of—

(a) the amount of that relief, and

(b) the excess,

but this subsection does not apply to a disposal to which [*section 1028(5)* or *1031M(5)*][1] relates.

(2) In relation to shares in respect of which relief has been given and not withdrawn, any question—

(a) as to which of any such shares issued to a person at different times a disposal relates, or

(b) whether a disposal relates to such shares or to other shares,

shall for the purposes of capital gains tax be determined as for the purposes of *section 496*.

(3) Where an individual holds ordinary shares in a company and the relief has been given in respect of some of the shares but not others, then, if there is a reorganisation (within the meaning of *section 584*) affecting those shares, *section 584(3)* shall apply separately to the shares in respect of which the relief has been given and to the other shares (so that the shares of each kind shall be treated as a separate holding of original shares and identified with a separate new holding).

(4) There shall be made all such adjustments of capital gains tax, whether by means of assessment or by means of discharge or repayment of tax, as may be required in consequence of the relief being given or withdrawn.][2]

Amendments

[1] Substituted by F(No.3)A11 sched1(140). Shall have effect from 27 July 2011.

[2] Substituted by FA11 s33(1)(a). Has effect in respect of shares issued on or after 25 November 2011.

Note

FA12 s26(2) amends FA11 s33 and provides:

(b) This section does not have effect in respect of shares issued before 25 November 2011 and, for all the purposes of Part 16 in connection with those shares, the Principal Act has effect as if this section had not been enacted.

(c) This section does not have effect in respect of shares issued on or after 25 November 2011 and on or before 31 December 2011 where—

(i) the company issuing the shares, or

(ii) where the shares are acquired by an investment fund, the fund acquiring the shares,

elects by notice in writing to the Revenue Commissioners on or before 31 December 2011 that, for all the purposes of Part 16 in connection with those shares, the Principal Act has effect as if this section had not been enacted.

Cross References

From Section 504

Section 496 Disposals of shares.

Section 584 Reorganisation or reduction of share capital.

Section 1028 Married persons.

To Section 504

Section 489 The relief.

Section 493 Seed capital relief.

505 Application to subsidiaries

[(1) A qualifying company may in the relevant period have one or more subsidiaries if—

(a) the conditions set out in *subsection (2)* are satisfied in respect of the subsidiary or each subsidiary and, except where provided in *subsection (3)*, continue to be so satisfied until the end of the relevant period, and

(b) the subsidiary or each subsidiary is a company—

(i) to which *section 494(3)(a)(i)* relates, or

(ii) which exists solely for the purpose of carrying on any trade which consists solely of any one or more of the following relevant trading activities—

(I) the purchase of goods or materials for use by the qualifying company or its subsidiaries,

(II) the sale of goods or materials produced by the qualifying company or its subsidiaries, or

(III) the rendering of services to or on behalf of the qualifying company or its subsidiaries.

(2) The conditions referred to in *subsection (1)(a)* are—

(a) that the subsidiary is a 51 per cent subsidiary of the qualifying company,

(b) that no other person has control of the subsidiary within the meaning of *section 11*, and

(c) that no arrangements are in existence by virtue of which the conditions in *paragraphs (a)* and *(b)* could cease to be satisfied.

(3) The conditions referred to in *subsection (1)(a)* shall not be regarded as ceasing to be satisfied by reason only of the fact that the subsidiary or the qualifying company is wound up or dissolved without winding up if—

(a) it is shown that the winding up or dissolution is for bona fide commercial reasons and not part of a scheme or arrangement the main purpose or one of the main purposes of which is the avoidance of tax, and

(b) the net assets, if any, of the subsidiary or, as the case may be, the qualifying company are distributed to its members before the end of the relevant period or, in the case of a winding up, the end (if later) of 3 years from the commencement of the winding up.

(4) Where a qualifying company has one or more subsidiaries in the relevant period, this Part shall apply subject to Schedule 10.][1]

Amendments

[1] Substituted by FA11 s33(1)(a). Has effect in respect of shares issued on or after 25 November 2011.

Note

FA12 s26(2) amends FA11 s33 and provides:

(b) This section does not have effect in respect of shares issued before 25 November 2011 and, for all the purposes of Part 16 in connection with those shares, the Principal Act has effect as if this section had not been enacted.

(c) This section does not have effect in respect of shares issued on or after 25 November 2011 and on or before 31 December 2011 where—

(i) the company issuing the shares, or

(ii) where the shares are acquired by an investment fund, the fund acquiring the shares,

elects by notice in writing to the Revenue Commissioners on or before 31 December 2011 that, for all the purposes of Part 16 in connection with those shares, the Principal Act has effect as if this section had not been enacted.

Cross References

From Section 505

Section 11 Meaning of "control" in certain contexts.
Section 494 Qualifying companies.

To Section 505

Section 488 Interpretation (Part 16).
Section 491 Restriction on relief where amounts raised exceed permitted maximum.
Section 494 Qualifying companies.
Section 498 Replacement capital.
Schedule 10 Relief for Investment in Corporate Trades: Subsidiaries
Schedule 29 Provisions Referred to in Sections 1052, 1053 and 1054

506 Nominees and designated funds

[(1) Shares subscribed for, issued to, held by or disposed of for an individual by a nominee shall be treated for the purposes of this Part as subscribed for, issued to, held by or disposed of by that individual.

(2) (a) Relief shall be given, and *section 490(1)(a)* does not apply, in respect of an amount subscribed as nominee for an individual by a person or persons having the management of an investment fund designated by the Revenue Commissioners for the purposes of this section (in this Part referred to as the "*managers of a designated fund*") where the amount so subscribed forms part of the fund.

(b) Except where provided by *paragraph (a)*, relief shall not be given in respect of an amount subscribed as nominee for an individual by a person or persons having the management of an investment fund where the amount so subscribed forms part of the fund.

(3) The Revenue Commissioners may, if they think fit, having regard to the facts of the particular case and after such consultation, if any, as may seem to them to be necessary with such person or body of persons as in their opinion may be of assistance to them, and subject to such conditions, if any, as they think proper to attach to the designation, designate an investment fund for the purposes of this Part.

(4) (a) The Revenue Commissioners may, by notice in writing given to the managers of a designated investment fund, withdraw the designation given for the purposes of this section to the fund in accordance with *subsection (3)* and, on the giving of the notice, the fund ceases to be a designated fund as respects any subscriptions made after the date of the notice referred to in *paragraph (b)*.

(b) Where the Revenue Commissioners withdraw the designation of any fund for the purposes of this section, notice of the withdrawal shall be published as soon as may be in *Iris Oifigiúil*.

(5) Where an individual claims relief in respect of eligible shares in a company which have been issued to the managers of a designated fund as nominee for the individual, then *section 501(2)* applies as if it required—

(a) the certificate referred to in that section to be issued by the company to the managers, and

(b) the claim for relief to be accompanied by a certificate issued by the managers, in such form as the Revenue Commissioners may authorise, furnishing such information as the Revenue Commissioners may require and certifying that the managers hold certificates issued to them by the companies concerned, for the purposes of *section 501(2)* in respect of the holdings of eligible shares shown on the managers' certificate.

(6) The managers of a designated fund may be required by a notice given to them by an inspector or other officer of the Revenue Commissioners to deliver to the officer within the time limited by the notice a return of the holdings of eligible shares shown on certificates issued by them in accordance with *subsection (5)* in the year of assessment to which the return relates.

(7) *Section 501(6)* does not apply in relation to any certificate issued by the managers of a designated fund for the purposes of *subsection (5)*.

(8) Without prejudice to the generality of *subsection (3)*, the Revenue Commissioners shall designate a fund for the purposes of this Part only if they are satisfied that—

(a) the fund is established under irrevocable trusts for the sole purpose of enabling individuals who qualify for the relief (in this subsection referred to as "*qualifying individuals*") to invest in eligible shares of a qualifying company, and

(b) under the terms of the trusts it is provided that—

(i) the entire fund is to be invested without undue delay in eligible shares,

(ii) the fund is to subscribe only for shares which, subject to the circumstances of the qualifying individuals participating in the fund (in this subsection referred to as "*participants*"), qualify those participants for relief,

(iii) pending investment in eligible shares, any moneys subscribed for the purchase of shares are to be placed on deposit in a separate account with a bank licensed to transact business in the State,

(iv) any amounts received by means of dividends or interest are, subject to a commission in respect of management expenses at a rate not exceeding a rate which shall be specified in the deed of trust under which the fund has been established, to be paid without undue delay to the participants,

(v) any charges to be made by means of management or other expenses in connection with the establishment, the running, the winding down or the termination of the fund shall be at a rate not exceeding a rate which shall be specified in the deed of trust under which the fund is established,

(vi) audited accounts of the fund are submitted annually to the Revenue Commissioners as soon as may be after the end of each period for which accounts of the fund are made up,

(vii) the managers, the trustees of the fund and any of their associates are not for the time being connected either directly or indirectly with any company whose shares comprise part of the fund,

(viii) any discounts on eligible shares received by the trustees or managers of the fund are accepted solely for the benefit of the participants,

(ix) the fund is a closed fund and the closing date for participation precedes the making of the first investment,

(x) if a limit is placed on the size of the fund or a minimum amount for investment is stipulated, any subscriptions not accepted are to be returned without undue delay, and

(xi) no participant is allowed to have any shares in any company in which the fund has invested transferred into his or her name until 3 years have elapsed from the date of the issue of the shares to the fund.

(9) The Revenue Commissioners may nominate in writing an inspector or other officer to perform any acts and discharge any functions authorised by this Part to be performed or discharged by the Revenue Commissioners.][1]

Amendments

[1] Substituted by FA11 s33(1)(a). Has effect in respect of shares issued on or after 25 November 2011.

Note

FA12 s26(2) amends FA11 s33 and provides:

(b) This section does not have effect in respect of shares issued before 25 November 2011 and, for all the purposes of Part 16 in connection with those shares, the Principal Act has effect as if this section had not been enacted.

(c) This section does not have effect in respect of shares issued on or after 25 November 2011 and on or before 31 December 2011 where—

(i) the company issuing the shares, or

(ii) where the shares are acquired by an investment fund, the fund acquiring the shares,

elects by notice in writing to the Revenue Commissioners on or before 31 December 2011 that, for all the purposes of Part 16 in connection with those shares, the Principal Act has effect as if this section had not been enacted.

Cross References

From Section 506

Section 490 Limits on the relief.
Section 501 Claims.

To Section 506

Section 489 The relief.
Section 490 Limits on the relief.
Section 491 Restriction on relief where amounts raised exceed permitted maximum.

507 Reporting of relief

[(1) A person (being a qualifying company or the managers of a designated fund) shall, when required to do so by notice in writing by the Revenue Commissioners, furnish the Revenue Commissioners within such time as may be specified in the notice (not being less than 30 days) with such information, in relation to the relief provided for in this Part, as the Revenue Commissioners may reasonably require from that person for the purpose of the annual reports required in accordance with [*section* 5.4 of the Community Guidelines on State aid to promote risk finance investments OJ No. C 19, 22.1.2014, p. 4.][1]

(2) Notwithstanding any obligation as to secrecy imposed on them by the Tax Acts or the Official Secrets Act 1963, the Revenue Commissioners may furnish the information obtained in accordance with *subsection (1)* to the person submitting the annual reports referred to in that subsection.

(3) The Revenue Commissioners may nominate any of their officers to discharge any function authorised by this section to be discharged by the Revenue Commissioners.

(4) No obligation as to secrecy imposed by statute or otherwise shall preclude the Revenue Commissioners from publishing information obtained by them in accordance with *subsection (1)*.

(5) Where any person fails to comply with a requirement to furnish the information in accordance with *subsection (1)*, that person shall be liable to a penalty of €2,000 and, if that failure continues after the period of 30 days referred to in that subsection, a further penalty of €50 for each day on which the failure so continues.][2]

Amendments

[1] Substituted by FA14 s27(1)(g). Comes into operation on such day or days as the Minister for Finance may by order or orders appoint and different days may be appointed for different purposes or different provisions.

[2] Substituted by FA11 s33(1)(a). Has effect in respect of shares issued on or after 25 November 2011.

Note

FA12 s26(2) amends FA11 s33 and provides:

(b) This section does not have effect in respect of shares issued before 25 November 2011 and, for all the purposes of Part 16 in connection with those shares, the Principal Act has effect as if this section had not been enacted.

(c) This section does not have effect in respect of shares issued on or after 25 November 2011 and on or before 31 December 2011 where—

(i) the company issuing the shares, or

(ii) where the shares are acquired by an investment fund, the fund acquiring the shares,

elects by notice in writing to the Revenue Commissioners on or before 31 December 2011 that, for all the purposes of Part 16 in connection with those shares, the Principal Act has effect as if this section had not been enacted.

508 Nominees and designated funds [Repealed]

Repealed by FA11 s33(1)(a). Has effect in respect of shares issued on or after 25 November 2011.

Note

FA12 s26(2) amends FA11 s33 and provides:

(b) This section does not have effect in respect of shares issued before 25 November 2011 and, for all the purposes of Part 16 in connection with those shares, the Principal Act has effect as if this section had not been enacted.

(c) This section does not have effect in respect of shares issued on or after 25 November 2011 and on or before 31 December 2011 where—

(i) the company issuing the shares, or

(ii) where the shares are acquired by an investment fund, the fund acquiring the shares,

elects by notice in writing to the Revenue Commissioners on or before 31 December 2011 that, for all the purposes of Part 16 in connection with those shares, the Principal Act has effect as if this section had not been enacted.

508A Reporting of relief [Repealed]

Repealed by FA11 s33(1)(a). Has effect in respect of shares issued on or after 25 November 2011.

Note

FA12 s26(2) amends FA11 s33 and provides:

(b) This section does not have effect in respect of shares issued before 25 November 2011 and, for all the purposes of Part 16 in connection with those shares, the Principal Act has effect as if this section had not been enacted.

(c) This section does not have effect in respect of shares issued on or after 25 November 2011 and on or before 31 December 2011 where—

(i) the company issuing the shares, or

(ii) where the shares are acquired by an investment fund, the fund acquiring the shares,

elects by notice in writing to the Revenue Commissioners on or before 31 December 2011 that, for all the purposes of Part 16 in connection with those shares, the Principal Act has effect as if this section had not been enacted.

PART 17

Profit Sharing Schemes and Employee Share Ownership Trusts

CHAPTER 1

Profit Sharing Schemes

509 Interpretation (Chapter 1)

[FA82 s50]

(1) In this Chapter and in *Schedule 11*—

"*the appropriate percentage*", in relation to any shares, shall be construed in accordance with *section 511(3)*;

"*approved scheme*" shall be construed in accordance with *section 510(1)*;

"*the company concerned*" has the meaning assigned to it by *paragraph 3(1)* of *Schedule 11*;

"*group scheme*" and, in relation to such a scheme, "*participating company*" have the meanings respectively assigned to them by *paragraph 3(2)* of *Schedule 11*;

"*initial market value*", in relation to any shares, shall be construed in accordance with *section 510(2)*;

"*locked-in value*", in relation to any shares, shall be construed in accordance with *section 512(1)*;

"*market value*", in relation to any shares, shall be construed in accordance with *section 548*;

"*participant*" shall be construed in accordance with *section 510(1)(a)*;

"*the period of retention*" has the meaning assigned to it by *section 511(1)(a)*;

"*the release date*" has the meaning assigned to it by *section 511(2)*;

["*shares*" includes stock and specified securities;

"*specified securities*" means securities (within the meaning of *Schedule 12*), other than ordinary shares, which—

(a) were transferred to the trustees of an approved scheme by the trustees of an employee share ownership trust to which *section 519* applies, and

(b) were—

(i) securities issued to the trustees of the employee share ownership trust referred to in *paragraph (a)* in an exchange to which *section 586* applies,

(ii) securities (in this subparagraph referred to as "*similar securities*") similar to the securities referred to in *subparagraph (i)* and which were acquired by those trustees using dividends received in respect of the securities so referred to or in respect of similar securities so acquired,

(iii) securities issued to those trustees as a result of a reorganisation or reduction of share capital (in accordance with *section 584*) which occurred subsequent to the exchange referred to in *subparagraph (i)* and which securities represent the securities issued in that exchange and the similar securities (if any) referred to in *subparagraph (ii)*, or

(iv) securities (in this subparagraph referred to as "*similar securities*") similar to the securities first-mentioned in *subparagraph (iii)* and which were acquired by those trustees using dividends received in respect of the securities so mentioned in *subparagraph (iii)* or in respect of similar securities so acquired,

but subject to the condition that, where the company which issued the securities in the exchange referred to in *paragraph (b)* is a company limited by shares (within the meaning of section 5 of the Companies Act, 1963), the trustees of the employee share ownership trust have, as a result of the exchange, acquired such percentage of the ordinary share capital of the company which issued the securities that is not less than the percentage of the ordinary share capital of the company which the trustees held immediately prior to the exchange;][1]

"*the trust instrument*", in relation to an approved scheme, means the instrument referred to in *paragraph 3(3)(c)* of *Schedule 11*;

"*the trustees*", in relation to an approved scheme or a participant's shares, means the body of persons for the establishment of which the scheme shall provide as mentioned in *paragraph 3(3)* of *Schedule 11*.

(2) Any provision of this Chapter with respect to—

(a) the order in which any of a participant's shares are to be treated as disposed of for the purposes of this Chapter, or

(b) the shares in relation to which an event is to be treated as occurring for any such purpose,

shall apply notwithstanding any direction given to the trustees with respect to shares of a particular description or to shares appropriated to the participant at a particular time.

(3) For the purposes of capital gains tax—

(a) no deduction shall be made from the consideration for the disposal of any shares by reason only that an amount determined under this Chapter is chargeable to income tax,

(b) any charge to income tax by virtue of *section 513* shall be disregarded in determining whether a distribution is a capital distribution within the meaning of *section 583*, and

(c) nothing in any provision referred to in *subsection (2)* shall affect the rules applicable to the computation of a gain accruing on a part disposal of a holding of shares or other securities which were acquired at different times.

[(4) The Revenue Commissioners may nominate any of their officers to perform any acts and discharge any functions authorised by this Chapter or by *Schedule 11* to be performed or discharged by them.][2]

Amendments

[1] Substituted by FA02 s13(1)(a)(i). This section shall apply and have effect as on and from 16 April 2001.

[2] Inserted by FA02 s13(1)(a)(ii). This section shall apply and have effect as on and from 16 April 2001.

Revenue Briefings

Tax Briefing

Tax Briefing December 2003 – Issue 54 pg 13 – Approved Profit Sharing Schemes

Tax Briefing July 2004 – Issue 56 pg 20 – Approved Profit Sharing Schemes

Tax Briefing December 2008 – Issue 70 – Salary Sacrifice
Tax Briefing April 2009 – Issue 71 – Review of Practices Relating to the Approved Profit Sharing Scheme (APSS)

Revenue Information Notes

IT 62 – A Guide to Profit Sharing Schemes

Cross References

From Section 509

Section 510 Approved profit sharing schemes: appropriated shares.
Section 511 The period of retention, release date and appropriate percentage.
Section 512 Disposals of scheme shares.
Section 513 Capital receipts in respect of scheme shares.
Section 519 Employee share ownership trusts.
Section 548 Valuation of assets.
Section 583 Capital distributions by companies.
Section 584 Reorganisation or reduction of share capital.
Section 586 Company amalgamations by exchange of shares.
Schedule 11 Profit Sharing Schemes
Schedule 12 Employee Share Ownership Trusts

To Section 509

Section 81A Restriction of deductions for employee benefit contributions.
Section 118B Revenue approved salary sacrifice agreements.
Section 122A Notional loans relating to shares, etc.
Section 177 Conditions as to residence and period of ownership.
Schedule 11 Profit Sharing Schemes
Schedule 12 Employee Share Ownership Trusts

510 Approved profit sharing schemes: appropriated shares

[FA82 s51(1) to (7)]

(1) In this Chapter, references to an approved scheme are references to a scheme approved of as is mentioned in *subsection (3)* and, in relation to such a scheme—

(a) any reference to a participant is a reference to an individual to whom the trustees of the scheme have appropriated shares, and

(b) subject to *section 514*, any reference to a participant's shares is a reference to the shares which have been appropriated to the participant by the trustees of an approved scheme.

(2) Any reference in this Chapter to the initial market value of any of a participant's shares is a reference to the market value of those shares determined—

(a) except where *paragraph (b)* applies, on the date on which the shares were appropriated to the participant, and

(b) if the Revenue Commissioners and the trustees of the scheme agree in writing, on or by reference to such earlier date or dates as may be provided for in the agreement.

(3) This section shall apply where the trustees of a profit sharing scheme approved of in accordance with *Part 2* of *Schedule 11* appropriate shares—

(a) which have previously been acquired by the trustees, and

(b) as to which the conditions in *Part 3* of that Schedule are fulfilled,

to an individual who participates in the scheme.

(4) Notwithstanding anything in the Income Tax Acts, a charge to tax shall not be made on any individual in respect of the receipt of a right to receive the beneficial interest in shares passing or to be passed to that individual by virtue of such an appropriation of shares as is mentioned in *subsection (3)*.

(5) Notwithstanding anything in the approved scheme concerned or in the trust instrument or in *section 511*, for the purposes of capital gains tax a participant shall be treated as absolutely entitled to his or her shares as against the trustees.

[(5A) (a) This subsection shall apply where—

(i) the trustees of an approved profit sharing scheme make an appropriation of shares, to which *section 510(3)* applies, to a participant,

(ii) the shares concerned were transferred to the trustees of the approved scheme concerned by the trustees of an employee share ownership trust to which *section 519* applies, and

(iii) the shares were transferred at a date later than that on which the shares could have first been transferred in accordance with the terms of the employee share ownership trust deed or any other document but, for whatever reason, were not transferred on that earlier date.

(b) Where this subsection applies, the appropriation to the participant concerned shall, for the purposes of capital gains tax, be deemed to have taken place on the day following the day on which those shares could have first been transferred by the trustees of the employee share ownership trust concerned, in accordance with the terms of the trust deed under which that trust was established or any other document.][1]

(6) Where the trustees of an approved scheme acquire any shares as to which the conditions in *Part 3* of *Schedule 11* are fulfilled and, within the period of 18 months beginning with the date of their acquisition, those shares are appropriated in accordance with the scheme—

(a) *section 805* shall not apply to income consisting of dividends on those shares received by the trustees, and

(b) any gain accruing to the trustees on the appropriation of those shares shall not be a chargeable gain,

and, for the purpose of determining whether any shares are appropriated within that period of 18 months, shares which were acquired at an earlier time shall be taken to be appropriated before shares of the same class which were acquired at a later time.

(7) The Revenue Commissioners may by notice in writing require any person to furnish to them, within such time as they may direct (but not being less than 30 days), such information as they think necessary for the purposes of their functions under this Chapter, including in particular information to enable them—

(a) to determine whether to approve of a scheme or withdraw an approval already given, and

(b) to determine the liability to tax, including capital gains tax, of any participant in an approved scheme.

[(8) Without prejudice to *subsection (7)* the trustees of an approved scheme shall as respects any year, prepare and deliver to the Revenue Commissioners on or before 31 March in the year following that year, a return in the prescribed form (within the meaning of [*Chapter 3* of *Part 41A*][2]) of such particulars relating to the approved scheme for that year as may be required by the prescribed form and *sections 1052* and *1054* shall apply to a failure by the trustees to deliver a return in accordance with this subsection as they apply to a failure to deliver a return referred to in *section 1052*.][3]

Amendments

[1] Inserted by FA99 s69(1)(a)(i). Shall apply as respects an appropriation of shares made by the trustees of an approved scheme on or after the date of 25 March 1999

[2] Substituted by FA12 sched4(part 2)(g).

[3] Inserted by FA08 s19(1)(a). Applies as on and from 1 January 2009.

Revenue Briefings

Tax Briefing

Tax Briefing December 2008 – Issue 70 – Salary Sacrifice

Revenue Precedents

Where shares are purchased by Trustees over a period of time the average purchase price can be used as the initial market value of the shares at the date of appropriation provided the purchase period does not exceed 30 days. PS 16

Cross References

From Section 510

Section 510 Approved profit sharing schemes: appropriated shares.
Section 511 The period of retention, release date and appropriate percentage.
Section 514 Company reconstructions, amalgamations, etc.
Section 519 Employee share ownership trusts.
Section 805 Surcharge on certain income of trustees.
Section 951 Obligation to make a return.
Section 1052 Penalties for failure to make certain returns, etc.
Section 1054 Penalties in the case of a secretary of a body of persons.
Schedule 11 Profit Sharing Schemes

To Section 510

Section 118B Revenue approved salary sacrifice agreements.
Section 509 Interpretation (Chapter 1).
Section 510 Approved profit sharing schemes: appropriated shares.
Section 511 The period of retention, release date and appropriate percentage.
Section 511A Shares acquired from an employee share ownership trust.
Section 531AM Charge to universal social charge.
Schedule 11 Profit Sharing Schemes
Schedule 29 Provisions Referred to in Sections 1052, 1053 and 1054

511 The period of retention, release date and appropriate percentage

[FA82 s52; FA86 s11; FA97 s50(a)]

(1) (a) In this Chapter, "*the period of retention*", in relation to any of a participant's shares, means the period beginning on the date on which those shares are appropriated to the participant and ending on the second anniversary of that date or, if it is earlier—

(i) the date on which the participant ceases to be an employee or director of a relevant company by reason of injury or disability or on account of his or her being dismissed by reason of redundancy (within the meaning of the [Redundancy Payments Acts, 1967 to 2003][1]),

(ii) the date on which the participant reaches pensionable age (within the meaning of section 2 of the [Social Welfare Consolidation Act 2005,][2] or

(iii) the date of the participant's death.

(b) In *paragraph (a)*, "*relevant company*" means the company concerned or, if the scheme in question is a group scheme, a participating company and, in the application of *paragraph (a)* to a participant in a group scheme, the participant shall not be treated as ceasing to be an employee or director of a relevant company until such time as he or she is no longer an employee or director of any of the participating companies.

(2) In this Chapter, "*the release date*", in relation to any of a participant's shares, means—

(a) as on and from the 10th day of May, 1997, the third anniversary of the date on which the shares were appropriated to the participant, and

(b) before the 10th day of May, 1997, the fifth anniversary of the date on which the shares were appropriated to the participant.

(3) Subject to *section 515(4)*, for the purposes of the provisions of this Chapter charging an individual to income tax under Schedule E by reason of the occurrence of an event relating to any of the individual's shares, any reference to the appropriate percentage in relation to those shares shall be determined according to the time of that event, as follows—

(a) as respects such an occurrence as on and from the 10th day of May, 1997—

(i) if the event occurs before the third anniversary of the date on which the shares were appropriated to the participant and *subparagraph (ii)* does not apply, the appropriate percentage shall be 100 per cent, and

(ii) if, in a case where at the time of the event the participant—

(I) has ceased to be an employee or director of a relevant company as mentioned in *subsection (1)(a)(i)*, or

(II) has reached pensionable age (within the meaning of section 2 of the [Social Welfare Consolidation Act 2005,][3]

the event occurs before the third anniversary of the date on which the shares were appropriated to the participant, the appropriate percentage shall be 50 per cent, and

(b) as respects such an occurrence before the 10th day of May, 1997—

(i) if the event occurs before the fourth anniversary of the date on which the shares were appropriated to the participant and *subparagraph (iii)* does not apply, the appropriate percentage shall be 100 per cent,

(ii) if the event occurs on or after the fourth anniversary and before the fifth anniversary of the date on which the shares were appropriated to the participant and *subparagraph (iii)* does not apply, the appropriate percentage shall be 75 per cent, and

(iii) if, in a case where at the time of the event the participant—

(I) has ceased to be an employee or director of a relevant company as mentioned in *subsection (1)(a)(i)*, or

(II) has reached pensionable age (within the meaning of section 2 of the [Social Welfare Consolidation Act 2005,][4]

the event occurs before the fifth anniversary of the date on which the shares were appropriated to the participant, the appropriate percentage shall be 50 per cent.

(4) No scheme shall be approved of as is mentioned in *section 510(3)* unless the Revenue Commissioners are satisfied that, whether under the terms of the scheme or otherwise, every participant in the scheme is bound in contract with the company concerned—

(a) to permit his or her shares to remain in the hands of the trustees throughout the period of retention,

(b) not to assign, charge or otherwise dispose of his or her beneficial interest in his or her shares during that period,

(c) if he or she directs the trustees to transfer the ownership of his or her shares to him or her at any time before the release date, to pay to the trustees before the transfer takes place a sum equal to income tax at the standard rate on the appropriate percentage of the locked-in value of the shares at the time of the direction, and

(d) not to direct the trustees to dispose of his or her shares at any time before the release date in any other way except by sale for the best consideration in money that can reasonably be obtained at the time of the sale.

(5) No obligation placed on the participant by virtue of *subsection (4)(c)* shall be construed as binding his or her personal representatives to pay any sum to the trustees.

(6) Any obligation imposed on a participant by virtue of *subsection (4)* shall not prevent the participant from—

(a) directing the trustees to accept an offer for any of his or her shares (in this paragraph referred to as "*the original shares*") if the acceptance or agreement will result in a new holding (within the meaning of *section 584*) being equated with the original shares for the purposes of capital gains tax,

(b) directing the trustees to agree to a transaction affecting his or her shares or such of those shares as are of a particular class, if the transaction would be entered into pursuant to a compromise, arrangement or scheme applicable to or affecting—

(i) all the ordinary share capital of the company in question or, as the case may be, all the shares of the class in question, or

(ii) all the shares, or shares of the class in question, held by a class of shareholders identified otherwise than by reference to their employment or their participation in an approved scheme,

(c) directing the trustees to accept an offer of cash, with or without other assets, for his or her shares if the offer forms part of a general offer made to holders of shares of the same class as his or her shares or of shares in the same company and made in the first instance on a condition such that if it is satisfied the person making the offer will have control (within the meaning of *section 11*) of that company, or

(d) agreeing, after the expiry of the period of retention, to sell the beneficial interest in his or her shares to the trustees for the same consideration as in accordance with *subsection (4)(d)* would be required to be obtained for the shares themselves.

(7) If in breach of his or her obligation under *subsection (4)(b)* a participant assigns, charges or otherwise disposes of the beneficial interest in any of his or her shares, the participant shall as respects those shares be treated for the purposes of this Chapter as if, at the time they were appropriated to him or her, he or she was ineligible to participate in the scheme, and *section 515* shall apply accordingly.

Amendments

[1] Substituted by FA12 sched6(1)(f). Has effect as on and from 31 March 2012.

[2, 3, 4] Substituted by FA07 sched4(1)(q). Shall have effect as on and from 2 April 2007

Cross References

From Section 511

Section 11 Meaning of "control" in certain contexts.
Section 510 Approved profit sharing schemes: appropriated shares.
Section 515 Excess or unauthorised shares.
Section 584 Reorganisation or reduction of share capital.

To Section 511

Section 509 Interpretation (Chapter 1).
Section 510 Approved profit sharing schemes: appropriated shares.
Section 511A Shares acquired from an employee share ownership trust.
Section 512 Disposals of scheme shares.
Section 516 Assessment of trustees in respect of sums received.
Schedule 11 Profit Sharing Schemes

511A Shares acquired from an employee share ownership trust

[(1) This section applies where, on or after the passing of the Finance Act, 1998—

(a) the trustees of an approved scheme make an appropriation of shares to which *section 510(3)* applies to a participant,

(b) the shares concerned had been transferred to the trustees of the approved scheme by the trustees of an employee share ownership trust to which *section 519* applies, and

(c) the participant concerned was a beneficiary (within the meaning of *paragraph 11* or *11A*, as the case may be, of *Schedule 12*) under the employee share ownership trust concerned at all times (other than any period which forms part of the 30 day period referred to in *paragraph 12A(b)* of *Schedule 11*) during the period (in this section referred to as the "*holding period*")—

(i) beginning on—

(I) the day the shares concerned were acquired by that employee share ownership trust, or

(II) if later, the day that participant last became such a beneficiary,

and

(ii) ending on the day those shares were appropriated to that participant.

(2) Where this section applies, then, notwithstanding *section 511*—

(a) the period of retention, in relation to the participant and the shares concerned, ends—

(i) in the case where the holding period is 2 years or more, on the day following the end of the holding period, and

(ii) in any other case, on the day following the end of a period which, when added to the holding period, forms a period of 2 years, or, if it is earlier, on the date referred to in *subparagraph (i)*, *(ii)* or *(iii)*, as the case may be, of *section 511(1)(a)*,

and

(b) the release date, in relation to the participant and the shares concerned, means—

(i) in the case where the holding period is 3 years or more, the day following the end of the holding period, and

(ii) in any other case, the day following the end of a period which, when added to the holding period, forms a period of 3 years.][1]

Amendments

[1] Substituted by FA02 s13(1)(b). This section shall apply and have effect as on and from 16 April 2001.

Revenue Briefings

Tax Briefing

Tax Briefing April 2002 – Issue 47 pg 9 – Approved Profit Sharing Schemes and Employee Ownership Trusts

Cross References

From Section 511A

Section 510 Approved profit sharing schemes: appropriated shares.
Section 511 The period of retention, release date and appropriate percentage.
Section 519 Employee share ownership trusts.
Schedule 11 Profit Sharing Schemes
Schedule 12 Employee Share Ownership Trusts

512 Disposals of scheme shares

[FA82 s53]

(1) Subject to *sections 514* and *515(6)*, any reference in this Chapter to the locked-in value of any of a participant's shares at any time shall be construed as follows:

(a) if before that time the participant has become chargeable to income tax by virtue of *section 513* on a percentage of the amount or value of any capital receipt (within the meaning of that section) which is referable to those shares, the locked-in value of the shares shall be the amount by which their initial market value exceeds the amount or value of that capital receipt or, if there has been more than one such receipt, the aggregate of those receipts, and

(b) in any other case, the locked-in value of the shares shall be their initial market value.

(2) Where the trustees dispose of any of a participant's shares at any time before the release date or, if it is earlier, the date of the participant's death, the participant shall, subject to *subsections (3)* and *(4)*, be chargeable to income tax under Schedule E for the year of assessment in which the disposal takes place on the appropriate percentage of the locked-in value of the shares at the time of the disposal.

(3) Subject to *subsection (4)*, if on a disposal of shares within *subsection (2)* the proceeds of the disposal are less than the locked-in value of the shares at the time of the disposal, *subsection (2)* shall apply as if that locked-in value were reduced to an amount equal to the proceeds of the disposal.

(4) Where at any time before the disposal of any of a participant's shares a payment was made to the trustees to enable them to exercise rights arising under a rights issue, *subsections (2)* and *(3)* shall, subject to *subsection (5)(b)*, apply as if the proceeds of the disposal were reduced by an amount equal to that proportion of that payment or, if there was more than one such payment, of the aggregate of those payments which, immediately before the disposal, the market value of the

shares disposed of bore to the market value of all the participant's shares held by the trustees at that time.

(5) (a) In this subsection, "*shares*", in relation to shares allotted or to be allotted on a rights issue, includes securities and rights of any description.

(b) For the purposes of *subsection (4)*—

(i) no account shall be taken of any payment to the trustees if or to the extent that it consists of the proceeds of a disposal of rights arising under a rights issue, and

(ii) in relation to a particular disposal, the amount of the payment or, as the case may be, of the aggregate of the payments referred to in that subsection shall be taken to be reduced by an amount equal to the total of the reduction (if any) previously made under that subsection in relation to earlier disposals,

and any reference in *subsection (4)* or *subparagraph (i)* to the rights arising under a rights issue is a reference to rights conferred in respect of a participant's shares, being rights to be allotted, on payment, other shares in the same company.

(6) Where the disposal referred to in *subsection (2)* is made from a holding of shares appropriated to the participant at different times, then, in determining for the purposes of this Chapter—

(a) the initial market value and the locked-in value of each of those shares, and

(b) the percentage which is the appropriate percentage in relation to each of those shares,

the disposal shall be treated as being of shares appropriated earlier before those appropriated later.

(7) Where at any time the participant's beneficial interest in any of his or her shares is disposed of, the shares in question shall be treated for the purposes of this Chapter as having been disposed of at that time by the trustees for (subject to *subsection (8)*) the like consideration as was obtained for the disposal of the beneficial interest, and for the purpose of this subsection there shall be no disposal of the participant's beneficial interest if and at the time when that interest becomes vested in any person on the insolvency of the participant or otherwise by operation of the law of the State.

(8) Where—

(a) a disposal of shares within *subsection (2)* is a transfer to which *section 511(4)(c)* applies,

(b) the Revenue Commissioners are of the opinion that any other disposal within that subsection is not at arm's length and accordingly direct that this subsection shall apply, or

(c) a disposal of shares within that subsection is one which is treated as taking place by virtue of *subsection (7)* and takes place within the period of retention,

the proceeds of the disposal for the purposes of this Chapter shall be taken to be equal to the market value of the shares at the time of the disposal.

Cross References

From Section 512

Section 511 The period of retention, release date and appropriate percentage.
Section 513 Capital receipts in respect of scheme shares.
Section 514 Company reconstructions, amalgamations, etc.
Section 515 Excess or unauthorised shares.

To Section 512

Section 496 Disposals of shares.
Section 509 Interpretation (Chapter 1).
Section 513 Capital receipts in respect of scheme shares.
Section 514 Company reconstructions, amalgamations, etc.
Section 515 Excess or unauthorised shares.

513 Capital receipts in respect of scheme shares

[FA82 s54]

(1) Subject to this section, where, in respect of or by reference to any of a participant's shares, the trustees become or the participant becomes entitled, before the release date, to receive any money or money's worth (in this section referred to as a "*capital receipt*"), the participant shall be chargeable to income tax under Schedule E for the year of assessment in which the entitlement arises on the appropriate percentage (determined as at the time when the trustees become or the participant becomes so entitled) of the amount or value of the receipt.

(2) Money or money's worth shall not be a capital receipt for the purposes of this section if or, as the case may be, to the extent that—

(a) it constitutes income in the hands of the recipient for the purposes of income tax,

(b) it consists of the proceeds of a disposal within *section 512*, or

(c) it consists of new shares within the meaning of *section 514*.

(3) Where, pursuant to a direction given by or on behalf of the participant or any person in whom the beneficial interest in the participant's shares is for the time being vested, the trustees—

(a) dispose of some of the rights arising under a rights issue within the meaning of *section 512(5)(b)*, and

(b) use the proceeds of that disposal to exercise other such rights,

the money or money's worth which constitutes the proceeds of that disposal shall not be a capital receipt for the purposes of this section.

(4) Where apart from this subsection the amount or value of a capital receipt would exceed the sum which, immediately before the entitlement to the receipt arose, was the locked-in value of the shares to which the receipt is referable, *subsection (1)* shall apply as if the amount or value of the receipt were equal to that locked-in value.

(5) *Subsection (1)* shall not apply in relation to a receipt if the entitlement to it arises after the death of the participant to whose shares it is referable.

(6) *Subsection (1)* shall not apply in relation to any receipt the amount or value of which (after any reduction under *subsection (4)*) does not exceed [€13][1].

Amendments

[1] Substituted by FA01 sched5.

Cross References

From Section 513

Section 512 Disposals of scheme shares.

Section 514 Company reconstructions, amalgamations, etc.

To Section 513

Section 509 Interpretation (Chapter 1).

Section 512 Disposals of scheme shares.

Section 514 Company reconstructions, amalgamations, etc.

Schedule 11 Profit Sharing Schemes

514 Company reconstructions, amalgamations, etc

[FA82 s55]

(1) In this section—

"*new shares*" means shares comprised in the new holding which were issued in respect of, or otherwise represent, shares comprised in the original holding;

"*the corresponding shares*", in relation to any new shares, means those shares in respect of which the new shares were issued or which the new shares otherwise represent.

(2) This section shall apply where there occurs in relation to any of a participant's shares (in this section referred to as "*the original holding*") a transaction (in this section referred to as a "*company reconstruction*") which results in a new holding (within the meaning of *section 584*) being equated with the original holding for the purposes of capital gains tax.

(3) (a) Where shares are issued as part of a company reconstruction in circumstances such that *section 131(2)* applies, those shares shall be treated for the purposes of this section as not forming part of the new holding.

(b) Nothing in this Chapter shall affect the application of *section 130(2)(c)* or *132(2)*.

(4) Subject to this section, references in this Chapter to a participant's shares shall be construed, after the time of the company reconstruction, as being or, as the case may be, as including, references to any new shares, and for the purposes of this Chapter—

(a) a company reconstruction shall be treated as not involving a disposal of shares comprised in the original holding,

(b) the date on which any new shares are to be treated as having been appropriated to the participant shall be the date on which the corresponding shares were appropriated, and

(c) the conditions in *Part 3* of *Schedule 11* shall be treated as fulfilled with respect to any new shares if those conditions were (or were treated as) fulfilled with respect to the corresponding shares.

(5) In relation to shares comprised in the new holding, *section 512(1)* shall apply as if the references in that section to the initial market value of the shares were references to their locked-in value immediately after the company reconstruction, which shall be determined by—

(a) ascertaining the aggregate amount of locked-in value immediately before the reconstruction of those shares comprised in the original holding which had at that time the same locked-in value, and

(b) distributing that amount proportionately among—

(i) such of those shares as remain in the new holding, and

(ii) any new shares in relation to which those shares are the corresponding shares,

according to their market value immediately after the date of the reconstruction, and *section 512(1)(a)* shall apply only to capital receipts after the date of the reconstruction.

(6) For the purposes of this Chapter, where as part of a company reconstruction the trustees become entitled to a capital receipt (within the meaning of *section 513*), their entitlement to the capital receipt shall be taken to arise before the new holding comes into being and, for the purposes of *subsection (5)*, before the date on which the locked-in value of any shares comprised in the original holding falls to be ascertained.

(7) In relation to a new holding, any reference in this section to shares includes securities and rights of any description which form part of the new holding for the purposes of *section 584*.

Revenue Precedents

Will relief under section 514 TCA 1997 be allowed in a company reconstruction where only cash is on offer to employees for their shares? The relief will be applied where: (A) under the terms of the reconstruction shares can be exchanged for cash only, (B) the scheme will be continued by the new company, (C) all the cash is retained by the Trustees and not passed to the participants, and, (D) the total sums are reinvested by the Trustees in shares in the new company, without delay. GM

Cross References

From Section 514

Section 130 Matters to be treated as distributions.
Section 131 Bonus issues following repayment of share capital.
Section 132 Matters to be treated or not treated as repayments of share capital.
Section 512 Disposals of scheme shares.
Section 513 Capital receipts in respect of scheme shares.
Section 584 Reorganisation or reduction of share capital.
Schedule 11 Profit Sharing Schemes

To Section 514

Section 510 Approved profit sharing schemes: appropriated shares.
Section 512 Disposals of scheme shares.
Section 513 Capital receipts in respect of scheme shares.
Section 515 Excess or unauthorised shares.
Schedule 11 Profit Sharing Schemes

515 Excess or unauthorised shares

[FA82 s56; FA95 s16]

[(1) Subject to subsection (2B), where the total of the initial market values of all the shares appropriated to an individual in any one year of assessment (whether under a single approved scheme or under 2 or more such schemes) exceeds—

(a) [€12,700][1], or

(b) [€38,100][2] where the conditions in *subsection (2A)* are satisfied,

subsections (4) to *(7)* shall apply to any excess shares, that is, any share which caused the applicable limit to be exceeded and any share appropriated after the applicable limit was exceeded.

(2) For the purposes of subsection (1), where a number of shares is appropriated to an individual at the same time under 2 or more approved schemes, the same proportion of the shares appropriated at that time under each scheme shall be regarded as being appropriated before the limit of [€12,700][3] or the limit of [€38,100][4], as the case may be, is exceeded.

(2A) The conditions referred to in *paragraph (b)* of *subsection (1)* are—

(a) the shares appropriated to such individual have been transferred to the trustees of the approved scheme concerned by the trustees of an employee share ownership trust to which *section 519* applies,

(b) at each given time in the [period of 5 years, or such lesser period as the Minister for Finance may by order prescribe,][5] commencing with the date of the establishment of the employee share ownership trust 50 per cent, or such lesser percentage as the Minister for Finance may by order prescribe, of the securities retained by the trustees at the time were pledged by them as security for borrowings,

(c) at the time of transfer referred to in *paragraph (a)* [a period of at least 10 years, or such lesser period (not being less than the period referred to in paragraph (*b*)) as the Revenue Commissioners may allow,][6] commencing on the date the employee share ownership trust was established and ending at the time when all the shares pledged as security for borrowings by the trustees of the employee share ownership trust became unpledged (hereafter in this section referred to as the "*encumbered period*") has elapsed, and

(d) no shares which were pledged, at any time since the trust was established, as security for borrowings by the trustees of the employee share ownership trust were previously transferred to the trustees of the approved scheme because they remained so pledged during the encumbered period.

(2B) The limit of [€38,100][7] in *paragraph (b)* of *subsection (1)* may only be applied in the first year of assessment during which the encumbered period has elapsed and then only in respect of shares appropriated after that period has so elapsed.][8]

(3) Where the trustees of an approved scheme appropriate shares to an individual at a time when the individual is ineligible to participate in the scheme by virtue of *Part 4* of *Schedule 11*, *subsections (4)* to *(7)* shall apply in relation to those shares, and in those subsections those shares are referred to as "*unauthorised shares*".

(4) For the purposes of any provision of this Chapter charging an individual to income tax under Schedule E by reason of the occurrence of an event relating to any of the individual's shares—

(a) the appropriate percentage in relation to excess shares or unauthorised shares shall in every case be 100 per cent, and

(b) without prejudice to *section 512(6)*, the event shall be treated as relating to shares which are not excess shares or unauthorised shares before shares which are.

(5) Excess shares or unauthorised shares which have not been disposed of before the release date, or if it is earlier, the date of the death of the participant whose shares they are, shall be treated for the purposes of this Chapter as having been disposed of by the trustees immediately before the release date or, as the case may require, the date of the participant's death, for a consideration equal to their market value at that time.

(6) The locked-in value at any time of any excess shares or unauthorised shares shall be their market value at that time.

(7) Where there has been a company reconstruction to which *section 514* applies, a new share (within the meaning of that section) shall be treated as an excess share or unauthorised share if the corresponding share (within the meaning of that section) or, if there was more than one corresponding share, each of them was an excess share or an unauthorised share.

[(8) Where an order is proposed to be made under subsection (2A)*(b)*, a draft of the order shall be laid before Dáil Éireann, and the order shall not be made until a resolution approving of the draft has been passed by Dáil Éireann.][9]

Amendments

[1, 2, 3, 4, 7] Substituted by FA01 sched5.

[5] Substituted by FA00 s24(a).

[6] Substituted by FA08 s14(1). Applies as on and from 31 January 2008.

[8] Substituted by FA99 s69(1)(a)(iii).

[9] Inserted by FA00 s24(b).

Cross References

From Section 515

Section 512 Disposals of scheme shares.
Section 514 Company reconstructions, amalgamations, etc.
Section 519 Employee share ownership trusts.
Schedule 11 Profit Sharing Schemes

To Section 515

Section 177 Conditions as to residence and period of ownership.
Section 511 The period of retention, release date and appropriate percentage.
Section 512 Disposals of scheme shares.
Schedule 11 Profit Sharing Schemes

516 Assessment of trustees in respect of sums received

[FA82 s57]

Where in connection with a direction to transfer the ownership of a participant's shares to which *paragraph (c)* of *section 511(4)* applies the trustees receive such a sum as is referred to in that paragraph—

(a) the trustees shall be chargeable to income tax under Case IV of Schedule D on an amount equal to the appropriate percentage of the locked-in value of the shares at the time of the direction, and

(b) the amount on which the participant is to be charged to income tax as a result of the transfer shall be deemed to be an amount from which income tax has been deducted at the standard rate pursuant to *section 238*.

Cross References

From Section 516

Section 238 Annual payments not payable out of taxed income.
Section 511 The period of retention, release date and appropriate percentage.

517 Payments to trustees of approved profit sharing scheme

[FA82 s58; FA83 s24; FA84 s31(b); FA97 s146(1) and Sch9 PtI par12(3)]

(1) Subject to *subsections (3)* and *(4)*, as respects any accounting period, any sum expended in that accounting period by the company concerned or, in the case of

a group scheme, by a participating company in making a payment or payments to the trustees of an approved scheme shall be included—

(a) in the sums to be deducted in computing for the purposes of Schedule D the profits or gains for that accounting period of a trade carried on by that company, or

(b) if that company is an investment company within the meaning of *section 83* or a company in the case of which that section applies by virtue of *section 707*, in the sums to be deducted under *section 83(2)* as expenses of management in computing the profits of the company for that accounting period for the purposes of corporation tax,

only if one of the conditions in *subsection (2)(b)* is fulfilled.

(2) (a) In this subsection, "*the relevant period*" means the period of 9 months beginning on the day following the end of the period of account in which the sum mentioned in *subsection (1)* is charged as an expense of the company incurring the expenditure or such longer period as the Revenue Commissioners may allow by notice in writing given to that company.

(b) The conditions referred to in *subsection (1)* are—

(i) that before the expiry of the relevant period the sum mentioned in *subsection (1)* is applied by the trustees in the acquisition of shares for appropriation to individuals who are eligible to participate in the scheme by virtue of their being or having been employees or directors of the company making the payment, and

(ii) that the sum is necessary to meet the reasonable expenses of the trustees in administering the scheme.

(3) (a) In this subsection, "*trading income*", in relating to any trade, means the income from the trade computed in accordance with the rules applicable to Case I of Schedule D before any deduction under this Chapter and after any set-off or reduction of income by virtue of *section 396* or *397*, and after any deduction or addition by virtue of *section 307* or *308*, and after any deduction by virtue of *section 666*.

(b) No deduction shall be allowed under this section or under any other provision of the Tax Acts in respect of so much of any sum or the aggregate amount of any sums expended by a participating company in an accounting period in the manner referred to in *subsection (1)* as exceeds the company's—

(i) trading income for that accounting period, in the case of a company to which *paragraph (a)* of that subsection applies, or

(ii) income for that accounting period, in the case of a company to which *paragraph (b)* of that subsection applies, after taking into account any sums which apart from this section are to be deducted under *section 83(2)* as expenses of management in computing the profits of the company for the purposes of corporation tax.

(4) The deduction to be allowed under this section or under any other provision of the Tax Acts in respect of any sum or the aggregate amount of any sums expended by a participating company in an accounting period in the manner referred to in *subsection (1)* shall not exceed such sum as is in the opinion of the Revenue Commissioners reasonable, having regard to the number of employees

or directors of the company making the payment who have agreed to participate in the scheme, the services rendered by them to that company, the levels of their remuneration, the length of their service or similar factors.

(5) For the purposes of this section, the trustees of an approved scheme shall be taken to apply sums paid to them in the order in which the sums are received by them.

Cross References

From Section 517

Section 83 Expenses of management of investment companies.
Section 307 Corporation tax: allowances and charges in taxing a trade.
Section 308 Corporation tax: manner of granting, and effect of, allowances made by means of discharge or repayment of tax.
Section 396 Relief for trading losses other than terminal losses.
Section 397 Relief for terminal loss in a trade.
Section 666 Deduction for increase in stock values.
Section 707 Management expenses.

518 Costs of establishing profit sharing schemes

[FA82 s58A; FA97 s50(b)]

(1) This section shall apply to a sum expended on or after the 10th day of May, 1997, by a company in establishing a profit sharing scheme which the Revenue Commissioners approve of in accordance with *Part 2* of *Schedule 11* and under which the trustees acquire no shares before such approval is given.

(2) A sum to which this section applies shall be included—

(a) in the sums to be deducted in computing for the purposes of Schedule D the profits or gains of a trade carried on by the company, or

(b) if the company is an investment company within the meaning of *section 83* or a company in the case of which that section applies by virtue of *section 707*, in the sums to be deducted under *section 83(2)* as expenses of management in computing the profits of the company for the purposes of corporation tax.

(3) In a case where—

(a) *subsection (2)* applies, and

(b) the approval is given after the end of the period of 9 months beginning on the day following the end of the accounting period in which the sum is expended,

then, for the purpose of *subsection (2)*, the sum shall be treated as expended in the accounting period in which the approval is given and not in the accounting period mentioned in *paragraph (b)*.

Cross References

From Section 518

Section 83 Expenses of management of investment companies.
Section 707 Management expenses.
Schedule 11 Profit Sharing Schemes

Chapter 2

Employee Share Ownership Trusts

519 Employee share ownership trusts

[FA97 s51]

(1) (a) This section shall apply to an employee share ownership trust which the Revenue Commissioners have approved of as a qualifying employee share ownership trust in accordance with *Schedule 12* and which approval has not been withdrawn.

(b) This section shall be construed together with *Schedule 12*.

(2) Where, in an accounting period of a company, the company expends a sum—

(a) in establishing a trust to which this section applies, or

(b) in making a payment by means of contribution to the trustees of a trust which at the time the sum is expended is a trust to which this section applies, and—

(i) at that time the company or a company which it then controls has employees who are eligible to benefit under the terms of the trust deed, and

(ii) before the expiry of the expenditure period the sum is expended by the trustees for one or more of the qualifying purposes,

then, the sum shall be included—

(I) in the sums to be deducted in computing for the purposes of Schedule D the profits or gains for the accounting period of a trade carried on by that company, or

(II) if the company is an investment company within the meaning of *section 83* or a company in the case of which that section applies by virtue of *section 707*, in the sums to be deducted under *section 83(2)* as expenses of management in computing the profits of the company for that accounting period for the purposes of corporation tax.

(3) Where—

(a) *subsection (2)(a)* applies, and

(b) the trust is established after the end of the period of 9 months beginning on the day following the end of the accounting period in which the sum is expended by the company,

then, for the purposes of *subsection (2)*, the sum shall be treated as expended in the accounting period in which the trust is established and not in the accounting period mentioned in *paragraph (b)*.

(4) For the purposes of *subsection (2)(b)(i)*, the question whether one company is controlled by another shall be construed in accordance with *section 432*.

(5) For the purposes of *subsection (2)(b)(ii)*—

(a) each of the following shall be a qualifying purpose—

(i) the acquisition of shares in the company which established the trust,

(ii) the repayment of sums borrowed,

(iii) the payment of interest on sums borrowed,

(iv) the payment of any sum to a person who is a beneficiary under the terms of [the trust deed,][1]

[(iva) the payment of any sum or the transfer of securities to the personal representatives of a deceased beneficiary under the terms of the trust deed, and][2]

(v) the meeting of expenses,

and

(b) the expenditure period shall be the period of 9 months beginning on the day following the end of the accounting period in which the sum is expended by the company or such longer period as the Revenue Commissioners may allow by notice given to the company.

(6) For the purposes of this section, the trustees of an employee share ownership trust shall be taken to expend sums paid to them in the order in which the sums are received by them, irrespective of the number of companies making payments.

[(7) The trustees of a trust to which this section applies shall not be chargeable to income tax in respect of income consisting of dividends in respect of securities held by the trust if, and to the extent that, the income is expended within the expenditure period (within the meaning of paragraph 13 of *Schedule 12*) by the trustees for one or more of the qualifying purposes referred to in that paragraph[…][3].][4]

[(7A) Where the trustees of a trust to which this section applies—

(a) sell securities on the open market, or

(b) receive a sum on the redemption of securities,

any gain accruing to such trustees shall not be a chargeable gain if, and to the extent that the proceeds of such sale or redemption, as the case may be, are used—

(i) to repay moneys borrowed by those trustees,

(ii) to pay interest on such borrowings, or

(iii) to pay a sum to the personal representatives of a deceased beneficiary.][5]

(8) Where the trustees of a trust to which this section applies transfer securities to the trustees of a profit sharing scheme approved under *Part 2* of *Schedule 11*, any gain accruing to those first-mentioned trustees on that transfer shall not be a chargeable gain.

[(8A) Where the trustees of a trust to which this section applies transfer securities to the personal representatives of a deceased beneficiary, any gain accruing to the trustees on that transfer shall not be a chargeable gain.

(8B) The payment of any sum as is referred to in [*subsection (7A)(iii)*][6] or the transfer of any securities to which *subsection (8A)* applies shall, notwithstanding any other provision of the Income Tax Acts, be exempt from income tax.][7]

(9) Notwithstanding anything in [*subsections (1)* to *(8B)*][8], where the Revenue Commissioners in accordance with *Schedule 12* withdraw approval of an employee share ownership trust as a qualifying employee share ownership trust, then, as on and from the date from which that withdrawal has effect, this section shall not apply in relation to—

(a) any sum expended by a company in making a payment to that trust,

[(b) income consisting of dividends in respect of securities held by that trust,

(c) the transfer of securities to a profit sharing scheme approved under Part 2 of [*Schedule 11*,][9]

[(ca) the payment of any sum or the transfer of securities to the personal representatives of a deceased beneficiary of the trust, or][10]

[(d) the gain accruing to the trustees of that trust from—

(i) the sale on the open market, or

(ii) the redemption,

of securities.][11]][12]

[(10) For the purposes of this section—

"*deceased beneficiary*" means a person who on the date of such person's death—

(a) would have been eligible to have [securities][13] appropriated to him or her, had such [securities][14] been available for appropriation, under a scheme approved of by the Revenue Commissioners under *Schedule 11* and for which approval has not been withdrawn, and

(b) was a beneficiary under the terms of a trust deed of an employee share ownership trust approved of by the Revenue Commissioners under *Schedule 12* and for which approval has not been withdrawn and which trust deed contained provision for the transfer of securities to the trustees of the scheme referred to in *paragraph (a)* and for the payment of sums and for the transfer of securities to the personal representatives of deceased beneficiaries.][15]

Amendments

[1] Substituted by FA01 s13(a)(i)(I).

[2] Inserted by FA01 s13(a)(i)(II).

[3] Repealed by FA00 sched2.

[4] Substituted by FA98 s36(1)(b). Shall apply as on and from the date of 27 March 1998

[5] Substituted by FA02 s13(1)(c)(i). This section shall apply and have effect as on and from 16 April 2001.

[6] Substituted by FA04 sched3(1)(n). This section shall have effect as on and from 25 March 2004

[7] Inserted by FA01 s13(a)(iii).

[8] Substituted by FA01 s13(a)(iv)(I).

[9] Substituted by FA01 s13(a)(iv)(II).

[10] Inserted by FA01 s13(a)(iv)(III).

[11] Substituted by FA02 s13(1)(c)(ii). This section shall apply and have effect as on and from 16 April 2001.

[12] Substituted by FA99 s69(1)(b)(ii). Shall apply as respects employee share ownership trusts approved on or after the date of 25 March 1999

[13, 14] Substituted by FA02 s13(1)(c)(iii). This section shall apply and have effect as on and from 16 April 2001.

[15] Inserted by FA01 s13(a)(v).

Cross References

From Section 519

Section 83 Expenses of management of investment companies.

Section 432 Meaning of "associated company" and "control".

Section 707 Management expenses.

Schedule 11 Profit Sharing Schemes

Schedule 12 Employee Share Ownership Trusts

To Section 519

Section 130 Matters to be treated as distributions.
Section 509 Interpretation (Chapter 1).
Section 510 Approved profit sharing schemes: appropriated shares.
Section 511A Shares acquired from an employee share ownership trust.
Section 515 Excess or unauthorised shares.
Schedule 11 Profit Sharing Schemes
Schedule 12 Employee Share Ownership Trusts

CHAPTER 3

Approved Savings-Related Share Option Schemes

519A Approved savings-related share option schemes

[(1) (a) The provisions of this section shall apply where an individual obtains a right to acquire shares in a body corporate—

(i) by reason of the individual's office or employment as a director or employee of that or any other body corporate, and

(ii) that individual obtains that right in accordance with the provisions of a savings-related share option scheme approved under *Schedule 12A* on or after the 6th day of April, 1999, and in respect of which approval has not been withdrawn.

(b) This section shall be construed together with *Schedule 12A*.

(2) Tax shall not be chargeable under any provision of the Tax Acts in respect of the receipt of the right referred to in *subsection (1)*.

(3) Subject to *subsection (4)* if the individual exercises the right in accordance with the provisions of the scheme at a time when it is approved tax shall not be chargeable under any provision of the Tax Acts in respect of any gain realised by the exercise of the right.

[(3A) (a) Where, in exercising a right in accordance with the provisions of the scheme at a time when it is approved, the individual acquires scheme shares from a relevant body, neither a chargeable gain nor an allowable loss shall accrue to the relevant body on the disposal of the scheme shares, and the individual shall, notwithstanding *section 547(1)(a)*>, be deemed for the purposes of the Capital Gains Tax Acts to have acquired the scheme shares for a consideration equal to the amount paid for their acquisition.

(b) In this subsection and in *section 519B*—

"*relevant body*" means a trust or a company which exists for the purpose of acquiring and holding scheme shares;

"*schemes shares*" has the meaning assigned to it by paragraph 10 of *Schedule 12A*.][1]

(4) *Subsection (3)* shall not apply in respect of a right obtained by a person under a scheme which is exercised within 3 years of its being obtained by virtue of a provision included in a scheme pursuant to paragraph 22 of *Schedule 12A*.

(5) In this section "savings-related share option scheme" has the meaning assigned to it by *Schedule 12A*.][2]

Amendments

[1] Inserted by FA00 s51(a)(i).

[2] Inserted by FA99 s68(a).

Revenue Briefings

Tax Briefing

Tax Briefing June 2000 – Issue 40 pg 29 – Savings-Related Share Option Schemes
Tax Briefing December 2000 – Issue 42 pg 30 – Savings-Related Share Option Schemes
Tax Briefing June 2002 – Issue 48 pg 18 – Savings-Related Share Option Schemes and Unpaid Leave

Revenue Information Notes

A Guide to Approved Savings Related Share Option Schemes

Cross References

From Section 519A

Section 519B Costs of establishing savings-related share option schemes.
Section 547 Disposals and acquisitions treated as made at market value.
Schedule 12A Approved Savings-Related Share Option Schemes

To Section 519A

Section 531AM Charge to universal social charge.
Schedule 12A Approved Savings-Related Share Option Schemes

519B Costs of establishing savings-related share option schemes

[(1) [Subject to *subsection (2A)* this section shall apply][1] to a sum expended on or after the 6th day of April, 1999, by a company in establishing a savings-related share option scheme which the Revenue Commissioners approve of in accordance with the provisions of *Schedule 12A* and under which no employee or director obtains rights before such approval is given.

(2) A sum to which this section applies shall be included—

(a) in the sums to be deducted in computing for the purposes of Schedule D the profits or gains of a trade carried on by the company, or

(b) if the company is an investment company within the meaning of *section 83* or a company in the case of which that section applies by virtue of *section 707*, in the sums to be deducted under *section 83(2)* as expenses of management in computing the profits of the company for the purposes of corporation tax.

[(2A) Notwithstanding any provision of the Tax Acts, any sum expended by the company, either directly or indirectly, to enable a relevant body to acquire scheme shares shall not be included—

(a) in the sums to be deducted in computing for the purposes of Schedule D the profits or gains of a trade carried on by the company, or

(b) if the company is an investment company within the meaning of *section 83* or a company in the case of which that section applies by virtue of *section 707*, in the sums to be deducted under *section 83(2)* as expenses of management in computing the profits of the company for the purposes of corporation tax.][2]

(3) In a case where—

(a) *subsection (2)* applies, and

(b) the approval is given after the end of the period of 9 months beginning on the day following the end of the accounting period in which the sum is expended, then, for the purpose of *subsection (2)*, the sum shall be treated as expended in the accounting period in which the approval is given and not the accounting period mentioned in *paragraph (b)*.][3]

Amendments

[1] Substituted by FA00 s51(a)(ii)(I).

[2] Inserted by FA00 s51(a)(ii)(II).

[3] Inserted by FA99 s68(a).

Revenue Briefings

Tax Briefing

Tax Briefing June 2000 – Issue 40 pg 29 – Savings-Related Share Option Schemes

Tax Briefing December 2000 – Issue 42 pg 30 – Savings-Related Share Option Schemes

Cross References

From Section 519B

Section 83 Expenses of management of investment companies.

Section 707 Management expenses.

Schedule 12A Approved Savings-Related Share Option Schemes

To Section 519B

Section 519A Approved savings-related share option schemes.

519C Interest, etc. under certified contractual savings schemes

[(1) In this section—

"*qualifying savings institution*" means any of the following persons—

(a) a person who is a holder of a licence granted under section 9 of the Central Bank Act, 1971, or a person who holds a licence or other similar authorisation under the law of any other Member State of the European Communities which corresponds to a licence granted under that section,

(b) a building society within the meaning of *section 256*,

(c) a trustee savings bank within the meaning of the Trustee Savings Banks Act, 1989,

[...][1]

[...][2]

(g) the Post Office Savings Bank,

(h) a credit union within the meaning of the Credit Union Act, 1997, or

(i) such other person as the Minister for Finance may by order prescribe.

(2) Any terminal bonus or interest paid by a qualifying savings institution to an individual under a certified contractual savings scheme shall be exempt from income tax and shall not be reckoned in computing total income for the purposes of the Income Tax Acts.

(3) Any terminal bonus or interest paid by a qualifying savings institution under a certified contractual savings scheme shall not, where the qualifying savings institution is a relevant deposit taker within the meaning of *section 256*, be relevant interest for the purposes of that section and accordingly shall not be subject to deduction of appropriate tax under *section 257*.

(4) In this section "*certified contractual savings scheme*" means a scheme—

(a) which provides for periodical contributions to be made by individuals for a specified period to a qualifying savings institution where the deposit represented by such contributions would, but for subsection (3), constitute a relevant deposit within the meaning of *section 256* if the qualifying savings institution were a relevant deposit taker within the meaning of that section,

(b) where the individuals referred to in *paragraph (a)*—

(i) are eligible to participate in, that is to say, to obtain and exercise rights under, an approved savings-related share option scheme, and

(ii) whose contributions under the scheme are to be used in accordance with paragraph 17 of *Schedule 12A*,

and

(c) which is certified by the Revenue Commissioners as qualifying for exemption under this section by reference to requirements specified by the Minister for Finance in accordance with *Schedule 12B*.

(5) *Schedule 12B* to this Act which contains provisions supplementing this section shall have effect.

(6) This section shall apply in relation to any terminal bonus or interest paid by a qualifying savings institution on or after the 6th day of April, 1999, under a certified contractual savings scheme.][3]

Amendments

[1] Repealed by ACC BA01 s12 and S.I. No 69 of 2002 with effect from 28 February 2002.

[2] Repealed by ICC BA00 s7 and ICC BA00 (Sections 5 and 7) (Commencement) Order S.I. No 46 of 2001 with effect from 12 February 2001.

[3] Inserted by FA99 s68(a).

Cross References

From Section 519C

Section 256 Interpretation (Chapter 4).
Section 257 Deduction of tax from relevant interest.
Schedule 12A Approved Savings-Related Share Option Schemes
Schedule 12B Certified Contractual Savings Schemes

To Section 519C

Schedule 12A Approved Savings-Related Share Option Schemes
Schedule 12B Certified Contractual Savings Schemes

Chapter 4

Approved Share Option Schemes

519D Approved share option schemes

[(1) The provisions of this section shall apply where an individual obtains a right to acquire shares in a body corporate—

(a) by reason of the individual's office or employment as a director or employee of that or any other body corporate, and

(b) that individual obtains the right in accordance with the provisions of a share option scheme approved under *Schedule 12C* and in respect of which approval has not been withdrawn.

(2) Tax shall not be chargeable under any provision of the Tax Acts in respect of the receipt of the right referred to in *subsection (1)*.

(3) Subject to *subsection (4)* (except where *paragraph 18(2)* of *Schedule 12C* applies), if the individual exercises the right in accordance with the provisions of the scheme at a time when it is approved—

(a) tax shall not be chargeable under any provision of the Tax Acts in respect of any gain realised by the exercise of the right, and

(b) notwithstanding *section 547(1)(a)*, the individual shall be deemed for the purposes of the Capital Gains Tax Acts to have acquired the shares, acquired by the exercise of the right, for a consideration equal to the amount paid for their acquisition.

(4) *Subsection (3)* shall not apply in relation to the exercise by any individual of a right in accordance with the provisions of a scheme if the period beginning with his or her obtaining the right and ending with his or her disposal of any of—

(a) the shares acquired by the exercise of the right, or

(b) in a case where *section 584*, *586* or *587* applies, the shares received in exchange for the shares so acquired,

is less than 3 years.

(5) (a) Where, in exercising a right in accordance with the provisions of the scheme at a time when it is approved, the individual acquires scheme shares from a relevant body, neither a chargeable gain nor an allowable loss shall accrue to the relevant body on the disposal of the scheme shares, and the individual shall, notwithstanding *section 547(1)(a)*, be deemed for the purposes of the Capital Gains Tax Acts to have acquired the scheme shares for a consideration equal to the amount paid for their acquisition.

(b) In this subsection and in *subsection (6)*—

"*relevant body*" means a trust or a company which exists for the purpose of acquiring and holding scheme shares;

"*scheme shares*" has the meaning assigned to it by *paragraph 11* of *Schedule 12C*.

(6) (a) Subject to *paragraph (c)*, this subsection applies to a sum expended by a company in establishing a share option scheme which the Revenue Commissioners approve of in accordance with the provisions of *Schedule 12C* and under which, subject to *subsection (7)*, no employee or director obtains rights before such approval is given.

(b) A sum to which this subsection applies shall be included—

(i) in the sums to be deducted in computing for the purposes of Schedule D the profits or gains of a trade carried on by the company, or

(ii) if a company is an investment company within the meaning of *section 83* or a company in the case of which that section applies by virtue of *section 707*, in the sums to be deducted under *section 83(2)* as expenses of management in computing the profits of the company for the purposes of corporation tax.

(c) Notwithstanding *paragraph (b)* or any other provision of the Tax Acts, any sum expended by a company, either directly or indirectly, to enable a relevant body to acquire scheme shares shall not be included—

(i) in the sums to be deducted in computing for the purposes of Schedule D the profits or gains of a trade carried on by the company, or

(ii) if the company is an investment company within the meaning of *section 83* or a company in the case of which that section applies by virtue of *section 707*, in the sums to be deducted under *section 83(2)* as expenses of management in computing the profits of the company for the purposes of corporation tax.

(d) In a case where—

(i) *paragraph (b)* applies, and

(ii) the approval is given after the end of the period of 9 months beginning on the day following the end of the accounting period in which the sum is expended,

then, for the purposes of *paragraph (b)*, the sum shall be treated as expended in the accounting period in which approval is given and not the accounting period mentioned in *subparagraph (ii)*.

(7) (a) Where a share option scheme is approved by the Revenue Commissioners under Schedule 12C and, prior to such approval, an individual had obtained under the scheme a right which meets the conditions of *paragraph (b)*, that right shall be treated for all the purposes of this section and *Schedule 12C* as if it had been obtained under an approved scheme.

(b) The conditions of this paragraph are—

(i) the right was exercised on or after 15 February 2001,

(ii) the scheme is approved by the Revenue Commissioners under Schedule 12C on or before 31 December 2001, and

(iii) at the time—

(I) the right was obtained, and

(II) the right was exercised, if such exercise occurred before the scheme was approved under *Schedule 12C*,

the scheme would, at each of those times, have been capable of approval under *Schedule 12C* if that Schedule had been in force from the time the right was obtained.

[(8) The exemption from income tax authorised by *subsection (2)* in respect of the receipt of the right referred to in *subsection (1)* shall not apply where the right is received on or after 24 November 2010.

(9) The exemption from income tax authorised by *subsection (3)* in respect of any gain realised by the exercise of the right referred to in *subsection (1)* shall not apply where the gain from the exercise of the right is realised on or after 24 November 2010.][1]][2]

Amendments

[1] Inserted by FA11 s10(b).

[2] Inserted by FA01 s15. Applies with effect from 30 March 2001

Revenue Briefings

Tax Briefing

Tax Briefing April 2001 – Issue 43 pg 15 – Approved Share Option Schemes

eBrief

eBrief No. 17/2011 – Share-Based Remuneration – Finance Act 2011 Changes

Revenue Information Notes

A Guide to the New Approved Share Options Schemes

Cross References

From Section 519D

Section 83 Expenses of management of investment companies.
Section 547 Disposals and acquisitions treated as made at market value.
Section 584 Reorganisation or reduction of share capital.
Section 586 Company amalgamations by exchange of shares.
Section 587 Company reconstructions and amalgamations.
Section 707 Management expenses.
Schedule 12C Approved Share Option Schemes

To Section 519D

Section 531AM Charge to universal social charge.
Schedule 12C Approved Share Option Schemes

PART 18

Payments in Respect of Professional Services by Certain Persons and Payments to Subcontractors in Certain Industries

CHAPTER 1

Payments in Respect of Professional Services by Certain Persons

520 Interpretation (Chapter 1)

[FA87 s13; FA88 s8(a)(i) and (ii); FA92 s10]

(1) In this Chapter—

"*accountable person*" has the meaning assigned to it by *section 521*;

"*appropriate tax*", in relation to a relevant payment, means—

(a) where such payment does not include value-added tax, a sum representing income tax on the amount of that payment at the standard rate in force at the time of payment, and

(b) where such payment includes value-added tax, a sum representing income tax at the standard rate in force at the time of payment on the amount of that payment exclusive of the value-added tax;

"*authorised insurer*" has the same meaning as in *section 470*;

"*basis period for a year of assessment*", in relation to a specified person, means—

(a) where a relevant payment is to be included in a computation of profits or gains of that person for the purposes of Case I or II of Schedule D, the period on the profits or gains of which income tax for that year is to be finally computed for the purposes of Case I or II of Schedule D, and—

[(i) where 2 basis periods overlap, then, subject to *subsection (3)*, the period common to both shall be deemed for the purposes of this Chapter to fall in the second basis period only,][1]

(ii) where there is an interval between the end of the basis period for one year of assessment and the basis period for the next year of assessment, the interval shall be deemed to be part of the second basis period, and

(iii) the reference in *subparagraph (i)* to the overlapping of 2 periods shall be construed as including a reference to the coincidence of 2 periods or to the inclusion of one period in another, and the reference to the period common to both shall be construed accordingly,

and

(b) in any other case, the year of assessment;

"*contract of insurance*" means a contract between an authorised insurer and a subscriber in respect of such insurance as is referred to in the definition of "*relevant contract*" in *section 470(1)*;

["*income tax month*" means—

(a) in relation to a period prior to 6 December 2001, a month beginning on the 6th day of a month and ending on the 5th day of the next month,

(b) the period beginning on 6 December 2001 and ending on 31 December 2001, and

(c) thereafter, a calendar month;][2]

"*member*", in relation to a contract of insurance, means a person who is named in the relevant policy of insurance and who has been accepted for insurance by an authorised insurer;

["*partnership trade or profession*" means a trade or profession carried on by two or more persons in partnership;][3]

"*practitioner*" has the same meaning as in *section 469*;

["*precedent partner*", in relation to a partnership and a partnership trade or profession, has the same meaning as in section 1007;][4]

"*professional services*" includes—

(a) services of a medical, dental, pharmaceutical, optical, aural or veterinary nature,

(b) services of an architectural, engineering, quantity surveying or surveying nature, and related services,

(c) services of accountancy, auditing or finance and services of financial, economic, marketing, advertising or other consultancies,

(d) services of a solicitor or barrister and other legal services,

(e) geological services, and

(f) training services provided on behalf of An Foras Áiseanna Saothair;

"*relevant medical expenses*" means expenses incurred in respect of professional services provided by a practitioner, being expenses that are or may become the subject of a claim for their reimbursement or discharge in whole or in part under a contract of insurance but not including any such expenses that—

(a) under the terms of the contract of insurance may (except in the case of certain expenses that in the opinion of the authorised insurer concerned are unusually large) be the subject of a claim for their discharge or reimbursement only—

(i) after the expiry of a stated period of 12 months in which the expenses are incurred, and

(ii) to the extent that the aggregate of the expenses and any other expenses incurred in that period exceeds a stated amount,

or

(b) are incurred in respect of professional services provided by a practitioner outside the State;

"*relevant payment*" means a payment made by—

(a) an accountable person in respect of professional services whether or not such services are provided to the accountable person making the payment,

or

(b) an authorised insurer to a practitioner in accordance with *section 522*, or otherwise, in the discharge of a claim in respect of relevant medical expenses under a contract of insurance,

but excludes—

(i) emoluments within the scope of *Chapter 4* of *Part 42* to which that Chapter [applies,][5] [(ii) relevant payments as defined for the purpose of *Chapter 2* of this Part,][6]

[(iii) a payment by one accountable person to another in reimbursement of a relevant [payment, and][7]][8]

[(iv) a payment by one accountable person to—

(I) another accountable person being a person whose income is exempt from corporation tax or is disregarded for the purposes of the Tax Acts, or

(II) a body which has been granted an exemption from tax for the purposes of *section 207*;][9]

["*specified person*", in relation to a relevant payment, means the person to whom that payment is made but, in a case where the relevant payment (including a payment to which *section 522* applies) is in relation to a professional service that is provided in the conduct of a partnership trade or profession, means each person who is a partner in the partnership;][10]

"*subscriber*", in relation to a contract of insurance, means a person (other than an authorised insurer) who is a party to the contract and in whose name the relevant policy of insurance is registered.

(2) For the purposes of this Chapter—

(a) any reference in this Chapter to the amount of a relevant payment shall be construed as a reference to the amount which would be the amount of that payment if no appropriate tax were to be deducted from that payment, and

(b) in relation to a specified person, appropriate tax referable to—

(i) an accounting period, or

(ii) a basis period for a year of assessment,

means the appropriate tax deducted from a relevant payment which is taken into account in computing the specified person's profits or gains for that period and where there is more than one such relevant payment in that period the aggregate of the appropriate tax deducted from such payments.

[(3) Where, by virtue of the application of *subsections (2)(a)* and *(3B)* of *section 65*, a specified person's basis period for the year of assessment 2002, being a 12 month period ending in the period from 1 January 2002 to 5 April 2002, is also treated as the specified person's basis period for the year of assessment 2001, that basis period shall be deemed for the purposes of this Chapter to be the basis period for the year of assessment 2001 only.][11]

Amendments

[1] Substituted by FA01 sched2(28)(a)(i).

[2] Substituted by FA01 sched2(28)(a)(ii).

[3, 4] Inserted by FA13 s93(1)(a). Applies from 27 March 2013.

[5] Substituted by FA03 s10(1)(a)(i).

[6] Substituted by FA11 s(20)(1)(a).

[7] Substituted by FA05 s15(1)(b). This section comes into operation with effect as on and from 25 March 2005

[8] Inserted by FA03 s10(1)(a)(iii).

[9] Inserted by FA05 s15(1)(c). This section comes into operation with effect as on and from 25 March 2005

[10] Substituted by FA13 s93(1)(b). Applies from 27 March 2013.

[11] Inserted by FA01 sched2(28)(b).

Revenue Briefings

Tax Briefing

Tax Briefing July 1994 – Issue 15 pg 4 – Professional Services – Withholding Tax – Contracts Performed Abroad by Non-Residents

Tax Briefing June 1996 – Issue 22 pg 15 – Professional Services Withholding Tax (PSWT) – Commencement and Cessations

Tax Briefing April 1998 – Issue 31 pg 13 – Tax Treatment of Interest Paid under the Prompt Payment of Accounts Act 1997

Tax Briefing June 2002 – Issue 44 pg 26 – Professional Services Withholding Tax

Tax Briefing April 2002 – Issue 47 pg 19 – Professional Services Withholding Tax

Tax Briefing May 2003 – Issue 52 pg 25 – Late Payment in Commercial Transactions – Professional Services Withholding Tax

Tax Briefing August 2003 – Issue 53 pg 20 – Professional Services Withholding Tax (FA 2003)

Tax Briefing July 2004 – Issue 56 pg 12 – Professional Services Withholding Tax Credit

Tax Briefing August 2005 – Issue 60 pg 22 – Professional Services Withholding Tax (FA 2005)

Revenue Information Notes

IT 19 – Professional Services Withholding Tax (PSWT)

IT 61 – A Revenue Guide to Professional Services Withholding Tax (PSWT) for Accountable Persons and Specified Persons

Explanatory Note for non-resident persons on how to claim a refund of Professional Service Withholding Tax (PSWT)

Revenue Precedents

What is the treatment of grants paid by accountable persons? General grants are not subject to PSWT. Grants for specific professional services are subject to PSWT. WHT09

Statements of Practice

Professional Services Withholding Tax (the "Daly" case) – SP IT/01/95

Withholding Tax – Interim Refunds – SP IT/03/90

Cross References

From Section 520

Section 65 Cases I and II: basis of assessment.

Section 207 Rents of properties belonging to hospitals and other charities.

Section 469 Relief for health expenses.

Section 470 Relief for insurance against expenses of illness.

Section 521 Accountable persons.

Section 522 Obligation on authorised insurers.

Section 960 Date for payment of income tax other than under self assessment.

Section 983 Interpretation (Chapter 4).

To Section 520

Section 444 Exclusion of mining and construction operations.

Section 904 Power of inspection: tax deduction from payments to certain subcontractors.

Section 904J Power of inspection: tax deduction from payments in respect of professional services by certain persons.

Section 912B Questioning of suspects in Garda Síochána custody in certain circumstances.

Section 1003 Payment of tax by means of donation of heritage items.

Section 1003A Payment of tax by means of donation of heritage property to an Irish heritage trust.

Schedule 13 Accountable Persons for Purposes of Chapter 1 of Part 18

Schedule 31 Consequential Amendments

521 Accountable persons

[FA87 s14; FA92 s11(1)]

(1) In this Chapter, "*accountable person*" means, subject to *subsection (2)*, a person specified in *Schedule 13*.

[(2) Where any of the persons specified in *Schedule 13* is a body corporate, "*accountable person*" includes—

(a) any subsidiary of that body corporate where such subsidiary is resident in the State and, for the purposes of this subsection, "*subsidiary*" has the meaning assigned to it by *section 155* of the Companies Act 1963, and

(b) a company, resident in the State, of which more than one accountable person are members if the accountable persons—

(i) control the composition of its board of directors,

(ii) hold more than half in nominal value of its equity share capital, or

(iii) hold more than half in nominal value of its shares carrying voting rights (other than voting rights which arise only in specified circumstances).][1]

(3) For the purposes of this Chapter, the Minister for Finance may by regulations extend or restrict the meaning of "*accountable person*" by adding or deleting one or more persons to or from, as the case may be, the list of persons specified in *Schedule 13.*

(4) Where regulations are proposed to be made under *subsection (3)*, a draft of the regulations shall be laid before Dáil Éireann and the regulations shall not be made until a resolution approving of the draft has been passed by Dáil Éireann.

Amendments

[1] Substituted by F(No.2)A13 s17(1)(a). Comes into operation on 1 January 2014.

Cross References

From Section 521

Schedule 13 Accountable Persons for Purposes of Chapter 1 of Part 18

To Section 521

Section 520 Interpretation (Chapter 1).

Section 904J Power of inspection: tax deduction from payments in respect of professional services by certain persons.

Schedule 13 Accountable Persons for Purposes of Chapter 1 of Part 18

522 Obligation on authorised insurers

[FA87 s14A; FA88 s 8(c)]

Subject to *section 523(1)*, where under a contract of insurance a claim is made to an authorised insurer in respect of relevant medical expenses—

[(a) the insurer shall, subject to *section 529A*, discharge the claim by making payment to the extent of the amount of the benefit, if any, due under the contract—

(i) to the practitioner who provided the professional services to the subscriber or member concerned to whom the relevant medical expenses relate, or

(ii) to the employer of the practitioner who provided the professional services to the subscriber or member concerned, where the professional services to which the claim relates were provided by the practitioner in the practitioner's capacity as employee rather than on the practitioner's own account,

and][1]

(b) the subscriber or member, as the case may be, shall be acquitted and discharged of such amount as is represented by the payment as if the subscriber or member had made such payment.

Amendments

[1] Substituted by F(No.2)A13 s17(1)(b). Comes into operation on 1 January 2014.

Revenue Briefings

eBrief

eBrief No. 83/2014 – Application of Professional Services Withholding Tax (PSWT) to payments made to Medical Practitioners under a contract of insurance in respect of relevant medical expenses

Cross References

From Section 522

Section 523 Deduction of tax from relevant payments.

To Section 522

Section 520 Interpretation (Chapter 1).

Section 523 Deduction of tax from relevant payments.

523 Deduction of tax from relevant payments

[FA87 s15; FA88 s8(d)]

(1) (a) An accountable person making a relevant payment shall deduct from the amount of the payment the appropriate tax in relation to the payment.

(b) [The specified person or, where *section 529A* applies, the partnership][1] to whom the amount is payable shall allow such deduction on receipt of the residue of the payment.

(c) The accountable person making the deduction and, if the accountable person is an authorised insurer, any subscriber or member on whose behalf the accountable person is making the relevant payment shall be acquitted and discharged of such amount as is represented by the deduction, as if the amount had actually been paid.

(2) Where—

[(a) in accordance with *section 522* or *529A*, a relevant payment has been made to a [practitioner, an employer][2] or, as the case may be, a partnership by an authorised insurer, and][3]

(b) in accordance with *subsection (1)*, [the recipient][4] has allowed a deduction of appropriate tax in respect of that payment and a subscriber or member has been acquitted and discharged of so much money as is represented by the deduction,

[the recipient shall][5], if any amount in respect of the relevant medical expenses to which the relevant payment relates has been paid by the subscriber or member, pay to the subscriber or member, as the case may be, an amount equal to the amount by which the aggregate of the amount paid by the subscriber or member and the amount of the relevant payment exceeds the relevant medical expenses.

(3) (a) The Minister for Finance may make such regulations as that Minister considers necessary or expedient for the purpose of giving full effect to this Chapter in so far as it relates to authorised insurers and the making of payments under contracts of insurance in respect of relevant medical expenses, and, in particular but without prejudice to the generality of the foregoing, regulations under this subsection may—

(i) specify the circumstances and the manner in which a payment (other than a relevant payment) may be made or claimed in respect of relevant medical expenses, and

(ii) provide for the indemnification of an individual against claims in respect of relevant medical expenses, or any other claims arising out of acts done or omitted to be done by the individual pursuant to this Chapter or regulations made under this subsection in so far as this Chapter relates or those regulations relate to authorised insurers and the making of payments under contracts of insurance in respect of relevant medical expenses.

(b) Every regulation made under this subsection shall be laid before Dáil Éireann as soon as may be after it is made and, if a resolution annulling the regulation is passed by Dáil Éireann within the next 21 days on which Dáil Éireann has sat after the regulation is laid before it, the regulation shall be annulled accordingly, but without prejudice to the validity of anything previously done thereunder.

(4) The provisions of the Tax Acts relating to the computation of profits or gains shall not be affected by the deduction of appropriate tax from relevant payments in accordance with *subsection (1)*, and accordingly the amount of such relevant payments shall be taken into account in computing the profits or gains of the specified person for tax purposes.

Amendments

[1] Substituted by FA13 s93(1)(d). Applies from 27 March 2013.

[2] Substituted by F(No.2)A13 s17(1)(c)(i). Comes into operation on 1 January 2014.

[3] Substituted by FA13 s93(1)(e). Applies from 27 March 2013.

[4] Substituted by F(No.2)A13 s17(1)(c)(ii). Comes into operation on 1 January 2014.

[5] Substituted by F(No.2)A13 s17(1)(c)(iii). Comes into operation on 1 January 2014.

Cross References

From Section 523

Section 522 Obligation on authorised insurers.

To Section 523

Section 522 Obligation on authorised insurers.

Revenue Briefings

eBrief

eBrief No. 34/2013 – Partnerships - Professional Services Withholding Tax (PSWT)

524 Identification of, and issue of documents to, specified persons

[FA87 s16]

(1) [Subject to *subsection (1A)*, the specified person][1] shall furnish to the accountable person concerned—

(a) in the case of a specified person resident in the State or a person having a permanent establishment or fixed base in the State—

(i) details of the specified person's income tax or corporation tax number, as may be appropriate, and

(ii) if the relevant payment includes an amount in respect of value-added tax, the specified person's value-added tax registration number, and

(b) in the case of a specified person other than a person mentioned in *paragraph (a)*, details of the specified person's country of residence and the specified person's tax reference in that country.

[(1A) (a) Where a relevant payment (including a payment to which *section 522* applies) is made in accordance with *section 529A(1)*, the precedent partner shall furnish the tax number of the partnership to the accountable person.

(b) For the purposes of *paragraph (a)*, "*tax number*" in relation to a partnership means—

(i) the registration number allocated by an inspector in relation to the operation by the partnership of value-added tax, or any other tax, or the reference number stated on any return, form or notice issued by an inspector in relation to the partnership, or

(ii) where appropriate, the tax reference of the partnership in another country.][2]

(2) Where the specified person has complied with *subsection (1)*, [or, as the case may be, the precedent partner has complied with *subsection (1A)*,][3] the accountable person, on making a relevant payment, shall give to such person in a form prescribed by the Revenue Commissioners particulars of—

(a) the name and address of the specified person [or, as the case may be, of the partnership][4],

(b) the specified person's tax reference as furnished in accordance with *paragraph (a)(i)* or *(b)* of *subsection (1)* [or, as the case may be, the partnership's tax number as furnished in accordance with *subsection (1A)*,][5]

(c) the amount of the relevant payment,

(d) the amount of the appropriate tax deducted from that payment, and

(e) the date on which the payment is made.

[(3) For the purposes of this section, an accountable person may—

(a) require a specified person or, as the case may be, a precedent partner to provide evidence from the Revenue Commissioners that the income tax or corporation tax number of the specified person or, as the case may be, the tax number (referred to in *subsection (1A)(b)(i)*) of the partnership, that is provided to the accountable person, relates to that specified person or, as the case may be, that partnership, or

(b) request confirmation from the Revenue Commissioners as to whether the income tax or corporation tax number that is provided to the accountable person by a specified person or, as the case may be, the tax number (referred to in *subsection (1A)(b)(i)*) of a partnership that is provided by a precedent partner, relates to that specified person or, as the case may be, that partnership.][6]

Amendments

[1] Substituted by F(No.2)A13 sched(1)(f). Has effect on and from 18 December 2013.

[2] Inserted by FA13 s93(1)(h). Applies from 27 March 2013.

[3] Inserted by FA13 s93(1)(i)(i). Applies from 27 March 2013.

[4] Inserted by FA13 s93(1)(i)(ii). Applies from 27 March 2013.

[5] Inserted by FA13 s93(1)(i)(iii). Applies from 27 March 2013.

[6] Inserted by FA13 s93(1)(j). Applies from 27 March 2013.

Cross References

To Section 524

Section 526 Credit for appropriate tax borne.

Section 527 Interim refunds of appropriate tax.

525 Returns and collection of appropriate tax

[FA87 s17]

(1) Within [14 days][1] from the end of every income tax month, an accountable person shall remit to the Collector-General all amounts of appropriate tax which the accountable person is liable under this Chapter to deduct from relevant payments made by the accountable person during that income tax month.

(2) Each remittance under *subsection (1)* shall be accompanied by a return containing, in relation to each specified person [or, where *section 529A* applies, each partnership][2] to whom a relevant payment has been made in the income tax month concerned, the particulars required by the return.

(3) A return shall be required to be made by an accountable person for an income tax month notwithstanding that no relevant payments were made by the accountable person in that income tax month.

(4) Every return shall be in a form prescribed by the Revenue Commissioners and shall include a declaration to the effect that the return is correct and complete.

(5) The Collector-General shall give the accountable person a receipt for the total amount so remitted.

[(6) The provisions of *Chapter 2* relating to the assessment, collection and recovery of tax deductible under [that Chapter][3] shall apply to the assessment, collection and recovery of appropriate tax.][4]

Amendments

[1] Substituted by FA01 sched2(29). Applies as on and from 1 January 2002.

[2] Inserted by FA13 s93(1)(k). Applies from 27 March 2013.

[3] Substituted by FA11 s(20)(1)(b).

[4] Substituted by FA03 s10(1)(b).

Cross References

From Section 525

Section 531 Payments to subcontractors in certain industries.

To Section 525

Section 904J Power of inspection: tax deduction from payments in respect of professional services by certain persons.

526 Credit for appropriate tax borne

[FA87 s18]

(1) Where in relation to an accounting period a specified person is within the charge to corporation tax and has borne appropriate tax referable to that accounting period, the specified person may, subject to *section 529*, claim to have the amount of appropriate tax specified in *subsection (4)* set against corporation tax chargeable for that accounting period and, where such appropriate tax exceeds such corporation tax, to have the excess refunded to the specified person.

(2) Where in relation to a year of assessment a specified person is within the charge to income tax and has borne appropriate tax referable to the basis period for that year of assessment, the specified person may, subject to *section 529*, claim to have the amount of appropriate tax specified in *subsection (4)* set against the income tax chargeable for the year of assessment and, where such appropriate tax exceeds such income tax, to have the excess refunded to the specified person.

[(3) The specified person shall, where requested by the appropriate inspector, furnish the following in respect of each amount of appropriate tax included in a claim under *subsection (1)* or *(2)*—

(a) the form given to the specified person by an accountable person in accordance with *section 524(2)*, or

(b) in the case of a specified person who is a partner in relation to a partnership trade or profession, the documentation referred to in *section 529A(3)*.][1]

(4) The amount of the appropriate tax to be set against corporation tax for an accounting period or against income tax for a year of assessment in accordance with *subsection (1)* or *(2)* shall be the total of the appropriate tax referable to the accounting period or to the basis period for the year of assessment, as the case may be, [which is included in relation to the specified person in the forms or, as the case may be, the documentation referred to in *subsection (3)*][2] and not repaid under this Chapter.

[(5) References in this section to corporation tax chargeable and to income tax chargeable shall be construed in accordance with the definition of "*amount of tax chargeable*" in *section 959A*.][3]

Amendments

[1] Substituted by FA13 s93(1)(l). Applies from 27 March 2013.

[2] Substituted by FA13 s93(1)(m). Applies from 27 March 2013.

[3] Inserted by FA13 s93(1)(n). Applies from 27 March 2013.

Revenue Briefings

Tax Briefing

Tax Briefing July 2004 – Issue 56 pg 12 – Professional Services Withholding Tax Credit

eBrief

eBrief No. 68/2012 – Preliminary Tax Requirements for 2012 – Interaction with Credit for Withholding Taxes

Cross References

From Section 526

Section 524 Identification of, and issue of documents to, specified persons.
Section 529 Limitation on credits or interim refunds of appropriate tax.

To Section 526

Section 528 Apportionment of credits or interim refunds of appropriate tax.
Section 529 Limitation on credits or interim refunds of appropriate tax.

527 Interim refunds of appropriate tax

[FA87 s19]

(1) A specified person may make a claim for an interim refund of the whole or part of the appropriate tax referable to an accounting period or to a basis period for a year

of assessment, as the case may be (in this section referred to as "*the first-mentioned period*"), and the inspector shall, if he or she is satisfied that the specified person making the claim has complied with the requirements of *subsection (2)*, make such refund as is specified in *subsection (3)* and, subject to those requirements as modified by *subsection (4)(a)*, [make an offset or interim refund][1] as is specified in that subsection.

(2) The requirements of this subsection are—

(a) that the profits or gains for the accounting period or for the basis period for the year of assessment, as the case may be, immediately preceding the first-mentioned period have been finally determined for tax purposes,

(b) that the amount of tax which was payable for that accounting period or year of assessment corresponding to that basis period has been paid [...][2], and

(c) that the specified person shall, in respect of each relevant payment included in the claim, furnish to the inspector the form given to the specified person by an accountable person in accordance with *section 524(2)* [or, in the case of a specified person who is a partner in relation to a partnership trade or profession, the documentation referred to in *section 529A(3)*][3]

[(3) (a) The amount of the tax available for offset or interim refund shall be the excess of the total of the appropriate tax not already repaid under the provisions of this section, which is included in relation to the specified person in the forms or, as the case may be, the documentation referred to in *subsection (2)(c)*, over an amount equivalent to the amount of tax referred to in *subsection (2)(b)*.

(b) Where an excess arises in accordance with *paragraph (a)*, the excess shall be offset under *section 960H* to the extent that the specified person has a liability (within the meaning of that section) and any balance of the excess shall, subject to the Acts, be refunded to the specified person.][4]

[(3A) Where a specified person makes a claim for an interim refund of the whole or part of the appropriate tax referable to the basis period for the year of assessment 2001 or the year of assessment 2002, subsection (3) shall apply as if the reference in that subsection to the amount of tax referred to in *subsection (2)(b)* were a reference to—

(a) in the case where the claim relates to the basis period for the year of assessment 2001, 74 per cent, and

(b) in the case where the claim relates to the basis period for the year of assessment 2002, 135 per cent,

of the amount of tax referred to in *subsection (2)(b)*.][5]

(4) (a) Where the first-mentioned period is the period in which the trade or profession of the specified person has been set up and commenced, *paragraphs (a)* and *(b)* of *subsection (2)* shall not apply and the inspector shall, in accordance with this subsection, [make an offset or interim refund][6] to the specified person in respect of appropriate tax deducted from relevant payments taken, or to be taken, into account in computing the profits or gains of the trade or profession.

(b) For the purposes of determining the amount of [the offset or interim refund][7], the inspector shall determine—

(i) an amount equal to the amount of tax at the standard rate on an amount determined by the formula—

$$E \times \frac{A}{B} \times \frac{C}{P}$$

where—

A is the estimated total amount of the relevant payments to be taken into account as income in computing for tax purposes the profits or gains of the first-mentioned period,

B is the estimated total sum of all amounts to be so taken into account as income in computing those profits or gains,

C is the estimated number of months or fractions of months comprised in the period in respect of which the claim to the refund is made,

E is the estimated amount to be laid out or expended wholly and exclusively by the specified person in the first-mentioned period for the purposes of the trade or profession, and

P is the estimated number of months or fractions of months comprised in the first-mentioned period,

and the inspector shall make the estimates referred to in this formula to the best of his or her knowledge and belief and in accordance with the information available to him or her, and

[(ii) the amount of appropriate tax deducted from relevant payments in relation to the specified person in respect of which forms or, as the case may be, the documentation have been furnished in accordance with *subsection (2)(c)* after deducting from that amount any amount of such tax already offset or refunded in relation to the period for which the claim to a refund is made.][8]

(c) The inspector shall [offset or refund][9] an amount of appropriate tax equal to the lesser of the amounts determined at *subparagraphs (i)* and *(ii)* of *paragraph (b)*.

[(5) Where the specified person claims and proves the presence of particular hardship, the Revenue Commissioners may waive, in whole or in part, one or more than one of the conditions for the making of an offset or refund specified in this section and, where they so waive such a condition or conditions, they shall determine, having regard to all the circumstances and taking into account the objects and intentions of *subsections (1)* to *(4)*, an amount of an offset or refund or a further offset or refund which they consider to be just and reasonable and they shall make such offset or refund or, as the case may be, such further offset or refund accordingly.][10]

(6) For the purposes of this section, the income of a specified person for an accounting period or a basis period for a year of assessment shall be the total of all amounts received or receivable by the specified person which are taken into account in computing the profits or gains of the specified person's trade or profession for that period.

Amendments

[1] Substituted by FA13 s93(1)(o). Applies from 27 March 2013.

[2] Deleted by FA13 s93(1)(p). Applies from 27 March 2013.

[3] Inserted by FA13 s93(1)(q). Applies from 27 March 2013.

[4] Substituted by FA13 s93(1)(r). Applies from 27 March 2013.

[5] Inserted by FA01 sched2(30).

[6] Substituted by FA13 s93(1)(s). Applies from 27 March 2013.

[7] Substituted by FA13 s93(1)(t). Applies from 27 March 2013.

[8] Substituted by FA13 s93(1)(u). Applies from 27 March 2013.

[9] Substituted by FA13 s93(1)(v). Applies from 27 March 2013.

[10] Substituted by FA13 s93(1)(w). Applies from 27 March 2013.

Cross References

From Section 527

Section 524 Identification of, and issue of documents to, specified persons.

Section 960 Date for payment of income tax other than under self assessment.

Section 983 Interpretation (Chapter 4).

To Section 527

Section 528 Apportionment of credits or interim refunds of appropriate tax.

Section 529 Limitation on credits or interim refunds of appropriate tax.

528 Apportionment of credits or interim refunds of appropriate tax

[FA87 s20]

Where the form referred to in either *section 526(3)* or *527(2)(c)* relates to 2 or more specified persons, any necessary apportionment shall be made for the purposes of giving effect to *sections 526* and *527*.

Cross References

From Section 528

Section 526 Credit for appropriate tax borne.

Section 527 Interim refunds of appropriate tax.

529 Limitation on credits or interim refunds of appropriate tax

[FA87 s21]

No amount of appropriate tax shall be set off or refunded more than once under this Chapter, and any amount of appropriate tax refunded in accordance with *section 527* shall not be available for set-off under *section 526*.

Cross References

From Section 529

Section 526 Credit for appropriate tax borne.

Section 527 Interim refunds of appropriate tax.

To Section 529

Section 526 Credit for appropriate tax borne.

529A Partnerships

[(1) Subject to the provisions of this section, where a professional service is provided in the conduct of a partnership trade or profession then, for the purposes of this Chapter, an accountable person may make a relevant payment (including a payment to which *section 522* applies) in relation to that service in the name of the partnership.

(2) Where a relevant payment (including a payment to which *section 522* applies) is in relation to a professional service that is provided in the conduct of a partnership trade or profession, then for the purposes of *sections 520(2), 526* and *527*—

(a) the relevant payment shall be deemed to have been made to each person who is a partner in the partnership in the proportion in which profits or gains of the partnership trade or profession for the chargeable period involved are to be apportioned amongst the partners, and

(b) appropriate tax deducted from the relevant payment shall be apportioned solely between the partners and in the same proportion referred to in *paragraph (a)*.

(3) Where an apportionment as referred to in *subsection (2)* applies to a relevant payment and to the appropriate tax deducted from that payment, the precedent partner shall, for the purposes of *sections 526* and *527*, provide details of the apportionment that applies to the payment and the appropriate tax deducted, and the basis for that apportionment, in a statement issued to each partner in the partnership, together with a copy of the form given to the precedent partner by the accountable person in accordance with *section 524(2)*.

(4) The statement referred to in *subsection (3)* may be issued in writing or by electronic means (within the meaning of *section 50 917EA*) and shall be in such form as may be approved by the Revenue Commissioners for that purpose.][1]

Amendments

[1] Inserted by FA13 s93(1)(x). Comes into operation on the making of an order by the Minister for Finance, that provision shall come into operation on such day or days as the Minister for Finance shall appoint either generally or with reference to any particular purpose or provision and different days may be so appointed for different purposes or different provisions.

Revenue Briefings

eBrief

eBrief No. 83/2014 – Application of Professional Services Withholding Tax (PSWT) to payments made to Medical Practitioners under a contract of insurance in respect of relevant medical expenses

CHAPTER 1A

Payments in Respect of Non-resident Artistes by Companies Qualifying for Relief for Investment in Films

529B Interpretation (Chapter 1A)

[(1) In this Chapter—

"*artiste*" means an individual who provides artistic services;

"*artistic services*" means the services of an individual, when provided within the State, in giving a performance in audio-visual works of any kind, including films and television content, which is or may be made available to the public or any section of the public;

"*appropriate tax*", in relation to a relevant payment, means—

(a) where such payment does not include value-added tax, a sum representing income tax on the amount of that payment at the standard rate in force at the time of payment, and

(b) where such payment includes value-added tax, a sum representing income tax at the standard rate in force at the time of payment on the amount of that payment exclusive of the value-added tax;

"*certificate of deduction*" means a certificate issued in accordance with *section 529D(2)*;

"*chargeable period*" means the period specified in a notice in writing given by the Revenue Commissioners to a person, being a period of one or more income tax months, in respect of which the person is required under *section 529E* to make a return to the Collector-General, or where no such notice issued, a calendar month;

"*due date*", in relation to a chargeable period, means the day that is 23 days after the end of that period;

"*EEA Agreement*" means the Agreement on the European Economic Area signed at Oporto on 2 May 1992, as adjusted by all subsequent amendments to that Agreement;

"*EEA State*" means a state which is a contracting party to the EEA Agreement;

"*electronic means*" has the meaning assigned to it in *section 917EA(1)*;

"*income tax month*" means a calendar month;

"*non-resident*" means an individual who is neither resident nor ordinarily resident in the State, in another Member State or in another EEA state;

"*qualifying company*" has the meaning assigned to it in *section 481*;

"*relevant payment*" means any payment of whatever nature made, whether directly or indirectly, by a qualifying company in a chargeable period in respect of artistic services provided by an artiste who is non-resident, whether or not the artistic services are provided directly or indirectly to the qualifying company including any payments relating to the exploitation of or compensation for any rights held by or on behalf of or in respect of the artiste who is non-resident, but excludes emoluments to which *Chapter 4* of *Part 42* applies;

"*Revenue officer*" means an officer of the Revenue Commissioners;

"*specified person*" means a person to whom a relevant payment is due.

(2) For the purposes of this Chapter any reference to the amount of a relevant payment shall be construed as a reference to the amount which would be the amount of that payment as if no appropriate tax were required to be deducted from that payment.][1]

Amendments

[1] Inserted by F(No.2)A13 s25(1). Comes into operation on such day as the Minister for Finance may appoint by order.

529C Deduction of tax from relevant payments

[(1) (a) A qualifying company making a relevant payment shall deduct from the amount of the payment the appropriate tax in relation to the payment.

(b) The specified person shall allow such deduction on the receipt of the residue of the payment.

(c) The qualifying company shall be acquitted and discharged of such amount as is represented by the deduction, as if that amount had actually been paid to the specified person.

(2) (a) A specified person shall be entitled to have the amount of the relevant payment reduced by the amount of expenditure, which was not reimbursed or is not reimbursable, that was incurred in the provision of artistic services to a qualifying company.

(b) The amount of expenditure referred to in *paragraph (a)* shall be computed as if the artistic services provided to the qualifying company was a separate trade and the expenditure was incurred for the purposes of that trade.

(c) A specified person may make a claim to the Revenue Commissioners in respect of expenditure defrayed in accordance with *paragraph (b)*.

(d) Where a Revenue officer is satisfied that the amount of expenditure claimed under *paragraph (c)* would not have been disallowed under *section 81* if the specified person had provided the services directly to the qualifying company by carrying on a trade or profession chargeable to tax under Case I or Case II, then a Revenue officer shall issue a notification to the qualifying company specifying the amount of expenditure that shall be allowed as a deduction under *paragraph (a)*.

(e) On receipt of a notification issued under *paragraph (d)*, the qualifying company shall deduct the appropriate tax from the amount of the relevant payment after allowing the deduction in the notification issued under *paragraph (d)*.

(3) A qualifying company which makes a relevant payment to a specified person in circumstances other than those referred to in *subsection (1)* shall—

(a) be liable to pay tax to the Revenue Commissioners at the standard rate on the amount of the relevant payment, and

(b) without prejudice to any other penalty to which the qualifying company may be liable and without prejudice to *section 1078*, be liable to a penalty of €5,000 or the amount of the tax payable under *paragraph (a)*, whichever is the lesser.][1]

Amendments

[1] Inserted by F(No.2)A13 s25(1). Comes into operation on such day as the Minister for Finance may appoint by order.

529D Identification of, and issue of documents to, specified persons

[(1) A specified person shall furnish to a qualifying company details of the specified person's country of residence, address and tax reference in the country of residence.

(2) Where the specified person has complied with *subsection (1)* the qualifying company, on making a relevant payment, shall give to such person a certificate of deduction in a form prescribed by the Revenue Commissioners with particulars of—

(a) the name and address of the specified person,

(b) the specified person's tax reference as furnished in accordance with *subsection (1)*,

(c) the amount of the relevant payment,

(d) the amount of the appropriate tax deducted from that payment, and

(e) the date on which the payment is made.][1]

Amendments

[1] Inserted by F(No.2)A13 s25(1). Comes into operation on such day as the Minister for Finance may appoint by order.

529E Returns by qualifying company

[(1) On or before the due date relating to a chargeable period, a qualifying company shall make a return to the Collector-General of all relevant payments made by the qualifying company during that chargeable period and shall specify on that return the amount of the qualifying company's tax liability under this Chapter.

(2) A return required under this section shall be made by electronic means and the relevant provisions of *Chapter 6* of *Part 38* shall apply.

(3) Where a qualifying company fails to submit the return due under *subsection (1)*, the qualifying company shall, without prejudice to any other penalty to which the qualifying company may be liable and without prejudice to *section 1078*, be liable to a penalty of €5,000 or the amount of the tax due under *subsection (2)*, whichever is the lesser.

(4) The Revenue Commissioners shall make regulations for the purposes of this section and such regulations may provide for—

(a) the manner by which qualifying companies shall communicate electronically with the Revenue Commissioners,

(b) the particulars to be included in the return required under this section, and

(c) any other matters relating to returns under this section by a qualifying company.][1]

Amendments

[1] Inserted by F(No.2)A13 s25(1). Comes into operation on such day as the Minister for Finance may appoint by order.

529F Payment of tax by qualifying company

[On or before the due date relating to a chargeable period, a qualifying company shall remit to the Collector-General all amounts of appropriate tax which the qualifying company is liable under this Chapter to deduct from relevant payments made by the qualifying company during that chargeable period.][1]

Amendments

[1] Inserted by F(No.2)A13 s25(1). Comes into operation on such day as the Minister for Finance may appoint by order.

529G Assessment by Revenue officer

[(1) Where a Revenue officer has reason to believe that there is an amount of appropriate tax in relation to a relevant payment that ought to have been but has not been included in a return under *section 529E(1)*, or where the Revenue officer is dissatisfied with any such return, the Revenue officer may make an assessment on the qualifying company to the best of the officer's judgement of the amount of the appropriate tax which in the opinion of the officer is due and payable by the qualifying company for the chargeable period or periods.

(2) Without prejudice to *section 529E* but subject to *subsection (4)*, the amount of tax specified in an assessment under *subsection (1)* shall be due and payable to the Revenue Commissioners from the qualifying company so assessed.

(3) (a) A Revenue officer may, where the officer considers this necessary, amend an assessment of tax made under *subsection (1)*, and where, in accordance with this section, the Revenue officer makes or amends an assessment, the officer shall give notice to the qualifying company assessed showing the total amount of tax due and payable in accordance with the assessment.

(b) Without prejudice to anything in this section, the provisions of *Chapter 5* of *Part 41A*, including those relating to time limits shall, with any necessary modifications, apply to the making and amending of an assessment under this section.

(c) The Revenue officer may issue the notice of assessment or of amended assessment by electronic means.

(4) (a) Where a notice is given to a qualifying company under *subsection (3)*, the qualifying company may, if the qualifying company claims that the total amount of tax assessed is excessive, on giving notice in writing to the Revenue officer within the period of 30 days from the date of the notice, appeal to the Appeal Commissioners.

(b) A qualifying company to whom notice is given under *subsection (3)*, shall not be entitled to appeal to the Appeal Commissioners—

(i) in the case of a qualifying company who has made a return under *section 529E*, until that qualifying company has paid the tax due and payable on the basis of the qualifying company's return together with the related interest due under *section 529H*, and

(ii) in any other case, until the qualifying company has made a return under *section 529E* for the return period concerned and has paid the tax due and payable on the basis of that return together with the related interest due under *section 529H*.

(c) The Appeal Commissioners shall hear and determine an appeal made to them under this subsection as if it were an appeal against an assessment to income tax and the provisions of the Income Tax Acts relating to such appeals and to the rehearing of an appeal and to the statement of a case for the opinion of the High Court on a point of law shall apply accordingly with any necessary modifications.][1]

Amendments

[1] Inserted by F(No.2)A13 s25(1). Comes into operation on such day as the Minister for Finance may appoint by order.

529H Interest on late payment of appropriate tax

[(1) Where an amount of tax which a qualifying company is liable to pay under this Chapter to the Collector-General is not paid by the due date concerned, simple interest on the amount outstanding shall be paid by the qualifying company to the Collector-General and shall be calculated from the due date concerned until payment, for any day or part of a day during which the amount remains unpaid at the rate specified in *section 1080*.

(2) *Subsections (3)* to *(5)* of *section 1080* shall apply in relation to interest payable under *subsection (1)* as they apply in relation to interest payable under that section.][1]

Amendments

[1] Inserted by F(No.2)A13 s25(1). Comes into operation on such day as the Minister for Finance may appoint by order.

529I Repayment of appropriate tax

[(1) Notwithstanding anything in the Tax Acts—

(a) subject to *paragraph (d)*, no repayment of appropriate tax in respect of any relevant payment shall be made to any specified person receiving or entitled to the relevant payment,

(b) the amount of any relevant payment shall be deemed to be income of the specified person and chargeable to income tax under Case IV of *Schedule*

D and under no other Case or Schedule, and shall be taken into account in computing the total income of the person entitled to that amount but in relation to such a person—

(i) except for the purposes of a claim to repayment under *paragraph (d)*, the specified amount within the meaning of *section 188(2)* shall, as respects the year of assessment for which the person is to be charged to income tax in respect of the relevant payment, be increased by that amount, and

(ii) where the taxable income of that person includes a relevant payment then the part of the taxable income, equal to that relevant payment, shall be chargeable to tax at the rate at which tax was deducted from the relevant payment,

(c) *section 59* shall apply as if a reference to appropriate tax deductible by virtue of this Chapter were contained in *paragraph (a)* of that section,

(d) (i) a specified person shall be entitled in computing the income chargeable under Case IV, in accordance with *paragraph (b)*, to a deduction in respect of expenditure, which was not reimbursed or is not reimbursable, incurred in the provision of artistic services to a qualifying company,

(ii) the amount of expenditure referred to in *subparagraph (i)* shall be computed as if the artistic services provided to the qualifying company was a separate trade or profession and the expenditure was incurred for the purposes of that trade or profession,

(iii) a specified person may make a claim for repayment of appropriate tax to the Revenue Commissioners in respect of expenditure incurred in accordance with *subparagraph (ii)*,

(iv) on receipt of a claim under *subparagraph (iii)* a Revenue officer shall make a determination on an amount that is equal to the expenditure that would not have been disallowed as a deduction under *section 81* if the specified person had provided the services directly to the qualifying company by carrying on a trade or profession chargeable to tax under Case I or Case II,

(v) a repayment of the appropriate tax charged on the amount determined by a Revenue officer under *subparagraph (iv)* shall be made to the specified person,

(vi) following a determination under *subparagraph (iv)* and the application of *subparagraph (v)* the Revenue Commissioners shall notify the specified person of the repayment, if any, that is due,

(vii) a claim may not be made under this section where the relevant payment has been reduced, in respect of expenditure incurred, under *section 529C(2)*.

(2) On receipt of a notice of a determination made under *subsection (1)(d)(iv)*, a specified person who is aggrieved by the determination may, by notice in writing given to the Revenue Commissioners within 30 days of the date of the determination, appeal to the Appeal Commissioners.

(3) The Appeal Commissioners shall hear and determine an appeal made to them under *subsection (2)* as if it were an appeal against an assessment to income tax and the provisions of the Income Tax Acts relating to such appeals and to

the rehearing of an appeal and to the statement of a case for the opinion of the High Court on a point of law shall apply accordingly with any necessary modifications.

(4) The Revenue Commissioners shall make regulations for the purposes of this section and such regulations may provide for—

(a) the manner by which specified persons shall communicate with the Revenue Commissioners,

(b) the particulars to be included in a claim for a repayment under this section,

(c) the transmission of information in connection with appeals,

(d) any other matters related to repayments under this section.][1]

Amendments

[1] Inserted by F(No.2)A13 s25(1). Comes into operation on such day as the Minister for Finance may appoint by order.

529J Obligation on specified person

[Every specified person shall furnish to a qualifying company, on request, all such information or particulars as are required by the qualifying company to enable the qualifying company to comply with this Chapter.]

Amendments

[1] Inserted by F(No.2)A13 s25(1). Comes into operation on such day as the Minister for Finance may appoint by order.

529K Record keeping and inspection of records

[(1) Without prejudice to any other provision of the Tax Acts each qualifying company shall keep and maintain a record of all relevant payments made and the record shall state, in relation to each such payment, the name, address and tax reference of the specified person or the artiste, as appropriate, the date of the payment, the amount of the payment and the amount of appropriate tax deducted from the payment.

(2) The obligations contained in *subsections (3)* and *(4)* of *section 886* to keep and retain records and linking documents apply to all records, documents and other data created or maintained manually or by any electronic means for the purposes of this Chapter.

(3) (a) Without prejudice to other provisions of the Tax Acts, any person, or any employee of a person, who has made or received a relevant payment, shall produce to a Revenue officer for inspection all documents and records relating to the relevant payment as are in the power, possession or procurement of such person or employee, as the case may be, which have been requested by the Revenue officer.

(b) For the purposes of *subsection (1)*, any Revenue officer who exercises powers or performs duties, as the case may be, under this section shall be authorised in writing by the Revenue Commissioners to exercise those powers or perform those duties.

(c) An authorised officer when exercising powers or performing duties under this section shall, on request, produce evidence of the officer's authorisation.][1]

Amendments

[1] Inserted by F(No.2)A13 s25(1). Comes into operation on such day as the Minister for Finance may appoint by order.

529L Civil penalties

[*Chapter 3A* of *Part 47* applies, with any necessary modification, to a penalty arising under *section 529C(3)* or *529E(3)*.][1]

Amendments

[1] Inserted by F(No.2)A13 s25(1). Comes into operation on such day as the Minister for Finance may appoint by order.

529M Miscellaneous

[(1) Regulations made under this Chapter shall be laid before Dáil Éireann as soon as may be after they are made and, if a resolution annulling those regulations is passed by Dáil Éireann within the next 21 days on which Dáil Éireann has sat after the regulations are laid before it, the regulations shall be annulled accordingly, but without prejudice to the validity of anything previously done under them.

(2) (a) Anything required to be done by a qualifying company under this Chapter or under regulations made under this Chapter may be done by another person acting under the authority of the qualifying company.

(b) Where anything is done by such other person under the authority of a qualifying company, this Chapter shall apply as if it had been done by the qualifying company.

(c) Anything purporting to have been done by or on behalf of a qualifying company shall for the purposes of this Chapter be deemed to have been done by the qualifying company or under the qualifying company's authority, as the case may be, unless the contrary is proved.

(3) Anything to be done by or under this Chapter by the Revenue Commissioners, other than the making of regulations, may be done by any Revenue officer or may, if appropriate, be done through such electronic systems as the Revenue Commissioners may put in place for the time being for any such purpose.][1]

Amendments

[1] Inserted by F(No.2)A13 s25(1). Comes into operation on such day as the Minister for Finance may appoint by order.

CHAPTER 2

Payments to Subcontractors in Certain Industries

530 Interpretation (Chapter 2)

[FA70 s17(1) and (13); FA72 Sch1 PtIII par4; FA76 s21; FA92 s28(a); FA95 s18(1)(a); FA96 s41(a); FA97 s13(1)(a), s146(1) and Sch9 PtI par5(3)]

(1) In this Chapter—

"*certificate of authorisation*" means a certificate issued under *section 531(11)*;

"*certificates of deduction*" has the meaning assigned to it by *section 531(6)(f)*;

["*certified subcontractor*", in relation to a principal, means a subcontractor—

(a) in respect of whom the principal holds, at the time of making a payment under a relevant contract to the subcontractor, a relevant payments card for the year in which the payment is made, and

(b) in respect of whom the principal has not received a notice under *paragraph (a)* of *subsection (13)* of *section 531*;][1]

["*chargeable period*" has the same meaning as in *section 321(2)*;][2]

"*construction operations*" means operations of any of the following descriptions—

(a) the construction, alteration, repair, extension, demolition or dismantling of buildings or structures,

(b) the construction, alteration, repair, extension or demolition of any works forming, or to form, part of the land, including walls, roadworks, power lines, [telecommunication apparatus,][3] aircraft runways, docks and harbours, railways, inland waterways, pipelines, reservoirs, water mains, wells, sewers, industrial plant and installations for purposes of land drainage,

[(c) the installation, alteration or repair in any building or structure of systems of heating, lighting, air-conditioning, sound proofing, ventilation, power supply, drainage, sanitation, water supply, or burglar or fire protection,][4]

[(ca) the installation, alteration or repair in or on any building or structure of systems of telecommunications,][5]

(d) the external cleaning of buildings (other than cleaning of any part of a building in the course of normal maintenance) or the internal cleaning of buildings and structures, in so far as carried out in the course of their construction, alteration, extension, repair or restoration,

(e) operations which form an integral part of, or are preparatory to, or are for rendering complete such operations as are described in *paragraphs (a)* to *(d)*, including site clearance, earth-moving, excavation, tunnelling and boring, laying of foundations, erection of scaffolding, site restoration, landscaping and the provision of roadways and other access works,

(f) operations which form an integral part of, or are preparatory to, or are for rendering complete, the drilling for or extraction of minerals, oil, natural gas or the exploration for, or exploitation of, natural resources,

(g) the haulage for hire of materials, machinery or plant for use, whether used or not, in any of the construction operations referred to in *paragraphs (a)* to *(f)*;

"*the contractor*" has the meaning assigned to it by the definition of "*relevant contract*";

["*deducted tax*" has the meaning given to it in *section 530P*;

"*deduction authorisation*" has the meaning given to it in *section 530D*;

'*deduction summary*', in relation to a return period, means a statement (adjusted as appropriate in accordance with regulations made under this Chapter) which the Revenue Commissioners cause to be issued to a registered principal setting out, in summary form—

(a) details in respect of each relevant payment notified by that principal under *section 530C* which is, in accordance with regulations made under this Chapter, the subject of a valid deduction authorisation at the time of issue of the deduction summary, and

(b) the aggregate amount of tax that is, based on the details referred to in *paragraph (a)*, payable by the principal in respect of the return period,

and includes a statement to the effect that no such relevant payments were notified, where that is the case;][6]

"*director*" means—

(a) in relation to a body corporate the affairs of which are managed by a board of directors or similar body, a member of that board or body,

(b) in relation to a body corporate the affairs of which are managed by a single director or similar person, that director or person,

(c) in relation to a body corporate the affairs of which are managed by the members themselves, a member of the body corporate,

and includes any person who is or has been a director;

["*due date*", in relation to a return period, means—

(a) the day that is 14 days after the end of that return period, or

(b) the day that is 23 days after the end of that return period, in a case where the return for that period is made by electronic means in accordance with Chapter 6 of Part 38 and the remittance of the amount of tax that the person was liable to remit to the Collector-General under this Chapter in respect of that period is made by such electronic means as are required by the Revenue Commissioners, if the return and the remittance concerned are made by that day;

"*electronic means*" has the same meaning as in *section 917EA(1)*;][7]

"*employee*", in relation to a body corporate, includes any person taking part in the management of the affairs of the body corporate who is not a director, and includes a person who is to be or has been an employee;

"*forestry operations*" means operations of any of the following descriptions—

(a) the thinning, lopping or felling of trees in woods, forests or other plantations,

(b) with effect from the 6th day of October, 1997, the planting of trees in woods, forests or other plantations,

(c) with effect from the 6th day of October, 1997, the maintenance of woods, forests and plantations and the preparation of land, including woods or forests which have been harvested, for planting,

(d) the haulage or removal of thinned, lopped or felled trees,

(e) the processing (including cutting or preserving) of wood from thinned, lopped or felled trees in sawmills or other like premises,

(f) the haulage for hire of materials, machinery or plant for use, whether used or not, in any of the operations referred to in *paragraphs (a)* to *(e)*;

["*income tax month*" means—

(a) in relation to a period prior to 6 December 2001, a month beginning on the 6th day of a month and ending on the 5th day of the next month,

(b) the period beginning on 6 December 2001 and ending on 31 December 2001, and

(c) thereafter, a calendar month;][8]

["*meat processing operations*" means operations of any of the following descriptions—

(a) the slaughter of cattle, sheep, pigs, domestic fowl, turkeys, guinea-fowl, ducks or geese,

(b) the catching of domestic fowl, turkeys, guinea-fowl, ducks or geese,

(c) the division (including cutting or boning), sorting, packaging (including vacuum packaging), rewrapping or branding of, or the application of any other similar process to, the carcasses or any part of the carcasses (including meat) of slaughtered cattle, sheep, pigs, domestic fowl, turkeys, guinea-fowl, ducks or geese,

(d) the application of methods of preservation (including cold storage) to the carcasses or any part of the carcasses (including meat) of slaughtered cattle, sheep, pigs, domestic fowl, turkeys, guinea-fowl, ducks or geese,

(e) the loading or unloading of the carcasses or part of the carcasses (including meat) of slaughtered cattle, sheep, pigs, domestic fowl, turkeys, guinea-fowl, ducks or geese at any establishment where any of the operations referred to in *paragraphs (a)*, *(c)* and *(d)* are carried on,

(f) the haulage of the carcasses or any part of the carcasses (including meat) of slaughtered cattle, sheep, pigs, domestic fowl, turkeys, guinea-fowl, ducks or geese from any establishment where any of the operations referred to in *paragraphs (a)*, *(c)* and *(d)* are carried on,

[(fa) the rendering of the carcasses or any part of the carcasses of slaughtered cattle, sheep, pigs, domestic fowl, turkeys, guinea-fowl, ducks or geese,][9]

(g) the cleaning down of any establishment where any of the operations referred to in *paragraphs (a)*, *(c)* and *(d)* are carried on,

(h) the grading, sexing and transport of day-old chicks of domestic fowl, turkeys, guinea-fowl, ducks or geese,

(i) the haulage for hire of cattle, sheep, pigs, domestic fowl, turkeys, guinea-fowl, ducks or geese or of any of the materials, machinery or plant for use, whether used or not, in any of the operations referred to in *paragraphs (a)* to *(h)*.][10]

["*NAMA*" and "*NAMA group entity*" have the same meanings, respectively, as they have in the National Asset Management Agency Act 2009;][11]

"*the principal*" has the meaning assigned to it by the definition of "*relevant contract*";

"*proprietary director*", means a director of a company who is either the beneficial owner of, or able, either directly or through the medium of other companies or by any other indirect means, to control, more than 15 per cent of the ordinary share capital of the company;

"*proprietary employee*" means an employee who is either the beneficial owner of, or able, either directly or through the medium of other companies or by any other indirect means, to control, more than 15 per cent of the ordinary share capital of the company;

["*qualifying period*" means the period of 3 years, or such shorter period as the inspector may allow, ending on [31 December][12] in the year preceding the year of assessment which is the first year of assessment of the period, in respect of which a certificate of authorisation is sought together with the period, if any, from [1 January][13] in the said first year of assessment to the date on which the application for the said certificate is received by the Revenue Commissioners;][14]

["*registered principal*" means a principal included in a register of principals kept and maintained by the Revenue Commissioners for the purposes of this Chapter;][15]

"*relevant contract*" means a contract (not being a contract of employment[, or a contract between NAMA and a NAMA group entity or a contract between a NAMA group entity and another NAMA group entity][16]) whereby a person (in this Chapter referred to as "*the contractor*") is liable to another person (in this Chapter referred to as "*the principal*")—

(a) to carry out relevant operations,

(b) to be answerable for the carrying out of such operations by others, whether under a contract with the contractor or under other arrangements made or to be made by the contractor, or

[(c) to furnish the contractor's own labour or the labour of others in the carrying out of relevant operations or to arrange for the labour of others to be furnished for the carrying out of such operations,][17]

but, as respects relevant contracts entered into on or after the 15th day of May, 1996, a separate relevant contract shall be deemed to exist between the principal and each individual member of a gang or group of persons, [including persons in patrnership][18], where relevant operations are performed collectively by the gang or group, notwithstanding that any payment or part of a payment in respect of such relevant operations is made by the principal to one or more of the gang or group or to some other person;

"*relevant operations*" means construction operations, forestry operations or meat processing operations, as the case may be;

["*relevant payment*" means a payment made by a principal to whom *section 530A* applies in respect of a relevant contract;][19]

"*relevant payments card*" has the meaning assigned to it by *section 531(12)*;

"*relevant tax deduction card*" has the meaning assigned to it by *section 531(6)(c)(ii)*;

["*return period*", in relation to the principal concerned, means the period specified in a notice in writing given by the Revenue Commissioners to that principal, being a period of one or more income tax months, in respect of which the principal is required under *section 531(3A)* to make a return to the Collector-General[, or where no such period is specified, an income tax month][20];][21]

["*Revenue officer*" means any officer of the Revenue Commissioners;][22]

["*subcontractor*" means the contractor under a relevant contract where the principal under that contract is a person to whom *section 530A* applies;][23]

['*technology systems failure*' means circumstances in which the electronic system put in place by the Revenue Commissioners for the efficient operation of this Chapter is not functioning or is not functioning properly at any particular time such that a person is unable to comply with an obligation under this Chapter or regulations made under this Chapter, or circumstances where a person concerned is unable to use the electronic system at any particular time because of a general or partial systems failure of an internet service provider or of an electricity service provider, occurring in the general locality of the person's place of business;][24]

["*uncertified subcontractor*" means a subcontractor who is not a certified subcontractor.][25]

['*unreported payment notification*' means a notification to the Revenue Commissioners of a relevant payment which has not been made in accordance with *section 530C* and where a deduction authorisation has not been issued in accordance with *section 530D*;][26]

(2) In relation to a case where a subcontractor is chargeable to corporation tax, unless the context otherwise requires, references in this Chapter to tax shall

include references to corporation tax and references to a year of assessment shall include references to an accounting period.

(3) For the purposes of the definition of "*proprietary director*" and "*proprietary employee*", ordinary share capital which is owned or controlled as referred to in those definitions by a person, being [a spouse, a civil partner, a minor child or a minor child of the civil partner,][27] of a director or employee, or by a trustee of a trust for the benefit of a person or persons, being or including any such person or such director or employee, shall be deemed to be owned or controlled by such director or employee and not by any other person.

[(4) This Chapter applies in relation to relevant operations which are carried out in the State regardless of whether or not one or more of the following circumstances apply in respect of those operations:

(a) that either or both the principal and the subcontractor under the relevant contract under which the operations are so carried out—

(i) is not or are not resident in the State for the year of assessment or accounting period, as may be appropriate, in which the operations are carried out, or

(ii) in relation to those relevant operations, is not or are not, or not deemed to be, carrying on in the State—

(I) through a branch or agency or otherwise, a trade in respect of which the principal or subcontractor, as the case may be, is liable to income tax or corporation tax, as may be appropriate, or

(II) through a permanent establishment, within the meaning of arrangements having the force of law by virtue of [*section 826(1)*][28], a business;

(b) that the relevant contract under which the relevant operations are carried out is not subject to the law of the State;

(c) that payment in respect of the relevant operations is made outside the State.][29]

Amendments

[1] Inserted by FA01 s28(a).

[2] Inserted by FA11 s(20)(1)(c).

[3] Inserted by FA02 s51(1)(a)(i). Shall apply as on and from 1 April 2002.

[4] Substituted by FA12 s22(1)(a). Comes into operation on and from 31 March 2012.

[5] Substituted by FA12 s22(1)(b). Comes into operation on and from 31 March 2012.

[6] Substituted by FA12 s22(1)(c). Comes into operation on and from 31 March 2012.

[7] Inserted by FA11 s(20)(1)(e).

[8] Substituted by FA01 s28(a).

[9] Inserted by FA02 s51(1)(a)(ii). Shall apply as on and from 1 April 2002.

[10] Substituted by FA98 s37(1)(a). This section shall apply as on and from the 6th day of October, 1998.

[11, 16] Inserted by the National Asset Management Agency Act 2009 Sched 3 part 10.

[12, 13, 23] Inserted by FA01 s28(b).

[14] Substituted by FA99 s18(1)(a)(i). Shall apply as respects the year 1999-2000 and subsequent years of assessment.

[15] Inserted by FA11 s(20)(1)(f).

[17] Substituted by FA99 s18(1)(a)(iii). Shall apply as respects the year 1999-2000 and subsequent years of assessment.

[18] Substituted by FA12 s22(1)(d). Comes into operation on and from 31 March 2012.

[19] Inserted by FA11 s(20)(1)(g).

[20] Inserted by FA11 s(20)(1)(h).

[21] Inserted by FA10 s29(1). Deemed to have come into force and takes effect as on and from 1 January 2010.

[22] Inserted by FA11 s(20)(1)(i).

[23] Substituted by FA11 s(20)(1)(j).

[24] Inserted by FA12 s22(1)(e). Comes into operation on and from 31 March 2012.

[26] Inserted by FA14 s17(a). Comes into operation on 1 January 2015.

[27] Substituted by F(No.3)A11 sched1(143).

[28] Substituted by FA07 sched2(1)(p). Has effect as on and from 2 April 2007

[29] Inserted by FA06 s43. Applies with effect from 7 March 2006.

Note

FA11 s20(4)(b) – Section 531 and regulations made under that section shall not apply as regards payments made on or after the day referred to in paragraph (a) under a relevant contract, as defined in section 530.

Revenue Briefings

Tax Briefing

Tax Briefing August 2006 – Issue 64 – Business Tax Registration
Tax Briefing August 2006 – Issue 64 – Construction Industry

eBrief

eBrief No. 91/2010 – Important end of year information for Relevant Contracts Tax (RCT) Contractors
eBrief No. 98/2010 – Important end of year information for Relevant Contracts Tax Contractors
eBrief No. 09/2013 – Amended Regulations for Relevant Contracts Tax (RCT)
eBrief No. 46/2014 – Relevant Contracts Tax – Clarification on the installation of water meters and the hire of plant and machinery

Revenue Information Notes

Code of Practice for Determining Employment or Self-Employment Status of Individuals

Revenue Precedents

Whether, under Regulation 12 of the RCT Regulations 1971 as amended, an Inspector can make more than one estimated assessment in a tax year for a principal? Under Regulation 12, an Inspector cannot make more than one estimated assessment in a tax year for a principal. IT952549

Whether payments for cold storage facilities in respect of meat products fall within the RCT scheme? Such payments do fall within the RCT scheme. The activity comes within the definition of meat processing operations. IT952560

Cross References

From Section 530

Section 321 Provisions of general application in relation to the making of allowances and charges.
Section 530A Principal to whom relevant contracts tax applies.
Section 530D Deduction authorisation.
Section 530P Credit for deducted tax.
Section 531 Payments to subcontractors in certain industries.
Section 826 Agreements for relief from double taxation.
Section 917EA Mandatory electronic filing and payment of tax.

To Section 530

Section 21A Higher rate of corporation tax.
Section 444 Exclusion of mining and construction operations.
Section 530U Civil penalties.
Section 531 Payments to subcontractors in certain industries.
Section 644A Relief from income tax in respect of income from dealing in residential development land.
Section 904 Power of inspection: tax deduction from payments to certain subcontractors.
Section 912B Questioning of suspects in Garda Síochána custody in certain circumstances.
Section 1003 Payment of tax by means of donation of heritage items.

Section 1003A Payment of tax by means of donation of heritage property to an Irish heritage trust.
Section 1077E Penalty for deliberately or carelessly making incorrect returns, etc.
Schedule 31 Consequential Amendments

530A Principal to whom relevant contracts tax applies

[(1) Subject to *subsections (2)* and *(3)*, this section applies to a principal who is—

(a) in respect of the whole or any part of a relevant contract, the contractor under another relevant contract,

(b) a person—

(i) carrying on a business that includes the erection of buildings or the development of land (within the meaning of *section 639(1)*) or the manufacture, treatment or extraction of materials for use, whether used or not, in construction operations,

(ii) carrying on a business of meat processing operations in an establishment approved and inspected in accordance with the European Communities (Fresh Meat) Regulations, 1997 (S.I. No. 434 of 1997) or, as the case may be, the European Communities (Fresh Poultry-meat) Regulations, 1996 (S.I. No. 3 of 1996), or

(iii) carrying on a business that includes the processing (including cutting and preserving) of wood from thinned or felled trees in sawmills or other like premises or the supply of thinned or felled trees for such processing,

(c) a person connected with a company carrying on a business mentioned in *paragraph (b)*,

(d) a local authority, a public utility society (within the meaning of section 2 of the Housing Act 1966) or a body referred to in subparagraph (i) or (ii) of section 12(2)(*a*) of that Act or *section 19* or *45* of that Act,

(e) a Minister of the Government,

(f) any board or body established by or under statute or any board or body established by or under royal charter and funded wholly or mainly out of moneys provided by the Oireachtas, or […][1]

(g) a person who carries on any gas, water, electricity, hydraulic power, dock, canal or railway [undertaking, or][2].

[(*h*) a person who carries out the installation, alteration or repair in or on any building or structure of systems of telecommunications.][3]

(2) A person carrying on a business shall not be deemed to be a person of a kind specified in *subsection (1)(b)* by reason only of the fact that in the course of that business such person erects buildings or develops land for the use or occupation of such person or employees of such person.

(3) (a) Subject to *paragraph (b)*, a person shall be deemed not to be a principal of a kind specified in *subsection (1)(c)* where the following conditions are met—

(i) in the performance of a relevant contract, the person makes a payment to a subcontractor solely in connection with construction operations carried out in or on buildings or land to be used or occupied by such person or the employees of such person, and

(ii) the person does not carry on a business of the type mentioned in *subsection (1)(b)(i)*.

(b) Where a person is a principal of a kind specified in *subsection (1)(c)* by reason of the fact that such person is connected with a company carrying on a business of the type mentioned in *subsection (1)(b)(i), paragraph (a)* shall apply only where in addition to the conditions specified in that paragraph such person is a company.][4]

Amendments

[1] Deleted by FA12 s22(1)(f). Comes into operation on and from 31 March 2012.

[2] Substituted by FA12 s22(1)(f). Comes into operation on and from 31 March 2012.

[3] Inserted by FA12 s22(1)(f). Comes into operation on and from 31 March 2012.

[4] Inserted by FA11 s20(1)(k). With effect from 1 January 2012 per S.I. No. 660 of 2011.

Revenue Briefings

eBrief

eBrief No. 55/2011 – Changes to the operation of Relevant Contracts Tax (RCT)
eBrief No. 79/2011 – Commencement of the Modernised e-based scheme of Relevant Contracts Tax (RCT)
eBrief No. 83/2011 – Important end of year information for Relevant Contracts Tax Contractors
eBrief No. 38/2013 – Relevant Contracts Tax – Clarification on Connected Persons Rule

Cross References

From Section 530A

Section 45 Exemption of non-interest-bearing securities.
Section 639 Interpretation (Chapter 1).

To Section 530A

Section 530 Interpretation (Chapter 2).
Section 530B Notification of contract by principal.
Section 530F Obligation on principals to deduct tax.

530B Notification of contract by principal

[(1) Upon entering into a relevant contract, and in a case where *subsection (2)* applies, a principal to whom *section 530A* applies shall provide to the Revenue Commissioners—

[(a) information in relation to—

(i) the identity of the subcontractor, including name and tax reference number,

(ii) the estimated contract value,

(iii) the estimated contract duration, including the estimated start date and estimated end date of the contract,

(iv) the location or locations at which relevant operations under the contract are to take place, and

(v) whether or not a contract is a labour only contract,][1]

and

(b) a declaration stating that the principal is satisfied, if that is the case having regard to guidelines published by the Revenue Commissioners as to the distinction between contracts of employment and relevant contracts, that the named subcontractor is not performing the contract or any part of it as an employee of the principal.

[(1A) (a) Before providing the information and declaration referred to in *subsection (1)*, a principal shall be satisfied as to the identity of the subcontractor concerned.

(b) For the purposes of *paragraph (a)*, a principal shall require documentary evidence of identity from the subcontractor and shall make and retain a copy of the documentary evidence provided, or record and retain relevant details from the documentary evidence given.][2]

(2) Where a relevant contract was entered into prior to commencement of this section, a principal to whom *section 530A* applies shall provide the information and declaration referred to in *subsection (1)* if a payment is outstanding under that contract, or under that contract as amended, on such commencement.

(3) The information and declaration required under *subsection (1)* shall be provided by electronic means, and the relevant provisions of *Chapter 6* of *Part 38* shall apply.

[(4) The Revenue Commissioners shall make regulations for the purposes of this section and such regulations may—

(a) specify the manner by which principals shall communicate electronically with the Revenue Commissioners,

(b) in the case of a labour only contract, provide for the submission of additional information in relation to the contract,

(c) provide for the issuing of an acknowledgement by the Revenue Commissioners to a principal following notification by the principal of a contract under *subsection (1)* and for the manner by which such acknowledgement may issue,

(d) provide for notification to a subcontractor by the Revenue Commissioners of details of a contract, including changes to the terms of a contract, in respect of which a principal has notified the Revenue Commissioners under *subsection (1)* that the subcontractor is a party and for the manner by which such notification may issue,

(e) provide for notification to the Revenue Commissioners by a principal of changes to the terms of a contract which has been notified under *subsection (1)*,

(f) provide for a principal to notify a subcontractor where the Revenue Commissioners are unable to verify the identity of the subcontractor by reference to the name and tax reference number supplied to the Revenue Commissioners by the principal under *subsection (1)*, and

(g) provide for any other related matters.][3][4]

Amendments

[1] Substituted by FA12 s22(1)(g). Comes into operation on and from 31 March 2012.

[2] Inserted by FA12 s22(1)(h). Comes into operation on and from 31 March 2012.

[3] Substituted by FA12 s22(1)(i). Comes into operation on and from 31 March 2012.

[4] Inserted by FA11 s20(1)(k). With effect from 1 January 2012 per S.I. No. 660 of 2011.

Revenue Briefings

eBrief

eBrief No. 12/2011 – Changes to the operation of Relevant Contracts Tax (RCT)
eBrief No. 79/2011 – Commencement of the Modernised e-based scheme of Relevant Contracts Tax (RCT)
eBrief No. 58/2012 – RCT for Principal Contractors. Extension of transitional arrangement.
eBrief No. 65/2012 – Important Information for eRCT Customers
eBrief No. 26/2013 – RCT for Principal Contractors Transitional Arrangement

Cross References

From Section 530B

Section 530A Principal to whom relevant contracts tax applies.

To Section 530B

Section 530J Register of principals.

530C Notification of relevant payment by principal

[(1) Immediately before a principal makes a relevant payment to a subcontractor, the principal shall notify the Revenue Commissioners of his or her intention to make such a payment to the subcontractor and of the amount of that payment.

(2) The notification required under *subsection (1)* shall be given by electronic means and the relevant provisions of *Chapter 6* of *Part 38* shall apply.

[(3) The Revenue Commissioners shall make regulations for the purposes of this section and such regulations may—

(a) specify the manner by which principals shall communicate electronically with the Revenue Commissioners,

(b) provide for the details to be supplied by a principal in relation to a payment referred to in *subsection (1)*,

(c) specify the circumstances in which and the means by which a principal may cancel a notification given under *subsection (1)*,

(d) specify the circumstances in which notification under this section is deemed not to have been given,

(e) provide for notification to a subcontractor where a payment notification is cancelled, and

(f) provide for any other related matters.][1]][2]

Amendments

[1] Substituted by FA12 s22(1)(j). Comes into operation on and from 31 March 2012.

[2] Inserted by FA11 s20(1)(k). With effect from 1 January 2012 per S.I. No. 660 of 2011.

Revenue Briefings

eBrief

eBrief No. 12/2011 – Changes to the operation of Relevant Contracts Tax (RCT)

eBrief No. 79/2011 – Commencement of the Modernised e-based scheme of Relevant Contracts Tax (RCT)

eBrief No. 58/2012 – RCT for Principal Contractors. Extension of transitional arrangement

eBrief No. 65/2012 – Important Information for eRCT Customers

Cross References

To Section 530C

Section 530D Deduction authorisation.

Section 530K Return by principal.

Section 530M Late returns and amendments.

Section 530S Record keeping.

530D Deduction authorisation

[(1) Where a principal notifies the Revenue Commissioners in accordance with *section 530C*, the Revenue Commissioners shall issue a deduction authorisation to the principal in respect of the relevant payment to which the notification relates.

(2) A deduction authorisation issued under *subsection (1)* shall—

(a) specify, in accordance with *section 530E*, the rate of tax to be deducted from the payment, including, as appropriate, zero, and

(b) authorise the principal concerned to deduct a specified sum of tax or no tax from the relevant payment.

(3) At the end of each return period, the Revenue Commissioners shall issue a deduction summary to each registered principal in respect of that return period.

(4) The Revenue Commissioners shall issue deduction authorisations and deduction summaries by electronic means.

[(5) The Revenue Commissioners shall make regulations for the purposes of this section and such regulations may—

(a) specify the manner by which the Revenue Commissioners shall communicate electronically with a principal,

(b) provide for the circumstances in which a deduction authorisation shall be valid and for the period of validity of a deduction authorisation,

(c) specify the details to be contained in a deduction summary,

(d) specify the obligations on a principal to ensure that a deduction summary accurately reflects the details of all relevant payments made, and tax deducted, by a principal in a return period, and

(e) provide for any other related matters.][1]][2]

Amendments

[1] Substituted by FA12 s22(1)(k). Comes into operation on and from 31 March 2012.

[2] Inserted by FA11 s20(1)(k). With effect from 1 January 2012 per S.I. No. 660 of 2011.

Revenue Briefings

eBrief

eBrief No. 12/2011 – Changes to the operation of Relevant Contracts Tax (RCT)
eBrief No. 79/2011 – Commencement of the Modernised e-based scheme of Relevant Contracts Tax (RCT)

Cross References

From Section 530D

Section 530C Notification of relevant payment by principal.
Section 530E Rates of tax.

To Section 530D

Section 530 Interpretation (Chapter 2).
Section 530E Rates of tax.
Section 530F Obligation on principals to deduct tax.
Section 530K Return by principal.

530E Rates of tax

[(1) For the purpose of *section 530D(2)*, the rate of tax—

(a) shall be zero where the Revenue Commissioners have made a determination that the subcontractor is a person to whom *section 530G* applies,

(b) shall be the standard rate (within the meaning of *section 3*) in force at the time of payment where the Revenue Commissioners have made a determination that the subcontractor is a person to whom *section 530H* applies,

[(c) shall be 35 per cent where the Revenue Commissioners have made a determination that the subcontractor is a person to whom neither *section 530G* nor *section 530H* apply, and (*d*) shall, in the case of a partnership, be the highest rate that would apply to any of the individual partners following a determination by the Revenue Commissioners under *section 530I*.][1]

(2) Any reference to a determination in *subsection (1)* is to the most recent determination made by the Revenue Commissioners under *section 530I* or as determined on appeal in accordance with that section, in respect of the subcontractor concerned.][2]

Amendments

[1] Substituted by FA12 s22(1)(l). Comes into operation on and from 31 March 2012.

[2] Inserted by FA11 s20(1)(k). With effect from 1 January 2012 per S.I. No. 660 of 2011.

Revenue Briefings

eBrief

eBrief No. 79/2011 – Commencement of the Modernised e-based scheme of Relevant Contracts Tax (RCT)

eBrief No. 14/2012 – New RCT System – Freezing of subcontractors' rates for first three months in 2012

eBrief No. 58/2012 – RCT for Principal Contractors. Extension of transitional arrangement.

eBrief No. 65/2012 – Important Information for eRCT Customers

eBrief No. 17/2014 – eRCT Bulk Rate Review

Cross References

From Section 530E

Section 3 Interpretation of Income Tax Acts.
Section 530D Deduction authorisation.
Section 530G Zero rate subcontractor.
Section 530H Standard rate subcontractor.
Section 530I Determination of rates.

To Section 530E

Section 530D Deduction authorisation.
Section 530I Determination of rates.

530F Obligation on principals to deduct tax

[(1) A principal to whom a deduction authorisation is issued under *section 530D* shall deduct tax from the relevant payment concerned only in accordance with the terms of the deduction authorisation.

[(2) A principal to whom *section 530A* applies who makes a relevant payment to a subcontractor in circumstances other than those referred to in *subsection (1)* shall, without prejudice to *section 1078*, be liable to a penalty of—

(a) 35 per cent of the relevant payment, where the person to whom the relevant payment was made was a subcontractor who has not had a determination made by the Revenue Commissioners under *section 530I*,

(b) 20 per cent of the relevant payment, where the person to whom the relevant payment was made was a subcontractor who has had a determination made by the Revenue Commissioners under *section 530I* and where neither *section 530G* nor *section 530H* applies to the subcontractor concerned,

(c) 10 per cent of the relevant payment, where the person to whom the relevant payment was made was a subcontractor to whom *section 530H* applies, and

(d) 3 per cent of the relevant payment, where the person to whom the relevant payment was made was a subcontractor to whom *section 530G* applies.][1]

[(3) (a) Where *subsection (2)* applies, a principal shall submit an unreported payment notification to the Revenue Commissioners.

(b) The Revenue Commissioners shall make regulations for the purposes of this subsection and such regulations may—

(i) specify the manner by which principals shall submit an unreported payment notification to the Revenue Commissioners, and

(ii) provide for the details to be supplied to the Revenue Commissioners by a principal in relation to an unreported payment notification.][2]

[(4) Where, in making a relevant payment to a subcontractor, a principal deducts tax from the payment, the principal shall—

(a) provide the subcontractor with a copy of the deduction authorisation related to that payment, or

(b) arrange for the following details from the deduction authorisation to be given to the subcontractor by written or electronic means:

(i) the name and tax reference number of the principal,

(ii) the name and tax reference number of the subcontractor,

(iii) the gross amount of the payment, including the amount of tax deducted,

(iv) the amount of tax deducted,

(v) the rate at which tax was deducted,

(vi) the date of the payment, and

(vii) the unique reference number issued by the Revenue Commissioners on the deduction authorisation.][3]

(5) The amount of tax which a principal is liable to deduct under *subsection (1)* from a relevant payment shall be due and payable by the principal concerned to the Revenue Commissioners in respect of the return period in which the payment is made.

[...][4]

[(7) Where, due to a persistent technology systems failure, a principal is unable to give notification to the Revenue Commissioners under *section 530C(1)* and has no option but to make a relevant payment without complying with that provision, *subsection (2)* shall not apply to that payment if the principal—

(a) deducts tax from that payment at the rate last notified to the principal in respect of the subcontractor concerned, or if there was no such notification, deducts tax at a rate of 35 per cent from that payment,

(b) immediately upon rectification of the technology systems failure notifies the Revenue Commissioners, in accordance with this Chapter or regulations made under this Chapter, that the payment has been made,

(c) provides all details in relation to the payment that the Revenue Commissioners may require, and

(d) pays the tax deducted in accordance with *paragraph (a)* to the Revenue Commissioners on or before the due date for the making of a return for the period within which the principal notifies the Revenue Commissioners under *paragraph (b)*.

(8) Where a principal complies with the requirements of *subsection (7)*—

(a) the principal shall be deemed to have deducted tax from a relevant payment in accordance with the terms of a valid deduction authorisation, and

(b) for the purposes of *section 530K*, the payment shall be deemed to have been made in the return period in which the principal notifies the Revenue Commissioners under *subsection (7)(b)*.

(9) A principal shall, on request, provide the Revenue Commissioners with information in relation to the circumstances and details of a persistent technology systems failure under *subsection (7)*][5].

Amendments

[1] Substituted by FA14 s17(b)(i). Comes into operation on 1 January 2015.

[2] Substituted by FA14 s17(b)(ii). Comes into operation on 1 January 2015.

[3] Substituted by FA12 s22(1)(p). Comes into operation on and from 31 March 2012.

[4] Deleted by FA14 s17(b)(iii). Comes into operation on 1 January 2015.

[5] Inserted by FA12 s22(1)(q). Comes into operation on and from 31 March 2012.

Revenue Briefings

eBrief

eBrief No. 12/2011 – Changes to the operation of Relevant Contracts Tax (RCT)
eBrief No. 79/2011 – Commencement of the Modernised e-based scheme of Relevant Contracts Tax (RCT)
eBrief No. 39/2012 – Important information for subcontractors on the electronic Relevant Contracts Tax (RCT) system

Cross References

From Section 530F

Section 530A Principal to whom relevant contracts tax applies.
Section 530D Deduction authorisation.
Section 530I Determination of rates.
Section 530K Return by principal.
Section 1078 Revenue offences.

To Section 530F

Section 530K Return by principal.
Section 530M Late returns and amendments.
Section 530N Assessment by Revenue officer.
Section 530O Computation of subcontractor's profit.
Section 530P Credit for deducted tax.
Section 530S Record keeping.
Section 530U Civil penalties.

530G Zero rate subcontractor

[(1) Subject to *subsections (2)* and *(3)*, this section applies to a person in relation to whom the Revenue Commissioners are satisfied that the person—

(a) is or is about to become a subcontractor engaged in the business of carrying out relevant operations,

(b) carries on or will carry on business from a fixed place established in a permanent building and has or will have such equipment, stock and other facilities as in the opinion of the Revenue Commissioners are required for the purposes of the business,

(c) properly and accurately keeps and will keep any business records to which *section 886(2)* refers and any other records normally kept in connection with such a business,

(d) has throughout the previous 3 years complied with all the obligations imposed by the Tax Acts, the Capital Gains Tax Acts and the Value-Added Tax Acts, in relation to—

(i) the payment or remittance of taxes, interest and penalties,

(ii) the delivery of returns, and

(iii) the supply, on request, of accounts or other information to a Revenue officer,

and

(e) in the case of a person who was resident outside the State at some time during the previous 3 years, has throughout that period complied with all the obligations comparable to those mentioned in *paragraphs (c)* and *(d)* imposed by the laws of the country in which that person was resident at any time during that period.

(2) This section does not apply to a person—

[(a) engaged in the business of carrying out relevant contracts in partnership unless the partnership business itself has complied with the obligations referred to in *subsection (1)* and the Revenue Commissioners are satisfied that it will continue to comply with those obligations,][1]

(b) which is a company, unless each director of the company and any person who is either the beneficial owner of, or able, directly or indirectly, to control more than 15 per cent of the ordinary share capital of the company, are persons to which *paragraphs (c)* and *(d)* of *subsection (1)* refer,

(c) who is or was a proprietary director or proprietary employee of a company engaged in the business of carrying out relevant contracts unless the company is a person to whom *paragraphs (c)* and *(d)* of *subsection (1)* refer,

(d) who, for good reason, the Revenue Commissioners consider unlikely to comply in the future with the obligations referred to in *paragraph (c)*or*(d)* of *subsection (1)*, or

(e) if relevant operations (being construction operations, forestry operations or meat processing operations, as the case may be) similar to those being carried out or to be carried out by that person were previously, or are being, carried out by another person (in this subsection referred to as the "*second-mentioned person*"), and the second-mentioned person—

(i) is a company connected (within the meaning of *section 10* as it applies for the purposes of the Tax Acts) with the first-mentioned person or would have been such a company but for the fact that the company has been wound up or dissolved without being wound up,

(ii) is a company and the first-mentioned person is a partner in a partnership in which—

(I) a partner is or was able, or

(II) where more than one partner is a share-holder, those partners together are or were able,

directly or indirectly, whether with or without a connected person or connected persons (within the meaning of *section 10* as it applies for the purposes of the Tax Acts), to control more than 15 per cent of the ordinary share capital of the company, or

(iii) is a partnership and the first-mentioned person is a company in which—

(I) a partner is or was able, or

(II) where more than one partner is a share-holder, those partners together are or were able,

directly or indirectly, whether with or without a connected person or connected persons (within the meaning of *section 10* as it applies for the purposes of the Tax Acts), to control more than 15 per cent of the ordinary share capital of the company,

but this paragraph does not apply if the second-mentioned person concerned is a person to whom *paragraphs (c)* and *(d)* of *subsection (1)* refer.

(3) This section also applies to a person who satisfies the Revenue Commissioners that, in all the circumstances, the matter or matters referred to in *subsection (1)* or *(2)*, which would otherwise cause such person not to be a person to whom this section applies, ought to be disregarded for the purposes of this section.][2]

Amendments

[1] Substituted by FA12 s22(1)(r). Comes into operation on and from 31 March 2012.

[2] Inserted by FA11 s20(1)(k). With effect from 1 January 2012 as per S.I. No. 660 of 2011.

Revenue Briefings

eBrief

eBrief No. 79/2011 – Commencement of the Modernised e-based scheme of Relevant Contracts Tax (RCT)
eBrief No. 39/2012 – Important information for subcontractors on the electronic Relevant Contracts Tax (RCT) system
eBrief No. 78/2014 – eRCT Bulk Rate Review

Cross References

From Section 530G

Section 10 Connected persons.
Section 886 Obligation to keep certain records.

To Section 530G

Section 530E Rates of tax.
Section 530I Determination of rates.
Section 980 Deduction from consideration on disposal of certain assets.

530H Standard rate subcontractor

[(1) Subject to *subsection (2)*, this section applies to a person in relation to whom the Revenue Commissioners are satisfied that the person—

(a) is or is about to become a subcontractor engaged in the business of carrying out relevant operations,

(b) carries on or will carry on business from a fixed place established in a permanent building and has or will have such equipment, stock and other facilities as in the opinion of the Revenue Commissioners are required for the purposes of the business,

(c) properly and accurately keeps and will keep any business records to which *section 886(2)* refers and any other records normally kept in connection with such a business,

(d) has throughout the previous 3 years complied substantially with the obligations imposed by the Tax Acts, the Capital Gains Tax Acts and the Value-Added Tax Acts,

(e) in the case of a person who was resident outside the State at some time during the previous 3 years, has throughout that period complied with the obligations comparable to those mentioned in *paragraph (c)* and has throughout that period complied substantially with the obligations comparable to those mentioned in *paragraph (d)* imposed by the laws of the country in which that person was resident at any time during that period,

(f) has provided to the Revenue Commissioners whatever information is required by them to register the person for tax purposes, and

(g) is not a person to whom *section 530G* applies.

(2) For the purposes of *subsection (1)(d)*, the Revenue Commissioners may make regulations identifying matters to be taken into account by them, including—

(a) the payment or remittance of taxes, interest and penalties,

(b) the delivery of returns,

(c) the supply, on request, of accounts or other information to a Revenue officer, and

(d) the extent to which any non-compliance is being addressed.

(3) This section does not apply to—

[(a) a person engaged in the business of carrying out relevant contracts in partnership unless the partnership business itself has complied with the obligations referred to in *subsection (1)* and the Revenue Commissioners are satisfied that it will continue to comply with those obligations, or][1]

(b) a person if the Revenue Commissioners form an opinion that deductions from relevant payments at the standard rate of tax for the year of assessment will be insufficient to fully satisfy the income tax liability of the person for that year.][2]

[(4) This section also applies to a person who satisfies the Revenue Commissioners that, in all the circumstances, the matter or matters referred to in *subsection (1), (2)* or *(3)*, which would otherwise cause such person not to be a person to whom this section applies, ought to be disregarded for the purposes of this section.][3]

Amendments

[1] Substituted by FA12 s22(1)(s). Comes into operation on and from 31 March 2012.

[2] Inserted by FA11 s20(1)(k). With effect from 1 January 2012 per S.I. No. 660 of 2011.

[3] Inserted by FA12 s22(1)(t). Comes into operation on and from 31 March 2012.

Revenue Briefings

eBrief

eBrief No. 79/2011 – Commencement of the Modernised e-based scheme of Relevant Contracts Tax (RCT)

eBrief No. 39/2012 – Important information for subcontractors on the electronic Relevant Contracts Tax (RCT) system

eBrief No. 78/2014 – eRCT Bulk Rate Review

Cross References

From Section 530H

Section 30G

Section 886 Obligation to keep certain records.

To Section 530H

Section 530E Rates of tax.

Section 530I Determination of rates.

530I Determination of rates

[(1) For the purpose of establishing the rate of tax referred to in *section 530E(1)*, the Revenue Commissioners shall, from time to time, determine whether a subcontractor is a person to whom *section 530G* applies, a person to whom *section 530H* applies or a person to whom neither *section 530G* nor *530H* applies.

[(2) Following a determination under *subsection (1)*, the Revenue Commissioners shall notify the subcontractor of the determination and the rate of tax resulting from such determination.][1]

(3) (a) On receipt of a notification under *subsection (2)*, a subcontractor who is aggrieved by the determination of the Revenue Commissioners may, by notice in writing given to the Revenue Commissioners within 30 days of the date of the determination, appeal to the Appeal Commissioners.

(b) The Appeal Commissioners shall hear and determine an appeal made to them under this subsection as if it were an appeal against an assessment to income tax and the provisions of the Income Tax Acts relating to such appeals and to the rehearing of an appeal and to the statement of a case for the opinion of the High Court on a point of law shall apply accordingly with any necessary modifications.

(c) Pending the determination of an appeal under this section, the Revenue Commissioners may issue a deduction authorisation under this Chapter and—

(i) nothing in this subsection shall prejudice the validity of any such deduction authorisation issued, and

(ii) the principal concerned shall comply with the terms of any such deduction authorisation.][2]

[(4) The Revenue Commissioners shall not be obliged to make a determination under *subsection (1)*—

(a) until after a period of 30 days has elapsed following the previous determination made by the Revenue Commissioners in respect of a subcontractor,

(b) if an appeal by a subcontractor is awaiting determination under *subsection (3)*, or

(c) until a period of 30 days has elapsed following determination of an appeal under *subsection (3)*.][3]

Amendments

[1] Substituted by FA12 s22(1)(u). Comes into operation on and from 31 March 2012.

[2] Inserted by FA11 s20(1)(k). With effect from 1 January 2012 as per S.I. No. 660 of 2011.

[3] Inserted by FA12 s22(1)(v). Comes into operation on and from 31 March 2012.

Revenue Briefings

eBrief

eBrief No. 79/2011 – Commencement of the Modernised e-based scheme of Relevant Contracts Tax (RCT)
eBrief No. 78/2014 – eRCT Bulk Rate Review

Cross References

From Section 530I

Section 530E Rates of tax.
Section 530G Zero rate subcontractor.
Section 530H Standard rate subcontractor.

To Section 530I

Section 530E Rates of tax.
Section 530F Obligation on principals to deduct tax.
Section 980 Deduction from consideration on disposal of certain assets.

530J Register of principals

[(1) The Revenue Commissioners shall keep and maintain a register of principals for the purposes of this Chapter.

(2) Every principal to whom *section 530B* applies shall register as a principal with the Revenue Commissioners, unless he or she stands registered under *section 531* immediately before the commencement of this section.

[(3) The Revenue Commissioners shall make regulations for the purposes of this section and such regulations may provide for—

(a) keeping and maintaining the register,

(b) registration and time for registration,

(c) the particulars to be submitted to the Revenue Commissioners for the purposes of registering a person as a principal,

(d) notification of change in relevant details,

(e) notification of cessation as a principal,

(f) cancellation of registration,

(g) the use of electronic means in connection with the registration process, and

(h) any other related matters.][1]

Amendments

[1] Substituted by FA12 s22(1)(w). Comes into operation on and from 31 March 2012.

Revenue Briefings

eBrief

eBrief No. 79/2011 – Commencement of the Modernised e-based scheme of Relevant Contracts Tax (RCT)

Cross References

From Section 530J

Section 530B Notification of contract by principal.
Section 531 Payments to subcontractors in certain industries.

530K Return by principal

[(1) On or before the due date relating to a return period, a principal shall make a return to the Collector-General of all relevant payments made by him or her during that return period and shall specify on that return the amount of his or her tax liability under this Chapter.

[(2) (a) For the purposes of *subsection (1)*, where the Revenue Commissioners issue, under *section 530D(3)*, a deduction summary to a principal for a return period, the details on that summary shall, for the purposes of the Tax Acts, be deemed to be a return made by the principal to the Collector-General in respect of the return period and the amount of tax specified on that summary shall be deemed to be the amount specified by the principal of his or her tax liability under this Chapter in respect of that return period.

(b) *Paragraph (a)* does not apply where a principal is required to amend the details on a deduction summary in accordance with regulations made under this section and to submit a return under *subsection (1)* in accordance with those amended details, and so submits the required return.][1]

(3) Without prejudice to *section 530F*, the amount of tax specified in a return made or deemed to have been made under this section shall be due and payable by the principal concerned to the Revenue Commissioners.

(4) A return required under this section, including a return to which *section 530M* applies, shall be made by electronic means and the relevant provisions of Chapter 6 of Part 38 shall apply.

[(5) The Revenue Commissioners shall make regulations for the purposes of this section and such regulations may provide for—

(a) the manner by which principals shall communicate electronically with the Revenue Commissioners,

(b) the particulars to be included in the return required under this section,

(c) the obligations on, and the actions to be taken by, a principal to ensure that any relevant payment made by a principal relating to a return period and the tax liability related to that payment are accurately reflected on the return required under this section,

(d) notification to a subcontractor in relation to actions taken by a principal as referred to in *paragraph (c)*, and

(e) any other related matters.][2]][3]

Amendments

[1] Substituted by FA12 s22(1)(x). Comes into operation on and from 31 March 2012.

[2] Substituted by FA12 s22(1)(y). Comes into operation on and from 31 March 2012.

[3] Inserted by FA11 s20(1)(k). With effect from 1 January 2012 as per S.I. No. 660 of 2011.

Revenue Briefings

eBrief

eBrief No. 79/2011 – Commencement of the Modernised e-based scheme of Relevant Contracts Tax (RCT)

Cross References

From Section 530K

Section 530C Notification of relevant payment by principal.
Section 530D Deduction authorisation.
Section 530F Obligation on principals to deduct tax.
Section 530M Late returns and amendments.

To Section 530K

Section 530F Obligation on principals to deduct tax.
Section 530M Late returns and amendments.
Section 530N Assessment by Revenue officer.

530L Payment of tax by principal

[(1) Tax due and payable in accordance with this Chapter shall be paid to the Collector-General not later than the due date relating to the return period concerned.

(2) Where tax is due and payable for a period covering more than one return period by virtue of *section 530N*, the due date relating to that tax shall be the due date relating to the earliest return period covered by the relevant assessment or return.

(3) A surcharge arising by virtue of *section 530M* shall be due and payable to the Revenue Commissioners and shall be payable at the same time as the amount of tax to which it relates is payable.][1]

Amendments

[1] Inserted by FA11 s20(1)(k). With effect from 1 January 2012 as per S.I. No. 660 of 2011.

Revenue Briefings

eBrief

eBrief No. 79/2011 – Commencement of the Modernised e-based scheme of Relevant Contracts Tax (RCT)

Cross References

From Section 530L

Section 530M Late returns and amendments.
Section 530N Assessment by Revenue officer.

530M Late returns and amendments

[[(1) Notwithstanding the requirements of *section 530K(1)*, and without prejudice to any penalty to which the principal may be liable, a principal may, as appropriate—

(a) make a return required under *section 530K(1)* after the due date relating to the relevant return period, or

(b) amend a return after the making of the return or the deemed making of a return under *section 530K(2)* but—

(i) no amendment may be made in relation to any payment which has been the subject of a deduction authorisation under *section 530D*, and

(ii) no amendment may be made to a return where a Revenue officer has commenced an audit or other investigation in relation to the tax affairs of the principal to whom the return relates for the chargeable periodinwhich the return period falls.][1]

(2) Without prejudice to *section 530F*, where a principal makes or amends a return in accordance with *subsection (1)*, then—

(a) the amount of tax specified on that return shall be due and payable by that principal to the Revenue Commissioners, and

(b) that principal shall be subject to a surcharge of €100.

(3) The Revenue Commissioners shall serve notice on the principal of the total amount of tax and surcharge due and payable under this section for the return period or periods concerned.

(4) Where enforcement action for the recovery of tax specified in a return made or deemed made under *section 530K* has been taken, this section shall not apply until that action has been completed, unless the Revenue Commissioners otherwise direct.

[(5) The Revenue Commissioners shall make regulations for the purposes of this section and such regulations may provide for—

(a) the manner by which principals shall communicate electronically with the Revenue Commissioners,

(b) the particulars to be included in a return under this section,

(c) the actions to be taken by a principal to ensure that any relevant payment made by a principal relating to a return period and the tax liability related to that payment are accurately reflected on a return under this section,

(d) the format of a return which can be made in a case where a principal is appealing an assessment under *section 530N*, and

(e) any other related matters.][2]][3]

Amendments

[1] Substituted by FA12 s22(1)(z). Comes into operation on and from 31 March 2012.

[2] Substituted by FA12 s22(1)(aa). Comes into operation on and from 31 March 2012.

[3] Inserted by FA11 s20(1)(k). With effect from 1 January 2012 as per S.I. No. 660 of 2011.

Revenue Briefings

eBrief

eBrief No. 12/2011 – Changes to the operation of Relevant Contracts Tax (RCT)

eBrief No. 79/2011 – Commencement of the Modernised e-based scheme of Relevant Contracts Tax (RCT)

Cross References

From Section 530M

Section 530C Notification of relevant payment by principal.

Section 530F Obligation on principals to deduct tax.

Section 530K Return by principal.

Section 530N Assessment by Revenue officer.

To Section 530M

Section 530K Return by principal.

Section 530L Payment of tax by principal.

Section 530N Assessment by Revenue officer.

530N Assessment by Revenue officer

[(1) Where, in respect of a return period, a Revenue officer has reason to believe that a principal has not made a return under *section 530K* or *530M* or that the amount of tax due and payable by a principal under this Chapter for a return period was greater than the amount of tax, if any, specified in a return made or deemed to have been made by that principal for that return period, then, without prejudice to any other action which may be taken, the officer may make an assessment in one sum of the total amount of tax which in his or her opinion is due and payable by the principal in respect of that return period.

(2) Without prejudice to *section 530F*, but subject to *subsection (5)*, the amount of tax specified in an assessment under *subsection (1)* shall be due and payable to the Revenue Commissioners from the person so assessed.

(3) (a) A Revenue officer may, where he or she considers it necessary, amend an assessment of tax made under *subsection (1)*.

(b) Without prejudice to anything in this Chapter, the provisions of [*Chapter 5* of *Part 41A* and *section 1048*][1] (including those relating to time limits) shall, with any necessary modifications, apply to the making and amending of an assessment under this section.

(4) (a) Where, in accordance with this section, the Revenue officer makes or amends an assessment, he or she shall give notice to the person assessed showing the total amount of tax due and payable in accordance with the assessment.

(b) Where the person assessed is a registered principal, the Revenue officer shall issue the notice of assessment or of amended assessment by electronic means.

(5) (a) Subject to *paragraph (b)*, where notice is given to a person under *subsection (4)*, the person may, if he or she claims that the total amount of tax assessed is excessive, on giving notice in writing to the Revenue officer within the period of 30 days from the date of the notice, appeal to the Appeal Commissioners.

(b) A person to whom notice is given under *subsection (4)*, shall not be entitled to appeal to the Appeal Commissioners—

(i) in the case of a person who has made a return (including a deemed return) under *section 530K* or a return under *section 530M*, until that person has paid the tax and any surcharge due and payable on the basis of his or her return together with the related interest due under *section 530Q*, and

(ii) in any other case, until the person has made a return under *section 530M* for the return period concerned and has paid the tax and surcharge due and payable on the basis of that return together with the related interest due under *section 530Q*.

(c) The provisions of the Tax Acts relating to appeals shall, with any necessary modifications, apply to appeals against assessments made under this section as if those appeals were appeals against an assessment to income tax.

(d) On the determination of an appeal, the tax contained in an assessment or in an amended assessment shall, subject to *section 530F*, be due and payable by the person assessed to the Revenue Commissioners.

(6) A Revenue officer may make an assessment for a return period or for any number of consecutive return periods and an assessment may be issued before the end of the period to which it relates.

(7) (a) Subject to *paragraph (b)*, where a Revenue officer makes an assessment for a number of consecutive return periods, the person to whom notice is given shall not be entitled to appeal to the Appeal Commissioners until such a time as the person—

(i) makes the return required in respect of each return period covered by the assessment, or

(ii) elects to make one return covering the full period assessed and makes that return,

and *subsection (5)* shall apply with any necessary modifications.

(b) Where *paragraph (a)*(ii) applies, a hearing of the Appeal Commissioners shall be in respect of the full period assessed.

(8) The Revenue Commissioners shall make regulations for the purposes of this section and such regulations may provide for—

(a) the issuing of notices of assessment or amended assessment including the means by which such notices shall be issued,

(b) the transmission of information in connection with appeals,

(c) the format and transmission of returns in connection with appeals,

(d) the procedures to apply to give effect to *subsection (7)*, and

(e) any other related matters.][2]

Amendments

[1] Substituted by FA12 sched4(part 2)(g).

[2] Inserted by FA11 s20(1)(k). With effect from 1 January 2012 as per S.I. No. 660 of 2011.

Revenue Briefings

eBrief

eBrief No. 12/2011 – Changes to the operation of Relevant Contracts Tax (RCT)

eBrief No. 79/2011 – Commencement of the Modernised e-based scheme of Relevant Contracts Tax (RCT)

Cross References

From Section 530N

Section 530F Obligation on principals to deduct tax.

Section 530K Return by principal.

Section 530M Late returns and amendments.

Section 530Q Interest.

Section 955 Amendment of and time limit for assessments.

Section 956 Inspector's right to make enquiries and amend assessments.

Section 1048 Assessment of executors and administrators.

To Section 530N

Section 530L Payment of tax by principal.

Section 530M Late returns and amendments.

530O Computation of subcontractor's profit

[In computing, for the purposes of Schedule D, the profits or gains arising or accruing to a subcontractor who receives a payment from which tax has been deducted in accordance with *section 530F*, the payment shall be treated as being of an amount equal to the aggregate of the net amount received after deduction of the tax and the amount of the tax deducted.][1]

Amendments

[1] Inserted by FA11 s20(1)(k). With effect from 1 January 2012 as per S.I. No. 660 of 2011.

Revenue Briefings

eBrief

eBrief No. 79/2011 – Commencement of the Modernised e-based scheme of Relevant Contracts Tax (RCT)

Cross References

From Section 530O

Section 530F Obligation on principals to deduct tax.

530P Treatment of deducted tax

[(1) Where a principal deducts tax from a payment to a subcontractor in accordance with *section 530F*, such tax shall be treated as a payment on account by the subcontractor—

(a) of income tax for that tax year, where the tax was deducted in the basis period for a tax year, or

(b) of corporation tax for that accounting period, where the tax was deducted in an accounting period of a company.

(2) For the purposes of this Chapter, tax treated in accordance with *subsection (1)* shall be known as deducted tax.

(3) (a) Deducted tax shall be available for offset by the Revenue Commissioners against other tax liabilities of a subcontractor and in this subsection 'tax' has the same meaning as in *section 960A*.

(b) The Revenue Commissioners shall notify a subcontractor of the amount of deducted tax, if any, which is offset against other tax liabilities of the subcontractor.

(4) Where an assessment to income tax or, as the case may be, corporation tax has been made in relation to a subcontractor for a chargeable period, then deducted tax related to that period less any amount which is either—

(a) required to meet the income tax or, as the case may be, corporation tax liability of the subcontractor, or

(b) offset against other tax liabilities of the subcontractor under *subsection (3)*,

may, subject to *section 865*, be repaid to the subcontractor.

(5) No repayment of deducted tax shall be made, except in accordance with *subsection (4)*.

(6) No amount of deducted tax shall be treated as a payment on account, set off or refunded more than once and no amount of deducted tax set off under *subsection (3)* or refunded under *subsection (4)* shall be treated as a payment on account.][1]

Amendments

[1] Substituted by FA12 s22(1)(ab). Comes into operation on and from 31 March 2012.

530Q Interest

[Where an amount of tax or surcharge which a person is liable to pay under this Chapter to the Collector-General is not paid by the due date concerned, simple interest on the amount outstanding shall be paid by the person to the Collector-General and shall be calculated from the due date concerned until payment, for any day or part of a day during which the amount remains unpaid, at the rate of 0.0274 per cent.][1]

Amendments

[1] Inserted by FA11 s20(1)(k). With effect from 1 January 2012 as per S.I. No. 660 of 2011.

Revenue Briefings

eBrief

eBrief No. 79/2011 – Commencement of the Modernised e-based scheme of Relevant Contracts Tax (RCT)

Cross References

To Section 530Q

Section 530N Assessment by Revenue officer.
Section 1089 Status of interest on certain unpaid taxes and duties.

530R Partnerships

[[(1) As respects relevant contracts, where relevant operations are performed by a gang or group of persons (including persons in partnership), notwithstanding that any payment or part of a payment in respect of such relevant operations is made by the principal to one or more of the gang or group or to some other person, then, for the purposes of *section 530P*, such payment or part of a payment shall be deemed to have been made by the principal to the individual members of that gang or group in the proportions in which the payment or any amount in respect of the payment is to be divided amongst them [, and the provisions of *section 530P* shall, with any necessary modifications, apply.][1]

[(2) Except where the principal concerned makes a separate payment to each member of the gang or group, a person authorised by the gang or group, or in the case of a partnership, the precedent partner, shall, in respect of tax deducted from relevant payments to the gang or group, give to the Revenue Commissioners—

(a) the name, address and tax reference number of every person in the gang or group, and

(b) details of the proportion of the tax deducted to which each person, named by virtue of this provision, is entitled.][2]

(3) The Revenue Commissioners shall make regulations for the purposes of this section and such regulations may provide for the manner in which the information referred to in *subsection (2)* is to be given and the steps to be taken by the Revenue Commissioners on receipt of such information.

(4) Without prejudice to the duties and obligations of partners in a partnership, in a case where the principal is a partnership, all things required to be done by the principal under this Chapter shall be done by the precedent partner within the meaning of Part 43.][3]

Amendments

[1] Inserted by FA12 s22(1)(ac). Comes into operation on and from 31 March 2012.

[2] Substituted by FA12 s22(1)(ad). Comes into operation on and from 31 March 2012.

[3] Inserted by FA11 s20(1)(k). With effect from 1 January 2012 as per S.I. No. 660 of 2011.

Revenue Briefings

eBrief

eBrief No. 79/2011 – Commencement of the Modernised e-based scheme of Relevant Contracts Tax (RCT)

Cross References

From Section 530R

Section 530P Credit for deducted tax.

530S Record keeping

[[(1) Before giving a notification to the Revenue Commissioners under *section 530C*, a principal shall obtain from the subcontractor concerned a statement setting out appropriate details of the work giving rise to the payment, and the cost of the work, and such statement shall bear the subcontractor's name, business address and tax reference number.][1]

(2) Where a relevant contract is being performed by a gang or group of persons (including persons in partnership), the invoice required under *subsection (1)* shall bear the name, business address and tax reference number of the gang or group and the names of the individual members of the gang or group.

(3) Every subcontractor shall furnish to a principal, on request, all such information or particulars as are required by the principal to enable the principal to comply with this Chapter.

(4) (a) Without prejudice to other provisions of the Tax Acts, each subcontractor shall keep and maintain a record of all relevant payments received by him or her and the record shall state, in relation to each such payment, the date of the payment, the amount of the payment, the amount of tax, if any, deducted from the payment by the principal and the name of the person from whom the payment was received.

[(b) Each subcontractor shall keep and maintain—

(i) a copy of each deduction authorisation supplied by a principal under *section 530F(4)(a)*, or

(ii) a copy of any details given under *section 530F(4)(b)*.][2]

(5) Without prejudice to other provisions of the Tax Acts, the obligations contained in *subsections (3)* and *(4)* of *section 886* to keep and retain records and linking documents apply to all records, documents or other data created or maintained manually or by any electronic means for the purposes of this Chapter.

(6) The Revenue Commissioners may make Regulations for the purposes of this section and such Regulations may provide for—

(a) the creation, keeping and retention of records by principals by electronic or other means, and

(b) the creation, keeping and retention of records by subcontractors by electronic or other means.][3]

Amendments

[1] Substituted by FA12 s22(1)(ae). Comes into operation on and from 31 March 2012.

[2] Substituted by FA12 s22(1)(af). Comes into operation on and from 31 March 2012.

[3] Inserted by FA11 s20(1)(k). With effect from 1 January 2012 as per S.I. No. 660 of 2011.

Revenue Briefings

eBrief

eBrief No. 79/2011 – Commencement of the Modernised e-based scheme of Relevant Contracts Tax (RCT)

Cross References

From Section 530S

Section 530C Notification of relevant payment by principal.
Section 530F Obligation on principals to deduct tax.
Section 886 Obligation to keep certain records.

530T Inspection of records

[Without prejudice to other provisions of the Tax Acts, any person, or any employee of a person, who has made or received a relevant payment, shall produce to a Revenue officer for inspection all documents and records relating to the relevant payment as are in such person's power, possession or procurement which have been requested by the Revenue officer.][1]

Amendments

[1] Inserted by FA11 s20(1)(k). With effect from 1 January 2012 as per S.I. No. 660 of 2011.

Revenue Briefings

eBrief

eBrief No. 79/2011 – Commencement of the Modernised e-based scheme of Relevant Contracts Tax (RCT)

530U Civil penalties

[(1) In proceedings for the recovery of a penalty under *section 530F* or the recovery of a penalty under *section 1052*, *1054* or *1077E* in relation to matters arising under this Chapter—

(a) a certificate signed by a Revenue officer which certifies that he or she has inspected the relevant records of the Revenue Commissioners and that it appears from them that a deduction authorisation, deduction summary or other notice, statement or described document, was duly given to a stated person by stated means, including electronic means, on a stated day shall be evidence until the contrary is proved that that person received that deduction authorisation, deduction summary or other notice, statement or described document in the ordinary course,

(b) a certificate signed by a Revenue officer which certifies that he or she has inspected the relevant records of the Revenue Commissioners and that it appears from them that on a stated day or within a stated period, a stated person was a registered principal (within the meaning of *section 530*) shall be evidence until the contrary is proved that on a stated day or within a stated period, a stated person was a registered principal (within the meaning of *section 530*), and

(c) a certificate certifying as provided for in *paragraph* (*a*) or (*b*)of this subsection and purporting to be signed by a Revenue officer may be tendered in evidence without proof and shall be deemed until the contrary is proved to have been signed by such officer.

(2) Chapter 3A of Part 47 applies, with any necessary modifications, to a penalty arising under *section 530F*.][1]

Amendments

[1] Inserted by FA11 s20(1)(k). With effect from 1 January 2012 as per S.I. No. 660 of 2011.

Revenue Briefings

eBrief

eBrief No. 79/2011 – Commencement of the Modernised e-based scheme of Relevant Contracts Tax (RCT)

Cross References

From Section 530U

Section 530 Interpretation (Chapter 2).

Section 530F Obligation on principals to deduct tax.

Section 1052 Penalties for failure to make certain returns, etc.

Section 1054 Penalties in the case of a secretary of a body of persons.

Section 1077E Penalty for deliberately or carelessly making incorrect returns, etc.

To Section 530U

Section 1078 Revenue offences.

530V Miscellaneous

[[(1) Regulations made under this Chapter may contain such incidental, supplemental or consequential provisions as appear to the Revenue Commissioners to be necessary or expedient—

(a) to enable persons to fulfil their obligations under this Chapter or under regulations made under this Chapter, or

(b) to give effect to the proper implementation and efficient operation of the provisions of this Chapter or regulations made under this Chapter.

(1A) Regulations made under this Chapter shall be laid before Dáil Éireann as soon as may be after they are made and, if a resolution annulling those regulations is passed by Dáil Éireann within the next 21 days on which Dáil Éireann has sat after the regulations are laid before it, the regulations shall be annulled accordingly, but without prejudice to the validity of anything previously done under them.

(1B) (a) Anything required to be done by a principal under this Chapter or under regulations made under this Chapter may be done by another person acting under the authority of the principal.

(b) Where anything is done by such other person under the authority of the principal, this Chapter shall apply as if it had been done by the principal.

(c) Anything purporting to have been done by or on behalf of a principal shall for the purposes of this Chapter be deemed to have been done by the principal or by the principal's authority, as the case may be, unless the contrary is proved.][1]

(2) On the death of a principal, anything which the principal would have been liable to do under this Chapter shall be done by the personal representative of the principal.

[(3) Anything to be done by or under this Chapter by the Revenue Commissioners, other than the making of regulations, may be done by any Revenue officer or may, if appropriate, be done through such electronic systems as the Revenue Commissioners may put in place for the time being for any such purpose.][2]

(4) (a) Notwithstanding the provisions of any other enactment, the provisions of this Chapter shall, subject to *paragraphs* (*b*) and (*c*) apply to a relevant payment made to a liquidator or a receiver.

(b) Where tax is deducted under this Chapter from a relevant payment made to a liquidator or receiver in respect of a relevant contract which is entered into by that liquidator or receiver after his or her appointment as such, the tax so deducted shall be treated as a payment on account of tax for the chargeable period concerned after the appointment of the liquidator or receiver.

(c) Where tax is deducted under this Chapter from a relevant payment made to a liquidator or receiver in respect of a relevant contract which was entered into prior to his or her appointment as such, the tax so deducted shall be treated as a payment on account of tax for the chargeable period prior to the appointment of the liquidator or receiver.][3]

Amendments

[1] Substituted by FA12 s22(1)(ag). Comes into operation on and from 31 March 2012.

[2] Substituted by FA12 s22(1)(ah). Comes into operation on and from 31 March 2012.

[3] Inserted by FA11 s20(1)(k). With effect from 1 January 2012 as per S.I. No. 660 of 2012.

Revenue Briefings

eBrief

eBrief No. 79/2011 – Commencement of the Modernised e-based scheme of Relevant Contracts Tax (RCT)

531 Payments to subcontractors in certain industries

[FA70 s17(2) to (12) and (14) to (17); FA76 s21; FA78 s46; FA81 s7; FA90 s131; FA92 s28(b) to (h); FA95 s18(1)(b) and (c); FA96 s41(b), (c) and (d); FA97 s13(1)(b) and (c)]

(1) Subject to this section, where in the performance of a relevant contract in the case of which the principal is—

(a) a person who, in respect of the whole or any part of the relevant operations to which the contract relates, is the contractor under another relevant contract,

(b) a person—

(i) carrying on a business which includes the erection of buildings or[the development of land (within the meaning of *section 639(1)*) or][1] the manufacture, treatment or extraction of materials for use, whether used or not, in construction operations,

[(ii) carrying on a business of meat processing operations in an establishment approved and inspected in accordance with the European Communities (Fresh Meat) Regulations, 1997 (S.I. No. 434 of 1997) or, as the case may be, the European Communities (Fresh Poultry-meat) Regulations, 1996 (S.I. No. 3 of 1996), or][2]

(iii) carrying on a business which includes the processing (including cutting and preserving) of wood from thinned or felled trees in sawmills or other like premises or the supply of thinned or felled trees for such processing,

(c) a person connected with a company carrying on a business mentioned in *paragraph (b)*,

(d) a local authority, a public utility society (within the meaning of section 2 of the Housing Act, 1966) or a body referred to in subparagraph (i) or (ii) of section 12(2)(a) or section 19 or 45 of that Act,

(e) a Minister of the Government,

(f) any board established by or under statute[or any board or body established by or under royal charter and funded wholly or mainly out of moneys provided by the Oireachtas][3], or

(g) a person who carries on any gas, water, electricity, hydraulic power, dock, canal or railway undertaking,

the principal makes a payment, or as respects relevant contracts entered into on or after the 15th day of May, 1996, is deemed to make a payment pursuant to *subsection (3)*, to another person (whether the contractor or not and in this section referred to as "*the subcontractor*"), the principal shall deduct from the payment and pay to the Collector-General tax at the rate of 35 per cent of the amount of such payment.

(2) A person carrying on a business shall not be deemed to be a person of a kind specified in *subsection (1)(b)* by reason only of the fact that in the course of that business such person erects buildings[or develops land][4] for the use or occupation of such person or employees of such person.

[(2A) (a) Subject to *paragraph (b)*, a person shall be deemed not to be a principal of a kind specified in *subsection (1)(c)* where the following conditions are met—

(i) in the performance of a relevant contract, the person makes a payment to a subcontractor solely in connection with construction operations carried out in or on buildings or land to be used or occupied by such person or the employees of such person, and

(ii) the person does not carry on a business of the type mentioned in *subsection (1)(b)(i)*.

(b) Where a person is a principal of a kind specified in *subsection (1)(c)* by reason of the fact that such person is connected with a company carrying on a business of the type mentioned in *subsection (1)(b)(i)*, *paragraph (a)* shall apply only where in addition to the conditions specified in that paragraph such person is a company.][5]

(3) As respects relevant contracts entered into on or after the 15th day of May, 1996, where relevant operations are performed by a gang or group of persons, including a partnership in respect of which the principal has not received a relevant payments card, and notwithstanding that any payment or part of a payment in respect of such relevant operations is made by the principal to one or more of the gang or group or to some other person, then, for the purposes of this section and any regulations made under this section, such payment or part of a payment shall be deemed to have been made by the principal to the individual members of that gang or group in the proportions in which the payment or any amount in respect of the payment is to be divided amongst them.

[(3A) (a) Not later than 14 days after the end of a return period, a principal or any person who was previously a principal and who has been required to do so by notice in writing from the Revenue Commissioners, shall—

(i) make a return to the Collector-General, on the prescribed form, of the amount, if any, of tax which that person was liable under this section to deduct from payments made to uncertified subcontractors during that return period, and

(ii) remit to the Collector-General the amount of the tax, if any, which the person was so liable to deduct.][6]

(b) The Collector-General shall furnish the person concerned with a receipt in respect of the payment; such a receipt shall consist of whichever of the following the Collector-General considers appropriate, namely—

(i) a separate receipt on the prescribed form in respect of each such payment, or

(ii) a receipt on the prescribed form in respect of all such payments that have been made within a period specified in the receipt.][7]

[(c) The Revenue Commissioners may make regulations with respect to the provision to them, by a principal or other person as is referred to in *paragraph (a)*, of such information as may be specified in the regulations in relation to the constituent elements of the amount (if any) referred to in *paragraph (a)(i)*.][8]

[(3AA) Where a return and remittance referred to, respectively, in *subparagraphs (a)*(i) and *(a)*(ii) of *subsection (3A)* are—

(a) as respects the return, made by electronic means and in accordance with *Chapter 62* of *Part 38*, and

(b) as respects the remittance, made by such electronic means (within the meaning of *section 917EA*) as are required by the Revenue Commissioners,

[then *subsection (3A)* shall apply and have effect as if "23 days" were substituted for "14 days"][9]; but where that return or remittance is made after the day provided for in this subsection the Income Tax Acts shall apply and have effect without regard to the provisions of this subsection.][10]

[(3B) (a) Subject to *paragraph (b)*, where a principal or any person who was previously a principal makes a remittance of tax in respect of a year of assessment or a period comprised in a year of assessment and details of the remittance are not included in a return required to be made under *subsection (3A)*, the amount comprised in the remittance shall be deemed to be a remittance in respect of the first income tax month of the year of assessment.

(b) Where, within 1 month of interest being demanded of a person by the Collector-General under *subsection (9)* by virtue of the application of *paragraph (a)*, the person makes a return to the Collector-General under *subsection (3A)* for [return period or periods][11] to which the remittance of tax relates and of the amount comprised in the remittance for each of [those return periods][12], *paragraph (a)* shall be deemed not to have applied and the remittance shall be treated for the purposes of this section as a remittance or, as the case may be, remittances of tax for the respective [return period or periods][13].][14]

(4) In computing for the purposes of Schedule D the profits or gains arising or accruing to a subcontractor who receives a payment from which tax has been deducted in accordance with *subsection (1)*, the payment shall be treated as being of an amount equal to the aggregate of the net amount received after deduction of the tax and the amount of the tax deducted.

(5) In so far as a subcontractor is chargeable to tax in respect of any profits or gains arising or accruing to the subcontractor from a trade or vocation, the subcontractor shall be treated as having paid on account of tax so chargeable any tax which was deducted from payments taken into account in the computation of those profits or gains and which has not been repaid or for which a set-off has not been made, and the Revenue Commissioners shall make regulations for giving effect to this subsection and those regulations shall, in particular, include provision—

(a) as to the manner in which, and the periods for which, tax deducted under this section is to be taken into account as a sum paid on account of the liability to tax of a sub-contractor,

(b) for repayment, on due claim made for a period (in this paragraph referred to as "*the repayment period*") [commencing on the 1st day of a year of assessment and ending on the last day of the income tax month in which the payment was made][15], of such portion of the tax deducted from payments received by a subcontractor during the repayment period (reduced by any amount of such tax repaid or set off) as appears to the Revenue Commissioners to exceed the proportionate part of the amount of tax for which the subcontractor is liable or is estimated to be liable for that year of assessment, and

(c) for repayment in cases where the total of the tax deducted from payments received by a subcontractor and not repaid to the subcontractor exceeds the aggregate of—

(i) the amount of tax for which the subcontractor is liable, and

(ii) any amount which the subcontractor is liable to remit—

(I) under the Value-Added Tax Consolidation Act 2010,

(II) under the Capital Gains Tax Acts,

(III) under *Chapter 4* of *Part 42*, and

(IV) in respect of—

(A) employment contributions and self-employment contributions under the Social Welfare Acts,

(B) health contributions under the Health Contributions Act, 1979, and

(C) Employment and Training Levy under the Youth Employment Agency Act, 1981, as amended by the Labour Services Act, 1987.

[(5A) A claim to repayment under regulations made in accordance with *paragraph (b)* or *(c)* of *subsection (5)* shall not be allowed at a time at which a claim to repayment in respect of the chargeable period (within the meaning of *section 321*), within which the period for which the claim to repayment relates falls, would not be allowed under *section 865(4)*.][16]

[(5B) Where a claim to repayment, under regulations made in accordance with *paragraph (b)* or *(c)* of *subsection (5)*, is based on tax deducted from a payment made to a subcontractor under *subsection (1)*, the date of payment of that tax shall be deemed to be the date on which the certificate of deduction issued by a principal under regulation 6 of the Income Tax (Relevant Contracts) Regulations 2000 in respect of such tax is submitted to the Revenue Commissioners and the provisions of the Tax Acts shall apply accordingly.][17]

(6) The Revenue Commissioners shall make regulations with respect to the [assessment (including estimated assessment), estimation, charge, collection and recovery of tax deductible under *subsection (1)*][18] and the regulations may, in relation to such tax, include any matters which might be included in regulations under *section 986* in relation to tax deductible under *Chapter 4* of *Part 42* and, without prejudice to the generality of the foregoing, regulations under this subsection may include provision for—

(a) (i) the issue for [a period covering not more than 2 years of assessment][19], or, in relation to such class or classes of subcontractor as may be specified in the regulations, for such longer period as may be so specified, of certificates of authorisation,

(ii) the refusal to issue, appeal against refusal to issue, recall or cancellation of certificates of authorisation and the surrender of such certificates, and

(iii) the production of documents or other material, including a photograph of the subcontractor or, in a case where the subcontractor is not an individual, a photograph of the individual by whom the certificate of authorisation will be produced in accordance with *subsection (12)(a)*, in support of an application for a certificate of authorisation;

(b) (i) the making, before the entering into of a relevant contract, by the persons who intend to enter into such a contract [(other than where one of such persons comes within a class or classes of persons as may be specified in the regulations)][20] of a declaration, in a specified form, to the effect that, having regard to guidelines published by the Revenue Commissioners for the information of such persons as to the distinctions between contracts of employment and relevant contracts and without prejudice to the question of whether a particular contract is a contract of employment or a relevant contract, they have satisfied themselves that in their opinion the contract which they propose to enter into is not a contract of employment,

(ii) the publication of guidelines by the Revenue Commissioners for the purposes of *subparagraph (i)*, [...][21]

(iii) the keeping by principals of every such declaration and the inspection of any or all such [declarations, and][22]

[(iv) the delivery by principals of any or all such declarations to the Revenue Commissioners;][23]

[(ba) (i) the setting up by the Revenue Commissioners and the maintenance by them of a register containing details of every person who is a principal within the meaning of *section 530(1)*, and

(ii) requiring every such person as is specified in the regulations, to notify the Revenue Commissioners within the period and in such manner as is provided for in the said regulations, that that person is a principal for the purposes of this Chapter;][24]

(c) the keeping by principals of—

(i) such records as may be specified in the regulations,

(ii) relevant payments cards and the entry on those cards of such particulars as may be specified in the regulations,

(iii) cards (in this Chapter referred to as "*relevant tax deduction cards*") in such form as may be prescribed by the regulations and containing particulars of any deductions under *subsection (1)* and the entry on those cards of such other particulars as may be specified in the regulations;

(d) the making to the Revenue Commissioners of such returns relating to the payments made by principals as may be specified in the regulations and the inspection of the records referred to in *paragraph (c)* (including the cards referred to in that paragraph);

(e) the keeping by subcontractors of such records as may be specified in the regulations containing particulars of payments received by them, and the inspection of such records;

(f) the completion by principals of certificates of tax deducted (in this Chapter referred to as "*certificates of deduction*") from payments made to subcontractors and, as respects relevant contracts entered into on or after the 15th day of May, 1996, the entry on certificates of deduction of such particulars as may be specified in the regulations;

(g) the furnishing by subcontractors to principals of all such information or particulars as are required by principals to enable principals to comply with any provision of regulations made under this section;

(h) the sending to subcontractors, in cases where tax was deducted under *subsection (1)* from payments made to them, of statements containing particulars of their liability (if any) to tax for a year of assessment.

(7) Every regulation made under this section shall be laid before Dáil Éireann as soon as may be after it is made and, if a resolution annulling the regulation is passed by Dáil Éireann within the next 21 days on which Dáil Éireann has sat after the regulation is laid before it, the regulation shall be annulled accordingly, but without prejudice to the validity of anything previously done thereunder.

(8) The provisions of every enactment and of [the Income Tax (Relevant Contracts) Regulations 2000 (S.I. No. 71 of 2000)][25] which apply to the recovery of any amount of tax which a principal of the kind referred to in *subsection (1)* is liable under this section and those Regulations to pay to the Collector-General shall apply to the recovery of any amount of interest payable on that tax as if that amount of interest were a part of that tax.

[(9) Where the amount of tax which a person who is or is deemed to be a principal of the kind referred to in *subsection (1)* is liable under this section and any regulations under *subsection (6)* to pay to the Collector-General is not so paid, simple interest on the amount shall be paid by the person to the Collector-General and shall be calculated from the date on which the amount became due and payable until payment—

(a) for any day or part of a day before 1 August 1978 during which the amount remains unpaid, at a rate of 0.0492 per cent,

(b) for any day or part of a day on or after 1 August 1978 and before 1 April 1998 during which the amount remains unpaid, at a rate of 0.0410 per cent,

(c) for any day or part of a day on or after 1 April 1998 and before 1 July 2009 during which the amount remains unpaid, at a rate of 0.0322 per cent, and

(d) for any day or part of a day on or after 1 July 2009 during which the amount remains unpaid, at a rate of 0.0274 per cent.][26]

[(10) *Subsection (9)* shall apply to tax recoverable from a person by virtue of a notice issued under the Income Tax (Construction Contracts) Regulations, 1971 (S.I. No. 1 of 1971), as if the tax were tax which the person was liable under *subsection (3A)* to remit—

(i) where the notice relates to [a][27] [return period or periods][28], for the respective [return period or periods][29] referred to in the notice, and

[(ii) where the notice relates to a year of assessment, for the first income tax month in the year of assessment to which the notice relates, but where the inspector determines, or, on appeal against the notice, the Appeal Commissioners determine, the amount of tax which the person was liable to remit, but had not remitted, for [each return period][30] comprised in the year of assessment, interest shall be calculated and payable in respect of each amount so determined in accordance with *subsection (9)* as if that amount were included in a notice in respect of [the return period][31] in question.][32][33]

(11) (a) [Subject to *subsection (11A)*, the Revenue Commissioners shall][34], on application to them in that behalf by a person, issue to the person a certificate (in this section referred to as a "*certificate of authorisation*") if they are satisfied—

(i) that the person is or is about to become a subcontractor engaged in the business of carrying out relevant contracts,

(ii) that the business is or will be carried on from a fixed place of business established in a permanent building and has or will have such equipment, stock and other facilities as in the opinion of the Revenue Commissioners are required for the purposes of the business,

(iii) that in connection with the business records to which *section 886(2)* refers are being or will be kept, and any other records normally kept in connection with such a business are being or will be kept properly and accurately,

(iv) that—

(I) the person, any partnership in which the person is or was a partner and any company (within the meaning of the Companies Act, 1963) of which the person is or was a proprietary director or proprietary employee,

(II) in a case where the person is a partnership, each partner, and

(III) in a case where the person is a company, each director of the company and any person who is either the beneficial owner of, or able, directly or indirectly, to control, more than 15 per cent of the ordinary share capital of the company,

has throughout the qualifying period complied with all the obligations imposed by the Tax Acts, the Capital Gains Tax Acts or the Value-Added Tax Consolidation Act 2010, in relation to—

(A) the payment or remittance of the [taxes, interest and penalties][35] required to be paid or remitted under those Acts,

(B) the delivery of returns, and

(C) requests to supply to an inspector accounts of, or other information about, any business carried on,

by that individual, partnership or company, as the case may be, [...][36]

[(v) that there is good reason to expect that that person, partnership or company will comply with the obligations referred to in *subparagraphs (iii)* and *(iv)* in relation to periods ending after the date of termination of the qualifying period, and][37]

[(vi) in the case of a person who was resident outside the State at some time during the qualifying period, that the person has throughout the qualifying period complied with all the obligations comparable to those mentioned in *subparagraph (iv)* imposed by the laws of the country in which that person was resident at any time during the qualifying period.][38]

(b) [A person referred to in *paragraph (a)* in respect of whom the Revenue Commissioners are not satisfied in relation to the matters specified in *subparagraph (i)* to *(iv)* and *(vi)* of that paragraph][39] shall nevertheless, for the purposes of the issue of a certificate of authorisation, be treated as a person in respect of whom they are so satisfied if the Revenue Commissioners are of the opinion that in all the circumstances such person's failure to satisfy them in relation to such matter or matters ought to be disregarded for those purposes.

[(ba) Notwithstanding *paragraph (a)*, where the Revenue Commissioners have issued a certificate of authorisation to a person under the provisions of that paragraph or *paragraph (b)*, the Revenue Commissioners may issue a further certificate of authorisation to that person without a requirement that the person make a further application to them in that behalf, where they are satisfied, in respect of that person, in relation to the matters specified in *subparagraphs (i)* to *(vi)* of *paragraph (a)*, or, as the case may be, where the provisions of *paragraph (b)* apply.][40]

(c) A certificate of authorisation issued under this subsection shall be valid for such period as the Revenue Commissioners may provide by regulations made pursuant to *subsection (6)*.

[(11A) Where a person applies for a certificate of authorisation in accordance with *subsection (11)* (in this subsection referred to as the "*first-mentioned person*") and relevant operations (being construction operations, forestry operations or meat processing operations, as the case may be) similar to those being carried out or to be carried out by that person were previously, or are being, carried out by another person (in this subsection referred to as the "*second-mentioned person*"), and the second-mentioned person—

(a) is a company connected (within the meaning of *section 10* as it applies for the purposes of the Tax Acts) with the first-mentioned person or would have been such a company but for the fact that the company has been wound up or dissolved without being wound up,

(b) is a company and the first-mentioned person is a partnership in which—

(I) a partner is or was able, or

(II) where more than one partner is a shareholder, those partners together are or were able,

directly or indirectly, whether with or without a connected person or connected persons (within the meaning of *section 10* as it applies for the purposes of the Tax Acts), to control more than 15 per cent of the ordinary share capital of the company, or

(c) the second-mentioned person is a partnership and the first-mentioned person is a company in which—

(I) a partner is or was able, or

(II) where more than one partner is a shareholder, those partners together are or were able,

directly or indirectly, whether with or without a connected person or connected persons (within the meaning of *section 10* as it applies for the purposes of the Tax Acts), to control more than 15 per cent of the ordinary share capital of the company,

then, a certificate of authorisation shall not be issued under *subsection (11)* to the first-mentioned person unless the second-mentioned person is in compliance with the obligations imposed on that person by the Tax Acts, the Capital Gains Tax Acts and the Value-Added Tax Consolidation Act 2010 in relation to the matters specified in *paragraphs (a)(iii)* and *(iv)* of *subsection (11)*.][41]

[(12) (a) Where a subcontractor to whom a certificate of authorisation has been issued produces it to a principal, the principal shall apply to the Revenue Commissioners for a card (in this Chapter referred to as a "*relevant payments card*") in respect of the subcontractor.

(b) Notwithstanding *paragraph (a)*, where—

(i) a subcontractor has notified the Revenue Commissioners of details of the bank account, held in the State in the name of the subcontractor or in the case of a subcontractor who is not resident in the State, held either in the State or in the State in which the subcontractor is resident, into which payments in respect of relevant contracts are to be made (hereafter in this subsection referred to as "*the nominated bank account*"), and

(ii) the principal undertakes to make all payments to the subcontractor in question directly to the nominated bank account,

the principal may apply to the Revenue Commissioners for a relevant payments card where the subcontractor has provided details of the certificate of authorisation to the principal together with details of the nominated bank account into which payments are to be made by the principal.

[(c) Notwithstanding *paragraphs (a)* and *(b)*, a principal may apply for a relevant payments card in respect of a subcontractor for a year of assessment where—

(i) the principal has been issued with a relevant payments card in respect of the subcontractor for the immediately preceding year of assessment,

(ii) the relevant contract between the principal and the subcontractor in relation to which the relevant payments card is required is likely to be ongoing at the end of that preceding year, and

(iii) the principal has obtained from the subcontractor details of the subcontractor's certificate of authorisation for the year of assessment to which the application for the relevant payments card relates.][42][43]

[(d) Subject to the following provisions of this subsection and to *subsection (13)*, where, on the making to them by a principal of an application under *paragraph (a)*, *(b)* or *(c)*, the Revenue Commissioners are satisfied that a relevant payments card in respect of the subcontractor concerned ought to be issued, they shall issue such a card to the principal who, on receiving the card, shall, during the year of assessment (or the unexpired portion of the year of assessment) to which the relevant payments card relates, be entitled, subject to any limit imposed on the card in accordance with *paragraph (e)*, to make payment, without deduction of tax, to the subcontractor named on the card but, in the case of an application to which *paragraph (b)* applies, or an application to which *paragraph (c)* applies where the relevant payments card mentioned in *subparagraph (i)* of that paragraph was issued following an application made under and in accordance with *paragraph (b)*, any such payments shall be made by the principal directly to the nominated bank account.

(e) Where it appears requisite to them to do so for the protection of the revenue, the Revenue Commissioners may, by specifying the amount thereof on a relevant payments card, impose a limit (in this section referred to as the "*specified limit*") on the amount of the payments that a principal may make, without deduction of tax, to the subcontractor named on the card.

[(f) Where a specified limit has been applied by them for a year of assessment in relation to a relevant payments card by virtue of *paragraph (e)*, the Revenue Commissioners, either at the request of the subcontractor named on the card or otherwise, may, as they consider it appropriate, amend the limit by reducing, increasing or removing it.][44]

(g) Where, in accordance with *paragraph (f)*, the Revenue Commissioners amend a specified limit applied to a relevant payments card, they shall issue to the principal, and the principal shall thereafter use, a new relevant payments card.

(h) Where a specified limit is applied to a relevant payments card, the subcontractor named on the card shall, at the same time as the card is issued to the principal, be notified in writing by the Revenue Commissioners of the application of the limit and the amount, or revised amount, thereof, as the case may be.

(i) Where, in a year of assessment, the aggregate of the amount of the payments made by a principal to a subcontractor exceeds the specified limit, if any, imposed on the relevant payments card, or the amended relevant payments card, as the case may be, issued in respect of that subcontractor, the principal shall deduct from such excess, and pay to the Collector-General, tax in accordance with *subsection (1)*.][45]

(13) (a) Where it appears to the Revenue Commissioners that—

(i) a certificate of authorisation was issued on the basis of false or misleading information,

(ii) a certificate of authorisation would not have been issued if information obtained subsequent to its issue had been available at the date of its issue,

(iii) a person to whom a certificate of authorisation was issued has permitted it to be misused,

(iv) in the case of a certificate issued to a company, there has been a change in control (within the meaning of *section 432*) of the company,

(v) a person to whom a certificate of authorisation was issued has failed to comply with any of the obligations imposed on such person by the Tax Acts, the Capital Gains Tax Acts, the Value-Added Tax Consolidation Act 2010, or by any regulations made thereunder in relation to—

(I) the payment or remittance of the taxes required to be paid or remitted under any of those Acts,

(II) the delivery of returns, and

(III) requests to supply to an inspector accounts of, or other information about, any business carried on by such person,

or

(vi) the business of carrying out relevant contracts in relation to which the certificate of authorisation was issued has ceased to be carried on by the person to whom the certificate was issued,

the Revenue Commissioners may at any time cancel the certificate and give notice in writing to that effect to any principal.

(b) Where a principal receives a notice under *paragraph (a)*, the principal shall—

(i) deduct tax in accordance with *subsection (1)* from any payments made to the person to whom the notice relates on or after the date of receipt of the notice, and

(ii) return to the Revenue Commissioners any relevant payments cards issued to the principal in relation to that person and any relevant tax deduction card kept by the principal in relation to that person.

(c) The Revenue Commissioners shall advise a person in relation to whom a notice under *paragraph (a)* was issued of the issue of such notice and shall require such person to return to them forthwith the certificate of authorisation issued to such person.

(14) (a) Where any person—

(i) for the purpose of obtaining a certificate of authorisation or a relevant payments card makes any false statement or furnishes any document which is false in a material particular,

(ii) disposes of a certificate of authorisation otherwise than by the return of the certificate to the Revenue Commissioners,

(iii) fails to return a certificate of authorisation to the Revenue Commissioners when required to do so in accordance with *subsection (13)(c)*,

(iv) is in possession of a certificate of authorisation that was not issued to such person by the Revenue Commissioners, or

(v) produces to a principal a certificate of authorisation after such person has been advised by the Revenue Commissioners of the issue of a notice under *subsection (13)(c)*,

such person shall be guilty of an offence and shall be liable on summary conviction to a fine of [€5,000][46] or, at the discretion of the court, to imprisonment for a term not exceeding 6 months or to both the fine and the imprisonment.

(b) Any person who aids, abets, counsels or procures—

(i) the obtaining of a certificate of authorisation by means of a false statement,

(ii) the use by any person, other than the person to whom it was issued by the Revenue Commissioners, of a certificate of authorisation, or

(iii) the production to a principal of a document that is not a certificate of authorisation but purports to be such a certificate,

shall be guilty of an offence and shall be liable on summary conviction to a fine of [€5,000][47] or, at the discretion of the court, to imprisonment for a term not exceeding 6 months or to both the fine and the imprisonment.

(c) Any person who—

(i) fails to enter on a relevant payments card or relevant tax deduction card such particulars as are required to be entered on that card by virtue of this section and any regulations made under this section,

(ii) fails to return to the Revenue Commissioners the relevant payments card or relevant tax deduction card in accordance with *subsection (13)(b)*,

(iii) returns to the Revenue Commissioners any such card on which are entered particulars which are incorrect in any material particular,

(iv) fails to comply with any provision of regulations made under this section requiring such person—

(I) to make any declaration,

(II) to provide any information or particulars to principals, [...][48]

(III) to keep or produce any records, documents or [declarations, or][49]

[(IV) to deliver declarations to the Revenue Commissioners,][50]

(v) fails to give a subcontractor from whom tax has been deducted under *subsection (1)* a certificate of deduction in the prescribed form containing such particulars as are required to be entered in that certificate by virtue of any regulations made under this section, or

(vi) being a company to which a certificate of authorisation has been issued under *subsection (11)*, fails to notify the Revenue Commissioners of a change in control (within the meaning of *section 432*) of the company,

shall be guilty of an offence and shall be liable on summary conviction to a fine of [€5,000][51].

(15) Notwithstanding any other enactment, summary proceedings in respect of offences under this section may be instituted within 10 years of the commission of the offence.

(16) *Section 987*(4), *subsection (4)* of *section 1052* (other than as that subsection applies in relation to proceedings for the recovery of a penalty in relation to a return referred to in *sections 879* and *880*), [*subsections (9)* and *(17)* of *section 1077E*][52] and *sections 1068* and *1069* shall, with any necessary modifications, apply for the purposes of this section and any regulations made under this section as they apply for the purposes of those provisions.

(17) Any person who is aggrieved by a refusal by the Revenue Commissioners to issue a certificate of authorisation under this section may, by notice in writing to that effect given to the Revenue Commissioners within 30 days from the date of such refusal, apply to have such person's application heard and determined by the Appeal Commissioners.

[(17A) Any person who is aggrieved by the cancellation of a certificate of authorisation by the Revenue Commissioners in accordance with *subsection (13)* may, by notice in writing to that effect given to the Revenue Commissioners within 30 days from the date of such cancellation, appeal against such cancellation to the Appeal Commissioners but, pending the decision of the Appeal Commissioners in the matter, unless the Revenue Commissioners, on application to them, reinstate the certificate of authorisation pending the making of that decision, the certificate shall remain cancelled.][53]

[(17B) Any person who is aggrieved by the imposition by the Revenue Commissioners, under *subsection (12)*, of a specified limit in relation to a relevant payments card, or an amended relevant payments card, as the case may be, may, by notice in writing to that effect given to the Revenue Commissioners within 30 days from the date of issue of the relevant payments card concerned, appeal against the imposition of such a limit to the Appeal Commissioners, but, pending the decision of the Appeal Commissioners in the matter, the limit shall remain in place.][54]

(18) The Appeal Commissioners shall hear and determine an appeal made to them under [*subsection (17)*, *(17A)* or *(17B)*][55] as if it were an appeal against an assessment to income tax and, subject to *subsection (19)*, the provisions of the Income Tax Acts relating to such an appeal (including the provisions relating to the rehearing of an appeal and to the statement of a case for the opinion of the High Court on a point of law) shall apply accordingly with any necessary modifications.

(19) On the hearing of an appeal made under [*subsection (17)* or *(17B)*][56], the Appeal Commissioners shall have regard to all matters to which the Revenue Commissioners may or are required to have regard under this section.

(20) For the purposes of the hearing or rehearing of an appeal under [*subsection (17), (17A)* or *(17B)*][57], the Revenue Commissioners may nominate any of their officers to act on their behalf.

Amendments

[1] Inserted by FA07 s31(1)(b)(i)(I). Has effect as respects relevant contracts entered into on or after 1 May 2007.

[2] Substituted by FA98 s37(1)(b). This section shall apply as on and from the 6th day of October, 1998.

[3] Inserted by FA07 s31(1)(b)(i)(II). Has effect as respects relevant contracts entered into on or after 1 May 2007.

[4] Inserted by FA07 s31(1)(b)(ii). Has effect as respects relevant contracts entered into on or after 1 May 2007.

[5] Inserted by FA08 s35(1)(a). Has effect as on and from 13 March 2008.

[6] Substituted by FA10 s29(2)(a). Deemed to have come into force and takes effect as on and from 1 January 2010.

[7] Inserted by FA99 s18(1)(b)(i). Shall apply as respects the year 1999–2000 and subsequent years of assessment.

[8] Inserted by FA10 s29(2)(b). Deemed to have come into force and takes effect as on and from 1 January 2010.

[9] Substituted by FA10 s29(2)(c). Deemed to have come into force and takes effect as on and from 1 January 2010.

[10] Inserted by F(No.2)A08 sched3(1)(b). Have effect as on and from 1 January 2009.

[11, 13] Substituted by FA10 s29(2)(d)(i). Deemed to have come into force and takes effect as on and from 1 January 2010.

[12] Substituted by FA10 s29(2)(d)(ii). Deemed to have come into force and takes effect as on and from 1 January 2010.

[14] Inserted by FA03 s33(1)(a). Applies as respects the year of assessment 2003 and subsequent years of assessment.

[15] Substituted by FA01 sched2(32)(b). Applies as on and from 1 January 2002.

[16] Inserted by FA06 s44(1)(a). Applies as on and from the passing of this Act. FA06 31 March 2006

[17] Inserted by FA11 s20(2).

[18] Substituted by FA99 s18(1)(b)(ii). Shall apply as respects the year 1999–2000 and subsequent years of assessment.

[19] Substituted by FA10 s29(2)(e). Deemed to have come into force and takes effect as on and from 1 January 2010.

[20] Inserted by FA08 s35(1)(b). Has effect as on and from 13 March 2008.

[21] Deleted by FA07 s31(1)(b)(iii)(I). Has effect as on and from the date of passing of this Act. FA07 2 April 2007

[22] Substituted by FA07 s31(1)(b)(iii)(I). Has effect as on and from the date of passing of this Act. FA07 2 April 2007

[23] Inserted by FA07 s31(1)(b)(iii)(II). Has effect as on and from the date of passing of this Act. FA07 2 April 2007

[24] Inserted by FA04 s20(1)(a). Applies as and from the date of passing of this Act. FA04 25 March 2004

[25] Substituted by FA02 s51(1)(b)(i). Shall be deemed to have come into operation as on and from 6 April 2000.

[26] Substituted by FA09 s29(1)(d). Applies as respects any unpaid tax or duty, as the case may be, that has not been paid before 1 July 2009 regardless of whether that tax or duty became due and payable before, on or after that date.

[27] Substituted by FA11 sched3(1)(g). Has effect as on and from 6 February 2011.

[28, 29] Substituted by FA10 s29(2)(f). Deemed to have come into force and takes effect as on and from 1 January 2010.

[30] Substituted by FA10 s29(2)(g)(i). Deemed to have come into force and takes effect as on and from 1 January 2010.

[31] Substituted by FA10 s29(2)(g)(ii). Deemed to have come into force and takes effect as on and from 1 January 2010.

[32] Substituted by FA03 s33(1)(b). Applies as respects the year of assessment 2003 and subsequent years of assessment.

[33] Substituted by FA99 s18(1)(b)(iii). Shall apply as respects the year 1999–2000 and subsequent years of assessment.

[34] Substituted by FA06 s44(1)(b)(i)(I). Applies as respects applications, for certificates of authorisation, made on or after 2 February 2006.

[35] Substituted by FA02 s51(1)(b)(iii)(I). Shall apply as on and from 1 April 2002.

[36] Deleted by FA99 s18(1)(b)(iv)(I). Shall apply as respects the year 1999–2000 and subsequent years of assessment.

[37] Substituted by FA06 s44(1)(b)(i)(II). Applies as respects applications, for certificates of authorisation, made on or after 2 February 2006.

[38] Inserted by FA99 s18(1)(b)(iv)(III). Shall apply as respects the year 1999–2000 and subsequent years of assessment.

[39] Substituted by FA06 s44(1)(b)(ii). Applies as respects applications, for certificates of authorisation, made on or after 2 February 2006.

[40] Inserted by FA04 s20(1)(b). Applies as on and from 1 January 2004.

[41] Inserted by FA06 s44(1)(c). Applies as respects applications, for certificates of authorisation, made on or after 2 February 2006.

[42] Substituted by FA03 s33(1)(c)(i). Applies as respects on or after the date of 28 March 2003

[43] Substituted by FA99 s18(1)(b)(v). Shall apply as respects applications for relevant payments cards made on or after the 6th day of October, 1999.

[44] Substituted by FA10 s29(2)(h). Deemed to have come into force and takes effect as on and from 1 January 2010.

[45] Substituted by FA06 s44(1)(d). Applies as respects applications for relevant payments cards, made on or after 2 February 2006.

[46, 47, 51] Substituted by FA08 s138(1)(a). Applies as respects an offence committed on a day after 13 March 2008.

[48] Deleted by FA07 s31(1)(b)(iv)(I). Has effect as on and from the date of passing of this Act. FA07 2 April 2007

[49] Substituted by FA07 s31(1)(b)(iv)(I). Has effect as on and from the date of passing of this Act. FA07 2 April 2007

[50] Inserted by FA07 s31(1)(b)(iv)(II). Has effect as on and from the date of passing of this Act. FA07 2 April 2007

[52] Substituted by F(No.2)A08 sched5(part2)(1)(f). The enactments specified in Schedule 5 are amended or repealed to the extent and manner specified in that Schedule and, unless the contrary is stated, shall come into effect after 24 December 2008.

[53] Inserted by FA99 s18(1)(b)(vi). Shall apply as respects the year 1999–2000 and subsequent years of assessment.

[54] Inserted by FA06 s44(1)(e). Applies as respects applications for relevant payments cards, made on or after 2 February 2006.

[55] Substituted by FA06 s44(1)(f). Applies as respects applications for relevant payments cards, made on or after 2 February 2006.

[56] Substituted by FA06 s44(1)(g). Applies as respects applications for relevant payments cards, made on or after 2 February 2006.

[57] Substituted by FA06 s44(1)(h). Applies as respects applications for relevant payments cards, made on or after 2 February 2006.

Revenue Briefings

Tax Briefing

Tax Briefing December 2004 – Issue 58 pg 1 – New Registration Procedures for Principal Contractors
Tax Briefing August 2006 – Issue 64 – Construction Industry
Tax Briefing July 2007 – Issue 66 – Relevant Contracts Tax – Clarification of Scope of Section 531(2) Taxes Consolidation Act 1997
Tax Briefing September 2008 – Issue 69 – Relevant Contracts Tax – Clarification about Claiming Offsets/Repayments
Tax Briefing April 2009 – Issue 71 – Relevant Contracts Tax (RCT) – Clarification on Connected Party Rules (Section 531(1)(c) TCA, 1997) and Construction operations carried out in a private capacity by a sole trader or partnership

eBrief

eBrief No. 91/2010 – Important end of year information for Relevant Contracts Tax (RCT) Contractors
eBrief No. 98/2010 – Important end of year information for Relevant Contracts Tax Contractors
eBrief No. 03/2011 – Relevant Contracts Tax (RCT) in Liquidation, Receivership or Examinership
eBrief No. 47/2013 – Amended Regulations for Relevant Contracts Tax (RCT)

Revenue Precedents

The Inspector is not entitled to be present at a hearing in accordance with Regulation 17 of the RCT regulations. IT952004

A principal contractor who makes a payment in kind rather than a payment of money to subcontractor is obliged to operate RCT on the payment in kind. RCT applies to payments in kind in the same way as it applies to payments of money. "Payment" in section 531(1) TCA 1997 can include payment other than in money form. The value of the payment in kind is the market value. This can be determined at appeal, if necessary. IT972514

A supplier of Liquified Petroleum Gas is a person carrying on a gas undertaking for the purposes of section 531(1)(g) TCA 1997. IT922030

Cross References

From Section 531

Section 10 Connected persons.
Section 321 Provisions of general application in relation to the making of allowances and charges.
Section 432 Meaning of "associated company" and "control".
Section 530 Interpretation (Chapter 2).
Section 639 Interpretation (Chapter 1).
Section 865 Repayment of tax.
Section 879 Returns of income.
Section 880 Partnership returns.
Section 886 Obligation to keep certain records.
Section 917EA Mandatory electronic filing and payment of tax.
Section 960 Date for payment of income tax other than under self assessment.
Section 983 Interpretation (Chapter 4).
Section 986 Regulations.
Section 987 Penalties for breach of regulations.
Section 1052 Penalties for failure to make certain returns, etc.
Section 1068 Failure to act within required time.
Section 1069 Evidence of income.
Section 1077E Penalty for deliberately or carelessly making incorrect returns, etc.

To Section 531

Section 477A Relief for energy efficient works.
Section 525 Returns and collection of appropriate tax.
Section 530 Interpretation (Chapter 2).
Section 530J Register of principals.
Section 1089 Status of interest on certain unpaid taxes and duties.

LEVIES

PART 18A

Income Levy

531A Definitions (Part 18A)

[(1) In this Part—

["*aggregate income for the year of assessment*", in relation to an individual and a year of assessment, means the aggregate of the individual's relevant emoluments in the year of assessment, including relevant emoluments that are paid in whole or in part for a year of assessment other than the year of assessment during which the payment is made, and relevant income for the year of assessment;][1]

"*Collector-General*" means the Collector-General appointed under *section 851*;

"*employee*" and "*employer*" have the same meanings as in *section 983*;

"*excluded emoluments*" means emoluments which have been gifted to the Minister for Finance under *section 483*;

"*income levy*" has the meaning assigned to it by *section 531B*;

"*income tax month*" means a calendar month;

"*PAYE Regulations*" means the Income Tax (Employments) (Consolidated) Regulations 2001 (S.I. No. 559 of 2001);

"*relevant emoluments*" and "*relevant income*" shall be construed in accordance with *paragraphs (a)* and *(b)*, respectively, of the Table to *section 531B(1)*;

"*similar type payments*" means payments which are of a similar character to payments made under the Social Welfare Acts but which are made by—

(a) the Health Service Executive,

(b) the Department of Community, Rural and Gaeltacht Affairs,

(c) the Department of Enterprise, Trade and Employment,

(d) the Department of Education and Science,

(e) the Department of Agriculture, Fisheries and Food,

(f) An Foras Áiseanna Saothair, in respect of schemes mentioned in clauses (I), (II) and (III) of *section 472A(1)(b)(i)*, or

(g) any other state or territory;

"*social welfare payments*" means payments made under the Social Welfare Acts;

"*year of assessment*" means a year of assessment within the meaning of the Tax Acts.

(2) Words and expressions used in this Part have, except where otherwise provided or where the context otherwise requires, the same meaning as in the Tax Acts.][2]

Amendments

[1] Substituted by FA09 s2(1)(a). This section applies for the year of assessment 2009 and subsequent years of assessment.

[2] Inserted by F(No.2)A08 s2(a). This section is deemed to have come into force and takes effect as on and from 1 January 2009.

Revenue Briefings

eBrief

eBrief No. 33/2010 – Income Levy

Revenue Information Notes

Income Levy – Frequently Asked Questions

Cross References

From Section 531A

Section 472A Relief for the long-term unemployed.

Section 483 Relief for certain gifts.

Section 531B Charge to income levy.

Section 851 Collector-General.

Section 983 Interpretation (Chapter 4).

531B Charge to income levy

[(1) With effect from 1 January 2009, there shall be charged, levied and paid, in accordance with the provisions of this Part, a tax to be known as "income levy" in respect of the income specified in paragraphs *(a)* and *(b)* of the Table to this subsection.

TABLE

[(a) The income described in this paragraph, to be known as "*relevant emoluments*", is emoluments to which *Chapter 4* of *Part 42* applies or is applied—

(i) other than social welfare payments and similar type payments,

(ii) other than excluded emoluments,

(iii) disregarding expenses, in respect of which an employee may be entitled to relief from income tax, which fall within Regulation 10(3) of the PAYE Regulations,

(iv) having regard to any relief under *section 201(5)(a)* and *paragraphs 6* and *8* of *Schedule 3*, and

(v) excluding emoluments of an individual who is resident in a territory with which arrangements have been made under *subsection (1)(a)(i)* or *(1B)(a)(ii)* of *section 826* in relation to affording relief from double taxation, where those emoluments are the subject of a notification issued under *section 984(1)*.][1]

(b) [The income described in this paragraph, to be known as "*relevant income*", is income, without regard to any amount deductible from or deductible in computing total income, from all sources as estimated in accordance with the Tax Acts, other than relevant emoluments, social welfare payments and similar type payments and excluded emoluments, and—][2]

(i) as if *sections 140, 141, 142, 143, 195, 231, 232, 233, 234* and *664* were never enacted,

(ii) without regard to any deduction—

(I) in respect of double rent allowance under *section 324(2), 333(2), 345(3)* or *354(3)*,

(II) under *section 372AP*, in computing the amount of a surplus or deficiency in respect of rent from any premises,

(III) under *section 372AU*, in computing the amount of a surplus or deficiency in respect of rent from any premises,

(IV) under *section 847A*, in respect of a relevant donation (within the meaning of that section), or

(V) under *section 848A*, in respect of a relevant donation (within the meaning of that section),

(iii) excluding gains, income or payments to which any of the following provisions apply:

(I) Chapter 4 of Part 8;

(II) Chapter 5 of Part 8;

(III) Chapter 7 of Part 8;

(IV) Chapter 5 of Part 26;

(V) Chapter 6 of Part 26;

(VI) Chapter 1A of Part 27;

(VII) Chapter 4 of Part 27,

[...][3]

(iv) having regard to a deduction for any payment to which *section 1025* applies, made by an individual pursuant to a maintenance arrangement (within the meaning of that section) relating to the marriage for the benefit of the other party to the marriage, unless *section 1026* applies in respect of [such payment,][4]

[(iva) having regard to any reduction arising by virtue of *section 825A*, and][5]

[(ivb) having regard to any allowances due under *section 659* arising from the obligations under Council Directive 91/676/EEC of 12 December 1991* concerning the protection of waters against pollution caused by nitrates from agricultural sources.][6]

*OJ No. L375, 31.12.1991, p.1

[...][7]

(2) The income levy shall not be payable, for a year of assessment, by an individual who—

[(a) subject to subsection (3), proves to the satisfaction of the Revenue Commissioners that his or her aggregate income for the year of assessment does not exceed €15,028,][8]

(b) by virtue of section 45 of the Health Act 1970 or Council Regulation (EEC) No. 1408/71* of 14 June 1971 has full eligibility for services under Part IV of that Act, or

*OJ No. L149, 5.7.1971, p.2

(c) following receipt of a claim made in a manner approved or provided by the Revenue Commissioners, proves to their satisfaction that his or her aggregate income for the year of assessment does not exceed €20,000 and who has achieved the age of 65 years or over at any time during that year of assessment.

[(3) For the purposes of determining an individual's aggregate income for the year of assessment 2009 for the purposes of subsection (2)(*a*), any payment of relevant emoluments from which income levy was not deducted by an employer, made in the period from 1 January 2009 to 30 April 2009, to which the appropriate portion of €18,304 was applied in that period, shall be disregarded.

(4) (a) This subsection applies to emoluments paid to an individual in the period 1 January 2009 to 30 April 2009 in the form of any taxable exgratia payment made on the occasion of the redundancy of that individual, which is chargeable to income tax under the provisions of *section 123*.

(b) Notwithstanding any other provision of this Part and subject to *paragraph (c)*, to the extent that emoluments are emoluments to which this subsection applies, those emoluments—

(i) shall be charged to income levy for the year of assessment 2009 at the rate of—

(I) 1 per cent on the first €100,100 of such emoluments,

(II) 2 per cent on the next €150,020 of such emoluments, and

(III) 3 per cent on the remainder of such emoluments,

and

(ii) shall not be reckoned in computing relevant emoluments for that year for any other purpose of this Part.

(c) This subsection shall not apply to emoluments paid to an individual if that individual so elects by notice in writing to an inspector after the end of the year of assessment 2009.][9]][10]

Amendments

[1] Substituted by FA10 s3(1)(a). Applies as respects for the year of assessment 2009 and subsequent years.

[2] Substituted by FA09 s2(1)(b). This section applies for the year of assessment 2009 and subsequent years of assessment.

[3] Deleted by FA09 s2(1)(c). This section applies for the year of assessment 2009 and subsequent years of assessment.

[4] Substituted by FA09 s2(1)(d). This section applies for the year of assessment 2009 and subsequent years of assessment.

[5] Inserted by FA10 s3(1)(b). Applies as respects for the year of assessment 2009 and subsequent years.

[6] Inserted by FA10 s3(1)(c). Applies as respects for the year of assessment 2010 and subsequent years.

[7] Deleted by FA10 s3(1)(d). Applies as respects for the year of assessment 2009 and subsequent years.

[8] Substituted by FA09 s2(1)(f). This section applies for the year of assessment 2009 and subsequent years of assessment.

[9] Inserted by FA09 s2(1)(g). This section applies for the year of assessment 2009 and subsequent years of assessment.

[10] Inserted by F(No.2)A08 s2(a). This section is deemed to have come into force and takes effect as on and from 1 January 2009.

Revenue Briefings

eBrief

eBrief No. 42/2011 – Agent access to Income Levy details via ROS

eBrief No. 82/2011 – Universal Social Charge (USC) and Income Levy – employees resident and working in non tax treaty countries

Cross References

From Section 531B

Section 123 General tax treatment of payments on retirement or removal from office or employment.

Section 140 Distributions out of profits or gains from stallion fees, stud greyhound services fees and occupation of certain woodlands.

Section 141 Distributions out of income from patent royalties.

Section 142 Distributions out of profits of certain mines.

Section 143 Distributions out of profits from coal, gypsum and anhydrite mining operations.

Section 195 Exemption of certain earnings of writers, composers and artists.

Section 201 Exemptions and reliefs in respect of tax under section 123.

Section 231 Profits or gains from stallion fees.

Section 232 Profits from occupation of certain woodlands.

Section 233 Stud greyhound service fees.

Section 234 Certain income derived from patent royalties.
Section 324 Double rent allowance in respect of rent paid for certain business premises.
Section 333 Double rent allowance in respect of rent paid for certain business premises.
Section 345 Double rent allowance in respect of rent paid for certain business premises.
Section 354 Double rent allowance in respect of rent paid for certain business premises.
Section 372AP Relief for lessors.
Section 372AU Saver for relief due, and for clawback of relief given under, old schemes.
Section 659 Farming: allowances for capital expenditure on the construction of farm buildings, etc. for control of pollution.
Section 664 Relief for certain income from leasing of farm land.
Section 825A Reduction in income tax for certain income earned outside the State.
Section 826 Agreements for relief from double taxation.
Section 847A Donations to certain sports bodies.
Section 848A Donations to approved bodies.
Section 960 Date for payment of income tax other than under self assessment.
Section 983 Interpretation (Chapter 4).
Section 984 Application.
Section 1025 Maintenance in case of separated spouses.
Section 1026 Separated and divorced persons: adaptation of provisions relating to married persons.

To Section 531B

Section 531A Definitions (Part 18A).
Section 531K Repayments.
Section 531AL Definitions (Part 18D).

531C Rate of charge

[(1) For the year of assessment 2009, an individual shall be charged to income levy on the individual's aggregate income for the year of assessment at the rates specified in the Table to this subsection.

TABLE

Part of aggregate income	Rate of income levy
The first €75,036	1.67%
The next €25,064	3%
The next €74,880	3.33%
The next €75,140	4.67%
The remainder	5%

(2) For the year of assessment 2010, and subsequent years of assessment, an individual shall be charged to income levy on the individual's aggregate income for the year of assessment at the rates specified in the Table to this subsection.

TABLE

Part of aggregate income	Rate of income levy
The first €75,036	2%
The next €99,944	4%
The remainder	6%

.][1]

Amendments

[1] Substituted by FA09 s2(1)(h). This section applies for the year of assessment 2009 and subsequent years of assessment.

531D Deduction and payment of income levy on relevant emoluments

[(1) An employer shall be liable in the first instance to pay income levy due in respect of any payment of relevant emoluments.

[(2) (a) As respects any payment of relevant emoluments made to or on behalf of an employee in the period beginning on 1 January 2009 and ending on 30 April 2009, income levy shall be deducted from such emoluments by the employer at any or all of the following rates—

(i) 1 per cent where the amount of the relevant emoluments does not exceed €1,925, in the case where the period in respect of which the payment is being made is a week, or a corresponding amount, where the period is greater or less than a week,

(ii) 2 per cent on the amount of the excess where the amount of relevant emoluments exceeds €1,925, but does not exceed €4,810, in the case where the period in respect of which the payment is being made is a week, or a corresponding amount, where the period is greater or less than a week,

(iii) 3 per cent on the amount of the excess where the amount of relevant emoluments exceeds €4,810, in the case where the period in respect of which the payment is being made is a week, or a corresponding amount, where the period is greater or less than a week.

(b) As respects any payment of relevant emoluments made to or on behalf of an employee on or after 1 May 2009, income levy shall be deducted from such emoluments by the employer at any or all of the following rates—

(i) 2 per cent where the amount of the relevant emoluments does not exceed €1,443, in the case where the period in respect of which the payment is being made is a week, or a corresponding amount, where the period is greater or less than a week,

(ii) 4 per cent on the amount of the excess where the amount of relevant emoluments exceeds €1,443, but does not exceed €3,365, in the case where the period in respect of which the payment is being made is a week, or a corresponding amount, where the period is greater or less than a week,

(iii) 6 per cent on the amount of the excess where the amount of relevant emoluments exceeds €3,365, in the case where the period in respect of which the payment is being made is a week, or a corresponding amount, where the period is greater or less than a week.][1]

(3) The provisions of Part 4 of the PAYE Regulations, with any necessary modifications, shall apply to income levy in respect of relevant emoluments, and income levy payable by an employee shall only be recoverable from him or her by his or her employer by deduction in accordance with those provisions.

(4) (a) (i) Within 14 days of the end of every income tax month the employer shall remit to the Collector-General the total of all amounts of income levy which the employer was liable to deduct from relevant emoluments paid by the employer during that income tax month.

(ii) The Collector-General may, in writing, and unless the employer objects, authorize the employer to remit to the Collector-General, within 14 days from the end of such longer period (if any) but not exceeding one year, as may be so authorised, the total of all amounts of income levy which the employer was liable to deduct from relevant emoluments paid by the employer during that longer period.

(iii) Where a remittance referred to in *subparagraph (i)* is made by such electronic means (within the meaning of *section 917EA*) as are approved by the Revenue Commissioners, subparagraph (i) shall apply and have effect as if "Within 23 days of the end of every income tax month" were substituted for "Within 14 days of the end of every income tax month" but, where the said remittance is not made within that period of 23 days, *subparagraph (i)* shall apply and have effect without regard to the provisions of this subparagraph.

(b) On payment of income levy, the Collector-General may furnish the employer concerned with a receipt in respect of the payment which shall consist of whichever of the following the Collector-General considers appropriate, namely—

(i) a separate receipt in respect of each such payment, or

(ii) a receipt for all such payments made within the period specified in the receipt.

(5) (a) Within 46 days from the end of a year of assessment, or from the date the employer ceases permanently to be an employer to whom Regulation 7(1) of the PAYE Regulations applies, whichever is the earlier, the employer shall send to the Collector-General—

(i) a return, in a form provided or approved of by the Revenue Commissioners, in respect of each individual to whom payment of relevant emoluments was made during that year showing—

(I) the total amount of income levy payable as respects the individual in that year,

(II) the dates of commencement and cessation within that year of the employment of the individual, where applicable,

(III) the rate of income levy payable as respects the individual, and

(IV) the total relevant emoluments paid to the individual in that year,

and

(ii) a statement, declaration and certificate, in such form as may be provided or approved of by the Revenue Commissioners, showing the total amount of income levy which the employer was liable to remit in respect of every individual to whom payment of relevant emoluments was made in the year of assessment.

(b) Where the employer is a body corporate, the declaration and certificate referred to in *paragraph (a)(ii)* shall be signed either by the secretary or a director of the body corporate.

(6) (a) (i) Within 46 days from the end of a year of assessment, the employer shall give to every employee who is in the employer's employment on the last day of the year of assessment and from whose relevant emoluments any income levy has been deducted during that year, a certificate showing—

(I) the total amount of income levy deducted from the relevant emoluments of the employee during that year,

(II) the date of commencement within that year of the employment of the employee, where applicable,

(III) the rate of income levy payable as respects the employee, and

(IV) the total relevant emoluments paid to the employee in that year.

(ii) The certificate specified in *subparagraph (i)* shall be in such form as may be provided or approved by the Revenue Commissioners.

(b) (i) An employer shall, in the case of an employee to whom he or she makes a payment of relevant emoluments, give to the employee, on the cessation of the period of employment to which the payment of income levy in respect of the employee relates, a certificate showing—

(I) the total income levy as respects the employee which the employer was liable to remit for the year of assessment in which the cessation occurs up to and including the date of cessation,

(II) the dates of commencement (where applicable) and cessation within that year of the employment of the individual,

(III) the rate of income levy payable as respects the employee, and

(IV) the total relevant emoluments paid to the employee in that year up to and including the date of cessation.

(ii) The certificate specified in *subparagraph (i)* shall be in such form as may be provided or approved of by the Revenue Commissioners.][2]

Amendments

[1] Substituted by FA09 s2(1)(i). This section applies for the year of assessment 2009 and subsequent years of assessment.

[2] Inserted by F(No.2)A08 s2(a). This section is deemed to have come into force and takes effect as on and from 1 January 2009.

Revenue Briefings

eBrief

eBrief No. 60/2010 – Income Levy

Cross References

From Section 531D

Section 917EA Mandatory electronic filing and payment of tax.

531E Record keeping

[(1) An employer shall record the following particulars in respect of each employee to whom payment of relevant emoluments has been made in a year of assessment—

(a) the amount of each payment of relevant emoluments,

(b) the amount of income levy deducted from each such payment,

(c) the total amount of income levy which the employer is liable to remit in respect of each such payment, and

(d) the dates of commencement and cessation within the year of assessment of the employment of the individual, where applicable.

(2) The records specified in *subsection (1)* shall be in a form approved of by the Revenue Commissioners and shall be retained by employers for not less than 6 years after the end of the year of assessment to which they relate.][1]

Amendments

[1] Inserted by F(No.2)A08 s2(a). This section is deemed to have come into force and takes effect as on and from 1 January 2009.

Cross References

To Section 531E

Section 531F Power of inspection.

531F Power of inspection

[The provisions of *section 903* and Regulation 32 of the PAYE Regulations, in relation to inspection of records, with any necessary modifications, shall apply to the particulars recorded pursuant to *section 531E* as they apply to the records specified in those provisions.][1]

Amendments

[1] Inserted by F(No.2)A08 s2(a). This section is deemed to have come into force and takes effect as on and from 1 January 2009.

Cross References

From Section 531F

Section 531E Record keeping.

Section 903 Power of inspection: PAYE.

531G Estimation of income levy due for income tax months and for year

[*Sections 989, 990* and *990A* shall apply to income levy as they apply to income tax.][1]

Amendments

[1] Inserted by F(No.2)A08 s2(a). This section is deemed to have come into force and takes effect as on and from 1 January 2009.

Cross References

From Section 531G

Section 989 Estimation of tax due for income tax months.

Section 990 Estimation of tax due for year.

Section 990A Generation of estimates by electronic, photographic or other process.

531H Assessment, collection, payment and recovery of income levy on aggregate income for the year of assessment

[(1) Income levy payable for a year of assessment in respect of aggregate income for the year of assessment shall be assessed, charged and paid in all respects as if it was an amount of income tax assessed and charged under the Tax Acts, but without regard to *section 1017*, and may be stated in one sum (in this section referred to as the "*aggregate sum*") with the amount of income tax contained in any computation of, or assessment or assessments to, income tax made by or on the individual by whom the income levy is payable for the year of assessment.

(2) Where, but for this subsection, no assessment to income levy would be made on an individual for a year of assessment, then an officer of the Revenue Commissioners shall make an assessment to income levy on the individual to the best of the officer's judgement of the amounts chargeable to income levy, and the provisions of the Tax Acts, including in particular those provisions relating to the assessment, collection and recovery of tax and the payment of interest on

unpaid tax, shall apply as respects any assessment to income levy made on the individual by virtue of this subsection, other than any such provisions in so far as they relate to the granting of any allowance, deduction or relief.

(3) Where income levy is payable for the year of assessment 2009 in respect of aggregate income for the year of assessment, *section 958* shall apply and have effect as if, in accordance with this Part, income levy had been payable for the year of assessment 2008.

(4) The Revenue Commissioners may make regulations for the purposes of the proper administration and implementation of this Part, and those regulations may, in particular and without prejudice to the generality of the foregoing, include provision for assessment, collection, recovery and repayment of income levy for any year of assessment to which this Part applies.][1]

Amendments

[1] Substituted by FA09 s2(1)(j). This section applies for the year of assessment 2009 and subsequent years of assessment.

Cross References

From Section 531H

Section 958 Date for payment of tax.

Section 1017 Assessment of husband in respect of income of both spouses.

531I Married couples

[Where an election has been made or is deemed to have been made under *section 1018* and has effect for a year of assessment, income levy payable by one spouse shall be charged, collected and recovered as if it were income levy payable by the spouse assessable under *section 1017*.][1]

Amendments

[1] Inserted by F(No.2)A08 s2(a). This section is deemed to have come into force and takes effect as on and from 1 January 2009.

Cross References

From Section 531I

Section 1017 Assessment of husband in respect of income of both spouses.

Section 1018 Election for assessment under section 1017.

531J False statements

[The provisions of *section 1056* in relation to the making of returns, declarations or statements shall apply, with any necessary modifications, in relation to income levy.][1]

Amendments

[1] Inserted by F(No.2)A08 s2(a). This section is deemed to have come into force and takes effect as on and from 1 January 2009.

Cross References

From Section 531J

Section 1056 Penalty for false statement made to obtain allowance.

531K Repayments

[(1) In any case of underpayment or overpayment of income levy to the Collector-General, payment of the amount not paid or repayment of the amount overpaid, as the case may be, shall be made to or by the Collector-General, as appropriate.

(2) In the case of an individual to whom *paragraph (a), (b)* or *(c)* of *section 531B(2)* applies, any income levy deducted from his or her income shall be repaid to the individual by the Revenue Commissioners on receipt of a valid claim made in such manner as may be approved by the Revenue Commissioners, and for the purposes of such repayment the income levy shall be deemed to be income tax.

(3) Where, at the end of a year of assessment, married persons assessed to tax for the year of assessment under *section 1017*, one or both of whom have reached the age of 65 years or over at any time during the year of assessment, prove to the satisfaction of the Revenue Commissioners that their aggregate income from all sources is not in excess of twice the limit set out in *section 531B(2)(c)*, then the Revenue Commissioners shall repay such income levy, if any, as has been deducted from that income during that year of assessment.][1]

Amendments

[1] Inserted by F(No.2)A08 s2(a). This section is deemed to have come into force and takes effect as on and from 1 January 2009.

Cross References

From Section 531K

Section 531B Charge to income levy.

Section 1017 Assessment of husband in respect of income of both spouses.

531L Restriction on deduction

[(1) Income levy paid in respect of a year of assessment is in addition to, and does not reduce, any liability which an individual may have in respect of income tax or other taxes under the Tax Acts.

(2) Excess tax credits or reliefs which are available to an individual may not be set against any charge to income levy which is due and payable for a year of assessment.][1]

Amendments

[1] Inserted by F(No.2)A08 s2(a). This section is deemed to have come into force and takes effect as on and from 1 January 2009.

531M Application of provisions relating to income tax

[(1) The provisions of Chapter 1 of Part 40, in relation to appeals, shall apply to income levy as they apply to income tax.

(2) The provisions of Part 47, in relation to penalties, offences, interest and other sanctions, shall apply in relation to income levy as they apply to income tax.

(3) *Section 865* shall apply to any repayment of income levy as it applies to income tax.

(4) *Section 987* shall apply, with any necessary modifications, to income levy as it applies to income tax.][1]

Amendments

[1] Inserted by F(No.2)A08 s2(a). This section is deemed to have come into force and takes effect as on and from 1 January 2009.

Cross References

From Section 531M

Section 865 Repayment of tax.
Section 987 Penalties for breach of regulations.

531N Care and management

[Income levy is under the care and management of the Revenue Commissioners and Part 37 shall apply to income levy as it applies to income tax.][1]

Amendments

[1] Inserted by F(No.2)A08 s2(a). This section is deemed to have come into force and takes effect as on and from 1 January 2009.

531NA Cessation of charge to income levy

[Subject to *section 531AY*, income levy shall cease to be charged, in accordance with this Part, for the year of assessment 2011 and subsequent years of assessment.][1]

Amendments

[1] Inserted by FA11 s2. Deemed to have come into force and takes effect as on and from 1 January 2011.

Cross References

From Section 531NA

Section 531AY Recovery of unpaid universal social charge.

PART 18B
Parking Levy in Urban Areas

531O Interpretation (Part 18B)

[In this Part—

"*car*" means a mechanically propelled road vehicle designed, constructed or adapted for the carriage of the driver or the driver and one or more other persons, other than—

(a) a motor-cycle (within the meaning of *section 121*),

(b) an official vehicle,

(c) a van (within the meaning of *section 121A*) where an employee is required by the employer to use the van in the performance of the duties of his or her office or employment, or

(d) a vehicle, other than a van, of a type not commonly used as a private vehicle and unsuitable to be so used;

"*disabled person's parking permit*" means a permit granted in accordance with Article 43 of the Road Traffic (Traffic and Parking) Regulations 1997 (S.I. No. 182 of 1997);

"*emoluments*" means emoluments to which Chapter 4 of Part 42 applies;

"*employee*" has the same meaning as it has for the purposes of the PAYE Regulations;

"*employer*" has the same meaning as it has for the purposes of the PAYE Regulations;

"*entitlement to use a parking space*" shall be construed in accordance with *section 531Q*;

"*fire authority*" has the same meaning as it has for the purposes of the Fire Services Act 1981;

"*maternity leave*" means the period of leave referred to in section 8 (as amended by section 2 of the Maternity Protection (Amendment) Act 2004 and by the Maternity Protection Act 1994 (Extension of Periods of Leave) Order 2006) of the Maternity Protection Act 1994;

"*mechanically propelled road vehicle*" includes a vehicle the means of propulsion of which is electrical or partly electrical and partly mechanical;

"*Minister*" means the Minister for Finance;

"*net emoluments*" means emoluments (less allowable contributions (within the meaning of Regulation 41 of the PAYE Regulations)) after the deduction, in accordance with—

(a) the PAYE Regulations, of income tax,

(b) the Social Welfare (Consolidated Contributions and Insurability) Regulations 1996 (S.I. No. 312 of 1996), of a contribution within the meaning of those regulations,

(c) the Health Contributions Regulations 1979 (S.I. No. 107 of 1979), of a health contribution, and

(d) Part 18A (as inserted by the *Finance (No. 2) Act 2008*), of income levy;

"*official vehicle*" means a vehicle which is owned or provided by the State or by a State authority where an employee of the State or of such an authority is required by the employer to use the vehicle in the performance of the duties of his or her office or employment;

"*parking levy*" means the tax, provided for in *section 531T*, on an entitlement to use a parking space in an urban area;

"*parking space*" means any area or part of an area on, at, or in which it is possible to park a vehicle and includes any part of a building, erection or structure (including a moveable structure);

"*PAYE Regulations*" means the Income Tax (Employments) (Consolidated) Regulations 2001 (S.I. No. 559 of 2001);

"*personal public service number*" has the same meaning as in section 262 of the Social Welfare Consolidation Act 2005;

"*public sector employee*" means a person whose emoluments are paid, funded or partly funded directly or indirectly by the State;

"*relevant local authority*" means the city council (within the meaning of section 2 of the Local Government Act 2001) of Cork, Dublin, Galway, Limerick or Waterford;

"*State authority*" means the Garda Síochána, the Defence Forces, the Health Service Executive (in so far as it relates to the ambulance service), the Revenue Commissioners (in so far as it relates to the Customs service), a fire authority or such other body as may be prescribed by order of the Minister under *section 531P(1)*;

"*urban area*" means an area or areas designated by order of the Minister under *section 531P(1)*;

"*year of assessment*" means a calendar year.][1]

Amendments

[1] Inserted by F(No.2)A08 s3(1)(a). This section is deemed to have come into force and takes effect as on and from 1 January 2009.

Note

In accordance with section 531P the Minister may by order provide for the date from which this Part shall have effect.

Cross References

From Section 531O

Section 121 Benefit of use of car.
Section 121A Benefit of use of van.
Section 531P Urban areas to which parking levy applies and making of orders by the Minister.
Section 531Q Entitlement to use a parking space.
Section 531T Charge to parking levy.

531P Urban areas to which parking levy applies and making of orders by the Minister

[(1) The Minister may, following consultation with any other Minister of the Government as he or she considers appropriate in the circumstances, by order—

(a) designate that an area or areas which is or are within the administrative area (within the meaning of section 2 of the Local Government Act 2001) of a relevant local authority shall be an urban area for the purposes of this Part,

(b) prescribe that a body shall be a State authority for the purposes of this Part, and

(c) provide for the date from which this Part shall have effect.

(2) Every order made by the Minister under subsection (1) shall be laid before Dáil Éireann as soon as may be after it is made and, if a resolution annulling the order is passed by Dáil Éireann within the next 21 days on which Dáil Éireann has sat after the order is laid before it, the order shall be annulled accordingly, but without prejudice to the validity of anything previously done thereunder.][1]

Amendments

[1] Inserted by F(No.2)A08 s3(1)(a). This section is deemed to have come into force and takes effect as on and from 1 January 2009.

Cross References

To Section 531P

Section 531O Interpretation (Part 18B).

531Q Entitlement to use a parking space

[(1) An employee shall be regarded as having an entitlement to use a parking space for the purposes of this Part where any one or more of the following circumstances apply:

(a) the employee holds or has been issued with an authorisation in the form of a badge, permit, sticker or any other form of authorisation to use a parking space or is otherwise given permission (including oral permission) to use a parking space;

(b) the employee holds or has been issued with any form or means of access to a parking space;

(c) the employee has been allocated a dedicated parking space;

(d) the employee has been allocated a parking space on a shared basis or other similar arrangement;

(e) the availability of a parking space to the employee is on the basis of a system commonly known as on a first-come — first-served basis.

(2) (a) An employee shall not be regarded as having an entitlement to use a parking space for the purposes of this Part where the use of the space by the employee arises as a result of authorisation, permission or access occasionally given to the employee and the total number of days—

(i) covered by such authorisation, permission or access, and

(ii) of actual use of the space by the employee,

is not more than 10 days in a year of assessment.

(b) For the purposes of paragraph *(a)*—

(i) authorisation, permission or access given for part of a day shall be regarded as given for a full day, and

(ii) use of a parking space for part of a day shall be regarded as use of the space for a full day.

(3) An employee shall cease to be regarded as having an entitlement to use a parking space for the purposes of this Part where—

(a) (i) he or she disclaims, in writing or in an electronic format, entitlement to use a parking space, as referred to in subsection (1), or

(ii) the entitlement to use a parking space lapses or such entitlement is withdrawn,

(b) if relevant, the employee returns to the employer, or to the person who provides the parking space as appropriate, either or both the form of authorisation and the form or means of access which he or she holds or which was issued to him or her, and

(c) the employee ceases to use a parking space provided directly or indirectly by his or her employer.

(4) For the purposes of *subsection (1)(a)*, permission to use a parking space shall be regarded as given to an employee where an employer enters into an arrangement or agreement with the employee or any other person whereby a parking space is provided for the use of the employee.][1]

Amendments

[1] Inserted by F(No.2)A08 s3(1)(a). This section is deemed to have come into force and takes effect as on and from 1 January 2009.

Note

In accordance with section 531P the Minister may by order provide for the date from which this Part shall have effect.

Cross References

To Section 531Q

Section 531O Interpretation (Part 18B).
Section 531U Rate of charge to parking levy.
Section 531X Records and regulations.

531R Provision of parking space by employer

[For the purposes of this Part, a parking space shall be regarded as provided directly or indirectly by an employer for the use of an employee where—

(a) the employer provides the parking space on, at or in any premises which is owned or occupied by the employer,

(b) the parking space is provided on, at or in any premises which is owned or occupied by a person connected (within the meaning of *section 10*) with the employer,

(c) the employer enters into an arrangement or agreement with an employee or any other person whereby a parking space is provided for the use of that employee or any other employee of the employer, or

(d) in the case of a public sector employee to whom *paragraph (a), (b)* or *(c)* does not apply, the person who provides the parking space to that employee is funded or part funded directly or indirectly by the employer of that employee.][1]

Amendments

[1] Inserted by F(No.2)A08 s3(1)(a). This section is deemed to have come into force and takes effect as on and from 1 January 2009.

Note

In accordance with section 531P the Minister may by order provide for the date from which this Part shall have effect.

Cross References

From Section 531R

Section 10 Connected persons.

To Section 531R

Section 531S Exemption for certain persons.
Section 531X Records and regulations.

531S Exemption for certain persons

[The parking levy provided for under this Part shall not apply—

(a) to an employee who is the holder of a valid disabled person's parking permit,

(b) to the use of a parking space by an employee of a State or civil emergency service where the use of that space relates solely to a response, required of the employee by the employer, to an emergency situation, or

(c) to occasional use of a parking space by a retired person where that person's former employer or, where *section 531R(d)* applies, the person who provided the parking space to the retired person before he or she retired, continues to make a parking space available to him or her.][1]

Amendments

[1] Inserted by F(No.2)A08 s3(1)(a). This section is deemed to have come into force and takes effect as on and from 1 January 2009.

Note

In accordance with section 531P the Minister may by order provide for the date from which this Part shall have effect.

Cross References

From Section 531S

Section 531R Provision of parking space by employer.

To Section 531S

Section 531T Charge to parking levy.
Section 531X Records and regulations.

531T Charge to parking levy

[Subject to *section 531S*, where—

(a) an employee has an entitlement to use a parking space in an urban area for the parking of a car, and

(b) such space is provided directly or indirectly by his or her employer,

then a tax to be known as "parking levy" shall be charged, levied and paid in accordance with this Part in relation to such entitlement.][1]

Amendments

[1] Inserted by F(No.2)A08 s3(1)(a). This section is deemed to have come into force and takes effect as on and from 1 January 2009.

Note

In accordance with section 531P the Minister may by order provide for the date from which this Part shall have effect.

Cross References

From Section 531T

Section 531S Exemption for certain persons.

To Section 531T

Section 531O Interpretation (Part 18B).
Section 531V Deduction of levy by employer.

531U Rate of charge to parking levy

[(1) Subject to the subsequent provisions of this section, the amount of the parking levy in relation to each employee—

(a) shall be €200 in relation to each year of assessment, or

(b) in relation to the year of assessment in which this Part takes effect, shall be €200 reduced to an amount which bears the same proportion to €200 as the period consisting of the part of that year in which this Part has effect bears to the full year of assessment.

(2) Where an employee has been allocated a parking space on a shared basis, or other similar arrangement including on a first-come — first-served basis as referred to in *section 531Q(1)(e)*, the amount of the parking levy shall—

(a) where the ratio of employees sharing a parking space to a space is less than two to one, be the appropriate amount referred to in *subsection (1)*, and

(b) where the ratio of employees sharing a parking space to a space is two to one or more than two to one, be reduced to 50 per cent of the appropriate amount referred to in *subsection (1)*.

(3) Where the normal pattern of work required of an employee involves the employee working only a portion of the full working week or year, then the amount of the parking levy determined in accordance with *subsection (1)* or *(2)* shall be reduced to an amount which bears the same proportion to the amount so determined as the portion of the full working week or year required to be worked by the employee bears to the full working week or year, subject to the amount of the levy being not less than 50 per cent of the amount determined in accordance with *subsection (1)* or *(2)* as the case may be.

(4) Where an employee's entitlement to use a parking space applies for part of a year of assessment or part of the period referred to in *subsection (1)(b)*, then the amount of the parking levy determined in accordance with *subsection (1)*, *(2)* or *(3)*, as the case may be, shall be reduced to an amount which bears the same proportion to the amount so determined as the part of the year or period during which the employee has such entitlement bears to the full period or year.

(5) An employee's entitlement to use a parking space for the period during which the employee is on maternity leave and for a period of 10 weeks immediately prior to the date the employee commences such leave shall be disregarded for the purposes of *subsection (4)*.

(6) Where the pattern of work required of an employee involves starting or finishing work after 9 o'clock in the evening or before 7 o'clock in the morning, that part of a year of assessment or that part of the period referred to in *subsection (1)(b)* in which such pattern of work applies shall be disregarded for the purposes of subsection (4).][1]

Amendments

[1] Inserted by F(No.2)A08 s3(1)(a). This section is deemed to have come into force and takes effect as on and from 1 January 2009.

Note

In accordance with section 531P the Minister may by order provide for the date from which this Part shall have effect.

Cross References

From Section 531U

Section 531Q Entitlement to use a parking space.

To Section 531U

Section 531V Deduction of levy by employer.
Section 531X Records and regulations.

531V Deduction of levy by employer

[(1) Where *section 531T* applies, an employer shall—

(a) deduct the amount of the parking levy, determined in accordance with *section 531U*, from the employee's net emoluments for the period during which he or she has an entitlement to use a parking space and such deduction shall be made at a time and frequency which corresponds with the payment of the employee's emoluments,

(b) be accountable for the amount of the parking levy deductible, and liable to pay that amount to the Revenue Commissioners as if it were an amount of income tax deductible in accordance with the PAYE Regulations, and

(c) remit to the Collector-General the total of all amounts of parking levy which the employer was liable to deduct from employees and such remittance shall be made at the same time and in the same manner as the employer is required under Regulation 28 or, as the case may be, under Regulation 29 of the PAYE Regulations to remit amounts of tax which the employer was liable to deduct from emoluments paid to employees.

(2) Where an amount of parking levy is, in accordance with this Part, deducted by an employer from the net emoluments of an employee—

(a) the employee shall allow such deduction on the receipt of the residue of the net emoluments, and

(b) the employer shall be acquitted and discharged of such amount as is represented by the deduction, as if the amount had actually been paid.][1]

Amendments

[1] Inserted by F(No.2)A08 s3(1)(a). This section is deemed to have come into force and takes effect as on and from 1 January 2009.

Note

In accordance with section 531P the Minister may by order provide for the date from which this Part shall have effect.

Cross References

From Section 531V

Section 531T Charge to parking levy.
Section 531U Rate of charge to parking levy.

To Section 531V

Section 531X Records and regulations.
Section 531Y Payment, collection and recovery.
Section 531Z Penalties.

531W No relief for any payment in relation to parking levy

[Notwithstanding any provision of the Tax Acts, no sum shall—

(a) in the case of an employee, be allowed to the employee in relation to a parking levy payable under this Part—

(i) as a deduction under *section 114*, or

(ii) as a credit against any liability arising under the Tax Acts,

or

(b) in the case of an employer—

(i) be deducted in computing the amount of profits or gains chargeable to tax under Schedule D, or

(ii) be included in computing any expenses of management in respect of which a deduction may be claimed under *section 83* or *707*,

in relation to any amount which is paid by the employer to an employee in compensation for, or in re-imbursement of, the payment of a parking levy under this Part.][1]

Amendments

[1] Inserted by F(No.2)A08 s3(1)(a). This section is deemed to have come into force and takes effect as on and from 1 January 2009.

Note

In accordance with section 531P the Minister may by order provide for the date from which this Part shall have effect.

Cross References

From Section 531W

Section 83 Expenses of management of investment companies.

Section 114 General rule as to deductions.

Section 707 Management expenses.

531X Records and regulations

[(1) Subject to *subsection (2)*, where a parking space in an urban area to which this Part applies is provided directly or indirectly by an employer for the use of one or more employees for the parking of a car, the employer shall in respect of each year of assessment and the period referred to in *section 531U(1)(b)* keep in a permanent form a full and true record of the following:

(a) details of the locations at which each such parking space is provided,

(b) the name and personal public service number of each employee who has an entitlement to use a parking space,

(c) where *section 531Q(3)* applies, the name and personal public service number of each employee who ceased to have an entitlement to use a parking space and the date from which the entitlement ceased,

(d) where *section 531S(a)* applies, the name and personal public service number of each employee to which that section applies, and

(e) such other records specified in regulations by the Revenue Commissioners as may reasonably be required by them for the purposes of this Part.

(2) Where a parking space in an urban area to which this Part applies is provided by a person referred to in *section 531R(d)* for the use of one or more public sector employees for the parking of a car, that person shall in respect of each year of assessment and the period referred to in *section 531U(1)(b)*—

(a) keep in a permanent form a full and true record of the information referred to in *paragraphs (a)* to *(e)* of *subsection (1)*, and

(b) (i) transmit in sufficient time to the employer of such employee or employees, such details as are necessary for the employer to comply with the requirements of *section 531V(1)*, and

(ii) make a record of the details so transmitted.

(3) The Revenue Commissioners may make regulations for the purposes of the administration and implementation of this Part and without prejudice to the generality of the foregoing, such regulations may include provision in relation to such records as are referred to in *subsection (1)(e)* and such matters as are referred to in *subsection (2)(b)*.

(4) For the purposes of this Part, the definition of "*records*" in *section 903* shall be treated as including the records referred to in *subsections (1)* and *(2)* and the provisions of *section 903* shall accordingly apply to such records.][1]

Amendments

[1] Inserted by F(No.2)A08 s3(1)(a). This section is deemed to have come into force and takes effect as on and from 1 January 2009.

Note

In accordance with section 531P the Minister may by order provide for the date from which this Part shall have effect.

Cross References

From Section 531X

Section 531Q Entitlement to use a parking space.
Section 531R Provision of parking space by employer.
Section 531S Exemption for certain persons.
Section 531U Rate of charge to parking levy.
Section 531V Deduction of levy by employer.
Section 903 Power of inspection: PAYE.

To Section 531X

Section 531Z Penalties.

531Y Payment, collection and recovery

[(1) The parking levy provided for under this Part is placed under the care and management of the Revenue Commissioners and *section 849* shall apply as if "parking levy" were included in the definition of "*tax*" in that section.

(2) The provisions of Chapter 4 of Part 42 and Part 5 of the PAYE Regulations shall, with any necessary modifications, apply to the payment, collection and recovery of the parking levy as they apply to the payment, collection and recovery of income tax in accordance with the said Part 42 and those Regulations and without prejudice to the generality of the foregoing—

(a) the definition of "*the regulations*" in *section 989* applies as if it included a reference to the provisions of this Part, and

(b) *sections 989, 990, 991* and *991A* apply as if the respective references to income tax or tax in those sections included a reference to the parking levy payable under this Part.

(3) In any case of underpayment or overpayment of the parking levy to the Collector-General by an employer, payment of the amount not paid or repayment of the

amount overpaid, as the case may be, shall be made to or by the Collector-General, as appropriate.

(4) In the case of an employer to whom *section 531V(1)* applies, the employer shall include the following details on the form which is required to be sent to the Collector-General under Regulation 31 of the PAYE Regulations:

(a) the total number of employees to whom the parking levy applied in the year of assessment, and

(b) the total amount of parking levy deducted by the employer from employees in the year of assessment.][1]

Amendments

[1] Inserted by F(No.2)A08 s3(1)(a). This section is deemed to have come into force and takes effect as on and from 1 January 2009.

Note

In accordance with section 531P the Minister may by order provide for the date from which this Part shall have effect.

Cross References

From Section 531Y

Section 531V Deduction of levy by employer.
Section 849 Taxes under care and management of Revenue Commissioners.
Section 989 Estimation of tax due for income tax months.
Section 990 Estimation of tax due for year.
Section 991 Interest.
Section 991A Payment of tax by direct debit.

To Section 531Y

Section 531Z Penalties.

531Z Penalties

[(1) Where an employer fails to—

(a) deduct or remit the parking levy in accordance with *section 531V(1)*,

(b) keep records in accordance with *section 531X(1)*, or

(c) include the details referred to in *paragraphs (a)* and *(b)* of *section 531Y(4)* on the form which is required to be sent to the Collector-General under Regulation 31 of the PAYE Regulations,

that person shall be liable to a penalty of €3,000.

(2) Where a person to whom *section 531X(2)* applies fails to—

(a) keep records in accordance with *paragraphs (a)* and *(b)(ii)* of that section, or

(b) provide details to an employer in accordance with *paragraph (b)(i)* of that section,

that person shall be liable to a penalty of €3,000.

(3) *Subsections (3)* and *(4)* of *section 987* apply to the penalties provided for in *subsections (1)* and *(2)* of this section as they apply to the penalties provided for in *section 987*.][1]

Amendments

[1] Inserted by F(No.2)A08 s3(1)(a). This section is deemed to have come into force and takes effect as on and from 1 January 2009.

Note

In accordance with section 531P the Minister may by order provide for the date from which this Part shall have effect.

Cross References

From Section 531Z

Section 531V Deduction of levy by employer.
Section 531X Records and regulations.
Section 531Y Payment, collection and recovery.
Section 987 Penalties for breach of regulations.

PART 18C

Domicile Levy

531AA Interpretation (Part 18C)

[(1) In this Part—

"*close company*" has the meaning assigned to it by *section 430*;

"*discretionary trust*" means any disposition whereby, or by virtue or in consequence of which, property is held on trust to apply, or with a power to apply, the income or capital or part of the income or capital of the property for the benefit of any person or persons or of any one or more of a number or of a class of persons whether at the discretion of trustees or any other person and notwithstanding that there may be a power to accumulate all or any part of the income and for the purposes of this definition "*disposition*" includes any disposition whether by deed or otherwise and any covenant, agreement or arrangement whether effected with or without writing;

"*domicile levy*" has the meaning assigned to it by *section 531AB*;

"*final decision*" means a decision against which no appeal lies or against which an appeal lies within a period which has expired without an appeal having been brought;

"*foundation*" means any legal entity, wherever established, to which an individual disposes of, or transfers, property, irrespective of—

(a) how that entity is described in the place of establishment, and

(b) the name by which that entity is called in the place of establishment;

"*holding company*" and "*subsidiary*" have the same meanings as in section 155 of the Companies Act 1963;

"*Irish property*", in relation to an individual and a valuation date, means all property, situate in the State, to which the individual is beneficially entitled in possession on the valuation date, but does not include—

(a) shares in a company which exists wholly or mainly for the purpose of carrying on a trade or trades,

(b) shares in a holding company which derive the greater part of their value from subsidiaries which wholly or mainly carry on a trade or trades;

"*liability to income tax*", in relation to an individual and a tax year, means the amount of income tax due and payable by the individual for the tax year in accordance with the Tax Acts and in respect of which a final decision has been made;

"*market value*", in relation to property, means the price which such property would fetch if sold on the open market on the valuation date in such manner and subject to such conditions as might reasonably be calculated to obtain for the vendor the best price for the property;

"*minor child*" means a child who has not attained the age of 18 years and is not and has not been [married or is not and has not been a civil partner][1];

"*property*" includes rights and interests of every description;

"*relevant individual*", in relation to a tax year, means an individual—

(a) who is domiciled in [...][2] the State in the tax year,

(b) whose world-wide income for the tax year is more than €1,000,000,

(c) whose liability to income tax in the State for the tax year is less than €200,000, and

(d) the market value of whose Irish property on the valuation date in the tax year is in excess of €5,000,000;

"*return*" means such a return as is referred to in *section 531AF*;

"*tax year*" means a year of assessment for income tax purposes;

"*world-wide income*", in relation to an individual, means the individual's income, without regard to any amount deductible from or deductible in computing total income, from all sources as estimated in accordance with the Tax Acts and as if any provision of those Acts providing for any income, profits or gains to be exempt from income tax or to be disregarded or not reckoned for the purposes of income tax or of those Acts were never enacted, and—

(a) without regard to any deduction—

(i) in respect of double rent allowance under *section 324(2), 333(2), 345(3)* or *354(3)*,

(ii) under *section 372AP*, in computing the amount of a surplus or deficiency in respect of rent from any premises,

(iii) under *section 372AU*, in computing the amount of a surplus or deficiency in respect of rent from any premises,

(iv) under *section 847A*, in respect of a relevant donation (within the meaning of that section),

(v) under *section 848A*, in respect of a relevant donation (within the meaning of that section),

and

[(b) having regard to a deduction for—

(i) any payment to which *section 1025* applies made by an individual pursuant to a maintenance arrangement (within the meaning of that section) relating to the marriage for the benefit of the other party to the marriage, unless *section 1026* applies in respect of such payment,

(ii) a payment of a similar nature to a payment referred to in *subparagraph (i)* pursuant to a maintenance arrangement (within the meaning of *section 1025*) relating to the marriage for the benefit of the other party to the marriage which attracts substantially the same tax treatment as such a payment,

(iii) any payment to which *section 1031J* applies made by an individual pursuant to a maintenance arrangement (within the meaning of that section) relating to the civil partnership for the benefit of the other party to the civil partnership, unless *section 1031K* applies in respect of such payment,

(iv) a payment of a similar nature to a payment referred to in *subparagraph (iii)*, pursuant to an order of a court under the law of another territory that, had it been made by a court in the State, would be a maintenance arrangement (within the meaning of *section 1031J*), relating to the civil partnership for the benefit of the other party to the civil partnership which attracts substantially the same tax treatment as such a payment, or

(v) any payment to which *section 1031Q* applies made by an individual pursuant to a maintenance arrangement (within the meaning of that section) where a relationship between cohabitants ends,][3]

determined on the basis that the individual, if not otherwise resident in the State for the year, was resident in the State for the tax year;

"*valuation date*", in relation to a tax year, means 31 December in that year.

(2) Subject to *subsection (3)*, for the purposes of the definition of "*Irish property*" in *subsection (1)*, an individual shall be deemed to be beneficially entitled in possession on the valuation date to—

(a) all property situate in the State which the individual has transferred [to his or her spouse, civil partner or minor children, or to the minor children of his or her civil partner,][4] for less than market value, on or after 18 February 2010,

(b) all property situate in the State which the individual has disposed of, or transferred, to a discretionary trust, for less than market value, on or after 18 February 2010, and

(c) all property situate in the State which the individual has disposed of, or transferred, to a foundation, for less than market value, on or after 18 February 2010.

(3) (a) *Subsection (2)(a)* shall not apply to a maintenance arrangement (within the meaning of [*section 1025, 1031]* or *1031Q*][5]).

(b) *Subsection (2)(b)* and *(c)* shall not apply to a discretionary trust or a foundation, as the case may be, which is shown, to the satisfaction of the Revenue Commissioners, to have been created exclusively—

(i) for purposes which, in accordance with the law of the State, are charitable, or

(ii) for the benefit of one or more named individuals and for the reason that such individual, or all such individuals, is or are, because of age or improvidence, or of physical, mental or legal incapacity, incapable of managing that individual's or those individuals' affairs.

(4) For the purposes of this Part, where the whole or the greater part of the market value of any share in a company incorporated outside the State that would be a close company if it were incorporated in the State is attributable, directly or indirectly, to property situate in the State, that share shall be deemed to be property situate in the State.

(5) In estimating the market value of any property for the purposes of this Part, no deduction shall be made from the market value for any debts or encumbrances.

(6) References in this Part to the Revenue Commissioners shall be construed as including references to any of their officers.][6]

Amendments

[1] Substituted by F(No.3)A11 sched1(144).

[2] Deleted by FA12 s136(1). Applies to domicile levy chargeable for the year 2012 and subsequent years.

[3] Substituted by F(No.3)A11 sched1(145). Shall have effect from 27 July 2011.

[4] Substituted by F(No.3)A11 sched1(146). Shall have effect from 27 July 2011.

[5] Substituted by F(No.3)A11 sched1(147).

[6] Inserted by FA10 s150(1). This section shall apply for the year of assessment 2010 and subsequent years.

Revenue Briefings

eBrief

eBrief No. 56/2011 – Domicile Levy
eBrief No. 72/2014 – Domicile Levy

Cross References

From Section 531AA

Section 324 Double rent allowance in respect of rent paid for certain business premises.
Section 333 Double rent allowance in respect of rent paid for certain business premises.
Section 345 Double rent allowance in respect of rent paid for certain business premises.
Section 354 Double rent allowance in respect of rent paid for certain business premises.
Section 372AP Relief for lessors.
Section 372AU Saver for relief due, and for clawback of relief given under, old schemes.
Section 430 Meaning of "close company".
Section 531AB Charge to domicile levy.
Section 531AF Delivery of returns.
Section 847A Donations to certain sports bodies.
Section 848A Donations to approved bodies.
Section 1025 Maintenance in case of separated spouses.
Section 1026 Separated and divorced persons: adaptation of provisions relating to married persons.

To Section 531AA

Section 531AG Opinion of Revenue Commissioners.

531AB Charge to domicile levy

[Subject to this Part, with effect from 1 January 2010 a levy, to be known as "*domicile levy*", shall be charged, levied and paid annually by every relevant individual and the amount of such levy shall be €200,000.][1]

Amendments

[1] Inserted by FA10 s150(1). This section shall apply for the year of assessment 2010 and subsequent years.

Revenue Briefings

eBrief

eBrief No. 56/2011 – Domicile Levy
eBrief No. 72/2014 – Domicile Levy

Cross References

To Section 531AB

Section 531AA Interpretation (Part 18C).

531AC Credit for income tax paid

[A relevant individual's liability to income tax for a tax year shall be allowable as a credit in arriving at the amount of domicile levy chargeable for that year, but only to the extent that such income tax has been paid at the same time as, or before, domicile levy for that year is paid.][1]

Amendments

[1] Inserted by FA10 s150(1). This section shall apply for the year of assessment 2010 and subsequent years.

531AD Valuation procedures

[(1) If the Revenue Commissioners are not satisfied with the market value of property estimated in a return, or if they consider it necessary to do so, they may estimate the value of that property and, where the market value as so estimated by the Revenue Commissioners exceeds the market value estimated in the return, any charge to tax shall be made by reference to the market value estimated by the Revenue Commissioners and not by reference to the market value estimated in the return.

(2) The market value of any property for the purposes of *subsection (1)* shall be ascertained by the Revenue Commissioners in such manner and by such means as they think fit and they may authorise a person suitably qualified for that purpose to inspect any property and report to them the value of such property for the purposes of this Part and the person having custody or possession of that property shall permit the person so authorised to inspect it at such reasonable times as the Revenue Commissioners consider necessary.

(3) Where the Revenue Commissioners require a valuation to be made by a person authorised by them for the purposes of *subsection (2)* the costs of such valuation shall be defrayed by the Revenue Commissioners.][1]

Amendments

[1] Inserted by FA10 s150(1). This section shall apply for the year of assessment 2010 and subsequent years.

531AE Appeals regarding value of real property

[If a relevant individual is aggrieved by a decision of the Revenue Commissioners as to the market value of any real property, the individual may appeal against the decision in the manner prescribed by section 33 of the Finance (1909-10) Act 1910, and the provisions as to appeals under that section shall apply accordingly with any necessary modifications.][1]

Amendments

[1] Inserted by FA10 s150(1). This section shall apply for the year of assessment 2010 and subsequent years.

531AF Delivery of returns

[(1) A relevant individual shall, as respects a tax year, on or before 31 October in the year after the valuation date, prepare and deliver to the Revenue Commissioners a full and true return, together with the payment of domicile levy, of all such matters and particulars in relation to the determination of liability to domicile levy as the Revenue Commissioners may require.

[(1A) Where the Revenue Commissioners have reason to believe that an individual is chargeable to domicile levy for any year on the basis that he or she is a relevant individual for that year, the Revenue Commissioners may, by notice in writing, request the individual to deliver, within 30 days of the date of the notice, a full and true return, together with the payment of domicile levy, of all such matters and particulars in relation to the determination of liability to domicile levy as the Revenue Commissioners may require.][1]

(2) A return under this section shall—

(a) be in such form as the Revenue Commissioners may require,

(b) be signed by the relevant individual, and

(c) include a declaration by the individual who signed the return that the return is, to the best of that individual's knowledge, information and belief, correct and complete.][2]

Amendments

[1] Inserted by FA14 s85(a).

---

[2] Inserted by FA10 s150(1). This section shall apply for the year of assessment 2010 and subsequent years.

Cross References

To Section 531AF

Section 531AA Interpretation (Part 18C).

Section 531AH Making and amending of assessments by Revenue Commissioners.

531AG Opinion of Revenue Commissioners

[(1) On an application to the Revenue Commissioners by an individual who is considering the making of a significant investment in the State, they may give an opinion to the individual as to whether or not, in the tax year in which the application is made, the individual would be likely to be regarded as an individual to whom *paragraph (a)* of the definition of "*relevant individual*" in *section 531AA(1)* applies.

(2) An application for an opinion under *subsection (1)* shall be in such form and contain such information and particulars as the Revenue Commissioners may require in relation to such an application.

(3) Nothing in this section shall be construed as obliging the Revenue Commissioners to give the opinion referred to in *subsection (1)*.][1]

Amendments

[1] Inserted by FA10 s150(1). This section shall apply for the year of assessment 2010 and subsequent years.

Cross References

From Section 531AG

Section 531AA Interpretation (Part 18C).

531AH Making and amending of assessments by Revenue Commissioners

[(1) Where—

(a) a return under *section 531AF(1)* is not delivered to the Revenue Commissioners by an individual on or before 31 October in the year following the valuation date, or

(b) the Revenue Commissioners are dissatisfied with a return delivered to them under *section 531AF(1)*,

the Revenue Commissioners may make an assessment or an amending assessment upon an individual who they have reason to believe is chargeable to domicile levy on the basis that the individual is a relevant individual.

(2) The Revenue Commissioners may withdraw an assessment made under *subsection (1)* and make an assessment of the amount of domicile levy payable on the basis of a return which, in their opinion, represents reasonable compliance with their requirements and which is delivered to them within 30 days after the date of the assessment made by them pursuant to *subsection (1)*.][1]

Amendments

[1] Inserted by FA10 s150(1). This section shall apply for the year of assessment 2010 and subsequent years.

Cross References

From Section 531AH

Section 531AF Delivery of returns.

531AI Right of Revenue Commissioners to make enquiries and amend assessments

[(1) [*Section 959Z*][1] shall apply, with any necessary modifications, for the purposes of this Part as it applies for the purposes of income tax.

(2) For the purposes of making an enquiry or taking such actions, as referred to in [*section 959Z*][2] or for the purposes of making, amending or further amending an assessment on an individual in relation to domicile levy, the Revenue Commissioners shall have all such powers as an inspector would have under that section in relation to making enquiries or taking such actions as he or she considers necessary to satisfy himself or herself as to the accuracy or otherwise of any statement or particular contained in a return delivered for the purposes of income tax.][3]

Amendments

[1, 2] Substituted by FA12 sched4(part 2)(g).

[3] Inserted by FA10 s150(1). This section shall apply for the year of assessment 2010 and subsequent years.

Cross References

From Section 531AI

Section 956 Inspector's right to make enquiries and amend assessments.

531AJ Application of provisions relating to income tax

[(1) The provisions of *Chapter 1* of *Part 40*, in relation to appeals, shall apply to domicile levy as they apply to income tax.

(2) *Chapter 1* of *Part 47* shall apply to domicile levy as it applies to income tax.

(3) *Section 1080* shall apply to domicile levy as it applies to income tax.][1]

Amendments

[1] Inserted by FA10 s150(1). This section shall apply for the year of assessment 2010 and subsequent years.

Cross References

From Section 531AJ

Section 932 Prohibition on alteration of assessment except on appeal.

Section 1052 Penalties for failure to make certain returns, etc.

Section 1080 Interest on overdue income tax, corporation tax and capital gains tax.

531AK Care and management

[Domicile levy is under the care and management of the Revenue Commissioners and *Part 37* applies to domicile levy as it applies to income tax.][1]

Amendments

[1] Inserted by FA10 s150(1). This section shall apply for the year of assessment 2010 and subsequent years.

Cross References

From Section 531AK

Section 849 Taxes under care and management of Revenue Commissioners.

PART 18D

Universal Social Charge

531AL Definitions (Part 18D)

[In this Part—

"*aggregate income for the tax year*", in relation to an individual and a tax year, means the aggregate of the individual's—

(a) relevant emoluments in the tax year, including relevant emoluments that are paid in whole or in part for a tax year other than the tax year during which the payment is made, and

(b) relevant income for the tax year;

"*Collector-General*" means the Collector-General appointed under *section 851*;

"*employee*" and "*employer*" have the same meanings as in *section 983*;

"*excluded emoluments*" means emoluments which have been gifted to the Minister for Finance under *section 483*;

"*income levy*" has the meaning assigned to it by *section 531B*;

"*income tax month*" means a calendar month;

"*inspector*" means an inspector of taxes or other officer of the Revenue Commissioners;

"*PAYE Regulations*" means the Income Tax (Employments) (Consolidated) Regulations 2001 (S.I. No. 559 of 2001);

"*relevant emoluments*" and "*relevant income*" shall be construed in accordance with *paragraphs (a)* and *(b)*, respectively, of the Table to *section 531AM(1)*;

['*similar type payments*' means payments which are of a similar character to social welfare payments but which are made by—

(a) the Department of Education and Skills,

(b) the Department of Agriculture, Food and the Marine,

(c) the Health Service Executive,

(d) an education and training board in relation to attendance at a non-craft training course funded by An tSeirbhis Oideachais Leanúnaigh agus Scileanna,

(e) a sponsor in respect of participation in programmes known as the Community Employment Scheme and the Jobs Initiative Scheme, or

(f) any other state or territory;][1]

"*social welfare payments*" means payments made under the Social Welfare Acts;

"*tax year*" means a year of assessment within the meaning of the Tax Acts;

"*universal social charge*" has the meaning assigned to it by *section 531AM*.][2]

Amendments

[1] Substituted by FA14 s2(a). Comes into operation on 1 January 2015.

[2] Inserted by FA11 s3(1)(a). Applies for the year of assessment 2011 and each subsequent year of assessment.

Revenue Information Notes

IT 22 – Taxation of Illness Benefit and Occupational Injury Benefit

Cross References

From Section 531AL

Section 472A Relief for the long-term unemployed.

Section 483 Relief for certain gifts.

Section 531B Charge to income levy.

Section 531AM Charge to universal social charge.
Section 851 Collector-General.
Section 983 Interpretation (Chapter 4).

531AM Charge to universal social charge

[(1) With effect from 1 January 2011, there shall be charged, levied and paid, in accordance with the provisions of this Part, a tax to be known as "*universal social charge*" in respect of the income specified in *paragraphs* (*a*) and (*b*) of the Table to this subsection.

TABLE

(a) The income described in this paragraph (in this Part referred to as "*relevant emoluments*") is emoluments to which *Chapter 4* of *Part 42* applies or is applied, including—

(i) any allowable contributions referred to in Regulations 41 and 42 of the PAYE Regulations,

(ii) the initial market value (within the meaning of *section 510(2)*) of any shares, excluded from the charge to income tax by virtue of *section 510(4)*, appropriated in accordance with *Chapter 1* of *Part 17* [except where such shares were held by an employee share ownership trust, approved in accordance with *Schedule 12*, before 1 January 2011,][1]

(iii) the market value (determined in accordance with *section 548*) of the right referred to in *section 519A(1)* or *519D(1)*, [...][2]

[(iv) any gain exempted from income tax by virtue of *section 519A(3)* or *519D(3)* after such a gain is reduced by the market value of the right referred to in *subparagraph (iii)*, and,][3]

[(v) the '*specified amount*' as defined in *section 825C*,][4]

but not including—

(I) social welfare payments and similar type payments,

(II) excluded emoluments,

(III) emoluments disregarded by an employer on the direction of an inspector in accordance with Regulation 10(3) of the [PAYE Regulations, [...][5]][6]

(IV) any amount in respect of which relief is due under *section 201(5)(a)* and *paragraphs 6* and *8* of [*Schedule 3*, and][7]

[(V) any amount transferred by an administrator under section 782A(3).][8]

[...][9]

(b) The income described in this paragraph (in this Part referred to as "*relevant income*") is income, without regard to any amount deductible from or deductible in computing total income, from all sources as estimated in accordance with the Tax Acts, other than—

(i) relevant emoluments,

(ii) any emoluments, payments, expenses or other amounts referred to in *subparagraphs (I)* to *(V)*][10] of *paragraph* (*a*)[...][11] of this Table,

(iii) any gains, income or payments to which any of the following provisions apply—

(I) Chapter 4 of Part 8;

(II) Chapter 5 of Part 8;

(III) Chapter 7 of Part 8;
(IV) Chapter 5 of Part 26;
(V) Chapter 6 of Part 26;
(VI) Chapter 1A of Part 27;
(VII) Chapter 4 of Part 27,

(iv) where *section 825A* applies in respect of an individual for a tax year, an amount equal to the difference between—

(I) the individual's total income for the tax year had that section not applied for that year, and

(II) the amount of total income which if charged to income tax for the year would have given an amount of income tax payable equal to that which would be payable by virtue of the operation of that section,

(v) where *section 1025* applies in respect of an individual, the amount of any deduction for any payment to which that section applies, made by an individual pursuant to a maintenance arrangement (within the meaning of that section) relating to the marriage for the benefit of the other party to the marriage unless *section 1026* applies in respect of such payment,

[(va) where *section 1031J* applies in respect of an individual, the amount of any deduction for any payment to which that section applies, made by an individual pursuant to a maintenance arrangement (within the meaning of that section) for the benefit of his or her civil partner or former civil partner unless *section 1031K* applies in respect of such payment,

(vb) where *section 1031Q* applies in respect of an individual, the amount of any deduction for any payment to which that section applies, made by a qualified cohabitant pursuant to a maintenance arrangement (within the meaning of that section) for the benefit of the other qualified cohabitant,][12]

(vi) where *section 382* applies in respect of an individual carrying on a trade or profession, an amount equal to the amount referred to in [*section 531AU(1)*,][13]

(vii) where *section 272, 284, 658* or *659* applies in respect of an individual carrying on a trade or profession, an amount equal to the amount referred to in [*section 531AU(2)*, and][14]

[(viii) where *section 372AP* applies in respect of an individual, the amount that the individual is deemed to have received as rent in accordance with *subsection (7)* of that section where the individual received, or was entitled to receive, the deduction referred to in *subsection (2)* of that section on or after 1 January 2012,][15]

and—

(I) as if *sections 140, 141, 142, 143, 195, 232, 234* and *664* were never [enacted,][16]

(II) without regard to any deduction—

(A) in respect of double rent allowance under *section 324(2), 333(2), 345(3)* or *354(3)*,

(B) under *section 372AP*, in computing the amount of a surplus or deficiency in respect of rent from any premises,

(C) under *section 372AU*, in computing the amount of a surplus or deficiency in respect of rent from any premises,

(D) under *section 847A*, in respect of a relevant donation (within the meaning of that section), or

(E) under *section 848A*, in respect of a relevant donation [(within the meaning of that section).][17]

[(III) including a balancing charge in respect of any amount that would have been deducted by virtue of *subparagraph (vii)*.][18]

(2) Universal social charge shall not be payable for a tax year by an individual who proves to the satisfaction of the Revenue Commissioners that his or her aggregate income for the tax year does not exceed [€12,012].[19]][20]

Amendments

[1] Inserted by FA12 s2(1)(a). Deemed to have had effect as on and from 1 January 2011.

[2] Deleted by FA12 s2(1)(b). Deemed to have come into force and takes effect on and from 1 January 2012.

[3] Substituted by FA12 s2(1)(c). Deemed to have had effect as on and from 1 January 2011.

[4] Inserted by FA12 s2(1)(d). Deemed to have come into force and takes effect on and from 1 January 2012.

[5] Deleted by FA13 s2(a). Deemed to have come into force and takes effect on and from 1 January 2013.

[6] Substituted by FA12 s(1)(e). Deemed to have come into force and takes effect on and from 1 January 2012.

[7] Substituted by FA13 s2(a). Deemed to have come into force and takes effect on and from 1 January 2013.

[8] Inserted by FA13 s2(b). Deemed to have come into force and takes effect on and from 1 January 2013.

[9] Deleted by FA12 s2(1)(g). Deemed to have come into force and takes effect on and from 1 January 2012.

[10] Substituted by FA13 s2(c). Deemed to have come into force and takes effect on and from 1 January 2013.

[11] Deleted by FA12 s2(1)(h)(ii). Deemed to have had effect as on and from 1 January 2011.

[12] Inserted by F(No.3)A11 sched1(148).

[13] Substituted by FA12 s2(1)(i). Deemed to have come into force and takes effect on and from 1 January 2012.

[14] Substituted by FA12 s2(1)(j). Deemed to have come into force and takes effect on and from 1 January 2012.

[15] Inserted by FA12 s2(1)(k). Deemed to have come into force and takes effect on and from 1 January 2012.

[16, 17] Substituted by FA13 s2(d). Deemed to have come into force and takes effect on and from 1 January 2013.

[18] Inserted by FA13 s2(e). Deemed to have come into force and takes effect on and from 1 January 2013.

[19] Substituted by FA14 s2(b). Comes into operation on 1 January 2015.

[20] Inserted by FA11 s3(1)(a). Applies for the year of assessment 2011 and each subsequent year of assessment.

Revenue Briefings

Tax Briefing

Tax Briefing April 2011 – Issue 02 – Share-Based Remuneration - Finance Act 2011 Changes

Tax Briefing December 2011 – Issue 06 – Tax and Universal Social Charge (USC) treatment of income arising from having or exercising the public office of director of an Irish incorporated company

eBrief

eBrief No. 17/2011 – Share-Based Remuneration – Finance Act 2011 Changes

eBrief No. 26/2011 – Preliminary Tax for 2011 and Universal Social Charge (USC)

eBrief No. 54/2011 – Change to the operation of the Universal Social Charge from 1 January 2012

eBrief No. 80/2011 – Universal Social Charge Regulations 2011 (S.I. 658 of 2011)

eBrief No. 81/2011 – "Cross-Border" Workers and Universal Social Charge (USC)
eBrief No. 82/2011 – Universal Social Charge (USC) and Income Levy – employees resident and working in non tax treaty countries
eBrief No. 05/2012 – The Application of Universal Social Charge (USC) to Social Welfare-type Payments
eBrief No. 12/2012 – Universal social charge and capital allowances – 2011 Form 11
eBrief No. 27/2012 – Tax and Universal Social Charge (USC) treatment of employment income arising to flight crew members
eBrief No. 08/2013 – Universal Social Charge
eBrief No. 52/2014 – USC – Split Year Residence, Payment of arrears and bonuses

Revenue Information Notes

Universal Social Charge – Frequently Asked Questions

Cross References

From Section 531AM

Section 140 Distributions out of profits or gains from stallion fees, stud greyhound services fees and occupation of certain woodlands.
Section 141 Distributions out of income from patent royalties.
Section 142 Distributions out of profits of certain mines.
Section 143 Distributions out of profits from coal, gypsum and anhydrite mining operations.
Section 195 Exemption of certain earnings of writers, composers and artists.
Section 201 Exemptions and reliefs in respect of tax under section 123.
Section 232 Profits from occupation of certain woodlands.
Section 234 Certain income derived from patent royalties.
Section 272 Writing-down allowances.
Section 284 Wear and tear allowances.
Section 324 Double rent allowance in respect of rent paid for certain business premises.
Section 333 Double rent allowance in respect of rent paid for certain business premises.
Section 345 Double rent allowance in respect of rent paid for certain business premises.
Section 354 Double rent allowance in respect of rent paid for certain business premises.
Section 372AP Relief for lessors.
Section 372AU Saver for relief due, and for clawback of relief given under, old schemes.
Section 382 Right to carry forward losses to future years.
Section 510 Approved profit sharing schemes: appropriated shares.
Section 519A Approved savings-related share option schemes.
Section 519D Approved share option schemes.
Section 531AU Capital allowances and losses.
Section 548 Valuation of assets.
Section 658 Farming: allowances for capital expenditure on construction of buildings and other works.
Section 659 Farming: allowances for capital expenditure on the construction of farm buildings, etc. for control of pollution.
Section 664 Relief for certain income from leasing of farm land.
Section 825A Reduction in income tax for certain income earned outside the State.
Section 826 Agreements for relief from double taxation.
Section 847A Donations to certain sports bodies.
Section 848A Donations to approved bodies.
Section 984 Application.
Section 1025 Maintenance in case of separated spouses.
Section 1026 Separated and divorced persons: adaptation of provisions relating to married persons.

To Section 531AM

Section 531AAB Regulations.
Section 531AL Definitions (Part 18D).
Section 531AU Capital allowances and losses.
Section 531AW Repayments.

531AN Rate of charge

[[(1) For each tax year an individual shall be charged to universal social charge on his or her aggregate income for the tax year—

(a) at the rate specified in [*column (2)* of *Part 1* of the Table to this section corresponding to the *part* of aggregate income specified in *column (1)* of *Part 1* of that Table][1] where the individual is—

(i) aged under 70 years, or

(ii) aged 70 years or over at any time during the tax year and has aggregate income that exceeds €60,000,

or

(b) at the rate specified in [*column (2)* of *Part 2* of the Table to this section corresponding to the part of aggregate income specified in *column (1)* of *Part 2* of that Table][2] where the individual is aged 70 years or over at any time during the tax year and has aggregate income that does not exceed €60,000.][3]

[(2) Notwithstanding *subsection (1)* and the Table to this section, where an individual has relevant income that exceeds €100,000, the individual shall, instead of being charged to universal social charge on the amount of the excess at the rate provided for in [*column (2)* of *Part 1* of that Table, be charged on the amount of that excess at the rate of 11 per cent][4].][5]

[(2A) For the purposes of *subsection (2)*, relevant income shall not include any amount in respect of which an individual is chargeable to tax under Schedule E in accordance with *section 128(2)*.][6]

(3) [Notwithstanding *subsection (1)* and the Table to this section, where an individual is in receipt of aggregate income which does not exceed €60,000, is aged under 70 years][7] and has full eligibility for services under Part IV of the Health Act 1970, by virtue of sections 45 and 45A of that Act or Council Regulation (EC) No. 883/2004 of 29 April 2004*][8], the individual shall, instead of being charged to universal social charge on the part of aggregate income for the tax year concerned that [exceeds €17,576 at the rate provided for in *column (2)* of *Part 1* of that Table, be charged on the amount of the excess at the rate of 3.5 per cent].[9]

* OJ No. L166 30.4.2004, p.1

[(3A) Where an individual is chargeable to income tax under Case IV of Schedule D in respect of an encashment amount, or a deemed encashment amount, as the case may be, under *section 787TA*, then—

(a) notwithstanding *subsection (1)* and the Table to this section, the individual shall be charged to universal social charge for the tax year in which the income tax is charged on the full amount so charged to income tax at the rate of [3.5 per cent][10], and

(b) the amount so chargeable to income tax shall not be regarded as relevant income for the purposes of *subsection (2)*.][11]

[(4) *Subsection (3)* shall cease to have effect for the tax year 2018 and subsequent tax years.][12]

TABLE

PART 1

[Part of aggregate income (1)	Rate of universal social charge (2)
The first €12,012	1.5 per cent
The next €5,564	3.5 per cent
The next €52,468	7 per cent
The remainder	8 per cent

PART 2

Part of aggregate income (1)	Rate of universal social charge (2)
The first €12,012	1.5 per cent
The remainder	3.5 per cent][13]

Amendments

[1] Substituted by FA14 s2(c)(i). Comes into operation on 1 January 2015.

[2] Substituted by FA14 s2(c)(ii). Comes into operation on 1 January 2015.

[3] Substituted by FA13 s3(a). Applies as respects the year of assessment 2013 and subsequent year of assessment.

[4] Substituted by FA14 s2(c)(iii). Comes into operation on 1 January 2015.

[5] Substituted by FA13 s3(b). Applies as respects the year of assessment 2013 and subsequent year of assessment.

[6] Inserted by FA12 s2(3)(a). Deemed to have had effect as on and from 1 January 2011.

[7] Substituted by FA13 s3(c). Applies as respects the year of assessment 2013 and subsequent year of assessment.

[8] Substituted by FA12 s2(3)(b). Deemed to have had effect as on and from 1 January 2011.

[9] Substituted by FA14 s2(c)(iv). Comes into operation on 1 January 2015.

[10] Substituted by FA14 s2(c)(v). Comes into operation on 1 January 2015.

[11] Inserted by FA12 s2(3)(c). Deemed to have come into force and takes effect on and from 1 January 2012.

[12] Substituted by FA14 s2(c)(vi). Comes into operation on 1 January 2015.

[13] Substituted by FA14 s2(c)(vii). Comes into operation on 1 January 2015.

Revenue Briefings

eBrief

eBrief No. 81/2011 – "Cross-Border" Workers and Universal Social Charge (USC)

Revenue Information Notes

Universal Social Charge – Frequently Asked Questions

Cross References

To Section 531AN

Section 531AAD Excess bank remuneration charge.

531AO Deduction and payment of universal social charge on relevant emoluments

[(1) An employer shall be liable in the first instance to pay universal social charge due in respect of any payment of relevant emoluments.

[…][1]

[(1A) Where—

(a) an employer pays relevant emoluments to an employee in the form of shares (including stock), or

(b) an employee realises a gain by the exercise of a right in accordance with the provisions of a scheme approved under *Schedule 12A*,

and where, by reason of an insufficiency of payments actually made to or on behalf of the employee, the employer is unable to deduct the amount (or full amount) of the universal social charge required to be deducted under this Part and regulations made under this Part in respect of those shares or that gain, as the case may be, that employer shall be entitled to withhold and to realise sufficient shares to meet that universal social charge liability.

(1B) Where *subsection (1A)* applies—

(a) the employee shall allow such withholding as is referred to in that subsection, and

(b) the employer shall be acquitted and discharged of so much of the universal social charge liability as is represented by the shares withheld as if the value of those shares had been paid to the employee.

(1C) *Subsection (1A)* shall not apply where the employee has otherwise made good to the employer the amount of the universal social charge required to be deducted under this Part and regulations made under this Part in respect of those shares or that gain, as the case may be, as is referred to in that subsection.][2]

Amendments

[1] Deleted by FA12 s2(4)(a). Deemed to have come into force and takes effect on and from 1 January 2012.

[2] Inserted by FA12 s2(4)(b). Deemed to have come into force and takes effect on and from 1 January 2012.

Revenue Information Notes

Universal Social Charge – Frequently Asked Questions

eBrief

eBrief No. 35/2013 - Employer P30 and P35 Returns

Cross References

From Section 531AO

Section 531AAB Regulations.

Section 917EA Mandatory electronic filing and payment of tax.

To Section 531AO

Section 531AAD Excess bank remuneration charge.

531AP Record keeping [Deleted]

Deleted by FA12 s2(5). Deemed to have come into force and takes effect on and from 1 January 2012.

531AQ Power of inspection [Deleted]

Deleted by FA12 s2(5). Deemed to have come into force and takes effect on and from 1 January 2012.

531AR Estimation of universal social charge due

[*Sections 989*, *990* and *990A* shall apply to universal social charge as they apply to income tax.][1]

Amendments

[1] Inserted by FA11 s3(1)(a). Applies for the year of assessment 2011 and each subsequent year of assessment.

Revenue Information Notes

Universal Social Charge – Frequently Asked Questions

Cross References

From Section 531AR

Section 989 Estimation of tax due for income tax months.

Section 990 Estimation of tax due for year.

Section 990A Generation of estimates by electronic, photographic or other process.

531AS Universal social charge payable by chargeable persons (within the meaning of Part 41)

[(1) Universal social charge payable for a tax year in respect of an individual's aggregate income for a tax year, being an individual who is a chargeable person (within the meaning of [*Part 41A*][1], shall be due and payable in all respects as if it were an amount of income tax due and payable by the chargeable person under the Income Tax Acts, but without regard to [*section 1017* or *1031C*][2].

[(1A) For the purposes of *subsection (1)* and, as respects a gain realised by an individual by the exercise of a right to acquire shares in a company, *section 128B* shall, with any necessary modifications, apply to universal social charge as it applies to income tax and for this purpose—

(a) '*relevant tax*' as referred to in *section 128B* shall include universal social charge,

(b) '*B*' in the formula in *section 128B(2)* shall be the percentage which is equal to the highest rate set out in [*column (2)* of *Part 1* or *column (2)* of *Part 2*][3], as the case may be, of the Table to *section 531AN* that is in force for the tax year in which the individual realises a gain by the exerciseof a right to acquire shares in a company, and

(c) where the Revenue Commissioners are satisfied that the individual is likely to be chargeable to universal social charge for a tax year at a rate other than whichever of the rates set out in [*column (2)* of *Part 1* or *column (2)* of *Part 2*][4], as the case may be, of the Table to *section 531AN* is the highest such rate, *section 128B(14)* shall apply as if the reference to the standard rate was a reference to that other rate.][5]

(2) An individual who, by virtue of *section 140, 141, 142, 143, 195, 232, 234*, or 664, would not be treated as a chargeable person (within the meaning of [*Part 41A*][6]) in respect of the individual's aggregate income for a tax year, shall be treated as such a chargeable person for the purposes of this Part.

(3) Universal social charge may be stated in one sum (in this section referred to as the "*aggregated sum*") with the amount of income tax contained in any computation of, or any assessment or assessments to, income tax made by or on such an individual as is referred to in *subsection (1)*.

(4) For the purposes of *subsection (2)* universal social charge may be so stated as referred to in *subsection (3)* notwithstanding that there is no amount of income tax contained in the computation, assessment or assessments, and all the provisions of the Tax Acts, other than any such provisions in so far as they relate to the granting of any allowance, deduction or relief, shall apply as if the aggregated sum were a single sum of income tax.

(5) Where universal social charge is payable for the tax year 2011 in respect of an individual's aggregate income for a tax year, being an individual who is a chargeable person (within the meaning of [*Part 41A*][7]), [*Chapter 7* of *Part 41A*][8] shall apply and have effect as if, in accordance with this Part, universal social charge had been payable for the tax year 2010 and as if income levy had not been payable for that tax year.][9]

Amendments

[1] Substituted by FA12 sched4(part 2)(g).

[2] Substituted by F(No.3)A11 sched1(149).

[3] Substituted by FA14 s2(d)(i). Comes into operation on 1 January 2015.

[4] Substituted by FA14 s2(d)(ii). Comes into operation on 1 January 2015.

[5] Inserted by FA12 s2(6). Deemed to have come into force and takes effect on and from 1 January 2012.

[6] Substituted by FA12 sched4(part 2)(g).

[7] Substituted by FA12 sched4(part 2)(g).

[8] Substituted by FA12 sched4(part 2)(g).

[9] Inserted by FA11 s3(1)(a). Applies for the year of assessment 2011 and each subsequent year of assessment.

Revenue Briefings

Tax Briefing

Tax Briefing April 2011 – Issue 02 – Share-Based Remuneration – Finance Act 2011 Changes

Revenue Information Notes

Universal Social Charge – Frequently Asked Questions

Cross References

From Section 531AS

Section 140 Distributions out of profits or gains from stallion fees, stud greyhound services fees and occupation of certain woodlands.

Section 141 Distributions out of income from patent royalties.

Section 142 Distributions out of profits of certain mines.

Section 143 Distributions out of profits from coal, gypsum and anhydrite mining operations.

Section 195 Exemption of certain earnings of writers, composers and artists.

Section 232 Profits from occupation of certain woodlands.

Section 234 Certain income derived from patent royalties.

Section 958 Date for payment of tax.

Section 1017 Assessment of husband in respect of income of both spouses.

To Section 531AS

Section 531AT Universal social charge payable by persons other than chargeable persons (within the meaning of Part 41).

531AT Universal social charge payable by persons other than chargeable persons (within the meaning of Part 41)

[(1) Universal social charge payable for a tax year in respect of an individual's aggregate income for a tax year, being an individual who is not a chargeable person (within the meaning of [*Part 41A*][1]), shall be assessed, charged and paid in all respects as if it were an amount of income tax due and payable under the Income Tax Acts, but without regard to [*section 1017* or *1031C*][2].

[(2) *Subsections (3)* and *(4)* of *section 531AS*, as they relate to the aggregation of universal social charge and income tax, shall apply for the purposes of this section, with any necessary modifications, as they apply to universal social charge due and payable by a chargeable person and as if 'For the purposes of *subsection (2)*' were deleted in subsection (4).][3]][4]

Amendments

[1] Substituted by FA12 sched4(part 2)(g).

[2] Substituted by F(No.3)A11 sched1(150).

[3] Substituted by FA12 s2(7). Deemed to have had effect as on and from 1 January 2011.

[4] Inserted by FA11 s3(1)(a). Applies for the year of assessment 2011 and each subsequent year of assessment.

Revenue Information Notes

Universal Social Charge – Frequently Asked Questions

Cross References

From Section 531AT

Section 531AS Universal social charge payable by chargeable persons (within the meaning of Part 41).

Section 1017 Assessment of husband in respect of income of both spouses.

531AU Capital allowances and losses

[(1) Where an individual who has sustained a loss in a trade or profession for which relief from income tax has not been wholly given in an earlier tax year carries forward any unrelieved portion of that loss to a later tax year in accordance with *section 382*, the amount referred to in *section 531AM(1)(b)(vi)* is an amount equal to the amount of the carried forward loss that is deducted from or set off against the amount of profits or gains on which the individual is assessed to income tax under Schedule D in respect of that trade or profession for that later tax year.

(2) The amount referred to in *section 531AM(1)(b)(vii)* is—

(a) in the case of an individual who is entitled to an allowance for a tax year under *section 284(1)*,

(b) in the case of an individual who is entitled to an allowance for a tax year under *subsection (3)* of *section 272* of an amount determined in accordance with *paragraph* (*a*), (*b*), (*c*)(iii), (*da*), (*db*), (*e*) or (*g*) of that subsection,

(c) in the case of an individual who is entitled to an allowance for a tax year under *subsection (2)* of *section 658* of an amount determined in accordance with *paragraph* (*b*) of that subsection, or

(d) in the case of an individual who is entitled to an allowance for a tax year under *section 659(2)(a)* determined in accordance with *subsection (3A), (3AA), (3B)* or *(3BA)* of that section,

an amount equal to the aggregate of—

(i) the amount of the allowance made in the tax year to which effect is given in taxing the individual's trade or profession for that tax year, other than where effect is given by making a claim under *section 381* by virtue of *section 392*, and

(ii) any unrelieved allowance, or part of an allowance, carried forward from a previous tax year in accordance with *section 304(4)* to which effect is given in the tax year,

other than where such an allowance is made on a lessor or where such an allowance is made on an individual who is not an active partner (within the meaning of *section 409A*).][1]

Amendments

[1] Inserted by FA11 s3(1)(a). Applies for the year of assessment 2011 and each subsequent year of assessment.

Revenue Information Notes

Universal Social Charge – Frequently Asked Questions

Cross References

From Section 531AU

Section 272 Writing-down allowances.
Section 284 Wear and tear allowances.
Section 304 Income tax: allowances and charges in taxing a trade, etc.
Section 381 Right to repayment of tax by reference to losses.
Section 382 Right to carry forward losses to future years.
Section 392 Option to treat capital allowances as creating or augmenting a loss.
Section 409A Income tax: restriction on use of capital allowances on certain industrial buildings and other premises.
Section 531AM Charge to universal social charge.
Section 658 Farming: allowances for capital expenditure on construction of buildings and other works.
Section 659 Farming: allowances for capital expenditure on the construction of farm buildings, etc. for control of pollution.

To Section 531AU

Section 531AM Charge to universal social charge.

531AUA Universal social charge and approved profit sharing scheme

[Where universal social charge is charged on the initial market value of shares in accordance with *subparagraph (a)(ii)* of the Table to *section 531AM(1)*, it shall not be charged—

(a) where there is a disposal of shares, or a deemed disposal of shares, as referred to in *subsections (2)* and *(7)*, respectively, of *section 512*, on the appropriate percentage of the locked-in value of those shares as construed in accordance with *subsection (1)* of that section, or

(b) where there is a capital receipt within the meaning of *section 513(1)*, on the appropriate percentage of the amount or value, as the case may be, of that capital receipt.][1]

Amendments

[1] Inserted by FA12 s2(8). Deemed to have had effect as on and from 1 January 2011.

531AV Married couples

[Where an election has been made or is deemed to have been made under [*section 1018* or *1031D*][1] and has effect for a tax year, universal social charge payable by [one spouse or civil partner][2] shall be charged, collected and recovered as if it were universal social charge payable by the spouse assessable under [*section 1017* or nominated civil partner assessable under *section 1031C*][3].][4]

Amendments

[1] Substituted by F(No.3)A11 sched1(151).

[2] Substituted by F(No.3)A11 sched1(152).

[3] Substituted by F(No.3)A11 sched1(153).

[4] Inserted by FA11 s3(1)(a). Applies for the year of assessment 2011 and each subsequent year of assessment.

Revenue Information Notes

Universal Social Charge – Frequently Asked Questions

Cross References

From Section 531AV

Section 1017 Assessment of husband in respect of income of both spouses.

Section 1018 Election for assessment under section 1017.

531AW Repayments

[(1) In any case of underpayment or overpayment of universal social charge to the Collector-General, payment of the amount not paid or repayment of the amount overpaid, as the case may be, shall be made to or by the Collector-General, as appropriate.

(2) In the case of an individual to whom *section 531AM(2)* applies, any universal social charge deducted from his or her income shall be repaid to the individual by the Revenue Commissioners on receipt of a valid claim made in such manner as may be approved by the Revenue Commissioners, and for the purposes of such repayment universal social charge shall be deemed to be income tax.][1]

Amendments

[1] Inserted by FA11 s3(1)(a). Applies for the year of assessment 2011 and each subsequent year of assessment.

Revenue Information Notes

Universal Social Charge – Frequently Asked Questions

Cross References

From Section 531AW

Section 531AM Charge to universal social charge.

531AX Restriction on deduction

[(1) Universal social charge paid in respect of a tax year is in addition to, and does not reduce, any liability which an individual may have in respect of income tax or other taxes under the Tax Acts.

(2) Excess tax credits or reliefs which are available to an individual may not be set against any charge to universal social charge which is due and payable for a tax year.][1]

Amendments

[1] Inserted by FA11 s3(1)(a). Applies for the year of assessment 2011 and each subsequent year of assessment.

Revenue Information Notes

Universal Social Charge – Frequently Asked Questions

531AY Recovery of unpaid universal social charge

[(1) Where any universal social charge in relation to an employee, remains unpaid for a tax year and is not otherwise recovered (in this section referred to as the "*underpayment*"), the employer shall be treated, on receipt of a notice from an inspector to the effect that this section applies, as making a payment of relevant emoluments to the employee in the subsequent tax year of an amount equal to the amount determined by *subsection (2)* (in this section referred to as "*notional emoluments*").

(2) The amount of the notional emoluments shall be an amount that would produce an amount of universal social charge equal to the amount of the under-payment and which amount shall be set out in the notice issued under *subsection (1)*.

(3) Where an employer is treated as making a payment of notional emoluments in accordance with *subsections (1)* and *(2)*, the amount of the notional emoluments for the subsequent tax year shall be apportioned over that tax year to each week, in a case where relevant emoluments are paid weekly, or such corresponding period where relevant emoluments are paid for a period either greater or less than a week, and the employer shall deduct universal social charge by reference to the part of the notional emoluments for the tax year apportioned to each such week or a corresponding amount where the period is greater or less than a week.

(4) Where any universal social charge remains unpaid after the end of a tax year, the amount of tax credits (within the meaning of the PAYE Regulations) and the standard rate cut-off point (within that meaning) appropriate to an employee for any subsequent tax year may be adjusted as necessary by an inspector to collect unpaid universal social charge which is not otherwise recovered.

(5) Where, but for this subsection, no assessment to universal social charge would be made on an individual for a tax year, then an inspector may make

an assessment to universal social charge on the individual to the best of the inspector's judgement of the amounts chargeable to universal social charge, and the provisions of the Tax Acts, including in particular those provisions relating to the assessment, collection and recovery of tax and the payment of interest on unpaid tax, shall apply as respects any assessment to universal social charge made on the individual by virtue of this subsection, other than any such provisions in so far as they relate to the granting of any allowance, deduction or relief.][1]

Amendments

[1] Inserted by FA11 s3(1)(a). Applies for the year of assessment 2011 and each subsequent year of assessment.

Revenue Information Notes

Universal Social Charge – Frequently Asked Questions

Cross References

To Section 531AY

Section 531NA Cessation of charge to income levy.

Section 531AAB Regulations.

Section 531AZ Repayments of, and recovery of unpaid, income levy.

531AZ Repayments of, and recovery of unpaid, income levy

[(1) Where any income levy in relation to an employee, remains unpaid for the tax year 2009 or 2010 and is not otherwise recovered, the provisions of *section 531AY* in relation to—

(a) the making of notional emoluments and the apportionment of those emoluments, and

(b) the adjustment of tax credits and the standard rate cut-off point,

shall apply to the recovery of any under-payment of income levy as they apply to the recovery of any underpayment of universal social charge.

(2) Repayments of income levy paid for the tax years 2009 and 2010 shall, to the extent that insufficient income levy has been paid in 2011 or a later year, be made out of universal social charge.][1]

Amendments

[1] Inserted by FA11 s3(1)(a). Applies for the year of assessment 2011 and each subsequent year of assessment.

Revenue Information Notes

Universal Social Charge – Frequently Asked Questions

Cross References

From Section 531AZ

Section 531AY Recovery of unpaid universal social charge.

531AAA Application of provisions relating to income tax

[The provisions of—

[(a) *Chapter 1* of *Part 38*, in relation to the making of returns of income, [Chapter 3 of that Part, in relation to the obligation to keep records, and Chapter 4][1] of that Part, in relation to the making of enquiries and the exercise of the powers, duties and responsibilities provided for by that Chapter,][2]

(b) [*Part 41A*][3], in relation to the making of assessments of [income tax and the right of a Revenue officer to make enquiries][4],

(c) [*Chapters*][5] *1* and *3* of *Part 40*, in relation to appeals,

(d) [*Chapters 1* and *4*][6] of *Part 42*, in relation to the collection and recovery of unpaid income tax, and

(e) *Part 47*, in relation to penalties, offences, interest and other sanctions,

shall apply, with any necessary modifications, to universal social charge as those provisions apply to income tax.][7]

Amendments

[1] Substituted by FA13 s4(a). Deemed to have come into force and takes effect on and from 1 January 2013.

[2] Substituted by FA12 s2(9)(a). Deemed to have had effect as on and from 1 January 2011.

[3] Substituted by FA12 sched4(part 2)(g).

[4] Substituted by FA13 s4(b). Deemed to have come into force and takes effect on and from 1 January 2013.

[5] Substituted by FA12 s2(9)(b). Deemed to have had effect as on and from 1 January 2011.

[6] Substituted by FA13 s4(c). Deemed to have come into force and takes effect on and from 1 January 2013.

[7] Inserted by FA11 s3(1)(a). Applies for the year of assessment 2011 and each subsequent year of assessment.

531AAB Regulations

[(1) The Revenue Commissioners may make regulations for the purposes of the proper implementation and administration of this Part, and those regulations may, in particular and without prejudice to the generality of the foregoing, include provision—

(a) for requiring any employer who pays relevant emoluments exceeding the limit specified in *section 531AM(2)* to notify the Revenue Commissioners within the period specified in the regulations that that employer is such an employer;

(b) for requiring any employer making any payment of relevant emoluments, when that employer makes the payment, to make a deduction or repayment of universal social charge calculated by reference to such rate or rates of charge for the tax year as may be specified;

(c) for the deduction of universal social charge at whatever rate or rates are specified for a tax year in such cases or classes of cases as may be provided for by the regulations;

(d) for specifying the manner in which deductions or repayments of universal social charge are to be made from any payment of relevant emoluments made by an employer;

(e) for rendering persons who are required to make any deduction or repayment of universal social charge accountable, in the case of a deduction (whether or not made), for the amount of universal social charge deductible and liable to pay that amount to the Revenue Commissioners and entitled, in the case of a repayment, (if a repayment has been made) to be paid it, or given credit for it, by the Revenue Commissioners;

(f) for treating persons who are not employers as employers in such cases or classes of cases as may be provided for by the regulations;

(g) for the manner in which employers are to remit payments of universal social charge to the Revenue Commissioners, including remittance by electronic means, and the manner in which the Revenue Commissioners are to acknowledge such payments;

(h) for the period within which payment of universal social charge is to be remitted to the Revenue Commissioners;

(i) for requiring any employer making any payment of relevant emoluments to provide the Revenue Commissioners, within a period specified in the regulations, and in such form as the Revenue Commissioners may approve or provide, with information in relation to payments of relevant emoluments and universal social charge deducted from such relevant emoluments, and such other information as the Revenue Commissioners consider appropriate, and in what-ever form they consider appropriate;

(j) for requiring any employer making any payment of relevant emoluments to provide his or her employees, within a period specified in the regulations or on the occurrence of a particular event such as the cessation of an employee's employment, and in such form as the Revenue Commissioners may approve or provide, with information in relation to payments of relevant emoluments and universal social charge deducted from such relevant emoluments;

(k) for requiring every employer who pays relevant emoluments exceeding the limits specified in *section 531AM(2)* to keep and maintain a register of that employer's employees in such manner as may be specified in the regulations and, on being required to do so on receipt of a notice from the Revenue Commissioners, to deliver the register to the Revenue Commissioners within the period specified in the notice;

(l) for the production to, and inspection by, persons authorised by the Revenue Commissioners of payroll records and other documents and records for the purpose of satisfying themselves that universal social charge in respect of relevant emoluments has been and is being duly deducted, repaid and accounted for;

(m) for the collection and recovery, whether by deduction from relevant emoluments paid in any tax year or otherwise, of universal social charge in respect of relevant emoluments which has not been deducted or otherwise recovered during the tax year;

(n) for the collection and recovery, to the extent that the Revenue Commissioners consider appropriate, and the employee does not object, of universal social charge in respect of income other than relevant emoluments, which has not otherwise been recovered during the tax year;

(o) for the collection and recovery, from the employee rather than from the employer, of any amount of universal social charge that the Revenue Commissioners consider should have been deducted by the employer from the relevant emoluments of the employee;

(p) for the collection and recovery from an employee of any amount of interest and penalties due from the employee that has not otherwise been recovered;

(q) for the repayment to an employer of a payment or remittance (including part of such a payment or remittance) that is in excess of the amount of liability due and payable under this Part against which it is credited provided that a claim for such repayment is made by the employer within 4 years after the end of the tax year to which the claim applies, [...][1]

(r) for appeals with respect to matters arising under the regulations that would not otherwise be the subject of an [appeal;][2]

[(s) with respect to the deduction, collection and recovery of amounts to be accounted for in respect of notional payments, and

(t) for the making available by the Revenue Commissioners of an electronic system or systems to allow employers and employees to fulfil their obligations under this Chapter and regulations made under this Chapter and to allow for electronic communications between the Revenue Commissioners, officers of the Revenue Commissioners, employers, employees and other persons pursuant to obligations under those provisions and for the provision of enhancements or other changes to that system or those systems, as the case may be, and for any replacement for such system or systems.][3]

(2) Any reference in regulations under this section to a payment of relevant emoluments shall include a reference to an amount referred to in *section 531AY* as "*notional emoluments*".

(3) Regulations under this section shall apply notwithstanding anything in this Part, but shall not affect any right of appeal that a person would have apart from the regulations.

(4) Notwithstanding any other provision of this section, where the Revenue Commissioners are satisfied that it is unnecessary or is not appropriate for an employer to comply with any of the regulations made under *subsection (1)* they may notify the employer accordingly.

(5) Every regulation made under this section shall be laid before Dáil Éireann as soon as may be after it is made and, if a resolution annulling the regulation is passed by Dáil Éireann within the next 21 days on which Dáil Éireann has sat after the regulation is laid before it, the regulation shall be annulled accordingly, but without prejudice to the validity of anything previously done thereunder.][4]

Amendments

[1] Deleted by FA12 s2(10)(a). Deemed to have come into force and takes effect on and from 1 January 2012.

[2] Substituted by FA12 s2(10)(b). Deemed to have come into force and takes effect on and from 1 January 2012.

3 Inserted by FA12 s2(10)(c). Deemed to have come into force and takes effect on and from 1 January 2012.

[4] Inserted by FA11 s3(1)(a). Applies for the year of assessment 2011 and each subsequent year of assessment.

Cross References

From Section 531AAB

Section 531AM Charge to universal social charge.

Section 531AY Recovery of unpaid universal social charge.

To Section 531AAB

Section 531AO Deduction and payment of universal social charge on relevant emoluments.

Section 531AP Record keeping.

Section 531AQ Power of inspection.

531AAC Care and management

[Universal social charge is under the care and management of the Revenue Commissioners and Part 37 shall apply to universal social charge as it applies to income tax.][1]

Amendments

[1] Inserted by FA11 s3(1)(a). Applies for the year of assessment 2011 and each subsequent year of assessment.

531AAD Excess bank remuneration charge

[(1) In this section—

"*excess bank remuneration charge*" shall be construed in accordance with *subsection (7)*;

"*relevant employee*", in relation to a specified institution, means an employee of the specified institution—

(a) who is resident in the State (within the meaning of *Part 34*) in a tax year for the purposes of the Acts, or

(b) the duties of whose employment in that specified institution are at any time in the tax year concerned performed wholly or partly in the State;

"*relevant remuneration*", in relation to a relevant employee, means, subject to *subsection (2)*, relevant emoluments that are not regular salary or wages or a regular benefit or perquisite;

"*regular*", in relation to any salary, wages, fees, benefit or perquisite of a relevant employee, means so much of the amount of such salary, wages, fees, benefit or perquisite that does not vary according to—

(a) the performance of, or any part of—

(i) any business of the specified institution, or

(ii) any business of a person connected with the specified institution,

(b) the contribution made by the relevant employee to the performance of, or of any part of, any business referred to in *subparagraph (i)* or *(ii)* of *paragraph* (*a*), or

(c) the performance by the relevant employee of any of the duties of the employment,

or any similar consideration;

"*specified institution*" means an institution, specified by order of the Minister for Finance made under section 6(1) of the Credit Institutions (Financial Support) Act 2008, that has received financial support under either or both that Act and the National Pensions Reserve Fund Act 2000.

(2) This section does not apply in respect of a relevant employee to whom or in respect of whom relevant remuneration of not more than €20,000 is awarded during a tax year.

(3) For the purposes of this section, relevant remuneration is awarded during a tax year if—

(a) a contractual obligation to pay or provide it arises during the tax year, or

(b) the relevant remuneration is paid or provided during the tax year without any such obligation having arisen during the tax year.

(4) The amount of any relevant remuneration is—

(a) if it is money, its amount when awarded, or

(b) if it is money's worth, the amount of the money's worth when awarded.

(5) Where the market value (within the meaning of *section 548*) of any relevant remuneration at the time it is awarded exceeds, or would exceed, what would otherwise be its amount, its amount is that market value.

(6) (a) Where anything constituting relevant remuneration is or would be when awarded subject to any restriction the restriction is to be ignored in arriving at its amount.

(b) For the purpose of *paragraph* (*a*) "*restriction*" means any condition, restriction or other similar provision that causes the market value of the relevant remuneration to be less than it would otherwise be.

(7) A relevant employee, instead of being charged to universal social charge at the rates provided for in *section 531AN* on that part of his or her aggregate income for a tax year that constitutes relevant remuneration awarded during the tax year to or in respect of the relevant employee by reason of his or her employment as an employee of the specified institution, shall be charged to universal social charge (to be known, for the purposes of this section, as "*excess bank remuneration charge*") on the amount of that relevant remuneration at the rate of 45 per cent for that tax year.

(8) Notwithstanding *section 531AO(2)*, as respects any award of relevant remuneration made to or in respect of a relevant employee in the period beginning on the date of the passing of the *Finance Act 2011* and ending on 31 December 2011 and in each subsequent tax year, excess bank remuneration charge shall be deducted from relevant remuneration by the employer at the rate of 45 per cent.

(9) An employer shall for each award of relevant remuneration from which excess bank remuneration charge has not been deducted in the period beginning on 1 January 2011 and ending on the date of the passing of the *Finance Act 2011* make and deliver to the Revenue Commissioners on or before 30 June 2011 a return, in such form as may be provided or approved by the Revenue Commissioners, including the following information in respect of each such payment—

(a) the name, address and Personal Public Service Number (within the meaning of section 262 of the Social Welfare Consolidation Act 2005) of the relevant employee to whom the relevant remuneration was awarded,

(b) the amount of the relevant remuneration awarded,

(c) the amount, if any, of universal social charge deducted and remitted to the Collector-General in respect of that relevant remuneration, and

(d) such other details or information as may be specified by the Revenue Commissioners in the return.

(10) Within 46 days from the end of a tax year an employer shall for each award of relevant remuneration made to or in respect of a relevant employee in the period beginning on the date of the passing of the *Finance Act 2011* and ending on 31 December 2011 and in each subsequent tax year make and deliver to the Revenue Commissioners a return, in such form as may be provided or approved by the Revenue Commissioners, including the following information in respect of each such payment—

(a) the name, address and Personal Public Service Number (within the meaning of section 262 of the Social Welfare Consolidation Act 2005) of the relevant employee to whom the relevant remuneration was awarded,

(b) the amount of the relevant remuneration awarded,

(c) the amount, if any, of excess bank remuneration charge deducted and remitted to the Collector-General in respect of that relevant remuneration, and

(d) such other details or information as may be specified by the Revenue Commissioners in the return.][1]

Amendments

[1] Inserted by FA11 s3(1)(a). Applies for the year of assessment 2011 and each subsequent year of assessment.

Cross References

From Section 531AAD

Section 531AN Rate of charge.

Section 531AO Deduction and payment of universal social charge on relevant emoluments.

Section 548 Valuation of assets.

531AAE Property relief surcharge

[(1) In this section—

'*aggregate of the specified property reliefs*', in relation to a tax year and an individual, means the aggregate of the amounts of specified property reliefs used by the individual in respect of the tax year;

'*amount of specified property relief* ', in relation to a specified relief used by an individual in respect of a tax year, means the amount of the specified property relief used by the individual in respect of the tax year, determined by reference to the entry in *column (3)* of *Schedule 25B* opposite the reference to the specified relief concerned in *column (2)* of that Schedule;

'*area-based capital allowance*', in relation to a tax year and an individual, means any allowance, or part of such allowance, made under Chapter 1 of Part 9 as that Chapter is applied—

(a) by *section 323, 331, 332, 341, 342, 343, 344, 352, 353, 372C, 372D, 372M, 372N, 372V, 372W,* [*372AC, 372AD* or *372AAC,*][1] or

(b) by virtue of *paragraph 11* of *Schedule 32,*

for the tax year, including any such allowance, or part of any such allowance, made for a previous tax year and carried forward from that previous tax year in accordance with Part 9;

'*balancing allowance*' means any allowance made under *section 274*;

'*specified capital allowance*', in relation to a tax year and an individual, means any specified relief that is—

(a) a writing down allowance or a balancing allowance made for the tax year, or

(b) an allowance, or part of such allowance, made under *Chapter 1* of *Part 9* as that Chapter is applied by *section 372AX, 372AY, 843* or *843A* for the tax year,

including any such allowance or part of such allowance made for a previous tax year and carried forward from that tax year in accordance with *Part 9*;

'*specified individual*', in relation to a tax year, means an individual whose aggregate income for the tax year is €100,000 or more;

'*specified property relief* ', in relation to a tax year and an individual, means—

(a) any allowance, or part of any allowance, specified in the definition of 'area-based capital allowance' or 'specified capital allowance', as the case may be, or

(b) any eligible expenditure within the meaning of *Chapter 11* of *Part 10*, to which *section 372AP* applies, which is to be taken into account in computing under *section 97(1)* a deficiency in respect of any rent from a qualifying premises or a special qualifying premises, within the meaning of *section 372AK*;

'*specified relief*', in relation to a tax year and an individual, means any relief arising under, or by virtue of, any of the provisions set out in column (2) of *Schedule 25B*;

'*writing down allowance*' means any allowance made under *section 272* and includes any such allowance as increased under *section 273*.

(2) Any reference in this section to any specified property relief being used in respect of any tax year shall be a reference to that part of that specified property relief to which full effect has been given for that tax year.

(3) The amount of universal social charge which is to be charged on the aggregate income for the tax year concerned of a specified individual under this Part shall be increased by an amount equal to 5 per cent of that part of that aggregate income in relation to which an amount of specified property relief or, as the case may be, the aggregate of the specified property reliefs, has been used by the specified individual in that tax year.

(4) For the purposes of this section—

(a) *section 485C(3)* and *Schedule 25C* (as if the references to the tax years 2006 and 2007 in that Schedule were references to the tax years 2011 and 2012, respectively) shall apply in determining the amount of any specified property relief to be carried forward from any tax year to each subsequent tax year, and

(b) any specified relief, which is a specified property relief, shall be treated as used in any tax year in priority to a specified relief which is not a specified property relief.

(5) Where universal social charge is payable for the tax year 2012 in respect of a specified individual's aggregate income for a tax year, being an individual who is a chargeable person (within the meaning of *Part 41*), *section 958* shall apply and have effect as if, in accordance with this section, universal social charge had been payable for the tax year 2011.][2]

Amendments

[1] Substituted by FA13 s30(1)(c). Comes into operation on such day as the Minister for Finance may by order appoint.

[2] Inserted by FA12 s3(1). Applies for the year of assessment 2012 and each subsequent year of assessment.

531AAF Delegation of functions and discharge of functions by electronic means

[Any act to be performed or function to be discharged by the Revenue Commissioners that is authorised or required by this Part or by regulations made under this Part may be performed or discharged by any one or more of their officers acting under their authority or may, if appropriate, be performed or discharged through such electronic systems as the Revenue Commissioners may put in place for the time being for any such purpose.][1]

Amendments

[1] Inserted by FA12 s2(11). Deemed to have come into force and takes effect on and from 1 January 2012.

TAXATION OF CHARGEABLE GAINS

PART 19

Principal Provisions Relating to Taxation of Chargeable Gains

CHAPTER 1

Assets and Acquisitions and Disposals of Assets

532 Assets

[CGTA75 s7(1); FA80 s62(a)]

All forms of property shall be assets for the purposes of the Capital Gains Tax Acts whether situated in the State or not, including—

(a) options, debts and incorporeal property generally,

(b) any currency other than [the currency of the State][1], and

(c) any form of property created by the person disposing of it, or otherwise becoming owned without being acquired.

Amendments

[1] Substituted by FA13 s44(a). Deemed to have come into force and takes effect on and from 1 January 2013.

Case Law

In O'Brien v Benson's Hosiery (Holdings) Ltd 1979 STC 735 it was held that a sum of money paid to a company by the director in consideration of the company releasing him from his obligations under a service agreement was a capital sum derived from that service agreement, and that the service agreement in question was an asset of the company, notwithstanding that the company could not transfer the service agreement to any other party without the agreement of the employee.

In Marren v Ingles 1980 STC 500 the Court held that the right to receive a sum was an asset for the purposes of CGT.

In Zim Properties Ltd v Proctor 1985 STC 90 the Court accepted Revenue's argument that the right to compensation derived from an asset, being Zim's "right to sue" their legal advisors, was an asset for CGT purposes.

In Kirby v Thorn EMI plc 1987 STC 621 the UK Court of Appeal established that assets are synonymous with "property" and held that the right or freedom to trade, or to compete, is not "property" and, therefore, is not an asset for CGT purposes.

Cross References

To Section 532

Section 267N Interpretation.

Section 693 Exploration expenditure: allowances and charges.

Section 828 Capital gains tax: double taxation relief.

Schedule 14 Capital Gains Tax: Leases

533 Location of assets

[CGTA75 s48]

The situation of assets specified in this section shall, except where otherwise provided by *section 29*, be determined for the purposes of the Capital Gains Tax Acts in accordance with the following provisions:

(a) the situation of rights or interests (otherwise than by means of security) in or over immovable property shall be that of the immovable property;

(b) subject to this section, the situation of rights or interests (otherwise than by means of security) in or over tangible movable property shall be that of the tangible movable property;

(c) subject to this section, a debt, secured or unsecured, shall be situated in the State only if the creditor is resident in the State;

(d) shares or securities issued by any municipal or governmental authority, or by any body created by such an authority, shall be situated in the country of that authority;

[(da) subject to *paragraph (d)*, shares in, or securities of, a company incorporated in the State shall be situated in the State and, for the purposes of this paragraph, 'shares' includes warrants in respect of shares (including share warrants (within the meaning of *section 88* of the Companies Act 1963)) and any other instrument or security the value of which is derived from, or calculated by reference to, shares;][1]

(e) [subject to *paragraphs (d)* and *(da)*][2], registered shares or securities shall be situated where they are registered and, if registered in more than one register, where the principal register is situated;

(f) a ship or aircraft shall be situated in the State only if the owner is resident in the State, and an interest or right in or over a ship or aircraft shall be situated in the State only if the person entitled to the interest or right is resident in the State;

(g) the situation of goodwill as a trade, business or professional asset shall be at the place where the trade, business or profession is carried on;

(h) patents, trade marks and designs shall be situated where they are registered and, if registered in more than one register, where each register is situated, and copyright, franchises, rights and licences to use any copyright material, patent, trade mark or design shall be situated in the State if they, or any rights derived from them, are exercisable in the State;

(i) a judgment debt shall be situated where the judgment is recorded.

Amendments

[1] Inserted by FA12 s56(1)(a). Applies as on and from 8 February 2012.

[2] Substituted by FA12 s56(1)(b). Applies as on and from 8 February 2012.

Cross References

From Section 533

Section 29 Persons chargeable.

534 Disposals of assets

[CGTA75 s8(1)]

For the purposes of the Capital Gains Tax Acts—

(a) references to a disposal of an asset include, except where the context otherwise requires, references to a part disposal of an asset, and

(b) there shall be a part disposal of an asset where an interest or right in or over the asset is created by the disposal, as well as where it subsists before the disposal, and, generally, there shall be a part disposal of an asset where, on a person making a disposal, any description of property derived from the asset remains undisposed of.

Revenue Briefings

Tax Briefing

Tax Briefing September 2000 – Issue 41 pg 34 – Topical Questions

Cross References

To Section 534

Section 5 Interpretation of Capital Gains Tax Acts.

Section 538 Disposals where assets lost or destroyed or become of negligible value.

Section 540 Options and forfeited deposits.

535 Disposals where capital sums derived from assets

[CGTA75 s8(2) and (7)]

(1) In this section, "*capital sum*" means any money or money's worth not excluded from the consideration taken into account in the computation of the gain under *Chapter 2* of this Part.

(2) (a) Subject to *sections 536* and *537(1)* and to any other exceptions in the Capital Gains Tax Acts, there shall be for the purposes of those Acts a disposal of an asset by its owner where any capital sum is derived from the asset notwithstanding that no asset is acquired by the person paying the capital sum, and this paragraph shall apply in particular to—

(i) capital sums received by means of compensation for any kind of damage or injury to an asset or for the loss, destruction or dissipation of an asset or for any depreciation or risk of depreciation of an asset,

(ii) capital sums received under a policy of insurance of the risk of any kind of damage or injury to, or the loss or depreciation of, an asset,

(iii) capital sums received in return for forfeiture or surrender of a right or for refraining from exercising a right, and

(iv) capital sums received as consideration for use or exploitation of an asset.

(b) Without prejudice to *paragraph (a)(ii)* but subject to *paragraph (c)*, neither the rights of the insurer nor the rights of the insured under any policy of insurance, whether the risks insured relate to property or not, shall constitute an asset on the disposal of which a gain may accrue, and in this paragraph "*policy of insurance*" does not include a policy of assurance on human life.

(c) *Paragraph (b)* shall not apply where the right to any capital sum within *paragraph (a)(ii)* is assigned after the event giving rise to the damage or injury to, or the loss or depreciation of, an asset has occurred, and for the purposes of the Capital Gains Tax Acts such an assignment shall be deemed to be a disposal of an interest in the asset concerned.

Case Law

A company whose businesses included mining of fireclay received compensation for loss of mining rights. The land continued to be held by the company and it was held that the compensation payment was for the loss of a capital asset. Glenboig Union Fireclay Company Ltd 1921 12 TC 427

Payment of statutory compensation for disturbance of rights under a lease was not derived from an asset but by reason of statute. Davis v Powell 1977 STC 32

In Davenport v Chilver 1983 STC 426 a payment under a statutory compensation fund was held to be a capital sum derived from an asset.

Compensation for loss of trading stock, damage to and loss of contents, loss of profits and for improvements, was held to be compensation in respect of loss of profits and therefore it was an income receipt. Lang v Rice 1984 STC 172

Revenue Briefings

eBrief

eBrief No. 76/09 – Negligible Value Claim – Shares in Anglo Irish Bank

Revenue Precedents

A premium payable by the E.C. in respect of grubbing up of orchards is a capital receipt. G125(3).
Where such policies are cross-assigned by partners/directors, no liability to CGT will arise on a disposal of an interest in the policy or on the sums becoming payable under the policy. G11(3)

Cross References

From Section 535

Section 536 Capital sums: receipt of compensation and insurance moneys not treated as a disposal in certain cases.
Section 537 Mortgages and charges not to be treated as disposals.
Section 544 Interpretation and general (Chapter 2).

To Section 535

Section 536 Capital sums: receipt of compensation and insurance moneys not treated as a disposal in certain cases.
Section 540 Options and forfeited deposits.
Section 542 Time of disposal and acquisition.
Section 564 Woodlands.

536 Capital sums: receipt of compensation and insurance moneys not treated as a disposal in certain cases

[CGTA75 s29(1) to (3) and (5)]

(1) (a) Subject to *paragraph (b)*, where the recipient so claims, receipt of a capital sum within *subparagraph (i), (ii), (iii)* or *(iv)* of *section 535(2)(a)* derived from an asset which is not lost or destroyed shall not be treated as a disposal of the asset if—

(i) the capital sum is wholly applied in restoring the asset, or

(ii) the capital sum is applied in restoring the asset except for a part of the capital sum which is not reasonably required for the purpose and which is small as compared with the whole capital sum;

but, if the receipt is not treated as a disposal, all sums which, if the receipt had been so treated, would have been taken into account as consideration for that disposal in the computation of a gain accruing on the disposal shall be deducted from any expenditure allowable under *Chapter 2* of this Part as a deduction in computing a gain on the subsequent disposal of the asset.

(b) *Paragraph (a)* shall not apply to cases within *subparagraph (ii)* of that paragraph if immediately before the receipt of the capital sum there is no expenditure attributable to the asset under *paragraphs (a)* and *(b)* of *section 552(1)* or if the consideration for the part disposal deemed to be effected on receipt of the capital sum exceeds that expenditure.

(2) Where an asset is lost or destroyed and a capital sum received as compensation for the loss or destruction, or under a policy of insurance of the risk of the loss or destruction, is, within one year of receipt or such longer period as the inspector may allow, applied in acquiring an asset in replacement of the asset lost or destroyed, the owner shall on due claim be treated for the purposes of the Capital Gains Tax Acts as if—

(a) the consideration for the disposal of the old asset were (if otherwise of a greater amount) of such amount as would secure that on the disposal neither a loss nor a gain accrued to such owner, and

(b) the amount of the consideration for the acquisition of the new asset were reduced by the excess of the amount of the capital sum received as compensation or under the policy of insurance, together with any residual or scrap value, over the amount of the consideration which such owner is treated as receiving under *paragraph (a)*.

(3) A claim shall not be made under *subsection (2)* if part only of the capital sum is applied in acquiring the new asset; but, if all of that capital sum except for a part which is less than the amount of the gain (whether all chargeable gain or not) accruing on the disposal of the old asset is so applied, the owner shall on due claim be treated for the purposes of the Capital Gains Tax Acts as if—

(a) the amount of the gain so accruing were reduced to the amount of that part of the capital sum not applied in acquiring the new asset (and, if not all chargeable gain, with a proportionate reduction in the amount of the chargeable gain), and

(b) the amount of the consideration for the acquisition of the new asset were reduced by the amount by which the gain is reduced under *paragraph (a)*.

(4) This section shall not apply in relation to a wasting asset.

Revenue Briefings

eBrief

eBrief No. 50/2008 – Decommissioning of Fishing Vessels

Revenue Precedents

In strictness, no relief is due as in law, the building and the land on which it stands are one asset. However, in practice, the 'old' and the 'new' buildings may be treated as distinct assets separate from the land on which they stand and relief may be allowed under s536(2). This practice does not apply to leasehold with less than 50 years to run. G130.

Cross References

From Section 536

Section 535 Disposals where capital sums derived from assets.
Section 544 Interpretation and general (Chapter 2).
Section 552 Acquisition, enhancement and disposal costs.

To Section 536

Section 535 Disposals where capital sums derived from assets.
Section 556 Adjustment of allowable expenditure by reference to consumer price index.

537 Mortgages and charges not to be treated as disposals

[CGTA75 s8(4), (5) and (6)]

(1) The conveyance or transfer as security of an asset or of an interest or right in or over an asset, or the transfer of a subsisting interest or right as security in or over an asset (including a retransfer on redemption of the security), shall not be treated for the purposes of the Capital Gains Tax Acts as involving any acquisition or disposal of the asset.

(2) Where a person entitled to an asset as security or to the benefit of a charge or incumbrance on an asset deals with the asset for the purpose of enforcing or giving effect to the security, charge or incumbrance, such person's dealings with the asset

shall be treated for the purposes of the Capital Gains Tax Acts as if they were done through such person as nominee by the person entitled to the asset subject to the security, charge or incumbrance, and this subsection shall apply to the dealings of any person appointed to enforce or give effect to the security, charge or incumbrance as receiver and manager or judicial factor as it applies to the dealings of the person so entitled.

(3) An asset shall be treated as having been acquired free of any interest or right as security subsisting at the time of any acquisition of the asset, and as being disposed of free of any such interest or right subsisting at the time of the disposal and, where an asset is acquired subject to any such interest or right, the full amount of the liability thereby assumed by the person acquiring the asset shall form part of the consideration for the acquisition and disposal in addition to any other consideration.

Case Law

In Bank of Ireland Finance Ltd v Revenue Commissioners 1989 IV ITR 217 on a disposal of a property held on mortgage, the purchaser retained 15% of the consideration in the absence of a clearance certificate. The bank was held not to be entitled to a refund of the payment.

Cross References

To Section 537

Section 535 Disposals where capital sums derived from assets.

Section 571 Chargeable gains accruing on disposals by liquidators and certain other persons.

538 Disposals where assets lost or destroyed or become of negligible value

[CGTA75 s12(3), (4) and (5)]

(1) Subject to the Capital Gains Tax Acts and in particular to *section 540*, the occasion of the entire loss, destruction, dissipation or extinction of an asset shall for the purposes of those Acts constitute a disposal of the asset whether or not any capital sum as compensation or otherwise is received in respect of the destruction, dissipation or extinction of the asset.

(2) Where on a claim by the owner of an asset the inspector is satisfied that the value of an asset has become negligible, the inspector may allow the claim, and thereupon the Capital Gains Tax Acts shall apply as if the claimant had sold and immediately reacquired the asset for a consideration of an amount equal to the value specified in the claim.

[(2A) (a) Where as a result of the dissolution of a body corporate, property of the body corporate becomes property of the State by virtue of Part III of the State Property Act, 1954, and the Minister for Finance, in accordance with that Part of that Act, waives the right of the State to that property in favour of a person who holds or has held shares in the body corporate, then, notwithstanding *section 31* and subject to *paragraph (c)*, any allowable loss (in this subsection referred to as a "claimed loss") accruing to the person by virtue of a claim made under subsection (2) in respect of those shares shall not be allowable as a deduction from chargeable gains in any year of assessment earlier than the year of assessment in which the property is disposed of by the person and any necessary adjustments may be made [by way of assessment or amended assessment][1] to give effect to this paragraph.

(b) Paragraph *(a)* shall apply in relation to a body corporate which has no share capital as if references to shares included references to any interest in the body corporate possessed by members of the body corporate.

(c) For the purposes of *paragraph (a)*—

(i) where in a year of assessment there is a part disposal (within the meaning of *section 534*) of property, only so much of the claimed loss shall be allowable as a deduction from chargeable gains in that year of assessment as bears to the amount of the claimed loss the same proportion as the market value, when acquired, of the part of the property which is disposed of bears to the market value of the whole of that property when acquired,][2]

[(ii) the year of assessment in which property is disposed of by a person—

(I) where the disposal, being a disposal to the husband or wife of the person, is a disposal to which *section 1028(5)* applies, or

(II) where the disposal, being a disposal to the civil partner of the person, is a disposal to which *section 1031M(5)* applies,

shall mean the year of assessment in which the property is subsequently disposed of by the person's wife, husband or civil partner, as the case may be, where the subsequent disposal is a disposal to which *section 1028(5)* or *1031M(5)*, as the case may be, does not apply.][3]

(3) For the purposes of *subsections (1)* and *(2)*, a building and any permanent or semi-permanent structure in the nature of a building may be regarded as an asset separate from the land on which it is situated; but, where either of those subsections applies in accordance with this subsection, the person deemed to make the disposal of the building shall be treated as if such person had also sold and immediately reacquired the site of the building or structure (including in the site any land occupied for purposes ancillary to the use of the building or structure) for a consideration equal to its market value at that time.

Amendments

[1] Substituted by FA12 sched4(part 2)(g).

[2] Inserted by FA98 s67(1). This section shall apply as respects a waiver of the right of the State to property on or after the 12th day of February, 1998.

[3] Substituted by F(No.3)A11 sched1(154). Shall have effect from 27 July 2011.

Case Law

The loss is deemed to arise in the tax year in which the claim is lodged. Williams v Bullivant 1983 STC 107 Harper v R&C Commrs 2009 TC 00317 explored the requirement that the value of an asset must have "become negligibile" for a claim for loss relief to succeed.

Revenue Briefings

Tax Briefing

Tax Briefing May 2003 – Issue 52 pg 19 – Losses – Assets with Negligible Value

eBrief

eBrief No. 76/09 – Negligible Value Claim – Shares in Anglo Irish Bank

Revenue Precedents

On a strict interpretation a loss arising on a deemed disposal under section 538(2) is allowable only in the year of claim. However, in practice, a claim made within twelve months of the end of the year of assessment or accounting period for which relief is sought will be admitted, provided that the asset was of negligible value in the year of assessment or account period concerned. G35(2).

Where a partnership has written off goodwill in the balance sheet and a partner makes a subsequent disposal of his share in partnership assets, including goodwill, the partner is treated as realising a loss on the goodwill if he has a cost greater than nil. G36(A).

Cross References

From Section 538

Section 31 Amount chargeable.
Section 534 Disposals of assets.
Section 540 Options and forfeited deposits.
Section 1028 Married persons.

To Section 538

Section 581 Disposals of shares or securities within 4 weeks of acquisition.
Section 621 Depreciatory transactions in group.
Section 730K Disposal of foreign life policy.
Section 747E Disposal of an interest in offshore funds.
Schedule 20 Offshore Funds: Computation of Offshore Income Gains
Schedule 25A Exemption from Tax in the Case of Gains on Certain Disposals of Shares

539 Disposals in cases of hire purchase and similar transactions

[CGTA75 s10(2)]

[(1) A hire purchase or other transaction under which the use and enjoyment of an asset is obtained by a person for a period at the end of which the property in the asset will or may pass to such person shall be treated for the purposes of the Capital Gains Tax Acts, both in relation to such person and in relation to the person from whom the use and enjoyment of the asset is obtained, as if it amounted to an entire disposal of the asset to such person at the beginning of the period for which such person obtains the use and enjoyment of the asset, but subject to such adjustments of tax, whether by means of repayment or discharge of tax or otherwise, as may be required where the period for which such person has the use and enjoyment of the asset terminates without the property in the asset passing to such person.][1]

[(2) *Subsection (4)* or *(6)* of *section 865* shall not prevent the Revenue Commissioners from repaying an amount of tax as a consequence of an adjustment of tax made under this section, where a claim for any such adjustment is made within 4 years from the end of the chargeable period (within the meaning of *section 321*) in which the termination referred to in *subsection (1)* occurs.][2]

Amendments

[1, 2] Inserted and renumbered by FA08 sched6(1)(g). Applies as on and from 31 January 2008.

Cross References

From Section 539

Section 321 Provisions of general application in relation to the making of allowances and charges.
Section 865 Repayment of tax.

540 Options and forfeited deposits

[CGTA75 s47(1) to (6) and (8) to (11); FA92 s63]

(1) In this section—

"*quoted option*" means an option which at the time of abandonment or other disposal is quoted and dealt in on a stock exchange in the State or elsewhere in the same manner as shares;

"*traded option*" means an option which at the time of abandonment or other disposal is quoted on a stock exchange or a futures exchange in the State or elsewhere;

references to an option include references to an option binding the grantor to grant a lease for a premium or to enter into any other transaction which is not a sale, and references to buying and selling in pursuance of an option shall be construed accordingly.

(2) Without prejudice to *sections 534* and *535*, the grant of an option, including—

(a) the grant of an option binding the grantor to sell an asset the grantor does not own and, because the option is abandoned, never has occasion to own, and

(b) the grant of an option binding the grantor to buy an asset which, because the option is abandoned, the grantor does not acquire,

shall constitute the disposal of an asset (being the option) for the purposes of the Capital Gains Tax Acts, but subject to the following provisions of this section as to treating the grant of an option as part of a larger transaction.

(3) Where an option is exercised, the grant of the option and the transaction entered into by the grantor in fulfilment of the grantor's obligations under the option shall be treated as a single transaction, and accordingly for the purposes of the Capital Gains Tax Acts—

(a) if the option binds the grantor to sell, the consideration for the option shall be part of the consideration for the sale, and

(b) if the option binds the grantor to buy, the consideration for the option shall be deducted from the cost of acquisition incurred by the grantor in buying in pursuance of the grantor's obligations under the option.

(4) The exercise of an option by the person for the time being entitled to exercise it shall not constitute the disposal of an asset for the purposes of the Capital Gains Tax Acts by that person; but, if an option is exercised, the acquisition of the option (whether directly from the grantor or not) and the transaction entered into by the person exercising the option in exercise of that person's rights under the option shall be treated as a single transaction, and accordingly for the purposes of the Capital Gains Tax Acts—

(a) if the option binds the grantor to sell, the cost of acquiring the option shall be part of the cost of acquiring the asset which is sold, and

(b) if the option binds the grantor to buy, the cost of the option shall be treated as a cost incidental to the disposal of the asset which is bought by the grantor of the option.

(5) (a) The abandonment of an option by the person for the time being entitled to exercise it shall constitute the disposal of an asset (being the option) for the purposes of the Capital Gains Tax Acts by that person.

(b) Subject to *subsections (7)* and *(8)(a)*, the abandonment of an option by the person for the time being entitled to exercise it shall not for the purposes of the Capital Gains Tax Acts give rise to an allowable loss.

(6) In relation to the disposal by means of transfer of an option binding the grantor to sell or buy shares or securities which have a quoted market value on a stock exchange in the State or elsewhere, the option shall be regarded for the purposes of the Capital Gains Tax Acts as a wasting asset the life of which ends when the right to exercise the option ends, or when the option becomes valueless, whichever is the earlier, but without prejudice to the application of the provisions of *Chapter 2* of this Part relating to wasting assets to other descriptions of options.

(7) Where an option, being an option to acquire assets exercisable by a person intending to use the assets, if acquired, for the purposes of a trade carried on by that person or which that person commences to carry on within 2 years of that person's acquisition of the option, is disposed of or abandoned, then—

(a) if the option is abandoned, *subsection (5)(b)* shall not apply, and

(b) *section 560(3)* shall not apply.

(8) (a) Where—

(i) a quoted option to subscribe for shares in a company, or

(ii) a traded option,

is disposed of or abandoned, then—

(I) if the option is abandoned, *subsection (5)(b)* shall not apply, and

(II) *section 560(3)* and *subsection (6)* shall not apply.

(b) Where a quoted option to subscribe for shares in a company is dealt in within 3 months after the taking effect, with respect to the company granting the option, of any reorganisation, reduction, conversion or amalgamation to which *section 584, 585, 586* or *587* applies (or within such longer period as the Revenue Commissioners may by notice in writing allow), the option shall for the purposes of *section 584, 585, 586* or *587* be regarded as the shares which could be acquired by exercising the option, and *section 548(3)* shall apply for determining its market value.

(9) This section shall apply in relation to an option binding the grantor both to sell and to buy as if it were 2 separate options with 50 per cent of the consideration attributed to each option.

(10) This section shall apply in relation to a forfeited deposit of purchase money or other consideration money for a prospective purchase or other transaction which is abandoned as it applies in relation to the consideration for an option which binds the grantor to sell and which is not exercised.

Case Law

The abandonment of an option for consideration was not a real abandonment and therefore was liable to capital gains tax. Dillen v Kearns 1993 IV ITR 547

In calculating the consideration for grant of an option, payment for release from a restrictive covenant was not deductible. Garner v Pounds 1999 STC 18

Revenue Briefings

Tax Briefing

Tax Briefing May 2006 – Issue 63 pg 18 – Unapproved Share Option Schemes

Tax Briefing September 2009 – Issue 73 – 'Rent to Buy' (and similar) Schemes

eBrief

eBrief No. 45/09 – 'Rent-to-Buy' (and similar) Schemes

Cross References

From Section 540

Section 534 Disposals of assets.

Section 535 Disposals where capital sums derived from assets.

Section 544 Interpretation and general (Chapter 2).

Section 548 Valuation of assets.

Section 560 Wasting assets.

Section 584 Reorganisation or reduction of share capital.

Section 585 Conversion of securities.

Section 586 Company amalgamations by exchange of shares.

Section 587 Company reconstructions and amalgamations.

To Section 540

Section 538 Disposals where assets lost or destroyed or become of negligible value.
Section 588 Demutualisation of assurance companies.
Schedule 16 Building Societies: Change of Status

540A Disposal of certain emissions allowances

[(1) In this section—

'*Agency*' means the Environmental Protection Agency, being a competent authority designated under Article 18 of the Directive;

'*aircraft operator*' has the same meaning as in Article 3 of the Directive;

'*Directive*' means Directive 2003/87/EC of the European Parliament and of the Council of 13 October 2003* (as amended by Directive 2004/101/EC of the European Parliament and of the Council of 27 October 2004†, Directive 2008/101/EC of the European Parliament and of the Council of 19 November 2008†† and Directive 2009/29/EC of the European Parliament and of the Council of 23 April 2009**);

*OJ No. L275, 25.10.2003, p.32
†OJ No. L338, 13.11.2004, p.18
††OJ No. L8, 13.1.2009, p.3
**OJ No. L140, 5.6.2009, p.63

'*emissions allowance*' means an allowance within the meaning of Article 3 of the Directive;

'*installation*' and '*operator*' have the same meanings respectively as in Article 3 of the Directive;

'*permit*' means a greenhouse gas emissions permit within the meaning of Article 3 of the Directive;

'*relevant person*' means—

(a) a person to whom a permit has been issued in accordance with Articles 5 and 6 of the Directive in respect of an installation in relation to which the person is an operator, or

(b) an aircraft operator;

'*relevant scheme*' means—

(a) a scheme of reconstruction or amalgamation in relation to which *section 615* applies,

(b) a transfer of an asset in relation to which *section 617* applies, or

(c) a transfer of a trade, or part of a trade, in relation to which *section 631* applies.

(2) (a) Subject to *paragraphs (b)*, *(c)* and *(d)* and notwithstanding *section 110* or any other provision of the Tax Acts, where—

(i) a relevant person sells, transfers or otherwise disposes of an emissions allowance (in this section referred to as a '*relevant emissions allowance*') received or receivable free of charge by that person from the Agency in accordance with the Directive, or

(ii) a company sells, transfers or otherwise disposes of a relevant emissions allowance which the company acquired under, or as part of, a relevant scheme,

such a sale, transfer or disposal shall constitute the disposal of an asset for the purposes of the Capital Gains Tax Acts and be treated as not being a disposal of trading stock for such purposes.

(b) References in *paragraph (a)* to the sale, transfer or disposal of a relevant emissions allowance shall include references to the sale, transfer or disposal of any interest or rights in or over such an allowance.

(c) *Paragraph (a)* shall not apply to a surrender and cancellation of an emissions allowance in accordance with Article 12 of 40 the Directive.

(d) *Paragraph (a)(ii)* shall not apply to any sale, transfer or disposal of a relevant emissions allowance where, at any time before that event, the relevant emissions allowance was transferred from one company to another company in circumstances where the transfer was not made under, or as part of, a relevant scheme.

(3) For the purposes of the computation under this Part of any gain accruing to a relevant person or a company, as the case may be, on a disposal referred to in *subsection (2)*—

(a) no sum shall, notwithstanding *section 547* or *552*, be allowed as a deduction from the consideration for the disposal apart from incidental costs to the person or company making the disposal, and

(b) emissions allowances other than relevant emissions allowances shall be deemed to have been disposed of before relevant emissions allowances are disposed of by the person or company.

(4) *Section 596* shall not apply where a relevant emissions allowance acquired by a person is appropriated as trading stock of the trade carried on by the person.][1]

Amendments

[1] Inserted by FA12 s44(1)(b). Applies to disposals, referred to in *section 540A* made on or after 8 February 2012.

Revenue Briefings

Tax Briefing

Tax Briefing July 2012 – Issue 03 – EU Emissions Trading Scheme

541 Debts

[CGTA75 s46; FA80 s62(b); FA96 s61(1); FA97 s78]

(1) (a) For the purposes of the Capital Gains Tax Acts but subject to *paragraph (b)*, where a person incurs a debt to another person (being the original creditor), whether in [the currency of the State][1] or in some other currency, no chargeable gain shall accrue to that creditor or to that creditor's personal representative or legatee on a disposal of the debt.

(b) *Paragraph (a)* shall not apply in the case of a debt on a security within the meaning of *section 585*.

(2) Subject to *subsection (1)* and *sections 585* and *586*, the satisfaction of a debt or part of a debt (including a debt on a security within the meaning of *section 585*) shall be treated for the purposes of the Capital Gains Tax Acts as a disposal of the debt or of that part by the creditor made at the time when the debt or that part is satisfied.

(3) Where property is acquired by a creditor in satisfaction of the creditor's debt or part of that debt, then, subject to *sections 585* and *586*, the property shall not be treated for the purposes of the Capital Gains Tax Acts as disposed of by the debtor or acquired by the creditor for a consideration greater than its market

value at the time of the creditor's acquisition of it; but, if under *subsection (1)* (and in a case not within either *section 585* or *586*) no chargeable gain is to accrue on a disposal of the debt by the original creditor and a chargeable gain accrues to that creditor on a disposal by that creditor of the property, the amount of the chargeable gain shall (where necessary) be reduced so as not to exceed the chargeable gain which would have accrued if that creditor had acquired the property for a consideration equal to the amount of the debt or that part of the debt.

(4) For the purposes of the Capital Gains Tax Acts, a loss accruing on the disposal of a debt acquired by the person making the disposal from the original creditor or the original creditor's personal representative or legatee at a time when the creditor or the creditor's personal representative or legatee is a person connected with the person making the disposal, and so acquired either directly or by one or more than one purchase through persons all of whom are connected with the person making the disposal, shall not be an allowable loss.

(5) Where the original creditor is a trustee and the debt when created is settled property, *subsections (1)* and *(4)* shall apply as if for the references to the original creditor's personal representative or legatee there were substituted references to any person becoming absolutely entitled as against the trustee to the debt on its ceasing to be settled property and to that person's personal representative or legatee.

(6) This section shall not apply to a debt owed by a bank which is not in [the currency of the State][2] and which is represented by a sum standing to the credit of a person in an account in the bank, unless it represents currency acquired by the holder for the personal expenditure outside the State of the holder or [his or her family, dependants or civil partner, or any child of his or her civil partner][3] (including expenditure on the maintenance of any residence outside the State).

(7) For the purposes of this section, a debenture issued by any company shall be deemed to be a security (within the meaning of *section 585*) if it is issued—

(a) on a reorganisation referred to in *section 584(2)* or in pursuance of the debenture's allotment on any such reorganisation,

(b) in exchange for shares in or debentures of another company where the requirements of *section 586(2)* are satisfied in relation to the exchange,

(c) under any arrangements referred to in *section 587(2)*,

(d) in connection with any transfer of assets referred to in *section 631*,

(e) in connection with any disposal of assets referred to in *section 632*,

(f) in the course of a transaction which is the subject of an application under *section 637*, or

(g) in pursuance of rights attached to any debenture within *paragraph (a), (b), (c), (d), (e)* or *(f)*.

(8) *Paragraphs (d), (e)* and *(f)*, and (in so far as it relates to debentures within those paragraphs) *paragraph (g)*, of *subsection (7)* shall apply as respects the disposal of a debenture on or after the 26th day of March, 1997.

Amendments

[1,2] Substituted by FA13 s44(b). Deemed to have come into force and takes effect on and from 1 January 2013.

[3] Substituted by F(No.3)A11 sched1(155).

Case Law

A debt on a security must be marketable or at least have such characteristics to enable it to be dealt in and converted into shares or other securities. Aberdeen Construction Group Ltd v IRC 1978 STC 127

Loan notes which require the consent of the issuer for their transfer, and were redeemable at the option of the issuer before redemption, were held not to be debts on a security. Tarmac Roadstone Holdings Ltd v Williams 1996 SpC 409

Convertibility is sufficient to render the loan a debt on a security. Mooney v McSweeney 1997 V ITR 163

Cross References

From Section 541

Section 584 Reorganisation or reduction of share capital.
Section 585 Conversion of securities.
Section 586 Company amalgamations by exchange of shares.
Section 587 Company reconstructions and amalgamations.
Section 631 Transfer of assets generally.
Section 632 Transfer of assets by company to its parent company.
Section 637 Other transactions.

To Section 541

Section 541A Treatment of debts on a change in currency.
Section 590 Attribution to participators of chargeable gains accruing to non-resident company.
Schedule 17 Reorganisation into Companies of Trustee Savings Banks

541A Treatment of debts on a change in currency

[(1) Where on any day a debt (to which *section 541* does not apply by virtue of *subsection (6)* of that section) owed to a person in a currency other than [the currency of the State][1], becomes a debt in Irish currency as a result of the currency of a State being substituted by another currency, which other currency also on that day becomes Irish currency, then, subject to *subsection (2)*, that debt shall be deemed, for the purposes of the Capital Gains Tax Acts, on the day preceding that day, to be disposed of by the person and immediately reacquired by the person at its market value.

(2) [Subject to *subsection (4)* and notwithstanding any other provision of the Capital Gains Tax Acts][2], where in respect of a debt a chargeable gain accrues to a person by virtue of *subsection (1)*, that chargeable gain shall be assessed and charged as if it were a chargeable gain which accrued to the person at the time of the disposal of the debt and shall not be assessed and charged otherwise.

(3) For the purposes of *subsection (2)*, in relation to a debt owed to a person, the satisfaction of the debt or part of the debt shall be treated as a disposal of the debt or of that part at the time when the debt or that part is satisfied.

[(4) (a) In this subsection—

"*assurance company*" has the meaning assigned to it in *section 706*;

"*life business fund*" has the meaning assigned to it in *section 719*;

"*special investment fund*" has the meaning assigned to it in *section 723*;

"*special investment scheme*" has the meaning assigned to it in *section 737*;

"*undertaking for collective investment*" has the meaning assigned to it in *section 738*.

(b) Where the person referred to in *subsection (1)* is a company and either—

(i) the company is an assurance company and the debt referred to in that subsection is an asset of the company's life business fund, or

(ii) the company is an undertaking for collective investment and the debt referred to in that subsection is an asset of the undertaking, subsection (1) shall not apply and where the day (in this paragraph referred to as "*the deemed disposal day*") on which, but for this paragraph, the debt would be deemed to be disposed of and reacquired in accordance with *subsection (1)*, is not the day on which an accounting period of the company ends—

(I) in case of an assurance company, *section 719(2)* shall apply in respect of the debt as if, for this purpose only, the deemed disposal day was the day on which an accounting period of the company ends and the chargeable gain or allowable loss thereby accruing shall be included in the net amount (within the meaning of *section 720*) in respect of the accounting period in which the deemed disposal day falls, and

(II) in case of an undertaking for collective investment, *section 738(4)(a)* shall apply in respect of the debt as if, for this purpose only, the deemed disposal day was the day on which an accounting period of the company ends and the chargeable gain or allowable loss thereby accruing shall be included in the net amount (within the meaning of *section 738(4)(b)*) in respect of the accounting period in which the deemed disposal day falls.

(c) Where the person referred to in *subsection (1)* is an undertaking for collective investment and is not a company, *subsection (2)* shall not apply but the chargeable gain or allowable loss which accrues to the undertaking by virtue of *subsection (1)* shall be treated as accruing to the undertaking by virtue of *paragraph (a)* of *section 738(4)* and the provisions of that section shall apply accordingly.

(d) *Subsection (2)* shall not apply to a debt which is—

(i) an asset of a special investment fund of an assurance company, or

(ii) an asset which is subject to any trust created pursuant to a special investment scheme.][3]][4]

Amendments

[1] Substituted by FA13 s44(c). Deemed to have come into force and takes effect on and from 1 January 2013.

[2] Substituted by FA99 s87(1)(a). This section shall be deemed to have applied as on and from the 31st day of December, 1998.

[3] Inserted by FA99 s87(1)(b). This section shall be deemed to have applied as on and from the 31st day of December, 1998.

[4] Inserted by FA98 sched2(9). With effect from 31 December 1998 per S.I. 502 of 1998.

Cross References

From Section 541A

Section 541 Debts.
Section 706 Interpretation and general (Part 26).
Section 719 Deemed disposal and reacquisition of certain assets.
Section 720 Gains or losses arising by virtue of section 719.
Section 723 Special investment policies.
Section 737 Special investment schemes.
Section 738 Undertakings for collective investment.

541B Restrictive covenants

[(1) Where—

(a) a person gives an undertaking (whether absolute or qualified and whether legally valid or not), the tenor or effect of which is to restrict the person as to the person's conduct or activities,

(b) in respect of the giving of that undertaking by the person, or of the total or partial fulfilment of that undertaking by the person, any sum is paid either to the person or to any other person, and

(c) that sum is neither—

(i) treated, for the purposes of the Tax Acts, as profits or gains chargeable to tax under Schedule D or Schedule E, nor

(ii) treated as consideration for the disposal of an asset for the purposes of the Capital Gains Tax Acts,

the amount of the sum shall be deemed for the purposes of the Capital Gains Tax Acts to be the amount of a chargeable gain accruing to the person to whom it is paid (for the year of assessment in which it is paid) on the disposal of a chargeable asset.

(2) Where valuable consideration otherwise than in the form of money is given in respect of the giving of, or the total or partial fulfilment of, any undertaking, *subsection (1)* applies as if a sum had instead been paid equal to the value of that consideration.][1]

Amendments

[1] Inserted by FA03 s70(1). Applies as respects the giving of an undertaking by a person on or after 6 February 2003.

541C Tax treatment of certain venture fund managers

[(1) In this section—

"*carried interest*", in relation to a qualifying venture capital fund, means the share of profits (where the share ratio was agreed at the commencement of the qualifying venture capital fund) referred to in *paragraph (b)* of the definition of "*total profits*" that are received by a company, partnership or individual in respect of the management of the qualifying venture capital fund;

"*carried interest to which this section applies*", in relation to a qualifying venture capital fund, means an amount of carried interest which is not greater than 20 per cent of the total profits of a qualifying venture capital fund and which is a proportion of carried interest derived from the relevant investment;

"*EEA Agreement*" means the Agreement on the European Economic Area signed in Oporto on 2 May 1992, as adjusted by all subsequent amendments to that Agreement;

"*EEA State*" means a state which is a contracting party to the EEA Agreement;

"*innovation activities*" means development of new technological, telecommunication, scientific or business processes;

"*investor*", in relation to a relevant investment, means a person other than a person entitled to carried interest or a person connected with that person;

"*proportion of carried interest derived from the relevant investment*" means an amount of carried interest determined by the formula—

$$A \times \frac{B}{C}$$

where—

A is carried interest,

B is the value of all relevant investments in an EEA State (including the State) of the qualifying venture capital fund, and

C is the value of all relevant investments of the qualifying venture capital fund;

"*qualifying venture capital fund*" means an entity structured in the form of a partnership the main purpose of which is to make relevant investments and where the individuals, companies or partnerships which invest in the partnership are either limited partners or general partners (as defined in the partnership agreement) who are obliged under a legally binding agreement to provide capital sums for investment purposes over a period of time;

"*relevant investment*" means any investment made in unquoted shares or securities of a private trading company on or after 1 January 2009, where the qualifying venture capital fund retains the shares or securities in the company for a period of at least 3 years from the date of the initial investment and that company is—

(a) carrying on a business of research and development activities or innovation activities, and

(b) not carrying on an excepted trade within the meaning of *section 21A*;

"*research and development activities*" has the same meaning as in *section 766(1)*;

"*total profits*", in relation to a qualifying venture capital fund, means the sum of—

(a) the profits which are attributable to investors in the fund by reference to an agreed initial rate of return, and

(b) the balance of the profits of the fund over and above those calculated by reference to the agreed initial rate of return.][1]

(2) (a) Notwithstanding any other provision of the Tax Acts or the Capital Gains Tax Acts, carried interest to which this section applies and which is received by [an individual or][2] a partnership shall be deemed to be an amount of chargeable gains to which *section 28(1)* applies.

(b) Notwithstanding any other provision of the Tax Acts or the Capital Gains Tax Acts, carried interest to which this section applies and which is received by a company shall be deemed to be an amount of chargeable gains to which *section 28(1)* applies.

(3) (a) Notwithstanding any other provision of the Tax Acts or the Capital Gains Tax Acts, the rate of capital gains tax in respect of chargeable gains to which subsection (2)(*a*) apply shall be 15 per cent.

(b) Notwithstanding any other provision of the Tax Acts or the Capital Gains Tax Acts, the rate of corporation tax in respect of chargeable gains to which *subsection (2)(b)* apply shall be 12.5 per cent.][3]

Amendments

[1] Substituted by FA13 s46(a). Deemed to have come into force and takes effect on and from 1 January 2013.

[2] Inserted by FA13 s46(b). Deemed to have come into force and takes effect on and from 1 January 2013.

[3] Inserted by F(No.2)A08 s41. This section is deemed to have come into force and takes effect as on and from 1 January 2009.

Cross References

From Section 541C

Section 21A Higher rate of corporation tax.
Section 28 Taxation of capital gains and rate of charge.
Section 766 Tax credit for research and development expenditure.

542 Time of disposal and acquisition

[CGTA75 s10(1) and (3)]

(1) (a) Subject to *paragraph (b)* and *subsection (2)*, for the purposes of the Capital Gains Tax Acts, where an asset is disposed of and acquired under a contract, the time at which the disposal and acquisition is made shall be the time at which the contract is made (and not, if different, the time at which the asset is conveyed or transferred).

(b) Where the contract is conditional (and in particular where it is conditional on the exercise of an option), the time at which the disposal and acquisition is made shall be the time at which the condition is satisfied.

(c) For the purposes of the Capital Gains Tax Acts, where an interest in land is acquired, otherwise than under a contract, by an authority possessing compulsory purchase powers, the time at which the disposal and acquisition is made shall be the time at which the compensation for the acquisition is agreed or otherwise determined (variations on appeal being disregarded for this purpose) or, if earlier, the time at which the authority enters on the land in pursuance of its powers.

[(d) Notwithstanding *paragraph (c)*, for the purposes of the Capital Gains Tax Acts, where a person makes a disposal of land to an authority possessing compulsory purchase powers, and the disposal would not have been made but for the exercise of those powers or the giving by the authority of formal notice of its intention to exercise those powers, then the chargeable gain (if any) on the disposal shall be deemed to accrue—

(i) on the day on which the payment of the compensation amount is received by the person making the disposal, or

(ii) at a time immediately before the person's death if the consideration has not been received at the date of his or her death.][1]

(2) For the purposes of *subparagraphs (i)* to *(iv)* of *section 535(2)(a)*, the time of disposal shall be the time at which any capital sum is received.

Amendments

[1] Substituted by FA10 s56(1). This section applies to disposals made on or after 4 February 2010.

Case Law

The meaning of "conditional" was considered in Lyon v Pettigrew 1985 STC 369

In O'Connor v Coady 2004 IESC 54 the condition providing that the sale was subject to obtaining planning permission was a condition subsequent and not a condition precedent.

Revenue Briefings

Tax Briefing

Tax Briefing September 2000 – Issue 41 pg 32 – Topical Questions
Tax Briefing April 2002 – Issue 47 pg 15 – Finance Act 2002 changes

eBrief

eBrief No. 4/2004 – Capital Gains Tax – Time of Disposal of Conditional Contracts
eBrief No. 20/2008 – Capital Gains Tax – Due Dates for Payment

eBrief No. 50/2008 – Decommissioning of Fishing Vessels
eBrief No. 86/09 – Capital Gains Tax – Compulsory Purchase – Section 542(1)(d) Tax Consolidation Act 1997

Cross References

From Section 542

Section 535 Disposals where capital sums derived from assets.

543 Transfers of value derived from assets

[CGTA75 s45]

(1) Without prejudice to the generality of the provisions of the Capital Gains Tax Acts as to the transactions which are disposals of assets, any transaction which under this section is to be treated as a disposal of an asset—

(a) shall be so treated (with a corresponding acquisition of an interest in the asset) notwithstanding that there is no consideration, and

(b) in so far as, on the assumption that the parties to the transaction were at arm's length, the party making the disposal could have obtained consideration or additional consideration for the disposal, shall be treated as not being at arm's length, and the consideration so obtainable, added to the consideration actually passing, shall be treated as the market value of what is acquired.

(2) (a) Where a person having control of a company exercises that control so that value passes out of shares in the company owned by such person or a person with whom such person is connected, or out of rights over the company exercisable by such person or by a person with whom such person is connected, and passes into other shares in or rights over the company, that exercise of such person's control shall be a disposal of the shares or rights out of which the value passes by the person by whom they were owned or exercisable.

(b) References in *paragraph (a)* to a person include references to 2 or more persons connected with one another.

(3) Where, after a transaction which results in the owner of land or of any other description of property becoming the lessee of the property, there is any adjustment of the rights and liabilities under the lease (whether or not involving the grant of a new lease) which as a whole is favourable to the lessor, that shall constitute a disposal by the lessee of an interest in the property.

(4) Where an asset is subject to any description of right or restriction, the extinction or abrogation in whole or in part of the right or restriction by the person entitled to enforce it shall constitute a disposal by that person of the right or restriction.

Case Law

In Floor v Davis 1979 STC 379 it was held that control was exercised where a resolution was passed, and as a result value passed out of shares, even though the taxpayers were absent and consequently did not vote in favour of the resolution.

CHAPTER 2

Computation of Chargeable Gains and Allowable Losses

544 Interpretation and general (Chapter 2)

[CGTA75 s51(2), Sch1 pars1 and 5(3) and Sch4 par13; CGT(A)A78 s17 and Sch2]

(1) In this Chapter, "*renewals allowance*" means a deduction allowable in computing profits, gains or losses for the purposes of the Income Tax Acts by reference to the cost of acquiring an asset in replacement of another asset, and for the purposes of this Chapter a renewals allowance shall be regarded as a deduction allowable in respect of the expenditure incurred on the asset which is being replaced.

(2) References in this Chapter to sums taken into account as receipts or as expenditure in computing profits, gains or losses for the purposes of the Income Tax Acts shall include references to sums which would be so taken into account but for the fact that any profits or gains of a trade, profession or employment are not chargeable to income tax or that losses are not allowable for those purposes.

(3) References in this Chapter to income or profits charged or chargeable to tax include references to income or profits taxed or, as the case may be, taxable by deduction at source.

(4) No deduction shall be allowable in a computation under the Capital Gains Tax Acts more than once from any sum or from more than one sum.

(5) For the purposes of any computation under this Chapter of a gain accruing on a disposal, any necessary apportionment shall be made of any consideration or of any expenditure, and the method of apportionment adopted shall, subject to this Chapter, be such method as appears to the inspector or on appeal the Appeal Commissioners to be just and reasonable.

(6) *Section 557* and the other provisions of the Capital Gains Tax Acts for apportioning on a part disposal expenditure which is deductible in computing a gain shall be operated before the operation of and without regard to—

- (a) *section 1028(5)*,
- (b) *section 597*, and
- (c) any other provision making an adjustment to secure that neither a gain nor a loss accrues on a disposal.

(7) Any assessment to income tax or any decision on a claim under the Income Tax Acts, and any decision on an appeal under the Income Tax Acts against such an assessment or decision, shall be conclusive in so far as under any provision of the Capital Gains Tax Acts liability to tax depends on the provisions of the Income Tax Acts.

(8) In so far as the provisions of the Capital Gains Tax Acts require the computation of a gain by reference to events before the 6th day of April, 1974, all those provisions, including the provisions fixing the amount of the consideration deemed to be given on a disposal or an acquisition, shall apply except in so far as expressly excluded.

Cross References

From Section 544

Section 557 Part disposals.
Section 597 Replacement of business and other assets.
Section 1028 Married persons.

To Section 544

Section 535 Disposals where capital sums derived from assets.
Section 536 Capital sums: receipt of compensation and insurance moneys not treated as a disposal in certain cases.
Section 540 Options and forfeited deposits.
Section 594 Foreign life assurance and deferred annuities: taxation and returns.
Section 828 Capital gains tax: double taxation relief.
Schedule 14 Capital Gains Tax: Leases

545 Chargeable gains

[CGTA75 s7(2) and s11; CGT(A)A78 s17 and Sch2]

(1) Where under the Capital Gains Tax Acts an asset is not a chargeable asset, no chargeable gain shall accrue on its disposal.

(2) The amount of the gain accruing on the disposal of an asset shall be computed in accordance with this Chapter, and subject to the other provisions of the Capital Gains Tax Acts.

(3) Except where otherwise expressly provided by the Capital Gains Tax Acts, every gain shall be a chargeable gain.

Cross References

To Section 545

Section 5 Interpretation of Capital Gains Tax Acts.
Section 950 Interpretation (Part 41).

546 Allowable losses

[CGTA75 s7(2) and s12(1), (2), (6) and (7); CGT(A)A78 s16 and Sch1 par7]

(1) Where under the Capital Gains Tax Acts an asset is not a chargeable asset, no allowable loss shall accrue on its disposal.

(2) Except where otherwise expressly provided, the amount of a loss accruing on a disposal of an asset shall be computed in the same way as the amount of a gain accruing on a disposal is computed.

(3) Except where otherwise expressly provided, the provisions of the Capital Gains Tax Acts which distinguish gains which are chargeable gains from those which are not, or which make part of a gain a chargeable gain and part not, shall apply also to distinguish losses which are allowable losses from those which are not, and to make part of a loss an allowable loss and part not, and references in the Capital Gains Tax Acts to an allowable loss shall be construed accordingly.

(4) A loss accruing to a person in a year of assessment for which the person is neither resident nor ordinarily resident in the State shall not be an allowable loss for the purposes of the Capital Gains Tax Acts unless under *section 29(3)* the person would be chargeable to capital gains tax in respect of a chargeable gain if there had been a gain instead of a loss on that occasion.

(5) Except where provided by *section 573*, an allowable loss accruing in a year of assessment shall not be allowable as a deduction from chargeable gains in any

earlier year of assessment, and relief shall not be given under the Capital Gains Tax Acts—

(a) more than once in respect of any loss or part of a loss, and

(b) if and in so far as relief has been or may be given in respect of that loss or part of a loss under the Income Tax Acts.

(6) For the purposes of *section 31*, where, on the assumption that there were no allowable losses to be deducted under that section, a person would be chargeable under the Capital Gains Tax Acts at more than one rate of tax for a year of assessment, any allowable losses to be deducted under that section shall be deducted—

(a) if the person would be so chargeable at 2 different rates, from the chargeable gains which would be so chargeable at the higher of those rates and, in so far as they cannot be so deducted, from the chargeable gains which would be so chargeable at the lower of those rates, and

(b) if the person would be so chargeable at 3 or more rates, from the chargeable gains which would be so chargeable at the highest of those rates and, in so far as they cannot be so deducted, from the chargeable gains which would be so chargeable at the next highest of those rates, and so on.

Cross References

From Section 546

Section 29 Persons chargeable.

Section 31 Amount chargeable.

Section 573 Death.

To Section 546

Section 5 Interpretation of Capital Gains Tax Acts.

Section 128E Tax treatment of directors of companies and employees who acquire forfeitable shares.

Section 571 Chargeable gains accruing on disposals by liquidators and certain other persons.

Section 581 Disposals of shares or securities within 4 weeks of acquisition.

Section 595 Life assurance policy or deferred annuity contract entered into or acquired by company.

Section 730K Disposal of foreign life policy.

Section 739 Taxation of unit holders in undertakings for collective investment.

Section 747E Disposal of an interest in offshore funds.

Schedule 20 Offshore Funds: Computation of Offshore Income Gains

546A Restrictions on allowable losses

[(1) In this section—

"*arrangements*" includes any agreement, understanding, scheme, transaction or series of transactions (whether or not legally enforceable);

"*tax advantage*" means—

(a) relief or increased relief from tax,

(b) repayment or increased repayment of tax,

(c) the avoidance or reduction of a charge to tax or an assessment to tax, or

(d) the avoidance of a possible assessment to tax;

"*tax*" means capital gains tax or corporation tax on chargeable gains.

(2) For the purposes of the Capital Gains Tax Acts, a loss shall not be an allowable loss if—

(a) it accrues to the person directly or indirectly in consequence of, or otherwise in connection with, any arrangements, and

(b) the main purpose, or one of the main purposes, of the arrangements is to secure a tax advantage.

(3) For the purposes of *subsection (2)*, it shall not be relevant—

(a) whether or not the loss accrues at a time when there are no chargeable gains from which it could otherwise have been deducted, or

(b) whether or not the tax advantage is secured for the person to whom the loss accrues or for any other person.][1]

Amendments

[1] Inserted by FA10 s59(1). This section applies to disposals made on or after 4 February 2010.

Revenue Briefings

Tax Briefing

Tax Briefing July 2011 – Issue 03 – Restriction on the allowance of Capital Losses

eBrief

eBrief No. 40/2011 – Restriction on the allowance of Capital Losses

547 Disposals and acquisitions treated as made at market value

[CGTA75 s9; FA82 s62; FA92 s62]

(1) Subject to the Capital Gains Tax Acts, a person's acquisition of an asset shall for the purposes of those Acts be deemed to be for a consideration equal to the market value of the asset where—

(a) the person acquires the asset otherwise than by means of a bargain made at arm's length (including in particular where the person acquires it by means of a gift),

(b) the person acquires the asset by means of a distribution from a company in respect of shares in the company, or

(c) the person acquires the asset wholly or partly—

(i) for a consideration that cannot be valued,

(ii) in connection with the person's own or another person's loss of office or employment or diminution of emoluments, or

(iii) otherwise in consideration for or in recognition of the person's or another person's services or past services in any office or employment or of any other service rendered or to be rendered by the person or another person.

[(1A) (a) Notwithstanding subsection (1), where, by virtue of section 31 of the State Property Act, 1954, the Minister for Finance waives, in favour of a person, the right of the State to property, the person's acquisition of the property shall for the purposes of the Capital Gains Tax Acts be deemed to be for a consideration equal to the amount (including a nil amount) of the payment of money made by the person as one of the terms of that waiver.][1]

(2) (a) In this subsection, "*shares*" includes stock, debentures and any interests to which *section 587(3)* applies and any option in relation to such shares, and references in this subsection to an allotment of shares shall be construed accordingly.

(b) Notwithstanding *subsection (1)* and *section 584(3)*, where a company, otherwise than by means of a bargain made at arm's length, allots shares in the company (in this subsection referred to as "*the new shares*") to a person connected with the company, the consideration which the person gives or becomes liable to give for the new shares shall for the purposes of the Capital Gains Tax Acts be deemed to be an amount (including a nil amount) equal to the lesser of—

(i) the amount or value of the consideration given by the person for the new shares, and

(ii) the amount by which the market value of the shares in the company which the person held immediately after the allotment of the new shares exceeds the market value of the shares in the company which the person held immediately before the allotment or, if the person held no such shares immediately before the allotment, the market value of the new shares immediately after the allotment.

(3) *Subsection (1)* shall not apply to the acquisition of an asset where—

(a) there is no corresponding disposal of the asset, and

(b) (i) there is no consideration in money or money's worth for the asset, or

(ii) the consideration for the asset is of an amount or value which is lower than the market value of the asset.

(4) (a) Subject to the Capital Gains Tax Acts, a person's disposal of an asset shall for the purposes of those Acts be deemed to be for a consideration equal to the market value of the asset where—

(i) the person disposes of the asset otherwise than by means of a bargain made at arm's length (including in particular where the person disposes of it by means of a gift), or

(ii) the person disposes of the asset wholly or partly for a consideration that cannot be valued.

(b) *Paragraph (a)* shall not apply to a disposal by means of a gift made before the 20th day of December, 1974, and any loss incurred on a disposal by means of a gift made before that date shall not be an allowable loss.

Amendments

[1] Inserted by FA98 s68(1). This section shall apply as respects a waiver of the right of the State to property on or after the 12th day of February, 1998.

Case Law

In Spectros International plc v Madden 1997 STC 114 the purchasing company had agreed to discharge an overdraft. It was held that the amount of the overdraft should be included in the sales consideration. Shares sold at undervalue did not mean that the bargain was otherwise than at arm's length. Bullivant Holdings v IRC 1998 STC 905

Revenue Briefings

Tax Briefing

Tax Briefing May 2006 – Issue 63 pg 18 – Unapproved Share Options

Cross References

From Section 547

Section 584 Reorganisation or reduction of share capital.
Section 587 Company reconstructions and amalgamations.

To Section 547

Section 519A Approved savings-related share option schemes.
Section 519D Approved share option schemes.
Section 549 Transactions between connected persons.

Section 611 Disposals to State, public bodies and charities.
Section 737 Special investment schemes.
Section 738 Undertakings for collective investment.
Section 838 Special portfolio investment accounts.
Schedule 32 Transitional Provisions

548 Valuation of assets

[CGTA75 s49(1) to (6); CTA76 s140(2) and Sch2 PtII par7]

(1) Subject to this section, in the Capital Gains Tax Acts, "*market value*", in relation to any assets, means the price which those assets might reasonably be expected to fetch on a sale in the open market.

(2) In estimating the market value of any assets, no reduction shall be made in the estimate on account of the estimate being made on the assumption that the whole of the assets is to be placed on the market at the same time.

(3) (a) The market value of shares or securities quoted on a stock exchange in the State or in the United Kingdom shall, except where in consequence of special circumstances the prices quoted are by themselves not a proper measure of market value, be as follows—

(i) in relation to shares or securities listed in the Stock Exchange Official List-Irish—

(I) the price shown in that list at which bargains in the shares or securities were last recorded (the previous price), or

(II) where bargains other than bargains done at special prices were recorded in that list for the relevant date, the price at which the bargains were so recorded or, if more than one such price was so recorded, a price halfway between the highest and the lowest of such prices,

taking the amount under *clause (I)* if less than under *clause (II)* or if no such business was recorded on the relevant date, and taking the amount under *clause (II)* if less than under *clause (I)*, and

(ii) in relation to shares or securities listed in the Stock Exchange Daily Official List—

(I) the lower of the 2 prices shown in the quotations for the shares or securities on the relevant date plus 25 per cent of the difference between those 2 figures, or

(II) where bargains other than bargains done at special prices were recorded in that list for the relevant date, the price at which the bargains were so recorded or, if more than one such price was so recorded, a price halfway between the highest and the lowest of such prices,

taking the amount under *clause (I)* if less than under *clause (II)* or if no such bargains were recorded for the relevant date, and taking the amount under *clause (II)* if less than under *clause (I)*.

(b) Notwithstanding *paragraph (a)*—

(i) where the shares or securities are listed in both of the Official Lists referred to in that paragraph for the relevant date, the lower of the 2 amounts as ascertained under *subparagraphs (i)* and *(ii)* of that paragraph shall be taken,

(ii) this subsection shall not apply to shares or securities for which some other stock exchange affords a more active market, and

(iii) if the stock exchange concerned, or one of the stock exchanges concerned, is closed on the relevant date, the market value shall be ascertained by reference to the latest previous date or earliest subsequent date on which it is open, whichever affords the lower market value.

(4) Where shares and securities are not quoted on a stock exchange at the time at which their market value is to be determined by virtue of *subsection (1)*, it shall be assumed for the purposes of such determination that in the open market which is postulated for the purposes of *subsection (1)* there is available to any prospective purchaser of the asset in question all the information which a prudent prospective purchaser of the asset might reasonably require if such prospective purchaser were proposing to purchase it from a willing vendor by private treaty and at arm's length.

(5) In the Capital Gains Tax Acts, "*market value*", in relation to any rights of unit holders in any unit trust (including any unit trust legally established outside the State) the buying and selling prices of which are published regularly by the managers of the trust, means an amount equal to the buying price (that is, the lower price) so published on the relevant date or, if none was published on that date, on the latest date before that date.

(6) If and in so far as any appeal against an assessment to capital gains tax or against a decision on a claim under the Capital Gains Tax Acts involves the question of the value of any shares or securities in a company resident in the State, other than shares or securities quoted on a stock exchange, that question shall be determined in the like manner as an appeal against an assessment made on the company.

(7) *Subsection (6)* shall apply for the purposes of corporation tax as it applies for the purposes of capital gains tax.

Revenue Briefings

Tax Briefing

Tax Briefing December 2001 – Issue 46 pg 26 – Calculation of Base Cost of Eircom Shares and Vodafone Shares

eBrief

eBrief No. 39/2014 – Tax Treatment of Return of Value to Vodafone Shareholders

Cross References

To Section 548

Section 5 Interpretation of Capital Gains Tax Acts.
Section 55 Taxation of strips of securities.
Section 119 Valuation of benefits in kind.
Section 122A Notional loans relating to shares, etc.
Section 128 Tax treatment of directors of companies and employees granted rights to acquire shares or other assets.
Section 128A Deferral of payment of tax under section 128.
Section 128C Tax treatment of directors and employees who acquire convertible shares.
Section 128D Tax treatment of directors of companies and employees who acquire restricted shares.
Section 128E Tax treatment of directors of companies and employees who acquire forfeitable shares.
Section 130 Matters to be treated as distributions.
Section 409 Capital allowances: room ownership schemes.
Section 479 Relief for new shares purchased on issue by employees.
Section 488 Interpretation (Part 16).
Section 509 Interpretation (Chapter 1).

Section 531AAD Excess bank remuneration charge.
Section 531AM Charge to universal social charge.
Section 540 Options and forfeited deposits.
Section 627 Deemed disposal of assets.
Section 706 Interpretation and general (Part 26).
Section 736 Option for non-application of section 735.
Section 737 Special investment schemes.
Section 739 Taxation of unit holders in undertakings for collective investment.
Section 743 Material interest in offshore funds.
Section 745 Charge to income tax or corporation tax of offshore income gain.
Section 784A Approved retirement fund.
Section 787A Interpretation and supplemental.
Section 787O Interpretation and general (Chapter 2C).
Section 817 Schemes to avoid liability to tax under Schedule F.
Section 838 Special portfolio investment accounts.
Section 841 Voluntary Health Insurance Board: restriction of certain losses and deemed disposal of certain assets.
Schedule 12A Approved Savings-Related Share Option Schemes
Schedule 12C Approved Share Option Schemes

549 Transactions between connected persons

[CGTA75 s33(1) to (6); FA89 s87]

(1) This section shall apply for the purposes of the Capital Gains Tax Acts where a person acquires an asset and the person making the disposal is connected with the person acquiring the asset.

(2) Without prejudice to the generality of *section 547*, the person acquiring the asset and the person making the disposal shall be treated as parties to a transaction otherwise than by means of a bargain made at arm's length.

(3) Where on the disposal a loss accrues to the person making the disposal, the loss shall not be deductible except from a chargeable gain accruing to that person on some other disposal of an asset to the person acquiring the asset mentioned in *subsection (1)*, being a disposal made at a time when they are connected persons.

(4) *Subsection (3)* shall not apply to a disposal by means of a gift in settlement if the gift and the income from it are wholly or primarily applicable for educational, cultural or recreational purposes, and the persons benefiting from the application for those purposes are confined to members of an association of persons for whose benefit the gift was made, not being persons all or most of whom are connected persons.

(5) Where the asset mentioned in *subsection (1)* is an option to enter into a sale or other transaction given by the person making the disposal, a loss accruing to a person acquiring the asset shall not be an allowable loss unless it accrues on a disposal of the option at arm's length to a person not connected with the person acquiring the asset.

[(6) Where the asset mentioned in subsection (1) is subject to any right or restriction enforceable by the person making the disposal or by a person connected with that person, then that market value shall, where the amount of the consideration for the acquisition is in accordance with subsection (2) deemed to be equal to the market value of the asset, be what its market value would be if not subject to the right or restriction, reduced—

(a) by the lesser of—

(i) the market value of the right or restriction, and

(ii) the amount by which its extinction would enhance the value of the asset to its owner, or

(b) by the market value of the right or restriction, where the market value referred to in paragraph *(a)*(i) and the amount referred to in paragraph *(a)*(ii) are equal.][1]

(7) Where the right or restriction referred to in *subsection (6)*—

(a) is of such a nature that its enforcement would or might effectively destroy or substantially impair the value of the asset without bringing any countervailing advantage either to the person making the disposal or a person connected with that person,

(b) is an option or other right to acquire the asset, or

(c) in the case of incorporeal property, is a right to extinguish the asset in the hands of the person giving the consideration by forfeiture or merger or otherwise,

then, the market value of the asset shall be determined, and the amount of the gain accruing on the disposal shall be computed, as if the right or restriction did not exist.

[(7A) (a) This subsection applies where the asset mentioned in subsection (1) is subject to any right or restriction enforceable by the person making the disposal or by the person connected with that person, and the market value of the asset at the date of its acquisition (without reference to any right or restriction) is greater than the consideration, in money or money's worth, given in payment for that asset.

(b) Where, on a subsequent disposal of an asset to which paragraph *(a)* applies by the person who acquired that asset, subsection (7) has the effect (without taking account of this subsection) of—

(i) increasing a loss, or

(ii) substituting a loss for a gain,

then that subsection shall not apply.][2]

(8) (a) Where a person disposes of an asset to another person in such circumstances that—

(i) *subsection (7)* would but for this subsection apply in determining the market value of the asset, and

(ii) the person is not chargeable to capital gains tax under *section 29* or *30* in respect of any gain accruing on the person's disposal of the asset,

then, as respects any subsequent disposal of the asset by the other person, that other person's acquisition of the asset shall for the purposes of the Capital Gains Tax Acts be deemed to be for an amount equal to the market value of the asset determined as if *subsection (7)* had not been enacted.

(b) This subsection shall apply—

(i) to disposals made on or after the 25th day of January, 1989, and

(ii) for the purposes of the determination of any deduction to be made from a chargeable gain accruing on or after the 25th day of January, 1989, in respect of an allowable loss, notwithstanding that the loss accrued or but for this section would have accrued on a disposal made before that day.

(9) *Subsections (6)* and *(7)* shall not apply to a right of forfeiture or other right exercisable on breach of a covenant contained in a lease of land or other property, or to any right or restriction under a mortgage or other charge.

Amendments

[1] Substituted by F(No.2)A08 s43(1)(a). Applies to disposals made on or after 20 November 2008.

[2] Inserted by F(No.2)A08 s43(1)(b). Applies to disposals made on or after 20 November 2008.

Revenue Precedents

Occasions of charge arise on disposals between partners. A change in asset-sharing ratios involves a disposal/acquisition, most commonly on retirement of a partner or admission of a new partner. Where (1) no consideration is involved, (2) there is no revaluation of assets, (3) other than as partners, the individuals are not connected persons within the meaning of S.10 TCA 1997 (4) the transaction is a bona fide commercial arrangement not forming part of a tax avoidance scheme – no gain is triggered and a re-allocation of balance sheet values is acceptable. G36

Cross References

From Section 549

Section 29 Persons chargeable.

Section 30 Partnerships.

Section 547 Disposals and acquisitions treated as made at market value.

550 Assets disposed of in series of transactions

[CGTA75 s34]

Where a person is given, or acquires from one or more persons with whom such person is connected, by means of 2 or more transactions, assets of which the aggregate market value, when considered separately in relation to the separate other transactions, is less than the aggregate market value of those assets when considered together, then, for the purposes of the Capital Gains Tax Acts, the market value of the assets where relevant shall be taken to be the larger market value and that value shall be apportioned rateably to the respective disposals.

551 Exclusion from consideration for disposals of sums chargeable to income tax

[CGTA75 s51(1) and Sch1 par2; CTA76 s140(2) and Sch2 PtII par8]

(1) In this section, *"rent"* includes any rent charge, fee farm rent and any payment in the nature of a rent.

(2) There shall be excluded from the consideration for a disposal of an asset taken into account in the computation under this Chapter of the gain accruing on that disposal any money or money's worth charged to income tax as income of, or taken into account as a receipt in computing income, profits, gains or losses for the purposes of the Income Tax Acts of, the person making the disposal; but the exclusion from consideration under this subsection shall not be taken as applying to a computation in accordance with Case I of Schedule D for the purpose of restricting relief in respect of expenses of management under *section 707*.

(3) *Subsection (2)* shall not be taken as excluding from the consideration so taken into account any money or money's worth taken into account in the making of a balancing charge under *Part 9* or under *Chapter 1* of *Part 29*.

(4) This section shall not preclude the taking into account in a computation under this Chapter of the gain, as consideration for the disposal of an asset,

of the capitalised value of a rent (as in a case where rent is exchanged for some other asset), or of a right of any other description to income or to payments in the nature of income over a period, or to a series of payments in the nature of income.

Cross References

From Section 551

Section 268 Meaning of "industrial building or structure".

Section 707 Management expenses.

Section 754 Interpretation (Chapter 1).

To Section 551

Section 644 Provisions supplementary to section 643.

Section 693 Exploration expenditure: allowances and charges.

Section 707 Management expenses.

Section 726 Investment income.

Section 747 Deduction of offshore income gain in determining capital gain.

Schedule 14 Capital Gains Tax: Leases

552 Acquisition, enhancement and disposal costs

[CGTA75 s51(1) and Sch1 par3(1) to (5); CTA76 s140(2) and Sch2 PtII par9]

(1) Subject to the Capital Gains Tax Acts, the sums allowable as a deduction from the consideration in the computation under this Chapter of the gain accruing to a person on the disposal of an asset shall be restricted to—

(a) the amount or value of the consideration in money or money's worth given by the person or on the person's behalf wholly and exclusively for the acquisition of the asset, together with the incidental costs to the person of the acquisition or, if the asset was not acquired by the person, any expenditure wholly and exclusively incurred by the person in providing the asset,

(b) the amount of any expenditure wholly and exclusively incurred on the asset by the person or on the person's behalf for the purpose of enhancing the value of the asset, being expenditure reflected in the state or nature of the asset at the time of the disposal, and any expenditure wholly and exclusively incurred by the person in establishing, preserving or defending the person's title to, or to a right over, the asset, and

(c) the incidental costs to the person of making the disposal.

[(1A) (a) In this subsection "*rate of exchange*" means a rate at which 2 currencies might reasonably be expected to be exchanged for each other by persons dealing at arm's length.

(b) For the purposes of *subsection (1)* where a sum allowable as a deduction was incurred in a currency other than the currency of the State, it shall be expressed in terms of the currency of the State by reference to the rate of exchange of the currency of the State for the other currency at the time that the sum was incurred.][1]

[(1B) (a) In this subsection—

"*connected person*" has the same meaning as in *section 10*;

"*debt*" means a debt or debts, in respect of borrowed money, whether incurred by the person making the disposal of an asset or by a connected person;

"*group*" and "member of a group" have the same meanings, respectively, as in *section 616*.

(b) Where—

(i) the amount or value of the consideration referred to in *subsection (1)(a)*, or

(ii) the amount of any expenditure referred to in *subsection (1)(b)*,

was defrayed either directly or indirectly out of borrowed money, the debt in respect of which is released in whole or in part (whether before, on or after the disposal of the asset), that amount shall be reduced by the lesser of the amount of the debt which is released or the amount of the allowable loss which, but for this subsection, would arise.

(c) For the purposes of *paragraph (b)*, the date on which the whole or part of a debt is released shall be determined on the same basis as the release of the whole or part of a specified debt is treated as having been effected in *section 87B(4)*.

(d) Where a debt is released in whole or in part in a year of assessment after the year of assessment in which the disposal of the asset takes place (such that the release of the debt was not taken into account in the computation of a chargeable gain or allowable loss on the disposal of the asset) then for the purposes of the Capital Gains Tax Acts a chargeable gain, equal to the amount of the reduction that would have been made under *paragraph (b)* had the release been effected in the year of assessment in which the disposal of the asset took place, shall be deemed to accrue to the person who disposed of the asset on the date on which the debt is released but, where the disposal is to a connected person, any gain under this subsection shall be treated for the purposes of *section 549(3)* as if it accrued on the disposal of an asset to that connected person.

(e) A chargeable gain under *paragraph (d)* shall not be deemed to accrue where, had a gain accrued on the disposal of the asset, it would not have been a chargeable gain or it would have qualified for relief from capital gains tax.

(f) Where a debt released is in respect of money borrowed by a member of a group of companies from another member of the group, the amount or value of the consideration referred to in *subsection (1)(a)*, or the amount of any expenditure referred to in *subsection (1)(b)*, shall not be reduced by the amount of that debt which is released under *paragraph (b)* or a chargeable gain in respect of the release of that debt shall not be deemed to accrue under *paragraph (d)*.][2]

(2) For the purposes of the Capital Gains Tax Act as respects the person making the disposal, the incidental costs to the person of the acquisition of the asset or of its disposal shall consist of expenditure wholly and exclusively incurred by that person for the purposes of the acquisition or, as the case may be, the disposal, being fees, commission or remuneration paid for the professional services of any surveyor, valuer, auctioneer, accountant, agent or legal advisor and costs of transfer or conveyance (including stamp duty), together with—

(a) in the case of the acquisition of an asset, costs of advertising to find a seller, and

(b) in the case of a disposal, costs of advertising to find a buyer and costs reasonably incurred in making any valuation or apportionment required for the purposes of the computation under this Chapter of the gain, including in particular expenses reasonably incurred in ascertaining market value where required by the Capital Gains Tax Acts.

(3) (a) Where—

(i) a company incurs expenditure on the construction of any building, structure or works, being expenditure allowable as a deduction under *subsection (1)* in computing a gain accruing to the company on the disposal of the building, structure or works, or of any asset comprising the building, structure or works,

(ii) that expenditure was defrayed out of borrowed money,

(iii) the company charged to capital all or any part of the interest on that borrowed money referable to a period ending on or before the disposal, and

(iv) the company is chargeable to capital gains tax in respect of the gain,

then, the sums so allowable under *subsection (1)* shall include the amount of that interest charged to capital except in so far as such interest has been taken into account for the purposes of relief under the Income Tax Acts, or could have been so taken into account but for an insufficiency of income or profits or gains.

(b) Subject to *paragraph (a)*, no payment of interest shall be allowable as a deduction under this section.

(4) Without prejudice to *section 554*, there shall be excluded from the sums allowable as a deduction under this section any premium or other payment made under a policy of insurance of the risk of any kind of damage or injury to, or loss or depreciation of, the asset.

(5) In the case of a gain accruing to a person on the disposal of, or of a right or interest in or over, an asset to which the person became absolutely entitled as legatee or as against the trustees of settled property—

(a) any expenditure within *subsection (2)* incurred by the person in relation to the transfer of the asset to the person by the personal representatives or trustees, and

(b) any such expenditure incurred in relation to the transfer of the asset by the personal representatives or trustees,

shall be allowable as a deduction under this section.

Amendments

[1] Inserted by FA98 sched2(10). With effect from 31 December 2008 per S.I. 502 of 1998.

[2] Inserted by F(No.2)A13 s42. Comes into operation on 1 January 2014.

Case Law

In Loffland Bros North Sea Inc v Goodbrand 1998 STC 930 it was held that consideration is to be converted at date of contract and not date of receipt and that no bad debt relief can be claimed for the exchange loss between date of contract and date of receipt.

The case of Oram v Johnson 1980 STC 222 established that expenditure on the cost, or enhancement, of an asset does not include the notional cost of the taxpayer's own labour.

Where the acquisition and disposal cost of an asset are in a foreign currency, the computation of the chargeable gain or allowable loss must include any foreign exchange gain or loss. Bentley v Pike 1981 STC 360

Fees paid to a valuer which were attributable to negotiations with the UK Revenue and to the conduct of an appeal, were not allowed as a deduction for the purpose of the capital gains tax computation. Couch v Caton's Administrators 1996 STC 201

Revenue Briefings

Tax Briefing

Tax Briefing May 2006 – Issue 63 pg 18 – Unapproved Share Option Schemes

Cross References

From Section 552

Section 554 Exclusion of expenditure by reference to income tax.

To Section 552

Section 128 Tax treatment of directors of companies and employees granted rights to acquire shares or other assets.
Section 128C Tax treatment of directors and employees who acquire convertible shares.
Section 128D Tax treatment of directors of companies and employees who acquire restricted shares.
Section 267O Treatment of credit return.
Section 479 Relief for new shares purchased on issue by employees.
Section 536 Capital sums: receipt of compensation and insurance moneys not treated as a disposal in certain cases.
Section 553 Interest charged to capital.
Section 554 Exclusion of expenditure by reference to income tax.
Section 555 Restriction of losses by reference to capital allowances and renewals allowances.
Section 556 Adjustment of allowable expenditure by reference to consumer price index.
Section 557 Part disposals.
Section 559 Assets derived from other assets.
Section 560 Wasting assets.
Section 561 Wasting assets qualifying for capital allowances.
Section 562 Contingent liabilities.
Section 577A Relinquishing of a life interest by the person entitled.
Section 580 Shares, securities, etc: identification.
Section 588 Demutualisation of assurance companies.
Section 589 Shares in close company transferring assets at undervalue.
Section 594 Foreign life assurance and deferred annuities: taxation and returns.
Section 600 Transfer of business to company.
Section 603 Wasting chattels.
Section 611 Disposals to State, public bodies and charities.
Section 631 Transfer of assets generally.
Schedule 14 Capital Gains Tax: Leases

553 Interest charged to capital

[CTA76 s128]

Where—

(a) a company incurs expenditure on the construction of any building, structure or works, being expenditure allowable as a deduction under *section 552* in computing a gain accruing to the company on the disposal of the building, structure or works, or of any asset comprising the building, structure or works,

(b) that expenditure was defrayed out of borrowed money, and

(c) the company charged to capital all or any of the interest on that borrowed money referable to a period or part of a period ending on or before the disposal,

then, the sums so allowable shall, notwithstanding *section 552(3)(b)*, include the amount of that interest charged to capital.

Cross References

From Section 553

Section 552 Acquisition, enhancement and disposal costs.

554 Exclusion of expenditure by reference to income tax

[CGTA75 s51(1) and Sch1 par4]

(1) There shall be excluded from the sums allowable under *section 552* as a deduction any expenditure allowable as a deduction in computing the profits or gains or losses of a trade or profession for the purposes of income tax or allowable as a deduction in computing any other income or profits or gains or losses for the purposes of the Income Tax Acts and any expenditure which, although not so allowable as a deduction in computing any losses, would be so allowable but for an insufficiency of income or profits or gains, and this subsection shall apply irrespective of whether effect is or would be given to the deduction in computing the amount of tax chargeable or by discharge or repayment of tax or in any other way.

(2) Without prejudice to *subsection (1)*, there shall be excluded from the sums allowable under *section 552* as a deduction any expenditure which, if the assets or all the assets to which the computation relates were, and had at all times been, held or used as part of the fixed capital of a trade the profits or gains of which were chargeable to income tax, would be allowable as a deduction in computing the profits or gains or losses of the trade for the purposes of the Income Tax Acts.

Cross References

From Section 554

Section 552 Acquisition, enhancement and disposal costs.

To Section 554

Section 78 Computation of companies' chargeable gains.
Section 479 Relief for new shares purchased on issue by employees.
Section 481 Relief for investment in films.
Section 489 The relief.
Section 493 Seed capital relief.
Section 552 Acquisition, enhancement and disposal costs.
Section 555 Restriction of losses by reference to capital allowances and renewals allowances.
Section 644 Provisions supplementary to section 643.

555 Restriction of losses by reference to capital allowances and renewals allowances

[CGTA75 s51(1) and Sch1 par 5(1), (2) and (4)]

(1) *Section 554* shall not require the exclusion from the sums allowable as a deduction under *section 552* of any expenditure as being expenditure in respect of which a capital allowance or renewals allowance is made but, in the computation of the amount of a loss accruing to the person making the disposal, there shall be excluded from the sums allowable as a deduction any expenditure to the extent to which any capital allowance or renewals allowance has been or may be made in respect of that expenditure.

(2) Where the person making the disposal acquired the asset—

(a) by a transfer to which *section 289(6)* or *295* applies, or

(b) by a transfer by means of a sale in relation to which an election under *section 312(5)* was made, then, this section shall apply as if any capital allowance made to the transferor in respect of the asset had (except in so far as any loss to the transferor was restricted under those sections) been made to the person making the disposal (being the transferee) and, where the transferor acquired the asset by such a transfer, capital allowances which by virtue of this subsection may be taken into account in relation to the transferor shall also be taken into account in relation to the transferee, and so on for any series of transfers before the disposal.

(3) The amount of capital allowances to be taken into account under this section in relation to a disposal includes any allowances to be made by reference to the event which is the disposal, and there shall be deducted from the amount of the allowances the amount of any balancing charge to which effect has been or is to be given by reference to the event which is the disposal, or any earlier event, and of any balancing charge to which effect might have been so given but for the making of an election under *section 290.*

Cross References

From Section 555

Section 289 Calculation of balancing allowances and balancing charges in certain cases.
Section 290 Option in case of replacement.
Section 295 Option in case of succession under will or intestacy.
Section 312 Special provisions as to certain sales.
Section 552 Acquisition, enhancement and disposal costs.
Section 554 Exclusion of expenditure by reference to income tax.

To Section 555

Section 372AP Relief for lessors.
Section 557 Part disposals.
Section 619 Disposals or acquisitions outside group.
Section 693 Exploration expenditure: allowances and charges.

556 Adjustment of allowable expenditure by reference to consumer price index

[CGT(A)A78 s3, s16 and Sch1 par1; S.I. No. 157 of 1997]

(1) In this section—

"*the consumer price index number*" means the All Items Consumer Price Index Number compiled by the Central Statistics Office;

"the consumer price index number relevant to any year of assessment" means the consumer price index number at the [mid-November][1] before the commencement of that year expressed on the basis that the consumer price index at mid-November, 1968, was 100.

(2) (a) For the purposes of computing the chargeable gain accruing to a person on the disposal of an asset, each sum (in this section referred to as "*deductible expenditure*") allowable as a deduction from the consideration for the disposal under *paragraphs (a)* and *(b)* of *section 552(1)* shall be adjusted by multiplying it by the figure (in this section referred to as "*the multiplier*") [specified in *subsection (5)*, determined under *subsection (6)* or specified in *subsection (6A)*, as the case may be.][2]

(b) This subsection shall not apply in relation to deductible expenditure where the person making the disposal had incurred the expenditure in the period of 12 months ending on the date of the disposal.

(3) For the purposes of the Capital Gains Tax Acts, it shall be assumed that an asset held by a person on the 6th day of April, 1974, was sold and immediately reacquired by such person on that date, and there shall be deemed to have been given by such person as consideration for the reacquisition an amount equal to the market value of the asset at that date.

(4) *Subsections (2)* and *(3)* shall not apply in relation to the disposal of an asset if as a consequence of the application of those subsections—

(a) a gain would accrue on that disposal to the person making the disposal and either a smaller gain or a loss would so accrue if those subsections did not apply, or

(b) a loss would so accrue and either a smaller loss or a gain would accrue if those subsections did not apply,

and accordingly, in a case to which *paragraph (a)* or *(b)* applies, the amount of the gain or loss accruing on the disposal shall be computed without regard to *subsections (2)* and *(3)*; but, in a case where this subsection would otherwise substitute a loss for a gain or a gain for a loss, it shall be assumed in relation to the disposal that the relevant asset was acquired by the owner for a consideration such that neither a gain nor a loss accrued to the owner on making the disposal.

(5) In relation to the disposal of an asset made in the year 1997-98, the multiplier shall be the figure mentioned in *column (2)* of the Table to this subsection opposite the mention in *column (1)* of that Table of the year of assessment in which the deductible expenditure was incurred.

TABLE

Year of assessment in which deductible expenditure incurred (1)	Multiplier (2)
1974-75	6.112
1975-76	4.936
1976-77	4.253
1977-78	3.646
1978-79	3.368
1979-80	3.039
1980-81	2.631
1981-82	2.174
1982-83	1.829
1983-84	1.627
1984-85	1.477
1985-86	1.390
1986-87	1.330
1987-88	1.285
1988-89	1.261
1989-90	1.221
1990-91	1.171
1991-92	1.142

TABLE

Year of assessment in which deductible expenditure incurred (1)	Multiplier (2)
1992-93	1.101
1993-94	1.081
1994-95	1.063
1995-96	1.037
1996-97	1.016

(6) (a) The Revenue Commissioners shall make regulations specifying the multipliers, determined in accordance with *paragraph (b)*, in relation to the disposal of an asset made in the year 1998-99 and shall make corresponding regulations in relation to the disposal of an asset made [[in each subsequent year][3] of assessment up to and including the year of assessment 2003.][4]

(b) The multiplier, in relation to the disposal of an asset made in the year 1998-99 or [any subsequent year of assessment up to and including the year of assessment 2003,][5] shall be the quotient, rounded up to 3 decimal places, obtainable by dividing the consumer price index number relevant to the year of assessment in which the disposal is made by the consumer price index number relevant to the year of assessment in which the deductible expenditure was incurred.

[(6A) In relation to the disposal of an asset made in the year 2004 or any subsequent year of assessment, the multiplier shall be the figure mentioned in column (2) of the Table to this subsection opposite the mention in column (1) of that Table of the year of assessment in which the deductible expenditure was incurred.

TABLE

Year of assessment in which deductible expenditure incurred (1)	Multiplier (2)
1974-75	7.528
1975-76	6.080
1976-77	5.238
1977-78	4.490
1978-79	4.148
1979-80	3.742
1980-81	3.240
1981-82	2.678
1982-83	2.253
1983-84	2.003
1984-85	1.819
1985-86	1.713
1986-87	1.637

TABLE

Year of assessment in which deductible expenditure incurred (1)	Multiplier (2)
1987-88	1.583
1988-89	1.553
1989-90	1.503
1990-91	1.442
1991-92	1.406
1992-93	1.356
1993-94	1.331
1994-95	1.309
1995-96	1.277
1996-97	1.251
1997-98	1.232
1998-99	1.212
1999-00	1.193
2000-01	1.144
2001	1.087
2002	1.049
2003 and subsequent years	1.000]6

(7) Every regulation made under this section shall be laid before Dáil Éireann as soon as may be after it is made and, if a resolution annulling the regulation is passed by Dáil Éireann within the next 21 days on which Dáil Éireann has sat after the regulation is laid before it, the regulation shall be annulled accordingly, but without prejudice to the validity of anything previously done thereunder.

(8) A capital sum which under *section 536(1)(a)* is to be deducted from any expenditure allowable as a deduction in computing a gain on the disposal of an asset shall be deducted from the sum applied in restoring the asset before *subsection (2)* is applied to the residue, if any, of that sum.

(9) An amount determined in accordance with *subsection (3)* in respect of an asset shall be reduced by any expenditure within *section 565* which relates to the asset and which was incurred before the 6th day of April, 1974, and *subsection (2)* shall apply to the residue of that amount.

Amendments

[1] Substituted by FA01 sched2(33). Applies as on and from 1 January 2002.

[2] Substituted by FA03 s65(a).

[3] Substituted by FA05 sched6(1)(i). Applies as on and from 25 March 2005.

[4] Substituted by FA03 s65(b).

[5] Substituted by FA03 s65(c).

[6] Inserted by FA03 s65(d).

Cross References

From Section 556

Section 536 Capital sums: receipt of compensation and insurance moneys not treated as a disposal in certain cases.
Section 552 Acquisition, enhancement and disposal costs.
Section 565 Expenditure reimbursed out of public money.

To Section 556

Section 403 Restriction on use of capital allowances for certain leased assets.
Section 580 Shares, securities, etc: identification.
Section 582 Calls on shares.
Section 584 Reorganisation or reduction of share capital.
Section 591 Relief for individuals on certain reinvestment.
Section 594 Foreign life assurance and deferred annuities: taxation and returns.
Section 597 Replacement of business and other assets.
Section 600A Replacement of qualifying premises.
Section 611A Treatment of certain disposals made by The Pharmaceutical Society of Ireland.
Section 615 Company reconstruction or amalgamation: transfer of assets.
Section 619 Disposals or acquisitions outside group.
Section 633 Company reconstruction or amalgamation: transfer of development land.
Section 651 Restriction of indexation relief in relation to relevant disposals.
Section 711 Chargeable gains of life business.
Section 737 Special investment schemes.
Section 738 Undertakings for collective investment.
Section 739 Taxation of unit holders in undertakings for collective investment.
Section 747E Disposal of an interest in offshore funds.
Section 838 Special portfolio investment accounts.
Schedule 20 Offshore Funds: Computation of Offshore Income Gains

557 Part disposals

[CGTA75 s51(1) and Sch1 par6]

(1) Where a person disposes of an interest or rights in or over an asset and, generally wherever on the disposal of an asset, any description of property derived from that asset remains undisposed of, the sums which under *paragraphs (a)* and *(b)* of *section 552(1)* are attributable to the asset shall be apportioned both for the purposes of the computation under this Chapter of the gain accruing on the disposal and for the purpose of applying this Chapter in relation to the property which remains undisposed of.

(2) Such portion of the expenditure shall be allowable as a deduction in computing under this Chapter the amount of the gain accruing on the disposal as bears the same proportion to the total of those sums as the value of the consideration for the disposal bears to the aggregate of that value and the market value of the property which remains, and the balance of the expenditure shall be attributed to the property which remains undisposed of.

(3) Any apportionment to be made in pursuance of this section shall be made before the operation of *section 555* and, if after a part disposal there is a subsequent disposal of an asset, the capital allowances or renewals allowances to be taken into account in pursuance of that section in relation to the subsequent disposal shall, subject to *subsection (4)*, be those referable to the sums which under *paragraphs (a)* and *(b)* of *section 552(1)* are attributable to the asset whether before or after the part disposal, but those allowances shall be reduced by the amount (if any) by which the loss on the earlier disposal was restricted under that section.

(4) This section shall not be taken as requiring the apportionment of any expenditure which on the facts is wholly attributable to the asset or part of the asset which is disposed of or wholly attributable to the asset or part of the asset which remains undisposed of.

Revenue Briefings

Tax Briefing

Tax Briefing September 2000 – Issue 41 pg 34 – Partition of Joint Tenancy or Tenancy in Common
Tax Briefing December 2000 – Issue 42 pg 48 – CGT Treatment of Capital Sum Derived from Shares
Tax Briefing May 2003 – Issue 52 pg 18 – Part Disposal of Development Land

Cross References

From Section 557

Section 552 Acquisition, enhancement and disposal costs.
Section 555 Restriction of losses by reference to capital allowances and renewals allowances.

To Section 557

Section 544 Interpretation and general (Chapter 2).
Section 558 Part disposals before 6th day of April, 1978.
Section 616 Groups of companies: interpretation.
Section 719 Deemed disposal and reacquisition of certain assets.
Section 747 Deduction of offshore income gain in determining capital gain.
Schedule 14 Capital Gains Tax: Leases

558 Part disposals before 6th day of April, 1978

[CGT(A)A78 s16 and Sch1 par10(1) and (2)]

(1) Where on or after the 6th day of April, 1974, but before the 6th day of April, 1978, a person made a disposal (to which paragraph 6 of Schedule 1 to the Capital Gains Tax Act, 1975, applied) of an asset held by such person on the 6th day of April, 1974, and—

(a) the amount of the chargeable gain which accrued on that disposal was determined under paragraph 18 of Schedule 1 to the Capital Gains Tax Act, 1975, and

(b) any property derived from that asset remained undisposed of on the 6th day of April, 1978,

then, for the purpose of determining the balance of the expenditure which under *section 557* is to be attributed to the property which remains undisposed of, it shall be assumed that on the disposal the amount of the chargeable gain referred to in *paragraph (a)* had been determined, not under paragraph 18 of Schedule 1 to the Capital Gains Tax Act, 1975, but on the assumption that the asset was disposed of and immediately reacquired by the person on the 6th day of April, 1974.

(2) Where on or after the 6th day of April, 1974, but before the 6th day of April, 1978, a person made a disposal (to which paragraph 6 of Schedule 1 to the Capital Gains Tax Act, 1975, applied) of an asset acquired by such person on a death which occurred on or after the 6th day of April, 1974, and—

(a) the amount of the chargeable gain which accrued on that disposal was determined on the basis that the asset had been acquired by such person on a date earlier than the date of that death, and

(b) any property derived from that asset remained undisposed of on the 6th day of April, 1978,

then, notwithstanding *subsection (1)*, for the purpose of determining the balance of the expenditure which under *section 557* is to be attributed to the property which remains undisposed of, it shall be assumed that on the disposal the amount of the chargeable gain referred to in *paragraph (a)* had been determined as if section 14(1) of the Capital Gains Tax Act, 1975 (as amended by section 6 of the Capital Gains Tax (Amendment) Act, 1978) or, as the case may be, section 15(4)*(b)* of the Capital Gains Tax Act, 1975 (as amended by section 7 of the Capital Gains Tax (Amendment) Act, 1978) had applied at the date of that disposal.

Cross References

From Section 558

Section 557 Part disposals.

559 Assets derived from other assets

[CGTA75 s51(1) and Sch1 par7]

(1) If and in so far as, in a case where assets have been merged or divided or have changed their nature, or rights or interests in or over assets have been created or extinguished, the value of an asset is derived from any other asset in the same ownership, an appropriate proportion of the sums allowable as a deduction in respect of the other asset under *paragraphs (a)* and *(b)* of *section 552(1)* shall, both for the purpose of the computation of a gain accruing on the disposal of the first-mentioned asset and, if the other asset remains in existence, on a disposal of that other asset, be attributed to the first-mentioned asset.

(2) The appropriate proportion shall be computed by reference to the market value at the time of disposal of the assets (including rights or interests in or over the assets) which have not been disposed of and the consideration received in respect of the assets (including rights or interests in or over the assets) disposed of.

Cross References

From Section 559

Section 552 Acquisition, enhancement and disposal costs.

560 Wasting assets

[CGTA75 s51(1) and Sch1 pars 8 and 9]

(1) In this Chapter—

"*the residual or scrap value*", in relation to a wasting asset, means the predictable value, if any, which the wasting asset will have at the end of its predictable life as estimated in accordance with this section;

"*wasting asset*" means an asset with a predictable life not exceeding 50 years, but so that—

(a) freehold land shall not be a wasting asset whatever its nature and whatever the nature of the buildings or works on that land,

(b) "*life*", in relation to any tangible movable property, means useful life, having regard to the purpose for which the tangible assets were acquired or provided by the person making the disposal,

(c) plant [(other than plant that is a work of art)][1] and machinery shall in every case be regarded as having a predictable life of less than 50 years, and in estimating that life it shall be assumed that its life will end when it is finally put out of use as being unfit for further use and that it will be used in the normal manner and to the normal extent and will be so used throughout its life as so estimated, and

(d) a life interest in settled property shall not be a wasting asset until the predictable expectation of life of the life tenant is 50 years or less, and the predictable life of life interests in settled property and of annuities shall be ascertained from actuarial tables approved by the Revenue [Commissioners;][2]

['*work of art*' includes a picture, print, book, manuscript, sculpture, piece of jewellery, furniture or similar object;][3]

(2) The question as to what is the predictable life of an asset, and the question as to what is its predictable residual or scrap value, if any, at the end of that life, shall, in so far as

those questions are not immediately answered by the nature of the asset, be taken in relation to any disposal of the asset as they were known or ascertainable at the time when the asset was acquired or provided by the person making the disposal.

(3) In the computation under this Chapter of the gain accruing on the disposal of a wasting asset, it shall be assumed—

(a) that any expenditure attributable to the asset under *section 552(1)(a)*, after deducting the residual or scrap value, if any, of the asset, is written off at a uniform rate from its full amount at the time when the asset is acquired or provided to nil at the end of its life, and

(b) that any expenditure attributable to the asset under *section 552(1)(b)* is written off at a uniform rate from the full amount of that expenditure at the time when that expenditure is first reflected in the state or nature of the asset to nil at the end of its life.

(4) Where any expenditure attributable to the asset under *section 552(1)(b)* creates or increases a residual or scrap value of the asset, the residual or scrap value to be deducted under *subsection (3)(a)* shall be the residual or scrap value so created or increased.

(5) Any expenditure written off under this section shall not be allowable as a deduction under *section 552*.

Amendments

[1] Inserted by FA14 s47(1)(a)(i). Applies to disposals made on or after 23 December 2014.

[2] Substituted by FA14 s47(1)(a)(ii). Applies to disposals made on or after 23 December 2014.

[3] Inserted by FA14 s47(1)(b). Applies to disposals made on or after 23 December 2014.

Cross References

From Section 560

Section 552 Acquisition, enhancement and disposal costs.

To Section 560

Section 5 Interpretation of Capital Gains Tax Acts.
Section 540 Options and forfeited deposits.
Section 561 Wasting assets qualifying for capital allowances.
Section 602 Chattel exemption.
Schedule 14 Capital Gains Tax: Leases

561 Wasting assets qualifying for capital allowances

[CGTA75 s51(1) and Sch1 par10]

(1) *Subsections (3)* to *(5)* of *section 560* shall not apply in relation to a disposal of an asset—

(a) which, from the beginning of the period of ownership of the person making the disposal to the time when the disposal is made, is used solely for the purposes of a trade or profession and in respect of which that person has claimed or could have claimed any capital allowance in respect of any expenditure attributable to the asset under *paragraph (a)* or *(b)* of *section 552(1)*, or

(b) on which the person making the disposal has incurred any expenditure which has otherwise qualified in full for any capital allowance.

(2) In the case of the disposal of an asset which in the period of ownership of the person making the disposal has been used partly for the purposes of a trade or profession and partly for other purposes, or has been used for the purposes of

a trade or profession for part of that period, or which has otherwise qualified in part only for capital allowances—

(a) the consideration for the disposal and any expenditure attributable to the asset under *paragraph (a)* or *(b)* of *section 552(1)* shall be apportioned by reference to the extent to which that expenditure qualified for capital allowances,

(b) the computation under this Chapter of the gain on the disposal shall be made separately in relation to the apportioned parts of the expenditure and consideration,

(c) *subsections (3)* to *(5)* of *section 560* shall not apply for the purposes of the computation in relation to the part of the consideration apportioned to use for the purposes of the trade or profession or to the expenditure qualifying for capital allowances,

(d) if an apportionment of the consideration for the disposal has been made for the purposes of making any capital allowance to the person making the disposal or for the purpose of making any balancing charge on that person, that apportionment shall be employed for the purposes of this section, and

(e) subject to *paragraph (d)*, the consideration for the disposal shall be apportioned for the purposes of this section in the same proportions as the expenditure attributable to the asset is apportioned under *paragraph (a)*.

Cross References

From Section 561

Section 552 Acquisition, enhancement and disposal costs.
Section 560 Wasting assets.

To Section 561

Schedule 14 Capital Gains Tax: Leases

562 Contingent liabilities

[CGTA75 s51(1) and Sch1 par11]

(1) No allowance shall be made under *section 552*—

(a) in the case of a disposal by means of assigning a lease of land or other property, for any liability remaining with or assumed by the person making the disposal by means of assigning the lease which is contingent on a default in respect of liabilities thereby or subsequently assumed by the assignee under the terms and conditions of the lease;

(b) for any contingent liability of the person making the disposal in respect of any covenant for quiet enjoyment or other obligation assumed—

(i) as vendor of land or of any estate or interest in land,

(ii) as a lessor, or

(iii) as grantor of an option binding that person to sell land or an interest in land or to grant a lease of land;

(c) for any contingent liability in respect of a warranty or representation made on a disposal by means of a sale or lease of any property other than land.

(2) Where it is shown to the satisfaction of the inspector that any contingent liability mentioned in *subsection (1)* has become enforceable and is being or has been enforced, [and this is so shown within 4 years from the end of the chargeable period (within the meaning of *section 321*) in which the contingent liability has become enforceable][1] such adjustment, whether by means of discharge or repayment of tax or otherwise, shall be made as may be necessary.

[(2A) No adjustment shall be made in accordance with *subsection (2)* unless it is shown to the satisfaction of the inspector that the assignor, vendor, lessor or grantor of an option, as the case may be, has paid an amount equal to the amount of the contingent liability in respect of that liability.][2]

[(3) *Subsection (2)* shall apply notwithstanding any limitation in *section 865(4)* on the time within which a claim for repayment of tax is required to be made. *Section 865(6)* shall not prevent the Revenue Commissioners from repaying an amount of tax as a consequence of any adjustment made in accordance with *subsection (2)*.][3]

Amendments

[1] Inserted by FA08 sched6(1)(h)(i). Applies as on and from 31 January 2008.

[2] Inserted by FA12 s57(1). Applies to disposals made on or after 8 February 2012.

[3] Inserted by FA08 sched6(1)(h)(ii). Applies as on and from 31 January 2008.

Cross References

From Section 562

Section 321 Provisions of general application in relation to the making of allowances and charges.
Section 552 Acquisition, enhancement and disposal costs.
Section 865 Repayment of tax.

563 Consideration due after time of disposal

[CGTA75 s44(2); CTA76 s140(2) and Sch2 PtII par6]

(1) (a) In the computation of a chargeable gain, consideration for the disposal shall be taken into account without any discount for postponement of the right to receive any part of the consideration and without regard to a risk of any part of the consideration being irrecoverable or to the right to receive any part of the consideration being contingent.

(b) Where any part of the consideration taken into account in accordance with *paragraph (a)* is shown to the satisfaction of the inspector to be irrecoverable, such adjustment, whether by means of discharge or repayment of tax or otherwise, shall be made as the case may require. [Subsection (4) or (6) of section 865 shall not prevent the Revenue Commissioners from repaying an amount of tax as a consequence of any such adjustment.][1]

(2) *Subsection (1)* shall apply for the purposes of corporation tax as it applies for the purposes of capital gains tax.

Amendments

[1] Inserted by FA08 sched6(1)(i). Applies as on and from 31 January 2008.

Case Law

Consideration shall not be taken into account where the consideration is wholly uncertain in amount. Marson v Marriage 1980 STC 177

Fielder v Vedlynn 1992 STC 553 examined the meaning of "consideration" and the judge held that consideration was equal to the sum of money specified, with no account for future guarantees

Loss on foreign exchange is not irrecoverable consideration. Goodbrand v Loffland Bros North Sea 1998 STC 930

Cross References

From Section 563

Section 865 Repayment of tax.

564 Woodlands

[CGTA75 s51(1) and Sch1 par12]

(1) In the computation under this Chapter of the gain accruing on the disposal by an individual of woodland, there shall be excluded—

(a) consideration for the disposal of trees growing on the land, and

(b) notwithstanding *section 535(2)*, capital sums received under a policy of insurance in respect of the destruction of or damage or injury to trees by fire or other hazard on such land.

(2) In the computation under this Chapter of the gain, so much of the cost of woodland as is attributable to trees growing on the land shall be disregarded.

(3) References in this section to trees include references to saleable underwood.

Cross References

From Section 564

Section 535 Disposals where capital sums derived from assets.

565 Expenditure reimbursed out of public money

[CGTA75 s51(1) and Sch1 par3(7)]

There shall be excluded from the computation under this Chapter of a gain accruing on a disposal any expenditure which has been or is to be met directly or indirectly by any government, by any board established by statute or by any public or local authority whether in the State or elsewhere.

Cross References

To Section 565

Section 556 Adjustment of allowable expenditure by reference to consumer price index.

566 Leases

[CGTA75 s51(1)]

Schedule 14 shall apply for the purposes of the Capital Gains Tax Acts.

Cross References

From Section 566

Schedule 14 Capital Gains Tax: Leases

To Section 566

Schedule 14 Capital Gains Tax: Leases

CHAPTER 3

Assets Held in a Fiduciary or Representative Capacity, Inheritances and Settlements

567 Nominees, bare trustees and agents

[CGTA75 s8(3), s15(10), s51(1) and Sch4 par2; FA73 s33(4) and (7)]

(1) References in the Capital Gains Tax Acts to any asset held by a person as trustee for another person absolutely entitled as against the trustee are references to a case where that other person has the exclusive right, or would have such a right if that other person were not an infant or other person under disability, subject only to satisfying

any outstanding charge, lien or right of the trustees to resort to the asset for payment of duty, taxes, costs or other outgoings, to direct how that asset shall be dealt with.

(2) In relation to assets held by a person (in this subsection referred to as "*the first-mentioned person*") as nominee for another person, or as trustee for another person absolutely entitled as against the trustee, or for any person who would be so entitled but for being an infant or other person under disability (or for 2 or more persons who are or would be jointly so entitled), the Capital Gains Tax Acts shall apply as if the property were vested in, and the acts of the first-mentioned person in relation to the assets were the acts of, the person or persons for whom the first-mentioned person is the nominee or trustee (acquisitions from or disposals to the first-mentioned person by that person or those persons being disregarded accordingly).

[(3) Where exploration or exploitation activities are carried on by a person on behalf of the holder of a licence or lease granted under the Petroleum and Other Minerals Development Act, 1960, such holder shall for the purpose of an assessment to capital gains tax be deemed to be the agent of that person.][1]

(4) *Schedule 1* shall apply for the purpose of supplementing *subsection (3)*.

Amendments

[1] Substituted by FA01 s44(b).

Case Law

In Boothe v Ellard 1980 I WLR 1443 it was held that since the family retained the right to direct the trustees what to do with the shares they were absolutely entitled as against the trustees.

"Absolutely entitled" is not necessarily restricted to beneficial entitlement. Bond v Pickford 1983 STC 517

The word "jointly" is not confined to joint tenants; it can mean two or more. Kidson v MacDonald & Another 1974 STC 54

"Person" includes an unincorporated association. Frampton and Another v IRC 1985 STC 186

Cross References

From Section 567

Schedule 1 Supplementary Provisions Concerning the Extension of Charge to Tax to Profits and Income Derived from Activities Carried On and Employments Exercised on the Continental Shelf

To Section 567

Section 5 Interpretation of Capital Gains Tax Acts.
Section 568 Liability of trustees, etc.
Section 572 Funds in court.
Section 576 Person becoming absolutely entitled to settled property.
Section 579A Attribution of gains to beneficiaries.
Section 588 Demutualisation of assurance companies.
Section 731 Chargeable gains accruing to unit trusts.
Schedule 1 Supplementary Provisions Concerning the Extension of Charge to Tax to Profits and Income Derived from Activities Carried On and Employments Exercised on the Continental Shelf
Schedule 16 Building Societies: Change of Status

568 Liability of trustees, etc

[CGTA75 s51(1) and Sch4 par12]

(1) Capital gains tax chargeable in respect of chargeable gains accruing to the trustees of a settlement or capital gains tax due from the personal representatives of a deceased person may be assessed and charged on and in the name of one or more of those trustees or personal representatives.

(2) Subject to *section 567(2)*, chargeable gains accruing to the trustees of a settlement or to the personal representatives of a deceased person, and capital gains tax

chargeable on or in the name of such trustees or personal representatives, shall not be regarded for the purposes of the Capital Gains Tax Acts as accruing to or chargeable on any other person, nor shall any trustee or personal representative be regarded for the purposes of those Acts as an individual.

Cross References

From Section 568

Section 567 Nominees, bare trustees and agents.

569 Assets of insolvent person

[(1) In this section—

"*deed of arrangement*" means a deed of arrangement to which the Deeds of Arrangement Act 1887 applies;

"*insolvent person*" means an individual who is insolvent and who has entered into a Debt Settlement Arrangement or a Personal Insolvency Arrangement (both within the meaning of *section 2* of the Personal Insolvency Act 2012) with his or her creditors;

"*relevant person*" means a personal insolvency practitioner (within the meaning of the Personal Insolvency Act 2012) who holds the assets of an insolvent person in trust for the benefit of creditors of that insolvent person under a Debt Settlement Arrangement or a Personal Insolvency Arrangement (both within the meaning aforesaid).

(2) In relation to assets held by a person as trustee or assignee in bankruptcy or under a deed of arrangement or by a relevant person, the Capital Gains Tax Acts shall apply as if the assets were vested in, and the acts of the trustee, assignee or relevant person in relation to the assets were the acts of, the bankrupt, debtor or insolvent person (acquisitions from or disposals to such person by the bankrupt, debtor or insolvent person being disregarded accordingly), and tax in respect of any chargeable gains which accrue to any such trustee, assignee or relevant person shall be assessable on and recoverable from such trustee, assignee or relevant person.

(3) Assets held by a trustee or assignee in bankruptcy or under a deed of arrangement or by a relevant person at the death of the bankrupt, debtor or insolvent person shall for the purposes of the Capital Gains Tax Acts be regarded as held by a personal representative of the deceased, and—

(a) *subsection (2)* shall not apply after the death, and

(b) *section 573(2)* shall apply as if any assets held by a trustee or assignee in bankruptcy or under a deed of arrangement or by a relevant person at the death of the bankrupt, debtor or insolvent person were assets of which the deceased was competent to dispose and which then devolved on the trustee or assignee in bankruptcy or the relevant person as if the trustee or assignee in bankruptcy or the relevant person were a personal representative.

(4) Assets vesting in a trustee in bankruptcy or a relevant person after the death of the bankrupt, debtor or insolvent person shall for the purposes of the Capital Gains Tax Acts be regarded as held by a personal representative of the deceased, and *subsection (2)* shall not apply.][1]

Amendments

[1] Substituted by FA13 s100(1)(e). Applies to disposals made on or after 27 March 2013.

Cross References

From Section 569

Section 573 Death.

570 Company in liquidation

[CGTA75 s41]

Where assets of a company are vested in a liquidator under section 230 of the Companies Act, 1963, or otherwise, the Capital Gains Tax Acts shall apply as if the assets were vested in, and the acts of the liquidator in relation to the assets were acts of, the company (acquisitions from or disposals to the liquidator by the company being disregarded accordingly).

Cross References

To Section 570

Section 571 Chargeable gains accruing on disposals by liquidators and certain other persons.

571 Chargeable gains accruing on disposals by liquidators and certain other persons

[FA83 s56]

(1) In this section—

"*accountable person*" means—

(a) a liquidator of a company, or

(b) any person entitled to an asset by means of security or to the benefit of a charge or encumbrance on an asset or, as the case may be, any person appointed to enforce or give effect to the security, charge or encumbrance;

"*the company*" has the meaning assigned to it by *subsection (6)*;

"*the debtor*" has the meaning assigned to it by *subsection (5)*;

"*referable capital gains tax*" has the meaning assigned to it by *subsection (2)*;

"*referable corporation tax*" has the meaning assigned to it by *subsection (3)*;

"*relevant disposal*" has the same meaning as in *section 648*.

(2) In this section—

(a) in a case where no chargeable gains other than the chargeable gains mentioned in *subsection (5)(a)* (in this subsection referred to as "*the referable gains*") accrued to the debtor in the year of assessment, "*referable capital gains tax*" means the amount of capital gains tax which apart from *subsection (5)* would be assessable on the debtor in respect of the referable gains;

(b) in a case where, in addition to the referable gains, other chargeable gains accrued to the debtor in the year of assessment and, in charging all of those gains to capital gains tax without regard to *subsection (5)*, the same rate of tax would apply, and either—

(i) none of the disposals on which the chargeable gains accrued is a relevant disposal, or

(ii) each of the disposals is a relevant disposal,

"*referable capital gains tax*" means an amount of tax determined by the formula—

$$\frac{A}{B} \times C$$

where—

A is the amount of capital gains tax which apart from *subsection (5)* would be assessable on the debtor in respect of the referable gains if no other chargeable gains accrued to the debtor in the year of assessment and if no deductions or reliefs were to be allowed against the referable gains,

B is the amount of capital gains tax which apart from *subsection (5)* would be assessable on the debtor in respect of all chargeable gains, including the referable gains, which accrued to the debtor in the year of assessment, if no deductions or reliefs were to be allowed against those chargeable gains, and

C is the amount of capital gains tax which apart from *subsection (5)* would be assessable on the debtor in respect of the total amount of chargeable gains, including the referable gains, which accrued to the debtor in the year of assessment;

(c) in any other case, "*referable capital gains tax*" means the amount of capital gains tax which apart from *subsection (5)* and taking into account—

(i) all other chargeable gains accruing to the debtor in the year of assessment, and

(ii) where appropriate, *sections 546(6), 601(3)* and *653*,

would be the amount of capital gains tax appropriate to the referable gains.

(3) In this section—

(a) in a case where no chargeable gains other than—

(i) the chargeable gains mentioned in *subsection (6)(a)* (in this subsection referred to as "*the referable gains*"), or

(ii) any chargeable gains accruing on a relevant disposal,

accrued to the company in the accounting period, "*referable corporation tax*" means the amount of capital gains tax which apart from *subsection (6)* would be assessable on the company in respect of the referable gains on the assumptions that—

(I) notwithstanding any provision to the contrary in the Corporation Tax Acts, capital gains tax was to be charged in respect of the refereable gains in accordance with the Capital Gains Tax Acts, and

(II) accounting periods were years of assessment,

or, if it is less, the amount of corporation tax which apart from *subsection (6)* would be assessable on the company for the accounting period;

(b) in a case where, in addition to the referable gains, other chargeable gains (not being chargeable gains accruing on a relevant disposal) accrued to the company in the accounting period and, on the assumptions made in *paragraph (a)*, in charging all of those gains to capital gains tax without regard to *subsection (6)*, the same rate of tax would apply, "*referable corporation tax*" means an amount of tax determined by the formula—

$$\frac{D}{E} \times F$$

where—

D is the amount of capital gains tax which, apart from *subsection (6)* and on the assumptions made in *paragraph (a)*, would be assessable on the company in respect of the referable gains if no other chargeable gains accrued to the company in the accounting period and if no deductions or reliefs were to be allowed against the referable gains,

E is the amount of capital gains tax which, apart from *subsection (6)* and on the assumptions made in *paragraph (a)*, would be assessable on the company in respect of all chargeable gains including the referable gains (but not including chargeable gains accruing on a relevant disposal) which accrued to the company in the accounting period, if no deductions or reliefs were to be allowed against those chargeable gains, and

F is the amount (in this subsection referred to as "*the notional amount*") of capital gains tax which apart from *subsection (6)* would in accordance with *section 78(2)* be calculated in relation to the company for the accounting period in respect of all chargeable gains including the referable gains or, if it is less, the amount of corporation tax which apart from *subsection (6)* would be assessable on the company for the accounting period;

(c) (i) in any other case, "*referable corporation tax*" means, subject to *subparagraph (ii)*, the amount of capital gains tax which, apart from *subsection (6)* and on the assumptions made in *paragraph (a)*, and taking into account—

(I) all other chargeable gains (not being chargeable gains accruing on a relevant disposal) accruing to the company in the accounting period, and

(II) where appropriate, *sections 546(6)* and *653*,

would be the amount of capital gains tax appropriate to the referable gains;

(ii) in any case in which *subparagraph (i)* applies, if the notional amount is greater than the amount of corporation tax which apart from *subsection (6)* would be assessable on the company for the accounting period, "*referable corporation tax*" shall mean an amount determined by the formula—

$$\frac{G}{H} \times K$$

where—

G is the amount which under *subparagraph (i)* would be the referable corporation tax,

H is the notional amount, and

K is the amount of corporation tax which apart from *subsection (6)* would be assessable on the company for the accounting period.

(4) (a) In any case where, in calculating an amount of referable capital gains tax or referable corporation tax under *subsection (2)(c)* or *(3)(c)*, deductions or reliefs were to be allowed against chargeable gains accruing in a year of assessment or in an accounting period and apart from this subsection those deductions or reliefs (or part of them) would be set against 2 or more chargeable gains chargeable at the same rate of capital gains tax, then, those deductions or reliefs (or, as the case may be, that part of them) shall, in so far as is necessary to calculate the amount of referable capital gains tax or referable corporation tax, be apportioned between the chargeable gains chargeable at the same rate in proportion to the amounts of those chargeable gains.

(b) In the case of chargeable gains accruing to a company (not being chargeable gains accruing on a relevant disposal), any reference in *paragraph (a)* to a rate of tax shall be construed as a reference to the rate of capital gains tax which would be applicable to those gains on the assumptions made in *subsection (3)(a)*.

(5) Where *section 537(2)* or *570* applies in respect of the disposal of an asset in a year of assessment by an accountable person, then, notwithstanding any provision of the Capital Gains Tax Acts—

(a) any referable capital gains tax in respect of any chargeable gains which accrue on the disposal shall be assessable on and recoverable from the accountable person,

(b) the referable capital gains tax shall be treated as a necessary disbursement out of the proceeds of the disposal and shall be paid by the accountable person out of those proceeds, and

(c) referable capital gains tax paid by the accountable person shall discharge a corresponding amount of the liability to capital gains tax, for the year of assessment in which the disposal is made, of the person (in this section referred to as "*the debtor*") who apart from this subsection is the chargeable person in relation to the disposal.

(6) Where *section 78(8)* or *537(2)* applies in respect of the disposal (not being a relevant disposal) of an asset in an accounting period of a company by an accountable person, then, notwithstanding any provision of the Corporation Tax Acts—

(a) any referable corporation tax in respect of any chargeable gains which accrue on the disposal shall be assessable on and recoverable from the accountable person,

(b) the referable corporation tax shall be treated as a necessary disbursement out of the proceeds of the disposal and shall be paid by the accountable person out of those proceeds, and

(c) referable corporation tax paid by the accountable person shall discharge a corresponding amount of the liability to corporation tax, for the accounting period in which the disposal is made, of the company (in this section referred to as "*the company*") which apart from this subsection is the chargeable person in relation to the disposal.

(7) Notwithstanding any provision of the Capital Gains Tax Acts or of the Corporation Tax Acts, the amount of referable capital gains tax or referable corporation tax, as the case may be, which under this section is assessable on an accountable person in relation to a disposal, shall be recoverable by an assessment on the accountable

person to income tax under Case IV of Schedule D for the year of assessment in which the disposal occurred on an amount the income tax on which at the standard rate for that year of assessment is equal to the amount of the referable capital gains tax or referable corporation tax, as the case may be.

(8) Where tax is paid by an accountable person under this section and it is established that the amount of tax paid is excessive, appropriate relief by means of repayment or otherwise shall be given to the accountable person.

(9) Subject to *subsections (5)(c)* and *(6)(c)*, nothing in this section shall affect the amount of chargeable gains on which—

(a) the debtor is chargeable to capital gains tax, or

(b) the company is chargeable to corporation tax.

Cross References

From Section 571

Section 78 Computation of companies' chargeable gains.
Section 537 Mortgages and charges not to be treated as disposals.
Section 546 Allowable losses.
Section 570 Company in liquidation.
Section 601 Annual exempt amount.
Section 648 Interpretation (Chapter 2).
Section 653 Restriction of relief for losses, etc. in relation to relevant disposals.

572 Funds in court

[CGTA75 s42]

(1) In this section—

"*the Accountant*" means the Accountant attached to the court or a deputy appointed by the Minister for Justice, Equality and Law Reform;

"*court*" means the High Court except where the reference is to the Circuit Court;

"*funds in court*" means any moneys (and investments representing such moneys), annuities, stocks, shares or other securities standing or to be placed to the account of the Accountant in the books of the Bank of Ireland or any company, and includes boxes and other effects.

(2) For the purposes of *section 567(2)*, funds in court shall be regarded as held by the Accountant as nominee for the persons entitled to or interested in the funds or, as the case may be, for their trustees.

(3) Where funds in court standing to an account in the books of the Accountant are invested or after investment are realised, the method by which the Accountant effects the investment or the realisation of investments shall not affect the question as to whether there is for the purposes of the Capital Gains Tax Acts an acquisition or, as the case may be, a disposal of an asset representing funds in court standing to that account, and in particular there shall for those purposes be an acquisition or disposal of assets notwithstanding that the investment of funds in court standing to an account in the books of the Accountant, or the realisation of funds which have been so invested, is effected by setting off in the Accountant's accounts investment in one account against realisation of investments in another.

(4) This section shall apply with any necessary modifications to funds in the Circuit Court as it applies to funds in court.

Cross References

From Section 572

Section 567 Nominees, bare trustees and agents.

573 Death

[CGTA75 s14; CGT(A)A78 s6(1)]

(1) In this section, references to assets of which a deceased person was competent to dispose are references to assets of the deceased which the deceased could if of full age and capacity have disposed of by will, assuming that all the assets were situated in the State and that the deceased was domiciled in the State, and include references to the deceased's severable share in any assets to which immediately before his or her death he or she was beneficially entitled as a joint tenant.

(2) For the purposes of the Capital Gains Tax Acts, the assets of which a deceased person was competent to dispose—

(a) shall be deemed to be acquired on his or her death by the personal representatives or other person on whom they devolve for a consideration equal to their market value at the date of the death; but

(b) shall not be deemed to be disposed of by him or her on his or her death (whether or not they were the subject of a testamentary disposition).

(3) Allowable losses sustained by an individual in the year of assessment in which he or she dies may, in so far as they cannot be deducted from chargeable gains accruing in that year, be deducted from chargeable gains accruing to the deceased in the 3 years of assessment preceding the year of assessment in which the death occurs, taking chargeable gains accruing in a later year before those accruing in an earlier year, and there shall be made all such amendments of assessments or repayments of tax as may be necessary to give effect to this subsection.

(4) In relation to property forming part of the estate of a deceased person, the personal representatives shall for the purposes of the Capital Gains Tax Acts be treated as being a single and continuing body of persons (distinct from the persons who may from time to time be the personal representatives), and that body shall be treated as having the deceased's residence, ordinary residence and domicile at the date of death.

(5) Where any asset is acquired by a person as legatee no chargeable gain shall accrue to the personal representatives, but the legatee shall be treated as if the personal representatives' acquisition of the asset had been the legatee's acquisition of the asset.

(6) Where not more than 2 years, or such longer period as the Revenue Commissioners may by notice in writing allow, after a death any of the dispositions of the property of which the deceased was competent to dispose, whether effected by will or under the law relating to intestacies or otherwise, are varied by a deed of family arrangement or similar instrument, this section shall apply as if the variations made by the deed or other instrument were effected by the deceased, and no disposition made by the deed or other instrument shall constitute a disposal for the purposes of the Capital Gains Tax Acts.

Cross References

To Section 573

Section 546 Allowable losses.

Section 569 Assets of insolvent person.

Section 594 Foreign life assurance and deferred annuities: taxation and returns.
Section 741 Disposals of material interests in non-qualifying offshore funds.
Section 747B Interpretation and application.

574 Trustees of settlement

[CGTA75 s15(1), (9) and (11)]

(1) (a) In relation to settled property, the trustees of a settlement shall for the purposes of the Capital Gains Tax Acts be treated as being a single and continuing body of persons (distinct from the persons who may from time to time be the trustees) and, subject to *paragraph (b)*, that body shall be treated as being resident and ordinarily resident in the State unless the general administration of the trusts is ordinarily carried on outside the State and the trustees or a majority of them for the time being are not resident or not ordinarily resident in the State.

(b) A person carrying on a business which consists of or includes the management of trusts, and acting as trustees of a trust in the course of that business, shall be treated in relation to that trust as not resident in the State if the whole of the settled property consists of or derives from property provided by a person not at the time (or, in the case of a trust arising under a testamentary disposition or on an intestacy or partial intestacy, at his or her death) domiciled, resident or ordinarily resident in the State and, if in such a case the trustees or a majority of them are or are treated in relation to that trust as not resident in the State, the general administration of the trust shall be treated as ordinarily carried on outside the State.

(2) Where any amount of capital gains tax assessed on the trustees or any one trustee of a settlement in respect of a chargeable gain accruing to the trustee is not paid within 6 months from the date when it becomes payable by the trustees or trustee and, before or after the expiration of that period of 6 months, the asset in respect of which the chargeable gain accrued, or any part of the proceeds of sale of that asset, is transferred by the trustees to a person who as against the trustees is absolutely entitled to it, then, that person may, at any time within 2 years from the time when that amount of tax became payable, be assessed and charged (in the name of the trustees) to an amount of capital gains tax not exceeding the amount of capital gains tax chargeable on an amount equal to the amount of the chargeable gain and, where part only of the asset or of the proceeds was transferred, not exceeding a proportionate part of that amount.

(3) For the purposes of this section, where part of the property comprised in a settlement is vested in one trustee or set of trustees and part in another trustee or set of trustees […][1], they shall be treated as together constituting and, in so far as they act separately, as acting on behalf of a single body of trustees.

Amendments

[1] Deleted by the the Land and Conveyancing Law Reform Act 2009 Sched 1. This Act shall come into operation on such day or days as the Minister may appoint by order or orders either generally or with reference to any particular purpose or provision and different days may be so appointed for different purposes and different provisions

Cross References

To Section 574

Section 177 Conditions as to residence and period of ownership.
Section 731 Chargeable gains accruing to unit trusts.

575 Gifts in settlement

[CGTA75 s15(2)]

A gift in settlement, whether revocable or irrevocable, shall be a disposal of the entire property thereby becoming settled property notwithstanding that the donor has some interest as a beneficiary under the settlement and notwithstanding that the donor is a trustee or the sole trustee of the settlement.

576 Person becoming absolutely entitled to settled property

[CGTA75 s15(3) and (8)]

(1) On the occasion when a person becomes absolutely entitled to any settled property as against the trustee, all the assets forming part of the settled property to which the person becomes so entitled shall be deemed for the purposes of the Capital Gains Tax Acts to have been disposed of by the trustee, and immediately reacquired by the trustee in the trustee's capacity as a trustee within *section 567(2)*, for a consideration equal to their market value.

(2) On the occasion when a person becomes absolutely entitled to any settled property as against the trustee, any allowable loss which has accrued to the trustee in respect of property which is, or is represented by, the property to which that person becomes so entitled (including any allowable loss carried forward to the year of assessment in which that occasion falls), being a loss which cannot be deducted from chargeable gains accruing to the trustee in that year, but before that occasion, shall be treated for the purposes of the Capital Gains Tax Acts as if it were an allowable loss accruing at that time to the person becoming so entitled, instead of to the trustee.

Case Law

Begg MacBrearty v Stilwell (Trustee of the Croke Settlement) 1996 STC 413 considered the time that the beneficiary acquired the interest under the trust.

Cross References

From Section 576

Section 567 Nominees, bare trustees and agents.

To Section 576

Section 577 Termination of life interest on death of person entitled.
Section 577A Relinquishing of a life interest by the person entitled.
Section 578 Death of annuitant.
Section 588 Demutualisation of assurance companies.
Section 611 Disposals to State, public bodies and charities.
Section 613 Miscellaneous exemptions for certain kinds of property.
Schedule 16 Building Societies: Change of Status

577 Termination of life interest on death of person entitled

[CGTA75 s15(4), (5), (5A), (6) and (12); CGT(A)A78 s7(1); FA97 s73(1)]

(1) (a) In this section, "*life interest*", in relation to a settlement—

(i) includes a right under the settlement to the income of, or the use or occupation of, settled property for the life of a person (or for the lives of persons) other than the person entitled to the right,

(ii) does not include any right which is contingent on the exercise of the discretion of the trustee or the discretion of some other person, and

(iii) does not include an annuity, notwithstanding that the annuity is payable out of or charged on settled property or the income of settled property except where some or all of the settled property is appropriated by the trustees as a fund out of which the annuity is payable and there is no right of recourse to settled property not so appropriated, or to the income of settled property not so appropriated.

(b) Without prejudice to *subsection (4)(b)*, where under *paragraph (a)(iii)* an annuity is to be treated as a life interest in relation to a settlement, the settled property or the part of the settled property appropriated by the trustees as a fund out of which the annuity is payable shall, while the annuity is payable and on the occasion of the death of the annuitant, be treated for the purposes of *subsection (3)* as being settled property under a separate settlement.

(2) Where by virtue of *section 576(1)* the assets forming part of any settled property are deemed to be disposed of and reacquired by the trustee on the occasion when a person becomes absolutely entitled to the assets as against the trustee, then, if that occasion is the termination of a life interest by the death of the person entitled to that interest—

(a) no chargeable gain shall accrue on the disposal, and

(b) the reacquisition under that section shall be deemed to be for a consideration equal to the market value of the assets at the date of the death.

(3) On the termination of a life interest in possession in all or any part of settled property, the whole or a corresponding part of each of the assets forming part of the settled property and not ceasing at that time to be settled property shall be deemed for the purposes of the Capital Gains Tax Acts at that time to be disposed of by the trustee, and immediately reacquired by the trustee, for a consideration equal to the whole or a corresponding part of the market value of the asset.

(4) For the purposes of *subsection (3)*—

(a) a life interest which is a right to part of the income of settled property shall be treated as a life interest in a corresponding part of the settled property, and

(b) if there is a life interest in a part of the settled property and, where that interest is a life interest in income, there is no right of recourse to, or to the income of, the remainder of the settled property, the part of the settled property in which the life interest subsists shall while it subsists be treated for the purposes of this subsection as being settled property under a separate settlement.

(5) (a) Subject to *paragraph (b)*, where—

(i) as a consequence of a termination, on the death of the person entitled to it, of a life interest in settled property, *subsection (3)* applies, and

(ii) an asset which forms the whole or any part of that settled property—

(I) is comprised in an inheritance (within the meaning of the Capital Acquisitions Tax Consolidation Act 2003) taken on the death, and

(II) is exempt from tax in relation to the inheritance under section 77 of that Act, or that section as applied by section 77(6) and (7) of the Capital Acquisitions Tax Consolidation Act 2003, that asset shall for the purposes of *subsection (3)*, be excluded from the assets deemed to be disposed of and immediately reacquired.

(b) Where, in a year of assessment, in respect of an asset an exemption from tax in relation to an inheritance referred to in *paragraph (a)* ceases to apply, then, the chargeable gain which but for *paragraph (a)* would have accrued to the trustee on the termination of the life interest in accordance with *subsection (3)* shall be deemed to accrue to the trustee in that year of assessment and shall accordingly be included in the return required to be made by the trustee concerned under [*Chapter 3* of *Part 41A*][1] for that year of assessment.

Amendments

[1] Substituted by FA12 sched4(part 2)(g).

Cross References

From Section 577

Section 576 Person becoming absolutely entitled to settled property.

Section 951 Obligation to make a return.

To Section 577

Section 577A Relinquishing of a life interest by the person entitled.

Section 578 Death of annuitant.

Section 611 Disposals to State, public bodies and charities.

577A Relinquishing of a life interest by the person entitled

[Where by virtue of *section 576(1)* the assets forming part of any settled property are deemed to be disposed of and immediately reacquired by the trustee on the occasion when a person becomes absolutely entitled to the assets as against the trustee, then, in case that occasion is the relinquishing of a life interest (within the meaning of *section 577*) by the person entitled to that interest, the trustee shall be given such relief as would be given under *sections 598* and *599* to the person who relinquished the life interest—

(a) if the person had become absolutely entitled to the assets as against the trustee at the commencement of the life interest and had continued to be so entitled throughout the period (in this section referred to as the "life interest period") that the life interest subsisted, and

(b) as if any expenditure of the kind referred to in *paragraph (b)* of *section 552(1)* that was incurred on the assets during the life interest period by the trustee had been incurred by the person.][1]

Amendments

[1] Inserted by FA98 s69(1). This section shall apply as respects a disposal deemed to be made on or after the 12th day of February, 1998.

Cross References

From Section 577A

Section 552 Acquisition, enhancement and disposal costs.

Section 576 Person becoming absolutely entitled to settled property.

Section 577 Termination of life interest on death of person entitled.

Section 598 Disposals of business or farm on "retirement".

Section 599 Disposals within family of business or farm.

578 Death of annuitant

[CGTA75 s15(7)]

Sections 576(1) and *577(3)* shall apply where an annuity which is not a life interest within the meaning of *section 577* is terminated by the death of the annuitant as they apply on the termination of a life interest (within the meaning of that section) by the death of the person entitled to that life interest.

Cross References

From Section 578

Section 576 Person becoming absolutely entitled to settled property.

Section 577 Termination of life interest on death of person entitled.

To Section 578

Section 731 Chargeable gains accruing to unit trusts.

579 Non-resident trusts

[CGTA75 s37]

(1) This section shall apply as respects chargeable gains accruing to the trustees of a settlement where the trustees are not resident and not ordinarily resident in the State, and where the settlor or one of the settlors is [...][1] either resident or ordinarily resident in the State, or was [...][2] either resident or ordinarily resident in the State when such settlor made the settlement.

(2) (a) Any beneficiary under the settlement who is domiciled and either resident or ordinarily resident in the State in any year of assessment shall be treated for the purposes of the Capital Gains Tax Acts as if an apportioned part of the amount, if any, on which the trustees would have been chargeable to capital gains tax under *section 31*, if domiciled and either resident or ordinarily resident in the State in that year of assessment, had been chargeable gains accruing to the beneficiary in that year of assessment.

[(b) Notwithstanding *paragraph (a)*, where a beneficiary under the settlement was neither resident nor ordinarily resident in the State in a year of assessment during which again accrued to the trustees, but was so resident or ordinarily resident in an earlier and subsequent year of assessment, the gain which would have accrued to that beneficiary if *paragraph (a)* had applied shall be treated as accruing in the first year of assessment in which he or she subsequently becomes resident or ordinarily resident in the State.

(c) Notwithstanding *paragraph (a)*, where a person was excluded as a beneficiary under the settlement for a period of time but was subsequently included as a beneficiary of that settlement and a gain accrued to the trustees during a year of assessment when that beneficiary was so excluded, a gain which would have accrued to the beneficiary if *paragraph (a)* had applied shall be treated as accruing in the first year of assessment in which that person was subsequently included as a beneficiary of the settlement concerned.

(d) Notwithstanding *paragraph (a)*, if a beneficiary is not treated under the provisions of *paragraph (a)*, *(b)* or *(c)* as if any apportioned part of a gain accrued to him or her in a year of assessment and—

(i) the trustees have earlier realised a chargeable gain, and

(ii) the beneficiary receives a capital payment (within the meaning of *section 579A(1)*) from the trust during a year of assessment in which he or she is either resident or ordinarily resident in the State,

then, the beneficiary shall be treated as if an amount equal to—

(I) the capital payment, or

(II) the apportioned gain which would have accrued to him or her if *paragraphs (a)*, *(b)* or *(c)* had applied,

whichever is less, were a chargeable gain accruing to him or her in the year of assessment in which the capital payment is received.

(e) For the purposes of this section, any amount referred to in *paragraph (a)*, *(b)* or *(c)* shall be apportioned in such manner as is just and reasonable between persons having interests in the settled property, whether the interest is a life interest or an interest in reversion, and so that the chargeable gain is apportioned as near as may be according to the respective values of those interests, disregarding in the case of a defeasible interest the possibility of defeasance.][3]

(3) For the purposes of this section—

(a) where in any of the 5 years ending with that in which the chargeable gain accrues a person has received a payment or payments out of the income of the settled property made in exercise of a discretion, such person shall be regarded, in relation to that chargeable gain, as having an interest in the settled property of a value equal to that of an annuity of a yearly amount equal to 20 per cent of the total of the payments so received by such person in those 5 years,

[...][4]

(4) In the case of a settlement made before the 28th day of February, 1974—

(a) *subsection (2)* shall not apply to a beneficiary whose interest is solely in the income of the settled property and who cannot, by means of the exercise of any power of appointment or power of revocation or otherwise, obtain for himself or herself, whether with or without the consent of any other person, any part of the capital represented by the settled property, and

(b) payment of capital gains tax chargeable on a gain apportioned to a beneficiary in respect of an interest in reversion in any part of the capital represented by the settled property may be postponed until that person becomes absolutely entitled to that part of the settled property, or disposes of the whole or any part of his or her interest, unless he or she can, by any means described in *paragraph (a)*, obtain for himself or herself any of it at any earlier time,

and, for the purposes of this subsection, property added to a settlement after the settlement is made shall be regarded as property under a separate settlement made at the time when the property is so added.

(5) In any case in which the amount of any capital gains tax payable by a beneficiary under a settlement in accordance with this section is paid by the trustees of the settlement, such amount shall not for the purposes of income tax or capital gains tax be regarded as a payment to such beneficiary.

(6) This section shall not apply in relation to a loss accruing to the trustees of the settlement.

Amendments

[1, 2] Deleted by FA12 s66(1)(a). Applies to disposals made on or after 8 February 2012.

[3] Substituted by FA12 s66(1)(b). Applies to disposals made on or after 8 February 2012.

[4] Deleted by FA12 s66(1)(c). Applies to disposals made on or after 8 February 2012.

Case Law

In Leedale v Lewis 1982 STC 169 the beneficiaries held both a discretionary interest and a fixed interest and were assessed on their fixed interest without receiving anything from the non resident trust.

Cross References

From Section 579

Section 31 Amount chargeable.

To Section 579

Section 579A Attribution of gains to beneficiaries.
Section 746 Offshore income gains accruing to persons resident or domiciled abroad.
Section 917 Returns relating to non-resident companies and trusts.
Section 959 Miscellaneous (Part 41).

579A Attribution of gains to beneficiaries

[(1) (a) For the purposes of this section and the following sections of this Chapter, "*capital payments*" means any payment which is not chargeable to income tax on the recipient or, in the case of a recipient who is neither resident nor ordinarily resident in the State, any payment received otherwise than as income, but does not include a payment under a transaction entered into at arm's length.

(b) In *paragraph (a)* references to a payment include references to the transfer of an asset and the conferring of any benefit, and to any occasion on which settled property becomes property to which *section 567(2)* applies.

(c) The amount of a capital payment made by way of loan, and of any other capital payment which is not an outright payment of money, shall be taken to be equal to the value of the benefit conferred by it.

(d) A capital payment shall be treated as received by a beneficiary from the trustees of a settlement if—

(i) the beneficiary receives it from the trustees directly or indirectly,

(ii) it is directly or indirectly applied by the trustees in payment of any debt of the beneficiary or is otherwise paid for the benefit of the beneficiary, or

(iii) it is received by a third party at the beneficiary's direction.

[(2) (a) This section shall apply to a settlement for any year of assessment (beginning on or after 6 April 1999) during which the trustees are at no time resident or ordinarily resident in the State, and—

(i) the settlor does not have an interest in the settlement at any time in that year of assessment, or

(ii) the settlor does have an interest in the settlement but—

(I) was not domiciled in the State, and

(II) was neither resident nor ordinarily resident in the State,

in that year of assessment, or when the settlor made the settlement.

(b) *Section 579* shall not apply as respects chargeable gains accruing after 5 April 1999 to trustees of a settlement to which this section applies; and references in *subsections (4)* and *(5)* to capital payments received by beneficiaries do not include references to any payments received before 11 February 1999 or any payments received on or after that date so far as they represent a chargeable gain which accrued to the trustees in respect of a disposal by the trustees before 11 February 1999.

(c) For the purposes of this subsection a settlor has an interest in a settlement if—

(i) any relevant property which is, or may at any time become, comprised in the settlement is, or will or may become, applicable for the benefit of or payable in any circumstances to, a relevant beneficiary,

(ii) any relevant income which arises, or may arise, under the settlement is, or will or may become, applicable for the benefit of or payable in any circumstances to, a relevant beneficiary, or

(iii) a relevant beneficiary enjoys a benefit directly or indirectly from any relevant property which is comprised in the settlement or any relevant income arising under the settlement.

(d) In this subsection—

"*relevant beneficiary*" means—

(i) the settlor,

(ii) the [spouse or civil partner][1] of the settlor,

(iii) a company controlled by either or both the settlor and the [spouse or civil partner][2] of the settlor, or

(iv) a company associated with a company referred to in *paragraph (iii)* of this definition;

"*relevant income*" means income originating from the settlor;

"*relevant property*" means property originating from the settlor.

(e) For the purposes of this subsection—

(i) references to property originating from a person are references to property provided by that person, and property representing that property,

(ii) references to income originating from a person are references to income from property originating from that person and income provided by that person,

(iii) whether a company is controlled by a person or persons shall be construed in accordance with *section 432* without regard to *subsection (6)* of that section,

(iv) whether a company is associated with another company shall be construed in accordance with *section 432* without regard to *subsection (6)* of that section, and

(v) references to relevant property comprised in a settlement being, or becoming, applicable for the benefit of or payable in any circumstances to, a relevant beneficiary, do not include references to the repayment of, or obligation to repay, a loan to a settlor which loan was provided by the settlor to the trustees of the settlement on terms that it would be repaid.

(f) Where, for the year of assessment 2002 or any subsequent year of assessment, chargeable gains are treated as accruing to a beneficiary under a settlement by virtue of *section 579*, then notwithstanding that section such chargeable gains, in so far as they are in respect of a disposal made on or after 7 March 2002 by the trustees of the settlement, shall be treated as accruing to the settlor in relation to the settlement and not to any other person, if the settlor is resident or ordinarily resident in the State, whether or not the settlor is the beneficiary.][3]

(3) There shall be computed in respect of every year of assessment for which this section applies the amount on which the trustees would have been chargeable to capital gains tax under *section 31* if they had been resident and ordinarily resident in the State in the year of assessment and that amount, together with the corresponding amount in respect of any earlier such year of assessment, so far as not already treated under *subsection (4)* or *section 579F(2)* as chargeable gains accruing to beneficiaries under the settlement, is in this section referred to as "*the trust gains for the year of assessment*".

(4) Subject to this section, the trust gains for a year of assessment shall be treated for the purposes of the Capital Gains Tax Acts as chargeable gains accruing in the year of assessment to beneficiaries of the settlement who receive capital payments from the trustees in the year of assessment or have received such payments in any earlier year of assessment.

(5) The attribution of chargeable gains to beneficiaries under *subsection (4)* shall be made in proportion to, but shall not exceed, the amounts of capital payments received by them.

(6) A capital payment shall be left out of account for the purposes of *subsections (4)* and *(5)* to the extent that chargeable gains have, by reason of the payment, been treated as accruing to the recipient in an earlier year of assessment.

(7) A beneficiary shall not be charged to tax on chargeable gains treated by virtue of *subsection (4)* as accruing to him or her in any year of assessment unless he or she is domiciled in the State at some time in that year of assessment.

(8) For the purposes of this section a settlement arising under a will or intestacy shall be treated as made by the testator or, as the case may be, intestate at the time of death.

(9) In any case in which the amount of any capital gains tax payable by a beneficiary under a settlement in accordance with this section is paid by the trustees of the settlement, such amount shall not for the purposes of income tax or capital gains tax be regarded as a payment to the beneficiary.

[…][4]][5]

Amendments

[1, 2] Substituted by F(No.3)A11 sched1(156).

[3] Substituted by FA02 s47(1)(a). This section is deemed to have applied as on and from 11 February 1999.

[4] Deleted by FA02 s47(1)(b). This section is deemed to have applied as on and from 11 February 1999.

[5] Inserted by FA99 s88(1). This section shall apply as on and from the 11th day of February, 1999.

Cross References

From Section 579A

Section 31 Amount chargeable.
Section 432 Meaning of "associated company" and "control".
Section 567 Nominees, bare trustees and agents.
Section 579 Non-resident trusts.
Section 579F Migrant settlements.

To Section 579A

Section 579F Migrant settlements.
Section 746 Offshore income gains accruing to persons resident or domiciled abroad.
Section 807A Liability of nontransferors.

579B Trustees ceasing to be resident in the State

[(1) In this section and in the following sections of this Chapter—

"*arrangements*" means arrangements having the force of law by virtue of [*section 826(1)*][1] (as extended to capital gains tax by *section 828*);

"*the new assets*" and "*the old assets*" have the meaning assigned, respectively, to them by *section 597(4)*.

(2) This section shall apply where the trustees of a settlement become at any time (hereafter in this section referred to as the "*relevant time*") neither resident nor ordinarily resident in the State.

(3) The trustees to whom this section applies shall, for the purposes of the Capital Gains Tax Acts, be deemed—

(a) to have disposed of the defined assets immediately before the relevant time, and

(b) immediately to have reacquired them,

at their market value at that time.

(4) Subject to *subsections (5)* and (6), the defined assets are all assets constituting settled property of the settlement immediately before the relevant time.

(5) If immediately after the relevant time—

(a) the trustees carry on a trade in the State through a branch or agency, and

(b) any assets are situated in the State and either used in or for the purposes of the trade or used or held for the purposes of the branch or agency,

the assets falling within *paragraph (b)* shall not be defined assets.

(6) Assets shall not be defined assets if—

(a) they are of a description specified in any arrangements, and

(b) the trustees would, were they to dispose of them immediately before the relevant time, fall to be regarded for the purposes of the arrangements as not being liable in the State to tax on gains accruing to them on the disposal.

(7) Notwithstanding anything in that section—

(a) *section 597* shall not apply where the trustees—

(i) have disposed of the old assets, or their interest in them, before the relevant time, and

(ii) acquire the new assets, or their interest in them, after the relevant time, and

(b) where under *section 597* a chargeable gain accruing on a disposal of old assets is treated as not accruing until a time later (being the time that the new assets cease to be used for the purposes of a trade or other purposes as referred to in *subsection (2)* of that section) than the time of the disposal, and, but for this subsection, the later time would fall after the relevant time, the chargeable gain shall be treated as accruing immediately before the relevant time,

unless the new assets are excepted from the application of this subsection by *subsection (8)*.

(8) If at the time when the new assets are acquired—

(a) the trustees carry on a trade in the State through a branch or agency, and

(b) any new assets, which immediately after the relevant time, are situated in the State and either used in or for the purposes of the trade or used or held for the purposes of the branch or agency, the assets falling within *paragraph (b)* shall be excepted from the application of *subsection (7)*.][2]

Amendments

[1] Substituted by FA07 sched2(1)(q). Has effect as on and from 2 April 2007

[2] Inserted by FA99 s88(1). This section shall apply as on and from the 11th day of February, 1999.

Cross References

From Section 579B

Section 597 Replacement of business and other assets.
Section 826 Agreements for relief from double taxation.
Section 828 Capital gains tax: double taxation relief.

To Section 579B

Section 579C Death of trustee: special rules.
Section 579D Past trustees: liability for tax.
Section 613A Supplementary provisions.

579C Death of trustee: special rules

[(1) *Subsection (2)* applies where—

(a) *section 579B* applies as a result of the death of a trustee of a settlement, and

(b) within the period of 6 months beginning with the death, the trustees of the settlement become resident and ordinarily resident in the State.

(2) *Section 579B* shall apply as if the defined assets were restricted to such assets (if any) as—

(a) would be defined assets apart from this section, and

(b) fall within *subsection (3)*.

(3) Assets fall within this subsection if they were disposed of by the trustees in the period which—

(a) begins with the death, and

(b) ends when the trustees become resident and ordinarily resident in the State.

(4) Where—

(a) at any time the trustees of a settlement become resident and ordinarily resident in the State as a result of the death of a trustee of the settlement, and

(b) *section 579B* applies as regards the trustees of the settlement in circumstances where the relevant time (within the meaning of that section) falls within the period of 6 months beginning with the death,

that section shall apply as if the defined assets were restricted to such assets (if any)—

(i) as would be defined assets but for this section, and

(ii) which the trustees acquired in the period beginning with the death and ending with the relevant time.][1]

Amendments

[1] Inserted by FA99 s88(1). This section shall apply as on and from the 11th day of February, 1999.

Cross References

From Section 579C

Section 579B Trustees ceasing to be resident in the State.

579D Past trustees: liability for tax

[(1) In this section "*specified period*", in relation to a year of assessment, means the period beginning with the specified return date for the year of assessment (within the meaning of [*section 959A*][1]) and ending 3 years after the time [when a return under [*Chapter 3* of *Part 41A*][2] for the chargeable period is delivered to the Collector-General][3].

(2) For the purposes of this section—

(a) where the relevant time (within the meaning of *section 579B*) falls within the period of 12 months beginning with the 11th day of February, 1999, the relevant period is the period beginning with that day and ending with the relevant time, and

(b) in any other case, the relevant period is the period of 12 months ending with the relevant time.

(3) This section shall apply at any time on or after the 11th day of February, 1999, where—

(a) *section 579B* applies as regards the trustees (in this section referred to as "*migrating trustees*") of a settlement, and

(b) any tax, which is payable by the migrating trustees in respect of a chargeable gain accruing to them for a year of assessment (in this section referred to as "*the year of assessment concerned*") by virtue of section 579B(3), is not paid within 6 months after the date on or before which the tax is due and payable.

(4) The Revenue Commissioners may, at any time before the end of the specified period in relation to the year of assessment concerned, serve on any person to whom *subsection (5)* applies, a notice—

(a) stating the amount which remains unpaid of the tax payable by the migrating trustees for the year of assessment concerned, and

(b) requiring that person to pay that amount within 30 days of the service of the notice.

(5) This subsection applies to any person who, at any time within the relevant period, was a trustee of the settlement, other than such a person who—

(a) ceased to be a trustee of the settlement before the end of the relevant period, and

(b) shows that, when he or she (or in the case of a company, the company) ceased to be a trustee of the settlement, there was no proposal that the trustees might become neither resident nor ordinarily resident in the State.

(6) Any amount which a person is required to pay by a notice under this section—

(a) may be recovered by that person from the migrating trustees,

(b) shall not be allowed as a deduction in computing income, profits, gains or losses for any tax purposes, and

(c) may be recovered from that person as if it were tax due by such person.][4]

Amendments

[1,2] Substituted by FA12 sched4(part 2)(g).

[3] Substituted by FA01 s78(2)(b). Applies as respects the year of assessment 2001 and subsequent years and as respects accounting periods of companies ending on or after 1 April 2001.

[4] Inserted by FA99 s88(1). This section shall apply as on and from the 11th day of February, 1999.

Cross References

From Section 579D

Section 579B Trustees ceasing to be resident in the State.

Section 950 Interpretation (Part 41).

Section 951 Obligation to make a return.

579E Trustees ceasing to be liable to Irish tax

[(1) This section shall apply where the trustees of a settlement, while continuing to be resident and ordinarily resident in the State, become at any time (in this section referred to as "*the time concerned*") on or after the 11th day of February, 1999, trustees who fall to be regarded for the purposes of any arrangements—

(a) as resident in a territory outside the State, and

(b) as not liable in the State to tax on gains accruing on disposals of assets (in this section referred to as "*relevant assets*") which constitute settled property of the settlement and fall within descriptions specified in the arrangements.

(2) The trustees shall be deemed for all the purposes of the Capital Gains Tax Acts—

(a) to have disposed of their relevant assets immediately before the time concerned, and

(b) immediately to have reacquired them,

at their market value at that time.

(3) Notwithstanding anything in that section—

(a) *section 597* shall not apply where—

(i) the new assets are, or an interest in them is, acquired by the trustees of a settlement,

(ii) at the time of the acquisition the trustees are resident and ordinarily resident in the State and fall to be regarded for the purposes of any arrangements as resident in a territory outside the State,

(iii) the assets are of a description specified in those arrangements, and

(iv) the trustees would, were they to dispose of the assets immediately after the acquisition, fall to be regarded for the purposes of the arrangements as not being liable in the State to tax on gains accruing to them on the disposal,

and

(b) where under *section 597* a chargeable gain accruing on a disposal of the old assets is treated as not accruing until a time later (being the time that the new assets cease to be used for the purposes of a trade or other purposes as set out in *subsection (2)* of that section) than the time of the disposal, and but for this paragraph, the latter time would fall after the time concerned, the chargeable gain shall be treated as accruing immediately before the time concerned, if—

(i) the new assets are of a description specified in any arrangements, and

(ii) the trustees would, were they to dispose of the new assets immediately after the time concerned, fall to be regarded for the purposes of those arrangements as not being liable in the State to tax on gains accruing to them on the disposal.][1]

Amendments

[1] Inserted by FA99 s88(1). This section shall apply as on and from the 11th day of February, 1999.

Cross References

From Section 579E

Section 597 Replacement of business and other assets.

To Section 579E

Section 613A Supplementary provisions.

579F Migrant settlements

[(1) Where a period (in this section referred to as "*a non-resident period*") of one or more years of assessment for which *section 579A* applies to a settlement, succeeds a period (in this section referred to as "*a resident period*") of one or more years of assessment for each of which *section 579A* does not apply to the settlement, a capital payment received by a beneficiary in the resident period shall be disregarded for the purposes of *section 579A* if it was not made in anticipation of a disposal made by the trustees in the non-resident period.

(2) Where—

(a) a non-resident period is succeeded by a resident period, and

(b) the trust gains for the last year of assessment of the non-resident period are not, or not wholly, treated as chargeable gains accruing to beneficiaries,

then, subject to *subsection (3)*, those trust gains, or the outstanding part of them, shall be treated as chargeable gains accruing in the first year of assessment of the resident period, to beneficiaries of the settlement who receive capital payments from the trustees in that year of assessment, and so on for the second and subsequent years until the amount treated as accruing to the beneficiaries is equal to the amount of the trust gains for the last year of assessment of the non-resident period.

(3) *Subsections (5)* and *(7)* of *section 579A* shall apply in relation to *subsection (2)* as they apply in relation to *subsection (4)* of that section.][1]

Amendments

[1] Inserted by FA99 s88(1). This section shall apply as on and from the 11th day of February, 1999.

Cross References

From Section 579F

Section 579A Attribution of gains to beneficiaries.

To Section 579F

Section 579A Attribution of gains to beneficiaries.
Section 746 Offshore income gains accruing to persons resident or domiciled abroad.
Section 807A Liability of nontransferors.
Section 917 Returns relating to non-resident companies and trusts.

CHAPTER 4

Shares and Securities

580 Shares, securities, etc: identification

[CGT(A)A78 s16 and Sch1 par4]

(1) For the purposes of identifying shares acquired with shares subsequently disposed of, in so far as the shares are of the same class, shares acquired at an earlier time shall for the purposes of the Capital Gains Tax Acts be deemed to have been disposed of before shares acquired at a later time.

(2) Shares shall not be treated for the purposes of this section as being of the same class unless, if dealt with on a stock exchange, they would be so treated, but shall be treated in accordance with this section notwithstanding that they are identified in a different way by a disposal or by the transfer or delivery giving effect to the disposal.

(3) This section shall apply to securities as it applies to shares.

(4) This section apart from *subsection (2)* shall apply in relation to any assets as it applies in relation to shares where the assets are of a nature to be dealt in without identifying the particular assets disposed of or acquired.

(5) (a) This subsection shall apply in relation to the disposal of any assets to which paragraph 13 of Schedule 1 to the Capital Gains Tax Act, 1975, applied, where—

(i) any such assets were on the 6th day of April, 1978, comprised in a holding of the kind referred to in that paragraph,

(ii) the holding consisted of assets acquired on different dates, and

(iii) before the 6th day of April, 1978, there had been a disposal of assets which if that disposal had not taken place would have been comprised in the holding on that date.

(b) For the purposes of applying *subsection (1)* in relation to each disposal to which this subsection applies—

(i) shares acquired on different dates shall be treated as if they were distinguishable parts of a single asset (in this subsection referred to as "*the holding*") acquired respectively on the separate dates on which they were acquired and for the consideration for which they were acquired, and

(ii) it shall be assumed that, on each occasion before the 6th day of April, 1978, on which a disposal was made of shares in the holding, each of the distinguishable parts of the holding as it existed immediately before the disposal was reduced, both as regards the number of shares comprised in that part and the expenditure attributable to that part under *paragraphs (a)* and *(b)* of *section 552(1)*, in the same proportion as the number of shares so disposed of bears to the number of shares comprised in the holding immediately before that disposal, and

(iii) the number of shares comprised in each such part on the 6th day of April, 1978, and the expenditure attributable (apart from *section 556*) to that part under *paragraphs (a)* and *(b)* of *section 552(1)* shall, in relation to a disposal made on or after that date, be the number and expenditure respectively determined in accordance with this subsection.

(c) Nothing in this subsection shall affect the computation of any chargeable gain or allowable loss in relation to any disposal of assets made before the 6th day of April, 1978.

(6) This section shall apply subject to *section 581*.

Revenue Briefings

Tax Briefing

Tax Briefing June 2000 – Issue 40 pg 17 – CGT and Disposal of Shares

Cross References

From Section 580

Section 552 Acquisition, enhancement and disposal costs.

Section 556 Adjustment of allowable expenditure by reference to consumer price index.

Section 581 Disposals of shares or securities within 4 weeks of acquisition.

To Section 580

Section 737 Special investment schemes.

Section 739 Taxation of unit holders in undertakings for collective investment.

Section 838 Special portfolio investment accounts.

581 Disposals of shares or securities within 4 weeks of acquisition

[CGTA75 s51(1) and Sch1 par14(1) to (5)]

(1) For the purposes of the Capital Gains Tax Acts, where the same person in the same capacity disposes of shares of the same class as shares which such person acquired within 4 weeks preceding the disposal, the shares disposed of shall be identified with the shares so acquired within those 4 weeks.

(2) For the purposes of the Capital Gains Tax Acts, where the quantity of shares of the same class disposed of exceeds the quantity of shares of the same class acquired within the period of 4 weeks preceding the disposal, the excess shall be identified with shares of the same class acquired otherwise than within the period of 4 weeks.

(3) Where a loss accrues to a person on the disposal of shares and such person reacquires shares of the same class within 4 weeks after the disposal, that loss shall not be allowable under *section 538* or *546* otherwise than by deduction from a chargeable gain accruing to such person on the disposal of the shares reacquired; but, if the quantity of shares so reacquired is less than the quantity so disposed of, such proportion of the loss shall be allowable under *section 538* or *546* as bears the same proportion to the loss on the disposal as the quantity not reacquired bears to the quantity disposed of.

(4) In the case of [a man and his wife living with him, or civil partners living together][1]—

(a) *subsections (1)* and *(2)* shall, with the necessary modifications, apply where shares are acquired by one of them and shares of the same class are disposed of within 4 weeks by the other, and

(b) *subsection (3)* shall, with the necessary modifications, apply also where a loss on the disposal accrues to one of them and the acquisition after the disposal is made by the other.

(5) This section shall apply to securities as it applies to shares.

Amendments

[1] Substituted by F(No.3)A11 sched1(157). Shall have effect from 27 July 2011.

Cross References

From Section 581

Section 538 Disposals where assets lost or destroyed or become of negligible value.
Section 546 Allowable losses.

To Section 581

Section 580 Shares, securities, etc: identification.
Section 711 Chargeable gains of life business.
Section 737 Special investment schemes.
Section 738 Undertakings for collective investment.

582 Calls on shares

[CGT(A)A78 s16 and Sch1 par3]

Where, as respects an issue of shares in or debentures of a company, a person gives any consideration on a date which is more than 12 months after the date on which the shares or debentures were allotted, the consideration shall, in the computation of a gain accruing to such person on a disposal of the shares or debentures, be deemed for the purposes of *section 556* to be expenditure incurred on the date on which the consideration was given.

Cross References

From Section 582

Section 556 Adjustment of allowable expenditure by reference to consumer price index.

583 Capital distributions by companies

[CGTA75 s51(1) and Sch2 par1]

(1) In this section, "*capital distribution*" means any distribution from a company (including a distribution in the course of dissolving or winding up the company) in money or money's worth except a distribution which in the hands of the recipient constitutes income for the purposes of income tax.

(2) Where a person receives or becomes entitled to receive in respect of shares in a company any capital distribution from the company (other than a new holding within the meaning of *section 584*), such person shall be treated for the purposes of the Capital Gains Tax Acts as if such person had in consideration of that capital distribution disposed of an interest in the shares.

Cross References

From Section 583

Section 584 Reorganisation or reduction of share capital.

To Section 583

Section 509 Interpretation (Chapter 1).
Section 584 Reorganisation or reduction of share capital.
Section 598 Disposals of business or farm on "retirement".
Section 614 Capital distribution derived from chargeable gain of company: recovery of tax from shareholder.
Section 617 Transfers of assets, other than trading stock, within group.
Section 977 Recovery of capital gains tax from shareholder.

584 Reorganisation or reduction of share capital

[CGTA75 s51(1) and Sch2 par2(1) to (7) and (9); CGT(A)A78 s16 and Sch1 par5]

(1) In this section—

"*new holding*", in relation to any original shares, means the shares in and debentures of the company which as a result of the reorganisation or reduction of capital represent the original shares (including such, if any, of the original shares as remain);

"*original shares*" means shares held before and concerned in the reorganisation or reduction of capital;

references to a reorganisation of a company's share capital include—

(a) any case where persons are, whether for payment or not, allotted shares in or debentures of the company in respect of and in proportion to (or as nearly as may be in proportion to) their holdings of shares in the company or of any class of shares in the company, and

(b) any case where there is more than one class of shares and the rights attached to shares of any class are altered;

references to a reduction of share capital do not include the paying off of redeemable share capital and, where shares in a company are redeemable by the company otherwise than by the issue of shares or debentures (with or without other consideration) and otherwise than in a liquidation, the shareholder shall be treated as disposing of the shares at the time of the redemption.

(2) This section shall apply for the purposes of the Capital Gains Tax Acts in relation to any reorganisation or reduction of a company's share capital.

(3) [Subject to *subsections (4)* to [*(10)*][1]][2], a reorganisation or reduction of a company's share capital shall not be treated as involving any disposal of the original shares or any acquisition of the new holding or any part of it; but the original shares (taken as a single asset) and the new holding (taken as a single asset) shall be treated as the same asset acquired as the original shares were acquired.

(4) (a) Where on a reorganisation or reduction of a company's share capital a person gives or becomes liable to give any consideration for such person's new holding or any part of it, that consideration shall, in the computation of a gain accruing to such person on a disposal of the new holding or any part of it, be deemed for the purposes of *section 556* to be expenditure incurred on the date the consideration was given and, if the new holding or part of it is disposed of with a liability attaching to it in respect of that consideration, the consideration given for the disposal shall be adjusted accordingly.

(b) Notwithstanding *paragraph (a)*, there shall not be treated as consideration given for the acquisition of the new holding—

(i) any surrender, cancellation or other alteration of the original shares or of the rights attached to the original shares, or

(ii) any consideration consisting of any application, in paying up the shares or debentures or any part of them, of any assets of the company, or of any dividend or other distribution declared out of those assets but not made;

but, if *section 816* applies in relation to the issue of any of the shares, the sum in cash which the person would have received if the person had not exercised the option to receive additional share capital instead of a sum in cash shall be treated for the purposes of this subsection as consideration given for those shares.

(5) Where on a reorganisation or reduction of a company's share capital a person receives (or is deemed to receive), or becomes entitled to receive, any consideration other than the new holding for the disposal of an interest in the original shares, and in particular—

(a) where under *section 583* such person is to be treated as if such person had in consideration of a capital distribution disposed of an interest in the original shares, or

(b) where such person receives (or is deemed to receive) a consideration from other shareholders in respect of a surrender of rights derived from the original shares,

such person shall be treated as if the new holding resulted from such person having for that consideration disposed of an interest in the original shares (but without prejudice to the original shares and the new holding being treated in accordance with *subsection (3)* as the same asset).

(6) Where, for the purpose of computing the gain or loss accruing to a person from the acquisition and disposal of any part of the new holding, it is necessary to apportion the cost of acquisition of any of the original shares between the part which is disposed of and the part which is retained, the apportionment shall be made by reference to market value at the date of the disposal (with such adjustment of the market value of any part of the new holding as may be required to offset any liability attaching to the new holding but forming part of the cost to be apportioned), and any corresponding apportionment for the purposes of *subsection (5)* shall be made in the like manner.

(7) Notwithstanding *subsection (6)*—

(a) where a new holding—

(i) consists of more than one class of shares in or debentures of the company and one or more of those classes is of shares or debentures which, at any time not later than the end of the period of 3 months beginning on the date on which the reorganisation or reduction of capital took effect, or of such longer period as the Revenue Commissioners may by notice in writing allow, had quoted market values on a recognised stock exchange in the State or elsewhere, or

(ii) consists of more than one class of rights of unit holders and one or more of those classes is of rights the prices of which were published regularly by the managers of the scheme at any time not later than the end of that period of 3 months (or longer if so allowed), and

(b) where, for the purpose of computing the gain or loss accruing to a person from the acquisition and disposal of the whole or any part of any class of shares or securities or rights of unit holders forming part of a new holding of the kind referred to in *paragraph (a)*, it is necessary to apportion costs of acquisition between the part that is disposed of and the part that is retained,

then, the cost of acquisition of the new holding shall first be apportioned between the entire classes of shares or debentures or rights of which it consists by reference to market value on the first day (whether that day fell before the reorganisation or reduction of capital took effect or later) on which market values or prices were quoted or published for the shares, debentures or rights mentioned in *paragraph (a)* or *(b)* (with such adjustment of the market value of any class as may be required to offset any liability attaching thereto but forming part of the cost to be apportioned) and, for the purposes of this subsection, the day on which a reorganisation of share capital involving the allotment of shares or debentures or unit holders' rights takes effect shall be the day following the day on which the right to renounce any allotment expires.

(8) Where a person receives or becomes entitled to receive in respect of any shares in or debentures of a company a provisional allotment of shares in or debentures of the company and such person disposes of such person's rights, *section 583* shall apply as if the amount of the consideration for the disposal were a capital distribution received by such person from the company in respect of the first-mentioned shares, and as if such person had, instead of disposing of the rights, disposed of an interest in those shares.

[(9) *Subsection (3)* shall not apply to the extent that the new holding comprises debentures, loan stock or other similar securities issued or allotted on or after 4 December 2002, unless—

(a) they were so issued or allotted pursuant to a binding written agreement made before that date, or

(b) this section has application by virtue of *section 586*.][3]

[(10) (a) In this subsection, '*investment undertaking*' and '*unit*' have the same meanings respectively as in *section 739B*.

(b) *Subsection (3)* shall not apply where the new holding comprises units in an investment undertaking, being a company.][4]

Amendments

[1] Substituted by FA12 s58(1)(a). Applies to any shares or debentures issued by a company on or after 22 February 2012.

[2] Substituted by FA03 s66(a)(i).

[3] Inserted by FA03 s66(a)(ii).

[4] Inserted by FA12 s58(1)(b). Applies to any shares or debentures issued by a company on or after 22 February 2012.

Case Law

Gains and losses should be computed by reference to the consideration paid when an asset comes into the group and the consideration received when an asset leaves the group. NAP Holdings UK Ltd v Whittles 1994 STC 979

All increases in share capital which constitute a reorganisation of share capital are not defined exhaustively in ss(1). Young Austen v Dunstan 1989 STC 69

Revenue Briefings

Tax Briefing

Tax Briefing December 2000 – Issue 42 pg 48 – Topical Questions – Capital Gains Tax

Tax Briefing August 2003 – Issue 53 pg 3 – First Active PLC – CGT

Tax Briefing August 2003 – Issue 53 pg 21 – Jefferson Smurfit Shares – CGT

Tax Briefing December 2006 – Issue 65 – The Calculation of Base Cost of Fyffes Shares and Blackrock International Land shares

Tax Briefing July 2007 – Issue 66 pg 16 – Calculation of Base Cost of Fyffes Shares and Total Produce shares

Cross References

From Section 584

Section 556 Adjustment of allowable expenditure by reference to consumer price index.

Section 583 Capital distributions by companies.

Section 586 Company amalgamations by exchange of shares.

Section 816 Taxation of shares issued in place of cash dividends.

To Section 584

Section 128D Tax treatment of directors of companies and employees who acquire restricted shares.

Section 177 Conditions as to residence and period of ownership.

Section 249 Rules relating to recovery of capital and replacement loans.
Section 479 Relief for new shares purchased on issue by employees.
Section 496 Disposals of shares.
Section 504 Capital gains tax.
Section 509 Interpretation (Chapter 1).
Section 511 The period of retention, release date and appropriate percentage.
Section 514 Company reconstructions, amalgamations, etc.
Section 519D Approved share option schemes.
Section 540 Options and forfeited deposits.
Section 541 Debts.
Section 547 Disposals and acquisitions treated as made at market value.
Section 583 Capital distributions by companies.
Section 585 Conversion of securities.
Section 586 Company amalgamations by exchange of shares.
Section 587 Company reconstructions and amalgamations.
Section 588 Demutualisation of assurance companies.
Section 626B Exemption from tax in the case of gains on disposals of shares.
Section 733 Reorganisation of units in unit trust scheme.
Section 741 Disposals of material interests in non-qualifying offshore funds.
Section 742 Offshore funds operating equalisation arrangements.
Section 744 Non-qualifying offshore funds.
Section 747 Deduction of offshore income gain in determining capital gain.
Section 751A Exchange of shares held as trading stock.
Section 884 Returns of profits.
Section 913 Application of income tax provisions relating to returns, etc.
Section 980 Deduction from consideration on disposal of certain assets.
Schedule 11 Profit Sharing Schemes
Schedule 12 Employee Share Ownership Trusts
Schedule 25A Exemption from Tax in the Case of Gains on Certain Disposals of Shares

585 Conversion of securities

[CGTA75 s51(1) and Sch2 par3]

(1) In this section—

"*conversion of securities*" includes—

(a) a conversion of securities of a company into shares in the company,

[(b) a conversion at the option of the holder of the securities converted as an alternative to the redemption of those securities for cash where the conversion takes place before 4 December 2002, or where the conversion takes place after that date pursuant to a binding written agreement made before that date, and][1]

(c) any exchange of securities effected in pursuance of any enactment which provides for the compulsory acquisition of any shares or securities and the issue of securities or other securities instead;

['*investment undertaking*' and '*unit*' have the same meanings respectively as in *section 739B*;][2]

"*security*" includes any loan stock or similar security, whether of any government or of any public or local authority or of any company and whether secured or unsecured but excluding securities within *section 607*.

[(1A) For the purposes of this section, a conversion of securities shall not include a conversion of securities into units in an investment undertaking, being a company.][3]

(2) *Section 584* shall apply with any necessary modifications in relation to the conversion of securities as it applies in relation to the reorganisation or reduction of a company's share capital.

Amendments

[1] Substituted by FA03 s66(b).

[2] Inserted by FA12 s58(1)(c). Applies to any shares or debentures issued by a company on or after 22 February 2012.

[3] Inserted by FA12 s58(1)(d). Applies to any shares or debentures issued by a company on or after 22 February 2012.

Cross References

From Section 585

Section 584 Reorganisation or reduction of share capital.

Section 607 Government and certain other securities.

To Section 585

Section 177 Conditions as to residence and period of ownership.

Section 540 Options and forfeited deposits.

Section 541 Debts.

Section 733 Reorganisation of units in unit trust scheme.

Section 742 Offshore funds operating equalisation arrangements.

Section 744 Non-qualifying offshore funds.

586 Company amalgamations by exchange of shares

[CGTA75 s51(1) and Sch2 par4; FA82 s63(1)(a) and (2)]

(1) Subject to *section 587*, where a company issues shares or debentures to a person in exchange for shares in or debentures of another company, *section 584* shall apply with any necessary modifications as if the 2 companies were the same company and the exchange were a reorganisation of its share capital.

(2) This section shall apply only where—

(a) the company issuing the shares or debentures has, or in consequence of the exchange will have, control of the other company, or

(b) the first-mentioned company issues the shares or debentures in exchange for shares as the result of a general offer made to members of the other company or any class of them (with or without exceptions for persons connected with the first-mentioned company), the offer being made in the first instance on a condition such that if it were satisfied the first-mentioned company would have control of the other company.

(3) (a) In this subsection, "*shares*" includes stock, debentures and any interests to which *section 587(3)* applies and also includes any option in relation to such shares.

(b) This section shall not apply to the issue by a company of shares in the company by means of an exchange referred to in *subsection (1)* unless it is shown that the exchange is effected for bona fide commercial reasons and does not form part of any arrangement or scheme of which the main purpose or one of the main purposes is avoidance of liability to tax.

[(c) This section shall not apply where, on or after 4 December 2002, a company issues debentures, loan stock or other similar securities to a person in exchange for shares of another company unless—

(i) such issue is pursuant to a binding written agreement made before that date, or

(ii) the company issuing the debentures, loan stock or other similar securities and the person to whom they are issued are members of the same group (within the meaning of *section 616*) throughout the period commencing one year before and ending one year after the day the debentures, loan stock or other similar securities are issued, or

(iii) the other company is a company quoted on a recognised stock exchange and its board of directors had, before 4 December 2002, made a public announcement that they had agreed the terms of a recommended offer to be made for the company's entire issued, and to be issued, ordinary share capital.][1]

[(d) This section shall not apply where the company issuing the shares or debentures is an investment undertaking within the meaning of *section 739B*.][2]

Amendments

[1] Inserted by FA03 s66(c).

[2] Inserted by FA12 s58(1)(e). Applies to any shares or debentures issued by a company on or after 22 February 2012.

Revenue Briefings

Tax Briefing

Tax Briefing June 2002 – Issue 48 pg 15 – Capital Gains Tax – Company Amalgamations by Exchange of Shares

Revenue Precedents

Where part of the consideration for a takeover consists of shares or securities to be issued at a future date if a contingency is satisfied, the earn out element will be treated as a security and relief under S.586 may be due. This will apply only insofar as the earn-out element does not or could not take the form of cash. G111(A).

Cross References

From Section 586

Section 584 Reorganisation or reduction of share capital.
Section 587 Company reconstructions and amalgamations.
Section 616 Groups of companies: interpretation.

To Section 586

Section 177 Conditions as to residence and period of ownership.
Section 249 Rules relating to recovery of capital and replacement loans.
Section 509 Interpretation (Chapter 1).
Section 519D Approved share option schemes.
Section 540 Options and forfeited deposits.
Section 541 Debts.
Section 584 Reorganisation or reduction of share capital.
Section 587 Company reconstructions and amalgamations.
Section 598 Disposals of business or farm on "retirement".
Section 625 Shares in subsidiary member of group.
Section 733 Reorganisation of units in unit trust scheme.
Section 741 Disposals of material interests in non-qualifying offshore funds.
Section 742 Offshore funds operating equalisation arrangements.
Section 744 Non-qualifying offshore funds.
Section 884 Returns of profits.
Section 913 Application of income tax provisions relating to returns, etc.
Schedule 11 Profit Sharing Schemes
Schedule 12 Employee Share Ownership Trusts
Schedule 25A Exemption from Tax in the Case of Gains on Certain Disposals of Shares

587 Company reconstructions and amalgamations

[CGTA75 s51(1) and Sch2 par5; FA82 s63(1)(b) and (2)]

(1) In this section, "*scheme of reconstruction or amalgamation*" means a scheme for the reconstruction of any company or companies or the amalgamation of any 2 or more companies, and references to shares or debentures being retained include their being retained with altered rights or in an altered form, whether as the result of reduction, consolidation, division or otherwise.

(2) Where under any arrangement between a company and the persons holding shares in or debentures of the company or any class of such shares or debentures, being an arrangement entered into for the purposes of or in connection with a scheme of reconstruction or amalgamation, another company issues shares or debentures to those persons in respect of and in proportion to (or as nearly as may be in proportion to) their holdings of the first-mentioned shares or debentures, but the first-mentioned shares or debentures are either retained by those persons or cancelled, then, those persons shall be treated as exchanging the first-mentioned shares or debentures for those held by them in consequence of the arrangement (any shares or debentures retained being for this purpose regarded as if they had been cancelled and replaced by a new issue), and accordingly *section 586(1)* shall apply to such exchange of shares or debentures.

(3) *Subsection (2)* shall apply in relation to a company which has no share capital as if references to shares in or debentures of a company included references to any interests in the company possessed by members of the company, and *sections 584* and *586* shall apply accordingly.

(4) (a) In this subsection, "*shares*" has the same meaning as in *section 586(3)*.

(b) This section shall not apply to the issue by a company of shares in the company under a scheme of reconstruction or amalgamation referred to in *subsection (2)* unless it is shown that the reconstruction or amalgamation is effected for bona fide commercial reasons and does not form part of any arrangement or scheme of which the main purpose or one of the main purposes is avoidance of liability to tax.

[(c) This section shall not apply to any person to whom, under a scheme of reconstruction or amalgamation, a company issues debentures, loan stock or other similar securities on or after 4 December 2002, unless—

(i) they were issued pursuant to a binding written agreement made before that date, or

(ii) that person and the company are members of the same group (within the meaning of *section 616*) throughout the period commencing one year before and ending one year after the day the debentures, loan stock or other similar securities were issued, or

(iii) they were issued pursuant to a scheme or arrangement, the principal terms of which had been brought to the attention of the Revenue Commissioners and the Revenue Commissioners had acknowledged in writing before 4 December 2002, to the effect that the scheme or arrangement was a scheme of reconstruction and amalgamation.][1]

[(d) This section shall not apply where the company issuing the shares or debentures is an investment undertaking within the meaning of *section 739B*.][2]

Amendments

[1] Inserted by FA03 s66(d).

[2] Inserted by FA12 s58(1)(f). Applies to any shares or debentures issued by a company on or after 22 February 2012.

Revenue Briefings

Tax Briefing

Tax Briefing June 2001 – Issue 44 pg 34 – Partition of Family Trading Companies
Tax Briefing April 2002 – Issue 47 pg 17 – Retirement Relief and Reconstructions
Tax Briefing June 2002 – Issue 48 pg 15 – Capital Gains Tax – Company Amalgamations by Exchange of Shares
Tax Briefing May 2002 – Issue 52 pg 13 – Finance Act 2003 – Capital Gains Tax

Revenue Precedents

Where a family trading company (or group of companies) is broken up into separate individual trading companies, such an event will not be regarded as a disposal for CGT purposes provided that the value of each individual's holding in the company or group remains strictly unaltered and also provided certain other conditions are met. Prior approval and formal undertakings will be required. G12.

Cross References

From Section 587

Section 584 Reorganisation or reduction of share capital.
Section 586 Company amalgamations by exchange of shares.
Section 616 Groups of companies: interpretation.

To Section 587

Section 177 Conditions as to residence and period of ownership.
Section 479 Relief for new shares purchased on issue by employees.
Section 488 Interpretation (Part 16).
Section 519D Approved share option schemes.
Section 540 Options and forfeited deposits.
Section 541 Debts.
Section 547 Disposals and acquisitions treated as made at market value.
Section 586 Company amalgamations by exchange of shares.
Section 588 Demutualisation of assurance companies.
Section 598 Disposals of business or farm on "retirement".
Section 625 Shares in subsidiary member of group.
Section 633C Treatment of securities on a merger.
Section 741 Disposals of material interests in non-qualifying offshore funds.
Section 751A Exchange of shares held as trading stock.
Section 884 Returns of profits.
Section 913 Application of income tax provisions relating to returns, etc.
Schedule 11 Profit Sharing Schemes
Schedule 25A Exemption from Tax in the Case of Gains on Certain Disposals of Shares

588 Demutualisation of assurance companies

[CGTA75 s51(1) and Sch2 par5A; FA97 s70]

(1) In this section—

["*assurance company*" means—

(a) an assurance company within the meaning of section 3 of the Insurance Act 1936, or

(b) a person that holds an authorisation within the meaning of the European Communities (Life Assurance) Framework Regulations 1994 (S.I. No. 360 of 1994);][1]

"*free shares*", in relation to a member of the assurance company, means any shares issued by the successor company to that member in connection with the arrangement but for no new consideration;

"*member*", in relation to the assurance company, means a person who is or has been a member of it, in that capacity, and any reference to a member includes a reference to a member of any particular class or description;

"*new consideration*" means consideration other than—

(a) consideration provided directly or indirectly out of the assets of the assurance company or the successor company, or

(b) consideration derived from a member's shares or other rights in the assurance company or the successor company.

(2) This section shall apply as on and from the 21st day of April, 1997, in respect of an arrangement between a company and its members, being an arrangement to which *subsection (2)* of *section 587* applies by virtue of *subsection (3)* of that section, and where the company is an assurance company which carries on a mutual life business.

(3) Where in connection with the arrangement there is conferred on a member of the assurance company concerned any rights—

(a) to acquire shares in another company (in this section referred to as the "*successor company*") in priority to other persons,

(b) to acquire shares in the successor company for consideration of an amount or value lower than the market value of the shares, or

(c) to free shares in the successor company,

then, any such rights so conferred on a member shall be regarded for the purposes of capital gains tax as an option (within the meaning of *section 540*) granted to and acquired by such member for no consideration and having no value at the time of that grant and acquisition.

(4) Where in connection with the arrangement shares in the successor company are issued to a member of the assurance company concerned, and such shares are treated under *section 587* as having been exchanged by the member for the interest in the company possessed by the member, those shares shall, notwithstanding *section 584*, be regarded for the purposes of *section 552(1)*—

(a) as having been issued to the member for a consideration given by the member of an amount or value equal to the amount or value of any new consideration given by the member for the shares or, if no new consideration is given, as having been issued for no consideration, and

(b) as having, at the time of their issue to the member, a value equal to the amount or value of the new consideration so given or, if no new consideration is given, as having no value;

but this subsection is without prejudice to the operation where applicable of *subsection (3)*.

(5) *Subsection (6)* shall apply in any case where—

(a) in connection with the arrangement, shares in the successor company are issued by that company to trustees on terms which provide for the transfer of those shares to members of the assurance company concerned for no new consideration, and

(b) the circumstances are such that in the hands of the trustees the shares constitute settled property.

(6) (a) Where this subsection applies, then, for the purposes of capital gains tax—

(i) the shares shall be regarded as acquired by the trustees for no consideration,

(ii) the interest of any member in the settled property constituted by the shares shall be regarded as acquired by the member for no consideration and as having no value at the time of its acquisition, and

(iii) where on the occasion of a member becoming absolutely entitled as against the trustees to any of the settled property, both the trustees and the member shall be treated as if, on the member becoming so entitled, the shares in question had been disposed of and immediately reacquired by the trustees, in their capacity as trustees within *section 567(2)*, for a consideration of such an amount as would secure that on the disposal neither a gain nor a loss would accrue to the trustees, and accordingly *section 576(1)* shall not apply in relation to that occasion.

(b) Reference in *paragraph (a)* to the case where a member becomes absolutely entitled to settled property as against the trustees shall be taken to include reference to the case where the member would become so entitled but for being a minor or otherwise under a legal disability.

[(7) Where in connection with the arrangements there is conferred on a member of an assurance company a right to acquire shares in a successor company, or a right to a distribution of assets (including cash) of the assurance company, the assurance company shall, within 30 days of the arrangements being effected or within such longer period as the Revenue Commissioners may on request allow, make a return to the Revenue Commissioners in such electronic format as they require, which, in respect of each such member, specifies—

(a) the name of the member,

(b) the address of the member,

(c) the number of shares in the successor company which the member has a right to acquire,

(d) the amount of new consideration which the member is required to give to acquire those shares,

(e) the value of any assets of the assurance company to which the member has a right, and

(f) such other information that the Revenue Commissioners advise the assurance company that they require.][2]

Amendments

[1] Substituted by FA06 s59(1)(a). This section is deemed to have applied as on and from 20 December 2000.

[2] Inserted by FA06 s76.

Cross References

From Section 588

Section 540 Options and forfeited deposits.

Section 552 Acquisition, enhancement and disposal costs.

Section 567 Nominees, bare trustees and agents.
Section 576 Person becoming absolutely entitled to settled property.
Section 584 Reorganisation or reduction of share capital.
Section 587 Company reconstructions and amalgamations.

589 Shares in close company transferring assets at undervalue

[CGTA75 s35(1) to (3) and (5); CTA76 s140(2) and Sch 2 PtII par3(1)]

(1) Where a close company transfers an asset to any person otherwise than by means of a bargain made at arm's length and for a consideration of an amount or value less than the market value of the asset, an amount equal to the difference shall be apportioned among the issued shares of the company, and the holders of those shares shall be treated in accordance with *subsections (2)* and *(3)*.

(2) For the purposes of the computation of a chargeable gain accruing on the disposal of any of those shares by the person owning them on the date of transfer, an amount equal to the amount so apportioned to that share shall be excluded from the expenditure allowable as a deduction under *section 552(1)(a)* from the consideration for the disposal.

(3) Where the person owning any of those shares at the date of transfer is itself a close company, an amount equal to the amount apportioned to the shares so owned under *subsection (1)* to that close company shall be apportioned among the issued shares of that close company, and the holders of those shares shall be treated in accordance with *subsection (2)*, and so on through any number of close companies.

(4) This section shall apply to a company within *section 590* as it applies to a close company.

Cross References

From Section 589

Section 552 Acquisition, enhancement and disposal costs.
Section 590 Attribution to participators of chargeable gains accruing to non-resident company.

To Section 589

Section 616 Groups of companies: interpretation.

590 Attribution to participators of chargeable gains accruing to non-resident company

[(1) In this section—

(a) "*participator*", in relation to a company, has the meaning assigned to it by *section 433(1)*;

(b) references to a person's interest as a participator in a company are references to the interest in the company which is represented by all the factors by reference to which the person falls to be treated as such a participator; and

(c) references to the extent of such an interest are references to the proportion of the interests as participators of all the participators in the company (including any who are not resident or ordinarily resident in the State) which on a just and reasonable apportionment is represented by that interest.

(2) For the purposes of this section, where—

(a) the interest of any person in a company is wholly or partly represented by an interest (in this subsection referred to as the "*person's beneficial interest*") which the person has under any settlement, and

(b) the person's beneficial interest is the factor, or one of the factors, by reference to which the person would be treated, apart from this subsection, as having an interest as a participator in the company,

the interest as a participator in the company which would be that person's shall be deemed, to the extent that it is represented by the person's beneficial interest, to be an interest of the trustees of the settlement, and not an interest of the person's, and references in this section, in relation to a company, to a participator shall be construed accordingly.

(3) This section shall apply as respects chargeable gains accruing to a company—

(a) which is not resident in the State, and

(b) which would be a close company if it were resident in the State.

(4) Subject to this section, every person who at the time when the chargeable gain accrues to the company is resident or ordinarily resident in the State, who, if an individual, is domiciled in the State, and who is a participator in the company, shall be treated for the purposes of the Capital Gains Tax Acts as if a part of the chargeable gain had accrued to that person.

(5) The part of the chargeable gain referred to in *subsection (4)* shall be equal to the proportion of that gain that corresponds to the extent of the participator's interest as a participator in the company.

(6) *Subsection (4)* shall not apply in the case of any participator in the company to which the gain accrues where the aggregate amount falling under that subsection to be apportioned to the participator and to persons connected with the participator does not exceed one-twentieth of the gain.

(7) This section shall not apply in relation to—

[(a) a chargeable gain accruing on the disposal of assets, being—

(i) tangible property, whether movable or immovable, or a lease of such property, or

(ii) specified intangible assets within the meaning of *section 291A(1)*,

where the assets were used, and used only, for the purposes of a trade carried on by a company, or by another company which is a member of the same group (within the meaning of *subsection (16)*) as the first-mentioned company, wholly outside the State,][1]

(b) a chargeable gain accruing on the disposal of currency or of a debt within *section 541(6)*, where the currency or debt is or represents money in use for the purposes of a trade carried on by the company wholly outside the State, or

(c) a chargeable gain in respect of which the company is chargeable to capital gains tax by virtue of *section 29* or to corporation tax by virtue of *section 25(2)(b)*.

(8) Where—

(a) any amount of capital gains tax is paid by a person in pursuance of *subsection (4)*, and

(b) an amount in respect of the chargeable gain is distributed, whether by way of dividend or distribution of capital or on the dissolution of the company, within 2 years from the time when the chargeable gain accrued to the company,

that amount of tax, so far as neither reimbursed by the company nor applied as a deduction under *subsection (9)*, shall be applied for reducing or extinguishing any liability of the person to income tax in respect of the distribution or (in the case of a distribution falling to be treated as a disposal on which a chargeable gain accrues to the person) to any capital gains tax in respect of the distribution.

(9) The amount of capital gains tax paid by a person in pursuance of *subsection (4)*, so far as neither reimbursed by the company nor applied under *subsection (8)* for reducing any liability to tax, shall be allowable as a deduction in the computation under the Capital Gains Tax Acts of a gain accruing on the disposal by the person of any asset representing the person's interest as a participator in the company.

(10) In ascertaining for the purposes of *subsection (8)* the amount of income tax chargeable on any person for any year of assessment on or in respect of a distribution, any such distribution mentioned in that subsection which falls to be treated as income of that person for that year of assessment shall be regarded as forming the highest part of the income on which the person is charged to tax for the year of assessment.

(11) To the extent that it would reduce or extinguish chargeable gains accruing by virtue of this section to a person in a year of assessment, this section shall apply in relation to a loss accruing to the company on the disposal of an asset in that year of assessment as it would apply if a gain instead of a loss had accrued to the company on the disposal, but shall only apply in relation to that person; and, subject to the preceding provisions of this subsection, this section shall not apply in relation to a loss accruing to the company.

(12) Where the person who is a participator in the company at the time when the chargeable gain accrued to the company is itself a company which is not resident in the State but which would be a close company if it were resident in the State, an amount equal to the amount apportioned under *subsection (5)* out of the chargeable gain to the participating company's interest as a participator in the company to which the gain accrues shall be further apportioned among the participators in the participating company according to the extent of their respective interests as participators, and *subsection (4)* shall apply to them accordingly in relation to the amounts further apportioned, and so on through any number of companies.

(13) The persons treated by this section as if a part of a chargeable gain accruing to a company had accrued to them shall include trustees who are participators in the company, or in any company amongst the participators in which the gain is apportioned under *subsection (12)*, if when the gain accrued to the company the trustees are neither resident nor ordinarily resident in the State.

(14) Where any tax payable by any person by virtue of *subsection (4)* is paid by the company to which the chargeable gain accrues, or in a case under *subsection (12)* is paid by any such other company, the amount so paid shall not, for the purposes of income tax, capital gains tax or corporation tax, be regarded as a payment to the person by whom the tax was originally payable.

(15) For the purposes of this section, the amount of the gain or loss accruing at any time to a company which is not resident in the State shall be computed (where it is not the case) as if the company were within the charge to corporation tax on capital gains.

(16) (a) In this subsection—

"*group*" shall be construed in accordance with *subsections (1)* (excluding *paragraph (a)*), *(3)* and *(4)* of *section 616*;

"non-resident group" of companies—

(i) in the case of a group none of the members of which is resident in the State, means that group, and

(ii) in the case of a group 2 or more members of which are not resident in the State, means the members not resident in the State.

(b) For the purposes of this section—

(i) [*section 617* (other than *paragraphs (b)* and *(c)* of *subsection (1)*), *section 618* (with the omission of the words "to which this section applies" in *subsections (1)(a)* and *(2)*, of "such" in *subsection (1)(c)* and of *subsection (3)*), *section 619(2)* (with the substitution for "in the course of a disposal to which *section 617* applies" of "at a time when both were members of the group") and *section 620(2)* (with the omission of the words "to which this section applies")][2] shall apply in relation to non-resident companies which are members of a non-resident group of companies as they apply in relation to companies resident in the State which are members of a group of companies, and

(ii) *sections 623* [(apart from *paragraphs (c)* and *(d)* of *subsection (2)*)][3] and *625* shall apply as if for any reference in those sections to a group of companies there were substituted a reference to a non-resident group of companies, and as if references to companies were references to companies not resident in the State.][4]

Amendments

[1] Substituted by FA10 s57(1). This section applies to disposals made on or after 4 February 10 2010.

[2] Substituted by FA01 s39(1)(a). This section applies in cases in which section 617, 618, 619(2) or 620(2), as the case may be, have effect as amended by this Act.

[3] Inserted by FA01 s39(1)(b). This section applies in cases in which section 617, 618, 619(2) or 620(2), as the case may be, have effect as amended by this Act.

[4] Substituted by FA99 s89(1). This section shall apply as respects chargeable gains accruing to a company on or after the 11th day of February, 1999.

Cross References

From Section 590

Section 25 Companies not resident in the State.
Section 29 Persons chargeable.
Section 291A Intangible assets.
Section 433 Meaning of "participator", "associate", "director" and "loan creditor".
Section 541 Debts.
Section 616 Groups of companies: interpretation.
Section 617 Transfers of assets, other than trading stock, within group.
Section 618 Transfers of trading stock within group.
Section 619 Disposals or acquisitions outside group.
Section 620 Replacement of business assets by members of group.
Section 623 Company ceasing to be member of group.
Section 625 Shares in subsidiary member of group.

To Section 590

Section 589 Shares in close company transferring assets at undervalue.
Section 746 Offshore income gains accruing to persons resident or domiciled abroad.
Section 917 Returns relating to non-resident companies and trusts.

591 Relief for individuals on certain reinvestment

[FA93 s27(1) to (5) (apart from proviso to (5)) and (6) to (13); FA94 s65(b); FA95 s74(1);FA96 s62(1); FA97 s75(1)]

(1) In this section—

"*director*" has the same meaning as in *section 116*;

"*eligible shares*" and "*ordinary shares*" have the same meanings respectively as in *section 488*;

"*full-time director*", "*full-time employee*", "*part-time director*" and "*part-time employee*" have the same meanings respectively as in *section 250*;

"*holding company*" means a company whose business consists wholly or mainly in the holding of shares in, or securities of, one or more companies which are trading companies and which are its 51 per cent subsidiaries;

"*material disposal*" has the meaning assigned to it by *subsection (5)*;

"*ordinary share capital*" has the same meaning as in *section 2*;

"*the original holding*" has the meaning assigned to it by *subsection (2)*;

"*qualifying company*" has the meaning assigned to it by *subsection (7)*;

"*qualifying investment*" has the meaning assigned to it by *subsection (6)*;

"*the reinvestor*" has the meaning assigned to it by *subsection (2)*;

"*the specified period*" has the meaning assigned to it by *subsection (6)(b)*;

"*trade*" includes a profession, and "*trading company*", "*trading group*", "*qualifying trade*" (within the meaning of *subsection (8)*) and "*qualifying trading operations*" (within the meaning of that subsection) shall be construed accordingly;

"*trading company*" means a company whose business consists wholly or mainly of the carrying on of a trade or trades;

"*trading group*" means a holding company and one or more trading companies which are 51 per cent subsidiaries of the holding company;

"*unquoted company*" means a company none of whose shares, stocks or debentures are listed in the official list of a stock exchange or quoted on an unlisted securities market of a stock exchange;

"*51 per cent subsidiary*" has the meaning assigned to it by *section 9*.

(2) (a) Subject to this section, where the consideration which an individual (in this section referred to as "*the reinvestor*") [obtains for any material disposal, before 4 December 2002, by][1] him or her of shares in or securities of any company (in this section referred to as "*the original holding*") is applied by him or her within the period of 3 years from the date of that disposal in acquiring a qualifying investment, the reinvestor shall, on making a claim in that behalf, be treated for the purposes of the Capital Gains Tax Acts as if the chargeable gain accruing on the disposal of the original holding did not accrue until he or she disposes of the qualifying investment.

(b) Notwithstanding *paragraph (a)*, where—

(i) the disposal of the qualifying investment is a material disposal for the purposes of this section, and

(ii) the consideration for that disposal is applied by the reinvestor within the period of 3 years from the date of that disposal in acquiring another qualifying investment,

the reinvestor shall be treated as if the chargeable gain accruing on the disposal of the original holding did not accrue until he or she disposes of the other qualifying investment and any further qualifying investment which is acquired in a similar manner.

(3) (a) Where an individual is not entitled to be treated in accordance with *subsection (2)* solely by reason of not having satisfied the requirements of either or both *paragraphs (a)* and *(e)* of *subsection (6)*, and—

(i) all the other requirements of this section have been satisfied,

(ii) the capital gains tax on the disposal of the original holding has been paid in full, and

(iii) the individual has, throughout a period of 2 years beginning within the specified period, been a full-time employee or a full-time director of the qualifying company,

then, the individual—

(I) shall be entitled on making a claim in that behalf to such repayment of capital gains tax as would secure that the tax which is ultimately borne by the individual does not exceed the tax which would have been borne by the individual if he or she had been entitled to be treated in accordance with *subsection (2)*, and

(II) shall be treated for the purposes of the Capital Gains Tax Acts as if the chargeable gain accruing on the disposal of the original holding did not accrue until the individual disposes of the qualifying investment, and *subsection (2)(b)* shall apply for the purposes of this subsection as it applies for the purposes of *subsection (2)*.

(b) No repayment of tax under this subsection shall carry interest.

(4) *Subsection (2)* shall not apply if part only of the amount or value of the consideration for the material disposal of the original holding is applied, within the period of 3 years from the date of that disposal, in acquiring a qualifying investment but, if all of the amount of that consideration except for a part which is less than the amount of the gain accruing on the disposal is so applied, the reinvestor shall, on making a claim in that behalf, be treated for the purposes of the Capital Gains Tax Acts as if the amount of the gain accruing on the disposal were reduced to the amount of the consideration not applied in acquiring a qualifying investment, and the balance of the gain shall be treated as if it did not accrue until the reinvestor disposes of the qualifying investment.

(5) For the purposes of this section, the disposal of shares in or securities of a company shall be a material disposal if—

(a) throughout the period of 3 years ending with the date of the disposal, or

(b) in a case where the company commenced to trade at any time in the period mentioned in *paragraph (a)*, throughout the period beginning at that time and ending with the date of the disposal,

the following conditions are satisfied—

(i) the company has been a trading company or a holding company, and

(ii) the reinvestor has been a full-time employee, part-time employee, full-time director or part-time director of the company or, if that company is a member of a trading group, of one or more companies which are members of the trading group.

(6) For the purposes of this section, an individual shall be regarded as acquiring a qualifying investment where he or she acquires any eligible shares in a qualifying company if—

(a) he or she holds not less than 5 per cent of the ordinary share capital of the company at any time in the period (in this subsection referred to as "*the initial period*") beginning on the date of the acquisition of the eligible shares and ending on the date which is one year after the date of the disposal of the original holding,

(b) he or she holds not less than 15 per cent of the ordinary share capital of the company at any time in the period (in this section referred to as "*the specified period*") beginning on the date of the acquisition of the eligible shares and ending on the date which is 3 years after the date of the disposal of the original holding,

(c) within the specified period, the company uses the money raised through the issue of the eligible shares for the purposes of enabling it, or enlarging its capacity, to undertake qualifying trading operations (within the meaning of *subsection (8)*),

(d) the company is not—

(i) the company in which the original holding has subsisted, or

(ii) a company that was a member of the same trading group as that company,

and

(e) he or she becomes at any time within the initial period, and is throughout the period beginning at that time and—

(i) ending at the end of the specified period, or

(ii) in a case where the company is wound up or dissolved without winding up and the conditions mentioned in *subsection (7)(d)* are satisfied, ending at the time of the commencement of the winding up or dissolution of the company,

a full-time employee or a full-time director of the company.

(7) (a) For the purposes of this section and subject to *paragraphs (b)* to *(d)*, a company shall be a qualifying company if it is incorporated in the State and if—

(i) it is throughout the specified period—

(I) an unquoted company resident in the State and not resident elsewhere, and

(II) a company which exists wholly for the purposes of carrying on wholly or mainly in the State of one or more qualifying trades,

and

(ii) it is not at any time in the specified period—

(I) under the control of another company (or of another company and any person connected with that other company), or

(II) without being under the control of another company, a 51 per cent subsidiary of that other company.

(b) A company shall be deemed not to have ceased to be a qualifying company solely by virtue of shares in the company commencing, at any time in the specified period, to be quoted on the market known as the Developing Companies Market of the Irish Stock Exchange.

(c) A company shall cease to be a qualifying company if at any time in the specified period a resolution is passed, or an order is made, for the winding up of the company (or in the case of a winding up otherwise than under the Companies Act, 1963, any other act is done for the like purpose) or the company is dissolved without winding up.

(d) Notwithstanding *paragraph (c)*, a company shall be deemed not to have ceased to be a qualifying company solely by virtue of the application of that paragraph where—

(i) it is shown that the winding up or dissolution is for bona fide commercial reasons and does not form part of a scheme or arrangement the main purpose or one of the main purposes of which is the avoidance of income tax, corporation tax or capital gains tax, and

(ii) the company's net assets, if any, are distributed to its members within 3 years from the commencement of the dissolution or the winding up.

(8) (a) In this subsection, "*qualifying trading operations*", in relation to a trade, means all the operations of the trade excluding those of dealing in shares, securities, land, currencies, futures or traded options.

(b) A trade shall be a qualifying trade for the purposes of *subsection (7)* if throughout the specified period the trade—

(i) is conducted on a commercial basis and with a view to the realisation of profits, and

(ii) consists wholly or mainly of qualifying trading operations,

and a trade which during the specified period consists partly of qualifying trading operations and partly of other trading operations shall be regarded for the purposes of this subsection as a trade which consists wholly or mainly of qualifying trading operations only if the total amount receivable in the specified period by the company carrying on the trade from sales made and services rendered in the course of qualifying trading operations is not less than 75 per cent of the total amount receivable by the company from all sales made and services rendered in the course of the trade in the specified period.

(9) A claim for relief under this section may be made after the making of a material disposal and the acquisition of eligible shares in a qualifying company if all the conditions for the relief are or will be satisfied, but the relief shall be withdrawn if, by reason of the subsequent happening of any event or failure of an event to happen which at the time the relief was claimed was expected to happen, the individual by whom the relief was claimed is not entitled to the relief so claimed.

(10) The withdrawal of relief under *subsection (9)* shall be made—

(a) for the year of assessment in which the happening or failure to happen, as the case may be, of the event giving rise to the withdrawal of the relief occurred, and

(b) in accordance with *subsection (11)*,

and both—

(i) details of the happening or the failure to happen, as the case may be, of the event giving rise to the withdrawal of relief, and

(ii) the amount to be treated as a gain under *subsection (11)*,

shall be included in the return required to be made by the individual concerned under [*Chapter 3* of *Part 41A*][2] for that year of assessment.

(11) (a) Notwithstanding any other provision of the Capital Gains Tax Acts, where relief is to be withdrawn under *subsection (9)* for any year of assessment,

such amount (in this subsection referred to as "*the relevant amount*") of the chargeable gain which accrued to the reinvestor on the disposal of the original holding as was treated under *subsection (2)* or *(4)* as not accruing at that time—

(i) reduced in accordance with *paragraph (b)*, and

(ii) increased in accordance with *paragraph (c)*,

shall be treated as a gain which accrued in that year of assessment.

(b) The amount by which the relevant amount is to be reduced under *paragraph (a)(i)* is an amount equal to the aggregate of—

(i) to the extent that such excess has not been deducted in years of assessment subsequent to the year of assessment in which the disposal of the original holding occurred, the excess of the amount of the losses which would have been deducted under *section 31* in the year of assessment in which the disposal of the original holding occurred, if relief under this section had not been claimed, over the amount of such losses which were so deducted in that year, and

(ii) any amount of chargeable gains in the year of assessment in which the disposal of the original holding occurred in respect of which the reinvestor would not by virtue of *section 601* have been charged to capital gains tax if relief under this section had not been claimed.

(c) The amount by which the relevant amount is to be increased under *paragraph (a)(ii)* is an amount determined by the formula—

$$G \times \frac{R}{100} \times M$$

where—

G is the relevant amount reduced in accordance with *paragraph (b)*,

R [is 0.083][3], and

M is the number of months in the period beginning on the date on which capital gains tax for the year of assessment in which the disposal of the original holding occurred was due and payable and ending on the date on which capital gains tax for the year of assessment for which the withdrawal of relief is to be made is due and payable.

(12) A chargeable gain or the balance of a chargeable gain which under *subsection (2)* or *(4)*, as may be appropriate, is treated as accruing at a date later than the date of the disposal on which it accrued shall not be so treated for the purposes of *section 556*.

(13) Without prejudice to the provisions of the Capital Gains Tax Acts providing generally for apportionments, where consideration is given for the acquisition or disposal of any assets some or part of which are shares or other securities to the acquisition or disposal of which a claim under this section relates and some or part of which are not, the consideration shall be apportioned in such manner as is just and reasonable.

(14) This section shall not apply unless the acquisition of a qualifying investment was made for bona fide commercial reasons and not wholly or partly for the purposes of realising a gain from the disposal of the qualifying investment.

Amendments

[1] Substituted by FA03 s67(1)(a).

[2] Substituted by FA12 sched4(part 2)(g).

[3] Substituted by FA05 sched5. Applies to any unpaid income tax, corporation tax or capital gains tax, as the case may be, that has not been paid before 1 April 2005 regardless of when that tax becomes due and payable and notwithstanding anything to the contrary in any other enactment other than section 1082 of TCA97. Does not apply to the part, if any, before 1 January 1963 of any period of delay within the meaning of section 1080 of TCA97.

Cross References

From Section 591

Section 2 Interpretation of Tax Acts.
Section 9 Subsidiaries.
Section 31 Amount chargeable.
Section 116 Interpretation (Chapter 3).
Section 250 Extension of relief under section 248 to certain individuals in relation to loans applied in acquiring interest in certain companies.
Section 488 Interpretation (Part 16).
Section 556 Adjustment of allowable expenditure by reference to consumer price index.
Section 601 Annual exempt amount.
Section 951 Obligation to make a return.

591A Dividends paid in connection with disposals of shares or securities

[(1) For the purposes of this section, a dividend paid, or a distribution made, by a company to a person in respect of shares or securities of the company in connection with a disposal of shares in the company shall be treated as being abnormal if the amount or value of the dividend, or as the case may be the distribution, exceeds the amount that could reasonably have been expected to be paid, or as the case may be made, in respect of the shares or securities of the company if there were no such disposal of the shares or securities.

(2) Where, in connection with the disposal by a person of any shares or securities of a company, there exists any scheme, arrangement or understanding by virtue of which, either directly or indirectly, an abnormal dividend is paid, or an abnormal distribution is made—

(a) where the person is a company, to that person or to any company connected (within the meaning of section 10) with that person, and

(b) where the person is not a company, to any company connected (within the meaning of section 10) with the person,

then, for the purposes of the Capital Gains Tax Acts, the amount or value of the dividend paid, or distribution made, to the person or, as the case may be, to the connected person, shall be treated as consideration received by the person for the disposal of the shares or securities, and shall be ignored for the purposes of the Tax Acts.

(3) Subsection (2) does not apply if it is shown that the scheme, arrangement or understanding is effected for bona fide commercial reasons and is not, or does not form part of, any scheme, arrangement or understanding of which the main purpose or one of the main purposes is avoidance of liability to tax.][1]

Amendments

[1] Inserted by FA08 s51(1). Applies as respects a dividend paid, or a distribution made, on or after 19 February 2008.

Cross References

From Section 591A

Section 10 Connected persons.

592 Reduced rate of capital gains tax on certain disposals of shares by individuals [Repealed]

Repealed by FA98 s70(1). This section shall apply as respects disposals made on or after the 3rd day of December, 1997.

CHAPTER 5

Life Assurance and Deferred Annuities

593 Life assurance and deferred annuities

[CGTA75 s20]

(1) This section shall apply for the purposes of the Capital Gains Tax Acts as respects any policy of assurance or contract for a deferred annuity on the life of any person.

(2) No chargeable gain shall accrue on the disposal of or of an interest in the rights under any such policy of assurance or contract except where the person making the disposal is not the original beneficial owner and acquired the rights or interests for a consideration in money or money's worth.

(3) Subject to *subsection (2)*, the occasion of the payment of the sum or sums assured by a policy of assurance or of the first instalment of a deferred annuity, and the occasion of the surrender of a policy of assurance or of the rights under a contract for a deferred annuity, shall be the occasion of a disposal of the rights under the policy of assurance or contract for a deferred annuity, and the amount of the consideration for the disposal of a contract for a deferred annuity shall be the market value at that time of the right to the first and further instalments of the annuity.

(4) In *subsection (3)*, the reference to payment of the sum assured shall include a reference to the transfer of investments or other assets to the owner of the policy in accordance with the policy.

Cross References

To Section 593

Section 594 Foreign life assurance and deferred annuities: taxation and returns.

Section 595 Life assurance policy or deferred annuity contract entered into or acquired by company.

594 Foreign life assurance and deferred annuities: taxation and returns

[CGTA75 s20A; FA93 s24; FA95 s68; FA97 s74(1)]

(1) (a) (i) For the purposes of this section, a policy of assurance or contract for a deferred annuity on the life of any person, being a policy issued or a contract made before the 20th day of May, 1993, shall be treated as a policy issued or contract made, as the case may be, after that date if there is a variation of the policy or contract on or after that date which directly or indirectly increases the benefits secured by, or extends the term of, the policy or contract, as the case may be.

(ii) For the purposes of *subparagraph (i)*, where a policy of assurance issued or a contract made before the 20th day of May, 1993, provides an option to have another policy or contract substituted for it or to have any of its terms changed, any change in the terms of the policy or contract made in pursuance of the option shall be deemed to be a variation of the policy or contract, as the case may be.

(b) Subject to *subsection (2)*, this section shall be construed together with *subsections (3)* and *(4)* of *section 593* as if *subsection (3)* of that section were not subject to *subsection (2)* of that section.

(c) (i) In this paragraph and in *subsection (3)*—

["*assurance company*" means—

(I) an assurance company within the meaning of section 3 of the Insurance Act 1936, or

(II) a person that holds an authorisation within the meaning of the European Communities (Life Assurance) Framework Regulations 1994 (S.I. No. 360 of 1994);][1]

"*excluded policy*" means a policy of assurance or contract for a deferred annuity on the life of any person where the policy is issued to or the contract is made with, as the case may be, a person who did not continuously reside outside the State throughout the period of 6 months commencing on the date of issue or the date of contract, as the case may be;

"*life assurance fund*" has the same meaning as in the Insurance Acts 1909 to 1969;

"*relevant company*" means a company which is—

(I) resident in the State, or

(II) chargeable under Case III of Schedule D by virtue of *section 726* in respect of its income from the investment of its life assurance fund.

(ii) *Subsection (2)* shall apply to any policy of assurance or contract for a deferred annuity on the life of any person which is a policy issued or a contract made, as the case may be, […][2]—

(I) otherwise than by an assurance company which is a relevant company, or

(II) being a policy or contract which is an excluded policy issued or made, as the case may be, by a relevant company to which *section 710(2)* applies.

[(iii) *Subsection (2)* shall apply as if *section 573(2)(b)* had not been enacted.

(iv) For the purposes of *subsection (2)*—

(I) there shall be a disposal of or of an interest in the rights of a policy of assurance, where benefits are payable under the policy, and

(II) where at any time, a policy of assurance, or an interest therein, gives rise to benefits in respect of death or disability, either on or before maturity of the policy, the amount or value of such benefits which shall be taken into account for the purposes of determining the amount of a gain under that subsection shall be the excess of the value of the policy or, as the case may be, the interest therein, immediately before that time, over the value of the policy or, as the case may be, the interest therein, immediately after that time.

(v) For the purposes of *subparagraph (iv)*, the value of a policy or of an interest therein at any time means—

(I) in the case of a policy which has a surrender value, the surrender value of the policy or, as the case may be, of the interest therein, at that time, and,

(II) in the case of a policy which does not have a surrender value, the market value of the rights or other benefits conferred by the policy or, as the case may be, the interest therein, at that time.][3]

(2) (a) In this subsection, "*relevant gain*" means a chargeable gain arising on a disposal of or of an interest in the rights under any policy of assurance or contract for a deferred annuity to which this subsection applies, including a disposal by a person who is not the original beneficial owner of those rights and who acquired them or an interest in them for a consideration in money or money's worth.

(b) *Section 593(2)* shall not apply in respect of any disposal of or of any interest in the rights under any policy of assurance or contract for a deferred annuity to which this subsection applies.

(c) A relevant gain shall be computed as if *section 556* had not been enacted.

(d) Notwithstanding *section 31*, the total amount of chargeable gains accruing to a person chargeable in a year of assessment after deducting any allowable losses shall not be less than the total amount of any relevant gains accruing to the person in that year, and accordingly any deduction for allowable losses made in computing the total amount of chargeable gains so accruing shall not exceed the total amount of chargeable gains so accruing which are not relevant gains.

(e) Notwithstanding *section 601* or *1028(4)*, an individual shall be charged to capital gains tax on the amount of any relevant gains accruing to the individual.

[(f) Notwithstanding *subsection (3)* of *section 28*, the rate of capital gains tax in respect of a relevant gain accruing to a person shall be 40 per cent][4]

[(g) Where a policy was issued or a contract made before 20 May 1993, only so much of the gain on disposal as accrued on or after 20 March 2001 shall be a chargeable gain][5]

[…][6]

(4)

[(a) in this subsection, "*reinsurance contract*" means any contract or other agreement for reassurance or reinsurance in respect of—

(i) any policy of assurance on the life of any person, or

(ii) any class of such policies, not being new basis business within the meaning of section 730A.][7]

(b) Where apart from this paragraph a reinsurance contract would not be a policy of assurance on the life of any person for the purposes of the Capital Gains Tax Acts, it shall be deemed to be such a policy for those purposes.

(c) *Subsections (2)* and *(3)* shall not apply to, and shall be deemed never to have applied to, reinsurance contracts; but, where apart from this paragraph a reinsurance contract would not be a relevant policy within the meaning of *section 595* for the purposes of that section, it shall be deemed not to be such a policy for those purposes.

(d) (i) Subject to *paragraph (e)*, where *subsection (2)* would (apart from *paragraph (c)*) apply to a reinsurance contract in respect of any policy of assurance on the life of any person, being a policy issued on or after the 1st day of January, 1995, *section 593(2)* shall not apply in respect of any disposal or deemed disposal on or after the 1st day of January, 1995, of, or of any interest in, rights of the insured company under the reinsurance contract to the extent that—

(I) those rights refer to that policy, and

(II) the insured company could receive, otherwise than on the death, disablement or disease of any person or one of a class of persons to whom that policy refers, payment on a disposal of those rights the aggregate amount of which would exceed the aggregate amount of payment made by it in respect of those rights.

(ii) *Subparagraph (i)* shall apply as if—

(I) as respects any reinsurance contract made before the 20th day of May, 1993, that contract were made on that day, and

(II) as respects any reinsurance contract made or modified on or after the 1st day of January, 1995, there were deleted from *subparagraph (i)* "being a policy issued on or after the 1st day of January, 1995,".

(iii) *Subparagraphs (i)* and *(ii)* of *subsection (1)(a)* shall apply for the purposes of this paragraph as if for "the 20th day of May, 1993" there were substituted "the 1st day of January, 1995".

(e) *Paragraph (d)* shall not apply to any disposal of or of any interest in rights under a reinsurance contract, being a disposal resulting directly from the death, disablement or disease of a person or one of a class of persons to whom the reinsurance contract refers; but in computing any gain or loss in respect of a disposal or deemed disposal of or of any interest in rights of the insured company under a reinsurance contract—

(i) there shall be excluded from the sums allowable under *section 552* so much of any payment made by the insured company under the reinsurance contract as is paid in respect of an entitlement to a payment on the death, disablement or disease of a person, or one of a class of persons, and

(ii) there shall be added to the consideration taken into account under *Chapter 2* of this Part the market value of an entitlement for any period, commencing on or after the most recent acquisition or deemed acquisition by the insured company of those rights, to a payment on the death, disablement or disease of a person, or one of a class of persons, to the extent that the insured company held the entitlement for that period in place of any return which would otherwise have accrued under the reinsurance contract and increased that consideration.

Amendments

[1] Substituted by FA06 s59(1)(b). This section is deemed to have applied as on and from 20 December 2000.

[2] Deleted by FA01 s66(1)(a)(i). Applies as on and from 20 March 2001.

[3] Inserted by FA01 s66(1)(a)(ii). Applies as on and from 20 March 2001.

[4] Inserted by FA98 s65(1)(b). Applies as respects in relation to disposals made on or after the 12th day of February, 1998.

[5] Inserted by FA01 s66(1)(a)(iii). Applies as on and from 20 March 2001.

[6] Deleted by FA01 s66(1)(b). Applies in respect of any chargeable period commencing on or after 15 February 2001.

[7] Substituted by FA01 s66(1)(c). Shall be deemed to have applied as on and from 1 January 2001.

Cross References

From Section 594

Section 28 Taxation of capital gains and rate of charge.
Section 31 Amount chargeable.
Section 544 Interpretation and general (Chapter 2).
Section 552 Acquisition, enhancement and disposal costs.
Section 556 Adjustment of allowable expenditure by reference to consumer price index.
Section 573 Death.
Section 593 Life assurance and deferred annuities.
Section 595 Life assurance policy or deferred annuity contract entered into or acquired by company.
Section 601 Annual exempt amount.
Section 710 Profits of life business.
Section 726 Investment income.
Section 1028 Married persons.

To Section 594

Section 595 Life assurance policy or deferred annuity contract entered into or acquired by company.
Section 720 Gains or losses arising by virtue of section 719.
Section 730K Disposal of foreign life policy.

595 Life assurance policy or deferred annuity contract entered into or acquired by company

[CGTA75 s20B; FA94 s58]

(1) (a) In this section—

"*relevant disposal*" means a disposal of or an interest in the rights under any relevant policy, other than—

(i) a disposal by a person who is not the original beneficial owner of those rights and who acquired them or an interest in them for a consideration in money or money's worth, or

(ii) a disposal resulting directly from the death, disablement or disease of a person, or one of a class of persons, specified in the terms of the policy;

"*relevant gain*" means a chargeable gain arising on a relevant disposal;

["*relevant policy*" means a policy of life assurance or a contract for a deferred annuity on the life of a person, entered into or acquired by a company on or after 11 April 1994, which is not—

(a) a policy to which *section 594* applies, or

(b) new basis business within the meaning of *section 730A* (inserted by the Finance Act, 2000).][1]

(b) (i) For the purposes of this section, a policy of assurance or a contract for a deferred annuity on the life of any person, entered into by a company before the 11th day of April, 1994, shall be treated as a policy or contract, as the case may be, entered into on or after that date if there is a variation of the policy or contract on or after that date which directly or indirectly increases the benefits secured by, or extends the term of, the policy or contract, as the case may be.

(ii) For the purposes of *subparagraph (i)*, where a policy or contract entered into by a company before the 11th day of April, 1994, provides an option to have another policy or contract substituted for it or to have any of its terms changed, any change in the terms of the policy or contract which is made in pursuance of the option shall be deemed to be a variation of the policy or contract, as the case may be.

(c) Subject to *subsection (2)*, this section shall be construed together with *subsections (3)* and *(4)* of *section 593*, as if *subsection (3)* of that section were not subject to *subsection (2)* of that section.

(2) *Section 593(2)* shall not apply in respect of any relevant disposal.

(3) (a) For the purposes of the Corporation Tax Acts—

(i) any relevant gain arising to a company shall be treated as if it were the net amount of a gain from the gross amount of which corporation tax has been deducted at the standard rate (within the meaning of *section 3*) of income tax,

(ii) the amount to be taken into account in respect of the relevant gain in computing in accordance with *section 78* the company's chargeable gains, for the accounting period in which the relevant gain arises, shall be that gross amount, and

(iii) the corporation tax treated as deducted from that gross amount shall—

(I) be set off against the corporation tax assessable on the company for that accounting period, or

(II) in so far as it cannot be set off in accordance with *clause (I)*, be repaid to the company.

(b) *Paragraph (a)* shall be disregarded for the purposes of *section 546(2)*.

(c) This subsection shall be construed together with the Corporation Tax Acts.

(4) For the purposes of this section, a contract, being a policy of life assurance or a contract for a deferred annuity on the life of any person, shall be treated as having been entered into by a company before the 11th day of April, 1994, if—

(a) (i) a document referable to the contract was served on the company in pursuance of section 52 of the Insurance Act, 1989, before the 11th day of April, 1994, and

(ii) the company entered into the contract on or before the 22nd day of April, 1994,

or

(b) (i) the contract was entered into before the 30th day of June, 1994, by the company,

(ii) before the 11th day of April, 1994—

(I) there was in existence a binding agreement in writing under which the company was obliged to acquire land, and

(II) preliminary commitments or agreements had been entered into by the company—

(A) to obtain a loan, which was to be secured on the land, to defray money applied in acquiring the land, and

(B) to enter into the contract primarily for the purpose of repaying the loan,

and

(iii) the agreement under which the loan was advanced obliges the company to apply any payment made to it under the contract to the repayment of the loan before any other application by it of such payment.

Amendments

[1] Substituted by FA00 s55.

Revenue Briefings

Tax Briefing

Tax Briefing September 2000 – Issue 41 pg 21 – Life Assurance Companies – New Regime

Cross References

From Section 595

Section 3 Interpretation of Income Tax Acts.

Section 78 Computation of companies' chargeable gains.

Section 546 Allowable losses.

Section 593 Life assurance and deferred annuities.

Section 594 Foreign life assurance and deferred annuities: taxation and returns.

Section 730A Profits of life business: new basis.

To Section 595

Section 594 Foreign life assurance and deferred annuities: taxation and returns.

CHAPTER 6

Transfer of Business Assets

596 Appropriations to and from stock in trade

[CGTA75 s51(1) and Sch1 par15; FA90 s86]

(1) Where an asset acquired by a person otherwise than as trading stock of a trade carried on by the person is appropriated by that person for the purposes of the trade as trading stock (whether on the commencement of the trade or otherwise) and, if that person had then sold the asset for its market value, a chargeable gain or allowable loss would have accrued to that person, that person shall be treated for the purposes of the Capital Gains Tax Acts as having by such appropriation disposed of the asset by selling it for its then market value.

(2) Where at any time an asset forming part of the trading stock of a person's trade is appropriated by the person for any other purpose or is retained by the person on that person ceasing to carry on the trade, that person shall be treated for the purposes of the Capital Gains Tax Acts as having acquired the asset at that time for a consideration equal to the amount brought into the accounts of the trade in respect of the asset for the purposes of income tax on the appropriation or on that person ceasing to carry on the trade, as the case may be.

(3) *Subsection (1)* shall not apply in relation to a person's appropriation of an asset for the purposes of a trade if the person is chargeable to income tax in respect of the profits of the trade under Case I of Schedule D, and instead elects that the market value of the asset at the time of the appropriation shall, in computing the profits of the trade for the purposes of income tax, be treated as reduced by the amount of the chargeable gain or increased by the amount of the allowable loss referred to in that subsection and, where that subsection does not apply by reason of such an election, the profits of the trade shall be computed accordingly; but—

(a) if a person making an election under this subsection is at the time of the appropriation carrying on the trade in partnership with others, the election shall not have effect unless concurred in by the others, and

(b) an election under this subsection shall not be made in any case where the application of *subsection (1)* would give rise to an allowable loss.

Cross References

To Section 596

Section 380R Relocation allowance.
Section 618 Transfers of trading stock within group.
Section 644 Provisions supplementary to section 643.
Section 1028 Married persons.
Schedule 25A Exemption from Tax in the Case of Gains on Certain Disposals of Shares

597 Replacement of business and other assets

[CGTA75 s28; CGT(A)A78 s9]

(1) In this section, "*farming*", "*trade*", "*profession*", "*office*" and "*employment*" have the same meanings respectively as in the Income Tax Acts, but not so as to apply the provisions of those Acts as to the circumstances in which, on a change in the persons carrying on a trade, a trade is to be regarded as discontinued or as set up and commenced, and "a trade of dealing in or developing land" shall include a business of dealing in or developing land regarded as a trade under those Acts.

(2) This section shall apply with the necessary modifications in relation to—

(a) the discharge of the functions of a public authority,

(b) the occupation of woodlands where the woodlands are managed by the occupier on a commercial basis and with a view to the realisation of profits,

(c) a profession, office or employment,

(d) such of the activities of a body of persons whose activities are carried on otherwise than for profit and are wholly or mainly directed to the protection or promotion of the interests of its members in the carrying on of their trade or profession as are so directed,

(e) the activities of a body of persons, being a body not established for profit whose activities are wholly or mainly carried on otherwise than for profit, but in the case of assets within *subsection (3)(b)* only if they are both occupied and used by the body and in the case of other specified assets only if they are used by the body,

(f) such of the activities of a body of persons established for the sole purpose of promoting athletic or amateur games or sports as are directed to that purpose, and

(g) farming,

as it applies in relation to a trade.

(3) The following shall be assets for the purpose of this section—

(a) plant or machinery;

(b) except where the trade is a trade of dealing in or developing land, or of providing services for the occupier of land in which the person carrying on the trade has an estate or interest—

(i) any building or part of a building and any permanent or semi-permanent structure in the nature of a building occupied (as well as used) only for the purposes of the trade,

(ii) any land occupied (as well as used) only for the purposes of the trade, provided that where the trade is a trade of dealing in or developing land, but a profit on the sale of any land held for the purposes of the trade would not form part of the trading profits, the trade shall be treated for the purposes of this subsection as if it were not a trade of dealing in or developing land;

[(c) goodwill,

(d) any financial assets owned by a body of persons referred to in *paragraph (f)* of *subsection (2)*; for the purposes of this paragraph "*financial assets*" means shares of any company and stocks, bonds and obligations of any government, municipal corporation, company or other body corporate.][1]

(4) (a) Where—

(i) the consideration which a person carrying on a trade [obtains for the disposal, before 4 December 2002, of,][2] or of that person's interest in, assets (in this section referred to as "*the old assets*") used only for the purposes of the trade throughout the period of ownership is applied by that person in acquiring other assets, or an interest in other assets (in this section referred to as "*the new assets*"),

(ii) the new assets on their acquisition are taken into use and used only for the purposes of the trade, and

(iii) the old assets and the new assets are assets of a kind specified in *subsection (3)*,

then, the person carrying on the trade shall on making a claim in that behalf be treated for the purposes of the Capital Gains Tax Acts as if the chargeable gain accruing on the old assets did not accrue until that person ceases to use the new assets for the purposes of the trade.

(b) Where the consideration for the disposal of the new assets is applied in acquiring other new assets which on the acquisition are taken into use and used only for the purposes of the trade and are assets specified in *subsection (3)*, then, the person carrying on the trade shall be treated as if the chargeable gain accruing on the disposal of the old assets did not accrue until that person ceases to use the other new assets for the purposes of the trade and any further new assets which are acquired in a similar manner, taken into use, and used only, for the purposes of the trade and are assets specified in *subsection (3)*.

(5) *Subsection (4)* shall not apply if part only of the amount or value of the consideration for the disposal of or of the interest in the old assets is applied as described in that subsection, but if all of the amount or value of the consideration except for a part which is less than the amount of the gain (whether all chargeable gain or not) accruing on the disposal of or of the interest in the old assets is so applied, then, the person carrying on the trade shall on making a claim in that behalf be treated for the purposes of the Capital Gains Tax Acts as if the amount of the gain accruing on the disposal of the old assets were reduced to the amount of consideration not applied in the acquisition of the new assets (and if not all chargeable gain with a proportionate reduction in the amount of the chargeable gain) and the balance of the gain (or chargeable gain) shall be treated as if it did not accrue until that person ceases to use the new assets for the purposes of the trade.

(6) A chargeable gain or the balance of a chargeable gain which under *subsection (4)* or *(5)*, as may be appropriate, is treated as accruing on a date later than the date of the disposal on which it accrued shall not be so treated for the purposes of *section 556*.

(7) This section shall apply only if the acquisition of or of the interest in the new assets takes place, or an unconditional contract for the acquisition is entered into, in the period beginning 12 months before and ending 3 years after the disposal of or of the interest in the old assets, or at such earlier or later time as the Revenue Commissioners may by notice in writing allow; but, where an unconditional contract for the acquisition is so entered into, this section may be applied on a provisional basis without waiting to ascertain whether the new assets are, or the interest in the new assets is, acquired in pursuance of the contract, and when that fact is ascertained all necessary adjustments shall be made by making assessments or by repayment or discharge of tax, and shall be so made notwithstanding any limitation in the Capital Gains Tax Acts on the time within which assessments may be made [or any limitation in section 865(4) on the time within which a claim for a repayment of tax is required to be made][3].

(8) This section shall not apply unless the acquisition of or of the interest in the new assets was made for the purpose of their use in the trade, and not wholly or partly for the purpose of realising a gain from the disposal of or of the interest in the new assets.

(9) Where over the period of ownership or any substantial part of the period of ownership part of a building or structure is, and part is not, used for the purposes of a trade, this section shall apply as if the part so used, together with any land occupied for purposes ancillary to the occupation and use of that part of the building or structure, were a separate asset, and subject to any necessary apportionments of consideration for an acquisition or disposal of or of an interest in the building or structure and other land.

(10) Where the old assets were not used for the purposes of the trade throughout the period of ownership, this section shall apply as if a part of the asset representing its use for the purposes of the trade, having regard to the time and extent to which it was and was not used for those purposes, were a separate asset which had been wholly used for the purposes of the trade, and this subsection shall apply in relation to that part subject to any necessary apportionment of consideration for an acquisition or disposal of or of the interest in the asset.

(11) (a) This section shall apply in relation to a person who carries on 2 or more trades which are in different localities, but which are concerned wholly or mainly with goods or services of the same kind, as if, in relation to the assets used for the purposes of the trades, the trades were the same trade.

(b) This section shall apply in relation to a person who ceases to carry on a trade or trades (in this paragraph referred to as "*the old trade or trades*") which the person has carried on for a period of 10 years or more and commences to carry on another trade or trades (in this paragraph referred to as "*the new trade or trades*") within a period of 2 years from the date on which the person ceased to carry on the old trade or trades as if, in relation to the old assets used for the purposes of one of the old trades and the new assets used for the purposes of the new trade, the 2 trades were the same trade.

(12) Without prejudice to the provisions of the Capital Gains Tax Acts providing generally for apportionments, where consideration is given for the acquisition or disposal of assets some or part of which are assets in relation to which a claim under *subsection (4)* or *(5)* applies, and some or part of which are not, the consideration shall be apportioned in such manner as is just and reasonable.

Amendments

[1] Substituted by FA98 s71(1). This section shall apply as respects disposals made on or after 27 March 1998

[2] Substituted by FA03 s67(1)(b). does not apply— as respects paragraph (b), to a disposal by a person, on or after 4 December 2002 and on or before 31 December 2003, of an asset used for the purposes of the person's trade (or any other activity of the person as is referred to in section 597(2)), where the person claims that, but for the provisions of subsection (1)(b),the person would have been entitled to claim that the chargeable gain accruing on that disposal could not accrue to the person until assets, which were acquired by the person before 4 December 2002 or acquired under an unconditional contract entered into by the person before that date, ceased to be used for the purposes of that trade of the person, or, as the case may be, that other activity of the person,

[3] Inserted by FA08 sched6(1)(j). Applies as on and from 31 January 2008.

Revenue Precedents

Where a trade is carried on for less than 10 years and commencement of a similar trade, strictly, relief is not due as section 597(ii)(b) requires that the old trade be carried on for at least 10 years. However, section 597(ii)(a) allows relief where two trades, wholly or mainly concerned with goods or services of the same kind are carried on. This is read as applying where the trades are carried on simultaneously or successively, thus covering a cessation of one trade and the commencement of a similar trade. G10(E).

Cross References

From Section 597

Section 556 Adjustment of allowable expenditure by reference to consumer price index.
Section 865 Repayment of tax.

To Section 597

Section 544 Interpretation and general (Chapter 2).
Section 579B Trustees ceasing to be resident in the State.
Section 579E Trustees ceasing to be liable to Irish tax.
Section 598 Disposals of business or farm on "retirement".
Section 620 Replacement of business assets by members of group.
Section 620A Deemed disposal in certain circumstances.
Section 623 Company ceasing to be member of group.
Section 627 Deemed disposal of assets.
Section 652 Non-application of reliefs on replacement of assets in case of relevant disposals.
Section 689 Restriction of relief for losses on certain disposals.
Section 978 Gifts: recovery of capital gains tax from donee.

Schedule 17 Reorganisation into Companies of Trustee Savings Banks
Schedule 26 Replacement of Harbour Authorities by Port Companies

597A Entrepreneur relief

[(1) In this section—

'*chargeable business asset*' means an asset, including goodwill but not including shares (other than shares mentioned in *paragraph (b)*), securities or other assets held as investments, where that asset is acquired at a cost of not less than €10,000 on or after 1 January 2014 but on or before 31 December 2018 and which—

(a) is, or is an interest in, an asset used wholly for the purposes of a new business carried on by a qualifying enterprise, or

(b) is a holding of new ordinary shares, issued on or after 1 January 2014—

(i) in a qualifying company carrying on new business, or

(ii) in a holding company which owns 100 per cent of the ordinary share capital of a qualifying company carrying on new business,

of which an individual claiming relief under this section—

(I) owns not less than 15 per cent of the ordinary share capital of the qualifying company or the holding company, and

(II) is a full-time working director of the qualifying company,

other than an asset on the disposal of which no gain accruing would be a chargeable gain;

'*full-time working director*', in relation to a qualifying company, means a director required to devote substantially the whole of his or her time to the service of the company in a managerial or technical capacity;

'*holding company*' means a company that is not listed on the official list of any stock exchange whose business consists wholly of holding shares in a qualifying company;

'*initial risk finance investment*' means the funding of the qualifying enterprise for the purpose of new business which funding—

(a) must not exceed a total of €15 million,

(b) is provided in full within 6 months of the commencement of the new business, and

(c) includes equity or investment or both;

'*new business*' means relevant trading activities carried on—

(a) by a qualifying enterprise (to which *paragraph (a)* of the definition of 'qualifying enterprise' applies) that were not, prior to 1 January 2014, carried on by that qualifying enterprise or by any person connected (within the meaning of *section 10*) with that qualifying 10 enterprise, or

(b) by a qualifying enterprise (to which *paragraph (b)* of the definition of 'qualifying enterprise' applies) that were not, prior to 1 January 2014, carried on by that qualifying enterprise or by any person connected (within the meaning of *section 10*) with that qualifying enterprise,

but shall not include any relevant trading activities the products, goods or services of which are substantially the same as products, goods or services previously provided by any individual claiming relief under this section or by any person connected with that individual;

'*qualifying company*' is a company that is a qualifying enterprise and which, at the time of the making of the initial risk finance investment, is not listed on the official list of any stock exchange;

'*qualifying enterprise*' means an enterprise which, at the time of the making of the initial risk finance investment, is a micro, small or medium-sized enterprise, as defined in Article 2 of the Annex to Commission Recommendation 2003/361/EC of 6 May 2003* and which—

*OJ No. L124, 20.5.2003, p.36

(a) has not been carrying on any business, trade or profession, or

(b) has been carrying on a business, trade or profession for less than 7 years;

'*relevant trading activities*' has the same meaning as it has in *section 488* and includes farming (within the meaning of *section 654*).

(2) An individual who—

(a) on or after 1 January 2010, has made a disposal of an asset on which capital gains tax has been paid, and

(b) on or after 1 January 2014 but on or before 31 December 2018, applies an amount equal to all or part of the consideration received on that disposal (after deducting any capital gains tax paid on that disposal) as an initial risk finance investment in acquiring chargeable business assets,

shall be entitled to a tax credit against capital gains tax liability arising on a subsequent disposal of, or of an interest in, those chargeable business assets made more than 3 years after they were acquired, in an amount equal to the lower of—

(i) that part of the capital gains tax paid on the disposal of the first-mentioned asset in the proportion that the amount applied as an initial risk finance investment bears to the consideration received on the first-mentioned disposal (after deducting any capital gains tax paid), and

(ii) 50 per cent of the capital gains tax payable on the disposal of the chargeable business asset.

(3) Where on a subsequent disposal of the chargeable business assets referred to in *subsection (2)*, an amount equal to all or part of the consideration (after deducting any capital gains tax paid on that disposal) applied as initial risk finance investment is, in turn, applied as an initial risk finance investment on or after 1 January 2014 but on or before 31 December 2018, in acquiring other chargeable business assets (in this subsection referred to as 'the new chargeable business assets'), the individual shall similarly be entitled to a tax credit against capital gains tax liability arising on a subsequent disposal of, or of an interest in, those new chargeable business assets made more than 3 years after they were acquired, in an amount equal to the lower of—

(a) that part of the capital gains tax paid on the disposal of the first- mentioned chargeable business asset in the proportion that the amount applied as an initial risk finance investment bears to the consideration received on that disposal (after deducting any capital gains tax paid), and

(b) 50 per cent of the capital gains tax payable on the disposal of the new chargeable business asset.

(4) Where for *bona fide* commercial reasons, a person making a disposal of a chargeable business asset first transfers that asset to a wholly owned company followed immediately by the disposal of the shares in that company to the person making the acquisition, the tax credit under *subsection (2)* or *(3)*, as appropriate, shall apply to the disposal of the shares in the company to which the chargeable business asset was transferred as it would have applied if the chargeable business asset had been disposed of directly to the person making the acquisition.

(5) *Subsection (4)* shall not apply where the transfer of the chargeable business asset to a wholly owned company is an arrangement or part of an arrangement the main purpose or one of the main purposes of which is to secure a tax advantage within the meaning of *section 546A*.][1]

Amendments

[1] Substituted by FA14 s52(1). Comes into operation with effect from 1 January 2014.

598 Disposals of business or farm on "*retirement*"

[CGTA75 s26(1) to (6); FA90 s84(c)(iii); FA91 s42(b); FA95 s71(1); FA96 s60(1)]

(1) (a) In this section and in *section 599*—

["*certificate*" has the same meaning as it has for the purposes of Regulation 8(8)(*c*)(ii) of the European Communities (Milk Quota) Regulations 2000 (S.I. No. 94 of 2000) as amended or extended from time to time;][1]

"*chargeable business asset*" means an asset (including goodwill but not including shares or securities or other assets held as investments) which is, or is an interest in, an asset used for the purposes of farming, or a trade, profession, office or employment, carried on by—

(i) the individual,

(ii) the individual's family company, or

(iii) a company which is a member of a trading group of which the holding company is the individual's family company,

other than an asset on the disposal of which no gain accruing would be a chargeable gain;

"*family company*", in relation to an individual, means, subject to *paragraph (b)*, a company the voting rights in which are—

(i) as to not less than 25 per cent, exercised by the individual, or

(ii) as to not less than 75 per cent, [exercisable by the individual, his or her civil partner, a member of the individual's family, or a member of the family of the civil partner of the individual, and,][2] as to not less than 10 per cent, exercisable by the individual himself or herself;

"*family*", in relation to an individual, means the husband or wife of the individual, and a relative of the individual or of the individual's husband or wife, and "*relative*" means brother, sister, ancestor or lineal descendant;

["*family of the civil partner*", in relation to an individual, means any brother, sister, ancestor or lineal descendant of the civil partner;][3]

"*full-time working director*" means a director required to devote substantially the whole of his or her time to the service of the company in a managerial or technical capacity;

"*holding company*" means a company whose business (disregarding any trade carried on by it) consists wholly or mainly of the holding of shares or securities of one or more companies which are its 75 per cent subsidiaries;

["*milk production partnership*" has the meaning assigned to it by the European Communities (Milk Quota) Regulations 2000 (S.I. No. 94 of 2000) as amended or extended from time to time;

"*payment entitlement*" has the same meaning as it has for the purposes of [Regulation (EU) No. 1307/2013 of the European Parliament and of the Council of 17 December 2013*][4];][5]

* OJ No. L347 of 20.12.2013, p.608

"*qualifying assets*", in relation to a disposal, includes—

[(i) the chargeable business assets of the individual which apart from tangible moveable property he or she has owned for a period of not less than 10 years ending with the disposal and which have been his or her chargeable business assets throughout the period of 10 years ending with that disposal,][6]

[(ii) (I) the shares or securities, which the individual has owned for a period of not less than 10 years ending with the disposal, being shares or securities of a relevant company that is a company—

(A) which has been a trading company, or a farming company, and the individual's family company, or

(B) which has been a member of a trading group, of which the holding company is the individual's family company,

during a period of not less than 10 years ending with the disposal and the individual has been a working director of the relevant company for a period of not less than 10 years during which period he or she has been a full-time working director of the relevant company for a period of not less than 5 years, and

(II) land, machinery or plant (if any) which the individual has owned for a period of not less than 10 years ending with the disposal, and which—

(A) was used throughout that period for the purposes of the relevant company, and

(B) is disposed of at the same time and to the same person as the shares or securities referred to in *subparagraph (I)*,

[(iia) payment entitlements, where they are disposed of at the same time and to the same person as land to the extent that the land would support a claim to payment in respect of those payment entitlements,][7]

(iii) land used for the purposes of farming carried on by the individual which he or she has owned and used for that purpose for a period of not less than 10 years ending with the transfer of an interest in that land for the purposes of complying with the terms of the Scheme, [...][8]

(iv) land which has been let by the individual at any time in the period of 5 years ending with the disposal, where—

(I) immediately before the time the land was first let in that period, the land was owned by the individual and used for the purposes of farming carried on by the individual for a period of not less than 10 years ending at that time, and

(II) the disposal is a disposal referred to in [*section 652(5)(a)*, and][9]][10]

[(v) land which has been let by the individual at any time in the period of 25 years ending with the disposal where—

(I) immediately before the time the land was first let in that period of 25 years, the land was owned by the individual and used for the purposes of farming carried on by the individual for a period of not less than 10 years ending at that time, and

(II) the disposal is—

(A) to a child (within the meaning of *section 599*) of the individual,

(B) to an individual, other than a child referred to in *clause (A)*, where that disposal occurs on or before 31 December 2016, or

(C) to an individual, other than a child referred to in *clause (A)*, provided the land was let to a person for the purposes of farming during the period of 25 years referred to in *subparagraph (I)* and each letting of the land was for a period of not less than 5 consecutive years;][11]

["*the Scheme*" means the scheme known as—

(i) the Scheme of Early Retirement From Farming introduced by the Minister for Agriculture and Food for the purpose of implementing Council Regulation (EEC) No. 2079/92 of 30 June 1992*, […][12]

* OJ No. L.215, of 30.7.92, p.91.

(ii) the Scheme of Early Retirement From Farming introduced by the Minister for Agriculture, Food and Rural Development for the purpose of implementing Council Regulation (EC) No. 1257/1999 of 17 May 1999*, [or][13]][14]

* OJ No. L.160, of 26.6.99, p.80.

[(iii) the Scheme of Early Retirement From Farming introduced by the Minister for Agriculture and Food for the purpose of implementing Council Regulation (EC) No. 1698/2005 of 20 September 2005*;][15]

* OJ No. L277 of 21 October 2005, p.1

"*trade*", "*farming*", "*profession*", "*office*" and "*employment*" have the same meanings respectively as in the Income Tax Acts;

"*trading company*" means a company whose business consists wholly or mainly of the carrying on of one or more trades or professions;

"*trading group*" means a group of companies consisting of the holding company and its 75 per cent subsidiaries, the business of whose members taken together consists wholly or mainly of the carrying on of one or more trades or professions;

"*75 per cent subsidiary*" has the meaning assigned to it by *section 9*.

(b) For the purposes of the definition of "*family company*", where a company which is a holding company would not but for this paragraph be an individual's family company, but would be such a company if the individual had not at any time on or after the 6th day of April, 1987, and before the 6th day of April, 1990, disposed of shares in the company to a child (within the meaning of *section 599*) of the individual, the company shall be deemed to be the individual's family company.

(c) In this section, references to the disposal of the whole or part of an individual's qualifying assets include references to the disposal of the whole or part of the assets provided or held for the purposes of an office or employment by the individual exercising that office or employment.

(d) For the purposes of the definition of "*qualifying assets*", there shall be taken into account—

[(i) (I) the period of ownership of an asset by a [spouse or civil partner][16] of an individual as if it were a period of ownership of the asset by the individual, and

(II) where a [spouse or civil partner][17] of an individual has died, the period of use of an asset by the [spouse or civil partner][18] as if it were a period of use of the asset by the individual,][19]

(ii) where the chargeable business assets are new assets within the meaning of *section 597*, the period of ownership of the old assets as if it were a period of ownership of the new assets,

[(iia) the period for which an individual was a director or, as the case may be, a full-time working director of the following companies as if it were a period for which the individual was a director of a "relevant company" (which, for the purposes of this subparagraph, means a company referred to in *paragraph (ii)* of the definition of qualifying assets in *subsection (1)(a)*):

(I) a company that was treated as being the same company as the relevant company for the purposes of *section 586*,

(II) a company involved in the same scheme of reconstruction or amalgamation under *section 587* with the relevant company,][20]

[(iib) the period of use of land by an individual as a partner in a milk production partnership as if it were also a period of use by the [spouse or civil partner][21] of the individual where the [spouse or civil partner][22]—

(I) is a co-owner of the land,

(II) used the land for a period ending on the date the milk production partnership commenced, and

(III) was issued with a certificate by the Minister for Agriculture and Food,][23]

(iii) where the qualifying assets are shares or securities in a family company to which *section 600* applies, the period immediately before the transfer to the company of chargeable business assets during which those assets were owned by the individual as if it were a period of ownership of the individual of the qualifying assets or a period throughout which he or she was a full-time working director, as may be appropriate, and

(iv) a period immediately before the death of the [spouse or civil partner][24] of the individual throughout which the deceased was a full-time working director as if it were a period throughout which the individual was a full-time working director.

[(e) For the purposes of *paragraph (v)(II)(C)* in the definition of 'qualifying assets', land let under one or more than one conacre agreement before 31 December 2016 shall not affect entitlement to relief under this section, where a letting of the land for a period of 30 not less than 5 consecutive years commences on or before 31 December 2016.][25]

[(2) (a) Subject to this section, where an individual who has attained the age of 55 years but has not attained the age of 66 years disposes of the whole or part of his or her qualifying assets, then—

(i) if the amount or value of the consideration for the disposal does not exceed €750,000, relief shall be given in respect of the full amount of capital gains tax chargeable on any gain accruing on the disposal;

(ii) if the amount or value of the consideration for the disposal exceeds €750,000, the amount of capital gains tax chargeable on the gain accruing on the disposal shall not exceed 50 per cent of the difference between the amount of that consideration and €750,000.

(b) Subject to this section, where an individual who has attained the age of 66 years disposes of the whole or part of his or her qualifying assets on or before 31 December 2013, then—

(i) if the amount or value of the consideration for the disposal does not exceed €750,000, relief shall be given in respect of the full amount of capital gains tax chargeable on any gain accruing on the disposal;

(ii) if the amount or value of the consideration for the disposal exceeds €750,000, the amount of capital gains tax chargeable on the gain accruing on the disposal shall not exceed 50 per cent of the difference between the amount of that consideration and €750,000.

(c) Subject to this section, where an individual who has attained the age of 66 years disposes of the whole or part of his or her qualifying assets on or after 1 January 2014, then—

(i) if the amount or value of the consideration for the disposal does not exceed €500,000, relief shall be given in respect of the full amount of capital gains tax chargeable on any gain accruing on the disposal;

(ii) if the amount or value of the consideration for the disposal exceeds €500,000, the amount of capital gains tax chargeable on the gain accruing on the disposal shall not exceed 50 per cent of the difference between the amount of that consideration and €500,000.

(d) For the purposes of *paragraphs (a)*, *(b)* and *(c)*, the amount of capital gains tax chargeable in respect of the gain shall be the amount of tax which would not have been chargeable but for that gain.][26]

(3) For the purposes of *subsection (2)*, the consideration on the disposal of qualifying assets by the individual shall be aggregated, and nothing in this section shall affect the computation of gains accruing on the disposal of assets other than qualifying assets.

[(3A) Where compensation has been received by a person under the scheme for compensation in respect of the decommissioning of fishing vessels implemented by the Minister for Agriculture, Fisheries and Food in accordance with Council Regulation (EC) No. 1198/2006 of 27 July 2006*, relief under subsection (2) shall apply as if the period referred to in paragraph (i) of the definition of "*qualifying assets*" in subsection (1)(*a*) were 6 years and the age referred to in subsection (2) were 45 years.][27]

* OJ No. L223, 15 August 2006, p.1

(4) Where a disposal of qualifying assets includes a disposal of shares or securities of the individual's family company, the amount of the consideration to be taken into account for the purposes of *subsection (2)* in respect of those shares or securities shall be the proportion of the consideration for those shares or securities which is equal to—

(a) in a case where the individual's family company is not a holding company, the proportion which the part of the value of the company's chargeable assets at the time of the disposal which is attributable to the value of the company's chargeable business assets bears to the whole of that value, and

(b) in a case where the individual's family company is a holding company, the proportion which the part of the value of the chargeable assets of the trading group (excluding shares or securities of one member of the group held by another member of the group) at the time of the disposal which is attributable to the value of the chargeable business assets of the trading group bears to the whole of that value;

but nothing in this section shall affect liability on any gains calculated by reference to the balance of the consideration for the disposal of those shares or securities.

(5) For the purposes of *subsection (4)*, every asset shall be a chargeable asset except one on the disposal of which by the company or a member of the trading group, as the case may be, at the time of the disposal of the shares or securities, no gain accruing to the company or member of the trading group, as the case may be, would be a chargeable gain.

(6) (a) The total of the amounts of relief given under this section for any year of assessment and all years of assessment before such year shall not exceed such amount as would reduce the total amount of capital gains tax chargeable for all those years of assessment below the amount which would be chargeable if the disposals of qualifying assets had all been made in the year of assessment.

(b) Where at any time the relief given under this section exceeds the amount of relief which would be given if the disposals of qualifying assets for the year of assessment and all years of assessment before such year had been made in the year of assessment, any necessary adjustment may be made [by means of assessment or assessment amended][28] [...][29] after the end of the year of assessment in which the last of such disposals is made.

(c) For the purposes of this subsection, [a disposal of qualifying assets other than a disposal of the whole of such assets, by a husband to a wife or by a wife to a husband, or by an individual to his or her civil partner, shall, notwithstanding *section 1028(5)* or *section 1031M(5)*, as the case may be,][30] be taken into account at the market value of the assets.

(7) *Subsection (2)* shall apply where under *section 583* an individual is treated as disposing of interests in shares or securities of his or her family company in consideration of a capital distribution from the company (not being a distribution consisting of chargeable business assets) in the course of dissolving or winding up the company as it applies where he or she disposes of shares or securities of the company.

[(7A) (a) In this subsection "*relevant payment*" means a payment made by a company on the redemption, repayment or purchase of its own shares which, by virtue of *section 176*, is not treated as a distribution for the purposes of *Chapter 2* of *Part 6*.

(b) *Subsection (2)* shall apply where an individual disposes of shares in his or her family company and receives a relevant payment in exchange for that disposal.][31]

[(8) This section shall not apply to a disposal of qualifying assets unless it is shown that the disposal is made for bona fide commercial reasons and does not form part of any arrangement or scheme of which the main purpose or one of the main purposes is the avoidance of liability to tax.][32]

Amendments

[1] Inserted by FA06 s70(1)(a)(i).

[2] Substituted by F(No.3)A11 sched1(158).

[3] Inserted by F(No.3)A11 sched1(159).

[4] Substituted by FA14 sched3(1)(e). Has effect as respects disposals made on or after 1 January 2015.

[5] Inserted by FA06 s70(1)(a)(ii).

[6] Substituted by FA98 s72(1)(a)(i). This section shall apply as respects a disposal of an asset on or after the 6th day of April, 1998.

[7] Inserted by FA06 s70(1)(a)(iii).

[8, 9] Deleted by FA07 s52(1)(a)(i)(I). Applies as respects disposals made on or after the date of 2 April 2007

[10] Substituted by FA02 s59.

[11] Substituted by FA14 s50(1)(a). Applies to disposals made on or after 1 January 2015.

[12] Deleted by F(No.2)A08 sched6(1)(b)(i). This paragraph is deemed to have come into force and have taken effect as respects a disposal of an asset on or after 13 June 2007.

[13] Inserted by F(No.2)A08 sched6(1)(b)(i). This paragraph is deemed to have come into force and have taken effect as respects a disposal of an asset on or after 13 June 2007.

[14] Substituted by FA03 s68(1)(a). This is deemed to have applied as respects a disposal of an asset on or after 27 November 2000.

[15] Inserted by F(No.2)A08 sched6(1)(b)(ii). This paragraph is deemed to have come into force and have taken effect as respects a disposal of an asset on or after 13 June 2007.

[16, 17, 18, 21, 22, 24] Substituted by F(No.3)A11 sched1(160).

[19] Substituted by FA03 s68(1)(b). Applies as respects a disposal of an asset on or after 6 February 2003.

[20] Inserted by FA03 s68(1)(c). Applies as respects a disposal of an asset on or after 6 February 2003.

[23] Inserted by FA06 s70(1)(b).

[25] Inserted by FA14 s50(1)(b). Applies to disposals made on or after 1 January 2015.

[26] Substituted by FA12 s59. Deemed to have come into force and takes effect on and from 1 January 2012.

[27] Inserted by FA08 s54(1)(a)(i). With effect from 1 May 2008 as per S.I. No. 105 of 2008.

[28] Substitued by FA12 sched4(part 2)(g).

[29] Deleted by FA14 s45(1)(a). Applies to disposals giving rise to a clawback of relief under section 598, 599 or 611 where such disposals are made on or after 23 December 2014.

[30] Substituted by F(No.3)A11 sched1(161).

[31] Inserted by FA10 s58(1). This section applies to disposals made on or after 4 February 2010.

[32] Inserted by FA08 s54(1)(a)(ii). Applies to disposals made on or after 31 January 2008.

Case Law

Palmer v Moloney and anor 1999 STC 890 considered the meaning of "full-time working officer" or "employee".

Disposal of milk quota nearly a year after disposing of farm and ceased farming did not constitute a disposal of the whole or part of a business. Wase v Bourke 1996 STC 18

In Davenport v Hasslacher 1997 STC 254 it was held that the phrase "during a period" meant "throughout the entire period of 10 years, and not "at any time during that 10 year period".

Revenue Briefings

Tax Briefing

Tax Briefing April 1997 – Issue 26 pg 17 – Retirement Relief and Liquidations

Tax Briefing June 1999 – Issue 36 pg 14 – Disposal of a Taxi Plate & Land let on Con-Acre

Tax Briefing April 2002 – Issue 47 pg 17 – Retirement Relief and Reconstructions

Tax Briefing August 2005 – Issue 60 – Retirement Relief – Individual disposes of 'qualifying assets' before 55th birthday

Tax Briefing November 2005 – Issue 61 – Tax Implications of the Single Payment Scheme

eBrief

eBrief No.14/2005 – Retirement Relief – Individual disposes of 'qualifying assets' before 55th birthday

eBrief No. 50/2008 – Decommissioning of Fishing Vessels

Revenue Precedents

Revenue accepted that the requirement of S.598 was met in one case where very exceptional circumstances applied. A sole trader was terminally ill. The business required a high level of personal input by him. His wife did not consider that she could manage the business in the period of some months before his death. Had a request made to Revenue without the traders knowledge. The assets had been in the traders' possession for nine years. 4107/97.

In strictness, relief is not due on the transfer of a trade to subsidiary in 10 years prior to disposal as the holding company has not been a holding company throughout the 10 years ending with the disposal. In practice, relief will be allowed where all other requirements of the section are met. G6(N)

A "look through" approach may be taken and the taxpayer will be treated as satisfying both conditions where a holding company is interposed or removed during the 10 years prior to disposal. G6(N)(I)

The shares held by a limited company funded by the International Fund for Ireland with the object of creating employment in a disadvantaged area should be ignored in the determination of whether or not a company is a holding company within the meaning of Section 598(1) Taxes Consolidation Act, 1997. DTX209MISC

Whilst the old lease and the new lease are separate assets, in practice the periods of ownership may be aggregated for the purpose of the 10 year ownership requirement. G6(Q)

Cross References

From Section 598

Section 9 Subsidiaries.

Section 129 Irish resident company distributions not generally chargeable to corporation tax.

Section 130 Matters to be treated as distributions.

Section 176 Purchase of unquoted shares by issuing company or its subsidiary.

Section 583 Capital distributions by companies.

Section 586 Company amalgamations by exchange of shares.

Section 587 Company reconstructions and amalgamations.

Section 597 Replacement of business and other assets.

Section 599 Disposals within family of business or farm.

Section 600 Transfer of business to company.

Section 652 Non-application of reliefs on replacement of assets in case of relevant disposals.
Section 1028 Married persons.

To Section 598

Section 577A Relinquishing of a life interest by the person entitled.
Section 599 Disposals within family of business or farm.
Section 601 Annual exempt amount.

598A Relief on dissolution of farming partnerships

[(1) In this section—

"*farming*" and "*trade*" have the same meanings as in the Income Tax Acts;

"*farming partnership*" means a partnership comprised of individuals which carries on or has carried on the trade of farming; "*relevant asset*" means an asset which is jointly owned by the partners in a farming partnership;

"*relevant disposal*" means a disposal which arises on the occasion of the partition of a relevant asset.

(2) This section applies where a relevant asset has been owned and used for the purposes of farming by the farming partnership for a period of not less than 10 years ending with the relevant disposal.

(3) Notwithstanding subsection (2), where one of the partners acquired his or her share of a relevant asset by way of inheritance, the period of ownership and use of that asset shall be deemed to have commenced on the date on which the person entered into partnership with the other partner or partners in the farming partnership.

(4) Where a relevant disposal arises in respect of a relevant asset, a gain shall not be treated as accruing in respect of that disposal and the relevant asset shall be treated for the purposes of the Capital Gains Tax Acts as having been acquired at the same time and for the same consideration as it was originally acquired by the partner who disposed of that asset.

(5) This section shall not apply if, until the disposal, the asset formed part of the trading stock of the farming trade carried on by the farming partnership or, if the asset is acquired as trading stock, for the purposes of a trade carried on by the partner acquiring the asset.][1]

Amendments

[1] Inserted by FA08 s54(1)(b). Applies to disposals made on or after 13 March 08 and will apply until 31 December 2013.

599 Disposals within family of business or farm

[CGTA75 s27; CGT(A)A78 s8; FA90 s85; FA95 s72; FA96 s132(2) and Sch5 Pt II]

[(1) (a) In this section "*child*", in relation to a disposal for which relief is claimed under this section, includes—

(i) a child of a deceased child,

(ii) a nephew or a niece who has worked substantially on a full-time basis, for the period of 5 years ending with the disposal, in carrying on, or assisting in the carrying on of, the trade, business or profession concerned or the work of, or connected with, the office or employment concerned, and

(iii) an individual (in this [subparagraph][1] referred to as "*the first-mentioned individual*") who resided with, was under the care of and was maintained at the expense of the individual making the disposal throughout—

(I) a period of 5 years, or

(II) periods which together comprised at least 5 years,

before the first-mentioned individual attained the age of 18 years but only if such claim is not based on the uncorroborated testimony of one witness.][2]

[(b) Subject to this section—

(i) where an individual who has attained the age of 55 years but has not attained the age of 66 years disposes of the whole or part of his or her qualifying assets to his or her child, relief shall be given in respect of the capital gains tax chargeable on any gain accruing on the disposal;

(ii) where an individual who has attained the age of 66 years disposes of the whole or part of his or her qualifying assets to his or her child on or before 31 December 2013, relief shall be given in respect of the capital gains tax chargeable on any gain accruing on the disposal;

[(iia) where an individual who has attained the age of 66 years disposes of the whole or part of his or her qualifying assets to his or her child on or after 1 January 2014 and the market value of the qualifying assets is €3,000,000 or less, relief shall be given in respect of the capital gains tax chargeable on any gain accruing on the disposal;][3]

(iii) where an individual who has attained the age of 66 years disposes of the whole or part of his or her qualifying assets to his or her child on or after 1 January 2014 and the market value of the qualifying assets is greater than €3,000,000, relief shall be given in respect of the capital gains tax chargeable on any gain accruing on the disposal as if the consideration for the disposal had been €3,000,000.][4]

[(c) For the purposes of *paragraph (b)*, the capital gains tax chargeable in respect of the gain shall be the amount of tax which would not have been chargeable but for that gain, but nothing in that paragraph shall affect the computation of gains accruing on the disposal of assets other than qualifying assets by an individual who makes a disposal to which that paragraph applies.][5]

[(d) Where the qualifying asset is land used for the purposes of farming and the consideration for its disposal consists in whole or in part of other such land, a gain shall not be treated as arising on the disposal of that other land by the child concerned but that other land shall be treated for the purposes of the Capital Gains Tax Acts as having been acquired by the individual at the same time and for the same value and used by the individual for the same purposes as it was originally acquired and used by the child concerned.][6]

[(2) The consideration on the disposal of qualifying assets by the individual referred to in *subparagraph (iii)* of *subsection (1)(b)* on or after 1 January 2014 shall be aggregated for the purposes of that subparagraph.][7]

(3) *Section 598(4)* shall apply to a disposal within *subsection (1)* as it applies to a disposal within *section 598(2)*.

(4) (a) Where assets comprised in a disposal to a child in respect of which relief has been granted under this section are, within 6 years of the disposal by the individual concerned, disposed of by the child, the capital gains tax which if *subsection (1)* had not applied would have been charged on the individual on his or her disposal of those assets to the child shall be assessed and charged on the child, in addition to any capital gains tax chargeable in respect of the gain accruing to the child on the child's disposal of those assets.

[...][8]

(5) The consideration on a disposal within *subsection (1)* shall not be taken into account for the purposes of aggregation under *section 598(3)*.

[(6) Relief under this section may be claimed, if all other conditions of this section have been met, where a disposal is made to—

(a) a child of the civil partner of the individual,

(b) a child of a deceased child of the civil partner of the individual,

(c) a child of the civil partner of a deceased child of the individual, or

(d) a child of the civil partner of a deceased child of the civil partner of the individual.][9]

Amendments

[1] Substituted by FA13 s47(a). Deemed to have come into force and takes effect on and from 1 January 2013.

[2] Substituted by FA07 s52(1)(b)(i). Applies as respects disposals made on or after the date of 2 April 2007.

[3] Inserted by FA13 s47(b). Deemed to have come into force and takes effect on and from 1 January 2013.

[4] Substituted by FA12 s60. Deemed to have come into force and takes effect on and from 1 January 2012.

[5] Substituted by FA13 s47(c). Deemed to have come into force and takes effect on and from 1 January 2013.

[6] Inserted by FA07 s52(1)(b)(ii). Applies as respects disposals made on or after the date of 2 April 2007.

[7] Substituted by FA13 s47(d). Deemed to have come into force and takes effect on and from 1 January 2013.

[8] Deleted by FA14 s45(1)(b). Applies to disposals giving rise to a clawback of relief under section 598, 599 or 611 where such disposals are made on or after 23 December 2014.

[9] Inserted by F(No.3)A11 sched1(162).

Revenue Briefings

Tax Briefing

Tax Briefing October 2004 – Issue 57 pg 7 – New Time Limits

Tax Briefing August 2005 – Issue 60 – Retirement Relief – Individual disposes of 'qualifying assets' before 55th birthday

Tax Briefing November 2005 – Issue 61 – Tax Implications of the Single Payment Scheme

eBrief

eBrief No.14/2005 – Retirement Relief – Individual disposes of 'qualifying assets' before 55th birthday

Revenue Precedents

If the "share for share" reorganisation comes within S.584 TCA 1997, it will not constitute a disposal for the purposes of S.599(4).

Cross References

From Section 599

Section 598 Disposals of business or farm on "retirement".

To Section 599

Section 577A Relinquishing of a life interest by the person entitled.
Section 598 Disposals of business or farm on "retirement".
Section 601 Annual exempt amount.

600 Transfer of business to company

[CGTA75 s51(1) and Sch2 par6; FA92 s61]

(1) In this section—

"*net chargeable gains*" means chargeable gains less allowable losses;

references to the business, in relation to shares or consideration received in exchange for the business, include references to assets of the business referred to in *subsection (2)*.

(2) This section shall apply for the purposes of the Capital Gains Tax Acts where a person who is not a company transfers to a company a business as a going concern, together with the whole of the assets of the business or together with the whole of those assets other than cash, and the business is so transferred wholly or partly in exchange for shares (in this section referred to as "*the new assets*") issued by the company to the person transferring the business.

(3) The amount determined under *subsection (5)* shall be deducted from the aggregate (in this section referred to as "*the gain on the old assets*") of the net chargeable gains.

(4) For the purpose of computing any chargeable gain accruing on the disposal of any new asset—

(a) the amount determined under *subsection (5)* shall be apportioned between the new assets as a whole, and

(b) the sums allowable as a deduction under *section 552(1)(a)* shall be reduced by the amount apportioned to the new asset under *paragraph (a)*,

and, if the shares which comprise the new assets are not all of the same class, the apportionment between the shares under *paragraph (a)* shall be in accordance with their market values at the time they were acquired by the transferor.

(5) (a) In this subsection, "*the cost of the new assets*" means any sums which would be allowable as a deduction under *section 552(1)(a)* if the new assets were disposed of as a whole in circumstances giving rise to a chargeable gain.

(b) The amount referred to in *subsections (3)* and *(4)(a)* shall be such portion of the gain on the old assets as bears the same proportion to the total of such gains as the cost of the new assets bears to the value of the whole of the consideration received by the transferor in exchange for the business.

(6) This section shall not apply to the transfer by a person of a business to a company wholly or partly in exchange for shares issued by the company, unless it is shown that the transfer is effected for bona fide commercial reasons and does not form part of any arrangement or scheme of which the main purpose or one of the main purposes is avoidance of liability to tax.

Revenue Precedents

Liabilities of the business included in the transfer rank as consideration for the transfer because the discharge of liabilities of the transferor by the transferee is equivalent to the payment of cash by the transferee to the transferor. In practice, however, where an individual transfers a business to a company, in exchange for shares only and assets exceed liabilities, bona fide trade creditors taken over will not be treated as consideration. G5(1).

Cross References

From Section 600

Section 552 Acquisition, enhancement and disposal costs.

To Section 600

Section 177 Conditions as to residence and period of ownership.
Section 598 Disposals of business or farm on "retirement".
Section 747 Deduction of offshore income gain in determining capital gain.
Schedule 20 Offshore Funds: Computation of Offshore Income Gains

600A Replacement of qualifying premises

[(1) In this section—

"*qualifying premises*", in relation to a person, means a building or part of a building, or an interest in a building or a part of a building—

[(a) in which there is one or more residential units,][1]

(b) in respect of which the person is entitled to a rent or to receipts from any easement, and

(c) in respect of which all the requirements of the Regulations are complied with;

"*Regulations*" means—

(i) the Housing (Standards for Rented Houses) Regulations, 1993 (S.I. No. 147 of 1993),

(ii) the Housing (Rent Books) Regulations, 1993 (S.I. No. 146 of 1993), and

(iii) the Housing (Registration of Rented Houses) Regulations, 1996, as amended by the Housing (Registration of Rented Houses) (Amendment) Regulations, 2000 (S.I. No. 12 of 2000);

"*replacement premises*", in relation to a person, means a building or part of a building, or an interest in a building or a part of a building—

(a) which the person acquires with the consideration obtained by the person from the disposal of a qualifying premises,

[(b) in which the number of residential units is—

(i) not less than 3, and

(ii) not less than the number of residential units in the qualifying premises,][2]

(c) in respect of which the person is entitled to a rent or to receipts from any easement, and

(d) in respect of which all the requirements of the Regulations are complied with;

"*residential unit*" means a separately contained part of a residential premises used or suitable for use as a dwelling.

(2) (a) Where the consideration which a person obtains [for the disposal, before 4 December 2002, of][3] a qualifying premises, which was a qualifying premises throughout the period of its ownership by the person, is applied by that person in acquiring a replacement premises, then the person shall, subject to *paragraph (b)*, be treated for the purposes of the Capital

Gains Tax Acts as if the chargeable gain accruing on the disposal of the qualifying premises did not accrue until—

(i) that person disposes of the replacement premises, or

(ii) the replacement premises ceases to be a replacement premises.

(b) Where the consideration for the disposal of the replacement premises is applied by a person in acquiring a further replacement premises then, the person shall be treated as if the chargeable gain accruing on the disposal of the qualifying premises did not accrue until that person disposes of the further replacement premises or any other further replacement premises which are acquired in a similar manner, or that further replacement premises or any other further replacement premises which are acquired in a similar manner, cease to be a replacement premises.

(3) *Subsection (2)* shall not apply if part only of the amount or value of the consideration for the disposal of the qualifying premises is applied as described in that subsection; but if all of the amount or value of the consideration except for a part which is less than the amount of the gain (whether all chargeable or not) accruing on the disposal of the qualifying premises is so applied, then, the person shall on making a claim in that behalf be treated for the purposes of the Capital Gains Tax Acts—

(a) as if the amount of the gain accruing on the disposal of the qualifying premises were reduced to the amount of consideration not applied in the acquisition of the replacement premises (and if not all chargeable gain with a proportionate reduction in the amount of the chargeable gain), and

(b) in respect of the balance of the gain or chargeable gain as if it did not accrue until that person disposes of the replacement premises or the replacement premises ceases to be a replacement premises.

(4) A chargeable gain or the balance of a chargeable gain which under *subsection (2)* or *(3)*, as may be appropriate, is treated as accruing on a date later than the date of the disposal on which it accrued shall not be so treated for the purposes of *section 556*.

(5) This section shall apply only if the acquisition of the replacement premises takes place, or an unconditional contract for the acquisition is entered into, in the period beginning 12 months before and ending 3 years after the disposal of the qualifying premises, or at such earlier or later time as the Revenue Commissioners may by notice in writing allow; but, where an unconditional contract for the acquisition is so entered into, this section may be applied on a provisional basis without waiting to ascertain whether the replacement premises is acquired in pursuance of the contract, and when that fact is ascertained all necessary adjustments shall be made by making assessments or by repayment or discharge of tax, and shall be so made notwithstanding any limitation in the Capital Gains Tax Acts on the time within which assessments may be made [or any limitation in section 865(4) on the time within which a claim for a repayment of tax is required to be made][4].

(6) This section shall not apply if the acquisition of the replacement premises was wholly or partly for the purpose of realising a gain from the disposal of the replacement premises.

(7) Where the qualifying premises was not a qualifying premises throughout the period of ownership of a person making a claim under this section, the section

shall apply as if a part of the qualifying premises representing the period for which it was a qualifying premises was a separate asset, and this section shall apply in relation to that part subject to any necessary apportionments of consideration for an acquisition or disposal of the interest in the premises.

(8) Without prejudice to the provisions of the Capital Gains Tax Acts providing generally for apportionments, where consideration is given for the acquisition or disposal of assets some or part of which are assets in relation to which a claim under *subsection (2)* or *(3)* applies, and some or part of which are not, the consideration shall be apportioned in such manner as is just and reasonable.][5]

Amendments

[1] Substituted by FA02 s60(a).

[2] Substituted by FA02 s60(b).

[3] Substituted by FA03 s67(1)(c). does not apply—to a disposal by a person, on or after 4 December 2002 and on or before 31 December 2003, of a qualifying premises (within the meaning of section 600A) where the person claims that, but for the provisions of subsection (1)(c),the person would have been entitled to claim that the chargeable gain accruing on that disposal could not accrue to the person until a replacement premises (within that meaning) which were acquired by the person before 4 December 2002, or acquired by the person under an unconditional contract entered into before that date— (i) was disposed of by the person, or (ii) ceased to be a replacement premises,

[4] Inserted by FA08 sched6(1)(k). Applies as on and from 31 January 2008.

[5] Inserted by FA01 s92(1). Shall apply to disposals on or after 5 January 2001.

Revenue Briefings

Tax Briefing

Tax Briefing April 2001 – Issue 43 pg 19 – Rollover Relief on Certain Investment Property
Tax Briefing April 2002 – Issue 47 pg 15 – Finance Act 2002
Tax Briefing May 2003 – Issue 52 pg 13 – Finance Act 2003

Cross References

From Section 600A

Section 556 Adjustment of allowable expenditure by reference to consumer price index.
Section 865 Repayment of tax.

CHAPTER 7

Other Reliefs and Exemptions

601 Annual exempt amount

[CGTA75 s16; CGT(A)A78 s16, s17, Sch1 par8 and Sch2; FA92 s59]

(1) An individual shall not be chargeable to capital gains tax for a year of assessment if the amount on which he or she is chargeable to capital gains tax under *section 31* for that year does not exceed [€1,270][1].

(2) Where the amount on which an individual is chargeable to capital gains tax under *section 31* for a year of assessment exceeds [€1,270][2], only the excess of that amount over [€1,270][3] shall be charged to capital gains tax for that year.

(3) Where, on the assumption that *subsection (2)* did not apply, an individual would be chargeable under the Capital Gains Tax Acts at more than one rate of tax for a year of assessment, the relief to be given under that subsection in respect of the first [€,1270][4] of chargeable gains shall be given—

(a) if the individual would be so chargeable at 2 different rates, in respect of the chargeable gains which would be so chargeable at the higher of those rates and, in so far as relief cannot be so given, in respect of the chargeable gains which would be so chargeable at the lower of those rates, and

(b) if the individual would be so chargeable at 3 or more rates, in respect of the chargeable gains which would be so chargeable at the highest of those rates and, in so far as relief cannot be so given, in respect of the chargeable gains which would be so chargeable at the next highest of those rates, and so on.

(4) In the case of an individual who dies in the year of assessment, this section shall apply with the substitution for the reference to the individual of a reference to his or her personal representatives, and the amount of chargeable gains shall be that on which the personal representatives are chargeable in respect of gains accruing before death.

(5) Relief shall not be given under this section where relief is allowed under *section 598* or *599*.

Amendments

1, 2, 3, 4 Substituted by FA01 sched5.

Cross References

From Section 601

Section 31 Amount chargeable.

Section 598 Disposals of business or farm on "retirement".

Section 599 Disposals within family of business or farm.

To Section 601

Section 571 Chargeable gains accruing on disposals by liquidators and certain other persons.

Section 591 Relief for individuals on certain reinvestment.

Section 594 Foreign life assurance and deferred annuities: taxation and returns.

Section 838 Special portfolio investment accounts.

602 Chattel exemption

[CGTA75 s17]

(1) In this section, tangible movable property shall not include a wasting asset within the meaning of *section 560*.

(2) Subject to this section, a gain accruing on a disposal by an individual of an asset which is tangible movable property shall not be a chargeable gain if the amount or value of the consideration for the disposal does not exceed [€2,540][1].

(3) (a) The amount of capital gains tax chargeable in respect of a gain accruing on a disposal within *subsection (2)* for a consideration the amount or value of which exceeds [€2,540][2] shall not exceed 50 per cent of the difference between the amount of that consideration and [€2,540][3].

(b) For the purposes of this subsection, the capital gains tax chargeable in respect of the gain shall be the amount of tax which would not have been chargeable but for that gain.

(4) *Subsections (2)* and *(3)* shall not affect the amount of an allowable loss accruing on the disposal of an asset, but for the purposes of computing under the Capital Gains Tax Acts the amount of a loss accruing on the disposal by an individual of tangible movable property the consideration for the disposal shall, if less than [€2,540][4], be deemed to be [€2,540][5] and the losses which are allowable losses shall be restricted accordingly.

(5) Where 2 or more assets which have formed part of a set of articles of any description all owned at one time by one person are disposed of by that person—

(a) to the same person, or

(b) to persons who are acting in concert or who are connected persons,

whether on the same or different occasions, the 2 or more transactions shall be treated as a single transaction disposing of a single asset, but with any necessary apportionments of the reductions in tax and in allowable losses under *subsections (3)* and *(4)*, and this subsection shall also apply where the assets or some of the assets are disposed of on different occasions, and one of those occasions falls after the 28th day of February, 1974, but before the 6th day of April, 1974, but not so as to make any gain accruing on a disposal before the 6th day of April, 1974, a chargeable gain.

(6) Where the disposal is of a right or interest in or over tangible movable property, then—

(a) in the first instance, *subsections (2)* to *(4)* shall be applied in relation to the asset as a whole, taking the consideration as including, in addition to the consideration for the disposal (in this subsection referred to as "the actual consideration"), the market value of what remains undisposed of,

(b) if the sum of the actual consideration and that market value exceeds [€2,540][6], the limitation on the amount of tax in *subsection (3)* shall be to 50 per cent of the difference between that sum and [€2,540][7] multiplied by the fraction equal to the actual consideration divided by that sum, and

(c) if that sum is less than [€2,540][8], any loss shall be restricted under *subsection (4)* by deeming the consideration to be the actual consideration plus that fraction of the difference between that sum and [€2,540][9].

(7) This section shall not apply—

(a) in relation to a disposal of commodities of any description by a person dealing on a terminal market or dealing with or through a person ordinarily engaged in dealing on a terminal market, or

(b) in relation to a disposal of currency of any description.

Amendments

1, 2, 3, 4, 5, 6, 7, 8, 9 Substituted by FA01 sched5.

Cross References

From Section 602

Section 560 Wasting assets.

603 Wasting chattels

[CGTA75 s18]

(1) Subject to this section, no chargeable gain shall accrue on the disposal of or of an interest in an asset which is tangible movable property and a wasting asset.

(2) *Subsection (1)* shall not apply to a disposal of or of an interest in an asset where—

(a) from the beginning of the period of ownership of the person making the disposal to the time when the disposal is made, the asset has been used and used solely for the purposes of a trade or profession and that person has claimed or could have claimed any capital allowance in respect of any expenditure attributable to the asset or interest under *paragraph (a)* or *(b)* of *section 552(1)*, or

(b) the person making the disposal has incurred any expenditure on the asset or interest which has otherwise qualified in full for any capital allowance.

(3) In the case of the disposal of or of an interest in an asset which, in the period of ownership of the person making the disposal, has been used partly for the purposes of a trade or profession and partly for other purposes, or has been used for the purposes of a trade or profession for part of that period, or which has otherwise qualified in part only for capital allowances—

(a) the consideration for the disposal and any expenditure attributable to the asset or interest under *paragraph (a)* or *(b)* of *section 552(1)* shall be apportioned by reference to the extent to which that expenditure qualified for capital allowances,

(b) the computation of the gain shall be made separately in relation to the apportioned parts of the expenditure and consideration, and

(c) *subsection (1)* shall not apply to any gain accruing by reference to the computation in relation to the part of the consideration apportioned to use for the purposes of the trade or profession, or to the expenditure qualifying for capital allowances.

(4) *Subsection (1)* shall not apply to a disposal of commodities of any description by a person dealing on a terminal market or dealing with or through a person ordinarily engaged in dealing on a terminal market.

Case Law

Burnham (Inspector of Taxes) v Westminister Press Ltd 1982 STC 669 considered a case for the wasting chattel exemption where plant was sold after capital allowances were claimed. The exemption was granted on the basis that the capital allowances claimed had been withdrawn.

Cross References

From Section 603

Section 552 Acquisition, enhancement and disposal costs.

603A Disposal of site to child

[(1) In this section "*child of a parent*", in relation to a disposal for which relief is claimed under this section, includes an individual who resided with, was under the care of and was maintained at the expense of the person making the disposal throughout—

(a) a period of 5 years, or

(b) periods which together comprised at least 5 years,

before the first-mentioned individual attained the age of 18 years but only if such claim is not based on the uncorroborated testimony of one witness, and a disposal by a parent to a child of a parent shall be construed accordingly.

[(1A) This section applies to the disposal of land which at the date of the disposal—

(a) has a market value that does not exceed [€500,000][1], and

(b) comprises—

(i) the area of land on which a dwelling house referred to in *subsection (2)(b)* is to be constructed, and

(ii) an area of land for occupation and enjoyment with that dwelling house as its garden or grounds which, exclusive of the area referred to in *subparagraph (i)*, does not exceed 0.4047 hectare.][2][3]

(2) Subject to this section, a chargeable gain shall not accrue on a disposal of land to which this section applies where the disposal—

(a) is by a [parent or the civil partner of a parent to a child of the parent][4], and

(b) is for the purpose of enabling the child to construct a dwelling house on the land which dwelling house is to be occupied by the child as his or her only or main residence.

[(2A) For the purposes of subsection (2) "disposal" includes a simultaneous disposal by both parents.][5]

(3) Where a child—

(a) at any time disposes of the land or a part of the land referred to in *subsection (2)*, other than to his or her [spouse or civil partner][6], and

(b) the land being disposed of does not contain a dwelling house which—

(i) was constructed by the child since the time of acquisition of the land, and

(ii) has been occupied by the child as his or her only or main residence for a period of 3 years,

the chargeable gain which, but for *subsection (2)*, would have accrued on the disposal of that land to the child, shall be treated as accruing to the child at the time of the disposal referred to in *paragraph (a)*.

(4) Where *subsection (2)* applies to a disposal of land by a parent to a child, it shall not apply to any such subsequent disposal to that child unless, by virtue of *subsection (3)*, the full amount of the chargeable gain which, but for *subsection (2)* would have accrued to the parent, is treated as accruing to the child.][7]

[(5) (a) This section applies to the disposal of a site to a child of an individual's civil partner if all other conditions of this section have been met.

(b) For the purposes of *paragraph (a)*, "*disposal*" includes a simultaneous disposal by both civil partners concerned.][8]

Amendments

[1] Substituted by FA08 s55(1)(a). Applies to disposals made on or after 5 December 2007.

[2] Substituted by FA07 s53(1). Applies to disposals made on or after 1 February 2007.

[3] Substituted by FA06 s72(1). This section applies to disposals made on or after the date of 31 March 2006

[4] Substituted by F(No.3)A11 sched1(163).

[5] Inserted by FA08 s55(1)(b). Shall be deemed to have applied from 6 December 2000.

[6] Substituted by F(No.3)A11 sched1(164).

[7] Inserted by FA01 s93(1)(a). Shall apply to disposals on or after 6 December 2000.

[8] Inserted by F(No.3)A11 sched1(165).

Revenue Briefings

Tax Briefing

Tax Briefing April 2001 – Issue 43 pg 19 – Transfer of Site from Parent to Child

604 Disposals of principal private residence

[CGTA75 s25; FA79 s35; FA80 s61(c); FA84 s67; FA97 s146(1) and Sch9 PtI par9(2)]

(1) In this section, "the period of ownership"—

(a) where the individual has had different interests at different times, shall be taken to begin from the first acquisition taken into account in determining the expenditure which under the Capital Gains Tax Acts is allowable as a deduction in computing the amount of the gain to which this section applies, and

(b) for the purposes of *subsections (3)* to *(5)*, shall not include any period before the 6th day of April, 1974.

(2) This section shall apply to a gain accruing to an individual on the disposal of or of an interest in—

(a) a dwelling house or part of a dwelling house which is or has been occupied by the individual as his or her only or main residence, or

(b) land which the individual has for his or her own occupation and enjoyment with that residence as its garden or grounds up to an area (exclusive of the site of the dwelling house) not exceeding one acre;

but, where part of the land occupied with a residence is and part is not within this subsection, then, that part shall be taken to be within this subsection which, if the remainder were separately occupied, would be the most suitable for occupation and enjoyment with the residence.

(3) The gain shall not be a chargeable gain if the dwelling house or the part of a dwelling house has been occupied by the individual as his or her only or main residence throughout the period of ownership or throughout the period of ownership except for all or any part of the last 12 months of that period.

(4) Where *subsection (3)* does not apply, such portion of the gain shall not be a chargeable gain as represents the same proportion of the gain as the length of the part or parts of the period of ownership during which the dwelling house or the part of a dwelling house was occupied by the individual as his or her only or main residence, but inclusive of the last 12 months of the period of ownership in any event, bears to the length of the period of ownership.

(5) (a) In this subsection, "*period of absence*" means a period during which the dwelling house or part of a dwelling house was not the individual's only or main residence and throughout which he or she had no residence or main residence eligible for relief under this section.

(b) For the purposes of *subsections (3)* and *(4)*—

(i) any period of absence throughout which the individual worked in an employment or office all the duties of which were performed outside the State, and

(ii) in addition, any period of absence not exceeding 4 years (or periods of absence which together did not exceed 4 years) throughout which the individual was prevented from residing in the dwelling house or the part of a dwelling house in consequence of the situation of the individual's place of work or in consequence of any condition imposed by the individual's employer requiring the individual to reside elsewhere, being a condition reasonably imposed to secure the effective performance by the employee of the employee's duties,

shall be treated as if in that period of absence the dwelling house or the part of a dwelling house was occupied by the individual as his or her only or main residence if both before and after the period the dwelling house (or the part in question) was occupied by the individual as his or her only or main residence.

(6) Where the gain accrues from the disposal of a dwelling house or part of a dwelling house part of which is used exclusively for the purposes of a trade, business or profession, the gain shall be apportioned and *subsections (2)* to *(5)* shall apply in relation to the part of the gain apportioned to the part which is not exclusively used for those purposes.

(7) Where at any time in the period of ownership there is a change in the dwelling house or the part of it which is occupied as the individual's residence, whether on account of a reconstruction or conversion of a building or for any other reason, or there have been changes as regards the use of part of the dwelling house for the purpose of a trade, business or profession or for any other purpose, the relief given by this section may be adjusted in such manner as the inspector and the individual may agree, or as the Appeal Commissioners may on an appeal consider to be just and reasonable.

(8) For the purposes of this section, an individual shall not be treated as having more than one main residence at any one time and in so far as it is necessary to determine which of 2 or more residences is an individual's main residence for any period—

(a) that question may be determined by agreement between the inspector and the individual on the latter giving notice in writing to the inspector by the end of the year 1975–76 or within 2 years from the beginning of that period if that is later, and

(b) failing such agreement, the question shall be determined by the inspector, whose determination may be as respects either the whole or specified parts of the period of ownership in question,

and notice of any determination by the inspector under *paragraph (b)* shall be given to the individual who may appeal to the Appeal Commissioners against that determination within 21 days of service of the notice.

(9) In the case of [a man and his wife living with him, or civil partners living together][1]—

(a) there may be for the purposes of this section only one residence or main residence for both so long as they are living together and, where a notice under *subsection (8)(a)* affects [both the husband and his wife or both civil partners][2], it must be made by both,

(b) if the one disposes of, or of his or her interest in, the dwelling house or part of a dwelling house which is their only or main residence to the other, or if it passes on death to the other as legatee, the other's period of ownership shall begin with the beginning of the period of ownership of the one making the disposal or from whom it passes on death,

(c) if *paragraph (b)* applies but the dwelling house or part of a dwelling house was not the only or main residence of both throughout the period of ownership of the one making the disposal, account shall be taken of any part of that period during which it was the only or main residence of the one as if it was also the only or main residence of the other, and

(d) any notice under *subsection (8)(b)* which affects a residence [owned by the husband and a residence owned by the wife, or a residence owned by one civil partner and a residence owned by the other civil partner,][3] shall be given to each and either may appeal under that subsection.

(10) This section shall also apply in relation to a gain accruing to a trustee on a disposal of settled property, being an asset within *subsection (2)*, where during the period of ownership of the trustee the dwelling house or the part of a dwelling

house mentioned in that subsection has been the only or main residence of an individual entitled to occupy it under the terms of the settlement, and in this section as so applied—

(a) references to the individual shall be taken as references to the trustee except in relation to the occupation of the dwelling house or the part of a dwelling house, and

(b) the notice which may be given to the inspector under *subsection (8)(a)* shall be a joint notice by the trustee and the person entitled to occupy the dwelling house or the part of a dwelling house.

(11) [(a) In this subsection '*dependent relative*', in relation to an individual, means a relative of the individual, or of the wife or husband of the individual, who is incapacitated by old age or infirmity from maintaining himself or herself, or a person, whether or not he or she is so incapacitated, and—

(i) who is the widowed father or widowed mother of the individual or of the wife or husband of the individual, or

(ii) who is the father or mother of the individual or of the wife or husband of the individual and is a surviving civil partner who has not subsequently married or entered into another civil partnership.][4]

(b) Where as respects a gain accruing to an individual on the disposal of, or of an interest in, a dwelling house or part of a dwelling house which is, or has at any time in his or her period of ownership been, the sole residence of a dependent relative of the individual, provided rent-free and without any other consideration, the individual so claims, such relief shall be given in respect of it and of its garden or grounds as would be given under this section if the dwelling house (or part of the dwelling house) had been the individual's only or main residence in the period of residence by the dependent relative, and shall be so given in addition to any relief available under this section apart from this subsection; but no more than one dwelling house (or part of a dwelling house) may qualify for relief as being the residence of a dependent relative of the claimant at any one time.

[(c) Relief under *paragraph (b)* shall also be given where all other conditions of this section have been met but the residence concerned has been the sole residence of a dependent relative of the civil partner of the individual.][5]

(12) (a) In this subsection—

"*base date*", in relation to an asset disposed of by an individual, means the date of acquisition by the individual of the asset or, if the asset was held by the individual on the 6th day of April, 1974, that date;

"*base value*", in relation to an asset disposed of by an individual, means the amount or value of the consideration, in money or money's worth, given by the individual or on his or her behalf wholly and exclusively for the acquisition of the asset exclusive of the incidental costs to the individual of the acquisition or, if the asset was held by the individual on the 6th day of April, 1974, the market value of the asset on that date;

"*current use value*" and "*development land*" have the same meanings respectively as in *section 648*.

(b) Where—

(i) a gain accrues to an individual on the disposal of or of an interest in an asset which is development land, and

(ii) apart from this subsection relief would be given under this section in respect of the disposal of that asset (being an asset within *subsection (2)* or *(11)*),

then, subject to *paragraph (c)*, that relief shall be given in respect of the gain (or where appropriate in respect of a portion of the gain) only to the extent (if any) to which such relief would be given if, in computing the chargeable gain accruing on the disposal (notwithstanding that the disposal was a disposal of development land), there were excluded from the computation—

(I) the amount (if any) by which the base value of the asset exceeds the current use value of the asset on the base date,

(II) the amount by which the consideration for the disposal of the asset exceeds the current use value of the asset on the date of the disposal,

(III) if the asset was not held by the individual on the 6th day of April, 1974, such proportion (if any) of the incidental costs to the individual of the acquisition of the asset as would be referable to the amount (if any) referred to in *subparagraph (I)*, and

(IV) such proportion of the incidental costs to the individual of the disposal of the asset as would be referable to the amount referred to in *subparagraph (II)*.

(c) *Paragraph (b)* shall not apply to a disposal made by an individual in any year of assessment if the total consideration in respect of all disposals made by that individual in that year and to which that paragraph would otherwise apply does not exceed [€19,050][6].

(13) Apportionments of consideration shall be made wherever required by this section and in particular where a person disposes of a dwelling house only part of which is the person's only or main residence.

(14) This section shall not apply in relation to a gain if the acquisition of or of the interest in the dwelling house or the part of the dwelling house was made wholly or mainly for the purpose of realising a gain from the disposal of it, and shall not apply in relation to a gain in so far as the gain is attributable to any expenditure which was incurred after the beginning of the period of ownership and wholly or mainly for the purpose of realising a gain from the disposal.

Amendments

[1] Substituted by F(No.3)A11 sched1(166). Shall have effect from 27 July 2011.

[2] Substituted by F(No.3)A11 sched1(167). Shall have effect from 27 July 2011.

[3] Substituted by F(No.3)A11 sched1(168). Shall have effect from 27 July 2011.

[4] Substituted by FA12 s134(1)(d). Has effect as if it had come into operation for the year of assessment (within the meaning of the Income Tax Acts and the Capital Gains Tax Acts) 2011 and each subsequent year of assessment.

[5] Inserted by F(No.3)A11 sched1(169). Shall have effect from 27 July 2011.

[6] Substituted by FA01 sched5.

Case Law

Gardens sold after the disposal of the residence will not qualify for relief. Varty v Lyons 1976 STC 508

A caravan with all the normal services was a principal private residence in Makins v Elson 1977 STC 46. However, in Moore v Thompson 1986 STC 170 a caravan was not a dwelling capable of being regarded as a principal private residence.

In Batey v Wakefield 1981 STC 326 a caretaker bungalow formed part of the main residence. The fact that the bungalow was physically separate from the main house was irrelevant. Similarly in Williams v Merrylees 1987 STC 445 a caretaker lodge was regarded as part of the taxpayer's dwelling house for the purpose of the relief. However in Lewis v Lady Rood 1992 STC 171 it was held that a cottage occupied by a gardener did not form part of the main residence. Also, a bungalow built on the estate, but situated a considerable distance from the main house, did not qualify for the relief in Markey v Saunders 1987 STC 256.

In Goodwin v Curtis 1998 STC 475 a residence used for temporary occupation, where it never had been the taxpayer's intention to occupy the property as his permanent residence, did not qualify for the relief.

Cross References

From Section 604

Section 648 Interpretation (Chapter 2).

To Section 604

Section 216A Rent-a-room relief.
Section 216C Childcare services relief.
Section 605 Disposals to authority possessing compulsory purchase powers.
Section 643 Tax to be charged under Case IV on gains from certain disposals of land.
Schedule 31 Consequential Amendments

604A Relief for certain disposals of land or buildings

[(1) In this section—

'*EEA Agreement*' means the Agreement on the European Economic Area signed at Oporto on 2 May 1992, as adjusted by the Protocol signed in Brussels on 17 March 1993;

'*EEA State*' means a state which is a contracting party to the EEA Agreement.

(2) This section applies to land or buildings situated in any EEA State (including the State)—

(a) which—

(i) were acquired for a consideration equal to their market value in the period commencing on [31 December 2014][1] and ending on 31 December 2013, or

(ii) were acquired in the period referred to in *subparagraph (i)* from a relative (within the meaning of *section 10*) and the consideration was not less than 75 per cent of their market value at the date they were acquired,

and

(b) which continue in the ownership of the person who acquired that land or those buildings for a period of at least 7 years from the date they were acquired.

(3) On a disposal of land or buildings to which this section applies, such portion of the gain shall not be a chargeable gain as represents the same proportion of the gain as 7 years bears to the period of ownership of such land or buildings.

(4) Relief under *subsection (3)* shall not apply—

(a) to land or buildings to which this section applies unless any income or profits or gains derived from the land or buildings concerned in the period of 7 years from the date they were acquired by the person who acquired them is income or profits or gains to which the Income Tax Acts or the Corporation Tax Acts apply, or

(b) where arrangements (within the meaning of *section 546A*) have been put in place and it can be shown that relief (apart from the relief given under *subsection (3)*) would be less if the arrangements had not been put in place.][2]

Amendments

[1] Substituted by F(No.2)A13 s44. Comes into operation on 1 January 2014.

[2] Inserted by FA12 s64. Deemed to have come into force and takes effect on and from 1 January 2012.

604B Relief for farm restructuring

[(1) (a) In this section—

['*agricultural land*' means land used for the purposes of farming but does not include buildings on the land;][1]

"*exchange of farm land*" means an exchange under which an interest in agricultural land is conveyed or transferred by a farmer to another farmer in exchange for receiving, by way of conveyance or transfer, an interest in agricultural land from that other farmer and includes an exchange where the agricultural land is conveyed or transferred by or to joint owners where all the joint owners (other than the spouse or civil partner of a joint owner) are farmers; and the date of the exchange shall be the date on which the conveyance or transfer is executed;

"*farm restructuring certificate*" means a certificate issued for the purposes of this section by Teagasc to a farmer in relation to a sale and purchase or an exchange of qualifying land where—

(i) the first sale or purchase of qualifying land occurs in the relevant period and the subsequent sale or purchase of that land occurs within the period of 24 months commencing on or after the date of the first sale or purchase of such land, or

(ii) the exchange occurs in the relevant period,

and which identifies the land concerned, the owner or owners of such land and certifies that Teagasc is satisfied, on the basis of information available to Teagasc at the time of so certifying, that the sale and purchase or the exchange of qualifying land complies, or will comply, with the conditions relating to farm restructuring set down in the guidelines;

"*farmer*" means an individual who spends not less than 50 per cent of that individual's normal working time farming;

"*guidelines*" means guidelines made and published pursuant to *paragraph (b)(i)*;

"*interest in qualifying land*" means an interest in qualifying land which is not subject to any power on the exercise of which the qualifying land, or any part of any interest in the qualifying land, may be revested in the person from whom it was purchased or exchanged or in any person on behalf of such person;

"*purchase of qualifying land*" means a conveyance or transfer of an interest in qualifying land to a farmer and includes a conveyance or transfer where the qualifying land is conveyed or transferred to joint owners where all the joint owners (other than the spouse or civil partner of a joint owner) are farmers; and the date of purchase of qualifying land shall be the date on which the conveyance or transfer is executed;

"*qualifying land*" means agricultural land in respect of which a farm restructuring certificate has been issued by Teagasc and that certificate has not been withdrawn;

"*relevant period*" means the period commencing on 1 January 2013 and ending on [31 December 2016][2];

"*sale of qualifying land*" means a conveyance or transfer of an interest in qualifying land by a farmer and includes a conveyance or transfer where the qualifying land is conveyed or transferred by joint owners where all the joint owners (other than the spouse or civil partner of a joint owner) are farmers; and the date of the sale of qualifying land shall be the date on which the conveyance or transfer is executed;

"*Teagasc*" means Teagasc — the Agricultural and Food Development Authority.

(b) For the purposes of this section—

(i) theMinister for Agriculture, Food and the Marine with the consent of the Minister for Finance may make and publish guidelines, from time to time, setting out—

(I) how an application for a farm restructuring certificate, in relation to a sale and purchase, or exchange, of agricultural land, is to be made,

(II) the documentation required to accompany such an application,

(III) the conditions relating to farm restructuring, and

(IV) such other information as may be required in relation to such application,

(ii) where an application is made in that regard, Teagasc shall issue a farm restructuring certificate in respect of a sale and purchase, or an exchange, of agricultural land, where they are satisfied, on the basis of the information available to Teagasc at that time, that the sale and purchase or exchange of such land complies, or will comply, with the conditions relating to farm restructuring, and

(iii) Teagasc may, by notice in writing, withdraw any farm restructuring certificate already issued.

(2) A gain shall not be a chargeable gain on a sale or exchange of qualifying land by an individual or individuals where the consideration for the qualifying land that is purchased or the other qualifying land that is exchanged is equal to or exceeds the consideration for the qualifying land that is sold or exchanged by the individual or individuals concerned.

(3) Where the consideration for the qualifying land that is purchased or exchanged by an individual or individuals is less than the consideration for the qualifying land that is sold or the other qualifying land that is exchanged by the individual or individuals concerned, the chargeable gain that accrues in respect of the sale or exchange of the qualifying land shall be reduced in the same proportion that the consideration for the qualifying land that is purchased or exchanged bears to the consideration for the qualifying land that is sold or the other qualifying land that is exchanged.

(4) Where qualifying land in respect of which relief has been given under *subsection (2)* or *(3)* is disposed of within the period of 5 years from the date of the purchase or exchange of that qualifying land, capital gains tax shall be charged on the individual

or individuals concerned as if the relief in those provisions had not applied.

(5) *Subsection (4)* shall not apply where the disposal arises as a consequence of a compulsory acquisition.

(6) Relief under *subsection (2)* or *(3)* shall be by means of discharge or repayment of tax or otherwise.][3]

Amendments

[1] Substituted by FA14 s49(a). Comes into operation on 1 January 2015.

[2] Substituted by FA14 s49(b). Comes into operation on 1 January 2015.

[3] Inserted by FA13 s48(1). With effect from 6 June 2013 as per S.I. No. 193 of 2013.

604C Exemption of certain payment entitlements

[(1) In this section—

'*farmer*' and '*payment entitlement*' have the same meanings, respectively, as they have for the purposes of Council Regulation (EC) No. 73/2009 of 19 January 2009*;

*OJ No. L30, 31.1.2009, p.16

'*scheme year 2013*' means the period beginning on 16 May 2012 and ending on 15 May 2013;

'*scheme year 2014*' means the period beginning on 16 May 2013 and ending on 15 May 2014.

(2) The disposal by farmers in the scheme year 2014 of payment entitlements that have, together with the land on which eligibility for the payment entitlements is based, been fully leased in the scheme year 2013 shall be exempt from capital gains tax.][1]

Amendments

[1] Inserted by FA14 s51. Comes into operation on 1 January 2015.

605 Disposals to authority possessing compulsory purchase powers

[CGT(A)A78 s5]

(1) [Where a person makes a disposal, before 4 December 2002, of][1] or of an interest in property situate in the State (in this section referred to as "the original assets") to an authority possessing compulsory purchase powers and claims and proves to the satisfaction of the Revenue Commissioners that—

(a) the disposal would not have been made but for—

(i) the exercise of those powers, or

(ii) the giving by the authority of formal notice of its intention to exercise those powers,

(b) the whole of the consideration for the disposal and no more is applied in acquiring other property situate in the State or an interest in such other property (in this section referred to as "the replacement assets"), and

[(c) subject to *subsection (4A)*, the original assets and the replacement assets are within one, and the same one, of the classes of assets specified in *subsection (5)*,][2]

then, for the purposes of the Capital Gains Tax Acts, the disposal shall not be treated as involving any disposal of the original assets and the acquisition shall not be treated as involving any acquisition of the replacement assets or any part of those assets, but the original assets and the replacement assets shall be treated as the same assets acquired as the original assets were acquired.

(2) In a case where *subsection (1)* would apply but for the fact that an amount in excess of the amount or value of the consideration for the disposal concerned is applied as described in *paragraph (b)* of that subsection—

(a) the person making the disposal shall be treated for the purposes of the Capital Gains Tax Acts as if, in consideration of that excess, that person had acquired at the time of the acquisition of the replacement assets a portion of those assets which bears to the whole the same proportion as the amount of the excess bears to the amount or value of the consideration applied in acquiring the replacement assets, and

(b) *subsection (1)* shall apply to the remainder of those assets and to the original assets.

(3) In a case where *subsection (1)* would apply but for the fact that part of the amount or value of the consideration for the disposal concerned is not applied as described in *paragraph (b)* of that subsection—

(a) the person making the disposal shall be treated for the purposes of the Capital Gains Tax Acts as if, in consideration of that part, that person had disposed of an interest in the original assets, and

(b) *subsection (1)* shall apply to the remainder of those assets and to the replacement assets.

(4) This section shall apply only if the acquisition of the replacement assets takes place, or an unconditional contract for the acquisition is entered into, in the period beginning 12 months before and ending 3 years after the disposal of the original assets, or at such earlier or later time as the Revenue Commissioners may by notice in writing allow; but, where an unconditional contract for the acquisition is so entered into, this section may be applied on a provisional basis without ascertaining whether the replacement assets are acquired in pursuance of the contract, and when that fact is ascertained all necessary adjustments shall be made by making assessments or by repayment or discharge of tax, and shall be so made notwithstanding any limitation in the Capital Gains Tax Acts on the time within which assessments may be made [or any limitation in section 865(4) on the time within which a claim for a repayment of tax is required to be made][3].

[(4A) Where the original assets is land which has been let by the person making the disposal at any time in the period of 5 years ending with the disposal and, immediately before the time the land was first let in that period, the land was owned by that person and used by that person for farming (within the meaning of *section 654*) for a period of not less than 10 years ending with the time the land was first so let, the land may be treated as being within Class 1, which is referred to in *subsection (5)*.][4]

(5) The classes of assets referred to in *subsection (1)* shall be as follows:

Class 1

Assets of a trade carried on by the person making the disposal which consist of—

(a) plant or machinery;

(b) except where the trade is a trade of dealing in or developing land, or of providing services for the occupier of land in which the person carrying on the trade has an estate or interest—

(i) any building or part of a building and any permanent or semi-permanent structure in the nature of a building occupied (as well as used) only for the purposes of the trade,

(ii) any land occupied (as well as used) only for the purposes of the trade, provided that where the trade is a trade of dealing in or developing land, but a profit on the sale of any land held for the purposes of the trade would not form part of the trading profits, the trade shall be treated for the purposes of this subsection as if it were not a trade of dealing in or developing land;

(c) goodwill.

Class 2

Any land or buildings, not being land or buildings within Class 1, but excluding a dwelling house or part of a dwelling house in relation to which the person making the disposal would be entitled to claim relief under *section 604*.

Amendments

[1] Substituted by FA03 s67(1)(d). does not apply to a disposal by a person, on or after 4 December 2002 and on or before 31 December 2003, of original assets (within the meaning of section 605 to the satisfaction of the Revenue Commissioners that, but for the provisions of subsection (1)(d), the person would have been entitled to claim that that disposal would not be treated as a disposal for the purposes of the Capital Gains Tax Acts by virtue of the person having, before 4 December 2002, acquired, or entered into an unconditional contract to acquire, new assets (within that meaning).

[2] Substituted by FA02 s61(a).

[3] Inserted by FA08 sched6(1)(l). Applies as on and from 31 January 2008.

[4] Inserted by FA02 s61(b).

Revenue Briefings

Tax Briefing

Tax Briefing April 2002 – Issue 47 pg 15 – Finance Act 2002

Tax Briefing May 2003 – Issue 52 pg 13 – Finance Act 2003

Cross References

From Section 605

Section 604 Disposals of principal private residence.

Section 654 Interpretation (Part 23).

Section 865 Repayment of tax.

To Section 605

Section 652 Non-application of reliefs on replacement of assets in case of relevant disposals.

606 Disposals of work of art, etc., loaned for public display

[FA91 s43(1) and (2)]

(1) This section shall apply to an object, being any picture, print, book, manuscript, sculpture, piece of jewellery or work of art which—

(a) in the opinion of the Revenue Commissioners, after such consultation (if any) as may seem to them to be necessary with such person or body of persons as in their opinion may be of assistance to them, has a market value of not less than [€31,740][1] at the date when the object is [loaned to the Trust (within the meaning of *section 1003A*) or to a gallery or museum][2] in the State, being a gallery or museum approved of by the Revenue Commissioners for the purposes of this section, and

(b) is the subject of or included in a display to which the public is afforded reasonable access in the gallery or museum to which it has been loaned for a period (in this section referred to as "the qualifying period") of [not less than 10 years][3] from the date the object is so loaned.

(2) Where after the end of the qualifying period a disposal of an object to which this section applies is made by the person who had loaned the object in the circumstances described in *subsection (1)*, the disposal shall be treated for the purposes of the Capital Gains Tax Acts as being made for such consideration as to secure that neither a gain nor a loss accrues on the disposal.

Amendments

[1] Substituted by FA01 sched5.

[2] Substituted by FA06 s73(1)(a).

[3] Substituted by FA06 s73(1)(b). Applies to a loan made on or after 2 February 2006.

Cross References

From Section 606

Section 1003 Payment of tax by means of donation of heritage items.

To Section 606

Section 236 Loan of certain art objects.

607 Government and certain other securities

[CGTA75 s19; FA82 s41(a); FA84 s66; FA88 s70(2); FA89 s32 and s95(2); FA92 s24(2); FA96 s39(1) and (5)]

(1) The following shall not be chargeable assets—

(a) securities (including savings certificates) issued under the authority of the Minister for Finance,

(b) stock issued by—

(i) a local authority, or

(ii) a harbour authority mentioned in the First Schedule to the Harbours Act, 1946,

(c) land bonds issued under the Land Purchase Acts,

(d) debentures, debenture stock, certificates of charge or other forms of security issued by the Electricity Supply Board, Bord Gáis Éireann, [the company established pursuant to *section 5* of the Gas Regulation Act 2013,][1] [Irish Water][2] Radio Telefís Éireann, […][3], […][4] Córas Iompair Éireann, […][5], Bord na Móna, [or Dublin Airport Authority,][6]

(e) securities issued by the Housing Finance Agency under section 10 of the Housing Finance Agency Act, 1981,

(f) securities issued by a body designated under section 4(1) of the Securitisation (Proceeds of Certain Mortgages) Act, 1995,

[…][7]

(g) securities issued in the State, with the approval of the Minister for Finance, by the European Community, the European Coal and Steel Community, the International Bank for Reconstruction and Development, the European Atomic Energy Community or the European Investment Bank, and

(h) securities issued by An Post and guaranteed by the Minister for Finance.

(2)

[(a) All futures contracts which—

(i) are unconditional contracts for the acquisition or disposal of any of the instruments referred to in *subsection (1)* or any other instruments to which this section applies by virtue of any other enactment (whenever enacted),

(ii) require delivery of the instruments in respect of which the contracts are made, and

(iii) meet the requirements of *paragraph (c)* of this subsection,

shall not be chargeable assets.][8]

(b) The requirement in *paragraph (a)* that the instrument be delivered shall be treated as satisfied where a person who has entered into a futures contract dealt in or quoted on a futures exchange or stock exchange closes out the futures contract by entering into another futures contract, so dealt in or quoted, with obligations which are reciprocal to those of the contract so closed out and are thereafter settled in respect of both futures contracts by means (if any) of a single cash payment or receipt.

[(c) Where a profit or loss on a futures contract is calculated, either directly or indirectly, by reference to the acquisition cost or disposal proceeds of an instrument to which *subparagraph (i)* of *subsection (2)(a)* applies, then—

(i) that acquisition cost shall be the market value of the instrument at the date of acquisition, and

(ii) those disposal proceeds shall be the market value of the instrument at the date of disposal.][9]

Amendments

[1] Inserted by FA14 s25(1)(b). Has effect as respects any securities issued by the company established pursuant to section 5 of the Gas Regulation Act 2013 on or after 23 October 2014.

[2] Inserted by F(No.2)A13 s29(1)(b). Has effect as respects any securities issued by Irish Water on or after 24 October 2013.

[3] Repealed by ICC BA00 s7 and the ICC BA00 (Commencement) (Sections 5 and 7) Order 01 (S.I. 396/2001).

[4] Deleted by FA01 s241(1)(b). Has effect as respects any securities issued by Bord Telecom Éireann or Irish Telecommunications Investments plc. on or after 15 February 2001.

[5] Repealed by ACC BA01 s12 and S.I. No 69 of 2002.

[6] Substituted by FA08 sched8(1)(h). Has effect as on and from 31 January 2008.

[7] Deleted by NTMA(A)A14 part4(8).

[8] Substituted by FA10 s60(1)(a). This section applies to disposals made on or after 4 February 2010.

[9] Inserted by FA10 s60(1)(b). This section applies to disposals made on or after 4 February 2010.

Cross References

To Section 607

Section 55 Taxation of strips of securities.
Section 585 Conversion of securities.
Section 711 Chargeable gains of life business.
Section 719 Deemed disposal and reacquisition of certain assets.
Section 732 Special arrangements for qualifying unit trusts.
Section 737 Special investment schemes.
Section 738 Undertakings for collective investment.
Section 749 Dealers in securities.
Section 815 Taxation of income deemed to arise on certain sales of securities.
Section 838 Special portfolio investment accounts.
Section 898B Interpretation (Chapter 3A).
Section 913 Application of income tax provisions relating to returns, etc.

608 Superannuation funds

[CGTA75 s21; FA88 s30(1) and (2)(b); FA91 s38]

(1) (a) In this subsection, "financial futures" and "traded options" mean respectively financial futures and traded options for the time being dealt in or quoted on any futures exchange or any stock exchange, whether or not that exchange is situated in the State.

(b) For the purposes of *subsection (2)*, a contract entered into in the course of dealing in financial futures or traded options shall be regarded as an investment.

[(2) A gain shall not be a chargeable gain if accruing to a person from the person's disposal of assets held by that person as part of a fund approved under *section 774*, *784(4)* or *785(5)* or held by that person as PRSA assets (within the meaning of section 787A).][1]

[(2A) A gain shall not be a chargeable gain if accruing to a person who is exempt from income tax under *section 790B*.][2]

(3) Where part only of a fund is approved under a section referred to in *subsection (2)*, the gain shall be exempt from being a chargeable gain to the same extent only as income derived from the assets would be exempt under that section.

(4) For the purposes of this section, the fund set up under section 6A of the Oireachtas (Allowances to Members) Act, 1938 (inserted by the Oireachtas (Allowances to Members) and Ministerial and Parliamentary Offices (Amendment) Act, 1960), shall be deemed to be a fund approved under *section 774*.

Amendments

[1] Substituted by FA03 s14(1)(a). Has effect as on and from the passing of this Act. FA03 28 March 2003

[2] Inserted by FA05 s58.

Cross References

From Section 608

Section 774 Certain approved schemes: exemptions and reliefs.

Section 784 Retirement annuities: relief for premiums.

Section 785 Approval of contracts for dependants or for life assurance.

Section 790 Liability of certain pensions, etc. to tax.

609 Charities

[CGTA75 s22]

(1) Subject to *subsection (2)*, a gain shall not be a chargeable gain if it accrues to a charity and is applicable and applied for charitable purposes.

(2) Where property held on charitable trusts ceases to be subject to charitable trusts—

(a) the trustees shall be treated as if they had disposed of and immediately reacquired the property for a consideration equal to its market value, any gain on the disposal being treated as not accruing to a charity, and

(b) if and in so far as any of that property represents directly or indirectly the consideration for the disposal of assets by the trustees, any gain accruing on that disposal shall be treated as not having accrued to a charity,

and an assessment to capital gains tax chargeable by virtue of *paragraph (b)* may be made at any time not more than 10 years after the end of the year of assessment in which the property ceases to be subject to charitable trusts.

Revenue Information Notes

CHY 1 – Applying for Relief from Tax on the Income and Property of Charities

610 Other bodies

[CGTA75 s23; FA89 s33; FA91 s20(2) and s44; FA94 s32(5); FA95 s44(1) and (3); FA96 s39(1) and (6) and s64; FA97 s49(1) and (3)]

(1) A gain shall not be a chargeable gain if it accrues to a body specified in *Part 1* of *Schedule 15.*

(2) A gain shall not be a chargeable gain if it accrues to a body specified in *Part 2* of *Schedule 15* in respect of a disposal by that body of an asset to the Interim Board established under the Milk (Regulation of Supply) (Establishment of Interim Board) Order, 1994 (S.I. No. 408 of 1994).

Cross References

From Section 610

Schedule 15 List of Bodies for Purposes of Section 610

To Section 610

Schedule 15 List of Bodies for Purposes of Section 610

610A Exemption for proceeds of disposal by sports bodies

[(1) Subject to *subsection (2)*, a gain shall not be a chargeable gain if it accrues to an approved body to the extent that the proceeds of the disposal giving rise to the gain or, if greater, the consideration for the disposal under the Capital Gains Tax Acts have, within 5 years of the receipt of the proceeds of the disposal or the consideration, as the case may be, been applied for the sole purpose of promoting athletic or amateur games or sports.

(2) A gain shall not be a chargeable gain if it accrues to an approved body to the extent that the proceeds of the disposal (or part thereof) giving rise to the gain or, if greater, the consideration for the disposal (or part thereof) have, within 5 years of the receipt of the proceeds of the disposal or the consideration, as the case may be, been donated for charitable purposes to a person or body of persons and—

(a) application has been made to the Minister for Finance specifying the person or body of persons to which the approved body proposes to make a donation and he or she has approved the making of the donation to the person or body of persons specified in the application,

(b) the donation is evidenced by a deed which stipulates that the donation is applicable and must be applied for the purposes of the charity only, and

(c) neither the donor nor a person connected to the donor receives a benefit in consequence of making the donation, either directly or indirectly.

(3) The Minister for Finance may refuse to approve the donation to the person or body of persons referred to in *subsection (2)* if he or she believes that the public good would not be served if the donation were made.

(4) The Revenue Commissioners may allow an extension of the period of 5 years referred to in *subsection (1)* for the application of proceeds for sporting purposes if they are satisfied that an approved body is in the process of applying proceeds for that purpose.

(5) The Revenue Commissioners may allow an extension of the period of 5 years referred to in *subsection (2)* for the making of a donation for charitable purposes if they are satisfied that an approved body is in the process of making such a donation.

(6) In this section 'approved body' means an approved body of persons within the meaning of *section 235(1)*.][1]

Amendments

[1] Inserted by FA12 s67(1)(a). Subsections (2), (3) and (5) of section 610A shall be deemed to have had effect in respect of disposals on or after 1 January 2005.

611 Disposals to State, public bodies and charities

[CGTA75 s39; CGT(A)A78 s10]

(1) (a) [Subject to *section 848A*, where a disposal of an asset][1] is made otherwise than under a bargain at arm's length—

(i) to the State,

(ii) to a charity, or

[(iii) to the Chester Beatty Library, the Crawford Art Gallery Cork, the Irish Museum of Modern Art, the National Archives, the National Concert Hall, the National Gallery of Ireland, the National Library of Ireland, the National Museum of Ireland, the Friends of the National Collections of Ireland, [the Local Government Computer Services Board, the Local Government Management Services Board, the Affordable Homes Partnership, Irish Water Safety, Limerick Northside Regeneration Agency, Limerick Southside Regeneration Agency,][2] a local authority or a joint body within the meaning of section 2(1) of the Local Government Act 2001 and any university in the State,][3]

section 547 shall not apply but, if the disposal is for no consideration or for a consideration not exceeding the sums which would be allowable as a deduction under *sections 552* and *828(4)* for the purposes of computing a chargeable gain, then—

(I) the disposal and acquisition shall be treated for the purposes of the Capital Gains Tax Acts as being made for such consideration as to secure that neither a gain nor a loss accrues on the disposal, and

(II) where the disposal is to a person within *subparagraph (ii)* or *(iii)* and the asset is later disposed of by that person in such circumstances that if a gain accrued on the later disposal it would be a chargeable gain, the capital gains tax which would have been chargeable in respect of the gain accruing on the earlier disposal if *section 547* had applied in relation to it shall be assessed and charged on the person making the later disposal in addition to any capital gains tax chargeable in respect of the gain accruing to that person on the later disposal.

(b) Where relief was given under this subsection in respect of a disposal to a person of an asset, being a disposal made before the 20th day of December, 1978, and there is a later disposal of the asset by the person on or after that date, *paragraph (a)(II)* shall apply as if the first-mentioned disposal were the earlier disposal referred to in that paragraph.

[...][4]

(d) For the purposes of *paragraph (a)(II)*, the amount of the capital gains tax which would have been chargeable in respect of the gain accruing on the earlier disposal shall be the amount of tax which would not have been chargeable but for that gain.

(2) Where under *section 576(1)* or *577(3)* any assets or parts of any assets forming part of settled property are deemed to be disposed of ad reacquired by the trustee, and—

(a) where the assets deemed to be disposed of under *section 576(1)* are reacquired on behalf of the State, a charity or a body [referred to in *paragraph (a)(iii)* of *subsection (1)*,][5] or

(b) the assets which or parts of which are deemed to be disposed of and reacquired under *section 577(3)* are held for the purposes of the State, a charity or a body [referred to in *paragraph (a)(iii)* of *subsection (1)*,][6]

then, if no consideration is received by any person for or in connection with any transaction by virtue of which the State, the charity or other body becomes so entitled or the assets are so held, the disposal and acquisition of the assets to which the State, the charity or other body becomes so entitled or of the assets which are held as mentioned in *paragraph (b)* shall be treated for the purposes of Capital Gains Tax Acts as made for such consideration as to secure that neither a gain nor a loss accrues on the disposal.

Amendments

[1] Substituted by FA06 s20(1)(a). Applies as on and from 1 January 2006.

[2] Inserted by FA12 s61(1). Applies to disposals made on or after 8 February 2012.

[3] Substituted by FA10 s61(1)(a). This section applies to disposals made on or after 4 February 2010.

[4] Deleted by FA14 s45(1)(c). Applies to disposals giving rise to a clawback of relief under section 598, 599 or 611 where such disposals are made on or after 23 December 2014.

[5, 6] Substituted by FA10 s61(1)(b). This section applies to disposals made on or after 4 February 2010.

Cross References

From Section 611

Section 547 Disposals and acquisitions treated as made at market value.
Section 552 Acquisition, enhancement and disposal costs.
Section 576 Person becoming absolutely entitled to settled property.
Section 577 Termination of life interest on death of person entitled.
Section 828 Capital gains tax: double taxation relief.
Section 848A Donations to approved bodies.

To Section 611

Section 848A Donations to approved bodies.

611A Treatment of certain disposals made by The Pharmaceutical Society of Ireland

[(1) In this section—

"*new Society*" means Cumann Cógaisceoirí na hÉireann or, in the English language, The Pharmaceutical Society of Ireland established by section 5(2) of the Pharmacy Act 2007;

"*old Society*" means the Pharmaceutical Society of Ireland constituted and incorporated by section 4 of the Pharmacy (Ireland) Act 1875.

(2) An asset disposed of by the new Society which it acquired from the old Society by virtue of section 5 of the Pharmacy Act 2007 shall be deemed to have been acquired by the new Society at the same time and for the same consideration that it was acquired by the old Society, and the provisions of section 556 shall apply accordingly.][1]

Amendments

[1] Inserted by F(No.2)A08 s45(1). Applies to disposals made on or after 20 November 2008.

Cross References

From Section 611A

Section 556 Adjustment of allowable expenditure by reference to consumer price index.

612 Scheme for retirement of farmers

[CGTA75 s30]

For the purposes of the Capital Gains Tax Acts, an amount by means of capital sum or premium provided under the European Communities (Retirement of Farmers) Regulations, 1974 (S.I. No. 116 of 1974), whether or not an annuity is granted in place of such capital sum or premium, shall not be deemed to form part of the consideration for the disposal in relation to which such capital sum or premium is provided.

613 Miscellaneous exemptions for certain kinds of property

[CGTA75s24]

(1) The following shall not be chargeable gains—

(a) any bonus payable under an instalment saving scheme within the meaning of section 53 of the Finance Act, 1970;

(b) any prize under section 22 of the Finance (Miscellaneous Provisions) Act, 1956;

(c) any sum obtained by means of compensation or damages for any wrong or injury suffered by an individual in his or her person or in his or her [profession][1]

[(d) any payment to which *section 205A* applies.][2]

(2) Winnings from betting (including pool betting), lotteries, sweepstakes or games with prizes shall not be chargeable gains, and rights to winnings obtained by participating in any pool betting, lottery, sweepstake or game with prizes shall not be chargeable assets.

(3) No chargeable gain shall accrue on the disposal of a right to or to any part of—

(a) any allowance, annuity or capital sum payable out of any superannuation fund, or under any superannuation scheme, established solely or mainly for persons employed in a profession, trade, undertaking or employment, and their dependants,

(b) an annuity granted otherwise than under a contract for a deferred annuity by a company as part of its business of granting annuities on human life, whether or not including instalments of capital, or

(c) annual payments due under a covenant made by any person and not secured on any property.

(4) (a) [Subject to *subsection (5)*, no chargeable gain][3] shall accrue on the disposal of an interest created by or arising under a settlement (including in particular an annuity or life interest and the reversion to an annuity or life interest)—

(i) by the person for whose benefit the interest was created by the terms of the settlement, or

(ii) by any other person except one who acquired, or derives that person's title from one who acquired, the interest for a consideration in money or money's worth, other than consideration consisting of another interest under the settlement.

(b) Subject to *paragraph (a)*, where a person who has acquired an interest in settled property (including in particular the reversion to an annuity or life interest) becomes as the holder of that interest absolutely entitled as against the trustee to any settled property, the person shall be treated as disposing of the interest in consideration of obtaining that settled property, but without prejudice to any gain accruing to the trustee on the disposal of that property deemed to be effected by the trustee under *section 576(1)*.

[(5) *Subsection (4)(a)* shall not apply—

(a) to the disposal of an interest in settled property, other than such a disposal treated under *subsection (4)(b)* as made in consideration of obtaining the settled property, if at the time of the disposal the trustees are neither resident nor ordinarily resident in the State,

(b) if the settlement falls within *subsection (6)*, or

(c) the property comprised in the settlement is or includes property that is derived directly or indirectly from a settlement falling within *subsection (6)*.

(6) (a) In this subsection "*arrangements*" means arrangements having the force of law by virtue of [*section 826(1)*][4] (as extended to capital gains tax by *section 828*).

(b) A settlement falls within this subsection if there has been a time when the trustees of the settlement—

(i) were neither resident nor ordinarily resident in the State, or

(ii) fell to be regarded for the purposes of any arrangements as resident in a territory outside the State.][5]

[(7) No chargeable gain shall arise on the receipt of an amount of compensation whether in money or money's worth under the Cessation of Turf Cutting Compensation Scheme administered by the Minister for Arts, Heritage and the Gaeltacht relating to the cessation of turf cutting on raised bog Special Areas of Conservation or Natural Heritage Areas, as required under the European Communities (Birds and Natural Habitats) Regulations 2011 (S.I. No. 477 of 2011) or the Wildlife (Amendment) Act 2000.][6]

Amendments

[1] Substituted by F(No.2)A13 s77(1)(b)(i). Applies to payments to which section 205A applies made on or after 1 August 2013.

[2] Inserted by F(No.2)A13 s77(1)(b)(ii). Applies to payments to which section 205A applies made on or after 1 August 2013.

[3] Substituted by FA99 s90(1)(a)(i). This section shall apply as respects the disposal on or after the 11th day of February, 1999, of an interest created by or arising under a settlement.

[4] Substituted by FA07 sched2(1)(r). Has effect as on and from the passing of this Act. FA07 2 April 2007

[5] Inserted by FA99 s90(1)(a)(ii). This section shall apply as respects the disposal on or after the 11th day of February, 1999, of an interest created by or arising under a settlement.

[6] Inserted by FA12 s62. Deemed to have come into force and takes effect on and from 1 January 2012.

Cross References

From Section 613

Section 576 Person becoming absolutely entitled to settled property.
Section 826 Agreements for relief from double taxation.
Section 828 Capital gains tax: double taxation relief.

To Section 613

Section 613A Supplementary provisions.
Section 726 Investment income.
Section 913 Application of income tax provisions relating to returns, etc.

613A Supplementary provisions

[(1) Subject to this section, *subsection (2)* shall apply where—

(a) *section 579B* applies as regards the trustees of a settlement,

(b) after the relevant time (within the meaning of that section) a person disposes of an interest created by or arising under the settlement and the circumstances are such that *subsection (4)(a)* of *section 613* does not apply by virtue of *subsection (5)(a)* of that section, and

(c) the interest was created for the benefit of the person making the disposal or that person otherwise acquired it, before the relevant time.

(2) For the purposes of calculating any chargeable gain accruing on the disposal of the interest, the person disposing of it shall be treated as having—

(a) disposed of it immediately before the relevant time, and

(b) immediately reacquired it,

at its market value at that time.

(3) *Subsection (2)* shall not apply if *section 579E* applied as regards the trustees in circumstances where the time concerned (within the meaning of that section) fell before the time when the interest was created for the benefit of the person disposing of it or when the person otherwise acquired it.

(4) *Subsection (6)* applies where—

(a) *section 579B* applies as regards the trustees of a settlement,

(b) after the relevant time (within the meaning of that section) a person disposes of an interest created by or arising under the settlement and the circumstances are such that *subsection (4)(a)* of *section 613* does not apply by virtue of *subsection (5)(a)* of that section,

(c) the interest was created for the person's benefit, or the person otherwise acquired it, before the relevant time, and

(d) *section 579E* applied as regards the trustees in circumstances where the time concerned (within the meaning of that section) fell in the relevant period.

(5) The relevant period is the period which—

(a) begins when the interest was created for the benefit of the person disposing of it or when the person otherwise acquired it, and

(b) ends with the relevant time.

(6) For the purposes of calculating any chargeable gain accruing on the disposal of the interest, the person disposing of it shall be treated as having—

(a) disposed of it immediately before the time determined in accordance with *subsection (7)*, and

(b) immediately reacquired it,

at its market value at that time.

(7) The time mentioned in *subsection (6)* is—

(a) where there is only one such time, the time concerned, or

(b) where there is more than one time concerned, because *section 579E* applied more than once, the earliest time concerned.

(8) Where *subsection (2)* applies, *subsection (6)* shall not apply.][1]

Amendments

[1] Inserted by FA99 s90(1)(b). This section shall apply as respects the disposal on or after the 11th day of February, 1999, of an interest created by or arising under a settlement.

Cross References

From Section 613A

Section 579B Trustees ceasing to be resident in the State.

Section 579E Trustees ceasing to be liable to Irish tax.

Section 613 Miscellaneous exemptions for certain kinds of property.

PART 20

Companies' Chargeable Gains

CHAPTER 1

General

614 Capital distribution derived from chargeable gain of company: recovery of tax from shareholder

[CTA76 s126]

(1) In this section, "*capital distribution*" has the same meaning as in *section 583*.

(2) This section shall apply where a person connected with a company resident in the State receives or becomes entitled to receive in respect of shares in the company any capital distribution from the company, other than a capital distribution representing a reduction of capital, and—

(a) the capital so distributed derives from the disposal after the 5th day of April, 1976, of assets in respect of which a chargeable gain accrues to the company, or

(b) the distribution constitutes such a disposal of assets.

(3) Where the corporation tax assessed on the company for the accounting period in which the chargeable gain accrues included any amount in respect of chargeable gains, and any of the tax assessed on the company for that period is not paid within 6 months from the date when it becomes payable by the company, the person referred to in *subsection (2)* may by an assessment made within 2 years from that date be assessed and charged (in the name of the company) to an amount of that corporation tax—

(a) not exceeding the amount or value of the capital distribution which that person has received or became entitled to receive, and

(b) not exceeding a proportion equal to that person's share of the capital distribution made by the company of corporation tax on the amount and at the rate charged in respect of that gain in the assessment in which that tax was charged.

(4) A person paying any amount of tax under this section shall be entitled to recover a sum equal to that amount from the company.

(5) This section is without prejudice to any liability of the person receiving or becoming entitled to receive the capital distribution in respect of a chargeable gain accruing to such person by reference to the capital distribution as constituting a disposal of an interest in shares in the company.

Cross References

From Section 614

Section 583 Capital distributions by companies.

To Section 614

Section 626A Restriction on set-off of pre-entry losses.

615 Company reconstruction or amalgamation: transfer of assets

[CTA76 s127; CGT(A)A78 s13]

(1) In this section—

"*scheme of reconstruction or amalgamation*" means a scheme for the reconstruction of any company or companies or the amalgamation of any 2 or more companies;

"*trading stock*" has the same meaning as in *section 89*.

[(2) (a) Subject to this section, where—

(i) any scheme of reconstruction or amalgamation involves the transfer of the whole or part of a company's business to another company,

(ii) (I) the company acquiring the assets is resident in the State at the time of the acquisition, or the assets are chargeable assets in relation to that company immediately after that time, and

(II) the company from which the assets are acquired is resident in the State at the time of the acquisition, or the assets are chargeable assets in relation to that company immediately [before that time,][1]

(iii) the first-mentioned company receives no part of the consideration for the transfer (otherwise than by the other company taking over the whole or part of the liabilities [of the business), and][2]

[(iv) the company acquiring the assets is not an authorised investment company (within the meaning of Part XIII of the Companies Act 1990) that is an investment undertaking (within the meaning of section 739B),][3]

then, in so far as relates to corporation tax on chargeable gains, both companies shall be treated as if any assets included in the transfer were acquired by the one company from the other company for a consideration of such amount as would secure that on the disposal by means of the transfer neither a gain nor a loss would accrue to the company making the disposal, and for the purposes of *section 556* the acquiring company shall be treated as if the respective acquisitions of the assets by the other company had been the acquiring company's acquisition of the assets.

(b) For the purposes of paragraph *(a)*—

(i) an asset is a "*chargeable asset*" in relation to a company at any time if, were the asset to be disposed of by the company at that time, any gain accruing to the company would be a chargeable gain, and

(ii) a reference to a company shall apply only to a company which, by virtue of the law of a [relevant Member State][4], is resident for the purposes of tax in such a Member State, and for this purpose "tax", in relation to a [relevant Member State][5] other than the State, means any tax imposed in the Member State which corresponds to corporation tax in the State.][6]

(3) This section shall not apply in relation to an asset which until the transfer formed part of trading stock of a trade carried on by the company making the disposal, or in relation to an asset which is acquired as trading stock for the purposes of a trade carried on by the company acquiring the asset.

[(4) (a) This section shall not apply in relation to the transfer of a specified intangible asset within the meaning of section 291A where the company acquiring the asset and the company from which the asset is acquired jointly so elect by giving notice, not later than 12 months from the end of the accounting period in which the company acquired the asset, to the Collector-General in such manner as the Revenue Commissioners may require.

(b) Where—

(i) an election is made under paragraph *(a)* in relation to the transfer of a specified intangible asset, and

(ii) that transfer is not a transfer to which section 400(6) applies,

then, for the purposes of computing any chargeable gain, the transfer of that asset shall be treated, as respects—

(I) the disposal by the company from which the asset was acquired, and

(II) the acquisition by the company acquiring the asset,

as having been made for a consideration equal to the market value of the asset on the date of that transfer.][7]

Amendments

[1, 2] Substituted by FA08 s42(1)(a)(i). Applies as respects a transfer, or as the case may be a disposal, on or after 18 February 2008.

[3] Inserted by FA08 s42(1)(a)(ii). Applies as respects a transfer, or as the case may be a disposal, on or after 18 February 2008.

[4, 5] Substituted by FA02 s36(a).

[6] Substituted by FA01 s38(1)(a). Applies as respects a disposal on or after 15 February 2001.

[7] Inserted by FA09 s13(1)(e). Applies to expenditure incurred by a company after 7 May 2009.

Revenue Briefings

Tax Briefing

Tax Briefing June 2001 – Issue 44 pg 34 – Partition of Family Trading Companies
Tax Briefing April 2002 – Issue 47 pg 17 – Retirement Relief and Reconstructions
Tax Briefing June 2002 – Issue 48 pg 16 – Capital Gains Tax – Transfer of Business Assets
Tax Briefing January 2003 – Issue 51 pg 6 – Family Trading Companies

Revenue Precedents

Where a family trading company (or group of companies) is broken up into separate individual trading companies, such an event will not be regarded as a disposal for CGT purposes provided that the value of each individual's holding in the company or group remains strictly unaltered and also provided certain other conditions are met. Prior approval and formal undertakings will be required. Requests for this treatment should be addressed to the Technical Services (CGT) area in the office of the Chief Inspector of Taxes. G.12.

Cross References

From Section 615

Section 89 Valuation of trading stock at discontinuance of trade.
Section 291A Intangible assets.
Section 400 Company reconstructions without change of ownership.
Section 556 Adjustment of allowable expenditure by reference to consumer price index.
Section 739B Interpretation and application.

To Section 615

Section 291A Intangible assets.
Section 620A Deemed disposal in certain circumstances.
Section 633 Company reconstruction or amalgamation: transfer of development land.
Section 633A Formation of SE or SCE by merger — leaving assets in the State.

616 Groups of companies: interpretation

[CTA76 s129(1) to (6)(b); FA90 s58]

(1) For the purposes of this section and of the following sections [of this Chapter][1] —

[(a) subject to *section 621(1)*, a reference to a company or companies shall apply only to a company or companies, as limited by *subsection (2)*, being a company or, as the case may be, companies which, by virtue of the law of a [relevant Member State][2], is or are resident for the purposes of tax in such a Member State, and for this purpose "tax", in relation to a [relevant Member State][3] other than the State, means any tax imposed in the Member State which corresponds to corporation tax in the State, and references to a member or members of a group of companies shall be construed accordingly;][4]

(b) a company is an effective 75 per cent subsidiary of another company (in this paragraph referred to as "*the parent*") at any time if at that time—

(i) the company is a 75 per cent subsidiary (within the meaning of *section 9*) of the parent,

(ii) the parent is beneficially entitled to not less than 75 per cent of any profits available for distribution to equity holders of the company, and

(iii) the parent would be beneficially entitled to not less than 75 per cent of the assets of the company available for distribution to its equity holders on a winding up,

and *sections 413* to *419* shall apply for the purposes of this paragraph as they apply for the purposes of *Chapter 5* of *Part 12*;

(bb) a principal company and all its effective 75 per cent subsidiaries shall form a group, and where a principal company is a member of a group as being itself an effective 75 per cent subsidiary that group shall comprise all its effective 75 per ent subsidiaries;

(c) "*principal company*" means a company of which another company is an effective 75 per cent subsidiary;][5]

(d) in applying the definition of "*75 per cent subsidiary*" in *section 9*, any share capital of a registered industrial and provident society shall be treated as ordinary share capital;

(e) "group" and "subsidiary" shall be construed with any necessary modifications where applied to a company incorporated under the law of a country outside the [State;][6]

[(f) an asset is a "*chargeable asset*" in relation to a company at any time if, were the asset to be disposed of by the company at that time, any gain accruing to the company would be a chargeable gain.][7]

[(g) Notwithstanding *paragraph (b)*—

(i) a company (in this paragraph referred to as the "*first-mentioned company*") shall be an effective 75 per cent subsidiary of the National Asset Management Agency where that Agency directly owns any part of the ordinary share capital of that company, and

(ii) any other company which is an effective 75 per cent subsidiary of the first-mentioned company shall be an effective 75 per cent subsidiary of the National Asset Management Agency.][8]

(2) For the purposes of this section and of the following sections of this Part, references to a company shall apply only to—

(a) a company within the meaning of the Companies Act, 1963,

(b) a company constituted under any other Act or a charter or letters patent or [...][9] formed under the law of a country or territory outside the State,

(c) a registered industrial and provident society, being a society within the meaning of *section 698*, and

(d) a building society incorporated or deemed by virtue of section 124(2) of the Building Societies Act, 1989, to be incorporated under that Act.

(3) For the purposes of this section and of the following sections of this Part, a group shall remain the same group so long as the same company remains the principal company of the group and, if at any time the principal company of a group becomes [an effective 75 per cent subsidiary][10] of another company, the group of which it was the principal company before that time shall be regarded as the same as the group of which that other company is the principal company or [an effective 75 per cent subsidiary][11], and the question whether or not a company has ceased to be a member of a group shall be determined accordingly.

[(3A) Where at any time the principal company of a group—

(a) (i) becomes an SE by reason of being the acquiring company in the formation of an SE by merger by acquisition (in accordance with Articles 2(1), 17(2)(*a*) and 29(1) of the SE Regulation (within the meaning of *section 630*)),

(ii) becomes a subsidiary of a holding SE (formed in accordance with Article 2(2) of that Regulation), or

(iii) is transformed into an SE (in accordance with Article 2(4) of that Regulation),

or

(b) becomes an SCE in the course of a merger in accordance with Article 2 of the SCE Regulation (within the meaning of *section 630*),

then the group of which it was the principal company before that time and any group of which the SE, or as the case may be the SCE, is a member on formation shall be regarded as the same, and the question of whether or not a company has ceased to be a member of a group shall be determined accordingly.][12]

(4) For the purposes of this section and of the following sections of this Part, the passing of a resolution or the making of an order or any other act for the winding up of a company shall not be regarded as the occasion of that company or of any [effective 75 per cent subsidiary][13] of that company ceasing to be a member of a group of companies.

(5) (a) The following sections of this Part, except in so far as they relate to the recovery of tax, shall also apply in relation to bodies from time to time established by or under any enactment for the carrying on of any industry or part of an industry, or of any undertaking, under national ownership or control as if—

(i) such bodies were companies within the meaning of those sections,

(ii) any such bodies charged with related functions and subsidiaries of any of them formed a group, and

(iii) any 2 or more such bodies charged at different times with the same or related functions were members of a group.

(b) *Paragraph (a)* shall apply subject to any enactment by virtue of which property, rights, liabilities or activities of one such body mentioned in that paragraph are to be treated for corporation tax as those of another such body.

(6) For the purposes of this Part—

(a) *section 557* and all other provisions for apportioning on a part disposal expenditure which is deductible in computing a gain shall be operated before the operation of and without regard to—

(i) *section 617(1)*, and

(ii) any other enactment making an adjustment to secure that neither a gain nor a loss occurs on a disposal;

(b) *section 589* shall not apply where the transfer is a disposal to which *section 617(1)* applies.

[(7) For the purposes of this Part—

"*EEA Agreement*" means the Agreement on the European Economic Area signed at Oporto on 2 May 1992, as adjusted by the Protocol signed at Brussels on 17 March 1993;

"*EEA State*" means a state which is a contracting party to the EEA Agreement;

"*relevant Member State*" means—

(a) a Member State of the European Communities, or

(b) not being such a Member State, an EEA State which is a territory with the government of which arrangements having the force of law by virtue of [*section 826(1)*][14] have been made;][15]

Amendments

[1] Substituted by FA99 s56(1)(a)(i). Applies as respects accounting periods ending on or after the 1st day of July, 1998.

[2, 3] Substituted by FA02 s36(b)(i).

[4] Substituted by FA01 s38(1)(b)(i)(I).

[5] Substituted by FA99 s56(1)(a)(ii). Applies as respects accounting periods ending on or after the 1st day of July, 1998.

[6] Substituted by FA01 s38(1)(b)(i)(II).

[7] Inserted by FA01 s38(1)(b)(i)(III).

[8] Inserted by the National Asset Management Agency Act 2009 Sched 3 part 10.

[9] Deleted by FA01 s38(1)(b)(ii).

[10, 11] Substituted by FA99 s56(1)(b)(i). Applies in any other case as on and from the 11th day of February, 1999.

[12] Inserted by FA06 s60(c).

[13] Substituted by FA99 s56(1)(b)(ii). Applies in any other case as on and from the 11th day of February, 1999.

[14] Substituted by FA07 sched2(1)(s). Has effect as on and from 2 April 2007

[15] Inserted by FA02 s36(b)(ii).

Cross References

From Section 616

Section 9 Subsidiaries.

Section 381 Right to repayment of tax by reference to losses.

Section 410 Group payments.

Section 413 Profits or assets available for distribution.
Section 419 The relevant accounting period, etc.
Section 557 Part disposals.
Section 589 Shares in close company transferring assets at undervalue.
Section 617 Transfers of assets, other than trading stock, within group.
Section 621 Depreciatory transactions in group.
Section 630 Interpretation (Part 21).
Section 698 Interpretation (Chapter 1).
Section 826 Agreements for relief from double taxation.

To Section 616

Section 494 Qualifying companies.
Section 586 Company amalgamations by exchange of shares.
Section 587 Company reconstructions and amalgamations.
Section 590 Attribution to participators of chargeable gains accruing to non-resident company.
Section 623A Transitional provisions in respect of section 623
Section 624 Exemption from charge under section 623 in case of certain mergers.
Section 625A Transitional provisions in respect of section 625.
Section 626B Exemption from tax in the case of gains on disposals of shares.
Section 629 Tax on non-resident company recoverable from another member of group or from controlling director.
Section 644AB Treatment of profits or gains from land rezonings
Section 649 Companies chargeable to capital gains tax in respect of chargeable gains accruing on relevant disposals.
Section 649B Windfall gains from rezonings: rate of charge.
Section 817D Interpretation and general (Chapter 3).
Schedule 18A Restriction on Set-off of Pre-entry Losses

617 Transfers of assets, other than trading stock, within group

[CTA76 s130]

[(1) Notwithstanding any provision in the Capital Gains Tax Acts fixing the amount of the consideration deemed to be received on a disposal or given on an acquisition, where—

(a) a member of a group of companies disposes of an asset to another member of the group,

(b) the company making the disposal is resident in the State at the time of the disposal or the asset is a chargeable asset in relation to that company immediately before that time, and

[(c) the other company—

(i) is resident in the State at the time of the disposal or the asset is a chargeable asset in relation to that company immediately after that time, and

[(ii) is not—

(I) an authorised investment company (within the meaning of Part XIII of the Companies Act 1990) that is an investment undertaking (within the meaning of *section 739B*), or

(II) a Real Estate Investment Trust (within the meaning of *section 705A*) or a member of a group Real Estate Investment Trust (within the meaning of *section 705A*),][1]][2]

both members shall, except where provided by [subsections (2), (3) and (4)][3], be treated, in so far as relates to corporation tax on chargeable gains, as if the asset acquired by the member to whom the disposal is made were acquired for a consideration of such amount as would secure that on the other member's disposal neither a gain nor a loss would accrue to that other member; but, where it is assumed for any purpose that a member of a group of companies has sold or acquired an asset, it shall be assumed also that it was not a sale to or acquisition from another member of the group.][4]

(2) *Subsection (1)* shall not apply where the disposal is—

(a) a disposal of a debt from a member of a group of companies effected by satisfying the debt or part of it, or

(b) a disposal of redeemable shares in a company on the occasion of their redemption,

and the reference in that subsection to a member of a group of companies disposing of an asset shall not apply to anything which under *section 583* is to be treated as a disposal of an interest in shares in a company in consideration for a capital distribution (within the meaning of that section) from that company, whether or not involving a reduction of capital.

(3) For the purposes of *subsection (1)*, in so far as the consideration for the disposal consists of money or money's worth by means of compensation for any kind of damage or injury to assets, or for the destruction or dissipation of assets or for anything which depreciates or might depreciate an asset, the disposal shall be treated as being to the person who, whether as an insurer or otherwise, ultimately bears the burden of furnishing that consideration.

[(4) Where a member of a group of companies disposes of a specified intangible asset within the meaning of section 291A to another member of the group, subsection (1) shall not apply to the disposal of that asset where the companies jointly so elect by giving notice, not later than 12 months from the end of the accounting period in which the other member of the group acquired the asset, to the Collector-General in such manner as the Revenue Commissioners may require.][5]

Amendments

[1] Substituted by FA14 s29(1)(a). Applies as respects any disposal on or after 23 October 2014.

[2] Substituted by FA08 s42(1)(b). Applies as respects a transfer, or as the case may be a disposal, on or after 18 February 2008.

[3] Substituted by FA09 s13(1)(f). Applies to expenditure incurred by a company after 7 May 2009.

[4] Substituted by FA01 s38(1)(c). Applies as respects a disposal on or after 15 February 2001.

[5] Inserted by FA09 s13(1)(g). Applies to expenditure incurred by a company after 7 May 2009.

Revenue Precedents

Under section 617 certain assets can be transferred within a capital gains tax group without a chargeable gain arising. Instead, the transferee company takes the asset at the same time and cost at which it was originally acquired by the transferor company. The definition of a capital gains tax group in S.616 confines this relief to such group companies where both companies are resident in the State. In practice Revenue will allow similar relief in circumstances involving transfers within a non-resident CGT group where assets are transferred as part of a transfer of a trade carried on in the State where profits of the trade, including chargeable gains, are chargeable to Corporation Tax. The assets must be in use for the purpose of the trade and there must be no discontinuance of the trade i.e. the transferee will continue to carry on the trade. The transfer must also be for bona fide commercial reasons and not to avoid tax. To avail of this treatment a formal submission must be made to the Technical Services (CGT) area of the Office of the Chief Inspector of Taxes. This will involve formal undertakings from the transferee and the group parent in relation to the asset transferred. G60.

Cross References

From Section 617

Section 291A Intangible assets.
Section 583 Capital distributions by companies.
Section 739B Interpretation and application.

To Section 617

Section 291A Intangible assets.
Section 486C Relief from tax for certain start-up companies.
Section 590 Attribution to participators of chargeable gains accruing to non-resident company.
Section 616 Groups of companies: interpretation.
Section 619 Disposals or acquisitions outside group.
Section 620A Deemed disposal in certain circumstances.
Section 622 Dividend stripping.
Section 632 Transfer of assets by company to its parent company.
Section 649 Companies chargeable to capital gains tax in respect of chargeable gains accruing on relevant disposals.
Schedule 18A Restriction on Set-off of Pre-entry Losses

618 Transfers of trading stock within group

[CTA76 s131]

[(1) Where—

(a) a company which is a member of a group of companies acquires an asset as trading stock of a trade to which this section applies,

(b) the acquisition is from another company which is a member of the group, and

(c) the asset did not form part of the trading stock of any such trade carried on by the other company,

the company acquiring the asset shall be treated for the purposes of *section 596* as having acquired the asset otherwise than as trading stock and immediately appropriated it for the purposes of the trade as trading stock.][1]

(2) Where a member of a group of companies disposes of an asset to another member of the group and the asset formed part of the trading stock of a trade[to which this section applies][2] carried on by the member disposing of the asset but is acquired by the other member otherwise than as trading stock of a trade carried on by that other member, the member disposing of the asset shall be treated for the purposes of *section 596* as having immediately before the disposal appropriated the asset for some purpose other than the purpose of use as trading stock.

[(3) This section applies to—

(a) a trade carried on by a company which is resident in the State, and

(b) a trade carried on in the State through a branch or agency by a company which is not so resident.][3]

Amendments

[1] Substituted by FA01 s38(1)(d)(i). Applies as respects an acquisition or disposal on or after 15 February 2001.

[2] Inserted by FA01 s38(1)(d)(ii). Applies as respects an acquisition or disposal on or after 15 February 2001.

[3] Inserted by FA01 s38(1)(d)(iii). Applies as respects an acquisition or disposal on or after 15 February 2001.

Cross References

From Section 618

Section 596 Appropriations to and from stock in trade.

To Section 618

Section 590 Attribution to participators of chargeable gains accruing to non-resident company.
Section 649 Companies chargeable to capital gains tax in respect of chargeable gains accruing on relevant disposals.
Schedule 25A Exemption from Tax in the Case of Gains on Certain Disposals of Shares

619 Disposals or acquisitions outside group

[CTA76 s132; CGT(A)A78 s14; FA92 s73]

(1) Where a company which is or has been a member of a group of companies disposes of an asset which it acquired from another member of the group [in the course of a disposal to which *section 617* applies][1], *section 555* shall apply in relation to any capital allowances made to the other member (in so far as not taken into account in relation to a disposal of the asset by that other member), and so on as respects previous transfers of the asset between members of the group, but this shall not be taken as affecting the consideration for which an asset is deemed under *section 617(1)* to be acquired.

(2) (a) *Section 556* shall apply in relation to a disposal of an asset by a company which is or has been a member of a group of companies, and which acquired the asset from another member of the group [in the course of a disposal to which *section 617* applies][2], as if all members of the group for the time being were the same person, and as if the acquisition or provision of the asset by the group, so taken as a single person, had been the acquisition or provision of the asset by the member disposing of the asset.

(b) Notwithstanding *paragraph (a)*, where at any time after the asset was acquired or provided by the group so taken as a single person and before the 24th day of April, 1992, there was an acquisition (in this paragraph referred to as "the later acquisition") of the asset by a member of the group from another member of the group as a result of a relevant disposal (within the meaning of *section 648*), this subsection shall apply as if the reference in *paragraph (a)* to the acquisition or provision of the asset by the group were a reference to the later acquisition or, where there was more than one, the last such acquisition.

Amendments

[1, 2] Substituted by FA01 s38(1)(e). Applies as respects an acquisition on or after 15 February 2001.

Cross References

From Section 619

Section 555 Restriction of losses by reference to capital allowances and renewals allowances.
Section 556 Adjustment of allowable expenditure by reference to consumer price index.
Section 617 Transfers of assets, other than trading stock, within group.
Section 648 Interpretation (Chapter 2).

To Section 619

Section 590 Attribution to participators of chargeable gains accruing to non-resident company.
Section 632 Transfer of assets by company to its parent company.

620 Replacement of business assets by members of group

[(1) For the purposes of this section "*old assets*" and "*new assets*" have the same meanings as in *section 597*.

(2) Subject to *subsection (4)*, for the purposes of *section 597* all the trades to which this section applies carried on by members of a group of companies shall be treated as a single trade (except in a case of one member of the group acquiring, or acquiring the interest in, the new assets from another member or disposing of, or disposing of the interest in, the old assets to another member).

(3) This section applies to—

(a) any trade carried on by a company which is resident in the State, and

(b) any trade carried on in the State through a branch or agency of a company which is not so resident.

(4) This section shall not apply unless—

(a) the company disposing of the old assets is resident in the State at the time of the disposal, or the assets are chargeable assets in relation to that company immediately before that time, and

(b) the company acquiring the new assets is resident in the State at the time of acquisition, or the assets are chargeable assets in relation to that company immediately after that time.][1]

Amendments

[1] Substituted by FA01 s38(1)(f). Applies in relation to cases in which either the disposal or acquisition is on or after 15 February 2001, or both the disposal and acquisition are on or after that date.

Cross References

From Section 620

Section 597 Replacement of business and other assets.

To Section 620

Section 590 Attribution to participators of chargeable gains accruing to non-resident company.

Section 620A Deemed disposal in certain circumstances.

620A Deemed disposal in certain circumstances

[(1) This section applies in relation to a company where—

(a) at any time on or after 15 February 2001 an asset ceases to be a chargeable asset in relation to the company—

(i) where at the time of the acquisition of the asset by the company the asset consisted of shares deriving their value or the greater part of their value from assets specified in *paragraph (a)* or *(b)* of *section 29(3)*, by virtue of the assets ceasing to so derive their value or the greater part of their value, or

(ii) by virtue of the asset becoming situated outside the State,

and

(b) (i) the company acquired the asset in the course of—

(I) a transfer to which *section 615* applies, or

(II) a disposal to which *section 617* applies,

or

(ii) by virtue of *section 620* the asset constitutes new assets for the purposes of *section 597*.

(2) Where this section applies in relation to a company, the company shall be deemed for the purposes of the Capital Gains Tax Acts and the Corporation Tax Acts—

(a) to have disposed of the asset immediately before the time when it ceased to be a chargeable asset in relation to the company, and

(b) immediately to have reacquired it,

at its market value at that time.][1]

Amendments

[1] Inserted by FA01 s38(1)(g). This section applies from 15 February 2001.

Cross References

From Section 620A

Section 29 Persons chargeable.

Section 597 Replacement of business and other assets.

Section 615 Company reconstruction or amalgamation: transfer of assets.
Section 617 Transfers of assets, other than trading stock, within group.
Section 620 Replacement of business assets by members of group.

621 Depreciatory transactions in group

[CTA76 s138]

(1) For the purposes of this section—

"securities" includes any loan stock or similar security whether secured or unsecured;

references to the disposal of assets include references to any method by which one company which is a member of a group appropriates the goodwill of another member of the group;

[a "group of companies" may consist of companies some or all of which are not resident for the purposes of tax in a [relevant Member State][1].][2]

(2) References in this section to the disposal of shares or securities include references to the occasion of the making of a claim under *section 538(2)* that the value of shares or securities has become negligible, and references to a person making a disposal shall be construed accordingly.

(3) This section shall apply as respects a disposal of shares in or securities of a company (in this section referred to as an "ultimate disposal") if the value of the shares or securities has been materially reduced by a depreciatory transaction effected on or after the 6th day of April, 1974, and for this purpose "*depreciatory transaction*" means—

(a) any disposal of assets at other than market value by one member of a group of companies to another, or

(b) any other transaction satisfying the conditions of *subsection (4)*;

but a transaction shall not be treated as a depreciatory transaction to the extent that it consists of a payment which is required to be or has been taken into account, for the purposes of corporation tax on chargeable gains, in computing a chargeable gain or allowable loss accruing to the person making the ultimate disposal.

(4) The conditions referred to in *subsection (3)(b)* are—

(a) that the company, the shares in which or securities of which are the subject of the ultimate disposal, or any [effective 75 per cent subsidiary][3] of that company, was a party to the transaction, and

(b) that the parties to the transaction were or included 2 or more companies which at the time of the transaction were members of the same group of companies.

(5) Without prejudice to the generality of *subsection (3)*, the cancellation of any shares in or securities of one member of a group of companies under section 72 of the Companies Act, 1963, shall, to the extent that immediately before the cancellation those shares or securities were the property of another member of the group, be taken to be a transaction fulfilling the conditions in *subsection (4)*.

(6) Where the person making the ultimate disposal is or has at any time been a member of the group of companies referred to in *subsection (3)* or *(4)*, any allowable loss accruing on the disposal shall be reduced to such extent as appears to the inspector, or on appeal the Appeal Commissioners, or on a rehearing by a judge of the Circuit Court, that judge, to be just and reasonable having regard to the depreciatory transaction; but, if the person making the ultimate disposal is not a member of that group when disposing of the shares or securities, no

reduction of the loss shall be made by reference to a depreciatory transaction which took place when that person was not a member of that group.

(7) The inspector, the Appeal Commissioners or the judge of the Circuit Court shall make the decision under *subsection (6)* on the basis that the allowable loss ought not to reflect any diminution in the value of the company's assets attributable to a depreciatory transaction, but allowance may be made for any other transaction on or after the 6th day of April, 1974, which has enhanced the value of the company's assets and depreciated the value of the assets of any other member of the group.

(8) (a) Where under *subsection (6)* a reduction is made in an allowable loss, any chargeable gain accruing on a disposal of the shares in or securities of any other company which was a party to the depreciatory transaction by reference to which the reduction was made, being a disposal not later than 10 years after the depreciatory transaction, shall be reduced to such extent as appears to the inspector, or on appeal to the Appeal Commissioners, or on a rehearing by a judge of the Circuit Court, that judge, to be just and reasonable having regard to the effect of the depreciatory transaction on the value of those shares or securities at the time of their disposal.

(b) Notwithstanding *paragraph (a)*, the total amount of any one or more reductions in chargeable gains made by reference to a depreciatory transaction shall not exceed the amount of the reductions in allowable losses made by reference to that depreciatory transaction.

(c) All such adjustments, whether by means of discharge or repayment of tax or otherwise, as are required to give effect to this subsection may be made at any time.

Amendments

[1] Substituted by FA02 s36(c).

[2] Substituted by FA01 s38(1)(h). Applies as respects a case in which the depreciatory transaction (within the meaning of section 621) is on or after 15 February 2001.

[3] Substituted by FA99 s56(1)(c). Applies in any other case as on and from the 11th day of February, 1999.

Case Law

In Tesco plc v Crimmin 1997 STC 981 a loss arising on the disposal of a subsidiary by a parent company was eliminated as it was held to have been a depreciatory transaction.

Cross References

From Section 621

Section 538 Disposals where assets lost or destroyed or become of negligible value.

To Section 621

Section 616 Groups of companies: interpretation.

Section 622 Dividend stripping.

Section 649 Companies chargeable to capital gains tax in respect of chargeable gains accruing on relevant disposals.

622 Dividend stripping

[CTA76 s139]

(1) This section shall apply where one company (in this section referred to as "the first company") has a holding in another company (in this section referred to as "the second company") and the following conditions are fulfilled—

(a) that the holding amounts to, or is an ingredient in a holding amounting to, 10 per cent of all holdings of the same class in the second company,

(b) that the first company is not a dealing company in relation to the holding,

(c) that a distribution is or has been made on or after the 6th day of April, 1974, to the first company in respect of the holding, and

(d) that the effect of the distribution is that the value of the holding is or has been materially reduced.

(2) (a) Where this section applies in relation to a holding, *section 621* shall apply in relation to any disposal of any shares or securities comprised in the holding, whether the disposal is by the first company or by any other company to which the holding is transferred by a transfer to which *section 617* applies, as if the distribution were a depreciatory transaction and, if the companies concerned are not members of a group of companies, as if they were.

(b) Notwithstanding *paragraph (a)*, the distribution shall not be treated as a depreciatory transaction to the extent that it consists of a payment which is required to be or has been taken into account, for the purposes of corporation tax on chargeable gains, in computing a chargeable gain or allowable loss accruing to the person making the ultimate disposal.

(3) This section shall be construed together with *section 621*.

(4) For the purposes of this section, a company shall be a dealing company in relation to a holding if a profit on the sale of the holding would be taken into account in computing the company's trading profits.

(5) References in this section to a holding in a company are references to a holding of shares or securities by virtue of which the holder may receive distributions made by the company, but so that—

(a) a company's holdings of different classes in another company shall be treated as separate holdings, and

(b) holdings of shares or securities which differ in the entitlements or obligations they confer or impose shall be regarded as holdings of different classes.

(6) For the purposes of *subsection (1)*—

(a) all a company's holdings of the same class in another company shall be treated as ingredients constituting a single holding, and

(b) a company's holding of a particular class shall be treated as an ingredient in a holding amounting to 10 per cent of all holdings of that class if the aggregate of that holding and other holdings of that class held by connected persons amounts to 10 per cent of all holdings of that class.

Cross References

From Section 622

Section 617 Transfers of assets, other than trading stock, within group.

Section 621 Depreciatory transactions in group.

623 Company ceasing to be member of group

[CTA76 s135 and FA96 s51]

(1) For the purposes of this section—

(a) 2 or more companies shall be associated companies if by themselves they would form a group of companies;

(b) a chargeable gain shall be deferred on a replacement of business assets if, by one or more claims under *section 597*, a chargeable gain on the disposal of those assets is treated as not accruing until the new assets within the meaning of that section cease to be used for the purpose of a trade carried on by the company making the claim;

(c) an asset acquired by the chargeable company shall be treated as the same as an asset owned at a later time by that company or an associated company if the value of the second asset is derived in whole or in part from the first asset, and in particular where the second asset is a freehold, and the first asset was a leasehold and the lessee has acquired the reversion;

(d) references to a company ceasing to be a member of a group of companies shall not apply to cases where a company ceases to be a member of a group by being wound up or dissolved or in consequence of another member of the group being wound up or dissolved where the winding up or dissolution of the member or the other member, as the case may be, is for bona fide commercial reasons and is not part of a scheme or arrangement the main purpose or one of the main purposes of which is the avoidance of tax.

[(2) [Subject to *subsection (2A)*, this section applies where—][1]

(a) a company (in this section referred to as the "*chargeable company*") which is a member of a group of companies acquires an asset from another company which at the time of acquisition was a member of the group,

(b) the chargeable company ceases to be a member of the group within the period of 10 years after the time of the acquisition,

(c) the chargeable company is resident in the State at the time of acquisition of the asset, or the asset is a chargeable asset in relation to that company immediately after that time, and

(d) the other company is resident in the State at the time of that acquisition, or the asset is a chargeable asset in relation to that company immediately before that time.][2]

[(2A) (a) This section does not apply to a bank asset where that asset is acquired on or after the establishment day by—

(i) NAMA, or

(ii) a company to which *section 616(1)(g)* relates from that Agency or a company to which that paragraph relates.

(b) In this subsection "*bank asset*", "*establishment day*" and "*NAMA*" have the same meanings, respectively, as they have in the National Asset Management Agency Act 2009.][3]

(3) (a) Where 2 or more associated companies (in this subsection referred to as "the associated companies") cease to be members of a group at the same time—

(i) *subsection (2)* shall not apply as respects an acquisition by one from another of the associated companies, and

(ii) where—

(I) a dividend has been paid or a distribution has been made by one of the associated companies to a company which is not one of the associated companies, and

(II) the dividend so paid or the distribution so made has been paid or made, as the case may be, wholly or partly out of profits which derive from the disposal of any asset by one to another of the associated companies,

the amount of the dividend paid or the amount or value of the distribution made, to the extent that it is paid or made, as the case may be, out of those profits, shall be deemed for the purposes of the Capital Gains Tax Acts to be consideration (in addition to any other consideration) received by the member of the group or former member of the group in respect of a disposal, being a disposal which gave rise to or was caused by the associated companies ceasing to be members of the group.

(b) *Paragraph (a)(ii)* shall not apply to a distribution other than a dividend where a company ceases to be a member of a group of companies before the 23rd day of April, 1996.

(4) If when the chargeable company ceases to be a member of the group the chargeable company, or an associated company also leaving the group, owns otherwise than as trading stock—

(a) the asset referred to in *subsection (2)*, or

(b) property on the acquisition of which a chargeable gain in relation to the asset has been deferred on a replacement of business assets,

the chargeable company shall be treated for the purposes of the Capital Gains Tax Acts as if immediately after its acquisition of the asset it had sold and immediately reacquired the asset at market value at that time ["and, solely for the purpose of determining when such tax is due and payable, as if any tax charged in respect of a chargeable gain that accrued from such a sale and reacquisition were tax for the accounting period of the chargeable company in which it ceases to be a member of the group"][4].

(5) Where any of the corporation tax assessed on a company in consequence of this section is not paid within 6 months from the date when it becomes payable, then—

(a) a company which on that date, or immediately after the chargeable company ceased to be a member of the group, was the principal company of the group, and

(b) a company which owned the asset on that date or when the chargeable company ceased to a member of the group,

may, at any time within 2 years from the time when the tax became payable, be assessed and charged (in the name of the chargeable company) to all or any part of that tax, and a company paying any amount of tax under this subsection shall be entitled to recover a sum of that amount from the chargeable company.

(6) Notwithstanding any limitation on the time for making assessments, an assessment to corporation tax chargeable in consequence of this section may be made at any time within 10 years from the time when the chargeable company ceased to be a member of the group, and where under this section the chargeable company is to be treated as having disposed of and reacquired an asset, all such recomputations

of liability in respect of other disposals, and all such adjustments of tax, whether by means of assessment or by means of discharge or repayment of tax, as may be required in consequence of this section shall be made.

Amendments

[1] Substituted by the National Asset Management Agency Act 2009 Sched 3 part 10.

[2] Substituted by FA01 s38(1)(i). Applies as respects an asset acquired on or after 15 February 2001.

[3] Inserted by the National Asset Management Agency Act 2009 Sched 3 part 10.

[4] Inserted by FA14 s41. Comes into operation on 1 January 2015.

Case Law

There was a deemed disposal of assets previously acquired by an intra-group transaction where the holding company ceased to be a member of a group by reason of its subsidiaries becoming non-resident. Lion v Inspector of Taxes 1997 SpC 115

Revenue Briefings

Tax Briefing

Tax Briefing June 2002 – Issue 48 pg 17 – Exemption from Section 623 for Certain Mergers (Section 624 TCA 1997)

Cross References

From Section 623

Section 597 Replacement of business and other assets.

To Section 623

Section 590 Attribution to participators of chargeable gains accruing to non-resident company.
Section 623A Transitional provisions in respect of section 623
Section 624 Exemption from charge under section 623 in case of certain mergers.
Section 649 Companies chargeable to capital gains tax in respect of chargeable gains accruing on relevant disposals.
Schedule 25A Exemption from Tax in the Case of Gains on Certain Disposals of Shares

623A Transitional provisions in respect of section 623

[(1) In this section "*the new definition*" means *section 616* as amended by *section 56* of the *Finance Act, 1999,* and "the old definition" means that section as it had effect on the 10th day of February, 1999.

(2) Where—

(a) on the 11th day of February, 1999, a company ceases, for the purposes of *section 616* and the provisions of this Part subsequent to that section, to be a member of a group by reason only of the substitution for the old definition of the new definition, and

(b) in consequence of ceasing to be such a member the company would, apart from this section, be treated by virtue of *section 623(4)* as selling an asset at any time,

the company shall not be treated as selling the asset at that time unless the conditions in *subsection (3)* become satisfied, assuming for that purpose that the old definition applies.

(3) The conditions referred to in *subsection (2)* are—

(a) that for the purposes of *section 623*, the company ceases at any time (in this subsection referred to as the "*relevant time*") to be a member of the group referred to in *subsection (2)(a)*,

(b) that, at the relevant time, the company (or an associated company also ceasing to be a member of that group at that time) owns, otherwise than as trading stock, the asset, or property on the acquisition of which a chargeable gain in relation to the asset has been deferred on a replacement of business assets, and

(c) that the time of acquisition of the asset referred to in *section 623(2)* fell within the period of 10 years ending with the relevant time.][1]

Amendments

[1] Inserted by FA99 s56(1)(d). Applies in any other case as on and from the 11th day of February, 1999.

Cross References

From Section 623A

Section 56 Tax on quarries, mines and other concerns chargeable under Case I(b) of Schedule D.

Section 616 Groups of companies: interpretation.

Section 623 Company ceasing to be member of group.

624 Exemption from charge under section 623 in case of certain mergers

[CTA76 s136]

(1) *Section 623* shall not apply in a case where—

(a) as part of a merger a company (in this section referred to as "company A") ceases to be a member of a group of companies (in this section referred to as "the A group"), and

(b) it is shown that the merger was carried out for bona fide commercial reasons and that the avoidance of liability to tax was not the main or one of the main purposes of the merger.

(2) In this section, "*merger*" means an arrangement (including a series of arrangements)—

(a) whereby one or more companies (in this section referred to as "the acquiring company" or, as the case may be, "the acquiring companies") none of which is a member of the A group acquires or acquire, otherwise than with a view to their disposal, one or more interests in the whole or part of the business which, before the arrangement took effect, was carried on by company A,

(b) whereby one or more members of the A group acquires or acquire, otherwise than with a view to their disposal, one or more interests in the whole or part of the business or each of the businesses which, before the arrangement took effect, was carried on either by the acquiring company or acquiring companies or by a company at least 90 per cent of the ordinary share capital of which was then beneficially owned by 2 or more of the acquiring companies, and

(c) in respect of which the conditions in *subsection (4)* are fulfilled.

(3) For the purposes of *subsection (2)*, a member of a group of companies shall be treated as carrying on as one business the activities of that group.

(4) The conditions referred to in *subsection (2)(c)* are—

(a) that not less than 25 per cent by value of each of the interests acquired as mentioned in *paragraphs (a)* and *(b)* of *subsection (2)* consists of a holding of ordinary share capital, and the remainder of the interest or, as the case may be, of each of the interests acquired as mentioned in *paragraph (b)* of that subsection consists of a holding of share capital (of any description) or debentures or both,

(b) that the value or, as the case may be, the aggregate value of the interest or interests acquired as mentioned in *subsection (2)(a)* is substantially the same as the value or, as the case may be, the aggregate value of the interest or interests acquired as mentioned in *subsection (2)(b)*, and

(c) that the consideration for the acquisition of the interest or interests acquired by the acquiring company or acquiring companies as mentioned in *subsection (2)(a)*, disregarding any part of that consideration which is small by comparison with the total, either consists of, or is applied in the acquisition of, or consists partly of and as to the balance is applied in the acquisition of, the interest or interests acquired by members of the A group as mentioned in *subsection (2)(b)*,

and for the purposes of this subsection the value of an interest shall be determined as at the date of its acquisition.

(5) Notwithstanding *section 616(1)(a)*, references in this section to a company shall include references to [a company which is not resident in a [relevant Member State][1]][2].

Amendments

[1] Substituted by FA02 s36(d).

[2] Substituted by FA01 s38(1)(j). Applies from 15 February 2001.

Cross References

From Section 624

Section 616 Groups of companies: interpretation.

Section 623 Company ceasing to be member of group.

625 Shares in subsidiary member of group

[CTA76 s137]

(1) (a) This section shall apply if a company (in this section referred to as "the subsidiary") ceases to be a member of a group of companies, and on an earlier occasion shares in the subsidiary were disposed of by another company (in this section referred to as "the chargeable company") which was then a member of that group in the course of an amalgamation or reconstruction in the group, but only if that earlier occasion fell within the period of 10 years ending on the date on which the subsidiary ceases to be a member of the group.

(b) References in this section to a company ceasing to be a member of a group of companies shall not apply to cases where a company ceases to be a member of a group by being wound up or dissolved or in consequence of another member of the group being wound up or dissolved.

(2) The chargeable company shall be treated for the purposes of the Capital Gains Tax Acts as if immediately before the earlier occasion it had sold and immediately reacquired the shares referred to in *subsection (1)(a)* at market value at that time.

(3) Where before the subsidiary ceases to be a member of the group the chargeable company has ceased to exist, or a resolution has been passed, or an order made, for the winding up of the company, or any other act has been done for the like purpose, any corporation tax to which, if the chargeable company had continued in existence, it would have been chargeable in consequence of this section may be

assessed and charged (in the name of the chargeable company) on the company which is, at the time when the subsidiary ceases to be a member of the group, the principal company of the group.

(4) Where any of the corporation tax assessed on a company in consequence of this section, or in pursuance of *subsection (3)*, is not paid within 6 months from the date when it becomes payable, then—

(a) a company which is on that date, or was on the earlier occasion, the principal company of the group, and

(b) any company taking an interest in the subsidiary as part of the amalgamation or reconstruction in the group, may at any time within 2 years from the time when the tax became payable, be assessed and charged (in the name of the chargeable company) to all or any part of that tax, and a company paying any amount of tax under this subsection shall be entitled to recover a sum of that amount from the chargeable company or, as the case may be, from the company assessed under *subsection (3)*.

(5) Notwithstanding any limitation on the time for making assessments, an assessment to corporation tax chargeable in consequence of this section may be made at any time within 10 years from the time when the subsidiary ceased to be a member of the group and, in relation to any disposal of the property after the earlier occasion, there shall be made all such adjustments of tax, whether by means of assessment or by means of discharge or repayment of tax, as may be required in consequence of this section.

(6) For the purposes of this section, there shall be a disposal of shares in the course of an amalgamation or reconstruction in a group of companies if—

(a) *section 586* or *587* applies to shares in a company so as to equate them with shares in or debentures of another company, and

(b) the companies are members of the same group, or become members of the same group as a result of the amalgamation or reconstruction.

(7) Where by virtue of *section 587* shares are to be treated as cancelled and replaced by a new issue, references in this section to a disposal of shares include references to the occasion of the shares being so treated.

Cross References

From Section 625

Section 586 Company amalgamations by exchange of shares.

Section 587 Company reconstructions and amalgamations.

To Section 625

Section 590 Attribution to participators of chargeable gains accruing to non-resident company.

Section 625A Transitional provisions in respect of section 625.

625A Transitional provisions in respect of section 625

[(1) In this section—

"*the subsidiary*" and "*the chargeable company*" have the same meanings, respectively, assigned to them by 625(1);

"*the new definition*" means *section 616* as amended by section 56 of the Finance Act, 1999, and "*the old definition*" means that section as it had effect on the 10th day of February, 1999.

(2) Where—

(a) on the 11th day of February, 1999, the subsidiary company ceases, for the purposes of *section 616* and the provisions of this Part subsequent to that section, to be a member of a group by reason only of the substitution for the old definition of the new definition, and

(b) in consequence of ceasing to be such a member the chargeable company would, apart from this section, be treated by virtue of *section 625(2)* as selling shares in the subsidiary at any time,

the chargeable company shall not be treated as selling the shares at that time unless the conditions in subsection (3) become satisfied assuming for that purpose that the old definition applies.

(3) The conditions referred to in subsection (2) are—

(a) that for the purposes of *section 625* the subsidiary ceases at any time (in this subsection referred to as "*the relevant time*") to be a member of the group referred to in *subsection (2)(a)*, and

(b) that the time of the earlier occasion referred to in *section 625(1)(a)* fell within the period of 10 years ending with the relevant time.][1]

Amendments

[1] Inserted by FA99 s56(1)(e). Applies in any other case as on and from the 11th day of February, 1999.

Cross References

From Section 625A

Section 616 Groups of companies: interpretation.

Section 625 Shares in subsidiary member of group.

626 Tax on company recoverable from other members of group

[CTA76 s134]

(1) Where at any time a chargeable gain accrues to a company which at that time is a member of a group of companies and any of the corporation tax assessed on the company for the accounting period in which the chargeable gain accrues is not paid within 6 months from the date when it becomes payable by the company, then, if the tax so assessed included any amount in respect of chargeable gains—

(a) a company which at the time when the gain accrued was the principal company of the group, and

(b) any other company which in any part of the period of 2 years ending with that time was a member of that group of companies and owned the asset disposed of or any part of it or, where the asset is an interest or right in or over another asset, owned either asset or any part of either asset,

may at any time within 2 years from the time when the tax became payable be assessed and charged (in the name of the company to whom the chargeable gain accrued) to an amount of that corporation tax not exceeding corporation tax on the amount and at the rate charged in respect of that gain in the assessment on the company to which the chargeable gain accrued.

(2) A company paying any amount of tax under *subsection (1)* shall be entitled to recover a sum of that amount—

(a) from the company to which the chargeable gain accrued, or

(b) if that company is not the company which was the principal company of the group at the time when the chargeable gain accrued, from that principal company, and a company paying any amount under *paragraph (b)* shall be entitled to recover a sum of that amount from the company to which the chargeable gain accrued and, in so far as it is not so recovered, to recover from any company which is for the time being a member of the group and which has while a member of the group owned the asset disposed of or any part of that asset (or, where that asset is an interest or right in or over another asset, owned either asset or any part of either asset) such proportion of the amount unrecovered as is just having regard to the value of the asset at the time when the asset, or an interest or right in or over that asset, was disposed of by that company.

Cross References

To Section 626

Section 649 Companies chargeable to capital gains tax in respect of chargeable gains accruing on relevant disposals.

626A Restriction on set-off of pre-entry losses

[For the purposes of *Part 20*, Schedule 18A (which makes provision in relation to losses accruing to a company before the time when it becomes a member of a group of companies and losses accruing on assets held by any company at such a time) shall apply.][1]

Amendments

[1] Inserted by FA99 s56(1)(f). Applies in any other case as on and from the 11th day of February, 1999.

Cross References

From Section 626A

Section 614 Capital distribution derived from chargeable gain of company: recovery of tax from shareholder.

626B Exemption from tax in the case of gains on disposals of shares

[(1) (a) In this section, *section 626C* and Schedule 25A—

"*investor company*" and "*investee company*" have the meanings assigned by *subsection (2)*;

"*relevant territory*" means—

(i) a Member State of the European Communities, [...][1]

(ii) not being such a Member State, a territory with the government of which arrangements having the force of law by virtue of [*section 826(1)*][2] [have been made, or][3]

[(iii) not being a territory referred to in subparagraph (i) or (ii), a territory with the government of which arrangements have been made which on completion of the procedures set out in section 826(1) will have the force of law;][4]

[...][5]

"*tax*" in relation to a relevant territory other than the State means any tax imposed in that territory which corresponds to income tax or corporation tax in the State;

"2 year period" means a period ending on the day before the second anniversary of the day on which the period began.

(b) For the purposes of this section, *section 626C* and Schedule 25A—

(i) a company shall only be a parent company in relation to another company at any time if that time falls within an uninterrupted period of not less than 12 months throughout which it directly or indirectly holds shares in that company by virtue of which—

(I) it holds not less than [5 per cent][6] of the company's ordinary share capital,

(II) it is beneficially entitled to not less than [5 per cent][7] of the profits available for distribution to equity holders of the company, and

(III) it would be beneficially entitled on a winding up to not less than [5 per cent][8] of the assets of the company available for distribution to equity holders,

and for the purposes of this subparagraph—

(A) *subsections (2)* to *(10)* of *section 9* shall apply with any necessary modifications, and

(B) *sections 413* to *419* shall apply as they apply for the purposes of *Chapter 5* of *Part 12* but as if "in a relevant territory" were substituted for "in the State" in *subparagraph (iii)* of *section 413(3)(a)* and as if *paragraph (c)* of *section 411(1)*, other than that paragraph as it applies by virtue of [*clauses (I)* and *(II)* of *subparagraph (i)*][9], were disregarded,

(ii) in determining whether the conditions in *paragraph (a)* of *subsection (2)* are satisfied, a company that is a member of a group shall be treated as holding so much of any shares held by any other company in the group and as having so much of the entitlement of any such company to any rights enjoyed by virtue of holding shares—

(I) as the company would not, apart from this paragraph, hold or have, and

(II) as are not part of a life business fund within the meaning of *section 719*,

and, for the purposes of this subparagraph, "*group*" means a company which has one or more 51 per cent subsidiaries together with those subsidiaries,

(iii) in determining whether the treatment provided for in *subsection (2)* applies, the question of whether there is a disposal shall be determined without regard to *section 584* or that section as applied by any other section: and, to the extent to which an exemption under *subsection (2)* does apply in relation to a disposal, *section 584* shall not apply in relation to the disposal,

(iv) where assets of a company are vested in a liquidator under section 230 of the Companies Act 1963 or otherwise, the assets shall be deemed to be vested in, and the acts of liquidation in relation to the assets shall be deemed to be the acts of, the company (and acquisitions from, and disposals to, the liquidator shall be disregarded accordingly),

(v) *section 616* shall not apply.

(2) A gain accruing to a company (in this section referred to as the "*investor company*") on a disposal of shares in another company (in this section referred to as the "*investee company*") is not a chargeable gain if—

[(a) the disposal by the investor company is at a time—

(i) when the investor company is a parent company of the investee company, or

(ii) within the 2 year period beginning on the most recent day on which the investor company was a parent company of the investee company,][10]

(b) the investee company is, by virtue of the law of a relevant territory, resident for the purposes of tax in the relevant territory at the time of the disposal, and

(c) at the time of the disposal—

(i) the investee company is a company whose business consists wholly or mainly of the carrying on of a trade or trades, or

(ii) the business of—

(I) the investor company,

(II) each company of which the investor company is the parent company, and

(III) the investee company, if it is not a company referred to in clause (II), and any company of which the investee company is the parent company,

taken together consists wholly or mainly of the carrying on of a trade or trades.

(3) The treatment of a gain, as not being a chargeable gain, provided by this section and *section 626C* shall not apply—

(a) to a disposal that by virtue of any provision relating to chargeable gains is deemed to be for a consideration such that no gain or loss accrues to the person making the disposal,

(b) to a disposal a gain on which would, by virtue of any provision other than this section or *section 626C*, not be a chargeable gain,

(c) to disposals, including deemed disposals, of shares which are part of a life business fund within the meaning of *section 719*,

(d) to a disposal of shares deriving their value or the greater part of this value directly or indirectly from assets specified in [paragraphs (*a*) and (*b*) of subsection (3) of section 29 and subsection (6) of that section][11][,][12]

[(e) to deemed disposals under *section 627*.][13]

[(3A) (a) In this subsection 'relevant treatment of a gain' means the treatment, provided by this section or *section 626C*, of a gain as not being a chargeable gain.

(b) Notwithstanding any provision of *section 590*, the relevant treatment of a gain shall not apply for the purposes of *section 590*, but this is subject to *paragraph (c)*.

(c) The relevant treatment of a gain shall apply for the purposes of *section 590* where the participator (within the meaning of that section) is a company.][14]

(4) Schedule 25A shall have effect for the purposes of supplementing this section and *section 626C*.][15]

Amendments

[1] Deleted by F(No.2)A08 s33(g)(i). This section is deemed to have come into force and takes effect as on and from 1 January 2009.

[2] Substituted by FA07 sched2(1)(t). Has effect as on and from 2 April 2007

[3] Substituted by F(No.2)A08 s33(g)(i). This section is deemed to have come into force and takes effect as on and from 1 January 2009.

[4] Inserted by F(No.2)A08 s33(g)(ii). This section is deemed to have come into force and takes effect as on and from 1 January 2009.

[5] Deleted by FA05 s54(1)(a). Applies as on and from 2 February 2004.

[6, 7, 8] Substituted by FA05 s54(1)(b). Applies as on and from 2 February 2004.

[9] Substituted by F(No.2)A13 sched(1)(g). Has effect on and from 18 December 2013.

[10] Substituted by FA05 s54(1)(c). Applies as on and from 2 February 2004.

[11] Substituted by FA09 s12(1). Applies to disposals made on or after 7 May 2009.

[12] Substituted by FA06 s64(1)(a).

[13] Inserted by FA06 s64(1)(b).

[14] Inserted by FA14 s44(1). Applies as respects disposals on or after 18 November 2014.

[15] Inserted by FA04 s42(1)(a). This section comes into operation on such day as the Minister for Finance may appoint by order. With effect from 2 February 2002 per S.I. 551 of 2004.

Revenue Briefings

Tax Briefing

Tax Briefing April 2004 – Issue 55 pg 8 – Finance Act 2004 – Capital Gains Tax
Tax Briefing July 2007 – Issue 66 – Capital Gains Tax – Holding Company Regime

Cross References

From Section 626B

Section 9 Subsidiaries.
Section 29 Persons chargeable.
Section 381 Right to repayment of tax by reference to losses.
Section 410 Group payments.
Section 411 Surrender of relief between members of groups and consortia.
Section 413 Profits or assets available for distribution.
Section 419 The relevant accounting period, etc.
Section 584 Reorganisation or reduction of share capital.
Section 616 Groups of companies: interpretation.
Section 626C Treatment of assets related to shares.
Section 627 Deemed disposal of assets.
Section 719 Deemed disposal and reacquisition of certain assets.
Section 826 Agreements for relief from double taxation.

To Section 626B

Section 21B Tax treatment of certain dividends.
Section 249 Rules relating to recovery of capital and replacement loans.
Section 626C Treatment of assets related to shares.
Schedule 25A Exemption from Tax in the Case of Gains on Certain Disposals of Shares

626C Treatment of assets related to shares

[(1) For the purposes of this section—

(a) an asset is related to shares in a company if it is—

(i) an option to acquire or dispose of shares in that company,

(ii) a security to which are attached rights by virtue of which the holder is or may become entitled, whether by conversion or exchange or otherwise, to acquire or dispose of—

(I) shares in that company,

(II) an option to acquire or dispose of shares in that company, or

(III) another security falling within this paragraph,

or

(iii) an option to acquire or dispose of any security within *subparagraph (ii)* or an interest in any such security,

(b) in determining whether a security is within *paragraph (a)(ii)*, no account shall be taken—

(i) of any rights attached to the security other than rights relating, directly or indirectly, to shares of the company in question, or

(ii) of rights as regards which, at the time the security came into existence, there was no more than a negligible likelihood that they would in due course be exercised to a significant extent.

(2) A gain accruing to a company (in this subsection referred to as the "*first-mentioned company*") on the disposal of an asset related to shares in another company is not a chargeable gain if—

(a) (i) immediately before the disposal the first-mentioned company holds shares in the other company, and

(ii) any gain accruing to the first-mentioned company on a disposal at that time of the shares would, by virtue of *section 626B*, not be a chargeable gain,

or

(b) (i) immediately before the disposal the first-mentioned company does not hold shares in the other company but is a member of a group and another member of that group does hold shares in the other company, and

(ii) if the first-mentioned company, rather than the other member of the group, held the shares, any gain accruing to the first-mentioned company on a disposal at that time of the shares would, by virtue of *section 626B*, not be a chargeable gain;

and for the purposes of this paragraph "*group*" means a company which has one or more 51 per cent subsidiaries together with those subsidiaries.][1]

Amendments

[1] Inserted by FA04 s42(1)(a). This section comes into operation on such day as the Minister for Finance may appoint by order. With effect from 2 February 2002 per S.I. 551 of 2004.

Revenue Briefings

Tax Briefing

Tax Briefing April 2004 – Issue 55 pg 8 – Finance Act 2004 – Capital Gains Tax

Cross References

From Section 626C

Section 626B Exemption from tax in the case of gains on disposals of shares.

To Section 626C

Section 626B Exemption from tax in the case of gains on disposals of shares.

CHAPTER 2

Provisions Where Companies Cease to be Resident in the State

627 Deemed disposal of assets

[FA97 s42]

(1) (a) In this section and in *section 628*—

"*designated area*", "exploration or exploitation activities" and "exploration or exploitation rights" have the same meanings respectively as in *section 13*;

"*exploration or exploitation assets*" means assets used or intended for use in connection with exploration or exploitation activities carried on in the State or in a designated area;

"market value" shall be construed in accordance with *section 548*;

"the new assets" and "the old assets" have the meanings respectively assigned to them by *section 597*.

(b) For the purposes of this section and *section 628*, a company shall not be regarded as ceasing to be resident in the State by reason only that it ceases to exist.

(2) (a) In this subsection—

"control" shall be construed in accordance with *subsections (2)* to *(6)* of *section 432* as if in *subsection (6)* of that section for "5 or fewer participators" there were substituted "persons resident in a relevant territory";

"excluded company" means a company of which not less than 90 per cent of its issued share capital is held by a foreign company or foreign companies, or by a person or persons directly or indirectly controlled by a foreign company or foreign companies;

"foreign company" means a company which—

(i) is not resident in the State,

(ii) is under the control of a person or persons resident in a relevant territory, and

(iii) is not under the control of a person or persons resident in the State;

["*relevant territory*" means a territory with the government of which arrangements having the force of law by virtue of [*section 826(1)*][1] have been made.][2]

(b) Subject to *paragraph (c)*, this section and *section 628* shall apply to a company (in this section referred to as a "relevant company") if at any time (in this section and in *section 628* referred to as "the relevant time") on or after the 21st day of April, 1997, the company ceases to be resident in the State.

(c) This section and *section 628* shall not apply to a company which is an excluded company.

(3) A relevant company shall be deemed for the purposes of the Capital Gains Tax Acts—

(a) to have disposed of all its assets, other than assets excepted from this subsection by *subsection (5)*, immediately before the relevant time, and

(b) to have immediately reacquired them,

at the market value of the assets at that time.

(4) *Section 597* shall not apply where a relevant company—

(a) has disposed of the old assets, or of its interest in those assets, before the relevant time, and

(b) acquires the new assets, or its interest in those assets, after the relevant time, unless the new assets are excepted from this subsection by *subsection (5)*.

(5) Where at any time after the relevant time a relevant company carries on a trade in the State through a branch or agency—

(a) any assets which, immediately after the relevant time, are situated in the State and are used in or for the purposes of the trade, or are used or held for the purposes of the branch or agency, shall be excepted from *subsection (3)*, and

(b) any new assets which, after that time, are so situated and are so used or so held shall be excepted from *subsection (4)*,

and references in this subsection to assets situated in the State include references to exploration or exploitation assets and to exploration or exploitation rights.

Amendments

[1] Substituted by FA07 sched2(1)(u). Has effect as on and from 2 April 2007

[2] Substituted by FA98 sched3(5).

Cross References

From Section 627

Section 13 Extension of charge to income tax to profits and income derived from activities carried on and employments exercised on the Continental Shelf.
Section 432 Meaning of "associated company" and "control".
Section 548 Valuation of assets.
Section 597 Replacement of business and other assets.
Section 628 Postponement of charge on deemed disposal under section 627.
Section 826 Agreements for relief from double taxation.

To Section 627

Section 626B Exemption from tax in the case of gains on disposals of shares.
Section 628 Postponement of charge on deemed disposal under section 627.
Section 629 Tax on non-resident company recoverable from another member of group or from controlling director.

628 Postponement of charge on deemed disposal under section 627

[FA97 s43]

(1) (a) In this section—

"*deemed disposal*" means a disposal which by virtue of *section 627(3)* is deemed to have been made;

"*foreign assets*" of a company means any assets of the company which immediately after the relevant time are situated outside the State and are used in or for the purposes of a trade carried on by the company outside the State.

(b) For the purposes of this section, a company shall be a 75 per cent subsidiary of another company if and so long as not less than 75 per cent of its ordinary share capital (within the meaning of *section 2*) is owned directly by that other company.

(2) Where—

(a) immediately after the relevant time a company (in this section referred to as "the company") to which this section applies by virtue of *section 627* is a 75 per cent subsidiary of another company (in this section referred to as "the principal company") which is resident in the State, and

(b) the principal company and the company jointly so elect by notice in writing given to the inspector within 2 years after the relevant time,

the Capital Gains Tax Acts shall apply subject to *subsections (3)* to *(6)*.

(3) Any allowable losses accruing to the company on a deemed disposal of foreign assets shall be set off against the chargeable gains so accruing and—

(a) that deemed disposal shall be treated as giving rise to a single chargeable gain equal to the aggregate of those gains after deducting the aggregate of those losses, and

(b) the whole of that single chargeable gain shall be treated as not accruing to the company on that disposal but an equivalent amount (in this section referred to as "the postponed gain") shall be taken into account in accordance with *subsections (4)* and *(5)*.

(4) (a) In this subsection, "*the appropriate proportion*" means the proportion which the chargeable gain taken into account in determining the postponed gain in respect of the part of the relevant assets disposed of bears to the aggregate of the chargeable gains so taken into account in respect of the relevant assets held immediately before the time of the disposal.

(b) Where at any time within 10 years after the relevant time the company disposes of any assets (in this subsection referred to as "relevant assets") the chargeable gains on which were taken into account in determining the postponed gain, there shall be deemed to accrue to the principal company as a chargeable gain at that time the whole or the appropriate proportion of the postponed gain in so far as not already taken into account under this subsection or *subsection (5)*.

(5) Where at any time within 10 years after the relevant time—

(a) the company ceases to be a 75 per cent subsidiary of the principal company, or

(b) the principal company ceases to be resident in the State,

there shall be deemed to accrue to the principal company as a chargeable gain—

(i) where *paragraph (a)* applies, at that time, and

(ii) where *paragraph (b)* applies, immediately before that time,

the whole of the postponed gain in so far as not already taken into account under this subsection or *subsection (4)*.

(6) Where at any time—

(a) the company has allowable losses which have not been allowed as a deduction from chargeable gains, and

(b) a chargeable gain accrues to the principal company under *subsection (4)* or *(5)*,

then, if and to the extent that the principal company and the company jointly so elect by notice in writing given to the inspector within 2 years after that time, those losses shall be allowed as a deduction from that gain.

Cross References

From Section 628

Section 2 Interpretation of Tax Acts.

Section 627 Deemed disposal of assets.

To Section 628

Section 627 Deemed disposal of assets.

Section 629 Tax on non-resident company recoverable from another member of group or from controlling director.

628A Deferral of exit tax

[(1) In this section—

"*chargeable period*" means a year of assessment or an accounting period, as the case may be;

"*disposal of assets*" means a disposal of migrated assets;

"*EEA Agreement*" means the Agreement on the European Economic Area signed at Oporto on 2 May 1992, as adjusted by all subsequent amendments to that Agreement;

"*EEA State*" means a state which is a contracting party to the EEA Agreement;

"*electronic means*" has the meaning assigned to it in *section 917EA(1)*;

"*migrated assets*" means the assets of a migrating company, the chargeable gain on the deemed disposal of which was taken into account in determining the amount of relevant tax;

"*migrating company*" means a company which ceases to be resident in the State and becomes resident, under the law of a relevant territory, in that territory for the purposes of tax;

"*migration date*" means the date, on or after 1 January 2014, on which a company ceases to be resident in the State;

"*relevant event*" means—

(a) the appointment of a liquidator to the migrating company,

(b) any event under the law of a relevant territory corresponding to the event specified in *paragraph (a)*,

(c) the migrating company ceasing to be resident, under the law of a relevant territory, in that territory for the purposes of tax, and not becoming so resident in another relevant territory for that purpose, or

(d) any failure to pay relevant tax by the date that it becomes due and payable;

"*relevant period*", in respect of which a statement under *paragraph (b)* of *subsection (4)* is to be made, is the calendar year immediately preceding the 21-day period in which the statement is to be made, except that in respect of the first such statement of the 5 or 9 statements, as the case may be, referred to in that subsection, such period shall be the period commencing at the migration date and ending on the last day before the beginning of the calendar year in respect of which the next such statement is to be made;

"*relevant tax*" means tax payable, other than tax in respect of the amount of any postponed gain under *section 628*, which but for *section 627* would not be payable by a migrating company for a chargeable period;

"*relevant territory*" means a Member State (other than the State) or an EEA State;

'*specified date*' means—

(a) in relation to corporation tax, the last day of the period of 9 months starting on the day immediately following the migration date, but in any event not later than day 23 of the month in which that period of 9 months ends, or

(b) in relation to capital gains tax payable in respect of a year of assessment in which the migration date occurs, 31 October in the tax year following that year;

"*tax*", in relation to a relevant territory other than the State, means any tax imposed in that territory which corresponds to income tax or corporation tax.

(2) Subject to the provisions of this section, a migrating company may elect to pay relevant tax—

(a) in 6 equal instalments at yearly intervals, the first instalment of which shall be due and payable on the specified date, and the remaining 5 instalments shall be due and payable respectively on each of the next 5 anniversaries of the specified date, or

(b) not later than 60 days after the date of disposal of assets.

(3) Where a migrating company makes an election to pay relevant tax—

(a) in accordance with *paragraph (a)* of *subsection (2)*, relevant tax shall be payable in 6 equal instalments at yearly intervals in accordance with that paragraph, or

(b) in accordance with *paragraph (b)* of *subsection (2)*—

(i) so much of the relevant tax shall be paid on the disposal of assets by the company as bears the same proportion to the relevant tax as the chargeable gains, computed on the deemed disposal of those assets at the migration date, bears to the aggregate of the chargeable gains computed on the deemed disposal of the assets by the company at the migration date, and

(ii) any relevant tax which is not due and payable within a period of 10 years from the migration date, shall be deemed to become due and payable on the tenth anniversary of the migration date.

(4) (a) An election under *subsection (2)* shall—

(i) be made in the return under *section 959I*—

(I) where the relevant tax is corporation tax, for the accounting period which ends on the migration date for the company, or

(II) where the relevant tax is capital gains tax, for the year of assessment in which the migration date for the company occurs,

and that return shall be made by electronic means (in accordance with *Chapter 6* of *Part 38*);

(ii) specify—

(I) the date on which the company ceased to be resident in the State,

(II) the relevant territory in which the migrating company has become resident,

(III) the amount of the relevant tax, and

(IV) whether the election is being made to pay relevant tax in accordance with *paragraph (a)* or *(b)* of *subsection (2)*;

and

(iii) provide such other information as may be required by the Revenue Commissioners for the purposes of this section.

(b) Where an election is made to pay relevant tax in accordance with—

(i) *subsection (2)(a)*, the migrating company shall within 21 days of the end of each of the 5 calendar years which follow the year in which the migration date occurs, or

(ii) *subsection (2)(b)*, the migrating company shall within 21 days of the end of each of the 9 calendar years which follow the year in which the migration date occurs,

deliver to the Revenue Commissioners a statement, notwithstanding that the migrating company has not received a notice to prepare and deliver such a statement, by such electronic means and in such form and format as the Revenue Commissioners may specify, in respect of the relevant period, for the purposes of relevant tax—

(I) specifying whether the company is treated under the laws of a relevant territory as resident for the purposes of tax in that territory throughout that relevant period,

(II) where the company has made an election to pay relevant tax in accordance with *subsection (2)(b)*—

(A) stating whether any relevant tax became due and payable during that relevant period,

(B) specifying the amount of that tax, the amount of the related interest charge and whether that tax and interest has been paid, and

(C) setting out the computation of that tax and interest, in accordance with *subsections (3)(b)(i)* and *(6)*,

and

(III) providing such other information as may be required by the Revenue Commissioners for the purposes of this section.

(5) Notwithstanding *subsections (2)* and *(3)* if, at any time within 10 years of the migration date, a relevant event occurs, then any amount of relevant tax which has not been paid at the time of the relevant event, and any interest charged on that amount in accordance with *subsection (6)*, shall become due and payable on the occurrence of the relevant event.

(6) (a) Where relevant tax becomes due and payable at any time under this section, simple interest shall be payable on the amount of that relevant tax and shall be calculated, from the specified date until payment, for any day or part of a day during which the amount of relevant tax remains unpaid, at the prevailing rate specified in the Table to *subsection (2)(c)(ii)* of *section 1080*, and such interest shall be due and payable when the relevant tax concerned is due and payable.

(b) Interest charged on the relevant tax shall be added to each of the instalments mentioned in *subsection (2)(a)* or, where *subsection (2)(b)*, *(3)(b)(ii)* or *(5)* applies, added to the amount of relevant tax, and shall be paid at the same time as such instalment is due or at the same time as relevant tax is payable in accordance with *subsection (2)(b)*, *(3)(b)(ii)* or *(5)*, as the case may be.

(7) The Revenue Commissioners may, where it appears to them that the deferral of tax would otherwise present a serious risk to collection of the tax, require a migrating company which has made an election under *subsection (2)* to give security, or further security, of such amounts and in such form and manner as they may determine, for the payment of relevant tax, within 30 days from the date of service on the company of a notice in writing.

(8) All amounts of relevant tax and interest shall be paid to the Collector-General.

(9) Any amount of relevant tax and interest payable in accordance with this section shall be payable without the making of an assessment.

(10) (a) The Collector-General may, at any time before the end of the period beginning with the date on which that tax was due and payable by reference to this section and ending 3 years after the time when a statement under *subsection (4)(b)*, specifying the amount of that tax, is made and delivered to the Collector-General, serve on—

(i) a company which is, or during the period of 12 months ending with the date when relevant tax became due and payable was, a member of the same group (within the meaning of *section 629(1)*) as the migrating company, or

(ii) a person who is, or during the period mentioned in *subparagraph (i)* was, a controlling director (within the meaning of *section 629(1)*) of the migrating company or of a company which has, or within that period had, control over the migrating company,

a notice—

(I) stating the amount which remains unpaid of the relevant tax payable by the migrating company and the date on which the tax became due and payable, and

(II) requiring the company referred to in *subparagraph (i)* or the person referred to in *subparagraph (ii)*, as the case may be, to pay that amount within 30 days of service of the notice,

and in the event of the serving of such notice the amount referred to in *subparagraph (I)* shall be so payable by the company or person concerned, as the case may be.

(b) Any amount which a person is required to pay by a notice under this subsection may be recovered from the person as if it were tax due by such person, and such person may recover any such amount paid on foot of a notice under this section from the migrating company.

(c) A payment in pursuance of a notice under this subsection shall not be allowed as a deduction in computing income, profits or losses for any tax purposes.

(11) Without prejudice to the provisions of this section, the provisions of the Corporation Tax Acts and the Capital Gains Tax Acts, as appropriate, relating to the collection and recovery of corporation tax, capital gains tax, and interest, shall apply, with any necessary modifications, to the collection and recovery of relevant tax and interest payable in accordance with this section as they apply to any other corporation tax, capital gains tax, and interest.][1]

Amendments

[1] Inserted by F(No.2)A13 s35(1). Comes into operation on 1 January 2014.

629 Tax on non-resident company recoverable from another member of group or from controlling director

[FA97 s44]

(1) In this section—

"*chargeable period*" means a year of assessment or an accounting period, as the case may be;

"*controlling director*", in relation to a company, means a director of the company who has control of the company (construing control in accordance with *section 432*);

"*director*", in relation to a company, has the same meaning as in *section 116*, and includes any person within section *433(4)*;

"*group*" has the meaning which would be given by *section 616* if in that section references to residence in [relevant Member State][1] were omitted and for references to "75 per cent subsidiaries" there were substituted references to "51 per cent subsidiaries", and references to a company being a member of a group shall be construed accordingly;

"*specified period*", in relation to a chargeable period, means the period beginning with the specified return date for the chargeable period (within the meaning of [*section 959A*][2]) and ending 3 years after the time [when a return under [*Chapter 3* of *Part 41A*][3] for the chargeable period is delivered to the Collector-General][4];

"*tax*" means corporation tax or capital gains tax, as the case may be.

(2) This section shall apply at any time on or after the 21st day of April, 1997, where tax payable (being tax which but for *section 627* or *628* would not be payable) by a company (in this section referred to as "the taxpayer company") for a chargeable period (in this section referred to as "the chargeable period concerned") is not paid within 6 months after the date on or before which the tax is due and payable.

(3) The Revenue Commissioners may, at any time before the end of the specified period in relation to the chargeable period concerned, serve on any person to whom *subsection (4)* applies a notice—

(a) stating the amount which remains unpaid of the tax payable by the taxpayer company for the chargeable period concerned and the date on or before which the tax became due and payable, and

(b) requiring that person to pay that amount within 30 days of the service of the notice.

(4) (a) This subsection shall apply to any person, being—

(i) a company which is, or during the period of 12 months ending with the time when the gain accrued was, a member of the same group as the taxpayer company, and

(ii) a person who is, or during that period was, a controlling director of the taxpayer company or of a company which has, or within that period had, control over the taxpayer company.

(b) This subsection shall apply in any case where the gain accrued before the 21st day of April, 1998, with the substitution in *paragraph (a)(i)* of "beginning with the 21st day of April, 1997, and" for "of 12 months".

(5) Any amount which a person is required to pay by a notice under this section may be recovered from the person as if it were tax due by such person, and such person may recover any such amount paid on foot of a notice under this section from the taxpayer company.

(6) A payment in pursuance of a notice under this section shall not be allowed as a deduction in computing any income, profits or losses for any tax purposes.

Amendments

[1] Substituted by FA02 s36(e).

[2, 3] Substituted by FA12 sched4(part 2)(g).

[4] Substituted by FA01 s78(2)(b). Applies as respects the year of assessment 2001 and subsequent years and as respects accounting periods of companies ending on or after 1 April 2001.

Cross References

From Section 629

Section 116 Interpretation (Chapter 3).
Section 432 Meaning of "associated company" and "control".
Section 616 Groups of companies: interpretation.
Section 627 Deemed disposal of assets.
Section 628 Postponement of charge on deemed disposal under section 627.
Section 950 Interpretation (Part 41).
Section 951 Obligation to make a return.

629A Company ceasing to be resident on formation of SE or SCE

[If at any time a company ceases to be resident in the State in the course of—

(a) the formation of an SE by merger, or

(b) the formation of an SCE,

then, whether or not the company continues to exist after the formation of the SE or (as the case may be) the SCE, the Tax Acts and the Capital Gains Tax Acts shall apply to any obligations of the company under this Act in relation to liabilities accruing and matters arising before that time—

(i) as if the company were still resident in the State, and

(ii) where the company has ceased to exist, as if the SE or (as the case may be) the SCE were the company.][1]

Amendments

[1] Inserted by FA06 s60(d).

PART 21

Mergers, Divisions, Transfers of Assets and Exchanges of Shares Concerning Companies of Different Member States

630 Interpretation (Part 21)

[FA92 s64]

In this Part—

"*bilateral agreement*" means arrangements having the force of law by virtue of [*section 826(1)*][1];

"*company*" means a company from a Member State;

"company from a Member State" has the meaning assigned to it by Article 3 of the Directive;

["*the Directive*" means Council Directive 2009/133/EC of 19 October 2009*, as amended, on the common system of taxation applicable to mergers, divisions, partial divisions, transfers of assets and exchanges of shares concerning companies of different Member States and to the transfer of the registered office of an SE or SCE between Member States;][2]

*OJ No. L310, 25.11.2009, p.34

"*Member State*" means a Member State of the European Communities;

"*receiving company*" means the company to which the whole or part of a trade is transferred in the course of a transfer;

["*SE Regulation*" means Council Regulation (EC) No. 2157/2001 of 8 October 2001, on the Statute for a European Company (SE)*;

* OJ No. L294, 10.11.2001, p.1

"*SCE Regulation*" means Council Regulation (EC) No. 1435/2003 of 22 July 2003 on the Statute for a European Cooperative Society (SCE)*;][3]

* OJ No. L207, 18.8.2003, p.1

"*securities*" means shares and debentures;

"shares" includes stock;

"*transfer*" means the transfer by a company of the whole or part of its trade in the circumstances set out in *section 631(1)* or *634(2)*, as the case may be;

"*transferring company*" means the company by which the whole or part of a trade is transferred in the course of a transfer.

Amendments

1 Substituted by FA07 sched2(1)(v). Has effect as on and from 2 April 2007

2 Substituted by F(No.2)A13 sched(1)(h). Has effect on and from 1 July 2013.

3 Inserted by FA06 s60(e)(i)(III).

Cross References

From Section 630

Section 631 Transfer of assets generally.

Section 634 Credit for tax.

Section 826 Agreements for relief from double taxation.

To Section 630

Section 616 Groups of companies: interpretation.

Schedule 18A Restriction on Set-off of Pre-entry Losses

631 Transfer of assets generally

[FA92 s65]

(1) (a) This section shall apply where a company transfers the whole of a trade carried on by it in the State to another company and the consideration for the transfer consists solely of the issue to the transferring company of securities (in this section referred to as "the new assets") in the receiving company.

(b) A company which transfers part of a trade to another company shall be treated for the purposes of this section as having carried on that part of its trade as a separate trade.

(2) (a) The transfer shall not be treated as giving rise to any allowance or charge provided for by *section 307* or *308*.

(b) There shall be made to or on the receiving company in accordance with *sections 307* and *308* all such allowances and charges as would, if the transferring company had continued to carry on the trade and had continued to use the transferred assets for the purposes of the trade, have been made to or on the transferring company in respect of any assets transferred in the course of the transfer, and the amount of any such allowance or charge shall be computed as if the receiving company had been carrying on the trade since the transferring company began to do so and as if everything done to or by the transferring company had been done to or by the receiving company.

(c) This subsection shall not apply as respects assets transferred in the course of a transfer if in consequence of the transfer, or a transaction of which the transfer is a part, the Corporation Tax Acts are to apply subject to *subsections (6)* to *(9)* of *section 400*.

(3) For the purposes of the Capital Gains Tax Acts and, in so far as they apply to chargeable gains, the Corporation Tax Acts—

(a) the transfer shall not be treated as involving any disposal by the transferring company, and

(b) the receiving company shall be treated as if the assets transferred to it in the course of the transfer were acquired by it at the same time and for the same consideration at which they were acquired by the transferring company and as if all things done by the transferring company relating to the assets transferred in the course of the transfer had been done by the receiving company.

(4) Where, at any time within a period of 6 years commencing on the day on which the assets were transferred in the course of the transfer, the transferring company disposes of the new assets then, for the purposes of the Capital Gains Tax Acts and, in so far as they apply to chargeable gains, the Corporation Tax Acts, in computing any chargeable gain on the disposal of any new assets—

(a) the aggregate of the chargeable gains less allowable losses which but for *subsection (3)(a)* would have been chargeable on the transferring company shall be apportioned between the new assets as a whole, and

(b) the sums allowable as a deduction under *section 552(1)(a)* shall be reduced by the amount apportioned to the new asset under *paragraph (a)*,

and, if the securities which comprise the new assets are not all of the same type, the apportionment between the securities under *paragraph (a)* shall be in accordance with their market value at the time they were acquired by the transferring company.

(5) *Subsections (2)* to *(4)* shall not apply if—

(a) immediately after the time of the transfer—

(i) the assets transferred in the course of the transfer are not used for the purposes of a trade carried on by the receiving company in the State,

(ii) the receiving company would not be chargeable to corporation tax or capital gains tax in respect of any chargeable gains accruing to it on a disposal, if it were to make such a disposal, of any assets (other than cash) acquired in the course of the transfer, or

(iii) any of the assets are assets in respect of which, by virtue of being of a description specified in a bilateral agreement, the receiving company is to be regarded as not liable in the State to corporation tax or capital gains tax on gains accruing to it on a disposal,

or

(b) the transferring company and the receiving company jointly so elect by notice in writing to the inspector, and such notice shall be made by the time by which a return is to be made by the transferring company under [*Chapter 3* of *Part 41A*][1] for the accounting period in which the transfer takes place.

Amendments

[1] Substituted by FA12 sched4(part 2)(g).

Case Law

Kofoed v Skatteministeriet – Case C 321/05 2008 STC 1202 considered whether a dividend payment could be included in the calculation of a "cash payment" for the purpose of the parent-subsidiary directive.

Cross References

From Section 631

Section 307 Corporation tax: allowances and charges in taxing a trade.

Section 308 Corporation tax: manner of granting, and effect of, allowances made by means of discharge or repayment of tax.

Section 400 Company reconstructions without change of ownership.

Section 552 Acquisition, enhancement and disposal costs.

Section 951 Obligation to make a return.

To Section 631

Section 486C Relief from tax for certain start-up companies.

Section 541 Debts.

Section 630 Interpretation (Part 21).

Section 632 Transfer of assets by company to its parent company.

Section 633 Company reconstruction or amalgamation: transfer of development land.

Section 635 Avoidance of tax.

Section 636 Returns.

632 Transfer of assets by company to its parent company

[FA92 s66]

(1) Where a company disposes of an asset used for the purposes of a trade carried on by it in the State to another company which holds all of the securities representing the company's capital and but for this section the companies would not be treated in accordance with *section 617* in respect of the asset, then, if—

(a) immediately after the disposal the company acquiring the asset commences to use the asset for the purposes of a trade carried on by it in the State, and

(b) the disposal is not, or does not form part of, a transfer to which *section 631* applies,

sections 617 to *619* shall apply as if the companies were resident in the State.

(2) *Subsection (5)* of *section 631* shall apply with any necessary modification for the purposes of this section as if references in that subsection to *subsections (2)* to *(4)* of that section were references to *subsection (1)* of this section.

Cross References

From Section 632

Section 617 Transfers of assets, other than trading stock, within group.
Section 619 Disposals or acquisitions outside group.
Section 631 Transfer of assets generally.

To Section 632

Section 541 Debts.
Section 635 Avoidance of tax.
Section 636 Returns.

633 Company reconstruction or amalgamation: transfer of development land

[FA92 s67]

Where a company, for the purposes of or in connection with a scheme of reconstruction or amalgamation (within the meaning of *section 615*), disposes of an asset which consists of development land (within the meaning of *section 648*) to another company and—

(a) the disposal is not made in the course of a transfer to which *section 631* applies, and

(b) the company disposing of the asset and the company acquiring the asset would, if—

(i) the definition of "*chargeable gains*" in *section 78(4)*, and

(ii) *section 649(1)*,

were deleted, be treated in accordance with *section 615(2)* in respect of that asset,

then, the companies shall be treated for the purposes of the Capital Gains Tax Acts as if the asset was acquired by the one company from the other company for a consideration of such amount as would secure that on the disposal neither a gain nor a loss would accrue to the company making the disposal, and for the purposes of *section 556* the acquiring company shall be treated as if the acquisition of the asset by the other company had been the acquiring company's acquisition of the asset.

Cross References

From Section 633

Section 78 Computation of companies' chargeable gains.
Section 556 Adjustment of allowable expenditure by reference to consumer price index.
Section 615 Company reconstruction or amalgamation: transfer of assets.
Section 631 Transfer of assets generally.
Section 648 Interpretation (Chapter 2).
Section 649 Companies chargeable to capital gains tax in respect of chargeable gains accruing on relevant disposals.

To Section 633

Section 635 Avoidance of tax.
Section 636 Returns.

633A Formation of SE or SCE by merger — leaving assets in the State

[(1) For the purposes of this section an asset is a qualifying transferred asset if—

(a) the asset is transferred to an SE or an SCE as part of the process of the merger forming it,

(b) (i) the transferor in relation to the asset is resident in the State at the time of the transfer, or

(ii) any gain that would have accrued to the transferor in respect of the asset, had it disposed of the asset immediately before the time of the transfer, would have been a chargeable gain,

and

(c) (i) the transferee SE or SCE in relation to the asset is resident in the State on formation, or

(ii) any gain that would have accrued to the transferee SE or SCE in respect of the asset, if it disposed of the asset immediately after the transfer, would be a chargeable gain.

(2) For the purposes of this section and section 633B, a company is treated as resident for the purposes of tax in a Member State (other than the State) if—

(a) it is so treated by virtue of the law of the Member State, and

(b) it is not treated, for the purposes of double taxation relief arrangements to which the Member State is a party, as resident for the purposes of tax in a territory which is not a Member State, and for this purpose "tax", in relation to a Member State other than the State, means any tax imposed in the Member State which corresponds to corporation tax in the State.

(3) This section applies where—

(a) (i) an SE is formed by the merger of 2 or more companies in accordance with Articles 2(1) and 17(2)(*a*) or (*b*) of the SE Regulation, or

(ii) an SCE is formed by a merger in accordance with Article 2 of the SCE Regulation,

(b) each merging company is resident for the purposes of tax in a Member State,

(c) the merging companies are not all resident for the purposes of tax in the same Member State, and

(d) *section 615* does not apply to any qualifying transferred assets.

(4) Where this section applies, qualifying transferred assets shall be treated for the purpose of the Capital Gains Tax Acts and, in so far as they apply to chargeable gains, the Corporation Tax Acts as if acquired by the SE, or as the case may be the SCE, for a consideration resulting in neither gain or loss for the transferor.

(5) Where this section applies—

(a) the transfer of assets in the course of the merger shall be treated as not giving rise to any allowance or charge provided for by *section 307* or *308*,

(b) there shall be made to or on the SE or (as the case may be) the SCE in accordance with *sections 307* and *308* all such allowances and charges as would, if the transferring company had continued to use the transferred assets for the purposes of its trade, have been made to or on the transferring company in respect of any assets transferred in the course of the merger, and the amount of any such allowance or charge shall be computed as if the SE or (as the case may be) the SCE had been carrying on the trade carried on by the transferring company since the transferring company began to do so and as if everything done to or by the transferring company had been done to or by the SE or (as the case may be) the SCE.][1]

Amendments

[1] Inserted by FA06 s60(e)(ii).

Cross References

From Section 633A

Section 307 Corporation tax: allowances and charges in taxing a trade.

Section 308 Corporation tax: manner of granting, and effect of, allowances made by means of discharge or repayment of tax.

Section 615 Company reconstruction or amalgamation: transfer of assets.

To Section 633A

Section 635 Avoidance of tax.

Section 636 Returns.

633B Formation of SE or SCE by merger — not leaving assets in the State

[(1) This section applies where—

(a) (i) an SE is formed by the merger of 2 or more companies in accordance with Articles 2(1) and 17(2)*(a)* or *(b)* of the SE Regulation, or

(ii) an SCE is formed by a merger in accordance with Article 2 of the SCE Regulation,

(b) each merging company is resident for the purposes of tax in a Member State,

(c) the merging companies are not all resident for the purposes of tax in the same Member State,

(d) in the course of the merger a company resident in the State transfers to a company resident in a Member State other than the State all assets and liabilities of a trade which the company resident in the State carried on in a Member State (other than the State) through a branch or agency, and

(e) the aggregate of the chargeable gains accruing to the company resident in the State on the transfer exceeds the aggregate of any allowable losses so accruing.

(2) Where this section applies, for the purposes of the Capital Gains Tax Acts and, in so far as they apply to chargeable gains the Corporation Tax Acts—

(a) the allowable losses accruing to the company resident in the State on the transfer shall be set off against the chargeable gains so accruing, and

(b) the transfer shall be treated as giving rise to a single chargeable gain equal to the aggregate of those gains after deducting the aggregate of those losses.

(3) Where this section applies, *section 634* shall also apply.][1]

Amendments

[1] Inserted by FA06 s60(e)(ii).

Cross References

From Section 633B

Section 634 Credit for tax.

To Section 633B

Section 636 Returns.

633C Treatment of securities on a merger

[(1) This section applies where—

(a) (i) an SE is formed by the merger of 2 or more companies in accordance with Articles 2(1) and 17(2)(*a*) or (*b*) of the SE Regulation, or

(ii) an SCE is formed by a merger in accordance with Article 2 of the SCE Regulation,

(b) each merging company is resident for the purposes of tax in a Member State,

(c) the merging companies are not all resident for the purposes of tax in the same Member State, and

(d) the merger does not constitute or form part of a scheme of reconstruction or amalgamation within the meaning of *section 587*.

(2) Where this section applies, the merger shall be treated for the purposes of *section 587* as if it were a scheme of reconstruction.][1]

Amendments

[1] Inserted by FA06 s60(e)(ii).

Cross References

From Section 633C

Section 587 Company reconstructions and amalgamations.

To Section 633C

Section 635 Avoidance of tax.

Section 636 Returns.

633D Mergers where a company is dissolved without going into liquidation

[The transfer of all the assets and liabilities of a company which is a wholly owned subsidiary of another company (in this section referred to as the 'parent company') to the parent company, on that subsidiary company being dissolved without going into liquidation, shall not be treated as involving a disposal by the parent company of the share capital which it held in the subsidiary company immediately before the dissolution.][1]

Amendments

[1] Inserted by FA12 s51(1). Has effect in respect of assets and liabilities transferred on or after 1 January 2012.

634 Credit for tax

[FA92 s69]

(1) In this section—

"law of the Member State which has the effect of deferring a charge to tax on a gain" means any law of the Member State concerned which provides—

(a) that the gain accruing to the transferring company on the disposal of the assets in the course of the transfer is to be treated as not accruing until the disposal of the assets by the receiving company,

(b) that the receiving company is to be treated as having acquired the assets for a consideration of such amount as would secure that, for the purposes of charging the gain on the disposal to tax in that Member State, neither a gain nor a loss would accrue to the transferring company on the transfer and the receiving company is to be treated as if the acquisition of the assets by the transferring company had been the receiving company's acquisition of the assets, or

(c) such other deferral of a charge to tax as corresponds to *paragraph (a)* or *(b)*;

"relevant certificate given by the tax authorities of a Member State" means a certificate so given and which states—

(a) whether gains accruing to the transferring company on the transfer would have been chargeable to tax under the law of the Member State but for—

(i) the Directive, or

(ii) any provision of the law of the Member State which has the effect of deferring a charge to tax on a gain in the case of such a transfer,

(b) if those gains accruing would have been so chargeable, the amount of tax which would have been payable under that law if, in so far as is permitted under that law, any losses arising on the transfer are set against any gains so arising and any deductions and reliefs available to the transferring company under that law other than the provisions mentioned in *paragraph (a)* had been claimed.

(2) Where—

(a) a company resident in the State transfers the whole or part of a trade which immediately before the time of the transfer it carried on in a Member State (other than the State) through a branch or agency to a company not resident in the State,

(b) the transfer includes the whole of the assets of the transferring company used for the purposes of the trade or the part of the trade or the whole of those assets other than cash, and

(c) the consideration for the transfer consists wholly or partly of the issue to the transferring company of securities in the receiving company,

then, tax specified in a relevant certificate given by the tax authorities of the Member State in which the trade was so carried on shall be treated for the purposes of *Chapter 1* of *Part 35* as tax—

(i) payable under the law of that Member State, and

(ii) in respect of which credit may be allowed under a bilateral agreement.

[(3) (a) Where—

(i) a company which is not resident in the State transfers the whole of a trade carried on by it, or a part of such a trade, to another company and the consideration for the transfer consists solely of the issue to the transferring company of securities in the receiving company, and

(ii) for the purposes of computing the income or gains of any person (in this subsection referred to as the "*relevant person*") who is chargeable to tax in the State, income or gains of the transferring company are treated as being income, or as the case may be chargeable gains, of the relevant person and as not being income or chargeable gains of the transferring company,

then, in computing any liability to tax of the relevant person in respect of the transfer, an appropriate part of tax specified in a relevant certificate given by the tax authorities of the Member State in which the trade was so carried on shall be treated for the purposes of *Chapter 1* of *Part 35* as tax—

(I) payable under the law of that Member State, and

(II) in respect of which credit may be allowed under a bilateral agreement.

(b) For the purposes of this subsection, the appropriate part of tax on income or gains specified in a certificate in relation to a relevant person shall be so much of that tax as bears to the amount of that tax the same proportion as the part of any income, or as the case may be gains, of the transferring company in respect of the transfer which is treated as income, or as the case may be gains, of the relevant person bears to the amount of that income, or as the case may be gains, of the transferring company.][1]

Amendments

[1] Inserted by FA06 s60(e)(iii).

Cross References

From Section 634

Section 826 Agreements for relief from double taxation.

To Section 634

Section 630 Interpretation (Part 21).

Section 633B Formation of SE or SCE by merger — not leaving assets in the State.

Section 635 Avoidance of tax.

Section 636 Returns.

635 Avoidance of tax

[FA92 s70]

Notwithstanding any other provision of the Tax Acts or the Capital Gains Tax Acts, [*sections 631*, *632*, *633*, *633A*, *633C* and *634*][1] shall not apply [as respects a transfer, disposal or the formation of an SE or an SCE by merger unless it is shown that the transfer, disposal or merger, as the case may be][2], is effected for bona fide commercial reasons and does not form part of any arrangement or scheme of which the main purpose or one of the main purposes is avoidance of liability to income tax, corporation tax or capital gains tax.

Amendments

[1] Substituted by FA06 s60(e)(iv)(I).

[2] Substituted by FA06 s60(e)(iv)(II).

Cross References

From Section 635

Section 631 Transfer of assets generally.

Section 632 Transfer of assets by company to its parent company.

Section 633 Company reconstruction or amalgamation: transfer of development land.

Section 633A Formation of SE or SCE by merger — leaving assets in the State.

Section 633C Treatment of securities on a merger.

Section 634 Credit for tax.

636 Returns

[FA92 s71]

[...][1]

(2) Where [*section 631*, *632*, *633*, *633A*, *633B*, *633C* or *634*][2] applies in relation to a transfer or disposal, the transferring company shall make a return of the transfer or disposal, as the case may be, to the appropriate inspector in such form as the Revenue Commissioners may require.

(3) Where corporation tax or capital gains tax payable by a company is to be reduced by virtue of *section 634*, a return under this section shall include a relevant certificate given by the tax authorities of the Member State in which the trade was carried on immediately before the time of the transfer.

(4) A company shall make a return under this section within 9 months from the end of the accounting period in which the transfer occurs.

Amendments

[1] Deleted by FA12 sched5(1)(f).

[2] Substituted by FA06 s60(e)(v).

Cross References

From Section 636

Section 631 Transfer of assets generally.

Section 632 Transfer of assets by company to its parent company.

Section 633 Company reconstruction or amalgamation: transfer of development land.

Section 633A Formation of SE or SCE by merger — leaving assets in the State.

Section 633B Formation of SE or SCE by merger — not leaving assets in the State.

Section 633C Treatment of securities on a merger.

Section 634 Credit for tax.

Section 950 Interpretation (Part 41).

637 Other transactions

[FA92 s72]

(1) The Revenue Commissioners may, on an application being made to them in writing in respect of a transaction—

(a) of a type specified in the Directive, and

(b) to which this Part does not apply,

give such relief as appears to them to be just and reasonable for the purposes of giving effect to the Directive.

(2) An application under this section shall be made in such form as the Revenue Commissioners may require.

Cross References

To Section 637

Section 541 Debts.

638 Apportionment of amounts

[FA92 s74]

Where for the purposes of this Part any sum is to be apportioned and at the time of the apportionment it appears that it is material as respects the liability to tax (for whatever period) of 2 or more companies, any question which arises as to the manner in which the sum is to be apportioned shall be determined for the purposes of the tax of all those companies by the Appeal Commissioners who shall determine the question in the like manner as if it were an appeal against an assessment, and the provisions of the Income Tax Acts relating to the rehearing of an appeal and to the statement of a case for the opinion of the High Court on a point of law shall apply accordingly with any necessary modifications, and all those companies shall be entitled to appear and be heard by the Appeal Commissioners or to make representations to them in writing.

TRANSACTIONS IN LAND

PART 22

Provisions Relating to Dealing in or Developing Land and Disposals of Development Land

CHAPTER 1

Income Tax and Corporation Tax: Profits or Gains from Dealing in or Developing Land

639 Interpretation (Chapter 1)

[F(MP)A68 s16(1), (2) and (4)]

(1) In this Chapter, except where the context otherwise requires—

"company" includes any body corporate;

"*development*", in relation to any land, means—

(a) the construction, demolition, extension, alteration or reconstruction of any building on the land, or

(b) the carrying out of any engineering or other operation in, on, over or under the land to adapt it for materially altered use,

and "developing" and "developed" shall be construed accordingly;

"*market value*", in relation to any property, means the price which that property might reasonably be expected to fetch if sold in the open market;

"*trading stock*" has the same meaning as in *section 89*;

any reference to the disposal of an interest in land includes a reference to the creation of an interest, and any reference to the acquisition of an interest in land includes a reference to the acquisition of an interest which ceases on the acquisition.

(2) For the purposes of this Chapter—

(a) a person shall not be regarded as disposing of an interest in land by reason of the person conveying or transferring the interest by means of security or of the person granting a lease of the land on terms which do not require the payment of any fine, premium or like sum, and

(b) an option or other right to acquire or dispose of any interest in any land shall be deemed to be an interest in the land.

(3) This Chapter shall apply notwithstanding *Chapter 8* of *Part 4*.

Revenue Briefings

Tax Briefing

Tax Briefing September 2009 – Issue 73 – "Rent to Buy" (and similar) Schemes

eBrief

eBrief No. 45/2009 – "Rent to Buy" (and similar) Schemes

Cross References

From Section 639

Section 52 Persons chargeable.
Section 89 Valuation of trading stock at discontinuance of trade.
Section 96 Interpretation (Chapter 8).

To Section 639

Section 21A Higher rate of corporation tax.
Section 530A Principal to whom relevant contracts tax applies.
Section 531 Payments to subcontractors in certain industries.

640 Extension of charge under Case I of Schedule D to certain profits from dealing in or developing land

[F(MP)A68 s17; FA81 s28]

(1) For the purposes of *subsection (2)*—

(a) a dealing in land shall be regarded as taking place where a person having an interest in any land disposes, as regards the whole or any part of the land, of that interest or of an interest which derives from that interest, and

(b) a person who secures the development of any land shall be regarded as developing that land.

(2) (a) Where apart from this section all or some of the activities of a business of dealing in or developing land would not be regarded as activities carried on in the course of a trade within Schedule D but would be so regarded if every disposal of an interest in land included among such activities (including a disposal of an interest in land which apart from this section is a disposal of the full interest in the land which the person carrying on the business had acquired) were treated as fulfilling the conditions specified in *paragraph (b)*, the business shall be deemed to be wholly a trade within Schedule D or, as the case may be, part of such a trade, and the profits or gains of that business shall be charged to tax under Case I of Schedule D accordingly.

(b) The conditions referred to in *paragraph (a)* are—

(i) that the disposal was a disposal of the full interest in the land which the person carrying on the business had acquired, and

(ii) that the interest disposed of had been acquired by such person in the course of the business.

(3) Where an interest in land is disposed of in the course of the winding up of a company, the company shall for the purposes of this section be deemed not to have ceased to carry on the trade or business which it carried on before the commencement of the winding up until the completion of the disposal, or of the last such disposal where there is more than one, and the question whether any such disposal was made in the course of a business of dealing in or developing land which is, or is to be deemed to be, a trade or part of a trade shall accordingly be determined without regard to the fact that the company is being wound up.

641 Computation under Case I of Schedule D of profits or gains from dealing in or developing land

[F(MP)A68 s18; FA81 s29(2)(a)]

(1) Where a business of dealing in or developing land is, or is to be regarded as, a trade within Schedule D or a part of such a trade, the provisions applicable to

Case I of that Schedule shall, as respects the computation of the profits or gains of the business, apply subject to *subsections (2)* to *(4)*.

(2) (a) Any consideration (other than rent or an amount treated as rent under *section 98*) for the disposal of an interest in any land or in a part of any land shall be treated as a consideration for the disposal of trading stock and accordingly shall be taken into account as a trading receipt.

(b) Any interest in any land which is held by a person carrying on a trade (in this section referred to as "the trader") and which has become trading stock of the trade shall thereafter, until the discontinuance of the trade, continue to be such trading stock.

(c) Where the trader has acquired an interest in any land otherwise than for consideration in money or money's worth, the trader shall, subject to *paragraph (d)*, be deemed to have purchased the interest for a consideration equal to its market value at the time of acquisition.

(d) Where at the time of acquisition of an interest in any land the trade had not been commenced or the interest was not then appropriated as trading stock, the trader shall be deemed to have purchased the interest for a consideration equal to its market value at the time of its appropriation as trading stock.

(e) Any consideration (other than receipts within *section 75(1)(b)* the profits or gains arising from which are by virtue of that section chargeable to tax under Case V of Schedule D) for the granting by the trader of any right in relation to the development of any land shall be taken into account as a trading receipt.

(3) Account shall not be taken of any sum (in this subsection referred to as "the relevant sum") which is paid or is payable at any time by the trader as consideration for the forfeiture or surrender of the right of any person to an annuity or other annual payment unless—

(a) the annuity or other annual payment arises under—

(i) a testamentary disposition, or

(ii) a liability incurred for—

(I) valuable and sufficient consideration all of which is required to be taken into account in computing for the purposes of income tax or corporation tax the income of the person to whom that consideration is given, or

(II) consideration given to a person who—

(A) has not at any time carried on a business of dealing in or developing land which is, or is to be regarded as, a trade or a part of a trade, and

(B) is not and was not at any time connected with any of the following persons—

(aa) the trader,

(bb) a person who is or was at any time connected with the trader, and (cc) any other person who, in the course of a business of dealing in or developing land which is, or is to be regarded as, a trade or a part of a trade, holds or held an interest in land on which the annuity or other annual payment was charged or reserved,

or

(b) the relevant sum is required to be taken into account in computing for the purposes of income tax or corporation tax the profits or gains of a trade of dealing in or developing land carried on by the person to whom the relevant sum is payable.

(4) (a) *Paragraph (b)* shall apply where—

(i) a sum (in this subsection referred to as "the relevant sum") is payable—

(I) by a person (in this subsection referred to as "the relevant person") who is not the trader, and

(II) as consideration for the forfeiture or surrender of the right (in this subsection referred to as "the right") of any person to an annuity or other annual payment,

(ii) the relevant sum is not required to be taken into account in computing for the purposes of income tax or corporation tax the profits or gains of a trade of dealing in or developing land carried on by the person to whom the relevant sum is payable, and

(iii) the trader incurs expenditure (in this subsection referred to as "the cost") in acquiring any interest (in this subsection referred to as "the interest") in land on which the annuity or other annual payment had been reserved or charged.

(b) Where this paragraph applies—

(i) the trader shall be treated as having expended in acquiring the interest an amount equal to the amount which would have been expended if the right had not been forfeited or surrendered, and

(ii) the excess of the cost over the amount determined in accordance with *subparagraph (i)* shall be treated for the purposes of *subsection (3)* as having been payable by the trader as consideration for the forfeiture or surrender of the right.

(c) For the purposes of this subsection, all such apportionments and valuations shall be made as appear to the inspector or on appeal to the Appeal Commissioners to be just and reasonable.

(d) This subsection shall not apply where the relevant person carries on a trade of dealing in or developing land and pays the relevant sum in the course of carrying on that trade.

Revenue Briefings

Tax Briefing

Tax Briefing September 2000 – Issue 73 – "Rent to Buy" (and similar) Schemes

eBrief

eBrief No. 45/2009 – "Rent to Buy" (and similar) Schemes

Cross References

From Section 641

Section 75 Case V: basis of assessment.

Section 98 Treatment of premiums, etc. as rent.

642 Transfers of interests in land between certain associated persons

[F(MP)A68 s19]

(1) Where an interest in land is disposed of by any person (in this subsection referred to as "the disponer") to a person connected with the disponer (in this subsection referred to as "the transferee") and—

(a) the interest is disposed of at a price greater than its market value, and

(b) the price—

(i) is not to be taken into account in relation to the disponer in computing for tax purposes the profits or gains of a trade which is or includes a business of dealing in or developing land, but

(ii) is to be so taken into account in relation to the transferee,

the transferee shall for tax purposes be deemed to have acquired the interest at a price equal to the market value of the interest at the time of its acquisition by the transferee.

(2) (a) Where an interest in land is disposed of by any person (in this subsection referred to as "the disponer") to a person connected with the disponer (in this subsection referred to as "the transferee") and—

(i) the interest is disposed of at a price less than its market value, and

(ii) the price—

(I) is not to be taken into account in relation to the transferee in computing for tax purposes the profits or gains of a trade which is or includes a business of dealing in or developing land, but

(II) is to be so taken into account in relation to the disponer,

the disponer shall for tax purposes be deemed to have disposed of the interest at a price equal to the market value of the interest at the time of the disposal by the disponer.

(b) A disposal by means of gift shall be regarded for the purposes of this subsection as being a disposal at a nominal price.

(3) In the application of this section to a case in which a lease is granted, any reference to price shall be construed as a reference to the fine, premium or like sum payable for the grant of the lease.

643 Tax to be charged under Case IV on gains from certain disposals of land

[F(MP)A68 s20; FA81 s29(3)]

(1) In this section and in *section 644*—

"*capital amount*" means any amount in money or money's worth which apart from this section is not to be included in any computation of income for the purposes of the Tax Acts, and other expressions which include the word "capital" shall be construed accordingly;

"*chargeable period*" means an accounting period of a company or a year of assessment;

"land" includes any interest in land, and references to the land include references to all or any part of the land;

"share" includes stock;

references to property deriving its value from land include references to—

(a) any shareholding in a company, or any partnership interest, or any interest in settled property, deriving its value or the greater part of its value directly or indirectly from land, and

(b) any option, consent or embargo affecting the disposition of land.

(2) This section shall not apply to a gain accruing to an individual which by virtue of *section 604* is exempt from capital gains tax or which would be so exempt but for *subsection (14)* of that section.

(3) This section shall apply in any case where—

(a) land or any property deriving its value from land is acquired with the sole or main object of realising a gain from disposing of the land,

(b) land is held as trading stock, or

(c) land is developed by a company with the sole or main object of realising a gain from disposing of the land when developed,

and any gain of a capital nature is obtained from disposing of the land—

(i) by the person acquiring, holding or developing the land, or by a person connected with that person, or

(ii) where any arrangement or scheme is effected as respects the land which enables the gain to be realised directly or indirectly by any transaction, or by any series of transactions, by any person who is a party to or concerned in the arrangement or scheme,

and this subsection shall apply whether that gain is obtained by any such person for that person's benefit or for the benefit of any other person.

(4) Where this section applies, the whole of any gain mentioned in *subsection (3)* shall for the purposes of the Tax Acts be treated—

(a) as being income which arises at the time when the gain is realised and which constitutes profits or gains chargeable to tax under Case IV of Schedule D for the chargeable period in which the gain is realised, and

(b) subject to *subsections (5)* to *(17)*, as being income of the person by whom the gain is realised.

(5) For the purposes of this section, land shall be treated as disposed of if, by any one or more transactions or by any arrangement or scheme, whether concerning the land or property deriving its value from the land, the property in the land or control over the land is effectively disposed of, and references in *subsection (3)* to the acquisition or development of land or property with the sole or main object of realising a gain from disposing of the land shall be construed accordingly.

(6) For the purposes of this section—

(a) where, whether by a premature sale or otherwise, a person directly or indirectly makes available to another person the opportunity of realising a gain, the gain of that other person shall be treated as having been obtained for that other person by the first-mentioned person, and

(b) any number of transactions may be regarded as constituting a single arrangement or scheme if a common purpose is discerned in those transactions or if there is other sufficient evidence of a common purpose.

(7) In applying this section, account shall be taken of any method, direct or indirect, by which—

(a) any property or right is transferred or transmitted to another person, or

(b) the value of any property or right is enhanced or diminished,

and accordingly the occasion of the transfer or transmission of any property or right by whatever method and the occasion when the value of any property or right is enhanced may be treated as an occasion on which tax becomes chargeable under this section.

(8) *Subsection (7)* shall apply in particular to—

(a) sales, contracts and other transactions made otherwise than for full consideration or for more than full consideration,

(b) any method by which any property or right, or the control of any property or right, is transferred or transmitted to any person by assigning—

(i) share capital or other rights in a company,

(ii) rights in a partnership, or

(iii) an interest in settled property,

(c) the creation of any option or consent or embargo affecting the disposition of any property or right, and to the consideration given for the option, or for the giving of the consent or the release of the embargo, and

(d) the disposal of any property or right on the winding up, dissolution or termination of any company, partnership or trust.

(9) For the purposes of this section, such method of computing a gain shall be adopted as is just and reasonable in the circumstances, taking into account the value of what is obtained for disposing of the land and allowing only such expenses as are attributable to the land disposed of, and in applying this subsection—

(a) where an interest in land is acquired and the reversion is retained on disposal, account may be taken of the way in which the profits or gains under Case I of Schedule D of a person dealing in land are computed in such a case, and

(b) account may be taken of the adjustments to be made in computing such profits or gains under *sections 99(2)* and *100(4)*.

(10) *Paragraph (c)* of *subsection (3)* shall not apply to so much of any gain as is fairly attributable to the period, if any, before the intention to develop that land was formed, and which would not be within *paragraph (a)* or *(b)* of that subsection, and in applying this subsection account shall be taken of the treatment under Case I of Schedule D of a person who appropriates land as trading stock.

(11) If all or any part of the gain accruing to any person is derived from value, or an opportunity of realising a gain, provided directly or indirectly by some other person (whether or not put at the disposal of the first-mentioned person), *subsection (4)(b)* shall apply to the gain or that part of the gain with the substitution of that other person for the person by whom the gain was realised.

(12) Where there is a disposal of shares in—

(a) a company which holds land as trading stock, or

(b) a company which owns directly or indirectly 90 per cent or more of the ordinary share capital of another company which holds land as trading stock,

and all the land so held is disposed of in the normal course of its trade by the company which held the land, and so as to procure that all opportunity of profit in respect of the land arises to that company, then, notwithstanding *subsection (3) (i)*, this section shall not apply to any gain accruing to the holder of shares as being a gain on property deriving value from that land (but without prejudice to any liability under *subsection (3)(ii)*).

(13) In ascertaining for the purposes of this section the intentions of any person, the objects and powers of any company, partners or trustees, as set out in any memorandum or articles of association or other document, shall not be conclusive.

(14) For the purposes of ascertaining whether and to what extent the value of any property or right is derived from any other property or right, value may be traced through any number of companies, partnerships and trusts, and the property held by any company, partnership or trust shall be attributed to the shareholders, partners or beneficiaries at each stage in such manner as is just and reasonable.

(15) In applying this section—

(a) any expenditure, receipt, consideration or other amount may be apportioned by such method as is just and reasonable, and

(b) all such valuations shall be made as may be necessary to give effect to this section.

(16) For the purposes of this section, partners, trustees of settled property or personal representatives may be regarded as persons distinct from the individuals or other persons who are for the time being partners, trustees or personal representatives.

(17) This section shall apply to a person, whether resident in the State or not, if all or any part of the land in question is situated in the State.

Cross References

From Section 643

Section 99 Charge on assignment of lease granted at undervalue.
Section 100 Charge on sale of land with right to reconveyance.
Section 604 Disposals of principal private residence.
Section 644 Provisions supplementary to section 643.

To Section 643

Section 644 Provisions supplementary to section 643.
Section 644A Relief from income tax in respect of income from dealing in residential development land.
Section 644B Relief from corporation tax in respect of income from dealing in residential development land.
Section 645 Power to obtain information.

644 Provisions supplementary to section 643

[F(MP)A68 s21; FA81 s29(3)]

(1) (a) Where a person (in this subsection referred to as "the first-mentioned person") is assessed to tax under *section 643* and that assessment to tax arises in consequence of and in respect of consideration receivable by another person (in this subsection referred to as "the second-mentioned person")—

(i) the first-mentioned person shall be entitled to recover from the second-mentioned person any part of that tax which the first-mentioned person has paid,

(ii) if any part of that tax remains unpaid at the expiration of 6 months from the date when it became due and payable, it shall be recoverable from the second-mentioned person as though the second-mentioned person were the person so assessed, but without prejudice to the right to recover the tax from the first-mentioned person, and

(iii) for the purposes of *subparagraph (i)*, the inspector shall on request furnish a certificate specifying the amount of income in respect of which tax has been paid and the amount of tax so paid, and the certificate shall be evidence until the contrary is proved of any facts stated in the certificate.

(b) For the purposes of this subsection, any amount which by virtue of *section 643* is treated as the income of a person shall, notwithstanding any other provision of the Tax Acts, be treated as the highest part of the person's income.

(2) Where it appears to the Revenue Commissioners that any person entitled to any consideration or other amount chargeable to tax under *section 643* is not resident in the State, they may direct that *section 238* shall apply to any payment forming part of that amount as if the payment were an annual payment charged with tax under Schedule D, but without prejudice to the final determination of the liability of that person, including any liability under *subsection (1)(a)(ii)*.

(3) *Section 643* shall apply subject to any provision of the Tax Acts deeming income to be income of a particular person.

(4) Where by virtue of *section 643(3)(c)* any person is charged to tax on the realisation of a gain, and by virtue of *section 643(10)* the computation of the gain proceeded on the basis that the land or some other property was appropriated at any time as trading stock, that land or other property shall also be treated on that basis for the purposes of *section 596*.

(5) Where by virtue of *section 643(11)* the person charged to tax is a person other than the person for whom the capital amount was obtained or the person by whom the gain was realised and the tax has been paid, then, for the purposes of *sections 551* and *554*, the person for whom the capital amount was obtained or the person by whom the gain was realised, as may be appropriate, shall be regarded as having been charged to the tax so paid.

Cross References

From Section 644

Section 238 Annual payments not payable out of taxed income.

Section 551 Exclusion from consideration for disposals of sums chargeable to income tax.

Section 554 Exclusion of expenditure by reference to income tax.

Section 596 Appropriations to and from stock in trade.

Section 643 Tax to be charged under Case IV on gains from certain disposals of land.

To Section 644

Section 643 Tax to be charged under Case IV on gains from certain disposals of land.

Section 645 Power to obtain information.

644A Relief from income tax in respect of income from dealing in residential development land

[(1) In this section—

"*basis period*" has the same meaning as in *section 127(1)*;

"*construction operations*", in relation to residential development land, means operations of any of the descriptions referred to in the definition of "*construction operations*" in *section 530(1)* other than such operations as consist of—

(a) the demolition or dismantling of any building or structure on the land,

(b) the construction or demolition of any works forming part of the land, being roadworks, water mains, wells, sewers or installations for the purposes of land drainage, or

(c) any other operations which are preparatory to residential development on the land other than the laying of foundations for such development;

"residential development" includes any development which is ancillary to the development and which is necessary for the proper planning and development of the area in question;

"*residential development land*" means land—

(a) disposed of to—

(i) a housing authority (within the meaning of section 23 of the Housing (Miscellaneous Provisions) Act, 1992),

(ii) the National Building Agency Limited (being the company referred to in section 1 of the National Building Agency Limited Act, 1963), or

(iii) a body standing approved of for the purposes of section 6 of the Housing (Miscellaneous Provisions) Act, 1992,

which land is specified in a certificate in writing given by a housing authority or the National Building Agency Limited, as appropriate, as land being required for the purposes of the Housing Acts, 1966 to 1998,

(b) in respect of which permission for residential development has been granted under [the Local Government (Planning and Development) Acts 1963 to 1999 or the Planning and Development Act 2000,][1] and such permission has not ceased to exist, or

(c) which is, in accordance with a development objective (as indicated in the development plan of the planning authority concerned), for use solely or primarily for residential purposes.

(2) This section applies to profits or gains being—

(a) profits or gains arising from dealing in or developing residential development land in the course of a business consisting of or including dealing in or developing land which is, or is regarded as, a trade within Schedule D or a part of such a trade, or

(b) any gain of a capital nature arising from the disposing of residential development land which, by virtue of *section 643*, constitutes profits or gains chargeable to tax under Case IV of Schedule D.

(3) Notwithstanding any other provision of the Tax Acts and subject to *subsections (4)* and *(5)*—

(a) to the extent to which profits or gains of a basis period for a year of assessment consist of profits or gains to which this section applies, those profits or gains—

(i) shall be chargeable to income tax for that year at the rate of 20 per cent, and

(ii) shall not be reckoned in computing total income for that year for the purposes of the Income Tax Acts,

and

(b) the provisions of [section 188][2], and the reductions specified in Part 2 of the Table to *section 458* shall not apply as regards income tax so charged.

(4) For the purposes of this section—

(a) where a trade consists partly of dealing in residential development land and partly of other operations or activities, the part of the trade consisting of dealing in residential development land and the part of the trade consisting of other operations or activities shall each be treated as a separate trade, and the total amount receivable from sales made and services rendered in the course of the trade, and of expenses incurred in the trade, shall be apportioned to each such part,

(b) in computing the profits or gains to which this section applies, no account shall be taken, in determining those profits or gains, of that part, if any, of profits or gains which are attributable to construction operations on the land, and

(c) where, in order to give effect to the provisions of this section, an apportionment of profits and gains, amounts receivable or expenses incurred is required to be made, such apportionment shall be made in a manner that is just and reasonable.

(5) This section shall not apply to profits or gains arising to a person in a year of assessment if that person so elects by notice in writing to the inspector on or before the specified return date for the chargeable period (within the meaning of *section 950*).

[(6) This section shall not apply to profits or gains arising to a person in the year of assessment 2009 or in any subsequent year of assessment.][3]][4]

Amendments

[1] Substituted by FA04 s83(1)(a).

[2] Substituted by FA08 s5(f).

[3] Inserted by FA09 s6(a). This section is deemed to have come into force and takes effect as on and from 1 January 2009.

[4] Inserted by FA00 s52(1).

Revenue Briefings

Tax Briefing

Tax Briefing June 2000 – Issue 40 pg 1 – Residential Development Land – Income Tax

Tax Briefing October 2001 – Issue 45 pg 11 – PRSI/Health Contribution & Residential Development Land

Cross References

From Section 644A

Section 127 Tax treatment of restrictive covenants.

Section 188 Age exemption and associated marginal relief.

Section 458 Deductions allowed in ascertaining taxable income and provisions relating to reductions in tax.

Section 530 Interpretation (Chapter 2).

Section 643 Tax to be charged under Case IV on gains from certain disposals of land.

Section 950 Interpretation (Part 41).

To Section 644A

Section 21A Higher rate of corporation tax.

Section 644C Relief from corporation tax for losses from dealing in residential development land.

Section 644AA Treatment of losses from dealing in residential development land.

644AA Treatment of losses from dealing in residential development land

[(1) In this section—

"*adjusted income*" for a tax year means a person's income from all sources for the tax year after taking into account any allowance, charge, deduction or loss attributable to a specific source to which the person is entitled in taxing the income from the source or which is required to be made in taxing the person's income from the source, but without taking into account any allowance, charge, deduction or loss to which the person is entitled, or which is required to be made, in taxing the person's income from all sources;

"*adjusted profits or gains*" in relation to a trade for a tax year means the amount, if any, of the profits or gains from the trade after taking into account any allowance, charge, deduction or loss to which a person is entitled in taxing the trade or which is required to be made in taxing the trade, and references to the adjusted profits or gains from the combined trade or from the non-specified trade shall be construed accordingly;

"*combined trade*" means a trade comprising partly of a specified trade and partly of a non-specified trade;

"*non-specified trade*", in relation to a combined trade, means the activities and operations of the combined trade that are the part of the trade that is not a specified trade;

"*relevant loss*", in relation to a tax year, means—

(a) in the case of a specified trade, the full amount of a loss sustained in the specified trade in the tax year, and

(b) in the case of a combined trade, so much of the amount of a loss sustained in the combined trade in the tax year as is attributable to a specified trade;

"*specified trade*" means, as the case may be, a trade, or the part of a combined trade, the profits or gains, if any, of which, for a tax year before the tax year 2009, were chargeable to tax in accordance with section 644A(3) (other than by virtue of subsection (5) of that section);

"*tax*" means income tax;

"*tax year*" means a year of assessment.

(2) For the purposes of subsections (3) to (8), where a trade is a combined trade, the part of the trade which is a specified trade and the part of the trade which is a non-specified trade shall each be treated as a separate trade and where, in order to give effect to the provisions of subsections (3) to (8), an apportionment of the total amount receivable from sales made and services rendered in the course of a combined trade and of expenses incurred in that trade is required to be made, such apportionment shall be made in a manner that is just and reasonable.

(3) Where, in respect of a tax year before the tax year 2009, a claim is made by a person (in this subsection and subsections (4) to (7) referred to as the "claimant") in accordance with subsection (6) of section 381, which claim is in respect of, or includes, a relevant loss, then, notwithstanding subsection (1) of that section, unless the claim is made to and received by the Revenue Commissioners before 7 April 2009, that subsection shall not apply to so much of the loss as is a relevant loss and the claimant shall instead be entitled as regards the relevant loss to such repayment of tax as is provided for by subsection (4).

(4) (a) In relation to the relevant loss referred to in subsection (3), the repayment of tax to which the claimant is entitled shall be such amount as is necessary

to secure that the aggregate amount of tax for the tax year ultimately borne by the claimant does not exceed the amount which would have been borne by the claimant if the interim amount of tax payable by the claimant for the tax year had been reduced by the amount (in this section referred to as the "tax credit") determined in accordance with subsection (5).

(b) For the purposes of this subsection and subsections (6)(*a*) and (7)(*a*), the references to the "interim amount of tax payable by the claimant for the tax year" shall be taken to mean the tax which would have been borne by that person for that tax year following any reduction in the income of that person for that tax year, to which the person is entitled in accordance with section 381(1), by—

(i) so much of the amount of a loss arising in a combined trade as is attributable to the non-specified trade, and

(ii) the amount of any other loss (other than the amount of the relevant loss).

(5) The tax credit referred to in subsection (4) shall be an amount equivalent to the amount determined by the formula—

$$A \times \frac{20}{100}$$

where A is the amount of the relevant loss.

(6) (a) Notwithstanding section 382, to the extent that relief has not been fully given under subsection (4) in respect of a relevant loss due to the interim amount of tax payable by the claimant for the tax year being less than the tax credit provided by that subsection, the claimant may claim that the unused portion of the tax credit (in this section referred to as the "excess tax credit") shall be carried forward and, insofar as may be, used to reduce the amount of tax payable on the profits or gains on which that person is assessed under Schedule D in respect of the combined trade for any subsequent tax year.

(b) Any relief under this subsection shall be given as far as possible from the tax payable for the first subsequent tax year and, in so far as it cannot be so given, from the tax payable for the next tax year and so on.

(7) (a) For the purposes of subsection (6)(*a*) but subject to paragraph (*b*), where in a subsequent tax year to which an excess tax credit is carried forward a person's income comprises profits or gains from a combined trade and other income, the amount of tax payable on the profits or gains from the combined trade for the tax year shall be taken to be an amount equivalent to the amount determined by the formula—

$$B \times \frac{C}{D}$$

where—

B is the interim amount of tax payable by the claimant for the tax year,

C is the adjusted profits or gains from the combined trade for the tax year, and

D is the claimant's adjusted income for the tax year.

(b) For the purposes of subsection (6)(*a*), where the tax year to which an excess tax credit is carried forward is a tax year before the tax year 2009, any excess tax credit shall be used to reduce—

(i) firstly, the amount of tax, if any, payable in accordance with section 644A(3) on the profits or gains of the specified trade for that tax year, and

(ii) secondly, where following the application of subparagraph (i), all or part of the excess tax credit remains unused, the amount of tax payable on the non-specified trade calculated in accordance with paragraph (*a*) but on the assumption that the following definition was substituted for the definition of C in the formula in that paragraph:

"C is the adjusted profits or gains from the non-specified trade for the tax year, and".

(8) (a) Where a claim under section 382 is made in respect of a relevant loss, or part of a relevant loss, sustained in a tax year before the tax year 2009 (other than a relevant loss to which a claimant is entitled to a repayment of tax under subsection (4)) then, notwithstanding subsection (1) of that section, unless the claim is made to and received by the Revenue Commissioners before 7 April 2009, that subsection shall not apply, and instead the claimant shall, in relation to the amount of the relevant loss to which the claim relates, be entitled to carry forward a tax credit determined in accordance with paragraph (*b*).

(b) The amount of the tax credit referred to in paragraph (*a*) shall be an amount equivalent to the amount determined by the formula—

$$E \times \frac{20}{100}$$

where E is the relevant loss, or the part of the relevant loss, in respect of which the claim under section 382 relates.

(c) The amount of the tax credit a claimant is entitled to carry forward in accordance with paragraph (*a*) shall be treated as an excess tax credit of the kind referred to in subsection (6)(*a*).

(9) (a) Where a claim to relief under section 385 is made in respect of a terminal loss sustained in a combined trade, then, for the purposes of subsection (1) of that section, unless the claim is made to and received by the Revenue Commissioners before 7 April 2009, that subsection shall apply in relation to so much of the terminal loss as is attributable to the period before 1 January 2009, as if the part of the combined trade which was a specified trade and the part of the combined trade which was a non-specified trade were each separate trades and sections 386 to 389 shall apply accordingly.

(b) Where, in order to give effect to the provisions of paragraph (*a*), an apportionment of the total amount receivable from sales made and services rendered in the course of a combined trade and of expenses incurred in that trade is required to be made, such apportionment shall be made in a manner that is just and reasonable.][1]

Amendments

[1] Inserted by FA09 s6(b). This section is deemed to have come into force and takes effect as on and from 1 January 2009.

Cross References

From Section 644AA

Section 381 Right to repayment of tax by reference to losses.
Section 382 Right to carry forward losses to future years.
Section 385 Terminal loss.
Section 386 Determination of terminal loss.
Section 389 Determination of claim for terminal loss.
Section 644A Relief from income tax in respect of income from dealing in residential development land.

644AB Treatment of profits or gains from land rezonings

[(1) In this section—

"*basis period*" has the same meaning as in section 127(1);

"*company*" has the same meaning as in section 4;

"*construction operations*", in relation to land, means operations of any of the descriptions referred to in the definition of "*construction operations*" in section 530(1);

"*development land-use*" means residential, commercial or industrial uses or a mixture of such uses;

"*distribution*" has the same meaning as in section 130(2);

"*non-development land-use*" means a land-use which is agricultural, open space, recreational or amenity use or a mixture of such uses;

"*qualifying land*" means land which is disposed of at any time in the course of a business, being land—

(a) disposed of to an authority possessing compulsory purchasing powers where the Revenue Commissioners are satisfied that the disposal would not have been made but for the exercise of those powers or the giving by the authority of formal notice of its intention to exercise those powers, [...][1]

(b) disposed of by a company referred to in [*section 616(1)(g)*, or][2];

[(c) consisting of a site of 0.4047 hectares or less whose market value at the date of disposal does not exceed €250,000 (notwithstanding that a planning authority may have granted permission in respect of that site in accordance with section 34(1) of the Planning and Development Act 2000), other than where the disposal by the person making it, or by a person connected with that person, forms part of a larger transaction or series of transactions,][3]

[...][4]

["*relevant planning decision*", in relation to land and in accordance with the Planning and Development Act 2000 (in this definition referred to as the "Act of 2000"), means—

(a) a change in the zoning of land in a development plan or a local area plan made or varied under Part II of the Act of 2000 from non-development land-uses to development land-uses or from one development land-use to another development land-use including a mixture of such uses, or

(b) a decision to grant permission, in accordance with section 34(6) or 37(2) of the Act of 2000, for a development that would materially contravene a development plan;][5]

(2) This section applies to—

(a) profits or gains arising from dealing in, or developing, land in the course of a business consisting of or including dealing in or developing land which is, or is regarded as, a trade within Schedule D or part of such a trade, or

(b) any gain of a capital nature arising directly or indirectly from the disposal of land which, by virtue of section 643, constitutes profits or gains chargeable to tax under Case IV of Schedule D,

to the extent to which the profits or gains are attributable to [a relevant planning decision][6].

(3) Notwithstanding any provision to the contrary in the Corporation Tax Acts, but subject to this section, a company shall not be chargeable to corporation tax in respect of profits or gains to which this section applies and, accordingly, such profits or gains shall not be regarded as profits or gains of the company for the purposes of corporation tax.

(4) Notwithstanding any other provision of the Tax Acts and subject to *subsections (6)* and *(7)*, to the extent to which profits or gains of a basis period for a year of assessment consist of profits or gains to which this section applies—

(a) those profits or gains shall be chargeable to income tax for such year at the rate of 80 per cent, and

(b) those profits or gains shall be disregarded for all the purposes of the Tax Acts, other than those relating to the assessment, collection and recovery of income tax and of any interest or penalties on that tax.

(5) (a) To the extent that a loss is attributable to [a relevant planning decision][7] referred to in *subsection (2)*, that loss—

(i) may be carried forward and may only be deducted from or set off against the amount of profits or gains to which this section applies for any subsequent year of assessment, and

(ii) in the case of a company, shall be disregarded for the purposes of the Corporation Tax Acts.

(b) Any relief under this subsection shall be given as far as possible against the profits or gains for the first subsequent year of assessment and, in so far as it cannot be so given, from the profits or gains for the next year of assessment and so on for succeeding years.

(6) Where an individual is chargeable to tax in accordance with *subsection (4)* in respect of profits or gains, the profits or gains shall not be included in reckonable income—

(a) within the meaning of section 2(1) of the Social Welfare Consolidation Act 2005, or

(b) within the meaning of section 1 of the Health Contributions Act 1979,

for the purposes of those Acts or any regulations made under those Acts.

(7) For the purposes of the Tax Acts in computing the profits or gains to which this section applies, no account shall be taken, in determining those profits or gains, of that part, if any, of profits or gains which are attributable to (*a*) construction operations on the land, or (*b*) qualifying land.

(8) Where, in order to give effect to the provisions of *subsections (2)*, *(4)* and *(7)*, an apportionment of profits and gains, amounts receivable or expenses incurred is required to be made, such apportionment shall be made in a manner that is just and reasonable.

(9) Where a distribution is made by a company in part out of profits or gains to which this section applies and in part out of other profits or gains, then the distribution shall be treated as if it consisted of 2 distributions respectively made out of the profits or gains to which this section applies and out of other profits or gains.

(10) So much of any distribution as has been made out of profits or gains to which this section applies shall not be regarded as income for any purpose of the Income Tax Acts or be included in reckonable income—

(a) within the meaning of section 2(1) of the Social Welfare Consolidation Act 2005, or

(b) within the meaning of section 1 of the Health Contributions Act 1979,

for the purposes of those Acts or any regulations made under those Acts.

[(11) This section shall apply as respects the years of assessment 2010 to 2014.][8]][9]

Amendments

[1] Deleted by FA10 s25(1)(a). Applies as respects disposals made on or after 30 October 2009.

[2] Substituted by FA10 s25(1)(a). Applies as respects disposals made on or after 30 October 2009.

[3] Inserted by FA10 s25(1)(a). Applies as respects disposals made on or after 30 October 2009.

[4] Deleted by FA10 s25(1)(b). Applies as respects changes or decisions made on or after 4 February 2010.

[5] Inserted by FA10 s25(1)(b). Applies as respects changes or decisions made on or after 4 February 2010.

[6] Substituted by FA10 s25(1)(c). Applies as respects changes or decisions made on or after 4 February 2010.

[7] Substituted by FA10 s25(1)(d). Applies as respects changes or decisions made on or after 4 February 2010.

[8] Substituted by FA14 s31(a). Comes into operation on 1 January 2015.

[9] Inserted by the National Asset Management Agency Act 2009 Sched 3 part 10. This section shall apply as respects the year of assessment 2010 and subsequent years of assessment.

Cross References

From Section 644AB

Section 616 Groups of companies: interpretation.

644B Relief from corporation tax in respect of income from dealing in residential development land

[(1) In this section—

"*excepted trade*" has the same meaning as in section 21A;

"*residential development*" and "*residential development land*" have the same meaning as each has in section 644A.

(2) (a) Where in an accounting period a company carries on an excepted trade the operations or activities of which consist of or include dealing in land which, at the time at which it is disposed of by the company, is residential development land, the corporation tax payable by the company for the accounting period, in so far as it is referable to trading income from dealing in residential development land, shall be reduced by one-fifth.

(b) For the purposes of *paragraph (a)*—

(i) the corporation tax payable by a company for an accounting period which is referable to trading income from dealing in residential development land shall be such amount as bears to the amount of corporation tax for the period referable to income of an excepted trade the same proportion as—

(I) the amount receivable by the company in the accounting period from the disposal in the course of the excepted trade of residential development land, exclusive of so much of that amount as is attributable to construction operations (within the meaning of section 21A) carried out by or for the company on the land, bears to

(II) the total amount receivable by the company in the accounting period, exclusive of so much of that amount as is attributable to construction operations (within the meaning of section 21A) carried out by or for the company on land disposed of by it, in the course of the excepted trade,

and

(ii) corporation tax referable to income from an excepted trade for an accounting period shall be such sum as bears to the amount of corporation tax charged for the period in accordance with section 21A at the rate of 25 per cent the same proportion as the amount of the company's profits treated under section 21A as consisting of income from the excepted trade bears to the total amount of the profits of the company for the period so charged at the rate of 25 per cent.

(3) (a) Where in an accounting period income of a company which is chargeable under Case IV of Schedule D by virtue of *section 643* consists of or includes an amount in respect of a gain obtained from disposing of land which, at the time of its disposal, is residential development land, the corporation tax payable by the company for the accounting period, in so far as it is referable to that gain, shall be reduced by one-fifth.

(b) For the purposes of *paragraph (a)*—

(i) the corporation tax payable by a company for an accounting period which is referable to a gain from disposing of residential development land shall be such amount as bears to the amount of corporation tax for the accounting period referable to a gain charged to tax in accordance with *section 643* the same proportion as so much of the amount (in this subparagraph referred to as the "*specified amount*") of the last-mentioned gain as is attributable to the disposal of residential development land (exclusive of any part of the gain as is referable to construction operations, within the meaning of section 644A, carried out by the company) bears to the specified amount, and

(ii) corporation tax referable to a gain from disposing of land which is treated by virtue of *section 643* as income chargeable under Case IV of Schedule D shall be such sum as bears to the amount of corporation tax charged for the accounting period in accordance with section 21A at the rate of 25 per cent the same proportion as the amount of the company's profits which consists of income chargeable under Case IV of Schedule D by virtue of *section 643* bears to the total amount of the profits of the company for the period so charged at the rate of 25 per cent.

(4) (a) Where a company makes a claim in that behalf, the corporation tax payable by the company for an accounting period ending before 1 January 2001 shall be computed as if *subparagraph (ii)* of *paragraph (a)* of the definition

of excepted operations in section 21A did not have effect in relation to residential development land.

(b) For the purposes of this subsection where an accounting period of a company begins before 1 January 2001 and ends on or after that day, it shall be divided into two parts, one beginning on the day on which the accounting period begins and ending on 31 December 2000 and the other beginning on 1 January 2001 and ending on the day on which the accounting period ends, and both parts shall be treated for the purpose of this section as if they were separate accounting periods of the company.][1]

[(5) (a) This section shall not apply to an accounting period ending after 31 December 2008.

(b) Where an accounting period of a company begins before 31 December 2008 and ends after that day, it shall be divided into 2 parts, one beginning on the day on which the accounting period begins and ending on 31 December 2008 and the other beginning on 1 January 2009 and ending on the day on which the accounting period ends, and both parts shall be treated for the purposes of this section as if they were separate accounting periods of the company.][2]

Amendments

[1] Inserted by FA00 s52(1), applies (a)(i) as respects income tax, in relation to profits or gains arising on or after 1 December 1999, and (ii) as respects corporation tax, in relation to accounting periods ending on or after 1 January 2000. (b) For the purposes of this section where an accounting period of a company begins before 1 January 2000 and ends on or after that day, it shall be divided into two parts, one beginning on the day on which the accounting period begins and ending on 31 December 1999 and the other beginning on 1 January 2000 and ending on the day on which the accounting period ends, and both parts shall be treated for the purpose of this section as if they were separate accounting periods of the company.

[2] Inserted by FA09 s11(1)(a). Applies as on and from 1 January 2009.

Revenue Briefings

Tax Briefing

Tax Briefing June 2000 – Issue 40 pg 1 – Residential Development Land – Corporation Tax

Cross References

From Section 644B

Section 643 Tax to be charged under Case IV on gains from certain disposals of land.

To Section 644B

Section 448 Relief from corporation tax.

Section 486C Relief from tax for certain start-up companies.

Section 644C Relief from corporation tax for losses from dealing in residential development land.

Schedule 24 Relief from Income Tax and Corporation Tax by Means of Credit in Respect of Foreign Tax

644C Relief from corporation tax for losses from dealing in residential development land

[(1) (a) In this section—

"*corporation tax referable to dealing in residential development land*", in relation to an accounting period of a company, means the corporation tax referable to trading income from dealing in residential development land within the meaning of subsection (2) of section 644B as reduced under that section;

"*relevant corporation tax*", in relation to an accounting period of a company, means the corporation tax which would be chargeable on the company for the accounting period apart from—

(i) this section and sections 239, 241, 420B, 440 and 441, and

(ii) where the company carries on a life business (within the meaning of section 706), any corporation tax which would be attributable to policyholders' profits;

"*relevant trading income*" has the same meaning as it has in section 243A;

"*residential development land*" has the same meaning as it has in section 644A(1).

(b) Where an accounting period of a company begins before 31 December 2008 and ends after that day, it shall be divided into 2 parts, one beginning on the day on which the accounting period begins and ending on 31 December 2008 and the other beginning on 1 January 2009 and ending on the day on which the accounting period ends, and both parts shall be treated for the purpose of this section as if they were separate accounting periods of the company.

(2) Notwithstanding subsection (1) of section 396, where a company claims that a loss incurred in a trade, the operations or activities of which consist of or include dealing in residential development land, in an accounting period ending on or before 31 December 2008 be set off against trading income of an accounting period beginning after that date, the said subsection (1) shall apply as if the amount of the loss so far as it relates to dealing in residential development land were reduced by 20 per cent.

(3) Notwithstanding subsection (2) of section 396, for the purposes of that subsection the amount of a loss incurred by a company in an accounting period in a trade, the operations or activities of which consist of or include dealing in residential development land, shall be deemed to be reduced—

(a) where the accounting period falls wholly before 1 January 2009, by the lesser of—

(i) the amount of the loss, and

(ii) the amount of the loss which relates to dealing in residential development land,

and

(b) where the accounting period begins before 1 January 2009 and ends on or after that day, by the lesser of—

(i) the amount of the loss, and

(ii) the amount of the loss which relates to dealing in residential development land,

incurred in the period beginning when the accounting period begins and ending on 31 December 2008.

(4) The computation of the amount of the loss which relates to dealing in residential development land for the purposes of subsections (2), (3)(*a*)(ii), (3)(*b*)(ii), (13)(*b*), (14)(*a*)(ii), (14)(*b*)(ii), (20)(*b*)(i)(II) and (20)(*b*)(ii)(II) shall take into account receipts and purchases, changes in values of stock and other expenses referable to residential development land and a proportion (determined on a just and reasonable basis) of receipts and expenses partly referable to dealing in residential development land and partly to other land or activities of the trade.

(5) Subsections (6) to (12) shall apply to the amount by which a loss in an accounting period is restricted under subsection (3) as if it were a loss (hereinafter in this section referred to as a "*relevant loss*") incurred by the company in that accounting period in carrying on a separate trade of dealing in residential development land.

(6) Where in an accounting period a company incurs a relevant loss, the company may make a claim requiring that the loss be set off against profits of the company, being—

(a) income specified in section 21A(4)(*b*),

(b) relevant trading income,

(c) income to which section 21A(3) does not apply by virtue of section 21B, and

(d) profits attributable to chargeable gains,

of that accounting period and, if the company was then carrying on the trade, the losses of which are restricted under subsection (3), and if the claim so requires, of preceding accounting periods ending within the time specified in subsection (7), and subject to that subsection and any relief for an earlier trading loss, to the extent that the profits of any of those accounting periods consists of or includes profits or income specified in paragraphs (*a*) to (*d*), those profits or that income shall then be reduced by the amount of the loss to which this section applies or by so much of that amount as cannot be relieved against profits of a later accounting period.

(7) For the purposes of subsection (6), the time referred to in that subsection shall be a time immediately preceding the accounting period first mentioned in subsection (6) equal in length to the accounting period in which the loss is incurred, but the amount of the reduction which may be made under subsection (3) in the profits of an accounting period falling partly before that time shall not exceed a part of those profits proportionate to the part of the period falling within that time.

(8) Where in any accounting period a company incurs a relevant loss and the amount of that loss exceeds an amount equal to the aggregate of the amounts which could, if a timely claim for such set off had been made by the company, have been set off in respect of that loss for the purposes of corporation tax against profits of the company of that accounting period and any preceding accounting period in accordance with subsection (6), then the company may claim relief under this subsection in respect of the excess.

(9) Where for any accounting period a company claims relief under subsection (8) in respect of the excess, the relevant corporation tax of the company for that accounting period and, if the company was then carrying on the trade, the losses of which are reduced under subsection (3), and the claim so requires, for preceding accounting periods ending within the time specified in subsection (10) and subject to that subsection, shall be reduced by an amount equal to 20 per cent of the excess or so much of that amount as cannot be relieved against relevant corporation tax of a later accounting period.

(10) For the purposes of subsection (9), the time referred to in that subsection shall be a time immediately preceding the accounting period first mentioned in subsection (9) equal in length to the accounting period in which the loss is incurred, but the amount of the reduction which may be made under subsection (9) in the relevant corporation

tax for an accounting period falling partly before that time shall not exceed a part of that corporation tax proportionate to the part of the period falling within that time.

(11) (a) Where a company makes a claim for relief for any accounting period under subsection (8) in respect of a relevant loss, an amount (which shall not exceed the amount of the excess in respect of which a claim under subsection (8) may be made), determined in accordance with paragraph (*b*), shall be treated for the purposes of the Tax Acts as an amount of loss relieved against profits of that accounting period.

(b) Subject to paragraph (*c*), the amount determined in accordance with this paragraph in relation to an accounting period is an amount equal to:

$$T \times \frac{100}{20}$$

where—

T is the amount by which the relevant corporation tax payable is reduced by virtue of subsection (9).

(c) (i) In this paragraph "*relevant amount*" means an amount (not being an amount incurred by a company for the purposes of a trade carried on by it) of charges on income, expenses of management or other amount (not being an allowance to which effect is given under section 308(4)) which is deductible from, or may be treated as reducing, profits of more than one description.

(ii) For the purposes of paragraph (*b*), where as respects an accounting period of a company a relevant amount is deductible from, or may be treated as reducing, profits of more than one description, the amount by which corporation tax is reduced by virtue of subsection (9) shall be deemed to be the amount by which it would have been reduced if no relevant amount were so deductible or so treated.

(12) Subsections (3) to (11) shall apply in respect of any claim to relief under section 396(2) in respect of a loss in a trade, the operations or activities of which consist of or include dealing in residential development land and the claim is made on or after 7 April 2009.

(13) Notwithstanding subsection (1) of section 397, where, on or before 31 December 2008, a company ceasing to carry on a trade, the operations or activities of which include dealing in residential development land, has incurred a loss in the trade, in any accounting period falling wholly or partly within the period of 12 months ending on the day the company ceased to carry on the trade, then, for the purposes of subsection (1) of that section, the amount of that loss shall be deemed to be reduced by the lesser of—

(a) the amount of the loss, and

(b) the amount of the loss which relates to dealing in residential development land.

(14) Notwithstanding subsection (1) of section 397, where, on or after 1 January 2009, a company ceasing to carry on a trade, the operations or activities of which include dealing in residential development land, has incurred a loss in the trade, in any

accounting period falling wholly or partly within the period of 12 months ending on the day the company ceased to carry on the trade, and falling wholly or partly before 1 January 2009, then, for the purposes of subsection (1) of that section, the amount of that loss shall be deemed to be reduced—

(a) where the accounting period falls wholly before 1 January 2009, by the lesser of—

(i) the amount of the loss, and

(ii) the amount of the loss which relates to dealing in residential development land,

and

(b) where the accounting period begins before 1 January 2009 and ends on or after that day, by the lesser of—

(i) the amount of the loss, and

(ii) the amount of the loss which relates to dealing in residential development land,

incurred in the period beginning when the accounting period begins and ending on 31 December 2008.

(15) Where a company ceasing to carry on a trade, the operations or activities of which include dealing in residential development land, makes a claim under section 397 in respect of a loss incurred in that trade and the loss is reduced under subsection (13) or (14) for an accounting period, then, subject to subsection (17) and to any relief for earlier losses, the company may claim relief under this subsection for that accounting period in respect of the amount by which the loss has been reduced.

(16) Where for any accounting period a company claims relief under subsection (15) in respect of a loss to which that subsection applies, the corporation tax paid by the company in respect of the income of the trade which is corporation tax referable to dealing in residential development land of the company for accounting periods falling wholly or partly within the 3 years preceding the period of 12 months mentioned in subsection (13) or (14) (or within any shorter period throughout which the company has carried on the trade) shall be reduced by an amount equal to 20 per cent of the loss, or by so much of that amount as cannot be relieved under this subsection against corporation tax of a later accounting period.

(17) (a) Relief shall not be given under subsection (16) in respect of any loss in so far as the loss has been or can be otherwise taken into account so as to reduce or relieve any charge to tax.

(b) Where a loss is incurred in an accounting period falling partly outside the period of 12 months mentioned in subsection (13) or (14), relief shall be given under subsection (16) in respect of a part only of that loss proportionate to the part of the period falling within that period of 12 months, and the amount of the reduction which may be made under that subsection in the corporation tax for an accounting period falling partly outside the 3 years mentioned in subsection (16) shall not exceed a part of that corporation tax proportionate to the part of the period falling within those 3 years.

(18) Where relief is claimed under section 397 in respect of an accounting period and the amount of loss, in respect of which relief is claimed, is reduced by virtue of [*subsection (13)* or *(14)*][1], then, for the purposes of granting relief under that section—

(a) the income from the trade for the accounting period shall be deemed to be reduced by an amount determined by the formula—

$$U \times \frac{100}{20}$$

where—

U is the amount of the corporation tax referable to dealing in residential development land payable by the company for the accounting period before relief given under subsection (16),

and

(b) the corporation tax paid by the company shall be deemed to be reduced by any corporation tax referable to dealing in residential development land paid by the company and not repaid to it for that accounting period.

(19) Subsections (13) to (18) shall apply in any case where a claim for relief under section 397 is made on or after 7 April 2009 in respect of a loss in a trade, the operations or activities of which include dealing in residential development land.

(20) (a) Notwithstanding subsections (1) and (6) of section 420 and section 421, where in an accounting period ending before 31 December 2009 the surrendering company has incurred a loss in a trade, the operations or activities of which consist of or include dealing in residential development land, then an amount of the loss, determined in accordance with paragraph (*b*), may not be set off for the purposes of corporation tax against the total profits of the claimant company for its corresponding accounting period.

(b) The amount determined in accordance with this paragraph in relation to an accounting period is an amount equal to—

(i) where the accounting period ends on or before 31 December 2008, the lesser of—

(I) the amount of the loss, and

(II) the amount of the loss which relates to dealing in residential development land,

and

(ii) where the accounting period begins before 1 January 2009 and ends after that date, the lesser of—

(I) the amount of the loss, and

(II) the amount of the loss which relates to dealing in residential development land, incurred in the period beginning when the accounting period begins and ending on 31 December 2008.

(21) (a) Where in any accounting period the surrendering company has incurred a loss in a trade, the operations and activities of which consist of or include dealing in residential development land, and an amount of the loss (hereinafter in this section referred to as the "*restricted loss*") may not be set off for the purposes of corporation tax against the total profits of the claimant company for its corresponding accounting period by virtue of subsection (20), then the corporation tax (if any) of the claimant company which is referable to dealing in residential development land for its corresponding accounting period may be reduced by 20 per cent of the restricted loss for that period.

(b) Where for any accounting period a company claims relief under this subsection, the surrendering company shall be treated as having surrendered, and the claimant company shall be treated as having claimed relief for, trading losses of an amount determined by the formula—

$$V \times \frac{100}{20}$$

where—

V is the amount by which the relevant corporation tax payable for the accounting period is reduced by virtue of paragraph (*a*).

(22) (a) Where in any accounting period the surrendering company has incurred a loss in a trade, the operations and activities of which consist of or include dealing in residential development land, the restricted loss as reduced by any amount treated as relieved by subsection (21)(*b*), may be set off for the purposes of corporation tax against—

(i) income specified in section 21A(4)(*b*),

(ii) relevant trading income,

(iii) income to which section 21A(3) does not apply by virtue of section 21B, and

(iv) profits attributable to chargeable gains,

of the claimant company for its corresponding accounting period as reduced by any amounts allowed as deductions against that income under section 243A or set off against that income under section 396A.

(b) Paragraph (*a*) shall not apply—

(i) to so much of a loss as is excluded from section 396(2) by section 396(4) or 663, or

(ii) so as to reduce the profits of a claimant company which carries on life business (within the meaning of section 706) by an amount greater than the amount of such profits (before a set off under this subsection) computed in accordance with Case I of Schedule D and section 710(1).

(23) Group relief allowed under subsection (22) shall reduce the income from a trade of the claimant company for an accounting period—

(a) before relief granted under section 397 in respect of a loss incurred in a succeeding accounting period or periods, and

(b) after the relief granted under section 396 in respect of a loss incurred in a preceding accounting period or periods.

(24) For the purposes of subsections (21) and (22), in the case of a claim made by a company as a member of a consortium only a fraction of a restricted loss may be set off, and that fraction shall be equal to that member's share in the consortium, subject to any further reduction under section 422(2).

(25) Where in any accounting period the surrendering company has incurred a loss in a trade the operations or activities of which consists of or includes dealing in residential development land, and the restricted loss is greater than an amount equal to the aggregate of the amounts which could, if timely claims had been made for such set off, have been set off in respect of that loss for the purposes of corporation tax against—

(a) the profits of the company in accordance with subsection (6), or

(b) profits of any other company in accordance with subsections (21) and (22),

the claimant company may claim relief under subsection (26) for its corresponding accounting period in respect of the amount (hereinafter in this section referred to as the "*relievable loss*") by which the [restricted loss][2] is greater than that aggregate.

(26) (a) Where for any accounting period a company claims relief under subsection (25) in respect of a relievable loss, the relevant corporation tax of the company for the accounting period shall be reduced by an amount equal to 20 per cent of that loss.

(b) Where for any accounting period a company claims relief under this section in respect of any relievable loss, the surrendering company shall be treated as having surrendered, and the claimant company shall be treated as having claimed relief for, trading losses of an amount determined by the formula—

$$W \times \frac{100}{20}$$

where—

W is the amount by which the relevant corporation tax payable for the accounting period is reduced by virtue of paragraph (*a*).

(27) Chapter 5 of Part 12 shall apply as if subsections (20) to (26) were contained in that Chapter.

(28) Subsections (20) to (27) shall apply in any case where a claim for group relief is made on or after 7 April 2009 in respect of a loss in a trade, the operations or activities of which consist of or include dealing in residential development land.][3]

Amendments

[1] Substituted by FA10 sched(4)(1)(g)(i). Has effect as on and from 3 April 2010.

[2] Substituted by FA10 sched(4)(1)(g)(ii). Has effect as on and from 3 April 2010.

[3] Inserted by FA09 s11(1)(b). Applies as on and from 1 January 2009.

Cross References

From Section 644C

Section 21A Higher rate of corporation tax.
Section 21B Tax treatment of certain dividends.
Section 239 Income tax on payments by resident companies.
Section 241 Income tax on payments by non-resident companies.
Section 243A Restriction of relevant charges on income.
Section 308 Corporation tax: manner of granting, and effect of, allowances made by means of discharge or repayment of tax.
Section 396 Relief for trading losses other than terminal losses.
Section 396A Relief for relevant trading losses.
Section 397 Relief for terminal loss in a trade.
Section 420 Losses, etc. which may be surrendered by means of group relief.
Section 420B Group relief: Relief for certain losses on a value basis.
Section 421 Relation of group relief to other relief.
Section 422 Corresponding accounting periods.
Section 440 Surcharge on undistributed investment and estate income.
Section 441 Surcharge on undistributed income of service companies.
Section 644A Relief from income tax in respect of income from dealing in residential development land.
Section 644B Relief from corporation tax in respect of income from dealing in residential development land.

Section 663 Corporation tax: restriction of relief for losses in farming or market gardening.
Section 706 Interpretation and general (Part 26).
Section 710 Profits of life business.

645 Power to obtain information

[F(MP)A68 s22; FA81 s29(3)]

(1) The inspector may by notice in writing require any person to furnish him or her within such time as may be specified in the notice (not being less than 30 days) with such particulars as the inspector thinks necessary for the purposes of *sections 643* and *644*.

(2) The particulars which a person is obliged to furnish under this section, if required by notice to do so, shall include particulars as to—

(a) transactions or arrangements with respect to which the person is or was acting on behalf of others,

(b) transactions or arrangements which in the opinion of the inspector should properly be examined for the purposes of *sections 643* and *644*, notwithstanding that in the opinion of the person to whom the notice is given no liability to tax arises under those sections, and

(c) whether the person to whom the notice is given has taken or is taking any transactions or arrangements of a description specified in the notice and, if so, what transactions or arrangements, and what part the person has taken or is taking in those transactions or arrangements.

(3) Notwithstanding anything in *subsection (2)*, a solicitor shall not be deemed for the purposes of *subsection (2)(c)* to have taken part in any transaction or arrangements by reason only that he or she has given professional advice to a client in connection with the transaction or arrangements, and shall not, in relation to anything done by him or her on behalf of a client, be compellable under this section, except with the consent of the client, to do more than state that he or she is or was acting on behalf of a client, and give the name and address of the client.

Cross References

From Section 645

Section 643 Tax to be charged under Case IV on gains from certain disposals of land.
Section 644 Provisions supplementary to section 643.

To Section 645

Schedule 29 Provisions Referred to in Sections 1052, 1053 and 1054

646 Postponement of payment of income tax to be permitted in certain cases

[F(MP)A68 s23(1) to (3) and (5)]

(1) In this section, "*basis period*", in relation to any year of assessment, means the period on the profits or gains of which income tax for that year is finally computed under Case I of Schedule D in respect of the trade or, where by virtue of the Income Tax Acts the profits or gains of any other period are taken to be the profits or gains of that period, that other period.

(2) Where—

(a) a person (in this section referred to as "the vendor") carrying on a trade of dealing in or developing land (in this section referred to as "the trade") disposes in the course of the trade of the full interest acquired by the person in any land,

(b) the person to whom the disposition is made (in this section referred to as "the purchaser") is not connected with the vendor,

(c) the terms subject to which the disposition is made provide for the grant of a lease of the land by the purchaser to the vendor,

(d) a sum representing the value of the vendor's right to be granted a lease is to be taken into account as a consideration for the disposal in computing the profits or gains of the trade, and

(e) within 6 months after the time of the disposition, a lease of the land in accordance with those terms is granted by the purchaser to the vendor,

subsections (3) and *(4)* shall apply in relation to income tax for a year of assessment in the basis period for which the disposition is made.

(3) Where, at the time when any amount of income tax charged by an assessment in respect of the profits or gains of the trade would but for this subsection become due and payable, the vendor—

(a) retains the leasehold interest acquired by the vendor from the purchaser, and

(b) has not disposed, as regards the whole or any part of the land, of an interest derived from that leasehold interest,

then, a part of that amount of income tax equal to 90 per cent of so much of such tax as would not have been chargeable if no sum had to be taken into account as mentioned in *subsection (2)(d)* shall be payable in 9 equal instalments at yearly intervals the first of which is payable on the 1st day of January in the year following that in which but for this subsection that amount of income tax would have been payable.

(4) Where, in a case in which the postponement of payment of any amount of income tax has been authorised by *subsection (3)*, the vendor—

(a) ceases to retain the leasehold interest acquired by the vendor from the purchaser,

(b) disposes, as regards the whole or any part of the land, of an interest derived from that leasehold interest,

(c) being an individual, dies, or

(d) being a company, commences to be wound up,

then, that amount of income tax or, as the case may be, so much of that amount of income tax as has not already become due and payable shall become due and payable forthwith.

Cross References

To Section 646

Section 647 Postponement of payment of corporation tax to be permitted in certain cases.

647 Postponement of payment of corporation tax to be permitted in certain cases

[CTA76 s150]

(1) Where—

(a) for any accounting period the profits of a company consist of or include income from a trade of dealing in or developing land in the course of which the company disposes of the full interest acquired by it in any land,

(b) in relation to that disposal, the conditions specified in *paragraphs (b)* to *(e)* of *section 646(2)* are satisfied, and

(c) at the time when any amount of corporation tax charged by an assessment for that accounting period would but for this section become due and payable the company—

(i) retains the leasehold interest acquired by it from the person to whom the disposition is made, and

(ii) has not disposed, as regards the whole or any part of the land, of an interest derived from that leasehold interest,

then, a part of that amount of corporation tax equal to 90 per cent of so much of that amount as would not have been chargeable if no sum had to be taken into account as mentioned in *section 646(2)(d)* shall be payable in 9 equal instalments at yearly intervals the first of which shall be payable on the expiration of 12 months from the date on which but for this section that amount of corporation tax would have been payable.

(2) Where, in a case in which the postponement of payment of any amount of corporation tax has been authorised by *subsection (1)*, the company—

(a) ceases to retain the leasehold interest acquired by it,

(b) disposes, as regards the whole or any part of the land, of an interest derived from that leasehold interest, or

(c) commences to be wound up,

then, that amount of corporation tax or, as the case may be, so much of that amount of corporation tax as has not already become due and payable shall become due and payable forthwith.

Cross References

From Section 647

Section 646 Postponement of payment of income tax to be permitted in certain cases.

CHAPTER 2

Capital Gains Tax: Disposals of Development Land

648 Interpretation (Chapter 2)

[FA82 s36(1)]

In this Chapter—

"*the Act of 1963*" means the Local Government (Planning and Development) Act, 1963;

["*the Act of 2000*" means the Planning and Development Act 2000;][1]

"*compulsory disposal*" means a disposal to an authority possessing compulsory purchase powers, which is made pursuant to the exercise of those powers or the giving of formal notice of intention to exercise those powers, other than a disposal to which section 29 of the Act of 1963 applies;

"current use value"—

(a) in relation to land at any particular time, means the amount which would be the market value of the land at that time if the market value were calculated on the assumption that it was at that time and would remain unlawful to carry out any development [(within the meaning of section 3 of the Act of 1963, or, on or after 21 January 2002, within the meaning of section 3 of the Act of 2000)][2] in relation to the land other than development of a minor nature, and

(b) in relation to shares in a company (being shares deriving their value or the greater part of their value directly or indirectly from land, other than shares quoted on a stock exchange) at any particular time, means the amount which would be the market value of the shares at that time if the market value were calculated on the same assumption, in relation to the land from which the shares so derive value, as is mentioned in *paragraph (a)*;

"*development land*" means land in the State the consideration for the disposal of which, or the market value of which at the time at which the disposal is made, exceeds the current use value of that land at the time at which the disposal is made, and includes shares deriving their value or the greater part of their value directly or indirectly from such land, other than shares quoted on a Stock Exchange;

["*development of a minor nature*" means development (not being development by a local authority or a statutory undertaker within the meaning of section 2 of the Act of 1963, or, on or after 11 March 2002, within the meaning of section 2 of the Act of 2000) which, under or by virtue of section 4 of the Act of 1963, or, on or after 11 March 2002, under or by virtue of section 4 of the Act of 2000, is exempted development for the purposes of the Local Government (Planning and Development) Acts 1963 to 1999 or the Act of 2000;][3]

"*relevant disposal*" means a disposal of development land made on or after the 28th day of January, 1982.

Amendments

[1] Inserted by FA04 s83(1)(b)(i). This section is deemed to have applied as on and from 21 January 2002.

[2] Substituted by FA04 s83(1)(b)(ii). This section is deemed to have applied as on and from 21 January 2002.

[3] Substituted by FA04 s83(1)(b)(iii). This section is deemed to have applied as on and from 11 March 2002.

Cross References

To Section 648

Section 78 Computation of companies' chargeable gains.

Section 571 Chargeable gains accruing on disposals by liquidators and certain other persons.

Section 604 Disposals of principal private residence.

Section 619 Disposals or acquisitions outside group.

Section 633 Company reconstruction or amalgamation: transfer of development land.

649 Companies chargeable to capital gains tax in respect of chargeable gains accruing on relevant disposals

[FA82 s36(4) to (6); FA92 s68(a)]

(1) Notwithstanding any provision to the contrary in the Corporation Tax Acts, a company shall not be chargeable to corporation tax in respect of chargeable gains accruing to it on relevant disposals, and accordingly—

(a) such gains shall not be regarded as profits of the company for the purposes of corporation tax, and

(b) the company shall be chargeable to capital gains tax under the Capital Gains Tax Acts in respect of those gains.

(2) *Sections 617* and *621* to *626* shall apply with any necessary modifications in relation to capital gains tax to which a company is chargeable on chargeable gains accruing to the company on a relevant disposal as they apply in relation to corporation tax on chargeable gains, and references in those sections to corporation tax shall be construed as including references to capital gains tax.

(3) (a) Where a company which is or has been a member of a group of companies (within the meaning of *section 616*) makes a relevant disposal of an asset which, as a result of a disposal which was not a relevant disposal, the company had acquired from another member of that group at a time when both were members of the group, the amount of the chargeable gain accruing on the relevant disposal and the capital gains tax on that gain shall be computed as if all members of the group for the time being were the same person and as if the acquisition or provision of the asset by the group, so taken as a single person, had been the acquisition or provision of the asset by the member disposing of the asset.

(b) Notwithstanding *paragraph (a)*, where under *section 618(2)* or *623* a member of the group (in this paragraph referred to as "the first-mentioned member") had been treated as having acquired or reacquired the asset at a time later than the original acquisition or provision of the asset by the first-mentioned member or by another member of the group, as the case may be, *paragraph (a)* shall apply as if the reference in that paragraph to the acquisition or provision of the asset by the group were a reference to its acquisition or reacquisition so treated as having been made by the first-mentioned member.

Cross References

From Section 649

Section 616 Groups of companies: interpretation.
Section 617 Transfers of assets, other than trading stock, within group.
Section 618 Transfers of trading stock within group.
Section 621 Depreciatory transactions in group.
Section 623 Company ceasing to be member of group.
Section 626 Tax on company recoverable from other members of group.

To Section 649

Section 21 The charge to corporation tax and exclusion of income tax and capital gains tax.
Section 633 Company reconstruction or amalgamation: transfer of development land.

649A Relevant disposals: rate of charge

[(1) Notwithstanding *section 28(3)* and subject to *subsection (2)*, the rate of capital gains tax in respect of a chargeable gain accruing to a person on a relevant disposal shall be—

[(a) in the case of a relevant disposal made in the period from 3 December 1997 to 30 November 1999, 40 per cent, and][1]

[(b) in the case of a relevant disposal made on or after 6 December 2012, 33 per cent.][2]

[…][3]

(2) (a) *Subsection (1)* shall not apply to a relevant disposal to which this subsection applies and, accordingly, the rate of capital gains tax in respect of a chargeable gain on such a relevant disposal shall be 20 per cent.

(b) This subsection shall apply to the following:

[...][4]

(ii) a relevant disposal made in the period from 23 April 1998 to 30 November 1999, being a disposal of land to a housing authority (within the meaning of section 23 of the Housing (Miscellaneous Provisions) Act, 1992) which land is specified in a certificate given by the housing authority as land required for the purposes of the Housing Acts, 1966 to 1998;

(iii) a relevant disposal made in the period from 10 March 1999 to 30 November 1999, being a disposal of land to the National Building Agency Limited or to a body approved for the purposes of section 6 of the Housing (Miscellaneous Provisions) Act, 1992, which land is specified in a certificate given by a housing authority or the National Building Agency Limited, as appropriate, as land required for the purposes of the Housing Acts, 1966 to 1998;

(iv) a relevant disposal made in the period from 23 April 1998 to 30 November 1999, being a disposal of land in respect of the whole of which, at the time at which the disposal is made, permission for residential development has been granted under section 26 of the Local Government (Planning and Development) Act, 1963, and such permission has not ceased to exist, other than a disposal to which *paragraph (c)* applies;

(v) a relevant disposal made in the period from 10 March 1999 to 30 November 1999, being a disposal of land in respect of the whole of which, at the time at which the disposal is made, is, in accordance with a development objective (as indicated in the development plan of the planning authority concerned), for use solely or primarily for residential purposes other than a disposal to which *paragraph (c)* applies.

(c) This paragraph shall apply to a relevant disposal being a disposal—

(i) by a person (in this paragraph referred to as the "*disponer*") to a person who is connected with the disponer, or

(ii) of land under a relevant contract in relation to the disposal.][5]

(3) In this section—

"*development plan*" has the meaning assigned to it by the Local Government (Planning and Development) Act, 1963;

"*planning authority*" has the meaning assigned to it by section 2(2) of the Local Government (Planning and Development) Act, 1963;

"*relevant contract*", in relation to a disposal of land, means a contract or other arrangement under which the land is disposed of which is conditional on permission for development, other than permission for residential development, being granted under section 26 of the Local Government (Planning and Development) Act, 1963, in respect of the land;

"*residential development*" includes any development which is ancillary to the development and which is necessary for the proper planning and development of the area in question.][6]][7]

Amendments

[1] Substituted by FA01 s94(a).

[2] Substituted by FA13 s43(1)(b). Applies to disposals made on or after 6 December 2012.

[3] Deleted by FA01 s94(b).

[4] Deleted by F(No.2)A08 s44(1)(b)(ii). Applies to disposals made on or after 15 October 2008.

[5] Substituted by FA00 s86.

[6] Substituted by FA98No2 s3.

[7] Inserted by FA98 s65(1)(c). Applies as respects in relation to disposals made on or after the 3rd day of December, 1997.

Revenue Briefings

Tax Briefing

Tax Briefing March 2000 – Issue 39 pg 17 – Development Land

Tax Briefing May 2003 – Issue 52 pg 18 – Part Disposal of Development Land

Cross References

From Section 649A

Section 28 Taxation of capital gains and rate of charge.

649B Windfall gains from rezonings: rate of charge

[(1) In this section—

"*development land-use*" means residential, commercial or industrial uses or a mixture of such uses;

"*loss arising on rezoning*" means a loss realised on or after 30 October 2009 on a disposal of land to the extent to which that loss is attributable solely to a decrease in the market value of the land arising on a rezoning, and which loss has not otherwise been effectively relieved;

"*non-development land-use*" means a land-use which is agricultural, open space, recreational or amenity use or a mixture of such uses;

[…][1]

["*relevant planning decision*", in relation to land and in accordance with the Planning and Development Act 2000 (in this definition referred to as the "Act of 2000"), means—

(a) a change in the zoning of land in a development plan or a local area plan made or varied under Part II of the Act of 2000 from non-development land-uses to development land-uses or from one development land-use to another development land-use including a mixture of such uses, or

(b) a decision to grant permission, in accordance with section 34(6) or 37(2) of the Act of 2000, for a development that would materially contravene a development plan;][2]

"*windfall gain*" means any increase in the market value of land which is attributable to [a relevant planning decision][3].

(2) This section applies to a relevant disposal[…][4] where the disposal consists of land that—

(a) has been the subject of [a relevant planning decision][5] since its acquisition by the person making the disposal,

(b) was acquired from a connected person and the acquisition cost for the purposes of the Capital Gains Tax Acts was other than market value, where the [relevant planning decision][6] took place during the ownership period of either person, or

(c) was the subject of a sequence of transfers between connected persons, if the [relevant planning decision][7] took place during the period between the date of disposal and the latest date at which the acquisition cost, at any step in the sequence, was market value.

(3) Notwithstanding section 28(3), the rate of capital gains tax in respect of a chargeable gain, being the lesser of the gain arising on the disposal and the windfall gain, accruing to a person on a relevant disposal to which this section applies shall be 80 per cent.

(4) This section shall not apply to a disposal of land to which *subsection (2)* relates where—

(a) the land is disposed of to an authority possessing compulsory purchasing powers, but only if the Revenue Commissioners are satisfied that the disposal would not have been made but for the exercise of those powers or the giving by the authority of formal notice of its intention to exercise those powers,[...][8]

(b) the disposal is a disposal by a company referred to in [*section 616(1)(g)*, or][9]

[(c) the disposal is the disposal of a site of 0.4047 hectares or less whose market value at the date of disposal does not exceed €250,000 (notwithstanding that a planning authority may have granted permission in respect of that site in accordance with section 34(1) of the Planning and Development Act 2000), other than where the disposal by the person making it, or by a person connected with that person, forms part of a larger transaction or series of transactions,][10]

and, accordingly, the rate of capital gains tax in respect of a chargeable gain on a relevant disposal referred to in *paragraphs (a)* to *(c)* shall be the rate specified in section 28(3).

(5) Notwithstanding any provision to the contrary in the Capital Gains Tax Acts, any loss accruing on any disposal shall not be deducted from a chargeable gain to which this section applies except a loss arising on a [relevant planning decision][11].

[(6) This section shall apply to relevant disposals made in the period beginning on 30 October 2009 and ending on 31 December 2014.][12]][13]

Amendments

[1] Deleted by FA10 s25(1)(e). Applies as respects changes or decisions made on or after 4 February 2010.

[2] Inserted by FA10 s25(1)(e). Applies as respects changes or decisions made on or after 4 February 2010.

[3] Substituted by FA10 s25(1)(f). Deemed to have come into force and takes effect as on and from 1 January 2010.

[4] Deleted by FA10 s25(1)(g)(i). Applies as on and from 4 February 2010.

[5,6,7] Substituted by FA10 s25(1)(g)(ii). Applies as respects changes or decisions made on or after 4 February 2010.

[8] Deleted by FA10 s25(1)(h). Applies as respects disposals made on or after 30 October 2009.

[9] Substituted by FA10 s25(1)(h). Applies as respects disposals made on or after 30 October 2009.

[10] Inserted by FA10 s25(1)(h). Applies as respects disposals made on or after 30 October 2009.

[11] Substituted by FA10 s25(1)(i). Applies as respects changes or decisions made on or after 4 February 2010.

[12] Substituted by FA14 s31(b). Comes into operation on 1 January 2015.

[13] Inserted by the National Asset Management Agency Act 2009 Sched 3 part 10.

Cross References

From Section 649B

Section 616 Groups of companies: interpretation.

650 Exclusion of certain disposals

[FA82 s37]

Sections 651 to *654* shall not apply to a relevant disposal made by an individual in any year of assessment if the total consideration in respect of all relevant disposals made by that individual in that year does not exceed [€19,050][1].

Amendments

[1] Substituted by FA01 sched5.

Cross References

From Section 650

Section 651 Restriction of indexation relief in relation to relevant disposals.

Section 654 Interpretation (Part 23).

651 Restriction of indexation relief in relation to relevant disposals

[FA82 s38]

For the purposes of computing the chargeable gain accruing to a person on a relevant disposal, the adjustment of sums allowable as deductions from the consideration for the disposal which under *section 556(2)* would otherwise be made shall be made only to—

(a) such part of the amount or value of the consideration in money or money's worth given by the person or on the person's behalf wholly and exclusively for the acquisition of the asset, together with the incidental costs to the person of the acquisition, as is equal to the current use value of the asset at the date of the acquisition together with such proportion of the incidental costs to the person of the acquisition as would be referable to such value, or

(b) in the case of an asset to which *section 556(3)* applies, such part of the market value of the asset on the 6th day of April, 1974, as is equal to the current use value of the asset on that date.

Revenue Precedents

Compensation for suspension of milk quota is regarded as a capital receipt. IT892037

Cross References

From Section 651

Section 556 Adjustment of allowable expenditure by reference to consumer price index.

To Section 651

Section 650 Exclusion of certain disposals.

652 Non-application of reliefs on replacement of assets in case of relevant disposals

[FA82 s39; FA95 s73(1); FA97 s77(1)]

(1) Consideration obtained for a relevant disposal shall not be regarded for the purposes of relief under *section 597* as having been obtained for the disposal of old assets within the meaning of that section.

(2) [(a) In this subsection 'the relevant local authority', in relation to a relevant disposal, means the local authority for the purposes of the Local

Government Act 2001 (as amended by the *Local Government Reform Act 2014*) in whose functional area the land being disposed of is situated.][1]

(b) *Subsection (1)* shall not apply to a relevant disposal where the relevant local authority gives a certificate in writing to the person making the disposal stating that the land being disposed of is subject to a use which, on the basis of guidelines issued by the Minister for the Environment and Local Government, is inconsistent with the protection and improvement of the amenities of the general area within which that land is situated or is otherwise damaging to the local environment.

(3) (a) In this subsection—

"*assets of an authorised racecourse*" means assets of a racecourse which is an authorised racecourse where the assets are used for the provision of appropriate facilities or services to carry on horseracing at race meetings or to accommodate persons associated with horseracing, including members of the public;

"*authorised racecourse*" has the same meaning as in section 2 of the Irish Horseracing Industry Act, 1994.

(b) Subject to *paragraph (c)*, *subsection (1)* shall not apply to consideration obtained for a relevant disposal where—

(i) throughout a period of 5 years ending with the time of disposal the old assets, and

(ii) the new assets within the meaning of *section 597*,

are assets of an authorised racecourse.

(c) *Section 597* shall apply in relation to assets of an authorised racecourse as if—

(i) references in *subsection (4)* and (5) of that section to new assets ceasing to be used for the purposes of a trade included a reference to new assets ceasing to be assets of an authorised racecourse, and

(ii) *subsection (11)(b)* had not been enacted.

[(3A) (a) In this subsection—

"*greyhound race*", "*greyhound race track*" and "*greyhound race track licence*" have the same meanings respectively as in section 2 of the Greyhound Industry Act, 1958;

"*assets of an authorised greyhound race track*" means assets of a greyhound race track which is an authorised greyhound race track where the assets are used for the provision of appropriate facilities or services to hold greyhound races or to accommodate persons associated with greyhound racing, including members of the public;

"*authorised greyhound race track*" means a greyhound race track in respect of which a greyhound race track licence has been granted, and that licence has not been revoked.

(b) Subject to *paragraph (c)*, *subsection (1)* shall not apply to consideration obtained for a relevant disposal where—

(i) throughout a period of 5 years ending with the time of disposal the old assets, and

(ii) the new assets within the meaning of *section 597*,

are assets of an authorised greyhound race track.

(c) *Section 597* shall apply in relation to assets of an authorised greyhound race track as if—

(i) references in *subsections (4)* and (5) of that section to new assets ceasing to be used for the purposes of a trade included a reference to new assets ceasing to be assets of an authorised greyhound race track, and

(ii) *subsection (11)(b)* had not been enacted.

(3B) *Subsection (1)* shall not apply to consideration obtained for a relevant disposal effected by an order made under section 28(1) of the Dublin Docklands Development Authority Act, 1997.][2]

(4) *Section 605* shall not apply to a relevant disposal.

[(5) (a) *Subsection (4)* shall not apply to a relevant disposal made to an authority possessing compulsory purchase powers where the disposal is made—

(i) for the purposes of enabling the authority to construct, widen or extend a road or part of a road, or

(ii) for a purpose connected with or ancillary to the construction, widening or extension of a road or part of a road by the authority.

(b) Where *section 605* applies to a relevant disposal by virtue of this subsection that section shall be construed as if for *subsection (4)* of that section the following were substituted:

"(4) This section shall apply only if the acquisition of the replacement assets takes place, or an unconditional contract for the acquisition is entered into, in the period beginning 2 years before and ending 8 years after the disposal of the original assets, or at such earlier or later time as the Revenue Commissioners may by notice in writing allow; but, where an unconditional contract for the acquisition is so entered into, this section may be applied on a provisional basis without ascertaining whether the replacement assets are acquired in pursuance of the contract, and when that fact is ascertained all necessary adjustments shall be made by making assessments or by repayment or discharge of tax, and shall be so made notwithstanding any limitation in the Capital Gains Tax Acts on the time within which assessments may be made [or any limitation in section 865(4) on the time within which a claim for a repayment of tax is required to be made][3].".][4]

(6) *Subsections (1)* and *(4)* shall not apply to a relevant disposal made by a body of persons established for the sole purpose of promoting athletic or amateur games or sports, being a disposal which is made in relation to such of the activities of that body as are directed to that purpose.

Amendments

[1] Substituted by LGRA14 sched2(part5).

[2] Inserted by FA98 s73(1). This section shall apply in respect of relevant disposals made on or after the 6th day of April, 1998.

[3] Inserted by FA08 sched6(1)(m). Applies as on and from 31 January 2008.

[4] Substituted by FA01 s95(1). Applies to relevant disposals made on or after 6 December 2000.

Revenue Precedents

S.652(5) effectively allows relief under S.605 on the disposal of development land to a local authority possessing compulsory purchase powers in certain circumstances. The land in question must be land occupied and used only for the purpose of farming. There is no requirement that the person making the disposal has to have farmed the land him/herself and thus, let land can qualify as long as it has been occupied and used by the lessor for the purposes of farming. G85 (A)(14)

Cross References

From Section 652

Section 597 Replacement of business and other assets.
Section 605 Disposals to authority possessing compulsory purchase powers.
Section 865 Repayment of tax.

To Section 652

Section 598 Disposals of business or farm on "retirement".

653 Restriction of relief for losses, etc. in relation to relevant disposals

[FA82 s40(1) and (2)]

(1) Notwithstanding any provision to the contrary in the Capital Gains Tax Acts, any losses accruing on disposals which are not relevant disposals shall not, in the computation of a person's liability to capital gains tax in respect of chargeable gains accruing on relevant disposals, be deducted from the amount of those chargeable gains.

(2) In the computation of the amount on which under *section 31* capital gains tax is to be charged on chargeable gains accruing on relevant disposals, any allowable losses accruing on relevant disposals may be deducted in accordance with that section but, in so far as they are so deducted, they shall not be treated as relevant allowable losses within the meaning of *section 78(4)* for the purposes of the calculation required to be made under *section 78(2),* and for the purposes of this subsection [any necessary assessments may, as appropriate, be made or amended][1].

Amendments

[1] Substituted by FA12 sched4(part 2)(g).

Cross References

From Section 653

Section 31 Amount chargeable.
Section 78 Computation of companies' chargeable gains.

To Section 653

Section 571 Chargeable gains accruing on disposals by liquidators and certain other persons.

OTHER SPECIAL PROVISIONS

PART 23

Farming and Market Gardening

CHAPTER 1

Interpretation and General

654 Interpretation (Part 23)

[ITA67 s54(1); FA74 s13(1); FA75 s12; FA78 s12(1); FA83 s120 and Sch4]

In this Part other than in *section 664*—

"*farming*" means farming farm land, that is, land in the State wholly or mainly occupied for the purposes of husbandry, other than market garden land;

"*market garden land*" means land in the State occupied as a nursery or garden for the sale of the produce (other than land used for the growth of hops), and "market gardening" shall be construed accordingly;

"*occupation*", in relation to any land other than market garden land, means having the use of that land or having the right by virtue of any easement (within the meaning of *section 96*) to graze livestock on that land.

Revenue Briefings

Tax Briefing

Tax Briefing November 2005 – Issue 61 – Tax Implications of the Single Payment Scheme

Revenue Precedents

Whether bee-keeping falls within the definition of husbandry? Revenue accepts CCJ decision that bee-keeping is to be regarded as husbandry. 2293/85

Mushroom growing in tunnels is not regarded as farming within the meaning of section 654 Taxes Consolidation Act 1997. It is regarded as market gardening. As a consequence, farm buildings allowance, income averaging and stock relief is not available. An industrial buildings allowance is available at the rate of 10%. 959

Cross References

From Section 654

Section 96 Interpretation (Chapter 8).
Section 654 Interpretation (Part 23).
Section 664 Relief for certain income from leasing of farm land.

To Section 654

Section 53 Cattle and milk dealers.
Section 268 Meaning of "industrial building or structure".
Section 404 Restriction on use of capital allowances for certain leased machinery or plant.
Section 605 Disposals to authority possessing compulsory purchase powers.
Section 650 Exclusion of certain disposals.
Section 654 Interpretation (Part 23).
Section 1092 Disclosure of certain information to rating authorities, etc.
Schedule 31 Consequential Amendments

655 Farming and market gardening profits to be charged to tax under Schedule D

[ITA67 s54(2)(a); FA69 s65(1) and Sch5 PtI; FA74 s15; FA83 s11]

(1) For the purposes of the Tax Acts, farming shall be treated as the carrying on of a trade or, as the case may be, of part of a trade, and the profits or gains of farming shall be charged to tax under Case I of Schedule D.

(2) Notwithstanding anything to the contrary in *Part 43*, farming carried on by any person, whether solely or in partnership, shall be treated as the carrying on of a single trade; but this subsection shall not prejudice or restrict the operation of *Chapter 3* of *Part 4* where a partnership trade of farming is set up and commenced or is permanently discontinued.

(3) Market gardening shall, for the purposes of the Tax Acts in relation to the person by whom it is carried on, be treated as a trade, and the profits or gains of market gardening shall be charged to tax under Case I of Schedule D.

Revenue Briefings

eBrief

eBrief No. 45/2012 – Advice for Farmers Making Their Form 11 Return – Poor Quality Completion of Forms Draws Unnecessary Attention from Revenue

Revenue Precedents

The taxation treatment of sheep headage and ewe premium payments – all headage payments and ewe premia are trading receipts for tax purposes. IT913063

How are the payments received under the EEC Scheme of Installation Aid for Young Farmers taxed? The scheme, which was introduced by EEC Council Regulation No. 797/85, provides for the payment to farmers of a single premium. Such a payment may be treated as a capital sum which will not give rise to a charge to Capital Gains Tax as there is no disposal of an asset. IT903118

Payments from the Department of Agriculture under the Flood Damage Relief Scheme 1995 are chargeable to Income Tax. It is the Revenue view that these payments, which are in respect of the loss of livestock or fodder, are income receipts liable to income tax in the hands of the recipient. IT953512

Where compensation is paid for the non-allocation of a milk quota to a partnership each of the partners cannot claim the reduction outlined in article 1.3 of Tax Briefing No. 14. The reductions outlined in the article should be applied to the compensation amount received by the partnership with the reduced amount forming part of the trading income of the partnership for the year of receipt. IT953538

What is the commencement date for the review procedure for the valuation of broodmares? The review procedure outlined in the article titled "Book value of Brood Mares" in Issue 25 of Tax Briefing operates in respect of accounting periods ending on or after 1 December 1994. IT973008

Cross References

From Section 655

Section 52 Persons chargeable.
Section 65 Cases I and II: basis of assessment.
Section 1007 Interpretation (Part 43).

To Section 655

Section 658 Farming: allowances for capital expenditure on construction of buildings and other works.
Section 659 Farming: allowances for capital expenditure on the construction of farm buildings, etc. for control of pollution.

656 Farming: trading stock of discontinued trade

[ITA67 s 62(1) proviso; FA96 s11]

(1) In this section, "*specified return date for the chargeable period*" has the same meaning as in [*section 959A*][1].

(2) Where trading stock of a trade of farming is transferred by a farmer (in this subsection referred to as "the transferor") to another farmer (in this subsection

referred to as "the transferee"), the transferor and the transferee may jointly elect that—

(a) *section 89(2)(b)* shall not apply, and

(b) in computing their respective profits or gains from farming, the transferor and the transferee shall include such stock at the value at which the stock is included in the accounts of the transferor at the date of discontinuance,

and such election shall be made in writing on or before the specified return date for the chargeable period in which the stock is transferred.

Amendments

[1] Substituted by FA12 sched4(part 2)(g).

Cross References

From Section 656

Section 89 Valuation of trading stock at discontinuance of trade.

Section 950 Interpretation (Part 41).

657 Averaging of farm profits

[FA74 s16(1) to (2) and (4) to (5) and s20B (apart from proviso to *subsection (2)(b)*); FA75 s14(1)(a) and (b); FA77 s10; FA81 s10; FA83 s120 and Sch4; FA90 s20(2); FA97 s146(2) and Sch9 PtII]

(1) In this section—

"an individual to whom *subsection (1)* applies" means an individual carrying on farming in a year of assessment and—

(a) who at any time in the year of assessment is also carrying on either solely or in partnership another trade or profession,

(b) [whose spouse, in a case where the individual is a married person, or whose civil partner, in a case where the individual is in a civil partnership,][1] is at any time in the year of assessment also carrying on either solely or in partnership another trade or profession, other than a trade consisting solely of the provision of accommodation in buildings on the farm land occupied by the individual, the provision of such accommodation being ancillary to the farming of that farm land,

(c) who at any time in the year of assessment is a director of a company carrying on a trade or profession and is either the beneficial owner of, or able, either directly or through the medium of other companies or by any other means, to control, more than 25 per cent of the ordinary share capital of the company, or

(d) [whose spouse, in a case where the individual is a married person, or whose civil partner, in a case where the individual is in a civil partnership,][2] is at any time in the year of assessment a director of a company carrying on a trade or profession and is either the beneficial owner of, or able, either directly or through the medium of other companies or by any other means, to control, more than 25 per cent of the ordinary share capital of the company,

[but—

(i) a reference to a trade in *paragraphs (a)* and *(b)* does not include a trade—

(I) which is ancillary to the trade of farming, and

(II) which is carried on by the individual or his or her spouse or civil partner on the farm land (within the meaning of *section 664*) used by the individual for the trade of farming,

and

(ii) *paragraphs (b)* and *(d)* shall not apply in a case where the wife of an individual is treated for tax purposes as not living with her husband, or the civil partner of an individual is treated for tax purposes as not living with his or her civil partner;][3]

"*company*" means a company within the meaning of the Companies Act, 1963;

"director" includes a person holding any office or employment under a company.

(2) The definition of "an individual to whom *subsection (1)* applies" shall apply in the case of [a married person whose wife is carrying on farming or a civil partner whose civil partner is carrying on farming][4], and shall apply in such a case as if the references to the individual were references to the [individual's wife or civil partner][5].

(3) For the purposes of *paragraphs (c)* and *(d)* of the definition of "an individual to whom *subsection (1)* applies", ordinary share capital which is owned or controlled in the manner referred to in those paragraphs by a person, being [the spouse or civil partner, or a minor child or minor child of the civil partner,][6] of a director, or by the trustee of a trust for the benefit of a person or persons, being or including any such person or such director, shall be deemed to be owned or controlled by such director and not by any other person.

(4) (a) Subject to *paragraph (b)*, where an assessment in respect of profits or gains from farming is made for any year of assessment on an individual, other than an individual to whom *subsection (1)* applies, the individual may on giving notice in writing to that effect to the inspector within 30 days after the date of the notice of assessment elect to be charged to income tax for that year in respect of those profits or gains in accordance with *subsection (5)*, and—

(i) the Income Tax Acts shall apply in relation to the assessment as if the notice given to the inspector were a notice of appeal against the assessment under *section 933*, and

(ii) the assessment shall be amended as necessary so as to give effect to the election so made by the individual.

(b) This subsection shall not apply as respects any year of assessment where for [any of the 4][7] immediately preceding years of assessment the individual was not charged to tax in respect of profits or gains from farming in accordance with *section 65(1)*.

[(4A) Where an individual was first charged to tax in accordance with *subsection (5)* for the year of assessment 2014, then the individual shall be charged to tax for the year of assessment 2015 in accordance with that subsection as if a reference in that subsection to 5 years was a reference to 4 years.][8]

(5) (a) An individual who is to be charged to income tax for a year of assessment in respect of profits or gains from farming in accordance with this subsection shall be so charged under Case I of Schedule D on the full amount of those profits or gains determined on a fair and just average of the profits or gains from farming of the individual in each of the [5 years][9] ending on the date in the year of assessment to which it has been customary to make up accounts or, where it has not been customary to make up accounts, on [31 December][10] in the year of assessment.

[(aa) As respects the year of assessment 2001, this subsection shall apply as if in *paragraph (a)* "74 per cent of the full amount of those profits or gains" were substituted for "the full amount of those profits or gains".

(ab) For the purposes of *paragraph (a)*, where an individual makes up annual accounts to a date in the period from 1 January 2002 to 5 April 2002, those accounts shall, in addition to being accounts made up to a date in the year of assessment 2002, be treated as accounts made up to a date in the year of assessment 2001.][11]

(b) Any profits or gains arising to, and any loss sustained by, the individual in the [5 years][12] referred to in *paragraph (a)* in the carrying on of farming shall be aggregated for the purposes of this subsection.

(6) (a) Subject to *paragraph (b)* and *subsection (7)*, where as respects a year of assessment an individual duly elects in accordance with *subsection (4)*, the individual shall be charged to income tax for that year and for each subsequent year of assessment in respect of profits or gains from farming in accordance with *subsection (5)*.

(b) This subsection shall not apply for any year of assessment in which the individual—

(i) is an individual to whom *subsection (1)* applies, or

(ii) is not chargeable to tax on profits or gains from farming.

[(7) Subject to *subsection (7A)*, where for a year of assessment an individual is by virtue of *subsection (6)* chargeable to income tax in respect of profits or gains from farming in accordance with *subsection (5)* and the individual was so chargeable for each of the 5 years of assessment immediately preceding the year of assessment, he or she may, on including a claim in that behalf with the return required under *Chapter 3* of *Part 41A* for the year of assessment, elect to be charged to tax for that year of assessment in accordance with *Chapter 3* of *Part 4*; but where in the case of an individual *subsection (6)* does not apply for any year of assessment by reason of *paragraph (b)(i)* of that subsection, the individual shall be deemed to be entitled to elect and to have duly elected, as respects that year of assessment, in accordance with this subsection.][13]

[(7A) (a) Where as respects the year of assessment 2015 an individual duly elects or is deemed to have elected in accordance with *subsection (7)* that subsection shall be construed as if a reference to 5 years in that subsection was a reference to 3 years, and

(b) where as respects the year of assessment 2016 an individual duly elects or is deemed to have elected in accordance with *subsection (7)* that subsection shall be construed as if a reference to 5 years in that subsection was a reference to 4 years.][14]

(8) Where as respects a year of assessment an individual duly elects or is deemed to have elected in accordance with *subsection (7)*—

(a) the individual shall be charged to income tax for that year and for each subsequent year of assessment in accordance with *Chapter 3* of *Part 4*, and

[(b) there shall be made such assessment or assessments, if any, as may be necessary to secure that the amount of profits or gains from farming on which the individual who, in respect of the year of assessment 2015 duly elects or is deemed to have elected in accordance with *subsection (7)* is charged for each of the years of assessment 2012 and 2013, shall be not less than the amount on which the individual was charged by virtue of *subsection (6)* in accordance with *subsection (5)* for the year of assessment 2014,][15]

[(c) notwithstanding *section 959Z*, there shall be made such assessment or assessments, if any, as may be necessary to secure that the amount of profits or gains from farming on which the individual, in the case of an individual referred to in *subsection (4A)*, is charged to tax for each of the 3 years immediately preceding the year preceding the year of assessment as respects which the individual elects or is deemed to have elected in accordance with *subsection (7)*, shall be not less than the amount on which the individual is charged by virtue of *subsection (6)* in accordance with *subsection (5)* for the preceding year of assessment, and

(d) in any other case, notwithstanding *section 959Z*, there shall be made such assessment or assessments, if any, as may be necessary to secure that the amount of profits or gains from farming on which the individual is charged to tax for each of the 4 years immediately preceding the year preceding the year of assessment as respects which the individual elects or is deemed to have elected in accordance with *subsection (7)*, shall be not less than the amount on which the individual is charged by virtue of *subsection (6)* in accordance with *subsection (5)* for the preceding year of assessment.][16]

[(8A) Where as respects the year of assessment 2002 an individual duly elects or is deemed to have elected in accordance with *subsection (7)*, *subsection (8)* shall apply as if the following were substituted for *paragraph (b)* of that subsection:

"(b) there shall be made such assessment or assessments, if any, as may be necessary to secure that the amount of the profits or gains from farming on which the individual is charged for each of the years of assessment 1999-2000 and 2000-2001 shall be not less than 135 per cent of the amount on which the individual is charged by virtue of *subsection (6)* in accordance with *subsection (5)* for the year of assessment 2001."

(8B) Where as respects the year of assessment 2003 an individual duly elects or is deemed to have elected in accordance with *subsection (7)*, *subsection (8)* shall apply as if the following were substituted for *paragraph (b)* of that subsection:

"(b) there shall be made such assessment or assessments, if any, as may be necessary to secure that the amount of the profits or gains from farming on which the individual is charged for the year of assessment 2000-2001 and the year of assessment 2001 shall be—

(i) in the case of the year of assessment 2000-2001, not less than, and

(ii) in the case of the year of assessment 2001, not less than 74 per cent of,

the amount on which the individual is charged by virtue of *subsection (6)* in accordance with *subsection (5)* for the year of assessment 2002."

(8C) Where as respects the year of assessment 2004 an individual duly elects or is deemed to have elected in accordance with *subsection (7)*, *subsection (8)* shall apply as if the following were substituted for *paragraph (b)* of that subsection:

"(b) there shall be made such assessment or assessments, if any, as may be necessary to secure that the amount of the profits or gains from farming on which the individual is charged for each of the years of assessment 2001 and 2002 shall be—

(i) in the case of the year of assessment 2001, not less than 74 per cent of, and

(ii) in the case of the year of assessment 2002, not less than,

the amount on which the individual is charged by virtue of *subsection (6)* in accordance with *subsection (5)* for the year of assessment 2003."][17]

(9) In determining for any year of assessment what capital allowances, balancing allowances or balancing charges are to be made to or on an individual in taxing a trade of farming in accordance with *subsection (5)*, the individual shall be deemed to be chargeable for that year of assessment in respect of the profits or gains of the trade in accordance with *section 65(1)*.

(10) Nothing in this section shall prejudice or restrict the operation of *section 67* in any case where a trade of farming is permanently discontinued.

[(10A) Where the commencement of a partnership to which European Communities (Milk Quota) (Amendment) Regulations 2002 (S.I. No. 97 of 2002) apply, would otherwise result in the permanent discontinuation of another trade of farming then, notwithstanding subsection (10) and solely for the purposes of the application of this section, the partnership trade shall be treated as a continuation of that other trade.][18]

[(11) Where for any year of assessment a loss is aggregated with profits or gains in accordance with *subsection (5)(b)* and the amount of the loss is in excess of the profits or gains—

(a) in the case of an individual referred to in *subsection (4A)*, one-quarter of the amount of such excess shall be deemed for the purposes of *Chapter 1* of *Part 12* to be a loss sustained in the trade of farming in the final year of the 4 years, and

(b) in any other case, one-fifth of the amount of such excess shall be deemed for the purposes of *Chapter 1* of *Part 12* to be a loss sustained in the trade of farming in the final year of the 5 years,

on the average of the profits or gains of which the individual is to be charged to tax for that year of assessment, and any loss so aggregated shall not be eligible for relief under any provision of the Income Tax Acts apart from this subsection.][19]

[(11A) As respects the year of assessment 2001, *subsection (11)* shall apply as if in that subsection "74 per cent of one-third of the amount of such excess" were substituted for "one-third of the amount of such excess" and, where this subsection applies, the individual may claim that 26 per cent of one-third of the amount of the excess referred to in *subsection (11)* shall, notwithstanding anything to the contrary in that subsection, be carried forward under *section 382* for deduction from or set-off against the profits or gains of the individual from farming for any subsequent year of assessment.][20]

(12) The profits or gains from farming on which an individual is to be charged to tax for any year of assessment by virtue of *subsection (6)* in accordance with *subsection (5)* shall be deemed to be the profits or gains from farming of that individual in determining his or her total income for that year for the purposes of the Income Tax Acts apart from this section, and any provision of those Acts relating to the delivery of any return, account (including balance sheet), statement, declaration, book, list or other document or the furnishing of any particulars shall apply as if this section had not been enacted.

Amendments

[1, 2] Substituted by F(No.3)A11 sched1(170). Shall have effect from 27 July 2011.

[3] Substituted by FA14 s20(a)(i). Comes into operation on 1 January 2015.

[4] Substituted by F(No.3)A11 sched1(172). Shall have effect from 27 July 2011.

[5] Substituted by F(No.3)A11 sched1(173). Shall have effect from 27 July 2011.

[6] Substituted by F(No.3)A11 sched1(174). Shall have effect from 27 July 2011.

[7] Substituted by FA14 s20(a)(ii). Comes into operation on 1 January 2015.

[8] Inserted by FA14 s20(a)(iii). Comes into operation on 1 January 2015.

[9, 12] Substituted by FA14 s20(a)(iv). Comes into operation on 1 January 2015.

[10] Substituted by FA01 sched2(37)(a)(i).

[11] Inserted by FA01 sched2(37)(a)(ii).

[13] Substituted by FA14 s20(a)(v). Comes into operation on 1 January 2015.

[14] Inserted by FA14 s20(a)(vi). Comes into operation on 1 January 2015.

[15] Substituted by FA14 s20(a)(vii)(I). Comes into operation on 1 January 2015.

[16] Inserted by FA14 s20(a)(vii)(II). Comes into operation on 1 January 2015.

[17] Inserted by FA01 sched2(37)(b).

[18] Inserted by FA08 s15.

[19] Substituted by FA14 s20(a)(viii). Comes into operation on 1 January 2015.

[20] Inserted by FA01 sched2(37)(c).

Revenue Precedents

Qualification for income averaging – (i) losses incurred (ii) commencement of farming in partnership. (i) the fact that a farmer incurs a loss while on income averaging does not affect his entitlement to be on income averaging (ii) Where a farmer trading as a sole trader on income averaging starts trading as a partner, Revenue would be prepared to allow income averaging to continue for existing farming activities; once the partnership trade had been in existence for sufficiently long to be assessed for two years in accordance with section 65(1) TCA 1997, the farmer could opt for averaging in respect of this trade. 892000

A father and son farm in partnership. If the father decides to retire and the son continues to farm as a sole trader, is the son entitled to continue on income averaging? What review procedure applies in these circumstances? The cessation of a partnership trade and the commencement of a sole trade will not affect an individual's entitlement to income averaging. Section 657(6)(a) Taxes Consolidation Act 1997 provides that once an individual elects for income averaging he is charged to tax for each year of assessment in respect of profits based on a 3 year average. He will continue to be charged in this manner until either of the following applies: (a) he is an individual to whom subsection (1) applies, in which case he is deemed to elect to opt out of averaging (b) he is not chargeable to tax on farming profits (c) he elects to opt out of averaging (d) he is deemed to elect to opt out of averaging. This only applies in the case of (a). A review, for the purposes of section 657(8)(b), will therefore not be required in these circumstances as the individual has not elected or deemed to have elected out of averaging. A review will however be necessary under section 67 Taxes Consolidation Act 1997 of both the father's and son's assessments. IT973010

Where there is a farming loss but a balancing charge arises the taxpayer is not charged to tax in respect of profits or gains from farming for that year for the purposes of section 657(4)(b). GD97084

The taxable amount of "Mulder compensation", as computed in accordance with Article 1.3 of Tax Briefing No. 14, can be averaged in the normal way. IT963507

What is the position regarding averaging in situations where a farmer is a sole trader and also farming in partnership? Where a taxpayer has farming income as a sole trader and also income from a farming partnership, on an ongoing basis, the income averaging rules should be applied to both businesses in view of the fact that under section 655 all farming carried on by any person whether solely or in partnership is treated as the carrying on of a single trade. IT943512

A farmer, by notice in writing, elected to be charged to tax for a year of assessment in accordance with the provisions of section 657 Taxes Consolidation Act 1997. Is there any concession by which he may be regarded as not having made the election? Section 657 Taxes Consolidation Act 1997 does not provide for the reversal of an election. There is no non-statutory practice whereby this election may be regarded as not having been made. IT973014

Where a farmer, who is on income averaging in respect of a sole trade of farming, commences to carrying on farming in partnership, will he be entitled to elect for averaging in respect of the partnership trade? An individual who, in addition to carrying on a sole trade of farming, the profits of which are charged to tax by virtue of section 657 Taxes Consolidation Act 1997, commences to carry on farming in partnership – so that part of his profits from the single trade of farming are charged to tax under income averaging and part are charged in accordance with the provisions of section 66(1), Taxes Consolidation Act 1997 – might not, strictly speaking, be entitled to a elect for income averaging. In practice, however, each part of the overall trade would be looked at separately, so that the income averaging could continue to be allowed in respect of the sole trade, and income averaging could be claimed as soon as the partnership had been assessed in accordance with section 65(1), Income Tax Act 1967, for the requisite two preceding years." IT923027

A farmer elects for income averaging for a year of assessment. The following year he commences to carry on another trade. A review is therefore required under section 657(8)(b) Taxes Consolidation Act 1997. Given that averaging was only in operation for one year would the revision apply to the averaged year only? Section 657(8)(b) Taxes Consolidation Act 1997 provides that where an individual is deemed to have elected out of income averaging, the amount of profits or gains from farming upon which he is charged for each of the two years of assessment immediately preceding the year preceding the year of assessment in which he is deemed to have elected out will be reviewed. The Act makes no provision for a lesser review period where the person was not charged to tax by virtue of the provisions of section 657 for three or more years. IT923036

A farmer availed of income averaging for a number of years and then ceased to trade. On the discontinuance of the trade a review of the penultimate year is required. Is the revision based on a comparison of the actual profits and the current year profits or with the "averaged" profits? Subsection (10) of section 657 Taxes Consolidation Act 1997 ensures that the provisions of section 67 Taxes Consolidation Act 1997 will operate, even where an election has been made for income averaging. If the actual profits of the penultimate year exceed the "averaged" profit on which the person has been charged, the person will instead be charged on the actual profits or gains of that year. IT913024

Will a surviving spouse be entitled to continue on income averaging where the deceased spouse had formerly been on such income averaging? Where, on the death of a spouse, who was on income averaging, the farming trade passes in its entirety to the person's surviving spouse, that spouse will be regarded as continuing on income averaging. IT923034

A farmer's trading profits for a year of assessment are nil due to stock relief. Profits arose in the two years prior to that year. Is the farmer entitled to claim income averaging for the year subsequent to the year in which the stock relief was claimed? An individual is not entitled to elect to be charged to tax, for a year of assessment, in respect of farming profits, under section 657 Taxes Consolidation Act 1997, where the individual was not charged to tax in either of the two immediately preceding years in respect of profits from farming on the current year basis (i.e. in accordance with section 65(1) TCA 1997.) Stock relief is given as a deduction in computing an individual's trading profits. An individual cannot be regarded as being charged to tax in respect of profits if no trading profits arise. IT963009

Cross References

From Section 657

Section 52 Persons chargeable.
Section 65 Cases I and II: basis of assessment.
Section 67 Special basis on discontinuance of trade or profession.
Section 381 Right to repayment of tax by reference to losses.
Section 382 Right to carry forward losses to future years.
Section 933 Appeals against assessment.
Section 951 Obligation to make a return.

To Section 657

Section 657A "Taxation of certain farm payments.
Schedule 31 Consequential Amendments

657A "Taxation of certain farm payments

[(1) In this section—

"*relevant individual*" means an individual who is in receipt of—

(a) a relevant payment or relevant payments, and

(b) a payment under the EU Single Payment Scheme operated by the Department of Agriculture and Food under Council Regulation No. 1782/2003 of 29 September 2003*,

* OJ No. L270 of 21.10.2003, p. 1

in respect of both of which the individual would be, apart from this section, chargeable to income tax on the profits or gains from farming for [the same year of assessment][1], but does not include an individual who in [that year of assessment][2] is chargeable to income tax in respect of profits or gains from farming in accordance with *subsection (5)* of *section 657*;

"*relevant payment*" means a payment made at any time in the calendar year 2005 to an individual under any of the EU schemes specified in the Table to this section.

(2) A relevant individual may elect to have the aggregate of all relevant payments made to the individual treated in accordance with *subsections (3)* to *(6)*, and each such election shall be made in such form and contain such information as the Revenue Commissioners may require.

[(3) Notwithstanding any other provision of the Income Tax Acts apart from *subsection (4)*, where an individual elects in accordance with *subsection (2)*, then the relevant payment or relevant payments shall—

(a) be disregarded as respects the "same year of assessment" referred to in the definition of "relevant individual" in *subsection (1)*, and

(b) instead be treated for the purposes of the Income Tax Acts as arising in equal instalments in the year of assessment that is such same year of assessment and in the 2 immediately succeeding years of assessment.][3]

(4) Where a trade of farming is permanently discontinued, tax shall be charged under Case IV of Schedule D for the year of assessment in which such discontinuation takes place in respect of the amount of any relevant payment which would, but for such discontinuance, be treated by virtue of *subsection (3)* as arising in a year of assessment or years of assessment ending after such discontinuance.

[(5) An election under *subsection (2)* by a person to whom this section applies, shall be made by notice in writing on or before 31 October in the year following the "same year of assessment" referred to in the definition of "relevant individual" in *subsection (1)*, and shall be included in the annual statement required to be delivered on or before that date under the Income Tax Acts of the profits or gains from farming for the year of assessment that is such same year of assessment.][4]

(6) Subject to *subsection (4)* an election made under *subsection (2)* cannot be altered or varied during the period to which it refers.

TABLE

1. Special Beef Premium Schemes.
2. Suckler Cow Premium Scheme.
3. Ewe Premium Schemes.
4. Extensification Payments Scheme.
5. Slaughter Premium Scheme.
6. Arable Aid Schemes.
7. National Envelope Top-Ups.][5]

Amendments

[1, 2] Substituted by FA07 s22(a).

[3] Substituted by FA07 s22(b).

[4] Substituted by FA07 s22(c).

[5] Inserted by FA05 s29.

Revenue Briefings

Tax Briefing

Tax Briefing August 2006 – Issue 64 – Single Payment Scheme (Farming)

eBrief

eBrief No. 34/2014 - Capital Gains Tax - Exemption on Disposal of Single Farm Payment Entitlements in Certain Circumstances

Cross References

From Section 657A

Section 657 Averaging of farm profits.

657B Restructuring and diversification aid for sugar beet growers

[(1) In this section—

"*specified individual*" means an individual who carries on in the year of assessment 2007 or in any subsequent year of assessment the trade of farming in respect of which the individual is within the charge to tax under Case I of Schedule D;

"*specified payment*" means a payment to a specified individual under the EU temporary scheme for the restructuring of the sugar industry in the Community, operated by the Department of Agriculture, Fisheries and Food under any of Articles 3(6) first indent, 6 and 7 of Council Regulation (EC) No. 320/2006 of 20 February 2006* (as amended by Council Regulation (EC) No. 1261/2007 of 9 October 2007†) in respect of which the specified individual would, apart from this section, be chargeable to income tax on the profits or gains from farming for the year of assessment 2007 or for any subsequent year of assessment.

* OJ No. L58, 28 February 2006, p.42

† OJ No. L283, 27 October 2007, p.8

(2) A specified individual may elect to have the aggregate of all specified payments made to the individual which would, apart from this section, be chargeable to income tax for a year of assessment treated in accordance with subsections (3) to (6), and each such election shall be made in such form and contain such information as the Revenue Commissioners may require.

(3) Notwithstanding any other provision of the Income Tax Acts apart from subsection (4), where a specified individual elects in accordance with subsection (2), the specified payment or specified payments shall be disregarded as respects the year of assessment referred to in subsection (2) and shall instead be treated for the purposes of the Income Tax Acts as chargeable in equal instalments for the year of assessment so referred to in subsection (2) and for the 5 succeeding years of assessment.

(4) Where a trade of farming is permanently discontinued, tax shall be charged under Case IV of Schedule D for the year of assessment in which such discontinuation takes place in respect of the amount of any specified payment which would, but for such discontinuance, be treated by virtue of subsection (3) as chargeable for a year of assessment or years of assessment ending after such discontinuance.

(5) An election under subsection (2) by an individual to whom this section applies, shall be made by notice in writing on or before 31 October in the year of assessment following the year of assessment referred to in subsection (2).

(6) Subject to subsection (4), an election made under subsection (2) shall not be altered or varied during the period to which it relates.][1]

Amendments

[1] Substituted by FA08 s20.

658 Farming: allowances for capital expenditure on construction of buildings and other works

[FA74 s22(1) to (3) and (5) to (11); CTA76 s21(1) and Sch1 par70; FA83 s15; FA93 s34(2); FA94 s23]

(1) This section shall apply to any person carrying on farming, the profits or gains of which are chargeable to tax in accordance with *section 655*.

(2) (a) Where a person to whom this section applies incurs, for the purpose of a trade of farming land occupied by such person, any capital expenditure on the construction of farm buildings (excluding a building or part of a building used as a dwelling), fences, roadways, holding yards, drains or land reclamation or other works, there shall be made to such person during a writing-down period of 7 years beginning with the chargeable period related to that expenditure, writing-down allowances (in this section referred to as "farm buildings allowances") in respect of that expenditure and such allowances shall be made in taxing the trade.

(b) As respects each of the first 6 years of the writing-down period, the farm buildings allowance to be made under this subsection shall be 15 per cent of the capital expenditure referred to in *paragraph (a)* and, as respects the last year of the writing-down period, the farm buildings allowance to be made under this subsection shall be 10 per cent of that expenditure.

(c) Where the capital expenditure referred to in *paragraph (a)* was incurred before the 27th day of January, 1994, this section shall apply subject to *paragraph 23* of *Schedule 32*.

(3) For the purposes of the application to this section of *section 321*, "*basis period*" has the meaning assigned to it by *section 306*.

(4) Where for any year of assessment an individual is not chargeable to income tax in respect of profits or gains from farming in accordance with *Chapter 3* of *Part 4*, and that year is a year of assessment in respect of which, if the individual had been so chargeable, he or she could have claimed a farm buildings allowance under this section, that allowance shall for the purposes of this section be deemed to have been made for that year of assessment and shall not be carried forward and set off against profits or gains chargeable for any subsequent year of assessment.

(5) Any capital expenditure incurred by a person about to carry on farming but before commencing farming shall for the purposes of this section be treated as if it had been incurred on the first day on which the person commences farming.

(6) Any claim for a farm buildings allowance to be made to a person under this section shall be included in the annual statement required to be delivered by the person under the Income Tax Acts of the profits or gains from farming, and *section 304(4)* shall apply in relation to the allowance as it applies in relation to allowances to be made under *Part 9*.

(7) Any claim for a farm buildings allowance under this section shall be made to and determined by the inspector, but any person aggrieved by any decision of the inspector on any such claim may, on giving notice in writing to the inspector within 21 days after the notification to that person of the decision, appeal to the Appeal Commissioners.

(8) The Appeal Commissioners shall hear and determine an appeal to them made under *subsection (7)* as if it were an appeal against an assessment to tax, and the provisions of the Income Tax Acts relating to the rehearing of an appeal and to

the statement of a case for the opinion of the High Court on a point of law shall apply accordingly with any necessary modifications.

(9) Subject to *subsection (10)*, where a person who is entitled to a farm buildings allowance under this section in respect of capital expenditure incurred for the purpose of farming farm land transfers such person's interest in that farm land or any part of that farm land to another person, that other person shall, to the exclusion of the first-mentioned person, be entitled to the allowances under this section for the chargeable periods following the chargeable period in which the transfer of interest took place.

(10) Where the transfer of interest to which *subsection (9)* refers takes place in relation to part of the farm land, *subsection (9)* shall apply to so much of the allowance as is properly referable to that part of the land as if it were a separate allowance.

(11) Where expenditure is incurred partly for the purposes of farming and partly for other purposes, *subsection (2)* shall apply to so much only of that expenditure as on a just apportionment ought fairly to be treated as incurred for the purposes of farming.

(12) No farm buildings allowance shall be made by virtue of this section in respect of any expenditure if for the same or any other chargeable period an allowance is or has been made in respect of that expenditure under *Chapter 1* of *Part 9*.

(13) Expenditure shall not be regarded for the purposes of this section as having been incurred by a person in so far as it has been or is to be met directly or indirectly by the State or by any person other than the first-mentioned person.

Revenue Precedents

If a farmer retires and leases his buildings to another farmer he cannot continue to claim the remaining farm buildings allowances in respect of the buildings. In order to qualify for the farm buildings allowances he must be carrying on farming, the profits or gains of which are chargeable in accordance with section 655. IT943518

A farmer proposes to transfer his farm to a trust under which he would retain a life interest with remainder interests to a discretionary settlement in favour of his children. The issue arising is whether the person would not be regarded as having transferred his interest to another person for the purposes of section 658(9) Taxes Consolidation Act 1997, having regard to the retention of a life interest in that asset and to the fact that it is he, rather than the trust, which will be continuing the trade of farming on the land. Where a person transfers a farm to a trust, with the retention of a life interest, there will be a transfer for the purposes of section 658(9) Taxes Consolidation Act 1997. IT923025

Farmer lets farm building to partnership in which he is a partner; is Farm Buildings allowance due? Yes, provided the building is let at market value and the payment is not in respect of services to the partnership. If the farmer introduces the buildings into the partnership, the capital allowances would go to the partnership. IT922026

If a Local Authority carries out accommodation works such as fencing as part of the compensation given for land acquired under a compulsory purchase order is the farmer entitled to farm buildings allowance in respect of that expenditure. Section 658 Taxes Consolidation Act 1997 provides that a farm buildings allowance will be made where a farmer incurs any capital expenditure on the construction of farm buildings. The agreement of the compensation terms arising under the Compulsory Purchase Order does not amount to a contract under which a farmer may be regarded as having incurred expenditure. Accordingly, such allowances are not available. 961

Cross References

From Section 658

Section 52 Persons chargeable.
Section 65 Cases I and II: basis of assessment.
Section 268 Meaning of "industrial building or structure".
Section 304 Income tax: allowances and charges in taxing a trade, etc.
Section 306 Meaning of basis period.

Section 321 Provisions of general application in relation to the making of allowances and charges.
Section 655 Farming and market gardening profits to be charged to tax under Schedule D.
Schedule 32 Transitional Provisions

To Section 658

Section 309 Companies not resident in the State.
Section 319 Adjustment of allowances by reference to value-added tax.
Section 321 Provisions of general application in relation to the making of allowances and charges.
Section 531AM Charge to universal social charge.
Section 531AU Capital allowances and losses.
Section 659 Farming: allowances for capital expenditure on the construction of farm buildings, etc. for control of pollution.
Schedule 32 Transitional Provisions

659 Farming: allowances for capital expenditure on the construction of farm buildings, etc. for control of pollution

[FA97 s20(1) to (13)]

(1) This section shall apply to any person—

(a) carrying on farming, the profits or gains of which are chargeable to tax in accordance with *section 655*,

(b) for whom, in respect of capital expenditure to which *paragraph (c)* refers and in respect of farm land occupied by him or her, a farm nutrient management plan has been drawn up by an agency or planner approved to draw up such plans by the Department of Agriculture and Food, and drawn up in accordance with—

(i) the guidelines in relation to such plans entitled "Farm Nutrient Management Plan" issued by the Department of Agriculture, Food and Forestry on the 21st day of March, 1997, or

(ii) a plan drawn up under the scheme known as the Rural Environment Protection Scheme (REPS) or the scheme known as the Erne Catchment Nutrient Management Scheme, both being schemes administered by the Department of Agriculture and Food,

and

(c) who incurs capital expenditure on or after the 6th day of April, 1997, and before the [1 January 2011][1], on the construction of those farm buildings (excluding a building or part of a building used as a dwelling) or structures specified in the Table to this section in the course of a trade of farming land occupied by such person where such building or structures are constructed in accordance with that farm nutrient management plan and are certified as being necessary by that agency or planner for the purpose of securing a reduction in or the elimination of any pollution arising from the trade of farming.

[(2) (a) Subject to the provisions of Article 6 of Council Regulation (EEC) No. 2328/91 of 15 July 1991*, on improving the efficiency of agricultural structures, as amended, and subject to *subsections (3)* and *(3A)*, where a person to whom this section applies—

* OJ No. L218, 6.8.1991, p.1

(i) has delivered to the Department of Agriculture, Food and Rural Development a farm nutrient management plan referred to in *subsection (1)(b)*, and

(ii) incurs capital expenditure to which *subsection (1)* applies,

there shall be made to such person during the writing-down periods, specified in *paragraph (b)*, writing-down allowances (in this section referred to as "*farm pollution control allowances*") in respect of that expenditure and such allowances shall be made in taxing the trade.

(b) The writing-down periods referred to in *paragraph (a)* shall be—

(i) 8 years beginning with the chargeable period related to the capital expenditure, where that expenditure is incurred before [6 April 2000,][2]

(ii) 7 years beginning with the chargeable period related to the capital expenditure, where that expenditure is incurred on or after [6 April 2000 but before 1 January 2005, or][3]][4]

[(iii) 3 years beginning with the chargeable period related to the capital expenditure, where that expenditure is incurred on or after 1 January 2005.][5]

(3) The farm pollution control allowances to be made in accordance with *subsection (2)* in respect of capital expenditure incurred in a chargeable period shall be—

[(a) as respects the first year of the writing-down period referred to in *subsection (2)(b)(i)*, where the capital expenditure was incurred—

(i) before 6 April 1998, an amount equal to 50 per cent of that expenditure or [€12,700][6], whichever is the lesser,

(ii) on or after 6 April 1998 and before 6 April 2000, an amount equal to 50 per cent of that expenditure or [€19,050][7], whichever is the lesser,][8]

(b) as respects the next 6 years of that writing-down period, an amount equal to 15 per cent of the balance of that expenditure after deducting the amount of any allowance made by virtue of *paragraph (a)*, and

(c) as respects the last year of that writing-down period, an amount equal to 10 per cent of the balance of that expenditure after deducting the amount of any allowance made by virtue of *paragraph (a)*.

[(3A) The farm pollution control allowances to be made in accordance with *subsection (2)* during the writing-down period referred to in *subsection (2)(b)(ii)*, in respect of capital expenditure incurred in a chargeable period, where that expenditure is incurred [on or after 6 April 2000 but before 1 January 2005 shall,][9] subject to *subsection (3B)*, be an amount equal to—

(a) 15 per cent of that expenditure incurred for each of the first 6 years of the writing-down period, and

(b) 10 per cent of that expenditure for the last year of the writing-down period.

[(3AA) The farm pollution control allowances to be made in accordance with *subsection (2)* during the writing-down period referred to in *subsection (2)(b)(iii)* in respect of capital expenditure incurred in a chargeable period, shall where that expenditure is incurred on or after 1 January 2005, and subject to *subsection (3BA)*, be an amount equal to 33 per cent of that expenditure incurred for each of the 3 years of the writing-down period.][10]

(3B) (a) [In this subsection and *subsection (3BA)*][11]—

["*residual amount*", in relation to capital expenditure incurred in a chargeable period, means an amount equal to 50 per cent of that expenditure or—

(i) €31,750, where incurred in a chargeable period ending before 1 January 2006, and

(ii) €50,000, in any other case,

whichever is the lesser;][12]

"*specified amount*", in relation to capital expenditure incurred in a chargeable period, means the balance of that expenditure after deducting the [residual amount.][13]

[…][14]

(b) Notwithstanding *subsection (3A)*, where farm pollution control allowances are to be made to a person in accordance with that subsection during the writing-down period referred to in *subsection (2)(b)(ii)*, such person may elect to have those allowances made in accordance with this subsection and, where such person so elects, the allowances shall be made in accordance with this subsection only.

(c) Where *paragraph (b)* applies to a person, the farm pollution control allowances to be made to such person during the writing-down period referred to in *subsection (2)(b)(ii)* shall be an amount equal to—

(i) 15 per cent of the specified amount for each of the first 6 years of the writing-down period, and

(ii) 10 per cent of the specified amount for the last year of the writing-down period, and

(iii) subject to *paragraph (d)*, the whole or any part of the residual amount, as is specified by the person to whom the allowances are to be made, in any year of the writing-down period.

(d) The allowances to be made in accordance with *subparagraphs (i)* and *(iii)* of *paragraph (c)* or *subparagraphs (ii)* and *(iii)* of that paragraph, as the case may be, for any year of the writing-down period, shall not in the aggregate exceed the residual amount.

[(3BA) (a) Notwithstanding *subsection (3AA)*, where farm pollution control allowances are to be made to a person in accordance with that subsection during the writing-down period referred to in *subsection (2)(b)(iii)*, such person may elect to have those allowances made in accordance with this subsection and, where such person so elects, the allowances shall be made in accordance with this subsection only.

(b) Where *paragraph (a)* applies to a person, the farm pollution control allowance to be made to such person during the writing-down period referred to in *subsection (2)(b)(iii)* shall be an amount equal to—

(i) 331/3 per cent of the specified amount for each of the 3 years of the writing-down period, and

(ii) subject to *paragraph (c)*, the whole or any part of the residual amount, as is specified by the person to whom the allowances are to be made, in any year of the writing-down period.

(c) The allowances to be made in accordance with *paragraph (b)* for any year of the writing-down period, shall not in the aggregate exceed the residual amount.][15]

[(3C) (a) An election by a person to whom this section applies in relation to the farm pollution control allowances claimed in *subsection (3B)* or *(3BA)*, as the case may be, shall be made in writing on or before the specified return date for the chargeable period (within the meaning of *section 950*) in which the expenditure is incurred and shall be included in the annual statement required to be delivered under the Income Tax Acts of the profits or gains from farming as set out in *subsection (5)*.][16]

(b) An election made under the provisions of *paragraph (a)* cannot be altered or varied during the writing-down period to which it refers.][17]

(4) For the purposes of the application to this section of *section 321*, "*basis period*" has the meaning assigned to it by *section 306*.

(5) Any claim by a person for a farm pollution control allowance to be made to such person shall be included in the annual statement required to be delivered under the Income Tax Acts of the profits or gains from farming, and *section 304(4)* shall apply in relation to the allowance as it applies in relation to allowances to be made under *Part 9*.

(6) Any claim for a farm pollution control allowance shall be made to and determined by the inspector, but any person aggrieved by any decision of the inspector on any such claim may, on giving notice in writing to the inspector within 21 days after the notification to the person of the decision, appeal to the Appeal Commissioners.

(7) The Appeal Commissioners shall hear and determine an appeal to them made under *subsection (6)* as if it were an appeal against an assessment to tax, and the provisions of the Income Tax Acts relating to the rehearing of an appeal and to the statement of a case for the opinion of the High Court on a point of law shall apply accordingly with any necessary modifications.

(8) Subject to *subsection (9)*, where a person who is entitled to farm pollution control allowances in respect of farm land occupied by the person transfers his or her interest in that farm land or any part of that farm land to another person, that other person shall, to the exclusion of the first-mentioned person, be entitled to the allowances under this section for the chargeable periods following the chargeable period in which the transfer of interest took place.

(9) Where the transfer of interest to which *subsection (8)* refers took place in relation to part of the farm land, *subsection (8)* shall apply to so much of the farm pollution control allowance as is properly referable to that part of the land as if it were a separate allowance.

(10) Where expenditure is incurred partly for a purpose for which a farm pollution control allowance is to be made and partly for another purpose, *subsection (2)* shall apply to so much only of that expenditure as on a just apportionment ought fairly to be treated as incurred for the first-mentioned purpose.

(11) No farm pollution control allowance shall be made in respect of any expenditure if for the same or any other chargeable period an allowance is or has been made in respect of that expenditure under [Chapter 1 or Chapter 2][18] of *Part 9* or *section 658*.

(12) Expenditure shall not be regarded for the purposes of this section as having been incurred by a person in so far as it has been or is to be met directly or indirectly by the State or by any person other than the first-mentioned person.

(13) For the purposes only of determining, in relation to a claim for a farm pollution control allowance, whether and to what extent capital expenditure incurred on the construction of a building or structure to which this section applies is incurred or not incurred in the period specified in *subsection (1)(c)*, only such an amount of that capital expenditure as is properly attributable to work on the construction of the building or structure actually carried out during that period shall (notwithstanding any other provision of the Tax Acts as to the time when any capital expenditure is or is to be treated as incurred) be treated as having been incurred in that period.

TABLE

Farm Buildings and Structures to Which Allowances for the Control of Pollution Apply

1. Waste storage facilities including slurry tanks.
2. Soiled water tanks.
3. Effluent tanks.
4. Tank fences and covers.
5. Dungsteads and manure pits.
6. Yard drains for storm and soiled water removal.
7. Walled silos, silage bases and silo aprons.
8. Housing for cattle, including drystock accommodation, byres, loose houses, slatted houses, sloped floor houses and kennels, roofed feed or exercise yards where such houses or structures eliminate soiled water.
9. Housing for sheep and unroofed wintering structures for sheep and sheep dipping tanks.

Amendments

[1] Substituted by F(No.2)A08 s17. This section is deemed to have come into force and takes effect as on and from 1 January 2009.

[2] Substituted by FA05 s30(b)(i).

[3] Substituted by FA05 s30(b)(ii).

[4] Substituted by FA00 s60(b)(i).

[5] Inserted by FA05 s30(b)(iii).

[6, 7] Substituted by FA01 s240 and sched5 part1.

[8] Substituted by FA00 s60(b)(ii).

[9] Substituted by FA05 s30(c).

[10] Inserted by FA05 s30(d).

[11, 15] Substituted by FA05 s30(e)(i).

[12] Substituted by FA06 s19.

[13] Substituted by FA05 s30(e)(ii).

[14] Deleted by FA05 s30(e)(iii).

[16] Substituted by FA05 s30(g).

[17] Inserted by FA00 s60(b)(iii).

[18] Substituted by FA05 s30(h).

Cross References

From Section 659

Section 268 Meaning of "industrial building or structure".
Section 304 Income tax: allowances and charges in taxing a trade, etc.
Section 306 Meaning of basis period.
Section 321 Provisions of general application in relation to the making of allowances and charges.
Section 655 Farming and market gardening profits to be charged to tax under Schedule D.
Section 658 Farming: allowances for capital expenditure on construction of buildings and other works.
Section 950 Interpretation (Part 41).

To Section 659

Section 319 Adjustment of allowances by reference to value-added tax.
Section 531B Charge to income levy.
Section 531AM Charge to universal social charge.
Section 531AU Capital allowances and losses.

660 Farming: wear and tear allowances deemed to have been made in certain cases

[FA74 s25; CTA76 s21(1) and Sch1 par71; FA78 s14(c)]

(1) In this section—

"balancing allowance" and "balancing charge" have the same meanings respectively as in *Chapter 2* of *Part 9*;

"wear and tear allowance" means an allowance made under *section 284*.

(2) In determining whether any, and if so what, wear and tear allowance, balancing allowance or balancing charge in respect of machinery or plant is to be made to or on any person for any chargeable period in taxing a trade of farming, there shall be deemed to have been made to that person, for every previous chargeable period in which the machinery or plant belonged to that person and which is a chargeable period to be taken into account for the purpose of this section, such wear and tear allowance or greater wear and tear allowance, if any, in respect of the machinery or plant as would have been made to that person if, in relation to every such previous chargeable period—

(a) the profits or gains from farming had been chargeable to tax under Case I of Schedule D,

(b) those profits or gains had been charged to tax in accordance with section 58 of the Income Tax Act, 1967, and not in an amount determined under section 21 of the Finance Act, 1974,

(c) farming had been carried on by that person since the date on which that person acquired the machinery or plant,

(d) the machinery or plant had been used by that person solely for the purposes of farming since that date, and

(e) a proper claim had been duly made by that person for wear and tear allowance in respect of the machinery or plant for every relevant chargeable period.

(3) There shall be taken into account for the purposes of this section every previous chargeable period in which the machinery or plant concerned belonged to the person and—

(a) during which the machinery or plant was not used by the person for the purposes of farming,

(b) in respect of which the person was charged to tax on an amount determined in accordance with section 21 of the Finance Act, 1974,

(c) during which farming was not carried on by the person, or

(d) during which farming was carried on by the person in such circumstances that the full amount of the profits or gains of farming was not liable to be charged to tax under Case I of Schedule D.

(4) In the case of a company (within the meaning of *section 4(1)*), *subsection (2)(c)* shall not alter the periods which are to be taken as chargeable periods but, if during any period after the 5th day of April, 1976, and after the company acquired the machinery or plant, the company has not been within the charge to corporation tax, any year of assessment or part of a year of assessment falling within that period shall be taken as a chargeable period as if it had been an accounting period of the company.

(5) Nothing in this section shall affect *section 288(4)*.

Cross References

From Section 660

Section 4 Interpretation of Corporation Tax Acts.
Section 268 Meaning of "industrial building or structure".
Section 283 Initial allowances.
Section 284 Wear and tear allowances.
Section 288 Balancing allowances and balancing charges.

To Section 660

Section 309 Companies not resident in the State.
Section 321 Provisions of general application in relation to the making of allowances and charges.

661 Farming: restriction of relief in respect of certain losses

[FA78 s15(1) and (2); FA83 s120 and Sch4]

(1) This section shall apply to a loss sustained by a person in the carrying on of farming in any year of assessment, being a year for which such person was not chargeable to tax in respect of profits or gains from farming.

(2) No relief shall be given under *section 382* in respect of a loss to which this section applies by deducting such loss from or setting it off against the amount of the profits or gains from farming assessed for any year of assessment.

Cross References

From Section 661

Section 382 Right to carry forward losses to future years.

662 Income tax: restriction of relief for losses in farming or market gardening

[FA74 s27(1) to (6); FA75 s33(2) and Sch1 PtII; FA96 s132(2) and Sch5 PtII]

(1) In this section—

"*prior 3 years*", in relation to a loss incurred in a year of assessment, means the last 3 years of assessment before that year;

"*prior period of loss*" means the prior 3 years or, if losses were incurred in successive years of assessment amounting in the aggregate to a period longer than 3 years (and ending when the prior 3 years end), that longer period.

(2) (a) Any loss (including any amount in respect of allowances which by virtue of *section 392* is to be treated as a loss) incurred in a trade of farming or market gardening shall not be available for relief under *section 381* unless

it is shown that, for the year of assessment in which the loss is claimed to have been incurred, the trade was being carried on on a commercial basis and with a view to the realisation of profits in the trade.

(b) Without prejudice to *paragraph (a)*, any loss (including any amount in respect of allowances which by virtue of *section 392* is to be treated as a loss) incurred in any year of assessment in a trade of farming or market gardening shall not be available for relief under *section 381* if in each of the prior 3 years a loss was incurred in carrying on that trade.

(c) For the purposes of this section, the fact that a trade of farming or market gardening was being carried on at any time so as to afford a reasonable expectation of profit shall be conclusive evidence that it was then being carried on with a view to the realisation of profits.

(d) This subsection shall not restrict relief for any loss or any capital allowance where it is shown by the claimant—

(i) that the whole of the claimant's farming or market gardening activities in the year following the prior 3 years are of such a nature, and carried on in such a way, as would have justified a reasonable expectation of the realisation of profits in the future if those activities had been undertaken by a competent farmer or market gardener, and

(ii) that if such farmer or market gardener had undertaken those activities at the beginning of the prior period of loss, such farmer or market gardener could not reasonably have expected those activities to become profitable until after the end of the year following the prior period of loss.

(e) This subsection shall not restrict relief where the carrying on of the trade forms part of and is ancillary to a larger trading undertaking.

(3) In ascertaining for the purposes of this section whether a loss was incurred in any year, the rules applicable to Case I of Schedule D shall be applied.

(4) Where a trade of farming or market gardening is or is to be treated as being carried on for a part only of a year of assessment by reason of its being set up and commenced, or discontinued, or both, in that year, *subsection (2)* shall apply in relation to that trade as regards that part of that year.

(5) *Subsection (2)* shall not restrict relief for any loss or capital allowance if the trade was set up and commenced within the prior 3 years, and for the purposes of this subsection a trade shall be treated as discontinued and a new trade set up in any event which under the Income Tax Acts is to be treated as equivalent to the permanent discontinuance or setting up of a trade.

(6) Notwithstanding *subsection (5)*, where at any time there has been a change in the persons engaged in carrying on a trade of farming or market gardening, this section shall apply to any person who was engaged in carrying on the trade immediately before and immediately after the change as if the trade were the same before and after the change without any discontinuance and as if a person and another person with whom such person is connected were the same person.

Revenue Precedents Losses can be claimed in the fourth year in a commencement situation. Section 662(5) indicates that the restriction on relief for losses does not apply for a year of assessment if the trade was set up and commenced within the last three years of assessment before that year. IT943513

Trade of farming is regarded as forming part of and being ancillary to the larger trade of dealing in land for the purposes of claiming relief for farm losses in the fourth consecutive year. Section 662(2)(e) of the Taxes Consolidation Act 1997 provides that relief is not to be denied where the loss making farm is part of and ancillary to a larger undertaking. The subsection is designed to meet cases such as that of a butcher who makes a practice of fattening bullocks for his business, or a manufacturer who grows his own raw materials or a seedsman, a chemical manufacturer or a fertiliser manufacturer who runs a farm for testing or improving his products. The phrase "part of and ancillary to" is interpreted strictly. Ancillary means subservient and annexed to (Croom – Johnson J in Cross v Emery at 31TC198). It implies a close operating link with and contribution to the larger undertaking. The question of whether the carrying on of the trade of farming forms part of the trade of dealing in land is a matter of fact. Prima facie, it is highly unlikely that it could form such a part. The farming operations are not sufficiently linked to the trade of dealing in land nor do they contribute to that trade. The trade of farming cannot therefore be regarded as being ancillary to the trade of dealing in land. IT973007

Cross References

From Section 662

Section 381 Right to repayment of tax by reference to losses.

Section 392 Option to treat capital allowances as creating or augmenting a loss.

663 Corporation tax: restriction of relief for losses in farming or market gardening

[CTA76 s17]

(1) In this section—

"*prior 3 years*", in relation to a loss incurred in an accounting period, means the last 3 years before the beginning of the accounting period.

"*prior period of loss*" means the prior 3 years or, if losses were incurred in successive accounting periods amounting in all to a period longer than 3 years (and ending when the prior 3 years end), that longer period.

(2) (a) Any loss incurred in a trade of farming or market gardening shall not be available for relief under *section 396(2)* unless it is shown that, for the accounting period in which the loss is claimed to have been incurred, the trade was being carried on on a commercial basis and with a view to the realisation of profits in the trade.

(b) (i) In this paragraph, "*loss computed without regard to capital allowances*" means a loss ascertained in accordance with the rules of Case I of Schedule D but so that, notwithstanding *sections 307* and *308*, no account shall be taken of any allowance or charge which otherwise would be taken into account under those sections.

(ii) Without prejudice to *paragraph (a)*, any loss incurred in any accounting period in a trade of farming or market gardening shall not be available for relief under *section 396(2)* if a loss computed without regard to capital allowances was incurred in carrying on that trade in that accounting period and in each of the accounting periods wholly or partly comprised in the prior 3 years.

(c) For the purposes of this section, the fact that a trade of farming or market gardening was being carried on at any time so as to afford a reasonable expectation of profit shall be conclusive evidence that it was then being carried on with a view to the realisation of profits.

(d) This subsection shall not restrict relief for any loss where it is shown by the claimant company—

(i) that the whole of its farming or market gardening activities in the year following the prior 3 years are of such a nature, and carried on in such a way, as would have justified a reasonable expectation of the realisation of profits in the future if those activities had been undertaken by a competent farmer or market gardener, and

(ii) that if such farmer or market gardener had undertaken those activities at the beginning of the prior period of loss, such farmer or market gardener could not reasonably have expected those activities to become profitable until after the end of the year following the prior period of loss.

(e) This subsection shall not restrict relief where the carrying on of the trade forms part of and is ancillary to a larger trading undertaking.

(3) *Subsection (2)* shall not restrict relief for any loss if the trade was set up and commenced within the prior 3 years, and for the purposes of this subsection a trade shall be treated as discontinued and a new trade set up in any event which under the Tax Acts is to be treated as equivalent to the permanent discontinuance or setting up of a trade; but a trade shall not be treated as discontinued if under *section 400(6)* it is not to be treated as discontinued for the purpose of capital allowances and charges.

(4) Where a trade of farming or market gardening is or is to be treated as being carried on for a part only of an accounting period by reason of its being set up and commenced, or discontinued, or both, in that accounting period, *subsection (2)* shall apply in relation to that trade as regards that part of that accounting period.

(5) Notwithstanding *subsection (3)*, where at any time there has been a change in the persons engaged in carrying on a trade of farming or market gardening, this section shall apply to any person, who was engaged in carrying on the trade immediately before and immediately after the change as if the trade were the same before and after the change without any discontinuance and as if a person and another person with whom such person is connected were the same person, and accordingly relief from corporation tax may be restricted under this section by reference to losses some of which are incurred in years of assessment and some, computed without regard to capital allowances, are incurred in a company's accounting periods.

Cross References

From Section 663

Section 307 Corporation tax: allowances and charges in taxing a trade.

Section 308 Corporation tax: manner of granting, and effect of, allowances made by means of discharge or repayment of tax.

Section 396 Relief for trading losses other than terminal losses.

Section 400 Company reconstructions without change of ownership.

To Section 663

Section 420 Losses, etc. which may be surrendered by means of group relief.

Section 420A Group relief: relevant losses and charges.

Section 644C Relief from corporation tax for losses from dealing in residential development land.

664 Relief for certain income from leasing of farm land

[ITA67 s195B(3) and (6); FA85 s10, FA87 s2, FA91 s10; FA93 s10(1); FA96 s10, s132(1) and Sch5 PtI par14]

(1) (a) In this section—

"*farm land*" means land in the State wholly or mainly occupied for the purposes of husbandry and includes a building (other than a building or part of a building used as a dwelling) situated on the land and used for the purposes of farming that land;

"lease", "lessee", "lessor" and "rent" have the same meanings respectively as in *Chapter 8* of *Part 4*;

"*qualifying lease*" means a lease of farm land which is—

(i) in writing or evidenced in writing,

(ii) for a definite term of 5 years or more, and

(iii) made on an arm's length basis between a qualifying lessor or qualifying lessors and a lessee or lessees who is, or each of whom is, a qualifying lessee in relation to the qualifying lessor or the qualifying lessors;

['*qualifying lessee*', in relation to a qualifying lessor or qualifying lessors, means, as the case may be—

(i) an individual who—

(I) is not connected with the qualifying lessor or with any of the qualifying lessors, and

(II) uses any farm land leased from the qualifying lessor or the qualifying lessors for the purpose of a trade of farming carried on solely or in partnership,

or

(ii) a company which—

(I) is not connected with the qualifying lessor or with any of the qualifying lessors,

(II) is not controlled either directly or indirectly by any person who is connected with the qualifying lessor or with any of the qualifying lessors, and

(III) uses any farm land leased from the qualifying lessor or the qualifying lessors for the purpose of a trade of farming carried on solely or in partnership;][1]

"*qualifying lessor*" means an individual who—

[...][2]

(ii) has not after the 30th day of January, 1985, leased the farm land which is the subject of the qualifying lease from a person or persons, who is or are, or one of whom is, connected with him or her, on terms which are not such as might have been expected to be included in a lease if the negotiations for the lease had been at arm's length;

"*the specified amount*", in relation to any surplus or surpluses (within the meaning of *section 97(1)*) arising in respect of the rent or the rents from any farm land let under a qualifying lease or qualifying leases, means, subject to *paragraph (b)*, the lesser of—

(i) the amount of that surplus or the aggregate amount of those surpluses,

(ii) as respects a qualifying lease or qualifying leases made—

(I) in the period beginning on the 6th day of April, 1985, and ending on the 19th day of January, 1987, [€2,539.48][3],

(II) in the period beginning on the 20th day of January, 1987, and ending on the 31st day of December, 1987, [€3,555.27][4],

(III) in the period beginning on the 1st day of January, 1988, and ending on the 29th day of January, 1991, [€2,539.48][5],

(IV) in the period beginning on the 30th day of January, 1991, and ending on the 22nd day of January, 1996—

(A) [€5,078.95][6], in a case where the qualifying lease or qualifying leases is or are for a definite term of 7 years or more, and

(B) [€3,809.21][7], [in any other case,][8]

[(V) in the period beginning on 23 January 1996, and ending on 31 December 2003—

(A) €7,618.43, in a case where the qualifying lease or qualifying leases is or are for a definite term of 7 years or more, and

(B) €5,078.95, in any other case,

[...][9]][10]

[(VI) in the period beginning on 1 January 2004 and ending on 31 December 2005—

(A) €10,000, in a case where the qualifying lease or qualifying leases is or are for a definite term of 7 years or more, and

(B) €7,500, in any other case,

[...][11]

[(VII) in the period beginning on 1 January 2006 and ending on 31 December 2006—

(A) €15,000, in a case where the qualifying lease or qualifying leases is or are for a definite term of 7 years or more, and

(B) €12,000, in any other case,

or

(VIII) ["in the period beginning on 1 January 2007 and ending on 31 December 2014"][12]

(A) €20,000, in a case where the qualifying lease or qualifying leases is or are for a definite term of 10 years or more,

(B) €15,000, in a case where the qualifying lease or qualifying leases is or are for a definite term of 7 years or more, other than a case to which clause (A) applies, and

(C) €12,000, in any other case,][13]][14]

[(IX) on or after 1 January 2015—

(A) €40,000, in a case where the qualifying lease or qualifying leases is or are for a definite term of 15 years or more,

(B) €30,000, in a case where the qualifying lease or qualifying leases is or are for a definite term of 10 years or more, other than a case to which *clause (A)* applies,

(C) €22,500, in a case where the qualifying lease or qualifying leases is or are for a definite term of 7 years or more, other than a case to which either *clause (A)* or *clause (B)* applies, and

(D) €18,000, in any other case,][15]

and

(iii) where the rent or rents was or were not receivable in respect of a full year's letting or lettings, such amount as bears to the amount determined in accordance with [*subparagraph (I), (II), (III), (IV), (V), (VI), (VII)*[, *(VIII)* or *(IX)*,][16] as may be appropriate, of *paragraph (ii)* of this definition][17] the same proportion as the amount of the rent or the aggregate amount of the rents bears to the amount of the rent or the aggregate amount of the rents which would be receivable for a full year's letting or lettings.

(b) Where the income of a qualifying lessor consists of or includes rent or rents—

(i) from a qualifying lease or qualifying leases made in the period beginning on the 20th day of January, 1987, and ending on the 31st day of December, 1987, and from a qualifying lease made—

(I) in the period beginning on the 6th day of April, 1985, and ending on the 19th day of January, 1987, or

(II) in the period beginning on the 1st day of January, 1988, and ending on the 29th day of January, 1991,

the specified amount shall not exceed [€3,555.27][18];

(ii) from a qualifying lease or qualifying leases made in the period beginning on the 30th day of January, 1991, and ending on the 22nd day of January, 1996, and from a qualifying lease made before the 30th day of January, 1991, the specified amount shall not exceed—

(I) [€5,078.95][19], in a case where the qualifying lease or qualifying leases is or are for a definite term of 7 years or more, and

(II) [€3,809.21][20], in any other case;

[(iii) from a qualifying lease or qualifying leases made in the period beginning on 23 January 1996, and ending on 31 December 2003, and from a qualifying lease made before 23 January 1996, the specified amount shall not exceed—

(I) €7,618.43, in a case where the qualifying lease or qualifying leases is or are for a definite term of 7 years or more, and

(II) €5,078.95, in any other case;

[(iv) from a qualifying lease or qualifying leases made in the period beginning on 1 January 2004, and ending on 31 December 2005, and from a qualifying lease made before 1 January 2004, the specified amount shall not exceed—

(I) €10,000, in a case where the qualifying lease or qualifying leases is or are for a definite term of 7 years or more, and

(II) €7,500, in any other case;

[(v) from a qualifying lease or qualifying leases made in the period beginning on 1 January 2006 and ending on 31 December 2006, and from a qualifying lease made before 1 January 2006, the specified amount shall not exceed—

(I) €15,000, in a case where the qualifying lease or qualifying leases is or are for a definite term of 7 years or more, and

(II) €12,000, in any other case;

[(vi) from a qualifying lease or qualifying leases made in the period beginning on 1 January 2007 and ending on 31 December 2014, and from a qualifying lease made before 1 January 2007, the specified amount shall not exceed—

(I) €20,000, in a case where the qualifying lease or qualifying leases is or are for a definite term of 10 years or more,

(II) €15,000, in a case where the qualifying lease or qualifying leases is or are for a definite term of 7 years or more, other than a case to which *clause (I)* applies, and

(III) €12,000, in any other case;

(vii) from a qualifying lease or qualifying leases made on or after 1 January 2015, and from a qualifying lease made at any other time, the specified amount shall not exceed—

(I) €40,000, in a case where the qualifying lease or qualifying leases is or are for a definite term of 15 years or more,

(II) €30,000, in a case where the qualifying lease or qualifying leases is or are for a definite term of 10 years or more, other than a case to which *clause (I)* applies,

(III) €22,500, in a case where the qualifying lease or qualifying leases is or are for a definite term of 7 years or more, other than a case to which either *clause (I)* or *clause (II)* applies, and

(IV) €18,000, in any other case.][21]][22]][23]][24]

(2) Where for any year of assessment—

(a) the total income of a qualifying lessor consists of or includes any profits or gains chargeable to tax under Case V of Schedule D, and

(b) any surplus or surpluses (within the meaning of *section 97(1)*) arising in respect of the rent or rents from any farm land let under a qualifying lease or qualifying leases has been or have been taken into account in computing the amount of those profits or gains,

the qualifying lessor shall in determining that total income be entitled to a deduction of the lesser of—

(i) the specified amount in relation to the surplus or surpluses, and

(ii) the amount of the profits or gains.

[(3) The amount of any deduction due under *subsection (2)* shall—

(a) where by virtue of *section 1017* a woman's income is deemed to be her husband's income, be determined separately as regards the part of his income which is his by virtue of that section and the part which is his apart from that section,

(b) where by virtue of *section 1017* a man's income is deemed to be his wife's income, be determined separately as regards the part of her income which is hers by virtue of that section and the part which is hers apart from that section, or

(c) where by virtue of *section 1031C* an individual's income is deemed to be his or her civil partner's income, be determined separately as regards the part of his or her income which is his or hers by virtue of that section and the part which is his or hers apart from that section,

and where *section 1023* or *1031H*, as the case may be, applies, any deduction allowed by virtue of *subsection (2)* shall be allocated to the person and to his or her spouse or civil partner as if they were not married or civil partners.][25]

(4) (a) For the purposes of *subsection (2)*, where a single qualifying lease relates to both farm land and other property, goods or services, only such amount, if any, of the surplus arising in respect of the rent payable under the lease as is determined by the inspector and after such apportionments of rent, expenses and other deductions as are necessary, according to the best of the inspector's knowledge and judgment, to be properly attributable to the lease of the farm land shall be treated as a surplus arising in respect of a rent from farm land let under a qualifying lease.

(b) Any amount which by virtue of *paragraph (a)* is determined by the inspector may be amended by the Appeal Commissioners or by the Circuit Court on the hearing or the rehearing of an appeal against that determination.

(5) For the purposes of determining the amount of any relief to be granted under this section, the inspector may by notice in writing require the lessor to furnish such information as the inspector considers necessary.

(6) (a) *Subsections (1)* and *(2)* of *section 459* and *section 460* shall apply to a deduction under this section as they apply to any allowance, deduction, relief or reduction under the provisions specified in the Table to *section 458*.

(b) *Subsections (3)* and *(4)* of *section 459* and *paragraph 8* of *Schedule 28* shall, with any necessary modifications, apply in relation to a deduction under this section.

[(7) Notwithstanding any other provisions of the Tax Acts, for the purposes of determining the amount of any relief to be granted under this section, any payment received by the lessor, relating to the leasing of farm land under a qualifying lease, which is in consequence of the receipt or the expected receipt by the lessee of a payment relating to that farm land under the EU Single Payment Scheme operated by the Department of Agriculture and Food under Council Regulation (EC) No. 1782/2003 of 29 September 2003*, will be treated as rent from farm land.][26]

* OJ No. L270 of 21.10.2003, p.1

Amendments

[1] Substituted by FA14 s20(b)(i). Comes into operation on 1 January 2015.

[2] Deleted by FA14 s20(b)(ii). Comes into operation on 1 January 2015.

[3, 4, 5, 6, 7, 18, 19, 20] Substituted by FA01 s240 and sched5 part1.

[8] Substituted by FA04 s14(1)(a)(ii)(I). Applies and has effect as on and from 1 January 2004.

[9] Deleted by FA06 s12(1)(a)(i).

[10] Substituted by FA04 s14(1)(a)(ii)(II). Applies and has effect as on and from 1 January 2004.

[11] Deleted by FA07 s16(1)(a)(i). Applies as on and from 1 January 2007.

[12] Substituted by FA14 s20(b)(iii). Comes into operation on 1 January 2015.

[13] Substituted by FA07 s16(1)(a)(ii). Applies as on and from 1 January 2007.

[14] Substituted by FA06 s12(1)(a)(ii).

[15] Inserted by FA14 s20(b)(iv). Comes into operation on 1 January 2015.

[16] Substituted by FA14 s20(b)(v). Comes into operation on 1 January 2015.

[17] Substituted by FA07 s16(1)(a)(iii). Applies as on and from 1 February 2007.

[21] Substituted by FA14 s20(c). Comes into operation on 1 January 2015.

[22] Substituted by FA07 s16(1)(b). Applies as on and from 1 January 2007.

[23] Substituted by FA06 s12(1)(b).

[24] Substituted by FA04 s14(1)(b). Applies and has effect as on and from 1 January 2004.

[25] Substituted by F(No.3)A11 sched1(175).

[26] Inserted by FA06 s12(1)(c). Applies and has effect as on and from 1 January 2005.

Revenue Briefings

Tax Briefing

Tax Briefing December 2006 – Issue 65 – Single Farm Payment – Finance Act 2006 Amendments

Tax Briefing July 2007 – Issue 66 – Finance Act 2007 – Section 16 amends section 664 of the Taxes Consolidation Act 1997

Revenue Precedents

A verbal agreement was made to lease land for a five year period. A written agreement evidencing the verbal agreement was drawn up at the commencement of the final year of the lease. The issue is whether relief can be claimed for all years since the commencement of the verbal agreement. The Commissioners would consider granting relief under section 664 Taxes Consolidation Act 1997 if – (a) the lessor could prove to the satisfaction of the Inspector of Taxes that the farmland had actually been leased in the period and that he had received rental income from the leasing and had returned same for income tax purposes, and (b) all the other conditions provided for in section 664 Taxes Consolidation Act, 1997 had been met. IT923012

A niece or nephew is not connected with an uncle or aunt for the purposes of this section. IT943037

Cross References

From Section 664

Section 52 Persons chargeable.
Section 96 Interpretation (Chapter 8).
Section 97 Computational rules and allowable deductions.
Section 458 Deductions allowed in ascertaining taxable income and provisions relating to reductions in tax.
Section 459 General provisions relating to allowances, deductions and reliefs.
Section 460 Rate of tax at which repayments are to be made.
Section 1017 Assessment of husband in respect of income of both spouses.
Section 1023 Application for separate assessments.
Schedule 28 Statements, Lists and Declarations

To Section 664

Section 531B Charge to income levy.
Section 531AM Charge to universal social charge.
Section 654 Interpretation (Part 23).

664A Relief for increase in carbon tax on farm diesel

[(1) In this section—

'*accounting period*', in relation to a person, means—

(a) where the person is a company, an accounting period determined in accordance with *section 27*, or

(b) where the person is not a company, a period of one year ending on the date to which the accounts of the person are usually made up,

but, where accounts have not been made up or where accounts have been made up for a greater or lesser period than one year, the accounting period shall be such period not exceeding one year as the Revenue Commissioners may determine;

'*carbon tax*' means the carbon charge referred to in *section 96(1A)* (inserted by *section 64(1)(f)* of the Finance Act 2010) of the Finance Act 1999;

'*farm diesel*' means the mineral oil described as 'other heavy oil' in *Schedule 2A* to the Finance Act 1999 used by a person in the carrying on of a trade of farming, but does not include such oil used for the purpose of home heating;

'*relevant carbon tax*' means an amount equivalent to the amount determined by the formula—

$$A - B$$

where—

A is the amount of the carbon tax included in a deduction in respect of farm diesel in the computation by a person of the amount of the profits or gains of that person to be charged to tax under Case I of Schedule D, and

B is the amount of the carbon tax that would have been included in that deduction if the amount of the carbon tax had been calculated at the rate of €41.30 per 1,000 litres of farm diesel.

(2) Where—

(a) a person carries on in an accounting period a trade of farming in respect of which the person is within the charge to tax under Case I of Schedule D, and

(b) in the computation of the amount of the profits or gains of that trade the person is, apart from this section, entitled to any deduction on account of farm diesel,

then such person shall be entitled in that computation to a further deduction for farm diesel of an amount equal to the relevant carbon tax.][1]

Amendments

[1] Inserted by FA12 s20(a). Deemed to have come into force and takes effect on and from 1 January 2012.

CHAPTER 2

Farming: Relief for Increase in Stock Values

665 Interpretation (Chapter 2)

[FA96 s133]

In this Chapter—

"*accounting period*", in relation to a person, means—

(a) where the person is a company, an accounting period determined in accordance with *section 27*, or

(b) where the person is not a company, a period of one year ending on the date to which the accounts of the person are usually made up,

but, where accounts have not been made up or where accounts have been made up for a greater or lesser period than one year, the accounting period shall be such period not exceeding one year as the Revenue Commissioners may determine;

"*chargeable period*" has the same meaning as in *section 321(2)*;

"*company*" has the same meaning as in *section 4*;

"*period of account*", in relation to a person, means a period for which the accounts of the person have been made up;

[…][1]

"*specified return date for the chargeable period*" has the same meaning as in [*section 959A*][2]

"*trading income*", in relation to the trade of farming, means—

(a) where the person is a company, the income from the trade computed in accordance with the rules applicable to Case I of Schedule D, or

(b) in the case of any other person, the profits or gains of the trade computed in accordance with the rules applicable to Case I of Schedule D;

"*trading stock*", in relation to the trade of farming, has the same meaning as in *section 89* and, in determining the value of a person's trading stock at any time for the purposes of a deduction under *section 666*, to the extent that at or before that time any payments on account have been received by the person in respect of any trading stock, the value of that stock shall be reduced accordingly.

Amendments

[1] Deleted by FA01 s46.

[2] Substituted by FA12 sched4(part 2)(g).

Revenue Briefings

Tax Briefing

Tax Briefing September 2010 – Issue 12 – Share Farming

Revenue Precedents

Does the definition of trading stock for the purposes of stock relief include such items as fertilisers, pesticides, purchased feeds, home produced feeds, diesel and machinery parts? The definition of trading stock in section 89 Taxes Consolidation Act 1997 includes "materials such as are used in the manufacture, preparation, or construction of property such as is sold in the ordinary course of that trade". Stock relief should therefore be allowed on items which are inputs to the property which is sold in the ordinary course of the business (e.g. feed, fertiliser, seeds, etc). It should not be allowed on expense stocks such as machine parts, diesel etc. IT903005

Is deer farming regarded as a separate trade from farming?. Are deer regarded as trading stock for the purposes of stock relief? A person involved in deer farming is regarded as carrying on the trade of farming. Where deer farming is carried on in conjunction with another farming enterprise; the two enterprises are regarded as one trade for the purposes of tax. Deer are regarded as trading stock for the purposes of stock relief. IT923019

Cross References

From Section 665

Section 4 Interpretation of Corporation Tax Acts.
Section 27 Basis of, and periods for, assessment.
Section 89 Valuation of trading stock at discontinuance of trade.
Section 321 Provisions of general application in relation to the making of allowances and charges.
Section 666 Deduction for increase in stock values.
Section 950 Interpretation (Part 41).

666 Deduction for increase in stock values

[FA96 s134; FA97 s18]

(1) Subject to this Chapter, where—

(a) a person carries on in an accounting period the trade of farming in respect of which the person is within the charge to tax under Case I of Schedule D, and

(b) the value of the person's trading stock of that trade at the end of the accounting period (in this Chapter referred to as its "*closing stock value*") exceeds the value of the trading stock of that trade at the beginning of the accounting period (in this Chapter referred to as its "*opening stock value*"),

the person shall, in the computation for the purposes of tax of the trading income of that trade, be entitled to a deduction under this section equal to 25 per cent of the amount of that excess as if the deduction were a trading expense incurred in the accounting period, and the amount of that excess is referred to in this Chapter as the person's "increase in stock value".

(2) In the case of a company—

(a) the amount of the deduction under this section in an accounting period shall not exceed the amount of the company's trading income for that period after all reductions of income for that period by virtue of *sections 396* and *397* and after all deductions and additions for that period by virtue of *sections 307* and *308* and before any deduction allowed by virtue of this section, and

(b) where a deduction allowed by virtue of this section in computing the company's income from the trade of farming for an accounting period applies for an accounting period (in this subsection referred to as "*the relevant period*"), the company shall not be entitled to—

(i) a deduction under *section 307* or *308* for any accounting period later than the relevant period in respect of any allowance treated as a trading loss of the trade before the commencement of the relevant period,

(ii) a set-off of a loss under *section 396* for any accounting period later than the relevant period in respect of a loss sustained in the trade before the commencement of the relevant period, or

(iii) a set-off of a loss under *section 397* for any accounting period earlier than the relevant period in respect of a loss sustained in the trade.

(3) In the case of a person other than a company, where a deduction allowed by virtue of this section in computing the person's trading profits of the trade of farming for an accounting period applies for a year of assessment (in this subsection referred to as "*the relevant year*")—

(a) the person shall not be entitled to relief—

(i) under *section 382* for any year of assessment later than the relevant year in respect of a loss sustained in the trade before the commencement of the relevant year, or

(ii) under *section 385* for any year of assessment earlier than the relevant year in respect of a loss sustained in the trade,

(b) *section 304(4)* or that section as applied by any other provision of the Income Tax Acts shall not apply as respects a capital allowance or part of a capital allowance which is or is deemed to be all or part of a capital allowance for the relevant year and to which full effect has not been given in that year because there were no profits or gains chargeable for that year or there was an insufficiency of profits or gains chargeable for that year,

(c) *section 392* shall not apply to the capital allowances or any part of such allowances for the relevant year, and

(d) the amount of any deduction given under this section shall not exceed the amount of the person's trading income from the trade of farming for the relevant year before any deduction allowed by virtue of this section.

[(4) (a) A deduction shall not be allowed under this section in computing a company's trading income for any accounting period which ends after [31 December 2015][1].

(b) Any deduction allowed by virtue of this section in computing the profits or gains of the trade of farming for an accounting period of a person other than a company shall not apply for any purpose of the Income Tax Acts for any year of assessment later than the [year 2015][2].][3]

(5) A person shall not be entitled to a deduction under this section for any chargeable period unless a written claim for such a deduction is made on or before the specified return date for that chargeable period.

(6) This section shall apply to a trade of farming carried on by a partnership as it applies to a trade of farming carried on by a person.

Amendments

[1] Substituted by FA13 s20(1)(a)(i). With effect from 3 October 2013 per S.I. No. 378 of 2013.

[2] Substituted by FA13 s20(1)(a)(ii). With effect from 3 October 2013 per S.I. No. 378 of 2013.

[3] Substituted by FA05 s31(1). This section comes into operation on 3 February 2005.

Cross References

From Section 666

Section 304 Income tax: allowances and charges in taxing a trade, etc.
Section 307 Corporation tax: allowances and charges in taxing a trade.
Section 308 Corporation tax: manner of granting, and effect of, allowances made by means of discharge or repayment of tax.
Section 382 Right to carry forward losses to future years.
Section 385 Terminal loss.
Section 392 Option to treat capital allowances as creating or augmenting a loss.
Section 396 Relief for trading losses other than terminal losses.
Section 397 Relief for terminal loss in a trade.

To Section 666

Section 517 Payments to trustees of approved profit sharing scheme.
Section 665 Interpretation (Chapter 2).

Section 667 Special provisions for qualifying farmers.
Section 667A Further provisions for qualifying farmers.
Section 667B New arrangements for qualifying farmers.
Section 668 Compulsory disposals of livestock.
Section 669 Supplementary provisions (Chapter 2).
Section 669K Miscellaneous (Chapter 4).

667 Special provisions for qualifying farmers

[FA94 Sch6; FA96 s135; FA97 s19]

(1) [In this section, but subject to *section 667A*,][1] "*qualifying farmer*" means an individual who—

(a) in the year 1993-94 or any subsequent year of assessment first qualifies for grant aid under the Scheme of Installation Aid for Young Farmers operated by the Department of Agriculture and Food under Council Regulation (EEC) No. 797/85 of 12 March 1985* or that Regulation as may be revised from time to time, or

* O.J. No. L93 of 30.3.1985, p.6.

(b) (i) first becomes chargeable to income tax under Case I of Schedule D in respect of profits or gains from the trade of farming for the year 1993-94 or any subsequent year of assessment,

(ii) has not attained the age of 35 years at the commencement of the year of assessment referred to in *subparagraph (i)*, and

(iii) at any time in the year of assessment so referred to—

(I) is the holder of a qualification set out in the Table to this section (in this subparagraph referred to as "the Table") and, in the case of a qualification set out in *subparagraph (c), (d), (e), (f)* or *(g)* of *paragraph 3*, or in *paragraph 4*, of the Table, is also the holder of a certificate issued by Teagasc — The Agricultural and Food Development Authority (in this section referred to as "Teagasc") certifying that such person has satisfactorily attended a course of training in farm management the aggregate duration of which exceeded 80 hours; but, where Teagasc certifies that any other qualification corresponds to a qualification set out in the Table, that other qualification shall for the purposes of this subsection be treated as if it were the corresponding qualification so set out,[or][2]

(II) (A) has satisfactorily attended full-time a course at a third-level institution in any discipline for a period of not less than 2 years' duration, and

(B) is the holder of a certificate issued by Teagasc certifying satisfactory attendance at a course of training in either or both agriculture and horticulture the aggregate duration of which exceeded [180 hours.][3]

[...][4]

[...][5]

(2) In the case of a qualifying farmer—

(a) *section 666(1)* shall apply as if "100 per cent" were substituted for "25 percent";

(b) *paragraph (a)* shall apply in computing a person's trading profits for an accounting period in the case of an individual who becomes a qualifying farmer—

(i) on or after the 6th day of April, 1993, and before the 6th day of April, 1995, for the year of assessment 1995-96 and for each of the 3 immediately succeeding [years of assessment, or][6]

[(ii) on or after 6 April 1995 and on or before 31 December 2004, for the year of assessment in which the individual becomes a qualifying farmer and for each of the 3 immediately succeeding years of assessment.][7]

TABLE

1. Qualifications awarded by Teagasc:

(a) Certificate in Farming;

(b) Diploma in Commercial Horticulture;

(c) Diploma in Amenity Horticulture;

(d) Diploma in Pig Production;

(e) Diploma in Poultry Production.

2. Qualifications awarded by the Farm Apprenticeship Board:

(a) Certificate in Farm Management;

(b) Certificate in Farm Husbandry;

(c) Trainee Farmer Certificate.

3. Qualifications awarded by a third-level institution:

(a) Degree in Agricultural Science awarded by the National University of Ireland through the National University of Ireland, Dublin;

(b) Degree in Horticultural Science awarded by the National University of Ireland through the National University of Ireland, Dublin;

(c) Degree in Veterinary Science awarded by the National University of Ireland through the National University of Ireland, Dublin;

(d) Degree in Rural Science awarded by the National University of Ireland through the National University of Ireland, Cork or by the University of Limerick;

(e) Diploma in Rural Science awarded by the National University of Ireland through the National University of Ireland, Cork;

(f) Degree in Dairy Science awarded by the National University of Ireland through the National University of Ireland, Cork;

(g) Diploma in Dairy Science awarded by the National University of Ireland through the National University of Ireland, Cork.

4. Certificates awarded by the National Council for Educational Awards:

(a) National Certificate in Agricultural Science studied through Kildalton Agricultural College and Waterford Regional Technical College;

(b) National Certificate in Business Studies (Agribusiness) studied through the Franciscan Brothers Agricultural College, Mountbellew, and Galway Regional Technical College.

Amendments

[1] Substituted by FA04 s13(1)(a)(i). Applies and has effect as on and from 1 January 2004.

[2] Inserted by FA04 s13(1)(a)(ii)(I). Applies and has effect as on and from 1 January 2004.

[3] Substituted by FA04 s13(1)(a)(ii)(II). Applies and has effect as on and from 1 January 2004.

[4] Deleted by FA04 s13(1)(a)(ii)(II). Applies and has effect as on and from 1 January 2004.

[5] Deleted by FA04 s13(1)(a)(ii)(III). Applies and has effect as on and from 1 January 2004.

[6] Substituted by FA98 s39(a).

[7] Substituted by FA03 s19(1). With effect from 1 January 2003 as per S.I. No. 427 of 2004.

Revenue Precedents

Is a young farmer regarded as being a holder of a qualification in the year he completes his Teagasc course or in the year he receives his certificate? An individual would be regarded as holding a qualification once he has been conferred with a degree/diploma or presented with a certificate. The Certificate in Farming qualification is presented in September or October each year. IT963010

Cross References

From Section 667

Section 666 Deduction for increase in stock values.

Section 667A Further provisions for qualifying farmers.

To Section 667

Section 667A Further provisions for qualifying farmers.

667A Further provisions for qualifying farmers

[(1) In this section "*qualifying farmer*" means an individual who—

(a) in the year 2004 or any subsequent year of assessment first qualifies for grant aid under the Scheme of Installation Aid for Young Farmers operated by the Department of Agriculture and Food under Council Regulation (EEC) No. 797/85 of 12 March 1985* or that Regulation as may be revised from time to time, or

* OJ No. L93, 30.3.1985, p.6

(b) (i) first becomes chargeable to income tax under Case I of Schedule D in respect of profits or gains from the trade of farming for the year 2004 or any subsequent year of assessment,

(ii) has not attained the age of 35 years at the commencement of the year of assessment referred to in *subparagraph (i)*, and

(iii) at any time in the year of assessment so referred to satisfies the conditions set out in *subsection (2)*, *(3)* or *(4)*.

(2) The conditions required by this subsection are that the individual, referred to in the definition of "*qualifying farmer*" in *subsection (1)*, is the holder of a qualification set out in the Table to this section (in this section referred to as the "*Table*"), and—

(a) in the case of a qualification set out in *paragraph 1(f)* or *paragraph 2(h)* of the Table, is also the holder of a certificate awarded by the Further Education and Training Awards Council for achieving the minimum stipulated standard in assessments completed in a course of training, approved by Teagasc—

(i) in either or both agriculture and horticulture, the aggregate duration of which exceeded 100 hours, and

(ii) in farm management, the aggregate duration of which exceeded 80 hours,

or

(b) in the case of a qualification set out in *subparagraph (b)*, *(c)* or *(d)* of *paragraph 3* of the Table, is also the holder of a certificate awarded by the Further Education and Training Awards Council for achieving the minimum stipulated standard in assessments completed in a course of training, approved by Teagasc, in farm management, the aggregate duration of which exceeded 80 hours.

(3) The conditions required by this subsection are that the individual, referred to in the definition of "*qualifying farmer*" in *subsection (1)*—

(a) has achieved the required standard for entry into the third year of a full-time course of 3 or more years" duration in any discipline at a third-level institution and that has been confirmed by that institution, and

(b) is the holder of a certificate awarded by the Further Education and Training Awards Council for achieving a minimum stipulated standard in assessments completed in a course of training, approved by Teagasc—

(i) in either or both agriculture and horticulture, the aggregate duration of which exceeded 100 hours, and

(ii) in farm management, the aggregate duration of which exceeded 80 hours.

(4) The conditions required by this subsection are that the individual, referred to in the definition of "*qualifying farmer*" in *subsection (1)*, is the holder of a letter of confirmation from Teagasc confirming satisfactory completion of a course of training, approved by Teagasc, for persons who in the opinion of Teagasc are restricted in their learning capacity due to physical, sensory, mental health or intellectual disability.

(5) For the purposes of *subsection (2)* where Teagasc certifies that—

(a) any other qualification corresponds to a qualification set out in the Table, and

(b) that other qualification is deemed by the National Qualifications Authority of Ireland to be at least at a standard equivalent to that of the qualification set out in the Table,

then that other qualification shall be treated as if it were the qualification set out in the Table.

(6) In the case of a qualifying farmer—

(a) *section 666(1)* shall apply as if "100 per cent" were substituted for "25 per cent", and

(b) *paragraph (a)* shall apply in computing a person's trading profits for an accounting period in the case of an individual who becomes a qualifying farmer at any time in the period beginning on or after 1 January 2004 and ending on or before [31 December 2008][1], for the year of assessment in which the individual becomes a qualifying farmer and for each of the 3 immediately succeeding years of assessment.

(7) For the purposes of this section, an individual who, before 1 January 2004—

(a) is the holder of a qualification set out in the Table to *section 667* or a qualification certified by Teagasc as corresponding to such a qualification so set out, in respect of which—

(i) satisfactory attendance at a course of training in farm management, the aggregate duration of which exceeded 80 hours, is required in order for the conditions of *paragraph (b)(iii)* of the definition of "*qualifying farmer*" in *section 667(1)* to be satisfied, shall be deemed to be the holder of a qualification corresponding to that set out in *paragraph 3(b)* of the Table, or

(ii) satisfactory attendance at a course of training is not required in order for the conditions of *paragraph (b)(iii)* of the definition of "*qualifying farmer*" in *section 667(1)* to be satisfied, shall be deemed to be the holder of a qualification corresponding to that set out in *paragraph 2(a)* of the Table,

(b) satisfies the requirements set out in *paragraph (b)(iii)(II)(A)* of the definition of "*qualifying farmer*" in *section 667(1)*, shall be deemed to satisfy the requirements set out in *subsection (3)(a)*, and

(c) is the holder of a certificate issued by Teagasc certifying satisfactory attendance at a course of training—

(i) in farm management, the aggregate duration of which exceeded 80 hours, shall be deemed to be the holder of a certificate referred to in *subsection (2)(b)*, or

(ii) in either or both agriculture and horticulture, the aggregate duration of which exceeded 180 hours, shall be deemed to be the holder of a certificate referred to in *subsection (2)(a)*.

TABLE

1. Qualifications awarded by the Further Education and Training Awards Council:

(a) Vocational Certificate in Agriculture — Level 3;

(b) Advanced Certificate in Agriculture;

(c) Vocational Certificate in Horticulture — Level 3;

(d) Vocational Certificate in Horse Breeding and Training — Level 3;

(e) Vocational Certificate in Forestry — Level 3;

(f) Awards other than those referred to in *subparagraphs (a)* to *(e)* which are, at least, at a standard equivalent to that of the award referred to in *subparagraph (a)*.

2. Qualifications awarded by the Higher Education and Training Awards Council:

(a) National Certificate in Agriculture;

(b) National Diploma in Agriculture;

(c) National Certificate in Science in Agricultural Science;

(d) National Certificate in Business Studies in Agri-Business;

(e) National Certificate in Technology in Agricultural Mechanisation;

(f) National Diploma in Horticulture;

(g) National Certificate in Business Studies in Equine Studies;

(h) National Certificate or Diploma awards other than those referred to in *subparagraphs (a)* to *(g)*.

3. Qualifications awarded by other third-level institutions:

(a) Primary degrees awarded by the faculties of General Agriculture and Veterinary Medicine at University College Dublin;

(b) Bachelor of Science (Education) in Biological Sciences awarded by the University of Limerick;

(c) Bachelor of Science in Equine Science awarded by the University of Limerick;

(d) Diploma or Certificate in Science (Equine Science) awarded by the University of Limerick.

Amendments

[1] Substituted by FA07 s24(1)(b). This section comes into operation on the making of an order to that effect by the Minister for Finance.

Cross References

From Section 667A

Section 666 Deduction for increase in stock values.

Section 667 Special provisions for qualifying farmers.

To Section 667A

Section 667 Special provisions for qualifying farmers.

Section 667B New arrangements for qualifying farmers.

667B New arrangements for qualifying farmers

[(1) In this section "*qualifying farmer*" means an individual—

(a) (i) who in the year of assessment 2007 or any subsequent year of assessment first qualifies for grant aid under the scheme of Installation Aid for Young Farmers operated by the Department of Agriculture, Food and the Marine under Council Regulation (EEC) No. 797/85 of 12 March 1985* or that Regulation as may be revised from time to time, or

*OJ No. L93, 30.3.1985, p.6

(ii) who—

(I) first becomes chargeable to income tax under Case I of Schedule D in respect of profits or gains from the trade of farming for the year of assessment 2007 or any subsequent year of assessment,

(II) has not attained the age of 35 years at the commencement of the year of assessment referred to in clause (I), and

(III) at any time in the year of assessment so referred to satisfies the conditions set out in *subsection (2)* or *(3)*,

and

(b) who, where the requirements of *subparagraph (i)* or *(ii)* of *paragraph (a)* are first satisfied in the year of assessment 2012 or any subsequent year of assessment (in this paragraph referred to as the "*first year of assessment*"), submits a business plan to—

(i) Teagasc, for the purpose of this section, or

(ii) Teagasc or the Minister for Agriculture, Food and the Marine, for any other purpose,

on or before 31 October in the year following the first year of assessment.][1]

(2) The conditions required by this subsection are that the individual, referred to in the definition of "*qualifying farmer*" in *subsection (1)*, is the holder of a qualification set out in the Table to this section (in this section referred to as the "*Table*").

(3) The conditions required by this subsection are that the individual, referred to in the definition of "*qualifying farmer*" in *subsection (1)*, is the holder of a letter of confirmation from Teagasc confirming satisfactory completion of a course of training, approved by Teagasc, for persons who in the opinion of Teagasc are restricted in their learning capacity due to physical, sensory, or intellectual disability or to mental health.

(4) For the purposes of *subsection (2)* where Teagasc certifies that—

(a) any other qualification corresponds to a qualification set out in the Table, and

(b) that other qualification is deemed by [the Qualifications and Quality Assurance Authority of Ireland][2] to be at least at a level equivalent to that of the qualification set out in the Table,

then that other qualification will be treated as if it were the qualification set out in the Table.

(5) In the case of a qualifying farmer—

(a) *section 666(1)* will apply as if "100 per cent" were substituted for "25 per cent", and

(b) *paragraph (a)* will apply in computing a person's trading profits for an accounting period in the case of an individual who becomes a qualifying farmer at any time in the period beginning on or after 1 January 2007 and ending on or before [31 December 2015][3], for the year of assessment in which the individual becomes a qualifying farmer and for each of the 3 immediately succeeding years of assessment.

[(5A) (a) In this subsection—

"*qualifying period*", in relation to a qualifying farmer, means the year of assessment in which an individual becomes a qualifying farmer and each of the 3 immediately succeeding years of assessment;

"*relevant tax*" means any income tax or universal social charge;

"*relief* " means an amount equivalent to an amount determined by the formula—

$$A - B$$

where—

A is the amount of relevant tax that would be payable by a qualifying farmer for a year of assessment falling within the qualifying period computed as if *subsection (5)* had not been enacted, and

B is the amount of relevant tax payable by the qualifying farmer for that year of assessment.

(b) Where a qualifying period commences in the year of assessment 2012 or any subsequent year of assessment, the qualifying farmer shall be entitled to relief in respect of deductions under *section 666(1)*, by virtue of *subsection (5)*, of an amount not exceeding—

(i) in the aggregate in the qualifying period, €70,000, and

(ii) in any one year of assessment falling within the qualifying period, €40,000.][4]

(6) An individual who, at any time before 31 March 2008, satisfies the conditions referred to in *paragraph (b)(iii)* of the definition of "*qualifying farmer*" in *section 667A (1)* will be deemed to satisfy the conditions referred to [in *paragraph (a)(ii)(III)* of the definition of "*qualifying farmer*" in *subsection (1)*][5].

[(7) This section shall apply to a qualifying farmer who comes within the definition of "*small and medium-sized enterprises*" in Article 2 of Commission Regulation (EC) No. 1857/2006 of 15 December 2006*, and in respect of whom subsection (5) applies for the year of assessment 2012 or any subsequent year of assessment.][6]

*OJ No. L358, 16.12.2006, p.7

TABLE

1. [Qualifications awarded by the Qualifications and Quality Assurance Authority of Ireland][7]:

(a) Level 6 Advanced Certificate in Farming;

(b) Level 6 Advanced Certificate in Agriculture;

(c) Level 6 Advanced Certificate in Dairy Herd Management;

(d) Level 6 Advanced Certificate in Drystock Management;

(e) Level 6 Advanced Certificate in Agricultural Mechanisation;

(f) Level 6 Advanced Certificate in Farm Management;

(g) Level 6 Advanced Certificate in Machinery and Crop Management;

(h) Level 6 Advanced Certificate in Horticulture;

(i) Level 6 Advanced Certificate in Forestry;

(j) Level 6 Advanced Certificate in Stud Management;

(k) Level 6 Advanced Certificate in [Horsemanship;][8]

[(l) Level 6 Specific Purpose Certificate in Farm Administration.][9]

2. [Qualifications awarded by the Qualifications and Quality Assurance Authority of Ireland][10]:

(a) Higher Certificate in Agriculture;

(b) Bachelor of Science in Agriculture;

(c) Higher Certificate in Agricultural Science;

(d) Bachelor of Science in Agricultural Science;

(e) Bachelor of Science (Honours) in Land Management, Agriculture;

(f) Bachelor of Science (Honours) in Land Management, Horticulture;

(g) Bachelor of Science (Honours) in Land Management, Forestry;

(h) Higher Certificate in Engineering in Agricultural Mechanisation;

(i) Bachelor of Science in Rural Enterprise and Agri-Business;

(j) Bachelor of Science in Agriculture and Environmental Management;

(k) Bachelor of Science in Horticulture;

(l) Bachelor of Arts (Honours) in Horticultural Management;

(m) Bachelor of Science in Forestry;

(n) Higher Certificate in Business in Equine Studies;

(o) Bachelor of Science in [Equine Studies;][11]

[(p) Higher Certificate in Science [Applied Agriculture,][12]][13]

[(q) Bachelor of Science (Honours) in Sustainable Agriculture.][14]

3. Qualifications awarded by other third level institutions:

(a) Bachelor of Agricultural Science — Animal Crop Production awarded by University College Dublin;

[(aa) Bachelor of Agricultural Science — Agri-Environmental Science awarded by University College Dublin;][15]

(b) Bachelor of Agricultural Science — Animal Science awarded by University College Dublin;

[(ba) Bachelor of Agricultural Science – Animal Science Equine awarded by University College *Dublin;*

(bb) Bachelor of Agricultural Science – Dairy Business awarded by University College Dublin;][16]

(c) Bachelor of Agricultural Science — Food and Agribusiness Management awarded by University College Dublin;

(d) Bachelor of Agricultural Science — Forestry awarded by University College Dublin;

(e) Bachelor of Agricultural Science — Horticulture, Landscape and Sportsturf Management awarded by University College Dublin;

(f) Bachelor of Veterinary Medicine awarded by University College Dublin;

(g) Bachelor of Science in Equine Science awarded by the University of Limerick;

(h) Diploma in Equine Science awarded by the University of Limerick.".][17]

Amendments

[1] Substituted by FA13 s20(1)(b). With effect from 3 October 2013 per S.I. No. 378 of 2013.

[2] Substituted by F(No.2)A13 s20(1)(a). Applies with effect from 6 November 2012.

[3] Substituted by FA13 s20(1)(c). With effect from 3 October 2013 per S.I. No. 378 of 2013.

[4] Inserted by FA13 s20(1)(d). With effect from 3 October 2013 per S.I. No. 378 of 2013.

[5] Substituted by FA13 s20(1)(e). With effect from 3 October 2013 per S.I. No. 378 of 2013.

[6] Inserted by FA13 s20(1)(f). With effect from 3 October 2013 per S.I. No. 378 of 2013.

[7] Substituted by F(No.2)A13 s20(1)(b)(i). Applies with effect from 6 November 2012.

[8] Substituted by FA12 s20(b). Deemed to have come into force and takes effect on and from 1 January 2012.

[9] Inserted by FA12 s20(c). Deemed to have come into force and takes effect on and from 1 January 2012.

[10] Substituted by F(No.2)A13 s20(1)(b)(ii). Applies with effect from 6 November 2012.

[11] Substituted by F(No.2)A13 s20(1)(b)(iii)(I). Comes into operation on 1 January 2014.

[12] Substituted by FA14 s20(d)(i). Comes into operation on 1 January 2015.

[13] Inserted by F(No.2)A13 s20(1)(b)(iii)(II). Comes into operation on 1 January 2014.

[14] Inserted by FA14 s20(d)(ii). Comes into operation on 1 January 2015.

[15] Inserted by FA10 s14. Deemed to have come into force and takes effect as on and from 1 January 2010.

[16] Inserted by F(No.2)A13 s20(1)(b)(iv). Comes into operation on 1 January 2014.

[17] Inserted by FA07 s24(1)(c). This section comes into operation on the making of an order to that effect by the Minister for Finance.

Cross References

From Section 667B

Section 666 Deduction for increase in stock values.
Section 667A Further provisions for qualifying farmers.

667C Special Provisions for registered farm paternerships

[(1) In this section—

'*qualifying farmer*' has the meaning assigned to it by *section 667B*;

["*registered farm partnership*" means—

(a) a milk production partnership within the meaning of the European Communities (Milk Quota) Regulations 2008 (S.I. No. 227 of 2008), and

(b) a farm partnership included on a register of farm partnerships established by regulations made under *subsection (4A)*.][1]

(2) [Subject to *subsection (3) and (3A)*][2], where a person is a partner in a registered farm partnership, *section 666* shall apply as if in that section—

(a) in *subsection (1)* '50 per cent' were substituted for '25 per cent', and

(b) the following was substituted for *subsection (4)*—

'(4) (a) A deduction shall not be allowed under this section in computing a company's trading income for any accounting period which ends after 31 December 2015.

(b) Any deduction allowed by virtue of this section in computing the profits or gains of a trade of farming for an accounting period of a person other than a company shall not apply for any purpose of the Income Tax Acts for any year of assessment later than the year 2015.'

(3) Where a person referred to in *subsection (2)* is a qualifying farmer, *section 667B* shall apply for the purposes of this section as if in *subsection (5)(a)* of that section '50 per cent' were substituted for '25 per cent'.

[(3A) (a) In this subsection—

"*qualifying period*", in relation to a specified person—

(i) means an accounting period in respect of which that person is entitled to a relevant deduction and each subsequent accounting period where the accounting periods in aggregate do not exceed 36 months where the specified person is a company, and

(ii) where the specified person is not a company, means a year of assessment in which that person is entitled to a relevant deduction and each of the 2 immediately succeeding years of assessment where the specified person is not a company;

"*relevant deduction*" means a deduction under *section 666(1)*, in accordance with *subsection (2)(a)* of this section;

"*relevant tax*", in relation to a specified person—

(i) where the specified person is a company, means any corporation tax, and

(ii) where the specified person is not a company, means any income tax or universal social charge;

"*relief*" means an amount equivalent to an amount determined by the formula—

$$A - B$$

where—

A is the amount of relevant tax that would be payable by a specified person for a year of assessment or an accounting period, as the case may be, falling within the qualifying period computed as if *subsection (2)* had not been enacted, and

B is the amount of relevant tax payable by the specified person for that year of assessment or accounting period, as the case may be;

"*specified person*" means a person referred to in *subsection (2)*, other than a person entitled to a deduction under *subsection (1)* of section 666 equal to 100 per cent of the excess referred to in the said *subsection (1)*.

[(b) Subject to *paragraph (c)*, a specified person shall be entitled to relief in respect of relevant deductions of an amount not exceeding €7,500 in the aggregate in the qualifying period.

(c) In the case of a qualifying period commencing on or after 1 January 2014, a specified person shall be entitled to relief in respect of relevant deductions of an amount not exceeding €15,000 in the aggregate in that qualifying period.][3]][4]

[(4) This section shall apply in respect of any accounting period which begins on or after 1 January 2012 and ends on or before 31 December 2015.][5]

[(4A) (a) The Minister for Agriculture, Food and the Marine (in this subsection referred to as the "*Minister*"), after consultation with and with the approval of the Minister for Finance, may by regulations establish and maintain a register of farm partnerships (in this subsection referred to as the "*register*") and those regulations may provide for—

(i) the form and manner of registration of a farm partnership on the register,

(ii) the conditions with which a farm partnership shall comply,

(iii) the minimum and maximum number of persons who may participate in a farm partnership,

(iv) the assignment of a unique identifier to a farm partnership included on the register,

(v) procedures for addressing non-compliance with the conditions referred to in *subparagraph (ii)*, and

(vi) such supplemental and incidental matters as appear to the Minister to be necessary and appropriate.

(b) Every regulation made under this subsection shall be laid before Dáil Éireann as soon as may be after it is made and, if a resolution annulling the regulation is passed by Dáil Éireann within the next 21 days on which Dáil Éireann has sat after the regulation is laid before it, the regulation shall be annulled accordingly but without prejudice to the validity of anything previously done under the regulation.][6]

(5) This section comes into operation on such day as the Minister for Finance may appoint by order.][7]

Amendments

[1] Substituted by FA13 s20(1)(g). Has effect from 27 March 2013.

[2] Substituted by F(No.2)A13 s20(2)(a). Comes into operation on 1 January 2014.

[3] Substituted by FA14 s20(e). Comes into operation on 1 January 2015.

[4] Inserted by F(No.2)A13 s20(2)(b). Comes into operation on 1 January 2014.

[5] Substituted by F(No.2)A13 s20(2)(c). Comes into operation on 1 January 2014.

[6] Inserted by FA13 s20(1)(h). Has effect from 27 March 2013.

[7] Inserted by FA12 s20(d). Comes into operation on 1st day of January 2012 as per S.I. No. 455 of 2014.

668 Compulsory disposals of livestock

[FA96 s136]

(1) In this section—

"*excess*" means the excess of the relevant amount over the value of the stock to which this section applies at the beginning of the accounting period in which the disposal takes place;

"*relevant amount*" means the amount of any income received by a person as a result or in consequence of a disposal of stock to which this section applies;

["*stock to which this section applies*" means—

(a) all cattle forming part of the trading stock of the trade of farming, where such cattle are compulsorily disposed of on or after 6 April 1993, under any statute [...][1], and for the purposes of this section all cattle shall be regarded as compulsorily disposed of where, in the case of any disease eradication scheme relating to the eradication or control of brucellosis in livestock, all eligible cattle for the purposes of any such scheme, together with such other cattle as are required to be disposed of, are disposed of, or

(b) animals and poultry of a kind specified in Parts I and II, respectively, of the First Schedule to the Diseases of Animals Act, 1966, forming part of the trading stock of the trade of farming, where all animals or poultry of the particular kind forming part of that trade of farming are disposed of on or after 6 December 2000, in such circumstances that compensation is paid by the Minister for Agriculture, Food and Rural Development in respect of that disposal.][2]

(2) Where stock to which this section applies is disposed of in an accounting period by a person carrying on the trade of farming, the person may elect to have the excess treated in accordance with *subsections (3)* to *(5)*, and such election shall be made in such form and contain such information as the Revenue Commissioners may require.

(3) (a) Notwithstanding any other provision of the Tax Acts apart from [*paragraph (b)* and *subsection (3A)*][3], where a person elects in accordance with *subsection (2)*, the excess shall be disregarded as respects the accounting period in which it arises and shall instead be treated for the purposes of the Tax Acts as arising in equal instalments in each of [the 4 immediately succeeding accounting periods][4].

(b) [Notwithstanding *paragraph (a)* but subject to *subsection (3A)*][5], where the person further elects, the excess shall be treated as arising in such equal instalments in the accounting period in which it arises and in [the 3 immediately succeeding accounting periods][6].

[(3A) Where a trade of farming is permanently discontinued, tax shall be charged under Case IV of Schedule D for the chargeable period in which such discontinuation takes place in respect of the amount of the excess which would, but for such discontinuance, be treated by virtue of *subsection (3)* as arising in an accounting period or accounting periods ending after such discontinuance.][7]

[(4) Subject to *subsection (4A)*, where, not later than the end of the period over which the excess is treated as arising under *subsection (3)*, the person incurs or intends to incur expenditure on the replacement of stock to which this section applies in an amount not less than the relevant amount, then the person shall, in substitution for any deduction to which the person might otherwise be entitled under *section 666* as a result of incurring an amount of expenditure equal to the relevant amount, be deemed to be entitled to a deduction under that section—

(a) where *subsection (3)(a)* applies, for each of the 4 immediately succeeding accounting periods referred to in that subsection, and

(b) where *subsection (3)(b)* applies, for the accounting period in which the excess arises and each of the 3 immediately succeeding accounting periods referred to in that subsection,

and the amount of that deduction shall be an amount equal to the amount treated as arising in each accounting period under *subsection (3)(a)* or *(3)(b)*, as the case may be, and *section 666* shall apply with any necessary modifications in order to give effect to this subsection.

(4A) Where it subsequently transpires that the expenditure actually incurred, on the replacement of stock to which this section applies, by the end of the period over which the excess is treated as arising under *subsection (3)*, was less than the relevant amount, then—

(a) the aggregate deduction to which the person is deemed by *subsection (4)* to be entitled under *section 666* in respect of the 4 accounting periods referred to in *paragraph (a)* or *(b)*, as the case may be, of that subsection shall be reduced to an amount that bears the same proportion to that aggregate deduction as the expenditure actually incurred in those 4 accounting periods bears to the relevant amount, and

(b) the reduction to be made in accordance with *paragraph (a)* shall, as far as possible, be made in a later accounting period in priority to an earlier accounting period.][8]

(5) An election under this section shall be made by notice in writing made on or before the specified return date for the chargeable period in which the stock to which this section applies is compulsorily disposed of.

[(6) Where—

(a) by virtue of the operation of *section 65*, the profits or gains of both the year of assessment 2001 and the year of assessment 2002 are computed on the basis of an accounting period of one year ending in the period from 1 January 2002 to 5 April 2002, and

(b) an instalment referred to in *subsection (3)* is treated as arising in that accounting period,

then, notwithstanding any other provision of the Tax Acts—

(i) an amount equal to 74 per cent of that instalment shall be taken to be part of the profits or gains of the trade of farming for the year of assessment 2001, and

(ii) an amount equal to 26 per cent of that instalment shall be taken to be part of the profits or gains of the trade of farming for the year of assessment 2002.

(7) Where, by virtue of *subsection (4)*, a person is deemed to be entitled to a deduction under *section 666* in respect of the accounting period referred to in *subsection (6)*, then—

(a) 74 per cent of such deduction shall be granted for the year of assessment 2001, and

(b) 26 per cent of such deduction shall be granted for the year of assessment 2002.][9]

Amendments

[1] Deleted by FA08 s33.

[2] Substituted by FA01 s49.

[3, 4] Substituted by FA02 s29(1)(a)(i). Apply as respects disposals made on or after 21 February 2001.

[5, 6] Substituted by FA02 s29(1)(a)(ii). Apply as respects disposals made on or after 21 February 2001.

[7] Inserted by FA02 s29(1)(b). Apply as respects disposals made on or after 21 February 2001.

[8] Substituted by FA02 s29(1)(c). Apply as respects disposals made on or after 21 February 2001.

[9] Inserted by FA02 s29(1)(d). This section is deemed to have applied as on and from 6 April 2001.

Revenue Briefings

Tax Briefing

Tax Briefing April 2002 – Issue 47 pg 11 – Disposal of Livestock due to Disease Eradication Measures
Tax Briefing October 2002 – Issue 50 pg 3 – Farming Issues – Compulsory Disposals of Livestock

Revenue Precedents

Under the Brucellosis Eradication Scheme all female cattle and certain male cattle are required to be disposed of. A person may elect to avail of the 100% compulsory disposal stock relief in respect of them. Is the ordinary 25% stock relief available in respect of an increase in the stock which is not required to be disposed of? If a person elects to claim a 100% stock relief deduction under section 668 in respect of cattle compulsory disposed of, they are not entitled to a further deduction in respect of those cattle under section 666 for that year. 956

If a loss arises in a year as a result of an election made under this section is the loss available for set off against income? Yes – subject to the usual restrictions in section 662. IT953560

The section defines 'relevant amount' as the amount of income received as a result of a disposal of stock. In the context of this definition to what does the word 'income' refer? The reference to income in the definition is a reference to the total proceeds received in respect of the cattle which are compulsorily disposed of. GD94069A

Do the provisions of the section apply if a partial disposal of cattle held by a farmer takes place? No – partial disposals do not come within the provisions of the section, apart from those in relation to brucellosis as outlined in the section. GD94069

Taxpayer received BSE compensation and elected under section 668 of the Taxes Consolidation Act, 1997 to have the excess treated as arising in each of the 2 immediately succeeding accounting periods on a 50/50 basis for the years ended 31 March 2000 and 31 March 2001. Taxpayer successfully restocked during the year ended 31 March 2000 but was prevented from doing so during the year ending 31 March 2001 due to the onset of foot and mouth disease. As the difficulties which prevented the taxpayer restocking were due to foot and mouth disease and could not have been provided for under the provisions of section 668. The taxpayer was allowed to concessionally: have the second installment of the profit on disposal of cattle from BSE compensation normally taxable in the year ending 31 March 2001 to be deferred and taxed in the following year ending 31 March 2002. The taxpayer was entitled to the balance of the stock relief in respect of his accounts to year ending 31 March 2002. 946

Does the 100% stock relief apply to stock which has been disposed of due to B.S.E.? Cattle which have been disposed of due to Bovine Spongiform Encephalopathy (BSE) are regarded as cattle compulsorily disposed of under a statute relating to the eradication or control of diseases in livestock for the purposes of the definition of "stock to which this section applies" in section 668(1) Taxes Consolidation Act 1997.GD90.112

Cross References

From Section 668

Section 65 Cases I and II: basis of assessment.
Section 666 Deduction for increase in stock values.

669 Supplementary provisions (Chapter 2)

[FA96 s137]

(1) (a) Where a person has acquired or disposed of trading stock otherwise than in the normal conduct of the trade of farming, the person shall be treated for the purposes of this Chapter as having, at the beginning or end of the relevant period of account, trading stock of such value as appears to the inspector (or on appeal to the Appeal Commissioners) to be just and reasonable having regard to all the circumstances of the case.

(b) Where the value of a person's trading stock at the beginning of a period of account is not calculated on the basis used for the calculation of the value of the trading stock at the end of that period, the value of the trading stock at the beginning of that period shall for the purposes of this Chapter be treated as being what it would have been if it had been calculated on that basis.

(2) (a) In any case where a person's accounting period does not coincide with a period of account or with 2 or more consecutive periods of account, the person's increase in stock value in the accounting period shall be determined for the purposes of *section 666* not in accordance with *subsection (1)* of that section but by reference to a period (in this section referred to as "the reference period") determined in accordance with this subsection.

(b) In any case where the beginning of a person's accounting period does not coincide with the beginning of a period of account, the reference period shall begin at the beginning of the period of account which is current at the beginning of the person's accounting period.

(c) In any case where the end of the person's accounting period does not coincide with the end of a period of account, the reference period shall end at the end of the period of account which is current at the end of the person's accounting period.

(d) In any case where *paragraph (b)* does not apply, the reference period shall begin at the beginning of the person's accounting period and, in any case where *paragraph (c)* does not apply, the reference period shall end at the end of the person's accounting period.

(3) (a) In any case where *subsection (2)(a)* applies, a person's increase in stock value in the accounting period shall be determined for the purposes of *section 666* by the formula—

$$\frac{A \times (C - O)}{N}$$

where—

A is the number of months in the person's accounting period,

C is the value of the person's trading stock at the end of the reference period,

O is the value of the person's trading stock at the beginning of the reference period, and

N is the number of months in the reference period.

(b) In any case where a person's increase in stock value in an accounting period is to be determined in accordance with *paragraph (a)*, then, in *section 666* and in *subsections (4)* to *(6)*, any reference to the person's closing stock value shall be construed as a reference to the value of the person's trading stock at the end of the reference period.

(4) (a) A person shall not be entitled to a deduction under *section 666* for an accounting period if that accounting period ends by virtue of the person ceasing to—

(i) carry on the trade of farming,

(ii) be resident in the State, or

(iii) be within the charge to tax under Case I of Schedule D in respect of that trade.

(b) In any case where a person's increase in stock value in an accounting period is to be determined in accordance with *subsection (3)(a)*, *paragraph (a)* shall apply as if the reference in that paragraph to the person's accounting period were a reference to any of the accounting periods comprised in the person's reference period.

(5) (a) Subject to *paragraphs (b)* to *(d)*, where a person claims a deduction under *section 666* and, immediately before the beginning of an accounting period, the person was not carrying on the trade to which the claim relates, then, unless—

(i) the person acquired the initial trading stock of that trade on a sale or transfer from another person on that person's ceasing to carry on that trade, and

(ii) the stock so acquired is or is included in the person's trading stock as valued at the beginning of the accounting period,

the person shall be treated for the purposes of *section 666* and *subsections (1)* to *(4)* as having at the beginning of the accounting period trading stock of such value as appears to the inspector to be just and reasonable.

(b) In determining for the purposes specified in *paragraph (a)* the value of trading stock to be attributed to a person at the beginning of the accounting period, the inspector shall have regard to all the relevant circumstances of the case and in particular to—

(i) movements during the person's accounting period in the costs of items of a kind comprised in the person's trading stock during that period, and

(ii) changes during that period in the volume of the trade in question carried on by the person.

(c) The Appeal Commissioners dealing with an appeal from the decision of an inspector on a claim in a case where in accordance with *paragraph (a)* the inspector has attributed to a person at the beginning of an accounting period trading stock of a particular value shall, in hearing and determining the appeal in so far as it relates to the value of the trading stock to be so attributed, determine such value as appears to the Appeal Commissioners to be just and reasonable, having regard to those factors to which the inspector is required to have regard by virtue of *paragraph (b)*.

(d) In any case where *subsection (2)(a)* applies to a person's accounting period, for any reference in *paragraphs (a)* to *(c)* to that accounting period there shall be substituted a reference to the reference period.

(6) In any case where a person's accounting period or reference period consists of a number of complete months and a fraction of a month, any reference in this section to the number of months in the period shall be construed as including that fraction of a month (and in any case where any such period is less than one month any such reference shall be construed as a reference to that fraction of a month of which the period consists).

Cross References

From Section 669

Section 666 Deduction for increase in stock values.

CHAPTER 3

Milk Quotas

669A Interpretation

[In this Chapter—

[…][1]

"*levy*" means the levy referred to in Council Regulation (EEC) No. 3950 of 28 December 1992*, as amended;

* O.J. No. L405, 31.12.1992, p.1

"*milk*" means the produce of the milking of one or more cows and "*other milk products*" includes cream, butter and cheese;

"*milk quota*" means—

(a) the quantity of a milk or other milk products which may be supplied by a person carrying on farming, in the course of a trade of farming land occupied by such person to a purchaser in a milk quota year without that person being liable to pay a levy, or

(b) the quantity of a milk or other milk products which may be sold or transferred free for direct consumption by a person carrying on farming, in the course of a trade of farming land occupied by such person in a milk quota year without that person being liable to pay a levy;

"*milk quota restructuring scheme*" means a scheme introduced by the Minister for Agriculture, Food and Rural Development under the provisions of Article 8(*b*) of Council Regulation (EEC) No. 3950 of 28 December 1992, as amended;

"*milk quota year*" means a twelve month period beginning on 1 April and ending on the following 31 March;

"*purchaser*" has the meaning assigned to it under Council Regulation (EEC) No. 3950 of 28 December 1992;

"*qualifying expenditure*" means—

(a) in the case of milk quota to which *paragraph (a)* of the definition of "*qualifying quota*" refers, the amount of the capital expenditure incurred on the purchase of that qualifying quota, and

(b) in the case of milk quota to which *paragraph (b)* of the definition of "*qualifying quota*" refers, the lesser of—

(i) the amount of capital expenditure incurred on the purchase of that qualifying quota, or

[(ii) the amount of capital expenditure which would have been incurred on the purchase of that milk quota if the price paid were set otherwise than by the Minister for Agriculture and Food for the purposes of a Milk Quota Restructuring Scheme in the area in which the land, with which that milk quota is associated, is situated;][2]

"*qualifying quota*" means–

(a) a milk quota purchased by a person on or after 1 April 2000 under a Milk Quota Restructuring Scheme, or [(b) any other milk quota purchased on or after 1 April 2000;][3]

"*writing-down period*" has the meaning assigned to it by section 669B(2).][4]

Amendments

[1] Deleted by FA02 s30(1)(a). This section shall be deemed to have applied as on and from 6 April 2000.

[2] Substituted by FA07 s25.

[3] Substituted by FA02 s30(1)(b). This section shall be deemed to have applied as on and from 6 April 2000.

[4] Inserted by FA00 s61(b). With effect from 1 November 2001 per S.I. 505 of 2001.

669B Annual allowances for capital expenditure on purchase of milk quota

[(1) Where, on or after 6 April 2000, a person incurs qualifying expenditure on the purchase of a qualifying quota, there shall, subject to and in accordance with this Chapter, be made to that person writing-down allowances during the writing-down period as specified in *subsection (2)*; but no writing-down allowance shall be made to a person in respect of any qualifying expenditure unless the allowance is to be made to the person in taxing the person's trade of farming.

(2) The writing-down period referred to in *subsection (1)* shall be 7 years commencing with the beginning of the chargeable period related to the qualifying expenditure.

(3) The writing-down allowances to be made during the writing-down period referred to in *subsection (2)* in respect of qualifying expenditure shall be determined by the formula—

$$A \times \frac{B}{C}$$

where—

[A is the amount of the qualifying expenditure incurred on the purchase of the milk quota,][1]

B is the length of the part of the chargeable period falling within the writing-down period, and

C is the length of the writing-down period.][2]

Amendments

[1] Substituted by FA03 sched6(1)(f). This section shall be deemed to have come into force and take effect as on and from 1 November 2001.

[2] Inserted by FA00 s61(b). With effect from 1 November 2001 per S.I. 505 of 2001.

669C Effect of sale of quota

[(1) Where a person incurs qualifying expenditure on the purchase of a qualifying quota and, before the end of the writing-down period, any of the following events occurs—

(a) the person sells the qualifying quota or so much of the quota as the person still owns;

(b) the qualifying quota comes to an end or ceases altogether to be used;

(c) the person sells part of the qualifying quota and the net proceeds of the sale (in so far as they consist of capital sums) are not less than the amount of the qualifying expenditure remaining unallowed;

no writing-down allowance shall be made to that person for the chargeable period related to the event or any subsequent chargeable period.

(2) Where a person incurs qualifying expenditure on the purchase of a qualifying quota and, before the end of the writing-down period, either of the following events occurs—

(a) the qualifying quota comes to an end or ceases altogether to be used;

(b) the person sells all of the qualifying quota or so much of that quota as the person still owns, and the net proceeds of the sale (in so far as they consist of capital sums) are less than the amount of the qualifying expenditure remaining unallowed;

there shall, subject to and in accordance with this Chapter, be made to that person for the [chargeable period][1] related to the event an allowance (in this Chapter referred to as a "*balancing allowance*") equal to—

(i) if the event is the qualifying quota coming to an end or ceasing altogether to be used, the amount of the qualifying expenditure remaining unallowed, and

(ii) if the event is a sale, the amount of the qualifying expenditure remaining unallowed less the net proceeds of the sale.

(3) Where a person who has incurred qualifying expenditure on the purchase of a qualifying quota sells all or any part of that quota and the net proceeds of the sale (in so far as they consist of capital sums) exceed the amount of the qualifying expenditure remaining unallowed, if any, there shall, subject to and in accordance with this Chapter, be made on that person for the chargeable period related to the sale a charge (in this Chapter referred to as a "*balancing charge*") on an amount equal to—

(a) the excess, or

(b) where the amount of the qualifying expenditure remaining unallowed is nil, the net proceeds of the sale.

(4) Where a person who has incurred qualifying expenditure on the purchase of a qualifying quota sells a part of that quota and *subsection (3)* does not apply, the amount of any writing-down allowance made in respect of that expenditure for the chargeable period related to the sale or any subsequent chargeable period shall be the amount determined by—

(a) subtracting the net proceeds of the sale (in so far as they consist of capital sums) from the amount of the expenditure remaining unallowed at the time of the sale, and

(b) dividing the result by the number of complete years of the writing-down period which remained at the beginning of the chargeable period related to the sale,

and so on for any subsequent sales.

(5) References in this section to the amount of any qualifying expenditure remaining unallowed shall in relation to any event be construed as references to the amount of that expenditure less any writing-down allowances made in respect of that expenditure for chargeable periods before the chargeable period related to that event, and less also the net proceeds of any previous sale by the person who incurred the expenditure of any part of the qualifying quota acquired by the expenditure, in so far as those proceeds consist of capital sums.

(6) Notwithstanding *subsections (1)* to *(5)*—

(a) no balancing allowance shall be made in respect of any expenditure unless a writing-down allowance has been, or, but for the happening of the event giving rise to the balancing allowance, could have been, made in respect of that expenditure, and

(b) the total amount on which a balancing charge is made in respect of any expenditure shall not exceed the total writing-down allowances actually made in respect of that expenditure less, if a balancing charge has previously been made in respect of that expenditure, the amount on which that charge was made.][2]

Amendments

[1] Substituted by FA01 s27.

[2] Inserted by FA00 s61(b). With effect from 1 November 2001 per S.I. 505 of 2001.

669D Manner of making allowances and charges

[An allowance or charge under this Chapter shall be made to or on a person in taxing the profits or gains from farming but only if at any time in the chargeable period or its basis period the qualifying quota in question was used for the purposes of that trade.][1]

Amendments

[1] Inserted by FA00 s61(b). With effect from 1 November 2001 per S.I. 505 of 2001.

669E Application of Chapter 4 of Part 9

[(1) Subject to *subsection (2)*, *Chapter 4* of *Part 9* shall apply as if this Chapter were contained in that Part.

(2) In *Chapter 4* of *Part 9*, as applied by virtue of *subsection (1)* to a qualifying quota, the reference in *section 312(5)(a)(i)* to the sum mentioned in *paragraph (b)* shall in the case of a qualifying quota be construed as a reference to the amount of the qualifying expenditure on the acquisition of the qualifying quota remaining unallowed, computed in accordance with section 669C.][1]

Amendments

[1] Inserted by FA00 s61(b). With effect from 1 November 2001 per S.I. No. 505 of 2001.

669F Commencement (Chapter 3)

[This Chapter shall come into operation on such day as the Minister for Finance, with the consent of the Minister for Agriculture, Food and Rural Development, may, by order, appoint.][1]

Amendments

[1] Inserted by FA00 s61(b). With effect from 1 November 2001 per S.I. 505 of 2001.

CHAPTER 4

Taxation of Stallion Profits and Gains

669G Interpretation (Chapter 4)

[In this Chapter—

"*excess relief*" has the same meaning as in *section 485C*;

"*initial value*" in relation to a stallion means its market value on—

(a) 1 August 2008, or

(b) the day it is either acquired for, or appropriated to, stud activities, as the case may be,

whichever is later, and any reference to a stallion includes a reference to an interest in a stallion;

"*market value*", at any time in relation to a stallion, means the price which the stallion might reasonably be expected to fetch on a sale in the open market and in a case where a person (the "*purchaser*") acquires the stallion from another person (the "*vendor*")—

(a) at arm's length, and

(b) the purchaser and the vendor are not connected persons (within the meaning of *section 10*),

then the market value is the price paid;

"*relevant amount*", in relation to a year of assessment and an individual, means an amount determined by the formula—

$$A - B$$

where—

A is the amount of income tax payable by the individual for the year of assessment, and

B is the amount of income tax which would be payable by the individual for the year of assessment if—

(a) the entry at Reference Number 6 of Schedule 25B had not been enacted, and

(b) for the purposes of the entry at Reference Number 1 of Schedule 25B the definition of "*exempt profits*" in *section 140(1)* did not include profits or gains which by virtue of *section 231* were not charged to tax;

"*relevant excess relief*", in relation to a year of assessment and an individual, means an amount determined by the formula—

$$C - D$$

where—

C is the amount of excess relief which is carried forward to the next year of assessment and which the individual is entitled to deduct from his or her total income for that year, and

D is the amount of excess relief which would be carried forward to the next year of assessment and which the individual would be entitled to deduct from his or her total income for that year if—

(a) the entry at Reference Number 6 of Schedule 25B had not been enacted, and

(b) for the purposes of the entry at Reference Number 1 of Schedule 25B the definition of "*exempt profits*" in *section 140(1)* did not include profits or gains which by virtue of *section 231* were not charged to tax;

"*residual value*", in relation to a stallion, at any time, means—

(a) an amount equal to the initial value of the stallion, or

(b) if less, the amount by which the initial value of the stallion exceeds—

(i) the amount which has been allowed as a deduction under *section 669I* for a chargeable period ending before that time, or

(ii) where there is more than one such amount, the aggregate of such amounts.][1]

Amendments

[1] Inserted by FA07 s26(1)(b). With effect from 1 August 2008 per S.I. No. 160 of 2008.

Cross References

From Section 669G

Section 10 Connected persons.

Section 140 Distributions out of profits or gains from stallion fees, stud greyhound services fees and occupation of certain woodlands.

Section 231 Profits or gains from stallion fees.

Section 485C Interpretation (Chapter 2A).

Section 669I Provisions as to deductions.

669H Charging provisions

[(1) The profits or gains arising in any chargeable period to the owner or part-owner of a stallion from the sale of services of mares by the stallion or rights to such services shall be chargeable to income tax or corporation tax, as the case may be, in accordance with *subsection (2)*.

(2) (a) In a case in which the owner or part-owner of a stallion carries on in the chargeable period referred to in *subsection (1)* the trade of farming in respect of which the owner or part-owner is within the charge to tax under Case I of Schedule D, the profits or gains referred to in *subsection (1)* and any amount chargeable under *subsection (3)(c)* of *section 669I* shall be chargeable under that Case of that Schedule as part of that trade.

(b) In a case, other than one referred to in *paragraph (a)*, the profits or gains referred to in *subsection (1)* and any amount chargeable under *subsection (3)(c)* of *section 669I* shall be chargeable under Case IV of Schedule D.][1]

Amendments

[1] Inserted by FA07 s26(1)(b). With effect from 1 August 2008 per S.I. No. 160 of 2008.

Cross References

From Section 669H

Section 669I Provisions as to deductions.

To Section 669H

Section 669I Provisions as to deductions.

Section 669K Miscellaneous (Chapter 4).

669I Provisions as to deductions

[(1) Where any person acquires ownership or part-ownership of a stallion, the profits or gains in relation to which are chargeable in accordance with *section 669H(2)*, then that person, in computing the amount of income to be charged to tax under the Tax Acts for any chargeable period, shall not be entitled, other than in accordance with *subsection (2)*, to any deduction in respect of expenditure incurred on such acquisition.

(2) (a) Where the profits or gains referred to in *subsection (1)* are chargeable in accordance with *section 669H(2)(a)*, for each of 4 consecutive chargeable periods, the first of which begins with the chargeable period in which—

(i) 1 August 2008 occurs, in a case where the stallion is owned or part-owned on that day, or

(ii) in any other case, the stallion is either acquired for, or appropriated to, stud activities, as the case may be,

the owner or part-owner of the stallion shall, in computing for the purposes of tax the trading income of the trade of farming referred to in that section, be entitled to a deduction under this section equal to 25 per cent of the initial value of the stallion, as if the deduction were a trading expense incurred in the chargeable period.

(b) Subject to *section 669K(3)*, where the profits or gains referred to in *subsection (1)* are chargeable in accordance with section *669H(2)(b)*, in determining the amount of income to be charged to tax under Case IV of Schedule D, such income shall be computed in accordance with the provisions applicable to Case I of Schedule D, taking into account this Chapter.

(3) Where, in any chargeable period a stallion to which this Chapter applies is disposed of or dies, then—

(a) no deduction which would otherwise be allowed under *subsection (2)(a)* or *(2)(b)*, as the case may be, in respect of the initial value of that stallion shall be allowed for that chargeable period or for any subsequent chargeable period,

(b) a deduction of an amount equal to the residual value of the stallion at the time of its disposal or death shall be allowed for that chargeable period as if it were a deduction under *subsection (2)(a)*, and

(c) the owner or part-owner of the stallion shall be chargeable to income tax or corporation tax, as the case may be, on—

(i) the amount received in money or money's worth, in respect of its disposal or death, or

(ii) in the case of a disposal, if greater, the price which the stallion might reasonably have been expected to fetch at the time of its disposal on a sale, at arm's length between persons who are not connected (within the meaning of *section 10*), in the open market.][1]

Amendments

[1] Inserted by FA07 s26(1)(b). With effect from I August 2008 per S.I. No. 160 of 2008.

Cross References

From Section 669I

Section 10 Connected persons.
Section 669H Charging provisions.
Section 669K Miscellaneous (Chapter 4).

To Section 669I

Section 669G Interpretation (Chapter 4).
Section 669H Charging provisions.

669J Credit for tax paid

[(1) Subject to the provisions of this section, any individual, to whom Chapter 2A of *Part 15* applies for any year of assessment, who has made a payment which includes a relevant amount in respect of that year of assessment shall, without prejudice to the payment so made, be treated as having made a payment on account of income tax of an amount equal to the relevant amount.

(2) So much of a payment of tax (referred to in this section as the "deemed payment on account of tax") for a year of assessment by an individual as is treated in accordance with *subsection (1)* shall, in so far as possible, be set against any liability to income tax of the individual, for the year of assessment following the first-mentioned year of assessment.

(3) To the extent that the deemed payment on account of tax has not been set off in accordance with *subsection (2)*, the balance remaining shall be set off against a liability to income tax for any subsequent year of assessment of the individual who is treated as having made the payment, in the order of being set off against a liability for an earlier period in priority to a liability for a later period.

(4) Only the excess of an overpayment of income tax for any year of assessment over the deemed payment on account of tax to be made for that year of assessment by virtue of this section may be repaid and interest shall not be payable in respect of any part of such overpayment other than the excess.

(5) Where in any year of assessment *section 485E* applies to an individual, then for the purposes of *section 485F* the excess relief for the year shall be reduced by an amount equal to the amount of the relevant excess relief.][1]

Amendments

[1] Inserted by FA07 s26(1)(b). With effect from 1 August 2008 per S.I. No. 160 of 2008.

Cross References

From Section 669J

Section 458 Deductions allowed in ascertaining taxable income and provisions relating to reductions in tax.
Section 485E Recalculation of taxable income for purposes of limiting reliefs.
Section 485F Carry forward of excess relief.

669K Miscellaneous (Chapter 4)

[(1) For the purposes of determining the market value of a stallion to which this Chapter applies, the Revenue Commissioners may consult with such person or body of persons as, in their opinion, may be of assistance to them.

(2) Notwithstanding any other provisions of the Tax Acts, trading stock comprising stallions shall be disregarded for all purposes of *section 666*.

(3) In a case in which in any chargeable period the computation of the amount of income of a person to be charged to tax under Case IV of Schedule D under

this Chapter results in a loss, then, notwithstanding *section 383*, the amount of the loss may not be deducted from or set off against other income charged to tax under Case IV of Schedule D arising in that chargeable period, and any loss, when carried forward to a subsequent chargeable period, may only be deducted from or set off against income to which *section 669H(2)(b)* applies arising in that subsequent chargeable period.][1]

Amendments

[1] Inserted by FA07 s26(1)(b). With effect from 1 August 2008 per S.I. No 160 of 2008.

Cross References

From Section 669K

Section 383 Relief under Case IV for losses.

Section 666 Deduction for increase in stock values.

Section 669H Charging provisions.

To Section 669K

Section 669I Provisions as to deductions.

PART 24

Taxation of Profits of Certain Mines and Petroleum Taxation

CHAPTER 1

Taxation of Profits of Certain Mines

670 Mine development allowance

[ITA67 s245; CTA76 s21(1) and Sch1 par10; FA80 s17(3); FA96 s132(2) and Sch5 PtII]

(1) In this section—

"*mine*" means a mine operated for the purpose of obtaining, whether by underground or surface working, any scheduled mineral, mineral compound or mineral substance within the meaning of section 2 of the Minerals Development Act, 1940, but, in relation to capital expenditure incurred before the 6th day of April, 1960, "*mine*" means an underground excavation made for the purpose of getting minerals;

references to capital expenditure incurred in connection with a mine shall be construed as references to capital expenditure incurred—

(a) in the development of the mine on searching for, or on discovering and testing, mineral deposits or winning access to such deposits, or

(b) on the construction of any works which are of such a nature that when the mine has ceased to be operated they are likely to have so diminished in value that their value will be nil or almost nil,

but as excluding references to—

(i) any expenditure on the acquisition of the site of the mine or of the site of any such works or of rights in or over any such site,

(ii) any expenditure on the acquisition of, or of rights over, the deposits, or

(iii) any expenditure on works constructed wholly or mainly for subjecting the raw product of the mine to any process except a process designed for preparing the raw product for use as such;

references to assets representing capital expenditure incurred in connection with a mine shall be construed as including—

(a) in relation to expenditure on searching for, discovering and testing deposits, references to any information or other results obtained from any search, exploration or enquiry on which the expenditure was incurred,

(b) references to any part of such assets, and

(c) in the case of any such assets destroyed or damaged, references to any insurance moneys or other compensation moneys in respect of such destruction or damage.

(2) Expenditure shall not for the purposes of this section be regarded as having been incurred by a person carrying on the trade of working a mine in so far as the expenditure has been or is to be met directly or indirectly out of moneys provided by the Oireachtas or by any other person (not being a person who has carried on the trade of working that mine).

(3) Any person who carries on the trade of working a mine and who has on or after the 6th day of April, 1946, incurred any capital expenditure in connection

with the mine may apply for an allowance (in this section referred to as a "mine development allowance") in respect of that capital expenditure.

(4) Application for a mine development allowance for any chargeable period may be made to the inspector not later than 24 months after the end of that period.

(5) (a) Subject to *paragraph (b)*, the following provisions shall apply in relation to the amount of a mine development allowance for any chargeable period in respect of any capital expenditure incurred in connection with a mine:

(i) the inspector shall estimate to the best of his or her judgment the life (in this subsection referred to as "the estimated life") of the deposits, but shall not estimate such life at more than 20 years;

(ii) the inspector shall then estimate the amount of the difference (in this subsection referred to as "the estimated difference") between the capital expenditure incurred in connection with the mine and the amount which in his or her opinion the assets representing that capital expenditure are likely to be worth at the end of the estimated life;

(iii) the inspector shall, subject to this section, allow as the mine development allowance for that chargeable period an amount equal to a sum which bears to the estimated difference the same proportion as the length of that chargeable period bears to the length of the estimated life;

(iv) if capital expenditure incurred in connection with the mine was incurred during that chargeable period, then, that chargeable period shall for the purposes of *subparagraph (iii)* be taken to comprise so much only of that chargeable period as is subsequent to the date on which the capital expenditure was incurred.

(b) The total of the mine development allowances shall not exceed the estimated difference.

(6) A mine development allowance to any person carrying on the trade of working a mine shall be made in taxing that trade, and *section 304(4)* shall apply in relation to the allowance as it applies in relation to allowances to be made under *Part 9*.

(7) A mine development allowance shall not be made in respect of any capital expenditure incurred in connection with a mine in any case where the asset representing that capital expenditure is an asset in respect of which an allowance may be made under *section 284*.

(8) Where a mine development allowance for any chargeable period has been made in respect of capital expenditure incurred in connection with a mine, then, for that chargeable period *section 85* shall not apply as respects any such asset.

(9) Any capital expenditure incurred on or after the 6th day of April, 1946, in connection with a mine by a person about to carry on the trade of working the mine but before commencing such trade shall be treated for the purposes of this section as if it had been incurred on the first day of the commencement of such trade.

(10) Where mine development allowances in respect of any capital expenditure incurred in connection with a mine have been made and the mine has finally ceased to be operated, the following provisions shall apply:

(a) the inspector shall review the mine development allowances;

(b) if on such review it appears that the amount of the difference (in this subsection referred to as "the difference") between the capital expenditure incurred in connection with the mine and the amount which the assets representing that capital expenditure at such cessation were worth at such cessation exceeds the total of the mine development allowances, then, further mine development allowances equal to the excess may be made for any chargeable period (being the chargeable period in which the mine has finally ceased to be operated or any previous chargeable period), but the total of such further mine development allowances shall not amount to more than the excess and if necessary [(and notwithstanding any limitation in section 865(4) on the time within which a claim for a repayment of tax is required to be made)][1] effect may be given to this paragraph by means of repayment;

(c) if on such review it appears that the difference is less than the total of the mine development allowances, then, the deficiency or the total of the mine development allowances, whichever is the less, shall be treated as a trading receipt of the trade of working the mine accruing immediately before such cessation.

(11) Where the person (in this subsection referred to as "the vendor") carrying on the trade of working a mine sells to any other person (not being a person who succeeds the vendor in that trade) any asset representing capital expenditure incurred in connection with the mine and by reference to which mine development allowances have been made, the following provisions shall apply:

(a) if the total of the mine development allowances when added to the sum realised on the sale of that asset is less than that capital expenditure by any amount (in this subsection referred to as "the unexhausted allowance"), then, further mine development allowances may be granted to the vendor in respect of any chargeable period (being the chargeable period of such sale or any previous chargeable period), but the total of such further mine development allowances shall not exceed the unexhausted allowance;

(b) if the total of the mine development allowances when added to the sum realised on the sale of that asset exceeds that capital expenditure, then, the amount of such excess or the total of the mine development allowances, whichever is the less, shall be treated as a trading receipt of the trade accruing immediately before the sale.

(12) Where—

(a) mine development allowances in respect of any capital expenditure incurred in connection with a mine have been made to a person (in this subsection referred to as "the original trader") carrying on the trade of working the mine, and

(b) another person (in this subsection referred to as "the successor") succeeds to that trade,

mine development allowances may continue to be made in respect of that capital expenditure to the successor, but in no case shall the amount of such allowances exceed the amount to which the original trader would have been entitled if the original trader had continued to carry on that trade.

(13) Where for any chargeable period a company was entitled to relief from tax by virtue of Chapter II or Chapter III of Part XXV of the Income Tax Act, 1967, then, for the purposes of *subsections (5)* and *(10)* to *(12)*, there shall be deemed to have been made for that chargeable period in respect of any expenditure the full mine development allowance which on due claim could have been made for that chargeable period in respect of that expenditure, unless that allowance has in fact been made.

(14) An appeal to the Appeal Commissioners shall lie on any question arising under this section in the like manner as an appeal would lie against an assessment, and the provisions of the Income Tax Acts relating to appeals shall apply accordingly.

Amendments

[1] Inserted by FA08 sched6(1)(n). Applies as on and from 31 January 2008.

Cross References

From Section 670

Section 85 Deduction for certain industrial premises.
Section 268 Meaning of "industrial building or structure".
Section 284 Wear and tear allowances.
Section 304 Income tax: allowances and charges in taxing a trade, etc.
Section 865 Repayment of tax.

To Section 670

Section 80A Taxation of certain short-term leases plant and machinery.
Section 267O Treatment of credit return.
Section 267P Treatment of credit transaction.
Section 267S Treatment of certificate owner.
Section 270 Meaning of "expenditure on construction of building or structure".
Section 309 Companies not resident in the State.
Section 311 Apportionment of consideration and exchanges and surrenders of leasehold interests.
Section 312 Special provisions as to certain sales.
Section 319 Adjustment of allowances by reference to value-added tax.
Section 321 Provisions of general application in relation to the making of allowances and charges.
Section 413 Profits or assets available for distribution.
Section 428 Exclusion of double allowances, etc.
Section 672 Interpretation (sections 672 to 683).
Section 673 Allowance in respect of development expenditure and exploration expenditure.
Section 677 Investment allowance in respect of exploration expenditure.
Section 679 Exploration expenditure.
Section 680 Annual allowance for mineral depletion.
Section 692 Development expenditure: allowances and charges.
Section 693 Exploration expenditure: allowances and charges.
Section 695 Abandonment expenditure: allowances and loss relief.
Section 697A Interpretation (Part 24A).
Schedule 17 Reorganisation into Companies of Trustee Savings Banks
Schedule 22 Dividends Regarded as Paid Out of Profits Accumulated Before Given Date
Schedule 26 Replacement of Harbour Authorities by Port Companies
Schedule 32 Transitional Provisions

671 Marginal coal mine allowance

[FA74 s74; CTA76 s140(1), s164, Sch2 PtI par48 and Sch3 PtII]

(1) In this section, "*marginal coal mine*" means a coal mine in the State being worked for the purpose of the production of coal and in respect of which the [Minister for Communications, Energy and Natural Resources][1] gives a certificate stating that that Minister is satisfied that the profits derived or to be derived from the working of that mine are such that, if tax is to be charged on those profits in accordance with the Income Tax Acts, other than this section, the mine is unlikely to continue to be worked.

(2) The Minister for Finance, after consultation with the [Minister for Communications, Energy and Natural Resources,][2] may direct in respect of a marginal coal mine that for any particular year of assessment the tax chargeable on the profits of that mine shall be reduced to such amount (including nil) as may be specified by the Minister for Finance.

(3) Where a person is carrying on the trade of working a coal mine in respect of which the Minister for Finance gives a direction under *subsection (2)* in respect of a year of assessment, an allowance shall be made as a deduction in charging the profits of that trade to tax for that year of assessment of such amount as will ensure that the tax charged in respect of the profits of that trade shall equal the amount specified by that Minister.

(4) This section shall apply for corporation tax as it applies for income tax, and references to the Income Tax Acts, to years of assessment and to a deduction in charging the profits of a trade shall apply as if they were or included respectively references to the Corporation Tax Acts, to accounting periods and to a deduction made in computing the trading income for corporation tax.

Amendments

[1] Substituted by FA08 sched8(1)(i)(i). Has effect as on and from 13 March 2008.

[2] Substituted by FA08 sched8(1)(i)(ii). Has effect as on and from 13 March 2008.

672 Interpretation (sections 672 to 683)

[F(TPCM)A74 s1(1), (2), (6) and (7); CTA76 s21(1) and Sch1 par63; FA96 s132(1) and Sch5 PtI par8]

(1) In this section and in *sections 673* to *683*, except where otherwise provided or the context otherwise requires—

"*development expenditure*" means capital expenditure—

(a) on the development of a qualifying mine, or

(b) on the construction of any works in connection with a qualifying mine which are of such a nature that, when the mine ceases to be operated, they are likely to have so diminished in value that their value will be nil or almost nil,

and includes interest on money borrowed to meet such capital expenditure, but does not include expenditure on—

(i) the acquisition of the site of the mine or the site of any such works or of rights in or over any such site,

(ii) the acquisition of a scheduled mineral asset, or

(iii) works constructed wholly or mainly for subjecting the raw product of the mine to any process except a process designed for preparing the raw product for use as such;

"*exploration expenditure*" means capital expenditure on searching in the State for deposits of scheduled minerals or on testing such deposits or winning access to such deposits, and includes capital expenditure on systematic searching for areas containing scheduled minerals and searching by drilling or other means for scheduled minerals in those areas, but does not include expenditure on operations in the course of working a qualifying mine or expenditure which is development expenditure;

"*mine development allowance*" has the same meaning as in *section 670*;

"*qualifying mine*" means a mine being worked for the purpose of obtaining scheduled minerals;

"*scheduled mineral asset*" means a deposit of scheduled minerals or land comprising such a deposit or an interest in or right over such deposit or land;

"*scheduled minerals*" means minerals specified in the Table to this section occurring in non-bedded deposits of such minerals.

(2) Except where provided for in *sections 674* to *676*, expenditure shall not be regarded for the purposes of this section and *sections 673* to *683* as having been incurred by a person carrying on the trade of working a qualifying mine in so far as the expenditure has been or is to be met directly or indirectly out of moneys provided by the Oireachtas or by any other person (not being a person who has carried on the trade of working that mine).

(3) The Minister for Finance may by regulations add minerals occurring in non-bedded deposits of such minerals to the Table to this section.

(4) Every regulation made under *subsection (3)* shall be laid before Dáil Éireann as soon as may be after it is made and, if a resolution annulling the regulation is passed by Dáil Éireann within the next 21 days on which Dáil Éireann has sat after the regulation is laid before it, the regulation shall be annulled accordingly, but without prejudice to the validity of anything previously done thereunder.

TABLE

SCHEDULED MINERALS

Barytes
Felspar
Serpentinous marble
Quartz rock
Soapstone
Ores of copper
Ores of gold
Ores of iron
Ores of lead
Ores of manganese
Ores of molybdenum
Ores of silver
Ores of sulphur
Ores of zinc.

Cross References

From Section 672

Section 670 Mine development allowance.
Section 673 Allowance in respect of development expenditure and exploration expenditure.
Section 674 Expenditure on abortive exploration.
Section 676 Expenditure incurred by person not engaged in trade of mining.
Section 683 Charge to tax on sums received from sale of scheduled mineral assets.

To Section 672

Section 309 Companies not resident in the State.
Section 675 Exploration expenditure incurred by certain bodies corporate.
Section 676 Expenditure incurred by person not engaged in trade of mining.
Section 679 Exploration expenditure.
Section 684 Interpretation (Chapter 2).

673 Allowance in respect of development expenditure and exploration expenditure

[F(TPCM)A74 s2(1) and (4); CTA76 s21(1) and Sch1 par64; FA90 s39(a)]

(1) Subject to *subsections (2)* and *(3)*, where a person carrying on the trade of working a qualifying mine incurs on or after the 6th day of April, 1974, any development expenditure or exploration expenditure and makes application under *section 670* for a mine development allowance for a chargeable period in respect of such expenditure—

(a) that expenditure shall be deemed to be expenditure in respect of which that allowance may be granted, whether or not in the case of exploration expenditure a deposit of scheduled minerals is found as a result of the expenditure,

(b) the amount of such allowance for that chargeable period shall be equal to the total amount of—

(i) the exploration expenditure, and

(ii) in the case of development expenditure, the amount of the difference between that expenditure and the amount which in the opinion of the inspector the assets representing that expenditure are likely to be worth at the end of the estimated life of the qualifying mine, and

(c) in relation to a case in which this section has applied, any reference in the Tax Acts to an allowance made under *section 670* shall be construed as including a reference to an allowance made under that section by virtue of this section.

(2) For the purposes of this section, no account shall be taken of exploration expenditure incurred before the 1st day of April, 1990, as a result of which a deposit of scheduled minerals is not found if the expenditure was incurred more than 10 years before the date on which the person carrying on the trade of working a qualifying mine commenced to carry on that trade.

(3) No allowance shall be made under *subsection (1)* in respect of expenditure incurred before the 6th day of April, 1974, whether or not such expenditure is by virtue of any provision of the Tax Acts deemed to have been incurred on or after that date.

Cross References

From Section 673

Section 670 Mine development allowance.

To Section 673

Section 413 Profits or assets available for distribution.
Section 672 Interpretation (sections 672 to 683).
Section 674 Expenditure on abortive exploration.
Section 675 Exploration expenditure incurred by certain bodies corporate.
Section 677 Investment allowance in respect of exploration expenditure.
Section 679 Exploration expenditure.
Section 680 Annual allowance for mineral depletion.

674 Expenditure on abortive exploration

[F(TPCM)A74 s3(2) to (5); CTA76 s21(1) and Sch1 par65; FA90 s39(b)]

(1) (a) Where a person who commences to carry on a trade of working a qualifying mine has incurred exploration expenditure and that expenditure was not incurred in connection with the qualifying mine, then, subject to

paragraph (b), in taxing the trade for the chargeable period in which the person commences to carry on the trade, there shall be made an allowance of an amount equal to the amount of that expenditure.

(b) For the purposes of *paragraph (a)*, no account shall be taken of exploration expenditure incurred before the 1st day of April, 1990, if the expenditure was incurred more than 10 years before the date on which the person commences to carry on the trade of working the qualifying mine.

(2) Where in a case referred to in *subsection (1)* the person concerned is a body corporate and there was or is, after all or part of the expenditure referred to in that subsection had been incurred by the body corporate, a change in ownership (within the meaning of *Schedule 9*) of the body corporate or of a body corporate that is a parent body or a wholly-owned subsidiary (within the meaning of *section 675*) of the first-mentioned body corporate, no allowance shall be made under this section in respect of any part of that expenditure incurred before the date of the change in ownership; but, in any case where part of the ordinary share capital of any body corporate is acquired by a Minister of the Government, such acquisition shall be disregarded in determining whether or not there was or is such a change in ownership.

(3) Where a person commences to carry on the trade of working a qualifying mine but has not incurred the exploration expenditure incurred in connection with that mine, no allowance shall be made under this section or by virtue of *section 673* in respect of exploration expenditure incurred by that person before the date on which that person commences to carry on that trade.

(4) Subject to *paragraphs 16* and *18* of *Schedule 32*, a person shall not be entitled to an allowance in respect of the same expenditure both under this section and under some other provision of the Tax Acts.

Cross References

From Section 674

Section 673 Allowance in respect of development expenditure and exploration expenditure.
Section 675 Exploration expenditure incurred by certain bodies corporate.
Schedule 9 Change in Ownership of Company: Disallowance of Trading Losses
Schedule 32 Transitional Provisions

To Section 674

Section 413 Profits or assets available for distribution.
Section 672 Interpretation (sections 672 to 683).
Section 675 Exploration expenditure incurred by certain bodies corporate.
Section 679 Exploration expenditure.

675 Exploration expenditure incurred by certain bodies corporate

[F(TPCM)A74 s4; CTA76 s21(1) and Sch1 par66; FA90 s39(c)]

(1) Subject to *subsection (2)*, where exploration expenditure, in respect of which an allowance may be claimed by virtue of *section 673* or *674*, or (as respects expenditure incurred on or after the 1st day of April, 1990) by virtue of *section 673* as applied by *section 679*, is or has been incurred by a body corporate (in this section referred to as "the exploration company") and—

(a) another body corporate is or is deemed to be a wholly-owned subsidiary of the exploration company, or

(b) the exploration company is or is deemed to be a wholly-owned subsidiary of another body corporate,

then, the expenditure or so much of it as the exploration company specifies—

(i) in the case referred to in *paragraph (a)*, may at the election of the exploration company be deemed to have been incurred by such other body corporate (being a body corporate which is or is deemed to be a wholly-owned subsidiary of the exploration company) as the exploration company specifies,

(ii) in the case referred to in *paragraph (b)*, may at the election of the exploration company be deemed to have been incurred by the body corporate (in this paragraph referred to as "the parent body") of which the exploration company was, at the time the expenditure was incurred, a wholly-owned subsidiary or by such other body corporate (being a body corporate which is or is deemed to be a wholly-owned subsidiary of the parent body) as the exploration company specifies,

and, in a case where that expenditure was incurred on a date before the incorporation of the body corporate so specified, *sections 672* to *683* shall apply in relation to the granting of any allowance in respect of that expenditure as if that body corporate had been in existence at the time the expenditure was incurred and had incurred the expenditure at that time.

(2) (a) The same expenditure shall not be taken into account in relation to more than one trade by virtue of this section.

(b) Subject to *paragraphs 16* and *18* of *Schedule 32*, an allowance shall not be granted in respect of the same expenditure both by virtue of this section and under some other provision of the Tax Acts.

(3) A body corporate shall for the purposes of *subsection (1)* be deemed to be a wholly-owned subsidiary of another body corporate if and so long as all of its ordinary share capital is owned by that other body corporate, whether directly or through another body corporate or other bodies corporate or partly directly and partly through another body corporate or other bodies corporate; but, where part of the ordinary share capital of any body corporate is held by a Minister of the Government and the remainder of the ordinary share capital of that body corporate is held by another body corporate, the first-mentioned body corporate shall for the purposes of *subsection (1)* be deemed to be a wholly owned subsidiary of the last-mentioned body corporate.

(4) *Subsections (5)* to *(10)* of *section 9* shall apply for the purpose of determining the amount of ordinary share capital held in a body corporate through other bodies corporate.

Cross References

From Section 675

Section 9 Subsidiaries.

Section 672 Interpretation (sections 672 to 683).

Section 673 Allowance in respect of development expenditure and exploration expenditure.

Section 674 Expenditure on abortive exploration.

Section 679 Exploration expenditure.

Section 683 Charge to tax on sums received from sale of scheduled mineral assets.

Schedule 32 Transitional Provisions

To Section 675

Section 674 Expenditure on abortive exploration.
Section 677 Investment allowance in respect of exploration expenditure.
Section 679 Exploration expenditure.

676 Expenditure incurred by person not engaged in trade of mining

[F(TPCM)A74 s5; CTA76 s21(1) and Sch1 par67]

(1) Where—

(a) a person incurs exploration expenditure which results in the finding of a deposit of scheduled minerals, and

(b) without having carried on any trade which consists of or includes the working of that deposit and without any allowance or deduction under or by virtue of *sections 672* to *683* having been made to the person in respect of that expenditure, the person sells any assets representing that expenditure to another person,

then, if that other person carries on such a trade in connection with that deposit, that other person shall for the purposes of *sections 672* to *683* be deemed to have incurred, for the purposes of the trade and in connection with the deposit, exploration expenditure equal to the lesser of—

(i) the amount of the exploration expenditure represented by the assets, and

(ii) the price paid by that other person for the assets,

and that expenditure shall be deemed to have been incurred by that other person on the date on which that other person commences to carry on that trade.

(2) A person who by virtue of *subsection (1)* is deemed to have incurred an amount of exploration expenditure shall be deemed not to have incurred that amount of expenditure unless the working of the deposit results in the production of scheduled minerals in reasonable commercial quantities.

(3) Subject to *paragraphs 16* and *18* of *Schedule 32*, a deduction or allowance in respect of the same expenditure shall not be made both under this section and under some other provision of the Tax Acts.

(4) *Section 677* shall not apply to expenditure in respect of which an allowance is made by virtue of this section.

Cross References

From Section 676

Section 672 Interpretation (sections 672 to 683).
Section 677 Investment allowance in respect of exploration expenditure.
Section 683 Charge to tax on sums received from sale of scheduled mineral assets.
Schedule 32 Transitional Provisions

To Section 676

Section 672 Interpretation (sections 672 to 683).
Section 679 Exploration expenditure.

677 Investment allowance in respect of exploration expenditure

[F(TPCM)A74 s6; CTA76 s21(1) and Sch1 par68]

(1) Where a person carrying on the trade of working a qualifying mine incurs on or after the 6th day of April, 1974, [and before 1 January 2011,][1] exploration expenditure in relation to which *section 673* applies, there shall, in addition to any mine development allowance made in respect of such expenditure, be made to the person in taxing the trade for the chargeable period for which such

mine development allowance is made an allowance (which shall be known as an "exploration investment allowance") equal to 20 per cent of such expenditure, and *section 670(6)* shall apply to an exploration investment allowance as it applies to a mine development allowance.

(2) (a) No allowance shall be made under this section in respect of exploration expenditure—

(i) incurred before the 6th day of April, 1974, whether or not such expenditure is by virtue of any provision of the Tax Acts deemed to have been incurred on or after that date, or

(ii) which is deemed to be incurred by a person other than the person who incurred the expenditure.

(b) *Paragraph (a)* shall not apply in respect of expenditure deemed under *section 675* to have been incurred by a body corporate other than the body corporate which incurred the expenditure.

Amendments

[1] Inserted by FA11 s27(a). Deemed to have come into force and takes effect as on and from 1 January 2011.

Cross References

From Section 677

Section 670 Mine development allowance.
Section 673 Allowance in respect of development expenditure and exploration expenditure.
Section 675 Exploration expenditure incurred by certain bodies corporate.

To Section 677

Section 413 Profits or assets available for distribution.
Section 676 Expenditure incurred by person not engaged in trade of mining.
Section 679 Exploration expenditure.

678 Allowance for machinery and plant

[F(TPCM)A74 s7(1), (3) and (4); CTA76 s21 and Sch1 pars57, 58, 59 and 69; FA71 s22(3) and (4), s23, s24 and s25; FA97 s146(1) and Sch9 PtI par7(1)]

(1) Where on or after the 6th day of April, 1974, new machinery or new plant (other than vehicles suitable for the conveyance by road of persons or goods or the haulage by road of other vehicles) is provided for use for the purposes of the trade of working a qualifying mine, that machinery or plant shall, if it is not qualifying machinery or plant, be deemed for the purpose of *section 285* to be qualifying machinery or plant.

(2) Where on or after the 6th day of April, 1974, [and before 1 January 2011,][1] a person carrying on the trade of working a qualifying mine incurs capital expenditure on the provision of new machinery or new plant (other than vehicles suitable for the conveyance by road of persons or goods or the haul-age by road of other vehicles) for the purposes of that trade, there shall be made to the person for the chargeable period related to the expenditure an allowance equal to 20 per cent of the expenditure, and such allowance shall be made in taxing the trade.

(3) For the purposes of ascertaining the amount of any allowance to be made to any person under *section 284* in respect of expenditure incurred during a chargeable period on any qualifying machinery or plant, no account shall be taken of an allowance under *subsection (2)* in respect of that expenditure, and in *section 284(4)* "the allowances on that account" and "the allowances" where it occurs before "exceed" shall each be

construed as not including a reference to any allowance made under *subsection (2)* to the person by whom the trade of working a qualifying mine is carried on.

(4) Where an allowance under *subsection (2)* has been made to any person in respect of expenditure incurred on the provision of qualifying machinery or plant and the machinery or plant is sold by that person without the machinery or plant having been used by that person for the purposes of the trade of working a qualifying mine or before the expiration of the period of 2 years from the day on which the machinery or plant began to be so used, the allowance shall be withdrawn [and assessments shall be made or amended][2] as may be necessary for or in consequence of the withdrawal of the allowance.

(5) For the purposes of this section—

(a) the day on which any expenditure is incurred shall be taken to be the day when the sum in question becomes payable,

(b) expenditure shall not be regarded as having been incurred by a person in so far as it has been or is to be met directly or indirectly by the State, by any board established by statute or by any public or local authority,

(c) any expenditure incurred for the purposes of a trade by a person about to carry on the trade shall be treated as if that expenditure had been incurred by that person on the first day on which that person carries on the trade,

(d) capital expenditure shall not include any expenditure which is allowed to be deducted in computing for the purposes of tax the profits or gains of a trade carried on by the person incurring the expenditure, and

(e) *subsections (2)* and *(3)* of *section 306* shall apply in determining the chargeable period (being a year of assessment) for which an allowance is to be made under this section.

(6) For the purposes of the Income Tax Acts, any claim by a person for an allowance under this section in taxing the person's trade shall be included in the annual statement required to be delivered under those Acts of the profits or gains of the person's trade and shall be accompanied by a certificate signed by the claimant (which shall be deemed to form part of the claim) stating that the expenditure was incurred on the provision of qualifying machinery or plant and giving such particulars as show that the allowance is to be made.

(7) *Section 304(4)* shall apply in relation to an allowance under *subsection (2)* as it applies in relation to allowances to be made under *Part 9*.

Amendments

[1] Inserted by FA11 s27(b). Deemed to have come into force and takes effect as on and from 1 January 2011.

[2] Substituted by FA12 sched4(part 2)(g).

Cross References

From Section 678

Section 268 Meaning of "industrial building or structure".

Section 284 Wear and tear allowances.

Section 285 Acceleration of wear and tear allowances.

Section 304 Income tax: allowances and charges in taxing a trade, etc.

Section 306 Meaning of basis period.

To Section 678

Section 309 Companies not resident in the State.

Section 679 Exploration expenditure.

679 Exploration expenditure

[F(TPCM)A 74 s7A; FA90 s39(d)]

(1) (a) In this section—

"*exploration company*" means a company, the business of which for the time being consists primarily of exploring for scheduled minerals;

"*exploring for scheduled minerals*" means searching in the State for deposits of scheduled minerals or testing such deposits or winning access to such deposits, and includes the systematic searching for areas containing scheduled minerals and searching by drilling or other means for scheduled minerals within those areas, but does not include operations which are operations in the course of developing or working a qualifying mine.

(b) This section shall apply as respects expenditure incurred on or after the 1st day of April, 1990.

(2) Subject to *subsections (3)* to *(5)*, for as long as a company—

(a) is an exploration company,

(b) does not carry on a trade of working a qualifying mine, and

(c) incurs capital expenditure (including such expenditure incurred on the provision of plant and machinery) for the purposes of exploring for scheduled minerals,

the company shall be deemed for the purposes of *sections 673, 674(3), 677* and *678* and the other provisions of the Tax Acts, apart from *section 672, subsections (1), (2)* and *(4)* of *section 674* and *sections 675, 676, 680, 681, 682* and *683*—

(i) to be carrying on a trade of working a qualifying mine,

(ii) to come within the charge to corporation tax in respect of that trade when it first incurs the capital expenditure referred to in *paragraph (c)*, and

(iii) to incur for the purposes of that trade that expenditure incurred on the provision of plant and machinery,

so that all allowances or charges to be made for an accounting period by virtue of this subsection and *section 673, 677* or *678* shall be given effect by treating the amount of any allowance as a trading expense of that trade in the period and by treating the amount on which any such charge is to be made as a trading receipt of that trade in the period.

(3) Where by virtue of *subsection (2)* a company is to be treated as incurring a loss in a trade in an accounting period, the company—

(a) shall be entitled to relief in respect of the loss under […][1] *subsections (1)* to *(3)* of *section 396* and *subsections (1)* and *(2)* of *section 397* as if for "trading income from the trade" or "trading income", wherever occurring in *sections 396* and *397*, there were substituted "profits (of whatever description)", and

(b) subject to *subsection (4)(b)(ii)*, shall not otherwise be entitled to relief in respect of the loss or to surrender relief under *section 420(1)* in respect of the loss.

(4) (a) Any asset representing exploration expenditure in respect of which an allowance or deduction has been made to a company by virtue of *subsection (2)* and *section 673* shall for the purposes of *section 670(11)* be treated as an asset representing capital expenditure incurred in connection with the mine which the company is deemed to be working by virtue of *subsection (2)*, and the company shall not cease to be deemed to be carrying on the trade

of working that mine, so as to be within the charge to corporation tax in respect of that trade, before any sale of such an asset in the event of such a sale.

(b) Subject to *paragraph (c)*, where a company begins at any time (in this paragraph and in *paragraph (c)* referred to as "the relevant time") to carry on a trade of working a qualifying mine and accordingly ceases to be deemed to carry on such a trade, the company shall be treated as carrying on the same trade before and after that time for the purposes of—

(i) any allowance, charge or trade receipt treated as arising by reference to any capital expenditure incurred before the relevant time, and

(ii) relief, other than by virtue of *subsection (3)*, under *section 396(1)* for any losses arising before the relevant time, in so far as relief has not already been given for those losses by virtue of this section.

(c) *Paragraph (b)* shall not apply where there is a change in the ownership of the company within a period of—

(i) 12 months ending at the relevant time, or

(ii) 24 months beginning at the relevant time.

(d) *Schedule 9* shall apply for the purposes of supplementing this subsection.

(5) (a) Notwithstanding any other provision of the Tax Acts, where an allowance or deduction has been given by virtue of this section in respect of any expenditure, no other allowance or deduction shall be given by virtue of any provision of the Tax Acts, including this section, in respect of that expenditure.

(b) *Paragraph (b)* of *section 261* shall apply to a company for as long as it is deemed by virtue of *subsection (2)* to be carrying on a trade of working a qualifying mine as if "who is not a company within the charge to corporation tax in respect of the payment" were deleted from that paragraph.

Amendments

[1] Deleted by FA03 s41(1)(i). This section applies as respects accounting periods ending on or after 6 February 2003.

Cross References

From Section 679

Section 261 Taxation of relevant interest, etc.
Section 396 Relief for trading losses other than terminal losses.
Section 397 Relief for terminal loss in a trade.
Section 420 Losses, etc. which may be surrendered by means of group relief.
Section 670 Mine development allowance.
Section 672 Interpretation (sections 672 to 683).
Section 673 Allowance in respect of development expenditure and exploration expenditure.
Section 674 Expenditure on abortive exploration.
Section 675 Exploration expenditure incurred by certain bodies corporate.
Section 676 Expenditure incurred by person not engaged in trade of mining.
Section 677 Investment allowance in respect of exploration expenditure.
Section 678 Allowance for machinery and plant.
Section 680 Annual allowance for mineral depletion.
Section 681 Allowance for mine rehabilitation expenditure.
Section 682 Marginal mine allowance.
Section 683 Charge to tax on sums received from sale of scheduled mineral assets.
Schedule 9 Change in Ownership of Company: Disallowance of Trading Losses

To Section 679

Section 675 Exploration expenditure incurred by certain bodies corporate.

Schedule 9 Change in Ownership of Company: Disallowance of Trading Losses

680 Annual allowance for mineral depletion

[F(TPCM)A74 s8; CTA76 s140 and Sch2 PtI par37]

(1) Where a person carrying on the trade of working a qualifying mine incurs after the 31st day of March, 1974, capital expenditure on the acquisition of a scheduled mineral asset entitling such person to work deposits of scheduled minerals and in connection with that trade commences to work those deposits, such person shall be entitled to mine development allowances under *section 670* in respect of that capital expenditure to the extent that such person would have been entitled to such allowances if that capital expenditure had been capital expenditure incurred in the development of the mine, but *section 673* shall not apply in respect of any such expenditure.

(2) Where a person who commences to carry on the trade of working a qualifying mine [at any time][1] on or after the 6th day of April, 1974, incurred capital expenditure before that [time][2] on the acquisition of a scheduled mineral asset in connection with that mine, such person shall for the purposes of this section be deemed to have incurred that expenditure on the day on which such person commences to carry on that trade, and *subsection (1)* shall apply accordingly.

Amendments

[1] Inserted by FA98 s40(a).

[2] Substituted by FA98 s40(b).

Cross References

From Section 680

Section 670 Mine development allowance.

Section 673 Allowance in respect of development expenditure and exploration expenditure.

To Section 680

Section 413 Profits or assets available for distribution.

Section 679 Exploration expenditure.

681 Allowance for mine rehabilitation expenditure

[F(TPCM)A74 s8A(1) to (9); FA96 s34; FA97 s146(1) and Sch9 PtI par7(2)]

(1) (a) In this section—

"*integrated pollution control licence*" means a licence granted under section 83 of the Environmental Protection Agency Act, 1992;

"*mine rehabilitation fund*", in relation to a qualifying mine, means a fund—

(i) which consists of amounts paid by a person carrying on the trade of working a qualifying mine to another person (in this section referred to as "the fund holder") not connected with the first-mentioned person,

(ii) which is obliged to be maintained under the terms—

(I) of a State mining facility, or

(II) of any other agreement in writing to which the Minister is a party and to which the State mining facility is subject,

(iii) the sole purpose of which is to have available at the time a qualifying mine ceases to be worked such amount as is specified in a certificate given by the Minister under *subsection (2)* as being the amount which in the Minister's opinion could reasonably be expected to be necessary to meet rehabilitation expenditure in relation to the qualifying mine, and

(iv) no part of which may be paid to the person, or a person connected with that person, who is working or has worked the qualifying mine except where—

(I) the fund holder has been authorised in writing by the Minister, and by either or both the relevant local authority and the Environmental Protection Agency, to make a payment to the person or the connected person, as the case may be, for the purposes of incurring rehabilitation expenditure in relation to the qualifying mine, or

(II) an amount may be paid to the person or the connected person, as the case may be, after a certificate of completion of rehabilitation in relation to the qualifying mine has been submitted to and approved by—

(A) the Minister, and

(B) either or both the relevant local authority and the Environmental Protection Agency;

"*the Minister*" means the [Minister for Communications, Energy and Natural Resources;][1]

"*qualifying mine*" means a mine being worked for the purpose of obtaining scheduled minerals, dolomite and dolomitic [fireclay, coal][2], calcite and gypsum, or any of those minerals;

"*rehabilitation expenditure*" means expenditure incurred in connection with the rehabilitation of the site of a mine or part of a mine, being expenditure incurred by a person who has ceased to work the mine in order to comply with any condition—

(i) of a State mining facility,

(ii) subject to which planning permission for development consisting of the mining and working of minerals was granted, or

(iii) subject to which an integrated pollution control licence for an activity specified in the First Schedule to the Environmental Protection Agency Act, 1992, was granted;

"rehabilitation" includes landscaping and the carrying out of any activities which take place after the mine ceases to be worked and which are required by a condition subject to which planning permission for development consisting of the mining and working of minerals, or an integrated pollution control licence, was granted;

['*relevant local authority*', in relation to a qualifying mine disposal, means the local authority for the purposes of the Local Government Act 2001 (as amended by the *Local Government Reform Act 2014*) in whose functional area the mine being disposed of is situated;][3]

"*relevant payments*" means payments specified in accordance with *paragraph (b)(iii)* of *subsection (2)* in a certificate given under that subsection and which are paid at or about the time specified in the certificate;

"*State mining facility*", in relation to a mine, means a State mining lease, a State mining licence or a State mining permission granted by the Minister in relation to the mine.

(b) For the purposes of this section—

(i) any reference to the site of a mine includes a reference to land used in connection with the working of the mine, and

(ii) the net cost to any person of the rehabilitation of the site of a mine shall be the excess, if any, of rehabilitation expenditure over any receipts attributable to the rehabilitation (whether for spoil or other assets removed from the site or for tipping rights or otherwise).

(c) For the purposes of this section, *subsections (2)* and *(3)* of *section 306* shall apply in determining the chargeable period (being a year of assessment) for which an allowance is to be made under this section.

(2) (a) Where in relation to a fund the Minister is of the opinion that—

(i) the matters set out in *paragraphs (i), (ii)* and *(iv)* of the definition of "mine rehabilitation fund" are satisfied, and

(ii) the sole purpose of the fund is to have available at the time a qualifying mine ceases to be worked such amount as could reasonably be expected to be necessary to meet rehabilitation expenditure in relation to the qualifying mine,

the Minister may give a certificate to that effect.

(b) A certificate given under *paragraph (a)* shall, in addition to the information specified in that paragraph, specify—

(i) the number of years, being the Minister's opinion of the life (in this section referred to as "the estimated life") of the mine remaining at the time the certificate is given,

(ii) the amount which in the Minister's opinion could reasonably be expected to be necessary to meet rehabilitation expenditure in relation to the qualifying mine, and

(iii) the amounts (in this section referred to as "the scheduled payments") required to be paid to the fund holder, and the times at which such amounts are to be paid, so as to achieve the purpose specified in *paragraph (a)(ii)*.

(c) The Minister may, by notice in writing given to a person to whom a certificate has been given under this section, amend the certificate.

(3) (a) An allowance equal to so much of any rehabilitation expenditure in relation to a qualifying mine as does not exceed the net cost of the rehabilitation of the site of the mine shall be made to a person under this section for the chargeable period related to the expenditure.

(b) Expenditure incurred by a person after the person ceases to carry on the trade of working a qualifying mine shall be treated as having been incurred on the last day on which the person carried on the trade.

(4) (a) Subject to *paragraphs (b)* and *(c)*, where the Minister has issued a certificate under *subsection (2)* in respect of a mine rehabilitation fund related to a qualifying mine, an allowance shall be made to the person who—

(i) is working the qualifying mine, and

(ii) is obliged to make relevant payments to the fund holder in relation to the fund, for any chargeable period which falls wholly or partly in the period (in this subsection referred to as "the funding period") commencing on the date on which the Minister gives the certificate and ending at the end of the estimated life of the mine, and the amount of the allowance shall be an amount determined by the formula—

$$E \times \frac{N}{12} \times \frac{1}{L}$$

where—

E is the aggregate of the scheduled payments,

N is the number of months in the chargeable period, or the part of the chargeable period falling in the funding period, and

L is the number of years in the estimated life of the mine.

(b) The aggregate of the amounts of allowances under this subsection for a chargeable period and all preceding chargeable periods shall not exceed the aggregate of the amounts of relevant payments made in the chargeable period or its basis period and in all preceding chargeable periods or their basis periods.

(c) Where effect cannot be given to an allowance or part of an allowance under this subsection for a chargeable period by virtue of *paragraph (b)*, the allowance or the part of the allowance, as the case may be, shall be added to the amount of an allowance under this subsection for the following chargeable period and, subject to *paragraph (b)*, shall be deemed to be part of the allowance for that period or, if there is no such allowance for that period, shall be deemed to be the allowance for that period, and so on for succeeding periods.

(5) Where the Minister by notice in writing amends a certificate under *subsection (2)(c)* in a chargeable period or its basis period—

(a) if the aggregate of the amounts of allowances made under *subsection (4)* for the chargeable period and all preceding chargeable periods exceeds the aggregate of the amounts of allowances which would have been made under that subsection for those chargeable periods if the certificate had been amended in accordance with the notice at the time the certificate was given, an amount equal to the amount of the excess shall be treated as a trading receipt of the chargeable period in which, or in the basis period for which, the certificate was amended, and

(b) if the aggregate of the amounts of allowances which would have been made under *subsection (4)* for the chargeable period and all preceding chargeable periods if the certificate had been amended in accordance with the notice at the time the certificate was given exceeds the aggregate of the amounts of allowances made under that subsection for those chargeable periods, the allowance under *subsection (4)* for the chargeable period shall, subject to *subsection (4)(b)*, be increased by an amount equal to the excess.

(6) (a) Subject to *paragraph (b)*, an amount received by a person who is working or has worked a qualifying mine, or by a person connected with such a person, from the fund holder of a mine rehabilitation fund in relation to the qualifying mine, or otherwise in connection with the mine rehabilitation fund, shall be treated as trading income of the person in accordance with this section.

(b) The amount to be treated as trading income for a chargeable period shall not exceed the excess of the aggregate of the amounts of allowances made under *subsections (4)* and *(5)* in that chargeable period and in any preceding chargeable periods over the aggregate amounts treated under this subsection or *subsection (5)* as trading income for all preceding chargeable periods.

(c) An amount to be treated under this subsection as trading income of a person shall be treated as income of—

(i) where the amount is received at any time when the person is working the qualifying mine, the chargeable period in which, or in the basis period for which, the amount is received, and

(ii) in any other case, the chargeable period in which the mine ceases to be worked.

(d) Notwithstanding *paragraph (c)*, where an amount is to be treated as income of a chargeable period in accordance with *subparagraph (ii)* of that paragraph, the amount shall be assessed for the chargeable period in which, or in the basis period for which, the amount is received, and details of the receipt of the amount shall be included in the return required to be made by the person under [*Chapter 3* of *Part 41A*][4] for that chargeable period.

(7) Where a person (in this subsection referred to as "the first-mentioned person") ceases to work a qualifying mine and any obligations of the first-mentioned person to rehabilitate the site of the mine are transferred to any other person, that other person shall be treated for the purposes of this section as if that other person had worked the qualifying mine and as if everything done to or by the first-mentioned person had been done to or by that other person.

(8) As respects any person who incurs rehabilitation expenditure in respect of which an allowance is made under *subsection (3)*—

(a) rehabilitation expenditure shall not otherwise be deductible in computing income of the person for any purpose of income tax or corporation tax,

(b) an allowance shall not be made in respect of the expenditure under any provision of the Tax Acts other than this section, and

(c) to the extent that any receipts are taken into account under *subsection (1)(b)(ii)* to determine the net cost of the rehabilitation of the site of a mine, those receipts shall not constitute income of the person for any purpose of income tax or corporation tax.

(9) An allowance under this section made to a person who is carrying on a trade of working a mine shall be made in taxing that trade, and *section 304(4)* shall apply in relation to an allowance under *subsection (4)* as it applies in relation to allowances to be made under *Part 9*.

Amendments

[1] Substituted by FA08 sched8(1)(j). Has effect as on and from 13 March 2008.

[2] Inserted by FA98 s41.

[3] Substituted by LGRA14 sched2(part5).

[4] Substituted by FA12 sched4(part 2)(g).

Cross References

From Section 681

Section 268 Meaning of "industrial building or structure".

Section 304 Income tax: allowances and charges in taxing a trade, etc.

Section 306 Meaning of basis period.
Section 951 Obligation to make a return.

To Section 681

Section 679 Exploration expenditure.

682 Marginal mine allowance

[F(TPCM)A74 s10; CTA76 s140(1), s164, Sch2 PtI par38 and Sch3 PtII]

(1) In this section, "*marginal mine*" means a qualifying mine in respect of which the [Minister for Communications, Energy and Natural Resources][1] gives a certificate stating that that Minister is satisfied that the profits derived or to be derived from the working of that mine are such that, if tax is to be charged on those profits in accordance with the Income Tax Acts, other than this section, the mine is unlikely to be worked or to continue to be worked.

(2) The Minister for Finance, after consultation with the [Minister for Communications, Energy and Natural Resources,][2] may direct in respect of a marginal mine that for any particular year of assessment the tax chargeable on the profits of that qualifying mine shall be reduced to such amount (including nil) as may be specified by the Minister for Finance.

(3) Where a person is carrying on the trade of working a qualifying mine in respect of which the Minister for Finance gives a direction under *subsection (2)* in respect of a year of assessment, an allowance (which shall be known as a "marginal mine allowance") shall be made as a deduction in charging the profits of that trade to income tax for that year of assessment of such amount or amounts as will ensure that the tax charged in respect of the profits of that trade shall equal the amount specified by that Minister.

(4) This section shall apply for corporation tax as it applies for income tax, and the references to the Income Tax Acts, to a year of assessment and to charging the profits of that trade to income tax shall apply as if they were respectively references to the Corporation Tax Acts, to an accounting period and to computing the profits of that trade for the purposes of corporation tax.

Amendments

[1] Substituted by FA08 sched8(1)(k)(i). Has effect as on and from 13 March 2008.

[2] Substituted by FA08 sched8(1)(k)(ii). Has effect as on and from 13 March 2008.

Cross References

To Section 682

Section 679 Exploration expenditure.

683 Charge to tax on sums received from sale of scheduled mineral assets

[F(TPCM)A74 s11; CTA76 s140(1) and Sch2 PtI par39; FA81 s9(e)]

(1) In this section—

"*chargeable period*" means an accounting period of a company or a year of assessment;

any reference to the sale of a right to a scheduled mineral asset includes a reference to the grant of a licence to work scheduled minerals.

(2) Where a person resident in the State sells any scheduled mineral asset and the net proceeds of the sale consist wholly or partly of a capital sum, the person shall, subject to this section, be charged to tax under Case IV of Schedule D for the

chargeable period in which the sum is received by the person on an amount equal to that sum; but where the person is an individual who, not later than 24 months after the end of the year of assessment in which the sum is paid, elects by notice in writing to the inspector to be charged to tax for that year of assessment and for each of the 5 succeeding years of assessment on an amount equal to one-sixth of that sum, the person shall be so charged.

(3) (a) In this subsection, "*tax*" shall mean income tax, unless the seller of the scheduled mineral asset, being a company, would be within the charge to corporation tax in respect of any proceeds of the sale not consisting of a capital sum.

(b) Subject to *paragraph (c)*, where a person not resident in the State sells any scheduled mineral asset and the net proceeds of the sale consist wholly or partly of a capital sum, then—

(i) the person shall be charged to tax in respect of that sum under Case IV of Schedule D for the chargeable period in which the sum is received by the person, and

(ii) *section 238* shall apply to that sum as if it were an annual payment payable otherwise than out of profits or gains brought into charge to tax.

(c) Where the person referred to in *paragraph (b)* is an individual who, not later than 24 months after the end of the year of assessment in which the sum is paid elects by notice in writing to the Revenue Commissioners that the sum shall be treated for the purpose of tax for that year and for each of the 5 succeeding years as if one-sixth of that sum were included in his or her income chargeable to tax for each of those years respectively, it shall be so treated, and all such repayments and assessments of tax for each of those years shall be made as are necessary to give effect to the election; but—

(i) the election shall not affect the amount of tax to be deducted and accounted for under *section 238*,

(ii) where any sum is deducted under *section 238*, any adjustments necessary to give effect to the election shall be made by means of repayment of tax, and

(iii) those adjustments shall be made year by year and as if one-sixth of the sum deducted had been deducted in respect of tax for each year, and no repayment of, or of any part of, that portion of the tax deducted which is to be treated as deducted in respect of tax for any year shall be made unless and until it is ascertained that the tax ultimately to be paid for that year is less than the amount of tax paid for that year.

(4) Where the scheduled mineral asset sold by a person was acquired by the person by purchase and the price paid consisted wholly or partly of a capital sum, *subsections (2)* and *(3)* shall apply as if any capital sum received by the person when the person sells the asset were reduced by the amount of that sum; but nothing in this subsection shall affect the amount of tax to be deducted and accounted for under *section 238* by virtue of *subsection (3)*, and where any sum is deducted under *section 238* any adjustment necessary to give effect to this subsection shall be made by means of repayment of tax.

(5) Where by virtue of an order made by the [Minister for Communications, Energy and Natural Resources][1] under section 14 of the Minerals Development Act, 1940, scheduled minerals or rights to work such minerals are acquired and that Minister pays compensation to any person in respect of such acquisition, that person shall be deemed for the purposes of this section to have sold a scheduled mineral asset for a capital sum equal to the amount of compensation paid to that person, and *subsections (2)* to *(4)* shall apply to the compensation as they apply to a capital sum received in respect of a sale of a scheduled mineral asset.

Amendments

[1] Substituted by FA08 sched8(1)(l). Has effect as on and from 13 March 2008.

Revenue Precedents

If an individual disposes of mineral rights in land but retains ownership of the land, the proceeds are liable to Income Tax under Schedule D, Case IV. IT943033

Cross References

From Section 683

Section 238 Annual payments not payable out of taxed income.

To Section 683

Section 672 Interpretation (sections 672 to 683).
Section 675 Exploration expenditure incurred by certain bodies corporate.
Section 676 Expenditure incurred by person not engaged in trade of mining.
Section 679 Exploration expenditure.

CHAPTER 2

Petroleum Taxation

684 Interpretation (Chapter 2)

[FA92 s75; FA95 s42(a)]

(1) In this Chapter—

"*abandonment activities*", in relation to a relevant field or any part of it, means those activities of a person, whether carried on by the person or on behalf of the person, which comply with the requirements of a petroleum lease held by the person, or, if the person is a company, held by the company or a company associated with it, in respect of—

(a) the closing down, decommissioning or abandonment of the relevant field or the part of it, as the case may be, or

(b) the dismantlement or removal of the whole or a part of any structure, plant or machinery which is not situated on dry land and which has been brought into use for the purposes of transporting as far as dry land petroleum won from the relevant field or from the part of it, as the case may be;

"*abandonment expenditure*", in relation to a relevant field or any part of it, means expenditure incurred on abandonment activities in relation to the field or the part of it, as the case may be;

"*chargeable period*" means an accounting period of a company or a year of assessment;

"*designated area*" means an area designated by order under section 2 of the Continental Shelf Act, 1968;

"*development expenditure*" means capital expenditure incurred in connection with a relevant field on the provision for use in carrying on petroleum extraction activities of—

(a) machinery or plant,

(b) any works, buildings or structures, or

(c) any other assets,

which are of such a nature that when the relevant field ceases to be worked they are likely to be so diminished in value that their value will be nil or almost nil, but does not include—

(i) expenditure on any vehicle suitable for the conveyance by road of persons or goods or the haulage by road of other vehicles,

(ii) expenditure on any building or structure for use as a dwelling house, shop or office or for any purpose ancillary to the purposes of a dwelling house, shop or office,

(iii) (I) expenditure incurred on petroleum exploration activities, and

(II) payments made to the [Minister for Communications, Energy and Natural Resources][1] on the application for, or in consideration of the granting of, a licence (other than a petroleum lease) or other payments made to that Minister in respect of the holding of the licence,

(iv) expenditure on the acquisition of the site of a relevant field, or of the site of any works, buildings or structures or of rights in or over any such site,

(v) expenditure on the acquisition of, or of rights in or over, deposits of petroleum,

(vi) expenditure on—

(I) machinery or plant, or

(II) works, buildings or structures,

provided for the processing or storing of petroleum won in the course of carrying on petroleum extraction activities, other than the initial treatment and storage of such petroleum,

or

(vii) any interest payment,

and "assets representing development expenditure" shall be construed accordingly and shall include any results obtained from any search or enquiry on which the expenditure was incurred;

"*dry land*" means land not permanently covered by water;

"*exploration expenditure*" means—

(a) capital expenditure incurred on petroleum exploration activities, and

(b) payments made to the [Minister for Communications, Energy and Natural Resources][2] on the application for, or in consideration of the granting of, a licence (other than a petroleum lease) or other payments made to that Minister in respect of the holding of the licence,

but does not include any interest payment, and "assets representing exploration expenditure" shall be construed accordingly and shall include any results obtained from any search, exploration or enquiry on which the expenditure was incurred;

"initial treatment and storage", in relation to petroleum won from a relevant field, means the doing of any of the following—

(a) subjecting petroleum so won to any process of which the sole purpose is to enable the petroleum to be safely stored, safely loaded into a tanker or safely accepted for refining,

(b) separating petroleum so won and consisting of gas from other petroleum so won,

(c) separating petroleum won and consisting of gas of a kind that is transported and sold in normal commercial practice from other petroleum so won and consisting of gas,

(d) liquefying petroleum so won and consisting of gas of such a kind as is mentioned in *paragraph (c)* for the purpose of transporting such petroleum,

(e) subjecting petroleum so won to any process so as to secure that petroleum disposed of without having been refined has the quality that is normal for petroleum so disposed of from the relevant field, or

(f) storing petroleum so won before its disposal or its appropriation to refining or to any use, except use in—

(i) winning petroleum from a relevant field, including searching in that field for and winning access to such petroleum, or

(ii) transporting as far as dry land petroleum that is won from a place not on dry land,

but does not include any activity carried on as part of or in association with the refining of petroleum;

"*licence*" means—

(a) an exploration licence,

(b) a lease undertaking,

(c) a licensing option,

(d) a petroleum prospecting licence,

(e) a petroleum lease, or

(f) a reserved area licence,

granted in respect of an area in the State or a designated area under the Petroleum and Other Minerals Development Act, 1960, and which was granted subject to—

(i) the licensing terms set out in the Notice entitled "Ireland Exclusive Offshore Licensing Terms" presented to each House of the Oireachtas on the 29th day of April, 1975,

(ii) licensing terms presented to each House of the Oireachtas on a day or days which fall after the 29th day of April, 1975, or

(iii) licensing terms to which *paragraph (i)* or *(ii)* relates, as amended or varied from time to time;

"*licensed area*" means an area in respect of which a licence is in force;

"*mining trade*" means a trade consisting only of working a mine which is a qualifying mine or, in the case of a trade consisting partly of such an activity and partly of one or more other activities, the part of the trade consisting only of working such a mine which is treated by virtue of *section 685* as a separate trade;

"*petroleum*" means petroleum (within the meaning of section 2(1) of the Petroleum and Other Minerals Development Act, 1960) won or capable of being won under the authority of a licence;

"*petroleum activities*" means any one or more of the following activities—

(a) petroleum exploration activities,

(b) petroleum extraction activities, and

(c) the acquisition, enjoyment or exploitation of petroleum rights;

"*petroleum exploration activities*" means activities of a person carried on by the person or on behalf of the person in searching for deposits of petroleum in a licensed area, in testing or appraising such deposits or in winning access to such deposits for the purposes of such searching, testing or appraising, where such activities are carried on under a licence (other than a petroleum lease) authorising the activities and held by the person or, if the person is a company, held by the company or a company associated with it;

"petroleum extraction activities" means activities of a person carried on by the person or on behalf of the person under a petroleum lease authorising the activities and held by the person or, if the person is a company, held by the company or a company associated with it in—

(a) winning petroleum from a relevant field, including searching in that field for and winning access to such petroleum,

(b) transporting as far as dry land petroleum so won from a place not on dry land, or

(c) effecting the initial treatment and storage of petroleum so won from the relevant field;

"petroleum profits", in relation to a company which is chargeable to corporation tax on its profits, means the income of the company from petroleum activities and any amount to be included in its total profits in respect of chargeable gains accruing to the company from disposals of petroleum-related assets;

"*petroleum-related asset*" means any of the following assets or any part of such an asset—

(a) any petroleum rights,

(b) any asset representing exploration expenditure or development expenditure,

(c) shares deriving their value or the greater part of their value, whether directly or indirectly, from petroleum activities, other than shares dealt in on a stock exchange;

"*petroleum rights*" means rights to petroleum to be extracted or to interests in, or to the benefit of, petroleum, and includes an interest in a licence;

"*petroleum trade*" means a trade consisting only of trading activities which are petroleum activities or, in the case of a trade consisting partly of such activities and partly of other activities, the part of the trade consisting only of trading activities which are petroleum activities which is treated by virtue of *section 685* as a separate trade;

"*qualifying mine*" has the same meaning as in *section 672*;

"*relevant field*" means an area in respect of which a licence, being a petroleum lease, is in force.

(2) For the purposes of this Chapter, 2 companies shall be associated with one another if—

(a) one company is a 51 per cent subsidiary of the other company,

(b) each company is a 51 per cent subsidiary of a third company, or

(c) one company is owned by a consortium of which the other company is a member,

and for the purposes of *paragraph (c)* a company shall be owned by a consortium if all the ordinary share capital of that company is directly and beneficially owned between them by 5 or fewer companies, which companies are in this Chapter referred to as "the members of the consortium".

Amendments

[1] Substituted by FA08 sched8(1)(m)(i). Has effect as on and from 13 March 2008.

[2] Substituted by FA08 sched8(1)(m)(ii). Has effect as on and from 13 March 2008.

Cross References

From Section 684

Section 672 Interpretation (sections 672 to 683).

Section 685 Separation of trading activities.

To Section 684

Section 696B Interpretation and application (Chapter 3).

Section 697A Interpretation (Part 24A).

Schedule 32 Transitional Provisions

685 Separation of trading activities

[FA92 s76]

(1) Where a person carries on any petroleum activities as part of a trade and those activities apart from any other activity would constitute a trade, those activities shall be treated for the purposes of the Tax Acts and the Capital Gains Tax Acts as a separate trade distinct from all other activities carried on by the person as part of the trade, and any necessary apportionment shall be made of receipts and expenses.

(2) Where a person works a qualifying mine as part of a trade, that activity shall be treated for the purposes of this Chapter as a separate trade distinct from all other activity carried on by the person as part of the trade, and any necessary apportionment shall be made of receipts and expenses.

Cross References

To Section 685

Section 684 Interpretation (Chapter 2).

686 Reduction of corporation tax [Repealed]

Repealed by FA05 s55. Has effect as respects accounting periods ending on or after 3 February 2005.

Cross References

From Section 687

Section 305 Income tax: manner of granting, and effect of, allowances made by means of discharge or repayment of tax.

Section 308 Corporation tax: manner of granting, and effect of, allowances made by means of discharge or repayment of tax.

Section 381 Right to repayment of tax by reference to losses.

Section 383 Relief under Case IV for losses.

Section 396 Relief for trading losses other than terminal losses.

Section 399 Losses in transactions from which income would be chargeable under Case IV or V of Schedule D.

To Section 687

Section 696B Interpretation and application (Chapter 3).

687 Treatment of losses

[FA92 s78]

(1) Notwithstanding *sections 381* and *396(2)*—

(a) as respects a loss incurred by a person in a petroleum trade, relief shall not be given—

(i) under *section 381* against any income other than income arising from petroleum activities, or

(ii) under *section 396(2)* against any profits other than petroleum profits,

and

(b) as respects any loss, other than a loss incurred in a petroleum or a mining trade, incurred by a person, relief shall not be given—

(i) under *section 381* against income arising from petroleum activities, or

(ii) under *section 396(2)* against petroleum profits.

(2) Notwithstanding *sections 383* and *399(1)*, the amount of any income of a person which is within the charge to tax under Case IV of Schedule D, and which is income arising from petroleum activities, shall not be reduced by the amount of any loss which may be relieved under *section 383* or *399(1)*, other than a loss incurred in petroleum activities, and the amount of any loss so incurred shall not be treated under either of those sections as reducing the amount of any income other than income arising from petroleum activities.

(3) Notwithstanding *sections 305(1)(b)* and *308(4)*, a capital allowance which is to be given by discharge or repayment of tax, or in charging income under Case V of Schedule D, shall not to any extent be given effect—

(a) under *section 305* against income arising from petroleum activities, or

(b) under *section 308(4)* against petroleum profits.

Cross References

From Section 687

Section 305 Income tax: manner of granting, and effect of, allowances made by means of discharge or repayment of tax.

Section 308 Corporation tax: manner of granting, and effect of, allowances made by means of discharge or repayment of tax.

Section 381 Right to repayment of tax by reference to losses.

Section 383 Relief under Case IV for losses.

Section 396 Relief for trading losses other than terminal losses.

Section 399 Losses in transactions from which income would be chargeable under Case IV or V of Schedule D.

To Section 687

Section 696B Interpretation and application (Chapter 3).

688 Treatment of group relief

[FA92 s79]

(1) In this section, "*claimant company*" and "*surrendering company*" have the meanings respectively assigned to them by *section 411*.

(2) On a claim for group relief made by a claimant company in relation to a surrendering company, group relief shall not be allowed against any petroleum profits of the claimant company except to the extent that the claim relates to—

(a) a loss incurred by the surrendering company in a petroleum or mining trade, or

(b) charges on income paid, other than to a connected person, by the surrendering company which consist of payments made wholly and exclusively for the purposes of such a trade,

and group relief in respect of any such loss incurred by the surrendering company, or in respect of any charge on income paid by the surrendering company which is a payment made wholly and exclusively for the purposes of the petroleum or mining trade, shall not be allowed against any profits of the claimant company other than its petroleum profits.

Cross References

From Section 688

Section 411 Surrender of relief between members of groups and consortia.

689 Restriction of relief for losses on certain disposals

[FA92 s80(1) and (2)]

(1) Notwithstanding any provision of the Capital Gains Tax Acts or of the Corporation Tax Acts relating to the deduction of allowable losses for the purposes of capital gains tax or of corporation tax on chargeable gains—

(a) an allowable loss accruing on a disposal of an asset other than a petroleum-related asset shall not be deducted from the amount of a chargeable gain accruing on a disposal of a petroleum-related asset, and

(b) an allowable loss accruing on a disposal of a petroleum-related asset shall not be deducted from the amount of a chargeable gain accruing on a disposal of an asset other than a petroleum-related asset.

(2) *Subsection (11)* of *section 597* shall apply as respects the application of that section to a disposal of assets which have been used by the person disposing of them for the purposes of a petroleum trade as if each reference in that subsection to a "trade" or "trades" were respectively a reference to a "petroleum trade" or "petroleum trades" within the meaning of this Chapter.

Cross References

From Section 689

Section 597 Replacement of business and other assets.

690 Interest and charges on income

[FA92 s81(1) to (5) and (7)]

(1) In computing the amount of—

(a) a person's profits or gains for the purposes of income tax, or

(b) a person's income for the purposes of corporation tax,

arising from a petroleum trade, no deduction shall be made in respect of—

(i) any interest payable by the person to a connected person to the extent that the amount of the interest exceeds for whatever reason the amount which, having regard to all the terms on which the money in respect of which it is payable was borrowed and the standing of the borrower, might have been expected to be payable if the lender and the borrower had been independent parties dealing at arm's length,

(ii) interest payable by the person on any money borrowed to meet expenditure incurred on petroleum exploration activities, or

(iii) interest payable by the person on any money borrowed to meet expenditure incurred in acquiring petroleum rights from a connected person.

(2) *Section 130(2)(d)(iv)* shall not apply to so much of any interest as—

(a) would but for *section 130(2)(d)(iv)* be deductible in computing the amount of a company's income from a petroleum trade,

(b) would not be precluded by *subsection (1)* from being so deducted, and

(c) is interest payable to a company which is a resident [...][1]of a territory with the government of which arrangements having the force of law by virtue of [*section 826(1)*][2] have been made,

and for the purposes of *paragraph (c)* [...][3] a company shall be regarded as being a resident of a territory[...][4] if it is so regarded under arrangements made with the government of that territory and having the force of law by virtue of [*section 826(1)*][5].

(3) Notwithstanding *section 243*—

(a) no deduction shall be allowed from that part of a company's profits which consists of petroleum profits in respect of—

(i) a charge on income paid by the company to a connected person, or

(ii) any other charge on income paid by the company unless it is a payment made wholly and exclusively for the purposes of a petroleum or mining trade carried on by the company,

and

(b) no deduction shall be allowed from that part of a company's profits which consists of profits other than petroleum profits in respect of any charge on income paid by the company which is a payment made wholly and exclusively for the purposes of a petroleum trade carried on by the company.

(4) In applying *section 237* to any annual payment made by a person whose profits or gains for the purposes of income tax arise wholly or partly from petroleum activities—

(a) the profits or gains arising from those activities shall not be treated as profits or gains which have been brought into charge to income tax—

(i) where the annual payment is made to a connected person, or

(ii) unless (but subject to *subparagraph (i)*) the payment is made wholly and exclusively for the purposes of a petroleum or mining trade carried on by the person making the payment,

and

(b) profits or gains, other than profits or gains arising from petroleum activities, shall not be treated as profits or gains which have been brought into charge to income tax where the annual payment is made wholly and exclusively for the purposes of a petroleum trade carried on by the person making the payment.

(5) Relief shall not be allowed—

(a) under *section 396(7)* in respect of a payment to which *subsection (3)(a)(i)* applies, or

(b) under *section 390* in respect of a payment to which *subsection (4)(a)(i)* applies,

where the payment is made wholly and exclusively for the purposes of a petroleum trade.

(6) In any case where for an accounting period of a company charges on income paid by the company are allowable under *section 243*—

(a) such amount of those charges as, by virtue of *subsection (3)*—

(i) is not allowable against a part of the company's profits, but

(ii) is allowable against the remaining part (in this subsection referred to as "other profits") of its profits,

exceeds the other profits, and

(b) the amount of that excess is greater than the amount, if any, by which the total of the charges on income which, subject to *subsection (3)*, are allowable to the company under *section 243* exceeds the total of the company's profits, then, for the purpose of enabling the company to surrender the excess referred to in *paragraph (a)* by means of group relief, *section 420(6)* shall apply as if—

(I) the reference in that section to the amount paid by the surrendering company by means of charges on income were a reference to so much of that amount as by virtue of *subsection (3)* is allowable only against the company's other profits, and

(II) the reference in that section to the surrendering company's profits were a reference to its other profits only.

Amendments

[1] Deleted by FA98 sched3(6)(a).

[2, 5] Substituted by FA07 sched2(1)(w). Has effect as on and from 2 April 2007.

[3] Deleted by FA98 sched3(6)(b).

[4] Deleted by FA98 sched3(6)(c).

Cross References

From Section 690

Section 130 Matters to be treated as distributions.
Section 237 Annual payments payable wholly out of taxed income.
Section 243 Allowance of charges on income.
Section 390 Amount of assessment made under section 238 to be allowed as a loss for certain purposes.
Section 396 Relief for trading losses other than terminal losses.
Section 420 Losses, etc. which may be surrendered by means of group relief.
Section 826 Agreements for relief from double taxation.

To Section 690

Section 696B Interpretation and application (Chapter 3).

691 Restriction of set-off of advance corporation tax [Deleted]

Deleted by FA03 s41(1)(q). This section applies as respects accounting periods ending on or after 6 February 2003.

692 Development expenditure: allowances and charges

[FA92 s83; FA96 s132(1) and Sch5 PtI par18]

(1) Subject to *subsection (4)*, the provisions of the Tax Acts relating to allowances and charges in respect of capital expenditure shall apply in relation to a petroleum trade as if each reference in those provisions to machinery or plant included a reference to assets, not being machinery or plant, representing development expenditure.

(2) In relation to assets representing development expenditure, *section 284(2)* shall, subject to *subsection (3)*, apply [as if the reference to *paragraph (a)(i)* of that section to 15 per cent were a reference to 100 per cent][1].

(3) Assets representing development expenditure shall not be treated for the purposes of *section 284(1)* as being in use for the purposes of a petroleum trade at the end of any chargeable period or its basis period which ends before the commencement of production of petroleum in commercial quantities from the relevant field in connection with which the assets were provided.

(4) The following provisions shall not apply as respects development expenditure—

(a) *Chapters 1* and *3* of *Part 9*,

(b) *section 283*,

(c) *section 670*,

(d) *Chapter 1* of *Part 29*,

(e) *sections 763* to *765*, and

(f) *section 768*.

(5) (a) For the purposes of this section, assets representing development expenditure shall be deemed to include assets (in this subsection referred to as "leased assets") provided for leasing to a person carrying on a petroleum trade where such leased assets would, if they had been provided by that person, be assets representing development expenditure, and where this paragraph applies—

(i) *section 284* shall apply as if the trade for the purposes of which the leased assets are (or would under *section 298(1)* be regarded as being) in use were a petroleum trade carried on by the lessor, and

(ii) *section 403* shall apply as if each reference in that section to machinery or plant included a reference to assets, not being machinery or plant, representing development expenditure.

(b) For the purposes of *subsection (4)*, capital expenditure on the provision of leased assets shall be deemed to be development expenditure.

Amendments

[1] Substituted by FA03 s23(1)(c). This section applies as on and from 4 December 2002.

Cross References

From Section 692

Section 268 Meaning of "industrial building or structure".
Section 283 Initial allowances.
Section 284 Wear and tear allowances.
Section 298 Allowances to lessors.
Section 302 Interpretation (Chapter 3).
Section 403 Restriction on use of capital allowances for certain leased assets.
Section 670 Mine development allowance.
Section 754 Interpretation (Chapter 1).
Section 763 Interpretation (sections 764 and 765).
Section 765 Allowances for capital expenditure on scientific research.
Section 768 Allowance for know-how.

693 Exploration expenditure: allowances and charges

[FA92 s84; FA97 s146(1) and Sch9 PtI par16(2)]

(1) Subject to *subsections (5)* and *(16)*, where a person carrying on a petroleum trade has incurred any exploration expenditure (not being expenditure which has been or is to be met directly or indirectly by any other person) there shall be made to the person for the chargeable period related to the expenditure an allowance equal to the amount of the expenditure.

(2) (a) Subject to *paragraph (b)*, where a person carrying on a petroleum trade has incurred any exploration expenditure in respect of which an allowance has been made to the person under *subsection (1)* and disposes of assets representing any amount of that expenditure, a charge (in this section referred to as a "balancing charge") equal to the net amount or value of the consideration in money or money's worth received by the person on the disposal shall be made on the person for the chargeable period related to the disposal

or, if the disposal occurs after the date on which the trade is permanently discontinued, for the chargeable period related to the discontinuance.

(b) The amount on which a balancing charge is made shall not exceed the amount of the allowance made to the person under *subsection (1)* in respect of the amount of exploration expenditure represented by the assets disposed of.

(3) Where any assets representing exploration expenditure are destroyed, those assets shall for the purposes of *subsection (2)* be treated as if they had been disposed of immediately before their destruction, and any sale, insurance, salvage or compensation moneys received in respect of the assets by the person carrying on the petroleum trade shall be treated as if those moneys were consideration received on that disposal.

(4) Where a person disposes of any assets representing exploration expenditure incurred by the person in connection with an area which at the time of the disposal is, or which subsequently becomes, a relevant field (or part of such a field), the person who acquires the assets shall, if that person carries on a petroleum trade which consists of or includes the working of the relevant field (or, as the case may be, the part of the relevant field), be deemed for the purposes of this section to have incurred—

(a) on the day on which that person acquires the assets, or

(b) if later, on the day on which that person commences to work the area connected with the assets as a relevant field (or, as the case may be, as part of the relevant field),

an amount of exploration expenditure equal to the lesser of—

(i) the amount of the exploration expenditure represented by the assets, and

(ii) the amount or value of the consideration given by that person on the acquisition of the assets.

(5) (a) Any exploration expenditure incurred by a person before the person commences to carry on a petroleum trade shall be treated for the purposes of *subsection (1)* as if that expenditure had been incurred by that person on the first day on which that person carries on the petroleum trade.

(b) Notwithstanding *paragraph (a)*, no account shall be taken for the purposes of this subsection of expenditure incurred in connection with an area which is not a relevant field, or part of such a field, being worked in the course of carrying on the petroleum trade, if the expenditure was incurred more than 25 years before that first day.

(6) Where a person incurs exploration expenditure before commencing to carry on a petroleum trade and *subsection (5)* applies as respects that expenditure and, before the person commences to carry on that trade, the person disposes of assets representing any amount of that expenditure, the allowance to be made to the person under this section in respect of that expenditure shall be reduced by the net amount or value of any consideration in money or money's worth received by the person on that disposal.

(7) For the purposes of this section other than for the purposes of *subsections (4)* and *(5)(a)*, the day on which any expenditure is incurred shall be taken to be the day on which the sum in question becomes payable.

(8) Any allowance or balancing charge made to or on a person under this section shall be made to or on the person in taxing the person's petroleum trade but,

subject to *subsection (4)*, such allowance shall not be made in respect of the same expenditure in taxing more than one such trade.

(9) *Section 304(4)* shall apply in relation to an allowance under this section as it applies in relation to an allowance to be made under *Part 9*.

(10) *Section 307(2)(a)* shall apply for the purposes of this section, and *subsections (2)* to *(7)* of *section 321* shall apply for the interpretation of this section.

(11) *Subsections (2)* and *(3)* of *section 306* shall apply in determining the chargeable period (being a year of assessment) for which an allowance or a balancing charge is to be made under this section.

(12) References to capital expenditure in *Part 9* and in *section 670*, *Chapter 1* of *Part 29* and *sections 763* to *765* shall be deemed not to include references to expenditure which is exploration expenditure, and exploration expenditure shall be deemed not to be expenditure on know-how for the purposes of *section 768*.

(13) Notwithstanding *subsection (12)*, the following provisions—

(a) *section 312*,

(b) *subsections (1)* and *(2)* of *section 316*,

(c) *section 317(2)*,

(d) *section 318*, and

(e) *subsections (4)* and *(5)* of *section 320*,

shall, with any necessary modifications, apply for the purposes of this section as they apply for the purposes of *Part 9* and *Chapter 1* of *Part 29*.

(14) *Part 19* shall apply as if—

(a) the reference in *section 551(3)* to a balancing charge included a reference to a balancing charge under this section, and

(b) references in *section 555* to a capital allowance (or capital allowances) and to a balancing charge included references respectively to an allowance (or allowances) and a balancing charge under this section.

(15) *Section 319* shall apply as if *subsections (1)* and *(2)* of that section included references to this section.

(16) For the purposes of this section, a person shall be deemed not to be carrying on a petroleum trade unless and until the person is carrying on in the course of that trade trading activities which are petroleum extraction activities.

(17) Any reference in this section to assets representing any exploration expenditure shall be construed as including a reference to a part of or share in any such assets, and any reference in this section to a disposal or acquisition of any such assets shall be construed as including a reference to a disposal or acquisition of a part of or share in any such assets.

Cross References

From Section 693

Section 268 Meaning of "industrial building or structure".

Section 304 Income tax: allowances and charges in taxing a trade, etc.

Section 306 Meaning of basis period.

Section 307 Corporation tax: allowances and charges in taxing a trade.

Section 312 Special provisions as to certain sales.

Section 316 Interpretation of certain references to expenditure and time when expenditure is incurred.

Section 317 Treatment of grants.

Section 318 Meaning of "sale, insurance, salvage or compensation moneys".

Section 319 Adjustment of allowances by reference to value-added tax.

Section 320 Other interpretation (Part 9).
Section 321 Provisions of general application in relation to the making of allowances and charges.
Section 532 Assets.
Section 551 Exclusion from consideration for disposals of sums chargeable to income tax.
Section 555 Restriction of losses by reference to capital allowances and renewals allowances.
Section 670 Mine development allowance.
Section 754 Interpretation (Chapter 1).
Section 763 Interpretation (sections 764 and 765).
Section 765 Allowances for capital expenditure on scientific research.
Section 768 Allowance for know-how.

To Section 693

Section 694 Exploration expenditure incurred by certain companies.
Section 695 Abandonment expenditure: allowances and loss relief.

694 Exploration expenditure incurred by certain companies

[FA92 s85]

(1) For the purposes of *section 693*, where exploration expenditure (not being expenditure which has been or is to be met directly or indirectly by any other person) is incurred by a company (in this section referred to as an "exploration company") and—

(a) another company is a wholly-owned subsidiary of the exploration company, or

(b) the exploration company is at the time the exploration expenditure is incurred a wholly-owned subsidiary of another company (in this section referred to as "the parent company"),

then, the expenditure or so much of it as the exploration company specifies—

(i) in the case referred to in *paragraph (a)*, may at the election of the exploration company be deemed to have been incurred by such other company (being a wholly-owned subsidiary of the exploration company) as the exploration company specifies, and

(ii) in the case referred to in *paragraph (b)*, may at the election of the exploration company be deemed to have been incurred by the parent company or by such other company (being a wholly-owned subsidiary of the parent company) as the exploration company specifies.

(2) Where under *subsection (1)* exploration expenditure incurred by an exploration company is deemed to have been incurred by another company (in this subsection referred to as "the other company")—

(a) the expenditure shall be deemed to have been incurred by the other company at the time at which the expenditure was actually incurred by the exploration company,

(b) in a case where the expenditure was incurred at a time before the incorporation of the other company, that company shall be deemed to have been in existence at the time the expenditure was incurred, and

(c) in the application of *section 693* to a petroleum trade carried on by the other company, the expenditure shall be deemed—

(i) to have been incurred by the other company for the purposes of that trade, and

(ii) not to have been met directly or indirectly by the exploration company.

(3) The same expenditure shall not be taken into account in relation to more than one trade by virtue of this section.

(4) A deduction or allowance shall not be made in respect of the same expenditure both by virtue of this section and under some other provision of the Tax Acts.

(5) A company shall for the purposes of *subsection (1)* be deemed to be a wholly-owned subsidiary of another company if and so long as all of its ordinary share capital is owned by that other company, whether directly or through another company or other companies, or partly directly and partly through another company or other companies, and *paragraph 6* of *Schedule 9* shall apply for the purposes of supplementing this subsection as if the reference in that paragraph to that Schedule were a reference to this subsection.

Cross References

From Section 694

Section 693 Exploration expenditure: allowances and charges.

Schedule 9 Change in Ownership of Company: Disallowance of Trading Losses

To Section 694

Section 696D Provisions relating to groups (Chapter 3).

695 Abandonment expenditure: allowances and loss relief

[FA92 s86]

(1) In this section, "*abandonment losses*" means so much of a loss in a petroleum trade incurred by a person in a chargeable period as does not exceed the total amount of allowances which—

(a) are to be made to the person for that chargeable period under this section, and

(b) have been taken into account in determining the amount of that loss in the petroleum trade.

(2) Subject to *subsections (5)* to *(9)*, where in a chargeable period a person, who is or has been carrying on in relation to a relevant field or a part of it petroleum extraction activities other than effecting the initial treatment and storage of petroleum that is won from the relevant field, incurs abandonment expenditure (not being expenditure which has been or is to be met directly or indirectly by any other person) in relation to the field or the part of it, as the case may be, there shall be made to the person for the chargeable period an allowance equal to the amount of the expenditure.

(3) (a) Subject to *paragraph (b)*, as respects so much of a loss in a petroleum trade incurred by a person in a chargeable period as is an abandonment loss, the person shall be entitled on making a claim in that behalf to such repayment of income tax as is necessary to secure that the aggregate amount of income tax for the chargeable period and the 3 chargeable periods immediately preceding it will not exceed the amount which would have been borne by the person if the person's income arising from petroleum activities for each of those chargeable periods had been reduced by the lesser of—

(i) the abandonment loss, and

(ii) so much of the abandonment loss as could not on that claim be treated as reducing such income of a later chargeable period.

(b) Relief under *paragraph (a)* in respect of a loss shall be deemed for the purposes of the Tax Acts to be relief given under *section 381(1)* such that—

(i) no further relief shall be given under *section 381(1)* in respect of so much of an abandonment loss as is an amount in respect of which relief has been given under *paragraph (a)*, and

(ii) *subsections (3)* to *(7)* of *section 381* and *section 392* shall apply to relief under *paragraph (a)* as they apply to relief under *section 381*.

(c) As respects so much of a loss in a petroleum trade incurred by a person in a chargeable period as is an abandonment loss, *subsections (2)* and *(3)* of *section 396* shall apply as if the time specified in *subsection (3)* of that section were a period of 3 years ending immediately before the chargeable period in which the loss is incurred.

(4) So much of the abandonment losses, if any, incurred by a person on or before the day on which the person permanently discontinues to carry on a petroleum trade (in this subsection referred to as "the first-mentioned trade") as would not apart from this subsection be allowed against or treated as reducing the person's or any other person's income or profits, shall be treated as incurred by the person in the first chargeable period of the first petroleum trade (in this section referred to as "the new trade") to be carried on by the person after the permanent discontinuance of the first-mentioned trade as a trading expense of the new trade.

(5) Where a petroleum trade carried on by a person has been permanently discontinued, any abandonment expenditure incurred by the person after the discontinuance shall be treated for the purposes of *subsection (2)* as if that expenditure had been incurred by the person on the last day on which the person carries on the petroleum trade.

(6) For the purposes of this section other than *subsections (4)* and *(5)*, the day on which any expenditure is incurred shall be taken to be the day on which the sum in question becomes payable.

(7) Any allowance made to a person under this section shall be made in taxing the person's petroleum trade, but such allowance shall not be made in respect of the same expenditure in taxing more than one trade.

(8) References to capital expenditure in *Part 9* and in *section 670*, *Chapter 1* of *Part 29* and *sections 763* to *765* shall be deemed not to include references to expenditure which is abandonment expenditure; but *subsections (1)* and *(2)* of *section 316* and *sections 317(2)* and *320(5)* shall, with any necessary modifications, apply for the purposes of this section as they apply for the purposes of *Part 9* and *Chapter 1* of *Part 29*.

(9) *Subsections (9)* to *(11)* and *(15)* of *section 693* shall apply for the purposes of this section as they apply for the purposes of that section.

Cross References

From Section 695

Section 268 Meaning of "industrial building or structure".
Section 316 Interpretation of certain references to expenditure and time when expenditure is incurred.
Section 317 Treatment of grants.
Section 320 Other interpretation (Part 9).
Section 381 Right to repayment of tax by reference to losses.
Section 392 Option to treat capital allowances as creating or augmenting a loss.
Section 396 Relief for trading losses other than terminal losses.
Section 670 Mine development allowance.
Section 693 Exploration expenditure: allowances and charges.
Section 754 Interpretation (Chapter 1).

Section 763 Interpretation (sections 764 and 765).
Section 765 Allowances for capital expenditure on scientific research.

696 Valuation of petroleum in certain circumstances

[FA92 s87]

(1) Where a person disposes, otherwise than by means of a sale at arm's length, of petroleum acquired by the person by virtue of petroleum activities carried on by the person, then, for the purposes of the Tax Acts the disposal of the petroleum and its acquisition by the person to whom the disposal was made shall be treated as having been for a consideration equal to the market value of the petroleum at the time the disposal was made.

(2) (a) In this subsection, "*relevant appropriation*", in relation to any petroleum won or otherwise acquired in the course of the carrying on by a person of petroleum activities, means the appropriation of that petroleum to refining or to any use except use for petroleum extraction activities carried on by the person, and "relevantly appropriated" shall be construed accordingly.

(b) Where a person who carries on in the course of a trade petroleum activities and other activities makes a relevant appropriation of any petroleum won or otherwise acquired by the person in the course of the petroleum activities without disposing of the petroleum, then, for the purposes of the Tax Acts the person shall be treated as having at the time of the appropriation—

(i) sold the petroleum in the course of the petroleum trade carried on by the person, and

(ii) bought the petroleum in the course of a separate trade consisting of the activities other than the petroleum activities,

and as having so sold and bought the petroleum at a price equal to its market value at the time the petroleum was relevantly appropriated.

(3) For the purposes of this section, the market value at any time of any petroleum shall be the price which that petroleum might reasonably be expected to fetch on a sale of that petroleum at that time if the parties to the transaction were independent parties dealing at arm's length.

696A Treatment of certain disposals

[[FA92 s88]

(1) In this section, "*relevant period*", as respects a disposal, means the period beginning 12 months before and ending 3 years after the disposal, or such longer period as the [Minister for Communications, Energy and Natural Resources][1] may, on the application of the person making the disposal, certify to be in that Minister's opinion reasonable having regard to the proper exploration, delineation or development of any licensed area.

(2) This section shall apply where on or after the 14th day of January, 1985, a person, with the consent of the [Minister for Communications, Energy and Natural Resources,][2] makes a disposal of an interest in a licensed area (including the part disposal of such an interest or the exchange of an interest owned by the person in one licensed area for an interest in another licensed area) and the disposal is shown to the satisfaction of that Minister to have been made for the sole purpose of ensuring the proper exploration, delineation or development of any licensed area.

(3) Where this section applies as respects a disposal by a person (neither being nor including an exchange referred to in *subsection (2)*) and the consideration received by the person is in the relevant period wholly and exclusively applied (whether by the person, or on that person's behalf by the person acquiring the asset disposed of) for the purposes of either or both of the following—

(a) petroleum exploration activities, and

(b) searching for or winning access to petroleum in a relevant field,

then, for the purposes of the Capital Gains Tax Acts, if the person making the disposal makes a claim in that behalf, the disposal shall not be treated as involving any disposal of an asset but the consideration shall not, as respects any subsequent disposal of any asset acquired or brought into being or enhanced in value by the application of that consideration, be deductible from the consideration for that subsequent disposal in the computation of the chargeable gain accruing on that disposal.

(4) (a) Where this section applies as respects an exchange referred to in *subsection (2)*, then, for the purposes of the Capital Gains Tax Acts, if the person making such an exchange makes a claim in that behalf, the exchange shall not be treated as involving any disposal or acquisition by that person of an asset, but the asset given by that person and the asset acquired by that person in the exchange shall be treated as the same asset acquired as the asset given by that person was acquired.

(b) Notwithstanding *paragraph (a)*—

(i) where the person receives for the exchange any consideration in addition to the interest in the other licensed area, this subsection shall not apply as respects the claim made by that person unless the additional consideration is applied in the relevant period in the manner referred to in *subsection (3)* but, where that additional consideration is so applied and the person makes a claim that this subsection should apply, it shall so apply as if the asset given by that person in exchange were such portion only of that asset as is equal in value to the interest in the other licensed area taken by that person in the exchange, and *subsection (3)* shall apply as if the remaining portion of the asset so given by that person were disposed of by that person for that additional consideration, and

(ii) where the person gives for the exchange any consideration in addition to the interest in a licensed area given by that person in the exchange, this subsection shall apply as respects the claim made by that person as if the interest in the other licensed area taken by that person in the exchange were such portion only of that interest as is equal in value to the interest in the licensed area given by that person in the exchange.][3]

Amendments

[1] Substituted by FA08 sched8(1)(n)(i). Has effect as on and from 13 March 2008.

[2] Substituted by FA08 sched8(1)(n)(ii). Has effect as on and from 13 March 2008.

[3] Renumbered by FA08 s45(1)(a). Arising from an apparent drafting error in FA08 s45, this amendment is being applied to s696A rather than to s697 as the legislation directs

CHAPTER 3

Profit Resource Rent Tax

696B Interpretation and application (Chapter 3)

[(1) In this Chapter—

"*cumulative field expenditure*", in relation to an accounting period of a company in respect of a taxable field, means the aggregate of the taxable field expenditure of the company in respect of the taxable field—

(a) for that accounting period, and

(b) for any preceding accounting period beginning on or after 1 January 2007;

"*cumulative field profits*", in relation to an accounting period of a company in respect of a taxable field, means the aggregate of the net taxable field profits of the company in respect of the taxable field—

(a) for that accounting period, and

(b) for any preceding accounting period beginning on or after 1 January 2007,

after deducting the amount of any loss incurred in respect of the taxable field for any such period;

"*net taxable field profits*", in relation to an accounting period of a company, means the taxable field profits of the company for the accounting period after deducting the amount of corporation tax (if any) which would, apart from this Chapter, be payable by the company for the accounting period if the tax were computed on the basis of those profits;

"*profit ratio*", in relation to an accounting period of a company in respect of a taxable field, means an amount determined by the formula—

$$\frac{A}{B}$$

where—

A is the cumulative field profits of the company in respect of the taxable field in relation to that accounting period, and

B is the cumulative field expenditure of the company in respect of the taxable field in relation to that accounting period;

"*profit resource rent tax*" has the meaning given to it in section 696C;

"*specified licence*" means—

(a) an exploration licence, or a reserved area licence, that is granted on or after 1 January 2007, or

(b) a licensing option;

"*taxable field*" means an area in respect of which a petroleum lease entered into following on from a specified licence is in force;

"*taxable field expenditure*", in relation to an accounting period of a company, means the aggregate of the amounts of capital expenditure which consist of—

(a) abandonment expenditure,

(b) development expenditure, and

(c) exploration expenditure,

incurred by the company for the accounting period in respect of a taxable field;

"taxable field profits", in relation to an accounting period of a company, means the amount of the petroleum profits of the company in respect of a taxable field, after making all deductions and giving or allowing all reliefs that for the purposes of corporation tax are made from, or given or allowed against, or are treated as reducing—

(a) those profits, or

(b) income or chargeable gains, if any, included in those profits.

(2) For the purposes of this Chapter—

(a) the interpretations in section 684 shall apply, with any necessary modifications, in relation to expenditure and activities carried on under a specified licence as they would apply in relation to expenditure and activities carried on under a licence within the meaning of section 684 if such a licence was a specified licence, and

(b) capital expenditure incurred on or after 1 January 2007 by a company in an area which is not a taxable field but which subsequently becomes a taxable field (or part of such a field) shall be treated as if it had been incurred by the company on the day on which the area first becomes a taxable field (or part of such a field).

(3) (a) Where a company carries on a petroleum trade and that petroleum trade includes petroleum activities carried on under a specified licence, such activities shall, for the purposes of this Chapter, be treated in respect of each taxable field as a separate petroleum trade distinct from all other activities carried on by the company as part of the trade.

(b) For the purposes of paragraph (*a*), any necessary apportionment shall be made in computing taxable field profits or taxable field expenditure of a company and the method of apportionment adopted shall be such method as appears to the inspector or on appeal the Appeal Commissioners to be just and reasonable.

(c) Subject to paragraph (*d*) the provisions of sections 687 to 690 shall apply for the purposes of this Chapter in relation to any activities treated under paragraph (*a*) as a separate trade as they apply to a petroleum trade within the meaning of those sections.

(d) For the purposes of applying this Chapter, in relation to an accounting period of a company in respect of a taxable field, no account shall be taken of any charges paid, interest payable or a loss incurred—

(i) by any other company, or

(ii) by the first-mentioned company,

in respect of activities other than activities in relation to that field.][1]

Amendments

[1] Inserted by FA08 s45(1)(b). This section is deemed to have applied in the case of profits in respect of any petroleum lease entered into following on from a licensing option or from an exploration licence, or a reserved area licence, awarded by the Minister for Communications, Energy and Natural Resources after 1 January 2007.

Cross References

From Section 696B

Section 684 Interpretation (Chapter 2).

Section 687 Treatment of losses.

Section 690 Interest and charges on income.
Section 696C Charge to profit resource rent tax.

696C Charge to profit resource rent tax

[(1) Where for an accounting period of a company the profit ratio of the company in relation to a taxable field is equal to 1.5 or more, an additional duty of corporation tax (in this Chapter referred to as a "*profit resource rent tax*") shall be charged on the profits of the company in accordance with the provisions of this Chapter.

(2) Profit resource rent tax shall be charged on the profits to which this Chapter applies of a company for an accounting period at the rate of—

(a) 5 per cent, where the profit ratio is less than 3,

(b) 10 per cent, where the profit ratio is equal to or greater than 3 and less than 4.5,

(c) 15 per cent, where the profit ratio is equal to or greater than 4.5.

(3) The profits to which this Chapter applies as respects any taxable field for an accounting period of a company shall—

(a) in respect of any accounting period in relation to which—

(i) the profit ratio is equal to or greater than 1.5, and

(ii) the profit ratio for the immediately preceding accounting period was less than 1.5,

be determined by the formula—

$$\{A - (B \times 1.5)\} \times \frac{100}{100 - R}$$

where—

A is the cumulative field profits of the company in respect of the taxable field in relation to the accounting period,

B is the cumulative field expenditure of the company in respect of the taxable field in relation to the accounting period, and

R is the rate per cent specified in section 21A(3),

and

(b) in respect of any other accounting period of the company, be the taxable field profits of the company in respect of the taxable field for the accounting period.][1]

Amendments

[1] Inserted by FA08 s45(1)(b). This section is deemed to have applied in the case of profits in respect of any petroleum lease entered into following on from a licensing option or from an exploration licence, or a reserved area licence, awarded by the Minister for Communications, Energy and Natural Resources after 1 January 2007.

Cross References

From Section 696C

Section 21A Higher rate of corporation tax.

To Section 696C

Section 696B Interpretation and application (Chapter 3).
Section 696F Collection and general provisions.

696D Provisions relating to groups (Chapter 3)

[(1) Where taxable field expenditure in respect of a taxable field is incurred by a company (in this section referred to as the "*first company*") and

(a) another company is a wholly-owned subsidiary of the first company, or

(b) the first company is, at the time the taxable field expenditure is incurred, a wholly-owned subsidiary of another company (in this section referred to as the "*parent company*"),

then, the expenditure or so much of it as the first company specifies, may at the election of that company be deemed to be taxable field expenditure in respect of the taxable field incurred—

(i) in the case referred to in paragraph (*a*), by such other company (being a wholly-owned subsidiary of the first company) as the first company specifies, and

(ii) in the case referred to in paragraph (*b*), by the parent company or by such other company (being a wholly-owned subsidiary of the parent company) as the first company specifies.

(2) Where under subsection (1) taxable field expenditure incurred by a first company is deemed to have been incurred by another company (in this subsection referred to as the "*other company*")—

(a) the expenditure shall be deemed to have been incurred by the other company at the time at which the expenditure was actually incurred by the first company, and

(b) in the application of this Chapter the expenditure shall—

(i) be deemed to have been incurred by the other company for the purposes of determining the cumulative field expenditure of that company, and

(ii) be deemed not to have been incurred by the first company for the purposes of determining the cumulative field expenditure of that company.

(3) The same expenditure shall not be taken into account in relation to the determination of cumulative expenditure for more than one taxable field by virtue of this section.

(4) Subsection (5) of section 694 applies for the purposes of subsection (1) as it applies for the purposes of that subsection.][1]

Amendments

[1] Inserted by FA08 s45(1)(b). This section is deemed to have applied in the case of profits in respect of any petroleum lease entered into following on from a licensing option or from an exploration licence, or a reserved area licence, awarded by the Minister for Communications, Energy and Natural Resources after 1 January 2007.

Cross References

From Section 696D

Section 694 Exploration expenditure incurred by certain companies.

696E Returns (Chapter 3)

[(1) In this section "*prescribed form*" means a form prescribed by the Revenue Commissioners or a form used under the authority of the Revenue Commissioners, and includes a form which involves the delivery of a statement by any electronic, photographic or other process approved of by the Revenue Commissioners.

(2) A company carrying on petroleum activities under a specified licence shall, in addition to the return required to be delivered under section 951, prepare and deliver to the Collector-General at the same time as, and together with, the return required under [*Chapter 3* of *Part 41A*][1] on or before the specified return date for the chargeable period a full and true statement in a prescribed form of the details required by the form in respect of—

(a) the amounts constituting the aggregate of the cumulative field expenditure for each field,

(b) the amounts constituting the aggregate of the cumulative field profits for each field,

(c) the breakdown of the amounts specified in paragraphs (*a*) and (*b*), and

(d) the amount of profit resource rent tax, if any, payable in respect of each field,

and of such further particulars in relation to this Chapter as may be required by the prescribed form.

(3) An officer of the Revenue Commissioners may make such enquiries or take such actions within his or her powers as he or she considers necessary for the purposes of determining the accuracy or otherwise of any details or particulars contained in the statement referred to in subsection (2).

(4) [*Subsection (5)* of *section 959I* and *subsections (2)* and *(3)* of *section 959O*][2] shall apply to a statement required to be delivered under this section as they apply to a return required to be [delivered under *Chapter 3* of *Part 41A*][3], and for that purpose a reference in those subsections to a return, other than a reference to the specified return date for the chargeable period, shall be construed as a reference to a statement under this section.

(5) Section 1052 shall apply to a failure by a person to deliver a statement under this section or the details or particulars referred to in subsection (3) as it applies to a failure to deliver a return referred to in section 1052.][4]

Amendments

[1, 2, 3] Substituted by FA12 sched4(part 2)(g).

[4] Inserted by FA08 s45(1)(b). This section is deemed to have applied in the case of profits in respect of any petroleum lease entered into following on from a licensing option or from an exploration licence, or a reserved area licence, awarded by the Minister for Communications, Energy and Natural Resources after 1 January 2007.

Cross References

From Section 696E

Section 951 Obligation to make a return.

Section 1052 Penalties for failure to make certain returns, etc.

696F Collection and general provisions

[(1) The provisions of the Corporation Tax Acts relating to—

(a) assessments to corporation tax,

(b) appeals against such assessments (including the rehearing of appeals and the statement of a case for the opinion of the High Court), and

(c) the collection and recovery of corporation tax,

shall apply in relation to a profit resource rent tax charged under section 696C as they apply to corporation tax charged otherwise than under this Chapter.

(2) (a) Any amount of profit resource rent tax payable in accordance with this Chapter without the making of an assessment shall carry interest at the rate of 0.0273 per cent for each day or part of a day from the date when the amount becomes due and payable until payment.

(b) Section 1080 shall apply in relation to interest payable under paragraph (*a*) as it applies in relation to interest payable under section 1080.][1]

Amendments

[1] Inserted by FA08 s45(1)(b). This section is deemed to have applied in the case of profits in respect of any petroleum lease entered into following on from a licensing option or from an exploration licence, or a reserved area licence, awarded by the Minister for Communications, Energy and Natural Resources after 1 January 2007.

Cross References

From Section 696F

Section 696C Charge to profit resource rent tax.

Section 1080 Interest on overdue income tax, corporation tax and capital gains tax.

697 Treatment of certain disposals [Renumbered]

Renumbered as 696A by FA08 s45.

PART 24A

Shipping: Tonnage Tax

697A Interpretation (Part 24A)

[(1) In this Part and in Schedule 18B—

"*bareboat charter terms*", in relation to the charter of a ship, means the letting on charter of a ship for a stipulated period on terms which give the charterer possession and control of the ship, including the right to appoint the master and crew;

"*chartered in*" means—

(a) in relation to a single company, the letting on charter of a ship to the company otherwise than on bareboat charter terms, and

(b) in relation to a group of companies, the letting on charter of a ship otherwise than on bareboat charter terms to a qualifying company that is a member of the group by a person who is not a qualifying company that is a member of the group;

"*company election*" and "*group election*" have the meanings respectively assigned to them by *section 697D(1)*;

["*commencement date*" means the date of the passing of the *Finance Act 2003*;][1]

"*control*" shall be construed in accordance with *subsections (2)* to *(6)* of *section 432*;

"*initial period*" has the meaning assigned to it by *paragraph 2* of Schedule 18B;

"*group of companies*" means—

(a) all the companies of which an individual has control, or

(b) where a company that is not controlled by another person controls one or more other companies, that company and all the companies of which that company has control,

and references to membership of a group and group shall be construed accordingly;

"*Member State*" means a Member State of the European Communities;

"*qualifying company*" means a company—

(a) within the charge to corporation tax,

(b) that operates qualifying ships, and

(c) which carries on the strategic and commercial management of those ships in the State;

"*qualifying group*" means a group of companies of which one or more members are qualifying companies;

"*qualifying ship*" means, subject to *subsection (2)*, a self-propelled seagoing vessel (including a hovercraft) of 100 tons or more gross tonnage which is certificated for navigation at sea by the competent authority of any country or territory, but does not include a vessel (in this Part and in Schedule 18B referred to as a "*vessel of an excluded kind*") which is—

(a) a fishing vessel or a vessel used for subjecting fish to a manufacturing or other process on board the vessel,

[(b) a vessel, other than a vessel operated for bona fide commercial purposes and with an overnight passenger capacity (not including crew) of not less than 50 persons, of a kind whose primary use is for the purposes of sport or recreation,][2]

(c) a harbour, estuary or river ferry,

(d) an offshore installation, including a mobile or fixed rig, a platform or other installation of any kind at sea,

(e) a tanker used for petroleum extraction activities (within the meaning of *Chapter 2* of *Part 24*),

(f) a dredger, including a vessel used primarily as a floating platform for working machinery or as a diving platform,

(g) a tug in respect of which a certificate has not been given by the Minister for the Marine and Natural Resources certifying that in the opinion of the Minister the tug is capable of operating in seas outside the portion of the seas which are, for the purposes of the Maritime Jurisdiction Act, 1959, the territorial seas of the State;

"*tonnage tax*" has the meaning assigned to it in *section 697B*;

"*tonnage tax activities*", in relation to a tonnage tax company, means activities carried on by the company in the course of a trade which consists of one or more than one of the activities described in [*paragraphs (a)* to *(g)* and *paragraphs (i)* and *(j)*][3] of the definition of "*relevant shipping income*";

"*tonnage tax asset*" means an asset used wholly and exclusively for the purposes of the tonnage tax activities of a tonnage tax company;

"*tonnage tax company*" and "*tonnage tax group*" mean, respectively, a company or group in relation to which a tonnage tax election has effect;

"*tonnage tax election*" has the meaning assigned to it in *section 697D(1)*;

"*tonnage tax profits*", in relation to a tonnage tax company, means the company's profits for an accounting period calculated in accordance with *section 697C*;

"*tonnage tax trade*", in relation to a tonnage tax company, means a trade carried on by the company the income from which is within the charge to corporation tax and which consists solely of the carrying on of tonnage tax activities or, in the case of a trade consisting partly of the carrying on of such activities and partly of other activities, that part of the trade consisting solely of the carrying on of tonnage tax activities and which is treated under *section 697L* as a separate trade carried on by the company;

"*relevant shipping income*", in relation to a tonnage tax company, means the company's income from—

(a) the carriage of passengers by sea in a qualifying ship operated by the company[…][4],

(b) the carriage of cargo by sea in a qualifying ship operated by the company[…][5],

[(c) towage, salvage or other marine assistance by a qualifying ship operated by the company, but does not include income from any such work undertaken in a port or an area under the jurisdiction of a port authority,][6]

(d) transport in connection with other services of a kind necessarily provided at sea by a qualifying ship operated by the company,

[(e) the provision on board a qualifying ship operated by the company of goods or services ancillary to the carriage of passengers or cargo, but only to the extent that such goods or services are provided for consumption on board the qualifying ship,][7]

(f) the granting of rights by virtue of which another person provides or will provide such ancillary services on board a qualifying ship operated by the company,

(g) other ship-related activities that are a necessary and integral part of the business of operating the company's qualifying ships,

[...][8]

(i) the letting on charter of a qualifying ship for use for the carriage by sea of passengers and cargo where the operation of the ship and the crew of the ship remain under the direction and control of the company,

(j) the provision of ship management services for qualifying ships operated by the company,

(k) a dividend or other distribution of a company not resident in the State (in this Part referred to as the "*overseas company*") in respect of which the conditions set out in *section 697H(1)* are met,

(l) gains treated as income by virtue of *section 697J*,

[...][9]

"*relevant shipping profits*", in relation to a tonnage tax company, means—

(a) the company's relevant shipping income, and

(b) so much of the company's chargeable gains as are excluded from the charge to tax by *section 697N*;

"*renewal election*" has the meaning assigned to it in *paragraph 6* of *Schedule 18B*;

[...][10]

(2) A vessel is not a qualifying ship for the purposes of this Part if the main purpose for which it is used is the provision of goods or services of a kind normally provided on land.

(3) (a) References in this Part and in Schedule 18B to a company or group entering or leaving tonnage tax are references to its becoming or ceasing to be a tonnage tax company or group.

(b) References in this Part and in Schedule 18B to a company or group of companies being subject to tonnage tax are references to the company or group being entitled to calculate its profits in accordance with the provisions of this Part and that Schedule.

(4) Schedule 18B shall apply for the purposes of this Part.][11]

Amendments

[1] Substituted by FA03 s62(1)(a)(i). Applies as on and from 28 March 2003

[2] Substituted by FA06 s67(1)(a)(i). This section comes into operation on 2 February 2006.

[3] Substituted by FA07 sched4(1)(s). Apply to accounting periods ending on or after 1 January 2007.

[4] Deleted by FA03 s62(1)(a)(ii)(I). Applies as on and from 28 March 2003

[5] Deleted by FA03 s62(1)(a)(ii)(II). Applies as on and from the date of the passing of this Act. FA03 28 March 2003

[6] Substituted by FA03 s62(1)(a)(ii)(III). Applies as on and from 28 March 2003

[7] Substituted by FA03 s62(1)(a)(ii)(IV). Applies as on and from the date of the passing of this Act. FA03 28 March 2003

[8, 9] Deleted by FA03 s62(1)(a)(ii)(V). Applies as on and from the date of the passing of this Act. FA03 28 March 2003

[10] Deleted by FA06 s67(1)(a)(ii). This section come into operation on such day or days as the Minister for Finance may by order or orders appoint and different days may be appointed for different purposes or different provisions.

[11] Inserted by FA02 s53(1). Per FA03 s62(2), with effect from the date of passing of Finance Act 2003; 28 March 2003.

Revenue Briefings

Tax Briefing

Tax Briefing May 2003 – Issue 52 pg 12 – Finance Act 2003 – Tonnage Tax
Tax Briefing December 2006 – Issue 65 – Tonnage Tax

Cross References

From Section 697A

Section 432 Meaning of "associated company" and "control".
Section 670 Mine development allowance.
Section 684 Interpretation (Chapter 2).
Section 697B Application.
Section 697C Calculation of profits of tonnage tax company.
Section 697D Election for tonnage tax.
Section 697H Relevant shipping income: distributions of overseas shipping companies.
Section 697J Relevant shipping income: foreign currency gains.
Section 697L Tonnage tax trade.
Section 697N Chargeable gains.

To Section 697A

Section 21 The charge to corporation tax and exclusion of income tax and capital gains tax.
Section 697H Relevant shipping income: distributions of overseas shipping companies.
Section 697J Relevant shipping income: foreign currency gains.
Schedule 18B Tonnage Tax

697B Application

[Notwithstanding any other provision of the Tax Acts or the Capital Gains Tax Acts, this Part and Schedule 18B shall apply to provide an alternative method (in this Part referred to as "*tonnage tax*") for computing the profits of a qualifying company for the purposes of corporation tax.][1]

Amendments

[1] Inserted by FA02 s53(1). FA03 s62 amends FA03s53 to provide that Part 24A will take effect from the date of passing of FA03, 28 March 2003.

Cross References

To Section 697B

Section 697A Interpretation (Part 24A).

697C Calculation of profits of tonnage tax company

[(1) The tonnage tax profits of a tonnage tax company shall be charged to corporation tax in place of the company's relevant shipping profits.

(2) Where the profits of a tonnage tax company would be relevant shipping income, any loss accruing to the company in respect of its tonnage tax activities or any loss which would, but for this subsection, be taken into account by virtue of *section 79* in computing the trading income of the company shall not be brought into account for the purposes of corporation tax.

(3) A company's tonnage tax profits for an accounting period in respect of each qualifying ship operated by the company shall be calculated in accordance with this section by reference to the net tonnage of each qualifying ship operated by the company and, for this purpose, the net tonnage of a ship shall be rounded down (if necessary) to the nearest multiple of 100 tons.

(4) The daily profit to be attributed to each qualifying ship operated by the company shall be determined by reference to the net tonnage of the ship as follows:

(a) for each 100 tons up to 1,000 tons, €1.00,

(b) for each 100 tons between 1,000 and 10,000 tons, €0.75,

(c) for each 100 tons between 10,000 and 25,000 tons, €0.50, and

(d) for each 100 tons above 25,000 tons, €0.25.

(5) The profit to be attributed to each qualifying ship for the accounting period shall be determined by multiplying the daily profit as determined under *subsection (4)* by—

(a) the number of days in the accounting period, or

(b) if the ship was operated by the company as a qualifying ship for only part of the period, by the number of days in that part of the accounting period.

(6) The amount of the company's tonnage tax profits for the accounting period shall be the aggregate of the profit determined in respect of each qualifying ship operated by the company in accordance with *subsection (5)*.

(7) If 2 or more companies are to be regarded as operators of a ship by virtue of a joint interest in the ship, or in an agreement for the use of the ship, the tonnage tax profits of each company shall be calculated as if each were entitled to a share of the profits proportionate to its share of that interest.

(8) If 2 or more companies are to be treated as the operator of a ship otherwise than as mentioned in *subsection (7)*, the tonnage tax profits of each shall be computed as if each were the only operator.][1]

Amendments

[1] Inserted by FA02 s53(1). FA03 s62 amends FA03 s53 to provide that Part 24A will take effect from the date of passing of FA03, 28 March 2003.

Cross References

From Section 697C

Section 79 Foreign currency: computation of income and chargeable gains.

To Section 697C

Section 697A Interpretation (Part 24A).

697D Election for tonnage tax

[(1) Tonnage tax shall apply only if an election (in this Part and Schedule 18B referred to as a "*tonnage tax election*") under this Part to that effect is made by a qualifying single company (in this Part and in Schedule 18B referred to as a "*company election*") or by a qualifying group of companies (in this Part and in Schedule 18B referred to as a "*group election*").

(2) (a) Tonnage tax shall only apply to a company which is a member of a group of companies if the company joins in a group election which shall be made jointly by all the qualifying companies in the group.

(b) A group election shall have effect in relation to all qualifying companies in the group.

(3) A tonnage tax election shall be made only if the requirements of [*section 697F*][1] are met.

(4) Part 1 of Schedule 18B shall apply for the purposes of making and giving effect to an election under this Part.][2]

Amendments

[1] Substituted by FA06 s67(1)(b). This section comes into operation on such day or days as the Minister for Finance may by order or orders appoint and different days may be appointed for different purposes or different provisions.

[2] Inserted by FA02 s53(1). FA03 s62 amends FA03 s53 to provide that Part 24A will take effect from the date of passing of FA03, 28 March 2003.

Cross References

From Section 697D

Section 697F Requirement not to enter into tax avoidance arrangements.

To Section 697D

Section 697A Interpretation (Part 24A).
Schedule 18B Tonnage Tax

697E Requirement that not more than 75 per cent of fleet tonnage is chartered in [Deleted]

Deleted by FA06 s67(1)(c).

697F Requirement not to enter into tax avoidance arrangements

[(1) It shall be a condition of remaining within tonnage tax that a company is not a party to any transaction or arrangement that is an abuse of the tonnage tax regime.

(2) A transaction or arrangement shall be such an abuse as is referred to in *subsection (1)* if in consequence of its being, or having been, entered into the provisions of this Part and Schedule 18B may be applied in a way that results (or would but for this subsection result) in—

(a) a tax advantage (within the meaning of [*section 811,* or *section 811C,* as the case may be][1]) being obtained for—

(i) a company other than a tonnage tax company, or

(ii) a tonnage tax company in respect of its non-tonnage tax activities, or

(b) the amount of the tonnage tax profits of a tonnage tax company being artificially reduced.

(3) If a tonnage tax company is a party to any such transaction or arrangement as is referred to in *subsection (1)*, the Revenue Commissioners may—

(a) if it is a single company, give notice excluding it from tonnage tax;

(b) if it is a member of a group, subject to *paragraph 22* of *Schedule 18B*, give notice to the tonnage tax company excluding the group from tonnage tax.

(4) The effect of such a notice as is referred to in *subsection (3)*—

(a) in the case of a single company, is that the company's tonnage tax election shall cease to be in force from the beginning of the accounting period in which the transaction or arrangement was entered into, and

(b) in the case of a group, is that the group's tonnage tax election shall cease to be in force from such date as may be specified in the notice, but the date so specified shall not be earlier than the beginning of the earliest accounting period in which any member of the group entered into the transaction or arrangement in question.

(5) The provisions of *sections 697P* apply where a company ceases to be a tonnage tax company by virtue of this section.]²

Amendments

¹ Substituted by FA14 sched1(4).

² Inserted by FA02 s53(1). FA03 s62 amends FA03 s53 to provide that Part 24A will take effect from the date of passing of FA03, 28 March 2003.

Cross References

From Section 697F

Section 697P Withdrawal of relief etc. on company leaving tonnage tax.

Section 811 Transactions to avoid liability to tax.

To Section 697F

Section 697D Election for tonnage tax.

Section 697G Appeals.

Section 697P Withdrawal of relief etc. on company leaving tonnage tax.

697G Appeals

[Any person aggrieved by the giving of such a notice as is referred to in [*section 697F*]¹ may by notice in writing to that effect made to the Revenue Commissioners within 30 days from the date of the giving of the first-mentioned notice appeal to the Appeal Commissioners. In the case of a notice given to a tonnage tax company which is a member of a group of companies only one appeal may be brought, but it may be brought jointly by 2 or more members of the group concerned.]²

Amendments

¹ Substituted by FA06 s67(1)(d). This section shall come into operation on such day or days as the Minister for Finance may by order or orders appoint and different days may be appointed for different purposes or different provisions.

² Inserted by FA02 s53(1). FA03 s62 amends FA03 s53 to provide that Part 24A will take effect from the date of passing of FA03, 28 March 2003.

Cross References

From Section 697G

Section 697F Requirement not to enter into tax avoidance arrangements.

697H Relevant shipping income: distributions of overseas shipping companies

[(1) The conditions referred to in *paragraph (k)* of the definition of "*relevant shipping income*" in *section 697A* are—

(a) that the overseas company operates qualifying ships;

(b) that more than 50 per cent of the voting power in the overseas company is held by a company resident in a Member State, or that 2 or more companies each of which is resident in a Member State hold in aggregate more than 50 per cent of that voting power;

[…]¹

(d) that all the income of the overseas company is such that, if it were a tonnage tax company, it would be relevant shipping income;

(e) that the distribution is paid entirely out of profits arising at a time when—

(i) the conditions in *paragraphs (a)* to *(d)* were met, and

(ii) the tonnage tax company was subject to tonnage tax;

and

(f) the profits of the overseas company out of which the distribution is paid are subject to a tax on profits (in the country of residence of the company or elsewhere, or partly in that country and partly elsewhere).

(2) A dividend or other distribution of an overseas company which is made out of profits which are referable to a dividend or other distribution in relation to which the conditions of *subsection (1)* are met shall be deemed for the purposes of this Part to be a dividend or other distribution in respect of which the conditions in *subsection (1)* are met.

(3) *Section 440* shall not apply to dividends and other distributions of an overseas company which is relevant shipping income of a tonnage tax company.][2]

Amendments

[1] Deleted by FA06 s67(1)(e). This section shall come into operation on such day or days as the Minister for Finance may by order or orders appoint and different days may be appointed for different purposes or different provisions.

[2] Inserted by FA02 s53(1). FA03 s62 amends FA03 s53 to provide that Part 24A will take effect from the date of passing of FA03, 28 March 2003.

Cross References

From Section 697H

Section 440 Surcharge on undistributed investment and estate income.

Section 697A Interpretation (Part 24A).

To Section 697H

Section 697A Interpretation (Part 24A).

Section 697K General exclusion of investment income.

697I Relevant shipping income: cargo and passengers [Deleted]

Deleted by FA03 s62(1)(b). Applies as on and from the date of the passing of this Act. FA03 28 March 2003

697J Relevant shipping income: foreign currency gains

[(1) This section shall apply to—

(a) any gain, whether realised or unrealised, attributable to a relevant monetary item (within the meaning of *section 79*) which would but for this Part be taken into account in computing the trading income of a company's tonnage tax trade in accordance with *section 79*, and

(b) any gain, whether realised or unrealised, attributable to a relevant contract (within the meaning of *section 79*) which would but for this Part be taken into account in computing the trading income of a company's tonnage tax trade in accordance with *section 79*.

(2) Where this section applies to any gain, the gain shall be treated as income for the purposes of the definition of "*relevant shipping income*" in *section 697A*.][1]

Amendments

[1] Inserted by FA02 s53(1). FA03 s62 amends FA03 s53 to provide that Part 24A will take effect from the date of passing of FA03, 28 March 2003.

Cross References

From Section 697J

Section 79 Foreign currency: computation of income and chargeable gains.
Section 697A Interpretation (Part 24A).

To Section 697J

Section 697A Interpretation (Part 24A).

697K General exclusion of investment income

[(1) Income from investments shall not be relevant shipping income, and for this purpose "*income from investments*" includes any income chargeable to tax under Case III, IV or V of Schedule D or under Schedule F.

(2) To the extent that an activity gives rise to income from investments it shall not be regarded as part of a company's tonnage tax activities.

(3) *Subsection (1)* shall not apply to income that is relevant shipping income under [*sections 697H*.][1]][2]

Amendments

[1] Substituted by FA07 sched4(1)(t). Apply to accounting periods ending on or after 1 January 2007.

[2] Inserted by FA02 s53(1). FA03 s62 amends FA03 s53 to provide that Part 24A will take effect from the date of passing of FA03, 28 March 2003.

Cross References

From Section 697K

Section 20 Schedule F.
Section 697H Relevant shipping income: distributions of overseas shipping companies.

697L Tonnage tax trade

[(1) Subject to *section 697M*, where in an accounting period a tonnage tax company carries on as part of a trade tonnage tax activities, those activities shall be treated for the purposes of the Corporation Tax Acts (other than any provision of those Acts relating to the commencement or cessation of a trade) as a separate trade distinct from all other activities carried on by the company as part of the trade.

(2) An accounting period of a company shall end (if it would not otherwise do so) when the company enters or leaves tonnage tax.

[(3) A company to which *subsection (1)* applies shall, as respects any activities which are treated by virtue of that subsection as a separate trade distinct from all other activities carried on by that company as part of its trade, comply with all the requirements of the Tax Acts and the Capital Gains Tax Acts as respects those activities regarding the computation of tax and the keeping of records separate from any other activity carried on by that company.][1]][2]

Amendments

[1] Inserted by FA03 s62(1)(c). Applies as on and from the date of the passing of this Act. FA03 28 March 2003

[2] Inserted by FA02 s53(1). FA03 s62 amends FA03 s53 to provide that Part 24A will take effect from the date of passing of FA03, 28 March 2003.

Cross References

From Section 697L

Section 697M Exclusion of reliefs, deductions and set-offs.

To Section 697L

Section 697A Interpretation (Part 24A).

697LA Transactions between associated persons and between tonnage tax trade and other activities of same company

[(1) In this section—

"control" shall be construed in accordance with *section 11*;

"*losses*" includes amounts in respect of which relief may be given in accordance with *section 83(3)* and *Part 12*; "*transaction*" includes any agreement, arrangement or understanding of any kind (whether or not it is, or is intended to be, legally enforceable).

(2) Where—

(a) provision is made or imposed as between a tonnage tax company and another company by means of a transaction,

(b) the results of the transaction are taken into account in computing the tonnage tax company's relevant shipping income,

(c) at the time of the transaction—

(i) one of the companies is directly or indirectly under the control of the other, or

(ii) both of the companies are, directly or indirectly, under the control of the same person or persons,

and

(d) the relevant shipping income of the tonnage tax company is greater than it would be if the parties to the transaction had been independent parties dealing at arm's length,

then, the income or losses of both companies shall be computed for any purpose of the Tax Acts as if the consideration in the transaction had been that which would have obtained if the transaction had been a transaction between independent persons dealing at arm's length.

(3) *Subsection (2)* shall apply in relation to a tonnage tax company where provision is made or imposed as between the company's tonnage tax trade and other activities carried on by the company as if—

(a) that trade and those other activities were carried on by two different persons,

(b) those persons had entered into a transaction, and

(c) the two persons were both controlled by the same person at the time of the making or imposition of the provision.

(4) A company to which *subsection (2)* or *(3)* applies shall keep for a period not less than 6 years sufficient documentation to prove how prices and terms have been determined in a transaction to which that subsection applies, including a written and detailed explanation of the pricing principles it has applied in relation to any such business transaction.

(5) An officer of the Revenue Commissioners may by notice in writing require a company to which *subsection (2)* or *(3)* applies to furnish him or her with such information, particulars or documentation as may be necessary for that officer to establish whether or not the company has complied with this section.

(6) *Section 1052* shall apply to a failure to comply with *subsection (5)* as it applies to a failure to deliver a return referred to in that section.

(7) *Sections 900* and *901* shall apply to records under this section as if they were books, records or documents within the meaning of *section 900*.

(8) Nothing in this section is to be construed as affecting the computation of a company's tonnage tax profits.][1]

Amendments

[1] Inserted by FA03 s62(1)(d). Applies as on and from the date of the passing of this Act. FA03 28 March 2003

Cross References

From Section 697LA

Section 11 Meaning of "control" in certain contexts.
Section 83 Expenses of management of investment companies.
Section 381 Right to repayment of tax by reference to losses.
Section 900 Power to call for production of books, information, etc.
Section 901 Application to High Court: production of books, information, etc.
Section 1052 Penalties for failure to make certain returns, etc.

697LB Treatment of finance costs

[(1) (a) In this section—

"*deductible finance costs outside the tonnage tax trade*" means—

(i) in relation to a tonnage tax company, the total of the amounts that may be taken into account in respect of finance costs in calculating for the purpose of corporation tax the company's profits other than relevant shipping profits, and

(ii) in relation to a group of companies, so much of the group's finance costs as may be taken into account in calculating for the purposes of corporation tax—

(I) in the case of a group member which is a tonnage tax company, the company's profits other than relevant shipping profits, and

(II) in the case of a group member which is not a tonnage tax company, the company's profits;

"*finance costs*", in relation to a company, means the cost of debt finance for that company, including—

(i) any interest expense which gives rise to a deduction under *section 81* or relief under *Part 8*,

(ii) any gain or loss referred to in *section 79* in relation to debt finance,

(iii) the finance cost implicit in a payment under a finance lease,

(iv) the finance cost payable on debt factoring or on any similar transaction, and

(v) any other costs arising from what would be considered on generally accepted accounting practice to be a financing transaction;

"*finance lease*", in relation to finance costs, means any arrangements that provide for machinery or plant to be leased or otherwise made available by a person (in this definition referred to as the "*lessor*") to another person such that, in cases where the lessor and persons connected with the lessor are all companies resident in the State—

(i) the arrangements, or

(ii) the arrangements in which they are comprised,

fall, in accordance with generally accepted accounting practice, to be treated in the accounts, including any consolidated group accounts relating to two or more companies of which that company is one, of one or more of those companies as a finance lease or as a loan;

"*total finance costs*" means—

(i) in relation to a tonnage tax company, so much of the company's finance costs as could, if there were no tonnage tax election, be taken into account in calculating the company's profits for the purposes of corporation tax, and

(ii) in relation to a group of companies, so much of the group's finance costs as could, if there were no tonnage tax election, be taken into account in calculating for the purposes of corporation tax the profits of any group member.

(b) For the purposes of this section, where, in the case of a group of companies, an accounting period of a company does not coincide with the corresponding accounting period of another group company or companies, then the periods shall be matched on whatever basis appears to be just and reasonable.

(2) Where it appears, in relation to an accounting period of a tonnage tax company (not being a member of a group of companies) which carries on tonnage tax activities and which also carries on other activities, that the company's deductible finance costs outside the tonnage tax trade exceed a fair proportion of the company's total finance costs, then an adjustment as determined in accordance with *subsection (3)* shall be made in computing the company's profits for corporation tax purposes for that accounting period.

(3) (a) The proportion of the company's deductible finance costs outside the tonnage tax trade which are to be treated as exceeding a fair proportion of the company's total finance costs shall be determined on a just and reasonable basis.

(b) The just and reasonable determination referred to in *paragraph (a)* shall be made by reference to the extent to which the debt finance of the company, in respect of which the company's total finance costs are incurred, is applied in such a way that any profits arising, directly or indirectly, would be relevant shipping profits.

(4) Where an adjustment is to be made under *subsection (2)*, an amount equal to the excess determined in accordance with *subsection (3)* shall be taken into account in computing the trading income of the company's non-tonnage tax activities for the accounting period in respect of which the adjustment arises.

(5) Where it appears, in relation to an accounting period of a tonnage tax company (being a member of a tonnage tax group) where the activities carried on by the members of the group include activities other than the carrying on of a tonnage tax trade or tonnage tax trades, that the group's deductible finance costs outside the tonnage tax trade exceed a fair proportion of the group's total finance costs, then an adjustment as determined in accordance with *subsection (6)* shall be made in computing the company's profits for corporation tax purposes for that accounting period.

(6) (a) The proportion of the group's deductible finance costs outside the tonnage tax trade which are to be treated as exceeding a fair proportion of the company's total finance costs shall be determined on a just and reasonable basis.

(b) The just and reasonable determination referred to in *paragraph (a)* shall be made by reference to the extent to which the debt finance of the group, in respect of which the group's total finance costs are incurred, is applied in such a way that any profits arising, directly or indirectly, would be relevant shipping profits.

(7) Where an adjustment is to be made under *subsection (5)*, an amount equal to the proportion of the excess determined in accordance with *subsection (6)* which the company's tonnage tax profits bears to the tonnage tax profits of all the members of the group shall be taken into account in computing the trading income of the company's non-tonnage tax activities for the accounting period in respect of which the adjustment arises.

(8) No adjustment shall be made under this section if—

(a) in calculating for a period a company's deductible finance costs outside the tonnage tax trade of the company, or

(b) in calculating for a period a group's deductible finance costs outside the tonnage tax trades of the group,

the amount taken into account in respect of costs and losses is exceeded by the amount taken into account in respect of profits and gains.][1]

Amendments

[1] Inserted by FA03 s62(1)(d). Applies as on and from the date of the passing of this Act. FA03 28 March 2003

Cross References

From Section 697LB

Section 79 Foreign currency: computation of income and chargeable gains.

Section 81 General rule as to deductions.

Section 237 Annual payments payable wholly out of taxed income.

697M Exclusion of reliefs, deductions and set-offs

[(1) No relief, deduction or set-off of any description is allowed against the amount of a company's tonnage tax profits.

(2) (a) When a company enters tonnage tax, any losses that have accrued to it before entry and are attributable—

(i) to activities that under tonnage tax become part of the company's tonnage tax trade, or

(ii) to a source of income that under tonnage tax becomes relevant shipping income,

shall not be available for loss relief in any accounting period beginning on or after the company's entry into tonnage tax.

(b) Any apportionment necessary to determine the losses so attributable shall be made on a just and reasonable basis.

(c) In *paragraph (a)* "*loss relief*" includes any means by which a loss might be used to reduce the amount in respect of which that company, or any other company, is chargeable to tax.

(3) (a) Any relief or set-off against a company's tax liability for an accounting period shall not apply in relation to so much of that tax liability as is attributable to the company's tonnage tax profits.

(b) Relief to which this subsection applies includes, but is not limited to, any relief or set-off under *section 826*, *828* or Part 2 of *Schedule 24*.

(c) This subsection shall not apply to any set-off under *section 24(2)* or *25(3)*.][1]

Amendments

[1] Inserted by FA02 s53(1). FA03 s62 amends FA03 s53 to provide that Part 24A will take effect from the date of passing of FA03, 28 March 2003.

Cross References

From Section 697M

Section 24 Companies resident in the State: income tax on payments made or received.
Section 25 Companies not resident in the State.
Section 826 Agreements for relief from double taxation.
Section 828 Capital gains tax: double taxation relief.
Schedule 24 Relief from Income Tax and Corporation Tax by Means of Credit in Respect of Foreign Tax

To Section 697M

Section 697L Tonnage tax trade.

697N Chargeable gains

[(1) Where for one or more continuous periods of at least 12 months part of an asset has been used wholly and exclusively for the purposes of the tonnage tax activities of a tonnage tax company and part has not, this section shall apply as if the part so used were a separate asset.

(2) Where *subsection (1)* applies, any necessary apportionment of the gain or loss on the disposal of the whole asset shall be made on a just and reasonable basis.

(3) (a) When an asset is disposed of that is or has been a tonnage tax asset—

(i) any gain or loss on the disposal, which but for this paragraph would have been the amount of the chargeable gain or the allowable loss, shall be a chargeable gain or allowable loss only to the extent (if any) to which it is referable to periods during which the asset was not a tonnage tax asset, and

(ii) any such chargeable gain or allowable loss on a disposal by a tonnage tax company shall be treated as arising otherwise than in the course of the company's tonnage tax trade.

(b) For the purposes of *paragraph (a)*, the proportion of the gain or loss referable to periods during which the asset was not a tonnage tax asset shall be determined by the formula:

$$\frac{(P - T)}{P}$$

where

P is the total length of the period since the asset was created or, if later, the last third-party disposal, and

T is the length of the period (or the aggregate length of the periods) since—

(I) the asset was created, or

(II) if later, the last third-party disposal,

during which the asset was a tonnage tax asset.

(c) In *paragraph (b)* a "*third-party disposal*" means a disposal (or deemed disposal) that is not treated as one on which neither a gain nor a loss accrues to the person making the disposal.

(4) A tonnage tax election shall not affect the deduction under *section 31* as applied by *section 78(2)* of relevant allowable losses (within the meaning of *section 78*) that accrued to a company before it became a tonnage tax company.][1]

Amendments

[1] Inserted by FA02 s53(1). FA03 s62 amends FA03 s53 to provide that Part 24A will take effect from the date of passing of FA03, 28 March 2003.

Cross References

From Section 697N

Section 31 Amount chargeable.

Section 78 Computation of companies' chargeable gains.

To Section 697N

Section 697A Interpretation (Part 24A).

Section 697P Withdrawal of relief etc. on company leaving tonnage tax.

697O Capital allowances: general

[(1) A company's tonnage tax trade shall not be treated as a trade for the purposes of determining the company's entitlement to capital allowances under *Part 9* or under any other provision which is to be construed as one with that Part, but nothing in this subsection shall be taken as preventing the making of a balancing charge under those provisions as applied by Schedule 18B.

(2) Notwithstanding any other provision of the Tax Acts, *Part 9* insofar as it relates to machinery or plant shall not apply to machinery or plant provided for leasing by a lessor (within the meaning of *section 403*) who is an individual to a lessee (within the meaning of *section 403*) for use in a tonnage tax trade carried on or to be carried on by the lessee.

(3) *Part 3* of Schedule 18B shall apply for the purposes of applying the provisions of *Part 9* or any other provision which is to be construed as one with that Part for the purposes of a tonnage tax trade of a tonnage tax company.][1]

Amendments

[1] Inserted by FA02 s53(1). FA03 s62 amends FA03 s53 to provide that Part 24A will take effect from the date of passing of FA03, 28 March 2003.

Cross References

From Section 697O

Section 32 Interpretation (Chapter 1).

Section 268 Meaning of "industrial building or structure".

Section 403 Restriction on use of capital allowances for certain leased assets.

To Section 697O

Schedule 18B Tonnage Tax

697P Withdrawal of relief etc. on company leaving tonnage tax

[(1) This section shall apply where a company ceases to be a tonnage tax company—

(a) on ceasing to be a qualifying company for reasons relating wholly or mainly to tax, or

(b) under *section 697F*.

(2) Where this section applies, *section 697N* shall apply in relation to chargeable gains (within the meaning of the Capital Gains Tax Acts), but not losses, on all

relevant disposals as if the company had never been a tonnage tax company and for this purpose a "*relevant disposal*" means a disposal—

(a) on or after the day on which the company ceases to be a tonnage tax company, or

(b) at any time during the period of 6 years immediately preceding that day when the company was a tonnage tax company.

(3) Where *subsection (2)* operates to increase the amount of the chargeable gain on a disposal made at a time within the period mentioned in *subparagraph (2)(b)*, the gain is treated to the extent of the increase—

(a) as arising immediately before the company ceased to be a tonnage tax company, and

(b) as not being relevant shipping profits of the company.

(4) No relief, deduction or set-off of any description shall be allowed against the amount of that increase or the corporation tax charged on that amount.

(5) Where this section applies and in a relevant accounting period during which the company was a tonnage tax company the company was liable to a balancing charge in relation to which *paragraph 16* or *17*, as appropriate, of *Schedule 18B* applied to reduce the amount of the charge, then the company shall be treated as having received an additional amount of profits chargeable to corporation tax equal to the aggregate of the amounts by which those balancing charges were reduced.

(6) For the purposes of *subsection (5)* a "*relevant accounting period*" means an accounting period ending not more than 6 years before the day on which the company ceased to be a tonnage tax company.

(7) The additional profits referred to in *subsection (5)* shall be treated—

(a) as arising immediately before the company ceased to be a tonnage tax company, and

(b) as not being relevant shipping profits of the company.

(8) No relief, deduction or set-off of any description shall be allowed against those profits or against the corporation tax charged on them.][1]

Amendments

[1] Inserted by FA02 s53(1). FA03 s62 amends FA03 s53 to provide that Part 24A will take effect from the date of passing of FA03, 28 March 2003.

Cross References

From Section 697P

Section 697F Requirement not to enter into tax avoidance arrangements.
Section 697N Chargeable gains.

To Section 697P

Section 697F Requirement not to enter into tax avoidance arrangements.
Schedule 18B Tonnage Tax

697Q Ten year disqualification from re-entry into tonnage tax

[(1) This section shall apply in every case where a company ceases to be a tonnage tax company otherwise than on the expiry of a tonnage tax election.

(2) Where this section applies—

(a) a company election made by a former tonnage tax company shall be ineffective if made before the end of the period of 10 years beginning with the date on which the company ceased to be a tonnage tax company, and

(b) a group election that—

(i) is made in respect of a group whose members include a former tonnage tax company, and

(ii) would result in that company becoming a tonnage tax company,

shall be ineffective if made before the end of the period of 10 years beginning with the date on which that company ceased to be a tonnage tax company.

(3) This section shall not prevent a company becoming a tonnage tax company under and in accordance with the rules in Part 4 of Schedule 18B.

(4) In this section "*former tonnage tax company*" means a company that is not a tonnage tax company but has previously been a tonnage tax company.][1]

Amendments

[1] Inserted by FA02 s53(1). FA03 s62 amends FA03 s53 to provide that Part 24A will take effect from the date of passing of FA03, 28 March 2003.

Cross References

To Section 697Q

Schedule 18B Tonnage Tax

PART 25

Industrial and Provident Societies, Building Societies, and Trustee Savings Banks

CHAPTER 1

Industrial and Provident Societies

698 Interpretation (Chapter 1)

[ITA67 s218; FA75 s33(2) and Sch1 PtII]

In this Chapter, except where the context otherwise requires—

"*loan interest*", in relation to a society, means any interest payable by the society in respect of any mortgage, loan, loan stock or deposit;

"*share interest*", in relation to a society, means any interest, dividend, bonus or other sum payable to a shareholder of the society by reference to the amount of the shareholder's holding in the share capital of the society;

"*society*" means a society registered under the Industrial and Provident Societies Acts, 1893 to 1978;

references to the payment of share interest or loan interest include references to the crediting of such interest.

Cross References

To Section 698

Section 430 Meaning of "close company".

Section 616 Groups of companies: interpretation.

699 Deduction as expenses of certain sums, etc

[ITA67 s219(1) and (4)(b) and (c); FA74 s47; CTA76 s30(5)(a)]

(1) In computing for the purposes of Case I of Schedule D the profits or gains of a society, there shall be deducted as expenses any sums which—

(a) represent a discount, rebate, dividend or bonus granted by the society to members of the society or other persons in respect of amounts paid or payable by or to them on account of their transactions with the society, being transactions taken into account in that computation and calculated by reference to those amounts or to the magnitude of those transactions and not by reference to the amount of any share or interest in the capital of the society;

(b) are share interest or loan interest paid by the society, being interest wholly and exclusively laid out or expended for the purposes of the trade.

(2) (a) Where for the year 1962-63 or any previous year of assessment an annual allowance, balancing allowance or balancing charge in respect of capital expenditure on the construction of a building or structure might have been made to or on a society under Part V of the Finance Act, 1959, but for the circumstance that the society was exempt from tax under Schedule D, any writing down allowance, balancing allowance or balancing charge to be made in respect of the expenditure under *Part 9* for any chargeable period

shall be computed as if every annual allowance, balancing allowance and balancing charge which might have been so made had been made; but nothing in this paragraph shall affect *section 274(8)*.

(b) Where for the year 1962-63 or any previous year of assessment an annual allowance in respect of capital expenditure on the purchase of patent rights might have been made to or on a society under Part V of the Finance Act, 1959, but for the circumstance that the society was exempt from tax under Schedule D, the amount of the expenditure remaining unallowed (within the meaning of *section 756*) shall, in relation to any balancing allowance or balancing charge under *Chapter 1* of *Part 29* to be made to or on the society in respect of the expenditure for any chargeable period, be computed as if every annual allowance which might have been so made had been made.

Cross References

From Section 699

Section 268 Meaning of "industrial building or structure".
Section 274 Balancing allowances and balancing charges.
Section 754 Interpretation (Chapter 1).
Section 756 Effect of lapse of patent rights.

To Section 699

Section 700 Special computational provisions.

700 Special computational provisions

[CTA76 s30(2) to (4); FA78 s19]

(1) Notwithstanding anything in the Tax Acts, [other than Chapter 5 of Part 8,][1] any share or loan interest paid by a society—

(a) shall be paid without deduction of income tax and shall be charged under Case III of Schedule D, and

(b) shall not be treated as a distribution;

but *paragraph (a)* shall not apply to any share interest or loan interest payable to a person whose usual place of abode is not in the State.

[(1A) For the purposes of *subsection (1)*, "*society*" shall include a credit union which is—

(a) registered as such under the Credit Union Act, 1997, or

(b) deemed to be so registered by virtue of section 5(3) of that Act.][2]

(2) In computing the corporation tax payable for any accounting period of a society, *section 243* shall apply subject to the deletion of "yearly" in *subsection (4)(a)* of that section.

(3) On or before the [31 January][3] in each year, every society shall deliver to the inspector a return in such form as the Revenue Commissioners may prescribe specifying—

(a) the name and place of residence of every person to whom share interest or loan interest amounting to the sum of [€90][4] or more has been paid by the society in the year of assessment which ended before that date, and

(b) the amount of such share interest or loan interest paid in that year to each of those persons,

and, if such a return is not fully made as respects any year of assessment, the society shall not be entitled to any deduction under *section 97(2)(e)*, *243* or *699(1)* in respect of any payments of share interest or loan interest which it was required to include in the return, [and assessments shall, as necessary, be made or amended][5] to give effect to this subsection.

Amendments

[1] Inserted by FA01 s57(1)(b). With effect from 1 January 2002 as per S.I. No. 596 of 2001.

[2] Inserted by FA00 s32(1). This section shall be deemed to have come into operation as on and from 6 April 1999.

[3] Substituted by FA01 sched2(39)(a). Applies as respects the year of assessment 2001 or any subsequent year of assessment.

[4] Substituted by FA01 s240 and sched5 part1.

[5] Substituted by FA12 sched4(part 2)(g).

Cross References

From Section 700

Section 97 Computational rules and allowable deductions.
Section 243 Allowance of charges on income.
Section 699 Deduction as expenses of certain sums, etc.

To Section 700

Section 246 Interest payments by companies and to non-residents.

701 Transfer of shares held by certain societies to members of society

[FA93 s 35(1)(a) and (2) to (6); FA97 s146(1) and Sch9 PtI par17(2)]

(1) In this section—

"*company*" has the meaning assigned to it by *section 5(1)*;

"*consideration*" means consideration in money or money's worth;

"*control*", in relation to a company, shall be construed in accordance with *section 432*;

"*society*" means a society registered under the Industrial and Provident Societies Acts, 1893 to 1978, which is an agricultural society or a fishery society within the meaning of [*section 133(1)(a)*][1].

(2) (a) In this subsection and in *subsection (4)*, "*the appropriate number*", in relation to a member's original shares, means such portion (or as near as may be to such portion) of the total number of the referable shares owned by the member at the time of the transfer as bears to that number the same proportion as the total number of shares in the company which are subject to the transfer bears to the total number of shares in the company owned by the society immediately before the transfer, and the number of the referable shares owned by a member shall be an amount determined by the formula—

$$\frac{A \times B}{C} \times \frac{D}{B}$$

where—

A is the market value of the shares in the company owned by the society immediately before the transfer,

B is the total number of the shares in the society in issue immediately before the transfer,

C is the market value of the total assets (including the shares in the company) of the society immediately before the transfer, and

D is the number of shares in the society owned by the member immediately before the transfer.

(b) Where on or after the 6th day of April, 1993, a society, being a society which at any time on or after that date controls or has had control of a company, transfers to the members of the society shares owned by it in the company (in this section referred to as "*the transfer*") and—

(i) the transfer, in so far as it relates to any member, is in respect of and in proportion to, or as nearly as may be in proportion to, that member's holding of shares (in this section referred to as "*the original shares*") in the society immediately before the transfer,

(ii) no consideration (apart from the consideration given by the members represented by the cancellation of the original shares referred to in *subparagraph (iii)*) for, or in connection with, the transfer is given to or received from any member (or any person connected with that member) by the society (or any person connected with the society), and

(iii) on the transfer or as soon as possible after the transfer, the original shares (or the appropriate number of those shares) of each member are cancelled without any consideration (apart from the consideration given to the members represented by the transfer to the members of the shares in the company) for or in connection with such cancellation being given to or received from any member (or any person connected with that member) by the society (or any person connected with the society) and, where the original shares (or the appropriate number of those shares) have been issued to a member at different times, any cancellation of such shares shall involve those issued earlier rather than those issued later,

then, subject to *subsection (5)*, *subsections (3)* and *(4)* shall apply.

(3) For the purposes of the Corporation Tax Acts, the transfer shall be treated as—

(a) not being a distribution within the meaning of *Part 6*, and

(b) being for a consideration of such amount as would secure that, for the purposes of charging the gain on the disposal by the society of the shares owned by it in the company, neither a gain nor a loss would accrue to the society.

(4) For the purposes of the Capital Gains Tax Acts—

(a) the cancellation of the original shares (or the appropriate number of those shares) shall not be treated as involving any disposal of those shares, and

(b) each member shall be treated as if the shares transferred to that member in the course of the transfer were acquired by that member at the same time and for the same consideration at which the original shares (or the appropriate number of those shares) were acquired by that member and, for the purposes of giving effect to this paragraph, where the original shares (or the appropriate number of those shares) have been issued to a member at different times, there shall be made all such apportionments as are in the circumstances just and reasonable.

(5) This section shall not apply unless it is shown that the transfer is effected for bona fide commercial reasons and does not form part of any arrangement or scheme of which the main purpose or one of the main purposes is avoidance of liability to corporation tax or capital gains tax.

(6) In a case where this section applies, the society concerned shall include in the return required to be made by it under *section 884* a statement of the total number of shares cancelled in accordance with *subsection (2)(b)(iii)*.

Amendments

[1] Substituted by FA12 sched1(23).

Cross References

From Section 701

Section 5 Interpretation of Capital Gains Tax Acts.
Section 129 Irish resident company distributions not generally chargeable to corporation tax.
Section 432 Meaning of "associated company" and "control".
Section 443 Meaning of "goods".
Section 884 Returns of profits.

CHAPTER 2

Building Societies

702 Union or amalgamation of, transfer of engagement between, societies

[CTA76 s31(5) and (8)]

(1) In this section, "*building society*" means a building society within the meaning of the Building Societies Acts, 1874 to 1989.

(2) Where in the course of or as part of a union or amalgamation of 2 or more building societies or a transfer of engagements from one building society to another building society there is a disposal of an asset by one society to another society, both societies shall be treated for the purposes of corporation tax in respect of chargeable gains as if the asset were acquired from the society making the disposal for a consideration of such amount as would secure that on the disposal neither a gain nor a loss would accrue to the society making the disposal.

Cross References

To Section 702

Section 430 Meaning of "close company".

703 Change of status of society

[FA90 s57]

(1) In this section and in *Schedule 16*—

"*building society*" means a building society incorporated or deemed by section 124(2) of the Building Societies Act, 1989, to be incorporated under that Act, and references to "*society*" shall be construed accordingly;

"*successor company*" means a successor company within the meaning of Part XI of the Building Societies Act, 1989.

(2) *Schedule 16* shall apply where a society converts into a successor company in accordance with Part XI of the Building Societies Act, 1989.

Cross References

From Section 703

Schedule 16 Building Societies: Change of Status

To Section 703

Schedule 16 Building Societies: Change of Status

CHAPTER 3

Trustee Savings Banks

704 Amalgamation of trustee savings banks

[FA90 s59]

(1) In this Chapter and in *Schedule 17*, "*trustee savings bank*" has the same meaning as in the Trustee Savings Banks Act, 1989.

(2) Where any assets or liabilities of a trustee savings bank are transferred or deemed to be transferred to another trustee savings bank in accordance with Part IV of the Trustee Savings Banks Act, 1989, those banks shall be treated for the purposes of the Tax Acts and the Capital Gains Tax Acts as if they were the same person.

Cross References

From Section 704

Schedule 17 Reorganisation into Companies of Trustee Savings Banks

705 Reorganisation of trustee savings banks into companies

[FA90 s60]

Schedule 17 shall apply to the reorganisation in accordance with section 57 of the Trustee Savings Banks Act, 1989, of—

(a) one or more trustee savings banks into a company, or

(b) a company referred to in *subparagraph (i)* of *subsection (3)(c)* of that section into a company referred to in *subparagraph (ii)* of that subsection.

Cross References

From Section 705

Schedule 17 Reorganisation into Companies of Trustee Savings Banks

To Section 705

Schedule 17 Reorganisation into Companies of Trustee Savings Banks

PART 25A

Real Estate Investment Trusts

705A Interpretation and application

[In this Part—

"*aggregate income*", in relation to a company or group, means the aggregate profits of the company or group, as the case may be, as—

(a) reduced by the aggregate net gains of the company or group, as the case may be, where aggregate net gains arise, or

(b) increased by the aggregate net losses of the company or group, as the case may be, where aggregate net losses arise;

"*aggregate net gains*", in relation to a company or group, means the amount by which the sum of the gains recognised in arriving at the aggregate profits of the company or group, as the case may be, being gains which arise on the revaluation or disposal of investment property or other non-current assets, exceeds the sum of the losses so recognised, being losses which arise on such revaluation or disposal;

"*aggregate net losses*", in relation to a company or group, means the amount by which the sum of the losses recognised in arriving at the aggregate profits of the company or group, as the case may be, being losses which arise on the revaluation or disposal of investment property or other non-current assets, exceeds the sum of the gains so recognised, being gains which arise on such revaluation or disposal;

"*aggregate profits*", in relation to a company or group, means the profit that is stated in accounts of the company or consolidated accounts of the group, as the case may be, being accounts made up in accordance with relevant accounting standards, or, where such accounts or consolidated accounts, as the case may be, have not been made up, the profits which would be so stated if such accounts or consolidated accounts, as the case may be, were made up in accordance with those standards;

"*authorised officer*" means an officer of the Revenue Commissioners authorised by them in writing to exercise the powers conferred by this Part;

"*control*" shall be construed in accordance with *section 432*;

"*distribution*" has the same meaning as in the Corporation Tax Acts;

"*group*" means a group of companies comprising a holding company and its whollyowned subsidiaries and a reference to a member of a group shall be construed as a reference to any company in the group;

"*group Real Estate Investment Trust*" means a group, where—

(a) the principal company of that group:

  (i) has given a notice under *section 705E*, and

  (ii) complies with the conditions in *section 705B(1)(a)*,

and

(b) the group complies with the conditions in *section 705B(1)(b)*,

and any references to "*group REIT*" shall be construed accordingly;

"*holding company*" means a company that holds another company as its wholly-owned subsidiary and, for the purpose of this definition and for the purpose of the [definition of "*group*"][1], a company shall be a wholly-owned subsidiary of another company if and so long as 100 per cent of its ordinary share capital is directly owned by that other company;

"*market value*" shall be construed in accordance with *section 548*;

"*principal company*" means the company within a group that gives a notice to the Revenue Commissioners under *section 705E(2)*;

"*property income*", in relation to a company or group, means the property profits of the company or group, as the case may be, as—

(a) reduced by the property net gains of the company or group, as the case may be, where property net gains arise, or

(b) increased by the property net losses of the company or group, as the case may be, where property net losses arise;

"*property income dividend*" means a dividend paid by a REIT or the principal company of a group REIT, as the case may be, from its property income;

"*property net gains*", in relation to a company or group, means the amount by which the sum of the gains recognised in arriving at the aggregate profits of the company or group, as the case may be, being gains which arise on the revaluation or disposal of investment property or other non-current assets which are assets of the property rental business, exceeds the sum of the losses so recognised, being losses which arise on such revaluation or disposal;

"*property net losses*", in relation to a company or group, means the amount by which the sum of the losses recognised in arriving at the aggregate profits of the company or group, as the case may be, being losses which arise on the revaluation or disposal of investment property or other non-current assets which are assets of the property rental business, exceeds the sum of the gains so recognised, being gains which arise on such revaluation or disposal;

"*property profits*", in relation to a company or group, means an amount which is the lesser of—

(a) the amount which would be the aggregate profits of the company or group, as the case may be, if the residual business, if any, of the company or group, as the case may be, were disregarded, and

(b) the aggregate profits of that company or group, as the case may be;

"*property rental business*" means a business which is carried on by a REIT or a group REIT, as the case may be, for the sole purpose of generating rental income in the State or outside the State, and, for the purpose of this definition, such businesses of a group are to be treated as a single business;

"*qualifying investor*" in relation to a REIT or a group REIT, as the case may be, means—

(a) an investment undertaking within the meaning of *section 739B(1)*, or

(b) a person referred to in *paragraph (a)*, *(b)*, *(f)* or *(ka)* of *section 739D(6)*;

"*Real Estate Investment Trust*" means a company which—

(a) has given a notice under *section 705E*, and

(b) complies with the conditions in *section 705B(1)*,

and any references to "*REIT*" shall be construed accordingly;

"*recognised stock exchange*" means a stock exchange in a Member State, being a stock exchange which—

(a) is regulated by the appropriate regulatory authority of that Member State, and

(b) other than in the case of the Irish Stock Exchange, has substantially the same level of recognition in that Member State as the Irish Stock Exchange has in the State;

"*relevant accounting standards*" has the meaning assigned to it in Schedule 17A;

"*rental income*" means any rent-charge or payment in the nature of rent in respect of—

(a) residential premises within the meaning of *section 96(1)*, and

(b) any building other than such residential premises;

"*residual business*", in relation to a REIT or a group REIT, means any business carried on by the REIT or group REIT, as the case may be, which is not property rental business;

"*specified accounting period*" means the accounting period in which the company or principal company, as the case may be, gives a notice under *section 705E*;

"*specified debt*" means any debt incurred by a REIT or group REIT in respect of monies borrowed by, or advanced to, the REIT or group REIT, as the case may be;

"*specified return date for the accounting period*" has the same meaning as in *section 959A*;

"*the Acts*" means the Tax Acts and the Capital Gains Tax Acts.]²

Amendments

¹ Substituted by F(No.2)A13 s36(a). Comes into operation on 1 January 2014.

² Inserted by FA13 s41(c). Deemed to have come into force and takes effect on and from 1 January 2013.

705B Conditions for notice under section 705E

[(1) Subject to *subsections (2)* and *(3)*, the notice referred to in *section 705E* shall contain a statement to the effect that—

(a) each of the following conditions, in relation to a REIT or the principal company of a group REIT, as the case may be, is met throughout the specified accounting period, namely—

(i) it is resident in the State and not resident in another territory,

(ii) it is incorporated under the Companies Acts,

(iii) its shares are listed on the main market of a recognised stock exchange in a Member State, and

(iv) it is not a close company within the meaning of *Chapter 1* of *Part 13*,

and

(b) each of the following conditions, in relation to a REIT or group REIT, as the case may be, is reasonably expected to be met at the end of the specified accounting period, namely—

(i) at least 75 per cent of the aggregate income of the REIT or group REIT derives from carrying on property rental business,

(ii) it conducts property rental business consisting of at least three properties, the market value of no one of which is more than 40 per cent of the total market value of the properties constituting the property rental business,

(iii) it maintains a property financing costs ratio (within the meaning of *section 705H(1)*) of at least 1.25:1,

(iv) at least 75 per cent of the aggregate market value of the assets of the REIT or group REIT relates to assets of the property rental business of the REIT or group REIT, as the case may be,

(v) it ensures that the aggregate of the specified debt shall not exceed an amount equal to 50 per cent of the aggregate market value of the assets of the business or businesses of the REIT or group REIT, as the case may be, and

(vi) subject to having sufficient distributable reserves, it distributes to the shareholders of the REIT or the shareholders of the principal company of the group REIT, as the case may be, at least 85 per cent of the property income for each accounting period of the REIT or group REIT, as the case may be, by way of property income dividend, on or before the specified return date for the accounting period in relation to the REIT, or the principal company of the group REIT, as the case may be.

(2) Each of the conditions in *subparagraphs (iii)* and *(iv)* of *subsection (1)(a)* shall be regarded as having been met throughout the specified accounting period if that condition is met within the period of three years commencing on the date on which the company or group becomes a REIT, or group REIT, as the case may be.

(3) The condition in *subparagraph (ii)* of *subsection (1)(b)* shall be regarded as having been met at the end of the specified accounting period if that condition is met within the period of three years commencing on the date on which the company or group becomes a REIT, or group REIT, as the case may be.

(4) *Subparagraph (iv)* of *subsection (1)(a)* shall not apply to a REIT or a group REIT, as the case may be, which is under the control of persons who are qualifying investors.][1]

Amendments

[1] Inserted by FA13 s41(c). Deemed to have come into force and takes effect on and from 1 January 2013.

705C Conditions regarding shares

[(1) In this section—

"*ordinary shares*" means shares other than preference shares;

"*preference shares*" means shares which do not carry any right to dividends other than dividends at a rate per cent of the nominal value of the shares which is fixed, and which carry rights in respect of dividends and capital which are comparable with those general for fixed-dividend shares quoted on a stock exchange in the State.

(2) Each share issued by a REIT or the principal company of a group REIT, as the case may be, shall either—

(a) form part of its ordinary share capital, or

(b) be a preference share with no voting rights attaching to it.

(3) No more than one class of ordinary share shall be issued by a REIT or by the principal company of a group REIT, as the case may be.][1]

Amendments

[1] Inserted by FA13 s41(c). Deemed to have come into force and takes effect on and from 1 January 2013.

705D Conditions regarding an accounting period

[Subject to *subsections (2)* and *(3)* of *section 705B*, where a notice has been given under *section 705E* by—

(a) a company, all of the conditions in *section 705B(1)* must continue to be met by that company for each accounting period following the specified accounting period until a notice has been issued in accordance with *section 705O*,

(b) a principal company in respect of a group, the conditions in *section 705B(1)(a)* must continue to be met by that principal company for each accounting period following the specified accounting period until a notice has been issued in accordance with *section 705O*, and

(c) a principal company in respect of a group, the conditions in *section 705B(1)(b)* must continue to be met by that group for each accounting period following the specified accounting period until a notice has been issued in accordance with *section 705O*.][1]

Amendments

[1] Inserted by FA13 s41(c). Deemed to have come into force and takes effect on and from 1 January 2013.

705E Notice to become a Real Estate Investment Trust

[(1) A company shall not be a REIT unless it gives a notice to the Revenue Commissioners under this section.

(2) A group shall not be a group REIT unless a company (in this Part referred to as the "*principal company*") which is a member of that group gives a notice to the Revenue Commissioners under this section.

(3) (a) A notice under this section is a notice in writing specifying a date on or after 1 January 2013—

(i) from which the company is to be a REIT, or

(ii) from which the group is to be a group REIT,

being a date that is not earlier than the date of the notice given under *subsection (1)* or *subsection (2)*, as the case may be, and

(b) the notice shall, in the case of a group REIT, list all of the members of the group, to each of which the group REIT designation will apply.

[(3A) (a) Where at any time a company becomes a member of a group subsequent to the date of a notice given under *subsection (2)* by the principal company of that group, the principal company shall give an amended notice to the Revenue Commissioners within the period of 30 days after the date on which that company became a member of the group.

(b) An amended notice under this section is a notice in writing—

(i) specifying a date from which that company is to be a member of the group REIT, which date shall not be a date earlier than the date of the amended notice, and

(ii) containing a statement that each of the conditions in *paragraph (b)* of *section 705B(1)* in relation to the group REIT is reasonably expected to be met at the end of the accounting period in which the principal company gives the amended notice.

(c) An amended notice shall list all of the members of the group, to each of which the group REIT designation will apply.

(d) Where the principal company does not, in accordance with this subsection, give to the Revenue Commissioners an amended notice, the provisions of *section 705O* shall apply as if the group REIT had given a notice under *subsection (1)* of that section specifying the date at the end of the period specified in *paragraph (a)* as the date from which it would cease to be a group REIT.][1]

(4) The date from which a company or group shall be a REIT or a group REIT, as the case may be, shall be the date—

(a) on or after 1 January 2013, as specified in a notice under [this section][2], and

(b) from which the company or group, as the case may be, meets, or is regarded as having met, the conditions of *section 705B*.][3]

Amendments

[1] Inserted by FA14 s29(1)(b)(i). Comes into operation on 1 January 2015.

[2] Substituted by FA14 s29(1)(b)(ii). Comes into operation on 1 January 2015.

[3] Inserted by FA13 s41(c). Deemed to have come into force and takes effect on and from 1 January 2013.

705F Duration of Real Estate Investment Trust

[A company or group shall not be a REIT or a group REIT, as the case may be, after the date specified in a notice issued in accordance with *section 705O* to the company or group, as the case may be.][1]

Amendments

[1] Inserted by FA13 s41(c). Deemed to have come into force and takes effect on and from 1 January 2013.

705G Charge to tax

[(1) Notwithstanding anything in the Acts, but subject to the provisions of this Part, a company which is a REIT or a member of a group REIT shall not be chargeable to tax in respect of—

(a) income of its property rental business, or

(b) chargeable gains accruing on the disposal of assets of that property rental business.

(2) Where a company or group, which is, or which, subsequent to such acquisition, becomes, a REIT or group REIT, as the case may be, acquires an asset which is used, or subsequent to such acquisition is used, for the purposes of its property rental business, and following that acquisition—

(a) the asset is developed, the cost of which development exceeds 30 per cent of the market value of the asset at the date of commencement of the development, and

(b) the asset is disposed of within the period of three years beginning with the completion of the development,

then, notwithstanding the provisions of *subsection (1)*, the profits arising therefrom, computed in accordance with the Tax Acts, shall be chargeable to corporation tax at the rate specified in *section 21A*.][1]

[(3) Notwithstanding *Chapter 4* of *Part 8*, that Chapter shall apply to a deposit (within the meaning of that Chapter) to which a REIT or a member of a group REIT is for the time being entitled as if such deposit were not a relevant deposit within the meaning of that Chapter.][2]

Amendments

[1] Inserted by FA13 s41(c). Deemed to have come into force and takes effect on and from 1 January 2013.

[2] Inserted by FA14 s29(1)(c). Comes into operation on 1 January 2015.

705H Profit: financing cost ratio

[(1) In this section—

"*property financing costs*" means costs, being costs of debt finance or finance leases for the purposes of property rental business, which are taken into account in arriving at aggregate profits, including amounts in respect of—

(a) interest, discounts, premiums, or net swap or hedging costs, and

(b) fees or other expenses associated with raising debt finance or arranging finance leases;

"*property financing costs ratio*" means the ratio of the sum of property income and property financing costs of a company or group to the property financing costs of the company or group, as the case may be.

(2) This section applies to a REIT or a group REIT if the property financing costs ratio of the REIT or group REIT, as the case may be, is less than 1.25:1 for an accounting period.

(3) (a) Subject to *paragraph (b)*, the REIT or the principal company of the group REIT, as the case may be, shall be charged to corporation tax under Case IV of Schedule D for the accounting period in respect of the amount by which the property financing costs of the REIT or group REIT, as the case may be, would have to be reduced for the property financing costs ratio to equal 1.25:1 for that accounting period.

(b) The amount mentioned in *paragraph (a)* shall not exceed 20 per cent of the property income of the REIT or group REIT, as the case may be.

(4) No loss, deficit, expense or allowance may be set off against the first-mentioned amount in *subsection (3)(a)* in charging that amount to corporation tax.][1]

Amendments

[1] Inserted by FA13 s41(c). Deemed to have come into force and takes effect on and from 1 January 2013.

705I Funds awaiting reinvestment

[(1) This section applies where—

(a) a REIT or group REIT disposes of a property of its property rental business, or

(b) a REIT or a principal company, in the case of a group REIT, raises cash from the issue of ordinary share capital,

and the REIT or group REIT, as the case may be, holds the proceeds.

(2) (a) Profits arising from the investment of such proceeds, other than in property for the property rental business, shall be treated as property profits during the period of 24 months commencing on—

(i) date of disposal, where *subsection (1)(a)* applies, or

(ii) date of issue of ordinary share capital, where *subsection (1)(b)* applies,

and as not being property profits thereafter.

(b) Any apportionment of profits for the purpose of *paragraph (a)* shall be made in accordance with *section 4(6)*.

(3) Where the proceeds are held at any time after the date on which the period referred to in *subsection (2)* ends, the proceeds are to be treated as being assets of the residual business after that date.][1]

Amendments

[1] Inserted by FA13 s41(c). Deemed to have come into force and takes effect on and from 1 January 2013.

705J Taxation of shareholders

[(1) This section applies where a REIT or group REIT, as the case may be, pays a property income dividend.

(2) Subject to *subsection (3)*, a shareholder within the charge to corporation tax shall, notwithstanding any other provision of the Tax Acts, be chargeable to corporation tax under Case IV of Schedule D in respect of a distribution referred to in *subsection (1)*.

(3) A property income dividend, received by a company which is a member of a group REIT from a company which is a member of the same group REIT, shall not be chargeable to corporation tax and the property income dividend shall not be taken into account in computing income for corporation tax of the first-mentioned company.

(4) Notwithstanding the provisions of *subsection (2)*, and subject to *subsection (3)*, a shareholder within the definition of "*qualifying company*" in *section 110(1)* shall be chargeable to corporation tax under Case III of Schedule D in respect of a distribution referred to in *subsection (1)*.

(5) Where, but for *subsection (2)* and *section 129*, a property income dividend would be income of a company which is income chargeable to tax under Case I of Schedule D, it shall be so chargeable notwithstanding those provisions.][1]

Amendments

[1] Inserted by FA13 s41(c). Deemed to have come into force and takes effect on and from 1 January 2013.

705K Taxation of certain shareholders

[(1) In this section, and subject to *subsection (2)*, "*holder of excessive rights*" means a person, other than a qualifying investor, who—

(a) is beneficially entitled, directly or indirectly, to at least 10 per cent of the distribution referred to in [*section 705B(1)(b)(vi),* or][1]

(b) is beneficially entitled to, or controls directly or indirectly—

(i) at least 10 per cent of the share capital of, or voting rights in, the REIT, or

(ii) in the case of a group REIT, to at least 10 per cent of the share capital of, or voting rights in, the principal company.

(2) Where a shareholder becomes a holder of excessive rights in a company as a result of that company becoming a REIT or the principal company of a group REIT, then the provisions of *subsection (3)* will not apply for a period of three years commencing from the date specified by that company in accordance with *section 705E(4)*.

(3) Where a REIT or group REIT makes a distribution to a holder of excessive rights and the REIT or group REIT, as the case may be, has not taken reasonable steps to prevent the distribution to such a person being made, the REIT or the principal company of the group REIT, as the case may be, shall, notwithstanding the provisions of *section 705G,* be treated as receiving an amount of income equal to the amount of the distribution.

(4) The amount of income referred to in *subsection (3)* shall be chargeable to corporation tax under Case IV of Schedule D and shall be treated as income—

(a) arising in the accounting period in which the distribution is made, and

(b) against which no loss, deficit, expense or allowance may be set off.][2]

Amendments

[1] Substituted by F(No.2)A13 s36(b). Comes into operation on 1 January 2014.

[2] Inserted by FA13 s41(c). Deemed to have come into force and takes effect on and from 1 January 2013.

705L Transfer of assets

[(1) Where a company becomes a REIT, the assets of the company before it becomes a REIT shall be deemed, for the purposes of the Capital Gains Tax Acts, to have been—

(a) sold by the company immediately before it becomes a REIT, and

(b) reacquired by the company immediately on becoming a REIT,

and such deemed sale and reacquisition shall be treated as being for a consideration equal to the market value of the assets on the date specified by the company, in accordance with *section 705E(3)(a)*, in a notice under that section.

(2) Where a group becomes a group REIT, the assets of each member of the group before it becomes a group REIT shall be deemed for the purposes of the Capital Gains Tax Acts, to have been—

(a) sold by that member of the group immediately before the group becomes a group REIT, and

(b) reacquired by that member of the group immediately on the group becoming a group REIT,

and such deemed sale and reacquisition shall be treated as being for a consideration equal to the market value of the assets on the date specified by the principal company of the group, in accordance with *section 705E(3)(a)*, in a notice under that section.

(3) Where an asset of a REIT or group REIT […][1] which is used for the purposes of the property rental business of the REIT or group REIT, as the case may be, ceases to be used for such purposes and begins to be used for the purposes of the residual business of the REIT or group REIT, as the case may be, the asset shall be deemed for the purposes of the Capital Gains Tax Acts, to have been—

(a) sold by the REIT, or the relevant member of the group REIT, as the case may be, for that property rental business, and

(b) acquired by the REIT, or the relevant member of the group REIT, as the case may be, for that residual business,

at the date on which it ceases to be so used.

(4) The deemed sale and acquisition in *subsection (3)* shall be treated as being for a consideration equal to the market value of the asset at the date referred to in *subsection (3)*. A gain accruing to the property rental business as a result of *subsection (3)* shall, notwithstanding the provisions of *section 705G*, be a chargeable gain for the purposes of the Capital Gains Tax Acts.

(5) Where an asset of a REIT or group REIT […][2] which is used for the purposes of the residual business, ceases to be used for such purposes and begins to be

used for the purposes of the property rental business, the asset shall be deemed for the purposes of the Capital Gains Tax Acts, to have been—

(a) sold by the REIT, or the relevant member or members of the group REIT, as the case may be, for that residual business, and

(b) acquired by the REIT, or the relevant member or members of the group REIT, as the case may be, for that property rental business,

at the date on which it ceases to be so used, for a consideration equal to the market value of the asset on that date.][3]

Amendments

[1] Deleted by F(No.2)A13 s36(c)(i). Comes into operation on 1 January 2014.

[2] Deleted by F(No.2)A13 s36(c)(ii). Comes into operation on 1 January 2014.

[3] Inserted by FA13 s41(c). Deemed to have come into force and takes effect on and from 1 January 2013.

705M Annual statement to Revenue

[(1) Every REIT, or principal company in respect of a group REIT, shall, in respect of each accounting period, by 28 February in the year following the year in which the accounting period ends, make a statement to the Revenue Commissioners in electronic format approved by them, confirming that the conditions in *section 705D* have been met in relation to the REIT or group REIT, as the case may be, throughout the accounting period specified in the statement.

(2) Where a REIT or principal company in respect of a group REIT, as the case may be, cannot make the statement referred to in *subsection (1)*, it shall notify the authorised officer of the Revenue Commissioners and that notification shall—

(a) state the date or dates on which the condition or conditions first ceased to be met and the date or dates (if any) on which the condition or conditions was or were met again,

(b) give a description of the respects in which the condition or conditions was or were not met, and

(c) give details of the steps (if any) taken to prevent a recurrence of the condition or conditions not being met.

(3) Where a REIT, or principal company in respect of a group REIT—

(a) within a reasonable time determined by the authorised officer, fails to secure that a condition referred to in *subsection (2)* is met, or

(b) fails to make a statement required under *subsection (1)*,

then, the Revenue Commissioners may treat the REIT or group REIT, as the case may be, as having ceased to be a REIT or group REIT at the end of the accounting period immediately prior to the accounting period in which the failure to meet the condition, or make the statement required, began and may apply the provisions of *section 705O*.

(4) Where a REIT, or principal company in respect of a group REIT—

(a) makes an incorrect or incomplete statement under *subsection (1)*, or

(b) fails, without reasonable excuse, to make a statement under that subsection,

then, the REIT, or principal company in respect of a group REIT, as the case may be, shall be liable to a penalty of €3,000. For the purposes of the recovery of a penalty under this subsection, *section 1061* shall apply in the same manner as it applies for the purposes of the recovery of a penalty under any of the sections referred to in that section.][1]

Amendments

[1] Inserted by FA13 s41(c). Deemed to have come into force and takes effect on and from 1 January 2013.

705N Breach of conditions regarding distributions

[Where for an accounting period a REIT or group REIT does not comply with the provisions of [*section 705B(1)(b)(vi)*][1] in respect of the requirement to distribute at least 85 per cent of its property income—

(a) the REIT or the principal company of the group REIT, as the case may be, shall be charged to corporation tax under Case IV of Schedule D in respect of an amount calculated by subtracting the amount of property income distributed in respect of that accounting period from the amount equal to 85 per cent of the property income of that accounting period, and

(b) no loss, deficit, expense or allowance may be set off against the first-mentioned amount in paragraph (a) in charging that amount to corporation tax,

but, where a company is restricted from making a distribution by reason of any provision of the Companies Acts, regard shall be had to such restriction in determining the amount, if any, chargeable to tax by virtue of *paragraph (a)*.][2]

Amendments

[1] Substituted by F(No.2)A13 s36(d). Comes into operation on 1 January 2014.

[2] Inserted by FA13 s41(c). Deemed to have come into force and takes effect on and from 1 January 2013.

705O Cessation Notice

[(1) *Subsection (2)* shall apply if a REIT or group REIT gives a notice in writing to the Revenue Commissioners specifying a date from which it will cease to be a REIT or group REIT, as the case may be.

(2) The company or group shall cease to be a REIT or group REIT, as the case may be, at the date specified in the notice referred to in *subsection (1)*.

(3) The specified date shall be a date on or after the date of the notice referred to in *subsection (1)*.

(4) In accordance with *section 705M(3)*, the authorised officer may by written notice state that any company or group shall cease to be a REIT or group REIT, as the case may be.

(5) The date the company or group ceases to be a REIT or group REIT, as the case may be, shall be a date specified by the authorised officer in the notice referred to in *subsection (4)*.

(6) Where a notice is given under *subsection (4)*, the REIT or group REIT to which the notice is given may, within 30 days from the date of such notice, appeal to the Appeal Commissioners and the Appeal Commissioners shall hear the appeal in all respects as if it were an appeal against an assessment.

(7) The notice of appeal referred to in *subsection (6)* shall be given in writing to the authorised officer.][1]

Amendments

[1] Inserted by FA13 s41(c). Deemed to have come into force and takes effect on and from 1 January 2013.

705P Effect of cessation

[(1) Where a notice is given under *subsection (1)* or *(4)* of *section 705O*, a company or group that has ceased to be a REIT or group REIT is to be treated for corporation tax purposes as having ceased, at the date specified in the notice, to be a REIT or group REIT, as the case may be.][1]

(2) Where a notice is given under [*subsection (1) or (4) of section 705O*][2], the assets of the REIT or group REIT [...][3] shall be deemed to have been disposed of by the REIT or the members of the group REIT, as the case may be, immediately before the cessation date and reacquired by the post-cessation company or members of the group, as the case may be, immediately after the cessation date, at the market value on that cessation date.][4]

Amendments

[1] Substituted by F(No.2)A13 s36(e)(i). Comes into operation on 1 January 2014.

[2] Substituted by F(No.2)A13 s36(e)(ii)(I). Comes into operation on 1 January 2014.

[3] Deleted by F(No.2)A13 s36(e)(ii)(II). Comes into operation on 1 January 2014.

[4] Inserted by FA13 s41(c). Deemed to have come into force and takes effect on and from 1 January 2013.

705Q Antiavoidance provision

[(1) This Part shall not apply to any transaction engaged in by, or on behalf of, a REIT or group REIT, or to which it is directly, or indirectly, a party unless the transaction has been undertaken for bona fide commercial reasons and does not form part of any arrangement or scheme of which the main purpose, or one of the main purposes, is the avoidance of liability to tax.

(2) Where appropriate, a reference in *subsection (1)* to a REIT or a group REIT includes a reference to a company or a group before it has become, or after it has ceased to be, a REIT or a group REIT and, in the case of a group REIT, a company before it has become, or after it has ceased to be, a member of the group REIT.

Amendments

[1] Inserted by FA13 s41(c). Deemed to have come into force and takes effect on and from 1 January 2013.

PART 26

Life Assurance Companies

CHAPTER 1

General Provisions

706 Interpretation and general (Part 26)

[CTA76 s36A(7) and s50(2) to (4); FA79 s28(5); FA86 s59(d); FA93 s11(f) and (k); FA96 s132(1) and Sch5 PtI par10(2) and (3)]

(1) In this Part, unless the context otherwise requires—

"*actuary*" has the same meaning as in section 3 of the Insurance Act, 1936;

"*annuity business*" means the business of granting annuities on human life;

"*annuity fund*" means, where an annuity fund is not kept separately from the life assurance fund of an assurance company, such part of the life assurance fund as represents the liability of the company under its annuity contracts, as stated in its periodical returns;

["*assurance company*" means—

(a) an assurance company within the meaning of section 3 of the Insurance Act 1936, or

(b) a person that holds an authorisation within the meaning of the European Communities (Life Assurance) Framework Regulations 1994 (S.I. No. 360 of 1994);][1]

"*excluded annuity business*", in relation to an assurance company, means annuity business which—

(a) is not pension business, or the liability of the company in respect of which is not taken into account in determining the foreign life assurance fund (within the meaning of *section 718(1)*) of the company, and

(b) arises out of a contract for the granting of an annuity on human life, being a contract effected, extended or varied on or after the 6th day of May, 1986, and which fails to satisfy any one or more of the following conditions—

(i) that the annuity shall be payable (whether or not its commencement is deferred for any period) until the end of a human life or for a period ascertainable only by reference to the end of a human life (whether or not continuing after the end of a human life),

(ii) that the amount of the annuity shall be reduced only on the death of a person who is an annuitant under the contract or by reference to a bona fide index of prices or investment values, and

(iii) that the policy document evidencing the contract shall expressly and irrevocably prohibit the company from agreeing to commutation in whole or in part of any annuity arising under the contract;

"*general annuity business*" means any annuity business which is not—

(a) excluded annuity business, or

(b) pension business,

and "*pension business*" shall be construed in accordance with *subsections (2)* and *(3)*;

"*life business*" includes "*life assurance business*" and "*industrial assurance business*", which have the same meanings respectively as in section 3 of the Insurance Act, 1936, and where a company carries on both businesses may mean either;

"*life assurance fund*" and "*industrial assurance fund*" have the same meanings respectively as in the Insurance Acts, 1909 to 1969, and "*life assurance fund*", in relation to industrial assurance business, means the industrial assurance fund;

"*market value*" shall be construed in accordance with *section 548*;

"*overseas life assurance company*" means an assurance company having its head office outside the State but carrying on life assurance business through a branch or agency in the State;

"*pension fund*" and "*general annuity fund*" shall be construed in accordance with *subsection (2)*;

"*periodical return*", in relation to an assurance company, means a return deposited with the Minister for Enterprise, Trade and Employment under the Assurance Companies Act, 1909, and the Insurance Act, 1936;

"*policy*" and "*premium*" have the same meanings respectively as in section 3 of the Insurance Act, 1936;

"*special investment business*", "*special investment fund*" and "*special investment policy*" have the meanings respectively assigned to them by *section 723*;

"*valuation period*" means the period in respect of which an actuarial report is made under section 5 of the Assurance Companies Act, 1909, as extended by section 55 of the Insurance Act, 1936.

(2) Any division to be made between general annuity business, pension business and other life assurance business shall be made on the principle of—

(a) referring to pension business any premiums within *subsection (3)*, together with the incomings, outgoings and liabilities referable to those premiums, and the policies and contracts under which they are or have been paid, and

(b) allocating to general annuity business all other annuity business except excluded annuity business,

and references to "*pension fund*" and "*general annuity fund*" shall be construed accordingly, whether or not such funds are kept separately from the assurance company's life assurance fund.

(3) The premiums to be referred to pension business shall be those payable under contracts which are (at the time when the premium is payable) within one or other of the following descriptions—

(a) any contract with [an individual who, at the time the contract is made, is][2], or but for an insufficiency of profits or gains would be, chargeable to income tax in respect of relevant earnings (within the meaning of *section 783*) from a trade, profession, office or employment carried on or held by him or her, being a contract approved by the Revenue Commissioners under *section 784* or *785* or any contract under which there is payable an annuity in relation to which *section 786(3)* applies;

(b) any contract (including a contract of assurance) entered into for the purposes of, and made with the persons having the management of, an exempt approved scheme (within the meaning of *Chapter 1* of *Part 30*), being a contract so framed that the liabilities undertaken by the assurance company under the contract correspond with liabilities against which the contract is intended to secure the scheme;

(c) any contract with the trustees or other persons having the management of a scheme approved under *section 784* or *785* or under both of those sections, being a contract which—

(i) was entered into for the purposes only of that scheme, and

(ii) in the case of a contract entered into or varied on or after the 6th day of April, 1958, is so framed that the liabilities undertaken by the assurance company under the contract correspond with liabilities against which the contract is intended to secure the scheme;

[(d) (i) any PRSA contract (within the meaning of Chapter 2A of *Part 30*), and

(ii) any contract with a PRSA provider (within that meaning) being a contract which was entered into for the purposes only of the PRSA concerned;][3]

and, in this subsection and in *subsection (2)*, "*premium*" includes any consideration for an annuity.

(4) (a) In this subsection, "*deduction*" means any deduction, relief or set-off which may be treated for the purposes of corporation tax as reducing profits of more than one description.

(b) For the purposes of the Corporation Tax Acts, any deduction from the profits of an assurance company, being profits of more than one class of life assurance business referred to in *section 707(2)*, shall be treated as reducing the amount of the profits of each such class of business by an amount which bears the same proportion to the amount of the deduction as the amount of the profits of that class of business, before any deduction, bears to the amount of the profits of the company brought into charge to corporation tax.

Amendments

[1] Substituted by FA06 s59(1)(c). This section is deemed to have applied as on and from 20 December 2000.

[2] Substituted by FA03 s54(a).

[3] Substituted by FA03 s54(b).

Cross References

From Section 706

Section 548 Valuation of assets.
Section 706 Interpretation and general (Part 26).
Section 707 Management expenses.
Section 718 Foreign life assurance funds.
Section 723 Special investment policies.
Section 770 Interpretation and supplemental (Chapter 1).
Section 783 Interpretation and general (Chapter 2).
Section 784 Retirement annuities: relief for premiums.
Section 785 Approval of contracts for dependants or for life assurance.
Section 786 Approval of certain other contracts.

To Section 706

Section 29 Persons chargeable.
Section 79 Foreign currency: computation of income and chargeable gains.
Section 98A Taxation of reverse premiums.

Section 396 Relief for trading losses other than terminal losses.
Section 396B Relief for certain trading losses on a value basis.
Section 420 Losses, etc. which may be surrendered by means of group relief.
Section 420A Group relief: relevant losses and charges.
Section 420B Group relief: Relief for certain losses on a value basis.
Section 446 Certain trading operations carried on in Custom House Docks Area.
Section 487 Corporation tax: credit for bank levy.
Section 541A Treatment of debts on a change in currency.
Section 644C Relief from corporation tax for losses from dealing in residential development land.
Section 706 Interpretation and general (Part 26).
Section 739D Gain arising on a chargeable event.
Section 784A Approved retirement fund.
Section 832 Provisions in relation to Convention for reciprocal avoidance of double taxation in the State and the United Kingdom of income and capital gains.
Section 845 Corporation tax: treatment of tax-free income of non-resident banks, insurance businesses, etc.
Section 848B Interpretation.
Section 904C Power of inspection (returns and collection of appropriate tax): assurance companies.
Schedule 2B Investment Undertakings: Declarations

707 Management expenses

[CTA76 s33(1) to (2); FA86 s59(a); FA92 s44(a); FA93 s11(a) and (b)]

(1) Subject to *sections 709* and *710*, *section 83* shall apply for computing the profits of a company carrying on life business, whether mutual or proprietary (and not charged to corporation tax in respect of it under Case I of Schedule D), whether or not the company is resident in the State, as that section applies in relation to an investment company, except that—

(a) there shall be deducted from the amount treated as expenses of management for any accounting period—

(i) any repayment or refund receivable in the period of the whole or part of a sum disbursed by the company for that period or any earlier period as expenses of management, including commissions (in whatever manner described),

(ii) reinsurance commissions earned by the company in the period, and

(iii) the amount of any fines or fees receivable in the period or profits arising from reversions in the period,

and in calculating profits arising from reversions the company may set off against those profits any losses arising from reversions in any previous accounting period during which any enactment granting this relief was in operation in so far as they have not already been so set off, and

[(b) no deduction shall be made under *section 83(2)(b)* other than in respect of the amount of any income (other than receipts from premiums) which, if the profits of the company were chargeable to corporation tax under Case I of Schedule D, would be taken into account in computing those profits and any such deduction from the amount treated as expenses of management under that section shall not be regarded as reducing acquisition expenses within the meaning of *section 708*.][1]

(2)

[(a) Where the life assurance business of an assurance company includes more than one of the following classes of business—

(i) pension business,

(ii) general annuity business, and

(iii) life assurance business (excluding such pension business and general annuity business),

then, for the purposes of the Corporation Tax Acts, the business of each such class shall be treated as though it were a separate business, and *subsection (1)* shall apply separately to each such class of business as if it were the only business of the company.][2]

(b) Any amount of an excess referred to in *section 83(3)* which is carried forward from an accounting period ending before the 27th day of May, 1986, may for the purposes of *section 83(2)* be deducted in computing the profits of the company for a later accounting period in respect of such of the classes of business referred to in *paragraph (a)* as the company may elect; but any amount so deducted in computing the profits from one of those classes of business shall not be deducted in computing the profits of the company from another of those classes of business.

[(c) Any amount of excess referred to in *section 83(3)* in relation to special investment business, which is available to be carried forward from an accounting period ending in 2002, may for the purposes of that section, be carried forward to the succeeding accounting period and treated as relating to life assurance business, other than new basis business (within the meaning of section 730A(1)).][3]

[...][4]

(4) Relief under *subsection (1)* shall not be given to any such company in so far as it would, if given in addition to all other reliefs to which the company is entitled, reduce the corporation tax borne by the company on the income and gains of its life business for any accounting period to less than would have been paid if the company had been charged to tax at the rate specified in *section 21(1)* in respect of that business under Case I of Schedule D and, where relief has been withheld in respect of any accounting period by virtue of this subsection, the excess to be carried forward by virtue of *section 83(3)* shall be increased accordingly.

(5) (a) For the purposes of *subsection (4)*—

[...][5]

[...][6]

[...][7]

(iv) *sections 709(2), 710* and *714* shall, and *section 396(5)(b)* shall not, apply for the purposes of computing the profits of the life assurance business or the industrial assurance business, as the case may be, which would have been charged to tax under Case I of Schedule D.

(b) The reference in *section 551(2)* to computing income or profits or gains or losses shall not be taken as applying to a computation of a company's income for the purposes of *subsection (4)*.

Amendments

[1] Substituted by FA99 s86(1). This section shall be deemed to have applied as respects income accruing for accounting periods commencing on or after the 1st day of January, 1999.

[2] Substituted by FA03 s52(1)(a)(i)(I). This section applies as respects accounting periods ending in 2003 and subsequent years.

[3] Inserted by FA03 s52(1)(a)(i)(II). This section applies as respects accounting periods ending in 2003 and subsequent years.
[4] Deleted by FA99 sched6.
[5, 6] Deleted by FA00 sched2.
[7] Deleted by FA03 s52(1)(a)(ii). This section applies as respects accounting periods ending in 2003 and subsequent years.

Cross References

From Section 707

Section 21 The charge to corporation tax and exclusion of income tax and capital gains tax.
Section 83 Expenses of management of investment companies.
Section 396 Relief for trading losses other than terminal losses.
Section 551 Exclusion from consideration for disposals of sums chargeable to income tax.
Section 708 Acquisition expenses.
Section 709 Companies carrying on life business.
Section 710 Profits of life business.
Section 714 Life business: computation of profits.

To Section 707

Section 127 Tax treatment of restrictive covenants.
Section 375 Limit on renewals allowance for cars.
Section 420 Losses, etc. which may be surrendered by means of group relief.
Section 517 Payments to trustees of approved profit sharing scheme.
Section 518 Costs of establishing profit sharing schemes.
Section 519 Employee share ownership trusts.
Section 519B Costs of establishing savings-related share option schemes.
Section 519D Approved share option schemes.
Section 531W No relief for any payment in relation to parking levy.
Section 551 Exclusion from consideration for disposals of sums chargeable to income tax.
Section 706 Interpretation and general (Part 26).
Section 708 Acquisition expenses.
Section 710 Profits of life business.
Section 711 Chargeable gains of life business.
Section 715 Annuity business: separate charge on profits.
Section 718 Foreign life assurance funds.
Section 728 Expenses of management.
Section 751A Exchange of shares held as trading stock.
Section 774 Certain approved schemes: exemptions and reliefs.
Section 787J Allowance to employer.
Section 814 Taxation of income deemed to arise from transactions in certificates of deposit and assignable deposits.
Section 832 Provisions in relation to Convention for reciprocal avoidance of double taxation in the State and the United Kingdom of income and capital gains.
Section 840 Business entertainment.
Schedule 32 Transitional Provisions

708 Acquisition expenses

[CTA76 s33A(1) to (5) and (7) to (8); FA92 s44(c); FA93 s23; FA96 s46; FA97 s156(3)]

(1) For the purposes of this section and subject to *subsections (2)* to *(4)*, the acquisition expenses for any period of an assurance company carrying on life assurance business shall be such of the following expenses of management, including commissions (in whatever manner described) and excluding any payment of rent in respect of which a deduction is to be made twice by virtue of *section 324*, *333* or *345* in the computation of profits or gains, as are for that period attributable to the company's life assurance business (excluding pension business and general annuity business)—

(a) expenses of management which are disbursed solely for the purpose of the acquisition of business, and

(b) so much of any other expenses of management which are disbursed partly for the purpose of the acquisition of business and partly for other purposes as are properly attributable to the acquisition of business,

reduced by—

(i) any repayment or refund receivable in the period of the whole or part of management expenses within *paragraph (a)* or *(b)* and disbursed by the company for that period or any earlier period, and

(ii) reinsurance commission earned by the company in that period which is referable to life assurance business (excluding pension business and general annuity business).

(2) *Subsection (1)* shall not apply to acquisition expenses in respect of policies of life assurance issued before the 1st day of April, 1992, but without prejudice to the application of that subsection to any commission (in whatever manner described) attributable to a variation on or after that date in a policy of life assurance issued before that date, and for this purpose the exercise of any rights conferred by a policy shall be regarded as a variation of the policy.

(3) In *subsection (1)*, "*the acquisition of business*" includes the securing on or after the 1st day of April, 1992, of the payment of increased or additional premiums in respect of a policy of assurance which has already been issued before, on or after that date.

(4) For the purposes of *subsection (1)* and in relation to any period, the expenses of management attributable to a company's life assurance business (excluding pension business and general annuity business) shall be expenses—

(a) which are disbursed for that period (disregarding any treated as so disbursed by *section 83(3)*), and

(b) which, disregarding *subsection (5)*, are deductible as expenses of management of such life assurance business in accordance with *section 707*.

(5) Notwithstanding anything in *section 707*, only one-seventh of the acquisition expenses for any accounting period (in this section referred to as "*the base period*") shall be treated as deductible under that section for the base period, and in *subsections (6)* and *(7)* any reference to the full amount of the acquisition expenses for the base period is a reference to the amount of those expenses which would be deductible for that period apart from this subsection.

(6) Where by virtue of *subsection (5)* only a fraction of the full amount of the acquisition expenses for the base period is deductible under *section 707* for that period, then, subject to *subsection (7)*, a further one-seventh of the full amount shall be so deductible for each succeeding accounting period after the base period until the whole of the full amount has become so deductible, except that for any accounting period of less than a year the fraction of one-seventh shall be proportionately reduced.

[(6A) Acquisition expenses for any accounting period ending on or before 31 December 2002 which relate to special investment business shall, for the purposes of *subsection (6)*, be treated as acquisition expenses which relate to life assurance business (excluding pension business and general annuity business).][1]

(7) For any accounting period for which the fraction of the full amount of the acquisition expenses for the base period which would otherwise be deductible in accordance with *subsection (6)* exceeds the balance of those expenses which has

not become deductible for earlier accounting periods, only that balance shall be deductible.

Amendments

[1] Inserted by FA03 s52(1)(b). This section applies as respects accounting periods ending in 2003 and subsequent years.

Cross References

From Section 708

Section 83 Expenses of management of investment companies.
Section 324 Double rent allowance in respect of rent paid for certain business premises.
Section 333 Double rent allowance in respect of rent paid for certain business premises.
Section 345 Double rent allowance in respect of rent paid for certain business premises.
Section 707 Management expenses.

To Section 708

Section 707 Management expenses.
Section 711 Chargeable gains of life business.

709 Companies carrying on life business

[CTA76 s34]

(1) Where an assurance company carries on life business in conjunction with insurance business of any other class, the life business shall for the purposes of corporation tax be treated as a separate business from any other class of business carried on by the company.

(2) In ascertaining for the purposes of *section 396* or *397* whether and to what extent a company has incurred a loss on its life business, any profits derived from the investments of its life assurance fund (including franked investment income of a company resident in the State) shall be treated as part of the profits of that business.

Cross References

From Section 709

Section 396 Relief for trading losses other than terminal losses.
Section 397 Relief for terminal loss in a trade.

To Section 709

Section 109 Payments in respect of redundancy.
Section 707 Management expenses.

710 Profits of life business

[CTA76 s35; FA91 s30; FA94 s60; FA97 s67]

(1) Where the profits of an assurance company in respect of its life business are for the purposes of the Corporation Tax Acts computed in accordance with the provisions applicable to Case I of Schedule D, the following provisions shall apply:

(a) such part of those profits as belongs or is allocated to, or is expended on behalf of, policyholders or annuitants shall be excluded in making the computation;

(b) such part of those profits as is reserved for policyholders or annuitants shall also be excluded in making the computation but, if any profits so excluded as being so reserved cease at any time to be so reserved and are not allocated to, or expended on behalf of, policyholders or annuitants, those profits shall be treated as profits of the company for the accounting period in which they ceased to be so reserved.

(2) (a) Subject to *paragraph (b)*, [where a company's trading operations on 31 December 2000 consisted solely of foreign life assurance business][1] (within the meaning of *section 451(1)*) the following provisions shall apply:

(i) subject to this subsection, the company shall be chargeable to corporation tax in respect of the profits of that business under Case I of Schedule D;

(ii) notwithstanding *subsection (1)(b)*, where apart from this subparagraph any part of those profits would be excluded in computing the income chargeable under Case I of Schedule D solely by virtue of that part being reserved for policyholders or annuitants, that part shall not be excluded in computing the income so chargeable;

[...][2]

[...][3]

[(b) Where a company would be chargeable to corporation tax in respect of the profits of a life business in accordance with *subsection (2)(a)* but for the fact that—

(i) *section 446* has been deleted, and

(ii) that section referred to time limits in respect of certificates to which the section related,

then, notwithstanding that deletion and those time limits, those profits shall be chargeable to corporation tax in accordance with *subsection (2)(a)*, and the other provisions of this section shall apply with any modifications necessary to give effect to this subsection.][4]

(3) (a) In this subsection—

"*policy of assurance*" means—

(i) a policy of assurance issued by a company (to which *subsection (2)* applies) to an individual who on the date the policy is issued resides outside the State and who continuously so resides throughout a period of not less than 6 months commencing on that date, or

(ii) a policy issued or a contract made which is not a retirement benefits policy solely by virtue of the age condition not being complied with;

"*relevant amount*"—

(i) in relation to a policy of assurance, means the amount determined by the formula—

$$V - P$$

and

(ii) in relation to a retirement benefits policy, means the amount determined by the formula—

$$(V - P) \times \frac{75}{100}$$

where—

V is the amount or the aggregate of amounts by which the market value of all the entitlements under the policy of assurance or the retirement benefits policy, as the case may be, increased during any period or periods in which the policyholder was residing in the State, and

P is the amount of premiums or like sums paid in respect of the policy of assurance or the retirement benefits policy, as the case may be, during any period or periods in which the policyholder was residing in the State;

"*retirement benefits policy*" means a policy issued or a contract made by a company (to which *subsection (2)* applies)—

(i) to or with, as the case may be, an individual who, on the date the policy is issued or the contract is made, resides outside the State and who continuously so resides throughout a period of not less than 6 months commencing on that date, and

(ii) on terms which include the condition (in this subsection referred to as "*the age condition*") that the main benefit secured by the policy or contract is the payment by the company (otherwise than on the death or disability of the individual) of a sum to the individual on or after the individual attains the age of 60 years and before the individual attains the age of 70 years and that condition is complied with.

(b) Where, in respect of a policy of assurance or a retirement benefits policy, a sum is payable by a company (otherwise than by reason of death or disability of the policyholder) to a policyholder who is resident or ordinarily resident in the State (within the meaning of *Part 34*), then—

(i) the company shall be deemed for the purposes of the Corporation Tax Acts to have made, in the year of assessment in which the sum is payable, an annual payment of an amount equal to the relevant amount in relation to the policy of assurance or the retirement benefits policy, as the case may be, and *section 239* shall apply for the purposes of the charge, assessment and recovery of such tax,

(ii) the company shall be entitled to deduct the tax out of the sum otherwise payable,

(iii) the recipient of the sum payable shall not be entitled to repayment of, or credit for, such tax so deducted, and

(iv) the sum paid, or any part of the sum paid, shall not be reckoned in computing total income of the recipient of the sum paid for the purposes of the Income Tax Acts.

(4) Where an assurance company carries on both life assurance business and industrial assurance business, the business of each such class shall for the purposes of the Corporation Tax Acts be treated as though it were a separate business, and *section 707* shall apply separately to each such class of business.

(5) (a) Where under section 25(1) of the Insurance Act, 1989, an assurance company amalgamates its industrial assurance and life assurance funds, *subsection (4)* shall not apply to that company for any accounting period ending on or after the completion of the amalgamation and before the recommencement, if any, of a separate industrial assurance or life assurance fund.

(b) For the purposes of applying *section 707*, in so far as it is affected by—

(i) management expenses or charges on income which apart from *section 83(3)* would be treated as respectively incurred for or paid in an accounting period ending before the day on which the amalgamation is completed, or

(ii) any loss incurred in such a period,

to a company which has amalgamated its industrial assurance and life assurance funds, *subsection (4)* shall apply as if the company had not amalgamated its funds.

(6) For the purposes of *subsections (2)* and *(5)*, where an accounting period of an assurance company begins before the day (in this subsection referred to as "*the day of amalgamation*") on which the company completes the amalgamation of its industrial assurance and life assurance funds and ends on or after the day of amalgamation, that period shall be divided into one part beginning on the day on which the accounting period begins and ending on the day before the day of amalgamation and another part beginning on the day of amalgamation and ending on the day on which the accounting period ends, and both parts of the accounting period shall be treated as if they were separate accounting periods.

Amendments

[1] Substituted by FA00 s56(1)(a). This section shall apply as respects the financial year 2001 and subsequent financial years.

[2, 3] Deleted by FA00 s56(1)(b). This section shall apply as respects the financial year 2001 and subsequent financial years.

[4] Substituted by FA12 sched1(24).

Revenue Briefings

Tax Briefing

Tax Briefing September 2000 – Issue 41 pg 19 – Life Assurance Companies – New Taxation Regime

Tax Briefing April 2001 – Issue 43 pg 8 – New Life Assurance Regime

Cross References

From Section 710

Section 83 Expenses of management of investment companies.

Section 239 Income tax on payments by resident companies.

Section 446 Certain trading operations carried on in Custom House Docks Area.

Section 451 Treatment of income and gains of certain trading operations carried on in Custom House Docks Area from investments held outside the State.

Section 707 Management expenses.

Section 818 Interpretation (Part 34).

To Section 710

Section 420 Losses, etc. which may be surrendered by means of group relief.

Section 420A Group relief: relevant losses and charges.

Section 594 Foreign life assurance and deferred annuities: taxation and returns.

Section 644C Relief from corporation tax for losses from dealing in residential development land.

Section 707 Management expenses.

Section 713 Investment income reserved for policyholders.

Section 715 Annuity business: separate charge on profits.

Section 730A Profits of life business: new basis.

Section 734 Taxation of collective investment undertakings.

711 Chargeable gains of life business

[CTA76 s35A; FA93 s11(d); FA96 s47(1)]

[(1) For the purposes of computing corporation tax on chargeable gains accruing to a fund or funds maintained by an assurance company in respect of its life business—

(a) (i) *section 556*, and

(ii) *section 607*,

shall not apply,

(b) *section 581* shall, as respects—

(i) subsections (1) and (2) of that section, and

(ii) subsection (3) of that section, in so far as a chargeable gain is not thereby disregarded for the purposes of that subsection,

apply as if *paragraph 24* of *Schedule 32*, *section 719*, *section 723(7)(a)* and *paragraph (a)(ii)* had not been enacted,

(c) the amount of capital gains tax computed for the purposes of *section 78(2)* [...][1] is the amount so computed as if, notwithstanding *section 28(3)*, the rate of capital gains tax were—

(i) throughout the financial year 1999, subject to *paragraph (d)*, 40 per cent, and

(ii) throughout each subsequent financial year, the rate of corporation tax specified in *section 21(1)* for that financial year,

and

(d) where for an accounting period the expenses of management (within the meaning of section 83 as applied by *section 707*), deductible exceeds the amount of profits from which they are deductible, the reference in *paragraph (c)(i)* to 40 per cent shall be a reference to the rate of corporation tax referred to in *section 21(1)* for the financial year 1999.][2]

(2) (a) In this subsection—

"the appropriate amount in respect of the interest" means the appropriate amount in respect of the interest which would be determined in accordance with *Schedule 21* if a company were the first buyer and carried on a trade to which *section 749(1)* applies but, in so determining the appropriate amount in respect of the interest in accordance with *Schedule 21*, *paragraph 3(4)* of that Schedule shall apply as if "in the opinion of the Appeal Commissioners" were deleted;

"*securities*" has the same meaning as in *section 815*.

(b) Where in an accounting period a company disposes of any securities and in the following accounting period interest becoming payable in respect of the securities is receivable by the company, the gain or loss accruing on the disposal shall be computed as if the price paid by the company for the securities was reduced by the appropriate amount in respect of the interest; but where for an accounting period this paragraph applies so as to reduce the price paid for securities, the amount by which the price paid for the securities is reduced shall be treated as a loss arising in the immediately following accounting period from the disposal of the securities.

(3) Subject to *section 720*, where an assurance company, in the course of carrying on a class of life assurance business mentioned in *subparagraph (iii)* or *(iv)* of *section 707(2)(a)*, disposes of or is deemed to dispose of assets in an accounting period, the amount, if any, for each such class of business by which the aggregate of allowable losses exceeds the aggregate of chargeable gains on the disposals or deemed disposals in the course of that class of business in the accounting period shall be—

(a) disregarded for the purposes of *section 31*, and

(b) treated for the purposes of the Corporation Tax Acts as a sum disbursed by the company in the accounting period as an expense of management, other than an acquisition expense (within the meaning of *section 708*), incurred in the course of carrying on that class of business.

(4) For the purposes of *subsection (3)*, any amount which apart from *paragraph 24* of *Schedule 32* would be treated as a chargeable gain or an allowable loss of an accounting period of a company by virtue of *section 720* shall also be treated as arising on a disposal of assets by the company in the accounting period so that each such amount shall be taken into account in determining the amount, if any, by which the aggregate of allowable losses exceeds the aggregate of chargeable gains on disposals of assets by the company in the course of carrying on life assurance business [(excluding pension business and general annuity business)][3] in the accounting period.

Amendments

[1] Deleted by FA03 s52(1)(c)(i). This section applies as respects accounting periods ending in 2003 and subsequent years.

[2] Substituted by FA00 s81(1)(a). This section is deemed to apply for the financial year 1999 and subsequent financial years.

[3] Substituted by FA03 s52(1)(c)(ii). This section applies as respects accounting periods ending in 2003 and subsequent years.

Cross References

From Section 711

Section 21 The charge to corporation tax and exclusion of income tax and capital gains tax.
Section 28 Taxation of capital gains and rate of charge.
Section 31 Amount chargeable.
Section 78 Computation of companies' chargeable gains.
Section 556 Adjustment of allowable expenditure by reference to consumer price index.
Section 581 Disposals of shares or securities within 4 weeks of acquisition.
Section 607 Government and certain other securities.
Section 707 Management expenses.
Section 708 Acquisition expenses.
Section 719 Deemed disposal and reacquisition of certain assets.
Section 720 Gains or losses arising by virtue of section 719.
Section 723 Special investment policies.
Section 749 Dealers in securities.
Section 815 Taxation of income deemed to arise on certain sales of securities.
Schedule 21 Purchase and Sale of Securities: Appropriate Amount in Respect of the Interest
Schedule 32 Transitional Provisions

712 Distributions received from Irish resident companies

[CTA76 s33B; FA93 s11(c)]

(1) [*Section 129* and *subsections (4)* and *(5)* of *section 153*][1] shall not apply as respects a distribution received by an assurance company in connection with that part of its life business the profits of which are charged to corporation tax otherwise than under Case I or IV of Schedule D[...][2].

[...][3]

Amendments

[1] Substituted by FA99 s28(2). This section shall apply as respects distributions made on or after the 6th day of April, 1999.

[2, 3] Deleted by FA00 sched2.

Cross References

From Section 712

Section 129 Irish resident company distributions not generally chargeable to corporation tax.

Section 153 Distributions to certain nonresidents.

713 Investment income reserved for policyholders

[CTA76 s36; FA93 s11(e); FA96 s48(1); FA97 s68]

(1) For the purposes of this section—

(a) "*unrelieved profits*" means the amount of profits on which corporation tax falls finally to be borne;

(b) the amount of tax which is or would be chargeable on a company shall be taken to be the amount of tax which is or would be so chargeable after allowance of any relief to which the company is or would be entitled otherwise than under this section […][1].

[…][2]

[(3) Notwithstanding *sections 21(1)* and 21A and subject to *subsection (6)(b)*, corporation tax shall be charged in respect of the part specified in *subsection (6)(a)* of unrelieved profits of an accounting period of an assurance company from investments referable to life business, […][3] at the rate determined by the formula—

$$\frac{(N2 \times SR1) + (N3 \times SR2)}{N1}$$

where—

N1 is the number of months in the accounting period,

N2 is the number of months from the day of the commencement of the accounting period to the earlier of—

(a) the end of the year of assessment (in this subsection referred to as the "*first year of assessment*") in which that day falls, and

(b) the end of the accounting period,

N3 is N1 reduced by N2,

SR1 is the standard rate for the first year of assessment, and

SR2 is the standard rate for the year of assessment immediately subsequent to the first year of assessment.][4]

[…][5]

(5) (a) Subject to *paragraph (b)*, the franked investment income from investments held in connection with a company's life business shall be apportioned between—

(i) policyholders or annuitants, and

(ii) shareholders,

by attributing to policyholders or annuitants such fraction of that income as the fraction (in this subsection referred to as "*the appropriate fraction*") of the profits of the company's life business which, on a computation of such profits in accordance with the provisions applicable to Case I of Schedule D (whether or not the company is in fact charged to tax under that Case for the relevant accounting period or periods), would be excluded under *section 710(1)*.

(b) Where the franked investment income referred to in *paragraph (a)* exceeds the profits of the company's life business as computed in accordance with the provisions applicable to Case I of Schedule D other than *section 710*, the part of the franked investment income attributable to policy holders or annuitants shall be the aggregate of—

(i) the appropriate fraction of the franked investment income in so far as not exceeding those profits, and

(ii) the amount of the excess of the franked investment income over those profits.

(6) [(a) Where the aggregate of the unrelieved profits and the shareholders' part of the franked investment income exceeds the profits of the company in respect of its life business for the relevant accounting periods computed in accordance with the provisions of Case I of Schedule D, reduced by the aggregate of the amounts of—

(i) relevant trading charges on income under *section 243A*,

(ii) a relevant trading loss under *section 396A*, and

(iii) a loss or excess under *section 420A*,

to which the company is entitled for the relevant accounting periods, as extended by *sections 710* and *714* (whether or not the company is charged to tax under that Case), the part referred to in *subsection (3)* shall be the lesser of—

(I) the amount of that excess, and

(II) the unrelieved profits,

and][6]

(b) where the aggregate referred to in *paragraph (a)* is less than the profits of the company's life business as so computed, *subsection (3)* shall not apply.

(7) This section shall apply subject to *paragraph 24* of *schedule 32*.

Amendments

[1] Deleted by FA00 sched2.

[2] Deleted by FA00 s81(1)(b)(i). This section is deemed to have effect for the financial year 2000 and subsequent financial years.

[3] Deleted by FA03 s52(1)(d). This section applies as respects accounting periods ending in 2003 and subsequent years.

[4] Substituted by FA00 s81(1)(b)(ii). This section is deemed to have effect for the financial year 2000 and subsequent financial years.

[5] Deleted by FA00 s81(1)(b)(iii). This section is deemed to have effect for the financial year 2000 and subsequent financial years.

[6] Substituted by FA06 s54(1). This section applies as respects all claims made on or after 2 February 2006.

Cross References

From Section 713

Section 21 The charge to corporation tax and exclusion of income tax and capital gains tax.
Section 243A Restriction of relevant charges on income.
Section 396A Relief for relevant trading losses.
Section 420A Group relief: relevant losses and charges.
Section 710 Profits of life business.
Section 714 Life business: computation of profits.
Schedule 32 Transitional Provisions

To Section 713

Section 714 Life business: computation of profits.
Schedule 24 Relief from Income Tax and Corporation Tax by Means of Credit in Respect of Foreign Tax
Schedule 32 Transitional Provisions

714 Life business: computation of profits

[CTA76 s38; FA93 s11(g)]

(1) For the purposes of [*section 713*][1], the exclusion by *section 129* from the charge to corporation tax of franked investment income shall not prevent such income of a company resident in the State attributable to the investments of the company's life assurance fund from being taken into account as part of the profits in computing trading income in accordance with the provisions applicable to Case I of Schedule D.

[...][2]

Amendments

[1] Substituted by FA00 sched2(n).

[2] Deleted by FA00 sched2.

Cross References

From Section 714

Section 129 Irish resident company distributions not generally chargeable to corporation tax.
Section 713 Investment income reserved for policyholders.

To Section 714

Section 707 Management expenses.
Section 713 Investment income reserved for policyholders.

715 Annuity business: separate charge on profits

[CTA76 s39; FA86 s59(b); FA96 s131(2) and Sch5 Pt2]

(1) Except in the case of an assurance company charged to tax in accordance with the provisions applicable to Case I of Schedule D in respect of the profits of its life assurance business, profits arising to an assurance company from pension business or general annuity business shall be treated as annual profits or gains within Schedule D and shall be chargeable to corporation tax under Case IV of that Schedule, and for that purpose—

(a) the business of each such class shall be treated separately, and

(b) subject to *paragraph (a)* and *subsection (2)*, the profits from each such class of business shall be computed in accordance with the provisions applicable to Case I of Schedule D.

(2) In making the computation in accordance with the provisions applicable to Case I of Schedule D—

[(a) (i) subject to *subparagraphs (ii)*, *(iii)* and *(iv)*, *subsection (1)* of *section 710* shall apply with the necessary modifications and in particular shall apply as if there were deleted from that subsection all references to policyholders other than holders of policies referable to pension business,

(ii) where apart from this subparagraph any profits would be excluded in making the computation solely by virtue of that part being reserved for holders of policies referable to pension business, that part shall not be so excluded,

(iii) in relation to investments of any fund representing the amount of the liabilities of the company to policyholders in respect of its pension business or general annuity business, as the case may be,

(I) any increase in value of those investments (whether realised or unrealised) shall be taken into account as a receipt, and

(II) any decrease in value of those investments (whether realised or unrealised) shall be taken into account as an expense,

to the extent that the increase or decrease, as the case may be, is included in the value of those liabilities as valued by the actuary to the company, and

(iv) where the profits of an assurance company for an accounting period (in this subparagraph referred to as "the first accounting period") are computed in accordance with *subparagraph (iii)* and the profits of the most recent preceding accounting period are not so computed, the increase or decrease in the value of investments referred to in *subparagraph (iii)* shall as respects the first accounting period be computed by reference to the cost of the investments at the time they were acquired by the company and such increase or decrease shall be treated as a receipt or as an expense, as the case may be.][1]

(b) no deduction shall be allowed in respect of any expense, being an expense of management referred to in *section 707*, and

(c) there may be set off against the profits of pension business or general annuity business any loss, to be computed on the same basis as the profits, which was sustained in the same class of business in any previous accounting period while the company was within the charge to corporation tax in respect of that class of business in so far as that loss not already been so set off.

(3) *Section 399* shall not be taken as applying to a loss sustained by a company on its general annuity business or pension business.

(4) The treatment of an annuity as containing a capital element for the purposes of *section 788* shall not prevent the full amount of the annuity from being deductible in computing profits or from being treated as a charge on income for the purposes of the Corporation Tax Acts.

(5) Notwithstanding any other provision of the Corporation Tax Acts, any annuity paid by a company and referable to its excluded annuity business—

(a) shall not be treated as a charge on income for the purposes of the Corporation Tax Acts, and

(b) shall be deductible in computing for the purposes of Case I of Schedule D the profits of the company in respect of its life assurance business.

Amendments

[1] Substituted by FA98 s64(1). This section shall apply as respects an accounting period of a company ending on or after the 4th day of March, 1998.

Cross References

From Section 715

Section 399 Losses in transactions from which income would be chargeable under Case IV or V of Schedule D.

Section 707 Management expenses.
Section 710 Profits of life business.
Section 788 Capital element in certain purchased annuities.

To Section 715

Section 716 General annuity business.
Section 717 Pension business.
Section 718 Foreign life assurance funds.
Section 727 General annuity and pension business.
Section 729 Income tax, foreign tax and tax credit.
Section 845 Corporation tax: treatment of tax-free income of non-resident banks, insurance businesses, etc.

716 General annuity business

[CTA76 s40; FA86 s59(c)]

(1) In this section, "*taxed income*" means income charged to corporation tax, otherwise than under *section 715*, and franked investment income.

(2) In the case of a company carrying on general annuity business, the annuities paid by the company, in so far as referable to that business and in so far as they do not exceed the taxed income of the part of the annuity fund so referable, shall be treated as charges on income.

(3) Notwithstanding any other provision of the Corporation Tax Acts, any annuities which under *subsection (2)* are treated as charges on income of a company (in this subsection referred to as "*the first-mentioned company*") for an accounting period shall not be allowed as deductions against any profits (whether of the first-mentioned company or of any other company) other than against that part of the total profits […][1] arising in that accounting period to the first-mentioned company from its general annuity business.

(4) In computing under *section 715* the profits arising to an assurance company from general annuity business—

- (a) taxed income shall not be taken into account as part of those profits, and
- (b) of the annuities paid by the company and referable to general annuity business—
  - (i) those which under *subsection (2)* are treated as charges on income shall not be deductible, and
  - (ii) those which are not so treated shall, notwithstanding *section 76*, be deductible.

(5) A company not resident in the State which carries on through a branch or agency in the State any general annuity business shall not be entitled to treat any part of the annuities paid by it which are referable to that business as paid out of profits or gains brought into charge to income tax.

Amendments

[1] Deleted by FA03 s41(1)(j). This section applies as respects accounting periods ending on or after 6 February 2003.

Cross References

From Section 716

Section 76 Computation of income: application of income tax principles.
Section 715 Annuity business: separate charge on profits.

717 Pension business

[CTA76 s41; FA88 s30(1) and (2)(c); FA91 s38]

(1) Exemption from corporation tax shall be allowed in respect of income from, and chargeable gains in respect of, investments and deposits of so much of an assurance company's life assurance fund and separate annuity fund, if any, as is referable to pension business.

(2) (a) In this subsection, "*financial futures*" and "*traded options*" mean respectively financial futures and traded options which are for the time being dealt in or quoted on any futures exchange or any stock exchange, whether or not that exchange is situated in the State.

(b) For the purposes of *subsection (1)*, a contract entered into in the course of dealing in financial futures or traded options shall be regarded as an investment.

(3) The exemption from tax conferred by *subsection (1)* shall not exclude any sums from being taken into account as receipts in computing profits or losses for any purpose of the Corporation Tax Acts.

(4) Subject to *subsection (5)*, the exclusion by *section 129* from the charge to corporation tax of franked investment income shall not prevent such income being taken into account as part of the profits in computing under *section 715* income from pension business.

(5) (a) Where for any accounting period there is apart from this subsection a profit arising to an assurance company from pension business (computed in accordance with *section 715*) and the company so elects as respects all or any part of its franked investment income arising in that period, being an amount of franked investment income not exceeding the amount of the profit arising from pension business, *subsections (1)* and *(4)* shall not apply to the franked investment income to which the election relates.

(b) An election under *paragraph (a)* shall be made by notice in writing given to the inspector not later than 2 years after the end of the accounting period to which the election relates or within such longer period as the Revenue Commissioners may by notice in writing allow.

(6) In computing under *section 715* the profits from pension business, annuities shall be deductible notwithstanding *section 76(5)*, and a company shall not be entitled to treat as paid out of profits or gains brought into charge to income tax any part of the annuities paid by the company which is referable to pension business.

Cross References

From Section 717

Section 76 Computation of income: application of income tax principles.

Section 129 Irish resident company distributions not generally chargeable to corporation tax.

Section 715 Annuity business: separate charge on profits.

To Section 717

Section 729 Income tax, foreign tax and tax credit.

718 Foreign life assurance funds

[CTA76 s42(1) to (5) and (8)]

(1) In this section, "*foreign life assurance fund*" means—

(a) any fund representing the amount of the liability of an assurance company in respect of its life business with policyholders and annuitants residing outside the State whose proposals were made to, or whose annuity contracts were granted by, the company at or through a branch or agency outside the State, and

(b) where such a fund is not kept separately from the life assurance fund of the company, such part of the life assurance fund as represents the liability of the company under such policies and annuity contracts, such liability being estimated in the same manner as it is estimated for the purposes of the periodical returns of the company.

(2) Corporation tax under Case III of Schedule D on income arising from securities and possessions in any place outside the State which form part of the investments of the foreign life assurance fund of an assurance company shall be computed on the full amount of the actual sums received in the State from remittances payable in the State, or from property imported, or from money or value arising from property not imported, or from money or value so received on credit or on account in respect of such remittances, property, money or value brought into the State without any deduction or abatement.

(3) Where—

(a) any securities issued by the Minister for Finance with a condition in the terms specified in *section 43*, or

(b) any stocks or other securities to which *section 49* applies and which are issued with either or both of the conditions specified in *subsection (2)* of that section,

for the time being form part of the investments of the foreign life assurance fund of an assurance company, the income arising from any of those stocks or securities, if applied for the purposes of that fund or reinvested so as to form part of that fund, shall not be liable to corporation tax.

(4) Where the Revenue Commissioners are satisfied that any income arising from the investments of the foreign life assurance fund of an assurance company has been remitted to the State and invested as part of the investments of that fund in any stocks or securities of a type referred to in *subsection (3)*, that income shall not be liable to corporation tax and any such tax paid on that income shall if necessary be repaid to the company on the making of a claim.

(5) Where income from investments of the foreign life assurance fund of an assurance company has been relieved from corporation tax in accordance with this section, a corresponding reduction shall be made—

(a) in the relief granted under *section 707* in respect of expenses of management, and

(b) in any amount on which the company is chargeable to corporation tax by virtue of *section 715*—

(i) in respect of general annuity business, or

(ii) in respect of pension business,

in so far as the investment income relieved is referable to general annuity business or pension business, as the case may be.

(6) Where this section applies in relation to income arising from investments of any part of an assurance company's life assurance fund, it shall apply in the like manner in relation to chargeable gains accruing from the disposal of any such investments, and losses so accruing shall not be allowable losses.

Cross References

From Section 718

Section 43 Certain securities issued by Minister for Finance.

Section 49 Exemption of certain securities.

Section 707 Management expenses.

Section 715 Annuity business: separate charge on profits.

To Section 718

Section 706 Interpretation and general (Part 26).

Section 719 Deemed disposal and reacquisition of certain assets.

719 Deemed disposal and reacquisition of certain assets

[CTA76 s46A; FA92 s44(d); FA93 s11(j); FA97 s69]

(1) In this section and in *section 720*—

"*average*", in relation to 2 amounts, means 50 per cent of the aggregate of those 2 amounts;

"*closing*", in relation to an accounting period, means the position at the end of the valuation period which coincides with that accounting period or in which that accounting period falls;

"*foreign life assurance fund*" has the same meaning as in *section 718*;

"*investment reserve*", in relation to an assurance company, means the excess of the value of the assets of the company's life business fund over the liabilities of the life business;

"*life business fund*" means the fund or funds maintained by an assurance company in respect of its life business [...][1];

"*linked assets*" means assets of an assurance company identified in its records as assets by reference to the value of which benefits provided for under a policy or contract are to be determined;

"*linked liabilities*" means liabilities in respect of benefits to be determined by reference to the value of linked assets;

"*opening*", in relation to an accounting period, means the position at the beginning of the valuation period which coincides with that accounting period or in which that accounting period falls;

"*with-profits liabilities*" means liabilities in respect of policies or contracts under which the policy holders or annuitants are eligible to participate in surplus.

(2) Each asset of the life business fund of an assurance company on the day on which an accounting period of the company ends shall, subject to this section, be deemed to have been disposed of and immediately reacquired by the company on that day at the asset's market value on that day.

(3) *Subsection (2)* shall not apply to—

(a) (i) assets to which *section 607* applies, other than, with effect as on and from the 26th day of March, 1997, where such assets are held in connection with a contract or other arrangement which secures the future exchange of the assets for other assets to which that section does not apply, and

(ii) assets which are strips within the meaning of *section 55*,

(b) assets linked solely to pension business or [...][2], or

(c) assets of the foreign life assurance fund,

and, in relation to other assets which are not assets linked solely to life assurance business [(excluding pension business and general annuity business)][3], shall apply only to the relevant chargeable fraction for an accounting period of each class of asset.

(4) In *subsection (3)*, "the relevant chargeable fraction for an accounting period"—

(a) in relation to linked assets, means the fraction of which—

(i) the denominator is the average of such of the opening and closing life business liabilities as are liabilities in respect of benefits to be determined by reference to the value of linked assets other than—

[(I) assets linked solely to life assurance business (excluding pension business and general annuity business), or pension business, and][4]

(II) assets of the foreign life assurance fund, and

(ii) the numerator is the average of such of the opening and closing liabilities within *subparagraph (i)* as are liabilities of business the profits of which are not charged to tax under Case I or IV of Schedule D, and

(b) in relation to assets other than linked assets, means the fraction of which—

(i) the denominator is the aggregate of—

(I) the average of the opening and closing life business liabilities, other than liabilities in respect of benefits to be determined by reference to the value of linked assets and liabilities of the foreign life assurance business [...][5], and

(II) the average of the opening and closing amounts of the investment reserve, and

(ii) the numerator is the aggregate of—

(I) the average of such of the opening and closing liabilities within *subparagraph (i)* as are liabilities of business the profits of which are not charged to tax under Case I or IV of Schedule D, and

(II) the average of the appropriate parts of the opening and closing amounts of the investment reserve.

(5) (a) In this subsection, "liabilities" does not include the liabilities of the foreign life assurance business[...][6].

(b) In *subsection (4)*, "*appropriate part*", in relation to the investment reserve, means—

(i) where none, or only an insignificant proportion, of the liabilities of the life business are with-profits liabilities, the part of that reserve which bears to the whole the same proportion as the amount of the liabilities of business, the profits of which are not charged to tax under Case I or IV of Schedule D, which are not linked liabilities bears to the whole amount of the liabilities of the life business which are not linked liabilities, and

(ii) in any other case, the part of that reserve which bears to the whole the same proportion as the amount of the with-profits liabilities of business, the profits of which are not charged to tax under Case I or IV of Schedule D, bears to the whole amount of the with-profits liabilities of the life business.

(6) For the purposes of this section, in applying *section 557* to the computation of gains accruing to an assurance company on the disposal, on the day on which an accounting period of the company ends, of assets which are not linked solely to life assurance business [(excluding pension business, general annuity business or special investment business)][7], the company shall be deemed to have acquired all of the assets of its life business fund, other than the assets it acquired in that accounting period, at their respective market values on the day immediately before the day on which that period began.

[(7) For the purposes of this section, assets of the foreign life assurance fund and liabilities of the foreign life assurance business shall be disregarded in determining the investment reserve.][8]

Amendments

[1] Deleted by FA03 s52(1)(e)(i). This section applies as respects accounting periods ending in 2003 and subsequent years.

[2] Deleted by FA03 s52(1)(e)(ii)(I). This section applies as respects accounting periods ending in 2003 and subsequent years.

[3] Substituted by FA03 s52(1)(e)(ii)(II). This section applies as respects accounting periods ending in 2003 and subsequent years.

[4] Substituted by FA03 s52(1)(e)(iii)(I). This section applies as respects accounting periods ending in 2003 and subsequent years.

[5] Deleted by FA03 s52(1)(e)(iii)(II). This section applies as respects accounting periods ending in 2003 and subsequent years.

[6] Deleted by FA03 s52(1)(e)(iv). This section applies as respects accounting periods ending in 2003 and subsequent years.

[7] Substituted by FA03 s52(1)(e)(v). This section applies as respects accounting periods ending in 2003 and subsequent years.

[8] Substituted by FA03 s52(1)(e)(vi). This section applies as respects accounting periods ending in 2003 and subsequent years.

Cross References

From Section 719

Section 55 Taxation of strips of securities.
Section 557 Part disposals.
Section 607 Government and certain other securities.
Section 718 Foreign life assurance funds.
Section 720 Gains or losses arising by virtue of section 719.

To Section 719

Section 541A Treatment of debts on a change in currency.
Section 626B Exemption from tax in the case of gains on disposals of shares.
Section 711 Chargeable gains of life business.
Section 720 Gains or losses arising by virtue of section 719.
Schedule 18A Restriction on Set-off of Pre-entry Losses

720 Gains or losses arising by virtue of section 719

[CTA76 s46B; FA92 s44(d); FA95 s69; FA96 s50]

(1) Subject to *subsections (2)* to *(4)*, chargeable gains or allowable losses which would otherwise accrue on disposals deemed by virtue of *section 719* to have been made in a company's accounting period (other than a period in which the company

ceased to carry on life business) shall be treated, subject to *paragraphs (b)* and *(c)*, as not accruing to the company, but instead—

(a) there shall be ascertained the difference (in this section referred to as "*the net amount*") between the aggregate of those gains and the aggregate of those losses,

(b) one-seventh of the net amount shall be treated as a chargeable gain or, where it represents an excess of losses over gains, as an allowable loss accruing to the company in the accounting period, and

(c) a further one-seventh shall be treated as a chargeable gain or, as the case may be, as an allowable loss accruing in each succeeding accounting period until the whole amount has been accounted for.

(2) As respects chargeable gains or allowable losses accruing on disposals of rights under reinsurance contracts (within the meaning of *section 594(4)*) deemed by virtue of *section 719* to have been made in the accounting period or part of an accounting period falling wholly within the year ending on—

(a) the 31st day of December, 1997, this section shall not apply to three-sevenths,

(b) the 31st day of December, 1998, this section shall not apply to two-sevenths, or

(c) the 31st day of December, 1999, this section shall not apply to one-seventh,

of those chargeable gains and allowable losses.

(3) For any accounting period of less than one year, the fraction of one-seventh referred to in *subsection (1)(c)* shall be proportionately reduced and, where this subsection has applied in relation to any accounting period before the last for which *subsection (1)(c)* applies, the fraction treated as accruing in that last accounting period shall be reduced so as to secure that no more than the whole of the net amount has been accounted for.

(4) Where a company ceases to carry on life business before the beginning of the last of the accounting periods for which *subsection (1)(c)* would apply in relation to a net amount, the fraction of that amount which is treated as accruing in the accounting period in which the company ceases to carry on life business shall be such as to secure that the whole of the net amount has been accounted for.

(5) Where in an accounting period a company incurs a loss on the disposal (in this subsection referred to as the "*first-mentioned disposal*") of an asset the gain or loss in respect of a deemed disposal of which was included in a net amount to which *subsection (1)(b)* applied for any preceding accounting period, then, so much of the allowable loss on the first-mentioned disposal as is equal to the excess of the amount of the loss over the amount which, if *section 719* had not been enacted, would have been the allowable loss on the first-mentioned disposal shall be treated for the purposes of this section as an allowable loss which would otherwise accrue on disposals deemed by virtue of *section 719* to have been made in the company's accounting period.

Cross References

From Section 720

Section 594 Foreign life assurance and deferred annuities: taxation and returns.

Section 719 Deemed disposal and reacquisition of certain assets.

To Section 720

Section 541A Treatment of debts on a change in currency.
Section 711 Chargeable gains of life business.
Section 719 Deemed disposal and reacquisition of certain assets.
Schedule 18A Restriction on Set-off of Pre-entry Losses
Schedule 32 Transitional Provisions

721 Life policies carrying rights not in money

[CTA76 s48]

Where any investments or other assets are, in accordance with a policy issued in the course of life business carried on by an assurance company, transferred to the policyholder, the policyholder's acquisition of the assets and the disposal of the assets to the policyholder shall be deemed to be for a consideration equal to the market value of the assets—

(a) for the purposes of the Capital Gains Tax Acts, and

(b) for the purposes of computing income in accordance with Case I or IV of Schedule D.

722 Benefits from life policies issued before 6th April, 1974

[CTA76 s49]

(1) This section shall apply in relation to policies of life assurance issued before the 6th day of April, 1974, by a company carrying on life business, being policies which—

(a) provide for benefits consisting to any extent of investments of a specified description or of a sum of money to be determined by reference to the value of such investments, but

(b) do not provide for the deduction from those benefits of any amount by reference to tax chargeable in respect of chargeable gains.

(2) Where—

(a) the investments of the company's life assurance fund, in so far as referable to those policies, consist wholly or mainly of investments of the description so specified, and

(b) on the company becoming liable under any of those policies for any such benefits (including benefits to be provided on the surrender of a policy), a chargeable gain accrues to the company from the disposal, in meeting or for the purpose of meeting that liability, of investments of that description forming part of its life assurance fund, or would so accrue if the liability were met by or from the proceeds of such a disposal,

then, the company shall be entitled as against the person receiving the benefits to retain out of the benefits a part of the benefits not exceeding in amount or value corporation tax at the full rate in respect of the chargeable gain referred to in *paragraph (b)* computed without regard to any amount retained under this subsection and reduced in accordance with *section 78(1)*.

Cross References

From Section 722

Section 78 Computation of companies' chargeable gains.

CHAPTER 2

Special Investment Policies

723 Special investment policies

[CTA76 s36A(1) to (6) and (8); FA93 s11(f); FA94 s33; FA96 s49]

(1) In this section—

"*excluded shares*" means—

(a) shares in an investment company within the meaning of Part XIII of the Companies Act, 1990,

(b) shares in an undertaking for collective investment in transferable securities within the meaning of the European Communities (Undertakings for Collective Investment in Transferable Securities) Regulations, 1989 (S.I. No. 78 of 1989), or

(c) shares in a company, being shares the market value of which may be expected to approximate at all times to the market value of the proportion of the assets of the company which they represent;

"*inspector*", in relation to any matter, means an inspector of taxes appointed under *section 852*, and includes such other officers as the Revenue Commissioners shall appoint in that behalf;

"*mortality cover*" means any amount payable under a policy of life assurance in the event of the death of a person specified in the terms of that policy;

"*ordinary shares*" means shares forming part of a company's ordinary share capital;

"*qualifying shares*" means ordinary shares—

(a) in a company resident in the State, or

(b) (i) listed in the official list of the Irish Stock Exchange, or

(ii) dealt in on the smaller companies market, or the unlisted securities market, of the Irish Stock Exchange,

other than excluded shares;

[…][1]

"*special investment business*" means so much of the life business of an assurance company as is connected with special investment policies;

["*special investment fund*" means a fund in respect of which the conditions specified in *subsection (2)* are satisfied as respects accounting periods ending on or before 31 December 2002, of the assurance company concerned;][2]

["*special investment policy*" means a policy of life assurance issued by an assurance company to an individual on or after 1 February 1993 and before 1 January 2001, in respect of which—

[(a) the conditions specified in *subsection (3)* are satisfied as respects accounting periods ending on or before 31 December 2002, of the assurance company concerned, and][3]

(b) a declaration of the kind specified in *subsection (4)* has been made to the assurance company;][4]

"*specified qualifying shares*", in relation to a special investment fund, means qualifying shares in a company the issued share capital of which has a market value of less than [€255,000,000][5] when the shares are acquired for the fund.

(2) The conditions referred to in the definition of "*special investment fund*" are as follows:

(a) the fund shall be owned by an assurance company;

(b) the fund shall be kept separately from its other funds, if any, by the assurance company;

(c) the fund shall represent only the liabilities of the assurance company in respect of its special investment business, and accordingly there shall not be any arrangements whereby any asset of the fund is connected directly or indirectly with any business of the company other than its special investment business;

(d) the aggregate of the consideration given for shares which are at any time before the 1st day of February, 1994, assets of the fund shall not be less than—

(i) as respects qualifying shares, 40 per cent, and

(ii) as respects specified qualifying shares, 6 per cent, of the aggregate of the consideration given for the assets which are assets of the fund at that time;

(e) the aggregate of the consideration given for shares which are at any time within the year ending on the 31st day of January, 1995, assets of the fund shall not be less than—

(i) as respects qualifying shares, 45 per cent, and

(ii) as respects specified qualifying shares, 9 per cent,

of the aggregate of the consideration given for the assets which are assets of the fund at that time;

(f) the aggregate of the consideration given for shares which are at any time within the year ending on the 31st day of January, 1996, assets of the fund shall not be less than—

(i) as respects qualifying shares, 50 per cent, and

(ii) as respects specified qualifying shares, 10 per cent,

of the aggregate of the consideration given for the assets which are assets of the fund at that time;

[(g) the aggregate of consideration given for shares which are, at any time on or after 1 February 1996 and before 31 December 2000, assets of the fund shall not be less than—

(i) as respects qualifying shares, 55 per cent, and

(ii) as respects specified qualifying shares, 10 per cent,

of the aggregate of the consideration given for the assets which are assets of the fund at that time,][6]

(3) The conditions referred to in the definition of "*special investment policy*" are as follows:

(a) the policy of life assurance concerned shall be designated by the assurance company concerned as a special investment policy;

(b) any payments received by the company in respect of the policy shall not, or shall not in the aggregate if there is more than one such payment, exceed [€63,500][7];

[…][8]

(d) the policy shall not be issued to or owned by an individual who is not of full age;

(e) the policy shall be issued to an individual—

(i) who is beneficially entitled to, and

(ii) to whom there shall be paid,

all amounts, other than mortality cover, payable under the policy by the company;

(f) except in the case of a policy issued to and owned jointly only by a couple married to each other, the policy shall not be a joint policy;

(g) unless the policy is issued to and owned jointly only by a couple married to each other, the policy shall be the only such policy owned by the individual;

(h) if the policy is to be issued to and owned jointly only by a couple married to each other, it shall be the only such policy, or one of 2 only such policies, owned only by them;

and for the purposes of *paragraphs (d)* to *(h)* references to ownership of a policy shall be construed as references to beneficial ownership of the policy.

(4) The declaration referred to in *paragraph (b)* of the definition of "*special investment policy*" shall be a declaration in writing to an assurance company which—

(a) (i) is made by the individual (in this section referred to as "*the declarer*") to whom any amounts, other than mortality cover, are payable by the assurance company in respect of the policy in respect of which the declaration is made, and

(ii) is signed by the declarer,

(b) is made in such form as may be prescribed or authorised by the Revenue Commissioners,

(c) declares that at the time when the declaration is made the conditions referred to in *paragraphs (d)* to *(h)* of *subsection (3)* are satisfied in relation to the policy in respect of which the declaration is made,

(d) contains the full name and address of the individual beneficially entitled to any amounts, other than mortality cover, payable in respect of the policy in respect of which the declaration is made,

(e) contains an undertaking by the declarer that, if any of the conditions specified in *paragraphs (d)* to *(h)* of *subsection (3)* cease to be satisfied in respect of the policy in respect of which the declaration is made, the declarer will notify the assurance company accordingly, and

(f) contains such other information as the Revenue Commissioners may reasonably require for the purposes of this section.

(5) (a) An assurance company shall—

(i) keep and retain for not less than the longer of the following periods—

(I) a period of 6 years, and

(II) a period which, in relation to the policy in respect of which the declaration is made, ends not earlier than 3 years after the date on which the company ceases to have any liability in respect of the policy, and

(ii) on being so required by notice given to it in writing by an inspector, make available to the inspector within the time specified in the notice,

all declarations of the kind specified in *subsection (4)* which have been made to the company.

(b) The inspector may examine and take copies of or of extracts from a declaration made available to him or her under *paragraph (a)*.

[…][9]

[…][10]

Amendments

[1] Deleted by FA01 s68(1)(a). This section shall be deemed to have applied as on and from 1 January 2001.

[2] Substituted by FA03 s52(1)(f)(i)(I). This section applies as respects accounting periods ending in 2003 and subsequent years.

[3] Substituted by FA03 s52(1)(f)(i)(II). This section applies as respects accounting periods ending in 2003 and subsequent years.

[4] Substituted by FA00 s62.

[5, 7] Substituted by FA01 s240 and sched5 part1.

[6] Substituted by FA01 s68(1)(b). This section shall be deemed to have applied as on and from 1 January 2001.

[8] Deleted by FA01 s68(1)(c). This section shall be deemed to have applied as on and from 1 January 2001.

[9, 10] Deleted by FA03 s52(1)(f)(i)(III). This section applies as respects accounting periods ending in 2003 and subsequent years.

Cross References

From Section 723

Section 852 Inspectors of taxes.

To Section 723

Section 541A Treatment of debts on a change in currency.
Section 706 Interpretation and general (Part 26).
Section 711 Chargeable gains of life business.
Section 725 Special investment policies: breaches of conditions.
Section 737 Special investment schemes.
Section 839 Limits to special investments.
Schedule 24 Relief from Income Tax and Corporation Tax by Means of Credit in Respect of Foreign Tax

724 Transfer of assets into or out of special investment fund

[CTA76 s36B; FA93 s11(f)]

[Where, in an accounting period ending on or before 31 December 2002, an assurance company transfers][1] the whole or part of an asset (any interest in or rights over an asset being regarded for the purposes of this section as part of the asset)—

(a) which it owned before the transfer, or which was created by the transfer, into, or

(b) which it owns after the transfer, out of,

its special investment fund, the company shall be deemed to have disposed of and immediately reacquired the asset or the part of the asset, as the case may be, at the market value of the asset or the part of the asset, as the case may be, at the time of the transfer.

Amendments

[1] Substituted by FA03 s52(1)(g). This section applies as respects accounting periods ending in 2003 and subsequent years.

725 Special investment policies: breaches of conditions

[CTA76 s36C; FA93 s11(f)]

(1) For the purposes of this section, a policy of life assurance held by an individual, whether married or not, shall not be a special investment policy [at any particular time on or before 31 December 2002,][1] if—

(a) as respects the policy—

(i) a declaration of the kind specified in *section 723(4)* has not been made, or

(ii) any of the conditions referred to in *section 723(3)* is not satisfied at that time,

or

(b) as respects the individual, he or she has at that time a beneficial interest prohibited by *section 839* in classes of investment mentioned in *paragraphs (a)* to *(d)* of *subsection (1)* of that section.

(2) Where an assurance company becomes aware [at any time on or before 31 December 2002,][2] that a policy of life assurance which it has treated as a special investment policy is not such a policy—

(a) the assurance company shall ensure that in accordance with *section 723(2)(c)* its special investment fund does not after that time represent its liability in respect of the policy, and

(b) for the purposes of the Tax Acts other than *section 958(4)*, the liability to corporation tax of the company for the accounting period in which it became aware that the policy was not a special investment policy shall be increased by an amount determined by the formula—

$$(A - B) \times \frac{10}{9} \times \frac{S - 10}{100}$$

where—

A is the amount which was the assumed liability, other than the liability, if any, in respect of mortality cover, of the company in respect of the policy immediately before it became aware that the policy was not a special investment policy,

B is—

(i) the amount which was the liability, other than the liability, if any, in respect of mortality cover, of the company in respect of the policy when the policy ceased to be a special investment policy, or

(ii) if the policy was never a special investment policy, the amount of the aggregate of the payments received and not repaid by the company in respect of the policy, and

S is the standard rate per cent for the year of assessment in which that accounting period ends.

Amendments

[1] Substituted by FA03 s52(1)(h)(i). This section applies as respects accounting periods ending in 2003 and subsequent years.

[2] Substituted by FA03 s52(1)(h)(ii). This section applies as respects accounting periods ending in 2003 and subsequent years.

Cross References

From Section 725

Section 723 Special investment policies.
Section 839 Limits to special investments.
Section 958 Date for payment of tax.

CHAPTER 3

Provisions Applying to Overseas Life Assurance Companies

726 Investment income

[CTA76 s43; FA93 s11(h); FA95 s64; FA96 s132(2) and Sch5 PtII]

(1) Any income of an overseas life assurance company from the investments of its life assurance fund (excluding the pension fund, general annuity fund and special investment fund, if any), wherever received, shall, to the extent provided in this section, be deemed to be profits comprised in Schedule D, and shall be charged to corporation tax under Case III of Schedule D.

(2) Distributions received from companies resident in the State shall be taken into account under this section notwithstanding their exclusion from the charge to corporation tax.

(3) Where an overseas life assurance company is entitled to an amount (in this subsection referred to as "*the first amount*"), being an amount which corresponds to a tax credit, by virtue of having received a distribution from a company not resident in the State, the distribution shall be treated for the purposes of this section as representing income equal to the aggregate of the amount or value of that distribution and the first amount.

(4) A portion only of the income from the investments of the life assurance fund (excluding the pension fund, general annuity fund and special investment fund, if any) shall be charged in accordance with *subsection (1)*, and for any accounting period that portion shall be determined by the formula—

$$\frac{A \times B}{C}$$

where—

A is the total income from those investments for that period,

B is the average of the liabilities for that period to policyholders resident in the State and to policyholders resident outside the State whose proposals were made to the company at or through its branch or agency in the State, and

C is the average of the liabilities for that period to all the company's policyholders,

but any reference in this subsection to liabilities does not include liabilities in respect of special investment, general annuity or pension business.

(5) For the purposes of this section—

(a) the liabilities of an assurance company attributable to any business at any time shall be ascertained by reference to the net liabilities of the company as valued by an actuary for the purposes of the relevant periodical return, and

(b) the average of any liabilities for an accounting period shall be taken as 50 per cent of the aggregate of the liabilities at the beginning and end of the valuation period which coincides with that accounting period or in which that accounting period falls.

(6) (a) For the purposes of this subsection—

(i) "the average of branch liabilities for an accounting period" means the aggregate of the amounts represented by B in *subsection (4)*, B in *section 727(2)* and the average of the liabilities attributable to pension business for the accounting period, and

(ii) "the assets to which this subsection applies" are assets the gains from the disposal of which are chargeable to corporation tax by virtue of *subsections (3)* and *(6)* of *section 29* together with assets the gains from the disposal of which would be so chargeable but for *sections 551(607)* and *613*.

(b) Where the average of branch liabilities for an accounting period exceeds the mean value for the accounting period of the assets to which this subsection applies, the amount to be included in profits under *section 78(1)* shall be an amount determined by the formula—

$$\frac{A \times B}{C}$$

where—

A is the amount which apart from this subsection would be so included in profits,

B is the average of branch liabilities for the accounting period, and

C is the mean value for the accounting period of the assets to which this subsection applies.

(7) *Section 70(1)* as applied to corporation tax shall not apply to income to which *subsection (1)* applies.

Cross References

From Section 726

Section 29 Persons chargeable.

Section 70 Case III: basis of assessment.

Section 78 Computation of companies' chargeable gains.

Section 551 Exclusion from consideration for disposals of sums chargeable to income tax.

Section 613 Miscellaneous exemptions for certain kinds of property.

Section 727 General annuity and pension business.

To Section 726

Section 43 Certain securities issued by Minister for Finance.

Section 49 Exemption of certain securities.

Section 50 Securities of Irish local authorities issued abroad.

Section 594 Foreign life assurance and deferred annuities: taxation and returns.

Section 729 Income tax, foreign tax and tax credit.

Section 832 Provisions in relation to Convention for reciprocal avoidance of double taxation in the State and the United Kingdom of income and capital gains.

Section 845 Corporation tax: treatment of tax-free income of non-resident banks, insurance businesses, etc.

727 General annuity and pension business

[CTA76 s44]

(1) Nothing in the Corporation Tax Acts shall prevent the distributions of companies resident in the State from being taken into account as part of the profits in computing under *section 715* the profits arising from pension business and general annuity business to an overseas life assurance company.

(2) Any charge to tax under *section 715* for any accounting period on profits arising to an overseas life assurance company from general annuity business shall extend only to a portion of the profits arising from that business, and that portion shall be determined by the formula—

$$\frac{A \times B}{C}$$

where—

A is the total amount of those profits,

B is the average of the liabilities attributable to that business for the relevant accounting period in respect of contracts with persons resident in the State or contracts with persons resident outside the State whose proposals were made to the company at or through its branch or agency in the State, and

C is the average of the liabilities attributable to that business for that accounting period in respect of all contracts.

(3) For the purposes of this section—

(a) the liabilities of an assurance company attributable to general annuity business at any time shall be ascertained by reference to the net liabilities of the company as valued by an actuary for the purposes of the relevant periodical return, and

(b) the average of any liabilities for an accounting period shall be taken as 50 per cent of the aggregate of the liabilities at the beginning and end of the valuation period which coincides with that accounting period or in which that accounting period falls.

Cross References

From Section 727

Section 715 Annuity business: separate charge on profits.

To Section 727

Section 726 Investment income.

Section 729 Income tax, foreign tax and tax credit.

728 Expenses of management

[CTA76 s33(3); FA92 s44(b)]

The relief under *section 707* available to an overseas life assurance company in respect of its expenses of management shall be limited to expenses attributable to the life assurance business carried on by the company at or through its branch or agency in the State.

Cross References

From Section 728

Section 707 Management expenses.

729 Income tax, foreign tax and tax credit

[CTA76 s45; FA88 s31(2) and Sch2 PtI par2(2); FA97 s37 and Sch2 pars1 and 2]

(1) *Section 77(6)* shall not affect the liability to tax of an overseas life assurance company in respect of the investment income of its life assurance fund under *section 726* or in respect of the profits of its annuity business under *sections 715*, *717* and *727*.

(2) For the purposes of *section 25(3)* as it applies to life business, the amount of the income tax referred to in that section which shall be available for set-off under that section in an accounting period shall be limited in accordance with *subsections (3)* and *(4)*.

(3) Where the company is chargeable to corporation tax for an accounting period in accordance with *section 726* in respect of the income from the investments of its life assurance fund, the amount of income tax available for set-off against any corporation tax assessed for that period on that income shall not exceed an amount equal to income tax at the standard rate on the portion of income from investments which is chargeable to corporation tax by virtue of *subsection (4)* of that section.

(4) Where the company is chargeable to corporation tax for an accounting period in accordance with *section 727* on a proportion of the total amount of the profits arising from its general annuity business, the amount of income tax available for set-off against any corporation tax assessed for that period on those profits shall not exceed an amount equal to income tax at the standard rate on the like proportion of the income from investments included in computing those profits.

[...][1]

(6) *Section 828(4)* shall not affect the liability to tax under *section 726* of an overseas life assurance company in respect of gains from the disposal of investments held in connection with its life business.

[...][2]

Amendments

[1, 2] Deleted by FA00 sched2.

Cross References

From Section 729

Section 25 Companies not resident in the State.
Section 77 Miscellaneous special rules for computation of income.
Section 715 Annuity business: separate charge on profits.
Section 717 Pension business.
Section 726 Investment income.
Section 727 General annuity and pension business.
Section 828 Capital gains tax: double taxation relief.

To Section 729

Section 25 Companies not resident in the State.

730 Tax credit in respect of distributions [Repealed]

Repealed by FA00 sched2.

Cross References

To Section 730

Schedule 19 Offshore Funds: Distributing Funds

CHAPTER 4

Taxation of Assurance Companies — New Basis

730A Profits of life business: new basis

[(1) In this Chapter and Chapter 5 of this Part—

"*assurance company*" means an assurance company chargeable to corporation tax;

["*credit union*" has the meaning assigned to it in section 2 of the Credit Union Act 1997;

"*financial institution*" means—

(a) a person who holds a licence under section 9 of the Central Bank Act 1971,

(b) a person referred to in section 7(4) of the Central Bank Act 1971, or

(c) a credit institution duly authorised by virtue of Directive No. 2000/12/EC of 20 March 2000*;][1]

* OJ No. L.126, of 26 May 2000, p.1

"*new basis business*" means—

(a) where an assurance company was carrying on life business on 1 April 2000, other than where the assurance company's trading operations at that time consisted solely of foreign life assurance business within the meaning of section 451(1)—

[(i) all policies and contracts commenced by the assurance company on or after 1 January 2001 except those which refer to industrial assurance business, and][2]

(ii) all policies and contracts commenced by the assurance company before that date in so far as they relate to—

(I) pension business and general annuity business, and

(II) permanent health insurance, in respect of which the profits arising to the assurance company were before 1 January 2001 charged to tax under Case I of Schedule D,

(b) where an assurance company was carrying on life business on 1 April 2000, and the assurance company's trading operations at that time consisted solely of foreign life assurance business within the meaning of section 451(1), all policies and contracts commenced by the assurance company on or after 1 January 2001, and

(c) where an assurance company was not carrying on life business on 1 April 2000, subject to *subsection (2)*, all policies and contracts commenced by the assurance company [from the time it began to carry on life business;][3]

["*Service*" means the Courts Service;][4]

["*sinking fund or capital redemption business*" has the same meaning as in section 3 of the Insurance Act, 1936.][5]

(2) Where an assurance company begins to carry on life business after 1 April 2000 and before 31 December 2000, the assurance company may elect that all policies and contracts commenced by it before 31 December 2000 be treated as not being new basis business in so far as they relate to life business (other than pension business and general annuity business).

(3) Life business of an assurance company, in so far as it comprises new basis business, shall for the purposes of the Corporation Tax Acts be treated as though it were a separate business, that is, a business separate from other business (if any) carried on by the assurance company.

(4) Notwithstanding Chapters 1 and 3 of this Part, an assurance company shall be charged to corporation tax in respect of the profits of new basis business under Case I of Schedule D and those profits shall, subject to *subsection (5)*, be computed in accordance with the provisions applicable to that Case of that Schedule.

(5) Where all or part of the profits of an assurance company are, under this Chapter, to be computed in accordance with the provisions applicable to Case I of Schedule D, the following provisions shall also apply—

(a) such part of those profits as belongs or is allocated to, or is expended on behalf of, policyholders or annuitants shall be excluded in making the computation, and

(b) there shall not be excluded in making the computation any remaining part of those profits reserved for policyholders or annuitants.

[(6) Notwithstanding the provisions of *Chapter 3* of *Part 12*, where an assurance company incurs a loss in respect of new basis business, the amount of the loss which may be set off against profits of any other business of the company shall not exceed such amount of those profits computed under the provisions of Case 1 of Schedule D and *section 710*.

(7) (a) This subsection applies to a company carrying on any mutual life assurance business.

(b) Subject to *paragraph (c)*, in respect of each accounting period of a company to which this subsection applies, one-twentieth of the amount determined under *subsection (8)(c)* shall be treated as annual profits or gains within Schedule D and shall be chargeable to corporation tax under Case III of that Schedule.

(c) Where for an accounting period the value referred to in *subsection (8)(c)(ii)* is not less than such value at 31 December 2000, but exceeds the value referred to in *subsection (8)(c)(i)*, an amount equal to one-twentieth of the excess may be deducted from annual profits or gains chargeable to corporation tax by virtue of *paragraph (b)*, of the previous accounting period (so long as it commences on or after 1 January 2001) or a subsequent accounting period.

(8) (a) In this subsection "*statutory accounts*", in relation to a company means—

(i) in the case of a company (in this definition referred to as the "*resident company*") resident in the State, the profit and loss account and balance sheet of that company, and

(ii) in the case of a company (in this definition referred to as the "*non-resident company*") not resident in the State but carrying on a trade in the State through a branch or agency, the profit and loss account and balance sheet of the company,

a report in respect of which is required to be made to the members of the company by an auditor appointed under section 160 of the Companies Act, 1963, or under the law of the State in which the resident company or non-resident company is incorporated and which corresponds to that section.

(b) For the purposes of this subsection the liabilities of an assurance company attributable to any business at any time shall be ascertained by reference to the net liabilities of the company as valued by an actuary for the purposes of the statutory accounts in relation to the company.

(c) The amount referred to in *subsection (7)(b)* is—

(i) the total value at the end of the accounting period, less—

(ii) the total value at the beginning of the accounting period,

of all funds the allocation of which to policyholders has not been determined; but in the case of an overseas life assurance company, the values referred to in *subparagraphs (i)* and *(ii)* at a time shall be multiplied by the following fraction—

$$\frac{A}{B}$$

where—

A is the liabilities at that time to policyholders whose proposals were made to the company at or through its branch or agency in the State, and

B is the liabilities at that time to all the company's policyholders.][6]][7]

Amendments

[1] Inserted by FA03 s57(a)(i).

[2] Substituted by FA01 s69(1)(a)(i). This section shall apply as respects accounting periods commencing on or after 1 January 2001.

[3] Substituted by FA01 s69(1)(a)(ii). This section shall apply as respects accounting periods commencing on or after 1 January 2001.

[4] Inserted by FA03 s57(a)(ii).

[5] Inserted by FA01 s69(1)(b). This section shall apply as respects accounting periods commencing on or after 1 January 2001.

[6] Inserted by FA01 s69(1)(c). This section shall apply as respects accounting periods commencing on or after 1 January 2001.

[7] Inserted by FA00 s53.

Revenue Briefings

Tax Briefing

Tax Briefing September 2000 – Issue 41 pg 19 – Life Assurance Companies – New Taxation Regime

Tax Briefing April 2001 – Issue 43 pg 8 – New Life Assurance Regime – Tax Computations

Cross References

From Section 730A

Section 381 Right to repayment of tax by reference to losses.

Section 396 Relief for trading losses other than terminal losses.

Section 451 Treatment of income and gains of certain trading operations carried on in Custom House Docks Area from investments held outside the State.

Section 710 Profits of life business.

To Section 730A

Section 595 Life assurance policy or deferred annuity contract entered into or acquired by company.

Section 730C Chargeable event.

CHAPTER 5

Policyholders — New basis

730B Taxation of policyholders

[(1) In this Chapter "*return*" means a return under section 730G.

[(2) Subject to *subsection (3)*, this Chapter applies for the purpose of imposing certain charges to tax in respect of a policy (in this Chapter referred to as a "*life policy*") which is—

(a) a policy of assurance on the life of any person, or

(b) a policy in respect of sinking fund or capital redemption business,

where the life policy is new basis business of the assurance company which commenced the life policy.][1]

(3) This Chapter does not apply to a life policy which relates to pension business, general annuity business or permanent health insurance business, of an assurance company.

[(4) For the purposes of this Chapter—

(a) where a policyholder is a person entrusted to pay all premiums (in this subsection referred to as "*group premiums*") in respect of a life policy (in this subsection referred to as a "*group policy*"), out of money under the control or subject to the order of any Court, this Chapter shall apply as if the group policy comprised separate life policies (in this subsection referred to as "*separate life policies*"),

(b) each person beneficially entitled to any part of the rights conferred by the group policy shall be treated as being the policyholder of a separate life policy,

(c) the premiums paid in respect of each separate life policy shall be such amount of the said money included in group premiums paid, which is beneficially owned by the policyholder of the separate life policy,

(d) a gain which, but for the provisions of *section 730D(2)*, would have arisen on the happening of a chargeable event in relation to the group policy shall be treated as if it were a gain arising on a chargeable event in relation to any separate policy where, and to the extent that, the gain is beneficially owned by the policyholder of that separate policy,

(e) *subsections (2)*, *(3)* and *(4)* of *section 730F*, *sections 730G* and *730GA* and *section 904C* apply as if references in those subsections and sections to an assurance company were to read as references to the Service, and

(f) the Service shall in respect of each year of assessment, on or before 28 February in the year following the year of assessment, make a return (including where it is the case, a nil return) to the Revenue Commissioners in electronic format approved by them, which in respect of each year of assessment—

(i) specifies the total amount of gains (in this section referred to as the "*total gains*") arising in respect of the group policy, and

(ii) specifies in respect of each policyholder of a separate policy—

(I) where available, the name and address of the policyholder,

(II) the amount of the total gains to which the person has beneficial entitlement, and

(III) such other information as the Revenue Commissioners may require.][2]][3]

Amendments

[1] Substituted by FA01 s70(1)(a). Applies as on and from 1 January 2001.

[2] Inserted by FA03 s57(b).

[3] Inserted by FA00 s53.

Revenue Briefings

Tax Briefing

Tax Briefing September 2000 – Issue 41 pg 19 – Life Assurance Companies – New Taxation Regime

Cross References

To Section 730B

Section 739BA Personal portfolio investment undertaking.

Section 904C Power of inspection (returns and collection of appropriate tax): assurance companies.

730BA Personal portfolio life policy

[(1) In this section—

"*building society*" has the same meaning as in *section 256*;

"*foreign life policy*" has the same meaning as in section 730H;

"*internal linked fund*", in relation to an assurance company, means a fund maintained by the assurance company to which fund the assurance company appropriates certain linked assets and which fund may be subdivided into subdivisions the value of each of which is determined by the assurance company by reference to the value of such linked assets;

"*investment undertaking*" has the same meaning as in section 739B;

"*land*" includes an interest in land and also includes shares deriving their value or the greater part of their value directly or indirectly from land other than shares quoted on a recognised stock exchange;

"*linked asset*", in relation to an assurance company, means an asset of the assurance company which is identified in the records of the assurance company as an asset by reference to the value of which asset the benefits provided for under a life policy are to be determined;

"*policyholder*" has the same meaning as it has for the purposes of section 730E;

"*prices*" index' means—

(a) the all items consumer price index compiled by the Central Statistics Office,

(b) any general index of prices corresponding to such consumer price index and duly published by or on behalf of any state other than the State, or

(c) any published index of prices of shares listed on a recognised stock exchange;

"*public*" means individuals generally, companies generally, or a combination of these, as the case may be;

"*units*" has the same meaning as in section 739B.

(2) In this Chapter and in Chapter 6 of this Part "*personal portfolio life policy*" means, subject to *subsection (4)*, a life policy or a foreign life policy, as the case may be, under whose terms—

(a) (i) some or all of the benefits conferred by the policy are or were determined by reference to the value of, or the income from, property of any description (whether or not specified in the policy), or

(ii) some or all of the benefits conferred by the policy are or were determined by reference to fluctuations in, or fluctuations in an index of, the value of property of any description (whether or not specified in the policy),

and

(b) some or all of the property or the index may be or was selected by or the selection of some or all of the property or index may be or was influenced by—

(i) the policyholder,

(ii) a person acting on behalf of the policyholder,

(iii) a person connected (within the meaning of *section 10*) with the policyholder,

(iv) a person connected (within that meaning) with a person acting on behalf of the policyholder,

(v) the policyholder and a person connected (within that meaning) with the policyholder, or

(vi) a person acting on behalf of both the policyholder and a person connected (within that meaning) with the policyholder.

(3) For the purposes of *paragraph (b)* of *subsection (2)* and without prejudice to the application of that provision, the terms of a life policy or a foreign life policy shall be treated as permitting the selection referred to in that paragraph where—

(a) the terms of the policy or any other agreement between any person referred to in that paragraph and the assurance company concerned—

(i) allow the exercise of an option by any person referred to in that paragraph to make the selection referred to in that paragraph,

(ii) give the assurance company discretion to offer any person referred to in that paragraph the right to make the selection referred to in that paragraph, or

(iii) allow any of the persons referred to in that paragraph the right to request, subject to the agreement of the assurance company, a change in the terms of the policy such that the selection referred to in that paragraph may be made by any of those persons,

or

(b) the policyholder is unable under the terms of the policy to select any of the property so as to determine the benefits under the policy, but any of the persons referred to in that paragraph has or had the option of requiring the assurance company to appoint an investment advisor (no matter how such a person is described) in relation to the selection of the property which is to determine the benefits under the policy.

(4) A life policy or a foreign life policy is not a personal portfolio life policy if—

(a) (i) the only property which may be or has been selected is—

(I) property which the assurance company concerned has appropriated to an internal linked fund,

(II) property consisting of any of the following—

(A) units in an investment undertaking, or

(B) cash, including cash deposited in a bank account or similar account (including cash deposited in a share account with a building society) except where the acquisition of the cash was made wholly or partly for the purpose of realising a gain from the disposal of the cash, or

(III) property consisting of a combination of the property specified in clauses (I) and (II),

and the property satisfies the condition specified in *subsection (5)*, or

(ii) the only index which may be or has been selected is of a description specified in *subsection (6)*,

and

(b) as respects a life policy or a foreign life policy commenced on or after 5 December 2001 (other than a policy in respect of which the only property which may be selected is property described in *paragraph (a)(i)(II)(B)* or a policy in respect of which marketing or other promotional literature was published before that date) the terms under which the policy is offered meet the requirements of *subsection (7)*.

(5) The condition specified in this subsection is that at the time when the property is or was available to be selected the opportunity to select—

(a) in the case of land, that property, and

(b) in any other case, property of the same description as the first-mentioned property,

is or was available to the public on terms which provide or provided that the opportunity to select the property is or was available to any person falling within the terms of the opportunity and that opportunity is or was clearly identified to the public, in marketing or other promotional literature published at that time by the assurance company concerned, as available generally to any person falling within the terms of the opportunity.

(6) The description of index specified by this subsection is an index consisting of a prices' index or a combination of prices' indices where at the time the index is or was available to be selected the opportunity to select the same index is or was available to the public on terms which provide or provided that the opportunity to select the index is or was available to any person falling within the terms of the opportunity and that opportunity is or was clearly identified to the public, in marketing or other promotional literature published at that time by the assurance company concerned, as available generally to any person falling within the terms of the opportunity.

(7) The requirements of this subsection are that—

(a) the assurance company concerned does not subject any person to any treatment in connection with the opportunity which is different or more burdensome than any treatment to which any other person is or may be subject, and

(b) where the terms of the opportunity referred to in *subsection (5)* include terms—

(i) which set out the capital requirement of the opportunity and this requirement is identified to the public in the marketing or other promotional material published by the assurance company at the time the property is available to be selected, and

(ii) indicating that 50 per cent or more by value of the property referred to in that subsection is or is to be land,

the amount any one person may invest in the policy shall not represent more than 1 per cent of the capital requirement (exclusive of any borrowings) of the opportunity as so identified.][1]

Amendments

[1] Inserted by FA02 s40(1)(a). shall apply as respects— (i) the happening of a chargeable event in relation to a life policy (within the meaning of Chapter 5 of Part 26), or (ii) the receipt by a person of a payment in respect of a foreign life policy (within the meaning of Chapter 6 of that Part) or the disposal in whole or in part of a foreign life policy (within that meaning), on or after 26 September 2001.

Cross References

From Section 730BA

Section 10 Connected persons.

Section 256 Interpretation (Chapter 4).

To Section 730BA

Section 739BA Personal portfolio investment undertaking.

730C Chargeable event

[(1) Subject to the provisions of this section, in this Chapter—

(a) "*chargeable event*", in relation to a life policy, means—

(i) the maturity of the life policy (including where payments are made on death or disability, which payments result in the termination of the life policy),

(ii) the surrender in whole or in part of the rights conferred by the life policy (including where payments are made on death or disability, which payments do not result in the termination of the life policy),

(iii) the assignment in whole or in part, of those rights,

[(iv) the ending of a relevant period, where such ending is not otherwise a chargeable event within the meaning of this section, and for the purposes of this subparagraph "*relevant period*", in relation to a life policy, means a period of 8 years beginning with the inception of the policy and each subsequent period of 8 years beginning immediately after the preceding relevant period,][1]

and

(b) in the case of a life policy issued by an assurance company which could have made an election under *section 730A(2)*, but did not so do, a chargeable event shall be deemed to happen on 31 December 2000, where the life policy was commenced before that date.

(2) No account shall be taken for the purposes of *subsection (1)* of an assignment in whole or in part effected—

(a) by way of security for a debt, or the discharge of a debt secured by the rights concerned, where the debt is a debt due to a financial institution […][2],

(b) [between a husband and wife or between civil partners][3],

[(c) (i) between the spouses or former spouses concerned (as the case may be), by virtue of or in consequence of an order made under Part III of the Family Law (Divorce) Act 1996, on or following the granting of a decree of divorce, or

(ii) between the civil partners or former civil partners concerned (as the case may be), by virtue of or in consequence of an order made under Part 12 of the Civil Partnership and Certain Rights and Obligations of Cohabitants Act 2010, on or following the granting of a decree of dissolution,][4]

(d) between the spouses concerned, by virtue or in consequence of an order made under Part II of the Family Law Act, 1995, on or following the granting of a decree of judicial separation within the meaning of that Act, or

[(e) (i) between the spouses or former spouses concerned (as the case may be), by virtue of an order or other determination of like effect, which is analogous to an order referred to in *paragraph (c)(i)* or *(d)*, of a court under the law of a territory other than the State made under or in consequence of the dissolution of a marriage or the legal separation of the spouses, being a dissolution or legal separation that is entitled to be recognised as valid in the State, or

(ii) between the civil partners or former civil partners concerned (as the case may be), by virtue of an order or other determination of like effect, which is analogous to an order referred to in *paragraph (c)(ii)*, of a court under the law of a territory other than the State made under or in consequence of the dissolution of a civil partnership, being a dissolution that is entitled to be recognised as valid in the State.][5]

(3) (a) Where at any time a life policy, or an interest therein, gives rise to benefits in respect of death or disability, the amount or value of such benefits which shall be taken into account for the purposes of determining the amount of a gain under *section 730D* shall be the excess of the value of the policy or, as the case may be, the interest therein, immediately before that time, over the value of the policy or, as the case may be, the interest therein, immediately after that time.

(b) For the purposes of *paragraph (a)*, the value of a policy or of an interest therein at a time means—

(i) in the case of a policy which has a surrender value, the surrender value of the policy or, as the case may be, of the interest therein, at that time, and

(ii) in the case of a policy which does not have a surrender value, the market value of the rights or other benefits conferred by the policy or, as the case may be, the interest therein, at that time.

(c) In determining the amount or value of benefits payable under a life policy for the purposes of *paragraph (a)* or *(b)*, no account shall be taken of any amount of appropriate tax which may be required by this Chapter to be deducted from such benefits.][6]

Amendments

[1] Substituted by FA07 s43(1)(a). Applies and has effect as respects any chargeable event occurring on or after the passing of this Act. FA07 2 April 2007

[2] Deleted by FA03 s57(c).

[3] Substituted by F(No.3)A11 sched1(176).

[4] Substituted by F(No.3)A11 sched1(177).

[5] Substituted by F(No.3)A11 sched1(178).

[6] Substituted by FA01 s70(1)(b). Applies as on and from 15 February 2001.

Revenue Briefings

Tax Briefing

Tax Briefing September 2000 – Issue 41 pg 19 – Life Assurance Companies – New Taxation Regime

Cross References

From Section 730C

Section 730A Profits of life business: new basis.

Section 730D Gain arising on a chargeable event.

To Section 730C

Section 730D Gain arising on a chargeable event.

Section 730F Deduction of tax on the happening of a chargeable event.

Section 904C Power of inspection (returns and collection of appropriate tax): assurance companies.

730D Gain arising on a chargeable event

[(1) On the happening of a chargeable event in relation to a life policy, there shall, [subject to *subsections (1A)* and *(2)*][1], be treated as arising—

(a) if the chargeable event is the maturity of the life policy or the surrender in whole of the rights thereby conferred, a gain in the amount determined under *subsection (3)(a)*,

(b) if the chargeable event is an assignment of the whole of the rights conferred by the life policy, a gain in the amount determined under *subsection (3)(b)*,

(c) if the chargeable event is the surrender of part of the rights conferred by the life policy, a gain in the amount determined under *subsection (3)(c)*,

(d) if the chargeable event is the assignment of part of the rights conferred by the life policy, a gain in the amount determined under *subsection (3)(d)* […][2]

[(da) if the chargeable event is the ending of a relevant period in accordance with section 730C(1)(*a*)(iv), a gain in the amount determined under *subsection (3)(da)*, and][3]

(e) if the chargeable event is deemed to happen on 31 December 2000 under section 730C(1)(*b*), a gain in the amount determined under *subsection (3)(e)*.

[(1A) (a) Where—

(i) a chargeable event occurs in relation to a life policy, and

(ii) a chargeable event within the meaning of *section 730C(1)(a)(iv)* occurred previously in relation to that policy,

then the gain arising on the chargeable event referred to in *subparagraph (i)* shall be determined as if *section 730C(1)(a)(iv)* had not been enacted.

(b) Where *paragraph (a)* applies and the chargeable event referred to in subparagraph (i) of that paragraph is not the surrender or assignment of part of the rights conferred by the life policy, any first tax (within the meaning of *section 730F(1A)*) shall, for the purposes of *subsection (3)*, be added to the value of the rights or other benefits conferred by that policy immediately before the chargeable event.

(c) Where *paragraph (a)* applies and the chargeable event referred to in *subparagraph (i)* of that paragraph is the surrender or assignment of part of the rights conferred by the life policy, any first tax (within the meaning of *section 730F(1A)*) shall, for the purposes of *subsection (3)*, be deducted from the amount of premiums taken into account in determining the gain on the happening of the chargeable event.][4]

[(2) A gain shall not be treated as arising on the happening of a chargeable event in relation to a life policy where—

(a) immediately before the chargeable event, the assurance company which commenced the life policy—

(i) is in possession of a declaration, in relation to the life policy, of a kind referred in *section 730E(2)*, and

(ii) is not in possession of any information which would reasonably suggest that—

(I) the information contained in that declaration is not, or is no longer, materially correct,

(II) the policyholder (within the meaning of *section 730E*) failed to comply with the undertaking referred to in *section 730E(2)(f)*, or

(III) immediately before the chargeable event the policyholder (within the said meaning) is resident or ordinarily resident in the State,

[(b) immediately before the chargeable event, the policyholder is—

(i) a company carrying on life business,

(ii) an investment undertaking (within the meaning of *section 739B*),

(iii) (I) a person who is entitled to exemption from income tax under Schedule D by virtue of *section 207(1)(b)*, or

(II) a person who is entitled to exemption from corporation tax by virtue of *section 207(1)(b)* as it applies for the purposes of corporation tax under *section 76(6)*,

(iv) a PRSA provider (which has the same meaning as that assigned to it in Chapter 2A (inserted by the Pensions (Amendment) Act 2002) of *Part 30*),

(v) a credit union, […][5]

(vi) a person entrusted to pay all premiums payable, in respect of the life policy, out of money under the control or subject to the order of [any Court,][6]

[(vii) the National Asset Management Agency,][7]

[(viii) a pension scheme being an exempt approved scheme within the meaning of *section 774* or a trust scheme to which *section 784* or *785* applies, or

(ix) an approved retirement fund within the meaning of *section 784A* or an approved minimum retirement fund within the meaning of *section 784C*,][8]

and the assurance company which commenced the life policy is in possession of a declaration, in relation to the life policy, of a kind referred to in [*section 730E(3)*,][9]][10]

(c) where the life policy is an asset held in a special savings incentive account within the meaning of *section 848B* (inserted by the *Finance Act, 2001*) and the assurance company which commenced the life policy is in possession of a declaration of a kind referred to in [*section 730E(3A)*,][11]][12]

[(ca) where the life policy is an asset held by the National Treasury Management Agency or the State acting through the National Treasury Management Agency, and the National Treasury Management Agency has made a declaration to that effect to the assurance company, or

(cb) where the life policy is an asset held by a Fund investment vehicle (within the meaning of *section 37* of the *National Treasury Management Agency (Amendment) Act 2014*) of which the Minister for Finance is the sole beneficial owner, and the National Treasury Management Agency has made a declaration to that effect to the assurance company.][13]

[…][14]

[…][15]

[(2A) (a) In this subsection—

"*EEA Agreement*" means the Agreement on the European Economic Area signed at Oporto on 2 May 1992, as adjusted by the Protocol signed at Brussels on 17 March 1993;

"*EEA state*" means a State, other than the State, which is a Contracting Party to the EEA Agreement;

"*offshore state*" means a State, other than the State, which is—

(a) a Member State of the European Communities, or

(b) a State which is an EEA state.

(b) A gain shall not be treated as arising on the happening of a chargeable event in relation to a life policy where—

[(i) (I) (A) the assurance company which commenced the life policy has established a branch in an off-shore state, and

(B) the commitment represented by that life policy is covered by that branch,

or

(II) (A) the assurance company which commenced the life policy underwrites the business from the State on a freedom of services basis under Regulation 50 of the European Communities (Life Assurance) Framework Regulations 1994 (S.I. No. 360 of 1994) or other equivalent arrangement in an EEA state, and

(B) the policyholder resides in an offshore state,

and][16]

[...][17]

(iii) the assurance company has received written approval from the Revenue Commissioners, to the effect that the provisions of *subsection (2)(a)* need not apply to the life policy, and that approval has not been withdrawn.

(c) The Revenue Commissioners may give the approval referred to in *paragraph (b)(iii)* subject to such conditions as they consider necessary.

(d) The Revenue Commissioners may nominate in writing an inspector or other officer to perform any acts and discharge any functions authorised by this subsection to be performed or discharged by the Revenue Commissioners.][18]

(3) The amount referred to—

(a) in *subsection (1)(a)* is the amount determined by the formula—

$$B - P,$$

(b) in *subsection (1)(b)* is the amount determined by the formula—

$$V - P,$$

(c) in *subsection (1)(c)* is the amount determined by the formula—

$$B \quad - \quad \frac{(P \times B)}{V},$$

(d) in *subsection (1)(d)* is the amount determined by the formula—

$$A \quad - \quad \frac{(P \times A)}{V},$$

[...][19]

[(da) in *subsection (1)(da)* is the amount determined by the formula—

$$V - P$$

and][20]

(e) in *subsection (1)(e)* is the amount determined by the formula—

$$V - P,$$

where—

B is the amount or value of the sum payable and other benefits arising by reason of the chargeable event,

P is subject to *subsection (4)*, an amount of premiums (in this section referred to as "*allowable premiums*") being the total of all premiums paid in respect of the life policy immediately before the chargeable event, to the extent that they have not been taken into account in determining a gain on the previous happening [of a chargeable event (not being a chargeable event within the meaning of *section 730C(1)(a)(iv)*),][21]

V is the value of the rights and other benefits conferred by the life policy immediately before the chargeable event, and

A is the value of the part of the rights and other benefits conferred by the life policy, which has been assigned,

without having regard to any amount of appropriate tax (within the meaning of section 730F) in connection with the chargeable event.

(4)

[(a) For the purposes of *subsection (3)*, the amount of premiums taken into account in determining a gain on the happening of a chargeable event, is where the gain is, or would but for *subsection (2)* be determined—

(i) under *paragraph (c)* of *subsection (3)*, an amount equal to the lesser of B and—

$$\frac{(P \times B)}{V},$$

and

(ii) under *paragraph (d)* of *subsection (3)*, an amount equal to the lesser of A and—

$$\frac{(P \times A)}{V}$$]22

(b) Where a chargeable event in relation to a life policy is deemed to happen on 31 December 2000 then, for the purposes of determining a gain arising on the happening of a subsequent chargeable event, the allowable premiums immediately after 31 December 2000 shall be deemed to be the greater of—

(i) an amount equal to the value of the policy immediately after 31 December 2000, and

(ii) the allowable premiums immediately before 31 December 2000.

[...]23

(c) Where a chargeable event in relation to a life policy is an assignment of the whole of the rights conferred by the life policy then, for the purposes of determining a gain arising on the happening of a subsequent chargeable event, the allowable premiums immediately after the time of assignment shall be deemed to be the greater of—

(i) an amount equal to the value of the policy immediately after the time of the assignment, and

(ii) the allowable premiums immediately before the assignment.

(d) Where a chargeable event in relation to a life policy is the assignment of part of the rights conferred by the life policy then the policy shall, for the purposes of determining a gain arising on the happening of any subsequent chargeable event, be treated as if it were comprised of 2 policies, that is—

(i) one policy conferring the part of the rights assigned, the allowable premiums in respect of which immediately after the assignment are an amount equal to the value of the policy immediately after the assignment, and

(ii) the other policy conferring the rights which were not assigned, the allowable premiums in respect of which immediately after the assignment are the amount of the allowable premiums immediately before the assignment reduced by the amount of premiums taken into account in determining a gain on the assignment.

[(5) (a) Where at any time—

(i) a chargeable event, being a chargeable event (in this subsection referred to as a "relevant event") within the meaning of section

730C(1)(*a*)(iv), occurs in relation to a life policy which commenced before [1 May 2006][24],

(ii) immediately before that time the assurance company that commenced the life policy does not have in its possession a declaration in relation to the policy of the kind referred to in *subsection (2)*, and

(iii) the permanent address of the policy-holder, as stated in the policy, is not in the State and the assurance company does not have reasonable grounds to believe that the policyholder is resident in the State,

then the assurance company may elect to be treated in relation to that chargeable event for the purposes of *subsection (2)* as if, immediately before that time, the assurance company was in possession of a declaration in relation to the policy of the kind referred to in that subsection.

(b) Where at any time—

(i) a relevant event occurred in relation to a life policy and a chargeable event, not being a relevant event, subsequently occurs in relation to the policy,

(ii) this subsection applied to the relevant event in accordance with *paragraph (a)*, and

(iii) immediately before that time the assurance company that commenced the life policy does not have in its possession a declaration in relation to the policy of the kind referred to in *subsection (2)*,

then *paragraph (a)* shall be deemed not to have applied to the relevant event and any appropriate tax payable by virtue of a gain arising under this section shall be due and payable as if *paragraph (a)* had not been enacted.][25]][26]

Amendments

[1] Substituted by FA06 s48(1)(b)(i). Applies and has effect as respects any chargeable event occurring on or after 31 March 2006

[2] Deleted by FA05 s42(1)(b)(i)(I). Per FA06 s48(2) applies and has effect as respects any chargeable event (within the meaning of section 730C(1)(a)(iv)) occurring from the time immediately before 31 March 2006.

[3] Inserted by FA05 s42(1)(b)(i)(II). Per FA06 s48(2) applies and has effect as respects any chargeable event (within the meaning of section 730C(1)(a)(iv)) occurring from the time immediately before 31 March 2006.

[4] Substituted by FA07 s43(1)(b). Applies and has effect as respects any chargeable event occurring on or after 2 April 2007

[5] Deleted by the National Asset Management Agency Act 2009 Sched 3 part 10.

[6] Substituted by FA12 s29(a). Deemed to have come into force and takes effect on and from 1 January 2012.

[7] Inserted by the National Asset Management Agency Act 2009 Sched 3 part 10.

[8] Inserted by FA12 s29(b). Deemed to have come into force and takes effect on and from 1 January 2012.

[9] Inserted by the the Financial Measures (Miscellaneous Provisions) Act 2009 Sched2(6)(2)

[10] Substituted by FA03 s57(d)(i).

[11] Inserted by the the Financial Measures (Miscellaneous Provisions) Act 2009 Sched2(6)(3)

[12] Substituted by FA01 s70(1)(c)(i). Applies as on and from 1 January 2001.

[13] Inserted by NTMA(A)A14 part4(9)(a).

[14] Deleted by NTMA(A)A14 part4(9)(b).

[15] Deleted by NTMA(A)A14 part4(9)(c).

[16] Substituted by FA08 s38(1)(a). Applies on and from 13 March 2008.

[17] Deleted by FA08 s38(1)(b). Applies on and from 13 March 2008.

[18] Inserted by FA02 s48(1)(b).

[19] Deleted by FA05 s42(1)(b)(ii)(I). Per FA06 s48(2) applies and has effect as respects any chargeable event (within the meaning of section 730C(1)(a)(iv)) occurring from the time immediately before 31 March 2006.

[20] Inserted by FA05 s42(1)(b)(ii)(II). Per FA06 s48(2) applies and has effect as respects any chargeable event (within the meaning of section 730C(1)(a)(iv)) occurring from the time immediately before 31 March 2006.

[21] Substituted by FA07 s43(1)(c). Applies and has effect as respects any chargeable event occurring on or after 2 April 2007

[22] Substituted by FA01 s70(1)(c)(ii). Applies as on and from 1 January 2001.

[23] Deleted by FA06 s48(1)(b)(iii). Applies and has effect as respects any chargeable event occurring on or after 31 March 2006

[24] Substituted by FA06 s48(1)(b)(iv). Applies and has effect as respects any chargeable event occurring on or after 31 March 2006

[25] Inserted by FA05 s42(1)(b)(iv). Per FA06 s48(2) applies and has effect as respects any chargeable event (within the meaning of section 730C(1)(a)(iv)) occurring from the time immediately before 31 March 2006.

[26] Inserted by FA00 s53.

Cross References

From Section 730D

Section 76 Computation of income: application of income tax principles.
Section 207 Rents of properties belonging to hospitals and other charities.
Section 730C Chargeable event.
Section 730E Declarations.
Section 730F Deduction of tax on the happening of a chargeable event.
Section 770 Interpretation and supplemental (Chapter 1).
Section 848B Interpretation.

To Section 730D

Section 730C Chargeable event.
Section 730E Declarations.
Section 730F Deduction of tax on the happening of a chargeable event.

730E Declarations

[(1) In this section and in *section 730F*, "*policyholder*", in relation to a life policy, at any time means—

(a) where the rights conferred by the life policy are vested at that time in a person as beneficial owner, such person,

(b) where the rights conferred by the life policy are held at that time on trusts created by a person, such person, and

(c) where the rights conferred by the life policy are held at that time as security for a debt owed by a person, such person.

(2) The declaration referred to in [*section 730D(2)(a)*][1] in relation to a life policy is, subject to *subsection (4)*, a declaration in writing to the assurance company which—

[(a) is made by the policyholder[at or about the time of the inception of the life policy][2],][3]

(b) is signed by the policyholder,

(c) is made in such form as may be prescribed or authorised by the Revenue Commissioners,

[(d) declares that the policyholder is not resident and not ordinarily resident in the State at the time of making the declaration,][4]

(e) contains—

(i) the name of the policyholder,

(ii) the address of the principal place of residence of the policyholder,

(f) contains an undertaking by the policyholder that if the policyholder becomes resident in the State, the policyholder will notify the assurance company accordingly, and

(g) contains such other information as the Revenue Commissioners may reasonably require for the purposes of this Chapter.

[(3) The declaration referred to in *section 730D(2)(b)* in relation to a life policy is, subject to *subsection (4)*, a declaration in writing to the assurance company which—

(a) is made by the policyholder,

(b) is signed by the policyholder,

(c) is made in such form as may be prescribed or authorised by the Revenue Commissioners,

(d) contains the name and address of the policyholder,

[(e) declares that the policyholder, at the time the declaration is made, is—

(i) a company carrying on life business,

(ii) an investment undertaking (which has the same meaning as that assigned to it in *section 739B*),

(iii) (I) a person who is entitled to exemption from income tax under Schedule D by virtue of *section 207(1)(b)*, or

(II) a person who is entitled to exemption from corporation tax by virtue of *section 207(1)(b)* as it applies for the purposes of corporation tax under *section 76(6)*,

(iv) a PRSA provider (which has the same meaning as that assigned to it in Chapter 2A (inserted by the Pensions (Amendment) Act 2002) of *Part 30*),

(v) a credit union, […][5]

(vi) a person entrusted to pay all premiums payable, in respect of the life policy, out of money under the control or subject to the order of [any Court,][6]

[(vii) the National Asset Management Agency,][7]

[(viii) a pension scheme being an exempt approved scheme within the meaning of *section 774* or a trust scheme to which *section 784* or *785* applies, or

(ix) an approved retirement fund within the meaning of *section 784A* or an approved minimum retirement fund within the meaning of *section 784C*,][8]

(f) contains an undertaking that should the policyholder cease to be a person referred to in [*paragraph (e)*][9], the assurance company will be advised accordingly, and][10]

(g) contains such other information as the Revenue Commissioners may reasonably require for the purposes of this Chapter.

(3A) The declaration referred to in *section 730D(2)(c)* in relation to a life policy is a declaration in writing to the assurance company which—

(a) is made by a qualifying savings manager (in this paragraph referred to as the "*declarer*") within the meaning of *section 848B* (inserted by the *Finance Act, 2001*), in respect of the life policy which is an asset held in a special savings incentive account,

(b) is signed by the declarer,

(c) is made in such form as may be prescribed or authorised by the Revenue Commissioners,

(d) declares that, at the time the declaration is made, the life policy in respect of which the declaration is made—

(i) is an asset held in a special savings investment account, and

(ii) is managed by the declarer for the individual who is beneficially entitled to the life policy,

(e) contains the name and the address, and the PPS Number (within the meaning of [section 262 of the Social Welfare Consolidation Act 2005][11]), of the individual referred to in *paragraph (d)*,

(f) contains an undertaking by the declarer that if the life policy ceases to be an asset held in the special savings incentive account, the declarer will notify the assurance company accordingly, and

(g) contains such other information as the Revenue Commissioners may reasonably require for the purposes of this Chapter.][12]

(4) Where, immediately before the happening of a chargeable event, the rights conferred by a life policy were vested beneficially in 2 or more persons, or were held on trusts created, or as security for a debt owed, by 2 or more persons, this section and section 730D shall have effect in relation to each of those persons as if he or she had been the sole owner, settlor or, as the case may be, debtor, but with references to the amount of the gain construed as references to the part of it proportionate to his or her share in the rights at the time of the event, or, as the case may require, when the trusts were created.

[(5) An insurance company shall keep and retain declarations referred to in this section for a period of 6 years from the time the life policy in respect of which the declaration was made ceases.][13][14]

Amendments

[1] Substituted by FA01 s70(1)(d)(i)(I). Applies as on and from 1 January 2001.

[2] Inserted by FA05 s42(1)(c). Per FA06 s48(2) applies as respects any policy taken out on or after 1 May 2006.

[3] Substituted by FA01 s70(1)(d)(i)(II). Applies as on and from 1 January 2001.

[4] Substituted by FA01 s70(1)(d)(i)(III). Applies as on and from 1 January 2001.

[5] Deleted by the National Asset Management Agency Act 2009 Sched 3 part 10.

[6] Substituted by FA12 s29(a). Deemed to have come into force and takes effect on and from 1 January 2012.

[7] Inserted by the National Asset Management Agency Act 2009 Sched 3 part 10.

[8] Inserted by FA12 s29(d). Deemed to have come into force and takes effect on and from 1 January 2012.

[9] Substituted by the National Asset Management Agency Act 2009 Sched 3 part 10.

[10] Substituted by FA03 s57(e)(i).

[11] Substituted by FA07 sched4(1)(u). Shall have effect as on and from 2 April 2007

[12] Substituted by FA01 s70(1)(d)(ii). Applies as on and from 1 January 2001.

[13] Inserted by FA03 s57(e)(ii).

[14] Inserted by FA00 s53.

Cross References

From Section 730E

Section 76 Computation of income: application of income tax principles.
Section 207 Rents of properties belonging to hospitals and other charities.
Section 730D Gain arising on a chargeable event.
Section 730F Deduction of tax on the happening of a chargeable event.
Section 770 Interpretation and supplemental (Chapter 1).
Section 848B Interpretation.

To Section 730E

Section 730D Gain arising on a chargeable event.
Section 904C Power of inspection (returns and collection of appropriate tax): assurance companies.

730F Deduction of tax on the happening of a chargeable event

[(1) [Subject to *subsection (1B)*, in the section][1], and in *section 730G*, "*appropriate tax*", in connection with a chargeable event in relation to a life policy, means a sum representing income tax on the amount of the gain treated in accordance with *section 730D* as thereby arising—

[(a) subject to *paragraph (b)*, where the chargeable event falls on or after 1 January 2001, at the rate of—

(i) 25 per cent where the policyholder is a company, and

(ii) [41 per cent][2] in the case of any other policyholder,][3]

[(b) where, in the case of a personal portfolio life policy, the chargeable event falls on or after 26 September 2001, [at the rate of 60 per cent][4], and

(c) where the chargeable event falls on or before 31 December 2000, at a rate of 40 per cent.][5]

[(1A) (a) In this subsection—

"*first tax*", in relation to a life policy, means the appropriate tax that was accounted for and paid in accordance with *section 730G* in respect of a chargeable event [within the meaning of *section 730C(1)(a)(iv)* in relation to the life policy and which has not been repaid;][6]

["*new gain*", in relation to a life policy, means a gain referred to in *section 730D(1A)(a)* determined in accordance with *section 730D* in relation to the life policy;][7]

"*second tax*" means appropriate tax calculated in accordance with *subsection (1)* in respect of that new gain.

(b) (i) Where at any time [*section 730D(1A)(a)*][8] applies in respect of a life policy commenced by an assurance company, a proportion (in this subsection referred to as the "*relevant proportion*") of first tax shall be set off against any amount of second tax.

(ii) Where such relevant proportion exceeds such second tax, an amount equal to the amount of the excess shall, [...][9]—

(I) be paid by the assurance company to the policy holder in relation to the life policy,

(II) be included in a return under *section 730G(2)*, and

(III) be treated as an amount which may be set off against appropriate tax payable by the assurance company in respect of any chargeable event in the period for which such a return is to be made, or any subsequent period.

[...][10]

(c) For the purposes of this subsection, the "*relevant proportion*" is determined by the formula—

$$A \times \frac{B}{C}$$

where—

A is the first tax,

B is the new gain, and

C is a gain determined in accordance with *section 730D* if the policy matured at that time.][11]

[(1B) Where the policyholder is a company—

(a) the rate specified in *subsection (1)(a)(i)* shall not apply unless the policyholder has made the declaration referred to in *paragraph (b)*, and

(b) the rate specified in *subsection (1)(a)(ii)* shall apply unless immediately before the chargeable event, the life assurance company is in possession of a declaration from the policyholder to the effect that the policyholder is a company and which includes the company's tax reference number (within the meaning of s*ection 891B(1)*).][12]

(2) An assurance company shall account for appropriate tax in accordance with *section 730G*.

(3) (a) An assurance company which is liable to account for appropriate tax in connection with a chargeable event in relation to a life policy shall, at the time of the chargeable event, be entitled—

(i) where the chargeable event is the maturity or surrender whether in whole or in part of the rights conferred by the life policy, to deduct from the proceeds payable to the policyholder on maturity, or as the case may be, surrender in whole or in part, an amount equal to the appropriate tax,

(ii) where the chargeable event—

(I) is the assignment, in whole or in part, of the rights conferred by the life policy, or

[(Ia) is the ending of a relevant period in accordance with *section 730C(1)(a)(iv)*, or][13]

(II) is deemed to happen on 31 December 2000 under *section 730C(1)(b)*,

to appropriate and realise sufficient assets underlying the life policy, to meet the amount of appropriate tax for which the assurance company is liable to account,

(b) the policyholder shall allow such deduction or, as the case may be, such appropriation, and

(c) the assurance company shall be acquitted and discharged of so much as is represented by the deduction or, as the case may be, the appropriation as if the amount of the deduction or the value of the appropriation had been paid to the policyholder.

[(4) Where in the period commencing on 26 September 2001 and ending on 5 December 2001 in connection with a chargeable event in relation to a personal portfolio life policy—

(a) an assurance company which is entitled to deduct an amount equal to the appropriate tax in accordance with *subsection (3)(a)(i)*, or to appropriate and realise sufficient assets to meet the amount of appropriate tax for which the assurance company is liable to account for in accordance with *subsection (3)(a)(ii)*, and

(b) the assurance company fails to deduct an amount equal to the appropriate tax due or fails to appropriate and realise sufficient assets to account for the amount of appropriate tax due,

then, for the purposes of regulating the time and manner in which any appropriate tax, which has not been accounted for or paid, shall be accounted for and paid, *section 730FA* shall apply to the exclusion of *section 730G* (apart from *subsection (7)*) and *section 730GA*.][14]][15]

Amendments

[1] Substituted by FA13 s39(1)(a). Deemed to have come into force and takes effect on and from 1 January 2013.

[2] Substituted by F(No.2)A13 s30(1)(a). Applies and has effect as respects the happening of a chargeable event in relation to a life policy (within the meaning of Chapter 5 of Part 26) on or after 1 January 2014.

[3] Substituted by FA12 s28(1)(a). Has effect as respects the happening of a chargeable event in relation to a life policy (within the meaning of Chapter 5 of Part 26) on or after 1 January 2012.

[4] Substituted by F(No.2)A13 s30(1)(b). Applies and has effect as respects the happening of a chargeable event in relation to a life policy (within the meaning of Chapter 5 of Part 26) on or after 1 January 2014.

[5] Substituted by FA02 s40(1)(b)(i). Shall apply as respects the happening of a chargeable event in relation to a life policy on or after 26 September 2001.

[6] Substituted by FA07 s43(1)(d)(i). Applies and has effect as respects any chargeable event occurring on or after 2 April 2007

[7] Substituted by FA07 s43(1)(d)(ii). Applies and has effect as respects any chargeable event occurring on or after 2 April 2007

[8] Substituted by FA07 s43(1)(d)(iii). Applies and has effect as respects any chargeable event occurring on or after 2 April 2007

[9] Deleted by FA07 s43(1)(d)(iv). Applies and has effect as respects any chargeable event occurring on or after 2 April 2007

[10] Deleted by FA07 s43(1)(d)(v). Applies and has effect as respects any chargeable event occurring on or after 2 April 2007

[11] Inserted by FA06 s48(1)(c). Applies and has effect as respects any chargeable event occurring on or after 31 March 2006

[12] Inserted by FA13 s39(1)(b). Deemed to have come into force and takes effect on and from 1 January 2013.

[13] Inserted by FA05 s42(1)(d). Per FA06 s48(2) applies and has effect as respects any chargeable event (within the meaning of section 730C(1)(a)(iv)) occurring from the time immediately before 31 March 2006.

[14] Inserted by FA02 s40(1)(b)(ii). Shall apply as respects the happening of a chargeable event in relation to a life policy on or after 26 September 2001.

[15] Inserted by FA00 s53.

Cross References

From Section 730F

Section 4 Interpretation of Corporation Tax Acts.
Section 730C Chargeable event.
Section 730D Gain arising on a chargeable event.
Section 730FA Assessment of appropriate tax where tax not deducted under section 730F.
Section 730G Returns and collection of appropriate tax.
Section 730GA Repayment of appropriate tax.

To Section 730F

Section 730D Gain arising on a chargeable event.
Section 730E Declarations.
Section 730GA Repayment of appropriate tax.
Section 904C Power of inspection (returns and collection of appropriate tax): assurance companies.

730FA Assessment of appropriate tax where tax not deducted under section 730F

[(1) Where section 730F(4)(*b*) applies then, notwithstanding any other provision of the Tax Acts or the Capital Gains Tax Acts, this section shall apply for the purposes of regulating the time and manner in which any appropriate tax which remains to be accounted for and paid in connection with a chargeable event, which happened in the period commencing on 26 September 2001 and ending on 5 December 2001, in relation to a personal portfolio life policy shall be assessed, accounted for and paid.

(2) An assurance company shall for each personal portfolio life policy in respect of which it has not—

(a) deducted an amount equal to the amount of appropriate tax, for which the assurance company is liable to account, in accordance with *subsection (3)(a)(i)* of section 730F, or

(b) appropriated and realised sufficient assets to meet the amount of appropriate tax, for which the assurance company is liable to account, in accordance with *subsection (3)(a)(ii)* of section 730F,

make and deliver to the inspector to whom it is customary for the assurance company to make a return under *section 951* a return on or before 31 December 2001 containing in each case—

(i) the name, address and, if appropriate, the registered office, of the policyholder,

(ii) the amount of the gain arising on the happening of the chargeable event in relation to the policy, including details of all amounts referred to in *subsections (3)* and *(4)* of section 730D which are relevant to the determination of the gain arising on the chargeable event in question,

(iii) the amount actually deducted in accordance with section 730F(3)(*a*)(i) or the amount actually realised in accordance with section 730F(3)(*a*)(ii),

(iv) the method of payment of the benefits under the policy,

(v) if payment was made to a person other than the policyholder, details of the name and address of that person, and

(vi) details of the property which is a linked asset in relation to the personal portfolio life policy.

(3) An assurance company which fails to deliver, within the time specified in *subsection (2)*, the return referred to in that subsection or which fails to deliver such a return which is correct may, in addition to any penalty to

which it may be liable, be made liable for the payment of any appropriate tax due in respect of a personal portfolio life policy to which that subsection applies which remains unpaid. An inspector may make an assessment on the assurance company to the best of his or her judgement of the appropriate tax so unpaid.

(4) Where, in connection with a chargeable event in relation to a personal portfolio life policy, an assurance company—

(a) fails to deduct an amount equal to the appropriate tax which should have been deducted in accordance with *subsection (3)(a)(i)* of section 730F, or

(b) fails to appropriate and realise sufficient assets to meet the full amount of appropriate tax for which the assurance company is liable to account for in accordance with *subsection (3)(a)(ii)* of section 730F,

then the policyholder or the person to whom the payment referred to in *subsection (2)* was made shall be liable for the payment of any appropriate tax due in relation to the personal portfolio life policy which remains unpaid. An inspector may make an assessment on the policyholder or the person concerned to the best of his or her judgement of the appropriate tax so unpaid.

(5) Where an inspector makes an assessment under *subsection (3)* or *(4)* it shall not be necessary to set out in the notice of assessment any particulars other than particulars as to the amount of appropriate tax to be paid by the assurance company or the policyholder, as appropriate.

(6) (a) An inspector may at any time amend or further amend an assessment made on a person under *subsection (3)* or *(4)* by making such alterations in or additions to the assessment as he or she considers necessary and the inspector shall give notice to the person of the assessment so amended or so further amended.

(b) After the end of a period of 6 years starting from 31 December 2001, no assessment shall be made under *subsection (3)* or *(4)* or no assessment made under either of those subsections shall be amended or further amended.

(7) For the purposes of making an assessment under *subsection (3)* or *(4)* or for the purposes of amending or further amending such an assessment an inspector may make such enquiries or take such action within his or her powers as he or she considers necessary—

(a) to satisfy himself or herself as to the accuracy or otherwise of the return referred to in *subsection (2)*, or

(b) where no such return is made or an incorrect return is made, for the purposes of ascertaining the information which should have been included in such a return.

(8) Appropriate tax specified in an assessment made under *subsection (3)* or *(4)* or in an amended assessment made under *subsection (6)* shall be due and payable within one month after the issue of the notice of assessment or the amended assessment, as appropriate, subject to any appeal against the assessment.][1]

Amendments

[1] Inserted by FA02 s40(1)(c). Shall apply as respects the happening of a chargeable event in relation to a life policy on or after 26 September 2001.

Cross References

From Section 730FA

Section 951 Obligation to make a return.

To Section 730FA

Section 730F Deduction of tax on the happening of a chargeable event.

Section 904C Power of inspection (returns and collection of appropriate tax): assurance companies.

Schedule 29 Provisions Referred to in Sections 1052, 1053 and 1054

730G Returns and collection of appropriate tax

[(1) Notwithstanding any other provision of the Tax Acts, this section shall apply for the purposes of regulating the time and manner in which appropriate tax in connection with a chargeable event in relation to a life policy shall be accounted for and paid.

(2) An assurance company shall for each financial year make to the Collector-General—

(a) a return of the appropriate tax[, and amounts which may be credited under section 730F(1A),][1] in connection with chargeable events happening on or prior to 30 June, within 30 days of that date, and

(b) a return of appropriate tax[, and amounts which may be credited under section 730F(1A),][2] in connection with chargeable events happening between 1 July and 31 December, within 30 days of that later date, and

where it is the case, the return shall specify that there is no appropriate tax for the period in question.

(3) The appropriate tax in connection with a chargeable event which is required to be included in a return[(reduced by any amount which is to be credited in accordance with *subsection 730F(1A)*)][3] shall be due at the time by which the return is to be made and shall be paid by the assurance company to the Collector-General, and the appropriate tax so due shall be payable by the assurance company without the making of an assessment; but appropriate tax which has become so due may be assessed on the assurance company (whether or not it has been paid when the assessment is made) if that tax or any part of it is not paid on or before the due date.

(4) Where it appears to the inspector that there is an amount of appropriate tax in relation to a chargeable event which ought to have been but has not been included in a return, or where the inspector is dissatisfied with any return, the inspector may make an assessment on the assurance company to the best of his or her judgement, and any amount of appropriate tax in connection with a chargeable event due under an assessment made by virtue of this subsection shall be treated for the purposes of interest on unpaid tax as having been payable at the time when it would have been payable if a correct return had been made.

[(5) Where—

(a) any item has been incorrectly included in a return as appropriate tax, the inspector may make such assessments, adjustments or set-offs as may in his or her judgement be required for securing that the resulting liabilities to tax, including interest on unpaid tax, whether of the assurance company making the return or of any other person, are in so far as possible the same as they would have been if the item had not been included, or

(b) any item has been correctly included in a return, but within one year of the making of the return the assurance company proves to the satisfaction of the Revenue Commissioners that it is just and reasonable that an amount of appropriate tax (included in the return) which has been paid, should be repaid to the assurance company, such amount may be repaid to the assurance company.][4]

(6) (a) Any appropriate tax assessed on an assurance company shall be due within one month after the issue of the notice of assessment (unless that tax is due earlier under *subsection (3)*) subject to any appeal against the assessment, but no appeal shall affect the date when any amount is due under *subsection (3)*.

(b) On determination of the appeal against an assessment under this Chapter, any appropriate tax overpaid shall be repaid.

(7) (a) The provisions of the Income Tax Acts relating to—

(i) assessments to income tax,

(ii) appeals against such assessments (including the rehearing of appeals and the statement of a case for the opinion of the High Court), and

(iii) the collection and recovery of income tax,

shall, in so far as they are applicable, apply to the assessment, collection and recovery of appropriate tax.

[(b) Any amount of appropriate tax shall carry interest from the date when the amount becomes due and payable until payment—

(i) for any day or part of a day before 1 July 2009 during which the amount remains unpaid, at a rate of 0.0322 per cent, and

(ii) for any day or part of a day on or after 1 July 2009 during which the amount remains unpaid, at a rate of 0.0274 per cent.][5]

(c) [*Subsections (3)* to *(5)* of *section1080*][6] shall apply in relation to interest payable under *paragraph (b)* as they apply in relation to interest payable under *section 1080*.

(d) In its application to any appropriate tax charged by any assessment made in accordance with this Chapter, *section 1080* shall apply as if [*subsection (2) (b)*][7] of that section were deleted.

(8) Every return shall be in a form prescribed by the Revenue Commissioners and shall include a declaration to the effect that the return is correct and complete.][8]

Amendments

[1] Inserted by FA06 s48(1)(d)(i)(I). Applies and has effect as respects any chargeable event occurring on or after 31 March 2006

[2] Inserted by FA06 s48(1)(d)(i)(II). Applies and has effect as respects any chargeable event occurring on or after 31 March 2006

[3] Inserted by FA06 s48(1)(d)(ii). Applies and has effect as respects any chargeable event occurring on or after 31 March 2006

[4] Substituted by FA07 sched4(1)(v). Shall have effect as on and from 1 January 2007.

[5] Substituted by FA09 s29(1)(e). Applies as respects any unpaid tax or duty, as the case may be, that has not been paid before 1 July 2009 regardless of whether that tax or duty became due and payable before, on or after that date.

[6, 7] Substituted by FA05 sched5.

[8] Inserted by FA00 s53.

Cross References

From Section 730G

Section 1080 Interest on overdue income tax, corporation tax and capital gains tax.

To Section 730G

Section 730F Deduction of tax on the happening of a chargeable event.
Section 904C Power of inspection (returns and collection of appropriate tax): assurance companies.
Schedule 29 Provisions Referred to in Sections 1052, 1053 and 1054

730GA Repayment of appropriate tax

[For the purposes of a claim to relief, under *section 189*, *189A* or *192*, or a repayment of income tax in consequence thereof, the amount of a payment made to a policyholder by an assurance company shall be treated as a net amount of income from the gross amount of which has been deducted income tax, of an amount equal to the amount of appropriate tax (within the meaning of *section 730F*) deducted from the payment, and such amount of gross income shall be treated as chargeable to tax under Case III of Schedule D.][1]

Amendments

[1] Inserted by FA01 s70(1)(f). Applies as on and from 1 January 2001.

Cross References

From Section 730GA

Section 189 Payments in respect of personal injuries.
Section 189A Special trusts for permanently incapacitated individuals.
Section 192 Payments in respect of thalidomide children.
Section 730F Deduction of tax on the happening of a chargeable event.

To Section 730GA

Section 730F Deduction of tax on the happening of a chargeable event.

730GB Capital Acquisitions Tax Consolidation Act set-off

Where on the death of a person, an assurance company is liable to account for appropriate tax (within the meaning of section 730F(1)) in connection with a gain arising on a chargeable event in relation to a life policy, the amount of such tax, in so far as it does not exceed the amount of appropriate tax to which the assurance company would be liable if that tax was calculated in accordance with section 730F(1)(a), shall be treated as an amount of capital gains tax paid for the purposes of section 104 of the Capital Acquisitions Tax Consolidation Act 2003.][1]

Amendments

[1] Substituted by FA03 s57(f).

CHAPTER 6

Certain Foreign Life Policies — Taxation and Returns

730H Interpretation and application

[(1) In this Chapter—

"*chargeable period*" has the same meaning as in *section 321(2)*;

["*deemed disposal*" means a disposal of the type provided for in section 730K(6);][1]

"*EEA Agreement*" means the Agreement on the European Economic Area signed at Oporto on 2 May 1992, as adjusted by the Protocol signed at Brussels on 17 March 1993;

"*EEA state*" means a State, other than the State, which is a Contracting Party to the EEA Agreement;

"*foreign life policy*" means a policy of assurance on the life of a person commenced—

(a) by a branch or agency, carrying on business in an offshore state, of an assurance company, or

(b) by an assurance company carrying on business in an offshore state, other than by its branch or agency carrying on business in the State;

"*OECD*" means the organisation known as the Organisation for Economic Co-operation and Development;

"*offshore state*" means a State other than the State which is—

(i) a Member State of the European Communities,

(ii) a State which is an EEA state, or

(iii) a State which is a member of the OECD, the government of which have entered into arrangements having the force of law by virtue of [*section 826(1)*][2];

["*relevant event*" means the ending of a relevant [period;][3]

["*relevant period*" in relation to a foreign life policy means a period of 8 years beginning with the inception of the policy and each subsequent period of 8 years beginning immediately after the preceding relevant period;][4][5]

"*relevant payment*" means any payment made to a person in respect of a foreign life policy where such payments are made annually or at more frequent intervals, other than a payment made in consideration of the disposal, in whole or in part, of the foreign life policy;

"*return of income*" has the meaning assigned to it by *section 1084*;

"specified return date for the chargeable period" has the meaning assigned to it by [*section 959A*][6]

"*standard rate per cent*" has the meaning assigned to it by *section 4*.

(2) For the purposes of this Chapter—

(a) there shall be a disposal of an asset if there would be such a disposal for the purposes of the Capital Gains Tax Acts,

(b) an income shall be correctly included in a return made by a person, only where that income is included in a return of income made by the person on or before the specified return date for the chargeable period in which the income arises, and

(c) details of a disposal shall be correctly included in a return made by a person, only where details of the disposal are included in a return of income made by the person or, where the person has died, his or her executor or administrator, on or before the specified return date for the chargeable period in which the disposal is made.][7]

Amendments

[1] Inserted by FA06 s49(1)(a)(i). This section applies as respects any relevant event occurring on or after the passing of this Act in respect of a foreign life policy taken out on or after 1 January 2001.

---

[2] Substituted by FA07 sched2(1)(x). Has effect as on and from 2 April 2007

[3] Substituted by FA07 s42(1)(a). Applies as respects any relevant event occurring on or after the passing of this Act in respect of a foreign life policy taken out on or after 1 January 2001.

[4] Substituted by FA07 s42(1)(b). Applies as respects any relevant event occurring on or after the passing of this Act in respect of a foreign life policy taken out on or after 1 January 2001.

[5] Inserted by FA06 s49(1)(a)(ii). This section applies as respects any relevant event occurring on or after the passing of this Act in respect of a foreign life policy taken out on or after 1 January 2001.
[6] Substituted by FA12 sched4(part 2)(g).

[7] Inserted by FA01 s67. This section shall be deemed to have applied as on and from 1 January 2001.

Cross References

From Section 730H

Section 4 Interpretation of Corporation Tax Acts.
Section 321 Provisions of general application in relation to the making of allowances and charges.
Section 730K Disposal of foreign life policy.
Section 826 Agreements for relief from double taxation.
Section 950 Interpretation (Part 41).
Section 1084 Surcharge for late returns.

730I Returns on acquisition of foreign life policy

[Where in any chargeable period a person acquires a foreign life policy, the person shall, notwithstanding anything to the contrary in [*Part 41A* or *section 1084*][1] be deemed for that chargeable period to be a chargeable person for the purposes of [*Chapter 3* of *Part 41A* and *section 1084*][2], and the return of income to be delivered by the person for that chargeable period shall include the following particulars—

(a) the name and address of the person who commenced the foreign life policy,

(b) a description of the terms of the foreign life policy including premiums payable, and

(c) the name and address of the person through whom the foreign life policy was acquired.][3]

Amendments

[1, 2] Substituted by FA12 sched4(part 2)(g).

[3] Inserted by FA01 s67. This section shall be deemed to have applied as on and from 1 January 2001.

Cross References

From Section 730I

Section 950 Interpretation (Part 41).
Section 951 Obligation to make a return.
Section 1084 Surcharge for late returns.

To Section 730I

Section 896 Returns in relation to certain offshore products.

730J Payment in respect of foreign life policy

[Where on or after 1 January 2001 a person who has a foreign life policy is in receipt of a payment in respect of the foreign life policy, then—

[(a) where the person is not a company—

(i) the rate of income tax to be charged on the income represented by the payment, where the payment is not made in consideration of the disposal, in whole or in part, of the foreign life policy, shall, notwithstanding *section 15*, be—

(I) subject to *subparagraph (ii)*, in the case of a foreign life policy which is a personal portfolio life policy, at the rate of 60 per cent, and

(II) in any other case, at the rate of 41 per cent,

and

(ii) in the case of a foreign life policy which is a personal portfolio life policy and the income represented by the payment is not correctly included in a return made by the person, the income shall, notwithstanding *section 15*, be charged to income tax at the rate of 80 per cent,][1]

(b) where the person is a company, the income represented by the payment shall be charged to tax under Case III of Schedule D.][2]

Amendments

[1] Substituted by FA14 s35(1)(a). Comes into operation on 1 January 2015.

[2] Inserted by FA01 s67. This section shall be deemed to have applied as on and from 1 January 2001.

Cross References

From Section 730J

Section 15 Rate of charge.

To Section 730J

Section 485C Interpretation (Chapter 2A).

730K Disposal of foreign life policy

[(1) Where on or after 1 January 2001 a person disposes, in whole or in part, of a foreign life policy, and the disposal gives rise to a gain computed in accordance with *subsection (2)*, [then, notwithstanding *section 594,* the amount of the gain shall be treated as an amount of income chargeable to tax under Case IV of *Schedule D*, and where the person is not a company the rate of income tax to be charged on that income shall, notwithstanding *section 15*, be—

(a) (i) subject to *paragraph (b)*, in the case of a foreign life policy which is a personal portfolio life policy, at the rate of 60 per cent, and

(ii) in any other case, at the rate of 41 per cent,

and

(b) in the case of a foreign life policy which is a personal portfolio life policy and the details of the disposal are not correctly included in a return made by the person, at the rate of 80 per cent.][1]

(2) The amount of the gain accruing on a disposal referred to in *subsection (1)* is the amount of the relevant gain (within the meaning of *section 594(2)*) which would be computed if the gain accruing on the disposal were computed for the purposes of that section.

[(3) (a) Notwithstanding *sections 538* and *546*, where apart from this subsection the effect of any computation under *subsection (2)* would be to produce a loss, the gain on the disposal referred to in *subsection (1)* shall be treated as nil and accordingly for the purposes of this Chapter no loss shall be treated as accruing on such disposal.][2]

[(b) Where in respect of a foreign life policy—

(i) a gain on a disposal is treated as nil in accordance with *paragraph (a)*,

(ii) that disposal is not a deemed disposal, and

(iii) a person was chargeable to tax in respect of an earlier deemed disposal of the policy,

then the provisions of *section 865* (apart from *subsection (4)*) shall apply and the inspector may make such repayment or set-off as is necessary for securing that the aggregate of tax payable in respect of the policy under this section does not exceed the tax that would have been so payable in respect of the policy if *subsection (6)* had not been enacted.][3]

(4) Where, as a result of a disposal by a person, an amount of income is chargeable to tax under Case IV of Schedule D in accordance with *subsection (1)*, that amount shall not be reduced by a claim made by the person—

(a) where the person is not a company, under *section 381* or *383*, or

(b) where the person is a company, under *section 396* or *399*.

[(5) Where an individual is chargeable to tax in accordance with *subsection (1)* in respect of an amount of income the tax there by payable, in so far as it is paid, shall be treated as an amount of capital gains tax paid for the purposes of *section 104* of the Capital Acquisitions Tax Consolidation Act 2003.][4]

[(6) Where a person has a foreign life policy and a relevant event occurs in respect of that policy, then the person shall be deemed for the purposes of this section to have disposed of the whole of the policy immediately before the time of that relevant event and immediately to have reacquired it at its market value at that time.][5][6]

Amendments

[1] Substituted by FA14 s35(1)(b). Comes into operation on 1 January 2015.

[2] Renumbered by FA06 s49(1)(b)(i)(I). This section applies as respects any relevant event occurring on or after the passing of this Act in respect of a foreign life policy taken out on or after 1 January 2001.

[3] Inserted by FA06 s49(1)(b)(i)(II). This section applies as respects any relevant event occurring on or after the passing of this Act in respect of a foreign life policy taken out on or after 1 January 2001.

[4] Substituted by FA12 sched6(1)(g). Has effect as on and from 31 March 2012.

[5] Inserted by FA06 s49(1)(b)(ii). This section applies as respects any relevant event occurring on or after the passing of this Act in respect of a foreign life policy taken out on or after 1 January 2001.

[6] Inserted by FA01 s67. This section shall be deemed to have applied as on and from 1 January 2001.

Cross References

From Section 730K

Section 104 Taxation of certain rents and other payments.
Section 381 Right to repayment of tax by reference to losses.
Section 383 Relief under Case IV for losses.
Section 396 Relief for trading losses other than terminal losses.
Section 399 Losses in transactions from which income would be chargeable under Case IV or V of Schedule D.

Section 538 Disposals where assets lost or destroyed or become of negligible value.
Section 546 Allowable losses.
Section 594 Foreign life assurance and deferred annuities: taxation and returns.
Section 865 Repayment of tax.

To Section 730K

Section 485C Interpretation (Chapter 2A).
Section 730H Interpretation and application.

PART 27

Unit Trusts and Offshore Funds

CHAPTER 1

Unit Trusts

731 Chargeable gains accruing to unit trusts

[CGTA75 s31; FA77 s34; FA79 s37(1); FA93 s19; FA94 s64]

(1) In this section, "*capital distribution*" means any distribution from a unit trust, including a distribution in the course of terminating the unit trust, in money or money's worth except a distribution which in the hands of the recipient constitutes income for the purposes of income tax.

(2) For the purposes of the Capital Gains Tax Acts and without prejudice to *section 567* and *sections 574* to *578*, chargeable gains accruing to a unit trust in any year of assessment shall be assessed and charged on the trustees of the unit trust.

(3) The trustees of a unit trust shall for the purposes of the Capital Gains Tax Acts be treated as being a single and continuing body of persons (distinct from the persons who may from time to time be the trustees), and that body shall be treated as being resident and ordinarily resident in the State unless the general administration of the unit trust is ordinarily carried on outside the State and the trustees or a majority of them for the time being are not resident or not ordinarily resident in the State.

(4) Where a person receives or becomes entitled to receive in respect of units in a unit trust any capital distribution from the unit trust, such person shall be treated as having in consideration of that capital distribution disposed of an interest in the units.

[(5) (a) (i) Where throughout a year of assessment all the issued units in a unit trust which neither is, nor is deemed to be, an authorised unit trust scheme (within the meaning of the Unit Trusts Act 1990) are assets such that if those units were disposed of by the unit holder any gain accruing would be wholly exempt from capital gains tax (otherwise than by reason of residence or by virtue of *section 739(3)*), then gains accruing to the unit trust in that year shall not be chargeable gains.

(ii) Where the trustees, or any persons duly authorised to act on their behalf, of a unit trust to which *subparagraph (i)* applies are satisfied that, throughout a year of assessment, all the issued units in the unit trust are assets referred to in *subparagraph (i)*, then they shall, in respect of that year of assessment, make a declaration to that effect.

(iii) The trustees, or any persons duly authorised to act on their behalf, of every unit trust to which *subparagraph (i)* applies shall in respect of each year of assessment, on or before 28 February in the year following the year of assessment, make a statement to the Revenue Commissioners in electronic format approved by them, which in respect of that year of assessment—

(I) states whether a declaration as referred to in *subparagraph (ii)* has, or has not, been made, and

(II) specifies in respect of each person who is a unit holder—

(A) the name and address of the person, and

(B) such other information as the Revenue Commissioners may require.

(iv) Where the trustees, or any persons duly authorised to act on their behalf, of a unit trust—

(I) make an incorrect or incomplete statement under *subparagraph (iii)*, or

(II) fail, without reasonable excuse, to make such a statement,

then the trustees of that unit trust shall be liable to a penalty of €3,000. For the purposes of the recovery of a penalty under this subparagraph, *section 1061* shall apply in the same manner as it applies for the purposes of the recovery of a penalty under any of the sections referred to in that section.][1]

(b) For the purposes of any assessment to capital gains tax, *paragraph (a)* shall not apply as respects a unit trust to which *subsection (6)* applies.

[(c) Where, by virtue of *paragraph (a)*, gains accruing to a unit trust in a year of assessment are not chargeable gains, then—

(i) the unit trust shall not be chargeable to income tax for that year of assessment, and

(ii) a deposit (within the meaning of *section 256(1)*), which is an asset of the unit trust, shall not be a relevant deposit (within the meaning of that section) for the purposes of *Chapter 4* of *Part 8*, for that year of assessment.][2]

(6) Gains accruing on the disposal of units in a unit trust shall not be chargeable gains for the purposes of the Capital Gains Tax Acts where—

(a) the trustees of the unit trust have at all times (but not taking into account any time before the 6th day of April, 1974) been resident and ordinarily resident in the State, and

(b) the unit trust is a scheme which is established for the purpose or has the effect, solely or mainly, of providing facilities for the participation by the public as beneficiaries under a trust in profits or income arising from the acquisition, holding, management or disposal of securities or any other property whatever and which is administered by the holder of a licence under the Insurance Act, 1936, and for participation in which, in respect of units first issued after the 14th day of June, 1973, a policy of assurance on human life is required to be effected (but so that the units do not become the property of the owner of the policy either as benefits or otherwise).

(7) (a) Subject to *paragraph (b)*, where there is a disposal in any year of assessment of units in a unit trust—

(i) not being an undertaking for collective investment (within the meaning of *section 738*) which began carrying on business on or after the 25th day of May, 1993,

(ii) all the assets of which were throughout the year of assessment 1993-94 assets, whether mentioned in section 19 of the Capital Gains Tax Act, 1975, or in any other provision of the Capital Gains Tax Acts, to which that section applied, and

(iii) the person disposing of the units acquired the units before the 6th day of April, 1994,

then, the chargeable gain on the disposal shall be computed as if the units had been sold and immediately reacquired by that person on the 5th day of April, 1994, at their market value at that date.

(b) *Paragraph (a)* shall not apply in relation to the disposal of units—

(i) if as a consequence of the application of that paragraph a gain would accrue on that disposal to the person making the disposal and either a smaller gain or a loss would so accrue if that paragraph did not apply, or

(ii) if as a consequence of the application of that paragraph a loss would so accrue and either a smaller loss or a gain would accrue if that paragraph did not apply,

and accordingly in a case to which *subparagraph (i)* or *(ii)* applies, the amount of the gain or loss accruing on the disposal shall be computed without regard to this subsection (other than this paragraph) but, in a case where this paragraph would otherwise substitute a loss for a gain or a gain for a loss, it shall be assumed in relation to the disposal that the units were acquired by the person disposing of them for a consideration such that neither a gain nor a loss accrued to that person on making the disposal.

Amendments

1 Substituted by FA10 s30(1). This section shall apply for the year of assessment 2010 and subsequent years of assessment.

2 Inserted by FA01 s71(1)(b). This section shall be deemed to have applied as respects paragraph (b), for the year of assessment 2000-2001 and subsequent years of assessment.

Cross References

From Section 731

Section 237 Annual payments payable wholly out of taxed income.
Section 256 Interpretation (Chapter 4).
Section 567 Nominees, bare trustees and agents.
Section 574 Trustees of settlement.
Section 578 Death of annuitant.
Section 738 Undertakings for collective investment.
Section 739 Taxation of unit holders in undertakings for collective investment.
Section 1061 Recovery of penalties.

To Section 731

Section 172C Exemption from dividend withholding tax for certain persons.
Section 246 Interest payments by companies and to non-residents.
Section 734 Taxation of collective investment undertakings.
Section 736 Option for non-application of section 735.
Section 738 Undertakings for collective investment.
Section 739B Interpretation and application.
Section 739D Gain arising on a chargeable event.
Section 848H Termination of special savings incentive account.
Section 891B Returns of certain payments made by certain persons.
Section 904D Power of inspection (returns and collection of appropriate tax): investment undertakings.

Schedule 2A Dividend Withholding Tax
Schedule 2B Investment Undertakings: Declarations
Schedule 19 Offshore Funds: Distributing Funds
Schedule 20 Offshore Funds: Computation of Offshore Income Gains
Schedule 31 Consequential Amendments

732 Special arrangements for qualifying unit trusts

[CGTA75 s32; FA77 s35; CGT(A)A78 s16 and Sch1 par9; FA97 s146(2) and Sch9 PtII]

(1) In this section—

"*securities*" includes securities within *section 607* and stocks, shares, bonds and obligations of any government, municipal corporation, company or other body corporate;

"*quoted securities*" means securities which, at any time at which they are to be taken into account for the purposes of this section, or at any time in the period of 6 years immediately before such time, have or have had quoted market values on a stock exchange in the State or elsewhere.

(2) This section shall apply—

(a) to a unit trust (in this section referred to as a "*qualifying unit trust*")—

(i) which is a registered unit trust scheme (within the meaning of section 3 of the Unit Trusts Act, 1972),

(ii) the trustees of which are resident and ordinarily resident in the State,

(iii) the prices of units in which are published regularly by the managers,

(iv) all the units in which are of equal value and carry the same rights, and

(v) which, at all times since it was registered in the register established under the Unit Trusts Act, 1972, but subject to *subsection (7)*, satisfied the conditions specified in *subsection (6)*, and

(b) to disposals of assets which are units in a qualifying unit trust (in this section referred to as "*qualifying units*").

(3) Chargeable gains accruing to a qualifying unit trust in any year of assessment shall be chargeable to capital gains tax at one-half of the rate specified in *section 28(3)*.

(4) Chargeable gains which derive from the disposal of qualifying units and accrue to a person chargeable to capital gains tax shall be chargeable to tax at one-half of the rate at which those gains would be chargeable under the Capital Gains Tax Acts apart from this subsection.

(5) For any accounting period of a company, being an accounting period for which the company is chargeable to corporation tax in respect of chargeable gains—

(a) where the total amount of chargeable gains accruing to the company for the accounting period derives from the disposal of qualifying units, the amount which apart from this section would be included in respect of chargeable gains in the company's total profits for the accounting period under *section 78(1)* shall be reduced by 50 per cent,

(b) where the total amount of chargeable gains accruing to the company for the accounting period includes—

(i) an amount in respect of such chargeable gains on the disposal of qualifying units, and

(ii) an amount in respect of such chargeable gains on the disposal of assets other than qualifying units, the amount which apart from this section would be included in respect of chargeable gains in the company's total profits for the accounting period under *section 78(1)* shall be reduced by such amount as bears to the amount to be so included the same proportion as one-half of the amount referred to in *subparagraph (i)* bears to the total of the amounts referred to in *subparagraphs (i)* and *(ii)*.

(6) The conditions referred to in *subsection (2)(a)(v)* are that—

(a) not less than 80 per cent of the units were held by persons who acquired them pursuant to an offer made to the general public,

(b) the number of unit holders was not less than 50 and no one unit holder was the beneficial owner of more than 5 per cent of the units in issue at any time, and for the purposes of this paragraph a person and any persons with whom such person is connected shall be treated as one unit holder,

(c) the value of quoted securities held by the trustees on behalf of the unit trust was not less than 80 per cent by value of the assets so held by the trustees, and

(d) the securities held by the trustees on behalf of the unit trust in any one company did not exceed 15 per cent by value of the total securities so held by the trustees.

(7) The Revenue Commissioners may treat a unit trust as a qualifying unit trust for the purposes of this section notwithstanding that one or more of the conditions specified in *subsection (6)* was or were not complied with in relation to the unit trust—

(a) for the period ending on the 5th day of April, 1978, in the case where the unit trust became registered in the register established under the Unit Trusts Act, 1972, before the 6th day of April, 1976, and

(b) for the period ending on a date not more than 2 years after the date on which the unit trust became registered in that register, in the case where the unit trust became so registered on or after the 6th day of April, 1976.

Cross References

From Section 732

Section 28 Taxation of capital gains and rate of charge.
Section 78 Computation of companies' chargeable gains.
Section 607 Government and certain other securities.

To Section 732

Section 734 Taxation of collective investment undertakings.
Section 737 Special investment schemes.

733 Reorganisation of units in unit trust scheme

[CGTA75 s51(1) and Sch2 par2A; FA90 s87]

(1) In this section, references to a reorganisation of units in a trust scheme include—

(a) any case where persons are, whether for payment or not, allotted units in the scheme in respect of and in proportion to (or as nearly as may be in proportion to) their holdings of units in the scheme or of any class of units in the scheme, and

(b) any case where there is more than one class of units and the rights attached to units of any class are altered.

(2) (a) Subject to *paragraph (b)*, *section 584* shall apply with any necessary modification in relation to a reorganisation or reduction of units in any unit trust scheme registered under the Unit Trusts Act, 1972, or authorised under the European Communities (Undertakings for Collective Investment in Transferable Securities) Regulations, 1989 (S.I. No. 78 of 1989), as if (except as respects *subsection (7)* of that section)—

(i) that scheme were a company, and

(ii) the units in that scheme were shares in the company.

(b) Where but for this paragraph this section would apply to any reorganisation or reduction of units in a unit trust scheme in a year of assessment so that units which are deemed not to be chargeable assets for that year for the purposes of the Capital Gains Tax Acts would be treated as "*original shares*" or a "*new holding*" within the meaning of *section 584*, that section shall not apply to that reorganisation or reduction of units in the unit trust scheme.

(3) The references in *subsection (2)* to *section 584* do not include references to that section as applied by *section 585* or *586*.

Cross References

From Section 733

Section 584 Reorganisation or reduction of share capital.
Section 585 Conversion of securities.
Section 586 Company amalgamations by exchange of shares.

To Section 733

Section 742 Offshore funds operating equalisation arrangements.

734 Taxation of collective investment undertakings

[FA89 s18(1) to (9), (11), (11A) and (12); FA91 s19 (1) and (2); FA93 s20(a); FA94 s25(1); S.I. No. 227 of 1994; FA95 s38; FA96 s35(1); FA97 s32]

(1) (a) In this section and in *Schedule 18*—

"*accounting period*", in relation to a collective investment undertaking, means the chargeable period or its basis period (within the meaning of *section 321(2)*) on the income or profits of which the undertaking is chargeable to income tax or corporation tax, as the case may be, for any chargeable period (within the meaning of that section), or would be so chargeable but for an insufficiency of income or profits, and—

(i) where 2 basis periods overlap, the period common to both shall be deemed to fall in the first basis period only,

(ii) where there is an interval between the end of the basis period for one chargeable period and the basis period for the next chargeable period, the interval shall be deemed to be part of the second basis period, and

(iii) the reference in *paragraph (i)* to the overlapping of 2 periods shall be construed as including a reference to the coincidence of 2 periods or to the inclusion of one period in another, and the reference to the period common to both shall be construed accordingly;

"*the Acts*" means the Tax Acts and the Capital Gains Tax Acts;

"*the airport*" has the same meaning as in the Customs-Free Airport Act, 1947;

"*appropriate tax*", in relation to the amount of any relevant payment made by a collective investment undertaking or in relation to any amount of undistributed relevant income of such an undertaking, as the case may be, means a sum representing tax on the amount of the payment or the amount of the undistributed relevant income, as appropriate, at a rate equal to the standard rate of income tax in force at the time of the payment or at the end of the accounting period to which the undistributed relevant income relates, as the case may be, after making a deduction from that sum of an amount equal to, or to the aggregate of—

(i) in the case of a relevant payment—

(I) in so far as it is made wholly or partly out of relevant income which at a previous date had been or formed part of the undistributed relevant income of the undertaking, the amount of any appropriate tax deducted—

(A) from the relevant income, or

(B) where the payment, or that part of the payment which is made out of relevant income, is less than the relevant income, from such part of the relevant income as is represented by the payment, or that part of the payment, as the case may be, and

(II) any other amount or amounts of tax deducted—

(A) from the relevant profits out of which the relevant payment is made, or

(B) where the payment is less than the profits, from such part of the profits as is represented by the payment,

under any of the provisions of the Acts apart from this section and which is or are not repayable to the collective investment undertaking,

or

(ii) in the case of an amount of undistributed relevant income, any amount or amounts of tax deducted from the income under any of the provisions of the Acts apart from this section and which is or are not repayable to the collective investment undertaking,

but the amount of the deduction shall not exceed the amount of the sum;

"*the Area*" has the same meaning as it has for the purposes of *section 446*;

"*chargeable gain*" has the same meaning as in the Capital Gains Tax Acts;

"collective investor", in relation to an authorised investment company (within the meaning of Part XIII of the Companies Act, 1990), means an investor, being a life assurance company, pension fund or other investor—

(i) who invests in securities or any other property whatever with moneys contributed by 50 or more persons—

(I) none of whom has at any time directly or indirectly contributed more than 5 per cent of such moneys, and

(II) each of a majority of whom has contributed moneys to the investor with the intention of being entitled, otherwise than on the death of any person or by reference to a risk of any kind to any person or property, to receive from the investor—

(A) a payment which, or

(B) payments the aggregate of which,

exceeds those moneys by a part of the profits or income arising to the investor,

and

(ii) who invests in the authorised investment company primarily for the benefit of those persons;

"*collective investment undertaking*" means, subject to *paragraph (b)*—

(i) a unit trust scheme which is or is deemed to be an authorised unit trust scheme (within the meaning of the Unit Trusts Act, 1990) and which has not had its authorisation under that Act revoked,

(ii) any other undertaking which is an undertaking for collective investment in transferable securities within the meaning of the relevant Regulations, being an undertaking which holds an authorisation, which has not been revoked, issued pursuant to the relevant Regulations,

[(iii) a limited partnership (other than an investment limited partnership within the meaning of the Investment Limited Partnerships Act 1994) which—][1]

(I) has as its principal business, as expressed in the partnership agreement establishing the limited partnership, the investment of its funds in property, and

(II) has been authorised to carry on that business, under any enactment which provides for such authorisation, by the Central Bank of Ireland,

and where, in addition to being a collective investment undertaking, it is also a specified collective investment undertaking, and

(iv) any authorised investment company (within the meaning of Part XIII of the Companies Act, 1990)—

(I) which has not had its authorisation under that Part of that Act revoked, and

(II) (A) which has been designated in that authorisation as an investment company which may raise capital by promoting the sale of its shares to the public and has not ceased to be so designated, or

(B) (aa) which is not a qualified company,

(bb) which in addition to being a collective investment undertaking is also a specified collective investment undertaking, and

(cc) where all the holders of units who must be resident outside the State, for the company to be a specified collective investment undertaking, are collective investors;

"*distribution*" has the same meaning as in the Corporation Tax Acts;

"*qualified company*" has, in relation to any business of a collective investment undertaking carried on in—

(i) the airport, the same meaning as it has for the purposes of *section 445*, or

(ii) the Area, the same meaning as it has for the purposes of *section 446*;

"qualifying management company", in relation to a collective investment undertaking, means a qualified company which in the course of relevant trading operations carried on by the qualified company manages the whole or any part of the investments and other activities of the business of the undertaking;

"*relevant gains*", in relation to a collective investment undertaking, means gains accruing to the undertaking, being gains which would constitute chargeable gains in the hands of a person resident in the State;

"*relevant income*", in relation to a collective investment undertaking, means any amounts of income, profits or gains which arise to or are receivable by the collective investment undertaking, being amounts of income, profits or gains—

(i) which are or are to be paid to unit holders as relevant payments,

(ii) out of which relevant payments are or are to be made to unit holders, or

(iii) which are or are to be accumulated for the benefit of, or invested in transferable securities for the benefit of, unit holders,

and which if they arose to an individual resident in the State would in the hands of the individual constitute income for the purposes of income tax;

"*relevant payment*" means a payment made to a unit holder by a collective investment undertaking by reason of rights conferred on the unit holder as a result of holding a unit or units in the collective investment undertaking, other than a payment made in respect of the cancellation, redemption or repurchase of a unit;

"*relevant profits*", in relation to a collective investment undertaking, means the relevant income and relevant gains of the undertaking;

"*relevant Regulations*" means the European Communities (Undertakings for Collective Investment in Transferable Securities) Regulations, 1989 (S.I. No. 78 of 1989);

"relevant trading operations" has, in relation to any business of a collective investment undertaking carried on by a qualified company in—

(i) the airport, the same meaning as it has for the purposes of *section 445*, or

(ii) the Area, the same meaning as it has for the purposes of *section 446*;

"*return*" means a return under *paragraph 1(2)* of *Schedule 18*;

"*specified collective investment undertaking*" means, subject to *paragraph (c)*, a collective investment undertaking—

(i) most of the business of which, to the extent that it is carried on in the State—

(I) (A) is carried on in the Area by the undertaking or by a qualifying management company of the undertaking or by the undertaking and the qualifying management company of the undertaking, or

(B) is not so carried on in the Area but—

(aa) is so carried on in the State,

(bb) would be so carried on in the Area but for circumstances outside the control of the person or persons carrying on the business, and

(cc) is so carried on in the Area when those circumstances cease to exist,

or

(II) is carried on in the airport by the undertaking or by a qualifying management company of the undertaking or by the undertaking and the qualifying management company of the undertaking,

and

(ii) in which, except to the extent that such units are held by the undertaking itself, the qualifying management company of the undertaking, a company referred to in *section 710(2)*, a specified company or another specified collective investment undertaking, all the holders of units in the undertaking are persons resident outside the State,

and includes any company limited by shares or guarantee which—

(iii) is wholly owned by such a collective investment undertaking or its trustees, if any, for the benefit of the holders of units in that undertaking,

(iv) is so owned solely for the purpose of limiting the liability of that undertaking or its trustees, as the case may be, in respect of futures contracts, options contracts or other financial instruments with similar risk characteristics, by enabling it or its trustees, as the case may be, to invest or deal in such investments through the company, and

(v) would, if references to an undertaking in *paragraph (i)* were to be construed as including references to a company limited by shares or guarantee, satisfy the condition set out in *paragraph (i)*;

"*specified company*" means a company—

(i) which is—

(I) a qualified company carrying on relevant trading operations (within the meaning of *section 446*), or

(II) a qualified company carrying on relevant trading operations (within the meaning of *section 445*) so long as those relevant trading operations could be certified by the Minister for Finance as relevant trading operations for the purposes of *section 446* if they were carried on in the Area rather than in the airport,

and

[(ii) (I) not more than 25 per cent of the share capital of which is owned directly or indirectly by persons resident in the State, or

(II) all of the share capital of which is owned directly by another company resident in the State and not more than 25 per cent of the share capital of that other company is owned directly or indirectly by persons resident in the State,][2]

"*tax*" means income tax, corporation tax or capital gains tax, as may be appropriate;

"*transferable securities*" has the same meaning as in the relevant Regulations;

"*undistributed relevant income*", in relation to a collective investment undertaking, means any relevant income arising to or receivable by the undertaking in an accounting period of the undertaking and which at the end of the accounting period has not been paid to the unit holders and from which appropriate tax has not previously been deducted;

"unit" includes any investment, such as a subscription for shares or a contribution of capital, in a collective investment undertaking, being an investment which entitles the investor—

(i) to a share of the investments or relevant profits of, or

(ii) to receive a distribution from,

the collective investment undertaking;

"*unit holder*", in relation to a collective investment undertaking, means any person who by reason of the holding of a unit, or under the terms of a unit, in the undertaking is entitled to a share of any of the investments or relevant profits of, or to receive a distribution from, the undertaking.

(b) References in this section to a collective investment undertaking, apart from such references in the definition of "specified collective investment undertaking", shall include references to a company limited by shares or guarantee which is a specified collective investment undertaking.

[(c) Where, a collective investment undertaking would not be chargeable to tax in respect of relevant profits, but the relevant profits would be chargeable to tax in the hands of the unit holder, including the undertaking, to whom a relevant payment of, or out of the relevant profits is made in accordance with *subsection (3)* but for the fact that—

(i) *sections 445* and *446* have been deleted, and

(ii) those sections referred to time limits in respect of certificates to which each section related,

then, notwithstanding those deletions and time limits, the collective investment undertaking shall not be so chargeable to tax in respect of relevant profits, but the relevant profits shall be so chargeable to tax in the hands of the unit holder, including the undertaking, to whom a relevant payment of, or out of the relevant profits is made and the other provisions of this section shall apply with any modifications necessary to give effect to this subsection.][3]

(2) For the purposes of this section—

(a) where any payment is made out of relevant profits or out of any part of such profits from which any tax including appropriate tax has been deducted and the payment is less than the relevant profits or that part of such profits, the amount of the tax so deducted which is referable to the part of the profits represented by the payment shall be the amount which bears to the total amount of the tax deducted from the relevant profits or the part of such profits, the same proportion as the amount of the payment bears to the amount of the relevant profits or the part of such profits, as the case may be, and

(b) any reference in this section to the amount of a relevant payment shall be construed as a reference to the amount which would be the amount of the relevant payment if the appropriate tax were not to be deducted from the relevant payment or from any undistributed relevant income out of which the relevant payment or any part of such payment is made.

(3) Notwithstanding anything in the Acts but subject to *subsection (5)*, a collective investment undertaking shall not be chargeable to tax in respect of relevant profits, but the relevant profits shall be chargeable to tax in the hands of any unit holder, including the undertaking, to whom a relevant payment of or out of the relevant profits is made if and to the extent that the unit holder would be chargeable to tax in the State on such relevant profits, or on such part of the relevant profits as is represented by the payment, on the basis that and in all respects as if, subject to *subsections (4)* and *(6)*, the relevant profits or that part of the relevant profits had arisen or accrued to the unit holder without passing through the hands of the undertaking.

(4) Where in accordance with *subsection (3)* a unit holder is to be charged to tax on a relevant payment made by a collective investment undertaking which is not a specified collective investment undertaking—

(a) in so far as any amount of the relevant payment on which the unit holder is to be so charged is or is made out of relevant income, the unit holder shall be charged to tax on that amount under Case IV of Schedule D as if it were an amount of income arising to the unit holder at the time the payment is made, and

(b) in so far as any amount of the relevant payment on which the unit holder is to be so charged is or is made out of relevant gains, it shall be treated as a capital distribution within the meaning of *section 731* and, if it is not already the case, the Capital Gains Tax Acts shall apply in all respects as if the amount of the relevant payment were a capital distribution made by a unit trust and the unit or units in respect of which it is paid were a unit or units in a unit trust.

(5) (a) Where a collective investment undertaking which is not a specified collective investment undertaking—

(i) makes a relevant payment of or out of relevant profits to a unit holder resident in the State, or

(ii) has at the end of an accounting period of the undertaking any undistributed relevant income,

it shall deduct out of the amount of the relevant payment or the amount of the undistributed relevant income, as the case may be, the appropriate tax.

(b) Where appropriate tax is deducted in accordance with *paragraph (a)*—

(i) the unit holder to whom the relevant payment is made or the unit holder or unit holders entitled to the relevant income, as the case may be, shall allow the deduction, and

(ii) the collective investment undertaking shall, on the making of the relevant payment to the unit holder or on the making of any relevant payment out of the undistributed relevant income to any unit holder, as the case may be, be acquitted and discharged of so much money as is represented—

(I) by the deduction, or

(II) where the relevant payment is less than the amount of the undistributed relevant income, by so much of the deduction as is referable to the relevant payment,

as if the amount of money had actually been paid to the unit holder.

(c) *Schedule 18* shall apply for the purposes of supplementing this subsection.

(6) (a) Where a unit holder receives a relevant payment from a collective investment undertaking which is not a specified collective investment undertaking and appropriate tax has been deducted from the payment, or from the relevant profits or part of those profits out of which the payment is made, then, the unit holder shall—

(i) if the unit holder is not resident in the State for tax purposes at the time the payment is made, be entitled, on due claim and on proof of the facts, to repayment of the appropriate tax, or so much of it as is referable to the relevant payment, as the case may be, or

(ii) in any other case, be entitled—

(I) to have the unit holder's liability to tax under any assessment made in respect of the relevant payment or any part of the relevant payment reduced by a sum equal to so much, if any, of the appropriate tax as is referable to the amount of the relevant payment contained in the assessment, and

(II) where the appropriate tax so referable exceeds the unit holder's liability to tax in respect of the relevant payment, or in respect of that part of the relevant payment contained in the assessment, to repayment of the excess.

(b) For the purposes of *paragraph (a)(ii)*, the inspector or on appeal the Appeal Commissioners shall make such apportionment of the appropriate tax deducted from a relevant payment, or from the relevant profits out of which the relevant payment or any part of the relevant payment is made, as is just and reasonable to determine the amount of the appropriate tax, if any, referable to any part of the relevant payment contained in an assessment.

(7) *Section 732* shall not apply as on and from—

(a) the 24th day of May, 1989, to—

(i) a qualifying unit trust (within the meaning of *section 732*), and

(ii) the disposal of qualifying units (within the meaning of that section) in such a qualifying unit trust,

where the qualifying unit trust is also a specified collective investment undertaking, and

(b) (i) the 6th day of April, 1990, or

(ii) where this section applies by virtue of *subsection (12)(b)* on an earlier day to a qualifying unit trust which is a collective investment undertaking, such earlier day in respect of the qualifying unit trust,

to such a qualifying unit trust or to the disposal of such qualifying units in the qualifying unit trust, where the qualifying unit trust is a collective investment undertaking without also being a specified collective investment undertaking.

(8) *Section 805* shall not apply to a collective investment undertaking if but for this subsection it would otherwise apply.

(9) As respects any collective investment undertaking which is a company (within the meaning of the Corporation Tax Acts)—

(a) a relevant payment made out of the relevant profits of the undertaking or a payment made in respect of the cancellation, redemption or repurchase of a unit in the undertaking shall not be treated as a distribution for any of the purposes of the Tax Acts, and

(b) if but for this subsection *section 440* would otherwise apply, it shall not apply to the collective investment undertaking.

(10) Notwithstanding *section 1034*, a person not resident in the State shall not by virtue of that section be assessable and chargeable in the name of an agent in respect of a relevant payment made out of the relevant profits of a collective investment undertaking.

(11) For the purposes of the Tax Acts, a unit holder other than a qualifying management company shall not be treated as carrying on a trade in the State through a branch or agency or otherwise where that unit holder would not be so treated if the unit holder did not hold any units in a specified collective investment undertaking.

(12) This section shall apply as on and from—

(a) in the case of a specified collective investment undertaking, the 24th day of May, 1989, and

(b) in the case of any other collective investment undertaking, the 6th day of April, 1990, or such earlier day, not being earlier than the 6th day of April, 1989, as the Revenue Commissioners may agree to in writing with any such other collective investment undertaking in respect of that undertaking.

Amendments

[1] Substituted by FA13 s42(1)(b). Applies in respect of an investment limited partnership that has been granted an authorisation under section 8 of the Investment Limited Partnerships Act 1994 on or after 13 February 2013.

[2] Substituted by FA98 s42.

[3] Substituted by FA12 sched1(25).

Revenue Precedents

Investment by Lloyds syndicates, some of whose members are resident in Ireland for tax purposes would not prejudice the tax exempt status of the fund as Lloyds syndicates are regarded as non-resident investors and there is no look through to the individual Lloyds "names". 5019/96

The take-over of a foreign fund, with Irish resident investors, by an SCIU would not prejudice the tax exempt status of the SCIU provided the Irish investors are removed from the fund within 3 months of the date of the take-over. 2577/93

The holding of units by an Irish resident nominee company on behalf of non-residents would not prejudice the exempt status of the SCIU provided the nominee company is in the business of holding shares in a nominee capacity and advance approval is received from the Revenue Commissioners. 1579/89

Cross References

From Section 734

Section 321 Provisions of general application in relation to the making of allowances and charges.
Section 440 Surcharge on undistributed investment and estate income.
Section 445 Certain trading operations carried on in Shannon Airport.
Section 446 Certain trading operations carried on in Custom House Docks Area.
Section 710 Profits of life business.
Section 731 Chargeable gains accruing to unit trusts.
Section 732 Special arrangements for qualifying unit trusts.
Section 805 Surcharge on certain income of trustees.
Section 1034 Assessment.

Schedule 18 Accounting for and Payment of Tax Deducted from Relevant Payments and Undistributed Relevant Income

To Section 734

Section 172A Interpretation.
Section 198 Certain interest not to be chargeable.
Section 246 Interest payments by companies and to non-residents.
Section 446 Certain trading operations carried on in Custom House Docks Area.
Section 735 Certain unit trusts not to be collective investment undertakings.
Section 736 Option for non-application of section 735.
Section 737 Special investment schemes.
Section 738 Undertakings for collective investment.
Section 739B Interpretation and application.
Section 739D Gain arising on a chargeable event.
Schedule 18 Accounting for and Payment of Tax Deducted from Relevant Payments and Undistributed Relevant Income
Schedule 29 Provisions Referred to in Sections 1052, 1053 and 1054
Schedule 31 Consequential Amendments

735 Certain unit trusts not to be collective investment undertakings

[FA90 s35(1) and (2)]

(1) This section shall apply to any unit trust scheme (within the meaning of the Unit Trusts Act, 1972) where there is or was at any time in respect of any or all units issued after the 14th day of June, 1973, a requirement for participation in that unit trust scheme that a policy of assurance on human life be effected (but without those units becoming the property of the owner of the policy either as benefits or otherwise).

(2) Notwithstanding *section 734*, a unit trust scheme to which this section applies shall be deemed not to be a collective investment undertaking for the purposes of that section and *Schedule 18*.

Cross References

From Section 735

Section 734 Taxation of collective investment undertakings.
Schedule 18 Accounting for and Payment of Tax Deducted from Relevant Payments and Undistributed Relevant Income

To Section 735

Section 736 Option for non-application of section 735.

736 Option for non-application of section 735

[FA92 s36]

(1) Where the trustees of a unit trust scheme (within the meaning the Unit Trusts Act, 1990), which apart from *section 735* would be a collective investment undertaking for the purposes of *section 734* and *Schedule 18*, have not later than the 1st day of November, 1992—

(a) paid the capital gains tax which would have been chargeable on them if—

(i) on the 31st day of March, 1992, they had disposed of all the assets of the unit trust scheme, and

(ii) the resulting chargeable gains were chargeable to tax at one-half of the rate at which they would have been chargeable under the Capital Gains Tax Acts apart from this subparagraph,

and

(b) given notice in writing to the Revenue Commissioners that they have paid that tax in accordance with *paragraph (a)*,

then, notwithstanding *section 735*, the unit trust scheme (in this section referred to as "*the relevant unit trust*") shall be deemed to be and to have been a collective investment undertaking for the purposes of *section 734* and *Schedule 18* with effect from the 1st day of April, 1992.

(2) (a) Where units in a relevant unit trust were held by a person on the 31st day of March, 1992, they shall be treated, for the purposes of computing chargeable gains accruing to the person on or after the 1st day of April, 1992, as having been acquired by the person on the 31st day of March, 1992.

(b) *Section 731(6)* shall not apply to disposals on or after the 1st day of April, 1992, of units in a relevant unit trust.

(3) Where the consideration received for a disposal, or given for an acquisition, of an asset on the 31st day of March, 1992, is to be determined as a result of this section, it shall be deemed to be an amount equal to the market value of the asset on that day, and for this purpose "*market value*", in relation to any asset, shall be construed in accordance with *section 548*.

Cross References

From Section 736

Section 548 Valuation of assets.

Section 731 Chargeable gains accruing to unit trusts.

Section 734 Taxation of collective investment undertakings.

Section 735 Certain unit trusts not to be collective investment undertakings.

Schedule 18 Accounting for and Payment of Tax Deducted from Relevant Payments and Undistributed Relevant Income

737 Special investment schemes

[FA93 s13; FA94 s34(a); FA96 s36]

(1) (a) In this section—

"*inspector*", "*ordinary shares*", and "*qualifying shares*" have the same meanings respectively as in *section 723*;

"*authorised unit trust scheme*" means a unit trust scheme which is or is deemed to be an authorised unit trust scheme (within the meaning of the Unit Trusts Act, 1990) and which has not had its authorisation under that Act revoked;

"*market value*" shall be construed in accordance with *section 548*;

[...][1]

"*special investment scheme*" means an authorised unit trust scheme in respect of which the conditions specified in *subsection (2)* are satisfied;

["*special investment units*" means units sold to an individual on or after 1 February 1993 and before 1 January 2001 by the management company or trustee under an authorised unit trust scheme in respect of which—

(a) the conditions specified in *subsection (3)* are satisfied, and

(b) a declaration of the kind specified in *subsection (4)* has been made to the management company or trustee;][2]

"*specified qualifying shares*", in relation to a special investment scheme, means qualifying shares in a company which, when the shares are acquired for the scheme, has an issued share capital the market value of which is less than [€255,000,000][3];

"*units*", in relation to an authorised unit trust scheme, means any units (whether described as units or otherwise) into which are divided the beneficial interests in the assets subject to any trust created under the scheme.

(b) A reference in this section to the management company or trustee under an authorised unit trust scheme shall be construed as a reference to the person in whom are vested the powers of management relating to property for the time being subject to any trust created pursuant to the scheme or, as the case may be, to the person in whom such property is or may be vested in accordance with the terms of the trust.

(2) (a) The conditions referred to in the definition of "*special investment scheme*" are as follows:

(i) the beneficial interests in the assets subject to any trust created under the authorised unit trust scheme concerned shall be divided into special investment units;

(ii) the aggregate of the consideration given for shares which are at any time before the 1st day of February, 1994, assets subject to any trust created under the scheme shall not be less than—

(I) as respects qualifying shares, 40 per cent, and

(II) as respects specified qualifying shares, 6 per cent, of the aggregate of the consideration given for the assets which are at that time subject to any such trust;

(iii) the aggregate of the consideration given for shares which are at any time within the year ending on the 31st day of January, 1995, assets subject to any trust created under the scheme shall not be less than—

(I) as respects qualifying shares, 45 per cent, and

(II) as respects specified qualifying shares, 9 per cent,

of the aggregate of the consideration given for the assets which are at that time subject to any such trust;

(iv) the aggregate of the consideration given for shares which are at any time within the year ending on the 31st day of January, 1996, assets subject to any trust created under the scheme shall not be less than—

(I) as respects qualifying shares, 50 per cent, and

(II) as respects specified qualifying shares, 10 per cent,

of the aggregate of the consideration given for the assets which are at that time subject to any such trust;

[(v) the aggregate of consideration given for shares which are, at any time on or after 1 February 1996 and before 31 December 2000, assets subject to any trust created under the scheme shall not be less than—

(I) as respects qualifying shares, 55 per cent, and

(II) as respects specified qualifying shares, 10 per cent,

of the aggregate of the consideration given for the assets which are at that time subject to any such trust.][4]

(b) For the purposes of *subparagraphs (ii)* to *(v)* of *paragraph (a)*, the amount of the consideration given for assets subject to any trust created under the scheme shall be determined in accordance with *sections 547* and *580.*

(3) (a) The conditions referred to in the definition of "*special investment units*" are as follows:

(i) the special investment units shall be so designated in the trusts created under the authorised unit trust scheme concerned;

(ii) the aggregate of payments made on or before any day to the management company or trustee under the scheme by or on behalf of an individual in respect of special investment units owned, whether jointly or otherwise, by the individual on that day shall not exceed [€63,500][5];

[…][6]

(iv) special investment units shall not be sold to or owned by an individual who is not of full age;

(v) special investment units shall only be sold to an individual—

(I) who shall be beneficially entitled to, and

(II) to whom there shall be paid,

all amounts payable in respect of those units by the management company or trustee under the scheme;

(vi) except in the case of special investment units sold to and owned jointly only by a couple married to each other, units shall not be jointly owned;

(vii) except in the case of special investment units bought by and owned jointly only by a couple married to each other, an individual who owns such units of an authorised unit trust scheme shall not buy or own such units of another authorised unit trust scheme;

(viii) where a couple married to each other buy and jointly own special investment units of an authorised unit trust scheme, they shall not buy or own such units in any other such scheme either individually or jointly, other than units which they buy and jointly own in one other such scheme.

(b) For the purposes of *subparagraphs (ii)* to *(iv)* and *(vi)* to *(viii)* of *paragraph (a)*, references to ownership of special investment units shall be construed as references to beneficial ownership of the units.

(c) For the purposes of *subparagraphs (ii)* and *(iii)* of *paragraph (a)*, a disposal of special investment units of an authorised unit trust scheme acquired by an individual at different times shall be assumed to be a disposal of units acquired later, rather than of units acquired earlier, by the individual.

(4) The declaration referred to in the definition of "*special investment units*" is a declaration in writing to the management company or trustee under an authorised unit trust scheme which—

(a) (i) is made by the individual (in this section referred to as "*the declarer*") to whom any amounts are payable by the management company or trustee in respect of units in respect of which the declaration is made, and

(ii) is signed by the declarer,

(b) is made in such form as may be prescribed or authorised by the Revenue Commissioners,

(c) declares that at the time when the declaration is made the conditions specified in *subparagraphs (iv)* to *(viii)* of *subsection (3)(a)* are satisfied in relation to the units in respect of which the declaration is made,

(d) contains the full name and address of the individual beneficially entitled to any amounts payable in respect of the units in respect of which the declaration is made,

(e) contains an undertaking by the declarer that, if any of the conditions referred to in *subparagraphs (iv)* to *(viii)* of *subsection (3)(a)* ceases to be satisfied in respect of the units in respect of which the declaration is made, the declarer will notify the management company or trustee accordingly, and

(f) contains such other information as the Revenue Commissioners may reasonably require for the purposes of this section.

(5) (a) The management company or trustee under an authorised unit trust scheme shall—

(i) keep and retain for not less than the longer of the following periods—

(I) a period of 6 years, and

(II) a period which, in relation to the units in respect of which the declaration is made, ends 3 years after the earliest date on which all of those units stand cancelled, redeemed or bought by the management company or trustee, and

(ii) on being so required by notice given to it in writing by an inspector, make available to the inspector within the time specified in the notice,

all declarations of the kind specified in *subsection (4)* which have been made to it.

(b) The inspector may examine and take copies of or of extracts from a declaration made available to him or her under *paragraph (a)*.

(6) (a) Notwithstanding *section 734*, a special investment scheme shall not be a collective investment undertaking for the purposes of that section and *Schedule 18*; but a special investment scheme shall continue to be treated as a collective investment undertaking (within the meaning of *section 734*) for the purposes of section 206(*a*) of the Finance Act, 1992.

(b) Notwithstanding any other provision of the Tax Acts or the Capital Gains Tax Acts but subject to *paragraphs (c)* and *(d)*—

(i) income tax in respect of income arising to a special investment scheme shall be chargeable at the standard rate, and such income shall not be charged to an additional duty of income tax under *section 805*, and

(ii) capital gains tax in respect of chargeable gains accruing to a special investment scheme shall be chargeable at the rate specified in *section 28(3)*.

[(c) Any income tax or capital gains tax chargeable in accordance with *paragraph (b)* shall be the amount of such tax, before it is reduced by any credit, relief or other deduction under the Tax Acts or the Capital Gains

Tax Acts apart from this section, which is 20 per cent of income arising or chargeable gains accruing, as the case may be, to the scheme.][7]

(d) Only so much of income arising or gains accruing to the scheme shall be chargeable to income tax or capital gains tax, as the case may be, in accordance with *paragraph (b)* as is or is to be—

(i) paid to, or

(ii) accumulated or invested for the benefit of,

holders of special investment units or as would be so paid, accumulated or invested if any gains accruing to the scheme by virtue of *subsection (8)* were gains on an actual disposal of the assets concerned.

(7)[…][8]

[…][9]

(c) Notwithstanding *Chapter 4* of *Part 8*, that Chapter shall apply to a deposit (within the meaning of that Chapter) for the time being subject to any trust created pursuant to a special investment scheme as if such a deposit were not a relevant deposit (within the meaning of that Chapter).

(8) (a) Notwithstanding the Capital Gains Tax Acts, for the purposes of computing chargeable gains arising to a special investment scheme—

(i) each asset which on [31 December][10] is subject to any trust created pursuant to the scheme shall be deemed to have been disposed of and immediately reacquired by the management company or trustee under the scheme on that day at the asset's market value on that day,

(ii) *section 556* shall not apply,

(iii) *section 607* shall not apply,

(iv) without prejudice to the treatment of losses on such shares as allowable losses, gains accruing on the disposal or deemed disposal of eligible shares (within the meaning of *Part 16*) in a qualifying company (within the meaning of that Part) shall not be chargeable gains, and

(v) as respects *section 581*—

(I) *subsections (1)* and *(2)* of that section, and

(II) *subsection (3)* of that section, in so far as a chargeable gain is not thereby disregarded for the purposes of that subsection,

shall apply as if *subparagraphs (i)* and *(iii)* had not been enacted.

(b) Where in a year of assessment the management company or trustee under a special investment scheme incurs allowable losses on disposals or deemed disposals of assets subject to any trust created pursuant to the scheme, the amount, if any, by which the aggregate of such allowable losses exceeds the aggregate of chargeable gains on such disposals in the year of assessment shall be—

(i) disregarded for the purposes of *section 31*,

(ii) treated as reducing the income chargeable to income tax arising to the scheme in that year of assessment, and

(iii) to the extent that it is not treated as reducing income arising to the scheme in that year of assessment, treated for the purposes of the Capital Gains Tax Acts and this paragraph as an allowable loss incurred in the next year of assessment on a disposal of an asset subject to a trust created pursuant to the scheme.

[(bb) Where in a year of assessment (in this section referred to as the "year of cessation") the business of a special investment scheme ceases and an amount, but for that cessation, would under *paragraph (b)(iii)* be treated as an amount of allowable loss incurred in the next year of assessment, that amount may be deducted from chargeable gains accruing to the special investment scheme in the 3 years of assessment preceding the year of cessation taking chargeable gains accruing in a later year before those accruing in an earlier year, and there shall be made all such amendments of assessments or repayments as may be necessary to give effect to this paragraph.][11]

(c) (i) In this paragraph—

"the appropriate amount in respect of the interest" means the appropriate amount in respect of the interest which would be determined in accordance with *Schedule 21* if the management company or the trustee was the first buyer and the management company or the trustee carried on a trade to which *section 749(1)* applies but, in determining the appropriate amount in respect of the interest in accordance with *Schedule 21*, *paragraph 3(4)* of that Schedule shall apply as if "*in the opinion of the Appeal Commissioners*" were deleted;

"*securities*" has the same meaning as in *section 815*.

(ii) Where in a year of assessment (in this paragraph referred to as "*the first year of assessment*") any securities which are assets subject to any trust created pursuant to a special investment scheme are disposed of and in the following year of assessment interest becoming payable in respect of the securities is receivable by the special investment scheme, then, for the purposes of computing the chargeable gains for the first year of assessment, the price paid by the management company or the trustee for the securities shall be treated as reduced by the appropriate amount in respect of the interest.

(iii) Where for a year of assessment *subparagraph (ii)* applies so as to reduce the price paid for securities, the amount by which the price paid for the securities is reduced shall be treated as a loss arising in the following year of assessment from the disposal of the securities.

(9) (a) In this subsection, "*eligible shares*" means eligible shares within the meaning of *Part 16* in a qualifying company within the meaning of that Part.

(b) Distributions received by the management company or trustee under a special investment scheme in respect of eligible shares which are subject to any trust created in pursuance of the scheme shall not be chargeable to income tax[...][12]

(c) Notwithstanding *section 508*, the Revenue Commissioners shall not designate a special investment scheme for the purposes of *Part 16*.

(10) (a) Any payment made to a holder of special investment units by the management company or trustee under the special investment scheme concerned by reason of rights conferred on the holder as a result of holding such units shall not be reckoned in computing total income for the purposes of the Income Tax Acts.

(b) *Section 732* shall not apply to a special investment scheme or the disposal of special investment units.

(c) No chargeable gain shall accrue on the disposal of, or of an interest in, special investment units.

(d) Notwithstanding any other provision of the Income Tax Acts or the Capital Gains Tax Acts, the holder of special investment units of a special investment scheme shall not be entitled to any credit for or payment of any income tax or capital gains tax paid in respect of income arising to, or capital gains accruing to, the scheme.

Amendments

[1] Deleted by FA01 s73(1)(a). This section shall be deemed to have applied as on and from 1 January 2001.

[2] Substituted by FA00 s57(a).

[3, 5] Substituted by FA01 s240 and sched5 part1.

[4] Substituted by FA01 s73(1)(b). This section shall be deemed to have applied as on and from 1 January 2001.

[6] Deleted by FA01 s73(1)(c). This section shall be deemed to have applied as on and from 1 January 2001.

[7] Substituted by FA99 s63(1)(c). Shall apply as on and from the 6th day of April, 1999.

[8, 9, 12] Deleted by FA00 sched2.

[10] Substituted by FA01 sched2(40). Applies as respects the year of assessment 2001 and subsequent years of assessment.

[11] Inserted by FA03 s50.

Revenue Precedents

An investor cannot invest more than £75,000 in one SIP even if amounts are held under different account numbers and no amount in one account exceeds £75,000. The legislation provides that the aggregate of payments made under the scheme shall not exceed £75,000. GD93011B

Cross References

From Section 737

Section 28 Taxation of capital gains and rate of charge.
Section 31 Amount chargeable.
Section 237 Annual payments payable wholly out of taxed income.
Section 256 Interpretation (Chapter 4).
Section 488 Interpretation (Part 16).
Section 547 Disposals and acquisitions treated as made at market value.
Section 548 Valuation of assets.
Section 556 Adjustment of allowable expenditure by reference to consumer price index.
Section 580 Shares, securities, etc: identification.
Section 581 Disposals of shares or securities within 4 weeks of acquisition.
Section 607 Government and certain other securities.
Section 723 Special investment policies.
Section 732 Special arrangements for qualifying unit trusts.
Section 734 Taxation of collective investment undertakings.
Section 749 Dealers in securities.
Section 805 Surcharge on certain income of trustees.
Section 815 Taxation of income deemed to arise on certain sales of securities.
Schedule 18 Accounting for and Payment of Tax Deducted from Relevant Payments and Undistributed Relevant Income
Schedule 21 Purchase and Sale of Securities: Appropriate Amount in Respect of the Interest

To Section 737

Section 246 Interest payments by companies and to non-residents.
Section 541A Treatment of debts on a change in currency.
Section 738 Undertakings for collective investment.
Section 739B Interpretation and application.
Section 839 Limits to special investments.

738 Undertakings for collective investment

[FA93 s17; FA94 s57(a); FA96 s38(1); FA97 s35]

(1) (a) In this section and in *section 739*—

"*chargeable period*" means an accounting period of an undertaking for collective investment which is a company or, as respects such an undertaking which is not a company, a year of assessment;

"*designated assets*" means—

(i) land, or

(ii) shares in a company resident in the State which are not shares—

(I) listed in the official list, or

(II) dealt in on the smaller companies market or the unlisted securities market,

of the Irish Stock Exchange;

"designated undertaking for collective investment" means an undertaking for collective investment which, on the 25th day of May, 1993, owned designated assets for which that undertaking gave consideration (determined in accordance with *section 547*) the aggregate of which is not less than 80 per cent of the aggregate of the consideration (as so determined) which that undertaking gave for the total assets it owned at that date;

"*distribution*" has the same meaning as in the Corporation Tax Acts;

"guaranteed undertaking for collective investment" means an undertaking for collective investment all of the issued units of which, on the 25th day of May, 1993, are units in respect of each of which the undertaking will make one payment only, being a payment—

(i) to be made on a specified date in cancellation of those units, and

(ii) which is the aggregate of—

(I) a fixed amount, and

(II) an amount, which may be nil, determined by a stock exchange index or indices;

"*relevant Regulations*" means the European Communities (Undertakings for Collective Investment in Transferable Securities) Regulations, 1989 (S.I. No. 78 of 1989);

"*undertaking for collective investment*" means, subject to *paragraph (b)*—

(i) a unit trust scheme, other than—

(I) a unit trust mentioned in *section 731(5)(a)*, or

(II) a special investment scheme (within the meaning of *section 737*),

which is or is deemed to be an authorised unit trust scheme (within the meaning of the Unit Trusts Act, 1990) and has not had its authorisation under that Act revoked,

(ii) any other undertaking which is an undertaking for collective investment in transferable securities within the meaning of the relevant Regulations, being an undertaking which holds an authorisation, which has not been revoked, issued pursuant to the relevant Regulations, or

(iii) any authorised investment company (within the meaning of Part XIII of the Companies Act, 1990) which—

(I) has not had its authorisation under that Part of that Act revoked, and

(II) has been designated in that authorisation as an investment company which may raise capital by promoting the sale of its shares to the public and has not ceased to be so designated,

which is neither a specified collective investment undertaking (within the meaning of *section 734(1)*) nor an offshore fund (within the meaning of *section 743*);

"*unit*" includes a share and any other instrument granting an entitlement—

(i) to a share of the investments or relevant profits of, or

(ii) to receive a distribution from,

an undertaking for collective investment;

"*unit holder*", in relation to an undertaking for collective investment, means any person who by reason of the holding of a unit, or under the terms of a unit, in the undertaking is entitled to a share of any of the investments or relevant profits of, or to receive a distribution from, the undertaking;

"*standard rate*" has the same meaning as in *section 3(1)*;

"*standard rate per cent*" has the same meaning as in *section 4(1)*.

(b) For the purposes of this section and *section 739*, references to an undertaking for collective investment (other than in this paragraph) shall be construed so as to include a reference to a trustee, management company or other such person who—

(i) is authorised to act on behalf, or for the purposes, of the undertaking, and

(ii) habitually does so,

to the extent that such construction brings into account for the purposes of this section and *section 739* any matter relating to the undertaking, being a matter which would not otherwise be brought into account for those purposes.

(c) For the purposes of this section—

(i) as respects an undertaking for collective investment which is a company, where an accounting period of the company begins before the 6th day of April, 1994, and ends on or after that day, it shall be divided into 2 parts, one beginning on the day on which the accounting period begins and ending on the 5th day of April, 1994, and the other beginning on the 6th day of April, 1994, and ending on the day on which the accounting period ends, and both parts shall be treated as if they were separate accounting periods of the company, and

(ii) without prejudice to *section 815(2)*, any attribution of income or chargeable gains of such an undertaking to periods treated as separate accounting periods by virtue of *subparagraph (i)* shall be made—

(I) as respects such income, on the basis of the time that income arises to the undertaking, and

(II) as respects such capital gains, on the basis of the time of disposal of the assets concerned,

and *section 4(6)* shall not apply for the purpose of such attribution.

(2) (a) Other than in the case of *subsections (7)* to *(9)* of *section 734*, that section shall not apply, and the following provisions of this section shall apply, to an undertaking for collective investment as respects the chargeable periods of the undertaking ending on or after—

(i) the 6th day of April, 1994, if the undertaking was carrying on a collective investment business on the 25th day of May, 1993, or

(ii) the 25th day of May, 1993, if the undertaking was not carrying on such a business at that date.

[(b) (i) Subject to *subparagraph (ii)*, as respects an undertaking for collective investment which is a company, the corporation tax which is chargeable on its profits on which corporation tax falls finally to be borne for a chargeable period beginning on or after 8 February 2012 shall, for the purposes of the Tax Acts, be such tax, before it is reduced by any credit, relief or other reduction under those Acts, computed as if the rate of corporation tax were 30 per cent.

(ii) For the purposes of this paragraph, as respects an undertaking for collective investment which is a company, where an accounting period of the company begins before 8 February 2012 and ends on or after that date, it shall be divided into 2 parts, one beginning on the date on which the accounting period begins and ending on 7 February 2012, and the other beginning on 8 February 2012 and ending on the date on which the accounting period ends, and both parts shall be treated as if they were separate accounting periods of the company and the corporation tax for the chargeable period ending on 7 February 2012 shall be computed as if the rate of corporation tax were 20 per cent.][1]

(c) In computing profits for the purposes of *paragraph (b)*, *section 78(2)* shall apply as if the rate per cent of capital gains tax specified in *section 28(3)*, were [the rate per cent of corporation tax specified in *section 21(1)*][2].

(d) As respects an undertaking for collective investment which is not a company—

[(i) the income tax which is chargeable on the income arising, and the capital gains tax which is chargeable on the chargeable gains accruing, in a year of assessment to the undertaking shall be the amount of such tax, before it is reduced by any credit, relief or other deduction under any provision, other than under this section, of the Tax Acts or the Capital Gains Tax Acts, which is the rate of 30 per cent of the income arising, and the chargeable gains accruing to the undertaking, but, in relation to the year of assessment commencing on 1 January 2012, payments made and gains realised in the period from 1 January 2012 to 7 February 2012 shall be chargeable to income tax or capital gains tax, as the case may be, at the rate of 20 per cent, and][3]

(ii) only so much of income arising or gains accruing to the undertaking shall be chargeable to income tax or capital gains tax, as the case may be, as is or is to be—

(I) paid to, or

(II) accumulated or invested for the benefit of,

unit holders in the undertaking or as would be so paid, accumulated or invested if any gains accruing to the scheme by virtue of *subsection (4)* were gains on an actual disposal of the assets concerned.

(3) (a) (i) *Section 129* shall not apply as respects a distribution received by an undertaking for collective investment which is a company[…][4]

[…][5]

[…][6]

(c) Notwithstanding *Chapter 4* of *Part 8*, that Chapter shall apply to a deposit (within the meaning of that Chapter) which is for the time being beneficially owned by an undertaking for collective investment which is not a company as if such a deposit were not a relevant deposit (within the meaning of that Chapter).

(4) (a) (i) Every asset of an undertaking for collective investment on the day on which a chargeable period of the undertaking ends shall, subject to *subparagraph (ii)* and *paragraphs (b)* to *(e)*, be deemed to have been disposed of and immediately reacquired by the undertaking at the asset's market value on that day.

(ii) *Subparagraph (i)* shall not apply to—

(I) assets to which *section 607* applies other than where such assets are held in connection with a contract or other arrangement which secures the future exchange of the assets for other assets to which that section does not apply, and

(II) assets which are strips within the meaning of *section 55*.

(b) Subject to *paragraphs (c)* and *(d)*, chargeable gains or allowable losses, which would otherwise accrue to an undertaking for collective investment on disposals deemed by virtue of *paragraph (a)* to have been made in a chargeable period (other than a period in which the collective investment business of the undertaking concerned ceases) of the undertaking, shall be treated, subject to *subparagraphs (ii)* and *(iii)*, as not accruing to it, and instead—

(i) there shall be ascertained the difference (in this subsection referred to as "*the net amount*") between the aggregate of those gains and the aggregate of those losses,

(ii) one-seventh of the net amount shall be treated as a chargeable gain or, where it represents an excess of losses over gains, as an allowable loss accruing to the undertaking on disposals of assets deemed to be made in the chargeable period, and

(iii) a further one-seventh shall be treated as a chargeable gain or, as the case may be, as an allowable loss accruing on disposals of assets deemed to be made in each succeeding chargeable period until the whole amount has been accounted for.

(c) For any chargeable period of less than one year, the fraction of one-seventh referred to in *paragraph (b)(iii)* shall be proportionately reduced and, where this paragraph has applied in relation to any chargeable period before the last such period for which *paragraph (b)(iii)* applies, the fraction treated as accruing in that last chargeable period shall be reduced so as to secure that no more than the whole of the net amount has been accounted for.

(d) Where the collective investment business of the undertaking concerned ceases before the beginning of the last of the chargeable periods for which *paragraph (b)(iii)* would apply in relation to a net amount, the fraction of that amount that is treated as accruing in the chargeable period in which the business ceases shall be such as to secure that the whole of the net amount has been accounted for.

(e) Where in a chargeable period an undertaking for collective investment incurs a loss on the disposal (in this paragraph referred to as "*the first-mentioned disposal*") of an asset the gain or loss in respect of a deemed disposal of which was included in a net amount to which *paragraph (b)(ii)* applied for any preceding chargeable period, so much of the allowable loss on the first-mentioned disposal as is equal to the excess of the amount of the loss over the amount which but for *paragraph (a)* would have been the allowable loss on the first-mentioned disposal shall be treated for the purposes of *paragraph (b)* as an allowable loss which would otherwise accrue to the undertaking for collective investment on disposals deemed by virtue of *paragraph (a)* to have been made in the chargeable period.

(5) Notwithstanding the Capital Gains Tax Acts, for the purposes of computing chargeable gains accruing to an undertaking for collective investment—

(a) (i) *section 556*, and

(ii) *section 607*,

shall not apply,

(b) *section 581* shall as respects—

(i) *subsections (1)* and *(2)* of that section, and

(ii) *subsection (3)* of that section, in so far as a chargeable gain is not thereby disregarded for the purposes of that subsection,

apply as if *subsection (4)*, *paragraph (a)(ii)* and *paragraph (c)* had not been enacted, and

(c) if the undertaking was carrying on a collective investment business on the 25th day of May, 1993, it shall be deemed to have acquired each of the assets it holds on the 5th day of April, 1994, apart from assets to which *section 607* applies, at the asset's market value on that date.

(6) Subject to *subsection (4)(b)*, where an undertaking for collective investment incurs allowable losses on disposals or deemed disposals of assets in a chargeable period, the amount (if any) by which the aggregate of such allowable losses exceeds the aggregate of chargeable gains on such disposals in the chargeable period shall—

(a) be disregarded for the purposes of *section 31*,

(b) be treated as reducing the income chargeable to income tax or corporation tax arising to the undertaking in that chargeable period, and

(c) to the extent that it is not treated as reducing income arising to the undertaking in that chargeable period, be treated for the purposes of the Capital Gains Tax Acts and this subsection as an allowable loss incurred on a disposal of an asset deemed to be made in the next chargeable period.

(7) (a) In this subsection—

"the appropriate amount in respect of the interest" means the appropriate amount in respect of the interest which would be determined in accordance with *Schedule 21* if the undertaking for collective investment was the first buyer and it carried on a trade to which *section 749(1)* applies but, in determining the appropriate amount in respect of the interest in accordance with *Schedule 21, paragraph 3(4)* of that Schedule shall apply as if "in the opinion of the Appeal Commissioners" were deleted;

"*securities*" has the same meaning as in *section 815*.

(b) Where in a chargeable period an undertaking for collective investment disposes of any securities and in the following chargeable period or its basis period interest becoming payable in respect of the securities is receivable by the undertaking for collective investment, then, the gain or loss accruing on the disposal shall be computed as if the price paid by the undertaking for collective investment for the securities was reduced by the appropriate amount in respect of the interest.

(c) Where for a chargeable period *paragraph (b)* applies so as to reduce the price paid for securities, the amount by which the price paid for the securities is reduced shall be treated as a loss arising in the following chargeable period from the disposal of the securities.

(8) Notwithstanding any provision of the Tax Acts or the Capital Gains Tax Acts other than *section 739*, unit holders in an undertaking for collective investment shall not be entitled to any credit for or repayment of any income tax, capital gains tax or corporation tax paid in respect of income arising to, capital gains accruing to or profits of the undertaking.

(9) (a) Notwithstanding *subsection (2)* but subject to *paragraph (b)*, *subsections (1)* to *(8)* and *section 739* shall be construed as respects designated undertakings for collective investment and guaranteed undertakings for collective investment as if every reference in those subsections and in that section—

(i) to the 5th day of April, 1994, were a reference to the 5th day of April, 1998, and

(ii) to the 6th day of April, 1994, were a reference to the 6th day of April, 1998,

and, as respects such an undertaking, those subsections and *section 739* shall not apply except as so construed.

(b) Where—

(i) the aggregate of the consideration (determined in accordance with *section 547*) given for the designated assets owned at any time after the 25th day of May, 1993, and before the 5th day of April, 1997, by a designated undertaking for collective investment is less than 80 per cent of the aggregate of the consideration (as so determined) given for the total assets owned by the undertaking at that time, or

(ii) at any time before the 5th day of April, 1997, a guaranteed undertaking for collective investment makes any payment to unit holders in the undertaking which is not a payment in cancellation of those units,

paragraph (a) shall be construed as respects that undertaking as if each reference in that paragraph—

(I) to the 5th day of April, 1998, were a reference to the 5th day of April, and

(II) to the 6th day of April, 1998, were a reference to the 6th day of April, subsequent to the time referred to in *subparagraph (i)* or *(ii)*, as the case may be.

Amendments

[1] Substituted by FA12 s30(1)(a). Deemed to have come into force and takes effect on and from 1 January 2012.

[2] Substituted by FA98 s49(1).

[3] Substituted by FA12 s30(1)(b). Deemed to have come into force and takes effect on and from 1 January 2012.

[4, 5, 6] Deleted by FA00 sched2.

Cross References

From Section 738

Section 3 Interpretation of Income Tax Acts.
Section 4 Interpretation of Corporation Tax Acts.
Section 21 The charge to corporation tax and exclusion of income tax and capital gains tax.
Section 28 Taxation of capital gains and rate of charge.
Section 31 Amount chargeable.
Section 55 Taxation of strips of securities.
Section 78 Computation of companies' chargeable gains.
Section 129 Irish resident company distributions not generally chargeable to corporation tax.
Section 237 Annual payments payable wholly out of taxed income.
Section 256 Interpretation (Chapter 4).
Section 547 Disposals and acquisitions treated as made at market value.
Section 556 Adjustment of allowable expenditure by reference to consumer price index.
Section 581 Disposals of shares or securities within 4 weeks of acquisition.
Section 607 Government and certain other securities.
Section 731 Chargeable gains accruing to unit trusts.
Section 734 Taxation of collective investment undertakings.
Section 737 Special investment schemes.
Section 739 Taxation of unit holders in undertakings for collective investment.
Section 743 Material interest in offshore funds.
Section 749 Dealers in securities.
Section 815 Taxation of income deemed to arise on certain sales of securities.
Schedule 21 Purchase and Sale of Securities: Appropriate Amount in Respect of the Interest

To Section 738

Section 172A Interpretation.
Section 541A Treatment of debts on a change in currency.
Section 731 Chargeable gains accruing to unit trusts.
Section 739A Reorganisation of undertakings for collective investment.
Section 739B Interpretation and application.
Section 815 Taxation of income deemed to arise on certain sales of securities.
Schedule 18A Restriction on Set-off of Pre-entry Losses
Schedule 24 Relief from Income Tax and Corporation Tax by Means of Credit in Respect of Foreign Tax

739 Taxation of unit holders in undertakings for collective investment

[FA93 s18; FA94 s57(b)]

(1) Subject to this section, as respects a payment made on or after the 6th day of April, 1994, in money or money's worth to a unit holder by reason of rights conferred on the holder as a result of holding units in an undertaking for collective investment—

(a) where the holder is not a company, the payment shall not be reckoned in computing the total income of the holder for the purposes of the Income Tax Acts, and

(b) where apart from this paragraph the payment would be taken into account for the purposes of computing income chargeable to corporation tax, such payment shall be treated as if it were the net amount of an annual payment chargeable to tax under Case IV of Schedule D from the gross amount of which income tax has been deducted at the [rate of 30 per cent][1].

(2) (a) This subsection shall apply to a payment which—

(i) is made on or after the 6th day of April, 1994, in money or money's worth, by reason of rights conferred on a unit holder as a result of holding units in an undertaking for collective investment, and

(ii) apart from *subsection (1)* would be charged to corporation tax under Case I of Schedule D.

(b) *Subsection (1)* shall not apply to a payment to which this subsection applies.

(c) For the purposes of the Tax Acts other than *paragraphs (d)* and *(e)*—

(i) the income for a chargeable period attributable to a payment to which this subsection applies shall be increased by an amount determined by reference to *paragraph (d)*, and

(ii) the amount so determined shall be deemed to be an amount of income tax which shall—

(I) be set off against corporation tax assessable on the unit holder for the chargeable period, or

(II) in so far as it cannot be set off in accordance with *clause (I)*, be repaid to the unit holder.

(d) The amount referred to in *paragraph (c)*, by which the income attributable to a payment to which this subsection applies is to be increased, shall be determined by the formula—

$$I \times \frac{A}{100 - A}$$

where—

I is the income attributable to a payment to which this subsection applies, and

A [is 30][2]

(e) For the purposes of this subsection, in computing income attributable to a payment—

(i) an amount shall be deducted from the payment if the payment arises on a sale or other transfer of ownership, or on a cancellation, redemption or repurchase by the undertaking for collective investment, of units or an interest in units, and an amount shall not be deducted otherwise,

(ii) subject to *subparagraphs (iii)* to *(v)*, the amount of the consideration in money or money's worth given by or on behalf of the unit holder for the acquisition of units or an interest in units for which the payment is made, and not any other amount, shall be deducted from the payment,

(iii) where units are acquired by the unit holder before the 6th day of April, 1994, in an undertaking for collective investment carrying on business on the 25th day of May, 1993, the consideration for the acquisition of the units shall be deemed to be the amount of their market value (within the meaning of *section 548*) on the 6th day of April, 1994, if that amount is greater than the consideration given, or deemed by virtue of *subparagraph (iv)* to be given, by the unit holder for their acquisition,

(iv) where units are acquired by a unit holder for a consideration which is less than the market value (within the meaning of *section 548*) of the units on the day the unit holder acquired them, the consideration given by the unit holder for those units shall be deemed to be that market value, and

(v) the amount of consideration given for units shall be determined in accordance with *section 580*.

(3) (a) Subject to *paragraph (b)* and *subsections (5)* and *(6)*, as respects a disposal on or after the 6th day of April, 1994, of units in an undertaking for collective investment by a person other than a company—

(i) no chargeable gain shall accrue on the disposal if the person disposing of the units acquired them on or after that date, and

(ii) if the person disposing of the units acquired them before that date, the chargeable gains on the disposal shall be computed as if—

(I) the consideration for the disposal were the market value of the units on the 5th day of April, 1994, and

(II) for the purposes of selecting the appropriate multiplier (within the meaning of *section 556*) and of applying *paragraph 25* of *Schedule 32* the disposal were made in the year 1993-94,

and for the purposes of this subsection and *subsection (4)* references to units shall be construed as including a reference to an interest in units, and accordingly this subsection and *subsection (4)* shall apply with any necessary modifications.

(b) *Clause (I)* of *paragraph (a)(ii)* shall not apply in relation to the disposal of units if as a consequence of the application of that clause—

(i) a gain would accrue on that disposal to the person making the disposal and either a smaller gain or loss would so accrue if that clause did not apply, or

(ii) a loss would so accrue and either a smaller loss or a gain would accrue if that clause did not apply,

and accordingly, in a case to which *subparagraph (i)* or *(ii)* applies, the amount of the gain or loss accruing on the disposal shall be computed without regard to *clause (I)* of *paragraph (a)(ii)* but, in a case where this paragraph would otherwise substitute a loss for a gain or a gain for a loss, it shall be assumed in relation to the disposal that the units were acquired by the person disposing of them for a consideration such that neither a gain nor a loss accrued to that person on making the disposal.

(4) (a) Subject to *paragraph (b)* and *subsections (5)* and *(6)*, as respects a disposal by a company on or after the 6th day of April, 1994, of units in an undertaking for collective investment, for the purposes of the Corporation Tax Acts—

(i) any chargeable gain accruing on the disposal shall, notwithstanding *section 21(3)*, be treated as if it were the net amount of a gain from the gross amount of which capital gains tax has been deducted at the [rate of 30 per cent][3].

(ii) the amount to be taken into account in respect of the chargeable gain in computing in accordance with *section 78* the company's chargeable gains for the accounting period in which the company disposes of the units shall be the gross amount of the chargeable gain, and

(iii) the capital gains tax treated as deducted from the gross amount of the chargeable gain shall—

(I) be set off against the corporation tax assessable on the company for the accounting period, or

(II) in so far as it cannot be set off in accordance with *clause (I)*, be repaid to the company.

(b) As respects a disposal by a company of units which it acquired before the 6th day of April, 1994, in an undertaking for collective investment carrying on business on the 25th day of May, 1993, *paragraph (a)* shall apply only to so much of the chargeable gain accruing to the company on that disposal of units as does not exceed the chargeable gain which would have accrued on that disposal had the company sold and immediately reacquired those units on the 5th day of April, 1994, at their market value on that day.

(c) This subsection shall be disregarded for the purposes of *section 546(2)*.

(5) (a) Where a person (in this subsection referred to as "*the disponer*") disposing of units in an undertaking for collective investment acquired them—

(i) on or after the 6th day of April, 1994, and

(ii) in such circumstances that by virtue of any enactment other than *section 556(4)* the disponer and the person from whom the disponer acquired them (in this subsection referred to as "*the previous owner*") were to be treated for the purposes of the Capital Gains Tax Acts as if the disponer's acquisition were for a consideration of such an amount as would secure that, on the disposal under which the disponer acquired them, neither a gain nor a loss accrued to the previous owner,

then, the previous owner's acquisition of the interest shall be treated as the disponer's acquisition of the interest.

(b) Where the previous owner acquired the units disposed of on or after the 6th day of April, 1994, and in circumstances similar to those referred to in *paragraph (a)*, the acquisition of the units by the previous owner's predecessor shall be treated for the purposes of this section as the previous owner's acquisition, and so on back through previous acquisitions in similar circumstances until the first such acquisition before the 6th day of April, 1994, or, as the case may be, until an acquisition on a disposal on or after that date.

(6) Where an undertaking for collective investment was not carrying on a collective investment business on the 25th day of May, 1993, this section shall apply as respects payments by, or disposals of units in, that undertaking as if—

(a) "on or after the 6th day of April, 1994," were deleted from *subsections (1), (2), (3)* and *(4)*, and

(b) *paragraphs (a)(ii)* and *(b)* were deleted from *subsection (3)*.

Amendments

[1] Substituted by FA12 s30(1)(c). Applies as respects payments made on or after 8 February 2012.

[2] Substituted by FA12 s30(1)(d). Applies as respects payments made on or after 8 February 2012.

[3] Substituted by FA12 s30(1)(e). Applies as respects any disposal made on or after 8 February 2012.

Cross References

From Section 739

Section 21 The charge to corporation tax and exclusion of income tax and capital gains tax.
Section 78 Computation of companies' chargeable gains.
Section 546 Allowable losses.
Section 548 Valuation of assets.
Section 556 Adjustment of allowable expenditure by reference to consumer price index.
Section 580 Shares, securities, etc: identification.
Schedule 32 Transitional Provisions

To Section 739

Section 731 Chargeable gains accruing to unit trusts.
Section 738 Undertakings for collective investment.
Section 739B Interpretation and application.
Schedule 2B Investment Undertakings: Declarations

739A Reorganisation of undertakings for collective investment

[(1) (a) In this section "*undertaking for collective investment*" has the meaning assigned to it in *section 738(1)*.

(b) Where an undertaking for collective investment (in this section referred to as the "*first undertaking*") disposes of assets (in this section referred to as "*transferred assets*") to another undertaking for collective investment in exchange for the issue of units to the first undertaking by that other undertaking for collective investment, no chargeable gains shall accrue to the first undertaking on that disposal.

(2) For the purposes of computing a gain accruing to the first undertaking on a disposal or first deemed disposal, under *section 738(4)(a)(i)*, of the units referred to in *subsection (1)*, notwithstanding any other provision of the Capital Gains Tax Acts, the amount or value of the consideration in money or money's worth given by the first undertaking for the acquisition of the units is—

(a) where the transferred assets fell within *section 738(4)(a)(i)*, the value of the transferred assets on their latest deemed disposal by the first undertaking under that section, and

(b) where the transferred assets did not fall within *section 738(4)(a)(i)*, the cost incurred by the first mentioned undertaking in acquiring the transferred assets.][1]

Amendments

[1] Inserted by FA00 s57(c).

Cross References

From Section 739A

Section 738 Undertakings for collective investment.

CHAPTER 1A

Investment Undertakings

739B Interpretation and application

[(1) In this Chapter and in Schedule 2B—

"*the Acts*" means the Tax Acts and the Capital Gains Tax Acts;

"*approved minimum retirement fund*" has the meaning assigned to it in section 784C;

"*approved retirement fund*" has the meaning assigned to it in section 784A;

"*chargeable event*", in relation to an investment undertaking in respect of a unit holder, means—

(a) the making of a relevant payment by the investment undertaking,

(b) the making of any other payment by the investment undertaking to a person, by virtue of that person being a unit holder (whether or not in respect of the cancellation, redemption or repurchase of a unit) [...][1],

(c) the transfer by a unit holder, by way of sale or otherwise [...][2], of entitlement to a unit in the investment undertaking[...][3]

[(cc) the appropriation or cancellation of units of a unit holder by an investment undertaking for the purposes of meeting the amount of appropriate tax payable on any gain arising by virtue of *paragraph (c)*, [...][4]][5]

[(ccc) the ending of a relevant period, [where such ending is not otherwise a chargeable event within the meaning of this section,][6] and for the purposes of this paragraph "*relevant period*", in relation to a unit in an investment undertaking, means a period of 8 years beginning with the acquisition of that unit by a unit holder and each subsequent period of 8 years beginning immediately after the preceding relevant period, and][7]

(d) a chargeable event shall be deemed to happen on 31 December 2000 in respect of all unit holders (if any) at that date in relation to an investment undertaking—

(i) which commenced on or after 1 April 2000, or

(ii) which was on 31 March 2000 a specified collective investment undertaking,

but does not include—

[(I) any exchange by a unit holder, effected by way of a bargain made at arm's length by an investment undertaking which is an umbrella scheme, of units in a sub-fund of the investment undertaking, for units in another sub-fund of the investment undertaking,

(II) any exchange by a unit holder, effected by way of a bargain made at arm's length by an investment undertaking, of units in the investment undertaking for other units in the investment undertaking,

[(IIa) any transaction in relation to, or in respect of, relevant units (within the meaning of *subsection (2A)(a)*) in an investment undertaking which transaction arises only by virtue of a change of court funds manager for that undertaking,][8]

(III) any transaction in relation to, or in respect of, units which are held in a recognised clearing system, and

(IV) the transfer by a unit holder of entitlement to a unit where the transfer is—

(A) [between a husband and wife or between civil partners][9],

(B) between the spouses or former spouses concerned (as the case may be), by virtue or in consequence of an order made under Part III of the Family Law (Divorce) Act, 1996, on or following the granting of a decree of divorce,

[(BA) between the civil partners or former civil partners concerned (as the case may be), by virtue of or in consequence of an order made under Part 12 of the Civil Partnership and Certain Rights and Obligations of Cohabitants Act 2010, on or following the granting of a decree of dissolution,][10]

[(C) between the spouses concerned, by virtue or in consequence of an order made under Part II of the Family Law Act 1995, on or following the granting of a decree of judicial separation within the meaning of that Act,

(D) between the spouses or former spouses concerned (as the case may be), by virtue of an order or other determination of like effect, which is analogous to an order referred to in *subparagraph (B)* or *(C)*, of a court under the law of a territory other than the State made under or in consequence of the dissolution of a marriage or the legal separation of the spouses, being a dissolution or legal separation that is entitled to be recognised as valid in the State, or

(DA) between the civil partners or former civil partners concerned (as the case may be), by virtue of an order or other determination of like effect, which is analogous to an order referred to in *subparagraph (BA)*, of a court under the law of a territory other than the State made under or in consequence of the dissolution of a civil partnership, being a dissolution that is entitled to be recognised as valid in the State,][11]

but on the happening of a chargeable event following such a transfer, the then unit holder shall be treated as having acquired the unit transferred at the same cost as the person who transferred the unit;][12]

"*collective investor*", in relation to an authorised investment company (within the meaning of Part XIII of the Companies Act, 1990), means an investor, being a life assurance company, pension fund or other investor—

(a) who invests in securities or any other property whatever with moneys contributed by 50 or more persons—

(i) none of whom has at any time directly or indirectly contributed more than 5 per cent of such moneys, and

(ii) each of a majority of whom has contributed moneys to the investor with the intention of being entitled, otherwise than on death of any person or by reference to a risk of any kind to any person or property, to receive from the investor—

(I) a payment which, or

(II) payments the aggregate of which,

exceeds those moneys by a part of the profits or income arising to the investor,

and

(b) who invests in the authorised investment company primarily for the benefit of those persons;

["*courtfunds manager*" means a person appointed by the Service to set up and administer an investment undertaking with money under the control or subject to the order of any Court;][13]

["*credit union*" has the meaning assigned to it in section 2 of the Credit Union Act 1997;][14]

"*distribution*" has the same meaning as in the Corporation Tax Acts;

"*intermediary*" means a person who—

(a) carries on a business which consists of, or includes, the receipt of payments from an investment undertaking on behalf of other persons, or

(b) holds units in an investment undertaking on behalf of other persons;

"*investment undertaking*" means—

(a) a unit trust scheme, other than—

(i) a unit trust mentioned in section 731(5)(*a*), or

(ii) a special investment scheme,

which is or is deemed to be an authorised unit trust scheme (within the meaning of the Unit Trusts Act, 1990) and has not had its authorisation under that Act revoked,

(b) any other undertaking which is an undertaking for collective investment in transferable securities within the meaning of the relevant Regulations, being an undertaking which holds an authorisation, which has not been revoked, issued pursuant to the relevant Regulations, [and][15]

(c) any authorised investment company (within the meaning of Part XIII of the Companies Act, 1990)—

(i) which has not had its authorisation under that Part of that Act revoked, and

(ii) (I) which has been designated in that authorisation as an investment company which may raise capital by promoting the sale of its shares to the public and has not ceased to be so designated, or

(II) each of the shareholders of which is a collective investor,

[...][16]

[...][17]

which is not an offshore fund (within the meaning of section 743); but includes any company limited by shares or guarantee which—

(A) is wholly owned by such an investment undertaking or its trustees, if any, for the benefit of the holders of units in that undertaking, and

(B) is so owned solely for the purpose of limiting the liability of that undertaking or its trustees, as the case may be, in respect of futures contracts, options contracts or other financial instruments with similar risk characteristics, by enabling it or its trustees, as the case may be, to invest or deal in such investments through the company,

which is not an offshore fund (within the meaning of *section 743*);

["*money market fund*" has the same meaning as it has in Regulation (EC) No. 2423/2001 of the European Central Bank of 22 November 2001*;][18]

* OJ No. L333 of 17 December 2001, p.1

"*pension scheme*" means an exempt approved scheme within the meaning of *section 774* or a retirement annuity contract or a trust scheme to which *section 784* or *785* applies;

"*qualifying fund manager*" has the meaning assigned to it in section 784A;

["*qualifying management company*", in relation to an investment undertaking, means a company which, in the course of a trade of managing investments, manages the whole or any part of the investments and other activities of the business of the undertaking;][19]

["*qualifying savings manager*" has the meaning assigned to it in *section 848B* (inserted by the *Finance Act, 2001*);][20]

[…][21]

"*relevant gains*", in relation to an investment undertaking, means gains accruing to the investment undertaking, being gains which would constitute chargeable gains in the hands of a person resident in the State including gains which would so constitute chargeable gains if all assets concerned were chargeable assets and no exemption from capital gains tax applied;

"*relevant income*", in relation to an investment undertaking, means any amounts of income, profits or gains which arise to or are receivable by the investment undertaking, being amounts of income, profits or gains—

(a) which are or are to be paid to unit holders as relevant payments,

(b) out of which relevant payments are or are to be made to unit holders, or

(c) which are or are to be accumulated for the benefit of, or invested for the benefit of, unit holders,

and which if they arose to an individual resident in the State would in the hands of the individual constitute income for the purposes of income tax;

"*relevant payment*" means a payment including a distribution made to a unit holder by an investment undertaking by reason of rights conferred on the unit holder as a result of holding a unit or units in the investment undertaking, where such payments are made annually or at more frequent intervals, other than a payment made in respect of the cancellation, redemption or repurchase of a unit;

"*relevant profits*", in relation to an investment undertaking, means the relevant income and relevant gains of the investment undertaking;

["*relevant Regulations*" means the European Communities (Undertaking for Collective Investment in Transferable Securities) Regulations 1989 (S.I. No. 78 of 1989) as amended or extended from time to time and any other regulations that may be construed as one with those Regulations;][22]

"*return*" means a return under section 739F;

["*Service*" means the Courts Service;][23]

"*specified collective investment undertaking*" and "*specified company*" have, respectively, the meanings assigned to them in *section 734(1)*;

"*special investment scheme*" has the same meaning as in *section 737*;

["*special savings incentive account*" has the meaning assigned to it by *section 848B* (inserted by the *Finance Act, 2001*);][24]

"*standard rate*" has the same meaning as in *section 3(1)*;

"*umbrella scheme*" means an investment undertaking—

(a) which is divided into a number of sub-funds, and

(b) in which the unit holders are entitled to exchange units in one sub-fund for units in another;

"unit" includes any investment made by a unit holder, such as a subscription for shares or a contribution of capital, in an investment undertaking, being an investment which entitles the investor—

(a) to a share of the investments or relevant profits of, or

(b) to receive a relevant payment from,

the investment undertaking;

"*unit holder*", in relation to an investment undertaking, means any person who by reason of the holding of a unit, or under the terms of a unit, in the investment undertaking is entitled to a share of any of the investments or relevant profits of, or to receive a relevant payment from, the investment undertaking.

[(1A) The definition of "*recognised clearing system*" in section 246A(2) applies for the purposes of this section as it applies for the purposes of section 246A.][25]

(2) For the purposes of this Chapter, Schedule 2B and section 904D, references to an investment undertaking (other than in this subsection) shall be construed so as to include a reference to a trustee, management company or other such person who—

(a) is authorised to act on behalf, or for the purposes, of the investment undertaking, and

(b) habitually does so,

to the extent that such construction brings into account for the purposes of this Chapter, Schedule 2B and section 904D any matter relating to the investment undertaking, being a matter which would not otherwise be brought into account for those purposes; but such construction shall not render the trustee, management company or other such person liable in a personal capacity to any tax imposed by this Chapter on an investment undertaking.

[(2A) (a) Where money under the control or subject to the order of any Court is applied to acquire units (in this section referred to as "*relevant units*") in an investment undertaking, *subsections (2)* and *(3)* of *section 739E*, *section 739F* and *section 904D* shall apply as if references in those sections and subsections to the investment undertaking were to read as references to the Service.

(b) The Service shall in respect of each year of assessment, on or before 28 February in the year following the year of assessment, make a return (including where it is the case, a nil return) to the Revenue Commissioners in electronic format approved by them, which in respect of each year of assessment—

(i) specifies the total amount of gains (in this section referred to as the "*total gains*") arising to the investment undertaking in respect of relevant units, and

(ii) specifies in respect of each person who is or was beneficially entitled to those units—

(I) where available, the name and address of the person,

(II) the amount of the total gains to which the person has beneficial entitlement, and

(III) such other information as the Revenue Commissioners may require.][26]

[(3) This Chapter applies to an investment undertaking and the unit holders in relation to that investment undertaking where the investment undertaking—

(a) is on 31 March 2000 a specified collective investment undertaking, from 1 April 2000,

(b) first issued units on or after 1 April 2000, from the day of such first issue, or

(c) was a unit trust mentioned in *section 731(5)(a)*, from the day on which the unit trust became an investment undertaking.][27]

(4) Where this Chapter applies to an investment undertaking, *sections 734*, *738* and *739* shall not apply to that investment undertaking or to unit holders in relation to that investment undertaking.

(5) Schedule 2B has effect for the purposes of supplementing this Chapter.

(6) For the purposes of this Chapter and Schedule 2B, where a holder of units in an investment undertaking is—

(a) an investment undertaking,

(b) a special investment scheme, or

(c) a unit trust to which *section 731(5)(a)* applies,

the unit holder shall be treated as being entitled to the units so held.][28]

Amendments

[1] Deleted by FA01 s74(1)(a)(i)(I)(A). Applies on or after 15 February 2001.

[2] Deleted by FA01 s74(1)(a)(i)(I)(B). Applies on or after 15 February 2001.

[3] Deleted by FA04 s29(1)(a)(i). This section applies as respects the appropriation or cancellation of a unit on or after 4 February 2004.

[4] Deleted by FA06 s50(1)(a)(i). This section applies and has effect as respects any chargeable event occurring on or after 31 March 2006

[5] Inserted by FA04 s29(1)(a)(ii). This section applies as respects the appropriation or cancellation of a unit on or after 4 February 2004.

[6] Inserted by FA08 s39(1)(a). Applies and has effect as respects any chargeable event (within the meaning of section 739B(1)) occurring on or after 13 March 08.

[7] Inserted by FA06 s50(1)(a)(ii). This section applies and has effect as respects any chargeable event occurring on or after 31 March 2006

[8] Inserted by FA05 s40(a)(i).

[9] Substituted by F(No.3)A11 sched1(179).

[10] Inserted by F(No.3)A11 sched1(180).

[11] Substituted by F(No.3)A11 sched1(181).

[12] Substituted by FA01 s74(1)(a)(i)(I)(C). Applies on or after 15 February 2001.

[13] Inserted by FA05 s40(a)(ii).

[14] Inserted by FA03 s53(a)(i)(I).

[15] Inserted by FA13 s42(1)(c)(i). Applies in respect of an investment limited partnership that has been granted an authorisation under section 8 of the Investment Limited Partnerships Act 1994 on or after 13 February 2013.

[16] Deleted by FA13 s42(1)(c)(ii). Applies in respect of an investment limited partnership that has been granted an authorisation under section 8 of the Investment Limited Partnerships Act 1994 on or after 13 February 2013.

[17] Deleted by FA13 s42(1)(c)(iii). Applies in respect of an investment limited partnership that has been granted an authorisation under section 8 of the Investment Limited Partnerships Act 1994 on or after 13 February 2013.

[18] Inserted by FA03 s53(a)(i)(II).

[19] Substituted by FA10 s31(1)(a). Has effect as on and from 3 April 2010.

[20] Inserted by FA01 s74(1)(a)(i)(II). Applies on or after 15 February 2001.

[21] Deleted by FA03 s49(3)(c)(i). Shall apply as on and from the date of 28 March 2003

[22] Substituted by FA03 s53(a)(i)(III).

[20] Inserted by FA03 s53(a)(i)(IV).

[21] Inserted by FA01 s74(1)(a)(i)(III). Applies on or after 15 February 2001.

[22] Inserted by FA03 s49(3)(c)(ii). Shall apply as on and from the date of 28 March 2003

[23] Inserted by FA03 s53(a)(ii).

[24] Substituted by FA01 s74(1)(a)(ii). Applies on or after 1 April 2000.

[25] Inserted by FA00 s58(a).

Revenue Briefings

Tax Briefing

Tax Briefing December 2000 – Issue 42 pg 29 – Investment Undertakings

Cross References

From Section 739B

Section 3 Interpretation of Income Tax Acts.
Section 731 Chargeable gains accruing to unit trusts.
Section 734 Taxation of collective investment undertakings.
Section 737 Special investment schemes.
Section 738 Undertakings for collective investment.
Section 739 Taxation of unit holders in undertakings for collective investment.
Section 743 Material interest in offshore funds.
Section 774 Certain approved schemes: exemptions and reliefs.
Section 784 Retirement annuities: relief for premiums.
Section 785 Approval of contracts for dependants or for life assurance.

To Section 739B

Section 172A Interpretation.
Section 246 Interest payments by companies and to non-residents.
Section 615 Company reconstruction or amalgamation: transfer of assets.
Section 617 Transfers of assets, other than trading stock, within group.
Section 739D Gain arising on a chargeable event.
Section 739E Deduction of tax on the occurrence of a chargeable event.
Section 739G Taxation of unit holders in investment undertakings.Taxation of unit holders in investment undertakings.
Section 747G Tax treatment of relevant UCITS.
Section 790B "Exemption of cross-border scheme.
Section 848B Interpretation.
Section 891B Returns of certain payments made by certain persons.
Section 904D Power of inspection (returns and collection of appropriate tax): investment undertakings.
Schedule 2 Machinery for Assessment, Charge and Payment of Tax under Schedule C and, in Certain Cases, Schedule D

739BA Personal portfolio investment undertaking

[(1) In this section—

"*investor*" means—

(a) in relation to an investment undertaking, a unit holder in the investment undertaking who is an individual, and

(b) in relation to an offshore fund to which Chapter 4 applies, an individual who has a material interest in the offshore fund;

"*land*" has the same meaning as in *section 730BA*;

"*material interest*" shall be construed in accordance with *section 743*;

"*offshore fund*" has the meaning assigned to it by *section 743*;

"*public*" has the same meaning as in *section 730BA*.

(2) In this Chapter and in Chapter 4 of this Part "personal portfolio investment undertaking" means—

(a) in relation to an investor in an investment undertaking, an investment undertaking, and

(b) in relation to an investor in an offshore fund to which Chapter 4 applies, such an offshore fund,

under the terms of which some or all of the property of the undertaking or, as the case may be, the offshore fund, may be, or was, selected by, or the selection of some or all of the property may be, or was, influenced by—

(i) the investor,

(ii) a person acting on behalf of the investor,

(iii) a person connected with the investor,

(iv) a person connected with a person acting on behalf of the investor,

(v) the investor and a person connected with the investor, or

(vi) a person acting on behalf of both the investor and a person connected with the investor,

where "*person connected*" in this subsection means a person connected within the meaning of *section 10*.

(3) For the purposes of *subsection (2)* and without prejudice to the application of that subsection, the terms of an investment undertaking or an offshore fund, as the case may be, shall be treated as permitting the selection referred to in that subsection where—

(a) the terms of such undertaking or offshore fund, or any other agreement between any person referred to in that subsection and such undertaking or offshore fund concerned—

(i) allow the exercise of an option by any person referred to in that subsection to make the selection referred to in that subsection,

(ii) give such undertaking or offshore fund discretion to offer any person referred to in that subsection the right to make the selection referred to in that subsection, or

(iii) allow any of the persons referred to in that subsection the right to request, subject to the agreement of such undertaking or offshore fund, a change in those terms such that the selection referred to in that subsection may be made by any of those persons,

or

(b) the investor is unable under those terms to select any of the property but any of the persons referred to in that subsection has or had the option of requiring such undertaking or offshore fund to appoint an investment advisor (no matter how such a person is described) in relation to the selection of the property.

(4) An investment undertaking or an offshore fund, as the case may be, is not a personal portfolio investment undertaking if—

(a) the only property which may be or has been selected satisfies the condition specified in *subsection (5)*, and

(b) the terms under which such undertaking or offshore fund is offered meet the requirements of *subsection (6)*.

(5) The condition specified in this subsection is that at the time when the property is or was available to be selected the opportunity to select—

(a) in the case of land, that property, and

(b) in any other case, property of the same description as the first-mentioned property,

is or was available to the public on terms which provide or provided that the opportunity to select the property is or was available to any person falling within the terms of the opportunity and that opportunity is or was clearly identified to the public, in marketing or other promotional literature published at that time by the investment undertaking or offshore fund concerned, as available generally to any person falling within the terms of the opportunity.

(6) The requirements of this subsection are that—

(a) the investment undertaking or offshore fund concerned does not subject any person to any treatment in connection with the opportunity which is different or more burdensome than any treatment to which any other person is or may be subject, and

(b) where the terms of the opportunity referred to in *subsection (5)* include terms—

(i) which set out the capital requirement of the opportunity and this requirement is identified to the public in the marketing or other promotional material published by the investment undertaking or offshore fund at the time the property is available to be selected, and

(ii) indicating that 50 per cent or more by value of the property referred to in that subsection is or is to be land,

then the amount any one person may invest in the investment undertaking or offshore fund shall not represent more than 1 per cent of the capital requirement (exclusive of any borrowings) of the opportunity as so identified.][1]

Amendments

[1] Inserted by FA07 s40(1) and applies as respects (a) the occurrence of a chargeable event in relation to an investment undertaking (within the meaning of Chapter 1A of Part 27), (b) the receipt by a person of a payment in respect of a material interest in an offshore fund (within the meaning of Chapter 4 of Part 27), and (c) the disposal in whole or in part of a material interest in an offshore fund (within that meaning), on or after 20 February 2007.

Cross References

From Section 739BA

Section 10 Connected persons.
Section 730B Taxation of policyholders.
Section 730BA Personal portfolio life policy.
Section 743 Material interest in offshore funds.

739C Charge to tax

[(1) Notwithstanding anything in the Acts, an investment undertaking shall, […][1] not be chargeable to tax in respect of relevant profits otherwise than to the extent provided for in this Chapter.

[…][2]][3]

(2) Notwithstanding *Chapter 4* of *Part 8*, that Chapter shall apply to a deposit (within the meaning of that Chapter) to which an investment undertaking is for the time being entitled as if such deposit were not a relevant deposit within the meaning of that Chapter.][4]

Amendments

[1] Deleted by FA05 s44(c)(i).

[2] Deleted by FA05 s44(c)(ii).

[3] Substituted by FA03 s53(b).

[4] Inserted by FA00 s58(a).

Cross References

From Section 739C

Section 237 Annual payments payable wholly out of taxed income.
Section 256 Interpretation (Chapter 4).

739D Gain arising on a chargeable event

[(1) [In this Chapter and Schedule 2B][1]—

[(a) references to an investment undertaking being associated with another investment undertaking are references to both investment undertakings being set up and promoted by the same person,][2]

(b) references to an amount invested by a unit holder in an investment undertaking for the acquisition of a unit (in this paragraph referred to as the "*original unit*"), where the original unit is a unit in a sub-fund of an umbrella scheme and the original unit has been exchanged for a unit or units of another sub-fund of the umbrella scheme, are references to the amount invested by the unit holder for the acquisition of the original unit,[…][3]

[(bb) references to an amount invested by a unit holder in an investment undertaking for the acquisition of a unit (in this paragraph referred to as the "*original unit*"), where the original unit has been exchanged for a unit or units in a transaction of the type referred to in *paragraph (IIa)* of the definition of "*chargeable event*" in *section 739B(1)*, are references to the amount invested by the unit holder for the acquisition of the original unit, and][4]

(c) references to an amount invested by a unit holder in an investment undertaking for the acquisition of a unit shall, where the investment undertaking was on 31 March 2000 a specified collective investment undertaking and the unit was at that time a unit (within the meaning of *section 734(1)*) held by the unit holder as a unit holder (within the meaning of the said section) in relation to the specified collective investment undertaking, be references to the amount invested by the unit holder for the acquisition of the unit (within the said meaning) of the specified collective investment undertaking, or where that unit was otherwise acquired by the unit holder, the value of that unit at its date of acquisition by the unit holder.

(2) On the happening of a chargeable event in relation to an investment undertaking in respect of a unit holder, there shall, subject to this section [and in accordance with *subsection (2A)*][5], be treated as arising to the investment undertaking a gain in the amount of—

(a) where the chargeable event is the making of a relevant payment, the amount of the relevant payment,

(b) where the chargeable event is the making of any other payment by the investment undertaking to a person, by virtue of that person being a unit holder, otherwise than on the cancellation, redemption or repurchase of a unit, the amount of the payment,

(c) where the chargeable event is the making of a payment by the investment undertaking to a unit holder, on the cancellation, redemption or repurchase of a unit—

(i) the amount determined under *subsection (3)*, or

(ii) where the investment undertaking has made an election under *subsection (5)*, the amount of the payment reduced by the amount invested by the unit holder in the investment undertaking in acquiring the unit, and where the unit was otherwise acquired by the unit holder, the amount so invested shall be the value of the unit at the time of its acquisition by the unit holder,

(d) where the chargeable event is the transfer by a unit holder of entitlement to a unit,

(i) the amount determined under *subsection (4)*, or

(ii) where the investment undertaking has made an election under *subsection (5)*, the value of the unit transferred at the time of transfer reduced by the amount invested by the unit holder in the investment undertaking in acquiring the unit, and where the unit was otherwise acquired by the unit holder, the amount so invested shall be the value of the unit at the time of its acquisition by the unit holder, […][6]

[(dd) where the chargeable event is the appropriation or cancellation of units by an investment undertaking as a consequence of the transfer by a unit holder of entitlement to a unit, [except as a consequence of a gain arising on a chargeable event within the meaning of *paragraph (ccc)* in *section 739B(1)*,][7] the amount determined under *subsection (5A)*, […][8]][9]

[(ddd) where the chargeable event is the ending of a relevant period in relation to a unit of a unit holder—

(i) the excess (if any) of the value of the unit, without having regard to any amount of appropriate tax (within the meaning of *section 739E*) thereby arising, held by the unit holder on the day of that ending over the total amount invested in the investment undertaking by the unit holder for the acquisition of the unit, and where the unit was otherwise acquired by the unit holder, the amount so invested to acquire that unit shall be the value of the unit at the time of its acquisition by the unit holder, or

(ii) in a case where the investment undertaking has made an election under *subsection (5B)*, the amount determined under that subsection, and][10]

(e) where the chargeable event is deemed to happen on 31 December 2000, the excess (if any) of the value of the units held by the unit holder on that day over the total amount invested in the investment undertaking by the unit holder for the acquisition of the units, and where any unit was otherwise acquired by the unit holder, the amount so invested to acquire that unit shall be the value of the unit at the time of its acquisition by the unit holder.

[(2A) Where—

[(a) a chargeable event occurs in relation to an investment undertaking in respect of a unit holder, and][11]

(b) a chargeable event within the meaning of *paragraph (ccc)* of the definition of chargeable event in *section 739B(1)* occurred previously in relation to an investment undertaking in respect of a unit holder,

then the gain arising on the chargeable event referred to in *paragraph (a)* shall be determined as if *section 739B(1)(ccc)* had not been enacted.][12]

[(3) The amount referred to in *subsection (2)(c)* is the amount determined by the formula—

$$P - \frac{(C \times P)}{V}$$

where—

P is the amount in money or money's worth payable to the unit holder on the cancellation, redemption or repurchase of units, without having regard to any amount of appropriate tax (within the meaning of *section 739E*) thereby arising,

C is the total amount invested by the unit holder in the investment undertaking to acquire the units held by the unit holder immediately [before the chargeable event, reduced by any amount of first tax (within the meaning of *section 739E (1A)(a)*),][13] and—

(a) where any unit was otherwise acquired by the unit holder, or

(b) where a chargeable event was deemed to happen on 31 December 2000 in respect of the unit holder of that unit,

the amount so invested to acquire the unit is—

(i) where *paragraph (a)* applies, the value of the unit at the time of its acquisition by the unit holder, and

(ii) where *paragraph (b)* applies, the greater of the cost of first acquisition of the unit by the unit holder and the value of the unit on 31 December 2000, without having regard to any amount of appropriate tax (within the meaning of *section 739E*) thereby arising,

and

V is the total value of the units held by the unit holder immediately before the chargeable event.

(4) The amount referred to in *subsection (2)(d)* is the amount determined by the formula—

$$V1 - \frac{(C \times V1)}{V2}$$

where—

V1 is the value of the units transferred, at the time of transfer, without having regard to any amount of appropriate tax (within the meaning of *section 739E*) thereby arising,

C is the total amount invested by the unit holder in the investment undertaking to acquire the units held by the unit holder immediately [before the chargeable event, reduced by any amount of first tax (within the meaning of *section 739E (1A)(a)*),][14] and—

(a) where any unit was otherwise acquired by the unit holder, or

(b) a chargeable event was deemed to happen on 31 December 2000 in respect of the unit holder of that unit,

the amount so invested to acquire the unit is—

(i) where *paragraph (a)* applies, the value of the unit at the time of its acquisition by the unit holder, and

(ii) where *paragraph (b)* applies, the greater of the cost of first acquisition of the unit by the unit holder and the value of the unit on 31 December 2000, without having regard to any amount of appropriate tax (within the meaning of *section 739E*) thereby arising,

and

V2 is the total value of the units held by the unit holder immediately before the chargeable event.

(5) (a) The election referred to in *paragraphs (c)* and *(d)* of *subsection (2)* is an irrevocable election made by an investment undertaking in respect of all its unit holders at the time of the election or at any other time, so that, for the purposes of identifying units acquired with units subsequently disposed of by a unit holder, units acquired at an earlier time are deemed to have been disposed of before units acquired at a later time.

(b) On the first occasion that an investment undertaking is required to compute a gain on the happening of a chargeable event in respect of a unit holder on the cancellation, redemption, repurchase or transfer of a unit, and—

(i) the gain is computed in accordance with *paragraph (a)*, the investment undertaking will be deemed to have made the election specified in that paragraph, or

(ii) the gain is not computed in accordance with *paragraph (a)*, an election under *paragraph (a)* shall not be made.][15]

[(5A) [Subject to *subsection (5AA)*, the amount][16] referred to in *subsection (2)(dd)* is the amount determined—

(a) where the unit holder is a company, by the formula—

$$A \times G \times \frac{100}{100 - (G \times 25)}$$

and

(b) in any other case, by the formula—

$$A \times G \times \frac{100}{100 - [(G \times 41)]^{17}}$$

where in relation to the formula in *paragraphs (a)* and *(b)*—

A is the appropriate tax payable on the transfer by a unit holder of entitlement to a unit in accordance with *subsection (2)(d)*, and

G is the amount of the gain on that transfer of that unit divided by the value of that unit.][18]

[(5AA) Where the unit holder is a company—

(a) the formula specified in *subsection (5A)(a)* shall not apply unless the unit holder has made the declaration referred to in *paragraph (b)*, and

(b) the formula specified in *subsection (5A)(b)* shall apply unless immediately before the chargeable event, the investment undertaking is in possession of a declaration from the unit holder to the effect that the unit holder is a company and which includes the company's tax reference number (within the meaning of *section 891B(1)*).][19]

[(5B) (a) The election referred to in *paragraph (ddd)* of *subsection (2)* is an irrevocable election made by an investment undertaking in respect of all its unit holders at the time of the election or at any other time and the amount is as determined by the formula—

$$A1 - A2$$

where—

A1 is the value of the unit at the later of 30 June or 31 December prior to the date of the chargeable event,

and

A2 is—

(i) the total amount invested in the investment undertaking by the unit holder for the acquisition of the unit, and where the unit was otherwise acquired by the unit holder, the amount so invested to acquire that unit shall be the value of the unit at the time of its acquisition by the unit holder, or

(ii) if a chargeable event to which *paragraph (ccc)* of *section 739B(1)* refers has previously occurred, the value of the unit at the later of 30 June or 31 December prior to the date of the latest of such chargeable events.

(b) On the first occasion that the investment undertaking is required to compute a gain on the happening of a chargeable event within the meaning of *paragraph (ccc)* in *section 739B(1)* in respect of a unit holder, and—

(i) the gain is computed in accordance with *paragraph (a)*, the investment undertaking will be deemed to have made the election specified in that paragraph, or

(ii) the gain is not computed in accordance with *paragraph* (*a*), an election under *paragraph* (*a*) shall not be made.][20]

(6) A gain shall not be treated as arising to an investment undertaking on the happening of a chargeable event in respect of a unit holder where, immediately before the chargeable event, the unit holder—

(a) is a pension scheme which has made a declaration to the investment undertaking in accordance with *paragraph 2* of *Schedule 2B*,

(b) is a company carrying on life business within the meaning of *section 706*, and which company has made a declaration to the investment undertaking in accordance with *paragraph 3* of *Schedule 2B*,

(c) is another investment undertaking which has made a declaration to the investment undertaking in accordance with *paragraph 4* of *Schedule 2B*,

[(cc) is an investment limited partnership within the meaning of *section 739J* which has made a declaration to the investment undertaking in accordance with *paragraph 4A* of Schedule 2B,][21]

(d) is a special investment scheme which has made a declaration to the investment undertaking in accordance with *paragraph 5* of *Schedule 2B*,

(e) is a unit trust to which *section 731(5)(a)* applies, and the unit trust has made a declaration to the investment undertaking in accordance with *paragraph 6* of *Schedule 2B*,

[(f) (i) is a person who—

(I) is exempt from income tax under Schedule D by virtue of *section 207(1)(b)*, or

(II) is exempt from corporation tax by virtue of *section 207(1)(b)* as it applies for the purposes of corporation tax under *section 76(6)*,

and

(ii) has made a declaration to the investment undertaking in accordance with *paragraph 7* of *Schedule 2B*,][22]

(g) is a qualifying management company or a specified company and has made a declaration to the investment undertaking in accordance with *paragraph 8* of [*Schedule 2B*,][23]

[(h) is a person who is entitled to exemption from income tax and capital gains tax by virtue of *section 784A(2)* (as amended by the Finance Act, 2000) or by virtue of *section 848E* (inserted by the *Finance Act, 2001*) and the units held are assets of an approved retirement fund, an approved minimum retirement fund or, as the case may be, a special savings incentive account, and the qualifying fund manager, or, as the case may be, the qualifying savings manager has made a declaration to the investment undertaking in accordance with *paragraph 9* of [Schedule 2B, or][24]][25]

[(i) is a person who is entitled to exemption from income tax and capital gains tax by virtue of section 787I (as inserted by *section 4* of the *Pensions (Amendment) Act, 2002*) and the units held are assets of a PRSA (within the meaning of Chapter 2A of *Part 30*) and the PRSA administrator (within the meaning of that Chapter 2A) has made a declaration to the investment undertaking in accordance with *paragraph 9A* of *Schedule 2B*,][26] [(j) is a credit union that has made a declaration to the investment undertaking in accordance with *paragraph 9B* of *Schedule 2B*, [...][27]

(k) (I) is a company that—

(A) is or will be within the charge to corporation tax in accordance with *section 739G(2)* [...][28], in respect of payments made to it by the investment undertaking,

(B) has made a declaration to that effect and has provided the investment undertaking with the company's tax reference number (within the meaning of *section 885*),

and

(II) the investment undertaking is a money market fund,][29]

[(ka) is the National Asset Management Agency and has made a declaration to that effect to the investment undertaking,][30]

[(kb) is the National Treasury Management Agency or a Fund investment vehicle (within the meaning of *section 37* of the *National Treasury Management Agency (Amendment) Act 2014*) of which the Minister for Finance is the sole beneficial owner, or the State acting through the National Treasury Management Agency, and the National Treasury Management Agency has made a declaration to that effect to the investment undertaking, or][31]

[...][32]

(m) is a company that—

(i) is or will be within the charge to corporation tax in accordance with *section 110(2)*, in respect of payments made to it by the investment undertaking, and

(ii) has made a declaration to that effect and has provided the investment undertaking with the company's tax reference number (within the meaning of *section 885*),][33]

and the investment undertaking is in the possession of the declaration immediately before the chargeable event.

(7) Subject to *subsection (8)*, a gain shall not be treated as arising to an investment undertaking on the happening of a chargeable event in respect of a unit holder where, immediately before the chargeable event, the investment undertaking—

(a) is in possession of a declaration of a kind referred to in—

(i) *paragraph 10* of *Schedule 2B*, or

(ii) where the unit holder is not a company, *paragraph 11* of that Schedule, and

(b) is not in possession of any information which would reasonably suggest that—

(i) the information contained in that declaration is not, or is no longer, materially correct,

(ii) the unit holder failed to comply with the undertaking referred to in *paragraph 10(g)* or *11(f)*, as the case may be, of Schedule 2B, or

(iii) immediately before the chargeable event the unit holder is resident or ordinarily resident in the State.

[(7A) Where an investment undertaking is in possession of—

(a) a declaration made by a unit holder who is a person referred to in *subsection (6)*, or

(b) a declaration made by a unit holder of the kind referred to in *subsection (7)* and *paragraph (b)* of that subsection is satisfied,

which unit holder is entitled to the units in respect of which the declaration was made, a gain shall not be treated as arising—

(i) to the investment undertaking on the happening of a chargeable event in respect of the unit holder in relation to any other units in the investment undertaking to which the unit holder becomes entitled, or

(ii) to another investment undertaking which is associated with the investment undertaking referred to in *subparagraph (i)*, on the happening of a chargeable event in respect of the unit holder in relation to units in that other investment undertaking to which the unit holder becomes entitled.][34]

[(7B) (a) A gain shall not be treated as arising to an investment undertaking on the happening of a chargeable event in respect of a unit holder where, immediately before the chargeable event, the investment undertaking is in possession of written notice of approval from the Revenue Commissioners to the effect that [*subsection (7)* or *(9)*, as the case may be,][35] is deemed to have been complied with in respect of the unit holder, and that approval has not been withdrawn.

(b) The Revenue Commissioners may give to an investment undertaking the approval, referred to in *paragraph (a)*, that [*subsection (7)* or *(9)*, as the case may be,][36] is deemed to have been complied with—

(i) as respects any unit holder or class of unit holder, and

(ii) subject to such conditions as they consider necessary so as to satisfy themselves that, at the time the approval is granted, appropriate equivalent measures have been put in place by the investment undertaking to ensure that unit holders in that investment undertaking are not resident or ordinarily resident in the State.

(c) (i) The Revenue Commissioners may by notice in writing withdraw any approval given under *paragraph (b)* if an investment undertaking has failed to comply with any of the conditions subject to which the approval was given.

(ii) Where approval is withdrawn in accordance with *subparagraph (i)*, *paragraph (a)* shall not apply from such date, and in respect of such unit holder or class of unit holder, as may be specified in the notice.

(d) The Revenue Commissioners may nominate in writing an inspector or other officer to perform any acts and discharge any functions authorised by this subsection to be performed or discharged by the Revenue Commissioners.][37]

[(8) (a) A gain shall not be treated as arising to an investment undertaking on the happening of a chargeable event in respect of a unit holder where the investment undertaking was on 31 March 2000 a specified collective investment undertaking and—

(i) the unit holder was a unit holder (within the meaning of *section 734(1)*) in relation to that specified collective investment undertaking at that time and the investment undertaking on or before 30 June 2000 makes to the Collector-General a declaration in accordance with *paragraph 12* of *Schedule 2B*, or

(ii) the unit holder otherwise became a unit holder on or before 30 September 2000 and the investment undertaking forwarded to the Collector-General, on or before 1 November 2000, a list containing the name and address of each such unit holder who is resident in the State,

otherwise than, subject to *paragraph (b)*, in respect of a unit holder (in this subsection and in *section 739G* referred to as an "*excepted unit holder*")—

(I) whose name is included in the schedule to the declaration referred to in *paragraph 12(d)* of *Schedule 2B* or the list referred to in *subparagraph (ii)*, and

(II) who has not made a declaration of a kind referred to in *subsection (6)* to the investment undertaking.

(b) A gain shall not be treated as arising to an investment undertaking on the happening of a chargeable event in respect of an excepted unit holder where a chargeable event is deemed to happen on 31 December 2000.

(8A) Where under *subsection (8)(a)* a gain is not treated as arising to an investment undertaking on the happening of a chargeable event in respect of a unit holder who acquired units on or before 30 September 2000, a gain shall not be treated as arising—

(a) to the investment undertaking on the happening of a chargeable event in respect of the unit holder in relation to any other units in the investment undertaking to which the unit holder becomes entitled, or

(b) to another investment undertaking which is associated with the investment undertaking referred to in *paragraph (a)*, on the happening of a chargeable event in respect of the unit holder in relation to units in that other investment undertaking to which the unit holder becomes entitled.

(8B) A gain shall not be treated as arising to an investment undertaking on the happening of a chargeable event in respect of a unit holder where—

(a) the investment undertaking was a unit trust mentioned in *section 731(5)(a)*,

(b) the unit holder held units in that unit trust at the time that it became an investment undertaking, and

(c) within 30 days of that time, the investment undertaking forwards to the Collector-General a list containing the name and address of each such unit holder and such other information as the Revenue Commissioners reasonably require.

(8C) (a) In this section a "*scheme of amalgamation*" means an arrangement whereby a unit holder in a unit trust referred to in *section 731(5)(a)* exchanges units so held, for units in an investment undertaking.

(b) A gain shall not be treated as arising to an investment undertaking on the happening of a chargeable event in respect of a unit holder where—

(i) the unit holder acquires units in the investment undertaking in exchange for units held in a unit trust referred to in *section 731(5)(a)*, under a scheme of amalgamation, and

(ii) within 30 days of the scheme of amalgamation taking place, the investment undertaking forwards to the Collector-General a list containing, in respect of each unit holder who so acquired units in the investment undertaking, the name and address and such other information as the Revenue Commissioners may reasonably require.

(8D)

[(a) In this subsection—

"*offshore fund*" means any of the following—

(i) a company not resident in the State,

(ii) a unit trust scheme, the trustees of which are neither resident nor ordinarily resident in the State, and

(iii) any arrangements not within *subparagraphs (i)* or *(ii)* which take effect by virtue of the law of a territory outside the State and which under that law create rights in the nature of co-ownership without restricting that expression to its meaning in the law of the State),

in which persons have an interest and which is established for the purposes of collective investment by such persons and references in this subsection to an offshore fund shall be construed as a reference to any such company, unit trust scheme or arrangements, in which such persons have an interest;

['*scheme of migration and amalgamation*' means an arrangement whereby the assets of an offshore fund are transferred to an investment undertaking in exchange for the issue by the investment undertaking of units—

(i) to each of the persons who have an interest in the offshore fund, in proportion to the value of that interest, and as a result of which the value of that interest becomes negligible, or

(ii) to that offshore fund.][38]

(b) [Subject to *paragraph (d)*, a gain shall not be treated as arising][39] to an investment undertaking on the happening of a chargeable event in respect of a unit holder where—

(i) under a scheme of migration and amalgamation the unit holder acquires units in the investment undertaking in exchange for the unit holder's interest in an offshore fund, and

(ii) within 30 days of the scheme of migration and amalgamation taking place, the investment undertaking forwards to the [inspector or other officer of the Revenue Commissioners nominated under *subsection (7B)(d)*][40] a declaration of a kind referred to in *paragraph (c)*,

otherwise than in respect of a unit holder whose name is included in the schedule referred to in *paragraph (c)(ii)*.][41]

(c) The declaration referred to in *paragraph (b)* is a declaration in writing made and signed by the investment undertaking which—

(i) declares to the best of the investment undertaking's knowledge and belief that at the time of the scheme of migration and amalgamation it did not issue units to a person who was resident in the State at that time, other than such persons whose names and addresses are set out on the schedule to the declaration, and

(ii) contains a schedule which sets out the name and address of each person who was resident in the State at the time that the person was issued units by the investment undertaking under the scheme of migration and amalgamation.][42]

[(d) A gain which, by virtue of *paragraph (b)*, would not otherwise be treated as arising to an investment undertaking on the happening of a chargeable event in respect of a unit holder shall nevertheless be treated as so arising where, immediately before the chargeable event, the investment undertaking is in possession of any information which would reasonably suggest that the unit holder is resident in the State.][43]

[(8E) (a) In this subsection—

'*relevant jurisdiction*' has the same meaning as in *section 256F(1)* of the Companies Act 1990;

'*scheme of migration*' means either of the following—

(i) a migrating company (within the meaning of *section 256F* of the Companies Act 1990) which holds an authorisation from the Central Bank of Ireland to carry on business in the State under Part XIII of that Act, and which authorisation has not been revoked, or

(ii) a unit trust which has migrated from a relevant jurisdiction and which holds an authorisation from the Central Bank of Ireland to carry on business in the State as an authorised unit trust scheme under the Unit Trusts Act 1990 or as a unit trust within the meaning of the relevant Regulations, and which authorisation has not been revoked.

(b) Where, under a scheme of migration, a company or a unit trust, as the case may be, comes within the definition of 'investment undertaking' in *section 739B(1)*, the following provisions apply—

(i) subject to *subparagraph (iii)*, a gain shall not be treated as arising to that investment undertaking on the happening of a chargeable event in respect of a unit holder holding units in that investment undertaking at the time of the scheme of migration, otherwise than in respect of a unit holder whose name is included in the schedule referred to in *subparagraph (ii)*, where the investment undertaking, within 30 days of the scheme of migration taking place, forwards to the inspector or other officer of the Revenue Commissioners nominated under *subsection (7B)(d)*, a declaration of a kind referred to in *subparagraph (ii)*,

(ii) the declaration referred to in *subparagraph (i)* is a declaration in writing made and signed by the investment undertaking which—

(I) declares to the best of the investment undertaking's knowledge and belief that at the time of the scheme of migration no units in that investment undertaking were held by a person who was resident in the State, other than the persons whose names and addresses are set out in the schedule to the declaration, and

(II) contains a schedule which sets out the name and address of each person who, at the time of the scheme of migration, was resident in the State,

and

(iii) a gain which, by virtue of *subparagraph (i)*, would not otherwise be treated as arising to that investment undertaking on the happening of a chargeable event in respect of a unit holder shall nevertheless be treated as so arising where, immediately before the chargeable event, the investment undertaking is in possession of any information which would reasonably suggest that the unit holder is resident in the State.][44]

[(9) A gain shall not be treated as arising to an investment undertaking on the happening of a chargeable event in respect of a unit holder, where immediately before the chargeable event the investment undertaking or an investment undertaking associated with the first-mentioned investment undertaking—

(a) is, in relation to the units concerned, in possession of a declaration of a kind referred to in *paragraph 13* of *Schedule 2B*, and

(b) is not in possession of any information which would reasonably suggest that—

(i) the information contained in that declaration is not, or is no longer, materially correct,

(ii) the intermediary failed to comply with the undertaking referred to in *paragraph 13(e)* of *Schedule 2B*, or

(iii) any of the persons, on whose behalf the intermediary holds units of, or receives payments from, the investment undertaking, is resident or ordinarily resident in the State.

(9A) A gain shall not be treated as arising to an investment undertaking on the happening of a chargeable event in respect of a unit holder where immediately before the chargeable event the investment undertaking or an investment undertaking associated with the first-mentioned investment undertaking—

(a) is, in relation to the units concerned, in possession of a declaration of a kind referred to in *paragraph 14* of *Schedule 2B*, and

(b) is not in possession of any information which would reasonably suggest that—

(i) the information contained in that declaration is not, or is no longer, materially correct,

(ii) the intermediary failed to comply with the undertaking referred to in *paragraph 14(e)* of *Schedule 2B*, or

(iii) any of the persons, on whose behalf the intermediary holds units of, or receives payment from, the investment undertaking, is not a person referred to in [*paragraphs (a)* to *(k)*][45] of *section 739D(6)*.][46]

[(10) An investment undertaking shall keep and retain declarations made to it in accordance with *Schedule 2B* for a period of 6 years from the time the unit holder of the units in respect of which the declaration was made, ceases to be both such a unit holder and a unit holder in all investment undertakings which are associated with the investment undertaking.][47]][48]

Amendments

[1] Substituted by FA02 s44(a).

[2] Substituted by FA01 s74(1)(b)(i). Applies on or after 1 April 2000.

[3] Deleted by FA05 s40(b)(i).

[4] Inserted by FA05 s40(b)(ii).

[5] Inserted by FA06 s50(1)(b)(i)(I). This section applies and has effect as respects any chargeable event occurring on or after 31 March 2006

[6] Deleted by FA04 s29(1)(b)(i). This section applies as respects the appropriation or cancellation of a unit on or after 4 February 2004.

[7] Inserted by FA08 s39(1)(b)(i)(I). Applies and has effect as respects any chargeable event (within the meaning of section 739B(1)) occurring on or after 13 March 08.

[8] Deleted by FA06 s50(1)(b)(i)(II). This section applies and has effect as respects any chargeable event occurring on or after 31 March 2006

[9] Inserted by FA04 s29(1)(b)(ii). This section applies as respects the appropriation or cancellation of a unit on or after 4 February 2004.

[10] Substituted by FA08 s39(1)(b)(i)(II). Applies and has effect as respects any chargeable event (within the meaning of section 739B(1)) occurring on or after 13 March 08.

[11] Substituted by FA08 s39(1)(b)(ii). Applies and has effect as respects any chargeable event (within the meaning of section 739B(1)) occurring on or after 13 March 08.

[12] Inserted by FA06 s50(1)(b)(ii). This section applies and has effect as respects any chargeable event occurring on or after 31 March 2006

[13] Substituted by FA08 s39(1)(b)(iii). Applies and has effect as respects any chargeable event (within the meaning of section 739B(1)) occurring on or after 13 March 08.

[14] Substituted by FA08 s39(1)(b)(iv). Applies and has effect as respects any chargeable event (within the meaning of section 739B(1)) occurring on or after 13 March 08.

[15] Substituted by FA01 s74(1)(b)(ii). Applies on or after 1 April 2000.

[16] Substituted by FA13 s39(2)(a). Deemed to have come into force and takes effect on and from 1 January 2013.

[17] Substituted by F(No.2)A13 s30(4)(a). Applies and has effect as respects the happening of a chargeable event in relation to an investment undertaking (within the meaning of section 739B(1)) on or after 1 January 2014.

[18] Substituted by FA12 s28(4)(a). Has effect as respects the happening of a chargeable event in relation to an investment undertaking (within the meaning of section 739B(1)) on or after 1 January 2012.

[19] Inserted by FA13 s39(2)(b). Deemed to have come into force and takes effect on and from 1 January 2013.

[20] Inserted by FA08 s39(1)(b)(v). Applies and has effect as respects any chargeable event (within the meaning of section 739B(1)) occurring on or after 13 March 08.

[21] Inserted by FA13 s42(1)(d). Applies in respect of an investment limited partnership that has been granted an authorisation under section 8 of the Investment Limited Partnerships Act 1994 on or after 13 February 2013.

[22] Substituted by FA02 s44(b).

[23] Substituted by PAA02 s4(1)(c)(i).

[24] Substituted by FA03 s53(c)(i).

[25] Substituted by FA01 s74(1)(b)(iii). Applies on or after 1 April 2000.

[26] Inserted by PAA02 s4(1)(c)(iii).

[27] Deleted by FA07 s41(a).

[28] Deleted by FA07 s41(b).

[29] Inserted by FA03 s53(c)(ii).

[30] Inserted by the National Asset Management Agency Act 2009 Sched 3 part 10.

[31] Inserted by NTMA(A)A14 part4(10)(a).

[32] Deleted by NTMA(A)A14 part4(10)(b).

[33] Inserted by FA07 s41(c).

[34] Inserted by FA01 s74(1)(b)(iv). Applies on or after 1 April 2000.

[35, 36] Substituted by FA12 s31(a). Deemed to have come into force and takes effect on and from 1 January 2012.

[37] Inserted by FA10 s31(1)(b). Has effect as on and from 3 April 2010.

[38] Substituted by FA12 s35(a). Deemed to have come into force and takes effect on and from 1 January 2012.

[39] Substituted by FA12 s35(b). Deemed to have come into force and takes effect on and from 1 January 2012.

[40] Substituted by FA12 s35(c). Deemed to have come into force and takes effect on and from 1 January 2012.

[41] Substituted by FA02 s44(c).

[42] Substituted by FA01 s74(1)(b)(v). Applies on or after 1 April 2000.

[43] Inserted by FA12 s35(d). Deemed to have come into force and takes effect on and from 1 January 2012.

[44] Inserted by FA12 s31(b). Deemed to have come into force and takes effect on and from 1 January 2012.

[45] Substituted by FA03 s53(d).

[46] Substituted by FA02 s44(d).

[47] Substituted by FA01 s74(1)(b)(vii). Applies on or after 1 April 2000.

[48] Inserted by FA00 s58(a).

Cross References

From Section 739D

Section 76 Computation of income: application of income tax principles.
Section 110 Securitisation.
Section 207 Rents of properties belonging to hospitals and other charities.
Section 706 Interpretation and general (Part 26).
Section 731 Chargeable gains accruing to unit trusts.
Section 734 Taxation of collective investment undertakings.
Section 739B Interpretation and application.
Section 739E Deduction of tax on the occurrence of a chargeable event.
Section 770 Interpretation and supplemental (Chapter 1).
Section 784A Approved retirement fund.
Section 848E Payment of tax credit.
Section 885 Obligation to show tax reference number on receipts.

To Section 739D

Section 739E Deduction of tax on the occurrence of a chargeable event.
Schedule 2B Investment Undertakings: Declarations

739E Deduction of tax on the occurrence of a chargeable event

[(1) [Subject to *subsection (1B)* in this section][1] and *sections 739F* and *739G*, "*appropriate tax*", in connection with a chargeable event in relation to an investment undertaking in respect of a unit holder, means a sum representing income tax on the amount of the gain arising to an investment undertaking—

[(a) subject to *paragraph (ba)*, where the amount of the gain is provided by *section 739D(2)(a)*, at the rate of—

(i) 25 per cent where the unit holder is a company, and

(ii) [41 per cent][2] in any other case,][3]

[(b) subject to *paragraph (ba)*, where the chargeable event happens on or after 1 January 2001 and the amount of the gain is provided by *paragraph (b)*, *(c)*, *(d)*, *(dd)* or *(ddd)* of *section 739D(2)*, at the rate of—

(i) 25 per cent where the unit holder is a company, and

(ii) [41 per cent][4] in any other case,][5]

(ba) where in the case of a personal portfolio investment undertaking, the chargeable event happens on or after 20 February 2007, [at the rate of 60 per cent][6], and][7]

(c) where the chargeable event happens in the period commencing on 1 April 2000 and ending on 31 December 2000 and the amount of the gain is provided by *paragraph (b), (c), (d)* or *(e)* of *section 739D(2)*, at a rate of 40 per cent.

[(1A) (a) In this subsection—

["*first tax*", in relation to a unit of a unit holder, means the appropriate tax that was accounted for and paid in accordance with [section 739F or, as the case may be, in accordance with *subsection (2A)(b)(iii)* and *section 739G(2A)*][8] in respect of a chargeable event within the meaning of *paragraph (ccc)* of the definition of "*chargeable event*" in *section 739B(1)* in relation to an investment undertaking in respect of the unit and which has not been repaid;][9]

["*new gain*", in relation to a unit of the unit holder, means a gain referred to in *section 739D(2A)* in respect of that unit;][10]

"*second tax*" means appropriate tax calculated in accordance with *subsection (1)* in respect of that new gain.

(b) (i) Where at any time *subsection 739D(2A)* applies in respect of a unit of a unit holder in an investment undertaking a proportion (in this subsection referred to as the "*relevant proportion*") of first tax shall be set off against any amount of second tax.

[(ii) Where such relevant proportion exceeds such second tax, an amount equal to the amount of the excess shall—

(I) (A) be paid by the investment undertaking to the unit holder in respect of the unit,

(B) be included in a return under *section 739F(2)*, and

(C) be treated as an amount which may be set off against appropriate tax payable by the investment undertaking in respect of any chargeable event in the period for which such a return is made, or any subsequent period,

or

(II) if the investment undertaking so elects, in writing to the Revenue Commissioners, be paid by the Revenue Commissioners to the unit holder in respect of the unit on receipt of a claim by the unit holder but only if immediately before the chargeable event the value of the number of units of the investment undertaking in respect of which, if a gain had arisen, would be treated as arising to the investment undertaking on the happening of a chargeable event does not exceed 15 per cent of the value of the total number of units of the investment undertaking at that time,

and where the investment undertaking has advised the unit holder, in writing, that clause (II) applies and has supplied the unit holder with the necessary information to enable the claim to be made to the Revenue Commissioners, then the investment undertaking shall be deemed to have made the election specified in that clause; otherwise the election under that clause shall not be made.][11]

[…][12]

(c) For the purposes of this subsection, "*relevant proportion*" is determined by the formula—

$$A \times \frac{B}{C}$$

where—

A is the first tax,

B is the new gain, and

C is a gain determined in accordance with *section 739D* if the unit to which the first tax applied was cancelled at that time.][13]

[(1B) Where the unit holder is a company—

(a) the rate specified in *paragraph (a)(i)* or *paragraph (b)(i)*, as the case may be, of *subsection (1)* shall not apply unless the unit holder has made the declaration referred to in *paragraph (b)*, and

(b) the rate specified in *paragraph (a)(ii)* or *paragraph (b)(ii)*, as the case may be, of *subsection (1)* shall apply unless immediately before the chargeable event, the investment undertaking is in possession of a declaration from the unit holder to the effect that the unit holder is a company and which includes the company's tax reference number (within the meaning of *section 891B(1)*).][14]

(2) [Subject to *subsection (2A)*, an investment undertaking][15] shall account for the appropriate tax in connection with a chargeable event in relation to a unit holder in accordance with *section 739F*.

[(2A) (a) *Subsection (2)* shall not apply in relation to a chargeable event to which *paragraph (ccc)* in *section 739B(1)* refers where—

(i) immediately before the chargeable event the value of the number of units in the investment undertaking, or if an umbrella scheme exists in the sub-fund concerned, in respect of which any gains arising would be treated as arising to the investment undertaking, or the sub-fund as the case may be, on the happening of a chargeable event is less than 10 per cent of the value of the total number of units in the investment undertaking, or the sub-fund as the case may be, at that time, and

(ii) the investment undertaking has made an election, in writing, to the Revenue Commissioners that it will make in respect of each year of assessment a statement (including where it is the case, a statement with a nil amount) to the Revenue Commissioners in electronic format approved by them, on or before 31 March in the year following the year of assessment, which specifies in respect of each person who is a unit holder—

(I) the name and address of the person,

(II) the value at the end of the year of assessment of the units to which the person is entitled at that time, and

(III) such other information as the Revenue Commissioners may require.

(b) Where *paragraph (a)* applies—

(i) the investment undertaking shall advise the unit holder concerned, in writing, that paragraph (*a*) applies,

(ii) the statement specified in *paragraph (a)(ii)* shall be made by the investment undertaking in accordance with that paragraph, and

(iii) the unit holder shall be deemed for that chargeable period to be a chargeable person for the purposes of [*Chapter 3* of *Part 41A* and *1084*][16], and the return of income to be delivered by the person for that chargeable period shall include the following particulars:

(I) the name and address of the investment undertaking, and

(II) the gains arising on the chargeable event.][17]

(3) An investment undertaking which is liable to account for appropriate tax in connection with a chargeable event in relation to a unit holder shall, at the time of the chargeable event, where the chargeable event is—

(a) the making of a payment to a unit holder, be entitled to deduct from the payment an amount equal to the appropriate tax,

(b) (i) the transfer by a unit holder of entitlement to a unit, [...][18]

[(ia) the appropriation or cancellation of units as a consequence of the transfer by a unit holder of entitlement to a [unit,][19]][20]

[(ib) the ending of a relevant period, or][21]

(ii) deemed to happen on 31 December 2000,

be entitled to appropriate or cancel such units of the unit holder as are required to meet the amount of appropriate tax,

and the investment undertaking shall be acquitted and discharged of such deduction or, as the case may be, such appropriation or cancellation as if the amount of appropriate tax had been paid to the unit holder and the unit holder shall allow such deduction or, as the case may be, such appropriation or cancellation.][22]

Amendments

1 Substituted by FA13 s39(3)(a). Deemed to have come into force and takes effect on and from 1 January 2013.

2 Substituted by F(No.2)A13 s30(4)(b)(i). Applies and has effect as respects the happening of a chargeable event in relation to an investment undertaking (within the meaning of section 739B(1)) on or after 1 January 2014.

3 Substituted by FA12 s28(4)(b). Has effect as respects the happening of a chargeable event in relation to an investment undertaking (within the meaning of section 739B(1)) on or after 1 January 2012.

4 Substituted by F(No.2)A13 s30(4)(b)(ii). Applies and has effect as respects the happening of a chargeable event in relation to an investment undertaking (within the meaning of section 739B(1)) on or after 1 January 2014.

5 Substituted by FA12 s28(4)(c). Has effect as respects the happening of a chargeable event in relation to an investment undertaking (within the meaning of section 739B(1)) on or after 1 January 2012.

6 Substituted by F(No.2)A13 s30(4)(b)(iii). Applies and has effect as respects the happening of a chargeable event in relation to an investment undertaking (within the meaning of section 739B(1)) on or after 1 January 2014.

7 Substituted by FA07 s40(1) and applies as respects (a) the occurrence of a chargeable event in relation to an investment undertaking (within the meaning of Chapter 1A of Part 27), (b) the receipt by a person of a payment in respect of a material interest in an offshore fund (within the meaning of Chapter 4 of Part 27), and (c) the disposal in whole or in part of a material interest in an offshore fund (within that meaning), on or after 20 February 2007.

[8] Substituted by F(No.2)A08 s27(1)(c)(ii)(II). Applies and has effect as respects the happening of a chargeable event in relation to an investment undertaking (within the meaning of section 739B(1)) on or after 1 January 2009.

[9] Substituted by FA08 s39(1)(c)(i)(I)(A). Applies and has effect as respects any chargeable event (within the meaning of section 739B(1)) occurring on or after 13 March 08.

[10] Substituted by FA08 s39(1)(c)(i)(I)(B). Applies and has effect as respects any chargeable event (within the meaning of section 739B(1)) occurring on or after 13 March 08.

[11] Substituted by FA08 s39(1)(c)(i)(II)(A). Applies and has effect as respects any chargeable event (within the meaning of section 739B(1)) occurring on or after 13 March 08.

[12] Deleted by FA08 s39(1)(c)(i)(II)(B). Applies and has effect as respects any chargeable event (within the meaning of section 739B(1)) occurring on or after 13 March 08.

[13] Inserted by FA06 s50(1)(c)(i). This section applies and has effect as respects any chargeable event occurring on or after 31 March 2006

[14] Inserted by FA13 s39(3)(b). Deemed to have come into force and takes effect on and from 1 January 2013.

[15] Substituted by FA08 s39(1)(c)(ii). Applies and has effect as respects any chargeable event (within the meaning of section 739B(1)) occurring on or after 13 March 08.

[16] Substituted by FA12 sched4(part 2)(g).

[17] Inserted by FA08 s39(1)(c)(iii). Applies and has effect as respects any chargeable event (within the meaning of section 739B(1)) occurring on or after 13 March 08.

[18] Deleted by FA04 s29(1)(c)(ii)(I). This section applies as respects the appropriation or cancellation of a unit on or after 4 February 2004.

[19] Substituted by FA06 s50(1)(c)(iii)(I). This section applies and has effect as respects any chargeable event occurring on or after 31 March 2006

[20] Inserted by FA04 s29(1)(c)(ii)(II). This section applies as respects the appropriation or cancellation of a unit on or after 4 February 2004.

[21] Inserted by FA06 s50(1)(c)(iii)(II). This section applies and has effect as respects any chargeable event occurring on or after 31 March 2006

[22] Inserted by FA00 s58(a).

Cross References

From Section 739E

Section 4 Interpretation of Corporation Tax Acts.
Section 739B Interpretation and application.
Section 739D Gain arising on a chargeable event.
Section 739F Returns and collection of appropriate tax.
Section 739F
Section 739G Taxation of unit holders in investment undertakings.Taxation of unit holders in investment undertakings.
Section 951 Obligation to make a return.
Section 1084 Surcharge for late returns.

To Section 739E

Section 739D Gain arising on a chargeable event.
Section 739F Returns and collection of appropriate tax.
Section 739G Taxation of unit holders in investment undertakings.Taxation of unit holders in investment undertakings.
Section 904D Power of inspection (returns and collection of appropriate tax): investment undertakings.
Section 1078 Revenue offences.

739F Returns and collection of appropriate tax

[(1) Notwithstanding any other provision of the Tax Acts, this section shall apply for the purposes of regulating the time and manner in which appropriate tax in connection with a chargeable event in relation to a unit holder shall be accounted for and paid.

(2) An investment undertaking shall for each financial year make to the Collector-General—

(a) a return of the appropriate tax[, and amounts which may be credited under *section 739E(1A)*,][1] in connection with chargeable events happening on or prior to 30 June, within 30 days of that date, and

(b) a return of appropriate tax[, and amounts which may be credited under *section 739E(1A)*,][2] in connection with chargeable events happening between 1 July and 31 December, within 30 days of that later date,

and where it is the case, the return shall specify that there is no appropriate tax for the period in question.

(3) The appropriate tax in connection with a chargeable event which is required to be included in a return [(reduced by any amount which is to be credited in accordance with *section 739E(1A)*)][3] shall be due at the time by which the return is to be made and shall be paid by the investment undertaking to the Collector-General, and the appropriate tax so due shall be payable by the investment undertaking without the making of an assessment; but appropriate tax which has become so due may be assessed on the investment undertaking (whether or not it has been paid when the assessment is made) if that tax or any part of it is not paid on or before the due date.

(4) Where it appears to the inspector that there is an amount of appropriate tax in relation to a chargeable event which ought to have been but has not been included in a return, or where the inspector is dissatisfied with any return, the inspector may make an assessment on the investment undertaking to the best of his or her judgement, and any amount of appropriate tax in connection with a chargeable event due under an assessment made by virtue of this subsection shall be treated for the purposes of interest on unpaid tax as having been payable at the time when it would have been payable if a correct return had been made.

[(5) Where—

(a) any item has been incorrectly included in a return as appropriate tax, the inspector may make such assessments, adjustments or set-offs as may in his or her judgement be required for securing that the resulting [liabilities to tax][4], including interest on unpaid tax, whether of the investment undertaking making the return or of any other person, are in so far as possible the same as they would have been if the item had not been included, or

(b) any item has been correctly included in a return, but within one year of the making of the return the investment undertaking proves to the satisfaction of the Revenue Commissioners that it is just and reasonable that an amount of appropriate tax (included in the return) which has been paid, should be repaid to the investment undertaking, such amount may be repaid to the investment undertaking.][5]

(6) (a) Any appropriate tax assessed on an investment undertaking shall be due within one month after the issue of the notice of assessment (unless that tax is due earlier under *subsection (3)*) subject to any appeal against the assessment, but no appeal shall affect the date when any amount is due under *subsection (3)*.

(b) On determination of the appeal against an assessment under this Chapter, any appropriate tax overpaid shall be repaid.

(7) (a) The provisions of the Income Tax Acts relating to—

(i) assessments to income tax,

(ii) appeals against such assessments (including the rehearing of appeals and the statement of a case for the opinion of the High Court), and

(iii) the collection and recovery of income tax,

shall, in so far as they are applicable, apply to the assessment, collection and recovery of appropriate tax.

[(b) Any amount of appropriate tax shall carry interest from the date when the amount becomes due and payable until payment—

(i) for any day or part of a day before 1 July 2009 during which the amount remains unpaid, at a rate of 0.0322 per cent, and

(ii) for any day or part of a day on or after 1 July 2009 during which the amount remains unpaid, at a rate of 0.0274 per cent.][6]

[(c) [*Subsections (3)* to *(5)* of *section1080*][7] shall apply in relation to interest payable under *paragraph (b)* as they apply in relation to interest payable under *section 1080*.][8]

(d) In its application to any appropriate tax charged by any assessment made in accordance with this Chapter, *section 1080* shall apply as if [*subsection (2) (b)*][9] of that section were deleted.

(8) Every return shall be in a form prescribed by the Revenue Commissioners and shall include a declaration to the effect that the return is correct and complete.][10]

Amendments

[1] Inserted by FA06 s50(1)(d)(i)(I). This section applies and has effect as respects any chargeable event occurring on or after 31 March 2006

[2] Inserted by FA06 s50(1)(d)(i)(II). This section applies and has effect as respects any chargeable event occurring on or after 31 March 2006

[3] Inserted by FA06 s50(1)(d)(ii). This section applies and has effect as respects any chargeable event occurring on or after 31 March 2006

[4] Substituted by FA07 sched4(1)(w). Shall have effect as on and from 1 January 2007.

[5] Substituted by FA01 s74(1)(c). Applies on or after 1 April 2000.

[6] Substituted by FA09 s29(1)(f). Applies as respects any unpaid tax or duty, as the case may be, that has not been paid before 1 July 2009 regardless of whether that tax or duty became due and payable before, on or after that date.

[7, 9] Substituted by FA05 sched5.

[8] Substituted by FA01 s74(1)(d). Applies on or after 1 April 2000.

[10] Inserted by FA00 s58(a).

Cross References

From Section 739F

Section 739E Deduction of tax on the occurrence of a chargeable event.

Section 1080 Interest on overdue income tax, corporation tax and capital gains tax.

To Section 739F

Section 739E Deduction of tax on the occurrence of a chargeable event.

Section 904D Power of inspection (returns and collection of appropriate tax): investment undertakings.

Section 1078 Revenue offences.

Schedule 29 Provisions Referred to in Sections 1052, 1053 and 1054

739G Taxation of unit holders in investment undertakings

[(1) Where a chargeable event in relation to an investment undertaking in respect of a unit holder is deemed to happen on 31 December 2000 and the unit holder is an excepted unit holder referred to in section 739D(8), the unit holder shall be treated for all the purposes of the Capital Gains Tax Acts as if the amount of the gain which, but for section 739D(8)(*b*), would have arisen to the investment undertaking on the happening of the chargeable event, were a chargeable gain accruing to the unit holder at that time and notwithstanding section 28, the rate of capital gains tax in respect of that chargeable gain shall be 40 per cent.

(2) As respects a payment in money or money's worth to a unit holder by reason of rights conferred on the unit holder as a result of holding units in an investment undertaking to which this Chapter applies—

(a) where the unit holder is not a company and the payment is a payment from which appropriate tax has been deducted, the payment shall not be reckoned in computing the total income of the unit holder for the purposes of the Income Tax Acts and shall not be treated as giving rise to a chargeable gain under the Capital Gains Tax Acts,

[(b) where the unit holder is not a company and the payment is a payment from which appropriate tax has not been deducted, the payment shall be treated as if it were a payment from an offshore fund to which the provisions of Chapter 4 of this Part apply, and the provisions of *section 747D*, or *section 747E* apply as appropriate,][1]

(c) where the unit holder is a company, the payment is a relevant payment and appropriate tax has been deducted from the payment, the amount received by the unit holder shall, subject to *paragraph (g)*, be treated for the purposes of the Tax Acts as the net amount of an annual payment chargeable to tax under Case IV of Schedule D from the gross amount of which income tax has been deducted [at the rate [specified in][2] [*section 739E(1)(a)*[*(i)*,][3]][4]

(d) where the unit holder is a company, the payment is a relevant payment and appropriate tax has not been deducted from the payment, the amount of the payment shall, subject to *paragraph (g)*, be treated for the purposes of the Tax Acts as income arising to the unit holder, constituting profits or gains chargeable to tax under Case IV of Schedule D,

[(e) where the unit holder is a company, the payment is not a relevant payment and appropriate tax has been deducted from the payment, the amount received by the unit holder shall, subject to *paragraph (g)*, be treated for the purposes of the Tax Acts as the net amount of an annual payment chargeable to tax under Case IV of Schedule D from the gross amount of which income tax has been deducted at the rate specified in *section 739E(1)(b)(i)*,][5]

(f) where the unit holder is a company, the payment is not a relevant payment and appropriate tax has not been deducted from the payment, the amount of such payment shall, subject to *paragraph (g)*, be treated for the purposes of the Tax Acts as income arising to the unit holder, constituting profits or gains chargeable to tax under Case IV of Schedule D; but where the payment is in respect of the cancellation, redemption, repurchase or transfer of units, such income shall be reduced by the amount of the consideration in money or money's worth given by the unit holder for the acquisition of those units,][6]

(g) where the unit holder is a company chargeable to tax on the payment under Case I of Schedule D[, or is a qualifying company within the meaning of *section 110* that is chargeable to tax on the payment under Case III of Schedule D][7]—

(i) subject to *subparagraph (ii)*, the amount received by the unit holder increased by the amount (if any) of appropriate tax deducted shall be income of the unit holder for the chargeable period in which the payment is made,

(ii) where the payment is made on the cancellation, redemption or repurchase of units by the investment undertaking, such income shall be reduced by the amount of the consideration in money or money's worth given by the unit holder for the acquisition of those units, and

(iii) the amount (if any) of appropriate tax deducted shall be set off against corporation tax assessable on the unit holder for the chargeable period in which the payment is made,

[(h) the amount of a payment made to a unit holder—

(i) by an investment undertaking, or

(ii) arising from the transfer by way of sale, or otherwise, of an entitlement to a unit in an investment undertaking,

shall not be chargeable to income tax or capital gains tax where the unit holder is a company which is not resident in the State or the unit holder, not being a company, is neither resident nor ordinarily resident in the State,][8]

[(i) otherwise than by virtue of *section 739F(5)* or *paragraph (j)*, no repayment of appropriate tax shall be made to any person who is not a company within the charge to corporation tax, and

(j) notwithstanding *paragraph (a)*, for the purposes of a claim to relief, under *section 189*, 189A or *192*, or a repayment of income tax in consequence thereof, the amount of a payment made to a unit holder shall be treated as a net amount of income from the gross amount of which has been deducted income tax (of an amount equal to the amount of appropriate tax deducted in making the payment), and such gross amount of income shall be treated as chargeable to tax under Case III of Schedule D.][9]

[(2A) Where a gain arises on a chargeable event to which paragraph (*ccc*) in section 739B(1) refers, and section 739E(2) does not apply to that chargeable event by virtue of subsection (2A) of that section, then such gain—

(a) shall be treated for the purposes of the Tax Acts as arising to the unit holder, constituting profits or gains chargeable to tax under Case IV of Schedule D at the rate specified in section 739E(1)(*b*), and

(b) shall not be reckoned in computing total income for the purposes of the Tax Acts,

and section 188, and the reductions specified in Part 2 of the Table to section 458, shall not apply as regards the tax so charged.][10]

[(3) References in *subsection (2)* to payments, from which appropriate tax has not been deducted, made to a unit holder by an investment undertaking, include references to payments made to a unit holder who holds units which are held in a recognised clearing system.

(4) Where the units of an investment undertaking are denominated in a currency other than the currency of the State (in this subsection referred to as "*foreign currency*"), then for the purposes of the Capital Gains Tax Acts the amount of foreign currency given by a unit holder to the investment undertaking for the acquisition of a unit in the investment undertaking shall be deemed to have been disposed of and reacquired by the unit holder—

(a) immediately before it was so given, and

(b) immediately after the unit holder receives payment for the cancellation, redemption or repurchase of, or as the case may be, transfer of, his or her units.

(5) Where appropriate tax is payable as a result of the death of a person, the amount of such tax, in so far as it has been paid, shall be treated as an amount of capital gains tax paid, for the purposes of section 104 of the Capital Acquisitions Tax Consolidation Act 2003.][11]][12]

Amendments

[1] Substituted by FA03 s53(e).

[2] Substituted by FA09 s10(4)(e). Applies and has effect as respects the happening of a chargeable event in relation to an investment undertaking (within the meaning of section 739B(1)) on or after 8 April 2009.

[3] Substituted by FA12 s28(4)(e). Has effect as respects the happening of a chargeable event in relation to an investment undertaking (within the meaning of section 739B(1)) on or after 1 January 2012.

[4] Substituted by F(No.2)A08 s27(1)(c)(iii). Applies and has effect as respects the happening of a chargeable event in relation to an investment undertaking (within the meaning of section 739B(1)) on or after 1 January 2009.

[5] Substituted by FA12 s28(4)(f). Has effect as respects the happening of a chargeable event in relation to an investment undertaking (within the meaning of section 739B(1)) on or after 1 January 2012.

[6] Substituted by FA01 s74(1)(e)(i)(II). Applies on or after 1 April 2000.

[7] Inserted by FA06 s52(b).

[8] Substituted by FA12 s32. Deemed to have come into force and takes effect on and from 1 January 2012.

[9] Substituted by FA01 s74(1)(e)(i)(IV). Applies on or after 1 April 2000.

[10] Inserted by FA08 s39(1)(d). Applies and has effect as respects any chargeable event (within the meaning of section 739B(1)) occurring on or after 13 March 08.

[11] Inserted by FA01 s74(1)(e)(ii). Applies on or after 1 April 2000.

[12] Inserted by FA00 s58(a).

Cross References

From Section 739G

Section 12 The charge to income tax.
Section 110 Securitisation.
Section 188 Age exemption and associated marginal relief.
Section 189 Payments in respect of personal injuries.
Section 192 Payments in respect of thalidomide children.
Section 458 Deductions allowed in ascertaining taxable income and provisions relating to reductions in tax.
Section 739B Interpretation and application.
Section 739E Deduction of tax on the occurrence of a chargeable event.

To Section 739G

Section 739E Deduction of tax on the occurrence of a chargeable event.

739H Investment undertakings: reconstructions and amalgamations

[(1) In this section—

"*exchange*", in relation to a scheme of reconstruction or amalgamation, means the issue of units (in this section referred to as "*new units*") by an investment undertaking (in this section referred to as the "*new undertaking*") to the unit holders of another investment undertaking (in this section referred to as the "*old undertaking*") in respect of and in proportion to (or as nearly as may be in proportion to) their holdings of units (in this section referred to as "*old units*") in the old undertaking in exchange for the transfer by the old undertaking of all its assets and liabilities to the new undertaking where the exchange is entered into for the purposes of or in connection with a scheme of reconstruction or amalgamation;

"*scheme of reconstruction or amalgamation*" means a scheme for the reconstruction of any investment undertaking or investment undertakings or the amalgamation of any 2 or more investment undertakings.

[(1A) For the purposes of subsection (1) a reference in the definition of "*exchange*" to an investment undertaking includes a reference to a sub-fund of an umbrella scheme where the exchange concerned is between 2 or more sub-funds of different umbrella schemes.

(1B) Subsection (1A) shall not apply unless the exchange concerned is effected for bona fide commercial reasons and not primarily for the purpose of avoiding liability to taxation.][1]

[(2) The cancellation of old units arising from an exchange in relation to a scheme of reconstruction or amalgamation shall not be a chargeable event and the amount invested by a unit holder for, and the date of, the acquisition of the new units shall for the purposes of this Chapter be the amount invested by the unit holder for, and the date of, the acquisition of the old units.][2]

[(3) (a) This section applies to a scheme for the reconstruction of a common contractual fund or funds (within the meaning of *section 739I(1)(a)(i)*) or to the amalgamation of 2 or more such funds as it would apply to a scheme of reconstruction or amalgamation if "*investment undertaking*" included a common contractual fund within the meaning of *section 739I(1)(a)(i)*.

(b) For the purposes of this subsection the definitions of "*investment undertaking*", "*unit*" and "*unit holder*" shall apply, with any necessary modifications, to a common contractual fund within the meaning of *section 739I(1)(a)(i)* as they apply to an investment undertaking within the meaning of *paragraph (b)* of the definition of "*investment undertaking*".][3][4]

Amendments

[1] Inserted by FA08 s39(1)(e)(i). Applies and has effect as respects any exchange (within the meaning of section 739H(1)) in relation to a scheme of reconstruction or amalgamation occurring on or after 13 March 08.

[2] Substituted by FA08 s39(1)(e)(ii). Applies and has effect as respects any exchange (within the meaning of section 739H(1)) in relation to a scheme of reconstruction or amalgamation occurring on or after 13 March 08.

[3] Inserted by FA06 s45(a).

[4] Inserted by FA00 s58(a).

Cross References

From Section 739H

Section 739I Common contractual funds.

739HA Investment undertakings: amalgamations with offshore funds

[(1) In this section—

'material interest' shall be construed in accordance with *section 743*;

'offshore fund' has the meaning assigned to it by *section 743*;

'offshore state' has the same meaning as in *section 747B(1)*;

'scheme of amalgamation' means an arrangement whereby the assets of an investment undertaking are transferred to an offshore fund of an offshore state in exchange for the issue by the offshore fund of an offshore state of a material interest in that offshore fund to each of the unit holders in the investment undertaking, in proportion to the value of the units held by each unit holder, and as a result of which the value of those units becomes negligible.

(2) The cancellation of units in an investment undertaking arising from an exchange in relation to a scheme of amalgamation shall not be a chargeable event and the amount invested by a unit holder for, and the date of, the acquisition of a material interest in an offshore fund of an offshore state under that scheme shall for the purposes of *Chapter 4* be the amount invested by the unit holder for, and the date of, the acquisition of those units in the investment undertaking.][1]

Amendments

[1] Inserted by FA12 s33(a). Deemed to have come into force and takes effect on and from 1 January 2012.

739I Common contractual funds

[(1) (a) In this section "*common contractual fund*" means—

[(i) a collective investment undertaking being an unincorporated body established by a management company under which the participants by contractual arrangement participate and share in the property of the collective investment undertaking as co-owners, where it is expressly stated in its deed of constitution to be established pursuant to the Investment Funds, Companies and Miscellaneous Provisions Act 2005 and which holds an authorisation issued in accordance with that Act and which is not established pursuant to Council Directive No. 85/611/EEC of 20 December 1985*, as amended from time to time, or][1]

* OJ No. L375, 31.12.1985, p.3

(ii) an investment undertaking within the meaning of *paragraph (b)* of the definition of "*investment undertaking*" which is constituted otherwise than under trust law or statute law.

(b) For the purposes of this section the definitions of "*relevant gains*", "*relevant income*", "*relevant payment*", "*relevant profits*", "*unit*" and "*unit holder*" shall apply, with any necessary modifications, to a collective investment undertaking within the meaning of *paragraph (i)* of the definition of "*common contractual fund*" as they apply to an investment undertaking within the meaning of *paragraph (b)* of the definition of "*investment undertaking*".

(2) (a) Notwithstanding anything in the [Acts][2] and subject to *subsections (3)* and *(4)*, a common contractual fund shall not be chargeable to tax in respect of relevant profits.

(b) For the purposes of the [Tax Acts][3], relevant income and relevant gains in relation to a common contractual fund shall be treated as arising, or as the case may be, accruing, to each unit holder of the common contractual fund in proportion to the value of the units beneficially owned by the unit holder, as if the relevant income and relevant gains had arisen or, as the case may be, accrued, to the unit holders in the common contractual fund without passing through the hands of the common contractual fund.

(3) *Subsection (2)* shall only apply where each of the units of the common contractual fund—

(a) is an asset of a pension fund or beneficially owned by a person other than an individual, or

(b) is held by a custodian or trustee for the benefit of a person other than an individual.

(4) Every common contractual fund shall in respect of each year of assessment, on or before 28 February in the year following the year of assessment, make a statement (including where it is the case, a statement with a nil amount) to the Revenue Commissioners in electronic format approved by them, which in respect of each year of assessment—

(a) specifies the total amount of relevant profits arising to the common contractual fund in respect of units in that fund, and

(b) specifies in respect of each person who is a unit holder—

(i) the name and address of the person,

(ii) the amount of the relevant profits to which the person is entitled, and

(iii) such other information as the Revenue Commissioners may require.

(5) Notwithstanding *Chapter 4* of *Part 8*, that Chapter shall apply to a deposit (within the meaning of that Chapter) to which a common contractual fund is for the time being entitled as if such deposit were not a relevant deposit within the meaning of that Chapter.

Amendments

[1] Substituted by FA06 s45(b).

[2, 3] Substituted by FA14 sched3(1)(f). Has effect on and from 23 December 2014.

Cross References

From Section 739I

Section 237 Annual payments payable wholly out of taxed income.
Section 256 Interpretation (Chapter 4).

To Section 739I

Section 172A Interpretation.
Section 246 Interest payments by companies and to non-residents.
Section 739H Investment undertakings: reconstructions and amalgamations.

739J Investment limited partnerships

[(1) (a) In this section "*investment limited partnership*" means an investment limited partnership within the meaning of the Investment Limited Partnerships Act 1994.

(b) For the purposes of this section the definitions of "*relevant gains*", "*relevant income*", "*relevant payment*", "*relevant profits*", "*unit*" and "*unit holder*" shall apply, with any necessary modifications, to an investment limited partnership as they apply to an investment undertaking.

(2) (a) Notwithstanding anything in the Acts and subject to *subsection (3)*, an investment limited partnership shall not be chargeable to tax in respect of relevant profits.

(b) For the purposes of the Acts, relevant income and relevant gains in relation to an investment limited partnership shall be treated as arising, or as the case may be, accruing, to each unit holder of the investment limited partnership in proportion to the value of the units beneficially owned by the unit holder, as if the relevant income and relevant gains had arisen or, as the case may be, accrued, to the unit holders in the investment limited partnership without passing through the hands of the investment limited partnership.

(3) Every investment limited partnership shall in respect of each year of assessment, on or before 28 February in the year following the year of assessment, make a statement (including, where it is the case, a statement with a nil amount) to the Revenue Commissioners in electronic format approved by them which in respect of each year of assessment—

(a) specifies the total amount of relevant profits arising to the investment limited partnership in respect of units in the investment limited partnership, and

(b) specifies in respect of each person who is a unit holder—

(i) the name and address of the person,

(ii) the amount of the relevant profits to which the person is entitled, and

(iii) such other information as the Revenue Commissioners may require.

(4) Notwithstanding *Chapter 4* of *Part 8*, that Chapter shall apply to a deposit (within the meaning of that Chapter) to which an investment limited partnership is for the time being entitled as if such deposit were not a relevant deposit within the meaning of that Chapter.][1]

Amendments

[1] Inserted by FA13 s42(1)(e). Applies in respect of an investment limited partnership that has been granted an authorisation under section 8 of the Investment Limited Partnerships Act 1994 on or after 13 February 2013.

CHAPTER 2

Offshore Funds

740 Interpretation (Chapter 2 and Schedules 19 and 20)

[FA90 s62]

In this Chapter and in *Schedules 19* and *20*—

"*account period*" shall be construed in accordance with *subsections (8)* to *(10)* of *section 744*;

"*disposal*" shall be construed in accordance with *section 741(2)*;

"*distributing fund*" shall be construed in accordance with *subsections (2)* and *(3)* of *section 744*;

"*the equalisation account*" has the meaning assigned to it by *section 742(1)*;

"*Irish equivalent profits*" has the meaning assigned to it by *paragraph 5* of *Schedule 19*;

"*material interest*" shall be construed in accordance with *section 743(2)*;

"*non-qualifying fund*" has the meaning assigned to it by *section 744(1)*;

"*offshore fund*" has the meaning assigned to it by *section 743(1)*;

"*offshore income gain*" shall be construed in accordance with *paragraphs 5* and *6(1)* of *Schedule 20*.

Revenue Briefings

Tax Briefing

Tax Briefing December 2006 – Issue 65 pg 4 – Offshore Funds Legislation
Tax Briefing July 2007 – Issue 66 – Offshore Funds – Finance Act 2007 changes
Tax Briefing April 2008 – Issue 68 – Offshore Funds

Cross References

From Section 740

Section 741 Disposals of material interests in non-qualifying offshore funds.
Section 742 Offshore funds operating equalisation arrangements.
Section 743 Material interest in offshore funds.
Section 744 Non-qualifying offshore funds.
Schedule 19 Offshore Funds: Distributing Funds
Schedule 20 Offshore Funds: Computation of Offshore Income Gains

To Section 740

Section 747A Capital gains tax: rate of charge.
Section 747AA Treatment of certain offshore funds.

741 Disposals of material interests in non-qualifying offshore funds

[FA90 s63]

(1) This Chapter shall apply to a disposal by any person of an asset if at the time of the disposal—

(a) the asset constitutes a material interest in an offshore fund which is or has at any material time been a non-qualifying offshore fund, or

(b) the asset constitutes an interest in a company resident in the State or in a unit trust scheme, the trustees of which are at that time resident in the State and at a material time on or after the 1st day of January, 1991, the company or unit trust scheme was a non-qualifying offshore fund and the asset constituted a material interest in that fund,

and, for the purpose of determining whether the asset disposed of is within *paragraph (b)*, *subsection (3)* of *section 584* shall apply as it applies for the purposes of the Capital Gains Tax Acts.

(2) Subject to *subsections (3)* to *(7)* and *section 742*, there shall be a disposal of an asset for the purposes of this Chapter if there would be such a disposal for the purposes of the Capital Gains Tax Acts.

(3) Notwithstanding anything in *paragraph (b)* of *section 573(2)*, where a person dies and the assets of which he or she was competent to dispose include an asset which is or has at any time been a material interest in a non-qualifying offshore fund, then, for the purposes of this Chapter (other than *section 742*) that interest shall, immediately before the acquisition referred to in *paragraph (a)* of *section 573(2)*, be deemed to be disposed of by the deceased for such a consideration as is mentioned in that paragraph; but nothing in this subsection shall affect the determination in accordance with *subsection (1)* of the question whether that deemed disposal is one to which this Chapter applies.

(4) Subject to *subsection (3)*, *section 573* shall apply for the purposes of this Chapter as it applies for the purposes of the Capital Gains Tax Acts, and the reference

in that subsection to the assets of which a deceased person was competent to dispose shall be construed in accordance with *subsection (1)* of that section.

(5) Notwithstanding anything in *section 586* or *587*, in any case where—

(a) a company (in this subsection referred to as "*the acquiring company*") issues shares or debentures in exchange for shares in or debentures of another company (in this subsection referred to as "*the acquired company*") and the acquired company is or was at a material time a non-qualifying offshore fund and the acquiring company is not such a fund, or

(b) persons are to be treated in consequence of an arrangement as exchanging shares, debentures or other interests in or of an entity which is or was at a material time a non-qualifying offshore fund for assets which do not constitute interests in such a fund,

then, *section 586(1)* shall not apply for the purposes of this Chapter.

(6) In any case where (apart from *subsection (5)*) *section 586(1)* would apply, the exchange concerned of shares, debentures or other interests in or of a non-qualifying fund shall for the purposes of this Chapter constitute a disposal of interests in the offshore fund for a consideration equal to their market value at the time of the exchange.

(7) (a) In this subsection, "*relevant consideration*" means consideration which, assuming the application to the disposal of the Capital Gains Tax Acts, would be taken into account in determining the amount of the gain or loss accruing on the disposal, whether that consideration was given by or on behalf of the person making the disposal or by or on behalf of a predecessor in title of the person making the disposal whose acquisition cost represents directly or indirectly the whole or any part of the acquisition cost of the person making the disposal.

(b) For the purposes of this section, a material time in relation to the disposal of an asset shall be any time on or after—

(i) the 6th day of April, 1990, where the asset was acquired on or before that date, or

(ii) where the asset was not so acquired, the earliest date on which any relevant consideration was given for the acquisition of the asset.

Revenue Precedents

Under general law gains arising from the disposal of a material interest in an offshore fund held under a trust form part of the capital of the trust and accordingly are not available for distribution to the beneficiary. Therefore, they are assessable on the trustee. IT972507

Cross References

From Section 741

Section 573 Death.
Section 584 Reorganisation or reduction of share capital.
Section 586 Company amalgamations by exchange of shares.
Section 587 Company reconstructions and amalgamations.
Section 742 Offshore funds operating equalisation arrangements.

To Section 741

Section 740 Interpretation (Chapter 2 and Schedules 19 and 20).
Section 742 Offshore funds operating equalisation arrangements.
Section 747 Deduction of offshore income gain in determining capital gain.
Section 747A Capital gains tax: rate of charge.
Schedule 20 Offshore Funds: Computation of Offshore Income Gains

742 Offshore funds operating equalisation arrangements

[FA90 s64]

(1) For the purposes of this Chapter, an offshore fund operates equalisation arrangements if and at a time when arrangements are in existence which have the result that where—

(a) a person acquires by means of initial purchase a material interest in the fund at some time during a period relevant to the arrangements, and

(b) the fund makes a distribution for a period which begins before the date of the acquisition of that interest,

the amount of that distribution paid to the person (assuming the person is still retaining that interest) will include a payment of capital debited to an account (in this Chapter and in *Schedules 19* and *20* referred to as "*the equalisation account*") maintained under the arrangements and determined by reference to the income which had accrued to the fund at the date of the person's acquisition.

(2) For the purposes of this section, a person shall acquire an interest in an offshore fund by means of initial purchase if the person's acquisition is by—

(a) subscription for or allotment of new shares, units or other interests issued or created by the fund, or

(b) direct purchase from the persons concerned with the management of the fund and their sale to that person is made in their capacity as managers of the fund.

(3) Without prejudice to *section 741(1)*, this Chapter shall apply, subject to *subsections (4)* to *(6)*, to a disposal by any person of an asset if—

(a) at the time of the disposal the asset constitutes a material interest in an offshore fund which at that time is operating equalisation arrangements,

(b) the fund is not and has not at any material time (within the meaning of *section 741(7)*) been a non-qualifying offshore fund, and

(c) the proceeds of the disposal are not to be taken into account as a trading receipt.

(4) This Chapter shall not by virtue of *subsection (3)* apply to a disposal if—

(a) the disposal takes place during the period mentioned in *subsection (1)(a)*, and

(b) throughout so much of that period as precedes the disposal the income of the offshore fund concerned has been of the nature referred to in *paragraph 3(1)* of *Schedule 19*.

(5) An event which apart from *section 584(3)* would constitute a disposal of an asset shall constitute such a disposal for the purpose of determining whether by virtue of *subsection (3)* there is a disposal to which this Chapter applies.

(6) The reference in *subsection (5)* to *section 584(3)* shall be deemed to include a reference to that section as applied by *section 586* or *733* but not as applied by *section 585*.

Cross References

From Section 742

Section 584 Reorganisation or reduction of share capital.
Section 585 Conversion of securities.
Section 586 Company amalgamations by exchange of shares.
Section 733 Reorganisation of units in unit trust scheme.
Section 741 Disposals of material interests in non-qualifying offshore funds.
Schedule 19 Offshore Funds: Distributing Funds
Schedule 20 Offshore Funds: Computation of Offshore Income Gains

To Section 742

Section 740 Interpretation (Chapter 2 and Schedules 19 and 20).
Section 741 Disposals of material interests in non-qualifying offshore funds.
Section 747 Deduction of offshore income gain in determining capital gain.
Schedule 19 Offshore Funds: Distributing Funds
Schedule 20 Offshore Funds: Computation of Offshore Income Gains

743 Material interest in offshore funds

[FA90 s65]

(1) In this Chapter, references to a material interest in an offshore fund shall be construed as references to such an interest in any of the following—

(a) a company resident outside the State,

(b) a unit trust scheme the trustees of which are not resident in the State, and

(c) any arrangements not within *paragraph (a)* or *(b)* which take effect by virtue of the law of a territory outside the State and which under that law create rights in the nature of co-ownership (without restricting that expression to its meaning in the law of the State),

and any reference in this Chapter to an offshore fund shall be construed as a reference to any such company, unit trust scheme or arrangements in which any person has an interest which is a material interest.

(2) Subject to *subsections (3)* to *(9)*, a person's interest in a company, unit trust scheme or arrangements shall be a material interest if at the time when the person acquired the interest it could be reasonably expected that at some time during the period of 7 years beginning at the time of the acquisition the person would be able to realise the value of the interest (whether by transfer, surrender or in any other manner).

(3) For the purposes of *subsection (2)*, a person shall be deemed to be able to realise the value of an interest if the person can realise an amount which is reasonably approximate to that portion which the interest represents (directly or indirectly) of the market value of the assets of the company or, as the case may be, of the assets subject to the scheme or arrangements.

(4) For the purposes of *subsections (2)* and *(3)*—

(a) a person shall be deemed to be able to realise a particular amount if the person is able to obtain that amount either in money or in the form of assets to the value of that amount, and

(b) if at any time an interest in an offshore fund has a market value which is substantially greater than the portion which the interest represents, as mentioned in *subsection (3)*, of the market value at that time of the assets concerned, the ability to realise such a market value of the interest shall not be regarded as an ability to realise such an amount as is referred to in that subsection.

(5) An interest in a company, scheme or arrangements shall be deemed not to be a material interest if it is either—

(a) an interest in respect of any loan capital or debt issued or incurred for money which in the ordinary course of business of banking is loaned by a person carrying on that business, or

(b) a right arising under a policy of insurance.

(6) Shares in a company within *subsection (1)(a)* (in this section referred to as "*the overseas company*") shall not constitute a material interest if—

(a) the shares are held by a company and the holding of them is necessary or desirable for the maintenance and development of a trade carried on by the company or a company associated with it,

(b) the shares confer at least 10 per cent of the total voting rights in the overseas company and a right in the event of a winding up to at least 10 per cent of the assets of that company remaining after the discharge of all liabilities having priority over the shares,

(c) not more than 10 persons hold shares in the overseas company and all the shares in that company confer both voting rights and a right to participate in the assets on a winding up, and

(d) at the time of its acquisition of the shares the company had such a reasonable expectation as is referred to in *subsection (2)* by reason only of the existence of either or both—

(i) an arrangement under which, at some time within the period of 7 years beginning at the time of acquisition, that company may require the other participators to purchase its shares, and

(ii) provisions of either an agreement between the participators or the constitution of the overseas company under which the company will be wound up within a period which is or is reasonably expected to be shorter than the period referred to in *subsection (2)*,

and in this paragraph "*participators*" means the persons holding shares which are within *paragraph (c)*.

(7) For the purposes of *subsection (6)(a)*, a company shall be associated with another company if one company has control (within the meaning of *section 432*) of the other company or both companies are under the control (within the meaning of that section) of the same person or persons.

(8) An interest in a company within *subsection (1)(a)* shall be deemed not to be a material interest at any time when the following conditions are satisfied—

(a) that the holder of the interest has the right to have the company wound up, and

(b) that in the event of a winding up the holder is, by virtue of the interest and any other interest which the holder then holds in the same capacity, entitled to more than 50 per cent of the assets remaining after the discharge of all liabilities having priority over the interest or interests concerned.

(9) The market value of any asset for the purposes of this Chapter shall be determined in the like manner as it would be determined for the purposes of the Capital Gains Tax Acts except that, in the case of an interest in an offshore fund for which there are separate published buying and selling prices, *section 548(5)* shall apply with any necessary modifications for determining the market value of the interest for the purposes of this Chapter.

Cross References

From Section 743

Section 432 Meaning of "associated company" and "control".

Section 548 Valuation of assets.

To Section 743

Section 172A Interpretation.
Section 738 Undertakings for collective investment.
Section 739B Interpretation and application.
Section 739BA Personal portfolio investment undertaking.
Section 740 Interpretation (Chapter 2 and Schedules 19 and 20).
Section 744 Non-qualifying offshore funds.
Section 747B Interpretation and application.
Section 747G Tax treatment of relevant UCITS.
Section 747AA Treatment of certain offshore funds.
Section 896 Returns in relation to certain offshore products.
Schedule 19 Offshore Funds: Distributing Funds

744 Non-qualifying offshore funds

[FA90 s66]

(1) For the purposes of this Chapter, an offshore fund shall be a non-qualifying fund except during an account period of the fund in respect of which the fund is certified by the Revenue Commissioners as a distributing fund.

(2) An offshore fund shall not be certified as a distributing fund in respect of an account period unless with respect to that period the fund pursues a full distribution policy within the meaning of *Part 1* of *Schedule 19*.

(3) Subject to *Part 2* of *Schedule 19*, an offshore fund shall not be certified as a distributing fund in respect of any account period if at any time during that period—

(a) more than 5 per cent by value of the assets of the fund consists of interests in other offshore funds,

(b) subject to *subsections (4)* and *(5)*, more than 10 per cent by value of the assets of the fund consists of interests in a single company,

(c) the assets of the fund include more than 10 per cent of the issued share capital of any company or of any class of that share capital, or

(d) subject to *subsection (6)*, there is more than one class of material interest in the offshore fund and they do not all receive proper distribution benefits within the meaning of *subsection (7)*.

(4) For the purposes of *subsection (3)(b)*, in any account period the value, expressed as a percentage of the value of all the assets of an offshore fund, of that portion of the assets of the fund which consists of an interest in a single company shall be determined as at the most recent occasion (whether in that account period or an earlier one) on which the fund acquired an interest in that company for consideration in money or in money's worth; but for this purpose there shall be disregarded any occasion—

(a) on which the interest acquired constituted the new holding for the purposes of *section 584*, including that section as applied by *section 585* or *586*, and

(b) on which no consideration fell to be given for the interest acquired, other than the interest which constituted the original shares for the purposes of *section 584*, including that section as so applied.

(5) Except for the purpose of determining the total value of the assets of an offshore fund, an interest in a company shall be disregarded for the purposes of *subsection (3)(b)* if—

(a) the company carries on a banking business in the State or elsewhere which provides current or deposit account facilities in any currency for members of the public and bodies corporate, and

(b) the interest consists of a current or deposit account provided in the normal course of the company's banking business.

(6) There shall be disregarded for the purposes of *subsection (3)(d)* any interests in an offshore fund which—

(a) are held solely by persons employed or engaged in or about the management of the assets of the fund,

(b) carry no right or expectation to participate directly or indirectly in any of the profits of the fund, and

(c) on a winding up or on redemption carry no right to receive anything other than the return of the price paid for the interests.

(7) Where in any account period of an offshore fund there is more than one class of material interests in the fund, the classes of interests shall not (for the purposes of *subsection (3)(d)*) all receive proper distribution benefits unless, were each class of interests and the assets which that class represents interests in and assets of a separate offshore fund, each of those separate funds would (with respect to that period) pursue a full distribution policy within the meaning of *Part 1* of *Schedule 19*.

(8) For the purposes of this Chapter and *Schedule 19*, an account period of an offshore fund shall begin—

(a) on the 6th day of April, 1990, or, if it is later, whenever the fund begins to carry on its activities, and

(b) whenever an account period of the fund ends without the fund then ceasing to carry on its activities.

(9) For the purposes of this Chapter and *Schedule 19*, an account period of an offshore fund shall end on the first occurrence of any of the following—

(a) the expiration of 12 months from the beginning of the period;

(b) an accounting date of the fund or, if there is a period for which the fund does not make up accounts, the end of that period;

(c) the fund ceasing to carry on its activities.

(10) For the purposes of this Chapter and *Schedule 19*—

(a) an account period of an offshore fund which is a company within *section 743(1)(a)* shall end if and at the time when the company ceases to be resident outside the State, and

(b) an account period of an offshore fund which is a unit trust scheme within *section 743(1)(b)* shall end if and at the time when the trustees of the scheme become resident in the State.

(11) *Parts 3* and *4* of *Schedule 19* shall apply with respect to the procedure for and in connection with the certification of an offshore fund as a distributing fund.

Cross References

From Section 744

Section 584 Reorganisation or reduction of share capital.
Section 585 Conversion of securities.
Section 586 Company amalgamations by exchange of shares.
Section 743 Material interest in offshore funds.
Schedule 19 Offshore Funds: Distributing Funds

To Section 744

Section 740 Interpretation (Chapter 2 and Schedules 19 and 20).

Schedule 19 Offshore Funds: Distributing Funds

745 Charge to income tax or corporation tax of offshore income gain

[FA90 s67]

(1) Where a disposal to which this Chapter applies gives rise, in accordance with *Schedule 20*, to an offshore income gain, then, subject to this section, the amount of that gain shall be treated for the purposes of the Tax Acts as—

(a) income arising at the time of the disposal to the person making the disposal, and

(b) constituting profits or gains chargeable to tax under Case IV of Schedule D for the chargeable period (within the meaning of *section 321(2)*) in which the disposal is made.

(2) Subject to *subsection (3)*, *sections 25(2)(b)*, *29* and *30* shall apply in relation to income tax or corporation tax in respect of offshore income gains as they apply in relation to capital gains tax or corporation tax in respect of chargeable gains.

(3) In the application of *sections 29* and *30* in accordance with *subsection (2)*, *section 29(3)(c)* shall apply with the deletion of "situated in the State".

(4) In the case of individuals resident or ordinarily resident but not domiciled in the State, *subsections (4)* and *(5)* of *section 29* shall apply in relation to income tax chargeable by virtue of *subsection (1)* on an offshore income gain as they apply in relation to capital gains tax in respect of gains accruing to such individuals from the disposal of assets situated outside the State.

(5) (a) In this subsection, "*charity*" has the same meaning as in *section 208*, and "*market value*" shall be construed in accordance with *section 548*.

(b) A charity shall be exempt from tax in respect of an offshore income gain if the gain is applicable and applied for charitable purposes; but, if the property held on charitable trusts ceases to be subject to charitable trusts and that property represents directly or indirectly an offshore income gain, the trustees shall be treated as if they had disposed of and immediately reacquired that property for a consideration equal to its market value, any gain (calculated in accordance with *Schedule 20*) accruing being treated as an offshore income gain not accruing to a charity.

(6) In any case where—

(a) a disposal to which this Chapter applies is a disposal of settled property within the meaning of the Capital Gains Tax Acts, and

(b) for the purposes of the Capital Gains Tax Acts, the general administration of the trusts is ordinarily carried on outside the State and the trustees or a majority of them for the time being are not resident or not ordinarily resident in the State,

then, *subsection (1)* shall not apply in relation to any offshore income gain to which the disposal gives rise.

Cross References

From Section 745

Section 25 Companies not resident in the State.

Section 29 Persons chargeable.

Section 30 Partnerships.
Section 208 Lands owned and occupied, and trades carried on by, charities.
Section 321 Provisions of general application in relation to the making of allowances and charges.
Section 548 Valuation of assets.
Schedule 20 Offshore Funds: Computation of Offshore Income Gains

To Section 745

Section 189 Payments in respect of personal injuries.
Section 189A Special trusts for permanently incapacitated individuals.
Section 192 Payments in respect of thalidomide children.
Section 746 Offshore income gains accruing to persons resident or domiciled abroad.
Section 747E Disposal of an interest in offshore funds.
Schedule 20 Offshore Funds: Computation of Offshore Income Gains

746 Offshore income gains accruing to persons resident or domiciled abroad

[FA90 s68]

[(1) Subject to *subsection (2)*, *sections 579* and *579A* shall apply in relation to their application to offshore income gains as if—

(a) for any references to a chargeable gain there were substituted a reference to an offshore income gain,

(b) in *subsection (2)* of *section 579* and *subsection (4)* of *section 579A* for "the Capital Gains Tax Acts" there were substituted "the Tax Acts",

(c) in *subsection (2)* of *section 579* and *subsection (3)* of *section 579A* for "capital gains tax under *section 31*" there were substituted "income tax by virtue of *section 745*, and

(d) in *subsection (5)* of *section 579* and *subsection (9)* of *section 579A*—

(i) for "any capital gains tax payable" there were substituted "any income tax or corporation tax payable", and

(ii) for "for the purposes of income tax" there were substituted "for the purposes of income tax, corporation tax".][1]

(2) Where in any year of assessment—

(a) under *section 579(3)*, as it applies apart from *subsection (1)*, a chargeable gain is to be attributed to a beneficiary, and

(b) under *section 579(3)*, as applied by *subsection (1)*, an offshore income gain is also to be attributed to the beneficiary,

section 579 shall apply as if it required offshore income gains to be attributed before chargeable gains.

[(2A) Where in any year of assessment—

(a) under *section 579A(4)*, as it applies apart from *subsection (1)*, a chargeable gain is to be attributed to a beneficiary, and

(b) under *section 579A(4)*, as applied by *subsection (1)*, an offshore income gain is also to be attributed to the beneficiary,

section 579A shall apply as if it required offshore income gains to be attributed before chargeable gains.][2]

(3) *Section 590* shall apply in relation to its application to offshore income gains as if—

(a) for any reference to a chargeable gain there were substituted a reference to an offshore income gain, [(b) for the reference in *subsection (9)* of that section to capital gains tax there were substituted a reference to income tax or corporation tax, and

(c) *paragraphs (a)* and *(b)* of *subsection (7)*, and *subsection (11)*, of that section were deleted.][3]

(4) *Section 917* shall apply in relation to offshore income gains as if—

(a) for "chargeable gains" there were substituted "offshore income gains", and

[(b) for "capital gains tax under *sections 579* to *579F* or *section 590*" there were substituted "income tax or corporation tax under *sections 579* to *579F* or *section 590*, as applied by *section 746*".][4]

(5) Subject to *subsection (6)*, for the purpose of determining whether an individual [resident or ordinarily resident][5] in the State has a liability for income tax in respect of an offshore income gain arising on a disposal to which this Chapter applies where the disposal is made by a person resident or domiciled out of the State—

(a) [*sections 806, 807, 807A, 807B* and *807C*][6] shall apply as if the offshore income gain arising to the person resident or domiciled out of the State constituted income becoming payable to such person, and

(b) accordingly any reference in [*sections 806, 807, 807A, 807B* and *807C*][7] to income of, or payable or arising to, such person shall include a reference to the offshore income gain arising to such person by reason of the disposal to which this Chapter applies.

(6) To the extent that an offshore income gain is treated by virtue of *subsection (1)* or *(3)* as having accrued to any person resident or ordinarily resident in the State, that gain shall not be deemed to be the income of any individual for the purposes of [*sections 806, 807, 807A, 807B* and *807C*][8] or *Part 31*.

Amendments

[1] Substituted by FA99 s58(1)(a). This section shall apply as on and from the 11th day of February, 1999.

[2] Inserted by FA99 s58(1)(b). This section shall apply as on and from the 11th day of February, 1999.

[3] Substituted by FA99 s58(1)(c). This section shall apply as on and from the 11th day of February, 1999.

[4] Substituted by FA99 s58(1)(d). This section shall apply as on and from the 11th day of February, 1999.

[5] Substituted by FA07 s55(1)(a). Applies as on and from 1 February 2007.

[6, 7, 8] Substituted by FA07 s55(1)(b). Applies as on and from 1 February 2007.

Cross References

From Section 746

Section 31 Amount chargeable.
Section 579 Non-resident trusts.
Section 579A Attribution of gains to beneficiaries.
Section 579F Migrant settlements.
Section 590 Attribution to participators of chargeable gains accruing to non-resident company.
Section 745 Charge to income tax or corporation tax of offshore income gain.
Section 746 Offshore income gains accruing to persons resident or domiciled abroad.
Section 791 Income under revocable dispositions.
Section 806 Charge to income tax on transfer of assets abroad.
Section 807 Deductions and reliefs in relation to income chargeable to income tax under section 806.
Section 807A Liability of nontransferors.
Section 807B Certain transitional arrangements in relation to transfer of assets abroad.
Section 807C Supplementary provisions in relation to section 806 — apportionment in certain cases.
Section 917 Returns relating to non-resident companies and trusts.

To Section 746

Section 746 Offshore income gains accruing to persons resident or domiciled abroad.

747 Deduction of offshore income gain in determining capital gain

[FA90 s69(1) to (7)]

(1) This section shall apply where a disposal (being a disposal to which this Chapter applies) gives rise to an offshore income gain and, if that disposal also constitutes the disposal of the interest concerned for the purposes of the Capital Gains Tax Acts, that disposal is referred to in this section as "the disposal for the purposes of the Capital Gains Tax Acts".

(2) So far as relates to an offshore income gain which arises on a material disposal (within the meaning of *Part 1* of *Schedule 20*), *subsections (3)* and *(4)* shall apply in relation to the disposal for the purposes of the Capital Gains Tax Acts in substitution for *section 551(2)*.

(3) Subject to *subsections (4)* to *(7)*, in the computation in accordance with the Capital Gains Tax Acts of any gain accruing on the disposal for the purposes of those Acts, a sum equal to the offshore income gain shall be deducted from the sum which would otherwise constitute the amount or value of the consideration for the disposal.

(4) Where the disposal for the purposes of the Capital Gains Tax Acts is of such a nature that by virtue of *section 557* an apportionment is to be made of certain expenditure, no deduction shall be made by virtue of *subsection (3)* in determining for the purposes of the apportionment in *section 557(2)* the amount or value of the consideration for the disposal.

(5) Where the disposal for the purposes of the Capital Gains Tax Acts forms part of a transfer to which *section 600* applies, then, for the purposes of *subsection (5)(b)* of that section, the value of the whole of the consideration received by the transferor in exchange for the business shall be taken to be what it would be if the value of the consideration (other than shares so received by the transferor) were reduced by a sum equal to the offshore income gain.

(6) Where the disposal to which this Chapter applies constitutes such a disposal by virtue of *section 741(6)* or *742(5)*, the Capital Gains Tax Acts shall apply as if an amount equal to the offshore income gain to which the disposal gives rise were given (by the person making the exchange concerned) as consideration for the new holding (within the meaning of *section 584(1)*).

(7) In any case where—

(a) a disposal to which this Chapter applies by virtue of *subsection (3)* of *section 742* is made otherwise than to the offshore fund concerned or to the persons referred to in *subsection (2)(b)* of that section,

(b) subsequently a distribution which is referable to the asset disposed of is paid either to the person who made the disposal or to a person connected with such person, and

(c) the disposal gives rise (in accordance with *Part 2* of *Schedule 20*) to an offshore income gain,

then, for the purposes of the Tax Acts, the amount of the first distribution within *paragraph (b)* shall be taken to be reduced or, as the case may be, extinguished by deducting from such amount an amount equal to the offshore income gain referred to in *paragraph (c)* and, if that amount exceeds the amount of that first distribution, the balance shall be set against the second and, where necessary, any subsequent distribution within *paragraph (b)* until the balance is exhausted.

Cross References

From Section 747

Section 1 Interpretation of this Act.
Section 12 The charge to income tax.
Section 551 Exclusion from consideration for disposals of sums chargeable to income tax.
Section 557 Part disposals.
Section 584 Reorganisation or reduction of share capital.
Section 600 Transfer of business to company.
Section 741 Disposals of material interests in non-qualifying offshore funds.
Section 742 Offshore funds operating equalisation arrangements.
Schedule 20 Offshore Funds: Computation of Offshore Income Gains

To Section 747

Section 747E Disposal of an interest in offshore funds.

CHAPTER 3

Offshore Funds: Supplementary Provisions

747A Capital gains tax: rate of charge

[(1) In this section "*material interest*", "*non-qualifying fund*" and "*offshore fund*" shall have the same meaning as is assigned to them in *Chapter 2* of this Part.

(2) This section shall apply to a disposal, on or after the 12th day of February, 1998, by a person of an asset, if at the time of the disposal—

(a) the asset constitutes a material interest in an offshore fund which is not nor was at any material time a non-qualifying offshore fund, or

(b) the asset constitutes an interest in a company resident in the State or in a unit trust scheme, the trustees of which are at that time resident in the State and at a material time on or after the 1st day of January, 1991, the company or unit trust scheme was an offshore fund other than a non-qualifying offshore fund and the asset constituted a material interest in that fund.

(3) *Subsections (2)* to *(7)* of *section 741* shall apply for the purposes of this section as if references in those subsections to a non-qualifying offshore fund were references to an offshore fund.

(4) Notwithstanding *subsection (3)* of *section 28*, the rate of capital gains tax in respect of chargeable gains accruing to a person on the disposal of an asset to which this section applies shall be 40 per cent.][1]

Amendments

[1] Inserted by FA98 s66.

Amendments

[1] Inserted by FA98 s66.

Cross References

From Section 747A

Section 28 Taxation of capital gains and rate of charge.

Section 740 Interpretation (Chapter 2 and Schedules 19 and 20).

Section 741 Disposals of material interests in non-qualifying offshore funds.

To Section 747A

Section 747AA Treatment of certain offshore funds.

747AA Treatment of certain offshore funds

[Without prejudice to "*offshore fund*" having the meaning assigned to it by *section 743* for the purposes of Chapter 4, where that Chapter does not apply to an offshore fund by virtue of *subsection (2A)* of *section 747B*, then *Chapter 2* and *section 747A* shall not apply in respect of that offshore fund.][1]

Amendments

[1] Inserted by FA07 s39(1)(b). Applies as respects income arising or gains accruing on or after 20 February 2007.

Cross References

From Section 747AA

Section 740 Interpretation (Chapter 2 and Schedules 19 and 20).

Section 743 Material interest in offshore funds.

Section 747A Capital gains tax: rate of charge.

Section 747B Interpretation and application.

CHAPTER 4

Certain Offshore Funds — Taxation and Returns

747B Interpretation and application

[(1) In this Chapter—

"chargeable period" has the same meaning as in *section 321(2)*;

["*deemed disposal*" means a disposal of the type provided for in *section 747E(6)*;][1]

"EEA Agreement" means the Agreement on the European Economic Area signed at Oporto on 2 May 1992, as adjusted by the Protocol signed at Brussels on 17 March 1993;

"EEA state" means a State, other than the State, which is a Contracting Party to the EEA Agreement;

"material interest" shall be construed in accordance with *section 743*;

"OECD" means the organisation known as the Organisation for Economic Co-operation and Development;

"offshore fund" has the meaning assigned to it by *section 743*;

"offshore state" means a State, other than the State, which is—

(i) a Member State of the European Communities,

(ii) a State which is an EEA state, or

(iii) a State which is a member of the OECD, the government of which have entered into arrangements having the force of law by virtue of [*section 826(1)*][2];

["*relevant event*" means the ending of a relevant period, where "*relevant period*" in relation to an offshore fund means a period of 8 years beginning with the acquisition of a material interest in the fund and each subsequent period of 8 years beginning immediately after the preceding relevant period;][3]

"relevant payment" means any payment including a distribution made to a person in respect of a material interest in an offshore fund, where such payments are made annually or at more frequent intervals, other than a payment made in consideration of the disposal of an interest in the offshore fund;

"return of income" has the meaning assigned to it by *section 1084*;

"specified return date for the chargeable period" has the meaning assigned to it by [*section 959A*][4]

"standard rate per cent" has the meaning assigned to it by *section 4*.

(2) [Subject to *subsection (2A)*, this Chapter][5] applies to an offshore fund which—

(a) being a company, the company is resident in,

(b) being a unit trust scheme, the trustees of the unit trust scheme are resident in, or

(c) being any arrangements referred to in *section 743(1)*, those arrangements take effect by virtue of the law of,

an offshore state.

[(2A) This Chapter does not apply to an offshore fund other than an offshore fund which—

(a) (i) is an undertaking for collective investment formed under the law of an offshore state,

(ii) is similar in all material respects to an investment limited partnership (within the meaning of the Investment Limited Partnership Act 1994), and

(iii) holds a certificate authorising it to act as such an undertaking, being a certificate issued by the authorities of that state under laws providing for the proper and orderly regulation of such undertakings,

(b) is authorised by or under any measures duly taken by a Member State for the purposes of giving effect to—

(i) Council Directive 85/611/EEC on the coordination of laws, regulations and administrative provisions relating to undertakings for collective investment in transferable securities (UCITS), or

(ii) any amendment to that Directive,

(c) (i) is a company formed under the law of an offshore state,

(ii) is similar in all material respects to an authorised investment company (within the meaning of Part XIII of the Companies Act 1990),

(iii) holds an authorisation issued by the authorities of that state under laws providing for the proper and orderly regulation of such companies and that authorisation has not ceased to have effect, and

(iv) is an investment company—

(I) which raises capital by promoting the sale of its shares to the public, or

(II) each of the shareholders of which is an investor which, if the company were an authorised investment company within the meaning of Part XIII of the Companies Act 1990 would be a collective investor within the meaning of section 739B,

or

(d) (i) is a unit trust scheme, the trustees of which are not resident in the State,

(ii) is similar in all material respects to an authorised unit trust scheme (within the meaning of the Unit Trusts Act 1990),

(iii) holds an authorisation issued by the authorities of that offshore state under laws providing for the proper and orderly regulation of such schemes and that authorisation has not ceased to have effect, and

(iv) provides facilities for the participation by the public, as beneficiaries under the trust, in profits or income arising from the acquisition, holding, management or disposal of securities or any other property whatsoever.][6]

(3) For the purposes of this Chapter—

(a) (i) there shall be a disposal of an asset if there would be such a disposal for the purposes of the Capital Gains Tax Acts, and

(ii) where, on the death of a person, an asset which the person was competent to dispose, is a material interest in an offshore fund to which this Chapter applies, then, notwithstanding *section 573(2)(b)*, such material interest shall be deemed to be disposed of and reacquired by the person immediately before the death of the person for a consideration equal to its then market value,

(b) an income shall be correctly included in a return made by a person, only where that income is included in a return of income made by the person on or before the specified return date for the chargeable period in which the income arises, and

(c) details of a disposal shall be correctly included in a return made by a person, only where details of the disposal are included in a return of income made by the person or, where the person has died, his or her executor or administrator, on or before the specified return date for the chargeable period in which the disposal is made.][7]

Amendments

[1] Inserted by FA06 s51(1)(a)(i). This section applies as respects any relevant event occurring on or after the passing of this Act in respect of a material interest in an offshore fund acquired on or after 1 January 2001.

[2] Substituted by FA07 sched2(1)(y). Has effect as on and from 2 April 2007

[3] Inserted by FA06 s51(1)(a)(ii). This section applies as respects any relevant event occurring on or after the passing of this Act in respect of a material interest in an offshore fund acquired on or after 1 January 2001.

[4] Substituted by FA12 sched4(part 2)(g).

[5] Substituted by FA07 s39(1)(a)(i). Applies as respects income arising or gains accruing on or after 20 February 2007.

[6] Inserted by FA07 s39(1)(a)(ii). Applies as respects income arising or gains accruing on or after 20 February 2007.

[7] Inserted by FA01 s72(1). This section shall be deemed to have applied as on and from 1 January 2001.

Revenue Briefings

Tax Briefing

Tax Briefing December 2006 – Issue 65 pg 4 – Offshore Funds Legislation

Cross References

From Section 747B

Section 4 Interpretation of Corporation Tax Acts.
Section 321 Provisions of general application in relation to the making of allowances and charges.
Section 573 Death.
Section 743 Material interest in offshore funds.
Section 747E Disposal of an interest in offshore funds.
Section 826 Agreements for relief from double taxation.
Section 950 Interpretation (Part 41).
Section 1084 Surcharge for late returns.

To Section 747B

Section 747AA Treatment of certain offshore funds.

747C Return on acquisition of material interest

[Where in any chargeable period a person acquires a material interest in an offshore fund, the person shall, notwithstanding anything to the contrary in [*Part 41A* or *section 1084*][1] be deemed for that chargeable period to be a chargeable person for the purposes of [*Chapter 3* of *Part 41A* and *sections 1084*][2], and the return of income to be delivered by the person for that chargeable period shall include the following particulars—

(a) the name and address of the offshore fund,

(b) a description, including the cost to the person, of the material interest acquired, and

(c) the name and address of the person through whom the material interest was acquired.][3]

Amendments

[1, 2] Substituted by FA12 sched4(part 2)(g).

[3] Inserted by FA01 s72(1). This section shall be deemed to have applied as on and from 1 January 2001.

Cross References

From Section 747C

Section 950 Interpretation (Part 41).
Section 951 Obligation to make a return.
Section 1084 Surcharge for late returns.

To Section 747C

Section 896 Returns in relation to certain offshore products.

747D Payment in respect of offshore funds

[Where on or after 1 January 2001 a person who has a material interest in an offshore fund, is in receipt of a payment from the offshore fund, then—

[(a) where the person is not a company—

(i) the rate of income tax to be charged on the income represented by the payment, where the payment is not made in consideration of the disposal of an interest in the offshore fund, shall, notwithstanding *section 15*, be—

(I) subject to *subparagraph (ii)*, in the case of an offshore fund which is a personal portfolio investment undertaking, at the rate of 60 per cent,

and

(II) in any other case, at the rate of 41 per cent, and

(ii) in the case of an offshore fund which is a personal portfolio investment undertaking and the income represented by the payment is not correctly included in a return made by the person, the income shall, notwithstanding *section 15*, be charged to income tax at the rate of 80 per cent,][1]

and

[(b) where the person is a company and the payment is not taken into account as a receipt of a trade carried on by the company, the income represented by the payment shall be charged to tax under Case III of Schedule D.][2]][3]

Amendments

[1] Substituted by FA14 s35(2)(a). Comes into operation on 1 January 2015.

[2] Substituted by FA02 s46(1)(a). This section shall be deemed to have applied as on and from 1 January 2001.

[3] Inserted by FA01 s72(1). This section shall be deemed to have applied as on and from 1 January 2001.

Cross References

From Section 747D

Section 15 Rate of charge.

To Section 747D

Section 485C Interpretation (Chapter 2A).

747E Disposal of an interest in offshore funds

[(1) [Subject to *subsection 1(A)*, where on or after][1] 1 January 2001 a person who has a material interest in an offshore fund, disposes of an interest in the offshore fund and the disposal gives rise to a gain computed in accordance with *subsection (2)* then, notwithstanding *sections 745* and *747*, where the gain is not taken into account in computing the profits or gains of a trade carried on by a company, the amount of that gain shall be treated as an amount of income chargeable to tax under Case IV of Schedule D, and—

[…][2]

[(b) where the person is not a company, the rate of income tax to be charged on that income shall, notwithstanding *section 15*, be—

(i) in the case of an offshore fund which is a personal portfolio investment undertaking—

(I) subject to *clause (II)*, at the rate of 60 per cent, and

(II) where the details of the disposal are not correctly included in a return made by the person, at the rate of 80 per cent,

and

(ii) in any other case, at the rate of 41 per cent.][3]][4]

[(1A) (a) In this subsection—

'*umbrella scheme*' means an offshore fund—

(i) which is divided into a number of sub-funds, and

(ii) in which each person who has a material interest in a sub-fund is entitled to exchange the whole or part of such interest for an interest in another sub-fund of the offshore fund.

(b) A disposal under *subsection (1)* does not include any exchange by a person who has a material interest in a sub-fund of an offshore fund which is an umbrella scheme, effected by way of a bargain made at arm's length by that offshore fund, of the whole or part of such interest for an interest in another sub-fund of that offshore fund.

(c) Any exchange referred to in *paragraph (b)* shall not be regarded as a disposal by a person of a material interest in an offshore fund which is an umbrella scheme.][5]

(2) The amount of the gain accruing on a disposal referred to in *subsection (1)* is the amount which would be the amount of a gain accruing on the disposal for the purposes of the Capital Gains Tax Acts, if it were computed without regard to—

(a) any charge to tax by virtue of this section, and

(b) *section 556(2).*

(3) [(a) Notwithstanding *sections 538* and *546*, where apart from this subsection the effect of any computation under *subsection (2)* would be to produce a loss, the gain on the disposal referred to in *subsection (1)* shall be treated as nil and [for the purposes of the Tax Acts and the Capital Gains Tax Acts][6] no loss shall be treated as accruing on such disposal.][7]

[(b) Where in respect of a material interest in an offshore fund—

(i) a gain on a disposal is treated as nil in accordance with *paragraph (a)*,

(ii) that disposal is not a deemed disposal, and

(iii) a person was chargeable to tax in respect of an earlier deemed disposal of a material interest in the fund,

then the provisions of *section 865* (apart from *subsection (4)*) shall apply and the inspector may make such repayment or set-off as is necessary for securing that the aggregate of tax payable in respect of the material interest in the fund under this section does not exceed the tax that would have been so payable in respect of the material interest in the fund if *subsection (6)* had not been enacted.][8]

(4) Where, as a result of a disposal by a person, an amount of income is chargeable to tax under Case IV of Schedule D, that amount shall not be reduced by a claim made by the person—

(a) where the person is not a company, under *section 381* or *383*, or

(b) where the person is a company, under [*section 396, 396B*][9] or *399*.

[(5) Where an individual is chargeable to tax in accordance with *subsection (1)* in respect of an amount of income the tax thereby payable, in so far as it is paid, shall be treated as an amount of capital gains tax paid for the purposes of *section 104* of the Capital Acquisitions Tax Consolidation Act 2003.][10]

[(6) Where a person has a material interest in an offshore fund and a relevant event occurs in respect of that fund, then the person shall be deemed for the purposes of this section to have disposed of the whole of the material interest immediately before the time of that relevant event and immediately to have reacquired it at its market value at that time.][11]][12]

Amendments

[1] Substituted by FA12 s34(a). Deemed to have come into force and takes effect on and from 1 January 2012.

[2] Deleted by FA12 s28(5)(f). Has effect as respects the disposal in whole or in part by a person of a material interest in an offshore fund (within the meaning of Chapter 4 of Part 27) on or after 1 January 2012.

[3] Substituted by FA14 s35(2)(b). Comes into operation on 1 January 2015.

[4] Substituted by FA07 s40(1)(d). Applies as respects on or after 20 February 2007.

[5] Inserted by FA12 s34(b). Deemed to have come into force and takes effect on and from 1 January 2012.

[6] Substituted by FA05 s43(1). This section applies as respects the disposal of an interest in an offshore fund on or after 3 February 2005.

[7] Renumbered by FA06 s51(1)(b)(i)(I). This section applies as respects any relevant event occurring on or after the passing of this Act in respect of a material interest in an offshore fund acquired on or after 1 January 2001.

[8] Inserted by FA06 s51(1)(b)(i)(II). This section applies as respects any relevant event occurring on or after the passing of this Act in respect of a material interest in an offshore fund acquired on or after 1 January 2001.

[9] Substituted by FA04 s30(a).

[10] Substituted by FA12 sched6(1)(h). Has effect as on and from 31 March 2012.

[11] Inserted by FA06 s51(1)(b)(ii). This section applies as respects any relevant event occurring on or after the passing of this Act in respect of a material interest in an offshore fund acquired on or after 1 January 2001.

[12] Inserted by FA01 s72(1). This section shall be deemed to have applied as on and from 1 January 2001.

Cross References

From Section 747E

Section 15 Rate of charge.
Section 21 The charge to corporation tax and exclusion of income tax and capital gains tax.
Section 381 Right to repayment of tax by reference to losses.
Section 383 Relief under Case IV for losses.
Section 396 Relief for trading losses other than terminal losses.
Section 396B Relief for certain trading losses on a value basis.
Section 399 Losses in transactions from which income would be chargeable under Case IV or V of Schedule D.
Section 538 Disposals where assets lost or destroyed or become of negligible value.
Section 546 Allowable losses.
Section 556 Adjustment of allowable expenditure by reference to consumer price index.
Section 745 Charge to income tax or corporation tax of offshore income gain.
Section 747 Deduction of offshore income gain in determining capital gain.
Section 865 Repayment of tax.

To Section 747E

Section 189 Payments in respect of personal injuries.
Section 189A Special trusts for permanently incapacitated individuals.
Section 192 Payments in respect of thalidomide children.
Section 485C Interpretation (Chapter 2A).
Section 747B Interpretation and application.

747F Reconstructions and amalgamations in offshore funds

[(1) In this section "*scheme of reconstruction or amalgamation*" means an arrangement under which each person who has a material interest in an offshore fund (in this section referred to as an "*old interest*") receives in place of that old interest a material interest in another offshore fund (in this section referred to as the "*new interest*") in respect of or in proportion to, or as nearly as may be in proportion to, the value of the old interest and as a result of which the value of that old interest becomes negligible.

(2) Where, in connection with a scheme of reconstruction or amalgamation, a person disposes of an old interest and receives in place of that old interest a new interest, the disposal of the old interest shall not give rise to a gain but the new interest shall for the purposes of section 747E(2) be treated as acquired at the same time and at the same cost as the old interest.][1]

Amendments

[1] Inserted by FA04 s30(b).

747FA Offshore funds: amalgamations with investment undertaking

[(1) In this section—

'*investment undertaking*' has the same meaning as in *section 739B(1)*;

'*scheme of amalgamation*' means an arrangement whereby the assets of an offshore fund are transferred to an investment undertaking in exchange for the issue by the investment undertaking of units to each of the persons who have a material interest in the offshore fund, in proportion to the value of that interest, and as a result of which the value of that interest becomes negligible.

(2) Where, in connection with a scheme of amalgamation, a person disposes of a material interest in an offshore fund and receives, in place of that interest, units in an investment undertaking, the disposal of the interest in the offshore fund shall not give rise to a gain but the units acquired in the investment undertaking under that scheme shall for the purposes of *Chapter 1A* be treated as acquired at the same time and at the same cost as the interest in the offshore fund.][1]

Amendments

[1] Inserted by FA12 s33(b). Deemed to have come into force and takes effect on and from 1 January 2012.

CHAPTER 5

Relevant UCITS and Relevant AIF

747G Tax treatment of a relevant UCITS or a relevant AIF

[(1) In this section—

'*AIF*' means an alternative investment fund within the meaning of the relevant AIFM Directives;

'*AIFM*' means alternative investment fund manager;

'*alternative investment fund manager*' means a person whose regular business is managing one, or more than one, AIF;

'*branch or agency*' has the same meaning as in *section 4*;

'*EEA state*' has the same meaning as in *section 747B*;

'*management company*', in relation to a relevant UCITS, means a management company within the meaning of the relevant UCITS Directives;

'*relevant AIF*' means an AIF which is formed under the laws of a jurisdiction other than the State and which is not an investment undertaking within the meaning of *section 739B*;

'*relevant AIFM Directives*' means Directive 2011/61/EU of the European Parliament and of the Council of 8 June 2011* on Alternative Investment Fund Managers and any Directive amending that Directive;

*OJ No. L174, 1.7.2011, p.1

'*relevant profits*', in relation to a relevant UCITS or a relevant AIF, means the profits which would be relevant profits (within the meaning of *section 739B*) if the relevant UCITS or the relevant AIF were an investment undertaking (within the meaning of that section);

'*relevant UCITS*' means an undertaking for collective investment in transferable securities—

(a) to which the relevant UCITS Directives apply, and

(b) which is formed under the laws of any Member State other than the State and which is not an investment undertaking within the meaning of *section 739B*;

'*relevant UCITS Directives*' means Directive 2009/65/EC of the European Parliament and of the Council of 13 July 2009* on the coordination of laws, regulations and administrative provisions relating to undertakings for collective investment in transferable securities (UCITS), and any Directive amending that Directive.

*OJ No. L302, 17.11.2009, p.32

(2) Notwithstanding anything in the Tax Acts and the Capital Gains Tax Acts—

(a) a relevant UCITS which is managed by a management company authorised under any laws of the State which implement the relevant UCITS Directives, or

(b) a relevant AIF which is managed—

(i) by an AIFM authorised under any laws of the State which implement the relevant AIFM Directives, or

(ii) through a branch or agency in the State of an AIFM authorised under the laws of an EEA state,

shall not be chargeable to tax under those Acts in respect of so much of relevant profits as would be, apart from this subsection, so chargeable solely by virtue of the relevant UCITS or the relevant AIF, as the case may be, being so managed.

(3) An interest in a relevant UCITS or a relevant AIF shall be treated for the purposes of this Part as an interest in a company, scheme or arrangement specified in *section 743(1)*.][1]

Amendments

[1] Substituted by FA14 s30. Comes into operation on 1 January 2015.

PART 28

Purchase and Sale of Securities

CHAPTER 1

Purchase and Sale of Securities

748 Interpretation and application (Chapter 1)

[ITA67 s367; F(MP)A68 s3(2) and Sch PtI; CTA76 s140(1) and Sch2 PtI par17]

(1) In this Chapter and in *Schedule 21*—

"*distribution*" has the same meaning as in the Corporation Tax Acts;

"*interest*" includes a distribution and any dividend which is not such a distribution and, in applying references to interest in relation to such a distribution, "*gross interest*" or "*gross amount*" means the distribution together with the tax credit to which the recipient of the distribution is entitled in respect of it and "*net interest*" means the distribution exclusive of any such tax credit;

"*person*" includes any body of persons, and references to a person entitled to any exemption from income tax include, in a case of an exemption expressed to apply to income of a trust or fund, references to the persons entitled to make claims for the granting of that exemption;

"*securities*" includes stocks and shares;

securities shall be deemed to be similar if they entitle their holders to the same rights against the same persons as to capital and interest and the same remedies for the enforcement of those rights, notwithstanding any difference in the total nominal amounts of the respective securities or in the form in which they are held or the manner in which they can be transferred.

(2) Subject to this section, this Chapter shall apply in the case of a purchase by a person (in this Chapter referred to as "*the first buyer*") of any securities and their subsequent sale by the first buyer, where the result of the transaction is that interest becoming payable in respect of the securities (in this Chapter referred to as "*the interest*") is receivable by the first buyer.

(3) This Chapter shall not apply in the case where—

(a) the time elapsing between the purchase by the first buyer and the first buyer's taking steps to dispose of the securities exceeds 6 months, or

(b) that time exceeds one month and in the opinion of the Revenue Commissioners the purchase and sale were each effected at the current market price and the sale was not effected in pursuance of an agreement or arrangement made before or at the time of the purchase.

(4) An appeal shall lie to the Appeal Commissioners with respect to any opinion of the Revenue Commissioners under *subsection (3)(b)* in the like manner as an appeal would lie against an assessment to income tax, and the provisions of the Income Tax Acts relating to appeals shall apply accordingly.

(5) The reference in *subsection (3)* to the first buyer taking steps to dispose of the securities shall be construed—

(a) if the first buyer sold the securities in the exercise of an option the first buyer had acquired, as a reference to the first buyer's acquisition of the option, and

(b) in any other case, as a reference to the first buyer selling the securities.

(6) (a) For the purposes of this Chapter but subject to *paragraph (b)*, a sale of securities similar to, and of the like nominal amount as, securities previously bought (in this subsection referred to as "*the original securities*") shall be equivalent to a sale of the original securities and *subsection (5)* shall apply accordingly, and, where the first buyer bought parcels of similar securities at different times, a subsequent sale of any of the securities shall, in so far as may be, be related to the last of the parcels to be bought, and then to the last but one, and so on.

(b) A person shall be under no greater liability to tax by virtue of this subsection than would have been the case if instead of selling the similar securities the person had sold the original securities.

(7) Where, at the time when a trade is or is deemed to be set up and commenced, any securities form part of the trading stock belonging to the trade, those securities shall be treated for the purposes of this section as having been sold at that time in the open market by the person to whom they belonged immediately before that time and as having been purchased at that time in the open market by the person thereafter engaged in carrying on the trade, and, subject to this subsection, where there is a change in the persons engaged in carrying on a trade which is not a change on which the trade is deemed to be discontinued, this section shall apply in relation to the person so engaged after the change as if anything done to or by that person's predecessor had been done to or by that person.

Cross References

From Section 748

Schedule 21 Purchase and Sale of Securities: Appropriate Amount in Respect of the Interest

To Section 748

Section 400 Company reconstructions without change of ownership.

749 Dealers in securities

[ITA67 s368]

(1) Subject to this section, where the first buyer is engaged in carrying on a trade which consists of or comprises dealings in securities, then, in computing for any of the purposes of the Tax Acts the profits arising from or loss sustained in the trade, the price paid by the first buyer for the securities shall be reduced by the appropriate amount in respect of the interest determined in accordance with *Schedule 21*.

(2) Where in the opinion of the Revenue Commissioners the first buyer is bona fide carrying on the business of a discount house in the State, or where the first buyer is a member of a stock exchange in the State who is recognised by the committee of that stock exchange as carrying on the business of a dealer, *subsection (1)* shall not apply in relation to securities bought in the ordinary course of such business.

[(2A) (a) *Subsection (1)* shall not apply for a chargeable period if the securities are overseas securities purchased by the first buyer in the ordinary course of the first buyer's trade as a dealer in securities and the following conditions are satisfied—

(i) that the interest payable in respect of all such overseas securities to which this Chapter applies is brought into account in computing, for the purposes of the Tax Acts, the profits or gains arising from, or losses sustained in, the trade for the chargeable period, and

(ii) where credit against tax would, but for this section, fall to be allowed for the chargeable period in respect of that interest by virtue of *Part 14* or *35* or *Schedule 24*, that the first buyer elects by notice in writing, on or before the specified return date for the chargeable period, that such credit shall not be so allowed.

(b) In this subsection—

"*foreign local authority*" means an authority, corresponding in substance to a local authority for the purposes of the Local Government Act 2001, which is established outside the State and whose functions are carried on primarily outside the State;

"*foreign local government*" means any local or regional government in any jurisdiction outside the State;

"*foreign public authority*" means an authority, corresponding in substance to a public authority for the purposes of the Local Government Act 2001, which is established outside the State and whose functions are carried on primarily outside the State;

overseas securities' means securities issued—

(i) by a government of a territory outside of the State,

(ii) by a foreign local authority, foreign local government or foreign public authority, or

(iii) by any other body of persons not resident in the State;

"*specified return date for the chargeable period*" has the same meaning as in [*section 959A*][1].

(2B) Where an election is made in accordance with *subsection (2A)(a)(ii)*—

(a) then, notwithstanding *Parts 14* and *35* and *Schedule 24*, credit against tax in respect of the interest shall not be allowed by virtue of either of those Parts or, as the case may be, that Schedule,

(b) that election shall be included in the return, required to be made by the first buyer under [*Chapter 3* of *Part 41A*][2], for the chargeable period, and

(c) that election shall have effect only for the chargeable period for which it is made.

(2C) *Subsection (1)* shall not apply for a chargeable period if the securities are securities, which are not chargeable assets for the purposes of the Capital Gains Tax Acts by virtue of *section 607*, purchased by the first buyer in the ordinary course of the first buyer's trade as a dealer in securities and the interest payable in respect of all such securities to which this Chapter applies is brought into account in computing, for the purposes of the Tax Acts, the profits or gains arising from, or losses sustained in, the trade for the chargeable period.][3]

(3) *Subsection (1)* shall not apply if the interest is to any extent required to be taken into account under *section 752* as if it were a trading receipt which had not borne tax or would to any extent be so required to be taken into account but for *paragraph 2* of *Schedule 22*.

Amendments

[1,2] Substituted by FA12 sched4(part 2)(g).

[3] Inserted by FA03 s31(1). Applies as respects securities purchased on or after 1 January 2003.

Cross References

From Section 749

Section 442 Interpretation (Part 14).
Section 607 Government and certain other securities.
Section 752 Purchases of shares by financial concerns and persons exempted from tax.
Section 826 Agreements for relief from double taxation.
Section 950 Interpretation (Part 41).
Section 951 Obligation to make a return.
Schedule 21 Purchase and Sale of Securities: Appropriate Amount in Respect of the Interest
Schedule 22 Dividends Regarded as Paid Out of Profits Accumulated Before Given Date
Schedule 24 Relief from Income Tax and Corporation Tax by Means of Credit in Respect of Foreign Tax

To Section 749

Section 711 Chargeable gains of life business.
Section 737 Special investment schemes.
Section 738 Undertakings for collective investment.
Section 751 Traders other than dealers in securities.
Section 838 Special portfolio investment accounts.
Schedule 21 Purchase and Sale of Securities: Appropriate Amount in Respect of the Interest
Schedule 22 Dividends Regarded as Paid Out of Profits Accumulated Before Given Date

750 Persons entitled to exemption

[ITA67 s369(1); CTA76 s140(1) and Sch 2 Pt1 par18]

Where the first buyer is entitled under any enactment to an exemption from tax which apart from this section would extend to the interest, then, subject to this section, the exemption shall not extend to an amount equal to the appropriate amount in respect of the interest determined in accordance with *Schedule 21*; but, if the first buyer is so entitled and any annual payment is payable by the first buyer out of the interest, the annual payment shall be deemed as to the whole of that payment—

(a) to be paid out of profits or gains not brought into charge to tax, and *section 238* shall apply accordingly, and

(b) for the purposes of corporation tax, not to be a payment which is a charge on income.

Cross References

From Section 750

Section 238 Annual payments not payable out of taxed income.
Schedule 21 Purchase and Sale of Securities: Appropriate Amount in Respect of the Interest

To Section 750

Schedule 21 Purchase and Sale of Securities: Appropriate Amount in Respect of the Interest

751 Traders other than dealers in securities

[ITA67 s370; CTA76 Sch2 Pt1 par19]

(1) Where the first buyer carries on a trade not within *section 749*, then, in ascertaining—

(a) for the purposes of income tax, whether any, and if so what, repayment of tax is to be made to the first buyer under *section 381* by reference to any loss sustained in the trade for the year of assessment the first buyer's income for which includes the interest, there shall be disregarded—

(i) the appropriate amount in respect of the interest determined in accordance with *Schedule 21*, and

(ii) any tax paid on that amount;

(b) for the purposes of corporation tax, the income or profits against which the loss may be set off under [...][1] *396*, there shall be disregarded the appropriate amount in respect of the interest determined in accordance with *Schedule 21*.

(2) Where the first buyer is a body corporate and carries on a trade not within *section 749* or a business consisting mainly in the making of investments, then, if any annual payment payable by the body corporate is to any extent payable out of the interest, that annual payment shall be deemed to that extent—

(a) for the purposes of income tax, not to be payable out of profits or gains brought into charge to tax, and *section 238* shall apply accordingly, and

(b) for the purposes of corporation tax, not to be a payment which is a charge on income.

Amendments

[1] Deleted by FA03 s41(1)(k). This section applies as respects accounting periods ending on or after 6 February 2003.

Cross References

From Section 751

Section 238 Annual payments not payable out of taxed income.

Section 381 Right to repayment of tax by reference to losses.

Section 396 Relief for trading losses other than terminal losses.

Section 749 Dealers in securities.

Schedule 21 Purchase and Sale of Securities: Appropriate Amount in Respect of the Interest

To Section 751

Schedule 21 Purchase and Sale of Securities: Appropriate Amount in Respect of the Interest

751A Exchange of shares held as trading stock

[(1) In this section—

"*new holding*", in relation to original shares, and "*original shares*" have, respectively, the same meanings as in *section 584(1)*.

(2) *Subsections (4)* and *(5)* shall apply where a transaction to which this section applies occurs in relation to any original shares—

(a) to which a person carrying on a business consisting wholly or partly of dealing in securities is beneficially entitled, and

(b) which are such that a profit on their sale would form part of the trading profits of that business.

(3) This section applies to any transaction, being a disposal of original shares which, if the original shares were not such as are mentioned in *subsection (2)* would result in the disposal not being treated as a disposal by virtue of *sections 584* to *587*; but does not apply to any transaction in relation to which *section 751B* applies.

(4) Subject to *subsection (5)*, in making any computation in accordance with the provisions of the Tax Acts applicable to trading profits chargeable to tax under Case I of Schedule D—

(a) the transaction to which this section applies shall be treated as not involving any disposal of the original shares, and

(b) the new holding shall be treated as the same asset as the original shares.

(5) Where, under a transaction to which this section applies, the person concerned receives or becomes entitled to receive any consideration in addition to the new holding, *subsection (4)* shall have effect as if the references to the original shares were references to the proportion of them which the market value of the new holding at the time of the transaction bears to the aggregate of that value and the market value at that time (or, if it is cash, the amount) of that consideration.

(6) *Subsections (4)* and *(5)* shall have effect with the necessary modifications in relation to any computation made for the purposes of *section 707(4)* in a case where the original shares held by the company concerned and the new holding are treated as the same asset by virtue of any of *sections 584* to *587*.][1]

Amendments

[1] Inserted by FA99 s59(1). Applies as respects section 751A inserted by subsection (1), as on and from the 11th day of February, 1999.

Cross References

From Section 751A

Section 584 Reorganisation or reduction of share capital.
Section 587 Company reconstructions and amalgamations.
Section 707 Management expenses.
Section 751B Exchange of Irish Government bonds.

751B Exchange of Irish Government bonds

[(1) In this section—

"*chargeable period*" has the same meaning as in *section 321(2)*;

"*the exchange*" in relation to an investor, means the exchange of old securities for new securities under the Exchange Programme in Irish Government bonds as designated by the National Treasury Management Agency;

"*investor*" means any person who as beneficial owner of securities exchanges them for new securities under the exchange;

"*last payment day*" in relation to old securities, means the last day, before the day on which the exchange takes place, on which interest is payable in respect of the old securities; and in a case where a payment of such interest may be made on a number of days, that interest shall be treated as payable on the first of those days; but if there has not been any day upon which interest in respect of old securities has been payable before the day on which the exchange takes place, the last payment day means the day of issue of the old securities;

"*old securities*" means the first-mentioned securities in the definition of "*investor*";

"*new securities*" means the securities issued to an investor in exchange for old securities under the exchange;

"*securities*" means securities to which *section 36* applies.

(2) (a) *Subsections (3)* and *(5)* shall apply as respects an investor who is a person carrying on a trade or business which consists wholly or partly of dealing in securities in respect of which any profits or gains are chargeable to tax under Case I of Schedule D.

(b) *Subsection (6)* shall apply as respects any investor other than an investor referred to in *paragraph (a)*.

(3) There shall be computed for the chargeable period in which the exchange by an investor to whom this subsection applies takes place, an amount of tax (in this

section referred to as "*the deferred tax*") where the deferred tax is found by the formula—

(a) in a case where the investor is chargeable to tax in the chargeable period in respect of interest received in the chargeable period—

$$A - B - C, \text{ and}$$

(b) in any other case—

$$A - B$$

where—

A is the amount of tax which, apart from this section, would finally fall to be borne by the investor for that chargeable period;

B is the amount of tax which, apart from this section, would finally fall to be borne by the investor for that chargeable period if the exchange were not taken into account in computing that tax, but, in a case to which *paragraph (b)* applies, includes the tax on interest which has accrued in respect of old securities from the beginning of that chargeable period, or the day on which the old securities were acquired by the investor, whichever is later, to the day on which the exchange took place; and

C is the amount representing the tax on accrued interest for that chargeable period in respect of old securities which is included in A.

(4) For the purposes of *subsection (3)* the accrued interest in respect of old securities is the interest accrued on such securities from—

(a) the last payment day in respect of the old securities, or

(b) the day on which the old securities were acquired by an investor,

whichever is later.

(5) Where an investor to whom this section applies so elects, the amount of tax which, apart from this subsection, finally falls to be borne for the chargeable period in which the exchange takes place, shall be reduced by the amount of the deferred tax and the amount of the deferred tax shall be deemed to be an amount of tax which finally falls to be borne for the chargeable period (in this subsection referred to as "*the later chargeable period*") in which the new securities are disposed of in addition to any tax, which apart from this subsection, finally falls to be borne for the later chargeable period and the provisions of [*Part 41A*][1] shall apply accordingly.

(6) (a) Subject to *paragraph (b)*, the amount of capital gains tax, which apart from this subsection, would be chargeable on chargeable gains accruing to an investor to whom this subsection applies, on the disposal of old securities, after such chargeable gains have been reduced by any allowable losses under *section 31*, shall, if the investor so elects, be deemed to be an amount of capital gains tax chargeable on chargeable gains which are deemed to accrue to the investor in the chargeable period (in this subsection referred to as "*the later chargeable period*") in which the new securities are disposed of (and not in any other chargeable period) in addition to any capital gains tax chargeable on chargeable gains accruing to the investor in the later chargeable period and the provisions of [*Part 41A*][2] shall apply accordingly.

(b) *section 815* shall apply to the disposal of the old securities to which *paragraph (a)* applies as if—

(i) there were inserted, in *subsection (3)(b)* of that section after "profits of the trade", "unless the trade consists wholly or partly of a life business the profits of which are not assessed to corporation tax under Case I of Schedule D for that accounting period", and

(ii) *subsection (3)(c)* of that section were deleted.

(7) The election referred to in *subsections (5)* and *(6)* shall be made within a period of two years after the end of the chargeable period in which the disposal of the old securities takes place.][3]

Amendments

[1,2] Substituted by FA12 sched4(part 2)(g).

[3] Inserted by FA99 s59(1). Applies as respects section 751B inserted by subsection (1), to an exchange of old securities for new securities (within the meaning of the said section 751B) in the period beginning on the 11th day of February, 1999, and ending before the 1st day of January, 2000.

CHAPTER 2

Purchases of Shares by Financial Concerns and Persons Exempted from Tax, and Restriction on Relief for Losses by Repayment of Tax in Case of Dividends Paid Out of Accumulated Profits

752 Purchases of shares by financial concerns and persons exempted from tax

[ITA67 s371; F(MP)A68 s3(2) and Sch PtI; CTA76 s140(1), s164, Sch2 Pt1 par20 and Sch3 PtI]

(1) For the purposes of this Chapter and *Schedule 22*—

(a) references to a dividend shall, except where the context otherwise requires, be construed as including references to a distribution, and to an amount which under any enactment is to be treated as a distribution, made on or after the 6th day of April, 1976,

(b) in relation to such a distribution, including an amount to be so treated as a distribution, references to a dividend being paid or becoming payable or being received or becoming receivable on shares shall be construed as references to a distribution or an amount to be so treated as a distribution being made or received in respect of shares or securities, and

(c) in applying references to a dividend in relation to a distribution, "*gross amount*" or "*gross dividend*" means the distribution together with the tax credit to which the recipient of the distribution is entitled in respect of it, and "*net amount*" or "*net dividend*" means the distribution exclusive of any such tax credit,

and in this subsection "*distribution*" has the same meaning as in the Corporation Tax Acts.

(2) (a) In this section and in *Schedule 22*—

"*company*" includes any body corporate, but does not include a company not resident in the State;

"*control*", in relation to a body corporate, means the power of a person to secure—

(i) by means of the holding of shares or the possession of voting power in or in relation to that or any other body corporate, or

(ii) by virtue of any powers conferred by the articles of association or other document regulating that or any other body corporate,

that the affairs of the first-mentioned body corporate are conducted in accordance with the wishes of that person and, in relation to a partnership, means the right to a share of more than 50 per cent of the assets, or of more than 50 per cent of the income, of the partnership;

"*person*" includes any body of persons, and references to a person entitled to any exemption from tax include, in a case of an exemption expressed to apply to income of a trust or fund, references to the persons entitled to make claims for the granting of that exemption;

"*share*" includes stock other than debenture or loan stock;

"shares of a class to which this section applies" means shares of any class forming part of a company's share capital, other than a class of fully-paid preference shares carrying only a right to dividends at a rate per cent of the nominal value of the shares which is fixed and which in the opinion of the Appeal Commissioners does not substantially exceed the yield generally obtainable on preference shares the prices of which are quoted on stock exchanges in the State.

(b) For the purposes of this section and *Schedule 22*—

(i) shares shall be regarded as of different classes if the rights and obligations respectively attached to them are distinguishable as regards the payment of dividends or the amount paid up or in any other respect;

(ii) any reference to shares acquired in right of other shares includes a reference to shares acquired in pursuance of an offer or invitation which was restricted to holders of those other shares;

(iii) 2 trades shall be regarded as under the same control if they are carried on by persons one of whom is a body of persons over whom the other has control or both of whom are bodies of persons under the control of a third person, and several trades shall be regarded as under the same control if each is under the same control as all of the others, and in this subparagraph "*body of persons*" includes a partnership.

(3) Where a person engaged in carrying on a trade which consists of or comprises dealings in shares or other investments becomes entitled to receive a dividend on a holding of shares of a class to which this section applies, being shares sold or issued to that person or otherwise acquired by that person not more than 10 years before the date on which the dividend becomes payable, and the dividend is to any extent paid out of profits accumulated before the date on which the shares were so acquired, then, if those shares, or those shares together with—

(a) any other shares the dividend on which is payable to that person and which were sold or issued to that person or otherwise acquired by that person not more than 10 years before the date on which the dividend becomes payable,

(b) in a case where the trade is under the same control as another trade which consists of or comprises dealings in shares or other investments, any shares the dividend on which is payable to the person engaged in carrying on that other trade and which were sold or issued to that person or otherwise acquired by that person not more than 10 years before the date on which the dividend becomes payable, and

(c) any shares to be taken into account under *subsection (5)*,

amount to 10 per cent or more of the issued shares of that class, the net amount of the dividend received on the shares in the holding shall, to the extent to which it was paid out of profits accumulated before the shares were acquired, be taken into account in computing for the purposes of the Tax Acts the profits or gains or losses of the trade as if it were a trading receipt which had not borne tax.

(4) Where a person entitled under the Tax Acts to an exemption from tax which extends to dividends on shares becomes entitled to receive a dividend on a holding of shares of a class to which this section applies, being shares sold or issued to that person or otherwise acquired by that person not more than 10 years before the date on which the dividend becomes payable, and the dividend is to any extent paid out of the profits accumulated before the date on which the shares were so acquired, then, if those shares, or those shares together with—

(a) any other shares the dividend on which is payable to that person and which were sold or issued to that person or otherwise acquired by that person not more than 10 years before the date on which the dividend becomes payable, and

(b) any shares to be taken into account under *subsection (5)*,

amount to 10 per cent or more of the issued shares of that class, the exemption shall, to an extent proportionate to the extent to which the dividend is paid out of profits accumulated before the date on which the shares were acquired, not apply to the dividend; but, if any annual payment is payable by that person out of the dividend, that annual payment shall be deemed as to the whole of that payment—

(i) to be paid out of profits or gains not brought into charge to tax and *section 238* shall apply accordingly, and

(ii) for the purposes of corporation tax, not to be a payment which is a charge on income.

(5) Where 2 or more persons, being persons engaged in carrying on trades of the kind mentioned in *subsection (3)* or entitled to an exemption of the kind mentioned in *subsection (4)*, have each acquired shares in a company and the transactions in pursuance of which the acquisition was made were either transactions entered into by those persons acting in concert or transactions together comprised in any arrangements made by any person, then, in the application of either of those subsections in relation to a dividend payable to one of those persons on shares which include shares so acquired (or shares acquired in right of those shares), there shall be taken into account under *subsection (3)(c)* or, as the case may be, *subsection (4)(b)* any shares the dividend on which is payable to any other of those persons, being shares so acquired by that other person (or shares acquired in right of those shares).

(6) Where any shares have been sold or otherwise disposed of by a person who held shares of that kind acquired at different times, it shall be assumed for the

purposes of this section that shares which have been held for a longer time have been disposed of before shares which have been held for a shorter time.

(7) Where, at the time when a trade is or is deemed to be set up and commenced, any shares form part of the trading stock belonging to the trade, those shares shall be regarded for the purposes of this section as having been acquired at that time by the person then engaged in carrying on the trade, and, subject to this subsection, where there is a change in the persons engaged in carrying on a trade which is not a change on which the trade is deemed to be discontinued, this section shall apply in relation to the person so engaged after the change as if anything done to or by that person's predecessor had been done to or by that person.

(8) *Schedule 22* shall apply for the purpose of ascertaining whether a dividend is to be regarded as paid to any extent out of profits accumulated before a particular date.

Cross References

From Section 752

Section 238 Annual payments not payable out of taxed income.

Schedule 22 Dividends Regarded as Paid Out of Profits Accumulated Before Given Date

To Section 752

Section 749 Dealers in securities.

Section 753 Restriction on relief for losses by repayment of tax in case of dividends paid out of accumulated profits.

Schedule 22 Dividends Regarded as Paid Out of Profits Accumulated Before Given Date

753 Restriction on relief for losses by repayment of tax in case of dividends paid out of accumulated profits

[ITA67 s372; CTA76 s140(1) and Sch2 Pt1 par21(1)]

Where a person or a body of persons carries on a trade, other than such a trade mentioned in *section 752(3)*, and the person's or the body of persons' income for any year of assessment or, as the case may be, accounting period includes a dividend the net amount of which would, if the trade were such a trade mentioned in *section 752(3)*, be required to any extent to be taken into account as a trading receipt which has not borne tax, then, in ascertaining—

(a) for the purposes of income tax, whether any or what repayment of tax is to be made to that person or body of persons under *section 381* by reference to any loss sustained in the trade for that year of assessment, there shall be disregarded—

(i) the gross amount corresponding to so much of that net amount as would have been required to be taken into account as a trading receipt which has not borne tax, and

(ii) any tax credit in respect of the amount required to be disregarded under *subparagraph (i)*;

(b) for the purposes of corporation tax, the income or profits against which the loss may be set off under […][1] *396*, there shall be disregarded the gross amount corresponding to so much of that net amount as would have been required to be taken into account as a trading receipt which has not borne tax.

Amendments

[1] Deleted by FA03 s41(1)(l). This section applies as respects accounting periods ending on or after 6 February 2003.

Cross References

From Section 753

Section 381 Right to repayment of tax by reference to losses.

Section 396 Relief for trading losses other than terminal losses.

Section 752 Purchases of shares by financial concerns and persons exempted from tax.

PART 29

Patents, Scientific and Certain Other Research, Know-How and Certain Training

CHAPTER 1

Patents

754 Interpretation (Chapter 1)

[ITA67 s284; CTA76 s21(1) and Sch1 par35; FA97 s146(1) and Sch9 PtI par1(19)]

(1) In this Chapter—

"*the commencement of the patent*", in relation to a patent, means the date from which the patent rights become effective;

"*income from patents*" means—

(a) any royalty or other sum paid in respect of the user of a patent, and

(b) any amount on which tax is payable for any chargeable period by virtue of this Chapter;

"*Irish patent*" means a patent granted under the laws of the State;

"*patent rights*" means the right to do or to authorise the doing of anything which but for that right would be an infringement of a patent;

"*the writing-down period*" has the meaning assigned to it by *section 755(2)*.

(2) In this Chapter, any reference to the sale of part of patent rights includes a reference to the grant of a licence in respect of the patent in question, and any reference to the purchase of patent rights includes a reference to the acquisition of a licence in respect of a patent; but, if a licence granted by a person entitled to any patent rights is a licence to exercise those rights to the exclusion of the grantor and all other persons for the whole of the remainder of the term for which the rights subsist, the grantor shall be treated for the purposes of this Chapter as thereby selling the whole of the rights.

(3) Where, under section 77 of the Patents Act, 1992, or any corresponding provisions of the law of any country outside the State, an invention which is the subject of a patent is made, used, exercised or vended by or for the service of the State or the government of the country concerned, this Chapter shall apply as if the making, user, exercise or vending of the invention had taken place in pursuance of a licence, and any sums paid in respect thereof shall be treated accordingly.

Cross References

From Section 754

Section 755 Annual allowances for capital expenditure on purchase of patent rights.

To Section 754

Section 2 Interpretation of Tax Acts.
Section 80A Taxation of certain short-term leases plant and machinery.
Section 267O Treatment of credit return.
Section 267P Treatment of credit transaction.
Section 267S Treatment of certificate owner.
Section 391 Interpretation (Chapter 2).

Section 401 Change in ownership of company: disallowance of trading losses.
Section 428 Exclusion of double allowances, etc.
Section 551 Exclusion from consideration for disposals of sums chargeable to income tax.
Section 692 Development expenditure: allowances and charges.
Section 693 Exploration expenditure: allowances and charges.
Section 695 Abandonment expenditure: allowances and loss relief.
Section 699 Deduction as expenses of certain sums, etc.
Section 1007 Interpretation (Part 43).
Schedule 17 Reorganisation into Companies of Trustee Savings Banks
Schedule 22 Dividends Regarded as Paid Out of Profits Accumulated Before Given Date
Schedule 26 Replacement of Harbour Authorities by Port Companies

755 Annual allowances for capital expenditure on purchase of patent rights

[ITA67 s285; CTA76 s21(1) and Sch1 par36]

(1) Where a person incurs capital expenditure on the purchase of patent rights, there shall, subject to and in accordance with this Chapter, be made to that person writing-down allowances in respect of that expenditure during the writing-down period; but no writing-down allowance shall be made to a person in respect of any expenditure unless—

(a) the allowance is to be made to the person in taxing the person's trade, or

(b) any income receivable by the person in respect of the rights would be liable to tax.

(2) (a) Subject to *paragraphs (b)* to *(d)*, the writing-down period shall be the 17 years beginning with the chargeable period related to the expenditure.

(b) Where the patent rights are purchased for a specified period, *paragraph (a)* shall apply with the substitution for the reference to 17 years of a reference to 17 years or the number of years comprised within that period, whichever is the less.

(c) Where the patent rights purchased begin one complete year or more after the commencement of the patent and *paragraph (b)* does not apply, *paragraph (a)* shall apply with the substitution for the reference to 17 years of a reference to 17 years less the number of complete years which, when the rights begin, have elapsed since the commencement of the patent or, if 17 complete years have so elapsed, of a reference to one year.

(d) For the purposes of this subsection, any expenditure incurred for the purposes of a trade by a person about to carry on the trade shall be treated as if that expenditure had been incurred by that person on the first day on which that person carries on the trade unless before that first day that person has sold all the patent rights on the purchase of which the expenditure was incurred.

[(3) Subject to subsection (4), this section shall not apply to a company within the charge to corporation tax.

(4) (a) Subject to paragraph (*b*), where a company elects in writing, this section shall apply to capital expenditure, specified in the election, incurred by it on the purchase of patent rights after 7 May 2009 and before 7 May 2011.

(b) An election under paragraph (*a*) shall be made in the return required to be made under section 951 for the accounting period of the company in which the expenditure is incurred and shall not be made later than 12 months from the end of the accounting period in which the capital expenditure, giving rise to the claim, is incurred.][1]

Amendments

[1] Inserted by FA09 s13(1)(h). Applies to expenditure incurred by a company after 7 May 2009.

Cross References

From Section 755

Section 951 Obligation to make a return.

To Section 755

Section 754 Interpretation (Chapter 1).

756 Effect of lapse of patent rights

[ITA67 s286; CTA76 s21(1) and Sch1 par37]

(1) Where a person incurs capital expenditure on the purchase of patent rights and, before the end of the writing-down period, any of the following events occurs—

(a) the rights come to an end without being subsequently revived;

(b) the person sells all those rights or so much of those rights as the person still owns;

(c) the person sells part of those rights and the net proceeds of the sale (in so far as they consist of capital sums) are not less than the amount of the capital expenditure remaining unallowed;

no writing-down allowance shall be made to that person for the chargeable period related to the event or for any subsequent chargeable period.

(2) Where a person incurs capital expenditure on the purchase of patent rights and, before the end of the writing-down period, either of the following events occurs—

(a) the rights come to an end without being subsequently revived;

(b) the person sells all those rights or so much of those rights as the person still owns, and the net proceeds of the sale (in so far as they consist of capital sums) are less than the amount of the capital expenditure remaining unallowed;

there shall, subject to and in accordance with this Chapter, be made to that person for the chargeable period related to the event an allowance (in this Chapter referred to as a "*balancing allowance*") equal to—

(i) if the event is the rights coming to an end, the amount of the capital expenditure remaining unallowed, and

(ii) if the event is a sale, the amount of the capital expenditure remaining unallowed less the net proceeds of the sale.

(3) Where a person who has incurred capital expenditure on the purchase of patent rights sells all or any part of those rights and the net proceeds of the sale (in so far as they consist of capital sums) exceed the amount of the capital expenditure remaining unallowed, if any, there shall, subject to and in accordance with this Chapter, be made on that person for the chargeable period related to the sale a charge (in this Chapter referred to as a "*balancing charge*") on an amount equal to—

(a) the excess, or

(b) where the amount of the capital expenditure remaining unallowed is nil, the net proceeds of the sale.

(4) Where a person who has incurred capital expenditure on the purchase of patent rights sells a part of those rights and *subsection (3)* does not apply, the amount of any writing-down allowance made in respect of that expenditure for the

chargeable period related to the sale or any subsequent chargeable period shall be the amount determined by—

(a) subtracting the net proceeds of the sale (in so far as they consist of capital sums) from the amount of the expenditure remaining unallowed at the time of the sale, and

(b) dividing the result by the number of complete years of the writing-down period which remained at the beginning of the chargeable period related to the sale,

and so on for any subsequent sales.

(5) References in this section to the amount of any capital expenditure remaining unallowed shall in relation to any event be construed as references to the amount of that expenditure less any writing-down allowances made in respect of that expenditure for chargeable periods before the chargeable period related to that event, and less also the net proceeds of any previous sale by the person who incurred the expenditure of any part of the rights acquired by the expenditure, in so far as those proceeds consist of capital sums.

(6) Notwithstanding *subsections (1)* to *(5)*—

(a) no balancing allowance shall be made in respect of any expenditure unless a writing-down allowance has been, or, but for the happening of the event giving rise to the balancing allowance, could have been, made in respect of that expenditure, and

(b) the total amount on which a balancing charge is made in respect of any expenditure shall not exceed the total writing-down allowances actually made in respect of that expenditure less, if a balancing charge has previously been made in respect of that expenditure, the amount on which that charge was made.

[(7) This section shall not apply to patent rights in respect of which an allowance has been made to a company under section 284 as applied by section 291A.][1]

Amendments

[1] Inserted by FA09 s13(1)(i). Applies to expenditure incurred by a company after 7 May 2009.

Cross References

From Section 756

Section 284 Wear and tear allowances.

Section 291A Intangible assets.

To Section 756

Section 699 Deduction as expenses of certain sums, etc.

Section 762 Application of Chapter 4 of Part 9.

757 Charges on capital sums received for sale of patent rights

[ITA67 s288; CTA76 s21(1) and Sch1 par38]

(1) (a) Subject to *paragraphs (b)* and *(c)*, where a person resident in the State sells any patent rights and the net proceeds of the sale consist wholly or partly of a capital sum, that person shall, subject to this Chapter, be charged to tax under Case IV of Schedule D for the chargeable period in which the sum is received by that person and for successive chargeable periods, being charged in each period on the same fraction of the sum as the period is of 6 years (or such less fraction as has not already been charged).

(b) Where the person by notice in writing served on the inspector not later than 12 months after the end of the chargeable period in which the capital sum was received elects that the whole of that sum shall be charged to tax for the chargeable period in which the sum is received, it shall be charged to tax accordingly.

(c) Where the person by notice in writing served on the inspector not later than 12 months after the end of the chargeable period in which the capital sum was received applies to have the fraction referred to in *paragraph (a)* determined as being other than the same fraction as the chargeable period is of 6 years, then, if it appears to the Revenue Commissioners that hardship is likely to arise having regard to all the circumstances of the case unless a direction is given under this paragraph, they may direct that the fraction shall be the same fraction of the sum as the chargeable period is of a number of years other than 6 years, and that the charge shall be spread accordingly.

(2) (a) Where a person not resident in the State sells any patent rights and the net proceeds of the sale consist wholly or partly of a capital sum, and the patent is an Irish patent, then, subject to this Chapter—

(i) the person shall be chargeable to tax in respect of that sum under Case IV of Schedule D, and

(ii) *section 238* shall apply to that sum as if it were an annual payment payable otherwise than out of profits or gains brought into charge to tax.

(b) Where, not later than 12 months after the end of the year of assessment in which the sum referred to in *paragraph (a)* is paid, the person to whom it is paid, by notice in writing to the Revenue Commissioners, elects that the sum shall be treated for the purpose of income tax for that year and for each of the 5 succeeding years as if one-sixth of that sum were included in that person's income chargeable to tax for all those years respectively, it shall be so treated, and all such repayments and assessments of tax for each of those years shall be made as are necessary to give effect to the election; but—

(i) the election shall not affect the amount of tax to be deducted and accounted for under *section 238*,

(ii) where any sum is deducted under *section 238*, any adjustments necessary to give effect to the election shall be made by means of repayment of tax, and

(iii) those adjustments shall be made year by year and as if one-sixth of the sum deducted had been deducted in respect of tax for each year, and no repayment of or of any part of that portion of the tax deducted which is to be treated as deducted in respect of tax for any year shall be made unless and until it is ascertained that the tax ultimately to be paid for that year is less than the amount of tax paid for that year.

(3) (a) In *subsection (2)*, "*tax*" shall mean income tax, unless the seller of the patent rights, being a company, would be within the charge to corporation tax in respect of any proceeds of the sale not consisting of a capital sum.

(b) Where *paragraph (a)* of *subsection (2)* applies to charge a company to corporation tax in respect of a sum paid to it, *paragraph (b)* of that subsection shall not apply; but—

(i) the company may, by notice in writing given to the Revenue Commissioners not later than 12 months after the end of the accounting period in which the sum is paid, elect that the sum shall be treated as arising rateably in the accounting periods ending not later than 6 years from the beginning of the accounting period in which the sum is paid (being accounting periods during which the company remains within the charge to corporation tax by virtue of *subsection (2)(a)*), and

(ii) there shall be made all such repayments of tax and assessments to tax as are necessary to give effect to any such election.

(4) Where the patent rights sold by a person, or the rights out of which the patent rights sold by a person were granted, were acquired by the person by purchase and the price paid consisted wholly or partly of a capital sum, *subsections (1)* to *(3)* shall apply as if any capital sum received by the person on the sale of the rights were reduced by the amount of that sum; but—

(a) where between the purchase and the sale the person has sold part of the patent rights acquired by the person and the net proceeds of that sale consist wholly or partly of a capital sum, the amount of the reduction to be made under this subsection in respect of the subsequent sale shall itself be reduced by the amount of that sum, and

(b) nothing in this subsection shall affect the amount of tax to be deducted and accounted for under *section 238* by virtue of *subsection (2)* and, where any sum is deducted under *section 238*, any adjustment necessary to give effect to this subsection shall be made by means of repayment of tax.

(5) This section shall apply in relation to any sale of part of any patent rights as it applies in relation to sales of patent rights.

Cross References

From Section 757

Section 238 Annual payments not payable out of taxed income.

To Section 757

Section 390 Amount of assessment made under section 238 to be allowed as a loss for certain purposes.
Section 759 Spreading of revenue payments over several years.
Section 760 Capital sums: effect of death, winding up and partnership changes.
Section 762 Application of Chapter 4 of Part 9.
Section 1011 Provision as to charges under section 757.

758 Relief for expenses

[ITA67 s290(1) to (3); CTA76 s21(1) and Sch1 par39]

(1) Notwithstanding *section 81*, in computing the profits or gains of any trade, there shall be allowed to be deducted as expenses any fees paid or expenses incurred in obtaining for the purposes of the trade the grant of a patent or an extension of the term of a patent.

(2) Where—

(a) a person, otherwise than for the purposes of a trade carried on by the person, pays any fees or incurs any expenses in connection with the grant or maintenance of a patent or the obtaining of an extension of a term of a patent, and

(b) those fees or expenses would, if they had been paid or incurred for the purposes of a trade, have been allowable as a deduction in estimating the profits or gains of the trade,

there shall be made to the person for the chargeable period in which those fees or expenses were paid or incurred an allowance equal to the amount of those fees or expenses.

(3) Where a patent is granted in respect of any invention, an allowance equal to so much of the net amount of any expenses incurred by an individual who, whether alone or in conjunction with any other person, actually devised the invention as is properly ascribable to the devising of that invention (not being expenses in respect of which, or of assets representing which, an allowance is to be made under any other provision of the Tax Acts) shall be made to that individual for the year of assessment in which the expenses were incurred.

Cross References

From Section 758

Section 81 General rule as to deductions.

759 Spreading of revenue payments over several years

[ITA67 s195B(3) and (6) and s291; CTA76 s21(1) and Sch1 par40; FA93 s10(1)]

(1) In this section, any reference to the tax payable by a person includes, in cases where the income of an individual's [spouse or civil partner][1] is deemed to be the income of the individual, references to the income tax payable by the individual's [spouse or civil partner][2].

(2) Where a royalty or other sum to which *section 237* or *238* applies is paid in respect of the user of a patent and that user extended over a period of 6 complete years or more, the person receiving the payment may require that the tax payable by that person by reason of the receipt of that sum shall be reduced so as not to exceed the total amount of tax which would have been payable by that person if that royalty or sum had been paid in 6 equal instalments at yearly intervals, the last of which was paid on the date on which the payment was in fact made.

(3) *Subsection (2)* shall apply in relation to a royalty or other sum where the period of the user is 2 complete years or more but less than 6 complete years as it applies to the royalties and sums mentioned in that subsection, but with the substitution for the reference to 6 equal instalments of a reference to so many equal instalments as there are complete years comprised in that period.

(4) Nothing in this section shall apply to any sum to which *section 238* applies by virtue of *section 757*.

Amendments

[1, 2] Substituted by F(No.3)A11 sched1(182).

Cross References

From Section 759

Section 237 Annual payments payable wholly out of taxed income.
Section 238 Annual payments not payable out of taxed income.
Section 757 Charges on capital sums received for sale of patent rights.

760 Capital sums: effect of death, winding up and partnership changes

[ITA67 s195B(3) and (6) and s293; CTA76 s21(1) and Sch1 par42; FA93 s10(1)]

(1) In this section, any references to tax paid or borne or payable or to be paid or borne by a person include, in cases where the income of an individual's [spouse or civil partner][1] is deemed to be income of the individual, references to the income tax paid or borne, or payable or to be paid or borne, by the individual's [spouse or civil partner][2].

(2) Where a person on whom, by reason of the receipt of a capital sum, a charge is to be, or would otherwise be, made under *section 757* dies or, being a body corporate, commences to be wound up—

(a) no sums shall be charged under that section on that person for any chargeable period subsequent to that in which the death takes place or the winding up commences, and

(b) the amount to be charged for the chargeable period in which the death occurs or the winding up commences shall be increased by the total amounts which but for the death or winding up would have been charged for subsequent chargeable periods.

(3) (a) In the case of a death, the personal representatives may, by notice in writing served on the inspector not later than 21 days after notice has been served on them of the charge to be made by virtue of this section, require that the tax payable out of the estate of the deceased by reason of the increase provided for by this section shall be reduced so as not to exceed the amount determined in accordance with *paragraph (b)*.

(b) The amount referred to in *paragraph (a)* shall be the total amount of tax which would have been payable by the deceased or out of his or her estate by reason of the operation of *section 757* in relation to the capital sum if, instead of the amount to be charged for the year in which the death occurs being increased by the whole amount of the sums charged for subsequent years, the several amounts to be charged for the years beginning with that in which the capital sum was received and ending with that in which the death occurred had each been increased by that whole amount divided by the number of those years.

(4) (a) In this subsection, "*the relevant period*" has the same meaning as in *Part 43*.

(b) Where, under *Chapter 4* of *Part 9* as modified by *Part 43*, charges under *section 757* are to be made on 2 or more persons as being the persons for the time being carrying on a trade, and the relevant period comes to an end, *subsection (2)* shall apply in relation to the ending of the relevant period as it applies where a body corporate commences to be wound up.

(c) Where *paragraph (b)* applies—

(i) the additional sums which under *subsection (2)* are to be charged for the year in which the relevant period ends shall be aggregated and apportioned among the members of the partnership immediately before the ending of the relevant period according to their respective interests in the partnership profits at that time and each partner (or, if that partner is dead, his or her personal representatives) charged for his or her proportion, and

(ii) each partner (or, if that partner is dead, his or her personal representatives) shall have the same right to require a reduction of the total tax payable by him or her or out of his or her estate by reason of the increase provided for by this section as would have been exercisable by the personal representatives under *subsection (3)* in the case of a death, and that subsection shall apply accordingly but as if the reference to the amount of tax which would have been payable by the deceased or out of his or her estate in the event mentioned in that subsection were a reference to the amount of tax which would in that event have been paid or borne by the partner in question or out of his or her estate.

Amendments

[1, 2] Substituted by F(No.3)A11 sched1(183).

Cross References

From Section 760

Section 268 Meaning of "industrial building or structure".
Section 304 Income tax: allowances and charges in taxing a trade, etc.
Section 757 Charges on capital sums received for sale of patent rights.
Section 1007 Interpretation (Part 43).

761 Manner of making allowances and charges

[ITA67 s292; CTA76 s21(1) and Sch1 par41]

(1) An allowance or charge under this Chapter shall be made to or on a person in taxing the person's trade if—

(a) the person is carrying on a trade the profits or gains of which are, or, if there were any, would be, chargeable to tax under Case I of Schedule D for the chargeable period for which the allowance or charge is made, and

(b) at any time in the chargeable period or its basis period the patent rights in question, or other rights out of which they were granted, were or were to be used for the purposes of that trade;

but nothing in this subsection shall affect the preceding provisions of this Chapter allowing a deduction as expenses in computing the profits or gains of a trade or requiring a charge to be made under Case IV of Schedule D.

(2) Except where provided for in *subsection (1)*, an allowance under this Chapter shall be made by means of discharge or repayment of tax and shall be available against income from patents, and a charge under this Chapter shall be made under Case IV of Schedule D.

Cross References

To Section 761

Section 762 Application of Chapter 4 of Part 9.

762 Application of Chapter 4 of Part 9

[ITA67 s299(4)(b)(iii) and s303(1); CTA76 s21(1) and Sch1 par46 and par49]

(1) Subject to *subsection (2)*, *Chapter 4* of *Part 9* shall apply as if this Chapter were contained in that Part, and any reference in the Tax Acts to any capital allowance to be given by means of discharge or repayment of tax and to be available or available primarily against a specified class of income shall include a reference to any capital allowance given in accordance with *section 761(2)*.

(2) In *Chapter 4* of *Part 9*, as applied by virtue of *subsection (1)* to patent rights—

(a) the reference in *section 312(5)(a)(i)* to the sum mentioned in *paragraph (b)* shall in the case of patent rights be construed as a reference to the amount of the capital expenditure on the acquisition of the patent rights remaining unallowed, computed in accordance with *section 756*, and

(b) the reference in *section 316(1)* to any expenditure or sum in the case of which a deduction of tax is to be or may be made under *section 237* or *238* shall not include a sum in the case of which such a deduction is to be or may be so made by virtue of *section 757*.

Cross References

From Section 762

Section 237 Annual payments payable wholly out of taxed income.
Section 238 Annual payments not payable out of taxed income.
Section 268 Meaning of "industrial building or structure".
Section 304 Income tax: allowances and charges in taxing a trade, etc.
Section 312 Special provisions as to certain sales.
Section 316 Interpretation of certain references to expenditure and time when expenditure is incurred.
Section 756 Effect of lapse of patent rights.
Section 757 Charges on capital sums received for sale of patent rights.
Section 761 Manner of making allowances and charges.

CHAPTER 2

Scientific and Certain Other Research

763 Interpretation (sections 764 and 765)

[ITA67 s244(1), (8) and (9); CTA76 s21(1) and Sch1 par9; FA92 s39]

(1) In this section—

"*designated area*" means an area designated by order under section 2 of the Continental Shelf Act, 1968;

"*exploring for specified minerals*" means searching in the State for deposits of specified minerals or testing such deposits or winning access to such deposits, and includes the systematic searching for areas containing specified minerals and searching by drilling or other means for specified minerals within those areas, but does not include operations in the course of developing or working a mine;

"*licence*" means—

(a) an exploration licence,

(b) a petroleum prospecting licence,

(c) a petroleum lease, or

(d) a reserved area licence, duly granted before the 11th day of June, 1968, in respect of an area in the State, or on or after the 11th day of June, 1968, in respect of either or both a designated area and an area in the State, and which was or may be so granted subject to such licensing terms as were presented to each House of the Oireachtas, and includes any such licence the terms of which have been duly amended or varied from time to time;

"*licensed area*" means an area in respect of which a licence is in force;

"*mine*" means an underground excavation for the purpose of getting specified minerals;

"*petroleum*" includes—

(a) any mineral oil or relative hydrocarbon and natural gas and other liquid or gaseous hydrocarbons and their derivatives or constituent substances existing in its natural condition in strata (including, without limitation, distillate, condensate, casinghead gasoline and such other substances as are ordinarily produced from oil and gas wells), and

(b) any other mineral substance contained in oil or natural gas brought to the surface with them in the normal process of extraction, but does not include coal and bituminous shales and other stratified deposits from which oil can be extracted by distillation,

won or capable of being won under the authority of a licence;

"*petroleum exploration activities*" means activities of a person carried on by the person or on behalf of the person in searching for deposits in a licensed area, in testing or appraising such deposits or in winning access to such deposits for the purposes of such searching, testing and appraising, where such activities are carried on under a licence (other than a petroleum lease) authorising the activities and held by the person or, if the person is a company, held by the company or a company associated with it;

"*petroleum extraction activities*" means activities of a person carried on by the person or on behalf of the person under a petroleum lease authorising the activities and held by the person or, if the person is a company, held by the company or a company associated with it in—

(a) winning petroleum from a relevant field, including searching in that field for, and winning access to, such petroleum,

(b) transporting as far as dry land petroleum so won from a place not on dry land, or

(c) effecting the initial treatment and storage of petroleum so won from the relevant field;

"*relevant field*" means an area in respect of which a licence, being a petroleum lease, is in force;

"*specified minerals*" means the following minerals occurring in non-bedded deposits of such minerals, that is, barytes, felspar, serpentinous marble, quartz rock, soapstone, ores of copper, ores of gold, ores of iron, ores of lead, ores of manganese, ores of molybdenum, ores of silver, ores of sulphur and ores of zinc.

(2) In *sections 764* and *765*—

"*asset*" includes part of an asset;

"*expenditure on scientific research*" does not include any expenditure incurred in the acquisition of rights in or arising out of scientific research;

"*scientific research*" means, subject to *subsections (3)* and *(4)*, any activities in the fields of natural or applied science for the extension of knowledge.

(3) For the purposes of the definition of "*scientific research*", that definition shall, subject to *subsection (4)*, be construed as including and be deemed always to have included a provision excluding from that definition the following activities—

(a) exploring for specified minerals,

(b) petroleum exploration activities, and

(c) petroleum extraction activities.

(4) As respects activities carried on before the 29th day of January, 1992, *subsection (3)* shall not apply for the purpose of computing any charge to income tax or corporation tax on a person who has before the 3rd day of December, 1991, made a claim in respect of expenditure incurred in exploring for specified minerals or in respect of petroleum exploration activities or in respect of petroleum extraction activities.

(5) For the purposes of *sections 764* and *765*, expenditure shall not be regarded as incurred by a person in so far as it is or is to be met directly or indirectly out

of moneys provided by the Oireachtas or by any person other than the first-mentioned person.

(6) The same expenditure shall not be taken into account for any of the purposes of *section 764* or *765* in relation to more than one trade.

Case Law

In Texaco (Ireland) Ltd v Murphy 1992 IV ITR 91 exploring for oil and gas was considered "scientific research".

Cross References

From Section 763

Section 764 Deduction for revenue expenditure on scientific research.
Section 765 Allowances for capital expenditure on scientific research.

To Section 763

Section 692 Development expenditure: allowances and charges.
Section 693 Exploration expenditure: allowances and charges.
Section 695 Abandonment expenditure: allowances and loss relief.

764 Deduction for revenue expenditure on scientific research

[ITA67 s244(2) and (2A); CTA76 s21(1) and Sch1 par9]

(1) Where a person carrying on a trade either—

(a) incurs non-capital expenditure on scientific research relating to the trade, or

(b) pays any sum to—

(i) a body carrying on scientific research and approved for the purposes of this section by the Minister for Finance, or

(ii) an Irish university,

in order that such body or university may undertake scientific research,

then, the expenditure so incurred or the sum so paid shall be deducted as an expense in computing the profits or gains of the trade.

(2) Where a person carrying on a trade—

(a) incurs non-capital expenditure on scientific research or pays any sum to a body or university referred to in *subsection (1)(b)* in order that the body or university may undertake scientific research, and

(b) the expenditure so incurred or the sum so paid is not deductible as an expense under *subsection (1)* because the scientific research is not related to any trade being carried on by the person,

then, the expenditure so incurred or the sum so paid shall be deducted as an expense in computing the profits or gains of the person's trade.

Cross References

To Section 764

Section 309 Companies not resident in the State.
Section 311 Apportionment of consideration and exchanges and surrenders of leasehold interests.
Section 312 Special provisions as to certain sales.
Section 319 Adjustment of allowances by reference to value-added tax.
Section 321 Provisions of general application in relation to the making of allowances and charges.
Section 763 Interpretation (sections 764 and 765).
Section 766 Tax credit for research and development expenditure.
Section 848A Donations to approved bodies.

765 Allowances for capital expenditure on scientific research

[ITA67 s244(3), (4), (5), (6) and (7); CTA76 s21(1) and Sch1 par9; FA80 s17(3); FA96 s132(2) and Sch5 PtII]

(1) Where a person—

(a) incurs capital expenditure on scientific research,

(b) (i) is then carrying on a trade to which such expenditure relates, or

(ii) subsequently sets up and commences a trade which is related to such research,

(c) applies to the inspector for an allowance under this subsection in respect of such expenditure, and

(d) so applies—

(i) in the case where the expenditure was incurred while carrying on the trade, within 24 months after the end of the chargeable period in which it was incurred, or

(ii) in the case where the expenditure was incurred before the setting up and commencement of the trade, within 24 months after the end of the chargeable period in which the trade was set up and commenced,

then, subject to this section, there shall be made in taxing the trade for the chargeable period mentioned in whichever of *subparagraphs (i)* and *(ii)* of *paragraph (d)* is applicable an allowance equal to the amount of the expenditure.

(2) Where a person carrying on a trade incurs capital expenditure on scientific research in respect of which an allowance may not be made under *subsection (1)* because the scientific research is not related to any trade being carried on by that person, there shall be made in taxing that person's trade for the chargeable period in which the expenditure was incurred an allowance equal to the amount of the expenditure.

(3) Where an asset representing capital expenditure on scientific research ceases at any time from any cause whatever to be used for such research, relating to the trade carried on by the person who incurred the expenditure, then—

(a) an amount equal to the allowance made under this section in respect of that expenditure, or, if the value of the asset immediately before the cessation is less than that allowance, equal to that value, shall be treated as a trading receipt of the trade accruing immediately before the cessation, and

(b) in the application of *section 284* to an allowance made in respect of the asset for any chargeable period after that in which the cessation takes place, the actual cost of the asset shall be treated as being reduced by the amount of the allowance effectively made.

(4) Where an allowance under this section is made to a person for any chargeable period in respect of expenditure represented wholly or partly by assets, no allowance in respect of those assets shall be made to that person under *section 85* or *284* for that chargeable period.

(5) *Section 304(4)* shall apply in relation to an allowance under *subsection (1)* or *(2)* as it applies in relation to allowances to be made under *Part 9*.

Cross References

From Section 765

Section 85 Deduction for certain industrial premises.

Section 268 Meaning of "industrial building or structure".

Section 284 Wear and tear allowances.
Section 304 Income tax: allowances and charges in taxing a trade, etc.

To Section 765

Section 270 Meaning of "expenditure on construction of building or structure".
Section 288 Balancing allowances and balancing charges.
Section 309 Companies not resident in the State.
Section 311 Apportionment of consideration and exchanges and surrenders of leasehold interests.
Section 312 Special provisions as to certain sales.
Section 319 Adjustment of allowances by reference to value-added tax.
Section 321 Provisions of general application in relation to the making of allowances and charges.
Section 413 Profits or assets available for distribution.
Section 428 Exclusion of double allowances, etc.
Section 692 Development expenditure: allowances and charges.
Section 693 Exploration expenditure: allowances and charges.
Section 695 Abandonment expenditure: allowances and loss relief.
Section 763 Interpretation (sections 764 and 765).
Schedule 17 Reorganisation into Companies of Trustee Savings Banks
Schedule 22 Dividends Regarded as Paid Out of Profits Accumulated Before Given Date
Schedule 26 Replacement of Harbour Authorities by Port Companies

766 Tax credit for research and development expenditure

[(1) (a) In this section—

[...][1]

["*authorised officer*" means an officer of the Revenue Commissioners authorised by them in writing for the purposes of this section;][2]

"*EEA Agreement*" means the Agreement on the European Economic Area signed at Oporto on 2 May 1992 as adjusted by the Protocol signed at Brussels on 17 March 1993;

"*expenditure on research and development*", in relation to a company, means expenditure, other than expenditure on a building or structure, incurred by the company [wholly and exclusively][3] in the carrying on by it of research and development activities in a relevant Member State, being expenditure—

[(i) which—

(I) is allowable for the purposes of tax in the State as a deduction in computing income from a trade (otherwise than by virtue of *section 307*), or would be so allowable but for the fact that for accounting purposes it is brought into account in determining the value of an intangible asset, or

(II) is relieved under *Part 8*,][4]

(ii) on machinery or plant [(other than a specified intangible asset within the meaning of *section 291A* treated as machinery or plant by virtue of *subsection (2)* of that section)][5] which qualifies for any allowance under *Part 9* or this Chapter, or

(iii) which qualifies for an allowance under *section 764*,

but—

(I) expenditure on research and development shall not include a royalty or other sum paid by a company in respect of the user of an invention—

(A) if the royalty or other sum is paid to a person who is connected with the company within the meaning of *section 10* and is income from a qualifying patent within the meaning of *section 234*, or

(B) to the extent to which the royalty or other sum exceeds the royalty or other sum which would have been paid if the payer of the royalty or other sum and the beneficial recipient of the royalty or other sum were independent persons acting at arm's length,

[...][6]

[(IA) expenditure by a company on research and development shall not include any amount of interest notwithstanding that such interest is brought into account by the company in determining the value of an asset,[...][7]][8]

[(IB) expenditure on research and development shall not include—

(A) except as provided for in *subparagraphs (vii)* and *(viii)* of *subsection (1)(b)*, any amount paid to another person to carry on research and development activities, or

(B) expenditure incurred by a company in the management or control of research and development activities where such activities are carried on by another person,

and 'in the carrying on by it of research and development activities' shall be construed accordingly, and][9]

(II) expenditure incurred by a company which is resident in the State shall not be expenditure on research and development if it—

(A) may be taken into account as an expense in computing income of the company,

(B) is expenditure in respect of which an allowance for capital expenditure may be made to the company, or

(C) may otherwise be allowed or relieved in relation to the company,

for the purposes of tax in a territory other than the State;

"*group expenditure on research and development*", in relation to a relevant period of a group of companies, means the aggregate of the amounts of expenditure on research and development incurred in the relevant period by qualified companies which for the relevant period are members of the group: but—

(i) expenditure incurred by a company which is a member of a group for a part of a relevant period shall only be included in group expenditure on research and development if the expenditure is incurred at a time when the company is a member of the group, and

(ii) expenditure on research and development incurred by a company which has been included in group expenditure on research and development in relation to a group shall not be included in group expenditure on research and development in relation to any other group;

['*key employee*' has the meaning ascribed to it by *section 472D*;][10]

"*qualified company*", in relation to a relevant period, means a company which—

(i) throughout the relevant period—

(I) carries on a trade,

(II) is a 51 per cent subsidiary of a company which carries on a trade, or

(III) is a 51 per cent subsidiary of a company whose business consists wholly or mainly of the holding of stocks, shares or securities of a company which carries on a trade or more than one such company,

[(ii) carries out research and development activities in the relevant period,

(iii) maintains a record of expenditure incurred by it in the carrying out by it of those activities, and

(iv) in the case of a company which is a member of a group of companies that carries on research and development activities in separate geographical locations, maintains separate records of expenditure incurred in respect of the activities carried on at each location;][11]

['*qualifying group expenditure on research and development*', in relation to—

(a) relevant periods commencing on or after 1 January 2015, shall have the same meaning as that assigned to 'group expenditure on research and development', and

(b) a relevant period commencing on or before 31 December 2014, shall be determined by the following formula—][12]

$$A + B$$

where—

A is so much of the amount of group expenditure on research and development in relation to a relevant period as does not exceed [€300,000][13], and

B is the amount equal to the excess of the amount of group expenditure on research and development in relation to the relevant period over the threshold amount in relation to the relevant period,

but the amount of qualifying group expenditure on research and development in relation to a relevant period shall not exceed the amount of group expenditure on research and development in relation to that relevant period;][14]

"*relevant Member State*" means a state which is a Member State of the European Communities or, not being such a Member State, a state which is a contracting party to the EEA Agreement;

"*relevant period*" means—

(i) in the case of companies which are members of a group the respective ends of the accounting periods of the members of which coincide, the period of 12 months throughout which one or more members of the group carries on a trade and ending at the end of the first accounting period which commences on or after 1 January 2004, and

(ii) in the case of companies which are members of a group the respective ends of the accounting periods of which do not coincide, the period specified in a notice in writing made jointly by companies which are members of the group and given to the appropriate inspector within a period of 9 months after the end of the period so specified, being a period of 12 months throughout which one or more members of the group carries on a trade and ending at the end of the first accounting period of a company which is a member of the group which accounting period commences on or after 1 January 2004, and each subsequent period of 12 months commencing immediately after the end of the preceding relevant period;

"*research and development activities*" means systematic, investigative or experimental activities in a field of science or technology, being one or more of the following—

(i) basic research, namely, experimental or theoretical work undertaken primarily to acquire new scientific or technical knowledge without a specific practical application in view,

(ii) applied research, namely, work undertaken in order to gain scientific or technical knowledge and directed towards a specific practical application, or

(iii) experimental development, namely, work undertaken which draws on scientific or technical knowledge or practical experience for the purpose of achieving technological advancement and which is directed at producing new, or improving existing, materials, products, devices, processes, systems or services including incremental improvements thereto: but activities will not be research and development activities unless they—

(I) seek to achieve scientific or technological advancement, and

(II) involve the resolution of scientific or technological uncertainty;

["*research and development centre*" means a fixed base or bases, established in buildings or structures, which are used for the purpose of the carrying on by a company of research and development activities;][15]

['*specified amount*' means an amount—

(i) paid by the Revenue Commissioners in accordance with *subsection (4B)* of this section or *section 766A(4B)*, as the case may be, or

(ii) surrendered in accordance with *subsection (2A)*,

and a claim in respect of a specified amount shall be construed accordingly;][16]

["*threshold amount*", in relation to a relevant period of a group of companies, means the aggregate of the amounts of expenditure on research and development incurred in the period of one year ending on a date in the year 2003, which corresponds with the date on which the relevant period ends by all companies which are members of the group in the threshold period, in relation to the relevant period concerned: [but—][17];][18]

[(i) expenditure incurred by a company which is a member of the group for a part of the threshold period shall only be included in the threshold amount if the expenditure is incurred at a time when the company is a member of the group, and

(ii) subject to *subsection (7C)(a)*—

(I) where at any time during the threshold period, a group of companies carried on research and development activities in more than one research and development centre and each centre is in a separate geographical location, and

(II) at a time (referred to in this section as the "*cessation time*") after the end of the threshold period, a research and development centre ceases to be used for the purposes of a trade by a company which is a member of the group of companies and is not so used by any other company which is a member of the group,

then expenditure incurred in relation to that research and development centre shall not be taken into account in calculating the threshold amount in relation to any relevant period which commences after the cessation time][19]

"*threshold period*", in relation to a relevant period, means the period of one year referred to in the definition of "*threshold amount*";

"*university or institute of higher education*" means—

(i) a college or institution of higher education in the State which—

(I) provides courses to which a scheme approved by the Minister for Education and Science under the Local Authorities (Higher Education Grants) Acts 1968 to 1992 applies, or

(II) operates in accordance with a code of standards which from time to time may, with the consent of the Minister for Finance, be laid down by the Minister for Education and Science, and which the Minister for Education and Science approves for the purposes of *section 473A*;

(ii) any university or similar institution of higher education in a relevant Member State (other than the State) which—

(I) is maintained or assisted by recurrent grants from public funds of that or any other relevant Member State (including the State), or

(II) is a duly accredited university or institution of higher education in the Member State in which it is situated.

(b) For the purposes of this section—

(i) 2 companies shall be deemed to be members of a group if one company is a 51 per cent subsidiary of the other company or both companies are 51 per cent subsidiaries of a third company: but in determining whether one company is a 51 per cent subsidiary of another company, the other company shall be treated as not being the owner of—

(I) any share capital which it owns directly in a company if a profit on a sale of the shares would be treated as a trading receipt of its trade, or

(II) any share capital which it owns indirectly, and which is owned directly by a company for which a profit on a sale of the shares would be a trading receipt;

(ii) *sections 412* to *418* shall apply for the purposes of this paragraph as they would apply for the purposes of *Chapter 5* of *Part 12* if—

(I) "51 per cent subsidiary" were substituted for "75 per cent subsidiary" in each place where it occurs in that Chapter, and

(II) *paragraph (c)* of *section 411(1)* were deleted;

(iii) a company and all its 51 per cent subsidiaries shall form a group and, where that company is a member of a group as being itself a

51 per cent subsidiary, that group shall comprise all its 51 per cent subsidiaries and the first-mentioned group shall be deemed not to be a group: but a company which is not a member of a group shall be treated as if it were a member of a group which consists of that company;

(iv) in determining whether a company was a member of a group of companies (in this subparagraph referred to as the "*threshold group*") for the purposes of determining the threshold amount in relation to a relevant period of a group of companies (in this subparagraph referred to as the "*relevant group*"), the threshold group shall be treated as the same group as the relevant group notwithstanding that one or more of the companies in the threshold group is not in the relevant group, or vice versa, where any person or group of persons which controlled the threshold group is the same as, or has a reasonable commonality of identity with, the person or group of persons which controls the relevant group;

(v) expenditure shall not be regarded as having been incurred by a company if it has been or is to be met directly or indirectly by grant assistance or any other assistance which is granted [by or through—

(I) the State or another relevant Member State, or

(II) any board established by statute, any public or local authority or any other agency of the State or another relevant Member State;][20]

(vi) where a company—

(I) incurs expenditure on research and development at a time when the company is not carrying on a trade, being expenditure which, apart from this subparagraph, is not included in group expenditure on [research and development,][21]

[(II) begins to carry on a trade after that time, and][22]

[(III) makes a claim in respect of expenditure incurred at a time referred to in clause (I),][23]

[the expenditure shall be treated—

(A) for the purpose only of *subsection (5)*, as incurred at the time the company begins to carry on the trade, and

(B) for the purposes of *subsection (2)*, as it would if the company had commenced to carry on a trade at the time the expenditure was incurred, and the amount of any credit computed thereon shall be carried forward in accordance with *subsection (4)* and treated as an amount by which the corporation tax of the first accounting period which commenced on or after the time the company begins to trade is reduced;][24]

(vii) where in any period a company—

(I) incurs expenditure on research and development, and

(II) pays a sum to a university or institute of higher education in order for that university or institute to carry on research and development activities in a relevant Member State, so much of the sum so paid as does not exceed [the greater of 5 per cent of that expenditure or €100,000, shall, to the extent that it does not exceed the expenditure referred to in clause (I), be treated as if it were expenditure incurred by the company in the carrying on by it of research and development activities;][25]

[(viii) where in any period a company—

(I) incurs expenditure on research and development, and

(II) pays a sum (not being a sum referred to in clause (II) of *subparagraph (vii)*) to a person, other than to a person who is connected (within the meaning of *section 10*) with the company, in order for that person to carry on research and development activities, and notifies that person in writing that the payment is a payment to which this clause applies and that the person may not make a claim under this section in respect of such research and development activities,

then, so much of the sum so paid as does not exceed the greater of [15 per cent][26] of that expenditure or €100,000, shall, to the extent that it does not exceed the expenditure referred to in clause (I), be treated as if it were expenditure incurred by the company in the carrying on by it of research and development activities and expenditure incurred by that other person in connection with the activities referred to in clause (II) shall not be expenditure on research and development;][27]

[(ix) A research and development centre used by a company which is a member of a group of companies will be treated as being in a separate geographical location to another research and development centre used by the company or another company which is a member of the group if it is not less than a distance of 20 kilometres from that other research and development centre.][28]

[(1A) (a) Where expenditure is incurred by a company on machinery or plant which qualifies for any allowance under *Part 9* or this Chapter and the machinery or plant will not be used by the company wholly and exclusively for the purposes of research and development, the amount of the expenditure attributable to research and development shall be such portion of that expenditure as appears to the inspector (or on appeal the Appeal Commissioners) to be just and reasonable, and such portion of the expenditure shall be treated for the purposes of *subsection (1)(a)* as incurred by the company wholly and exclusively in carrying on research and development activities.

(b) Where, at any time, the apportionment made under *paragraph (a)*, or a further apportionment made under this paragraph, ceases to be just and reasonable, then—

(i) such further apportionment shall be made at that time as appears to the inspector (or on appeal the Appeal Commissioners) to be just and reasonable,

(ii) any such further apportionment shall supersede any earlier apportionment, and

(iii) any such adjustments, assessments or repayments of tax shall be made as are necessary to give effect to any apportionment under this subsection.][29]

(2) [Subject to subsection (2A) where][30] for any accounting period a company makes a claim in that behalf to the appropriate inspector, the corporation tax of the company for that accounting period shall be reduced by an amount equal to [25 per cent][31] of qualifying expenditure attributable to the company as is referable to the accounting period.

[(2A) (a) Subject to *paragraph (c)*, where as respects any accounting period a company is entitled to reduce the corporation tax of that accounting period by an amount, in accordance with *subsection (2)*, the company may instead on making a claim in that behalf to the appropriate inspector surrender all or part of that amount to one or such number of key employees as the company may specify but the aggregate of such amounts, attributable to such employees, may not exceed the amount so surrendered.

(b) The part of that amount that may be surrendered by the company may not exceed the corporation tax of the accounting period, which would be chargeable, if no claim could be made in accordance with *subsection (2)*.

(c) A company may not make a claim under this subsection where, at the time of making such a claim the company has a liability (within the meaning of *section 960H*) in respect of the corporation tax of the accounting period referred to in *subsection (2)* or a previous accounting period.

(d) A claim in accordance with this subsection shall be made in such form as the Revenue Commissioners may prescribe and the company shall notify the key employee, in writing, of any amount surrendered to that employee.

(2B) Where as respects any accounting period a company makes a claim under *subsections (2)* and *(2A)* and in accordance with that claim—

(a) the corporation tax of an accounting period is reduced and an amount is surrendered, and

(b) either or both the amount so reduced or surrendered, as the case may be, is subsequently found not to have been as is authorised by this section,

then, the amount which is not so authorised shall be first attributable to a claim under *subsection (2)* in priority to a claim under *subsection (2A)*.

(2C) Where in respect of an accounting period, a company makes a claim under *subsection (2A)* and it is subsequently found that the amount surrendered in accordance with that claim (hereafter in this section referred to as the 'initial amount') is not as authorised by this section, then, in relation to each key employee, the amount surrendered, which is authorised by this section, shall be an amount (hereafter in this section referred to as the 'relevant authorised amount') determined by the formula—

$$A \times \frac{B}{C}$$

where—

A is the portion of the initial amount attributable to that key employee in accordance with the claim under *subsection (2A)*,

B is the aggregate amount that may be surrendered by the company for that accounting period as is authorised by this section, and

C is the initial amount,

and the company shall notify the key employee in writing of the relevant authorised amount.][32]

(3) For the purposes of *subsection (2)*—

(a) qualifying expenditure attributable to a company in relation to a relevant period shall be so much of the amount of qualifying group expenditure on research and development in the relevant period as is attributed to the company in the manner specified in a notice made jointly in writing to the appropriate inspector by the qualified companies that are members of the group: but where no such notice is given means an amount determined by the formula—

$$Q \times \frac{C}{G}$$

where—

Q is the qualifying group expenditure on research and development in the relevant period,

C is the amount of expenditure on research and development incurred by the company in the relevant period at a time when the company is a member of the group, and

G is the group expenditure on research and development in the relevant period,

(b) where a relevant period coincides with an accounting period of a company, the amount of qualifying expenditure on research and development attributable to the company as is referable to the accounting period of the company shall be the full amount of that expenditure, and

(c) where the relevant period does not coincide with an accounting period of the company—

(i) the qualifying expenditure on research and development attributable to the company shall be apportioned to the accounting periods which fall wholly or partly in the relevant period, and

(ii) the amount so apportioned to an accounting period shall be treated as the amount of qualifying expenditure on research and development attributable to the company as is referable to the accounting period of the company.

(4) [...][33] [Subject to *subsections (4A)* and *(4B)*, where][34] as respects any accounting period of a company the amount by which the company is entitled to reduce corporation tax of the accounting period exceeds the corporation tax of the company for the accounting period, the excess shall be carried forward and treated as an amount by which corporation tax for the next succeeding accounting period may be reduced, and so on for succeeding accounting periods.

[(4A) (a) Where as respects any accounting period of a company the amount by which the company is entitled to reduce corporation tax of the accounting period exceeds the corporation tax of the company for the accounting period, the company may make a claim requiring the corporation tax of the preceding accounting period ending within the time specified in *paragraph (b)* to be reduced by the amount of the excess.

(b) The time referred to in *paragraph (a)* shall be a time immediately preceding the accounting period first mentioned in that paragraph, equal in length to that accounting period, but the amount of the reduction which may be made under paragraph *(a)* in the corporation tax of an accounting period falling partly before that time shall not exceed the corporation tax referable to the part of those profits proportionate to the part of the period falling within that time.

(4B) (a) Where a claim under *subsection (4A)(a)* has been made, and the amount of the excess referred to in *subsection (4A)(a)* exceeds the corporation tax of the preceding accounting periods ending within the time specified in *subsection (4A)(b)* or where no corporation tax arises for those preceding accounting periods, the company may make a claim to have any excess remaining paid to the company by the Revenue Commissioners.

(b) Subject to section 766B, on receipt of a claim the Revenue Commissioners shall pay any excess remaining to the company, in 3 instalments—

(i) the first instalment shall be paid by the Revenue Commissioners not earlier than the date provided for in paragraph (*b*) of the definition of "*specified return date for the chargeable period*" as defined in section 950(1), for the accounting period in which the expenditure on research and development was incurred and shall equal 33 per cent of the excess remaining,

(ii) in respect of the second instalment—

(I) the excess remaining, as reduced by the first instalment under subparagraph (i), shall be first treated as an amount by which the corporation tax of the accounting period next succeeding the accounting period in which the expenditure giving rise to the claim under this subsection was incurred, is reduced in accordance with subsection (4), and

(II) the second instalment shall be paid by the Revenue Commissioners not earlier than 12 months immediately following the date referred to in subparagraph (i) and shall equal 50 per cent of the amount [of the excess remaining as reduced][35] by the aggregate of the first instalment under *subparagraph (i)* and the amount treated as reducing the corporation tax of an accounting period under clause (I),

and

(iii) in respect of the last instalment—

(I) the excess remaining, as reduced by the first and second instalments and by the amount treated as reducing the corporation tax of an accounting period under clause (I) of subpara-graph (ii), shall be first treated as an amount by which the corporation tax of the accounting period next succeeding the accounting period referred to in clause (I) of subpara-graph (ii) is reduced in accordance with *subsection (4)*, and

(II) the last instalment shall be paid by the Revenue Commissioners not earlier than 24 months immediately following the date referred to in *subparagraph (i)* and shall equal the amount by which the excess remaining is reduced by the first and second instalments and by the total of the amounts by which the corporation tax of an accounting period is reduced under clause (I) of *subparagraph (ii)* and under clause (I) of this subparagraph.][36]

[(4C) Where a company (in this section and *section 766A* referred to as the 'predecessor') which has made a claim in accordance with this section ceases to carry on a trade which includes the carrying on by it of research and development activities and another company (in this section and *section 766A* referred to as the 'successor') commences to carry on the trade and those research and development activities (the cessation and commencement referred to in this section and *section 766A* as the 'event') and—

(a) both the predecessor and successor were, at the time of the event, members of the same group of companies within the meaning of *section 411(1)*, and

(b) on or at any time within 2 years after the event the trade and the research and development activities are not carried on otherwise than by the successor,

then the successor may, to the extent that the predecessor has not used an amount to reduce the corporation tax of an accounting period in accordance with *subsection (2)*, surrendered an amount in accordance with *subsection (2A)* or made a claim under *subsection (4A)* or *(4B)*, carry forward any excess that the predecessor would have been entitled to carry forward in accordance with *subsection (4)*.][37]

[(5) Any claim under this section shall be made within 12 months from the end of the accounting period in which the expenditure on research and development, giving rise to the claim, is incurred.][38]

(6) (a) The Minister for Enterprise, Trade and Employment, in consultation with the Minister for Finance, may make regulations for the purposes of this section providing—

(i) that such categories of activities as may be specified in the regulations are not research and development activities, and

(ii) that such other categories of activities as may be specified in the regulations are research and development activities.

(b) Where regulations are to be made under this subsection, a draft of the regulations shall be laid before Dáil Éireann and the regulations shall not be made until a resolution approving the draft has been passed by Dáil Éireann.][39]

[(7) (a) The Revenue Commissioners may in relation to a claim by a company under this section or *section 766A*—

(i) consult with any person who in their opinion may be of assistance to them in ascertaining whether the expenditure incurred by the company was incurred in the carrying on by it of research and development activities, and

(ii) notwithstanding any obligation as to secrecy or other restriction on the disclosure of information imposed by, or under, the Tax Acts or any other statute or otherwise, but subject to *paragraph (b)*, disclose any detail in the company's claim under this section, or under *section 766A*, which they consider necessary for the purposes of such consultation.

(b) (i) Before disclosing information to any person under *paragraph (a)*, the Revenue Commissioners shall make known to the company—

(I) the identity of the person who they intend to consult, and

(II) the information they intend to disclose to the person.

(ii) Where the company shows to the satisfaction of the Revenue Commissioners (or on appeal to the Appeal Commissioners) that disclosure of such information to that person could prejudice the company's business, then the Revenue Commissioners shall not make such disclosure.

[(7A) Any amount payable by virtue of subsection (4B) shall not be income of the company or another company for any tax purpose.

[(7B) (a) Any amount payable by the Revenue Commissioners to the company or another company by virtue of *subsection (4B)* shall be deemed to be an overpayment of corporation tax, for the purposes only of *section 960H(2)*.

(b) Any claim in respect of a specified amount shall be deemed for the purposes of *section 1077E* to be a claim in connection with a credit and, for the purposes of determining an amount in accordance with *section 1077E(11)* or *1077E(12)*, a reference to an amount of tax that would have been payable for the relevant periods by the person concerned shall be read as if it were a reference to a specified amount.

[(c) (i) Subject to *subparagraph (ii)*, where a company makes a claim in respect of a specified amount and it is subsequently found that the claim is not as authorised by this section or by *section 766A*, as the case may be, then the company may be charged to tax under Case IV of *Schedule D* for the accounting period in respect of which the payment was made or the amount surrendered, as the case may be, in an amount equal to 4 times so much of the specified amount as is not so authorised.

(ii) Where a company makes a claim under *subsection (2A)* and it is subsequently found that the claim is deliberately false or overstated and that the amount surrendered in accordance with that claim is not as authorised by this section, then *subparagraph (i)* shall not apply and the company shall be charged to tax under Case IV of *Schedule D* for the accounting period in respect of which the amount was surrendered in an amount equal to 8 times so much of the amount surrendered as is not so authorised.][40]

(d) Where in accordance with *paragraph (c)* an inspector makes an assessment in respect of a specified amount, the amount so charged shall for the purposes of *section 1080* be deemed to be tax due and payable and shall carry interest as determined in accordance with *subsection (2)(c)* of *section 1080* as if a reference to the date when the tax became due and payable were a reference to the date the amount was paid by the Revenue Commissioners, or a reference to the date the corporation tax of the company for the accounting period in respect of which the amount was surrendered, was payable, as the case may be.][41]

[(7C) (a) *Subparagraph (ii)* of the definition of "*threshold amount*" shall not apply in relation to a relevant period [commencing on or after 1 January 2010][42] (in this paragraph referred to as the "*first-mentioned relevant period*") or any relevant period subsequent to that relevant period, where, at a time during that first-mentioned relevant period or any later relevant period, being a time subsequent to the cessation time—

(i) the research and development centre referred to in clause (II) of *subparagraph (ii)* of the definition of "*threshold amount*" is used for the purposes of a trade by a company which is a member of the group, or

(ii) activities substantially the same as the research and development activities which were carried on in that research and development centre at any time in the 48 months immediately preceding the cessation time are carried on [in the State][43] by a company which is a member of the group of companies.

(b) Where—

(i) by virtue of *subparagraph (ii)* of the definition of "*threshold amount*", expenditure incurred in the threshold period is not taken into account in calculating the threshold amount in relation to a relevant period, and

(ii) by virtue of *paragraph (a)* of this subsection, *subparagraph (ii)* of that definition does not apply in relation to a subsequent relevant period,

then, in respect of the accounting period commencing at the same time as that subsequent relevant period or where no accounting period commences at that time, the first accounting period commencing after that time, the company referred to in *subparagraph (i)* or *(ii)* of *paragraph (a)*, as the case may be, shall be charged to tax under Case IV of Schedule D on an amount equal to the aggregate of the amounts by which the qualifying group expenditure on research and development has been increased, as a result of a reduction in the threshold amount by virtue of *subparagraph (ii)* of the definition of threshold amount, for relevant periods, taking account of each relevant period in respect of which the qualifying group expenditure on research and development was so increased.

(c) Where—

(i) by virtue of *subparagraph (ii)* of the definition of "*threshold amount*", expenditure incurred in the threshold period by a company which is a member of a group of companies is not taken into account in calculating the threshold amount in relation to a relevant period, and

(ii) at any time during the period of 10 years commencing on the date on which the research and development centre ceased to be used, no company which is a member of the group is carrying on a trade which is within the charge to corporation tax,

then, in respect of the final accounting period for which a company which is a member of the group is chargeable to corporation tax in respect of its trade, that company shall be charged to tax under Case IV of Schedule D on an amount equal to the aggregate of the amounts by which the qualifying group expenditure on research and development has been increased, as a result of a reduction in the threshold amount by virtue of *subparagraph (ii)* of the definition of threshold amount, for relevant periods, taking account of each relevant period in respect of which the qualifying group expenditure on research and development was so increased, as reduced by any amount charged to tax in accordance with *paragraph (b)*.][44]

(8) Any functions which are authorised by *subsection (7)* to be performed or discharged by the Revenue Commissioners may be performed or discharged by an authorised officer and any references in *subsection (7)* to the Revenue Commissioners shall,

with any necessary modifications, be construed as including references to the authorised officer.][45]

Amendments

[1] Deleted by FA12 sched (1)(g).

[2] Inserted by FA06 s66(1)(a)(i). This section applies for accounting periods ending on or after 2 February 2006.

[3] Inserted by FA06 s66(1)(a)(ii). This section applies for accounting periods ending on or after 2 February 2006.

[4] Substituted by FA05 s48(1)(f)(i). This section applies as respects any period of account beginning on or after 1 January 2005. With effect from 1 January 2005 per S.I. 434 of 2004.

[5] Inserted by FA11 s41. Deemed to have come into force and takes effect as on and from 1 January 2011.

[6] Deleted by FA05 s48(1)(f)(ii). This section applies as respects any period of account beginning on or after 1 January 2005. With effect from 1 January 2005 per S.I. 434 of 2004.

[7] Deleted by FA12 s27(1)(a). Applies to accounting periods commencing on or after 1 January 2012.

[8] Inserted by FA05 s48(1)(f)(ii). This section applies as respects any period of account beginning on or after 1 January 2005. With effect from 1 January 2005 per S.I. 434 of 2004.

[9] Inserted by FA12 s27(1)(a). Applies to accounting periods commencing on or after 1 January 2012.

[10] Inserted by FA12 s27(1)(b). Applies to accounting periods commencing on or after 1 January 2012.

[11] Substituted by FA10 s54(1)(a). Applies to relevant periods commencing on or after 1 January 2010.

[12] Substituted by FA14 s26(a). Comes into operation on 1 January 2015.

[13] Substituted by F(No.2)A13 s21(1)(a). Applies to accounting periods commencing on or after 1 January 2014.

[14] Substituted by FA12 s27(1)(c). Applies to accounting periods commencing on or after 1 January 2012.

[15] Inserted by FA10 s54(1)(b). Applies to relevant periods commencing on or after 1 January 2010.

[16] Inserted by FA12 s27(1)(d). Applies to accounting periods commencing on or after 1 January 2012.

[17, 19] Substituted by FA10 s54(1)(c). Deemed to have come into force and takes effect as on and from 1 January 2010.

[18] Substituted by F(No.2)A08 s34(1)(a). Applies to expenditure incurred in accounting periods commencing on or after 1 January 2009.

[20] Substituted by FA12 s27(1)(e). Applies to accounting periods commencing on or after 1 January 2012.

[21] Substituted by FA10 s54(1)(d). Deemed to have come into force and takes effect as on and from 1 January 2010.

[22] Substituted by FA10 s54(1)(e). Deemed to have come into force and takes effect as on and from 1 January 2010.

[23] Inserted by FA10 s54(1)(f). Deemed to have come into force and takes effect as on and from 1 January 2010.

[24] Substituted by FA10 s54(1)(g). Applies to accounting periods commencing on or after 1 January 2010.

[25] Substituted by FA12 s27(1)(f). Applies to accounting periods ending on or after 1 January 2012.

[26] Substituted by F(No.2)A13 s21(1)(b). Applies to accounting periods commencing on or after 1 January 2014.

[27] Substituted by FA12 s27(1)(g). Applies to accounting periods ending on or after 1 January 2012.

[28] Inserted by FA10 s54(1)(i). Deemed to have come into force and takes effect as on and from 1 January 2010.

[29] Inserted by FA06 s66(1)(b). This section applies for accounting periods ending on or after 2 February 2006.

[30] Substituted by FA12 s27(1)(h). Applies to accounting periods commencing on or after 1 January 2012.

[31] Substituted by F(No.2)A08 s34(1)(b). Applies to expenditure incurred in accounting periods commencing on or after 1 January 2009.

[32] Inserted by FA12 s27(1)(i). Applies to accounting periods commencing on or after 1 January 2012.

[33] Deleted by F(No.2)A08 s34(1)(c). Applies to expenditure incurred in accounting periods commencing on or after 1 January 2009.

[34] Substituted by F(No.2)A08 s34(1)(c). Applies to expenditure incurred in accounting periods commencing on or after 1 January 2009.

[35] Substituted by FA10 s54(1)(j). Applies and has effect from 1 January 2010.

[36] Inserted by F(No.2)A08 s34(1)(d). Applies to expenditure incurred in accounting periods commencing on or after 1 January 2009.

[37] Inserted by FA12 s27(1)(j). Applies to accounting periods commencing on or after 1 January 2012.

[38] Substituted by F(No.2)A08 s34(1)(e). Applies to claims under section 766 made on or after 1 January 2009.

[39] Substituted by FA04 s33(1)(a). This section comes into operation on such day as the Minister for Finance may appoint by order and has effect as respects expenditure incurred on or after that day. With effect from 1 January 2004 per S.I. 425 of 2004.

[40] Substituted by F(No.2)A13 s21(1)(c). Applies to accounting periods commencing on or after 1 January 2014.

[41] Substituted by FA12 s27(1)(k). Applies to accounting periods commencing on or after 1 January 2012.

[42] Inserted by FA14 s26(b)(i). Comes into operation on 1 January 2015.

[43] Inserted by FA14 s26(b)(ii). Comes into operation on 1 January 2015.

[44] Inserted by FA10 s54(1)(l). Deemed to have come into force and takes effect as on and from 1 January 2010.

[45] Inserted by FA06 s66(1)(c). This section applies for accounting periods ending on or after 2 February 2006.

Revenue Briefings

Tax Briefing

Tax Briefing April 2004 – Issue 55 pg 6 – Finance Act 2004 – Research and Development Credit
Tax Briefing April 2005 – Issue 59 pg 20 – Research and Development Tax Credit
Tax Briefing July 2007 – Issue 66 – Claiming a Tax Credit for Research & Development
Tax Briefing December 2007 – Issue 67 – Claims for Research and Development Tax Credit
Tax Briefing December 2008 – Issue 70 – Finance (No 2) Bill 2008 changes – Research and Development
Tax Briefing April 2009 – Issue 71 – Research and Development (R&D) Tax Credit
Tax Briefing December 2009 – Issue 83 – Research and Development (R&D) Tax Credits

eBrief

eBrief No. 42/2007 – Claims for Research and Development (R&D) tax credit in respect of projects approved for Research Technology & Innovation (RTI) grants from Enterprise Ireland
eBrief No. 14/2008 – Revenue Guidelines for Research and Development Tax Credits
eBrief No. 63/2008 – Finance (No.2) Bill 2008 – Research and Development
eBrief No. 02/2009 – Research and Development protective claims – follow up to eBrief 63/2008
eBrief No. 14/2009 – Research and Development – Finance (No.2) Act 2008
eBrief No. 36/2009 – Accounting Treatment of Research and Development Tax Credits
eBrief No. 89/2009 – Research and Development (R&D) Tax Credits
eBrief No. 32/2014 – Relief for key employees engaged in Research and Development activities
eBrief No. 89/2014 – R&D – Clarification of the treatment of threshold expenditure in certain circumstances
eBrief No. 94/2014 – CT 1 2014 and claims for the set back of excess Trading Losses and excess Research & Development Credit

Revenue Information Notes

Revenue Guidelines for Research and Development Tax Credit

Cross References

From Section 766

Section 10 Connected persons.
Section 234 Certain income derived from patent royalties.
Section 237 Annual payments payable wholly out of taxed income.
Section 268 Meaning of "industrial building or structure".
Section 291A Intangible assets.
Section 307 Corporation tax: allowances and charges in taxing a trade.
Section 381 Right to repayment of tax by reference to losses.
Section 410 Group payments.
Section 411 Surrender of relief between members of groups and consortia.

Section 412 Qualification for entitlement to group relief.
Section 418 Beneficial percentage.
Section 473A Relief for fees paid for third level education, etc.
Section 764 Deduction for revenue expenditure on scientific research.
Section 766A Tax credit on expenditure on buildings or structures used for research and development.
Section 766B Limitation of tax credits to be paid under section 766 or 766A.
Section 950 Interpretation (Part 41).
Section 960H Offset between taxes.

To Section 766

Section 141 Distributions out of income from patent royalties.
Section 488 Interpretation (Part 16).
Section 489 The relief.
Section 493 Seed capital relief.
Section 541C Tax treatment of certain venture fund managers.
Section 766A Tax credit on expenditure on buildings or structures used for research and development.
Section 766B Limitation of tax credits to be paid under section 766 or 766A.

766A Tax credit on expenditure on buildings or structures used for research and development

[(1) (a) In this section—

"*qualified company*", "*relevant member State*" and "*research and development activities*" have the same meanings as in *section 766*;

["*qualifying building*" means a building or structure, which is to be used for the purpose of the carrying on by the company of research and development activities in a relevant Member State, where, for the specified relevant period in relation to that building or structure, the proportion of use of the building or structure attributable to the research and development activities carried on by the company, as calculated in accordance with *subsection (6)*, is not less than 35 per cent;][1]

"*refurbishment*", in relation to a building or structure, means any work of construction, reconstruction, repair or renewal including the provision of water, sewerage or heating facilities carried out in the course of the repair or restoration, or maintenance in the nature of repair or restoration, of the building or structure;

"*relevant expenditure*" on a building or structure, in relation to a company, means expenditure incurred by the company on the construction of a [qualifying building][2], being expenditure which qualifies for an allowance under *Part 9* or this Part: but expenditure incurred by a company which is resident in the State shall not be relevant expenditure if it—

(i) may be taken into account as an expense in computing income of the company,

(ii) is expenditure in respect of which an allowance for capital expenditure may be made to the company, or

(iii) may otherwise be allowed or relieved in relation to the company,

for the purposes of tax in a territory other than the State.

["*specified relevant expenditure*" means the same proportion of relevant expenditure as the research and development activities carried on in the qualifying building by the company for the specified relevant period bears to the total of all activities carried on by the company in that building for that period;

"*specified relevant period*" means—

(i) in the case of the construction of a qualifying building, the period of 4 years, commencing with the date on which the building or structure is first brought into use for the purposes of a trade,

(ii) in the case of the refurbishment of a qualifying building, the period of 4 years, commencing with the date on which the refurbishment is completed or, such earlier period of 4 years, as the company may elect, beginning not earlier than the date on which the refurbishment commences;][3]

['*specified time*' in relation to a building or structure means the period of 10 years commencing at the beginning of the accounting period in which the predecessor incurs relevant expenditure on that building or structure;][4]

(b) For the purposes of this section—

(i) expenditure shall not be regarded as having been incurred by a company if it has been or is to be met directly or indirectly [by or through—

(I) the State or another relevant Member State, or

(II) any board established by statute, any public or local authority or any other agency of the State or of another relevant Member State;][5]

(ii) a reference to expenditure incurred on the construction of a building or structure includes expenditure on the refurbishment of the building or structure, but does not include—

(I) any expenditure incurred on the acquisition of, or of rights in or over, any land,

(II) any expenditure on the provision of machinery or plant or on any asset treated for any chargeable period as machinery or plant, or

(III) any expenditure on research and development within the meaning of *section 766*;

(iii) where a building or structure which is to be used for the purposes of the carrying on of research and development activities forms part of a building or is one of a number of buildings in a single development, or forms a part of a building which is itself one of a number of buildings in a single development, there shall be made such apportionment as is necessary of the expenditure incurred on the construction of the whole building or number of buildings, as the case may be, for the purpose of determining the expenditure incurred on the construction of the building or structure which is to be used for the purposes of carrying on of research and development activities,

(iv) *paragraphs (i)* to *(iii)* of *section 766(1)(b)* shall apply.

[(2) Where in an accounting period a qualified company incurs relevant expenditure, the corporation tax of the company for that accounting period shall be reduced by an amount equal to 25 per cent of the specified relevant expenditure.][6]

[(3) Where—

(a) in an accounting period a company incurs relevant expenditure on a building or structure,

(b) in relation to that expenditure the corporation tax of the company or another company is reduced under *subsection (2)* or *(4A)*, or a payment has been made to the company or another company by the Revenue Commissioners by virtue of *subsection (4B)*, and

(c) at any time in the period of 10 years commencing at the beginning of that accounting period the building or structure is sold or ceases to be used by the company for the purpose of research and development activities or for the purpose of the same trade that was carried on by the company at the beginning of the specified relevant period, in connection with which the research and development activities were carried on,

[then, subject to *subsection (3A)*, the company][7]—

(i) and in relation to that expenditure, another company, shall not be entitled to reduce corporation tax under *subsection (2)* for any accounting period ending after the time specified in *paragraph (c)*, and

(ii) shall be charged to tax under Case IV of Schedule D for the accounting period in which the building or structure is sold or ceases to be used for the purpose of research and development activities or for the purpose of the trade, in an amount equal to 4 times the aggregate amount by which, in respect of the company or in relation to that expenditure, another company, the corporation tax payable is reduced under *subsections (2)*, *(4)* and *(4A)*, and payments are made under *subsection (4B)*.][8]

[(3A) Where an event referred to in *section 766(4C)* occurs and—

(a) in connection with the event the predecessor transfers to the successor a building or structure in respect of which—

(i) the predecessor had made a claim under [this section][9]

(ii) the transfer is a transfer to which *section 617* applies, and

(iii) at the time of the transfer either or both the specified relevant period and the specified time had not expired,

(b) on, or at any time within 2 years after, the event, the trade and research and development activities are not carried on otherwise than by the successor, and

(c) the building or structure in respect of which relevant expenditure was incurred by the predecessor—

(i) in a case where the specified relevant period had not expired, would continue to be a qualifying building if a reference, in the definition of '*qualifying building*' to activities carried on by the company were construed as a reference to activities carried on by the company and the successor, and

(ii) continues to be used by the successor throughout the remainder of the '*specified time*' for the purposes of research and development activities, then—

(I) *subparagraphs (i)* and *(ii)* of *subsection (3)* shall not apply in relation to the transfer by the predecessor,

(II) the successor may, to the extent that the predecessor has not used an amount to reduce the corporation tax of an accounting period in accordance with *subsection (2)* or made a claim under *subsection (4A)* or *(4B)* carry forward any excess that the predecessor would have been entitled to carry forward, in accordance with *subsection (4)*, and

(III) *subsection (3)* shall have effect as if a reference to the company in *subsection (3)(c)* and thereafter in *subsection (3)* were a reference to the successor.][10]

(4) (a) Subject to *paragraphs (b)* and *(c)* [and *subsections (4A)* and *(4B)*,][11] where as respects any accounting period of a company the amount by which the company is entitled under this section to reduce corporation tax of the accounting period exceeds the relevant corporation tax of the company for the accounting period, the excess shall be carried forward and treated as an amount by which corporation tax for the next succeeding accounting period may be reduced, and so on for succeeding accounting periods.

(b) Where the company referred to in *paragraph (a)* is a member of a group of companies, the company may specify that the excess specified in *paragraph (a)*, or any part of that excess, is to be treated as an amount by which corporation tax payable by another company which is a member of that group for that other company's corresponding accounting period is to be reduced.

(c) So much of the excess specified under *paragraph (a)* as is treated under *paragraph (b)* as an amount by which tax payable by another company is to be reduced shall not be carried forward under *paragraph (a)*.

[(4A) (a) Where as respects any accounting period of a company the amount by which the company is entitled to reduce corporation tax of the accounting period exceeds the corporation tax of the company for the accounting period, the company may make a claim requiring the corporation tax of the preceding accounting periods ending within the time specified in *paragraph* (*b*) to be reduced by the amount of the excess.

(b) The time referred to in *paragraph* (*a*) shall be a time immediately preceding the accounting period first mentioned in that paragraph, equal in length to that accounting period, but the amount of the reduction which may be made under that paragraph in the corporation tax of an accounting period falling partly before that time shall not exceed the corporation tax referable to the part of those profits proportionate to the part of the period falling within that time.

(4B) (a) Where a claim under *subsection (4A)*(*a*) has been made, and the amount of the excess referred to in *subsection (4A)*(*a*) exceeds the corporation tax of the preceding accounting periods ending within the time specified in *subsection (4A)*(*b*) or where no corporation tax arises for those preceding accounting periods, the company may make a claim to have any excess remaining paid to the company by the Revenue Commissioners.

(b) Subject to section 766B, on receipt of a claim the Revenue Commissioners shall pay any excess remaining to the company, in 3 instalments—

(i) the first instalment shall be paid by the Revenue Commissioners not earlier than the date provided for in [*paragraph (b)(i)* of the definition of "*specified return date for the chargeable period*" as defined in *section 959A*][12], for the accounting period in which the expenditure on research and development was incurred and shall equal 33 per cent of the excess remaining,

(ii) in respect of the second instalment—

(I) the excess remaining, as reduced by the first instalment under *subparagraph (i)*, shall be first treated as an amount by which the corporation tax of the accounting period next succeeding the accounting period in which the expenditure giving rise to the claim under this subsection was incurred, is reduced in accordance with *subsection (4)*, and

(II) the second instalment shall be paid by the Revenue Commissioners not earlier than 12 months immediately following the date referred to in [*subparagraph (i)*][13] and shall equal 50 per cent of the amount [of the excess remaining as reduced][14] by the aggregate of the first instalment under *subparagraph (i)* and the amount treated as reducing the corporation tax of an accounting period under clause (I),

and

(iii) in respect of the last instalment—

(I) the excess remaining, as reduced by the first and second instalments and by the amount treated as reducing the corporation tax of an accounting period under clause (I) of *subparagraph (ii)*, shall be first treated as an amount by which the corporation tax of the accounting period next succeeding the accounting period referred to in clause (I) of *subparagraph (ii)* is reduced in accordance with *subsection (4)*, and

(II) the last instalment shall be paid by the Revenue Commissioners not earlier than 24 months immediately following the date referred to in *subparagraph (i)* and shall equal the amount by which the excess remaining is reduced by the first and second instalments and by the total of the amounts by which the corporation tax of an accounting period is reduced under clause (I) of *subparagraph (ii)* and under clause (I) of this subparagraph.][15]

[(5) Any claim under this section shall be made within 12 months from the end of the accounting period in which the relevant expenditure, giving rise to the claim, is incurred.][16]

[(6) (a) Where expenditure is incurred by a company on a building or structure and the building or structure will not be used by the company wholly and exclusively for the purposes of research and development, the proportion of the use of the building or the amount of the expenditure, attributable to research and development shall be such portion of the use of the building or the expenditure as appears to the inspector (or on appeal the Appeal Commissioners) to be just and reasonable.

(b) Where, at any time, any apportionment referred to in *paragraph* (*a*), or a further apportionment made under this paragraph, ceases to be just and reasonable, then—

(i) such further apportionment shall be made at that time as appears to the inspector (or on appeal the Appeal Commissioners) to be just and reasonable,

(ii) any such further apportionment shall supersede any earlier apportionment, and

(iii) any such adjustments, assessments or repayments of tax shall be made as are necessary to give effect to any apportionment under this subsection.

(7) Any amount payable by virtue of subsection (4B) shall not be income of the company or another company, for any tax purpose.

(8) Any amount payable by the Revenue Commissioners to the company or another company by virtue of subsection (4B) shall be deemed to be an overpayment of corporation tax, for the purposes only of [*section 960H(2)*][17].][18][19]

Amendments

[1] Inserted by F(No.2)A08 s35(1)(a)(i). Comes into operation as respects expenditure incurred after 24 September 2009 and in any accounting period commencing on or after 1 January 2009 as per S.I. No. 392/2009.

[2] Substituted by F(No.2)A08 s35(1)(a)(ii). Comes into operation as respects expenditure incurred after 24 September 2009 and in any accounting period commencing on or after 1 January 2009 as per S.I. No. 392/2009.

[3] Inserted by F(No.2)A08 s35(1)(a)(iii). Comes into operation as respects expenditure incurred after 24 September 2009 and in any accounting period commencing on or after 1 January 2009 as per S.I. No. 392/2009.

[4] Inserted by FA12 s27(1)(l). Applies to accounting periods commencing on or after 1 January 2012.

[5] Substituted by FA12 s27(1)(m). Applies to accounting periods commencing on or after 1 January 2012.

[6] Substituted by F(No.2)A08 s35(1)(b). Comes into operation as respects expenditure incurred after 24 September 2009 and in any accounting period commencing on or after 1 January 2009 as per S.I. No. 392/2009.

[7] Substituted by FA12 s27(1)(n). Applies to accounting periods commencing on or after 1 January 2012.

[8] Substituted by F(No.2)A08 s35(1)(c). Comes into operation as respects expenditure incurred after 24 September 2009 and in any accounting period commencing on or after 1 January 2009 as per S.I. No. 392/2009.

[9] Substituted by FA13 sched2(1)(g). Has effect on and from 27 March 2013.

[10] Inserted by FA12 s27(1)(o). Applies to accounting periods commencing on or after 1 January 2012.

[11] Inserted by F(No.2)A08 s35(1)(d). Comes into operation as respects expenditure incurred after 24 September 2009 and in any accounting period commencing on or after 1 January 2009 as per S.I. No. 392/2009.

[12] Substituted by FA12 sched4(part 2)(g).

[13] Substituted by FA11 sched3(1)(h). Has effect as on and from 6 February 2011.

[14] Substituted by FA10 sched(4)(1)(h)(i). Has effect as on and from 3 April 2010.

[15] Inserted by F(No.2)A08 s35(1)(e). Comes into operation as respects expenditure incurred after 24 September 2009 and in any accounting period commencing on or after 1 January 2009 as per S.I. No. 392/2009.

[16] Substituted by F(No.2)A08 s35(1)(f). Comes into operation as respects expenditure incurred after 24 September 2009 and in any accounting period commencing on or after 1 January 2009 as per S.I. No. 392/2009.

[17] Substituted by FA10 sched(4)(1)(h)(ii). Has effect as on and from 3 April 2010.

[18] Inserted by F(No.2)A08 s35(1)(g). Comes into operation as respects expenditure incurred after 24 September 2009 and in any accounting period commencing on or after 1 January 2009 as per S.I. No. 392/2009.

[19] Substituted by FA04 s33(1)(a). This section comes into operation on such day as the Minister for Finance may appoint by order and has effect as respects expenditure incurred on or after that day. With effect from 1 January 2004 per S.I. 425 of 2004.

Revenue Briefings

Tax Briefing

Tax Briefing April 2004 – Issue 55 pg 6 – Finance Act 2004 – Research and Development Credit
Tax Briefing December 2008 – Issue 70 – Finance (No. 2) Bill 2008 changes – Research and Development
Tax Briefing April 2009 – Issue 71 – Research and Development (R&D) Tax Credit
Tax Briefing December 2009 – Issue 83 – Research and Development (R&D) Tax Credits

eBrief

eBrief No. 63/2008 – Finance (No.2) Bill 2008 – Research and Development
eBrief No. 02/2009 – Research and Development protective claims – follow up to eBrief 63/2008
eBrief No. 14/2009 – Research and Development – Finance (No.2) Act 2008
eBrief No. 36/2009 – Accounting Treatment of Research and Development Tax Credits
eBrief No. 89/2009 – Research and Development (R&D) Tax Credits
eBrief No. 94/2014 – CT 1 2014 and claims for the set back of excess Trading Losses and excess Research & Development Credit

Revenue Information Notes

Revenue Guidelines for Research and Development Tax Credit

Cross References

From Section 766A

Section 268 Meaning of "industrial building or structure".
Section 766 Tax credit for research and development expenditure.
Section 766B Limitation of tax credits to be paid under section 766 or 766A.
Section 950 Interpretation (Part 41).
Section 960H Offset between taxes.

To Section 766A

Section 766 Tax credit for research and development expenditure.
Section 766B Limitation of tax credits to be paid under section 766 or 766A.

766B Limitation of tax credits to be paid under section 766 or 766A

[(1) In this section—

"*payroll liabilities*" means—

(a) the amount of income tax which the company is required, by or under Chapter 4 of Part 42, to remit to the Collector-General for the relevant payroll period in respect of emoluments, as defined in section 983, paid to, or on account of, all employees and directors,

(b) the amount of Pay Related Social Insurance Contributions in respect of the reckonable earnings and reckonable emoluments of all directors and employees which the company is required to remit to the Collector-General for the relevant payroll period by or under the Social Welfare Acts, and

(c) any other amount of levies or charges the company is required, by or under Parts 18A, 18B or 18D, to remit to the Collector-General for the relevant payroll period;

"*relevant payroll period*" means the period—

(a) beginning at the time the period immediately preceding, and equal in length to, the accounting period in which the expenditure was incurred begins, and

(b) ending at the time that accounting period ends.][1]

(2) For the purpose of subsection (1), Pay Related Social Insurance includes Pay Related Social Insurance Contributions payable under the Social Welfare Acts, Health Contributions payable under the Health Contributions Act 1979, and levies payable under the National Training Fund Act 2000.

(3) Where in respect of expenditure in an accounting period a company makes a claim under section 766(4B) or 766A(4B), then the aggregate amount payable by the Revenue Commissioners to that company under those sections shall not exceed the greater of—

(a) the aggregate of the corporation tax paid by the company in respect of accounting periods ending in the 10 years immediately preceding the time specified in subsection (4A)(*b*) of section 766, in relation to the accounting period in which the expenditure was incurred, as reduced by any amounts payable to the company in respect of claims made under section 766(4B) or 766A(4B), as the case may be, in respect of expenditure in a previous accounting period, or

[(b) the aggregate of the amounts payable by the company in respect of payroll liabilities for the relevant payroll period in which the expenditure was incurred as reduced by the lesser of—

(i) the amount by which the aggregate of any amounts payable to the company in respect of claims made under section 766(4B) or 766A(4B), as the case may be, in respect of expenditure incurred in a previous accounting period, exceeds the payroll liabilities in respect of the period—

(I) beginning at the time that the accounting period in respect of which the first such claim was made begins, and

(II) ending at the time the accounting period immediately preceding the accounting period in which the expenditure was incurred ends,

and

(ii) the amount of the payroll liabilities for the period—

(I) beginning at the time at which the relevant payroll period begins, and

(II) ending at the time the accounting period immediately preceding the accounting period in which the expenditure was incurred ends.][2][3]

Amendments

[1] Substituted by F(No.2)A11 s1(1)(a). This section applies to accounting periods commencing on or after the passing of this Act.

[2] Substituted by F(No.2)A11 s1(1)(b). This section applies to accounting periods commencing on or after the passing of this Act.

[3] Inserted by F(No.2)A08 s36. This section is deemed to have come into force and takes effect as on and from 1 January 2009.

Revenue Briefings

Tax Briefing

Tax Briefing December 2008 – Issue 70 – Finance (No. 2) Bill 2008 changes – Research and Development

Tax Briefing April 2009 – Issue 71 – Research and Development (R&D) Tax Credit

eBrief

eBrief No. 32/2014 – Relief for key employees engaged in Research and Development activities

Cross References

From Section 766B

Section 766 Tax credit for research and development expenditure.

Section 766A Tax credit on expenditure on buildings or structures used for research and development.

To Section 766B

Section 766 Tax credit for research and development expenditure.

Section 766A Tax credit on expenditure on buildings or structures used for research and development.

767 Payment to universities and other approved bodies for research in, or teaching of, approved subjects [Repealed]

Repealed by TCA97 s848A, as inserted by FA01 s45.

Cross References

To Section 767

Section 848A Donations to approved bodies.

CHAPTER 3

Know-How and Certain Training

768 Allowance for know-how

[FA68 s2]

(1) In this section—

"*control*" has the same meaning as in *section 312*;

"*know-how*" means industrial information and techniques likely to assist in the manufacture or processing of goods or materials, or in the carrying out of any agricultural, forestry, fishing, mining or other extractive operations;

references to a body of persons include references to a partnership.

(2) (a) For the purposes of this subsection, a person incurring expenditure on know-how before the setting up and commencement of the trade in which it is used shall be treated as incurring it on that setting up and commencement.

(b) Where a person incurs expenditure on know-how for use in a trade carried on by the person or, having incurred expenditure on know-how, sets up and commences a trade in which it is used, there shall, subject to this section, be allowed to be deducted as expenses, in computing for the purposes of Case I of Schedule D the profits or gains of the trade, such part of the expenditure as would but for this section not be allowed to be so deducted.

[(3) (a) Where a person acquires a trade or part of a trade and, together with the trade or the part of the trade, know-how used in the trade or part of the trade, then no amount shall be allowed to be deducted under this section in respect of expenditure incurred on the acquisition of the know-how.

(b) Subject to paragraph (*c*), where—

(i) a person acquires a trade or part of a trade, and

(ii) a person connected (within the meaning of section 10) with the person acquires knowhow used in the trade or the part of the trade, then—

(I) the amount of expenditure incurred on the know-how by the person referred to in subparagraph (ii) shall be allowed as a deduction against profits of the trade, carried on by that person, in which the know-how is used (in this subsection referred to as a "*relevant trade*") but not against any other income or profits of whatever description,

(II) no amount of any royalty or other sum paid by the person referred to in subparagraph (i), or by any person connected (within the meaning of section 10) with that person, for the know-how acquired by the person referred to in subparagraph (ii) shall be allowed to be deducted in computing the profits of any description, or to be treated as a charge on income, of the person making such payment, and

(III) no amount shall be allowed to be deducted under this section where, at any time, the trade or part of the trade referred to in subparagraph (i) is transferred to the person referred to in subparagraph (ii).

(c) Where as respects any chargeable period of a person carrying on a relevant trade, the amount by which a deduction available to be made under paragraph (*b*)(I) exceeds the profits of the relevant trade but for that deduction, the excess shall be carried forward and treated as an amount deductible under paragraph (*b*)(I) for succeeding chargeable periods and (so long as the person continues to carry on the trade) its profits from the trade in any succeeding chargeable period shall then be treated as reduced by the amount of the excess, or by so much of that excess as cannot be relieved against profits of the trade of an earlier chargeable period.][1]

(3A) The amount which shall be allowed to be deducted under this section in respect of expenditure incurred by a person on know-how shall be limited to the amount which has been incurred wholly and exclusively on the acquisition of know-how for bona fide commercial reasons and was not incurred as part of a scheme or arrangement the main purpose or one of the main purposes of which is the avoidance of tax.][2]

(4) *Subsection (2)* shall not apply on any sale of know-how where the buyer is a body of persons over whom the seller has control, or the seller is a body of persons over whom the buyer has control, or both the seller and the buyer are bodies of persons and some other person has control over both of them.

[(5) (a) The Revenue Commissioners may, in relation to a claim by a person that expenditure is allowed to be deducted in accordance with subsection (2)—

(i) consult with any person (in this subsection referred to as an "*expert*") who in their opinion may be of assistance in ascertaining the extent to which such expenditure is incurred on know-how, and

(ii) notwithstanding any obligation as to secrecy or other restriction on the disclosure of information imposed by, or under, the Tax Acts or any other statute or otherwise, but subject to paragraph (*b*), disclose any detail in the person's claim under this section which they consider necessary for such consultation.

(b) (i) Before disclosing information to any expert under paragraph (*a*), the Revenue Commissioners shall make known to the person—

(I) the identity of the expert who they intend to consult, and

(II) the information they intend to disclose to the expert.

(ii) Where the person shows to the satisfaction of the Revenue Commissioners (or on appeal to the Appeal Commissioners) that disclosure of such information to that expert could prejudice the person's trade, then the Revenue Commissioners shall not make such disclosure.][3]

[(6) Where any relief has been claimed under this section which is subsequently found not to have been due, that relief shall be withdrawn by making an assessment to tax, under Case IV of Schedule D, for the chargeable period or chargeable periods in which relief was claimed and, notwithstanding anything in the Tax Acts, such an assessment may be made at any time.][4]

[(7) Subject to subsection (8), this section shall not apply to a company within the charge to corporation tax.

(8) (a) Subject to paragraph (*b*), where a company elects in writing, this section shall apply to expenditure, specified in the election, incurred by it on know-how after 7 May 2009 and before 7 May 2011.

(b) An election under paragraph (*a*) shall be made in the return required to be made under section 951 for the accounting period of the company in which the expenditure is incurred and shall not be made later than 12 months from the end of the accounting period in which the capital expenditure, giving rise to the claim, is incurred.][5]

Amendments

[1] Substituted by F(No.2)A08 s30(1)(a). Applies as respects any chargeable period (within the meaning of section 321(2)) ending on or after 31 December 2008.

[2] Substituted by FA08 s40(1)(a). This section applies as respects any chargeable period (within the meaning of section 321(2)) ending on or after 31 January 2008.

[3] Inserted by FA08 s40(1)(b). This section applies as respects any chargeable period (within the meaning of section 321(2)) ending on or after 31 January 2008.

[4] Inserted by F(No.2)A08 s30(1)(b). Applies as respects any chargeable period (within the meaning of section 321(2)) ending on or after 31 December 2008.

[5] Inserted by FA09 s13(1)(j). Applies to expenditure incurred by a company after 7 May 2009.

Cross References

From Section 768

Section 10 Connected persons.
Section 312 Special provisions as to certain sales.
Section 951 Obligation to make a return.

To Section 768

Section 291A Intangible assets.
Section 692 Development expenditure: allowances and charges.
Section 693 Exploration expenditure: allowances and charges.

769 Relief for training of local staff before commencement of trading

[ITA67 s305; CTA76 s21(1) and Sch1 par51; FA93 s34(1)(c)]

(1) Where, before the day of the setting up or commencement of a trade consisting of the production for sale of manufactured goods, a person who is about to carry on the trade incurs or has incurred expenditure on the recruitment and training, with a view to their employment in the trade, of persons all or a majority of whom are Irish citizens, there shall be made to such person allowances in respect

of that expenditure during a writing-down period of 3 years beginning on that day, and such allowances shall be made in taxing the trade.

(2) For the purposes of this section—

(a) expenditure shall not include any expenditure incurred by a person in respect of which no deduction would have been allowable to the person, in computing the profits or gains of the trade under the provisions of the Tax Acts applicable to Case I of Schedule D, if it had been incurred on or after the day of the setting up or commencement of the trade;

(b) expenditure shall not be regarded as having been incurred by a person in so far as it has been or is to be met directly or indirectly by the State or by any person other than the first-mentioned person;

(c) the date on which any expenditure is incurred shall be taken to be the date on which the sum in question becomes payable.

(3) *Section 304(4)* shall apply in relation to an allowance under *subsection (1)* as it applies in relation to an allowance to be made under *Part 9*.

(4) For the purposes of the Income Tax Acts, any claim by a person for an allowance under this section shall be included in the annual statement required to be delivered under those Acts of the profits or gains of the person's trade and shall be accompanied by a certificate signed by the claimant (which shall be deemed to form part of the claim) stating that the expenditure was incurred on the recruitment and training, with a view to their employment in the trade, of persons all or a majority of whom are Irish citizens and giving such particulars as show that the allowance is to be made.

Cross References

From Section 769

Section 268 Meaning of "industrial building or structure".

Section 304 Income tax: allowances and charges in taxing a trade, etc.

To Section 769

Section 309 Companies not resident in the State.

Section 319 Adjustment of allowances by reference to value-added tax.

Section 321 Provisions of general application in relation to the making of allowances and charges.

Schedule 17 Reorganisation into Companies of Trustee Savings Banks

Schedule 26 Replacement of Harbour Authorities by Port Companies

CHAPTER 4

Transmission Capacity Rights

769A Interpretation (Chapter 4)

[(1) In this Chapter—

"*capacity rights*" means the right to use wired, radio or optical transmission paths for the transfer of voice, data or information;

["control" shall be construed in accordance with *section 432*;

"*qualifying expenditure*" means capital expenditure incurred on the purchase of capacity rights, but does not include expenditure incurred on or after 6 February 2003 which consists of a licence fee or other payment paid to the Commission for Communications Regulation in respect of a licence or permission granted by that Commission on or after that date under—

(a) the Wireless Telegraphy Acts 1926 to 1988, or

(b) the Postal and Telecommunications Services Act 1983;][1]

"*writing-down period*" has the meaning assigned to it by *section 769B(2)*.

(2) In this Chapter, any reference to the sale of part of capacity rights includes a reference to the grant of a licence in respect of the capacity rights in question, and any reference to the purchase of capacity rights includes a reference to the acquisition of a licence in respect of capacity rights; but, if a licence granted by a company entitled to any capacity rights is a licence to exercise those rights to the exclusion of the grantor and all other persons for the whole of the remainder of the term for which the rights subsist, the grantor shall be treated for the purposes of this Chapter as thereby selling the whole of the rights.][2]

Amendments

[1] Inserted by FA03 s20(1)(a). This section applies as on and from the date of 28 March 2003

[2] Inserted by FA00 s64.

Cross References

From Section 769A

Section 432 Meaning of "associated company" and "control".

Section 769B Annual allowances for capital expenditure on purchase of capacity rights.

769B Annual allowances for capital expenditure on purchase of capacity rights

[(1) Where, on or after 1 April 2000, a company incurs [qualifying expenditure][1] on the purchase of capacity rights, there shall, subject to and in accordance with this Chapter, be made to that company writing-down allowances, in respect of that expenditure during the writing-down period; but no writing-down allowance shall be made to a company in respect of any expenditure unless—

(a) the allowance is to be made to the company in taxing the company's trade, or

(b) any income receivable by the company in respect of the rights would be liable to tax.

(2) (a) Subject to *paragraph (c)*, the writing-down period shall be—

(i) a period of 7 years, or

(ii) where the capacity rights are purchased for a specified period which exceeds 7 years, the number of years for which the capacity rights are purchased,

commencing with the beginning of the accounting period related to the expenditure.

(b) For the purposes of this section, writing-down allowances shall be determined by the formula—

$$A \times \frac{B}{C}$$

where—

A is the amount of the [...][2] [qualifying expenditure][3] incurred on the purchase of the capacity rights,

B is the length of the part of the chargeable period falling within the writing-down period, and

C is the length of the writing-down period.

(c) For the purposes of this subsection, any expenditure incurred for the purposes of a trade by a company about to carry on the trade shall be treated as if that expenditure had been incurred by that company on the first day on which that company carries on the trade unless before that day the company has sold all the capacity rights on the purchase of which the expenditure was incurred.][4]

[(3) (a) Notwithstanding any other provisions of this Chapter, where a company (in this paragraph referred to as the "*buyer*") incurs qualifying expenditure on the purchase from another company (in this paragraph referred to as the "*seller*") of capacity rights, no allowances shall be made under this Chapter to the buyer in respect of that expenditure if both companies are companies within a group of companies, unless an allowance had been made under this Chapter to the seller (or would have been made to the seller if it had not sold those rights) in respect of the capital expenditure it incurred on the purchase of those rights.

(b) For the purposes of this subsection—

(i) a "*group of companies*" means a company and any other companies of which it has control or with which it is associated, and

(ii) a company is associated with another company where it could reasonably be considered that—

(I) any person or any group of persons or groups of persons having a reasonable commonality of identity has or have, as the case may be, or had the means or power, either directly or indirectly, to determine the trading operations carried on or to be carried on by both companies, or

(II) both companies are under the control of any person or any group of persons or groups of persons having a reasonable commonality of identity.][5]

Amendments

[1, 2, 3] Substituted by FA03 s20(1)(b)(i). This section applies as on and from the date of FA03 28 March 2003

[4] Inserted by FA00 s64.

[5] Inserted by FA03 s20(1)(b)(ii). This section applies as on and from the date of 28 March 2003

Cross References

To Section 769B

Section 769A Interpretation (Chapter 4).

769C Effect of lapse of capacity rights

[(1) Where a company incurs [qualifying expenditure][1] on the purchase of capacity rights and, before the end of the writing-down period, any of the following events occurs—

(a) the rights come to an end without provision for their subsequent renewal or the rights cease altogether to be exercised;

(b) the company sells all those rights or so much of them as it still owns;

(c) the company sells part of those rights and the amount of net proceeds of the sale (in so far as they consist of capital sums) are not less than the amount of the [qualifying expenditure][2] remaining unallowed;

no writing-down allowance shall be made to that company for the chargeable period related to the event or for any subsequent chargeable period.

(2) Where a company incurs [qualifying expenditure][3] on the purchase of capacity rights and, before the end of the writing-down period, either of the following events occurs—

(a) the rights come to an end without provision for their subsequent renewal or the rights cease altogether to be exercised;

(b) the company sells all those rights or so much of them as it still owns, and the amount of the net proceeds of the sale (in so far as they consist of capital sums) are less than the amount of the [qualifying expenditure][4] remaining unallowed;

there shall, subject to and in accordance with this Chapter, be made to that company for the accounting period related to the event an allowance (in this Chapter referred to as a "*balancing allowance*") equal to—

(i) if the event is one referred to in *paragraph (a)*, the amount of the [qualifying expenditure][5] remaining unallowed, and

(ii) if the event is one referred to in *paragraph (b)*, the amount of the [qualifying expenditure][6] remaining unallowed less the amount of the net proceeds of the sale.

(3) Where a company which has incurred [qualifying expenditure][7] on the purchase of capacity rights sells all or any part of those rights and the amount of the net proceeds of the sale (in so far as they consist of capital sums) exceeds the amount of the [qualifying expenditure][8] remaining unallowed, if any, there shall, subject to and in accordance with this Chapter, be made on that company for the chargeable period related to the sale a charge (in this Chapter referred to as a "*balancing charge*") on an amount equal to—

(a) the excess, or

(b) where the amount of the [qualifying expenditure][9] remaining unallowed is nil, the amount of the net proceeds of the sale.

(4) Where a company which has incurred [qualifying expenditure][10] on the purchase of capacity rights sells a part of those rights and *subsection (3)* does not apply, the amount of any writing-down allowance made in respect of that expenditure for the chargeable period related to the sale or any subsequent chargeable period shall be the amount determined by—

(a) subtracting the amount of the net proceeds of the sale (in so far as they consist of capital sums) from the amount of the expenditure remaining unallowed at the time of the sale, and

(b) dividing the result by the number of complete years of the writing-down period which remained at the beginning of the chargeable period related to the sale,

and so on for any subsequent sales.

(5) References in this section to the amount of any [qualifying expenditure][11] remaining unallowed shall in relation to any event aforesaid be construed as references to the amount of that expenditure less any writing-down allowances made in respect of

that expenditure for chargeable periods before the chargeable period related to that event, and less also the amount of the net proceeds of any previous sale by the company which incurred the expenditure of any part of the rights acquired by the expenditure, in so far as those proceeds consist of capital sums.

(6) Notwithstanding *subsections (1)* to *(5)*—

(a) no balancing allowance shall be made in respect of any expenditure unless a writing-down allowance has been, or, but for the happening of the event giving rise to the balancing allowance, could have been, made in respect of that expenditure, and

(b) the total amount on which a balancing charge is made in respect of any expenditure shall not exceed the total writing-down allowances actually made in respect of that expenditure less, if a balancing charge has previously been made in respect of that expenditure, the amount on which that charge was made.][12]

Amendments

1, 2, 3, 4, 5, 6, 7, 8, 9, 10, 11 Substituted by FA03 s20(1)(c). This section applies as on and from the date of 28 March 2003

12 Inserted by FA00 s64.

Cross References

To Section 769C

Section 769E Application of Chapter 4 of Part 9.

769D Manner of making allowances and charges

[(1) An allowance or charge under this Chapter shall be made to or on a company in taxing the company's trade if—

(a) the company is carrying on a trade the profits or gains of which are or, if there were any, would be, chargeable to corporation tax for the chargeable period for which the allowance or charge is made, and

(b) at any time in the chargeable period or its basis period the capacity rights in question, or other rights out of which they were granted, were used for the purposes of that trade.

(2) Except where provided for in *subsection (1)*, an allowance under this Chapter shall be made by means of discharge or repayment of tax and shall be available against income from capacity rights, and a charge under this Chapter shall be made under Case IV of Schedule D.][1]

Amendments

1 Inserted by FA00 s64.

Cross References

To Section 769D

Section 769E Application of Chapter 4 of Part 9.

769E Application of Chapter 4 of Part 9

[(1) Subject to *subsection (2)*, *Chapter 4* of *Part 9* shall apply as if this Chapter were contained in that Part, and any reference in the Tax Acts to any capital allowance to be given by means of discharge or repayment of tax and to be available or available primarily against a specified class of income shall include a reference to any capital allowance given in accordance with *section 769D(2)*.

(2) In *Chapter 4* of *Part 9*, as applied by virtue of *subsection (1)* to capacity rights, the reference in *section 312(5)(a)(i)* to the sum mentioned in *paragraph (b)* shall in the case of capacity rights be construed as a reference to the amount of the [qualifying expenditure][1] on the acquisition of the capacity rights remaining unallowed, computed in accordance with *section 769C*.][2]

Amendments

[1] Substituted by FA03 s20(1)(d). This section applies as on and from the date of 28 March 2003

[2] Inserted by FA00 s64.

Cross References

From Section 769E

Section 268 Meaning of "industrial building or structure".
Section 304 Income tax: allowances and charges in taxing a trade, etc.
Section 312 Special provisions as to certain sales.
Section 769C Effect of lapse of capacity rights.
Section 769D Manner of making allowances and charges.

769F Commencement (Chapter 4)

[This Chapter shall come into operation [on the date of the passing of the *Finance Act 2003*][1].][2]

Amendments

[1] Substituted by FA03 s20(1)(e). This section applies as on and from the date of 28 March 2003

[2] Inserted by FA00 s64.

PART 30

Occupational Pension Schemes, Retirement Annuities, Purchased Life Annuities and Certain Pensions

CHAPTER 1

Occupational Pension Schemes

770 Interpretation and supplemental (Chapter 1)

[FA72 s13(1), (2) and (4); FA74 s86 and Sch2 PtII]

(1) In this Chapter, except where the context otherwise requires—

["*additional voluntary contributions*" means voluntary contributions made to a scheme by an employee which are—

(i) contributions made under a rule or part of a rule, as the case may be, of a retirement benefits scheme (in this definition referred to as the "*main scheme*") which provides specifically for the payment of members' voluntary contributions, other than contributions made at the rate or rates specified for members' contributions in the rules of the main scheme, or

(ii) contributions made under a separately arranged scheme for members' voluntary contributions which is associated with the main scheme;][1]

["*administrator*", in relation to a retirement benefits scheme, means the person or persons, established in a Member State of the European Communities, having the management of the scheme, and references to the administrator of a scheme shall be deemed to include the person mentioned in *section 772(2)(c)(ii)*;][2]

"*approved scheme*" means a retirement benefits scheme for the time being approved by the Revenue Commissioners for the purposes of this Chapter;

"*company*" includes any body corporate or unincorporated body of persons other than a partnership;

["*approved retirement fund*" has the meaning assigned to it by *section 784A*;

"*approved minimum retirement fund*" has the meaning assigned to it by *section 784C*;][3]

"*director*", in relation to a company, includes—

(a) in the case of a company the affairs of which are managed by a board of directors or similar body, a member of that board or body,

(b) in the case of a company the affairs of which are managed by a single director or similar person, that director or person,

(c) in the case of a company the affairs of which are managed by the members themselves, a member of that company,

and includes a person who is to be or has been a director;

"*employee*"—

(a) in relation to a company, includes an officer of the company, any director of the company and any other person taking part in the management of the affairs of the company, and

(b) in relation to any employer, includes a person who is to be or has been an employee, and "employer" and other cognate expressions shall be construed accordingly;

"*exempt approved scheme*" has the meaning assigned to it by *section 774*;

"*final remuneration*" means the average annual remuneration of the last 3 years' service;

["*overseas pension scheme*" means a retirement benefits scheme, other than a state social security scheme, which is—

(a) operated or managed by an Institution for Occupational Retirement Provision as defined by Article 6(*a*) of Directive 2003/41/EC of the European Parliament and of the Council of 3 June 2003*, and

* OJ No. L235, 23.9.2003, p.10

(b) established in a Member State of the European Communities, other than the State, which has given effect to that Directive in its national law;][4]

"*pension*" includes annuity;

["*pension adjustment order*" means an order made in accordance with section 12 of the Family Law Act 1995, section 17 of the Family Law (Divorce) Act 1996, or section 121 of the Civil Partnership and Certain Rights and Obligations of Cohabitants Act 2010;][5]

["*proprietary director*" means a director who, [either alone or together with his or her spouse and minor children or, as the case may be, his or her civil partner, his or her minor children and the minor children of his or her civil partner][6] is or was, at any time within 3 years of the date of—

(i) the specified normal retirement date,

(ii) an earlier retirement date, where applicable,

(iii) leaving service, or

(iv) in the case of a pension or part of a pension payable in accordance with a pension adjustment order, the relevant date in relation to that order,

the beneficial owner of shares which, when added to any shares held by the trustees of any settlement to which the director or [his or her spouse or civil partner][7] had transferred assets, carry more than 5 per cent of the voting rights in the company providing the benefits or in a company which controls that company;][8]

["*Personal Retirement Savings Account*" or "*PRSA*" has the same meaning as in *Chapter 2A* of this Part;][9]

"*relevant benefits*" means any pension, lump sum, gratuity or other like benefit—

(a) given or to be given on retirement or on death or in anticipation of retirement or, in connection with past service, after retirement or death, or

(b) to be given on or in anticipation of or in connection with any change in the nature of the service of the employee in question,

but does not include any benefit which is to be afforded solely by reason of the death or disability of a person resulting from an accident arising out of or in the course of his or her office or employment and for no other reason;

["*relevant date*" means, in relation to a pension adjustment order, the date on which [the decree of separation, the decree of divorce, or the decree of dissolution,][10] as the case may be, was granted, by reference to which the pension adjustment order in question was made;][11]

["*retirement benefits scheme*" has the meaning assigned to it by *section 771*;][12]

"*service*" means service as an employee of the employer in question and other expressions, including "*retirement*", shall be construed accordingly;

["*state social security scheme*" means a system of mandatory protection put in place by the Government of a country or territory, other than the State, to provide a minimum level of retirement income or other benefits, the level of which is determined by that Government;][13]

"*statutory scheme*" means a retirement benefits scheme established by or under any enactment.

(2) Any reference in this Chapter to the provision of relevant benefits, or of a pension, for employees of an employer includes a reference to the provision of those benefits or that pension by means of a contract between the administrator or the employer and a third person.

(3) [*Schedules 23* and *23C*][14] shall apply for the purposes of supplementing this Chapter and shall be construed as one with this Chapter.

Amendments

[1] Inserted by FA00 s23(1)(a)(i). Shall apply as on and from 6 April 2000.

[2] Substituted by FA05 s21(1)(a)(i)(I). Applies as respects any retirement benefits scheme approved on or after 1 January 2005.

[3] Inserted by FA99 s19(1)(a)(i)(I). Paragraph (a) of subsection (1) shall apply as respects any retirement benefits scheme (within the meaning of section 771) approved on or after the 6th day of April, 1999.

[4] Inserted by FA05 s21(1)(a)(i)(II). Applies as respects any retirement benefits scheme approved on or after 1 January 2005.

[5] Substituted by F(No.3)A11 sched1(184).

[6] Substituted by F(No.3)A11 sched1(185).

[7] Substituted by F(No.3)A11 sched1(186).

[8] Substituted by FA01 s18(a)(i)(II).

[9] Inserted by PAA02 s4(1)(d)(i).

[10] Substituted by F(No.3)A11 sched1(187).

[11] Inserted by FA01 s18(a)(i)(III).

[12] Inserted by FA05 s21(1)(a)(i)(III). Applies as respects any retirement benefits scheme approved on or after 1 January 2005.

[13] Inserted by FA05 s21(1)(a)(i)(IV). Applies as respects any retirement benefits scheme approved on or after 1 January 2005.

[14] Substituted by FA13 s17(1)(a). Has effect from 27 March 2013.

Case Law

In Venables and others v Hornby 2004 STC 84 it was held a person could retire as an employee while remaining a director.

Revenue Briefings

Tax Briefing

Tax Briefing September 2000 – Issue 41 pg 23 – New Pension Options – Finance Act 2000 changes

eBrief

eBrief No. 24/2006 – Pensions

eBrief No. 65/2008 – Deferral of Annuity Purchase

Revenue Information Notes

IT 14 – Tax relief for investment in a pension and approved retirement fund options

Cross References

From Section 770

Section 771 Meaning of "retirement benefits scheme".

Section 772 Conditions for approval of schemes and discretionary approval.

Section 774 Certain approved schemes: exemptions and reliefs.

Section 784A Approved retirement fund.
Section 784C Approved minimum retirement fund.
Schedule 23 Occupational Pension Schemes

To Section 770

Section 81A Restriction of deductions for employee benefit contributions.
Section 118 Benefits in kind: general charging provision.
Section 128 Tax treatment of directors of companies and employees granted rights to acquire shares or other assets.
Section 128C Tax treatment of directors and employees who acquire convertible shares.
Section 128D Tax treatment of directors of companies and employees who acquire restricted shares.
Section 128E Tax treatment of directors of companies and employees who acquire forfeitable shares.
Section 185 Associated persons.
Section 201 Exemptions and reliefs in respect of tax under section 123.
Section 430 Meaning of "close company".
Section 431 Certain companies with quoted shares not to be close companies.
Section 433 Meaning of "participator", "associate", "director" and "loan creditor".
Section 706 Interpretation and general (Part 26).
Section 730D Gain arising on a chargeable event.
Section 730E Declarations.
Section 739D Gain arising on a chargeable event.
Section 787A Interpretation and supplemental.
Section 787O Interpretation and general (Chapter 2C).
Section 790AA Taxation of lump sums in excess of the tax free amount.
Section 805 Surcharge on certain income of trustees.
Section 848V Interpretation (Part 36B).
Section 897A Returns by employers in relation to pension products.
Section 897B Returns of information in respect of awards of shares to directors and employees.
Section 985A Application of section 985 to certain perquisites, etc.
Schedule 2A Dividend Withholding Tax
Schedule 2B Investment Undertakings: Declarations
Schedule 23 Occupational Pension Schemes
Schedule 31 Consequential Amendments

771 Meaning of "*retirement benefits scheme*"

[FA72 s14]

(1) In this Chapter, "*retirement benefits scheme*" means, subject to this section, a scheme for the provision of benefits consisting of or including relevant benefits, but does not include any scheme under the [Social Welfare Consolidation Act 2005][1] providing such benefits.

(2) References in this Chapter to a scheme include references to a [contract,][2] deed, agreement, series of agreements or other arrangements providing for relevant benefits, notwithstanding that it relates or they relate only to—

(a) a small number of employees or to a single employee, or

(b) the payment of a pension starting immediately on the making of the arrangements.

(3) The Revenue Commissioners may if they think fit treat a retirement benefits scheme relating to employees of 2 or more different classes or descriptions as being for the purposes of this Chapter 2 or more separate retirement benefits schemes relating respectively to such one or more of those classes or descriptions of those employees as the Revenue Commissioners think fit.

(4) For the purposes of this Chapter—

(a) employees may be regarded as belonging to different classes or descriptions if they are employed by different employers, and

(b) a particular class or description of employee may consist of a single employee or any number of employees.

Amendments

[1] Substituted by FA07 sched4(1)(x). Shall have effect as on and from 2 April 2007

[2] Inserted by FA05 s21(1)(a)(ii). Applies as respects any retirement benefits scheme approved on or after 1 January 2005.

Cross References

To Section 771

Section 770 Interpretation and supplemental (Chapter 1).
Section 787O Interpretation and general (Chapter 2C).
Section 790AA Taxation of lump sums in excess of the tax free amount.

772 Conditions for approval of schemes and discretionary approval

[FA72 s15(1) to (7); FA74 s64(1); FA92 s6(a); FA96 s131(2) and Sch5 PtII; FA97 s146(1) and Sch9 PtI par5(1)]

(1) Subject to this section, the Revenue Commissioners shall approve any retirement benefits scheme for the purposes of this Chapter if it satisfies all of the prescribed conditions, namely—

(a) the conditions set out in *subsection (2)*, and

(b) the conditions as respects benefits set out in *subsection (3)*.

(2) The conditions referred to in *subsection (1)(a)* are—

(a) that the scheme is bona fide established for the sole purpose of providing relevant benefits in respect of service as an employee, being benefits payable to, or to [the widow, widower, surviving civil partner, children or dependants, or personal representatives, of the employee, or children of the surviving civil partner of the employee;][1]

(b) that the scheme is recognised by the employer and employees to whom it relates, and that every employee who is or has a right to be a member of the scheme has been given written particulars of all essential features of the scheme which concern the employee;

[(c) that in relation to the discharge of all duties and obligations imposed on the administrator of a scheme [by this Chapter and [, *Chapter 2C* and section 125B of the Stamp Duties Consolidation Act 1999][2]][3]—

(i) the administrator of an overseas pension scheme has entered into a contract with the Revenue Commissioners enforceable in a Member State of the European Communities in relation to the discharge of those duties and obligations and in entering into such a contract the parties to the contract have acknowledged and agreed in writing that—

(I) it is governed solely by the laws of the State, and

(II) that the courts of the State have exclusive jurisdiction in determining any dispute arising under it,

or

(ii) there is a person resident in the State, appointed by the administrator, who will be responsible for the discharge of all of those duties and obligations and the administrator shall notify the Revenue Commissioners of the appointment of that person and the identity of that person;][4]

(d) that the employer is a contributor to the scheme;

(e) that the scheme is established in connection with some trade or undertaking carried on in the State by a person resident in the State;

(f) that no amount can be paid, whether during the subsistence of the scheme or later, by means of repayment of an employee's contributions under the scheme.

(3) The conditions as respects benefits referred to in *subsection (1)(b)* are—

(a) that any benefit for an employee is a pension on retirement at a specified age not earlier than 60 years and not later than 70 years, or on earlier retirement through incapacity, which does not exceed one-sixtieth of the employee's final remuneration for each year of service up to a maximum of 40 years;

[(b) that any pension for [any widow, widower, surviving civil partner, children or dependants, or children of the surviving civil partner, of an employee][5] who dies before retirement shall be a pension or pensions payable on the employee's death of an amount that does not or, as the case may be, do not in aggregate exceed any pension or pensions which, consonant with the condition in *paragraph (a)*, could have been provided for the employee on retirement on attaining the specified age, if the employee had continued to serve until the employee attained that age at an annual rate of remuneration equal to the employee's final remuneration;][6]

(c) that any lump sums provided for [any widow, widower, surviving civil partner, children or dependants, or personal representatives, of an employee, or children of the surviving civil partner of an employee][7] who dies before retirement shall not exceed in the aggregate 4 times the employee's final remuneration;

[(d) that any benefit for [any widow, widower, surviving civil partner, children or dependants, or children of the surviving civil partner of an employee][8] payable on the employee's death after retirement is a pension or pensions such that the aggregate amount of such pension or, as the case may be, pensions so payable does not exceed any pension or pensions payable to the employee;][9]

[...][10]

(f) [that, subject to *subsection (3A)*,][11] no pension is capable in whole or in part of surrender, commutation or assignment, except in so far as the scheme allows an employee on retirement to obtain by commutation of the employee's pension a lump sum or sums not exceeding in all three-eightieths of the employee's final remuneration for each year of service up to a maximum of 40 years;

(g) that no other benefits are payable under the scheme.

[(3A) (a) Subject to *paragraph (aa)*, the Revenue Commissioners shall not approve a retirement benefits scheme for the purposes of this Chapter unless it appears to them that the scheme provides for any individual entitled to a pension under the scheme or, as the case may be, where the pension or part of the pension is payable in accordance with a pension adjustment order, the [spouse or former spouse, or civil partner or former civil partner,][12] of such an individual to whom the pension or part of the pension is so payable (in this subsection referred to as the "*relevant individual*"), to opt, on or before the date on which that pension would otherwise become payable, for the transfer, on or after that date, to—

(i) the relevant individual, or

(ii) an approved retirement fund,

of an amount equivalent to the amount determined by the formula—

A – B

where—

[A is—

(I) the amount equal to the value of the relevant individual's accrued rights under the scheme (including accrued rights which relate to additional voluntary contributions under the scheme) exclusive of any lump sum paid in accordance with *subsection (3) (f)*, or

(II) the amount equal to the value of the relevant individual's accrued rights under the scheme which relate to additional voluntary contributions paid by that individual exclusive of any part of that amount paid by way of lump sum in accordance with *subsection (3)(f)* in conjunction with the scheme rules, and][13]

B is the amount or value of assets which the trustees, administrators or other person charged with the management of the scheme (in this section referred to as "*the trustees*") would, if the assumptions in *paragraph* (*b*) were made, be required, in accordance with *section 784C*, to transfer to an approved minimum retirement fund held in the name of the relevant individual or to apply in purchasing an annuity payable to the relevant individual with effect from the date of the exercise of the option.][14]

[(aa) In the case of a retirement benefits scheme that is a defined benefit arrangement within the meaning of *section 787O(1)*, *paragraph (a)* shall, with any necessary modifications, apply in relation to an individual entitled to a pension under the scheme (other than a proprietary director of a company to which the scheme relates) as if—

(i) the reference in that paragraph to any relevant individual entitled to a pension under the scheme were a reference to any individual entitled to a pension under the scheme who is an individual entitled to rights arising from additional voluntary contributions to the scheme, and

[(ii) clause (I) of the construction of 'A' in the formula in *paragraph (a)* had never been enacted.][15]

(ab) (i) In this paragraph "*deferred annuity option*" means the option provided to an individual who is a member of a retirement benefits scheme to defer, in accordance with Revenue e-Brief No. 65/08 entitled 'Deferral of Annuity Purchase' issued by the Revenue Commissioners on 22 December 2008, the purchase of an annuity from a company carrying on the business of granting annuities on human life.

(ii) An individual entitled to a pension under a retirement benefits scheme approved by the Revenue Commissioners before the date of passing of the *Finance Act 2011* who, before that date, has exercised a deferred annuity option may opt in accordance with *paragraph (a)* within the period of one month from that date, where on or after that date the rules of the scheme are altered to enable such an option.

(iii) For the purposes of this paragraph, where an individual has exercised a deferred annuity option, the purchase of the annuity may be further deferred for a period of one month from the date of passing of the *Finance Act 2011*.][16]

(b) The assumptions in this paragraph are—

[(i) that the retirement benefits scheme or, as the case may be, the relevant part of the scheme was an annuity contract approved in accordance with *section 784*,][17]

(ii) that the trustees of the retirement benefit scheme were a person lawfully carrying on the business in the State of providing annuities on human life with whom the said contract had been made, and

(iii) that the individual had opted in accordance with *subsection (2A)* of *section 784*.

(3B) Where an individual opts in accordance with *subsection (3A)* then—

(a) the provisions of *subsection (2B)* of *section 784* and of *sections 784A, 784B, 784C, 784D* and *784E* shall, with any necessary modifications, apply as if—

(i) any reference in those sections to the person lawfully carrying on in the State the business of granting annuities on human life were a reference to the trustees of the retirement benefit scheme,

(ii) any reference in those sections to the annuity contract were references to the retirement benefit scheme, [...][18]

[...][19]

[(iia) in the case of an individual referred to in *subsection (3A)(ab)(ii)* (in this paragraph referred to as the "*first-mentioned individual*")—

(I) the reference in *subsection (2)(ii)* of *section 784C* to an amount equivalent to the amount determined by the formula in that subsection were a reference to an amount equal to €63,500,

(II) the reference in *subsection (4)(a)* of *section 784C* to specified income per annum of an amount equal to the amount determined by the formula in that subsection were a reference to specified income per annum of €12,700, and

(III) the reference in *subsection (6A)* of *section 784C* to the individual were a reference to the first-mentioned individual and the reference in that subsection to the transfer, before the date of passing of the *Finance Act 2011*, of the amount referred to as B in the formula in *section 784(2A)* to an approved minimum retirement fund in respect of the individual, were a reference to the transfer, within the period of time referred to in *subsection (3A)(ab)(ii)*, of the amount referred to as B in the formula in *subsection (3A)(a)* to an approved minimum retirement fund in respect of the first-mentioned individual.][20]

(b) [other than in the case of an individual referred to in clause (II) of the construction of 'A' in the formula in *subsection (3A)(a)* and an individual referred to in *subsection (3A)(aa)*,][21] *paragraph (f)* of *subsection (3)* shall apply as if the reference to "a lump sum or sums not exceeding in all three-eightieths of the employee's final remuneration for each year of service up to a maximum of 40 years' were a reference to "a lump sum not exceeding 25 per cent of the value of the pension which would otherwise be payable".][22]

[(3C) Where the rules of a retirement benefits scheme provide for the purchase of an annuity from a company carrying on the business of granting annuities on human life, references in *subsection (3A)* to the date on which a pension would otherwise become payable shall, in relation to that retirement benefits scheme, be construed as references to the latest date on which such an annuity must be purchased in accordance with those rules.][23]

[(3D) A retirement benefits scheme shall not cease to be an approved scheme because of any provision in the rules of the scheme whereby, either or both—

(a) a member's entitlements under the scheme, other than an amount referred to in *paragraph (b)*, may, either on the member's changing employment or on the scheme being wound up, be transferred to one or more than one PRSA to which that member is the contributor if the following conditions are satisfied, that is to say—

(i) benefits have not become payable to the member under the scheme, and

(ii) the period or the aggregate of the periods for which the individual has been a member of the scheme or of any other scheme related to that individual's employment with, or with any person connected with, the employer immediately before the said transfer is 15 years or less,

(b) an amount equal to the accumulated value of a member's contributions to the scheme, which consist of additional voluntary contributions made by the member, may be transferred to one or more than one PRSA to which that member is the contributor.][24]

[(3E) A retirement benefits scheme shall neither cease to be an approved scheme nor shall the Revenue Commissioners be prevented from approving a retirement benefits scheme for the purposes of this Chapter because of any provision in the rules of the scheme which makes provision for borrowing by the scheme.][25]

[(3F) A retirement benefits scheme shall neither cease to be an approved scheme nor shall the Revenue Commissioners be prevented from approving a retirement benefits scheme for the purposes of this Chapter because of any provision in the rules of the scheme whereby a member's entitlement under the scheme may be commuted, to such extent as may be necessary, for the purpose of discharging a tax liability in connection with that entitlement under the provisions of *Chapter 2C* of this Part.][26]

[(3G) A retirement benefits scheme shall not cease to be an approved scheme where the trustees of the scheme, notwithstanding anything contained in the rules of the scheme as approved, discharge liabilities of the scheme under *section 59(3)* of the [Pensions Act 1990][27] (inserted by section 43 of the Social Welfare and Pensions Act 2010).][28]

[(3H) A retirement benefits scheme shall neither cease to be an approved scheme nor shall the Revenue Commissioners be prevented from approving a retirement benefits scheme for the purposes of this Chapter because of any provision in the rules of the scheme allowing a member who comes within the provisions of *section 787TA* to exercise an option in accordance with that section requiring an amount representing the value of, or part of the value of, the member's accrued rights under the scheme at the date of the exercise of the option to be transferred by the trustees of the scheme to the member.][29]

[(3I) A retirement benefits scheme shall not cease to be an approved scheme where the trustees of the scheme, notwithstanding anything contained in the rules of the scheme as approved, allow a member or, as the case may be, where the scheme is subject to a pension adjustment order, the spouse or former spouse or civil partner or former civil partner of the member, to avail of an option in accordance with section 782A.][30]

(4) (a) The Revenue Commissioners may if they think fit having regard to the facts of a particular case and subject to such conditions, if any, as they think proper to attach to the approval, approve a retirement benefits scheme for the purposes of this Chapter, notwithstanding that it does not satisfy one or more of the prescribed conditions.

(b) The Revenue Commissioners may in particular approve by virtue of this subsection a scheme which—

(i) exceeds the limits imposed by the prescribed conditions as respects benefits for less than 40 years' service,

(ii) allows benefits to be payable on retirement within 10 years of the specified age or on earlier incapacity,

(iii) provides for the return in certain contingencies of employees' contributions and payment of interest (if any) on the contributions, or

(iv) relates to a trade or undertaking carried on only partly in the State and by a person not resident in the State.

[(c) Notwithstanding *paragraphs (a)* and *(b)*, the Revenue Commissioners shall not approve a scheme unless it appears to them that the scheme complies with the provisions of *subsection (3A)*.][31]

(5) Where in the opinion of the Revenue Commissioners the facts concerning any scheme or its administration cease to warrant the continuance of their approval of the scheme, they may at any time, by notice in writing to the administrator, withdraw their approval on such grounds, and from such date, as may be specified in the notice.

(6) Where an alteration has been made in a retirement benefits scheme, no approval given as regards the scheme before the alteration shall apply after the date of the alteration unless the alteration has been approved by the Revenue Commissioners.

(7) For the purpose of determining whether a retirement benefits scheme, in so far as it relates to a particular class or description of employees, satisfies or continues to satisfy the prescribed conditions, that scheme shall be considered in conjunction with any other retirement benefits scheme or schemes relating to employees of that class or description, and, if those conditions are satisfied in the case of both or all of those schemes taken together, they shall be taken to be satisfied in the case of each of them but otherwise those conditions shall be taken to be satisfied in the case of none of them.

Amendments

[1] Substituted by F(No.3)A11 sched1(188).

[2] Substituted by F(No.2)A11 s4(2)(a).

[3] Substituted by FA06 s14(1)(a)(i)(I).

[4] Substituted by FA05 s21(1)(a)(iii). Applies as respects any retirement benefits scheme approved on or after 1 January 2005.

[5] Substituted by F(No.3)A11 sched1(189).

[6] Substituted by FA02 s10(1)(a)(i)(I). Applies from 25 March 2002.

[7] Substituted by F(No.3)A11 sched1(190).

[8] Substituted by F(No.3)A11 sched1(191).

[9] Substituted by FA02 s10(1)(a)(i)(II). Applies from 25 March 2002.

[10] Deleted by FA02 s10(1)(a)(i)(III). Applies from 25 March 2002.

[11] Substituted by FA99 s19(1)(a)(ii)(I). Paragraph (a) of subsection (1) shall apply as respects any retirement benefits scheme (within the meaning of section 771) approved on or after the 6th day of April, 1999.

[12] Substituted by F(No.3)A11 sched1(192).

[13] Substituted by FA12 s18(1)(a). Has effect from 6 February 2011.

[14] Substituted by FA11 s(19)(1)(a). Has effect as on and from 6 February 2011.

[15] Substituted by FA12 s18(1)(b). Has effect from 6 February 2011.

[16] Inserted by FA11 s(19)(1)(b). Has effect as on and from 6 February 2011.

[17] Substituted by FA00 s23(1)(b)(ii). Shall apply as on and from 6 April 2000.

[18] Deleted by FA11 s(19)(1)(c). Has effect as on and from 6 February 2011.

[19] Deleted by FA00 s23(1)(b)(iii)(I). Shall apply as regards an approved retirement fund or an approved minimum retirement fund, as the case may be, where the assets in the fund were first accepted into the fund by the qualifying fund manager on or after 6 April 2000.

[20] Inserted by FA11 s(19)(1)(d). Has effect as on and from 6 February 2011.

[21] Substituted by FA12 s18(1)(c). Has effect from 6 February 2011.

[22] Inserted by FA99 s19(1)(a)(ii)(II). Paragraph (a) of subsection (1) shall apply as respects any retirement benefits scheme (within the meaning of section 771) approved on or after the 6th day of April, 1999.

[23] Inserted by FA00 s23(1)(b)(iv). Shall be deemed to have come into force and shall take effect as on and from 6 April 1999.

[24] Inserted by PAA02 s4(1)(d)(ii). With effect from 7 November 2002 per S.I. 502 of 2002.

[25] Inserted by FA04 s16(1). Applies as on and from 25 March 2004.

[26] Inserted by FA06 s14(1)(a)(i)(II).

[27] Substituted by FA12 sched6(1)(i). Deemed to have come into force and have taken effect on and from 21 December 2010.

[28] Inserted by SWAPA10 s44.

[29] Inserted by FA12 s18(1)(d). Has effect from 8 February 2012.

[30] Inserted by FA13 s17(1)(b). Has effect from 27 March 2013.

[31] Inserted by FA99 s19(1)(a)(ii)(III). Paragraph (a) of subsection (1) shall apply as respects any retirement benefits scheme (within the meaning of section 771) approved on or after the 6th day of April, 1999.

Case Law

In R v IRC (ex parte Roux Waterside Inn Ltd) 1997 STC 781 there was a transfer from one pension scheme to another. Approval was withdrawn from the scheme as Revenue considered that the transfer was devised to avoid restrictions imposed as a condition of approval.

Revenue Precedents

While the question of taxation of the emoluments is a matter for the appropriate District dealing with the employees, any arrangement under which an employee waived an entitlement to remuneration (salary sacrifice) or accepted a reduction in remuneration in return for a corresponding payment by the employer into the pension scheme to enhance the employees pension benefits would be regarded as an application of the employees income. PREC/31

All employee contributions do not qualify for PRSI relief. Purely as a consequence of the operation of the net pay arrangement the ordinary annual contribution is relieved from PRSI. Special Contributions (those paid directly by the employee to the scheme) do not qualify for PRSI relief. PREC/27

A residual Widows/Widowers/Dependant pension can only be commuted when they come into payment. PREC/19

Normal Retirement ages from age 55 are acceptable for firemen. PREC

Irish Insurance Companies can appoint foreign fund managers who are resident in EU States. PREC/29

A scheme capable of approval can be established after the point of retirement but only to the extent that it provides for benefits for the ex-employee in a non commutable form. PREC/20

If the individual would be resident in the UK subsequent to termination of service then funds can be transferred to a UK buy out bond PREC/10

Tax free lump sums in commutation of foreign pensions are not taxable in Ireland should the individual come to reside in this country following their retirement. PREC/28

In the case of Directors engaged as moneybroker/dealers or as managers responsible for such dealers, normal retirement age of 55 and upwards is acceptable. PREC

Normal Retirement age can be later than 70 only where it is customary for employees in a particular occupation to retire at an age later than 70. PREC

Contributions paid during absence on career break to be treated as "special contributions" and allowable on a spread forward basis .Thus, relief becomes available when the individual re-commences the employment. PREC/22

Where an insurance company has undertaken to continue to pay long term disability payments in cases where employments have been effectively terminated then there will be no Revenue objection to the continuation of those members in the employers pension scheme, and for the continuation of appropriate funding through the relevant amounts received for such purposes under the disability scheme. PREC/21

Advance payments of contributions which are due and payable in subsequent accounting periods should be disallowed. Neither can they be treated as special contributions and spread forward, as such special contributions are only allowable to fund for past service or to augment benefits already secured or to make up an actuarial deficiency. PREC/24

Revenue Practice would not permit the splitting of member's total benefits so that part of such benefits would be dealt with by a transfer payment and a part held by the trustees of the scheme as a deferred benefit. PREC

The provisions in Practice Note 4.4 apply to one man insured arrangements only and not one member schemes. PREC/23

An employer can make further contributions to a scheme after benefits for ex-employee have been transferred to a buy out bond, if within approvable limits, and it is likely that the maximum approvable lump sum element of benefits would be taken from the buy out bond, the further benefits arising would need to be in pension form only. PREC/11

A non-Irish national seconded to work in Ireland can remain in his home country scheme and get relief from Irish tax on his contributions to that scheme, provided that the secondment here is for a period of less than 10 years, the scheme is a trust scheme, and the benefits to be provided by the overseas scheme are within Irish approval limits. PREC/30

Tax relief may be granted on contributions made by employees on or shortly after leaving service. This is intended to cater for special circumstances where there might be an unavoidable delay in the employee making a special contribution, for example, in many public sector schemes retiring employees have deductions made from lump sums to pay for spouses benefits which qualify for relief. Strictly speaking contributions should only be paid by "employees" and not ex-employees. PREC/26

Remuneration for pension purposes is not reduced by virtue of the deduction for income earned outside the State (Sec 823 TCA). The remuneration figure on which benefits are based is the remuneration before the deduction for income earned abroad (excluding the United Kingdom). PREC

An employer can make payments to employees to compensate for changes in the benefit structure of a pension scheme free of tax, if the situation is a bone fide one, for example, arising out of Labour Relations recommendation and ultimately a Labour Court ruling. Each case would have to be judged on its merits. PREC/32

The following may be included for final remuneration purposes in fluctuating emoluments: benefits in kind chargeable under section 118 TCA, expenses allowances chargeable under section 117 TCA, preferential loans chargeable under section 112 TCA (net amount after interest relief), share options/ share participation schemes chargeable under section 128 TCA (only the amount actually charged). PREC

The restrictions outlined in Practice Notes 9.3 and 9.4 do not apply in cases where benefits are deferred to Normal Retirement Age. PREC/9

Cross References

From Section 772

Section 784 Retirement annuities: relief for premiums.
Section 784A Approved retirement fund.
Section 784B Conditions relating to an approved retirement fund.
Section 784C Approved minimum retirement fund.
Section 784D Conditions relating to an approved minimum retirement fund.
Section 784E Returns, and payment of tax, by qualifying fund managers.
Section 787O Interpretation and general (Chapter 2C).

To Section 772

Section 84 Expenses in relation to establishment or alteration of superannuation schemes.
Section 770 Interpretation and supplemental (Chapter 1).
Section 772A Approval of retirement benefits products.
Section 773 General Medical Services: scheme of superannuation.
Section 774 Certain approved schemes: exemptions and reliefs.
Section 781 Charge to income tax: commutation of entire pension.
Section 783 Interpretation and general (Chapter 2).
Section 787E Extent of relief.
Section 787G Taxation of payments from a PRSA.
Section 787O Interpretation and general (Chapter 2C).
Section 790AA Taxation of lump sums in excess of the tax free amount.
Schedule 23 Occupational Pension Schemes
Schedule 23B Limit on Tax-Relieved Pension Funds

772A Approval of retirement benefits products

[(1) In this section—

"*promoter*" means a person lawfully carrying on the business of granting annuities on human life and, where that person—

(a) is not resident in the State, or

(b) is not trading in the State through a fixed place of business,

that person is an insurance undertaking authorised to transact insurance business in the State under Directive 2002/83/EC of the European Parliament and of the Council of 5 November 2002 *;

* OJ No. L345, 19.12.2002, p.1

"*retirement benefits product*" means a product for the provision of relevant benefits in respect of which an application for approval has been made by a promoter to the Revenue Commissioners under this section and under which, if and when approved, a single member retirement benefits scheme may be established by way of a contract entered into with the promoter to secure the scheme;

"*single member retirement benefits scheme*", in relation to a retirement benefits product, means a retirement benefits scheme that relates to a single employee;

"*terms and rules*", in relation to a retirement benefits product, means the provisions governing a retirement benefits scheme to be established under the product, by whatever name such provisions are called.

(2) Subject to this section, the Revenue Commissioners may, if they think fit, and subject to such conditions, if any, as they think proper to attach to the approval, approve a retirement benefits product for the purposes of this Chapter.

(3) Subject to *subsection (6)*, a retirement benefits scheme, established under a retirement benefits product for the time being approved by the Revenue Commissioners

under *subsection (2)*, shall be taken to be a retirement benefits scheme for the time being approved by the Revenue Commissioners for the purposes of this Chapter, and the provisions of this Chapter shall apply accordingly, except as otherwise provided for by this section.

(4) For the purposes of approval under *subsection (2)*, the promoter of a retirement benefits product shall make an application to the Revenue Commissioners in writing and the application shall be in such form and contain such information and particulars as the Revenue Commissioners may from time to time determine.

(5) The Revenue Commissioners shall not approve a retirement benefits product unless the terms and rules provide that—

(a) contributions to be paid in any year, whether by an employee or by, or on behalf of, an employer in respect of that employee, may not, when aggregated, exceed the aggregate amount of annual contributions allowed to be deducted in any year by an individual in accordance with *section 774(7)(c)*, and

(b) the provisions of *section 772(3A)* apply.

(6) Where an alteration has been made to the terms and rules governing a retirement benefits scheme established under a retirement benefits product for the time being approved by the Revenue Commissioners under *subsection (2)*, then no approval taken to be given to the scheme for the time being under *subsection (3)* before the date of the alteration shall apply after the date of the alteration unless the alteration has been approved by the Revenue Commissioners.

(7) Where in the opinion of the Revenue Commissioners the facts concerning any retirement benefits product cease to warrant the continuance of their approval of the product, then they may at any time, by notice in writing to the promoter, withdraw their approval on such grounds, and from such date, as may be specified in the notice.

(8) Where approval of a product is withdrawn pursuant to *subsection (7)*, there shall be made such assessments or amendment of assessments as may be appropriate for the purpose of withdrawing any relief given under this Chapter consequent on the grant of the approval.

(9) Where an alteration has been made to a retirement benefits product, then no approval given as regards the product before the alteration shall apply after the date of the alteration unless the alteration has been approved by the Revenue Commissioners.][1]

Amendments

[1] Inserted by FA07 s17(1)(a).

Revenue Briefings

Tax Briefing

Tax Briefing July 2007 – Issue 66 – Finance Act 2007

Cross References

From Section 772A

Section 772 Conditions for approval of schemes and discretionary approval.

Section 774 Certain approved schemes: exemptions and reliefs.

773 General Medical Services: scheme of superannuation

[FA91 s12]

(1) The Revenue Commissioners may, if they think fit and subject to any undertakings and conditions that they think proper to attach to the approval, approve for the purposes of this Chapter a scheme of superannuation provided for under an

agreement for the provision of services under section 58 of the Health Act, 1970 (in this section referred to as a "*relevant scheme*") as if it were a retirement benefits scheme within the meaning of this Chapter and notwithstanding that it does not satisfy one or more of the conditions set out in *subsections (2)* and *(3)* of *section 772*.

(2) As respects a relevant scheme approved under this section, this Chapter and *Schedule 23* shall apply subject to any necessary modifications and in particular as if in this Chapter and in that Schedule—

(a) "*employee*" included a registered medical practitioner providing services under an agreement for the provision of services under section 58 of the Health Act, 1970 (in this section referred to as an "*agreement*"),

(b) "*service*" included services by a registered medical practitioner under an agreement and an "*office or employment*" included the provision of such services, and

(c) a reference to Schedule E were a reference to Case II of Schedule D except in *section 779*.

(3) *Chapter 2* of this Part shall apply as if a member of a relevant scheme were the holder of a pensionable office or employment and such member's income assessable to tax under Case II of Schedule D arising from an agreement were remuneration from such an office or employment.

Revenue Briefings

Tax Briefing

Tax Briefing October 1997 – Issue 28 pg 10 – GMS Superannuation Plan – Retirement Relief
Tax Briefing September 2010 – Issue 11 – Tax Relief for Pension Contributions: Application of Earnings Limit in the case of Doctors with General Medical Services (GMS) and private practice income

eBrief

eBrief No. 62/10 – Tax Relief for Pension Contributions: Application of Earnings Limit in the case of Doctors with General Medical Services (GMS) and private practice income

Cross References

From Section 773

Section 772 Conditions for approval of schemes and discretionary approval.
Section 779 Charge to income tax of pensions under Schedule E.
Section 783 Interpretation and general (Chapter 2).
Schedule 23 Occupational Pension Schemes

774 Certain approved schemes: exemptions and reliefs

[FA72 s16(1) to (5) and (7); CTA76 s164 and Sch3 PtI; FA88 s30(1) and (2)(a); FA91 s38; FA97 s41(1)(a) and (3)]

[(1) This section shall apply as respects—

(a) any approved scheme shown to the satisfaction of the Revenue Commissioners to be established under irrevocable trusts,

(b) any approved scheme which is an overseas pension scheme, or

(c) any other approved scheme as respects which the Revenue Commissioners, having regard to any special circumstance, direct that this section shall apply,

and any scheme which is for the time being within *paragraph (a)*, *(b)* or *(c)* is in this Chapter referred to as an "exempt approved scheme".][1]

(2) This section shall apply only as respects income arising or contributions paid at a time when a scheme is an exempt approved scheme.

(3) Exemption from income tax shall, on a claim being made in that behalf, be allowed in respect of income derived from investments or deposits of a scheme

if, or to such extent as the Revenue Commissioners are satisfied that, it is income from investments or deposits held for the purposes of the scheme.

(4) (a) In this subsection, "*financial futures*" and "*traded options*" mean respectively financial futures and traded options for the time being dealt in or quoted on any futures exchange or any stock exchange, whether or not that exchange is situated in the State.

(b) For the purposes of *subsection (3)*, a contract entered into in the course of dealing in financial futures or traded options shall be regarded as an investment.

(5) Exemption from income tax shall, on a claim being made in that behalf, be allowed in respect of underwriting commissions if, or to such extent as the Revenue Commissioners are satisfied that, the underwriting commissions are applied for the purposes of the scheme, and in respect of which the trustees of the scheme would but for this subsection be chargeable to tax under Case IV of Schedule D.

(6) (a) For the purposes of this section and *section 775*—

(i) a reference to a "*chargeable period*" shall be construed as a reference to a "chargeable period or its basis period" (within the meaning of *section 321*), and

(ii) in relation to an employer whose chargeable period is a year of assessment, "*basis period*" means the period on the profits or gains of which income tax for that year of assessment is to be finally computed for the purposes of Case I or II of Schedule D in respect of the trade, profession or vocation of the employer.

(b) Any sum paid by an employer by means of contribution under the scheme shall for the purposes of Case I or II of Schedule D and of *sections 83* and *707(4)* be allowed to be deducted as an expense, or expense of management, incurred in the chargeable period in which the sum is paid but no other sum shall for those purposes be allowed to be deducted as an expense, or expense of management, in respect of the making, or any provision for the making, of any contributions under the scheme.

(c) The amount of an employer's contributions which may be deducted under *paragraph (b)* shall not exceed the amount contributed by that employer under the scheme in respect of employees in a trade or undertaking in respect of the profits of which the employer is assessable to income tax or corporation tax, as the case may be.

(d) A sum not paid by means of an ordinary annual contribution shall for the purposes of *paragraph (b)* be treated, as the Revenue Commissioners may direct, either as an expense incurred in the chargeable period in which the sum is paid, or as an expense to be spread over such period of years as the Revenue Commissioners think proper.

(e) In the case of any employer for a chargeable period, being—

(i) where the chargeable period is an accounting period of a company, an accounting period ending on or before the 21st day of April, 1997, and

(ii) where the chargeable period is a year of assessment, any year of assessment the employer's basis period for which ends on or before that date, this subsection shall apply subject to *paragraph 26* of *Schedule 32*.

(7) (a) Any ordinary annual contribution paid under the scheme by an employee shall, in assessing income tax under Schedule E, be allowed to be deducted as an expense incurred in the year in which the contribution is paid.

(b) Any contribution, which is not an ordinary annual contribution, paid or borne by an employee under the scheme may, as the Revenue Commissioners think proper—

(i) be treated, as respects the year in which it is paid, as an ordinary annual contribution paid in that year, or

[(ii) in the case of—

(I) such a contribution made on retirement, following an application in writing made before 6 February 2003 by the employee in response to an invitation in writing under the scheme, pursuant to the rules of the scheme—

(A) to contribute towards the purchase for superannuation purposes of relevant benefits, consisting of only a pension on retirement not exceeding one-eightieth of the employee's final remuneration for each year of service up to a maximum of 40 years and a lump sum not exceeding three-eightieths of the employee's final remuneration for each year of service up to a maximum of 40 years, in respect of actual service by the employee before becoming a member of the scheme, and

(B) to make such purchase by way of such a contribution either on retirement or otherwise,

and as a consequence of which application the employee opted, or was treated by the scheme as opting, to make the contribution on retirement, for the purposes of receiving relevant benefits under the scheme in excess of the benefits which, if the application referred to had not been made, the employee would otherwise have been entitled to receive under those rules, or

(II) a contribution to which *paragraph (ba)* applies,

be apportioned among such years as the Revenue Commissioners direct, and the amount of the contribution attributed thereby to any year shall be treated as an ordinary annual contribution paid in that year.][2]

[(ba) This paragraph applies to a contribution, which is not an ordinary annual contribution, and which—

(i) is required by the rules of the scheme to be made, in respect of a benefit to which *section 772(3)(b)* applies, by way of deduction from a lump sum payable to the employee in accordance with *section 772(3)(f)*, or

(ii) is, following resumption of or change of employment, made, on retirement, in connection with the repayment by the employee to the scheme of superannuation contributions previously refunded to the employee or of relevant benefits provided to the employee on the employee's leaving an employment in relation to service in which the superannuation contributions or, as the case may be, the relevant benefits related.][3]

[(c) The aggregate amount of annual contributions (whether ordinary annual contributions or contributions treated as ordinary annual contributions) allowed to be deducted in any year shall not exceed—

(i) in the case of an individual who at any time during the year of assessment was of the age of 30 years or over but had not attained the age of 40 years, 20 per cent,

(ii) in the case of an individual who at any time during the year of assessment was of the age of 40 years or over but had not attained the age of 50 years, 25 per cent,

[...][4]

[(iii) in the case of an individual who at any time during the year of assessment was of the age of 50 years or over but had not attained the age of 55 years, 30 per cent,

(iv) in the case of an individual who at any time during the year of assessment was of the age of 55 years or over but had not attained the age of 60 years, 35 per cent,

(v) in the case of an individual who at any time during the ear of assessment was of the age of 60 years or over, 40 per cent, and

(vi) in any other case, 15 per cent,][5]

of the remuneration for that year of the office or employment in respect of which the contributions are paid.][6]

[(d) Where in any year of assessment a reduction or a greater reduction would be made under this section in the remuneration of an individual but for an insufficiency of remuneration, the amount of the reduction which would have been made but for that reason, less the amount of the reduction which is made in that year, shall be carried forward to the next year of assessment, and shall be treated for the purposes of relief under this section as the amount of an annual contribution paid in the next year of assessment.

(e) In so far as an amount once carried forward under *paragraph (d)* (and treated as an amount of an annual contribution paid in the next year of assessment) is not deducted from or set off against the individual's remuneration for that year of assessment, it shall be carried forward again to the following year of assessment (and treated as the amount of an annual contribution paid in that year of assessment) and so on for succeeding years.][7]

[(7A) Subsection (7)(*b*)(ii) shall operate notwithstanding any limitation in section 865(4) on the time within which a claim for a repayment of tax is required to be made where the officer or employee makes a claim for relief in respect of a contribution which is not an ordinary annual contribution within 4 years from the end of the year of assessment in which such contribution is paid or borne by the officer or employee. Section 865(6) shall not prevent the Revenue Commissioners from making a repayment of tax as a consequence of such a claim, where a valid claim for a repayment of tax (within the meaning of section 865(1)(*b*)) has been made by the officer or employee.][8]

[(8) Subject to *paragraphs (b)* and *(ba)* of *subsection (7)* where in relation to a year of assessment any contribution, which is not an ordinary annual contribution, is paid by an employee under the scheme after the end of the year of assessment but before the specified return date for the chargeable period (within the meaning of [*Part 41A*][9], the contribution may, if the individual so elects on or before that date, be treated for the purposes of this section as paid in the earlier year (and not in the year in which it is paid); but where the amount of that contribution, together with any other contribution to the scheme paid by the individual in the year to which the contribution relates (or treated as so paid by virtue of any previous election under this subsection), exceeds the maximum amount of contributions allowed to be deducted in that year, the election shall have no effect as respects the excess.][10]

Amendments

[1] Substituted by FA05 s21(1)(a)(iv). Applies as respects any retirement benefits scheme approved on or after 1 January 2005.

[2] Substituted by FA04 s16(2). Has applied as on and from 6 February 2003.

[3] Inserted by FA03 s14(1)(b)(i)(II). Shall be taken to have come into force and has effect as on and from 6 February 2003

[4] Deleted by FA06 s14(1)(a)(ii)(I).

[5] Inserted by FA06 s14(1)(a)(ii)(II).

[6] Substituted by FA02 s10(1)(a)(ii). Applies as respects the year of assessment 2002 and subsequent years of assessment.

[7] Inserted by FA03 s14(1)(b)(i)(III). Shall be taken to have come into force and has effect as on and from 6 February 2003.

[8] Inserted by FA08 sched6(1)(o). Applies as on and from 31 January 2008.

[9] Substituted by FA12 sched4(part 2)(g).

[10] Inserted by FA03 s14(1)(b)(i)(IV). Shall be taken to have come into force and has effect as on and from 6 February 2003.

Case Law

The exercise of the Pensions Board discretion as to how contributions were treated could not be reviewed by the Appeal Commissioners . Kelsall v Investment Chartwork Ltd 1994 STC 33

In Clarke(HMIT) v British Telecom Pension Scheme Trustees and others 2000 STC 222 it was held that the sub-underwriting commissions applied for the purpose of the scheme would have been taxable under the UK equivalent of Schedule D Case IV and not as trading income.

Revenue Briefings

Tax Briefing

Tax Briefing June 2002 – Issue 48 pg 10 – Occupational Pension Schemes

eBrief

eBrief No. 61/09 – Tax Relief for Pension Contributions – Late Elections

Revenue Precedents

For the purposes of Sections 774/776 "remuneration" does not include payments which are chargeable to tax under Section 123. PREC

Cross References

From Section 774

Section 83 Expenses of management of investment companies.
Section 321 Provisions of general application in relation to the making of allowances and charges.
Section 707 Management expenses.
Section 772 Conditions for approval of schemes and discretionary approval.
Section 775 Certain approved schemes: provisions supplementary to section 774(6).
Section 865 Repayment of tax.
Section 950 Interpretation (Part 41).
Schedule 32 Transitional Provisions

To Section 774

Section 83 Expenses of management of investment companies.
Section 172A Interpretation.
Section 256 Interpretation (Chapter 4).
Section 608 Superannuation funds.
Section 739B Interpretation and application.
Section 770 Interpretation and supplemental (Chapter 1).
Section 772A Approval of retirement benefits products.
Section 775 Certain approved schemes: provisions supplementary to section 774(6).
Section 787N Qualifying overseas pension plans: relief for contributions.
Section 790A Limit on earnings.
Section 790B "Exemption of cross-border scheme.
Section 823 Deduction for income earned outside the State.
Section 897A Returns by employers in relation to pension products.
Schedule 2A Dividend Withholding Tax
Schedule 2B Investment Undertakings: Declarations
Schedule 31 Consequential Amendments
Schedule 32 Transitional Provisions

775 Certain approved schemes: provisions supplementary to section 774(6)

[FA72 s16A; FA97 s41(1)(b)]

(1) Where—

(a) after the 21st day of April, 1997, there is an actual payment by an employer of a contribution under an exempt approved scheme,

(b) apart from this section that payment would be allowed to be deducted as an expense, or expense of management, of the employer in relation to any chargeable period, and

(c) the total of previously allowed deductions exceeds the relevant maximum,

then, the amount allowed to be so deducted in respect of the payment mentioned in *paragraph (a)* and of any other actual payments of contributions under the scheme which, having been made after the 21st day of April, 1997, are within *paragraph (b)* in relation to the same chargeable period shall be reduced by whichever is the lesser of the excess and the amount which reduces the deduction to nil.

(2) In relation to any such actual payment by an employer of a contribution under an exempt approved scheme as would be allowed to be deducted as mentioned in *subsection (1)* in relation to any chargeable period—

(a) the reference in that subsection to the total of previously allowed deductions is a reference to the aggregate of every amount in respect of the making, or any provision for the making, of that or any other contribution under the scheme, which has been allowed to be deducted as an expense, or expense of management, of that person in relation to all previous chargeable periods, and

(b) the reference to the relevant maximum is a reference to the amount which would have been that aggregate if the restriction on deductions for sums other than actual payments imposed by virtue of *section 774(6)* had been applied in relation to every previous chargeable period,

and for the purposes of this subsection an amount the deduction of the whole or any part of which is to be taken into account as allowed in relation to more than one chargeable period shall be treated as if the amount allowed were a different amount in the case of each of those periods.

(3) For the purposes of this section, any payment which is treated under *paragraph (d)* of *section 774(6)* as spread over a period of years shall be treated as actually paid at the time when it is treated as paid in accordance with that paragraph.

Cross References

From Section 775

Section 774 Certain approved schemes: exemptions and reliefs.

To Section 775

Section 774 Certain approved schemes: exemptions and reliefs.

776 Certain statutory schemes: exemptions and reliefs

[FA72 s17(1) and (2)]

(1) This section shall apply to any statutory scheme established under a public statute.

(2) (a) Any ordinary annual contribution paid under a scheme to which this section applies by any officer or employee shall, in assessing income tax under Schedule E, be allowed to be deducted as an expense incurred in the year in which the contribution is paid.

(b) [Subject to *paragraph (bb)*, any contribution][1] which is not an ordinary annual contribution, paid or borne by an officer or employee under a scheme to which this section applies may, as the Revenue Commissioners think proper—

(i) be treated, as respects the year in which it is paid, as an ordinary annual contribution paid in that year, or

[(ii) in the case of—

(I) such a contribution made on retirement, following an application in writing made before 6 February 2003 by the employee in response to an invitation in writing under the scheme, pursuant to the rules of the scheme—

(A) to contribute towards the purchase for superannuation purposes of relevant benefits, consisting of only a pension on retirement not exceeding one-eightieth of the employee's final remuneration for each year of service up to a maximum of 40 years and a lump sum not exceeding three-eightieths of the employee's final remuneration for each year of service up to a maximum of 40 years, in respect of actual service by the employee before becoming a member of the scheme, and

(B) to make such purchase by way of such a contribution either on retirement or otherwise,

and as a consequence of which application the employee opted, or was treated by the scheme as opting, to make the contribution on retirement, for the purposes of receiving relevant benefits under the scheme in excess of the benefits which, if the application referred to had not been made, the employee would otherwise have been entitled to receive under those rules, or

(II) a contribution to which *paragraph (ba)* applies,

be apportioned among such years as the Revenue Commissioners direct, and the amount of the contribution attributed thereby to any year shall be treated as an ordinary annual contribution paid in that year.][2]

[(ba) This paragraph applies to a contribution, which is not an ordinary annual contribution, and which—

(i) is required by the statute under which the scheme is established or by any other statute or regulation to be made in respect of the provision of a pension for [any widow, widower, surviving civil partner, children or dependants, or children of the surviving civil partner, of the officer or employee][3] by way of a deduction from a lump sum payable to the employee on [retirement or from the balance of a lump sum payable to the employee in accordance with *paragraph 5* of *Appendix A* of the Department of Finance Circular 12/09, dated 30 April 2009, entitled "*Incentivised Scheme of Early Retirement*", or][4]

(ii) is, following resumption of or on change of employment, made, on retirement, in connection with the repayment by the officer or employee to the scheme of superannuation contributions previously refunded to the officer or employee or of relevant benefits provided to the officer or employee on the officer or employee's leaving the office or employment in relation to service in which the superannuation contributions or, as the case may be, the relevant benefits related.][5]

[(bb) (i) In this paragraph—

'*fixed-term employee*' has the meaning assigned to it by *section 2* of the Protection of Employees (Fixed-Term Work) Act 2003;

'*NUIG*' means the National University of Ireland, Galway;

'*NUIG scheme*' means, as the case may be—

(I) the National University of Ireland, Galway (Closed) Pension Scheme 2010 (Joint Pension Scheme), or

(II) the National University of Ireland, Galway Pension Scheme 2005 (Model Scheme);

'*qualifying period*' means the period beginning on 1 July 2008 and ending on 31 December 2018;

'*relevant period*' means the period beginning on 14 July 2003 and ending on 30 June 2008;

'*relevant year*' means any year which falls wholly or partially within the relevant period;

'*specified employee*' means an individual who was a fixed-term employee of NUIG during the relevant period under a contract of employment which is governed by the Protection of Employees (Fixed-Term Work) Act 2003.

(ii) This paragraph applies to a contribution, which is not an ordinary annual contribution, paid or borne by a specified employee under the NUIG scheme during the qualifying period in respect of a relevant year, other than such a contribution which is—

(I) treated as an ordinary annual contribution in accordance with *subparagraph (i)* or *(ii)(II)* of *paragraph (b)*, or

(II) following an election under *subsection (3)*, is treated for the purposes of this section as paid in the year prior to the year in which it is paid.

(iii) Any contribution to which this paragraph applies, which has not otherwise been deducted as an expense in assessing income tax under *Schedule E* for any year, shall be treated as an ordinary annual contribution paid in the relevant year.][6]

[(c) The aggregate amount of annual contributions (whether ordinary annual contributions or contributions treated as ordinary annual contributions) allowed to be deducted in any year shall not exceed—

(i) in the case of an individual who at any time during the year of assessment was of the age of 30 years or over but had not attained the age of 40 years, 20 per cent,

(ii) in the case of an individual who at any time during the year of assessment was of the age of 40 years or over but had not attained the age of 50 years, 25 per cent,

[…][7]

[(iii) in the case of an individual who at any time during the year of assessment was of the age of 50 years or over but had not attained the age of 55 years, 30 per cent,

(iv) in the case of an individual who at any time during the year of assessment was of the age of 55 years or over but had not attained the age of 60 years, 35 per cent,

(v) in the case of an individual who at any time during the year of assessment was of the age of 60 years or over, 40 per cent, and

(vi) in any other case, 15 per cent,][8]

of the remuneration for that year of the office or employment in respect of which the contributions are paid.][9]

[(d) Where in any year of assessment a reduction or a greater reduction would be made under this section in the remuneration of an individual but for an insufficiency of remuneration, the amount of the reduction which would have been made but for that reason, less the amount of the reduction which is made in that year, shall be carried forward to the next year of assessment, and shall be treated for the purposes of relief under this section as the amount of an annual contribution paid in the next year of assessment.

(e) In so far as an amount once carried forward under *paragraph (d)* (and treated as an amount of an annual contribution paid in the next year of assessment) is not deducted from or set off against the individual's remuneration for that year of assessment, it shall be carried forward again to the following year of assessment (and treated as the amount of an annual contribution paid in that year of assessment) and so on for succeeding years.][10]

[(2A) (a) *Paragraphs (b)(ii)* and *(bb)* of *subsection (2)* shall operate notwithstanding any limitation in *section 865(4)* on the time within which a claim for a repayment of tax is required to be made where the officer or employee makes a claim for relief in respect of a contribution which is not an ordinary annual contribution within 4 years from the end of the year of assessment in which such contribution is paid or borne by the officer or employee and *section 865(6)* shall not prevent the Revenue Commissioners from making a repayment of tax as a consequence of such a claim, where a valid claim for a repayment of tax (within the meaning of *section 865(1)(b)*) has been made by the officer or employee.

(b) For the purposes of this subsection, where a contribution to which *subsection (2)(bb)* applies has been paid or borne by a specified employee before 1 January 2015, it shall be treated as having been paid or borne by the employee in the year of assessment 2014.][11]

[(3) Subject to *paragraphs (b), (ba)* and *(bb)* of *subsection (2)*,[12] where in relation to a year of assessment any contribution, which is not an ordinary annual contribution, is paid by an employee under the scheme after the end of the year of assessment but before the specified return date for the chargeable period (within the meaning of [*Part 41A*][13], the contribution may, if the individual so elects on or before that date, be treated for the purposes of this section as paid in the earlier year (and not in the year in which it is paid); but where the amount of that contribution, together with any other contribution to the scheme paid by the individual in the year to which the contribution relates (or treated as so paid by virtue of any previous election under this subsection), exceeds the maximum amount of contributions allowed to be deducted in that year, the election shall have no effect as respects the excess.][14]

Amendments

[1] Substituted by FA14 s19(1)(a)(i). Has effect on and from 1 January 2015.

[2] Substituted by FA04 s16(3). Has applied as on and from 6 February 2003.

[3] Substituted by F(No.3)A11 sched1(193).

[4] Substituted by F(No.2)A13 s18(1)(a). Applies as respects the balance of a lump sum referred to in section 776(2)(ba)(i) paid on or after 1 May 2009.

[5] Inserted by FA03 s14(1)(b)(ii)(II). Shall be taken to have come into force and has effect as on and from 6 February 2003.

[6] Inserted by FA14 s19(1)(a)(ii). Has effect on and from 1 January 2015.

[7] Deleted by FA06 s14(1)(a)(iii)(I).

[8] Inserted by FA06 s14(1)(a)(iii)(II).

[9] Substituted by FA02 s10(1)(a)(iii). Applies as respects the year of assessment 2002 and subsequent years of assessment.

[10] Inserted by FA03 s14(1)(b)(ii)(III). Shall be taken to have come into force and has effect as on and from 6 February 2003.

[11] Substituted by FA14 s19(1)(b). Has effect on and from 1 January 2015.

[12] Substituted by FA14 s19(1)(c). Has effect on and from 1 January 2015.

[13] Substituted by FA12 sched4(part 2)(g).

[14] Inserted by FA03 s14(1)(b)(ii)(IV). Shall be taken to have come into force and has effect as on and from 6 February 2003.

Revenue Briefings

eBrief

eBrief No. 61/09 – Tax Relief for Pension Contributions – Late Elections

Revenue Precedents

For the purposes of Sections 774/776 "remuneration" does not include payments which are chargeable to tax under Section 123. PREC

An individual who had previously taken a refund of superannuation contributions subsequently repays the refund. The individual is charged "interest" to restore the actuarial value of the refund received. The "interest" is a superannuation contribution and qualifies for relief when paid. IT 95 1503

Cross References

From Section 776

Section 865 Repayment of tax.

Section 951 Obligation to make a return.

To Section 776
Section 790A Limit on earnings.
Section 897A Returns by employers in relation to pension products.
Schedule 31 Consequential Amendments

777 Charge to income tax in respect of certain relevant benefits provided for employees

[FA72 s18(1)(a), (2), (3), (4) and (5); FA97 s146(1) and Sch9 PtI par5(2)]

(1) Subject to this Chapter, where pursuant to a retirement benefits scheme the employer in any year of assessment pays a sum with a view to the provision of any relevant benefits for any employee of that employer, then (whether or not the accrual of the benefits is dependent on any contingency), the sum paid, if not otherwise chargeable to income tax as income of the employee, shall be deemed for the purposes of the Income Tax Acts to be income of that employee for that year of assessment and assessable to income tax under Schedule E.

(2) Subject to this Chapter, where—

(a) the circumstances in which any relevant benefits under a retirement benefits scheme are to accrue are not such as will render the benefits assessable to income tax as emoluments of the employee in respect of whom the benefits are paid, and

(b) the provision of those benefits is not, or is not fully, secured by the payment of sums by the employer with a view to the provision of those benefits,

then (whether or not the accrual of the benefits is dependent on any contingency), an amount equal to the cost, estimated in accordance with *subsection (3)*, of securing the provision by a third person of the benefits or, as the case may be, of the benefits in so far as not already secured by the payment of sums mentioned in *subsection (1)* shall be deemed for the purposes of the Income Tax Acts to be income of the employee for the year or years of assessment specified in *subsection (3)* and assessable to income tax under Schedule E.

(3) The cost referred to in *subsection (2)* shall be estimated either—

(a) as an annual sum payable in each year of assessment in which the scheme in question is in force or the employee is serving, up to and including the year of assessment in which the benefits accrue or there ceases to be any possibility of the accrual of the benefits, or

(b) as a single sum payable in the year of assessment in which falls the date when the employee acquired the right to the relevant benefits or the date when the employee acquired the right to any increase in the relevant benefits,

as may be more appropriate in the circumstances of the case.

(4) Where the employer pays any sum mentioned in *subsection (1)* in relation to more than one employee, the sum so paid shall for the purpose of that subsection be apportioned among those employees by reference to the separate sums which would have had to be paid to secure the separate benefits to be provided for them respectively, and the part of the sum apportioned to each of them shall be deemed for that purpose to have been paid separately in relation to that one of them.

(5) Any reference in this section to the provision for an employee of relevant benefits shall include a reference to the provision of benefits payable to the employee's [spouse, civil partner, widow, widower, surviving civil partner, children, dependants, personal representatives or children of the surviving civil partner.][1]

Amendments

[1] Substituted by F(No.3)A11 sched1(194).

Cross References

To Section 777

Section 201 Exemptions and reliefs in respect of tax under section 123.

Section 778 Exceptions to charge to tax under section 777.

778 Exceptions to charge to tax under section 777

[FA72 s19]

(1) Neither *subsection (1)* nor *subsection (2)* of *section 777* shall apply where the retirement benefits scheme in question is—

(a) an approved scheme,

(b) a statutory scheme, or

(c) a scheme set up by a Government outside the State for the benefit, or primarily for the benefit, of its employees.

(2) Neither *subsection (1)* nor *subsection (2)* of *section 777* shall apply for any year of assessment where apart from those subsections the employee is under the Income Tax Acts either not assessable to income tax in respect of the emoluments of his or her employment or is so assessable in respect of those emoluments on the basis of the amount received in the State.

(3) Where, in respect of the provision for an employee of any relevant benefits, a sum has been deemed to be income of the employee by virtue of *subsection (1)* or *(2)* of *section 777*, and subsequently the employee proves to the satisfaction of the Revenue Commissioners—

(a) that no payment in respect of or in substitution for the benefits has been made, and

(b) that some event has occurred by reason of which no such payment will be made,

and the employee makes application for relief under this subsection within 6 years from the time when that event occurred, the Revenue Commissioners shall give relief in respect of tax on that sum by repayment or otherwise as may be appropriate, and, if the employee satisfies the Revenue Commissioners in relation to some particular part of the benefits but not the whole of the benefits, the Revenue Commissioners may give such relief as may seem to them just and reasonable.

Cross References

From Section 778

Section 777 Charge to income tax in respect of certain relevant benefits provided for employees.

To Section 778

Section 201 Exemptions and reliefs in respect of tax under section 123.

Section 787N Qualifying overseas pension plans: relief for contributions.

Schedule 3 Reliefs in Respect of Income Tax Charged on Payments on Retirement, Etc

779 Charge to income tax of pensions under Schedule E

[FA72 s20]

[(1) Subject to *subsection (2)*, pensions paid under any scheme, including an overseas pension scheme, which is approved or is being considered for approval under this Chapter shall, notwithstanding anything in *section 18* or *19*, be charged to tax under Schedule E, and *Chapter 4* of *Part 42* shall apply accordingly.][1]

(2) In respect of any scheme which is approved or is being considered for approval under this Chapter, the Revenue Commissioners may direct that until such date as they may specify pensions under the scheme shall be charged to tax as annual payments under Case III of Schedule D, and tax shall be deductible under *section 237* or *238* accordingly.

Amendments

[1] Substituted by FA05 s21(1)(a)(v). Applies as respects any retirement benefits scheme approved on or after 1 January 2005.

Cross References

From Section 779

Section 237 Annual payments payable wholly out of taxed income.
Section 238 Annual payments not payable out of taxed income.
Section 960 Date for payment of income tax other than under self assessment.
Section 983 Interpretation (Chapter 4).

To Section 779

Section 439 Effect of release, etc. of debt in respect of loan under section 438.
Section 773 General Medical Services: scheme of superannuation.

779A Transactions deemed to be pensions in payment

[(1) Where the assets of a retirement benefits scheme, which is approved, or is being considered for approval, under this Chapter (in this section referred to as the "*scheme*"), are used in connection with any transaction which would, if the assets were the assets of an approved retirement fund, be regarded under *section 784A* as giving rise to a distribution for the purposes of that section, the use of the assets shall be regarded as a pension paid under the scheme and the amount so regarded shall be calculated in accordance with that section.

(2) An amount which has been regarded as a pension paid under the scheme, in accordance with this section, shall not be regarded as an asset in the scheme for any purpose.

(3) Any property, the acquisition or sale of which is regarded as giving rise to a pension payment under the scheme, shall not be regarded as an asset of the scheme.][1]

Amendments

[1] Inserted by FA06 s14(1)(a)(iv). Has effect as on and from 2 February 2006.

Cross References

From Section 779A

Section 784A Approved retirement fund.

780 Charge to income tax on repayment of employees' contributions

[FA72 s21(1) to (5)(a) and (6) and (7); FA73 s18; FA92 s6(b)]

(1) In this section and in *section 781*, "*employee*", in relation to a statutory scheme, includes an officer.

(2) Subject to this section, tax shall be charged under this section on any repayment to an employee during his or her lifetime of any contribution (including interest on contributions, if any) if the payment is made under—

(a) a scheme which is or has at any time been an exempt approved scheme, or

(b) a statutory scheme established under a public statute.

[(2A) This section shall not apply to the extent that any repayment of contributions is transferred by the administrator of the scheme to the administrator of a PRSA, by way of contribution to a PRSA to which the employee is the contributor.][1]

(3) This section shall not apply where the employee's employment was carried on outside the State.

(4) *Subsection (2)(a)* shall not apply in relation to a contribution made after the scheme ceases to be an exempt approved scheme unless it again becomes an exempt approved scheme.

(5) Where any payment is chargeable to tax under this section, the administrator of the scheme shall be charged to income tax under Case IV of Schedule D and, subject to *subsection (7)*, the rate of the tax shall be [the standard rate in force at the time of payment][2]; but, in the case of any repayment under a statutory scheme established under a public statute, the administrator of the scheme shall be entitled to deduct the tax chargeable in respect of that repayment from the amount of that repayment.

(6) The tax shall be charged on the amount paid or, if the administrator is entitled under the rules of the relevant scheme or otherwise to deduct the tax before payment, on the amount before deduction of tax, and the amount so charged to tax shall not be treated as income for any other purpose of the Income Tax Acts.

(7) (a) The Minister for Finance may by order from time to time increase or decrease the rate of tax under *subsection (5)*.

(b) Every order under *paragraph (a)* shall be laid before Dáil Éireann as soon as may be after it is made and, if a resolution annulling the order is passed by Dáil Éireann within the next 21 days on which Dáil Éireann has sat after the order is laid before it, the order shall be annulled accordingly, but without prejudice to the validity of anything previously done thereunder.

Amendments

[1] Inserted by PAA02 s4(1)(d)(iii). With effect from 7 November 2002 per S.I. 502 of 2002.

[2] Substituted by FA02 s10(1)(a)(iv). Applies to any repayment of contributions referred to in section 780 which is made on or after 5 December 2001.

Cross References

From Section 780

Section 781 Charge to income tax: commutation of entire pension.

To Section 780

Section 781 Charge to income tax: commutation of entire pension.
Section 787F Transfers to PRSAs.
Schedule 23 Occupational Pension Schemes

781 Charge to income tax: commutation of entire pension

[FA72 s22(1) to (4); FA92 s6(c)]

(1) Where—

(a) a scheme which is or has at any time been an approved scheme, or

(b) a statutory scheme established under a public statute,

contains a rule allowing in special circumstances a payment in commutation of an employee's entire pension, and any pension is commuted, whether wholly or not, under the rule, tax shall be charged on the amount by which the sum receivable exceeds—

(i) the largest sum which would have been receivable in commutation of any part of the pension if the scheme had contained a rule providing that the aggregate value of the relevant benefits payable to an employee on or after retirement, excluding any pension which was not commutable, should not exceed three-eightieths of the employee's final remuneration for each year of service up to a maximum of 40 years, or

(ii) the largest sum which would have been receivable in commutation of any part of the pension under any rule of the scheme authorising the commutation of part (but not the whole) of the pension, or which would have been so receivable but for those circumstances,

whichever gives the lesser amount chargeable to tax.

(2) This section shall not apply where the employee's employment was carried on outside the State.

(3) Where any amount is chargeable to tax under this section, the administrator of the scheme shall be charged to income tax under Case IV of Schedule D on that amount and, subject to *subsection (6)* of *section 780* which shall apply as it applies to tax chargeable under that section, the rate of tax shall be 10 per cent.

(4) In applying *paragraph (i)* or *(ii)* of *subsection (1)*—

(a) the same considerations shall be taken into account, including the provisions of any other relevant scheme, as would have been taken into account by the Revenue Commissioners in applying *section 772*, and

(b) where the scheme has ceased to be an approved scheme, account shall only be taken of the rules of the scheme at the date of the cesser.

Cross References

From Section 781

Section 772 Conditions for approval of schemes and discretionary approval.

Section 780 Charge to income tax on repayment of employees' contributions.

To Section 781

Section 780 Charge to income tax on repayment of employees' contributions.

Section 790AA Taxation of lump sums in excess of the tax free amount.

Schedule 23 Occupational Pension Schemes

782 Charge to tax: repayments to employer

[FA72 s23]

(1) Where any payment is made or becomes due to an employer out of funds which are or have been held for the purposes of a scheme which is or has at any time been an exempt approved scheme, then—

(a) if the scheme relates to a trade or profession carried on by the employer, the payment shall be treated for the purposes of the Tax Acts as a receipt of that trade or profession receivable when the payment is due or on the last day on which the trade or profession is carried on by the employer, whichever is the earlier;

(b) if the scheme does not relate to such a trade or profession, the employer shall be charged to tax on the amount of the payment under Case IV of Schedule D, but only in proportion to the extent that the payment represents contributions by the employer under the scheme which were allowable as deductions for tax purposes.

(2) This section shall not apply to a payment which was due before the scheme became an exempt approved scheme.

(3) References in this section to any payment include references to any transfer of assets or other transfer of money's worth.

782A Pre-retirement access to AVCs

[(1) (a) In this section—

"*accumulated value*", in relation to relevant AVC contributions, means—

(i) where the contributions are contributions of a kind referred to in *paragraph (i)* of the definition of "*relevant AVC contributions*", the amount which the administrator determines to be equal to the realisable value of the portion of the resources of the scheme that, in accordance with the rules of the scheme, represents those contributions, less the amount of so much of the expenses of the scheme as, under the rules of the scheme, are to be discharged out of that portion, and

(ii) where the contributions are contributions of a kind referred to in *paragraph (ii)* of the definition of "*relevant AVC contributions*", the amount which the PRSA administrator determines to be equal to the realisable value of the resources of the PRSA contract that, in accordance with the terms of the contract, represents those contributions, less the amount of the expenses of the contract as, under the terms of the contract, are to be discharged out of the realisable value;

"*administrator*", in relation to an AVC fund, means the person or persons having the management of the scheme to which the relevant AVC contributions comprising the AVC fund have been made or, as the case may be, the PRSA administrator;

"*AVC fund*" means the accumulated value of relevant AVC contributions made by a member, other than the accumulated value of relevant AVC contributions of a kind referred to in *paragraph (ii)* of the definition of that term where benefits have become payable to the member under the main scheme;

"*designated benefit*" and "*pension adjustment order*" have the meanings assigned to them in *section 787O(5)(a)*;

"*member*", in relation to a scheme, means any person who, having been admitted to membership under the rules of the scheme, remains entitled to any benefit under the scheme;

"*PRSA administrator*" has the meaning assigned to it in *section 787A(1)*;

"*PRSA contract*" has the meaning assigned to it in *section 787A*;][1]

"*relevant AVC contributions*" means—

(i) additional voluntary contributions within the meaning of *section 770(1)*, and

(ii) additional voluntary PRSA contributions within the meaning of *section 787A(1)*, made for the purpose of providing relevant benefits on retirement and include such additional voluntary contributions representing a transfer of additional voluntary contributions from a retirement benefits scheme or a PRSA, as the case may be, but shall not include such additional voluntary contributions made under a purchase of notional service scheme;

"*relevant individual*" means a member of a scheme who has an AVC fund and, as the case may be, where the AVC fund is subject to a pension adjustment order includes the spouse or former spouse or civil partner or former civil partner of the member;

"*scheme*" means an approved scheme or a statutory scheme;

"*specified period*" means the period of 3 years from the date of passing of the *Finance Act 2013*.

(b) For the purposes of this section, where an AVC fund is subject to a pension adjustment order, each relevant individual shall be deemed to have a separate AVC fund the value of which shall be determined as if the designated benefit pursuant to the order was payable at the time of the transfer provided for in *subsection (3)*.

(c) For the purposes of this section, relevant AVC contributions shall not include—

(i) any sum paid by means of contribution, howsoever described, at any time by an employer (within the meaning of *section 787A*) to a scheme or to a PRSA,

(ii) contributions (which are not voluntary contributions) made at any time by a member to a scheme at the rate or rates specified for member's contributions in the rules of the scheme or otherwise, or

(iii) contributions (which are not additional voluntary contributions of a kind referred to in *subparagraph (ii)* of the definition of "*relevant AVC contributions*") made at any time by a member to a PRSA.

[(2) Notwithstanding—

(a) *section 32* of the Pensions Act 1990,

(b) the rules of a scheme of which a relevant individual is a member or the terms of a PRSA contract to which a relevant individual is party, or

(c) the provisions of a pension adjustment order made in relation to a relevant individual,

a relevant individual may during the specified period irrevocably instruct in writing the administrator of his or her AVC fund to exercise, on one occasion only, the option (in this section referred to as the 'pre-retirement access option') provided for in *subsection (3)*.][2]

(3) The pre-retirement access option is the transfer by the administrator to the relevant individual, before retirement, of an amount not exceeding 30 per cent of the value, at the time of the transfer, of the relevant individual's AVC fund.

(4) (a) The amount transferred by an administrator to a relevant individual in accordance with *subsection (3)* shall, notwithstanding *section 780*, be treated as a payment to the individual of emoluments to which Schedule E applies and accordingly the provisions of *Chapter 4* of *Part 42* shall apply to any such payment, and

(b) the administrator shall deduct tax from the amount transferred at the higher rate for the year of assessment in which the payment is made unless the administrator has received from the Revenue Commissioners a certificate of tax credits and standard rate cut-off point or a tax deduction card for that year in respect of the individual.

(5) Where an administrator receives an irrevocable instruction referred to in *subsection (2)* the administrator shall keep and retain for a period of 6 years each such instruction and on being so required by notice given to the administrator in writing by an officer of the Revenue Commissioners make available within the time specified in the notice such instructions as may be required by the notice.

(6) Where a pre-retirement access option is exercised in respect of a relevant individual in accordance with *subsection (3)* the amount transferred shall not be a benefit crystallisation event (within the meaning of *section 787O(1)*) for the purposes of *Chapter 2C* and *Schedule 23B*.][3]

Amendments

[1] Inserted by F(No.2)A13 s18(1)(b)(i). Deemed to have effect from 27 March 2013.

[2] Substituted by F(No.2)A13 s18(1)(b)(ii). Deemed to have effect from 27 March 2013.

[3] Inserted by FA13 s17(1)(c). Has effect from 27 March 2013.

CHAPTER 2

Retirement Annuities

783 Interpretation and general (Chapter 2)

[ITA67 s195B(3) and (6), s235(6) to (9) and s238(3) and (4); FA69 s65(1) and Sch5 PtI; FA72 Sch1 PtIII par4; FA93 s10(1); FA96 s132(2) and Sch5 PtII; FA97 s146(1) and Sch9 PtI par 5(3)]

(1) (a) [In this Chapter][1]—

["*approved retirement fund*" has the meaning assigned to it by *section 784A*;

["*close company*" has the same meaning as in *section 430*;

"*connected person*" has the same meaning as in *section 10*;][2]

"*approved minimum retirement fund*" has the meaning assigned to it by *section 784C*;][3]

"*director*" means—

(i) in relation to a body corporate the affairs of which are managed by a board of directors or similar body, a member of that board or body,

(ii) in relation to a body corporate the affairs of which are managed by a single director or similar person, that director or person,

(iii) in relation to a body corporate the affairs of which are managed by the members themselves, a member of the body corporate,

and includes any person who is or has been a director;

["*earnings limit*" shall be construed in accordance with *section 790A*;][4]

"*employee*", in relation to a body corporate, includes any person taking part in the management of the affairs of the body corporate who is not a director, and includes a person who is or has been an employee;

"*investment company*" means a company the income of which consists mainly of investment income;

"*investment income*", in relation to a company, means income which, if the company were an individual, would not be earned income;

["*participator*" has the same meaning as in *section 433*;][5]

"*proprietary director*" means a director of a company who is either the beneficial owner of, or able, either directly or through the medium of other companies or by any other indirect means, to control, more than 15 per cent of the ordinary share capital of the company;

"*proprietary employee*", in relation to a company, means an employee who is the beneficial owner of, or able, either directly or through the medium of other companies or by any other indirect means, to control, more than 15 per cent of the ordinary share capital of the company;

"*sponsored superannuation scheme*" means a scheme or arrangement relating to service in particular offices or employments and having for its object or one of its objects the making of provision in respect of persons serving in those offices or employments against—

(i) future retirement or partial retirement,

(ii) future termination of service through death or disability, or

(iii) similar matters,

being a scheme or arrangement under which any part of the cost of the provision so made is or has been borne otherwise than by those persons by reason of their service (whether it is the cost or part of the cost of the benefits provided, or of paying premiums or other sums in order to provide those benefits, or of administering or instituting the scheme or arrangement).

(b) For the purposes of the definitions of "*proprietary director*" and "*proprietary employee*", ordinary share capital which is owned or controlled as is specified in those definitions by a person, being a [spouse, civil partner, infant child or infant child of the civil partner][6] of a director or employee, or by the trustee of a trust for the benefit of a person or persons, being or including any such person or such director or employee, shall be deemed to be owned or controlled by such director or employee and not by any other person.

(c) For the purposes of the definition of "*sponsored superannuation scheme*", a person shall be treated as bearing by reason of his or her service the cost of any payment made or agreed to be made in respect of his or her service if that payment or the agreement to make it is treated under the Income Tax Acts as increasing the person's income or would be so treated if he or she were chargeable to tax under Schedule E in respect of his or her emoluments from that service.

(2) (a) For the purposes of this Chapter, an office or employment shall be a pensionable office or employment only if service in it is service to which a sponsored superannuation scheme relates (not being a scheme under which the benefits provided in respect of that service are limited to [benefits of a kind referred to in *paragraphs (b)* and *(c)* of *section 772(3)*, including any similar benefit provided under a statutory scheme established under a public statute,][7] or disability before the age of 70 years or some lower age); but references to a pensionable office or employment apply whether or not the duties are performed wholly or partly in the State or the holder is chargeable to tax in respect of the office or employment.

(b) For the purposes of *paragraph (a)*, service in an office or employment shall not be treated as service to which a sponsored superannuation scheme relates by reason only of the fact that the holder of the office or employment might (though he or she does not) participate in the scheme by exercising or refraining from exercising an option open to him or her by virtue of that service.

[(c) For the purposes of calculating the amount of any reduction in net relevant earnings in respect of any qualifying premium or of any PRSA contribution (within the meaning of *Chapter 2A* of this Part) this Chapter and *Chapter 2A* shall apply as if any contribution by an employee to a sponsored superannuation scheme relating to service in an office or employment, which is not a pensionable office or employment within the meaning of *paragraph (a)*, were a payment of a qualifying premium for which relief had been given under this Chapter.][8]

(3) For the purposes of this Chapter but subject to *subsection (4)*, "*relevant earnings*", in relation to an individual, means any income of the individual chargeable to tax for the year of assessment in question, being either—

(a) income arising in respect of remuneration from an office or employment of profit held by the individual, other than a pensionable office or employment,

(b) income from any property which is attached to or forms part of the emoluments of any such office or employment of profit held by the individual, or

(c) income which is chargeable under Schedule D and is immediately derived by the individual from the carrying on or exercise by the individual of his or her trade or profession either as an individual or, in the case of a partnership, as a partner personally acting in the partnership;

but does not include any remuneration from an investment company of which the individual is a proprietary director or a proprietary employee.

(4) For the purposes of this Chapter, the relevant earnings of an individual shall not be treated as the relevant earnings of his or her [spouse or civil partner][9], notwithstanding that the individual's income chargeable to tax is treated as his or her [spouse's or civil partner's][10] income.

(5) The Revenue Commissioners may make regulations prescribing the procedure to be adopted in giving effect to this Chapter in so far as such procedure is not otherwise provided for and, without prejudice to the generality of the foregoing, may by such regulations—

(a) prescribe the manner and form in which claims for relief from or repayment of tax are to be made,

(b) prescribe the time limit for the making of any such claim,

(c) require the trustees or other persons having the management of an approved trust scheme to deliver from time to time such information and particulars as the Revenue Commissioners may reasonably require for the purposes of this Chapter, and

(d) apply for purposes of this Chapter or of the regulations any provision of the Income Tax Acts (with or without modifications).

(6) Where any person, for the purpose of obtaining for that person or for any other person any relief from or repayment of tax under this Chapter,[...][11] makes any false statement or false representation, that person shall be liable to a penalty of [€3,000][12].

Amendments

[1] Substituted by FA03 s14(1)(c)(i)(I)(A). Shall be taken to have come into force and has effect as on and from 6 February 2003.

[2] Inserted by FA03 s14(1)(c)(i)(I)(B). Shall be taken to have come into force and has effect as on and from 6 February 2003.

[3] Inserted by FA99 s19(1)(b)(i). Paragraph (b), other than subparagraph (vi), of subsection (1) shall apply as respects any annuity contract for the time being approved by the Revenue Commissioners under section 784 entered into on or after the 6th day of April, 1999.

[4] Inserted by FA06 s14(1)(b)(i). Has effect as on and from 1 January 2006.

[5] Inserted by FA03 s14(1)(c)(i)(I)(C). Shall be taken to have come into force and has effect as on and from 6 February 2003.

[6] Substituted by F(No.3)A11 sched1(195).

[7] Substituted by FA03 s14(1)(c)(i)(II)(a). Applies as on and from 1 January 2003.

[8] Inserted by FA03 s14(1)(c)(i)(II)(b). Applies as on and from 1 January 2003.

[9] Substituted by F(No.3)A11 sched1(196).

[10] Substituted by F(No.3)A11 sched1(197).

[11] Deleted by F(No.2)A08 sched5(part2)(1)(g)(i). The enactments specified in Schedule 5 are amended or repealed to the extent and manner specified in that Schedule and, unless the contrary is stated, shall come into effect after 24 December 2008.

[12] Substituted by F(No.2)A08 sched5(part2)(1)(g)(ii). The enactments specified in Schedule 5 are amended or repealed to the extent and manner specified in that Schedule and, unless the contrary is stated, shall come into effect after 24 December 2008.

Case Law

'Relevant earnings' do not include profits of an individual who owns but who does not carry on a trade. Koenigsberger v Mellor 1995 STC 547

A pension paid to a retired partner did not qualify as 'relevant earnings'. It was held that the pension was derived from the contractual liability of the existing partners. Pegler v Abell 1975 STC 23

Revenue Briefings

Tax Briefing

Tax Briefing May 2003 – Issue 52 pg 9 – Finance Act 2003 – Pension products and retirement funds

Tax Briefing July 2007 – Issue 66 – Finance Act 2007 changes – Tax Treatment of various Pension Products

eBrief

eBrief No. 24/2006 – Pensions – Claiming a Personal Fund Threshold

eBrief No. 29/2007 – Approved Retirement Funds

Revenue Precedents

The earliest retirement age for jockeys is aged 50. PREC/12

Income payable under an approved Permanent Health Benefit policy is regarded as relevant earnings for RAC purposes if the contributions to the scheme are not maintained by the policy. PREC/18

An employer can pay retirement annuity premiums on behalf of the employee but it is chargeable to PAYE, PRSI and Levies. Relief is due to the individual subject to the 15% limit. PREC/13

Income which qualifies for the artists' exemption is not "chargeable to tax" and is not a source of relevant earnings so the individual is not entitled to affect an RAC. PREC/14

If an individual goes abroad on a temporary basis (for periods up to 3 years) and it is clear that the intention is to return and resume in the occupation which constituted the source of relevant earnings then premiums can continue to be paid after the individual becomes non resident. The life office should advise Retirement Benefits District of individual cases. PREC/15

Funds cannot be transferred between Retirement annuity contracts except at the point of maturity as outlined in section 786 of TCA97. PREC/16

Relevant earnings are not reduced to take account of income earned outside the State. PREC

What is the earliest retirement age for different classes of occupations under retirement annuity contracts? Badminton Players, Boxers, Cricketers, Croupiers, Cyclists, Dancers, Divers, Footballers, Golfers (Tournament earnings), Jockeys Flat racing and National Hunt, Motor Cylclist (Competitive), Motor racing drivers, Off shore Riggers, Rugby players (professional), Speedway Riders, Squash players, Table Tennis Players, Tennis Players, Trapeze Artists, Wrestlers can retire at 50. Air Pilots, Brass Instrumentalists, Distant Water trawlermen, Firemen (Part-time), Inshore fishermen, Moneybroker dealers, Singers can retire at 55. PREC/17

Cross References

From Section 783

Section 10 Connected persons.
Section 430 Meaning of "close company".
Section 433 Meaning of "participator", "associate", "director" and "loan creditor".
Section 772 Conditions for approval of schemes and discretionary approval.
Section 784A Approved retirement fund.
Section 784C Approved minimum retirement fund.
Section 790A Limit on earnings.

To Section 783

Section 3 Interpretation of Income Tax Acts.
Section 706 Interpretation and general (Part 26).
Section 773 General Medical Services: scheme of superannuation.
Section 787A Interpretation and supplemental.
Section 787E Extent of relief.
Section 787L Transfers to and from PRSA.
Section 788 Capital element in certain purchased annuities.
Section 1061 Recovery of penalties.
Schedule 31 Consequential Amendments

784 Retirement annuities: relief for premiums

[ITA67 s235(1) to (5) and (10); FA74 s65]

[(1) (a) Where an individual, being an individual referred to in *paragraph (b)*, pays a premium or other consideration under an annuity contract for the time being approved by the Revenue Commissioners as being a contract by which the main benefit secured is, or would, but for the exercise of an option by the individual under *subsection (2A)*, be a life annuity for the individual in his or her old age or under a contract for the time being approved under *section 785* (in this Chapter referred to as a "*qualifying premium*"), relief from income tax may be given in respect of the qualifying premium under *section 787*.

(b) An individual referred to in this paragraph is an individual who is or was (or but for an insufficiency of profits or gains would be or would have been) for any year of assessment chargeable to tax in respect of relevant earnings from any trade, profession, office or employment carried on or held by him or her and who paid a qualifying premium in that year.][1]

(2) (a) [Subject to *subsections (2A)* and *(3)* and to *section 786*,][2], the Revenue Commissioners shall not approve a contract unless it appears to them to satisfy the following conditions—

[(i) that it is made by the individual with a person lawfully carrying on the business of granting annuities on human life, and, where that person—

(I) is not resident in the State, or

(II) is not trading in the State through a fixed place of business,

that person is an insurance undertaking authorised to transact insurance business in the State under Directive 2002/83/EC of the European Parliament and of the Council of 5 November 2002*,][3]

* OJ No. L345, 19.12.2002, p.1

(ii) that it includes provision securing that no annuity payable under it shall be capable in whole or in part of surrender, commutation or assignment, and

(iii) that it does not—

(I) provide for the payment by that person during the life of the individual of any sum except sums payable by means of annuity to the individual,

(II) provide for the annuity payable to the individual to commence before the individual attains the age of 60 years or after he or she attains the age of [75 years][4],

(III) provide for the payment by that person of any other sums except sums payable by means of annuity to the individual's [widow, widower or surviving civil partner][5] and any sums which, in the event of no annuity becoming payable either to the individual or to a [widow, widower or surviving civil partner][6], are payable to the individual's personal representatives by means of return of premiums, reasonable interest on premiums or bonuses out of profits,

(IV) provide for the annuity, if any, payable to a [widow, widower or surviving civil partner][7] of the individual to be of a greater annual amount than that paid or payable to the individual, or

(V) provide for the payment of any annuity otherwise than for the life of the annuitant.

[(b) Notwithstanding *paragraph (a)*—

(i) the contract may provide for the payment to the individual, at the time the annuity commences to be payable or, where the individual opts in accordance with *subsection (2A)*, at the time of the transfer referred to in that subsection, of a lump sum by means of commutation of part of the annuity where the individual elects, at or before the time when the annuity first becomes payable to him or her or before the date of such transfer, to be paid the lump sum, and

(ii) the amount payable under *subparagraph (i)* shall not exceed 25 per cent of the value of the annuity payable or the value of the annuity which would have been payable if the individual had not opted in accordance with *subsection (2A)*.

(c) The reference in *paragraph (b)(i)* to the commutation of part of the annuity shall, in a case where the individual has opted in accordance with *subsection (2A)*, be construed as a reference to the commutation of the annuity which would, but for such election, be payable if the individual opted to have the annuity paid with effect from the date of the transfer referred to in that subsection.][8]

[(2A) The Revenue Commissioners shall not approve a contract unless it appears to them that the contract provides for the individual entitled to an annuity under the contract to exercise, on or before the date on which that annuity would otherwise become payable, an option for the transfer by the person with whom the contract is made, on or after that date, to—

(a) the individual, or

(b) an approved retirement fund,

of an amount equivalent to the amount determined by the formula—

$$A - B$$

where—

A is the amount equal to the value of the individual's accrued rights under the contract exclusive of any lump sum paid in accordance with *paragraph (b)* of *subsection (2)*, and

B is the amount or value of assets which the person with whom the contract is made is required, in accordance with *section 784C*, to transfer to an approved minimum retirement fund held in the name of the individual or to apply in purchasing an annuity payable to the individual with effect from the date of the exercise of the said option.

[(2B) (a) Where an individual opts in accordance with *subsection (2A)*, any amount paid to the individual by virtue of that subsection, other than an amount payable by virtue of *paragraph (b)* of *subsection (2)*, [shall, notwithstanding anything in *section 18* or *19*,][9] be regarded as a payment of emoluments to which Schedule E applies and, accordingly, the provisions of *Chapter 4* of *Part 42* shall, subject to *paragraph (b)*, apply to any such payment.

(b) The person making a payment to which *paragraph (a)* refers shall deduct tax from the payment at the higher rate for the year of assessment in which the payment is made unless that person has received from the Revenue Commissioners a [certificate of tax credits and standard rate cut-off point][10] or a tax deduction card for that year in respect of the individual beneficially entitled to the payment.][11]][12]

[(2C) Notwithstanding anything contained in this Part, a retirement annuity contract shall not cease to be an approved contract because of any provision in law, whether or not contained in the contract, whereby the parties to the contract may cancel the contract and effect a transfer of assets into one or more than one PRSA of which the individual who is a party to that approved contract is the contributor.][13]

[(2D) Notwithstanding any other provisions in this Chapter, a retirement annuity contract shall neither cease to be an annuity contract for the time being approved by the Revenue Commissioners nor shall the Revenue Commissioners be prevented from approving such a contract notwithstanding that the contract provides for the annuity secured by the contract for an individual to be commuted to such extent as may be necessary for the purpose of discharging a tax liability in respect of the individual, under the provisions of *Chapter 2C* of this Part, in connection with the annuity.][14]

[(2E) Notwithstanding any other provision of this Chapter, a retirement annuity contract shall not cease to be an annuity contract for the time being approved by the Revenue Commissioners, nor shall the Revenue Commissioners be prevented from approving such a contract, notwithstanding that the contract provides for the annuity secured by the contract for an individual to be commuted, where the individual comes within the provisions of *section 787TA*, to such extent as may be necessary for the purpose of the exercise of an option by the individual in accordance with that section requiring an amount representing the value of, or part of the value of, the individual's accrued rights under the contract at the date of the exercise of the option to be transferred to the individual by the person with whom the contract is made.][15]

(3) The Revenue Commissioners may, if they think fit and subject to any conditions they think proper to impose, approve a contract otherwise satisfying the conditions referred to in *subsection (2)*, notwithstanding that the contract provides for one or more of the following matters—

(a) the payment after the individual's death of an annuity to a dependant, not being the [widow, widower or surviving civil partner][16] of the individual;

(b) the payment to the individual of an annuity commencing before he or she attains the age of 60 years, where the annuity is payable on the individual becoming permanently incapable through infirmity of mind or body of carrying on his or her own occupation or any occupation of a similar nature for which he or she is trained or fitted;

(c) where the individual's occupation is one in which persons customarily retire before attaining the age of 60 years, the annuity to commence before the individual attains that age (but not before he or she attains the age of 50 years);

[…][17]

(e) the annuity payable to any person to continue for a term certain (not exceeding 10 years) notwithstanding his or her death within that term, or the annuity payable to any person to terminate, or be suspended, on [marriage or remarriage or on entering into a civil partnership or a new civil partnership][18] or in other circumstances;

(f) in the case of an annuity which is to continue for a term certain, the annuity to be assignable by will and, in the event of any person dying entitled to the annuity, the annuity to be assignable by his or her personal representatives in the distribution of the estate so as to give effect to a testamentary disposition, or to the rights of those entitled on intestacy or to an appropriation of the annuity to a legacy or to a share or interest in the estate.

(4) *Subsections (1)* to *(3)* shall apply in relation to a contribution under a trust scheme or part of a trust scheme approved by the Revenue Commissioners as they apply in relation to a premium under an annuity contract so approved, with the modification that for the condition in *subsection (2)(a)(i)* there shall be substituted a condition that the scheme (or the part of the scheme)—

(a) is established under the law of and administered in the State,

(b) is established for the benefit of individuals engaged in or connected with a particular occupation (or one or other of a group of occupations) and for the purpose of providing retirement annuities for those individuals with or without subsidiary benefits for their [families, civil partners, dependants or the children of their civil partners][19], and

(c) is so established under irrevocable trusts by a body of persons comprising or representing the majority of the individuals so engaged in the State,

and with the necessary modifications of other references to the contract or the person with whom it is made, and exemption from income tax shall be allowed in respect of income derived from investments or deposits of any fund maintained for the purpose referred to in *paragraph (b)* under a scheme or part of a scheme for the time being approved under this subsection.

[(4A) At any time when the person referred to in *subsection (2)(a)(i)* or in *section 785(1)*—

(a) is not resident in the State, or

(b) is not trading in the State through a fixed place of business,

the person shall, in relation to the discharge of all duties and obligations imposed [by this section or, as the case may be, by *section 785*[, by *Chapter 2C* and by section 125B of the Stamp Duties Consolidation Act 1999][20]][21]—

(i) enter into a contract with the Revenue Commissioners enforceable in a Member State of the European Communities in relation to the discharge of those duties and obligations and in entering into such a contract the parties to the contract shall acknowledge and agree in writing that—

(I) it is governed solely by the laws of the State, and

(II) that the courts of the State shall have exclusive jurisdiction in determining any dispute arising under it,

or

(ii) ensure that there is a person resident in the State (referred to in this paragraph as the "appointed person"), appointed by the person, to be responsible for the discharge of those duties and obligations and the person shall notify the Revenue Commissioners of the appointment of the appointed person and the identity of the appointed person.

(4B) The Revenue Commissioners may by notice in writing require the person to whom premiums are payable under any contract for the time being approved under this section or under *section 785*, or the appointed person referred to in *subsection (4A)(ii)*, as the case may be, to provide, within 30 days of the date of such notice, such information and particulars as may be specified in the notice as they may reasonably require for the purposes of this Chapter, and, without prejudice to the generality of the foregoing, such information and particulars may include—

(a) the name, address and PPS Number (within the meaning of *section 787A(1)*) of the individual with whom the contract has been made,

(b) the name, address and PPS Number (within that meaning) of the individual or individuals to whom any payment of an annuity in respect of the contract has been made, and

(c) the amount of the annuity payments referred to in *paragraph (b)*.][22]

(5) The Revenue Commissioners may at any time, by notice in writing given to the persons by and to whom premiums are payable under any contract for the time being approved under this section or to the trustees or other persons having the management of any trust scheme so approved, withdraw that approval on such grounds and from such date (including a date before the date of the notice) as may be specified in the notice and, where any approval is so withdrawn, there shall be made such assessments as may be appropriate for the purpose of withdrawing any reliefs given under this Chapter consequent on the approval.

(6) Nothing in *sections 4* and *6* of the Policies of Assurance Act, 1867, shall be taken to apply to any contract approved under this section.

[(7) Notwithstanding anything in *section 18* or *section 19*, any payment of an annuity made on or after 1 January 2002 in respect of an annuity contract approved under this section or under *section 785* shall be regarded as a pension chargeable to tax under Schedule E, and *Chapter 4* of *Part 42* shall apply accordingly.][23]

Amendments

[1] Substituted by FA02 s10(1)(b). Applies as respects the year of assessment 2002 and subsequent years of assessment.

[2] Substituted by FA99 s19(1)(b)(ii)(II)(A). Paragraph (b), other than subparagraph (vi), of subsection (1) shall apply as respects any annuity contract for the time being approved by the Revenue Commissioners under section 784 entered into on or after the 6th day of April, 1999.

[3] Substituted by FA05 s21(1)(b)(i)(I). Applies as respects any annuity contract for the time being approved by the Revenue Commissioners entered into on or after 1 January 2005.

[4] Substituted by FA99 s19(1)(b)(ii)(II)(B). Paragraph (b), other than subparagraph (vi), of subsection (1) shall apply as respects any annuity contract for the time being approved by the Revenue Commissioners under section 784 entered into on or after the 6th day of April, 1999.

[5, 6, 7] Substituted by F(No.3)A11 sched1(198).

[8] Substituted by FA99 s19(1)(b)(ii)(III). Paragraph (b), other than subparagraph (vi), of subsection (1) shall apply as respects any annuity contract for the time being approved by the Revenue Commissioners under section 784 entered into on or after the 6th day of April, 1999.

[9] Substituted by FA05 s21(1)(b)(i)(II). Applies as respects any annuity contract for the time being approved by the Revenue Commissioners entered into on or after 1 January 2005.

[10] Substituted by FA03 sched6(1)(g). This section shall be deemed to have come into force and take effect as on and from 6 April 2001.

[11] Substituted by FA00 s23(1)(c).

[12] Inserted by FA99 s19(1)(b)(ii)(IV). Paragraph (b), other than subparagraph (vi), of subsection (1) shall apply as respects any annuity contract for the time being approved by the Revenue Commissioners under section 784 entered into on or after the 6th day of April, 1999.

[13] Inserted by PAA02 s4(1)(d)(iv). With effect from 7 November 2002 per S.I. 502 of 2002.

[14] Inserted by FA06 s14(1)(b)(ii)(I). Has effect as on and from 1 January 2006.

[15] Inserted by FA12 s18(2). Has effect from 8 February 2012.

[16] Substituted by F(No.3)A11 sched1(199).

[17] Deleted by FA99 s19(1)(b)(ii)(V). Paragraph (b), other than subparagraph (vi), of subsection (1) shall apply as respects any annuity contract for the time being approved by the Revenue Commissioners under section 784 entered into on or after the 6th day of April, 1999.

[18] Substituted by F(No.3)A11 sched1(200).

[19] Substituted by F(No.3)A11 sched1(201).

[20] Substituted by F(No.2)A11 s4(2)(b).

[21] Substituted by FA06 s14(1)(b)(ii)(II). Has effect as on and from 1 January 2006.

[22] Inserted by FA05 s21(1)(b)(i)(III). Applies as respects any annuity contract for the time being approved by the Revenue Commissioners entered into on or after 1 January 2005.

[23] Inserted by FA01 s18(b)(i).

Revenue Briefings

Tax Briefing

Tax Briefing December 2005 – Issue 62 – Tax Relief on Pension Contributions to EU based Pension Schemes

Revenue Precedents

Earliest age for retirement for musicians is 60 with the exception of brass instrumentalists, who can retire from age 55. PREC

Cross References

From Section 784

Section 784C Approved minimum retirement fund.
Section 785 Approval of contracts for dependants or for life assurance.
Section 786 Approval of certain other contracts.
Section 787 Nature and amount of relief for qualifying premiums.
Section 787A Interpretation and supplemental.
Section 960 Date for payment of income tax other than under self assessment.
Section 983 Interpretation (Chapter 4).

To Section 784

Section 172A Interpretation.
Section 256 Interpretation (Chapter 4).
Section 608 Superannuation funds.
Section 706 Interpretation and general (Part 26).
Section 739B Interpretation and application.
Section 772 Conditions for approval of schemes and discretionary approval.
Section 784B Conditions relating to an approved retirement fund.
Section 784C Approved minimum retirement fund.
Section 784D Conditions relating to an approved minimum retirement fund.
Section 785 Approval of contracts for dependants or for life assurance.
Section 786 Approval of certain other contracts.
Section 787H Approved Retirement Fund option.
Section 787N Qualifying overseas pension plans: relief for contributions.
Section 787O Interpretation and general (Chapter 2C).
Section 788 Capital element in certain purchased annuities.
Section 790AA Taxation of lump sums in excess of the tax free amount.
Section 848V Interpretation (Part 36B).
Section 897A Returns by employers in relation to pension products.
Schedule 2A Dividend Withholding Tax
Schedule 2B Investment Undertakings: Declarations
Schedule 23B Limit on Tax-Relieved Pension Funds
Schedule 31 Consequential Amendments

784A Approved retirement fund

[(1) (a) In this section—

"*approved retirement fund*" means a fund which is managed by a qualifying fund manager and which complies with the conditions of *section 784B*;

"*qualifying fund manager*" means—

[(a) a person who is a holder of a licence granted under section 9 of the Central Bank Act, 1971, or a person who holds a licence or other similar authorisation under the law of any other Member State of the European Communities which corresponds to a licence granted under that section,][1]

(b) a building society within the meaning of *section 256*,

(c) a trustee savings bank within the meaning of the Trustee Savings Banks Act, 1989,

[…][2]

[…][3]

(g) the Post Office Savings Bank,

(h) a credit union within the meaning of the Credit Union Act, 1997,

(i) a collective investment undertaking within the meaning of *section 172A*, [(j) the holder of—

(i) an authorisation issued by the Minister for Enterprise, Trade and Employment under the European Communities (Life Assurance) Framework Regulations of 1984 (S.I. No. 57 of 1984) as amended, or

(ii) an authorisation granted by the authority charged by law with the duty of supervising the activities of insurance undertakings in a Member State other than the State in accordance with Article 6 of Directive No. 79/267/EEC*, who is carrying on the business of life assurance in the State, or

* OJ No. L63, 13.3.1979, p.1

(iii) an official authorisation to undertake insurance in Iceland, Liechtenstein and Norway pursuant to the EEA Agreement within the meaning of the European Communities (Amendment) Act, 1993, and who is carrying on the business of life assurance in the State,][4]

(k) a person—

(i) which is an authorised member firm of the Irish Stock Exchange, within the meaning of the Stock Exchange Act, 1995, or a member firm (which carries on a trade in the State through a branch or agency) of a stock exchange of any other Member State of the European Communities, and

(ii) which has sent to the Revenue Commissioners a notification of its name and address and of its intention to act as a qualifying fund manager,

or

[(l) a firm approved under section 10 of the Investment Intermediaries Act, 1995, which is authorised to hold client money, other than a firm authorised as a Restricted Activity Investment Product Intermediary, where the firm's authorisation permits it to engage in the proposed activities, or a business firm which has been authorised to provide similar investment business services under the laws of a Member State of the European Communities which correspond to that Act;][5]

"*tax reference number*", in relation to an individual, has the meaning assigned to it by *section 885* in relation to a specified person within the meaning of that section.

(b) For the purposes of this Chapter, references to an approved retirement fund shall be construed as a reference to assets in an approved retirement fund which are managed for an individual by a qualifying fund manager and which are beneficially owned by the individual.

[(c) Nothing in this Part shall be construed as authorising or permitting a person who is a qualifying fund manager to provide any services which that person would not otherwise be authorised or permitted to provide in the State.

(d) Any reference in this section to a distribution in relation to an approved retirement fund shall be construed as including any payment or transfer of assets out of the fund [or any assignment of the fund or of assets out of the fund by any person,][6] for "Any contribution, including a payment, transfer or assignment to the individual beneficially entitled to the assets, other than a payment, transfer or assignment to another approved retirement fund the beneficial owner of the assets in which is the individual who is beneficially entitled to the assets in the first-mentioned approved retirement fund, whether or not the payment, transfer or assignment is made to the said individual.][7]

[(e) For the purposes of this section, any distribution in relation to an approved retirement fund shall be deemed to have been made by the qualifying fund manager.][8]

[(1A) Without prejudice to the generality of *subsection (1)(d)*, where assets of an approved retirement fund are used in connection with any of the transactions referred to in *subsection (1B)*, the transaction shall be regarded as a distribution for the purposes of this section of the amount specified in that subsection.

(1B) The transactions referred to in *subsection (1A)* and the amount to be regarded as a distribution in relation to any such transaction are as follows—

(a) in the case of a loan made to the individual beneficially entitled to the assets in an approved retirement fund or to any person connected with that individual, the amount to be regarded as a distribution for the purposes of this section is an amount equal to the value of the assets of the approved retirement fund used to make such a loan or used as security for such a loan,

(b) in the case of the acquisition of property from the individual beneficially entitled to the assets in an approved retirement fund or from any person connected with that individual, the amount to be regarded as a distribution for the purposes of this section is an amount equal to the value of the assets in the approved retirement fund used in or in connection with that acquisition,

(c) in the case of the sale of any asset in an approved retirement fund to the individual beneficially entitled to the assets in an approved retirement fund or to any person connected with that individual, the amount to be regarded as a distribution for the purposes of this section is an amount equal to the value of the asset sold,

(d) in the case of the acquisition of—

(i) any property which is to be used as holiday property, or

(ii) property which is to be used as a residence,

by the individual beneficially entitled to the assets in the approved retirement fund or by any person connected with that individual, the amount to be regarded as a distribution for the purposes of this section is an amount equal to the value of the assets in the approved retirement fund used in or in connection with that acquisition, but where property is acquired, on or after 6 February 2003, in relation to the acquisition of which a distribution is not treated as arising under this Chapter and that property commences to be used for one of the purposes mentioned in *subparagraphs (i)* or *(ii)* of this *paragraph*, the distribution shall be treated as arising at the date such use commences and the amount to be regarded as a distribution for the purposes of this section is an amount equal to the value of the assets of the approved retirement fund used in or in connection with the acquisition together with any assets used in or in connection with any expenditure on the improvement or repair of the property in question,

(e) in the case of the acquisition of shares or any other interest in a company, which is a close company or which would be a close company but for the fact that the company is not resident in the State, in relation to which the individual beneficially entitled to the assets in the approved retirement fund or a person connected with that individual is a participator, the amount to be regarded as a distribution for the purposes of this section is an amount equal to the value of assets in the approved retirement fund used in or in connection with that acquisition, […][9]

(f) in the case of the acquisition of tangible moveable property, the amount to be regarded as a distribution for the purposes of this section is an amount equal to the value of the assets in the approved retirement fund used in or in connection [with that acquisition,][10]

[(g) in the case of the acquisition of property which is to be used in connection with any business of the individual beneficially entitled to the assets in the approved retirement fund or in connection with any business of any person connected with that individual, the amount to be regarded as a distribution for the purposes of this section is an amount equal to the value of the assets in the approved retirement fund used in or in connection with that acquisition, but where property is acquired, on or after 2 February 2006, in relation to the acquisition of which a distribution is not treated as arising under this Chapter and that property commences to be used for the purpose mentioned in this paragraph, the distribution shall be treated as arising at the date such use commences and the amount to be regarded as a distribution for the purposes of this section is an amount equal to the value of the assets of the approved retirement fund used in or in connection with the acquisition together with any assets used in or in connection with any expenditure on the improvement or repair of the [property in question, and][11]][12]

[(h) in the case of the acquisition by the individual beneficially entitled to the assets in the approved retirement fund (in this paragraph referred to as the 'ARF investor') of any interest (whether solely or jointly with another person or persons) in units or shares of any description or class (in this paragraph referred to as 'units') in any fund, trust or scheme (in this paragraph referred to as a 'relevant fund'), or sub-fund, sub-trust or sub-scheme of any such relevant fund (in this paragraph referred to as a 'relevant sub-fund'), whether acquired directly or indirectly, then where the circumstances set out in both of the following subparagraphs (in this paragraph referred to as the 'circumstances') arise, namely—

(i) where a relevant pension arrangement (within the meaning of *section 787O(1)*), a member or holder of which is a person connected (within the meaning of *section 10* as it applies for the purposes of the Capital Gains Tax Acts) with the ARF investor, (in this paragraph referred to as the 'pension investor'), acquires, at any time, any interest (whether solely or jointly with another person or persons) in units in the same relevant fund or relevant sub-fund or in any other relevant fund or relevant sub- fund, whether directly or indirectly, and

(ii) there is any arrangement whereby the value of the units held by the pension investor increases, or may increase in the future, and that increase is attributable in whole or in part, directly or indirectly, to the units held by the ARF investor,

the amount to be regarded as a distribution for the purposes of this section (at the time the circumstances arise) is an amount equal to the value of the assets in the approved retirement fund used in or in connection with the acquisition of the units by the ARF investor.][13]

[...][14]

(1C) An amount which has been regarded as a distribution from an approved retirement fund, [other than a specified amount referred to in [*section 790 D(4)*][15],][16] shall not be regarded as an asset in that approved retirement fund for any purpose.

(1D) Any property, the acquisition or sale of which is regarded as giving rise to a distribution of assets in an approved retirement fund, shall not be regarded as an asset in that approved retirement fund.

(1E) [For the purposes of [*subsection (1B)*][17] references to the value of an asset in an approved retirement fund shall, except where the asset is cash, be construed as references to the market value of the asset, within the meaning of *section 548*.][18]

[(2) Subject to *subsections (3)* and *(4)*, exemption from income tax and capital gains tax shall be allowed in respect of the income and chargeable gains arising in respect of assets held in an approved retirement fund.

(3) [Subject to *subsections (3A)* and *(4)*][19]—

(a) the amount or value of any distribution by a qualifying fund manager in respect of assets held in an approved retirement fund [shall, notwithstanding anything in *section 18* or *19*,][20] be treated as a payment to the person beneficially entitled to the assets in the fund of emoluments to which Schedule E applies and, accordingly, the provisions of *Chapter 4* of *Part 42* shall apply to any such distribution, and

(b) the qualifying fund manager shall deduct tax from the distribution at the higher rate for the year of assessment in which the distribution is made unless the qualifying fund manager has received from the Revenue Commissioners a certificate of tax free allowances or a tax deduction card for that year in respect of the person referred to in *paragraph (a)*.

[(3A) *Subsection (3)* shall not apply where the distribution referred to in that subsection is made for the purpose of—

(a) reimbursing, in whole or in part, an administrator (within the meaning of *section 787O(1)*) in respect of the payment by that administrator of income tax charged on a chargeable excess in respect of the person beneficially entitled to the assets in the fund, or

(b) payment by the qualifying fund manager of the amount, or part of the amount, of the appropriate share (within the meaning of *section 787R(2A)(b)*) of a non-member (within the meaning of *section 787O(1)*) (being the person beneficially entitled to the assets in the fund) of income tax charged on a chargeable excess, under the provisions of *Chapter 2C* of this Part.][21]

(4) (a) Where the distribution referred to in *subsection (3)* is made following the death of the individual who was prior to death beneficially entitled to the assets of the approved retirement fund, the amount or value of the distribution shall be treated as the income of that individual for the year of assessment in which that individual dies and, subject to *paragraph (b)*, *subsection (3)* shall apply accordingly.

(b) *Subsection (3)* shall not apply to a distribution made following the death of the individual who was prior to death beneficially entitled to the assets in an approved retirement fund where the distribution is made—

(i) to another such fund (hereafter in this subsection referred to as "*the second-mentioned fund*") the beneficial owner of the assets in which is the [spouse or civil partner][22] of the said individual, or

(ii) to, or for the sole benefit of, [any child of the individual or any child of the civil partner of the individual][23].

(c) Where, in a case referred to in *paragraph (b)*, the distribution is made—

(i) to a person who had attained the age of 21 years at the date of death of the individual beneficially entitled to the assets in the approved retirement fund, or

(ii) following the death of the beneficial owner of the second-mentioned fund, not being a distribution to or for the sole benefit of [a child or child of the civil partner][24] of that owner who at the time of death of that person had not attained the age of 21 years,

[the qualifying fund manager shall deduct income tax from the distribution under Case IV of Schedule D at a rate of 30 per cent, and—

(I) the amount so charged to tax—

(A) shall not be reckoned in computing total income for the purposes of the Tax Acts, and

(B) shall be computed without regard to any amount deductible from, or deductible in computing, total income for the purposes of the Tax Acts,

(II) the charging of the distribution in such manner shall be without any relief or reduction specified in the Table to *section 458*, or any other deduction from that distribution, and

(III) *section 188* shall not apply as regards the amount so charged.

(d) Where a qualifying fund manager deducts tax in accordance with *paragraph (c)*, *subsections (8)* to *(15)* of *section 790AA* shall, with any necessary modifications, apply as if any reference in those subsections—

(i) to the administrator were a reference to the qualifying fund manager,

(ii) to a relevant pension arrangement were a reference to an approved retirement fund, and

(iii) to an excess lump sum were a reference to a distribution of a kind referred to in *paragraph (c)*.][25]

(5) For the purposes of this section, *Chapter 1* of *Part 26* shall apply as if references in that Chapter to pension business were references to moneys held in an approved retirement fund.

(6) Notwithstanding *Chapter 4* of *Part 8*, that Chapter shall apply to a deposit (within the meaning of that Chapter) where the deposit consists of money held by a qualifying fund manager in that capacity as if such a deposit were not a relevant deposit (within the meaning of that Chapter).

(7)

[(a) At any time when the qualifying fund manager—

(i) is not resident in the State, or

(ii) is not trading in the State through a fixed place of business,

the qualifying fund manager shall, in relation to the discharge of all duties and obligations relating to approved retirement funds which are imposed on the qualifying fund manager by virtue of this Chapter—

(I) enter into a contract with the Revenue Commissioners enforceable in a Member State of the European Communities in relation to the discharge of those duties and obligations and in entering into such a contract the parties to the contract shall acknowledge and agree in writing that—

(A) it shall be governed solely by the laws of the State, and

(B) that the courts of the State shall have exclusive jurisdiction in determining any dispute arising under it,

or

(II) ensure that there is a person resident in the State, appointed by the qualifying fund manager, who will be responsible for the discharge of all of those duties and obligations and shall notify the Revenue Commissioners of the appointment of that person and the identity of that person.][26]

(b) A qualifying fund manager shall be liable to pay to the Collector-General income tax which the fund manager is required to deduct from any distribution by virtue of this Chapter and the individual beneficially entitled to assets held in an approved retirement fund, including the personal representatives of a deceased individual who was so entitled prior to that individual's death, shall allow such deduction; but where there are no funds or insufficient funds available out of which the qualifying fund manager may satisfy the tax required to be deducted, the amount of such tax for which there are insufficient funds available shall be a debt due to the qualifying fund manager from the individual beneficially entitled to the asset in the approved retirement fund or from the estate of the deceased individual, as the case may be.][27]

[(8) (a) Within one month of commencing to act as manager of approved retirement funds, a qualifying fund manager shall give notice to that effect to the Revenue Commissioners.

(b) A qualifying fund manager who commenced to act as manager of an approved retirement fund prior to the passing of the *Finance Act 2003* shall give notice to that effect to the Revenue Commissioners within three months of the passing of that Act.

(c) A notice under *paragraph (a)* or *(b)* shall specify the date the qualifying fund manager commenced to so act.][28]

[(9) The Revenue Commissioners may by notice in writing require a qualifying fund manager or the person appointed under *subsection (7)(a)(II)*, as the case may be, to provide within 30 days of the date of such notice, such information and particulars as may be specified in the notice as they may reasonably require for the purposes of this Chapter, and without prejudice to the generality of the foregoing, such information and particulars may include—

(a) the name, address and tax reference number of the individual in whose name the approved retirement fund is or was held,

(b) the name, address and tax reference number of any individual to whom any distribution has been made, and

(c) the amount of any distributions referred to in *paragraph (b)*.][29]

Amendments

[1] Substituted by FA00 s23(1)(d)(i)(I).

[2] Repealed by ACC BA01 s12 and S.I. No 69 of 2002 with effect from 28 February 2002.

[3] Repealed by ICC BA00 s7 and ICC BA00 (Sections 5 and 7) (Commencement) Order S.I. No 46 of 2001 with effect from 12 February 2001.

[4] Substituted by FA00 s23(1)(d)(i)(II).

[5] Substituted by FA00 s23(1)(d)(i)(III).

[6] Substituted by FA14 s19(2)(a)(i). Has effect on and from 23 October 2014.

[7] Inserted by FA00 s23(1)(d)(ii).

[8] Inserted by FA14 s19(2)(a)(ii). Has effect on and from 23 October 2014.

[9] Deleted by FA06 s14(1)(b)(iii)(I)(A). Has effect as on and from 2 February 2006.

[10] Substituted by FA14 s19(2)(a)(iii)(I). Has effect on and from 23 October 2014.

[11] Substituted by FA14 s19(2)(a)(iii)(II). Has effect on and from 23 October 2014.

[12] Inserted by FA06 s14(1)(b)(iii)(I)(C). Has effect as on and from 2 February 2006.

[13] Inserted by FA14 s19(2)(a)(iii)(III). Has effect on and from 23 October 2014.

[14] Deleted by FA12 s18(3)(a). Has effect from 1 January 2012.

[15] Substituted by FA12 s18(3)(b). Has effect from 1 January 2012.

[16] Inserted by FA06 s14(1)(b)(iii)(III). Has effect as on and from 1 January 2006.

[17] Substituted by FA12 s18(3)(c). Has effect from 1 January 2012.

[18] Inserted by FA03 s14(1)(c)(ii). Shall be taken to have come into force and has effect as on and from 6 February 2003.

[19] Substituted by FA12 s18(3)(d). Has effect from 8 February 2012.

[20] Substituted by FA05 s21(1)(b)(ii)(I). Applies as respects any annuity contract for the time being approved by the Revenue Commissioners entered into on or after 1 January 2005.

[21] Substituted by FA14 s19(2)(a)(iv). Has effect on and from 1 January 2015.

[22] Substituted by F(No.3)A11 sched1(202).

[23] Substituted by FA12 s134(1)(e). Has effect as if it had come into operation for the year of assessment (within the meaning of the Income Tax Acts and the Capital Gains Tax Acts) 2011 and each subsequent year of assessment.

[24] Substituted by F(No.3)A11 sched1(203).

[25] Substituted by FA12 s18(3)(f). Has effect as on and from 31 March 2012.

[26] Substituted by FA05 s21(1)(b)(ii)(II). Applies as respects any annuity contract for the time being approved by the Revenue Commissioners entered into on or after 1 January 2005.

[27] Substituted by FA00 s23(1)(d)(iii). Shall apply as regards an approved retirement fund or an approved minimum retirement fund, as the case may be, where the assets in the fund were first accepted into the fund by the qualifying fund manager on or after 6 April 2000.

[28] Inserted by FA03 s14(1)(c)(iii). Has effect as on and from 28 March 2003

[29] Inserted by FA05 s21(1)(b)(ii)(III). Applies as respects any annuity contract for the time being approved by the Revenue Commissioners entered into on or after 1 January 2005.

Revenue Briefings

eBrief

eBrief No. 29/2007 – Approved Retirement Funds
eBrief No. 72/2011 – The extended "ARF option" and Buy-Out-Bonds

Cross References

From Section 784A

Section 172A Interpretation.
Section 237 Annual payments payable wholly out of taxed income.
Section 256 Interpretation (Chapter 4).
Section 548 Valuation of assets.
Section 706 Interpretation and general (Part 26).
Section 784B Conditions relating to an approved retirement fund.
Section 784C Approved minimum retirement fund.
Section 885 Obligation to show tax reference number on receipts.
Section 960 Date for payment of income tax other than under self assessment.
Section 983 Interpretation (Chapter 4).

To Section 784A

Section 172A Interpretation.
Section 739D Gain arising on a chargeable event.
Section 770 Interpretation and supplemental (Chapter 1).
Section 772 Conditions for approval of schemes and discretionary approval.
Section 779A Transactions deemed to be pensions in payment.
Section 783 Interpretation and general (Chapter 2).
Section 784C Approved minimum retirement fund.
Section 787A Interpretation and supplemental.
Section 787G Taxation of payments from a PRSA.
Section 787H Approved Retirement Fund option.
Section 787O Interpretation and general (Chapter 2C).
Section 788 Capital element in certain purchased annuities.
Schedule 29 Provisions Referred to in Sections 1052, 1053 and 1054

784B Conditions relating to an approved retirement fund

[(1) The conditions of this section are—

(a) an approved retirement fund shall be held by a qualifying fund manager in the name of the individual who is beneficially entitled to the assets in the fund,

(b) assets held in an approved retirement fund shall consist of and only of one or more of—

(i) assets transferred to the fund by virtue of an option exercised by the individual in accordance with *section 784(2A)*,

(ii) assets which were previously held in another approved retirement fund held in the name of the individual or the individual's deceased [spouse or civil partner][1], and

(iii) assets derived from such assets as are referred to in *subparagraphs (i)* and *(ii)*,

(c) the individual referred to in *paragraph (a)* shall, on the opening of an approved retirement fund, make a declaration of the kind mentioned in *paragraph (d)* to the qualifying fund manager, and

(d) the declaration referred to in *paragraph (c)* shall be a declaration, in writing, to the qualifying fund manager which—

(i) is made by the individual who is beneficially entitled to the assets in the approved retirement fund,

(ii) is made in such form as may be prescribed or authorised by the Revenue Commissioners,

(iii) contains the full name, address and tax reference number of the individual referred to in *subparagraph (i)*,

(iv) declares that the assets included in the fund consist only of assets referred to in *paragraph (b)* to which the individual was beneficially entitled, and

(v) contains such other information as the Revenue Commissioners may reasonably require for the purposes of this Act.

(2) A qualifying fund manager shall not accept any assets into an approved retirement fund unless the fund manager receives a certificate to which *subsection (3)* applies in relation to those assets from a person lawfully carrying on in the State the business of granting annuities on human life or from another qualifying fund manager.

(3) A certificate to which this subsection applies is a certificate stating—

(a) that the assets in relation to which the certificate refers are assets to which the individual named on the certificate is beneficially entitled and which are being transferred to the approved retirement fund, or have previously been transferred to an approved retirement fund, in accordance with *subsection (2A)* of *section 784*,

(b) that the assets in relation to which the certificate is given do not form part of an approved minimum retirement fund within the meaning of *section 784C*, and

(c) the amount of the balance on the income and gains account, and the residue in relation to the approved retirement fund, the assets of which are being transferred or assigned to the qualifying fund manager.

(4) *Subsection (2)* of *section 263* shall apply to a declaration made in accordance with *subsection (1)(c)* or a certificate to which *subsection (3)* applies as it applies in relation to declarations of a kind mentioned in that section.

(5) The Minister for Finance may by order specify requirements regarding the operation of approved retirement funds.][2]

Amendments

[1] Substituted by F(No.3)A11 sched1(204).

[2] Inserted by FA99 s19(1)(b)(iii). Paragraph (b), other than subparagraph (vi), of subsection (1) shall apply as respects any annuity contract for the time being approved by the Revenue Commissioners under section 784 entered into on or after the 6th day of April, 1999.

Cross References

From Section 784B

Section 263 Declarations relating to deposits of non-residents.
Section 784 Retirement annuities: relief for premiums.
Section 784C Approved minimum retirement fund.

To Section 784B

Section 772 Conditions for approval of schemes and discretionary approval.
Section 784A Approved retirement fund.
Section 784C Approved minimum retirement fund.

784C Approved minimum retirement fund

[(1) In this section, "*an approved minimum retirement fund*" means a fund managed by a qualifying fund manager (within the meaning of *section 784A*) and which complies with the conditions of *section 784D*.

(2) Subject to *subsections (3)* and *(4)*, where an individual, who has not attained the age of 75 years, exercises an option in accordance with *subsection (2A)* of *section 784*, the amount referred to as B in the formula in the said subsection which the person with whom the annuity contract is made shall—

(a) transfer to an approved minimum retirement fund in respect of that individual, or

[(b) apply in the purchase of an annuity payable to the individual,

[shall be the lesser of—

(i) the amount referred to as A in that formula, and

(ii) €63,500.][1]][2]

(3) Where the individual has already exercised an option in accordance with *subsection (2A)* of *section 784*, the amount referred to as B in the formula in *subsection (2A)* shall be such amount as will result in the aggregate of the amount required in respect of all such options, in accordance with *subsection (2A)*, to be transferred to an approved minimum retirement fund or applied in the purchase of an annuity payable to the individual being the lesser of—

(a) the aggregate of the amount referred to as A in that formula in relation to each contract, [and][3]

[(b) €63,500.][4]

(4) [(a) Where, at the date of exercise of an option under *section 784(2A)*, the individual by whom the option is exercised is in receipt of specified income amounting to €12,700 per annum, the amount referred to as B in the formula in that section shall be nil.][5]

(b) For the purposes of this subsection, "*specified income*" means a pension or annuity which is payable for the life of the individual, including a pension payable under the [Social Welfare Consolidation Act 2005,][6] and any pension to which the provisions of section 200 apply.

(5) Subject to *subsection (6)*, the qualifying fund manager shall not make any payment or transfer of assets out of the approved minimum retirement fund [, including any distribution or amount regarded under this Chapter as a distribution, other than—][7]

(a) a transfer of all the assets of the fund to another qualifying fund manager to be held as an approved minimum retirement fund, or

[(b) a payment or transfer, on one occasion only, in any tax year (being a year of assessment for tax purposes) to the individual beneficially entitled to the assets in the fund of an amount that does not exceed 4 per cent of the value of the assets of the fund at the time of the payment or transfer.][8]

[(6) Where the individual referred to in *subsection (2)*—

(a) attains the age of 75 years,

(b) is in receipt of specified income referred to in *subsection (4)* at any date (in this paragraph referred to as the "*first-mentioned date*") after the date of the exercise of an option under *section 784(2A)* of an amount which would, if the option had been exercised on the first-mentioned date, have resulted in B in the formula in *section 784(2A)* being nil, or

(c) dies,

the approved minimum retirement fund shall, thereupon, become an approved retirement fund and *section 784A*, *subsections (1)* and *(5)* of *section 784B* and *section 784E* shall apply accordingly.][9]

[(6A) Where before the date of passing of the *Finance Act 2011*, the individual referred to in *subsection (2)* has exercised an option in accordance with *section 784(2A)* and the person with whom the annuity contract is made has, before that date, transferred the amount referred to as B in the formula in that section to an approved minimum retirement fund in respect of that individual, *subsection (6)* shall apply for the period of 3 years from the date of passing of the *Finance Act 2011* as if the following paragraph were substituted for *paragraph (b)* of that subsection:

'(b) is in receipt of specified income of €12,700 at any time in the period of 3 years from the date of passing of the *Finance Act 2011*, or'.][10]

[(7) The provisions of *section 784A* shall, with any necessary modifications, apply to income and chargeable gains arising from, and to distributions in respect of assets, held in an approved minimum retirement fund as they apply to assets held in an approved retirement fund.][11]

[...][12][13]

Amendments

[1] Substituted by FA13 s17(2)(a). Shall apply as respects the exercise of an option in accordance with section 772(3A)(a), 784(2A) or 787H(1) on or after 27 March 2013.

[2] Substituted by FA11 s(19)(2)(b). Shall apply as respects the exercise of an option in accordance with section 772(3A)(a), 784(2A) or 787H(1) on or after 6 February 2011.

[3] Substituted by FA11 s(19)(2)(c). Shall apply as respects the exercise of an option in accordance with section 772(3A)(a), 784(2A) or 787H(1) on or after 6 February 2011.

[4] Substituted by FA13 s17(2)(b). Shall apply as respects the exercise of an option in accordance with section 772(3A)(a), 784(2A) or 787H(1) on or after 27 March 2013.

[5] Substituted by FA13 s17(2)(c). Shall apply as respects the exercise of an option in accordance with section 772(3A)(a), 784(2A) or 787H(1) on or after 27 March 2013.

[6] Substituted by FA07 sched4(1)(y). Shall have effect as on and from 2 April 2007

[7] Substituted by FA03 s14(1)(c)(iv). Shall be taken to have come into force and has effect as on and from 6 February 2003.

[8] Substituted by FA14 s19(2)(b). Has effect on and from 1 January 2015.

[9] Substituted by FA11 s(19)(2)(f). Deemed to have effect on and from 6 February 2011 as per FA13s17(5).

[10] Inserted by FA11 s(19)(2)(g). Has effect as on and from 6 February 2011.

[11] Substituted by FA00 s23(1)(e)(i). Shall apply as regards an approved retirement fund or an approved minimum retirement fund, as the case may be, where the assets in the fund were first accepted into the fund by the qualifying fund manager on or after 6 April 2000.

[12] Deleted by FA00 s23(1)(e)(ii). Shall apply as regards an approved retirement fund or an approved minimum retirement fund, as the case may be, where the assets in the fund were first accepted into the fund by the qualifying fund manager on or after 6 April 2000.

[13] Inserted by FA99 s19(1)(b)(iii). Paragraph (b), other than subparagraph (vi), of subsection (1) shall apply as respects any annuity contract for the time being approved by the Revenue Commissioners under section 784 entered into on or after the 6th day of April, 1999.

Special Note

FA13 s17(6) which cannot be consolidated provides as follows:

(6) (a) In this subsection—

"approved minimum retirement fund" has the meaning assigned to it by section 784C(1)

"non ring-fenced amount", in relation to a vested PRSA, means the amount or value of assets in the vested PRSA that the PRSA administrator can make available to, or pay to, the PRSA contributor or to any other person;

"Personal Retirement Savings Account", "contributor" and "PRSA administrator" have the meanings assigned to them by section 787A(1)

"relevant option" means an option exercised in accordance with section 772(3A)(a), 784(2A) or 787H(1);

"ring-fenced amount", in relation to a vested PRSA, means an amount retained within the vested PRSA by the PRSA administrator equivalent to the amount which the PRSA administrator would, if an option had been exercised in accordance with section 787H(1), have had to transfer to an approved minimum retirement fund in accordance with section 784C and by virtue of section 787H(3);

"specified income" has the meaning assigned to it by section 784C(4)(b);

"vested PRSA" means a Personal Retirement Savings Account in respect of which assets have first been made available to, or paid to, the contributor by the PRSA administrator on or after 6 February 2011, and the term

"vesting of a PRSA" shall be construed accordingly.

(b) Where on or after 6 February 2011 and before the date of passing of this Act one or more than one relevant option is exercised by an individual, or an individual has one or more than one vested PRSA, and in the exercise of the relevant option or options or in the vesting of the PRSA or PRSAs, an amount or value of assets is transferred to an approved minimum retirement fund (by way of one or more than one transfer) or, as the case may be, is a ringfenced amount (in this paragraph referred to as the "relevant amount", and where this term is used in the context of a ring-fenced amount it shall, where there is more than one ring-fenced amount, be construed as meaning the aggregate of the ring-fenced amounts), then where the individual—

(i) has specified income of not less than €12,700 on or after the date of passing of this Act—

(I) the approved minimum retirement fund shall thereupon become an approved retirement fund (in respect of which section 784A and subsections (1) and (5) of section 784B of the Principal Act shall accordingly apply), or

(II) the ring-fenced amount or, as the case may be, each ring-fenced amount shall thereupon become a non ring-fenced amount,

(ii) has specified income of less than €12,700 on the date of passing of this Act in circumstances where the relevant amount is greater than €63,500—

(I) the approved minimum retirement fund shall, to the extent of the excess of the relevant amount over €63,500, thereupon become an approved retirement fund (in respect of which section 784A and subsections (1) and (5) of section 784B of the Principal Act shall accordingly apply), or

(II) the ring-fenced amount or, as the case may be, so much of each ring-fenced amount determined in accordance with *paragraph (c)* shall, to the extent of the excess of the relevant amount over €63,500 thereupon become a non ring-fenced amount.

(c) For the purposes of giving effect to *paragraph (b)(ii)(II)*, where more than one vested PRSA has a ring-fenced amount the individual shall determine how much of each ring-fenced amount shall become a non ring-fenced amount.

Cross References

From Section 784C

Section 784 Retirement annuities: relief for premiums.
Section 784A Approved retirement fund.
Section 784B Conditions relating to an approved retirement fund.
Section 784D Conditions relating to an approved minimum retirement fund.
Section 784E Returns, and payment of tax, by qualifying fund managers.

To Section 784C

Section 172A Interpretation.
Section 770 Interpretation and supplemental (Chapter 1).
Section 772 Conditions for approval of schemes and discretionary approval.
Section 783 Interpretation and general (Chapter 2).
Section 784 Retirement annuities: relief for premiums.
Section 784A Approved retirement fund.
Section 784B Conditions relating to an approved retirement fund.
Section 784D Conditions relating to an approved minimum retirement fund.
Section 787A Interpretation and supplemental.
Section 787H Approved Retirement Fund option.
Section 787O Interpretation and general (Chapter 2C).

784D Conditions relating to an approved minimum retirement fund

[(1) The conditions of this section are—

(a) an approved minimum retirement fund shall be held in the name of the individual who is beneficially entitled to the assets in the fund,

(b) assets held in an approved minimum retirement fund shall consist of one or more of the following—

(i) assets transferred to the fund by virtue of an option exercised by the individual in accordance with *section 784(2A)*,

(ii) assets which were previously held in another approved minimum retirement fund held in the name of the individual, and

(iii) assets derived from such assets as are referred to in *subparagraphs (i)* and *(ii)*,

(c) the individual referred to in *paragraph (a)* shall make a declaration of the kind mentioned in *paragraph (d)* to the qualifying fund manager,

(d) the declaration referred to in *paragraph (c)* shall be a declaration, in writing, to the qualifying fund manager which—

(i) is made by the individual who is beneficially entitled to the assets in the approved minimum retirement fund,

(ii) is made in such form as may be prescribed or authorised by the Revenue Commissioners,

(iii) contains the full name, address and tax reference number of the individual referred to in *subparagraph (i)*,

(iv) declares that assets included in the fund consist only of assets referred to in *paragraph (b)* to which the individual was beneficially entitled in accordance with *section 784(2A)*, and

(v) contains such other information as the Revenue Commissioners may reasonably require for the purposes of this Act.

(2) A qualifying fund manager shall not accept any assets into an approved minimum retirement fund unless the fund manager receives a certificate to which *subsection (3)* applies in relation to those assets from a person lawfully carrying on in the State the business of granting annuities on human life or from another qualifying fund manager.

(3) A certificate to which this subsection applies is a certificate stating—

(a) that the assets in relation to which the certificate is given are the assets of an approved minimum retirement fund to which the individual named on the certificate is beneficially entitled and which are being transferred to the approved minimum retirement fund or have previously been transferred to such a fund in accordance with *subsection (2A)* of *section 784*,

(b) in the case of assets transferred by another qualifying fund manager, the amount or value of assets transferred to the approved minimum retirement fund for the purposes of *subsection (3)* of *section 784C*.

(4) *Subsection (2)* of *section 263* shall apply to a declaration made in accordance with *subsection (1)(c)* or a certificate to which *subsection (3)* applies as it applies in relation to declarations of a kind mentioned in that section.

(5) The Minister for Finance may specify requirements regarding the operation of approved minimum retirement funds.][1]

Amendments

[1] Inserted by FA99 s19(1)(b)(iii). Paragraph (b), other than subparagraph (vi), of subsection (1) shall apply as respects any annuity contract for the time being approved by the Revenue Commissioners under section 784 entered into on or after the 6th day of April, 1999.

Cross References

From Section 784D

Section 263 Declarations relating to deposits of non-residents.
Section 784 Retirement annuities: relief for premiums.
Section 784C Approved minimum retirement fund.

To Section 784D

Section 772 Conditions for approval of schemes and discretionary approval.
Section 784C Approved minimum retirement fund.
Section 787H Approved Retirement Fund option.

784E Returns, and payment of tax, by qualifying fund managers [Deleted]

Deleted by FA00 s23(1)(f). Shall apply as regards an approved retirement fund or an approved minimum retirement fund, as the case may be, where the assets in the fund were first accepted into the fund by the qualifying fund manager on or after 6 April 2000.

Cross References

To Section 784E

Section 772 Conditions for approval of schemes and discretionary approval.
Section 784C Approved minimum retirement fund.

785 Approval of contracts for dependants or for life assurance

[ITA67 s235A(1) to (6); FA74 s66]

(1) The Revenue Commissioners may approve for the purposes of this Chapter a contract made by an individual with a person (in *subsection (2)* referred to as "*the insurer*") lawfully carrying on in the State the business of granting annuities on human life if—

(a) the main benefit secured by the contract is the provision of an annuity for the [wife, husband or civil partner][1] of the individual or for any one or more dependants of the individual, or

(b) the sole benefit secured by the contract is the provision of a lump sum on the death of the individual before he or she attains the age of [75 years][2], being a lump sum payable to the individual's personal representatives.

[(1A) For the purposes of *subsection (1)*, the reference in *subsection (1)* to a person lawfully carrying on in the State the business of granting annuities on human life shall include a reference to an insurance undertaking, authorised to transact insurance business in the State under Directive 2002/83/EC of the European Parliament and of the Council of 5 November 2002*, that—

* OJ No. L345, 19.12.2002, p.1

(a) is not resident in the State, or

(b) is not trading in the State through a fixed place of business.][3]

(2) The Revenue Commissioners shall not approve a contract made by an individual with the insurer under *subsection (1)(a)* unless it appears to them to satisfy the following conditions—

(a) that any annuity payable to the [wife, husband, civil partner or dependant][4] of the individual commences on the death of the individual;

(b) that any annuity payable under the contract to the individual commences at a time after the individual attains the age of 60 years and, unless the individual's annuity is one to commence on the death of a person to whom an annuity would be payable under the contract if that person survived the individual, cannot commence after the time when the individual attains the age of [75 years][5];

(c) that the contract does not provide for the payment by the insurer of any sum, other than any annuity payable to the individual's [wife, husband, civil partner or dependant][6] or to the individual except, in the event of no annuity becoming payable under the contract, any sums payable to the individual's personal representatives by means of return of premiums, reasonable interest on premiums or bonuses out of profits;

(d) that the contract does not provide for the payment of any annuity otherwise than for the life of the annuitant;

(e) that the contract provides that no annuity payable under it shall be capable in whole or in part of surrender, commutation or assignment.

(3) The Revenue Commissioners may, if they think fit and subject to any conditions they think proper to impose, approve a contract under *subsection (1)(a)*, notwithstanding that in one or more respects it does not appear to them to satisfy the conditions specified in *subsection (2)*.

(4) *Subsections (2)* and *(3)* of *section 784* shall not apply to the approval of a contract under this section.

(5) The Revenue Commissioners may approve a trust scheme or part of a trust scheme otherwise satisfying the conditions specified in *paragraphs (a)* to *(c)* of *section 784(4)*, notwithstanding that its main purpose is to provide annuities for the [wives, husbands, civil partners and dependants][7] of the individuals, or lump sums payable to the individuals' personal representatives on death, and—

(a) *subsections (1)* to *(4)* shall apply with any necessary modifications in relation to such approval,

(b) this Chapter shall apply to the scheme or part of the scheme when so approved as it applies to a contract approved under this section, and

(c) the exemption from income tax provided in *section 784(4)* shall apply to the scheme or part of the scheme when so approved.

(6) Except where otherwise provided in this Chapter, any reference in the Income Tax Acts to a contract, scheme or part of a scheme approved under *section 784* shall include a reference to a contract, scheme or part of a scheme approved under this section.

Amendments

[1] Substituted by F(No.3)A11 sched1(205).

[2, 5] Substituted by FA99 s19(1)(b)(iv). Paragraph (b), other than subparagraph (vi), of subsection (1) shall apply as respects any annuity contract for the time being approved by the Revenue Commissioners under section 784 entered into on or after the 6th day of April, 1999.

[3] Inserted by FA05 s21(1)(b)(iv). Applies as respects any annuity contract for the time being approved by the Revenue Commissioners entered into on or after 1 January 2005.

[4] Substituted by F(No.3)A11 sched1(206).

[6] Substituted by F(No.3)A11 sched1(207).

[7] Substituted by F(No.3)A11 sched1(208).

Cross References

From Section 785

Section 784 Retirement annuities: relief for premiums.

To Section 785

Section 172A Interpretation.
Section 256 Interpretation (Chapter 4).
Section 608 Superannuation funds.
Section 706 Interpretation and general (Part 26).
Section 739B Interpretation and application.
Section 784 Retirement annuities: relief for premiums.
Section 786 Approval of certain other contracts.
Section 787 Nature and amount of relief for qualifying premiums.
Schedule 2A Dividend Withholding Tax
Schedule 2B Investment Undertakings: Declarations
Schedule 31 Consequential Amendments

786 Approval of certain other contracts

[FA79 s28(1) to (3)]

[(1) The Revenue Commissioners shall not approve an annuity contract under *section 784* unless the contract provides that the individual by whom it is made may require a sum representing the value of his or her accrued rights under the contract—

(a) to be paid by the person with whom it is made to such other person as the individual may specify, and

(b) to be applied by such other person in payment of the premium or other consideration under an annuity contract made between the individual and that other person and approved by the Revenue Commissioners under that section,

if the first-mentioned contract is otherwise to be approved by the Revenue Commissioners under that section.][1]

(2) References in *subsection (1)* to the individual by whom a contract is made include references to any [widow, widower, surviving civil partner or dependant][2] having accrued rights under the contract.

(3) Where, in accordance with a provision of the kind referred to in *subsection (1)* of an annuity contract approved under *section 784* or a corresponding provision of a contract approved under *section 785(1)(a)*, a sum representing the value of accrued rights under one contract (in this subsection referred to as "*the original contract*") is paid by means of premium or other consideration under another contract (in this subsection referred to as "*the substituted contract*"), any annuity payable under the substituted contract shall be treated as earned income of the annuitant to the same extent that an annuity under the original contract would have been so treated.

Amendments

[1] Substituted by FA99 s19(1)(b)(v). Paragraph (b), other than subparagraph (vi), of subsection (1) shall apply as respects any annuity contract for the time being approved by the Revenue Commissioners under section 784 entered into on or after the 6th day of April, 1999.

[2] Substituted by F(No.3)A11 sched1(209).

Cross References

From Section 786

Section 784 Retirement annuities: relief for premiums.

Section 785 Approval of contracts for dependants or for life assurance.

To Section 786

Section 706 Interpretation and general (Part 26).

Section 784 Retirement annuities: relief for premiums.

Section 788 Capital element in certain purchased annuities.

787 Nature and amount of relief for qualifying premiums

[ITA67 s236(1) to (2B), (3) to (9) and (11), s238(1) and (2); F(MP)A68 s3(2) and Sch PtI; FA74 s67(1) and (2); FA75 s33(2) and Sch1 PtII; FA78 s4; FA90 s27(1); FA96 s13(a)]

(1) For the purposes of relief under this section, an individual's relevant earnings shall be those earnings before giving effect to any deduction to be made from those earnings in respect of a loss or in respect of a capital allowance (within the meaning of *section 2*), and references to income in this section (other than references to total income) shall be construed similarly.

(2) For the purposes of this section, "*net relevant earnings*", in relation to an individual and subject to *subsections (3)* to *(5)*, means the amount of the individual's relevant earnings for the year of assessment in question less the amount of any deductions to be made from the relevant earnings in computing the individual's total income for that year, being either—

(a) deductions in respect of payments made by the individual, or

(b) deductions in respect of losses or of such allowances mentioned in *subsection (1)*, being losses or allowances arising from activities, profits or gains of which would be included in computing relevant earnings of the individual or of the individual's [spouse or civil partner][1] for the year of assessment.

[(2A) Notwithstanding *subsection (2)*, for the purposes of relief under this section an individual's net relevant earnings [shall not exceed the earnings limit][2] or such other amount as shall be specified in regulations made by the Minister for Finance.

(2B) Where regulations are proposed to be made under *subsection (2A)*, a draft of the regulations shall be laid before Dáil Éireann and the regulations shall not be made until a resolution approving of the draft has been passed by Dáil Éireann.][3]

(3) Where in any year of assessment for which an individual claims and is allowed relief under this section there is to be made in computing the total income of the individual or of the individual's [spouse or civil partner][4] a deduction in respect of any such loss or allowance of the individual referred to in *subsection (2)(b)*, and the deduction or part of it is to be so made from income other than relevant earnings, then, the amount of the deduction made from that other income shall be treated as reducing the individual's net relevant earnings for subsequent years of assessment and shall be deducted as far as may be from those of the following year, whether or not the individual claims or is entitled to claim relief under this section for that year, and in so far as it cannot be so deducted, then from those of the next year, and so on.

(4) Where an individual's income for any year of assessment consists partly of relevant earnings and partly of other income, then, as far as may be, any deductions to be made in computing the individual's total income, and which may be treated in whole or in part either as made from relevant earnings or as made from other income, shall be treated for the purposes of this section as being made from those relevant earnings in so far as they are deductions in respect of any such loss referred to in *subsection (2)(b)* and otherwise as being made from that other income.

(5) An individual's net relevant earnings for any year of assessment shall be computed without regard to any relief to be given for that year under this section either to the individual or to the individual's [spouse or civil partner][5].

(6) Where relief is to be given under this section in respect of any qualifying premium paid by an individual, the amount of that premium shall, subject to this section, be deducted from or set off against the individual's relevant earnings for the year of assessment in which the premium is paid.

(7) Where in relation to a year of assessment a qualifying premium is paid after the end of the year of assessment but [on or before the specified return date for the chargeable period (within the meaning of [*Part 41A*][6])][7], the premium may, if the individual so elects on or before that date, be treated for the purposes of this section as paid in the earlier year (and not in the year in which it is paid); but where—

(a) the amount of that premium, together with any qualifying premiums paid by the individual in the year to which the assessment relates (or treated as so paid by virtue of any previous election under this subsection), exceeds the maximum amount of the reduction which may be made under this section in the individual's relevant earnings for that year, or

(b) the amount of that premium itself exceeds the increase in that maximum amount which is due to taking into account the income on which the assessment is made,

the election shall have no effect as respects the excess.

[(8) Subject to this section, the amount which may be deducted or set off in any year of assessment (whether in respect of one or more qualifying premiums and whether or not including premiums in respect of a contract approved under *section 785*) shall not be more than—

(a) in the case of an individual who at any time during the year of assessment was of the age of 30 years or over but had not attained the age of 40 years, 20 per cent,

(b) in the case of an individual who at any time during the year of assessment was of the age of 40 years or over but had not attained the age of 50 years, 25 per cent,

[…][8]

[(c) in the case of an individual who at any time during the year of assessment was of the age of 50 years or over but had not attained the age of 55 years or who for the year of assessment was a specified individual, 30 per cent,

(d) in the case of an individual who at any time during the year of assessment was of the age of 55 years or over but had not attained the age of 60 years, 35 per cent,

(e) in the case of an individual who at any time during the year of assessment was of the age of 60 years or over, 40 per cent, and

(f) in any other case, 15 per cent,][9]

of the individual's net relevant earnings for that year, and the amount to be deducted shall to the greatest extent possible include qualifying premiums in respect of contracts approved under *section 785*.

(8A) For the purposes of this section, "*specified individual*", in relation to a year of assessment, means an individual whose relevant earnings for the year of assessment were derived wholly or mainly from an occupation or profession specified in *Schedule 23A*.

(8B) The Minister for Finance may, after consultation with the Minister for Tourism, Sport and Recreation, by regulations extend or restrict the meaning of specified individual by adding or deleting one or more occupations or professions to or from, as the case may be, the list of occupations and professions specified in *Schedule 23A*.

(8C) Where regulations are proposed to be made under *subsection (8B)*, a draft of the regulations shall be laid before Dáil Éireann and the regulations shall not be made until a resolution approving of the draft has been passed by Dáil Éireann.][10]

[…][11]

[(10) Where in any year of assessment a reduction or a greater reduction would be made under this section in the relevant earnings of an individual but for an insufficiency of net relevant earnings, the amount of the reduction which would have been made but for that reason, less the amount of the reduction which is made in that year, shall be carried forward to the next year of assessment, and shall be treated for the purposes of relief under this section as the amount of a qualifying premium paid in the next year of assessment.][12]

(11) If and in so far as an amount once carried forward under *subsection (10)* (and treated as the amount of a qualifying premium paid in the next year of assessment) is not deducted from or set off against the individual's net relevant earnings for that year of assessment, it shall be carried forward again to the following year of assessment (and treated as the amount of a qualifying premium paid in that year of assessment), and so on for succeeding years.

[…][13]

(13) Where relief under this section for any year of assessment is claimed and allowed (whether or not relief is then to be given for that year), and afterwards there is made [any assessment, amendment of an assessment][14], or other adjustment of the claimant's liability to tax, there shall be made also such adjustments, if any, as are consequential thereon in the relief allowed or given under this section for that or any subsequent year of assessment.

(14) Where relief under this section is claimed and allowed for any year of assessment in respect of any payment, relief shall not be given in respect of that payment

under any other provision of the Income Tax Acts for the same or a later year of assessment nor (in the case of a payment under an annuity contract) in respect of any other premium or consideration for an annuity under the same contract.

(15) Relief shall not be given under this section in respect of a qualifying premium except on a claim made to and allowed by the inspector, but any person aggrieved by any decision of the inspector on any such claim may, on giving notice in writing to the inspector within 21 days after the notification to that person of the decision, appeal to the Appeal Commissioners.

(16) The Appeal Commissioners shall hear and determine an appeal to them under *subsection (15)* as if it were an appeal to them against an assessment to income tax, and the provisions of the Income Tax Acts relating to the rehearing of an appeal and to the statement of a case for the opinion of the High Court on a point of law shall, with the necessary modifications, apply accordingly.

Amendments

[1, 4, 5] Substituted by F(No.3)A11 sched1(210).

[2] Substituted by FA06 s14(1)(b)(iv)(I). Has effect as on and from 1 January 2006.

[3] Inserted by FA99 s19(1)(b)(vi)(I). Subparagraph (vi) of paragraph (b), and paragraph (c), of subsection (1) shall apply as respects the year of assessment 1999-2000 and subsequent years.

[6, 14] Substituted by FA12 sched4(part 2)(g).

[7] Substituted by FA98 s46.

[8] Deleted by FA06 s14(1)(b)(iv)(II). Has effect as on and from 1 January 2006.

[9] Inserted by FA06 s14(1)(b)(iv)(III). Has effect as on and from 1 January 2006.

[10] Substituted by FA99 s19(1)(b)(vi)(II). Subparagraph (vi) of paragraph (b), and paragraph (c), of subsection (1) shall apply as respects the year of assessment 1999-2000 and subsequent years.

[11] Deleted by FA01 s18(b)(iii)(I).

[12] Substituted by FA01 s18(b)(iii)(II).

[13] Deleted by FA01 s18(b)(iii)(III).

Revenue Briefings

Tax Briefing

Tax Briefing October 1997 – Issue 28 pg 10 – GMS Superannuation Plan – Retirement Relief
Tax Briefing July 2001 – Issue 44 pg 27 – Retirement Annuity Contracts

eBrief

eBrief No. 61/09 – Tax Relief for Pension Contributions – Late Elections

Cross References

From Section 787

Section 2 Interpretation of Tax Acts.
Section 785 Approval of contracts for dependants or for life assurance.
Section 950 Interpretation (Part 41).

To Section 787

Section 3 Interpretation of Income Tax Acts.
Section 480A Relief on retirement for certain income of certain sportspersons.
Section 784 Retirement annuities: relief for premiums.
Section 787N Qualifying overseas pension plans: relief for contributions.
Section 788 Capital element in certain purchased annuities.
Section 790A Limit on earnings.
Section 823 Deduction for income earned outside the State.
Section 847A Donations to certain sports bodies.
Section 848A Donations to approved bodies.

Schedule 23A Specified Occupations and Professions
Schedule 31 Consequential Amendments

CHAPTER 2A

Personal Retirement Savings Accounts

787A Interpretation and supplemental

[(1) In this Chapter, unless the context otherwise requires—

"*additional voluntary PRSA contributions*" means contributions made to a PRSA by an employee, who is a member of an approved scheme or of a statutory scheme, which are—

(i) contributions made under a rule or part of a rule, as the case may be, of a retirement benefits scheme (in this definition referred to as the "*main scheme*") which provides specifically for the payment of voluntary contributions to a PRSA by members of the main scheme, or

(ii) contributions made under a separately arranged scheme approved by the Revenue Commissioners which is associated with the main scheme and which provides for voluntary contributions to a PRSA by members of the main scheme;

"*approved scheme*" has the same meaning as in *Chapter 1* of this Part;

"*approved retirement fund*" has the meaning assigned to it by *section 784A*;

"*approved minimum retirement fund*" has the meaning assigned to it by *section 784C*;

"*contract of employment*" means—

(a) a contract of service or apprenticeship, or

(b) any other contract whereby an individual agrees with another person, who is carrying on the business of an employment agency (within the meaning of the Employment Agency Act, 1971) and is acting in the course of that business, to do or perform personally any work or service for a third person (whether or not the third person is party to the contract),

whether the contract is express or implied or if express, whether it is oral or in writing;

"*contributor*" means an individual who enters into a PRSA contract with a PRSA provider and an individual shall be regarded as a contributor to a PRSA notwithstanding that all contributions are made by that individual's employer;

"*director*", in relation to a company includes—

(a) in the case of a company the affairs of which are managed by a board of directors or similar body, a member of that board or body,

(b) in the case of a company the affairs of which are managed by a single director or similar person, that director or person,

(c) in the case of a company the affairs of which are managed by the members themselves, a member of that company,

and includes a person who is to be or has been a director;

"*distribution*" has the same meaning as in the Corporation Tax Acts;

["*earnings limit*" shall be construed in accordance with *section 790A*;][1]

"*employee*"—

(a) means a person of any age, who has entered into or works under (or where the employment has ceased, entered into or worked under) a contract of employment and references, in relation to an employer, to an employee shall be construed as references to an employee employed by that employer; and for the purposes of this Chapter, a person holding office under, or in the service of, the State (including a civil servant within the meaning of the Civil Service Regulation Act, 1956) shall be deemed to be an employee employed by the State or Government, as the case may be, and an officer or servant of a local authority for the purposes of the Local Government Act, 2001, or of a harbour authority, [the Health Service Executive][2] or [a member of staff of an education and training board][3] shall be deemed to be an employee employed by the authority, [...][4][the Executive or the committee][5], as the case may be), and

(b) in relation to a company, includes a director or other officer of the company and any other person taking part in the management of the affairs of the company;

"*employer*" means, in relation to an employee, the person with whom the employee has entered into, or for whom the employee works under (or, where the employment has ceased, entered into or worked under), a contract of employment, subject to the qualification that the person, who under a contract of employment referred to in *paragraph (b)* of the definition of "*contract of employment*" is liable to pay the wages of the individual concerned, in respect of the work or service concerned shall be deemed to be the individual's employer;

"*market value*" shall be construed in accordance with *section 548*;

"*PPS Number*", in relation to an individual, means that individual's Personal Public Service Number within the meaning of [section 262 of the Social Welfare Consolidation Act 2005;][6]

"*Personal Retirement Savings Account*" means a personal retirement savings account established by a contributor with a PRSA provider under the terms of a PRSA contract and the expression "*PRSA*" shall be construed accordingly;

"*PRSA administrator*" means the PRSA provider or a person to whom a PRSA provider delegates in pursuance of Part X of the Pensions Act, 1990, its administrative functions in relation to a PRSA, including a person appointed by the PRSA provider [in accordance with *section 787G(5)(ii)*][7];

"*PRSA assets*" means the assets held on behalf of a contributor in a PRSA and includes the value of any contributions made to that PRSA by any employer of the contributor;

"*PRSA contract*" means a contract entered into between a PRSA provider and a contributor in respect of a PRSA product;

"*PRSA contribution*" means a contribution within the meaning of Part X of the Pensions Act, 1990;

"*PRSA product*" means a PRSA product (within the meaning of Part X of the Pensions Act, 1990) that for the time being stands approved under section 94 of that Act;

"*PRSA provider*" has the same meaning as in Part X of the Pensions Act, 1990;

"*relevant payment*" in relation to a PRSA means any payment, including a distribution, made by reason of rights arising as a result of a PRSA contract and includes any annuity payable by reason of such rights;

"*retirement annuity contract*" means a contract approved by the Revenue Commissioners in accordance with *Chapter 2* of this Part;

"*retirement benefits scheme*" has the same meaning as in *Chapter 1* of this Part;

"*specified individual*", in relation to a year of assessment, means an individual whose relevant earnings for the year of assessment were derived wholly or mainly from an occupation or profession specified in *Schedule 23A*;

"*statutory scheme*" has the same meaning as in *Chapter 1* of this Part.

(2) Subject to *subsection (1)*, a word or expression that is used in this Chapter and is also used in Part X of the Pensions Act, 1990 has, except where the context otherwise requires, the same meaning in this Chapter as it has in that Part.][8]

Amendments

[1] Inserted by FA06 s14(1)(c)(i). Has effect as on and from 1 January 2006.

[2] Substituted by FA05 sched6(1)(l)(i). Applies as on and from 25 March 2005.

[3] Substituted by EATBA13 sched6(24).

[4] Deleted by FA05 sched6(1)(l)(ii). Applies as on and from 25 March 2005.

[5] Substituted by FA05 sched6(1)(l)(ii). Applies as on and from 25 March 2005.

[6] Substituted by FA07 sched4(1)(z). Shall have effect as on and from 2 April 2007.

[7] Substituted by FA05 s21(1)(c)(i). Applies as respects on or after 1 January 2005.

[8] Inserted by PAA02 s4(1)(d)(v). With effect from 7 November 2002 per S.I. 502 of 2002.

Note

EABTA13 made an amendment to the definition of employee in subsection 1 which cannot be consolidated.

Revenue Briefings

Tax Briefing

Tax Briefing April 2002 – Issue 47 pg 29 – Pensions (PRSA)
Tax Briefing October 2002 – Issue 50 pg 18 – Personal Retirement Savings Accounts

eBrief

eBrief No. 24/2006 – Pensions Personal Fund Threshold

Cross References

From Section 787A

Section 548 Valuation of assets.
Section 770 Interpretation and supplemental (Chapter 1).
Section 783 Interpretation and general (Chapter 2).
Section 784A Approved retirement fund.
Section 784C Approved minimum retirement fund.
Section 787G Taxation of payments from a PRSA.
Section 790A Limit on earnings.

To Section 787A

Section 172A Interpretation.
Section 784 Retirement annuities: relief for premiums.
Section 787O Interpretation and general (Chapter 2C).
Section 790AA Taxation of lump sums in excess of the tax free amount.
Section 897A Returns by employers in relation to pension products.

787B Relevant earnings and net relevant earnings

[(1) For the purposes of this Chapter but subject to *subsection (2)*, "*relevant earnings*", in relation to an individual, means any income of the individual chargeable to tax for the year of assessment in question, being any of the following—

(a) income arising in respect of remuneration from an office or employment of profit held by the individual,

(b) income from any property which is attached to or forms part of the emoluments of any such office or employment of profit held by the individual, or

(c) income which is chargeable under Schedule D and is immediately derived by the individual from the carrying on or exercise by the individual of his or her trade or profession either as an individual or, in the case of a partnership, as a partner personally acting in the partnership;

but does not include any remuneration from an investment company of which the individual is a proprietary director or a proprietary employee.

(2) For the purposes of this Chapter, the relevant earnings of an individual shall not be treated as the relevant earnings of his or her [spouse or civil partner][1], notwithstanding that the individual's income chargeable to tax is treated as his or her [spouse's or civil partner's][2] income.

(3) For the purposes of relief under this Chapter, an individual's relevant earnings shall be those earnings before giving effect to any deduction to be made from those earnings in respect of a loss or in respect of a capital allowance (within the meaning of *section 2*), and references to income in this Chapter (other than references to total income) shall be construed similarly.

(4) For the purposes of this Chapter, "*net relevant earnings*", in relation to an individual and subject to *subsections (5)* to *(7)*, means the amount of the individual's relevant earnings for the year of assessment in question less the amount of any deductions to be made from the relevant earnings in computing the individual's total income for that year, being either—

(a) deductions in respect of payments made by the individual, or

(b) deductions in respect of losses or of such allowances mentioned in *subsection (3)*, being losses or allowances arising from activities, profits or gains of which would be included in computing relevant earnings of the individual or of the individual's [spouse or civil partner][3] for the year of assessment.

(5) Where in any year of assessment for which an individual claims and is allowed relief under this Chapter there is to be made in computing the total income of the individual or of the individual's [spouse or civil partner][4] a deduction in respect of any such loss or allowance of the individual referred to in *subsection (4)(b)*, and the deduction or part of it is to be so made from income other than relevant earnings, then, the amount of the deduction made from that other income shall be treated as reducing the individual's net relevant earnings for subsequent years of assessment and shall be deducted as far as may be from those of the following year, whether or not the individual claims or is entitled to claim relief under this Chapter for that year, and in so far as it cannot be so deducted, then from those of the next year, and so on.

(6) Where an individual's income for any year of assessment consists partly of relevant earnings and partly of other income, then, as far as may be, any deductions to be made in computing the individual's total income, and which may be treated in whole or in part either as made from relevant earnings or as made from other income, shall be treated for the purposes of this section as being made from those relevant earnings in so far as they are deductions in respect of any such loss referred to in *subsection (4)(b)* and otherwise as being made from that other income.

(7) An individual's net relevant earnings for any year of assessment shall be computed without regard to any relief to be given for that year under this Chapter either to the individual or to the individual's [spouse or civil partner][5].

(8) Notwithstanding anything in this section, for the purposes of relief under this Chapter an individual's net relevant earnings [shall not exceed the earnings limit][6] but this subsection shall not apply as regards relief for additional voluntary PRSA contributions.][7]

Amendments

[1, 3, 4, 5] Substituted by F(No.3)A11 sched1(211).

[2] Substituted by F(No.3)A11 sched1(212).

[6] Substituted by FA06 s14(1)(c)(ii). Has effect as on and from 1 January 2006.

[7] Inserted by PAA02 s4(1)(d)(v). With effect from 7 November 2002 per S.I. 502 of 2002.

Cross References

From Section 787B

Section 2 Interpretation of Tax Acts.

787C PRSAs — method of granting relief for PRSA contributions

[(1) Subject to the provisions of this Chapter, relief from income tax shall be given in respect of contributions to a PRSA by an individual chargeable to tax in respect of relevant earnings from any trade, profession, office or employment carried on or held by that individual.

(2) Where relief is to be given under this Chapter in respect of any contribution made by an individual, the amount of that contribution shall, subject to this section, be deducted from or set off against the individual's relevant earnings for the year of assessment in which the contribution is paid.

(3) Where in relation to a year of assessment a contribution to a PRSA is made after the end of the year of assessment but on or before the specified return date for the chargeable period (within the meaning of [*Part 41A*][1]) the payment may, if the individual so elects on or before that date, be treated for the purposes of this section as paid in the earlier year (and not in the year in which it is paid); but where—

(a) the amount of that contribution, together with any contributions made by the individual in the year to which the assessment relates (or treated as so paid by virtue of any previous election under this subsection), exceeds the maximum amount of the reduction which may be made under this Chapter in the individual's relevant earnings for that year, or

(b) the amount of that PRSA contribution itself exceeds the increase in that maximum amount which is due to taking into account the income on which the assessment is made,

the election shall have no effect as respects the excess.

(4) Where in any year of assessment a reduction or a greater reduction would be made under this section in the relevant earnings of an individual but for an insufficiency of net relevant earnings, the amount of the reduction which would be made but for that reason, less the amount of any reduction which is made in that year, shall be carried forward to the next year of assessment, and shall be treated for the purposes of relief under this Chapter as the amount of a qualifying contribution paid in that next year of assessment.

(5) If and in so far as an amount once carried forward under *subsection (4)* (and treated as the amount of a qualifying payment made in the next year of assessment) is not deducted from or set off against the individual's net relevant earnings for that year of assessment, it shall be carried forward again to the following year of assessment (and treated as the amount of a qualifying payment made in that year of assessment), and so on for succeeding years.

(6) Where relief under this Chapter for any year of assessment is claimed and allowed (whether or not relief is then to be given for that years, and afterwards there is made [any assessment, amendment of an assessment][2], or other adjustment of the claimant's liability to tax, there shall be made also such adjustments, if any, as are consequential thereon in the relief allowed or given under this Chapter for that or any subsequent year of assessment.

(7) Where relief under this Chapter is claimed and allowed for any year of assessment in respect of any contribution, relief shall not be given in respect of that contribution under any other provision of the Income Tax Acts for the same or a later year of assessment.][3]

Amendments

[1, 2] Substituted by FA12 sched4(part 2)(g).

[3] Inserted by PAA02 s4(1)(d)(v). With effect from 7 November 2002 per S.I. 502 of 2002.

Revenue Briefings

eBrief

eBrief No. 61/09 – Tax Relief for Pension Contributions – Late Elections

Cross References

From Section 787C

Section 950 Interpretation (Part 41).

To Section 787C

Section 787N Qualifying overseas pension plans: relief for contributions.
Section 790A Limit on earnings.

787D Claims to relief

[(1) Relief shall not be given under this Chapter in respect of a contribution to a PRSA except on a claim made to and allowed by the inspector, but any person aggrieved by any decision of the inspector on any such claim may, on giving notice in writing to the inspector within 21 days after the notification to that person of the decision, appeal to the Appeal Commissioners.

(2) The Appeal Commissioners shall hear and determine an appeal to them under *subsection (1)* as if it were an appeal to them against an assessment to income tax, and the provisions of the Income Tax Acts relating to the rehearing of an appeal and to the statement of a case for the opinion of the High Court on a point of law shall, with the necessary modifications, apply accordingly.][1]

Amendments

[1] Inserted by PAA02 s4(1)(d)(v). With effect from 7 November 2002 per S.I. 502 of 2002.

787E Extent of relief

[(1) Subject to this section, the amount which may be deducted or set off in any year in respect of contributions made by, or deemed in accordance with *subsection (2)* to have been made by, an individual to one or more PRSA products, hereafter in this section referred to as the maximum allowable contribution, shall not be more than—

[(a) in the case of an individual who at any time during the year of assessment was of the age 30 years or over but had not attained the age of 40 years, 20 per cent,

(b) in the case of an individual who at any time during the year of assessment was of the age 40 years or over but had not attained the age of 50 years, 25 per cent,

[...][1]

[(c) in the case of an individual who at any time during the year of assessment was of the age of 50 years or over but had not attained the age of 55 years or who for the year of assessment was a specified individual, 30 per cent,

(d) in the case of an individual who at any time during the year of assessment was of the age of 55 years or over but had not attained the age of 60 years, 35 per cent,

(e) in the case of an individual who at any time during the year of assessment was of the age of 60 years or over, 40 per cent, and

(f) in any other case, 15 per cent,][2]][3]

of the individual's net relevant earnings for that year of assessment.

(2) Where for a year of assessment a sum is chargeable to tax in accordance with *section 118(5)* in respect of a contribution by an employer to a PRSA, the employee shall, in addition to any contributions actually made by the employee, be deemed, for the purposes of this section, to have made contributions to the said PRSA in that year of assessment equal to such sum.

(3) [Where during a year of assessment an individual is a member either of an approved scheme or of a statutory scheme (hereafter referred to as a "*scheme*") in relation to an office or employment, not being a scheme under which the benefits provided in respect of that service are limited to benefits of a kind referred to in *paragraphs (b)* and *(c)* of *section 772(3)*, including any similar benefit provided under a statutory scheme established under a public statute,][4] the following provisions shall apply, that is to say—

(a) relief shall be allowed under this Chapter as regards relevant earnings from that office or employment only in respect of contributions that are additional voluntary PRSA contributions,

(b) notwithstanding *subsection (1)*, the amount which may be deducted or set off in that year of assessment in respect of such contributions against the individual's net relevant earnings from that office or employment shall not be more than—

(i) in the case of an individual who at any time during the year of assessment was of the age of 30 years or over but had not attained the age of 40 years, 20 per cent,

(ii) in the case of an individual who at any time during the year of assessment was of the age of 40 years or over but had not attained the age of 50 years, 25 per cent,

[...][5]

[(iii) in the case of an individual who at any time during the year of assessment was of the age of 50 years or over but had not attained the age of 55 years, 30 per cent,

(iv) in the case of an individual who at any time during the year of assessment was of the age of 55 years or over but had not attained the age of 60 years, 35 per cent,

(v) in the case of an individual who at any time during the year of assessment was of the age of 60 years or over, 40 per cent, and

(vi) in any other case, 15 per cent,][6]

of the remuneration for that year of the office or employment in respect of which the contributions are made, reduced by the amount of any contributions of the individual in the year to any scheme related to the office or employment of which he or she is a member,

(c) the amount of the net relevant earnings of the individual in respect of which any other PRSA contributions are to be deducted or set off shall be reduced by the amount of the remuneration from such office or employment, and

(d) notwithstanding *sections 787K* and *787L*, the aggregate benefits under—

(i) all schemes, of which the individual is a member, related to the office or employment, and

(ii) all Personal Retirement Savings Accounts to which the individual is the contributor of additional voluntary PRSA contributions,

shall not exceed the maximum benefits that could be provided for the individual by reference to *section 772*.

(4) Notwithstanding *subsection (1)*, where the maximum allowable contribution would but for this subsection be less than €1,525, *subsection (1)* shall apply as if the said maximum allowable contribution were €1,525.

(5) Where an individual is entitled to relief for a year of assessment under *Chapter 2* of this Part in respect of a qualifying premium, the maximum allowable contribution for that year of assessment, other than additional voluntary PRSA contributions, shall be reduced by the amount of such relief.][7]

Amendments

[1] Deleted by FA06 s14(1)(c)(iii)(I)(A). Has effect as on and from 1 January 2006.

[2] Inserted by FA06 s14(1)(c)(iii)(I)(B). Has effect as on and from 1 January 2006.

[3] Substituted by FA03 s14(1)(d)(i). Applies as on and from 1 January 2003.

[4] Substituted by FA03 s14(1)(d)(ii). Applies as on and from 1 January 2003.

[5] Deleted by FA06 s14(1)(c)(iii)(II)(A). Has effect as on and from 1 January 2006.

[6] Inserted by FA06 s14(1)(c)(iii)(II)(B). Has effect as on and from 1 January 2006.

[7] Inserted by PAA02 s4(1)(d)(v). With effect from 7 November 2002 per S.I. 502 of 2002.

Revenue Briefings

eBrief

eBrief No. 36/2011 – Employer contributions to PRSAs – Income Tax, PRSI and USC

Cross References

From Section 787E

Section 118 Benefits in kind: general charging provision.
Section 772 Conditions for approval of schemes and discretionary approval.
Section 783 Interpretation and general (Chapter 2).
Section 787K Revenue approval of PRSA products.
Section 787L Transfers to and from PRSA.

To Section 787E

Section 787F Transfers to PRSAs.

Section 787N Qualifying overseas pension plans: relief for contributions.

Section 897A Returns by employers in relation to pension products.

787F Transfers to PRSAs

[To the extent that any contribution to one or more than one PRSA is made from—

(a) the value of accrued rights under a retirement annuity contract,

(b) the value of accrued rights under an approved scheme or a statutory scheme, or

(c) a repayment of contributions to which *section 780(2)* would, but for *subsection (2A)* (inserted by the *Pensions (Amendment) Act, 2002*) of that section, otherwise apply,

it shall not be taken into account for the purposes of *section 787E* and no relief shall be allowed under this Chapter in respect of such a contribution.][1]

Amendments

[1] Inserted by PAA02 s4(1)(d)(v). With effect from 7 November 2002 per S.I. 502 of 2002.

Cross References

From Section 787F

Section 780 Charge to income tax on repayment of employees' contributions.

Section 787E Extent of relief.

To Section 787F

Section 787N Qualifying overseas pension plans: relief for contributions.

787G Taxation of payments from a PRSA

[(1) Subject to *subsections (2), (3)* and *(4)*—

(a) the amount or value of any assets that a PRSA administrator makes available to, or pays to, a PRSA contributor or to any other person, including any annuity where the whole or part of the consideration for the grant of the annuity consisted of assets which, at the time of application of the said assets for the purchase of the annuity, were PRSA assets, [shall, notwithstanding anything in *section 18* or *19*,][1] be treated as a payment to the PRSA contributor of emoluments to which Schedule E applies and, accordingly, the provisions of *Chapter 4* of *Part 42* shall apply to any such payment or amount treated as a payment, and

(b) the PRSA administrator shall deduct tax from the assets at the higher rate for the year of assessment in which the assets are made available unless the PRSA administrator has received from the Revenue Commissioners a certificate of tax credits and standard rate cut-off point or a tax deduction card for that year in respect of the PRSA contributor.

(2) A PRSA administrator shall be liable to pay to the Collector-General the income tax which the PRSA administrator is required to deduct from any assets of a PRSA by virtue of this section and the individual beneficially entitled to assets held in a PRSA, including the personal representatives of a deceased individual who was so entitled prior to that individual's death, shall allow such deduction; but where there are no funds or insufficient funds available out of which the

PRSA administrator may satisfy the tax required to be deducted, the amount of such tax for which there are insufficient funds available shall be a debt due to the PRSA administrator from the individual beneficially entitled to the assets in the PRSA or from the estate of the deceased individual, as the case may be.

(3) *Subsection (1)* shall not apply where the assets made available from a PRSA are—

(a) an amount made available, at the time assets of the PRSA are first made available to the PRSA contributor, by way of lump sum not exceeding 25 per cent of the value of the assets in the PRSA at that time or, in the case of a PRSA to which additional voluntary PRSA contributions were made, an amount not exceeding the amount that may be paid by way of lump sum in accordance with *section 772(3)(f)* in conjunction with the rules of the scheme,

(b) an amount transferred to an approved retirement fund or to an approved minimum retirement fund in accordance with *section 787H*,

(c) an amount made available to the personal representatives of the PRSA contributor in accordance with *section 787K(1)(c)(iii)*,

(d) a transfer of assets from a PRSA to another PRSA, an approved scheme or a statutory scheme where—

(i) in relation to that other PRSA, approved scheme or statutory scheme the contributor to the first-mentioned PRSA is either a contributor or a member as the case may be, and

(ii) the first-mentioned PRSA is not a PRSA in respect of which a lump sum to which *paragraph (a)* applies has been paid [or made available,][2]

[(e) an amount referred to in [*section 787K(2A)*,][3]][4]

[(f) an amount made available from a PRSA, where the PRSA is a vested PRSA (within the meaning of *section 790D(1)*), for the purpose of—

(i) reimbursing, in whole or in part, an administrator (within the meaning of *section 787O(1)*) in respect of the payment by that administrator of income tax charged on a chargeable excess in respect of the PRSA contributor, or

(ii) payment by the PRSA administrator of the amount, or part of the amount, of the appropriate share (within the meaning of *section 787R(2A)(b)*) of a non-member (within the meaning of *section 787O(1)*) (being the PRSA contributor) of income tax charged on a chargeable excess,

under the provisions of *Chapter 2C* of this Part.][5]

(4) For the purposes of this Chapter, the circumstances in which a PRSA administrator shall be treated as making assets of a PRSA available to an individual shall include—

(a) the making of a relevant payment by the PRSA administrator,

(b) any circumstances whereby assets cease to be assets of the PRSA, and

(c) any circumstances whereby assets cease to be beneficially owned by the contributor to the PRSA.

[(4A) Without prejudice to the generality of *subsection (4)*, the circumstances in which a PRSA administrator shall, for the purposes of this Chapter, be treated as making assets of a PRSA [(including a vested PRSA within the meaning of *section 790D(1)*)][6] available to an individual shall include the use of those assets in connection with any transaction which would, if the assets were assets of an approved retirement fund, be regarded under *section 784A* as giving rise to a distribution for the purposes of that section and the amount to be regarded as made available shall be calculated in accordance with that section.][7]

[(5) At any time when a PRSA administrator—

(a) is not resident in the State, or

(b) is not trading in the State through a fixed place of business,

the PRSA administrator shall, in relation to the discharge of all duties and obligations relating to Personal Retirement Savings Accounts which are imposed on the PRSA administrator [by virtue of this Chapter[, *Chapter 2C* and section 125B of the Stamp Duties Consolidation Act 1999][8]][9]—

(i) enter into a contract with the Revenue Commissioners enforceable in a Member State of the European Communities in relation to the discharge of those duties and obligations and in entering into such a contract the parties to the contract shall acknowledge and agree in writing that—

(I) it shall be governed solely by the laws of the State, and

(II) that the courts of the State shall have exclusive jurisdiction in determining any dispute arising under it,

or

(ii) ensure that there is a person resident in the State, appointed by the PRSA administrator, who will be responsible for the discharge of all of those duties and obligations and shall notify the Revenue Commissioners of the appointment of that person and the identity of that person.][10]

[(5A) The Revenue Commissioners may by notice in writing require a PRSA administrator, a PRSA provider or the person appointed under *subsection (5) (ii)*, as the case may be, to provide, within 30 days of the date of such notice, such information and particulars as may be specified in the notice as they may reasonably require for the purposes of this Chapter, and, without prejudice to the generality of the foregoing, such information and particulars may include—

(a) the name, address and PPS Number of the PRSA contributor,

(b) the name, address and PPS Number of any person to whom any payments have been made, or to whom any assets have been made available, by the PRSA administrator or the PRSA provider, and

(c) the amount of any payments and the value of any assets referred to in *paragraph (b)*.][11]

(6) Notwithstanding *subsection (1)*, where assets of a PRSA are treated under *subsection (4)* as having been made available to an individual, the provisions of *section 784A(4)* shall apply as if assets of that PRSA at the time of death of that individual were assets of an approved retirement fund.][12]

Amendments

[1] Substituted by FA05 s21(1)(c)(ii)(I). Applies as respects on or after 1 January 2005.

[2] Substituted by FA06 s14(1)(c)(iv)(I)(A). Has effect as on and from 1 January 2006.

[3] Substituted by FA12 s18(4)(a). Has effect from 8 February 2012.

[4] Inserted by FA06 s14(1)(c)(iv)(I)(B). Has effect as on and from 1 January 2006.

[5] Substituted by FA14 s19(3)(a). Has effect on and from 1 January 2015.

[6] Inserted by FA14 s19(3)(b). Has effect on and from 23 October 2014.

[7] Inserted by FA03 s14(1)(d)(iii). Applies as on and from 1 January 2003.

[8] Substituted by F(No.2)A11 s4(2)(c).

[9] Substituted by FA06 s14(1)(c)(iv)(II). Has effect as on and from 1 January 2006.

[10] Substituted by FA05 s21(1)(c)(ii)(II). Applies as respects on or after 1 January 2005.

[11] Inserted by FA05 s21(1)(c)(ii)(III). Applies as respects on or after 1 January 2005.

[12] Inserted by PAA02 s4(1)(d)(v). With effect from 7 November 2002 per S.I. 502 of 2002.

Cross References

From Section 787G

Section 4 Interpretation of Corporation Tax Acts.
Section 772 Conditions for approval of schemes and discretionary approval.
Section 784A Approved retirement fund.
Section 787H Approved Retirement Fund option.
Section 787K Revenue approval of PRSA products.
Section 983 Interpretation (Chapter 4).

To Section 787G

Section 787A Interpretation and supplemental.
Section 787H Approved Retirement Fund option.
Section t Revenue approval of PRSA products.
Section 790AA Taxation of lump sums in excess of the tax free amount.

787H Approved Retirement Fund option

[(1) At any time assets of a PRSA are allowed to be made available to a beneficiary in accordance with *section 787K*, that individual may opt to have those assets transferred to an approved retirement fund and the PRSA administrator shall make that transfer.

(2) The assets that a PRSA administrator shall transfer to an approved retirement fund in accordance with *subsection (1)* shall be the assets available in the PRSA at the time the election under that subsection is made less—

(a) any lump sum the PRSA administrator is permitted to pay without deduction of tax in accordance with *section 787G(3)(a)*, and

(b) any amount the PRSA administrator is required to transfer to an approved minimum retirement fund in accordance with *section 784C*, by virtue of *subsection (3)*.

(3) Where an individual opts in accordance with *subsection (1)*, *sections 784A* to *784D* shall apply as if that option were an option in accordance with *section 784(2A)*.][1]

Amendments

[1] Inserted by PAA02 s4(1)(d)(v). With effect from 7 November 2002 per S.I. 502 of 2002.

Cross References

From Section 787H

Section 784 Retirement annuities: relief for premiums.
Section 784A Approved retirement fund.
Section 784C Approved minimum retirement fund.
Section 784D Conditions relating to an approved minimum retirement fund.
Section 787G Taxation of payments from a PRSA.
Section 787K Revenue approval of PRSA products.

To Section 787H

Section 787G Taxation of payments from a PRSA.
Section 787K Revenue approval of PRSA products.
Section 787O Interpretation and general (Chapter 2C).
Schedule 23B Limit on Tax-Relieved Pension Funds

787I Exemption of PRSA

[(1) Exemption from income tax shall, on a claim being made in that behalf, be allowed in respect of income derived from investments or deposits of a PRSA if, or to such extent as the Revenue Commissioners are satisfied that, it is income from investments or deposits held for the purposes of the PRSA.

(2) (a) In this subsection, "*financial futures*" and "*traded options*" mean respectively financial futures and traded options for the time being dealt in or quoted on any futures exchange or any stock exchange, whether or not that exchange is situated in the State.

(b) For the purposes of *subsection (1)*, a contract entered into in the course of dealing in financial futures or traded options shall be regarded as an investment.

(3) Exemption from income tax shall, on a claim being made in that behalf, be allowed in respect of underwriting commissions if, or to such extent as the Revenue Commissioners are satisfied that, the underwriting commissions are applied for the purposes of the PRSA, and in respect of which the administrator of the PRSA would, but for this subsection, be chargeable to tax under Case IV of Schedule D.][1]

Amendments

[1] Inserted by PAA02 s4(1)(d)(v). With effect from 7 November 2002 per S.I. 502 of 2002.

787J Allowance to employer

[(1) For the purposes of this section—

(a) a reference to a "*chargeable period*" shall be construed as a reference to a "*chargeable period or its basis period*" (within the meaning of *section 321*), and

(b) in relation to an employer whose chargeable period is a year of assessment, "*basis period*" means the period on the profits or gains of which income tax for that year of assessment is to be finally computed for the purposes of Case I or II of Schedule D in respect of the trade, profession or vocation of the employer.

(2) Subject to *subsection (3)*, any sum paid by an employer by way of contribution under a PRSA contract of an employee shall for the purposes of Case I or II of Schedule D and of *sections 83* and *707(4)* be allowed to be deducted as an expense, or expense of management, incurred in the chargeable period in which the sum is paid but no other sum shall for those purposes be allowed to be deducted as an expense, or expense of management, in respect of the making, or any provision for the making, of any contributions under the PRSA contract.

(3) The amount of an employer's contributions which may be deducted under *subsection (2)* shall not exceed the amount contributed by that employer to Personal Retirement Savings Accounts in respect of employees in a trade or undertaking in respect of the profits of which the employer is assessable to income tax or corporation tax, as the case may be.][1]

Amendments

[1] Inserted by PAA02 s4(1)(d)(v). With effect from 7 November 2002 per S.I. 502 of 2002.

Cross References

From Section 787J

Section 83 Expenses of management of investment companies.

Section 321 Provisions of general application in relation to the making of allowances and charges.

Section 707 Management expenses.

To Section 787J

Section 787N Qualifying overseas pension plans: relief for contributions.

787K Revenue approval of PRSA products

[(1) Subject to *subsection (2)* and to *sections 787H* and *787L*, the Revenue Commissioners shall not approve, for the purposes of section 94(3) of the Pensions Act, 1990, a PRSA product (within the meaning of Part X of that Act) unless it appears to them to satisfy the following conditions—

(a) that the arrangements in respect of that product will be entered into by an individual with a person lawfully carrying on in the State the business of a PRSA provider,

(b) that it includes provision securing that no annuity payable under it shall be capable in whole or in part of surrender, commutation or assignment, and

(c) that it does not—

(i) provide for the payment of any sum or the making available of PRSA assets, by that person during the life of the individual of any sum except—

(I) sums payable by means of annuity to the individual,

(II) a sum payable without deduction of tax by way of lump sum, in accordance with *section 787G(3)(a)*,

(III) assets transferred to an approved retirement fund or to an approved minimum retirement fund, in accordance with *section 787H(1)*, or

(IV) assets made available to the PRSA contributor by the PRSA administrator, where the PRSA administrator retains such assets as would be required to be transferred to an approved minimum retirement fund if the PRSA contributor opted in accordance with *section 787H(1)*,

(ii) provide for the annuity or other sums payable to the individual to commence or for assets to be made available to the individual before the individual attains the age of 60 years or after he or she attains the age of 75 years,

(iii) provide for the payment by that person of any other sums except sums payable by means of annuity to the individual's [widow, widower or surviving civil partner][1] and any sums which, in the event of no annuity or other benefits becoming payable either to the individual or to a widow or widower, are payable to the individual's personal representatives by way of transfer of the PRSA assets to the estate of the PRSA contributor,

(iv) provide for the annuity, if any, payable to a [widow, widower or surviving civil partner][2] of the individual to be of a greater annual amount than that paid or payable to the individual, or

(v) provide for the payment of any annuity otherwise than for the life of the annuitant.

(2) The Revenue Commissioners may, if they think fit and subject to any conditions they think proper to attach to the approval under section 94 of the Pensions Act, 1990, approve, for the purposes of section 94(3) of that Act, a product otherwise satisfying the conditions referred to in *subsection (1)*, notwithstanding that the product provides for one or more of the following matters—

(a) the payment to the individual of an annuity or other sums or the making available of assets of the PRSA to the individual commencing before he or she attains the age of 60 years, where the annuity or other sums are payable on the individual becoming permanently incapable through infirmity of mind or body of carrying on his or her own occupation or any occupation of a similar nature for which he or she is trained or fitted,

(b) in the case of an individual being an employee, the payment to the individual of an annuity or other sums or the making available of assets of the PRSA to the individual commencing on retirement at age 50 or over,

(c) where the individual's occupation is one in which persons customarily retire before attaining the age of 60 years, the payment of the annuity or other sums to commence or the making available of assets of the PRSA to commence before the individual attains that age (but not before he or she attains the age of 50 years),

(d) the annuity payable to any person to continue for a term certain (not exceeding 10 years) notwithstanding his or her death within that term, or the annuity payable to any person to terminate, or be suspended, [on marriage or remarriage or on entering into a civil partnership or a new civil partnership][3] or in other circumstances,

(e) in the case of an annuity which is to continue for a term certain, the annuity to be assignable by will and, in the event of any person dying entitled to the annuity, the annuity to be assignable by his or her personal representatives in the distribution of the estate so as to give effect to a testamentary disposition, or to the rights of those entitled on intestacy or to an appropriation of the annuity to a legacy or to a share or interest in the estate.

[(2A) A PRSA product (within the meaning of Part X of the Pensions Act 1990) shall neither cease to be an approved product under section 94 of that Act nor shall the Revenue Commissioners be prevented from approving a product under that section notwithstanding that the product permits the PRSA administrator to make available from the PRSA assets, to such extent as may be necessary, an amount for the purpose of discharging a tax liability in relation to a PRSA contributor, under the provisions of *Chapter 2C* of this Part, in connection with a relevant payment to the PRSA contributor.][4]

[(2B) A PRSA product (within the meaning of Part X of the Pensions Act 1990) shall neither cease to be an approved product under *section 94* of that Act nor shall the Revenue Commissioners be prevented from approving a product under that section notwithstanding that the product permits the PRSA administrator, where the PRSA contributor comes within the provisions of *section 787TA*, to make available from the PRSA assets to such extent as may be necessary an amount for the purposes of an option exercised by the PRSA contributor in accordance with that section requiring an amount representing the value of, or part of the value of, the PRSA contributor's accrued rights under the product at the date of the exercise of the option to be transferred to the PRSA contributor by the PRSA administrator.][5]

[(2C) A PRSA product (within the meaning of Part X of the Pensions Act 1990) approved under *section 94* of that Act, shall not cease to be an approved product where, notwithstanding anything contained in the terms of the product as approved, the PRSA administrator makes an amount available from the PRSA assets to the PRSA contributor or, as the case may be, where the PRSA is subject to a pension adjustment order, to the spouse or former spouse or civil partner or former civil partner of the

PRSA contributor (in this subsection referred to as the "*relevant individual*") on foot of the relevant individual availing of an option in accordance with *section 782A*.][6]

(3) Where, having regard to the provisions of this Chapter, the Revenue Commissioners are, at any time, of the opinion that approval of a product under section 94 of the Pensions Act, 1990, ought to be withdrawn they shall give notice in writing to the Pensions Board of that opinion and such a notice shall specify the grounds on which they formed that opinion.

(4) Where approval of a product is withdrawn pursuant to section 97 of the Pensions Act, 1990, there shall be made such assessments or amendment of assessments as may be appropriate for the purpose of withdrawing any relief given under this Chapter consequent on the grant of the approval.][7]

Amendments

[1] Substituted by F(No.3)A11 sched1(213).

[2] Substituted by FA12 s134(1)(f). Has effect as if it had come into operation for the year of assessment (within the meaning of the Income Tax Acts and the Capital Gains Tax Acts) 2011 and each subsequent year of assessment.

[3] Substituted by F(No.3)A11 sched1(214).

[4] Inserted by FA06 s14(1)(c)(v). Has effect as on and from 1 January 2006.

[5] Inserted by FA12 s18(4)(c). Has effect from 8 February 2012.

[6] Inserted by FA13 s17(3). Has effect from 27 March 2013.

[7] Inserted by PAA02 s4(1)(d)(v). With effect from 7 November 2002 per S.I. 502 of 2002.

Cross References

From Section 787K

Section 787G Taxation of payments from a PRSA.
Section 787H Approved Retirement Fund option.
Section 787L Transfers to and from PRSA.

To Section 787K

Section 787E Extent of relief.
Section 787G Taxation of payments from a PRSA.
Section 787H Approved Retirement Fund option.
Section 787L Transfers to and from PRSA.

787L Transfers to and from PRSA

[(1) In addition to the requirements imposed by *section 787K* for the granting of such approval, the Revenue Commissioners shall not approve, for the purposes of section 94(3) of the Pensions Act, 1990, a PRSA product (within the meaning of Part X of that Act) unless the product provides that the individual who has entered into the arrangements in respect of it may require a sum representing the value of his or her accrued rights under the product—

(a) to be paid by the person with whom the individual has entered into such arrangements to such other person as the individual may specify, and

(b) to be applied by such other person in payment either of a contribution under a PRSA contract made between the individual and that other person or a contribution under an approved scheme of which the individual is a member.

(2) Without prejudice to *subsection (1)*, the Revenue Commissioners shall not approve, for the purposes of section 94(3) of the Pensions Act, 1990, a PRSA product (within the meaning of Part X of that Act) unless the product provides that the PRSA provider may receive contributions from—

(a) another PRSA in respect of which the contributor to the first-mentioned PRSA is the contributor,

(b) either an approved scheme or a statutory scheme in respect of which the contributor to the first-mentioned PRSA is a member, or

(c) a contract approved by the Revenue Commissioners in accordance with *Chapter 2* of this Part to which the contributor to the first-mentioned PRSA is a party.

(3) References in *subsection (1)* to the individual by whom a contract is made include references to any [widow, widower, surviving civil partner or dependant][1] having accrued rights under the contract.][2]

Amendments

[1] Substituted by F(No.3)A11 sched1(215).

[2] Inserted by PAA02 s4(1)(d)(v). With effect from 7 November 2002 per S.I. 502 of 2002.

Cross References

From Section 787L

Section 783 Interpretation and general (Chapter 2).
Section 787K Revenue approval of PRSA products.

To Section 787L

Section 787E Extent of relief.
Section 787K Revenue approval of PRSA products.

CHAPTER 2B

Overseas Pension Plans: Migrant Member Relief

787M Interpretation and general (Chapter 2B)

[(1) In this Chapter, unless the context otherwise requires—

"*administrator*", in relation to an overseas pension plan, means the person or persons having the management of the plan;

"*contributions*" include premia;

"*certificate of contributions*" means a certificate obtained by the relevant migrant member from the administrator and provided to the Revenue Commissioners, in a form to be furnished by the Revenue Commissioners for that purpose, containing for each calendar year the following particulars in respect of the relevant migrant member of the plan—

(a) his or her name, address, PPS Number and policy reference number,

(b) the contributions paid by him or her under the plan in that year, and

(c) where relevant, the contributions, if any, paid under the plan in that year in respect of him or her by, or on behalf of, his or her employer;

"*overseas pension plan*" means a contract, an agreement, a series of agreements, a trust deed or other arrangements, other than a state social security scheme, which is established in, or entered into under the law of, a Member State of the European Communities, other than the State;

"*national of a Member State of the European Communities*" means any individual possessing the nationality or citizenship of a Member State of the European Communities;

"*policy reference number*" means the unique identifying number of a relevant migrant member in relation to an overseas pension plan;

"*PPS Number*" means a personal public service number within the meaning of [section 262 of the Social Welfare Consolidation Act 2005;][1]

"*qualifying overseas pension plan*" means an overseas pension plan—

(a) which is in good faith established for the sole purpose of providing benefits of a kind similar to those referred to in Chapters 1, 2, or 2A of this Part,

(b) in respect of which tax relief is available under the law of the Member State of the European Communities in which the plan is established in respect of any contributions paid under the plan, and

(c) in relation to which the relevant migrant member of the plan complies with the requirements of *subsection (2)*;

"*relevant migrant member*" means an individual who is a resident of the State and who is a member of a qualifying overseas pension plan and who, in relation to any contributions paid under the plan—

(a) was, at the time the individual first became a member of the pension plan, a resident of a Member State of the European Communities, other than the State, and entitled to tax relief in respect of contributions paid under the plan under the law of that Member State of the European Communities,

(b) was a member of the pension plan at the beginning of the period in which the individual became a resident of the State,

(c) was, immediately before the beginning of that period, resident outside of the State for a continuous period of 3 years, and

(d) (i) is a national of a Member State of the European Communities, or

(ii) not being such an individual, was a resident of a Member State of the European Communities, other than the State, immediately before becoming a resident of the State;

"*resident*" means—

(a) in the case of a Member State of the European Communities with the Government of which arrangements having the force of law by virtue of [*section 826(1)*][2] have been made, that the individual is regarded as being a resident of that State under those arrangements, and

(b) in any other case, that the individual is by virtue of the law of that State a resident of that State for the purposes of tax;

"*state social security scheme*" means a system of mandatory protection put in place by the Government of a country or territory, other than the State, to provide a minimum level of retirement income or other benefits, the level of which is determined by that Government;

"*tax reference number*" means, in relation to an institution operating or managing an overseas pension plan, the unique identification number allocated to the institution by a Member State of the European Communities, other than the State, for the purposes of taxation, and where more than one such number has been allocated, the reference number appropriate to the business in the course of which the overseas pension plan was issued.

(2) The requirements referred to in *paragraph (c)* of the definition of "*qualifying overseas pension plan*" in *subsection (1)* are that the relevant migrant member—

(a) obtains from the administrator of the plan and provides to the Revenue Commissioners in such form and manner as they may specify—

(i) such evidence as they may reasonably require to verify the position in relation to *paragraphs (a)* and *(b)* of the definition of "*qualifying overseas pension plan*" in *subsection (1)*, and

(ii) the following particulars in relation to the plan—

(I) the name, address and tax reference number of the institution operating or managing the plan,

(II) the policy reference number of the relevant migrant member of the plan,

(III) the date on which the relevant migrant member became a member of the plan,

(IV) the date on which contributions under the plan first became payable,

(V) the date on which benefits under the plan first become payable,

and

(b) has irrevocably instructed the administrator of the plan to provide to the Revenue Commissioners such information as they may reasonably require in relation to any payments made under the plan.][3]

Amendments

[1] Substituted by FA07 sched4(1)(aa). Shall have effect as on and from 2 April 2007

[2] Substituted by FA07 sched2(1)(z). Has effect as on and from 2 April 2007

[3] Inserted by FA05 s21(1)(d). Applies as respects contributions to a qualifying overseas pension plan made on or after 1 January 2005.

Revenue Briefings

Tax Briefing

Tax Briefing December 2005 – Issue 62 – Tax Relief on Pension Contributions to EU based Pension Plans

eBrief

eBrief No. 97/10 – Revenue Pensions Manual

Cross References

From Section 787M

Section 826 Agreements for relief from double taxation.

To Section 787M

Section 787N Qualifying overseas pension plans: relief for contributions.

Section 787O Interpretation and general (Chapter 2C).

787N Qualifying overseas pension plans: relief for contributions

[(1) Where in any year of assessment, contributions are paid to any qualifying overseas pension plan—

(a) by a relevant migrant member of that plan, or

(b) by, or on behalf of, an employer in respect of an employee (within the meaning of *Chapter 1*) who is a relevant migrant member of that plan,

then, where the relevant migrant member has provided a certificate of contributions, relief for that year of assessment [under the provisions of *subsections (6)*, *(7)* and *(8)* of *section 774* and *section 778(1)* of *Chapter 1*][1] (which relates to occupational pension schemes), or, as the case may be, *section 787* of *Chapter 2* (which relates to retirement annuities), or *sections 787C*, *787E*, *787F* or *787J* of *Chapter 2A* (which relates to personal retirement savings accounts), shall, with any necessary modifications, apply to those contributions as if—

(i) the qualifying overseas pension plan was an exempt approved scheme under *Chapter 1* or an annuity contract for the time being approved by the Revenue Commissioners under *Chapter 2*, or a PRSA product approved under *Chapter 2A* for the purposes of section 94(3) of the Pensions Act 1990, and

(ii) the relevant migrant member of the qualifying overseas pension plan was—

(I) an employee within the meaning of *Chapter 1*,

(II) an individual referred to in *section 784(1)* of *Chapter 2*, or

(III) an individual referred to in *Chapter 2A*.

(2) An individual who would be a relevant migrant member of a qualifying overseas pension plan but for the fact that he or she fails to meet the requirement in *paragraph (c)* of the definition of "*relevant migrant member*" in *section 787M* shall, notwithstanding that, be treated as a relevant migrant member if the Revenue Commissioners are of the opinion that in all the circumstances the failure of the individual to meet the condition ought to be disregarded for that purpose.

(3) (a) The Revenue Commissioners may by notice in writing require the administrator of a qualifying overseas pension plan who has received an irrevocable instruction as provided for in *section 787M(2)(b)*, to provide within 30 days of the date of such notice such information and particulars, in relation to payments under the plan, as the Revenue Commissioners may reasonably require for the purposes of this Chapter.

(b) The notice referred to in *paragraph (a)* shall specify—

(i) the information and particulars required by the Revenue Commissioners, and

(ii) the form and manner in which such information and particulars are to be provided.][2]

Amendments

[1] Substituted by FA06 s14(1)(d).

[2] Inserted by FA05 s21(1)(d). Applies as respects contributions to a qualifying overseas pension plan made on or after 1 January 2005.

Cross References

From Section 787N

Section 774 Certain approved schemes: exemptions and reliefs.
Section 778 Exceptions to charge to tax under section 777.
Section 784 Retirement annuities: relief for premiums.
Section 787 Nature and amount of relief for qualifying premiums.
Section 787C PRSAs — method of granting relief for PRSA contributions.
Section 787E Extent of relief.
Section 787F Transfers to PRSAs.
Section 787J Allowance to employer.
Section 787M Interpretation and general (Chapter 2B).

CHAPTER 2C

Limit on Tax-Relieved Pension Funds

787O Interpretation and general (Chapter 2C)

[(1) In this Chapter and *Schedule 23B*, unless the context otherwise requires—

["*accrued pension amount*", in relation to a benefit crystallisation event of the kind referred to in *paragraph 2(a)(i)* of *Schedule 23B* in respect of a relevant pension arrangement that is a defined benefit arrangement, means the part (if any), determined in accordance with *subsection (2A)*, of the amount represented by P in the formula in *paragraph 3(aa)* of that Schedule that had accrued to the individual under the arrangement on the specified date;][1]

"*administrator*", in relation to a relevant pension arrangement, means the person or persons having the management of the arrangement, and includes—

(a) an administrator, within the meaning of *section 770(1)*,

(b) a person mentioned in *section 784*, lawfully carrying on the business of granting annuities on human life, including the person mentioned in *section 784(4A)(ii)*,

(c) a PRSA administrator, within the meaning of *section 787A(1)*, and

(d) an administrator of a relevant pension arrangement of a kind described in *paragraphs (e)* and *(f)* of the definition of relevant pension arrangement, as may be specified by regulations under *section 787U*;

"*amount crystallised by a benefit crystallisation event*" shall be construed in accordance with *paragraph 3* of *Schedule 23B* and a reference to "*amount of the current event*" shall be construed as the amount crystallised by the benefit crystallisation event which is that event;

"*amount of uncrystallised pension rights on the specified date*", in relation to an individual, shall be determined in accordance with *paragraph 1* of *Schedule 23B*;

"*annual amount of a pension*" means the amount of pension payable to the individual in the period of 12 months beginning with the day on which the individual becomes entitled to the pension and on the assumption that there is no increase in the pension throughout that period;

['*applied*', in relation to a transfer amount, means the application of the transfer amount in accordance with—

(a) *subsection (5), (6), (8)* or *(9)* of *section 12* of the Family Law Act 1995,

(b) *subsection (5), (6), (8)* or *(9)* of *section 17* of the Family Law (Divorce) Act 1996, or

(c) *subsection (1), (3), (5)* or *(6)* of *section 123* of the Civil Partnership and Certain Rights and Obligations of Cohabitants Act 2010,

as the case may be;][2]

"*approved retirement fund*" has the meaning assigned to it by *section 784A*;

"*approved minimum retirement fund*" has the meaning assigned to it by *section 784C*;

"*benefit crystallisation event*" and the time when such an event occurs shall be construed in accordance with *paragraph 2* of *Schedule 23B*;

"*calculation A*", in relation to the annual amount of a pension, means a calculation that increases that annual amount at an annual percentage rate of 5 per cent for the whole of the period beginning with the month in which the individual became entitled to the pension and ending with the month in which the individual becomes entitled to payment of the pension at an increased annual amount;

"*calculation B*", in relation to the annual amount of a pension, means a calculation that increases that annual amount by 2 per cent plus the movement in the All Items Consumer Price Index Number compiled by the Central Statistics Office starting in the month in which the individual first became entitled to the pension and ending in the month when the individual becomes entitled to payment of the pension at an increased annual amount;

"*chargeable excess*" shall be construed in accordance with *section 787Q(4)*;

"*current event*" means a benefit crystallisation event occurring on or after the specified date;

"*date of the current event*" means the date on which—

(a) the individual acquires an actual entitlement to the payment of a benefit in respect of the current event under the relevant pension arrangement, whether or not the benefit is paid on, or commences to be paid on, that date,

(b) the annuity or, as the case may be, the pension would otherwise become payable under a relevant pension arrangement where the individual exercises an option in accordance with *section 772(3A)*, *784(2A)* or, as the case may be, *section 787H(1)*,

[(ba) the annuity would otherwise become payable under a PRSA of a kind referred to in *paragraph (c)* of the definition of "*relevant pension arrangement*" where an individual does not elect to exercise an option in accordance with *section 787H(1)* and instead retains the assets available in the PRSA at that date, in that PRSA or any other PRSA,][3]

(c) a payment or transfer is made to an overseas arrangement by direction of the individual under the provisions of the Occupational Pension Schemes and Personal Retirement Savings Accounts (Overseas Transfer Payments) Regulations 2003 (S.I. No. 716 of 2003), or

(d) the individual, having become entitled to a pension under a relevant pension arrangement on or after the specified date, becomes entitled to the payment of that pension at an increased annual amount which exceeds by more than the permitted margin the annual amount at which it was payable on the date the individual became entitled to it;

"*defined benefit arrangement*" means a relevant pension arrangement other than a defined contribution arrangement;

"*defined contribution arrangement*" means a relevant pension arrangement that provides benefits calculated by reference to an amount available for the provision of benefits to or in respect of the member, whether the amount so available is determined solely by reference to the contributions paid into the arrangement by or on behalf of the member and the investment return earned on those contributions or otherwise, and includes a relevant pension arrangement of the kind described in *paragraphs (b)* and *(c)* of the definition of "relevant pension arrangement";

['*designated benefit*', '*retirement benefit*' and '*transfer amount*' have the meaning assigned to them, respectively, in—

(a) *section 12* of the Family Law Act 1995,

(b) *section 17* of the Family Law (Divorce) Act 1996, or

(c) *section 121* of the Civil Partnership and Certain Rights and Obligations of Cohabitants Act 2010,

as the case may be;][4]

"*excepted circumstances*" means circumstances such that the increase in the annual amount of pension in payment to the individual is directly related to an increase in the rate of remuneration of all persons or of a class of persons employed in the sector in which the individual was employed and in respect of which employment the individual is entitled to the pension under the relevant pension arrangement;

"*market value*" shall be construed in accordance with *section 548*;

['*fund administrator*' means a qualifying fund manager of an approved retirement fund or an approved minimum retirement fund or the PRSA administrator of a vested PRSA (within the meaning of *section 790D(1)*), as the case may be, (in this definition referred to as the 'fund') the beneficial owner of which is a non-member and the assets of which consist, in whole or in part, of—

(a) assets transferred to the fund by virtue of the exercise by the non-member of a relevant option in relation to the transfer arrangement (in this definition referred to as the 'first-mentioned transfer'), or

(b) assets transferred to the fund which were previously held in another fund or funds the assets of which originated, in whole or in part, from the first mentioned transfer;][5]

"*maximum tax-relieved pension fund*", in relation to an individual, means the overall limit on the amount that may be crystallised by a benefit crystallisation event or, where there is more than one such event, the aggregate of all of such amounts on or after [7 December 2005][6] without giving rise to a chargeable excess;

"*member*", in relation to a relevant pension arrangement, means any individual who, having been admitted to membership under the rules of the arrangement, remains entitled to any benefit under the arrangement and includes an employee within the meaning of *section 770(1)*, the individual referred to in *section 784*, a PRSA contributor within the meaning of *Chapter 2A* and a relevant migrant member within the meaning of *section 787M(1)*;

['*non-member*', in relation to a relevant pension arrangement, means an individual (other than a dependent member of the family within the meaning of *section 2* of the Family Law Act 1995 and *section 2* of the Family Law (Divorce) Act 1996) in whose favour a pension adjustment order in respect of the retirement benefit of a member of the arrangement has been made;][7]

"*overseas arrangement*" means an arrangement for the provision of retirement benefits established outside the State;

['*pension adjustment order*' means an order made in accordance with—

(a) *section 12(2)* of the Family Law Act 1995,

(b) *section 17(2)* of the Family Law (Divorce) Act 1996, or

(c) *section 121(2)* of the Civil Partnership and Certain Rights and Obligations of Cohabitants Act 2010,

as the case may be, or any variation of such an order made by an order under—

(i) *section 18(2)* of the Family Law Act 1995,

(ii) *section 22(2)* of the Family Law (Divorce) Act 1996, or

(iii) *section 131(3)* of the Civil Partnership and Certain Rights and Obligations of Cohabitants Act 2010, as the case may be, the operation of which has not been suspended (or if suspended, or further suspended, has been revived) or discharged by an order made under any of the relevant provisions referred to in *subparagraph (i), (ii)* or *(iii)*;][8]

"*permitted margin*" means the amount by which the annual amount of the pension would be greater if it had been increased by whichever of calculation A and calculation B gives the greater amount;

"*personal fund threshold*", in relation to an individual for a year of assessment, means—

[(a) (i) where the individual is an individual to whom the Revenue Commissioners have issued a certificate or, as the case may be, a revised certificate in accordance with *section 787P* as that section applied at any time before the date of the passing of the *Finance (No. 2) Act 2013* (in this Chapter referred to as the 'earlier certificate'), the amount stated in the earlier certificate as being the individual's personal fund threshold, and][9]

(ii) [in any other case, for the year of assessment 2014, the lesser of—

(I) €2,300,000, and][10]

(II) (A) where no benefit crystallisation event in relation to the individual has occurred on or after 7 December 2005 and the individual has uncrystallised pension rights on the specified date, the amount of the uncrystallised pension rights on the specified date in relation to the individual, where the amount of those rights on that date exceed the standard fund threshold, or

(B) where one or more than one benefit crystallisation event in relation to the individual has occurred on or after 7 December 2005 and the individual has uncrystallised pension rights on the specified date, the aggregate of the amounts crystallised by those benefit crystallisation events and the amount of the uncrystallised pension rights on the specified date in relation to the individual, where the aggregate amount of those crystallised and uncrystallised rights exceed the standard fund threshold, and][11]

(b) for a year of assessment (in this paragraph referred to as the "*relevant year*") after the [year of assessment 2014][12], an amount equivalent to the amount determined by the formula—

$$A \times B$$

where—

A is the personal fund threshold for the year of assessment immediately preceding the relevant year, and

[B is—

(i) the earnings adjustment factor which may be designated in writing by the Minister for Finance in December of the year of assessment preceding the relevant year, a note of which shall be published as soon as practicable in the Iris *Iris Oifigiúil*, or

(ii) where no earnings adjustment factor is designated by the Minister for Finance, 1;][13]

"*previously used amount*", in relation to the standard fund threshold or, as the case may be, the personal fund threshold shall be construed in accordance with *paragraph 5* of *Schedule 23B*;

"*PPS Number*", in relation to an individual, means the individual's Personal Public Service Number within the meaning of section 262 of the Social Welfare Consolidation Act 2005;

['*relevant member*', in relation to a relevant pension arrangement, means—

(a) a member of a relevant pension arrangement in respect of whose retirement benefit under the arrangement a pension adjustment order has been made in favour of a non-member, or

(b) a member of a relevant pension arrangement to which a sum representing that member's accrued rights under the relevant pension arrangement referred to in *paragraph (a)* has been transferred, or subsequently transferred

'*relevant option*', in relation to a non-member and a transfer arrangement, means the option referred to in *section 772(3A)*, *784(2A)* or *787H(1)*, as the case may be, to the extent that those options refer to a transfer to an approved retirement fund, or where the transfer arrangement is a PRSA, the option to retain the assets of the transfer arrangement in that arrangement (or any other similar arrangement);][14]

"*relevant pension arrangement*" means—

(a) a retirement benefits scheme, within the meaning of *section 771*, for the time being approved by the Revenue Commissioners for the purposes of *Chapter 1*,

(b) an annuity contract or a trust scheme or part of a trust scheme for the time being approved by the Revenue Commissioners under *section 784*,

(c) a PRSA contract, within the meaning of *section 787A*, in respect of a PRSA product, within the meaning of that section,

(d) a qualifying overseas pension plan within the meaning of *Chapter 2B*,

(e) a public service pension scheme within the meaning of section 1 of the Public Service Superannuation (Miscellaneous Provisions) Act 2004, or

(f) a statutory scheme, within the meaning of *section 770(1)*, other than a public service pension scheme referred to in *paragraph (e)*;

"*relevant valuation factor*" has the meaning assigned to it by *subsection (2)*;

["*specified date*" means [1 January 2014][15];][16]

"*standard fund threshold*", in relation to an individual for a year of assessment, means—

[(a) for the year of assessment 2014, €2,000,000, and][17]

(b) for a year of assessment (in this paragraph referred to as the "*relevant year*") after the [year of assessment 2014][18], an amount equivalent to the amount determined by the formula—

$$A \times B$$

where—

A is the standard fund threshold for the year of assessment immediately preceding the relevant year, and

[B is—

(i) (i) the earnings adjustment factor which may be designated in writing by the Minister for Finance in December of the year of assessment preceding the relevant year, a note of which shall be published as soon as practicable in the Iris *Iris Oifigiúil*, or

(ii) (ii) where no earnings adjustment factor is designated by the Minister for Finance, 1;][19]

[*'subsequent administrator'* means the administrator of the transfer arrangement under which the non-member remains entitled to a retirement benefit under the arrangement or in respect of which the non-member's retirement benefit under the arrangement has crystallised;

'transfer arrangement' means a relevant pension arrangement—

(a) to which a transfer amount has been applied to provide a retirement benefit for or in respect of a non-member and includes the relevant pension arrangement of the relevant member where a retirement benefit for or in respect of the non-member is provided under that arrangement of the same actuarial value as the transfer amount, or

(b) to which a sum representing the non-member's accrued rights under an arrangement referred to in *paragraph (a)* has been transferred, or subsequently transferred;][20]

"*uncrystallised pension rights*", in relation to an individual on any date, means pension rights in respect of which the individual was not entitled to the payment of benefits in relation to those rights on that date.

[(2) (a) Subject to *paragraph (b)*, for the purposes of this Chapter and *Schedule 23B*, the relevant valuation factor in relation to a relevant pension arrangement that is a defined benefit arrangement (in this subsection referred to as the 'pension arrangement') is—

(i) on the specified date, 20, and

(ii) after the specified date, where at the date of the current event relating to the pension arrangement the individual has attained the age included in an entry in *column (1)* of the Table to *Schedule 23B*, the figure in *column (2)* of that Table opposite that entry (in this Chapter and *Schedule 23B* referred to as the 'relevant age-related factor').

(b) Where the administrator of a pension arrangement has, with the prior agreement of the Revenue Commissioners, used (before the specified date) a valuation factor (in this paragraph referred to as the 'first-mentioned factor') greater than the relevant valuation factor referred to in *paragraph (a)(i)* then, in such a case, for the purposes of this Chapter and *Schedule 23B*, the relevant valuation factor in relation to the pension arrangement is—

(i) on the specified date, the first-mentioned factor, and

(ii) after the specified date, the greater of the first-mentioned factor and the relevant age-related factor and the reference to the meaning of 'A' in the formula in *paragraph 3(a)* of *Schedule 23B* shall be construed accordingly.][21]

[(2A) For the purposes of this Chapter and *Schedule 23B*—

(a) where the individual has made a PFT notification (within the meaning of *section 787P*), the accrued pension amount shall be the annual amount of pension included in the statement from the administrator referred to in *subsection (2)(a)* of *section 787P*, and

(b) in any other case, the accrued pension amount shall be an amount equivalent to the annual amount of pension which would be represented by AP in the formula in *paragraph 1(2)(b)* of *Schedule 23B*, if the individual's uncrystallised pension rights under the arrangement on the specified date were being calculated.][22]

(3) For the purposes of this Chapter, where more than one benefit crystallisation event occurs in relation to an individual on the same day, the individual shall decide the order in which they are to be deemed to occur.

(4) *Schedule 23B* shall apply for the purposes of supplementing this Chapter and shall be construed as one with this Chapter.

[(5) For the purposes of this Chapter and *Schedule 23B*, where, on or after 7 December 2005, an individual is a relevant member of a relevant pension arrangement (in this subsection referred to as the 'arrangement') then, notwithstanding the pension adjustment order, the administrator of the arrangement shall, in calculating—

(a) the relevant member's pension rights (within the meaning of *section 787P(2)(a)(i)*) in respect of the arrangement for the purposes of the statement certifying those rights (referred to in that section), and

(b) the amount crystallised by a benefit crystallisation event occurring on or after 7 December 2005 in relation to the relevant member under the arrangement,

include in those calculations—

(i) the designated benefit payable pursuant to the order, or

(ii) where the transfer amount has been applied, the designated benefit that would otherwise have been payable pursuant to the order if the transfer amount had not been so applied,

as if the pension adjustment order had not been made, and where the administrator is the administrator of a relevant pension arrangement to which a sum representing the relevant member's accrued rights under the relevant pension arrangement in respect of which the pension adjustment order has been made, has been transferred, or subsequently transferred, in whole or in part, the calculations referred to in *paragraphs (a)* and *(b)* shall reflect the sum that would otherwise have been transferred, or subsequently transferred, if no pension adjustment order had been made.][23]

Amendments

[1] Inserted by F(No.2)A13 s18(2)(a)(i)(I). Has effect from 1 January 2014.

[2, 4, 5, 7, 8, 14, 20] Inserted by FA14 s19(4)(a)(i). Has effect on and from 1 January 2015.

[3] Inserted by FA10 s16(1)(b). Has effect as on and from 4 February 2010.

[6] Substituted by FA11 s(19)(3)(a). Has effect as on and from 7 December 2010.

[9] Substituted by F(No.2)A13 s18(2)(a)(i)(II)(A). Has effect from 1 January 2014.

[10] Substituted by F(No.2)A13 s18(2)(a)(i)(II)(B). Has effect from 1 January 2014.

[11] Substituted by FA11 s(19)(3)(b). Has effect as on and from 7 December 2010.

[12] Substituted by F(No.2)A13 s18(2)(a)(i)(II)(C). Has effect from 1 January 2014.

[13, 19] Substituted by F(No.2)A08 s16(1)(a). This section is deemed to have effect as on and from 7 December 2005.

[15] Substituted by F(No.2)A13 s18(2)(a)(i)(III). Has effect from 1 January 2014.

[16] Substituted by FA11 s(19)(3)(d). Has effect as on and from 7 December 2010.

[17] Substituted by F(No.2)A13 s18(2)(a)(i)(IV)(A). Has effect from 1 January 2014.

[18] Substituted by F(No.2)A13 s18(2)(a)(i)(IV)(B). Has effect from 1 January 2014.

[21] Substituted by F(No.2)A13 s18(2)(a)(ii). Has effect from 1 January 2014.

[22] Inserted by F(No.2)A13 s18(2)(a)(iii). Has effect from 1 January 2014.

[23] Substituted by FA14 s19(4)(a)(ii). Has effect on and from 1 January 2015.

Note

Note to FA11 Amendments – Nothwithstanding para (a) of the definition of "standard fund threshold" in section 787O(1) (as amended by subsection (3)(e)), for the purposes of the definition of "lump sum limit" in subsection (1)(a) of section 790AA (before the amendment of that section by subsection (4) (b)) of that Act, "standard fund threshold" shall mean €5,418,085 for the year of assessment 2010.

Revenue Briefings

eBrief

eBrief No. 24/2006 – Pensions Claiming a Personal Fund Threshold
eBrief No. 67/2007 – Earnings Adjustment Factor for the year of assessment 2008
eBrief No. 08/2014 – Pensions – Personal Fund Threshold Notification

Cross References

From Section 787O

Section 548 Valuation of assets.
Section 770 Interpretation and supplemental (Chapter 1).
Section 771 Meaning of "retirement benefits scheme".
Section 772 Conditions for approval of schemes and discretionary approval.
Section 784 Retirement annuities: relief for premiums.
Section 784A Approved retirement fund.
Section 784C Approved minimum retirement fund.
Section 787A Interpretation and supplemental.
Section 787H Approved Retirement Fund option.
Section 787M Interpretation and general (Chapter 2B).
Section 787P Maximum tax-relieved pension fund.
Section 787Q Chargeable excess.
Section 787U Regulations (Chapter 2C).

To Section 787O

Section 772 Conditions for approval of schemes and discretionary approval.
Section 787Q Chargeable excess.
Section 787U Regulations (Chapter 2C).
Section 790AA Taxation of lump sums in excess of the tax free amount.

787P Maximum tax-relieved pension fund

[(1) An individual's maximum tax-relieved pension fund shall not exceed—

(a) the standard fund threshold, or

(b) the personal fund threshold, where—

(i) the conditions set out in *subsection (2)* are met and the Revenue Commissioners have issued a certificate in accordance with *subsection (7)* or a revised certificate in accordance with *subsection (8)*, or

(ii) the Revenue Commissioners have issued an earlier certificate.

(2) The conditions referred to in *subsection (1)(b)(i)* are—

(a) that the individual requests and obtains from the administrator of each relevant pension arrangement of which he or she is a member a statement—

(i) certifying the amount of the crystallised or, as the case may be, uncrystallised pension rights in respect of the arrangement on the specified date, in relation to the individual (in this subsection referred to as the "*individual's pension rights*"), calculated in accordance with the provisions of this Chapter and *Schedule 23B*,

(ii) where the arrangement is a defined benefit arrangement, certifying the annual amount of pension represented by AP in the formula in *paragraph 1(2)(b)* of *Schedule 23B* included in the calculation of the individual's pension rights, and

(iii) where the arrangement is an arrangement of a kind described in *paragraph (a)* of the definition of 'relevant pension arrangement' in *section 787O(1)*, specifying the Revenue Approval Reference Number (in this subsection referred to as the 'reference number') of the arrangement,

and

(b) that the individual notifies the Revenue Commissioners, by such electronic means (within the meaning of *section 917EA*) as are required by the Commissioners, within the period of 12 months from the date the electronic means are made available by the Commissioners, or before the first benefit crystallisation event occurs after the specified date, whichever is the earlier, that he or she has a personal fund threshold and provides the following information (in this section referred to as the "*PFT notification*")—

(i) his or her full name, address, telephone number and PPS Number,

(ii) the following particulars of each relevant pension arrangement in respect of which the personal fund threshold arises:

(I) the name, address and telephone number of the administrator;

(II) the name and reference number of the arrangement;

(III) whether the arrangement is a defined benefit or defined contribution arrangement;

(IV) (A) the amount of the individual's pension rights in respect of the arrangement as certified by the administrator for the purposes of *paragraph (a)*, and

(B) where the arrangement is a defined benefit arrangement, the annual amount of pension referred to in *subsection (2)(a)(ii)* as certified by the administrator for the purposes of *paragraph (a)*;

and

(V) such other information and particulars as the Revenue Commissioners may reasonably require for the purposes of this Chapter and *Schedule 23B*.

(3) A statement referred to in *subsection (2)(a)* shall—

(a) be kept and retained by—

(i) the administrator, for the period of 6 years after the date of the benefit crystallisation event arising under the relevant pension arrangement or, where there is more than one such event, the date of the latest event, and

(ii) the individual, for the period of 6 years after the date of the last benefit crystallisation event arising in respect of the relevant pension arrangement or arrangements included in the PFT notification,

and

(b) on being so required by notice given to the administrator or, as the case may be, the individual in writing by an officer of the Revenue Commissioners, be made available to the officer within the time specified in the notice.

(4) Where a PFT notification is required to be made before the electronic means referred to in *subsection (2)(b)* are made available the notification shall be made in a manner approved by the Revenue Commissioners.

(5) A PFT notification made by electronic means shall be deemed to include a declaration to the effect that the notification is correct and complete.

(6) The administrator of each relevant pension arrangement of which an individual is a member shall comply with a request from the individual to provide a statement referred to in *subsection (2)(a)*.

(7) Subject to *subsection (8)*, the Revenue Commissioners, on receipt of a PFT notification, shall within 30 days of receipt, or such longer period as they may require for the purposes of this subsection, issue a certificate to the individual stating the amount of the personal fund threshold.

(8) The Revenue Commissioners may at any time withdraw a certificate issued in accordance with *subsection (7)* (in this subsection referred to as the 'first-mentioned certificate') and, where appropriate, issue a revised certificate if, following the issue of the first-mentioned certificate, the Commissioners are satisfied that—

(a) the information included in the PFT notification is incorrect, or

(b) the individual is not entitled to a certificate.][1]

Amendments

[1] Substituted by F(No.2)A13 s18(2)(b). Has effect from 1 January 2014.

Revenue Briefings

eBrief

eBrief No. 10/2011 – Pensions: Personal Fund Threshold Notification Form
eBrief No. 08/2014 – Pensions – Personal Fund Threshold Notification
eBrief No. 50/2014 – Pensions – Personal Fund Threshold – New Electronic Notification System

Cross References

To Section 787P

Section 787O Interpretation and general (Chapter 2C).
Section 787R Liability to tax and rate of tax on chargeable excess.

787Q Chargeable excess

[(1) Income tax shall be charged in accordance with *section 787R* where, on or after [7 December 2005][1], a benefit crystallisation event occurs (in this section referred to as the "*current event*") in relation to an individual who is a member of a relevant pension arrangement and either of the conditions in *subsection (2)* are met.

(2) The conditions referred to in *subsection (1)* are—

(a) that all or any part of the individual's standard fund threshold or, as the case may be, personal fund threshold is available at the date of the current event but the amount of that event exceeds the amount of the standard fund threshold or personal fund threshold which is available at that date, or

(b) that none of the individual's standard fund threshold or personal fund threshold, as the case may be, is available at the date of the current event.

(3) For the purposes of *subsection (2)*, the amount of an individual's standard fund threshold or, as the case may be, personal fund threshold that is available at the date of the current event shall be determined in accordance with *paragraph 4* of *Schedule 23B.*

(4) Subject to *subsection (5)*, where either of the conditions in *subsection (2)* are met, the amount of the current event or, as the case may be, the amount by which the amount of that event exceeds the amount of the standard fund threshold or personal fund threshold that is available at that date in relation to the individual, shall be known as the "*chargeable excess*".

(5) Where the amount of tax arising on a chargeable excess in accordance with *section 787R* is paid by the administrator of a relevant pension arrangement in whole or in part, then so much of the tax that is paid by the administrator shall itself be treated as forming part of the chargeable excess unless the individual's rights under the relevant pension arrangement are reduced so as to fully reflect the amount of tax so paid or the administrator is reimbursed by the individual in respect of any tax so paid.

[(5A) (a) Notwithstanding *section 59B* of the Pensions Act 1990, where, in accordance with *section 787S(3)*, a non-member's appropriate share (within the meaning of *section 787R(2A)(b)*) of tax arising on a chargeable excess is paid by the subsequent administrator, in whole or in part, and the non-member was in receipt of a pension benefit payable from the transfer arrangement at the date the subsequent administrator received the certificate referred to in *section 787R(3B)*, then so much of the tax that is paid by the subsequent administrator shall itself be treated as forming part of the non-member's appropriate share unless the non-member's pension benefit payable under the transfer arrangement is reduced so as to fully reflect the amount of tax so paid or the subsequent administrator is reimbursed by the non-member in respect of any tax so paid.

(b) Where, in accordance with *section 787S(3)*, a subsequent administrator or a fund administrator (in this paragraph referred to as the 'administrator') is liable to pay the amount of a non- member's appropriate share (within the meaning of *section 787R(2A)(b)*) of tax arising on a chargeable excess, or a part of that amount, the administrator shall, for the purposes of payment of the tax, be entitled to dispose of or appropriate such assets of—

(i) the transfer arrangement as represent the non-member's accrued rights under that arrangement, or

(ii) the approved retirement fund, approved minimum retirement fund (or where the non-member has an approved retirement fund and an approved minimum retirement fund, of both funds) or vested PRSA (or vested PRSAs, where the non-member has more than one vested PRSA), as the case may be, (in this subsection referred to as the 'fund'),

as are required to meet the amount of the tax so payable and the non-member shall allow such disposal or appropriation.

(c) Where in pursuance of this subsection and *section 787S(3)* a subsequent administrator reduces a non-member's pension benefit 5 or disposes of or appropriates an asset of the transfer arrangement, or a fund administrator disposes of or appropriates an asset of the fund, then no action shall lie against the subsequent administrator or the fund administrator in any court by reason of such reduction, disposal or appropriation.][2]

(6) Where the administrator of a relevant pension arrangement, of a kind described in *paragraphs (e)* and *(f)* of the definition of relevant pension arrangement in *section 787O(1)*, pays an amount of tax arising on a chargeable excess in accordance with *section 787S(3)*, then—

(a) the amount of tax so paid shall be a debt due to the administrator from the individual [...][3] and

[(b) the administrator shall be reimbursed by the individual for the tax so paid in accordance with *subsection (7)*.][4]

[(6A) Where the provisions of *section 787R(2A)* apply in relation to a relevant pension arrangement referred to in *subsection (6)*, then—

(a) where no transfer amount has been applied, or

(b) where a transfer amount has been applied to provide a retirement benefit for or in respect of the non-member under the arrangement of the same actuarial value as the transfer amount,

the provisions of *subsections (6)*, *(7)*, *(8)* and *(9)* shall apply, as if the references in those subsections to—

(i) the individual were a reference to the relevant member or the non-member, as the case may be, and

(ii) the rules of the scheme were a reference to the rules of the scheme having regard to the provisions of the pension adjustment order.][5]

[(7) An administrator referred to in *subsection (6)* shall be reimbursed for the payment of tax arising on a chargeable excess in the following manner—

(a) where the amount of tax paid is [20 per cent][6] or a lesser percentage of the amount of the lump sum payable to the individual under the rules of the relevant pension arrangement reduced by the amount of tax charged under *subsection (3)(a)(i)* or *(3)(b)(i)(I)* of *section 790AA* on an excess lump sum (within the meaning of *subsection (1)(e)* of that section), if any, in respect of that lump sum (in this subsection referred to as the 'net lump sum')—

(i) by appropriating that percentage of the net lump sum,

(ii) by payment by the individual of an amount to the administrator that is equal to the amount of tax paid, [...][7]

(iii) by a combination of *subparagraphs (i)* and *(ii)* such that the aggregate of the percentage of the net lump sum appropriated and the amount paid by the individual to the administrator is equal to the amount of tax [paid, or][8]

[(iv) by the individual exercising the option referred to in *subsection (8)*,][9]

(b) where the amount of tax paid is greater than [20 per cent][10] of the net lump sum [by the individual exercising the option referred to in *subsection (8)*, or][11]—

(i) (I) by appropriating not less than [20 per cent][12] of the net lump sum, or such higher percentage as the administrator and the individual may agree,

(II) by payment by the individual of an amount to the administrator that is not less than [20 per cent][13] of the net lump sum, or such higher amount as the administrator and the individual may agree, or

(III) by a combination of clauses (I) and (II) such that the aggregate of the percentage of the net lump sum appropriated and the amount paid by the individual to the administrator is not less than [20 per cent][14] of the net lump sum,

and

(ii) (I) by reducing the gross annual amount of pension payable to the individual under the rules of the relevant pension arrangement (in this subsection referred to as the 'pension reduction'), for a period agreed between the individual and the administrator that does not exceed [20 years][15] from the date of first payment of the pension (in this subsection referred to as the 'agreed period'), such that the pension reduction over the agreed period is sufficient to reimburse the administrator for that portion of the tax paid as was not reimbursed under *subparagraph (i)*, if any, (in this subsection referred to as the 'balance'),

(II) by payment by the individual of an amount equal to the balance to the administrator within the period of 3 months from the date of the benefit crystallisation event that gave rise to the chargeable excess,or

(III) by a combination of a pension reduction over an agreed period as provided for in clause (I) and payment of an amount by the individual as provided for in clause (II) where the aggregate of the amount of the reduction in the pension over the agreed period and the amount payable by the individual equals the balance,

[...][16][17]

[(8) The option referred to in *paragraphs (a)(iv)* and *(b)* of *subsection (7)* is the option to have the gross annual amount of pension payable to the individual under the rules of the relevant pension arrangement reduced for a period that does not exceed 20 years from the date of first payment of the pension, such that the reduction in the pension over the period is sufficient to reimburse the administrator for the tax paid.

(9) A payment by an individual to an administrator referred to in *subparagraphs (ii)* and *(iii)* of *paragraph (a)* of *subsection (7)* and in *clauses (II)* and *(III)* of *paragraph (b)(i)* of that subsection (in this subsection referred to as the 'first-mentioned payment') shall be made before the administrator pays the amount of the net lump sum or, as the case may be, such amount of the net lump sum as has not been appropriated to reimburse the administrator for the payment of tax arising on the chargeable excess and the administrator may withhold payment of that amount until such time as the first-mentioned payment is made by the individual.][18]

Amendments

[1] Substituted by FA11 s(19)(3)(n). Has effect as on and from 7 December 2010.

[2] Inserted by FA14 s19(4)(b)(i). Has effect on and from 1 January 2015.

[3] Deleted by FA12 s18(5)(a). Has effect from 8 February 2012.

[4] Substituted by FA12 s18(5)(b). Has effect from 8 February 2012.

[5] Inserted by FA14 s19(4)(b)(ii). Has effect on and from 1 January 2015.

[6, 10, 12, 13, 14] Substituted by F(No.2)A13 s18(2)(c)(i)(I). Has effect from 1 January 2014.

[7] Deleted by F(No.2)A13 s18(2)(c)(i)(II). Has effect from 1 January 2014.

[8] Substituted by F(No.2)A13 s18(2)(c)(i)(III). Has effect from 1 January 2014.

[9] Inserted by F(No.2)A13 s18(2)(c)(i)(IV). Has effect from 1 January 2014.

[11] Inserted by F(No.2)A13 s18(2)(c)(i)(V). Has effect from 1 January 2014.

[15] Substituted by F(No.2)A13 s18(2)(c)(i)(VI). Has effect from 1 January 2014.

[16] Deleted by F(No.2)A13 s18(2)(c)(i)(VII). Has effect from 1 January 2014.

[17] Inserted by FA12 s18(5)(c). Has effect from 8 February 2012.

[18] Inserted by F(No.2)A13 s18(2)(c)(ii). Has effect from 1 January 2014.

Cross References

From Section 787Q

Section 787O Interpretation and general (Chapter 2C).
Section 787R Liability to tax and rate of tax on chargeable excess.
Section 787S Payment of tax due on chargeable excess.

To Section 787Q

Section 787O Interpretation and general (Chapter 2C).
Section 787R Liability to tax and rate of tax on chargeable excess.

787R Liability to tax and rate of tax on chargeable excess

[(1) Without prejudice to any other provisions of the Tax Acts including, in particular, any other provision of those Acts relating to a charge to tax—

(a) the whole of the amount of a chargeable excess calculated in accordance with *section 787Q*, without any relief or reduction specified in the Table to *section 458* or any other deduction from that amount, shall be chargeable to income tax under Case IV of Schedule D [at the higher rate for the tax year (within the meaning of *section 787TA(1)*) in which the benefit crystallisation event giving rise to the chargeable excess occurs][1], and

(b) [section 188][2] shall not apply as regards income tax so charged.

[(2) [Subject to *subsection (2A)(d)*, the persons liable][3] for income tax charged under *subsection (1)* shall be the administrator of the relevant pension arrangement under which the benefit crystallisation event arises and the individual in relation to whom the benefit crystallisation event occurs and their liability shall be joint and several.][4]

[(2A) (a) Where an individual is a relevant member of a relevant pension arrangement, income tax charged under *subsection (1)* (in this subsection referred to as the 'tax') in respect of a chargeable excess arising on a benefit crystallisation event in respect of the relevant member under that arrangement shall be apportioned by the administrator between the relevant member and the non-member (in this subsection referred to as the 'relevant parties') in accordance with *paragraph (b)*, and the persons liable for the tax so apportioned and the extent of their liability shall be the persons referred to in *paragraph (d)* and the liabilities referred to therein.

(b) Subject to the assumption in *paragraph (c)*, the tax referred to in *paragraph (a)* shall be apportioned between the relevant parties such that each party's share of the tax (in this Chapter referred to as the 'appropriate share') shall not exceed such part of the tax as would bear to that tax the same proportion as each party's share of the retirement benefit (arising under the benefit crystallisation event giving rise to the tax) bears to that retirement benefit, having regard to the designated benefit payable to the non-member pursuant to the pension adjustment order.

(c) The assumption referred to in *paragraph (b)* is that, where a transfer amount has been applied to provide a retirement benefit for or in respect of the non-member, each party's share of the retirement benefit arising under the benefit crystallisation event giving rise to the tax shall be determined as follows:

(i) in the case of the non-member—

(I) where the relevant pension arrangement referred to in *paragraph (a)* is a defined benefit arrangement and is the arrangement in respect of which the pension adjustment order has been made, it shall be the designated benefit on which the transfer amount was calculated, and

(II) in any other case, it shall be the transfer amount, and

(ii) in the case of the relevant member, it shall be an amount equivalent to the amount determined by the formula—

$$A - B$$

where—

A is the retirement benefit arising under the benefit crystallisation event giving rise to the tax, and

B is the non-member's share determined in accordance with *clause (I)* or *(II)*, as the case may be, of *subparagraph (i)*.

(*d*) The persons liable for the tax apportioned in accordance with *paragraph (b)* and the extent of their liability shall be—

(i) the administrator and the relevant member in respect of the relevant member's appropriate share, and

(ii) (I) where no transfer amount has been applied to provide a retirement benefit for or in respect of the non-member (and notwithstanding the provisions of the pension adjustment order), the administrator and the non-member in respect of the non-member's appropriate share, or

(II) where a transfer amount has been applied to provide a retirement benefit for or in respect of the non-member and—

(A) the non-member's retirement benefit under the transfer arrangement has not crystallised at the date the subsequent administrator receives the certificate referred to in *subsection (3B)* or where the administrator and the subsequent administrator are the same person (in this section referred to as the 'alternative circumstance') at the date of the benefit crystallisation event giving rise to the chargeable excess (in this section referred to as the 'alternative date'), the subsequent administrator and the non-member in respect of the non-member's appropriate share, or

(B) the non-member's retirement benefit under the transfer arrangement has crystallised at the date the subsequent administrator receives the certificate referred to in *subsection (3B)* or where the alternative circumstance 15 arises at the alternative date and the non-member is in receipt of a pension payable from the transfer arrangement, the subsequent administrator and the non- member in respect of the non-member's appropriate share, or

(C) the non-member's retirement benefit under the transfer arrangement has crystallised at the date the subsequent administrator receives the certificate referred to in *subsection (3B)* or where the alternative circumstance arises at the alternative date and the non-member has exercised a relevant option under the transfer arrangement, the fund administrator and the non- member in respect of the non-member's appropriate share,

or

(III) in any other case, the non-member in respect of his or her appropriate share,

and the liability of the persons referred to in *subparagraph (i)* and in *clauses (I)* and *(II)* of *subparagraph (ii)* shall be joint and several.

(e) Notwithstanding *paragraph (d)(ii)(II)*, the liability of a subsequent administrator or a fund administrator shall not exceed the lesser of the non-member's appropriate share and—

(i) in the case of a subsequent administrator, the amount or value of the assets in the transfer arrangement (in this subparagraph referred to as the 'first-mentioned arrangement') representing the non-member's accrued rights under the arrangement at the time those rights are transferred to another relevant pension arrangement or at the time the non-member's retirement benefit under the first-mentioned arrangement crystallise, as the case may be, or

(ii) in the case of a fund administrator, the amount or value of the assets in the approved retirement fund, approved minimum retirement fund (or the aggregate of those amounts or values where the non-member has an approved retirement fund and an approved minimum retirement fund) or vested PRSA (or the aggregate of those amounts or values where the non-member has more than one vested PRSA), as the case may be, at the date the fund administrator receives the certificate or copy certificate referred to in *subsection (3C)*.][5]

[(3) A person referred to in *subsection (2)* or *paragraph (d)* of *subsection (2A)* shall be liable for any income tax charged in accordance with *subsection (1)* or, as the case may be, for the appropriate share of that tax, whether or not that person, or any other person who is liable to the charge, is resident or ordinarily resident in the State.][6]

[(3A) The references in *subsections (2)*, *(2A)(d)* and *(3)* to income tax charged under *subsection (1)* or to the appropriate share of that tax, shall be deemed to be references to the amount of income tax so charged or to the appropriate share of that tax, as the case may be, reduced, as appropriate, in accordance with *section 787RA*.

(3B) Where the provisions of *subsection (2A)* apply and a transfer amount has been applied, the administrator (other than where the alternative circumstance referred to in *subsection (2A)(d)(ii)(II)(A)* arises) shall establish the identity of the subsequent administrator and, within 21 days from the end of the month in which the benefit crystallisation event giving rise to the chargeable excess occurs, provide to the subsequent administrator a certificate stating—

(a) the name, address and telephone number of the administrator,

(b) details of the transfer arrangement, where known,

(c) details of the relevant pension arrangement under which the benefit crystallisation event giving rise to the chargeable excess occurred,

(d) the nature of the benefit crystallisation event referred to in *paragraph (c)* and the date on which it occurred,

(e) the full name, last known address and, where known, the PPS Number of the non-member,

(f) the amount of, and the basis of calculation of, the non-member's appropriate share, and

(g) such other information and particulars as the Revenue Commissioners may reasonably require for the purposes of this Chapter.

(3C) (a) Where—

(i) the provisions of *subsection (2A)* apply and a transfer amount has been applied, and

(ii) at the date the subsequent administrator receives the certificate referred to in *subsection (3B)* the non-member's retirement benefit under the transfer arrangement has crystallised and the non-member has exercised a relevant option under the transfer arrangement,

then, where the subsequent administrator and the fund administrator are not the same person, the subsequent administrator shall establish the identity of the fund administrator and, within 21 days from receipt of the certificate, forward a copy of the certificate (in this section referred to as the 'copy certificate') to the fund administrator.

(b) Where—

(i) the provisions of *subsection (2A)* apply and a transfer amount has been applied,

(ii) at the date of the benefit crystallisation event giving rise to the chargeable excess tax (in this paragraph referred to as the 'event') the non-member's retirement benefit under the transfer arrangement has crystallised and the non-member has exercised a relevant option under the transfer arrangement, and

(iii) the alternative circumstance referred to in *subsection (2A)(d)(ii)(II)(A)* arises,

then, where the administrator and the fund administrator are not the same person, the administrator shall establish the identity of the fund administrator and, within 21 days from the end of the month in which the event occurs, provide to the fund administrator the certificate referred to in *subsection (3B)*.

(3D) An administrator, subsequent administrator or fund administrator, as the case may be, shall within 21 days from—

(a) in the case of an administrator (including an administrator who is either or both the subsequent administrator and the fund administrator), the end of the month in which the benefit crystallisation event giving rise to the chargeable excess tax occurs, or

(b) in the case of a subsequent administrator or fund administrator, the date of receipt of a certificate or copy certificate, as the case may be,

inform the non-member by way of a notification in writing of the non-member's liability for the non-member's appropriate share of the chargeable excess tax and, where at the time the notification is due to be made the administrator or the subsequent administrator, as the case may be, is aware that the non-member is the person solely liable for the non-member's appropriate share, inform the non-member as part of the notification of that fact and of the fact that the tax is due and payable by the non-member to the Collector-General in accordance with *section 787S(3)* within 3 months of the date of the notification.

(3E) Where a notification referred to in *subsection (3D)* is sent to a non-member in circumstances where the non-member is solely liable for the non-member's appropriate share of the chargeable excess tax, a copy of the notice shall be sent by the administrator or the subsequent administrator, as the case may be, to the Revenue Commissioners at the same time.][7]

(4) Where a benefit crystallisation event is due to occur (in this subsection referred to as the "*future event*") in relation to an individual under a relevant pension arrangement […][8], the administrator of that arrangement may request the individual to make, before the date of the future event, a declaration in writing to the administrator, in such form as may be prescribed or authorised by the Revenue Commissioners for that purpose, which contains—

(a) the individual's full name, address and PPS Number,

(b) in respect of each benefit crystallisation event that has occurred in relation to the individual on or after [7 December 2005][9]—

(i) the date on which that event occurred, and

(ii) the amount crystallised by that event,

(c) in respect of a benefit crystallisation event or benefit crystallisation events that is or are due to occur from the date of the declaration made by the individual under this subsection up to and including the date of the future event—

(i) the expected date of each such event, and

(ii) the estimated amount to be crystallised by each such event,

(d) where relevant, the amount of the individual's personal fund threshold together with a copy of the certificate issued by the Revenue Commissioners under [*section 787P(7)* or, as the case may be, a copy of the revised certificate issued by the Commissioners under *section 787P(8)* (or, where relevant, a copy of the earlier certificate),][10]

[(e) where the administrator of the arrangement is an administrator of a kind referred to in *paragraph (d)* of the definition of 'administrator' in *section 787O(1)* and where relevant, details of the amount of unpaid tax required to be paid by the administrator and remitted to the Collector-General under *subsections (18)* and *(19)* of *section 787TA*, and][11].

(5) Where an individual has been requested to provide a declaration in writing to the administrator of a relevant pension arrangement in accordance with *subsection (4)* and fails to provide that declaration, the administrator may—

(a) where the benefit crystallisation event is an event of a kind described at *subparagraph (a)* or *(d)* of *paragraph 2* of *Schedule 23B*, withhold the payment of any benefit or, as the case may be, any increased annual amount of pension, and

(b) where the benefit crystallisation event is an event of a kind described at *subparagraph (b)* or *(c)* of *paragraph 2* of *Schedule 23B*, refuse to transfer an amount to the person, or any of the funds referred to in the said *subparagraph (b)* or, as the case may be, make a payment or transfer to an overseas arrangement,

until such time as a declaration in writing containing the information specified in [*paragraphs (a)* to *(f)*][12] of *subsection (4)* is provided to the administrator, in such form as may be prescribed or authorised by the Revenue Commissioners for the purposes of that subsection.

(6) An administrator of a relevant pension arrangement shall—

(a) keep and retain for a period of 6 years, and

(b) on being so required by notice given to the administrator in writing by an officer of the Revenue Commissioners, make available to the officer within the time specified in the notice,

a declaration, or declarations, of the kind mentioned in *subsections (4)* and *(5)*.][13]

[(6A) (a) A subsequent administrator or a fund administrator, as the case may be, shall keep and retain a certificate referred to in *subsection (3B)* or a copy certificate referred to in *subsection (3C)*, as appropriate, and

(b) an administrator, subsequent administrator and fund administrator shall keep and retain a copy of a notification referred to in *subsection (3D)*,

for a period of 6 years following—

(i) in the case of an administrator, the date of the benefit crystallisation event giving rise to the chargeable excess tax or, where a transfer amount has been applied and the administrator and the subsequent administrator are the same person, the later of that date and the date of crystallisation of the non-member's retirement benefit under the transfer arrangement,

(ii) in the case of a subsequent administrator in any other circumstance, the later of the date of crystallisation of the non-member's retirement benefit under the transfer arrangement and the date of receipt of the certificate, or

(iii) in the case of a fund administrator, where the administrator and the fund administrator are the same person, the date of the benefit crystallisation event giving rise to the chargeable excess tax, and in any other circumstance, the date of receipt of the certificate or copy certificate, as the case may be,

and on being so required by a notice given to the administrator in writing by an officer of the Revenue Commissioners make available to the officer within the time specified in the notice such certificates, copy certificates or notifications specified therein.][14]

Amendments

[1] Substituted by FA14 s19(4)(c)(i). Has effect on and from 1 January 2015.

[2] Substituted by FA08 s5(g).

[3] Substituted by FA14 s19(4)(c)(ii). Has effect on and from 1 January 2015.

[4] Substituted by FA11 s(19)(3)(o). Has effect as on and from 7 December 2010.

[5] Inserted by FA14 s19(4)(c)(iii). Has effect on and from 1 January 2015.

[6] Substituted by FA14 s19(4)(c)(iv). Has effect on and from 1 January 2015.

[7] Substituted by FA14 s19(4)(c)(v). Has effect on and from 1 January 2015.

[8] Deleted by FA11 s(19)(3)(p)(i). Has effect as on and from 7 December 2010.

[9] Substituted by FA11 s(19)(3)(p)(ii). Has effect as on and from 7 December 2010.

[10] Substituted by F(No.2)A13 s18(2)(d)(i). Has effect from 1 January 2014.

[11] Substituted by FA12 s18(6)(b). Has effect from 8 February 2012.

[12] Substituted by F(No.2)A13 s18(2)(d)(ii). Has effect from 1 January 2014.

[13] Inserted by FA06 s14(1)(e). Has effect as on and from 7 December 2005.

[14] Inserted by FA14 s19(4)(c)(vi). Has effect on and from 1 January 2015.

Revenue Briefings

eBrief

eBrief No. 38/2011 – Limit on Tax Relieved Pension Fund

eBrief No. 22/2014 – Pensions – Form 787S (Chargeable Excess Tax) and Form 790AA (Excess Lump Sum Tax)

Cross References

From Section 787R

Section 188 Age exemption and associated marginal relief.

Section 458 Deductions allowed in ascertaining taxable income and provisions relating to reductions in tax.

Section 787P Maximum tax-relieved pension fund.

Section 787Q Chargeable excess.

To Section 787R

Section 787Q Chargeable excess.

787RA Credit for tax paid on an excess lump sum

[(1) Where, on or after 1 January 2011, a benefit crystallisation event that gives rise to a chargeable excess in accordance with *section 787Q* occurs in relation to an individual in respect of a relevant pension arrangement [(including, where the provisions of *section 787R(2A)* apply, an individual who is a relevant member of a relevant pension arrangement)][1], then, in so far as income tax has been charged under *subsection (3)(a)(i)* or *(3)(b)(i)(I)* of *section 790AA* on an excess lump sum (within the meaning of *subsection (1)(e)* of that section) in respect of a lump sum paid, on or after that date, to the individual—

(a) by the administrator of that relevant pension arrangement (in this section referred to as the 'first-mentioned administrator'), whether under that relevant pension arrangement, orunder any other relevant pension arrangement administered by the first-mentioned administrator, or

(b) where the condition in *subsection (2)* is met, by the administrator of another relevant pension arrangement,

the income tax on the chargeable excess [or the relevant individual's appropriate share of that tax, as the case may be,][2] charged in accordance with *section 787R* (in this section referred to as the 'chargeable excess tax') shall be reduced by the aggregate of the amount of income tax charged under *subsection (3)(a)(i)* or *(3)(b)(i)(I)* of *section 790AA* on the excess lump sum and deducted by the first-mentioned administrator and the amount of such income tax charged on the excess lump sum and deducted by the other administrator (in this section referred to as the 'lump sum tax').

(2) The condition referred to in *subsection (1)(b)* is that the first-mentioned administrator obtains from the other administrator a certificate stating—

(a) the name and address of the administrator,

(b) the individual's full name, address and PPS Number,

(c) the relevant pension arrangement in respect of which the benefit crystallisation event giving rise to the excess lump sum arose,

(d) the date of payment of the lump sum in respect of which tax on the excess lump sum was deducted under *section 790AA* and the amount of the lump sum, and

(e) the amount of the lump sum tax in respect of the excess lump sum charged to tax in accordance with *subsection (3)(a)(i)* or *(3)(b)(i)(I)* of *section 790AA* and deducted by, and remitted to the Collector-General by the administrator in accordance with *subsection (8)* of that section.

(3) Subject to *subsection (4)*, where the lump sum tax referred to in *subsection (1)* is greater than the chargeable excess tax [or the appropriate share of that tax, as the case may be,][3] referred to in that subsection, the amount by which the lump sum tax exceeds the chargeable excess tax [or the appropriate share of that tax, as the case may be,][4] may be carried forward and aggregated with the lump sum tax on a lump sum (if any) paid to the individual under the next benefit crystallisation event that occurs in relation to that individual (in this section referred to as the 'tax balance') and, so far as may be, used to reduce the amount of the chargeable excess tax [or the appropriate share of that tax, as the case may be,][5] arising on that benefit crystallisation event (in this section referred to as the 'future chargeable excess tax') and so on in respect of each successive benefit crystallisation event until the tax balance is fully used.

(4) Where a future chargeable excess tax referred to in *subsection (3)* is in respect of a benefit crystallisation event under a relevant pension arrangement which is not administered by the first-mentioned administrator and the tax balance has not been fully used, the administrator of that relevant pension arrangement shall obtain from the first-mentioned administrator a certificate stating—

(a) the name and addressofthe first-mentioned administrator,

(b) the individual's full name, address and PPS Number, and

(c) the amount of the unused tax balance.

(5) Where an administrator receives a certificate referred to in *subsection (4)*, the future chargeable excess tax may be reduced by the aggregate of the amount of the unused tax balance referred to in that certificate and the lump sum tax, if any, charged by that administrator in respect of the benefit crystallisation event giving rise to the future chargeable excess tax.

(6) *Subsections (4)* and *(5)* shall apply as appropriate, and with any necessary modifications, on each successive occasion on which a benefit crystallisation event occurs in relation to the individual where the administrator of that benefit crystallisation event and the administrator of the immediately preceding benefit crystallisation event are not the same person.

(7) *Subsection (6)* of *section 787R* shall, with any necessary modifications, apply to an administrator who obtains a certificate under *subsection (2)* or *(4)* as if the reference in that *subsection (6)* to a declaration, or declarations were a reference to a certificate, or certificates, to which *subsection (2)* or *(4)* applies.

(8) Any lump sum tax or tax balance referred to in this section—
 (a) shall be used only once to reduce a chargeable excess tax [or the appropriate share of that tax, as the case may be,][6] and
 (b) shall be used for no other purpose.][7]

[(9) Where the provisions of *section 787R(2A)* apply, this section shall, 10 with any necessary modifications, apply to the non-member in respect of the non-member's appropriate share of the chargeable excess tax.][8]

Amendments

[1] Inserted by FA14 s19(4)(d)(i). Has effect on and from 1 January 2015.

[2] Inserted by FA14 s19(4)(d)(ii). Has effect on and from 1 January 2015.

[3, 4, 5] Inserted by FA14 s19(4)(d)(iii). Has effect on and from 1 January 2015.

[6] Inserted by FA14 s19(4)(d)(iv). Has effect on and from 1 January 2015.

[7] Inserted by FA12 s18(7)(a). Has effect from 1 January 2011.

[8] Inserted by FA14 s19(4)(d)(v). Has effect on and from 1 January 2015.

787S Payment of tax due on chargeable excess

[(1) The administrator of a relevant pension arrangement shall, [within 3 months from][1] the end of the month in which the benefit crystallisation event giving rise to the chargeable excess occurs, make a return to the Collector-General which shall contain—
 (a) the name and address of the administrator,
 (b) the name, address and PPS Number of the individual in relation to whom the benefit crystallisation event has occurred,
 (c) details of the relevant pension arrangement under which the benefit crystallisation event giving rise to the chargeable excess has occurred,
 (d) the amount of, and the basis of calculation of, the chargeable excess arising in respect of the benefit crystallisation event, and
 [(e) details of the tax which the administrator is required to account for in relation to the chargeable excess,

and where the administrator is the administrator of a relevant pension arrangement to which *section 787R(2A)* applies the return shall also contain—
 (i) where no transfer amount has been applied—
  (I) the name, address and PPS Number of the non-member, and
  (II) instead of the details referred to in *paragraph (e)*, details of the relevant member's and non-member's appropriate share of the tax which the administrator is required to account for in relation to the chargeable excess,

 and
 (ii) where a transfer amount has been applied—
  (I) other than where the administrator, subsequent administrator and fund administrator are the same person, the name, address and telephone number of the subsequent administrator or fund administrator, as the case may be,
  (II) the name, last known address and, where known, the PPS Number of the non-member, and

(III) instead of the details referred to in *paragraph (e)*, the amount of, and the basis of calculation of—

(A) the relevant member's appropriate share of the tax that the administrator is required to account for, and

(B) the non-member's appropriate share of the tax that the subsequent administrator or fund administrator, as the case may be, is required to account for by way of a separate return under this section.][2]

[(1A) Where the provisions of *section 787R(2A)* apply and a transfer amount has been applied, then—

(a) where the transfer arrangement is the relevant pension arrangement of the relevant member, the subsequent administrator, within 3 months from—

(i) the end of the month in which the benefit crystallisation event giving rise to the chargeable excess tax occurs where, at the date of that event, the non-member is in receipt of a pension payable from the transfer arrangement,

(ii) the end of the month in which a sum representing the non-member's accrued rights under the transfer arrangement (in this paragraph referred to as the 'first-mentioned arrangement') is transferred (in whole or in part) to another relevant pension arrangement, or

(iii) the end of the month in which the non-member's retirement benefit under the first-mentioned arrangement crystallises,

or

(b) where the transfer arrangement is not the relevant pension arrangement of the relevant member and the subsequent administrator has received a certificate referred to in *section 787R(3B)*, the subsequent administrator, within 3 months from—

(i) the end of the month in which the subsequent administrator receives the certificate where, at the date of receipt of the certificate, the non-member is in receipt of a pension payable from the transfer arrangement,

(ii) the end of the month in which a sum representing the non-member's accrued rights under the transfer arrangement (in this paragraph referred to as the 'first-mentioned arrangement') is transferred (in whole or in part) to another relevant pension arrangement, or

(iii) the end of the month in which the non-member's retirement benefit under the first-mentioned arrangement crystallises,

or

(c) where—

(i) the fund administrator has received a certificate or copy certificate referred to in *section 787R(3C)*, the fund administrator within 3 months from the end of the month in which the certificate or copy certificate is received, or

(ii) the fund administrator and the administrator of the pension arrangement in respect of which the benefit crystallisation event giving rise to the chargeable excess tax arises, are the same person, the fund administrator within 3 months from the end of the month in which the benefit crystallisation event occurs,

as the case may be, shall—

(i) make a return to the Collector-General which shall contain—

(I) the name, address and telephone number of the subsequent or fund administrator, as the case may be,

(II) the name, address and PPS Number of the non-member,

(III) the name, address and telephone number of the administrator of the relevant pension arrangement from which the transfer amount arose,

(IV) the amount of, and the basis of calculation of, the non-member's appropriate share of the tax, and

(V) the amount of the non-member's appropriate share of the tax which the subsequent or fund administrator, as the case may be, is required to account for,

and

(ii) where the amount of the non-member's appropriate share of the tax which the subsequent or fund administrator is required to account for is less than the amount of that share, notify the non-member in writing at the time the return to the Collector-General is made of that fact and that the balance (being the difference between the amount of the appropriate share and the amount of that share to be accounted for by the subsequent or fund administrator) is due and payable by the non-member to the Collector-General in accordance with this section within 3 months from the date of the notification.

(IB) Where a notification referred to in *subsection (1A)(ii)* is sent to a non- member, a copy of the notice shall be sent by the fund administrator or the subsequent administrator, as the case may be, to the Revenue Commissioners at the same time.

(IC) Where a non-member receives a notification referred to in *subsection (1A)(ii)* or a notification referred to in *section 787R(3D)* (in the circumstance referred to in *section 787R(3E))*, he or she shall within 3 months from the date of the notification make a return to the Collector-General which shall contain—

(a) the name, address and telephone number of the subsequent or fund administrator, as the case may be,

(b) the name, address and PPS Number of the non-member,

(c) the amount of the non-member's appropriate share of the tax,

(d) the amount of the non-member's appropriate share of the tax accounted for by the subsequent or fund administrator, as the case may be, and

(e) the amount of the non-member's appropriate share of the tax which the non-member is required to account for.][4]

[…][5]

(3) The tax [(including a relevant member's or non-member's appropriate share of that tax) which a person is required to account 10 for, in whole or in part,][6] in relation to a chargeable excess (in this section referred to as the "*appropriate tax*")

and which is required to be included in a return shall be due at the time by which the return is due to be made and shall be paid by that person to the Collector-General. The appropriate tax so due shall be payable by that person without the making of an assessment; but appropriate tax that has become so due may be assessed on that person (whether or not it has been paid when the assessment is made) if that tax or any part of it is not paid on or before the due date.

(4) Where it appears to an officer of the Revenue Commissioners that there is any amount of appropriate tax in relation to a chargeable excess which ought to have been but has not been included in a return, or where the officer is dissatisfied with any return, then the officer may make an assessment on the person liable for the appropriate tax to the best of his or her judgement, and any amount of appropriate tax in relation to a chargeable excess due under an assessment made by virtue of this subsection shall be treated for the purposes of interest on unpaid tax as having been payable at the time by which the return concerned was due to be made.

(5) Where any item has been incorrectly included in a return as a chargeable excess, then an officer of the Revenue Commissioners may make such assessments, adjustments or set-offs as may in his or her judgement be required for securing that the resulting liabilities to tax, including interest on unpaid tax, whether of the administrator of a relevant pension arrangement or the individual [or, where the provisions of *section 787R(2A)* apply, whether of the subsequent administrator, fund administrator, relevant member or non-member, as the case may be][7], are, so far as possible, the same as they would have been if the item had not been so included.

(6) (a) Any appropriate tax assessed on a person under this Chapter shall be due within one month after the issue of the notice of assessment (unless that tax is due earlier under *subsection (1)*) subject to—

(i) any appeal against the assessment, or

(ii) any application under *section 787T*,

but no such appeal or application, as the case may be, shall affect the date when any amount is due under *subsection (1)*.

(b) On the determination of an appeal against an assessment under this section, any appropriate tax overpaid shall be repaid.

(7) (a) The provisions of the Income Tax Acts relating to—

(i) assessments to income tax,

(ii) appeals against such assessments (including the rehearing of appeals and the statement of a case for the opinion of the High Court), and

(iii) the collection and recovery of income tax,

shall, in so far as they are applicable, apply to the assessment, collection and recovery of appropriate tax.

(b) Any amount of appropriate tax payable in accordance with this Chapter without the making of an assessment shall carry interest at the rate of [0.0219 per cent][8] for each day or part of a day from the date when the amount becomes due and payable until payment.

(c) *Subsections (3)* to *(5)* of *section 1080* shall apply in relation to interest payable under *paragraph (b)* as they apply in relation to interest payable under *section 1080*.

(d) In its application to any appropriate tax charged by any assessment made in accordance with this section, *section 1080* shall apply as if *subsection (2)(b)* of that section were deleted.

(8) Every return referred to in this section shall be in a form prescribed or authorised by the Revenue Commissioners and shall include a declaration to the effect that the return is correct and complete.][9]

Amendments

[1] Substituted by FA14 s19(4)(e)(i)(I). Has effect on and from 1 January 2015.

[2] Substituted by FA14 s19(4)(e)(i)(II). Has effect on and from 1 January 2015.

[3] Substituted by FA11 s(19)(3)(q). Has effect as on and from 7 December 2010.

[4] Inserted by FA14 s19(4)(e)(ii). Has effect on and from 1 January 2015.

[5] Deleted by FA11 s(19)(3)(r). Has effect as on and from 7 December 2010.

[6] Substituted by FA14 s19(4)(e)(iii). Has effect on and from 1 January 2015.

[7] Inserted by FA14 s19(4)(e)(iv). Has effect on and from 1 January 2015.

[8] Substituted by FA11 s(19)(3)(s). Has effect as on and from 7 December 2010.

[9] Inserted by FA06 s14(1)(e). Has effect as on and from 7 December 2005.

Revenue Briefings

eBrief

eBrief No. 22/2014 – Pensions – Form 787S (Chargeable Excess Tax) and Form 790AA (Excess Lump Sum Tax)

Cross References

From Section 787S

Section 787T Discharge of administrator from tax.

Section 1080 Interest on overdue income tax, corporation tax and capital gains tax.

To Section 787S

Section 787Q Chargeable excess.

787T Discharge of administrator from tax

[(1) Where the administrator of a relevant pension arrangement reasonably believed, in respect of a benefit crystallisation event, that—

(a) the benefit crystallisation event did not give rise to an income tax liability, or

(b) the amount of the income tax liability was less than the actual amount,

the administrator may apply to the Revenue Commissioners in writing to have that tax liability, or as the case may be, the amount of the difference between the amount which the administrator believed to be the amount of the tax liability and the actual amount (in this section referred to as the "*relevant tax liability*") discharged.

(2) Where, following receipt of an application referred to in *subsection (1)*, the Revenue Commissioners are of the opinion that in all of the circumstances it would not be just and reasonable for the administrator to be made liable to the relevant tax liability they may discharge the administrator from that liability and shall notify the administrator in writing of that decision.

(3) Without prejudice to any other circumstance in which an individual will be liable to discharge a tax liability due in respect of a chargeable excess, where an administrator of a relevant pension arrangement is discharged from a relevant tax liability in accordance with *subsection (2)*, the individual in respect of whom the income tax charge arises shall become liable for the charge.][1]

Amendments

[1] Inserted by FA06 s14(1)(e). Has effect as on and from 7 December 2005.

Cross References

To Section 787T

Section 787S Payment of tax due on chargeable excess.

787TA Encashment option

[(1) In this section—

'*active member*', in relation to a public sector scheme, means a member of the scheme who is in reckonable service within the meaning of *section 2(1)* of the Pensions Act 1990;

'*AMRF*' means an approved minimum retirement fund;

'*ARF*' means an approved retirement fund;

'*Personal Retirement Savings Account*' has the meaning assigned to it by *section 787A* and the expression 'PRSA' shall be construed accordingly;

'*private sector scheme*' means a relevant pension arrangement of a kind described in *paragraphs (a)* to *(d)* of the definition of 'relevant pension arrangement';

'*PRSA administrator*' has the meaning assigned to it by *section 787A*;

'*public sector scheme*' means a relevant pension arrangement of a kind described in *paragraphs (e)* and *(f)* of the definition of 'relevant pension arrangement';

'*qualifying fund manager*' has the meaning assigned to it by *section 784A*;

'*relevant individual*' means an individual who on 8 February 2012—

(a) (i) is a member of one or more than one private sector scheme or was such a member before that date and one or more than one benefit crystallisation event has occurred in respect of the scheme or schemes in the relevant period, and

(ii) is a member of one or more than one public sector scheme,

or

(b) is a member of one or more than one private sector scheme or becomes such a member after that date and who subsequently becomes a member of one or more than one public sector scheme,

and who continues as an active member of his or her public sector scheme until his or her retirement date;

'*relevant manager*', in relation to a relevant individual, means a qualifying fund manager of an ARF or an AMRF or, as the case may be, a PRSA administrator of a PRSA, the assets in which are beneficially owned by that individual;

'*relevant period*' means the period starting on 7 December 2005 and ending on 7 February 2012;

'*retirement date*', in relation to a public sector scheme, means the earlier of—

(a) the date on which a member of the scheme retires where that date is on or after the date on which the member reaches the age of 60 years, and

(b) the date on which a member of the scheme retires on grounds of incapacity under the rules of the scheme;

'*tax year*' means a year of assessment for income tax purposes.

(2) Subject to *subsection (11)*, this section shall apply in relation to a relevant individual where—

(a) no benefit crystallisation event has occurred in relation to the relevant individual in the relevant period,

(b) the aggregate of the amounts to be crystallised by benefit crystallisation events in relation to the relevant individual under his or her private sector scheme or schemes and his or her public sector scheme or schemes would, but for this section, exceed the standard fund threshold or, as the case may be, the relevant individual's personal fund threshold (in this section referred to as the 'specified amount'), and

(c) the benefit crystallisation events in relation to the public sector scheme or schemes of the relevant individual occur after the occurrence of all other benefit crystallisation events in relation to the private sector scheme or schemes of that individual.

(3) (a) Where the conditions set out in *subsection (4)* are met, an individual in relation to whom *subsection (2)* may apply may irrevocably instruct in writing the administrator of the private sector scheme or schemes to exercise the option (in this section referred to as the 'encashment option') provided for in *subsection (6)*.

(b) The encashment option may be exercised in respect of a relevant individual on one occasion only and on the same date in relation to each of the private sector schemes of the individual in respect of which he or she has irrevocably instructed the administrator to exercise the option.

(c) Where an administrator referred to in *paragraph (a)* or *subsection (11)(a)* or, as the case may be, a relevant manager referred to in *subsection (11)(a)* (in this paragraph referred to as the 'relevant administrator') receives an irrevocable instruction in writing from an individual the relevant administrator shall keep and retain for a period of 6 years each such instruction and on being so required by notice given to the relevant administrator in writing by an officer of the Revenue Commissioners make available within the time specified in the notice such instructions as may be required by the notice.

(4) The conditions are that the relevant individual—

(a) notifies the Revenue Commissioners in writing of his or her intention to have the encashment option exercised at least 3 months before the date on which the first benefit crystallisation event in relation to the public sector scheme or schemes is to occur and provides the following information—

(i) his or her full name, address and PPS Number,

(ii) an estimate of the value of the accrued rights in respect of which the encashment option is to be exercised or, as the case may be, the specified amount,

(iii) particulars of the private sector scheme or schemes in respect of which the encashment option is to be exercised,

(iv) the name, address and telephone number of the administrator of each such scheme, and

(v) such other information and particulars as the Revenue Commissioners may reasonably require for the purposes of this section,

and

(b) notifies the Revenue Commissioners in writing, within 7 working days of the exercise of the encashment option, that the option has been exercised and provides a schedule, with the notification, setting out the aggregate amount in respect of which the option was exercised and the amounts in respect of each of the private sector schemes concerned.

[(5) A notification referred to in *paragraph (a)* or *(b)* of *subsection (4)* shall be in such form as may be prescribed or authorised by the Revenue Commissioners and shall include a declaration to the effect that the notification is correct and complete.

(5A) An individual shall be taken to have satisfied the conditions in *subsection (4)* notwithstanding that the notification referred to in *paragraph (a)* or *(b)* of that subsection has been made after the time limited by the said *paragraph (a)* or *(b)*, as the case may be, has elapsed if the Revenue Commissioners consider that, in all of the circumstances, the failure of the individual to meet the conditions within the time limit concerned should be disregarded.][1]

(6) (a) The exercise of the encashment option is the transfer by the administrator of the private sector scheme or schemes to the relevant individual—

(i) where the relevant individual's retirement date is the date referred to in *paragraph (b)* of the definition of 'retirement date', on that date, or

(ii) in any other case, on or before the relevant individual's retirement date but not before the date on which the relevant individual attains the age of 60 years,

of the amount of the value of the relevant individual's accrued rights under the private sector scheme or schemes, including rights, if any, which relate to additional voluntary contributions under the scheme or schemes, equal to—

(i) where the condition referred to in *paragraph (b)* applies, the value of those rights, and

(ii) in any other case, the specified amount.

(b) The condition needed is that the amount to be crystallised by the benefit crystallisation events in relation to the relevant individual under his or her public sector scheme or schemes exceeds the standard fund threshold, or, as the case may be, the relevant individual's personal fund threshold.

(c) (i) In this paragraph—

'*rules*' means anything contained in the rules of a scheme or the terms and conditions of any contract in respect of a scheme;

'*tax-free lump sum*' means the lump sum of a kind that would under the rules have been payable tax-free to a relevant individual if *section 790AA* had never been enacted;

'*restricted tax-free lump sum*' means an amount equivalent to the amount determined by the formula—

$$A \times \frac{(1 - B)}{C}$$

where—

A is the amount of the tax-free lump sum,

B is—

(I) the specified amount, or

(II) where the encashment option is exercised in respect of any other private sector scheme or schemes of the relevant individual, an amount equivalent to the amount determined by the formula—

$$D - E$$

where—

D equals the specified amount, and

E equals the encashment amount or, as the case may be, the aggregate of the encashment amounts arising from the exercise of the encashment option in respect of the other private sector scheme or schemes,

and

C is the amount equal to the value of the relevant individual's accrued rights under the scheme.

(ii) Notwithstanding anything contained in this Part or anything contained in the rules, where an encashment option is exercised in respect of a scheme and—

(I) the encashment amount is equal to the value of the relevant individual's accrued rights under the scheme, the tax-free lump sum shall not be payable, or

(II) the encashment amount is less than the value of the relevant individual's accrued rights under the scheme, the tax-free lump sum shall be restricted to the restricted tax-free lump sum.

(7) Where an encashment option is exercised in respect of a relevant individual, the whole of the encashment amount in respect of each of the private sector schemes of the relevant individual in respect of which the encashment option is exercised shall be regarded as income of the individual for the tax year in which the amount is paid and shall be chargeable to income tax under Case IV of Schedule D.

(8) Income tax chargeable in accordance with *subsection (7)* shall be charged at the higher rate for the tax year in which the payment is made (in this section referred to as the 'encashment tax') and the administrator of each of the private sector schemes referred to in *subsection (7)* shall deduct the income tax due from the encashment amount and remit it to the Collector-General in accordance with *subsection (10)*.

(9) Where an encashment amount is regarded as income of the individual under *subsection (7)* and charged to tax in accordance with *subsection (8)*—

(a) such income shall be computed without regard to any amount deductible from, or deductible in computing, total income for the purposes of the Tax Acts,

(b) the charging of that income to tax in such manner shall be without any relief or reduction specified in the Table to *section 458*, or any other deduction from that income, and

(c) *section 188* shall not apply as regards the amount so charged.

(10) Where the administrator of a private sector scheme or, as the case may be, a relevant manager referred to in *subsection (16)* deducts encashment tax in accordance with *subsection (8)* or, as the case may be, *subsection (16)*, *subsections (1)* to *(8)* of *section 787S* shall, with any necessary modifications, apply as if any reference in those subsections—

(a) to an administrator included a reference to a relevant manager,

(b) to a relevant pension arrangement were a reference to a relevant individual's private sector scheme,

(c) to a benefit crystallisation event were a reference to an encashment option,

(d) to a chargeable excess were a reference to an encashment amount, or as the case may be, a deemed encashment amount, and

(e) to tax were a reference to encashment tax.

(11) (a) (i) Where the conditions set out in *subsection (4)*, as modified by *subsection (12)* (in this section referred to as the 'modified conditions'), are met, an individual in relation to whom the circumstances described in *paragraph (b)* may apply, may irrevocably instruct in writing the administrator or, as the case may be, the relevant manager of the private sector scheme or schemes to exercise the encashment option as if the benefit crystallisation event or events referred to in *subparagraph (i)* of *paragraph (b)* had not occurred.

(ii) Where the encashment option is exercised in respect of a private sector scheme or schemes of a kind referred to in *subparagraph (i)* of *paragraph (b)*, *subsection (6)(a)* shall apply as if the reference in that subsection to an administrator were a reference to a relevant manager.

(b) The circumstances referred to in *paragraph (a)* are that in relation to a relevant individual—

(i) one or more than one benefit crystallisation event has occurred within the relevant period in relation to one or more than one private sector scheme of that relevant individual, and

(ii) the aggregate of—

(I) the amounts so crystallised, and

(II) the amounts to be crystallised in the future by benefit crystallisation events in relation to the relevant individual—

(A) under his or her other private sector scheme or schemes, if any, and

(B) under his or her public sector scheme or schemes,

would, but for this section, exceed the standard fund threshold or, as the case may be, the relevant individual's personal fund threshold (referred to in *paragraph (a)(ii)* of *subsection (4)*, as modified by *subsection (12)*, and in the construction of 'B' in the formula in *subsection (15)(b)* as the 'other specified amount'), and

(iii) the benefit crystallisation events in relation to the public sector scheme or schemes of the relevant individual occur after the occurrence of all other benefit crystallisation events in relation to the private sector scheme or schemes of that individual.

(12) The modified conditions are that the individual complies with *subsection (4)* as if the following were substituted for *subparagraphs (ii)*, *(iii)* and *(iv)* of *paragraph (a)* of that subsection:

(ii) an estimate of the value of the accrued rights in respect of which the encashment option is to be exercised or, as the case may be, the other specified amount,

(iii) notwithstanding that one or more than one benefit crystallisation event has occurred in relation to one or more than one private sector scheme within the relevant period, particulars of the private sector scheme or schemes in respect of which the encashment option is to be exercised, and

(iv) the name, address and telephone number of the administrator or, as the case may be, the relevant manager of each such scheme,'.

(13) Where an encashment option is exercised in respect of an individual referred to in *subsection (11)(a)* being at that time a relevant individual, then in so far as the exercise of that option relates to—

(a) one or more than one private sector scheme of the individual in respect of which no benefit crystallisation event has occurred in the relevant period, *subsections (7)* to *(10)* shall apply, and

(b) one or more than one private sector scheme of the individual in respect of which one or more than one benefit crystallisation event has occurred in the relevant period, *subsection (14)* or *(15)*, as the case may be, shall apply.

(14) (a) Where an encashment option relates to a scheme referred to in *subsection (13)(b)*, the value of the individual's accrued rights under the scheme for the purposes of the exercise of the option shall be the amount crystallised by the benefit crystallisation events and where the encashment option has been exercised in respect of the whole of the scheme the part of the encashment amount from which encashment tax is to be deducted (in this section referred to as the 'deemed encashment amount') shall be the amount referred to in *paragraph (b)*.

(b) Where the benefit crystallisation event is—

(i) a lump sum paid under the rules of the scheme (of a kind that would, if *section 790AA* had never been enacted, have been paid tax-free to the individual and in this section referred to as the 'tax-free lump sum paid'), the deemed encashment amount shall be the amount of that tax-free lump sum paid,

(ii) the transfer of an amount to an ARF the assets in which are beneficially owned by the relevant individual, the deemed encashment amount shall be the lesser of the amount transferred to the ARF at the time the benefit crystallisation event occurred and the value of the assets in the ARF at the date of the exercise of the encashment option,

(iii) the transfer of an amount to an AMRF the assets in which are beneficially owned by the relevant individual, the deemed encashment amount shall be the lesser of the amount transferred to the AMRF at the time the benefit crystallisation event occurred and the value of the assets in the AMRF at the date of the exercise of the encashment option,

(iv) the retention of the assets of a PRSA in the PRSA (in this section referred to as the 'vested PRSA') beneficially owned by the relevant individual, the deemed encashment amount shall be the lesser of the value of the assets retained in the vested PRSA at the time the benefit crystallisation event occurred and the value of the assets in the vested PRSA at the date of the exercise of the encashment option, and

(v) in any other case, the deemed encashment amount shall be nil.

(c) The whole of the deemed encashment amount—

(i) shall be regarded as income of the individual for the tax year in which the encashment option is exercised, and

(ii) the amount so regarded as income shall be chargeable to income tax in accordance with *subsection (16)* or, as the case may be, *subsection (19)*.

(15) (a) Where an encashment option relates to a scheme referred to in *subsection (13) (b)* and that option is exercised in respect of only part of the scheme—

(i) the encashment amount shall be an amount equivalent to B in the formula in *paragraph (b)*, and

(ii) where the benefit crystallisation event was in respect of any one or more of the events described in *subsection (14)(b)*, the deemed encashment amount in respect of each of those events shall be an amount equivalent to the amount determined by that formula.

(b) The formula is—

$$A \times \frac{B}{C}$$

where—

A is—

(i) the amount of the tax-free lump sum paid,

(ii) the lesser of the amount transferred to the ARF at the time the benefit crystallisation event occurred and the value of the assets in the ARF at the date of the exercise of the encashment option (in this paragraph referred to as the 'encashment date'),

(iii) the lesser of the amount transferred to the AMRF at the time the benefit crystallisation event occurred and the value of the assets in the AMRF at the encashment date, or

(iv) the lesser of the value of the assets retained in the vested PRSA at the time the benefit crystallisation event occurred and the value of the assets in the vested PRSA at the encashment date,

B has the meaning assigned to it in the formula in the definition of 'restricted tax-free lump sum' in *subsection (6)(c)(i)* as if in that meaning a reference to specified amount were a reference to other specified amount,

and

C is the amount crystallised by the benefit crystallisation events under the scheme.

(c) *Paragraph (c)* of *subsection (14)* shall apply to the deemed encashment amounts referred to in *paragraph (a)*.

(16) (a) Any deemed encashment amount shall be charged to income tax under Case IV of Schedule D.

(b) The relevant manager shall deduct income tax from the deemed encashment amount at the higher rate for the tax year in which the encashment option is exercised and remit it to the Collector-General in accordance with *subsection (10)*.

(c) *Paragraphs (a)* to *(c)* of *subsection (9)* shall apply to a deemed encashment amount regarded as income of the relevant individual under *subsection (14) (c)* or *(15)(c)* and charged to income tax in accordance with *paragraph (a)*.

(d) (i) The deduction of income tax by a relevant manager in accordance with *paragraph (b)* shall include a deduction for a deemed encashment amount in respect of a tax-free lump sum paid under the rules of the private sector scheme from which the assets were, in whole or in part, transferred to the ARF or the AMRF or, as the case may be, in the case of a scheme that is a PRSA, with in which the assets were retained in whole or in part.

(ii) (I) In so far as income tax has been charged under *subsection (3)(a)(i)* or *(3)(b)(i)(I)* of *section 790AA* on an excess lump sum (within the meaning of *subsection (1)(e)* of that section) (in this paragraph referred to as the 'standard rate income tax') in respect of a lump sum referred to in *subparagraph (i)* and deducted by and remitted to the Collector-General by the administrator of the private sector scheme in accordance with *subsection (8)* of that section, the income tax to be deducted by the relevant manager from the deemed encashment amount in respect of the lump sum shall, where the condition in *subparagraph (iii)* is met, be reduced by the amount of the standard rate income tax, and

(II) where a deemed encashment amount in respect of a tax-free lump sum has been calculated in accordance with the formula in *subsection (15)*, then in so far as standard rate income tax has been charged in respect of the lump sum, the income tax to be deducted by the relevant manager from the deemed encashment amount shall, where the condition in *subparagraph (iii)* is met, be reduced by an amount of income tax equivalent to the amount determined by that formula if 'A' in the formula was the amount of the standard rate income tax.

(iii) The condition referred to in clauses (I) and (II) of *subparagraph (i)* is that the relevant manager obtains from the administrator of the private sector scheme a certificate giving the information set out in *paragraphs (a)* to *(e)* of *subsection (2)* of *section 787RA*.

(iv) Where income tax on a deemed encashment amount is reduced by an amount of standard rate income tax in accordance with clause (I) or (II) of *subparagraph (ii)*, that amount of standard rate income tax shall not be available for the purposes of *section 787RA*.

(v) *Subsection (6)* of *section 787R* shall, with any necessary modifications, apply to a relevant manager who obtains a certificate under *subparagraph (ii)* as if the reference in that subsection to a declaration, or declarations, were a reference to a certificate, or certificates, to which *subparagraph (ii)* applies.

(17) The tax required to be deducted by the relevant manager under *subsection (16)* shall be satisfied out of the funds in the ARF, the AMRF or, as the case may be, the vested PRSA beneficially owned by the relevant individual and the individual shall allow such deduction and where there are no funds or insufficient funds available out of which the relevant manager may satisfy the tax required to be deducted, the amount of such tax for which there are insufficient funds available (in this section referred to as the 'unpaid tax') shall be discharged in accordance with *subsection (18)*.

(18) (a) The unpaid tax referred to in *subsection (17)* shall be deemed to be tax on a chargeable excess inrespect of the relevant individual and shall be paid and remitted to the Collector-General by the administrator of the relevant individual's public sector scheme at the time of the occurrence of the first benefit crystallisation event in respect of the individual in relation to that scheme and the amount so paid shall be adebt due to the administrator from the individual, or where the individual is deceased, from his or her estate.

(b) The administrator referred to in *paragraph (a)* shall bereimbursed by the relevant individual for the payment of the unpaid tax that is deemed to be tax on a chargeable excess in the manner provided for in *paragraphs (a)* and *(b)* of *section 787Q(7)*.

(c) The deemed tax on a chargeable excess referred to in *paragraph (a)* shall not be tax on a chargeable excess for any other purpose of this Chapter.

(19) (a) Where an encashment option is exercised in relation to a private sector scheme of a relevant individual in circumstances where a tax-free lump sum was paid and the remainder of that individual's accrued rights under the scheme were applied by way of—

(i) the purchase of an annuity for the individual, or

(ii) the payment of a pension to the individual from the scheme, or

(iii) the transfer to the individual under the rules of the scheme of an amount on the exercise of an option by the individual under *section 772(3A)(a)* or *784(2A)* and taxed in accordance with *section 784(2B)* (or, as the case may be, taxed in accordance with that section by virtue of *section 772(3B)*), or an amount transferred to the individual at the time assets of the PRSA are first made available from the PRSA and taxed in accordance with *section 787G(1)*,

then income tax charged under *subsection (16)(a)* on the deemed encashment amount in relation to the tax-free lump sum shall be chargeable to tax at the higher rate for the tax year in which the encashment option is exercised and the encashment tax so charged shall, subject to *paragraph (c)*, be deemed to be unpaid tax for the purposes of *subsection (18)* and discharged in accordance with that subsection as if the reference in *paragraph (b)* of that subsection to *paragraphs (a)* and *(b)* of *section 787Q(7)* were a reference only to *paragraph (b)* of *section 787Q(7)*.

(b) *Subparagraphs (ii)* and *(iv)* of *paragraph (d)* of *subsection (16)* shall, with any necessary modifications, apply to encashment tax referred to in *paragraph (a)*, where the relevant individual obtains from the administrator of the private sector scheme a certificate giving the information set out in *paragraphs (a)* to *(e)* of *subsection (2)* of *section 787RA*.

(c) *Subsection (6)* of *section 787R* shall, with any necessary modifications, apply to a relevant individual who obtains a certificate under *paragraph (b)* as if the reference in that subsection to a declaration, or declarations, were a reference to a certificate, or certificates, to which *paragraph (b)* applies.

(20) Where a benefit crystallisation event has occurred in relation to a relevant individual under a private sector scheme in respect of which an encashment option is exercised and the benefit crystallisation event has resulted in the individual being the beneficial owner of the assets in an ARF, an AMRF or, as the case may be, a vested PRSA (in this subsection referred to as the 'fund'), then where the exercise of the option was in respect of—

(a) the whole of the private sector scheme, the value of the assets in the fund, or

(b) a part of the private sector scheme, the value of the assets in the fund that are deemed to be an encashment amount in accordance with *subsection (15)*,

shall for the purposes of this Part no longer be regarded as assets held in an ARF, an AMRF or, as the case may be, a vested PRSA from the date of the exercise of the option.

(21) Where an encashment option is exercised in respect of a relevant individual the encashment amount or, as the case may be, the deemed encashment amount shall not be—

(a) a benefit crystallisation event for the purposes of this Chapter and *Schedule 23B* and where that amount relates to a private sector scheme in respect of which one or more than one benefit crystallisation event has occurred before the exercise of the option such benefit crystallisation events or, as the case may be, the portion of such benefit crystallisation events represented by the amount of 'B' in the formula in *subsection (15)(b)*, shall be disregarded for the purposes of this Chapter and *Schedule 23B*,

(b) used by the relevant individual as a contribution to, or the payment of a premium under, a relevant pension arrangement, and

(c) regarded under the provisions of *Chapter 2* or *2A* as a distribution from an ARF or an AMRF or, as the case may be, as the making available to, or paying to, a PRSA contributor of assets of that amount or value from a PRSA.

(22) Where an encashment option is exercised in respect of a relevant individual in relation to a private sector scheme in respect of which one or more than one benefit crystallisation event has occurred in the relevant period and the deemed encashment amount is the amount of the tax-free lump sum paid or, as the case may be, a part of the tax-free lump sum paid, that amount, or that part, shall be disregarded in determining an excess lump sum (within the meaning of *subsection (1)(e)* of *section 790AA*) in respect of a lump sum (within the meaning of that section) that is paid to that individual on or after 8 February 2012.

(23) (a) The persons liable for income tax charged in accordance with *subsection (8)* or *(16)* shall be the relevant individual and the administrator of the private sector scheme, the relevant manager referred to in *subsection (16)* or, as the case may be, the administrator of the public sector scheme referred to in *subsection (18)* and their liability shall be joint and several.

(b) A person liable for income tax charged in accordance with *subsection (8)* or *(16)* shall be so liable whether or not that person or any other person who is liable for the charge is resident or ordinarily resident in the State.][2]

Amendments

[1] Substituted by F(No.2)A13 s18(2)(e). Has effect from 1 January 2014.

[2] Inserted by FA12 s18(7)(b). Has effect from 8 February 2012.

787TB Penalties

[A person who fails to comply with any of the obligations imposed on that person by this Chapter and any regulations made under it and by *Schedule 23B* shall, for each such failure, be liable to a penalty of €3,000.][1]

Amendments

[1] Inserted by F(No.2)A13 s18(2)(f). Has effect from 1 January 2014.

787U Regulations (Chapter 2C)

[(1) The Revenue Commissioners may make regulations prescribing the procedure to be adopted in giving effect to this Chapter, in so far as such procedure is not otherwise provided for, and providing generally as to the administration of this Chapter, and without prejudice to the generality of the foregoing, regulations under this section may include provision for specifying, for the purposes of this Chapter, the person who shall be treated as the administrator of a relevant pension arrangement of a kind described in *paragraphs (e)* and *(f)* of the definition of relevant pension arrangement in *section 787O(1)*.

(2) Every regulation made under this section shall be laid before Dáil Éireann as soon as may be after it is made and, if a resolution annulling the resolution is passed by Dáil Éireann within the next 21 days on which Dáil Éireann has sat after the regulation is laid before it, the regulation shall be annulled accordingly, but without prejudice to the validity of anything previously done thereunder.][1]

Amendments

[1] Inserted by FA06 s14(1)(e). Has effect as on and from 7 December 2005.

Cross References

From Section 787U

Section 787O Interpretation and general (Chapter 2C).

To Section 787U

Section 787O Interpretation and general (Chapter 2C).

CHAPTER 3

Purchased Life Annuities

788 Capital element in certain purchased annuities

[ITA67 s239; CTA76 s140(1) and Sch2 PtI par9; FA79 s28(4); FA96 s132(1) and Sch5 PtI par1(10) and (11); FA97 s146(1) and Sch9 PtI par1(15)]

(1) In this section—

"*life annuity*" means an annuity payable for a term ending with (or at a time ascertainable only by reference to) the end of a human life, whether or not there is provision for the annuity to end during the life on the expiration of a fixed term or on the happening of any event or otherwise, or to continue after the end of the life in particular circumstances;

"*purchased life annuity*" means a life annuity granted for a consideration in money or money's worth in the ordinary course of a business of granting annuities on human life.

(2) This section shall not apply to—

(a) any annuity which apart from this section would be treated for the purposes of the provisions of the Income Tax Acts relating to tax on annuities and other annual payments as consisting to any extent in the payment or repayment of a capital sum,

(b) any annuity purchased under or for the purposes of any sponsored superannuation scheme within the meaning of *section 783(1)*, or any scheme approved under *section 784*, or in pursuance of any obligation imposed or offer or invitation made under or in connection with any such scheme, or any other annuity purchased by any person in recognition of another's services (or past services) in any office or employment,

(c) any annuity payable under a substituted contract within the meaning of *section 786(3)*,

(d) any annuity where the whole or part of the consideration for the grant of the annuity consisted of sums satisfying the conditions for relief from tax under *section 787*, [...][1]

(e) any annuity purchased in pursuance of any direction in a will, or to provide for an annuity payable by virtue of a will or settlement out of income of property disposed of by the will or settlement (whether with or without resort to [capital),][2]

[(f) any annuity where the whole or part of the consideration for the grant of the annuity consisted of assets which, at the time of application of the said assets for the purchase of the annuity, were assets in an approved retirement fund, within the meaning of *section 784A*, or in an approved minimum retirement fund, within the meaning of *section 784*.][3]

[(g) any annuity where the whole or part of the consideration for the grant of the annuity consisted of assets which, at the time of the application of the said assets for the purchase of the annuity, were PRSA assets, within the meaning of *Chapter 2A* of this Part.][4]

(3) A purchased life annuity (not being of a description excepted by *subsection (2)*) shall, for the purposes of the provisions of the Income Tax Acts relating to tax on annuities and other annual payments, be treated as containing a capital element and, to the extent of the capital element, as not being an annual payment or in the nature of an annual payment; but the capital element in such an annuity shall be taken into account in computing profits or gains or losses for other purposes of the Income Tax Acts in any circumstances in which a lump sum payment would be taken into account.

(4) In the case of any purchased life annuity to which this section applies—

(a) the capital element shall be determined by reference to the amount or value of the payments made or other consideration given for the grant of the annuity,

(b) the proportion which the capital element in any annuity payment bears to the total amount of that payment shall be constant for all payments on account of the annuity,

(c) where neither the term of the annuity nor the amount of any annuity payment depends on any contingency other than the duration of a human life or lives, that proportion shall be the same proportion which the total amount or value of the consideration for the grant of the annuity bears to the actuarial value of the annuity payments as determined in accordance with *subsection (5)*, and

(d) where *paragraph (c)* does not apply, that proportion shall be such as may be just, having regard to that paragraph and to the contingencies affecting the annuity.

(5) For the purposes of *subsection (4)*—

(a) any entire consideration given for the grant of an annuity and for some other matter shall be apportioned as appears just (but so that a right to a return of premiums or other consideration for an annuity shall not be treated for this purpose as a distinct matter from the annuity),

(b) where it appears that the amount or value of the consideration purporting to be given for the grant of an annuity has affected, or has been affected by, the consideration given for some other matter, the aggregate amount or value of those considerations shall be treated as one entire consideration given for both and shall be apportioned under *paragraph (a)* accordingly, and

(c) the actuarial value of any annuity payments shall be taken to be their value as at the date when the first of those payments begins to accrue, that value being determined by reference to the prescribed tables of mortality and without discounting any payment for the time to elapse between that date and the date it is to be made.

(6) Where a person making a payment on account of any life annuity has been notified in the prescribed manner of any decision as to its being or not being a purchased life annuity to which this section applies or as to the amount of the capital element, if any, and has not been notified of any alteration of that decision, the notice shall be evidence until the contrary is proved as to those matters for the purpose of determining the amount of income tax which the person is entitled or required to deduct from the payment, or for which the person is liable in respect of the payment.

(7) Where a person making a payment on account of a purchased life annuity to which this section applies has not been notified in the prescribed manner of the amount of the capital element, the amount of income tax which the person is entitled or required to deduct from the payment, or for which the person is liable in respect of it, shall be the same as if the annuity were not a purchased life annuity to which this section applies.

(8) Any person, other than a company which is within the charge to corporation tax, carrying on a business of granting annuities on human life shall be entitled to repayment of any income tax borne by that person by deduction or otherwise for any year of assessment up to the amount of income tax which, if this section had not been enacted, that person would have been entitled to deduct and retain on making payments due in that year of assessment on account of life annuities and which in accordance with this section that person has not deducted.

(9) This section shall apply to life annuities whenever purchased or commencing, and the reference to *section 787* in *subsection (2)(d)* shall be construed accordingly.

Amendments

1 Deleted by FA99 s20(1)(a).

2 Substituted by PAA02 s4(1)(d)(vi)(I). With effect from 7 November 2002 per S.I. 502 of 2002.

3 Inserted by FA99 s20(1)(c).

4 Inserted by PAA02 s4(1)(d)(vi)(III). With effect from 7 November 2002 per S.I. 502 of 2002.

Cross References

From Section 788

Section 783 Interpretation and general (Chapter 2).
Section 784 Retirement annuities: relief for premiums.
Section 784A Approved retirement fund.
Section 786 Approval of certain other contracts.
Section 787 Nature and amount of relief for qualifying premiums.

To Section 788

Section 715 Annuity business: separate charge on profits.
Section 789 Supplementary provisions (Chapter 3).
Schedule 31 Consequential Amendments

789 Supplementary provisions (Chapter 3)

[ITA67 s240; F(MP)A68 s3(2) and Sch PtI]

(1) Any question as to whether an annuity is a purchased life annuity to which *section 788* applies, or what is the capital element in such an annuity, shall be determined by the inspector, but any person aggrieved by any decision of the inspector on any such question may appeal within the prescribed time to the Appeal Commissioners.

(2) Except where otherwise provided in this Chapter, the procedure to be adopted in giving effect to this Chapter shall be such as may be prescribed.

(3) The Revenue Commissioners may make regulations for prescribing anything which is to be prescribed under this Chapter, and the regulations may apply, for the purposes of this Chapter or of the regulations, any provision of the Income Tax Acts (with or without modifications), and in particular the provisions relating to the rehearing of an appeal and to the statement of a case for the opinion of the High Court on a point of law.

(4) Regulations under *subsection (3)* may in particular make provision as to the time limit for making any claim for relief from or repayment of tax under this Chapter and as to all or any of the following matters—

(a) the information to be given in connection with the determination of any question whether an annuity is a purchased life annuity to which *section 788* applies, or what is the capital element in an annuity, and the persons who may be required to give any such information;

(b) the manner of giving effect to the decision on any such question, and the making of assessments for the purpose on the person entitled to the annuity (notwithstanding anything in *section 237*);

(c) the extent to which any decision on any such question is to be binding and the circumstances in which it may be reviewed.

(5) Where any person, for the purpose of obtaining for that person or for any other person any relief from or repayment of tax under this Chapter,[...][1] makes any false statement or false representation, that person shall be liable to a penalty of [€3,000][2].

Amendments

[1] Deleted by F(No.2)A08 sched5(part2)(1)(h)(i). The enactments specified in Schedule 5 are amended or repealed to the extent and manner specified in that Schedule and, unless the contrary is stated, shall come into effect after 24 December 2008.

[2] Substituted by F(No.2)A08 sched5(part2)(1)(h)(ii). The enactments specified in Schedule 5 are amended or repealed to the extent and manner specified in that Schedule and, unless the contrary is stated, shall come into effect after 24 December 2008.

Cross References

From Section 789

Section 237 Annual payments payable wholly out of taxed income.
Section 788 Capital element in certain purchased annuities.

To Section 789

Section 1061 Recovery of penalties.

CHAPTER 4

Miscellaneous

790 Liability of certain pensions, etc. to tax

[ITA67 s225; FA97 s146(1) and Sch9 PtI par1(14)]

Where an individual has ceased to hold an office or employment and a pension, annuity or other annual payment is paid to the individual or to the individual's [widow, widower or surviving civil partner, or to the individual's child or the child of the surviving civil partner or any of the individual's relatives or dependants][1] by the person or the heirs, executors, administrators or successors of the person under whom the individual held such office or by whom the individual was so employed, such pension, annuity or other annual payment shall, notwithstanding that it is paid voluntarily or is capable of being discontinued, be deemed to be income for the purpose of assessment of income tax and shall be assessed and charged under Schedule D or E, as the case may require.

Amendments

[1] Substituted by F(No.3)A11 sched1(219).

Cross References

To Section 790

Section 608 Superannuation funds.

790A Limit on earnings

[(1) Notwithstanding anything in this Part, for the purposes of giving relief to an individual under—][1]

(a) *Chapter 1* in respect of an employee's contribution to a retirement benefits scheme,

(b) *Chapter 2* in respect of a qualifying premium under an annuity contract,

(c) *Chapter 2A* in respect of a PRSA contribution, and

[(d) *Chapter 2B* in respect of a contribution by a relevant migrant member to a qualifying overseas pension plan,][2]

the aggregate of the individual's remuneration, within the meaning of *Chapter 1* and that Chapter as applied by *Chapter 2B*, and net relevant earnings, within the meaning of *Chapters 2* and *2A* and those Chapters as applied by *Chapter 2B*, shall not exceed [€254,000 (in this section referred to as the "*earnings limit*").][3]

[(2) For a year of assessment (in this subsection referred to as the "*relevant year*") after the year of assessment 2006 the earnings limit shall be an amount equivalent to the amount determined by the formula—

$$A \times B$$

where—

A is the earnings limit for the year of assessment immediately preceding the relevant year, and

B is—

(i) the earnings adjustment factor which may be designated in writing by the Minister for Finance in December of the year of assessment preceding the relevant year, a note of which shall be published as soon as practicable in the *Iris Oifigiúil*, or

(ii) where no earnings adjustment factor is designated by the Minister for Finance, 1.][4]

[(3) Notwithstanding *subsection (2)*, for the purposes of *subsection (1)* the earnings limit for the year of assessment 2009 shall be €150,000.][5]][6]

[(4) Notwithstanding *subsection (2)*, for the purposes of *subsection (1)* the earnings limit for the year of assessment 2011 shall be €115,000.

(5) Notwithstanding *subsection (2)*, for the purposes of *subsection (1)* the earnings limit for the year of assessment 2010 shall be deemed to be €115,000 for the purpose of determining how much of a contribution or qualifying premium, as the case may be, paid by an employee or an individual in the year of assessment 2011, is to be treated by virtue of *section 774(8)*, *776(3)*, *787(7)* or *787C(3)*, as the case may be, as paid in the year of assessment 2010.][7]

Amendments

[1] Renumbered by FA06 s14(1)(f)(i)(I).

[2] Substituted by FA06 s14(1)(f)(i)(II).

[3] Substituted by FA06 s14(1)(f)(i)(III).

[4] Substituted by F(No.2)A08 s16(1)(b)(i). This section is deemed to have effect as on and from 1 January 2006.

[5] Inserted by F(No.2)A08 s16(1)(b)(ii). This section has effect as on and from 1 January 2009.

[6] Substituted by FA05 s21(1)(e)(i). Applies as on and from 1 January 2005.

[7] Inserted by FA11 s(19)(4)(a). Has effect as on and from 1 January 2011.

Revenue Briefings

Tax Briefing

Tax Briefing September 2009 – Issue 74 – Tax Relief for Pension Contributions: Application of Earnings Limit

Tax Briefing October 2009 – Issue 79 – Tax Relief for Pension Contributions: Application of Earnings Limit – Transitional Arrangements for 2008

Tax Briefing September 2010 – Issue 11 – Tax Relief for Pension Contributions: Application of Earnings Limit in the case of Doctors with General Medical Services (GMS) and private practice income

Tax Briefing October 2011 – Issue 05 – ROS Form 11 2010 – Retirement Annuity Relief

eBrief

eBrief No. 46/2009 – Tax Relief for Pensions Contributions: Application on Earnings Limit

eBrief No. 62/2010 – Tax Relief for Pension Contributions: Application of Earnings Limit in the case of Doctors with General Medical Services (GMS) and private practice income

Cross References

From Section 790A

Section 774 Certain approved schemes: exemptions and reliefs.

Section 776 Certain statutory schemes: exemptions and reliefs.

Section 787 Nature and amount of relief for qualifying premiums.

Section 787C PRSAs — method of granting relief for PRSA contributions.

To Section 790A

Section 783 Interpretation and general (Chapter 2).

Section 787A Interpretation and supplemental.

790AA Taxation of lump sums in excess of the tax free amount

[(1) (a) In this section—

"*administrator*", in relation to a relevant pension arrangement, means the person or persons having the management of the arrangement and, in particular, but without prejudice to the generality of the foregoing, references to the administrator of a relevant pension arrangement include—

(i) an administrator within the meaning of *section 770(1)*,

(ii) a person mentioned in *section 784*, lawfully carrying on the business of granting annuities on human life, including the appointed person mentioned in *section 784(4A)*(ii), and

(iii) a PRSA administrator within the meaning of *section 787A(1)*;

"*excess lump sum*" shall be construed in accordance with *paragraph (e)*;

"*relevant pension arrangement*" means any one or more of the following—

(i) a retirement benefits scheme, within the meaning of *section 771*, approved by the Revenue Commissioners for the purposes of Chapter 1,

(ii) an annuity contract or a trust scheme or part of a trust scheme approved by the Revenue Commissioners under *section 784*,

(iii) a PRSA contract, within the meaning of *section 787A*, in respect of a PRSA product, within the meaning of that section,

(iv) a qualifying overseas pension plan within the meaning of Chapter 2B,

(v) a public service pension scheme within the meaning of section 1 of the Public Service Superannuation (Miscellaneous Provisions) Act 2004,

(vi) a statutory scheme, within the meaning of *section 770(1)*, other than a public service pension scheme referred to in *paragraph (v)*;

"*specified date*" means 1 January 2011;

"*standard chargeable amount*" means the amount equivalent to the amount determined by the formula—

$$\frac{(SFT)}{4} - TFA$$

where—

SFT is the standard fund threshold, within the meaning of *section 787O(1)*, for the year of assessment in which the lump sum is paid, and

TFA is the tax free amount;

"*standard rate*" means the standard rate of income tax in force at the time the lump sum is paid;

"*tax free amount*" means €200,000;

"*tax year*" means a year of assessment within the meaning of the Tax Acts.

(b) (i) For the purposes of this section, a reference to a lump sum is a reference to a lump sum that is paid to an individual under the rules of a relevant pension arrangement by means of commutation of part of a pension or of part of an annuity or otherwise.

(ii) Without prejudice to the generality of *subparagraph (i)*, the reference in that subparagraph to the commutation of part of a pension or of part of an annuity shall, in a case where an individual opts in accordance with *section 772(3A)* or, as the case may be, *section 784(2A)*, be construed as a reference to the commutation of part of the pension or, as the case may be, part of the annuity which would, but for the exercise of that option, be payable to the individual.

(c) For the purposes of this section references to a lump sum that is paid to an individual include references to a lump sum that is obtained by, given to, or made available to, an individual and references to a lump sum which was, or has, or had been paid to an individual shall be construed accordingly.

(d) For the purposes of this section—

(i) a lump sum (in this subsection referred to as the "*first-mentioned lump sum*") shall be treated as paid before another lump sum (in this subsection referred to as the "*second-mentioned lump sum*") if the first-mentioned lump sum is paid before the second-mentioned lump sum on the same day, and

(ii) a lump sum shall not be treated as paid at the same time as one or more than one other lump sum and, where but for this subsection they would be so treated, the individual to whom the lump sums are paid shall decide on the order in which they are to be deemed to be paid.

(e) For the purposes of this section the excess lump sum, if any, in respect of a lump sum that is paid to an individual on or after the specified date (in this paragraph referred to as the "*current lump sum*") shall be—

(i) where no other lump sum has been paid to the individual on or after 7 December 2005, the amount by which the current lump sum exceeds the tax free amount, and

(ii) where, before the current lump sum was paid, one or more than one lump sum had been paid to the individual on or after 7 December 2005 (in this section referred to as the "*earlier lump sums*"), then—

(I) where the amount of the earlier lump sums is less than the tax free amount, the amount by which the aggregate of the amounts of the earlier lump sums and the current lump sum exceeds the tax free amount, and

(II) where the amount of the earlier lump sums is equal to or greater than the tax free amount, the amount of the current lump sum.

(2) Where a lump sum is paid to an individual on or after the specified date, the excess lump sum shall be regarded as income of the individual for the tax year in which the lump sum is paid and shall be chargeable to income tax in accordance with *subsection (3)*.

(3) Subject to *subsection (7)(b)*—

(a) where the excess lump sum arises in accordance with *subsection (1)(e)*(i), *(1)(e)(ii)(I)* or *(1)(e)(ii)(II)* (in so far as the amount of the earlier lump sums referred to in *subsection (1)(e)(ii)(II)* is equal to the tax free amount), then—

(i) so much of the excess lump sum as does not exceed the standard chargeable amount shall be charged to income tax under Case IV of Schedule D at the standard rate, and

(ii) so much of the excess lump sum, if any, as exceeds the standard chargeable amount shall be regarded as—

(I) profits or gains accruing from an office or employment (and accordingly tax under Schedule E shall be charged on those payments, and tax so chargeable shall be computed under *section 112(1)*), and

(II) emoluments to which Chapter 4 of Part 42 applies,

(in this section referred to as "*relevant emoluments*").

(b) Where the excess lump sum arises in accordance with *subsection (1)(e)(ii)(II)* (in so far as the amount of the earlier lump sums referred to in that subsection is greater than the tax free amount), then—

(i) where the amount by which the earlier lump sums is greater than the tax free amount (in this paragraph referred to as the "*first-mentioned amount*") is less than the standard chargeable amount—

(I) so much of the excess lump sum as does not exceed an amount equivalent to the difference between the standard chargeable amount and the first-mentioned amount shall be charged to income tax under Case IV of Schedule D at the standard rate, and

(II) so much of the excess lump sum, if any, as exceeds an amount equivalent to the difference between the standard chargeable amount and the first-mentioned amount, shall be relevant emoluments,

and

(ii) in any other case, the excess lump sum shall be relevant emoluments.

(4) The persons liable for income tax charged in accordance with *paragraph (a)(i)* or *(b)(i)(I)* of *subsection (3)* shall be the administrator of the relevant pension arrangement under which the lump sum arises and the individual in relation to whom the lump sum is paid and their liability shall be joint and several.

(5) A person referred to in *subsection (4)* shall be liable for any income tax referred to in that subsection whether or not that person, or any other person who is liable to the charge, is resident or ordinarily resident in the State.

(6) Where tax arising on an excess lump sum in accordance with *paragraph (a)(i)* or *(b)(i)(I)* of *subsection (3)* is paid—

(a) by the administrator of a relevant pension arrangement in whole or in part, then so much of the tax that is paid by the administrator shall itself be treated as forming part of the excess lump sum unless the lump sum paid to the individual under the relevant pension arrangement is reduced so as to fully reflect the amount of tax so paid or the administrator is reimbursed by the individual in respect of any tax so paid, or

(b) by the administrator of a relevant pension arrangement of a kind described in *paragraphs (v)* and *(vi)* of the definition of "*relevant pension arrangement*" in *subsection (1)*, then—

(i) the amount of tax so paid shall be a debt due to the administrator from the individual or, where the individual is deceased, from his or her estate, and

(ii) the administrator may appropriate so much of the individual's lump sum entitlements under that relevant pension arrangement, and the individual shall allow such appropriation, for the purposes of reimbursing the administrator in respect of the tax so paid.

(7) (a) The administrator of a relevant pension arrangement shall deduct tax from an excess lump sum payment in accordance with this section and remit such tax to the Collector-General.

(b) In so far as any part of an excess lump sum—

(i) is to be regarded as income of the individual for a tax year and charged to income tax at the standard rate in accordance with *paragraph (a)(i)* or *(b)(i)(I)* of *subsection (3)*—

(I) such income—

(A) shall not be reckoned in computing total income for the purposes of the Tax Acts, and

(B) shall be computed without regard to any amount deductible from, or deductible in computing, income for the purposes of the Tax Acts,

(II) the charging of that income in such manner shall be without any relief or reduction specified in the Table to *section 458* or any other deduction from that income, and

(III) *section 188* shall not apply as regards income so charged,

or

(ii) is to be regarded by virtue of this section as relevant emoluments, the administrator of the relevant pension arrangement under which the lump sum is paid shall deduct tax from the payment at the higher rate for the tax year in which the payment is made unless the administrator has received from the Revenue Commissioners a certificate of tax credits and standard rate cut-off point or a tax deduction card for that year in respect of the individual.

(8) The administrator of a relevant pension arrangement who deducts tax from an excess lump sum in accordance with *paragraph (a)(i)* or *(b)(i)(I)* of *subsection (3)* shall, within 3 months of the end of the month in which the lump sum giving rise to the excess lump sum is paid, make a return to the Collector-General which shall contain—

(a) the name and address of the administrator,

(b) the name, address and PPS Number of the individual in relation to whom the lump sum has been paid,

(c) details of the relevant pension arrangement under which the lump sum giving rise to the excess lump sum has been paid,

(d) the amount of, and the basis of calculation of, the excess lump sum arising in respect of the lump sum, and

(e) details of the tax which the administrator is required to account for in relation to the excess lump sum.

(9) The tax which the administrator of a relevant pension arrangement is required to account for in relation to an excess lump sum (hereinafter referred to as the "*relevant tax*") and which is required to be included in a return in accordance with *subsection (8)*, shall be due at the time by which the return is due to be made and shall be paid by the administrator to the Collector-General and the relevant tax so due shall be payable by the administrator without the making of an assessment; but relevant tax that has become so due may be assessed on any person liable for the tax (whether or not it has been paid when the assessment is made) if that tax or any part of it is not paid on or before the due date.

(10) Where it appears to an officer of the Revenue Commissioners that there is any amount of relevant tax in relation to an excess lump sum which ought to have been but has not been included in a return, or where the officer is dissatisfied with any return, then the officer may make an assessment on any person liable for the relevant tax to the best of his or her judgment, and any amount of relevant tax in relation to an excess lump sum due under an assessment made by virtue of this

subsection shall be treated for the purposes of interest on unpaid tax as having been payable at the time by which the return concerned was due to be made.

(11) Where any item has been incorrectly included in a return as an excess lump sum, then an officer of the Revenue Commissioners may make such assessments, adjustments or set-offs as may in his or her judgment be required for securing that the resulting liabilities to tax, including interest on unpaid tax, whether of the administrator of a relevant pension arrangement or the individual, are, so far as possible, the same as they would have been if the item had not been so included.

(12) Any relevant tax assessed on a person under this section shall be due within one month after the issue of the notice of assessment (unless that tax is due earlier under *subsection (9)*) subject to—

(a) any appeal against the assessment, or

(b) any application under *subsection (14)*,

but no such appeal or application, as the case may be, shall affect the date when any amount is due under *subsection (9)*.

(13) (a) The provisions of the Income Tax Acts relating to—

(i) assessments to income tax, and

(ii) appeals against such assessments (including the rehearing of appeals and the statement of a case for the opinion of the High Court),

shall, in so far as they are applicable, apply to the assessment of relevant tax.

(b) Any amount of relevant tax payable in accordance with this section without the making of an assessment shall carry interest at the rate of 0.0219 per cent for each day or part of a day from the date when the amount becomes due and payable until payment.

(c) *Subsections (3)* to *(5)* of *section 1080* shall apply in relation to interest payable under *paragraph (b)* as they apply in relation to interest payable under *section 1080*.

(d) In its application to any relevant tax charged by any assessment made in accordance with this section, *section 1080* shall apply as if *subsection (2)(b)* of that section were deleted.

(14) (a) Where the administrator of a relevant pension arrangement reasonably believed, in respect of a lump sum paid to an individual, that—

(i) the lump sum did not give rise to an income tax liability, or

(ii) the amount of the income tax liability arising on the excess lump sum was less than the actual amount,

the administrator may apply to the Revenue Commissioners in writing to have that tax liability or, as the case may be, the amount of the difference between the amount which the administrator believed to be the amount of the tax liability and the actual amount (in this subsection referred to as the "*referable tax liability*") discharged.

(b) Where, following receipt of an application referred to in *paragraph (a)*, the Revenue Commissioners are of the opinion that in all of the circumstances it would not be just and reasonable for the administrator to be made liable to the referable tax liability they may discharge the administrator from that liability and shall notify the administrator in writing of that decision.

(c) Without prejudice to any other circumstance in which an individual will be liable to discharge a tax liability due in respect of an excess lump sum, where an administrator of a relevant pension arrangement is discharged from a referable tax liability in accordance with *paragraph (b)*, the individual in respect of whom the income tax charge arises shall become liable for the tax.

(15) Every return referred to in this section shall be in a form specified or authorised by the Revenue Commissioners and shall include a declaration to the effect that the return is correct and complete.

(16) *Subsection (2)* of *section 787G* shall apply in respect of any income tax deducted from an excess lump sum by virtue of *subsection (3)* of this section, by an administrator of a relevant pension arrangement of a kind described in *paragraph (iii)* of the definition of "*relevant pension arrangement*" in *subsection (1)(a)* of this section, as it applies to income tax referred to in *subsection (2)* of *section 787G*.

(17) Where a lump sum is paid to an individual, on or after the specified date, under the rules of a relevant pension arrangement of a kind described in *paragraph (iv)* of the definition of "*relevant pension arrangement*" in *subsection (1)(a)*, the excess lump sum, if any, shall be charged to tax under Case IV of Schedule D for the tax year in which the lump sum is paid to that individual at the rate or rates determined in accordance with *subsection (3)*.

(18) This section shall not apply to—

[(a) a lump sum that is paid to—

(i) a widow or widower,

(ii) a surviving civil partner,

(iii) children,

(iv) dependants,

(v) personal representatives, or

(vi) children of the civil partner

of a deceased individual, or][1]

(b) the balance of a lump sum paid to an individual in accordance with *paragraph 5* of Appendix A of the Department of Finance Circular 12/09, dated 30 April 2009, entitled "Incentivised Scheme of Early Retirement".

(19) *Section 781* shall have effect notwithstanding the provisions of this section.][2]][3]

Amendments

[1] Substituted by F(No.3)A11 sched1(220).

[2] Substituted by FA11 s(19)(4)(b). Has effect as on and from 1 January 2011.

[3] Inserted by FA06 s14(1)(f)(ii). Has effect as on and from 7 December 2005.

Note

Note to FA11 Amendments – Nothwithstanding para (a) of the definition of "standard fund threshold" in section 787O(1) (as amended by subsection (3)(e)), for the purposes of the definition of "lump sum limit" in subsection (1)(a) of section 790AA (before the amendment of that section by subsection (4)(b)) of that Act, "standard fund threshold" shall mean €5,418,085 for the year of assessment 2010.

Revenue Briefings

eBrief

eBrief No. 27/2011 – Taxation of Retirement Lump Sums – New form where income tax is deducted under Case IV at the standard rate

eBrief No. 22/2014 – Pensions – Form 787S (Chargeable Excess Tax) and Form 790AA (Excess Lump Sum Tax)

Cross References

From Section 790AA

Section 112 Basis of assessment, persons chargeable and extent of charge.
Section 188 Age exemption and associated marginal relief.
Section 458 Deductions allowed in ascertaining taxable income and provisions relating to reductions in tax.
Section 770 Interpretation and supplemental (Chapter 1).
Section 771 Meaning of "retirement benefits scheme".
Section 772 Conditions for approval of schemes and discretionary approval.
Section 781 Charge to income tax: commutation of entire pension.
Section 784 Retirement annuities: relief for premiums.
Section 787A Interpretation and supplemental.
Section 787G Taxation of payments from a PRSA.
Section 787O Interpretation and general (Chapter 2C).
Section 1080 Interest on overdue income tax, corporation tax and capital gains tax.

790B Exemption of cross-border scheme

[(1) In this section—

"*competent authority*", in relation to the State, means the national authority designated to carry out the duties provided for in the Directive arising from the transposition of the Directive into the law of the State;

"*Directive*" means Directive 2003/41/EC of the European Council and of the Parliament of 3 June 2003* on the activities and supervision of institutions for occupational retirement provision;

* OJ No. L235, 23.9.2003, p.10

"*European undertaking*", in relation to a scheme, means an undertaking located in a European State which makes or proposes to make contributions to a scheme in respect of European members;

"*European members*" means individuals who are or have been employed or self-employed in a European State and in respect of which employment or self employment the trustees of the scheme have accepted or propose to accept contributions from the European undertaking;

"*European State*" means a Member State of the European Communities other than the State;

"*scheme*" means an occupational pension scheme established in the State under irrevocable trusts which provides, or is capable of providing, retirement benefits (within the meaning of Article 6(*d*) of the Directive) in relation to European members;

"*trustees*", in relation to a scheme, means the trustees of the scheme;

"*undertaking*" means any undertaking or other body, regardless of whether it includes or consists of one or more persons, which acts as an employer or as an association, or other representative body, of self employed persons.

(2) *Subsections (3)* and *(4)* shall apply to any scheme in respect of which, arising from the transposition of the Directive into the law of the State, the trustees have received from the competent authority—

(a) an authorisation, and

(b) an approval,

to accept contributions from a European undertaking in respect of European members, which authorisation has not been revoked.

(3) (a) Exemption from income tax shall, on a claim being made in that behalf, be allowed in respect of income derived from investments or deposits of a scheme, if or to such extent as the Revenue Commissioners are satisfied that, it is income from investments or deposits held for the purposes of the scheme.

(b) (i) In this subsection "*financial futures*" and "*traded options*" mean respectively financial futures and traded options for the time being dealt in or quoted on any futures exchange or any stock exchange, whether or not that exchange is situated in the State.

(ii) For the purposes of *paragraph (a)*, a contract entered into in the course of dealing in financial futures or traded options shall be regarded as an investment.

(c) Exemption from income tax shall, on a claim being made in that behalf, be allowed in respect of underwriting commissions if, or to such extent as the Revenue Commissioners are satisfied that, the underwriting commissions are applied for the purposes of the scheme, and in respect of which the trustees of the scheme would but for this subsection be chargeable to tax under Case IV of Schedule D.

(4) For the purposes of *sections 172A(1), 256(1)* and *739B(1)*, the reference to "an exempt approved scheme within the meaning of *section 774*" in the definition of "*pension scheme*" in those sections shall be deemed to include a reference to a scheme referred to in *subsection (2)*.

Amendments

Cross References

From Section 790B

Section 172A Interpretation.
Section 256 Interpretation (Chapter 4).
Section 739B Interpretation and application.
Section 774 Certain approved schemes: exemptions and reliefs.

790C Relief for deduction under Financial Emergency Measures in the Public Interest Act 2009.

[Any deduction made under the Financial Emergency Measures in the Public Interest Act 2009 in respect of a public servant (within the meaning of that Act) shall, in assessing income tax under Schedule E, be allowed to be deducted as an expense incurred in the year in which the deduction is made.][1]

Amendments

[1] Inserted by Financial Emergency Measures in the Public Interest Act 2009 s16(1)

790D Imputed distribution from certain funds

[(1) In this section—

'*additional voluntary PRSA contributions*' has the meaning assigned to it by *section 787A(1)*;

'*approved minimum retirement fund*' has the meaning assigned to it by *section 784C* and for the purposes of this section the expression 'AMRF' shall be construed accordingly;

'*approved retirement fund*' has the meaning assigned to it by *section 784A* and for the purposes of this section the expression 'ARF' shall be construed accordingly;

'*contributor*' has the meaning assigned to it by *section 787A*;

'*excluded distributions*' means one or more of the following:

(a) a specified amount regarded as a distribution or the making available of PRSA assets under *subsection (4)*;

(b) a payment, transfer or assignment of the assets of an ARF to another ARF the beneficial owner of the assets in which is the individual who is beneficially entitled to the assets in the first-mentioned ARF, whether or not the payment, transfer or assignment is made to the individual;

(c) a transaction regarded as a distribution for the purposes of *section 784A* by virtue of *subsection (1A)* of that section;

(d) a transfer referred to in *section 784C(5)(a)*;

(e) assets made available from a PRSA, being assets of a kind referred to in *section 787G(3)*;

(f) the circumstances set out in *section 787G(4A)* in which a PRSA administrator is treated as making assets of a PRSA available to an individual;

[(g) a distribution made for any of the purposes set out in *section 784A(3A)*;][1]

'*other manager*', in relation to an individual who has a relevant fund, means a person, other than the nominee, that is—

(a) a qualifying fund manager,

(b) a PRSA administrator, or

(c) both a qualifying fund manager and a PRSA administrator,

and which manages or administers, as the case may be, on the specified date—

(i) one or more than one ARF,

(ii) one or more than one vested PRSA, or

(iii) one or more than one ARF and one or more than one vested PRSA,

the assets in which are beneficially owned by the individual;

'*Personal Retirement Savings Account*' has the meaning assigned to it by *section 787A* and for the purposes of this section the expression 'PRSA' shall be construed accordingly;

'*PRSA administrator*' has the meaning assigned to it by *section 787A*;

'*qualifying fund manager*' has the meaning assigned to it by *section 784A*;

'*relevant distributions*', in relation to an individual, means the aggregate of the amount or value of—

(a) the distributions, if any, made during the tax year by a qualifying fund manager in respect of assets held in—

(i) an ARF, or, as the case may be, ARFs the assets of which are beneficially owned by the individual and managed by that qualifying fund manager, and

(ii) an AMRF, if any, the assets of which are beneficially owned by the individual and managed by that qualifying fund manager, (in this paragraph referred to as the 'funds') being funds the assets in which were first accepted into the funds by the qualifying fund manager on or after 6 April 2000,

and

(b) the assets, if any, that a PRSA administrator makes available to, or pays to, the individual or to any other person during the tax year from one or more than one vested PRSA that is beneficially owned by that individual and administered by that PRSA administrator,

less the aggregate of the amount or value of any excluded distributions made during the tax year in respect of assets which are beneficially owned by the individual;

'*relevant fund*' means all of the—

(a) ARFs, and

(b) vested PRSAs,

beneficially owned by the same individual on the specified date other than ARFs the assets in which were first accepted into the funds by the qualifying fund manager before 6 April 2000;

'*specified amount*', for a tax year, means an amount equivalent to the amount determined by the formula—

$$\frac{(A \times B)}{100} - C$$

where the amount so determined is greater than zero and where—

A is the value (in this section referred to as the 'relevant value') of the assets in a relevant fund on the specified date, excluding, where appropriate, the value of assets retained by the PRSA administrator as would be required to be transferred to an AMRF if the beneficial owner of the PRSA had opted in accordance with *section 787H(1)*,

[B is—

(a) where the relevant value is not greater than €2,000,000—

(i) 4, where the individual is not aged 70 years or over for the whole of the tax year, or

(ii) 5, where the individual is aged 70 years or over for the whole of the tax year,

or

(b) 6, where the relevant value is greater than €2,000,000,][2]

and

C is the amount or value of relevant distributions, if any, made in the tax year;

'*specified date*' means 30 November in the tax year;

'*tax year*' means a year of assessment for income tax purposes;

'*vested PRSA*' means—

(a) a PRSA in respect of which assets of the PRSA have been made available to, or paid to, the PRSA contributor or to any other person, by the PRSA administrator on or after 7 November 2002, other than assets of a kind referred to in *paragraphs (b), (c)* and *(d)* of *section 787G(3)*, and for the purposes of this definition the provisions of *subsections (4)* and *(4A)* of *section 787G* shall apply, and

(b) in the case of a PRSA that is a PRSA o which an individual is or was the contributor of additional voluntary PRSA contributions, such a PRSA where benefits become payable to the individual under the main scheme on or after 7 November 2002.

(2) For the purposes of this section, references to the value of an asset in a relevant fund shall, except where the asset is cash, be construed as a reference to the market value of the asset within the meaning of *section 548*.

(3) This section applies for any tax year in which an individual—

(a) has a relevant fund, and

(*b*) is aged 60 years or over for the whole of that tax year.

(4) Subject to the other provisions of this section, the specified amount shall for the purposes of *subsections (3)* and *(7)(b)* of *section 784A* or, as the case may be, *subsections (1)* and *(2)* of *section 787G* be regarded as—

(a) where the relevant fund comprises one or more than one ARF, a distribution of that amount from an ARF,

(b) where the relevant fund comprises one or more than one vested PRSA, the making available to, or paying to, the PRSA contributor of assets of that amount or value from a PRSA,

(c) where the relevant fund comprises one or more than one ARF and one or more than one vested PRSA and—

(i) the qualifying fund manager and the PRSA administrator of each ARF and of each PRSA concerned are the same person, a distribution of that amount from an ARF,

(ii) the nominee appointed in accordance with *subsection (5)* is a qualifying fund manager, a distribution of that amount from an ARF,

(iii) the nominee appointed in accordance with *subsection (5)* is a PRSA administrator, the making available to, or paying to, the PRSA contributor of assets of that amount or value from a PRSA, or

(iv) the nominee appointed in accordance with *subsection (5)* is both a qualifying fund manager and a PRSA administrator, a distribution of that amount from an ARF,

not later than the second month of the tax year following the tax year in respect of which the specified amount is determined.

(5) Where—

(a) an individual has a relevant fund and—

(i) the relevant value is €2,000,000 or less,

(ii) the relevant fund comprises—

(I) more than one ARF, or

(II) more than one vested PRSA, or

(III) one or more than one ARF and one or more than one vested PRSA,

and

(iii) in relation to each such relevant fund the qualifying fund manager of each ARF concerned and the PRSA administrator of each vested PRSA concerned are not the same person,

or

(b) where an individual has a relevant fund and the relevant value is greater than €2,000,000 and *subparagraphs (ii)* and *(iii)* of *subsection (a)* apply,

then the individual referred to in *paragraph (a)* may, and the individual referred to in *paragraph (b)* shall, appoint one of those persons (in this section referred to as the 'nominee') for the purposes of this section.

(6) Where an individual appoints a nominee in accordance with *subsection (5)* the individual shall—

(i) inform the other manager or the other managers, as the case may be, of such appointment for the purposes of this section,

(ii) where the appointment under *subsection (5)* is compulsory, advise the other manager or the other managers, as the case may be, of that fact, and

(iii) provide the other manager or the other managers, as the case may be, with the full name, address and telephone number of the nominee.

(7) Where an individual appoints a nominee in accordance with *subsection (5)*—

(a) the other manager or the other managers, as the case may be, shall within 14 days of the specified date provide the nominee with a certificate for that tax year stating the aggregate value (subject to *paragraph (b)*) of the assets on that date in, and the relevant distributions from—

(i) the ARF or ARFs, or

(ii) the vested PRSA or vested PRSAs, or

(iii) the ARF or ARFs and the vested PRSA or vested PRSAs,

managed or administered by the other manager or the other managers,

(b) the aggregate value of the assets referred to in *paragraph (a)* shall, where the assets are in one or more than one vested PRSA, exclude the value of such assets, if any, retained by the PRSA administrator as would be required to be transferred to an AMRF if the beneficial owner of the PRSA had opted in accordance with *section 787H(1)*, and

(c) the nominee shall keep and retain for a period of 6 years each certificate so provided and on being so required by notice given to the nominee in writing by an officer of the Revenue Commissioners, make available within the time specified in the notice such certificates as may be required by the notice.

(8) Where an individual appoints a nominee in accordance with *subsection (5)* and the nominee receives a certificate or, as the case may be, certificates provided in accordance with *subsection (7)(a)*, from the other manager or from one or more of the other managers, the specified amount shall be determined by the nominee as if the value of the assets and the relevant distributions stated in each certificate so received were the value of assets in and relevant distributions from an ARF or a vested PRSA managed or administered by the nominee in that tax year.

(9) Where an individual appoints a nominee in accordance with *subsection (5)* in respect of a relevant fund of a kind referred to in *paragraph (a)* of that subsection and—

(a) the nominee does not receive a certificate referred to in *subsection (7)(a)* from the other manager, or

(b) the nominee does not receive a certificate referred to in *subsection (7)(a)*—

(i) from any of the other managers, or

(ii) from any one or more of the other managers, but not all of them, then—

(I) where *paragraph (a)* or *(b)(i)* applies, the nominee and the other manager or, as the case may be, the nominee and each of the other managers, and

(II) where *paragraph (b)(ii)* applies, each of the other managers in respect of which the nominee has not received a certificate,

(in this subsection referred to as the 'relevant manager') shall determine the specified amount in accordance with this section as if the relevant fund of the individual was comprised solely, as the case may be, of—

(A) the ARF or ARFs,

(B) the vested PRSA or vested PRSAs, or

(C) the ARF or ARFs and the vested PRSA or vested PRSAs,

managed or administered by the relevant manager.

(10) Where an individual appoints a nominee in accordance with *subsection (5)* in respect of a relevant fund of a kind referred to in *paragraph (b)* of that subsection and *paragraph (a)* or *(b)* of *subsection (9)* applies, the specified amount shall be determined in accordance with *subsection (9)* as if B in the formula for the specified amount was 6.

(11) Where an individual has a relevant fund of a kind referred to in *subsection (5) (a)* and the individual opts not to appoint a nominee as provided for in that subsection, then each person who on the specified date is—

(a) a qualifying fund manager,

(b) a PRSA administrator, or

(c) both a qualifying fund manager and a PRSA administrator,

of one or more than one ARF, one or more than one vested PRSA or, as the case may be, one or more than one ARF and one or more than one vested PRSA comprised in that relevant fund shall determine the specified amount in accordance with this section as if the relevant fund was comprised solely, as the case may be, of—

(i) the ARF or ARFs, ... PRSAs, or

(ii) the vested PRS... and the vested PRSA or vested PRSAs,

(iii) the AR... by each such person.][3]

managed...

...A14 s19(5)(a)(i). Has effect on and from 1 January 2015.

...ated by FA14 s19(5)(a)(ii). Has effect on and from 1 January 2015.

[3] Inserted by FA12 s18(8). Has effect for the year of assessment 2012 and subsequent years of assessment.

790E Taxation of certain investment returns to relevant pension arrangements

[(1) Notwithstanding any other provisions of this Part or *Part 19*, where the amount to be regarded as a distribution for the purposes of *section 784A* is determined in accordance with *subsection (1B)(b)* of that section, then the provisions of *section 774(3)*, *784(4)*, *785(5)*, *787I(1)*, *608(2)* or *608(3)* shall not apply to any income or gains, to which those provisions would, but for this secti... otherwise apply, that arise to the pension investor (within the meaning of ...

section 784A) where the circumstances described in *subparagraphs (i)* 5 and *(ii)* of *subsection (1B)(b)* of *section 784A* arise.

(2) The income or gains referred to in *subsection (1)* shall be chargeable to tax on the trustees or administrator of the pension investor, referred to in that subsection, under Case IV of Schedule D.][1]

Amendments

[1] Inserted by FA14 s19(5)(b). Has effect on and from 23 October 2014.

PART 31

Taxation of Settlors, etc., in Respect of Settled or Transferred Income

CHAPTER 1

Revocable Dispositions for Short Periods and Certain Dispositions in Favour of Children

791 Income under revocable dispositions

[ITA67 s438 and s442]

(1) In this Chapter and in *paragraph 27* of *Schedule 32*, except where the context otherwise requires, "*disposition*" includes any trust, covenant, agreement or arrangement.

(2) Any income of which any person (in this subsection referred to as "*the first-mentioned person*") is able or has been able, without the consent of any other person by means of the exercise of any power of appointment, power of revocation or otherwise however by virtue or in consequence of a disposition made directly or indirectly by the first-mentioned person, to obtain for the first-mentioned person the beneficial enjoyment shall be deemed for the purposes of the Income Tax Acts to be the income of the person who is or was able to obtain such beneficial enjoyment, and not to be the income of any other person.

(3) Where any power referred to in *subsection (2)* may be exercised by a person with the consent of the [wife, husband or civil partner][1] of the person, the power shall for the purposes of *subsection (2)* be deemed to be exercisable without the consent of another person, except where the [husband and wife, or civil partners, are living apart][2] either by agreement or under an order of a court of competent jurisdiction.

(4) Where any power referred to in *subsection (2)* is exercisable by the [wife, husband or civil partner][3] of the person who made the disposition, the power shall for the purposes of *subsection (2)* be deemed to be exercisable by the person who made the disposition.

Amendments

[1,3] Substituted by F(No.3)A11 sched1(221). Shall have effect from the passing of this Act; 27 July 2011.

[2] Substituted by F(No.3)A11 sched1(222). Shall have effect from the passing of this Act; 27 July 2011.

Case Law

A nun transferred funds into a trust under which the income was to be used for charitable and religious purposes. In the event of the nun leaving the religious order she would take an absolute interest in the funds. It was held that the nun was the beneficial owner of the funds. Hughes v Smyth (Sister Mary Bernard) 1932 I ITR 411

The settlor was assessable on the trust income where the trust provided that the trustees were to advance the settlor funds on request. D'Ambrumenil v IRC 1940 TC 440

Revenue Briefings

Tax Briefing

Tax Briefing April 1998 – Issue 31 pg 31 – Charities – Deeds of Covenant

Revenue Precedents

Whether deed of covenant for period which exceeds or may exceed 6 years, where payments made for period less than 6 years; whether UK case law relevant in deciding if covenant for a sufficient period.

The fact that payments under deed are made for less than 6 years does not render the deed ineffective; UK case law is relevant, although the wording is different. IT932009

A covenant made in consideration of child minding services, where the parties are cohabiting is not an effective disposition of income. The payment is not pure income profit in the hands of the recipient. IT932022

Cross References

From Section 791

Schedule 32 Transitional Provisions

To Section 791

Section 746 Offshore income gains accruing to persons resident or domiciled abroad.

792 Income under dispositions for short periods

[ITA67 s439; FA95 s13(1)(a) and (2)]

(1) (a) In this subsection, "*relevant individual*" means an individual who is—

(i) permanently incapacitated by reason of mental or physical infirmity, or

(ii) aged 65 years or over.

(b) Any income which, by virtue of or in consequence of any disposition made directly or indirectly by any person (other than a disposition made for valuable and sufficient consideration), is payable to or applicable for the benefit of any other person, but excluding any income which—

(i) arises from capital of which the disponer by the disposition has divested absolutely himself or herself in favour of or for the benefit of the other person,

[…][1]

(iv) being payable to a relevant individual for the individual's own use, is so payable for a period which exceeds or may exceed 6 years, or

(v) being applicable for the benefit of a named relevant individual, is so applicable for a period which exceeds or may exceed 6 years,

shall be deemed for the purposes of the Income Tax Acts to be the income of the person, if living, by whom the disposition was made and not to be the income of any other person.

(2) (a) This subsection shall apply to a disposition or dispositions of a kind or kinds referred to in *subparagraphs (ii)* to *(v)* of *subsection (1)(b)* made directly or indirectly by a person being an individual (in this subsection referred to as "*the disponer*") except in so far as, by virtue or in consequence of such disposition or dispositions, income is payable or applicable in a year of assessment, in the manner referred to in *subparagraph (iv)* or *(v)* of that subsection, to or for the benefit of an individual referred to in *subsection (1)(a)(i)*.

(b) Notwithstanding *subsection (1)*, in relation to the disponer, any income which—

(i) is payable or applicable in a year of assessment by virtue or in consequence of a disposition or dispositions to which this subsection applies, and

(ii) is in excess of 5 per cent of the total income of the disponer for the year of assessment,

shall be deemed for the purposes of the Income Tax Acts to be the income of the disponer, if living, and not to be the income of any other person.

(c) Where *paragraph (b)* applies in relation to the disponer, for the purpose of determining for income tax purposes the amount of income which remains the income of persons other than the disponer for a year of assessment by virtue or in consequence of a disposition or dispositions to which this subsection applies, the aggregate of the income so remaining shall be apportioned amongst those other persons in proportion to their entitlements under such disposition or dispositions for that year.

[…][2]

(4) As respects the year of assessment 1997-98, this section shall apply subject to *paragraph 27* of *Schedule 32* in respect of a disposition to which that paragraph applies by a person in so far as, by virtue or in consequence of such a disposition, income is payable in that year of assessment to or for the benefit of an individual to whom that paragraph applies.

Amendments

[1, 2] Repealed by TCA97 s848A, as inserted by FA01 s45.

Case Law

A valid disposition could be made by a member of a religious order even if all the covenanted income was paid into a common fund. Revenue Commissioners v HI 1984 III ITR 242

The minimum payment is made from the date of the first payment to the date of the last payment as provided for in the investment. IRC v St Luke's Hostel Trustee 1930 TC 682

While the money must be applied for the covenantee's benefit, he does not need to have a beneficial interest in the payment. Action Aid v Revenue Commissioners 1997 V ITR 392

The definition of a settlor and a settlement was outlined in EG v MacSamhrain 1957 II ITR 352.

Revenue Briefings

Tax Briefing

Tax Briefing No. 1 1995 – Issue 17 – Income Tax Covenant Relief

Revenue Information Notes

IT 7 – Covenants to individuals

Cross References

From Section 792

Schedule 32 Transitional Provisions

To Section 792

Section 243 Allowance of charges on income.
Section 793 Recovery of tax from trustee and payment to trustee of excess tax recoupment.
Section 848A Donations to approved bodies.
Schedule 32 Transitional Provisions

793 Recovery of tax from trustee and payment to trustee of excess tax recoupment

[ITA67 s441; F(MP)A68 s3(2) and Sch PtI; FA74 s86 and Sch2 PtI; FA96 s132(2) and Sch5 PtII; FA97 s146(1) and Sch9 Pt1 par1(28)]

(1) Where by virtue of *section 792* any income tax becomes chargeable on and is paid by the person by whom the disposition was made, that person shall be entitled—

(a) to recover from any trustee or other person to whom the income is payable by virtue or in consequence of the disposition the amount of the tax so paid, and

(b) for that purpose to require the Revenue Commissioners to furnish to that person a certificate specifying the amount of the income in respect of which that person has so paid tax and the amount of the tax so paid, and any certificate so furnished shall be evidence until the contrary is proved of the matters of fact stated in that certificate.

(2) Where any person obtains in respect of any allowance or relief a repayment of income tax in excess of the amount of the repayment to which that person would but for *section 792* have been entitled, an amount equal to the excess shall be paid by that person to the trustee or other person to whom the income is payable by virtue or in consequence of the disposition or, where there are 2 or more such persons, shall be apportioned among those persons as the case may require.

(3) Where any question arises as to the amount of any payment or as to any apportionment to be made under *subsection (2)*, that question shall be decided by the Appeal Commissioners whose decision on that question shall be final.

(4) Any income which is deemed by virtue of this Chapter to be the income of any person shall be deemed to be the highest part of that person's income.

Cross References

From Section 793

Section 792 Income under dispositions for short periods.

CHAPTER 2

Settlements on Children Generally

794 Interpretation and application (Chapter 2)

[ITA67 s443(2), (3) and (5), s445 and s447; FA95 s12(1)(a)(ii) and (c)(i) and (ii)]

(1) In this Chapter—

"*income*" (except where in *sections 795(1)*, *796(2)(b)* and *subsections (4)* and *(5)* of *section 797* it is immediately preceded by "*as*" or "*that person's*" and except also in *section 798*) includes any income chargeable to income tax by deduction or otherwise and any income which would have been so chargeable if it had been received in the State by a person resident or ordinarily resident in the State;

"*settlement*" includes any disposition, trust, covenant, agreement or arrangement, and any transfer of money or other property or of any right to money or other property.

(2) This Chapter shall apply to every settlement wherever and whenever made or entered into.

(3) This Chapter shall not apply in relation to any income arising under a settlement in any year of assessment for which the settlor is not chargeable to income tax as a resident in the State, and references in this Chapter to income shall be construed accordingly.

(4) This Chapter shall not apply to any income which, by virtue or in consequence of a settlement and during the life of the settlor, is in any year of assessment paid to or for the benefit of a minor, [not being a child of the settlor or the settlor's civil partner][1], if such minor is permanently incapacitated by reason of mental or physical infirmity.

(5) For the purposes of this Chapter, the following provisions shall apply in relation to the construction of "irrevocable instrument":

(a) an instrument shall not be an irrevocable instrument if the trusts of the instrument provide for all or any one or more of the following matters—

(i) the payment or application to or for the settlor for the settlor's own benefit of any capital or income or accumulations of income in any circumstances whatever during the life of a person (in this paragraph referred to as a "*beneficiary*") to or for the benefit of whom any income or accumulations of income is or are or may be payable or applicable under the trusts of the instrument,

(ii) the payment or application during the life of the settlor to or for the [husband, wife or civil partner][2] of the settlor for his own or her own benefit of any capital or income or accumulations of income in any circumstances whatever during the life of any beneficiary,

(iii) the termination of the trusts of the instrument by the act or on the default of any person, and

(iv) the payment by the settlor of a penalty in the event of the settlor failing to comply with the instrument;

(b) an instrument shall not be prevented from being an irrevocable instrument by reason only that the trusts of the instrument include any one or more of the following provisions—

(i) a provision under which any capital or income or accumulations of income will or may become payable to or applicable for the benefit of the settlor or the [husband, wife or civil partner][3] of the settlor, on the bankruptcy of a person (in this paragraph referred to as a "*beneficiary*") to or for the benefit of whom any income or accumulations of income is or are or may be payable or applicable under the trusts of the instrument,

(ii) a provision under which any capital or income or accumulations of income will or may become payable to or applicable for the benefit of the settlor or the [husband, wife or civil partner][4] of the settlor, in the event of any beneficiary making an assignment of or charge on such capital or income or accumulations of income, and

(iii) a provision for the termination of the trusts of the instrument in such circumstances or manner that such termination would not, during the life of any beneficiary, benefit any person other than that beneficiary or that beneficiary's [husband, wife, civil partner or issue][5];

(c) "*irrevocable instrument*" includes instruments whenever made.

Amendments

[1] Substituted by F(No.3)A11 sched1(224).

[2, 3, 4] Substituted by F(No.3)A11 sched1(223).

[5] Substituted by F(No.3)A11 sched1(225).

Case Law

A mother who appointed part of her life interest in the income of a settlement under a revocable disposition to her baby daughter, was held to be the beneficial owner of the income. EG v MacSamhrain 1957 II ITR 352.

Cross References

From Section 794

Section 795 Income settled on children.

Section 796 Irrevocable instruments.

Section 797 Recovery of tax from trustee and payment to trustee of excess tax recoupment.
Section 798 Transfer of interest in trade to children.

To Section 794
Section 118 Benefits in kind: general charging provision.
Section 909 Power to require return of property.

795 Income settled on children

[ITA67 s443(1); FA95 s12(1)(a)(i) and (c)]

(1) Where, by virtue or in consequence of a settlement and during the life of the settlor, any income is in any year of assessment paid to or for the benefit of a person, such income shall, if at the time of payment such person is a minor, be treated for the purposes of the Income Tax Acts as income of the settlor for that year and not as income of any other person.

(2) For the purposes of this Chapter, but subject to *section 796*—

(a) income which, by virtue or in consequence of a settlement to which this Chapter applies, is so dealt with that it or assets representing it will or may become payable or applicable to or for the benefit of a person in the future (whether on the fulfilment of a condition, or on the happening of a contingency, or as the result of the exercise of a power or discretion conferred on any person, or otherwise) shall be deemed to be paid to or for the benefit of that person, and

(b) any income dealt with in the manner referred to in *paragraph (a)* which is not required by the settlement to be allocated, at the time when it is so dealt with, to any particular person or persons shall be deemed to be paid in equal shares to or for the benefit of each of the persons to or for the benefit of whom or any of whom the income or assets representing it will or may become payable or applicable.

Cross References

From Section 795
Section 796 Irrevocable instruments.

To Section 795
Section 794 Interpretation and application (Chapter 2).
Section 796 Irrevocable instruments.
Section 798 Transfer of interest in trade to children.

796 Irrevocable instruments

[ITA67 s444 and s447; FA71 s16(2) and (3); FA95 s12(1)(b)]

(1) In this section, "*property*" does not include any annual or other periodical payment secured by the covenant of the settlor, or by a charge made by the settlor on the whole or any part of the settlor's property or the whole or any part of the settlor's future income, or by both such covenant and such charge.

(2) Where by virtue of an irrevocable instrument property is vested in or held by trustees on such trusts that in any year of assessment *section 795* would but for this section apply to the income of such property, the following provisions shall apply:

(a) *section 795* shall not apply—

(i) in respect of any part of such income which is in that year of assessment accumulated for the benefit of a person, or

(ii) in respect of income arising in that year of assessment from accumulations of income referred to in *subparagraph (i)*;

(b) whenever in any year of assessment any sum whatever is paid under the trusts of such irrevocable instrument out of—

(i) such property,

(ii) the accumulations of the income of such property,

(iii) the income of such property, or

(iv) the income of those accumulations,

to or for the benefit of a person who at the time of payment is a minor, such sum shall, subject to the limitation in *paragraph (c)*, be deemed for the purposes of this Chapter to be paid as income;

(c) *paragraph (b)* shall not apply to so much of such sum as is equal to the amount by which the aggregate of such sum and all other sums (if any) paid after the 5th day of April, 1937, under the trusts of such irrevocable instrument to or for the benefit of that person or any other person (being a person who at the time of payment was a minor) exceeds the aggregate amount of the income arising after the 5th day of April, 1937, from such property together with the income arising after that date from those accumulations;

(d) for the purposes of *paragraph (c)*, the reference in that paragraph to another sum paid to or for the benefit of a person who at the time of payment was a minor shall be construed, in relation to a payment to which this paragraph applies of any such sum, as a reference to a sum so paid to or for the benefit of a person who at the beginning of the year of assessment in which such other sum was paid was a minor;

(e) *paragraph (d)* shall apply to any payment of any such sum—

(i) made before the 6th day of April, 1971, or

(ii) in the case of a payment to or for the benefit of a child born after the 6th day of April, 1971, and so made by virtue or in consequence of a settlement made before the 28th day of April, 1971, made in the year 1971–72;

(f) for the purposes of *paragraphs (c)* and *(d)*, references in those paragraphs to a person being at a particular time a minor shall, where that time is before the 6th day of April, 1986, be construed as references to a person who at that time was under the age of 21 years and was not or had not been married.

Case Law

A settlement includes a gift of shares Hood Barrs v IRC 1945 TC 385, a gift of money Thomas v Marshall 1952 TC 178, the surrender of a life interest IRC v Buchanan 1957 TC 365, and a series of non commercial transactions Copeman v Coleman 1939 22 TC 594.

Commercial transactions that have no element of bounty cannot constitute a settlement. Berry v Warnett 1980 STC 504, IRC v Plummer 1979 STC 793, Bulmer v IRC 1966 TC 1, IRC v Leiner 1964 TC 589

Revenue Precedents

Where there was no present debt, but an undertaking to make a series of payments, the payment under a deed of transfers would be treated as annual payments which would reduce the income of the payer and be income in the hands of the recipient. IT922047

Cross References

From Section 796

Section 795 Income settled on children.

To Section 796

Section 794 Interpretation and application (Chapter 2).
Section 795 Income settled on children.

797 Recovery of tax from trustee and payment to trustee of excess tax recoupment

[ITA67 s446; F(MP)A68 s3(2) and Sch PtI; FA74 s86 and Sch2 PtI; FA97 s146(1) and Sch9 PtI par1(29)]

(1) Where by virtue of this Chapter any income tax becomes chargeable on and is paid by a settlor, such settlor shall be entitled—

(a) to recover from any trustee or other person to whom the income is payable by virtue or in consequence of the settlement the amount of the tax so paid, and

(b) for that purpose to require the Revenue Commissioners to furnish to such settlor a certificate specifying the amount of the income in respect of which such settlor has so paid tax and the amount of the tax so paid, and every certificate so furnished shall be evidence until the contrary is proved of the matters of fact stated in the certificate.

(2) Where any person obtains in respect of any allowance or relief a repayment of income tax in excess of the amount of the repayment to which that person would but for this Chapter have been entitled, an amount equal to the excess shall be paid by that person to the trustee or other person to whom the income is payable by virtue or in consequence of the settlement and, where there are 2 or more such trustees or other persons, in such proportions as the circumstances may require.

(3) Where any question arises as to the amount of any payment or as to any apportionment to be made under *subsection (2)*, that question shall be decided by the Appeal Commissioners whose decision on that question shall be final.

(4) Any income which by virtue of this Chapter is treated as income of any person shall be deemed to be the highest part of that person's income.

(5) No repayment shall be made under *paragraph 21* of *Schedule 32* on account of tax paid in respect of any income which has by virtue of this Chapter been treated as income of a settlor.

Cross References

From Section 797

Schedule 32 Transitional Provisions

To Section 797

Section 794 Interpretation and application (Chapter 2).

798 Transfer of interest in trade to children

[ITA67 s448(1), (3) and (4)]

(1) Where by any means whatever (including indirect means or means consisting of a series of operations and whenever adopted) a trade, which at any time before the adoption of such means was carried on by any person solely or in partnership, becomes a trade carried on by one or more than one [child of such person or such person's civil partner][1] or by means of a partnership in which such person and one or more than one [child of such person or such person's civil partner][2] are partners, the following provisions shall apply:

(a) such means shall for the purposes of this Chapter be deemed to constitute a settlement as respects which such person shall be deemed to be the settlor;

(b) the profits or gains arising from the trade after the adoption of such means, in so far as they arise to one or, as the case may be, more than one [child of such person or such person's civil partner][3] shall for the purposes of this Chapter be deemed to be the same income as would have arisen to such person had such means not been adopted;

(c) "*income*" where it first occurs in *section 795* shall be deemed to include those profits or gains in so far as they arise to one or more than one [child of such person or such person's civil partner][4].

(2) The amount of the income of a person from the profits or gains of a trade deemed by virtue of *subsection (1)* to be income of another person shall, if the first-mentioned person is engaged actively in the carrying on of the trade, be the full amount of that income reduced by a sum (in *subsection (3)* referred to as "*the appropriate sum*") equal to the amount which would have been allowed in computing those profits or gains in respect of the first-mentioned person if that person, instead of being a person engaged in the carrying on of the trade, had been a person employed by a person or persons carrying on the trade.

(3) The appropriate sum shall be deemed to be profits or gains arising to the first-mentioned person referred to in *subsection (2)* from the exercise of an office or employment within the meaning of Schedule E.

Amendments

[1, 2, 3, 4] Substituted by F(No.3)A11 sched1(226). Shall have effect from the passing of this Act 27 July 2011.

Cross References

From Section 798

Section 795 Income settled on children.

To Section 798

Section 794 Interpretation and application (Chapter 2).

PART 32

Estates of Deceased Persons in Course of Administration and Surcharge on Certain Income of Trustees

CHAPTER 1

Estates of Deceased Persons in Course of Administration

799 Interpretation (Chapter 1)

[ITA67 s450; CTA76 s140 and Sch2 PtI par23; FA97 s146(1) and Sch9 PtI par1(30)]

(1) (a) In this Chapter—

"*administration period*" has the meaning assigned to it by *section 800(1)*;

"*charges on residue*", in relation to the estate of a deceased person, means the following liabilities properly payable out of the estate and interest payable in respect of those liabilities—

(i) funeral, testamentary, and administration expenses and debts,

(ii) general legacies, demonstrative legacies and annuities, and

(iii) any other liabilities of the deceased person's personal representatives as such,

but, in the case of any such liabilities which, as between persons interested under a specific disposition or in a legacy referred to in *paragraph (ii)* or in an annuity and persons interested in the residue of the estate, fall exclusively or primarily on the property that is the subject of the specific disposition or on the legacy or annuity, includes only such part (if any) of those liabilities as fall ultimately on the residue;

"*foreign estate*", as regards any year of assessment, means an estate other than an Irish estate;

"*Irish estate*", as regards any year of assessment, means an estate the income of which comprises only income which either has borne Irish income tax by deduction or in respect of which the personal representatives are directly assessable to Irish income tax, other than an estate any part of the income of which is income in respect of which the personal representatives are entitled to claim exemption from Irish income tax by reference to the fact that they are not resident or not ordinarily resident in the State;

"*personal representative*", in relation to the estate of a deceased person, means his or her personal representative within the meaning of section 3(1) of the Succession Act, 1965, and includes any person who takes possession of or intermeddles with the property of the deceased and also includes any person having, in relation to the deceased, under the law of another country any functions corresponding to the functions for administration purposes under the law of the State of a personal representative within the meaning of that section, and references to personal representatives as such shall be construed as references to personal representatives in their capacity as having such functions;

"*specific disposition*" means a specific devise or bequest made by a testator, and includes any disposition having, whether by virtue of any enactment or otherwise, under the law of the State or of another country an effect similar to that of a specific devise or bequest under the law of the State.

(b) For the purposes of this Chapter—

(i) references to the aggregate income of the estate of a deceased person for any year of assessment shall be construed, subject to *section 439(2)*, as references to the aggregate income from all sources for that year of the personal representatives of the deceased as such, treated as consisting of—

(I) any such income chargeable to Irish income tax by deduction or otherwise, such income being computed at the amount on which that tax falls to be borne for that year, and

(II) any such income which would have been so chargeable if it had arisen in the State to a person resident and ordinarily resident in the State, such income being computed at the full amount of that income actually arising during that year, less such deductions as would have been allowable if it had been charged to Irish income tax, but excluding any income from property devolving on the personal representatives otherwise than as assets for payment of the debts of the deceased;

(ii) references to sums paid include references to assets transferred or appropriated by a personal representative to himself or herself and to debts set off or released;

(iii) references to sums payable include references to assets as to which an obligation to transfer or a right of a personal representative to appropriate to himself or herself is subsisting on the completion of the administration and to debts as to which an obligation to release is set off, or a right of a personal representative so to do in his or her own favour, is then subsisting;

(iv) references to amount in relation to assets referred to in *subparagraphs (ii)* and *(iii)* shall be construed as references to the value of those assets at the date on which they were transferred or appropriated, or at the completion of the administration, as the case may require, and, in relation to such debts, as references to the amount of such debts.

(2) For the purposes of this Chapter—

(a) a person shall be deemed to have an absolute interest in the residue of the estate of a deceased person, or in a part of the residue of that estate, if and so long as the capital of the residue or of that part of the residue, as the case may be, would if the residue had been ascertained be properly payable to the person or to another in the person's right for the person's benefit, or is properly so payable, whether directly by the personal representatives, or indirectly through a trustee or other person;

(b) a person shall be deemed to have a limited interest in the residue of the estate of a deceased person, or in a part of the residue of that estate, during any period (other than a period during which the person has an absolute interest in the residue or in that part of the residue, as the case may be) where the income of the residue or of that part of the residue, as the case may be, for that period would, if the residue had been ascertained at the commencement of that period, be properly payable to the person, or to another person in the person's right, for the person's benefit, whether directly by the personal representatives, or indirectly through a trustee or other person;

(c) real estate included (either by a specific or a general description) in a residuary gift made by the will of a testator shall be deemed to be a part of the residue of the testator's estate and not to be the subject of a specific disposition.

(3) Where different parts of the estate of a deceased person are the subjects respectively of different residuary dispositions, this Chapter shall apply in relation to each such part with the substitution—

(a) for references to the estate of references to that part of the estate, and

(b) for references to the personal representatives of the deceased as such of references to those personal representatives in their capacity as having the functions referred to in the definition of "*personal representative*" in relation to that part of the estate.

Revenue Precedents

Whether, in view of the decision in Lynch v Burke Revenue can overturn a transfer of assets made prior to death where there is insufficient assets in the deceased person's estate to meet tax liabilities. It appears that Revenue would have a number of defences in cases where conveyances other than for good consideration were made to defeat Revenue claims, notwithstanding the Supreme Court decision in that case. In particular, in the case of a transferor who is still alive, it seems that resort to the Bankruptcy Act would enable such voluntary transfers to be overturned, where the transfer had been made in the previous five years. The Conveyancing Act 1634 could also be used to set aside such transfers. IT972011

Cross References

From Section 799

Section 439 Effect of release, etc. of debt in respect of loan under section 438.
Section 800 Limited interest in residue.

To Section 799

Section 5 Interpretation of Capital Gains Tax Acts.
Section 173 Interpretation (Chapter 9).
Section 244 Relief for interest paid on certain home loans.
Section 805 Surcharge on certain income of trustees.

800 Limited interest in residue

[ITA67 s451; F(MP)A68 s3(5) and Sch Pt IV; FA74 s11 and Sch1 PtII]

(1) This section shall apply in relation to a person who, during the period commencing on the death of a deceased person and ending on the completion of the administration of the estate of the deceased person (in this Chapter referred to as "*the administration period*") or during a part of that period, has a limited interest in the residue of that estate or in a part of the residue of that estate.

(2) When any sum has been paid during the administration period in respect of that limited interest, the amount of that sum shall, subject to *subsection (3)*, be deemed for the purposes of the Income Tax Acts to have been paid to that person as income for the year of assessment in which that sum was paid or, in the case of a sum paid in respect of an interest that has ceased, for the last year of assessment in which that interest was subsisting.

(3) On the completion of the administration of the estate—

(a) the aggregate amount of all sums paid before or payable on the completion of the administration in respect of that limited interest shall be deemed to have accrued due to that person from day to day during the administration period or the part of that period during which that person had that interest, as the case may be, and to have been paid to that person as it accrued due,

(b) the amount deemed to have been paid to that person by virtue of *paragraph (a)* in any year of assessment shall be deemed for the purposes of the Income Tax Acts to have been paid to that person as income for that year, and

(c) where the amount deemed to have been paid to that person as income for any year by virtue of this subsection is less or greater than the amount deemed to have been paid to that person as income for that year by virtue of *subsection (2)*, such adjustments shall be made as are provided in *section 804*.

(4) Any amount deemed to have been paid to that person as income for any year by virtue of this section shall—

(a) in the case of an Irish estate, be deemed to be income of such an amount as would after deduction of income tax at the standard rate of tax for that year be equal to the amount deemed to have been so paid and to be income that has borne income tax at that standard rate of tax;

(b) in the case of a foreign estate, be deemed to be income of the amount deemed to have been so paid, and shall be chargeable to income tax under Case III of Schedule D as if it were income arising from securities in a place outside the State.

(5) Where—

(a) a person has been charged to income tax for any year by virtue of this section in respect of an amount deemed to have been paid to that person as income in respect of an interest in a foreign estate, and

(b) any part of the aggregate income of that estate for that year has borne Irish income tax by deduction or otherwise,

the income in respect of which that person has been so charged to tax shall on proof of the facts be reduced by an amount bearing the same proportion thereto as the part of that aggregate income which has borne Irish income tax bears to the whole of that aggregate income.

(6) Where relief has been given in accordance with *subsection (5)*, such part of the amount in respect of which the person has been charged to income tax as corresponds to the proportion referred to in that subsection shall for the purpose of computing the person's total income be deemed to represent income of such an amount as would after deduction of income tax at the standard rate of tax be equal to that part of the amount charged.

Cross References

From Section 800

Section 804 Adjustments and information.

To Section 800

Section 799 Interpretation (Chapter 1).

Section 803 Special provisions as to certain interests.

801 Absolute interest in residue

[ITA67 s452; CTA76 s140(1) and Sch2 PtI par24]

(1) This section shall apply in relation to a person who during the administration period or a part of that period has an absolute interest in the residue of the estate of a deceased person or in a part of the residue of that estate.

(2) There shall be ascertained in accordance with *section 802* the amount of the residuary income of the estate for each whole year of assessment, and for each part of a year of assessment, during which—

(a) the administration period was current, and

(b) that person had that interest,

and the amount so ascertained in respect of any year or part of a year, or, in the case of a person having an absolute interest in a part of a residue, a proportionate part of that amount, is in this Chapter referred to as the "residuary income" of that person for that year of assessment.

(3) When any sum has or any sums have been paid during the administration period in respect of that absolute interest, the amount of that sum or the aggregate amount of those sums shall, subject to *subsection (4)*, be deemed for the purposes of the Income Tax Acts to have been paid to that person as income to the extent to which, and for the year or years of assessment for which, that person would have been treated for those purposes as having received income if—

(a) that person had had a right to receive in each year of assessment—

(i) in the case of an Irish estate, that person's residuary income for that year less income tax for that year at the standard rate of tax, or

(ii) in the case of a foreign estate, that person's residuary income for that year,

and

(b) that sum or the aggregate of those sums had been available for application primarily in or towards satisfaction of those rights as they accrued and had been so applied.

(4) In the case of an Irish estate, any amount deemed to have been paid to that person as income for any year by virtue of *subsection (3)* shall be deemed to be income of such an amount as would after deduction of income tax at the standard rate of tax for that year be equal to the amount deemed to have been so paid, and to be income which has borne income tax at the standard rate of tax.

(5) On the completion of the administration of the estate—

(a) the amount of the residuary income of that person for any year of assessment shall be deemed for the purposes of the Income Tax Acts to have been paid to that person as income for that year and, in the case of an Irish estate, shall be deemed to have borne tax by reference to the standard rate of tax, and

(b) where the amount deemed to have been paid to that person as income for any year by virtue of this subsection is less or greater than the amount deemed to have been paid to that person as income for that year by virtue of *subsection (3)* or *(4)*, such adjustments shall be made as are provided in *section 804*.

(6) In the case of a foreign estate, any amount deemed to have been paid to that person as income for any year by virtue of this section shall be deemed to be income of that amount, and shall be chargeable to income tax under Case III of Schedule D as if it were income arising from securities in a place outside the State.

(7) Where—

(a) a person has been charged to income tax for any year by virtue of this section in respect of an amount deemed to have been paid to that person as income in respect of an interest in a foreign estate, and

(b) any part of the aggregate income of that estate for that year has borne Irish income tax by deduction or otherwise, the income in respect of which that person has been so charged to tax shall on proof of the facts be reduced by an amount bearing the same proportion thereto as the part of that aggregate income which has borne Irish income tax bears to the whole of that aggregate income.

(8) Where relief has been given in accordance with *subsection (7)*, such part of the amount in respect of which the person has been charged to income tax as corresponds to the proportion referred to in that subsection shall for the purpose of computing the person's total income be deemed to represent income of such an amount as would after deduction of income tax at the standard rate of tax be equal to that part of the amount charged.

(9) For the purposes of any charge to corporation tax to which this section is applied, the residuary income of a company shall be computed in the first instance by reference to years of assessment, and the residuary income for any such year shall be apportioned between the accounting periods (if more than one) comprising that year.

Cross References

From Section 801

Section 802 Supplementary provisions as to absolute interest in residue.
Section 804 Adjustments and information.

To Section 801

Section 802 Supplementary provisions as to absolute interest in residue.

802 Supplementary provisions as to absolute interest in residue

[ITA67 s453]

(1) The amount of the residuary income of an estate for any year of assessment shall be ascertained by deducting from the aggregate income of the estate for that year—

(a) the amount of any annual interest, annuity or other annual payment for that year which is a charge on residue and the amount of any payment made in that year in respect of any such expenses incurred by the personal representatives as such in the management of the assets of the estate as, in the absence of any express provision in a will, would be properly chargeable to income, but excluding any such interest, annuity or payment allowed or allowable in computing the aggregate income of the estate, and

(b) the amount of any of the aggregate income of the estate for that year to which a person has on or after assent become entitled by virtue of a specific disposition either for a vested interest during the administration period or for a vested or contingent interest on the completion of the administration.

(2) (a) In this subsection, "*benefits received*", in relation to an absolute interest, means the following amounts in respect of all sums paid before, or payable on, the completion of the administration in respect of that interest—

(i) as regards a sum paid before the completion of the administration in the case of an Irish estate, such an amount as would, after deduction of income tax at the standard rate of tax for the year of assessment in which that sum was paid, be equal to that sum or, in the case of a foreign estate, the amount of that sum, and

(ii) as regards a sum payable on the completion of the administration in the case of an Irish estate, such an amount as would, after deduction of income tax at the standard rate of tax for the year of assessment in which the administration is completed, be equal to that sum or, in the case of a foreign estate, the amount of that sum.

(b) In the event of its appearing, on the completion of the administration of an estate in the residue of which, or in a part of the residue of which, a person had an absolute interest at the completion of the administration, that the aggregate of the benefits received in respect of that interest does not amount to as much as the aggregate for all years of the residuary income of the person having that interest, that person's residuary income for each year shall be reduced for the purpose of *section 801* by an amount bearing the same proportion thereto as the deficiency bears to the aggregate for all years of that person's residuary income.

(3) In the application of *subsection (2)* to a residue or a part of a residue in which a person, other than the person having an absolute interest at the completion of the administration, had an absolute interest at any time during the administration period, the aggregates mentioned in that subsection shall be computed in relation to those interests taken together, and the residuary income of that other person shall also be subject to reduction under that subsection.

Case Law

A taxpayer tried to argue that "benefits received" covered only payments to him of an income nature. IRC v Mardon 1956 TC 565. The Courts rejected this argument and held that the phrase covered benefits of both capital and of income.

Revenue Precedents

The question arose as to the extent of credit available to beneficiaries in respect of tax paid by executors. The executor is liable to tax at the standard rate on the gross income of the estate but can only make distributions out of the net income (gross income less management expenses). Form R185 issued by executors should reflect this, the executors should not issue certificates for the gross income received by them. IT902008

Cross References

From Section 802

Section 801 Absolute interest in residue.

To Section 802

Section 801 Absolute interest in residue.

803 Special provisions as to certain interests

[ITA67 s454]

(1) Where the personal representatives of a deceased person have as such a right in relation to the estate of another deceased person such that, if that right were vested in them for their own benefit, they would have an absolute interest or a limited interest in the residue of that estate or in part of the residue of that estate, the personal representatives shall be deemed to have that interest notwithstanding that that right is not vested in them for their own benefit, and any amount deemed to be paid to them as income by virtue of this Chapter shall be treated as part of the aggregate income of the estate of the person whose personal representatives they are.

(2) Where different persons have successively during the administration period absolute interests in the residue of the estate of a deceased person or in a part of the residue of that estate, sums paid during that period in respect of the residue or of that part of the residue, as the case may be, shall be treated for the purpose of this Chapter as having been paid in respect of the interest of the person who first had an absolute interest in that residue or that part of that residue up to the amount of—

(a) in the case of an Irish estate, the aggregate for all years of that person's residuary income less income tax at the standard rate of tax, or

(b) in the case of a foreign estate, the aggregate for all years of that person's residuary income,

and, as to any balance up to a corresponding amount, in respect of the interest of the person who next had an absolute interest in that residue or that part of that residue, as the case may be, and so on.

(3) Where on the exercise of a discretion any of the income of the residue of the estate of a deceased person for any period (being the administration period or a part of the administration period) would, if the residue had been ascertained at the commencement of that period, be properly payable to any person, or to another person in that person's right, for that person's benefit, whether directly by the personal representatives or indirectly through a trustee or other person—

(a) the amount of any sum paid pursuant to an exercise of the discretion in favour of that person shall be deemed for the purposes of the Income Tax Acts to have been paid to that person as income for the year of assessment in which it was paid, and

(b) *subsections (4)* to *(6)* of *section 800* shall apply in relation to an amount deemed to have been paid as income by virtue of *paragraph (a)*.

Cross References

From Section 803

Section 800 Limited interest in residue.

804 Adjustments and information

[ITA67 s455]

(1) Where on the completion of the administration of an estate any amount is deemed by virtue of this Chapter to have been paid to any person as income for any year of assessment and—

(a) that amount is greater than the amount previously deemed to have been paid to that person as income for that year by virtue of this Chapter, or

(b) no amount has previously been so deemed to have been paid to that person as income for that year,

[an assessment may be made on or by that person for that year or such an assessment may be amended][1] and tax charged accordingly or, on a claim being made for the purpose, any relief or additional relief to which that person may be entitled shall be allowed accordingly.

(2) Where on the completion of the administration of an estate any amount is deemed by virtue of this Chapter to have been paid to any person as income for any year of assessment and that amount is less than the amount that has previously been so deemed to have been paid to that person, then—

(a) if an assessment has already been made on that person for that year, such adjustments shall be made in that assessment as may be necessary for the purpose of giving effect to the provisions of this Chapter which take effect on the completion of the administration, and any tax overpaid shall be repaid, [notwithstanding any limitation in section 865(4) on the time within which a claim for a repayment of tax is required to be made,][2] and

(b) if—

(i) any relief has been allowed to that person by reference to the amount previously deemed by virtue of this Chapter to have been paid to that person as income for that year, and

(ii) the amount of that relief exceeds the amount of relief which could have been given by reference to the amount which, on the completion of the administration, is deemed to have been paid to that person as income for that year,

the relief so given in excess may, if not otherwise made good, be charged under Case IV of Schedule D and recovered from that person accordingly.

(3) Notwithstanding anything in the Income Tax Acts, the time within which—

(a) [an assessment may be made][3] for the purposes of this Chapter,

(b) [an assessment may be amended][4] for those purposes, or

(c) a claim for relief may be made by virtue of this Chapter,

shall not expire before the end of the third year following the year of assessment in which the administration of the estate in question was completed.

(4) The Revenue Commissioners may by notice in writing require any person, being or having been a personal representative of a deceased person, or having or having had an absolute interest or a limited interest in the residue of the estate of a deceased person or in a part of the residue of that estate, to furnish them within such time as they may direct (not being less than 28 days) with such particulars as they think necessary for the purposes of this Chapter.

Amendments

[1, 3, 4] Substituted by FA12 sched4(part 2)(g).

[2] Inserted by FA08 sched6(1)(q). Applies as on and from 31 January 2008.

Cross References

From Section 804

Section 865 Repayment of tax.

To Section 804

Section 800 Limited interest in residue.

Section 801 Absolute interest in residue.

Section 955 Amendment of and time limit for assessments.

Schedule 29 Provisions Referred to in Sections 1052, 1053 and 1054

CHAPTER 2

Surcharge on Certain Income of Trustees

805 Surcharge on certain income of trustees

[FA76 s13; FA90 s8]

(1) (a) In this section—

"*personal representative*" has the same meaning as in *section 799(1)*;

"*trustees*" does not include personal representatives, but where personal representatives, on or before the completion of the administration of the estate of a deceased person, pay to trustees any sum representing income which, if the personal representatives were trustees, would be income to which this section applies, that sum shall be deemed to be paid to the trustees as income and to have borne income tax at the standard rate.

(b) This subsection shall be construed together with *Chapter 1* of this Part.

(2) This section shall apply to income arising to trustees in any year of assessment in so far as it—

(a) is income which is to be accumulated or which is payable at the discretion of the trustees or any other person, whether or not the trustees have power to accumulate the income,

(b) is neither, before being distributed, the income of any person other than the trustees nor treated for any purpose of the Income Tax Acts as the income of a settlor,

(c) is not income arising under a trust established for charitable purposes only or income from investments, deposits or other property held for the purposes of a fund or scheme established for the sole purpose of providing relevant benefits within the meaning of *section 770*,

(d) exceeds the income applied in defraying the expenses of the trustees in that year which are properly chargeable to income, or would be so chargeable but for any express provisions of the trust, and

(e) is not distributed to one or more persons within that year of assessment or within 18 months after the end of that year of assessment in such circumstances that the income distributed is to be treated for the purposes of the Income Tax Acts as the income of the person or persons to whom it is distributed.

(3) (a) Income to which this section applies shall, in addition to being chargeable to income tax at the standard rate for the year of assessment for which it is so chargeable, be charged to an additional duty of income tax (in this section referred to as a "*surcharge*") at the rate of 20 per cent.

(b) A surcharge to be made on trustees under this section in respect of income arising in a year of assessment (in this subsection referred to as "the first year of assessment") shall—

(i) be charged on the trustees for the year of assessment in which a period of 18 months beginning immediately after the end of the first year of assessment ends, and

(ii) be treated as income tax chargeable for the year of assessment for which it is so charged.

(c) Subject to *subsection (4)*, the Income Tax Acts shall apply in relation to a surcharge made under this section as they apply to income tax charged otherwise than by virtue of this section.

(4) Where income in respect of which a surcharge is made is distributed, no relief from or repayment in respect of the surcharge shall be allowed or made to the person to whom the income is distributed.

(5) A notice given to trustees under any provision specified in *column 1* or *2* of *Schedule 29* may require that a return of the income arising to them shall include particulars of the manner in which the income has been applied, including particulars as to the exercise by them of any discretion and of the persons in whose favour that discretion has been so exercised.

Case Law

In Carver v Duncan 1985 STC 356 the Court held that the UK legislation should be given a secondary meaning. Firstly, there was the provision whereby the trust deed contained no express provisions concerning the allocation of expenses as between income and capital and secondly where the trust deed concerned express provisions regarding the allocating of income and capital. The court held the legislation was to be interpreted as allowing a deduction only for expense properly chargeable to income under general law disregarding the terms of the trust.

Receipts which are regarded as income for tax purposes but as capital for trust law purposes do not fall within section 805(2)(a). Howell and Anor v Trippier (Inspector of Taxes) 2004 STC 1245

Revenue Briefings

Tax Briefing

Tax Briefing September 1998 – Issue 33 pg 28 – Discretionary Trusts Surcharge

Cross References

From Section 805

Section 770 Interpretation and supplemental (Chapter 1).

Section 799 Interpretation (Chapter 1).

Schedule 29 Provisions Referred to in Sections 1052, 1053 and 1054

To Section 805

Section 510 Approved profit sharing schemes: appropriated shares.

Section 734 Taxation of collective investment undertakings.

Section 737 Special investment schemes.

PART 33

Anti-Avoidance

CHAPTER 1

Transfer of Assets Abroad

806 Charge to income tax on transfer of assets abroad

[FA74 s57 preamble and (1) to (7) and (8)(a), (b), (c), (e) and (f)]

(1) [In this section and *section 807A*—][1]

"*assets*" includes property or rights of any kind;

"*associated operation*", in relation to any transfer, means an operation of any kind effected by any person in relation to any of the assets transferred or any assets representing whether directly or indirectly any of the assets transferred, or to the income arising from any such assets, or to any assets representing whether directly or indirectly the accumulations of income arising from any such assets; [and for the purposes of this definition it is immaterial whether the operation is effected before, after, or at the same time as the transfer;][2]

"*benefit*" includes a payment of any kind;

"*company*" means any body corporate or unincorporated association;

"*transfer*", in relation to rights, includes the creation of those rights.

(2) [For the purposes of this section and *section 807A*—][3]

(a) any body corporate incorporated outside the State shall be treated as if it were resident out of the State whether it is so resident or not,

(b) a reference to an individual shall be deemed to include the [husband, wife or civil partner][4] of the individual, […][5]

(c) references to assets representing any assets, income or accumulations of income include references to shares in or obligations of any company to which, or obligations of any other person to whom, those assets, that income or those accumulations are or have been [transferred,][6]

[(d) the income that becomes payable to, or has become income of, a person resident or domiciled out of the State that is referred to in *subsection (3)* or *(5)* or in *section 807A(1)* includes any income which becomes payable to, or has become income of, the person by virtue or in consequence of—

(i) the transfer,

(ii) one or more associated operations, or

(iii) the transfer and one or more associated operations,

and

(e) the income which an individual has power to enjoy, as referred to in *subsection (4)*, includes any income which that individual has power to enjoy by virtue or in consequence of—

(i) the transfer,

(ii) one or more associated operations, or

(iii) the transfer and one or more associated operations.][7]

(3) This section shall apply for the purpose of preventing the avoidance by [individuals resident or ordinarily resident in the State][8] of liability to income tax by means of transfers of assets by virtue or in consequence of which, either alone or in conjunction with associated operations, income becomes payable to persons resident or domiciled out of the State.

(4) Where by virtue or in consequence of any such transfer, either alone or in conjunction with associated operations, such an individual has power to enjoy (within the meaning of this section), whether forthwith or in the future, any income of a person resident or domiciled out of the State which, if it were income of that individual received by that individual in the State, would be chargeable to tax by deduction or otherwise, that income shall, whether it would or would not have been chargeable to tax apart from this section, be deemed to be income of that individual for the purposes of the Income Tax Acts.

(5) (a) In this subsection, "*capital sum*" means—

(i) any sum paid or payable by means of loan or repayment of a loan, and

(ii) any other sum paid or payable otherwise than as income, being a sum not paid or payable for full consideration in money or money's worth.

(b) Where, whether before or after any such transfer, such an individual receives or is entitled to receive any capital sum the payment of which is in any way connected with the transfer or any associated operation, any income which, by virtue or in consequence of the transfer, either alone or in conjunction with associated operations, has become the income of a person resident or domiciled out of the State shall, whether it would or would not have been chargeable to tax apart from this section, be deemed to be the income of that individual for the purposes of the Income Tax Acts.

[(c) For the purposes of *paragraph (b)*, there shall be treated as a capital sum which an individual receives or is entitled to receive any sum which a third person receives or is entitled to receive at the individual's direction or by virtue of the assignment by the individual of the individual's right to receive it.][9]

[(5A) Nothing in *subsection (3)* shall be taken to imply that the provisions of *subsections (4)* and *(5)* apply only if—

(a) the individual in question was resident or ordinarily resident in the State at the time when the transfer was made, or

(b) the avoidance of liability to income tax is the purpose, or one of the purposes, for which the transfer was effected.][10]

(6) An individual shall for the purposes of this section be deemed to have power to enjoy income of a person resident or domiciled out of the State where—

(a) the income is in fact so dealt with by any person as to be calculated, at some point of time and whether in the form of income or not, to enure for the benefit of the individual,

(b) the receipt or accrual of the income operates to increase the value to the individual of any assets held by the individual or for the individual's benefit,

(c) the individual receives or is entitled to receive at any time any benefit provided or to be provided out of that income or out of moneys which are or will be available for the purpose by reason of the effect or successive effects of the associated operations on that income and on any assets which directly or indirectly represent that income,

(d) the individual has power, by means of the exercise of any power of appointment or power of revocation or otherwise, to obtain for himself or herself, whether with or without the consent of any other person, the beneficial enjoyment of the income, or may in the event of the exercise of any power vested in any other person become entitled to the beneficial enjoyment of the income, or

(e) the individual is able, in any manner whatever and whether directly or indirectly, to control the application of the income.

(7) In determining whether an individual has power to enjoy income within the meaning of this section, regard shall be had to the substantial result and effect of the transfer and any associated operations, and all benefits which may at any time accrue to the individual (whether or not the individual has rights at law or in equity in or to those benefits) as a result of the transfer and any associated operations shall be taken into account irrespective of the nature or form of the benefits.

(8) [Subject to *section 807B*, *subsections (4)* and *(5)*][11] shall not apply where the individual shows in writing or otherwise to the satisfaction of the Revenue Commissioners—

(a) that the purpose of avoiding liability to taxation was not the purpose or one of the purposes for which the transfer or associated operations or any of them was effected, or

(b) that the transfer and any associated operations were bona fide commercial transactions and were not designed for the purpose of avoiding liability to taxation.

(9) In any case where a person is aggrieved by a decision taken by the Revenue Commissioners in exercise of their functions under [*subsection (8)* or *(10)* or *section 807B* or *807C*][12], the person shall be entitled to appeal to the Appeal Commissioners against the decision of the Revenue Commissioners and the Appeal Commissioners shall hear and determine the appeal as if it were an appeal against an assessment to tax, and the provisions of the Income Tax Acts relating to the rehearing of an appeal and to the statement of a case for the opinion of the High Court on a point of law shall apply accordingly with any necessary modifications.

[(10) (a) In this subsection—

"*commercial transaction*" does not include—

(i) a transaction on terms other than those that would have been made between independent persons dealing at arm's length, or

(ii) a transaction that would not have been entered into between independent persons dealing at arm's length;

"*independent persons*" means persons who are not connected with each other (within the meaning of *section 10*);

"*relevant transactions*" means—

(i) the transfer, and

(ii) any associated operations.

(b) Subject to *section 807B*, *subsections (4)* and *(5)* shall not apply by reference to the relevant transactions where the individual shows in writing or otherwise to the satisfaction of the Revenue Commissioners—

(i) that it would not be reasonable to draw the conclusion, from all the circumstances of the case, that the purpose of avoiding liability to taxation was the purpose, or one of the purposes, for which the relevant transactions or any of them were effected, or

(ii) in a case where the condition in *subparagraph (i)* is not met, that—

(I) all the relevant transactions were genuine commercial transactions, and

(II) it would not be reasonable to draw the conclusion, from all the circumstances of the case, that any one or more of those transactions was more than incidentally designed for the purpose of avoiding liability to taxation.

(c) The intentions and purposes of any person who, whether or not for consideration—

(i) designs or effects the relevant transactions or any of them, or

(ii) provides advice in relation to the relevant transactions or any of them,

are to be taken into account in determining the purposes for which those transactions or any of them were effected.

(d) A relevant transaction is a commercial transaction only if it is effected—

(i) in the course of a trade or business, or

(ii) with a view to setting up and commencing a trade or business,

and, in either cases, for the purposes of such trade or business.

(e) For the purposes of *paragraph (d)*, the making and managing of investments, or the making or managing of investments, is not a trade or business except to the extent that—

(i) the person by whom it is done, and

(ii) the person for whom it is done,

are independent persons dealing at arm's length.

(f) Any associated operation that would not (apart from this paragraph) fall to be taken into account for the purposes of this subsection shall be taken into account for those purposes if, were it to be so taken into account, the conditions in *paragraph (b)* would be failed by reference to—

(i) that associated operation, or

(ii) that associated operation taken together with the transfer or any one or more other associated operations.][13]

Amendments

[1] Substituted by FA99 s60(1)(a)(i). Subparagraphs (i) and (ii) of paragraph (a) and paragraphs (c), (d) and (e), of subsection (1) shall apply as on and from the 11th day of February, 1999.

[2] Inserted by FA07 s44(1)(a)(i). Has effect as respects relevant transactions on or after 1 February 2007.

[3] Substituted by FA99 s60(1)(a)(ii). Subparagraphs (i) and (ii) of paragraph (a) and paragraphs (c), (d) and (e), of subsection (1) shall apply as on and from the 11th day of February, 1999.

[4] Substituted by F(No.3)A11 sched1(227). Shall have effect from the passing of this Act 27 July 2011.

[5] Deleted by FA07 s44(1)(a)(ii)(I). Has effect as respects relevant transactions on or after 1 February 2007.

[6] Substituted by FA07 s44(1)(a)(ii)(I). Has effect as respects relevant transactions on or after 1 February 2007.

[7] Inserted by FA07 s44(1)(a)(ii)(II). Has effect as respects relevant transactions on or after 1 February 2007.

[8] Substituted by FA98 s12(1)(a)(i). This section shall apply irrespective of when the transfer or associated operations took place but shall apply only to income arising on or after the 12th day of February, 1998.

[9] Inserted by FA99 s60(1)(a)(iii). Subparagraph (iii) of paragraph (a) of subsection (1) shall apply as respects any sum which a third person referred to in that subparagraph receives or becomes entitled to receive on or after the 11th day of February, 1999.

[10] Inserted by FA98 s12(1)(a)(ii). This section shall apply irrespective of when the transfer or associated operations took place but shall apply only to income arising on or after the 12th day of February, 1998.

[11] Substituted by FA07 s44(1)(a)(iii). Has effect as respects relevant transactions on or after 1 February 2007.

[12] Substituted by FA07 s44(1)(a)(iv). Has effect as respects relevant transactions on or after 1 February 2007.

[13] Inserted by FA07 s44(1)(a)(v). Has effect as respects relevant transactions on or after 1 February 2007.

Case Law

In Vestey's Executors v IRC 31 TC 1 the word "wife" was held not to include "widow".

Arising from Vestey V IRC 1980 STC 10 an individual could transfer assets abroad without becoming liable to tax under section 806 provided neither that individual nor his or her spouse could potentially benefit from the income attributable to that transfer.

In CIR v Shroder 1983 STC 480 it was held that an individual who had power to appoint trustees could not control the application of the income.

In Madigan & Madigan v AG 1984 ITR 127 the taxpayer argued that it was unconstitutional that his eligibility for relief from Residential Property Tax should depend on the income of the household over which he had no control. The Supreme Court held in reality the members of the household should contribute to the running of the family home.

Two brothers transferred assets to different non resident companies in exchange for shares and debentures in each of those companies. Each brother then executed a deed of gift of his shares and debentures to the other brother. Both brothers were held liable. Beatty's Exors v IRC TC 574

The Inland Revenue sought to tax three individuals who were both directors and shareholders of a company which had made a transfer of assets. The individuals between them only formed a minority of the board of directors and of the company's shareholders. It was held that it was the company and not the individuals that had made the transfer. IRC v Pratt 1982 STC 756

The power of trustees to transfer trust property could trigger "power to enjoy" provisions. IRC v Botnar 1999 STC 711

The UK case Herdman v IRC 1969 45 TC 394 dealt with the meaning of "associated operations". Under the UK equivalent of the Irish pre-2007 rules, the case established that it was only those associated operations which have to be taken into account upfront for the purposes of establishing a potential liability under section 806 TCA 1997 which were relevant.

The issue of transferring assets abroad was brought to attention in Willoughby v IRC 1997 STC 995. In this case, the taxpayer succeeded in proving that his motive for investing in an Isle of Man personal portfolio investment bond was not tax avoidance.

Under transfer of assets provisions, Revenue cannot take any amount of income into account more than once. R v Dimsey and Allen 1999 STC 846

In Carvill v IRC 2002 STC 1167 consideration was given as to whether the UK test in section 741 TA 1988 (equivalent to section 806(8) TCA 1997) was subjective or objective in nature.

An individual who transferred investments to a foreign company thereby increasing the value of the debt the company owed to him was held to have the power to enjoy the company's income. Ramsden v IRC 1957 TC 619

In Latilla v IRC 1943 TC 107 an individual who transferred assets to a foreign company in return for shares and non interest bearing debentures was held to have the power to enjoy the company's income where company profits were used to purchase the debenture.

An individual who had the power to appoint and remove directors held the power to enjoy the company's income. Lee v IRC 1941 TC 207

In Revenue Commissioners v ORMG 1982 ITR 28 there is a view that apportionment is not possible even in the case of joint incomes.

The question of when income arises should be decided by reference to normal Irish tax law principles. Chetwode v IRC 1977 STC 64

The UK case of McGuckian v CIR 1997 STC 908 established the principle that the equivalent UK section can apply even if the effect of the transfer of assets abroad would not have been successful in avoiding UK tax.

Revenue Briefings

Tax Briefing

Tax Briefing July 2007 – Issue 66 pg 21 Finance Act 2007: Transfer of assets abroad

Cross References

From Section 806

Section 10 Connected persons.

Section 807A Liability of nontransferors.
Section 807B Certain transitional arrangements in relation to transfer of assets abroad.
Section 807C Supplementary provisions in relation to section 806 — apportionment in certain cases.

To Section 806

Section 746 Offshore income gains accruing to persons resident or domiciled abroad.
Section 807 Deductions and reliefs in relation to income chargeable to income tax under section 806.
Section 807A Liability of nontransferors.
Section 807B Certain transitional arrangements in relation to transfer of assets abroad.
Section 807C Supplementary provisions in relation to section 806 — apportionment in certain cases.
Section 808 Power to obtain information.
Section 809 Saver.
Section 810 Application of Income Tax Acts.

807 Deductions and reliefs in relation to income chargeable to income tax under section 806

[FA74 s58]

(1) Income tax chargeable by virtue of *section 806* shall be charged under Case IV of Schedule D.

(2) In computing the liability to income tax of an individual chargeable by virtue of *section 806*, the same deductions and reliefs shall be allowed as would have been allowed if the income deemed to be income of the individual by virtue of that section had actually been received by the individual.

(3) Where an individual has been charged to income tax on any income deemed to be income of the individual by virtue of *section 806* and that income is subsequently received by the individual, it shall be deemed not to form part of the individual's income again for the purposes of the Income Tax Acts.

(4) In any case where an individual has for the purposes of *section 806* power to enjoy income of a person abroad by reason of receiving any such benefit referred to in *subsection (6)(c)* of that section, the individual shall be chargeable to income tax by virtue of that section under Case IV of Schedule D for the year of assessment in which the benefit is received on the whole of the amount or value of that benefit, except in so far as it is shown that the benefit derives directly or indirectly from income on which the individual has already been charged to income tax for that or a previous year of assessment.

[(5) An individual who is domiciled out of the State shall not be chargeable to income tax in respect of any income deemed to be the individual's by virtue of *section 806* if the individual would not, by reason of being so domiciled, have been chargeable to income tax in respect of it if it had in fact been the individual's income.][1]

Amendments

[1] Inserted by FA99 s60(1)(b). Paragraph (b) of subsection (1) shall be deemed to have applied as on and from the 12th day of February, 1998.

Case Law

Chetwode v IRC 1974 STC 474 considered if management expenses were deductible in computing income of the company.

Cross References

From Section 807

Section 806 Charge to income tax on transfer of assets abroad.

To Section 807

Section 746 Offshore income gains accruing to persons resident or domiciled abroad.
Section 808 Power to obtain information.

807A Liability of nontransferors

[(1) This section shall apply where—

(a) by virtue or in consequence of a transfer of assets, either alone or in conjunction with associated operations, income becomes payable to a person who is resident or domiciled out of the State, and

(b) an individual who is resident or ordinarily resident in the State and who is not liable to tax under *section 806* by reference to the transfer, receives a benefit provided out of assets which are available for the purpose by virtue or in consequence of the transfer or of any associated operations.

(2) Subject to the provisions of this section, the amount or value of any such benefit as is mentioned in *subsection (1)*, if not otherwise chargeable to income tax in the hands of the recipient, shall—

(a) to the extent to which it falls within the amount of relevant income of years of assessment up to and including the year of assessment in which the benefit is received, be treated for all the purposes of the Income Tax Acts as the income of the individual for that year of assessment,

(b) to the extent to which it is not by virtue of this subsection treated as the income of the individual for that year of assessment and falls within the amount of relevant income of the next following year of assessment, be treated for those purposes as the individual's income for the next following year of assessment,

and so on for subsequent years of assessment, taking the reference in *paragraph (b)* to the year of assessment mentioned in *paragraph (a)* as a reference to that year of assessment and any other year of assessment before the subsequent year of assessment in question.

(3) Subject to *subsection (8)*, the relevant income of a year of assessment, in relation to an individual, is any income which arises in that year of assessment to a person resident or domiciled out of the State and which by virtue or in consequence of the transfer or associated operations referred to in *subsection (1)* can directly or indirectly be used for providing a benefit for the individual or for enabling a benefit to be provided for the individual.

(4) Income tax chargeable by virtue of this section shall be charged under Case IV of Schedule D.

(5) An individual who is domiciled out of the State shall not, in respect of any benefit not received in the State, be chargeable to tax under this section by reference to relevant income which is such that, if the individual had received it, the individual would not, by reason of the individual being so domiciled, have been chargeable to income tax in respect of it, and *section 72* shall apply for the purposes of this subsection as it would apply for the purposes of *section 71 (3)* if the benefit were income arising from securities and possessions in any place outside the State.

(6) Where—

(a) the whole or part of the benefit received by an individual in a year of assessment is a capital payment within the meaning of *section 579A* or *579F(2)* (by virtue of not falling within the amount of relevant income referred to in *subsection (2)(a)*), and

(b) chargeable gains are by reason of that payment treated under either *section 579A* or *579F(2)* as accruing to the individual in that or a subsequent year of assessment, *subsection (2)(b)* shall apply in relation to any year of assessment (in this subsection referred to as "*a year of charge*") after one in which chargeable gains have been so treated as accruing to the individual, as if a part of the amount or value of the benefit corresponding to the amount of those gains had been treated under that subsection as income of the individual for a year of assessment before the year of charge.

(7) [*Subsections (8)*, *(9)* and *(10)*][1] of *section 806* shall apply for the purposes of this section as they apply for the purposes of *subsections (4)* and *(5)* of that section.

(8) This section shall apply irrespective of when the transfer or associated operations referred to in *subsection (1)* took place, but shall apply only to relevant income arising on or after the 11th day of February, 1999.][2]

Amendments

[1] Substituted by FA07 s44(1)(c). Has effect as respects relevant transactions on or after 1 February 2007.

[2] Inserted by FA99 s60(1)(c). Subparagraphs (i) and (ii) of paragraph (a) and paragraphs (c), (d) and (e), of subsection (1) shall apply as on and from the 11th day of February, 1999.

Cross References

From Section 807A

Section 71 Foreign securities and possessions.
Section 72 Charge to tax on sums applied outside the State in repaying certain loans.
Section 579A Attribution of gains to beneficiaries.
Section 579F Migrant settlements.
Section 806 Charge to income tax on transfer of assets abroad.

To Section 807A

Section 746 Offshore income gains accruing to persons resident or domiciled abroad.
Section 806 Charge to income tax on transfer of assets abroad.
Section 807B Certain transitional arrangements in relation to transfer of assets abroad.
Section 808 Power to obtain information.
Section 809 Saver.
Section 810 Application of Income Tax Acts.

807B Certain transitional arrangements in relation to transfer of assets abroad

[(1) In this section—

"*new transaction*" means a relevant transaction effected on or after the relevant date;

"*old transaction*" means a relevant transaction effected before the relevant date;

"*relevant date*" means 1 February 2007;

"*relevant transactions*" has the meaning assigned to it by *section 806(10)*.

(2) For the purposes of applying *subsection (3)* of this section and *subsections (8)* and *(10)* of *section 806*—

(a) if all the relevant transactions are old transactions, *section 806(8)* shall apply,

(b) if all the relevant transactions are new transactions, *section 806(10)* shall apply,

(c) if any one or more of the relevant transactions are old transactions and any one or more of the relevant transactions are new transactions, *sections 806* and *807A* shall apply subject to *subsection (3)*.

(3) (a) Where—

(i) the conditions in *section 806(8)* are failed by reference to the old transactions or any of them, or

(ii) the conditions in *section 806(10)(b)* are failed by reference to the new transactions or any of them, then, subject to *paragraph (b)*, *sections 806* and *807A* apply as they would have applied apart from any exemption by virtue of this section or by virtue of *section 806(8)* or *section 806(10)*.

(b) Where *paragraph (a)* applies by virtue only of *subparagraph (ii)* of that paragraph—

(i) for the purposes of *subsection (4)* or *(5)(b)* of *section 806* any income arising before the relevant date shall not be brought into account as income of the person resident or domiciled out of the State,

(ii) for the purposes of section *807A*—

(I) (A) where a benefit is received by an individual in a year of assessment ending after the relevant date, and

(B) relevant income (within the meaning of *section 807A(3)*) of years of assessment up to and including that year falls to be determined,

then years of assessment ending before the relevant date are to be brought into account as well as years of assessment ending after that date, and

(II) a benefit received by an individual in the year of assessment 2007 is to be left out of account to the extent that, on a time apportionment basis, it fell to be enjoyed in any part of the year that falls before the relevant date.][1]

Amendments

[1] Inserted by FA07 s44(1)(b). Has effect as respects relevant transactions on or after 1 February 2007.

Cross References

From Section 807B

Section 806 Charge to income tax on transfer of assets abroad.
Section 807A Liability of nontransferors.

To Section 807B

Section 746 Offshore income gains accruing to persons resident or domiciled abroad.
Section 806 Charge to income tax on transfer of assets abroad.
Section 808 Power to obtain information.

807C Supplementary provisions in relation to section 806 — apportionment in certain cases

[(1) In this section—

"*appropriate exemption*" means an exemption by virtue of *subsection (8)(b)* or *(10)(b)(ii)* of *section 806*;

"*exempt year of assessment*" means a year of assessment referred to in *subsection (2)(b)* in respect of which there was no earlier year of assessment where—

(a) the individual was liable to tax by virtue of *section 806*, or

(b) the individual would have been liable to tax by virtue of *section 806* if there had been any deemed income of such individual under that section;

"*relevant transactions*" has the meaning assigned to it by *section 806(10)*.

(2) This section applies where an individual is liable to income tax by virtue of *section 806* for a year of assessment and—

(a) the individual is so liable by virtue of the conditions in *section 806(10)(b)(ii)* not being met,

(b) since the making of the transfer there have been one or more years of assessment where the circumstances were such that, so far as relating to such of the relevant transactions as were effected before the end of the year of assessment concerned, the individual—

(i) was not liable to tax by virtue of *section 806* because an appropriate exemption applied, or

(ii) would not have been liable to tax by virtue of *section 806* if there had been any deemed income of such individual under that section because an appropriate exemption would have applied,

and

(c) the income by reference to which the individual is so liable is attributable—

(i) partly to relevant transactions by reference to which the appropriate exemption applied for the last exempt year of assessment, and

(ii) partly to associated operations not falling within *subparagraph (i)* (in this section referred to as "*chargeable operations*").

(3) Where this section applies, the liability of the individual shall be reduced as if it fell to be determined by reference to so much of the income as appears to the Revenue Commissioners, or such officer as the Revenue Commissioners may appoint, to be justly and reasonably attributable to chargeable operations in all the circumstances of the case.

(4) The facts and matters that may be taken into account in determining for the purposes of *subsection (3)* whether income may be regarded as justly and reasonably attributable to chargeable operations include whether, and to what extent, the chargeable operations or any of them directly or indirectly affect—

(a) the character, description or amount of any income of any person,

(b) any person's power to enjoy any income, or

(c) the character, description or amount of any income which a person has power to enjoy.][1]

Amendments

[1] Inserted by FA07 s44(1)(b). Has effect as respects relevant transactions on or after 1 February 2007.

Cross References

From Section 807C

Section 806 Charge to income tax on transfer of assets abroad.

To Section 807C

Section 746 Offshore income gains accruing to persons resident or domiciled abroad.

Section 806 Charge to income tax on transfer of assets abroad.

Section 808 Power to obtain information.

808 Power to obtain information

[FA74 s59(1) to (5); FA77 s3; FA97 s146(1) and Sch9 PtI par8(2)]

(1) In this section, "*settlement*" and "*settlor*" have the same meanings respectively as in *section 10*.

(2) The Revenue Commissioners or such officer as the Revenue Commissioners may appoint may by notice in writing require any person to furnish them within such time as they may direct (not being less than 28 days) with such particulars as they think necessary for the purposes of [*sections 806*, *807*, *807A*, *807B*, *807C* and *809*][1].

(3) The particulars which a person shall furnish under this section, if required by such a notice to do so, shall include particulars as to—

(a) transactions with respect to which the person is or was acting on behalf of others;

(b) transactions which in the opinion of the Revenue Commissioners, or of such officer as the Revenue Commissioners may appoint, it is proper that they should investigate for the purposes of [*sections 806, 807, 807A, 807B, 807C* and *809*][2], notwithstanding that in the opinion of the person to whom the notice is given no liability to tax arises under those sections;

(c) whether the person to whom the notice is given has taken or is taking any (and if so what) part in any (and if so what) transactions of a description specified in the notice.

(4) Notwithstanding anything in *subsection (3)*, a solicitor shall not be deemed for the purposes of *paragraph (c)* of that subsection to have taken part in a transaction by reason only that the solicitor has given professional advice to a client in connection with that transaction, and shall not, in relation to anything done by the solicitor on behalf of a client, be compellable under this section, except with the consent of the client, to do more than state that the solicitor is or was acting on behalf of a client, and specify the name and address of the client and also—

(a) in the case of anything done by the solicitor in connection with the transfer of any asset by or to [an individual resident or ordinarily resident in the State][3] to or by any body corporate mentioned in *subsection (5)*, or in connection with any associated operation in relation to any such transfer, to specify the names and addresses of the transferor and the transferee or of the persons concerned in the associated operation, as the case may be;

(b) in the case of anything done by the solicitor in connection with the formation or management of any body corporate mentioned in *subsection (5)*, to specify the name and address of the body corporate;

(c) in the case of anything done by the solicitor in connection with the creation, or with the execution of the trusts, of any settlement by virtue or in consequence of which income becomes payable to a person resident or domiciled out of the State, to specify the names and addresses of the settlor and of that person.

(5) The bodies corporate referred to in *subsection (4)* are bodies corporate resident or incorporated outside the State which are, or if resident in the State would be, close companies within the meaning of *sections 430* and *431*.

(6) Nothing in this section shall impose on any bank the obligation to furnish any particulars of any ordinary banking transactions between the bank and a customer carried out in the ordinary course of banking business, unless the bank has acted or is acting on behalf of the customer in connection with the formation or management of any body corporate mentioned in *subsection (4)(b)* or in connection with the creation, or with the execution of the trusts, of any settlement mentioned in *subsection (4)(c)*.

Amendments

[1, 2] Substituted by FA07 s44(1)(d). Has effect as respects relevant transactions on or after 1 February 2007.

[3] Substituted by FA98 s12(1)(b). This section shall apply irrespective of when the transfer or associated operations took place but shall apply only to income arising on or after the 12th day of February, 1998.

Cross References

From Section 808

Section 10 Connected persons.

Section 430 Meaning of "close company".
Section 431 Certain companies with quoted shares not to be close companies.
Section 806 Charge to income tax on transfer of assets abroad.
Section 807 Deductions and reliefs in relation to income chargeable to income tax under section 806.
Section 807A Liability of nontransferors.
Section 807B Certain transitional arrangements in relation to transfer of assets abroad.
Section 807C Supplementary provisions in relation to section 806 — apportionment in certain cases.
Section 809 Saver.

To Section 808

Schedule 29 Provisions Referred to in Sections 1052, 1053 and 1054

809 Saver

[FA74 s60]

Where any income of any person is by virtue of the Income Tax Acts, and in particular, but without prejudice to the generality of the foregoing, by virtue of [*sections 806* and *807A*][1], to be deemed to be income of any other person, that income shall not be exempt from tax either—

(a) as being derived from any stock or other security to which *section 43*, *47*, *49* or *50* applies, or

(b) by virtue of *section 35* or *63*,

by reason of the first-mentioned person not being resident, or not being ordinarily resident, or being neither domiciled nor ordinarily resident, in the State.

Amendments

[1] Substituted by FA99 s60(1)(e). Subparagraphs (i) and (ii) of paragraph (a) and paragraphs (c), (d) and (e), of subsection (1) shall apply as on and from the 11th day of February, 1999.

Cross References

From Section 809

Section 35 Securities of foreign territories.
Section 43 Certain securities issued by Minister for Finance.
Section 47 Certain securities of ACC Bank plc.
Section 49 Exemption of certain securities.
Section 50 Securities of Irish local authorities issued abroad.
Section 63 Exemption of dividends of non-residents.
Section 806 Charge to income tax on transfer of assets abroad.
Section 807A Liability of nontransferors.

To Section 809

Section 808 Power to obtain information.

810 Application of Income Tax Acts

[FA74 s61]

The provisions of the Income Tax Acts relating to the charge, assessment, collection and recovery of tax, to appeals against assessments and to cases to be stated for the opinion of the High Court shall apply to income tax chargeable by virtue of [*sections 806* and *807A*][1] subject to any necessary modifications.

Amendments

[1] Substituted by FA99 s60(1)(e). Subparagraphs (i) and (ii) of paragraph (a) and paragraphs (c), (d) and (e), of subsection (1) shall apply as on and from the 11th day of February, 1999.

Cross References

From Section 810

Section 806 Charge to income tax on transfer of assets abroad.
Section 807A Liability of nontransferors.

CHAPTER 2

Miscellaneous

811 Transactions to avoid liability to tax

[FA89 s86]

(1) (a) [In this section and *section 811A*—][1]

"*the Acts*" means—

(i) the Tax Acts,

(ii) the Capital Gains Tax Acts,

(iii) the Value-Added Tax Consolidation Act 2010, and the enactments amending or extending that Act,

(iv) the Capital Acquisitions Tax Consolidation Act 2003, and the enactments amending or extending that Act,

[...][2]

(vi) the statutes relating to stamp duty, [and][3]

[(vii) *Part 18 D*,][4]

and any instruments made thereunder;

"*business*" means any trade, profession or vocation;

"*notice of opinion*" means a notice given by the Revenue Commissioners under *subsection (6)*;

"*tax*" means any tax, duty, levy or charge which in accordance with the Acts is placed under the care and management of the Revenue Commissioners and any interest, penalty or other amount payable pursuant to the Acts;

"*tax advantage*" means—

(i) a reduction, avoidance or deferral of any charge or assessment to tax, including any potential or prospective charge or assessment, or

(ii) a refund of or a payment of an amount of tax, or an increase in an amount of tax, refundable or otherwise payable to a person, including any potential or prospective amount so refundable or payable,

arising out of or by reason of a transaction, including a transaction where another transaction would not have been undertaken or arranged to achieve the results, or any part of the results, achieved or intended to be achieved by the transaction;

"*tax avoidance transaction*" has the meaning assigned to it by *subsection (2)*;

"*tax consequences*", in relation to a tax avoidance transaction, means such adjustments and acts as may be made and done by the Revenue Commissioners pursuant to *subsection (5)* in order to withdraw or deny the tax advantage resulting from the tax avoidance transaction;

"*transaction*" means—

(i) any transaction, action, course of action, course of conduct, scheme, plan or proposal,

(ii) any agreement, arrangement, understanding, promise or undertaking, whether express or implied and whether or not enforceable or intended to be enforceable by legal proceedings, and

(iii) any series of or combination of the circumstances referred to in *paragraphs (i)* and *(ii)*,

whether entered into or arranged by one person or by 2 or more persons—

(I) whether acting in concert or not,

(II) whether or not entered into or arranged wholly or partly outside the State, or

(III) whether or not entered into or arranged as part of a larger transaction or in conjunction with any other transaction or transactions.

(b) In *subsections (2)* and *(3)*, for the purposes of the hearing or rehearing under *subsection (8)* of an appeal made under *subsection (7)* or for the purposes of the determination of a question of law arising on the statement of a case for the opinion of the High Court, the references to the Revenue Commissioners shall, subject to any necessary modifications, be construed as references to the Appeal Commissioners or to a judge of the Circuit Court or, to the extent necessary, to a judge of the High Court, as appropriate.

[(c) For the purposes of this section and section 811A, all appeals made under *section 811(7)* by, or on behalf of, a person against any matter or matters specified or described in the notice of opinion of the Revenue Commissioners that a transaction is a tax avoidance transaction, if they have not otherwise been so determined, shall be deemed to have been finally determined when—

(i) there is a written agreement, between that person and an officer of the Revenue Commissioners, that the notice of opinion is to stand or is to be amended in a particular manner,

(ii) (I) the terms of such an agreement that was not made in writing have been confirmed by notice in writing given by the person to the officer of the Revenue Commissioners with whom the agreement was made, or by such officer to the person, and

(II) 21 days have elapsed since the giving of the notice without the person to whom it was given giving notice in writing to the person by whom it was given that the first-mentioned person desires to repudiate or withdraw from the agreement, or

(iii) the person gives notice in writing to an officer of the Revenue Commissioners that the person desires not to proceed with an appeal against the notice of opinion.][5]

(2) For the purposes of this section and subject to *subsection (3)*, a transaction shall be a "tax avoidance transaction" if having regard to any one or more of the following—

(a) the results of the transaction,

(b) its use as a means of achieving those results, and

(c) any other means by which the results or any part of the results could have been achieved,

the Revenue Commissioners form the opinion that—

(i) the transaction gives rise to, or but for this section would give rise to, a tax advantage, and

(ii) the transaction was not undertaken or arranged primarily for purposes other than to give rise to a tax advantage, and references in this section to the Revenue Commissioners forming an opinion that a transaction is a tax avoidance transaction shall be construed as references to the Revenue Commissioners forming an opinion with regard to the transaction in accordance with this subsection.

(3) (a) Without prejudice to the generality of *subsection (2)*, in forming an opinion in accordance with that subsection and *subsection (4)* as to whether or not a transaction is a tax avoidance transaction, the Revenue Commissioners shall not regard the transaction as being a tax avoidance transaction if they are satisfied that—

(i) notwithstanding that the purpose or purposes of the transaction could have been achieved by some other transaction which would have given rise to a greater amount of tax being payable by the person, the transaction—

(I) was undertaken or arranged by a person with a view, directly or indirectly, to the realisation of profits in the course of the business activities of a business carried on by the person, and

(II) was not undertaken or arranged primarily to give rise to a tax advantage,

or

(ii) the transaction was undertaken or arranged for the purpose of obtaining the benefit of any relief, allowance or other abatement provided by any provision of the Acts and that the transaction would not result directly or indirectly in a misuse of the provision or an abuse of the provision having regard to the purposes for which it was provided.

(b) In forming an opinion referred to in *paragraph (a)* in relation to any transaction, the Revenue Commissioners shall have regard to—

(i) the form of that transaction,

(ii) the substance of that transaction,

(iii) the substance of any other transaction or transactions which that transaction may reasonably be regarded as being directly or indirectly related to or connected with, and

(iv) the final outcome and result of that transaction and any combination of those other transactions which are so related or connected.

(4) Subject to this section, the Revenue Commissioners as respects any transaction may at any time—

(a) form the opinion that the transaction is a tax avoidance transaction,

(b) calculate the tax advantage which they consider arises, or which but for this section would arise, from the transaction,

(c) determine the tax consequences which they consider would arise in respect of the transaction if their opinion were to become final and conclusive in accordance with *subsection (5)(e)*, and

(d) calculate the amount of any relief from double taxation which they would propose to give to any person in accordance with *subsection (5)(c)*.

(5) (a) Where the opinion of the Revenue Commissioners that a transaction is a tax avoidance transaction becomes final and conclusive, they may, notwithstanding any other provision of the Acts, make all such

adjustments and do all such acts as are just and reasonable (in so far as those adjustments and acts have been specified or described in a notice of opinion given under *subsection (6)* and subject to the manner in which any appeal made under *subsection (7)* against any matter specified or described in the notice of opinion has been finally determined, including any adjustments and acts not so specified or described in the notice of opinion but which form part of a final determination of any such appeal) in order that the tax advantage resulting from a tax avoidance transaction shall be withdrawn from or denied to any person concerned.

(b) Subject to but without prejudice to the generality of *paragraph (a)*, the Revenue Commissioners may—

(i) allow or disallow in whole or in part any deduction or other amount which is relevant in computing tax payable, or any part of such deduction or other amount,

(ii) allocate or deny to any person any deduction, loss, abatement, relief, allowance, exemption, income or other amount, or any part thereof, or

(iii) recharacterize for tax purposes the nature of any payment or other amount.

(c) Where the Revenue Commissioners make any adjustment or do any act for the purposes of *paragraph (a)*, they shall afford relief from any double taxation which they consider would but for this paragraph arise by virtue of any adjustment made or act done by them pursuant to *paragraphs (a)* and *(b)*.

(d) Notwithstanding any other provision of the Acts, where—

(i) pursuant to *subsection (4)(c)*, the Revenue Commissioners determine the tax consequences which they consider would arise in respect of a transaction if their opinion that the transaction is a tax avoidance transaction were to become final and conclusive, and

(ii) pursuant to that determination, they specify or describe in a notice of opinion any adjustment or act which they consider would be, or be part of, those tax consequences,

then, in so far as any right of appeal lay under *subsection (7)* against any such adjustment or act so specified or described, no right or further right of appeal shall lie under the Acts against that adjustment or act when it is made or done in accordance with this subsection, or against any adjustment or act so made or done that is not so specified or described in the notice of opinion but which forms part of the final determination of any appeal made under *subsection (7)* against any matter specified or described in the notice of opinion.

(e) For the purposes of this subsection, an opinion of the Revenue Commissioners that a transaction is a tax avoidance transaction shall be final and conclusive—

(i) if within the time limited no appeal is made under *subsection (7)* against any matter or matters specified or described in a notice or notices of opinion given pursuant to that opinion, or

(ii) as and when all appeals made under *subsection (7)* against any such matter or matters have been finally determined and none of the appeals has been so determined by an order directing that the opinion of the Revenue Commissioners to the effect that the transaction is a tax avoidance transaction is void.

[(5A) (a) In this subsection—

'assessment' includes a first assessment, an additional assessment, an additional first assessment and an estimate or estimation;

'amendment', in relation to an assessment, includes the adjustment, alteration or correction of the assessment.

(b) Where the opinion of the Revenue Commissioners, that a transaction is a tax avoidance transaction, becomes final and conclusive, then for the purposes of giving effect to this section, any time limit provided for by *Part 41* [or *41A*][6], or by any other provision of the Acts, on the making or amendment of an assessment or on the requirement or liability of a person to pay tax or to pay additional tax—

(i) shall not apply, and

(ii) shall not affect the collection and recovery of any amount of tax or additional tax that becomes due and payable.][7]

(6) (a) Where pursuant to *subsections (2)* and *(4)* the Revenue Commissioners form the opinion that a transaction is a tax avoidance transaction, they shall immediately on forming such an opinion give notice in writing of the opinion to any person from whom a tax advantage would be withdrawn or to whom a tax advantage would be denied or to whom relief from double taxation would be given if the opinion became final and conclusive, and the notice shall specify or describe—

(i) the transaction which in the opinion of the Revenue Commissioners is a tax avoidance transaction,

(ii) the tax advantage or part of the tax advantage, calculated by the Revenue Commissioners which would be withdrawn from or denied to the person to whom the notice is given,

(iii) the tax consequences of the transaction determined by the Revenue Commissioners in so far as they would refer to the person, and

(iv) the amount of any relief from double taxation calculated by the Revenue Commissioners which they would propose to give to the person in accordance with *subsection (5)(c)*.

(b) *Section 869* shall, with any necessary modifications, apply for the purposes of a notice given under this subsection or *subsection (10)* as if it were a notice given under the Income Tax Acts.

(7) Any person aggrieved by an opinion formed or, in so far as it refers to the person, a calculation or determination made by the Revenue Commissioners pursuant to *subsection (4)* may, by notice in writing given to the Revenue Commissioners within 30 days of the date of the notice of opinion, appeal to the Appeal Commissioners on the grounds and, notwithstanding any other provision of the Acts, only on the grounds that, having regard to all of the circumstances, including any fact or matter which was not known to the Revenue Commissioners when they formed their opinion or made their calculation or determination, and to this section—

(a) the transaction specified or described in the notice of opinion is not a tax avoidance transaction,

(b) the amount of the tax advantage or the part of the tax advantage, specified or described in the notice of opinion which would be withdrawn from or denied to the person is incorrect,

(c) the tax consequences specified or described in the notice of opinion, or such part of those consequences as shall be specified or described by the appellant in the notice of appeal, would not be just and reasonable in order to withdraw or to deny the tax advantage or part of the tax advantage specified or described in the notice of opinion, or

(d) the amount of relief from double taxation which the Revenue Commissioners propose to give to the person is insufficient or incorrect.

(8) The Appeal Commissioners shall hear and determine an appeal made to them under *subsection (7)* as if it were an appeal against an assessment to income tax and, subject to *subsection (9)*, the provisions of the Income Tax Acts relating to the rehearing of an appeal and to the statement of a case for the opinion of the High Court on a point of law shall apply accordingly with any necessary modifications; but on the hearing or rehearing of the appeal—

(a) it shall not be lawful to enquire into any grounds of appeal other than those specified in *subsection (7)*, and

(b) at the request of the appellants, 2 or more appeals made by 2 or more persons pursuant to the same opinion, calculation or determination formed or made by the Revenue Commissioners pursuant to *subsection (4)* may be heard or reheard together.

(9) (a) On the hearing of an appeal made under *subsection (7)*, the Appeal Commissioners shall have regard to all matters to which the Revenue Commissioners may or are required to have regard under this section, and—

(i) in relation to an appeal made on the grounds referred to in *subsection (7)(a)*, the Appeal Commissioners shall determine the appeal, in so far as it is made on those grounds, by ordering, if they or a majority of them—

(I) consider that the transaction specified or described in the notice of opinion or any part of that transaction is a tax avoidance transaction, that the opinion or the opinion in so far as it relates to that part is to stand,

(II) consider that, subject to such amendment or addition thereto as the Appeal Commissioners or the majority of them deem necessary and as they shall specify or describe, the transaction, or any part of it, specified or described in the notice of opinion, is a tax avoidance transaction, that the transaction or that part of it be so amended or added to and that, subject to the amendment or addition, the opinion or the opinion in so far as it relates to that part is to stand, or

(III) do not so consider as referred to in *clause (I)* or *(II)*, that the opinion is void,

(ii) in relation to an appeal made on the grounds referred to in *subsection (7)(b)*, they shall determine the appeal, in so far as it is made on those grounds, by ordering that the amount of the tax advantage or the part of the tax advantage specified or described in the notice of opinion be increased or reduced by such amount as they shall direct or that it shall stand,

(iii) in relation to an appeal made on the grounds referred to in *subsection (7)(c)*, they shall determine the appeal, in so far as it is made on those grounds, by ordering that the tax consequences specified or described in the notice of opinion shall be altered or added to in such manner as they shall direct or that they shall stand, or

(iv) in relation to an appeal made on the grounds referred to in *subsection (7)(d)*, they shall determine the appeal, in so far as it is made on those grounds, by ordering that the amount of the relief from double taxation specified or described in the notice of opinion shall be increased or reduced by such amount as they shall direct or that it shall stand.

(b) This subsection shall, subject to any necessary modifications, apply to the rehearing of an appeal by a judge of the Circuit Court and, to the extent necessary, to the determination by the High Court of any question or questions of law arising on the statement of a case for the opinion of the High Court.

(10) The Revenue Commissioners may at any time amend, add to or withdraw any matter specified or described in a notice of opinion by giving notice (in this subsection referred to as "*the notice of amendment*") in writing of the amendment, addition or withdrawal to each and every person affected thereby, in so far as the person is so affected, and *subsections (1)* to *(9)* shall apply in all respects as if the notice of amendment were a notice of opinion and any matter specified or described in the notice of amendment were specified or described in a notice of opinion; but no such amendment, addition or withdrawal may be made so as to set aside or alter any matter which has become final and conclusive on the determination of an appeal made with regard to that matter under *subsection (7)*.

(11) Where pursuant to *subsections (2)* and *(4)* the Revenue Commissioners form the opinion that a transaction is a tax avoidance transaction and pursuant to that opinion notices are to be given under *subsection (6)* to 2 or more persons, any obligation on the Revenue Commissioners to maintain secrecy or any other restriction on the disclosure of information by the Revenue Commissioners shall not apply with respect to the giving of those notices or to the performance of any acts or the discharge of any functions authorised by this section to be performed or discharged by them or to the performance of any act or the discharge of any functions, including any act or function in relation to an appeal made under *subsection (7)*, which is directly or indirectly related to the acts or functions so authorised.

(12) The Revenue Commissioners may nominate any of their officers to perform any acts and discharge any functions, including the forming of an opinion, authorised by this section to be performed or discharged by the Revenue Commissioners, and references in this section to the Revenue Commissioners shall with any necessary modifications be construed as including references to an officer so nominated.

(13) This section shall apply as respects any transaction where the whole or any part of the transaction is undertaken or arranged on or after the 25th day of January, 1989, and as respects any transaction undertaken or arranged wholly before that date in so far as it gives rise to, or would but for this section give rise to—

(a) a reduction, avoidance or deferral of any charge or assessment to tax, or part thereof, where the charge or assessment arises by virtue of any other transaction carried out wholly on or after a date, or

(b) a refund or a payment of an amount, or of an increase in an amount, of tax, or part thereof, refundable or otherwise payable to a person where that amount or increase in the amount would otherwise become first so refundable or otherwise payable to the person on a date,

which could not fall earlier than the 25th day of January, 1989.

[(14) This section shall only apply to a transaction which was commenced on or before 23 October 2014.][8]

Amendments

[1] Substituted by FA06 s126(a)(i).

[2] Deleted by FA13 s97(1)(a). Applies to any transaction (within the meaning of section 811(1)(a)) undertaken or arranged on or after 13 February 2013.

[3] Substituted by FA13 s97(1)(a). Applies to any transaction (within the meaning of section 811(1)(a)) undertaken or arranged on or after 13 February 2013.

[4] Inserted by FA13 s97(1)(a). Applies to any transaction (within the meaning of section 811(1)(a)) undertaken or arranged on or after 13 February 2013.

[5] Inserted by FA06 s126(a)(ii).

[6] Inserted by FA13 s92 and sched1(part 2)(e).

[7] Inserted by FA12 s130(1). Applies to any assessment to tax or any amendment of any assessment to tax which is made, on or after 28 February 2012, so that the tax advantage resulting from a tax avoidance transaction, in respect of which a notice of opinion has become final and conclusive, is withdrawn from or denied to any person concerned.

[8] Inserted by FA14 s87(1)(a). Applies to a transaction which was commenced on or before 23 October 2014.

Note:

FA13 s92 applies—

(a) in the case of a chargeable period (within the meaning of section 321(2)) which is an accounting period of a company, as respects chargeable periods that start on or after 1 January 2013, and

(b) in a case other than that referred to in paragraph (a), as respects the year of assessment (within the meaning of section 2(1)) 2013 and subsequent years of assessment.

Case Law

In CIR v Challenge Corporation 1986 STC 548 tax mitigation had to be distinguished from tax avoidance. The onus is on the taxpayer to establish that a general exemption applies, and in the context of section 811, the taxpayer needs to establish that the proposed use of any relief availed of is not a misuse or abuse. Revenue Commissioners v O'Flynn Construction Ltd et al 2006 77 ITR 81

In Trustees of Omega Group Pension Scheme v IRC 2001 STC 121 a fund manager sold shares under a share buy back and this fell to be treated as a distribution with a tax credit attached. At the time of the buyback the shares would have made a loss if sold on open market but a buyback resulted in repayment of an associated tax credit. A sale to the company of its own shares would yield a profit. One of main reasons to sell was to secure a tax advantage.

In IRC v Trustees of the Sema Group Pension Scheme 2002 STC 276 it was held that the taxpayer would not have sold their shares but for the tax credit that arose with the sale and therefore anti-avoidance was one of the main objectives of the transaction.

Once the steps which had no commercial purpose had been removed, the most appropriate taxing statute has to be applied. DTE Financial Services Ltd v Wilson 1999 STC 1061

The Australian General Anti-Avoidance rule contains a similar definition of 'transaction' as that in section 811. In the Australian case FCT v Peabody 94 ATC 4663, the High Court held that a 'transaction' does not include part of a transaction.

Revenue Commissioners v O'Flynn Construction & Ors 2011 IESC 47. In this landmark Irish anti-avoidance case, the Irish Supreme Court found in favour of the Revenue Commissioners and held that a scheme whereby ESR reserves were paid out as tax free dividends was a tax avoidance transaction and a misuse or abuse of the ESR provisions.

Cross References

From Section 811

Section 811 Transactions to avoid liability to tax.

Section 811A Transactions to avoid liability to tax: surcharge, interest and protective notification.

Section 869 Delivery, service and evidence of notices and forms.

To Section 811

Section 697F Requirement not to enter into tax avoidance arrangements.

Section 811 Transactions to avoid liability to tax.

Section 811A Transactions to avoid liability to tax: surcharge, interest and protective notification.

Section 817N Supplemental matters.

Section 1104 Short title and construction.

811A Transactions to avoid liability to tax: surcharge, interest and protective notification

[(1) (a) In this section references to tax being payable shall, except where the context requires otherwise, include references to tax being payable by a person to withdraw from that person so much of a tax advantage as is a refund of, or a payment of, an amount of tax, or an increase in an amount of tax, refundable, or otherwise payable, to the person.

(b) For the purposes of this section the date on which the opinion of the Revenue Commissioners that a transaction is a tax avoidance transaction becomes final and conclusive is—

(i) where no appeal is made under *section 811(7)* against any matter or matters specified or described in the notice of that opinion, 31 days after the date of the notice of that opinion, or

(ii) the date on which all appeals made under *section 811(7)* against any such matter or matters have been finally determined and none of the appeals has been so determined by an order directing that the opinion of the Revenue Commissioners to the effect that the transaction is a tax avoidance transaction is void.

(c) This section shall be construed together with *section 811* and shall have effect notwithstanding any of the provisions of *section 811*.

[(1A) Without prejudice to the generality of any provision of this section or section 811, [nothing in *section 959Z, 959AA* or *959AB* shall be construed][1] as preventing an officer of the Revenue Commissioners from—

(a) making any enquiry, or

(b) taking any action,

at any time in connection with this section or section 811.

(1B) Where the Revenue Commissioners have received from, or on behalf of, a person, on or before the relevant date (within the meaning of subsection (3)(*c*)) a notification (referred to in subsection (3) and (6) as a "*protective notification*") of full details of a transaction, then the Revenue Commissioners shall not form the opinion that the transaction is a tax avoidance transaction pursuant to subsections (2) and (4) of that section after the expiry of the period of 2 years commencing at—

(a) the relevant date, or

(b) if earlier, the date on which the notification was received by the Revenue Commissioners,

but this subsection shall not be construed as preventing an officer of the Revenue Commissioners from making any enquiry at any time in connection with this section or section 811.

[…][2]][3]

(2) Where, in accordance with adjustments made or acts done by the Revenue Commissioners under *section 811(5)*, on foot of their opinion (as amended, or added to, on appeal where relevant) that a transaction is a tax avoidance transaction having become final and conclusive, an amount of tax is payable by a person that would not have been payable if the Revenue Commissioners had not formed the opinion concerned, then, subject to *subsection (3)*—

(a) the person shall be liable to pay an amount (in this section referred to as the "*surcharge*") equal to [20 per cent][4] of the amount of that tax and the provisions of the Acts, including in particular *section 811(5)* and those provisions relating to the collection and recovery of that tax, shall apply to that surcharge, as if it were such tax, and

(b) for the purposes of liability to interest under the Acts on tax due and payable, the amount of tax, or parts of that amount, shall be deemed to be due and payable on the day or, as respects parts of that amount, days specified in the notice of opinion (as amended, or added to, on appeal where relevant) in accordance with *section 811(6)(a)(iii)* construed together with *subsection (4)(a)* of this section,

and the surcharge and interest shall be payable accordingly.

[(2A) (a) In this subsection 'qualifying avoidance disclosure' means a disclosure that the Revenue Commissioners are satisfied is a disclosure of complete information in relation to, and full particulars of, a transaction that is a tax avoidance transaction or that, had the Revenue Commissioners formed the opinion that the transaction was a tax avoidance transaction, would occasion a liability to tax pursuant to *section 811*, made in writing to the Revenue Commissioners and signed by or on behalf of that person and which is accompanied by—

(i) a declaration, to the best of that person's knowledge, information and belief, made in writing, that all matters contained in the disclosure are correct and complete, and

(ii) a payment of any tax due and payable in respect of any matter contained in the disclosure and the interest payable on the late payment of that tax.

(b) Where on or before 30 June 2015 the Revenue Commissioners receive a qualifying avoidance disclosure in relation to a transaction then—

(i) the surcharge referred to in subsection (2) shall not apply, and

(ii) the amount of any interest payable under the Acts shall be the amount that, apart from this subparagraph, would be so payable reduced by 20 per cent of that amount.][5]

(3) (a) Subject to *subsection (6)*, neither a surcharge nor interest shall be payable by a person in relation to a tax avoidance transaction finally and conclusively determined to be such a transaction if the Revenue Commissioners have received from, or on behalf of, that person, on or before the relevant date (within the meaning of *paragraph (c)*), notification (referred to in this subsection and *subsection (6)* as a "protective notification") of full details of that transaction.

(b) Where a person makes a protective notification, or a protective notification is made on a person's behalf, then the person shall be treated as making the protective notification—

(i) solely to prevent any possibility of [...][6] a surcharge or interest becoming payable by the person by virtue of subsection (2), and

(ii) wholly without prejudice as to whether any opinion that the transaction concerned was a tax avoidance transaction, if such an opinion were to be formed by the Revenue Commissioners, would be correct.

(c) Regardless of the type of tax concerned—

(i) where the whole or any part of the transaction, which is the subject of the protective notification, is undertaken or arranged on or after [19 February 2008][7], then the relevant date shall be—

(I) the date which is 90 days after the date on which the transaction commenced, or

(II) if it is later than the said 90 days, [19 May 2008][8],

(ii) where—

(I) the whole of the transaction is undertaken or arranged before 2 February 2006, and would give rise to, or would but for *section 811* give rise to, a reduction, avoidance, or deferral of any charge or assessment to tax, or part thereof, and

(II) that charge or assessment would arise only by virtue of one or more other transactions carried out wholly on or after 2 February 2006,

then the relevant date shall be the date which is 90 days after the date on which the first of those other transactions commenced, or

(iii) where—

(I) the whole of the transaction is undertaken or arranged before 2 February 2006, and would give rise to, or would but for *section 811* give rise to, a refund or a payment of an amount, or of an increase in an amount of tax, or part thereof, refundable or otherwise payable to a person, and

(II) that amount or increase in the amount would, but for *section 811*, become first so refundable or otherwise payable to the person on a date on or after 2 February 2006,

then the relevant date shall be the date which is 90 days after that date.

(d) Notwithstanding the receipt by the Revenue Commissioners of a protective notice, *paragraph (a)* shall not apply to any interest, payable in relation to a tax avoidance transaction finally and conclusively determined to be such a transaction, in respect of days on or after the date on which the opinion of the Revenue Commissioners in relation to that transaction becomes final and conclusive.

(4) (a) The determination of tax consequences, which would arise in respect of a transaction if the opinion of the Revenue Commissioners, that the transaction was a tax avoidance transaction, were to become final and conclusive, shall, for the purposes of charging interest, include the specification of—

(i) a date or dates, being a date or dates which is or are just and reasonable to ensure that tax is deemed to be due and payable not later than it would have been due and payable if the transaction had not been undertaken, disregarding any contention that another transaction would not have been undertaken or arranged to achieve the results, or any part of the results, achieved or intended to be achieved by the transaction, and

(ii) the date which, as respects such amount of tax as is due and payable by a person to recover from the person a refund of or a payment of tax, including an increase in tax refundable or otherwise payable, to the person, is the day on which the refund or payment was made, set off or accounted for,

and the date or dates shall be specified for the purposes of this paragraph without regard to—

(I) when an opinion of the Revenue Commissioners that the transaction concerned was a tax avoidance transaction was formed,

(II) the date on which any notice of that opinion was given, or

(III) the date on which the opinion (as amended, or added to, on appeal where relevant) became final and conclusive.

(b) Where the grounds of an appeal in relation to tax consequences refer to such a date or dates as are mentioned in *paragraph (a)*, *subsection (7)* of *section 811* shall apply, in that respect, as if the following paragraph were substituted for *paragraph (c)* of that subsection:

"(c) the tax consequences specified or described in the notice of opinion, or such part of those consequences as shall be specified or described by the appellant in the notice of appeal, would not be just and reasonable to ensure that tax is deemed to be payable on a date or dates in accordance with *subsection (4)(a)* of *section 811A*,"

and the grounds of appeal referred to in *section 811(8)(a)* shall be construed accordingly.

(5) A surcharge payable by virtue of *subsection (2)(a)* shall be due and payable on the date that the opinion of the Revenue Commissioners that a transaction is a tax avoidance transaction becomes final and conclusive and interest shall be payable in respect of any delay in payment of the surcharge as if the surcharge were an amount of that tax by reference to an amount of which the surcharge was computed.

(6) (a) A protective notification shall—

(i) be delivered in such form as may be prescribed by the Revenue Commissioners and to such office of the Revenue Commissioners as—

(I) is specified in the prescribed form, or

(II) as may be identified, by reference to guidance in the prescribed form, as the office to which the notification concerned should be sent, and

(ii) contain—

(I) full details of the transaction which is the subject of the protective notification, including any part of that transaction that has not been undertaken before the protective notification is delivered,

(II) full reference to the provisions of the Acts that the person, by whom, or on whose behalf, the protective notification is delivered, considers to be relevant to the treatment of the transaction for tax purposes, and

(III) full details of how, in the opinion of the person, by whom, or on whose behalf, the protective notification is delivered, each provision, referred to in the protective notification in accordance with clause (II), applies, or does not apply, to the transaction.

(b) Without prejudice to the generality of *paragraph (a)*, the specifying, under—

(i) section 81 of the Value-Added Tax Consolidation Act 2010,

(ii) section 46A of the Capital Acquisitions Tax Consolidation Act 2003,

(iii) section 8 of the Stamp Duties Consolidation Act 1999, or

(iv) [*section 959P*][9] of this Act,

of a doubt as to the application of law to, or the treatment for tax purposes of, any matter to be contained in a return shall not be regarded as being, or being equivalent to, the delivery of a protective notification in relation to a transaction for [the purposes of subsections (1B) and (3)][10].

(c) Where the Revenue Commissioners form the opinion that a transaction is a tax avoidance transaction and believe that a protective notification in relation to the transaction has not been delivered by a person in accordance with *subsection (6)(a)* by the relevant date (within the meaning of *subsection (3)(c)*) then, in giving notice under *section 811(6)(a)* to the person of their opinion in relation to the transaction, they shall give notice that they believe that a protective notification has not been so delivered by the person and *section 811* shall be construed, subject to any necessary modifications, as if—

(i) *subsection (7)* of that section included as grounds for appeal that a protective notification in relation to the transaction was so delivered by the person, and

(ii) *subsection (9)* of that section provided that an appeal were to be determined, in so far as it is made on those grounds, by ordering that a protective notification in relation to the transaction was so delivered or that a protective notification in relation to the transaction was not so delivered.

[(6A) The Revenue Commissioners may nominate any of their officers to perform any acts and discharge any functions authorised by this section to be performed or discharged by the Revenue Commissioners, and references in this section to the Revenue Commissioners shall with any necessary modifications be construed as including references to an officer so nominated.][11]

(7) This section shall apply—

(a) as respects any transaction where the whole or any part of the transaction is undertaken or arranged on or after [19 February 2008][12], and

(b) as respects any transaction, the whole of which was undertaken or arranged before that date, in so far as it gives rise to, or would but for *section 811* give rise to—

(i) a reduction, avoidance, or deferral of any charge or assessment to tax, or part thereof, where the charge or assessment arises only by virtue of another transaction or other transactions carried out wholly on or after [19 February 2008][13], or

(ii) a refund or a payment of an amount, or of an increase in an amount of tax, or part thereof, refundable or otherwise payable to a person where, but for *section 811*, that amount or increase in the amount would become first so refundable or otherwise payable to the person on or after [19 February 2008][14].][15]

[(8) This section shall only apply to a transaction which was commenced on or before 23 October 2014.][16]

Amendments

[1] Substituted by FA12 sched4(part 2)(d).

[2] Deleted by FA13 s97(1)(b)(i).

[3] Inserted by FA08 s140(1)(a).

[4] Substituted by FA08 s140(1)(b).

[5] Inserted by FA14 s87(1)(b)(i). Applies to a transaction which was commenced on or before 23 October 2014.

[6] Deleted by FA13 s97(1)(b)(ii).
[7] Substituted by FA08 s140(1)(c)(ii)(I).
[8] Substituted by FA08 s140(1)(c)(ii)(II).
[9] Substituted by FA12 sched4(part 2)(g).
[10] Substituted by FA08 s140(1)(d).
[11] Inserted by F(No2)A08 s95.
[12, 13, 14] Substituted by FA08 s140(1)(e).
[15] Inserted by FA06 s126(b).
[16] Inserted by FA14 s87(1)(b)(ii). Applies to a transaction which was commenced on or before 23 October 2014.

Note:

FA08 s140(1)

This section applies—

(a) as respects any transaction where the whole or any part of the transaction is undertaken or arranged on or after 19 February 2008, and

(b) as respects any transaction, the whole of which was undertaken or arranged before that date, in so far as it gives rise to, or would but for section 811 give rise to—

(i) a reduction, avoidance, or deferral of any charge or assessment to tax, or part thereof, where the charge or assessment arises only by virtue of another transaction or other transactions carried out wholly on or after 19 February 2008, or

(ii) a refund or a payment of an amount, or of an increase in an amount of tax, or part thereof, refundable or otherwise payable to a person where, but for section 811, that amount or increase in the amount would become first so refundable or otherwise payable to the person on or after 19 February 2008, but where as respects any transaction the Revenue Commissioners have before 19 February 2008 received from, or on behalf of, a person a notification (referred to in subsections (3) and (6) of section 811A as a "protective notification " and made on or before the relevant date, within the meaning of subsection (3)(c) of that section prior to any amendment made by this section) of full details of the transaction, then the said section 811A shall apply to that transaction as if this section had not been enacted.

FA13 s97(1)(b) applies as respects any transaction—

(i) where the whole or any part of the transaction is undertaken or arranged on or after 19 February 2008, or

(ii) the whole of which is undertaken or arranged before that date, in so far as it gives rise to, or would but for section 811 give rise to—

(I) a reduction, avoidance, or defral of any charge or assessment to tax, or part thereof, where the charge or assessment arises only by virtue of another transaction or other transactions carried out wholly on or after 19 February 2008, or

(II) a refund or payment of an amount, or of an increase in an amount of tax, or part thereof, refundable or otherwise payable to a person where, but for section 811, that amount or increase in the amount would become first so refundable or otherwise payable to the person on or after 19 February 2008.

Cross References

From Section 811A

Section 811 Transactions to avoid liability to tax.
Section 950 Interpretation (Part 41).
Section 955 Amendment of and time limit for assessments.
Section 956 Inspector's right to make enquiries and amend assessments.

To Section 811A

Section 811 Transactions to avoid liability to tax.
Section 817N Supplemental matters.

811B Tax treatment of loans from employee benefit schemes

[(1) In this section—

"*benefit scheme*", subject to *subsection (2)(c)*, means a trust, scheme or other arrangement and includes any settlement, disposition, covenant, agreement, transfer of money or transfer of other property or of any right to money or of any right to other property;

"*employee*" includes an office holder and any person who is an employee within the definition of "*employee*" in *section 983*;

"*employer*" includes any person connected with an employer and any person who is an employer within the definition of "*employer*" in *section 983* or connected with such employer;

"*loan*" means any loan, advance or any form of credit;

"*specified rate*" means the rate specified in *paragraph (iii)* of the definition of "*the specified rate*" in *section 122*.

(2) For the purposes of this section—

(a) any question whether a person is connected with another person shall be determined in accordance with *section 10* (as it applies for the purposes of the Tax Acts),

(b) the loan of, or the provision of the use of, an asset shall be deemed to be a loan of an amount equal to the value of that asset at the time such loan is made or at the time such asset is provided, and

(c) an arrangement or agreement under which a loan, the provision of a benefit or the loan of, or the provision of the use of, an asset is made to an employee by his or her employer shall not be an arrangement or agreement within the meaning of a benefit scheme where the provisions of *section 118, 118A, 121, 121A* or *122* apply to such loan, the provision of such benefit or to the loan, or provision, of such asset.

(3) Where, in the year of assessment 2013 or any subsequent year of assessment, an employee or former employee who holds or has held an office or employment the profits or gains from which are or were chargeable to tax under Schedule E or under Case III of Schedule D or any person connected with that employee or former employee receives, directly or indirectly, from a benefit scheme—

(a) a payment (including a loan),

(b) a benefit, or

(c) an asset (including the loan of, or the provision of the use of, an asset),

and that scheme was, directly or indirectly, provided, funded, subscribed to or otherwise made available by that employee's employer or former employer, then—

(i) the amount of that payment,

(ii) the cost of providing that benefit or the value of that benefit at the date of provision (whichever is the greater), or

(iii) the value of that asset,

shall, to the extent that it is not otherwise chargeable to income tax, be deemed to be income of that employee for that year of assessment chargeable to income tax under Case IV of Schedule D.

(4) Where, in the year of assessment 2013 or any subsequent year of assessment, an individual or any person connected with that individual receives, directly or indirectly, from a benefit scheme—

(a) a payment (including a loan),

(b) a benefit, or

(c) an asset (including the loan of, or the provision of the use of, an asset),

and that scheme was, directly or indirectly, provided, funded or otherwise made available by a person who subsequently becomes that individual's employer, then for the year of assessment in which the individual first holds with that employer an office or employment the profits or gains from which are chargeable to tax under Schedule E or under Case III of Schedule D—

(i) the amount of that payment,

(ii) the cost of providing that benefit or the value of that benefit at the date of provision (whichever is the greater), or

(iii) the value of that asset,

shall, to the extent that it is not otherwise chargeable to income tax or is not liable in a territory with the government of which arrangements are for the time being in force by virtue of *section 826(1)* (or in a territory with the government of which arrangements have been made which on completion of the procedures set out in *section 826(1)* will have the force of law) to a tax that corresponds to income tax, be deemed to be income of that individual chargeable to income tax under Case IV of Schedule D.

(5) For the purpose of *subsections (3)* and *(4)*, this section applies to the receipt, directly or indirectly, on or after 13 February 2013 of a payment (including a loan), a benefit or an asset (including the loan of, or the provision of the use of, an asset) from a benefit scheme.

(6) (a) Where an individual has paid all of the tax due by virtue of *subsection (3)* or *(4)* and that individual—

(i) repays all or part of a loan,

(ii) ceases, for a period of at least 12 months, to have use of an asset, or

(iii) ceases, for a period of at least 12 months, to have use of a benefit,

in respect of which those subsections applied, then, on foot of a claim in writing from that individual, relief shall be given by way of offset or repayment of an amount equal to the difference between—

(I) where a loan has been repaid in full or where the use of the asset or benefit has ceased—

(A) the tax paid by virtue of *subsection (3)* or *(4)*, and

(B) the tax that would have been payable by the individual as if *section 118, 118A, 121, 121A* or *122*, as appropriate, had applied to such loan or to the provision of such asset or benefit up to the date that that loan is repaid or to the date that such asset or benefit ceases to be available to that individual, as the case may be,

or

(II) where a loan has not been repaid in full—

(A) the amount of that tax paid by virtue of *subsection (3)* or *(4)* as is attributable to the amount of that loan repaid, and

(B) the tax that would have been payable as if *section 122* had applied in respect of the amount of the loan repaid up to the date that that amount is repaid.

(b) The relief referred to in *paragraph (a)* shall not apply where the loan, or part of the loan, referred to in that paragraph is, directly or indirectly—

(i) repaid by the individual referred to in that paragraph out of a payment (including a loan) or transfer of an asset to that individual, or to a person connected with that individual, from a benefit scheme that was, directly or indirectly, provided, funded, subscribed to or otherwise made available by the individual's employer or former employer, or

(ii) replaced by another loan that is directly or indirectly, provided, funded, subscribed to or otherwise made available by the individual's employer or former employer.

(c) Notwithstanding any limitation in *section 865(4)* on the time within which a claim for repayment of tax is required to be made or the provisions relating to the offset of tax in *section 865B*, a claim for the offset or repayment referred to in *paragraph (a)* shall be made within 4 years from the end of the year of assessment in which the loan, or part of the loan, is repaid or the use of the benefit or asset, as the case may be, ceases.

(7) (a) This subsection applies for the year of assessment 2013 and each subsequent year of assessment where—

(i) before 13 February 2013, an employee or former employee who holds or has held an office or employment the profits or gains of which are or were chargeable to tax under Schedule E or under Case III of Schedule D or any person connected with that employee or former employee received, directly or indirectly, from a benefit scheme—

(I) a loan, or

(II) the loan of, or the provision of the use of, an asset,

and that scheme was, directly or indirectly, provided, funded, subscribed to or otherwise made available by that employee's employer or former employer, and

(ii) at any time in the year of assessment—

(I) the loan referred to in *subparagraph (i)(I)*, or any part thereof, remains outstanding, or

(II) the employee or former employee continues to have the loan of or the use of the asset referred to in *subparagraph (i)(II)*.

(b) Where for any year of assessment that this subsection applies, then, in relation to a loan referred to in *paragraph (a)(i)(I)*, an amount equal to—

(i) if no interest is paid, the amount of interest that would have been payable in that year of assessment if interest had been payable at a rate equal to the specified rate, or

(ii) if interest is paid at a rate less than the specified rate, the difference between the aggregate amount of interest paid in that year of assessment and the amount of interest which would have been payable in that year if interest had been payable at a rate equal to the specified rate,

shall, if not otherwise chargeable to income tax, be deemed to be income of that employee or former employee for that year of assessment chargeable to income tax under Case IV of Schedule D and any reference to interest paid in *subparagraph (i)* or *(ii)* does not include an increase in the outstanding balance on the loan or loans or interest paid out of a further loan or advance made, directly or indirectly, by a benefit scheme or employer referred to in *paragraph (a)(i)*.

(c) Where for any year of assessment that this subsection applies, then, in relation to the provision of the loan of, or the provision of the use of, an asset referred to in *paragraph (a)(i)(II)*, there shall, if not otherwise chargeable to income tax, be deemed to be income of that employee or former employee for that year of assessment chargeable to income tax under Case IV of Schedule D an amount equal to an amount that would, if *section 118, 118A, 119, 121, 121A* or *122* had applied in respect of the loan of, or the provision of the use of, that asset be deemed to be an expense, emolument or perquisite chargeable to tax under Schedule E by virtue of those sections.

(8) This section shall not apply to a scheme approved for the purposes of *Part 17* or *30*.][1]

Amendments

[1] Inserted by FA13 s12. Deemed to have come into force and takes effect on and from 1 January 2013.

Revenue Briefings

eBrief

eBrief No. 39/2013 – Employee Benefit Schemes

811C Transactions to avoid liability to tax

[(1) (a) In this section and *section 811D*—

'*the Acts*' means—

(i) the Tax Acts,

(ii) the Capital Gains Tax Acts,

(iii) the Value-Added Tax Consolidation Act 2010, and the enactments amending or extending that Act,

(iv) the Capital Acquisitions Tax Consolidation Act 2003, and the enactments amending or extending that Act,

(v) the Stamp Duties Consolidation Act 1999, and the enactments amending or extending that Act, and

(vi) *Part 18D*,

and any instruments made thereunder;

'*assessment*' includes any assessment to tax made under any provision of the Acts including any amended assessment, correcting assessment and any estimate or estimation;

'*business*' means any trade, profession or vocation;

'*Revenue officer*' means an officer of the Revenue Commissioners;

'*tax*' means any tax, duty, levy or charge which in accordance with the Acts is placed under the care and management of the Revenue Commissioners and any interest or other amount payable pursuant to the Acts;

'*tax advantage*' means—

(i) a reduction, avoidance or deferral of any charge or assessment to tax, including any potential or prospective charge or assessment, or

(ii) a refund of or a payment of an amount of tax, or an increase in an amount of tax, refundable or otherwise payable to a person, including any potential or prospective amount so refundable or payable,

arising out of or by reason of a transaction, including a transaction where another transaction would not have been undertaken or arranged to achieve the results, or any part of the results, achieved or intended to be achieved by the transaction;

'*tax avoidance transaction*' has the meaning assigned to it by *subsection (2)*;

'*transaction*' means—

(i) any transaction, action, course of action, course of conduct, scheme, plan or proposal,

(ii) any agreement, arrangement, understanding, promise or undertaking, whether express or implied and whether or not enforceable or intended to be enforceable by legal proceedings, and

(iii) any series of or combination of the circumstances referred to in *paragraphs (i)* and *(ii)*,

whether entered into or arranged by one person or by 2 or more persons—

(I) whether acting in concert or not,

(II) whether or not entered into or arranged wholly or partly outside the State, or

(III) whether or not entered into or arranged as part of a larger transaction or in conjunction with any other transaction or transactions.

(b) This section and *section 811D* shall apply notwithstanding any other provision of the Acts.

(2) (a) Subject to *paragraph (b)*, for the purposes of this section a transaction shall be a 'tax avoidance transaction' if having regard to 5 the following matters—

(i) the form of that transaction,

(ii) the substance of that transaction,

(iii) the substance of any other transaction or transactions which that transaction may reasonably be regarded as being directly or indirectly related to or connected with, and

(iv) the final outcome of that transaction and any combination of those other transactions which are so related or connected,

and having regard to any one or more of the following matters—

(I) the results of the transaction,

(II) its use as a means of achieving those results,

(III) any other means by which the results or any part of the results could have been achieved,

it would be reasonable to consider that—

(A) the transaction gives rise to, or but for this section would give rise to, a tax advantage, and

(B) the transaction was not undertaken or arranged primarily for purposes other than to give rise to a tax advantage.

(b) For the purpose of this section, a transaction shall not be a tax avoidance transaction if, having regard to the matters set out in *paragraph (a)*—

(i) notwithstanding that the purpose or purposes of the transaction could have been achieved by some other transaction which would have given rise to a greater amount of tax being payable by the person, the transaction—

(I) was undertaken or arranged by a person with a view, directly or indirectly, to the realisation of profits in the course of the business activities of a business carried on by the person, and

(II) was not undertaken or arranged primarily to give rise to a tax advantage,

or

(ii) the transaction was undertaken or arranged for the purpose of obtaining the benefit of any relief, allowance or other abatement provided by any provision of the Acts and the transaction did not result directly or indirectly in a misuse of the provision or an abuse of the provision having regard to the purposes for which it was provided.

(3) A person shall not be entitled to any tax advantage arising out of or by reason of a tax avoidance transaction to which this section applies.

(4) (a) Where a person submits any return, declaration, statement or account or makes any claim which purports to obtain the benefit of a tax advantage arising out of or by reason of a tax avoidance transaction, a Revenue officer may at any time deny or withdraw the tax advantage.

(b) Without prejudice to the generality of *paragraph (a)*, it shall be a lawful exercise of the powers conferred by that paragraph to do one or more of the following acts, and accordingly that paragraph shall be read as permitting, for the purposes of that paragraph, a Revenue officer to do each of the following acts, namely to—

(i) make or amend an assessment,

(ii) allow or disallow in whole or in part any credit, deduction or other amount which is relevant in computing tax payable, or any part of such credit, deduction or other amount,

(iii) allocate or deny any credit, deduction, loss, abatement, relief, allowance, exemption, income or other amount, or any part thereof,

(iv) recharacterise, for tax purposes, the nature of any payment or other amount.

(c) In *paragraph (b)* a reference to the doing of an act includes a reference to the making of an adjustment.

(d) Where any adjustment is made or act is done to deny or withdraw a tax advantage, relief shall be afforded from any double taxation which would, or would but for this paragraph, arise by virtue of any such adjustment made or act done pursuant to this subsection.

(5) (a) For the purposes of this subsection, 'alternative assessment' means an assessment—

(i) not being an assessment made pursuant to *subsection (4)*, and

(ii) the effect of which is to withdraw or deny, in whole or in part, any tax advantage.

(b) Where a Revenue officer makes or amends an assessment to withdraw or deny a tax advantage pursuant to this section, it shall be lawful for a Revenue officer to make or have made or to amend or have amended an alternative assessment.

(c) No appeal shall lie against an assessment made pursuant to this section or an alternative assessment on the grounds that a Revenue officer has made or amended an assessment pursuant to this section, or an alternative assessment, as the case may be.

(d) Where an assessment is made pursuant to this section and an alternative assessment is made, then only one such assessment shall, by agreement with the person on whom the assessment and the alternative assessment were made or by way of determination on appeal, as the case may be, become final and conclusive.

(6) Except as provided for in *section 811D(4)(a)(i)*, this section and *section 811D* shall be read as enabling the doing of, and nothing in the Acts, in particular a provision stipulating a time limit, shall be read as preventing a Revenue officer from doing, each of the following, namely:

(a) making any enquiry;

(b) taking any action;

(c) making or amending an assessment;

(d) collecting or recovering any amount of tax;

at any time in connection with this section or *section 811D*.

(7) Where a tax advantage is withdrawn from or denied to 2 or more persons pursuant to this section, any obligation on the Revenue Commissioners to maintain secrecy or any other restriction on the disclosure of information by the Revenue Commissioners shall not apply with respect to the making of any adjustment, the performance of any other acts or the discharge of any functions authorised by this section to be made, performed or discharged by a Revenue officer or to the making of any adjustment, the performance of any other acts or the discharge of any functions (including any act or function in relation to an appeal made under *Part 40*) which is directly or indirectly related to the adjustment, acts or functions so authorised.

(8) A transaction shall not be a tax avoidance transaction for the purposes of this section if it was commenced on or before 23 October 2014.][1]

Amendments

[1] Inserted by FA14 s87(1)(c).

811D Transactions to avoid liability to tax: surcharge, interest and protective notifications

[(1) For the purposes of this section—

'*chargeable period*' has the meaning assigned to it in *Part 41A*;

'*disclosable transaction*' has the meaning assigned to it in *Chapter 3* of this Part but for the purposes of this section, a transaction shall not be a disclosable transaction if—

(a) the transaction was disclosable by a promoter, pursuant to Chapter 3 of this Part, and not by a person who enters into any transaction which is or forms part of a transaction which is disclosable under *section 817F*, *817G* or *817H*,

(b) by the specified return date, within the meaning of *Part 41A*, for a return referred to in *section 817HA(3)*, the transaction was not assigned a transaction number, within the meaning of *Chapter 3* of this Part, or the person, in whose name or on whose behalf a qualifying avoidance disclosure or a protective notification is made, was not provided with a transaction number by a promoter or marketer, within the meaning of *Chapter 3* of this Part,

(c) the person in whose name or on whose behalf a qualifying avoidance disclosure or a protective notification is made provides a Revenue officer with the specified information, within the meaning of *Chapter 3* of this Part, and

(d) the person in whose name or on whose behalf a qualifying avoidance disclosure or a protective notification is made, without unreasonable delay, provides a Revenue officer with any other information that the officer may reasonably require for the purposes of deciding if an application should be made to the relevant court under *section 817O(3)(a)*;

'*protective notification*' means a notification—

(a) which is delivered in such form as may be prescribed by the Revenue Commissioners and to such office of the Revenue Commissioners as—

(i) is specified in the prescribed form, or

(ii) as may be identified, by reference to guidance in the prescribed form, as the office to which the notification concerned should be sent,

(b) which contains—

(i) full details of the transaction which is the subject of the protective notification, including any part of that transaction that has not been undertaken before the protective notification is delivered,

(ii) full reference to the provisions of the Acts that the person, by whom, or on whose behalf, the protective notification is delivered, considers to be relevant to the treatment of the transaction for tax purposes,

(iii) full details of how, in the opinion of the person, by whom, or on whose behalf, the protective notification is delivered, each provision referred to in the protective notification in accordance with *subparagraph (ii)*, applies, or does not apply, to the transaction, and

(iv) full details of why, in the opinion of the person, by whom, or on whose behalf, the protective notification is delivered, section 811C does not apply,

(c) which includes copies of all documentation pertaining to the transaction which is the subject of the protective notification,

(d) which is received by the Revenue Commissioners on or before the relevant date, and

(e) which does not relate to a disclosable transaction,

and *subsection (2)* supplements this definition;

'*qualifying avoidance disclosure*' means a disclosure that a Revenue 5 officer is satisfied is a disclosure of complete information in relation to, and full particulars of, all matters occasioning a liability to tax that gives rise to a surcharge referred to in *subsection (3)*, made in writing to the Revenue officer and signed by or on behalf of that person and which is accompanied by—

(a) a declaration, to the best of that person's knowledge, information and belief, made in writing, that all matters contained in the disclosure are correct and complete, and

(b) a payment of any tax due and payable in respect of any matter contained in the disclosure and the interest payable on the late payment of that tax;

'*relevant date*' in relation to a transaction means the date which is 90 days after the date on which that transaction was commenced;

'*specific anti-avoidance provision*' means a provision specified in Schedule 33.

(2) (a) Where the condition set out in *paragraph (c)* of the definition of 'protective notification' in this section cannot be complied with by reason of the fact that part of the transaction is undertaken after the relevant date, the condition shall be deemed to have been complied with if copies of the documentation pertaining to that part of the transaction are delivered to the office referred to in *paragraph (a)* of that definition within 30 days from their execution.

(b) Without prejudice to the generality of *paragraph (a)* of the definition of 'protective notification', the specifying, under—

(i) *section 81* of the Value-Added Tax Consolidation Act 2010,

(ii) *section 46A* of the Capital Acquisitions Tax Consolidation Act 2003,

(iii) *section 8C* of the Stamp Duties Consolidation Act 1999, or

(iv) *section 959P* of this Act,

of a doubt as to the application of law to, or the treatment for tax purposes of, any matter to be contained in a return shall not be regarded as being, or being equivalent to, the delivery of a protective notification in relation to a transaction for the purposes of this section.

(3) (a) Subject to *subsections (4)* and *(5)*, where—

(i) a transaction has been undertaken or arranged which would, but for *section 811C* or a specific anti-avoidance provision, as the case may be, give rise to a tax advantage, and

(ii) a person submits any return, declaration, statement or account or makes any claim which purports to obtain the benefit of that tax advantage,

then that person shall be liable to pay an amount (in this section referred to as the 'surcharge') equal to 30 per cent of the amount of the tax advantage and the provisions of *Chapter 3A* of *Part 47*, as they apply to penalties, shall apply with any necessary modifications to that surcharge.

(b) *Paragraph (a)* shall not apply in relation to a transaction where a person has, in submitting any return, declaration, statement or account or making any claim which purports to obtain the benefit of that tax advantage, incurred a penalty under *section 1077E(2)* or *1077E(5)*, *section 116(2)* or *116(5)* of the Value-Added Tax Consolidation Act 2010, *section 134A* of the Stamp Duties Consolidation Act 1999 or *section 58* of the Capital Acquisitions Tax Consolidation Act 2003.

(4) (a) Where the Revenue Commissioners have received a protective notification from, or on behalf of, a person then in relation to the transaction which was the subject of the protective notification—

(i) *paragraphs (a)*, *(b)* and *(c)* of *section 811C(6)* shall not apply, and

(ii) where a Revenue officer, pursuant to *section 811C(4)*, makes or amends an assessment to withdraw or deny a tax advantage arising out of or by reason of a tax avoidance transaction—

(I) the surcharge referred to in *subsection (3)* shall not apply, and

(II) any tax due and payable by a person as a result of the tax advantage being withdrawn or denied shall be deemed to be due and payable not later than one month from the date of the assessment or amended assessment as appropriate.

(b) Where a notification which purports to be a protective notification has been received by the Revenue Commissioners and a Revenue officer determines that the notification is not a protective notification, because it does not comply with one or more of the requirements set out in the definition of protective notification in this section, and—

(i) commences carrying out enquiries as if *section 811C(6)(a)* applied, a taxpayer who is aggrieved by such enquiries, on the grounds that the person considers that the officer was precluded from making that enquiry by reason of *paragraph (a)(i)*, may appeal to the Appeal Commissioners and *subsections (5)* to *(8)* of *section 959Z* shall, with any necessary modifications, apply to that appeal, or

(ii) makes or amends an assessment as if *section 811C(6)(c)* applied, a taxpayer who is aggrieved by the making of such an assessment, or, as the case may be, such amendment, on the grounds that the person considers that the officer was precluded from making the assessment or, as the case may be, the amendment, by reason of *paragraph (a)(i)*, may appeal to the Appeal Commissioners and *subsections (2)* and *(3)* of *section 959AF* shall, with any necessary modifications, apply to that appeal.

(5) (a) Where a person makes a qualifying avoidance disclosure in relation to a transaction which is not a disclosable transaction, then—

(i) if a Revenue officer has not commenced any inquiry into the transaction and the disclosure is made within a period of 24 months from the end of the chargeable period in which the transaction was commenced, the surcharge referred to in *subsection (3)* shall not apply,

(ii) if a Revenue officer has not withdrawn or denied a tax advantage under *section 811C* or a specific anti-avoidance provision, as the case may be, the surcharge referred to in *subsection (3)* shall be 3 per cent,

(iii) if a Revenue officer has withdrawn or denied a tax advantage under *section 811C* or a specific anti-avoidance provision, as the case may be, and no appeal in relation to that withdrawal or denial has been made, the surcharge referred to in *subsection (3)* shall be 5 per cent,

(iv) if a person has made an appeal in relation to the withdrawal or denial of a tax advantage under *section 811C* or a specific anti-avoidance provision, as the case may be, and that appeal has not yet been heard by the Appeal Commissioners, the surcharge referred to in *subsection (3)* shall be 10 per cent,

and, if the case does not fall within any of *subparagraphs (i)* to *(iv)*, then the surcharge referred to in *subsection (3)* shall be 30 per cent.

(b) Where a person makes a qualifying avoidance disclosure in relation to a transaction which is a disclosable transaction, then—

(i) if a Revenue officer has not commenced any inquiry into the transaction and the disclosure is made within a period of 24 months from the end of the chargeable period in which the transaction was commenced, the surcharge referred to in *subsection (3)* shall be 3 per cent,

(ii) if a Revenue officer has not withdrawn or denied a tax advantage under *section 811C* or a specific anti-avoidance provision, as the case may be, the surcharge referred to in *subsection (3)* shall be 6 per cent,

(iii) if a Revenue officer has withdrawn or denied a tax advantage under *section 811C* or a specific anti-avoidance provision, as the case may be, and no appeal in relation to that withdrawal or denial has been made, the surcharge referred to in *subsection (3)* shall be 10 per cent,

(iv) if a person has made an appeal in relation to the withdrawal or denial of a tax advantage under *section 811C* or a specific anti-avoidance provision, as the case may be, and that appeal has not yet been heard by the Appeal Commissioners, the surcharge referred to in *subsection (3)* shall be 20 per cent,

and, if the case does not fall within any of *subparagraphs (i)* to *(iv)*, then the surcharge referred to in *subsection (3)* shall be 30 per cent.

(6) Where a person makes a protective notification, or a protective notification is made on a person's behalf, then the person shall be treated as making the protective notification—

(a) solely, by virtue of the operation of *subsection (4)(a)(ii)*, to prevent a surcharge or interest becoming payable by the person, and

(b) wholly without prejudice as to whether the transaction concerned was a tax avoidance transaction.

(7) This section shall not apply to a transaction if any part of it was commenced on or before 23 October 2014.][1]

Amendments

[1] Inserted by FA14 s87(1)(c).

812 Taxation of income deemed to arise from transfers of right to receive interest from securities

[ITA67 s449; CTA76 s140(1) and Sch2 PtI par22]

(1) In this section—

"*interest*" includes dividends, annuities and shares of annuities;

"*securities*" include stocks and shares of all descriptions.

(2) Where in any year of assessment or accounting period an owner (in this section referred to as "*the owner*") of any securities sells or transfers the right to receive any particular interest payable (whether before or after such sale or transfer) in respect of those securities without selling or transferring those securities, then, and in every such case, the following provisions shall apply:

(a) for the purposes of the Tax Acts that interest (whether it would or would not be chargeable to tax if this section had not been enacted)—

(i) shall be deemed to be the income of the owner or, where the owner is not the beneficial owner of the securities and some other person (in this section referred to as "*the beneficiary*") is beneficially entitled to the income arising from the securities, the income of the beneficiary,

(ii) shall be deemed to be income of the owner or the beneficiary, as the case may be, for that year of assessment or accounting period, as the case may be, [and][1]

[…][2]

(iv) shall, where the proceeds of the sale or transfer are chargeable to tax under Schedule C or under *Chapter 2* of *Part 4*, be deemed to be equal in amount to the amount of those proceeds;

[…][3]

(c) where the securities are of such character that the interest payable in respect of the securities may be paid without deduction of tax, then, unless the owner or beneficiary, as the case may be, shows that the proceeds of any sale or other realisation of the right to receive the interest, which is deemed to be income of the owner or of the beneficiary, as the case may be, by virtue of this section, have been charged to tax under Schedule C or under *Chapter 2* of *Part 4*, the owner or beneficiary, as the case may be, shall be chargeable to tax under Case IV of Schedule D in respect of that interest, but shall be entitled to credit for any tax which that interest is shown to have borne;

(d) where in any case to which *paragraph (c)* applies the computation of the tax in respect of the interest which is made chargeable under Case IV of Schedule D by that paragraph would, if that interest had been chargeable under Case III of Schedule D, have been made by reference to the amount received in the State, the tax chargeable pursuant to *paragraph (c)* shall be computed on the full amount of the sums received in the State in the year of assessment or in any subsequent year of assessment in which the owner remains the owner of the securities;

(e) nothing in this subsection shall affect any provision of the Tax Acts authorising or requiring the deduction of tax from any interest which is deemed by virtue of this subsection to be income of the owner or of the beneficiary or from the proceeds of any subsequent sale, transfer or other realisation mentioned in this subsection of the right to receive that particular interest.

(3) In relation to corporation tax—

(a) *subsection (2)(c)* shall apply (subject to the provisions of the Corporation Tax Acts relating to distributions) to any interest, whether or not the securities are of such character that the interest may be paid without deduction of tax, and as if ", but shall be entitled to credit for any tax which that interest is shown to have borne" were deleted, and

(b) *subsection (2)(d)* shall not apply.

(4) The Revenue Commissioners may by notice in writing require any person to furnish them, within such time (not being less than 28 days from the service of the notice) as shall be specified in the notice, with such particulars in relation to all securities of which such person was the owner at any time during the period specified in the notice as the Revenue Commissioners may consider to be necessary for the purposes of this section or for the purpose of discovering whether—

(a) tax has been borne in respect of the interest payable in respect of those securities, or

(b) the proceeds of any sale, transfer or other realisation of the right to receive the interest in respect of those securities has been charged to tax under Schedule C or under *Chapter 2* of *Part 4*.

[(5) This section shall not apply—

(a) where the interest would not be chargeable to tax in the State had it been received by the owner or the beneficiary, as the case may be, at any time in the period commencing with the date of the sale or transfer of the right to receive the interest and ending on the date the interest was paid, or

(b) where the owner or the beneficiary, as the case may be, is a person carrying on a trade, profession or business, the profits of which are chargeable to income tax or corporation tax computed in accordance with the provisions or principles applicable to Case I or Case II of *Schedule D*, and the consideration for the sale or transfer is taken into account in computing, for the purposes of assessment to income tax or corporation tax, the profits of that trade, profession or business.][4]

Amendments

[1] Inserted by FA06 s40(1)(a)(i). Applies in relation to a sale, transfer or other realisation, on or after 7 March 2006, of the right to receive any interest payable in respect of any securities.

[2] Deleted by FA06 s40(1)(a)(ii). Applies in relation to a sale, transfer or other realisation, on or after 7 March 2006, of the right to receive any interest payable in respect of any securities.

[3] Deleted by FA06 s40(1)(b). Applies in relation to a sale, transfer or other realisation, on or after 7 March 2006, of the right to receive any interest payable in respect of any securities.

[4] Inserted by FA14 s34(1). Applies to a sale or transfer of the right to receive particular interest payable where that sale or transfer takes place after 23 October 2014.

Cross References

From Section 812

Section 17 Schedule C.
Section 52 Persons chargeable.
Section 60 Interpretation (Chapter 2).

To Section 812

Schedule 29 Provisions Referred to in Sections 1052, 1053 and 1054

813 Taxation of transactions associated with loans or credit

[FA74 s41(1) to (6); CTA76 s140(1) and Sch2 PtI par45 and s164 and Sch3 PtII]

(1) This section shall apply as respects any transaction effected with reference to the lending of money or the giving of credit, or the varying of the terms on which money is loaned or credit is given, or which is effected with a view to enabling or facilitating any such arrangement concerning the lending of money or the giving of credit.

(2) *Subsection (1)* shall apply whether the transaction is effected between the lender or creditor and the borrower or debtor, or between either of them and a person connected with the other or between a person connected with one and a person connected with the other.

(3) Where the transaction provides for the payment of any annuity or other annual payment, not being interest but being a payment chargeable to tax under Schedule D, the payment shall be treated for the purposes of the Tax Acts as if it were a payment of annual interest.

(4) Where the transaction is one by which an owner of any securities or other property carrying a right to income (in this subsection referred to as "*the owner*") agrees to sell or transfer the property, and by the same or any collateral agreement—

(a) the purchaser or transferee (in this subsection referred to as "*the buyer*") or a person connected with the buyer agrees to sell or transfer at a later date the same or any other property to the owner or a person connected with the owner, or

(b) the owner or a person connected with the owner acquires an option, which the owner or the person connected with the owner subsequently exercises, to buy or acquire the same or any other property from the buyer or a person connected with the buyer,

then, without prejudice to the liability of any other person, the owner shall be chargeable to tax under Case IV of Schedule D on an amount equal to any income which arises from the first-mentioned property at any time before the repayment of the loan or the termination of the credit.

(5) Where under the transaction a person assigns, surrenders or otherwise agrees to waive or forego income arising from any property (without a sale or transfer of the property), then, without prejudice to the liability of any other person, the

first-mentioned person shall be chargeable to tax under Case IV of Schedule D on a sum equal to the amount of income assigned, surrendered, waived or foregone.

(6) Where credit is given for the purchase price of any property and the rights attaching to the property are such that during the subsistence of the debt the purchaser's rights to income from the property are suspended or restricted, the purchaser shall be treated for the purposes of *subsection (5)* as having surrendered a right to income of an amount equivalent to the income which the purchaser has in effect foregone by obtaining the credit.

(7) The amount of any income payable subject to deduction of tax at the standard rate shall be taken for the purposes of *subsection (5)* as the amount before deduction of that tax.

814 Taxation of income deemed to arise from transactions in certificates of deposit and assignable deposits

[FA74 s55; CTA76 s140(1) and Sch2 PtI par47; FA77 s42 and Sch1 PtIV par5]

(1) In this section—

"*assignable deposit*" means a deposit of money in any currency, which has been deposited with any person, whether it is to be repaid with or without interest and which at the direction of the depositor may be assigned with or without interest to another person;

"*certificate of deposit*" means a document relating to money in any currency, which has been deposited with the issuer or some other person, being a document which recognises an obligation to pay a stated amount to bearer or to order, with or without interest, and being a document by the delivery of which, with or without endorsement, the right to receive that stated amount, with or without interest, is transferable.

(2) This section shall apply to any right—

(a) to receive from any person an amount of money, with or without interest, which is stated in a certificate of deposit issued to the person who has deposited the money or to any other person, or

(b) to receive from any person an amount of money, with or without interest, being a right arising from an assignable deposit which may be assigned or transferred to another person by the person who has deposited the money or by any person who has acquired the right to do so.

(3) Where after the 3rd day of April, 1974, a person acquires a right to which this section applies, any gain arising to the person from the disposal of that right or, except in so far as it is a right to receive interest, from its exercise shall, if not to be taken into account as a trading receipt, be deemed for the purposes of the Tax Acts to be annual profits or gains chargeable to tax under Case IV of Schedule D and shall be charged to tax accordingly.

(4) Where on or before the 3rd day of April, 1974, a person acquired a right to which this section applies and disposes or disposed of, or exercises or exercised, the right after that date, so much of any gain arising to the person from that disposal, or, except in so far as it is a right to receive interest, from that exercise, as bears to the total amount of the gain the same proportion as the number of days from the 3rd day of April, 1974, to the date of the disposal or exercise bears to the total number of days from the date of the acquisition to the date of the

disposal or exercise, shall, if not to be taken into account as a trading receipt, be deemed for the purposes of the Tax Acts to be annual profits or gains chargeable to tax under Case IV of Schedule D and shall be charged to tax accordingly.

(5) Where a person sustains a loss in a transaction which if profits had arisen from it would be chargeable to tax by virtue of *subsection (3)* or *(4)*, then, if the person is chargeable to tax under Schedule C or D in respect of the interest payable on the amount of money the right to which has been disposed of, the amount of that interest shall be included in the amounts against which the person may claim to set off the amount of the loss under *section 383* or *399*, as the case may be.

(6) For the purposes of this section, profits or gains shall not be treated as falling to be taken into account as a trading receipt by reason only that they are included in the computation required by *section 707*.

Cross References

From Section 814

Section 17 Schedule C.

Section 383 Relief under Case IV for losses.

Section 399 Losses in transactions from which income would be chargeable under Case IV or V of Schedule D.

Section 707 Management expenses.

To Section 814

Section 399 Losses in transactions from which income would be chargeable under Case IV or V of Schedule D.

815 Taxation of income deemed to arise on certain sales of securities

[FA84 s29(1) to (3)(a) and (4) to (5); FA91 s27; FA93 s21; FA94 s26]

(1) In this section—

"*owner*", in relation to securities, means at any time the person who would be entitled, if the securities were redeemed at that time by the person who issued them, to the proceeds of the redemption;

"*securities*" includes—

(a) assets which are not chargeable assets for the purposes of capital gains tax by virtue of *section 607*, and

(b) stocks, bonds and obligations of any government, municipal corporation, company or other body corporate, whether creating or evidencing a charge on assets or not,

but does not include shares (within the meaning of the Companies Act, 1963) of a company (within the meaning of that Act) or similar body.

(2) (a) Subject to *paragraphs (b)* to *(d)* and *subsection (3)*, where the owner of a security (in this subsection referred to as "*the owner*") sells or transfers, or causes or authorises to be sold or transferred, the security and where any interest payable in respect of the security is receivable otherwise than by the owner, then, for the purposes of this section—

(i) interest payable in respect of the security shall be deemed for the purposes of the Tax Acts to have accrued on a day to day basis from the date on which the owner acquired the security, and

(ii) the owner shall be chargeable under Case IV of Schedule D on interest so deemed to have accrued from that date up to the date of the contract for sale or transfer of the security or the date of payment of the consideration in respect of the sale or transfer, whichever is the later.

(b) Where during the owner's period of ownership of the security the owner has received interest in respect of the security in respect of which the owner is chargeable to tax under any other provision of the Tax Acts, the amount of interest on which the owner is chargeable under this section shall be reduced by the amount in respect of which the owner is so chargeable under that other provision.

(c) Where under the terms of the sale or transfer of the security or an associated agreement, arrangement, understanding, promise or undertaking, whether express or implied, the owner—

(i) agrees to buy back or reacquire the security, or

(ii) acquires an option which the owner subsequently exercises to buy back or reacquire the security,

the charge to tax imposed under this section shall be based on the interest deemed to have accrued up to the next date after that sale or transfer on which interest is payable in respect of the security.

(d) Where the owner subsequently resells or retransfers, or causes or authorises to be resold or retransferred, the security, any further charge to tax under this section in respect of that subsequent resale or retransfer shall be based on interest deemed to have accrued from a date not earlier than that next payment date.

(3) This section shall not apply—

(a) where the security has been held by the same owner for a continuous period of at least 2 years immediately before the date of such contract for sale or transfer or the date of such payment of consideration, whichever is the later, as is referred to in *subsection (2)(a)*, the personal representatives of a deceased person whose estate is in the course of administration and the deceased person being regarded for the purposes of this paragraph as being the same owner,

(b) where the owner is a person carrying on a trade which consists wholly or partly of dealing in securities, the profits of which are chargeable to income tax or corporation tax under Case I of Schedule D for the year of assessment or, as the case may be, the accounting period in respect of which the consideration for the sale is taken into account in computing for the purposes of assessment to income tax or corporation tax for that year or accounting period the profits of the trade,

(c) where—

(i) the owner is an undertaking for collective investment (within the meaning of *section 738*), and

(ii) any gain or loss accruing to the owner on the sale or transfer is a chargeable gain or an allowable loss, as the case may be,

[(d) where the sale or transfer is a sale or transfer—

(i) by a wife to her husband at a time when she is treated as living with him for income tax purposes as provided in *section 1015*, or a sale or transfer by a husband to a wife at such time, or

(ii) by a civil partner to his or her civil partner at a time when one civil partner is treated as living with the other for income tax purposes as provided in *section 1031A*, the husband and the wife, or the civil partners, as the case may be, being regarded for the purposes of *paragraph (a)*, in the case of such a transaction or in the case of a sale or transfer by the husband or the wife, or either civil partner, as the case may be, to any other person after such a transaction or transactions, as being the same owner, or][1]

(e) where the security is a security the interest on which is treated as a distribution for the purposes of the Corporation Tax Acts.

(4) The reference in *subsection (2)(c)* to buying back or reacquiring the security shall be deemed to include references to buying or acquiring a similar security, and securities shall be so deemed to be similar if they entitle their holders to the same rights against the same persons as to capital and interest and the same remedies for the enforcement of those rights, notwithstanding any difference in the total nominal amounts of the respective securities or in the form in which they are held or the manner in which they can be transferred.

(5) (a) For the purposes of identifying securities acquired by an owner with securities included in a sale or transfer by the owner, in so far as the securities are of the same class, securities acquired at a later date shall be deemed to be so included before securities acquired at an earlier date.

(b) Securities shall be regarded as being of the same class where they entitle their owners to the same rights against the same person as to capital and interest and the same remedies for the enforcement of those rights.

(6) (a) Without prejudice to any other provision of the Tax Acts requiring the disclosure of information, an inspector may by notice in writing require any person to whom *paragraph (b)* applies to furnish within the time specified in the notice such particulars as the inspector considers necessary for the purposes of this section and for the purpose of determining whether a charge to tax arises under this section.

(b) This paragraph shall apply to—

(i) a person who issues a security,

(ii) any agent of such a person, and

(iii) an owner of a security.

Amendments

[1] Substituted by F(No.3)A11 sched1(228).

Revenue Precedents

Section 815(2)(b) cannot reduce the Case IV chargeable figure to a figure less than nil so as to create a loss. CTF 355

Cross References

From Section 815

Section 607 Government and certain other securities.
Section 738 Undertakings for collective investment.
Section 1015 Interpretation (Chapter 1).

To Section 815

Section 55 Taxation of strips of securities.
Section 711 Chargeable gains of life business.
Section 737 Special investment schemes.
Section 738 Undertakings for collective investment.
Section 751B Exchange of Irish Government bonds.
Section 838 Special portfolio investment accounts.
Schedule 29 Provisions Referred to in Sections 1052, 1053 and 1054

816 Taxation of shares issued in place of cash dividends

[FA74 s56(1), (2), (3)(b) and (c) and (4); FA93 s36]

[(1) In this section—

"*company*" means any body corporate;

"*quoted company*" means a company whose shares, or any class of whose shares—

(a) are listed in the official list of the Irish Stock Exchange or on any other stock exchange, or

(b) are quoted on the market known as the Developing Companies Market, or the market known as the Exploration Securities Market, of the Irish Stock Exchange or on any similar or corresponding market of any other stock exchange;

"*share*" means share in the share capital of a company and includes stock and any other interest in the company.

(2) Where any person as a consequence of the exercise (whether before, on or after the declaration of a distribution of profits by a company) of an option to receive in respect of shares in the company either a sum in cash or additional share capital of the company, receives such additional share capital, then, an amount equal to the amount which that person would have received if that person had received the distribution in cash instead of such share capital shall for the purposes of the Tax Acts—

(a) where the company is resident outside the State, be deemed to be income received by the person from the company, and such income shall be treated as income from securities and possessions outside the State and be assessed and charged to tax under Case III of Schedule D,

(b) where the company is resident in the State and is a quoted company—

(i) be treated as a distribution made by the company, and

(ii) be deemed to be a distribution received by the person,

and

(c) where the company is resident in the State and is not a quoted company, be deemed to be profits or gains of the person, being profits or gains not within any other Case of Schedule D and not charged by virtue of any other Schedule, and be assessed and charged to tax under Case IV of Schedule D.

(3) Where a company is treated under *subsection (2)(b)*(i) as making a distribution to a person, *section 152* shall apply with any necessary modifications as if the distribution were a dividend to which *subsection (1)* of that section applies.][1]

(4) For the purposes of this section, an option to receive either a dividend in cash or additional share capital shall be conferred on a person not only where that person is required to choose one or the other, but also where that person is offered the one subject to a right, however expressed, to choose the other instead, and a person's abandonment of, or failure to exercise, such a right shall be treated for those purposes as an exercise of the option.

Amendments

[1] Substituted by FA98 s43(1)(a). This section shall apply as respects shares issued by a company on or after the 3rd day of December, 1997.

Cross References

From Section 816

Section 152 Explanation of tax credit to be annexed to interest and dividend warrants.

To Section 816

Section 4 Interpretation of Corporation Tax Acts.
Section 20 Schedule F.
Section 130 Matters to be treated as distributions.
Section 172A Interpretation.
Section 584 Reorganisation or reduction of share capital.

817 Schemes to avoid liability to tax under Schedule F

[FA89 s88(1) to (7)]

(1) (a) In this section—

"*appeal*" means an appeal made in accordance with *section 933*;

"*close company*" has the same meaning as it has, by virtue of *sections 430* and *431*, for the purposes of the Corporation Tax Acts;

"*market value*" shall be construed in accordance with *section 548*;

"*new consideration*" has the same meaning as in *section 135*;

"*shares*" includes loan stock, debentures and any interest or rights in or over, or any option in relation to, shares, loan stock or debentures, and references to "*shareholder*" shall be construed accordingly.

(b) (i) For the purposes of this section, there shall be a disposal of shares by a shareholder where the shareholder disposes of shares or is treated under the Capital Gains Tax Acts as disposing of shares, and references to a disposal of shares shall include references to a part disposal of shares within the meaning of those Acts.

(ii) Where under any arrangement between a close company (in this subparagraph referred to as "*the first-mentioned company*") and its, or some of its, shareholders (being any arrangement similar to an arrangement entered into for the purposes of or in connection with a scheme of reconstruction or amalgamation) another close company issues shares to those shareholders in respect of or in proportion to (or as nearly as may be in proportion to) their holdings of shares in the first-mentioned company, but the shares in the first-mentioned company are either retained by the shareholders or are cancelled, then, those shareholders shall for the purposes of this section be treated as making a disposal or a part disposal, as the case may be, of the shares in the first-mentioned company in exchange for those shares held by them in consequence of such arrangement.

(c) For the purposes of this section, the interest of a shareholder in a trade or business shall not be significantly reduced following a disposal of shares, or the carrying out of a scheme or arrangement of which the disposal of shares is a part, only if at any time after the disposal the percentage of—

(i) the ordinary share capital of the close company carrying on the trade or business at such time which is beneficially owned by the shareholder at such time,

(ii) any profits, which are available for distribution to equity holders, of the close company carrying on the trade or business at such time to which the shareholder is beneficially entitled at such time, or

(iii) any assets, available for distribution to equity holders on a winding up, of the close company carrying on the trade or business at such time to which the shareholder would be beneficially entitled at such time on a winding up of the close company,

is not significantly less than the percentage of that ordinary share capital or those profits or assets, as the case may be, of the close company carrying on the trade or business at any time before the disposal—

(I) which the shareholder beneficially owned, or

(II) to which the shareholder was beneficially entitled,

at such time before the disposal, and *sections 413* to *415* and *section 418* shall apply, but without regard to *section 411(1)(c)* in so far as it relates to those sections, with any necessary modifications, to the determination for the purposes of this paragraph of the percentage of share capital or other amount which a shareholder beneficially owns or is beneficially entitled to, as they apply to the determination for the purposes of *Chapter 5* of *Part 12* of the percentage of any such amount which a company so owns or is so entitled to.

[(ca) For the purposes of this section, following a disposal of shares in a close company by a shareholder or the carrying out of a scheme or arrangement of which the disposal is a part, the interest of the shareholder in any trade or business which was carried on by the close company shall be deemed—

(i) to include the interest, or interests as the case may be, in that trade or business of one or more persons connected with the shareholder, if increasing that interest of the shareholder by such interest, or interests as the case may be, would result in the interest of the shareholder in the trade or business not having been significantly reduced,

(ii) notwithstanding *paragraph (c)*, not to have been significantly reduced where—

(I) the business carried on by the close company, taking account of any trade carried on by that company, consisted wholly or mainly of the holding of shares in another company carrying on a trade or business or in more than one such other company, and

(II) the interest of the shareholder in any such trade or business last-mentioned in clause (I), whether or not that trade or business continues to be carried on by such other company after the disposal, is not significantly reduced,

[(iii) notwithstanding *paragraph (c)*, not to have been significantly reduced where the gain realised, or the proceeds in either or both money or money's worth received, by the shareholder on that disposal is or are wholly or mainly attributable to payments or other transfers of value from another company or companies, which is or are controlled (within the meaning of *section 432*) by that shareholder or by that shareholder and persons connected with him or her, to the close company, and][1]

(iv) not to have been significantly reduced where—

(I) it would not have been so reduced if the shareholder were to be treated as beneficially entitled to any shares to which he or she could, at any time, become so entitled by the exercise of a discretion by trustees,

(II) the acquisition of those shares by the trustees was directly or indirectly related to a disposal, including a prior or subsequent disposal, of such shares by the shareholder, and

(III) the shares were acquired by the trustees with the direct or indirect financial assistance of a company or companies, which is or are controlled by the shareholder or by the shareholder and persons connected with the shareholder.][2]

(d) The value of any amount received in money's worth shall for the purposes of this section be the market value of the money's worth at the time of its receipt.

[(e) For the purposes of this section, the holding of money by a company shall be deemed to be a business carried on by the company, regardless of how that money was contributed to, or acquired by, the company.][3]

[(2) This section shall apply for the purposes of counteracting any scheme or arrangement undertaken or arranged by a close company, or to which the close company is a party, being a scheme or arrangement the purpose of which, or one of the purposes of which, is to secure that any shareholder in the close company avoids or reduces a charge or assessment to income tax under Schedule F by directly or indirectly extracting, or enabling such extracting of, either or both money and money's worth from the close company, for the benefit of the shareholder, without the close company paying a dividend, or (apart from *subsection (4)*) making a distribution, chargeable to tax under Schedule F.][4]

(3) Subject to *subsection (7)*, this section shall apply to a disposal of shares in a close company by a shareholder if, following the disposal or the carrying out of a scheme or arrangement of which the disposal is a part, the interest of the shareholder in any trade or business (in this section referred to as "*the specified business*") which was carried on by the close company at the time of the disposal, whether or not the specified business continues to be carried on by the close company after the disposal, is not significantly reduced.

(4) Subject to *subsection (5)* and notwithstanding *section 130(1)* or any provision of the Capital Gains Tax Acts, the amount of—

(a) the proceeds in either or both money and money's worth received by a shareholder in respect of a disposal of shares in a close company to which this section applies, or

(b) if it is less than those proceeds, the excess of those proceeds over any consideration, being consideration which—

(i) is new consideration received by the close company for the issue of those shares, and

(ii) has not previously been taken into account for the purposes of this subsection,

shall be treated for the purposes of the Tax Acts as a distribution (within the meaning of the Corporation Tax Acts) made at the time of the disposal by the close company to the shareholder.

(5) (a) In this subsection, "*capital receipt*" means, as appropriate in the circumstances, any amount of either or both money and money's worth (other than shares issued by a close company carrying on the specified business) which—

(i) is received by a shareholder in respect of a disposal of shares or by reason of any act done pursuant to a scheme or arrangement of which the disposal is a part, and

(ii) apart from this section is not chargeable to income tax in the hands of the shareholder.

(b) The amount which at any time may be treated under *subsection (4)* as a distribution made by a close company to a shareholder in respect of any disposal of shares in the close company shall not exceed the amount of the capital receipt, or the aggregate of the amounts of the capital receipts, which at such time has or have been received by the shareholder—

(i) in respect of the disposal, or

(ii) by reason of any act done pursuant to a scheme or arrangement of which the disposal is a part.

(c) A capital receipt received by a shareholder at any time on or after the disposal shall in respect of such time result in so much of the amount mentioned in *subsection (4)* being treated as a distribution (which is made by the close company to the shareholder at the time of the disposal) as does not exceed the amount of the capital receipt, or the aggregate of the amounts of such capital receipts, which at such time on or after the disposal has or have been received by the shareholder.

(d) Where as a result of a shareholder having received a capital receipt a close company is treated as having made a distribution to the shareholder under *subsection (4)*, any provision of the Income Tax Acts in respect of interest on unpaid tax shall apply for the purposes of tax due in respect of that distribution as if the tax were due and payable only from the day on which the shareholder received the capital receipt.

[…][5]

(7) This section shall not apply as respects a disposal of shares in a close company by a shareholder where it is shown to the satisfaction of the inspector or, on the hearing or the rehearing of an appeal, to the satisfaction of the Appeal Commissioners or a judge of the Circuit Court, as the case may be, that the disposal was made for bona fide commercial reasons and not as part of a scheme or arrangement the purpose or one of the purposes of which was the avoidance of tax.

Amendments

[1] Substituted by FA11 s28(1)(a). Has effect as respects any disposal of shares on or after 26 January 2011.

[2] Inserted by FA05 s39(1). This section applies and has effect as respects any disposal of shares on or after 1 March 2005.

[3] Inserted by FA11 s28(1)(b). Has effect as respects any disposal of shares on or after 26 January 2011.

[4] Substituted by FA06 s24(1). Applies and has effect as respects any disposal of shares on or after 21 February 2006.

[5] Deleted by FA03 s41(1)(m). This section applies as respects accounting periods ending on or after 6 February 2003.

Cross References

From Section 817

Section 20 Schedule F.

Section 130 Matters to be treated as distributions.

Section 135 Distributions: supplemental.

Section 381 Right to repayment of tax by reference to losses.

Section 410 Group payments.

Section 411 Surrender of relief between members of groups and consortia.

Section 413 Profits or assets available for distribution.

Section 415 Meaning of "the notional winding up".

Section 418 Beneficial percentage.
Section 430 Meaning of "close company".
Section 431 Certain companies with quoted shares not to be close companies.
Section 432 Meaning of "associated company" and "control".
Section 548 Valuation of assets.
Section 933 Appeals against assessment.

817A Restriction of relief for payments of interest

[(1) Relief shall not be given to any person under *Part 8* in respect of any payment of interest, including interest treated as a charge on income, if a scheme has been effected or arrangements have been made such that the sole or main benefit that might be expected to accrue to that person from the transaction under which the interest is paid is the obtaining of a reduction in tax liability by means of any such relief.

(2) Where relief in respect of interest paid, being interest treated as a charge on income, is claimed by virtue of *section 420(6)*, any question under this section as to what benefit might be expected to accrue from the transaction under which that interest is paid shall be determined by reference to the claimant company (within the meaning of *section 411(2)*) and the surrendering company (within the meaning of that section) taken together.][1]

Amendments

[1] Inserted by FA00 s73(1). This section applies, to interest paid, and to interest received, on or after 29 February 2000.

Cross References

From Section 817A

Section 237 Annual payments payable wholly out of taxed income.
Section 411 Surrender of relief between members of groups and consortia.
Section 420 Losses, etc. which may be surrendered by means of group relief.

817B Treatment of interest in certain circumstances

[(1) (a) In this section—

"*chargeable period*" means an accounting period of a company or a year of assessment, and a reference to a chargeable period or its basis period is a reference to the chargeable period if it is an accounting period and to the basis period for it if it is a year of assessment;

"*basis period*" means the period on the profits or gains of which income tax is to be finally computed under Schedule D or, where by virtue of the Income Tax Acts the profits or gains of any other period are to be taken to be the profits or gains of that period, that other period.

(b) For the purposes of this section, in relation to interest which is to be taken into account in computing income chargeable to tax under Case I of Schedule D—

(i) where 2 basis periods overlap, the period common to both shall be deemed to fall in the first basis period only,

(ii) where there is an interval between the end of the basis period for one year of assessment and the basis period for the next year of assessment, the interval shall be deemed to be part of the first basis period, and

(iii) the reference in *subparagraph (i)* to the overlapping of 2 periods shall be construed as including a reference to the coincidence of 2 periods or to the inclusion of one period in another, and the reference to the period common to both shall be construed accordingly.

(2) Notwithstanding any other provision of the Tax Acts, where, in relation to a chargeable period (in this subsection referred to as the "*earlier chargeable period*"), a person receives interest in the chargeable period or its basis period, so much of the amount of the interest as, apart from this section—

(a) would not be taken into account in computing the person's income chargeable to tax under Schedule D for the earlier chargeable period, and

(b) would be so taken into account for a subsequent chargeable period or subsequent chargeable periods,

shall be taken into account in computing the person's income so chargeable for the earlier chargeable period and shall not be so taken into account for the subsequent chargeable period or, as the case may be, the subsequent chargeable periods.][1]

Amendments

[1] Inserted by FA00 s73(1). This section applies, to interest paid, and to interest received, on or after 29 February 2000.

Cross References

To Section 817B

Section 817C Restriction on deductibility of certain interest.

817C Restriction on deductibility of certain interest

[(1) In this section—

"*chargeable period*" and "*basis period*" have the same meanings as they have for the purposes of *section 817B*;

"*relevant date*", in relation to a chargeable period, means the date on which the basis period for the chargeable period ends;

"*relevant liability*" means a liability of one person to another person.

(2) [Subject to *subsection (2A)*, this section applies where][1]—

(a) interest is payable by a person, directly or indirectly, to a connected person (being interest which, if it were paid, would be chargeable to tax under Schedule D),

(b) the interest would, apart from this section, be allowable in computing trading income of a trade carried on by the person, and

(c) (i) in a case where the connected person is chargeable to tax in respect of the interest, the interest does not fall to be taken into account, or

(ii) in any other case, if the connected person were resident in the State the interest would not fall to be taken into account,

in computing the trading income of a trade carried on by the connected person.

[(2A) (a) This section does not apply where the connected person referred to in *subsection (2)* is a company which—

(i) is not resident in the State, and

(ii) is not under the control, whether directly or indirectly, of a person who is, or persons who are, resident in the State.

(b) For the purposes of this subsection—

(i) "control" shall be construed in accordance with *subsections (2)* to *(6)* of *section 432* as if in *subsection (6)* of that section for "5 or fewer participators" there were substituted "persons resident in the State", and

(ii) a company shall not be treated as under the control whether directly or indirectly, of a person or persons if that person is or those persons are, in turn under the control of another person or other persons.][2]

(3) Where this section applies, so much of any interest payable, or treated under *subsection (4)* as payable, by a person, directly or indirectly, to a connected person in respect of a relevant liability shall not be allowable in computing trading income chargeable on the person for a chargeable period (in this subsection referred to as the "*first-mentioned chargeable period*") as is greater than the excess of A over B where—

A is the aggregate of amounts of interest on the relevant liability which are chargeable to tax as income of the connected person, or would be so chargeable but for the provisions of *section 198* or of arrangements having the force of law by virtue of [*826(1)*,][3] for all chargeable periods the basis periods for which end on or before the relevant date in relation to the first-mentioned chargeable period, and

B is the aggregate of the amounts of interest on the relevant liability which have been allowed as deductions in computing trading income for the purposes of tax for, or have otherwise been allowed or relieved for the purposes of tax in, chargeable periods the basis periods for which end before the relevant date in relation to the first-mentioned chargeable period.

(4) Interest which, by virtue of *subsection (3)*, is not allowable in computing trading income for a chargeable period shall be treated as being payable in the basis period for the following chargeable period.

(5) Where under arrangements made by any person (in this subsection referred to as the "*first person*")—

(a) interest is payable by the first person to another person such that this section does not apply by virtue only of the fact that the persons concerned are not connected, and

(b) interest is payable by some other person to a person (in this subsection referred to as the "*second person*") connected with the first person such that this section does not apply by virtue only of the fact that the other person and the second person are not connected,

then, *subsections (3)* and *(4)* shall apply as if the interest had been payable by the first person to the second person.][4]

Amendments

[1] Substituted by FA04 s32(1)(a). This section is deemed to have applied as respects any chargeable period ending on or after 6 February 2003.

[2] Inserted by FA04 s32(1)(b). This section is deemed to have applied as respects any chargeable period ending on or after 6 February 2003.

[3] Substituted by FA07 sched2(1)(aa). Has effect as on and from 2 April 2007

[4] Inserted by FA03 s44(1). This section applies as respects any chargeable period ending on or after 6 February 2003.

Cross References

From Section 817C

Section 198 Certain interest not to be chargeable.

Section 432 Meaning of "associated company" and "control".

Section 817B Treatment of interest in certain circumstances.

Section 826 Agreements for relief from double taxation.

CHAPTER 3

Mandatory Disclosure of Certain Transactions

817D Interpretation and general (Chapter 3)

[(1) In this Chapter, unless the context otherwise requires—

"*the Acts*" means—

(a) the Tax Acts,

(b) the Capital Gains Tax Acts,

[…][1]

(d) the Value-Added Tax Consolidation Act 2010, and the enactments amending or extending that Act,

(e) the Capital Acquisitions Tax Consolidation Act 2003, and the enactments amending or extending that Act,

(f) the Stamp Duties Consolidation Act 1999, and the enactments amending or extending that Act,

(g) the statutes relating to the duties of excise and to the management of those duties, [and][2]

[(h) *Part 18D*,][3]

and any instruments made thereunder and any instruments made under any other enactment relating to tax;

"*disclosable transaction*" means—

(a) any transaction, or

(b) any proposal for any transaction,

which—

(i) falls within any specified description,

(ii) enables, or might be expected to enable, any person to obtain a tax advantage, and

(iii) is such that the main benefit, or one of the main benefits, that might be expected to arise from the transaction or the proposal is the obtaining of that tax advantage,

whether the transaction or the proposal for the transaction relates to a particular person or to any person who may seek to take advantage of it;

['*emoluments*' means emoluments to which *Chapter 4* of *Part 42* applies;

'*employee*' means any person in receipt of emoluments;

'*employer*' means any person paying emoluments;][4]

"*marketer*", in relation to any disclosable transaction, means any person who is not a promoter but who has made a marketing contact in relation to the disclosable transaction;

"*marketing contact*", in relation to a disclosable transaction, means the communication by a person of the general nature of the disclosable transaction to another person with a view to that person or any other person considering whether—

(a) to ask for further details of the disclosable transaction, or

(b) to seek to have the disclosable transaction made available for implementation, and "makes a marketing contact" shall be construed accordingly;

"*PPS Number*", in relation to an individual, means the individual's personal public service number, within the meaning of section 262 of the Social Welfare Consolidation Act 2005;

"*promoter*", in relation to a disclosable transaction, means a person who in the course of a relevant business—

(a) is to any extent responsible for the design of the disclosable transaction,

(b) has specified information relating to the disclosable transaction and makes a marketing contact in relation to the disclosable transaction,

(c) makes the disclosable transaction available for implementation by other persons, or

(d) is to any extent responsible for the organisation or management of the disclosable transaction;

['*quarter*' means a period of 3 months ending on 31 March, 30 June, 30 September or 31 December;][5]

"*relevant business*" means any trade, profession, vocation or business which—

(a) includes the provision to other persons of services relating to taxation, or

(b) is carried on by a bank (within the meaning of section 124(1)(*a*) of the Stamp Duties Consolidation Act 1999),

and for the purposes of this definition—

(i) anything done by a company is to be taken to be done in the course of a relevant business if it is done for the purposes of a relevant business referred to in *paragraph (b)* carried on by another company, where both companies are members of the same group, and

(ii) "*group*" has the meaning that would be given by *section 616* if in that section references to residence in a relevant Member State were omitted and for references to "75 per cent subsidiaries" there were substituted references to "51 per cent subsidiaries", and references to a company being a member of a group shall be construed accordingly;

"*relevant date*", in relation to a disclosable transaction, means the earliest of the following dates—

(a) the date on which the promoter has specified information relating to the disclosable transaction and first makes a marketing contact in relation to the disclosable transaction,

(b) the date on which the promoter makes the disclosable transaction available for implementation by any other person, or

(c) the date on which the promoter first becomes aware of any transaction [which is or forms][6] part of the disclosable transaction having been implemented;

['*return*' means any return, claim, application, notification, election, declaration, nomination, statement, list, registration, particulars or other information, which a person is or may be required by the Acts to give to the Revenue Commissioners or any Revenue officer;

'*Revenue officer*' means an officer of the Revenue Commissioners;

'*specified date*' means—

(a) in relation to a promoter, the relevant date, and

(b) in relation to a person other than a promoter, the date the person first enters into any transaction which is or forms part of a disclosable transaction;][7]

"*specified description*" has the meaning assigned to it by [*section 817DA*];[8]

"*specified information*" means [, in respect of a disclosable transaction, the information set out in *subsection (2)(a)* and *subparagraphs (i)* to *(iii)*, as the case may be, of *subsection (2)(b)*];[9]

[...][10]

"*tax*" means any tax, duty, levy or charge which, in accordance with the Acts, is placed under the care and management of the Revenue Commissioners;

"*tax advantage*" means—

(a) relief or increased relief from, or a reduction, avoidance or deferral of, any assessment, charge or liability to tax, including any potential or prospective assessment, charge or liability,

(b) a refund or repayment of, or a payment of, an amount of tax, or an increase in an amount of tax refundable, repayable or otherwise payable to a person, including any potential or prospective amount so refundable, repayable or payable, or an advancement of any refund or repayment of, or payment of, an amount of tax to a person, or

(c) the avoidance of any obligation to deduct or account for tax,

arising out of or by reason of a transaction, including a transaction where another transaction would not have been undertaken or arranged to achieve the results, or any part of the results, achieved or intended to be achieved by the transaction;

"*tax reference number*", in relation to a person, means—

(a) in the case of a person who is an individual, the individual's PPS Number, and

(b) in any other case—

(i) the reference number stated in any return of income form or notice of assessment issued to the person by the Revenue Commissioners, or

(ii) the registration number of the person for the purposes of value-added tax;

"*transaction*" means—

(a) any transaction, action, course of action, course of conduct, scheme or plan,

(b) any agreement, arrangement, understanding, promise or undertaking, whether express or implied and whether or not enforceable or intended to be enforceable by legal proceedings, and

(c) any series of or combination of the circumstances referred to in *paragraphs (a)* and *(b)*,

whether entered into or arranged by one person or by two or more persons—

(i) whether acting in concert or not,

(ii) whether or not entered into or arranged wholly or partly outside the State, or

(iii) whether or not entered into or arranged as part of a larger transaction or in conjunction with any other transaction or transactions,

and any proposal for any transaction shall be construed accordingly.

['*transaction number*' means the number assigned to a transaction by the Revenue Commissioners under *section 817HB*;][11]

[(2) For the purposes of the definition of 'specified information' in the preceding subsection, the following provisions specify the information concerned:

(a) such information as might reasonably be expected to enable the manner in which the disclosable transaction operates, or is intended to operate, to be fully understood by a Revenue officer, and, in all cases, includes—

(i) full reference to the provisions of this Chapter by virtue of which the person by whom, or on whose behalf, the information is being provided considers that the transaction is disclosable,

(ii) a summary of the disclosable transaction and the name (if any) by which it is known,

(iii) full reference to the provisions of the Acts that are considered by the person to be relevant to the treatment of the disclosable transaction for tax purposes, and

(iv) full details of the disclosable transaction explaining each element of the transaction (including the way in which the transaction is structured) from which the tax advantage expected to be obtained under the transaction arises and how, in the opinion of the person by whom, or on whose behalf, the information is being provided, each provision of the Acts referred to in *subparagraph (iii)* applies, or as the case may be, does not apply to the transaction,

(b) where—

(i) the information is required to be disclosed by a promoter under *section 817E*, the following information, namely, the name, address, telephone number and tax reference number of the promoter,

(ii) the information is required to be disclosed by a person under *section 817F, 817H(1)* or *817L*, the following information, namely—

(I) the name, address, telephone number and tax reference number of the person, and

(II) the name, address and telephone number of the promoter,

or

(iii) the information is required to be disclosed by a person under *section 817G*, the following information, namely, the name, address, telephone number and tax reference number of the person;][12, 13]

Amendments

[1] Deleted by FA13 s97(1)(c).

[2] Substituted by FA13 s97(1)(c).

[3] Inserted by FA13 s97(1)(c).

[4] Inserted by FA14 s88(1)(a)(i). Applies to a transaction which is commenced after 23 October 2014.

[5] Inserted by FA14 s88(1)(a)(ii). Applies to a transaction which is commenced after 23 October 2014.

[6] Substituted by FA14 sched2(1). Applies to a transaction which is commenced after 23 October 2014.

[7] Inserted by FA14 s88(1)(a)(iii). Applies to a transaction which is commenced after 23 October 2014.

[8] Substituted by FA14 s88(1)(a)(iv). Applies to a transaction which is commenced after 23 October 2014.

[9] Substituted by FA14 s88(1)(a)(v). Applies to a transaction which is commenced after 23 October 2014.

[10] Deleted by FA14 s88(1)(a)(vi). Applies to a transaction which is commenced after 23 October 2014.

[11] Inserted by FA14 s88(1)(a)(vii). Applies to a transaction which is commenced after 23 October 2014.

[12] Substituted by FA14 s88(1)(a)(viii). Applies to a transaction which is commenced after 23 October 2014.
[13] Inserted by FA10 s149(1). Has effect as on and from 3 April 2010.

Note:

FA13 s97(1)(c) applies to—

(I) a promoter, in the case of any disclosable transaction in respect of which the relevant date falls on or after 13 February 2013, and

(II) a person referred to in section 817F, 817G or 817H(1) who enters into any transaction forming part of a disclosable transaction where the whole of the disclosable transaction is undertaken on or after 13 February 2013.

"disclosable transaction", "promoter" and "relevant date" have the same meaning as in Chapter 3 of Part 33.

Revenue Briefings

eBrief

eBrief No. 43/2010 – Mandatory Disclosure of Certain Transactions
eBrief No. 44/2010 – Mandatory Disclosure of Certain Transactions Consultation
eBrief No. 02/2011 – Mandatory Disclosure of Certain Transactions Regulations 2011 (S.I. No.7 of 2011)
eBrief No. 25/2011 – Mandatory Disclosure of Certain Transactions – Reminder

Cross References

From Section 817D

Section 616 Groups of companies: interpretation.
Section 817Q Regulations (Chapter 3).

To Section 817D

Section 817Q Regulations (Chapter 3).

817DA References to 'specified description'— classes of transaction for purposes of that expression

[(1) For the purposes of this Chapter, unless the context otherwise requires, a reference to a specified description shall be construed as a reference to a class of transaction to which any of *subsections (2)* to *(10)* applies.

(2) This subsection applies to a transaction, or any part of a transaction, where, but for the provisions of this Chapter, a promoter or person would, or might reasonably be expected to, wish to keep the transaction or any element of the transaction (including the way in which the transaction is structured) which gives rise to the tax advantage expected to be obtained, confidential from—

(a) the Revenue Commissioners, at any time after the specified date, and a purpose for doing so would be—

(i) to facilitate repeated or continued use of the same, or substantially the same, transaction in the future,

(ii) to prevent the Revenue Commissioners from using the information relating to the transaction to enquire into any return, or

(iii) to prevent the Revenue Commissioners from using the information relating to the transaction to withhold a refund or repayment of, or a payment of, any amount claimed separately from a return under any of the provisions of the Acts,

(b) any other promoter, at any time after the specified date, and a purpose for doing so would be to maintain competitive advantage.

(3) (a) This subsection applies to a transaction, or any part of a transaction, where it might reasonably be expected that a promoter, or a person connected (within the meaning of *section 10*) with a promoter, of transactions that are the same as, or substantially the same as, the transaction concerned, would,

but for the requirements of this Chapter, be able to obtain a premium fee from, or charge a premium fee to, a person implementing such transaction, being a person experienced in receiving services of the type being provided.

(b) For the purposes of this subsection—

'*premium fee*', in relation to a transaction, means a fee chargeable by virtue of the transaction from which the tax advantage expected to be obtained arises and which is—

(i) to a significant extent attributable to that tax advantage, or

(ii) to any extent contingent upon the obtaining of that tax advantage;

'*fee*', in relation to a transaction, includes any consideration, in whatever form, which is attributable to the provision of the transaction, whether the consideration is provided directly or indirectly.

(4) (a) This subsection applies to a transaction, or any part of a transaction, which is a standardised tax product.

(b) For the purposes of this subsection, a transaction is a standardised tax product if a promoter makes, or intends to make, the transaction available for implementation by more than one person and the transaction is—

(i) one which has, or is intended to have standardised, or substantially standardised, documentation—

(I) the purpose of which is to enable the implementation, by a person, of the transaction, and

(II) the form of which is determined by the promoter and not tailored, to any material extent, to reflect the circumstances of the person implementing the transaction,

and

(ii) one which requires the person implementing it to enter into a specific transaction, or series of transactions, that are standardised, or substantially standardised, in form.

(c) Notwithstanding *paragraphs (a)* and *(b)* and without prejudice to *subsection (2)* or *(3)*, a transaction shall not be a standardised tax product where it is a transaction of a kind specified in the Schedule to regulations made under *section 817Q*.

(5) This subsection applies to a transaction, or any part of a transaction, where the promoter expects more than one individual to implement the same, or substantially the same, transaction and the transaction is such that an informed observer, having examined it, could reasonably conclude—

(a) that a main outcome of the transaction that could be expected for some or all of the individuals participating in it is the provision of losses, and

(b) that those individuals would be expected to use such losses to reduce their liability to income tax or capital gains tax.

(6) (a) This subsection applies to a transaction, or any part of a transaction, where one of the parties to the transaction is a company that has, or expects to have, unrelieved losses at the end of an accounting period and an informed observer, having examined the transaction, could reasonably conclude that a main benefit of the transaction is—

(i) that the company transfers those losses to another party who would be expected to use them to reduce its corporation tax liability, or

(ii) that the company is able to use those losses to reduce its corporation tax liability.

(b) For the purposes of this subsection, 'unrelieved losses at the end of an accounting period' means trading losses in respect of which relief could not have been given (but for the transaction) for that, or any previous, accounting period.

(7) (a) This subsection applies to a transaction, or any part of a transaction, where a tax advantage is obtained, or might be expected to be obtained, by virtue of a transaction, or any part of a transaction, by way of a reduction in, or deferment of, liability to tax, by the employer or the employee or by any other person by reason of the employee's employment—

(i) where the tax advantage relates to employment income, in any year of assessment, or

(ii) in any other case, in any period of account.

(b) For the purposes of this subsection 'employment income' means salaries, fees, wages, perquisites, benefits or profits (by whatever name called, including expenses) from an office or employment.

(c) Notwithstanding *paragraph (a)* and without prejudice to *subsection (2)* or *(3)*, a transaction shall not be a transaction of a kind described in this subsection where it is a transaction of a kind specified in the Schedule to regulations made under *section 817Q*.

(8) (a) This subsection applies to a transaction where, as a consequence of the transaction, or part of the transaction, a person who would otherwise incur, or be expected to incur, a liability to income tax in any tax year, will—

(i) incur, or be expected to incur, a lesser or nil liability to income tax chargeable in that year, and

(ii) acquire an asset, the disposal of which would, in principle, give rise to a chargeable gain.

(b) For the purposes of *paragraph (a)* a chargeable gain includes a gain on the disposal of assets that are exempt from capital gains tax or relieved from capital gains tax under any of the provisions of the Acts.

(c) Notwithstanding *paragraph (a)* and without prejudice to *subsection (2)* or *(3)*, a transaction shall not be a transaction of a kind described in this subsection where it is a transaction of a kind specified in the Schedule to regulations made under *section 817Q*.

(9) This subsection applies to a transaction where, as a consequence of the transaction, or part of a transaction, a person who would otherwise incur, or be expected to incur, a liability to income tax in any tax year will—

(a) incur, or be expected to incur, a lesser or nil liability to income tax chargeable in that year, and

(b) be deemed to take a gift by virtue of *section 5(1)* of the Capital Acquisitions Tax Consolidation Act 2003.

(10) (a) This subsection applies to a transaction, or part of a transaction, where a party to that transaction is a trustee of a discretionary trust.

(b) Notwithstanding *paragraph (a)* and without prejudice to *subsection (2)* or *(3)*, a transaction shall not be a transaction of a kind described in this subsection where it is a transaction of a kind specified in the Schedule to regulations made under *section 817Q*.][1]

Amendments

[1] Inserted by FA14 s88(1)(b). Applies to a transaction which is commenced after 23 October 2014.

817E Duties of promoter

[Subject to this Chapter, a promoter shall—

(a) within 5 working days after the specified date, provide the Revenue Commissioners with specified information relating to any disclosable transaction, and

(b) provide any person—

  (i) to whom the promoter has made a disclosable transaction available for implementation, or

  (ii) who markets or seeks to market the disclosable transaction,

with the transaction number for that disclosable transaction within 5 working days after receipt of the transaction number from the Revenue Commissioners or within 5 working days after making the scheme available to the person, whichever is the later.][1]

Amendments

[1] Substituted by FA14 s88(1)(c). Applies to a transaction which is commenced after 23 October 2014.

Revenue Briefings

eBrief

eBrief No. 02/2011 – Mandatory Disclosure of Certain Transactions Regulations 2011 (S.I. No.7 of 2011)

Cross References

To Section 817E

Section 817G Duty of person where there is no promoter.
Section 817H Duty of person where legal professional privilege claimed.
Section 817K Supplemental information.
Section 817M Duty of promoter to provide client list.
Section 817O Penalties.

817F Duty of person where promoter is outside the State

[Any person who enters into any transaction [which is or forms][1] part of any disclosable transaction in relation to which—

(a) a promoter is outside the State, and

(b) no promoter is in the State,

shall, within [5 working days after the specified date][2], provide the Revenue Commissioners with specified information relating to the disclosable transaction.][3]

Amendments

[1] Substituted by FA14 sched2(2). Applies to a transaction which is commenced after 23 October 2014.

[2] Substituted by FA14 sched2(3). Applies to a transaction which is commenced after 23 October 2014.

[3] Inserted by FA10 s149(1). Has effect as on and from 3 April 2010.

Revenue Briefings

eBrief

eBrief No. 02/2011 – Mandatory Disclosure of Certain Transactions Regulations 2011 (S.I. No.7 of 2011)

Cross References

To Section 817F

Section 817G Duty of person where there is no promoter.
Section 817K Supplemental information.
Section 817O Penalties.

817G Duty of person where there is no promoter

[Any person who enters into any transaction [which is or forms][1] part of a disclosable transaction as respects which neither that person nor any other person in the State has an obligation to comply with *section 817E* or *817F* shall within [30 working days after the specified date][2] provide the Revenue Commissioners with specified information relating to the disclosable transaction.][3]

Amendments

[1] Substituted by FA14 sched2(4). Applies to a transaction which is commenced after 23 October 2014.

[2] Substituted by FA14 sched2(5). Applies to a transaction which is commenced after 23 October 2014.

[3] Inserted by FA10 s149(1). Has effect as on and from 3 April 2010.

Revenue Briefings

eBrief

eBrief No. 02/2011 – Mandatory Disclosure of Certain Transactions Regulations 2011 (S.I. No.7 of 2011)

Cross References

From Section 817G

Section 817E Duties of promoter.
Section 817F Duty of person where promoter is outside the State.

To Section 817G

Section 817I Pre-disclosure enquiry.
Section 817K Supplemental information.
Section 817O Penalties.

817H Duty of person where legal professional privilege claimed

[(1) Any person who enters into a transaction [which is or forms][1] part of a disclosable transaction as respects which the promoter, by virtue of *section 817J*, does not comply with *section 817E*, shall within [5 working days after the specified date][2], provide the Revenue Commissioners with specified information relating to the disclosable transaction.

(2) A promoter who by virtue of *section 817J* does not comply with *section 817E* shall inform each person to whom the promoter has made the disclosable transaction available for implementation of the obligations placed on that person by virtue of *subsection (1)*.

(3) A promoter who by virtue of *section 817J* does not comply with *section 817E* shall inform the Revenue Commissioners accordingly within [5 working days after the specified date][3].][4]

Amendments

[1] Substituted by FA14 sched2(6). Applies to a transaction which is commenced after 23 October 2014.

[2] Substituted by FA14 sched2(7). Applies to a transaction which is commenced after 23 October 2014.

[3] Substituted by FA14 sched2(8). Applies to a transaction which is commenced after 23 October 2014.

[4] Inserted by FA10 s149(1). Has effect as on and from 3 April 2010.

Case Law

Prudential plc & Anor, R (on the application of) v Special Commissioner of Income Tax & Anor 2013 UKSC 1 – the UK Supreme Court considered whether Legal Advice Privilege extends, or should be extended to apply to legal advice given by someone other than a member of the legal profession.

Revenue Briefings

eBrief

eBrief No. 02/2011 – Mandatory Disclosure of Certain Transactions Regulations 2011 (S.I. No.7 of 2011)

Cross References

From Section 817H

Section 817E Duties of promoter.
Section 817J Legal professional privilege.

To Section 817H

Section 817K Supplemental information.
Section 817O Penalties.

817HA Duty of person who obtains tax advantage

[(1) Any person who obtains or seeks to obtain a tax advantage from a disclosable transaction shall be a chargeable person for the purposes of *Part 41A*.

(2) A person who enters into any transaction which is or forms part of a disclosable transaction shall, in a timely manner, provide any other person who obtains or seeks to obtain a tax advantage from that disclosable transaction with the transaction number for that disclosable transaction so as to allow that person comply with their obligations under this section.

(3) A person who obtains or seeks to obtain a tax advantage from a disclosable transaction shall include the transaction number relating to the disclosable transaction in the return, within the meaning of *Part 41A*, for any chargeable period, within the meaning of *Part 41A*, in which the person—

(a) entered into any transaction which is or forms part of a disclosable transaction, or

(b) obtains, or seeks to obtain, a tax advantage from the disclosable transaction.

(4) Where a person who obtains or seeks to obtain a tax advantage from a disclosable transaction which was not assigned a transaction number, or where that person was not provided with a transaction number, then that person shall be deemed to have complied with the obligation under *subsection (3)* if that person—

(a) did not have an obligation to disclose that transaction under *section 817F*, *817G* or *817H*,

(b) provides a Revenue officer with the specified information in relation to that transaction, and

(c) without unreasonable delay, provides a Revenue officer with any other information that the officer may reasonably require for the purposes of deciding if an application should be made to the relevant court under *section 817O(3)(a)*.][1]

Amendments

[1] Inserted by FA14 s88(1)(d). Applies to a transaction which is commenced after 23 October 2014.

817HB Duty of Revenue Commissioners

[(1) Subject to *subsection (2)*, where the Revenue Commissioners receive specified information in relation to a disclosable transaction under *section 817E*, *817F*, *817G*, *817H* or *817L* they shall, within 90 days after such receipt—

(a) assign a unique transaction number to the disclosable transaction and notify the promoter, or the person who entered into the transaction, as the case may be, of that transaction number, or

(b) determine whether or not the transaction was a disclosable transaction and notify the promoter, or person who entered into the transaction, as the case may be, accordingly.

(2) Where the Revenue Commissioners request supplemental information in relation to a transaction under *section 817K*, the reference in 35 *subsection (1)* to 90 days after receipt of the specified information shall be construed as a reference to 90 days after the day on which the Revenue Commissioners receive all such supplemental information.][1]

Amendments

[1] Inserted by FA14 s88(1)(d). Applies to a transaction which is commenced after 23 October 2014.

817I Pre-disclosure enquiry

[(1) Where the Revenue Commissioners have reasonable grounds for believing that—

(a) a person is the promoter of a transaction that may be a disclosable transaction, or

(b) a person has entered into a transaction that may form part of a disclosable transaction, which if it were such a transaction would require the person to comply with *section 817G*,

the Commissioners may by written notice (in this Chapter referred to as a "*pre-disclosure enquiry*") require the person to state—

(i) whether, in that person's opinion, the transaction is a disclosable transaction, and

(ii) if in that person's opinion the transaction is not considered to be a disclosable transaction, the reasons for that opinion.

(2) A notice under *subsection (1)* shall specify the transaction to which it relates.

(3) The reasons referred to in *subsection (1)(ii)* (in this Chapter referred to as a "*statement of reasons*") shall demonstrate, by reference to this Chapter and regulations made under it, why the person holds the opinion that the transaction is not a disclosable transaction and, in particular, if the person asserts that the transaction does not fall within any specified description, the reasons shall provide sufficient information to enable the Revenue Commissioners to affirm the assertion.

(4) For the purposes of this section, it is not sufficient for the person to state that they have received an opinion given by a barrister or solicitor or a person referred to in *subparagraph (i)* or *(ii)* of *section 817P(5)(a)* to the effect that the transaction is not a disclosable transaction.

(5) A person to whom the Revenue Commissioners have issued a notice under *subsection (1)* shall comply with the notice within the period of time specified in the notice, not being less than 21 days from the date of the notice, or such longer period as the Commissioners may agree.][1]

Amendments

[1] Inserted by FA10 s149(1). Has effect as on and from 3 April 2010.

Revenue Briefings

eBrief

eBrief No. 02/2011 – Mandatory Disclosure of Certain Transactions Regulations 2011 (S.I. No.7 of 2011)

Cross References

From Section 817I

Section 817G Duty of person where there is no promoter.
Section 817P Appeal Commissioners.

To Section 817I

Section 817O Penalties.
Section 817P Appeal Commissioners.

817J Legal professional privilege

[Nothing in this Chapter shall be construed as requiring a promoter to disclose to the Revenue Commissioners information with respect to which a claim to legal professional privilege could be maintained by that promoter in legal proceedings.][1]

Amendments

[1] Inserted by FA10 s149(1). Has effect as on and from 3 April 2010.

Revenue Briefings

eBrief

eBrief No. 02/2011 – Mandatory Disclosure of Certain Transactions Regulations 2011 (S.I. No.7 of 2011)

Cross References

To Section 817J

Section 817H Duty of person where legal professional privilege claimed.

817K Supplemental information

[(1) Where a person has provided the Revenue Commissioners with information in purported compliance with *section 817E, 817F, 817G* or *817H(1)* and the Commissioners have reasonable grounds for believing that the person has not provided all of the specified information, the Commissioners may by notice in writing require the person to provide the information, specified in the notice, that the Commissioners have reasonable grounds for believing form part of the specified information.

(2) Where a person has provided the Revenue Commissioners with specified information in compliance with *section 817E, 817F, 817G* or *817H(1)* the Commissioners may by notice in writing require the person to provide such other information about,

or documents relating to, the disclosable transaction, as the Commissioners may reasonably require in support of or in explanation of the specified information.

(3) A person to whom the Revenue Commissioners have issued a notice under *subsection (1)* or *(2)* shall comply with the notice within the period of time specified in the notice, not being less than 21 days from the date of the notice, or such longer period as the Commissioners may agree.][1]

Amendments

[1] Inserted by FA10 s149(1). Has effect as on and from 3 April 2010.

Revenue Briefings

eBrief

eBrief No. 02/2011 – Mandatory Disclosure of Certain Transactions Regulations 2011 (S.I. No.7 of 2011)

Cross References

From Section 817K

Section 817E Duties of promoter.
Section 817F Duty of person where promoter is outside the State.
Section 817G Duty of person where there is no promoter.
Section 817H Duty of person where legal professional privilege claimed.

To Section 817K

Section 817O Penalties.
Section 817P Appeal Commissioners.

817L Duty of marketer to disclose

[(1) Where the Revenue Commissioners have reason to believe that a person is a marketer in relation to a transaction that may be a disclosable transaction, the Commissioners may by written notice require the person to provide the Commissioners with the name, address and, where known to the person, the tax reference number of each person who has provided that person with any information in relation to the transaction.

(2) A notice under subsection (1) shall specify the transaction to which it relates.

(3) A person to whom the Revenue Commissioners have issued a notice under *subsection (1)* shall comply with the notice within the period of time specified in the notice, not being less than 21 days from the date of the notice or such longer period as the Commissioners may agree.][1]

[(4) (a) Where a person is a marketer of a transaction that it would be reasonable to consider is a disclosable transaction and the promoter of that transaction has not provided the marketer with a transaction number for that transaction in accordance with *section 817E*, then within 30 working days from making the first marketing contact in relation to that transaction, the marketer shall provide the Revenue Commissioners with—

(i) the name and address of the promoter of the transaction,

(ii) details of the transaction, and

(iii) all materials, whether provided by the promoter or otherwise, used to make a marketing contact in relation to the transaction.

(b) Where a marketer provides information to Revenue in accordance with this subsection, then this shall be wholly without prejudice as to whether or not the transaction is a disclosable transaction.][2]

Amendments

[1] Inserted by FA10 s149(1). Has effect as on and from 3 April 2010.

[2] Inserted by FA14 s88(1)(e). Applies to a transaction which is commenced after 23 October 2014.

Revenue Briefings

eBrief

eBrief No. 02/2011 – Mandatory Disclosure of Certain Transactions Regulations 2011 (S.I. No.7 of 2011)

Cross References

To Section 817L

Section 817O Penalties.

817M Duty of promoter to provide client list

[(1) A person who is a promoter shall, subject to *subsection (2)*, in relation to each disclosable transaction in respect of which specified information has been provided by that promoter under *section 817E*, provide to the Revenue Commissioners—][1]

[(a) within the period of 30 days beginning on the day after the day on which—

(i) the promoter first makes the transaction concerned available to a person for implementation, or

(ii) in a case where the relevant date is the date referred to in *paragraph (c)* of the definition of 'relevant date', the promoter first becomes aware of any transaction which is or forms part of the disclosable transaction having been implemented,

and

(b) subject to *subsection (3)*, within the period of 5 days beginning on the day after the end of each quarter thereafter,][2]

the name, address and, where known to the person, the tax reference number of each person to whom that person has made the disclosable transaction available for implementation (in this Chapter referred to as the "*client list*").

[(2) A client list provided to the Revenue Commissioners under *paragraph (a)* or *(b)*, as the case may be, of *subsection (1)* shall not include the name, address or tax reference number of any person to whom the promoter has made the disclosable transaction available for implementation where the promoter is satisfied, at the time of providing the client list, that such person has not entered into any transaction forming part of the disclosable transaction.][3][4]

[(3) *Subsection (1)(b)* shall not apply to a quarter during which the promoter—

(a) has not made the disclosable transaction available to a person for implementation, or

(b) has provided the Revenue Commissioners with a client list in accordance with *subsection (1)(a)* and has not made the disclosable transaction available to any other person for implementation in the period from the date the client list was provided to the Revenue Commissioners to the last day of the quarter concerned.

(4) A client list required to be provided to the Revenue Commissioners in accordance with *subsection (1)(b)* (in this subsection referred to as the 'latest client list') shall not include the name, address and tax reference number of any person who has been included in a client list in respect of the disclosable transaction to which the latest client list relates, in any preceding quarter.][5]

Amendments

[1] Substituted by FA11 s72(1)(a) and (b). Applies as on and from 21 January 2011.

[2] Substituted by FA14 s88(1)(f)(i). Applies to a transaction which is commenced after 23 October 2014.

[3] Inserted by FA11 s72(1)(c). Applies as on and from 21 January 2011.

[4] Inserted by FA10 s149(1). Has effect as on and from 3 April 2010.

[5] Inserted by FA14 s88(1)(f)(ii). Applies to a transaction which is commenced after 23 October 2014.

Revenue Briefings

eBrief

eBrief No. 02/2011 – Mandatory Disclosure of Certain Transactions Regulations 2011 (S.I. No.7 of 2011)

Cross References

From Section 817M

Section 817E Duties of promoter.

Section 817Q Regulations (Chapter 3).

To Section 817M

Section 817O Penalties.

817N Supplemental matters

[(1) Where a promoter provides the Revenue Commissioners with specified information relating to a disclosable transaction and the client list in respect of that disclosable transaction, the provision of that information shall, as respects any person included on the client list who implements the transaction, be wholly without prejudice as to [whether or not the disclosable transaction concerned was a tax avoidance transaction within the meaning of *section 811C*.][1]

(2) Where a person, other than a promoter, provides the Revenue Commissioners with specified information relating to a disclosable transaction the person shall be treated as making that information available wholly without prejudice as to [whether or not the disclosable transaction concerned was a tax avoidance transaction within the meaning of *section 811C*.][2]

(3) Where a person provides the Revenue Commissioners with specified information relating to a disclosable transaction, the provision of that information shall not be regarded as being, or being equivalent to, the delivery of a protective notification by that person in relation to the transaction for the purposes of *section* [*811A or 811D*][3].

(4) Nothing in this Chapter shall be construed as preventing the Revenue Commissioners from—

(a) making any enquiry, or

(b) taking any action, at any time in connection with [*section 811, 811A, 811C or 811D*][4].][5]

Amendments

[1] Substituted by FA14 s88(1)(g)(i). Applies to a transaction which is commenced after 23 October 2014.

[2] Substituted by FA14 s88(1)(g)(ii). Applies to a transaction which is commenced after 23 October 2014.

[3] Substituted by FA14 s88(1)(g)(iii). Applies to a transaction which is commenced after 23 October 2014.

[4] Substituted by FA14 s88(1)(g)(iv). Applies to a transaction which is commenced after 23 October 2014.

[5] Inserted by FA10 s149(1). Has effect as on and from 3 April 2010.

Revenue Briefings

eBrief

eBrief No. 02/2011 – Mandatory Disclosure of Certain Transactions Regulations 2011 (S.I. No.7 of 2011)

Cross References

From Section 817N

Section 811 Transactions to avoid liability to tax.

Section 811A Transactions to avoid liability to tax: surcharge, interest and protective notification.

817O Penalties

[(1) A person who fails to comply with any of the obligations imposed on that person by this Chapter and any regulations made under it shall—

(a) where the failure relates to the obligation imposed on a person under *section 817H(2), [817H(3), 817HA(2), 817I,]*[1] *817K(2), 817L* or *817M*, be liable to—

(i) a penalty not exceeding €4,000, and

(ii) if the failure continues after a penalty is imposed under *subparagraph (i)* to a further penalty of €100 per day for each day on which the failure continues after the day on which the penalty is imposed [under that subparagraph,][2]

(b) where the failure relates to the obligation imposed on a person under *section 817E, 817F, 817G* or *817H(1)*, be liable to—

(i) a penalty not exceeding €500 for each day during the initial period, and

(ii) if the failure continues after a penalty is imposed under *subparagraph (i)* to a further penalty of €500 per day for each day on which the failure continues after the day on which the penalty is imposed under that [subparagraph,]

and

(c) where the failure relates to the obligation imposed on a person under *section 817HA(3)*, be liable to a penalty not exceeding €5,000.][3]

(2) In *subsection (1)(b)*—

"*the initial period*" means the period—

(a) beginning on the relevant day, and

(b) ending on the day on which an application referred to in *subsection (3)* is made;

"*relevant day*" means the first day after the specified period.

(3) (a) Notwithstanding *section 1077B*, the Revenue Commissioners shall, in relation to a failure referred to in *subsection (1)*, make an application to the relevant court for that court to determine whether the person named in the application has failed to comply with the obligation imposed on that person by a section referred to in [*subsection (1)(a), (b) or (c)*][4], as the case may be.

(b) In *paragraph (a)* "*relevant court*" means the District Court, the Circuit Court or the High Court, as appropriate, by reference to the jurisdictional limits for civil matters laid down in the Courts of Justice Act 1924, as amended, and the Courts (Supplemental Provisions) Act 1961, as amended.

(4) A copy of any application under *subsection (3)* shall be issued to the person to whom the application relates.

(5) The relevant court shall determine whether the person named in the application referred to in *subsection (3)* is liable to the penalty provided for in *subsection (1)* and the amount of that penalty, and in determining the amount of the penalty the court shall have regard to *paragraph (a)* or *(b)* of *subsection (6)*, as the case may be.

(6) In determining the amount of a penalty under *subsection (5)* the court shall have regard—

(a) in the case of a person who is a promoter, to the amount of any fees received, or likely to have been received, by the person in connection with the disclosable transaction, and

(b) in any other case, to the amount of any tax advantage gained, or sought to be gained, by the person from the disclosable transaction.

(7) *Section 1077C* shall apply for the purposes of a penalty under *subsection (1)*.

[...]][5][6]

Amendments

[1] Substituted by FA14 s88(1)(h)(i)(I). Applies to a transaction which is commenced after 23 October 2014.

[2] Substituted by FA14 s88(1)(h)(i)(II). Applies to a transaction which is commenced after 23 October 2014.

[3] Substituted by FA14 s88(1)(h)(ii). Applies to a transaction which is commenced after 23 October 2014.

[4] Substituted by FA14 s88(1)(h)(iii). Applies to a transaction which is commenced after 23 October 2014.

[5] Deleted by FA14 s88(1)(h)(iv). Applies to a transaction which is commenced after 23 October 2014.

[6] Inserted by FA10 s149(1). Has effect as on and from 3 April 2010.

Revenue Briefings

eBrief

eBrief No. 02/2011 – Mandatory Disclosure of Certain Transactions Regulations 2011 (S.I. No.7 of 2011)

Cross References

From Section 817O

Section 817E Duties of promoter.
Section 817F Duty of person where promoter is outside the State.
Section 817G Duty of person where there is no promoter.
Section 817H Duty of person where legal professional privilege claimed.
Section 817I Pre-disclosure enquiry.
Section 817K Supplemental information.
Section 817L Duty of marketer to disclose.
Section 817M Duty of promoter to provide client list.
Section 1077B Penalty notifications and determinations.
Section 1077C Recovery of penalties.
Section 1077D Proceedings against executor, administrator or estate.

817P Appeal Commissioners

[(1) The Revenue Commissioners may, by notice in writing, make an application to the Appeal Commissioners for a determination in relation to any of the following matters—

(a) requiring information or documents to be made available by a person in support of a statement of reasons (to the effect that a transaction is not a disclosable transaction) given by that person to the Revenue Commissioners in compliance with a notice under *section 817I*,

(b) requiring information, that the Revenue Commissioners have reasonable grounds for believing forms part of the specified information relating to a disclosable transaction, to be made available by a person to the Revenue Commissioners, following the failure of the person to comply with a notice under *section 817K(1)*,

(c) requiring information about, or documents relating to, a disclosable transaction to be made available by a person to the Revenue Commissioners, following the failure of the person to comply with a notice under *section 817K(2)*,

(d) that a transaction is to be treated as a disclosable transaction, or

(e) that a transaction is a disclosable transaction.

(2) On the hearing of an application made—

(a) on the grounds referred to in *subsection (1)(a)*, the Appeal Commissioners shall determine the application by ordering if they—

(i) consider that the information or documents should be so made available, that the information or documents should be so made available,

(ii) consider that the information or documents should not be so made available, that the information or documents should not be so made available,

(b) on the grounds referred to in *subsection (1)(b)*, the Appeal Commissioners shall determine the application by ordering if they—

(i) consider that the Revenue Commissioners have reasonable grounds for so believing, that the information be so made available to the Revenue Commissioners,

(ii) consider that the Revenue Commissioners do not have reasonable grounds for so believing, that the information not be made available to the Revenue Commissioners,

(c) on the grounds referred to in *subsection (1)(c)*, the Appeal Commissioners shall determine the application by ordering if they—

(i) consider that the information or documents (or, as the case may be, a part of that information or some of those documents) should be so made available, that the information or documents (or, as the case may be, a part of that information or some of those documents) should be so made available,

(ii) consider that the information or documents should not be so made available, that the information or documents should not be so made available,

(d) on the grounds referred to in *subsection (1)(d)*, the Appeal Commissioners shall determine the application by ordering if they—

(i) are satisfied that the Revenue Commissioners have taken all reasonable steps to establish whether the transaction is a disclosable transaction and have reasonable grounds for believing that the transaction may be disclosable, that the transaction is to be treated as a disclosable transaction,

(ii) are not satisfied that the Revenue Commissioners have taken all reasonable steps to establish whether the transaction is a disclosable transaction or have reasonable grounds for believing that the transaction may be disclosable, that the transaction is not to be treated as a disclosable transaction,

(e) on the grounds referred to in *subsection (1)(e)*, the Appeal Commissioners shall determine the application by ordering if they—

(i) are satisfied that the transaction is a disclosable transaction, that it is a disclosable transaction,

(ii) are satisfied that the transaction is not a disclosable transaction, that it is not a disclosable transaction.

(3) For the purposes of the hearing of an application made on the grounds referred to in *subsection (1)(d)*—

(a) reasonable steps may (but need not) include the making of a pre-disclosure enquiry or the making of an application by the Revenue Commissioners on the grounds referred to in *subsection (1)(a)*, and

(b) reasonable grounds for believing may include—

(i) the fact that the transaction falls within a specified description,

(ii) an attempt by the promoter to avoid or delay providing information or documents about the transaction on foot of a pre-disclosure enquiry or on foot of a determination of the Appeal Commissioners following the making of an application by the Revenue Commissioners on the grounds referred to in *subsection (1)(a)*,

(iii) the failure of the promoter to comply with a pre-disclosure enquiry or a determination of the Appeal Commissioners following the making of an application by the Revenue Commissioners on the grounds referred to in *subsection (1)(a)*, in relation to another transaction.

(4) An application under *subsection (1)* shall, with any necessary modifications, be heard by the Appeal Commissioners as if it were an appeal against an assessment to income tax.

[(5) Where the Appeal Commissioners make a determination in accordance with *paragraph (a)(i)*, *(b)(i)*, *(c)(i)*, *(d)(i)* or *(e)(i)*, as the case may be, of subsection (2)—

(a) the information or documents to be made available to the Revenue Commissioners by a person on foot of the determination (where the determination is made in accordance with *paragraph (a)(i)*, *(b)(i)* or *(c)(i)* of that subsection), or

(b) the specified information to be made available to the Revenue Commissioners by a person in consequence of the determination (where the determination is made in accordance with *paragraph (d)(i)* or *(e)(i)* of that subsection), shall be made available within the period of 5 days beginning on the day after the date of the determination.][1][2]

Amendments

[1] Substituted by FA14 s88(1)(i). Applies to a transaction which is commenced after 23 October 2014.

[2] Inserted by FA10 s149(1). Has effect as on and from 3 April 2010.

Revenue Briefings

eBrief

eBrief No. 02/11 – Mandatory Disclosure of Certain Transactions Regulations 2011 (S.I. No.7 of 2011)

Cross References

From Section 817P

Section 817I Pre-disclosure enquiry.

Section 817K Supplemental information.

To Section 817P

Section 817I Pre-disclosure enquiry.

817Q Regulations (Chapter 3)

[(1) The Revenue Commissioners may, with the consent of the Minister for Finance, make regulations—

[...][1]

(h) specifying the circumstances in which a person is not to be treated as a promoter in relation to a disclosable [transaction, and][2]

(i) specifying the procedure to be adopted in giving effect to this Chapter, in so far as such procedure is not otherwise provided for, and providing generally as to the administration of this Chapter including—

(i) the form and manner of delivery of information to be provided under the regulations, and

(ii) such supplemental and incidental matters as appear to the Revenue Commissioners to be [necessary, and][3]

[(j) specifying transactions which are not disclosable transactions.][4]

[...][5]

(3) Every regulation made under this section shall be laid before Dáil Éireann as soon as may be after it is made and, if a resolution annulling the regulation is passed by Dáil Éireann within the next 21 days on which Dáil Éireann has sat after the regulation is laid before it, the regulation shall be annulled accordingly but without prejudice to the validity of anything previously done under the regulation.][6]

Amendments

[1] Deleted by FA14 s88(1)(j)(i)(I). Applies to a transaction which is commenced after 23 October 2014.

[2] Substituted by FA14 s88(1)(j)(i)(II). Applies to a transaction which is commenced after 23 October 2014.

[3] Substituted by FA14 s88(1)(j)(i)(III). Applies to a transaction which is commenced after 23 October 2014.

[4] Inserted by FA14 s88(1)(j)(i)(IV). Applies to a transaction which is commenced after 23 October 2014.

[5] Deleted by FA14 s88(1)(j)(ii). Applies to a transaction which is commenced after 23 October 2014.

[6] Inserted by FA10 s149(1). Has effect as on and from 3 April 2010.

Revenue Briefings

eBrief

eBrief No. 02/2011 – Mandatory Disclosure of Certain Transactions Regulations 2011 (S.I. No.7 of 2011)

Cross References

From Section 817Q

Section 817D Interpretation and general (Chapter 3).

To Section 817Q

Section 817D Interpretation and general (Chapter 3).

Section 817M Duty of promoter to provide client list.

817R Nomination of Revenue Officers

[The Revenue Commissioners may nominate any of their officers to perform any acts and discharge any functions authorised by this Chapter and regulations made under it to be performed or discharged by the Revenue Commissioners, and references in this Chapter to the Revenue Commissioners shall with any necessary modifications be construed as including references to an officer so appointed.][1]

Amendments

[1] Inserted by FA10 s149(1). Has effect as on and from 3 April 2010.

CHAPTER 4

Payment Notices and Scheme Participants

817S Payment notices

[(1) In this Chapter—

'*assessment*' has the meaning given to it in *section 960A*;

'*disclosable transaction*' has the meaning given to it in *section 817D*;

'*Revenue officer*' means an officer of the Revenue Commissioners;

'*specified information*' has the meaning given to it in *section 817D*;

'*specific anti-avoidance provision*' means a provision specified in *Schedule 33*;

'*tax advantage*'—

(a) subject to *paragraph (b)*, has the meaning given to it in *section 817D*, or

(b) where this Chapter falls to be applied to a tax avoidance transaction, has the meaning given to it in *section 811C(1)*,

and a proposal for a transaction shall be construed accordingly;

'*tax avoidance transaction*' has the meaning given to it in *section 811C(1)*;

'*transaction*'—

(a) subject to *paragraph (b)*, has the meaning given to it in *section 817D*, or

(b) where this Chapter falls to be applied to a tax avoidance transaction, has the meaning given to it in *section 811C(1)*,

and a proposal for a transaction shall be construed accordingly;

'*transaction number*' has the meaning given to it in *section 817D*.

(2) This subsection applies where, as a result of a person entering into a transaction that is—

(a) a tax avoidance transaction,

(b) a disclosable transaction, or

(c) a transaction to which a specific anti-avoidance provision applies,

a Revenue officer makes or amends an assessment the effect of which is to deny or withdraw a tax advantage arising out of the transaction.

(3) Where—

(a) *subsection (2)* applies, and

(b) an assessment referred to in that subsection has been appealed to the Appeal Commissioners,

and—

(i) the Appeal Commissioners have determined the appeal, and

(ii) the Appeal Commissioners have made a determination other than one that the assessment should be reduced by the full amount of the tax advantage,

a Revenue officer may send, or cause to be sent, a notice (in this Chapter referred to as a 'payment notice') to the appellant requiring immediate payment of the amount stated in the payment notice.

(4) For the purpose of *subsection (3)*, the amount stated in the payment notice shall be the lower of—

(a) the amount charged by the assessment resulting from the denial or withdrawal of the tax advantage referred to in *subsection (2)*, or

(b) the tax that would be due and payable under an assessment if no notice was given under *section 941(2)* or *942(1)*.

(5) A person to whom a payment notice is sent shall pay the amount stated in a payment notice notwithstanding that that person may be entitled to require that, in relation to a determination referred to in *subsection (3)*—

(a) an appeal be reheard by a Judge of the Circuit Court, or

(b) the Appeal Commissioners state and sign a case for the opinion of the High Court.

(6) Where tax stated in a payment notice is paid and the assessment in respect of which the tax was paid subsequently becomes final and conclusive for a lower amount of tax than was paid—

(a) the amount overpaid shall be repaid with interest in accordance with *section 865A*, *section 159B* of the Stamp Duties Consolidation Act 1999, *section 105* of the Value-Added Tax Consolidation Act 2010 or *section 57(6)* of the Capital Acquisitions Tax Consolidation Act 2003, as if a valid claim to repayment was made on a day that is 93 days before the date payment was received by the Revenue Commissioners on foot of the payment notice, but no such repayment shall be made until such time as an assessment has become final and conclusive, and

(b) *section 865(4)*, *section 159A* of the Stamp Duties Consolidation Act 1999, *section 99(4)* of the Value-Added Tax Consolidation Act 2010 or *section 57(3)* of the Capital Acquisitions Tax Consolidation Act 2003 shall not apply in relation to any repayment to be made.

(7) *Section 960E(2)* shall apply as if a payment notice sent by a Revenue officer was a demand made by the Collector-General for tax that is due and payable.][1]

Amendments

[1] Inserted by FA14 s88(2).

817T Payment notices and scheme participants

[(1) In this section—

(a) a reference to a 'scheme' is a reference to a transaction to which *section 817S(2)* applies, and

(b) a reference to a 'scheme participant' is a reference to a person who enters into such transaction or a substantially similar transaction.

(2) For the purpose of this section, a transaction ('the second transaction') shall be the same transaction or substantially similar to another transaction ('the first transaction') where—

(a) *section 817S(3)* applies in relation to the first transaction and in the opinion of a Revenue officer, the provisions of the Acts or the principles and reasoning given by the Appeal Commissioners in making a determination in relation to the first transaction would, if applied in making a determination in an appeal against an assessment, being an assessment—

(i) made or amended by a Revenue officer in relation to the second transaction, and

(ii) the effect of which is to deny or withdraw a tax advantage arising out of the second transaction,

result in a determination other than one that that assessment should be reduced by the full amount of the tax advantage,

(b) both transactions were assigned the same transaction number under *section 817HB(1)(a)*,

(c) a transaction is one to which *section 817J* applies, and two or more transactions would have been assigned the same transaction number if they had been disclosed by a promoter under *section 817E* rather than by the person who entered into the transaction under *section 817H*, or

(d) specified information was not provided to the Revenue Commissioners and the transactions were not assigned a transaction number, but had they been assigned a transaction number, both transactions would have been assigned the same transaction number.

(3) Where a person to whom a Revenue officer may send, or cause to be sent, a payment notice under *section 817S(3)* is a scheme participant, a Revenue officer may send a payment notice to any other scheme participants notwithstanding that an assessment made in respect of those scheme participants has been appealed and the appeal has not yet been determined by the Appeal Commissioners.

(4) The payment notice referred to in *subsection (3)* shall—

(a) state the amount of the tax assessed on a scheme participant resulting from the denial or withdrawal of a tax advantage, having had regard to the determination referred to in *section 817S(3)*,

(b) state the transaction number, if any, which was assigned to the scheme,

(c) state the reasons why the transaction entered into by the scheme participant in receipt of the payment notice and the scheme participant who has received a determination from the Appeal Commissioners is the same or substantially similar, and

(d) have appended to it a copy of the determination.

(5) A scheme participant may request a Revenue officer to review the payment notice by submitting a notice (in this section referred to as a 'review notice') in

writing within 30 days from the payment notice giving reasons why the scheme participant does not consider a transaction entered into by that person to be the same as, or substantially similar to, the transaction in respect of which another scheme participant has received a payment notice under *section 817S(3)*.

(6) A Revenue officer shall consider a review notice received from a scheme participant and shall make a determination that either confirms or withdraws a payment notice.

(7) A scheme participant who is aggrieved by a determination referred to in *subsection (6)* may appeal the determination to the Appeal Commissioners by notice in writing to the Revenue officer within 30 days from the date of the determination, being a notice—

(a) that states the grounds for the appeal, and

(b) to which there is appended a copy of the determination.

(8) Where more than one scheme participant in the same scheme has submitted a notice of appeal under *subsection (7)*, the Appeal Commissioners may in adjudicating and determining an appeal if they consider it appropriate to do so—

(a) have regard to any determination previously made in respect of scheme participants,

(b) consolidate or hear together two or more appeals, or

(c) determine not to hold a hearing.

(9) The Appeal Commissioners' determination of an appeal made under *subsection (7)* shall be final and conclusive.

(10) Any obligation on the Revenue Commissioners to maintain secrecy or any other restriction on the disclosure of information by the Revenue Commissioners shall not apply with respect to the giving of a payment notice under *subsection (3)*.

(11) *Subsections (5)*, *(6)* and *(7)* of *section 817S* shall apply to a payment notice issued under this section as if it were a notice issued under *section 817S*.][1]

Amendments

[1] Inserted by FA14 s88(2).

PART 34

Provisions Relating to the Residence of Individuals

818 Interpretation (Part 34)

[FA94 s149]

In this Part other than in *section 825*—

"*the Acts*" means—

(a) the Tax Acts,

(b) the Capital Gains Tax Acts, and

(c) the Capital Acquisitions Tax Consolidation Act 2003, and the enactments amending or extending that Act,

and any instruments made thereunder;

["*authorised officer*" means an officer of the Revenue Commissioners;][1]

"*present in the State*", in relation to an individual, means the personal presence of the individual in the State;

"*tax*" means any tax payable in accordance with any provision of the Acts.

Amendments

[1] Substituted by FA08 s135.

Revenue Information Notes

Moving to Ireland Guide – Tax Residence

Coming to live in Ireland? A Guide to Irish Income Tax Liability based on some commonly asked questions.

Revenue Precedents

Revenue Precedents-Brief No. 3/2009 Finance (No 2) Act 2008 – Tax residence rules

Cross References

From Section 818

Section 818 Interpretation (Part 34).

Section 825 Residence treatment of donors of gifts to the State.

To Section 818

Section 2 Interpretation of Tax Acts.

Section 5 Interpretation of Capital Gains Tax Acts.

Section 472B Seafarer allowance, etc.

Section 710 Profits of life business.

Section 818 Interpretation (Part 34).

Section 825A Reduction in income tax for certain income earned outside the State.

Section 1104 Short title and construction.

819 Residence

[FA94 s150]

(1) For the purposes of the Acts, an individual shall be resident in the State for a year of assessment if the individual is present in the State—

(a) at any one time or several times in the year of assessment for a period in the whole amounting to [183 days][1] or more, or

(b) at any one time or several times—

(i) in the year of assessment, and

(ii) in the preceding year of assessment,

for a period (being a period comprising in the aggregate the number of days on which the individual is present in the State in the year of assessment and the number of days on which the individual was present in the State in the preceding year of assessment) in the aggregate amounting to [280 days][2] or more.

(2) Notwithstanding *subsection (1)(b)*, where for a year of assessment an individual is present in the State at any one time or several times for a period in the aggregate amounting to not more than [30 days][3]—

(a) the individual shall not be resident in the State for the year of assessment, and

(b) no account shall be taken of the period for the purposes of the aggregate mentioned in *subsection (1)(b)*.

(3) (a) Notwithstanding *subsections (1)* and *(2)*, an individual—

(i) who is not resident in the State for a year of assessment, and

(ii) to whom *paragraph (b)* applies,

may at any time elect to be treated as resident in the State for that year and, where an individual so elects, the individual shall for the purposes of the Acts be deemed to be resident in the State for that year.

(b) This paragraph shall apply to an individual who satisfies an authorised officer that the individual is in the State—

(i) with the intention, and

(ii) in such circumstances,

that the individual will be resident in the State for the following year of assessment.

[(4) For the purposes of this section—

(a) as respects the year of assessment 2008 and previous years of assessment, an individual shall be deemed to be present in the State for a day if the individual is present in the State at the end of the day, and

(b) as respects the year of assessment 2009 and subsequent years of assessment, an individual shall be deemed to be present in the State for a day if the individual is present in the State at any time during that day.][4]

Amendments

[1] Substituted by FA01 sched2(42)(a)(i). Shall apply only as respects the year of assessment 2001.

[2] Substituted by FA01 sched2(42)(a)(ii). Shall apply only as respects the year of assessment 2001 and the year of assessment 2002.

[3] Substituted by FA01 sched2(42)(b). Shall apply only as respects the year of assessment 2001.

[4] Substituted by F(No.2)A08 s15. This section is deemed to have come into force and takes effect as on and from 1 January 2009.

Case Law

The UK cases of Shepherd v Revenue & Customs Commissioners 2006 SpC 484 and Grace v Revenue and Customs Commissioners 2007 SpC 663 were brought to the Special Commissioner to conclude on the taxpayer's residence status. Both cases concerned pilots whose flying base was London airports. Both pilots had previously lived in the UK and both claimed to have ceased to be UK resident.

In Gaines-Cooper v R&C Commrs 2011 UKSC 47, This case examines the British residency rules and the UK tax authorities' guidance note which set out the circumstances in which an individual would or would not be treated as resident in the UK.

Revenue Briefings

eBrief

eBrief No. 3/2009 – Finance (No 2) Act 2008 – Tax Residence Rules

820 Ordinary residence

[FA94 s151]

(1) For the purposes of the Acts, an individual shall be ordinarily resident in the State for a year of assessment if the individual has been resident in the State for each of the 3 years of assessment preceding that year.

(2) An individual ordinarily resident in the State shall not for the purposes of the Acts cease to be ordinarily resident in the State for a year of assessment unless the individual has not been resident in the State in each of the 3 years of assessment preceding that year.

Case Law

In Gaines-Cooper v R&C Commrs 2011 UKSC 47, This case examines the British residency rules and the UK tax authorities' guidance note which set out the circumstances in which an individual would or would not be treated as resident in the UK.

Revenue Briefings

Tax Briefing

Tax Briefing July 1994 – Issue 15 – Residence of individuals
Tax Briefing No 1 1995 – Issue 17 pg 5 – Income Tax – Residence of individuals

eBrief

eBrief No. 3/2009 – Finance (No 2) Act 2008 – Tax Residence Rules

821 Application of sections 17 and 18(1) and Chapter 1 of Part 3

[FA94 s152; FA95 s169(1)]

(1) Where an individual is not resident but is ordinarily resident in the State, *sections 17* and *18(1)* and *Chapter 1* of *Part 3* shall apply as if the individual were resident in the State; but this section shall not apply in respect of—

(a) the income of an individual derived from one or more of the following—

(i) a trade or profession, no part of which is carried on in the State, and

(ii) an office or employment, all the duties of which are performed outside the State, and

(b) other income of an individual which in any year of assessment does not exceed [€3,810][1].

(2) In determining for the purposes of *subsection (1)* whether the duties of an office or employment are performed outside the State, any duties performed in the State, the performance of which is merely incidental to the performance of the duties of the office or employment outside the State, shall be treated as having been performed outside the State.

Amendments

[1] Substituted by FA01 sched5.

Revenue Briefings

Tax Briefing

Tax Briefing No 1 1995 – Issue 17 pg 5 – Income Tax – Ordinary residence
Tax Briefing February 1997 – Issue 25 pg 10 – Residence of individuals, section 152 Finance Act 1994

Revenue Precedents

Where the individual is chargeable to Irish tax by virtue of his/her ordinary residence status in Ireland, he/she may be 'fiscally domiciled' in Ireland, i.e. resident 'of' Ireland, for the purposes of a Double Taxation Convention, subject to tie breaker rules provided there is a 'fiscal domicile Article' within the relevant Double Taxation Convention. RT/364/94

Cross References

From Section 821

Section 17 Schedule C.
Section 32 Interpretation (Chapter 1).

822 Split year residence

[FA94 s153]

(1) For the purposes of a charge to tax on any income, profits or gains from an employment, where during a year of assessment (in this section referred to as "*the relevant year*")—

(a) (i) an individual who has not been resident in the State for the preceding year of assessment satisfies an authorised officer that the individual is in the State—

(I) with the intention, and

(II) in such circumstances,

that the individual will be resident in the State for the following year of assessment, or

(ii) an individual who is resident in the State satisfies an authorised officer that the individual is leaving the State, other than for a temporary purpose—

(I) with the intention, and

(II) in such circumstances,

that the individual will not be resident in the State for the following year of assessment,

and

(b) the individual would but for this section be resident in the State for the relevant year,

subsection (2) shall apply in relation to the individual.

(2) (a) An individual to whom *paragraphs (a)(i)* and *(b)* of *subsection (1)* apply shall be deemed to be resident in the State for the relevant year only from the date of his or her arrival in the State.

(b) An individual to whom *paragraphs (a)(ii)* and *(b)* of *subsection (1)* apply shall be deemed to be resident in the State for the relevant year only up to and including the date of his or her leaving the State.

(3) Where by virtue of this section an individual is resident in the State for part of a year of assessment, the Acts shall apply as if—

(a) income arising during that part of the year or, in a case to which *section 71(3)* applies, amounts received in the State during that part of the year were income arising or amounts received for a year of assessment in which the individual is resident in the State, and

(b) income arising or, as the case may be, amounts received in the remaining part of the year were income arising or amounts received in a year of assessment in which the individual is not resident in the State.

Revenue Briefings

Tax Briefing

Tax Briefing No 1 1995 – Issue 17 pg 5 – Income Tax – Split year treatment

eBrief

eBrief No. 52/2014 – USC – Split Year Residence, Payment of arrears and bonuses

Revenue Precedents

Return visits to Ireland for holidays will not affect the application of split year treatment, assuming of course that all the other conditions of section 822 TCA 1997 are satisfied. RT 300/94

An individual came to Ireland on 1 July 1994 to take up employment with an Irish subsidiary of a German company. He worked here for 1 week and then spent the following 3 months in Germany, finally returning to Ireland in October, 1994. His date of arrival for split year purposes was 1 July as he arrived in the State to take up employment with the intention and in such circumstances as to become permanently resident. RT 205/94

Cross References

From Section 822

Section 71 Foreign securities and possessions.

To Section 822

Section 472B Seafarer allowance, etc.

Section 823 Deduction for income earned outside the State.

Section 825A Reduction in income tax for certain income earned outside the State.

823 Deduction for income earned outside the State

[FA94 s154; FA95 s170(1)]

(1) In this section—

["*qualifying day*", in relation to an office or employment of an individual, means a day on or before 31 December 2003 which is one of at least 11 consecutive days throughout the whole of which the individual is absent from the State for the purposes of the performance of the duties of the office or employment or of those duties and the duties of other offices or employments of the individual outside the State and which (taken as a whole) are substantially devoted to the performance of such duties, but no day shall be counted more than once as a qualifying day;][1]

"*relevant period*", in relation to a year of assessment, means a continuous period of 12 months—

(a) part only of which is comprised in the year of assessment, and

(b) no part of which is comprised in another relevant period;

["*the specified amount*" in relation to an office or employment means an amount determined by the formula—

$$\frac{D \times E}{[365]^2}$$

where—

D is the number of qualifying days in relation to the office or employment in the year of assessment concerned, and

E is all the income, profits or gains from any office, employment or pension whether chargeable under Schedule D or E (including income from offices or employments the duties of which are performed in the State) of an individual in that year after deducting any contribution or qualifying premium in respect of which there is provision for a deduction under *section 774(7)* or *787* but excluding—

(a) any expense to which *section 118* applies,

(b) any amount treated as emoluments of an employment under *section 121(2)(b)(ii)* by virtue of a car being made available by reason of the employment,

(c) any sum treated for the purposes of *section 112* as a perquisite of an office or employment by virtue of *section 122*,

(d) any payment to which *section 123* applies,

(e) any sum deemed to be profits or gains arising or accruing from an office or employment by virtue of *section 127(2)*, or

(f) any gain to which *section 128* applies.][3]

(2) (a) Subject to *paragraph (b)*, this section shall apply to—

(i) an office of director of a company which is within the charge to corporation tax, or would be within the charge to corporation tax if it were resident in the State, and which carries on a trade or profession,

(ii) an employment other than—

(I) an employment the emoluments of which are paid out of the revenue of the State, or

(II) an employment with any board, authority or other similar body established by or under statute.

[(b) This section does not apply in any case where the income from an office or employment—

(i) is chargeable to tax in accordance with section 71(3), or

(ii) is income to which section 822 applies.][4]

[(2A) (a) In this subsection, "*qualifying employment*", "*qualifying individual*" and "*sea-going ship*" have the same meanings, respectively, as in *section 472B*.

(b) Where in any period of at least [11 consecutive days][5] in which a qualifying individual is absent from the State for the purposes of the performance of the duties of a qualifying employment, the sea-going ship on which he or she, in that period, performs those duties—

(i) visits a port in the United Kingdom, and

(ii) also visits a port other than a port in the State or in the United Kingdom,

then *subparagraph (ii)* of *subsection (2)(b)* shall not apply to the income, profits or gains from the qualifying employment for such period.][6]

(3) Where for any year of assessment an individual resident in the State makes a claim in that behalf to and satisfies an authorised officer that—

(a) the duties of an office or employment to which this section applies of the individual are performed wholly or partly outside the State, and

(b) either—

(i) the number of days in that year which are qualifying days in relation to the office or employment (together with any days which are qualifying days in relation to any other such office or employment of the individual), or

(ii) the number of such days referred to in *subparagraph (i)* in a relevant period in relation to that year,

amounts to at least 90 days [or, in the case where *subparagraph (i)* applies and the year of assessment concerned is the year of assessment 2001, 67 days][7],

there shall be deducted from the income, profits or gains from the office or employment to be assessed under Schedule D or E, as may be appropriate, an amount equal to the specified amount [in relation to that office or employment or the amount of the income, profits or gains .][8] [whichever is the lesser; but that amount, or the aggregate of those amounts where there is more than one such office or employment, shall not exceed [€31,750][9].][10]

(4) Notwithstanding anything in the Acts, the income, profits or gains from an office or employment shall for the purposes of this section be deemed not to include any amounts paid in respect of expenses incurred wholly, exclusively and necessarily in the performance of the duties of the office or employment.

Amendments

[1] Substituted by FA01 s31(1)(a)(i). Applies as on and from 26 January 2001.

[2] Substituted by FA01 s31(1)(a)(ii). Applies as respects the year of assessment 2001.

[3] Substituted by FA99 s21(1)(a). Applies as respects the year of assessment 1999-2000 and subsequent years of assessment.

[4] Substituted by FA08 s18(1)(b). Has effect as on and from 1 January 2008.

[5] Substituted by FA00 s47(1)(b). Shall apply as on and from 29 February 2000.

[6] Inserted by FA98 s14(1)(c).

[7] Inserted by FA01 s31(1)(b)(i).

[8] Inserted by FA99 s21(1)(b). Applies as respects the year of assessment 1998-99 to the extent that the income, profits or gains to be included in computing the specified amount accrues to an individual on or after the 10th day of March, 1999.

[9] Substituted by FA01 sched5.

[10] Substituted by FA00 s47(1)(c) applies (i) as respects the year of assessment 2000-2001 and subsequent years of assessment, and (ii) as respect the year of assessment 1999-2000, as if the reference to "that amount, or the aggregate of those amounts where there is more than one such office or employment" were a reference to "such portion of that amount, or such portion of the aggregate of those amounts where there is more than one such office or employment, which arises by virtue of income, profits or gains accuring or paid on or after 29 February 2000".

Case Law

When looking at a qualifying period for foreign earnings deduction, the question of non physical presence must be considered by looking at the current status of the individual and not his status in prior years. Carstairs (HMIT) v Sykes 2000 STC 1103

Revenue Briefings

Tax Briefing

Tax Briefing No 1 1995 – Issue 17 pg 8 – Income Tax Foreign Earnings Deduction
Tax Briefing April 1998 – Issue 31 pg 16 – Foreign Earnings Deduction Definition
Tax Briefing June 1999 – Issue 36 pg 15 – Foreign Earnings Deduction
Tax Briefing June 2000 – Issue 40 pg 11 – Foreign Earnings Deduction: Finance Act 2000 changes
Tax Briefing April 2001 – Issue 43 pg 16 – Finance Act 2001 Foreign Earnings Deduction

Cross References

From Section 823

Section 71 Foreign securities and possessions.
Section 112 Basis of assessment, persons chargeable and extent of charge.
Section 118 Benefits in kind: general charging provision.
Section 121 Benefit of use of car.
Section 122 Preferential loan arrangements.
Section 123 General tax treatment of payments on retirement or removal from office or employment.
Section 127 Tax treatment of restrictive covenants.
Section 128 Tax treatment of directors of companies and employees granted rights to acquire shares or other assets.
Section 472B Seafarer allowance, etc.
Section 774 Certain approved schemes: exemptions and reliefs.

Section 787 Nature and amount of relief for qualifying premiums.
Section 822 Split year residence.

To Section 823
Section 472B Seafarer allowance, etc.
Section 825A Reduction in income tax for certain income earned outside the State.

823A Deduction for income earned in certain foreign states

[(1) In this section—

'*qualifying day*', in relation to an office or employment of an individual, means a day on or after 1 January 2012 which is one of at least [3 consecutive days throughout the whole of which the individual is present in a relevant state for the purposes of the performance of the duties of the office or employment and where such consecutive days (taken as a whole) are substantially devoted to the performance of such duties, but no day shall be counted more than once as a qualifying day, and presence in a relevant state shall include the duration of time spent travelling directly from the State to a relevant state, and from a relevant state to the State or to another relevant state;][1]

'*relevant office or employment*' means an office or employment part of the duties of which are performed in a relevant state on a qualifying day;

'*relevant period*', in relation to a year of assessment, means a continuous period of 12 months part only of which is comprised in the year of assessment;

['*relevant state*' means, as regards the years of assessment 2012 to 2017, the Federative Republic of Brazil, the Russian Federation, the Republic of India, the People's Republic of China or the Republic of South Africa, and includes—

(a) as regards the years of assessment 2013 to 2017, the Arab Republic of Egypt, the People's Democratic Republic of Algeria, the Republic of Senegal, the United Republic of Tanzania, the Republic of Kenya, the Federal Republic of Nigeria, the Republic of Ghana and the Democratic Republic of the Congo, and

(b) as regards the years of assessment 2015 to 2017, Japan, the Republic of Singapore, the Republic of Korea, the Kingdom of Saudi Arabia, the United Arab Emirates, the State of Qatar, the Kingdom of Bahrain, the Republic of Indonesia, the Socialist Republic of Vietnam, the Kingdom of Thailand, the Republic of Chile, the Sultanate of Oman, the State of Kuwait, the United Mexican States and Malaysia;][2]

'*the specified amount*', in relation to a year of assessment and an individual, means an amount determined by the formula—

$$\frac{D \times E}{F}$$

where—

D is the number of qualifying days in the year of assessment in relation to the individual,

E is all the income, profits or gains that arise in the year of assessment from a relevant office or employment, whether chargeable under Schedule D or E, and includes so much of any gain to which *section 128* applies on which tax is payable in the State where such gain is realised by the exercise, assignment or release of a right obtained by the individual as an office holder or employee in the relevant office or employment, after deducting any contribution or qualifying premium in respect of which there is provision for a deduction under *section 774(7), 787, 787E* or *787N* but excluding—

(a) any expense to which *section 118* applies,

(b) any amount treated as emoluments of an employment under *section 121(2)(b)(ii)* by virtue of a car being made available by reason of the employment,

(c) any sum treated for the purposes of *section 112* as a perquisite of an office or employment by virtue of *section 122*,

(d) any payment to which *section 123* applies, or

(e) any sum deemed to be profits or gains arising or accruing from an office or employment by virtue of *section 127(2)*,

and

F is the aggregate number of days in the year of assessment that the individual held a relevant office or employment.

(2) (a) Subject to *paragraph (b)*, this section shall apply to—

(i) an office of director of a company which is within the charge to corporation tax, or would be within the charge to corporation tax if it were resident in the State, and which carries on a trade or profession,

(ii) an employment other than—

(I) an employment the emoluments of which are paid out of the revenue of the State, or

(II) an employment with any board, authority or other similar body established by or under statute.

(b) This section does not apply to income from an office or employment that—

(i) is chargeable to tax in accordance with *section 71(3)*, or

(ii) is income to which *section 472D, 822, 825A* or *825C* applies.

(3) Where for any year of assessment an individual resident in the State makes a claim in that behalf to and satisfies an authorised officer that either—

(a) the number of days in that year which are qualifying days in relation to an office or employment of the individual (together with any days which are qualifying days in relation to any other such office or employment of the individual), or

(b) the number of such days referred to in *paragraph (a)* in a relevant period in relation to that year and no part of which period is comprised in any other relevant period,

amounts to at least [60 days][3], there shall be deducted from the income, profits or gains of the individual from all offices or employments assessable under Schedule D or E, as may be appropriate, an amount equal to the specified amount in relation to that office or employment or those offices or employments but that amount, or the aggregate of those amounts where there is more than one such office or employment, shall not exceed €35,000.

(4) Notwithstanding anything in the Tax Acts, the income, profits or gains from an office or employment shall for the purposes of this section be deemed not to include any amounts paid in respect of expenses in respect of which a deduction would be due under *section 114*.

(5) Where for a year of assessment an individual is entitled to relief under *Part 35* for tax paid under the laws of a relevant state on the amount of income, profits or gains from a relevant office or employment attributable to the performance of the duties of the relevant office or employment on qualifying days in that relevant state, the specified amount shall be reduced by the amount of such income, profits or gains.][4]

[(6) This section shall continue to apply for the years of assessment 2015, 2016 and 2017.][5]

Amendments

[1] Substituted by FA14 s16(1)(a). Has effect for the years of assessment 2015, 2016 and 2017.

[2] Substituted by FA14 s16(1)(b).

[3] Substituted by FA14 s16(1)(c). Has effect for the years of assessment 2015, 2016 and 2017.

[4] Inserted by FA12 s12(1)(a). Applies as respects the years of assessment 2012, 2013 and 2014.

[5] Inserted by FA14 s16(1)(d).

Revenue Briefings

eBrief

eBrief No. 36/2012 – Deduction for income earned in certain foreign states (FED)

824 Appeals

[FA94 s156]

(1) An individual aggrieved by a decision of an authorised officer on any question arising under the provisions of this [Part][1] which require an individual to satisfy an authorised officer on such a question may, by notice in writing to that effect given to the authorised officer within 2 months from the date on which notice of the decision is given to the individual, make an application to have the question heard and determined by the Appeal Commissioners.

(2) Where an application is made under *subsection (1)*, the Appeal Commissioners shall hear and determine the question concerned in the like manner as an appeal made to them against an assessment, and the provisions of the Acts relating to such an appeal (including the provisions relating to the rehearing of an appeal and to the statement of a case for the opinion of the High Court on a point of law) shall apply accordingly with any necessary modifications.

Amendments

[1] Substituted by FA00 s160.

825 Residence treatment of donors of gifts to the State

[FA77 s53]

(1) In this section—

"*the Acts*" means—

(a) the Tax Acts,

(b) the Capital Gains Tax Acts, and

(c) the [Capital Acquisitions Tax Consolidation Act 2003][1];

"*donor*" means an individual who makes a gift to the State;

"*gift*" means a gift of property to the State which, on acceptance of the gift by the Government pursuant to the State Property Act, 1954, becomes vested pursuant to that Act in a State authority within the meaning of that Act;

"*Irish tax*" means any tax imposed by the Acts;

"*property*" includes interests and rights of any description;

"*relevant date*", in relation to an individual (being a donor or the spouse of a donor), means the date (not being earlier than the 1st day of September, 1974) on which the individual leaves the State for the purpose of residence (other than occasional residence) outside the State;

"*tax in that country*" means any tax imposed in that country which is identical with or substantially similar to Irish tax;

"*visits*" means—

(a) in relation to a donor, visits by the donor to the State after the relevant date for the purpose of advising on the management of the property which is the subject of the gift, being visits that are in the aggregate less than [182 days][2] in any year of assessment in which they are made, and

(b) in relation to the spouse of a donor, visits by that spouse when accompanying the donor on visits of the kind referred to in *paragraph (a)*.

(2) Where for any year of assessment a person (being a donor or the spouse of a donor) is resident in a country outside the State for the purposes of tax in that country and is chargeable to that tax without any limitation as to chargeability, then, notwithstanding anything to the contrary in the Tax Acts—

(a) as respects the year of assessment in which the relevant date occurs, that person shall not as from the relevant date be regarded as ordinarily resident in the State for the purposes of Irish tax, and

(b) as respects any subsequent year of assessment, in determining whether that person is resident or ordinarily resident in the State for the purposes of Irish tax, visits shall be disregarded.

[(3) This section ceases to have effect as respects a gift to the State made on or after 4 February 2010.][3]

Amendments

[1] Substituted by CATCA03 sched3.

[2] Substituted by FA01 sched2(44). Shall apply only as respects the year of assessment 2001.

[3] Inserted by FA10 s151. Has effect as on and from 3 April 2010.

Cross References

To Section 825

Section 818 Interpretation (Part 34).

825A Reduction in income tax for certain income earned outside the State

[(1) In this section—

"*authorised officer*" has the same meaning as in *section 818*;

"*proprietary director*" has the same meaning as in *section 472*;

"*qualifying employment*", in relation to a year of assessment, means an office (including an office of director of a company which would be within the charge to corporation tax if it were resident in the State, and which carries on a trade or profession) or employment which is held—

(a) outside the State in a territory with the Government of which arrangements are for the time being in force by virtue of [*826(1)*][1], and

(b) for a continuous period of not less than [13 weeks][2], but excluding any such office or employment—

(i) the emoluments of which are paid out of the revenue of the State,

(ii) with any board, authority or other similar body established in the State by or under statute;

"*the specified amount*" in relation to an individual means, as respects the year of assessment concerned, the amount of tax for that year determined by the formula—

$$\frac{A \times B}{C}$$

where—

A is the amount of tax which, apart from this section, would be chargeable on the individual for that year of assessment, other than tax charged in accordance with *section 16(2)*, and after taking account of any such reductions in tax as are specified in the provisions referred to in Part 2 of the Table to *section 458* but before credit for any foreign tax paid on any income, profits or gains assessed for that year,

B is the total income of the individual for that year but excluding any income, profits or gains from a qualifying employment for that year,

C is the total income of the individual for that year.

(2) This section shall not apply in any case where the income, profits or gains from a qualifying employment are—

(a) chargeable to tax in accordance with *section 71(3)*,

(b) income, profits or gains to which *section 822* applies, or

(c) income, profits or gains paid to a proprietary director or to the spouse of that person by a company of which that person is a proprietary director.

(3) Where for any year of assessment an individual resident in the State makes a claim in that behalf to an authorised officer and satisfies that officer that—

(a) he or she is in receipt of income, profits or gains from a qualifying employment,

(b) the duties of that qualifying employment are performed wholly outside the State in a territory, or territories, with the Government or Governments of which arrangements are for the time being in force by virtue of [*section 826(1)*][3],

(c) the full amount of the income, profits or gains from that qualifying employment is, under the laws of the territory in which the qualifying employment is held or of the territory or territories in which the duties of the qualifying employment are performed, subject to, and not exempt or otherwise relieved from, the charge to tax,

(d) the foreign tax due on that income, profits or gains from that qualifying employment has been paid and not repaid or entitled to be repaid, and

(e) during any week in which he or she is absent from the State for the purposes of the performance of the duties of the qualifying employment, he or she is present in the State for at least one day in that week,

he or she shall, where the amount of tax payable in respect of his or her total income for that year would, but for this section, exceed the specified amount, be entitled to have the amount of tax payable reduced to the specified amount.

(4) In determining for the purposes of *paragraph (b)* of *subsection (3)* whether the duties of a qualifying employment are exercised outside the State, any duties performed in the State, the performance of which is merely incidental to the performance of

the duties of the qualifying employment outside the State, shall be treated for the purposes of this section as having been performed outside the State.

(5) This section shall not apply in any case where the income, profits or gains of a qualifying employment are the subject of a claim for relief under—

(a) *section 472B*, or

(b) *section 823*.

(6) Where in any case an individual has the tax payable in respect of his or her total income for a year of assessment reduced in accordance with *subsection (3)*, that individual shall, notwithstanding anything in *Part 35*, not be entitled to a credit for foreign tax paid on the income, profits or gains from a qualifying employment in that year.

[(7) For the purposes of this section—

(a) as respects the year of assessment 2009 and previous years of assessment, an individual shall be deemed to be present in the State for a day if the individual is present in the State at the end of the day, and

(b) as respects the year of assessment 2010 and subsequent years of assessment, an individual shall be deemed to be present in the State for a day if the individual is present in the State at any time during that day.][4]

(8) Notwithstanding anything in the Tax Acts, the income, profits or gains from a qualifying employment shall for the purposes of this section be deemed not to include any amounts paid in respect of expenses incurred wholly, exclusively and necessarily in the performance of the duties of the qualifying employment.][5]

Amendments

[1] Substituted by FA07 sched2(1)(ab)(i). Has effect as on and from 2 April 2007

[2] Substituted by FA01 sched2(45). Shall apply only as respects the year of assessment 2001.

[3] Substituted by FA07 sched2(1)(ab)(ii). Has effect as on and from 2 April 2007

[4] Substituted by FA10 s11. Deemed to have come into force and takes effect as on and from 1 January 2010.

[5] Inserted by FA98 s13.

Revenue Briefings

Tax Briefing

Tax Briefing December 1998 – Issue 34 pg 28 – Transborder workers

Cross References

From Section 825A

Section 16 Income tax charged by deduction.

Section 71 Foreign securities and possessions.

Section 458 Deductions allowed in ascertaining taxable income and provisions relating to reductions in tax.

Section 472 Employee tax credit.

Section 472B Seafarer allowance, etc.

Section 818 Interpretation (Part 34).

Section 822 Split year residence.

Section 823 Deduction for income earned outside the State.

Section 826 Agreements for relief from double taxation.

To Section 825A

Section 531B Charge to income levy.

Section 531AM Charge to universal social charge.

825B Repayment of tax where earnings not remitted

[(1) In this section—

"*associated company*", in relation to a relevant employer, means a company which is that employer's associated company within the meaning of section 432 and which is incorporated or resident in a country or jurisdiction which is not a party to the EEA agreement, but with the government of which arrangements are for the time being in force by virtue of section 826(1);

"*EEA agreement*" means the Agreement on the European Economic Area signed at Oporto on 2 May 1992, as adjusted by the Protocol signed at Brussels on 17 March 1993;

"*emoluments*" has the same meaning as in Chapter 4 of Part 42;

"*relevant emoluments*", in relation to a tax year, means emoluments that are—

(a) paid by a relevant employer or an associated company of that relevant employer to a relevant employee, and

(b) within the charge to tax under Schedule E and to which Chapter 4 of Part 42 has been applied,

for that tax year;

"*relevant employee*" means an individual who, for a tax year—

(a) is resident in the State for tax purposes, and

(b) is not domiciled in the State,

and who, prior to becoming resident in the State for tax purposes—

(i) was a resident of, and resident in, a country or jurisdiction that is not a party to the EEA Agreement but with the government of which arrangements are for the time being in force by virtue of section 826(1),

(ii) was employed in that country or jurisdiction by the same relevant employer referred to in subsection (2) or by an associated company of that relevant employer, and

(iii) had exercised the greater part of his or her employment in that country or jurisdiction;

"*relevant employer*" means a company that is incorporated, and is resident, in a country or jurisdiction that is not a party to the EEA Agreement but with the government of which arrangements are for the time being in force by virtue of section 826(1);

"*Revenue officer*" means an officer of the Revenue Commissioners;

"*tax year*" means a year of assessment.

[(1A) As regards individuals who are not domiciled in the State and who, on or after 1 January 2010—

(a) become resident in the State for tax purposes for the first time, and

(b) exercise the duties of their employment in the State for the first time,

then, this section shall apply as if in *subsection (1)*—

(i) the words "which is not a party to the EEA agreement, but" were deleted from the definition of "*associated company*";

(ii) the words "that is not a party to the EEA Agreement but" were deleted from the definition of "*relevant employee*"; and

(iii) the words "that is not a party to the EEA Agreement but" were deleted from the definition of "*relevant employer*".][1]

[(1B) This section shall not apply for the tax year 2012 or any subsequent tax year.

(1C) Notwithstanding *subsection (1B)*, this section shall continue to apply—

(a) for the tax years 2012 and 2013 but only as respects relevant employees who had an entitlement to relief under this section for the first time in the tax year 2009,

(b) for the tax years 2012, 2013 and 2014 but only as respects relevant employees who had an entitlement to relief under this section for the first time in the tax year 2010, and

(c) for the tax years 2012, 2013, 2014 and 2015 but only as respects relevant employees who had an entitlement to relief under this section for the first time in the tax year 2011.

(1D) Where for a tax year a relevant employee makes a claim under this section, relief shall not be given under *section 823A, 825C* or *472D* for that tax year.][2]

(2) Where a relevant employee—

(a) becomes resident in the State for tax purposes,

(b) is required by his or her relevant employer to exercise the duties of his or her employment in the State,

(c) exercises those duties in the State on behalf of the relevant employer or on behalf of an associated company of the relevant employer for a period of at least [one year][3], and

(d) while so exercising those duties, continues to be paid relevant emoluments from abroad by his or her relevant employer or associated company,

then after the end of any tax year in respect of which relevant emoluments are paid, the relevant employee may apply to the Revenue Commissioners to have the tax due on the relevant emoluments computed for the tax year on the full amount of the greater of—

(i) the relevant emoluments earned and received in or remitted—

(I) either directly or indirectly,

(II) through any property imported,

(III) through any money or value received on credit or on account,

to the State in that tax year, and

(ii) an amount equal to €100,000 plus 50 per cent of the relevant emoluments in excess of €100,000, and any tax deducted [and not repaid][4] from the relevant emoluments in excess of the tax due as so computed shall be repaid on foot of a claim from the relevant employee.

(3) Section 72 shall, with any necessary modification, apply to this section.

(4) For the purposes of this section, where deductions under Chapter 4 of Part 42 are made from relevant emoluments, such deductions shall be deemed to be an amount of the relevant emoluments received in or remitted to the State for the year of assessment to which such deductions refer.

(5) (a) If relevant emoluments are remitted to the State in a tax year after the tax year in which they were earned, and the individual has received a repayment under subsection (2) of any tax originally deducted from those emoluments, the individual shall be liable to income tax on those emoluments[, computed by reference to *paragraphs (i)* and *(ii)* of *subsection (2)*,][5] from the date on which the tax was originally deducted.

(b) In a case in which paragraph (*a*) applies, section 924(2)(*b*) shall apply in the case of assessments or additional first assessments in respect of the emoluments referred to in paragraph (*a*) subject to a substitution of [a reference to the end of the tax year in which the emoluments were remitted for the reference to the end of the tax year to which the assessment relates][6].

(6) Where a relevant employee—

(a) has claimed a repayment of tax under subsection (2), and

(b) fails to comply with the [one year][7] limit contained in subsection (2)(*c*),

then that employee shall, whether or not requested to do so by a Revenue officer and within 2 months of that failure, repay to the Revenue Commissioners the tax repaid under subsection (2).

(7) If a Revenue officer is not satisfied with the information provided by a relevant employee making a claim under subsection (2), the officer may refuse the claim.][8]

Amendments

[1] Inserted by FA10 s10(a). As respects the year of assessment 2010 and subsequent years of assessment.

[2] Inserted by FA12 s13(a). Deemed to have come into force and takes effect on and from 1 January 2012.

[3] Substituted by FA10 s10(b)(i). As respects the year of assessment 2010 and subsequent years of assessment.

[4] Inserted by FA10 s10(b)(ii). As respects the year of assessment 2010 and subsequent years of assessment.

[5] Inserted by FA10 s10(c). As respects the year of assessment 2010 and subsequent years of assessment.

[6] Substituted by FA12 s13(b). Deemed to have come into force and takes effect on and from 1 January 2012.

[7] Substituted by FA10 s10(d). As respects the year of assessment 2010 and subsequent years of assessment.

[8] Inserted by F(No.2)A08 s13(1). This section shall apply for the year of assessment 2009 and subsequent years.

Cross References

From Section 825B

Section 72 Charge to tax on sums applied outside the State in repaying certain loans.
Section 432 Meaning of "associated company" and "control".
Section 826 Agreements for relief from double taxation.
Section 924 Additional assessments.

825C Special assignee relief programme

[(1) In this section—

'*associated company*', in relation to a relevant employer, means a company which is the relevant employer's associated company within the meaning of *section 432*;

['*PPS number*', in relation to an individual, means the individual's personal public service number within the meaning of section 262 of the Social Welfare Consolidation Act 2005;][1]

'*relevant employer*' means a company that is incorporated, and tax resident, in a country or jurisdiction with the government of which arrangements are for the time being in force by virtue of *subsection (1)* or *(1B)* of *section 826*;

'*relevant employment*', in relation to a relevant employee, means an employment held by the relevant employee with a relevant employer;

'*relevant income*', in relation to a relevant employee and a tax year, means the relevant employee's income, profits or gains for a tax year from an employment with a relevant employer or with an associated company, including any specified amount for which a deduction is claimed under *subsection (3)* but excluding the following:

(a) any expense to which *section 118* applies;

(b) any amount treated as emoluments of an employment under *section 121(2)(b)(ii)*;

(c) any sum treated for the purposes of *section 112* as a perquisite of an employment by virtue of *section 122*;

(d) any payment to which *section 123* applies;

(e) any sum deemed to be profits or gains arising or accruing from an employment by virtue of *section 127(2)*;

(f) [any bonus, commission or other similar payments][2], whether contractual or otherwise;

(g) any gain to which *section 128* applies;

(*h*) any shares or share based remuneration provided by or on behalf of the relevant employer or associated company of the relevant employer;

'*Revenue officer*' means an officer of the Revenue Commissioners;

[...][3]

'*tax year*' means a year of assessment for income tax purposes.

(2) (a) [In this section, in the case of an individual who arrives in the State in any of the tax years 2012, 2013 or 2014,][4] '*relevant employee*' means an individual who—

(i) for the whole of the 12 months immediately before his or her arrival in the State was a full time employee of a relevant employer and exercised the duties of his or her employment for that relevant employer outside the State,

(ii) arrives in the State [...][5], at the request of his or her relevant employer to—

(I) perform in the State the duties of his or her employment for that employer, or

(II) to take up employment in the State with an associated company,

(iii) performs the duties of his or her employment in the State for that relevant employer or for that associated company, as appropriate, for a minimum period of 12 consecutive months from the date he or she takes up residence in the State, and

(iv) was not resident in the State for the 5 tax years immediately preceding the tax year in which he or she first arrives in the State for the purposes of performing the duties referred to in *subparagraph (iii)*.

(b) In determining whether the duties of an employment [are performed in the State for the tax years 2012, 2013 and 2014,][6] any duties performed outside the State, the performance of which is merely incidental to the performance of those duties in the State, shall be treated as having been performed in the State.

[(2A) In this section, in the case of an individual who arrives in the State in any of the tax years 2015, 2016 or 2017, '*relevant employee*' means an individual—

(a) who for the whole of the 6 months immediately before his or her arrival in the State was a full time employee of a relevant employer and exercised the duties of his or her employment for that relevant employer outside the State,

(b) who arrives in the State at the request of his or her relevant employer to—

(i) perform in the State duties of his or her employment for that employer, or

(ii) to take up employment in the State with an associated company and to perform duties in the State for that company,

(c) who performs the duties referred to in *paragraph (b)* for a minimum period of 12 consecutive months from the date he or she first performs those duties in the State,

(d) who was not resident in the State for the 5 tax years immediately preceding the tax year in which he or she first arrives in the State for the purposes of performing the duties referred to in *paragraph (b)*, and

(e) in respect of whom the relevant employer or associated company certifies, in such form as the Revenue Commissioners may require, within 30 days from the employee's arrival in the State to perform the duties referred to in *paragraph (b)*, that the individual complies with the conditions set out in *paragraphs (a)*, *(b)* and *(c)*.

(2B) (a) In this section, 'specified amount', in relation to a relevant employee and a tax year, means an amount determined by the formula—

$$(A - B) \times 30 \text{ per cent.}$$

(b) For the purposes of *paragraph (a)*—

(i) 'A' is the amount of the relevant employee's income, profits or gains for the tax year from the employment referred to in *subsection (2)(a)(ii)* or *(2A)(b)*, as the case may be, excluding any amount that is not assessed to tax in the State, and after deducting—

(I) any contribution or qualifying premium in respect of which there is provision for a deduction under *section 774(7), 787, 787E* or *787N*, and

(II) any amount of income, profits or gains from that employment in respect of which the relevant employee is entitled to relief under *Part 35* for tax paid on such income, profits or gains under the laws of a territory other than the State, but in respect of the tax years 2012, 2013 and 2014 where this amount exceeds €500,000, 'A' shall be €500,000, and

(ii) 'B' is €75,000.

(c) Notwithstanding *paragraph (b)*—

(i) where, in the tax year for which a relevant employee is first entitled to relief under this section, the period from the date the relevant employee commences the performance in the State of duties of the employment with the relevant employer or associated company to the end of the tax year is less than the tax year, 'B' shall be reduced proportionately,

(ii) where, in the last tax year for which a relevant employee is entitled to relief under this section, the period from the start of the tax year to the date the relevant employee ceases the performance of duties in the State of the employment with the relevant employer or associated company is less than the tax year, 'B' shall be reduced proportionately.][7]

[(3) (a) Subject to *paragraph (b)*, where, for a tax year, a relevant employee—

(i) is resident in the State for tax purposes and is not resident elsewhere,

(ii) performs the duties referred to in *subsection (2)(a)(ii)* or *(2A)(b)*, and

(iii) has relevant income from his or her relevant employer or from the associated company, the annualised equivalent of which is not less than €75,000,

and makes a claim in that behalf, then that relevant employee shall be entitled to have an amount of income, profits or gains from his or her employment with a relevant employer or from his or her employment with an associated company equal to the specified amount deducted from the income, profits or gains to be assessed on that relevant employee for that tax year.

(b) With effect from the tax year 2015, *paragraph (a)(i)* shall apply as if the words 'and is not resident elsewhere' were deleted.

(c) A relevant employee shall only be entitled to relief under this section for 5 consecutive tax years commencing with the tax year for which the relevant employee is first entitled to relief under this section.][8]

[(4) For the purposes of *subsections (2B)(c)* and *(3)*, the tax year for which a relevant employee is first entitled to relief under this section means—

(a) in the case of a relevant employee who arrives in the State in 2012, 2013 or 2014—

(i) the first tax year in which the relevant employee arrives in the State for the purposes set out in *subsection (2)(a)(ii)* provided that for that tax year the relevant employee is resident in the State for tax purposes and not resident elsewhere, or

(ii) if not resident in the State for tax purposes for that first tax year, the tax year following that first tax year provided that for that following tax year the relevant employee is resident in the State and not resident elsewhere, or

(iii) where in that first tax year, he or she is resident in the State for tax purposes and is also resident elsewhere, the tax year following that first tax year provided that for that following tax year he or she is resident in the State for tax purposes and is not resident elsewhere,

but, as regards a relevant employee who arrives in the State in 2014, *subparagraph (ii)* shall apply as if the words 'and not resident elsewhere' were deleted, and *subparagraph (iii)* shall apply as if the words 'and is not resident elsewhere' were deleted,

(b) in the case of a relevant employee who arrives in the State in 2015, 2016 or 2017—

(i) the first tax year in which the employee arrives in the State for the purposes set out in *subsection (2A)(b)*, provided that for that tax year he or she is resident in the State for tax purposes, or

(ii) if not resident in the State for tax purposes for that first tax year, the tax year following that first year provided that for that following tax year he or she is resident in the State.][9]

[...][10]

(6) [In any tax year in respect of which][11] a relevant employee is entitled to make a claim for relief under *subsection (3)*, the payment or reimbursement by the relevant employer or by an associated company of—

(a) the reasonable costs associated with one return trip from the State for the relevant employee, his or her spouse or civil partner, and a child of the relevant employee or of the relevant employee's spouse or civil partner to—

(i) the country of residence of the relevant employee before his or her arrival in the State,

(ii) the country of residence of the relevant employee at the time of first employment by the relevant employer, or

(iii) the country of which the relevant employee or his or her spouse or civil partner is a national,

and

(b) the cost of fees, not exceeding €5,000 per annum in respect of each child of the relevant employee or each child of his or her spouse or civil partner, paid to a school established in the State and which has been approved by the Minister for Education and Skills for the purposes of providing primary or post-primary education to students, shall not be chargeable to tax.

(7) Where for a tax year a relevant employee makes a claim for relief under this section—

(a) relief shall not be given under *section 823A, 825A* or *472D* for that tax year, and

(b) *section 71(3)* shall not apply to any of the income, profits or gains from an employment with a relevant employer or with an associated company.

(8) Where for a tax year a relevant employee makes a claim for relief under this section, the relevant employee shall, not-withstanding anything to the contrary in [*Part 41A* or *section 1084*][12], be deemed for that tax year to be a chargeable person for the purposes of [*Part 41A*][13].

(9) Notwithstanding the requirement on a relevant employer or associated company, as the case may be, to deduct tax under *Chapter 4* of *Part 42* on the specified amount, no such tax deduction need be made where, [following an application, in such form as the Revenue Commissioners may require, by the relevant employer or associated company,][14] as appropriate, a Revenue officer confirms in writing that no such deduction need be made.

[(10) On or before 23 February following each tax year, a relevant employer or associated company shall deliver to the Revenue Commissioners an annual return, in such form as the Revenue Commissioners may require, setting out—

(a) in respect of each relevant employee—

(i) the name and PPS number,

(ii) nationality,

(iii) country in which the relevant employee worked for the relevant employer prior to his or her first arrival in the State to perform duties of the relevant employment,

(iv) job title and brief description of the role of the relevant employee while availing himself or herself of relief under this section, and

(v) where relevant, the amount of income, profits or gains in respect of which tax was not deducted in accordance with *subsection (9)*,

(b) details of the increase in the number of employees employed, or details of the number of employees retained, by the relevant employer or associated company as a result of the assignment to the State of the employees referred to in *paragraph (a)*, and

(c) the relevant employer's or associated company's employer registration number.][15]

[...][16]

(12) Notwithstanding anything in the Tax Acts, the income, profits or gains from an employment with a relevant employer or with an associated company shall, for the purposes of this section, be deemed not to include any amounts paid in respect of expenses for which deductions would be due under *section 114*.][17]

Amendments

1 Inserted by FA14 s15(a)(i). Comes into operation on 1 January 2015.

2 Substituted by FA14 s15(a)(ii). Comes into operation on 1 January 2015.

3 Deleted by FA14 s15(a)(iii). Comes into operation on 1 January 2015.

4 Substituted by FA14 s15(b)(i). Comes into operation on 1 January 2015.

5 Deleted by FA14 s15(b)(ii). Comes into operation on 1 January 2015.

6 Substituted by FA14 s15(b)(iii). Comes into operation on 1 January 2015.

7 Inserted by FA14 s15(c). Comes into operation on 1 January 2015.

8 Substituted by FA14 s15(d). Comes into operation on 1 January 2015.

9 Substituted by FA14 s15(e). Comes into operation on 1 January 2015.

10 Deleted by FA14 s15(f). Comes into operation on 1 January 2015.

11 Substituted by FA14 s15(g). Comes into operation on 1 January 2015.

12 Substituted by FA13 s92 and sched1(part 2)(f)(i).

13 Substituted by FA13 s92 and sched1(part 2)(f)(ii).

14 Substituted by FA14 s15(h). Comes into operation on 1 January 2015.

15 Substituted by FA14 s15(i). Comes into operation on 1 January 2015.

16 Deleted by FA14 s15(j). Comes into operation on 1 January 2015.

17 Inserted by FA12 s14. Deemed to have come into force and takes effect on and from 1 January 2012.

Note:

FA13 s92 applies—

(a) in the case of a chargeable period (within the meaning of section 321(2)) which is an accounting period of a company, as respects chargeable periods that start on or after 1 January 2013, and

(b) in a case other than that referred to in paragraph (a), as respects the year of assessment (within the meaning of section 2(1)) 2013 and subsequent years of assessment.

Revenue Briefings

eBrief

eBrief No. 29/2012 – Special Assignee Relief Programme (SARP)

eBrief No. 64/2012 – Return by employer of employees who availed of relief under the Special Assignee Relief Programme (SARP)

eBrief No. 52/2013 – Return by employer of employees who availed of relief under the Special Assignee Relief Programme (SARP)

PART 35

Double Taxation Relief

CHAPTER 1

Principal Reliefs

826 Agreements for relief from double taxation

[ITA67 s361; FA74 s86 and Sch2 PtI; CTA76 s22(2), s23(1) and s166(1) and Sch4 PtI; FA83 s47(4)]

[(1) Where—

(a) the Government by order declare that arrangements specified in the order have been made with the government of any territory outside the State in relation to—

(i) affording relief from double taxation in respect of—

(I) income tax,

(II) corporation tax in respect of income and chargeable gains (or, in the case of arrangements made before the enactment of the Corporation Tax Act 1976, corporation profits tax),

(III) capital gains tax,

(IV) any taxes of a similar character,

imposed by the laws of the State or by the laws of that territory, and

(ii) in the case of taxes of any kind or description imposed by the laws of the State or the laws of that territory—

(I) exchanging information for the purposes of the prevention and detection of tax evasion, [...][1]

(II) granting relief from taxation under the laws of that territory to persons who are resident in the State for the purposes of tax, [or][2]

[(III) collecting and recovering tax (including interest, penalties and costs in connection with such tax) for the purposes of the prevention of tax evasion,][3]

and that it is expedient that those arrangements should have the force of law, and

(b) the order so made is referred to in *Part 1* of *Schedule 24A*,

then, subject to this section and to the extent provided for in this section, the arrangements shall, notwithstanding any enactment, have the force of law as if each such order were an Act of the Oireachtas on and from the date of—

(A) the insertion of *Schedule 24A* into this Act, or

(B) the insertion of a reference to the order into *Part 1* of *Schedule 24A*,

whichever is the later.

(1A) Where—

(a) the Government by order declare that arrangements specified in the order have been made with the government of any territory outside the State in relation to affording relief from double taxation of air transport undertakings and their employees in respect of all taxes which are or may become chargeable on profits, income and capital gains imposed by the laws of the State or the laws of that territory, and that it is expedient that those arrangements should have the force of law, and

(b) the order so made is referred to in *Part 2* of *Schedule 24A*,

then, subject to this section and to the extent provided for in this section, the arrangements shall, notwithstanding any enactment, have the force of law as if each such order were an Act of the Oireachtas on and from the date of—

(i) the insertion of *Schedule 24A* into this Act, or

(ii) the insertion of a reference to the order into *Part 2* of *Schedule 24A*,

whichever is the later.

(1B) Where—

(a) the Government by order declare that arrangements specified in the order have been made with the government of any territory outside the State in relation to—

(i) exchanging information for the purposes of the prevention and detection of tax evasion in the case of taxes of any kind or description imposed by the law of the State or the laws of that territory,

(ii) such other matters relating to affording relief from double taxation as the Government consider appropriate,

and that it is expedient that those arrangements should have the force of law, and

(b) the order so made is specified in *Part 3* of *Schedule 24A*,

then, subject to this section, the arrangements shall, notwithstanding any enactment, have the force of law as if each such order were an Act of the Oireachtas on and from the date of the insertion of a reference to the order into *Part 3* of *Schedule 24A*.][4]

[(1C) Where—

(a) the Government by order declares that it has become a signatory to the Convention on Mutual Administrative Assistance in Tax Matters which was done at Strasbourg on the 25th day of January 1988, or any Protocol to the Convention, for the purposes of the prevention and detection of tax evasion in the case of taxes of any kind or description imposed by the laws of the State or the laws of the territories of the signatories other than the State to the Convention and that it is expedient that the Convention, or any Protocol to the Convention, should have the force of law, and

(b) the order so made is referred to in *Part 4* of *Schedule 24A*,

then, subject to this section, the Convention or any Protocol to the Convention shall, notwithstanding any enactment, have the force of law as if the order were an Act of the Oireachtas on and from the date of the insertion of a reference to the order into *Part 4* of *Schedule 24A*.][5]

(2) *Schedule 24* shall apply where arrangements which have the force of law by virtue of this section provide that tax payable under the laws of the territory concerned shall be allowed as a credit against tax payable in the State.

(3) Any arrangements to which the force of law is given under this section may include provision for relief from tax for periods before the passing of this Act or before the making of the arrangements and provisions as to income or

chargeable gains which is or are not subject to double taxation, and *subsections (1)* and *(2)* shall apply accordingly.

(4) For the purposes of *subsection (1)*, arrangements made with the head of a foreign state shall be regarded as made with the government of that state.

(5) Any order made under this section may be revoked by a subsequent order, and any such revoking order may contain such transitional provisions as appear to the Government to be necessary or expedient.

(6) Where an order is proposed to be made under this section, a draft of the order shall be laid before Dáil Éireann and the order shall not be made until a resolution approving of the draft has been passed by Dáil Éireann.

[(7) Where any arrangements have, or the Convention [or any Protocol to the Convention][6] has, the force of law by virtue of this section, the obligation as to secrecy imposed by any enactment shall not prevent the Revenue Commissioners or any authorised officer of the Revenue Commissioners from disclosing to any authorised officer of the government with which arrangements have been made, or of a party to the Convention [or any Protocol to the Convention][7], as the case may be, such information as is required to be disclosed for the purposes of the arrangements or the Convention [or any Protocol to the Convention][8].][9]

(8) The necessary apportionments as respects corporation tax shall be made where arrangements having the force of law by virtue of this section apply to the unexpired portion of an accounting period current at a date specified by the arrangements, and any such apportionment shall be made in proportion to the number of months or fractions of months in the part of the relevant accounting period before that date and in the remaining part of the relevant accounting period respectively.

(9) The Revenue Commissioners may from time to time make regulations generally for carrying out the provisions of this section or any arrangements having the force of law under this section and may in particular, but without prejudice to the generality of the foregoing, by those regulations provide—

(a) for securing that relief from taxation imposed by the laws of the territory to which any such arrangements relate does not enure to the benefit of persons not entitled to such relief, and

(b) for authorising, in cases where tax deductible from any periodical payment has, in order to comply with any such arrangements, not been deducted and it is discovered that the arrangements do not apply to that payment, the recovery of the tax by assessment on the person entitled to the payment or by deduction from subsequent payments.

Amendments

[1] Deleted by FA10 s157(a). Has effect as on and from 3 April 2010.

[2] Inserted by FA10 s157(a). Has effect as on and from 3 April 2010.

[3] Inserted by FA10 s157(b). Has effect as on and from 3 April 2010.

[4] Substituted by FA07 s35(1)(a). Has effect as on and from 2 April 2007

[5] Inserted by FA10 s157(c). Has effect as on and from 3 April 2010.

[6,7,8] Inserted by FA13 s99(1)(a). Applies as on and from 27 March 2013.

[9] Substituted by FA10 s157(d). Has effect as on and from 3 April 2010.

Case Law

Murphy (Inspector of Tax) v Asahi Synthetic Fibres (Ireland) Ltd 1986 IR 777 concerned an assessment for tax on interest paid on a loan from parent to subsidiary. The Court held there was no conflict between section 130 TCA 1997 and the double tax agreement. Tax is chargeable under Schedule F with no withholding tax.

A profit sharing agreement existed with a branch of a UK company. The taxpayer claimed double tax relief for the tax paid by the company. Training Consultant v Revenue & Customs Commissioners 2007 STC SCD

FKP Konzertproduktionen GmBH v Finanzamt Hamburg-Eimsbuttell C290/04 considered if an individual was only temporarily resident in Germany would a retention of tax at source on their income be against EU law.

In Compagnie de Saint-Gobain, Zweignierderlassung Deutschland and Finanzamt Aachen-Onenstadt 2000 STC 855 it was held that a member state must unilaterally give to a branch of an EU resident company the same benefits as a company resident in that State enjoys under the State's double tax agreement.

Revenue Briefings

Tax Briefing

Tax Briefing June 1998 – Issue 32 pg 15 – Double Tax Relief, Foreign Effective Rates
Tax Briefing July 2007 – Issue 66 – Finance Act 2007 Double Tax Relief
Tax Briefing December 2007 – Issue 67 – Double Tax Relief – Legal and General Case and Related Issues

eBrief

eBrief No. 26/2005 – Capital gains tax and the Ireland/Italy Double Tax Convention
eBrief No. 7/2006 – Competent Authority Agreement between Ireland and the United States
eBrief No. 12/2006 – Follow on from eBrief No 26/2005 CGT and Ireland/Italy Double Tax Agreement

Revenue Precedents

Where an individual is chargeable to Irish tax by virtue of his/her ordinary residence status in Ireland he/she may be "fiscally domiciled" in Ireland, i.e. resident "of" Ireland for the purpose of a Double Taxation Convention, subject to the tie breaker rules provided there is a "fiscal domicile Article" within the relevant Double Taxation Convention. RT/364/94

Article XIII Ireland/Germany DTA. Government Article. Are employees of the Goethe Institute posted to Ireland from Germany, considered to be engaged in the performance of a public function and exempt from Irish tax? Yes if the individual is a German National the exemption is allowed. RT 2401/82

An individual came to Ireland from N. Ireland on 1/9/90 for a research fellowship in T.C.D. scheduled to last until 31/12/91. His claim for exemption from Irish tax under Canadian D.T.A. was refused as the Irish/Canadian D.T.A. was not applicable as he was resident in the U.K. for almost 3 years prior to his Irish assignment. Thus he came to Ireland as an individual from the U.K. – no Teachers Article in Irl/U.K. D.T.A. RT 196/91

It was possible to have more than one teaching post and still benefit from the exemption under Article 19 Ireland/France DTA provided all other conditions of the Article are satisfied. RT 457/91

Training Fellowships T.C.D. Individual came to Ireland from France in October, 1992. Sought exemption on E.U. Training Scolarship in T.C.D. from 9/93 – 8/95 under Articles 19 & 17 of Irl/France D.T.A. and section 193 TCA 1997 Sch. 32 par2. This was refused as stay was intended to be in excess of 2 years and she was an "individual from Ireland" prior to her apointment with T.C.D. (and not an "individual from France" as specified in the D.T.A.). Art. 17 exemption – Refused as payments were not made from sources outside the State. Liable therefore to Irish tax. Section 193 exemption also did not apply as she was not studying for a higher degree. RT 42/94

Teacher/Researcher – Individual previously satisfied the conditions of Article 17, Ireland/Germany DTA, exemption granted. Does a return visit for employment to the same or similar institution cause the exemption that applied to be withdrawn retrospectively. As the terms of Article 17 of the DTA were satisfied at the time, the individual was correctly entitled to the exclusion order Oct. '92 to Oct '94. In the circumstances outlined in this case, the exemption was not revoked for the return visit. All cases of this nature should be examined on an individual basis. RT 166/97

Where an individual is not resident but is ordinarily resident, he/she is not entitled to a credit for foreign tax in accordance with section 826 where double taxation occurs. However, in practice a credit for foreign tax will be given. RT 353/96

Teagasc is regarded as a research institute for the purposes of Article 19 of the Irl/France DTA and an individual may qualify for the relief provided therein if he/she satisfies all other conditions of the Article. RT 22/97

Individual carried out French National Service in Dublin school. Exemption granted under Art. 13 of the Ireland/France DTA in respect of remuneration from the French Government. RT 168/97

The application for and the receipt of a British Passport by a Irish individual satisfies the conditions of section 2 British Nationality Act 1948 and therefore the provisions of article 3(1)(c)(ii) of the Ireland/UK DTA, if applied for prior to 2 June, 1976. RT 444/96

No credit is available in Ireland for UK composite rate tax which applied to interest payments on deposits from 6 April 1985 to 5 April 1991. IT932008

Statements of Practice

Tax Treatment of Share Options granted in respect of Employment and Directorships – SP IT/01/07

Cross References

From Section 826

Schedule 24 Relief from Income Tax and Corporation Tax by Means of Credit in Respect of Foreign Tax

To Section 826

Section 21B Tax treatment of certain dividends.
Section 23A Company residence.
Section 29A Temporary non-residents.
Section 42 Exemption of interest on savings certificates.
Section 44 Exemption from corporation tax of certain securities issued by Minister for Finance.
Section 81 General rule as to deductions.
Section 127B Tax treatment of flight crew in international traffic.
Section 130 Matters to be treated as distributions.
Section 153 Distributions to certain nonresidents.
Section 172A Interpretation.
Section 198 Certain interest not to be chargeable.
Section 222 Certain dividends from a non-resident subsidiary.
Section 246 Interest payments by companies and to non-residents.
Section 267G Interpretation (Chapter 6).
Section 410 Group payments.
Section 411 Surrender of relief between members of groups and consortia.
Section 430 Meaning of "close company".
Section 452 Application of section 130 to certain interest.
Section 481 Relief for investment in films.
Section 487 Corporation tax: credit for bank levy.
Section 530 Interpretation (Chapter 2).
Section 531B Charge to income levy.
Section 531AM Charge to universal social charge.
Section 579B Trustees ceasing to be resident in the State.
Section 613 Miscellaneous exemptions for certain kinds of property.
Section 616 Groups of companies: interpretation.
Section 626B Exemption from tax in the case of gains on disposals of shares.
Section 627 Deemed disposal of assets.
Section 630 Interpretation (Part 21).
Section 634 Credit for tax.
Section 690 Interest and charges on income.
Section 697M Exclusion of reliefs, deductions and set-offs.
Section 730H Interpretation and application.
Section 747B Interpretation and application.
Section 749 Dealers in securities.
Section 787M Interpretation and general (Chapter 2B).
Section 817C Restriction on deductibility of certain interest.
Section 825A Reduction in income tax for certain income earned outside the State.
Section 825B Repayment of tax where earnings not remitted.
Section 826A Unilateral relief from double taxation.
Section 827 Application to corporation tax of arrangements made in relation to corporation profits tax under old law.
Section 828 Capital gains tax: double taxation relief.
Section 829 Treatment for double taxation relief purposes of foreign tax incentive reliefs.

Section 830 Relief to certain companies liable to foreign tax.
Section 831 Implementation of Council Directive No. 90/435/EEC concerning the common system of taxation applicable in the case of parent companies and subsidiaries of different Member States.
Section 835A Interpretation.
Section 865 Repayment of tax.
Section 898M Credit for withholding tax.
Section 912A Information for tax authorities in other territories.
Section 917B Return by settlor in relation to non-resident trustees.
Schedule 3 Reliefs in Respect of Income Tax Charged on Payments on Retirement, Etc
Schedule 22 Dividends Regarded as Paid Out of Profits Accumulated Before Given Date
Schedule 24 Relief from Income Tax and Corporation Tax by Means of Credit in Respect of Foreign Tax
Schedule 24A Arrangements Made by the Government with the Government of any Territory Outside the State in Relation to Affording Relief from Double Taxation and Exchanging Information in Relation to Tax

826A Unilateral relief from double taxation

[Where relief from double taxation is not afforded by virtue of *section 826*, relief (known as "unilateral relief") from tax shall be given in respect of tax paid under the laws of a territory other than the State in accordance with *Schedule 24*.][1]

Amendments

[1] Inserted by FA07 s36(1)(a).

Revenue Briefings

Tax Briefing

Tax Briefing July 2007 – Issue 66 – Finance Act 2007 Foreign branch profits

Statement of Practice

SP-CT: Foreign Branch Double Taxation Relief

Cross References

From Section 826A

Section 826 Agreements for relief from double taxation.
Schedule 24 Relief from Income Tax and Corporation Tax by Means of Credit in Respect of Foreign Tax

827 Application to corporation tax of arrangements made in relation to corporation profits tax under old law

[CTA76 s22(1) and s23(1)]

Subject to any express amendments made by the Corporation Tax Acts and except in so far as arrangements made on or after the 31st day of March, 1976, provide otherwise, any arrangements made under section 361 of the Income Tax Act, 1967, or any earlier enactment corresponding to that section, in relation to corporation profits tax shall apply in relation to corporation tax and income and chargeable gains chargeable to corporation tax as they are expressed to apply in relation to corporation profits tax and profits chargeable to corporation profits tax, and not as they apply in relation to income tax; but this section shall not affect the operation, as they apply to corporation tax, of *section 826(7)* and *paragraph 12* of *Schedule 24*.

Cross References

From Section 827

Section 826 Agreements for relief from double taxation.
Schedule 24 Relief from Income Tax and Corporation Tax by Means of Credit in Respect of Foreign Tax

To Section 827

Section 448 Relief from corporation tax.
Section 486C Relief from tax for certain start-up companies.

828 Capital gains tax: double taxation relief

[CGTA75 s38, s51(1) and Sch1 PtI par3(6); FA97 s146(1) and Sch9 PtI par 9(3)]

(1) For the purposes of giving relief from double taxation in relation to capital gains tax charged under the law of any country outside the State, in *section 826* and *Schedule 24* as they apply for the purposes of income tax, for references to income there shall be substituted references to chargeable gains, for references to the Income Tax Acts there shall be substituted references to the Capital Gains Tax Acts and for references to income tax there shall be substituted references to capital gains tax meaning, as the context may require, tax charged under the law of the State or tax charged under the law of a country outside the State.

(2) In so far as capital gains tax charged under the law of a country outside the State may by virtue of this section be taken into account under *section 826* and *Schedule 24* as applied by this section, that tax, whether relief is given by virtue of this section in respect of it or not, shall not be taken into account for the purposes of those provisions as they apply apart from this section.

(3) *Section 826(7)* shall apply in relation to capital gains tax as it applies in relation to income tax.

(4) Subject to *subsections (1)* to *(3)* and the other provisions of the Capital Gains Tax Acts relating to double taxation, the tax chargeable under the law of any country outside the State on the disposal of an asset which is borne by the person making the disposal shall be allowable as a deduction in the computation under *Chapter 2* of *Part 19* of the gain accruing on the disposal.

Case Law

The domestic law of each Contracting State should be used to explain the meaning of terms not defined in the Tax Treaty. Kinsella v The Revenue Commissioners 2007 ITR 151

Revenue Briefings

eBrief

eBrief No. 26/2005 – Capital gains tax and the Ireland/Italy Double Tax Convention

Cross References

From Section 828

Section 532 Assets.

Section 544 Interpretation and general (Chapter 2).

Section 826 Agreements for relief from double taxation.

Schedule 24 Relief from Income Tax and Corporation Tax by Means of Credit in Respect of Foreign Tax

To Section 828

Section 579B Trustees ceasing to be resident in the State.

Section 611 Disposals to State, public bodies and charities.

Section 613 Miscellaneous exemptions for certain kinds of property.

Section 697M Exclusion of reliefs, deductions and set-offs.

Section 729 Income tax, foreign tax and tax credit.

Section 917B Return by settlor in relation to non-resident trustees.

829 Treatment for double taxation relief purposes of foreign tax incentive reliefs

[FA70 s57(2) to (4); CTA76 s166(1) and Sch4 PtI]

(1) This section shall apply to any relief given with a view to promoting industrial, commercial, scientific, educational or other development in a territory outside the State.

(2) For the purposes of *section 826* and *Schedule 24*, any amount of tax under the law of a territory outside the State which would have been payable but for a relief to which this section applies given under that law (being a relief with respect to which provision is made in arrangements for double taxation relief which are the subject of an order under [*section 826(1)*][1]) shall be treated as having been payable, and references in *section 826* and in *Schedule 24* to double taxation, tax payable or chargeable or tax not chargeable directly or by deduction shall be construed accordingly.

(3) The Revenue Commissioners may make regulations generally for carrying out the provisions of this section or any arrangements having the force of law under *section 826* and may in particular, but without prejudice to the generality of the foregoing, provide in the regulations—

(a) for the purposes of this section or of the regulations, for the application (with or without modifications) of any provision of the Tax Acts or any regulations made under those Acts, including the provisions relating to the rehearing of an appeal and to the statement of a case for the opinion of the High Court on a point of law, and

(b) that the whole or any part of a dividend paid out of profits or gains which consist of or include profits or gains in relation to which double taxation relief is given by virtue of this section is not to be regarded as income or profits for any purpose of the Tax Acts.

Amendments

[1] Substituted by FA07 sched2(1)(ac). Has effect as on and from 2 April 2007

Cross References

From Section 829

Section 826 Agreements for relief from double taxation.

Schedule 24 Relief from Income Tax and Corporation Tax by Means of Credit in Respect of Foreign Tax

CHAPTER 2

Miscellaneous

830 Relief to certain companies liable to foreign tax

[CTA76 s163]

(1) In this section—

"*accounting period*" includes a part of an accounting period;

"*external tax*" means a tax chargeable and payable under the law of the territory in which the paying company is resident, being a territory to which this section applies, and which corresponds to Irish corporation tax or income tax or both of those taxes, but a tax payable under the law of a province, state or other part of a country, or which is levied by or on behalf of a municipality or other local body, shall for the purposes of this subsection be deemed not to correspond to those taxes.

[(2) This section shall apply to every territory other than a territory with the government of which arrangements are for the time being in force by virtue of [*section 826(1)*][1].][2]

(3) Where a company (in this section referred to as "*the investing company*") has paid by deduction or otherwise, or is liable to pay, by reference to any part of its income arising in a territory to which this section applies, tax for any accounting period and it is shown to the satisfaction of the Revenue Commissioners that—

(a) that part of the investing company's income consists of a dividend or interest paid to it by a company resident in the territory (in this section referred to as "*the paying company*") not less than 50 per cent of the voting power in which is controlled directly or indirectly by the investing company,

(b) that dividend or interest arose from the investment in the paying company by the investing company, whether by means of loan or otherwise, of a sum or sums representing—

(i) profits the Irish tax referable to which was reduced to nil under—

(I) Part III of the Finance (Miscellaneous Provisions) Act, 1956,

(II) Chapter IV of Part XXV of the Income Tax Act, 1967, or

(III) Part IV of the Corporation Tax Act, 1976,

(ii) such proportion of profits the Irish tax referable to which was reduced otherwise than to nil under those provisions as is equal to the proportion by which that Irish tax has been so reduced, or

(iii) profits arising from exempted trading operations which by virtue of—

(I) Parts I and II of the Finance (Miscellaneous Provisions) Act, 1958,

(II) Chapter I of Part XXV of the Income Tax Act, 1967, or

(III) Part V of the Corporation Tax Act, 1976,

were not, in relation to the company by which such operations were carried on, taken into account for any purpose of—

(A) the Income Tax Acts,

(B) Part V of the Finance Act, 1920, and the enactments amending or extending that Part, or

(C) the Corporation Tax Acts,

and

(c) the investing company has paid external tax in the territory in respect of that part of its income,

then, the Revenue Commissioners may grant to the investing company in respect of that accounting period such relief as is just with a view to affording relief in respect of the double taxation of that part of the investing company's income, but not exceeding the lesser of—

(aa) 50 per cent of the total of the corporation tax which but for this section would be payable by the investing company in respect of that part of its income, and

(bb) the amount of the external tax paid or payable in the territory in respect of that part of its income after deduction of any relief to which the company may be entitled in that territory.

(4) (a) External tax paid by the paying company in respect of its profits shall be taken into account in considering whether any, and if so what, relief ought to be allowed in respect of a dividend paid by the paying company to the investing company, and for the purposes of this section (other

than this subsection) such tax or the appropriate part of such tax shall be regarded as external tax paid by the investing company.

(b) *Paragraph 8* of *Schedule 24* shall apply for the purpose of ascertaining the amount of the external tax paid by the paying company which is to be taken into account in relation to any dividend paid by the paying company to the investing company as it applies to the computation of foreign tax to be taken into account for the purposes of that paragraph.

(5) (a) Nothing in this section shall authorise the granting of relief under this section to any company in respect of any accounting period to such an extent as would reduce the aggregate amount (computed after deduction of any relief to which the company may be entitled in the territory) of the corporation tax and external tax payable by such company in respect of any part of its income of the kind described in *subsection (3)(a)* arising in a territory to which this section applies below the amount of corporation tax which would be payable by the company in respect of that part of its income if that part of its income had arisen in the State and had been liable in the hands of the investing company to corporation tax.

(b) In computing for the purposes of *paragraph (a)* the amount of corporation tax which would be so payable by the company in respect of that part of its income if that part had arisen in the State—

(i) no deduction for external tax shall be made from that part of its income, and

(ii) where pursuant to *subsection (4)* external tax paid by the paying company is regarded as external tax paid by the investing company, that part of the investing company's income shall be treated as increased by the amount of the external tax which is so regarded.

(6) Relief under this section shall be given as a credit against corporation tax chargeable by reference to the part of the investing company's income referred to in *subsection (3)(a)*.

(7) (a) Any claim for relief under this section shall be made in writing to the inspector not later than 6 years from the end of the accounting period to which it relates.

(b) An appeal to the Appeal Commissioners shall lie on any question arising under this section in the like manner as an appeal would lie against an assessment to corporation tax, and the provisions of the Tax Acts relating to appeals shall apply accordingly.

Amendments

[1] Substituted by FA07 sched2(1)(ad). Has effect as on and from 2 April 2007

[2] Substituted by FA98 sched3(9).

Cross References

From Section 830

Section 826 Agreements for relief from double taxation.

Schedule 24 Relief from Income Tax and Corporation Tax by Means of Credit in Respect of Foreign Tax

To Section 830

Schedule 24 Relief from Income Tax and Corporation Tax by Means of Credit in Respect of Foreign Tax

831 Implementation of Council Directive No. 90/435/EEC concerning the common system of taxation applicable in the case of parent companies and subsidiaries of different Member States

[FA91 s36]

(1) (a) In this section—

"*arrangements*" means arrangements having the force of law by virtue of [*section 826(1)*][1];

"*bilateral agreement*" means any arrangements, protocol or other agreement between the Government and the government of another Member State;

["*company*"[…][2] means a company of a Member State;][3]

"*company of a Member State*" has the meaning assigned to it by Article 2 of the Directive;

["*the Directive*" means Council Directive 2011/96/EU of 30 November 2011*, as amended, on the common system of taxation applicable in the case of parent companies and subsidiaries of different Member States;][4]

* OJ No. L345, 29.12.2011, p.8

"*distribution*" means income from shares or from other rights, not being debt claims, to participate in a company's profits, and includes any amount assimilated to income from shares under the taxation laws of the State of which the company making the distribution is resident;

"*foreign tax*" means any tax which—

(i) is payable under the laws of a Member State other than the State, and

(ii) (I) is specified in [Annex I, Part B][5] of the Directive, or

(II) is substituted for and is substantially similar to a tax so specified;

"*Member State*" means a Member State of the European Communities;

["*parent company*" means a company (referred to in this definition as the "*first-mentioned company*") being—

[(i) a company which owns at least 5 per cent of the share capital of another company which is not resident in the State, or][6]

(ii) a company not resident in the State which owns at least [5 per cent][7] of the share capital of another company which is resident in the State,

but where a bilateral agreement contains a provision to the effect—

(I) that a company shall only be a parent company during any uninterrupted period of at least 2 years throughout which at least [5 per cent][8] of the share capital of the other company is owned by the first-mentioned company, or

(II) that—

(A) the requirement (being the requirement for the purposes of this definition) that a company own at least [5 per cent][9] of the share capital of another shall be treated as a requirement that the first-mentioned company holds at least [5 per cent][10] of the voting rights in the other company, or

(B) that requirement shall be so treated and a company shall only be a parent company during any uninterrupted period of at least 2 years throughout which at least [5 per cent][11] of the voting rights in the other company is held by the first-mentioned company,

then, in its application to a company to which the provision in the bilateral agreement applies, this definition shall apply subject to that provision and shall be construed accordingly;

"*tax*", in relation to a relevant territory, means any tax imposed in that territory which corresponds to income tax or corporation tax in the State.][12]

(b) For the purposes of this section, a company shall be a subsidiary of another company which owns shares or holds voting rights in it where the other company's ownership of those shares or holding of those rights is sufficient for that other company to be a parent company.

(c) A word or expression used in this section and in the Directive has, unless the contrary intention appears, the same meaning in this section as in the Directive.

(2) Subject to *subsections (3)* and *(4)*, where a parent company [...][13] receives a distribution chargeable in the State to corporation tax, other than a distribution in a winding up, from its subsidiary— [which is a company not resident in the State][14]

(a) credit shall be allowed for—

[(i) any witholding tax charged on the distribution by a Member State pursuant to a derogation duly given from [Article 5][15] of the Directive,][16]

(ii) any foreign tax, not chargeable directly or by deduction in respect of the distribution, which is borne by the company making the distribution, and is properly attributable to the proportion of its profits which is represented by the distribution, in so far as that foreign tax exceeds so much of any tax credit in respect of the distribution as is payable to the parent company by the Member State in which the company making the distribution is [resident, and][17]

[(iii) any foreign tax borne by a company that would be allowed under *paragraph 9B* of *Schedule 24* if in *subparagraphs (2)* and *(3)* "and is connected with the relevant company" in each place where it occurs were deleted.][18]

against corporation tax in respect of the distribution to the extent that credit for such withholding tax and foreign tax would not otherwise be so allowed, and

(b) notwithstanding *Chapter 2* of *Part 4*, the distribution shall not be a dividend to which that Chapter applies.

[(2A) Subject to *subsections (3)* and *(4)*, where by virtue of the legal characteristics of a subsidiary (being a company which is not resident in the State) of a parent company, the parent company is chargeable to tax in the State on its share of the profits of the subsidiary company as they arise credit shall be allowed for so much of—

(a) any foreign tax borne by the subsidiary, and

(b) any foreign tax that would be treated as tax paid by the subsidiary company under *paragraph 9B* of *Schedule 24* if—

(i) the subsidiary company were the foreign company for the purposes of that paragraph, and

(ii) in *subparagraphs (2)* and *(3)* of that paragraph "and is connected with the relevant company" in both places where it occurs were deleted,

as is properly attributable to the proportion of the subsidiary's profits which are chargeable on the parent company in the State against corporation tax in respect of the profits so chargeable on the parent company to the extent that credit for such foreign tax would not otherwise be so allowed.][19]

(3) Where by virtue of *subsection (2)(a)* [or (2A)][20] a company is to be allowed credit for tax payable under the laws of a Member State other than the State, *Schedule 24* shall apply for the purposes of that subsection as if—

(a) the provisions of that subsection were arrangements providing that tax so payable shall be allowed as a credit against tax payable in the State, and

(b) references in *Schedule 24* to a dividend were references to a distribution within the meaning of this section.

(4) *Subsection (2)* shall apply without prejudice to any provision of a bilateral agreement.

[(5) *Chapter 8A* of *Part 6*, other than *section 172K*, shall not apply to a distribution made to a parent company which is not resident in the State by its subsidiary which is a company resident in the State.

[…][21]

(6) *Subsection (5)* shall not have effect in relation to a distribution made to a parent company if the majority of the voting rights in the parent company are controlled directly or indirectly by persons, other than persons who by virtue of the law of any relevant territory are resident for the purposes of tax in such a relevant territory (within the meaning assigned by *section 172A*), unless it is shown that the parent company exists for bona fide commercial reasons and does not form part of any arrangement or scheme of which the main purpose, or one of the main purposes, is the avoidance of liability to income tax (including dividend withholding tax under *Chapter 8A* of *Part 6)*, corporation tax or capital gains tax.][22]

Amendments

[1] Substituted by FA07 sched2(1)(ae). Has effect as on and from 2 April 2007

[2] Deleted by FA04 s34(a)(i).

[3] Substituted by FA00 s33(a). Applies as respects distributions made on or after 6 April 2000.

[4] Substituted by F(No.2)A13 sched(1)(i). Has effect on and from 1 July 2013.

[5] Substituted by FA12 sched6(1)(j)(i)(II). Has effect as on and from 31 March 2012.

[6] Substituted by FA04 s34(a)(iii)(I).

[7, 8, 9, 10, 11] Substituted by FA04 s34(a)(iii)(II).

[12] Substituted by FA99 s29(a).

[13] Deleted by FA04 s34(b)(i).

[14] Inserted by FA99 s29(b)(ii).

[15] Substituted by FA12 sched6(1)(j)(ii). Has effect as on and from 31 March 2012.

[16] Substituted by FA04 s34(b)(ii)(I).

[17] Substituted by FA04 s34(b)(ii)(II).

[18] Inserted by FA04 s34(b)(ii)(III).

[19] Inserted by FA04 s34(c).

[20] Inserted by FA04 s34(d).

[21] Deleted by FA04 s34(e).

[22] Inserted by FA99 s29(c).

Revenue Briefings

Tax Briefing

Tax Briefing April 2004 – Issue 55 pg 7 – Finance Act 2004 Parent and Subsidiary

Cross References

From Section 831

Section 52 Persons chargeable.
Section 60 Interpretation (Chapter 2).
Section 172A Interpretation.
Section 172K Returns, payment and collection of dividend withholding tax.
Section 826 Agreements for relief from double taxation.
Schedule 24 Relief from Income Tax and Corporation Tax by Means of Credit in Respect of Foreign Tax

To Section 831

Section 153 Distributions to certain nonresidents.
Section 172B Dividend withholding tax on relevant distributions.
Schedule 24 Relief from Income Tax and Corporation Tax by Means of Credit in Respect of Foreign Tax

831A Treatment of distributions to certain parent companies

[(1) (a) In this section—

"*company*", in relation to a company that is resident for the purposes of tax in Switzerland, means a company which—

(i) takes one of the forms specified in Article 15 of the Agreement attached to the Council Decision (2004/911/EC) of 2 June 2004 on the signing and conclusion of the Agreement between the European Community and the Swiss Confederation providing for measures equivalent to those laid down in Council Directive 2003/48/EC of 3 June 2003 on taxation of savings income in the form of interest payments and the accompanying Memorandum of Understanding*, and

* OJ No. L381, 28.12.2004, p.32

(ii) is subject to tax in Switzerland without being exempt;

"*parent company*" means a company which controls not less than 25 per cent of the voting power in another company;

"*tax*", in relation to Switzerland, means any tax imposed in Switzerland which corresponds to income tax or corporation tax in the State.

(b) For the purposes of this section a company shall be a subsidiary of another company which holds voting rights in it where the other company's holding of those rights is sufficient for that other company to be a parent company.

(2) *Chapter 8A* of *Part 6*, other than *section 172K*, shall not apply to a distribution made to a parent company which is, by virtue of the law of Switzerland, resident for the purposes of tax in Switzerland by its subsidiary which is a company resident in the State.][1]

Amendments

[1] Inserted by FA05 s51(1). This section applies as respects a distribution made on or after 1 July 2005.

Cross References

From Section 831A

Section 172K Returns, payment and collection of dividend withholding tax.

832 Provisions in relation to Convention for reciprocal avoidance of double taxation in the State and the United Kingdom of income and capital gains

[FA77 s39(1) and (3) to (5); FA96 s132(2) and Sch5 PtII]

(1) In this section—

"*the Convention*" means the Convention between the Government of Ireland and the Government of the United Kingdom for the avoidance of double taxation and the prevention of fiscal evasion with respect to taxes on income and capital gains, and the Protocol amending the Convention, both of which are set out in the Schedule to the Double Taxation Relief (Taxes on Income and Capital Gains) (United Kingdom) Order, 1976 [(S.I. No. 319 of 1976).][1]

[...][2]

[...][3]

(3) For the purpose of giving effect to the Convention, the Tax Acts shall, for any year for which the Convention is in force, apply subject to the modifications in *section 73*.

(4) (a) In applying *section 707* in the case of a society registered under the enactments for the time being in force in the United Kingdom corresponding to the Friendly Societies Acts, 1896 to 1977, only expenses of management attributable to the life business referable to contracts of assurance made on or after the 6th day of April, 1976, shall be taken into account.

(b) In applying *subsection (4)* of *section 726* in the case of a society referred to in *paragraph (a)*, there shall be excluded from the liabilities of which B in that subsection is the average any liabilities to policy holders arising from contracts made before the 6th day of April, 1976.

(c) This subsection shall be construed as one with *Part 26*.

Amendments

[1] Substituted by FA99 s67(1)(a)(i). Shall apply as on and from the 6th day of April, 1999, as respects income tax.

[2] Deleted by FA99 s67(1)(a)(ii). Shall apply as on and from the 6th day of April, 1999, as respects income tax.

[3] Deleted by FA99 s67(1)(b). Shall be deemed to apply as on and from the 1st day of January, 1999, as respects corporation tax.

Cross References

From Section 832

Section 73 Income from certain possessions in Great Britain or Northern Ireland.
Section 706 Interpretation and general (Part 26).
Section 707 Management expenses.
Section 726 Investment income.

833 Convention with United States of America [Deleted]

Deleted by FA98 sched3(10).

Cross References

To Section 833

Schedule 24 Relief from Income Tax and Corporation Tax by Means of Credit in Respect of Foreign Tax

834 Relief in respect of ships documented under laws of United States of America [Deleted]

Deleted by FA98 sched3(10).

835 Saver for arrangements made under section 362 of Income Tax Act, 1967

[FA87 s23(2)]

Notwithstanding the repeal of section 362 of the Income Tax Act, 1967, by section 23(1) of the Finance Act, 1987, where before the 9th day of July, 1987, an order was made under section 362 of the Income Tax Act, 1967, the arrangement to which the order relates shall continue to have the force of law.

PART 35A

Transfer Pricing

835A Interpretation

[(1) In this Part—

"*arrangement*" means any agreement or arrangement of any kind (whether or not it is, or is intended to be, legally enforceable);

"*authorised officer*" means an officer of the Revenue Commissioners authorised by them in writing for the purposes of this Part;

"*chargeable period*" has the same meaning as in *section 321(2)*;

"*Commission Recommendation*" means Commission Recommendation 2003/361/EC of 6 May 2003* concerning the definition of micro, small and medium-sized enterprises; "*double taxation relief arrangements*" means arrangements having effect by virtue of *section 826*;

* OJ No. L124, 20.05.2003, p.36

"*group*" means a company which has one or more 75 per cent subsidiaries together with those subsidiaries;

"*relevant activities*", in relation to a person who is one of the persons between whom an arrangement is made, means that person's activities—

(a) which comprise the activities in the course of which, or with respect to which, that arrangement is made, and

(b) which are not activities carried on either separately from the activities referred to in *paragraph (a)* or for the purpose of a different part of that person's business;

"*relevant person*", in relation to an arrangement, means a person who is within the charge to tax under Case I or II of Schedule D in respect of profits or gains or losses, the computation of which profits or gains or losses takes account of the results of the arrangement;

"*tax*" means income tax or corporation tax.

(2) References in this Part to "control", in relation to a company, shall be construed in accordance with *section 11*.][1]

Amendments

[1] Inserted by FA10 s42(1). This section applies for chargeable periods beginning on or after 1 January 2011 in relation to any arrangement (within the meaning of s835A(1)) other than any such arrangement the terms of which are agreed before 1 July 2010.

Revenue Briefings

eBrief

eBrief No. 62/2012 – Monitoring Compliance with Transfer Pricing rules contained in Part 35A TCA 1997

Cross References

From Section 835A

Section 11 Meaning of "control" in certain contexts.

Section 321 Provisions of general application in relation to the making of allowances and charges.

Section 826 Agreements for relief from double taxation.

To Section 835A

Section 835F Documentation and enquiries.

835B Meaning of associated

[(1) For the purposes of this Part—

(a) 2 persons are associated at any time if at that time—

(i) one of the persons is participating in the management, control or capital of the other, or

(ii) the same person is participating in the management, control or capital of each of the 2 persons,

and

(b) a person (in this paragraph referred to as the "*first person*") is participating in the management, control or capital of another person at any time only if that other person is at that time—

(i) a company, and

(ii) controlled by the first person.

(2) (a) For the purposes of this section a company shall be treated as controlled by an individual if it is controlled by the individual and persons connected with the individual.

(b) For the purposes of this subsection a person is connected with an individual if that person is a relative (within the meaning of *section 433(3)(a)*) of that individual.][1]

Amendments

1 Inserted by FA10 s42(1). This section applies for chargeable periods beginning on or after 1 January 2011 in relation to any arrangement (within the meaning of s835A(1)) other than any such arrangement the terms of which are agreed before 1 July 2010.

Cross References

From Section 835B

Section 433 Meaning of "participator", "associate", "director" and "loan creditor".

835C Basic rules on transfer pricing

[(1) Subject to this Part, this section applies to any arrangement—

(a) involving the supply and acquisition of goods, services, money or intangible assets,

(b) where, at the time of the supply and acquisition, the person making the supply (in this Part referred to as the "supplier") and the person making the acquisition (in this Part referred to as the "acquirer") are associated, and

(c) the profits or gains or losses arising from the relevant activities are within the charge to tax under Case I or II of Schedule D in the case of either the supplier or the acquirer or both.

(2) (a) If the amount of the consideration payable (in this Part referred to as the "actual consideration payable") under any arrangement to which this section applies exceeds the arm's length amount, then the profits or gains or losses of the acquirer that are chargeable to tax under Case I or II of Schedule D shall be computed as if the arm's length amount were payable instead of the actual consideration payable.

(b) If the amount of the consideration receivable (in this Part referred to as the "actual consideration receivable") under any arrangement to which this section applies is less than the arm's length amount, then the profits or gains or losses of the supplier that are chargeable to tax under Case I or II of Schedule D shall be computed as if the arm's length amount were receivable instead of the actual consideration receivable.

(3) For the purposes of this section the "arm's length amount" in relation to an arrangement is the amount of the consideration that independent parties would have agreed in relation to the arrangement had those independent parties entered into that arrangement.][1]

Amendments

[1] Inserted by FA10 s42(1). This section applies for chargeable periods beginning on or after 1 January 2011 in relation to any arrangement (within the meaning of s835A(1)) other than any such arrangement the terms of which are agreed before 1 July 2010.

Cross References

To Section 835C

Section 835D Principles for construing rules in accordance with OECD Guidelines.
Section 835F Documentation and enquiries.
Section 835G Elimination of double counting.
Section 835H Capital allowances.

835D Principles for construing rules in accordance with OECD Guidelines

[(1) In this section—

"*Article 9(1) of the OECD Model Tax Convention*" means the provisions which, at the date of the passing of the Finance Act 2010, were contained in Article 9(1) of the Model Tax Convention on Income and Capital published by the OECD;

"*OECD*" means the Organisation for Economic Cooperation and Development;

"*transfer pricing guidelines*" means the guidelines approved on 13 July 1995 by the Council of the OECD (in this definition referred to as the "*OECD Council*") as its Transfer Pricing Guidelines for Multinational Enterprises and Tax Administrations—

(a) supplemented by—

(i) the report on intangible property and services noted by the OECD Council on 11 April 1996,

(ii) the report on cost contribution arrangements noted by the OECD Council on 24 July 1997, and

(iii) such additional guidance, published by the OECD on or after the date of the passing of the Finance Act 2010, as may be designated by the Minister for Finance for the purposes of this Part by order made under *subsection (3)*,

and

(b) modified by updates approved by the OECD Council on 16 July 2009 [and 22 July 2010 and by the revision approved by the OECD Council on 22 July 2010.][1]

(2) For the purpose of computing profits or gains or losses chargeable to tax under Case I or II of Schedule D, this Part shall be construed to ensure, as far as practicable, consistency between—

(a) the effect which is to be given to *section 835C*, and

(b) the effect which, in accordance with the transfer pricing guidelines, would be given if double taxation relief arrangements incorporating Article 9(1) of the OECD Model Tax Convention applied to the computation of the profits or gains or losses, regardless of whether such double taxation relief arrangements actually apply,

but this section shall not apply for the purposes of construing this Part to the extent that such application of the section would be contrary to the provisions of double taxation relief arrangements that apply to the computation of those profits or gains or losses.

(3) The Minister for Finance may, for the purposes of this Part, by order designate any additional guidance referred to in *paragraph (a)(iii)* of the definition of "*transfer pricing guidelines*" in *subsection (1)* as being comprised in the transfer pricing guidelines.

(4) Every order made by the Minister for Finance under *subsection (3)* shall be laid before Dáil Éireann as soon as may be after it is made and, if a resolution annulling the order is passed by Dáil Éireann within the next 21 days on which Dáil Éireann has sat after the order is laid before it, the order shall be annulled accordingly, but without prejudice to the validity of anything previously done thereunder.][2]

Amendments

[1] Inserted by FA12 s48(1). Applies as on and from 31 March 2012.

[2] Inserted by FA10 s42(1). This section applies for chargeable periods beginning on or after 1 January 2011 in relation to any arrangement (within the meaning of s835A(1)) other than any such arrangement the terms of which are agreed before 1 July 2010.

Cross References

From Section 835D

Section 835C Basic rules on transfer pricing.

835E Small or medium-sized enterprise

[(1) This Part does not apply in computing for any chargeable period the profits or gains or losses of a person if that person is a small or medium-sized enterprise for that chargeable period.

(2) For the purposes of this section "*small or medium-sized enterprise*" means an enterprise which would fall within the category of micro, small and medium-sized enterprises as defined in the Annex to the Commission Recommendation (in this section referred to as the "*Annex*") if—

(a) in the case of an enterprise which is in liquidation or administration, the rights of the liquidator or administrator (in that capacity) were left out of account when applying Article 3(3)(*b*) of the Annex in determining for the purposes of this Part whether—

(i) that enterprise, or

(ii) any other enterprise (including that of the liquidator or administrator),

is a small or medium-sized enterprise,

(b) Article 3 of the Annex had effect with the omission of *paragraph 5* of that Article,

(c) the first sentence of Article 4(1) of the Annex had effect as if the data to apply to—

(i) the headcount of staff, and

(ii) the financial amounts,

were the data relating to the chargeable period referred to in *subsection (1)* (instead of the period described in the said first sentence of Article 4(1) of the Annex) and calculated on an annual basis, and

(d) Article 4 of the Annex had effect with the omission of the following provisions—
 (i) the second sentence of *paragraph 1* of that Article,
 (ii) *paragraph 2* of that Article, and
 (iii) *paragraph 3* of that Article.][1]

Amendments

[1] Inserted by FA10 s42(1). This section applies for chargeable periods beginning on or after 1 January 2011 in relation to any arrangement (within the meaning of s835A(1)) other than any such arrangement the terms of which are agreed before 1 July 2010.

835F Documentation and enquiries

[(1) A relevant person in relation to an arrangement to which *section 835C(1)* applies shall have available such records as may reasonably be required for the purposes of determining whether, in relation to the arrangement, the income of the person chargeable to tax under Case I or II of Schedule D has been computed in accordance with this Part.

(2) The records referred to in *subsection (1)* shall be prepared on a timely basis and *subsection (3)* of *section 886* shall apply to such records as it applies to records required by that section.

(3) *Sections 900* and *901* shall apply to records referred to in *subsection (1)* as if they were books, records or documents within the meaning of *section 900* and as if the reference to an authorised officer in *section 900* were a reference to an authorised officer within the meaning of *section 835A(1)*.

(4) Notwithstanding any other provisions of the Tax Acts, enquiries relating to compliance with this Part may only be initiated by an authorised officer.][1]

Amendments

[1] Inserted by FA10 s42(1). This section applies for chargeable periods beginning on or after 1 January 2011 in relation to any arrangement (within the meaning of s835A(1)) other than any such arrangement the terms of which are agreed before 1 July 2010.

Cross References

From Section 835F

Section 835A Interpretation.
Section 835C Basic rules on transfer pricing.
Section 886 Obligation to keep certain records.
Section 900 Power to call for production of books, information, etc.
Section 901 Application to High Court: production of books, information, etc.

835G Elimination of double counting

[(1) Where—

(a) the profits or gains or losses of a person (in this section referred to as the "*first-mentioned person*"), that are chargeable to tax under Case I or II of Schedule D, are, by virtue of *section 835C*, computed as if, instead of the actual consideration payable or receivable under the terms of an arrangement, the arm's length amount in relation to that arrangement were payable or receivable as the case may be, and

(b) the other party (in this section referred to as the "*affected person*") to the arrangement is within the charge to tax under Schedule D in respect of the profits or gains or losses arising from the relevant activities, then, subject to *subsections (2)* and *(3)*, on the making of a claim by the affected person, the profits or gains or losses of the affected person arising from the relevant activities that are chargeable to tax under Schedule D shall be computed as if, instead of the actual consideration receivable or payable by the affected person under the terms of the arrangement, the arm's length amount (determined in accordance with *section 835C*) in relation to that arrangement were receivable or payable as the case may be.

(2) (a) *Subsection (1)* shall not affect the credits to be brought into account by the affected person in respect of closing trading stocks, for any chargeable period.

(b) For the purposes of this subsection "trading stock", in relation to a trade, has the same meaning as it has for the purposes of *section 89*.

(3) *Subsection (1)* shall not apply in relation to an arrangement unless and until the tax due and payable by the first-mentioned person for the chargeable period, in respect of which the profits or gains or losses are, by virtue of *section 835C*, computed as if, instead of the actual consideration payable or receivable under the terms of an arrangement, the arm's length amount in relation to that arrangement were payable or receivable, as the case may be, has been paid.

(4) Where the profits or gains of an affected person are reduced by virtue of *subsection (1)* then the amount of foreign tax (if any) for which relief may be given under any double taxation relief arrangements or paragraph 9DA or 9FA of Schedule 24 shall be reduced by the amount of foreign tax which would not be or have become payable if, for the purposes of that tax, instead of the actual consideration payable or receivable under the terms of any arrangement to which *subsection (1)* applies, the arm's length amount (determined in accordance with *section 835C*) in relation to that arrangement were payable or receivable by the affected person as the case may be.

(5) (a) Where, in relation to an arrangement—

(i) the persons, who apart from this paragraph would be the affected person and the first-mentioned person, are members of the same group,

(ii) the arrangement is comprised of activities within the meaning of *paragraph (a)* of the definition of "*excepted operations*" in *section 21A*, and

(iii) the persons referred to in *subparagraph (i)* jointly elect that this section shall apply,

then *section 835C* and this section shall not apply in relation to that arrangement.

(b) An election under *paragraph (a)* shall be made by notice in writing to the inspector on or before the specified return date for the chargeable period (within the meaning of [*section 959A*][1]) for the chargeable period of the person who, apart from *paragraph (a)*, would be the first-mentioned person, and the notice shall set out the facts necessary to show that the persons referred to in *paragraph (a)(i)* are entitled to make the election.

(6) Any adjustments required to be made by virtue of this section may be made by the making of, or the amendment of, an assessment.][2]

Amendments

[1] Substituted by FA12 sched4(part 2)(g).

[2] Inserted by FA10 s42(1). This section applies for chargeable periods beginning on or after 1 January 2011 in relation to any arrangement (within the meaning of s835A(1)) other than any such arrangement the terms of which are agreed before 1 July 2010.

Cross References

From Section 835G

Section 21A Higher rate of corporation tax.
Section 89 Valuation of trading stock at discontinuance of trade.
Section 835C Basic rules on transfer pricing.
Section 950 Interpretation (Part 41).

835H Capital allowances

[*Section 835C* shall not apply in computing any deductions or additions to be made in taxing a trade under the provisions of the Tax Acts which relate to allowances and charges in respect of capital expenditure.][1]

Amendments

[1] Inserted by FA10 s42(1). This section applies for chargeable periods beginning on or after 1 January 2011 in relation to any arrangement (within the meaning of s835A(1)) other than any such arrangement the terms of which are agreed before 1 July 2010.

Cross References

From Section 835H

Section 835C Basic rules on transfer pricing.

PART 36

Miscellaneous Special Provisions

836 Allowances for expenses of members of Oireachtas

[Section 4 of the Oireachtas (Allowances to Members) and Ministerial and Parliamentary Offices (Amendment) Act, 1992]

(1) An allowance payable under section 3 of the Oireachtas (Allowances to Members) and Ministerial and Parliamentary Offices (Amendment) Act, 1992, shall be exempt from income tax and shall not be reckoned in computing income for the purposes of the Income Tax Acts.

[(1A) Subsection (1) shall apply to—

(a) an allowance payable under section 2 of the Oireachtas (Allowances to Members) Act, 1938, and section 5 of the Oireachtas (Allowances to Members) and Ministerial and Parliamentary Offices (Amendment) Act, 1964, in respect of travelling facilities within the meaning of the first-mentioned Act, and

(b) an allowance payable under section 1 or 2 of the Oireachtas (Allowances to Members) Act, 1962,

as it applies to an allowance payable under section 3 of the Oireachtas (Allowances to Members) and Ministerial and Parliamentary Offices (Amendment) Act, 1992.][1]

[(1B) Parliamentary standard allowance payable under section 3 of the Oireachtas (Allowances to Members) and Ministerial and Parliamentary Offices Act 2009 is exempt from income tax and shall not be reckoned in computing income for the purposes of the Income Tax Acts.][2]

(2) *Sections 114* and *115* shall not apply in relation to expenses in full settlement of which an allowance is payable under section 3 of the Oireachtas (Allowances to Members) and Ministerial and Parliamentary Offices (Amendment) Act, 1992, [or under section 3 of the Oireachtas (Allowances to Members) and Ministerial and Parliamentary Offices Act 2009 or any allowance or payment made in respect of any particular allowance or payment referred to in subsection (1) of that section][3] and no claim shall lie under those sections in respect of those expenses; but where a Minister of the Government, the Attorney General or a Minister of State, being—

(a) a member of Dáil Éireann for a constituency outside the county borough and the administrative county of Dublin, or

(b) a member of Seanad Éireann whose main residence is situated outside that county borough and administrative county,

is, arising out of the performance of his or her duties as an office holder or as a member of the Oireachtas, obliged to maintain a second residence in addition to his or her main residence, he or she shall be granted a deduction under *section 114* in respect of expenses incurred by him or her in maintaining that second residence [but such expenses shall not include local property tax payable under *section 16* of the Finance (Local Property Tax) Act 2012 or the charge for water services payable under *section 21* of the Water Services (No. 2) Act 2013][4].

Amendments

[1] Inserted by the Oireachtas (Allowances to Members) and Ministerial, Parliamentary, Judicial and Court Offices (Amendment) Act, 1998 s21(1). Subsection (1) shall be deemed to have come into operation on the 6th day of April, 1997.

[2] Inserted by the Oireachtas (Allowances to Members) and Ministerial and Parliamentary Offices Act 2009 Sec 3(7)(a)

[3] Inserted by the Oireachtas (Allowances to Members) and Ministerial and Parliamentary Offices Act 2009 Sec 3(7)(b)

[4] Inserted by FA14 s14. Comes into operation on 1 January 2015.

Cross References

From Section 836

Section 114 General rule as to deductions.

Section 115 Fixed deduction for certain classes of persons.

837 Members of the clergy and ministers of religion

[ITA67 s544(1); FA69 s65(1) and Sch5 PtI]

In assessing the income tax chargeable under any Schedule on a member of the clergy or minister of any religious denomination, the following deductions may be made from any profits, fees or emoluments of his or her profession—

(a) any sums of money paid or expenses incurred by him or her wholly, exclusively and necessarily in the performance of his or her duty as a member of the clergy or minister of any religious denomination;

(b) such part of the rent (not exceeding one-eighth), as the inspector by whom the assessment is made may allow, paid by him or her in respect of a dwelling house any part of which is used mainly and substantially for the purposes of his or her duty as a member of the clergy or minister of any religious denomination.

838 Special portfolio investment accounts

[FA93 s14 (other than proviso to sub(4)(c) and sub(6)(b)); FA94 s12(2) and s34(b); FA95 s11(2); FA96 s37(1); FA97 s31, s146(1) and Sch9 PtI par17(1)]

(1) (a) In this section—

"*designated broker*" means a person—

(i) which is a dealing member firm of the Irish Stock Exchange or a member firm (which carries on a trade in the State through a branch or agency) of a stock exchange of any other Member State of the European Communities, and

(ii) which has sent to the Revenue Commissioners a notification of its name and address and of its intention to accept specified deposits;

"*gains*" means chargeable gains within the meaning of the Capital Gains Tax Acts, including gains which but for *section 607* would be chargeable gains;

"*market value*" shall be construed in accordance with *section 548*;

"*ordinary shares*" means shares forming part of a company's ordinary share capital;

"*qualifying shares*" means ordinary shares in a company which are—

(i) listed in the official list of the Irish Stock Exchange, or

(ii) quoted on the market known as the Developing Companies Market, or the market known as the Exploration Securities Market, of the Irish Stock Exchange,

other than—

(I) shares in an investment company within the meaning of Part XIII of the Companies Act, 1990,

(II) shares in an undertaking for collective investment in transferable securities within the meaning of the European Communities (Undertakings for Collective Investment in Transferable Securities) Regulations, 1989 (S.I. No. 78 of 1989), or

(III) shares in a company, being shares the market value of which may be expected to approximate at all times to the market value of the proportion of the assets of the company which they represent;

"*relevant income or gains*" means the aggregate of the income and gains, including losses, arising from relevant investments, but only so much of income arising to or gains accruing to the special portfolio investment account shall be relevant income or gains as is or is to be—

(i) paid to, or

(ii) accumulated or invested for the benefit of,

the individual in whose name the special portfolio investment account is held, or would be so paid, accumulated or invested if any gains accruing to the account in accordance with *subsection (4)(e)* were gains on an actual disposal of the assets concerned;

"*relevant investment*" means an investment in [fully paid-up][1]—

(i) qualifying shares and specified qualifying shares, or

(ii) qualifying shares, specified qualifying shares and securities,

as the case may be, acquired by a designated broker [at market value][2] by the expenditure of money contributed by means of a specified deposit, and held by a designated broker in a special portfolio investment account;

[...][3]

"*securities*" means securities—

(i) issued under the authority of the Minister for Finance, or

(ii) issued by the Electricity Supply Board, Radio Telefís Éireann, [...][4], [...][5] Córas Iompair Éireann, [...][6] Bord na Móna, [or Dublin Airport Authority,][7]

which are listed in the official list of the Irish Stock Exchange;

"*special portfolio investment account*" means an account opened [on or after 1 February 1993 and before 6 April 2001][8], in which a relevant investment is held and in respect of which the conditions referred to in *paragraph (c)* are complied with;

"*specified deposit*" means a sum of money paid by an individual to a designated broker for the purpose of acquiring assets which will form part of a relevant investment;

"*specified qualifying shares*", in relation to a special portfolio investment account, means qualifying shares in a company which when the shares are acquired for the account has an issued share capital the market value of which is less than [€255,000,000][9].

(b) For the purposes of this section, *Chapter 4* of *Part 8* shall be construed as if—

(i) references to "*deposit*", "*interest*", "*relevant deposit*", "*relevant deposit taker*", "*relevant interest*" and "*special savings account*" were respectively references to "*specified deposit*", "*income or gains*", "*relevant investment*", "*designated broker*", "*relevant income or gains*" and "*special portfolio investment account*" within the meaning of this section, and

(ii) *subsections (4)* and *(5)* of *section 258* and *section 259* had not been enacted.

(c) Notwithstanding *subsection (3)*, *section 264* shall apply to a special portfolio investment account as if—

(i) *paragraphs (d)* to *(i)* of *subsection (1)* of that section had not been enacted, and

(ii) the conditions in *subsection (2)* of this section had been included in *subsection (1)* of that section.

(2) The conditions referred to in *subsection (1)(c)(ii)* are:

(a) each special portfolio investment account and all assets held in such an account shall be kept separately from all other investment accounts, if any, operated by a designated broker;

(b) the amount of a specified deposit or, if there is more than one, the aggregate of such amounts in respect of assets held at the same time as part of a special portfolio investment account shall not exceed—

(i) in the case of a special portfolio investment account in respect of which—

(I) the first specified deposit was made on or before the 5th day of April, 2000, and

(II) an amount (in this paragraph referred to as "*the particular amount*") equal to the whole or a part of the specified deposit or specified deposits has been used to acquire shares in a company quoted on the market known as the Developing Companies Market of the Irish Stock Exchange and those shares are at that time held as assets of the special portfolio investment account,

[€63,500][10] increased by the lesser of—

(A) the particular amount, and

(B) [€12,700][11],

and

(ii) in the case of any other special portfolio investment account, [€63,500][12];

[...][13]

(d) the aggregate of the consideration given for shares which are at any time before the 1st day of February, 1994, assets of a special portfolio investment account shall not be less than—

(i) as respects qualifying shares, 40 per cent, and

(ii) as respects specified qualifying shares, 6 per cent,

of the aggregate of the consideration given for the assets of the account at that time;

(e) the aggregate of the consideration given for shares which are at any time within the year ending on the 31st day of January, 1995, assets of a special portfolio investment account shall not be less than—

(i) as respects qualifying shares, 45 per cent, and

(ii) as respects specified qualifying shares, 9 per cent,

of the aggregate of the consideration given for the assets of the account at that time;

(f) the aggregate of the consideration given for shares which are at any time within the year ending on the 31st day of January, 1996, assets of a special portfolio investment account shall not be less than—

(i) as respects qualifying shares, 50 per cent, and

(ii) as respects specified qualifying shares, 10 per cent,

of the aggregate of the consideration given for the assets of the account at that time;

(g) the aggregate of the consideration given for shares which are at any time [on or after 1 February 1996 and before 31 December 2000][14], assets of a special portfolio investment account shall not be less than—

(i) as respects qualifying shares, 55 per cent, and

(ii) as respects specified qualifying shares, 10 per cent,

of the aggregate of the consideration given for the assets of the account at that time;

and for the purposes of—

(I) *paragraphs (b)* and *(c)*, a disposal of shares or securities, being shares or securities, as the case may be, of the same class acquired for a special portfolio investment account at different times, shall be assumed to be a disposal of shares or securities, as the case may be, acquired later, rather than of shares or securities, as the case may be, acquired earlier for the special portfolio investment account, and

(II) *paragraphs (d)* to *(g)*, the amount of the consideration given for shares shall be determined in accordance with *sections 547* and *580*.

(3) *Chapter 4* of *Part 8* (other than *section 259*) shall, subject to this section and with any other necessary modifications, apply to special portfolio investment accounts as it applies to special savings accounts[, and in particular the rate of appropriate tax specified in *section 256(1)* in relation to relevant interest payable in respect of a relevant deposit or relevant deposits held in a special savings account shall apply to special portfolio investment accounts][15].

(4) (a) *Paragraphs (b)* to *(h)* shall apply notwithstanding any other provision of the Tax Acts and the Capital Gains Tax Acts.

(b) Where for any year of assessment a loss arises from the computation of relevant income or gains, that loss shall be included in the computation of the relevant income or gains of the special portfolio investment account for the next year of assessment, and, in so far as relief for the loss cannot be so given, it shall be set against such relevant income or gains in the next year of assessment and, where appropriate, in each subsequent year of assessment in so far as it cannot be so relieved, and no further relief shall be allowed under any provision of the Tax Acts or the Capital Gains Tax Acts in respect of that loss.

[(bb) Notwithstanding *paragraph (b)*, where, at the time a special portfolio investment account is closed, a loss has not been relieved under that paragraph because of an insufficiency of relevant income or gains at that time, that loss shall for the purposes of *section 31* be treated as an allowable loss accruing at that time to the individual in whose name the special portfolio investment account was held.][16]

(c) *Sections 556*, *601*, *607* and *1028(4)* shall not apply in relation to any gains referable to a relevant investment.

(d) (i) In this paragraph—

"the appropriate amount in respect of the interest" means the appropriate amount in respect of the interest which would be determined in accordance with *Schedule 21* if the designated broker were the first buyer and the designated broker carried on a trade to which *section 749(1)* applies; but, in so determining the appropriate amount in respect of the interest in accordance with *Schedule 21*, *paragraph 3(4)* of that Schedule shall apply as if "in the opinion of the Appeal Commissioners" were deleted;

"*securities*" has the same meaning as in *section 815*.

(ii) Subject to *subparagraph (iii)*, where—

(I) in a year of assessment (in this subparagraph referred to as "the first year of assessment") securities which are assets of a special portfolio investment account are disposed of, and

(II) in the following year of assessment interest becoming payable in respect of the securities is receivable by the special portfolio investment account,

then, for the purposes of computing the relevant income or gains for the first year of assessment, the price paid by the designated broker for the securities shall be treated as reduced by the appropriate amount in respect of the interest.

(iii) Where for a year of assessment *subparagraph (ii)* applies so as to reduce the price paid for securities, the amount by which the price paid for the securities is reduced shall be treated as a loss arising in the following year of assessment from the disposal of the securities.

(e) For the purpose of computing relevant income or gains of a special portfolio investment account for a year of assessment, each asset of a special portfolio investment account on [31 December][17] in that year of assessment shall be deemed to have been disposed of and immediately reacquired by the designated broker on that day at the asset's market value on that day.

[(f) Subject to *subsection (5)*, where in a year of assessment the relevant income or gains of a special portfolio investment account includes a distribution from a company resident in the State, the amount or value of that distribution shall be taken into account in computing the relevant income or gains for that year of assessment.][18]

[…][19]

(h) Capital gains tax shall not be chargeable on the disposal of assets held as part of a relevant investment; but this paragraph shall not prevent any such disposals from being taken into account in computing the amount of relevant income or gains on which appropriate tax is payable.

(5) (a) In this subsection—

"*eligible shares*" has the same meaning as in *section 488*;

"*qualifying company*" has the meaning assigned to it by *section 495*.

(b) Without prejudice to the treatment of losses on eligible shares as allowable losses, gains accruing on the disposal or deemed disposal of eligible shares in a qualifying company shall not for the purposes of computing appropriate tax in accordance with *subsection (6)* be treated as gains.

(c) Distributions included in the relevant income or gains of a special portfolio investment account in respect of eligible shares in qualifying companies shall not be taken into account in computing appropriate tax in accordance with *subsection (6)*[...][20].

(6) (a) For the purposes of *sections 257* and *258*, a designated broker shall, in relation to each special portfolio investment account—

(i) be deemed to have made a payment on [31 December][21] in each year of assessment of the amount of relevant income or gains for that year of assessment, and

(ii) be liable to make a payment of appropriate tax in relation to such payment.

(b) The designated broker may deduct an amount on account of any such payment of appropriate tax and the individual beneficially entitled to the assets in the special portfolio investment account shall allow such deduction from any income or from the proceeds of the sale of any assets which the designated broker holds as part of the special portfolio investment account; but, where there are no such funds or insufficient funds available out of which the designated broker may satisfy the appropriate tax, the amount of such tax shall be an amount due to the designated broker from the person beneficially entitled to the relevant investment.

(c) For the purposes of this section, *section 258* shall apply as if in *subsection (2)* of that section "on or before [31 October][22] following that year of assessment" were substituted for "within 15 days from the end of the year of assessment".

(7) *Part 16* shall not apply in relation to any shares which form part of a relevant investment.

Amendments

[1] Inserted by FA99 s65(1)(a)(i). Shall be deemed to have applied, as respects paragraphs (a)(i), and (d) of subsection (1), as on and from the 1st day of December, 1998.

[2] Inserted by FA99 s65(1)(a)(ii). Shall be deemed to have applied, as respects paragraph (a)(ii) and paragraph (b) of subsection (1), as on and from the 1st day of February, 1993.

[3] Deleted by FA01 s56(a)(ii).

[4] Repealed by ICC BA00 s7 and the ICC BA00 (Sections 5 and 7) (Commencement) Order 2001 (S.I. 396/2001) as respects securities issued on or after 15 February 2001.

[5] Deleted by FA01 s241(1)(c). Has effect as respects any securities issued by Bord Telecom E´ireann or Irish Telecommunications Investments plc. on or after 15 February 2001.

[6] Repealed by ACCBA01 with effect from 28 February 2002 by S.I. 69 of 2002.

[7] Substituted by FA08 sched8(1)(p). Has effect as on and from 31 January 2008.

[8] Substituted by FA01 s56(a)(i).

[9, 10, 11, 12] Substituted by FA01 sched5.

[13] Deleted by FA01 s56(b)(i).

[14] Substituted by FA01 s56(b)(ii).

[15] Substituted by FA99 s65(1)(d). Shall be deemed to have applied, as respects paragraphs (a)(i), and (d) of subsection (1), as on and from the 1st day of December, 1998.

[16] Inserted by FA02 s50.

[17] Substituted by FA01 sched2(46)(a). Applies as respects the year of assessment 2001 and subsequent years of assessment.

[18] Substituted by FA00 sched2(o).

[19, 20] Repealed by FA00 sched2.

[21] Substituted by FA01 sched2(46)(b)(i). Applies as respects the year of assessment 2001 and subsequent years of assessment.

[22] Substituted by FA01 sched2(46)(b)(ii). Applies as respects the year of assessment 2001 and subsequent years of assessment.

Revenue Briefings

Tax Briefing

Tax Briefing September 1996 – Issue 23 pg 16 – Special Portfolio Investment Accounts

Revenue Precedents

If a SPIA holder gets income from the SPIA in the form of shares, the shares can be left in the SPIA without breaching the investment limit once the income is not taken out of the SPIA. The investment limit is breached only if the cash given to the designated broker for investment exceeds the limit. After 5 years the balance in the SPIA must be reduced to the prescribed limit. GD93011

The aggregate of the consideration given for shares which are at any time held in a SPIA must be, as respects specified qualifying shares, at least 10% of the aggregate of the consideration given for the assests of the SPIA at that time. GD93011A

Cross References

From Section 838

Section 31 Amount chargeable.

Section 237 Annual payments payable wholly out of taxed income.

Section 256 Interpretation (Chapter 4).

Section 257 Deduction of tax from relevant interest.

Section 258 Returns and collection of appropriate tax.

Section 259 Alternative amount on account of appropriate tax.

Section 264 Conditions and declarations relating to special savings accounts.

Section 488 Interpretation (Part 16).

Section 495 Specified individuals.

Section 547 Disposals and acquisitions treated as made at market value.

Section 548 Valuation of assets.

Section 556 Adjustment of allowable expenditure by reference to consumer price index.

Section 580 Shares, securities, etc: identification.

Section 601 Annual exempt amount.

Section 607 Government and certain other securities.

Section 749 Dealers in securities.

Section 815 Taxation of income deemed to arise on certain sales of securities.

Section 1028 Married persons.

Schedule 21 Purchase and Sale of Securities: Appropriate Amount in Respect of the Interest

To Section 838

Section 172A Interpretation.

Section 172C Exemption from dividend withholding tax for certain persons.

Section 839 Limits to special investments.

Schedule 2A Dividend Withholding Tax

839 Limits to special investments

[FA93 s16; FA94 s34(c) to (g)]

(1) Subject to *subsection (2)*, an individual shall not at the same time have a beneficial interest in investments of more than one of the following classes of investment—

(a) special savings accounts within the meaning of *section 256(1)* (such an account being referred to subsequently in this section as a "special savings account");

[...][1]

(c) special investment units within the meaning of *section 737*;

(d) special portfolio investment accounts within the meaning of *section 838*.

(2) (a) An individual, whether [married or not or in a civil partnership or not,][2] who does not have a joint interest in an investment of a class mentioned

(a) any person (in this definition referred to as "*the first-mentioned person*"),

(b) any person who is a member of the first-mentioned person's staff, or

(c) any person providing or performing any service for the first-mentioned person, the entertainment being entertainment that is provided in the course of, or is incidental to, the provision or performance of the service,

in connection with a trade carried on by the first-mentioned person, but does not include anything provided by that person for bona fide members of that person's staff unless its provision for them is incidental to its provision also for others;

a reference to expenses incurred in, or to the use of an asset for, providing entertainment includes a reference to expenses incurred in, or to the use of an asset for, providing anything incidental thereto;

a reference to a trade includes a reference to a business, profession or employment;

a reference to the members of a person's staff is a reference to persons employed by the person, directors of a company or persons engaged in the management of the company being for this purpose deemed to be persons employed by the company.

(2) In respect of any expenses incurred in providing business entertainment, no sum shall be—

(a) deducted in computing the amount of profits or gains chargeable to tax under Schedule D,

(b) included in computing any expenses of management in respect of which a deduction may be claimed under *section 83* or *707*, or

(c) allowed under *section 114*.

(3) (a) In this subsection, "*the specified provisions*" means the provisions of *Part 9* relating to machinery or plant.

(b) Where any asset is used or is provided for use wholly or partly for the purpose of providing business entertainment, no allowance under any of the specified provisions shall be made for any year of assessment or for any accounting period of a company in respect of the use of the asset or the expenditure incurred in the provision of the asset to the extent that it is used or is to be used for that business entertainment.

(4) The expenses to which *subsection (2)* applies include in the case of any person any sum paid by that person to, on behalf of or placed by that person at the disposal of a member of that person's staff for the purpose of defraying expenses incurred or to be incurred by the member of the staff in providing business entertainment.

(5) This section shall apply in relation to the provision of a gift as it applies in relation to the provision of entertainment.

(6) (a) Where by reason of the provision or performance of a service an amount is paid or payable to a person referred to in *paragraph (c)* of the definition of "*business entertainment*", so much of the amount as is equal to the cost of any business entertainment that is provided in the course of, or is incidental to the provision or performance of, the service shall be deemed to be incurred in providing business entertainment.

(b) The cost of any business entertainment shall be determined by the inspector according to the best of his or her knowledge and judgment.

(c) A determination made under *paragraph (b)* may be amended by the Appeal Commissioners or by the Circuit Court on the hearing or the rehearing of an appeal against any deduction (including a case where no deduction is granted) granted on the basis of the determination.

Revenue Precedents

The provision of accommodation for a foreign potential customer would appear to come within the definition of business entertainment and therefore would not be an allowable deduction. IT953505

Cross References

From Section 840

Section 83 Expenses of management of investment companies.

Section 114 General rule as to deductions.

Section 268 Meaning of "industrial building or structure".

Section 707 Management expenses.

840A Interest on loans to defray money applied for certain purposes

[(1) In this section—

"*asset*" means any asset other than—

(a) an asset that is treated by the provisions of *section 291A(2)* as machinery or plant for the purposes of *Chapters 2* and *4* of *Part 9*, or

(b) an asset acquired as trading stock;

"*trading stock*" has the same meaning as in *section 89*.

(2) Subject to *subsections (3), (6), (7)* and *(8)* in computing the amount of the profits or gains to be charged to corporation tax under Schedule D, no sum shall be deducted in respect of any interest payable on a loan to a company (in this section referred to as the "*investing company*") used in acquiring assets from a company which, at the time of the acquiring of the assets, was connected with the investing company if the loan is made to the investing company by a person who is connected with the investing company.

(3) Where, in an accounting period, interest is payable by an investing company on a loan to defray money applied in acquiring a trade (in this section referred to as an "*acquired trade*") which immediately before its acquisition by the investing company was carried on by a company which was not within the charge to corporation tax, then *subsection (2)* shall not apply to so much of that interest as does not exceed the amount of the profits or gains of the acquired trade for that accounting period which are chargeable to tax under Case I of Schedule D.

(4) This section shall apply where a company acquires part of a trade as if that part were a separate trade.

(5) Where the investing company begins to carry on the activities of an acquired trade as part of its trade, then that part of its trade shall for the purposes of *subsection (3)* be treated as a separate trade and any necessary apportionment shall be made so that profits or gains shall be attributed to the separate trade on a just and reasonable basis and the amount of those profits or gains shall not exceed the amount which would be attributed to a distinct and separate company, engaged in those activities, if it were independent of, and dealing at arm's length with, the investing company.

(6) (a) Where, in an accounting period, interest is payable by an investing company on a loan to defray money applied in acquiring an asset (in this subsection referred to as an "*acquired asset*") which is leased by the company for that accounting period in the course of a trade (in this paragraph referred to as the "*first-mentioned trade*") then, if immediately before that asset was acquired by the investing company it was not in use for the purposes of a trade carried on by a company which was within the charge to corporation tax, *subsection (2)* shall not apply to so much of that interest as does not

exceed the amount of the profits or gains of the first-mentioned trade for that accounting period as is attributable to the acquired asset.

(b) For the purposes of *paragraph (a)*, in arriving at the profits or gains of a trade attributable to an acquired asset, any necessary apportionment shall be made of the expenses and receipts of the trade.

(7) This section shall not apply to interest payable to a company (in this subsection referred to as the "*first-mentioned company*") by an investing company where the sole business of the first-mentioned company is the on-lending to the investing company of moneys which the first-mentioned company has borrowed from persons who are not connected with either or both the first-mentioned company and the investing company.

(8) This section shall not apply to any interest payable by a qualifying company (within the meaning of *section 110*).

(9) Where, as a part of, or in connection with, any scheme or arrangement for the making of a loan to the investing company by a person (in this subsection referred to as the "*first-mentioned person*") who is not connected with the investing company, another person who is connected with the investing company directly or indirectly makes a loan to, a deposit with, or otherwise provides funds to the first-mentioned person or to a person who is connected with the first-mentioned person, then the loan made to the investing company shall be treated for the purposes of *subsection (2)* as being a loan made to the investing company by a person with whom it is connected.][1]

Amendments

[1] Inserted by FA11 s36(1). This section shall apply in respect of a loan made on or after 21 January 2011 other than any such loan made in accordance with a binding written agreement made before that date.

Revenue Briefings

eBrief

eBrief No. 11/11 – Finance Act 2011 – Interest Payable on Loans

Cross References

From Section 840A

Section 89 Valuation of trading stock at discontinuance of trade.

Section 110 Securitisation.

Section 291A Intangible assets.

841 Voluntary Health Insurance Board: restriction of certain losses and deemed disposal of certain assets

[FA97 s61(1), (3) and (4)]

(1) In this section—

"*the Board*" means the Voluntary Health Insurance Board;

"*market value*" shall be construed in accordance with *section 548*.

(2) *Section 396* shall not apply to a loss incurred by the Board in an accounting period ending before the 1st day of March, 1997.

(3) Notwithstanding any other provision of the Tax Acts, bonds and shares held by the Board on the 28th day of February, 1997, in the course of the business of carrying out schemes of voluntary health insurance shall be deemed to have been disposed of and immediately reacquired by the Board on that date at the assets' market value on that date.

Cross References

From Section 841

Section 396 Relief for trading losses other than terminal losses.

Section 548 Valuation of assets.

842 Replacement of harbour authorities by port companies

[FA97 s48]

(1) In this section, "*relevant port company*" has the same meaning as in *paragraph 1* of Schedule 26.

(2) *Schedule 26* shall apply where assets are vested in, or transferred to, a relevant port company pursuant to the Harbours Act, 1996.

(3) This section and *Schedule 26* shall apply from the 1st day of March, 1997.

Cross References

From Section 842

Schedule 26 Replacement of Harbour Authorities by Port Companies

To Section 842

Schedule 26 Replacement of Harbour Authorities by Port Companies

843 Capital allowances for buildings used for third level educational purposes

[FA97 s25]

(1) In this section—

["*approved institution*" means—

(a) an institution of higher education within the meaning of section 1 of the Higher Education Authority Act, 1971, or

(b) an institution in the State in receipt of public funding which provides courses to which a scheme approved by the Minister for Education and Science under the Local Authorities (Higher Education Grants) Acts, 1968 to 1992, [[applies, or][1]][2];][3]

[(c) any body engaged in the provision of third level health and social services education or training which is approved by the Minister for Health and Children for the purposes of this section and is in receipt of public funding in respect of the provision of such education or training;][4]

"*qualifying expenditure*" means capital expenditure incurred on—

(a) the construction of a qualifying premises, or

(b) the provision of machinery or plant,

[which—

(i) in the case of an institution referred to in *paragraph (a)* or *(b)* of the definition of "*approved institution*", is, following the receipt of the advice of An tÚdarás, approved for that purpose by the Minister for Education and Science with the consent of the Minister for Finance, and

(ii) in the case of a body referred to in *paragraph (c)* of the definition of "*approved institution*", is approved for that purpose by the Minister for Health and Children with the consent of the Minister for Finance;][5]

["*qualifying period*" means the period commencing on 1 July 1997 and ending on [31 December 2006 or, where *subsection (1A)* applies, ending on 31 July 2008][6];][7]

"*qualifying premises*" means a building or structure which—

(a) apart from this section is not an industrial building or structure within the meaning of *section 268*, and

(b) (i) is in use for the purposes of third level education [or associated sporting or leisure activities][8] provided by an approved institution,

[(ii) is let to an approved institution,][9]

but does not include any part of a building or structure in use as or as part of a dwelling-house;

"*An tÚdarás*" means the Body established by section 2 of the Higher Education Authority Act, 1971.

[(1A) This subsection shall apply in relation to the construction of a qualifying premises where—

(a) the person who is constructing the qualifying premises has, on or before 31 December 2006, carried out work to the value of not less than 15 per cent of the actual construction costs of the qualifying premises, and

(b) the person referred to in *paragraph (a)* or, where the qualifying premises is sold by that person, the person who is claiming a deduction under *Part 9* in relation to the expenditure incurred, can show that the condition in *paragraph (a)* was satisfied.][10]

(2) [Subject to *subsections (2A)* to *(7)* and (as inserted by the *Finance Act 2006*) *sections 270(4)*, *270(5)*, *270(6)* and *316(2B)*][11], the provisions of the Tax Acts (other than *section 317(2)*) relating to the making of allowances or charges in respect of capital expenditure incurred on the construction of an industrial building or structure shall, notwithstanding anything to the contrary in those provisions, apply in relation to qualifying expenditure on a qualifying premises—

(a) as if the qualifying premises were, at all times at which it is a qualifying premises, a building or structure in respect of which an allowance is to be made for the purposes of income tax or corporation tax, as the case may be, under *Part 9* by reason of its use for a purpose specified in *section 268(1)(a)*, and

(b) where any activity carried on in the qualifying premises is not a trade, as if it were a trade.

[(2A) An allowance shall be given by virtue of *subsection (2)* in relation to any qualifying expenditure on a qualifying premises only in so far as that expenditure is incurred in the qualifying period.][12]

(3) In relation to [incurred in the qualifying period][13] on a qualifying premises *section 272* shall apply as if—

(a) in *subsection (3)(a)(ii)* of that section the reference to 4 per cent were a reference to 15 per cent, and

(b) in *subsection (4)(a)(ii)* of that section the reference to 25 years were a reference to 7 years.

(4) No allowance shall be made under *subsection (2)* unless, before the commencement of construction of a qualifying premises, the Minister for Finance certifies that—

(a) an approved institution has procured or otherwise secured a sum of money, none of which has been met directly or indirectly by the State, which sum is not less than 50 per cent of the qualifying expenditure to be incurred on the qualifying premises, and

(b) such sum is to be used solely by the approved institution for the following purposes—

(i) paying interest on money borrowed for the purpose of funding the construction of the qualifying premises,

(ii) paying any rent on the qualifying premises during such times as the qualifying premises is the subject of a letting on such terms as are referred to in *paragraph (b)(ii)* of the definition of "*qualifying premises*", and

(iii) purchasing the qualifying premises following the termination of the letting referred to in *subparagraph (ii)*.

(5) Notwithstanding *section 274(1)*, no balancing charge shall be made in relation to a qualifying premises by reason of any of the events specified in that section which occurs more than 7 years after the qualifying premises was first used.

(6) This section shall come into operation on the 1st day of July, 1997.

[(7) The Minister for Finance may not give a certificate under *subsection (4)* unless an application for certification was made before 1 January 2005.][14]

[(8) Notwithstanding the powers conferred and duties imposed—

(a) on the Minister for Education and Science and the Minister for Finance to approve or give consent to the approval of, respectively, certain capital expenditure by virtue of [*paragraph (i)* of the definition of "*qualifying expenditure*"][15] in *subsection (1)*, and

(b) [in so far as that expenditure is concerned,][16] on the Minister for Finance—

(i) to certify compliance with the requirements of *subsection (4)*, or

(ii) not to give a certificate under that subsection at any time later than a particular day by virtue of *subsection (7)*,

the Minister for Education and Science and the Minister for Finance may, [either generally in the case of institutions referred to in *paragraphs (a)* and *(b)* of the definition of "*approved institution*" or in respect of capital expenditure to be incurred on any particular type of qualifying premises to be used by any such institution][17], and subject to such conditions, if any, which they may see fit to impose, agree to delegate and may so delegate, in writing, to An tÚdarás the authority to exercise the powers and carry out the duties referred to in *paragraphs (a)* and *(b)* and where these Ministers of the Government so delegate that authority [, then, as respects the matters so delegated][18]—

[(I) the definition of "*qualifying expenditure*" in *subsection (1)* shall apply as if the reference in *paragraph (i)* of that definition to "is, following the receipt of the advice of An tÚdarás, approved for that purpose by the Minister for Education and Science with the consent of the Minister for Finance" were a reference to "is approved for that purpose by An tÚdarás, and"][19]

(II) *subsections (4)* and *(7)* shall apply as if the references in those subsections to "the Minister for Finance" were references to "An tÚdarás".][20]

[(9) For the purposes only of determining, in relation to a claim for an allowance by virtue of *subsection (2)*, whether and to what extent capital expenditure incurred on the construction of a qualifying premises is incurred or not incurred in the qualifying period, only such an amount of that capital expenditure as is properly attributable to work on the construction of the premises actually carried out during the qualifying period shall (notwithstanding any other provision of the

Tax Acts as to the time when any capital expenditure is or is to be treated as incurred) be treated as having been incurred in that period.][21]

Amendments

[1, 2] Substituted by FA01 s76(1)(a)(i)(I).

[3] Substituted by FA98 s44(a).

[4] Inserted by FA01 s76(1)(a)(i)(II).

[5] Substituted by FA01 s76(1)(a)(ii).

[6] Substituted by FA06 s34(1)(a). With effect from 26 June 2006 per S.I. 332 of 2006.

[7] Inserted by FA04 s27(a).

[8] Inserted by FA01 s76(1)(a)(iii). Shall be deemed to have come into operation as respects capital expenditure incurred on or after 1 October 1999.

[9] Substituted by FA98 s44(b).

[10] Inserted by FA06 s34(1)(b). With effect from 26 June 2006 per S.I. 332 of 2006.

[11] Substituted by FA06 s34(1)(c). With effect from 26 June 2006 per S.I. 332 of 2006.

[12] Inserted by FA04 s27(c).

[13] Inserted by FA04 s27(d).

[14] Substituted by FA05 s33.

[15] Substituted by FA01 s76(1)(c)(i).

[16] Inserted by FA01 s76(1)(c)(ii).

[17] Substituted by FA01 s76(1)(c)(iii).

[18] Inserted by FA01 s76(1)(c)(iv).

[19] Substituted by FA01 s76(1)(c)(v).

[20] Inserted by FA99 s51(b).

[21] Inserted by FA04 s27(e).

Revenue Briefings

Tax Briefing

Tax Briefing July 2001 – Issue 44 pg 41 – Topical Questions Industrial Buildings Allowance
Tax Briefing August 2005 – Issue 60 – Industrial and Commercial Buildings
Tax Briefing May 2006 – Issue 63 – Capital Allowances and Property Based Incentive Schemes
Tax Briefing August 2006 – Issue 64 – Capital Allowances and Property Based Incentive Schemes
Tax Briefing December 2006 – Issue 65 – Capital Allowances and Property Based Incentive Schemes

eBrief

eBrief No. 55/2006 – Property Based Incentive Schemes

Revenue Precedents

An approved institution within the meaning of section 843 [capital allowances for certain third level educational institutions] uses a subsidiary company to manage all its properties. It lets a premises to a subsidiary. A qualifying premises for the purpose of section 843 Taxes Consolidation Act 1997 means, inter alia, one which is let to an approved institution. A wholly owned subsidiary of an approved institution may be regarded as such an institution. Accordingly, if a company is a wholly owned subsidiary of the approved institution the premises may be let to the company and as long as it is used by the approved institution for the purposes of third level education it will be a qualifying premises. 00GM133

Cross References

From Section 843

Section 268 Meaning of "industrial building or structure".
Section 270 Meaning of "expenditure on construction of building or structure".
Section 272 Writing-down allowances.
Section 274 Balancing allowances and balancing charges.
Section 316 Interpretation of certain references to expenditure and time when expenditure is incurred.
Section 317 Treatment of grants.

To Section 843

Section 250A Restriction of relief to individuals in respect of loans applied in acquiring interest in companies.

Section 270 Meaning of "expenditure on construction of building or structure".

Section 409A Income tax: restriction on use of capital allowances on certain industrial buildings and other premises.

Section 409E Income tax: ringfence on use of certain capital allowances on certain industrial buildings and other premises.

Schedule 25B List of Specified Reliefs and Method of Determining Amount of Specified Relief Used in a Tax Year

843A Capital allowances for buildings used for certain childcare purposes

[(1) In this section—

"*pre-school child*" and "*pre-school service*" have the meanings respectively assigned to them by section 49 of the Child Care Act, 1991;

["*property developer*" means a person carrying on a trade which consists wholly or mainly of the construction or refurbishment of buildings or structures with a view to their sale;][1]

["*qualifying expenditure*" means capital expenditure incurred on the construction, conversion or refurbishment of a qualifying premises;][2]

["*qualifying period*" means the period commencing on 1 December 1999 and ending—

(a) on 30 September 2010, or

(b) where *subsection (6)(a)* applies, on 31 March 2011, or

(c) where *subsection (6)(b)* applies, on 31 March 2012;][3]

"*qualifying premises*" means a building or structure which—

(a) apart from this section is not an industrial building or structure within the meaning of *section 268*, and

(b) is in use for the purposes of providing—

(i) a pre-school service, or

(ii) a pre-school service and a day-care or other service to cater for children other than pre-school children,

and in respect of which it can be shown (to the extent that it is being used for the purposes of providing a pre-school service) that [the requirements of Regulation 10 or 11(1), as appropriate, of the Child Care (Pre-School Services) (No. 2) Regulations 2006 (S.I. No. 604 of 2006)][4], have been complied with,

but does not include any part of a building or structure in use as or as part of a dwelling-house.

(2) [Subject to *subsections (2A)* to *(5)*][5], the provisions of the Tax Acts relating to the making of allowances or charges in respect of capital expenditure incurred on the construction or refurbishment of an industrial building or structure shall, notwithstanding anything to the contrary in those provisions, apply in relation to qualifying expenditure on a qualifying premises—

(a) as if a qualifying premises were, at all times at which it is a qualifying premises, a building or structure in respect of which an allowance is to be made for the purposes of income tax or corporation tax, as the case may be, under *Part 9* by reason of its use for a purpose specified in *section 268(1)(a)*, and

(b) where any activity carried on in the qualifying premises is not a trade, as if it were a trade.

[(2A) An allowance shall be given by virtue of *subsection (2)* in relation to any qualifying expenditure on a qualifying premises only in so far as that expenditure is incurred in the qualifying period.][6]

(3) In relation to qualifying expenditure [incurred in the qualifying period][7] on a qualifying premises *section 272* shall apply as if—

(a) in *subsection (3)(a)(ii)* of that section the reference to 4 per cent were a reference to 15 per cent, […][8]

[(b) subject to *paragraph (c)*, in *subsection (4)(a)(ii)* of that section the reference to 25 years were a reference to 7 years, and

(c) in the case of a qualifying premises which—

(i) is first used on or after 1 February 2007, or

(ii) where qualifying expenditure on the refurbishment or conversion of the qualifying premises is incurred, is, subsequent to the incurring of that expenditure, first used on or after 1 February 2007,

in *subsection (4)(a)* of that section, the following were substituted for *subparagraph (ii)*:

(ii) 15 years beginning with the time when the building or structure was first used, or where capital expenditure on the refurbishment or conversion of the building or structure is incurred, 15 years beginning with the time when the building or structure was first used subsequent to the incurring of that expenditure.][9]

[(3A) For the purposes of the application, by *subsection (2)*, of *sections 271* and *273* in relation to qualifying expenditure incurred on or after 1 December 1999 on a qualifying premises—

(a) *section 271* shall apply—

(i) as if in *subsection (1)* of that section the definition of "*industrial development agency*" were deleted,

(ii) as if in *subsection (2)(a)*(i) of that section "to which *subsection (3)* applies" were deleted,

(iii) as if *subsection (3)* of that section were deleted,

(iv) as if the following subsection were substituted for *subsection (4)* of that section:

"(4) An industrial building allowance shall be an amount equal to 100 per cent of the capital expenditure mentioned in *subsection (2)*.",

and

(v) as if *subsection (5)* of that section were deleted,

and

(b) *section 273* shall apply—

(i) as if in *subsection (1)* of that section the definition of "*industrial development agency*" were deleted, and

(ii) as if *subsections (2)(b)* and *(3)* to *(7)* of that section were deleted.][10]

(4) Notwithstanding *section 274(1)*[, but subject to *subsection (4A)*][11], no balancing allowance or balancing charge shall be made in relation to a qualifying premises by reason of any event referred to in that section which occurs—

(a) more than 10 years after the qualifying premises was first used, or

(b) in a case where *section 276* applies, more than 10 years after the qualifying expenditure on refurbishment of the qualifying premises was incurred.

[(4A) In the case of a qualifying premises to which *subparagraph (i)* or *(ii)* of *subsection (3)(c)* applies, then notwithstanding *section 274(1)*, no balancing allowance or balancing charge shall be made in relation to a qualifying premises by reason of any event referred to in that section which occurs—

(a) where *subparagraph (i)* of *subsection (3)(c)* applies, more than 15 years after the qualifying premises was first used, or

(b) where *subparagraph (ii)* of *subsection (3)(c)* applies, more than 15 years after the qualifying premises was first used subsequent to the incurring of the qualifying expenditure on the refurbishment or conversion of the qualifying premises.][12]

[(5) Subsections (3) and (3A) shall not apply in respect of qualifying expenditure incurred on a qualifying premises on or after 1 January 2008—

(a) where a property developer or a person who is connected (within the meaning of section 10) with the property developer is entitled to the relevant interest, within the meaning of section 269, in that qualifying expenditure, and

(b) either of the persons referred to in paragraph (*a*) incurred the qualifying expenditure on that qualifying premises, or such expenditure was incurred by any other person connected (within the meaning of section 10) with the property developer.][13]

[(6) (a) For the purposes of *paragraph (b)* of the definition of "*qualifying period*", this paragraph applies where—

(i) capital expenditure is incurred on the construction, conversion or refurbishment of a qualifying premises,

(ii) the construction, conversion or refurbishment work on the qualifying premises represented by that expenditure is exempted development for the purposes of the Planning and Development Act 2000 by virtue of section 4 of that Act or by virtue of Part 2 of the Planning and Development Regulations 2001 (S.I. No. 600 of 2001) (in this subsection referred to as the "Regulations of 2001"), and

(iii) not less than 30 per cent of the total construction, conversion or refurbishment costs has been incurred on or before 30 September 2010.

(b) For the purposes of *paragraph (c)* of the definition of "*qualifying period*", this paragraph applies where—

(i) capital expenditure is incurred on the construction, conversion or refurbishment of a qualifying premises,

(ii) a planning application (not being an application for outline permission within the meaning of section 36 of the Planning and Development Act 2000), in so far as planning permission is required, in respect of the construction, conversion or refurbishment work on the qualifying premises represented by that expenditure, is made in accordance with the Regulations of 2001,

(iii) an acknowledgement of the application, which confirms that the application was received on or before 30 September 2010, is issued by the planning authority in accordance with article 26(2) of the Regulations of 2001, and

(iv) the application is not an invalid application in respect of which a notice was issued by the planning authority in accordance with article 26(5) of the Regulations of 2001.

(7) For the purposes only of determining, in relation to a claim for an allowance by virtue of *subsection (2)*, whether and to what extent capital expenditure incurred on the construction, conversion or refurbishment of a qualifying premises is incurred or not incurred in the qualifying period, only such an amount of that capital expenditure as is properly attributable to work on the construction, conversion or refurbishment of the premises actually carried out during the qualifying period shall (notwithstanding any other provision of the Tax Acts as to the time when any capital expenditure is or is to be treated as incurred) be treated as having been incurred in that period.][14]][15]

Amendments

[1] Inserted by FA00 s63(1)(a)(i). With effect from 21 June 2000 per S.I. 183 of 2000.

[2] Substituted by FA00 s63(1)(a)(ii). With effect from 21 June 2000 per S.I. 183 of 2000.

[3] Inserted by FA10 s26(a). Deemed to have come into force and takes effect as on and from 1 January 2010.

[4] Substituted by FA08 s29(1)(c)(i). Applies from 3 September 2007.

[5] Substituted by FA10 s26(b). Deemed to have come into force and takes effect as on and from 1 January 2010.

[6] Inserted by FA10 s26(c). Deemed to have come into force and takes effect as on and from 1 January 2010.

[7] Substituted by FA10 s26(d). Deemed to have come into force and takes effect as on and from 1 January 2010.

[8] Deleted by FA06 s38(a)(i).

[9] Substituted by FA06 s38(a)(ii).

[10] Inserted by FA00 s63(1)(c). With effect from 21 June 2000 per S.I. 183 of 2000.

[11] Inserted by FA06 s38(b).

[12] Inserted by FA06 s38(c).

[13] Substituted by FA08 s29(1)(c)(ii). Applies from 1 January 2008.

[14] Inserted by FA10 s26(e). Deemed to have come into force and takes effect as on and from 1 January 2010.

[15] Inserted by FA99 s49(b).

Revenue Briefings

Tax Briefing

Tax Briefing October 1999 – Issue 37 pg 11 – Childcare Services and BIK Capital Allowances

Tax Briefing September 2000 – Issue 41 pg 16 – Industrial and Commercial Buildings – Capital Allowances

Tax Briefing August 2005 – Issue 60 – Industrial and Commercial Buildings

Tax Briefing May 2006 – Issue 63 – Capital Allowances and Property Based Incentive Schemes

Tax Briefing August 2006 – Issue 64 – Capital Allowances and Property Based Incentive Schemes

Tax Briefing December 2006 – Issue 65 – Capital Allowances and Property Based Incentive Schemes

Tax Briefing September 2008 – Issue 69 – Property Developers and Capital Allowances

eBrief

eBrief No. 55/2006 – Property Based Incentive Schemes

Cross References

From Section 843A

Section 10 Connected persons.

Section 268 Meaning of "industrial building or structure".

Section 269 Meaning of "the relevant interest".

Section 271 Industrial building allowances.

Section 272 Writing-down allowances.

Section 273 Acceleration of writing-down allowances in respect of certain expenditure on certain industrial buildings or structures.

Section 274 Balancing allowances and balancing charges.

Section 276 Application of sections 272 and 274 in relation to capital expenditure on refurbishment.

To Section 843A

Section 268 Meaning of "industrial building or structure".

Section 274 Balancing allowances and balancing charges.

Schedule 25B List of Specified Reliefs and Method of Determining Amount of Specified Relief Used in a Tax Year

844 Companies carrying on mutual business or not carrying on a business

[CTA76 s29]

(1) Subject to *subsection (2)*, where a company carries on any business of mutual trading or mutual insurance or other mutual business, the provisions of the Corporation Tax Acts and of Schedule F relating to distributions shall apply to distributions made by the company, notwithstanding that they are made to persons participating in the mutual activities of that business and derive from those activities, but shall so apply only to the extent to which the distributions are made out of profits of the company which are brought into charge to corporation tax or out of franked investment income.

(2) In the case of a company carrying on any mutual life assurance business, the provisions of the Corporation Tax Acts and of Schedule F relating to distributions shall not apply to distributions made to persons participating in the mutual activities of that business and derived from those activities; but, if the business includes annuity business, the annuities payable in the course of that business shall not be treated as charges on the income of the company to any greater extent than if that business were not mutual but were being carried on by the company with a view to the realisation of profits for the company.

(3) Subject to *subsections (1)* and *(2)*, the fact that a distribution made by a company carrying on any such business is derived from the mutual activities of that business and the recipient is a person participating in those activities shall not affect the character which the payment or other receipt has for the purposes of corporation tax or income tax in the hands of the recipient.

(4) Where a company does not carry on and never has carried on a trade or a business of holding investments, and is not established for purposes which include the carrying on of a trade or of such a business, the provisions of the Corporation Tax Acts and of Schedule F relating to distributions shall apply to distributions made by the company only to the extent to which the distributions are made out of profits of the company which are brought into charge to corporation tax or out of franked investment income.

Cross References

From Section 844

Section 20 Schedule F.

845 Corporation tax: treatment of tax-free income of non-resident banks, insurance businesses, etc

[CTA76 s51(1), (2), (3)(a), (4), (5) and (6)]

(1) In this section, "*insurance business*" includes assurance business within the meaning of section 3 of the Insurance Act, 1936.

(2) In this section and in *section 846*, "*tax-free securities*" means securities to which *section 43*, *49* or *50* applies and which were issued with a condition regulating the treatment of the interest on the securities for tax purposes such that the interest on the securities is excluded in computing income or profits.

(3) (a) In this subsection, "*securities*" includes stocks and shares.

(b) Where a banking business, an insurance business or a business consisting wholly or partly in dealing in securities is carried on in the State by a person not resident in the State, then—

(i) in computing for the purposes of the Tax Acts the profits arising from, or loss sustained in, the business, and

(ii) in the case of an insurance business, also in computing the profits or loss from pension business and general annuity business under *section 715*, *section 76* shall not prevent the inclusion of interest, dividends and other payments to which *section 35* or *63* extends notwithstanding the exemption from tax conferred by those sections respectively.

(4) Where—

(a) any business referred to in *subsection (3)(b)* is carried on in the State by a person not ordinarily resident in the State, and

(b) in making any computation referred to in that subsection with respect to that business, interest on tax-free securities is excluded by virtue of a condition of the issue of such securities,

any expenses attributable to the acquisition or holding of, or to any transaction in, the securities (but not including in those expenses any interest on borrowed money), and any profits or losses so attributable, shall also be excluded in making that computation.

(5) In the case of an overseas life assurance company (within the meaning of *section 706*), in computing for the purposes of *section 726* the income from the investments of the life assurance fund of the company, any interest, dividends and other payments to which *section 35* or *63* extends shall be included notwithstanding the exemption from tax conferred by those sections respectively.

Cross References

From Section 845

Section 35 Securities of foreign territories.
Section 43 Certain securities issued by Minister for Finance.
Section 49 Exemption of certain securities.
Section 50 Securities of Irish local authorities issued abroad.
Section 63 Exemption of dividends of non-residents.
Section 76 Computation of income: application of income tax principles.
Section 706 Interpretation and general (Part 26).
Section 715 Annuity business: separate charge on profits.

Section 726 Investment income.
Section 846 Tax-free securities: exclusion of interest on borrowed money.

To Section 845
Section 846 Tax-free securities: exclusion of interest on borrowed money.

845A "Non-application of section 130 in the case of certain interest paid by banks

[(1) In this section, "bank" means—

(a) a person who is a holder of a licence granted under section 9 of the Central Bank Act, 1971, or

(b) a person who holds a licence or other similar authorisation under the law of any other Member State of the European Communities which corresponds to a licence granted under the said section 9.

(2) This subsection shall apply to so much of any interest as—

(a) is a distribution by virtue only of *section 130(2)(d)(iv)*,

(b) is payable by a bank carrying on a bona fide banking business in the State and would but for *section 130(2)(d)(iv)* be deductible as a trading expense in computing the amount of the bank's income from its banking business, and

(c) represents no more than a reasonable commercial return for the use of the principal in respect of which the interest is paid by the bank.

(3) Where a bank proves that *subsection (2)* applies to any interest payable by it for an accounting period and elects to have that interest treated as not being a distribution for the purposes of *section 130(2)(d)(iv)*, then, *section 130(2)(d)(iv)* shall not apply to that interest.

(4) An election under *subsection (3)* in relation to interest payable by a bank for an accounting period shall be made in writing to the inspector together with the bank's return of its profits for the period.".][1]

Amendments

[1] Inserted by FA01 s88.

Cross References

From Section 845A
Section 130 Matters to be treated as distributions.

To Section 845A
Section 130 Matters to be treated as distributions.
Section 243 Allowance of charges on income.

845B Set-off of surplus advance corporation tax

[(1) In this section—

"*surplus advance corporation tax*", in relation to an accounting period of a company, means an amount of advance corporation tax—

(a) to which the company was liable under *section 159* in respect of a distribution made before 6 April 1999,

(b) which was paid by the company and not repaid to it, and

(c) which was not set against the company's liability to corporation tax for any preceding accounting period.

(2) Where in the case of an accounting period of a company there is an amount of surplus advance corporation tax, that amount shall be set against the company's liability to corporation tax on any income charged to corporation tax for that accounting period and shall accordingly discharge a corresponding amount of that liability.

(3) For the purposes of this section—

(a) the income of a company charged to corporation tax for any accounting period shall be taken to be the amount of its profits for that period on which corporation tax falls finally to be borne exclusive of the part of the profits attributable to chargeable gains, and

(b) the part of the profits so attributable shall be taken to be the amount brought into the company's profits for that period for the purposes of corporation tax in respect of chargeable gains before any deduction for charges on income, expenses of management or other amounts which can be deducted from or set against or treated as reducing profits of more than one description.

(4) For the purposes of this section, a notice under *section 884* may require the inclusion in the return to be delivered by a company under that section of particulars of any surplus advance corporation tax carried forward in relation to that company under *subsection (2)*.

(5) Where an inspector discovers that any set-off of surplus advance corporation tax under this section ought not to have been made, or is or has become excessive, the inspector may make any such assessments as may in his or her judgment be required for recovering any tax that ought to have been paid and generally for securing that the resulting liabilities to tax (including interest on unpaid tax) of the person concerned are what they would have been if only such set-offs had been made as ought to have been made.][1]

Amendments

[1] Inserted by FA03 s41(1)(n). This section applies as respects accounting periods ending on or after 6 February 2003.

Cross References

From Section 845B

Section 159 Liability for advance corporation tax.

Section 884 Returns of profits.

846 Tax-free securities: exclusion of interest on borrowed money

[CTA76 s52(1) to (4) and (6)]

(1) This section shall apply where *section 845(4)* applies to a business for any accounting period.

(2) Up to the amount determined under this section (in this section referred to as "*the amount ineligible for relief*"), interest becoming due for payment on money borrowed for the purposes of the business—

(a) shall be excluded in any computation under the Tax Acts of the profits or loss arising from the business, and

(b) shall be excluded from the definition of "*charges on income*" in *section 243*.

(3) In determining the amount ineligible for relief, account shall be taken of all money borrowed for the purposes of the business outstanding in the accounting period up to the total cost of the tax-free securities held for the purposes of the business in that period; but account shall not be taken of any borrowed money

carrying interest which apart from *subsection (2)* would not be included in the computation under *paragraph (a)* of that subsection and would not be treated as a charge on income for the purposes of the Corporation Tax Acts.

(4) The amount ineligible for relief shall be equal to a year's interest on the amount of money borrowed which is to be taken into account under *subsection (3)* at a rate equal to the average rate of interest in the accounting period on money borrowed for the purposes of the business, except that in the case of an accounting period of less than 12 months interest shall be taken for that shorter period instead of for a year.

(5) For the purposes of this section, the cost of a holding of tax-free securities which has fluctuated in the accounting period shall be the average cost of acquisition of the initial holding, and of any subsequent acquisitions in the accounting period, applied to the average amount of the holding in the accounting period, and this subsection shall be applied separately to securities of different classes.

Cross References

From Section 846

Section 243 Allowance of charges on income.

Section 845 Corporation tax: treatment of tax-free income of non-resident banks, insurance businesses, etc.

To Section 846

Section 845 Corporation tax: treatment of tax-free income of non-resident banks, insurance businesses, etc.

847 Tax relief for certain branch profits

[FA95 s29]

(1) (a) In this section—

"*investment plan*" means a plan of a company resident in the State—

(i) which involves the investment by the company or by a company associated with it of substantial permanent capital in the State for the purposes of the creation before a date specified in the plan of substantial new employment in the State in trading operations carried on or to be carried on in the State by the company or the company associated with it, and

(ii) which has been submitted before the commencement of its implementation to the Minister by the company for the purpose of enabling it to obtain relief under this section;

"*the Minister*" means the Minister for Finance;

"*qualified company*" means a company to which the Minister, following consultation with the Minister for Enterprise and Employment, [has before 15 February 2001 given a certificate][1], which certificate has not been revoked, under *subsection (2)*;

"*qualified foreign trading activities*" means trading activities carried on by a qualified company through a branch or agency outside the State in a territory specified in the certificate given under *subsection (2)* to the company by the Minister following consultation with the Minister for Enterprise, Trade and Employment.

(b) For the purposes of this section—

(i) a company shall be associated with another company where one of the companies is a 75 per cent subsidiary of the other company or both companies are 75 per cent subsidiaries of a third company; but, in determining whether one company is a 75 per cent subsidiary of another company, the other company shall be treated as not being the owner of—

(I) any share capital which it owns directly in a company if a profit on the sale of the shares would be treated as a trading receipt of its trade, or

(II) any share capital which it owns indirectly and which is owned directly by a company for which a profit on the sale of the shares would be a trading receipt,

(ii) *sections 412* to *418* shall apply for the purposes of this paragraph as they would apply for the purposes of *Chapter 5* of *Part 12* if *section 411(1)(c)* were deleted,

(iii) where a trade carried on by a qualified company consists partly of qualified foreign trading activities and partly of other trading activities, the company shall be treated as if it were carrying on distinct trades consisting of such qualified foreign trading activities and of such other trading activities,

(iv) there shall be attributed to each trade carried on, or treated under *subparagraph (iii)* as carried on, such profits or gains or losses as might have been expected to be made if each trade had been carried on under the same or similar conditions by a person independent of, and dealing at arm's length with, the person carrying on the other trade, and

(v) there shall be made all necessary apportionments as are just and reasonable for the purposes of computing—

(I) profits or gains or losses arising from, and

(II) the amount of any charges on income, expenses of management or other amount which can be deducted from or set off against or treated as reducing profits of more than one description as is incurred for the purposes of,

a trade carried on, or treated under *subparagraph (iii)* as carried on, by a qualified company.

(2) Where a plan has been duly submitted by a company resident in the State and the Minister, following consultation with the Minister for Enterprise, Trade and Employment, is satisfied that—

(a) the plan is an investment plan,

(b) the company, or a company associated with it, will, before a date specified in the plan and approved by the Minister, make the substantial permanent capital investment in the State under the investment plan for the purposes of the creation of the substantial new employment in the State,

(c) the creation of substantial new employment in the State under the investment plan will be achieved, and

(d) the maintenance of the employment so created in trading operations in the State will be dependent on the carrying on by the company of qualified foreign trading activities,

then, the Minister may give a certificate certifying that the company is a qualified company with effect from a date specified in the certificate.

(3) (a) The Minister shall draw up guidelines for determining whether for the purposes of *subsection (2)* a company and companies associated with it will

create substantial new employment and will make a substantial permanent capital investment in the State.

(b) Without prejudice to the generality of *paragraph (a)*, guidelines under that paragraph may—

(i) include a requirement for specified levels of—

(I) employment in the State, and

(II) permanent capital investment in the State,

and

(ii) specify such criteria for the purposes of this subsection as the Minister considers appropriate.

(4) A certificate issued under *subsection (2)* may be given subject to such conditions as the Minister, following consultation with the Minister for Enterprise, Trade and Employment, considers proper and specifies in the certificate.

(5) Where in the case of a company in relation to which a certificate under *subsection (2)* has been given the Minister, following consultation with the Minister for Enterprise, Trade and Employment, forms the opinion that such certificate ought to be revoked because any condition subject to which the certificate was given has not been complied with, the Minister may by notice in writing served by registered post on the company revoke the certificate with effect from such date as may be specified in the notice.

(6) Notwithstanding [any provision of the Corporation Tax Acts other than this section][2]—

(a) profits or gains or losses arising from the carrying on of qualified foreign trading activities shall be disregarded for the purposes of those Acts, and

(b) no amount of any charges on income, expenses of management or other amount which apart from this paragraph may be deducted from or set off against or treated as reducing profits of more than one description, shall be so deducted, set off or treated, as is incurred for the purposes of a trade carried on, or treated under *subsection (1)(b)(iii)* as carried on, by a qualified company which consists of qualified foreign trading activities.

(7) A gain shall not be a chargeable gain for the purposes of the Capital Gains Tax Acts if it accrues to a qualified company on the disposal of an asset, other than an asset specified in *paragraphs (a)* to *(d)* of *section 980(2)*, used wholly and exclusively for the purposes of a trade carried on, or treated under *subsection (1)(b)(iii)* as carried on, by a qualified company which consists of qualified foreign trading activities.

(8) An inspector may by notice in writing require a qualified company to furnish him or her with such information or particulars as may be necessary for the purposes of giving relief under this section.

[(9) (a) The provisions of this section shall not apply to an accounting period ending after 31 December 2010.

(b) [For the purposes of this subsection and *subsection (10)*, where][3] an accounting period begins before 31 December 2010 and ends after that date, it shall be divided into 2 parts, one beginning on the date on which the accounting period begins and ending on 31 December 2010 and the other beginning on 1 January 2011 and ending on the date on which the accounting period ends, and both parts shall be treated as if they were separate accounting periods of the company.

[(10) (a) Notwithstanding *subsection (9)(a)*, where, in any accounting period, a qualified company incurred a loss (in this subsection referred to as a "*relevant loss*") on qualified foreign trading activities and that loss formed, or formed part of, the profits or gains or losses of the company which were disregarded for the purposes of the Corporation Tax Acts by virtue of *subsection (6)*, then the company may claim relief under *section 396(1)* in accordance with this subsection in respect of that loss for accounting periods beginning on or after 1 January 2011.

(b) For the purposes of a claim under *paragraph (a)* in respect of a relevant loss, the qualified foreign trading activities carried on by a qualified company through a branch or agency outside the State shall for all accounting periods be treated as a trade separate from all other activities carried on by the company and the company shall be treated as continuing to carry on that separate trade for so long as it continues to carry on those activities through that branch or agency and to permanently discontinue to carry on that trade when it ceases to carry on those activities through that branch or agency.

(c) Where a qualified company makes a claim under *paragraph (a)* in respect of a relevant loss then, subject to *paragraph (b)*, the company shall be entitled to such relief under *section 396(1)* for accounting periods beginning on or after 1 January 2011 as it would have been entitled to had the profits or gains or losses from qualified foreign trading activities carried on through the branch or agency not been disregarded for the purposes of the Corporation Tax Acts by virtue of *subsection (6)* and had relief been granted in respect of the relevant loss under *section 396(1)*, but not any other provision of the Corporation Tax Acts, for accounting periods ending before that date.][4]][5]

Amendments

[1] Substituted by FA01 s89.

[2] Substituted by FA10 s48(a). Deemed to have come into force and takes effect as on and from 1 January 2010.

[3] Substituted by FA10 s48(b). Deemed to have come into force and takes effect as on and from 1 January 2010.

[4] Inserted by FA10 s48(c). Deemed to have come into force and takes effect as on and from 1 January 2010.

[5] Inserted by FA04 sched3(1)(z). This section shall have effect as on and from 25 March 2004

Cross References

From Section 847

Section 381 Right to repayment of tax by reference to losses.
Section 396 Relief for trading losses other than terminal losses.
Section 410 Group payments.
Section 411 Surrender of relief between members of groups and consortia.
Section 412 Qualification for entitlement to group relief.
Section 418 Beneficial percentage.
Section 980 Deduction from consideration on disposal of certain assets.

847A Donations to certain sports bodies

[(1) In this section—

"*Acts*" means—

(a) the Tax Acts,

(b) the Capital Gains Tax Acts, and

(c) the Value-Added Tax Consolidation Act 2010 and the enactments amending or extending that Act, and any instruments made thereunder;

"*appropriate certificate*", in relation to a relevant donation by a donor who is an individual (other than an individual referred to in *subsection (9)*), means a certificate which is in such form as the Revenue Commissioners may prescribe and which contains—

(a) statements to the effect that—

(i) the donation satisfies the requirements of *subsection (5)*, and

(ii) the donor has paid or will pay to the Revenue Commissioners income tax of an amount equal to income tax at the standard rate or the higher rate or partly at the standard rate and partly at the higher rate, as the case may be, for the relevant year of assessment on the grossed up amount of the donation, but not being—

(I) income tax which the donor is entitled to charge against any other person or to deduct, retain or satisfy out of any payment which the donor is liable to make to any other person, or

(II) appropriate tax within the meaning of *Chapter 4* of *Part 8*,

(b) a statement specifying how much of the grossed up amount referred to in *paragraph (a)(ii)* has been or will be liable to income tax at the standard rate and the higher rate for the relevant year of assessment, and

(c) the identifying number, known as the Personal Public Service Number (PPSN) of the donor;

"*approved project*" means a project in respect of which the Minister has given a certificate under *subsection (4)*, which certificate has not been revoked under that subsection;

"*approved sports body*" means a body which is in possession of—

(a) a certificate from the Revenue Commissioners stating that in their opinion the body is a body of persons to which *section 235* applies, and

(b) a valid tax clearance certificate,

but does not include a body to whom the Revenue Commissioners have given a notice under *section 235(1)*;

"*Minister*" means the Minister for Tourism, Sport and Recreation;

"*project*", in relation to an approved sports body, means one or more of the following:

(a) the purchase, construction or refurbishment of a building or structure, or part of a building or structure, to be used for sporting or recreation activities provided by the approved sports body,

(b) the purchase of land to be used by the approved sports body in the provision of sporting or recreation facilities,

(c) the purchase of permanently based equipment (excluding personal equipment) for use by the approved sports body in the provision of sporting or recreation facilities,

(d) the improvement of the playing pitches, surfaces or facilities of the approved sports body, and

(e) the repayment of, or the payment of interest on, money borrowed by the approved sports body on or after 1 May 2002 for any of the purposes mentioned in *paragraphs (a)* to *(d)*;

"*relevant accounting period*", in relation to a relevant donation made by a company, means the accounting period in which that donation is made by the company;

"*relevant donation*" means a donation which satisfies the requirements of *subsection (5)* and takes the form of the payment by a person (in this section referred to as the "*donor*") of a sum or sums of money amounting to at least €250 to an approved sports body which is made—

(a) where the donor is an individual, in a year of assessment, and

(b) where the donor is a company, in an accounting period,

but where an accounting period of a company is less than 12 months in length the amount of €250 shall be proportionately reduced;

"*relevant year of assessment*", in relation to a relevant donation made by an individual, means the year of assessment in which that donation is made by the individual;

"*tax clearance certificate*" shall be construed in accordance with *subsection (3)*.

(2) For the purposes of this section and in relation to a donation by a donor who is an individual (other than an individual referred to in *subsection (9)*), references to the grossed up amount are to the amount which after deducting income tax at the standard rate or the higher rate or partly at the standard rate and partly at the higher rate, as the case may be, for the relevant year of assessment leaves the amount of the donation.

(3) (a) Where a body which is in compliance with the obligations imposed on it by the Acts in relation to—

(i) the payment or remittance of any taxes, interest or penalties required to be paid or remitted under the Acts to the Revenue Commissioners, and

(ii) the delivery of any returns required to be made under the Acts,

applies to the Collector-General in that behalf, the Collector-General shall issue to the body a certificate (in this section referred to as a "*tax clearance certificate*") for the purposes of this section stating that the body is in compliance with those obligations.

(b) *Subsections (5)* to *(9)* of *section 1094* shall apply to an application for a tax clearance certificate under this subsection as they apply to an application for a tax clearance certificate under that section.

(4) (a) The Minister, on the making of an application by an approved sports body in advance of the undertaking by that body of a project, may give a certificate to that body stating that the project to be undertaken by that body may be treated as an approved project for the purposes of this section.

(b) An application under this subsection shall be in such form and contain such information as the Minister may direct.

(c) The Minister may, by notice in writing given to the body, revoke the certificate given in respect of a project under *paragraph (a)*, and the project shall cease to be an approved project as respects any donations made to the body after the date of the Minister's notice.

(d) The Minister shall not give a certificate to any body in respect of a project under *paragraph (a)* if the aggregate cost of the project is, or is estimated to be, in excess of €40,000,000.

(5) A donation shall satisfy the requirements of this subsection if—

(a) it is made to the approved sports body for the sole purpose of funding an approved project,

(b) it is or will be applied by the approved sports body for that purpose,

(c) apart from this section, it is neither deductible in computing for the purposes of tax the profits or gains of a trade or profession nor an expense of management deductible in computing the total profits of a company,

(d) it is not a relevant donation to which *section 848A* applies,

(e) it is not subject to a condition as to repayment,

(f) neither the donor nor any person connected with the donor receives, either directly or indirectly, a benefit in consequence of making the donation, including, in particular, a right to membership of the approved sports body or a right to use the facilities of that body,

(g) it is not conditional on or associated with, or part of an arrangement involving, the acquisition of property by the approved sports body, otherwise than by way of gift, from the donor or a person connected with the donor, and

(h) in the case of a donation made by an individual, the individual—

(i) is resident in the State for the relevant year of assessment,

(ii) has (except in the case of an individual referred to in *subsection (9)*) given an appropriate certificate in relation to the donation to the approved sports body, and

(iii) has (except in the case of an individual referred to in *subsection (9)*) paid the tax referred to in such appropriate certificate and is not entitled to claim a repayment of that tax or any part of that tax.

(6) Where it is proved to the satisfaction of the Revenue Commissioners that a person has made a relevant donation, *subsection (7)*, *(9)* or *(11)*, as the case may be, shall apply.

(7) Where a company makes a relevant donation, other than a relevant donation to which *subsection (18)* applies, then, for the purposes of corporation tax, the amount of that donation shall be treated as—

(a) a deductible trading expense of a trade carried on by the company in, or

(b) an expense of management deductible in computing the total profits of the company for,

the relevant accounting period.

(8) A claim by a company under this section shall be made with the return required to be delivered by it under [*Chapter 3* of *Part 41A*][1] for the relevant accounting period.

(9) (a) Where a relevant donation, other than a relevant donation to which *subsection (18)* applies, is made by an individual who is a chargeable person (within the meaning of [*Part 41A*][2]) for the relevant year of assessment, then—

(i) the amount of the donation shall be deducted from or set off against any income of the individual chargeable to income tax for that year of assessment and tax shall, where necessary, be discharged or repaid accordingly, and

(ii) the total income of the individual or, where the individual's [spouse or civil partner][3] is assessed to income tax in accordance with [*section 1017* or *1031C*,][4] the total income of the [spouse or civil partner][5] shall be calculated accordingly.

(b) For the purposes of *paragraph (a)*, any such deduction or set-off shall not be taken into account in determining the net relevant earnings (within the meaning of *section 787*) of the individual or, as the case may be, the individual's [spouse or civil partner][6] for the relevant year of assessment.

(10) Where a relevant donation is made by an individual who is an individual referred to in *subsection (9)*, a claim under this section shall be made with the return required to be delivered by that individual under *section 951* for the relevant year of assessment.

(11) Where a relevant donation, other than a relevant donation to which *subsection (18)* applies, is made by an individual who is not an individual referred to in *subsection (9)*, the Tax Acts shall apply in relation to the approved sports body to which that donation is made as if—

(a) the grossed up amount of the donation were an annual payment which was the income of that body received by it under deduction of tax, in the amounts and at the rates specified in the statement referred to in *paragraph (b)* of the definition of "*appropriate certificate*", for the relevant year of assessment, and

(b) the provisions of the Tax Acts which apply in relation to a claim to repayment of tax applied in relation to any claim to repayment of such tax by that body;

but, if the total amount of the tax referred to in *paragraph (b)* of the definition of "*appropriate certificate*" is not paid, the amount of any repayment which would otherwise be made to that body in accordance with this section shall not exceed the amount of tax actually paid by that individual.

(12) The details contained in an appropriate certificate shall be given by the approved sports body to the Revenue Commissioners in an electronic format approved by the Revenue Commissioners in connection with the making of a claim to repayment of tax to which *subsection (11)(b)* refers and, where those details are so given, those details shall be accompanied by a declaration made by the approved sports body, on a form prescribed or authorised for that purpose by the Revenue Commissioners, to the effect that those details are correct and complete.

(13) Where the Revenue Commissioners are satisfied that an approved sports body does not have the facilities to give the details contained in an appropriate certificate in the electronic format referred to in *subsection (12)*, such details shall be given in writing in a form prescribed or authorised by the Revenue Commissioners and shall be accompanied by a declaration made by the approved sports body to the effect that the claim is correct and complete.

(14) Every approved sports body, when required to do so by notice in writing from the Minister, shall within the time limited by the notice prepare and deliver to the Minister a return containing particulars of the aggregate amount of relevant donations received by the body in respect of each approved project.

(15) Where any question arises as to whether for the purposes of this section a project is an approved project, or a donation is a relevant donation, the Revenue Commissioners may consult with the Minister.

(16) For the purposes of a claim to relief under this section, but subject to *subsection (17)*, an approved sports body shall, on acceptance of a relevant donation, give to the person making the relevant donation a receipt which shall—

(a) contain a statement that—

(i) it is a receipt for the purposes of this section,

(ii) the body is an approved sports body for the purposes of this section,

(iii) the donation in respect of which the receipt is given is a relevant donation for the purposes of this section, and

(iv) the project in respect of which the relevant donation has been made is an approved project,

(b) show—

(i) the name and address of the person making the relevant donation,

(ii) the amount of the relevant donation in both figures and words,

(iii) the date the relevant donation was made,

(iv) the full name of the approved sports body,

(v) the date on which the receipt was issued, and

(vi) particulars of the approved project in respect of which the relevant donation has been made,

and

(c) be signed by a duly authorised official of the approved sports body.

(17) An approved sports body shall not be required to give a receipt under *subsection (16)* to a donor—

(a) who is an individual but who is not an individual to which *subsection (9)* applies, or

(b) in respect of a relevant donation to which *subsection (18)* applies.

(18) Relief under this section shall not be given in respect of a relevant donation which is made at any time to an approved sports body in respect of an approved project if, at that time, the aggregate of the amounts of that relevant donation and all other relevant donations made to the approved sports body in respect of the approved project at or before that time exceeds €40,000,000.

(19) Where relief under this section has been granted in respect of a relevant donation and—

(a) that donation has not been used by the sports body concerned for the purpose of undertaking the approved project concerned, or

(b) which relief is otherwise found not to have been due,

section 235(2) shall not apply to the amount of that relevant donation.

(20) The Revenue Commissioners may nominate any of their officers to perform any acts and discharge any functions authorised by this section to be performed or discharged by them.][7]

Amendments

[1, 2] Substituted by FA12 sched4(part 2)(g).

[3, 5, 6] Substituted by F(No.3)A11 sched1(231).

[4] Substituted by F(No.3)A11 sched1(232).

[7] Inserted by FA02 s41(1). This section applies as on and from 1 May 2002.

Revenue Briefings

Tax Briefing

Tax Briefing April 2002 – Issue 47 pg 13 – Finance Act 2002 Donations to certain Sports Bodies

Cross References

From Section 847A

Section 235 Bodies established for promotion of athletic or amateur games or sports.
Section 237 Annual payments payable wholly out of taxed income.
Section 256 Interpretation (Chapter 4).
Section 787 Nature and amount of relief for qualifying premiums.
Section 848A Donations to approved bodies.
Section 951 Obligation to make a return.
Section 1017 Assessment of husband in respect of income of both spouses.
Section 1094 Tax clearance certificates in relation to certain licences.

To Section 847A

Section 531B Charge to income levy.
Section 531AA Interpretation (Part 18C).
Section 531AM Charge to universal social charge.
Section 1095 Tax clearance certificates: general scheme.
Schedule 25B List of Specified Reliefs and Method of Determining Amount of Specified Relief Used in a Tax Year

848 Designated charities: repayment of tax in respect of donations [Repealed]

Repealed by TCA97 s848A, as inserted by FA01 s45.

Cross References

To Section 848

Section 848A Donations to approved bodies.

848A Donations to approved bodies

[(1) (a) In this section—

[...][1]

["*annual certificate*", in relation to a relevant donation to an approved body by a donor who is an individual, means a certificate which is in such form as the Revenue Commissioners may prescribe and which contains—

(i) statements to the effect that—

(I) the donation satisfies the requirements of *subsection (3)*,

(II) the donor has paid or will pay to the Revenue Commissioners income tax of an amount equal to income tax at the specified rate for the relevant year of assessment on the grossed up amount of the donation, but not being—

(A) income tax which the donor is entitled to charge against any other person or to deduct, retain or satisfy out of any

payment which the donor is liable to make to any other person, or

(B) appropriate tax within the meaning of *Chapter 4* of *Part 8*,

and

(III) the donor acknowledges that the provisions of *subsection (9B)* apply to a repayment of tax to an approved body,

and

(ii) the personal public service number of the donor,

and includes a certificate which has been renewed by the donor with the approved body in a manner approved by the Revenue Commissioners for the subsequent year of assessment;][2]

"*approved body*" means a body specified in Part 1 of Schedule 26A;

["*designated securities*" means—

(i) shares (including stock), and

(ii) debentures,

of a class quoted on a recognised stock exchange;][3]

["*enduring certificate*", in relation to a relevant donation to an approved body by a donor who is an individual, means a certificate which is in such form as the Revenue Commissioners may prescribe and which contains—

(i) the year of assessment from which the certificate applies,

(ii) statements to the effect that the donor is aware that—

(I) a donation made during the specified period (in this definition referred to as the 'first specified period') has to satisfy the requirements of *subsection (3)*,

(II) income tax of an amount equal to income tax at the specified rate for the relevant year of assessment on the grossed up amount of a donation has been or will be paid to the Revenue Commissioners, but not being—

(A) income tax which the donor is entitled to charge against any other person or to deduct, retain or satisfy out of any payment which the donor is liable to make to any other person, or

(B) appropriate tax within the meaning of *Chapter 4* of *Part 8*,

and

(III) the donor acknowledges that the provisions of *subsection (9B)* apply to a repayment of tax to an approved body,

and

(iii) the personal public service number of the donor,

and includes a certificate which has been renewed by the donor with the approved body in a manner approved by the Revenue Commissioners for the specified period immediately succeeding the first specified period;

"*personal public service number*" has the same meaning as in *section 262* of the Social Welfare Consolidation Act 2005;][4]

"*relevant accounting period*" in relation to a relevant donation means the accounting period in which the relevant donation is made;

["*relevant donation*" means, subject to *subsection (3A)*, a donation which satisfies the requirements of *subsection (3)* and takes the form of the payment or the donation, as the case may be, by a person (in this section referred to as the "*donor*") of either or both—

(i) a sum or sums of money, and

(ii) designated securities, valued at their market value at the time the donation is made,

amounting to, in aggregate, at least €250 to an approved body which is made—

(I) where the donor is a company, in an accounting period, and

(II) where the donor is an individual, in a year of assessment;][5]

"*relevant year of assessment*", in relation to a relevant donation, means the year of assessment in which the relevant donation is made;

["*specified period*", in relation to an enduring certificate, means the year of assessment from which the certificate applies and each of the 4 immediately succeeding years of assessment;

"*specified rate*" means 31 per cent].[6]

[(b) For the purposes of this section and in relation to a donation by a donor who is an individual, references to the grossed up amount are to the amount which after deducting income tax at the specified rate for the relevant year of assessment leaves the amount of the donation.][7]

[(ba) An annual certificate renewed by a donor in the manner referred to in the definition of "*annual certificate*" shall be deemed to contain the statements referred to in *paragraph (i)* of that definition.

(bb) An enduring certificate renewed by a donor in the manner referred to in the definition of "*enduring certificate*" shall be deemed to contain the statements referred to in *paragraph (ii)* of that definition.][8]

(c) This section shall be construed together with *Schedule 26A*.

(2) Where it is proved to the satisfaction of the Revenue Commissioners that a person has made a relevant donation [the provisions of *subsection (4)* or *(9)*,][9] as the case may be, shall apply.

(3) A donation will satisfy the requirements of this section if—

(a) it is not subject to a condition as to repayment,

(b) neither the donor nor any person connected with the donor receives a benefit in consequence of making the donation, either directly or indirectly,

(c) it is not conditional on or associated with, or part of an arrangement involving, the acquisition of property by the approved body, otherwise than by way of gift, from the donor or a person connected with the donor,

(d) subject to *subsection (4)*—

(i) it would not be deductible in computing for the purposes of corporation tax the profits or gains of a trade or profession, and

(ii) it would not be an expense of management deductible in computing the total profits of a company,

(e) in respect of a donation made by an individual, the individual—

(i) is resident in the State for the relevant year of assessment,

[(ii) has given an annual certificate or, as the case may be, an enduring certificate in relation to the donation to the approved body, and

(iii) has, for the relevant year of assessment, paid the tax referred to in such annual certificate or enduring certificate, as the case may be, and is not entitled to claim a repayment of that tax or any part of that tax.][10]

[(3A) [(a) Notwithstanding any other provision of this section, where—

(i) the aggregate of the amounts of all donations made by an individual in any year of assessment to an approved body or approved bodies is in excess of €1,000,000, or

(ii) the aggregate of the amounts of all donations made by an individual in any year of assessment to an approved body or approved bodies with which the individual is associated is in excess of 10 per cent of the total income of the individual for that year of assessment,

the amount of the excess in each case shall not be treated as a relevant donation for the purposes of this section.][11]

(b) For the purposes of this subsection—

(i) an individual is associated with an approved body if, at the time the donation is made, the individual is an employee or member of, the approved body or another approved body which is associated with that approved body, and

(ii) an approved body is associated with another approved body if, at the time the donation is made, it could reasonably be considered that—

(I) any person or any group of persons or groups of persons having a reasonable commonality of identity has or have, or had the means or power, either directly or indirectly, to determine the activities carried on or to be carried on by both approved bodies, or

(II) any person or any group of persons or groups of persons having a reasonable commonality of identity exercises or exercise, or is or are able to exercise, control over the affairs of both approved bodies.][12]

[(3B) Where—

(a) the Revenue Commissioners withdraw the authorisation of an approved body by a notice in writing in accordance with *paragraph 7* of *Part 3* of *Schedule 26A*, and

(b) (i) a company, or

(ii) an individual who is a chargeable person (within the meaning of *Part 41A*) and who for a year of assessment is entitled to deduct or set off the amount of a relevant donation made to an approved body against any income of the individual chargeable to income tax for that year of assessment,

makes a donation in good faith to the approved body in the period beginning on the date specified in the notice from which the withdrawal of the authorisation applies and has effect and ending on the date of the notice,

the donation, notwithstanding the withdrawal of the authorisation, shall, subject to this section, be deemed to be a relevant donation made to an approved body.][13]

(4) Where a company makes a relevant donation in any accounting period and claims relief from tax by reference thereto, the amount thereof shall, for the purposes of corporation tax, be treated as—

(a) a deductible trading expense of a trade carried on by the company in, or

(b) an expense of management deductible in computing the total profits of the company for,

that accounting period.

(5) A claim by a company under this section shall be made with the return required to be delivered under [*Chapter 3* of *Part 41A*][14] for the accounting period in which the relevant donation is made.

(6) Where a relevant donation is made by a donor in an accounting period of a company [...][15] which is less than 12 months, the [amount][16] specified in the definition of "*relevant donation*" shall be proportionately reduced.

[...][17]

[(9) Where a donation is a relevant donation made to an approved body by a donor who is an individual, the Tax Acts shall apply in relation to the approved body as if—

(a) the grossed up amount of the donation were an annual payment which was the income of the approved body received by it under deduction of tax in the amount and at the specified rate of tax for the relevant year of assessment, and

(b) the provisions of those Acts which apply in relation to a claim to repayment of tax applied in relation to any claim to repayment of such tax by an approved body;

but, if the total amount of the tax referred to in *paragraph (i)* of the definition of "*annual certificate*" or *paragraph (ii)* of the definition of "*enduring certificate*", as the case may be, is not paid, the amount of any repayment which would otherwise be made to an approved body in accordance with this section shall not exceed the amount of tax actually paid by the donor.][18]

[(9A) *Section 611* does not apply to a disposal of an asset, being a relevant donation for the purposes of this section, where—

(a) a claim for relief from tax, or

(b) a claim for repayment of tax,

is made under this section in respect of that relevant donation.][19]

[(9B) Where a repayment of tax has been made to an approved body in accordance with this section, the amount of tax so repaid shall not be regarded as tax paid by the donor for the purposes of a repayment of tax to that donor under *section 865* or any other provision of the Income Tax Acts.][20]

(10) The details contained in an [annual certificate or enduring certificate, as the case may be,][21] shall be given by the approved body to the Revenue Commissioners in an electronic format approved by the Revenue Commissioners in connection with the making of a claim to repayment of tax to which *subsection (9)(b)* refers and where it is so given it shall be accompanied by a declaration made by the approved body, on a form prescribed or authorised for that purpose by the Revenue Commissioners, to the effect that the details are correct and complete.

(11) Where the Revenue Commissioners are satisfied that an approved body does not have the facilities to give the details contained in an [annual certificate or enduring certificate, as the case may be,][22] in the electronic format referred to in *subsection (10)*, such details shall be given in writing in a form prescribed or authorised by the Revenue Commissioners and shall be accompanied by a declaration made by the approved body to the effect that the claim is correct and complete.

(12) *Section 764* shall apply as if *subsection (1)(b)* were deleted and *subsection (2)* shall be construed accordingly.

(13) *Sections 88, 484, 485, 485A, 485B, 486, 486A* and *767*, *subparagraphs (ii)* and *(iii)* of *subsection (1)(b)*, and *subsection (3)*, of *section 792* and *section 848* are repealed.

(14) Where any body to which *Part 2* or *Part 3* of *Schedule 26A* relates has been approved or is the holder of an authorisation, as the case may be, under any enactment and, that approval or authorisation has not been withdrawn on the day prior to the coming into operation of this section, such body shall be deemed to be an approved body for the purposes of this section.][23]

Amendments

[1] Deleted by FA13 s19(1)(a). Shall apply as respects a relevant donation made on or after 1 January 2013.

[2,4,6] Inserted by FA13 s19(1)(b). Shall apply as respects a relevant donation made on or after 1 January 2013.

[3] Inserted by FA06 s20(1)(b)(i)(I). Applies as on and from 1 January 2006.

[5] Substituted by FA06 s20(1)(b)(i)(II). Applies as on and from 1 January 2006.

[7] Substituted by FA13 s19(1)(c). Shall apply as respects a relevant donation made on or after 1 January 2013.

[8] Inserted by FA13 s19(1)(d). Shall apply as respects a relevant donation made on or after 1 January 2013.

[9] Substituted by FA13 s19(1)(e). Shall apply as respects a relevant donation made on or after 1 January 2013.

[10] Substituted by FA13 s19(1)(f). Shall apply as respects a relevant donation made on or after 1 January 2013.

[11] Inserted by FA13 s19(1)(g). Shall apply as respects a relevant donation made on or after 1 January 2013.

[12] Inserted by FA03 s21(1)(b). Applies as respects donations made on or after 6 February 2003.

[13] Inserted by FA14 s18(1)(a). Has effect from 1 January 2015 as respects an authorisation issued, whether before, on or after that date, under paragraph 2 of Part 3 of Schedule 26A.

[14] Substituted by FA12 sched4(part 2)(g).

[15] Deleted by FA13 s19(1)(h)(i). Shall apply as respects a relevant donation made on or after 1 January 2013.

[16] Substituted by FA13 s19(1)(h)(iii). Shall apply as respects a relevant donation made on or after 1 January 2013.

[17] Deleted by FA13 s19(1)(ii). Shall apply as respects a relevant donation made on or after 1 January 2013.

[18] Substituted by FA13 s19(1)(j). Shall apply as respects a relevant donation made on or after 1 January 2013.

[19] Inserted by FA06 s20(1)(b)(ii). Applies as on and from 1 January 2006.

[20] Inserted by FA13 s19(1)(k). Shall apply as respects a relevant donation made on or after 1 January 2013.

[21] Substituted by FA13 s19(1)(l). Shall apply as respects a relevant donation made on or after 1 January 2013.

[22] Substituted by FA13 s19(1)(m). Shall apply as respects a relevant donation made on or after 1 January 2013.

[23] Inserted by FA01 s45(1).

Revenue Briefings

Tax Briefing

Tax Briefing June 2001 – Issue 44 pg 16 – Donations to Approved Bodies and Tax Relief
Tax Briefing May 2003 – Issue 52 pg 10 – Finance Act 2003 – Donations to Approved Bodies

eBrief

eBrief No. 55/2013 – Donations to Eligible Charities and other Approved Bodies

Revenue Information Notes

CHY2 Scheme of tax relief for donations of money or "designated securities" to "eligible charities" and other "approved bodies" under section 848A Taxes Consolidation Act 1997

Guidance Notes for Charities and Approved Bodies concerning what constitutes a relevant Donation under section 848A, Taxes Consolidation Act 1997

Eligible Charities and Approved Bodies as listed under the terms of Section 848A Taxes Consolidation Act, 1997

Cross References

From Section 848A

Section 88 Deduction for gifts to Enterprise Trust Ltd.
Section 256 Interpretation (Chapter 4).
Section 484 Relief for gifts for education in the arts.
Section 485 Relief for gifts to third-level institutions.
Section 485A Relief for gifts made to designated schools.
Section 485B Relief for gifts to the Scientific and Technological Education (Investment) Fund.
Section 486 Corporation tax: relief for gifts to First Step.
Section 486A Corporate donations to eligible charities.
Section 611 Disposals to State, public bodies and charities.
Section 764 Deduction for revenue expenditure on scientific research.
Section 767 Payment to universities and other approved bodies for research in, or teaching of, approved subjects.
Section 787 Nature and amount of relief for qualifying premiums.
Section 792 Income under dispositions for short periods.
Section 848 Designated charities: repayment of tax in respect of donations.
Section 950 Interpretation (Part 41).
Section 951 Obligation to make a return.
Section 1017 Assessment of husband in respect of income of both spouses.

To Section 848A

Section 531B Charge to income levy.
Section 531AA Interpretation (Part 18C).
Section 531AM Charge to universal social charge.
Section 611 Disposals to State, public bodies and charities.
Section 847A Donations to certain sports bodies.
Section 1024 Method of apportioning reliefs and charging tax in cases of separate assessments.
Schedule 25B List of Specified Reliefs and Method of Determining Amount of Specified Relief Used in a Tax Year
Schedule 26A Donations to approved bodies, etc.

848AA Tax treatment of return of value on certain shares

[(1) In this section—

'*company*' means Vodafone plc;

'*relevant legislation*' means *Part 26* of the Act of the British Parliament entitled the Companies Act 2006;

'*return of value*' means the special dividend paid in respect of fully paid bonus C shares issued to shareholders in the company in accordance with the terms of a return of value and related share consolidation, provided for by means of a scheme of arrangement under the relevant legislation, and which was completed by the company on or about 21 February 2014.

(2) Notwithstanding any other provision of this Act, the receipt by an individual who is a shareholder in the company of a return of value in an amount of not more than €1,000, shall be deemed, for the purposes of capital gains tax, to be the receipt of a capital sum derived from the individual's ordinary shares in the company and not to be income, unless the individual elects to have that return of value treated as income.

(3) An election referred to in *subsection (2)* to have a return of value treated as income shall be regarded as made by an individual by including the return of value as income in a return for the year ended 31 December 2014, required to be delivered under *section 879* or *959I*, as appropriate.][1]

Amendments

[1] Inserted by FA14 s48.

Note:

Due to a drafting error, FA14 s48 inserts a duplicate section reference, s 848AA, into this Act. This error is expected to be amended in the next Finance Act.

PART 36A

Special Savings Incentive Accounts

848B Interpretation

[(1) In this Part—

"*deposit account*" means an account beneficially owned by an individual, which is—

(a) an account into which a deposit (within the meaning of *section 256(1)*) is made, or

(b) an account with a relevant European institution into which repayable funds are lodged;

"*investment undertaking*" has the meaning assigned to it in *section 739B* and "*units in an "investment undertaking*" shall be construed accordingly;

"*PPS Number*", in relation to an individual, means that individual's Personal Public Service Number within the meaning of [section 262 of the Social Welfare Consolidation Act 2005;][1]

"*qualifying assets*", subject to *section 848G*, means—

(a) deposit accounts,

(b) shares within the meaning of section 2(1) of the Credit Union Act, 1997,

(c) units in an investment undertaking,

(d) units in, or shares of, a relevant UCITS,

(e) relevant life assurance policies,

(f) shares issued by a company, wherever incorporated, officially listed on a recognised stock exchange, and

(g) securities issued by or on behalf of a government;

"*qualifying individual*" means an individual who at the time of opening a special savings incentive account—

(a) is 18 years of age, or older, and

(b) is resident in the State;

"*qualifying savings manager*" means—

(a) a person who is a holder of a licence granted under section 9 of the Central Bank Act, 1971, or a person who holds a licence or other similar authorisation under the law of any other Member State of the European Communities which corresponds to a licence granted under that section,

(b) a building society within the meaning of *section 256*,

(c) a trustee savings bank within the meaning of the Trustee Savings Banks Act, 1989,

(d) ACC Bank plc,

(e) the Post Office Savings Bank,

(f) a credit union within the meaning of the Credit Union Act, 1997,

(g) an investment undertaking,

(h) the holder of—

(i) an authorisation issued by the Minister for Enterprise, Trade and Employment under the European Communities (Life Assurance) Regulations of 1984 (S.I. No. 57 of 1984), as amended, or,

(ii) an authorisation granted by the authority charged by law with the duty of supervising the activities of insurance undertakings in a Member State of the European Communities, other than the State, in accordance with Article 6 of Directive No. 79/267/EEC*, who is carrying on the business of life assurance in the State, or

* O.J. No. L63 of 13 March, 1979, P.1.

(iii) an official authorisation to undertake insurance in Iceland, Liechtenstein and Norway pursuant to the EEA Agreement within the meaning of the European Communities (Amendment) Act, 1993, and who is carrying on the business of life assurance in the State,

(i) a person which is an authorised member firm of the Irish Stock Exchange, within the meaning of the Stock Exchange Act, 1995, or a member firm (which carries on a trade in the State through a branch or agency) of a stock exchange of any other Member State of the European Communities,

(j) a firm approved under section 10 of the Investment Intermediaries Act, 1995, which is authorised to hold client money, other than a firm authorised as a Restricted Activity Investment Product Intermediary, where the firm's authorisation permits it to engage in the proposed activities, or a business firm which has been authorised to provide similar investment business services under the laws of a Member State of the European Communities which correspond to that Act, or

(k) the Minister for Finance, acting through the Agency (within the meaning of section (1) of the National Treasury Management Agency Act, 1990);

"*relevant European institution*" means an institution which is a credit institution (within the meaning of the European Communities (Licensing and Supervision of Credit Institutions) Regulations, 1992 (S.I. No. 395 of 1992)) which has been authorised by the Central Bank of Ireland to carry on business of a credit institution in accordance with the provisions of the supervisory enactments (within the meaning of those Regulations);

"*relevant UCITS*" means a UCITS situated in a Member State of the European Communities, other than the State, which has been authorised by the competent authorities of the Member State in which it is situated;

"*relevant life assurance policy*" means a policy of assurance which satisfies the conditions specified in *subsection (3)*;

"*special savings incentive account*" has the meaning assigned to it in *section 848C*;

"*tax credit*", in relation to a subscription, has the meaning assigned to it in *section 848D(1)*;

"*UCITS*" means undertakings for collective investment in transferable securities within the meaning of Article 1 of Council Directive 85/611* and references to—

* O.J. No. L375 of 31 December, 1985, P.3.

(a) "the Member State in which UCITS is situated"

and

(b) a UCITS which has been "authorised by the competent authorities of the Member State in which it is situated", shall have the same meanings as in Articles 3 and 4 respectively of that Directive;

"units in, or shares of, a relevant UCITS" means the rights or interests (however described) of the holder of units or shares in that relevant UCITS.

(2) Nothing in this Part shall be construed as authorising or permitting a person who is a qualifying savings manager to provide any services which that person would not otherwise be authorised or permitted to provide in the State.

(3) The conditions referred to in the definition of "relevant life assurance policy" in *subsection (1)* are that the policy of assurance is on the life of a person who beneficially owns the policy, and that the terms and conditions of the policy provide—

(a) for an express prohibition of any transfer of the policy, or the rights conferred by the policy or any share or interest in the policy or rights respectively, other than the cash proceeds from the termination of the policy or a partial surrender of the rights conferred by the policy, to that person,

(b) the policy, the rights conferred by the policy and any share or interest in the policy or rights respectively, shall not be capable of assignment, other than that the proceeds on the termination of the policy (other than on the death of the policyholder) may be transferred from a qualifying savings manager to another qualifying savings manager in accordance with the provisions of this Part, and

(c) the policy is not issued in the course of annuity business or pension business, within the meaning of *section 706*.][2]

Amendments

[1] Substituted by FA07 sched4(1)(ac). Shall have effect as on and from 2 April 2007

[2] Inserted by FA01 s33(1).

Revenue Briefings

Tax Briefing

Tax Briefing April 2001 – Issue 43 pg 25 – New Savings Schemes

Cross References

From Section 848B

Section 256 Interpretation (Chapter 4).

Section 706 Interpretation and general (Part 26).

Section 739B Interpretation and application.

Section 848C Special savings incentive account.

Section 848D Tax credits.

Section 848G Acquisition of qualifying assets.

To Section 848B

Section 172A Interpretation.

Section 730D Gain arising on a chargeable event.

Section 730E Declarations.

Section 848G Acquisition of qualifying assets.

Section 904H Power of inspection: qualifying savings managers.

848C Special savings incentive account

[A special savings incentive account is a scheme of investment commenced on or after 1 May 2001 and on or before 30 April 2002 by a qualifying individual with a qualifying savings manager (who is registered in accordance with *section 848R*) under terms which include the following—

(a) apart from tax credits, in relation to subscriptions, subscribed by the qualifying savings manager under *section 848E(1)(b)*(ii) only the qualifying individual, or the spouse of that individual, may subscribe to the account,

(b) such subscriptions are funded by the qualifying individual, or the spouse of that individual, from funds available to either or both of them out of their own resources without recourse to borrowing, or the deferral of repayment (whether in respect of capital or interest) of sums already borrowed,

(c) subject to *paragraph (d)*, such subscriptions, ignoring any amounts withdrawn from the account by the qualifying individual—

(i) in the month the account is commenced and in each of the 11 months immediately after that month, are of an amount agreed between the qualifying individual and the qualifying savings manager when the account is commenced, which amount shall not be less than [€12.50][1], and

(ii) in any one month, do not exceed [€254][2],

(d) such subscriptions, made in the month which is the month in which the fifth anniversary of the day of commencing the account falls, or thereafter, shall not be subscriptions for the purposes of *section 848D*,

(e) such subscriptions and tax credits, in relation to such subscriptions, are to be used, and used only, by the qualifying savings manager to acquire qualifying assets which—

(i) are held in the account and managed by the qualifying savings manager, and

(ii) are beneficially owned by the qualifying individual,

(f) all or any of the qualifying assets can not be assigned or otherwise pledged, as security for a loan,

(g) on commencing the account, the qualifying individual makes a declaration of a kind referred to in *section 848F*,

[(h) for the account to be treated as maturing (otherwise than in respect of the death of the qualifying individual) in accordance with *section 848H(1)*, the qualifying individual shall make a declaration of a kind referred to in *section 848I* at any time within the period of 3 months ending on the fifth anniversary of the end of the month in which a subscription was first made to the account,][3]

(i) that at the request of the qualifying individual, and within such time as shall be agreed, the account, with all rights and obligations of the parties thereto may be transferred to another qualifying savings manager in accordance with the provisions of this Part,

(j) that the qualifying savings manager will notify the qualifying individual if he or she ceases to be a qualifying savings manager, or ceases to be registered in accordance with *section 848R*, and

(k) that the qualifying savings manager will take reasonable measures—

(i) to establish that the PPS Number, contained in the declaration referred to in *paragraph (g)*, made by a qualifying individual, is the PPS Number in relation to that individual, and

(ii) to ensure that the terms, provided for in this section, under which the account is commenced are and continue to be complied with, and

(l) that the qualifying savings manager will retain a copy of all material used to establish the correctness of each PPS Number contained in a declaration in accordance with *paragraph (k)(i)*, for so long as the declaration is required to be retained under *section 848R(11)* and on being so required by an inspector, will make such material available for inspection.][4]

Amendments

[1] Substituted by FA01 s33(2)(a)(i). This subsection shall apply as on and from 1 January 2002.

[2] Substituted by FA01 s33(2)(a)(ii). This subsection shall apply as on and from 1 January 2002.

[3] Substituted by FA02 s49(a).

[4] Inserted by FA01 s33(1).

Cross References

From Section 848C

Section 848D Tax credits.
Section 848E Payment of tax credit.
Section 848F Declaration on commencement.
Section 848H Termination of special savings incentive account.
Section 848I Declaration on maturity.
Section 848R Registration etc.

To Section 848C

Section 848B Interpretation.
Section 848F Declaration on commencement.
Section 848H Termination of special savings incentive account.
Section 848I Declaration on maturity.
Section 848N Transfer of special savings incentive account.
Section 848Q Annual returns.
Section 848S Regulations.
Section 848U Disclosure of information.
Section 848V Interpretation (Part 36B).
Section 904H Power of inspection: qualifying savings managers.

848D Tax credits

[Where a qualifying individual, or the spouse of that individual, subscribes to a special savings incentive account—

(a) the qualifying individual shall be treated, for the purposes of the Tax Acts, as having paid a grossed up amount, which amount, after deducting income tax at the standard rate for the year of assessment 2001, leaves the amount of the subscription, and

(b) the qualifying individual shall be entitled to be credited with the amount of income tax (in this Part referred to as the "*tax credit*", in relation to the subscription) treated as having been so deducted, in accordance with the provisions of this Part and not under any other provision of the Tax Acts.][1]

Amendments

[1] Inserted by FA01 s33(1).

Cross References

To Section 848D

Section 848B Interpretation.
Section 848C Special savings incentive account.

848E Payment of tax credit

[(1) Where a qualifying individual subscribes to a special savings incentive account, and the qualifying savings manager of that account complies with the provisions of *section 848P* in relation to that subscription—

(a) the Revenue Commissioners shall, subject to that section, pay to the qualifying savings manager the tax credit in relation to that subscription, and

(b) that tax credit shall—

(i) be beneficially owned by the qualifying individual, and

(ii) on receipt, be immediately subscribed by the qualifying savings manager to the special savings incentive account.

(2) Subject to this Part, exemption from income tax and capital gains tax shall be allowed in respect of the income and chargeable gains arising in respect of qualifying assets held in a special savings incentive account.

(3) A deposit (within the meaning of *section 256(1)*) made to a deposit account which is a qualifying asset, shall not be a relevant deposit (within the meaning of that section) for the purposes of *Chapter 4* of *Part 8*.

[(3A) The provisions of *section 267B(2)* shall not apply to shares held in a special share account (within the meaning of *section 267A*) where the shares are a qualifying asset.][1]

(4) Notwithstanding *subsection (2)*, where in a year of assessment an individual commences a special savings incentive account, the individual is obliged to include in a return, required to be delivered by the individual under *section 951*, or as the case may be, *section 879*, in respect of that year of assessment, a statement to the effect that the individual has commenced such an account.][2]

Amendments

[1] Inserted by FA02 s49(b).

[2] Inserted by FA01 s33(1).

Cross References

From Section 848E

Section 237 Annual payments payable wholly out of taxed income.
Section 256 Interpretation (Chapter 4).
Section 267A Interpretation (Chapter 5).
Section 267B Election to open a special share account or a special term share account.
Section 848P Monthly returns.
Section 879 Returns of income.
Section 951 Obligation to make a return.

To Section 848E

Section 739D Gain arising on a chargeable event.
Section 848C Special savings incentive account.
Section 848H Termination of special savings incentive account.
Section 848J Gain on maturity.
Section 848S Regulations.

848F Declaration on commencement

[The declaration referred to in *section 848C(g)* is a declaration in writing made by the qualifying individual to the qualifying savings manager which—

(a) is made and signed by the qualifying individual,

(b) is made in such form—

(i) as may be prescribed or authorised by the Revenue Commissioners, and

(ii) which contains a reference to the offence of making a false declaration under *section 848T*,

(c) contains the qualifying individual's—

(i) name,

(ii) address of his or her permanent residence,

(iii) PPS Number, and

(iv) date of birth,

(d) declares at the time the declaration is made, that the qualifying individual—

(i) is resident in the State,

(ii) has not commenced another special savings incentive account,

(iii) is the person who will beneficially own the qualifying assets to be held in the account,

(iv) will subscribe to the account from funds available to him or her, or his or her spouse, from their own resources, without recourse to borrowing, or the deferral of repayment (whether in respect of capital or interest) of sums already borrowed, and

(v) will not assign or otherwise pledge qualifying assets to be held in the account as security for a loan,

and

(e) contains an undertaking that if at any time the declaration ceases to be materially correct, the qualifying individual will advise the qualifying savings manager accordingly.][1]

Amendments

[1] Inserted by FA01 s33(1).

Cross References

From Section 848F

Section 848C Special savings incentive account.
Section 848T Offences.

To Section 848F

Section 848C Special savings incentive account.
Section 848R Registration etc.
Section 848T Offences.
Section 904H Power of inspection: qualifying savings managers.

848G Acquisition of qualifying assets

[(1) Qualifying assets held in a special savings incentive account, managed by a qualifying savings manager and beneficially owned by a qualifying individual may not at any time—

(a) be purchased (or otherwise acquired) by the qualifying savings manager, otherwise than—

(i) out of money which the qualifying savings manager holds in the account, and

(ii) by way of a bargain made at arm's length,

(b) be purchased from the qualifying individual or any person connected with that individual (within the meaning of *section 10*), or

(c) be connected with any other asset or liability of the qualifying individual or any other person connected with that individual (within the meaning of *section 10*) and for this purpose a qualifying asset is connected with another asset or a liability if the terms under which either asset or the liability is acquired and held would be different if the qualifying asset, the other asset or the liability, had not been acquired and held.

(2) Shares fulfil the condition as to official listing in *paragraph (f)* of the definition of "*qualifying assets*" in *section 848B(1)* if in pursuance of a public offer, a qualifying savings manager applies for the allotment or allocation to him or her of shares in a company which are due to be admitted to such listing within 30 days of the allocation or allotment, and which, when admitted to such a listing, would be qualifying assets.][1]

Amendments

[1] Inserted by FA01 s33(1).

Cross References

From Section 848G

Section 10 Connected persons.

Section 848B Interpretation.

To Section 848G

Section 848B Interpretation.

848H Termination of special savings incentive account

[(1) A special savings incentive account is treated as maturing—

[(a) on the fifth anniversary of the end of the month in which a subscription was first made to the account where the qualifying individual has made a declaration of a kind referred to in *section 848I* and the qualifying savings manager is in possession of that declaration at that time, or,][1]

(b) on the day of the death of the qualifying individual,

whichever event first occurs.

(2) A special savings incentive account is treated as ceasing, where at any time before the account is treated as maturing—

(a) any of the terms referred to in *section 848C* are not complied with, or

(b) the qualifying individual is neither resident nor ordinarily resident in the State.

(3) Where a special savings incentive account is treated as maturing or ceasing—

(a) the account thereafter shall not be a special savings incentive account for the purposes of *section 848E*, and

(b) the assets remaining in the account after having regard to all liabilities to tax on gains treated as accruing to the account under this Part shall—

(i) where the assets are shares, securities, or units in, or shares of, a relevant UCITS, be treated for the purposes of the Capital Gains Tax Acts, as having been acquired by the qualifying individual at their then market value at that time,

(ii) where the asset is a relevant life assurance policy, be treated as if it were a policy commenced at that time and in respect of which premiums in an amount equal to the market value of the policy at that time had been paid at that time, for the purposes of *Chapter 5* of *Part 26*, and

(iii) where the asset is units in an investment undertaking, be treated as if the units had been acquired at that time, for their market value at that time, for the purposes of *Chapter lA* of *Part 27*.

[(4) Where at any time a special savings incentive account is treated as maturing or, as the case may be, ceasing, the amount of any income which accrues in respect of qualifying assets held in the account, in so far as it was not, but for this subsection, taken into account in determining a gain under *section 848J*, *848K* or *848L*, shall, when received, be treated as an amount of cash withdrawn from the account before the account is treated as maturing, or as the case may be, ceasing, and the qualifying savings manager shall be liable to tax in accordance with section *848M* on the gain thereby arising under section *848L*.][2]

[(5) Where a special savings incentive account is treated as maturing and the qualifying individual so requires for the purposes of *Part 36B*, the qualifying savings manager shall issue to the qualifying individual a "*maturity statement*", in relation to the account, being a statement which specifies—

(a) the name and address of the qualifying individual,

(b) the PPS Number of the qualifying individual,

(c) the maturity date in relation to the account, being the date on which the account was treated as maturing,

(d) the gross funds in relation to the account, being the value of the assets in the account immediately before the maturity date,

(e) the maturity tax in relation to the account, being the liability to tax on gains treated as accruing to the account on the maturity date,

(f) the net funds in relation to the account, being the value of the assets remaining in the account immediately after the maturity date and the maturity tax discharged, and

(g) the name and address of the qualifying savings manager.][3]][4]

Amendments

[1] Substituted by FA02 s49(c)(i).

[2] Inserted by FA02 s49(c)(ii).

[3] Inserted by FA06 s41(1). Applies as on and from 2 February 2006.

[4] Inserted by FA01 s33(1).

Cross References

From Section 848H

Section 731 Chargeable gains accruing to unit trusts.
Section 848C Special savings incentive account.
Section 848E Payment of tax credit.
Section 848I Declaration on maturity.
Section 848J Gain on maturity.
Section 848K Gain on cessation.
Section 848L Gain on withdrawal.
Section 848M Taxation of gains.

To Section 848H

Section 848C Special savings incentive account.
Section 848V Interpretation (Part 36B).

848I Declaration on maturity

[The declaration referred to in *section 848C(h)* is a declaration in writing made by the qualifying individual to the qualifying savings manager which—

(a) is made and signed by the qualifying individual,

(b) is made in such form—

(i) as may be prescribed or authorised by the Revenue Commissioners, and

(ii) which contains a reference to the offence of making a false declaration under *section 848T*,

(c) contains the qualifying individual's—

(i) name,

(ii) address of his or her permanent residence,

(iii) PPS Number, and

(iv) date of birth,

(d) declares that at all times in the period from which the account was commenced until the date the declaration is made, the qualifying individual—

(i) was the beneficial owner of the qualifying assets held in the account,

(ii) had only one special savings incentive account,

(iii) was resident or ordinarily resident in the State,

(iv) subscribed to the account from funds available to the qualifying individual or his or her spouse without recourse to borrowing, or the deferral of repayment (whether of capital or interest) of sums borrowed when the account was commenced, and

(v) did not assign or otherwise pledge qualifying assets held in the account as security for a loan.][1]

Amendments

[1] Inserted by FA01 s33(1).

Cross References

From Section 848I

Section 848C Special savings incentive account.
Section 848T Offences.

To Section 848I

Section 848C Special savings incentive account.
Section 848H Termination of special savings incentive account.
Section 848R Registration etc.
Section 848T Offences.
Section 904H Power of inspection: qualifying savings managers.

848J Gain on maturity

[(1) On the day on which a special savings incentive account is treated as maturing, a gain shall be treated as accruing on the account in an amount determined under *subsection (2)*.

(2) The amount of the gain referred to in *subsection (1)* is an amount equal to the aggregate market value of all assets (including cash) held in the account on the day the account is treated as maturing, less the sum of all subscriptions (including subscriptions made by the qualifying savings manager under *section 848E(1)(b)(ii)*), made to the account on or before that day to the extent that they have not previously been treated, in accordance with *subsection (3)*, as having been withdrawn from the account.

(3) For the purposes of *subsection (2)* where there is a withdrawal from an account, the amount withdrawn (before being reduced by any tax liability arising under

this Part in respect of any gain treated as accruing to the account as a result of the withdrawal) shall be treated as a withdrawal of subscriptions to the extent that the amount withdrawn does not exceed the total amount of subscriptions (including subscriptions made by the qualifying savings manager in accordance with *section 848E(1)(b)(ii)*) made to the account since commencement, reduced by the amount of such subscriptions previously treated as subscriptions withdrawn from the account under this subsection.

(4) For the purposes of *subsection (3)* where there is a withdrawal of assets (other than cash) from an account the amount withdrawn shall be the amount which is the market value of those assets at the time of their withdrawal.][1]

Amendments

[1] Inserted by FA01 s33(1).

Cross References

From Section 848J

Section 848E Payment of tax credit.

To Section 848J

Section 848H Termination of special savings incentive account.
Section 848Q Annual returns.

848K Gain on cessation

[(1) On the day on which a special savings incentive account is treated as ceasing, a gain shall be treated as accruing on the account in an amount determined under *subsection (2)*.

(2) The amount of the gain referred to in *subsection (1)* is an amount equal to the aggregate market value of all assets (including cash) held in the account on the day the account is treated as ceasing.][1]

Amendments

[1] Inserted by FA01 s33(1).

Cross References

To Section 848K

Section 848H Termination of special savings incentive account.
Section 848Q Annual returns.

848L Gain on withdrawal

[(1) Where before a special savings incentive account is treated as maturing or ceasing (as the case may be) a qualifying individual withdraws cash or other assets from the account, a gain shall be treated as accruing on the account in an amount determined under *subsection (2)*.

(2) The amount of the gain referred to in *subsection (1)* is—

(a) where the withdrawal is in cash, the amount of that cash, and

(b) where the withdrawal is of assets (other than cash) an amount equal to the market value of such assets on the day of withdrawal.][1]

Amendments

[1] Inserted by FA01 s33(1).

Cross References

To Section 848L

Section 848H Termination of special savings incentive account.

Section 848Q Annual returns.

848M Taxation of gains

[(1) A qualifying savings manager shall be liable to tax (in this Part referred to as "*relevant tax*") representing income tax on a gain treated under this Part as accruing to a special savings incentive account in an amount equal to 23 per cent of the amount of that gain.][1]

(2) A qualifying savings manager who becomes liable under *subsection (1)* to an amount of relevant tax shall be entitled to withdraw sufficient funds from the account to which the gain is treated as accruing to satisfy that liability and the qualifying individual shall allow such withdrawal; but where there are no funds or insufficient funds available in the account out of which the qualifying savings manager may satisfy, or fully satisfy, such liability, the amount of relevant tax for which there are insufficient funds so available shall be a debt due to the qualifying savings manager from the qualifying individual.

(3) Subject to *section 848P*, the relevant tax in respect of a gain which in accordance with that section, is required to be included in a return, shall be due at the time by which the return is to be made and shall be paid by the qualifying fund manager without the making of an assessment; but relevant tax which has become so due may be assessed on the qualifying savings manager (whether or not it has been paid when the assessment is made) if that tax or any part of it is not paid on or before the due date.

(4) Where it appears to the inspector that there is any amount of relevant tax which ought to have been, but has not been, included in a return, or where the inspector is dissatisfied with any return, the inspector may make an assessment on the qualifying savings manager [to the best of the inspector's judgement][2], and any amount of relevant tax due under an assessment made by virtue of this subsection shall be treated for the purposes of interest on unpaid tax as having been payable at the time when it would have been payable if a correct return had been made.

(5) (a) Any relevant tax assessed on a qualifying savings manager under this Chapter shall be due within one month after the issue of the notice of assessment (unless that tax is due earlier under *subsection (3)*) subject to any appeal against the assessment, but no such appeal shall affect the date when any amount is due under *subsection (3)*.

(b) On the determination of an appeal against an assessment under this section any relevant tax overpaid shall be repaid.

(6) (a) The provisions of the Income Tax Acts relating to—

(i) assessments to income tax,

(ii) appeals against such assessments (including the rehearing of appeals and the statement of a case for the opinion of the High Court), and

(iii) the collection and recovery of income tax,

shall, in so far as they are applicable, apply to the assessment, collection and recovery of relevant tax.

(b) Any amount of relevant tax payable in accordance with this Part without the making of an assessment shall carry interest at the rate of [0.0322 per cent for each day or part of a day][3] from the date when the amount becomes due and payable.

(c) [*Subsections (3)* to *(5)* of *section 1080*][4] shall apply in relation to interest payable under *paragraph (b)* as they apply in relation to interest payable under *section 1080*.

(d) In its application to any relevant tax charged by any assessment made in accordance with this section, *section 1080* shall apply as if [*subsection (2)(b)*][5] of that section were deleted.][6]

Amendments

[1] Substituted by FA02 s49(d)(i).

[2] Substituted by FA02 s49(d)(ii).

[3] Substituted by FA02 s129(1)(a). This section applies from 1 September 2002 to interest chargeable or payable in respect of an amount due to be paid or remitted or an amount to be repaid or retained, as the case may be, whether before, on or after that date in accordance with those provisions.

[4, 5] Substituted by FA05 sched5.

[6] Inserted by FA01 s33(1).

Cross References

From Section 848M

Section 848P Monthly returns.

Section 1080 Interest on overdue income tax, corporation tax and capital gains tax.

To Section 848M

Section 172A Interpretation.

Section 848H Termination of special savings incentive account.

848N Transfer of special savings incentive account

[(1) Where arrangements are made by a qualifying individual to transfer his or her special savings incentive account from one qualifying savings manager (in this section referred to as the "*transferor*") to another qualifying savings manager (in this section referred to as the "*transferee*") or the account is transferred in consequence of the transferor ceasing to act or to be a qualifying savings manager, the following provisions of this section shall apply.

(2) Where a transfer takes place under *subsection (1)*—

(a) all subscriptions to the special savings incentive account in so far as they have not been applied to acquire qualifying assets, and all qualifying assets in the account, must be made to a single transferee,

(b) the qualifying individual shall make a declaration of a kind referred to in *section 848O* to the transferee, and

(c) the transferee shall thereafter for the purposes of this Part be the qualifying savings manager of the special savings incentive account transferred.

(3) The transferor shall within 30 days after the date of transfer—

(a) give to the transferee a notice containing the information specified in *subsection (4)* and the declaration specified in *subsection (5)*, and

(b) pay to the transferee the aggregate of the amounts referred to in *subsection (4)(b)(vi)*.

(4) The information referred to in *subsection (3)* is—

(a) as regards the qualifying individual his or her—

(i) name,

(ii) address of permanent residence,

(iii) date of birth,

(iv) PPS Number,

and

(b) as respects the special savings incentive account transferred pursuant to this section—

(i) the date of transfer,

(ii) the date the account was commenced,

(iii) the identification of the assets held in the account,

(iv) the total of all subscriptions made to the account by the qualifying individual, or the spouse of that individual,

(v) the total of all tax credits, in relation to subscriptions, subscribed to the account,

(vi) the amount of any dividends, and other amounts payable in respect of qualifying assets held in the account and amounts of tax credits, which have not been received by the transferor at the date of transfer, and

(vii) the amount of each withdrawal from the account and the date of each such withdrawal.

(5) The declaration referred to in *subsection (3)* is a declaration in writing made and signed by the transferor to the effect that—

(a) the transferor has fulfilled all obligations under this Part,

(b) the transferor has transferred to the transferee all money and qualifying assets held in the account and that where registration of any such transfer is required, the transferor has taken the necessary steps to ensure that those qualifying assets can be registered in the name of the transferee, and

(c) that, to the best of the qualifying savings manager's knowledge and belief, the information contained in the notice referred to in *subsection (3)* is correct.

(6) Notwithstanding *section 848C*, where a special savings incentive account is being transferred in accordance with this section it shall not be treated as ceasing should, during the period of the transfer, the qualifying assets held in the account, temporarily cease to be managed by a qualifying savings manager, or a qualifying savings manager who is registered in accordance with *section 848R*.][1]

Amendments

[1] Inserted by FA01 s33(1).

Cross References

From Section 848N

Section 848C Special savings incentive account.
Section 848O Declaration on transfer.
Section 848R Registration etc.

To Section 848N

Section 848O Declaration on transfer.
Section 848R Registration etc.
Section 848T Offences.
Section 904H Power of inspection: qualifying savings managers.

848O Declaration on transfer

[The declaration referred to in *section 848N(2)(b)* is a declaration in writing made by the qualifying individual to the qualifying savings manager who is the transferee referred to in that section, which—

(a) is made and signed by the qualifying individual,

(b) is made in such form—

(i) as may be prescribed or authorised by the Revenue Commissioners, and

(ii) which contains a reference to the offence of making a false declaration under *section 848T*,

(c) contains the qualifying individual's—

(i) name,

(ii) address of his or her permanent residence,

(iii) PPS Number, and

(iv) date of birth,

and

(d) declares—

(i) at the time the declaration is made, that the qualifying individual—

(I) has not commenced another special savings incentive account, and

(II) is the person who beneficially owns the qualifying assets held in the account being transferred,

(ii) at the time the special savings incentive account was commenced, the qualifying individual was resident in the State,

(iii) that subscriptions to the account have been and will continue to be made from funds available to him or her, or his or her spouse, out of their own resources without recourse to borrowing, or the deferral of repayment (whether in respect of capital or interest) of sums borrowed when the account was commenced, and

(iv) has not and will not assign or otherwise pledge qualifying assets held in the account as security for a loan.][1]

Amendments

[1] Inserted by FA01 s33(1).

Cross References

From Section 848O

Section 848N Transfer of special savings incentive account.
Section 848T Offences.

To Section 848O

Section 848N Transfer of special savings incentive account.
Section 848R Registration etc.
Section 848T Offences.
Section 904H Power of inspection: qualifying savings managers.

848P Monthly returns

[A qualifying savings manager who is or was registered in accordance with *section 848R*, shall, within 15 days of the end of every month, make a return (including, where it is the case, a nil return) to the Revenue Commissioners, which—

(a) specifies in respect of all special savings incentive accounts managed by the qualifying savings manager in that month—

(i) the aggregate amount of tax credits, in relation to the aggregate of subscriptions made to those accounts in that month,

(ii) the aggregate amount of relevant tax to which the qualifying savings manager is liable in respect of gains treated as accruing on those accounts in that month, and

(iii) the net amount (being the difference between the amounts specified in *paragraphs (a)* and *(b)*) due from or, as the case may be, to, the Revenue Commissioners,

and

(b) contains a declaration in a form prescribed or authorised by the Revenue Commissioners that, to the best of the qualifying savings manager's knowledge and belief, the information referred to in *paragraph (a)* is correct.][1]

Amendments

[1] Inserted by FA01 s33(1).

Cross References

From Section 848P

Section 848R Registration etc.

To Section 848P

Section 848E Payment of tax credit.
Section 848M Taxation of gains.
Section 848R Registration etc.
Section 848S Regulations.
Section 904H Power of inspection: qualifying savings managers.

848Q Annual returns

[A qualifying savings manager who is or was registered in accordance with *section 848R* shall in respect of each year of assessment, on or before 28 February in the year following the year of assessment, make a return (including, where it is the case, a nil return), to the Revenue Commissioners which in respect of the year of assessment—

(a) specifies in respect of each special incentive savings account managed by the qualifying savings manager—

(i) the name of the qualifying individual,

(ii) the address of that individual's permanent residence,

(iii) the PPS Number of the individual,

(iv) the date the account was commenced,

(v) the total amount of subscriptions made by the qualifying individual, or the spouse of that individual, to the account,

(vi) the total amount of tax credits, in respect of subscriptions, subscribed to the account, and

(vii) in respect of each gain accruing on the account—

(I) the amount of relevant tax to which the qualifying savings manager has thereby become liable, and

(II) whether the gain accrued under *section 848J*, *848K* or *848L*,

and

(b) containing a declaration, in a form prescribed or authorised by the Revenue Commissioners, that to the best of the qualifying savings manager's knowledge and belief—

(i) in respect of each special savings incentive account referred to in the return, the terms referred to in *section 848C* have been and are being complied with, and

(ii) the information referred to in *paragraph (a)* and the declaration referred to in *subparagraph (i)* is correct.][1]

Amendments

[1] Inserted by FA01 s33(1).

Cross References

From Section 848Q

Section 848C Special savings incentive account.
Section 848J Gain on maturity.
Section 848K Gain on cessation.
Section 848L Gain on withdrawal.
Section 848R Registration etc.

To Section 848Q

Section 848R Registration etc.
Section 848S Regulations.
Section 904H Power of inspection: qualifying savings managers.

848QA Other returns

[A qualifying savings manager, who is or was registered in accordance with *section 848R*, shall when so required by the Revenue Commissioners, make a return to them in an electronic format specified by them, which sets out, in relation to all of the special savings incentive accounts managed by the qualifying savings manager, or such category of those accounts as may be specified by the Revenue Commissioners, such details in relation to each account as the Revenue Commissioners may specify.][1]

Amendments

[1] Inserted by FA07 s32.

Cross References

From Section 848QA

Section 848R Registration etc.

848R Registration etc

[(1) A person can not be a qualifying savings manager unless the person is included in a register maintained by the Revenue Commissioners of persons registered in accordance with *subsection (5)*.

(2) Where at any time a qualifying savings manager does not have a branch or business establishment in the State, or has such a branch or business establishment but does not intend to carry out all the functions as a qualifying savings manager at that branch or business establishment, the qualifying savings manager shall not be registered in accordance with *subsection (5)* unless the qualifying savings manager appoints for the time being a person, who—

(a) where an individual, is resident in the State, and

(b) where not an individual, has a business establishment in the State, to be responsible for securing the discharge of the obligations which fall to be discharged by the qualifying savings manager under this Part, and advises the Revenue Commissioners of the identity of that person and the fact of that person's appointment.

(3) Where a person has been appointed in accordance with *subsection (2)*, and subject to *subsection (4)* that person shall—

(a) be entitled to act on the qualifying savings manager's behalf for any of the purposes of the provisions of this Part,

(b) shall secure (where appropriate by acting on the qualifying savings manager's behalf) the qualifying savings manager's compliance with and discharge of the obligations under this Part, and

(c) shall be personally liable in respect of any failure of the qualifying savings manager to comply with or discharge any such obligations as if the obligations imposed on the qualifying savings manager were imposed jointly and severally on the qualifying savings manager and the person concerned.

(4) The appointment of a person in accordance with *subsection (2)* shall be treated as terminated in circumstances where—

(a) the Revenue Commissioners have reason to believe that the person concerned—

(i) has failed to secure the discharge of any of the obligations imposed on a qualifying savings manager under this Part, or

(ii) does not have adequate resources to discharge those obligations, and

(b) the Revenue Commissioners have notified the qualifying savings manager and that person that they propose to treat the appointment of that person as having terminated with effect from the date of the notice.

(5) If the Revenue Commissioners are satisfied that an applicant for registration is entitled to be registered, they shall register the applicant with effect from such date as may be specified by them.

(6) If it appears to the Revenue Commissioners at any time that a qualifying savings manager who is registered under this section—

(a) would not be entitled to be registered if it applied for registration at that time, or

(b) has not complied with the provisions of this Part,

the Revenue Commissioners may, by written notice given to the qualifying savings manager, cancel its registration with effect from such date as may be specified in the notice.

(7) Any qualifying savings manager who is aggrieved by the failure of the Revenue Commissioners to register it or by the cancellation of its registration, may, by notice given to the Revenue Commissioners before the end of the period of 30 days beginning with the date on which the qualifying savings manager was notified of the Revenue Commissioners decision, require the matter to be determined by the Appeal Commissioners and the Appeal Commissioners shall hear and determine the matter in like manner as an appeal.

(8) A qualifying savings manager shall give notice to the Revenue Commissioners and the qualifying individuals whose special savings incentive accounts he or she manages of his or her intention to cease to act as the qualifying savings manager

not less than 30 days before he or she so ceases so that his or her obligations to the Revenue Commissioners can be conveniently discharged at or about the time he or she ceases to so act, and the notice to the qualifying individuals shall inform them of their right to transfer their special savings incentive accounts under *section 848N*.

(9) Subject to *subsection (10)*, every return to be made by a qualifying savings manager under *section 848P* and *848Q* shall be made in electronic format approved by the Revenue Commissioners and shall be accompanied by a declaration made by the qualifying savings manager, in a form prescribed or authorised for that purpose by the Revenue Commissioners, to the effect that the return is correct.

(10) Where the Revenue Commissioners are satisfied that a qualifying savings manager does not have the facilities to make a return under *section 848P* or *848Q* in the format referred to in *subsection (9)*, such returns shall be made in writing in a form prescribed or authorised by the Revenue Commissioners, and shall be accompanied by a declaration made by the qualifying savings manager, on a form prescribed or authorised for that purpose by the Revenue Commissioners, to the effect that the return is correct.

(11) A qualifying savings manager shall retain—

(a) in respect of each special savings incentive account which is treated as maturing, the declarations of a kind referred to in *sections 848F*, *848I* and *848O* for a period of 3 years after the date on which the account was treated as maturing, and

(b) in respect of each special savings incentive account which is treated as ceasing, the declarations of a kind referred to in *sections 848F* and *848O* for a period of 3 years after the date on which the account was treated as ceasing,

and on being so required by notice given to him or her in writing by an inspector, make available for inspection all or any such declarations.][1]

Amendments

[1] Inserted by FA01 s33(1).

Cross References

From Section 848R

Section 848F Declaration on commencement.
Section 848I Declaration on maturity.
Section 848N Transfer of special savings incentive account.
Section 848O Declaration on transfer.
Section 848P Monthly returns.
Section 848Q Annual returns.

To Section 848R

Section 848C Special savings incentive account.
Section 848N Transfer of special savings incentive account.
Section 848P Monthly returns.
Section 848Q Annual returns.
Section 848QA Other returns.
Section 848S Regulations.
Section 904H Power of inspection: qualifying savings managers.

848S Regulations

[(1) The Revenue Commissioners shall make regulations providing generally as to the administration of this Part and those regulations may, in particular and without prejudice to the generality of the foregoing include provisions—

(a) as to the manner in which a qualifying savings manager is to register under *section 848R*,

(b) as to the manner in which a return is to be made under *section 848P*,

(c) as to the manner in which a return is to be made under *section 848Q*,

(d) as to the manner in which tax credits are to be paid under *section 848E(1)*, or the net amount referred to in *section 848P(a)(iii)*,

(e) as to the circumstances in which the Revenue Commissioners may require a qualifying savings manager to give a bond or guarantee to the Revenue Commissioners which is sufficient to indemnify the Commissioners against any loss arising by virtue of the fraud or negligence of the qualifying savings manager in relation to the operation of the provisions of this Part, and

(f) as to the manner in which a qualifying savings manager ensures compliance with the terms of special savings incentive accounts provided for in *section 848C*.

(2) Every regulation made under this section shall be laid before Dáil Éireann as soon as may be after it is made and, if a resolution annulling the regulation is passed by Dáil Éireann within the next 21 days on which Dáil Éireann has sat after the regulation is laid before it, the regulation shall be annulled accordingly but without prejudice to the validity of anything previously done thereunder.][1]

Amendments

[1] Inserted by FA01 s33(1).

Cross References

From Section 848S

Section 848C Special savings incentive account.
Section 848E Payment of tax credit.
Section 848P Monthly returns.
Section 848Q Annual returns.
Section 848R Registration etc.

848T Offences

[A person who makes a declaration under *section 848F*, *section 848I*, *section 848O* or *section 848N(5)* which is false, shall be guilty of an offence and shall be liable on summary conviction to a fine of [€1,900][1], or, at the discretion of the court, to imprisonment for a term not exceeding 6 months or to both the fine and the imprisonment.][2]

Amendments

[1] Substituted by FA01 s33(2)(a)(iii). This subsection shall apply as on and from 1 January 2002.

[2] Inserted by FA01 s33(1).

Cross References

From Section 848T

Section 848F Declaration on commencement.
Section 848I Declaration on maturity.
Section 848N Transfer of special savings incentive account.
Section 848O Declaration on transfer.

To Section 848T

Section 848F Declaration on commencement.
Section 848I Declaration on maturity.
Section 848O Declaration on transfer.

848U Disclosure of information

[Notwithstanding any obligation as to secrecy or other restriction upon disclosure of information imposed by or under statute or otherwise, where a qualifying savings manager has reasonable grounds to suspect that the terms, provided for under *section 848C*, under which a special savings incentive account was commenced, are not being complied with, the qualifying savings manager shall inform the Revenue Commissioners accordingly.][1]

Amendments

[1] Inserted by FA01 s33(1).

Cross References

From Section 848U

Section 848C Special savings incentive account.

PART 36B

Pensions: Incentive Tax Credits

848V Interpretation (Part 36B)

[In this Part—

"*additional voluntary contributions*" and "*retirement benefits scheme*" have, respectively, the meanings assigned to them in *section 770*;

"*administrator*" means, subject to section 848AD—

(a) in the case of a PRSA, a PRSA administrator,

(b) in the case of a retirement benefits scheme, an administrator within the meaning of *section 770*, and

(c) in the case of an annuity contract, a person mentioned in *section 784* who is lawfully carrying on the business of granting annuities on human life, including the person mentioned in *section 784(4A)(ii)*;

"*annuity contract*" means an annuity contract or a trust scheme or part of a trust scheme for the time being approved by the Revenue Commissioners under *section 784*;

"*gross funds*", "*maturity date*", "*maturity statement*", "*maturity tax*" and "*net funds*", in relation to a special savings incentive account have, respectively, the meanings assigned to them in *section 848H(5)*;

"*gross income*", in relation to an individual for a year of assessment, means the aggregate of—

(a) the income of the individual from all sources for the year of assessment before any reduction is made from that income in respect of allowances, losses, deductions and other reliefs, including reductions by virtue of *sections 372AP*, *372AR* and *372AU* and, otherwise than where such allowances are made in taxing a trade, allowances under *Part 9*, and

(b) the amount of income for the year of assessment which is exempt from tax under the Tax Acts;

"*PPS Number*", in relation to an individual, means the individual's Personal Public Service Number within the meaning of section 262 of the Social Welfare Consolidation Act 2005;

"*PRSA administrator*" and "*PRSA contribution*" have, respectively, the meanings assigned to them in *Chapter 2A* of Part 30;

"*special savings incentive account*" has the meaning assigned to it in *section 848C* and "*account*" shall be construed accordingly.][1]

Amendments

[1] Inserted by FA06 s42.

Cross References

From Section 848V

Section 268 Meaning of "industrial building or structure".
Section 372AP Relief for lessors.
Section 372AR Relief for owner-occupiers.
Section 372AU Saver for relief due, and for clawback of relief given under, old schemes.
Section 770 Interpretation and supplemental (Chapter 1).
Section 784 Retirement annuities: relief for premiums.
Section 848C Special savings incentive account.
Section 848H Termination of special savings incentive account.

848W Transfer of funds on maturity of SSIA

[This Part applies to an individual—

(a) whose gross income, for the year of assessment (in this section referred to as the "*previous year*") immediately before the year of assessment in which the maturity date of the individual's special savings incentive account falls, does not exceed €50,000, and

(b) none of whose taxable income for the previous year is chargeable to tax at the higher rate, or in the case of an individual who is married, none of whose taxable income for that year would be so chargeable if, where it is not the case, the individual had made an application under *section 1023* and that application had effect for that year,

and who—

(i) within the 3 month period commencing on the maturity date—

(I) furnishes his or her maturity statement to an administrator, and

(II) subscribes an amount (in this Part referred to as a "*pension subscription*") being equal to all or part of the net funds, in relation to his or her special savings incentive account, to the administrator—

(A) as an additional voluntary contribution,

(B) as a PRSA contribution, or

(C) as a premium under an annuity contract,

(ii) makes a declaration of a kind referred to in *section 848X*,

(iii) does not make a claim, under any provision of the Tax Acts, to a deduction for income tax purposes in respect of the pension subscription other than in respect of the amount by which it exceeds €7,500, the tax credit in relation to the pension subscription or the additional tax credit, and

(iv) does not reduce any amount which he or she is required to pay, in the year in which he or she becomes entitled to be credited with tax credits under *section 848Y*, under a retirement benefits scheme, or as a PRSA contribution or as a premium under an annuity contract.][1]

Amendments

[1] Inserted by FA06 s42.

Cross References

From Section 848W

Section 848X Declaration.
Section 848Y Entitlement to pension tax credit.
Section 1023 Application for separate assessments.

To Section 848W

Section 848X Declaration.

848X Declaration

[The declaration, referred to in *section 848W*, is a declaration in writing made by an individual to an administrator which—

(a) is made and signed by the individual,

(b) is made in such form—

(i) as may be prescribed or authorised by the Revenue Commissioners, and

(ii) which contains a reference to the offence of making a false declaration under section 848AF,

(c) contains the individual's—

(i) name,

(ii) address of his or her permanent residence,

(iii) PPS Number,

(iv) date of birth, and

(v) amount of pension subscription,

and

(d) declares that—

(i) the individual's gross income, for the year of assessment immediately before the year of assessment in which the maturity date of his or her special savings incentive account falls, does not exceed €50,000,

(ii) none of the individual's taxable income for the previous year is chargeable to tax at the higher rate, or in the case of an individual who is married, none of the individual's taxable income for that year would be so chargeable if, where it is not the case, the individual had made an application under *section 1023* and that application had effect for that year,

(iii) the individual will not make a claim under any provision of the Tax Acts, to a deduction for income tax purposes in respect of the pension subscription other than in respect of the amount by which it exceeds €7,500, the tax credit in relation to the pension subscription or the additional tax credit, and

(iv) the individual has not and will not reduce any amount which he or she is required to pay, in the year in which he or she becomes entitled to be credited with tax credits under *section 848Y*, under a retirement benefits scheme, or as a PRSA contribution or as a premium under an annuity contract.][1]

Amendments

[1] Inserted by FA06 s42.

Cross References

From Section 848X

Section 848W Transfer of funds on maturity of SSIA.
Section 848Y Entitlement to pension tax credit.
Section 1023 Application for separate assessments.

To Section 848X

Section 848W Transfer of funds on maturity of SSIA.
Section 848Y Entitlement to pension tax credit.
Section 848AF Offences (Part 36B).

848Y Entitlement to pension tax credit

[Where an individual has made a declaration of a kind referred to in *section 848X*, and furnished to the administrator a maturity statement and a pension subscription, the individual shall, when the pension subscription is irrevocable—

(a) subject to this Part, be treated for the purposes of the Tax Acts as having paid to the administrator a grossed up amount, which amount, after deducting income tax at the rate of 25 per cent, leaves the amount of the pension subscription, and

(b) subject to *section 848Z*, be entitled to be credited, in accordance with the provisions of this Part and not under any other provision of the Tax Acts, with the amount of income tax (in this Part referred to as the "*tax credit*", in relation to the pension subscription) treated as having been so deducted.][1]

Amendments

[1] Inserted by FA06 s42.

Cross References

From Section 848Y

Section 848X Declaration.

Section 848Z Tax credits.

To Section 848Y

Section 848W Transfer of funds on maturity of SSIA.

Section 848X Declaration.

848Z Tax credits

[(1) A tax credit in relation to a pension subscription shall not exceed €2,500.

(2) An individual, who is entitled to a tax credit in relation to his or her pension subscription, shall be entitled to be credited, in accordance with the provisions of this Part and not under any other provision of the Tax Acts, with a further amount (in this Part referred to as an "*additional tax credit*").

(3) The amount of the additional tax credit shall be determined by the formula—

$$\frac{(A \times C)}{B}$$

where—

A is the maturity tax in relation to the individual's account,

B is the net funds, in relation to the individual's account, and

C is the amount of the pension subscription.][1]

Amendments

[1] Inserted by FA06 s42.

Cross References

To Section 848Z

Section 848Y Entitlement to pension tax credit.

848AA Payment of tax credits

[Where an individual becomes entitled to a tax credit, in relation to his or her pension subscription, and an additional tax credit, and the administrator complies with *section 848AB*—

(a) the Revenue Commissioners shall, subject to that section, pay to the administrator, the tax credit and the additional tax credit,

(b) those tax credits shall, on receipt, be immediately treated by the administrator as an additional voluntary contribution, a PRSA contribution, or as the case may be, a premium under an annuity contract, made by the individual, and

(c) the pension subscription to the extent that it does not exceed €7,500 and the amount of those tax credits shall be disregarded for the purposes of any claim by the individual to relief under *Chapters 1, 2, 2A* and *2B* of *Part 30*.][1]

Amendments

[1] Inserted by FA06 s42.

Cross References

From Section 848AA

Section 848AB Monthly return.

To Section 848AA

Section 848ABA Withdrawal of tax credits.

848AB Monthly return

[An administrator who is or was registered in accordance with *section 848AD*, shall, within 15 days of the end of every month, make a return (including, where it is the case, a nil return) to the Revenue Commissioners, which—

(a) specifies in respect of all individuals who in the previous month became entitled, under this Part, to be credited with tax credits—

(i) the aggregate amount of tax credits in relation to pension subscriptions,

(ii) the aggregate amount of additional tax credits, and

(iii) the number of pension subscriptions concerned, distinguishing between additional voluntary contributions, PRSA contributions and premiums under an annuity contract,

and

(b) contains a declaration in a form prescribed or authorised by the Revenue Commissioners that, to the best of the administrator's knowledge and belief, the information referred to in *paragraph (a)* is correct.][1]

Amendments

[1] Inserted by FA06 s42.

Cross References

From Section 848AB

Section 848AD Registration and audit of administrators.

To Section 848AB

Section 848AA Payment of tax credits.
Section 848AD Registration and audit of administrators.
Section 848AE Regulations (Part 36B).
Section 848AF Offences (Part 36B).

848ABA Withdrawal of tax credits

[(1) In this section—

"*requested amount*" has the meaning assigned to it in *subsection (2)*;

"*retained amount*", in relation to a requested amount and subject to *subsection (4)*, means the amount determined by the formula—

$$R \times \frac{C}{S + C}$$

where—

R is the requested amount,

C is the aggregate of the tax credit and the additional tax credit, in relation to the pension subscription made by the individual, and

S is the amount of the pension subscription;

"*vesting day*", in relation to an individual's pension product, means the day on which an administrator, in accordance with *section 848AA*, treats tax credits as an additional voluntary contribution, a PRSA contribution, or as the case may be, a premium under an annuity contract, made by the individual.

(2) Where the vesting day in relation to an individual's pension product is on or after 29 September 2006, and, within a period of 1 year commencing on the vesting day, the individual requires the administrator to pay an amount (in this section referred to as a "*requested amount*") to him or her—

(a) where payment is to be made on or after 10 April 2007, the administrator shall deduct from the requested amount, the retained amount in relation to the requested amount, and

(b) where payment is made before 10 April 2007, the individual shall be assessed to income tax for the year of assessment 2007 in such an amount as would ensure that the individual is liable to pay to the Revenue Commissioners an amount equal to the retained amount, in relation to the requested amount.

(3) Where in accordance with *subsection (2)(a)* an administrator deducts a retained amount, the administrator is liable to pay that amount to the Revenue Commissioners in accordance with arrangements determined by them.

(4) The retained amount, in relation to any part of a requested amount or the aggregate of requested amounts that exceeds the aggregate of the tax credit, the additional tax credit and the pension subscription, shall be a nil amount.

(5) An administrator shall, when requested to do so by the Revenue Commissioners, furnish to them in respect of each individual who required the administrator to pay a requested amount—

(a) the name of the individual,

(b) the address of the individual,

(c) the PPS Number of the individual,

(d) the amount of tax credit in relation to the pension subscription made by the individual, that was claimed and paid,

(e) the amount of additional tax credit that was claimed and paid,

(f) the requested amount,

(g) the amount deducted by the administrator from the requested amount,

(h) the date on which payment was made to the individual, and

(i) such other information as the Revenue Commissioners may require.][1]

Amendments

[1] Inserted by FA07 s33.

Cross References

From Section 848ABA

Section 848AA Payment of tax credits.

848AC Other returns

[An administrator who is or was registered in accordance with *section 848AD*, shall, in respect of each of the 4 month periods ending on 30 September 2006, 31 January 2007, 31 May 2007 and 30 September 2007, on or before the 28th day of the month following the end of the period, make a return to the Revenue Commissioners (including, where it is the case, a nil return) which specifies—

(a) in respect of each individual for whom tax credits were claimed in the period—

(i) the name of the individual,

(ii) the address of the individual,

(iii) the PPS Number of the individual,

(iv) the maturity date in relation to the individual's special savings incentive account,

(v) the gross funds in relation to the account,

(vi) the net funds in relation to the account,

(vii) the maturity tax in relation to the account,

(viii) the amount of the pension subscription,

(ix) the amount of the tax credit in relation to the pension subscription that was claimed and paid,

(x) the amount of the additional tax credit that was claimed and paid, and

(xi) whether the tax credits were treated as an additional voluntary contribution, a PRSA contribution or a premium under an annuity contract,

and

(b) in relation to tax credits claimed in the period—

(i) the total amount of tax credits, in relation to pension subscriptions, and

(ii) the total amount of additional tax credits.][1]

Amendments

[1] Inserted by FA06 s42.

Cross References

From Section 848AC

Section 848AD Registration and audit of administrators.

To Section 848AC

Section 848AD Registration and audit of administrators.

Section 848AE Regulations (Part 36B).

848AD Registration and audit of administrators

[(1) A person cannot be an administrator for the purposes of this Part unless the person is included in a register maintained by the Revenue Commissioners for the purposes of this Part.

(2) The Revenue Commissioners may—

(a) audit the returns made by administrators under *sections 848AB* and *848AC*, and

(b) examine the procedures put in place by the administrator for the purpose of ensuring that the returns are correct.][1]

Amendments

[1] Inserted by FA06 s42.

Cross References

From Section 848AD

Section 848AB Monthly return.
Section 848AC Other returns.

To Section 848AD

Section 848AB Monthly return.
Section 848AC Other returns.
Section 848AE Regulations (Part 36B).

848AE Regulations (Part 36B)

[(1) The Revenue Commissioners may make regulations providing generally as to the administration of this Part and those regulations may, in particular and without prejudice to the generality of the foregoing, include provision—

(a) as to the manner in which an administrator is to be registered under *section 848AD*,

(b) as to the manner in which a return is to be made under *section 848AB*, and how errors in such a return are to be corrected,

(c) as to the manner in which a return is to be made under *section 848AC*, and how errors in such a return are to be corrected,

(d) as to the manner in which tax credits are to be claimed and paid,

(e) as to the period for which the documents referred to in [*section 848AG*][1] are required to be retained, and

(f) as to the manner in which the Revenue Commissioners may examine the procedures put in place by an administrator to ensure compliance with the provisions of this Part.

(2) Every regulation made under this section shall be laid before Dáil Éireann as soon as may be after it is made and, if a resolution annulling the regulation is passed by Dáil Éireann within the next 21 days on which Dáil Éireann has sat after the regulation is laid before it, the regulation shall be annulled accordingly but without prejudice to the validity of anything previously done thereunder.][2]

Amendments

[1] Substituted by FA07 sched4(1)(ab). This section is deemed to have come into force and have taken effect as on and from 1 January 2006.

[2] Inserted by FA06 s42.

Cross References

From Section 848AE

Section 848AB Monthly return.
Section 848AC Other returns.
Section 848AD Registration and audit of administrators.
Section 848AG Retention of declarations.

848AF Offences (Part 36B)

[A person who makes a declaration under section *848X* or *848AB* which is false, is liable on summary conviction to a fine of €3,000, or at the discretion of the court, to imprisonment for a term not exceeding 6 months or to both the fine and the imprisonment.][1]

Amendments

[1] Inserted by FA06 s42.

Cross References

From Section 848AF

Section 848X Declaration.

Section 848AB Monthly return.

848AG Retention of declarations

[An administrator shall retain in respect of each individual to whom this Part applies—

(a) the maturity statement in relation to the individual's special savings incentive account, and

(b) the declaration of a kind referred to in section 848X made by the individual,

for such period and in such form as the Revenue Commissioners may by regulation provide.][1]

Amendments

[1] Inserted by FA06 s42.

Cross References

To Section 848AG

Section 848AE Regulations (Part 36B).

MANAGEMENT PROVISIONS

PART 37

Administration

849 Taxes under care and management of Revenue Commissioners

[ITA67 s155; CGTA75 s51(1) and Sch4 pars 1(1) and (2); CTA76 s6(5); FA96 s132(1) and Sch5 PtI par10(1)]

(1) In this section, "*tax*" means income tax, corporation tax and capital gains tax.

(2) All duties of tax shall be under the care and management of the Revenue Commissioners.

(3) The Revenue Commissioners may do all such acts as may be deemed necessary and expedient for raising, collecting, receiving and accounting for tax in the like and in as full and ample a manner as they are authorised to do in relation to any other duties under their care and management and, unless the Minister for Finance otherwise directs, shall appoint such officers and other persons for collecting, receiving, managing and accounting for any duties of tax as are not required to be appointed by some other authority.

(4) All such appointments shall continue in force, notwithstanding the death, or the ceasing to hold office, of any Revenue Commissioner, and the holders shall have power to execute the duties of their respective offices and to enforce in the execution of those offices all laws and regulations relating to tax in every part of the State.

(5) The Revenue Commissioners may suspend, reduce, discharge or restore, as they see fit, any such officer or person.

(6) Any act or thing required or permitted by this or any other statute to be done by the Revenue Commissioners in relation to tax may be done by any one Revenue Commissioner.

Cross References

To Section 849

Section 531Y Payment, collection and recovery.

Section 531AK Care and management.

850 Appeal Commissioners

[ITA67 s156; F(MP)A68 s1(1), s3(2) and Sch PtI]

(1) The Minister for Finance shall appoint persons to be Appeal Commissioners for the purposes of the Income Tax Acts (in the Tax Acts and the Capital Gains Tax Acts referred to as "*Appeal Commissioners*") and the persons so appointed shall, by virtue of their appointment and without other qualification, have authority to execute such powers and to perform such duties as are assigned to them by the Income Tax Acts.

(2) Appeal Commissioners shall be allowed such sums in respect of salary and incidental expenses as the Minister for Finance directs.

(3) The Minister for Finance shall cause an account of all appointments of Appeal Commissioners and their salaries to be laid before each House of the Oireachtas within 20 days of their appointment or, in the case of a House not then sitting, within 20 days after the next sitting of that House.

(4) Anything required to be done under the Income Tax Acts by the Appeal Commissioners or any other Commissioners may, except where otherwise expressly provided by those Acts, be done by any 2 or more Commissioners.

Cross References

To Section 850

Section 2 Interpretation of Tax Acts.
Section 5 Interpretation of Capital Gains Tax Acts.
Schedule 31 Consequential Amendments

851 Collector-General

[ITA67 s162; FA74 s86 and Sch2 PtI; CGTA75 s51(1) and Sch4 par1(3); CTA76 s145(1); FA87 s52; FA97 s157]

(1) There shall be a Collector-General, who shall be appointed by the Revenue Commissioners from among their officers and who shall hold such office at their will and pleasure.

[…][1]

(3) (a) The Revenue Commissioners may nominate persons to exercise on behalf of the Collector-General any or all of the powers and functions conferred on the Collector-General by the Tax Acts and the Capital Gains Tax Acts.

(b) Those powers and functions, as well as being exercisable by the Collector-General, shall also be exercisable on his or her behalf by persons nominated under this subsection.

(c) A person shall not be nominated under this subsection unless he or she is an officer or employee of the Revenue Commissioners.

(4) If and so long as the office of Collector-General is vacant or the holder of that office is unable through illness, absence or other cause to fulfil his or her duties, a person nominated in that behalf by the Revenue Commissioners from among their officers shall act as the Collector-General, and any reference in this or any other Act to the Collector-General shall be construed as including, where appropriate, a reference to a person nominated under this subsection.

(5) The Revenue Commissioners may revoke a nomination under this section.

Amendments

[1] Deleted by F(No.2)A08 sched4(part1). Applies as respects any tax that becomes due and payable on or after 1 March 2009.

Case Law

When the Collector General is dealing with an application for tax clearance they cannot take account of a liquidated company with tax arrears, a common director, and a similar business. Melbarien Enterprises v Revenue Commissioners 1985 III ITR 290

If a new managing director is appointed to a company and an arrangement for payment to the Collector General is already in place, it still stands. Metal products Ltd (in receivership) v Hearn 1988 High Court

Revenue Briefings

eBrief

eBrief No. 87/10 – Mandatory Electronic Filing and Payment of tax – Notice of Defferal of Implementation Date Phase 3

Cross References

To Section 851

Section 2 Interpretation of Tax Acts.
Section 531A Definitions (Part 18A).
Section 531AL Definitions (Part 18D).
Schedule 31 Consequential Amendments

851A Confidentiality of taxpayer information

[(1) In this section,

"*agent*" means a member of a professional body;

"*investigation authority*" means a statutory body responsible for the investigation of alleged criminal offences;

"*professional body*" means—

(a) an accountancy body that comes within the supervisory remit of the Irish Auditing and Accounting Supervisory Authority,

(b) the Irish Auditing and Accounting Supervisory Authority, or

(c) the Irish Taxation Institute;

"*Revenue officer*" includes serving and former officers of the Revenue Commissioners;

["*service provider*" means any person engaged or formerly engaged by or on behalf of the Revenue Commissioners, or any person employed by such person, for the purposes of carrying out work relating to the administration of any taxes or duties under the care and management of the Revenue Commissioners by virtue of the Acts;][1]

["*taxpayer information*" means information of any kind and in any form relating to one or more persons that is—

(a) obtained by a Revenue officer or service provider for the purposes of the Acts,

(b) obtained by a Revenue officer or service provider purportedly for the purposes of the Acts, or

(c) prepared from information so obtained,

but does not include information that does not directly or indirectly reveal the identity of the person to whom it relates;][2]

"*the Acts*" means—

(a) the Tax Acts,

[(aa) the Customs Acts,][3]

(b) Parts 18A, 18B, 18C and 18D,

(c) the statutes relating to the duties of excise and to the management of those duties,

(d) the Capital Gains Tax Acts,

(e) the Value-Added Tax Acts,

[(f) the Capital Acquisitions Tax Consolidation Act 2003, and the enactments amending or extending that Act,

(g) the statutes relating to stamp duty and the management of that duty, and

(h) the *Finance (Local Property Tax) Act 2012*,][4]

and any instruments made thereunder and any instruments made under any other enactment and relating to tax.

(2) All taxpayer information held by the [Revenue Commissioners, a Revenue officer or a service provider][5] is confidential and may only be disclosed in accordance with this section or as is otherwise provided for by any other statutory provision.

(3) Except as authorised by this section, any [Revenue officer, service provider][6] [or any person to whom taxpayer information is disclosed][7] who knowingly—

(a) provides to any person any taxpayer information,

(b) allows to be provided to any person any taxpayer information,

(c) allows any person to have access to any taxpayer information, or

(d) uses any taxpayer information otherwise than in the course of administering or enforcing the Acts,

shall be guilty of an offence and shall be liable—

(i) on summary conviction to a fine of €3,000, and

(ii) on conviction on indictment to a fine of €10,000.

(4) Subject to *subsection (5)*, a [Revenue officer or service provider][8] shall not be required to give or produce evidence relating to taxpayer information in connection with any legal proceedings, notwithstanding anything to the contrary.

(5) *Subsection (2)* does not apply to—

(a) criminal proceedings, or

(b) any legal proceedings (including proceedings before the Appeal Commissioners) relating to the administration or enforcement of the Acts.

(6) (a) Where a Revenue officer has information that leads him or her to suspect that a criminal offence may have been committed, he or she may report the matter and provide such information, as is appropriate, to an investigation authority for investigation.

(b) Information received by an investigation authority may only be used in the detection or investigation of the matter reported to it.

(7) (a) A Revenue officer may disclose [taxpayer information][9] to a professional body where he or she is satisfied that the work of an agent does not meet the professional standards of a professional body.

(b) Information received by a professional body may only be used for the purposes of any investigation by the professional body.

(8) A Revenue officer may disclose information in the following circumstances—

(a) where disclosure of information is authorised by the Freedom of Information Act 1997 and the information is not taxpayer information,

(b) for the purposes of any enquiry under the Tribunal of Enquiry (Evidence) Acts 1921 to 2002,

(c) where the taxpayer information disclosed relates to the person to whom disclosure is made,

(d) where the taxpayer information is disclosed with the consent of the taxpayer to any other person,

(e) where disclosure is made to a person acting in a representative capacity, taxpayer information that is relevant to the person in that capacity,

(f) in relation to a charity, such information as a Revenue Commissioner may authorise in writing and which is in the possession of a revenue officer in relation to the name of a charity, its objectives, its governing documents and its principal officers,

(g) taxpayer information may be disclosed to an official of the Department of Finance solely for the purposes of the formulation or evaluation of fiscal policy,

(h) taxpayer information which may reasonably be regarded as necessary for the purposes of determining any tax, interest, penalty or other amount that is or may become payable by another person, or any refund or tax credit to which the other person is or may become entitled, may be disclosed to that other person,

(i) information which is not taxpayer information, [...][10]

(j) taxpayer information the disclosure of which is expressly authorised by another [enactment, and][11]

[(k) taxpayer information may be disclosed to a service provider for the purpose for which the service provider is engaged and that information shall not be used by that service provider for any other purpose.][12]

[(8A) Where a company is in receipt of relief from tax in relation to the production of a qualifying film under *section 481*, the Revenue Commissioners may disclose the following taxpayer information:

(a) the name of the company;

(b) the name of the film;

(c) the total cost of the production of the film;

(d) the amount of the tax relief given.][13]

(9) Nothing in this section shall prevent the due disclosure in the course of duties of taxpayer information by a [Revenue Commissioner, Revenue officer or service provider][14] to another Revenue Commissioner or Revenue officer.

(10) Section 13 of the Criminal Procedure Act 1967 shall apply in relation to an offence under this section as if, in place of the penalty provided for in subsection (3) of that section, there were specified in that subsection the penalty provided for by subsection (3)(i), and the reference in subsection (2)(a) of section 13 of the Criminal Procedure Act 1967 to the penalty provided for in subsection (3) of that section shall be construed and apply accordingly.][15]

Amendments

[1] Inserted by F(No.2)A13 s81(a)(i).

[2] Substituted by F(No.2)A13 s81(a)(ii).

[3] Inserted by FA12 s120(a). Deemed to have come into force and takes effect on and from 1 January 2012.

[4] Substituted by F(LPT)A 12 s158 & sched(1).

[5] Substituted by F(No.2)A13 s81(b).

[6] Substituted by F(No.2)A13 s81(c).

[7] Inserted by FA13 s102(a).

[8] Substituted by F(No.2)A13 s81(d).

[9] Substituted by FA12 s120(b). Deemed to have come into force and takes effect on and from 1 January 2012.

[10] Deleted by FA13 s102(b).

[11] Substituted by FA13 s102(b).

[12] Substituted by F(No.2)A13 s81(e).

[13] Inserted by FA14 s90.

[14] Substituted by F(No.2)A13 s81(f).

[15] Inserted by FA11 s77.

852 Inspectors of taxes

[ITA67 s161; FA86 s116]

(1) The Revenue Commissioners may appoint inspectors of taxes, and all such inspectors and all other officers or persons employed in the execution of [the Tax Acts and the Capital Gains Tax Acts][1] shall observe and follow the orders, instructions and directions of the Revenue Commissioners.

(2) The Revenue Commissioners may revoke an appointment made under this section.

(3) Inspectors of taxes appointed by the Minister for Finance before the 27th day of May, 1986, shall be deemed to have been appointed by the Revenue Commissioners.

Amendments

[1] Substituted by FA12 sched5(2)(a).

Case Law

The taxpayer companies were formed with a view to the commercial exploitation of an invention based on a car wash system. Revenue gave advance rulings (without knowing all the facts) to the effect that the grant of licenses to third companies and the income deriving from the patent qualified as income from a patent under the Taxes Consolidation Act 1997. It was held the advance ruling by Revenue could not be binding as they made it without being aware of all of the facts. Pandion Haliaetus Limited Ospreycare Ltd, Osprey Systems Design Ltd v The Revenue Commissioners 1987 ITR 670

Cross References

To Section 852

Section 2 Interpretation of Tax Acts.
Section 5 Interpretation of Capital Gains Tax Acts.
Section 173 Interpretation (Chapter 9).
Section 723 Special investment policies.
Schedule 31 Consequential Amendments

853 Governor and directors of Bank of Ireland [Deleted]

[Deleted by FA12 s38(1)(c). With effect from 1 January 2013 per S.I. No. 561 of 2012.]

854 Appointment of persons for purposes of assessment of certain public offices [Deleted]

[Deleted by FA12 sched5(2)(b).]

855 Declaration to be made by Commissioners [Deleted]

[Deleted by FA12 sched5(2)(b).]

856 Disqualification of Commissioners in cases of personal interest

[ITA67 s160; CTA76 s146(2)]

(1) Every Commissioner acting in the execution of the Income Tax Acts shall be chargeable with tax in the same manner as any other person, but shall take no part in the proceedings, and shall not be present, when any assessment, statement or schedule is under consideration, or any controversy or appeal is being determined, with reference to any case in which he or she is interested, either in his or her own right or in the right of any other person as his or her agent, except during the hearing of an appeal for the purpose of being examined orally by the Commissioners, and he or she shall withdraw during the consideration and determination of the controversy or appeal.

(2) A Commissioner who, in any case referred to in *subsection (1)*, takes any part in the determination of any such controversy or appeal, or fails to withdraw, shall incur a penalty of [€60][1] .

(3) For the purposes of corporation tax, where an Appeal Commissioner is interested in his or her own right or in the right of any other person in any matter under appeal, he or she shall not take part in, or be present at, the hearing or determination of the appeal.

Amendments

[1] Substituted by FA01 sched5.

857 Declarations on taking office

[ITA67 s163; F(MP)A68 s3(4) and Sch PtIII; CTA76 s147(5)]

(1) Every person appointed to one of the offices named in *Part 1* of *Schedule 27* shall, before he or she commences to act in the execution of [the Tax Acts and the Capital Gains Tax Acts][1] make and subscribe the declaration contained in that Part in respect of his or her office.

(2) The declaration [shall][2] be made before a Peace Commissioner.

(3) A person who acts in the execution of his or her office [...][3] before he or she has made the prescribed declaration shall forfeit the sum of [€125][4]

[...][5]

Amendments

[1] Substituted by FA12 sched5(2)(c). Applies as respects a person appointed after 31 March 2012.

[2] Substituted by FA12 sched5(2)(d). Applies as respects a person appointed after 31 March 2012.

[3] Deleted by FA12 sched5(2)(e). Applies as respects a person appointed after 31 March 2012.

[4] Substituted by FA01 sched5.

[5] Deleted by FA12 sched5(2)(f). Applies as respects a person appointed after 31 March 2012.

Cross References

From Section 857

Schedule 27 Forms of Declarations to be Made by Certain Persons

To Section 857

Schedule 27 Forms of Declarations to be Made by Certain Persons

858 Evidence of authorisation

[FA97 s159]

(1) In this section, except where the context otherwise requires—

"*the Acts*" means—

(a) (i) the Customs Acts,

(ii) the statutes relating to the duties of excise and to the management of those duties,

(iii) the Tax Acts,

(iv) the Capital Gains Tax Acts,

(v) the Value-Added Tax Consolidation Act 2010, and the enactments amending or extending that Act,

(vi) the Capital Acquisitions Tax Consolidation Act 2003, and the enactments amending or extending that Act,

(vii) the statutes relating to stamp duty and to the management of that duty,

[(viii) the *Finance (Local Property Tax) Act 2012*,][1]

and any instruments made thereunder or under any other enactment and relating to tax, and

(b) the European Communities (Intrastat) Regulations, 1993 (S.I. No. 136 of 1993);

"*authorised officer*" means an officer of the Revenue Commissioners who is authorised, nominated or appointed under any provision of the Acts to exercise or perform any functions under any of the specified provisions, and "*authorised*" and "*authorisation*" shall be construed accordingly;

"*functions*" includes powers and duties;

"*identity card*", in relation to an authorised officer, means a card which is issued to the officer by the Revenue Commissioners and which contains—

(a) a statement to the effect that the officer—

(i) is an officer of the Revenue Commissioners, and

(ii) is an authorised officer for the purposes of the specified provisions,

(b) a photograph and signature of the officer,

(c) a hologram showing the logo of the Office of the Revenue Commissioners,

(d) the facsimile signature of a Revenue Commissioner, and

(e) particulars of the specified provisions under which the officer is authorised;

"*specified provisions*", in relation to an authorised officer, means either or both the provisions of the Acts under which the authorised officer—

(a) is authorised and which are specified on his or her identity card, and

(b) exercises or performs functions under the Customs Acts or any statutes relating to the duties of excise and to the management of those duties;

"*tax*" means any tax, duty, levy or charge under the care and management of the Revenue Commissioners.

(2) Where, in the exercise or performance of any functions under any of the specified provisions in relation to him or her, an authorised officer is requested to produce or show his or her authorisation for the purposes of that provision, the production by the authorised officer of his or her identity card—

(a) shall be taken as evidence of authorisation under that provision, and

(b) shall satisfy any obligation under that provision which requires the authorised officer to produce such authorisation on request.

(3) This section shall come into operation on such day as the Minister for Finance may appoint by order.

Amendments

[1] Inserted by F(LPT)A 12 s158 & sched(2).

Cross References

To Section 858

Section 1104 Short title and construction.

859 Anonymity of authorised officers in relation to certain matters

[FA83 s19A; DCITPA96 s12; CABA96 s23]

(1) In this section—

"*authorised officer*" means an officer of the Revenue Commissioners nominated by them to be a member of the staff of the body;

"*the body*" has the meaning assigned to it by *section 58*;

"*proceedings*" includes any hearing before the Appeal Commissioners (within the meaning of the Revenue Acts);

"*the Revenue Acts*" means—

(a) the Customs Acts,

(b) the statutes relating to the duties of excise and to the management of those duties,

(c) the Tax Acts,

(d) the Capital Gains Tax Acts,

(e) the Value-Added Tax Consolidation Act 2010, and the enactments amending or extending that Act,

(f) the Capital Acquisitions Tax Consolidation Act 2003, and the enactments amending or extending that Act,

(g) the statutes relating to stamp duty and the management of that duty,

(h) Chapter IV of Part II of the Finance Act, 1992, and

(i) Part VI of the Finance Act, 1983,

[(j) the *Finance (Local Property Tax) Act 2012*,][1]

and any instruments made thereunder or under any other enactment and relating to tax;

"*tax*" means any tax, duty, levy or charge under the care and management of the Revenue Commissioners.

(2) Notwithstanding any requirement made by or under any enactment or any other requirement in administrative and operational procedures, including internal procedures, all reasonable care shall be taken to ensure that the identity of an authorised officer shall not be revealed.

(3) In particular and without prejudice to the generality of *subsection (2)*:

(a) where, for the purposes of exercising or performing his or her powers or duties under the Revenue Acts in pursuance of the functions of the body, an authorised officer may apart from this section be required to produce or show any written authority or warrant of appointment under those Acts or otherwise to identify himself or herself, the authorised officer shall—

(i) not be required to produce or show any such authority or warrant of appointment or to so identify himself or herself, for the purposes of exercising or performing his or her powers or duties under those Acts, and

(ii) be accompanied by a member of the Garda Síochána who shall, on request by a person affected, identify himself or herself as a member of the Garda Síochána and shall state that he or she is accompanied by an authorised officer;

(b) where, in pursuance of the functions of the body, an authorised officer exercises or performs in writing any of his or her powers or duties under the Revenue Acts or any provision of any other enactment, whenever passed, which relates to Revenue, such exercise or performance of his or her powers or duties shall be done in the name of the body and not in the name of the individual authorised officer involved, notwithstanding any provision to the contrary in any of those enactments;

(c) in any proceedings arising out of the exercise or performance, in pursuance of the functions of the body, of powers or duties by an authorised officer, any documents relating to such proceedings shall not reveal the identity of any authorised officer, notwithstanding any requirements to the contrary in any provision, and in any proceedings the identity of such officer other than as an authorised officer shall not be revealed other than to the judge or the Appeal Commissioner, as the case may be, hearing the case;

(d) where, in pursuance of the functions of the body, an authorised officer is required, in any proceedings, to give evidence and the judge or the Appeal Commissioner, as the case may be, is satisfied that there are reasonable grounds in the public interest to direct that evidence to be given by such authorised officer should be given in the hearing and not in the sight of any person, he or she may so direct.

Amendments

[1] Inserted by F(LPT)A 12 s158 & sched(3).

Cross References

From Section 859

Section 58 Charge to tax of profits or gains from unknown or unlawful source.

To Section 859

Section 1104 Short title and construction.

860 Administration of oaths

[ITA67 s164; F(MP)A68 s3(1) and (3) and Sch PtI; CTA76 s147(1) and (2)]

[(1) Subject to *subsection (2)*, a Peace Commissioner may administer an oath to be taken by any officer or person in any matter relating to the execution of the Tax Acts or the Capital Gains Tax Acts.][1]

(2) An Appeal Commissioner may administer an oath to be taken before the Appeal Commissioners under the Tax Acts by any officer or person in any matter relating to the execution of the Tax Acts.

Amendments

[1] Substituted by FA12 sched5(2)(g).

861 Documents to be in accordance with form prescribed by Revenue Commissioners

[ITA67 s165; CGTA75 s51(1) and Sch4 par2; CTA76 s143(12)(b) and (c) and s147(1) and (2)]

(1) Every assessment, charge, bond, warrant, notice of assessment or of demand, or other document required to be used in assessing, charging, collecting and levying income tax, corporation tax or capital gains tax shall be in accordance with the forms prescribed from time to time in that behalf by the Revenue Commissioners, and a document in the form prescribed and supplied or approved by them shall be valid and effectual.

(2) (a) In this subsection, "*return*" includes any statement, declaration or list.

(b) Any return [under the Tax Acts and the Capital Gains Tax Acts][1] shall be in such form as the Revenue Commissioners prescribe.

Amendments

[1] Substituted by FA12 sched5(2)(h).

862 Exercise of powers, etc. of Minister for Finance under Tax Acts

[ITA67 s166(2); CTA76 s147(1) and (2)]

Anything required [under the Tax Acts or the Capital Gains Tax Acts][1] to be done by the Minister for Finance may be signified under the hand of the Secretary General, [a Second Secretary General][2] or an Assistant Secretary of the Department of Finance.

Amendments

[1] Substituted by FA12 sched5(2)(i).

[2] Substituted by FA07 sched4(1)(ad). Shall have effect as on and from 2 April 2007.

863 Loss, destruction or damage of assessments and other documents

[ITA67 s188(1); CGTA75 s51(1) and Sch4 par2; CTA76 s147(1) and (2)]

(1) Subject to *subsection (2)*, where any assessment to income tax or capital gains tax for any year, or any assessment to corporation tax for any accounting period or any return or other document relating to income tax, corporation tax or capital gains tax has been lost or destroyed, or has been so defaced or damaged as to be illegible or otherwise useless, the Revenue Commissioners, the Collector-General, inspectors and other officers respectively having powers in relation to income tax, corporation tax or capital gains tax may, notwithstanding anything to the contrary in any enactment, do all such acts and things as they might have done, and all acts and things done under or in accordance with this section shall be as valid and effectual for all purposes as they would have been if the assessment had not been made, or the return or other document had not been made or furnished, or required to be made or furnished.

(2) Where any person who is charged with income tax, corporation tax or capital gains tax in consequence or by virtue of any act or thing done under or in accordance with this section proves to the satisfaction of the Revenue Commissioners that that person has already paid any income tax or capital gains tax for the same year, or corporation tax for the same accounting period, in respect of the subject matter and on the account in respect of and on which that person is so charged, relief shall be given to the extent to which the liability of that person has been discharged by the payments so made either by abatement from the charge or by repayment, as the case may require.

864 Making of claims, etc

[ITA67 s432(1) (part of); CGTA75 s51(1) and Sch4 par2; CTA76 s4 and s146(1); FA84 s6(a)]

(1) Notwithstanding any other provision of the Tax Acts or the Capital Gains Tax Acts—

[(a) all claims for exemption or for any allowance, credit or deduction under those Acts,][1]

(b) all claims for repayment of income tax, corporation tax or capital gains tax under those Acts, and

(c) (i) all claims to relief under those Acts where the relief is measured in the provision under which it is given, and

(ii) all matters and questions relating to any relief so measured,

in relation to which a right of appeal from a decision is, otherwise than by *section 949*, not specifically provided,

shall be stated in such manner and form as the Revenue Commissioners may prescribe, and shall be made to and determined by the Revenue Commissioners or such officer of the Revenue Commissioners (including an inspector) as they may authorise in that behalf.

(2) Effect shall be given—

(a) to *section 21(2)* and to that section as modified by *sections 24(2)* and *25(3)*, and

(b) in so far as the exemptions from income tax conferred by the Corporation Tax Acts call for repayment of tax, to those exemptions,

by means of a claim.

[(3) Any person who—

(a) makes or delivers to the Revenue Commissioners, or

(b) knowingly or carelessly assists in or induces another to make or deliver to the Revenue Commissioners,

any incorrect account, declaration, information, particulars, return or statement, including by means of approved electronic communications (within the meaning of *section 864A*), in connection with any claim for exemption or for any allowance, credit, deduction, relief or repayment shall be liable to a penalty of €3,000.][2]

Amendments

[1] Substituted by FA11 s21(a). Deemed to have come into force and takes effect as on and from 1 January 2011.

[2] Inserted by FA11 s21(b). Deemed to have come into force and takes effect as on and from 1 January 2011.

Case Law

In Thomas O'Callaghan v J.P. Clifford and others 1993 ITR 478 the Supreme Court queried the appropriateness of evidence to establish criminal culpability.

Cross References

From Section 864

Section 21 The charge to corporation tax and exclusion of income tax and capital gains tax.
Section 24 Companies resident in the State: income tax on payments made or received.
Section 25 Companies not resident in the State.
Section 864A Electronic claims.
Section 949 Appeals against determinations of certain claims, etc.

To Section 864

Section 208B Charities — miscellaneous.
Section 481 Relief for investment in films.
Section 865 Repayment of tax.
Section 949 Appeals against determinations of certain claims, etc.
Section 960Q Recovery of amounts received by a person following the lodgement of an incorrect account, etc.

864A Electronic claims

[(1) (a) In this section—

"*approved electronic communications*" means such form of electronic communications as the Revenue Commissioners approve of for the purposes of this section;

"*electronic communications*" means communication by electrical, digital, magnetic, optical, electromagnetic, biometric or photonic technology, and related technology, by means of which data is transmitted, including telephone apparatus, and "*electronic*" means shall be construed accordingly;

"*telephone apparatus*" means telegraphy apparatus designed or adapted for the purposes of transmitting and receiving, by way of a public telecommunications service, spoken messages or information or both of them.

(b) In *paragraph (a)*—

"*information*" has the meaning assigned to it by the Electronic Commerce Act 2000;

"*public telecommunications service*" has the meaning assigned to it by the European Communities (Telecommunications Infrastructure) Regulations 1997 (S.I. No. 338 of 1997).

(c) Except where the Revenue Commissioners otherwise direct, this section applies to a claim for an allowance, [credit,][1] deduction or relief which falls to be taken into account—

(i) in the making of deductions or repayments of tax under *Chapter 4* of *Part 42* and the regulations made under that Chapter, or

(ii) except in the case of a chargeable person (within the meaning of [*Part 41A*][2]), in relation to a repayment of tax deducted under that Chapter and those regulations.

(d) References in this section to "*a claim for an allowance, [credit,][3] deduction or relief*" include references to—

(i) the making of an election,

(ii) the giving of a notification or notice,

(iii) the amendment of a claim, election, notification or notice, and

(iv) the withdrawal of any claim, election, notification or notice,

in relation to an allowance, [credit,][4] deduction or relief, and also include references to an election, notice or application for the purposes of [*Chapter 1* of *Part 44* or *Chapter 1* of *Part 44A*][5] or a claim under Regulation 26(5) of the Income Tax (Employments) (Consolidated) Regulations 2001 (S.I. No. 559 of 2001).

(e) Notwithstanding any other enactment, references in this section to a claim in writing do not include a reference to a claim made by representing or reproducing words in visible form using electronic means.

(2) Notwithstanding any other provision of the Income Tax Acts or instruments made thereunder requiring claims to which this section applies to be made in writing or by notice or in such form as may be prescribed by the Revenue Commissioners, such claims as may be specified by the Revenue Commissioners may be made by an individual by means of approved electronic communications, but subject to such terms and conditions as the Revenue Commissioners may from time to time consider appropriate and specify for the purposes of this section.

(3) The Revenue Commissioners shall make known, in such manner as they think fit, any terms and conditions for the time being specified by them for the purposes of this section.

(4) Where terms and conditions specified by the Revenue Commissioners under this section are for the time being in force with respect to the making of claims to which this section applies, such claims that are made by electronic communications are required to be made in accordance with those terms and conditions.

(5) (a) Terms and conditions specified by the Revenue Commissioners for the purposes of this section shall not be capable of modifying any requirement by or under any enactment as to the period within which any claim is to be made, or as to the contents of any claim.

(b) Such terms and conditions may include provision as to how any requirement as to the contents of a claim is to be fulfilled when the claim is not produced in writing.

(6) Where a claim is made by a person in accordance with this section, the claim shall—

(a) unless and until the contrary is proved, be deemed to have been made by the person purporting to have made the claim, and

(b) be treated as having been made when it is acknowledged, howsoever, by the Revenue Commissioners as having been received by them.

(7) The making of a claim by a person in accordance with this section shall not prevent an officer of the Revenue Commissioners from enquiring into the claim in accordance with *section 886A* (inserted by the *Finance Act 2005*).

(8) Where a claim made in accordance with this section results in the issue to the claimant of a notice, or an amended notice, of determination of tax credits and standard rate cut-off point, the inspector shall, as may be appropriate, be deemed to have determined the amount of the tax credits and standard rate cutoff point appropriate to the claimant in accordance with Regulation 10, or amended the amount in accordance with Regulation 13, of the Income Tax (Employments) (Consolidated) Regulations 2001.

(9) *Section 917M* (as amended by the Finance Act 2001) shall apply in respect of proceedings in relation to this section, in the same manner as it applies in respect of proceedings in relation to *Chapter 6* of *Part 38*, subject to any necessary modifications including substituting in *section 917M* a reference to *section 864A* for a reference to *section 917F(1)* in each place where it occurs.

(10) Any act to be performed or function to be discharged by the Revenue Commissioners which is authorised by this section may be performed or discharged by any of their officers acting under their authority.][6]

Amendments

[1] Inserted by FA11 s21(c). Deemed to have come into force and takes effect as on and from 1 January 2011.

[2] Substituted by FA12 sched4(part 2)(g).

[3,4] Inserted by FA11 s21(d). Deemed to have come into force and takes effect as on and from 1 January 2011.

[5] Substituted by F(No.3)A11 sched1(235).

[6] Inserted by FA05 s23. Applies with effect from 25 March 2005.

Cross References

From Section 864A

Section 864A Electronic claims.
Section 876 Notice of liability to income tax.
Section 886A Retention and inspection of records in relation to claims by individuals.
Section 917F Electronic transmission of returns.
Section 917M Proceedings.
Section 950 Interpretation (Part 41).
Section 960 Date for payment of income tax other than under self assessment.
Section 983 Interpretation (Chapter 4).
Section 1015 Interpretation (Chapter 1).

To Section 864A

Section 864 Making of claims, etc.
Section 864A Electronic claims.

865 Repayment of tax

[(1) (a) In this section and *section 865A*—

['Acts' means the Tax Acts, the Capital Gains Tax Acts, *Part 18A*, *Part 18C* and *Part 18D* and instruments made thereunder;][1]

"*chargeable period*" has the meaning assigned to it by *section 321*;

"*correlative adjustment*" means an adjustment of profits under the terms of arrangements entered into by virtue of [*section 826(1)*][2]

['*tax*' means any income tax, corporation tax, capital gains tax, income levy, domicile levy or universal social charge and includes—

(i) any interest, surcharge or penalty relating to any such tax, levy or charge,

(ii) any sum arising from the withdrawal or clawback of a relief or an exemption relating to any such tax, levy or charge,

(iii) any sum required to be deducted or withheld by any person and paid or remitted to the Revenue Commissioners or the Collector-General, as the case may be, and

(iv) any amount paid on account of any such tax, levy or charge or paid in respect of any such tax, levy or charge;][3]

"*valid claim*" shall be construed in accordance with *paragraph (b).*

(b) For the purposes of *subsection (3)*—

[(i) where a person furnishes a statement or return which is required to be delivered by the person in accordance with any provision of the Acts for a chargeable period, such a statement or return shall be treated as a valid claim in relation to a repayment of tax where—

[(I) all the information which the Revenue Commissioners may reasonably require to enable them determine if and to what extent a repayment of tax is due to the person for that chargeable period is contained in the statement or return, and

(II) the repayment treated as claimed, if due—

(A) would arise out of the assessment to tax, made at the time the statement or return was furnished, on foot of the statement or return, or

(B) would have arisen out of the assessment to tax, that would have been made at the time the statement or return was furnished, on foot of the statement or return if an assessment to tax had been made at that time][4]][5][6]

and

(ii) where all information which the Revenue Commissioners may reasonably require, to enable them determine if and to what extent a repayment of tax is due to a person for a chargeable period, is not contained in such a statement or return as is referred to in *subparagraph (i)*, a claim to repayment of tax by that person for that chargeable period shall be treated as a valid claim when that information has been furnished by the person, and

(iii) to the extent that a claim to repayment of tax for a chargeable period arises from a correlative adjustment, the claim shall not be regarded as a valid claim until the quantum of the correlative adjustment is agreed in writing by the competent authorities of the two Contracting States.

(2) Subject to the provisions of this section, where a person has, in respect of a chargeable period, paid, whether directly or by deduction, an amount of tax which is not due from that person or which, but for an error or mistake in a return or statement made by the person for the purposes of an assessment to

[8] Substituted by F(No.2)A13 s75(1)(b).

[9] Substituted by F(No.2)A13 s75(1)(c).

[10] Inserted by FA05 s24(1)(c)(ii). Applies with effect from 25 March 2005.

[11] Inserted by FA06 sched2(1)(s). Has effect as on and from 31 March 2006.

[12] Substituted by FA03 s17(1)(a). Applies with effect from the day appointed by the Minister for Finance in accordance with different provisions.

[13] Inserted by F(No.2)A13 s75(1)(d).

Note:

F(No.2)A13 s75(1)(c) applies—(a) in the case of a chargeable period (within the meaning of section 321(2)) which is an accounting period of a company, as respects chargeable periods beginning on or after 1 January 2013, and

(b) in a case other than that referred to in paragraph (a), as respects the year of assessment 2013 and subsequent years of assessment.

Subsection (1)(c) does not affect the application of section 865(3A) which is amended by subsection (1)(c), as respects chargeable periods (within the said meaning) prior to those referred to above.

Case Law

Repayments are confined to statutorily prescribed periods. Deutsche Morgan Grenfell Group plc v Attorney General 2005 STC 329

The taxpayer had overpaid a large amount of tax which he wanted to recover but he was unable to satisfy the conditions for the statutory remedy and in judgment of the Chancellor no claim could be brought under general law. Monro v Revenue & Customs Commissioners 2008 STC 1815

The taxpayer's appeal was dismissed where he made an error for unclaimed deposits in his tax return. Gower Chemicals Ltd v Revenue and Customs Commissioners 2008 STC 1242

Revenue Briefings

Tax Briefing

Tax Briefing May 2003 – Issue 52 pg 10 – Finance Act 2003 Repayments, Interest and Time Limits
Tax Briefing July 2004 – Issue 56 pg 6 – Repayments, Interest and Time Limits
Tax Briefing October 2004 – Issue 57 pg 15 – Repayments, Interest and Time Limits
Tax Briefing April 2005 – Issue 59 pg 17 – Time Limits for Repayments
Tax Briefing September 2012 – Issue 05 – Revised arrangements for PAYE Tax Agency Services

eBrief

eBrief No. 74/2010 – 4 Year Limit on Tax Repayment Claims
eBrief No. 52/2012 – Revised arrangements for PAYE Tax Agency Services – Clarification
eBrief No. 61/2012 – Extension of eRepayment Facility

Cross References

From Section 865

Section 321 Provisions of general application in relation to the making of allowances and charges.
Section 826 Agreements for relief from double taxation.
Section 864 Making of claims, etc.
Section 865A Interest on repayments.
Section 949 Appeals against determinations of certain claims, etc.
Section 950 Interpretation (Part 41).
Section 983 Interpretation (Chapter 4).

To Section 865

Section 100 Charge on sale of land with right to reconveyance.
Section 101 Relief for amount not received.
Section 128E Tax treatment of directors of companies and employees who acquire forfeitable shares.
Section 438 Loans to participators, etc.
Section 480A Relief on retirement for certain income of certain sportspersons.
Section 482 Relief for expenditure on significant buildings and gardens.
Section 493 Seed capital relief.
Section 530P Credit for deducted tax.
Section 531 Payments to subcontractors in certain industries.
Section 531M Application of provisions relating to income tax.
Section 539 Disposals in cases of hire purchase and similar transactions.

Section 562 Contingent liabilities.
Section 563 Consideration due after time of disposal.
Section 597 Replacement of business and other assets.
Section 600A Replacement of qualifying premises.
Section 605 Disposals to authority possessing compulsory purchase powers.
Section 652 Non-application of reliefs on replacement of assets in case of relevant disposals.
Section 670 Mine development allowance.
Section 730K Disposal of foreign life policy.
Section 747E Disposal of an interest in offshore funds.
Section 774 Certain approved schemes: exemptions and reliefs.
Section 776 Certain statutory schemes: exemptions and reliefs.
Section 804 Adjustments and information.
Section 929 Double assessment.
Section 955 Amendment of and time limit for assessments.

865A Interest on repayments

[(1) Where a person is entitled to a repayment of tax for a chargeable period and that repayment, or part of the repayment, arises because of a mistaken assumption made by the Revenue Commissioners in the application of any provision of the Acts, that repayment or that part of the repayment shall, subject to [*section 960H(4)*][1], carry interest for each day or part of a day for the period commencing with the day after the end of the chargeable period or, as the case may be, the end of each of the chargeable periods for which the repayment is due or the date on which the tax was paid (whichever is the later) and ending on the day on which the repayment is made.

(2) Where, for any reason other than that mentioned in *subsection (1)*, a repayment of tax or a part of a repayment is due to a person for a chargeable period, that repayment or the part of the repayment shall, subject to [*section 960H(4)*][2], carry interest for the period beginning on the day which is [93 days][3] after the day on which the claim to repayment becomes a valid claim and ending on the day the repayment is made.

(3) (a) Interest payable in accordance with this section shall be simple interest payable at the rate of 0.011 per cent per day or part of a day.

(b) The Minister for Finance may, from time to time, make an order prescribing a rate for the purpose of paragraph (*a*).

(c) Every order made by the Minister for Finance under *paragraph (b)* shall be laid before Dáil Éireann as soon as may be after it is made and, if a resolution annulling the order is passed by Dáil Éireann within the next 21 days on which Dáil Éireann has sat after the order is laid before it, the order shall be annulled accordingly, but without prejudice to the validity of anything previously done under it.

(4) (a) Interest shall not be payable under this section if it amounts to less than €10.

(b) Income tax shall not be deductible on payment of interest under this section and such interest shall not be reckoned in computing income, profit or gains for the purposes of the Tax Acts.

(5) This section shall not apply in relation to any repayment or part of a repayment in respect of which interest is payable under any other provision of the Acts.][4]

Amendments

[1] Substituted by FA12 sched6(1)(k)(i). Has effect as on and from 31 March 2012.

[2] Substituted by FA12 sched6(1)(k)(ii). Has effect as on and from 31 March 2012.

[3] Substituted by FA07 s121(1). Applies as on or after 2 April 2007.

[4] Inserted by FA03 s17(1)(a). Applies with effect from the day appointed by the Minister for Finance in accordance with different provisions. With effect from 1 November 2003 per S.I. 508 of 2003.

Revenue Briefings

Tax Briefing

Tax Briefing May 2003 – Issue 52 pg 10 Finance Act 2003 Repayments, Interest and Time Limits
Tax Briefing July 2004 – Issue 56 pg 6 – Repayments, Interest and Time Limits
Tax Briefing October 2004 – Issue 57 pg 15 – Repayments, Interest and Time Limits
Tax Briefing April 2005 – Issue 59 pg 17 – Time Limits for Repayments

eBrief

eBrief No. 4/2007 – Electronic Refunds of Corporation Tax

Cross References

From Section 865A

Section 1006A Offset between taxes.

To Section 865A

Section 865 Repayment of tax.
Section 941 Statement of case for High Court.

865B No offset where repayment prohibited

[(1) In this section—

'*Acts*' means—

(a) the statutes relating to the duties of excise and to the management of those duties,

(b) the Tax Acts,

(c) the Capital Gains Tax Acts,

(d) *Parts 18A*, *18C* and *18D*,

(e) the Capital Acquisitions Tax Consolidation Act 2003 and the enactments amending or extending that Act,

(f) the Stamp Duties Consolidation Act 1999 and the enactments amending or extending that Act,

[(g) the Value-Added Tax Consolidation Act 2010 and the enactments amending or extending that Act,

(h) the *Finance (Local Property Tax) Act 2012,* and

(i) any instruments made under any of the statutes and enactments specified in paragraphs (a) to (h);][1]

'*relevant period*', in relation to a repayment, means—

(a) in the case of corporation tax, the accounting period of the company in respect of which the repayment arises,

(b) in the case of income tax, capital gains tax, income levy, universal social charge or domicile levy, the year of assessment in respect of which the repayment arises,

(c) in the case of stamp duties, the year of assessment or accounting period, as the case may be, within which falls the event in respect of which the repayment arises,

(d) in the case of gift tax or inheritance tax, the year of assessment or accounting period, as the case may be, within which falls the latest of the dates referred to in *section 57(3)* of the Capital Acquisitions Tax Consolidation Act 2003 and in respect of which the repayment arises, [(e) in the case of excise duty, the year of assessment or accounting period, as the case may be, within which falls the act or event in respect of which the repayment arises,

(f) in the case of value-added tax, the year of assessment or accounting period, as the case may be, within which falls the taxable period in respect of which the repayment arises, and

(g) in the case of local property tax, the year within which the repayment arises;][2]

'*repayment*' includes are fund;

['*tax*' means any income tax, corporation tax, capital gains tax, value-added tax, excise duty, stamp duty, gift tax, inheritance tax, income levy, domicile levy, universal social charge or local property tax and includes—][3]

(a) any interest, surcharge or penalty relating to any such tax, duty, levy or charge,

(b) any sum arising from the withdrawal or clawback of a relief or an exemption relating to any such tax, duty, levy or charge,

(c) any sum required to be deducted or withheld by any person and paid or remitted to the Revenue Commissioners or the Collector-General, as the case may be, and

(d) any amount paid on account of any such tax, duty, levy or charge or paid in respect of any such tax, duty, levy or charge;

'*taxable period*' has the same meaning as in section 2 of the Value-Added Tax Consolidation Act 2010.

(2) Subject to *subsections (3)* and *(4)*, where a repayment of any tax cannot be made to a person by virtue of the operation of—

(a) *section 865*,

(b) *section 105B* of the Finance Act 2001,

(c) section 99 of the Value-Added Tax Consolidation Act 2010,

(d) *section 159A* of the Stamp Duties Consolidation Act 1999,

(e) *section 57* of the Capital Acquisitions Tax Consolidation Act 2003, or

(f) any other provision of any of the Acts,

then, notwithstanding any other enactment or rule of law, that repayment shall not be set against any other amount of tax due and payable by, or from, that person.

(3) Where a repayment of tax cannot be made to a person in respect of a relevant period, it may be set against the amount of tax to which *paragraph (a)* of *subsection (4)* applies which is due and payable by the person in the circumstances set out in *paragraph (b)* of that subsection.

(4) (a) The amount of tax to which this paragraph applies is the amount, or so much of the amount, of tax that is due and payable by the person in respect of the relevant period as does not exceed the amount of the repayment that cannot be made to the person in respect of that relevant period.

(b) The circumstances set out in this paragraph are where tax is due and payable in respect of the relevant period by virtue of an assessment that is made or amended, or any other action that is taken for the recovery of tax, at a time that is 4 years or more after the end of the relevant period.

(5) No tax shall be set against any other amount of tax except as is provided for by the Acts.][4]

Amendments

[1] Substituted by F(LPT)A 12 s158 & sched(4)(a).

[2] Substituted by F(LPT)A 12 s158 & sched(4)(b).

[3] Substituted by F(LPT)A 12 s158 & sched(4)(c).

[4] Inserted by FA12 s128(1)(d). Shall apply as respects any tax (within the meaning of section 865B (inserted by subsection (1)(d))) paid or remitted to the Revenue Commissioners or the Collector-General, as the case may be, whether before, on or after 31 March 2012.

Revenue Briefings

eBrief

eBrief No. 25/2012 – Repayments, Time Limits and Offsets of Tax

866 Rules as to delivery of statements

[ITA67 s533; FA69 s65(1) and Sch5 PtI]

Any person who, on that person's own behalf or on behalf of another person or body of persons, delivers a statement of the amount of the profits [on which any income tax, Corporation tax or capital gains tax is chargeable][1] shall observe the rules and directions contained in *Schedule 28* in so far as those rules and directions are respectively applicable.

Amendments

[1] Substituted by FA12 sched5(2)(j).

Cross References

From Section 866

Schedule 28 Statements, Lists and Declarations

To Section 866

Schedule 28 Statements, Lists and Declarations

867 Amendment of statutory forms

[ITA67 s189]

It shall be lawful for the Revenue Commissioners from time to time to make such amendments of the forms of declarations, lists and statements contained in *Schedules 27* and *28* as appear to them to be necessary to give effect to [the Tax Acts and the Capital Gains Tax Acts][1].

Amendments

[1] Substituted by FA12 sched5(2)(k).

Cross References

From Section 867

Schedule 27 Forms of Declarations to be Made by Certain Persons
Schedule 28 Statements, Lists and Declarations

To Section 867

Schedule 27 Forms of Declarations to be Made by Certain Persons
Schedule 28 Statements, Lists and Declarations

868 Execution of warrants

[ITA67 s536; F(MP)A68 s3(4) and Sch PtIII, s3(5) and Sch PtIV; CTA76 s147(1) and (2)]

(1) Warrants issued under the authority of [the Tax Acts and the Capital Gains Tax Acts][1] shall be executed by the respective persons to whom they are directed.

(2) Members of the Garda Síochána shall aid in the execution of [the Tax Acts and the Capital Gains Tax Acts][2].

Amendments

1, 2 Substituted by FA12 sched5(2)(l).

869 Delivery, service and evidence of notices and forms

[ITA67 s542(2) and (4) to (7); F(MP)A68 s3(2) and Sch PtI; CGTA75 s51(1) and Sch4 par2; FA75 s25; CTA76 s147(1) and (2)]

(1) (a) In this subsection, except where in *paragraph (d)* the context otherwise requires, "*company*" means any body corporate.

(b) Any notice, form or other document which under the Tax Acts or the Capital Gains Tax Acts is to be given, served, sent or delivered to or on a person by the Revenue Commissioners or by an inspector or other officer of the Revenue Commissioners may be either delivered to the person or left—

(i) in a case where the person is a company, at the company's registered office or place of business, or

(ii) in any other case, at the person's usual or last known place of abode or place of business or, if the person is an individual, at his or her place of employment.

(c) Any notice, form or other document referred to in *paragraph (b)* may be served by post addressed—

(i) in a case where the person is a company, to the company at either of the places specified in *paragraph (b)(i)*, or

(ii) in any other case, to the person at any of the places specified in *paragraph (b)(ii)*.

(d) Without prejudice to *paragraphs (b)* and *(c)*, section 379 of the Companies Act, 1963, shall apply in relation to the service on a company of any notice, form or other document referred to in this subsection as it applies in relation to the service of documents under that section on a company within the meaning of that Act.

(2) Any notice which under the Tax Acts or the Capital Gains Tax Acts is authorised or required to be given by the Revenue Commissioners may be signed and given by any officer of the Revenue Commissioners authorised by them for the purpose of giving notices of the class to which the notice belongs and, where so signed and given, shall be as valid and effectual as if signed under the hands of the Revenue Commissioners and given by them.

[(3) Prima facie evidence of any notice given or served under the Tax Acts or the Capital Gains Tax Acts by the Revenue Commissioners or an inspector or other officer of the Revenue Commissioners may be given in any proceedings by the production of a document purporting—

(a) to be a copy of the notice, or

(b) if the details specified in the notice are contained in an electronic, photographic or other record maintained by the Revenue Commissioners, to reproduce those details in so far as they relate to the said notice,

and it shall not be necessary to prove the official positions or position of the persons or person by whom the notice purports to be given or served or, where it is signed, the signatures or signature or that the persons or person signing and giving or serving it were or was authorised to do so.][1]

(4) Notices to be given or delivered to, or served on, the Appeal Commissioners shall be valid and effectual if given or delivered to or served on their Clerk.

(5) This section shall apply notwithstanding any other provision of the Tax Acts or the Capital Gains Tax Acts.

Amendments

1 Substituted by FA99 s22.

Case Law

Effective service did not include service to the last known place of business Ex parte the debtor v IRC 1992 STC 751

Cross References

To Section 869

Section 811 Transactions to avoid liability to tax.

870 Effect of want of form, error, etc. on assessments, charges, warrants and other proceedings

[ITA67 s537; F(MP)A68 s3(2) and Sch PtI; CGTA75 s51(1) and Sch4 par2; CTA76 s147(1) and (2)]

(1) An assessment, charge, warrant or other proceeding which purports to be made in accordance with the Income Tax Acts, the Corporation Tax Acts or the Capital Gains Tax Acts shall not be quashed, or deemed to be void or voidable, for want of form, or be affected by reason of a mistake, defect, or omission therein, if the same is in substance and effect in conformity with or according to the intent and meaning of those Acts, and if the person or property charged or intended to be charged or affected thereby is designated therein according to common intent and understanding.

(2) For the purposes of the Tax Acts and the Capital Gains Tax Acts but subject to *subsection (3)*, an assessment or a charge made on an assessment shall not be impeached or affected—

(a) by reason of a mistake in the assessment or the charge made on the assessment as to—

(i) the name or surname of a person liable,

(ii) the description of any profits or property, or

(iii) the amount of the tax charged;

(b) by reason of any variance between the notice and the certificate of charge or assessment.

(3) In cases of charge, the notice of charge shall be duly served on the person intended to be charged, and the notice and certificate shall respectively contain, in substance and effect, the particulars on which the charge is made, and every such charge shall be heard and determined on its merits by the Appeal Commissioners.

Case Law

The taxpayer argued the assessments were invalid due to the erroneous description of his trade as a furniture manufacturer. They were held to be valid. M. Deighan v E. Hearne 1986 III ITR 533

871 Power to combine certain returns and assessments

[CGTA75 s51(1) and Sch4 par16]

Any return, assessment or other document relating to chargeable gains or capital gains tax may be combined with one relating to income or [income tax, or, as the case may be, with one relating to profits or corporation tax][1].

Amendments

[1] Substituted by FA12 sched5(2)(m).

872 Use of information relating to other taxes and duties

[FA28 s34(2); FA96 s130]

(1) Any information acquired, whether before or after the passing of this Act, in connection with any tax or duty under the care and management of the Revenue Commissioners may be used by them for any purpose connected with any other tax or duty under their care and management.

(2) The Revenue Commissioners or any of their officers may, for any purpose in connection with the assessment and collection of income tax, corporation tax or capital gains tax, make use of or produce in evidence any returns, correspondence, schedules, accounts, statements or other documents or information to which the Revenue Commissioners or any of their officers have or has had or may have lawful access for the purposes of the Acts relating to any tax, duty, levy or charge under the care and management of the Revenue Commissioners.

Cross References

To Section 872

Section 244A Application of section 244 (relief for interest paid on certain home loans) of Principal Act.
Section 472C Relief for trade union subscriptions.
Section 894A Returns by third parties in relation to personal reliefs.
Section 1104 Short title and construction.

873 Proof that person is a Commissioner or officer

[ITA67 s541; CTA76 s147(1) and (2)]

In any proceedings under or arising out of the Tax Acts before any court or person empowered to take evidence, prima facie proof of the fact that any person was a Commissioner or officer may be given by proving that, at the time when any matter in controversy in any such proceedings arose, that person was reputed to be or had acted as a Commissioner or officer.

874 Limitation of penalties on officers employed in execution of Tax Acts and Capital Gains Tax Acts

[ITA67 s519; CTA76 s147(1) and (2); CGTA75 s51(1) and Sch4 par3(2)]

(1) A Commissioner, sheriff, county registrar, clerk, inspector, [...][1] or Collector-General who acts, or is employed, in the execution of the Tax Acts or the Capital Gains Tax Acts shall not be liable to any penalty in respect of such execution other than as provided by those Acts.

(2) Where any civil or criminal proceeding against any officer or person employed in relation to any duty of income tax, corporation tax or capital gains tax on account of the seizure or detention of any goods is brought to trial, and a verdict or judgment is given against the defendant, then, if the court or judge certifies that there was probable cause for the seizure, the plaintiff shall not be entitled to any damages besides the goods seized, or the value of those goods, or to any costs, and the defendant shall not be liable to any punishment.

Amendments

[1] Deleted by FA12 sched5(2)(n).

874A Prescribing of forms etc.

[(1) In this section—

'the Acts' means—

(a) the Tax Acts,

(b) the Capital Gains Tax Acts,

(c) *Part 18C*,

(d) *Part 18D*,

(e) the Capital Acquisitions Tax Consolidation Act 2003, and the enactments amending or extending that Act,

[(f) the Stamp Duties Consolidation Act 1999, and the enactments amending or extending that Act,

(g) Chapter IV of Part II of the Finance Act 1992, and

(h) the *Finance (Local Property Tax) Act 2012*,][1]

and any instruments made under any of those Acts or Parts;

'form or other document' includes a form or other document for use, or capable of use, in a machine readable form.

(2) Where a provision of the Acts requires that a form or other document used for any purpose of the Acts is to be prescribed, authorised or approved by the Revenue Commissioners, other than in respect of any form which is required by the Acts to be prescribed by order or regulations made by the Revenue Commissioners, such form or other document may be prescribed, authorised or approved by—

(a) a Revenue Commissioner, or

(b) an officer of the Revenue Commissioners not below the grade or rank of Assistant Secretary authorised by them in writing for that purpose.

(3) Nothing in this section shall be read as restricting section 12 of the Interpretation Act 2005.][2]

Amendments

[1] Substituted by F(LPT)A 12 s158 & sched(5).

[2] Inserted by FA12 sched5(2)(o).

875 Exemption of appraisements and valuations from stamp duty [Deleted]

Deleted by FA99 s197 and Sched6 but continues to apply: (a) to instruments executed before the date of the passing of FA99 (25 March 1999), (b) to acts or omissions which occurred before the date of the passing of FA99 (25 March 1999), (c) to appeals against a decision of the Revenue Commissioners as to the value of any property for the purpose of an assessment being an assessment made before the date of the passing of FA99 (25 March 1999), and (d) in so far as they relate to section 18 of the Finance Act, 1943 , and section 969 of the Taxes Consolidation Act, 1997 , to persons committed to prison before the date of the passing of FA99 (25 March 1999), to such extent as if FA99 had not been enacted.

Cross References

To Section 875

Section 1104 Short title and construction.

PART 38

Returns of Income and Gains, Other Obligations and Returns, and Revenue Powers

CHAPTER 1

Income Tax: Returns of Income

876 Notice of liability to income tax

[F(MP)A68 s5(1)]

Every person who is chargeable to income tax for any year of assessment and who in relation to that year has not been given a notice under *section 877* or *879* and has not made a return of such person's total income shall, not later than one year after the end of the year of assessment, give notice to the inspector of taxes that such person is so chargeable.

Revenue Precedents

A non-resident individual who exercised employment in the State but did not have an Irish source of income was held to be liable to make a return of income. IT971502

Cross References

From Section 876

Section 877 Returns by persons chargeable.
Section 879 Returns of income.

To Section 876

Section 267T Reporting.
Section 864A Electronic claims.
Section 913 Application of income tax provisions relating to returns, etc.
Section 959 Miscellaneous (Part 41).
Section 1061 Recovery of penalties.
Section 1068 Failure to act within required time.
Schedule 29 Provisions Referred to in Sections 1052, 1053 and 1054

877 Returns by persons chargeable

[ITA67 s169; F(MP)A68 s6(2) and (3); FA69 s65(1) and Sch5 PtI; CTA76 s140(1) and Sch2 PtI par4; FA76 s11(5)]

(1) Every person chargeable under the Income Tax Acts, when required to do so by a notice given to such person by an inspector, shall, within the time limited by such notice, prepare and deliver to the inspector a statement in writing as required by the Income Tax Acts, signed by such person, containing the amount of the profits or gains arising to such person, from each and every source chargeable according to the respective schedules, estimated for the period specified in the notice and according to the Income Tax Acts.

[...][1]

(3) There shall be added to the statement referred to in *subsection (1)* a declaration that the amounts contained in that statement are estimated in respect of all the sources of income mentioned in the Income Tax Acts, describing those sources, after deducting only such sums as are allowed.

(4) Every such statement shall be made exclusive of any interest of money or other annual payment arising out of the property of any other person charged in respect of that interest of money or other annual payment.

(5) (a) Every person to whom a notice has been given by an inspector requiring such person to deliver a statement of any profits, gains or income in respect of which such person is chargeable under Schedule D or E shall deliver a statement in the form required by the notice, whether or not such person is so chargeable.

(b) The penalty imposed on any person proceeded against for not complying with this subsection who proves that such person was not chargeable to income tax shall not exceed [€5][2] for any one offence.

Amendments

[1] Deleted by FA00 sched2.
[2] Substituted by FA01 sched5.

Statements of Practice

Finance Act 1992 and Directors – SP IT/01/93
Preparation of Accounts for Revenue Purposes – SP IT/02/92

Cross References

To Section 877

Section 876 Notice of liability to income tax.
Section 878 Persons acting for incapacitated persons and non-residents.
Section 881 Returns by married persons.
Section 950 Interpretation (Part 41).
Section 951 Obligation to make a return.
Section 1052 Penalties for failure to make certain returns, etc.
Section 1054 Penalties in the case of a secretary of a body of persons.
Section 1084 Surcharge for late returns.
Schedule 29 Provisions Referred to in Sections 1052, 1053 and 1054

878 Persons acting for incapacitated persons and non-residents

[ITA67 s170; F(MP)A68 s6(4)]

(1) Every person (in this subsection referred to as "the first-mentioned person") acting in any character on behalf of any incapacitated person or person not resident in the State who, by reason of such incapacity or non-residence in the State, may not be personally charged under the Income Tax Acts shall, whenever required to do so by a notice given to the first-mentioned person by an inspector, within the time permitted by such notice and in any district in which the first-mentioned person may be chargeable on the first-mentioned person's own account, deliver a statement described in *section 877* of the profits or gains in respect of which income tax is to be charged on the first-mentioned person on account of that other person, together with the prescribed declaration.

(2) Where 2 or more such persons are liable to be charged for the same person—

(a) one statement only shall be required to be delivered which may be made by them jointly or by any one or more of them, and

(b) notice in writing may be given by any such persons to the inspector for each district in which they are called on for a statement stating in which district or districts they are respectively chargeable on their own account, and in which of those districts they desire to be charged on behalf of the person for whom they act, and they shall, if any one such person is liable to be charged on such person's own account in that district, be charged in that district accordingly by one assessment.

Cross References

From Section 878

Section 877 Returns by persons chargeable.

To Section 878

Section 913 Application of income tax provisions relating to returns, etc.
Schedule 29 Provisions Referred to in Sections 1052, 1053 and 1054

879 Returns of income

[ITA67 s172(1), (2), (4) and (6); FA74 s86 and Sch2 PtI; FA90 s23(2)]

(1) In this section, "*prescribed*" means prescribed by the Revenue Commissioners and, in prescribing forms for the purposes of this section, the Revenue Commissioners shall have regard to the desirability of securing in so far as may be possible that no individual shall be required to make more than one return annually of the sources of the individual's income and the amounts derived from those sources.

(2) Every individual, when required to do so by a notice given to him or her in relation to any year of assessment by an inspector, shall within the time limited by the notice prepare and deliver to the inspector a return in the prescribed form of—

(a) all the sources of his or her income for the year of assessment in relation to which the notice is given;

(b) the amount of income from each source for the year of assessment computed in accordance with *subsection (3)*;

(c) [such information, accounts, statements, and][1] further particulars for the purposes of income tax for the year of assessment as may be required by the notice or indicated by the prescribed form.

[(3) The amount of income from any source to be included in a return under this section shall be computed in accordance with the Income Tax Acts; but where under *Chapter 3* of *Part 4* the profits or gains (or, as respects the year of assessment 2001, 74 per cent of the profits or gains) of a particular 12 month period are to be taken to be the profits or gains of a year of assessment, the computation shall be made by reference to that period.][2]

(4) Where a person delivers to any inspector a return in a prescribed form, the person shall be deemed to have been required by a notice under this section to prepare and deliver that return.

Amendments

[1] Substituted by FA13 s95(a).

[2] Substituted by FA01 sched2(47).

Case Law

In Horner v Madden 1995 STC 802, the taxpayer submitted a formula from which his tax liability might be computed. It was held that the requirement to deliver a return was not satisfied.

Cross References

From Section 879

Section 52 Persons chargeable.
Section 65 Cases I and II: basis of assessment.

To Section 879

Section 531 Payments to subcontractors in certain industries.
Section 848E Payment of tax credit.
Section 876 Notice of liability to income tax.
Section 913 Application of income tax provisions relating to returns, etc.
Section 951 Obligation to make a return.
Section 1052 Penalties for failure to make certain returns, etc.
Schedule 29 Provisions Referred to in Sections 1052, 1053 and 1054

880 Partnership returns

[ITA67 s69(3) and s70(1) to (3A) and (5); FA74 s86 and Sch2 PtI; FA79 s30; FA90 s23(1)]

(1) In this section—

"*precedent partner*" has the same meaning as in *Part 43*;

"*prescribed*" means prescribed by the Revenue Commissioners.

(2) The precedent partner of any partnership, when required to do so by a notice given to that partner in relation to any year of assessment by an inspector, shall within the time limited by the notice prepare and deliver to the inspector a return in the prescribed form of—

(a) all the sources of income of the partnership for the year of assessment in relation to which the notice is given;

(b) the amount of income from each source for the year of assessment computed in accordance with *subsection (3)*;

(c) [such information, accounts, statements, and][1] further particulars for the purposes of income tax for the year of assessment as may be required by the notice or indicated by the prescribed form.

(3) The amount of income from any source to be included in a return under this section shall be computed in accordance with the Income Tax Acts; but where, in the case of a trade or profession, an account has been made up to a date within the year of assessment or more accounts than one have been made up to dates within that year, the computation shall be made by reference to the period, or to all the periods where there is more than one period, for which accounts have been so made up.

[(3A) For the purposes of *subsection (3)*, an account made up for a period of one year to a date falling in the period from 1 January 2002 to 5 April 2002 shall, in addition to being an account made up to a date in the year of assessment 2002, be deemed to be an account made up to a date within the year of assessment 2001.][2]

(4) Where a person delivers to any inspector a return in a prescribed form, the person shall be deemed to have been required by a notice under this section to prepare and deliver that return.

(5) The precedent partner of any partnership, when required to do so by a notice given to that partner by an inspector, shall within the time limited by such notice prepare and deliver to the inspector a statement in writing signed by that partner stating the amount of the profits or gains arising to the partnership from each and every source chargeable according to the respective schedules, estimated for the period specified in the notice and according to the Income Tax Acts.

(6) There shall be added to the statement referred to in *subsection (5)* a declaration that the amounts contained in that statement are estimated in respect of all the sources of income mentioned in the Income Tax Acts, describing those sources, after deducting only such sums as are allowed.

Amendments

[1] Substituted by FA13 s95(b).

[2] Inserted by FA01 sched2(48).

Cross References

From Section 880

Section 1007 Interpretation (Part 43).

To Section 880

Section 531 Payments to subcontractors in certain industries.
Section 913 Application of income tax provisions relating to returns, etc.
Section 951 Obligation to make a return.
Section 1010 Capital allowances and balancing charges in partnership cases.
Section 1052 Penalties for failure to make certain returns, etc.
Schedule 29 Provisions Referred to in Sections 1052, 1053 and 1054

881 Returns by married persons

[ITA67 s195B(3) and (6); FA76 s11(1) to (3); FA80 s19 and Sch1 PtIII par6; FA93 s10(1)]

(1) Where an individual is required by a notice given under *section 877* to deliver a statement in writing of the total income in respect of which the individual is chargeable to income tax and that income is or includes income of his or her [spouse or civil partner][1], the individual may, within 21 days from the date of the receipt of the notice, notify the inspector by whom the notice was given that the income in respect of which the individual is chargeable to income tax is or includes income of his or her [spouse or civil partner][2].

(2) Where an inspector receives a notification under *subsection (1)* or is of the opinion that the [spouse or civil partner][3] of the individual concerned is in receipt of income, the inspector may by notice given to the individual's [spouse or civil partner][4] require him or her to prepare and deliver to the inspector, within the time limited by the notice and in the form required by the notice, a statement in writing signed by him or her, setting out the amount of income arising to him or her from each and every source chargeable according to the respective schedules, estimated for the period specified in the notice and according to the Income Tax Acts, whether or not the individual's [spouse or civil partner][5] or the individual concerned is the person chargeable to income tax in respect of that income.

(3) The delivery of a statement under *subsection (2)* shall not affect [*Chapter 1* of *Part 44* or *Chapter 1* of *Part 44A*, as the case may be.][6]

Amendments

[1, 2, 3, 4, 5] Substituted by F(No.3)A11 sched1(236). Shall have effect from 27 July 2011.

[6] Substituted by F(No.3)A11 sched1(237). Shall have effect from 27 July 2011.

Cross References

From Section 881

Section 877 Returns by persons chargeable.
Section 1015 Interpretation (Chapter 1).

To Section 881

Section 950 Interpretation (Part 41).

Section 1084 Surcharge for late returns.

Schedule 29 Provisions Referred to in Sections 1052, 1053 and 1054

CHAPTER 2

Corporation Tax: Returns of Profits

882 Particulars to be supplied by new companies

[(1) (a) In this section—

"*secretary*" includes persons mentioned in *section 1044(2)* and, in the case of a company not resident in the State, the agent, manager, factor or other representative of the company;

"*settlor*" and "*settlement*" have the same meanings as in *section 10*;

"*tax*", in relation to a territory other than the State, means any tax imposed in that territory which corresponds to income tax or corporation tax;

"*ultimate beneficial owners*", in relation to a company, means—

(i) the individual or individuals who have control of the company, or

(ii) where a person, whether alone or together with other persons, who controls the company controls it in the capacity as the trustee of a settlement, any person who in relation to the settlement—

(I) is a settlor, or

(II) is, or can under any scheme or arrangement reasonably expect to become, a beneficiary under the settlement, or

(III) where such settlor or beneficiary, as the case may be, is a company, the ultimate beneficial owners of that company.

(b) For the purposes of this section, control shall be construed in accordance with *section 432*.

(2) Every company which is incorporated in the State or which commences to carry on a trade, profession or business in the State shall, in every case within 30 days of—

(a) the date on which it commences to carry on a trade, profession or business, wherever carried on,

(b) the date at which there is a material change in information previously delivered by the company under this section, and

(c) the giving of a notice to the company by an inspector requiring a statement under this section,

deliver to the Revenue Commissioners a statement in writing containing particulars of—

(i) in the case of every company—

(I) the name of the company,

(II) the address of the company's registered office,

(III) the address of its principal place of business,

(IV) the name and address of the secretary of the company,

(V) the date of commencement of the trade, profession or business,

(VI) the nature of the trade, profession or business,

(VII) the date up to which accounts relating to such trade, profession or business will be made up, and

(VIII) such other information as the Revenue Commissioners consider necessary for the purposes of the Tax Acts;

(ii) in the case of a company which is incorporated, but not resident, in the State—

(I) the name of the territory in which the company is, by virtue of the law of that territory, resident for tax purposes,

[…][1]

and

(iii) in the case of a company which is neither incorporated in the State nor resident in the State but which carries on a trade, profession or business in the State—

(I) the address of the company's principal place of business in the State,

(II) the name and address of the agent, manager, factor or other representative of the company, and

(III) the date of commencement of the company's trade, profession or business in the State.

[(3) Where a company fails to deliver a statement which it is required to deliver under this section, then, notwithstanding any obligations as to secrecy or other restriction upon disclosure of information imposed by or under any statute or otherwise—

(a) the Revenue Commissioners, or

(b) such officer of the Revenue Commissioners as is nominated by the Commissioners for the purposes of this section,

may give a notice in writing, or in such other form as the Revenue Commissioners may decide, to the registrar of companies (within the meaning of the Companies Act, 1963) stating that the company has so failed to deliver a statement under this section.][2]][3]

Amendments

[1] Deleted by FA14 s43(1)(b).

[2] Substituted by FA00 s78.

[3] Substituted by FA99 s83(1). This section shall apply— (a) in the case of companies which are incorporated on or after the 11th day of February, 1999, as on and from that day, and (b) in the case of companies which were incorporated before the 11th day of February, 1999, as on and from the 1st day of October, 1999.

Note:

Per FA14 s43(2) certain important conditions apply with reference to the company's ownership and date of incorporation. FA14 s43(2) cannot be consolidated but is reproduced here in full. References to the "Principal Act" are to TCA 97.

(a) Subject to paragraph (b), this section shall have effect from 1 January 2015. (b) As respects a company incorporated before 1 January 2015, this section shall have effect— (i) after 31 December 2020, or (ii) from the date, after 31 December 2014, of a change in ownership of the company where there is a major change in the nature or conduct of the business of the company within the relevant period, whichever is the earlier. (c) In paragraph (b) "relevant period" means a period— (i) beginning on the later of— (I) 1 January 2015, or (II) the date which occurs one year before the date of the change in ownership of the company referred to in that paragraph, and (ii) ending 5 years after the date of that change of ownership. (d) For the purposes of the references in paragraphs (b) and (c) to a change in ownership of a company, Schedule 9 (other than paragraph 4 of that Schedule) to the Principal Act shall apply as if references in that Schedule to section 401 or 679(4) of the Principal Act were references to the said paragraphs (b) and (c). (e) For the purposes of paragraph (b), "a major change in the nature or conduct of the business of the company" means— (i) a major change in the nature or conduct of a trade (within the meaning of section 401(1)(a) or (b) of the Principal Act) carried on by the company, (ii) the commencement by the company of a new trade, or (iii) a major change arising from the acquisition by the company of property or of an interest in, or right over, property.

Revenue Briefings

Tax Briefing

Tax Briefing October 1999 – Issue 37 pg 5 – Irish Registered Non-resident Companies – Update

Revenue Information Notes

IT48 – Starting in Business – A Revenue Guide

Cross References

From Section 882

Section 10 Connected persons.
Section 23A Company residence.
Section 432 Meaning of "associated company" and "control".
Section 1044 Bodies of persons.

To Section 882

Section 1073 Penalties for failure to furnish particulars required to be supplied by new companies.

883 Notice of liability to corporation tax

[CTA76 s142(1)]

Every company which is chargeable to corporation tax for any accounting period and which has not made a return of its profits for that accounting period shall, not later than one year after the end of that accounting period, give notice to the inspector that it is so chargeable.

Cross References

To Section 883

Section 1074 Penalties for failure to give notice of liability to corporation tax.

884 Returns of profits

[CTA76 s143(1) to (6), (7)(a), (b) and (d) and (12)(c); FA81 s16; FA83 s36; FA90 s54; FA92 s247]

(1) In this section, "*return*" includes any statement, declaration or list.

(2) A company may be required by a notice served on it by an inspector or other officer of the Revenue Commissioners to deliver to the officer within the time limited by the notice a return of—

(a) the profits of the company computed in accordance with the Corporation Tax Acts—

(i) specifying the income taken into account in computing those profits, with the amount from each source,

(ii) giving particulars of all disposals giving rise to chargeable gains or allowable losses under the Capital Gains Tax Acts and the Corporation Tax Acts and particulars of those chargeable gains or allowable losses, and

(iii) giving particulars of all charges on income to be deducted against those profits for the purpose of the assessment to corporation tax, other than those included in *paragraph (d)*,

[(aa) such information, accounts, statements, reports and further particulars—

(i) relevant to the tax liability of the company, or

(ii) otherwise relevant to the application of the Corporation Tax Acts to the company, as may be required by the notice or specified in the prescribed form in respect of the return,][1]

(b) the distributions received by the company from companies resident in the State […][2],

[…][3]

(d) payments made from which income tax is deductible and to which *subsections (3)* to *(5)* of *section 238* apply, and

(e) all amounts which under *section 438* are deemed to be annual payments.

[(2A) The authority under *subsection (2)* to require the delivery of accounts as part of a return is limited to such accounts, as, together with such documents as may be annexed thereto and such further information, statements, reports or further particulars as may be required by the notice referred to in *subsection (2)* or specified in the prescribed form in respect of the return, contain sufficient information to enable the chargeable profits of the company to be determined.][4]

[…][5]

(3) An event which, apart from *section 584(3)* as applied by *section 586* or *587*, would constitute the disposal of an asset giving rise to a chargeable gain or an allowable loss under the Capital Gains Tax Acts and the Corporation Tax Acts shall for the purposes of this section constitute such a disposal.

(4) A notice under this section may require a return of profits arising in any period during which the company was within the charge to corporation tax, together with particulars of distributions received in that period from companies resident in the State […][6].

(5) Every return under this section shall include a declaration to the effect that the return is correct and complete.

(6) A return under this section which includes profits which are payments on which the company has borne income tax by deduction shall specify the amount of income tax so borne.

(7) A notice under this section may require the inclusion in the return of particulars of management expenses, capital allowances and balancing charges which have been taken into account in determining the profits included in the return.

(8) *Subsections (3)*, *(4)* and *(5)(b)* of *section 913* shall apply in relation to a notice under this section as they apply in relation to a notice under any provision of the Income Tax Acts applied in relation to capital gains tax by *section 913*.

(9) (a) In this subsection, "*authorised officer*" means an inspector or other officer of the Revenue Commissioners authorised by them in writing to exercise the powers conferred by this subsection.

(b) Where a company which has been duly required to deliver a return under this section fails to deliver the return, or where the inspector is not satisfied with the return delivered by any such company, an authorised officer may serve on that company a notice or notices in writing requiring the company to do any of the following—

(i) to deliver to the inspector or to the authorised officer copies of such accounts (including balance sheets) of the company as may be specified or described in the notice, within such period as may be specified in the notice, including, where the accounts have been audited, a copy of the auditor's certificate;

(ii) to make available for inspection by an inspector or by an authorised officer within such time as may be specified in the notice all such books, accounts and documents in the possession or power of the company as may be specified or described in the notice, being books, accounts and documents which contain information as to profits, assets or liabilities of the company.

(c) The inspector or authorised officer may take copies of or extracts from any books, accounts or documents made available for his or her inspection under this subsection.

Amendments

[1] Substituted by FA12 s133(a).

[2, 6] Deleted by FA00 sched2.

[3] Deleted by FA03 s41(1)(o). This section applies as respects accounting periods ending on or after 6 February 2003.

[4] Substituted by FA14 s89(a)(i).

[5] Deleted by FA14 s89(a)(ii).

Revenue Briefings

Tax Briefing

Tax Briefing July 2012 – Issue 04 – Submission of Financial Statements in iXBRL

eBrief

eBrief No. 57/2012 – Update regarding the Submission of Financial Statements in iXBRL

eBrief No. 85/2014 – Important information regarding mandatory iXBRL filing for Corporation Tax payers

eBrief No. 90/2014 – Mandatory Filing of iXBRL Financial Statements

Statements of Practice

Company's Self Assessment, Return of Director's Details – SP CT/02/90
Preparation of Accounts for Revenue Purposes – SP IT/02/92

Cross References

From Section 884

Section 238 Annual payments not payable out of taxed income.
Section 438 Loans to participators, etc.
Section 584 Reorganisation or reduction of share capital.
Section 586 Company amalgamations by exchange of shares.
Section 587 Company reconstructions and amalgamations.
Section 913 Application of income tax provisions relating to returns, etc.

To Section 884

Section 182 Returns.
Section 234 Certain income derived from patent royalties.
Section 701 Transfer of shares held by certain societies to members of society.
Section 845B Set-off of surplus advance corporation tax.
Section 933 Appeals against assessment.
Section 950 Interpretation (Part 41).
Section 951 Obligation to make a return.
Section 1071 Penalties for failure to make certain returns.
Section 1072 Penalties for fraudulently or negligently making incorrect returns, etc.
Section 1084 Surcharge for late returns.

CHAPTER 3

Other Obligations and Returns

885 Obligation to show tax reference number on receipts

[FA83 s22(1) and (2)]

(1) In this section—

"*business*" means—

(a) a profession, or

(b) a trade consisting solely of the supply (within the meaning of the Value-Added Tax Consolidation Act 2010) of a service and includes, in the case of a trade part of which consists of the supply of a service, that part, and also includes, in the case of a trade the whole or part of which consists of the supply of a service which incorporates the supply of goods in the course of the supply of that service, that trade or that part, as the case may be;

"*specified person*", in relation to a business, means—

(a) where the business is carried on by an individual, that individual, and

(b) where the business is carried on by a partnership, the precedent partner;

"*tax reference number*", in relation to a specified person, means each of the following—

[(a) the Personal Public Service Number (PPSN) stated on any certificate of tax credits and standard rate cut-off point issued to that person by an inspector, not being a certificate issued to an employer in respect of an employee,][1]

(b) the reference number stated on any return of income form or notice of assessment issued to that person by an inspector, and

(c) the registration number of that person for the purposes of value-added tax.

(2) For the purposes of the Tax Acts and the Capital Gains Tax Acts, the specified person in relation to a business shall ensure that the specified person's tax reference number or, if the specified person has more than one tax reference number, one of those tax reference numbers or, if the specified person has no tax reference number, the specified person's full names and address is or are stated on any document (being an invoice, credit note, debit note, receipt, account, statement of account, voucher or estimate relating to an amount of [€7][2] or more) issued in the course of that business.

Amendments

[1] Substituted by FA01 sched1(1)(q). Applies as respects the year of assessment 2001 and subsequent years of assessment.

[2] Substituted by FA01 sched5.

Cross References

To Section 885

Section 172A Interpretation.
Section 246 Interest payments by companies and to non-residents.
Section 246A Interest in respect of wholesale debt instruments.

Section 256 Interpretation (Chapter 4).
Section 263B Declarations to the Revenue Commissioners relating to deposits of certain persons.
Section 263C Notifications by the Revenue Commissioners relating to deposits of certain persons.
Section 265 Deposits of companies and pensions schemes.
Section 265A Deposits of certain persons.
Section 477A Relief for energy efficient works.
Section 739D Gain arising on a chargeable event.
Section 784A Approved retirement fund.
Section 889 Returns of fees, commissions, etc. paid by certain persons.
Section 895 Returns in relation to foreign accounts.
Section 896 Returns in relation to certain offshore products.
Section 898H Returns of interest payments made to or secured for beneficial owners.
Section 980 Deduction from consideration on disposal of certain assets.
Schedule 2B Investment Undertakings: Declarations
Schedule 29 Provisions Referred to in Sections 1052, 1053 and 1054

886 Obligation to keep certain records

[FA68 s6(1) to (5); CTA76 s147(1) and (2); FA92 s231]

(1) In this section—

"*linking documents*" means documents drawn up in the making up of accounts and showing details of the calculations linking the records to the accounts;

"*records*" includes accounts, books of account, documents and any other data maintained manually or by any electronic, photographic or other process, relating to—

(a) all sums of money received and expended in the course of the carrying on or exercising of a trade, profession or other activity and the matters in respect of which the receipt and expenditure take place,

(b) all sales and purchases of goods and services where the carrying on or exercising of a trade, profession or other activity involves the purchase or sale of goods or services,

(c) the assets and liabilities of the trade, profession or other activity referred to in *paragraph (a)* or *(b)*, and

(d) all transactions which constitute an acquisition or disposal of an asset for capital gains tax purposes.

(2) (a) Every person who—

(i) on that person's own behalf or on behalf of any other person, carries on or exercises any trade, profession or other activity the profits or gains of which are chargeable under Schedule D,

(ii) is chargeable to tax under Schedule D or F in respect of any other source of income, or

(iii) is chargeable to capital gains tax in respect of chargeable gains,

shall keep, or cause to be kept on that person's behalf, such records as will enable true returns to be made for the purposes of income tax, corporation tax and capital gains tax of such profits or gains or chargeable gains.

(b) The records shall be kept on a continuous and consistent basis, that is, the entries in the records shall be made in a timely manner and be consistent from one year to the next.

(c) Where accounts are made up to show the profits or gains from any such trade, profession or activity, or in relation to a source of income, of any person, that person shall retain, or cause to be retained on that person's behalf, linking documents.

(d) Where any such trade, profession or other activity is carried on in partnership, the precedent partner (within the meaning of *section 1007*) shall for the purposes of this section be deemed to be the person carrying on that trade, profession or other activity.

(3) Records required to be kept or retained by virtue of this section shall be kept—

(a) in written form in an official language of the State, or

(b) subject to *section 887(2)*, by means of any electronic, photographic or other process.

(4) (a) [Notwithstanding any other law][1], linking documents and records kept in accordance with *subsections (2)* and *(3)* shall be retained by the person required to keep the records—

(i) for a period of 6 years after the completion of the transactions, acts or operations to which they relate, or

(ii) in the case of a person who fails to comply with [*Chapter 3* of *Part 41A*][2] requiring the preparation and delivery of a return on or before the specified return date for a year of assessment or an accounting period, as the case may be, until the expiry of a period of 6 years from the end of the year of assessment or accounting period, as the case may be, in which a return has been delivered showing the profits or gains or chargeable gains derived from those [transactions, acts or operations, or][3]

[(iii) where the transaction, act or operation is the subject of—

(I) an inquiry or investigation started by the Revenue Commissioners or by a Revenue officer into any matters to which this Act relates,

(II) a claim under a provision of this Act,

(III) proceedings relating to any matter to which this Act relates,

linking documents and records shall be retained by the person required to keep the records for the 6 year period and until such time as—

(A) the enquiry or investigation has been completed or the claim has been determined, and

(B) any appeal to Appeal Commissioners in relation to that enquiry or the determination of that claim or to any other matter to which the Act relates, has become final and conclusive, and

(C) any proceedings in relation to the outcome of the inquiry or investigation or the determination of that claim or that appeal, or to any other matter to which the Act relates, has been finally determined, and

(D) the time limit for instituting any appeal or proceedings or any further appeal or proceedings has expired.][4]

[…][5]

[(4A) For the purposes of this section—

(a) where a company is wound up, the liquidator, and

(b) where a company is dissolved without the appointment of a liquidator, the last directors, including any person occupying the position of director by whatever name called, of the company,

shall keep or retain the linking documents and records of the company for the period specified in [*subparagraph (i),* (ii) or *(iii)*][6], as appropriate, of *subsection (4)(a)*.][7]

[(4B) For the purposes of this section, where a person dies the executor or administrator of that deceased person shall keep or retain the linking documents and records of that deceased person for the period specified in *subparagraph (i), (ii)* or *(iii)*, as appropriate, of *subsection (4)(a)*.][8]

(5) [Any person who fails to comply with *subsection (2), (3),* [*(4), (4A)* or *(4B)*][9]][10] in respect of any records or linking documents in relation to a return for any year of assessment or accounting period shall be liable to a penalty of [€3,000][11]; but a penalty shall not be imposed under this subsection if it is proved that no person is chargeable to tax in respect of the profits or gains for that year of assessment or accounting period, as the case may be.

Amendments

[1] Substituted by FA12 s118(a). Deemed to have come into force and takes effect on and from 1 January 2012.

[2] Substituted by FA12 sched4(part 2)(g).

[3] Substituted by FA14 s91(a).

[4] Inserted by FA14 s91(b).

[5] Deleted by FA13 s98.

[6] Substituted by FA14 s91(c).

[7] Inserted by FA12 s118(c). Deemed to have come into force and takes effect on and from 1 January 2012.

[8] Inserted by FA14 s91(d).

[9] Substituted by FA14 s91(e).

[10] Substituted by FA12 s118(d). Deemed to have come into force and takes effect on and from 1 January 2012.

[11] Substituted by F(No.2)A08 sched5(part2)(1)(i). The enactments specified in Schedule 5 are amended or repealed to the extent and manner specified in that Schedule and, unless the contrary is stated, shall come into effect after 24 December 2008.

Case Law

Accounts prepared by an accountant as part of his workings were 'within the possession or power' of the taxpayer. Quigley v Burke 1995 V ITR 265

Revenue Briefings

Tax Briefing

Tax Briefing May 2003 – Issue 52 pg 19 – Retention of Records

Revenue Precedents

Personal bank statements are not "records" within the meaning of section 886 if they relate solely to personal transactions and are not such as would be used so as to enable true returns to be made of the profits or gains or chargeable gains of the trade, profession or other activity carried on by the person. IT923062

Statements of Practice

Revenue Powers Exercised in Places other than a Revenue Office – SP GEN/1/94 (Revised 02/2006)

Cross References

From Section 886

Section 20 Schedule F.

Section 887 Use of electronic data processing.

Section 951 Obligation to make a return.
Section 1007 Interpretation (Part 43).

To Section 886

Section 231 Profits or gains from stallion fees.
Section 232 Profits from occupation of certain woodlands.
Section 233 Stud greyhound service fees.
Section 481 Relief for investment in films.
Section 530G Zero rate subcontractor.
Section 530H Standard rate subcontractor.
Section 530S Record keeping.
Section 531 Payments to subcontractors in certain industries.
Section 835F Documentation and enquiries.
Section 904 Power of inspection: tax deduction from payments to certain subcontractors.
Section 1061 Recovery of penalties.
Schedule 31 Consequential Amendments

886A Retention and inspection of records in relation to claims by individuals

[(1) An individual who, in relation to a year of assessment, may wish to make a claim for an allowance, deduction or relief in relation to income tax shall keep and preserve all such records as may be requisite for the purpose of enabling the individual to make a correct and complete claim.

(2) The records which an individual is required to keep and preserve in accordance with subsection (1) shall be retained by the individual for the longer of the following periods—

(a) where enquiries into the claim or any amendment of the claim are made by an officer of the Revenue Commissioners, the period ending on the day on which those enquiries are treated as completed by the officer, and

(b) a period of 6 years beginning at the end of the year of assessment to which the claim relates.

(3) Subject to subsection (4), an individual who fails to comply with subsection (1) in relation to any claim which is made for a year of assessment, shall be liable to a penalty of €1,520 [...][1].

(4) Subsection (3) shall not apply where an officer of the Revenue Commissioners is satisfied that any facts which the officer reasonably requires to be proved, and which would have been proved by the records, are proved by other documentary evidence furnished to the officer.

(5) Subject to the provisions of [*section 959Z*][2], an officer of the Revenue Commissioners may enquire into—

(a) a claim made by an individual, or

(b) any amendment made by an individual of a claim made by the individual,

if, within 4 years from the end of the year of assessment in which the claim, or (as the case may be) any amendment of the claim, is made, the officer gives notice of his or her intention to do so to that individual.

(6) Where an officer of the Revenue Commissioners gives notice under subsection (5) to any individual (in this subsection referred to as the "claimant") of his or her intention to enquire into—

(a) a claim made by the claimant, or

(b) any amendment made by the claimant of such a claim,

then the officer may at the same or any subsequent time by notice in writing require the claimant, within such time (which shall not be less than 30 days) as may be specified in the notice—

(i) to produce to the officer such documents as are in the claimant's possession or power and as the officer may reasonably require for the purpose of determining whether and, if so, the extent to which the claim or amendment is correct, and

(ii) to furnish the officer with such accounts or particulars as the officer may reasonably require for that purpose.

(7) In complying with a notice under subsection (6) an individual may furnish to the officer copies of documents instead of originals, but—

(a) the copies must be photographic or other facsimiles, and

(b) the officer may by notice require the original to be produced for inspection.

(8) The officer may take copies of, or make extracts from, any document produced to him or her under this section.][3]

Amendments

[1] Deleted by FA12 sched6(1)(l). Applies as respects penalties incurred on or after 24 December 2008.

[2] Substituted by FA12 sched4(part 2)(g).

[3] Inserted by FA05 s25. Applies with effect from 25 March 2005.

Cross References

From Section 886A

Section 956 Inspector's right to make enquiries and amend assessments.
Section 1061 Recovery of penalties.

To Section 886A

Section 864A Electronic claims.

887 Use of electronic data processing

[(1) In this section—

"*the Acts*" means—

(a) the Tax Acts,

(b) the Capital Gains Tax Acts,

(c) the Value-Added Tax Consolidation Act 2010, and the enactments amending or extending that Act,

(d) the Capital Acquisitions Tax Consolidation Act 2003, and the enactments amending or extending that Act, and

(e) Part VI of the Finance Act, 1983,

and any instrument made under any of these enactments;

"*record*" means any document which a person is obliged by the Acts to keep, to issue or to produce for inspection, and any other written or printed material.

(2) For the purposes of the Acts, but subject to Chapter 2 of Part 9 of the Value-Added Tax Consolidation Act 2010, a record may be [generated,][1] stored, maintained, transmitted, reproduced or communicated, as the case may be, by any electronic, photographic or other process that—

(a) provides a reliable assurance as to the integrity of the record from the time when it was first generated in its final form by such electronic, photographic or other process,

(b) permits the record to be displayed in intelligible form and produced in an intelligible printed format,

(c) permits the record to be readily accessible for subsequent reference in accordance with paragraph (*b*), and

(d) conforms to the information technology and procedural requirements drawn up and published by the Revenue Commissioners in accordance with subsection (3).

(3) The Revenue Commissioners shall from time to time draw up and publish in *Iris Oifigiúil* the information technology and procedural requirements to which any electronic, photographic or other process used by a person for the storage, maintenance, transmission, reproduction and communication of any record shall conform.

(4) The authority conferred on the Revenue Commissioners by this section to draw up and publish requirements shall be construed as including the authority exercisable in a like manner to revoke and replace or to amend any such requirements.

(5) (a) Every person who preserves records by any electronic, photographic or other process, when required to do so by a notice in writing from the Revenue Commissioners, shall, within such period as is specified in the notice, not being less than 21 days from the date of service of the notice, supply to the Revenue Commissioners full particulars relating to the process used by that person, including full particulars relating to software (within the meaning of *section 912*).

(b) A person who fails or refuses to comply with a notice served on the person under paragraph (*a*) shall be liable to a penalty of [€3,000][2].

(6) (a) Subject to paragraph (*b*), where records are kept by a person (being a person who is obliged by the Acts to keep such records) by any electronic, photographic or other process which does not conform with the requirements referred to in paragraphs (*a*) to (*d*) of subsection (2), then the person shall be deemed to have failed to comply with that obligation and that person shall be liable to the same penalties as the person would be liable to if the person had failed to comply with any obligation under the Acts in relation to the keeping of records.

(b) Paragraph (*a*) shall not apply where the person referred to in that paragraph complies with any obligation under the Acts in relation to the keeping of records other than in accordance with the provisions of subsection (2).

(7) Where records are preserved by any electronic, photographic or other process, information contained in a document produced by any such process shall, subject to the rules of court, be admissible in evidence in any proceedings, whether civil or criminal, to the same extent as the records themselves.

(8) The Revenue Commissioners may nominate any of their officers to discharge any function authorised by this section to be discharged by the Revenue Commissioners.][3]

Amendments

[1] Inserted by F(No.2)A13 s76.

[2] Substituted by F(No.2)A08 sched5(part2)(1)(j). The enactments specified in Schedule 5 are amended or repealed to the extent and manner specified in that Schedule and, unless the contrary is stated, shall come into effect after 24 December 2008.

[3] Substituted by FA01 s232(1)(a). Applies as respects any chargeable period commencing on or after 15 February 2001.

Revenue Briefings

Tax Briefing

Tax Briefing December 2001 – Issue 46 pg 24 – Electronic Storage

eBrief

eBrief No. 06/2012 – Retention of Tax Records in Electronic Format

Cross References

From Section 887

Section 912 Computer documents and records.

To Section 887

Section 886 Obligation to keep certain records.

Section 903 Power of inspection: PAYE.

Section 1104 Short title and construction.

888 Returns, etc. by lessors, lessees and agents

[ITA67, 80(1) and s94; FA69 s33(1) and Sch4 PtI; FA92 s227(a); FA95 s14(1)]

[(1) In this section—

"*lease*", "*lessee*" and "*rent*" have the same meanings respectively as in Chapter 8 of Part 4;

"*premises*" means any lands, tenements or hereditaments.][1]

(2) For the purpose of obtaining particulars of profits or gains chargeable to tax under Case IV or V of Schedule D by virtue of *Chapter 8* of *Part 4*, [including, in the case of persons referred to in paragraph (*d*), of income which would be chargeable to tax under Case V of Schedule D if it had arisen in the State,][2] the inspector may by notice in writing require—

(a) any lessor or former lessor of premises to give, within the time limited by the notice, such information as may be specified in the notice as to the provisions of the lease, the terms subject to which the lease was granted and the payments made to or by that lessor or former lessor, as the case may be, in relation to the premises;

(b) any lessee, occupier or former lessee or occupier of premises (including any person having or having had the use of premises) to give such information as may be specified in the notice as to the terms applying to the lease, occupation or use of the premises and, where any of those terms are established by any written instrument, to produce the instrument to the inspector for inspection;

(c) any lessee or former lessee of premises to give such information as may be specified in the notice as to any consideration given for the grant to that lessee or former lessee, as the case may be, of the lease;

(d) any person who as an agent manages premises or is in receipt of rent or other payments arising from premises to prepare and deliver to the inspector a return containing—

(i) the full address of all such premises,

(ii) the name and address of every person to whom such premises belong,

(iii) a statement of all rents and other such payments arising from such premises, and

(iv) such other particulars relating to all such premises as may be specified in the notice;

(e) any Minister of the Government [who, or the Health Service Executive or any local authority][3] [for the purposes of the Local Government Act 2001 (as amended by the Local *Government Reform Act 2014*)][4] or other board or authority, or other similar body, established by or under statute which, makes any payment either in the nature of or for the purpose of rent or rent subsidy in relation to any premises to prepare and deliver to the inspector a return containing—

(i) the full address of all such premises,

(ii) the name and address of every person to whom such premises belong,

[(iia) the tax reference number of every such person,][5]

(iii) a statement of all such payments arising in respect of such premises, and

(iv) such other particulars relating to all such premises as may be specified in the notice.

[(3) (a) In this section "*tax reference number*" means—

(i) in the case of an individual, the individual's Personal Public Service Number within the meaning of section 262 of the Social Welfare Consolidation Act 2005, and

(ii) in the case of any other person, the reference number stated on any return form of income or profits, or notice of assessment, issued to that person by the Revenue Commissioners.

(b) Where a payment, either in the nature of or for the purpose of rent or rent subsidy in relation to any premises, is to be made by any body referred to in subsection (2)(*e*), that body shall request from every person to whom that premises belongs that the person furnish to the body—

(i) the person's tax reference number, or

(ii) where the person does not have a tax reference number, confirmation to that effect,

before the day on which the payment is to be made.

(c) A person to whom paragraph (*b*) relates shall comply with the request in a manner so as to enable the body to have that information before the day the payment is to be made.

(d) Where in making a return for the purposes of subsection (2)(*e*), the body is unable to provide the information required by subparagraph (ii*a*) of that subsection in respect of a person because the person failed to furnish the information in accordance with paragraph (*b*), then the body shall, unless it can otherwise duly provide the information, state that it cannot provide the information so required.][6]

Amendments

[1] Substituted by FA08 s136(a).

[2] Inserted by FA08 s136(b).

[3] Substituted by FA05 sched6(1)(n). Applies as on and from 25 March 2005.

[4] Substituted by LGRA14 sched2(part5).

[5] Inserted by FA07 s123(a)(i).

[6] Inserted by FA07 s123(a)(ii).

Revenue Briefings

eBrief

eBrief No. 39/2006 – Return of Third Party Information by Letting Agents and Managers of Premises

Statements of Practice

Revenue Powers Exercised in Places other than a Revenue Office – SP GEN/1/94 (Revised 02/2006)

Cross References

From Section 888

Section 52 Persons chargeable.
Section 96 Interpretation (Chapter 8).

To Section 888

Section 894 Returns of certain information by third parties.
Section 898A Format of returns etc.
Section 899 Inspector's right to make enquiries.
Section 913 Application of income tax provisions relating to returns, etc.
Section 950 Interpretation (Part 41).
Section 1084 Surcharge for late returns.
Schedule 29 Provisions Referred to in Sections 1052, 1053 and 1054

889 Returns of fees, commissions, etc. paid by certain persons

[ITA67 s173(1) to (7) and (9) to (10); FA82 s60; FA92 s227(b) and s248]

(1) In this section—

"tax reference number", in relation to a person, has the meaning assigned to it by *section 885* in relation to a specified person within the meaning of that section;

references to payments for services include references to payments in the nature of commission of any kind and references to payments in respect of expenses incurred in connection with rendering of services;

references to payments made include references to the giving of any valuable consideration, and the requirement imposed by *subsection (5)* to state the amount of a payment shall, in relation to any consideration given otherwise than in the form of money, be construed as a requirement to give particulars of the consideration.

(2) Every person carrying on a trade or business shall, if required to do so by notice from an inspector, make and deliver to the inspector a return of all payments of any kind specified in the notice made during the period so specified, being—

(a) payments made in the course of the trade or business, or of such part of the trade or business as may be specified in the notice, for services rendered in connection with the trade or business by persons ordinarily resident in the State and not employed in the trade or business,

(b) payments for services rendered in connection with the formation, acquisition, development or disposal of the trade or business, or any part of it, by persons ordinarily resident in the State and not employed in the trade or business, or

(c) periodical or lump sum payments made to persons ordinarily resident in the State in respect of any copyright.

(3) Every body of persons (which for the purposes of this section shall be deemed to include a Minister of the Government and any body established by or under statute) carrying on any activity which does not constitute a trade or business shall, if required to do so by a notice from an inspector, make and deliver to the

inspector a return of all payments of a kind specified in the notice made during the period specified in the notice, being—

(a) payments made in the course of carrying on the activity, or such part of the activity as may be specified in the notice, for services rendered in connection with the activity by persons ordinarily resident in the State and not employed by that body of persons, or

(b) periodical or lump sum payments made to persons ordinarily resident in the State in respect of any copyright.

(4) A return required under *subsection (2)* or *(3)* shall, if the trade or business or other activity is carried on by an unincorporated body of persons, be made and delivered by the person who is, or performs the duties of, secretary of the body, and the notice shall be framed accordingly.

(5) A return under this section shall give the name and tax reference number of the person to whom each payment was made, the amount of the payment and such other particulars as may be specified in the notice, including particulars as to—

(a) the services or rights in respect of which the payment was made,

(b) the period over which any services were rendered, and

(c) any business name and any business or home address of the person to whom payment was made.

(6) A return under this section shall include payments made by the person or body of persons in the course of the trade, business or activity on behalf of any other person.

(7) No person shall be required under this section to include in a return—

(a) particulars of any payment from which income tax is deductible,

(b) particulars of payments made to any one person where the total of the payments to that person which would otherwise have to be included in the return does not exceed [€635][1], or

(c) particulars of any payment made in a year of assessment ending more than 3 years before the service of the notice requiring the person to make the return.

(8) A person who fails to deliver, within the period limited in any notice served on the person under this section, a true and correct return which the person is required by the notice to deliver shall be liable to a penalty of [€3,000][2].

[...][3]

(10) In proceedings for the recovery of a penalty under this section, a certificate by an officer of the Revenue Commissioners which certifies that he or she has inspected the relevant records of the Revenue Commissioners and that it appears from them that during a stated period a stated return was not received from the defendant shall be evidence until the contrary is proved that the defendant did not during that period deliver that return, and any such certificate, purporting to be signed by an officer of the Revenue Commissioners, may be tendered in evidence without proof and shall be deemed until the contrary is proved to have been signed by an officer of the Revenue Commissioners.

Amendments

[1] Substituted by FA01 sched5.

[2] Substituted by F(No.2)A08 sched5(part2)(1)(k)(i). The enactments specified in Schedule 5 are amended or repealed to the extent and manner specified in that Schedule and, unless the contrary is stated, shall come into effect after 24 December 2008.

[3] Deleted by F(No.2)A08 sched5(part2)(1)(k)(ii). The enactments specified in Schedule 5 are amended or repealed to the extent and manner specified in that Schedule and, unless the contrary is stated, shall come into effect after 24 December 2008.

Case Law

Kennerley v Revenue & Customs Commissioner 2007 SpC 578 considered whether an assessment by Revenue was invalid on the basis that no Notice of Enquiry had been given by Revenue to the taxpayer.

Revenue Briefings

eBrief

eBrief No. 37/2013 – 46G Company Spreadsheet (Return of Third Party Information)
eBrief No. 66/2014 – 46G and 46G Company Spreadsheet (Return of Third Party Information)

Tax Briefing

Tax Briefing December 2005 – Issue 62 pg 11 – Third Party Returns Form 46G

Revenue Precedents

It was agreed that payments out of clients accounts need not be included on form 46G by solicitors. IT 902003

Statements of Practice

Return of Certain Information – Third party returns – SP IT/1/92
Revenue Powers Exercised in Places other than a Revenue Office – SP GEN/1/94 (Revised 02/2006)

Cross References

From Section 889

Section 885 Obligation to show tax reference number on receipts.

To Section 889

Section 894 Returns of certain information by third parties.
Section 899 Inspector's right to make enquiries.
Section 1064 Time for certain summary proceedings.

890 Returns by persons in receipt of income belonging to others

[ITA67 s176; F(MP)A68 s6(5); FA92 s227(c)]

(1) Every person (in this section referred to as "*the first-mentioned person*") who, in whatever capacity, is in receipt of any money or value, or of profits or gains arising from any of the sources mentioned in the Income Tax Acts, of or belonging to any other person who is chargeable in respect of such money, value, profits or gains, or who would be so chargeable if that other person were resident in the State and not an incapacitated person, shall, whenever required to do so by a notice given to the first-mentioned person by an inspector, prepare and deliver, within the period mentioned in such notice, a return in the prescribed form, signed by the first-mentioned person, containing—

(a) a statement of all such money, value, profits or gains;

(b) the name and address of every person to whom all such money, value, profits or gains belong;

(c) a declaration whether every such person is of full age, [a married person, a civil partner,][1] resident in the State or an incapacitated person.

(2) Where the first-mentioned person is acting jointly with any other person, the first-mentioned person shall, in the like manner, deliver a list of the names and addresses of all persons joined with the first-mentioned person at the time of delivery of the return mentioned in *subsection (1)*.

(3) No person shall be required under this section to include in a return particulars of receipts (to which *subsection (1)* applies) of or belonging to any one person where the total of the receipts relating to that person which would otherwise have to be included in the return does not exceed [€635][2].

Amendments

[1] Substituted by F(No.3)A11 sched1(238). Shall have effect from 27 July 2011.

[2] Substituted by FA01 sched5.

Case Law

In Fawcett v Special Commissioners & Lancaster Farmer's Auction Mart Co Ltd 1995 STC 61 it was held that an auctioneer of livestock was not obliged to deliver a return as the proceeds of sale held by him did not constitute "profits or gains" but were merely an element to be taken into account in ascertaining profits or gains.

Statements of Practice

Revenue Powers Exercised in Places other than a Revenue Office – SP GEN/1/94 (Revised 02/2006)

Cross References

To Section 890

Section 1050 Protection for trustees, agents and receivers.

Schedule 29 Provisions Referred to in Sections 1052, 1053 and 1054

891 Returns of interest paid or credited without deduction of tax

[ITA67 s175; FA83 s17(2); FA95 s168; Postal and Telecommunications Services Act, 1983 s8(1) and Sch4 PtI]

(1) Subject to *subsection (2)*, every person carrying on a trade or business who, in the ordinary course of the operations of the trade or business, receives or retains money in such circumstances that interest becomes payable on that money which is paid or credited without deduction of income tax, and in particular every person carrying on the trade or business of banking, shall, if required to do so by notice from an inspector, make and deliver to the inspector, within the time specified in the notice, a return of all interest so paid or credited by that person during a year specified in the notice in the course of that person's trade or business or any such part of that person's trade or business as may be so specified, giving the names and addresses of the persons to whom the interest was paid or credited and stating in each case the amount of the interest.

[(1A) (a) In this subsection, "*credit union*" means a society registered under the Credit Union Act, 1997, including a society deemed to be so registered under section 5(3) of that Act.

[(b) This section shall not apply in relation to any interest paid or credited by a credit union in respect of money received or retained by it, other than interest paid or credited by it in respect of a deposit to which subsection (1A) or (1B) of *section 256* refers.][1]][2]

(2) (a) No interest paid or credited to any person shall be required to be included in any return under *subsection (1)* where the total amount of the interest paid or credited to that person which would otherwise have had to be included in the return does not exceed [€65][3].

(b) The year specified in a notice under *subsection (1)* shall not be a year ending more than 3 years before the date of the service of the notice.

(3) Without prejudice to the generality of so much of *subsection (1)* as enables different notices to be served under that subsection in relation to different parts of a trade

or business, separate notices may be served under that subsection as respects the transactions carried on at any branch or branches respectively specified in the notices, and any such separate notice shall, if served on the manager or other person in charge of the branch or branches in question, be deemed to have been duly served on the person carrying on the trade or business and, where such a separate notice is so served as respects the transactions carried on at any branch or branches, any notice subsequently served under *subsection (1)* on the person carrying on the trade or business shall not be deemed to extend to any transaction to which that separate notice extends.

(4) (a) This section shall, with any necessary modifications, apply in relation to the Post Office Savings Bank as if it were a trade or business carried on by An Post.

(b) This subsection shall apply notwithstanding section 4 of the Post Office Savings Bank Act, 1861; but, subject to *paragraph (a)*, that section shall remain in full force and effect.

(5) *Subsections (1)* to *(4)* shall apply only to money received or retained in the State.

(6) (a) Subject to *paragraphs (b)* and *(c)*, where a person to whom any interest is paid or credited in respect of any money received or retained in the State by notice in writing served on the person paying or crediting the interest—

(i) declares that the person who was beneficially entitled to that interest when it was paid or credited was not then resident in the State, and

(ii) requests that the interest shall not be included in any return under this section,

the person paying or crediting the interest shall not be required to include the interest in any such return.

(b) Where the person on whom a notice under *paragraph (a)* is served is not satisfied that the person who served the notice was resident outside the State when the interest was paid or credited—

(i) there shall be given to the person on whom the notice is served an affidavit, made by the person who served the notice, stating that person's name and address and the country in which that person was resident when the interest was paid or credited, and

(ii) if the person who served the notice was not beneficially entitled to that interest when it was paid or credited, the affidavit shall state, in addition to the particulars specified in *subparagraph (i)*, the name and address of the person who was so entitled and the country in which that person was resident when the interest was paid or credited.

(c) Where the person on whom a notice under *paragraph (a)* is served is satisfied that the person who served the notice (in this paragraph referred to as "*the server*") was not resident in the State when the interest was paid or credited and, if the server declares in the notice, or in a subsequent notice served on the person on whom the first-mentioned notice was served, that the server was not beneficially entitled to the interest when it was paid or credited, the server shall, if the person so entitled (in this paragraph referred to as "*the beneficial owner*") is resident in the State, state in one of those notices or in a subsequent notice served on the person on whom the first-mentioned notice was served the name and address of the beneficial owner.

(7) A person to whom *subsection (1)* applies—

(a) shall keep and retain any notice served on that person in accordance with *subsection (6)*, and any affidavit that accompanied the notice, for a period of 6 years from the date of the service of the notice,

(b) shall, if requested in writing by the Revenue Commissioners to do so, inform the Revenue Commissioners within the time specified in the request whether a notice has been served on that person in accordance with *subsection (6)* by such person as is named, and whose address is stated, in the request, and

(c) shall, if requested in writing by the Revenue Commissioners to do so, furnish to the Revenue Commissioners within the time specified in the request such notice served on that person in accordance with *subsection (6)* as is specified in the request and the affidavit that accompanied that notice.

Amendments

[1] Substituted by FA07 s34(1)(g). Applies on and from 2 April 2007.

[2] Inserted by FA98 s131(1)(b). Shall apply as respects chargeable periods beginning on or after the 1st day of October, 1997.

[3] Substituted by FA01 sched5.

Cross References

From Section 891

Section 256 Interpretation (Chapter 4).

To Section 891

Section 246A Interest in respect of wholesale debt instruments.
Section 265 Deposits of companies and pensions schemes.
Section 265A Deposits of certain persons.
Section 266 Deposits of charities.
Section 891A Returns of interest paid to non-residents.
Section 891B Returns of certain payments made by certain persons.
Section 898A Format of returns etc.
Section 898H Returns of interest payments made to or secured for beneficial owners.
Schedule 29 Provisions Referred to in Sections 1052, 1053 and 1054

891A Returns of interest paid to non-residents

[(1) In this section—

[...][1]

"*chargeable period*" has the same meaning as in *section 321(2)*;

"*relevant interest*" means interest to which subsection (2) of *section 246* does not apply by virtue only of paragraph (*h*) (inserted by the *Finance Act, 1999*) of subsection (3) of that section;

"*relevant person*" has the same meaning as in *section 246*;

"*specified return date for the chargeable period*" has the same meaning as in *section 894(1)*.

(2) (a) Subject to paragraph (*c*), every relevant person who pays relevant interest in a chargeable period shall prepare and deliver to the appropriate inspector on or before the specified return date for the chargeable period a return of all relevant interest so paid by the relevant person in the chargeable period stating in the case of each person to whom that relevant interest was paid—

(i) the name and address of the person,

(ii) the amount of relevant interest paid to the person in the chargeable period, and

(iii) the territory in which the person is resident for tax purposes.

(b) *section 891* shall not apply, in respect of the payment of relevant interest, to any relevant person to whom paragraph (*a*) applies.

(c) *Sections 1052* and *1054* shall apply to a failure by a relevant person to deliver a return required by paragraph (*a*) and to each and every such failure, as they apply to a failure to deliver a return referred to in *section 1052*.][2]

Amendments

[1] Deleted by FA12 sched5(1)(h).

[2] Inserted by FA99 s40.

Cross References

From Section 891A

Section 246 Interest payments by companies and to non-residents.
Section 321 Provisions of general application in relation to the making of allowances and charges.
Section 891 Returns of interest paid or credited without deduction of tax.
Section 894 Returns of certain information by third parties.
Section 950 Interpretation (Part 41).
Section 1052 Penalties for failure to make certain returns, etc.
Section 1054 Penalties in the case of a secretary of a body of persons.

To Section 891A

Section 891B Returns of certain payments made by certain persons.
Section 898H Returns of interest payments made to or secured for beneficial owners.
Schedule 29 Provisions Referred to in Sections 1052, 1053 and 1054

891B Returns of certain payments made by certain persons

[(1) In this section—

"*assurance company*" means—

(a) an assurance company within the meaning of section 3 of the Insurance Act 1936, or

(b) a person that holds an authorisation within the meaning of the European Communities (Life Assurance) Framework Regulations 1994 (S.I. No. 360 of 1994);

[...][1]

"*financial institution*" means—

[(a) a person who holds or has held a licence under section 9 of the Central Bank Act 1971, or a person who holds or has held a licence or other 30 similar authorisation under the law of any other Member State of the European Communities which corresponds to a licence granted under that section,][2]

[(aa) an agent appointed by the National Treasury Management Agency to carry out certain functions of the National Treasury Management Agency in relation to State savings products,][3]

(b) a person referred to in section 7(4) of the Central Bank Act 1971, or

(c) a credit institution (within the meaning of the European Communities (Licensing and Supervision of Credit Institutions) Regulations, 1992 (S.I. No. 395 of 1992)) which has been authorised by the Central Bank of

Ireland to carry on business of a credit institution in accordance with the provisions of the supervisory enactments (within the meaning of those Regulations);

"*PPS Number*", in relation to an individual, means the individual's personal public service number (within the meaning of section 262 of the Social Welfare Consolidation Act 2005);

"*relevant payment*", in relation to a specified person, means—

(a) in the case of a specified person which is an assurance company, [...][4] or a financial institution—

(i) any payment of interest or in the nature of interest,

(ii) any payment in respect of any investment,

(iii) any payment made in the nature of a return on an investment, or

(iv) any other similar payment,

of a kind or kinds specified or defined in regulations which is made or credited by or through the specified person, and

(b) in the case of any other specified person, any payment of a kind or kinds specified or defined in regulations made or credited by or through the specified person;

"*relevant person*" means—

(a) any assurance company,

(b) any [financial institution, or][5]

[...][6]

(d) any Minister of the Government, any body established by or under statute, or any other body which undertakes the disbursement of public funds;

"*Revenue officer*" means an officer of the Revenue Commissioners;

"*specified person*" means a person who is a member of a class of relevant persons specified in regulations;

['*State savings products*' means savings products offered by the Minister for Finance through the National Treasury Management Agency, including Post Office Savings Bank accounts and prize bonds;][7]

"*tax*" means any tax provided for under the Tax Acts or the Capital Gains Tax Acts;

"*tax reference number*", in relation to a person, means—

(a) in the case of a person who is an individual, the individual's PPS Number, and

(b) in any other case—

(i) the reference number stated on any return of income form or notice of assessment issued to the person by a Revenue officer, or

(ii) the registration number of the person for the purposes of value-added tax.

(2) (a) For the purposes of this section and any regulations—

(i) any amount credited, or set off against any other amount, in respect of a relevant payment shall be treated as a payment and references in this section and in regulations to a payment shall be construed accordingly, and

(ii) any reference in this section and in regulations to the amount of a payment shall be construed as a reference to the amount which would be the amount of that payment if no tax were to be deducted from that payment.

(b) A reference in this section to a regulation or regulations shall be construed as a reference to a regulation or regulations made under subsection (3).

(3) The Revenue Commissioners, with the consent of the Minister for Finance, may by regulations provide that a specified person be required—

(a) to make to the Revenue Commissioners a return of information relating to relevant payments made by or through the specified person concerned for or by reference to such period or periods, other than a period beginning before 1 January 2005, as may be specified in the regulations, and

(b) subject to subsection (4)(*h*), to include in any such return the tax reference numbers of the persons to whom any such payments are made.

(4) Without prejudice to the generality of subsection (3), regulations may, in particular, include provision for—

(a) notifying a person that that person is a specified person, including the means by which such notification may be made,

(b) determining the date in any year by which a return required to be made under the regulations shall be made to the Revenue Commissioners,

(c) prescribing the office of the Revenue Commissioners to which returns should be delivered,

(d) specifying or defining the kind or kinds of relevant payments to be included in returns to be made under regulations,

(e) defining, for the purposes of determining the persons or classes of persons to be included in a return to be made under regulations, the persons or classes of persons to whom relevant payments may have been made,

(f) determining, for the purposes of including persons to whom relevant payments are made in a return to be made under regulations, the identity and place of residence or establishment of a person to whom a relevant payment is made,

(g) specifying the details relating to a relevant payment to be included in a return made under regulations,

(h) imposing an obligation on—

(i) specified persons to obtain a tax reference number from persons (in this paragraph referred to as "*customers*")—

(I) with whom they enter into contractual relationships,

(II) for whom they undertake any transaction, or

(III) in respect of whom they make a relevant payment,

on or after a date specified in regulations, which shall not be earlier than the date such regulations come into force, for the purposes of including that number in a return under regulations, and

(ii) customers to provide a specified person with their tax reference number on request by that specified person where—

(I) such customers enter into contractual relations with the specified person, or

(II) where the specified person undertakes any transaction,

on or after a date specified in regulations where the relationship or transaction may give rise to a relevant payment,

(i) defining "*books*" and "*records*" for the purposes of regulations,

(j) determining the manner of keeping records and setting the period for the retention of records so kept in relation to any of the matters specified in the preceding paragraphs,

(k) Revenue officers, authorised for the purpose, to—

(i) require—

(I) the production of books, records or other documents,

(II) the provision of information, explanations and particulars,

(III) persons to give all such assistance as may reasonably be required and as is specified in the regulations,

in relation to relevant payments and the persons to whom such payments were made within such time as may be specified in regulations, and

(ii) make extracts from or copies of books, records or other documents or require that copies of such books, records and documents be made available,

and

(l) such supplemental and incidental matters as appear to the Revenue Commissioners to be necessary—

(i) to enable persons to fulfil their obligations under regulations, or

(ii) for the general administration and implementation of any regulations, including—

(I) delegating to a Revenue officer the authority to perform any acts and discharge any functions authorised by regulations to be performed or discharged by the Revenue Commissioners, and

(II) the authorisation by the Revenue Commissioners of Revenue officers to exercise any powers, to perform any acts or to discharge any functions conferred by this section or by regulations.

(5) Every regulation made shall be laid before Dáil Éireann as soon as may be after it is made and, if a resolution annulling the regulation is passed by Dáil Éireann within the next 21 days on which Dáil Éireann has sat after the regulation is laid before it, the regulation shall be annulled accordingly, but without prejudice to the validity of anything previously done thereunder.

(6) A Revenue officer authorised for the purpose of regulations may at all reasonable times enter any premises or place of business of a specified person for the purposes of—

(a) determining whether information—

(i) included in a return made under regulations by that specified person was correct and complete, or

(ii) not included in such a return was correctly not so included,

or

(b) examining the procedures put in place by that specified person for the purposes of ensuring compliance with that person's obligations under regulations.

(7) (a) *Section 898O* shall apply to—

(i) a failure by a relevant person to deliver a return required under regulations, and to each and every such failure, and

(ii) the making of an incorrect or incomplete return under regulations,

as it applies to a failure to deliver a return or to the making of an incorrect or incomplete return referred to in *section 898O*.

(b) A person who does not comply with—

(i) the requirements of a Revenue officer in the exercise or performance of the officer's powers or duties under this section or under regulations, or

(ii) [...][8] any requirement of regulations made under subsection (3),

shall be liable to a penalty of €1,265 [...][9]

(8) A relevant payment shall not be included in a return to be made under regulations if such payment is included or would be liable to be included in a return made in accordance with *section 891A* or Chapter 3A.

(9) Where a return (in this subsection referred to as the "*first-mentioned return*") is furnished by a specified person under regulations a return shall not be required to be made by that person under *section 891*, notwithstanding the provisions of *section 894*, in respect of any payment included in the first-mentioned return.

[(10) Section 4 of the Post Office Savings Bank Act 1861 shall not apply to the disclosure of information required to be included in a return made under regulations made under this section and, accordingly, this section shall apply to information to which, but for this subsection, the said section 4 would apply.][10]][11]

Amendments

[1] Deleted by FA12 s121(a). Deemed to have come into force and takes effect on and from 1 January 2012.

[2] Substituted by F(No.2)A08 s92(a).

[3] Inserted by FA14 s92(a).

[4] Deleted by FA12 s121(b). Deemed to have come into force and takes effect on and from 1 January 2012.

[5] Substituted by FA12 s121(c)(i). Deemed to have come into force and takes effect on and from 1 January 2012.

[6] Deleted by FA12 s121(c)(ii). Deemed to have come into force and takes effect on and from 1 January 2012.

[7] Inserted by FA14 s92(b).

[8] Deleted by FA12 s121(d). Deemed to have come into force and takes effect on and from 1 January 2012.

[9] Deleted by FA12 sched6(1)(m).

[10] Inserted by FA08 s133. Has effect from 1 January 2008.

[11] Inserted by FA06 s125.

Revenue Briefings

eBrief

eBrief No. 78/2011 – Return of Payments (Insurance Undertakings) Regulations 2011

Cross References

From Section 891B

Section 731 Chargeable gains accruing to unit trusts.

Section 739B Interpretation and application.

Section 891 Returns of interest paid or credited without deduction of tax.

Section 891A Returns of interest paid to non-residents.

Section 894 Returns of certain information by third parties.

Section 898O Penalty for failure to make returns, etc.
Section 1061 Recovery of penalties.

To Section 891B

Section 263A Declarations to a relevant deposit taker relating to deposits of certain persons.
Section 263B Declarations to the Revenue Commissioners relating to deposits of certain persons.
Section 263C Notifications by the Revenue Commissioners relating to deposits of certain persons.
Section 265A Deposits of certain persons.
Section 267N Interpretation.

891C Returns of certain information by investment undertakings

[(1) In this section—

(a) '*investment undertaking*' has the same meaning as in *section 739B(1)* but does not include a common contractual fund within the meaning of [*section 739I* or an investment limited partnership within the meaning of *section 739J*][1];

(b) '*unit*' and '*unit holder*' have the same meanings respectively as in *section 739B(1)*;

(c) '*tax reference number*' has the same meaning as in *section 891B(1)*.

(2) A reference in this section to a regulation or regulations shall be construed as a reference to a regulation or regulations made under *subsection (3)*.

(3) The Revenue Commissioners, with the consent of the Minister for Finance, may by regulations provide that an investment undertaking be required—

(a) to make to the Revenue Commissioners a return of information relating to units of the investment undertaking concerned by reference to such date or dates, other than a date before 1 January 2012, as may be specified in the regulations, and

(b) subject to *subsection (5)(a)(vi)*, to include in any such return the tax reference numbers of the unit holders at that time.

(4) Information in relation to units shall not be included in a return to be made under regulations if information in relation to such units is included or would be liable to be included in a return made in accordance with *Chapter 3A*.

(5) For the purposes of this section—

(a) the provisions of *subsection (4)* of *section 891B* shall apply subject to the following modifications and any other necessary modifications:

(i) in *paragraph (a)* by substituting 'investment undertaking' for 'specified person';

(ii) in *paragraph (d)* by substituting 'the value of units' for 'the kind or kinds of relevant payments';

(iii) by substituting the following for *paragraph (e)*:

'(*e*) defining, for the purposes of determining the unit holders or classes of unit holders to be included in a return to be made under regulations, the unit holders or classes of unit holders';

(iv) by substituting the following for *paragraph (f)*:

'(*f*) determining for the purposes of including unit holders in a return to be made under regulations, the identity and place of residence or establishment of a unit holder';

(v) in *paragraph (g)* by substituting 'unit' for 'relevant payment';

(vi) in *paragraph (h)*—

(I) by substituting the following for *subparagraph (i)*:

'(i) investment undertakings to obtain a tax reference number from unit holders—

(I) with whom they enter into contractual relationships, or

(II) for whom they undertake any transaction,

on or after a date specified in regulations, which shall not be earlier than the date such regulations come into force, for the purposes of including that number in a return under regulations, and',

and

(II) in *subparagraph (ii)*—

(A) by substituting 'investment undertaking' for 'specified person' in each place,

(B) by substituting 'unit holders' for 'customers' in each place, and

(C) by deleting 'where the relationship or transaction may give rise to a relevant payment',

and

(vii) in *paragraph (k)* by substituting 'units and the unit holders' for 'relevant payments and the persons to whom such payments were made',

and

(b) the provisions of *subsections (6)* and *(7)* of *section 891B* shall apply subject to the modification that references in those subsections to 'person', 'relevant person' or 'specified person', as the case may be, shall be construed, where the context admits, as references to 'investment undertaking'.

(6) Every regulation made shall be laid before Dáil Éireann as soon as may be after it is made and, if a resolution annulling the regulation is passed by Dáil Éireann within the next 21 days on which Dáil Éireann has sat after the regulation is laid before it, the regulation shall be annulled accordingly, but without prejudice to the validity of anything previously done thereunder.][2]

Amendments

[1] Substituted by FA13 s42(1)(f). Applies in respect of an investment limited partnership that has been granted an authorisation under section 8 of the Investment Limited Partnerships Act 1994 on or after 13 February 2013.

[2] Inserted by FA12 s121(e). Deemed to have come into force and takes effect on and from 1 January 2012.

891D Returns of payment transactions by payment settlers

[(1) In this section—

'*authorised officer*' means an officer of the Revenue Commissioners authorised by them in writing to exercise the powers conferred by this section;

'*central organisation*' has the meaning assigned in the definition of 'electronic payment network';

'*electronic network transaction*' means any transaction which is settled through an electronic payment network;

'*electronic payment facilitator*' means any person, other than a payment settlement entity, acting on behalf of a payment settlement entity who submits instructions to transfer funds to the account of the merchant to settle the reportable payment transaction;

'*electronic payment network*' means any agreement or arrangement—

(a) which involves the establishment of accounts with a body (in this section referred to as a 'central organisation') by persons who—

(i) are unrelated to the central organisation,

(ii) provide goods or services, and

(iii) have agreed to settle transactions for the provision of such goods or services pursuant to such agreement or arrangement,

(b) which provides for standards and mechanisms for settling such transactions, and

(c) which guarantees persons providing goods or services pursuant to such agreement or arrangement that such persons will be paid for providing such goods or services,

but does not include any agreement or arrangement which provides for the issue of payment cards;

'*electronic settlement organisation*' means the central organisation which has the contractual obligation to make payment to merchants of electronic network transactions;

'*merchant*' means—

(a) in the case of a payment card transaction, any person having an address in the State who accepts a payment card as payment, and

(b) in the case of an electronic network transaction, any person having an address in the State who accepts payment from an electronic settlement organisation in settlement of such transaction;

'*merchant acquirer*' means the person who has the contractual obligation to make payment to merchants in settlement of payment card transactions;

'*payment card*' means any card which is issued pursuant to an agreement or arrangement which provides for—

(a) one or more issuers of such cards,

(b) a network of persons unrelated to each other, and to the issuer, who agree to accept such cards as payment, and

(c) standards and mechanisms for settling the transactions between the merchant acquirers and the persons who agree to accept such cards as payment,

and the acceptance as payment of any account number or other indicators associated with a payment card shall be treated for the purposes of this section in the same manner as accepting such payment card as payment;

'*payment card transaction*' means any transaction in which a payment card is accepted as payment;

'*payment settlement entity*' means—

(a) in the case of a payment card transaction, the merchant acquirer, and

(b) in the case of an electronic network transaction, the electronic settlement organisation;

'*PPS Number*', in relation to an individual, means the individual's personal public service number (within the meaning of *section 262* of the Social Welfare Consolidation Act 2005);

'*reportable payment transactions*' means, subject to regulations, any payment card transaction and any electronic network transaction;

'*services*', in relation to an electronic payment network, includes making arrangements directly or indirectly for persons to make voluntary payments with or without consideration for the benefit, in whole or in part, of another person;

'*tax reference number*', in relation to a person, means—

(a) in the case of a person who is an individual, the individual's PPS Number, and

(b) in any other case—

(i) the reference number stated on any return of income form or notice of assessment issued to the person by a Revenue officer, or

(ii) the registration number of that person for the purposes of the Value-Added Tax Acts.

(2) The Revenue Commissioners may by regulations provide that a payment settlement entity be required—

(a) to make to the Revenue Commissioners an electronic return for or by reference to such year or years, other than a year earlier than 2010, of reportable payment transactions and such other information as may be specified in the regulations, and

(b) subject to *subsection (4)(b)*, to include in any such return the tax reference numbers of merchants included in the return.

(3) Without prejudice to the generality of *subsection (2)*, regulations may, in particular, provide for—

(a) determining the date by which a return required to be made under the regulations shall be made to the Revenue Commissioners,

(b) prescribing the manner in which returns are to be made,

(c) specifying the type of reportable payment transactions to be included in the return,

(d) imposing an obligation on payment settlement entities to request, on or after a date specified in regulations, a tax reference number from merchants, which date shall not be earlier than the date such regulations come into force, for the purposes of including that number in a return under regulations,

(e) imposing an obligation on every merchant to provide the payment settlement entity concerned with the relevant tax reference number upon request being made by such payment settlement entity, and

(f) specifying the details relating to the reportable payment transactions to be included in the return, including, but not limited to, the following—

(i) account and reference numbers,

(ii) information concerning the business or service conducted by the merchant,

(iii) information relating to the terminals used by the merchant, such as the number of terminals in use, the serial numbers of such terminals and the location of such terminals,

(iv) information relating to the merchant, including name, address, email address and contact numbers, and

(v) bank account information of merchants to and from which funds are transferred by the payment settlement entity.

(4) (a) A payment settlement entity shall make all reasonable efforts to obtain from a merchant that person's tax reference number and the merchant shall provide to the payment settlement entity his or her tax reference number.

(b) Where the tax reference number provided for the purposes of this section is an individual's PPS Number, the payment settlement entity shall only use that number (as so provided) for the purpose of including it in the return to be made under *subsection (2)* and for no other purpose.

(5) An authorised officer may at all reasonable times enter any premises or place of business of a payment settlement entity for the purposes of—

(a) determining whether—

(i) information included in a return made by a payment settlement entity was correct and complete, or

(ii) information not included in such a return was correctly not so included, or

(b) examining the procedures put in place by that payment settlement entity for the purposes of ensuring compliance with that person's obligations under this section.

(6) (a) *Section 898O* shall apply to—

(i) a failure by a payment settlement entity to deliver a return, and to each and every such failure, and

(ii) the making of an incorrect or incomplete return,

as it applies to a failure to deliver a return or to the making of an incorrect or incomplete return referred to in *section 898O*.

(b) A payment settlement entity which does not comply with—

(i) the requirements of an authorised officer in the exercise or performance of the officer's powers or duties under this section or under regulations, or

(ii) any requirement imposed on the payment settlement entity by regulations made under *subsection (2)*,

shall be liable to a penalty of €3,000.][1]

Amendments

[1] Inserted by FA12 s122. Deemed to have come into force and takes effect on and from 1 January 2012.

891E Implementation of the Agreement to Improve Tax Compliance and Provide for Reporting and Exchange of Information concerning Tax Matters (United States of America) Order 2013

[(1) This section applies for the purpose of implementing the Agreement to Improve Tax Compliance and Provide for Reporting and Exchange of Information concerning Tax Matters (United States of America) Order 2013 (S.I. No. 33 of 2013).

(2) For the purposes of this section and the regulations made under this section—

"*Agreement*" means the Agreement Between the Government of Ireland and the Government of the United States of America to Improve International Tax Compliance and to Implement FATCA done at Dublin on 21 December 2012;

(I) with whom the institution enters into a contractual relationship, or

(II) for whom the institution undertakes any transaction,

on or after a date specified in the regulations, which shall not be earlier than the commencement of the regulations (and such persons are in this paragraph referred to as "*customers*") for the purposes of including that number in a return under the regulations, and

(ii) customers to provide a financial institution with their tax reference number on request by the financial institution where, on or after a date specified in the regulations—

(I) such customers enter into a contractual relationship with the financial institution, or

(II) the financial institution undertakes any transaction for such customers,

being respectively—

(A) a relationship which results in the opening, operation, administration or management of a financial account, or

(B) a transaction which arises in relation to a financial account,

(w) defining "*books*" and "*records*" for the purposes of the regulations,

(x) in relation to any of the matters specified in the preceding paragraphs, determining the manner of keeping records and setting the period for the retention of records so kept,

(y) enabling the authorisation of Revenue officers, for the purpose of such officers—

(i) requiring—

(I) the production of books, records or other documents,

(II) the provision of information, explanations and particulars, and

(III) persons to give all such assistance as may reasonably be required and as is specified in the regulations,

in relation to financial accounts within such time as may be specified in the regulations, and

(ii) making extracts from or copies of books, records or other documents or requiring that copies of such books, records and documents be made available,

and

(z) specifying such supplemental and incidental matters as appear to the Revenue Commissioners to be necessary—

(i) to enable persons to fulfill their obligations under the regulations, or

(ii) for the general administration and implementation of the regulations, including—

(I) delegating to a Revenue officer the authority to perform any acts and discharge any functions authorised by this section or the regulations to be performed or discharged by the Revenue Commissioners, and

(II) the authorisation by the Revenue Commissioners of Revenue officers to exercise any powers, to perform any acts or to discharge any functions conferred by this section or by the regulations.

(6) Every regulation made under this section shall be laid before Dáil Éireann as soon as may be after it is made and, if a resolution annulling the regulation is passed by Dáil Éireann within the next 21 days on which Dáil Éireann has sat after the regulation is laid before it, the regulation shall be annulled accordingly, but without prejudice to the validity of anything previously done thereunder.

(7) A Revenue officer authorised for the purpose of regulations under this section may at all reasonable times enter any premises or place of business of a financial institution for the purposes of—

(a) determining whether information—

(i) included ina return made under the regulations by the financial institution was correct and complete, or

(ii) not included in such a return was correctly not so included,

or

(b) examining the procedures put in place by the financial institution for the purposes of ensuring compliance with that institution's obligations under the regulations.

(8) (a) *Section 898O* shall apply to—

(i) a failure by a financial institution to deliver a return required under regulations under this section, and

(ii) the making of an incorrect or incomplete return under those regulations,

as it applies to a failure to deliver a return or to the making of an incorrect or incomplete return referred to in *section 898O*.

(b) A person who does not comply with—

(i) the requirements of a Revenue officer in the exercise or performance of the officer's powers or duties under this section or under regulations made under this section, or

(ii) any requirement of such regulations,

shall be liable to a penalty of €1,265.

(9) *Section 4* of the Post Office Savings Bank Act 1861 shall not apply to the disclosure of information required to be included in a return made under the regulations made under this section and, accordingly, this section shall apply to information to which, but for this subsection, the said *section 4* would apply.

(10) (a) Notwithstanding *section 851A*, the Revenue Commissioners are authorised to communicate to the competent authority information which is contained in a return required under regulations under this section.

(b) The Revenue Commissioners shall communicate the information referred to in *paragraph (a)* to the competent authority not later than the expiry of 9 months following the end of the tax year [to which the return relates][1].

(11) Where arrangements are entered into by any person and the main purpose or one of the main purposes of the arrangements, or any part of them, is the avoidance of any of the obligations imposed under this section or regulations thereunder,

then this section and those regulations shall apply as if the arrangements, or that part of them, had not been entered into.][2]

Amendments

[1] Substituted by F(No.2)A13 s27. Comes into operation on 1 January 2014.

[2] Inserted by FA13 s32. Deemed to have come into force and takes effect on and from 1 January 2013.

Revenue Briefings

eBrief

eBrief No. 88/2014 – Publication of Guidance Notes on the Implementation of FATCA in Ireland

891F Returns of certain information by financial institutions

[(1) This section provides for the collection and reporting of certain information in respect of financial accounts held by any person who is regarded by virtue of the laws of a jurisdiction other than the State as resident in that jurisdiction for the purposes of tax.

(2) In this section—

'*the standard*' means the Standard for Automatic Exchange of Financial Account Information approved on 15 July 2014 by the Council of the Organisation for Economic Cooperation and Development;

'*account holder*', '*financial account*', '*high value account*', '*lower value account*', '*reportable account*', '*reporting financial institution*' and '*TIN*' have the meanings respectively given to them by Section VIII of the standard.

(3) The Revenue Commissioners, with the consent of the Minister for Finance, may make regulations under this section with respect to the return by a reporting financial institution of information on reportable accounts held, managed or administered by that reporting financial institution.

(4) In addition to the specification in the regulations of a requirement that reporting financial institutions make a return to the Revenue Commissioners of information in relation to reportable accounts, regulations under this section may (without prejudice to the generality of *subsection (3)*) include provisions—

(a) determining the date by which a return required to be made under the regulations shall be made to the Revenue Commissioners,

(b) prescribing the manner in which returns are to be made,

(c) specifying the information to be reported in a return by the reporting financial institution, to the Revenue Commissioners, in relation to reportable accounts and, where different information is to be reported for different years, specifying the information to be reported for each of those years,

(d) specifying—

(i) the currency in which the reporting financial institution is required to report, and

(ii) the rules for conversion of amounts, denominated in another currency, into the currency, referred to in *subparagraph (i)*, for the purposes of a return under the regulations,

(e) requiring reporting financial institutions to identify reportable accounts,

(f) specifying the records and documents that must be examined or obtained by the reporting financial institution to enable the institution to identify reportable accounts,

(g) specifying the records and documents used to identify reportable accounts that must be retained by the reporting financial institution,

(h) specifying additional requirements in relation to the examination of high value accounts and lower value accounts,

(i) setting out the circumstances in which a reporting financial institution is required to aggregate financial accounts held by the same individual or entity for the purposes of identifying reportable accounts as high value accounts or lower value accounts,

(j) specifying the actions to be taken by a reporting financial institution where there is a change in circumstances with respect to the account holder of a financial account,

(k) setting out the conditions under which a reporting financial institution may appoint a third party as its agent to carry out the duties and obligations imposed on it by the regulations,

(l) setting out the circumstances in which a reporting financial institution may make a nil return,

(m) imposing an obligation on—

(i) a reporting financial institution to obtain a TIN from any person—

(I) with whom the institution enters into a contractual relationship, or

(II) for whom the institution undertakes any transaction, on or after a date specified in the regulations, which shall not be earlier than the commencement of the regulations (and such persons are in this paragraph referred to as 'customers') for the purposes of including that number in a return under the regulations,

and

(ii) customers to provide a reporting financial institution with their TIN on request by the reporting financial institution where, on or after a date specified in the regulations—

(I) such customers enter into a contractual relationship with the reporting financial institution, or

(II) the reporting financial institution undertakes any transaction for such customers,

being respectively—

(A) a relationship which results in the opening, operation, administration or management of a financial account, or

(B) a transaction which arises in relation to a financial account,

(n) defining 'books' and 'records' for the purposes of the regulations,

(o) in relation to any of the matters specified in the preceding paragraphs, determining the manner of keeping records and setting the period for the retention of records so kept,

(p) enabling the authorisation of Revenue officers, for the purpose of such officers—

(i) requiring—

(I) the production of books, records or other documents,

(II) the provision of information, explanations and particulars, and

(III) persons to give all such assistance as may reasonably be required and as is specified in the regulations,

in relation to financial accounts within such time as may be specified in the regulations, and

(ii) making extracts from or copies of books, records or other documents or requiring that copies of such books, records and documents be made available,

and

(q) specifying such supplemental and incidental matters as appear to the Revenue Commissioners to be necessary—

(i) to enable persons to fulfil their obligations under the regulations, or

(ii) for the general administration and implementation of the regulations, including—

(I) delegating to a Revenue officer the authority to perform any acts and discharge any functions authorised by this section or the regulations to be performed or discharged by the Revenue Commissioners, and

(II) the authorisation by the Revenue Commissioners of Revenue officers to exercise any powers, to perform any acts or to discharge any functions conferred by this section or by the regulations.

(5) Every regulation made under this section shall be laid before Dáil Éireann as soon as may be after it is made and, if a resolution annulling the regulation is passed by Dáil Éireann within the next 21 days on which Dáil Éireann has sat after the regulation is laid before it, the regulation shall be annulled accordingly, but without prejudice to the validity of anything previously done thereunder.

(6) A Revenue officer authorised for the purpose of regulations under this section may at all reasonable times enter any premises or place of business of a reporting financial institution for the purposes of—

(a) determining whether information—

(i) included in a return made under the regulations by the reporting financial institution was correct and complete, or

(ii) not included in such a return was correctly not so included,

or

(b) examining the procedures put in place by the reporting financial institution for the purposes of ensuring compliance with that institution's obligations under the regulations.

(7) (a) *Section 898O* shall apply to—

(i) a failure by a reporting financial institution to deliver a return required under regulations made under this section, and

(ii) the making of an incorrect or incomplete return under those regulations,

as it applies to a failure to deliver a return or to the making of an incorrect or incomplete return referred to in *section 898O*.

(b) A person who does not comply with—

(i) the requirements of a Revenue officer in the exercise or performance of the officer's powers or duties under this section or under regulations made under this section, or

(ii) any requirement of such regulations,

shall be liable to a penalty of €1,265.

(8) *Section 4* of the Post Office Savings Bank Act 1861 shall not apply to the disclosure of information required to be included in a return made under the regulations made under this section and, accordingly, this section shall apply to information to which, but for this subsection, the said *section 4* would apply.

(9) Where arrangements are entered into by any person and the main purpose or one of the main purposes of the arrangements, or any part of them, is the avoidance of any of the obligations imposed under this section or regulations thereunder, then this section and those regulations shall apply as if the arrangements, or that part of them, had not been entered into.

(10) Any word or expression which has a meaning given to it by *Section VIII* of the standard shall, where it is used in regulations made under this section and unless the contrary intention appears, have the same 30 meaning in those regulations as it has in that *Section VIII*.][1]

Amendments

[1] Inserted by FA14 s28. Comes into operation on 1 January 2015.

892 Returns by nominee holders of securities

[FA83 s21(1) and (2)]

(1) In this section, "*securities*" includes—

(a) shares, stocks, bonds, debentures and debenture stock of a company (within the meaning of *section 4(1)*) and also any promissory note or other instrument evidencing indebtedness issued to a loan creditor (within the meaning of *section 433(6)*) of a company,

(b) securities created and issued by the Minister for Finance under the Central Fund (Permanent Provisions) Act, 1965, or under any other statutory powers conferred on that Minister and any stock, debenture, debenture stock, certificate of charge or other security which is issued with the approval of the Minister for Finance given under any Act of the Oireachtas and in respect of which the payment of interest and the repayment of capital is guaranteed by the Minister for Finance under that Act, and

(c) securities of the government of any country or territory outside the State.

(2) Where for any purpose of the Tax Acts any person (in this subsection referred to as "*the holder*") in whose name any securities are registered is so required by notice in writing given by an inspector, the holder shall, within the time specified in the

notice, state whether or not the holder is the beneficial owner of the securities and, if not the beneficial owner of the securities or any of them, shall furnish in respect of each person on whose behalf the securities are registered in the holder's name—

(a) the name and address of such person,

(b) the nominal value of the securities so registered on behalf of such person and, in so far as the securities consist of shares in a company, the number and class of such shares, and

(c) the date on which each security was so registered in the holder's name on behalf of such person.

Statements of Practice

Revenue Powers Exercised in Places other than a Revenue Office – SP GEN/1/94 (Revised 02/2006)

Cross References

From Section 892

Section 4 Interpretation of Corporation Tax Acts.

Section 433 Meaning of "participator", "associate", "director" and "loan creditor".

To Section 892

Section 894 Returns of certain information by third parties.

Section 898A Format of returns etc.

Schedule 29 Provisions Referred to in Sections 1052, 1053 and 1054

893 Returns by certain intermediaries in relation to UCITS [Deleted]

Deleted by FA01 s232(1)(b). Applies as respects any chargeable period commencing on or after 15 February 2001.

Revenue Briefings

Tax Briefing

Tax Briefing October 1993 – Issue 12 – Third Party Returns

eBrief

eBrief No. 39/2006 – Return of Third Party Information by Letting Agents and Managers of Premises.

Revenue Information Notes

IT16 – Third Party Returns

Statements of Practice

Return of Certain Information – Third party returns – SP IT/01/92

Revenue Powers Exercised in Places other than a Revenue Office – SP GEN/1/94 (Revised 02/2006)

Cross References

To Section 893

Section 894 Returns of certain information by third parties.

894 Returns of certain information by third parties

[FA92 s226; FA95 s14(2)(i)]

(1) In this section—

"*appropriate inspector*", in relation to a person to whom this section applies, means—

(a) the inspector who has last given notice in writing to that person that he or she is the inspector to whom that person is required to deliver the return specified in *subsection (3)*,

(b) where there is no such inspector as is referred to in *paragraph (a)*, the inspector to whom it is customary for that person to deliver a [any return, statement, list or declaration][1], or

(c) where there is no such inspector as is referred to in *paragraphs (a)* and *(b)*, [the inspector of returns][2];

"*chargeable period*" has the same meaning as in *section 321(2)*;

"*relevant person*" has the meaning assigned to it by *subsection (2)*;

"*specified provisions*" means *paragraphs (d)* and *(e)* of *section 888(2)* and [*sections 889, 890, 891, 891A and 892*][3],

"*specified return date for the chargeable period*", in relation to a chargeable period, means—

[(a) (i) where the chargeable period is the year of assessment 2000-2001, 31 January 2002, and

(ii) where the chargeable period is the year of assessment 2001 or any subsequent year of assessment, 31 October in the year of assessment following that year,

and][4]

(b) where the chargeable period is an accounting period of a company, the last day of the period of 9 months commencing on the day immediately following the end of the accounting period.

(2) (a) Subject to *paragraphs (b)* to *(e)*, "*relevant person*" means any person who—

(i) has information of a kind,

(ii) makes a payment of a kind,

(iii) pays or credits interest of a kind, or

(iv) is in receipt of money or value or of profits or gains of a kind,

referred to in a specified provision.

(b) Subject to *paragraph (e)*, any person who would be excluded from making a return under a specified provision for a chargeable period shall not be a relevant person.

(c) A person with information of the kind referred to in *section 892* shall, subject to *paragraph (e)*, be a relevant person only where the person is not the beneficial owner of the securities referred to in that section.

[...][5]

(e) A person who is not a relevant person by virtue of any of the provisions of *paragraphs (b)* to *(d)* shall not be excluded from being a relevant person by virtue of any other provision of this subsection.

(3) Every relevant person shall as respects a chargeable period prepare and deliver to the appropriate inspector on or before the specified return date for the chargeable period a return of all such matters and particulars as would be required to be contained in a return delivered pursuant to a notice given to the relevant person by the appropriate inspector under any of the specified provisions for the chargeable period.

(4) An inspector may exclude any person from the application of this section by giving that person a notice in writing that that person is excluded from the application of this section, and the notice shall have effect for such chargeable period or periods, or until such chargeable period or the happening of such event, as shall be specified in the notice.

(5) Where it appears appropriate to an inspector, the inspector may notify any relevant person that a return to be made under this section may be confined to a particular type or category of information, payment or receipt and, where the

relevant person has been so notified, a return made on that basis shall satisfy this section.

(6) This section shall not affect the giving of a notice under any of the specified provisions and shall not remove from any person any obligation or requirement imposed on a person by such a notice, and the giving of a notice under any of the specified provisions to a person shall not remove from that person any obligation to prepare and deliver a return under this section.

(7) *Sections 1052* and *1054* shall apply to a failure by a relevant person to deliver a return required by *subsection (3)*, and to each and every such failure, as they apply to a failure to deliver a return referred to in *section 1052*.

Amendments

[1] Substituted by FA01 s78(2)(d). Applies as respects the year of assessment 2001 and subsequent years and as respects accounting periods of companies ending on or after 1 April 2001.

[2] Substituted by FA12 sched5(1)(l).

[3] Substituted by F(No.2)A13 sched(1)(j). Has effect on and from 18 December 2013.

[4] Substituted by FA03 s34(1)(b). This section is deemed to have come into operation as on and from 6 April 2001.

[5] Deleted by FA01 s232(1)(c). Applies as respects any chargeable period commencing on or after 15 February 2001.

Cross References

From Section 894

Section 321 Provisions of general application in relation to the making of allowances and charges.
Section 888 Returns, etc. by lessors, lessees and agents.
Section 889 Returns of fees, commissions, etc. paid by certain persons.
Section 892 Returns by nominee holders of securities.
Section 893 Returns by certain intermediaries in relation to UCITS.
Section 950 Interpretation (Part 41).
Section 1052 Penalties for failure to make certain returns, etc.
Section 1054 Penalties in the case of a secretary of a body of persons.

To Section 894

Section 246A Interest in respect of wholesale debt instruments.
Section 459 General provisions relating to allowances, deductions and reliefs.
Section 891A Returns of interest paid to non-residents.
Section 891B Returns of certain payments made by certain persons.
Schedule 29 Provisions Referred to in Sections 1052, 1053 and 1054

894A Returns by third parties in relation to personal reliefs

[(1) In this section—

"*PPS Number*", in relation to an individual, means the individual's Personal Public Service Number within the meaning of section 262 of the Social Welfare Consolidation Act 2005;

"*personal relief*" means a relief under any of the provisions specified in the Table to *section 458*.

(2) Where a person is in possession of information concerning expenditure defrayed by an individual that is relevant to establishing the title of that individual to a personal relief, or the amount of such a relief, that person may, notwithstanding anything contained in any other enactment or any obligation to maintain secrecy or other restriction on the disclosure of information, furnish details regarding the amount of such expenditure to the Revenue Commissioners if requested by them to do so.

(3) Information furnished to the Revenue Commissioners in accordance with subsection (2) shall, unless the Revenue Commissioners otherwise direct, be in

an electronic format approved by the Revenue Commissioners and shall contain the name and address and, where known, the PPS Number of the individual in relation to whom the information is being furnished.

(4) Notwithstanding any other provision to the contrary, for the purposes of making a return under subsection (3), a person not in possession of the PPS Number of an individual shall be entitled to request that number from the individual and shall inform the individual of the purpose for requesting the number.

(5) Information furnished to them in accordance with subsection (2) shall be used by the Revenue Commissioners only for the purpose of establishing the title of an individual to the personal relief concerned, or the amount of that relief and, notwithstanding *section 872*, shall be used for no other purpose.

(6) Any act to be performed or function to be discharged by the Revenue Commissioners, which is authorised by this section, may be performed or discharged by any of their officers acting under their authority.][1]

Amendments

[1] Inserted by FA07 s9(1)(e). Applies with effect from 2 April 2007.

Cross References

From Section 894A

Section 458 Deductions allowed in ascertaining taxable income and provisions relating to reductions in tax.

Section 872 Use of information relating to other taxes and duties.

To Section 894A

Section 477A Relief for energy efficient works.

895 Returns in relation to foreign accounts

[FA92 s230(1) to (6)]

(1) In this section—

"*appropriate inspector*", in relation to an intermediary or, as may be appropriate, a resident, means—

(a) the inspector who has last given notice in writing to the intermediary or, as the case may be, the resident that he or she is the inspector to whom the intermediary or, as the case may be, the resident is required [to deliver a return, statement, declaration or list by reason of a notice given to the person by the inspector][1],

(b) where there is no such inspector as is referred to in *paragraph (a)*, the inspector to whom it is customary for the intermediary or, as the case may be, the resident to deliver [such return, statement, declaration or list][2]

(c) where there is no such inspector as is referred to in *paragraphs (a)* and *(b)*, [the inspector of returns][3];

"*chargeable period*" has the same meaning as in *section 321(2)*;

"*deposit*" means a sum of money paid to a person on terms under which it will be repaid with or without interest and either on demand or at a time or in circumstances agreed by or on behalf of the person making the payment and the person to whom it is made;

"*foreign account*" means an account in which a deposit is held at a location outside the State;

"*intermediary*" means any person carrying on in the State a trade or business in the ordinary course of the operations of which that person provides a relevant service;

"*relevant person*" means a person who in the normal course of that person's trade or business receives or holds deposits;

"*relevant service*" means the acting in the State as an intermediary in or in connection with the opening of foreign accounts with relevant persons by or on behalf of residents;

"*resident*" means a person resident in the State;

"*specified return date for the chargeable period*", in relation to a chargeable period, means—

[(a) (i) where the chargeable period is a year of assessment for income tax or capital gains tax purposes, being the year of assessment 2000-2001, 31 January 2002, and

(ii) where the chargeable period is a year of assessment for income tax or capital gains tax purposes, being the year of assessment 2001 or any subsequent year of assessment, 31 October in the year of assessment following that year,

and][4]

(b) where the chargeable period is an accounting period of a company, the last day of the period of 9 months commencing on the day immediately following the end of the accounting period;

"*tax reference number*", in relation to a resident, has the meaning assigned to it by *section 885* in relation to a specified person within the meaning of that section.

(2) Every intermediary shall as respects a chargeable period prepare and deliver to the appropriate inspector on or before the specified return date for the chargeable period a return specifying in respect of every resident in respect of whom that intermediary has acted in the chargeable period as an intermediary in the opening of a foreign account—

(a) the full name and permanent address of the resident,

(b) the resident's tax reference number,

(c) the full name and address of the relevant person with whom the foreign account was opened,

(d) the date on which the foreign account was opened, and

(e) the amount of the deposit made in opening the foreign account.

(3) Where a resident requests an intermediary to provide the resident with a relevant service, the resident shall furnish to the intermediary the details which the intermediary is required to include in the return to the appropriate inspector in accordance with *subsection (2)* and the intermediary shall take all reasonable care (including, where necessary, the requesting of documentary evidence) to confirm that the details furnished are true and correct.

(4) (a) Where an intermediary fails—

(i) for any chargeable period to make a return required to be made by the intermediary in accordance with *subsection (2)*,

(ii) to include in such a return for a chargeable period details of any resident to whom the intermediary provided a relevant service in the chargeable period, or

(iii) to take reasonable care to confirm the details of the kind referred to in *subsection (2)* furnished to the intermediary by a resident to whom the intermediary has provided a relevant service in a chargeable period,

the intermediary shall, in respect of each such failure, be liable to a penalty of [€4,000][5].

[(b) Where a resident—

(i) fails to furnish details of the kind referred to in subsection (2) to an intermediary who has provided the resident with a relevant service, or

(ii) furnishes that intermediary with incorrect details of that kind,

the resident shall be liable to a penalty of €4,000.][6]

[...][7]

(6) Where in any chargeable period a resident opens, either directly or indirectly, a foreign account, or causes to be opened a foreign account in relation to which the resident is the beneficial owner of the deposit held in that account, the resident shall, notwithstanding anything to the contrary in [*Part 41A* or *section 1084*][8], be deemed for that chargeable period to be a chargeable person for the purposes of [*Chapter 3* of *Part 41A* and *section 1084*][9], and the return of income (within the meaning of *section 1084*) to be delivered by the resident for that chargeable period shall include the following particulars in relation to the account—

(a) the name and address of the relevant person with whom the account was opened,

(b) the date on which the account was opened,

(c) the amount of the deposit made in opening the account, and

(d) the name and address of the intermediary, if any, who provided a relevant service in relation to the opening of the account.

Amendments

[1] Substituted by FA01 s78(2)(e). Applies as respects the year of assessment 2001 and subsequent years and as respects accounting periods of companies ending on or after 1 April 2001.

[2] Substituted by FA01 s78(2)(f). Applies as respects the year of assessment 2001 and subsequent years and as respects accounting periods of companies ending on or after 1 April 2001.

[3] Substituted by FA12 sched5(1)(l).

[4] Substituted by FA03 s34(1)(c). This section is deemed to have come into operation as on and from 6 April 2001.

[5] Substituted by F(No.2)A08 sched5(part2)(1)(l)(i). The enactments specified in Schedule 5 are amended or repealed to the extent and manner specified in that Schedule and, unless the contrary is stated, shall come into effect after 24 December 2008.

[6] Substituted by F(No.2)A08 sched5(part2)(1)(l)(ii). The enactments specified in Schedule 5 are amended or repealed to the extent and manner specified in that Schedule and, unless the contrary is stated, shall come into effect after 24 December 2008.

[7] Deleted by F(No.2)A08 sched5(part2)(1)(l)(iii). The enactments specified in Schedule 5 are amended or repealed to the extent and manner specified in that Schedule and, unless the contrary is stated, shall come into effect after 24 December 2008.

[8, 9] Substituted by FA12 sched4(part 2)(g).

Revenue Briefings

Tax Briefing

Tax Briefing September 1996 – Issue 23 pg 14 – Returns to be made by Intermediaries in the Financial Services Area

Tax Briefing August 2002 – Issue 49 pg 18 – Returns by Intermediaries

Statements of Practice

Revenue Powers Exercised in Places other than a Revenue Office – SP GEN/1/94 (Revised 02/2006)

Cross References

From Section 895

Section 321 Provisions of general application in relation to the making of allowances and charges.
Section 885 Obligation to show tax reference number on receipts.
Section 950 Interpretation (Part 41).
Section 951 Obligation to make a return.
Section 1084 Surcharge for late returns.

To Section 895

Section 495 Specified individuals.
Section 896 Returns in relation to certain offshore products.
Section 950 Interpretation (Part 41).

896 Returns in relation to certain offshore products

[(1) In this section—

"*appropriate inspector*", in relation to an intermediary, means—

(a) the inspector who has last given notice in writing to the intermediary, that he or she is the inspector to whom the intermediary is required to deliver the return specified in subsection (2),

(b) where there is no such inspector as is referred to in paragraph (*a*), the inspector to whom it is customary for the intermediary to deliver a return or statement of income or profits, or

(c) where there is no such inspector as is referred to in paragraphs (*a*) or (*b*), [the inspector of returns][1];

"*chargeable period*" has the same meaning as in *section 321(2)*;

"*foreign life policy*" means a policy of assurance on the life of a person commenced—

(a) by a branch or agency (carrying on business in a State other than the State) of an assurance company, or

(b) by an assurance company (carrying on business in a State other than the State) other than by its branch or agency carrying on business in the State;

"*intermediary*" means any person carrying on in the State a trade or business in the course of operations of which that person provides relevant facilities;

"*material interest*" shall be construed in accordance with *section 743(2)*;

"*offshore fund*" has the meaning assigned to it by *section 743(1)*;

"*offshore product*" means—

(a) a material interest in an offshore fund, or

(b) a foreign life policy;

"*relevant facilities*" means—

(a) the marketing in the State of offshore products,

(b) the acting in the State as an intermediary in relation to the acquisition or disposal, in whole or in part, of offshore products by or on behalf of persons who are resident or ordinarily resident in the State, or

(c) the provision in the State of facilities for the making of payments from an offshore product to persons who are entitled to the offshore product, whether on the disposal, in whole or in part of the offshore product, or otherwise;

"*specified return date for the chargeable period*", in relation to a chargeable period, has the meaning assigned to it by *section 895(1)*;

"*tax reference number*" in relation to a person has the meaning assigned to it by *section 885* in relation to a specified person within the meaning of that section.

(2) Every intermediary shall as respects a chargeable period prepare and deliver to the appropriate inspector on or before the specified return date for the chargeable period a return specifying in respect of every person in respect of whom that intermediary has acted in the chargeable period as an intermediary—

(a) the full name and permanent address of the person,

(b) the person's tax reference number,

(c) a description of the relevant facilities provided, including a description of the offshore product concerned and the name and address of the person who provided the offshore product, and

(d) details of all payments made (directly or indirectly) by or to the person in respect of the offshore product.

(3) Where an intermediary fails—

(a) for any chargeable period to make a return required to be made by the intermediary in accordance with subsection (2),

(b) to include in such a return for a chargeable period details of any person to whom the intermediary provided relevant facilities in the chargeable period, or

(c) to take reasonable care to confirm the details of the kind referred to in subsection (2) furnished to the intermediary by a person to whom the intermediary has provided relevant facilities in the chargeable period,

the intermediary shall in respect of each such failure be liable to a penalty of [€4,000][2].

[(4) Where a person—

(a) fails to furnish details of the kind referred to in subsection (2) to an intermediary who has provided the person with relevant facilities, or

(b) furnishes that intermediary with incorrect details of that kind,

the person shall be liable to a penalty of €4,000.][3]

(5) Where in any chargeable period a person acquires an offshore product to which *section 730I* or *747C* (inserted by the *Finance Act, 2001*) does not relate, the person shall, notwithstanding anything to the contrary in [*Part 41A* or *section 1084*][4], be deemed for that chargeable period to be a chargeable person for the purposes of [*Chapter 3* of *Part 41A* and *section 1084*][5], and the return of income to be delivered by the person for that chargeable period shall include the following particulars—

(a) the name and address of the offshore fund or, as the case may be, the person who commenced the life policy,

(b) a description, including the cost to the person, of the material interest acquired or, as the case may be, a description of the terms of the life policy including premiums payable, and

(c) the name and address of the person through whom the offshore product was acquired.][6]

Amendments

[1] Substituted by FA12 sched5(1)(l).

[2] Substituted by F(No.2)A08 sched5(part2)(1)(m)(i). The enactments specified in Schedule 5 are amended or repealed to the extent and manner specified in that Schedule and, unless the contrary is stated, shall come into effect after 24 December 2008.

[3] Substituted by F(No.2)A08 sched5(part2)(1)(m)(ii). The enactments specified in Schedule 5 are amended or repealed to the extent and manner specified in that Schedule and, unless the contrary is stated, shall come into effect after 24 December 2008.

[4, 5] Substituted by FA12 sched4(part 2)(g).

[6] Substituted by FA01 s232(1)(d). Applies as respects any chargeable period commencing on or after 15 February 2001.

Revenue Briefings

Tax Briefing

Tax Briefing No 4 1995 – Issue 20 – Offshore Funds

Tax Briefing September 1996 – Issue 23 pg 14 – Returns to be made by Intermediaries in the Financial Services Area

Tax Briefing August 2002 – Issue 49 pg 18 – Returns by Intermediaries

Statements of Practice

Preparation of Accounts for Revenue Purposes – SP IT/02/92

Revenue Powers Exercised in Places other than a Revenue Office – SP GEN/1/94 (Revised 02/2006)

Cross References

From Section 896

Section 321 Provisions of general application in relation to the making of allowances and charges.

Section 730I Returns on acquisition of foreign life policy.

Section 743 Material interest in offshore funds.

Section 747C Return on acquisition of material interest.

Section 885 Obligation to show tax reference number on receipts.

Section 895 Returns in relation to foreign accounts.

Section 950 Interpretation (Part 41).

Section 951 Obligation to make a return.

Section 1084 Surcharge for late returns.

To Section 896

Section 899 Inspector's right to make enquiries.

Schedule 29 Provisions Referred to in Sections 1052, 1053 and 1054

896A Returns in relation to settlements and trustees

[(1) In this section—

"*authorised officer*" means an officer of the Revenue Commissioners authorised by them in writing to exercise the powers conferred on them by this section;

"*settlement*" and "*settlor*" have the same meanings respectively as in section 10.

(2) Where any person, in the course of a trade or profession carried on by that person, has been concerned with the making of a settlement and knows or has reason to believe that, at the time of the making of the settlement—

(a) the settlor was resident or ordinarily resident in the State, and

(b) the trustees of the settlement were not resident in the State, then that person shall, within the period specified in subsection (3), deliver to the appropriate inspector (within the meaning assigned by section 894(1)) a statement specifying—

(i) the name and address of the settlor,

(ii) the names and addresses of the persons who are the trustees of the settlement, and

(iii) the date on which the settlement was made or created.

(3) The statement referred to in subsection (2) shall be delivered—

(a) in a case where the settlement is one made on or after the date of the passing of the *Finance (No. 2) Act 2008*, within 4 months of the date of the making of the settlement, or

(b) in a case where the settlement is one made within the 5 year period prior to the passing of the *Finance (No. 2) Act 2008*, within 6 months of the date of the passing of the Act.

(4) For the purposes of this section trustees of a settlement shall be regarded as not resident in the State unless the general administration of the settlement is ordinarily carried on in the State and the trustees or a majority of each class of trustees are for the time being resident in the State.

(5) An authorised officer may by notice in writing require any person, whom the authorised officer has reason to believe has information relating to a settlement, to furnish to the authorised officer such information within such time as the authorised officer may direct.][1]

Amendments

[1] Inserted by F(No.2)A08 s93.

Cross References

To Section 896A

Schedule 29 Provisions Referred to in Sections 1052, 1053 and 1054

896B Provision of information by Commission for Taxi Regulation

[(1) In this section—

"*the Acts*" has the meaning assigned to it by *section 1078(1)*;

['*Authority*' means the National Transport Authority or, in the Irish language, An tÚdarás Náisiúnta Iompair.][1]

(2) The [Authority][2] shall, at such intervals as are specified by the Revenue Commissioners, supply to the Revenue Commissioners such information held by the [Authority][3] for the purposes of the Taxi Regulation Act 2003 as may be required for the performance of the functions of the Revenue Commissioners under the Acts.][4]

Amendments

[1] Substituted by FA12 sched6(1)(n)(i). Has effect as on and from 31 March 2012.

[2, 3] Substituted by FA12 sched6(1)(n)(ii). Has effect as on and from 31 March 2012.

[4] Inserted by FA10 s152. Has effect as on and from 3 April 2010.

Cross References

From Section 896B

Section 1078 Revenue offences.

896C

[(1) In this section—

'*Acts*' has the meaning assigned to it by *section 1078(1)*;

'*Agency*' means the Child and Family Agency.

(2) The Agency shall, at such intervals as are specified by the Revenue Commissioners, supply to the Revenue Commissioners such information held by the Agency for

the purposes of Part VIIA of the Child Care Act 1991 as may be required for the performance of the functions of the Revenue Commissioners under the Acts.][1]

Amendments

[1] Inserted by CFAA13 s96.

897 Returns of employees' emoluments, etc

[ITA67 s120(1) and (2), s123 and s178; F(MP)A68 s3(2) and Sch PtI; FA82 s4(7) and s8(6); FA97 s11(4)]

(1) (a) In this section, the references to payments made to persons in respect of their employment and to the remuneration of persons in their employment shall be deemed to include references to—

(i) any payments made to employed persons in respect of expenses,

(ii) any payments made on behalf of employed persons and not repaid, and

(iii) any payments made to the employees in a trade or business for services rendered in connection with the trade or business, whether the services were rendered in the course of their employment or not.

(b) The reference in *paragraph (a)(i)* to payments made to employed persons in respect of expenses includes a reference to sums put at the disposal of an employed person and paid away by the employed person.

(2) Every employer, when required to do so by notice from an inspector, shall within the time limited by the notice prepare and deliver to the inspector a return containing—

(a) the names and places of residence of all persons employed by that employer,

(b) particulars of any car (within the meaning of *section 121*) made available to those persons by reason of that employment,

(c) particulars of any preferential loan (within the meaning of *section 122*) made, released or written off by that employer in whole or in part and particulars of any interest released, written off or refunded by that employer in whole or in part and which was payable or paid on such loan,

(d) particulars of any relevant scholarships (within the meaning of *section 193*) in relation to those persons, not being a payment made before the 6th day of April, 1998, in respect of a scholarship (within the meaning of that section) awarded before the 26th day of March, 1997, and

(e) particulars of the payments made to those persons in respect of that employment, except persons who are not employed in any other employment and whose remuneration in the employment for the year does not exceed [€1,905][1].

(3) Where the employer is a body of persons, the secretary of the body or other officer (by whatever name called) performing the duties of secretary shall be deemed to be the employer for the purposes of this section, and any director (within the meaning of *section 116*) of a body corporate (including a company), or person engaged in the management of that body corporate, shall be deemed to be a person employed.

(4) Where an employer is a body corporate (including a company), that body corporate, as well as the secretary or other officer performing the duties of secretary of the body corporate, shall be liable to a penalty for failure to deliver a return under this section.

(5) An employer shall not be liable to any penalty for omitting from any return under *subsection (2)* the name or place of residence of any person employed by the

employer and not employed in any other employment, where it appears to the Revenue Commissioners that such person is entitled to total exemption from tax.

(6) Where for the purposes of a return under this section an employer apportions expenses incurred partly in or in connection with a particular matter and partly in or in connection with other matters—

(a) the return shall contain a statement that the sum included in the return is the result of such an apportionment,

(b) the employer, if required to do so by notice from the inspector, shall prepare and deliver to the inspector within the time limited by the notice a return containing full particulars as to the amount apportioned and the manner in which and the grounds on which the apportionment has been made, and

(c) where the inspector is dissatisfied with any such apportionment of expenses, the inspector may for the purposes of assessment apportion the expenses, but the employer may, on giving notice in writing to the inspector within 21 days after being notified of any such apportionment made by the inspector, appeal against that apportionment to the Appeal Commissioners.

(7) The Appeal Commissioners shall hear and determine an appeal to them under *subsection (6)* as if it were an appeal to them against an assessment to income tax, and the provisions of the Income Tax Acts relating to the rehearing of an appeal and to the statement of a case for the opinion of the High Court on a point of law shall, with the necessary modifications, apply accordingly.

Amendments

[1] Substituted by FA01 sched5.

Revenue Briefings

Tax Briefing

Tax Briefing March 2000 – Issue 39 pg 19 – Topical Questions, Schedule E – Fringe Benefits

Cross References

From Section 897

Section 116 Interpretation (Chapter 3).
Section 121 Benefit of use of car.
Section 122 Preferential loan arrangements.
Section 193 Income from scholarships.

To Section 897

Section 118 Benefits in kind: general charging provision.
Section 1052 Penalties for failure to make certain returns, etc.
Section 1054 Penalties in the case of a secretary of a body of persons.
Schedule 29 Provisions Referred to in Sections 1052, 1053 and 1054

897A Returns by employers in relation to pension products

[(1) In this section—

"*Consolidated Regulations*" means the Income Tax (Employments) (Consolidated) Regulations 2001 (S.I. No. 559 of 2001);

"*emoluments*" means emoluments to which *Chapter 4* of *Part 42* applies;

"*employee*"—

(a) in relation to an employee pension contribution, has the same meaning as it has for the purposes of *Chapter 1* of *Part 30*, and

(b) in relation to a PRSA contribution, has the same meaning as in subsection (1) of *section 787A*;

"employee pension contribution", in relation to a year of assessment and a scheme referred to in either *section 774* or *776*, means an allowable contribution within the meaning of paragraph (*b*) of Regulation 41 (inserted by the Income Tax (Employments) Regulations 2002 (S.I. No. 511 of 2002)) of the Consolidated Regulations;

"*employer*"—

(a) in relation to an employee pension contribution and an employer pension contribution, shall be construed for the purposes of this section in the same way as it is construed for the purposes of *Chapter 1* of *Part 30*, and

(b) in relation to a PRSA employee contribution and a PRSA employer contribution, has the same meaning as in *section 787A(1)*;

"*employer pension contribution*", in relation to a year of assessment and an exempt approved scheme (within the meaning of *section 774*), means any sum paid by an employer in the year of assessment by means of a contribution under the scheme in respect of employees in a trade or undertaking in respect of the profits of which the employer is assessable to tax;

"*PRSA*" shall be construed in accordance with *section 787A(1)*;

"*PRSA contribution*" has the meaning assigned to it by *section 787A(1)*;

"*PRSA employee contribution*", in relation to a year of assessment, means any PRSA contribution made by an employee in the year of assessment which is an allowable contribution within the meaning of paragraph (*c*) of Regulation 41 (inserted by the Income Tax (Employments) Regulations 2002) of the Consolidated Regulations;

"*PRSA employer contribution*", in relation to a year of assessment, means any PRSA contribution referred to in *section 787E(2)* made by an employer to a PRSA in the year of assessment;

"*RAC premium*", in relation to a year of assessment, means any qualifying premium (within the meaning of *section 784*) paid by an individual in the year of assessment which is an allowable contribution within the meaning of paragraph (*d*) (inserted by the Income Tax (Employments) Regulations 2003 (S.I. No. 613 of 2003)) of Regulation 41 of the Consolidated Regulations.

(2) Any person who, in relation to a year of assessment, is required by Regulation 31 of the Consolidated Regulations to send prescribed or approved forms to the Collector-General shall include, in one of those forms, details of the following matters in the manner specified in that form—

(a) the respective numbers of employees in respect of whom that person deducted—

(i) an employee pension contribution,

(ii) a PRSA contribution,

(iii) a RAC premium,

from emoluments due to the employee in the year of assessment in relation to which the return is being made,

(b) the respective numbers of employees in respect of whom that person made—

(i) an employer pension contribution,

(ii) a PRSA employer contribution,

in that year,

(c) the respective total amounts of—

(i) employee pension contributions,

(ii) PRSA contributions,

(iii) RAC premiums,

deducted by the person from emoluments due to the employees of that person in that year,

(d) the respective total amounts of—

(i) employer pension contributions,

(ii) PRSA employer contributions,

made by that person in respect of the employees of that person in that year.

(3) *Sections 1052* and *1054* shall apply to a failure by a person to make the return required by subsection (2) as they apply to a failure to deliver a return referred to in *section 1052*.][1]

Amendments

[1] Inserted by FA04 s86(1). Applies as respects the year of assessment 2005 and subsequent years of assessment.

Revenue Briefings

Tax Briefing

Tax Briefing April 2004 – Issue 55 pg 10 – Finance Act 2004 Information in respect of certain Tax Expenditure

Tax Briefing December 2004 – Issue 58 pg 15 – Pension Products, Employer Obligations

Cross References

From Section 897A

Section 770 Interpretation and supplemental (Chapter 1).

Section 774 Certain approved schemes: exemptions and reliefs.

Section 776 Certain statutory schemes: exemptions and reliefs.

Section 784 Retirement annuities: relief for premiums.

Section 787A Interpretation and supplemental.

Section 787E Extent of relief.

Section 960 Date for payment of income tax other than under self assessment.

Section 983 Interpretation (Chapter 4).

Section 1052 Penalties for failure to make certain returns, etc.

Section 1054 Penalties in the case of a secretary of a body of persons.

897B Returns of information in respect of awards of shares to directors and employees

[(1) In this section—

"*director*", "*employee*" and "*employer*" have the meanings, respectively, given to them by *section 770(1)*;

"*shares*" includes stock and securities within the meaning of *section 135*.

(2) (a) Where in any year of assessment an employer or other person awards shares to a director or employee and income tax under Schedule D or Schedule E may be chargeable on the director or employee in respect of the shares awarded, the employer or other person, as the case may be, shall deliver to the Revenue Commissioners on or before 31 March in the year of assessment following the year in which the award was made, particulars of all such awards.

(b) *Paragraph (a)* shall not apply where the employer or person, as the case may be, is obliged to provide such particulars under any other provision of the Income Tax Acts.][1]

Amendments

[1] Substituted by FA10 s18(1)(a). Applies as on and from 1 January 2010 in respect of shares awarded on or after 1 January 2009.

Cross References

From Section 897B

Section 135 Distributions: supplemental.

Section 770 Interpretation and supplemental (Chapter 1).

To Section 897B

Schedule 29 Provisions Referred to in Sections 1052, 1053 and 1054

898 Returns of copies of rates and production of certain valuations

[FA74 s73(1) to (4); CTA76 s147(1) and (2)]

[(1) In this section '*rating authority*' means—

(a) a county council,

(b) a city council, or

(c) a city and county council;][1]

(2) For the purpose of assessing tax chargeable under Schedule D, the secretary, clerk, or person acting as such, to a rating authority shall, when required by notice from an inspector, transmit to the inspector within such time as may be specified in the notice true copies of the last county rate or municipal rate made by the authority for its rating area or any part of that area.

(3) The Revenue Commissioners shall pay to any such person the expenses of making all such copies, not exceeding the rate of [€2][2] for every 100 ratings.

(4) Every person shall, at the request of any inspector or other officer acting in the execution of the Tax Acts, produce as soon as may be to such inspector or officer, as appropriate, any survey, valuation or record on which the rates for any rating area or part of any such area are assessed, made or collected, or any rate or assessment made under any Act relating to the county rate or municipal rate, which is in that person's custody or possession, and shall permit the inspector or other officer to inspect the same and to take copies of or extracts from any such survey, valuation or record, without any payment.

Amendments

[1] Substituted by LGRA14 sched2(part5).

[2] Substituted by FA01 sched5.

Cross References

To Section 898

Section 898A Format of returns etc.
Section 1092 Disclosure of certain information to rating authorities, etc.
Schedule 29 Provisions Referred to in Sections 1052, 1053 and 1054

898A Format of returns etc

[Where a person is required under this Chapter—

(a) to deliver a return, or

(b) to give or furnish information,

then such return or such information shall, be made, given, or as the case may be, furnished in such form as [...][1] [the Revenue Commissioners may require and in the case of such returns or information referred to in *paragraphs (d)* and *(e)* of *section 888(2)* and in *sections 891*, *892* and *898*, where the Revenue Commissioners so require, in an electronic format approved by them.][2]][3]

Amendments

[1] Deleted by FA07 s123(b).

[2] Substituted by FA07 s123(b).

[3] Inserted by FA02 s134.

Revenue Briefings

Tax Briefing

Tax Briefing May 2006 – Issue 63 pg 12 – EU Savings Directive

Cross References

From Section 898A

Section 888 Returns, etc. by lessors, lessees and agents.
Section 891 Returns of interest paid or credited without deduction of tax.
Section 892 Returns by nominee holders of securities.
Section 898 Returns of copies of rates and production of certain valuations.

CHAPTER 3A

Implementation of Council Directive 2003/48/EC of 3 June 2003 on Taxation of Savings Income in the Form of Interest Payments and Related Matters

898B Interpretation (Chapter 3A)

[(1) In this Chapter and in any regulations made under this Chapter, except where the context otherwise requires—

"*arrangements*" has the meaning assigned to it by *section 898P*;

"*beneficial owner*" has the meaning assigned to it by *section 898C(1)*;

"*building society*" and "*credit union*" have the same meanings, respectively, as in *section 256*;

"*certificate of residence for tax purposes*", in relation to a third country, means a certificate given by the competent authority of that country certifying that an individual is by virtue of the law of that country resident for the purposes of tax in that country, and references to a tax residence certificate shall be construed accordingly;

"*competent authority*" means—

(a) in relation to a Member State, the authority notified to the European Commission by the Member State for the purposes of the Directive, and

(b) in relation to a third country, the competent authority for the purposes of bilateral or multilateral tax conventions or, in the absence of any such authority, the authority competent in that country to issue certificates of residence for tax purposes;

"*deemed interest payment*" has the meaning assigned to it by *section 898E(7)(a)*;

"*deemed UCITS*" has the meaning assigned to it by *section 898D(3)(a)*;

["*the Directive*" means Council Directive 2003/48/EC of 3 June 2003* as amended;][1]

* OJ No. L157, 26.6.2003, p.38

"*electronic means*" includes electrical, digital, magnetic, optical, electromagnetic, biometric and photonic means of transmission of data and other forms of related technology by means of which data is transmitted;

"*interest payment*" has the meaning assigned to it by *section 898E*;

"*Member State*" means a Member State of the European Communities;

"*money*" includes money expressed in a currency other than euro;

"*money debt*" means a debt arising from a transaction for the lending of money and which may be settled by—

(a) the payment of money, or

(b) the transfer of a right to settlement under a debt which may be settled by the payment of money, whether or not the debt creates or evidences a charge on assets and whether or not the debt carries a right to participate in the profits of the debtor;

"*official identity card*" has the meaning assigned to it by *section 898G(1)*;

"*paying agent*" has the meaning assigned to it by *section 898D(1)*;

"*PPS number*", in relation to an individual resident in the State, means that individual's Personal Public Service Number within the meaning of [section 262 of the Social Welfare Consolidation Act 2005;][2]

"*residual entity*" has the meaning assigned to it by *section 898D(1)*;

"*relevant territory*" means—

(a) a Member State other than the State, or

(b) a territory with which arrangements have been made;

"*Revenue officer*" means an officer of the Revenue Commissioners;

"*securities*" includes—

(a) assets which are not chargeable assets for the purposes of capital gains tax by virtue of *section 607*,

(b) stocks, bonds and obligations of any government, municipal corporation, company or other body corporate, whether or not creating or evidencing a charge on assets, and

(c) any other money debts whether or not evidenced in writing,

but does not include shares (within the meaning of the Companies Act 1963) of a company (within the meaning of that Act) or similar body;

"*strip of a security*" shall be construed in accordance with *section 55*;

"*UCITS*" has the meaning assigned to it by *section 898D(2)(c)*;

"*UCITS Directive*" means Council Directive 85/611/EEC of 20 December 1985*;

* OJ No. L375, 31.12.1985, p.3

"*tax year*" means a year of assessment for income tax or capital gains tax, as appropriate;

"*third country*" means a territory other than a Member State;

"*TIN*", in relation to a relevant territory, means a unique identification number allocated by the relevant territory to an individual for the purposes of taxation and, in relation to the State, means an individual's PPS number.

(2) (a) Subject to *paragraph (b)*, for the purposes of this Chapter an individual's residence is to be treated as situated in the country in which the individual has his or her permanent address, and any reference in this Chapter to an individual being resident in a country shall be construed accordingly.

(b) *Paragraph (a)* shall not apply for the purposes of—

(i) the definition of "*certificate of residence for tax purposes*" in subsection (1) and any use of that definition or of the term tax residence certificate in this Chapter, and

(ii) *subsection (3)* and any reference in this Chapter to a person being a resident of a territory for tax purposes.

(3) For the purposes of this Chapter, a person is to be regarded as being a resident of a territory for tax purposes if the person is by virtue of the law of that territory resident for the purposes of tax in that territory.

(4) A word or expression that is used in this Chapter and is also used in the Directive has, unless the contrary intention appears, the meaning in this Chapter that it has in the Directive.][3]

Amendments

[1] Substituted by FA05 s144(1)(a). This section applies as on and from 25 March 2005.

[2] Substituted by FA07 sched4(1)(ae). Shall have effect as on and from 2 April 2007.

[3] Inserted by FA04 sched4.

Cross References

From Section 898B

Section 55 Taxation of strips of securities.
Section 256 Interpretation (Chapter 4).
Section 607 Government and certain other securities.
Section 898C Beneficial owner.
Section 898D Paying agent and residual entity.
Section 898E Interest payment.
Section 898G Obligations of paying agents in other contractual relations entered into.
Section 898P Arrangements with third countries and dependent and associated territories of Member States.

898C Beneficial owner

[(1) In this Chapter "*beneficial owner*", in relation to an interest payment, means an individual who receives the interest payment or an individual for whom the interest payment is secured, but does not include an individual to whom subsection (2) applies.

(2) This subsection applies to an individual (in this section referred to as the "*intermediary*") who provides evidence to the person making an interest payment to, or securing an interest payment for, the intermediary that, in relation to the interest payment, the intermediary—

(a) is a paying agent,

(b) acts on behalf of a person (not being an individual) or an undertaking referred to in *section 898D(2)*,

(c) acts on behalf of a residual entity, where both of the conditions set out in subsection (3) are met, or

(d) acts on behalf of another individual (in this section referred to as the "*other individual*") who receives the interest payment or for whom the interest payment is secured, where the condition set out in subsection (4) is met in relation to the other individual.

(3) The conditions of this subsection are that—

(a) the intermediary provides the name and address of the residual entity to the person making or securing the interest payment, and

(b) the person making the interest payment makes a return to the Revenue Commissioners within 3 months of the end of the tax year in which the information referred to in paragraph (*a*) is provided to the person of each name and address so provided in that tax year.

(4) The condition of this subsection is that the intermediary provides the person from whom he or she receives an interest payment with the identity of the other individual established in accordance with *section 898F* or *898G*, as appropriate.

(5) If a paying agent has information to the effect, or information indicating, that an individual is not the beneficial owner of an interest payment and paragraph (*a*), (*b*) or (*c*) of subsection (2) does not apply to that individual, the paying agent

shall take reasonable steps to identify the beneficial owner in accordance with the provisions of *section 898F* or *898G*, as appropriate.

(6) A paying agent shall treat an individual as the beneficial owner in relation to an interest payment received by, or secured for, the individual if the paying agent is otherwise unable to identify a beneficial owner.][1]

Amendments

[1] Inserted by FA04 sched4.

Cross References

From Section 898C

Section 898D Paying agent and residual entity.

Section 898F Obligations of paying agents where contractual relations entered into before 1 January 2004.

Section 898G Obligations of paying agents in other contractual relations entered into.

To Section 898C

Section 898B Interpretation (Chapter 3A).

898D Paying agent and residual entity

[(1) In this Chapter—

"*paying agent*", in relation to any interest payment, means a person who in the course of the person's business or profession carried on in the State makes the interest payment to, or secures the interest payment for, the immediate benefit of a beneficial owner and includes, in particular, a residual entity but only as respects a deemed interest payment, a Minister of the Government and any agency or body established by statute;

"*residual entity*", in relation to any interest payment, means a person or undertaking established in the State or in a relevant territory to which the interest payment is made for the benefit of a beneficial owner or for which the interest payment is secured for the benefit of a beneficial owner, unless the person making the payment is satisfied on the basis of evidence produced by the person or the undertaking that subsection (2) applies to that person or that undertaking.

(2) This subsection applies to a person or undertaking which—

(a) is a legal person (not being an individual) other than the legal persons referred to in Article 4.5 of the Directive,

(b) is a person within the charge to corporation tax or within the charge to a tax in a relevant territory which corresponds to corporation tax in the State, or

(c) is an undertaking for collective investment in transferable securities (in this Chapter referred to as a "*UCITS*") recognised as such under the UCITS Directive or an equivalent undertaking for collective investment established in a relevant territory other than a Member State.

(3) (a) A residual entity shall be entitled to elect for the purposes of this Chapter to be treated in the same manner as a UCITS recognised as such under the UCITS Directive is treated (in this Chapter referred to as a "*deemed UCITS*").

(b) Where this election is exercised a reference in this Chapter to a UCITS recognised as such under the UCITS Directive includes a reference to a residual entity which has elected to be treated in the same manner as such a UCITS.

(c) An election under this subsection shall not be valid unless the person or undertaking concerned presents a certificate issued to it by the competent authority of the relevant territory in which it is resident for tax purposes to the person making an interest payment to it, or securing an interest payment for it, certifying that the election provided for by this subsection has been made by the person or undertaking named on the certificate.

(d) As respects a person or undertaking to which this subsection applies who is resident in the State for tax purposes, the Revenue Commissioners shall make regulations—

(i) prescribing the form in which the election provided for by this subsection is to be made,

(ii) providing for the issue of a certificate to a person or undertaking exercising the election provided for by this subsection,

(iii) prescribing the details to be included on any such certificate,

(iv) requiring a residual entity making such an election to provide them with such information as respects its constitution, legal status, ownership, investments, income and customers as may be set out in such regulations, and

(v) providing for such incidental matters as may be necessary for the purposes of the preceding provisions of this paragraph.][1]

Amendments

[1] Inserted by FA04 sched4.

Cross References

To Section 898D

Section 898B Interpretation (Chapter 3A).
Section 898C Beneficial owner.
Section 898E Interest payment.

898E Interest payment

[(1) Subject to *section 898K*, in this Chapter "*interest payment*" means—

(a) any payment of interest of money, whether yearly or otherwise, including any bonus or interest payable under an instalment savings scheme (within the meaning of section 53 of the Finance Act 1970) and any accumulated interest payable in respect of any savings certificate referred to in *section 42*;

(b) any dividend or other distribution made in respect of shares in a building society;

(c) any dividend or other distribution made in respect of shares in a credit union;

(d) the excess of any amount received in respect of the redemption of a security, a unit of a security or a strip of a security over the amount paid for the security, unit or strip on issue;

(e) any prize attaching to a security, including a prize in respect of a prize bond issued under section 22 of the Finance (Miscellaneous Provisions) Act 1956;

(f) any amount realised on the sale, refund or redemption of a security, unit of a security, or a strip of a security, which is referable to accrued or capitalised interest, whether or not any such accrued or capitalised interest is separately identified;

(g) subject to *subsections (2), (5)* and *(6)*, income distributed by—

(i) a UCITS authorised in accordance with the UCITS Directive or an equivalent undertaking for collective investment established in a relevant territory other than a Member State,

(ii) a deemed UCITS, or

(iii) an undertaking for collective investment established in a territory other than a relevant territory,

which income derives from an interest payment within the meaning of any of the preceding paragraphs of this subsection and which income is received by any of these undertakings either directly or indirectly from a residual entity;

(h) subject to *subsections (2)* to *(6)*, income realised on the sale, refund or redemption of shares or units in—

(i) a UCITS authorised in accordance with the UCITS Directive or an equivalent undertaking for collective investment established in a relevant territory other than a Member State,

(ii) a deemed UCITS, or

(iii) an undertaking for collective investment established in a territory other than a relevant territory.

(2) Where a paying agent has no information with which to establish the proportion of any income referred to in *paragraphs (g)* and *(h)* of *subsection (1)* which is income derived from an interest payment that *paragraphs (a)* to *(f)* of that subsection relates, then the paying agent is to treat the full amount of any such income as an "*interest payment*" within the meaning of this section.

(3) (a) Income referred to in *paragraph (h)* of *subsection (1)* is only to be regarded as an interest payment where the UCITS or equivalent undertaking for collective investment established in a relevant territory other than a Member State, deemed UCITS or undertaking concerned has invested directly, or by way of the acquisition of shares or units in another such UCITS or equivalent undertaking, deemed UCITS or undertaking, more than 40 per cent of its assets in investments which produce or have the potential to produce interest or other income such as is referred to in *paragraphs (a)* to *(f)* of *subsection (1)*; but where a paying agent has no information with which to establish the percentage of such assets so invested, then for the purposes of this Chapter more than 40 per cent of such assets are to be treated as so invested.

(b) As on and from 1 January 2011, *paragraph (a)* shall apply with the substitution of "25 per cent" for "40 per cent" in both places in which it occurs.

(4) Where a paying agent is unable to determine the amount of income realised by a beneficial owner from the sale, refund or redemption of any shares or units referred to in *paragraph (h)* of *subsection (1)*, then the full proceeds from the sale, refund or redemption of the shares or units shall be treated as the amount of income realised by the beneficial owner for the purposes of that paragraph.

(5) Income referred to in *paragraphs (g)* and *(h)* of subsection (1) shall not be regarded as an interest payment in the case of such income from a UCITS (being an undertaking for collective investment in transferable securities within the meaning of the European Communities (Undertakings for Collective Investment in Transferable Securities) Regulations 1989 (S.I. No. 78 of 1989)) or a deemed

UCITS (being a person resident in the State) where the UCITS or deemed UCITS investment in assets referred to in *paragraphs (a)* to *(e)* of *subsection (1)* do not exceed 15 per cent of its total assets.

(6) (a) Income referred to in *paragraphs (g)* and *(h)* of *subsection (1)* shall not be regarded as an interest payment in the case of income from a UCITS authorised in accordance with the UCITS Directive or a deemed UCITS established in a Member State other than the State where the Member State concerned has exercised the option in paragraph 6 of Article 6 of the Directive to derogate from *subparagraphs (c)* and *(d)* of *paragraph 1* of that Article.

(b) Income referred to in *paragraphs (g)* and *(h)* of *subsection (1)* shall not be regarded as an interest payment in the case of income from an undertaking for collective investment which is equivalent to a UCITS or from a deemed UCITS established in a relevant territory not being a Member State where the relevant territory concerned has exercised, under arrangements, an option equivalent to the option in *paragraph 6* of Article 6 of the Directive to derogate from a provision equivalent to *subparagraphs (c)* and *(d)* of paragraph 1 of that Article.

(7) (a) An interest payment to a residual entity which has not elected to be treated as a UCITS in accordance with *section 898D(3)* shall, at the time the interest payment is received by the residual entity, be treated for the purposes of this Chapter as an interest payment (in this Chapter referred to as a "*deemed interest payment*") made by the residual entity at that time.

(b) This subsection shall not apply to—

(i) a residual entity resident in the State where the residual entity's investment in assets referred to in *subsection (1)* does not exceed 15 per cent of the total investments of the residual entity, and

(ii) (I) a residual entity established in a Member State other than the State where the Member State concerned has exercised the option in *paragraph 6* of Article 6 of the Directive to derogate from *paragraph 4* of that Article, or

(II) a residual entity established in a relevant territory not being a Member State where the relevant territory concerned has exercised, under arrangements, an option equivalent to the option in *paragraph 6* of Article 6 of the Directive to derogate from a provision equivalent to *paragraph 4* of that Article.

(8) For the purposes of this Chapter—

(a) the percentages referred to in *subsections (3)*, *(5)* and *(7)(b)(i)* shall be determined by reference to the most recent investment policy of the person or undertaking concerned as laid down in the instrument of incorporation of the person or the rules of the undertaking,

(b) in the absence of the information referred to in *paragraph (a)* or where a paying agent is in possession of information to suggest that the investment policy is not being implemented, the percentages shall be determined by the actual composition of the assets of the undertaking or the person.

(9) For the purposes of this Chapter any amount credited as interest shall be treated as a payment of interest, and references in this Chapter to interest being paid shall be construed accordingly.

(10) For the purposes of this Chapter any reference in this Chapter to the amount of an interest payment in a case where the interest payment is subject to deduction of tax shall be construed as a reference to the amount which would be the amount of that payment if no tax were to be deducted from that payment.

(11) For the purposes of this Chapter penalty charges for the late payment of any interest or other payment referred to in *paragraphs (a)* to *(f)* of *subsection (1)* shall not be regarded as an "*interest payment*" within the meaning of that subsection.][1]

Amendments

[1] Inserted by FA04 sched4.

Cross References

From Section 898E

Section 42 Exemption of interest on savings certificates.

Section 898D Paying agent and residual entity.

Section 898K Special arrangements for certain securities.

To Section 898E

Section 898B Interpretation (Chapter 3A).

Section 898H Returns of interest payments made to or secured for beneficial owners.

Section 898K Special arrangements for certain securities.

898F Obligations of paying agents where contractual relations entered into before 1 January 2004

[(1) This section applies for the purposes of enabling a paying agent to establish the identity and residence of an individual to whom the agent may make an interest payment or for whom the agent may secure an interest payment where the agent entered into contractual relations with the individual before 1 January 2004.

(2) A paying agent shall as respects contractual relations entered into before 1 January 2004 between the paying agent and an individual establish—

(a) the identity of each such individual consisting of his or her name and address in accordance with the procedure set out in *subsection (3)*, and

(b) the residence of each such individual in accordance with the procedure set out in *subsection (4)*.

(3) A paying agent shall establish the name and address of an individual using all relevant information at its disposal, in particular information it acquires by virtue of section 32 of the Criminal Justice Act 1994.

(4) A paying agent shall establish the residence of an individual using all relevant information at its disposal, in particular information it acquires by virtue of section 32 of the Criminal Justice Act 1994.

[(5) (a) A paying agent who establishes the identity and residence of an individual in accordance with this section shall retain or, in a case where the relevant documentation is held by another person, have access to—

(i) a copy of all materials used to identify the individual, and

(ii) a copy of all materials used to establish the residence of the individual,

for a period of at least 5 years after the relationship between the paying agent and the individual has ended.

(b) As respects any interest payment made to an individual referred to in *paragraph (a)* a paying agent shall retain the original documents or copies admissible in legal proceedings relating to the making of any interest payment to or securing of any interest payment for the individual where the payment is made or secured on or after 1 July 2005, for a period of at least 5 years after the interest payment was made or secured.][1]

(6) (a) Where a paying agent has established the identity and residence of an individual in accordance with the procedures set out in this section, the paying agent shall continue to treat that individual as so identified and so resident until such time as the paying agent is in possession, or aware, of information which can reasonably be taken to indicate that the individual has been incorrectly identified or is not so resident or has changed his or her residence.

(b) Where in accordance with *paragraph (a)* a paying agent becomes aware or has reason to believe that the individual's circumstances have changed or have been incorrectly established, the paying agent shall make all reasonable efforts to establish the individual's correct identity and residence in accordance with the procedures set out in *subsection (4)* or *(5)* of section *898G*, as appropriate.

(7) Where an individual informs a paying agent that his or her circumstances as established in accordance with the procedure set out in this section have changed, the paying agent shall establish his or her new circumstances in accordance with the procedure set out in *subsection (4)* or *(5)* of *898G*, as appropriate.][2]

Amendments

[1] Substituted by FA06 s124(1)(a). This section applies as on and from 31 March 2006.

[2] Inserted by FA04 sched4.

Cross References

From Section 898F

Section 898G Obligations of paying agents in other contractual relations entered into.

To Section 898F

Section 898C Beneficial owner.
Section 898H Returns of interest payments made to or secured for beneficial owners.
Section 898N Audit.
Section 898O Penalty for failure to make returns, etc.

898G Obligations of paying agents in other contractual relations entered into

[(1) In this section "*official identity card*", in relation to an individual resident in the State, means an official document issued by the Revenue Commissioners or the Minister for Social and Family Affairs which document contains the individual's name, address and PPS number and includes any other official document which may be specified in regulations made by the Revenue Commissioners.

(2) This section applies for the purposes of enabling a paying agent to establish the identity and residence of an individual to whom the agent may make an interest payment or for whom the agent may secure an interest payment where—

(a) the agent enters into contractual relations with the individual on or after 1 January 2004, or

(b) in the absence of contractual relations, the agent carries out a transaction on behalf of the individual on or after 1 January 2004,

but where, on the basis of documentary proof of identity and residence presented by the individual which is acceptable for the purposes of section 32 of the Criminal Justice Act 1994, the paying agent is satisfied that the individual is resident in the State this section shall not apply to that individual as respects contractual relations entered into or transactions carried out before 1 June 2004, but where the paying agent comes into possession of, or becomes aware of, information which can reasonably be taken to indicate that the individual is not, or may not be, so resident the paying agent shall make all reasonable efforts to determine the individual's correct identity and residence in accordance with the procedures set out in *subsections (4)* and *(5)*.

(3) A paying agent shall as respects contractual relations entered into, or as respects a transaction carried out in the absence of contractual relations, on or after 1 January 2004 between the paying agent and an individual establish—

(a) the identity of each such individual consisting of his or her—

(i) name,

(ii) address, and

(iii) in a case where the [territory][1] in which the individual is resident for tax purposes allocates a TIN, the individual's TIN,

in accordance with the procedure set out in *subsection (4)*, and

(b) the residence of each such individual in accordance with the procedure set out in *subsection (5)*.

(4) (a) A paying agent shall establish the name, address and, where relevant, the TIN of an individual by reference to the details of the person's name, address and TIN as set out in the person's passport or official identity card as presented by the individual.

(b) If an individual's address does not appear on his or her passport or official identity card the paying agent shall establish the individual's address on the basis of any other documentary proof of identity presented by the individual which is acceptable for the purposes of section 32 of the Criminal Justice Act 1994.

(c) If there is no TIN or if an individual's TIN does not appear on his or her passport, official identity card or any other documentary proof of identity referred to in *paragraph (b)* as presented by the individual, such as the individual's certificate of residence for tax purposes, the individual's identity as established in accordance with either or both *paragraphs (a)* and *(b)* shall be supplemented by the paying agent establishing the individual's date of birth and place of birth by reference to his or her passport or official identity card.

(5) A paying agent shall establish the residence of an individual—

(a) in the case of an individual who presents a passport or official identity card issued by a relevant territory and who at the time of such presentation claims to be resident in a third country, by reference to a tax residence certificate issued by the competent authority of the third country in which the individual claims to be so resident, and in the absence of such a certificate the individual is to be regarded as resident in the relevant territory which issued the passport or other official identity card presented,

(b) in any other case, by reference to the address of the individual as set out—

(i) in his or her passport,

(ii) in his or her official identity card, or

(iii) if the paying agent has reason to believe that the person's residence is other than that shown on his or her passport or official identity card, in any other documentary proof of identity presented by the individual which is acceptable for the purposes of section 32 of the Criminal Justice Act 1994.

[(6) (a) A paying agent who establishes the identity and residence of an individual in accordance with this section shall retain or, in a case where the relevant documentation is held by another person, have access to—

(i) a copy of all materials used to identify the individual, and

(ii) a copy of all materials used to establish the residence of the individual,

for a period of at least 5 years after the relationship between the paying agent and the individual has ended or, in the case of a transaction carried out in the absence of contractual relations, for a period of at least 5 years after the interest payment was made or secured.

(b) As regards any interest payment made to an individual referred to in *paragraph (a)* a paying agent shall retain the original documents or copies admissible in legal proceedings relating to the making of any interest payment to or securing of any interest payment for the individual where the payment is made or secured on or after 1 July 2005, for a period of at least 5 years after the interest payment was made or secured.][2]

(7) The Revenue Commissioners may make regulations governing the application of this section in a case where contractual relations are entered into, or any other transaction to which this section applies takes place, by postal, telephonic or electronic means. Any such regulations may provide for the use of notarised or certified copies of the documents referred to in this section.

(8) (a) Where a paying agent has established the identity and residence of an individual in accordance with the procedure set out in this section, the paying agent shall continue to treat that individual as so identified and so resident until such time as the paying agent is in possession, or aware, of information which can reasonably be taken to indicate that the individual has been incorrectly identified or is not so resident or has changed his or her residence.

(b) Where in accordance with *paragraph (a)* a paying agent becomes aware or has reason to believe that the individual's circumstances have changed or have been incorrectly established, the paying agent shall make all reasonable efforts to determine the individual's correct identity and residence in accordance with the procedures set out in this section.

(9) Where an individual informs a paying agent that his or her circumstances as established in accordance with the procedures set out in this section have changed, the paying agent shall establish his or her new circumstances in accordance with the procedure set out in *subsection (4)* or *(5)*, as appropriate.][3]

Amendments

[1] Substituted by FA05 s144(1)(c). This section applies as on and from 25 March 2005.

[2] Substituted by FA06 s124(1)(b). This section applies as on and from 31 March 2006.

[3] Inserted by FA04 sched4.

Cross References

To Section 898G

Section 898B Interpretation (Chapter 3A).
Section 898C Beneficial owner.
Section 898F Obligations of paying agents where contractual relations entered into before 1 January 2004.
Section 898H Returns of interest payments made to or secured for beneficial owners.
Section 898N Audit.
Section 898O Penalty for failure to make returns, etc.

898H Returns of interest payments made to or secured for beneficial owners

[(1) [Every paying agent shall, as respects an interest payment made for the immediate benefit of a beneficial owner on or after 1 July 2005 who is resident in a relevant territory, make and deliver to the Revenue Commissioners within 3 months of the end of a tax year (being the tax year 2005 and subsequent years) a return of all interest payments, as respects the tax year 2005, so made during the period 1 July 2005 to 31 December 2005 by that paying agent and, as respects any other tax year, so made by that paying agent during that year consisting of—][1]

(a) the details relating to the paying agent set out in subsection (2),

(b) the details relating to each beneficial owner to which an interest payment is so made as set out in subsection (3), and

(c) the details relating to the total amount of interest payments so made as set out in subsection (4).

(2) The details relating to the paying agent are—

(a) name,

(b) address (in the case of a company, the address of the company's registered office, if different), and

(c) tax reference number and for this purpose "*tax reference number*" has the meaning assigned to it by *section 885* in relation to a specified person within the meaning of that section.

(3) The details relating to a beneficial owner are—

(a) in a case where contractual relations were entered into before 1 January 2004—

(i) name,

(ii) address, and

(iii) residence (being the individual's country of residence),

as established in accordance with the procedure set out in *section 898F*, and

(b) in a case where contractual relations were entered into on or after 1 January 2004 or, as respects a transaction carried out on or after 1 January 2004, where there are no contractual relations—

(i) name,

(ii) address,

(iii) residence (being the individual's country of residence), and

(iv) (I) TIN, or

(II) if there is no TIN or the TIN has not been made available to the paying agent, date and place of birth,

as established in accordance with the procedure set out in *section 898G*.

(4) The details relating to an interest payment are—

(a) (i) the account number associated with the interest payment, or

(ii) in a case where there is no account number associated with the interest payment, information capable of identifying the asset giving rise to the interest payment,

[(b) (i) (I) the total amount of interest payments which are within the meaning of *paragraphs (a)*, *(b)*, *(c)*, *(d)*, *(e)* and *(g)* of *subsection (1)* of *section 898E*, and

(II) the total amount of interest payments which are within the meaning of *paragraphs (f)* and *(h)* of that subsection,

or

(ii) in a case where the paying agent is a residual entity—

(I) the total amount of deemed interest payments which are within the meaning of *paragraphs (a)*, *(b)*, *(c)*, *(d)*, *(e)* and *(g)* of *subsection (1)* of *section 898E*, and

(II) the total amount of deemed interest payments which are within the meaning of *paragraphs (f)* and *(h)* of that subsection.][2]

(5) *Sections 891* and *891A* shall not apply to an interest payment which has been included in a return made under this section.][3]

Amendments

[1] Substituted by FA05 s144(1)(d)(i). This section applies as on and from 25 March 2005.

[2] Substituted by FA05 s144(1)(d)(ii). This section applies as on and from 25 March 2005.

[3] Inserted by FA04 sched4. With effect from 1 July 2005 per S.I. 286 of 2005.

Cross References

From Section 898H

Section 885 Obligation to show tax reference number on receipts.
Section 891 Returns of interest paid or credited without deduction of tax.
Section 891A Returns of interest paid to non-residents.
Section 898E Interest payment.
Section 898F Obligations of paying agents where contractual relations entered into before 1 January 2004.
Section 898G Obligations of paying agents in other contractual relations entered into.

To Section 898H

Section 898J Exchange of information between Member States.
Section 898R Commencement (Chapter 3A).

898I Returns of interest payments to residual entities

[Every person who in the course of the person's business or profession carried on in the State makes an interest payment to, or secures an interest payment for, a residual entity in a tax year which residual entity is established in a relevant territory, shall make and deliver to the Revenue Commissioners within 3 months of the end of the tax year (being the tax year 2005 and subsequent tax years) a return consisting of—

(a) the name of the residual entity,

(b) the address of the residual entity, and

[(c) the total amount of the interest payments so made or so secured by it in the tax year (and for this purpose the tax year 2005 shall be deemed to begin on 1 July 2005 and end on 31 December 2005).][1]][2]

Amendments

[1] Substituted by FA05 s144(1)(e). This section applies as on and from 25 March 2005.

[2] Inserted by FA04 sched4. With effect from 1 July 2005 per S.I. 286 of 2005.

Cross References

To Section 898I

Section 898J Exchange of information between Member States.
Section 898R Commencement (Chapter 3A).

898J Exchange of information between Member States

[(1) The Revenue Commissioners are authorised to communicate information contained in a return made under *section 898H* in relation to a beneficial owner of any interest payment to the competent authority of the relevant territory of residence of the beneficial owner.

(2) The Revenue Commissioners are authorised to communicate information contained in a return made under *section 898I* in relation to a residual entity to the competent authority of the relevant territory in which the residual entity is resident.

(3) The Revenue Commissioners are to communicate the information referred to in *subsections (1)* and *(2)* to the relevant competent authority within 6 months of the end of the tax year in which an interest payment is made.][1]

Amendments

[1] Inserted by FA04 sched4. With effect from 1 July 2005 per S.I. 286 of 2005.

Cross References

From Section 898J

Section 898H Returns of interest payments made to or secured for beneficial owners.
Section 898I Returns of interest payments to residual entities.

To Section 898J

Section 898R Commencement (Chapter 3A).

898K Special arrangements for certain securities

[(1) Subject to *subsection (2)*, *section 898E* shall not apply to a security (being a security issued under a programme)—

(a) which issued before 1 March 2001, or

(b) where the issuing prospectus was approved before that date by the competent authorities of a Member State (within the meaning of Council Directive 80/390/EEC*) or by the responsible authorities of a third country.

* OJ No. L100, 17.4.1980, p.1

(2) *Subsection (1)* shall cease to apply—

(a) in the case of a security issued under a programme promoted by any Government or an entity referred to in the Annex to the Directive, to all securities issued under that programme if on or after 1 March 2002 any further security is issued under that programme, and

(b) in any other case, to any security issued under that programme on or after 1 March 2002.

[(3) This section shall cease to apply as on and from 31 December 2011.][1]

[...][2]][3]

Amendments

[1] Substituted by FA12 s123(a). Deemed to have come into force and takes effect on and from 1 January 2012.

[2] Deleted by FA12 s123(b).Deemed to have come into force and takes effect on and from 1 January 2012.

[3] Inserted by FA04 sched4.

Cross References

From Section 898K

Section 898E Interest payment.

To Section 898K

Section 898E Interest payment.

898L Certificate for the purposes of Article 13.2 of the Directive

[(1) Where an individual resident in the State for tax purposes makes an application to the Revenue Commissioners containing such information in relation to—

(a) the individual,

(b) the individual's contractual relations with a paying agent, and

(c) the identification of the asset which may give rise to an interest payment to be paid or secured by the paying agent,

as the Revenue Commissioners may require, the Revenue Commissioners shall, within 2 months of the receipt of the application, issue a certificate to the applicant containing details of—

(i) the name, address and PPS number of the applicant,

(ii) the name and address of the paying agent identified by the applicant, and

(iii) the account number or other information supplied by the applicant to identify the asset which may give rise to an interest payment to be paid or secured by the paying agent.

(2) A certificate issued in accordance with *subsection (1)* shall be valid—

(a) for a period of 3 years from its date of issue, or

(b) until such time as any of the information contained in the certificate becomes inaccurate.][1]

Amendments

[1] Inserted by FA04 sched4.

Cross References

To Section 898L

Section 898P Arrangements with third countries and dependent and associated territories of Member States.

Section 898R Commencement (Chapter 3A).

898M Credit for withholding tax

[(1) Subject to *subsections (3)* and *(4)*, where tax has been deducted from an interest payment in a relevant territory under provisions applicable in such territory in accordance with the Directive or the arrangements and—

(a) the interest payment is, or but for an exemption or relief from tax would be, taken into account in computing the total income of an individual for the tax year in which the tax was deducted for the purposes of income tax, and

(b) the individual is resident in the State for that tax year,

then—

(i) the individual may claim a credit for the tax deducted from the payment against any income tax chargeable on that individual for that year and, in determining the amount of tax payable on the individual's total income for that year, credit shall be given for the tax deducted from the interest payment and the amount of the credit shall be the amount of tax deducted from the interest payment, and

(ii) where—

(I) the tax deducted from the interest payment exceeds any such income tax chargeable, the excess shall be repaid, or

(II) no such income tax is chargeable, an amount equal to the tax deducted from the interest payment shall be repaid to the individual.][1]

[(2) Subject to *subsections (3)* and *(4)*, where tax has been deducted from an interest payment in a relevant territory under provisions applicable in such territory in accordance with the Directive or the arrangements and—

(a) the interest payment is, or but for an exemption or relief from tax would be, taken into account in computing the chargeable gains of an individual for the tax year in which the tax was deducted for the purposes of the Capital Gains Tax Acts, and

(b) the individual is resident in the State for that tax year,

then—

(i) the individual may claim a credit for the tax deducted from the payment against the capital gains tax chargeable on that individual for that year and, in determining the amount of tax payable on the chargeable gains of that individual for that year, credit shall be given for the tax deducted from the interest payment and the amount of the credit shall be the amount of tax deducted from the interest payment, and

(ii) where—

(I) the tax deducted exceeds any such capital gains tax, the excess shall be repaid to the individual, or

(II) no such capital gains tax is chargeable, an amount equal to the tax deducted shall be repaid to the individual.][2]

[(3) (a) The credit referred to in *subsection (1)* or *(2)*, as the case may be, shall apply only after the application of any other credit to which the individual may be entitled under any arrangement made under *section 826* in respect of any tax deducted from the payment under provisions other than those referred to in *subsection (1)* or *(2)*.

(b) *Subsection (1)* or *(2)* shall not apply where—

(i) the individual referred to in the subsection concerned has obtained relief under the law of a territory outside the State in respect of tax that has been deducted from an interest payment in a relevant territory under provisions applicable in such territory in accordance with the Directive or the arrangements, and

(ii) the individual was resident in that territory or was treated as being resident in that territory under arrangements made under *section 826* for the year of assessment in which the tax was deducted.][3]

(4) The credit or repayment referred to in *subsection (1)* or *(2)*, as the case may be, shall not be given—

(a) unless the individual claiming the credit or repayment—

(i) makes a claim in that behalf to the Revenue Commissioners,

(ii) makes a return in the prescribed form of the individual's total income or chargeable gains, as the case may be, for the tax year in which the interest payment is, or but for an exemption from tax would be, taken into account for the purposes of income tax or capital gains tax, as the case may be, and

(iii) provides to the Revenue Commissioners the statement referred to in *subsection (5)*, and

(b) the Revenue Commissioners are satisfied that tax has been deducted from the interest payment concerned under provisions applicable in the territory concerned in accordance with the Directive or the arrangements.

(5) The statement referred to in *subsection (4)* is a statement in writing given to the individual by the person who deducted the tax certifying—

(a) the name and address of the person deducting the tax,

(b) the name and address of the beneficial owner of the interest payment,

(c) the date of the interest payment,

(d) the amount of the interest payment, and

(e) the amount of tax deducted from the interest payment.][4]

Amendments

[1, 2, 3] Substituted by FA05 s144(1)(f). This section applies as on and from 25 March 2005.

[4] Inserted by FA04 sched4. With effect from 1 July 2005 per S.I. 286 of 2005.

Cross References

From Section 898M

Section 826 Agreements for relief from double taxation.

To Section 898M

Section 898P Arrangements with third countries and dependent and associated territories of Member States.

Section 898R Commencement (Chapter 3A).

898N Audit

[(1) In this section—

"*associated company*", in relation to a paying agent, means a company which is itself a paying agent and which is the paying agent's associated company within the meaning of *section 432*;

"*authorised officer*" means an officer of the Revenue Commissioners authorised by them in writing to exercise the powers conferred by this section;

"*books, records or other documents*" includes—

(a) any records used in the business of a paying agent or used in the transfer department of a paying agent acting as a registrar of securities, whether—

(i) comprised in bound volumes, loose-leaf binders or other loose-leaf filing system, loose leaf ledger sheets, pages, folios or cards, or

(ii) kept on microfilm, magnetic tape or in any non-legible form (by the use of electronics or otherwise) which is capable of being reproduced in a legible form,

(b) every electronic or other automated means, if any, by which any such thing in non-legible form is so capable of being reproduced,

(c) documents in manuscript, documents which are typed, printed, stencilled or created by any other mechanical or partly mechanical process in use from time to time and documents which are produced by any photographic or photostatic process,

(d) correspondence and records of other communications (including e-mails) between a paying agent and a beneficial owner or between a paying agent and a residual entity, and

(e) the materials and documents referred to in *sections 898F(5)* and *898G(6).*

(2) A Revenue officer may by notice in writing require a paying agent, or a person who appears to that officer to be a paying agent, to furnish him or her within such time, not being less than 14 days, as may be provided by the notice, with such information (including copies of any relevant books, records or other documents) as he or she may reasonably require for the purposes of determining whether information contained in a [return][1] under this Chapter by that paying agent was correct and complete.

(3) Any person who has been required by a notice under *subsection (2)* to furnish information (including copies of any relevant books, records or other documents) and that person fails to comply with the notice shall be liable to a penalty of [€3,000][2].

(4) An authorised officer may at all reasonable times enter any premises or place of business of a paying agent or a person who appears to that officer to be a paying agent for the purposes of determining whether information—

(a) included in a [return][3] under this Chapter by that paying agent was correct and complete, or

(b) not included in a [return][4] under this Chapter was correctly not so included.

(5) Without prejudice to the generality of subsection (4), an authorised officer may—

(a) examine the procedures put in place by the paying agent for the purpose of ensuring compliance by the paying agent with the paying agent's obligations under *sections 898F* and *898G,*

(b) check a sample of accounts or transactions in respect of which interest has been paid to a beneficial owner to determine whether—

(i) the procedures referred to in *paragraph (a)* have been observed in practice and whether they are adequate, and

(ii) the paying agent is, in respect of each account or transaction in the sample, in possession of the materials and documents referred to in *section 898F(5)* or *898G(6),* as appropriate.

(6) An authorised officer may require a paying agent or an employee of the paying agent to produce books, records or other documents and to furnish information, explanations and particulars and to give all assistance, which the authorised officer reasonably requires for the purposes of the determination and examination referred to in *subsections (4)* and *(5).*

(7) An authorised officer may require an associated company in relation to a paying agent or an employee of such an associated company to produce books, records or other documents and to furnish information, explanations and particulars and to give all assistance, which the authorised officer reasonably requires for the purposes of the determination and examination referred to in *subsections (4)* and *(5)*.

(8) An authorised officer may make extracts from or copies of all or any part of the books, records or other documents or other materials made available to him or her or require that copies of books, records or other documents be made available to him or her, in exercising or performing his or her powers under this section.

(9) An employee of a paying agent or of an associated company in relation to a paying agent who fails to comply with the requirements of an authorised officer in the exercise or performance of the authorised officer's powers or duties under this section shall be liable to a penalty of [€3,000][5].

(10) A paying agent or an associated company in relation to a paying agent which fails to comply with the requirements of the authorised officer in the exercise or performance of the authorised officer's powers or duties under this section shall be liable to a penalty of €19,045 and if that failure continues a further penalty of €2,535 for each day on which the failure continues.][6]

Amendments

[1] Substituted by FA07 sched4(1)(af)(i). Shall have effect as on and from 1 January 2007.

[2] Substituted by F(No.2)A08 sched5(part2)(1)(n)(i). The enactments specified in Schedule 5 are amended or repealed to the extent and manner specified in that Schedule and, unless the contrary is stated, shall come into effect after 24 December 2008.

[3, 4] Substituted by FA07 sched4(1)(af)(ii). Shall have effect as on and from 1 January 2007.

[5] Substituted by F(No.2)A08 sched5(part2)(1)(n)(ii). The enactments specified in Schedule 5 are amended or repealed to the extent and manner specified in that Schedule and, unless the contrary is stated, shall come into effect after 24 December 2008.

[6] Inserted by FA04 sched4.

Cross References

From Section 898N

Section 432 Meaning of "associated company" and "control".

Section 898F Obligations of paying agents where contractual relations entered into before 1 January 2004.

Section 898G Obligations of paying agents in other contractual relations entered into.

To Section 898N

Section 898O Penalty for failure to make returns, etc.

898O Penalty for failure to make returns, etc

[(1) Where any person required to make a return under this Chapter—

(a) fails, without reasonable excuse, to comply with any of the requirements of *section 898F* or *898G*,

(b) makes an incorrect or incomplete return under this Chapter, or

(c) fails, without reasonable excuse, to make such a return,

that person shall be liable to a penalty of €19,045 and, in the case of *paragraphs (a)* and *(c)*, if the failure continues that person shall be liable to a further penalty of €2,535 for each day on which the failure continues.][1]

[...][2]

(3) (a) A certificate signed by a Revenue officer which certifies that he or she has examined the relevant records and that it appears from those records that during a stated period a stated return was not received from the defendant shall be evidence until the contrary is proved that the defendant did not during that period deliver that return.

(b) A certificate certifying as provided for in *paragraph (a)* and purporting to be signed by a Revenue officer may be tendered in evidence without proof and shall be deemed until the contrary is proved to have been signed by such officer.][3]

Amendments

[1] Substituted by FA05 s144(1)(g). This section applies as on and from 25 March 2005.

[2] Deleted by FA12 sched6(1)(o). Applies as respects penalties incurred on or after 24 December 2008.

[3] Inserted by FA04 sched4.

Cross References

From Section 898O

Section 898F Obligations of paying agents where contractual relations entered into before 1 January 2004.
Section 898G Obligations of paying agents in other contractual relations entered into.
Section 898N Audit.
Section 1061 Recovery of penalties.

To Section 898O

Section 891B Returns of certain payments made by certain persons.
Section 898R Commencement (Chapter 3A).

898P Arrangements with third countries and dependent and associated territories of Member States

[(1) This Chapter shall apply for the purposes of implementing any arrangements made with a territory being a dependent or associated territory of a Member State (in this Chapter referred to as the "*arrangements*") in relation to the automatic exchange of information and the application of a withholding tax referred to in *paragraph 2(ii)* of Article 17 of the Directive.

(2) (a) In this subsection—

"Council Decision on signing of agreement with Andorra" means Council Decision (2004/828/EC) of 2 November 2004 concerning the signature of the Agreement between the European Community and the Principality of Andorra providing for measures equivalent to those laid down in Council Directive 2003/48/EC on taxation of savings income in the form of interest payments and the approval and signature of the accompanying Memorandum of Understanding*;

* OJ No. L359, 4.12.2004, p.32

"Council Decision on signing of agreement with Liechtenstein" means Council Decision (2004/897/EC) of 29 November 2004 on the signing of the Agreement between the European Community and the Principality of Liechtenstein providing for measures equivalent to those laid down in Council Directive 2003/48/EC on taxation of savings income in the form of interest payments and the approval and signing of the accompanying Memorandum of Understanding*;

* OJ No. L379, 24.12.2004, p.83

"Council Decision on signing of agreement with Monaco" means Council Decision (2005/35/EC) of 7 December 2004 on the signing of the Agreement between the European Community and the Principality of Monaco providing for measures equivalent to those laid down in Council Directive 2003/48/EC on taxation of savings income in the form of interest payments and the approval and signing of the accompanying Memorandum of Understanding*;

* OJ No. L19, 21.1.2005, p.53

"Council Decision on signing of agreement with San Marino" means Council Decision (2004/903/EC) of 29 November 2004 on the signing of the Agreement between the European Community and Republic of San Marino providing for measures equivalent to those laid down in Council Directive 2003/48/EC on taxation of savings income in the form of interest payments and the approval and signing of the accompanying Memorandum of Understanding*;

* OJ No. L381, 28.12.2004, p.32

"Council Decision on signing and conclusion of agreement with the Swiss Confederation" means Council Decision (2004/911/EC) of 2 June 2004 on the signing and conclusion of the Agreement between the European Community and the Swiss Confederation providing for measures equivalent to those laid down in Council Directive 2003/48/EC on taxation of savings income in the form of interest payments and the accompanying Memorandum of Understanding*.

* OJ No. L385, 29.12.2004, p.28

(b) (i) Article 12 (Exchange of information on request) of the agreement attached to the Council Decision on signing of agreement with Andorra,

(ii) Article 10 (Exchange of information) of the agreement attached to the Council Decision on signing of agreement with Liechtenstein,

(iii) Article 12 (Transmission of information on request) of the agreement attached to the Council Decision on signing of agreement with Monaco,

(iv) Article 13 (Exchange of information on request) of the agreement attached to the Council Decision on signing of agreement with San Marino, and

(v) Article 10 (Exchange of information) of the agreement attached to the Council Decision on signing and conclusion of agreement with the Swiss Confederation,

shall, notwithstanding any other enactment, have the force of law.

(c) *Section 898M* shall apply for the purposes of implementing—

(i) Article 10 (Elimination of double taxation) of the agreement attached to the Council Decision on signing of agreement with Andorra,

(ii) Article 9 (Elimination of double taxation) of the agreement attached to the Council Decision on signing of agreement with Liechtenstein,

(iii) Article 10 (Elimination of double taxation and/or repayment of withholding tax) of the agreement attached to the Council Decision on signing of agreement with Monaco,

(iv) Article 10 (Elimination of double taxation) of the agreement attached to the Council Decision on signing of agreement with San Marino, and

(v) Article 9 (Elimination of double taxation) of the agreement attached to the Council Decision on signing and conclusion of agreement with the Swiss Confederation,

in the same way as it applies for the purposes of the Directive or the arrangements, and references in that section to tax deducted from an interest payment in a relevant territory under provisions applicable in such territory in accordance with the Directive or the arrangements shall be construed as references to—

(I) in the case of Liechtenstein or the Swiss Confederation, as the case may be, a retention from an interest payment under provisions applicable in that country in accordance with the agreement, and

(II) in the case of Andorra, Monaco or San Marino, as the case may be, tax withheld from an interest payment under provisions applicable in that country in accordance with the agreement,

and references to tax deducted and cognate expressions shall be construed accordingly.

(d) (i) The Revenue Commissioners may make regulations generally for the purposes of implementing the provisions of any arrangements the Government may make with the Government of any of the countries referred to in article 17(2)(i) of the Directive for the purposes of supplementing *paragraph (b)*.

(ii) For the purposes of *subparagraph (i)*, arrangements made with the head of a State shall be regarded as made with the Government of that State.

(e) *Section 898L* shall apply for the purposes of Article 9 (Voluntary disclosure) of the agreement attached to the Council Decision on signing of agreement with Andorra in the same way as it applies for the purposes of the Directive.][1]

Amendments

[1] Substituted by FA05 s144(1)(h). This section applies as on and from 25 March 2005.

Cross References

From Section 898P

Section 898L Certificate for the purposes of Article 13.2 of the Directive.

Section 898M Credit for withholding tax.

To Section 898P

Section 898B Interpretation (Chapter 3A).

Section 912A Information for tax authorities in other territories.

898Q Miscellaneous and supplemental

[(1) Where a person is required under this Chapter or under regulations made under this Chapter to—

(a) deliver a return,

(b) give or furnish a certificate,

(c) make a declaration or election,

(d) make an application,

the return, certificate, declaration, election or application is to be made, given or furnished in such form as the Revenue Commissioners may require.

(2) The Revenue Commissioners may nominate any Revenue officer to perform any acts and discharge any functions authorised by this Chapter or by regulations made under this Chapter to be performed or discharged by the Revenue Commissioners apart from the making of regulations under this Chapter.

(3) Every regulation made under this Chapter shall be laid before Dáil Éireann as soon as may be after it is made and, if a resolution annulling the regulation is passed by Dáil Éireann within the next 21 days on which Dáil Éireann has sat after the regulation is laid before it, the regulation shall be annulled accordingly but without prejudice to the validity of anything previously done under the regulation.

(4) Regulations made by the Revenue Commissioners under this Chapter may contain such supplemental and incidental matters as appear to the Revenue Commissioners to be necessary—

(a) to enable persons to fulfil their obligations under this Chapter, or

(b) for the general administration of this Chapter.

[(5) (a) Where any person does not comply with any provision of regulations under this Chapter requiring that person to send any information, document or certificate to the Revenue Commissioners, that person shall be liable to a penalty of [€3,000][1].

(b) Where the person mentioned in *paragraph (a)* is a body of persons, the secretary of the body shall be liable to a separate penalty of [€3,000][2].

[…][3]

(d) In proceedings for recovery of a penalty under this section—

(i) a certificate signed by an officer of the Revenue Commissioners which certifies that he or she has inspected the relevant records of the Revenue Commissioners and that it appears from them that during a stated period any information, document or certificate referred to in *paragraph (a)* was not received from the defendant shall be evidence until the contrary is proved that the defendant did not during that period send that information, document or certificate to the Revenue Commissioners,

(ii) a certificate certifying as provided for in *subparagraph (i)* and purporting to be signed by an officer of the Revenue Commissioners may be tendered in evidence without proof and shall be deemed until the contrary is proved to have been signed by an officer of the Revenue Commissioners.][4][5]

Amendments

[1] Substituted by F(No.2)A08 sched5(part2)(1)(o)(i). The enactments specified in Schedule 5 are amended or repealed to the extent and manner specified in that Schedule and, unless the contrary is stated, shall come into effect after 24 December 2008.

[2] Substituted by F(No.2)A08 sched5(part2)(1)(o)(ii). The enactments specified in Schedule 5 are amended or repealed to the extent and manner specified in that Schedule and, unless the contrary is stated, shall come into effect after 24 December 2008.

[3] Deleted by F(No.2)A08 sched5(part2)(1)(o)(iii). The enactments specified in Schedule 5 are amended or repealed to the extent and manner specified in that Schedule and, unless the contrary is stated, shall come into effect after 24 December 2008.

[4] Inserted by FA06 s124(1)(c). This section applies as on and from 31 March 2006.

[5] Inserted by FA04 sched4.

898R Commencement (Chapter 3A)

[(1) This Chapter, other than sections *898H, 898I, 898J, 898L, 898M* and [*898O*][1], is deemed to have applied as on and from 1 January 2004.

[(2) *Section 898O* shall apply as respects an act or omission which takes place or begins on or after the date of the passing of the *Finance Act 2005*.][2]

(3) The provisions of *sections 898H, 898I, 898J, 898L* and *898M* shall come into operation on such day, being a day not earlier than [1 July 2005][3], as the Minister for Finance may specify by order.][4]

Amendments

[1] Substituted by FA05 s144(1)(i)(i). This section applies as on and from 25 March 2005.

[2] Substituted by FA05 s144(1)(i)(ii). This section applies as on and from 25 March 2005.

[3] Substituted by FA05 s144(1)(i)(iii). This section applies as on and from 25 March 2005.

[4] Inserted by FA04 sched4.

Cross References

From Section 898R

Section 898H Returns of interest payments made to or secured for beneficial owners.
Section 898I Returns of interest payments to residual entities.
Section 898J Exchange of information between Member States.
Section 898L Certificate for the purposes of Article 13.2 of the Directive.
Section 898M Credit for withholding tax.
Section 898O Penalty for failure to make returns, etc.

CHAPTER 4

Revenue Powers

899 Inspector's right to make enquiries

[FA92 s228; FA95 s14(2)(ii)]

(1) In this section, "*specified provisions*" means *paragraphs (d)* and *(e)* of *section 888(2)* [and *sections 889* to *896*][1].

(2) An inspector may make such enquiries or take such action within his or her powers as he or she considers necessary to satisfy himself or herself as to the accuracy or otherwise of any return, list, statement or particulars prepared and delivered under a specified provision.

[…][2]

Amendments

[1] Substituted by FA03 s158(a).

[2] Deleted by FA03 s158(b).

Case Law

The ability of the Inland Revenue to make enquiries in relation to a tax return was not restricted to positive entries made by the taxpayer. Nil returns were equally proper areas of investigation. Sokoya v Revenue & Customs Commissioners 2008 STC 51

Revenue Briefings

Tax Briefing

Tax Briefing August 2002 – Issue 49 pg 6 – Code of Practice Revenue Audits
Tax Briefing April 2005 – Issue 59 pg 21 – Clarification on Code of Practice for Revenue Audits

eBrief

eBrief No. 26/2005 Code of Practice for Revenue Auditors and Relevant Contracts Tax.

Revenue Information Notes

2010 Code of Practice for Revenue Audit
Code of Practice for Revenue Audit and Other Compliance Interventions

Statements of Practice

Revenue Powers Exercised in Places other than a Revenue Office – SP GEN/1/94 (Revised 02/2006)
Revenue Powers – SP GEN/1/99
Revenue Internal Review Procedures – Audit and Use of Powers – SP GEN/2/99

Cross References

From Section 899

Section 888 Returns, etc. by lessors, lessees and agents.
Section 889 Returns of fees, commissions, etc. paid by certain persons.
Section 896 Returns in relation to certain offshore products.

To Section 899

Section 1061 Recovery of penalties.
Section 1068 Failure to act within required time.

900 Power to call for production of books, information, etc

[(1) In this section and in *section 901*—

"*authorised officer*" means an officer of the Revenue Commissioners authorised by them in writing to exercise the powers conferred by this section, or as the case may be, *section 901*;

"books, records or other documents" includes—

(a) accounts (including balance sheets) relating to a trade or profession and where the accounts have been audited, a copy of the auditor's certificate,

(b) books, accounts, rolls, registers, papers and other documents, whether—

(i) comprised in bound volume, loose-leaf binders or other loose-leaf filing system, loose-leaf ledger sheets, pages, folios or cards, or

(ii) kept on microfilm, magnetic tape or in any non-legible form (by the use of electronics or otherwise) which is capable of being reproduced in a legible form,

(c) every electronic or other automatic means, if any, by which any such thing in non-legible form is so capable of being reproduced, and

(d) documents in manuscript, documents which are typed, printed, stencilled or created by any other mechanical or partly mechanical process in use from time to time and documents which are produced by any photographic or photostatic process;

"*judge*" means a judge of the High Court;

"*liability*" in relation to a person, means any liability in relation to tax to which the person is or may be, or may have been, subject, or the amount of such liability;

"*tax*" means any tax, duty, levy or charge under the care and management of the Revenue Commissioners.

(2) Subject to this section, an authorised officer may serve on a person a notice in writing, requiring the person, within such period as may be specified in the notice, not being less than 21 days from the date of the service of the notice, to do either or both of the following, namely—

(a) to deliver to, or to make available for inspection by, the authorised officer such books, records or other documents as are in the person's possession, power or procurement and as contain, or may (in the authorised officer's opinion formed on reasonable grounds) contain, information relevant to a liability in relation to the person,

(b) to furnish to the authorised officer, in writing or otherwise, such information, explanations and particulars as the authorised officer may reasonably require, being information, explanations and particulars that are relevant to any such liability, and which are specified in the notice.

(3) A notice shall not be served on a person under *subsection (2)* unless the person has first been given a reasonable opportunity to deliver, or as the case may be, to make available to the authorised officer concerned the books, records or other documents in question, or to furnish the information, explanations and particulars in question.

[(4) Nothing in this section shall be construed as requiring any person to disclose to an authorised officer—

(a) information with respect to which a claim to legal professional privilege could be maintained in legal proceedings,

(b) information of a confidential medical nature, or (c) professional advice of a confidential nature given to a client (other than advice given as part of a dishonest, fraudulent or criminal purpose).][1]

(5) Where, in compliance with the requirements of a notice served on a person under *subsection (2)*, the person makes available for inspection by an authorised officer, books, records or other documents, the person shall afford the authorised officer reasonable assistance, including information, explanations and particulars, in relation to the use of all the electronic or other automatic means, if any, by which the books, records or other documents, in so far as they are in a non-legible form, are capable of being reproduced in a legible form, and any data equipment or any associated apparatus or material.

(6) Where, under *subsection (2)*, a person makes books, records or other documents available for inspection by the authorised officer, the authorised officer may make extracts from or copies of all or any part of the books, records or other documents.

(7) A person who refuses or fails to comply with a notice served on the person under *subsection (2)* or fails to afford the assistance referred to in *subsection (5)* shall be liable to a penalty of [€4,000][2].][3]

Amendments

[1] Substituted by F(No.2)A08 s92(b).

[2] Substituted by F(No.2)A08 sched5(part2)(1)(p). The enactments specified in Schedule 5 are amended or repealed to the extent and manner specified in that Schedule and, unless the contrary is stated, shall come into effect after 24 December 2008.

[3] Substituted by FA99 s207(a).

Case Law

Accounts prepared by an accountant as part of his workings were 'within the possession or power' of the taxpayer. Therefore the nominal ledger should be produced to an Inspector on request as it is not part of an accountant's working papers. Quigley v Burke 1995 V ITR 265

In Jacques v Revenue & Customs Commissioners (No 2) 2007 STC 166 it was looked at whether documents required by the Revenue were needed to establish if the taxpayer's return was complete and correct.

Personal information should only be demanded where it is essential. Taylor v Bratherton 2004 SpC 448

The High Court will only in exceptional circumstances set aside a notice calling for documents. R v IRC ex parte Ulster Bank Ltd 1997 STC 832

Revenue Briefings

Tax Briefing

Tax Briefing June 1996 – Issue 22 – Audit Linking Documents

Tax Briefing August 2002 – Issue 49 pg 6 – Code of Practice Revenue Audits

Revenue Information Notes

2010 Code of Practice for Revenue Audit

Statements of Practice

Revenue Powers Exercised in Places other than a Revenue Office – SP GEN/1/94 (Revised 02/2006)

Revenue Powers (Finance Act 1999) – SP GEN/1/99

Revenue Internal Review Procedures – SP GEN/2/99

Cross References

From Section 900

Section 901 Application to High Court: production of books, information, etc.

To Section 900

Section 697LA Transactions between associated persons and between tonnage tax trade and other activities of same company.

Section 835F Documentation and enquiries.

Section 902 Information to be furnished by third party: request of an authorised officer.

Section 912A Information for tax authorities in other territories.

Section 913 Application of income tax provisions relating to returns, etc.

Section 1078 Revenue offences.

Section 1084 Surcharge for late returns.

Schedule 29 Provisions Referred to in Sections 1052, 1053 and 1054

901 Application to High Court: production of books, information, etc

[(1) An authorised officer may make an application to a judge for an order requiring a person, to do either or both of the following, namely—

(a) to deliver to the authorised officer, or to make available for inspection by the authorised officer, such books, records or other documents as are in the person's power, possession or procurement and as contain, or may (in the authorised officer's opinion formed on reasonable grounds) contain, information relevant to a liability in relation to the person,

(b) to furnish to the authorised officer such information, explanations and particulars as the authorised officer may reasonably require, being information, explanations and particulars that are relevant to any such liability,

and which are specified in the application.

(2) Where the judge, to whom an application is made under *subsection (1)*, is satisfied that there are reasonable grounds for the application being made, that judge may,

subject to such conditions as he or she may consider proper and specify in the order, make an order requiring the person to whom the application relates—

(a) to deliver to the authorised officer, or to make available for inspection by the authorised officer, such books, records or other documents, and

(b) to furnish to the authorised officer such information, explanations and particulars,

as may be specified in the order.

[(3) Nothing in this section shall be construed as requiring any person to disclose to an authorised officer—

(a) information with respect to which a claim to legal professional privilege could be maintained in legal proceedings,

(b) information of a confidential medical nature, or

(c) professional advice of a confidential nature given to a client (other than advice given as part of a dishonest, fraudulent or criminal purpose).][1]

[(4) Where in compliance with an order made under *subsection (2)*, a person makes available for inspection by an authorised officer, books, records or other documents, the person shall afford the authorised officer reasonable assistance, including information, explanations and particulars, in relation to the use of all the electronic or other automatic means, if any, by which the books, records or other documents, in so far as they are in a non-legible form, are capable of being reproduced in a legible form, and any data equipment or any associated apparatus or material.

(5) Where in compliance with an order made under *subsection (2)*, a person makes books, records or other documents available for inspection by the authorised officer, the authorised officer may make extracts from or copies of all or any part of the books, records or other documents.][2]][3]

Amendments

[1] Substituted by F(No.2)A08 s92(c).

[2] Inserted by FA02 s132(a).

[3] Substituted by FA99 s207(b).

Revenue Briefings

Tax Briefing

Tax Briefing August 2002 – Issue 49 pg 6 – Code of Practice Revenue Audits

Statements of Practice

Revenue Powers Exercised in Places other than a Revenue Office – SP GEN/1/94 (Revised 02/2006)

Revenue Powers (Finance Act 1999) – SP GEN/1/99

Revenue Internal Review Procedures – SP GEN/2/99

Cross References

To Section 901

Section 697LA Transactions between associated persons and between tonnage tax trade and other activities of same company.

Section 835F Documentation and enquiries.

Section 900 Power to call for production of books, information, etc.

Section 912A Information for tax authorities in other territories.

Section 1078 Revenue offences.

902 Information to be furnished by third party: request of an authorised officer

[(1) In this section and in *section 902A*—

"*authorised officer*" means an officer of the Revenue Commissioners authorised by them in writing to exercise the powers conferred by this section, or as the case may be, *section 902A*;

"*books, records or other documents*" and "*liability*", in relation to a person, have, respectively, the meaning assigned to them by *section 900(1)*.

(2) Notwithstanding any obligation as to secrecy or other restriction upon disclosure of information imposed by or under statute or otherwise, and subject to this section, an authorised officer may for the purpose of enquiring into a liability in relation to a person (in this section referred to as "*the taxpayer*") serve on any other person (not being a financial institution within the meaning of *section 906A*) a notice in writing requiring that other person, within such period as may be specified in the notice, not being less than 30 days from the date of the service of the notice, to do either or both of the following, namely—

(a) to deliver to, or make available for inspection by, the authorised officer, such books, records or other documents as are in the other person's power, possession or procurement and as contain, or may (in the authorised officer's opinion formed on reasonable grounds) contain, information relevant to a liability in relation to the taxpayer,

(b) to furnish to the authorised officer, in writing or otherwise, such information, explanations and particulars as the authorised officer may reasonably require, being information, explanations and particulars that are relevant to any such liability,

and which are specified in the notice.

(3) A notice shall not be served on a person under *subsection (2)* unless the authorised officer concerned has reasonable grounds to believe that the person is likely to have information relevant to the establishment of a liability in relation to the taxpayer.

(4) The persons who may be treated as a taxpayer for the purposes of this section include a company which has been dissolved and an individual who has died.

(5) A notice under *subsection (2)* shall name the taxpayer in relation to whose liability the authorised officer is enquiring.

(6) Where an authorised officer serves a notice under *subsection (2)*, a copy of such notice shall be given by the authorised officer to the taxpayer concerned.

(7) Where, under *subsection (2)*, a person has delivered any books, records or other documents and those books, records or other documents are retained by the authorised officer, the person shall, at all reasonable times and subject to such reasonable conditions as may be determined by the authorised officer, be entitled to inspect those books, records or other documents and to obtain copies of them.

(8) Where, under *subsection (2)*, a person makes books, records or other documents available for inspection by the authorised officer, the authorised officer may make extracts from or copies of all or any part of the books, records or other documents.

[(9) Nothing in this section shall be construed as requiring any person to disclose to an authorised officer—

(a) information with respect to which a claim to legal professional privilege could be maintained in legal proceedings,

(b) information of a confidential medical nature, or

(c) professional advice of a confidential nature given to a client (other than advice given as part of a dishonest, fraudulent or criminal purpose).][1]

(10) Where, in compliance with the requirements of a notice under *subsection (2)*, a person makes available for inspection by an authorised officer, books, records or other documents, the person shall afford the authorised officer reasonable assistance, including information, explanations and particulars, in relation to the use of all the electronic or other automatic means, if any, by which the books, records or other documents, in so far as they are in non-legible form, are capable of being reproduced in a legible form and any data equipment or any associated apparatus or material.

(11) A person who fails or refuses to comply with a notice served on the person under *subsection (2)* or to afford the assistance referred to in *subsection (10)* shall be liable to a penalty of [€4,000][2], but nothing in *section 1078* shall be construed as applying to such failure or refusal.][3]

Amendments

[1] Substituted by F(No.2)A08 s92(d).

[2] Substituted by F(No.2)A08 sched5(part2)(1)(q). The enactments specified in Schedule 5 are amended or repealed to the extent and manner specified in that Schedule and, unless the contrary is stated, shall come into effect after 24 December 2008.

[3] Substituted by FA99 s207(c).

Revenue Briefings

Tax Briefing

Tax Briefing August 2002 – Issue 49 pg 6 – Code of Practice Revenue Audits

Statements of Practice

Revenue Powers Exercised in Places other than a Revenue Office – SP GEN/1/94 (Revised 02/2006)

Revenue Powers (Finance Act 1999) – SP GEN/1/99

Revenue Internal Review Procedures – SP GEN/2/99

Cross References

From Section 902

Section 900 Power to call for production of books, information, etc.

Section 902A Application to High Court: information from third party.

Section 906A Information to be furnished by financial institutions.

Section 1078 Revenue offences.

To Section 902

Section 912A Information for tax authorities in other territories.

Section 1078 Revenue offences.

902A Application to High Court: information from third party

[(1) In this section—

"*the Acts*" has the meaning assigned to it by *section 1078(1)*;

"*judge*" means a judge of the High Court;

"*a taxpayer*" means any person including a person whose identity is not known to the authorised officer, and a group or class of persons whose individual identities are not so known.

(2) An authorised officer may make an application to a judge for an order requiring a person (other than a financial institution within the meaning of *section 906A*) to do either or both of the following, namely—

(a) to deliver to the authorised officer, or to make available for inspection by the authorised officer, such books, records or other documents as are in the person's power, possession or procurement and as contain, or may (in the authorised officer's opinion formed on reasonable grounds) contain, information relevant to a liability in relation to a taxpayer,

(b) to furnish to the authorised officer such information, explanations and particulars as the authorised officer may reasonably require, being information, explanations and particulars that are relevant to any such liability,

and which are specified in the application.

(3) An authorised officer shall not make an application under subsection (2) without the consent in writing of a Revenue Commissioner, and without being satisfied—

(a) that there are reasonable grounds for suspecting that the taxpayer, or, where the taxpayer is a group or class of persons, all or any one of those persons, may have failed or may fail to comply with any provision of the Acts,

(b) that any such failure is likely to have led or to lead to serious prejudice to the proper assessment or collection of tax (having regard to the amount of a liability in relation to the taxpayer, or where the taxpayer is a group or class of persons, the amount of a liability in relation to all or any one of those persons, that arises or might arise from such failure), and

(c) that the information—

(i) which is likely to be contained in the books, records or other documents to which the application relates, or

(ii) which is likely to arise from the information, explanations and particulars to which the application relates,

is relevant to the proper assessment or collection of tax.

(4) Where the judge, to whom an application is made under subsection (2), is satisfied that there are reasonable grounds for the application being made, that judge may, subject to such conditions as he or she may consider proper and specify in the order, make an order requiring the person to whom the application relates—

(a) to deliver to the authorised officer, or to make available for inspection by the authorised officer, such books, records or other documents, and

(b) to furnish to the authorised officer such information, explanations and particulars,

as may be specified in the order.

(5) The persons who may be treated as a taxpayer for the purposes of this section include a company which has been dissolved and an individual who has died.

[(6) Nothing in this section shall be construed as requiring any person to disclose to an authorised officer—

(a) information with respect to which a claim to legal professional privilege could be maintained in legal proceedings,

(b) information of a confidential medical nature, or

(c) professional advice of a confidential nature given to a client (other than advice given as part of a dishonest, fraudulent or criminal purpose).][1]

(7) Every hearing of an application for an order under this section and of any appeal in connection with that application shall be held in camera.][2]

Amendments

[1] Substituted by F(No.2)A08 s92(e).

[2] Inserted by FA99 s207(d).

Revenue Briefings

Tax Briefing

Tax Briefing August 2002 – Issue 49 pg 6 – Code of Practice Revenue Audits

Statements of Practice

Revenue Powers Exercised in Places other than a Revenue Office – SP GEN/1/94 (Revised 02/2006)
Revenue Powers (Finance Act 1999) – SP GEN/1/99
Revenue Internal Review Procedures – SP GEN/2/99

Cross References

From Section 902A

Section 906A Information to be furnished by financial institutions.
Section 1078 Revenue offences.

To Section 902A

Section 902 Information to be furnished by third party: request of an authorised officer.
Section 902B Powers of inspection: life policies.
Section 912A Information for tax authorities in other territories.

902B Powers of inspection: life policies

[(1) In this section—

["*assurance company*" means—

(a) an assurance company within the meaning of section 3 of the Insurance Act 1936, or

(b) a person that holds an authorisation within the meaning of the European Communities (Life Assurance) Framework Regulations 1994 (S.I. No. 360 of 1994);][1]

"*authorised officer*" means an officer of the Revenue Commissioners who is authorised by them in writing to exercise the powers conferred by this section;

"*policy*" and "*premium*" have the same meanings, respectively, as in section 3 of the Insurance Act 1936;

"*relevant records*", in relation to a policy, means any document or any other written or printed material in any form, and includes any information stored, maintained or preserved by means of any mechanical, photographic or electronic device whether or not stored, maintained or preserved in a legible form, but does not include so much of any record that is of a medical nature.

(2) A Revenue Commissioner may, subject to subsection (3) and for the purposes of subsection (7), direct an authorised officer to investigate a class or classes of policies issued by an assurance company and the policyholders to whom they were issued.

(3) Directions may be given by a Revenue Commissioner under subsection (2) where he or she forms the opinion that there are circumstances suggesting that a class of policy or classes of policies issued by an assurance company may have been issued to policyholders, some of whom have paid one or more than one premium in respect of any policy concerned out of income or gains which were required to be,

but were not, included in a return made by those policyholders under the Tax Acts or the Capital Gains Tax Acts; and for the purposes of this subsection the Revenue Commissioner may take into consideration information in relation to policies issued by other assurance companies and the policyholders of such policies.

(4) An authorised officer, when investigating a class or classes of policies and the policyholders to whom they were issued, may at all reasonable times, enter any premises or place of business of an assurance company to inspect the relevant records held by the assurance company in respect of a sample of policies of that class or those classes and the policy-holders of those policies.

(5) Where an authorised officer has entered any premises or place of business of an assurance company for the purposes of this section, he or she may require the assurance company, or any employee of the assurance company, to produce the relevant records in a form which is legible and to furnish such information and explanations as the authorised officer requires in relation to the relevant records.

(6) Where in accordance with this section an authorised officer inspects relevant records he or she may copy or make extracts from those records.

(7) Information obtained by an authorised officer from inspecting relevant records may only be used for the purposes of enabling an authorised officer, within the meaning of *section 902A*, to make an application under that section to a judge of the High Court.][2]

Amendments

[1] Substituted by FA06 s59(1)(d). Applies as on and from 31 March 2006.

[2] Inserted by FA05 s140.

Revenue Briefings

Tax Briefing

Tax Briefing August 2002 – Issue 49 pg 6 – Code of Practice Revenue Audits

Statements of Practice

Revenue Powers Exercised in Places other than a Revenue Office – SP GEN/1/94 (Revised 02/2006)
Revenue Powers (Finance Act 1999) – SP GEN/1/99
Revenue Internal Review Procedures – SP GEN/2/99

Cross References

From Section 902B

Section 902A Application to High Court: information from third party.

903 Power of inspection: PAYE

[ITA67 s127A; FA92 s233]

(1) In this section—

"*authorised officer*" means an officer of the Revenue Commissioners authorised by them in writing to exercise the powers conferred by this section;

"*emoluments*", "*employer*" and "*tax deduction card*" have the same meanings respectively as in *Chapter 4* of *Part 42*;

"*records*" means any personnel records relating to the payment of emoluments or the provision of benefits in kind or perquisites, payroll files, wages sheets, [certificates of tax credits and standard rate cut-off point][1], tax deduction cards, certificates issued in accordance with [Regulation 20 of the Income Tax (Employments) (Consolidated) Regulations 2001 (S.I. No. 559 of 2001)][2], including any data (within the meaning of *section 912*) [stored in accordance with *section 887*][3] or by any other means or any other information or documents which the authorised officer may reasonably require.

(2) An authorised officer may at all reasonable times enter any premises or place where the authorised officer has reason to believe that—

(a) an employer is or has been carrying on any activity as an employer,

(b) any person is or was either paying emoluments or providing benefits in kind or perquisites,

(c) any person is or was in receipt of emoluments, benefits in kind or perquisites, or

(d) records are or may be kept,

and the authorised officer—

(i) may require any employer or any other person who is on those premises or in that place, other than a person who is there to purchase goods or to receive a service, to produce any records which the authorised officer requires for the purposes of his or her enquiry,

(ii) may, if the authorised officer has reason to believe that any of the records he or she has required to be produced to him or her under *paragraph (i)* have not been so produced, search on those premises or in that place for those records, and

(iii) may examine, make copies of, take extracts from, remove and retain any records for further examination or for the purposes of any legal proceedings instituted by an officer of the Revenue Commissioners or for the purposes of any criminal proceedings.

[(2A) (a) An authorised officer shall not, without the consent of the occupier, enter any premises, or that portion of any premises, which is occupied wholly and exclusively as a private residence, except on production by such officer of a warrant issued by a Judge of the District Court expressly authorising the authorised officer to so enter.

(b) A Judge of the District Court may issue a warrant under paragraph (*a*) if satisfied by information on oath that it is proper to do so for the purposes of this section.".][4]

(3) An authorised officer may require any person, other than a person purchasing goods or receiving a service from an employer, to give the authorised officer all reasonable assistance, including providing information and explanations and furnishing documents required by the authorised officer.

(4) An authorised officer when exercising or performing his or her powers or duties under this section shall on request produce his or her authorisation for the purposes of this section.

(5) A person who does not comply with the requirements of an authorised officer in the exercise or performance of the authorised officer's powers or duties under this section shall be liable to a penalty of [€4,000][5] .

(6) The records referred to in this section shall be retained by the employer for a period of 6 years after the end of the year to which they refer or for such shorter period as the Revenue Commissioners may authorise in writing to the employer.

Amendments

[1] Substituted by FA01 sched1(1)(r). Applies as respects the year of assessment 2001 and subsequent years of assessment.

[2] Substituted by FA02 sched6(3)(n). Shall be deemed to have come into force and take effect as on and from 1 January 2002.

[3] Substituted by FA01 s232(1)(e). Applies as respects any chargeable period commencing on or after 15 February 2001.

[4] Inserted by FA05 s138.

[5] Substituted by F(No.2)A08 sched5(part2)(1)(r). The enactments specified in Schedule 5 are amended or repealed to the extent and manner specified in that Schedule and, unless the contrary is stated, shall come into effect after 24 December 2008.

Revenue Briefings

Tax Briefing

Tax Briefing August 2002 – Issue 49 pg 6 – Code of Practice Revenue Audits
Tax Briefing April 2005 – Issue 59 pg 21 – Code of Practice for Revenue Auditors
Tax Briefing June 2014 – Issue 05 – PAYE: Employer's obligation to keep, maintain and produce a Register of Employees

Revenue Information Notes

Compliance Code for PAYE Taxpayers

Statements of Practice

Revenue Powers Exercised in Places other than a Revenue Office – SP GEN/1/94 (Revised 02/2006)
Revenue Powers (Finance Act 1999) – SP GEN/1/99
Revenue Internal Review Procedures – SP GEN/2/99

Cross References

From Section 903

Section 887 Use of electronic data processing.
Section 912 Computer documents and records.
Section 960 Date for payment of income tax other than under self assessment.
Section 983 Interpretation (Chapter 4).

To Section 903

Section 531F Power of inspection.
Section 531X Records and regulations.
Section 906 Authorised officers and Garda Síochána.

904 Power of inspection: tax deduction from payments to certain subcontractors

[FA70 s17A; FA92 s235]

(1) In this section—

"*authorised officer*" means an officer of the Revenue Commissioners authorised by them in writing to exercise the powers conferred by this section;

"*principal*", "*relevant contract*", "*relevant operations*" and "*subcontractor*" have the same meanings respectively as in *Chapter 2* of *Part 18*;

"*records*" means those records required to be kept—

(a) under [*Chapter 2* of *Part 18* and regulations made under that Chapter][1], and

(b) under *section 886*.

(2) An authorised officer may at all reasonable times enter any premises or place where the authorised officer has reason to believe that—

(a) any relevant operations are or have been carried on,

(b) any person is making or has made payments to a subcontractor in connection with the performance by the subcontractor of a relevant contract in relation to which that person is the principal,

(c) any person is or has been in receipt of such payments, or

(d) records are or may be kept,

and the authorised officer may—

(i) require any principal or subcontractor, or any employee of, or any other person providing bookkeeping, clerical or other administrative services to, any principal or subcontractor, who is on that premises or in that place to produce any records which the authorised officer requires for the purpose of his or her enquiry,

(ii) if the authorised officer has reason to believe that any of the records he or she has required to be produced to him or her under this subsection have not been so produced, search on those premises or in that place for those records, and

(iii) examine, make copies of, take extracts from, remove and retain any records for a reasonable period for their further examination or for the purpose of any legal proceedings instituted by an officer of the Revenue Commissioners or for the purposes of any criminal proceedings.

[(2A) (a) An authorised officer shall not, without the consent of the occupier, enter any premises, or that portion of any premises, which is occupied wholly and exclusively as a private residence, except on production by such officer of a warrant issued by a Judge of the District Court expressly authorising the authorised officer to so enter.

(b) A Judge of the District Court may issue a warrant under *paragraph* (*a*) if satisfied by information on oath that it is proper to do so for the purposes of this section.][2]

(3) An authorised officer may require any principal or subcontractor, or any employee of, or any other person providing bookkeeping, clerical or other administrative services to, any principal or subcontractor, to give the authorised officer all reasonable assistance, including providing information and explanations and furnishing documents required by the authorised officer.

(4) An authorised officer when exercising or performing his or her powers or duties under this section shall on request produce his or her authorisation for the purposes of this section.

(5) A person who does not comply with the requirements of an authorised officer in the exercise or performance of the authorised officer's powers or duties under this section shall be liable to a penalty of [4,000][3].

(6) The records referred to in this section shall be retained for a period of 6 years after the end of the year to which they refer or for such shorter period as the Revenue Commissioners may authorise in writing.

Amendments

[1] Substituted by FA11 s20(1)(l). With effect from 1 January 2012 as per S.I. No 660 of 2012.

[2] Inserted by FA05 s139.

[3] Substituted by F(No.2)A08 sched5(part2)(1)(s). The enactments specified in Schedule 5 are amended or repealed to the extent and manner specified in that Schedule and, unless the contrary is stated, shall come into effect after 24 December 2008.

Revenue Briefings

Tax Briefing

Tax Briefing August 2002 – Issue 49 pg 6 – Code of Practice Revenue Audits

eBrief

eBrief No. 10/2007 – Code of Practice for Revenue Auditors: Relevant Contracts Tax

Statements of Practice

Revenue Powers Exercised in Places other than a Revenue Office – SP GEN/1/94 (Revised 02/2006)
Revenue Powers (Finance Act 1999) – SP GEN/1/99
Revenue Internal Review Procedures – SP GEN/2/99

Cross References

From Section 904

Section 520 Interpretation (Chapter 1).
Section 530 Interpretation (Chapter 2).
Section 886 Obligation to keep certain records.

To Section 904

Section 906 Authorised officers and Garda Síochána.
Schedule 29 Provisions Referred to in Sections 1052, 1053 and 1054

904A Power of inspection: returns and collection of appropriate tax

[(1) In this section—

"*amount on account of appropriate tax*", "*appropriate tax*", "*deposit*", "*interest*", "*relevant deposit taker*", "*relevant interest*" and "*return*" have, respectively, the meaning assigned to them by *section 256(1)*;

["*auditor*" means a person who is qualified, for the purposes of Part X of the Companies Act, 1990, for appointment as auditor of a company, or any other person whom the Revenue Commissioners consider suitable, having regard to his or her qualifications or experience, for appointment as an authorised officer;

"*authorised officer*" means—

(a) an officer of the Revenue Commissioners who is authorised by them in writing to exercise the powers conferred by this section, and

(b) an auditor who is authorised by the Revenue Commissioners in writing to exercise the powers conferred by this section in relation to an audit of the return of a named relevant deposit taker for a specified year or years of assessment;

"*associated company*", in relation to a relevant deposit taker, means a company which is itself a relevant deposit taker and which is the relevant deposit taker's associated company within the meaning of *section 432*;][1]

"books, records or other documents" includes—

(a) any records used in the business of a financial institution, or used in the transfer department of a financial institution acting as registrar of securities, whether—

(i) comprised in bound volume, loose-leaf binders or other loose-leaf filing system, loose-leaf ledger sheets, pages, folios or cards, or

(ii) kept on microfilm, magnetic tape or in any non-legible form (by the use of electronics or otherwise) which is capable of being reproduced in a legible form, and

(b) every electronic or other automatic means, if any, by which any such thing in non-legible form is so capable of being reproduced, and

(c) documents in manuscript, documents which are typed, printed, stencilled or created by any other mechanical or partly mechanical process in use from time to time and documents which are produced by any photographic or photostatic process, and

(d) correspondence and records of other communications between a relevant deposit taker and a person to whom it pays interest;

"*liability*" in relation to a person means any liability in relation to tax to which the person is or may be, or may have been, subject, or the amount of such liability;

"*tax*" means any tax, duty, levy or charge under the care and management of the Revenue Commissioners.

(2) An authorised officer, having regard to *Chapter 4* of *Part 8*, may at all reasonable times enter any premises or place of business of a relevant deposit taker for the purposes of auditing for a year of assessment—

(a) the return made by the relevant deposit taker of—

(i) the relevant interest paid by it in that year,

(ii) the appropriate tax in relation to the payment of that interest,

(iii) the amount of interest in respect of which an amount on account of appropriate tax is due and payable for that year, and

(iv) the amount on account of appropriate tax so due and payable, and

(b) whether payments of interest were properly made by the relevant deposit taker without deducting appropriate tax in relation to the payments.

(3) Without prejudice to the generality of subsection (2), the authorised officer may—

(a) examine the procedures put in place by the relevant deposit taker for the purpose of ensuring compliance by the relevant deposit taker with its obligations under *section 257(2)*, and

(b) check a sample of accounts into which deposits, which have not been treated by the relevant deposit taker as relevant deposits, have been paid, to determine whether—

(i) the procedures referred to in paragraph (*a*) have been observed in practice and whether they are adequate,

[(ii) the relevant deposit taker is, in respect of each deposit in the sample of deposits, in possession of—

(I) a declaration mentioned in [section 246A(3)(b)(ii)(III), 263 or 263A,][2]

(II) the number referred to in *paragraph (f)*(ii) or *(h)*(ii) of the definition of "*relevant deposit*" in *section 256*, or

(III) as respects a case within paragraph (*b*)(ii)(I) or (*b*)(ii)(II) of subsection (3) of *section 246A*, the tax reference number referred to in subsection (4) of that section,

as the case may be, and][3]

(iii) there is information in the relevant deposit taker's possession which can reasonably be taken to indicate that one or more of such deposits is or may be a relevant deposit.

(4) Where an authorised officer in exercising or performing his or her powers and duties under this section has reason to believe that in respect of one or more deposits, the relevant deposit taker has incorrectly treated them as not being

relevant deposits, the authorised officer may make such further enquiries as are necessary to establish whether there is a liability in relation to any person.

(5) An authorised officer may require a relevant deposit taker or an employee of the relevant deposit taker to produce books, records or other documents and to furnish information, explanations and particulars and to give all assistance, which the authorised officer reasonably requires for the purposes of his or her audit and examination under subsections (2) and (3), and, as the case may be, enquiries under subsection (4).

[(6) An authorised officer may require an associated company in relation to a relevant deposit taker or an employee of such an associated company to produce books, records or other documents and to furnish information, explanations and particulars and to give all assistance, which the authorised officer reasonably requires for the purposes of his or her audit and examination under subsections (2) and (3) and, as the case may be, enquiries under subsection (4).

(7) An authorised officer may make extracts from or copies of all or any part of the books, records or other documents or other material made available to him or her or require that copies of books, records, or other documents be made available to him or her, in exercising or performing his or her powers or duties under this section.

(8) An employee of a relevant deposit taker or of an associated company in relation to a relevant deposit taker, who fails to comply with the requirements of the authorised officer in the exercise or performance of the authorised officer's powers or duties under this section shall be liable to a penalty of [€1,265][4].

(9) A relevant deposit taker or an associated company in relation to a relevant deposit taker which fails to comply with the requirements of the authorised officer in the exercise or performance of the authorised officer's powers or duties under this section shall be liable to a penalty of [€19,045][5] and if that failure continues a further penalty of [€2,535][6] for each day on which the failure continues.][7][8]

Amendments

[1] Substituted by FA00 s68(a)(i).

[2] Substituted by FA07 s34(1)(h). Applies on and from 2 April 2007.

[3] Substituted by FA03 s49(4).

[4, 5, 6] Substituted by FA01 sched5.

[7] Substituted by FA00 s68(a)(ii).

[8] Inserted by FA99 s207(e).

Revenue Briefings

Tax Briefing

Tax Briefing August 2002 – Issue 49 pg 6 – Code of Practice Revenue Audits

Statements of Practice

Revenue Powers Exercised in Places other than a Revenue Office – SP GEN/1/94 (Revised 02/2006)
Revenue Powers (Finance Act 1999) – SP GEN/1/99
Revenue Internal Review Procedures – SP GEN/2/99

Cross References

From Section 904A

Section 237 Annual payments payable wholly out of taxed income.
Section 246A Interest in respect of wholesale debt instruments.
Section 256 Interpretation (Chapter 4).

Section 257 Deduction of tax from relevant interest.
Section 432 Meaning of "associated company" and "control".

To Section 904A

Section 267F Supplementary provisions (Chapter 5).
Section 904B Report to Committee of Public Accounts: publication etc.

904B Report to Committee of Public Accounts: publication etc

[(1) In this section—

"*appropriate tax*" and "*relevant deposit taker*" have, respectively, the meanings assigned to them by *section 256(1)*;

"*authorised officer*" has the meaning assigned to it by *section 904A*.

(2) Notwithstanding any obligation as to secrecy or other restriction upon disclosure of information imposed by or under statute or otherwise, the Revenue Commissioners—

(a) shall, before 1 November 2000, make a report in writing to the Committee of Public Accounts of Dáil Éireann, and

(b) may, at any time, cause to be made public a report, in such manner as they consider fit,

of the results (including interim results) of any audit carried out by an authorised officer under *section 904A* during the period from 25 March 1999 to the date the report is made.

(3) The report under subsection (2) shall be in respect of audits of relevant deposit takers for the years of assessment 1986-1987 to 1998-1999, and may specify, in respect of each such audit—

(a) the name of the relevant deposit taker concerned,

(b) the amount of additional appropriate tax payable by the relevant deposit taker as a result of the audit,

(c) the amount of interest payable in respect of any such amount,

(d) the amount of any fine or penalty imposed by a court on the relevant deposit taker under the Tax Acts, or accepted by the Revenue Commissioners in place of initiating proceedings for recovery of such fine or penalty,

(e) whether an assessment has been made in respect of appropriate tax and, if so, whether the assessment has been appealed,

(f) whether the audit has been completed as at the date of the report,

(g) the amount of any payment on account of appropriate tax paid by the relevant deposit taker in anticipation of an audit being carried out or during the course of an audit, and

(h) such further particulars as the Revenue Commissioners consider fit.][1]

Amendments

[1] Inserted by FA00 s68(b).

Cross References

From Section 904B

Section 256 Interpretation (Chapter 4).
Section 904A Power of inspection: returns and collection of appropriate tax.

904C Power of inspection (returns and collection of appropriate tax): assurance companies

[(1) In this section—

"*assurance company*" and "*life business*" have, respectively, the meanings assigned to them in *section 706*;

"*appropriate tax*" has the meaning assigned to it in *section 730F*;

"*authorised officer*" means an officer of the Revenue Commissioners authorised by them in writing to exercise the powers conferred by this section;

"books, records or other documents" includes—

(a) any records used in the business of an assurance company whether—

(i) comprised in bound volume, loose-leaf binders or other loose-leaf filing system, loose-leaf ledger sheets, pages, folios or cards, or

(ii) kept on microfilm, magnetic tape or in any non-legible form (by use of electronics or otherwise) which is capable of being reproduced in a legible form, and

(b) every electronic or other automatic means, if any, by which any such thing in non-legible form is so capable of being reproduced, and

(c) documents in manuscript, documents which are typed, printed, stencilled or created by any other mechanical means or partly mechanical process in use from time to time and documents which are produced by any photographic or photostatic process, and

(d) correspondence and records of other communications by, or on behalf of, policyholders with the assurance company carrying on life business;

"*chargeable event*", in relation to a life policy, has the meaning assigned to it by *section 730C*;

"*declaration*" means a declaration referred to in *section 730E*;

"*liability*", in relation to a person, means any liability in relation to tax to which the person is or may be, or may have been, subject, or the amount of such liability;

"*life policy*" has the meaning assigned to it in *section 730B*;

"*policyholder*" has the meaning assigned to it in *section 730E*;

["*return*" means a return under *section 730FA* or *section 730G*;][1]

"*tax*" means any tax, duty, levy or charge under the care and management of the Revenue Commissioners.

(2) An authorised officer may at all reasonable times enter any premises or place of business of an assurance company carrying on life business for the purposes of auditing for a financial year the returns made by the company of appropriate tax.

(3) Without prejudice to the generality of subsection (2) the authorised officer may—

(a) examine the procedures put in place by the assurance company for the purpose of ensuring compliance by the assurance company with its obligations under Chapter 5 of Part 26,

(b) examine all or a sample of the declarations made to the assurance company,

(c) examine a sample of life policies to determine whether—

(i) the procedures referred to in paragraph (*a*) have been observed in practice and whether they are adequate,

(ii) the assurance company has on the happening of chargeable events in relation to each life policy, paid the correct amount of appropriate tax in connection with the chargeable events, and

(iii) there is information in the assurance company's possession which can reasonably be taken to indicate that the assurance company incorrectly failed to pay appropriate tax in connection with a chargeable event.

(4) Where an authorised officer in exercising or performing his or her powers and duties under this section has reason to believe that in respect of one or more life policies, the assurance company has incorrectly failed to pay appropriate tax in connection with a chargeable event, the authorised officer may make such further enquiries as are necessary to establish whether there is a liability in relation to any person.

(5) An authorised officer may require an assurance company or an employee of the assurance company to produce books, records or other documents and to furnish information, explanations and particulars and to give all assistance, which the authorised officer reasonably requires for the purposes of his or her audit and examination under subsections (2) and (3), and, as the case may be, enquiries under subsection (4).

(6) An authorised officer may make extracts from or copies of all or any part of the books, records or other documents or other material made available to him or her or require that copies of books, records or other documents be made available to him or her, in exercising or performing his or her powers or duties under this section.

(7) An employee of an assurance company who fails to comply with the requirements of the authorised officer in the exercise or performance of the authorised officer's powers or duties under this section shall be liable to a penalty of [€1,265][2].

(8) An assurance company which fails to comply with the requirements of the authorised officer in the exercise or performance of the authorised officer's powers or duties under this section shall be liable to a penalty of [€19,045][3] and if that failure continues a further penalty of [€2,535][4] for each day on which the failure continues.][5]

Amendments

[1] Substituted by FA02 s40(3). Applies as on and from 5 December 2001.

[2, 3, 4] Substituted by FA01 sched5.

[5] Inserted by FA00 s68(b).

Revenue Briefings

Tax Briefing

Tax Briefing August 2002 – Issue 49 pg 6 – Code of Practice Revenue Audits

Statements of Practice

Revenue Powers Exercised in Places other than a Revenue Office – SP GEN/1/94 (Revised 02/2006)
Revenue Powers (Finance Act 1999) – SP GEN/1/99
Revenue Internal Review Procedures – SP GEN/2/99

Cross References

From Section 904C

Section 706 Interpretation and general (Part 26).
Section 730B Taxation of policyholders.
Section 730C Chargeable event.

Section 730E Declarations.
Section 730F Deduction of tax on the happening of a chargeable event.
Section 730FA Assessment of appropriate tax where tax not deducted under section 730F.
Section 730G Returns and collection of appropriate tax.

904D Power of inspection (returns and collection of appropriate tax): investment undertakings

[(1) In this section—

"*appropriate tax*" has the meaning assigned to it in *section 739E*;

"*authorised officer*" means an officer of the Revenue Commissioners authorised by them in writing to exercise the powers conferred by this section;

"books, records or other documents" includes—

(a) any records used in the business of an investment undertaking whether—

(i) comprised in bound volume, loose-leaf binders or other loose-leaf filing system, loose-leaf ledger sheets, pages, folios or cards, or

(ii) kept on microfilm, magnetic tape or in any non-legible form (by use of electronics or otherwise) which is capable of being reproduced in a legible form, and

(b) every electronic or other automatic means, if any, by which any such thing in non-legible form is so capable of being reproduced, and

(c) documents in manuscript, documents which are typed, printed, stencilled or created by any other mechanical means or partly mechanical process in use from time to time and documents which are produced by any photographic or photostatic process, and

(d) correspondence and records of other communications by, or on behalf of, unit holders with the investment undertaking;

"*declaration*" means a declaration referred to in Schedule 2B;

"*investment undertaking*" and "*unit holder*" have, respectively, the meanings assigned to them by *section 739B*;

"*liability*", in relation to a person, means any liability in relation to tax to which the person is or may be, or may have been, subject, or the amount of such liability;

"*return*" means a return under section *739F*;

"*tax*" means any tax, duty, levy or charge under the care and management of the Revenue Commissioners.

(2) An authorised officer may at all reasonable times enter any premises or place of business of an investment undertaking for the purposes of auditing for a financial year the returns made by the investment undertaking of appropriate tax.

(3) Without prejudice to the generality of subsection (2) the authorised officer may—

(a) examine the procedures put in place by the investment undertaking for the purpose of ensuring compliance by the investment undertaking with its obligations under *Chapter 1A* of *Part 27*,

(b) examine all or a sample of the declarations made to the investment undertaking,

(c) examine transactions in relation to a sample of unit holders to determine whether—

(i) the procedures referred to in paragraph (*a*) have been observed in practice and whether they are adequate,

(ii) the investment undertaking has, on the happening of a chargeable event in relation to a unit holder, paid the correct amount of appropriate tax in connection with the chargeable event, and

(iii) there is information in the investment undertaking's possession which can reasonably be taken to indicate that the investment undertaking incorrectly failed to pay appropriate tax in connection with a chargeable event.

(4) Where an authorised officer in exercising or performing his or her powers and duties under this section has reason to believe that in respect of one or more unit holders, the investment undertaking has incorrectly failed to pay appropriate tax in connection with a chargeable event, the authorised officer may make such further enquiries as are necessary to establish whether there is a liability in relation to any person.

(5) An authorised officer may require an investment undertaking or an employee of the investment undertaking to produce books, records or other documents and to furnish information, explanations and particulars and to give all assistance, which the authorised officer reasonably requires for the purposes of his or her audit and examination under *subsections (2)* and *(3)*, and, as the case may be, enquiries under *subsection (4)*.

(6) An authorised officer may make extracts from or copies of all or any part of the books, records or other documents or other material made available to him or her or require that copies of books, records or other documents be made available to him or her, in exercising or performing his or her powers or duties under this section.

(7) An employee of an investment undertaking who fails to comply with the requirements of the authorised officer in the exercise or performance of the authorised officer's powers or duties under this section shall be liable to a penalty of [€1,265][1].

(8) An investment undertaking which fails to comply with the requirements of the authorised officer in the exercise or performance of the authorised officer's powers or duties under this section shall be liable to a penalty of [€19,045][2] and if that failure continues a further penalty of [€2,535][3] for each day on which the failure continues.][4]

Amendments

[1, 2, 3] Substituted by FA01 sched5.

[4] Inserted by FA00 s68(b).

Revenue Briefings

Tax Briefing

Tax Briefing August 2002 – Issue 49 pg 6 – Code of Practice Revenue Audits

Statements of Practice

Revenue Powers Exercised in Places other than a Revenue Office – SP GEN/1/94 (Revised 02/2006)
Revenue Powers (Finance Act 1999) – SP GEN/1/99
Revenue Internal Review Procedures – SP GEN/2/99

Cross References

From Section 904D

Section 731 Chargeable gains accruing to unit trusts.
Section 739B Interpretation and application.
Section 739E Deduction of tax on the occurrence of a chargeable event.
Section 739F Returns and collection of appropriate tax.

904E Power of inspection: claims by authorised insurers

[(1) In this section—

["*authorised insurer*"—

(a) subject to *paragraph (b)*, has the same meaning as in *section 470*,

(b) in relation to a claim made under *section 470B(6)(b)(ii)*, has the same meaning as in *section 470B*;][1]

"*authorised officer*" means an officer of the Revenue Commissioners authorised by them in writing to exercise the powers conferred by this section.

(2) An authorised officer may at all reasonable times enter any premises or place of business of an authorised insurer for the purpose of auditing for a year of assessment claims made by the authorised insurer under *section 470(3)(b)(ii)* [or *470B(6)(b)(ii)*][2].

(3) Without prejudice to the generality of subsection (2), the authorised officer may—

(a) examine the procedures put in place by the authorised insurer in relation to the vouching of claims referred to in that subsection, and

(b) check a sample of the cases in respect of which such a claim has been made to determine whether the procedures referred to in paragraph (*a*) have been observed in practice and whether they are adequate.

(4) An authorised officer may require an authorised insurer or an employee of the authorised insurer to furnish information, explanations and particulars and to give all assistance which the authorised officer reasonably requires for the purposes of his or her audit and examination under subsections (2) and (3).

(5) An authorised officer when exercising or performing his or her powers or duties under this section shall, on request, produce his or her authorisation for the purposes of this section.

(6) An employee of an authorised insurer who fails to comply with the requirements of the authorised officer in the exercise or performance of the authorised officer's powers or duties under this section shall be liable to a penalty of [€1,265][3].

(7) An authorised insurer which fails to comply with the requirements of the authorised officer in the exercise or performance of the authorised officer's powers or duties under this section shall be liable to a penalty of [€19,045][4] and, if that failure continues, a further penalty of [€2,535][5] for each day on which the failure continues.][6]

Amendments

[1] Substituted by the Health Insurance (Miscellaneous Provisions) Act 2009 sec 23

[2] Inserted by the Health Insurance (Miscellaneous Provisions) Act 2009 sec 23

[3] Substituted by FA01 s22(2)(a). Applies as respects the year of assessment 2002 and subsequent years of assessment.

[4] Substituted by FA01 s22(2)(b)(i). Applies as respects the year of assessment 2002 and subsequent years of assessment.

[5] Substituted by FA01 s22(2)(b)(ii). Applies as respects the year of assessment 2002 and subsequent years of assessment.

[6] Inserted by FA01 s22(1). Applies as respects the year of assessment 2001 and subsequent years of assessment.

Revenue Briefings

Tax Briefing

Tax Briefing August 2002 – Issue 49 pg 6 – Code of Practice Revenue Audits

Statements of Practice

Revenue Powers Exercised in Places other than a Revenue Office – SP GEN/1/94 (Revised 02/2006)
Revenue Powers (Finance Act 1999) – SP GEN/1/99
Revenue Internal Review Procedures – SP GEN/2/99

Cross References

From Section 904E

Section 470 Relief for insurance against expenses of illness.
Section 470B Age-related relief for health insurance premiums.

904F Power of inspection: claims by qualifying lenders

[(1) In this section—

"*authorised officer*" means an officer of the Revenue Commissioners authorised by them in writing to exercise the powers conferred by this section;

"books, records or other documents" includes—

(a) any records used in the business of a qualifying lender whether—

(i) comprised in bound volume, loose-leaf binders or other looseleaf filing system, loose-leaf ledger sheets, pages, folios or cards, or

(ii) kept on microfilm, magnetic tape or in any non-legible form (by the use of electronics or otherwise) which is capable of being reproduced in a legible form, and

(b) every electronic or other automatic means, if any, by which any such thing in non-legible form is so capable of being reproduced, and

(c) documents in manuscript, documents which are typed, printed, stencilled or created by any other mechanical or partly mechanical process in use from time to time and documents which are produced by any photographic or photostatic process, and

(d) correspondence and records of other communications between a qualifying lender and an individual having a qualifying mortgage loan from that qualifying lender;

"*qualifying lender*" and "*qualifying mortgage loan*" have the same meanings respectively as in *section 244A*.

(2) An authorised officer may at all reasonable times enter any premises or place of business of a qualifying lender for the purpose of auditing for a year of assessment claims made by the qualifying lender under *section 244A(2)(b)(ii)*.

(3) Without prejudice to the generality of subsection (2), the authorised officer may—

(a) examine the procedures put in place by the qualifying lender in relation to the vouching of claims referred to in that subsection, and

(b) check a sample of the cases in respect of which such a claim has been made to determine whether the procedures referred to in *paragraph (a)* have been observed in practice and whether they are adequate.

(4) An authorised officer may require a qualifying lender or an employee of the qualifying lender to produce books, records or other documents and to furnish information, explanations and particulars and to give all assistance, which the authorised officer reasonably requires for the purposes of his or her audit and examination under subsections (2) and (3).

(5) An authorised officer may make extracts from or copies of all or any part of the books, records or other documents or other material made available to him or her or require that copies of books, records, or other documents be made available to him or her, in exercising or performing his or her powers or duties under this section.

(6) An authorised officer when exercising or performing his or her powers or duties under this section shall, on request, produce his or her authorisation for the purposes of this section.

(7) An employee of a qualifying lender who fails to comply with the requirements of the authorised officer in the exercise or performance of the authorised officer's powers or duties under this section shall be liable to a penalty of €1,265.

(8) A qualifying lender which fails to comply with the requirements of the authorised officer in the exercise or performance of the authorised officer's powers or duties under this section shall be liable to a penalty of €19,045 and if that failure continues a further penalty of €2,535 for each day on which the failure continues.][1]

Amendments

[1] Inserted by FA01 s22(3). Applies as respects the year of assessment 2002 and subsequent years of assessment.

Revenue Briefings

Tax Briefing

Tax Briefing August 2002 – Issue 49 pg 6 – Code of Practice Revenue Audits

Statements of Practice

Revenue Powers Exercised in Places other than a Revenue Office – SP GEN/1/94 (Revised 02/2006)
Revenue Powers (Finance Act 1999) – SP GEN/1/99
Revenue Internal Review Procedures – SP GEN/2/99

Cross References

From Section 904F

Section 244A Application of section 244 (relief for interest paid on certain home loans) of Principal Act.

904G Power of inspection: claims by qualifying insurers

[(1) In this section—

"*authorised officer*" means an officer of the Revenue Commissioners authorised by them in writing to exercise the powers conferred by this section;

"*qualifying insurer*" and "*qualifying long-term care policies*" have the same meanings respectively as in *section 470A*.

(2) An authorised officer may at all reasonable times enter any premises or place of business of a qualifying insurer for the purpose of auditing for a year of assessment claims made by the qualifying insurer under *section 470A(8)(b)(ii)*.

(3) Without prejudice to the generality of subsection (2), the authorised officer may—

(a) examine the procedures put in place by the qualifying insurer in relation to the vouching of claims referred to in that subsection, and

(b) check a sample of the cases in respect of which such a claim has been made to determine whether the procedures referred to in paragraph *(a)* have been observed in practice and whether they are adequate.

(4) An authorised officer may require a qualifying insurer or an employee of the qualifying insurer to furnish information, explanations and particulars and to give all assistance which the authorised officer reasonably requires for the purposes of his or her audit and examination under subsections (2) and (3).

(5) An authorised officer when exercising or performing his or her powers or duties under this section shall, on request, produce his or her authorisation for the purposes of this section.

(6) An employee of a qualifying insurer who fails to comply with the requirements of the authorised officer in the exercise or performance of the authorised officer's powers or duties under this section shall be liable to a penalty of [€1,265][1].

(7) A qualifying insurer which fails to comply with the requirements of the authorised officer in the exercise or performance of the authorised officer's powers or duties under this section shall be liable to a penalty of [€19,045][2] and, if that failure continues, a further penalty of [€2,535][3] for each day on which the failure continues.][4]

Amendments

[1] Substituted by FA01 s22(5)(a)(i). Applies as respects the year of assessment 2002 and subsequent years of assessment.

[2] Substituted by FA01 s22(5)(a)(ii)(I). Applies as respects the year of assessment 2002 and subsequent years of assessment.

[3] Substituted by FA01 s22(5)(a)(ii)(II). Applies as respects the year of assessment 2002 and subsequent years of assessment.

[4] Inserted by FA01 s22(4). Applies as respects the year of assessment 2001 and subsequent years of assessment.

Revenue Briefings

Tax Briefing

Tax Briefing August 2002 – Issue 49 pg 6 – Code of Practice Revenue Audits

Statements of Practice

Revenue Powers Exercised in Places other than a Revenue Office – SP GEN/1/94 (Revised 02/2006)
Revenue Powers (Finance Act 1999) – SP GEN/1/99
Revenue Internal Review Procedures – SP GEN/2/99

Cross References

From Section 904G

Section 470A Relief for premiums under qualifying long-term care policies.

904H Power of inspection: qualifying savings managers

[(1) In this section—

"*authorised officer*" means an officer of the Revenue Commissioners authorised by them in writing to exercise the powers conferred by this section;

"*qualifying savings manager*" has the same meaning as in *section 848B* (inserted by the *Finance Act, 2001*);

"*special savings incentive account*" has the same meaning as in *section 848B* (inserted by the *Finance Act, 2001*).

(2) An authorised officer may at all reasonable times enter any premises or place of business of a qualifying savings manager, or a person (in this section referred

to as an "*appointed person*") appointed by a qualifying savings manager in accordance with *section 848R* (inserted by the *Finance Act, 2001*), for the purposes of auditing compliance with the provisions of Part 36A (inserted by the *Finance Act, 2001*) and without prejudice to the generality of the foregoing the authorised officer may—

(a) audit the returns made in accordance with *sections 848P* and *848Q* (inserted by the *Finance Act, 2001*),

(b) examine the procedures put in place by the qualifying savings manager, or as the case may be, the appointed person, so as to ensure compliance with the obligations imposed by Part 36A (inserted by the *Finance Act, 2001*),

(c) examine all, or a sample of, special savings incentive accounts to determine—

(i) whether those procedures have been observed in practice,

(ii) whether the terms under which each such account was commenced and continues, are in accordance with the terms referred to in *section 848C* (inserted by the *Finance Act, 2001*), and

(iii) whether the qualifying savings manager, in respect of each such account, is, where appropriate, in possession of a declaration referred to in *sections 848F, 848I,* and *848O* (inserted by the *Finance Act, 2001*), and is not in possession of any information which would reasonably suggest that any such declaration is incorrect,

and

(d) examine any notice and declaration referred to in *section 848N(3)* (inserted by the *Finance Act, 2001*).

(3) An authorised officer may require a qualifying savings manager, or (as the case may be) the appointed person, or an employee of either such person, to produce all or any of the records relating to the management by him or her of special savings incentive accounts and furnish information, explanations and particulars and to give all assistance, which the authorised officer reasonably requires for the purposes of his or her audit and examination under subsection (2).

(4) An employee of a qualifying savings manager or of an appointed person who fails to comply with the requirements of the authorised officer in the exercise or performance of the authorised officer's powers or duties under this section shall be liable to a penalty of [€1,265][1].

(5) A qualifying savings manager or an appointed person who fails to comply with the requirements of the authorised officer in the exercise or performance of the authorised officer's powers or duties under this section shall be liable to a penalty of [€19,045][2] and, if that failure continues, a further penalty of [€2,535][3] for each day on which the failure continues.][4]

Amendments

[1] Substituted by FA01 s22(5)(b)(i). Applies as respects the year of assessment 2002 and subsequent years of assessment.

[2] Substituted by FA01 s22(5)(b)(ii)(I). Applies as respects the year of assessment 2002 and subsequent years of assessment.

[3] Substituted by FA01 s22(5)(b)(ii)(II). Applies as respects the year of assessment 2002 and subsequent years of assessment.

[4] Inserted by FA01 s22(4). Applies as respects the year of assessment 2001 and subsequent years of assessment.

Revenue Briefings

Tax Briefing

Tax Briefing August 2002 – Issue 49 pg 6 – Code of Practice Revenue Audits

Statements of Practice

Revenue Powers Exercised in Places other than a Revenue Office – SP GEN/1/94 (Revised 02/2006)

Revenue Powers (Finance Act 1999) – SP GEN/1/99

Revenue Internal Review Procedures – SP GEN/2/99

Cross References

From Section 904H

Section 848B Interpretation.

Section 848C Special savings incentive account.

Section 848F Declaration on commencement.

Section 848I Declaration on maturity.

Section 848N Transfer of special savings incentive account.

Section 848O Declaration on transfer.

Section 848P Monthly returns.

Section 848Q Annual returns.

Section 848R Registration etc.

904I Power of inspection: returns and collection of dividend withholding tax

[(1) In this section—

"*accountable person*" means—

(a) a company resident in the State which makes, and

(b) an authorised withholding agent who is treated under *section 172H* as making, a relevant distribution;

"*authorised withholding agent*", "*dividend withholding tax*", and "*relevant distribution*" have, respectively, the meanings assigned to them by *section 172A*;

"*authorised officer*" means an officer of the Revenue Commissioners, authorised by them in writing to exercise the powers conferred by this section;

"*records*" means all records which relate to compliance by an accountable person with obligations under *Chapter 8A* of *Part 6* including all declarations (and accompanying certificates) and notifications which are made, or, as the case may be, given to an accountable person in accordance with that Chapter of that Part and *Schedule 2A*.

(2) An authorised officer, having regard to Chapter 8A of Part 6, may at all reasonable times enter any premises or place of business of an accountable person for the purposes of auditing a return made by the accountable person under *section 172K*.

(3) Without prejudice to the generality of subsection (2), the authorised officer may—

(a) examine the procedures put in place by the accountable person for the purpose of ensuring compliance by the accountable person with its obligations under *Chapter 8A* of *Part 6*, and

(b) check all, or a sample of or a class of, the records in the power, possession or procurement of the accountable person to determine whether—

(i) the procedures referred to in paragraph *(a)* have been observed in practice and whether they are adequate, and

(ii) there is information in the accountable person's possession which can reasonably be taken to indicate that the information contained in one or more of the records is or may be incorrect.

(4) An authorised officer may require an accountable person or an employee of the accountable person to produce records and to furnish information, explanations and particulars and to give all assistance which the authorised officer reasonably requires for the purposes of his or her audit and examination under *subsections (2)* and *(3)*.

(5) An authorised officer may make extracts from or copies of all or any part of the records made available to him or her or require that copies of such records be made available to him or her, in exercising or performing his or her powers or duties under this section.

(6) An employee of an accountable person who fails to comply with the requirements of the authorised officer in the exercise or performance of the authorised officer's powers or duties under this section shall be liable to a penalty of €1,265.

(7) An accountable person who fails to comply with the requirements of the authorised officer in the exercise or performance of the authorised officer's powers or duties under this section shall be liable to a penalty of €19,045 and if that failure continues a further penalty of €2,535 for each day on which the failure continues.][1]

Amendments

[1] Inserted by FA02 s132(c).

Revenue Briefings

Tax Briefing

Tax Briefing August 2002 – Issue 49 pg 6 – Code of Practice Revenue Audits

Statements of Practice

Revenue Powers Exercised in Places other than a Revenue Office – SP GEN/1/94 (Revised 02/2006)
Revenue Powers (Finance Act 1999) – SP GEN/1/99
Revenue Internal Review Procedures – SP GEN/2/99

Cross References

From Section 904I

Section 172A Interpretation.
Section 172H Obligations of authorised withholding agent in relation to relevant distributions.
Section 172K Returns, payment and collection of dividend withholding tax.

904J Power of inspection: tax deduction from payments in respect of professional services by certain persons

[(1) In this section—

"*accountable person*" has the same meaning as in *section 521*;

"*authorised officer*" means an officer of the Revenue Commissioners authorised by them in writing to exercise the powers conferred by this section;

"books, records or other documents" includes—

(a) any records used in the business of an accountable person whether—

(i) comprised in bound volume, loose-leaf binders or other loose-leaf filing system, loose-leaf ledger sheets, pages, folios or cards, or

(ii) kept on microfilm, magnetic tape or in any non-legible form (by the use of electronics or otherwise) which is capable of being reproduced in a legible form,

and

(b) every electronic or other automatic means, if any, by which any such thing in non-legible form is so capable of being reproduced, and

(c) documents in manuscript, documents which are typed, printed, stencilled or created by any other mechanical or partly mechanical process in use from time to time and documents which are produced by any photographic or photostatic process, and

(d) correspondence and records of other communications between an accountable person and a specified person;

"*specified person*" has the same meaning as in *section 520*.

(2) An authorised officer may at all reasonable times enter any premises or place of business of an accountable person for the purpose of auditing for a year of assessment returns made by the accountable person under *section 525*.

(3) Without prejudice to the generality of subsection (2), the authorised officer may—

(a) examine the procedures put in place by the accountable person for the purpose of ensuring compliance by the accountable person with that person's obligations under *Chapter 1* of *Part 18*, and

(b) examine all or a sample of the returns made by the accountable person to determine whether the procedures referred to in paragraph (*a*) have been observed in practice and whether they are adequate.

(4) An authorised officer may require an accountable person or an employee of the accountable person to produce books, records or other documents and to furnish information, explanations and particulars and to give all assistance, which the authorised officer reasonably requires for the purposes of his or her audit and examination under subsections (2) and (3).

(5) An authorised officer may make extracts from or copies of all or any part of the books, records or other documents or other material made available to him or her or require that copies of books, records, or other documents be made available to him or her, in exercising or performing his or her powers or duties under this section.

(6) An authorised officer when exercising or performing his or her powers or duties under this section shall, on request, produce his or her authorisation for the purposes of this section.

(7) An employee of an accountable person who fails to comply with the requirements of the authorised officer in the exercise or performance of the authorised officer's powers or duties under this section is liable to a penalty of €1,265.

(8) An accountable person who fails to comply with the requirements of the authorised officer in the exercise or performance of the authorised officer's powers or duties under this section is liable to a penalty of €19,045 and if that failure continues a further penalty of €2,535 for each day on which the failure continues.][1]

Amendments

[1] Inserted by FA03 s159.

Revenue Briefings

Tax Briefing

Tax Briefing August 2002 – Issue 49 pg 6 – Code of Practice Revenue Audits

Statements of Practice

Revenue Powers Exercised in Places other than a Revenue Office – SP GEN/1/94 (Revised 02/2006)
Revenue Powers (Finance Act 1999) – SP GEN/1/99
Revenue Internal Review Procedures – SP GEN/2/99

Cross References

From Section 904J

Section 520 Interpretation (Chapter 1).
Section 521 Accountable persons.
Section 525 Returns and collection of appropriate tax.

904K Power of inspection: notices of attachment

[(1) In this section—

"*authorised officer*" means an officer of the Revenue Commissioners authorised by them in writing to exercise the powers conferred by this section;

"*books, records or other documents*" includes—

(a) any records used in the business of a relevant person whether—

(i) comprised in bound volume, loose-leaf binders or other loose-leaf filing system, loose-leaf ledger sheets, pages, folios or cards, or

(ii) kept on microfilm, magnetic tape or in any non-legible form (by the use of electronics or otherwise) which is capable of being reproduced in a legible form,

(b) every electronic or other automatic means, if any, by which any such thing in non-legible form is so capable of being reproduced,

(c) documents in manuscript, documents which are typed, printed, stencilled or created by any other mechanical or partly mechanical process in use from time to time and documents which are produced by any photographic or photostatic process, and

(d) correspondence and records of other communications between a qualifying lender and an individual having a qualifying mortgage loan from that qualifying lender;

"*relevant employee*" means an employee of a relevant person who by virtue of his or her employment—

(a) is in a position to produce or have produced, as appropriate, any books, records or other documents,

(b) is in a position to furnish or have furnished, as appropriate, any information, explanations or particulars relating to any books, records or other documents, or

(c) otherwise can give assistance for the purposes of *paragraph* (*a*) or (*b*),

to an authorised officer, as may be required under *subsection (3)*;

"*relevant person*" and "*return*" have the same meaning as in *section 1002*.

(2) An authorised officer may at all reasonable times enter any premises or place of business of a relevant person for the purpose of auditing a return.

(3) An authorised officer may require a relevant person or a relevant employee to produce books, records or other documents and to furnish information, explanations and particulars and to give all assistance, which the authorised officer reasonably requires for the purposes of his or her audit under *subsection (2)*.

(4) An authorised officer may make extracts from or copies of all or any part of the books, records or other documents or other material made available to him or her or require that copies of books, records, or other documents be made available to him or her, in exercising or performing his or her powers or duties under this section.

(5) An authorised officer when exercising or performing his or her powers or duties under this section shall, on request, produce his or her authorisation for the purposes of this section.

(6) A relevant employee who fails to comply with the requirements of the authorised officer in the exercise or performance of the authorised officer's powers or duties under this section shall be liable to a penalty of €1,265.

(7) A relevant person who fails to comply with the requirements of the authorised officer in the exercise or performance of the authorised officer's powers or duties under this section shall be liable to a penalty of €19,045 and if that failure continues a further penalty of €2,535 for each day on which the failure continues.][1]

Amendments

[1] Inserted by FA11 s74(c). Effective from date of passing of the Act.

Cross References

From Section 904K

Section 1002 Deduction from payments due to defaulters of amounts due in relation to tax.

905 Inspection of documents and records

[FA76 s34; FA92 s232]

(1) In this section—

"*authorised officer*" means an officer of the Revenue Commissioners authorised by them in writing to exercise the powers conferred by this section;

"*property*" means any asset relating to a tax liability;

["*records*" means any document or any other written or printed material in any form, and includes any information stored, maintained or preserved by means of any mechanical or electronic device, whether or not stored, maintained or preserved in a legible form—

(i) which relates to a business carried on by a person, or

(ii) which a person is obliged by any provision relating to tax to keep, retain, issue or produce for inspection or which may be inspected under any provision relating to tax;][1]

"*tax*" means any tax, duty, levy or charge under the care and management of the Revenue Commissioners;

"*tax liability*" means any existing liability to tax or further liability to tax which may be established by an authorised officer following the exercise or performance of his or her powers or duties under this section.

(2) (a) An authorised officer may at all reasonable times enter any premises or place where the authorised officer has reason to believe that—

(i) any trade, profession or other activity, the profits or gains of which are chargeable to tax, is or has been carried on,

(ii) anything is or has been done in connection with any trade, profession or other activity the profits or gains of which are chargeable to tax,

(iii) any records relating to—

(I) any trade, profession, other source of profits or gains or chargeable gains,

(II) any tax liability, or

(III) any repayments of tax in regard to any person,

are or may be kept, or

(iv) any property is or has been located,

and the authorised officer may—

(A) require any person who is on those premises or in that place, other than a person who is there to purchase goods or to receive a service, to produce any records or property,

(B) if the authorised officer has reason to believe that any of the records or property which he or she has required to be produced to him or her under this subsection have not been produced, search on those premises or in that place for those records or property,

(C) examine any records or property and take copies of or extracts from any records,

(D) remove any records and retain them for a reasonable time for the purposes of their further examination or for the purposes of any legal proceedings instituted by an officer of the Revenue Commissioners or for the purposes of any criminal proceedings, and

(E) examine property listed in any records.

(b) An authorised officer may in the exercise or performance of his or her powers or duties under this section require any person whom he or she has reason to believe—

(i) is or was carrying on any trade, profession or other activity the profits or gains of which are chargeable to tax,

(ii) is or was liable to any tax, or

(iii) has information relating to any tax liability,

to give the authorised officer all reasonable assistance, including providing information and explanations or furnishing documents and making available for inspection property as required by the authorised officer in relation to any tax liability or any repayment of tax in regard to any person.

[(c) Nothing in this section shall be construed as requiring any person to disclose to an authorised officer—

(i) information with respect to which a claim to legal professional privilege could be maintained in legal proceedings,

(ii) information of a confidential medical nature, or

(iii) professional advice of a confidential nature given to a client (other than advice given as part of a dishonest, fraudulent or criminal purpose).][2]

[…][3]

[(e) An authorised officer shall not, without the consent of the occupier, enter any premises, or that portion of any premises, which is occupied wholly and exclusively as a private residence, except on production by the officer of a warrant issued under subsection (2A).][4]

[…][5]

[(2A) (a) In this subsection "*the Acts*" has the meaning assigned to it by *section 1078(1)*.

(b) Without prejudice to any power conferred by subsection (2), if a Judge of the District Court is satisfied by information on oath that there are reasonable grounds for suspecting—

(i) that a person may have failed or may fail to comply with any provision of the Acts,

(ii) that any such failure is likely to have led or to lead to serious prejudice to the proper assessment or collection of tax (having regard to the amount of any tax liability that arises or might arise from such failure), and

(iii) that records, which are material to the proper assessment or collection of tax are likely to be kept or concealed at any premises or place,

the Judge may issue a search warrant.

(c) A search warrant issued under this subsection shall be expressed and shall operate to authorise an authorised officer accompanied by such other named officers of the Revenue Commissioners and such other named persons as the authorised officer considers necessary, at any time or times within one month of the date of issue of the warrant, to enter (if need be by force) the premises or other place named or specified in the warrant, to search such premises or other place, to examine anything found there, to inspect any records found there and, if there are reasonable grounds for suspecting that any records found there are material to the proper assessment or collection of tax, or that the records may be required for the purpose of any legal proceedings instituted by an officer of the Revenue Commissioners [...][6], remove such records and retain them for so long as they are reasonably required for the purpose aforesaid.][7]

(3) A person who does not comply with any requirement of an authorised officer in the exercise or performance of the authorised officer's powers or duties under this section shall be liable to a penalty of [€4,000][8].

(4) An authorised officer when exercising or performing his or her powers or duties under this section shall on request show his or her authorisation for the purposes of this section.

Amendments

[1] Substituted by FA02 s132(d).

[2] Substituted by F(No.2)A08 s92(f).

[3] Deleted by FA99 s207(f)(i).

[4] Substituted by FA07 s124(a)(i).

[5] Deleted by FA07 s124(a)(ii).

[6] Deleted by FA07 s124(b).

[7] Inserted by FA99 s207(f)(ii).

[8] Substituted by F(No.2)A08 sched5(part2)(1)(t). The enactments specified in Schedule 5 are amended or repealed to the extent and manner specified in that Schedule and, unless the contrary is stated, shall come into effect after 24 December 2008.

Case Law

The taxpayer had 30 days to produce documents as requested by Revenue . He offered that Revenue could view them at one minute to midnight at his home on the 30th day. The High Court held that he was not compliant. Johnson v IRC 1996 STI 270

Revenue Briefings

Tax Briefing

Tax Briefing August 2002 – Issue 49 pg 6 – Code of Practice Revenue Audits
Tax Briefing July 2007 – Issue 66 pg 27 – Finance Act 2007

Revenue Information Notes

2010 Code of Practice for Revenue Audit
Code of Practice for Revenue Audit and other Compliance Interventions

Statements of Practice

Revenue Powers Exercised in Places other than a Revenue Office – SP GEN/1/94 (Revised 02/2006)
Revenue Powers (Finance Act 1999) – SP GEN/1/99
Revenue Internal Review Procedures – SP GEN/2/99

Cross References

From Section 905

Section 1078 Revenue offences.

To Section 905

Section 906 Authorised officers and Garda Síochána.
Section 1078B Presumptions.
Section 1104 Short title and construction.
Schedule 31 Consequential Amendments

906 Authorised officers and Garda Síochána

[FA92 s236]

Where an authorised officer (within the meaning of *section 903*, *904* or *905*, as the case may be) in accordance with *section 903*, *904* or *905* enters any premises or place, the authorised officer may be accompanied by a member or members of the Garda Síochána, and any such member may arrest without warrant any person who obstructs or interferes with the authorised officer in the exercise or performance of his or her powers or duties under any of those sections.

Statements of Practice

Revenue Powers Exercised in Places other than a Revenue Office – SP GEN/1/94 (Revised 02/2006)
Revenue Powers (Finance Act 1999) – SP GEN/1/99
Revenue Internal Review Procedures – SP GEN/2/99

Cross References

From Section 906

Section 903 Power of inspection: PAYE.
Section 904 Power of inspection: tax deduction from payments to certain subcontractors.
Section 905 Inspection of documents and records.

To Section 906

Section 1104 Short title and construction.

906A Information to be furnished by financial institutions

[(1) In this section and in [*sections 907*, *907A* and *908*][1]—

"*the Acts*" has the meaning assigned to it by *section 1078(1)*;

"*authorised officer*" means an officer of the Revenue Commissioners authorised by them in writing to exercise the powers conferred by this section, or, as the case may be, [*section 907*, *907A* or *908*][2];

"books, records or other documents" includes—

(a) any records used in the business of a financial institution, or used in the transfer department of a financial institution acting as registrar of securities, whether—

(i) comprised in bound volume, loose-leaf binders or other loose-leaf filing system, loose-leaf ledger sheets, pages, folios or cards, or

(ii) kept on microfilm, magnetic tape or in any non-legible form (by the use of electronics or otherwise) which is capable of being reproduced in a legible form,

(b) every electronic or other automatic means, if any, by which any such thing in non-legible form is so capable of being reproduced,

(c) documents in manuscript, documents which are typed, printed, stencilled or created by any other mechanical or partly mechanical process in use from time to time and documents which are produced by any photographic or photostatic process, and

(d) correspondence and records of other communications between a financial institution and its customers;

"*connected person*" has the same meaning as in *section 10*; but an individual (other than in the capacity as a trustee of a settlement) shall be connected with another individual only if that other individual is [the spouse or civil partner of, or a minor child or minor child of the civil partner of, the first-mentioned individual][3];

"*deposit*" and "*interest*" have, respectively, the meaning assigned to them by *section 256(1)*;

["*financial institution*" means—

[(a) a person who holds or has held a licence under section 9 of the Central Bank Act 1971, or a 20 person who holds or has held a licence or other similar authorisation under the law of any other Member State of the European Communities which corresponds to a licence granted under that section,][4]

(b) a person referred to in section 7(4) of the Central Bank Act, 1971, or

(c) a credit institution (within the meaning of the European Communities (Licensing and Supervision of Credit Institutions) Regulations, 1992 (S.I. No. 395 of 1992)) which has been authorised by the Central Bank of Ireland to carry on business of a credit institution in accordance with the provisions of the supervisory enactments (within the meaning of those Regulations);][5]

"*liability*" in relation to a person means any liability in relation to tax to which the person is or may be, or may have been, subject, or the amount of such liability;

"*tax*" means any tax, duty, levy or charge under the care and management of the Revenue Commissioners.

(2) Notwithstanding any obligation as to secrecy or other restriction upon disclosure of information imposed by or under statute or otherwise, and subject to this section, an authorised officer may, for the purpose of enquiring into a liability in relation to a person (in this section referred to as the "*taxpayer*"), serve on a financial institution a notice in writing requiring the financial institution, within such period as may be specified in the notice, not being less than 30 days from the date of the service of the notice, to do either or both of the following, namely—

(a) to make available for inspection by the authorised officer such books, records or other documents as are in the financial institution's power, possession or procurement and as contain, or may (in the authorised officer's opinion formed on reasonable grounds) contain, information relevant to a liability in relation to the taxpayer,

(b) to furnish to the authorised officer, in writing or otherwise, such information, explanations and particulars as the authorised officer may reasonably require, being information, explanations and particulars that are relevant to any such liability,

and which are specified in the notice.

(3) Where, in compliance with the requirements of a notice under subsection (2), a financial institution makes available for inspection by an authorised officer, books, records or other documents, it shall afford the authorised officer reasonable assistance, including information, explanations and particulars, in relation to the use of all the electronic or other automatic means, if any, by which the books, records or other documents, in so far as they are in a non-legible form, are capable of being reproduced in a legible form and any data equipment or any associated apparatus or material.

(4) An authorised officer shall not serve a notice on a financial institution under subsection (2) without the consent in writing of a Revenue Commissioner and without having reasonable grounds to believe that the financial institution is likely to have information relevant to a liability in relation to the taxpayer.

(5) Without prejudice to the generality of subsection (2), the books, records or other documents which a financial institution may be required by notice under that subsection to deliver or to make available and the information, explanations and particulars which it may likewise be required to furnish, may include books, records or other documents and information, explanations and particulars relating to a person who is connected with the taxpayer.

(6) The persons who may be treated as a taxpayer for the purposes of this section include a company which has been dissolved and an individual who has died.

(7) A notice served under subsection (2) shall name the taxpayer in relation to whose liability the authorised officer is enquiring.

(8) Where an authorised officer serves a notice under subsection (2), a copy of such notice shall be given by the authorised officer to the taxpayer concerned.

(9) Where, in compliance with a notice served under subsection (2), a financial institution makes books, records or other documents available for inspection by an authorised officer, the authorised officer may make extracts from or copies of all or any part of the books, records or other documents.

(10) A financial institution which fails or refuses to comply with a notice issued under subsection (2) or which fails or refuses to afford reasonable assistance to an authorised officer as required under subsection (3), shall be liable to a penalty of [€19,045][6] and, if the failure or refusal to comply with such notice continues after the expiry of the period specified in the notice served under subsection (2), a further penalty of [€2,535][7] for each day on which the failure or refusal continues.][8]

Amendments

[1] Substituted by FA10 s153(a)(i). Has effect as on and from 3 April 2010.

[2] Substituted by FA10 s153(a)(ii). Has effect as on and from 3 April 2010.

[3] Substituted by F(No.3)A11 sched1(239). Shall have effect from 27 July 2011.

[4] Substituted by F(No.2)A08 s92(g).

[5] Substituted by FA00 s68(c).

[6, 7] Substituted by FA01 sched5.

[8] Inserted by FA99 s207(g).

Revenue Briefings

Tax Briefing

Tax Briefing August 2002 – Issue 49 pg 6 – Code of Practice Revenue Audits

Statements of Practice

Code of Practice for Revenue Audit

Cross References

From Section 906A

Section 10 Connected persons.
Section 256 Interpretation (Chapter 4).
Section 907 Application to Appeal Commissioners: information from financial institutions.
Section 907A Application to Appeal Commissioners: information from third party.
Section 908 Application to High Court seeking order requiring information: financial institutions.
Section 1078 Revenue offences.

To Section 906A

Section 246A Interest in respect of wholesale debt instruments.
Section 902 Information to be furnished by third party: request of an authorised officer.
Section 902A Application to High Court: information from third party.
Section 912A Information for tax authorities in other territories.

907 Application to Appeal Commissioners: information from financial institutions

[(1) In this section "*a taxpayer*" means any person including—

(a) a person whose identity is not known to the authorised officer, and a group or class of persons whose individual identities are not so known, and

(b) a person by or in respect of whom a declaration has been made under *section 263(1)* declaring that the person is beneficially entitled to all or part of the interest in relation to a deposit.

(2) An authorised officer may, subject to this section, make an application to the Appeal Commissioners for their consent, under subsection (5), to the service by him or her of a notice on a financial institution requiring the financial institution to do either or both of the following, namely—

(a) to make available for inspection by the authorised officer, such books, records or other documents as are in the financial institution's power, possession or procurement as contain, or may (in the authorised officer's opinion formed on reasonable grounds) contain, information relevant to a liability in relation to a taxpayer,

(b) to furnish to the authorised officer such information, explanations and particulars as the authorised officer may reasonably require, being information, explanations and particulars that are relevant to any such liability,

and which are specified in the application.

(3) An authorised officer shall not make an application under subsection (2) without the consent in writing of a Revenue Commissioner, and without being satisfied—

(a) that there are reasonable grounds for suspecting that the taxpayer, or where the taxpayer is a group or class of persons, all or any one of those persons, may have failed or may fail to comply with any provision of the Acts,

(b) that any such failure is likely to have led or to lead to serious prejudice to the proper assessment or collection of tax (having regard to the amount of a liability in relation to the taxpayer, or where the taxpayer is a group or class of persons, the amount of a liability in relation to all or any one of those persons, that arises or might arise from such failure), and

(c) that the information—

(i) which is likely to be contained in the books, records or other documents to which the application relates, or

(ii) which is likely to arise from the information, explanations and particulars to which the application relates,

is relevant to the proper assessment or collection of tax.

(4) Without prejudice to the generality of subsection (2), the authorised officer may make an application under that subsection to the Appeal Commissioners for their consent, under subsection (5), to the service by him or her of a notice on a financial institution in respect of the matters referred to in paragraphs (*a*) and (*b*) of subsection (2) in so far as they relate to a person who is connected with the taxpayer.

(5) Where the Appeal Commissioners determine that in all the circumstances there are reasonable grounds for the application being made, they may give their consent to the service by the authorised officer concerned of a notice on the financial institution, requiring the financial institution—

(a) to make available for inspection by the authorised officer, such books, records or other documents, and

(b) to furnish to the authorised officer such information, explanations and particulars,

of the kind referred to in subsection (2) as may, with the Appeal Commissioners" consent, be specified in the notice.

(6) The persons who may be treated as a taxpayer for the purposes of this section include a company which has been dissolved and an individual who has died.

(7) Where the Appeal Commissioners have given their consent in accordance with this section, the authorised officer shall, as soon as practicable, but not later than 14 days from the time that such consent was given, serve a notice on the financial institution concerned and stating that—

(a) such consent has been given, and

(b) the financial institution should, within a period of 30 days from the date of the service of the notice, comply with the requirements specified in the notice.

[(7A) Where in compliance with the requirements of a notice served under subsection (7), a financial institution makes available for inspection by an authorised officer, books, records or other documents, the financial institution shall afford the authorised officer reasonable assistance, including information, explanations and particulars, in relation to the use of all the electronic or other automatic means, if any, by which the books, records or other documents, in so far as they are in a non-legible form, are capable of being reproduced in a legible form, and any data equipment or any associated apparatus or material.

(7B) Where in compliance with the requirements of a notice served under subsection (7), a financial institution makes books, records or other documents available for inspection by the authorised officer, the authorised officer may make extracts from or copies of all or any part of the books, records or other documents.][1]

(8) (a) Subject to paragraph (*b*), an application by an authorised officer under subsection (2) shall, with any necessary modifications, be heard by the Appeal Commissioners as if it were an appeal against an assessment to income tax.

(b) Notwithstanding *section 933(4)*, a determination by the Appeal Commissioners under this section shall be final and conclusive.

(9) A financial institution which fails to comply with a notice served on the financial institution by an authorised officer in accordance with this section shall be liable to a penalty of [€19,045][2] and, if the failure continues after the expiry of the period specified in subsection (7)(*b*), a further penalty of [€2,535][3] for each day on which the failure so continues.][4]

Amendments

[1] Inserted by FA02 s132(e).

[2, 3] Substituted by FA01 sched5.

[4] Substituted by FA99 s207(h).

Revenue Briefings

Tax Briefing

Tax Briefing August 2002 – Issue 49 pg 6 – Code of Practice Revenue Audits

Statements of Practice

Revenue Powers Exercised in Places other than a Revenue Office – SP GEN/1/94 (Revised 02/2006)

Revenue Powers (Finance Act 1999) – SP GEN/1/99

Revenue Internal Review Procedures – SP GEN/2/99

Cross References

From Section 907

Section 263 Declarations relating to deposits of non-residents.

Section 933 Appeals against assessment.

To Section 907

Section 906A Information to be furnished by financial institutions.

Section 907A Application to Appeal Commissioners: information from third party.

Section 912A Information for tax authorities in other territories.

Section 1078 Revenue offences.

907A Application to Appeal Commissioners: information from third party

[(1) In this section—

"*taxpayer*" means a person whose identity is not known to the authorised officer, and a group or class of persons whose individual identities are not so known;

"*third party*" means a person whose identity has been furnished to an authorised officer by a financial institution in compliance with a notice issued under *section 907* or an order made under *section 908*.

(2) An authorised officer may, subject to this section, make application to the Appeal Commissioners for consent, to serve a notice on a third party, requiring the third party—

(a) to make available for inspection by the authorised officer, such books, records or other documents as are in the third party's power, possession or procurement as contain, or may (in the authorised officer's reasonable opinion) contain information relevant to a liability in relation to a taxpayer, or

(b) to furnish to the authorised officer such information, explanations and particulars as the authorised officer may reasonably require as being relevant to any such liability,

as may be specified in the application.

(3) An authorised officer shall not make application under *subsection (2)* without the consent in writing of a Revenue Commissioner, and without being satisfied—

(a) that there are reasonable grounds for suspecting that the taxpayer, or as the case may be, all or any of the taxpayers, may have failed or may fail to comply with any provision of the Acts,

(b) that any such failure is likely to have led or to lead to serious prejudice to the proper assessment or collection of tax, and

(c) that the information—

(i) which is likely to be contained in the books, records or other documents, or

(ii) which is likely to arise from the information, explanations and particulars,

to which the application relates, is relevant to the proper assessment or collection of tax.

(4) Without prejudice to the generality of *subsection (2)*, the authorised officer may make application to the Appeal Commissioners, for consent to serve a notice on a third party, in relation to books, records or other documents and information, explanations and particulars relating to a person who is connected with the taxpayer.

(5) Where the Appeal Commissioners determine that in all the circumstances there are reasonable grounds for making the application, they may give their consent to the authorised officer serving a notice on the third party, requiring the third party—

(a) to make available for inspection by the authorised officer, such books, records or other documents, and

(b) to furnish to the authorised officer such information, explanations and particulars,

as may, with the Appeal Commissioners' consent, be specified in the notice.

(6) The persons who may be treated as a taxpayer for the purposes of this section include a company which has been dissolved and an individual who has died.

(7) Nothing in this section shall be construed as requiring any person to disclose to an authorised officer—

(a) information with respect to which a claim to legal professional privilege could be maintained in legal proceedings,

(b) information of a confidential medical nature, or

(c) professional advice of a confidential nature given to a client (other than advice given as part of a dishonest, fraudulent or criminal purpose).

(8) Where the Appeal Commissioners have given their consent in accordance with this section, the authorised officer shall, as soon as practicable, but not later than 14 days from the time that such consent was made, serve a notice on the third party concerned and stating that—

(a) such consent has been given, and

(b) the third party should, within a period of 30 days, comply with the requirements as specified in the notice.

(9) (a) Subject to *paragraph (b)* an application by an authorised officer under *subsection (2)* shall with any necessary modifications be heard by the Appeal Commissioners as if it were an appeal against an assessment to income tax.

(b) Notwithstanding *section 933(4)*, a determination by the Appeal Commissioners under this section shall be final and conclusive.

(10) A third party which fails to comply with a notice served on the third party by an authorised officer in accordance with this section shall be liable to a penalty of €19,045 and, if the failure continues after the expiry of the period specified in *subsection (8)(b)*, a further penalty of €2,535 for each day on which the failure so continues.][1]

Amendments

[1] Inserted by FA10 s153(b). Has effect as on and from 3 April 2010.

Cross References

From Section 907A

Section 907 Application to Appeal Commissioners: information from financial institutions.

Section 908 Application to High Court seeking order requiring information: financial institutions.

Section 933 Appeals against assessment.

To Section 907A

Section 906A Information to be furnished by financial institutions.

908 Application to High Court seeking order requiring information: financial institutions

[(1) In this section—

"*judge*" means a judge of the High Court;

"*a taxpayer*" means any person including—

(a) a person whose identity is not known to the authorised officer, and a group or class of persons whose individual identities are not so known, and

(b) a person by or in respect of whom a declaration has been made under *section 263(1)* declaring that the person is beneficially entitled to all or part of the interest in relation to a deposit.

(2) An authorised officer may, subject to this section, make an application to a judge for an order requiring a financial institution, to do either or both of the following, namely—

(a) to make available for inspection by the authorised officer, such books, records or other documents as are in the financial institution's power, possession or procurement as contain, or may (in the authorised officer's opinion formed on reasonable grounds) contain information relevant to a liability in relation to a taxpayer,

(b) to furnish to the authorised officer such information, explanations and particulars as the authorised officer may reasonably require, being information, explanations and particulars that are relevant to any such liability,

and which are specified in the application.

(3) An authorised officer shall not make application under subsection (2) without the consent in writing of a Revenue Commissioner, and without being satisfied—

(a) that there are reasonable grounds for suspecting that the taxpayer, or, where the taxpayer is a group or class of persons, all or any one of those persons, may have failed or may fail to comply with any provision of the Acts,

(b) that any such failure is likely to have led or to lead to serious prejudice to the proper assessment or collection of tax (having regard to the amount of a liability in relation to the taxpayer, or where the taxpayer is a group or class of persons, the amount of a liability in relation to all or any one of them, that arises or might arise from such failure), and

(c) that the information—

(i) which is likely to be contained in the books, records or other documents to which the application relates, or

(ii) which is likely to arise from the information, explanations and particulars to which the application relates,

is relevant to the proper assessment or collection of tax.

(4) Without prejudice to the generality of *subsection (2)*, the authorised officer may make an application under that subsection to the judge for an order in respect of the matters referred to in *paragraphs (a)* and *(b)* of that subsection in so far as they relate to a person who is connected with the taxpayer.

(5) Where the judge, to whom an application is made under *subsection (2)*, is satisfied that there are reasonable grounds for the application being made, the judge may, subject to such conditions as he or she may consider proper and specify in the order, make an order requiring the financial institution—

(a) to make available for inspection by the authorised officer, such books, records or other documents, and

(b) to furnish to the authorised officer such information, explanations and particulars,

as may be specified in the order.

(6) The persons who may be treated as a taxpayer for the purposes of this section include a company which has been dissolved and an individual who has died.

[(6A) Where in compliance with an order made under *subsection (5)*, a financial institution makes available for inspection by an authorised officer, books, records or other documents, the financial institution shall afford the authorised officer reasonable assistance, including information, explanations and particulars, in relation to the use of all the electronic or other automatic means, if any, by which the books, records or other documents, in so far as they are in a non-legible form, are capable of being reproduced in a legible form, and any data equipment or any associated apparatus or material.

(6B) Where in compliance with an order made under *subsection (5)*, a financial institution makes books, records or other documents available for inspection by the authorised officer, the authorised officer may make extracts from or copies of all or any part of the books, records or other documents.][1]

(7) Every hearing of an application for an order under this section and of any appeal in connection with that application shall be held in camera.

(8) Where a judge makes an order under this section, he or she may also, on the application of the authorised officer concerned, make a further order prohibiting, for such period as the judge may consider proper and specify in the order, any transfer of, or any dealing with, without the consent of the judge, any assets or moneys of the person to whom the order relates that are in the custody of the financial institution at the time the order is made.

(9) (a) Where—

(i) a copy of any affidavit and exhibits grounding an application under subsection (2) or (8) and any order made under *subsection (5)* or (8) are to be made available to the taxpayer, or the taxpayer's solicitor or to the financial institution or the financial institution's solicitor, as the case may be, and

(ii) the judge is satisfied on the hearing of the application that there are reasonable grounds in the public interest that such copy of an affidavit, exhibits or order, as the case may be, should not include the name or address of the authorised officer,

such copy, or copies or order shall not include the name or address of the authorised officer.

(b) Where, on any application to the judge to vary or discharge an order made under this section, it is desired to cross-examine the deponent of any affidavit filed by or on behalf of the authorised officer and the judge is satisfied that there are reasonable grounds in the public interest to so order, the judge shall order either or both of the following—

(i) that the name and address of the authorised officer shall not be disclosed in court, and

(ii) that such cross-examination shall only take place in the sight and hearing of the judge and in the hearing only of all other persons present at such cross-examination.][2]

Amendments

[1] Inserted by FA02 s132(f).

[2] Substituted by FA99 s207(i).

Case Law

A prior demand for a return of income must have been made before any official application for an order is allowable. JB O'C v PCD and another 1984 III ITR 153

Walsh v National Irish Bank 2013 IESC 2 – The Irish Supreme Court considered the disclosure obligations under section 908 and the potential conflicts with a duty to retain confidentiality or to respect privacy in another jurisdiction. The Court found that this section only applies in Ireland and provides no legal basis for Revenue to make an order directly to the foreign jurisdiction.

Revenue Briefings

Tax Briefing

Tax Briefing August 2002 – Issue 49 pg 6 – Code of Practice Revenue Audits

Statements of Practice

Revenue Powers Exercised in Places other than a Revenue Office – SP GEN/1/94 (Revised 02/2006)

Revenue Powers (Finance Act 1999) – SP GEN/1/99

Revenue Internal Review Procedures – SP GEN/2/99

Cross References

From Section 908

Section 263 Declarations relating to deposits of non-residents.

To Section 908

Section 906A Information to be furnished by financial institutions.

Section 907A Application to Appeal Commissioners: information from third party.

Section 912A Information for tax authorities in other territories.

Section 1078 Revenue offences.

908A Revenue offence: power to obtain information from financial institutions

[(1) In this section—

["*the Acts*" means the Waiver of Certain Tax, Interest and Penalties Act, 1993, together with the meaning assigned to it by *section 1078(1)* and;][1]

"*authorised officer*" means an officer of the Revenue Commissioners authorised by them in writing to exercise the powers conferred by this section;

"books, records or other documents" includes—

(a) any records used in the business of a financial institution, or used in the transfer department of a financial institution acting as registrar of securities, whether—

(i) comprised in bound volume, loose-leaf binders or other loose-leaf filing system, loose-leaf ledger sheets, pages, folios or cards, or

(ii) kept on microfilm, magnetic tape or in any non-legible form (by the use of electronics or otherwise) which is capable of being reproduced in a legible form, and

(b) documents in manuscript, documents which are typed, printed, stencilled or created by any other mechanical or partly mechanical process in use from time to time and documents which are produced by any photographic or photostatic process;

"*judge*" means a judge of the Circuit Court or of the District Court;

["*financial institution*" means—

[(a) a person who holds or has held a licence under section 9 of the Central Bank Act 1971, or a person who holds or has held a licence or other similar authorisation under the law of any other Member State of the European Communities which corresponds to a licence granted under that section,][2]

(b) a person referred to in section 7(4) of the Central Bank Act, 1971, or

(c) a credit institution (within the meaning of the European Communities (Licensing and Supervision of Credit Institutions) Regulations, 1992 (S.I. No. 395 of 1992)) which has been authorised by the Central Bank of Ireland to carry on business of a credit institution in accordance with the provisions of the supervisory enactments (within the meaning of those Regulations);][3]

"*liability*" in relation to a person means any liability in relation to tax to which the person is or may be, or may have been, subject, or the amount of such liability;

["*offence*" means an offence falling within any provision of the Acts;][4]

"*tax*" means any tax, duty, levy or charge under the care and management of the Revenue Commissioners.

[(2) (a) In this subsection "*documentation*" includes information kept on microfilm, magnetic tape or in any non-legible form (by use of electronics or otherwise) which is capable of being reproduced in a permanent legible form.

(b) If, on application made by an authorised officer, with the consent in writing of a Revenue Commissioner, a judge is satisfied, on information given on oath by the authorised officer, that there are reasonable grounds for suspecting—

(i) that an offence, which would result (or but for its detection would have resulted) in serious prejudice to the proper assessment or collection of tax, is being, has been, or is about to be committed (having regard to the amount of a liability in relation to any person which might be, or might have been, evaded but for the detection of the relevant facts), and

(ii) that there is material in the possession of a financial institution specified in the application which is likely to be of substantial value (whether by itself or together with other material) to the investigation of the relevant facts,

the judge may make an order authorising the authorised officer to inspect and take copies of any entries in the books, records or other documents of the financial institution, and any documentation associated with or relating to an entry in such books, records or other documents, for the purposes of investigation of the relevant facts.][5]

(3) An offence the commission of which, if considered alone, would not be regarded as resulting in serious prejudice to the proper assessment or collection of tax for the purposes of this section may nevertheless be so regarded if there are reasonable grounds for suspecting that the commission of the offence forms part of a course of conduct which is, or but for its detection would be, likely to result in serious prejudice to the proper assessment or collection of tax.

(4) Subject to *subsection (5)*, a copy of any entry in books, records or other documents of a financial institution shall in all legal proceedings be received as prima facie evidence of such an entry, and of the matters, transactions, and accounts therein recorded.

(5) A copy of an entry in the books, records or other documents of a financial institution shall not be received in evidence in legal proceedings unless it is further proved that—

(a) in the case where the copy sought to be received in evidence has been reproduced in a legible form directly by either mechanical or electronic means, or both such means, from a financial institution's books, records or other documents maintained in a non-legible form, it has been so reproduced;

(b) in the case where the copy sought to be received in evidence has been made (either directly or indirectly) from a copy to which *paragraph (a)* would apply—

(i) the copy sought to be so received has been examined with a copy so reproduced and is a correct copy, and

(ii) the copy so reproduced is a copy to which *paragraph (a)* would apply if it were sought to have it received in evidence,

and

(c) in any other case, the copy has been examined with the original entry and is correct.

(6) Proof of the matters to which *subsection (5)* relates shall be given—

(a) in respect of *paragraph (a)* or *(b)(ii)* of that subsection, by some person who has been in charge of the reproduction concerned, and

(b) in respect of *paragraph (b)(i)* of that subsection, by some person who has examined the copy with the reproduction concerned, and

(c) in respect of *paragraph (c)* of that subsection, by some person who has examined the copy with the original entry concerned, and may be given either orally or by an affidavit sworn before any commissioner or person authorised to take affidavits.][6]

Amendments

[1] Inserted by FA02 s132(g)(i)(I).

[2] Substituted by F(No.2)A08 s92(h).

[3] Substituted by FA00 s68(c).

[4] Substituted by FA02 s132(g)(i)(II).

[5] Substituted by FA04 s88.

[6] Inserted by FA99 s207(j).

Revenue Briefings

Tax Briefing

Tax Briefing August 2002 – Issue 49 pg 6 – Code of Practice Revenue Audits

Statements of Practice

Revenue Powers Exercised in Places other than a Revenue Office – SP GEN/1/94 (Revised 02/2006)
Revenue Powers (Finance Act 1999) – SP GEN/1/99
Revenue Internal Review Procedures – SP GEN/2/99

Cross References

From Section 908A

Section 1078 Revenue offences.

908B Application to High Court seeking order requiring information: associated institutions

[(1) In this section—

"*the Acts*" has the meaning assigned to it by *section 1078(1)*;

"*associated institution*", in relation to a financial institution, means a person that—

(a) is controlled by the financial institution (within the meaning of *section 432*), and

(b) is not resident in the State;

"*authorised officer*" means an officer of the Revenue Commissioners authorised by them in writing to exercise the powers conferred by this section;

"books, records or other documents" includes—

(a) any records used in the business of an associated institution, or used in the transfer department of an associated institution acting as registrar of securities, whether—

(i) comprised in bound volume, loose-leaf binders or other loose-leaf filing system, loose-leaf ledger sheets, pages, folios or cards, or

(ii) kept on microfilm, magnetic tape or in any non-legible form (by the use of electronics or otherwise) which is capable of being reproduced in a legible form,

(b) every electronic or other automatic means, if any, by which any such thing in non-legible form is so capable of being reproduced,

(c) documents in manuscript, documents which are typed, printed, stencilled or created by any other mechanical or partly mechanical process in use from time to time and documents which are produced by any photographic or photostatic process, and

(d) correspondence and records of other communications between an associated institution and its customers;

"*financial institution*" means—

[(a) a person who holds or has held a licence under section 9 of the Central Bank Act 1971, or a person who holds or has held a licence or other similar authorisation under the law of any other Member State of the European Communities which corresponds to a licence granted under that section,][1]

(b) a person referred to in section 7(4) of the Central Bank Act 1971, or

(c) a credit institution (within the meaning of the European Communities (Licensing and Supervision of Credit Institutions) Regulations 1992 (S.I. No. 395 of 1992)) which has been authorised by the Central Bank and Financial Services Authority of Ireland to carry on business of a credit institution in accordance with the provisions of the supervisory enactments (within the meaning of those Regulations);

"*judge*" means a judge of the High Court;

"*liability*" in relation to a person means any liability in relation to tax which the person is or may be, or may have been, subject, or the amount of such liability;

"*tax*" means any tax, duty, levy or charge under the care and management of the Revenue Commissioners;

"*a taxpayer*" means any person including a person whose identity is not known to the authorised officer, and a group or class of persons whose individual identities are not so known.

(2) An authorised officer may, subject to this section, make an application to a judge for an order requiring a financial institution to do either or both of the following, namely—

(a) to make available for inspection by the authorised officer, such books, records or other documents as are in the power, possession or procurement of an associated institution, in relation to the financial institution, as contain, or may (in the authorised officer's opinion formed on reasonable grounds) contain information relevant to a liability in relation to a taxpayer, or

(b) to furnish to the authorised officer such information, explanations and particulars held by, or available from, the financial institution or an associated institution, in relation to the financial institution, as the authorised officer may reasonably require, being information, explanations or particulars that are relevant to any such liability,

and which are specified in the application.

(3) An authorised officer shall not make an application under subsection (2) without the consent in writing of a Revenue Commissioner, and without being satisfied—

(a) that there are reasonable grounds for suspecting that the taxpayer, or where the taxpayer is a group or class of persons, all or any one of those persons, may have failed or may fail to comply with any provision of the Acts,

(b) that any such failure is likely to have led or to lead to serious prejudice to the proper assessment or collection of tax (having regard to the amount of a liability in relation to the taxpayer, or where the taxpayer is a group or class of persons, the amount of a liability, in relation to all or any one of them, that arises or might arise from such failure), and

(c) that the information—

(i) which is likely to be contained in the books, records or other documents to which the application relates, or

(ii) which is likely to arise from the information, explanations and particulars to which the application relates,

is relevant to the proper assessment or collection of tax.

(4) Where the judge, to whom an application is made under subsection (2), is satisfied that there are reasonable grounds for the application being made, then the judge may, subject to such conditions as he or she may consider proper and specify in the order, make an order requiring the financial institution—

(a) to make available for inspection by the authorised officer, such books, records or other documents, and

(b) to furnish to the authorised officer such information, explanations and particulars,

as may be specified in the order.

(5) The persons who may be treated as a taxpayer for the purposes of this section include a company which has been dissolved and an individual who has died.

(6) Where in compliance with an order made under subsection (4) a financial institution makes available for inspection by an authorised officer, books, records or other documents, then the financial institution shall afford the authorised officer reasonable assistance, including information, explanations and particulars, in relation to the use of all the electronic or other automatic means, if any, by which the books, records or other documents, in so far as they are in a non-legible form, are capable of being reproduced in a legible form, and any data equipment or any associated apparatus or material.

(7) Where in compliance with an order made under subsection (4) a financial institution makes books, records or other documents available for inspection by the authorised officer, then the authorised officer may make extracts from or copies of all or any part of the books, records or other documents.

(8) Every hearing of an application for an order under this section and of any appeal in connection with that application shall be held in camera.][2]

Amendments

[1] Substituted by F(No.2)A08 s92(i).

[2] Inserted by FA04 s87.

Revenue Briefings

Tax Briefing

Tax Briefing August 2002 Issue 49 pg 6 – Code of Practice Revenue Audits

Statements of Practice

Revenue Powers Exercised in Places other than a Revenue Office – SP GEN/1/94 (Revised 02/2006)
Revenue Powers (Finance Act 1999) – SP GEN/1/99
Revenue Internal Review Procedures – SP GEN/2/99

Cross References

From Section 908B

Section 432 Meaning of "associated company" and "control".
Section 1078 Revenue offences.

908C Search warrants

[(1) In this section—

"*the Acts*" means the Waiver of Certain Tax, Interest and Penalties Act 1993 together with the meaning assigned to it in *section 1078(1)*;

"*authorised officer*" means an officer of the Revenue Commissioners authorised by them in writing to exercise the powers conferred by this section;

"*commission*", in relation to an offence, includes an attempt to commit the offence;

"*computer*" includes any electronic device capable of performing logical or arithmetical operations on data in accordance with a set of instructions;

"computer at the place which is being searched", includes any other computer, whether at that place or at any other place, which is lawfully accessible by means of that computer;

"*information in non-legible form*" means information which is kept (by electronic means or otherwise) on microfilm, microfiche, magnetic tape or disk or in any other non-legible form;

"*material*" means any books, documents, records or other things (including a computer);

"*offence*" means an offence under the Acts;

"*place*" includes any building (or part of a building), dwelling, vehicle, vessel, aircraft or hovercraft and any other place whatsoever;

"*record*" includes any information in non-legible form which is capable of being reproduced in a permanently legible form.

(2) If a judge of the District Court is satisfied by information given on oath by an authorised officer that there are reasonable grounds for suspecting—

(a) that an offence is being, has been or is about to be committed, and

(b) (i) that material which is likely to be of value (whether by itself or together with other information) to the investigation of the offence, or

(ii) that evidence of, or relating to the commission of, the offence,

is to be found in any place,

the judge may issue a warrant for the search of that place, and of any thing and any persons, found there.

(3) A warrant issued under this section shall be expressed and shall operate to authorise the authorised officer, accompanied by such other named officers of the Revenue Commissioners and such other named persons as the authorised officer considers necessary—

(a) to enter, at any time or times within one month from the date of issuing of the warrant (if necessary by the use of reasonable force), the place named in the warrant,

(b) to search, or cause to be searched, that place and any thing and any persons, found there, but no person shall be searched except by a person of the same sex unless express or implied consent is given,

(c) to require any person found there—

(i) to give his or her name, home address and occupation to the authorised officer, and

(ii) to produce to the authorised officer any material which is in the custody or possession of that person,

(d) to examine, seize and retain (or cause to be examined, seized and retained) any material found there, or in the possession of a person present there at the time of the search, which the authorised officer reasonably believes—

(i) is likely to be of value (whether by itself or together with other information) to the investigation of the offence, or

(ii) to be evidence of, or relating to the commission of, the offence, and

(e) to take any other steps which may appear to the authorised officer to be necessary for preserving any such material and preventing interference with it.

(4) The authority conferred by subsection (3)(*d*) to seize and retain (or to cause to be seized and retained) any material includes—

(a) in the case of books, documents or records, authority to make and retain a copy of the books, documents or records, and

(b) where necessary, authority to seize and, for as long as necessary, retain, any computer or other storage medium in which records are kept and to copy such records.

(5) An authorised officer acting under the authority of a warrant issued under this section may—

(a) operate any computer at the place which is being searched or cause any such computer to be operated by a person accompanying the authorised officer, and

(b) require any person at that place who appears to the authorised officer to be in a position to facilitate access to the information held in any such computer or which can be accessed by the use of that computer—

(i) to give to the authorised officer any password necessary to operate it,

(ii) otherwise to enable the authorised officer to examine the information accessible by the computer in a form in which the information is visible and legible, or

(iii) to produce the information in a form in which it can be removed and in which it is, or can be made, visible and legible.

(6) A person who—

(a) obstructs or attempts to obstruct the exercise of a right of entry and search conferred by virtue of a warrant issued under this section,

(b) obstructs the exercise of a right so conferred to examine, seize and retain material,

(c) fails to comply with a requirement under subsection (3)(*c*) or gives to the authorised officer a name, address or occupation that is false or misleading, or

(d) fails to comply with a requirement under subsection (5)(*b*),

is guilty of an offence and is liable on summary conviction to a fine not exceeding [€5,000][1] or imprisonment for a term not exceeding 6 months or to both the fine and the imprisonment.

(7) Where an authorised officer enters, or attempts to enter, any place in the execution of a warrant issued under subsection (2), the authorised officer may be accompanied by a member or members of the Garda Síochána, and any such member may arrest without warrant any person who is committing an offence under subsection (6) or whom the member suspects, with reasonable cause, of having done so.

(8) Any material which is seized under subsection (3) which is required for the purposes of any legal proceedings by an officer of the Revenue Commissioners or for the purpose of any criminal proceedings, may be retained for so long as it is reasonably required for the purposes aforesaid.][2]

Amendments

[1] Substituted by FA08 s138(1)(b). Applies as respects an offence committed on a day after 13 March 2008.

[2] Inserted by FA07 s124(c).

Revenue Briefings

Tax Briefing

Tax Briefing July 2007 Issue 66 pg 27 – Finance Act 2007

Cross References

From Section 908C

Section 1078 Revenue offences.

To Section 908C

Section 1078B Presumptions.

908D Order to produce evidential material

[(1) In this section—

"*the Acts*" means the Waiver of Certain Tax, Interest and Penalties Act 1993 together with the meaning assigned to it in *section 1078(1)*;

"*authorised officer*" means an officer of the Revenue Commissioners authorised by them in writing to exercise the powers conferred by this section;

"*commission*", in relation to an offence, includes an attempt to commit the offence;

"*computer*" includes any electronic device capable of performing logical or arithmetical operations on data in accordance with a set of instructions;

"*information in non-legible form*" means information which is kept (by electronic means or otherwise) on microfilm, microfiche, magnetic tape or disk or in any other non-legible form;

"*material*" means any books, documents, records or other things (including a computer);

"*offence*" means an offence under the Acts;

"*record*" includes any information in non-legible form which is capable of being reproduced in a permanently legible form.

(2) If a judge of the District Court is satisfied by information given on oath by an authorised officer that there are reasonable grounds for suspecting—

(a) that an offence is being, has been or is about to be committed, and

(b) that material—

(i) which is likely to be of value (whether by itself or together with other information) to the investigation of the offence, or

(ii) which constitutes evidence of, or relating to the commission of, the offence,

is in the possession or control of a person specified in the application,

the judge may order that the person shall—

(I) produce the material to the authorised officer for the authorised officer to take away, or

(II) give the authorised officer access to it,

either immediately or within such period as the order may specify.

(3) Where the material consists of or includes records contained in a computer, the order shall have effect as an order to produce the records, or to give access to them, in a form in which they are visible and legible and in which they can be taken away.

(4) An order under this section—

(a) in so far as it may empower an authorised officer to take away books, documents or records, or to be given access to them, shall also have effect as an order empowering the authorised officer to take away a copy of the books, documents or, as the case may be, records (and for that purpose the authorised officer may, if necessary, make a copy of them),

(b) shall not confer any right to production of, or access to, any document subject to legal privilege, and

(c) shall have effect notwithstanding any other obligation as to secrecy or other restriction on disclosure of information imposed by statute or otherwise.

(5) Any material taken away by an authorised officer under this section may be retained by the authorised officer for use as evidence in any criminal proceedings.

(6) (a) Information contained in books, documents or records which were produced to an authorised officer, or to which an authorised officer was given access, in accordance with an order under this section, shall be admissible in any criminal proceedings as evidence of any fact therein of which direct oral evidence would be admissible unless the information—

(i) is privileged from disclosure in such proceedings,

(ii) was supplied by a person who would not be compellable to give evidence at the instance of the prosecution,

(iii) was compiled for the purposes of, or in contemplation of, any—

(I) criminal investigation,

(II) investigation or inquiry carried out pursuant to or under any enactment,

(III) civil or criminal proceedings, or

(IV) proceedings of a disciplinary nature,

or unless the requirements of the provisions mentioned in *paragraph (b)* are not complied with.

(b) References in *sections 7* (notice of documentary evidence to be served on accused), *8* (admission and weight of documentary evidence) and *9* (admissibility of evidence as to credibility of supplier of information) of the Criminal Evidence Act 1992 to a document or information contained in it shall be construed as including references to books, documents and records mentioned in *paragraph (a)* and the information contained in them, and those provisions shall have effect accordingly with any necessary modifications.

(7) A judge of the District Court may, on the application of an authorised officer, or of any person to whom an order under this section relates, vary or discharge the order.

(8) A person who without reasonable excuse fails or refuses to comply with an order under this section is guilty of an offence and liable on summary conviction to a fine not exceeding [€5,000][1] or imprisonment for a term not exceeding 6 months or to both the fine and the imprisonment.][2]

Amendments

[1] Substituted by FA08 s138(1)(c). Applies as respects an offence committed on a day after 13 March 2008.

[2] Inserted by FA07 s124(c).

Revenue Briefings

Tax Briefing

Tax Briefing July 2007 Issue 66 pg 27 – Finance Act 2007

Cross References

From Section 908D

Section 7 Application to certain taxing statutes of Age of Majority Act, 1985.
Section 8 Construction of certain taxing statutes in accordance with Status of Children Act, 1987.
Section 9 Subsidiaries.
Section 1078 Revenue offences.

908E Order to produce documents or provide information

[(1) In this section and in *section 908F*—

'*authorised officer*' means an officer of the information. Revenue Commissioners authorised by them in writing to exercise the powers conferred by this section;

'*relevant offence*' means—

(a) an offence under *section 186* of the Customs Consolidation Act 1876,

(b) an offence under *section 139(5)* of the Finance Act 1992,

(c) an offence under *section 1056, 1078* or *1078A*,

(d) an offence under *subsection (1A), (1B) or (3)* of *section 102* of the Finance Act 1999,

(e) an offence under *section 119* of the Finance Act 2001,

(f) an offence under *section 79* of the Finance Act 2003,

(g) an offence under *section 78* of the Finance Act 2005.

(2) For the purposes of the investigation of a relevant offence, an authorised officer may apply to a judge of the District Court for an order under this section in relation to—

(a) the making available by a person of any particular documents or documents of a particular description, or

(b) the provision by a person of particular information by answering questions or making a statement containing the information,

or both.

(3) On an application under *subsection (2)*, a judge of the District Court, if satisfied by information on oath of the authorised officer making the application that—

(a) there are reasonable grounds for suspecting that a person has possession or control of particular documents or documents of a particular description,

(b) there are reasonable grounds for believing that the documents are relevant to the investigation of the relevant offence concerned,

(c) there are reasonable grounds for suspecting that the documents (or some of them) may constitute evidence of or relating to the commission of that relevant offence, and

(d) there are reasonable grounds for believing that the documents should be produced or that access to them should be given, having regard to the benefit likely to accrue to the investigation and any other relevant circumstances,

may order the person to—

(i) produce the documents to an authorised officer to take away and, if the judge considers it appropriate, to identify and categorise the documents to be so produced in the particular manner (if any) sought in the application or in such other manner as the judge may direct and to produce the documents in that manner, or

(ii) give such an officer access to them,

either immediately or within such period as the order may specify.

(4) On an application under *subsection (2)*, a judge of the District Court, if satisfied by information on oath of the authorised officer making the application that—

(a) there are reasonable grounds for suspecting that a person has information which he or she has failed or refused without reasonable excuse to give to the authorised officer having been requested to do so,

(b) there are reasonable grounds for believing that the information is relevant to the investigation of the relevant offence concerned,

(c) there are reasonable grounds for suspecting that the information (or some of it) may constitute evidence of or relating to the commission of that relevant offence, and

(d) there are reasonable grounds for believing that the information should be provided, having regard to the benefit likely to accrue to the investigation and any other relevant circumstances,

may, subject to *subsection (5)*, order the person to—

(i) provide the information to an authorised officer by answering the questions specified in the application or making a statement setting out the answers to those questions or both, and

(ii) make a declaration of the truth of the answers to such questions,

either immediately or within such period as the order may specify.

(5) The references in *subsections (2)(b)* and *(4)* to information that may be the subject of an order under this section are references to information that the person concerned has obtained in the ordinary course of business.

(6) An order under this section relating to documents in any place may, on the application of the authorised officer concerned under *subsection (2)*, require any person, being a person who appears to the judge of the District Court to be entitled to grant entry to the place, to allow an authorised officer to enter it so as to obtain access to the documents.

(7) Where the documents concerned are not in legible form, an order under this section shall have effect as an order—

(a) to give to an authorised officer any password necessary to make the documents legible and comprehensible,

(b) otherwise to enable the authorised officer to examine the documents in a form in which they are legible and comprehensible, or

(c) to produce the documents to the authorised officer in a form in which they can be removed and in which they are, or can be made, legible and comprehensible.

(8) An order under this section—

(a) in so far as it may empower an authorised officer to take away a document, or to be given access to it, shall also have effect as an order empowering the officer to make a copy of the document and to take the copy away,

(b) shall not confer any right to production of, or access to, any document subject to legal professional privilege, and

(c) shall have effect notwithstanding any other obligation as to secrecy or other restriction on disclosure of information imposed by statute or otherwise.

(9) (a) Where a document is, or may be, taken away by an authorised officer pursuant to an order under this section, any person to whom the order relates, or who is affected by the order, may request the authorised officer to permit the person to retain the document, or to have it returned to the person, while the officer takes or retains a copy of it.

(b) The authorised officer concerned may accede to a request under *paragraph (a)* but only if he or she is satisfied that—

(i) the document is required by the person for the purposes of his or her business or for some other legitimate purpose, and

(ii) the person undertakes in writing—

(I) to keep the document safely and securely, and

(II) when requested by the authorised officer to do so, to furnish it to the authorised officer in connection with any criminal proceedings for which it is required.

(c) A failure or refusal by a person to comply with an undertaking given by him or her under *paragraph (b)(ii)* shall not prejudice the admissibility in evidence in any criminal proceedings of a copy of the document concerned.

(10) Any documents taken away by an authorised officer pursuant to an order under this section may be retained by the officer for use as evidence in any criminal proceedings.

(11) A statement or admission made by a person pursuant to an order under this section shall not be admissible as evidence in proceedings brought against the person for an offence (other than an offence under *subsection (16), (17)* or *(18)*).

(12) (a) An order under this section providing that documents be produced, or that access to them be given, by a person may, if the judge of the District Court considers it appropriate to do so, require the person to furnish a certificate to an authorised officer affirming—

(i) the authenticity of the documents, and

(ii) in the case of documents in non-legible form that are reproduced in legible form, the system and manner of that reproduction,

either when the documents are produced, or access to them is given, or at such time thereafter as may be specified in the order.

(b) The Revenue Commissioners may make regulations for the purposes of this subsection specifying the manner in which documents of different types or classes, or copies of them, may be authenticated.

(13) Where a person who produces documents pursuant to an order under this section claims a lien on those documents or some of them, the production shall be without prejudice to the lien.

(14) A judge of the District Court may, on the application of any person to whom an order under this section relates or an authorised officer, vary or discharge the order.

(15) A judge of the District Court may, on the application of any person who is affected by an order under this section whose request for the return of documents under *subsection (9)* has not been acceded to, make an order regarding the return of the documents concerned to that person if the judge considers it appropriate to do so subject to such conditions (if any) as the judge may direct.

(16) A person who without reasonable excuse fails or refuses to comply with an order under this section shall be guilty of an offence and shall be liable—

(a) on summary conviction, to a class A fine or imprisonment for a term not exceeding 12 months or both, or

(b) on conviction on indictment, to a fine or imprisonment for a term not exceeding 2 years or both.

(17) A person who, in purported compliance with an order under this section provides information or makes a statement which is false or misleading in a material particular knowing it to be so false or misleading, or being reckless as to whether it is so, shall be guilty of an offence and shall be liable—

(a) on summary conviction, to a class A fine or imprisonment for a term not exceeding 12 months or both, or

(b) on conviction on indictment, to a fine or imprisonment for a term not exceeding 2 years or both.

(18) A person who without reasonable excuse fails or refuses to comply with an undertaking given by him or her under *subsection (9)(b)(ii)* shall be guilty of an offence and shall be liable on summary conviction to a class A fine or imprisonment for a term not exceeding 12 months or both.

(19) An application for an order under *subsection (2)* shall be made to a judge of the District Court who is assigned to the district court district in which the documents sought are located or the person from whom the documents or information are sought ordinarily resides or carries on any profession, business or occupation or, if that person is a company (within the meaning of the Companies Acts), the district court district in which the registered office of the company is situated or the company carries on any business.

(20) Nothing in this section shall affect the operation of a provision in any other enactment under which a court may order a person to produce any documents to a person in connection with the investigation of an offence.][1]

Amendments

[1] Inserted by FA12 s127. Deemed to have come into force and takes effect on and from 1 January 2012.

908F Privileged legal material

[(1) In this section 'privileged legal material' means a document which, in the opinion of the court concerned, a person is entitled to refuse to produce or to give access to it on the grounds of legal professional privilege.

(2) If a person refuses to produce a document or give access to it pursuant to an order of a judge of the District Court under *section 908E* on the grounds that the document is privileged legal material, an authorised officer may apply to a judge of that Court for a determination as to whether the document is privileged legal material.

(3) A person who refuses to produce a document or give access to it pursuant to an order of a judge of the District Court under *section 908E* on the grounds that the document is privileged legal material may apply to a judge of the District Court for a determination as to whether the document is privileged legal material.

(4) A person who refuses to produce a document or give access to it pursuant to an order of a judge of the District Court under *section 908E* on the grounds that the document is privileged legal material shall preserve the document and keep it in a safe and secure place pending the determination of an application under *subsection (2)* or *(3)* and shall, if it is so determined not to be privileged legal material, produce it in accordance with the order.

(5) Pending the making of a final determination of an application under *subsection (2)* or *(3)*, the judge of the District Court may give such interim or interlocutory directions as the judge considers appropriate including, without prejudice to the generality of the foregoing, in a case in which the volume of documents that are the subject of the application is substantial, directions as to the appointment of a person with suitable legal qualifications possessing the level of experience, and the independence from any interest falling to be determined between the parties concerned, that the judge considers to be appropriate for the purpose of—

(a) examining the documents, and

(b) preparing a report for the judge with a view to assisting or facilitating the judge in the making by him or her of his or her determination as to whether the documents are privileged legal material.

(6) An application under *subsection (2)*, *(3)* or *(5)* may, if the judge of the District Court so directs, be heard otherwise than in public.

(7) Notice of an application under *subsection (2)* shall be served on the person to whom the order concerned relates and notice of an application under *subsection (3)* shall be served on the authorised officer who seeks to compel the production of the document concerned or to be given access to it.

(8) An appeal against the determination of a judge of the District Court under this section shall lie to the Circuit Court and no further appeal shall lie from an order of the Circuit Court made on an appeal under this section.

(9) Rules of court may make provision for the expeditious hearing of applications to a judge of the District Court, and any appeals against the determinations of such a judge, under this section.][1]

Amendments

[1] Inserted by FA12 s127. Deemed to have come into force and takes effect on and from 1 January 2012.

909 Power to require return of property

[FA83 s20; FA92 s239]

(1) (a) In this section—

"*asset*" includes any interest in an asset;

"*limited interest*" means—

(i) an interest (other than a leasehold interest) for the duration of a life or lives or for a period certain, or

(ii) any other interest which is not an absolute interest;

"*prescribed*" means prescribed by the Revenue Commissioners;

"*property*" includes interests and rights of any description and, without prejudice to the generality of the foregoing, includes—

(i) in the case of a limited interest, the property in which the limited interest subsists or on which it is charged or secured or on which there exists a right to have it charged or secured,

(ii) an interest in expectancy,

(iii) an interest or share in a partnership, joint tenancy or estate of a deceased person,

(iv) stock or shares in a company which is in the course of liquidation,

(v) an annuity, and

(vi) property comprised in a settlement which the person concerned is empowered to revoke;

"*settlement*" has the same meaning as in *section 794*;

"*specified date*", in relation to a notice under *subsection (2)*, means the date specified in the notice;

"*tax*" means income tax and capital gains tax.

(b) For the purposes of this section, the cost of acquisition to a person of an asset shall include—

(i) the amount or value of the consideration, in money or money's worth, given by the person or on the person's behalf for the acquisition of the asset, together with the incidental costs to the person of the acquisition or, if the asset was not acquired by the person, any expenditure incurred by the person in providing the asset, and

(ii) the amount of any expenditure incurred on the asset by the person or on the person's behalf for the purpose of enhancing the value of the asset, being expenditure reflected in the state or nature of the asset at the specified date, and any expenditure incurred by the person in establishing, preserving or defending the person's title to, or to a right over, the asset.

(2) Where for the purposes of tax a person is required under any provision of the Tax Acts or the Capital Gains Tax Acts [to deliver a tax return, an inspector of taxes or [the inspector of returns][1], as the case may be,][2] may require—

(a) that person, by notice in writing given to that person, and

(b) where that person and his or her [spouse or civil partner][3] are, for the year of assessment to which the tax return relates, treated as living together for the purpose of [*section 1015* or *1031A*, as the case may be,][4] that person's [spouse or civil partner][5], by notice in writing given to the [spouse or civil partner][6],

to deliver to the inspector within the time specified in the notice or within such further period as the inspector may allow a statement of affairs in the prescribed form as at the date specified in the notice, and that person or that person's [spouse or civil partner][7] shall, if required by further notice or notices in writing by the inspector, deliver to the inspector within such time, not being less than 30 days, as may be specified in such further notice or notices, a statement verifying such statement of affairs together with such evidence, statement or documents required by the inspector in respect of any asset or liability shown on the statement of affairs, or in respect of any asset or liability which the inspector has reason to believe has been omitted from the statement of affairs.

(3) (a) In this section, "*statement of affairs*", in relation to a notice under *subsection (2)*, means—

(i) where the person to whom notice is given is an individual who is a chargeable person and the tax return concerned relates to income or capital gains in respect of which that individual is chargeable to tax otherwise than in a representative capacity or as a trustee, a statement of all the assets wherever situated to which that individual is beneficially entitled on the specified date and all the liabilities for which that individual is liable on the specified date,

(ii) where the person to whom notice is given is the [spouse or civil partner][8] of an individual referred to in *subparagraph (i)*, a statement of all the assets wherever situated to which that [spouse or civil partner][9] is beneficially entitled on the specified date and all the liabilities for which that [spouse or civil partner][10] is liable on the specified date,

(iii) where the person to whom notice is given is a chargeable person in a representative capacity and the tax return concerned relates to income or capital gains of a person (in this paragraph referred to as "*the second-mentioned person*") in respect of which that chargeable person is so chargeable, a statement of all the assets wherever situated to which the second-mentioned person is beneficially entitled and which give rise to income or capital gains in respect of which that chargeable person is chargeable to tax in a representative capacity and all the liabilities for which the second-mentioned person is liable, or which are assets or liabilities in relation to which that chargeable person performs functions or duties in such a capacity on the specified date, or

(iv) where the person to whom notice is given is a chargeable person as a trustee of a trust and the tax return concerned relates to income or capital gains of a trust, a statement of all the assets and liabilities comprised in the trust on the specified date.

(b) Any assets to which [a minor child of, or a minor child of the civil partner of, an individual referred to in *subparagraph (i)* or *(ii)* of *paragraph (a)*][11] is beneficially entitled shall be included in that individual's statement of affairs under this section where—

(i) such assets at any time before their acquisition by [that minor child][12] were disposed of by that individual whether to [that minor child][13] or not, or

(ii) the consideration for the acquisition of such assets by [that minor child][14] was provided directly or indirectly by that individual.

(4) (a) A statement of affairs delivered under this section shall contain in relation to each asset included in the statement—

(i) a full description,

(ii) its location on the specified date,

(iii) the cost of acquisition to the person beneficially entitled to that asset,

(iv) [the date of acquisition,][15]

(v) if it was acquired otherwise than by means of a bargain at arm's length, the name and address of the person from whom it was acquired and the consideration, if any, [given to that person in respect of its acquisition, and][16]

[(vi) details of all policies of insurance (if any) whereby the risk of any kind of damage or injury, or the loss or depreciation of the asset is insured.][17]

(b) A statement of affairs delivered under this section shall, in the case of an asset which is an interest other than an absolute interest, contain particulars of the title under which the beneficial entitlement arises.

(c) A statement of affairs delivered under this section shall be signed by the person by whom it is delivered and shall include a declaration by that person that it is to the best of that person's knowledge, information and belief correct and complete.

(d) The Revenue Commissioners may require the declaration mentioned in *paragraph (c)* to be made on oath.

Amendments

[1] Substituted by FA12 sched5(1)(l).

[2] Substituted by FA01 s78(2)(g). Applies as respects the year of assessment 2001 and subsequent years and as respects accounting periods of companies ending on or after 1 April 2001.

[3, 5, 6, 7] Substituted by F(No.3)A11 sched1(240). Shall have effect from 27 July 2011.

[4] Substituted by F(No.3)A11 sched1(241). Shall have effect from 27 July 2011.

[8, 9, 10] Substituted by F(No.3)A11 sched1(242). Shall have effect from 27 July 2011.

[11] Substituted by F(No.3)A11 sched1(243). Shall have effect from 27 July 2011.

[12, 13, 14] Substituted by F(No.3)A11 sched1(244). Shall have effect from 27 July 2011.

[15] Substituted by FA99 s207(k)(i).

[16] Substituted by FA99 s207(k)(ii).

[17] Inserted by FA99 s207(k)(iii).

Revenue Briefings

Tax Briefing

Tax Briefing August 2002 Issue 49 pg 6 – Code of Practice Revenue Audits

Statements of Practice

Revenue Powers Exercised in Places other than a Revenue Office – SP GEN/1/94 (Revised 02/2006)
Revenue Powers (Finance Act 1999) – SP GEN/1/99
Revenue Internal Review Procedures – SP GEN/2/99

Cross References

From Section 909

Section 794 Interpretation and application (Chapter 2).
Section 1015 Interpretation (Chapter 1).

To Section 909

Schedule 29 Provisions Referred to in Sections 1052, 1053 and 1054

910 Power to obtain information from Minister of the Government

[FA95 s175]

[(1) For the purposes of the assessment, charge, collection and recovery of any tax or duty placed under their care and management, the Revenue Commissioners may, by notice in writing, request any Minister of the Government or any body established by or under statute to provide them with such information in the possession of that Minister or body in relation to payments for any purposes made by that Minister or by that body, whether on that Minister's or that body's own behalf or on behalf of any other person, to such persons or classes of persons as the Revenue Commissioners may specify in the notice and a Minister of the Government or body of whom or of which such a request is made shall provide such information as may be so specified.][1]

(2) The Revenue Commissioners may nominate any of their officers to perform any acts and discharge any functions authorised by this section to be performed or discharged by the Revenue Commissioners.

[(3) Where information is to be provided to the Revenue Commissioners in accordance with subsection (1) it shall be provided, where the Revenue Commissioners so require, in an electronic format approved by them.][2]

Amendments

[1] Substituted by FA99 s208.

[2] Inserted by FA07 s123(c).

Cross References

To Section 910

Section 1104 Short title and construction.

911 Valuation of assets

[(1) In this section—

"*the Acts*" has the same meaning as in *section 1078*;

"*authorised person*" means—

(a) an inspector or other Revenue officer mentioned in *Part 41A*, or

(b) a person, suitably qualified for the purposes of ascertaining the value of an asset, authorised in writing by the Revenue Commissioners;

"*value*", in relation to any asset, means market value, current use value or such other value as the context requires for the purposes of the Acts.

(2) For the purposes of the Acts, an authorised person may inspect any asset (and where the asset is land enter on the land) for the purpose of ascertaining its value and reporting that value to the Revenue Commissioners, and the person having the custody or possession of that asset (or being the occupier in the case of premises) shall permit the authorised person, on producing if so requested evidence of his or her authorisation, to inspect the asset (and where the asset is land to enter on it) at such reasonable times as the Revenue Commissioners may consider necessary.

(3) (a) Notwithstanding *subsection (2)* an authorised person shall not, without the consent of the occupier, enter any premises, or that portion of any premises, which is occupied wholly and exclusively as a private residence, except on production by the authorised person of a warrant issued by a Judge of the District Court expressly authorising the authorised person to so enter.

(b) A Judge of the District Court may issue a warrant under *paragraph (a)* if satisfied by information on oath that it is proper to do so for the purposes of the Acts.

(4) Where the Revenue Commissioners require a valuation to be made by an authorised person, the costs of such valuation shall be defrayed by the Revenue Commissioners.][1]

Amendments

[1] Substituted by FA13 s101.

Cross References

From Section 911

Section 931 Making of assessments and application of income tax assessment provisions.

Section 1057 Fine for obstruction of officers in execution of duties.

912 Computer documents and records

[FA92 s237]

(1) In this section—

"*the Acts*" means—

(a) the Customs Acts,

(b) the statutes relating to the duties of excise and to the management of those duties,

(c) the Tax Acts,

(d) the Capital Gains Tax Acts,

(e) the Value-Added Tax Consolidation Act 2010, and the enactments amending or extending that Act,

(f) the Capital Acquisitions Tax Consolidation Act 2003, and the enactments amending or extending that Act, and

(g) Part VI of the Finance Act, 1983,

and any instruments made thereunder;

"*data*" means information in a form in which it can be processed;

"*data equipment*" means any electronic, photographic, magnetic, optical or other equipment for processing data;

"*processing*" means performing automatically logical or arithmetical operations on data, or the storing, maintenance, transmission, reproduction or communication of data;

"*records*" means documents which a person is obliged by any provision of the Acts to keep, issue or produce for inspection, and any other written or printed material;

"*software*" means any sequence of instructions used in conjunction with data equipment for the purpose of processing data or controlling the operation of the data equipment.

(2) Any provision under the Acts which—

(a) requires a person to keep, retain, issue or produce any records or cause any records to be kept, retained, issued or produced, or

(b) permits an officer of the Revenue Commissioners—

(i) to inspect any records,

(ii) to enter premises and search for any records, or

(iii) to take extracts from or copies of or remove any records,

shall, where the records are processed by data equipment, apply to the data equipment together with any associated software, data, apparatus or material as it applies to the records.

(3) An officer of the Revenue Commissioners may in the exercise or performance of his or her powers or duties require—

(a) the person by or on whose behalf the data equipment is or has been used, or

(b) any person having charge of, or otherwise concerned with the operation of, the data equipment or any associated apparatus or material,

to afford him or her all reasonable assistance in relation to the exercise or performance of those powers or duties.

Revenue Briefings

Tax Briefing

Tax Briefing August 2002 – Issue 49 pg 6 – Code of Practice Revenue Audits

Revenue Information Notes

2010 Code of Practice for Revenue Audit

Statements of Practice

Revenue Powers Exercised in Places other than a Revenue Office – SP GEN/1/94 (Revised 02/2006)
Revenue Powers (Finance Act 1999) – SP GEN/1/99
Revenue Internal Review Procedures – SP GEN/2/99

Cross References

To Section 912

Section 887 Use of electronic data processing.
Section 903 Power of inspection: PAYE.
Section 1104 Short title and construction.

912A Information for tax authorities in other territories

[(1) In this section—

["*foreign tax*" means a tax chargeable under the laws of a territory in relation to which—

(a) arrangements (in this section referred to as "*the arrangements*") having the force of law by virtue of *section 826* or *898P* of this Act or *section 106* of the Capital Acquisitions Tax Consolidation Act 2003 apply, or

(b) the Convention on Mutual Administrative Assistance in Tax Matters which was done at Strasbourg on 25 January 1988, or any Protocol to the Convention (such Convention or Protocol, as the case may be, referred to in this section as "*the Convention*"), having the force of law by virtue of *section 826*, applies;][1]

"*liability to foreign tax*", in relation to a person, means any liability in relation to foreign tax to which the person is or may be, or may have been, subject, or the amount of any such liability.

(2) For the purposes of complying with provisions with respect to the exchange of information contained [in the arrangements or in the Convention][2], *sections 900, 901, 902*, [*902A, 905*][3] *906A, 907* and *908* shall, subject to subsection (3), have effect—

(a) as if references in those sections to tax included references to foreign tax, and

(b) as if references in those sections to liability, in relation to a person, included references to liability to foreign tax, in relation to a person.][4]

[(3) Where *sections 902A, 905, 907* and *908* have effect by virtue only of this section, they shall have effect as if the references in those sections to—

(a) tax, were references to foreign tax, and

(b) any provision of the Acts, were references to any provision of the law of a territory in accordance with which foreign tax is charged or collected.][5]

Amendments

[1] Substituted by FA13 s99(1)(b). Applies as on and from 27 March 2013

[2] Substituted by FA13 s99(1)(c). Applies as on and from 27 March 2013.

[3] Substituted by FA12 s119(a). Deemed to have come into force and takes effect on and from 1 January 2012.

[4] Inserted by FA03 s38(b).

[5] Substituted by FA12 s119(b). Deemed to have come into force and takes effect on and from 1 January 2012.

Cross References

From Section 912A

Section 826 Agreements for relief from double taxation.

Section 898P Arrangements with third countries and dependent and associated territories of Member States.

Section 900 Power to call for production of books, information, etc.

Section 901 Application to High Court: production of books, information, etc.

Section 902 Information to be furnished by third party: request of an authorised officer.

Section 902A Application to High Court: information from third party.

Section 906A Information to be furnished by financial institutions.

Section 907 Application to Appeal Commissioners: information from financial institutions.

Section 908 Application to High Court seeking order requiring information: financial institutions.

912B Questioning of suspects in Garda Síochána custody in certain circumstances

[(1) In this section—

"*authorised officer*" means an officer of the Revenue Commissioners authorised by them in writing to exercise the powers conferred by this section;

"*specified offence*" means any offence under—

(a) the Customs Acts, including any offence under section 1078 or 1078A in so far as those sections relate to customs, and any instruments made there under and any instruments made under any other enactment and relating to customs,

(b) the statutes relating to the duties of excise and to the management of those duties, including any offence under section 1078 or 1078A in so far as those sections relate to excise, and any instruments made thereunder,

(c) (i) subsection (1A) and paragraphs (*c*), (*d*) and (*ii*) of subsection (2) of section 1078, and

(ii) section 1078A,

in so far as it is an offence relating to Chapter 2 of Part 18 and any instruments made under that Chapter, or

(d) (i) subsection (1A) and paragraphs (*c*) and (*d*) of subsection (2) of section 1078, and

(ii) section 1078A,

in so far as it is an offence relating to the Value-Added Tax Consolidation Act 2010, and the enactments amending or extending that Act and any instruments made thereunder,

which is an arrestable offence within the meaning of section 2 of the Criminal Law Act 1997.

(2) This section shall apply to a specified offence only.

(3) Where a member of the Garda Síochána arrests without warrant, whether in a Garda station or elsewhere, a person whom he or she, with reasonable cause, suspects of committing or of having committed a specified offence and the person has been taken to and detained in a Garda station, or if the person is arrested in a Garda station, has been detained in the station, pursuant to section 4 of the Criminal Justice Act 1984, an authorised officer or officers (but not more than 2 such officers) may, if and for so long as the officer or officers is, or are, accompanied by a member of the Garda Síochána, attend at, and participate in, the questioning of a person so detained in connection with the investigation of the specified offence, but only if the member of the Garda

Síochána requests the authorised officer or officers to do so and the member is satisfied that the attendance at, and participation in, such questioning of the authorised officer or officers is necessary for the proper investigation of the specified offence concerned.

(4) An authorised officer who attends at, and participates in, the questioning of a person in accordance with subsection (3) may not commit any act or make any omission which, if committed or made by a member of the Garda Síochána, would be a contravention of any regulation made under section 7 of the Criminal Justice Act 1984.

(5) An act committed or omission made by an authorised officer who attends at, and participates in, the questioning of a person in accordance with subsection (3) which, if committed or made by a member of the Garda Síochána, would be a contravention of any regulation made under section 7 of the Criminal Justice Act 1984 shall not of itself render the authorised officer liable to any criminal or civil proceedings or of itself affect the lawfulness of the custody of the detained person or the admissibility in evidence of any statement made by him or her.][1]

Amendments

[1] Inserted by FA08 s134. Has effect from 1 January 2008.

Cross References

From Section 912B

Section 520 Interpretation (Chapter 1).
Section 530 Interpretation (Chapter 2).
Section 1078 Revenue offences.
Section 1078A Concealing facts disclosed by documents.

CHAPTER 5

Capital Gains Tax: Returns, Information, etc.

913 Application of income tax provisions relating to returns, etc

[CGTA75 s51(1) and Sch4 par3(1), (2) (part of) and (3) to (5), par10(1) and par19; FA92 s246]

(1) The provisions of the Income Tax Acts relating to the making or delivery of any return, statement, declaration, list or other document, the furnishing of any particulars, the production of any document, the making of anything available for inspection, the delivery of any account or the making of any representation, shall, subject to any necessary modifications, apply in relation to capital gains tax as they apply in relation to income tax.

(2) In particular and without prejudice to *subsection (1)*, *sections 876* to *880*, *sections 888* and *900* and *paragraph 1* of *Schedule 1* shall, subject to any necessary modifications, apply in relation to capital gains tax.

(3) A notice under any provision of the Income Tax Acts as applied by this section may require particulars of any assets acquired by the person on whom the notice was served (or, if the notice relates to income or chargeable gains of some other person for whom the person who receives the notice is required to make a return under *section 878*, as so applied by this section, of any assets acquired by that other person) in the period specified in the notice, being a period beginning not earlier than the 6th day of April, 1974, but excluding—

(a) any assets exempted by *section 607* or *613*, or

(b) any assets acquired as trading stock.

(4) The particulars required under this section may include particulars of the person from whom the asset was acquired and of the consideration for the acquisition.

(5) (a) An event which, apart from *section 584(3)* as applied by *section 586* or *587*, would constitute the disposal of an asset shall for the purposes of this section constitute such a disposal.

(b) An event which, apart from *section 584(3)* as applied by *section 586* or *587*, would constitute the acquisition of an asset shall for the purposes of this section constitute such an acquisition.

(6) *Section 888* as applied by this section shall apply to property or leases of property other than premises as it applies to premises or leases of premises.

(7) A return of income of a partnership under *section 880* shall include—

(a) with respect to any disposal of partnership assets during a period to which any part of the return relates, the like particulars as if the partnership were liable to tax on any chargeable gain accruing on the disposal, and

(b) with respect to any acquisition of partnership assets, the particulars required by *subsection (3)*.

(8) A return under *section 879* as applied by this section in relation to chargeable gains accruing to a married woman in a year of assessment, or part of a year of assessment, during which she is a married woman and living with her husband may be required either from her or, if her husband is liable under *section 1028(1)*, from him.

Cross References

From Section 913

Section 584 Reorganisation or reduction of share capital.
Section 586 Company amalgamations by exchange of shares.
Section 587 Company reconstructions and amalgamations.
Section 607 Government and certain other securities.
Section 613 Miscellaneous exemptions for certain kinds of property.
Section 876 Notice of liability to income tax.
Section 878 Persons acting for incapacitated persons and non-residents.
Section 879 Returns of income.
Section 880 Partnership returns.
Section 888 Returns, etc. by lessors, lessees and agents.
Section 900 Power to call for production of books, information, etc.
Section 1028 Married persons.
Schedule 1 Supplementary Provisions Concerning the Extension of Charge to Tax to Profits and Income Derived from Activities Carried On and Employments Exercised on the Continental Shelf

To Section 913

Section 884 Returns of profits.
Section 959 Miscellaneous (Part 41).
Section 1014 Tax treatment of profits, losses and capital gains arising from activities of a European Economic Interest Grouping (EEIG).
Section 1077 Penalties for failure to make returns, etc. and for deliberately or carelessly making incorrect returns.
Section 1084 Surcharge for late returns.

914 Returns by issuing houses, stockbrokers, auctioneers, etc

[CGTA75 s51(1) and Sch4 par4; FA94 s63; FA95 s70]

(1) For the purpose of obtaining particulars of chargeable gains, an inspector may by notice in writing require a return under any provision of this section.

(2) (a) In this subsection, "*shares*" includes units in a unit trust.

(b) An issuing house or other person carrying on a business of effecting public issues of shares or securities in any company, or placings of shares or securities in any company, either on behalf of the company or on behalf of holders of blocks of shares or securities which have not previously been the subject of a public issue or placing, may be required to make a return of all such public issues or placings effected by that person in the course of the business in the period specified in the notice requiring the return, giving particulars of the persons to or with whom the shares or securities are issued, allotted or placed, and the number or amount of the shares or securities so obtained by them respectively.

(3) A person not carrying on such a business may be required to make a return as regards any such issue or placing effected by that person and specified in the notice, giving particulars of the persons to or with whom the shares or securities are issued, allotted or placed and the number or amount of the shares or securities so obtained by them respectively.

(4) A member of a stock exchange in the State may be required to make a return giving particulars of any transactions effected by that member in the course of that member's business in the period specified in the notice requiring the return and giving particulars of—

(a) the parties to the transactions,

(b) the number or amount of the shares or securities dealt with in the respective transactions, and

(c) the amount or value of the consideration.

(5) A person (other than a member of a stock exchange in the State) who acts as an agent in the State in transactions in shares or securities may be required to make a return giving particulars of—

(a) any such transactions effected by that person in the period specified in the notice,

(b) the parties to the transactions,

(c) the number or amount of the shares or securities dealt with in the respective transactions, and

(d) the amount or value of the consideration.

(6) An auctioneer and any person carrying on a trade of dealing in any description of tangible movable property, or of acting as an agent or intermediary in dealings in any description of tangible movable property, may be required to make a return giving particulars of any transactions effected by or through that auctioneer or that person, as the case may be, in which any asset which is tangible movable property is disposed of for a consideration the amount or value of which, in the hands of the recipient, exceeds—

(a) as respects transactions effected on or after the 6th day of April, 1994, but before the 6th day of April, 1995, [€6,350][1], and

(b) as respects transactions effected on or after the 6th day of April, 1995, [€19,050][2].

(7) No person shall be required under this section to include in a return particulars of any transaction effected more than 3 years before the service of the notice requiring that person to make the return.

[(8) Where a return is required to be made under this section, it shall be made, where the Revenue Commissioners so require, in an electronic format approved by the Revenue Commissioners.][3]

Amendments

[1, 2] Substituted by FA01 sched5.

[3] Inserted by FA07 s123(d).

Cross References

To Section 914

Section 1077 Penalties for failure to make returns, etc. and for deliberately or carelessly making incorrect returns.

915 Returns by nominee shareholders

[CGTA75 s51(1) and Sch4 par5]

(1) In this section, references to shares include references to securities and loan capital.

(2) Where, for the purpose of obtaining particulars of chargeable gains, any person in whose name any shares of a company are registered is so required by notice in writing by the Revenue Commissioners or by an inspector, that person shall state whether or not that person is the beneficial owner of those shares and, if that person is not the beneficial owner of those shares or any of them, shall furnish the name and address of the person or persons on whose behalf the shares are registered in that person's name.

Cross References

To Section 915

Section 1077 Penalties for failure to make returns, etc. and for deliberately or carelessly making incorrect returns.

916 Returns by party to a settlement

[CGTA75 s51(1) and Sch4 par6]

The Revenue Commissioners may by notice in writing require any person, being a party to a settlement, to furnish them within such time as they may direct (not being less than 28 days) with such particulars relating to the settlement as they think necessary for the purposes of the Capital Gains Tax Acts.

Cross References

To Section 916

Section 1077 Penalties for failure to make returns, etc. and for deliberately or carelessly making incorrect returns.

917 Returns relating to non-resident companies and trusts

[CGTA75 s51(1) and Sch4 par7]

A person who—

(a) holds shares or securities in a company not resident or ordinarily resident in the State, or

(b) is beneficially interested or acts as agent for or on behalf of a person who is beneficially interested in settled property under a settlement the trustees of which are not resident or ordinarily resident in the State,

may be required by a notice by the Revenue Commissioners to give such particulars as the Revenue Commissioners may consider are required to determine whether the company or trust is [within *sections 579* to *579F* and *section 590*][1], and whether any chargeable gains have accrued to that company, or to the trustees of that settlement, in respect of which the person to whom the notice is given is liable to capital gains tax [under *sections 579* to *579F* or *section 590*][2] .

Amendments

[1] Substituted by FA99 s92(1)(a)(i). This section shall apply as on and from the 11th day of February, 1999.

[2] Substituted by FA99 s92(1)(a)(ii). This section shall apply as on and from the 11th day of February, 1999.

Cross References

From Section 917

Section 579 Non-resident trusts.
Section 579F Migrant settlements.
Section 590 Attribution to participators of chargeable gains accruing to non-resident company.

To Section 917

Section 746 Offshore income gains accruing to persons resident or domiciled abroad.
Section 1077 Penalties for failure to make returns, etc. and for deliberately or carelessly making incorrect returns.

917A Return of property transfers to non-resident trustees

[[...][1]

(2) This section applies where—

(a) on or after the 11th day of February, 1999, a person (in this section referred to as the "*transferor*") transfers property to the trustees of a settlement otherwise than under a transaction entered into at arm's length,

(b) the trustees of the settlement are neither resident nor ordinarily resident in the State at the time the property is transferred, and

(c) the transferor knows or has reason to believe, that the trustees are not so resident and ordinarily resident.

(3) Where this section applies, the transferor shall, before the expiry of 3 months beginning with the day on which the transfer is made, deliver to the appropriate inspector a statement which—

(a) identifies the settlement, and

(b) specifies the property transferred, the day on which the transfer was made, and the consideration (if any) for the transfer.

(4) Where a transferor fails—

(a) to make a statement required to be made by the transferor in accordance with subsection (3), or

(b) to include in such a statement the details referred to in subsection (3),

the transferor shall in respect of each such failure be liable to a penalty of [€4,000][2].

[…][3]][4]

Amendments

[1] Deleted by FA12 sched5(1)(i).

[2] Substituted by F(No.2)A08 sched5(part2)(1)(u)(i). The enactments specified in Schedule 5 are amended or repealed to the extent and manner specified in that Schedule and, unless the contrary is stated, shall come into effect after 24 December 2008.

[3] Deleted by F(No.2)A08 sched5(part2)(1)(u)(ii). The enactments specified in Schedule 5 are amended or repealed to the extent and manner specified in that Schedule and, unless the contrary is stated, shall come into effect after 24 December 2008.

[4] Inserted by FA99 s92(1)(b). This section shall apply as on and from the 11th day of February, 1999.

Cross References

From Section 917A

Section 917B Return by settlor in relation to non-resident trustees.
Section 917C Return by certain trustees.
Section 950 Interpretation (Part 41).

917B Return by settlor in relation to non-resident trustees

[(1) In this section and in *section 917C* "*arrangements*" means arrangements having the force of law by virtue of [*section 826(1)*][1] (as extended to capital gains tax by *section 828*);

(2) This section applies where a settlement is created on or after the 11th day of February, 1999, and at the time it is created—

(a) the trustees are neither resident nor ordinarily resident in the State, or

(b) the trustees are resident and ordinarily resident in the State but fall to be regarded for the purposes of any arrangements as resident in a territory outside the State.

(3) Where this section applies, any person who—

(a) is a settlor in relation to the settlement at the time it is created, and

(b) at that time fulfils the condition mentioned in subsection (4),

shall, before the expiry of the period of 3 months beginning with the day on which the settlement is created, deliver to the appropriate inspector a statement specifying—

(i) the day on which the settlement was created;

(ii) the name and address of the person making the statement; and

(iii) the names and addresses of the persons who are the trustees immediately before the delivery of the statement.

(4) The condition is that the person concerned is domiciled in the State and is either resident or ordinarily resident in the State.

[(5) Where a person fails—

(a) to make a statement required to be made by the person in accordance with [subsection (3)][2], or

(b) to include in such a statement the details referred to in [subsection (3)][3],

then the person shall in respect of each such failure be liable to a penalty of €4,000.][4]

[...][5]][6]

Amendments

[1] Substituted by FA07 sched2(1)(ag). Has effect as on and from 2 April 2007.

[2,3] Substituted by FA13 sched2(1)(i). Has effect on and from 27 March 2013.

[4] Substituted by F(No.2)A08 sched5(part2)(1)(v)(i). The enactments specified in Schedule 5 are amended or repealed to the extent and manner specified in that Schedule and, unless the contrary is stated, shall come into effect after 24 December 2008.

[5] Deleted by F(No.2)A08 sched5(part2)(1)(v)(ii). The enactments specified in Schedule 5 are amended or repealed to the extent and manner specified in that Schedule and, unless the contrary is stated, shall come into effect after 24 December 2008.

[6] Inserted by FA99 s92(1)(b). This section shall apply as on and from the 11th day of February, 1999.

Cross References

From Section 917B

Section 826 Agreements for relief from double taxation.

Section 828 Capital gains tax: double taxation relief.

Section 917C Return by certain trustees.

To Section 917B

Section 917A Return of property transfers to non-resident trustees.

917C Return by certain trustees

[(1) This section applies where—

(a) the trustees of a settlement become at any time (in this section referred to as "*the relevant time*") on or after the 11th day of February, 1999, neither resident nor ordinarily resident in the State, or

(b) the trustees of a settlement, while continuing to be resident and ordinarily resident in the State, become at any time (in this section also referred to as "*the relevant time*") on or after the 11th day of February, 1999, trustees who fall to be regarded for the purposes of any arrangements as resident in a territory outside the State.

(2) Where this section applies, any person who was a trustee of the settlement immediately before the relevant time shall, before the expiry of the period of 3 months beginning with the day when the relevant time falls, deliver to the appropriate inspector a statement specifying—

(a) the day on which the settlement was created,

(b) the name and address of each person who is a settlor in relation to the settlement immediately before the delivery of the statement, and

(c) the names and addresses of the persons who are the trustees immediately before the delivery of the statement.

[(3) Where a person fails—

(a) to make a statement required to be made by the person in accordance with subsection (2), or

(b) to include in such a statement the details referred to in subsection (2),

then the person shall in respect of each such failure be liable to a penalty of €4,000.][1]

[...][2]][3]

Amendments

[1] Substituted by F(No.2)A08 sched5(part2)(1)(w)(i). The enactments specified in Schedule 5 are amended or repealed to the extent and manner specified in that Schedule and, unless the contrary is stated, shall come into effect after 24 December 2008.

[2] Deleted by F(No.2)A08 sched5(part2)(1)(w)(ii). The enactments specified in Schedule 5 are amended or repealed to the extent and manner specified in that Schedule and, unless the contrary is stated, shall come into effect after 24 December 2008.

[3] Inserted by FA99 s92(1)(b). This section shall apply as on and from the 11th day of February, 1999.

Cross References

To Section 917C

Section 917A Return of property transfers to non-resident trustees.

Section 917B Return by settlor in relation to non-resident trustees.

CHAPTER 6

Electronic Transmission of Returns of Income, Profits, etc., and of Other Revenue Returns

917D Interpretation (Chapter 6)

[(1) In this Chapter—

"*the Acts*" means—

(a) the statutes relating to the duties of excise and to the management of those duties,

[(aa) the Customs Acts,][1]

(b) the Tax Acts,

(c) the Capital Gains Tax Acts,

(d) the Value-Added Tax Consolidation Act 2010, and the enactments amending or extending that Act,

(e) the Capital Acquisitions Tax Consolidation Act 2003, and the enactments amending or extending that Act, and

(f) the [Stamp Duties Consolidation Act 1999,][2] and the enactments amending or extending that Act,

and any instruments made under any of the statutes and enactments referred to in paragraphs (*a*) to (*f*);

"*approved person*" shall be construed in accordance with *section 917G*;

"*approved transmission*" shall be construed in accordance with *section 917H*;

"*authorised person*" has the meaning assigned to it by [section 917G(3)(*a*);][3]

["*digital signature*", in relation to a person, means an advanced electronic signature (within the meaning of the Electronic Commerce Act, 2000) provided to the person by the Revenue Commissioners solely for the purpose of making an electronic transmission of information which is required to be included in a return to which this Chapter applies and for no other purpose and a qualified certificate (within the meaning of that Act) provided to the person by the Revenue Commissioners or a person appointed in that behalf by the Revenue Commissioners;][4]

["*electronic identifier*", in relation to a person, means—

(a) the person's digital signature, or

(b) such other means of electronic identification as may be specified or authorised by the Revenue Commissioners for the purposes of this Chapter;][5]

"*hard copy*", in relation to information held electronically, means a printed out version of that information;

["return" means any return, claim, application, notification, election, declaration, nomination, statement, list, registration, particulars or other information which a person is or may be required by the Acts to give to the Revenue Commissioners or any Revenue officer;][6]

"*revenue officer*" means the Collector-General, an inspector or other officer of the Revenue Commissioners (including an inspector or other officer who is authorised under any provision of the Acts (however expressed) to receive a return or to require a return to be prepared and delivered);

"*tax*" means any income tax, corporation tax, capital gains tax, value-added tax, gift tax, inheritance tax, [customs duty,][7] excise duty or stamp duty.

[...][8]

(3) Any references in this Chapter to the making of a return include references in any provision of the Acts to—

(a) the preparing and delivering of a return;

(b) the sending of a return;

(c) the furnishing of a return or of particulars;

(d) the delivering of a return;

(e) the presentation of a return;

(f) the rendering of a return;

(g) the giving of particulars or of any information specified in any provision; and

(h) any other means whereby a return is forwarded, however expressed.][9]

Amendments

[1] Inserted by F(No.2)A13 79(a).

[2] Substituted by FA08 sched8(1)(q)(i). Has effect as on and from 13 March 2008.

[3] Substituted by FA08 sched8(1)(q)(ii). Has effect as on and from 13 March 2008.

[4] Substituted by FA01 s235(a)(i)(I). Has effect from 15 February 2001.

[5] Inserted by FA05 s22(a). Applies with effect from 25 March 2005.

[6] Substituted by FA01 s235(a)(i)(II). Has effect from 15 February 2001.

[7] Substituted by F(No.2)A13 79(b).

[8] Deleted by FA01 s235(a)(ii). Has effect from 15 February 2001.

[9] Inserted by FA99 s209.

Revenue Briefings

Tax Briefing

Tax Briefing November 2007 – Issue 67 – Mandatory Electronic Filing of Returns

Tax Briefing September 2008 – Issue 69 – Consultations on Mandatory E-filing and E-paying – ROS

eBrief

eBrief No. 05/2005 – ROS Payments and Auditor Independence (US SEC Regulations)

eBrief No. 42/2008 – Mandatory Electronic Filing and Payment of Tax

eBrief No. 03/10 – Mandatory Electronic Filing and Payment of Tax – Clarification of Companies included in Phase 2

eBrief No. 50/10 – Proposed Extension of Mandatory E-Filing

eBrief No. 87/10 – Mandatory Electronic Filing and Payment of tax – Notice of Defferal of Implementation Date Phase 3

Cross References

From Section 917D

Section 917G Approved persons.

Section 917H Approved transmissions.

To Section 917D

Section 917EA Mandatory electronic filing and payment of tax.

917E Application

[This Chapter shall apply to a return if—

(a) the provision of the Acts under which the return is made is specified for the purpose of this Chapter by order made by the Revenue Commissioners, and

(b) the return is required to be made after the day appointed by such order in relation to returns to be made under the provision so specified.][1]

Amendments

[1] Inserted by FA99 s209.

Revenue Briefings

eBrief

eBrief No. 65/2014 – Electronic Filing – Board Orders made

Cross References

To Section 917E

Section 917EA Mandatory electronic filing and payment of tax.

917EA Mandatory electronic filing and payment of tax

[(1) In this section—

"*electronic means*" includes electrical, digital, magnetic, optical, electromagnetic, biometric, photonic means of transmission of data and other forms of related technology by means of which data is transmitted;

"*repayment of tax*" includes any amount relating to tax which is to be paid or repaid by the Revenue Commissioners;

"*specified person*" means any person, group of persons or class of persons specified in regulations made under this section for the purposes of either or both *paragraphs (a)* and *(b)* of *subsection (3)*;

"*specified return*" means a return specified in regulations made under this section;

"*specified tax liabilities*" means liabilities to tax including interest on unpaid tax specified in regulations made under this section.

(2) *Section 917D* shall apply for the purposes of regulations made under this section in the same way as it applies for the purposes of this Chapter.

(3) The Revenue Commissioners may make regulations—

(a) requiring the delivery by specified persons of a specified return by electronic means where an order under *section 917E* has been made in respect of that return,

(b) requiring the payment by electronic means of specified tax liabilities by specified persons, and

(c) for the repayment of any tax specified in the regulations to be made by electronic means.

(4) Regulations made under this section shall include provision for the exclusion of a person from the requirements of regulations made under this section where the Revenue Commissioners are satisfied that the person could not reasonably be expected to have the capacity to make a specified return or to pay the specified tax liabilities by electronic means, and allowing a person, aggrieved by a failure to exclude such person, to appeal that failure to the Appeal Commissioners.

(5) Regulations made under this section may, in particular and without prejudice to the generality of subsection (3), include provision for—

(a) the electronic means to be used to pay or repay tax,

(b) the conditions to be complied with in relation to the electronic payment or repayment of tax,

(c) determining the time when tax paid or repaid using electronic means is to be taken as having been paid or repaid,

(d) the manner of proving, for any purpose, the time of payment or repayment of any tax paid or repaid using electronic means, including provision for the application of any conclusive or other presumptions,

(e) notifying persons that they are specified persons, including the manner by which such notification may be made, and

(f) such supplemental and incidental matters as appear to the Revenue Commissioners to be necessary.

(6) The Revenue Commissioners may nominate any of their officers to perform any acts and discharge any functions authorised by regulation made under this section to be performed or discharged by the Revenue Commissioners.

(7) Where a specified person—

(a) makes a return which is a specified return for the purposes of regulations made under this section, or

(b) makes a payment of tax which is specified tax liabilities for the purposes of regulations made under this section,

in a form other than that required by any such regulation, the specified person shall be liable to a penalty of €1,520 [...][1].

(8) Every regulation made under this section shall be laid before Dáil Éireann as soon as may be after it is made and, if a resolution annulling the regulation is passed by Dáil Éireann within the next 21 days on which Dáil Éireann has sat after the regulation is laid before it, the regulation shall be annulled accordingly but without prejudice to the validity of anything previously done under the regulation.][2]

Amendments

[1] Deleted by FA12 sched6(1)(p). Applies as respects penalties incurred on or after 24 December 2008.

[2] Inserted by FA03 s164(1)(a). Has effect from such day as the Minister for Finance may appoint by order.

Revenue Briefings

Tax Briefing

Tax Briefing November 2007 – Issue 67 – Mandatory Electronic Filing of Returns

Tax Briefing September 2008 – Issue 69 – Consultations on Mandatory E-filing and E-paying – ROS

Tax Briefing July 2012 – Issue 04 – Submission of Financial Statements in iXBRL

eBrief

eBrief No. 42/2008 – Mandatory Electronic Filing and Payment of Tax

eBrief No. 03/2010 – Mandatory Electronic Filing and Payment of Tax – Clarification of companies included in Phase 2

eBrief No. 50/2010 – Proposed Extension of Mandatory E-Filing

eBrief No. 87/2010 – Mandatory Electronic Filing and Payment of Tax – Notice of Defferal of Implementation Date Phase 3

eBrief No. 04/2011 – Mandatory Electronic Filing and Payment of Tax – Implementation of Phase 3

eBrief No. 30/2011 – Form 46G(company) and Mandatory eFiling

eBrief No. 32/2011 – Mandatory Electronic Filing and Payment of Tax – Implementation of Phase 3A Update

eBrief No. 33/2011 – Stamp Duty – Mandatory Electronic Filing and Payment
eBrief No. 46/2011 – Mandatory Electronic Filing and Payment of Tax – Implementation of Phase 3B
eBrief No. 17/2012 – Mandatory Electronic Filing and Payment – Implementation of Phase 4
eBrief No. 26/2012 – Tax Returns and Payments (Mandatory Electronic Filing and Payment of Tax) Regulations 2012 (S.I. No. 156 of 2012)
eBrief No. 35/2012 – Tax Briefing Issue No. 04/12 – Submission of Financial Statements in iXBRL
eBrief No. 57/2012 – Update regarding the Submission of Financial Statements in iXBRL
eBrief No. 02/2013 – Revenue launches Direct Debit On-Line (DDOL facility) via ROS
eBrief No. 85/2014 – Important information regarding mandatory iXBRL filing for Corporation Tax payers

Cross References

From Section 917EA

Section 917D Interpretation (Chapter 6).
Section 917E Application.
Section 1061 Recovery of penalties.

To Section 917EA

Section 530 Interpretation (Chapter 2).
Section 531 Payments to subcontractors in certain industries.
Section 531D Deduction and payment of income levy on relevant emoluments.
Section 531AO Deduction and payment of universal social charge on relevant emoluments.
Section 950 Interpretation (Part 41).
Section 958 Date for payment of tax.

917F Electronic transmission of returns

[(1) Notwithstanding any other provision of the Acts, the obligation of any person to make a return to which this Chapter applies shall be treated as fulfilled by that person if information is transmitted electronically in compliance with that obligation, but only if—

(a) the transmission is made by an approved person or an authorised person,

(b) the transmission is an approved transmission,

[(c) the transmission bears the electronic identifier of that person, and][1]

(d) the receipt of the transmission is acknowledged in accordance with *section 917J*.

(2) In *subsection (1)*, the reference to the information which is required to be included in the return includes any requirement on a person to—

(a) make any statement,

(b) include [any information, accounts, statements, reports or further particulars][2], or

(c) make or attach any claim.

(3) Where the obligation of any person to make a return to which this Chapter applies is treated as fulfilled in accordance with *subsection (1)* then, any provision of the Acts which—

(a) requires that the return include or be accompanied by any description of declaration whatever by the person making the return, apart from a declaration of an amount,

(b) requires that the return be signed or accompanied by a certificate,

(c) requires that the return be in writing,

(d) authorises the return to be signed by a person acting under the authority of the person obliged to make the return,

(e) authorises the Revenue Commissioners to prescribe the form of a return or which requires a return to be in or on any prescribed form, or

(f) for the purposes of any claim for exemption or for any allowance, deduction or repayment of tax under the Acts which is required to be made with the return, authorises the Revenue Commissioners to prescribe the form of a claim,

shall not apply.

(4) Where the obligation of any person to make a return to which this Chapter applies is treated as fulfilled in accordance with *subsection (1)* then, the time at which any requirement under the Acts to make a return is fulfilled shall be the day on which the receipt of the information referred to in that subsection is acknowledged in accordance with *section 917J*.

[(5) Where an approved transmission is made by—

(a) an approved person on behalf of another person, or

(b) an authorised person on behalf of another person (not being the person who authorised that person),

a hard copy of the information shall be made and authenticated in accordance with *section 917K*.][3]

(6) (a) Where the obligation of any person to make a return to which this Chapter applies is treated as fulfilled in accordance with *subsection (1)* then, any requirement that—

(i) the return or any claim which is to be made with or attached to the return should be accompanied by any document (in this subsection referred to as a "*supporting document*") other than the return or the claim, and

(ii) the supporting document be delivered with the return or the claim,

shall be treated as fulfilled by the person subject to the requirement if the person or the approved person referred to in *subsection (1)(a)* retains the document for inspection on request by a revenue officer.

(b) Any person subject to the requirement referred to in *paragraph (a)* shall produce any supporting documents requested by a revenue officer within 30 days of that request.

(c) The references in this subsection to a document include references to any accounts, certificate, evidence, receipts, reports or statements.][4]

Amendments

[1] Substituted by FA05 s22(b). Applies with effect from 25 March 2005.

[2] Substituted by FA14 s89(b).

[3] Substituted by FA01 s235(b)(ii). Has effect from 15 February 2001.

[4] Inserted by FA99 s209.

Cross References

From Section 917F

Section 917J Acknowledgement of electronic transmissions.
Section 917K Hard copies.

To Section 917F

Section 864A Electronic claims.
Section 917K Hard copies.
Section 917L Exercise of powers.
Section 917M Proceedings.

917G Approved persons

[(1) A person shall be an approved person for the purposes of this Chapter if the person is approved by the Revenue Commissioners for the purposes of transmitting electronically information which is required to be included in a return to which this Chapter applies (in this section referred to as "*the transmission*") and [complies with the condition specified in subsection (3)(a) in relation to authorised persons and the condition specified in subsection (3)(b) in relation to the making of transmissions and the use of [electronic identifiers][1]][2].

(2) A person seeking to be approved under this section shall make application in that behalf to the Revenue Commissioners [by such means as the Revenue Commissioners may determine][3] for the purposes of this section.

[(3) The conditions referred to in subsection (1) are that—

(a) the person notifies the Revenue Commissioners in a manner to be determined by the Revenue Commissioners of the persons (each of whom is referred to in this section as an "authorised person"), in addition to the person, who are authorised to make the transmission, and

(b) the person and each person who is an authorised person in relation to that person in making the transmission complies with the requirements referred to in subsections (2) and (3) of *section 917H*.][4]

(4) A person seeking to be approved under this section shall be given notice by the Revenue Commissioners of the grant or refusal by them of the approval and, in the case of a refusal, of the reason for the refusal.

(5) An approval under this section may be withdrawn by the Revenue Commissioners by notice in writing or by such other means as the Revenue Commissioners may decide with effect from such date as may be specified in the notice.

(6) (a) A notice withdrawing an approval under the section shall state the grounds for the withdrawal.

(b) No approval under this section may be withdrawn unless an approved person or an authorised person has failed to comply with one or more of the requirements referred to in *section 917H(2)*.

(7) A person who is refused approval under this section or whose approval under this section is withdrawn may appeal to the Appeal Commissioners against the refusal or withdrawal.

(8) The appeal under subsection (7) shall be made by notice to the Revenue Commissioners before the end of the period of 30 days beginning with the day on which notice of the refusal or withdrawal was given to the person.

(9) The Appeal Commissioners shall hear and determine an appeal made to them under subsection (7) as if it were an appeal against an assessment to income tax, and the provisions of the Tax Acts relating to appeals shall apply accordingly.][5]

Amendments

[1] Substituted by FA05 s22(c). Applies with effect from 25 March 2005.

[2] Substituted by FA01 s235(c)(i). Has effect from 15 February 2001.

[3] Substituted by FA01 s235(c)(ii). Has effect from 15 February 2001.

[4] Substituted by FA01 s235(c)(iii). Has effect from 15 February 2001.

[5] Inserted by FA99 s209.

Cross References

From Section 917G

Section 917H Approved transmissions.

To Section 917G

Section 917D Interpretation (Chapter 6).

917H Approved transmissions

[(1) Where an approved person transmits electronically information which is required to be included in a return to which this Chapter applies the transmission shall not be an approved transmission unless it complies with the requirements of this section.

[(2) The Revenue Commissioners shall publish and make known to each approved person and each authorised person any requirement for the time being determined by them as being applicable to—

(a) the manner in which information which is required to be included in a return to which this Chapter applies is to be transmitted electronically, and

(b) the use of a person's [electronic identifier][1].

(3) The requirements referred to in subsection (2) include—

(a) requirements as to the software or type of software to be used to make a transmission,

(b) the terms and conditions under which a person may make a transmission, and

(c) the terms and conditions under which a person may use that person's [electronic identifier][2].][3]

[(4) For the purposes of subsection (3), the Revenue Commissioners may determine different terms and conditions in relation to different returns or categories of a return, different categories of persons and different returns or categories of a return made by different categories of persons.][4]][5]

Amendments

[1, 2] Substituted by FA05 s22(d)(i). Applies with effect from 25 March 2005.

[3] Substituted by FA01 s235(d). Has effect from 15 February 2001.

[4] Inserted by FA05 s22(d)(ii). Applies with effect from 25 March 2005.

[5] Inserted by FA99 s209.

Cross References

To Section 917H

Section 917D Interpretation (Chapter 6).

Section 917G Approved persons.

917I Digital signatures [Deleted]

Deleted by FA01 s235(e). Has effect from 15 February 2001.

917J Acknowledgement of electronic transmissions

[For the purposes of this Chapter, where an electronic transmission of information which is required to be included in a return to which this Chapter applies is received by the Revenue Commissioners, the Revenue Commissioners shall send an electronic acknowledgement of receipt of that transmission to the person from whom it was received.][1]

Amendments

[1] Inserted by FA99 s209.

Cross References

To Section 917J

Section 917F Electronic transmission of returns.

917K Hard copies

[(1) A hard copy shall be made in accordance with this subsection only if—

(a) the hard copy is made under processes and procedures which are designed to ensure that the information contained in the hard copy shall only be the information [transmitted or to be transmitted][1] in accordance with *section 917F(1)*,

(b) the hard copy is in a form approved by the Revenue Commissioners which is appropriate to the information so transmitted, and

(c) the hard copy is authenticated in accordance with subsection (2).

(2) For the purposes of this Chapter, a hard copy made in accordance with subsection (1) shall be authenticated only if the hard copy is signed by the person who would have been required to make the declaration, sign the return or furnish the certificate, as the case may be, but for paragraph *(a)*, *(b)* or *(d)* of *section 917F(3)*.][2]

Amendments

[1] Substituted by FA01 s235(f). Has effect from 15 February 2001.

[2] Inserted by FA99 s209.

Cross References

From Section 917K

Section 917F Electronic transmission of returns.

To Section 917K

Section 917F Electronic transmission of returns.

917L Exercise of powers

[(1) This section shall apply where the obligation of any person to make a return to which this Chapter applies is treated as fulfilled in accordance with *section 917F(1)*.

(2) Where this section applies the Revenue Commissioners and a revenue officer shall have all the powers and duties in relation to the information contained in the transmission as they or that officer would have had if the information had been contained in a return made by post.

(3) Where this section applies the person whose obligation to make a return to which this Chapter applies is treated as fulfilled in accordance with *section 917F(1)* shall have all the rights and duties in relation to the information contained in the transmission as the person would have had if that information had been contained in a return made by post.][1]

Amendments

[1] Inserted by FA99 s209.

Cross References

From Section 917L

Section 917F Electronic transmission of returns.

917M Proceedings

[(1) This section shall apply where the obligation of any person to make a return to which this Chapter applies is treated as fulfilled in accordance with *section 917F(1)*.

(2) In this section, "*proceedings*" means civil and criminal proceedings, and includes proceedings before the Appeal Commissioners or any other tribunal having jurisdiction by virtue of any provision of the Acts.

(3) Where this section applies a hard copy certified by a revenue officer to be a true copy of the information transmitted electronically in accordance with *section 917F(1)* shall be treated [for the purposes of the Acts][1] as if the hard copy—

(a) were a return or, as the case may be, a claim made by post, and

(b) contained any declaration, certificate or signature required by the Acts on such a return or, as the case may be, such a claim.

(4) For the purposes of any proceedings under the Acts, unless a Judge or any other person before whom proceedings are taken determines at the time of the proceedings that it is unjust in the circumstances to apply this provision, any rule of law restricting the admissibility or use of hearsay evidence shall not apply to a representation contained in a document recording information which has been transmitted in accordance with *section 917F(1)* in so far as the representation is a representation as to—

(a) the information so transmitted,

(b) the date on which, or the time at which, the information was so transmitted, or

(c) the identity of the person by whom or on whose behalf the information was so transmitted.][2]

Amendments

[1] Substituted by FA01 s235(g). Has effect from 15 February 2001.

[2] Inserted by FA99 s209.

Cross References

From Section 917M

Section 917F Electronic transmission of returns.

To Section 917M

Section 864A Electronic claims.

917N Miscellaneous

[The Revenue Commissioners may nominate any of their officers to perform any acts and discharge any functions authorised by this Chapter to be performed or discharged by the Revenue Commissioners.][1]

Amendments

[1] Inserted by FA99 s209.

PART 39

Assessments [Deleted]

Deleted by FA12 s129(2).

Note:

FA12 s129

Subject to the below, this section takes effect on and from 1 January 2013.

This section applies—

(a) in the case of a chargeable period (within the meaning of 45 *section 321(2)* TCA 97) which is an accounting period of a company, as respects chargeable periods that start on or after 1 January 2013, and

(b) in a case other than that referred to in *paragraph (a)*, as respects the year of assessment 2013 and subsequent years of assessment.

This section does not affect the application of the provisions of the TCA 97, which are amended or deleted by this section, as respects chargeable periods prior to those referred to above.

— Please refer to earlier editions of this publication for details of Part 39.

PART 40

Appeals

CHAPTER 1

Appeals Against Income Tax and Corporation Tax Assessments

932 Prohibition on alteration of assessment except on appeal

[ITA67 s415; CTA76 s146(1); FA83 s37]

[Except as provided in *Part 41A* or where otherwise expressly authorised][1] by the Tax Acts, an assessment to income tax or corporation tax shall not be altered before the time for hearing and determining appeals and then only in cases of assessments appealed against and in accordance with such determination, and if any person makes, causes, or allows to be made in any assessment any unauthorised alteration, that person shall incur a penalty of [€60][2].

Amendments

[1] Substituted by FA13 s92 and sched1(part 2)(g).

[2] Substituted by FA01 sched5.

Note:

FA13 s92 applies—

(a) in the case of a chargeable period (within the meaning of section 321(2)) which is an accounting period of a company, as respects chargeable periods that start on or after 1 January 2013, and

(b) in a case other than that referred to in paragraph (a), as respects the year of assessment (within the meaning of section 2(1)) 2013 and subsequent years of assessment.

Cross References

To Section 932

Section 531AJ Application of provisions relating to income tax.
Section 927 Rectification of excessive set-off, etc. of tax credit.
Schedule 31 Consequential Amendments

933 Appeals against assessment

[ITA67 s416(1) to (7)(f), (8) and (9); F(MP)A68 s3(1), s3(2) and Sch PtI; CTA76 s146(1); FA80 s54(1); FA83 s9(a)(i) and s37; FA95 s173(1)(a)]

(1) (a) A person aggrieved by any assessment to income tax or corporation tax made on that person by the inspector or such other officer as the Revenue Commissioners shall appoint in that behalf (in this section referred to as "*other officer*") shall be entitled to appeal to the Appeal Commissioners on giving, within 30 days after the date of the notice of assessment, notice in writing to the inspector or other officer.

(b) Where on an application under *paragraph (a)* the inspector or other officer is of the opinion that the person who has given the notice of appeal is not entitled to make such an appeal, the inspector or other officer shall refuse the application and notify the person in writing accordingly, specifying the grounds for such refusal.

(c) A person who has had an application under *paragraph (a)* refused by the inspector or other officer shall be entitled to appeal against such refusal by notice in writing to the Appeal Commissioners within 15 days of the date of issue by the inspector or other officer of the notice of refusal.

(d) On receipt of an application under *paragraph (c)*, the Appeal Commissioners shall request the inspector or other officer to furnish them with a copy of the notice issued to the person under *paragraph (b)* and, on receipt of the copy of the notice, they shall as soon as possible—

(i) refuse the application for an appeal by giving notice in writing to the applicant specifying the grounds for their refusal,

(ii) allow the application for an appeal and give notice in writing accordingly to both the applicant and the inspector or other officer, or

(iii) notify in writing both the applicant and the inspector or other officer that they have decided to arrange a hearing at such time and place specified in the notice to enable them determine whether or not to allow the application for an appeal.

(2) (a) The Appeal Commissioners shall from time to time appoint times and places for the hearing of appeals against assessments and the Clerk to the Appeal Commissioners shall give notice of such times and places to the inspector or other officer.

(b) The inspector or other officer shall give notice in writing to each person who has given notice of appeal of the time and place appointed for the hearing of that person's appeal; but—

(i) notice under this paragraph shall not be given in a case in which *subsection (3)(b)* applies either consequent on an agreement referred to in that subsection or consequent on a notice referred to in *subsection (3)(d)*, and

(ii) in a case where it appears to the inspector or other officer that an appeal may be settled by agreement under *subsection (3)*, he or she may refrain from giving notice under this paragraph or may by notice in writing and with the agreement of the appellant withdraw a notice already given.

(c) Where, on application in writing in that behalf to the Appeal Commissioners, a person who has given notice of appeal to the inspector or other officer in accordance with *subsection (1)(a)* satisfies the Appeal Commissioners that the information furnished to the inspector or other officer is such that the appeal is likely to be determined on the first occasion on which it comes before them for hearing, the Appeal Commissioners may direct the inspector or other officer to give the notice in writing first mentioned in *paragraph (b)* and the inspector or other officer shall comply forthwith with such direction, and accordingly *subparagraph (ii)* of that paragraph shall not apply to that notice of appeal.

(3) (a) This subsection shall apply to any assessment in respect of which notice of appeal has been given, not being an assessment the appeal against which has been determined by the Appeal Commissioners or which has become final and conclusive under *subsection (6)*.

(b) Where, in relation to an assessment to which this subsection applies, the inspector or other officer and the appellant come to an agreement, whether in writing or otherwise, that the assessment is to stand, is to be amended in a particular manner or is to be discharged or cancelled, the inspector or other officer shall give effect to the agreement and thereupon, if the agreement is that the assessment is to stand or is to be amended, the assessment or the amended assessment, as the case may be, shall have the same force and effect as if it were an assessment in respect of which no notice of appeal had been given.

(c) An agreement which is not in writing shall be deemed not to be an agreement for the purposes of *paragraph (b)* unless—

(i) the fact that an agreement was come to, and the terms agreed on, are confirmed by notice in writing given by the inspector or other officer to the appellant or by the appellant to the inspector or other officer, and

(ii) 21 days have elapsed since the giving of that notice without the person to whom it was given giving notice in writing to the person by whom it was given that the first-mentioned person desires to repudiate or withdraw from the agreement.

(d) Where an appellant desires not to proceed with the appeal against an assessment to which this subsection applies and gives notice in writing to that effect to the inspector or other officer, *paragraph (b)* shall apply as if the appellant and the inspector or other officer had, on the appellant's notice being received, come to an agreement in writing that the assessment should stand.

(e) References in this subsection to an agreement being come to with an appellant and the giving of notice to or by an appellant include references to an agreement being come to with, and the giving of notice to or by, a person acting on behalf of the appellant in relation to the appeal.

(4) All appeals against assessments to income tax or corporation tax shall be heard and determined by the Appeal Commissioners, and their determination on any such appeal shall be final and conclusive, unless the person assessed requires that that person's appeal shall be reheard under *section 942* or unless under the Tax Acts a case is required to be stated for the opinion of the High Court.

(5) An appeal against an assessment may be heard and determined by one Appeal Commissioner, and the powers conferred on the Appeal Commissioners by this Part may be exercised by one Appeal Commissioner.

(6) (a) In default of notice of appeal by a person to whom notice of assessment has been given, the assessment made on that person shall be final and conclusive.

(b) Where a person who has given notice of appeal against an assessment does not attend before the Appeal Commissioners at the time and place appointed for the hearing of that person's appeal, the assessment made on that person shall, subject to *subsection (8)*, have the same force and effect as if it were an assessment in respect of which no notice of appeal had been given.

(c) Where on the hearing of an appeal against an assessment—

(i) no application is or has been made to the Appeal Commissioners before or during the hearing of the appeal by or on behalf of the appellant for an adjournment of the proceedings on the appeal or such an application is or has been made and is or was refused, and

(ii) (I) a return of the appellant's income for the relevant year of assessment or, as the case may be, a return under *section 884* has not been made by the appellant, or

(II) such a return has been made but—

(A) all the statements of profits and gains, schedules and other evidence relating to such return have not been furnished by or on behalf of the appellant,

(B) information requested from the appellant by the Appeal Commissioners in the hearing of the appeal has not been supplied by the appellant,

(C) the terms of a precept issued by the Appeal Commissioners under *section 935* have not been complied with by the appellant, or

(D) any questions as to an assessment or assessments put by the Appeal Commissioners under *section 938* have not been answered to their satisfaction,

the Appeal Commissioners shall make an order dismissing the appeal against the assessment and thereupon the assessment shall have the same force and effect as if it were an assessment in respect of which no notice of appeal had been given.

(d) An application for an adjournment of the proceedings on an appeal against an assessment, being an application made before or during the hearing of the appeal, shall not be refused before the expiration of 9 months from the earlier of—

(i) the end of the year of assessment or, as the case may be, accounting period to which the assessment appealed against relates, and

(ii) the date on which the notice of assessment was given to the appellant.

(e) *Paragraph (c)* shall not apply if on the hearing of the appeal the Appeal Commissioners are satisfied that sufficient information has been furnished by or on behalf of the appellant to enable them to determine the appeal at that hearing.

(7) (a) A notice of appeal not given within the time limited by *subsection (1)* shall be regarded as having been so given where, on an application in writing having been made to the inspector or other officer in that behalf within 12 months after the date of the notice of assessment, the inspector or other officer, being satisfied that owing to absence, sickness or other reasonable cause the applicant was prevented from giving notice of appeal within the time limited and that the application was made thereafter without unreasonable delay, notifies the applicant in writing that the application under this paragraph has been allowed.

(b) Where on an application under *paragraph (a)* the inspector or other officer is not so satisfied, he or she shall by notice in writing inform the applicant that the application under this paragraph has been refused.

(c) Within 15 days after the date of a notice under *paragraph (b)* the applicant may by notice in writing require the inspector or other officer to refer the application to the Appeal Commissioners and, in relation to any application so referred, *paragraphs (a)* and *(b)* shall apply as if for every reference in those paragraphs to the inspector or other officer there were substituted a reference to the Appeal Commissioners.

(d) Notwithstanding *paragraph (a)*, an application made after the expiration of the time specified in that paragraph which but for that expiration would have been allowed under *paragraph (a)* may be allowed under that paragraph if at the time of the application—

(i) there has been made to the inspector or other officer a return of income or, as the case may be, a return under *section 884*, statements of profits and gains and such other information as in the opinion of the inspector or other officer would enable the appeal to be settled by agreement under *subsection (3)*, and

(ii) the income tax or corporation tax charged by the assessment in respect of which the application is made has been paid together with any interest on that tax chargeable under *section 1080*.

(e) Where on an application referred to in *paragraph (d)* the inspector or other officer is not satisfied that the information furnished would be sufficient to enable the appeal to be settled by agreement under *subsection (3)* or if the tax and interest mentioned in *paragraph (d)(ii)* have not been paid, the inspector or other officer shall by notice in writing inform the applicant that the application has been refused.

(f) Within 15 days after the date of a notice under *paragraph (e)* the applicant may by notice in writing require the inspector or other officer to refer the application to the Appeal Commissioners and, in relation to an application so referred, if—

(i) the application is one which but for the expiration of the period specified in *paragraph (a)* would have been allowed under *paragraph (c)* if the application had been referred to the Appeal Commissioners under that paragraph,

(ii) at the time the application is referred to the Appeal Commissioners the income tax or corporation tax charged by the assessment in respect of which the application is made, together with any interest on that tax chargeable under *section 1080*, has been paid, and

(iii) the information furnished to the inspector or other officer is such that in the opinion of the Appeal Commissioners the appeal is likely to be determined on the first occasion on which it comes before them for hearing,

the Appeal Commissioners may allow the application.

(8) In a case in which a person who has given notice of appeal does not attend before the Appeal Commissioners at the time and place appointed for the hearing of that person's appeal, *subsection (6)(b)* shall not apply if—

(a) at that time and place another person attends on behalf of the appellant and the Appeal Commissioners consent to hear that other person,

(b) on an application in that behalf having been made to them in writing or otherwise at or before that time, the Appeal Commissioners postpone the hearing, or

(c) on an application in writing having been made to them after that time the Appeal Commissioners, being satisfied that, owing to absence, sickness or other reasonable cause, the appellant was prevented from appearing before them at that time and place and that the application was made without unreasonable delay, direct that the appeal be treated as one the time for the hearing of which has not yet been appointed.

(9) (a) Where action for the recovery of income tax or corporation tax charged by an assessment has been taken, being action by means of the institution

of proceedings in any court or the issue of a certificate under [section 960L][1], neither *subsection (7)* nor *subsection (8)* shall apply in relation to that assessment until that action has been completed.

(b) Where, in a case within *paragraph (a)*, an application under *subsection (7)(a)* is allowed or, on an application under *subsection (8)(c)*, the Appeal Commissioners direct as provided in that subsection, the applicant shall in no case be entitled to repayment of any sum paid or borne by the applicant in respect of costs of any such court proceedings or, as the case may be, of any fees or expenses charged by the county registrar or sheriff executing a certificate under [section 960L][2].

Amendments

[1, 2] Substituted by F(No.2)A 08 sched4(part2). Applies as respects any tax that becomes due and payable on or after 1 March 2009.

Case Law

In Keogh v Criminal Assets Bureau, Revenue Commissioners 2003 VI ITR 635 the Supreme Court held that Revenue failed to inform the taxpayer of his statutory right of appeal. The taxpayer was reinstated to the same position as if the undertaking had in fact been met by Revenue. In response to this decision, the Revenue included an appeals section on all notices of assessment which outlines the thirty day time limit and the mandatory pre-requisites to the filing of an appeal.

Kennerley v Revenue & Customs Commissioners 2007 SpC 578 considered whether an assessment by Revenue was invalid on the basis that no Notice of Enquiry had been given by Revenue to the taxpayer.

In M Deighan v E Hearne and Others 1986 III ITR 533 the taxpayer argued the assessments were invalid as his trade was incorrectly described as a furniture wholesaler. The Court concluded that it did not matter that the trade was described incorrectly (immaterial) .

In O'Rourke v The Appeal Commissioners 2010 IEHC 264 the issue before the High Court was whether the decision of the Appeal Commissioners that each assessment was valid can be subject to an immediate appeal or whether any right to appeal arises only on a determination of the appeal against each assessment.

The jurisdiction of the Appeal Commissioners on appeal was to make a decision as to the final assessments to be made on the taxpayer. Until the final amount was determined, the appeal was not determined within the meaning of the Taxes Act. The State v Michael Smidic (Appeal Commissioners) 1938 I ITR 571

The onus is on the taxpayer to make clear that an appeal is being made under this section. Criminal Assets Bureau v D (K) 2002 VI ITR 445

If the taxpayer was prevented from making an appeal within the time limits due to absence, sickness or other reasonable cause, the Inspector is obliged to allow a reasonable period for the late appeal to be made. Criminal Assets Bureau v P McS 2001 VI ITR 421

In Criminal Assets Bureau v Sean and Rosaleen Hunt (nee) Maher 2003 VI ITR 559 the Supreme Court held that in enacting elaborate procedures for the determination of a taxpayer's liability by assessment and appeal, the Oireachtas provided exclusive machinery for the ascertainment of a taxpayer's liability.

Where an agreement is based on an erroneous view of the law, the parties could enter into a corrective agreement outside the 21 day limit. Tod v South Essex Motors 1988 STC 392.

Schutdenfrei v Hilton 1998 STC 404 considered the term 'agreement' and it was held that an error in an amended assessment followed by a taxpayer's silence was not an agreement.

The Court could amend an assessment which was based on an error in an agreement. Richart v Bass Holdings Ltd 1993 STC 122.

In Cassell v Crutchfiled 1995 STC 663 it was held that an accountant suspended from practice for criminal convictions had no right to an audience.

In Johnson v Walden 1996 STC 124 the taxpayer protested against the fact that the Appeal Commissioners had chosen to hear his case along with the case of another taxpayer where the transactions which formed the basis of the assessment for both taxpayers were the same transactions. The UK courts ruled that the Appeal Commissioners had a jurisdiction to make their own decision in the matter and were entitled to hear the two appeals together if they considered that neither taxpayer would suffer through the loss of privacy which was involved.

In R v IRC, ex parte Caglar 1995 STC 741 and Development Inc v CIR 1996 STC 440 it was held that it is only in exceptional circumstances that judicial review of an assessment would be entertained when the appeal procedure was in place.

Menolly Homes Limited v The Appeal Commissioners & Anor 2010 IEHC 49 considered if the taxpayer has a right to cross-examine a tax inspector on an appeal before the Appeal Commissioners.

Revenue Briefings

eBrief

eBrief No. 11/2013 – Revenue Complaint and Review Procedures

Cross References

From Section 933

Section 884 Returns of profits.
Section 935 Power to issue precepts.
Section 938 Questions as to assessments or schedules.
Section 942 Appeals to Circuit Court.
Section 960L Recovery by sheriff or county registrar.
Section 1080 Interest on overdue income tax, corporation tax and capital gains tax.

To Section 933

Section 657 Averaging of farm profits.
Section 817 Schemes to avoid liability to tax under Schedule F.
Section 907 Application to Appeal Commissioners: information from financial institutions.
Section 907A Application to Appeal Commissioners: information from third party.
Section 942 Appeals to Circuit Court.
Section 947 Appeals against determination under sections 98 to 100.
Section 949 Appeals against determinations of certain claims, etc.
Section 950 Interpretation (Part 41).
Schedule 31 Consequential Amendments

934 Procedure on appeals

[ITA67 s421; FA68 s16; CTA76 s146(1); FA80 s54(2); FA83 s9(a)(ii) and s37; FA90 s28; FA95 s173(1)(b)]

(1) The inspector or such other officer as the Revenue Commissioners shall authorise in that behalf (in this section referred to as "*other officer*") may attend every hearing of an appeal, and shall be entitled—

(a) to be present during all the hearing and at the determination of the appeal,

(b) to produce any lawful evidence in support of the assessment, and

(c) to give reasons in support of the assessment.

(2) (a) On any appeal, the Appeal Commissioners shall permit any barrister or solicitor to plead before them on behalf of the appellant or the inspector or other officer either orally or in writing and shall hear—

(i) any accountant, being any person who has been admitted a member of an incorporated society of accountants, or

[(ii) any person who has been admitted a member of the Irish Taxation Institute.][1]

(b) Notwithstanding *paragraph (a)*, the Appeal Commissioners may permit any other person representing the appellant to plead before them where they are satisfied that such permission should be given.

(3) Where on an appeal it appears to the Appeal Commissioners by whom the appeal is heard, or to a majority of such Appeal Commissioners, by examination of the appellant on oath or affirmation or by other lawful evidence that the appellant is overcharged by any assessment, the Appeal Commissioners shall abate or reduce the assessment accordingly, but otherwise the Appeal Commissioners shall determine the appeal by ordering that the assessment shall stand.

(4) Where on any appeal it appears to the Appeal Commissioners that the person assessed ought to be charged in an amount exceeding the amount contained in the assessment, they shall charge that person with the excess.

(5) Unless the circumstances of the case otherwise require, where on an appeal against an assessment which assesses an amount which is chargeable to income tax or corporation tax it appears to the Appeal Commissioners—

(a) that the appellant is overcharged by the assessment, they may in determining the appeal reduce only the amount which is chargeable to income tax or corporation tax,

(b) that the appellant is correctly charged by the assessment, they may in determining the appeal order that the amount which is chargeable to income tax or corporation tax shall stand, and

(c) that the appellant ought to be charged in an amount exceeding the amount contained in the assessment, they may charge the excess by increasing only the amount which is chargeable to income tax or corporation tax.

[(6) Where an appeal is determined by the Appeal Commissioners, the inspector or other officer shall, unless either—

(a) the person assessed requires that that person's appeal shall be reheard under *section 942*, or

(b) under the Tax Acts a case is required to be stated for the opinion of the High Court,

give effect to the Appeal Commissioners' determination and thereupon, if the determination is that the assessment is to stand or is to be amended, the assessment or the amended assessment, as the case may be, shall have the same force and effect as if it were an assessment in respect of which no notice of appeal had been given.][2]

(7) Every determination of an appeal by the Appeal Commissioners shall be recorded by them in the prescribed form at the time the determination is made and the Appeal Commissioners shall within 10 days after the determination transmit that form to the inspector or other officer.

Amendments

[1] Substituted by FA07 sched4(1)(ag). Shall have effect as on and from 2 April 2007.

[2] Substituted by FA07 s20(1)(a). Applies in relation to appeals determined by the Appeal Commissioners, or by a judge of the Circuit Court, on or after 2 April 2007.

Case Law

In Harris v Quigley & Irwin 2005 VI ITR 839 the Judge observed that although the determination of the Appeal Commissioners was not final, it was a lawful determination which then had to be put into effect. Therefore monies due to the taxpayer by Revenue pending the determination of the case stated to the High Court were lawfully due to be paid to the taxpayer. Subsequent legislative amendment to section 934 by FA 07 now provides that if a decision is subject to an appeal on a point of law to the High Court, no tax will be payable or repayable following a determination by the Circuit Court.

An Inspector was entitled to argue for an increase in an assessment he raised, although the UK equivalent of section 934 allows the Inspector only to give evidence and reasons which support the assessment. Glaxo Group v IRC 1996 STC 191

Menolly Homes Limited v The Appeal Commissioners & Anor 2010 IEHC 49 considered if the taxpayer has a right to cross-examine a tax inspector on an appeal before the Appeal Commissioners

Revenue Briefings

eBrief

eBrief No. 11/2013 – Revenue Complaint and Review Procedures

Cross References

From Section 934

Section 942 Appeals to Circuit Court.

To Section 934

Section 942 Appeals to Circuit Court.

935 Power to issue precepts

[ITA67 s422; F(MP)A68 s3(1), s3(2) and Sch PtI; CTA76 s146(1); FA83 s37; FA95 s173(1)(b)]

(1) Where notice of appeal has been given against an assessment, the Appeal Commissioners may, whenever it appears to them to be necessary for the purposes of the Tax Acts, issue a precept to the appellant ordering the appellant to deliver to them, within the time limited by the precept, a schedule containing such particulars for their information as they may demand under the authority of the Tax Acts in relation to—

(a) the property of the appellant,

(b) the trade, profession or employment carried on or exercised by the appellant,

(c) the amount of the appellant's profits or gains, distinguishing the particular amounts derived from each separate source, or

(d) any deductions made in determining the appellant's profits or gains.

(2) The Appeal Commissioners may issue further precepts whenever they consider it necessary for the purposes of the Tax Acts, until complete particulars have been furnished to their satisfaction.

(3) A precept may be issued by one Appeal Commissioner.

(4) A person to whom a precept is issued shall deliver the schedule required within the time limited by the precept.

(5) Any inspector or such other officer as the Revenue Commissioners shall authorise in that behalf may at all reasonable times inspect and take copies of or extracts from any such schedule.

Cross References

To Section 935

Section 933 Appeals against assessment.

Section 936 Objection by inspector or other officer to schedules.

Schedule 29 Provisions Referred to in Sections 1052, 1053 and 1054

936 Objection by inspector or other officer to schedules

[ITA67 s423; F(MP)A68 s3(2) and Sch PtI; CTA76 s146(1); FA95 s173(1)(b)]

(1) The inspector or such other officer as the Revenue Commissioners shall authorise in that behalf (in this section referred to as "*other officer*") may, within a reasonable time to be allowed by the Appeal Commissioners after examination by the inspector or other officer of any schedule referred to in *section 935*, object to that schedule or any part of that schedule, and in that case shall state in writing the cause of his or her objection according to the best of his or her knowledge or information.

(2) In every such case the inspector or other officer shall give notice in writing of his or her objection to the person chargeable in order that that person may, if that person thinks fit, appeal against the objection.

(3) A notice under *subsection (2)* shall be under cover and sealed, and addressed to the person chargeable.

(4) No assessment shall be confirmed or altered until any appeal against the objection has been heard and determined.

Cross References

From Section 936

Section 935 Power to issue precepts.

937 Confirmation and amendment of assessments

[ITA67 s424; F(MP)A68 s3(2) and Sch PtI; CTA76 s 146(1); FA95 s173(1)(b)]

Where—

(a) the Appeal Commissioners see cause to disallow an objection to a schedule by the inspector or such other officer as the Revenue Commissioners shall authorise in that behalf, or

(b) on the hearing of an appeal, the Appeal Commissioners are satisfied with the assessment, or if, after the delivery of a schedule, they are satisfied with the schedule and have received no information as to its insufficiency,

they shall confirm or alter the assessment in accordance with the schedule, as the case may require.

938 Questions as to assessments or schedules

[ITA67 s425; F(MP)A68 s3(2) and Sch PtI; CTA76 s146(1)]

(1) Whenever the Appeal Commissioners are dissatisfied with a schedule or require further information relating to a schedule, they may at any time and from time to time by precept put any questions in writing concerning the schedule, or any matter which is contained or ought to be contained in the schedule, or concerning any deductions made in arriving at the profits or gains, and the particulars thereof, and may require true and particular answers in writing signed by the person chargeable to be given within 7 days after the service of the precept.

(2) The person chargeable shall within the time limited either answer any such questions in writing signed by that person, or shall present himself or herself to be examined orally before the Appeal Commissioners, and may object to and refuse to answer any question; but the substance of any answer given by that person orally shall be taken down in writing in that person's presence and be read over to that person and, after that person has had liberty to amend any such answer, he or she may be required to verify the answer on oath to be administered to him or her by any one of the Appeal Commissioners, and the oath shall be subscribed by the person by whom it is made.

(3) Where any clerk, agent or servant of the person chargeable presents himself or herself on behalf of that person to be examined orally before the Appeal Commissioners, the same provisions shall apply to his or her examination as in the case of the person chargeable who presents himself or herself to be examined orally.

Cross References

To Section 938

Section 933 Appeals against assessment.

939 Summoning and examination of witnesses

[ITA67 s426; F(MP)A68 s3(2) and Sch PtI; CTA76 s146(1); FA82 s60(2)(c); FA92 s248]

(1) (a) The Appeal Commissioners may summon any person whom they think able to give evidence as respects an assessment made on another person to appear before them to be examined, and may examine such person on oath.

(b) The clerk, agent, servant or other person confidentially employed in the affairs of a person chargeable shall be examined in the same manner, and subject to the same restrictions, as in the case of a person chargeable who presents himself or herself to be examined orally.

(2) The oath shall be that the evidence to be given, touching the matter in question, by the person sworn shall be the truth, the whole truth and nothing but the truth, and the oath shall be subscribed by the person by whom it is made.

(3) A person who after being duly summoned—

(a) neglects or refuses to appear before the Appeal Commissioners at the time and place appointed for that purpose,

(b) appears but refuses to be sworn or to subscribe the oath, or

(c) refuses to answer any lawful question touching the matters under consideration,

shall be liable to a penalty of [€3,000][1]; but the penalty imposed in respect of any offence under *paragraph (b)* or *(c)* shall not apply to any clerk, agent, servant or other person referred to in *subsection (1)(b)*.

Amendments

[1] Substituted by F(No.2)A08 sched5(part2)(1)(x). The enactments specified in Schedule 5 are amended or repealed to the extent and manner specified in that Schedule and, unless the contrary is stated, shall come into effect after 24 December 2008.

940 Determination of liability in cases of default

[ITA67 s427; F(MP)A68 s3(2) and Sch PtI; CTA76 s146(1); FA95 s173(1)(b)]

Where—

(a) a person has neglected or refused to deliver a schedule in accordance with a precept of the Appeal Commissioners,

(b) any clerk, agent or servant of, or any person confidentially employed by, a person chargeable, having been summoned, has neglected or refused to appear before the Appeal Commissioners to be examined,

(c) the person chargeable or that person's clerk, agent or servant or any person confidentially employed by the person chargeable has declined to answer any question put to him or her by the Appeal Commissioners,

(d) an objection has been made to a schedule and the objection has not been appealed against, or

(e) the Appeal Commissioners decide to allow any objection made by the inspector or such other officer as the Revenue Commissioners shall authorise in that behalf,

the Appeal Commissioners shall ascertain and settle according to the best of their judgment the sum in which the person chargeable ought to be charged.

941 Statement of case for High Court

[ITA67 s428; F(MP)A68 s3(2) and Sch PtI; FA71 s19(2); CTA76 s146(1); FA83 s9(a)(iii) and s37; FA95 s173(1)(c)]

(1) Immediately after the determination of an appeal by the Appeal Commissioners, the appellant or the inspector or such other officer as the Revenue Commissioners shall authorise in that behalf (in this section referred to as "*other officer*"), if dissatisfied with the determination as being erroneous in point of law, may declare his or her dissatisfaction to the Appeal Commissioners who heard the appeal.

(2) The appellant or inspector or other officer, as the case may be, having declared his or her dissatisfaction, may within 21 days after the determination by notice in writing addressed to the Clerk to the Appeal Commissioners require the Appeal Commissioners to state and sign a case for the opinion of the High Court on the determination.

(3) The party requiring the case shall pay to the Clerk to the Appeal Commissioners a fee of [€25][1] for and in respect of the case before that party is entitled to have the case stated.

(4) The case shall set forth the facts and the determination of the Appeal Commissioners, and the party requiring it shall transmit the case when stated and signed to the High Court within 7 days after receiving it.

(5) At or before the time when the party requiring the case transmits it to the High Court, that party shall send notice in writing of the fact that the case has been stated on that party's application, together with a copy of the case, to the other party.

(6) The High Court shall hear and determine any question or questions of law arising on the case, and shall reverse, affirm or amend the determination in respect of which the case has been stated, or shall remit the matter to the Appeal Commissioners with the opinion of the Court on the matter, or may make such other order in relation to the matter, and may make such order as to costs as to the Court may seem fit.

(7) The High Court may cause the case to be sent back for amendment and thereupon the case shall be amended accordingly, and judgment shall be delivered after it has been amended.

(8) An appeal shall lie from the decision of the High Court to the Supreme Court.

[(9) If the amount of the assessment is altered by the order or judgment of the Supreme Court or the High Court, then—

(a) if too much tax has been paid, the amount over-paid shall be refunded with interest in accordance with *section 865A*, or

(b) if too little tax has been paid, the amount unpaid shall be deemed to be arrears of tax (except in so far as any penalty is incurred on account of arrears) and shall be paid and recovered accordingly.][2]

[(a) if too much tax has been paid, the amount over-paid shall be refunded with interest in accordance with the provisions of section 865A, or][3]

(b) if too little tax has been paid, the amount unpaid shall be deemed to be arrears of tax (except in so far as any penalty is incurred on account of arrears) and shall be paid and recovered accordingly.

Amendments

[1] Substituted by FA01 sched5.

[2] Substituted by FA07 s20(1)(b). Applies in relation to appeals determined by the Appeal Commissioners, or by a judge of the Circuit Court, on or after 2 April 2007.

[3] Substituted by FA03 s17(1)(b). Applies with effect from the day appointed by the Minister for Finance in accordance with different provisions. With effect from 1 November 2003 per S.I. 508 of 2003.

Case Law

In Harris v Quigley & Irwin 2005 VI ITR 839 the Judge observed that although the determination of the Appeal Commissioners was not final, it was a lawful determination which then had to be put into effect. Therefore monies due to the taxpayer by Revenue pending the determination of the case stated to the High Court were lawfully due to be paid to the taxpayer. Subsequent legislative amendment to section 934 by FA 07 now provides that if a decision is subject to an appeal on a point of law to the High Court, no tax will be payable or repayable following a determination by the Circuit Court.

In the case of fraud and negligence the initial burden is on the Revenue to show a loss of tax. Hurley v Taylor (Inspector of Taxes) 1998 STC 202

In O'Dwyer v Irish Exporters and Importers Ltd (in liquidation) 1942 I ITR 629 it was held that a retired Appeal Commissioner is entitled to sign a case.

The Court would not decline to entertain point not covered in the case stated where the point had already been argued before the Appeal Commissioners and Revenue had given due notice to the taxpayer of their intention to raise the point again Muir v CIR 1966 TC 367.

It is more appropriate for judicial review proceedings to deal with complaints that a taxpayer was not fairly treated in proceedings than the General Commissioners. Mellor v Gurney 1994 STC 1025 , Brittain v Gibb 1986 STC 418, Read v Rolliston 1982 STC 370

It is vital that the time limit for an appeal to the High Court is strictly complied with in order for the Court to hear the appeal. Petch v Gurney 1994 STC 689 and IRC v McGuckian 1994 STC 888

In it was held that a dissenting partner can declare dissatisfaction where the appellant is a partnership. Sutherland & Partners' v Barnes 1993 STC 399

Where a taxpayer failed to give a copy of the case and notice to the High Court within the required time the case was struck off. A & B v WJ Davies (Inspector of Taxes) 1942 II ITR 60

Revenue Briefings

Tax Briefing

Tax Briefing July 2004 Issue 56 pg 6 – Repayments, Interest and Time Limits

Tax Briefing October 2004 – Issue 57 pg 7 – New Time Limits

Tax Briefing October 2004 – Issue 57 pg 15 – Repayments, Interest and Time Limits – Correction

Revenue Precedents

The reference in section 941(9) to 'tax shall be paid in accordance with the determination of the Appeal Commissioners' does not entitle the taxpayer, demanding a case stated, to repayment. Repayment arises only in accordance with subsection 9 itself. Section 30(3) FA 1976 (now repealed and section 942(6)(b) do not apply where a case stated has been demanded. There is no obligation under section 934 Taxes Consolidation Act, 1997 on the Inspector to amend the assessment where there is an appeal from the Appeal Commissioners decision, since to amend the assessment in accordance with this section would give it the same force and effect as if it were an assessment in respect of which no appeal had been given. If it were such an assessment, section 942(6) and 941(9) would be redundant. IT962006

Cross References

From Section 941

Section 865A Interest on repayments.

To Section 941

Section 943 Extension of section 941.

Section 944 Communication of decision of Appeal Commissioners.

942 Appeals to Circuit Court

[ITA67 s416(10) and s429; F(MP)A68 s3(1), s3(2) and Sch PtI; FA71 s19(1); FA74 s69; CTA76 s146(1); FA83 s9(a)(iv) and (b)(i) and s37; FA95 s173(1)(d); FA97 s146(1) and Sch9 PtI par1(27)]

(1) Any person aggrieved by the determination of the Appeal Commissioners in any appeal against an assessment made on that person may, on giving notice in writing to the inspector or such other officer as the Revenue Commissioners shall authorise in that behalf (in this section referred to as "*other officer*") within 10 days after such determination, require that the appeal shall be reheard by the judge

of the Circuit Court (in this section referred to as "*the judge*") in whose circuit is situate, in the case of—

(a) a person who is not resident in the State,

(b) the estate of a deceased person,

(c) an incapacitated person, or

(d) a trust,

the place where the assessment was made and, in any other case, the place to which the notice of assessment was addressed, and the Appeal Commissioners shall transmit to the judge any statement or schedule in their possession which was delivered to them for the purposes of the appeal.

(2) At or before the time of the rehearing of the appeal by the judge, the inspector or other officer shall transmit to the judge the prescribed form in which the Appeal Commissioners' determination of the appeal is recorded.

(3) The judge shall with all convenient speed rehear and determine the appeal, and shall have and exercise the same powers and authorities in relation to the assessment appealed against, the determination, and all consequent matters, as the Appeal Commissioners might have and exercise, and the judge's determination shall, subject to *section 943*, be final and conclusive.

(4) *Section 934(2)* shall, with any necessary modifications, apply in relation to a rehearing of an appeal by a judge of the Circuit Court as it applies in relation to the hearing of an appeal by the Appeal Commissioners.

(5) The judge shall make a declaration in the form of the declaration required to be made by an Appeal Commissioner as set out in *Part 1* of *Schedule 27*.

[(6) Where an appeal is determined by the judge, the inspector or other officer shall, unless under the Tax Acts a case is required to be stated for the opinion of the High Court, give effect to the judge's determination and thereupon, if the determination is that the assessment is to stand or is to be amended, the assessment or the amended assessment, as the case may be, shall have the same force and effect as if it were an assessment in respect of which no notice of appeal had been given.][1]

[…][2]

(8) Where following an application for the rehearing of an appeal by a judge of the Circuit Court in accordance with *subsection (1)* there is an agreement within the meaning of *paragraphs (b)*, *(c)* and *(e)* of *section 933(3)* between the inspector or other officer and the appellant in relation to the assessment, the inspector shall give effect to the agreement and, if the agreement is that the assessment is to stand or is to be amended, the assessment or the amended assessment, as the case may be, shall have the same force and effect as if it were an assessment in respect of which no notice of appeal had been given.

(9) Every rehearing of an appeal by the Circuit Court under this section shall be held in camera.

[…][3]

Amendments

[1] Substituted by FA07 s20(1)(c). Applies in relation to appeals determined by the Appeal Commissioners, or by a judge of the Circuit Court, on or after 2 April 2007.

[2, 3] Deleted by FA05 sched6(1)(o). Applies as on and from 25 March 2005.

Case Law

The Appeal Commissioner made a determination, a circuit Court judge overruled it and then the Court refused to disturb the factual decision of the lower Court. O'Srianain v Lakeview Ltd 1984 III ITR 219

In Inspector of Taxes v Arida Ltd 1996 IV ITR 401 costs on an appeal from the Appeal Commissioners can be awarded by the Circuit Court judge.

In King v United Kingdom (No 3) 2005 STC 438 it was held that a delay in the conduct of an appeal was contrary to the Convention for protection of human rights 1950.

In Harris v Quigley & Irwin 2005 VI ITR 839 the Judge observed that although the determination of the Appeal Commissioners was not final, it was a lawful determination which then had to be put into effect. Therefore monies due to the taxpayer by Revenue pending the determination of the case stated to the High Court were lawfully due to be paid to the taxpayer. Subsequent legislative amendment to section 934 by FA 07 now provides that if a decision is subject to an appeal on a point of law to the High Court, no tax will be payable or repayable following a determination by the Circuit Court.

In O'Rourke v The Appeal Commissioners 2010 IEHC 264 the High Court rules that section 942 TCA 1997 prevents interim appeals on decisions of an interim ruling pending a determination of the Appeal Commissioners.

Revenue Briefings

Tax Briefing

Tax Briefing July 2004 – Issue 56 pg 6 – Repayments, Interest and Time Limits
Tax Briefing October 2004 – Issue 57 pg 7 – New Time Limits
Tax Briefing October 2004 – Issue 57 pg 15 – Repayments, Interest and Time Limits – Correction

Cross References

From Section 942

Section 933 Appeals against assessment.
Section 934 Procedure on appeals.
Section 943 Extension of section 941.
Schedule 27 Forms of Declarations to be Made by Certain Persons

To Section 942

Section 933 Appeals against assessment.
Section 934 Procedure on appeals.
Section 943 Extension of section 941.
Section 944 Communication of decision of Appeal Commissioners.
Schedule 27 Forms of Declarations to be Made by Certain Persons
Schedule 31 Consequential Amendments

943 Extension of section 941

[ITA67 s430; F(MP)A68 s3(2) and Sch PtI; CTA76 s146(1); FA83 s9(a)(v) and s37]

(1) *Section 941* shall, subject to this section, apply to a determination given by a judge pursuant to *section 942* in the like manner as it applies to a determination by the Appeal Commissioners, and any case stated by a judge pursuant to *section 941* shall set out the facts, the determination of the Appeal Commissioners and the determination of the judge.

(2) The notice in writing required under *section 941(2)* to be addressed to the Clerk to the Appeal Commissioners shall, in every case in which a judge is under the authority of this section required by any person to state and sign a case for the opinion of the High Court on the determination, be addressed by such person to the county registrar.

(3) The fee required under *section 941(3)* to be paid to the Clerk to the Appeal Commissioners shall in any case referred to in *subsection (2)* be paid to the county registrar.

Case Law

Revenue was entitled to proceed with collection on PAYE and PRSI assessments as there was a failure to express dissatisfaction. Bairead v Carr 1993 IV ITR 505

Cross References

From Section 943

Section 941 Statement of case for High Court.

Section 942 Appeals to Circuit Court.

To Section 943

Section 942 Appeals to Circuit Court.

Schedule 31 Consequential Amendments

944 Communication of decision of Appeal Commissioners

[ITA67 s431; F(MP)A68 s3(2) and Sch PtI; CTA76 s146(1); FA83 s37]

(1) Where the Appeal Commissioners have entertained an appeal against an assessment for any year of assessment or any accounting period and, after hearing argument on the appeal, have postponed giving their determination either for the purpose of considering the argument or for the purpose of affording to the appellant an opportunity of submitting in writing further evidence or argument, the Appeal Commissioners may, unless they consider a further hearing to be necessary, cause their determination to be sent by post to the parties to the appeal.

(2) Where the determination of an appeal by the Appeal Commissioners is sent to the parties by post under this section, a declaration of dissatisfaction under *section 941(1)* or a notice requiring a rehearing under *section 942(1)* may be made or given in writing within 12 days after the day on which the determination is so sent to the person making the declaration or giving the notice.

Cross References

From Section 944

Section 941 Statement of case for High Court.

Section 942 Appeals to Circuit Court.

To Section 944

Schedule 31 Consequential Amendments

944A Publication of determinations of Appeal Commissioners

[The Appeal Commissioners may make arrangements for the publication of reports of such of their determinations as they consider appropriate, but they shall ensure that any such report is in a form which, in so far as possible, prevents the identification of any person whose affairs are dealt with in the determination.][1]

Amendments

[1] Inserted by FA98 s134(1)(a). This section shall apply to appeals determined by the Appeal Commissioners after 27 March 1998.

CHAPTER 2

Appeals Against Capital Gains Tax Assessments

945 Appeals against assessments

[CGTA75 s51(1) and Sch4 par8; CGT(A)A78 s17 and Sch2; FA83 s55]

(1) A person aggrieved by any assessment under the Capital Gains Tax Acts made on the person by the inspector or other officer mentioned in [or other

Revenue officer mentioned in *Part 41A*][1] shall be entitled to appeal to the Appeal Commissioners on giving, within 30 days after the date of the notice of assessment, notice in writing to the inspector or other officer, and in default of notice of appeal by a person to whom notice of assessment has been given the assessment made on such person shall be final and conclusive.

(2) The provisions of the Income Tax Acts relating to—

(a) the appointment of times and places for the hearing of appeals,

(b) the giving of notice to each person who has given notice of appeal of the time and place appointed for the hearing of that person's appeal,

(c) the determination of an appeal by agreement between the appellant or the appellant's agent and an inspector of taxes or other officer mentioned in *section 931(1)*,

(d) the determination of an appeal by the appellant giving notice of the appellant's intention not to proceed with the appeal,

(e) the hearing, determination or dismissal of an appeal by the Appeal Commissioners, including the hearing, determination or dismissal of an appeal by one Appeal Commissioner,

[(ee) the publication of reports of determinations of the Appeal Commissioners,][2][3]

(f) the assessment having the same force and effect as if it were an assessment in respect of which no notice of appeal had been given where the person who has given notice of appeal does not attend before the Appeal Commissioners at the time and place appointed,

(g) the extension of the time for giving notice of appeal and the readmission of appeals by the Appeal Commissioners and the provisions which apply where action by means of court proceedings has been taken,

(h) the rehearing of an appeal by a judge of the Circuit Court and the statement of a case for the opinion of the High Court on a point of law, [and][4]

[…][5]

(j) the procedures for appeal,

shall, with any necessary modifications, apply to an appeal under any provision of the Capital Gains Tax Acts providing for an appeal to the Appeal Commissioners as if the appeal were an appeal against an assessment to income tax.

Amendments

[1] Substituted by FA12 sched4(part 2)(g).

[2,3] Inserted by FA98 s134(1)(b). This section shall apply to appeals determined by the Appeal Commissioners after 27 March 1998.

[4] Inserted by FA07 s20(1)(d). Applies in relation to appeals determined by the Appeal Commissioners, or by a judge of the Circuit Court, on or after 2 April 2007.

[5] Deleted by FA07 s20(1)(d). Applies in relation to appeals determined by the Appeal Commissioners, or by a judge of the Circuit Court, on or after 2 April 2007.

Revenue Briefings

eBrief

eBrief No. 11/2013 – Revenue Complaint and Review Procedures

Cross References

From Section 945

Section 931 Making of assessments and application of income tax assessment provisions.

To Section 945

Section 950 Interpretation (Part 41).

Section 1077 Penalties for failure to make returns, etc. and for deliberately or carelessly making incorrect returns.

946 Regulations with respect to appeals

[CGTA75 s51(1) and Sch4 par9]

(1) The Revenue Commissioners may make regulations—

(a) for the conduct of appeals against assessments and decisions on claims under the Capital Gains Tax Acts;

(b) entitling persons, in addition to those who would be so entitled apart from the regulations, to appear on such appeals;

(c) regulating the time within which such appeals or claims may be brought or made;

(d) where the market value of an asset on a particular date or an apportionment or any other matter may affect the liability to capital gains tax of 2 or more persons, enabling any such person to have the matter determined by the tribunal having jurisdiction to determine that matter if arising on an appeal against an assessment, and prescribing a procedure by which the matter is not determined differently on different occasions;

(e) authorising an inspector or other officer of the Revenue Commissioners, notwithstanding the obligation as to secrecy imposed by the Income Tax Acts or any other Act, to disclose—

(i) to a person entitled to appear on such an appeal, the market value of an asset as determined by an assessment or decision on a claim, or

(ii) to a person whose liability to tax may be affected by the determination of the market value of an asset on a particular date or an apportionment or any other matter, any decision on the matter made by an inspector or other officer of the Revenue Commissioners.

(2) Regulations under this section may contain such supplemental and incidental provisions as appear to the Revenue Commissioners to be necessary.

(3) Every regulation made under this section shall be laid before Dáil Éireann as soon as may be after it is made and, if a resolution annulling the regulation is passed by Dáil Éireann within the next 21 days on which Dáil Éireann has sat after the regulation is laid before it, the regulation shall be annulled accordingly, but without prejudice to the validity of anything previously done thereunder.

CHAPTER 3

Miscellaneous

947 Appeals against determination under sections 98 to 100

[FA75 s21(1) to (7); CTA76 s147(1) and (2)]

(1) Where it appears to the inspector that the determination of any amount on which a person may be chargeable to income tax or corporation tax by virtue of *section 98*, *99* or *100* may affect the liability to income tax or corporation tax of other persons, the inspector shall give notice in writing to those persons as well as to the first-mentioned person of the determination the inspector proposes to make and of the rights conferred on them by this section.

(2) Any person to whom such a notice is given may within 21 days after the date on which it is given object to the proposed determination by notice in writing given to the inspector, and *section 933(7)* shall apply, with any necessary modifications, in relation to any such notice as it applies in relation to a notice of appeal under *section 933*.

(3) (a) Subject to *paragraph (b)*, where notices have been given under *subsection (1)* and no notice of objection is duly given under *subsection (2)*, the inspector shall make the determination as proposed in his or her notices and the determination shall not be called in question in any proceedings.

(b) This subsection shall not operate to prevent any person to whom notice has not been given under *subsection (1)* from appealing against any such determination of the inspector which may affect that person's liability to income tax or corporation tax, as the case may be.

(4) Where a notice of objection is duly given, the amount mentioned in *subsection (1)* shall be determined in the like manner as an appeal and shall be so determined by the Appeal Commissioners.

(5) All persons to whom notices have been given under *subsection (1)* may take part in any proceedings under *subsection (4)* and in any appeal arising out of those proceedings and shall be bound by the determination made in the proceedings or on appeal, whether or not they have taken part in the proceedings, and their successors in title shall also be so bound.

(6) A notice under *subsection (1)* may, notwithstanding any obligation as to secrecy or other restriction on the disclosure of information, include a statement of the grounds on which the inspector proposes to make the determination.

(7) An inspector may by notice in writing require any person to give, within 21 days after the date of the notice or within such longer period as the inspector may allow, such information as appears to the inspector to be required for deciding whether to give a notice under *subsection (1)* to any person.

Cross References

From Section 947

Section 98 Treatment of premiums, etc. as rent.

Section 99 Charge on assignment of lease granted at undervalue.

Section 100 Charge on sale of land with right to reconveyance.

Section 933 Appeals against assessment.

To Section 947

Schedule 29 Provisions Referred to in Sections 1052, 1053 and 1054

948 Appeals against amount of income tax deducted under Schedule E

[ITA67 s113; F(MP)A68 s3(2) and Sch PtI]

(1) Any person charged to income tax under Schedule E may appeal to the Appeal Commissioners against the amount of tax deducted from that person's emoluments for any year.

(2) The Appeal Commissioners shall hear and determine an appeal to them under *subsection (1)* as if it were an appeal to them against an assessment to income tax, and the provisions of the Income Tax Acts relating to the rehearing of an appeal and to the statement of a case for the opinion of the High Court on a point of law shall, with the necessary modifications, apply accordingly.

949 Appeals against determinations of certain claims, etc

[ITA67 s432(1) (part only) and (2) to (4); F(MP)A68 s3(2) and Sch PtI; CGTA75 s51(1) and Sch4 par2; CTA76 s146(1) and s164 and Sch3 PtI; FA83 s37]

(1) Any person aggrieved by any determination by the Revenue Commissioners, or such officer of the Revenue Commissioners (including an inspector) as they may have authorised in that behalf, on any claim, matter or question referred to in *section 864* may, subject to [*Chapter 6* of *Part 41A*][1] and on giving notice in writing to the Revenue Commissioners or the officer within 30 days after notification to the person aggrieved of the determination, appeal to the Appeal Commissioners.

(2) The Appeal Commissioners shall hear and determine an appeal to them under *subsection (1)* as if it were an appeal against an assessment to income tax and the provisions of *section 933* with respect to such appeals, together with the provisions of the Tax Acts relating to the rehearing of an appeal and to the statement of a case for the opinion of the High Court on a point of law, shall apply accordingly with any necessary modifications.

(3) Where—

(a) a right of appeal to the Appeal Commissioners is given by any provision of the Tax Acts or the Capital Gains Tax Acts other than *section 1037*, and

(b) such provision, while applying the provisions of the Tax Acts relating to appeals against assessments, does not apply the provisions of those Acts relating to the rehearing of appeals,

such provision shall be deemed to apply those provisions relating to the rehearing of appeals.

(4) In a case in which—

(a) a notice of appeal is not given within the time limited by *subsection (1)*, or

(b) a person who has given notice of appeal does not attend before the Appeal Commissioners at the time and place appointed for the hearing of the person's appeal,

subsections (5) and *(7)* to *(9)* of *section 933* shall apply with any necessary modifications.

Amendments

[1] Substituted by FA12 sched4(part 2)(g).

Cross References

From Section 949

Section 864 Making of claims, etc.

Section 933 Appeals against assessment.

Section 957 Appeals.
Section 1037 Charge on percentage of turnover.

To Section 949

Section 235 Bodies established for promotion of athletic or amateur games or sports.
Section 481 Relief for investment in films.
Section 864 Making of claims, etc.
Section 865 Repayment of tax.
Section 960Q Recovery of amounts received by a person following the lodgement of an incorrect account, etc.

PART 41

Self Assessment [Deleted]

Deleted by FA12 s129(2).

Note:

FA12 s129

Subject to the below, this section takes effect on and from 1 January 2013.

This section applies—

(a) in the case of a chargeable period (within the meaning of 45 *section 321(2)* TCA 97) which is an accounting period of a company, as respects chargeable periods that start on or after 1 January 2013, and

(b) in a case other than that referred to in *paragraph (a)*, as respects the year of assessment 2013 and subsequent years of assessment.

This section does not affect the application of the provisions of the TCA 97, which are amended or deleted by this section, as respects chargeable periods prior to those referred to above.

— Please refer to earlier editions of this publication for details of Part 41.

PART 41A

Assessing Rules Including Rules for Self Assessment

CHAPTER 1

Interpretation (Part 41A)

959A Interpretation

[In this Part, except where the context otherwise requires—

'*Acts*' means—

(a) the Income Tax Acts,

(b) the Corporation Tax Acts,

(c) the Capital Gains Tax Acts,

(d) *Part 18C*,

(e) *Part 18D*,

and any instruments made under any of those Acts or Parts;

["*amount of tax chargeable*", in relation to a person and an Act, means the amount of tax chargeable on the person under the Act after taking into account—

(a) each allowance, deduction or relief that is authorised by the Act to be given to the person against income, profits or gains or, as applicable, chargeable gains, and

(b) in the case of an individual to whom *Chapter 2A* of *Part 15* applies, any increase in the taxable income of the individual by virtue of that Chapter;][1]

["*amount of tax payable*", in relation to a person and an Act, means the amount of tax payable by the person after reducing the amount of tax chargeable on the person under the Act by the amount of any tax credit that is authorised by the Act in relation to that person;][2]

'*appeal*' means an appeal under *section 933* or, as respects capital gains tax, an appeal under *section 945*;

'*assessment*', other than in *section 959G*, means an assessment to tax that is made under the Acts and, unless the context otherwise requires, includes a self assessment;

'*chargeable gain*' has the same meaning as in *section 545(3)*;

'*chargeable period*' means an accounting period of a company or a tax year;

'*chargeable person*' means, as respects a chargeable period, a person who is chargeable to tax for that period, whether on that person's own account or on account of some other person but, as respects income tax, does not include a person to whom *subsection (1)* of *section 959B* relates;

'*determination of the appeal*' means a determination by the Appeal Commissioners under *section 933(4)*, and includes an agreement referred to in *section 933(3)* and an assessment becoming final and conclusive by virtue of *section 933(6)*;

'*due date for the payment of an amount of preliminary tax*' has the meaning assigned to it by *Chapter 7*;

'*electronic means*' includes electronic, digital, magnetic, optical, electromagnetic, biometric, photonic means of transmission of data and other forms of related technology by means of which data is transmitted;

'*electronic record*' includes electronic, digital, magnetic, optical, electromagnetic, biometric, photonic means of storing data and other forms of related technology by means of which data is stored;

'*precedent partner*' has the same meaning as in Part 43;

'*prescribed form*' means a form prescribed by the Revenue Commissioners or a form used under the authority of the Revenue Commissioners;

'*preliminary tax*' means the amount of tax which a chargeable person is required to pay in accordance with *section 959AN*;

'*return*' means the return which is required to be prepared and delivered in accordance with *Chapter 3*;

'*Revenue assessment*' shall be construed in accordance with *section 959C*;

'*Revenue officer*' means an officer of the Revenue Commissioners;

'*self assessment*' means an assessment to tax made by a chargeable person, or in relation to a chargeable person, in accordance with *Chapter 4*;

'*specified provisions*' means *sections 877* to *881*, *section 884*, *paragraphs (a)* [and *(d)*][3] of *section 888(2)*, *section 1023*, and *section 1031H*;

'*specified return date for the accounting period*' shall be construed in accordance with *paragraph (b)* of the definition of specified return date for the chargeable period;

'*specified return date for the chargeable period*' means—

(a) in relation to a tax year for income tax or capital gains tax purposes, 31 October in the tax year following that year,

(b) in relation to an accounting period of a company—

(i) subject to *subparagraphs (ii)* and *(iii)*, the last day of the period of 9 months starting on the day immediately following the end of the accounting period, but in any event not later than day 21 of the month in which that period of 9 months ends,

(ii) where the accounting period ends on or before the date the winding up of the company starts and the specified return date in respect of that accounting period would, apart from this subparagraph, fall on a day after the date the winding up started but not within a period of 3 months after that date, the day which falls 3 months after the date the winding up started but in any event not later than day 21 of the month in which that period of 3 months ends, and

(iii) where, in relation to the accounting period, a return is made by electronic means in accordance with *Chapter 6* of *Part 38* and any payment which the company is required to make in accordance with the provisions of the Acts is made by such electronic means as are required by the Revenue Commissioners—

(I) in circumstances other than those referred to in *subparagraph (ii)*, the last day of the period of 9 months starting on the day immediately following the end of the accounting period, but in any event not later than day 23 of the month in which that period of 9 months ends provided that both the return and the payment is made by that day,

(II) in the circumstances referred to in *subparagraph (ii)*, the day which falls 3 months after the date the winding up started but in any event not later than day 23 of the month in which that period of 3 months ends provided that both the return and the payment is made by that day;

'*specified return date for the tax year*' shall be construed in accordance with *paragraph (a)* of the definition of specified return date for the chargeable period;

'*tax*', other than in *section 959G*, means any income tax, corporation tax, capital gains tax or any other levy or charge which under the Acts is placed under the care and management of the Revenue Commissioners;

["*tax credit*", in relation to a person and an Act, means an amount authorised by the Act to be given or set against, or deducted from, the amount of tax chargeable on the person under the Act;][4]

'*tax year*' means a year of assessment.][5]

Amendments

[1] Substituted by FA13 s92 and sched1(part 1)(a).

[2] Substituted by FA13 s92 and sched1(part 1)(b).

[3] Substituted by FA13 s92 and sched1(part 1)(c).

[4] Substituted by FA13 s92 and sched1(part 1)(d).

[5] Inserted by FA12 sched4(part1) and FA12s129.

Revenue Briefings

eBrief

eBrief No. 18/2014 – Exempt Childcare Services

Note:

FA12 s129

Subject to the below, this section takes effect on and from 1 January 2013.

This section applies—

(a) in the case of a chargeable period (within the meaning of section 321(2)) which is an accounting period of a company, as respects chargeable periods that start on or after 1 January 2013, and

(b) in a case other than that referred to in paragraph (a), as respects the year of assessment 2013 and subsequent years of assessment.

This section does not affect the application of the provisions of the TCA97, which are amended or deleted by this section, as respects chargeable periods prior to those referred to above.

FA13 s92 applies—

(a) in the case of a chargeable period (within the meaning of section 321(2)) which is an accounting period of a company, as respects chargeable periods that start on or after 1 January 2013, and

(b) in a case other than that referred to in paragraph (a), as respects the year of assessment (within the meaning of section 2(1)) 2013 and subsequent years of assessment.

959B Supplemental interpretation provisions

[(1) For the purposes of the meaning assigned to '*chargeable person*' in *section 959A*, it does not include a person—

(a) whose only source or sources of income for a tax year is or are sources the income from which consists of emoluments to which *Chapter 4* of *Part 42* applies, but for this purpose a person who, in addition to such source or sources of income, has another source or other sources of income shall be deemed for the tax year to be a person whose only source or sources of income for the tax year is or are sources the income from which consists of emoluments to which *Chapter 4* of *Part 42* applies [if the income from that other source or those other sources, which does not exceed €3,174 in total—

(i) is taken into account in determining the amount of his or her tax credits and standard rate cut-off point for the tax year applicable to those emoluments, or

(ii) is fully taxed at source under *section 261*,

and, for the purposes of deciding whether such income should be taken into account in determining the amount of tax credits and standard rate cut-off point for the tax year, the Revenue Commissioners may have regard to the amount for that, or any previous, tax year of the income of the person from that other source or those other sources before deductions, losses, allowances and other reliefs,][1]

(b) who for the tax year has been excluded by a Revenue officer from the requirements of Chapter 3 by reason of a notice given under *section 959N*, or

(c) who is chargeable to tax for the tax year by reason only of *section 237*, *238* or *239*,

but *paragraph (a)* shall not apply to a person who is a director or, in the case of a person to whom *section 1017* or *1031C* applies, whose spouse or civil partner is a director (within the meaning of *section 116*) of a body corporate other than a body corporate which during a period of 3 years ending on 5 April in the tax year—

(i) was not entitled to any assets other than cash on hands, or a sum of money on deposit within the meaning of *section 895*, not exceeding €130,

(ii) did not carry on a trade, business or other activity including the making of investments, and

(iii) did not pay charges on income within the meaning of *section 243*.

(2) (a) In the Acts (other than in this Part), any reference however expressed to a person being assessed to tax, to an assessment being made on a person, or to a person being charged to tax by an assessment, shall be construed as including a reference to a person being so assessed or so charged by a self assessment made under *Chapter 4*.

(b) For the purposes of *paragraph (a)*, the reference to assessment and self assessment includes an amended assessment and an amended self assessment.

(3) (a) Where any obligation or requirement is imposed on a person in any capacity under this Part and a corresponding obligation or requirement is imposed on that person in another capacity, the discharge of any one of those obligations or requirements shall not release the person from the other obligation or requirement.

(b) A person shall not in any capacity have an obligation or requirement imposed on that person under this Part by reason only that such obligation or requirement is imposed on that person in any other capacity.

(c) Where but for any of the subsequent provisions of this Part any such obligation or requirement would have been imposed on a person in more than one capacity, a release from such obligation or requirement under any of those provisions by reason of any fact or circumstance applying in relation to that person's liability to tax in any one capacity shall not release that person from such obligation or requirement as is imposed on that person in a capacity other than that in which that fact or circumstance applies.][2]

[(4) (a) References in this Part to tax payable, tax which would be payable or tax found to be payable shall be construed in accordance with the definition of "*amount of tax payable*" in *section 959A* and any related references shall also be construed accordingly.

(b) *Paragraph (a)* shall apply regardless of the type of tax to which the reference applies.][3]

Amendments

[1] Substituted by FA14 s86.

[2] Inserted by FA12 sched4(part1) and FA12 s129.

[3] Inserted by FA13 s92 and sched1(part 1)(e).

Note:

FA12 s129

Subject to the below, this section takes effect on and from 1 January 2013.

This section applies—

(a) in the case of a chargeable period (within the meaning of section 321(2)) which is an accounting period of a company, as respects chargeable periods that start on or after 1 January 2013, and

(b) in a case other than that referred to in paragraph (a), as respects the year of assessment 2013 and subsequent years of assessment.

This section does not affect the application of the provisions of the TCA97, which are amended or deleted by this section, as respects chargeable periods prior to those referred to above.

FA13 s92 applies—

(a) in the case of a chargeable period (within the meaning of section 321(2)) which is an accounting period of a company, as respects chargeable periods that start on or after 1 January 2013, and

(b) in a case other than that referred to in paragraph (a), as respects the year of assessment (within the meaning of section 2(1)) 2013 and subsequent years of assessment.

CHAPTER 2

Assessments: General Rules

959C Making of assessments: general rules

[(1) Any assessment made under the Acts, other that a self assessment, shall be made by or on behalf of the Revenue Commissioners and shall be known as a '*Revenue assessment*'.

(2) A Revenue assessment shall be made by a Revenue officer.

(3) An assessment made under an Act shall be an assessment to tax in relation to a person for a chargeable period and all tax that falls to be charged on the person under the Act for the chargeable period shall be included in one assessment.

(4) An assessment to tax in relation to a person shall be an assessment, in accordance with the Acts, for the chargeable period involved of—

(a) the amount of the income, profits or gains or, as the case may be, chargeable gains arising to the person for the period,

(b) the amount of tax chargeable on the person for the period,

(c) the amount of tax payable by the person for the period, and

(d) the balance of tax, taking account of any amount of tax paid directly by the person to the Collector-General for the period, which under the Acts—

(i) is due and payable by the person to the Revenue Commissioners for the period, or [(ii) is overpaid by the person for the period and which, subject to the Acts, is available for offset or repayment by the Revenue Commissioners.][1]

(5) Subject to *section 959E(5)*, an assessment to tax in relation to a person for a chargeable period may relate to—

(a) tax chargeable under more than one of the Acts, and

(b) an amount due under an enactment other than the Acts which by virtue of that enactment is to be assessed and charged as if it were an amount of income tax.

(6) An assessment to tax in relation to a person shall, where required under *section 1084*, include the amount of any surcharge due for the chargeable period.][2]

Amendments

[1] Substituted by FA13 s92 and sched1(part 1)(f).

[2] Inserted by FA12 sched4(part1).

Note:

FA13 s92 applies—

(a) in the case of a chargeable period (within the meaning of section 321(2)) which is an accounting period of a company, as respects chargeable periods that start on or after 1 January 2013, and

(b) in a case other than that referred to in paragraph (a), as respects the year of assessment (within the meaning of section 2(1)) 2013 and subsequent years of assessment.

959D Record of assessments and generation of notices by electronic means

[(1) The Revenue Commissioners shall keep a record of—

(a) each Revenue assessment made, and

(b) each self assessment made by a Revenue officer in relation to a chargeable person under *section 959U*.

(2) The requirements of *subsection (1)* shall be satisfied where a Revenue officer enters details of the assessment, including the tax charged in the assessment, in an electronic record.

(3) Where a Revenue officer—

(a) enters details of an assessment in accordance with *subsection (2)*, and

(b) a notice of assessment in the name of another Revenue officer is produced or generated by electronic means,

the Revenue officer whose name appears on the notice shall, for the purposes of the Acts, be deemed to have—

(i) other than where *section 959U(3)* applies, made the assessment to which the notice relates,

(ii) where the notice relates to a Revenue assessment, made the assessment to the best of his or her judgement, and

(iii) given the notice that was so issued, produced or generated.][1]

Amendments

[1] Inserted by FA12 sched4(part1).

959E Notice of assessment by Revenue officer

[(1) Where a Revenue assessment is made or a self assessment is made by a Revenue officer in relation to a chargeable person under *section 959U*, a Revenue officer shall give notice to the person assessed of the assessment made.

(2) Notice of an assessment, which is given by a Revenue officer, may be given in writing or by electronic means.

(3) Where a return is prepared and delivered in accordance with *section 959L* by another person acting under a chargeable person's authority, a copy of the notice of assessment shall be given to that other person.

(4) Subject to *subsection (5)* and *section 959AC*, a notice of assessment given by a Revenue officer to a person for a chargeable period shall include details of—

(a) the amount of the income, profits or gains or, as the case may be, chargeable gains arising to the person for the period,

(b) the amount of tax chargeable on the person for the period,

(c) the amount of tax payable by the person for the period,

(d) the balance of tax, taking account of any amount of tax paid directly by the person to the Collector-General for the period, which under the Acts—

(i) is due and payable by the person to the Revenue Commissioners for the period, or

[(ii) is overpaid by the person for the period and which, subject to the Acts, is available for offset or repayment by the Revenue Commissioners,][1]

(e) the amount of any surcharge which, under *section 1084*, is required to be included in the assessment,

(f) the name of the Revenue officer who is giving the notice and the address of the Revenue office at which that officer is based, and

(g) the time allowed for giving notice of appeal against the assessment to which the notice relates.

(5) (a) Where an assessment relates to tax chargeable under more than one of the Acts, the notice of assessment shall identify the amount of tax chargeable under each of the Acts.

(b) Where by virtue of an enactment other than the Acts, an amount due under that enactment is to be assessed and charged as if it were an amount of income tax, the notice of assessment shall identify the amount so chargeable by virtue of that enactment.

(6) A notice of assessment may include details of one or more of the following for the chargeable period involved:

(a) the Case or Schedule under which an amount of income, profits or gains has been charged in the assessment;

(b) the provision of the Act by virtue of which an amount of income, profits or gains or, as the case may be, chargeable gains has been charged in the assessment;

(c) the amount [of each][2] allowance, deduction, relief or tax credit to which the person assessed is entitled for the period;

(d) the calculation of the amount of tax chargeable on the person for the period;

(e) the calculation of the amount of tax payable by the person for the period;

(f) the calculation of the balance of tax payable by, or repayable to, the person for the period.][3]

Amendments

[1] Substituted by FA13 s92 and sched1(part 1)(g).

[2] Substituted by FA13 s92 and sched1(part 1)(h).

[3] Inserted by FA12 sched4(part1).

Note:

FA13 s92 applies—

(a) in the case of a chargeable period (within the meaning of section 321(2)) which is an accounting period of a company, as respects chargeable periods that start on or after 1 January 2013, and

(b) in a case other than that referred to in paragraph (a), as respects the year of assessment (within the meaning of section 2(1)) 2013 and subsequent years of assessment.

959F Double assessment

[(1) Where it appears to the satisfaction of the Revenue Commissioners that a person, either on the person's own account or on behalf of another person, has been assessed to tax more than once for the same chargeable period for the same cause and on the same account, they shall vacate the whole, or the part, of any assessment as appears to them to constitute a double assessment.

(2) A person who, either on the person's own account or on behalf of another person, has been assessed to tax and is again assessed for the same chargeable period for the same cause and on the same account, may apply for relief to the Revenue Commissioners who, on proof to their satisfaction of the double assessment, shall cause the assessment, or so much of the assessment as constitutes a double assessment, to be vacated.

[(3) Where it is proved to the satisfaction of the Revenue Commissioners that any double assessment has been made and that payment has been made on both assessments, they shall, subject to *section 865B*, offset the amount of the overpayment (in whole or in part as appropriate) against any other liability of that person in accordance with *section 960H* or, as the case may be but subject to *section 865*, repay the amount of the overpayment (or the balance of it after any offset) to the person on whom the double assessment has been made.][1]

(4) Where a person is aggrieved by a decision of the Revenue Commissioners not to grant relief under this section, the provisions of *section 949* shall apply to such decision as if it were a determination made on a matter referred to in *section 864*.

(5) Anything required to be done under this section by the Revenue Commissioners may be done by a Revenue officer.][2]

Amendments

[1] Substituted by FA13 s92 and sched1(part 1)(i).

[2] Inserted by FA12 sched4(part1).

Note:

FA13 s92 applies—

(a) in the case of a chargeable period (within the meaning of section 321(2)) which is an accounting period of a company, as respects chargeable periods that start on or after 1 January 2013, and

(b) in a case other than that referred to in paragraph (a), as respects the year of assessment (within the meaning of section 2(1)) 2013 and subsequent years of assessment.

959G Transmission to Collector-General of particulars of sums to be collected

[(1) In this section—

'*assessment*' has the same meaning as in *Chapter 1A* of *Part 42* and, by virtue of *section 959B(2)*, includes a self assessment;

'*tax*' has the same meaning as in *Chapter 1A* of Part 42.

(2) After assessments to tax have been made, a Revenue officer shall transmit particulars of the sums to be collected to the Collector-General or to a Revenue officer nominated in writing under *section 960B* for collection.

(3) The entering by a Revenue officer of details of an assessment to tax and of the tax charged in such an assessment in an electronic record from which the Collector-General or a Revenue officer nominated in writing under *section 960B* may extract such details by electronic means shall constitute transmission of such details by a Revenue officer to the Collector-General or to the Revenue officer nominated in writing under *section 960B*.][1]

Amendments

[1] Inserted by FA12 sched4(part1).

959H Amended assessment and notice of amended assessment

[For the purposes of the Acts, the other provisions of this Chapter shall with any necessary modifications apply in like manner to an amended assessment and a notice of an amended assessment as it applies to an assessment and a notice of assessment.][1]

Amendments

[1] Inserted by FA12 sched4(part1).

CHAPTER 3

Chargeable Persons: Returns

959I Obligation to make a return

[(1) Every chargeable person shall as respects a chargeable period prepare and deliver to the Collector-General on or before the specified return date for the chargeable period a return in the prescribed form.

(2) The prescribed form referred to in *subsection (1)* may include such matters in relation to gift tax and inheritance tax as may be required by that form.

(3) Where under this Chapter a person delivers a return to the Collector-General, the person shall be deemed to have been required by a notice under *section 877* to deliver a statement containing the matters and particulars contained in the return or to have been required by a notice under *section 879*, *880* or *884* to deliver the return, as the case may be.

(4) A chargeable person shall prepare and deliver to the Collector-General, a return for a chargeable period as required by this Chapter notwithstanding that the chargeable person has not received a notice to prepare and deliver a statement or return for that period under *section 877*, *879*, *880* or *884*, as the case may be.

(5) Nothing in the specified provisions or in a notice given under any of those provisions shall operate so as to require a chargeable person to deliver a return for a chargeable period on a date earlier than the specified return date for the chargeable period.][1]

Amendments

[1] Inserted by FA12 sched4(part1).

959J Requirements for returns for income tax and capital gains tax purposes

[In the case of a chargeable person who is chargeable to income tax or capital gains tax for a tax year, the return required by this Chapter shall include—

(a) all such matters and particulars as would be required to be contained in a statement delivered pursuant to a notice given to the chargeable person under *section 877*, if the period specified in such notice were the tax year,

(b) where the chargeable person is an individual who is chargeable to income tax or capital gains tax for a tax year, in addition to those matters and particulars referred to in *paragraph (a)*, all such matters and particulars as would be required to be contained in a return for the tax year delivered pursuant to a notice given to the chargeable person under *section 879*, and

(c) such further particulars, including particulars relating to the preceding tax year where the profits or gains of that preceding year are determined in accordance with *section 65(3)*, as may be required by the prescribed form.][1]

Amendments

[1] Inserted by FA12 sched4(part1).

959K Requirements for returns for corporation tax purposes

[In the case of a chargeable person who is chargeable to corporation tax for an accounting period, the return required by this Chapter shall include—

(a) all such [matters, information, accounts, statements, reports and further particulars][1] in relation to the accounting period as would be required to be contained in a return delivered pursuant to a notice given to the chargeable person under *section 884*, and

(b) such [such information, accounts, statements, reports and further particulars][2] as may be required by the prescribed form.][3]

Amendments

[1] Substituted by FA14 s89(c)(i).

[2] Substituted by FA14 s89(c)(ii).

[3] Inserted by FA12 sched4(part1).

959L Delivery of return by person acting under authority

[(1) A return required by this Chapter may be prepared and delivered by the chargeable person or by another person acting under the chargeable person's authority in that regard.

(2) Where a return is prepared and delivered by that other person, the Acts shall apply as if it had been prepared and delivered by the chargeable person.

(3) A return purporting to be prepared and delivered by or on behalf of any chargeable person shall for the purposes of the Acts be deemed to have been prepared and delivered by that person or by that person's authority, as the case may be, unless the contrary is proved.][1]

Amendments

[1] Inserted by FA12 sched4(part1).

959M Delivery of return by precedent partner

[The precedent partner of any partnership shall—

(a) be deemed to be a chargeable person for the purposes of this Chapter, and

(b) as respects any chargeable period, deliver to the Collector-General on or before the specified return date for that chargeable period the return which that partner would be required to deliver for that period under section 880, if notice under that section had been given [to that partner][1] before that specified date.][2]

Amendments

[1] Inserted by FA13 s92 and sched1(part 1)(j).

[2] Inserted by FA12 sched4(part1).

Note:

FA13 s92 applies—

(a) in the case of a chargeable period (within the meaning of section 321(2)) which is an accounting period of a company, as respects chargeable periods that start on or after 1 January 2013, and

(b) in a case other than that referred to in paragraph (a), as respects the year of assessment (within the meaning of section 2(1)) 2013 and subsequent years of assessment.

959N Exclusion from obligation to deliver a return

[(1) A Revenue officer may exclude a person from the application of this Chapter by giving the person a notice in writing stating that the person is excluded from its application.

(2) The notice shall have effect for such chargeable period or periods or until such chargeable period or until the happening of such event as is specified in the notice.

(3) Where a person who has been given a notice under this section is chargeable to capital gains tax for any chargeable period, this section shall not operate so as to remove the person's obligation under this Chapter to make a return of the person's chargeable gains for that chargeable period.][1]

Amendments

[1] Inserted by FA12 sched4(part1).

959O Failure to deliver a return

[(1) Any provision of the Acts relating to the taking of any action on the failure of a person to deliver a statement or return pursuant to a notice given under any of the sections referred to in *section 959I(3)* shall apply to a chargeable person in a case where such a notice has not been given as if the chargeable person had been given a notice on the specified return date for the chargeable period under such one or more of those sections as is appropriate to the provision in question.

(2) A certificate signed by a Revenue officer which certifies that he or she has examined the relevant records and that it appears from those records—

(a) that as respects a chargeable period a named person is a chargeable person, and

(b) that on or before the specified return date for the chargeable period a return in the prescribed form was not received from that chargeable person, shall be evidence until the contrary is proved that the person so named is a chargeable person as respects that chargeable period and that that person did not on or before the specified return date deliver that return.

(3) A certificate certifying as provided by *subsection (2)* and purporting to be signed by a Revenue officer may be tendered in evidence without proof and shall be deemed until the contrary is proved to have been signed by such officer.

(4) *Sections 1052* and *1054* shall apply to a failure by a chargeable person to deliver a return in accordance with this Chapter as they apply to a failure to deliver a return referred to in *section 1052*.][1]

Amendments

[1] Inserted by FA12 sched4(part1).

959P Expression of doubt

[(1) In this section—

'*law*' means one or more provisions of the Acts;

'*letter of expression of doubt*', in relation to a matter, means a communication by written or electronic means, as appropriate, which—

(a) sets out full details of the facts and circumstances of the matter,

[(b) specifies the doubt, the basis for the doubt and the law giving rise to the doubt,][1]

(c) identifies the amount of tax in doubt in respect of the chargeable period to which the expression of doubt relates,

[(d) lists or identifies the supporting documentation that is being submitted to the appropriate inspector in relation to the matter, and][2]

(e) is clearly identified as a letter of expression of doubt for the purposes of this section,

and reference to '*an expression of doubt*' shall be construed accordingly.

(2) Where a chargeable person is in doubt as to the correct application of the law to any matter to be contained in a return required for a chargeable period by this Chapter, which could—

(a) give rise to a liability to tax by that person, or

(b) affect that person's liability to tax or entitlement to an allowance, deduction, relief or tax credit,

then, the chargeable person may—

(i) prepare the return for the chargeable period to the best of that person's belief as to the correct application of the law to the matter, and deliver the return to the Collector-General, [...][3]

(ii) include a letter of expression of doubt with the [return, and][4]

[(iii) submit supporting documentation to the appropriate inspector in relation to the matter.][5]

[(3) This section applies only if—

(a) the return referred to in *subsection (2)* is delivered to the Collector-General, and

(b) the documentation referred to in *paragraph (iii)* of that subsection is delivered to the appropriate inspector,

on or before the specified return date for the chargeable period involved.][6]

[(3A) (a) The documentation referred to in *subsection (3)(b)* shall be delivered by electronic means where the return referred to in *subsection (2)* is delivered by electronic means.

(b) The electronic means by which the documentation referred to in *subsection (3)(b)* shall be delivered shall be such electronic means as may be specified by the Revenue Commissioners for that purpose.][7]

(4) Where a return is delivered in accordance with *subsection (2)*, a self assessment shall, where required under *section 959R*, be included in the return by reference to the particulars included in the return.

(5) Subject to *subsection (6)*, where a letter of expression of doubt is included with a return delivered by a chargeable person to the Collector-General for a chargeable period—

(a) that person shall be treated as making a full and true disclosure with regard to the matter involved, and

(b) any additional tax arising from the amendment of an assessment for the chargeable period by a Revenue officer to give effect to the correct application of the law to that matter shall be due and payable in accordance with *section 959AU(2)*.

(6) *Subsection (5)* does not apply where a Revenue officer does not accept as genuine an expression of doubt in respect of the application of the law to a matter, and an expression of doubt shall not be accepted as genuine in particular where—

[…][8]

[(b) the officer is of the opinion, having regard to any guidelines published by the Revenue Commissioners on the application of the law in similar circumstances and to any relevant supporting documentation delivered to the appropriate inspector in relation to the matter in accordance with *subsections (2)* and *(3)*, that the matter is sufficiently free from doubt as not to warrant an expression of doubt, or][9]

(c) the officer is of the opinion that the chargeable person was acting with a view to the evasion or avoidance of tax.

(7) Where a Revenue officer does not accept an expression of doubt as genuine, he or she shall notify the chargeable person accordingly and any additional tax arising from the amendment of an assessment for the chargeable period by a Revenue officer to give effect to the correct application of the law to the matter involved shall be due and payable in accordance with *section 959AU(1)*.

(8) Where a chargeable person is aggrieved by a decision of a Revenue officer that the person's expression of doubt is not genuine, the provisions of *section 949* shall apply to such decision as if it were a determination made on a matter referred to in *section 864*.][10]

Amendments

[1] Substituted by FA13 s92 and sched1(part 1)(k).

[2] Substituted by FA13 s92 and sched1(part 1)(l).

[3] Deleted by FA13 s92 and sched1(part 1)(m).

[4] Substituted by FA13 s92 and sched1(part 1)(m).

[5] Inserted by FA13 s92 and sched1(part 1)(m).

[6] Substituted by FA13 s92 and sched1(part 1)(n).

[7] Inserted by FA13 s92 and sched1(part 1)(o).

[8] Deleted by FA13 s92 and sched1(part 1)(p).

9 Substituted by FA13 s92 and sched1(part 1)(p).

10 Inserted by FA12 sched4(part1).

Note:

FA13 s92 applies—

(a) in the case of a chargeable period (within the meaning of section 321(2)) which is an accounting period of a company, as respects chargeable periods that start on or after 1 January 2013, and

(b) in a case other than that referred to in paragraph (a), as respects the year of assessment (within the meaning of section 2(1)) 2013 and subsequent years of assessment.

959Q Miscellaneous (Chapter 3)

[(1) (a) This Chapter does not affect the giving of a notice under any of the specified provisions and does not remove from any person any obligation or requirement imposed on the person by such a notice.

(b) The giving of a notice under any of the specified provisions to a person does not remove from that person any obligation to prepare and deliver a return under this Chapter.

(c) The giving by a chargeable person of a notice pursuant to *section 876* does not remove from the person an obligation to prepare and deliver a return under this Chapter.

(2) (a) The Collector-General may designate an address for the delivery of returns which in accordance with this Chapter are required to be delivered to the Collector-General.

(b) Where the Collector-General designates an address under *paragraph (a)*, that address shall be published in *Iris Oifigiúil* as soon as is practicable after such designation.][1]

Amendments

1 Inserted by FA12 sched4(part1).

CHAPTER 4

Chargeable Persons: Self-Assessments

959R Inclusion of self assessment in return

[(1) Subject to *sections 959S* and *959T*, every return prepared and delivered under *Chapter 3* in respect of a chargeable period shall include a self assessment by the chargeable person to whom the return relates.

(2) A self assessment shall be made in, and as part of, the return and shall include such details as the Revenue Commissioners may require.

(3) The details referred to in *subsection (2)* shall include an assessment by the chargeable person, in accordance with the Acts, for the chargeable period involved of—

(a) the amount of the income, profits or gains or, as the case may be, chargeable gains arising to the person for the period,

(b) the amount of tax chargeable on the person for the period,

(c) the amount of tax payable by the person for the period, and

(d) the balance of tax, taking account of any amount of tax paid directly by the person to the Collector-General for the period, which under the Acts—

(i) is due and payable by the person to the Revenue Commissioners for the period, or

[(ii) is overpaid by the person for the period and which, subject to the Acts, is available for offset or repayment by the Revenue Commissioners.][1]

(4) (a) Where a self assessment relates to tax chargeable on a person under more than one of the Acts, the self assessment shall identify the amount of tax chargeable under each of the Acts.

(b) Where by virtue of an enactment other than the Acts, an amount due under that enactment is to be assessed and charged as if it were an amount of income tax, the self assessment shall include such amount and shall identify the amount so chargeable by virtue of that enactment.

(c) A self assessment shall include and identify the amount of any surcharge which, under *section 1084*, is required to be included in the assessment for the chargeable period.

(5) Subject to *subsection (6)*, where the obligation to make a return for a chargeable period is treated as fulfilled under *Chapter 6* of *Part 38* and the chargeable person—

(a) includes a self assessment in the return in accordance with [such indicative tax calculation as may be provided by the electronic system][2] that is made available by the Revenue Commissioners for the purposes of that Chapter, and

(b) pays tax in accordance with that calculation,

then, in the event that the indicative tax calculation is incorrect—

(i) any additional tax due for the chargeable period that arises by reason of the indicative tax being incorrect shall be deemed to be due and payable not later than one month from the date of amendment of the self assessment, and

(ii) *Part 47* does not apply to the extent that the return included a self assessment that was in accordance with the indicative tax calculation.

(6) *Subsection (5)* applies where the chargeable person retains either an electronic or printed record of the indicative tax calculation and, on request from a Revenue officer, submits a copy of that record, and the various elements of the calculation are in accordance with the information, statements and particulars provided in the return.][3]

Amendments

[1] Substituted by FA13 s92 and sched1(part 1)(q).

[2] Substituted by F(No.2)A13 s74(a).

[3] Inserted by FA12 sched4(part1).

Note:

FA13 s92 applies—

(a) in the case of a chargeable period (within the meaning of section 321(2)) which is an accounting period of a company, as respects chargeable periods that start on or after 1 January 2013, and

(b) in a case other than that referred to in paragraph (a), as respects the year of assessment (within the meaning of section 2(1)) 2013 and subsequent years of assessment.

Revenue Briefings

Tax Briefing

Tax Briefing April 2014 – Issue 03 – Full Self-Assessment

eBrief

eBrief No. 45/2012 – Advice for Farmers Making Their Form 11 Return – Poor Quality Completion of Forms Draws Unnecessary Attention from Revenue

eBrief No. 15/2014 – Who must file a tax return and self-assessment under full self-assessment?

eBrief No. 24/2014 – Full Self-Assessment

959S Option for self assessment to be made by Revenue

[(1) An individual who is chargeable to income tax or capital gains tax for a tax year shall not be required to comply with *section 959R* where a return, which is delivered by means other than electronic means, is delivered on or before 31 August in the tax year following the tax year to which the return relates.

(2) Where *subsection (1)* applies, a Revenue officer shall make the self assessment on behalf of the chargeable person in accordance with *section 959U*.][1]

[(3) This section shall not apply to an individual who is, by virtue of *section 917EA*, a specified person who is required to deliver the return concerned by electronic means.][2]

[(4) Where the chargeable person is assessed to tax under *section 1023* or *1031H*, and his or her spouse or civil partner, as the case may be, is also a chargeable person, then, in relation to the return concerned, no self assessment shall be made under *subsection (2)* until such time as the spouse or civil partner, as the case may be, has delivered his or her return for the year of assessment.][3]

Amendments

[1] Inserted by FA12 sched4(part1).

[2] Inserted by FA13 s92 and sched1(part 1)(r).

[3] Inserted by F(No.2)A13 s74(b).

Note:

FA13 s92 applies—

(a) in the case of a chargeable period (within the meaning of section 321(2)) which is an accounting period of a company, as respects chargeable periods that start on or after 1 January 2013, and

(b) in a case other than that referred to in paragraph (a), as respects the year of assessment (within the meaning of section 2(1)) 2013 and subsequent years of assessment.

959T Self assessment by person acting under authority

[Where a return is prepared and delivered in accordance with *section 959L* by another person acting under the chargeable person's authority—

(a) the self assessment required under *section 959R* shall be made by that other person, and

(b) where the self assessment is so made by that other person—

(i) the Acts apply as if it had been made by the chargeable person, and

(ii) a self assessment purporting to have been made by or on behalf of any chargeable person shall for the purposes of the Acts be deemed to have been made by that person or by that person's authority, as the case may be, unless the contrary is proved.][1]

Amendments

[1] Inserted by FA12 sched4(part1).

959U Self assessment by Revenue officer in relation to chargeable person

[(1) Where a chargeable person, or a person to whom *section 959T* applies, delivers a return but does not include a self assessment in the return, a Revenue officer, subject to *section 959AA(1)*—

(a) shall, where *section 959S* applies, and

(b) may, in any other case,

make the self assessment in relation to the chargeable person.

(2) Where a self assessment is made under this section, a Revenue officer shall give notice of the assessment in accordance with *section 959E*.

(3) Any self assessment made by a Revenue officer under this section shall be deemed to be a self assessment made by the chargeable person and references in the Acts to the self assessment of a chargeable person shall be treated as including a self assessment made under this section.][1]

Amendments

[1] Inserted by FA12 sched4(part1).

959V Amendment by chargeable person of return and of self assessment in return

[(1) Subject to the provisions of this section, a chargeable person may, by notice to the Revenue Commissioners, amend the return delivered [by that person][1] for a chargeable period.

(2) Where a return is amended in accordance with *subsection (1)*, the chargeable person shall as part of that notice amend the self assessment for the chargeable period at the same time.

[(2A) A return and self assessment may be amended under this section only where such an amendment—

(a) arises from an allowance, credit, deduction or relief due under the Acts,

(b) is necessary to correct either an error or a mistake, or

(c) is necessary to comply with any other provision of the Acts,

and notice of an amendment under this section shall specify which of *paragraphs (a)*, *(b)* and *(c)* applies.][2]

(3) Subject to *subsection (4)*, notice under this section shall be given in writing to a Revenue officer in the Revenue office dealing with the tax affairs of the chargeable person.

[(4) (a) Notice under this section in relation to the amendment of a return and a self assessment shall be given by electronic means where the return was delivered by electronic means.

(b) The electronic means by which notice under this section shall be given shall be such electronic means as may be specified by the Revenue Commissioners for that purpose.][3]

[(c) This subsection shall not apply to an amendment to a return or self assessment in so far as it relates to capital gains tax.][4]

(5) Where another person, as referred to in *section 959L*, is acting under the chargeable person's authority—

(a) notice under *subsections (1)* and *(2)* may be given by that other person, and

(b) where notice is so given by that other person—

(i) the Acts apply as if the return and the self assessment had been amended by the chargeable person, and

(ii) a return and a self assessment purporting to have been amended by or on behalf of any chargeable person shall for the purposes of the Acts be deemed to have been amended by that person or by that person's authority, as the case may be, unless the contrary is proved.

[(6) (a) Subject to *paragraph (b)* and *subsection (7)*, notice under this section in relation to a return and a self assessment may only be given within a period of 4 years after the end of the chargeable period to which the return relates.

(b) Where a provision of the Acts provides that a claim for an exemption, allowance, credit, deduction, repayment or any other relief from tax is required to be made within a period shorter than the period of 4 years referred to in *paragraph (a)*, then notice of an amendment under this section shall not be given after the end of that shorter period where the amendment relates to either the making or adjustment of a claim for such exemption, allowance, credit, deduction, repayment or other relief.][5]

(7) Notice under this section shall not be given in relation to a return and a self assessment after a Revenue officer has started to make enquiries under *section 959Z* in relation to the return or self assessment or after he or she has commenced an audit or other investigation which relates to the tax affairs of the person to whom the return or self assessment relates for the chargeable period involved.][6]

Amendments

[1] Substituted by FA13 s92 and sched1(part 1)(s).

[2] Inserted by F(No.2)A13 s74(c)(i).

[3] Substituted by FA13 s92 and sched1(part 1)(t).

[4] Inserted by F(No.2)A13 s74(c)(ii).

[5] Substituted by FA13 s92 and sched1(part 1)(u).

[6] Inserted by FA12 sched4(part1).

Note:

FA13 s92 applies—

(a) in the case of a chargeable period (within the meaning of section 321(2)) which is an accounting period of a company, as respects chargeable periods that start on or after 1 January 2013, and

(b) in a case other than that referred to in paragraph (a), as respects the year of assessment (within the meaning of section 2(1)) 2013 and subsequent years of assessment.

Revenue Briefings

Tax Briefing

Tax Briefing April 2014 – Issue 03 – Full Self-Assessment

eBrief

eBrief No. 73/2014 - Amendment of tax returns by taxpayers and agents

959W Making of self assessment in accordance with return

[(1) A self assessment made by a chargeable person under *section 959R* shall be made by reference to the particulars contained in the chargeable person's return for the chargeable period involved.

(2) A self assessment amended by a chargeable person under *section 959V* shall be amended by reference to the particulars contained in the chargeable person's return, as amended by notice under that section, for the chargeable period involved.

(3) A self assessment made by a Revenue officer in relation to a chargeable person under *section 959U* shall be made by reference to the particulars contained in the chargeable person's return for the chargeable period involved.

(4) Nothing in this Chapter prevents a Revenue officer from making a Revenue assessment on a chargeable person under *Chapter 5* and where a Revenue officer makes an assessment under that Chapter any self assessment previously made under this Chapter shall, for the purposes of determining the chargeable person's liability to tax for the chargeable period, be treated as if it had not been made and shall be void for such purposes.

(5) Nothing in this Chapter prevents a Revenue officer from amending, under *Chapter 5*, a self assessment previously made under this Chapter.][1]

Amendments

[1] Inserted by FA12 sched4(part1).

959X Penalty for failure to make or amend self assessment

[(1) A person who is required under this Chapter to make a self assessment in a return prepared and delivered under *Chapter 3* for a chargeable period and who does not make the self assessment in the return shall be liable to a penalty of €250.

(2) A person who is required under this Chapter to amend a self assessment in a return amended by notice under *section 959V* for a chargeable period and who does not amend the self assessment in the return shall be liable to a penalty of €100.][1]

Amendments

[1] Inserted by FA12 sched4(part1).

CHAPTER 5

Revenue Assessments and Enquiries and Related Time Limits

959Y Chargeable person and other persons: assessment made or amended by Revenue officer

[(1) Subject to the provisions of this Chapter, a Revenue officer may at any time—

(a) make a Revenue assessment on a person for a chargeable period [in such amount][1] as, according to the officer's best judgment, ought to be charged on the person,

(b) amend a Revenue assessment on, or a self assessment in relation to, a person for a chargeable period in such manner as he or she considers necessary, notwithstanding that—

(i) tax may have been paid or repaid in respect of the assessment, or

(ii) the assessment may have been amended on a previous occasion or on previous occasions.

(2) For the purpose of making [any assessment on or in relation to][2] a chargeable person for a chargeable period or for the purpose of amending such an assessment, a Revenue officer—

(a) may accept either in whole or in part any statement or other particular con tained in a return delivered by the chargeable person for that chargeable period, and

(b) may assess any amount of income, profits or gains or, as the case may be, chargeable gains, or allow any allowance, deduction, relief or tax credit by reference to such statement or particular.

(3) The amendment of an assessment by a Revenue officer does not preclude that Revenue officer or any other Revenue officer from further amending the assessment in such manner as he or she considers necessary.

(4) (a) Where any amount of income, profits or gains or, as the case may be, chargeable gains is omitted from, or not properly reflected in, an assessment for a chargeable period or the tax stated in an assessment is less than the tax payable by the chargeable person for the chargeable period, then a Revenue officer may make such amendments to the assessment as are necessary to ensure that the assessment includes the correct amount or to ensure that the tax stated in the assessment is equal to the tax payable by the chargeable person for the chargeable period.

(b) For the purposes of *paragraph (a)*, the amendment of an assessment by a Revenue officer may include the addition of an amount of income, profits or gains or, as the case may be, chargeable gains that is not reflected in the assessment.][3]

Amendments

[1] Substituted by FA13 s92 and sched1(part 1)(v)(i).

[2] Substituted by FA13 s92 and sched1(part 1)(v)(ii).

[3] Inserted by FA12 sched4(part1).

Note:

FA13 s92 applies—

(a) in the case of a chargeable period (within the meaning of section 321(2)) which is an accounting period of a company, as respects chargeable periods that start on or after 1 January 2013, and

(b) in a case other than that referred to in paragraph (a), as respects the year of assessment (within the meaning of section 2(1)) 2013 and subsequent years of assessment.

959Z Right of Revenue officer to make enquiries

[(1) A Revenue officer may, subject to this section, make such enquiries or take such actions within his or her powers as he or she considers necessary to satisfy himself or herself as to—

(a) whether a person is chargeable to tax for a chargeable period,

(b) whether a person is a chargeable person as respects a chargeable period,

(c) the amount of income, profit or gains or, as the case may be, chargeable gains in relation to which a person is chargeable to tax for a chargeable period, or

(d) the entitlement of a person to any allowance, deduction, relief or tax credit for a chargeable period.

(2) The making of an assessment or the amendment of an assessment in accordance with *section 959Y(2)* by reference to any statement or particular referred to in *paragraph (a)* of that section does not preclude a Revenue officer from, subject to this section, making such enquiries or taking such actions within his or her powers as he or she considers necessary to satisfy himself or herself as to the accuracy or otherwise of that statement or particular.

(3) Subject to *subsection (4)*, any enquiries or actions to which either *subsection (1)* or *(2)* applies shall not be made in the case of a chargeable person for a chargeable period at any time after the expiry of the period of 4 years commencing at the

end of the chargeable period in which the chargeable person has delivered a return for the chargeable period.

(4) Enquiries and actions to which either *subsection (1)* or *(2)* applies may be made at any time in relation to a person or a return for a chargeable period where—

(a) any of the circumstances referred to in *paragraph (a)*, *(b)* or *(c)* of *section 959AC(2)* apply,

(b) a Revenue officer has reasonable grounds for believing, in accordance with *section 959AD(3)*, that any form of fraud or neglect has been committed by or on behalf of the person in connection with or in relation to tax due for the chargeable period.

(5) A chargeable person who is aggrieved by any enquiry made or action taken by a Revenue officer under this section for a chargeable period, after the expiry of the period referred to in *subsection (3)* in respect of that chargeable period, on the grounds that the chargeable person considers that the Revenue officer is precluded from making that enquiry or taking that action by reason of that subsection may, by notice in writing given to the Revenue officer within 30 days of the officer making that enquiry or taking that action, appeal to the Appeal Commissioners, and the Appeal Commissioners shall hear the appeal in all respects as if it were an appeal against an assessment.

(6) Any action required to be taken by the chargeable person and any further action proposed to be taken by a Revenue officer pursuant to the officer's enquiry or action shall be suspended pending the determination of the appeal.

(7) If on the hearing of the appeal the Appeal Commissioners determine that the Revenue officer was precluded from making the enquiry or taking action by reason of *subsection (3)*, then the chargeable person shall not be required to take any action pursuant to the officer's enquiry or action and the officer shall be prohibited from pursuing his enquiry or action.

(8) If on the hearing of the appeal the Appeal Commissioners determine that the Revenue officer was not precluded from making the enquiry or taking action by reason of *subsection (3)*, then the officer may continue with his or her enquiry or action.

(9) Nothing in this section affects the operation of [*section 811, 811A, 811C or 811D*][1].][2]

Amendments

[1] Substituted by FA14 sched1(1).

[2] Inserted by FA12 sched4(part1).

959AA Chargeable persons: time limit on assessment made or amended by Revenue officer

[(1) Where a chargeable person has delivered a return for a chargeable period and has made in the return a full and true disclosure of all material facts necessary for the making of an assessment for the chargeable period—

(a) an assessment for that period, or

(b) an amendment of an assessment for that period,

shall not be made by a Revenue officer on the chargeable person after the end of 4 years commencing at the end of the chargeable period in which the return is delivered and—

(i) no additional tax shall be payable by the chargeable person after the end of that period of 4 years, and

(ii) no tax shall be repaid after the end of a period of 4 years commencing at the end of the chargeable period for which the return is delivered,

by reason of any matter contained in the return.

(2) Nothing in this section prevents a Revenue officer from, at any time, amending an assessment for a chargeable period—

(a) where the return for the period does not contain a full and true disclosure of all material facts necessary for the making of an assessment for that period,

(b) to give effect to a determination on any appeal against an assessment or against a determination to which *section 949* applies,

(c) to take account of any fact or matter arising by reason of an event occurring after the return is delivered,

(d) to correct an error in calculation in the assessment, or

(e) to correct a mistake of fact whereby any matter in the assessment does not properly reflect the facts disclosed by the chargeable person,

and tax shall be paid or repaid (notwithstanding any limitation in *section 865(4)* on the time within which a claim for a repayment of tax is required to be made) where appropriate in accordance with any such amendment.

(3) Nothing in this section affects the operation of *section 804(3)*, [*811, 811A, 811C, 811D or*][1] *1048*.][2]

Amendments

[1] Substituted by FA14 sched1(2).

[2] Inserted by FA12 sched4(part1).

959AB Persons other than chargeable persons: time limit on Revenue assessment and amended assessment

[(1) Subject to the other provisions of this section [...][1], a Revenue assessment on a person other than a chargeable person may be made or amended by a Revenue officer at any time not later than 4 years after the end of the chargeable period to which the assessment relates.

(2) In a case in which emoluments to which *subsection (3)* applies are received in a year of assessment subsequent to that for which they are assessable, a Revenue assessment on a person other than a chargeable person may be made or amended by a Revenue officer [for the year of assessment for which the emoluments are assessable][2] at any time not later than 4 years after the end of the year of assessment in which the emoluments were received.

(3) The emoluments to which this subsection applies are emoluments within the meaning of *section 112(2)*, including any payments chargeable to tax by virtue of *section 123* and any sums which by virtue of *Chapter 3* of *Part 5* are to be treated as perquisites of a person's office or employment, being emoluments, payments or sums other than those taken into account in an assessment to income tax for the year of assessment in which they are received and, for the purposes of *subsection (2)*—

(a) any such payment shall, notwithstanding anything in *section 123(4)*, be treated as having been received at the time it was actually received, and

(b) any such sums which are not actually paid to that person shall be treated as having been received at the time when the relevant expenses were incurred or are treated for the purposes of *Chapter 3* of *Part 5* as having been incurred.

(4) Nothing in this section affects the operation of [*section 811, 811A, 811C or 811D*][3]][4]

Amendments

[1] Deleted by FA13 s92 and sched1(part 1)(w)(i).

[2] Inserted by FA13 s92 and sched1(part 1)(w)(ii).

[3] Substituted by FA14 sched1(3).

[4] Inserted by FA12 sched4(part1).

Note:

FA13 s92 applies—

(a) in the case of a chargeable period (within the meaning of section 321(2)) which is an accounting period of a company, as respects chargeable periods that start on or after 1 January 2013, and

(b) in a case other than that referred to in paragraph (a), as respects the year of assessment (within the meaning of section 2(1)) 2013 and subsequent years of assessment.

959AC Chargeable persons: Revenue assessment and amendment of assessments in absence of return, etc.

[(1) In this section 'information' includes information received from a member of the Garda Síochána.

(2) Notwithstanding *section 959AA*, where in absence of relation to a chargeable person—

(a) the person fails to deliver a return for a chargeable period,

(b) a Revenue officer is not satisfied with the sufficiency of a return delivered by the person having regard to any information received in that regard, or

(c) a Revenue officer has reasonable grounds for believing that a return delivered by the person does not contain a full and true disclosure of all material facts necessary for the making of an assessment for the chargeable period,

then a Revenue officer may, at any time, make a Revenue assessment on the chargeable person for the chargeable period in such sum as, according to the best of the officer's judgment, ought to be charged on that person.

(3) Where a Revenue officer makes a Revenue assessment on a chargeable person under this section in the event of the failure of the person to deliver a return, it shall not be necessary to set out in the notice of assessment any particulars other than the amount of tax payable by the person for the chargeable period on the basis on that assessment.

(4) In any of the circumstances referred to in *subsection (2)*, a Revenue officer may, at any time, amend a Revenue assessment on, or a self assessment in relation to, a chargeable person for the chargeable period involved in such manner as the officer considers necessary.][1]

Amendments

[1] Inserted by FA12 sched4(part1).

959AD Chargeable persons and other persons: Revenue assessment and amendment of assessments where there is fraud or neglect

[(1) In this section 'neglect' means negligence or a failure to give any notice, to make any return, statement or declaration, or to produce or furnish any list, document or other information required by or under the Acts.

(2) For the purposes of *subsection (1)*, a person shall be deemed not to have failed to do anything required to be done within a limited time if the person did it within such

further time, if any, as the Revenue Commissioners or Revenue officer concerned may have allowed and, where a person had a reasonable excuse for not doing anything required to be done, the person shall be deemed not to have failed to do it if the person did it without unreasonable delay after the excuse had ceased.

(3) Notwithstanding *sections 959AA* and *959AB*, where a Revenue officer has reasonable grounds for believing that any form of fraud or neglect has been committed by or on behalf of a person in connection with or in relation to tax due for a chargeable period, a Revenue officer may, at any time, make a Revenue assessment on that person for the chargeable period.

(4) An assessment to which this section applies shall be made by a Revenue officer in such sum as, according to the best of the officer's judgment, ought to be charged on the person involved.

(5) In the circumstances referred to in *subsection (3)*, a Revenue officer may, at any time, amend a Revenue assessment on, or a self assessment in relation to, a person for a chargeable period in such manner as the officer considers necessary.][1]

Amendments

[1] Inserted by FA12 sched4(part1).

959AE Other Revenue assessments and miscellaneous matters

[(1) Nothing in this Chapter prevents an inspector or other Revenue officer from making an assessment in accordance with—

(a) *section 960Q*,

(b) *section 977(3)* or *subsection (2)* or *(3)* of *section 978*, as appropriate, and, notwithstanding *Chapter7*, tax specified in such an assessment shall be due and payable in accordance with *section 979*,

(c) *subsection (5A)* or *(6)*, as appropriate, of *section 980* and, notwithstanding *Chapter 7*, tax specified in such an assessment shall be due and payable in accordance with that *section 980*, or

(d) *section 1042* and, notwithstanding *Chapter 7*, tax specified in such an assessment shall be due and payable in accordance with that section.

(2) Subject to *subsection (1)*, an assessment under this Chapter shall not be made on a chargeable person for a chargeable period at any time before the specified return date for the chargeable period unless at that time the chargeable person has delivered a return for the chargeable period.

(3) Nothing in this Chapter affects the right of an inspector or other Revenue officer to make or amend an assessment where a provision of the Acts (other than this Chapter) includes either a right to assess or charge a person to tax or a right to make or amend an assessment on a person.

(4) An assessment which is otherwise final and conclusive shall not for any purpose of the Acts be regarded as not final and conclusive or as ceasing to be final and conclusive by reason only of the fact that a Revenue officer has amended or may amend the assessment.][1]

Amendments

[1] Inserted by FA12 sched4(part1).

CHAPTER 6

Appeals

959AF Chargeable persons and other persons: appeal in relation to time limit on assessment made or amended by Revenue officer

[(1) A person who is aggrieved by an assessment made by a Revenue officer, or the amendment of an assessment by a Revenue officer, on the grounds that the person considers that the Revenue officer was precluded from making the assessment or, as the case may be, the amendment—

(a) in the case of a chargeable person, by reason of [*section 959AA*, *959C* or *959AD*][1], or

(b) in the case of a person other than a chargeable person, by reason of [*section 959AB* or *959AD*][2],

may appeal against the assessment or amended assessment on those grounds.

(2) If, on the hearing of the appeal, the Appeal Commissioners determine that the officer was precluded from making the assessment or, as the case may be, the amendment, the Acts apply as if the assessment or the amendment, as the case may be, had not been made, and the assessment or the amendment of the assessment as appropriate is void.

(3) If, on the hearing of the appeal, the Appeal Commissioners determine that the officer was not precluded from making the assessment or, as the case may be, the amendment, the assessment or the assessment as amended stands, except to the extent that any amount or matter in that assessment is the subject of a valid appeal on any other grounds.][3]

Amendments

1 Substituted by FA13 s92 and sched1(part 1)(x)(i).

2 Substituted by FA13 s92 and sched1(part 1)(x)(ii).

3 Inserted by FA12 sched4(part1).

Note:

FA13 s92 applies—

(a) in the case of a chargeable period (within the meaning of section 321(2)) which is an accounting period of a company, as respects chargeable periods that start on or after 1 January 2013, and

(b) in a case other than that referred to in paragraph (a), as respects the year of assessment (within the meaning of section 2(1)) 2013 and subsequent years of assessment.

Revenue Briefings

eBrief

eBrief No. 11/2013 – Revenue Complaint and Review Procedures

959AG Chargeable persons: no appeal against self assessment

[No appeal may be made against—

(a) a self assessment made under *section 959R*, *section 959T* or *section 959U*,

(b) a self assessment amended under *section 959V*,

(c) the amount of any income, profits or gains or, as the case may be, chargeable gains, or the amount of any allowance, deduction, relief or tax credit specified in such an assessment.][1]

Amendments

1 Inserted by FA12 sched4(part1).

959AH Chargeable persons: requirement to submit return and pay tax

[(1) Where a Revenue officer makes a Revenue assessment, no appeal lies against the assessment until such time as—

(a) where the assessment was made in default of the delivery of a return, the chargeable person delivers the return, and

(b) in all cases, the chargeable person pays or has paid an amount of tax on foot of the assessment which is not less than the tax which—

(i) is payable by reference to any self assessment included in the chargeable person's return, or

(ii) where no self assessment is included, would be payable on foot of a self assessment if the assessment were made in all respects by reference to the statements and particulars contained in the return delivered by the chargeable person.

(2) A Revenue officer shall refuse an application for an appeal unless the requirements of both *paragraph (a)* and *(b)* of *subsection (1)* have been satisfied within the time for bringing an appeal against the assessment.

(3) References in *subsection (1)* to an amount of tax shall be construed as including any amount of interest which would be due and payable under *section 1080* on that tax at the date of payment of the tax, together with any costs incurred or other amounts which may be charged or levied in pursuing the collection of the tax contained in the assessment or the assessment as amended, as the case may be.

(4) The requirements of this section apply in relation to an assessment as amended by a Revenue officer as they apply to a Revenue assessment made by a Revenue officer.][1]

Amendments

[1] Inserted by FA12 sched4(part1).

959AI Chargeable persons and other persons: no appeal against agreed amounts

[No appeal may be made against the amount of any income, profits or gains or, as the case may be, chargeable gains, or the amount of any allowance, deduction, relief or tax credit specified in an assessment or an amended assessment made on a person for a chargeable period where either—

(a) a Revenue officer has determined the amount by accepting without alteration of and without departing from the statement or statements, or the particular or particulars with regard to income, profits or gains or, as the case may be, chargeable gains, or allowances, deductions, reliefs or tax credits specified in the return delivered by the person for the chargeable period, or

(b) the amount has been agreed between the Revenue officer and the person, or any person authorised by the person in that behalf, before the making of the assessment or the amendment of the assessment, as the case may be.][1]

Amendments

[1] Inserted by FA12 sched4(part1).

959AJ Chargeable persons and other persons: grounds for appeal

[(1) Where an appeal is brought against an assessment or an amended assessment made on a person for any chargeable period, the person shall specify in the notice of appeal—

(a) each amount or matter in the assessment or amended assessment with which the person is aggrieved, and

(b) the grounds in detail of the person's appeal as respects each such amount or matter.

(2) Where, as respects an amount or matter to which a notice of appeal relates, the notice does not comply with *subsection (1)*, the notice is, in so far as it relates to that amount or matter, invalid and the appeal concerned shall, in so far as it relates to that amount or matter, be deemed not to have been brought.

(3) A person is not entitled to rely on any ground of appeal that is not specified in the notice of appeal unless the Appeal Commissioners, or the judge of the Circuit Court, as the case may be, are or is satisfied that the ground could not reasonably have been stated in the notice.][1]

Amendments

[1] Inserted by FA12 sched4(part1).

959AK Chargeable persons and other persons: appeal against amended assessment

[Subject to the other provisions of this Chapter, where an assessment is amended by a Revenue officer (not being an amendment made by reason of the determination of an appeal), the person assessed may appeal against the assessment as so amended in all respects as if it were an assessment made on the date of the amendment and the notice of the assessment as so amended were a notice of the assessment, except that the person shall have no further right of appeal, in relation to matters other than additions to, deletions from, or alterations in the assessment, made by reason of the amendment, than the person would have had if the assessment had not been amended.][1]

Amendments

[1] Inserted by FA12 sched4(part1).

959AL Persons other than chargeable persons: other rules

[Subject to the other provisions of this Chapter, where an appeal is brought against an assessment by a person who is not a chargeable person then, pending the determination of the appeal—

(a) an amount of tax shall be payable on the due date for the payment of tax under the assessment and shall be the amount which results when the appropriate tax credits (including personal tax credit where applicable) due to the person are allowed in calculating the tax charged in the assessment which does not relate to the amounts or matters with which the person assessed is aggrieved, and

(b) that amount of tax shall for the purposes of *sections 1080* and *1081* be deemed to be the tax due and payable under the assessment.][1]

Amendments

[1] Inserted by FA12 sched4(part1).

CHAPTER 7

Chargeable Persons: Preliminary Tax and Dates for Payment of Tax

959AM Interpretation and miscellaneous (Chapter 7)

[(1) In this Chapter—

'*accounting period*' means an accounting period of a company;

'*corresponding corporation tax for the preceding accounting period*', in relation to an accounting period and a company, means an amount determined by the formula—

$$T \times \frac{C}{P}$$

where—

T is the corporation tax payable for the preceding accounting period,

C is the number of days in the accounting period, and

P is the number of days in the preceding accounting period;

'*corresponding income tax for the preceding accounting period*', in relation to an accounting period and a company, means an amount determined by the formula—

$$I \times \frac{C}{P}$$

where—

I is the income tax payable under *section 239* or *241* for the preceding accounting period,

C is the number of days in the accounting period, and

P is the number of days in the preceding accounting period;

'*final instalment*' shall be construed in accordance with *section 959AS(1)*;

'*final relevant instalment*' shall be construed in accordance with *section 959AS(5)*;

'*initial instalment*' shall be construed in accordance with *section 959AS(1)*;

'*initial relevant instalment*' shall be construed in accordance with *section 959AS(5)*;

'*pre-preceding tax year*', in relation to income tax and a tax year, means the tax year next before the preceding tax year;

'*relevant accounting period*', in relation to an accounting period, means, subject to *subsection (2)*, an accounting period of a company other than a small company;

'*relevant accounting standards*' has the same meaning as in *Schedule 17A*;

'*relevant company*' means a company in respect of which profits or gains for the purposes of Case I or II of Schedule D are computed in accordance with relevant accounting standards, which are, or include, relevant accounting standards in relation to profits or gains or losses on financial assets or liabilities;

'*relevant limit*', in relation to an accounting period, means, subject to *subsection (3)*, €200,000;

'*small company*' shall be construed in accordance with *subsection (4)*;

'*tax payable for the initial period*', in relation to capital gains tax and a tax year, means the tax that would be payable by the chargeable person if the tax year ended on 30 November in the year instead of 31 December in that year;

'*tax payable for the later period*', in relation to capital gains tax and a tax year, means the tax payable by the chargeable person for the tax year less the tax payable for the initial period in relation to that year.

(2) An accounting period is not a relevant accounting period where, but for this subsection, the final instalment of preliminary tax would, by reason of the dates on which the accounting period starts and ends, be due and payable in accordance with *section 959AS(2)* on or before the date on which the initial instalment would be due and payable in accordance with that section.

(3) Where the length of an accounting period is less than 12 months, the relevant limit in relation to the accounting period shall be proportionately reduced.

(4) A company is a small company in relation to an accounting period if the corresponding corporation tax for the preceding accounting period does not exceed the relevant limit in relation to the accounting period.

(5) References in this Chapter to the due date for the payment of an amount of preliminary tax shall, in the case where that tax is due for an accounting period, other than a relevant accounting period, of a company, be construed in accordance with *section 959AR(1)*.

(6) References in this Chapter to the due date for the payment of the initial instalment, or the final instalment, of preliminary tax shall, in the case where that tax is due for a relevant accounting period, be construed in accordance with *section 959AS(2)*.

(7) The provisions of this Chapter apply as respects chargeable persons only.

(8) The provisions of this Chapter as respects due dates for payment of tax apply subject to *sections 579(4)(b)* and *981*.][1]

Amendments

[1] Inserted by FA12 sched4(part1).

959AN Obligation to pay preliminary tax

[(1) Every person who is a chargeable person as respects any chargeable period is liable to pay to the Collector-General in accordance with this Chapter the amount of that person's preliminary tax appropriate to that chargeable period.

(2) The amount of a chargeable person's preliminary tax appropriate to a chargeable period is the amount of tax which in the opinion of the chargeable person is likely to become payable by that person for the chargeable period by reason of either a self assessment under *Chapter 4* or a Revenue assessment under *Chapter 5*.

[(2A) Reference in *subsection (2)* to the amount of tax which in the opinion of the chargeable person is likely to become payable shall be construed in accordance with the definition of "*amount of tax payable*" in *section 959A*.][1]

(3) Any amount of preliminary tax appropriate to a chargeable period which is paid by and not repaid to a chargeable person in any capacity shall, to the extent of the amount of that payment or the extent of the amount of that payment less any amount that has been repaid, be treated as a payment on account of the tax payable by the chargeable person for the chargeable period.

(4) Where—

(a) the tax payable by a company for an accounting period does not exceed the relevant limit, and

(b) the accounting period started on the company coming within the charge to corporation tax,

then the preliminary tax appropriate to the accounting period shall be deemed to be nil and neither *subsection (3)* of *section 959AR* nor *subsection (4)* of *section 959AS* apply as respects that accounting period.

(5) This section does not apply to capital gains tax.][2]

Amendments

[1] Inserted by FA13 s92 and sched1(part 1)(y).

[2] Inserted by FA12 sched4(part1).

Note:

FA13 s92 applies—

(a) in the case of a chargeable period (within the meaning of section 321(2)) which is an accounting period of a company, as respects chargeable periods that start on or after 1 January 2013, and

(b) in a case other than that referred to in paragraph (a), as respects the year of assessment (within the meaning of section 2(1)) 2013 and subsequent years of assessment.

Revenue Briefings

eBrief

eBrief No. 68/2012 – Preliminary Tax Requirements for 2012 – Interaction with Credit for Withholding Taxes

eBrief No. 40/2013 – PRSI changes for modified rate employees (civil and public servants) with additional income

959AO Date for payment of income tax

[(1) Subject to *section 959AP*, preliminary tax appropriate to a tax year for income tax purposes is due and payable on or before October in the tax year.

(2) (a) Subject to *subsections (3)* to *(6)*, income tax payable by a chargeable person for a tax year shall be due and payable on or before the specified return date for the tax year whether or not an assessment is made on or by the chargeable person for the tax year on or before that date.

(b) Where an assessment to income tax for a tax year has not been made on or by a chargeable person on or before the specified return date for the tax year then [the amount of tax payable that is specified][1] in any subsequent assessment made on or by the chargeable person for that year shall be deemed to have been due and payable on or before the specified return date for the tax year.

(3) Income tax payable by a chargeable person for a tax year shall be deemed to have been due and payable on 31 October in the tax year where—

(a) the chargeable person has defaulted in the payment of preliminary tax for the tax year,

(b) the preliminary tax paid by the chargeable person for the tax year is less than, or less than the least of, as the case may be—

(i) 90 per cent of the income tax payable by the chargeable person for the tax year,

(ii) the income tax payable by the chargeable person for the preceding tax year, and

(iii) in the case of a chargeable person to whom *section 959AP* applies (other than a chargeable person in relation to whom the amount of income tax payable, or taken in accordance with *subsection (4)(a)* to be payable, for the pre-preceding tax year was nil), 105 per cent of the income tax payable by the chargeable person for the pre-preceding tax year, or

(c) the preliminary tax payable by the chargeable person for the tax year was not paid by 31 October in the tax year.

(4) For the purposes of *subparagraphs (ii)* and *(iii)* of *subsection (3)(b)*—

(a) subject to *subsection (5)*, where the chargeable person was not a chargeable person for the preceding tax year or for the pre-preceding tax year, the income tax payable for the preceding year or the pre-preceding year, as the case may be, shall be taken to be nil,

(b) where, after 31 October in a tax year, an amount of additional income tax for the preceding tax year or, in the case of a chargeable person to whom *section 959AP* applies, the pre-preceding tax year becomes payable, that additional income tax shall not be taken into account if it became due and payable one month following the amendment to the assessment or the determination of the appeal, as the case may be, by virtue of *section 959AU(2)* or *section 959AV(2)*, and

(c) the tax payable for the preceding tax year, or in the case of a chargeable person to whom *section 959AP* applies, the pre-preceding tax year, shall be determined without regard to any relief to which the chargeable person is or may become entitled for the preceding year or the pre-preceding year, as the case may be, under *section 481* or *Part 16*.

(5) Where, for a tax year, a chargeable person is assessed to income tax in accordance with *section 1017* or *1031C*, and that person was not so assessed for the preceding tax year or for the pre-preceding tax year or for both of those years either—

(a) because the person's spouse or civil partner was so assessed for either or both of those years, or

(b) because the person and the person's spouse or civil partner were assessed to income tax in accordance with *section 1016* or *1023*, or *section 1031B* or *1031H*, as the case may be, for either or both of those years,

subparagraphs (ii) and *(iii)* of *subsection (3)(b)* and *subsection (4)(a)* apply as if the person and the person's spouse or civil partner had elected in accordance with *section 1018*, *1019* or *1031D*, as the case may be, for the person to be assessed to income tax in accordance with *section 1017* or *1031C* for any of those years for which the person or the person's spouse or civil partner were entitled to so elect or, in the case of married persons, would have been so entitled if *section 1019* had applied.

(6) (a) Where, in relation to a tax year, the profits or gains of a corresponding period relating to the preceding tax year are taken to be the profits or gains of that preceding tax year in accordance with *section 65(3)*, then, notwithstanding that the assessment for that preceding tax year has not been amended, any income tax payable for that preceding tax year which exceeds the income tax due and payable for that year without regard to the operation of *section 65(3)* is due and payable on or before the specified return date for the tax year.

(b) An amount of income tax to which *paragraph (a)* applies shall not be taken into account for the purposes of *subsection (3).*

(c) Notwithstanding *section 959AU*, where, in relation to a tax year, any additional tax for the preceding tax year is due and payable by virtue of an amendment of the assessment for that year made in accordance with *section 65(3)*, then, such additional tax as specified in the amendment to the assessment for that year shall be deemed to have been due and payable on or before the specified return date for the tax year.][2]

Amendments

[1] Substituted by FA13 s92 and sched1(part 1)(z)(1).

[2] Inserted by FA12 sched4(part1).

Note:

FA13 s92 applies—

(a) in the case of a chargeable period (within the meaning of section 321(2)) which is an accounting period of a company, as respects chargeable periods that start on or after 1 January 2013, and

(b) in a case other than that referred to in paragraph (a), as respects the year of assessment (within the meaning of section 2(1)) 2013 and subsequent years of assessment.

959AP Payment of preliminary tax by direct debit

[(1) This section applies to a chargeable person who—

(a) authorises the Collector-General to collect preliminary tax for income tax purposes by the debiting of a bank account of that person in accordance with *subsection (2)*, and

(b) complies with such conditions as the Collector-General may reasonably impose to ensure that an amount of preliminary tax payable by a chargeable person for a tax year will be paid by the chargeable person in accordance with this section.

(2) Preliminary tax appropriate to a tax year for income tax purposes is due and payable in the case of a chargeable person to whom this subsection applies—

(a) as respects the first tax year for which the Collector-General is authorised in accordance with *subsection (1)* to debit that person's bank account, by way of a minimum of 3 equal monthly instalments in that year, and

(b) as respects any subsequent tax year in which the Collector-General is so authorised, by way of a minimum of 8 equal monthly instalments in that year,

and the Collector-General shall debit the bank account of that person with such instalments on day 9 of each month for which the Collector-General is so authorised.

(3) The Collector-General may, in any particular case, in order to facilitate the payment of preliminary tax in accordance with this section, agree at the Collector-General's discretion to vary the number of equal monthly instalments to be collected in a year or agree at the Collector-General's discretion to an increase or decrease in the amount to be collected in any subsequent instalment to be made in that year.

(4) A chargeable person shall not be treated as having paid an amount of preliminary tax in accordance with this subsection unless that person pays in the tax year the monthly instalments due in accordance with *subsection (2)* or *(3)*, as appropriate.

(5) For the purposes of *section 959AO*, a chargeable person who pays an amount of preliminary tax appropriate to a tax year in accordance with this section shall be deemed to have paid that amount of preliminary tax on 31 October in the tax year.][1]

Amendments

[1] Inserted by FA12 sched4(part1).

959AQ Date for payment of capital gains tax

[(1) Capital gains tax payable by a chargeable person for a tax year is, where an assessment has not been made on or by the chargeable person for the tax year, due and payable—

(a) as respects tax payable for the initial period, on or before 15 December in the tax year, and

(b) as respects tax payable for the later period, on or before 31 January in the next following tax year.

(2) Where the capital gains tax payable by a chargeable person for a tax year is due and payable in accordance with *subsection (1)*, then [the amount of tax payable that is specified][1] in any subsequent assessment made on or by the chargeable person for that year shall be deemed to have been due and payable—

(a) on or before 15 December in the tax year, as respects tax payable for the initial period, and

(b) on or before 31 January in the next following tax year, as respects tax payable for the later period.][2]

Amendments

[1] Substituted by FA13 s92 and sched1(part 1)(z)(2).

[2] Inserted by FA12 sched4(part1).

Note:

FA13 s92 applies—

(a) in the case of a chargeable period (within the meaning of section 321(2)) which is an accounting period of a company, as respects chargeable periods that start on or after 1 January 2013, and

(b) in a case other than that referred to in paragraph (a), as respects the year of assessment (within the meaning of section 2(1)) 2013 and subsequent years of assessment.

959AR Date for payment of corporation tax: companies other than with relevant accounting periods

[(1) Preliminary tax appropriate to an accounting period, other than a relevant accounting period, of a company is due and payable—

(a) subject to *paragraph (b)*, not later than the day (in this paragraph referred to as the 'first-mentioned day') which is 31 days before the day on which the accounting period ends, but where the first-mentioned day is later than day 21 of the month in which it occurs, the preliminary tax shall be due and pay able not later than—

(i) day 21 of the month in which that first-mentioned day occurs, or

(ii) where payment of the preliminary tax is made by day 23 of the month in which that first-mentioned day occurs by such electronic means as are required by the Revenue Commissioners, day 23 of the month in which that first-mentioned day occurs,

(b) in a case where the accounting period is less than one month and one day in length, not later than the last day of the accounting period, but where that day is later than day 21 of the month in which it occurs, the preliminary tax is due and payable not later than—

(i) day 21 of the month in which that last day occurs, or

(ii) where payment of the preliminary tax is made by day 23 of the month in which that last day occurs by such electronic means as are required by the Revenue Commissioners, day 23 of the month in which that last day occurs.

(2) (a) Subject to *subsections (3)* and *(4)*, tax payable by a chargeable person for an accounting period, other than a relevant accounting period, of a company shall be due and payable on or before the specified return date for the accounting period.

(b) Where the tax payable by a chargeable person for an accounting period, other than a relevant accounting period, of a company is due and payable in accordance with *paragraph (a)*, then [the amount of tax payable that is specified][1] in any subsequent assessment made on or by the chargeable person for that accounting period shall be deemed to have been due and payable on or before the specified return date for the accounting period.

(3) Subject to *subsection (4)*, the tax payable by a chargeable person for an accounting period, other than a relevant accounting period, of a company shall be deemed to have been due and payable on the due date for the payment of an amount of preliminary tax for the accounting period where—

(a) the chargeable person has defaulted in the payment of preliminary tax for the accounting period,

(b) in the case of a company that is a small company in relation to the accounting period, the preliminary tax paid by the chargeable person for the accounting period is less than, or less than the lower of—

(i) 90 per cent of the tax payable by the chargeable person for the accounting period, and

(ii) the sum of the corresponding corporation tax for the preceding accounting period and the corresponding income tax for the preceding accounting period,

(c) in the case of a company that is not a small company in relation to the accounting period, the preliminary tax paid by the chargeable person for the accounting period is less than 90 per cent of the tax payable by the charge able person for the accounting period, or

(d) the preliminary tax payable by the chargeable person for the accounting period was not paid by the date on which it was due and payable.

(4) Where as respects an accounting period, other than a relevant accounting period, of a company—

(a) the preliminary tax paid by the chargeable person for the accounting period in accordance with *subsection (1)* is less than 90 per cent of the tax payable by the chargeable person for the accounting period,

(b) the preliminary tax so paid by the chargeable person for the accounting period is not less than 90 per cent of [the amount of tax which][2] would be payable by the chargeable person for the accounting period if no amount were included in the company's profits for the accounting period—

(i) in respect of chargeable gains on the disposal of assets in the part of the accounting period which is after the date by which preliminary tax for the accounting period is payable in accordance with *subsection (1)*, or

(ii) in the case of a relevant company, in respect of profits or gains or losses accruing, and not realised, in the accounting period on financial assets or financial liabilities as are attributable to changes in value of those assets or liabilities in the part of the accounting period which is after the end of the month immediately preceding the month in which preliminary tax for the accounting period is payable in accordance with *subsection (1)*,

and

(c) the chargeable person makes a further payment of preliminary tax for the accounting period within one month after the end of the accounting period and the aggregate of that payment and the preliminary tax paid by the charge- able person for the accounting period in accordance with *subsection (1)* is not less than 90 per cent of the tax payable by the chargeable person for the accounting period,

then the further payment of preliminary tax paid by the chargeable person for the accounting period shall be treated for the purposes of *subsection (3)* as having been paid by the date by which it is due and payable.][3]

Amendments

[1] Substituted by FA13 s92 and sched1(part 1)(z)(3).

[2] Substituted by FA13 s92 and sched1(part 1)(z)(4).

[3] Inserted by FA12 sched4(part1).

Note:

FA13 s92 applies—

(a) in the case of a chargeable period (within the meaning of section 321(2)) which is an accounting period of a company, as respects chargeable periods that start on or after 1 January 2013, and

(b) in a case other than that referred to in paragraph (a), as respects the year of assessment (within the meaning of section 2(1)) 2013 and subsequent years of assessment.

959AS Date for payment of corporation tax: companies with relevant accounting periods

[(1) Preliminary tax appropriate to a relevant accounting period is due and payable in 2 instalments, the first of which is referred to in this section as the 'initial instalment' and the second of which is referred to in this section as the 'final instalment'.

(2) (a) The initial instalment is due and payable within a period of 6 months from the start of the accounting period, but where the last day of that period of months is later than day 21 of the month in which it occurs, the initial instalment is due and payable not later than—

(i) day 21 of the month in which that last day occurs, or

(ii) where payment of the initial instalment is made by day 23 of the month in which that last day occurs by such electronic means as are required by the Revenue Commissioners, day 23 of the month in which that last day occurs.

(b) The final instalment is due and payable not later than the day (in this paragraph referred to as the 'first-mentioned day') which is 31 days before the day on which the accounting period ends, but where the first-mentioned day is later than day 21 of the month in which it occurs, the final instalment is due and payable not later than—

(i) day 21 of the month in which that first-mentioned day occurs, or

(ii) where payment of the final instal ment is made by day 23 of the month in which that first-mentioned day occurs by such electronic means as are required by the Revenue Commissioners, day 23 of the month in which that first-mentioned day occurs.

(3) (a) Subject to *subsections (4)* to *(7)*, tax payable by a chargeable person for a relevant accounting period is due and payable on or before the specified return date for the accounting period.

(b) Where the tax payable by a chargeable person for a relevant accounting period is due and payable in accordance with *paragraph (a)*, then [the amount of tax payable that is specified][1] in any subsequent assessment made on or by the chargeable person for that accounting period shall be deemed to have been due and payable on or before the specified return date for the accounting period.

(4) Subject to *subsections (6)* and *(7)* and *section 959AT*, the tax payable by a chargeable person for a relevant accounting period shall be deemed to have been due and payable in accordance with subsection (5) where—

(a) the chargeable person has defaulted in the payment of the initial instalment or final instalment of preliminary tax for the accounting period,

(b) the initial instalment of preliminary tax paid by the chargeable person for the accounting period is less than, or less than the lower of—

(i) 45 per cent of the tax payable by the chargeable person for the accounting period, and

(ii) 50 per cent of the sum of the corresponding corporation tax for the preceding accounting period and the corresponding income tax for the preceding accounting period,

(c) in a case where the accounting period commenced on the company coming within the charge to corporation tax, the initial instalment of preliminary tax paid by the chargeable person for the accounting period is less than 45 per cent of the tax payable by the chargeable person for the accounting period,

(d) the aggregate of the initial instalment and the final instalment of preliminary tax paid by the chargeable person for the accounting period is less than 90 per cent of the tax payable by the chargeable person for the accounting period, or

(e) the initial instalment or the final instalment of preliminary tax payable by the chargeable person for the accounting period was not paid by the date on which it was due and payable.

(5) (a) Tax due and payable in accordance with this subsection by a chargeable person for a relevant accounting period is due and payable in 2 instalments, the first of which is referred to in this subsection as the 'initial relevant instalment' and the second of which is referred to in this subsection as the 'final relevant instalment'.

(b) The amount of the initial relevant instalment is 45 per cent of the tax payable by the chargeable person for the accounting period and the initial relevant instalment is due and payable not later than the day on which the initial instalment of preliminary tax is due and payable in accordance with *subsection (2)*.

(c) The amount of the final relevant instalment is an amount equal to the excess of the tax payable by the chargeable person for the accounting period over the amount of the initial relevant instalment and the final relevant instalment is due and payable not later than the day on which the final instalment of preliminary tax is due and payable in accordance with *subsection (2)*.

(6) Where as respects a relevant accounting period—

(a) the initial instalment of preliminary tax paid by the chargeable person for the accounting period in accordance with *subsection (2)* is less than 45 per cent of the tax payable by the chargeable person for the accounting period,

(b) the initial instalment of preliminary tax so paid by the chargeable person for the accounting period is not less than 45 per cent of [the amount of tax which][2] would be payable by the chargeable person for the accounting period if no amount were included in the company's profits for the accounting period—

(i) in respect of chargeable gains on the disposal of assets in the part of the accounting period which is after the date by which the initial instalment of preliminary tax for the accounting period is payable in accordance with *subsection (2)*, or

(ii) in the case of a relevant company, in respect of profits orgains or losses accruing, and not realised, in the accounting period on financial assets or financial liabilities as are attributable to changes in value of those assets or liabilities in the part of the accounting period which is after the end of the month immediately preceding the month in which the initial instalment of preliminary tax for the accounting period is payable in accordance with *subsection (2)*,

(c) the aggregate of the initial instalment and the final instalment of preliminary tax paid by the chargeable person for the accounting period in accordance with *subsection (2)* is not less than 90 per cent of the amount of tax which would be payable by the chargeable person for the accounting period if computed in accordance with *subsection (7)(b)*,

then the initial instalment of preliminary tax paid by the chargeable person for the accounting period shall be treated for the purposes of *subsection (4)* as having been paid by the date on which it is due and payable.

(7) Where as respects a relevant accounting period—

(a) the aggregate of the initial instalment and the final instalment of preliminary tax paid by the chargeable person for the accounting period in accordance with *subsection (2)* is less than 90 per cent of the tax payable by the chargeable person for the accounting period,

(b) the aggregate of the initial instalment and the final instalment of preliminary tax so paid by the chargeable person for the accounting period is not less than 90 per cent of [the amount of tax which][3] would be payable by the chargeable person for the accounting period if no amount were included in the company's profits for the accounting period—

(i) in respect of chargeable gains on the disposal of assets in the part of the accounting period which is after the date by which the final instalment of preliminary tax for the accounting period is payable in accordance with *subsection (2)*, or

(ii) in the case of a relevant company, in respect of profits or gains or losses accruing, and not realised, in the accounting period on financial assets or financial liabilities as are attributable to changes in value of those assets or liabilities in the part of the accounting period which is after the end of the month immediately preceding the month in which the final instalment of preliminary tax for the accounting period is payable in accordance with *subsection (2)*,

(c) the chargeable person makes a further payment of preliminary tax for the accounting period within one month after the end of the accounting period and the aggregate of that payment and the initial instalment and final instalment of preliminary tax paid by the chargeable person for the accounting period in accordance with *subsection (2)* is not less than 90 per cent of the tax payable by the chargeable person for the accounting period,

then the final instalment of preliminary tax paid by the chargeable person for the accounting period shall be treated for the purposes of *subsection (4)* as having been paid by the date on which it is due and payable.][4]

Amendments

[1] Substituted by FA13 s92 and sched1(part 1)(z)(5).

[2] Substituted by FA13 s92 and sched1(part 1)(z)(6).

[3] Substituted by FA13 s92 and sched1(part 1)(z)(7).

[4] Inserted by FA12 sched4(part1).

Note:

FA13 s92 applies—

(a) in the case of a chargeable period (within the meaning of section 321(2)) which is an accounting period of a company, as respects chargeable periods that start on or after 1 January 2013, and

(b) in a case other than that referred to in paragraph (a), as respects the year of assessment (within the meaning of section 2(1)) 2013 and subsequent years of assessment.

959AT Date for payment of corporation tax: groups

[(1) In this section—

'*initial balance*' means the amount represented by the formula—

$$A - B$$

where—

A is the amount of the initial instalment of preliminary tax paid by the surrendering company for the relevant period in accordance with *subsection (2)* of *section 959AS*, and

B is—

(a) where the relevant period started on the surrendering company coming within the charge to corporation tax—

(i) 45 per cent of the tax payable by the surrendering company for the relevant period, or

(ii) where *subsection (4)* of *section 959AN* applies in relation to that period, a nil amount,

or

(b) in any other case, the lower of—

(i) 45 per cent of the tax payable by the surrendering company for the relevant period, or

(ii) 50 per cent of the sum of the corresponding corporation tax for the preceding accounting period and the corresponding income tax for the preceding accounting period, which is payable by the surrendering company;

'*final balance*' means the amount represented by the formula—

C – D

where—

C is the amount of preliminary tax paid by the surrendering company for the relevant period in accordance with *section 959AR(1)* or *section 959AS(2)*, as the case may be, and

D is 90 per cent of the tax payable by the surrendering company for the relevant period, or, where *subsection (4)* of *section 959AN* applies in relation to that period, a nil amount;

'*relevant initial balance*' means that part of an initial balance that is specified in a notice given in accordance with *subsection (3)*;

'*relevant final balance*' means that part of a final balance that is specified in a notice given in accordance with *subsection (3)*.

(2) This section applies where—

(a) a company (in this section referred to as the 'surrendering company') which is a member of a group pays—

(i) an initial instalment of preliminary tax for an accounting period (in this subsection referred to as the 'relevant period') in accordance with *subsection (2)* of *section 959AS*, being an amount which exceeds, or exceeds the lower of—

(I) 45 per cent of the tax payable by that surrendering company for the relevant period, and

(II) 50 per cent of the sum of the corresponding corporation tax for the preceding accounting period and the corresponding income tax for the preceding accounting period, that is payable by the surrendering company,

(ii) an initial instalment of preliminary tax for a relevant period which started on the surrendering company coming within the charge to corporation tax, being an amount which exceeds 45 per cent of the tax payable by that company for the relevant period,

(iii) an amount of preliminary tax for a relevant period in accordance with *section 959AR(1)* or *section 959AS(2)*, as the case may be, being an amount which exceeds 90 per cent of the tax payable by the surrendering company for the relevant period, or

(iv) any amount of preliminary tax for a relevant period inrespect of which *subsection (4)* of *section 959AN* applies,

(b) another company (in this section referred to as the 'claimant company') which is a member of the group pays—

(i) an initial instalment of preliminary tax for an accounting period in accordance with *subsection (2)* of *section 959AS*, being an amount which is less than, or less than the lower of—

(I) 45 per cent of the tax payable by the claimant company for the accounting period, and

(II) 50 per cent of the sum of the corresponding corporation tax for the preceding accounting period and the corresponding income tax for the preceding accounting period, which is payable by the claimant company,

(ii) an initial instalment of preliminary tax for an accounting period which started on the claimant company coming within the charge to corporation tax, being an amount which is less than 45 per cent of the tax payable by that company for the relevant period, or

(iii) an amount of preliminary tax for an accounting period in accordance with *subsection (2)* of *section 959AS*, being an amount which is less than 90 per cent of the tax payable by the claimant company for the accounting period,

or

(c) the accounting period in *paragraph (b)* coincides with the relevant period, and

(d) the claimant company is not a small company in relation to the relevant period.

(3) Where this section applies, the 2 companies may, at any time on or before the specified return date for the accounting period of the surrendering company, jointly give notice to the Collector-General—

(a) that *subsection (4)(a)* is to have effect in relation to the relevant initial balance, or

(b) that *subsection (4)(b)* is to have effect in relation to the relevant final balance.

(4) (a) Where this subsection has effect in relation to any relevant initial balance—

(i) an additional amount of preliminary tax equal to the relevant initial balance shall be deemed for the purposes of *subsection (4)(b)* of *section 959AS* to have been paid by the claimant company on the due date for the payment of the initial instalment of preliminary tax of that company for the relevant period if 100 per cent of the tax payable by the claimant company for the relevant period, disregarding this subparagraph, is paid on or before the specified return date for the relevant period, and

(ii) the surrendering company shall for the purposes of this section be treated as having surrendered the relevant initial balance to the claimant company and that relevant initial balance shall not be available for use by any other company under this section.

(b) Where this subsection has effect in relation to any relevant final balance—

(i) an additional amount of preliminary tax equal to the relevant final balance shall be deemed for the purposes of *subsection (4)(d)* of *section 959AS* to have been paid by the claimant company on the due date for the payment of the final instalment of preliminary tax of that company for the relevant period if 100 per cent of the tax payable by the claimant company for the relevant period, disregarding this subparagraph, is paid on or before the specified return date for the relevant period, and

(ii) the surrendering company shall for the purposes of this section be treated as having surrendered the relevant final balance to the claimant company and that relevant final balance shall not be available for use by any other company under this section.

(5) A payment for a relevant initial balance or for a relevant final balance—

(a) shall not be taken into account in computing profits or losses of either company for corporation tax purposes, and

(b) shall not be regarded as a distribution or a charge on income for any of the purposes of the Corporation Tax Acts,

and, in this subsection, 'payment for a relevant initial balance or for a relevant final balance' means a payment made by the claimant company to the surrendering company in pursuance of an agreement between them as respects an amount surrendered in accordance with this section, being a payment not exceeding that amount.

(6) (a) This section does not affect the liability to pay corporation tax of any company to which the section relates.

(b) Where this section applies, the amount on which, but for this section, the claimant company is liable to pay interest in accordance with *section 1080* shall be reduced by—

(i) any relevant initial balance deemed to have been paid by that company in accordance with *subsection (4)(a)(i)*, or

(ii) any relevant final balance deemed to have been paid by that company in accordance with *subsection (4)(b)(i)*.

(7) For the purposes of this section, 2 companies are members of the same group if and only if they would be such members for the purposes of *section 411*.][1]

Amendments

[1] Inserted by FA12 sched4(part1).

959AU Date for payment of tax: amended assessments

[(1) Subject to *subsection (2)* and *section 959AV*, any additional tax due by reason of the amendment of an assessment for a chargeable period shall be deemed to be due and payable on the same day as the tax due under the assessment, before its amendment, was due and payable.

(2) Where—

(a) the assessment was made after the chargeable person had delivered a return containing a full and true disclosure of all material facts necessary for the making of the assessment, or

(b) the assessment had previously been amended following the delivery of the return containing such disclosure,

any additional tax due by reason of the amendment of the assessment shall be deemed to have been due and payable not later than one month from the date of the amendment.][1]

Amendments

[1] Inserted by FA12 sched4(part1).

959AV Date for payment of tax: determination of an appeal

[(1) Where, on the determination of an appeal against an assessment made on a chargeable person for a chargeable period, the amount of tax payable by the person for the period is in excess of the amount of the tax which the chargeable person had paid before the making of the appeal, the excess shall be deemed to be due and payable on the same date as the tax charged by the assessment is due and payable.

(2) Notwithstanding *subsection (1)*, where—

(a) [the amount of tax which][1] the chargeable person had paid before the making of the appeal is not less than 90 per cent of [the amount of tax found][2] to be payable on the determination of the appeal, and

(b) the tax charged by the assessment was due and payable in accordance with *section 959AO(2)*, *section 959AQ*, [*section 959AR(3)* or *section 959AS(3)*][3], as the case may be,

the excess referred to in *subsection (1)* shall be deemed to be due and payable not later than one month from the date of the determination of the appeal.][4]

Amendments

[1] Substituted by FA13 s92 and sched1(part 1)(z)(8).

[2] Substituted by FA13 s92 and sched1(part 1)(z)(9).

[3] Substituted by FA13 s92 and sched1(part 1)(z)(10).

[4] Inserted by FA12 sched4(part1).

Note:

FA13 s92 applies—

(a) in the case of a chargeable period (within the meaning of section 321(2)) which is an accounting period of a company, as respects chargeable periods that start on or after 1 January 2013, and

(b) in a case other than that referred to in paragraph (a), as respects the year of assessment (within the meaning of section 2(1)) 2013 and subsequent years of assessment.

PART 42

Collection and Recovery

CHAPTER 1

Income Tax

960 Date for payment of income tax other than under self assessment

[(1) Subject to *subsection (2)*, income tax contained in an assessment (other than an assessment [made on or by a person who is a chargeable person under *Part 41A*][1]) for any year of assessment shall be payable on or before 30 September in that year, except that income tax included in any such assessment for any year of assessment which is made on or after 30 September in that year shall be deemed to be due and payable not later than one month from the date on which the assessment is made.

(2) Where, for a year of assessment, any claim for exemption or for any allowance, credit, deduction, relief or repayment was granted on the basis of an incorrect account, declaration, information, particulars, return or statement or any other form of claim, then income tax contained in an assessment (other than an assessment [made on or by a person who is a chargeable person under *Part 41A*][2]) for the year of assessment or in a statement sent in accordance with Regulation 37 of the Income Tax (Employments) (Consolidated) Regulations 2001 (S.I. No. 559 of 2001) for the year of assessment shall be due and payable—

(a) on 1 July in the year of assessment, where the exemption, allowance, credit, deduction, relief or repayment was given in the year of assessment before that date,

(b) on 1 January in the year following the year of assessment, where the exemption, allowance, credit, deduction, relief or repayment was given in the year of assessment but on or after 1 July,

(c) on the date the allowance, credit, deduction, relief or repayment was given, where that date is after the end of the year of assessment.][1]

Amendments

[1, 2] Substituted by FA12 sched4(part 2)(g).

[3] Substituted by FA11 s21(e). Deemed to have come into force and takes effect as on and from 1 January 2011.

Cross References

To Section 960

Section 15 Rate of charge.
Section 124 Tax treatment of certain severance payments.
Section 125 Tax treatment of benefits received under permanent health benefit schemes.
Section 126 Tax treatment of certain benefits payable under Social Welfare Acts.
Section 127 Tax treatment of restrictive covenants.
Section 458 Deductions allowed in ascertaining taxable income and provisions relating to reductions in tax.
Section 472 Employee tax credit.
Section 520 Interpretation (Chapter 1).
Section 527 Interim refunds of appropriate tax.
Section 531 Payments to subcontractors in certain industries.
Section 531B Charge to income levy.

Section 779 Charge to income tax of pensions under Schedule E.
Section 784 Retirement annuities: relief for premiums.
Section 784A Approved retirement fund.
Section 864A Electronic claims.
Section 897A Returns by employers in relation to pension products.
Section 903 Power of inspection: PAYE.
Section 927 Rectification of excessive set-off, etc. of tax credit.
Section 950 Interpretation (Part 41).
Section 1078 Revenue offences.
Section 1079 Duties of relevant person in relation to certain revenue offences.
Section 1080 Interest on overdue income tax, corporation tax and capital gains tax.
Section 1084 Surcharge for late returns.
Schedule 31 Consequential Amendments

961 Issue of demand notes and receipts [Repealed]

Repealed by F(No.2)A08 sched4(part1). Applies as respects any tax that becomes due and payable on or after 1 March 2009.

962 Recovery by sheriff or county registrar [Repealed]

Repealed by F(No.2)A08 sched4(part1). Applies as respects any tax that becomes due and payable on or after 1 March 2009.

Cross References

To Section 962
Schedule 31 Consequential Amendments

963 Power of Collector-General and authorised officer to sue in Circuit Court or District Court [Repealed]

Repealed by F(No.2)A08 sched4(part1). Applies as respects any tax that becomes due and payable on or after 1 March 2009.

Cross References

To Section 963
Schedule 31 Consequential Amendments

964 Continuance of pending proceedings [Repealed]

Repealed by F(No.2)A08 sched4(part1). Applies as respects any tax that becomes due and payable on or after 1 March 2009.

Cross References

To Section 964
Schedule 31 Consequential Amendments

965 Evidence in proceedings in Circuit Court or District Court for recovery of income tax [Repealed]

Repealed by F(No.2)A08 sched4(part1). Applies as respects any tax that becomes due and payable on or after 1 March 2009.

966 High Court proceedings [Repealed]

Repealed by F(No.2)A08 sched4(part1). Applies as respects any tax that becomes due and payable on or after 1 March 2009.

Cross References

To Section 966

Schedule 31 Consequential Amendments

967 Evidence of electronic transmission of particulars of income tax to be collected in proceedings for recovery of tax [Repealed]

Repealed by F(No.2)A08 sched4(part1). Applies as respects any tax that becomes due and payable on or after 1 March 2009.

Cross References

To Section 967

Schedule 31 Consequential Amendments

968 Judgments for recovery of income tax [Repealed]

Repealed by F(No.2)A08 sched4(part1). Applies as respects any tax that becomes due and payable on or after 1 March 2009.

969 Duration of imprisonment for non-payment of income tax [Deleted]

Deleted by FA99 sched6.

970 Recovery of income tax charged on profits not distrainable [Repealed]

Repealed by F(No.2)A08 sched4(part1). Applies as respects any tax that becomes due and payable on or after 1 March 2009.

971 Priority of income tax debts over other debts [Repealed]

Repealed by F(No.2)A08 sched4(part1). Applies as respects any tax that becomes due and payable on or after 1 March 2009.

972 Duty of employer as to income tax payable by employees [Repealed]

Repealed by F(No.2)A08 sched4(part1). Applies as respects any tax that becomes due and payable on or after 1 March 2009.

CHAPTER 1A

Interpretation

960A Interpretation

[(1) In [*Chapters 1A, 1B, 1C* and *1D*][1], unless the contrary is expressly stated—

"*Acts*" means—

(a) the Tax Acts,

(b) the Capital Gains Tax Acts,

(c) the Value-Added Tax Consolidation Act 2010, and the enactments amending and extending that Act,

(d) the statutes relating to the duties of excise and to the management of those duties and the enactments amending and extending those statutes,

(e) the Stamp Duties Consolidation Act 1999 and the enactments amending and extending that Act,

(f) the Capital Acquisitions Tax Consolidation Act 2003 and the enactments amending and extending that Act,

[(g) Parts 18A, 18B and 18C and 18D,][2]

[(h) the *Finance (Local Property Tax) Act 2012*,][3]

and any instruments made under any of those Acts;

"*assessment*" means any assessment to tax made under any provision of the Acts, including any amended assessment, additional assessment, correcting assessment and any estimate made under *section 990* or under Regulation 13 or 14 of the RCT Regulations and any estimate made under section 110 of the Value-Added Tax Consolidation Act 2010;

"*emoluments*" has the same meaning as in *section 983*;

"*income tax month*" has the same meaning as in *section 983*;

"*PAYE Regulations*" means regulations made under *section 986*;

"*RCT Regulations*" means the Income Tax (Relevant Contracts) Regulations 2000 (S.I. No. 71 of 2000);

"*Revenue officer*" means any officer of the Revenue Commissioners;

['*tax*' means any income tax, corporation tax, capital gains tax, value-added tax, excise duty, stamp duty, gift tax, inheritance tax, local property tax or any other levy or charge which is placed under the care and management of the Revenue Commissioners and includes—][4]

(a) any interest, surcharge or penalty relating to any such tax, duty, levy or charge,

(b) any clawback of a relief or an exemption relating to any such tax, duty, levy or charge, and

(c) any sum which is required to be deducted or withheld by any person and paid or remitted to the Revenue Commissioners or the Collector-General, as the case may be, under any provision of the Acts;

"*tax due and payable*" means tax due and payable under any provision of the Acts.][5]

Amendments

[1] Substituted by FA13 sched 2(1)(j).

[2] Substituted by FA11 s3(1)(b). Applies for the year of assessment 2011 and each subsequent year of assessment.

[3] Inserted by F(LPT)A 12 s158 & sched(6)(a).

[4] Substituted by F(LPT)A 12 s158 & sched(6)(b).

[5] Inserted by F(No.2)A08 sched4(1)(b)(i). Applies as respects any tax that becomes due and payable on or after 1 March 2009.

Cross References

From Section 960A

Section 983 Interpretation (Chapter 4).

Section 986 Regulations.

Section 990 Estimation of tax due for year.

960B Discharge of Collector-General's functions

[The Revenue Commissioners may nominate in writing any Revenue officer to perform any acts and to discharge any functions authorised by [*Chapters 1B*, 1C and *1D*][1] to be performed or discharged by the Collector-General other than the acts and functions referred to in *subsections (1)* to *(4)* of *section 960N*, and references in this Part to "Collector-General" shall be read accordingly.][2]

Amendments

[1] Substituted by FA12 s125(b). Deemed to have come into force and takes effect on and from 1 January 2012.

[2] Inserted by F(No.2)A08 sched4(1)(b)(i). Applies as respects any tax that becomes due and payable on or after 1 March 2009.

Cross References

From Section 960B

Section 960N Continuance of pending proceedings and evidence in proceedings.

To Section 960B

Section 928 Transmission to Collector-General of particulars of sums to be collected.

Section 960N Continuance of pending proceedings and evidence in proceedings.

CHAPTER 1B

Collection of Tax, etc.

960C Tax to be due and payable to Revenue Commissioners

[Tax due and payable under the Acts shall be due and payable to the Revenue Commissioners.][1]

Amendments

[1] Inserted by F(No.2)A08 sched4(1)(b)(i). Applies as respects any tax that becomes due and payable on or after 1 March 2009.

Cross References

To Section 960C

Section 960E Collection of tax, issue of demands, etc.

960D Tax to be debt due to Minister for Finance

[Tax due and payable to the Revenue Commissioners shall be treated as a debt due to the Minister for Finance for the benefit of the Central Fund.][1]

Amendments

[1] Inserted by F(No.2)A08 sched4(1)(b)(i). Applies as respects any tax that becomes due and payable on or after 1 March 2009.

960E Collection of tax, issue of demands, etc.

[(1) Tax due and payable to the Revenue Commissioners by virtue of *section 960C* shall be paid to and collected by the Collector-General, including tax charged in all assessments to tax, particulars of which have been given to the Collector-General under [*section 959G*][1].

(2) The Collector-General shall demand payment of tax that is due and payable but remaining unpaid by the person from whom that tax is payable.

[(2A) (a) In this subsection 'approved person' shall be construed in accordance with *section 917G*.

(b) Without prejudice to the generality of *subsection (2)*, the Collector-General may issue a demand by electronic means (within the meaning of *section 917EA*) to an approved person or to a person who is required to deliver a return and pay tax in accordance with regulations made by the Revenue Commissioners under *section 917EA*.][2]

(3) Where tax is not paid in accordance with the demand referred to in *subsection (2)*, the Collector-General shall collect and levy the tax that is due and payable but remaining unpaid by the person from whom that tax is payable.

(4) On payment of tax, the Collector-General may [send, make available or cause to be made available][3] a receipt to the person concerned in respect of that payment and such receipt shall consist of whichever of the following the Collector-General considers appropriate, namely—

(a) a separate receipt in respect of each such payment, or

(b) a receipt for all such payments that have been made within the period specified in the receipt.][4]

Amendments

[1] Substituted by FA12 sched4(part 2)(g).

[2] Inserted by FA13 s96.

[3] Substituted by FA11 s78. Deemed to have come into force and takes effect as on and from 1 January 2011.

[4] Inserted by F(No.2)A08 sched4(1)(b)(i). Applies as respects any tax that becomes due and payable on or after 1 March 2009.

Cross References

From Section 960E

Section 928 Transmission to Collector-General of particulars of sums to be collected.

Section 960C Tax to be due and payable to Revenue Commissioners.

960EA Payment of tax by relevant payment methods

[(1) In this section—

"*prescribed*" means prescribed by the Revenue Commissioners in regulations made under *subsection (3)*;

"*relevant payment method*" means each of the following methods of payment:

(a) credit card,

(b) debit card,

(c) any other prescribed method or methods of payment;

"*relevant person*" means the Revenue Commissioners, the Collector-General or a Revenue officer, as the case may be.

(2) Where a person makes any payment of tax to a relevant person using a relevant payment method, the relevant person may refuse to accept such payment where, by accepting the payment made using such relevant payment method the Revenue Commissioners would, but for this section, incur any fees or charges (however described) in connection with any amount paid, using the relevant payment method concerned, to the relevant person, unless, at the time of making the payment, the person making the payment agrees to the payment of such additional charge or additional charges, as the case may be, as may be prescribed, by reason of the person's making payment by that relevant payment method.

(3) The Revenue Commissioners may make regulations—

(a) prescribing a relevant payment method or relevant payment methods or class or classes of relevant payment method or relevant payment methods for the purposes of this section,

(b) prescribing the additional charge or additional charges payable in respect of each relevant payment method or each class of relevant payment method or relevant payment methods and different additional charges may be prescribed for different relevant payment methods or classes of relevant payment methods, and

(c) specifying—

(i) the period of time within which or the time by which, and

(ii) the manner in which,

any such additional charge or additional charges as may be prescribed under *paragraph* (*b*) shall be paid.][1]

Amendments

[1] Inserted by FA11 s79.

Revenue Briefings

eBrief

eBrief No. 61/2011 – Payment of tax by Credit Card

eBrief No. 34/2012 – Credit Card Payments Using the Revenue On-Line Service

960F Moneys received for capital acquisitions tax and stamp duties and not appropriated to be recoverable

[(1) Any person who—

(a) having received a sum of money in respect of gift tax, inheritance tax or stamp duties, does not pay that sum to the Collector-General, and

(b) improperly withholds or detains such sum of money,

shall be accountable to the Revenue Commissioners for the pay... of that sum to the extent of the amount so received by that perso...

(2) The sum of money referred to in subsection ... treated as a debt due to the Minister for Finance for the be... ...al Fund and section 960I shall apply to any such sum ... ...ad payable.][1]

...pects any tax that becomes due and payable on or

...way of civil proceedings.

Amendments

[1] Inserted by F...

after 1 M...

...er to identify liability against which payment to be set...

...subsection (2), every person who makes a payment of tax ... the ... Commissioners or to the Collector-General shall identify the li... against which he or she wishes the payment to be set.

...Where payment of tax is received by the Revenue Commissi... or the Collector-General and the payment is accompanied by a pay sli... return, a tax demand or other document issued by the Revenue Commissioners or the Collector-General, the payment shall, unless the contrary intention is or has been clearly indicated, be treated as relating to the tax referred to in the document concerned.

(3) Where a payment is received by the Revenue Commissioners or the Collector-General from a person and it cannot reasonably be determined by the Revenue Commissioners or the Collector-General from the instructions, if any, which accompanied the payment which liabilities the person wishes the payment to be set against, then the Revenue Commissioners or the Collector-General may set the payment against any liability due by the person under the Acts.][1]

Amendments

[1] Inserted by F(No.2)A08 sched4(1)(b)(i). Applies as respects any tax that becomes due and payable on or after 1 March 2009.

960H Offset between taxes

[(1) In this section—

"*claim*" means a claim that gives rise to either or both a repayment of tax and a payment of interest payable in respect of such a repayment and includes part of such a claim;

"*liability*" means any tax due and payable which is unpaid and includes any tax estimated to be due and payable;

"*overpayment*" means a payment or remittance (including part of such a payment or remittance) which is in excess of the amount of the liability against which it is credited.

(2) Where the Collector-General is satisfied that a person has not complied with the obligations imposed on the person in relation to either or both—

(a) the payment of tax that is due and payable, and

(b) the delivery of returns required to be made,

then the Collector-General may, in a case where a repayment is due to the person in respect o[f] ... [c]laim or overpayment—

(i) where ... h (*a*) applies, or where paragraphs (*a*) and (*b*) apply, instead of making ... liability, and ... ment, set the amount of the repayment against any

(ii) where paragra... such time as the r... s, withhold making the repayment until ... e delivered have been delivered.

(3) (a) Where a person (refe... as the "*first-mentioned person*") has assigned, transferred ... overpayment to another person (referred to in this ... entioned person") and subsection (2)(*a*) applies, then ... in a case where a repayment would have been d... in respect of the claim or overpayment if he ... ed or sold his or her right to the claim or ... repayment to the second-mentioned pers... against tax that is due and payable by that fi...

(b) Where the first-mentioned person and the sec... connected persons within the meaning of sectio...

any, of the repayment referred to in paragraph (*a*) shall be set against tax due and payable by the second-mentioned person.

(4) Where the Collector-General has set or withheld a repayment by virtue of subsection (2) or (3), then he or she shall give notice in writing to that effect to the person or persons concerned and, where subsection (2)(ii) applies, interest shall not be payable under any provision of the Acts from the date of such notice in respect of any repayment so withheld.

(5) The Revenue Commissioners may make regulations for the purpose of giving effect to this section and, without prejudice to the generality of the foregoing, such regulations may provide for the order of priority of the liabilities to tax against which any claim or overpayment is to be set in accordance with subsection (2) or (3) or both.

(6) Every regulation made under this section is to be laid before Dáil Éireann as soon as may be after it is made and, if a resolution annulling the regulation is passed by Dáil Éireann within the next 21 days on which Dáil Éireann has sat after the regulation is laid before it, the regulation shall be annulled accordingly, but without prejudice to the validity of anything previously done under the regulation.

(7) The Taxes (Offset of Repayments) Regulations 2002 (S.I. No. 471 of 2002) shall have effect as if they were made under subsection (5) and had complied with subsection (6).][1]

Amendments

[1] Inserted by F(No.2)A08 sched4(1)(b)(i). Applies as respects any tax that becomes due and payable on or after 1 March 2009.

Revenue Briefings

eBrief

eBrief No. 31/2013 – VAT Return of Trader Details (RTD) – Enforcement of Statutory Filing Obligations under S960H Taxes Consolidation Act 1997

Cross References

From Section 960H

Section 10 Connected persons.

To Section 960H

Section 530P Credit for deducted tax.

Section 766 Tax credit for research and development expenditure.

Section 766A Tax credit on expenditure on buildings or structures used for research and development.

CHAPTER 1C

Recovery Provisions, Evidential Rules, etc.

960I Recovery of tax by way of civil proceedings

[(1) Without prejudice to any other means by which payment of tax may be enforced, any tax due and payable or any balance of such tax may be sued for and recovered by proceedings taken by the Collector-General in any court of competent jurisdiction.

(2) All or any of the amounts of tax due from any one person may be included in the same summons.

(3) The rules of court for the time being applicable to civil proceedings commenced by summary summons, in so far as they relate to the recovery of tax, shall apply to proceedings under this section.

(4) The acceptance of a part payment or a payment on account in respect of tax referred to in a summons shall not prejudice proceedings for the recovery of the balance of the tax due and the summons may be amended accordingly.

(5) (a) Proceedings under this section may be brought for the recovery of the total amount which an employer is liable, under Chapter 4 and the PAYE Regulations, to pay to the Collector-General for any income tax month without—

(i) distinguishing the amounts for which the employer is liable to pay by reference to each employee, and

(ii) specifying the employees in question.

(b) For the purposes of the proceedings referred to in paragraph (*a*), the total amount shall be one single cause of action or one matter of complaint.

(c) Nothing in this subsection shall prevent the bringing of separate proceedings for the recovery of each of the several amounts which the employer is liable to pay by reference to any income tax month and to the employer's several employees.

(6) For the purposes of subsection (5), any amount of tax—

(a) estimated under section 989, or

(b) estimated under section 990 or any balance of tax so estimated but remaining unpaid,

is deemed to be an amount of tax which any person paying emoluments was liable, under Chapter 4 and the PAYE Regulations, to pay to the Collector-General.][1]

Amendments

[1] Inserted by F(No.2)A08 sched4(1)(b)(i). Applies as respects any tax that becomes due and payable on or after 1 March 2009.

Cross References

From Section 960I

Section 989 Estimation of tax due for income tax months.

Section 990 Estimation of tax due for year.

To Section 960I

Section 960F Moneys received for capital acquisitions tax and stamp duties and not appropriated to be recoverable.

Section 960N Continuance of pending proceedings and evidence in proceedings.

960J Evidential and procedural rules

[(1) In proceedings for the recovery of tax, a certificate signed by the Collector-General to the effect that, before the proceedings were instituted, any one or more of the following matters occurred:

(a) the assessment to tax, if any, was duly made,

(b) the assessment, if any, has become final and conclusive,

(c) the tax or any specified part of the tax is due and outstanding,

(d) demand for the payment of the tax has been duly made,

shall be evidence until the contrary is proved of such of those matters that are so certified by the Collector-General.

(2) (a) Subsection (1) shall not apply in the case of tax to which Chapter 4 applies.

(b) In proceedings for the recovery of tax to which Chapter 4 applies, a certificate signed by the Collector-General that a stated amount of income tax under Schedule E is due and outstanding shall be evidence until the contrary is proved that the amount is so due and outstanding.

(3) In proceedings for the recovery of tax, a certificate purporting to be signed by the Collector-General certifying the matters or any of the matters referred to in subsection (1) or (2) may be tendered in evidence without proof and shall be deemed until the contrary is proved to have been duly signed by the person concerned.

(4) If a dispute relating to a certificate referred to in subsection (1), (2) or (3) arises during proceedings for the recovery of tax, the judge may adjourn the proceedings to allow the Collector-General or the Revenue officer concerned to attend and give oral evidence in the proceedings and for any register, file or other record relating to the tax to be produced and put in evidence in the proceedings.][1]

Amendments

[1] Inserted by F(No.2)A08 sched4(1)(b)(i). Applies as respects any tax that becomes due and payable on or after 1 March 2009.

960K Judgments for recovery of tax

[(1) In this section "judgment" includes any order or decree.

(2) Where, in any proceedings for the recovery of tax, judgment is given against a person and a sum of money is accepted from the person against whom the proceedings were brought on account or in part payment of the amount of which the judgment was given, then—

(a) such acceptance shall not prevent or prejudice the recovery under the judgment of the balance of that amount that remains unpaid,

(b) the judgment shall be capable of being executed and enforced in respect of the balance as fully in all respects and by the like means as if the balance were the amount for which the Fjudgment was given,

(c) the law relating to the execution and enforcement of the judgment shall apply in respect of the balance accordingly, and

(d) a certificate signed by the Collector-General stating the amount of the balance shall, for the purposes of the enforcement and execution of the judgment, be evidence until the contrary is proved of the amount of the balance.][1]

Amendments

[1] Inserted by F(No.2)A08 sched4(1)(b)(i). Applies as respects any tax that becomes due and payable on or after 1 March 2009.

960L Recovery by sheriff or county registrar

[(1) Where any person does not pay any sum in respect of tax for which he or she is liable under the Acts, the Collector-General may issue a certificate to the county registrar or sheriff of the county in which the person resides or has a place of business certifying the amount due and outstanding and the person from whom that amount is payable.

(2) (*a*) For the purposes of this subsection—

"*electronic*" has the meaning assigned to it by the Electronic Commerce Act 2000 and an "*electronic certificate*" shall be construed accordingly;

"*issued in non-paper format*" includes issued in facsimile.

(b) A certificate to be issued by the Collector-General under this section may—

(i) be issued in an electronic or other format, and

(ii) where the certificate is issued in a non-paper format, be reproduced in a paper format by the county registrar or sheriff or by persons authorised by the county registrar or sheriff to do so.

(c) A certificate issued in a non-paper format in accordance with paragraph (*b*) shall—

(i) constitute a valid certificate for the purposes of this section,

(ii) be deemed to have been made by the Collector-General, and

(iii) be deemed to have been issued on the date that the Collector-General caused the certificate to issue.

(d) (i) Where a certificate issued by the Collector-General is reproduced in a non-paper format in accordance with paragraph (*b*)(ii) and—

(I) the reproduction contains, or there is appended to it, a note to the effect that it is a copy of the certificate so issued, and

(II) the note contains the signature of the county registrar or sheriff or of the person authorised under paragraph (*b*)(ii) and the date of such signing,

then the copy of the certificate with the note so signed and dated shall, for all purposes, have effect as if it was the certificate itself.

(ii) A signature or date in a note, on a copy of, or appended to, a certificate issued in a non-paper format by the Collector-General, and reproduced in a paper format in accordance with paragraph (*b*)(ii), that—

(I) in respect of such signature, purports to be that of the county registrar or sheriff or of a person authorised to make a copy, shall be taken until the contrary is shown to be the signature of the county registrar or sheriff or of a person who at the material time was so authorised, and

(II) in respect of such date, shall be taken until the contrary is shown to have been duly dated.

(3) (a) Immediately on receipt of the certificate, the county registrar or sheriff shall proceed to levy the amount certified in the certificate to be in default by seizing all or any of the goods, animals or other chattels within his or her area of responsibility belonging to the defaulter.

(b) For the purposes of paragraph (*a*), the county registrar or sheriff shall (in addition to the rights, powers and duties conferred on him or her by this section) have all such rights, powers and duties as are for the time being vested in him or her by law in relation to the execution of a writ of *fieri facias* in so far as those rights, powers and duties are not inconsistent with the additional rights, powers and duties conferred on him or her by this section.

(4) A county registrar or sheriff executing a certificate under this section shall be entitled—

(a) if the sum certified in the certificate is in excess of €19,050, to charge and (where appropriate) to add to that sum and (in any case) to levy under the certificate such fees and expenses, calculated in accordance to the scales appointed by the Minister for Justice, Equality and Law Reform under section 14(1)(*a*) of the Enforcement of Court Orders Act 1926 and for the time being in force, as the county registrar or sheriff would be entitled so to charge or add and to levy if the certificate were an execution order, within the meaning of the Enforcement of Court Orders Act 1926 (in this section referred to as an "*execution order*"), of the High Court,

(b) if the sum referred to in the certificate to be in default exceeds €3,175 but does not exceed €19,050, to charge and (where appropriate) to add to that sum and (in any case) to levy under the certificate such fees and expenses, calculated according to the scales referred to in paragraph (*a*), as the county registrar or sheriff would be entitled so to charge or add and to levy if the certificate were an execution order of the Circuit Court, and

(c) if the sum certified in the certificate to be in default does not exceed €3,175 and (where appropriate) to add to that sum and (in any case) to levy under the certificate such fees and expenses, calculated according to the scales referred to in paragraph (*a*), as the county registrar or sheriff would be entitled so to charge or add and to levy if the certificate were an execution order of the District Court.][1]

Amendments

[1] Inserted by F(No.2)A08 sched4(1)(b)(i). Applies as respects any tax that becomes due and payable on or after 1 March 2009.

Cross References

To Section 960L

Section 933 Appeals against assessment.
Section 989 Estimation of tax due for income tax months.
Section 990 Estimation of tax due for year.
Section 1006 Poundage and certain other fees due to sheriffs or county registrars.

960M Taking by Collector-General of proceedings in bankruptcy

[(1) The Collector-General may in his or her own name apply for the grant of a bankruptcy summons under section 8 of the Bankruptcy Act 1988 or present a petition for adjudication under section 11 of that Act in respect of tax (except corporation tax) due and payable or any balance of such tax.

(2) Subject to this section, the rules of court for the time being applicable and the enactments relating to bankruptcy shall apply to proceedings under this section.][1]

Amendments

[1] Inserted by F(No.2)A08 sched4(1)(b)(i). Applies as respects any tax that becomes due and payable on or after 1 March 2009.

Cross References

To Section 960M

Section 960N Continuance of pending proceedings and evidence in proceedings.

960N Continuance of pending proceedings and evidence in proceedings

[(1) Where the Collector-General has instituted proceedings under section 960I(1) or 960M(1) for the recovery of tax or any balance of tax and, while such proceedings are pending, such Collector-General ceases for any reason to hold that office, the proceedings may be continued in the name of that Collector-General by any person (in this section referred to as the "*successor*") duly appointed to collect such tax in succession to that Collector-General or any subsequent Collector-General.

(2) In any case where subsection (1) applies, the successor shall inform the person or persons against whom the proceedings concerned are pending that those proceedings are being so continued and, on service of such notice, notwithstanding any rule of court, it shall not be necessary for the successor to obtain an order of court substituting him or her for the person who has instituted or continued proceedings.

(3) Any affidavit or oath to be made by a Collector-General for the purposes of the [Land and Conveyancing Law Reform Act 2009][1] may be made by a successor.

(4) Where the Collector-General duly appointed to collect tax in succession to another Collector-General institutes or continues proceedings under section 960I(1) or 960M(1) for the recovery of tax or any balance of tax, then the person previously appointed as Collector-General shall for the purposes of the proceedings be deemed until the contrary is proved to have ceased to be the Collector-General appointed to collect the tax.

(5) Where a Revenue officer nominated in accordance with section 960B has instituted proceedings under section 960I(1) or 960M(1) for the recovery of tax or the balance of tax, and while such proceedings are pending, such officer dies or otherwise ceases for any reason to be a Revenue officer—

(a) the right of such officer to continue proceedings shall cease and the right to continue proceedings shall vest in such other officer as may be nominated by the Revenue Commissioners,

(b) where such other officer is nominated he or she shall be entitled accordingly to be substituted as a party to the proceedings in the place of the first-mentioned officer, and

(c) where an officer is so substituted, he or she shall give notice in writing of the substitution to the defendant.

(6) In proceedings under section 960I(1) or 960M(1) taken by a Revenue officer nominated in accordance with section 960B, a certificate signed by the Revenue Commissioners certifying the following facts—

(a) that a person is an officer of the Revenue Commissioners,

(b) that he or she has been nominated by them in accordance with section 960B, and

(c) that he or she has been nominated by them in accordance with subsection (5)(*a*),

shall be evidence unless the contrary is proved of those facts.

(7) In proceedings under *[section]*[2] *960I(1)* or *960M(1)* taken by a Revenue officer nominated in accordance with *section 960B*, a certificate signed by the Revenue Commissioners certifying the following facts—

(a) that the plaintiff has ceased to be an officer of the Revenue Commissioners nominated by them in accordance with section 960B,

(b) that another person is a Revenue officer,

(c) that such other person has been nominated by them in accordance with section 960B, and

(d) that such other person has been nominated by them to take proceedings to recover tax,

shall be evidence until the contrary is proved of those facts.][3]

Amendments

[1] Substituted by FA10 sched(4)(1)(j)(i). Has effect as on and from 3 April 2010.

[2] Substituted by FA10 sched(4)(1)(j)(ii). Has effect as on and from 3 April 2010.

[3] Inserted by F(No.2)A08 sched4(1)(b)(i). Applies as respects any tax that becomes due and payable on or after 1 March 2009.

Cross References

From Section 960N

Section 960B Discharge of Collector-General's functions.
Section 960I Recovery of tax by way of civil proceedings.
Section 960M Taking by Collector-General of proceedings in bankruptcy.

To Section 960N

Section 960B Discharge of Collector-General's functions.

960O Winding-up of companies: priority for taxes

[(1) In this section—

"*Act of 1963*" means the Companies Act 1963;

"*Act of 2010*" means the Value-Added Tax Consolidation Act 2010;

"*relevant date*" has the same meaning as in section 285 of the Act of 1963;

"*relevant period*" means—

(a) in *paragraph (a)(i)* of *subsection (4)* and in *paragraphs* (*b*) and (*c*) of that subsection, the 12 month period next before the date that is 14 days after the end of the income tax month in which the relevant date occurred;

(b) in *subparagraphs (ii)* to *(v)* of *subsection (4)(a)*, the 12 month period referred to in the relevant subsection;

"*relevant subsection*" means *subsection (2)(a)(iii)* of section 285 of the Act of 1963.

(2) For the purposes of section 98 of the Act of 1963 and the relevant subsection, the amount referred to in the relevant subsection is deemed to include corporation tax and capital gains tax.

(3) (a) Any value-added tax, including interest payable on that value-added tax in accordance with section 114 of the Act of 2010, for which a company is liable for taxable periods (within the meaning of that Act) which ended within the period of 12 months next before the relevant date are to be included among the debts which under section 285 of the Act of 1963 are to be paid in priority to all other debts in the winding up of the company.

(b) For the purposes of section 98 of the Act of 1963, *paragraph (a)* is deemed to be included in section 285 of that Act.

(4) (a) For the purposes of section 98 of the Act of 1963 and the relevant subsection, the amount referred to in the relevant subsection is deemed to include—

(i) so much as is unpaid of an authorised employer's PAYE liability,

(ii) amounts of tax [due and payable under *Chapter 2* of *Part 18* and regulations made under that Chapter][1] that relate to a period or periods falling in whole or in part within the relevant period,

[...][2]

(iv) amounts of tax to which section 989 applies that relate to a period or periods falling in whole or in part within the relevant period,

(v) amounts of tax to which section 990 applies that relate to a period or periods falling in whole or in part within the relevant period.

(b) In the case of any amount referred to in *subparagraphs (ii)* to *(v)* of *paragraph (a)* for a period falling partly within and partly outside the relevant period, the total sum or amount is to be apportioned according to the respective lengths of the periods falling within the relevant period and outside of that period so as to determine the amount of tax that relates to the relevant period.

(c) For the purposes of *paragraph (a)(i)* "authorised employer's PAYE liability", in relation to an employer authorised under Regulation 29 of the PAYE Regulations, means the amount determined by the formula—

$$(A + B - C) + D$$

where—

A is any amount which, apart from Regulation 29 of the PAYE Regulations, would otherwise have been an amount due at the relevant date in respect of sums that the employer is liable under *Chapter 4* and the PAYE Regulations (other than Regulation 29 of those Regulations) to deduct from emoluments paid by the employer during the relevant period,

B is any amount which, apart from Regulation 29 of the PAYE Regulations, would otherwise have been an amount due at the relevant date in respect of sums that were not so deducted but which the employer was liable, in accordance with section 985A and any regulations under that section, to remit to the Collector-General in respect of notional payments made by the employer during the relevant period,

C is any amount which the employer was liable under *Chapter 4* and the PAYE Regulations to repay during the relevant period, and

D is any interest payable under section 991 in respect of the amounts referred to in the meanings of A and B.][3]

Amendments

[1] Substituted by FA11 s(20)(1)(m). With effect from 1 January 2012 as per S.I. No. 660 of 2011.

[2] Deleted by FA11 s20(1)(m). With effect from 1 January 2012 as per S.I. No. 660 of 2011.

[3] Inserted by F(No.2)A08 sched4(1)(b)(i). Applies as respects any tax that becomes due and payable on or after 1 March 2009.

Cross References

From Section 960O

Section 985A Application of section 985 to certain perquisites, etc.
Section 989 Estimation of tax due for income tax months.
Section 990 Estimation of tax due for year.
Section 991 Interest.

960P Bankruptcy: priority for taxes

[(1) In this section—

"*Act of 2010*" means the Value-Added Tax Consolidation Act 2010;

"*Act of 1988*" means the Bankruptcy Act 1988;

"*relevant period*", in relation to the distribution of the property of a bankrupt, arranging debtor or person dying insolvent, means the period of 12 months before the date on which the order for adjudication of the person as a bankrupt was made, the petition of arrangement of the person as a debtor was filed or, as the case may be, the person died insolvent.

[(2) For the purposes of *subsection (1)(a)* of *section 81* of the Act of 1988, the amount referred to in that subsection is deemed to include capital gains tax and local property tax.][1]

(3) The priority attaching to the taxes to which section 81 of the Act of 1988 applies shall also apply to—

(a) any value-added tax, including interest payable on value-added tax in accordance with section 114 of the Act of 2010, for which a person is liable for taxable periods (within the meaning of that Act) which have ended within the relevant period,

(b) so much as is unpaid of an employer's PAYE liability for the relevant period,

(c) amounts of tax [due and payable under Chapter 2 of Part 18 and regulations made under that Chapter][2] which relate to a period or periods falling in whole or in part within the relevant period,

[…][3]

(e) amounts of tax to which *section 989* applies which relate to a period or periods falling in whole or in part within the relevant period,

(f) amounts of tax to which *section 990* applies which relate to a period or periods falling in whole or in part within the relevant period.

(4) In the case of any amount referred to in *paragraphs* (*c*) to (*f*) of *subsection (3)* for a period falling partly within and partly outside the relevant period, the total sum or amount is to be apportioned according to the respective lengths of the periods falling within the relevant period and outside of that period in order to determine the amount of tax which relates to the relevant period.

(5) In *subsection (3)(b)* "*employer's PAYE liability for the relevant period*" means the amount determined by the formula—

$$(A + B - C) + D$$

where—

A is all sums which an employer was liable under Chapter 4 and the PAYE Regulations to deduct from emoluments paid by the employer during the relevant period,

B is all sums that were not so deducted but which an employer was liable, in accordance with section 985A and regulations under that section, to remit to the Collector-General in respect of notional payments made by the employer during the relevant period,

C is any amounts which the employer was liable under Chapter 4 and the PAYE Regulations to repay during the relevant period, and

D is any interest payable under section 991 in respect of the sums referred to in the meanings of A and B.",][4]

Amendments

[1] Substituted by F(LPT)A 12 s158 & sched(7).

[2] Substituted by FA11 s20(1)(n). With effect from 1 January 2012 as per S.I. No. 660 of 2011.

[3] Deleted by FA11 s20(1)(n). With effect from 1 January 2012 as per S.I. No. 660 of 2011.

[4] Inserted by F(No.2)A08 sched4(1)(b)(i). Applies as respects any tax that becomes due and payable on or after 1 March 2009.

Cross References

From Section 960P

Section 985A Application of section 985 to certain perquisites, etc.
Section 989 Estimation of tax due for income tax months.
Section 990 Estimation of tax due for year.
Section 991 Interest.

960Q Recovery of amounts received by a person following the lodgement of an incorrect account, etc.

[(1) All amounts of money received from the Revenue Commissioners by a person shall be repaid by that person to the Revenue Commissioners where those amounts arose from the making or delivery for any purpose of the Acts of any incorrect account, declaration, information, particulars, return or statement in connection with any claim for exemption or for any allowance, credit, deduction, relief or repayment.

(2) All amounts of money to be repaid to the Revenue Commissioners under *subsection (1)* shall—

(a) be determined by a Revenue officer,

(b) for the purposes of this Part, be deemed to be amounts of tax which are due and payable to the Revenue Commissioners.

(3) Notwithstanding anything in the Acts, the determination referred to in *subsection (2)(a)* may be made at any time.

(4) Where any person is aggrieved by a determination made by a Revenue officer under this section, *section 949* shall apply to such determination as if it were a determination made on a matter referred to in *section 864*.

(5) (a) Amounts of tax which, by virtue of *subsection (2)*, are due and payable to the Revenue Commissioners may be included in assessments made by an inspector or other Revenue officer.

(b) Where an assessment is made in accordance with *paragraph (a)*, an inspector or other Revenue officer shall give notice to the person assessed of the assessment made but it shall not be necessary to set out in the notice of assessment any particulars other than particulars as to the amount of tax to be paid by the person assessed.

(6) Notwithstanding anything in the Tax Acts, the assessment referred to in *subsection (5)* may be made at any time.][1]

Amendments

[1] Inserted by FA11 s21(f). Deemed to have come into force and takes effect as on and from 1 January 2011.

Cross References

From Section 960Q

Section 864 Making of claims, etc.
Section 949 Appeals against determinations of certain claims, etc.

CHAPTER 1D

960R Power to require statement of affairs, security, etc.

[(1) In this section—

'*asset*' includes any interest in an asset;

["*market value*", in relation to property, means the price which that property might reasonably be expected to fetch if sold in the open market;][1]

'*prescribed*' means prescribed by the Revenue Commissioners;

'*specified date*', in relation to a notice under *subsection (3)*, means the date specified in the notice.

(2) For the purposes of this section, the cost of acquisition to a person of an asset shall include—

(a) the amount or value of the consideration, in money or money's worth, given by the person or on the person's behalf for the acquisition of the asset, together with the incidental costs to the person of the acquisition or, if the asset was not acquired by the person, any expenditure incurred by the person in acquiring the asset, and

(b) the amount of any expenditure incurred on the asset by the person or on that person's behalf for the purpose of enhancing the value of the asset, being expenditure reflected in the state or nature of the asset at the specified date, and any expenditure incurred by the person in establishing, preserving or defending the person's title to, or to a right over, the asset.

(3) Where tax is due and outstanding by a person and that person has failed to discharge that tax, the Collector-General may require—

(a) that person, by notice in writing given to that person, and

(b) where that person and his or her spouse or civil partner are jointly assessed to income tax under *section 1017* or *1031C*, that person's spouse or civil partner, by notice in writing given to the spouse or civil partner,

to deliver to the Collector-General [within 30 days of the giving of the notice a statement of affairs][2] in the prescribed form as at the date specified in the notice.

(4) For the purposes of *subsection (3)*, a request in writing by the Collector-General to clarify any matter contained in the statement of affairs shall be deemed to be a requirement to deliver a statement of affairs.

(5) In this section 'statement of affairs', in relation to a notice under *subsection (3)*, means—

(a) where the person to whom notice is given is acting otherwise than in a representative capacity or as a trustee, a statement of all the assets wherever situated to which that person is beneficially entitled on the specified date and all the liabilities for which that person is liable on the specified date [and a statement of all the person's income and outgoings in respect of such period or periods as may be specified in the notice][3],

(b) where the person to whom notice is given is a person ('the first-mentioned person') acting in a representative capacity for a person ('the second-mentioned person'), a statement of all the assets wherever situated to which the second-mentioned person is beneficially entitled which give rise to tax in respect of which the first-mentioned person is liable in a representative capacity or are assets in respect of which the first-mentioned person performed functions or duties in a representative capacity and all the liabilities for which the first-mentioned person is liable on the specified date [and a statement of all the income and outgoings of the second-mentioned person in respect of such period or periods as may be specified in the notice][4],

(c) where the person to whom notice is given is a trustee of a trust, a statement of all the assets and liabilities comprised in the trust on the specified date [and a statement of all the income and outgoings of the trust in respect of such period or periods as may be specified in the notice][5], or

(d) where the person to whom notice is given is the spouse or civil partner referred to in *section (3)(b)*, a statement of all assets wherever situated to which that spouse or civil partner is beneficially entitled on the specified date and all the liabilities for which that spouse or civil partner is liable on the specified date [and a statement of all the person's income and outgoings in respect of such period or periods as may be specified in the notice][6].

(6) Any assets to which a minor child of, or a minor child of the civil partner of, the person referred to in *paragraph (a)* or *(b)* of *subsection (3)* is beneficially entitled shall be included in that person's statement of affairs under this section where—

(a) such assets at any time before their acquisition by the minor child were disposed of by that person whether to that minor child or not, or

(b) the consideration for the acquisition of such assets by the minor child was provided directly or indirectly by that person.

(7) A statement of affairs delivered under this section shall contain in respect of each asset included in the statement—

(a) a full description,

(b) its location on the specified date,

(c) the cost of acquisition to the person beneficially entitled to that asset,

(d) the date of acquisition,

[(e) its market value and details of any charges or encumbrances on that asset, and][7]

(f) details of all policies of insurance (if any) whereby the risk of any kind of damage or injury, or the loss or depreciation of the asset is insured.

[(7A) A statement of affairs delivered under this section shall contain in respect of each liability and each item of income or outgoings such information as the Collector-General may specify in the prescribed form.][8]

(8) A statement of affairs delivered under this section shall, in the case of an asset which is an interest other than an absolute interest, contain particulars of the title under which the beneficial entitlement arises.

(9) A statement of affairs delivered under this section shall be signed by the person by whom it is delivered and shall include a [statutory][9] declaration by that person that it is to the best of that person's knowledge, information and belief correct and complete.

[...][10][11]

Amendments

[1] Inserted by F(No.2)A13 s80(a).

[2] Substituted by F(No.2)A13 s80(b).

[3] Inserted by F(No.2)A13 s80(c)(i).

[4] Inserted by F(No.2)A13 s80(c)(ii).

[5] Inserted by F(No.2)A13 s80(c)(iii).

[6] Inserted by F(No.2)A13 s80(c)(iv).

[7] Substituted by F(No.2)A13 s80(d).

[8] Inserted by F(No.2)A13 s80(e).

[9] Inserted by F(No.2)A13 s80(f).

[10] Deleted by F(No.2)A13 s80(g).

[11] Inserted by FA12 s125(c). Deemed to have come into force and takes effect on and from 1 January 2012.

960S Security for certain taxes

[(1) In this section—

[…][1]

'*tax*' means—

(a) income tax deductible in accordance with *Chapter 4* of *Part 42* and any regulations made under that Chapter,

(b) tax deductible in accordance with *Chapter 2* of *Part 18* and any regulations made under that Chapter,

(c) universal social charge chargeable in accordance with *Part 18D*, or

[(d) value-added tax chargeable in accordance with the Value-Added Tax Acts, or

(e) local property tax deductible in accordance with the *Finance (Local Property Tax) Act 2012*.][2]

[(2) The Revenue Commissioners may, where it appears requisite to them to do so for the protection of the revenue, require a person carrying on a business, to give security, or further security, of such amount and in such manner and form as they may determine, for the payment of any tax which is, or may become, due from that person from the date of service on that person of a notice in writing to that effect.][3]

(3) Where a requirement under *subsection (2)* arises, the [Revenue Commissioners][4] shall cause a notice in writing to that effect to be served on the person.

(4) Where a person is served with a notice in accordance with *subsection (3)*, it shall be an offence for that person to engage in business until such security, or further security, is provided to the [Revenue Commissioners][5].

(5) Where a notice is served on a person in accordance with *subsection (3)*, the person may, on giving notice to the Revenue Commissioners within the period of 30 days from the date of the service of the notice, appeal the requirement of giving any security under *subsection (2)* to the Appeal Commissioners.

(6) Where a person gives a notice of appeal in accordance with *subsection (5)*, *subsection (4)* shall not apply until the Appeal Commissioners determine the matter.][2]

Amendments

[1] Deleted by FA14 s93(a).

[2] Substituted by F(LPT)A 12 s158 & sched(8).

[3] Substituted by FA14 s93(b).

[4, 5] Substituted by FA14 s93(c).

[6] Inserted by FA12 s126(1). Deemed to have come into force and takes effect on and from 1 January 2012.

Revenue Briefings

eBrief

eBrief No. 87/2014 – Collector-General's Requirement for Security Bonds – Section 960S TCA 1997

CHAPTER 2

Corporation Tax

973 Collection of corporation tax [Repealed]

Repealed by F(No.2)A08 sched4(part1). Applies as respects any tax that becomes due and payable on or after 1 March 2009.

974 Priority for corporation tax [Repealed]

Repealed by F(No.2)A08 sched4(part1). Applies as respects any tax that becomes due and payable on or after 1 March 2009.

975 Application of sections 964(2), 980(8) and 981 for purposes of corporation tax [Repealed]

Repealed by F(No.2)A08 sched4(part1). Applies as respects any tax that becomes due and payable on or after 1 March 2009.

CHAPTER 3

Capital Gains Tax

976 Collection of capital gains tax [Deleted]

Deleted by F(No.2)A08 sched4(part1). Applies as respects any tax that becomes due and payable on or after 1 March 2009.

977 Recovery of capital gains tax from shareholder

[CGTA75 s51(1) and Sch4 par17]

(1) In this section, "*capital distribution*" has the same meaning as in *section 583*.

(2) This section shall apply where a person (in this section referred to as "*the beneficiary*") connected with a company resident in the State receives or becomes entitled to receive in respect of shares in the company any capital distribution from the company, other than a capital distribution representing a reduction of capital, and—

(a) the capital so distributed derives from the disposal of assets in respect of which a chargeable gain accrues to the company, or

(b) the distribution constitutes such a disposal of assets.

(3) Where—

(a) the capital gains tax assessed on the company for the year of assessment in which the chargeable gain referred to in *subsection (2)* accrues includes any amount in respect of that chargeable gain, and

(b) any of the capital gains tax assessed on the company for that year is not paid within 6 months from the date when it becomes payable by the company,

the beneficiary may by an assessment made within 2 years from that date be assessed and charged (in the name of the company) to an amount of that capital gains tax—

(i) not exceeding the amount or value of the capital distribution which the beneficiary has received or became entitled to receive, and

(ii) not exceeding a proportion equal to the beneficiary's share of the capital distribution made by the company of capital gains tax on the amount of that gain at the rate in force when the gain accrued.

(4) A beneficiary paying any amount of tax under this section shall be entitled to recover a sum equal to that amount from the company.

(5) This section is without prejudice to any liability of the beneficiary receiving or becoming entitled to receive the capital distribution in respect of a chargeable gain accruing to that beneficiary by reference to the capital distribution as constituting a disposal of an interest in shares in the company.

Cross References

From Section 977

Section 583 Capital distributions by companies.

To Section 977

Section 954 Making of assessments.

Section 979 Time for payment of capital gains tax assessed under sections 977(3) or 978(2) and (3).

978 Gifts: recovery of capital gains tax from donee

[CGTA75 s51(1) and Sch4 par18]

(1) In this section—

"*old asset*" and "*new asset*" have the same meanings respectively as in *section 597*;

references to a donor include, in the case of an individual who has died, references to his or her personal representatives;

references to a gift include references to any transaction otherwise than by means of a bargain made at arm's length in so far as money or money's worth passes under the transaction without full consideration in money or money's worth, and "*donor*" and "*donee*" shall be construed accordingly.

(2) Where—

(a) a chargeable gain accrues in any year of assessment to any person on the disposal of an asset by means of a gift, and

(b) any amount of capital gains tax assessed on that person for that year of assessment is not paid within 12 months from the date when the tax becomes payable, the donee may by an assessment made not later than 2 years from the date when the tax became payable be assessed and charged (in the name of the donor) to capital gains tax on an amount—

(i) not exceeding the amount of the chargeable gain so accruing, and

(ii) not exceeding such an amount of chargeable gains as would, if charged at the rate provided in *section 28(3)*, result in liability to an amount of capital gains tax equal to that amount of capital gains tax which was not paid by the donor.

(3) Where the gift consists of a new asset, the donee may, in addition to being assessed and charged under *subsection (2)* in respect of the new asset, be assessed and charged as if the chargeable gain on the disposal of the old asset were a chargeable gain on the disposal of the new asset the capital gains tax in respect of which was not paid within 12 months from the date when the tax had become payable.

(4) (a) Where a person on whom capital gains tax is assessed and charged in respect of the disposal of an asset transfers directly or indirectly by means of a gift to a donee—

(i) the whole of the proceeds of the disposal, or

(ii) in a case where the asset is a new asset acquired by the use of the proceeds of the disposal of an old asset, the whole of the proceeds of the disposal of the new asset,

subsections (2) and *(3)* shall apply to the amount of capital gains tax so assessed and charged.

(b) Where a person on whom capital gains tax is assessed and charged in respect of the disposal of an asset transfers directly or indirectly by means of a gift to a donee—

(i) part of the proceeds of the disposal, or

(ii) in a case where the asset is a new asset acquired by the use of the proceeds of the disposal of an old asset, part of the proceeds of the disposal of the new asset,

subsections (2) and *(3)* shall apply to such part of the amount of capital gains tax so assessed and charged as bears to the whole of such tax the same proportion that that part of the proceeds bears to the whole of those proceeds.

(5) The donee of a gift paying any amount of tax in pursuance of this section shall, subject to any terms or conditions of the gift, be entitled to recover a sum of that amount from the donor of the gift as a simple contract debt in any court of competent jurisdiction.

(6) This section shall apply in relation to a gift made to 2 or more donees with any necessary modifications and subject to the condition that each such donee shall be liable to be assessed and charged in respect only of such part of the amount of capital gains tax payable by the donees by virtue of this section as bears to the whole of such tax the same proportion as the part of the gift made to that donee bears to the whole of the gift.

Cross References

From Section 978

Section 28 Taxation of capital gains and rate of charge.

Section 597 Replacement of business and other assets.

To Section 978

Section 954 Making of assessments.

Section 979 Time for payment of capital gains tax assessed under sections 977(3) or 978(2) and (3).

Section 980 Deduction from consideration on disposal of certain assets.

979 Time for payment of capital gains tax assessed under sections 977(3) or 978(2) and (3)

[CGTA75 s5(2); FA88 s13(7)(c); FA91 s48]

Capital gains tax assessed on any person under *section 977(3)* or *subsections (2)* and *(3)* of *section 978* in respect of gains accruing in any year shall be payable by that person at or before the expiration of 3 months following that year, or at the expiration of a period of 2 months beginning with the date of the making of the assessment, whichever is the later.

Cross References

From Section 979

Section 977 Recovery of capital gains tax from shareholder.

Section 978 Gifts: recovery of capital gains tax from donee.

To Section 979

Section 954 Making of assessments.

Section 1042 Charging and assessment of persons not resident or ordinarily resident: modification of general rules.

980 Deduction from consideration on disposal of certain assets

[CGTA75 s51(1) and Sch4 par11(1) to (10A); FA89 s29; FA95 s76; FA96 s59]

(1) In this section—

"*designated area*" means an area designated by order under section 2 of the Continental Shelf Act, 1968;

"*exploration or exploitation rights*" has the same meaning as in *section 13*;

"*shares*" includes stock and any security.

(2) This section shall apply to assets that are—

(a) land in the State,

(b) minerals in the State or any rights, interests or other assets in relation to mining or minerals or the searching for minerals,

(c) exploration or exploitation rights in a designated area,

(d) shares in a company deriving their value or the greater part of their value directly or indirectly from assets specified in *paragraph (a)*, *(b)* or *(c)*, other than shares quoted on a stock exchange,

(e) shares, other than shares quoted on a stock exchange, to which *section 584* applies, whether by virtue of that section or any other section, so that, as respects a person disposing of those shares, they are treated as the same shares as shares specified in *paragraph (d)*, acquired as the shares so specified were acquired, and

(f) goodwill of a trade carried on in the State.

(3) This section shall not apply where the amount or value of the consideration in money or money's worth on a disposal does not exceed the sum of [€500,000][1]; but if an asset owned at one time by one person, being an asset to which this section would but for this subsection apply, is disposed of by that person in parts—

(a) to the same person, or

(b) to persons who are acting in concert or who are connected persons,

whether on the same or different occasions, the several disposals shall for the purposes of this subsection, but not for any other purpose, be treated as a single disposal.

[(3A) This section shall not apply to a disposal by a body specified in *Schedule 15*.][2]

(4) (a) Subject to *paragraph (b)*, on payment of the consideration for acquiring an asset to which this section applies—

(i) the person by or through whom any such payment is made shall deduct from that payment a sum representing an amount of capital gains tax equal to 15 per cent of that payment,

(ii) the person to whom the payment is made shall allow such deduction on receipt of the residue of the payment, and

(iii) the person making the deduction shall, on proof of payment to the Revenue Commissioners of the amount so deducted, be acquitted and discharged of so much money as is represented by the deduction as if that sum had been actually paid to the person making the disposal.

[(b) Where the person disposing of the asset produces to the person acquiring the asset—

(i) a certificate issued under *subsection (8)* in relation to the disposal, or

(ii) if the asset concerned is land on which a new house has been built or land on which a new house is in the course of being built, a certificate issued under *subsection (8)* in relation to the disposal or one of the certificates specified in *subsection (8A)* which, in either case, has been issued to the person disposing of the asset,

no deduction referred to in *paragraph (a)* shall be made.

(c) In *paragraph (b)(ii)*—

"*house*" has the same meaning as it has in [*section 372AK*][3];

"*new house*" means a house which has been developed or is being developed by or on behalf of the person disposing of it and which has not been used at any time before its disposal.][4]

[(5) Where any payment referred to in *subsection (4)(a)* is made by or on behalf of any person, that person shall, within 30 days of the date of the payment, deliver to the Revenue Commissioners an account of the payment and of the amount deducted from the payment, and pay to the Collector-General an amount of capital gains tax equal to 15 per cent of the amount of the payment.

(5A) Capital gains tax which by virtue of *subsection (5)* is payable by a person who makes a payment shall—

(a) be payable by that person in addition to any capital gains tax which by virtue of any other provision of the Capital Gains Tax Acts is payable by that person,

(b) be due within 30 days of the time when the payment is made, and

(c) be payable by that person without the making of an assessment, but tax which has become so due may be assessed on the person making the payment (whether or not the tax has been paid when the assessment is made) if that tax or any part of that tax is not paid on or before the due date.][5]

(6) Where, in relation to any payment referred to in *subsection (4)(a)*, any person has made default in delivering an account required by this section, or where the inspector is not satisfied with the account, the inspector may estimate the amount of the payment to the best of his or her judgment and, notwithstanding *section 31*, may assess and charge that person to capital gains tax for the year of assessment in which the payment was made on the amount so estimated at the rate of 15 per cent.

[(7) Where the amount of capital gains tax which, by virtue of *subsection (5A)*, a person has become liable to pay to the Collector-General, has been so paid, appropriate relief shall, on a claim being made in that behalf, be given to the person chargeable in respect of the gain on the disposal, whether by discharge, repayment or otherwise.][6]

[(8) (a) A person chargeable to capital gains tax on the disposal of an asset to which this section applies, or another person (in this section referred to as an "*agent*") acting under the authority of such person, may apply to the inspector for a certificate that tax should not be deducted from the consideration for the disposal of the asset and that the person acquiring the asset should not be required to give notice to the Revenue Commissioners in accordance with *subsection (9)(a)*.

(b) If the inspector is satisfied that the person making the application is either the person making the disposal, or an agent, and that—

(i) the person making the disposal is resident in the State,

(ii) no amount of capital gains tax is payable in respect of the disposal, or

(iii) the capital gains tax chargeable for the year of assessment for which the person making the disposal is chargeable in respect of the disposal of the asset and the tax chargeable on any gain accruing in any earlier year of assessment (not being a year ending earlier than the 6th day of April, 1974) on a previous disposal of the asset has been paid,

the inspector shall issue the certificate to the person making the disposal or, as the case may be, the agent, and shall issue a copy of the certificate to the person acquiring the asset.

(c) Where an application is made under this subsection by an agent, it must include the name and address of the person making the disposal and where such person is resident in the State, that person's tax reference number (within the meaning of *section 885*).][7]

[(8A) (a) The certificates referred to in *subsection (4) (b)* are—

(i) a certificate of authorisation (within the meaning of *section 531*) issued for the purposes of that section, the period of validity of which, as provided for by regulations under *subsection (6)* of that section, has not expired,

(ii) a tax clearance certificate (within the meaning of *section 1094*) issued for the purposes of that section, the period of validity of which has not expired,

(iii) a tax clearance certificate (within the meaning of *section 1095*) issued for the purposes of that section, the period of validity of which has not expired, or

(iv) where a person has not been issued with such a certificate of authorisation or such a tax clearance certificate, a certificate such as is referred to in *paragraph (b)*.

(b) Where a person has not been issued with a certificate of authorisation or a tax clearance certificate such as is referred to in *subparagraph (i)*, *(ii)* or *(iii)* of *paragraph (a)*, the person disposing of an asset referred to in *subsection (4)(b)(ii)* may apply in that behalf, for the purposes of this paragraph, to the Collector-General for the issue of a certificate and such an application shall be deemed to be an application made under *section 1095* for the issuing of a tax clearance certificate thereunder and that section shall, accordingly, apply with the following and any other necessary modifications, that is to say, for the reference in *subsection (2)* of *section 1095* to the scheme there shall be substituted a reference to *subsection (4)(b)* of this section.][8]

[(c) For the purpose of this section, a notification issued, within the previous 12 months, by the Revenue Commissioners under *section 530I* that the named person is a person to whom *section 530G* applies shall be treated as a certificate for the purposes of this subsection.][9]

[(8B) *Subsection (8)* shall apply for corporation tax as it applies for capital gains tax, and references to capital gains tax in that [subsection][10] shall apply accordingly as if they were or included references to corporation tax.][11]

(9) (a) Where—

(i) after the 2nd day of June, 1995, a person acquires an asset to which this section applies and *section 978* does not apply,

(ii) the consideration for acquiring the asset is of such a kind that the deduction mentioned in *subsection (4)* cannot be made out of the consideration, and

[(iii) the person disposing of the asset does not, at or before the time at which the acquisition is made, produce to the person acquiring the asset a certificate under *subsection (8)* in relation to the disposal or one of the certificates specified in *subsection (8A)*, being a certificate which, in either case, has been issued to the person disposing of the asset,

the person acquiring the asset shall within 7 days of the time at which the acquisition is made—][12]

(I) notify the Revenue Commissioners of the acquisition in a notice in writing containing particulars of—

(A) the asset acquired,

(B) the consideration for acquiring the asset,

(C) the market value of that consideration estimated to the best of that person's knowledge and belief, and

(D) the name and address of the person making the disposal,

and

(II) pay to the Collector-General an amount of capital gains tax equal to 15 per cent of the market value of the consideration so estimated.

(b) Capital gains tax which by virtue of *paragraph (a)(II)* is payable by a person acquiring an asset shall—

(i) be payable by that person in addition to any capital gains tax which by virtue of any other provision of the Capital Gains Tax Acts is payable by that person,

(ii) be due within 7 days of the time at which that person acquires the asset, and

(iii) be payable by that person without the making of an assessment;

but tax which has become so due may be assessed on the person acquiring the asset (whether or not it has been paid when the assessment is made) if that tax or any part of that tax is not paid on or before the due date.

(c) Where any person acquiring an asset has in pursuance of *paragraph (a)(II)* paid any amount of capital gains tax by reference to the market value of the consideration for acquiring the asset, that person shall be entitled to recover a sum of that amount from the person disposing of the asset as a simple contract debt in any court of competent jurisdiction; but where a copy of a certificate under *subsection (8)* is issued to the person acquiring the asset, being a copy of a certificate in relation to the disposal by which the person acquired the asset, that person—

(i) shall not be entitled thereafter to so recover that sum, and

(ii) shall be repaid that amount of tax.

(d) This section shall apply in relation to the acquisition of an asset by 2 or more persons with any necessary modifications and subject to the condition that each such person shall be liable to be assessed and charged in respect only of such part of the amount of capital gains tax payable by those persons by virtue of *paragraph (b)* as bears to the whole of such tax the same proportion as the part of the asset acquired by that person bears to the whole of the asset.

[(e) Where a person acquiring an asset has paid to the Collector-General an amount of capital gains tax in accordance with *paragraph (a)(II)* and recovered a sum of that amount from the person disposing of the asset, then, on proof being given in that regard, appropriate relief shall be given to the person disposing of the asset, whether by discharge, repayment or otherwise.][13]

[…][14]

(11) (a) Subject to *paragraph (b)*, where there is a disposal of assets by virtue of a capital sum being derived from those assets, the person paying the capital sum shall, notwithstanding that no asset is acquired by that person, be treated for the purposes of this section as acquiring the assets disposed of for a consideration equal to the capital sum, whether that sum is paid in money or money's worth, and this section shall, subject to any necessary modifications, apply accordingly.

(b) *Paragraph (a)* shall not apply where there is a disposal of an asset by virtue of a capital sum being derived from the asset under a policy of insurance of the risk of any kind of damage to the asset.

[(12) The enforcement of a debt security by the National Asset Management Agency or by a company to which *section 616(1)(g)* relates does not constitute consideration for the purposes of this section.

(13) *Subsection (9)* does not apply to the National Asset Management Agency or to a company to which *section 616(1)(g)* relates.

(14) This section does not apply to a disposal by a company that would be a company to which *section 616(1)(g)* relates if the reference in that section to a 75 per cent subsidiary were a reference to a 51 per cent subsidiary.

(15) For the purposes of this section, the enforcement of a debt security by the National Asset Management Agency or by a company to which *section 616(1)(g)* relates shall not be treated as a disposal of an asset.][15]

[(16) In the case of a disposal to which this section applies, the person making the disposal shall provide details (if applicable) on application, if the form on which the application is made so requires, for a certificate referred to in *subsection (8)* relating to—

(a) whether or not the asset being disposed of was acquired by way of gift or inheritance,

(b) the market value of the asset on the date it was acquired, and

(c) whether or not gift tax or inheritance tax was paid in respect of the asset.][16]

Amendments

[1] Substituted by FA02 s63.

[2] Inserted by FA05 s56(1)(a). Applies as on and from 25 March 2005.

[3] Substituted by FA05 s56(1)(b). This section is deemed to have applied as on and from 25 March 2002.

[4] Substituted by FA00 s87(1)(b). This section shall apply as respects disposals made on or after 23 March 2000.

[5] Substituted by FA07 s56(1)(a). Applies to disposals made on or after 2 April 2007.

[6] Substituted by FA07 s56(1)(b). Applies to disposals made on or after 2 April 2007.

[7] Substituted by FA03 s71(1). Applies as respects applications made on or after 28 March 2003.

[8] Inserted by FA00 s87(1)(c). This section shall apply as respects disposals made on or after 23 March 2000.

[9] Inserted by FA11 s20(1)(o). With effect from 1 January 2012 as per S.I. No. 660 of 2011.

[10] Substituted by FA10 sched(4)(1)(k). Has effect as on and from 3 April 2010.

[11] Inserted by F(No.2)A08 sched4(1)(b)(ii). Applies as respects any tax that becomes due and payable on or after 1 March 2009.

[12] Substituted by FA00 s87(1)(d). This section shall apply as respects disposals made on or after 23 March 2000.

[13] Inserted by FA05 s56(1)(c). Applies as on and from 25 March 2005.

[14] Deleted by FA07 s56(1)(c). Applies to disposals made on or after 2 April 2007.

[15] Inserted by the National Asset Management Agency Act 2009 Sched 3 part 10.

[16] Inserted by FA10 s147(2)(b). Has effect as on and from 3 April 2010.

Case Law

A bank must get a certificate of clearance to avoid withholding tax when it is selling land from its mortgage. Bank of Ireland Finance Ltd v Revenue Commissioners 1989 IV ITR 217

Revenue Briefings

Tax Briefing

Tax Briefing March 1996 – Issue 21 pg 12 – Disposal of Certain Assets
Tax Briefing March 1999 – Issue 35 pg 22 – Procedure for obtaining CGT Clearance Certificates
Tax Briefing January 2003 – Issue 51 pg 5 – CG50
Tax Briefing May 2003 – Issue 52 pg 16 – Applications
Tax Briefing July 2004 – Issue 56 pg 5 – Deduction from Consideration on Disposal of Certain Assets
Tax Briefing December 2005 – Issue 62 pg 9 – CGT Clearance Certificates
Tax Briefing March 1996 – Issue 66 pg 23 – CGT Clearance Certificates
Tax Briefing December 2010 – Issue 13 – Capital Gains Tax
Tax Briefing March 2011 – Issue 01 – Tax exemption for New Start-up Companies

eBrief

eBrief No. 86/2014 – Tax Clearance Guidelines and Procedures Updated

Cross References

From Section 980

Section 13 Extension of charge to income tax to profits and income derived from activities carried on and employments exercised on the Continental Shelf.
Section 31 Amount chargeable.
Section 372AK Interpretation (Chapter 11).
Section 530G Zero rate subcontractor.
Section 530I Determination of rates.
Section 584 Reorganisation or reduction of share capital.
Section 885 Obligation to show tax reference number on receipts.
Section 978 Gifts: recovery of capital gains tax from donee.
Section 1094 Tax clearance certificates in relation to certain licences.
Section 1095 Tax clearance certificates: general scheme.
Schedule 15 List of Bodies for Purposes of Section 610

To Section 980

Section 847 Tax relief for certain branch profits.
Section 954 Making of assessments.
Section 1077 Penalties for failure to make returns, etc. and for deliberately or carelessly making incorrect returns.

981 Payment by instalments where consideration due after time of disposal

[CGTA75 s44(1)]

Where the consideration or part of the consideration taken into account in the computation of a chargeable gain is payable by instalments over a period beginning not earlier than the time when the disposal is made, being a period exceeding 18 months, then, if the person making the disposal satisfies the Revenue Commissioners that such person would otherwise suffer undue hardship, the capital gains tax [or corporation tax, as the case may be,][1] on such a chargeable gain accruing on a disposal may, at such person's option, be paid by such instalments as the Revenue Commissioners may allow over a period not exceeding 5 years and ending not later than the time at which the last of the first-mentioned instalments is payable.

Amendments

[1] Inserted by F(No.2)A08 sched4(1)(b)(iii). Applies as respects any tax that becomes due and payable on or after 1 March 2009.

Cross References

To Section 981

Section 959 Miscellaneous (Part 41).

982 Preferential payment [Repealed]

Repealed by F(No.2)A08 sched4(part1). Applies as respects any tax that becomes due and payable on or after 1 March 2009.

CHAPTER 4

Collection and Recovery of Income Tax on Certain Emoluments (PAYE System)

983 Interpretation (Chapter 4)

[ITA67 s124]

In this Chapter, except where the context otherwise requires—

"*emoluments*" means anything assessable to income tax under Schedule E, and references to payments of emoluments include references to payments on account of emoluments;

"*employee*" means any person in receipt of emoluments;

"*employer*" means any person paying emoluments;

["*income tax month*" means—

(a) in relation to a period prior to 6 December 2001, a month beginning on the 6th day of a month and ending on the 5th day of the next month,

(b) the period beginning on 6 December 2001 and ending on 31 December 2001, and

(c) thereafter, a calendar month;][1]

"*tax deduction card*" means a tax deduction card in the form prescribed by the Revenue Commissioners or such other document corresponding to a tax deduction card as may be authorised by the Revenue Commissioners in any particular case.

["*reliefs from income tax*" means allowances, deductions and tax credits; "*tax credits*" means personal tax credits and general tax credits;][2]

Amendments

[1] Substituted by FA01 sched2(53).

[2] Inserted by FA01 sched1(1)(s). Applies as respects the year of assessment 2001 and subsequent years of assessment.

Case Law

In Hearne v O'Cionna 1988 IV ITR 113 it was held that a person who paid emoluments on behalf of another was liable to account for PAYE thereon.

Even where a 'one off' payment is made, PAYE must be operated. Booth v Mirror Group of Newspapers plc 1992 STC 615

It was held in Kirkshell Timber Ltd v Revenue & Customs Commissioners 2006 SpC 559 that the assignment of book debts to a director constitutes payment subject to PAYE.

Revenue Briefings

Tax Briefing

Tax Briefing May 2006 – Issue 63 – New Simplified Filing Arrangements For Employers' PAYE/PRSI

Tax Briefing August 2006 – Issue 64 – Business Tax Registration

Tax Briefing August 2006 – Issue 64 – New Electronic Services for Employees – ROS

Tax Briefing August 2006 – Issue 64 – PAYE – Foreign Employments

Tax Briefing April 2009 – Issue 71 – Revenue Online Service (ROS) and PAYE Anytime

Tax Briefing December 2009 – Issue 82 – Individuals described as 'Locums' engaged in the Fields of Medicine, Health Care and Pharmacy

eBrief

eBrief No. 43/2005 – PAYE and Foreign Employments
eBrief No. 04/2006 – New Simplified Payment Arrangements for Employers PAYE/PRSI
eBrief No. 09/2006 – (further to eBrief No. 43/2005) 2005 Bonuses, Temporary Assignees, and Pension Contributions
eBrief No. 28/2006 – PAYE – Foreign Employments
eBrief No. 23/2007 – P35 Refunds and P35 Amendments
eBrief No. 58/2007 – 'Medical Insurance Paid By Employer' new field for completion on P35L
eBrief No. 59/2008 – Reduced frequency of Tax Returns and Payments for Employers PAYE/PRSI and VAT – Extension to Newly Eligible Customers
e-Brief No. 10/09 – Extended Date for Customers who Pay & File Electronically
eBrief No. 30/09 – Practitioner Access to PAYE Anytime
eBrief No. 78/2009: Reduced Frequency of Tax Returns and Payments for Employers PAYE/PRSI and VAT – Extension to Newly Eligible Customers
eBrief No. 85/2009 – Individuals described as 'Locums' engaged in the fields of Medicine, Health Care and Pharmacy
eBrief No. 05/2010 – Clarification of Certain Matters relating to Employment vs. Self Employment Status
eBrief No. 32/2010 – FAQs on the use of the ROS PAYE Service by Agents for Clients
eBrief No. 46/2010 – Agents ROS PAYE Service
eBrief No. 8/2011 – Taxation of Doctors engaged by General Practitioners (GPS) and Form P35 Filing Deadline
eBrief No. 07/2014 – Compliance Code for PAYE Taxpayers

Revenue Information Notes

Employer's Guide to PAYE
Employer's Guide to operating PAYE and PRSI for certain benefits (BIK)
Employers Guide to Benefit-in-Kind
IT11 – Employees' Guide to PAYE
IT 22 – Taxation of Illness Benefit and Occupational Injury Benefit
IT 67 – First Job – A Guide for First Time Entrants to the PAYE Tax System
IT 69 – eWorking and Tax
CG 6 – P35 – End of Year Returns
CG 7 – Direct Debit – PAYE/PRSI & VAT

Statements of Practice

Tax treatment of Remuneration of Members of State and State Sponsored Committees and Boards – SP IT/1/04
Tax treatment of the reimbursement of Expenses of Travel and Subsistence to Office Holders and Employees – SP IT/2/07
PAYE System – Employee payroll tax deductions in relation to non-Irish employments exercised in the State – SP IT/3/07

Cross References

To Section 983

Section 15 Rate of charge.
Section 124 Tax treatment of certain severance payments.
Section 125 Tax treatment of benefits received under permanent health benefit schemes.
Section 126 Tax treatment of certain benefits payable under Social Welfare Acts.
Section 127 Tax treatment of restrictive covenants.
Section 458 Deductions allowed in ascertaining taxable income and provisions relating to reductions in tax.
Section 459 General provisions relating to allowances, deductions and reliefs.
Section 470B Age-related relief for health insurance premiums.
Section 472 Employee tax credit.
Section 488 Interpretation (Part 16).
Section 520 Interpretation (Chapter 1).
Section 527 Interim refunds of appropriate tax.
Section 531 Payments to subcontractors in certain industries.
Section 531A Definitions (Part 18A).
Section 531B Charge to income levy.
Section 531AL Definitions (Part 18D).
Section 779 Charge to income tax of pensions under Schedule E.

Section 784 Retirement annuities: relief for premiums.
Section 784A Approved retirement fund.
Section 787G Taxation of payments from a PRSA.
Section 864A Electronic claims.
Section 865 Repayment of tax.
Section 897A Returns by employers in relation to pension products.
Section 903 Power of inspection: PAYE.
Section 950 Interpretation (Part 41).
Section 960A Interpretation.
Section 1001 Liability to tax, etc. of holder of fixed charge on book debts of company.
Section 1003 Payment of tax by means of donation of heritage items.
Section 1078 Revenue offences.
Section 1079 Duties of relevant person in relation to certain revenue offences.
Section 1084 Surcharge for late returns.
Schedule 31 Consequential Amendments

984 Application

[ITA67 s125; FA85 s6(1) and (2)]

(1) This Chapter shall apply to all emoluments except emoluments which are emoluments in respect of which the employer has been notified by the inspector that they are emoluments which arise from an office or employment and from which, in the opinion of the inspector, having regard to the circumstances of the office or employment or to the amount of the emoluments, the deduction of tax by reference to this Chapter is impracticable.

(2) The inspector may, if a change in the circumstances of the office or employment or in the amount of the emoluments so warrants, cancel a notification given under *subsection (1)* by notice in writing given to the employer, and this Chapter shall then apply to payments of emoluments arising from the office or employment made after the date of such notice.

(3) Any notice issued by or on behalf of the Revenue Commissioners under section 125 of the Income Tax Act, 1967, before the 6th day of April, 1986, shall not have effect in relation to emoluments arising in the year 1997-98 or any subsequent year of assessment.

Revenue Briefings

eBrief

eBrief No. 82/2011 – Universal Social Charge (USC) and Income Levy - employees resident and working in non tax treaty countries

Cross References

To Section 984

Section 124 Tax treatment of certain severance payments.
Section 126 Tax treatment of certain benefits payable under Social Welfare Acts.
Section 127 Tax treatment of restrictive covenants.
Section 531B Charge to income levy.
Section 531AM Charge to universal social charge.

985 Method of collection

[ITA67 s126; FA72 s46(1) and Sch4 PtI]

On the making of any payment of any emoluments to which this Chapter applies, income tax shall, subject to this Chapter and in accordance with regulations under this Chapter, be deducted or repaid by the person making the payment notwithstanding that—

(a) when the payment is made no assessment has been made in respect of the emoluments, or

(b) the emoluments are in whole or in part emoluments for some year of assessment other than that during which the payment is made.

Case Law

Weekly distribution of tips by the company director among waiters and other staff was held to be a payment of emoluments by the company to employees. The company was liable for PAYE due on the amounts distributed. Figael Ltd v Minister Fox 1992 STC 83

An employee was in receipt of sick pay net of PAYE from his employment. When he recovered damages from his insurance he only had to repay the net amount. British Railways Board v Franklin 1993 STC 487

Revenue Briefings

eBrief

eBrief No. 03/2012 – P35 Return Filing – Importance of Recording the Correct PPS Number for Employees

Cross References

To Section 985

Section 985A Application of section 985 to certain perquisites, etc.

985A Application of section 985 to certain perquisites, etc

[(1) [Subject to *subsection (1A)*, this section applies][1] to emoluments in the form of—

(a) perquisites and profits whatever which are chargeable to tax under *section 112* [...][2] including—

(i) an expense incurred by a body corporate in the provision of a benefit, other than a contribution to a PRSA (within the meaning of *Chapter 2A* of *Part 30*), for an employee which is treated as a perquisite for the purposes of *section 112* by virtue of *section 118*,

(ii) the benefit arising from a preferential loan which is treated as a perquisite for the purposes of *section 112* by virtue of *section 122*, and

(iii) a perquisite to which *section 112A* applies,

(b) the benefit of the private use of a car which is chargeable to tax by virtue of *section 121*, and

(c) the benefit of the private use of a van which is chargeable to tax by virtue of *section 121A*.

[(1A) [Subject to *subsection (1B)*, *subsection (1)*][3] shall not apply to emoluments in the form of perquisites or profits whatever received by an employee in the form of shares (including stock) being shares or stock in—

(a) the company in which the employee holds his or her office or employment, or

(b) a company which has control (within the meaning of *section 432*) of that company.][4]

[(1B) *Subsection (1A)* shall not apply to shares or stock referred to in that subsection received on or after 1 January 2011.][5]

(2) Where an employee is in receipt of any emolument to which this section applies, the employer shall be treated for the purposes of this Chapter and regulations under this Chapter as making a payment (in this section referred to as a "*notional payment*") of an amount equal to the amount referred to in *subsection (3)*.

(3) The amount referred to in this subsection, is the amount which, on the basis of the best estimate that can reasonably be made, is the amount of income likely to be chargeable to tax under Schedule E in respect of the emolument.

(4) Where, by reason of an insufficiency of payments actually made to or on behalf of an employee, the employer is unable to deduct the amount (or full amount) of the income tax required to be deducted by virtue of this Chapter and regulations made under this Chapter, the employer shall be liable to remit to the [Collector-General][6] at such time as may be prescribed by regulation an amount of income tax equal to the amount of income tax that the employer would be required, but is unable, to deduct.

[(4A) Any amount of tax which an employer remits in accordance with *subsection (4)* and any regulations made under that subsection in respect of a notional payment shall be treated as an amount of tax which, at the time the notional payment is made, is deducted in respect of the employee's liability to income tax.][7]

[(4B) Where—

(a) an employer pays emoluments to an employee in the form of shares (including stock),

(b) *subsection (4)* applies, and

(c) the employee has not made good to the employer the amount of the income tax required to be deducted under this Part and regulations made under this Part in respect of those shares,

then—

(i) the employer shall be entitled to withhold and to realise sufficient shares to meet that income tax liability,

(ii) the employee shall allow such withholding as is referred to in *paragraph (i)*, and

(iii) the employer shall be acquitted and discharged of such withholding as if the amount of income tax required to be deducted had been paid to the employee.][8]

(5) In any case where—

(a) an employee is in receipt of an emolument to which this section applies,

(b) the employer is required by virtue of this section and regulations made there-under to remit an amount of income tax (in this subsection referred to as the "*due amount*") in respect of that emolument, and

(c) the employee does not, before the end of the year of assessment, make good the due amount to the employer,

the employee shall be chargeable to tax under Schedule E in respect of the due amount for the next following year of assessment and the due amount shall be treated for that year as an emolument to which this section applies.

(6) The Revenue Commissioners may make regulations to make provision—

(a) with respect to the deduction, collection and recovery of amounts to be accounted for in respect of notional payments;

(b) applying (with or without modifications) any specified provisions of regulations for the time being in force in relation to deductions from actual payments to amounts to be accounted for in respect of any notional payments.

[(7) Every regulation made under this section shall be laid before Dáil Éireann as soon as may be after it is made and, if a resolution annulling the regulation is passed by Dáil Éireann within the next 21 days on which Dáil Éireann has sat after the regulation is laid before it, the regulation shall be annulled accordingly, but without prejudice to the validity of anything previously done thereunder.][9]][10]

Amendments

[1] Substituted by FA04 s9(1)(a)(i)(I).

[2] Deleted by FA04 s9(1)(a)(i)(II).

[3] Substituted by FA11 s10(c). Deemed to have come into force and takes effect as on and from 1 January 2011.

[4] Inserted by FA04 s9(1)(a)(ii).

[5] Inserted by FA11 s10(d). Deemed to have come into force and takes effect as on and from 1 January 2011.

[6] Substituted by FA08No.2 sched4(part2). Applies as respects any tax that becomes due and payable on or after 1 March 2009.

[7] Inserted by FA04 s9(1)(a)(iii). Applies as respects the year of assessment 2004 and subsequent years of assessment.

[8] Inserted by FA12 s4(1)(c). Deemed to have come into force and takes effect on and from 1 January 2012.

[9] Inserted by FA04 s9(1)(a)(iv).

[10] Inserted by FA03 s6(1)(d). This section applies and has effect as on and from 1 January 2004.

Revenue Briefings

Tax Briefing

Tax Briefing May 2003 – Issue 52 pg 8 – Income Tax, Benefits in Kind
Tax Briefing May 2006 – Issue 63 pg 22 – Restricted Stock Units, Income Tax

eBrief

eBrief No. 36/2011 - Employer contributions to PRSAs - Income Tax, PRSI and USC

Cross References

From Section 985A

Section 112 Basis of assessment, persons chargeable and extent of charge.
Section 112A Taxation of certain perquisites.
Section 118 Benefits in kind: general charging provision.
Section 121 Benefit of use of car.
Section 121A Benefit of use of van.
Section 122 Preferential loan arrangements.
Section 432 Meaning of "associated company" and "control".
Section 770 Interpretation and supplemental (Chapter 1).
Section 985 Method of collection.

To Section 985A

Section 196A State employees: foreign service allowances.
Section 196B Employees of certain agencies: foreign service allowances.
Section 960O Winding-up of companies: priority for taxes.
Section 960P Bankruptcy: priority for taxes.
Section 985D PAYE: employee of non-resident employer, etc.

985B PAYE settlement agreements

[(1) In this section "*qualifying emoluments*" means emoluments, other than emoluments in the form of a payment of money, which are—

(a) minor, as regards the amount or type of emolument involved, and

(b) irregular, as to the frequency in which or the times at which, the emoluments are provided.

(2) Subject to this section, the Revenue Commissioners may, on application in that behalf from an employer, enter into an agreement with the employer under which the employer shall account to them in accordance with the provisions of this section in respect of income tax in respect of qualifying emoluments for a year of assessment of one or more employees of the employer which the employer

would otherwise have to account for in accordance with the other provisions of this Chapter and any regulations made under those provisions.

(3) Where an employer accounts for income tax under an agreement made in accordance with this section—

(a) the employer shall not be liable to account for that tax under the other provisions of this Chapter and any regulations made under those provisions,

(b) qualifying emoluments covered by the agreement shall not be reckoned in computing, for the purposes of the Income Tax Acts, the total income of the employee concerned,

(c) the amount accounted for shall not be treated as having been deducted in accordance with the other provisions of this Chapter and any regulations under those provisions,

(d) an employee shall not be treated as having paid any part of the income tax accounted for by his or her employer and, accordingly, the employee shall not be entitled to a credit in respect of, or to claim or receive repayment of, any part of that tax, and

(e) emoluments covered by the agreement shall not be included in a return by the employer under Regulation 31 of the Income Tax (Employments) (Consolidated) Regulations 2001 (S.I. No. 559 of 2001).

(4) The amount in respect of income tax to be accounted for by an employer under an agreement entered into under this section shall be specified in the agreement and shall be—

(a) determined in accordance with the factors specified in *subsection (5)(a)*, and

(b) comprised of the amounts specified in *subsection (5)(b)*.

(5) (a) The factors specified for the purposes of *subsection (4)(a)* are—

(i) the aggregate amount of the qualifying emoluments covered by the agreement on which income tax is chargeable,

(ii) the total number of employees in receipt of qualifying emoluments covered by the agreement,

(iii) the number of those employees respectively chargeable to income tax—

(I) only at the standard rate for the year of assessment to which the agreement relates, and

(II) at both the standard rate and the higher rate for that year,

and

(iv) such other matters as are agreed by the Revenue Commissioners and the employer to be relevant in relation to the qualifying emoluments covered by the agreement.

(b) The amounts specified for the purposes of *subsection (4)(b)* are—

(i) an amount equal to income tax on the aggregate of the amounts computed in accordance with *paragraph (a)(i)*, calculated so as to take account of the factor specified in *paragraph (a)(iii)*, and

(ii) a further amount reflecting the income tax on the benefit to the employees of receiving the qualifying emoluments included in the agreement without liability to tax.

(6) Where an employer wishes to avail of this section for a year of assessment, the employer shall make application in writing in that behalf to the Revenue Commissioners which is received by them on or before 31 December in that year.

(7) If the amount of income tax which an employer is to account for in relation to a year of assessment in accordance with an agreement entered into under this section is not paid to the Collector-General within 46 days of the end of that year, the agreement shall be null and void and, accordingly, this Chapter and any regulations made thereunder shall apply as if this section had not been enacted.

(8) Any act to be performed or function to be discharged by the Revenue Commissioners which is authorised by this section may be performed or discharged by any of their officers acting under their authority.][1]

Amendments

[1] Inserted by FA04 s9(1)(a)(b). Has effect as on and from 25 March 2004.

985C PAYE: payment by intermediary

[(1) Subject to *subsection (2)*, where any payment of emoluments of an employee is made by an intermediary of the employer, the employer shall be treated, for the purposes of this Chapter and regulations made under this Chapter, as making a payment of such emoluments of an amount equal to the amount referred to in *subsection (3)*.

(2) *Subsection (1)* does not apply if the intermediary deducts income tax from the payment to the employee and accounts for it in accordance with this Chapter and regulations made under this Chapter.

(3) The amount referred to in this subsection is—

(a) if the amount of the payment made by the intermediary is an amount to which the recipient is entitled after deduction of any income tax, the aggregate of the amount of that payment and the amount of any income tax due, and

(b) in any other case, the amount of the payment made by the intermediary.

(4) For the purposes of this section, a payment of emoluments of an employee is made by an intermediary of the employer if it is made—

(a) by a person acting on behalf of the employer and at the expense of the employer or a person connected (within the meaning of *section 10*) with the employer, or

(b) by trustees holding property for any persons who include, or class of persons which includes, the employee.][1]

Amendments

[1] Inserted by FA06 s16. Applies with effect from 31 March 2006.

Statements of Practice

Tax Treatment of the Reimbursement of Expenses of Travel and Subsistence to Office Holders and Employees – SP IT/2/07

PAYE System – Employee Payroll Tax Deductions in relation to Non-Irish Employments exercised in the State – SP IT/3/07

Cross References

From Section 985C

Section 10 Connected persons.

985D PAYE: employee of non-resident employer, etc

[(1) In this section and *sections 985E* and *985F*, "*work*", in relation to an employee, means the performance of any duties of the office or employment of the employee and any reference to the employee working shall be construed accordingly.

(2) This subsection applies where—

(a) an employee, during any period, works for a person (in this section referred to as the "*relevant person*") who is not the employee's employer,

(b) any payment of emoluments of the employee in respect of work done in that period is made by a person who is the employer or an intermediary of the employer or of the relevant person,

(c) the person making the payment or, if that person makes the payment as an intermediary of the employer or of the relevant person, the employer is not resident in the State, and

(d) income tax is not deducted or accounted for in accordance with this Chapter and regulations made under this Chapter, by the person making the payment or, if that person makes the payment as an intermediary of the employer or of the relevant person, the employer.

(3) Where *subsection (2)* applies, the relevant person shall be treated, for the purposes of this Chapter and regulations made under this Chapter, as making a payment of emoluments of the employee of an amount equal to the amount referred to in *subsection (4)*.

(4) The amount referred to in this subsection is—

(a) if the amount of the payment, referred to in *subsection (2)*, actually made is an amount to which the recipient is entitled after deduction of any income tax, the aggregate of the amount of that payment and the amount of any income tax due, and

(b) in any other case, the amount of that payment actually made.

(5) Where, by virtue of *section 985A*, an employer is treated for the purposes of this Chapter and regulations made under this Chapter as making a payment of any amount to an employee, this section shall have effect—

(a) as if the employer were treated for the purposes of this section as making an actual payment of that amount, and

(b) as if *paragraph (a)* of *subsection (4)* were omitted.

(6) For the purposes of this section, a payment of emoluments of an employee is made by an intermediary of the employer or of the relevant person if it is made—

(a) by a person acting on behalf of the employer or the relevant person and at the expense of the employer or the relevant person or a person connected (within the meaning of *section 10*) with the employer or the relevant person, or

(b) by trustees holding property for any persons who include, or class of persons which includes, the employee.][1]

Amendments

[1] Inserted by FA06 s16. Applies with effect from 31 March 2006

Revenue Information Notes

Tax Treatment of the Reimbursement of Expenses of Travel and Subsistence to Office Holders and Employees – SP IT/2/07

PAYE System – Employee Payroll Tax Deductions in relation to Non-Irish Employments exercised in the State – SP IT/3/07

Statements of Practice

Tax Treatment of the Reimbursement of Expenses of Travel and Subsistence to Office Holders and Employees – SP IT/2/07

PAYE System – Employee Payroll Tax Deductions in relation to Non-Irish Employments exercised in the State – SP IT/3/07

Cross References

From Section 985D

Section 10 Connected persons.

Section 985A Application of section 985 to certain perquisites, etc.

Section 985E PAYE: employment not wholly exercised in State.

Section 985F PAYE: mobile workforce.

To Section 985D

Section 985E PAYE: employment not wholly exercised in State.

985E PAYE: employment not wholly exercised in State

[(1) (a) In this section "*appropriate person*" means the person designated by the employer for the purposes of this section, and if no person is so designated, the employer.

(b) In this section any reference to a payment made by the employer includes a reference to a payment made by a person acting on behalf of the employer and at the expense of the employer or a person connected (within the meaning of *section 10*) with the employer.

(2) This section applies in relation to an employee in a year of assessment only if the employee works or will work in the State and also works or is likely to work outside the State.

(3) Where in relation to any year of assessment it appears to an officer of the Revenue Commissioners that—

(a) some of the income of an employee to whom this section applies is assessable to income tax under Schedule E, but

(b) an as yet unascertainable proportion of the income may prove not to be so assessable,

then the officer may, on an application made by the appropriate person, give a direction for determining a proportion of any payment made in that year of, or on account of, income of the employee which shall be treated for the purposes of this Chapter and regulations made under this Chapter as a payment of emoluments of the employee.

(4) An application for a direction under *subsection (3)* shall provide such information as is available and is relevant to the giving of the direction.

(5) A direction under *subsection (3)*—

(a) shall specify the employee to whom and the year of assessment to which it relates,

(b) shall be given by notice to the appropriate person, and

(c) may be withdrawn by notice to the appropriate person from a date specified in the notice.

(6) The date specified under *subsection (5)(c)* may not be earlier than 30 days from the date on which the notice of the withdrawal is given.

(7) Where—

(a) a direction under *subsection (3)* has effect in relation to an employee to whom this section applies, and

(b) a payment of, or on account of, the income of the employee is made in the year of assessment to which the direction relates,

then the proportion of the payment determined in accordance with the direction shall be treated for the purposes of this Chapter and regulations made under this Chapter as a payment of emoluments of the employee.

(8) Where in any year of assessment—

(a) no direction under *subsection (3)* has effect in relation to an employee to whom this section applies, and

(b) any payment is made of, or on account of, the income of the employee,

then the entire payment shall be treated for the purposes of this Chapter and regulations made under this Chapter as a payment of emoluments of the employee.

(9) *Subsections (7)* and *(8)* are without prejudice to—

(a) any assessment in respect of the income of the employee in question, and

(b) any right to repayment of income tax overpaid and any obligation to pay income tax underpaid.

(10) In a case where *section 985D* applies—

(a) the references to the employer in *subsection (1)(a)* include references to the relevant person (within the meaning of that section), and

(b) any reference to a payment made by the employer includes a reference to a payment treated, for the purposes of this Chapter and regulations made under this Chapter, as made by the relevant person.][1]

Amendments

[1] Inserted by FA06 s16. Applies with effect from 31 March 2006.

Revenue Briefings

Tax Briefing

Tax Briefing August 2006 – Issue 64 – PAYE Foreign Employments

Statements of Practice

Tax Treatment of the Reimbursement of Expenses of Travel and Subsistence to Office Holders and Employees – SP IT/2/07

PAYE System – Employee Payroll Tax Deductions in relation to Non-Irish Employments exercised in the State – SP IT/3/07

Cross References

From Section 985E

Section 10 Connected persons.

Section 985D PAYE: employee of non-resident employer, etc.

To Section 985E

Section 985D PAYE: employee of non-resident employer, etc.

985F PAYE: mobile workforce

[(1) This section applies where it appears to the Revenue Commissioners that—

(a) a person (in this section referred to as the "*relevant person*") has entered into or is likely to enter into an agreement that employees of another person (in this section referred to as the "*contractor*") shall in any period work for, but not as employees of, the relevant person,

(b) payments of emoluments of the employees in respect of work done in that period are likely to be made by or on behalf of the contractor, and

(c) this Chapter and regulations made under this Chapter would apply on the making of such payments but it is likely that income tax will not be deducted or accounted for in accordance with this Chapter and such regulations.

(2) Where this section applies, the Revenue Commissioners may give a direction that if—

(a) any employees of the contractor work in any period for, but not as employees of, the relevant person, and

(b) any payment is made by the relevant person in respect of work done by the employees in that period,

income tax shall be deducted in accordance with this section by the relevant person on making that payment.

(3) A direction under *subsection (2)*—

(a) shall specify the relevant person and the contractor to whom it relates,

(b) shall be given by notice to the relevant person, and

(c) may at any time be withdrawn by notice to the relevant person.

(4) The Revenue Commissioners shall take such steps as are reasonably practicable to ensure that the contractor is supplied with a copy of any notice given under *subsection (3)* which relates to the contractor.

(5) Where—

(a) a direction under *subsection (2)* has effect, and

(b) any employees of the contractor specified in the direction work for, but not as employees of, the relevant person so specified,

income tax shall, subject to and in accordance with this Chapter and regulations made under this Chapter, be deducted by the relevant person on making any payment in respect of that work as if so much of the payment as is attributable to work done by each employee were a payment of emoluments of that employee.][1]

Amendments

[1] Inserted by FA06 s16. Applies with effect from 31 March 2006.

Statements of Practice

Tax Treatment of the Reimbursement of Expenses of Travel and Subsistence to Office Holders and Employees – SP IT/2/07

PAYE System – Employee Payroll Tax Deductions in relation to Non-Irish Employments exercised in the State – SP IT/3/07

Cross References

To Section 985F

Section 985D PAYE: employee of non-resident employer, etc.

986 Regulations

[ITA67 s127(1), (2), (3)(a)(i) and (b) (part of), (4), (5) and (7); FA72 s2(1); FA74 s11 and Sch1 PtII; FA93 s2(2) and Sch1 PtI par2; FA97 s6]

(1) The Revenue Commissioners shall make regulations with respect to the assessment, charge, collection and recovery of income tax in respect of emoluments to which this Chapter applies or of income tax for any previous year of assessment remaining unpaid, and those regulations may, in particular and without prejudice to the generality of the foregoing, include provision—

(a) for requiring any employer making any payment of emoluments to which this Chapter applies, when that employer makes the payment, to make a deduction or repayment of tax calculated by reference to such rate or rates of tax for the year as may be specified and any [reliefs from income tax][1] appropriate in the case of the employee as indicated by the particulars on the tax deduction card supplied in respect of the employee by the Revenue Commissioners;

(b) for rendering persons who are required to make any such deduction or repayment, in the case of a deduction (whether or not made), accountable for the amount of the tax and liable to pay that amount to the Revenue Commissioners and, in the case of a repayment, entitled (if a repayment has been made) to be paid it, or given credit for it, by the Revenue Commissioners;

(c) for the production to and inspection by persons authorised by the Revenue Commissioners of wages sheets and other documents and records for the purpose of satisfying themselves that tax in respect of emoluments to which this Chapter applies has been and is being duly deducted, repaid and accounted for;

(d) for the collection and recovery, whether by deduction from emoluments paid in any year or otherwise, of tax in respect of emoluments to which this Chapter applies which has not been deducted or otherwise recovered during the year;

(e) for appeals with respect to matters arising under the regulations which would not otherwise be the subject of an appeal;

(f) for the deduction of tax at the standard rate and at the higher rate in such cases or classes of cases as may be provided for by the regulations;

[(g) for requiring any employer making any payment of emoluments to which this Chapter applies, when making a deduction or repayment of tax in accordance with this Chapter and regulations under this Chapter, to make such deduction or repayment as would require to be made if the amount of emoluments were the emoluments reduced by the amount of any contributions payable by the employee and deductible by the employer from the emoluments being paid and which—

(i) by virtue of *section 471* are allowed as a deduction in ascertaining the amount of income on which the employee is to be charged to income tax, or

(ii) by virtue of [*Chapter 1*, *Chapter 2* or *Chapter 2A* of *Part 30*][2] are for the purposes of assessment under Schedule E allowed as a deduction from the emoluments;][3]

(h) for requiring every employer who pays emoluments to which this Chapter applies exceeding the limit specified in *subsection (5)* to notify the Revenue Commissioners within the period specified in the regulations that that employer is such an employer;

(i) for requiring every employer who pays emoluments to which this Chapter applies exceeding the limits specified in *subsection (5)* to keep and maintain a register of that employer's employees in such manner as may be specified in the regulations and, on being required to do so by the Revenue Commissioners, to deliver the register to the Revenue Commissioners within the period specified in the notice;

(j) for treating persons who are not employers as employers in such cases or classes of cases as may be provided for by the [regulations;][4]

[(k) for the collection and recovery, to the extent that the Revenue Commissioners deem appropriate and the employee does not object, of tax in respect of income other than emoluments to which this Chapter applies, which has not otherwise been recovered during the year;

(l) for the collection and recovery, from the employee rather than from the employer of any amount of tax that the Revenue Commissioners consider should have been deducted by the employer from the emoluments of the employee;

(m) for requiring any employer making any payment of emoluments to which this Chapter applies to provide, within a prescribed time, and on such form as the Revenue Commissioners may approve or prescribe, information in relation to payments of emoluments (including emoluments in the form of notional payments) and tax deducted from such emoluments, and such other information or documents as the Revenue Commissioners deem [appropriate,][5]][6]

[(n) for the making available by the Revenue Commissioners of an electronic system or systems to allow employers and employees to fulfil their obligations under this Chapter and regulations made under this Chapter and to allow further for electronic communications between the Revenue Commissioners, officers of the Revenue Commissioners, employers and employees and other persons pursuant to obligations under those provisions and for the provision of enhancements or other changes to that system or those systems, as the case may be, and for any replacement for any such system or systems,

(o) for requiring every employer who makes a payment to which this Chapter applies to an employee to notify the Revenue Commissioners within the period specified in the regulations of the employee particulars specified in the regulations,

(p) for requiring every employer who pays emoluments to which this Chapter applies exceeding the limit specified in *subsection (5)* to register with the Revenue Commissioners within the time limit specified in the regulations.][7]

(2) Regulations under this section shall apply notwithstanding anything in the Income Tax Acts, but shall not affect any right of appeal which a person would have apart from the regulations.

(3) (a) Tax deduction cards shall be prepared with a view to securing that in so far as may be practicable the total tax payable for the year of assessment in respect of any emoluments is deducted from the emoluments paid during that year.

(b) In *paragraph (a)*, any reference to the total tax payable for a year shall be construed as a reference to the total tax estimated to be payable for the year in respect of the emoluments, subject to a [provisional reliefs from income tax][8] and subject also, if necessary, to making an addition to that estimated amount (including a nil amount) for amounts remaining unpaid on account of income tax for any previous year of assessment and to making a deduction from that estimated amount for amounts overpaid on account of any such income tax.

(4) Notwithstanding any other provision of this section, when stating on a tax deduction card an amount in respect of [reliefs from income tax][9] the amount may be rounded up to a convenient greater amount and stated accordingly, and, as respects the amount of tax which is not deducted in the year of assessment as a result of such statement, the adjustment appropriate for its recovery shall be made in a subsequent year of assessment.

(5) (a) The limits referred to in *paragraphs (h)* and *(i)* of *subsection (1)* shall be emoluments at a rate equivalent to a rate of [€8][10] per week, or in the case of an employee with other employment, [€2][11] per week.

(b) In the case of employees paid monthly or at longer intervals, the references in *paragraph (a)* to a rate of [€8][12] per week and a rate of [€2][13] per week shall be treated as references to a rate of [€36][14] per month and a rate of [€9][15] per month respectively.

(6) (a) In this subsection—

"*domestic employee*" means an employee who is employed solely on domestic duties (including the minding of children) in the employer's private dwelling house;

"*domestic employment*" means employment by reference to which an employee is a domestic employee.

(b) Notwithstanding *subsection (5)*, as on and from the 6th day of June, 1997, regulations made in accordance with *paragraphs (h)* and *(i)* of *subsection (1)* shall not apply to an employer (being an individual) who pays emoluments to an employee engaged by that employer in a domestic employment where—

(i) the emoluments from that employment are less than [€40][16] per week, and

(ii) the employer has only one such employee.

[(6A) Notwithstanding any other provision of this section, where the Revenue Commissioners are satisfied that it is unnecessary or is not appropriate for an employer to comply with any of the regulations made under subsection (1) they may notify the employer accordingly.][17]

(7) Every regulation made under this section shall be laid before Dáil Éireann as soon as may be after it is made and, if a resolution annulling the regulation is passed by Dáil Éireann within the next 21 days on which Dáil Éireann has sat after the regulation is laid before it, the regulation shall be annulled accordingly, but without prejudice to the validity of anything previously done thereunder.

Amendments

[1] Substituted by FA01 sched1(1)(t)(i)(I). Applies as respects the year of assessment 2001 and subsequent years of assessment.

[2] Substituted by FA03 s14(1)(f). Has effect as on and from 28 March 2003.

[3] Substituted by FA01 sched1(1)(t)(i)(II). Applies as respects the year of assessment 2001 and subsequent years of assessment.

[4] Substituted by FA08 s17(a).

[5] Inserted by FA08 s17(b).

[6] Substituted by FA12 s15(a). Deemed to have come into force and takes effect on and from 1 January 2012.

[7] Inserted by FA12 s15(b). Deemed to have come into force and takes effect on and from 1 January 2012.

[8] Substituted by FA01 sched1(1)(t)(ii). Applies as respects the year of assessment 2001 and subsequent years of assessment.

[9] Substituted by FA01 sched1(1)(t)(iii). Applies as respects the year of assessment 2001 and subsequent years of assessment.

[10, 11, 12, 13, 14, 15, 16] Substituted by FA01 sched5.

[17] Inserted by FA08 s17(c).

Case Law

It was held that enforcement proceedings under the operation of PAYE regulations were valid. Director of Public Prosecutions v Downes 1987 III ITR 641

Cross References

From Section 986

Section 471 Relief for contributions to permanent health benefit schemes.

To Section 986

Section 481 Relief for investment in films.
Section 501 Claims.
Section 502 Assessments for withdrawing relief.
Section 531 Payments to subcontractors in certain industries.
Section 960A Interpretation.
Section 987 Penalties for breach of regulations.
Section 989 Estimation of tax due for income tax months.
Schedule 29 Provisions Referred to in Sections 1052, 1053 and 1054

987 Penalties for breach of regulations

[ITA67 s128(1), (1A), (2) and (4); FA72 s2(2); FA73 s43; FA76 s1; FA81 s4; FA82 s60; FA92 s234 and s248]

[(1) Where any person fails—

(a) to comply with any provision of regulations under this Chapter requiring that person to send any return, statement, notification or certificate, other than the end of year return required under Regulation 31 of the Income Tax (Employments) (Consolidated) Regulations 2001 (S.I. No. 559 of 2001),

(b) to remit income tax to the Collector-General, or

(c) to make any deduction or repayment in accordance with any regulation made pursuant to section 986(1)(*g*),

[(d) to register with the Revenue Commissioners in accordance with Regulation 7 of the Income Tax (Employment) (Consolidated) Regulations 2001 (S.I. No. 559 of 2001), or

(e) to keep and maintain a register of employees in accordance with Regulation 8 of the Income Tax (Employment) (Consolidated) Regulations 2001 (S.I. No. 559 of 2001),][1]

then that person shall be liable to a penalty of €4,000",][2]

[(1A) Where any person fails to send an end of year return to the Collector-General in accordance with [Regulation 31 of the Income Tax (Employments) (Consolidated) Regulations 2001 (S.I. No. 559 of 2001)][3], that person shall be liable to a penalty of [€1,000][4] for each month or part of a month during which the said return remains outstanding, subject to a maximum penalty of [€4,000][5].][6]

(2) Where the person mentioned in [*subsection (1)* or *(1A)*][7] is a body of persons, the secretary of the body shall be liable to a separate penalty of [€3,000][8].

[...][9]

(4) In proceedings for recovery of a penalty under this section—

(a) a certificate signed by an officer of the Revenue Commissioners which certifies that he or she has inspected the relevant records of the Revenue Commissioners and that it appears from them that during a stated period—

(i) a stated return, statement, notification or certificate was not received from the defendant,

(ii) stated wages sheets or other records or documents were not produced by the defendant,

(iii) the defendant did not remit stated tax to the Collector-General, or

(iv) the defendant did not make a stated deduction or repayment of tax,

shall be evidence until the contrary is proved that the defendant did not during that period send that return, statement, notification or certificate or did not produce those wages sheets or other records or documents or did not remit that tax to the Collector-General or did not make that deduction or repayment of tax;

(b) a certificate signed by an officer of the Revenue Commissioners which certifies that he or she has inspected the relevant records of the Revenue Commissioners and that it appears from them that a stated return or other document was duly sent to the defendant on a stated day shall be evidence until the contrary is proved that that person received that return or other document in the ordinary course;

(c) a certificate signed by an officer of the Revenue Commissioners which certifies that he or she has inspected the relevant records of the Revenue Commissioners and that it appears from them that during a stated period the defendant was an employer or a person whose name and address were registered in the register kept and maintained under [Regulation 7(4) of the Income Tax (Employments) (Consolidated) Regulations 2001 (S.I. No. 559 of 2001)][10], shall be evidence until the contrary is proved that the defendant was during that period an employer or, as the case may be, a person whose name and address were so registered;

(d) a certificate certifying as provided for in *paragraph (a)*, *(b)* or *(c)* and purporting to be signed by an officer of the Revenue Commissioners may be tendered in evidence without proof and shall be deemed until the contrary is proved to have been signed by an officer of the Revenue Commissioners.

Amendments

[1] Inserted by FA12 s15(c). Deemed to have come into force and takes effect on and from 1 January 2012.

[2] Substituted by F(No.2)A08 sched5(part2)(1)(y)(i). The enactments specified in Schedule 5 are amended or repealed to the extent and manner specified in that Schedule and, unless the contrary is stated, shall come into effect after 24 December 2008.

[3] Substituted by FA02 sched6(3)(p)(i). Shall be deemed to have come into force and take effect as on and from 1 January 2002.

[4] Substituted by F(No.2)A08 sched5(part2)(1)(y)(ii)(I). The enactments specified in Schedule 5 are amended or repealed to the extent and manner specified in that Schedule and, unless the contrary is stated, shall come into effect after 24 December 2008.

[5] Substituted by F(No.2)A08 sched5(part2)(1)(y)(ii)(II). The enactments specified in Schedule 5 are amended or repealed to the extent and manner specified in that Schedule and, unless the contrary is stated, shall come into effect after 24 December 2008.

[6] Inserted by FA99 s25(b).

[7] Substituted by FA99 s25(c).

[8] Substituted by F(No.2)A08 sched5(part2)(1)(y)(iii). The enactments specified in Schedule 5 are amended or repealed to the extent and manner specified in that Schedule and, unless the contrary is stated, shall come into effect after 24 December 2008.

[9] Deleted by F(No.2)A08 sched5(part2)(1)(y)(iv). The enactments specified in Schedule 5 are amended or repealed to the extent and manner specified in that Schedule and, unless the contrary is stated, shall come into effect after 24 December 2008.

[10] Substituted by FA02 sched6(3)(p)(ii). Shall be deemed to have come into force and take effect as on and from 1 January 2002.

Revenue Briefings

Tax Briefing

Tax Briefing June 2014 – Issue 05 – PAYE: Employer's obligation to keep, maintain and produce a Register of Employees

Cross References

From Section 987

Section 986 Regulations.

To Section 987

Section 531 Payments to subcontractors in certain industries.
Section 531M Application of provisions relating to income tax.
Section 531Z Penalties.
Section 988 Registration of certain persons as employers and requirement to send certain notifications.
Section 1064 Time for certain summary proceedings.
Section 1078 Revenue offences.
Schedule 31 Consequential Amendments

988 Registration of certain persons as employers and requirement to send certain notifications

[FA74 s72]

(1) Where the Revenue Commissioners have reason to believe that a person is liable to send them a notification under [Regulation 7 of the Income Tax (Employments) (Consolidated) Regulations 2001 (S.I. No. 559 of 2001)][1], and has not done so, they may register that person's name and address in the register kept and maintained under paragraph (4) of that regulation (in this section referred to as "*the register*") and serve a notice on that person stating that that person has been so registered.

(2) Where a notice is served under *subsection (1)* on a person, the following provisions shall apply:

(a) if the person claims to be not liable to send the notification referred to in *subsection (1)*, the person may, by giving notice in writing to the Revenue Commissioners within the period of 14 days from the service of the notice under *subsection (1)*, require the claim to be referred to the Appeal Commissioners and their decision on the claim shall be final and conclusive;

(b) if no such claim is, within the time specified in *paragraph (a)*, required to be referred, or if such claim is required to be referred and there is a determination by the Appeal Commissioners against the appellant, the appellant shall be regarded for the purposes of the Regulations referred to in *subsection (1)* as an employer who had sent a notification under paragraph (1) of regulation 8 of those Regulations;

(c) *if a claim is required to be referred and there is a determination by the Appeal Commissioners in favour of the appellant, the Revenue Commissioners shall on that determination delete the appellant's name and address from the register.*

(3) (a) Where a person whose name and address is registered in the register is not liable, under [Regulation 28][2] of the Regulations referred to in *subsection (1)*, to remit to the Collector-General any amount of tax for an income tax month, such person shall, within the period of 9 days from the end of that month, make a declaration to that effect in a form prescribed by the Revenue Commissioners and shall send that form to the Collector-General.

(b) Where a person whose name and address is registered in the register ceases to pay emoluments to which this Chapter applies, such person shall, within the period of 14 days from the date on which such person ceased to pay such emoluments, notify the Revenue Commissioners to that effect.

(4) *Section 987* shall apply to a non-compliance with *subsection (3)* as it applies to a non-compliance with regulations under this Chapter.

Amendments

[1] Substituted by FA02 sched6(3)(q)(i). Shall be deemed to have come into force and take effect as on and from 1 January 2002.

[2] Substituted by FA02 sched6(3)(q)(ii). Shall be deemed to have come into force and take effect as on and from 1 January 2002.

Cross References

From Section 988

Section 987 Penalties for breach of regulations.

989 Estimation of tax due for income tax months

[FA68 s7(1), (2), (4), (5) and (8); FA85 s9(a)]

(1) In this section and in *sections 990* and *991*, "*the regulations*" means any regulations under *section 986*.

(2) Where the Revenue Commissioners have reason to believe that a person was liable under the regulations to remit income tax in relation to any income tax month, and the person has not remitted any income tax in relation to that income tax month, they may—

(a) estimate the amount of tax which should have been remitted by the person within the period specified in the regulations for the payment of such tax, and

(b) serve notice on the person of the amount so estimated.

(3) Where a notice is served under *subsection (2)* on a person, the following provisions shall apply:

(a) the person, if claiming to be not liable to remit any tax for the income tax month to which the notice relates, may by giving notice in writing to the Revenue Commissioners within the period of 14 days from the service of the notice require the claim to be referred for decision to the Appeal Commissioners and their decision shall be final and conclusive;

(b) on the expiration of that period, if no such claim is required to be so referred or, if such claim is required to be referred, on final determination by the Appeal Commissioners against the claim, the estimated tax specified in the notice shall be recoverable in the like manner and by the like proceedings as if—

(i) the person were an employer, and

(ii) the amount specified in the notice were the amount of tax which the person was liable under the regulations to deduct from emoluments paid by the person during the income tax month specified in the notice reduced by any amounts which the person was liable under the regulations to repay during the income tax month;

(c) if at any time after the service of the notice the person furnishes a declaration of the amount which the person is liable under the regulations to remit in respect of the income tax month specified in the notice and pays the tax in accordance with the declaration together with any interest and costs which may have been incurred in connection with the default, the notice shall, subject to *paragraph (d)*, stand discharged and any excess of tax which may have been paid shall be repaid;

(d) where action for the recovery of tax specified in a notice under *subsection (2)* has been taken, being action by means of the institution of proceedings in any court or the issue of a certificate under [section 960L][1], *paragraph (c)* shall not, unless the Revenue Commissioners otherwise direct, apply in relation to that notice until that action [has been completed;][2]

[(e) where—

(i) the amount of tax estimated in the notice is remitted and a declaration referred to in *paragraph (c)* is not furnished, or

(ii) the Revenue Commissioners have reason to believe that the amount estimated in the notice is less than the amount which the person was liable to remit,

the Revenue Commissioners may amend the amount so estimated by increasing it and serve notice on the person concerned of the revised amount estimated and such notice shall supersede any previous notice issued under *subsection (2)*.][3]

(4) A notice given by the Revenue Commissioners under *subsection (2)* [or *subsection (3)(e)*][4] may extend to 2 or more consecutive income tax months.

(5) The Revenue Commissioners may nominate any of their officers to perform any acts and discharge any functions authorised by this section to be performed or discharged by the Revenue Commissioners.

Amendments

[1] Substituted by FA08No.2 sched4(part2). Applies as respects any tax that becomes due and payable on or after 1 March 2009.

[2] Substituted by FA03 s157(a)(i).

[3] Inserted by FA03 s157(a)(ii).

[4] Inserted by FA03 s157(a)(iii).

Case Law

In Kennedy v Hearne and others 1988 III ITR 590 it was held that enforcing liabilities, deducting PAYE, and charging interest is not unconstitutional.

Cross References

From Section 989

Section 960L Recovery by sheriff or county registrar.
Section 986 Regulations.
Section 990 Estimation of tax due for year.
Section 991 Interest.

To Section 989

Section 531G Estimation of income levy due for income tax months and for year.
Section 531Y Payment, collection and recovery.
Section 531AR Estimation of universal social charge due.
Section 960I Recovery of tax by way of civil proceedings.
Section 960O Winding-up of companies: priority for taxes.

Section 960P Bankruptcy: priority for taxes.
Section 990A Generation of estimates by electronic, photographic or other process.
Section 991 Interest.
Section 992 Appeals against estimates under section 989 or 990.

990 Estimation of tax due for year

[FA68 s8(1), (2) and (4); FA85 s9(b)]

(1) Where the inspector or such other officer as the Revenue Commissioners may nominate to exercise the powers conferred by this section (in this section referred to as "*other officer*") has reason to believe that the total amount of tax which an employer was liable under the regulations to remit in respect of the respective income tax months comprised in any year of assessment was greater than the amount of tax (if any) paid by the employer in respect of those months, then, without prejudice to any other action which may be taken, the inspector or other officer—

(a) may make an estimate in one sum of the total amount of tax which in his or her opinion should have been paid in respect of the income tax months comprised in that year, and

(b) may serve notice on the employer specifying—

(i) the total amount of tax so estimated,

(ii) the total amount of tax (if any) remitted by the employer in relation to the income tax months comprised in that year, and

(iii) the balance of tax remaining unpaid.

[(1A) (a) Where—

(i) a notice is served on an employer under *subsection (1)* in relation to a year of assessment (being the year of assessment 2000–2001 or a subsequent year of assessment), and

(ii) prior to the service of the notice, the employer had failed to submit to the Collector-General, in relation to that year of assessment, the return required by [Regulation 31 of the Income Tax (Employments) (Consolidated) Regulations 2001 (S.I. No. 559 of 2001)][1],

then, if, within 14 days after the service of the notice, the employer—

(I) sends that return to the Collector-General, and

(II) pays any balance of tax remaining unpaid for the year of assessment in accordance with the return, together with any interest and costs which may have been incurred in connection with the default,

the notice [may][2], subject to *paragraph (c)*, stand discharged and any excess of tax which may have been paid [may][3] be repaid.

(b) If, on expiration of the period referred to in *paragraph (a)*, the employer has not complied with *subparagraphs (I)* and *(II)* of *paragraph (a)*, the balance of tax remaining unpaid as specified in the notice shall become due and recoverable in the like manner as if the balance of tax had been charged on the employer under Schedule E.

(c) Where action for the recovery of tax specified in a notice under *subsection (1)* has been taken, being action by means of the institution of proceedings in any court or the issue of a certificate under [section 960L][4], so much of *paragraph (a)* as relates to the discharge of the notice shall not, unless the

Collector-General otherwise directs, apply in relation to that notice until that action has been completed.][5]

[(d) Where—

(i) the amount of tax estimated in a notice under *subsection (1)* is remitted and the return required by Regulation 31 of the Income Tax (Employments) (Consolidated) Regulations 2001 (S.I. No. 559 of 2001) is not submitted, or

(ii) the inspector or other officer has reason to believe that the amount estimated in the notice is less than the amount which the employer was liable to remit,

the inspector or other officer may amend the amount so estimated by increasing it and serve notice on the employer concerned of the revised amount estimated and such notice shall supersede any previous notice issued under *subsection (1)*.][6]

(2) Where a notice is served on an employer [under this section][7] [and prior to such service the employer had sent to the Collector-General the return required by][8][Regulation 31 of the Income Tax (Employments) (Consolidated) Regulations 2001 (S.I. No. 559 of 2001)][9]—

(a) the employer may, if claiming that the total amount of tax or the balance of tax remaining unpaid is excessive, on giving notice in writing to the inspector or other officer within the period of 30 days from the service of the notice, appeal to the Appeal Commissioners;

(b) on the expiration of that period, if no notice of appeal is received or, if notice of appeal is received, on determination of the appeal by agreement or otherwise, the balance of tax remaining unpaid as specified in the notice or the amended tax as determined in relation to the appeal shall become due and be recoverable in the like manner and by the like proceedings as if the balance of tax or the amended tax had been charged on the employer under Schedule E.

(3) A notice given by the inspector or other officer [under this section][10] may extend to 2 or more years of assessment.

Amendments

[1] Substituted by FA02 sched6(3)(r)(i). Shall be deemed to have come into force and take effect as on and from 1 January 2002.

[2, 3] Substituted by FA12 s15(d). Deemed to have come into force and takes effect on and from 1 January 2012.

[4] Substituted by FA08No.2 sched4(part2). Applies as respects any tax that becomes due and payable on or after 1 March 2009.

[5] Inserted by FA01 s237(a)(i).

[6] Inserted by FA03 s157(b).

[7] Substituted by FA12 s15(e). Deemed to have come into force and takes effect on and from 1 January 2012.

[8] Inserted by FA01 s237(a)(ii).

[9] Substituted by FA02 sched6(3)(r)(ii). Shall be deemed to have come into force and take effect as on and from 1 January 2002.

[10] Substituted by FA12 s15(f). Deemed to have come into force and takes effect on and from 1 January 2012.

Cross References

From Section 990

Section 960L Recovery by sheriff or county registrar.

To Section 990

Section 531G Estimation of income levy due for income tax months and for year.
Section 531Y Payment, collection and recovery.
Section 531AR Estimation of universal social charge due.
Section 960A Interpretation.
Section 960I Recovery of tax by way of civil proceedings.
Section 960O Winding-up of companies: priority for taxes.
Section 960P Bankruptcy: priority for taxes.
Section 989 Estimation of tax due for income tax months.
Section 990A Generation of estimates by electronic, photographic or other process.
Section 991 Interest.
Section 992 Appeals against estimates under section 989 or 990.

990A Generation of estimates by electronic, photographic or other process

[For the purposes of this Chapter—

(a) where the inspector, any officer of the Revenue Commissioners nominated by them for the purposes of *section 989 or 990* (in this section referred to as "*the nominated officer*") or any other officer of the Revenue Commissioners acting with the knowledge of the inspector or the nominated officer causes, for the purposes of *section 989* or *990*, to be issued, manually or by any electronic, photographic or other process, and to be served, a notice bearing the name of the inspector or the nominated officer, the estimate to which that notice relates shall be deemed—

(i) if that notice was issued for the purposes of *section 989*, to have been made by the nominated officer, and

(ii) if that notice was issued for the purposes of *section 990*, to have been made by the inspector or the nominated officer, as the case may be, to the best of his or her opinion,

and

(b) the provisions of [*section 959G*][1] shall, subject to any necessary modifications, apply in relation to estimates made in accordance with the provisions of *section 990* as they apply in relation to assessments to income tax.][2]

Amendments

[1] Substituted by FA12 sched4(part 2)(g).

[2] Inserted by FA99 s24. Shall apply as on and from the 6th day of April, 1999.

Cross References

From Section 990A

Section 928 Transmission to Collector-General of particulars of sums to be collected.
Section 989 Estimation of tax due for income tax months.
Section 990 Estimation of tax due for year.

To Section 990A

Section 531G Estimation of income levy due for income tax months and for year.
Section 531AR Estimation of universal social charge due.

991 Interest

[ITA67 s129; FA68 s9; FA73 s1(1); FA74 s71; FA75 s26; FA78 s46]

[(1) Where an amount of tax which an employer is liable under this Chapter and any regulations under this Chapter to pay to the Revenue Commissioners is not so paid, simple interest on the amount shall be paid by the employer to the Revenue Commissioners, and such interest shall be calculated from the expiration of the period specified in the regulations for the payment of the amount until payment—

(a) for any day or part of a day before 1 August 1978 during which the amount remains unpaid, at a rate of 0.0492 per cent,

(b) for any day or part of a day on or after 1 August 1978 and before 1 April 1998 during which the amount remains unpaid, at a rate of 0.0410 per cent,

(c) for any day or part of a day on or after 1 April 1998 and before 1 July 2009 during which the amount remains unpaid, at a rate of 0.0322 per cent, and

(d) for any day or part of a day on or after 1 July 2009 during which the amount remains unpaid, at a rate of 0.0274 per cent.][1]

[(1A) Notwithstanding anything in *subsection (1)* but subject to *subsection (1B)*, where an amount of tax (in this subsection referred to as "the relevant amount") in respect of a year of assessment (being the year of assessment 2000-2001 or a subsequent year of assessment) is paid later than 14 days after the end of that year of assessment, interest in accordance with *subsection (1)* shall be payable and calculated—

(a) where the relevant amount does not exceed 10 per cent of the total amount of tax which the employer was liable under this Chapter and any regulations made under this Chapter to pay to the Revenue Commissioners for that year of assessment, as if the due date for payment of the relevant amount was the 14th day immediately following the end of the year of assessment, and

(b) where the relevant amount exceeds 10 per cent of the amount so payable, as if the due date for payment of the relevant amount was—

(i) as respects the year of assessment 2000-2001, 31 October, 2000,

(ii) as respects the year of assessment 2001, 30 September, 2001, and

(iii) as respects the year of assessment 2002 and subsequent years of assessment, 31 July in the year.

(1B) Where, within 1 month of interest being demanded by the Collector-General in accordance with *subsection (1A)*, the employer declares in writing to the Collector-General the amounts of tax which he or she was liable to remit, but had not remitted, for each of the income tax months comprised in the year of assessment, interest shall be calculated and payable in respect of those amounts in accordance with *subsection (1)*, without regard to *subsection (1A)*.][2]

(2) This section shall apply—

(a) to tax recoverable by virtue of a notice under *section 989* as if the tax were tax which the person was liable under the regulations to pay for the respective income tax month or months referred to in the notice, and

(b) to tax recoverable by virtue of a notice under *section 990* as if the tax were tax which the person was liable under the regulations to remit for the last income tax month of the year of assessment to which the notice relates.

Amendments

[1] Substituted by FA09 s29(1)(g). Applies as respects any unpaid tax or duty, as the case may be, that has not been paid before 1 July 2009 regardless of whether that tax or duty became due and payable before, on or after that date.

[2] Inserted by FA01 s237(b).

Cross References

From Section 991

Section 989 Estimation of tax due for income tax months.
Section 990 Estimation of tax due for year.

To Section 991

Section 531Y Payment, collection and recovery.
Section 960O Winding-up of companies: priority for taxes.
Section 960P Bankruptcy: priority for taxes.
Section 989 Estimation of tax due for income tax months.
Section 991A Payment of tax by direct debit.
Section 1089 Status of interest on certain unpaid taxes and duties.

991A Payment of tax by direct debit

[Where, for a year of assessment (being the year of assessment 2000-2001 or a subsequent year of assessment)—

(a) an employer has been authorised by the Collector-General in accordance with [Regulation 29 of the Income Tax (Employments) (Consolidated) Regulations 2001 (S.I. No. 559 of 2001)][1], to remit income tax for a period longer than an income tax month, and

(b) such authorisation is subject to the condition that the employer is required each month to pay an amount to the Collector-General by direct debit from the employer's bank account,

then, the provisions of *section 991* shall apply to any tax in respect of that year of assessment which is paid by the employer after the end of that year.][2]

Amendments

[1] Substituted by FA02 sched6(3)(s). Shall be deemed to have come into force and take effect as on and from 1 January 2002.

[2] Inserted by FA01 s237(c).

Cross References

From Section 991A

Section 991 Interest.

To Section 991A

Section 531Y Payment, collection and recovery.

992 Appeals against estimates under section 989 or 990

[FA68 s10]

The provisions of the Income Tax Acts relating to appeals shall apply with any necessary modifications to claims and appeals under *sections 989(3)* and *990(2)* as if those claims or appeals were appeals against assessments to income tax but, in relation to claims under *section 989(3)*, only in so far as those provisions apply to appeals to the Appeal Commissioners.

Cross References

From Section 992

Section 989 Estimation of tax due for income tax months.

Section 990 Estimation of tax due for year.

993 Recovery of tax [Repealed]

Repealed by F(No.2)A08 sched4(part1). Applies as respects any tax that becomes due and payable on or after 1 March 2009.

Cross References

To Section 993

Schedule 31 Consequential Amendments

994 Priority in bankruptcy, etc. of certain amounts [Repealed]

Repealed by F(No.2)A08 sched4(part1). Applies as respects any tax that becomes due and payable on or after 1 March 2009.

995 Priority in winding up of certain amounts [Repealed]

Repealed by F(No.2)A08 sched4(part1). Applies as respects any tax that becomes due and payable on or after 1 March 2009.

996 Treatment for tax purposes of certain unpaid remuneration

[FA76 s17(1) to (3)(a) and (4)(b)]

(1) In this section—

"*accounting period*", in relation to a trade or profession, means a period of 12 months ending on the date up to which the accounts of the trade or profession are usually made up and, where accounts of the trade or profession have not been made up, such period not exceeding 12 months as the Revenue Commissioners may determine;

"*date of cessation*", in relation to an office or employment, means the date on which a person ceases to hold the office or employment;

"*date of commencement*", in relation to an office or employment, means the date on which a person commences to hold the office or employment;

"*period of account*", in relation to a trade or profession, means any period, other than an accounting period, for which the accounts of the trade or profession have been made up;

"*period of accrual*", in relation to remuneration in respect of an office or employment in a trade or profession, means the period beginning on the later of—

(a) the first day of an accounting period, or period of account, of the trade or profession, or

(b) the date of commencement of the office or employment,

and ending on the earlier of—

(i) the last day of an accounting period, or period of account, or

(ii) the date of cessation of the office or employment;

"*relevant date*" means—

(a) in relation to an accounting period, the last day of the period, and

(b) in relation to a period of account—

(i) where the period of account is less than 12 months, the last day of the period, and

(ii) where the period of account is more than 12 months, each [31st day of December][1] within the period and the last day of the period;

"*remuneration*" includes all salaries, fees, wages, perquisites or profits whatever from an office or employment.

(2) Where remuneration (in this section referred to as "*unpaid remuneration*") which is deductible as an expense in computing the profits or income of a trade or profession for an accounting period or period of account for the purposes of Schedule D is unpaid at a relevant date—

(a) the unpaid remuneration shall be deemed to be emoluments to which this Chapter applies and shall be deemed to have been paid in accordance with *subsection (3)*, and

(b) this Chapter and the regulations made under this Chapter shall, with any necessary modifications, apply to the unpaid remuneration as if it had been so paid.

(3) Unpaid remuneration shall be deemed to have accrued from day to day throughout the period of accrual and there shall be deemed to have been paid on each relevant date so much of that remuneration as accrued up to that date or, if it is earlier, the date of cessation of the office or employment in respect of which the unpaid remuneration is payable—

(a) where there was no preceding relevant date, from the beginning of the period of accrual or, if it is later, the date of commencement of the office or employment in respect of which the unpaid remuneration is payable, and

(b) where there was a preceding relevant date, from the day following that date or, if it is later, the date of commencement of the office or employment in respect of which the unpaid remuneration is payable.

(4) This section shall not apply to unpaid remuneration paid before—

(a) the date of expiry of 6 months after the date (in this subsection referred to as "*the deemed date*") on which that remuneration is by virtue of *subsection (3)* deemed to have been paid, or

(b) in the case where the period of account is one of more than 12 months, the date of expiry of 18 months from the first day of that period of account if the date of expiry is later than the deemed date.

Amendments

[1] Substituted by FA01 sched2(54).

Case Law

In Bedford (Collector General) v H 1968 II ITR 588 it was held that the Inspector had the power to make an assessment to assess remuneration under Schedule E in the year in which it was earned.

997 Supplementary provisions (Chapter 4)

[ITA67 s133; FA74 s11 and Sch1 PtII; FA93 s2(2) and Sch1 PtI par2]

(1) No assessment under Schedule E for any year of assessment need be made in respect of emoluments to which this Chapter applies except where—

(a) the person assessable, by notice in writing given to the inspector [...][1], requires an assessment to be made,

(b) the emoluments paid in the year of assessment are not the same in amount as the emoluments which are to be treated as the emoluments for that year, or

(c) there is reason to suppose that the emoluments would, if assessed, be taken into account in computing the total income of a person who is liable to tax at the higher rate or would be so liable if an assessment were made in respect of the emoluments;

but where any such assessment is made credit shall be given for the amount of any tax deducted […][2] from the emoluments [against the amount of tax chargeable in the assessment on the person 30 assessed][3].

[(1A) [Subject to *sections 959AB* and *959AD*][4] an assessment under Schedule E in respect of emoluments to which this Chapter applies shall not be made for any year of assessment—

(a) where *paragraph (a)* of that subsection applies, unless the person assessable has requested the assessment—

(i) in the case of any year of assessment prior to the year of assessment 2003, within 5 years, and

(ii) in the case of the year of assessment 2003 or any subsequent year of assessment, within 4 years,

from the end of the year of assessment concerned, and

(b) where *paragraph (b)* or *(c)* of that subsection applies, at any time later than 4 years from the end of the year of assessment concerned.][5]

(2) Where an employer pays to the Revenue Commissioners any amount of tax which, pursuant to this Chapter and any regulations under this Chapter, the employer has deducted from emoluments, the employer shall be acquitted and discharged of the sum represented by the payment as if the employer had actually paid that sum to the employee.

[(3) Where the inspector, in accordance with the provisions of Regulation 37 of the Income Tax (Employments) (Consolidated) Regulations 2001 (S.I. No. 559 of 2001) sends a statement of liability to an employee, that statement shall, if the inspector so directs and gives notice accordingly in or with the statement sent to the employee, be treated in all respects as if it were an assessment raised on the employee, and all the provisions of the Income Tax Acts relating to appeals against assessments and the collection and recovery of tax charged in an assessment shall accordingly apply to the statement.][6]

Amendments

[1] Deleted by FA03 s17(1)(i)(a)(i)(I). With effect from 1 January 2005 per S.I. 508 of 2003.

[2] Deleted by FA03 s17(1)(i)(a)(i)(II). With effect from 31 October 2003 per S.I. 508 of 2003.

[3] Inserted by FA13 s92 and sched1(part 2)(h).

[4] Substituted by FA13 s92 and sched1(part 2)(i).

[5] Inserted by FA03 s17(1)(i)(b). With effect from 1 January 2005 per S.I. 508 of 2003.

[6] Inserted by FA05 s26. Applies with effect from 25 March 2005.

Note:

FA13 s92 applies—

(a) in the case of a chargeable period (within the meaning of section 321(2)) which is an accounting period of a company, as respects chargeable periods that start on or after 1 January 2013, and

(b) in a case other than that referred to in paragraph (a), as respects the year of assessment (within the meaning of section 2(1)) 2013 and subsequent years of assessment.

Case Law

If the taxpayer does not require an assessment under section 997(1)(a), and there is no outstanding liability for the year concerned, the Inspector can use his discretion not to issue an assessment. The City of Limerick VEC v Lucy Carr and the Revenue Commissioners 2001 High Court

Revenue Briefings

Tax Briefing

Tax Briefing October 2004 – Issue 57 pg 9 – Time Limits – Schedule E Assessments

Cross References

To Section 997

Section 922 Assessment in absence of return.

Section 926 Estimation of certain amounts.

997A Credit in respect of tax deducted from emoluments of certain directors

[(1) (a) In this section—

"*control*" has the same meaning as in *section 432*;

"*ordinary share capital*", in relation to a company, means all the issued share capital (by whatever name called) of the company.

(b) For the purposes of this section—

(i) a person shall have a material interest in a company if the person, either on the person's own or with any one or more connected persons, or if any person connected with the person with or without any such other connected persons, is the beneficial owner of, or is able, directly or through the medium of other companies or by any other indirect means, to control, more than 15 per cent of the ordinary share capital of the company, and

(ii) the question of whether a person is connected with another person shall be determined in accordance with *section 10*.

(2) This section applies to a person to who, in relation to a company (hereafter in this section referred to as "the company"), has a material interest in the company.

(3) Notwithstanding any other provision of the Income Tax Acts or the regulations made under this Chapter, no credit for tax deducted from the emoluments paid by the company to a person to whom this section applies [shall be given against the amount of tax chargeable in any assessment][1] raised on the person or in any statement of liability sent to the person under Regulation 37 of the Income Tax (Employments) (Consolidated) Regulations 2001 (S.I. No. 559 of 2001) unless there is documentary evidence to show that the tax deducted has been remitted by the company to the Collector-General in accordance with the provisions of those regulations.

(4) Where the company remits tax to the Collector-General which has been deducted from emoluments [paid by the company in a year of assessment, the tax remitted for that year of assessment][2] shall be treated as having been deducted from emoluments paid to persons other than persons to whom this section applies in priority to tax deducted from persons to whom this section applies.

(5) Where, in accordance with *subsection (4)*, tax remitted to the Collector-General by the company is to be treated as having been deducted from emoluments paid by the company to persons to whom this section applies, the tax to be so treated shall, if there is more than one such person, be treated as having been deducted from the

emoluments paid to each such person in the same proportion as the emoluments paid to the person bears to the aggregate amount of emoluments paid by the company to all such persons.

[(6) Where, in accordance with *subsection (5)*, the tax to be treated as having been deducted from the emoluments paid to each person to whom this section applies exceeds the actual amount of tax deducted from the emoluments of each person, then the amount of credit to be given for tax deducted from those emoluments shall not exceed the actual amount of tax so deducted.][3][4]

[(7) Notwithstanding *section 960G* and for the purposes of the application of this section, where a company has an obligation to remit any amount by virtue of the provisions of—

(a) the Social Welfare Consolidation Act 2005 and regulations made under that Act, as respects employment contributions,

(b) *Part 18D* and regulations made under that Part, as respects universal social charge, and

(c) this Chapter and regulations made under this Chapter, as respects income tax,

any amount remitted by the company for a year of assessment shall be set—

(i) firstly against employment contributions,

(ii) secondly against universal social charge, and

(iii) lastly against income tax.

(8) Where any person is aggrieved by a decision of the Revenue Commissioners on a claim for credit for tax deducted from emoluments, in so far as that decision is made by reference to any provision of this section, the provisions of *section 949* shall apply to such decision as if it were a determination on a matter referred to in *section 864*][5].

Amendments

[1] Substituted by FA13 s92 and sched1(part 2)(j).

[2] Substituted by FA12 s15(g). Deemed to have come into force and takes effect on and from 1 January 2012.

[3] Inserted by FA10 s8. As respects the year of assessment 2010 and subsequent years of assessment.

[4] Inserted by FA05 s13. Applies as respects the year of assessment 2005 and subsequent years of assessment.

[5] Inserted by FA12 s15(h). Deemed to have come into force and takes effect on and from 1 January 2012.

Note:

FA13 s92 applies—

(a) in the case of a chargeable period (within the meaning of section 321(2)) which is an accounting period of a company, as respects chargeable periods that start on or after 1 January 2013, and

(b) in a case other than that referred to in paragraph (a), as respects the year of assessment (within the meaning of section 2(1)) 2013 and subsequent years of assessment.

Cross References

From Section 997A

Section 10 Connected persons.

Section 432 Meaning of "associated company" and "control".

CHAPTER 5

Miscellaneous Provisions

998 Recovery of moneys due [Repealed]

Repealed by F(No.2)A08 sched4(part1). Applies as respects any tax that becomes due and payable on or after 1 March 2009.

Cross References

To Section 998

Schedule 31 Consequential Amendments

999 Taking by Collector-General of proceedings in bankruptcy [Repealed]

Repealed by F(No.2)A08 sched4(part1). Applies as respects any tax that becomes due and payable on or after 1 March 2009.

1000 Priority in bankruptcy, winding up, etc. for sums recovered or deducted under sections 531, 989 or 990 [Repealed]

Repealed by F(No.2)A08 sched4(part1). Applies as respects any tax that becomes due and payable on or after 1 March 2009.

1001 Liability to tax, etc. of holder of fixed charge on book debts of company

[FA86 s115; FA95 s174]

(1) In this section, "*relevant amount*" means any amount which the company is liable to remit under—

[(a) *Chapter 4* of this Part,

(b) the Value-Added Tax Consolidation Act 2010, and

(c) the *Finance (Local Property Tax) Act 2012*.][1]

(2) Subject to this section, where a person holds a fixed charge (being a fixed charge created on or after the 27th day of May, 1986) on the book debts of a company (within the meaning of the Companies Act, 1963), such person shall, if the company fails to pay any relevant amount for which it is liable, become liable to pay such relevant amount on due demand, and on neglect or refusal of payment may be proceeded against in the like manner as any other defaulter.

(3) This section shall not apply—

(a) unless the holder of the fixed charge has been notified in writing by the Revenue Commissioners that a company has failed to pay a relevant amount for which it is liable and that by virtue of this section the holder of the fixed charge—

(i) may become liable for payment of any relevant amount which the company subsequently fails to pay, and

(ii) where *paragraph (c)* does not apply, has become liable for the payment of the relevant amount which the company has failed to pay,

(b) to any amounts received by the holder of the fixed charge from the company before the date on which the holder is notified in writing by the Revenue Commissioners in accordance with *paragraph (a)*, and [(c) where within 21 days of the creation of the fixed charge the holder of the fixed charge furnishes in writing to the Revenue Commissioners the following details in relation to the charge:

(i) the name of the company on whose book debts the charge has been created;

(ii) the registration number of the company as issued by the Companies Registration Office to that company;

(iii) the tax registration number of the company as issued by the Revenue Commissioners to that company;

(iv) the date the fixed charge was created; and

(v) the name and address of the holder of the fixed charge;

to any relevant amount which the company was liable to pay before the date on which the holder is notified in writing by the Revenue Commissioners in accordance with *paragraph (a)*.][2]

(4) The amount or aggregate amount which a person shall be liable to pay in relation to a company in accordance with this section shall not exceed the amount or aggregate amount which the person has, while the fixed charge on book debts in relation to the company is in existence, received directly or indirectly from that company in payment or in part payment of any debts due by the company to the person.

(5) The Revenue Commissioners may, at any time and by notice in writing given to the holder of the fixed charge, withdraw with effect from a date specified in the notice a notification issued by them in accordance with *subsection (3)*; but such withdrawal shall not—

(a) affect in any way any liability of the holder of the fixed charge under this section which arose before such withdrawal, or

(b) preclude the issue under *subsection (3)* of a subsequent notice to the holder of the fixed charge.

(6) The Revenue Commissioners may nominate any of their officers to perform any acts and discharge any functions authorised by this section to be performed or discharged by the Revenue Commissioners.

Amendments

[1] Substituted by F(LPT)A 12 s158 & sched(9).

[2] Substituted by FA07 s120. With effect from 2 April 2007.

Cross References

From Section 1001

Section 983 Interpretation (Chapter 4).

To Section 1001

Section 1104 Short title and construction.

1002 Deduction from payments due to defaulters of amounts due in relation to tax

[FA88 s73(1)(b) to (16) and (18); FA92 s241(a) to (d)]

(1) (a) In this section, except where the context otherwise requires—

"*the Acts*" means—

(i) the Customs Acts,

(ii) the statutes relating to the duties of excise and to the management of those duties,

(iii) the Tax Acts,

[(iiia) Parts 18A, 18B, 18C and 18D,][1]

(iv) the Capital Gains Tax Acts,

(v) the Value-Added Tax Consolidation Act 2010, and the enactments amending or extending that Act,

(vi) the Capital Acquisitions Tax Consolidation Act 2003, and the enactments amending or extending that Act, and

(vii) the [Stamp Duties Consolidation Act, 1999][2], and the enactments amending or extending that Act,

[(viii) the *Finance (Local Property Tax) Act 2012,*][3]

[…][4]

and any instruments made thereunder;

"*additional debt*", in relation to a relevant person who has received a notice of attachment in respect of a taxpayer, means any amount which, at any time after the time of the receipt by the relevant person of the notice of attachment but before the end of the relevant period in relation to the notice, would be a debt due by the relevant person to the taxpayer if a notice of attachment were received by the relevant person at that time;

"*debt*", in relation to a notice of attachment given to a relevant person in respect of a taxpayer and in relation to that relevant person and taxpayer, means, subject to *paragraphs (b)* to *(e)*, the amount or aggregate amount of any money which, at the time the notice of attachment is received by the relevant person, is due by the relevant person (whether on that person's own account or as an agent or trustee) to the taxpayer, irrespective of whether the taxpayer has applied for the payment (to the taxpayer or any other person) or for the withdrawal of all or part of the money;

"*deposit*" means a sum of money paid to a financial institution on terms under which it will be repaid with or without interest and either on demand or at a time or in circumstances agreed by or on behalf of the person making the payment and the financial institution to which it is made;

"*emoluments*" means anything assessable to income tax under Schedule E;

["*financial institution*" means—

(a) a person who holds or has held a licence under section 9 of the Central Bank Act 1971, or a person who holds or has held a licence or other similar authorisation under the law of any other Member State of the European Communities which corresponds to a licence granted under that section,

(b) a person referred to in section 7(4) of the Central Bank Act 1971,

(c) a credit institution (within the meaning of the European Communities (Licensing and Supervision of Credit Institutions) Regulations 1992 (S.I. No. 395 of 1992)) which has been authorised by the Central Bank and Financial Services Authority of Ireland to carry on business of a credit institution in accordance with the provisions of the supervisory enactments (within the meaning of those Regulations), or

(d) a branch of a financial institution which records deposits in its books as liabilities of the branch;][5]

"*further return*" means a return made by a relevant person under *subsection (4)*;

"*interest on unpaid tax*", in relation to a specified amount specified in a notice of attachment, means interest that has accrued to the date on which the notice of attachment is given under any provision of the Acts providing for the charging of interest in respect of the unpaid tax, including interest on an undercharge of tax which is attributable to fraud or neglect, specified in the notice of attachment;

"*notice of attachment*" means a notice under *subsection (2)*;

"*notice of revocation*" means a notice under *subsection (10)*;

"*penalty*" means a monetary penalty imposed on a taxpayer under a provision of the Acts;

"*relevant period*", in relation to a notice of attachment, means, as respects the relevant person to whom the notice of attachment is given, the period commencing at the time at which the notice is received by the relevant person and ending on the earliest of—

(i) the date on which the relevant person completes the payment to the Revenue Commissioners out of the debt, or the aggregate of the debt and any additional debt, due by the relevant person to the taxpayer named in the notice, of an amount equal to the specified amount in relation to the taxpayer,

(ii) the date on which the relevant person receives a notice of revocation of the notice of attachment, and

(iii) where the relevant person or the taxpayer named in the notice—

(I) is declared bankrupt, the date the relevant person or the taxpayer is so declared, or

(II) is a company which commences to be wound up, the relevant date within the meaning of section 285 of the Companies Act, 1963, in relation to the winding up;

"*relevant person*", in relation to a taxpayer, means a person whom the Revenue Commissioners have reason to believe may have, at the time a notice of attachment is received by such person in respect of a taxpayer, a debt due to the taxpayer;

"*return*" means a return made by a relevant person under *subsection (2)(a)(iii)*;

"*specified amount*" has the meaning assigned to it by *subsection (2)(a)(ii)*;

"*tax*" means any tax, duty, levy or charge which in accordance with any provision of the Acts is placed under the care and management of the Revenue Commissioners;

"*taxpayer*" means a person who is liable to pay, remit or account for tax to the Revenue Commissioners under the Acts.

(b) Where a relevant person is a financial institution, any amount or aggregate amount of money, including interest on that money, which at the time the notice of attachment is received by the relevant person is a deposit held by the relevant person—

(i) to the credit of the taxpayer for the taxpayer's sole benefit, or

(ii) to the credit of the taxpayer and any other person or persons for their joint benefit,

shall be regarded as a debt due by the relevant person to the taxpayer at that time.

[(c) Where the Revenue Commissioners issue a notice of attachment in respect of any amount of money due by the relevant person to the taxpayer as emoluments under a contract of service, the notice may provide for the payment by the relevant person of the amount of the default out of the emoluments, after taking account of statutory deductions, over a period specified in the notice.][6]

(d) Where there is a dispute as to an amount of money which is due by the relevant person to the taxpayer, the amount in dispute shall be disregarded for the purposes of determining the amount of the debt.

(e) In the case referred to in *paragraph (b)*, a deposit held by a relevant person which is a financial institution to the credit of the taxpayer and any other person or persons (in this paragraph referred to as "*the other party or parties*") for their joint benefit shall be deemed (unless evidence to the contrary is produced to the satisfaction of the relevant person within 10 days of the giving of the notices specified in *subsection (2)(e)*) to be held to the benefit of the taxpayer and the other party or parties to the deposit equally, and accordingly only the portion of the deposit so deemed shall be regarded as a debt due by the relevant person to the taxpayer at the time the notice of attachment is received by the relevant person and, where such evidence is produced within the specified time, only so much of the deposit as is shown to be held to the benefit of the taxpayer shall be regarded as a debt due by the relevant person to the taxpayer at that time.

[(f) A notice of attachment, notice of revocation and any other notice provided for by this section (including the obligation to notify a taxpayer or relevant person in accordance with *paragraph (b)* of *subsection (12)* but not including the notice referred to in *paragraph (a)* of that subsection) may be given to a taxpayer or to a relevant person, as the case may be, by electronic means (within the meaning of *section 917EA*).][7]

(2) (a) Subject to *subsection (3)*, where a taxpayer has made default whether before or after the passing of this Act in paying, remitting or accounting for any tax, interest on unpaid tax, or penalty to the Revenue Commissioners, the Revenue Commissioners may, if the taxpayer has not made good the default, give to a relevant person in relation to the taxpayer a notice in writing (in this section referred to as "*the notice of attachment*") in which is entered—

(i) the taxpayer's name and address,

(ii) (I) the amount or aggregate amount, or

(II) in a case where more than one notice of attachment is given to a relevant person or relevant persons in respect of a taxpayer, a portion of the amount or aggregate amount,

of the taxes, interest on unpaid taxes and penalties in respect of which the taxpayer is in default at the time of the giving of the notice or notices of attachment (the amount, aggregate amount, or portion of the amount or aggregate amount, as the case may be, being referred to in this section as "*the specified amount*"), and

(iii) a direction to the relevant person—

(I) subject to *paragraphs (b)* and *(c)*, to deliver to the Revenue Commissioners, within the period of 10 days from the time at which the notice of attachment is received by the relevant person, a return in writing specifying whether or not any debt is due by the relevant person to the taxpayer at the time the notice is received by the relevant person and, if any debt is so due, specifying the amount of the debt, and

(II) if the amount of any debt is so specified, to pay to the Revenue Commissioners within the period referred to in *clause (I)* a sum equal to the amount of the debt so specified.

(b) Where the amount of the debt due by the relevant person to the taxpayer is equal to or greater than the specified amount in relation to the taxpayer, the amount of the debt specified in the return shall be an amount equal to the specified amount.

(c) Where the relevant person is a financial institution and the debt due by the relevant person to the taxpayer is part of a deposit held to the credit of the taxpayer and any other person or persons to their joint benefit, the return shall be made within a period of 10 days from—

(i) the expiry of the period specified in the notices to be given under *paragraph (e)*, or

(ii) the production of the evidence referred to in *paragraph (e)(II)*.

(d) A relevant person to whom a notice of attachment has been given shall comply with the direction in the notice.

(e) Where a relevant person which is a financial institution is given a notice of attachment and the debt due by the relevant person to the taxpayer is part of a deposit held by the relevant person to the credit of the taxpayer and any other person or persons (in this paragraph referred to as "*the other party or parties*") for their joint benefit, the relevant person shall on receipt of the notice of attachment give to the taxpayer and the other party or parties to the deposit a notice in writing in which is entered—

(i) the taxpayer's name and address,

(ii) the name and address of the person to whom a notice under this paragraph is given,

(iii) the name and address of the relevant person, and

(iv) the specified amount,

and which states that—

(I) a notice of attachment under this section has been received in respect of the taxpayer,

(II) under this section a deposit is deemed (unless evidence to the contrary is produced to the satisfaction of the relevant person within 10 days of the giving of the notice under this paragraph) to be held to the benefit of the taxpayer and the other party or parties to the deposit equally, and

(III) unless such evidence is produced within the period specified in the notice given under this paragraph—

(A) a sum equal to the amount of the deposit so deemed to be held to the benefit of the taxpayer (and accordingly regarded as a debt due to the taxpayer by the relevant person) shall be paid to the Revenue Commissioners, where that amount is equal to or less than the specified amount, and

(B) where the amount of the deposit so deemed to be held to the benefit of the taxpayer (and accordingly regarded as a debt due to the taxpayer by the relevant person) is greater than the specified amount, a sum equal to the specified amount shall be paid to the Revenue Commissioners.

(3) An amount in respect of tax, interest on unpaid tax or a penalty, as respects which a taxpayer is in default as specified in *subsection (2)*, shall not be entered in a notice of attachment unless—

(a) a period of [14 days][8] has expired from the date on which such default commenced, and

(b) the Revenue Commissioners have given the taxpayer a notice in writing (whether or not the document containing the notice also contains other information being communicated by the Revenue Commissioners to the taxpayer), not later than 7 days before the date of the receipt by the relevant person or relevant persons concerned of a notice of attachment, stating that if the amount is not paid it may be specified in a notice or notices of attachment and recovered under this section from a relevant person or relevant persons in relation to the taxpayer.

(4) If, when a relevant person receives a notice of attachment, the amount of the debt due by the relevant person to the taxpayer named in the notice is less than the specified amount in relation to the taxpayer or no debt is so due and, at any time after the receipt of the notice and before the end of the relevant period in relation to the notice, an additional debt becomes due by the relevant person to the taxpayer, the relevant person shall within 10 days of that time—

(a) if the aggregate of the amount of any debt so due and the additional debt so due is equal to or less than the specified amount in relation to the taxpayer—

(i) deliver a further return to the Revenue Commissioners specifying the additional debt, and

(ii) pay to the Revenue Commissioners the amount of the additional debt,

and so on for each subsequent occasion during the relevant period in relation to the notice of attachment on which an additional debt becomes due by the relevant person to the taxpayer until—

(I) the aggregate amount of the debt and the additional debt or debts so due equals the specified amount in relation to the taxpayer, or

(II) *paragraph (b)* applies in relation to an additional debt, and

(b) if the aggregate amount of any debt and the additional debt or debts so due to the taxpayer is greater than the specified amount in relation to the taxpayer—

(i) deliver a further return to the Revenue Commissioners specifying such portion of the latest additional debt as when added to the aggregate of the debt and any earlier additional debts is equal to the specified amount in relation to the taxpayer, and

(ii) pay to the Revenue Commissioners that portion of the additional debt.

(5) Where a relevant person delivers, either fraudulently or negligently, an incorrect return or further return that purports to be a return or further return made in

accordance with this section, the relevant person shall be deemed to be guilty of an offence under *section 1078*.

(6) (a) Where a notice of attachment has been given to a relevant person in respect of a taxpayer, the relevant person shall not, during the relevant period in relation to the notice, make any disbursements out of the debt, or out of any additional debt, due by the relevant person to the taxpayer except to the extent that any such disbursement—

(i) will not reduce the debt or the aggregate of the debt and any additional debts so due to an amount that is less than the specified amount in relation to the taxpayer, or

(ii) is made pursuant to an order of a court.

(b) For the purposes of this section, a disbursement made by a relevant person contrary to *paragraph (a)* shall be deemed not to reduce the amount of the debt or any additional debts due by the relevant person to the taxpayer.

(7) (a) *Sections 1052* and *1054* shall apply to a failure by a relevant person to deliver a return required by a notice of attachment within the time specified in the notice or to deliver a further return within the time specified in *subsection (4)* as they apply to a failure to deliver a return referred to in *section 1052*.

(b) A certificate signed by an officer of the Revenue Commissioners which certifies that he or she has examined the relevant records and that it appears from those records that during a specified period a specified return was not received from a relevant person shall be evidence until the contrary is proved that the relevant person did not deliver the return during that period.

(c) A certificate certifying as provided by *paragraph (b)* and purporting to be signed by an officer of the Revenue Commissioners may be tendered in evidence without proof and shall be deemed until the contrary is proved to have been so signed.

(8) Where a relevant person to whom a notice of attachment in respect of a taxpayer has been given—

(a) delivers the return required to be delivered by that notice but fails to pay to the Revenue Commissioners within the time specified in the notice the amount specified in the return or any part of that amount, or

(b) delivers a further return under *subsection (4)* but fails to pay to the Revenue Commissioners within the time specified in that subsection the amount specified in the further return or any part of that amount,

the amount specified in the return or further return or the part of that amount, as the case may be, which the relevant person has failed to pay to the Revenue Commissioners may, if the notice of attachment has not been revoked by a notice of revocation, be sued for and recovered by action or other appropriate proceedings [by][9] the Revenue Commissioners in any court of competent jurisdiction.

(9) Nothing in this section shall be construed as rendering any failure by a relevant person to make a return or further return required by this section, or to pay to the Revenue Commissioners the amount or amounts required by this section to be paid by the relevant person, liable to be treated as a failure to which *section 1078* applies.

(10) (a) A notice of attachment given to a relevant person in respect of a taxpayer may be revoked by the Revenue Commissioners at any time by notice in

writing given to the relevant person and shall be revoked forthwith if the taxpayer has paid the specified amount to the Revenue Commissioners.

(b) Where in pursuance of this section a relevant person pays any amount to the Revenue Commissioners out of a debt or an additional debt due by the relevant person to the taxpayer and, at the time of the receipt by the Revenue Commissioners of that amount, the taxpayer has paid to the Revenue Commissioners the amount or aggregate amount of the taxes, interest on unpaid taxes and penalties in respect of which the taxpayer is in default at the time of the giving of the notice or notices of attachment, the first-mentioned amount shall be refunded by the Revenue Commissioners forthwith to the taxpayer.

(11) Where a notice of attachment or a notice of revocation is given to a relevant person in relation to a taxpayer, a copy of such notice shall be given by the Revenue Commissioners to the taxpayer forthwith.

(12) (a) Where in pursuance of this section any amount is paid to the Revenue Commissioners by a relevant person, the relevant person shall forthwith give the taxpayer concerned a notice in writing specifying the payment, its amount and the reason for which it was made.

(b) On the receipt by the Revenue Commissioners of an amount paid in pursuance of this section, the Revenue Commissioners shall forthwith notify the taxpayer and the relevant person in writing of such receipt.

(13) Where in pursuance of this section a relevant person pays to the Revenue Commissioners the whole or part of the amount of a debt or an additional debt due by the relevant person to a taxpayer, or any portion of such an amount, the taxpayer shall allow such payment and the relevant person shall be acquitted and discharged of the amount of the payment as if it had been paid to the taxpayer.

(14) Where in pursuance of this section a relevant person is prohibited from making any disbursement out of a debt or an additional debt due to a taxpayer, no action shall lie against the relevant person in any court by reason of a failure to make any such disbursement.

(15) Any obligation on the Revenue Commissioners to maintain secrecy or any other restriction on the disclosure of information by the Revenue Commissioners shall not apply in relation to information contained in a notice of attachment.

(16) A notice of attachment in respect of a taxpayer shall not be given to a relevant person at a time when the relevant person or the taxpayer is an undischarged bankrupt or a company being wound up.

(17) The Revenue Commissioners may nominate any of their officers to perform any acts and discharge any functions authorised by this section to be performed or discharged by the Revenue Commissioners.

Amendments

[1] Substituted by FA11 s3(1)(d). Applies for the year of assessment 2011 and each subsequent year of assessment.

[2] Substituted by SDCA99 sched4.

[3] Inserted by F(LPT)A 12 s158 & sched(10).

[4] Deleted by FA11 s3(1)(c). Applies for the year of assessment 2011 and each subsequent year of assessment.

[5] Substituted by F(No.2)A08 s92(j).

[6] Substituted by FA11 s74(a). Effective from 6 February 2011.

[7] Inserted by F(No.2)A13 s82.

[8] Substituted by FA01 s238.

[9] Substituted by FA11 s74(b). Effective from 6 February 2011.

Case Law

The taxpayer claimed that the notice procedure under section 1002 is unconstitutional in that it constituted an infringement on his right to earn a livelihood. The High Court rejected the taxpayer's argument and held that there is nothing in section 1002 which could be construed as inherently constituting an attack on the taxpayer's constitutional right to a livelihood. Orange v The Revenue Commissioners 1994 V ITR 70

Revenue Briefings

eBrief

eBrief No. 86/2011 – Attachment of Wages/Salaries

Revenue Information Notes

Collection Manual Guidelines for Attachment – reviewed 22 December 2011

Cross References

From Section 1002

Section 1052 Penalties for failure to make certain returns, etc.
Section 1054 Penalties in the case of a secretary of a body of persons.
Section 1078 Revenue offences.

To Section 1002

Section 904K Power of inspection: notices of attachment.
Section 1104 Short title and construction.
Schedule 29 Provisions Referred to in Sections 1052, 1053 and 1054
Schedule 31 Consequential Amendments

1003 Payment of tax by means of donation of heritage items

[FA95 s176; FA96 s139]

(1) (a) In this section—

"*the Acts*" means—

(i) the Tax Acts (other than *Chapter 8* of *Part 6*, *Chapter 2* of *Part 18* and *Chapter 4* of this Part),

(ii) the Capital Gains Tax Acts, and

(iii) the Capital Acquisitions Tax Consolidation Act 2003, and the enactments amending or extending that Act,

and any instruments made thereunder;

"*approved body*" means—

(i) the National Archives,

(ii) the National Gallery of Ireland,

(iii) the National Library of Ireland,

(iv) the National Museum of Ireland,

[(iva) the Crawford Art Gallery Cork Limited,][1]

(v) the Irish Museum of Modern Art, or

(vi) in relation to the offer of a gift of a particular item or collection of items, any other such body (being a body owned, or funded wholly or mainly, by the State or by any public or local authority) as may be approved, with the consent of the Minister for Finance, by the Minister for Arts, Heritage, Gaeltacht and the Islands for the purposes of this section;

"*arrears of tax*" means tax due and payable in accordance with any provision of the Acts (including any interest and penalties payable under any provision of the Acts in relation to such tax)—

(i) in the case of income tax, corporation tax or capital gains tax, in respect of the relevant period, or

(ii) in the case of gift tax or inheritance tax, before the commencement of the calendar year in which the relevant gift is made,

which has not been paid at the time a relevant gift is made;

"*current liability*" means—

(i) in the case of income tax or capital gains tax, any liability to such tax arising in the year of assessment in which the relevant gift is made,

(ii) in the case of corporation tax, any liability to such tax arising in the accounting period in which the relevant gift is made,

(iii) in the case of gift tax or inheritance tax, any liability to such tax which becomes due and payable in the calendar year in which the relevant gift is made;

"*designated officer*" means—

(i) the member of the selection committee who represents the appropriate approved body on that committee where the approved body is so represented, or

(ii) in any other case, a person nominated in that behalf by the Minister for Arts, Heritage, Gaeltacht and the Islands;

"*heritage item*" has the meaning assigned to it by *subsection (2)(a)*;

"*market value*" has the meaning assigned to it by *subsection (3)*;

"*relevant gift*" means a gift of a heritage item to an approved body in respect of which no consideration whatever (other than relief under this section) is received by the person making the gift, either directly or indirectly, from the approved body or otherwise;

"*relevant period*" means—

(i) in the case of income tax and capital gains tax, any year of assessment preceding the year in which the relevant gift is made, and

(ii) in the case of corporation tax, any accounting period preceding the accounting period in which the relevant gift is made;

"*selection committee*" means a committee consisting of—

[(i) an officer of the Minister for Arts, Sport and Tourism, who shall act as Chairperson of the committee,

(ii) the Chief Executive of the Heritage Council,

(iii) the Director of the Arts Council,

(iv) the Director of the National Archives,

(v) the Director of the National Gallery of Ireland,

(vi) the Director of the National Library of Ireland,

[(via) the Director of the Crawford Art Gallery Cork Limited,][2]

(vii) the Director of the National Museum of Ireland, and

(viii) the Director and Chief Executive of the Irish Museum of Modern Art,][3] and includes any person duly acting in the capacity of any of those persons as a result of the person concerned being unable to fulfil his or her duties for any of the reasons set out in *paragraph (b)(ii)*;

"*tax*" means income tax, corporation tax, capital gains tax, gift tax or inheritance tax, as the case may be, payable in accordance with any provision of the Acts;

"*valuation date*" means the date on which an application is made to the selection committee for a determination under *subsection (2)(a)*.

(b) (i) The selection committee may act notwithstanding one or more vacancies among its members and may regulate its own procedure.

(ii) If and so long as a member of the selection committee is unable through illness, absence or other cause to fulfil his or her duties, a person nominated in that behalf by the member shall act as the member of the committee in the place of the member.

[(iii) For the purposes of making a decision in relation to an application made to it for a determination under *subsection (2)(a)*, the selection committee shall not include the member of that committee who represents the approved body to which it is intended that the gift of the heritage item is to be made where that approved body is so represented but that member may participate in any discussion of the application by that committee prior to the making of the decision.][4]

(2) (a) In this section, "*heritage item*" means any kind of cultural item, including—

(i) any archaeological item, archive, book, estate record, manuscript and painting, and

(ii) any collection of cultural items and any collection of such items in their setting,

which, on application to the selection committee in writing in that behalf by a person who owns the item or collection of items, as the case may be, [is, subject to the provisions of *paragraphs (aa)* and *(ab)*, determined by the selection committee][5] to be an item or collection of items which is—

(I) an outstanding example of the type of item involved, pre-eminent in its class, whose export from the State would constitute a diminution of the accumulated cultural heritage of Ireland [or whose import into the State would constitute a significant enhancement of the accumulated cultural heritage of Ireland][6], and

(II) suitable for acquisition by an approved body.

[(aa) In considering an application under *paragraph (a)*, the selection committee shall—

(i) consider such evidence as the person making the application submits to it, and

(ii) seek and consider the opinion in writing in relation to the application of—

(I) the approved body to which it is intended the gift is to be made, and

(II) the Heritage Council, the Arts Council or such other person or body of persons as the committee considers to be appropriate in the circumstances.

(ab) Where an application under *paragraph (a)* is in respect of a collection of items, the selection committee shall not make a determination under that paragraph in relation to the collection unless, in addition to the making of a determination in relation to the collection as a whole, the selection committee is satisfied that, on the basis of its consideration of the application in accordance with *paragraph (aa)*, it could make a determination in respect of at least one item comprised in the collection, if such were required.][7]

[(ac) Paragraph (*ab*) shall not apply in the case of a collection of items, consisting wholly of archival material or manuscripts, which was either—

(i) created over time by one individual, family or organisation, or

(ii) was assembled by an individual, family or organisation,

and constitutes a collection of archival material or manuscripts where each item has been in such collection for a period of not less than 30 years and merits maintenance as a collection.][8]

(b) On receipt of an application for a determination under *paragraph (a)*, the selection committee shall request the Revenue Commissioners in writing to value the item or collection of items, as the case may be, in accordance with *subsection (3)*.

(c) The selection committee shall not make a determination under *paragraph (a)* where the market value of the item or collection of items, as the case may be, as determined by the Revenue Commissioners in accordance with *subsection (3)*, at the valuation date—

[(i) is less than,

(I) subject to clause (II), €150,000, and

(II) in the case of at least one item comprised in a collection of items, €50,000, or][9]

(ii) exceeds an amount (which shall not be less than [€150,000][10]) determined by the formula—

[€6,000,000][11] – M

where M is an amount (which may be nil) equal to the market value at the valuation date of the heritage item (if any) or the aggregate of the market values at the respective valuation dates of all the heritage items (if any), as the case may be, in respect of which a determination or determinations, as the case may be, under this subsection has been made by the selection committee in any one calendar year and not revoked in that year.

(d) (i) An item or collection of items shall cease to be a heritage item for the purposes of this section if—

(I) the item or collection of items is sold or otherwise disposed of to a person other than an approved body,

(II) the owner of the item or collection of items notifies the selection committee in writing that it is not intended to make a gift of the item or collection of items to an approved body, or

(III) the gift of the item or collection of items is not made to an approved body within the calendar year following the year in which the determination is made under *paragraph (a)*.

(ii) Where the selection committee becomes aware, at any time within the calendar year in which a determination under *paragraph (a)* is made in respect of an item or collection of items, that *clause (I)* or *(II)* of *subparagraph (i)* applies to the item or collection of items, the selection committee may revoke its determination with effect from that time.

[(2A) Notwithstanding subsection (2)(*c*), the selection committee may make a determination in respect of an item or collection of items, consisting wholly of archival material or manuscripts, and the market value limit in respect of any one item in such a collection at the valuation date as set out in subsection (2)(*c*)(i)(II) shall not apply.][12]

(3)

[(a) For the purposes of this section, the market value of any item or collection of items (in this subsection referred to as "*the property*") shall, subject to *paragraph (d)*, be estimated to be the lesser of—

(i) the price which, in the opinion of the Revenue Commissioners, the property would fetch if sold in the open market on the valuation date in such manner and subject to such conditions as might reasonably be calculated to obtain for the vendor the best price for the property, and

(ii) (I) the price which, in the opinion of the person making the gift of the property, the property would fetch on the valuation date if sold in the manner referred to in *subparagraph (i)*, or

(II) at the election of that person, the amount paid for the property by that person.][13]

(b) The market value of the property shall be ascertained by the Revenue Commissioners in such manner and by such means as they think fit, and they may authorise a person to inspect the property and report to them the value of the property for the purposes of this section, and the person having custody or possession of the property shall permit the person so authorised to inspect the property at such reasonable times as the Revenue Commissioners consider necessary.

(c) where within 21 days of the creation of the fixed charge the holder of the fixed charge furnishes in writing to the Revenue Commissioners the following details in relation to the charge:

(i) the name of the company on whose book debts the charge has been created;

(ii) the registration number of the company as issued by the Companies Registration Office to that company;

(iii) the tax registration number of the company as issued by the Revenue Commissioners to that company;

(iv) the date the fixed charge was created; and

(v) the name and address of the holder of the fixed charge;

to any relevant amount which the company was liable to pay before the date on which the holder is notified in writing by the Revenue Commissioners in accordance with *paragraph (a)*.

[(d) Where the property is acquired at auction by the person making the gift, the market value of the property shall, for the purposes of this section, be deemed to include the auctioneer's fees in connection with the auction together with—

(i) any amount chargeable under the Value-Added Tax Consolidation Act 2010, by the auctioneer to the purchaser of the property in respect of those fees and in respect of which the purchaser is not entitled to any deduction or refund under that Act or any other enactment relating to value-added tax, or

(ii) in the case of an auction in a country other than the State, the amount chargeable to the purchaser of the property in respect of a tax chargeable under the law of that country which corresponds to value-added tax in the State and in relation to which the purchaser is not entitled to any deduction or refund.][14]

(4) Where a relevant gift is made to an approved body—

(a) the designated officer of that body shall give a certificate to the person who made the relevant gift, in such form as the Revenue Commissioners may prescribe, certifying the receipt of that gift and the transfer of the ownership of the heritage item the subject of that gift to the approved body, and

(b) the designated officer shall transmit a duplicate of the certificate to the Revenue Commissioners.

(5) Subject to this section, where a person has made a relevant gift the person shall, on submission to the Revenue Commissioners of the certificate given to the person in accordance with *subsection (4)*, be treated as having made on the date of such submission a payment on account of tax of [an amount equal to 80 per cent of the market value][15] of the relevant gift on the valuation date.

(6) A payment on account of tax which is treated as having been made in accordance with *subsection (5)* shall be set in so far as possible against any liability to tax of the person who is treated as having made such a payment in the following order—

(a) firstly, against any arrears of tax due for payment by that person and against an arrear of tax for an earlier period in priority to a later period, and for this purpose the date on which an arrear of tax became due for payment shall determine whether it is for an earlier or later period, and

(b) only then, against any current liability of the person which the person nominates for that purpose,

and such set-off shall accordingly discharge a corresponding amount of that liability.

(7) To the extent that a payment on account of tax has not been set off in accordance with *subsection (6)*, the balance remaining shall be set off against any future liability to tax of the person who is treated as having made the payment which that person nominates for that purpose.

(8) Where a person has power to sell any heritage item in order to raise money for the payment of gift tax or inheritance tax, such person shall have power to make a relevant gift of that heritage item in or towards satisfaction of that tax and, except as regards the nature of the consideration and its receipt and application, any such relevant gift shall be subject to the same provisions and shall be treated for all purposes as a sale made in exercise of that power, and any conveyances or transfers made or purporting to be made to give effect to such a relevant gift shall apply accordingly.

(9) A person shall not be entitled to any refund of tax in respect of any payment on account of tax made in accordance with this section.

(10) Interest shall not be payable in respect of any overpayment of tax for any period which arises directly or indirectly by reason of the set-off against any liability for that period of a payment on account of tax made in accordance with this section.

(11) Where a person makes a relevant gift and in respect of that gift is treated as having made a payment on account of tax, the person concerned shall not be allowed relief under any other provision of the Acts in respect of that gift.

(12) (a) The Revenue Commissioners shall as respects each year compile a list of the titles (if any), descriptions and values of the heritage items (if any) in respect of which relief under this section has been given.

(b) Notwithstanding any obligation as to secrecy imposed on them by the Acts or the Official Secrets Act, 1963, the Revenue Commissioners shall include in their annual report to the Minister for Finance the list (if any) referred to in *paragraph (a)* for the year in respect of which the report is made.

Amendments

[1] Inserted by FA07 s125(a).

[2] Inserted by FA07 s125(b).

[3] Substituted by FA04 s85(a)(i). As respects determinations made under subsection (2)(a) of that section on or after 25 March 2004.

[4] Inserted by FA04 s85(a)(ii). As respects determinations made under subsection (2)(a) of that section on or after 25 March 2004.

[5] Substituted by FA04 s85(b)(i). As respects determinations made under subsection (2)(a) of that section on or after 25 March 2004.

[6] Inserted by FA02 s124(a).

[7] Inserted by FA04 s85(b)(ii). As respects determinations made under subsection (2)(a) of that section on or after 25 March 2004.

[8] Inserted by FA08 s131(a). Has effect from 1 January 2008.

[9] Substituted by FA04 s85(b)(iii)(I). As respects determinations made under subsection (2)(a) of that section on or after 25 March 2004.

[10] Substituted by FA04 s85(b)(iii)(II). As respects determinations made under subsection (2)(a) of that section on or after 25 March 2004.

[11] Substituted by FA02 s124(b)(ii).

[12] Inserted by FA08 s131(b). Has effect from 1 January 2008.

[13] Substituted by FA06 s121. Applies as respects the year of assessment 2006 and subsequent years of assessment.

[14] Inserted by FA02 s124(d).

[15] Substituted by F(No.2)A08 s94(1)(a). Applies in the case of paragraph (a) of that subsection, as respects any determination made under section 1003(2)(a) by the selection committee (within the meaning of that section), on or after 1 January 2009.

Revenue Information Notes

HET 1 – Relief for Donations of Heritage Items

Cross References

From Section 1003

Section 129 Irish resident company distributions not generally chargeable to corporation tax.
Section 159 Liability for advance corporation tax.
Section 520 Interpretation (Chapter 1).
Section 530 Interpretation (Chapter 2).
Section 983 Interpretation (Chapter 4).

To Section 1003

Section 606 Disposals of work of art, etc., loaned for public display.
Section 1104 Short title and construction.

1003A Payment of tax by means of donation of heritage property to an Irish heritage trust

[(1) In this section—

"*the Acts*" means—

(a) the Tax Acts (other than *Chapter 8* of *Part 6*, *Chapter 2* of *Part 18* and Chapter 4 of this Part),

(b) the Capital Gains Tax Acts, and

(c) the Capital Acquisitions Tax Consolidation Act 2003, and the enactments amending or extending that Act,

and any instruments made thereunder;

"*arrears of tax*" means tax due and payable in accordance with any provision of the Acts (including any interest and penalties payable under any provision of the Acts in relation to such tax)—

(a) in the case of income tax, corporation tax or capital gains tax, in respect of the relevant period, or

(b) in the case of gift tax or inheritance tax, before the commencement of the calendar year in which the relevant gift is made,

which has not been paid at the time a relevant gift is made;

"*contents of the building*" means furnishings historically associated with the building and in respect of which [the Minister is satisfied or, as appropriate, the Commissioners of Public Works in Ireland are satisfied][1] that they are important to establishing the historic or aesthetic context of the building;

"*current liability*" means—

(a) in the case of income tax or capital gains tax, any liability to such tax arising in the year of assessment in which the relevant gift is made,

(b) in the case of corporation tax, any liability to such tax arising in the accounting period in which the relevant gift is made,

(c) in the case of gift tax or inheritance tax, any liability to such tax which becomes due and payable in the calendar year in which the relevant gift is made;

"*heritage property*" has the meaning assigned to it by *subsection (2)(a)*;

"*market value*" has the meaning assigned to it by *subsection (3)*;

"*Minister*" means the [Minister for Arts, Heritage and the Gaeltacht][2]

["*relevant gift*" means a gift of heritage property to the Trust or, as appropriate, to the Commissioners of Public Works in Ireland in respect of which no consideration whatever (other than relief under this section) is received by the person making the gift, either directly or indirectly, from the Trust or from those Commissioners or otherwise;][3]

"*relevant period*" means—

(a) in the case of income tax and capital gains tax, any year of assessment preceding the year in which the relevant gift is made, and

(b) in the case of corporation tax, any accounting period preceding the accounting period in which the relevant gift is made;

"*tax*" means income tax, corporation tax, capital gains tax, gift tax or inheritance tax, as the case may be, payable in accordance with any provision of the Acts;

"*Trust*" means the company designated for the purposes of this section by the order referred to in *section 122(2)* of the Finance Act 2006;

"*valuation date*" means the date on which an application is made to the Minister for a determination under *subsection (2)(a)*.

[(2) (a) In this section "*heritage property*" means a building or a garden which, on application in writing to the Minister or, as appropriate, to the Commissioners of Public Works in Ireland in that behalf by a person who owns the building or the garden is, subject to the provisions of this subsection, determined by the Minister or, as appropriate, by those Commissioners to be a building or a garden which is—

(i) an outstanding example of the type of building or garden involved,

(ii) pre-eminent in its class,

(iii) intrinsically of significant scientific, historical, horticultural, national, architectural or aesthetic interest, and

(iv) suitable for acquisition by the Trust or, as appropriate, by the [Commissioners of Public Works in Ireland.][4]

[…][5]

[(aa) For the purposes of this section—

(i) a reference to "*building*" includes—

(I) any associated outbuilding, yard or land where the land is occupied or enjoyed with the building as part of its gardens or designed landscape and contributes to the appreciation of the building in its setting,

(II) the contents of the building, and

(III) land necessary for the provision of access to the building or for the provision of parking facilities for visitors to the building,

(ii) a reference to "*garden*" includes—

(I) any associated building, outbuilding, yard or land where the land is occupied or enjoyed with the garden and contributes to the appreciation of the garden in its setting, and

(II) land necessary for the provision of access to the garden or for the provision of parking facilities for visitors to the garden.

(ab) Where a heritage property is donated under this section and the Trust or, as appropriate, the Commissioners of Public Works in Ireland deem that lands outside of the ownership of the donor of the heritage property would be necessary for the provision of access to the heritage property or for the provision of parking facilities for visitors to the heritage property, such lands may be donated for such purpose to the Trust or, as appropriate, the Commissioners of Public Works in Ireland under the terms of this section and those lands shall be deemed to be a heritage property for the purpose of this section.][6]

(b) An application for a determination under this subsection shall be made to the Minister where it relates to a relevant gift to be made to the Trust or shall be made to the Commissioners of Public Works in Ireland where it relates to a relevant gift to be made to those Commissioners.

(c) In considering an application for a determination under this subsection, the Minister or, as appropriate, the Commissioners of Public Works in Ireland shall consider such evidence as the person making the application submits.

(d) On receipt of an application for a determination under this subsection, the Minister or, as appropriate, the Commissioners of Public Works in Ireland shall request the Revenue Commissioners in writing to value the property in accordance with *subsection (3)*.

(e) The Minister or, as appropriate, the Commissioners of Public Works in Ireland shall not, during any calendar year, make a determination under this subsection where the market value of the property, as determined by the Revenue Commissioners in accordance with *subsection (3)*, at the valuation date exceeds an amount determined by the formula—

$$€6,000,000 - M$$

where—

M is an amount (which may be nil) equal to the market value at the valuation date of the heritage property (if any) or the aggregate of the market values at the respective valuation dates of all the heritage properties (if any), as the case may be, in respect of which a determination has been made or determinations have been made, as the case may be, under this subsection whether by the Minister or by the Commissioners of Public Works in Ireland in that calendar year and not revoked in that calendar year.

(f) The Commissioners of Public Works in Ireland shall not make a determination under this subsection without the consent in writing of the [Minister for Public Expenditure and Refom][7] and any such determination shall be subject to such conditions as may be specified by the [Minister for Public Expenditure and Refom][8].

(g) The Minister and the Commissioners of Public Works in Ireland shall, as appropriate, consult with each other in connection with the general application of this section and in particular for the purposes of the application of *paragraph (e)*.

(h) (i) A property shall cease to be a heritage property for the purposes of this section if—

(I) the property is sold or otherwise disposed of to a person other than the Trust or, as appropriate, the Commissioners of Public Works in Ireland,

(II) the owner of the property notifies the Trust or, as appropriate, the Commissioners of Public Works in Ireland in writing that it is not intended to make a gift of the property to the Trust or, as appropriate, those Commissioners, or

(III) the gift of the property is not made to the Trust or, as appropriate, to the Commissioners of Public Works in Ireland by the end of the calendar year following the calendar year in which the determination is made under this subsection.

(ii) Where the Minister becomes aware or, as appropriate, the Commissioners of Public Works in Ireland become aware, at any time within the calendar year in which a determination under this subsection is made in respect of a property, that clause (I) or (II) of *subparagraph (i)* applies to the property, the Minister or, as appropriate, those Commissioners may revoke the determination with effect from that time.][9]

(3) (a) For the purposes of this section, the market value of any property shall be estimated to be the lesser of—

(i) the price which, in the opinion of the Revenue Commissioners, the property would fetch if sold in the open market on the valuation date in such manner and subject to such conditions as might reasonably be calculated to obtain for the vendor the best price for the property, and

(ii) (I) the price which, in the opinion of the person making the gift of the property, the property would fetch on the valuation date if sold in the manner referred to in *subparagraph (i)*, or

(II) at the election of that person, the amount paid for the property by that person.

(b) The market value of the property shall be ascertained by the Revenue Commissioners in such manner and by such means as they think fit, and they may authorise a person to inspect the property and report to them the value of the property for the purposes of this section, and the person having custody or possession of the property shall permit the person so authorised to inspect the property at such reasonable times as the Revenue Commissioners consider necessary.

(c) Where the Revenue Commissioners require a valuation to be made by a person authorised by them, the cost of such valuation shall be defrayed by the Revenue Commissioners.

[(4) Where a relevant gift is made to the Trust or, as appropriate, to the Commissioners of Public Works in Ireland—

(a) the Trust or, as appropriate, those Commissioners shall give a certificate to the person who made the relevant gift, in such form as the Revenue Commissioners may prescribe, certifying the receipt of that gift and the transfer of the ownership of the heritage property the subject of that gift to the Trust or, as appropriate, to the Commissioners of Public Works in Ireland, and

(b) the Trust or, as appropriate, the Commissioners of Public Works in Ireland shall transmit a duplicate of the certificate to the Revenue Commissioners.][10]

(5) Subject to this section, where a person has made a relevant gift the person shall, on submission to the Revenue Commissioners of the certificate given to the person in accordance with *subsection (4)*, be treated as having made on the date of such submission a payment on account of tax of [an amount equal to 50 per cent of the market value][11] of the relevant gift on the valuation date.

(6) A payment on account of tax which is treated as having been made in accordance with *subsection (5)* shall be set in so far as possible against any liability to tax of the person who is treated as having made such a payment in the following order—

(a) firstly, against any arrears of tax due for payment by that person and against an arrear of tax for an earlier period in priority to a later period, and for this purpose the date on which an arrear of tax became due for payment shall determine whether it is for an earlier or later period, and

(b) only then, against any current liability of the person which the person nominates for that purpose,

and such set-off shall accordingly discharge a corresponding amount of that liability.

(7) To the extent that a payment on account of tax has not been set off in accordance with *subsection (6)*, the balance remaining shall be set off against any future liability to tax of the person who is treated as having made the payment which that person nominates for that purpose.

(8) Where a person has power to sell any heritage property in order to raise money for the payment of gift tax or inheritance tax, such person shall have power to make a relevant gift of that heritage property in or towards satisfaction of that tax and, except as regards the nature of the consideration and its receipt and application, any such relevant gift shall be subject to the same provisions and shall be treated for all purposes as a sale made in exercise of that power, and any conveyances or transfers made or purporting to be made to give effect to such a relevant gift shall apply accordingly.

(9) A person shall not be en titled to any refund of tax in respect of any payment on account of tax made in accordance with this section.

(10) Interest shall not be payable in respect of any over-payment of tax for any period which arises directly or indirectly by reason of the set-off against any liability for that period of a payment on account of tax made in accordance with this section.

(11) Where a person makes a relevant gift and in respect of that gift is treated as having made a payment on account of tax, the person concerned shall not be allowed relief under any other provision of the Acts in respect of that gift.

[(11A) (a) In the event that Fota House in County Cork is acquired by the Trust, either by way of a relevant gift under this section or otherwise, and the collection referred to in *paragraph (b)* is acquired by the Trust by way of gift, relief under this section shall, subject to *paragraphs (c)* and *(d)*, be granted in respect of the collection on the basis that Fota House was acquired by the Trust by way of a relevant gift and the collection formed part of the contents of the building.

(b) The collection referred to in this paragraph (in this subsection referred to as the "*collection*") is a collection—

(i) of either or both Irish paintings and furniture which was displayed in Fota House in the period 1983 to 1990,

(ii) which is to be housed by the Trust in Fota House, and

(iii) in respect of which the Minister, after consulting with such person (if any) in the matter as the Minister may deem to be necessary, is satisfied that the collection is important to establishing the aesthetic context of Fota House.

(c) This subsection shall not apply unless the collection is gifted to the Trust before the end of [2008][12].

(d) Relief under this section, in respect of the market value of the collection as determined in accordance with *subsection (3)*, shall, where this subsection applies, be granted to the person making the gift to the Trust of the collection, notwithstanding that that person is not the person from whom Fota House was acquired by the Trust.][13]

(12) (a) The Revenue Commissioners shall as respects each year compile a list of the titles (if any), descriptions and values of the heritage properties (if any) in respect of which relief under this section has been given.

(b) Notwithstanding any obligation as to secrecy imposed on them by the Acts or the Official Secrets Act 1963, the Revenue Commissioners shall include in their annual report to the Minister for Finance the list (if any) referred to in *paragraph (a)* for the year in respect of which the report is made.][14]

Amendments

[1] Substituted by FA10 s28(1)(a). Deemed to have come into force and takes effect as on and from 1 January 2010.

[2] Substituted by FA13 s25(1)(a). Applies in respect of any determination made, on or after 27 March 2013.

[3] Substituted by FA10 s28(1)(b). Deemed to have come into force and takes effect as on and from 1 January 2010.

[4] Substituted by FA13 s25(1)(b)(i). Applies in respect of any determination made, on or after 27 March 2013.

[5] Deleted by FA13 s25(1)(b)(ii). Applies in respect of any determination made, on or after 27 March 2013.

[6] Inserted by FA13 s25(1)(c). Applies in respect of any determination made, on or after 27 March 2013.

[7] Substituted by FA13 s25(1)(d). Applies in respect of any determination made, on or after 27 March 2013.

[8] Substituted by FA13 s25(1)(d). Applies in respect of any determination made, on or after 27 March 2013.

[9] Substituted by FA10 s28(2). Deemed to have come into force and takes effect as on and from 1 January 2010.

[10] Substituted by FA10 s28(3). Deemed to have come into force and takes effect as on and from 1 January 2010.

[11] Substituted by FA13 s25(1)(e). Applies in respect of any determination made, on or after 27 March 2013.

[12] Substituted by FA08 s132(1). Applies as respects the year of assessment 2008.

[13] Inserted by FA07 s122(1).

[14] Inserted by FA06 s122(1). This section comes into operation on such day as the Minister for Finance may appoint by order. With effect from 5 October 2006 per S.I. 520 of 2006.

Cross References

From Section 1003A

Section 122 Preferential loan arrangements.
Section 129 Irish resident company distributions not generally chargeable to corporation tax.
Section 159 Liability for advance corporation tax.
Section 520 Interpretation (Chapter 1).
Section 530 Interpretation (Chapter 2).

1004 Unremittable income

[ITA67 s549; F(MP)A68 s3(2) and Sch PtI; FA74 s86 and Sch2 PtI; CTA76 s147(1) and (2)]

(1) In this section, "*particular income*" means income arising outside the State, the amount of which is or is included in the amount (in this section referred to as "*the relevant amount*") on which in accordance with the Tax Acts income tax or corporation tax is computed.

(2) Subject to *subsections (3)* to *(5)*, this section shall apply where income tax or corporation tax is charged by an assessment for any period and the tax has not been paid.

(3) In any case in which, on or after the date on which the income tax or corporation tax has become payable, such proof is given to the Revenue Commissioners as satisfies them that particular income cannot, by reason of legislation in the country in which it arises or of executive action of the government of that country, be remitted to the State, the Revenue Commissioners may for the purposes of collection treat the assessment as if the relevant amount did not include the particular income, but such treatment shall terminate on the Revenue Commissioners ceasing to be so satisfied.

(4) The Revenue Commissioners may for the purposes of this section call for such information as they consider necessary.

(5) Any person who is dissatisfied with a decision of the Revenue Commissioners under *subsection (3)* may, by giving notice in writing to the Revenue Commissioners within 21 days after the notification of the decision to that person, apply to have the matter referred to the Appeal Commissioners as if it were an appeal against an assessment, and the provisions of the Tax Acts relating to the rehearing of an appeal and to the statement of a case for the opinion of the High Court on a point of law shall apply accordingly with any necessary modifications.

1005 Unremittable gains

[CGTA75 s43]

(1) In this section, "*particular gains*" means chargeable gains accruing from the disposal of assets situated outside the State, the amount of which is or is included in the amount (in this section referred to as "*the relevant amount*") on which in accordance with the Capital Gains Tax Acts the tax is computed.

(2) Subject to *subsections (3)* to *(5)*, this section shall apply where capital gains tax has been charged by an assessment for the year in which the particular gains accrued and the tax has not been paid.

(3) In any case in which, on or after the date on which the capital gains tax has become payable, such proof is given to the Revenue Commissioners as satisfies them that particular gains cannot, by reason of legislation in the country in which they have accrued or of executive action of the government of that country, be remitted to the State, the Revenue Commissioners may for the purposes of collection treat the assessment as if the relevant amount did not include the particular gains, but such treatment shall terminate on the Revenue Commissioners ceasing to be so satisfied.

(4) The Revenue Commissioners may for the purposes of this section call for such information as they consider necessary.

(5) Any person who is dissatisfied with a decision of the Revenue Commissioners under *subsection (3)* may, by giving notice in writing to the Revenue Commissioners within 21 days after the notification of the decision to that person, apply to have the matter referred to the Appeal Commissioners as if it were an appeal against an assessment, and the provisions of the Income Tax Acts relating to the rehearing of an appeal and to the statement of a case for the opinion of the High Court on a point of law shall apply accordingly with any necessary modifications.

1006 Poundage and certain other fees due to sheriffs or county registrars

[FA88 s71(1) and (2)(a)]

(1) In this section—

"*the Acts*" means—

(a) the Tax Acts,

[(aa) Parts 18A, 18B, 18C and 18D,][1]

(b) the Capital Gains Tax Acts,

(c) the Value-Added Tax Consolidation Act 2010, and the enactments amending or extending that Act,

(d) the Capital Acquisitions Tax Consolidation Act 2003, and the enactments amending or extending that Act, and

(e) Part VI of the Finance Act, 1983, and the enactments amending or extending that Part,

[(f) the *Finance (Local Property Tax) Act 2012*,][2]

[…][3]

and any instruments made thereunder;

"*certificate*" means a certificate issued under [section 960L][4];

"*county registrar*" means a person appointed to be a county registrar under section 35 of the Court Officers Act, 1926;

"*defaulter*" means a person specified or certified in an execution order or certificate on whom a relevant amount specified or certified in the order or certificate is leviable;

"*execution order*" has the same meaning as in the Enforcement of Court Orders Act, 1926;

"*fees*" means the fees known as poundage fees payable under section 14(1) of the Enforcement of Court Orders Act, 1926, and orders made under that section for services in or about the execution of an execution order directing or authorising the execution of an order of a court by the seizure and sale of a person's property or, as may be appropriate, the fees corresponding to those fees payable under [section 960L][5] for the execution of a certificate;

"*interest on unpaid tax*" means interest which has accrued under any provision of the Acts providing for the charging of interest in respect of unpaid tax, including interest on an undercharge of tax which is attributable to fraud or neglect;

"*relevant amount*" means an amount of tax or interest on unpaid tax;

"*tax*" means any tax, duty, levy or charge which, in accordance with any provision of the Acts, is placed under the care and management of the Revenue Commissioners;

references, as respects an execution order, to a relevant amount include references to any amount of costs specified in the order.

(2) Where—

(a) an execution order or certificate specifying or certifying a defaulter and relating to a relevant amount is lodged with the appropriate sheriff or county registrar for execution,

(b) the sheriff or, as the case may be, the county registrar gives notice to the defaulter of the lodgment or of his or her intention to execute the execution order or certificate by seizure of the property of the defaulter to which it relates, or demands payment by the defaulter of the relevant amount, and

(c) the whole or part of the relevant amount is paid to the sheriff or, as the case may be, the county registrar or to the Collector-General, after the giving of that notice or the making of that demand,

then, for the purpose of the liability of the defaulter for the payment of fees and of the exercise of any rights or powers in relation to the collection of fees for the time being vested by law in sheriffs and county registrars—

(i) the sheriff or, as the case may be, the county registrar shall be deemed to have entered, in the execution of the execution order or certificate, into possession of the property referred to in *paragraph (b)*, and

(ii) the payment mentioned in *paragraph (c)* shall be deemed to have been levied, in the execution of the execution order or certificate, by the sheriff or, as the case may be, the county registrar,

and fees shall be payable by the defaulter to such sheriff or, as the case may be, country registrar accordingly in respect of the payment mentioned in *paragraph (c)*.

Amendments

[1] Substituted by FA11 s3(1)(f). Applies for the year of assessment 2011 and each subsequent year of assessment.

[2] Inserted by F(LPT)A 12 s158 & sched(11).

[3] Deleted by FA11 s3(1)(e). Applies for the year of assessment 2011 and each subsequent year of assessment.

[4, 5] Substituted by FA08No.2 sched4(part2). Applies as respects any tax that becomes due and payable on or after 1 March 2009.

Cross References

From Section 1006

Section 960L Recovery by sheriff or county registrar.

To Section 1006

Section 1104 Short title and construction.

1006A Offset between taxes. [Repealed]

Repealed by F(No.2)A08 sched4(part1). Applies as respects any tax that becomes due and payable on or after 1 March 2009.

Cross References

To Section 1006A

Section 480A Relief on retirement for certain income of certain sportspersons.

Section 865A Interest on repayments.

1006B Appropriation of payments. [Repealed]

Repealed by F(No.2)A08 sched4(part1). Applies as respects any tax that becomes due and payable on or after 1 March 2009.

PART 43

Partnerships and European Economic Interest Groupings (EEIG)

1007 Interpretation (Part 43)

[ITA67 s69; FA75 s33(2) and Sch1 PtII]

(1) In this Part—

"*annual payment*" means any payment from which, apart from any insufficiency of profits or gains of the persons making it, income tax is deductible under *section 237*;

"*balancing charge*" means a balancing charge under *Part 9* or *Chapter 1* of *Part 29*, as the case may be;

"*basis period*", in relation to a year of assessment, means the period on the profits or gains of which income tax for that year is to be finally computed under Case I of Schedule D in respect of the trade in question or, where by virtue of the Income Tax Acts the profits or gains of any other period are to be taken to be the profits or gains of that period, that other period;

"*partnership trade*" means a trade carried on by 2 or more persons in partnership;

"*precedent partner*", in relation to a partnership, means the partner who, being resident in the State—

(a) is first named in the partnership agreement,

(b) if there is no agreement, is named singly or with precedence over the other partners in the usual name of the firm, or

(c) is the precedent acting partner, if the person named with precedence is not an acting partner,

and any reference to precedent partner shall, in a case in which no partner is resident in the State, be construed as a reference to the agent, manager or factor of the firm resident in the State;

"*relevant period*", in relation to a partnership trade, means a continuous period the whole or part of which is after the 5th day of April, 1965—

(a) beginning at a time when either—

(i) the trade was not carried on immediately before that time by 2 or more persons in partnership, or

(ii) none of the persons then carrying on the trade in partnership was one of the persons who immediately before that time carried on the trade in partnership, and

(b) continuing only so long as there has not occurred a time when either—

(i) the trade is not carried on immediately after that time by 2 or more persons in partnership, or

(ii) none of the persons then carrying on the trade in partnership is one of the persons who immediately after that time carry on the trade in partnership,

subject to the condition that, in the case of any such period which apart from this condition would have begun before the 6th day of April, 1965, "*the relevant period*" shall be taken as having begun at the time, or at the last of 2 or more times, at which, a change having occurred in the partnership of persons then engaged in carrying on the trade, the persons so engaged immediately after the time were to be treated for the purposes of income tax as having set up or commenced the trade at that time.

(2) In relation to a case in which a partnership trade is from time to time during a relevant period carried on by 2 or more different partnerships of persons, any reference in this Part to the partnership shall, unless the context otherwise requires, be construed as including a reference to any partnership of persons by whom the trade has been carried on since the beginning of the relevant period and any reference to a partner shall be construed correspondingly.

(3) This Part shall, with any necessary modifications, apply in relation to professions as it applies in relation to trades.

Cross References

From Section 1007

Section 237 Annual payments payable wholly out of taxed income.
Section 268 Meaning of "industrial building or structure".
Section 754 Interpretation (Chapter 1).

To Section 1007

Section 267Q Treatment of deposit return.
Section 409A Income tax: restriction on use of capital allowances on certain industrial buildings and other premises.
Section 409B Income tax: restriction on use of capital allowances on certain hotels, etc.
Section 655 Farming and market gardening profits to be charged to tax under Schedule D.
Section 760 Capital sums: effect of death, winding up and partnership changes.
Section 880 Partnership returns.
Section 886 Obligation to keep certain records.
Section 950 Interpretation (Part 41).
Section 1034 Assessment.
Schedule 31 Consequential Amendments

1008 Separate assessment of partners

[ITA67 s71]

(1) In the case of a partnership trade, the Income Tax Acts shall, subject to this Part, apply in relation to any partner in the partnership as if for any relevant period—

(a) any profits or gains arising to that partner from the trade and any loss sustained by that partner in the trade were respectively profits or gains of, and loss sustained in, a trade (in this Part referred to as a "*several trade*") carried on solely by that partner, being a trade—

(i) set up or commenced at the beginning of the relevant period, or if that partner commenced to be engaged in carrying on the partnership trade at some time in the relevant period other than the beginning of that period, at the time when that partner so commenced, and

(ii) when that partner ceases to be engaged in carrying on the partnership trade either during the relevant period or at the end of that period, permanently discontinued at the time when that partner so ceases, and

(b) that partner had paid the part that partner was liable to bear of any annual payment paid by the partnership.

(2) (a)[(i)][1] For any year or period within the relevant period the amount of the profits or gains arising to any partner from that partner's several trade, or the amount of loss sustained by that partner in that trade, shall for the purposes of *subsection (1)* be taken to be so much of the full amount of the profits or gains of the partnership trade or, as the case

may be, of the full amount of the loss sustained in the partnership trade as would fall to that partner's share on an apportionment of those profits or gains or, as the case may be, of that loss made in accordance with the terms of the partnership agreement as to the sharing of profits and losses.

[(ii) Where for any year or period within the relevant period the aggregate of the respective amounts (in this subparagraph referred to as the "*aggregate*") of the profits or gains which under *subparagraph (i)* are taken as arising to each partner in the partnership is less than the full amount of the profits or gains of the partnership trade for that year or period, then the amount of the difference (in this subparagraph referred to as the "*balance*") between that full amount and the aggregate shall for the purposes of *subsection (1)* be apportioned in full between the partners—

(I) in the ratio which is expressed between the partners in relation to the apportionment of the balance, or

(II) where there is no such ratio expressed—

(A) in the same ratio as the ratio which applies between the respective amounts of the profits or gains which, under *subparagraph (i)*, were taken as arising to each partner, or

(B) where no amount of profits or gains was, under *subparagraph (i)*, taken as arising to any individual partner, in equal shares.][2]

(b) Where the year or period (in this paragraph referred to as "*the period of computation*") for which the profits or gains of, or the loss sustained in, the several trade of a partner is to be computed under this subsection is or is part of a year or period for which an account of the partnership trade has been made up, *sections 65* and *107* shall apply in relation to the partner as if an account of that partner's several trade had been made up for the period of computation.

(3) (a) For the purposes of *subsection (2)* and subject to *paragraph (b)*, the full amount of the profits or gains of the partnership trade for any year or period, or the full amount of the loss sustained in such trade in any year or period, shall, subject to *section 1012*, be determined by the inspector, and any such determination shall be made as it would have been made if the trade—

(i) had been set up or commenced at the beginning of the relevant period,

(ii) where the relevant period has come to an end, had been permanently discontinued at the end of that period, and

(iii) had at all times within the relevant period been carried on by one and the same person and everything done in the carrying on of the trade to or by the persons by whom it was in fact carried on had been done to or by that person.

(b) In a case in which the relevant period began at some time before the 6th day of April, 1965, and the trade was not treated for the purposes of income tax as having been set up or commenced at that time—

(i) the relevant period shall for the purposes of this subsection be deemed to have begun at the time at which the trade was treated for the purposes of income tax as having been set up or commenced, and

(ii) any profits or gains arising to any person from the trade, or any loss sustained by that person in the trade, for any year or period within the relevant period during which that person was engaged in the trade on that person's own account shall be deemed to be profits or gains arising to that person from, or, as the case may be, a loss sustained by that person in, a partnership trade in which that person was entitled during the year or period in question to the full amount of the profits or gains arising or was liable to bear the full amount of the loss.

[…][3]

(5) This section shall not cause any income which apart from this section is not earned income to become earned income.

Amendments

[1] Renumbered by FA07 s30(1)(a)(i). This section applies as respects the full amount of the profits or gains of a partnership trade for any year or period ending on or after 1 January 2007.

[2] Inserted by FA07 s30(1)(a)(ii). This section applies as respects the full amount of the profits or gains of a partnership trade for any year or period ending on or after 1 January 2007.

[3] Deleted by FA07 s30(1)(b). This section applies as respects the full amount of the profits or gains of a partnership trade for any year or period ending on or after 1 January 2007.

Revenue Precedents

A partnership determination is not necessary in the case of farmers trading in partnership. In view of section 655(2) TCA 1997, partnership determination is not required. IT892031

Whether section 1008(4) applies where the partners in a partnership decide not to allocate the full profits for a basis period to the partners? Section 1008(4) applies only where the profits to which the partners are entitled do not exhaust the profits for the period. In a case in which the partners are entitled to all of the profits but do not allocate them to any partner in particular, the sub-section does not apply. IT962007

In joint assessment cases, where income was previously returned as income of one spouse, whether a claim that both spouses are and have been in partnership can be sustained and tax treatment allowed accordingly? Whether a husband and wife are and have been in partnership is always a question of fact. Onus is on the claimants to show, as a point of fact that they are and were in partnership. IT972506

Cross References

From Section 1008

Section 65 Cases I and II: basis of assessment.
Section 107 Apportionment of profits.
Section 1012 Modification of provisions as to appeals.

To Section 1008

Section 293 Application to partnerships.
Section 388 Meaning of "permanently discontinued" for purposes of terminal loss.
Section 1009 Partnerships involving companies.
Section 1012 Modification of provisions as to appeals.

1009 Partnerships involving companies

[CTA76 s32 (apart from proviso to (3)(c))]

(1) In this section, profits shall not be taken as including chargeable gains.

(2) Subject to this section, *subsections (1)*, *(2)(a)* and *(3)* of *section 1008* shall apply for the purposes of corporation tax as they apply for the purposes of income tax.

(3) Where the whole or part of an accounting period of a company is or is part of a period for which an account of a partnership trade has been made up, any

necessary apportionment shall be made in computing the profits from or loss sustained in the company's several trade for the accounting period of the company.

(4) (a) In this subsection, "*the relevant amount*" means—

(i) where the year of assessment and the accounting period coincide, the whole amount of the appropriate share of the joint allowance or, as the case may be, the whole amount of the appropriate share of the joint charge, and

(ii) where part only of the year of assessment is within the accounting period, such portion of the appropriate share of the joint allowance or, as the case may be, such portion of the appropriate share of the joint charge as is apportioned to that part of the year of assessment which falls within the accounting period.

(b) Where a capital allowance equal to an appropriate share of a joint allowance would be made, if *section 21(2)* had not been enacted, in charging to income tax the profits of a company's several trade for any year of assessment, the relevant amount shall for corporation tax purposes be treated as a trading expense of the company's several trade for any accounting period of the company any part of which falls within that year of assessment.

(c) Where a balancing charge equal to an appropriate share of a joint charge would be made, if *section 21(2)* had not been enacted, in charging to income tax the profits of a company's several trade for any year of assessment, the relevant amount shall for corporation tax purposes be treated as a trading receipt of the company's several trade for any accounting period of the company any part of which falls within that year of assessment.

(d) Notwithstanding *section 1010(8)*, any reference in this subsection to a joint allowance for a year of assessment shall not include a reference to any capital allowance which is or could be brought forward from a previous year of assessment.

(5) Where under this section an amount is to be apportioned to—

(a) a part of an accounting period of a company,

(b) a part of a period for which an account of a partnership trade has been made up, or

(c) a part of a year of assessment,

the apportionment shall be made by reference to the number of months or fractions of months contained in that part and in the remainder of that accounting period, period or year, as the case may be.

Cross References

From Section 1009

Section 21 The charge to corporation tax and exclusion of income tax and capital gains tax.

Section 1008 Separate assessment of partners.

Section 1010 Capital allowances and balancing charges in partnership cases.

To Section 1009

Section 426 Partnerships involving companies: effect of arrangements for transferring relief.

Section 1014 Tax treatment of profits, losses and capital gains arising from activities of a European Economic Interest Grouping (EEIG).

1010 Capital allowances and balancing charges in partnership cases

[ITA67 s72; FA80 s17(2)]

(1) The provisions of the Income Tax Acts relating to the making of capital allowances and balancing charges in charging the profits or gains of a trade shall, in relation to the several trade of a partner in a partnership, apply subject to this section.

(2) Where for any year of assessment a claim has been made as provided by *subsection (9)* by the precedent partner for the time being of any partnership, there shall be made to any partner in the partnership in charging the profits or gains of that partner's several trade a capital allowance in respect of any expenditure or property equal to that partner's appropriate share of any capital allowance for that year, excluding any amount carried forward from an earlier year, (in this section referred to as a "*joint allowance*") which, apart from any insufficiency of profits or gains, might have been made in respect of that expenditure or property in charging the profits or gains of the partnership trade if the Income Tax Acts had provided that those profits should be charged by joint assessment on the persons carrying on the trade in the year of assessment as if—

(a) those persons had at all times been carrying on the trade and everything done to or by their predecessors in, or in relation to, the carrying on of the trade had been done to or by them, and

(b) the trade had been set up or commenced at the beginning of the relevant period and, where the relevant period has come to an end, had been permanently discontinued at the end of that period.

(3) There shall be made for any year of assessment on any partner in a partnership in charging the profits or gains of that partner's several trade a balancing charge equal to that partner's appropriate share of any balancing charge (in this section referred to as a "*joint charge*") which would have been made for that year in charging the profits or gains of the partnership trade if the Income Tax Acts had provided that those profits should be charged as specified in *subsection (2)*.

(4) Where at the end of the relevant period a person or a partnership of persons succeeds to a partnership trade and any property which immediately before the succession takes place was in use for the purposes of the partnership trade and, without being sold, is immediately after the succession takes place in use for the purposes of the trade carried on by the successor or successors, *section 313(1)* shall apply as it applies where by virtue of *section 69* a trade is to be treated as discontinued.

(5) Where for a partnership trade the relevant period began at some time before the 6th day of April, 1965, and the trade was not treated for the purposes of income tax as having been set up or commenced at that time, the relevant period shall for the purposes of *subsections (2)* and *(3)* be deemed to have begun at the time at which the trade was treated for the purposes of income tax as having been set up or commenced.

(6) (a) In relation to any partnership trade, the total amount of all joint allowances for any year of assessment and the total amount of all joint charges for that year shall, subject to *section 1012*, be determined by the inspector.

(b) Where after a determination has been made under *paragraph (a)* the inspector becomes aware of any facts or events by reference to which the determination is in his or her opinion incorrect, the inspector may from time to time and as often as appears to him or her to be necessary make a revised determination, and any such revised determination shall supersede any earlier determination [and any such assessments, amendments of assessments][1] or repayments of tax shall be made as may be necessary.

(7) (a) In this subsection, "*trading period*" means, where the relevant period begins or ends during the year of assessment for which the joint allowance or joint charge is computed, the part of that year of assessment which falls within the relevant period or, in any other case, that year of assessment.

(b) Subject to *paragraph (c)*, for any year of assessment the partners' appropriate shares of a joint allowance or of a joint charge shall be determined by apportioning the full amount of that allowance or charge between the partners on the same basis as a like amount of profits arising in the trading period from the partnership trade, and accruing from day to day over that period, would be apportioned in accordance with the terms of the partnership if any salary, interest on capital or other sum to which any partner was entitled without regard to the amount of the profits arising from the partnership trade had already been provided for.

(c) Where for any year of assessment all the partners (any deceased partner being represented by his or her legal representatives) allege, by notice in writing signed by them and sent to the inspector within 24 months after the end of the year of assessment, that hardship is caused to one or more partners by the apportionment of a joint allowance or joint charge on the basis set out in *paragraph (b)*, the Revenue Commissioners may, on being satisfied that hardship has been caused, give such relief as in their opinion is just by making a new apportionment of the joint allowance or joint charge, and any such new apportionment shall for the purposes of the Income Tax Acts apply as if it were an apportionment made under *paragraph (b)*, [and any such assessments, amendments of assessments][2] or repayments of tax shall be made as may be necessary.

(8) (a) In this subsection, "*capital allowance brought forward*" means—

(i) any capital allowance or part of a capital allowance due to be made to the partnership for the year 1964-65 or any earlier year of assessment which might, if Part VIII of the Finance Act, 1965, had not been enacted, have been carried forward and made as a deduction in charging the profits or gains of the partnership trade for the year 1965-66, and

(ii) any capital allowance or part of a capital allowance due to be made to a partner for the year 1965-66 or a later year of assessment which but for this subsection might have been carried forward and made as a deduction in charging the profits or gains of the several trade of the partner for a year of assessment subsequent to that for which the capital allowance was computed.

(b) For any year of assessment the aggregate amount of all capital allowances brought forward shall for the purposes of making the assessments on the partners be deemed to be a joint allowance for that year, and *subsection (7)* shall apply accordingly.

(9) In relation to a partnership trade—

(a) any claim for a joint allowance for any year of assessment shall be made by the precedent partner as if it were a claim for a capital allowance to be made to that partner and shall be included in the return delivered by that partner under *section 880* in relation to that year of assessment, and

(b) any claim for a joint allowance shall be deemed to be a claim by every partner for a capital allowance to be made to such partner, being a capital allowance equal to such partner's appropriate share of that joint allowance.

Amendments

1, 2 Substituted by FA12 sched4(part 2)(g).

Cross References

From Section 1010

Section 69 Changes of proprietorship.
Section 313 Effect, in certain cases, of succession to trade, etc.
Section 880 Partnership returns.
Section 1012 Modification of provisions as to appeals.

To Section 1010

Section 293 Application to partnerships.
Section 313 Effect, in certain cases, of succession to trade, etc.
Section 1009 Partnerships involving companies.
Section 1011 Provision as to charges under section 757.
Section 1012 Modification of provisions as to appeals.
Section 1014 Tax treatment of profits, losses and capital gains arising from activities of a European Economic Interest Grouping (EEIG).

1011 Provision as to charges under section 757

[ITA67 s74]

(1) Where for any year of assessment a charge under *section 757* (in this section referred to as a "*joint charge*") would have been made in charging the profits or gains of a partnership trade if the Income Tax Acts had provided that those profits or gains should be charged as specified in *section 1010(2)*, there shall be made on any partner in the partnership in charging the profits or gains of that partner's several trade a charge under *section 757* equal to that partner's appropriate share of the joint charge.

(2) A partner's appropriate share of a joint charge for the purposes of *subsection (1)* shall be determined in the same way as the partner's appropriate share of a joint charge within the meaning of *section 1010* is to be determined by virtue of *subsection (7)* of that section.

Cross References

From Section 1011

Section 757 Charges on capital sums received for sale of patent rights.
Section 1010 Capital allowances and balancing charges in partnership cases.

1012 Modification of provisions as to appeals

[ITA67 s73; F(MP)A68 s3(2) and Sch PtI]

(1) The inspector may give notice to the partnership concerned of any determination made by him or her under *section 1008(3)* or *1010(6)* by delivering a statement in writing of that determination to the precedent partner for the time being of the partnership, and the provisions of the Income Tax Acts relating to appeals against assessments to income tax shall, with any necessary modifications, apply in relation to any determination and any notice of a determination as if they were respectively such an assessment and notice of such an assessment.

(2) Where a determination has become final and conclusive or, in the case of a determination under *subsection (6)* of *section 1010* has become final and conclusive subject to *paragraph (b)* of that subsection, no question as to its correctness shall be raised on the hearing or on the rehearing of an appeal by any partner either against an assessment in respect of the profits or gains of that partner's several trade or against a determination by the inspector on a claim under *section 381*.

(3) Where on any appeal mentioned in *subsection (2)* any question arises as to an apportionment to be made under *section 1008(2)* or *1010(7)* and it appears that the question is material as respects the liability to income tax (for whatever year of assessment) of 2 or more persons, all those persons shall be notified of the time and place of the hearing and shall be entitled to appear and be heard by the Appeal Commissioners or to make representations to them in writing.

Cross References

From Section 1012

Section 381 Right to repayment of tax by reference to losses.
Section 1008 Separate assessment of partners.
Section 1010 Capital allowances and balancing charges in partnership cases.

To Section 1012

Section 1008 Separate assessment of partners.
Section 1010 Capital allowances and balancing charges in partnership cases.

1013 Limited partnerships

[FA86 s46(1) to (3) and (6), FA92 s23; FA94 s29]

(1) In this section—

["*active partner*", in relation to a partnership trade, means a partner who works for the greater part of his or her time on the day-to-day management or conduct of the partnership trade;][1]

"*the aggregate amount*", in relation to a trade, means—

(a) in the case of an individual, the aggregate of amounts given or allowed to the individual at any time under any of the specified provisions—

(i) in respect of a loss sustained by him or her in the trade, or of interest paid by him or her by reason of his or her participation in the trade, in any relevant year of assessment, or

(ii) as an allowance to be made to him or her for any relevant year of assessment either in taxing the trade or by means of discharge or repayment of tax to which he or she is entitled by reason of his or her participation in the trade,

and

(b) in the case of a company, the aggregate of amounts given or allowed to the company (in this section referred to as "*the partner company*") or to another company at any time under any of the specified provisions—

(i) in respect of a loss incurred by the partner company in the trade, or of charges paid by it or another company by reason of its participation in the trade, in any relevant accounting period, or

(ii) as an allowance to be made to the partner company for any relevant accounting period either in taxing the trade or by means of discharge or repayment of tax to which it is entitled by reason of its participation in the trade;

"*limited partner*", in relation to a trade, means—

(a) a person carrying on the trade as a limited partner in a limited partnership registered under the Limited Partnerships Act, 1907,

(b) a person carrying on the trade as a general partner in a partnership who is not entitled to take part in the management of the trade but is entitled to have the person's liabilities, or those liabilities beyond a certain limit, for debts or obligations incurred for the purposes of the trade, discharged or [reimbursed by some other person,][2]

(c) a person who carries on the trade jointly with others and, under the law of any territory outside the State, is not entitled to take part in the management of the trade and is not liable beyond a certain limit for debts or obligations [incurred for the purposes of the][3][trade,][4]

[(d) a person who carries on the trade as a general partner in a partnership otherwise than as an active [partner,][5]][6]

[(e) a person who carries on the trade as a partner in a partnership registered under the law of any territory outside the State, otherwise than as an active partner, or

(f) a person who carries on the trade jointly with others under any agreement, arrangement, scheme or understanding which is governed by the law of any territory outside the State, otherwise than as a person who works for the greater part of his or her time on the day-to-day management or conduct of that trade;][7]

"*relevant accounting period*" means an accounting period of the partner company which ends on or after the specified date and at any time during which it carried on the trade as a limited partner;

"*the relevant time*" means—

(a) in the case of an individual, the end of the relevant year of assessment in which the loss is sustained or the interest is paid, or for which the allowance is to be made (except that where the individual ceased to carry on the trade during that year of assessment it is the time when he or she so ceased), and

(b) in the case of a partner company, the end of the relevant accounting period in which the loss is incurred or the charges are paid, or for which the allowance is to be made (except that where the partner company ceases to carry on the trade during that accounting period it is the time when the partner company so ceased);

"*relevant year of assessment*" means a year of assessment which ends after the specified date and at any time during which the individual carried on the trade as a limited partner;

"*the specified date*" means the 22nd day of May, 1985;

"*the specified provisions*" means—

(a) in the case of an individual, *sections 245* to *255*, *305* and *381*, and

(b) in the case of a company, *sections 243*, *308(4)* and *396(2)* and *subsections (1)*, *(2)* and *(6)* of *section 420*.

(2) (a) Where, in the case of an individual who is a limited partner in relation to a trade, an amount may apart from this section be given or allowed under any of the specified provisions—

(i) in respect of a loss sustained by the individual in the trade, or of interest paid by him or her by reason of his or her participation in the trade, in a relevant year of assessment, or

(ii) as an allowance to be made to the individual for a relevant year of assessment either in taxing the trade or by means of discharge or repayment of tax to which he or she is entitled by reason of his or her participation in the trade,

such an amount may be given or allowed—

(I) as respects a contribution by a limited partner to the trade of the limited partnership made before the 24th day of April, 1992, otherwise than against income consisting of profits or [gains arising from the trade,][8]

(II) as respects such a contribution made on or after the 24th day of April, 1992, only against income consisting of [profits or gains arising from the][9][trade,][10],

[(III) where the individual is a limited partner in relation to a trade by virtue of *paragraph (d)* of the definition of "*limited partner*" and the relevant year of assessment is—

(A) in the case of such a partner where the activities of the trade include the activity of producing, distributing, or the holding of or of an interest in, films or video tapes or the activity of exploring for, or exploiting, oil or gas resources, the year of assessment 1997-1998 or any subsequent year of assessment, subject to *subsection (2A)*, or

(B) in any other case, the year of assessment 1999-2000 or any subsequent year of assessment, subject to *subsection (2B)*,

only against income consisting of profits or gains arising from the [trade, or][11]][12]

[(IV) where the individual is a limited partner in relation to a trade by virtue of *paragraph (e)* or *(f)* of the definition of "*limited partner*" and the relevant year of assessment is the year of assessment 2005 or any subsequent year of assessment, only against income consisting of profits or gains arising from the trade,][13]

and only to the extent that the amount given or allowed or, as the case may be, the aggregate amount in relation to that trade does not exceed the amount of his or her contribution to the trade at the relevant time.

(b) Where, in the case of a partner company which is a limited partner in relation to a trade, an amount may apart from this section be given or allowed under any of the specified provisions—

(i) in respect of a loss sustained by the partner company in the trade, or of charges paid by the partner company or another company by reason of its participation in the trade, in a relevant accounting period, or

(ii) as an allowance to be made to the partner company for a relevant accounting period either in taxing the trade or by means of discharge or repayment of tax to which it is entitled by reason of its participation in the trade, such an amount may be given or allowed to the partner company—

(I) as respects a contribution by a limited partner to the trade of the limited partnership made before the 24th day of April, 1992, otherwise than against profits or gains arising from the trade, or to another company, or

(II) as respects such a contribution made on or after the 24th day of April, 1992, only against profits or gains arising from the trade,

and only to the extent that the amount given or allowed or, as the case may be, the aggregate amount in relation to that trade does not exceed the partner company's contribution to the trade at the relevant time.

[(2A) [*Subparagraph (III)(A)*][14] of *subsection (2)(a)* shall not apply to—

(a) interest paid on or before the 27th day of February, 1998,

(b) an allowance to be made in respect of expenditure incurred on or before the 27th day of February, 1998, or

(c) a loss sustained in the year of assessment 1997-98 which would have been the loss sustained in that year if—

(i) that year of assessment had ended on the 27th day of February, 1998, and

(ii) the loss were determined only by reference to accounts made up in relation to the trade for the period commencing on the 6th day of April, 1997, or if later, the date the trade was set up and commenced, and ending on the 27th day of February, 1998, and not by reference to accounts made up for any other period.][15]

[(2B) *Subparagraph (III)(B)* of *subsection (2)(a)* shall not apply to—

(a) interest paid on or before 29 February 2000,

(b) an allowance to be made in respect of expenditure incurred on or before 29 February 2000, or

(c) a loss sustained in the year of assessment 1999-2000 which would have been the loss sustained in that year if—

(i) that year of assessment had ended on 29 February 2000, and

(ii) the loss were determined only by reference to accounts made up in relation to the trade for the period commencing on 6 April 1999 or, if later, the date the trade commenced and ending on 29 February 2000 and not by reference to accounts made up for any other period.

(2C) (a) In this subsection—

"*excepted expenditure*" means expenditure to which the provisions of *section 409A* apply and expenditure to which the provisions of that section or *section 409B* would apply but for the provisions of—

(i) *section 409A(5)*, or

(ii) *paragraph (a)* of the definition of "*specified building*" in *subsection (1)* or *(4)* of *section 409B*,

as the case may be;

"*specified deduction*" means the deduction referred to in *section 324(2)*, *333(2)*, *345(3)*, *354(3)*, *370(3)*, *372E(3)* or *372O(3)* as the "*second-mentioned deduction*" or in paragraph 13 of *Schedule 32* as the "*further deduction*";

"*specified individual*", in relation to a partnership trade, means an individual who is a limited partner in relation to the trade by virtue only of *paragraph (d)* of the definition of "*limited partner*", and a reference to a specified individual shall be construed accordingly.

(b) (i) *Subsection (2)(a)* shall not apply to a specified individual to which *paragraph (c), (d)* or *(e)*, as the case may be, applies to the extent that—

(I) the interest referred to in *subparagraph (i)* of *paragraph (a)* of that subsection is interest paid by the individual by reason of his or her participation in a trade referred to in *paragraph (c), (d)* or *(e)*, as the case may be, in a relevant year of assessment,

(II) the loss referred to in *subparagraph (i)* of *paragraph (a)* of that subsection is a loss sustained by the individual in a trade referred to in *paragraph (c), (d)* or *(e)*, as the case may be, in a relevant year of assessment,

(III) the allowance referred to in *subparagraph (ii)* of *paragraph (a)* of that subsection is an allowance to be made to the individual for a relevant year of assessment either in taxing a trade or by means of discharge or repayment of tax to which he or she is entitled by reason of his or her participation in a trade referred to in *paragraph (c), (d)* or *(e)*, as the case may be.

(ii) *Subsection (2)(a)* shall not apply to a specified individual to the extent that—

(I) the interest referred to in *subparagraph (i)* of *paragraph (a)* of that subsection is interest paid by the individual on a loan where the proceeds of the loan were used by the partnership to incur excepted expenditure in a relevant year of assessment,

(II) the loss referred to in *subparagraph (i)* of *paragraph (a)* of that subsection arises from the taking into account for the purposes of *section 392(1)* of an allowance to be made in respect of excepted expenditure, or

(III) the allowance referred to in *subparagraph (ii)* of *paragraph (a)* of that subsection is an allowance to be made to the individual for a relevant year of assessment in respect of excepted expenditure.

(c) This paragraph applies to a specified individual where—

(i) the partnership trade consists wholly of the leasing of machinery or plant to a qualifying company within the meaning of *section 486B*, and

(ii) the expenditure incurred on the provision of the machinery or plant was incurred under an obligation entered into by the lessor (within the meaning of *section 403*) and the lessee (within the meaning of *section 403*) before 1 March 2001.

(d) This paragraph applies to a specified individual where in charging the profits or gains of the individual's several trade an allowance in respect of capital expenditure on machinery or plant to which the provisions of *section 284(3A)* apply has been or is to be made to that individual; but this paragraph shall not apply to such an individual as respects—

(i) interest paid by that individual on a loan taken out on or after 4 September 2000,

(ii) an allowance to be made to that individual for capital expenditure incurred on or after 4 September 2000, or

(iii) a loss sustained in the trade in [the year of assessment 2002][16] or any subsequent year of assessment to the extent that the loss does not arise from the taking into account for the purposes of *section 392(1)* of an allowance to be made in accordance with the provisions of *section 284(3A)*.

(e) This paragraph applies to a specified individual where in computing the amount of the profits or gains, if any, of the partnership trade a specified deduction has been or is to be allowed in respect of a premises occupied by the partnership for the purposes of the partnership trade, and—

(i) the individual became a partner in the partnership before 29 February 2000,

(ii) the individual made a contribution to the partnership trade before that date, and

(iii) the qualifying lease in respect of which a specified deduction has been or is to be allowed was granted to or acquired by the partnership before that date;

but—

(I) subject to clause (II), this paragraph shall not apply to such an individual as respects—

(A) interest paid by that individual in,

(B) an allowance to be made to that individual for, or

(C) any loss sustained in the trade for,

any year of assessment for which a specified deduction in respect of the premises is not allowed in arriving at the amount of the profits or gains of the individual's several trade to be charged to tax or, as the case may be, the loss sustained therein or any subsequent year of assessment, and

(II) where in computing the amount of the profits or gains, if any, of the partnership trade a second-mentioned deduction (within the meaning of *section 354(3)*) may be made by virtue of *section 354(3)*, this paragraph shall not apply to such an individual as respects—

(A) interest paid by that individual on or after [1 January 2005][17],

(B) an allowance to be made to that individual for [the year of assessment 2005][18] or any subsequent year of assessment, or

(C) any loss sustained in that trade in [the year of assessment 2005][19] or any subsequent year of assessment.][20]

(3) (a) A person's contribution to a trade at any time shall be the aggregate of—

(i) the amount which the person has contributed to the trade as capital and has not subsequently, either directly or indirectly, drawn out or received back from the partnership or from a person connected with the partnership (other than anything, in relation to expenditure which the person has incurred on behalf of the partnership trade or in providing facilities for the partnership trade, which the person is or may be entitled so to draw out or receive back at any time when the person carries on the trade as a limited partner or which the person is or may be entitled to require another person to reimburse the person), and

(ii) the amount of any profits or gains of the trade to which the person is entitled but which the person has not received in money or money's worth.

(b) A person shall for the purposes of *paragraph (a)* be treated as having received back an amount contributed by the person to the partnership if—

(i) the person received consideration of that amount or value for the sale of the person's interest, or any part of the person's interest, in the partnership,

(ii) the partnership or any person connected with the partnership repays that amount of a loan or an advance from the person, or

(iii) the person receives that amount or value for assigning any debt due to the person from the partnership or from any person connected with the partnership.

(4) (a) This subsection shall apply, in relation to an amount given or allowed under any of the specified provisions, as respects a contribution by a partner to the trade of the partnership made on or after the 11th day of April, 1994.

(b) For the purposes of this section, where in connection with the making of a contribution to a partnership trade by a general partner in the partnership—

(i) there exists any agreement, arrangement, scheme or understanding under which the partner is required to cease to be a partner in the partnership at any time before the partner is entitled to receive back from the partnership the full amount of the partner's contribution to the trade, or

(ii) by virtue of any agreement, arrangement, scheme or understanding—

(I) any asset owned by the partner is exempt from execution on goods or from a process or mode of enforcement of a debt of the partner or the partnership, or

(II) any other limit or restriction is placed on the creditor's entitlement to recover any such debt from the partner,

the partner shall be treated as a person who is not entitled to take part in the management of the trade but is entitled to have the person's liabilities, or the person's liabilities beyond a certain limit, for debts or obligations incurred for the purposes of the trade, discharged or reimbursed by some other person.

(c) In determining whether an amount is given or allowed under any of the specified provisions as respects a contribution to a trade on or after the 11th day of April, 1994, any amount which would not otherwise have been given or allowed by virtue of this section but for a contribution to a trade on or after that date and on the basis that *paragraph (a)* had not been enacted shall be treated as given or allowed as respects such a contribution.

(5) (a) In determining whether an amount is given or allowed under any of the specified provisions as respects a contribution to a trade on or after the 24th day of April, 1992, any amount which would not otherwise have been given or allowed by virtue of this section but for a contribution to a trade

on or after that date and on the basis that *paragraphs (a)(II)* and *(b)(II)* of *subsection (2)* had not been enacted shall be treated as given or allowed as respects such a contribution.

(b) Notwithstanding *paragraph (a)* and *paragraphs (a)(II)* and *(b)(II)* of *subsection (2)*, this section shall apply in so far as the trade of a limited partnership consists of the management and letting of holiday cottages within the meaning of *section 268*, where—

(i) a written contract for the construction of the holiday cottages was signed and construction work had commenced before the 24th day of April, 1992, and

(ii) the construction work is completed before the 6th day of April, 1993,

as if references to on or after the 24th day of April, 1992, were references to on or after the 1st day of September, 1992.

Amendments

[1] Inserted by FA98 s50(1)(a)(i). This section shall apply as on and from the 28th day of February, 1998.

[2] Substituted by FA98 s50(1)(a)(ii)(I). This section shall apply as on and from the 28th day of February, 1998.

[3] Substituted by FA98 s50(1)(a)(ii)(II). This section shall apply as on and from the 28th day of February, 1998.

[4] Substituted by FA05 s37(a)(i).

[5] Substituted by FA05 s37(a)(ii).

[6] Substituted by FA00 s70(1)(a). This section shall apply as on and from 29 February 2000.

[7] Inserted by FA05 s37(a)(iii).

[8] Substituted by FA98 s50(1)(b)(i). This section shall apply as on and from the 28th day of February, 1998.

[9] Substituted by FA98 s50(1)(b)(ii). This section shall apply as on and from the 28th day of February, 1998.

[10] Substituted by FA05 s37(b)(i).

[11] Substituted by FA05 s37(b)(ii).

[12] Substituted by FA00 s70(1)(b). This section shall apply as on and from 29 February 2000.

[13] Inserted by FA05 s37(b)(iii).

[14] Substituted by FA00 s70(1)(c). This section shall apply as on and from 29 February 2000.

[15] Inserted by FA98 s50(1)(c). This section shall apply as on and from the 28th day of February, 1998.

[16] Substituted by FA01 sched2(55)(a).

[17] Substituted by FA01 sched2(55)(b)(i).

[18, 19] Substituted by FA01 sched2(55)(b)(ii).

[20] Inserted by FA00 s70(1)(d). This section shall apply as on and from 29 February 2000.

Cross References

From Section 1013

Section 243 Allowance of charges on income.
Section 245 Relief for certain bridging loans.
Section 255 Arrangements for payment of interest less tax or of fixed net amount.
Section 268 Meaning of "industrial building or structure".
Section 284 Wear and tear allowances.
Section 305 Income tax: manner of granting, and effect of, allowances made by means of discharge or repayment of tax.
Section 308 Corporation tax: manner of granting, and effect of, allowances made by means of discharge or repayment of tax.
Section 324 Double rent allowance in respect of rent paid for certain business premises.
Section 333 Double rent allowance in respect of rent paid for certain business premises.

Section 345 Double rent allowance in respect of rent paid for certain business premises.
Section 354 Double rent allowance in respect of rent paid for certain business premises.
Section 370 Double rent allowance in respect of rent paid for certain business premises.
Section 372E Double rent allowance in respect of rent paid for certain business premises.
Section 372O Double rent allowance in respect of rent paid for certain business premises.
Section 381 Right to repayment of tax by reference to losses.
Section 392 Option to treat capital allowances as creating or augmenting a loss.
Section 396 Relief for trading losses other than terminal losses.
Section 403 Restriction on use of capital allowances for certain leased assets.
Section 409A Income tax: restriction on use of capital allowances on certain industrial buildings and other premises.
Section 409B Income tax: restriction on use of capital allowances on certain hotels, etc.
Section 420 Losses, etc. which may be surrendered by means of group relief.
Schedule 32 Transitional Provisions

To Section 1013

Section 1014 Tax treatment of profits, losses and capital gains arising from activities of a European Economic Interest Grouping (EEIG).

1014 Tax treatment of profits, losses and capital gains arising from activities of a European Economic Interest Grouping (EEIG)

[FA90 s29(1), (2), (5) and (6)]

(1) In this section, "*grouping*" means a European Economic Interest Grouping formed on the terms, in the manner and with the effects laid down in—

(a) Council Regulation (EEC) No 2137/85 of 25 July 1985* on the European Economic Interest Grouping (EEIG), and

* O.J. L 119, 31.07.1985 p.1.

(b) the European Communities (European Economic Interest Groupings) Regulations, 1989 (S.I. No. 191 of 1989),

and references to members of a grouping shall be construed accordingly.

(2) Notwithstanding anything in the Tax Acts or in the Capital Gains Tax Acts, a grouping shall be neither—

(a) charged to income tax, corporation tax or capital gains tax, as the case may be, in respect of profits or gains or chargeable gains arising to it, nor

(b) entitled to relief for a loss sustained by it,

and any assessment required to be made on such profits or gains or chargeable gains, and any relief for a loss, shall as appropriate be made on and allowed to the members of a grouping in accordance with this section.

(3) This Part (other than *sections 1009*, *1010(8)* and *1013*) and *sections 30* and *913(7)* shall apply with any necessary modifications to the activities of a grouping in the same manner as they apply to a trade or profession carried on by 2 or more persons in partnership.

(4) In particular but without prejudice to the generality of *subsection (3)*, the provisions mentioned in that subsection shall in their application for the purposes of this section apply as if—

(a) references to a partnership agreement were references to the contract forming or providing for the formation of a grouping,

(b) references to a partner were references to a member of a grouping, and

(c) anything done or required to be done by the precedent acting partner was done or required to be done by the grouping.

Cross References

From Section 1014

Section 30 Partnerships.

Section 913 Application of income tax provisions relating to returns, etc.

Section 1009 Partnerships involving companies.

Section 1010 Capital allowances and balancing charges in partnership cases.

Section 1013 Limited partnerships.

To Section 1014

Section 4 Interpretation of Corporation Tax Acts.

Section 5 Interpretation of Capital Gains Tax Acts.

PART 44

Married, Separated and Divorced Persons

CHAPTER 1

Income Tax

1015 Interpretation (Chapter 1)

[ITA67 s192; FA80 s18]

(1) In this Chapter, "*the inspector*", in relation to a notice, means any inspector who might reasonably be considered by the person giving notice to be likely to be concerned with the subject matter of the notice or who declares himself or herself ready to accept the notice.

(2) A wife shall be treated for income tax purposes as living with her husband unless either—

(a) they are separated under an order of a court of competent jurisdiction or by deed of separation, or

(b) they are in fact separated in such circumstances that the separation is likely to be permanent.

(3) (a) In this Chapter, references to the income of a wife include references to any sum which apart from this Chapter would be included in computing her total income, and this Chapter shall apply in relation to any such sum notwithstanding that some enactment (including, except in so far as the contrary is expressly provided, an enactment passed after the passing of this Act) requires that that sum should not be treated as income of any person other than her.

(b) In the Income Tax Acts, a reference to a person who has duly elected to be assessed to tax in accordance with a particular section includes a reference to a person who is deemed to have elected to be assessed to tax in accordance with that section, and any reference to a person who is assessed to tax in accordance with *section 1017* for a year of assessment includes a reference to a case where the person and his or her spouse are assessed to tax for that year in accordance with *section 1023*.

(4) Any notice required to be served under any section in this Chapter may be served by post.

Case Law

The Supreme Court held that the provisions of the earlier legislation (ss 192 – 197 ITA 1967) insofar as these sections provide for the aggregation of the earned incomes of married couples and thereby impose a higher tax rate were repugnant to the Constitution and invalid. The State breeched its undertaking under the Constitution to guard with special care the institution of marriage and to protect it against attack. Supreme Court Decision. Murphy v The Attorney General 1980 V ITR 613

Revenue Information Notes

IT 2 – Taxation of Married Persons and Civil Partners

IT 3 – What to do about tax on the breakdown of a marriage, civil partnership or cohabiting relationship

Cross References

From Section 1015

Section 1017 Assessment of husband in respect of income of both spouses.
Section 1023 Application for separate assessments.

To Section 1015

Section 5 Interpretation of Capital Gains Tax Acts.
Section 128A Deferral of payment of tax under section 128.
Section 496 Disposals of shares.
Section 815 Taxation of income deemed to arise on certain sales of securities.
Section 864A Electronic claims.
Section 881 Returns by married persons.
Section 909 Power to require return of property.
Section 1025 Maintenance in case of separated spouses.
Schedule 31 Consequential Amendments

1016 Assessment as single persons

[ITA67 s193; FA80 s18]

(1) Subject to *subsection (2)*, in any case in which a wife is treated as living with her husband, income tax shall be assessed, charged and recovered, except as is otherwise provided by the Income Tax Acts, on the income of the husband and on the income of the wife as if they were not married.

(2) Where an election under *section 1018* has effect in relation to a husband and wife for a year of assessment, this section shall not apply in relation to that husband and wife for that year of assessment.

Revenue Briefings

eBrief

eBrief No. 76/2014 – Tax treatment of married, separated and divorced persons

Cross References

From Section 1016

Section 1018 Election for assessment under section 1017.

To Section 1016

Section 244 Relief for interest paid on certain home loans.
Section 473 Allowance for rent paid by certain tenants.
Section 477 Relief for service charges.
Section 477A Relief for energy efficient works.
Section 485C Interpretation (Chapter 2A).
Section 485FB Requirement to provide estimates and information.
Section 958 Date for payment of tax.
Section 1018 Election for assessment under section 1017.
Section 1084 Surcharge for late returns.

1017 Assessment of husband in respect of income of both spouses

[ITA67 s194; FA80 s18]

(1) Where in the case of a husband and wife an election under *section 1018* to be assessed to tax in accordance with this section has effect for a year of assessment—

(a) the husband shall be assessed and charged to income tax, not only in respect of his total income (if any) for that year, but also in respect of his wife's total income (if any) for any part of that year of assessment during which she is living with him, and for this purpose and for the purposes of the Income Tax Acts that last-mentioned income shall be deemed to be his income,

(b) the question whether there is any income of the wife chargeable to tax for any year of assessment and, if so, what is to be taken to be the amount of that income for tax purposes shall not be affected by this section, and

(c) any tax to be assessed in respect of any income which under this section is deemed to be income of a woman's husband shall, instead of being assessed on her, or on her trustees, guardian or committee, or on her executors or administrators, be assessable on him or, in the appropriate cases, on his executors or administrators.

(2) Any relief from income tax authorised by any provision of the Income Tax Acts to be granted to a husband by reference to the income or profits or gains or losses of his wife or by reference to any payment made by her shall be granted to a husband for a year of assessment only if he is assessed to tax for that year in accordance with this section.

Revenue Briefings

eBrief

eBrief No. 76/2014 – Tax treatment of married, separated and divorced persons

Cross References

From Section 1017

Section 1018 Election for assessment under section 1017.

To Section 1017

Section 3 Interpretation of Income Tax Acts.
Section 15 Rate of charge.
Section 122 Preferential loan arrangements.
Section 128A Deferral of payment of tax under section 128.
Section 244 Relief for interest paid on certain home loans.
Section 305 Income tax: manner of granting, and effect of, allowances made by means of discharge or repayment of tax.
Section 372AR Relief for owner-occupiers.
Section 381 Right to repayment of tax by reference to losses.
Section 409A Income tax: restriction on use of capital allowances on certain industrial buildings and other premises.
Section 461 Basic personal tax credit.
Section 464 Age tax credit.
Section 466A Home carer tax credit.
Section 467 Employed person taking care of incapacitated individual.
Section 468 Blind person's tax credit.
Section 469 Relief for health expenses.
Section 470 Relief for insurance against expenses of illness.
Section 470B Age-related relief for health insurance premiums.
Section 472 Employee tax credit.
Section 472C Relief for trade union subscriptions.
Section 473 Allowance for rent paid by certain tenants.
Section 473A Relief for fees paid for third level education, etc.
Section 476 Relief for fees paid for training courses.
Section 477 Relief for service charges.
Section 477A Relief for energy efficient works.
Section 481 Relief for investment in films.
Section 485FA Adaptation of provisions relating to taxation of married persons.
Section 490 Limits on the relief.
Section 502 Assessments for withdrawing relief.
Section 531H Assessment, collection, payment and recovery of income levy on aggregate income for the year of assessment.
Section 531I Married couples.
Section 531K Repayments.

Section 531AS Universal social charge payable by chargeable persons (within the meaning of Part 41).
Section 531AT Universal social charge payable by persons other than chargeable persons (within the meaning of Part 41).
Section 531AV Married couples.
Section 664 Relief for certain income from leasing of farm land.
Section 847A Donations to certain sports bodies.
Section 848A Donations to approved bodies.
Section 950 Interpretation (Part 41).
Section 958 Date for payment of tax.
Section 1015 Interpretation (Chapter 1).
Section 1018 Election for assessment under section 1017.
Section 1019 Assessment of wife in respect of income of both spouses.
Section 1020 Special provisions relating to year of marriage.
Section 1021 Repayment of tax in case of certain husbands and wives.
Section 1022 Special provisions relating to tax on wife's income.
Section 1023 Application for separate assessments.
Section 1084 Surcharge for late returns.

1018 Election for assessment under section 1017

[ITA67 s195; FA80 s18]

(1) A husband and his wife, where the wife is living with the husband, may at any time during a year of assessment, by notice in writing given to the inspector, jointly elect to be assessed to income tax for that year of assessment in accordance with *section 1017* and, where such election is made, the income of the husband and the income of the wife shall be assessed to tax for that year in accordance with that section.

(2) Where an election is made under *subsection (1)* in respect of a year of assessment, the election shall have effect for that year and for each subsequent year of assessment.

(3) Notwithstanding *subsections (1)* and *(2)*, either the husband or the wife may, in relation to a year of assessment, by notice in writing given to the inspector before the end of the year, withdraw the election in respect of that year and, on the giving of that notice, the election shall not have effect for that year or for any subsequent year of assessment.

(4) (a) A husband and his wife, where the wife is living with the husband and where an election under *subsection (1)* has not been made by them for a year of assessment (or for any prior year of assessment) shall be deemed to have duly elected to be assessed to tax in accordance with *section 1017* for that year unless before the end of that year either of them gives notice in writing to the inspector that he or she wishes to be assessed to tax for that year as a single person in accordance with *section 1016*.

(b) Where a husband or his wife has duly given notice under *paragraph (a)*, that paragraph shall not apply in relation to that husband and wife for the year of assessment for which the notice was given or for any subsequent year of assessment until the year of assessment in which the notice is withdrawn, by the person who gave it, by further notice in writing to the inspector.

Revenue Briefings

eBrief

eBrief No. 76/2014 – Tax treatment of married, separated and divorced persons

Cross References

From Section 1018

Section 1016 Assessment as single persons.
Section 1017 Assessment of husband in respect of income of both spouses.

To Section 1018

Section 485FA Adaptation of provisions relating to taxation of married persons.
Section 531I Married couples.
Section 531AV Married couples.
Section 958 Date for payment of tax.
Section 1016 Assessment as single persons.
Section 1017 Assessment of husband in respect of income of both spouses.
Section 1019 Assessment of wife in respect of income of both spouses.
Section 1020 Special provisions relating to year of marriage.
Section 1026 Separated and divorced persons: adaptation of provisions relating to married persons.
Schedule 31 Consequential Amendments

1019 Assessment of wife in respect of income of both spouses

[ITA67 s195B; FA93 s10(1)]

(1) In this section—

"*the basis year*", in relation to a husband and wife, means the year of marriage or, if earlier, the latest year of assessment preceding that year of marriage for which details of the total incomes of both the husband and the wife are available to the inspector at the time they first elect, or are first deemed to have duly elected, to be assessed to tax in accordance with *section 1017*;

"*year of marriage*", in relation to a husband and wife, means the year of assessment in which their marriage took place.

(2) *Subsection (3)* shall apply for a year of assessment where, in the case of a husband and wife who are living together—

(a) (i) an election (including an election deemed to have been duly made) by the husband and wife to be assessed to income tax in accordance with *section 1017* has effect in relation to the year of assessment, and

(ii) the husband and the wife by notice in writing jointly given to the inspector before [1 April][1] in the year of assessment elect that the wife should be assessed to income tax in accordance with *section 1017*,

or

(b) (i) the year of marriage is the year 1993-94 or a subsequent year of assessment,

(ii) not having made an election under *section 1018(1)* to be assessed to income tax in accordance with *section 1017*, the husband and wife have been deemed for that year of assessment, in accordance with *section 1018(4)*, to have duly made such an election, but have not made an election in accordance with *paragraph (a)(ii)* for that year, and

(iii) the inspector, to the best of his or her knowledge and belief, considers that the total income of the wife for the basis year exceeded the total income of her husband for that basis year.

(3) Where this subsection applies for a year of assessment, the wife shall be assessed to income tax in accordance with *section 1017* for that year, and accordingly references in *section 1017* or in any other provision of the Income Tax Acts, however expressed—

(a) to a husband being assessed, assessed and charged or chargeable to income tax for a year of assessment in respect of his own total income (if any) and his wife's total income (if any), and

(b) to income of a wife being deemed for income tax purposes to be that of her husband,

shall, subject to this section and the modifications set out in *subsection (6)* and any other necessary modifications, be construed respectively for that year of assessment as references—

(i) to a wife being assessed, assessed and charged or chargeable to income tax in respect of her own total income (if any) and her husband's total income (if any), and

(ii) to the income of a husband being deemed for income tax purposes to be that of his wife.

(4) (a) Where in accordance with *subsection (3)* a wife is by virtue of *subsection (2)(b)* to be assessed and charged to income tax in respect of her total income (if any) and her husband's total income (if any) for a year of assessment—

(i) in the absence of a notice given in accordance with *subsection (1)* or *(4)(a)* of *section 1018* or an application made under *section 1023*, the wife shall be so assessed and charged for each subsequent year of assessment, and

(ii) any such charge shall apply and continue to apply notwithstanding that her husband's total income for the basis year may have exceeded her total income for that year.

(b) Where a notice under *section 1018(4)(a)* or an application under *section 1023* is withdrawn and, but for the giving of such a notice or the making of such an application in the first instance, a wife would have been assessed to income tax in respect of her own total income (if any) and the total income (if any) of her husband for the year of assessment in which the notice was given or the application was made, as may be appropriate, then, in the absence of an election made in accordance with *section 1018(1)* (not being such an election deemed to have been duly made in accordance with *section 1018(4)*), the wife shall be so assessed to income tax for the year of assessment in which that notice or application is withdrawn and for each subsequent year of assessment.

(5) Where an election is made in accordance with *subsection (2)(a)(ii)* for a year of assessment, the election shall have effect for that year and each subsequent year of assessment unless it is withdrawn by further notice in writing given jointly by the husband and the wife to the inspector before [1 April][2] in a year of assessment and the election shall not then have effect for the year for which the further notice is given or for any subsequent year of assessment.

(6) For the purposes of the other provisions of this section and as the circumstances may require—

(a) a reference in the Income Tax Acts, however expressed, to an individual or a claimant, being a man, a married man or a husband shall be construed respectively as a reference to a woman, a married woman or a wife, and a reference in those Acts, however expressed, to a woman, a married woman or a wife shall be construed respectively as a reference to a man, a married man or a husband, and

(b) any provision of the Income Tax Acts shall, in so far as it may relate to the treatment of any husband and wife for the purposes of those Acts, be construed so as to give effect to this section.

Amendments

[1, 2] Substituted by FA01 sched2(56). Applies as respects the year of assessment 2002 and subsequent years of assessment.

Revenue Briefings

eBrief

eBrief No. 76/2014 – Tax treatment of married, separated and divorced persons

Cross References

From Section 1019

Section 1017 Assessment of husband in respect of income of both spouses.

Section 1018 Election for assessment under section 1017.

Section 1023 Application for separate assessments.

To Section 1019

Section 485FA Adaptation of provisions relating to taxation of married persons.

Section 958 Date for payment of tax.

Section 1022 Special provisions relating to tax on wife's income.

1020 Special provisions relating to year of marriage

[ITA67 s195A(1) to (6); FA83 s6; FA96 s132(1) and Sch5 PtI par1(8)]

(1) In this section—

["*income tax month*" means—

(a) in relation to a period prior to 6 December 2001, a month beginning on the 6th day of a month and ending on the 5th day of the next month,

(b) the period beginning on 6 December 2001 and ending on 31 December 2001, and

(c) thereafter, a calendar month;][1]

"*year of marriage*", in relation to a husband and wife, means the year of assessment in which their marriage took place.

(2) *Section 1018* shall not apply in relation to a husband and his wife for the year of marriage.

(3) Where, on making a claim in that behalf, a husband and his wife prove that the amount equal to the aggregate of the income tax paid and payable by the husband on his total income for the year of marriage and the income tax paid and payable by his wife on her total income for the year of marriage is in excess of the income tax which would have been payable by the husband on his total income and the total income of his wife for the year of marriage if—

(a) he had been charged to income tax for the year of marriage in accordance with *section 1017*, and

(b) he and his wife had been married to each other throughout the year of marriage,

they shall be entitled, subject to *subsection (4)*, to repayment of income tax of an amount determined by the formula—

$$A \times \frac{B}{[12]^2}$$

where—

A is the amount of the aforementioned excess, and

B is the number of income tax months in the period between the date on which the marriage took place and the end of the year of marriage, part of an income tax month being treated for this purpose as an income tax month in a case where the period consists of part of an income tax month or of one or more income tax months and part of an income tax month.

(4) Any repayment of income tax under *subsection (3)* shall be allocated to the husband and to the wife concerned in proportion to the amounts of income tax paid and payable by them, having regard to *subsection (2)*, on their respective total incomes for the year of marriage.

(5) Any claim for a repayment of income tax under *subsection (3)* shall be made in writing to the inspector after the end of the year of marriage and shall be made by the husband and wife concerned jointly.

(6) (a) *Subsections (1)* and *(2)* of *section 459* and *section 460* shall apply to a repayment of income tax under this section as they apply to any allowance, deduction, relief or reduction under the provisions specified in the Table to *section 458*.

(b) *Subsections (3)* and *(4)* of *section 459* and *paragraph 8* of *Schedule 28* shall, with any necessary modifications, apply in relation to a repayment of tax under this section.

Amendments

[1] Substituted by FA01 sched2(57)(a).

[2] Substituted by FA01 sched2(57)(b). Shall apply only as respects the year of assessment 2001.

Revenue Briefings

eBrief

eBrief No. 76/2014 – Tax treatment of married, separated and divorced persons

Cross References

From Section 1020

Section 458 Deductions allowed in ascertaining taxable income and provisions relating to reductions in tax.

Section 459 General provisions relating to allowances, deductions and reliefs.

Section 460 Rate of tax at which repayments are to be made.

Section 1017 Assessment of husband in respect of income of both spouses.

Section 1018 Election for assessment under section 1017.

Schedule 28 Statements, Lists and Declarations

To Section 1020

Section 502 Assessments for withdrawing relief.

1021 Repayment of tax in case of certain husbands and wives

[ITA67 s195C; FA93 s10(1)]

(1) This section shall apply for a year of assessment in the case of a husband and wife one of whom is assessed to income tax for the year of assessment in accordance with *section 1017* and to whom *section 1023* does not apply for that year.

(2) Where for a year of assessment this section applies in the case of a husband and wife, any repayment of income tax to be made in respect of the aggregate of the net tax deducted or paid under any provision of the Tax Acts [...][1] in respect of the total income (if any) of the husband and of the total income (if any) of the wife shall be allocated to the husband and the wife concerned in proportion to the net amounts of tax so deducted or paid in respect of their respective total incomes; but this subsection shall not apply where a repayment, which but for this subsection would not be made to a spouse, is less than [€25][2].

(3) Notwithstanding *subsection (2)*, where the inspector, having regard to all the circumstances of a case, is satisfied that a repayment or a greater part of a repayment of income tax arises by reason of some allowance or relief which, if *sections 1023* and *1024* had applied for the year of assessment, would have been allowed to one spouse only, the inspector may make the repayment to the husband and the wife in such proportions as the inspector considers just and reasonable.

Amendments

[1] Deleted by FA00 sched2.

[2] Substituted by FA01 sched5.

Cross References

From Section 1021

Section 1017 Assessment of husband in respect of income of both spouses.

Section 1023 Application for separate assessments.

Section 1024 Method of apportioning reliefs and charging tax in cases of separate assessments.

1022 Special provisions relating to tax on wife's income

[ITA67 s196; FA80 s18]

[(1)Where—

(a) an assessment to income tax (in this section referred to as the "*original assessment*") has been made for any year of assessment on an individual, or on an individual's trustee, guardian or committee (in this section referred to as the "*representative*"), or on an individual's executors or administrators,

(b) the Revenue Commissioners are of the opinion that, if an application for separate assessment under *section 1023* had been in force with respect to that year of assessment, an assessment in respect of or of part of the same income would have been made on, or on the representative of, or on the executors or administrators of, an individual who is the spouse of the individual referred to in *paragraph (a)* or who was the spouse of the individual referred to in *paragraph (a)* (in this subsection and in *subsection (2)* referred to as the "*spouse*") in that year of assessment, and (*c*) the whole or part of the amount payable under the original assessment has remained unpaid at the expiration of 28 days from the time when it became due,

the Revenue Commissioners may give to the spouse, or, if the spouse is dead, to the spouse's executors or administrators, or, if an assessment referred to in *paragraph (b)* could in the circumstances referred to in that paragraph have been made on the spouse's representative, to the spouse, or to the spouse's representative, a notice stating—

(i) particulars of the original assessment and of the amount remaining unpaid under that assessment, and

(ii) to the best of their judgement, particulars of the assessment (in this subsection referred to as the "*last-mentioned assessment*") which would have been so made,

and requiring the person to whom the notice is given to pay the lesser of—

(A) the amount which would have been payable under the last-mentioned assessment if it conformed with those particulars, and

(B) the amount remaining unpaid under the original assessment.][1]

(2) The same consequences as respects—

(a) the imposition of a liability to pay, and the recovery of, the tax with or without interest,

(b) priority for the tax in bankruptcy or in the administration of the estate of a deceased person,

(c) appeals to the Appeal Commissioners, the rehearing of such appeals and the stating of cases for the opinion of the High Court, and

(d) the ultimate incidence of the liability imposed,

shall follow on the giving of a notice under *subsection (1)* [to the spouse or to the spouse's representative, or to the spouse's executors or administrators, as would have followed on the making on the spouse, or on the spouse's representative, or on the spouse's executors or administrators][2], as the case may be, of an assessment referred to in *subsection (1)(b)*, being an assessment which—

(i) was made on the day of the giving of the notice,

(ii) charged the same amount of tax as is required to be paid by the notice,

(iii) fell to be made and was made by the authority who made the original assessment, and

(iv) was made by that authority to the best of that authority's judgment,

and the provisions of the Income Tax Acts relating to the matters specified in *paragraphs (a)* to *(d)* shall, with the necessary modifications, apply accordingly.

(3) Where a notice is given under *subsection (1)*, tax up to the amount required to be paid by the notice shall cease to be recoverable under the original assessment and, where the tax charged by the original assessment carried interest under *section 1080*, such adjustment shall be made of the amount payable under that section in relation to that assessment and such repayment shall be made of any amounts previously paid under that section in relation to that assessment as are necessary to secure that the total sum, if any, paid or payable under that section in relation to that assessment is the same as it would have been if the amount which ceases to be recoverable had never been charged.

(4) Where the amount payable under a notice under *subsection (1)* is reduced as the result of an appeal or of a case stated for the opinion of the High Court—

(a) the Revenue Commissioners shall, if having regard to that result they are satisfied that the original assessment was excessive, cause such relief to be given by means of repayment or otherwise as appears to them to be just; but

(b) subject to any relief so given, a sum equal to the reduction in the amount payable under the notice shall again become recoverable under the original assessment.

(5) The Revenue Commissioners and the inspector or other proper officer shall have the like powers of obtaining information with a view to the giving of, and otherwise in connection with, a notice under *subsection (1)* as they would have had with a view to the making of, and otherwise in connection with, an assessment referred to in *subsection (1)(b)* if the necessary conditions had been fulfilled for the making of such an assessment.

[(6) Where a husband or a wife dies (in this subsection and *subsections (7)* and *(8)* referred to as the "deceased spouse") and at any time before the death the husband and wife were living together, then the other spouse or, if the other spouse is dead, the executors or administrators of the other spouse may, not later than 2 months from the date of the grant of probate or letters of administration in respect of the deceased spouse's estate or, with the consent of the deceased spouse's executors or administrators, at any later date, give to the deceased spouse's executors or administrators and to the inspector a notice in writing declaring that, to the extent permitted by this section, the other spouse or the executors or administrators of the other spouse disclaim responsibility for unpaid income tax in respect of all income of the deceased spouse for any year of assessment or part of a year of assessment, being a year of assessment or a part of a year of assessment for which any income of the deceased spouse was deemed to be the income of the other spouse and in respect of which the other spouse was assessed to tax under *section 1017* or under that section as modified by *section 1019*.][3]

(7) A notice given to the inspector pursuant to *subsection (6)* shall be deemed not to be a valid notice unless it specifies the names and addresses of [the deceased spouse's executors or administrators][4].

(8) Where a notice under *subsection (6)* has been given to [a deceased spouse's executors or administrators][5] and to the inspector—

(a) it shall be the duty of the Revenue Commissioners and the Appeal Commissioners to exercise such powers as they may then or thereafter be entitled to exercise under *subsections (1)* to *(5)* in connection with any assessment made on or before the date when the giving of that notice is completed, being an assessment in respect of any of the income to which that notice relates, and

(b) the assessments (if any) to tax which may be made after that date shall, in all respects and in particular as respects the persons assessable and the tax payable, be the assessments which would have been made if—

(i) an application for separate assessment under *section 1023* had been in force in respect of the year of assessment in question, and

(ii) all assessments previously made had been made accordingly.

[(9) The Revenue Commissioners may nominate in writing any of their officers to perform any acts and discharge any functions authorised by this section to be [performed or discharged][6] by the Revenue Commissioners.][7]

Amendments

[1] Substituted by FA00 s29(1)(a). Shall apply as respects assessments made on or after 10 February 2000.

[2] Substituted by FA00 s29(1)(b). Shall apply as respects assessments made on or after 10 February 2000.

[3] Substituted by FA00 s29(1)(c). Shall apply as respects assessments made on or after 10 February 2000.

[4] Substituted by FA00 s29(1)(d). Shall apply as respects assessments made on or after 10 February 2000.

[5] Substituted by FA00 s29(1)(e). Shall apply as respects assessments made on or after 10 February 2000.

[6] Substituted by FA02 sched6(3)(u). Shall have effect as on and from 25 March 2002

[7] Inserted by FA00 s29(1)(f). Shall apply as respects assessments made before, on or after 10 February 2000

Cross References

From Section 1022

Section 1017 Assessment of husband in respect of income of both spouses.

Section 1019 Assessment of wife in respect of income of both spouses.

Section 1023 Application for separate assessments.

Section 1080 Interest on overdue income tax, corporation tax and capital gains tax.

To Section 1022

Section 1029 Application of section 1022 for purposes of capital gains tax.

1023 Application for separate assessments

[ITA67 s197; FA80 s18; FA97 s146(1) and Sch9 PtI par1(12)]

(1) In this section and in *section 1024*, "*personal reliefs*" means relief under any of the provisions specified in the Table to *section 458*, apart from relief under *sections* [*461A*][1], [*462B*][2] and *463*.

(2) Where an election by a husband and wife to be assessed to income tax in accordance with *section 1017* has effect in relation to a year of assessment and, in relation to that year of assessment, an application is made for the purpose under this section in such manner and form as may be prescribed by the Revenue Commissioners, either by the husband or by the wife, income tax for that year shall be assessed, charged and recovered on the income of the husband and on the income of the wife as if they were not married and the provisions of the Income Tax Acts with respect to the assessment, charge and recovery of tax shall, except where otherwise provided by those Acts, apply as if they were not married except that—

(a) the total deductions from [and reliefs][3] total income allowed to the husband and wife by means of personal reliefs shall be the same as if the application had not had effect with respect to that year,

(b) the total tax payable by the husband and wife for that year shall be the same as the total tax which would have been payable by them if the application had not had effect with respect to that year, and

(c) *section 1024* shall apply.

(3) An application under this section in respect of a year of assessment may be made—

(a) in the case of persons marrying during the course of that year, before the [1 April][4] in the following year, and

(b) in any other case, within 6 months before [1 April][5] in that year.

(4) Where an application is made under *subsection (2)*, that subsection shall apply not only for the year of assessment for which the application was made, but also for each subsequent year of assessment; but, in relation to a subsequent year of assessment, the person who made the application may, by notice in writing given to the inspector before [1 April][6] in that year, withdraw that election and, on the giving of that notice, *subsection (2)* shall not apply for the year of assessment in relation to which the notice was given or any subsequent year of assessment.

(5) A return of the total incomes of the husband and of the wife may be made for the purposes of this section either by the husband or by the wife but, if the Revenue Commissioners are not satisfied with any such return, they may require a return to be made by the wife or by the husband, as the case may be.

(6) The Revenue Commissioners may by notice require returns for the purposes of this section to be made at any time.

Amendments

[1] Inserted by FA00 sched1(6)(a).

[2] Substituted by F(No.2)A13 s7(1)(j). Applies for the year of assessment 2014 and subsequent years of assessment.

[3] Inserted by FA00 sched1(6)(b).

[4, 5, 6] Substituted by FA01 sched2(58). Applies as respects the year of assessment 2002 and subsequent years of assessment.

Revenue Briefings

eBrief

eBrief No. 09/2012 – Application for Separate Assessment

eBrief No. 76/2014 – Tax treatment of married, separated and divorced persons

Cross References

From Section 1023

Section 458 Deductions allowed in ascertaining taxable income and provisions relating to reductions in tax.
Section 461A Additional tax credit for certain widowed persons.
Section 462 One-parent family tax credit.
Section 463 Widowed parent tax credit.
Section 1017 Assessment of husband in respect of income of both spouses.
Section 1024 Method of apportioning reliefs and charging tax in cases of separate assessments.

To Section 1023

Section 244 Relief for interest paid on certain home loans.
Section 372AR Relief for owner-occupiers.
Section 473A Relief for fees paid for third level education, etc.
Section 476 Relief for fees paid for training courses.
Section 485FA Adaptation of provisions relating to taxation of married persons.
Section 664 Relief for certain income from leasing of farm land.
Section 848W Transfer of funds on maturity of SSIA.
Section 848X Declaration.
Section 950 Interpretation (Part 41).
Section 951 Obligation to make a return.
Section 958 Date for payment of tax.
Section 1015 Interpretation (Chapter 1).
Section 1019 Assessment of wife in respect of income of both spouses.
Section 1021 Repayment of tax in case of certain husbands and wives.
Section 1022 Special provisions relating to tax on wife's income.
Section 1024 Method of apportioning reliefs and charging tax in cases of separate assessments.
Section 1026 Separated and divorced persons: adaptation of provisions relating to married persons.
Section 1084 Surcharge for late returns.
Schedule 29 Provisions Referred to in Sections 1052, 1053 and 1054
Schedule 31 Consequential Amendments

1024 Method of apportioning reliefs and charging tax in cases of separate assessments

[ITA67 s198; FA80 s18; FA81 s5; FA92 s2(2)(a); FA97 s8(9) and s146(1) and Sch9 PtI par1(13)]

(1) This section shall apply where pursuant to an application under *section 1023* a husband and wife are assessed to tax for a year of assessment in accordance with that section.

(2) (a) Subject to *subsection (3)*, the benefit flowing from the personal reliefs for a year of assessment may be given either by means of reduction of the amount of the tax to be paid or by repayment of any excess of tax which has been paid, or by both of those means, as the case requires, and shall be allocated to the husband and the wife, in so far as it flows from—

[(i) relief under [*sections 244*, *372AR* and *372AAB*][1], in the proportions in which they incurred the expenditure giving rise to the relief;][2]

(ii) relief under *sections 461*, *464*, *465* (other than [*subsection (3)*][3]) and *468*, in the proportions of one-half and one-half;

(iii) relief in respect of a child under [*section 465(3)*][4] and relief in respect of a dependent relative under *section 466*, to the husband or to the wife according as he or she maintains the child or dependent relative;

(iv) relief under *section 467*, in the proportions in which they bear the cost of employing the person in respect of whom the relief is given;

(v) relief under *section 469*, in the proportions in which they bore the expenditure giving rise to the relief;

[(vi) relief under *sections 470*, *470A*[, *470B*][5] and *473*, to the husband or to the wife according as he or she made the payment giving rise to the relief;][6]

(vii) relief under *section 471*, in the proportions in which they incurred the expenditure giving rise to the relief;

[(viii) relief under *sections 472*, *472A* and *472B*, to the husband or to the wife according as the emoluments from which relief under those sections is granted are emoluments of the husband or of the wife;][7]

[(viiia) relief under *section 472C*, to the husband or the wife according as he or she is entitled to the relief under the said section;][8]

(ix) relief under *sections*, [[*473A*][9], *476*][10], *477*, *478* and *479*, in the proportions in which they incurred the expenditure giving rise to the relief;

(x) relief under *section 481*, in the proportions in which they made the relevant investment giving rise to the relief;

[(xa) relief under *section 848A(7)*, to the husband and wife according as he or she made the relevant donation giving rise to the relief;][11]

(xi) relief under *Part 16*, in the proportions in which they subscribed for the eligible shares giving rise to the relief;

(xii) relief under *paragraphs 12* and *20* of *Schedule 32*, in the proportions in which they incurred the expenditure giving rise to the relief.

(b) Any reduction of income tax to be made under *section 187(4)(b)* or *188(5)* for a year of assessment shall be allocated to the husband and to the wife in proportion to the amounts of income tax which but for *section 187(4)(b)* or *188(5)* would have been payable by the husband and by the wife for that year.

[(c) Subject to *subsection (4)*, Part 1 of the Table to *section 15* shall apply to each of the spouses concerned.][12]

(3) Where the amount of relief allocated to the husband under *subsection (2)(a)* exceeds the income tax chargeable on his income for the year of assessment, the balance shall be applied to reduce the income tax chargeable on the income of the wife for that year, and where the amount of relief allocated to the wife under that paragraph exceeds the income tax chargeable on her income for the year of assessment, the balance shall be applied to reduce the income tax chargeable on the income of the husband for that year.

[(4) Where the part of the taxable income of a spouse chargeable to tax in accordance with *subsection (2)(c)* at the standard rate is less than that of the other spouse and is less than the part of taxable income specified in *column (1)* of Part 1 of the Table to *section 15* (in this subsection referred to as the "*appropriate part*") in respect of which the first-mentioned spouse is so chargeable to tax at that rate, the part of taxable income of the other spouse which by virtue of *subsection (2)(c)* is to be charged to tax at the standard rate shall be increased, to an amount not exceeding the part of taxable income specified in *column (1)* of Part 3 of the Table to *section 15* in respect of which an individual to whom that Part applies is so chargeable at that rate, by the amount by which the taxable income of the first-mentioned spouse chargeable to tax at the standard rate is less than the appropriate part.][13]

Amendments

[1] Substituted by F(No.2)A13 s31(2)(b). Comes into operation on such date as the Minister for Finance may appoint by order.

[2] Substituted by FA02 sched2(2)(j).

[3] Substituted by FA02 sched6(3)(v)(i). Shall be deemed to have come into force and take effect as on and from 6 April 2001.

[4] Substituted by FA02 sched6(3)(v)(ii). Shall be deemed to have come into force and take effect as on and from 6 April 2001.

[5] Inserted by the Health Insurance (Miscellaneous Provisions) Act 2009 sec 24

[6] Substituted by FA01 s20(b).

[7] Substituted by FA00 sched1(7)(c).

[8] Inserted by FA01 s11(1)(c). Applies as respects the year of assessment 2001 and subsequent years of assessment.

[9] Substituted by FA02 sched6(3)(v)(iii). Shall be deemed to have come into force and take effect as on and from 6 April 2001.

[10] Substituted by FA00 s21(2). Applies as respects the year of assessment 2000-2001 and subsequent years of assessment.

[11] Substituted by FA02 sched6(3)(v)(iv). Shall be deemed to have come into force and take effect as on and from 6 April 2001.

[12] Substituted by FA00 s3(b)(i). Applies as respects the year of assessment 2000-2001 and subsequent years of assessment.

[13] Substituted by FA00 s3(b)(ii). Applies as respects the year of assessment 2000-2001 and subsequent years of assessment.

Cross References

From Section 1024

Section 15 Rate of charge.
Section 187 Exemption from income tax and associated marginal relief.
Section 188 Age exemption and associated marginal relief.
Section 244 Relief for interest paid on certain home loans.
Section 372AR Relief for owner-occupiers.
Section 461 Basic personal tax credit.
Section 464 Age tax credit.
Section 465 Incapacitated child tax credit.
Section 466 Dependent relative tax credit.
Section 467 Employed person taking care of incapacitated individual.
Section 468 Blind person's tax credit.
Section 469 Relief for health expenses.
Section 470 Relief for insurance against expenses of illness.
Section 470A Relief for premiums under qualifying long-term care policies.
Section 470B Age-related relief for health insurance premiums.
Section 471 Relief for contributions to permanent health benefit schemes.
Section 472 Employee tax credit.
Section 472A Relief for the long-term unemployed.
Section 472B Seafarer allowance, etc.
Section 472C Relief for trade union subscriptions.
Section 473 Allowance for rent paid by certain tenants.
Section 473A Relief for fees paid for third level education, etc.
Section 476 Relief for fees paid for training courses.
Section 477 Relief for service charges.
Section 478 Relief for payments made by certain persons in respect of alarm systems.
Section 479 Relief for new shares purchased on issue by employees.
Section 481 Relief for investment in films.
Section 488 Interpretation (Part 16).
Section 848A Donations to approved bodies.

Section 1023 Application for separate assessments.
Schedule 32 Transitional Provisions

To Section 1024

Section 502 Assessments for withdrawing relief.
Section 1021 Repayment of tax in case of certain husbands and wives.
Section 1023 Application for separate assessments.
Schedule 31 Consequential Amendments

1025 Maintenance in case of separated spouses

[FA83 s3; FA96 s132(1) and Sch5 PtI par13(1)]

(1) In this section—

"*maintenance arrangement*" means an order of a court, rule of court, deed of separation, trust, covenant, agreement, arrangement or any other act giving rise to a legally enforceable obligation and made or done in consideration or in consequence of—

(a) the dissolution or annulment of a marriage, or

(b) such separation of the parties to a marriage as is referred to in *section 1015(2)*,

and a maintenance arrangement relates to the marriage in consideration or in consequence of the dissolution or annulment of which, or of the separation of the parties to which, the maintenance arrangement was made or arises;

"*payment*" means a payment or part of a payment, as the case may be;

a reference to a child of a person includes a child in respect of whom the person was at any time before the making of the maintenance arrangement concerned entitled to [relief under *section 465*][1].

(2) (a) This section shall apply to payments made directly or indirectly by a party to a marriage under or pursuant to a maintenance arrangement relating to the marriage for the benefit of his or her child, or for the benefit of the other party to the marriage, being payments—

(i) which are made at a time when the wife is not living with the husband,

(ii) the making of which is legally enforceable, and

(iii) which are annual or periodical;

but this section shall not apply to such payments made under a maintenance arrangement made before the 8th day of June, 1983, unless and until such time as one of the following events occurs, or the earlier of such events occurs where both occur—

(I) the maintenance arrangement is replaced by another maintenance arrangement or is varied, and

(II) both parties to the marriage to which the maintenance arrangement relates, by notice in writing to the inspector, jointly elect that this section shall apply,

and where such an event occurs in either of those circumstances, this section shall apply to all such payments made after the date on which the event occurs.

(b) For the purposes of this section and of *section 1026* but subject to *paragraph (c)*, a payment, whether conditional or not, which is made directly or indirectly by a party to a marriage under or pursuant to a maintenance arrangement relating to the marriage (other than a payment of which the amount, or the method of calculating the amount, is specified in the maintenance arrangement and from which, or from the consideration for which, neither a child of the party to the marriage making the payment nor the other party to the marriage derives any benefit) shall be deemed to be made for the benefit of the other party to the marriage.

(c) Where the payment, in accordance with the maintenance arrangement, is made or directed to be made for the use and benefit of a child of the party to the marriage making the payment, or for the maintenance, support, education or other benefit of such a child, or in trust for such a child, and the amount or the method of calculating the amount of such payment so made or directed to be made is specified in the maintenance arrangement, that payment shall be deemed to be made for the benefit of such child, and not for the benefit of any other person.

(3) Notwithstanding anything in the Income Tax Acts but subject to *section 1026*, as respects any payment to which this section applies made directly or indirectly by one party to the marriage to which the maintenance arrangement concerned relates for the benefit of the other party to the marriage—

(a) the person making the payment shall not be entitled on making the payment to deduct and retain out of the payment any sum representing any amount of income tax on the payment,

(b) the payment shall be deemed for the purposes of the Income Tax Acts to be profits or gains arising to the other party to the marriage, and income tax shall be charged on that other party under Case IV of Schedule D in respect of those profits or gains, and

(c) the party to the marriage by whom the payment is made, having made a claim in that behalf in the manner prescribed by the Income Tax Acts, shall be entitled for the purposes of the Income Tax Acts to deduct the payment in computing his or her total income for the year of assessment in which the payment is made.

(4) Notwithstanding anything in the Income Tax Acts, as respects any payment to which this section applies made directly or indirectly by a party to the marriage to which the maintenance arrangement concerned relates for the benefit of his or her child—

(a) the person making the payment shall not be entitled on making the payment to deduct and retain out of the payment any sum representing any amount of income tax on the payment,

(b) the payment shall be deemed for the purposes of the Income Tax Acts not to be income of the child,

(c) the total income for any year of assessment of the party to the marriage who makes the payment shall be computed for the purposes of the Income Tax Acts as if the payment had not been made, and

(d) for the purposes of [*section 465(6)*][2], the payment shall be deemed to be an amount expended on the maintenance of the child by the party to the marriage who makes the payment and, notwithstanding that the payment is made to the other party to the marriage to be applied for or towards the maintenance of the child and is so applied, it shall be deemed for the purposes of that section not to be an amount expended by that other party on the maintenance of the child.

(5) (a) *Subsections (1)* and *(2)* of *section 459* and *section 460* shall apply to a deduction under *subsection (3)(c)* as they apply to any allowance, deduction, relief or reduction under the provisions specified in the Table to *section 458*.

(b) *Subsections (3)* and *(4)* of *section 459* and *paragraph 8* of *Schedule 28* shall, with any necessary modifications, apply in relation to a deduction under *subsection (3)(c)*.

Amendments

[1] Substituted by FA00 sched1(8).

[2] Substituted by FA13 sched2(1)(k). Has effect on and from 27 March 2013.

Revenue Briefings

eBrief

eBrief No. 76/2014 – Tax treatment of married, separated and divorced persons

Revenue Information Notes

IT 3 – What to do about tax on the breakdown of a marriage, civil partnership or cohabiting relationship

Revenue Precedents

Provision in deed of separation for part of retirement gratuity to be paid to separated spouse. It is not an annual or periodic payment. Therefore the spouse receiving the payment will not be assessable on it, and the spouse making the payment will not be entitled to a deduction. IT 97 1518

Cross References

From Section 1025

Section 458 Deductions allowed in ascertaining taxable income and provisions relating to reductions in tax.

Section 459 General provisions relating to allowances, deductions and reliefs.

Section 460 Rate of tax at which repayments are to be made.

Section 465 Incapacitated child tax credit.

Section 1015 Interpretation (Chapter 1).

Section 1026 Separated and divorced persons: adaptation of provisions relating to married persons.

Schedule 28 Statements, Lists and Declarations

To Section 1025

Section 531B Charge to income levy.

Section 531AA Interpretation (Part 18C).

Section 531AM Charge to universal social charge.

Section 1026 Separated and divorced persons: adaptation of provisions relating to married persons.

Schedule 31 Consequential Amendments

1026 Separated and divorced persons: adaptation of provisions relating to married persons

[FA83 s4; FA97 s5(a)]

(1) Where a payment to which *section 1025* applies is made in a year of assessment by a party to a marriage (being a marriage which has not been dissolved or annulled) and both parties to the marriage are resident in the State for that year, *section 1018* shall apply in relation to the parties to the marriage for that year of assessment as if—

(a) in *subsection (1)* of that section ", where the wife is living with the husband," were deleted, and

(b) *subsection (4)* of that section were deleted.

(2) Where by virtue of *subsection (1)* the parties to a marriage elect as provided for in *section 1018(1)*, then, as respects any year of assessment for which the election has effect—

(a) subject to *subsection (1)* and *paragraphs (b)* and *(c)*, the Income Tax Acts shall apply in the case of the parties to the marriage as they apply in the case of a husband and wife who have elected under *section 1018(1)* and whose election has effect for that year of assessment,

(b) the total income or incomes of the parties to the marriage shall be computed for the purposes of the Income Tax Acts as if any payments to which *section 1025* applies made in that year of assessment by one party to the marriage for the benefit of the other party to the marriage had not been made, and

(c) income tax shall be assessed, charged and recovered on the total income or incomes of the parties to the marriage as if an application under *section 1023* had been made by one of the parties and that application had effect for that year of assessment.

(3) Notwithstanding *subsection (1)*, where a payment to which *section 1025* applies is made in a year of assessment by a spouse who is a party to a marriage, that has been dissolved, for the benefit of the other spouse, and—

(a) the dissolution was under either—

(i) section 5 of the Family Law (Divorce) Act, 1996, or

(ii) the law of a country or jurisdiction other than the State, being a divorce that is entitled to be recognised as valid in the State,

(b) both spouses are resident in the State for tax purposes for that year of assessment, and

(c) neither spouse has entered into [another marriage or a civil partnership][1],

then, *subsections (1)* and *(2)* shall, with any necessary modifications, apply in relation to the spouses for that year of assessment as if their marriage had not been dissolved.

Amendments

[1] Substituted by F(No.3)A11 sched1(250). Shall have effect from the passing of this Act 27 July 2011.

Revenue Briefings

eBrief

eBrief No. 76/2014 – Tax treatment of married, separated and divorced persons

Revenue Information Notes

IT 3 – What to do about tax on the breakdown of a marriage, civil partnership or cohabiting relationship

Cross References

From Section 1026

Section 1018 Election for assessment under section 1017.
Section 1023 Application for separate assessments.
Section 1025 Maintenance in case of separated spouses.

To Section 1026

Section 531B Charge to income levy.
Section 531AA Interpretation (Part 18C).
Section 531AM Charge to universal social charge.
Section 1025 Maintenance in case of separated spouses.

1027 Payments pursuant to certain orders under Judicial Separation and Family Law Reform Act, 1989, Family Law Act, 1995, and Family Law (Divorce) Act, 1996, to be made without deduction of income tax

[Judicial Separation and Family Law Reform Act, 1989, s26; Family Law (Divorce) Act, 1996, s31; Family Law Act, 1995, s37]

Payment of money pursuant to—

(a) an order under Part II of the Judicial Separation and Family Law Reform Act, 1989,

(b) an order under the Family Law Act, 1995 (other than section 12 of that Act), and

(c) an order under the Family Law (Divorce) Act, 1996 (other than section 17 of that Act),

shall be made without deduction of income tax.

CHAPTER 2

Capital Gains Tax

1028 Married persons

[CGTA75 s13; FA80 s61(b); FA92 s59]

(1) Subject to this section, the amount of capital gains tax on chargeable gains accruing to a married woman in a year of assessment or part of a year of assessment during which she is a married woman living with her husband shall be assessed and charged on the husband and not otherwise; but this subsection shall not affect the amount of capital gains tax chargeable on the husband apart from this subsection or result in the additional amount of capital gains tax charged on the husband by virtue of this subsection being different from the amount which would otherwise have remained chargeable on the married woman.

(2) (a) Subject to *paragraph (b)*, *subsection (1)* shall not apply in relation to a husband and wife in any year of assessment where, before [1 April][1] in the year following that year of assessment, an application is made by either the husband or wife that *subsection (1)* shall not apply, and such an application duly made shall have effect not only as respects the year of assessment for which it is made but also for any subsequent year of assessment.

(b) Where the applicant gives, for any subsequent year of assessment, a notice withdrawing an application under *paragraph (a)*, that application shall not have effect with respect to the year for which the notice is given or any subsequent year; but such notice of withdrawal shall not be valid unless it is given before [1 April][2] in the year following the year of assessment for which the notice is given.

(3) In the case of a woman who during a year of assessment or part of a year of assessment is a married woman living with her husband, any allowable loss which under *section 31* would be deductible from the chargeable gains accruing in that year of assessment to the one spouse but for an insufficiency of chargeable gains shall for the purposes of that section be deductible from chargeable gains accruing in that year of assessment to the other spouse; but this subsection shall not apply in relation to losses accruing in a year of assessment to either spouse where an application that this subsection shall not apply is made by the husband or the wife before [1 April][3] in the year following that year of assessment.

[…][4]

(5) Where in any year of assessment in which or in part of which the married woman is a married woman living with her husband, the husband disposes of an asset to the wife, or the wife disposes of an asset to the husband, both shall be treated as if the asset was acquired from the spouse making the disposal for a consideration of such amount as would secure that on the disposal neither a gain nor a loss

would accrue to the spouse making the disposal; but this subsection shall not apply if until the disposal the asset formed part of trading stock of a trade carried on by the spouse making the disposal, or if the asset is acquired as trading stock for the purposes of a trade carried on by the spouse acquiring the asset.

(6) *Subsection (5)* shall apply notwithstanding *section 596* or any other provision of the Capital Gains Tax Acts fixing the amount of the consideration deemed to be given on a disposal or acquisition.

[(6A) *Subsection (5)* shall not apply where the spouse who acquired the asset could not be taxed in the State for the year of assessment in which the acquisition took place, in respect of a gain on a subsequent disposal in that year by that spouse of the asset, if that spouse had made such a disposal and a gain accrued on the disposal.][5]

(7) Where *subsection (5)* is applied in relation to a disposal of an asset by a husband to his wife, or by his wife to him, then, in relation to a subsequent disposal of the asset (not within that subsection), the spouse making the disposal shall be treated for the purposes of the Capital Gains Tax Acts as if the other spouse's acquisition or provision of the asset had been his or her acquisition or provision of the asset.

(8) An application or notice of withdrawal under this section shall be in such form and made in such manner as may be prescribed.

Amendments

[1, 2, 3] Substituted by FA01 sched2(59). Applies as respects the year of assessment 2002 and subsequent years of assessment.

[4] Deleted by FA98 s75. Applies as respects the year of assessment 1998-99 and subsequent years of assessment.

[5] Inserted by FA06 s75(1)(a). This section applies as respects the disposal of an asset by a spouse to the other spouse or former spouse concerned (as the case may be) made on or after 7 December 2005.

Revenue Information Notes

IT 3 – What to do about tax on the breakdown of a marriage, civil partnership or cohabiting relationship

Cross References

From Section 1028

Section 31 Amount chargeable.

Section 596 Appropriations to and from stock in trade.

To Section 1028

Section 481 Relief for investment in films.

Section 504 Capital gains tax.

Section 538 Disposals where assets lost or destroyed or become of negligible value.

Section 544 Interpretation and general (Chapter 2).

Section 594 Foreign life assurance and deferred annuities: taxation and returns.

Section 598 Disposals of business or farm on "retirement".

Section 838 Special portfolio investment accounts.

Section 913 Application of income tax provisions relating to returns, etc.

1029 Application of section 1022 for purposes of capital gains tax

[CGTA75 s51(1) and Sch4 par10(2)]

Section 1022 shall apply with any necessary modifications in relation to capital gains tax as it applies in relation to income tax.

Cross References

From Section 1029

Section 1022 Special provisions relating to tax on wife's income.

1030 Separated spouses: transfers of assets

[FA97 s72(1) to (3)]

(1) In this section, "*spouse*" shall be construed in accordance with section 2(2)(*c*) of the Family Law Act, 1995.

(2) Notwithstanding any other provision of the Capital Gains Tax Acts, where by virtue or in consequence of—

(a) an order made under Part II of the Family Law Act, 1995, on or following the granting of a decree of judicial separation within the meaning of that Act,

(b) an order made under Part II of the Judicial Separation and Family Law Reform Act, 1989, on or following the granting of a decree of judicial separation where such order is treated, by virtue of section 3 of the Family Law Act, 1995, as if made under the corresponding provision of the Family Law Act, 1995,

(c) a deed of separation, [...][1]

[(d) a relief order (within the meaning of the Family Law Act, 1995) made following the dissolution of a marriage or following the legal separation of spouses, or

(e) an order or other determination to like effect, which is analogous to an order referred to in *paragraph (d)*, of a court under the law of a territory other than the State made under or in consequence of the dissolution of a marriage or the legal separation of spouses, being a dissolution or legal separation that is entitled to be recognised as valid in the State,][2]

either of the spouses concerned disposes of an asset to the other spouse, then, subject to *subsection (3)*, both spouses shall be treated for the purposes of the Capital Gains Tax Acts as if the asset was acquired from the spouse making the disposal for a consideration of such amount as would secure that on the disposal neither a gain nor a loss would accrue to the spouse making the disposal.

[(2A) *Subsection (2)* shall not apply where the spouse who acquired the asset could not be taxed in the State for the year of assessment in which the acquisition took place, in respect of a gain on a subsequent disposal in that year by that spouse of the asset, if that spouse had made such a disposal and a gain accrued on the disposal.][3]

(3) *Subsection (2)* shall not apply if until the disposal the asset formed part of the trading stock of a trade carried on by the spouse making the disposal or if the asset is acquired as trading stock for the purposes of a trade carried on by the spouse acquiring the asset.

(4) Where *subsection (2)* applies in relation to a disposal of an asset by a spouse to the other spouse, then, in relation to a subsequent disposal of the asset (not being a disposal to which *subsection (2)* applies), the spouse making the disposal shall be treated for the purposes of the Capital Gains Tax Acts as if the other spouse's acquisition or provision of the asset had been his or her acquisition or provision of the asset.

Amendments

[1] Deleted by FA00 s88(1)(a). This section shall apply as respects disposals made on or after 10 February 2000.

[2] Substituted by FA00 s88(1)(b). This section shall apply as respects disposals made on or after 10 February 2000.

[3] Inserted by FA06 s75(1)(b). This section applies as respects the disposal of an asset by a spouse to the other spouse or former spouse concerned (as the case may be) made on or after 7 December 2005.

Revenue Information Notes

IT 3 – What to do about tax on the breakdown of a marriage, civil partnership or cohabiting relationship

1031 Divorced persons: transfers of assets

[Family Law (Divorce) Act, 1996, s35; FA97 s71(1) to (3)]

(1) In this section, "*spouse*" shall be construed in accordance with section 2(2)(*c*) of the Family Law (Divorce) Act, 1996.

(2) Notwithstanding any other provision of the Capital Gains Tax Acts, where by virtue or in consequence of an order made under Part III of the Family Law (Divorce) Act, 1996, on or following the granting of a decree of divorce, either of the spouses concerned disposes of an asset to the other spouse, then, subject to *subsection (3)*, both spouses shall be treated for the purpose of the Capital Gains Tax Acts as if the asset was acquired from the spouse making the disposal for a consideration of such amount as would secure that on the disposal neither a gain nor a loss would accrue to the spouse making the disposal.

[(2A) *Subsection (2)* shall not apply where the spouse who acquired the asset could not be taxed in the State for the year of assessment in which the acquisition took place, in respect of a gain on a subsequent disposal in that year by that spouse of the asset, if that spouse had made such a disposal and a gain accrued on the disposal.][1]

(3) *Subsection (2)* shall not apply if until the disposal the asset formed part of the trading stock of a trade carried on by the spouse making the disposal or if the asset is acquired as trading stock for the purposes of a trade carried on by the spouse acquiring the asset.

(4) Where *subsection (2)* applies in relation to a disposal of an asset by a spouse to the other spouse, then, in relation to a subsequent disposal of the asset (not being a disposal to which *subsection (2)* applies), the spouse making the disposal shall be treated for the purposes of the Capital Gains Tax Acts as if the other spouse's acquisition or provision of the asset had been his or her acquisition or provision of the asset.

Amendments

[1] Inserted by FA06 s75(1)(c). This section applies as respects the disposal of an asset by a spouse to the other spouse or former spouse concerned (as the case may be) made on or after 7 December 2005.

Revenue Information Notes

IT 3 – What to do about tax on the breakdown of a marriage, civil partnership or cohabiting relationship

PART 44A

Tax Treatment of Civil Partnerships

CHAPTER 1

Income Tax

1031A Interpretation (Chapter 1)

[(1) In this Chapter—

"*inspector*", in relation to a notice, means any inspector who might reasonably be considered by the individual giving notice to be likely to be concerned with the subject matter of the notice or who declares himself or herself ready to accept the notice;

"*nominated civil partner*", in relation to a civil partnership, means the civil partner who is nominated for the purposes of this Chapter in accordance with *section 1031D*;

"*other civil partner*", in relation to a civil partnership, means the civil partner who is not the nominated civil partner.

(2) A civil partner shall be treated for income tax purposes as living with his or her civil partner unless they are in fact [living separately][1] in circumstances where reconciliation is unlikely.

(3) (a) In this Chapter, references to the income of the other civil partner include references to any sum which apart from this Chapter would be included in computing that civil partner's total income, and this Chapter shall apply in relation to any such sum notwithstanding that an enactment (including, except in so far as the contrary is expressly provided, an enactment passed after 1 January 2011) requires that that sum should not be treated as income of any individual other than that civil partner.

(b) In the Income Tax Acts, a reference to an individual who has duly elected to be assessed to tax in accordance with a particular section includes a reference to an individual who is deemed to have elected to be assessed to tax in accordance with that section, and any reference to an individual who is assessed to tax in accordance with *section 1031C* for a year of assessment includes a reference to a case where the individual and his or her civil partner are assessed to tax for that year in accordance with *section 1031H*.

(4) Any notice required to be served under any section in this Chapter may be served by post.][2]

Amendments

[1] Substituted by FA12 s134(1)(g). Has effect as if it had come into operation for the year of assessment (within the meaning of the Income Tax Acts and the Capital Gains Tax Acts) 2011 and each subsequent year of assessment.

[2] Inserted by F(No.3)A11 s1(1). With effect for the year of assessment 2011 and subsequent years of assessment as appropriate.

1031B Assessment as single persons

[(1) Subject to *subsection (2)*, in any case in which civil partners are treated as living together, income tax shall be assessed, charged and recovered, except as is otherwise provided by the Income Tax Acts, on the income of each civil partner as if they were not in a civil partnership.

(2) Where an election under *section 1031D* has effect in relation to 2 individuals who are civil partners of each other for a year of assessment, this section shall not apply in relation to those civil partners for that year of assessment.][1]

Amendments

[1] Inserted by F(No.3)A11 s1(1). With effect for the year of assessment 2011 and subsequent years of assessment as appropriate.

Revenue Information Notes

IT 2 – Taxation of Married Persons and Civil Partners

1031C Assessment of nominated civil partner in respect of income of both civil partners

[(1) Where an election under *section 1031D* to be assessed to tax in accordance with this section has effect for a year of assessment—

(a) the nominated civil partner shall be assessed and charged to income tax, not only in respect of his or her total income (if any) for that year but also in respect of the other civil partner's total income (if any) for any part of that year of assessment during which they are living together, and for those purposes and for the purposes of the Income Tax Acts, that last-mentioned income shall be deemed to be the income of the nominated civil partner,

(b) the question of whether there is any income of the other civil partner chargeable to tax for any year of assessment and, if so, what is to be taken to be the amount of that income for tax purposes shall not be affected by this section, and

(c) any tax to be assessed in respect of any income which under this section is deemed to be income of the nominated civil partner shall, instead of being assessed on the other civil partner, or on his or her trustees, guardian or committee, or on his or her executors or administrators, be assessable on the nominated civil partner or, in the appropriate cases, on his or her executors or administrators.

(2) Any relief from income tax authorised by any provision of the Income Tax Acts to be granted to the nominated civil partner by reference to the income or profits or gains or losses of the other civil partner or by reference to any payment made by the other civil partner shall be granted to the nominated civil partner for a year of assessment only if the nominated civil partner is assessed to tax for that year in accordance with this section.][1]

Amendments

[1] Inserted by F(No.3)A11 s1(1). With effect for the year of assessment 2011 and subsequent years of assessment as appropriate.

Revenue Information Notes

IT 2 – Taxation of Married Persons and Civil Partners

1031D Election for assessment under section 1031C

[(1) (a) An individual and his or her civil partner who are living together may, at any time during a year of assessment, by notice in writing given to the inspector, jointly—

(i) elect to be assessed to income tax for that year of assessment in accordance with *section 1031C*, and

(ii) nominate which of them is to be the nominated civil partner for the purposes of this Chapter.

(b) If the notice under *paragraph (a)* does not nominate one of the civil partners to be the nominated civil partner, the Revenue Commissioners shall deem one of the civil partners to be the nominated civil partner.

(c) Where an election is made under *paragraph (a)*, the income of the nominated civil partner and the income of the other civil partner shall be assessed to tax for that year in accordance with *section 1031C*.

(2) Where an election is made under *subsection (1)* for a year of assessment, the election shall have effect for that year and for each subsequent year of assessment.

(3) Notwithstanding *subsections (1)* and *(2)*, either civil partner may, for a year of assessment, by notice in writing given to the inspector before the end of the year, withdraw the election for that year and, on the giving of that notice, the election shall not have effect for that year or for any subsequent year of assessment.

(4) (a) Where an individual and his or her civil partner are living together and an election under *subsection (1)* has not been made by them for a year of assessment (or for any prior year of assessment), the civil partners shall be deemed to have duly elected to be assessed to tax in accordance with *section 1031C* for that year and the Revenue Commissioners shall deem one of the civil partners to be the nominated civil partner, unless before the end of that year either of them gives notice in writing to the inspector that he or she wishes to be assessed to tax for that year as a single person in accordance with *section 1031B*.

(b) Where a civil partner has duly given notice under *paragraph (a)*, that paragraph shall not apply in relation to the civil partners concerned for the year of assessment for which the notice was given or for any subsequent year of assessment until the year of assessment in which the notice is withdrawn, by the civil partner who gave it, by further notice in writing to the inspector.][1]

Amendments

[1] Inserted by F(No.3)A11 s1(1). With effect for the year of assessment 2011 and subsequent years of assessment as appropriate.

Revenue Information Notes

IT 2 – Taxation of Married Persons and Civil Partners

1031E Special provisions relating to year of registration of civil partnership

[(1) In this section—

"*income tax month*" means a calendar month;

"*year of registration*", in relation to 2 individuals who are civil partners of each other, means—

(a) in the case of civil partners whose civil partnership was registered in the State, the year of assessment in which their civil partnership was registered, and

(b) in the case of civil partners whose legal relationship, entered into in another jurisdiction, is recognised pursuant to an order made under section 5 of the Civil Partnership and Certain Rights and Obligations of Cohabitants Act 2010, the year of assessment in which falls the day on which, by virtue of *subsection (2)* of that section, the civil partners are to be treated as civil partners under the law of the State,

and "*registered*" in relation to a civil partnership shall be construed accordingly.

(2) *Section 1031D* shall not apply in relation to civil partners for the year of registration.

(3) Where, on making a claim in that behalf, 2 individuals who are civil partners of each other prove that the amount equal to the aggregate of the income tax paid and payable by each of them on his or her total income for the year of registration is in excess of the income tax which would have been payable by one of the civil partners on his or her total income and the total income of his or her civil partner for the year of registration if—

(a) the civil partner had been charged to income tax as the nominated civil partner for the year of registration in accordance with *section 1031C*, and

(b) the civil partners had been civil partners of each other throughout the year of registration,

they shall be entitled, subject to *subsection (4)*, to repayment of income tax of an amount determined by the formula—

$$A \times \frac{B}{12}$$

where—

A is the amount of the excess, and

B is the number of income tax months in the period between the date on which the civil partnership was registered and the end of the year of registration, part of an income tax month being treated for this purpose as an income tax month in a case where the period consists of part of an income tax month or of one or more income tax months and part of an income tax month.

(4) Any repayment of income tax under *subsection (3)* shall be allocated to the civil partners concerned in proportion to the amounts of income tax paid and payable by them, having regard to *subsection (2)*, on their respective total incomes for the year of registration.

(5) Any claim for a repayment of income tax under *subsection (3)* shall be made in writing to the inspector after the end of the year of registration and shall be made by both civil partners concerned jointly.

(6) (a) *Subsections (1)* and *(2)* of *section 459* and *section 460* shall apply to a repayment of income tax under this section as they apply to any allowance, deduction, relief or reduction under the provisions specified in the Table to *section 458*.

(b) *Subsections (3)* and *(4)* of *section 459* and *paragraph 8* of *Schedule 28* shall, with any necessary modifications, apply in relation to a repayment of tax under this section.][1]

Amendments

[1] Inserted by F(No.3)A11 s1(1). With effect for the year of assessment 2011 and subsequent years of assessment as appropriate.

Revenue Information Notes

IT 2 – Taxation of Married Persons and Civil Partners

1031F Repayment of tax in case of certain civil partners

[(1) This section shall apply for a year of assessment in the case of civil partners who are assessed to income tax for the year of assessment in accordance with *section 1031C* and to whom *section 1031H* does not apply for that year.

(2) Where for a year of assessment this section applies in the case of civil partners, any repayment of income tax to be made in respect of the aggregate of the net tax deducted or paid under any provision of the Tax Acts in respect of the total income (if any) of the nominated civil partner and of the total income (if any) of the other civil partner shall be allocated to the civil partners concerned in proportion to the net amounts of tax so deducted or paid in respect of their respective total incomes; but this subsection shall not apply where a repayment, which but for this subsection would not be made to the other civil partner, is less than €25.

(3) Notwithstanding *subsection (2)*, where the inspector, having regard to all the circumstances of a case, is satisfied that a repayment or a greater part of a repayment of income tax arises by reason of some allowance or relief which, if *sections 1031H* and *1031I* had applied for the year of assessment, would have been allowed to one civil partner only, the inspector may make the repayment to the nominated civil partner and the other civil partner in such proportions as the inspector considers just and reasonable.][1]

Amendments

[1] Inserted by F(No.3)A11 s1(1). With effect for the year of assessment 2011 and subsequent years of assessment as appropriate.

1031G Special provisions relating to tax on individual's civil partner's income

[(1) Where—

(a) an assessment to income tax (in this section referred to as the "*original assessment*") has been made for any year of assessment on an individual, or on an individual's trustee, guardian or committee (in this section referred to as the "*representative*"), or on an individual's executors or administrators,

(b) the Revenue Commissioners are of the opinion that, if an application for separate assessment under *section 1031H* had been in force with respect to that year of assessment, an assessment in respect of or of part of the same income would have been made on, or on the representative of, or on the executors or administrators of, an individual who is the civil partner of the individual referred to in *paragraph (a)* or who was the civil partner of the individual referred to in *paragraph (a)* (in this subsection and in *subsection (2)* referred to as the "*other civil partner*") in that year of assessment, and

(c) the whole or part of the amount payable under the original assessment has remained unpaid at the expiration of 28 days from the time when it became due,

the Revenue Commissioners may give to the other civil partner, or, if the other civil partner is dead, to the other civil partner's executors or administrators, or, if an assessment referred to in *paragraph (b)* could in the circumstances referred to in that paragraph have been made on the other civil partner's representative, to the other civil partner, or to the other civil partner's executors or administrators, a notice stating—

(i) particulars of the original assessment and of the amount remaining unpaid under that assessment, and

(ii) to the best of their judgement, particulars of the assessment (in this subsection referred to as the "*last-mentioned assessment*") which would have been so made,

and requiring the other civil partner to whom the notice is given to pay the lesser of—

(I) the amount which would have been payable under the last-mentioned assessment if it conformed with those particulars, and

(II) the amount remaining unpaid under the original assessment.

(2) The same consequences as respects—

(a) the imposition of a liability to pay, and the recovery of, the tax with or without interest,

(b) priority for the tax in bankruptcy or in the administration of the estate of a deceased individual,

(c) appeals to the Appeal Commissioners, the rehearing of such appeals and the stating of cases for the opinion of the High Court, and

(d) the ultimate incidence of the liability imposed,

shall follow on the giving of a notice under *subsection (1)* to the other civil partner or to the other civil partner's representative, or to the other civil partner's executors or administrators, as would have followed on the making on the other civil partner, or on the other civil partner's representative, or on the other civil partner's executors or administrators, as the case may be, of an assessment referred to in *subsection (1)(b)*, being an assessment which—

(i) was made on the day of the giving of the notice,

(ii) charged the same amount of tax as is required to be paid by the notice,

(iii) fell to be made and was made by the authority who made the original assessment, and

(iv) was made by that authority to the best of that authority's judgment,

and the provisions of the Income Tax Acts relating to the matters specified in *paragraphs (a)* to *(d)* shall, with the necessary modifications, apply accordingly.

(3) Where a notice is given under *subsection (1)*, tax up to the amount required to be paid by the notice shall cease to be recoverable under the original assessment and, where the tax charged by the original assessment carried interest under *section 1080*, such adjustment shall be made of the amount payable under that section in relation to that assessment and such repayment shall be made of any amounts previously paid under that section in relation to that assessment as are necessary to secure that the total sum, if any, paid or payable under that section in relation to that assessment is the same as it would have been if the amount which ceases to be recoverable had never been charged.

(4) Where the amount payable under a notice under *subsection (1)* is reduced as the result of an appeal or of a case stated for the opinion of the High Court—

(a) the Revenue Commissioners shall, if having regard to that result they are satisfied that the original assessment was excessive, cause such relief to be given by means of repayment or otherwise as appears to them to be just, but

(b) subject to any relief given, a sum equal to the reduction in the amount payable under the notice concerned shall again become recoverable under the original assessment.

(5) The Revenue Commissioners and the inspector or other proper officer shall have the like powers of obtaining information with a view to the giving of, and otherwise in connection with, a notice under *subsection (1)* as they would have had with a view to the making of, and otherwise in connection with, an assessment referred to in *subsection (1)(b)* if the necessary conditions had been fulfilled for the making of such an assessment.

(6) Where a civil partner dies (in this subsection and *subsections (7)* and *(8)* referred to as the "*deceased civil partner*") and, at any time before the death, the deceased civil partner and his or her civil partner were living together, then the surviving civil partner or his or her executors or administrators (if he or she is also deceased) may, not later than 2 months from the date of the grant of probate or letters of administration in respect of the deceased civil partner's estate or, with the consent of the deceased civil partner's executors or administrators, at any later date, give to the deceased civil partner's executors or administrators and to the inspector a notice in writing declaring that, to the extent permitted by this section, the surviving civil partner, or his or her executors or administrators, as the case may be, disclaim responsibility for unpaid income tax in respect of all income of the deceased civil partner for any year of assessment or part of a year of assessment, being a year of assessment or a part of a year of assessment for which any income of the deceased civil partner was deemed to be the income of the surviving civil partner and in respect of which the surviving civil partner was assessed to tax under *section 1031C*.

(7) A notice given to the inspector pursuant to *subsection (6)* shall be deemed not to be a valid notice unless it specifies the names and addresses of the deceased civil partner's executors or administrators.

(8) Where a notice under *subsection (6)* has been given to a deceased civil partner's executors or administrators and to the inspector—

(a) it shall be the duty of the Revenue Commissioners and the Appeal Commissioners to exercise such powers as they may then or thereafter be entitled to exercise under *subsections (1)* to *(5)* in connection with any assessment made on or before the date when the giving of that notice is completed, being an assessment in respect of any of the income to which that notice relates, and

(b) the assessments (if any) to tax which may be made after that date shall, in all respects and in particular as respects the civil partners assessable and the tax payable, be the assessments which would have been made if—

(i) an application for separate assessment under *section 1031H* had been in force in respect of the year of assessment in question, and

(ii) all assessments previously made had been made accordingly.

(9) The Revenue Commissioners may nominate in writing any of their officers to perform any acts and discharge any functions authorised by this section to be performed or discharged by the Revenue Commissioners.][1]

Amendments

[1] Inserted by F(No.3)A11 s1(1). With effect for the year of assessment 2011 and subsequent years of assessment as appropriate.

1031H Application for separate assessments

[(1) In this section and in *section 1031I*, "*personal reliefs*" means relief under any of the provisions specified in the Table to *section 458*, apart from relief under *sections 461A*, [*462B*][1] and *463*.

(2) Where an election by civil partners to be assessed to income tax in accordance with *section 1031C* has effect for a year of assessment and, for that year of assessment, an application is made for the purpose under this section in such manner and form as may be prescribed by the Revenue Commissioners, by either civil partner, income tax for that year shall be assessed, charged and recovered on the income of each civil partner as if they were not civil partners of each other and the provisions of the Income Tax Acts with respect to the assessment, charge and recovery of tax shall, except where otherwise provided by those Acts, apply as if they were not civil partners of each other except that—

(a) the total deductions from total income and reliefs allowed to the civil partners by means of personal reliefs shall be the same as if the application had not had effect for that year,

(b) the total tax payable by the civil partners for that year shall be the same as the total tax which would have been payable by them if the application had not had effect for that year, and

(c) *section 1031I* shall apply.

(3) An application under this section for a year of assessment may be made—

(a) before 1 April in the following year—

(i) in the case of individuals whose civil partnership was registered in the State during the course of that year of assessment, and

(ii) in the case of civil partners whose legal relationship, entered into in another jurisdiction, is recognised pursuant to an order made under section 5 of the Civil Partnership and Certain Rights and Obligations of Cohabitants Act 2010, if the date on which the civil partners are to be treated as civil partners under the law of the State, by virtue of *subsection (2)* of that section, falls during the course of that year,

and

(b) in any other case, within 6 months before 1 April in that year.

(4) Where an application is made under *subsection (2)*, that subsection shall apply not only for the year of assessment for which the application was made, but also for each subsequent year of assessment; but, in relation to a subsequent year of assessment, the civil partner who made the application may, by notice in writing given to the inspector before 1 April in that year, withdraw that election and, on the giving of that notice, *subsection (2)* shall not apply for the year of assessment in relation to which the notice was given or any subsequent year of assessment.

(5) A return of the total incomes of both civil partners may be made for the purposes of this section by either civil partner concerned but, if the Revenue Commissioners are not satisfied with any such return, they may require a return to be made by the civil partner who did not make the return.

(6) The Revenue Commissioners may by notice require returns for the purposes of this section to be made at any time.][2]

Amendments

[1] Substituted by F(No.2)A13 s7(1)(k). Applies for the year of assessment 2014 and subsequent years of assessment.

[2] Inserted by F(No.3)A11 s1(1). With effect for the year of assessment 2011 and subsequent years of assessment as appropriate.

Revenue Information Notes

IT 2 – Taxation of Married Persons and Civil Partners

1031I Method of apportioning reliefs and charging tax in cases of separate assessments

[(1) This section shall apply where pursuant to an application under *section 1031H*, civil partners are assessed to tax for a year of assessment in accordance with that section.

(2) (a) Subject to subsection (3), the benefit flowing from the personal reliefs for a year of assessment may be given either by means of reduction of the amount of the tax to be paid or by repayment of any excess of tax which has been paid, or by both of those means, as the case requires, and shall be allocated to the civil partners—

(i) in so far as it flows from relief under [*sections 244, 372AR and 372AAB*][1], in the proportions in which they incurred the expenditure giving rise to the relief,

(ii) in so far as it flows from relief under *sections 461, 464, 465* (other than subsection (3)) and *468*, in the proportions of one-half and one-half,

(iii) in so far as it flows from relief in respect of a child under *section 465(3)* and relief in respect of a dependent relative under *section 466*, to the civil partner who maintains the child or dependent relative,

(iv) in so far as it flows from relief under *section 467*, in the proportions in which each civil partner bears the cost of employing the individual in respect of whom the relief is given,

(v) in so far as it flows from relief under *section 469*, in the proportions in which each civil partner incurred the expenditure giving rise to the relief,

(vi) in so far as it flows from relief under *sections 470, 470B* and *473*, to either civil partner according as he or she made the payment giving rise to the relief,

(vii) in so far as it flows from relief under *section 471*, in the proportions in which each civil partner incurred the expenditure giving rise to the relief,

(viii) in so far as it flows from relief under *sections 472, 472A* and *472B*, to either civil partner according as the emoluments from which relief under those sections is granted are emoluments of that civil partner,

(ix) in so far as it flows from relief under *sections 473A*, *476* and *477*, in the proportions in which each civil partner incurred the expenditure giving rise to the relief,

(x) in so far as it flows from relief under *section 481*, in the proportions in which each civil partner made the relevant investment giving rise to the relief,

(xi) in so far as it flows from relief under *section 848A(7)*, to each civil partner according as he or she made the relevant donation giving rise to the relief,

(xii) in so far as it flows from relief under Part 16, in the proportions in which each civil partner subscribed for the eligible shares giving rise to the relief, and

(xiii) in so far as it flows from relief under paragraphs 12 and 20 of Schedule 32, in the proportions in which each civil partner incurred the expenditure giving rise to the relief.

(b) Any reduction of income tax to be made under *section 188(5)* for a year of assessment shall be allocated to each civil partner in proportion to the amounts of income tax which but for *section 188(5)* would have been payable by both civil partners for that year.

(c) Subject to *subsection (4)*, Part 1 of the Table to section 15 shall apply to each of the civil partners concerned.

(3) Where the amount of relief allocated to a civil partner under subsection (2)(*a*) exceeds the income tax chargeable on his or her income for the year of assessment, the balance shall be applied to reduce the income tax chargeable on the income of his or her civil partner for that year, and where the amount of relief allocated to that civil partner under that paragraph exceeds the income tax chargeable on his or her income for the year of assessment, the balance shall be applied to reduce the income tax chargeable on the income of the first-mentioned civil partner for that year.

(4) Where the part of the taxable income of a civil partner chargeable to tax in accordance with subsection (2)(*c*) at the standard rate is less than that of his or her civil partner and is less than the part of taxable income specified in column (1) of Part 1 of the Table to section 15 (in this subsection referred to as the "*appropriate part*") in respect of which the first-mentioned civil partner is so chargeable to tax at that rate, the part of taxable income of the civil partner other than the first-mentioned civil partner which by virtue of subsection (2)(*c*) is to be charged to tax at the standard rate shall be increased, to an amount not exceeding the part of taxable income specified in column (1) of Part 3 of the Table to section 15 in respect of which an individual to whom that Part applies is so chargeable at that rate, by the amount by which the taxable income of the first-mentioned civil partner chargeable to tax at the standard rate is less than the appropriate part.][2]

Amendments

[1] Substituted by F(No.2)A13 s31(2)(c). Comes into operation on such date as the Minister for Finance may appoint by order.

[2] Inserted by F(No.3)A11 s1(1). With effect for the year of assessment 2011 and subsequent years of assessment as appropriate.

1031J Maintenance of civil partners living apart

[(1) In this section—

['*maintenance arrangement*' means—

(a) an order of a court under *Part 5* or *12* of the Civil Partnership and Certain Rights and Obligations of Cohabitants Act 2010, or

(b) a trust, covenant, agreement, arrangement or any other act giving rise to a legally enforceable obligation and made or done in consideration or in consequence of—

(i) the dissolution or annulment of a civil partnership, or

(ii) living separately in the circumstances referred to in *section 1031A(2)*,

and a maintenance arrangement relates to the civil partnership in consideration or in consequence of the dissolution or annulment of which, or of the living separately in the circumstances referred to in *section 1031A(2)* to which, the maintenance arrangement was made or arises;][1]

"*payment*" means a payment or part of a payment, as the case may be.

[(1A) In this section a reference to a child of a civil partner includes a child in respect of whom the civil partner was at any time before the making of the maintenance arrangement concerned entitled to relief under *section 465*.][2]

(2) (a) This section shall apply to payments made directly or indirectly by a civil partner under or pursuant to a maintenance arrangement [relating to the civil partnership for the benefit of his or her child, or for the benefit of the other civil partner being payments—

(i) which are made at a time when one civil partner is not living with the other,

(ii) the making of which is legally enforceable, and

(iii) which are annual or otherwise periodical.][3]

[(b) For the purposes of this section and *section 1031K*, but subject to *paragraph (c)*, a payment, whether conditional or not, which is made directly or indirectly by a civil partner or former civil partner under or pursuant to a maintenance arrangement relating to the civil partnership concerned (other than a payment of which the amount, or the method of calculating the amount, is specified in the maintenance arrangement and from which, or from the consideration for which, neither a child of the civil partner making the payment nor the other civil partner derives any benefit) shall be deemed to be made for the benefit of his or her civil partner or former civil partner.][4]

[(c) Where the payment, in accordance with the maintenance arrangement, is made or directed to be made for the use and benefit of a child of the civil partner making the payment, or for the maintenance, support, education or other benefit of such a child, or in trust for such a child, and the amount or the method of calculating the amount of such payment so made or directed to be made is specified in the maintenance arrangement, that payment shall be deemed to be made for the benefit of such child, and not for the benefit of any other person.][5]

(3) Notwithstanding anything in the Income Tax Acts but subject to *section 1031K*, as respects any payment to which this section applies made directly or indirectly by one civil partner or former civil partner under or pursuant to a maintenance arrangement for the benefit of his or her civil partner or former civil partner—

(a) the individual making the payment—

(i) shall not be entitled on making the payment to deduct and retain out of the payment any sum representing any amount of income tax on the payment, and

(ii) shall, if he or she makes a claim in that behalf in the manner prescribed by the Income Tax Acts, be entitled, for the purposes of those Acts, to deduct the payment in computing his or her total income for the year of assessment for which the payment is made,

and

(b) the payment shall be deemed for the purposes of the Income Tax Acts to be profits or gains arising to the individual receiving the payment, and income tax shall be charged on that individual under Case IV of Schedule D in respect of those profits or gains.

[(3A) Notwithstanding anything in the Income Tax Acts, as respects any payment to which this section applies made directly or indirectly by a civil partner to which the maintenance arrangement concerned relates for the benefit of his or her child—

(a) the person making the payment shall not be entitled on making the payment to deduct and retain out of the payment any sum representing any amount of income tax on the payment,

(b) the payment shall be deemed for the purposes of the Income Tax Acts not to be income of the child,

(c) the total income for any year of assessment of the civil partner who makes the payment shall be computed for the purposes of the Income Tax Acts as if the payment had not been made, and

(d) for the purposes of *section 465(6)*, the payment shall be deemed to be an amount expended on the maintenance of the child by the civil partner who makes the payment and, notwithstanding that the payment is made to the other civil partner to be applied for or towards the maintenance of the child and is so applied, it shall be deemed for the purposes of that section not to be an amount expended by that other civil partner on the maintenance of the child.][6]

(4) (a) *Subsections (1)* and *(2)* of *section 459* and *section 460* shall apply to a deduction under subsection (3)(*a*)(ii) as they apply to any allowance, deduction, relief or reduction under the provisions specified in the Table to *section 458*.

(b) *Subsections (3)* and *(4)* of *section 459* and *paragraph 8* of *Schedule 28* shall, with any necessary modifications, apply in relation to a deduction under *subsection (3)(a)(ii)*.][7]

Amendments

[1] Substituted by FA12 s134(1)(h). Has effect as if it had come into operation for the year of assessment (within the meaning of the Income Tax Acts and the Capital Gains Tax Acts) 2011 and each subsequent year of assessment.

[2] Inserted by FA13 s103(1)(a). Has effect as if it had come into operation for the year of assessment (within the meaning of the Income Tax Acts and Capital Gains Tax Acts) 2011 and each subsequent year of assessment.

[3] Inserted by FA13 s103(1)(b). Has effect as if it had come into operation for the year of assessment (within the meaning of the Income Tax Acts and Capital Gains Tax Acts) 2011 and each subsequent year of assessment.

[4] Substituted by FA13 s103(1)(c). Has effect as if it had come into operation for the year of assessment (within the meaning of the Income Tax Acts and Capital Gains Tax Acts) 2011 and each subsequent year of assessment.

[5] Inserted by FA13 s103(1)(d). Has effect as if it had come into operation for the year of assessment (within the meaning of the Income Tax Acts and Capital Gains Tax Acts) 2011 and each subsequent year of assessment.

[6] Inserted by FA13 s103(1)(e). Has effect as if it had come into operation for the year of assessment (within the meaning of the Income Tax Acts and Capital Gains Tax Acts) 2011 and each subsequent year of assessment.

[7] Inserted by F(No.3)A11 s1(1). With effect for the year of assessment 2011 and subsequent years of assessment as appropriate.

Revenue Information Notes

IT 3 – What to do about tax on the breakdown of a Marriage, Civil Partnership or Cohabiting relationship

1031K Dissolution or annulment of civil partnerships: adaptation of provisions relating to civil partners

[(1) Where a payment to which *section 1031J* applies is made in a year of assessment by a civil partner (whose civil partnership has not been dissolved or annulled) and both civil partners concerned are resident in the State for that year, *section 1031D* shall apply in relation to those civil partners for that year of assessment as if—

(a) the words "who are living together" in *subsection (1)(a)* of that section were deleted, and

(b) *subsection (4)* of that section were deleted.

(2) Where by virtue of *subsection (1)* both civil partners elect as provided for in *section 1031D(1)*, then, for any year of assessment for which the election has effect—

(a) subject to *subsection (1)* and *paragraphs (b)* and *(c)*, the Income Tax Acts shall apply in the case of the civil partners as they apply in the case of civil partners who have elected under *section 1031D(1)* and whose election has effect for that year of assessment,

(b) the total income or incomes of the civil partners shall be computed for the purposes of the Income Tax Acts as if any payments to which *section 1031J* applies made in that year of assessment by one civil partner for the benefit of his or her civil partner had not been made, and

(c) income tax shall be assessed, charged and recovered on the total income or incomes of the civil partners as if an application under *section 1031H* had been made by one of the civil partners and that application had effect for that year of assessment.

(3) Notwithstanding *subsection (1)*, where a payment to which *section 1031J* applies is made in a year of assessment by a civil partner whose civil partnership has been dissolved, for the benefit of the other civil partner, and—

(a) the dissolution was a dissolution under section 110 of the Civil Partnership and Certain Rights and Obligations of Cohabitants Act 2010, or deemed to be such a dissolution under section 5(4) of that Act,

(b) both civil partners are resident in the State for tax purposes for that year of assessment, and

(c) neither civil partner has entered into another civil partnership or a marriage, then, *subsections (1)* and *(2)* shall, with any necessary modifications, apply in relation to the civil partners for that year of assessment as if their civil partnership had not been dissolved.][1]

Amendments

[1] Inserted by F(No.3)A11 s1(1). With effect for the year of assessment 2011 and subsequent years of assessment as appropriate.

Revenue Information Notes

IT 3 – What to do about tax on the breakdown of a Marriage, Civil Partnership or Cohabiting relationship

CHAPTER 2

Capital Gains Tax

1031L Interpretation (Chapter 2)

[(1) In this Chapter—

"*inspector*", in relation to a notice, means any inspector who might reasonably be considered by the individual giving notice to be likely to be concerned with the subject matter of the notice or who declares himself or herself ready to accept the notice;

"*nominated civil partner*", in relation to a civil partnership, means the civil partner who is nominated for the purposes of this Chapter in accordance with *section 1031M*;

"*other civil partner*", in relation to a civil partnership, means the civil partner who is not the nominated civil partner.

(2) In the Capital Gains Tax Acts, a reference to an individual who has been duly nominated to be the nominated civil partner in accordance with *section 1031M* includes a reference to an individual who is deemed to be the nominated civil partner in accordance with that section.

(3) Any notice required to be served under any section in this Chapter may be served by post.][1]

Amendments

[1] Inserted by F(No.3)A11 s1(1). With effect for the year of assessment 2011 and subsequent years of assessment as appropriate.

1031M Civil partners

[(1) (a) An individual and his or her civil partner who are living together, may, for a year of assessment, by notice in writing given to the inspector on or before 1 April in the year following that year of assessment, jointly nominate which of them is to be the nominated civil partner for the purposes of this Chapter.

(b) If the notice under *paragraph (a)* is not given on or before the date mentioned in that paragraph, the Revenue Commissioners shall deem one of the civil partners to be the nominated civil partner.

(2) Subject to this section, the amount of capital gains tax on chargeable gains accruing to civil partners in a year of assessment or part of a year of assessment

during which they are living together shall be assessed and charged on the civil partner who is the nominated civil partner and not otherwise; but this subsection shall not affect the amount of capital gains tax chargeable on the nominated civil partner apart from this subsection or result in the additional amount of capital gains tax charged on the nominated civil partner by virtue of this subsection being different from the amount which would otherwise have remained chargeable on the other civil partner.

(3) (a) Subject to *paragraph (b)*, *subsection (2)* shall not apply in relation to a civil partner in any year of assessment where, on or before 1 April in the year following that year of assessment, an application is made by either civil partner that *subsection (2)* shall not apply, and such an application duly made shall have effect not only as respects the year of assessment for which it is made but also for any subsequent year of assessment.

(b) Where the applicant gives, for any subsequent year of assessment, a notice withdrawing an application under paragraph (*a*), that application shall not have effect with respect to the year for which the notice is given or any subsequent year; but such notice of withdrawal shall not be valid unless it is given before 1 April in the year following the year of assessment for which the notice is given.

(4) In the case of a civil partner who during a year of assessment or part of a year of assessment is a civil partner living with his or her civil partner, any allowable loss which under section 31 would be deductible from the chargeable gains accruing in that year of assessment to one civil partner but for an insufficiency of chargeable gains shall for the purposes of that section be deductible from chargeable gains accruing in that year of assessment to the other civil partner; but this subsection shall not apply in relation to losses accruing in a year of assessment to either civil partner where an application that this subsection shall not apply is made by either of them before 1 April in the year following that year of assessment.

(5) Where, in any year of assessment in which or in part of which a civil partner is living with his or her civil partner, either civil partner disposes of an asset to his or her civil partner, both civil partners shall be treated as if the asset was acquired from the civil partner making the disposal for a consideration of such amount as would secure that on the disposal neither a gain nor a loss would accrue to the civil partner making the disposal; but this subsection shall not apply if until the disposal the asset formed part of trading stock of a trade carried on by the civil partner making the disposal, or if the asset is acquired as trading stock for the purposes of a trade carried on by the civil partner acquiring the asset.

(6) *Subsection (5)* shall apply notwithstanding *section 596* or any other provision of the Capital Gains Tax Acts fixing the amount of the consideration deemed to be given on a disposal or acquisition.

(7) *Subsection (5)* shall not apply where the civil partner who acquired the asset could not be taxed in the State for the year of assessment in which the acquisition took place, in respect of a gain on a subsequent disposal in that year by that civil partner of the asset, if that civil partner had made such a disposal and a gain accrued on the disposal.

(8) Where *subsection (5)* is applied in relation to a disposal of an asset by a civil partner to his or her civil partner, then, in relation to a subsequent disposal of

the asset (not within that subsection), the civil partner making the disposal shall be treated for the purposes of the Capital Gains Tax Acts as if the acquisition or provision of the asset by his or her civil partner had been his or her own acquisition or provision of the asset.

(9) An application or notice of withdrawal under this section shall be in such form and made in such manner as may be prescribed by the Revenue Commissioners.][1]

Amendments

[1] Inserted by F(No.3)A11 s1(1). With effect for the year of assessment 2011 and subsequent years of assessment as appropriate.

Revenue Information Notes

IT 2 – Taxation of Married Persons and Civil Partners

1031N Application of section 1031G for purposes of capital gains tax

[*Section 1031G* shall apply with any necessary modifications in relation to capital gains tax as it applies in relation to income tax.][1]

Amendments

[1] Inserted by F(No.3)A11 s1(1). With effect for the year of assessment 2011 and subsequent years of assessment as appropriate.

1031O Transfers of assets where civil partnership dissolved

[(1) Notwithstanding any other provision of the Capital Gains Tax Acts, where by virtue or in consequence of—

(a) an order made under *Part 12* of the Civil Partnership and Certain Rights and Obligations of Cohabitants Act 2010, on or following the granting of a decree of dissolution or a dissolution deemed under *section 5(4)* of that Act to be a dissolution under *section 110* of that Act, or

(b) a deed of separation, agreement, arrangement or any other act giving rise to a legally enforceable obligation and made or done in consideration or in consequence of living separately in the circumstances referred to in *section 1031A(2)*,

either of the civil partners concerned disposes of an asset to the other civil partner, then, subject to *subsection (3)*, both civil partners shall be treated for the purposes of the Capital Gains Tax Acts as if the asset was acquired from the civil partner making the disposal for a consideration of such amount as would secure that on the disposal neither a gain nor a loss would accrue to the civil partner making the disposal.][1]

(2) *Subsection (1)* shall not apply where the civil partner who acquired the asset could not be taxed in the State for the year of assessment in which the acquisition took place, in respect of a gain on a subsequent disposal in that year by that civil partner of the asset, if that civil partner had made such a disposal and a gain accrued on the disposal.

(3) *Subsection (1)* shall not apply if until the disposal the asset formed part of the trading stock of a trade carried on by the civil partner making the disposal or if the asset is acquired as trading stock for the purposes of a trade carried on by the civil partner acquiring the asset.

(4) Where *subsection (1)* applies in relation to a disposal of an asset by a civil partner to his or her civil partner, then, in relation to a subsequent disposal of the asset (not being a disposal to which *subsection (1)* applies), the civil partner making the disposal shall be treated for the purposes of the Capital Gains Tax Acts as if the acquisition or provision of the asset by his or her civil partner had been his or her own acquisition or provision of the asset.][2]

Amendments

[1] Substituted by FA13 s103(1)(f). Has effect as if it had come into operation for the year of assessment (within the meaning of the Income Tax Acts and Capital Gains Tax Acts) 2011 and each subsequent year of assessment.

[2] Inserted by F(No.3)A11 s1(1). With effect for the year of assessment 2011 and subsequent years of assessment as appropriate.

Revenue Information Notes

IT 3 – What to do about tax on the breakdown of a Marriage, Civil Partnership or Cohabiting relationship

PART 44B

Tax Treatment of Cohabitants

CHAPTER 1

Income Tax

1031P Interpretation (Chapter 1)

[In this Part—

"*cohabitant*" has the same meaning as in section 172 of the Civil Partnership and Certain Rights and Obligations of Cohabitants Act 2010;

"*inspector*", in relation to a notice, means any inspector who might reasonably be considered by the individual giving notice to be likely to be concerned with the subject matter of the notice or who declares himself or herself ready to accept the notice;

"*qualified cohabitant*" has the same meaning as in section 172 of the Civil Partnership and Certain Rights and Obligations of Cohabitants Act 2010.][1]

Amendments

[1] Inserted by F(No.3)A11 s1(1). With effect for the year of assessment 2011 and subsequent years of assessment as appropriate.

1031Q Maintenance where relationship between cohabitants ends

[(1) In this section—

"*maintenance arrangement*" means an order of a court under section 175 of the Civil Partnership and Certain Rights and Obligations of Cohabitants Act 2010 giving rise to a legally enforceable obligation;

"*payment*" means a payment or part of a payment, as the case may be.

(2) (a) This section applies to payments made directly or indirectly by a qualified cohabitant under or pursuant to a maintenance arrangement.

(b) For the purposes of this section a payment, whether conditional or not, which is made directly or indirectly by a qualified cohabitant under or pursuant to a maintenance arrangement shall be deemed to be made for the benefit of the other qualified cohabitant.

(3) Notwithstanding anything in the Income Tax Acts, as respects any payment to which this section applies made directly or indirectly by an individual under or pursuant to a maintenance arrangement for the benefit of a qualified cohabitant—

(a) the individual making the payment—

(i) shall not be entitled on making the payment to deduct and retain out of the payment any sum representing any amount of income tax on the payment, and

(ii) shall, if he or she makes a claim in that behalf in the manner prescribed by the Income Tax Acts, be entitled, for the purposes of those Acts, to deduct the payment in computing his or her total income for the year of assessment in which the payment is made, and

(b) the payment shall be deemed for the purposes of the Income Tax Acts to be profits or gains arising to the qualified cohabitant, and income tax shall be charged on that qualified cohabitant under Case IV of Schedule D in respect of those profits or gains.

(4) (a) *Subsections (1)* and *(2)* of *section 459* and *section 460* shall apply to a deduction under *subsection (3)(a)(ii)* as they apply to any allowance, deduction, relief or reduction under the provisions specified in the Table to *section 458*.

(b) *Subsections (3)* and *(4)* of *section 459* and *paragraph 8* of *Schedule 28* shall, with any necessary modifications, apply in relation to a deduction under *subsection (3)(a)(ii)*.][1]

Amendments

[1] Inserted by F(No.3)A11 s1(1). With effect for the year of assessment 2011 and subsequent years of assessment as appropriate.

Revenue Information Notes

IT 3 – What to do about tax on the breakdown of a Marriage, Civil Partnership or Cohabiting relationship

CHAPTER 2

Capital Gains Tax

1031R Transfers of assets where relationship between cohabitants ends

[(1) Notwithstanding any other provision of the Capital Gains Tax Acts, where by virtue or in consequence of an order made under section 174 of the Civil Partnership and Certain Rights and Obligations of Cohabitants Act 2010, on or following the ending of a relationship between cohabitants, either of the cohabitants concerned disposes of an asset to the other cohabitant, then, subject to *subsections (2)* and *(3)*, both cohabitants shall be treated for the purposes of the Capital Gains Tax Acts as if the asset was acquired from the cohabitant making the disposal for a consideration of such amount as would secure that on the disposal neither a gain nor a loss would accrue to the cohabitant making the disposal.

(2) *Subsection (1)* shall not apply where the cohabitant who acquired the asset could not be taxed in the State for the year of assessment in which the acquisition took place, in respect of a gain on a subsequent disposal in that year by that cohabitant of the asset, if that cohabitant had made such a disposal and a gain accrued on the disposal.

(3) *Subsection (1)* shall not apply if until the disposal the asset formed part of the trading stock of a trade carried on by the cohabitant making the disposal or if the asset is acquired as trading stock for the purposes of a trade carried on by the cohabitant acquiring the asset.

(4) Where *subsection (1)* applies in relation to a disposal of an asset by a cohabitant to the other cohabitant, then, in relation to a subsequent disposal of the asset (not being a disposal to which *subsection (1)* applies), the cohabitant making the disposal shall be treated for the purposes of the Capital Gains Tax Acts as if the other cohabitant's acquisition or provision of the asset had been the acquisition or provision of the asset by the cohabitant who made the disposal.][1]

Amendments

[1] Inserted by F(No.3)A11 s1(1). With effect for the year of assessment 2011 and subsequent years of assessment as appropriate.

Revenue Information Notes

IT 3 – What to do about tax on the breakdown of a Marriage, Civil Partnership or Cohabiting relationship

PART 45

Charging and Assessing of Non-Residents

CHAPTER 1

Income Tax and Corporation Tax

1032 Restrictions on certain reliefs

[ITA67 s153; FA74 s6(2) and Sch 1 Pt I par1(vii)(d); FA94 s155; FA96 s132(1) and Sch5 PtI par1(7)]

(1) Except where otherwise provided by this section, an individual not resident in the State shall not be entitled to any of the allowances, deductions, reliefs or reductions under the provisions specified in the Table to *section 458.*

(2) Where an individual not resident in the State proves to the satisfaction of the Revenue Commissioners that he or she—

(a) is a citizen of Ireland,

(b) is resident outside the State for the sake or on account of his or her health or the health of a member of his or her family resident with him or her or because of some physical infirmity or disease in himself or herself or any such member of his or her family, and that previous to such residence outside the State he or she was resident in the State,

(c) is a citizen, subject or national of another Member State of the European Communities or of a country of which the citizens, subjects or nationals are for the time being exempted by an order under section 10 of the Aliens Act, 1935, from any provision of, or of an aliens order under, that Act, or

(d) is a person to whom one of the paragraphs (*a*) to (*e*) of the proviso to section 24 of the Finance Act, 1920, applied in respect of the year ending on the 5th day of April, 1935, or any previous year of assessment,

then, *subsection (1)* shall not apply to that individual, but the amount of any allowance, deduction or other benefit mentioned in that subsection shall, in the case of that individual, be reduced to an amount which bears the same proportion to the total amount of that allowance, deduction or other benefit as the portion of his or her income subject to Irish income tax bears to his or her total income from all sources (including income not subject to Irish income tax).

(3) Notwithstanding *subsection (2)*, where an individual not resident in the State proves to the satisfaction of the Revenue Commissioners that the individual is a resident of another Member State of the European Communities and that the proportion which the portion of the individual's income subject to Irish income tax bears to the individual's total income from all sources (including income not subject to Irish income tax) is 75 per cent or greater, *subsection (1)* or, as the case may be, *subsection (2)* shall not apply to that individual and he or she shall be entitled to the allowance, deduction or other benefit mentioned in *subsection (1)*.

Cross References

From Section 1032

Section 458 Deductions allowed in ascertaining taxable income and provisions relating to reductions in tax.

Revenue Briefings

eBrief

eBrief No. 76/2014 – Tax treatment of married, separated and divorced persons

1033 Entitlement to tax credit in respect of distributions [Repealed]

Repealed by FA99 s28(3). This section shall apply as respects distributions made on or after the 6th day of April, 1999.

1034 Assessment

[ITA67 s200]

A person not resident in the State, whether a citizen of Ireland or not, shall be assessable and chargeable to income tax in the name of any trustee, guardian, or committee of such person, or of any factor, agent, receiver, branch or manager, whether such factor, agent, receiver, branch or manager has the receipt of the profits or gains or not, in the like manner and to the like amount as such non-resident person would be assessed and charged if such person were resident in the State and in the actual receipt of such profits or gains; but, in the case of a partnership, the precedent partner (within the meaning of *section 1007*) or, if there is no precedent partner, the factor, agent, receiver, branch or manager shall be deemed to be the agent of a non-resident partner.

Case Law

A trade carried on in Australia was vested in trustees who resided in Ireland and the UK. The trade was managed by local agents appointed by the trustees. The High Court held that the Appeal Commissioners were incorrect to have concluded that the trustees were assessable under Schedule D, the important factor was not what the trustees had the power to do but rather what they had actually done. As control lay with the agents and the trade was carried on solely in Australia, it was outside the charge to Irish tax. The Executors and Trustees of AC Ferguson (deceased) v Donovan (Inspector of Taxes) 1927 I ITR 183

Revenue Precedents

Charge on non-resident partners – the partners are chargeable in the name of the precedent acting partner at the progressive rates i.e. the lower rate and at the higher rate. IT892038

Cross References

From Section 1034

Section 1007 Interpretation (Part 43).

To Section 1034

Section 734 Taxation of collective investment undertakings.
Section 1040 Application of sections 1034 to 1039 for purposes of corporation tax.
Section 1041 Rents payable to non-residents.
Section 1043 Application of sections 1034 and 1035 for purposes of capital gains tax.

1035 Profits from agencies, etc

[ITA67 s201]

[Subject to *section 1035A*, a non-resident person][1] shall be assessable and chargeable to income tax in respect of any profits or gains arising, whether directly or indirectly, through or from any factorship, agency, receivership, branch or management, and shall be so assessable and chargeable in the name of the factor, agent, receiver, branch or manager.

Amendments

[1] Substituted by FA03 s51(1)(a). This section is deemed to have applied in respect of chargeable periods commencing on or after 1 January 2002.

Cross References

From Section 1035

Section 1035A Relieving provision to section 1035.

To Section 1035

Section 1035A Relieving provision to section 1035.

Section 1043 Application of sections 1034 and 1035 for purposes of capital gains tax.

1035A Relieving provision to section 1035

[(1) In this section—

"*authorised agent*" means—

(a) a person acting as an investment business firm, or an authorised member firm—

(i) under an authorisation given by the Central Bank of Ireland under section 10(1) of the Investment Intermediaries Act 1995 or, as the case may be, section 18 of the Stock Exchange Act 1995 and not subsequently revoked, or

(ii) under an authorisation, which corresponds to either of the authorisations referred to in *subparagraph (i)*, given by a competent authority in another Member State for the purpose of Council Directive 93/22/EEC of 10 May 1993* as amended or extended from time to time, and not subsequently [revoked,][1]

* OJ No. L.141, of 11 June 1993, p.27.

(b) a credit institution duly authorised by virtue of Directive No. 2000/12/EC of 20 March 2000* which provides investment business services and in so doing does not exceed the terms of its authorisation and that authorisation has not been [revoked, or][2]

* OJ No. L.126, of 26 May 2000, p.1.

[(c) a company—

(i) authorised under any laws of the State that implement the relevant Directives, and

(ii) which carries on a trade which consists of or includes the management of unit trusts, common contractual funds or investment companies, or any combination thereof, each of which is a relevant UCITS,][3]

and "authorisation" shall be construed accordingly;

"*authorised member firm*" has the meaning assigned to it by section 3 of the Stock Exchange Act 1995;

"*competent authority*" has the meaning assigned to it by section 2 of the Investment Intermediaries Act 1995;

"*financial trade*" means a trade exercised in the State by a non-resident person through an authorised agent under and within the terms of the authorised agent's authorisation;

"*investment business firm*" has the meaning assigned to it by section 2 of the Investment Intermediaries Act 1995;

"*investment business services*" has the meaning assigned to it by section 2 of the Investment Intermediaries Act [1995][4][;][5]

["*relevant Directives*" means Directive 2009/65/EC of the European Parliament and of the Council of 13 July 2009* on the coordination of laws, regulations and administrative provisions relating to undertakings for collective investment in transferable securities (UCITS), and any Directive amending that Directive;

* OJ No. L302 of 17 November 2009, p.32

"*relevant UCITS*" means an undertaking for collective investment in transferable securities—

(i) to which the relevant Directives apply, and

(ii) which is formed under the laws of any of the Member States of the European Union other than the State.][6]

(2) For the purposes of this section—

(a) an authorised agent, through whom a non-resident person exercises a financial trade in the State, is independent in relation to the non-resident person for a chargeable period if throughout the chargeable period—

(i) the authorised agent does not otherwise act on behalf of the non-resident person,

(ii) the authorised agent, when acting on behalf of the non-resident person, does so in an independent capacity,

(iii) the authorised agent, when acting on behalf of the non-resident person, does so in the ordinary course of the authorised agent's business, and

(iv) the requirements referred to in *subsection (4)*, in relation to the financial trade, are satisfied,

(b) an authorised agent shall not be regarded as acting in an independent capacity when acting on behalf of a non-resident person unless, having regard to its legal, financial and commercial characteristics, the relationship between them is a relationship between persons carrying on independent businesses that deal with each other at arm's length, and

(c) references to an amount of profits or gains of a trade, exercised in the State by a non-resident person, to which another person has a beneficial entitlement are references to the amount of profits or gains of the trade to which the other person has, or may acquire, a beneficial entitlement by virtue of—

(i) any interest of the other person (whether or not an interest giving a right to an immediate payment of a share of the profits or gains of the trade) in property in which the whole or any part of the profits or gains of the trade are represented, or

(ii) any interest of the other person in, or other rights in relation to, the non-resident person.

(3) Notwithstanding section 18, a non-resident person shall not be assessable and chargeable to income tax in respect of any profits or gains arising or accruing for a chargeable period to the non-resident person from a financial trade exercised in the State solely through an authorised agent who throughout the chargeable period is independent in relation to the non-resident person.

(4) The requirements of this subsection are satisfied, at any time, in relation to a financial trade exercised in the State by a non-resident person through an authorised agent where at that time—

(a) the aggregate of the amount of the profits or gains of the trade, to which the authorised agent and persons, who are both resident in the State and connected with the authorised agent, have a beneficial entitlement, does not exceed 20 per cent of the amount of the profits or gains of the trade, or

(b) the Revenue Commissioners are satisfied that it is the intention of the authorised agent, that the aggregate of the amount of the profits or gains of the trade, to which the authorised agent and persons who are resident in the State and connected with the authorised agent have beneficial entitlement, does not exceed 20 per cent of the amount of the profits or gains of the trade and that the reasons for the failure to fulfill that intention, at that time, are of a temporary nature.

(5) The Revenue Commissioners may nominate any of their officers to perform any acts and discharge any functions authorised by this section to be performed or discharged by them.][7]

Amendments

[1, 2] Substituted by FA10 s32(1)(a). Has effect as on and from 3 April 2010.

[3] Inserted by FA10 s32(1)(a). Has effect as on and from 3 April 2010.

[4, 5] Substituted by FA10 s32(1)(b). Has effect as on and from 3 April 2010.

[6] Inserted by FA10 s32(1)(c). Has effect as on and from 3 April 2010.

[7] Inserted by FA03 s51(1)(b). This section is deemed to have applied in respect of chargeable periods commencing on or after 1 January 2002.

Revenue Briefings

eBrief

eBrief No. 36/2008 – Investment Intermediaries – Markets in Financial Instruments Directive (MiFID)

Cross References

From Section 1035A

Section 1035 Profits from agencies, etc.

1036 Control over residents

[ITA67 s202]

Where a non-resident person, not being a citizen of Ireland or an Irish firm or company, or a branch of a non-resident person, carries on business with a resident person, and it appears to the inspector that, owing to the close connection between the resident person and the non-resident person and to the substantial control exercised by the non-resident person over the resident person, the course of business between those persons can be so arranged and is so arranged that the business done by the resident person in pursuance of that person's connection with the non-resident person produces to the resident person either no profits or less than the ordinary profits which might be expected to arise from that business, then, the non-resident person shall be assessable and chargeable to income tax in the name of the resident person as if the resident person were an agent of the non-resident person.

1037 Charge on percentage of turnover

[ITA67 s203; F(MP)A68 s3(2) and Sch PtI]

(1) Where it appears to the inspector or on appeal to the Appeal Commissioners that the true amount of the profits or gains of any non-resident person chargeable with income tax in the name of a resident person cannot in any case be readily ascertained, the non-resident person may, if it is thought fit by the inspector or the Appeal Commissioners, be assessed and charged on a percentage of the turnover of the business done by the non-resident person through or with the resident person in whose name the non-resident person is so chargeable, and in such a case the provisions of the Income Tax Acts relating to the delivery of statements by persons acting on behalf of others shall extend so as to require returns to be given by the resident person of the business so done by the non-resident person through or with the resident person in the same manner as statements of profits or gains to be charged are to be delivered by persons acting for incapacitated or non-resident persons.

(2) The amount of the percentage under *subsection (1)* shall in each case be determined, having regard to the nature of the business, by the inspector by whom the assessment on the percentage basis is made, subject to appeal to the Appeal Commissioners.

(3) Where either the resident person or the non-resident person is dissatisfied with the percentage determined either in the first instance or by the Appeal Commissioners on appeal, that person may within 4 months of that determination require the inspector or the Appeal Commissioners, as the case may be, to refer the question of the percentage to a referee or board of referees to be appointed for the purpose by the Minister for Finance, and the decision of the referee or board of referees shall be final and conclusive.

Cross References

To Section 1037

Section 949 Appeals against determinations of certain claims, etc.

1038 Merchanting profit

[ITA67 s204; F(MP)A 68 s3(2) and Sch PtI]

Where a non-resident person is chargeable to income tax in the name of any branch, manager, agent, factor or receiver in respect of any profits or gains arising from the sale of goods or produce manufactured or produced outside the State by the non-resident person, the person in whose name the non-resident person is so chargeable may, if that person thinks fit, apply to—

(a) the inspector, or

(b) in case of an appeal, to the Appeal Commissioners,

to have the assessment to income tax in respect of those profits or gains made or amended on the basis of the profits which might reasonably be expected to have been earned by—

(i) a merchant, or

(ii) where the goods are retailed by or on behalf of the manufacturer or producer, by a retailer of the goods sold,

who had bought from the manufacturer or producer direct and, on proof to the satisfaction of the inspector or, as the case may be, the Appeal Commissioners of the amount of the profits on that basis, the assessment shall be made or amended accordingly.

1039 Restrictions on chargeability

[ITA67 s205]

(1) Nothing in this Chapter shall render a non-resident person chargeable in the name of—

(a) a broker or general commission agent, or

(b) an agent, not being—

(i) an authorised person carrying on the regular agency of the non-resident person, or

(ii) a person chargeable as if that person were an agent in pursuance of this Chapter,

in respect of profits or gains arising from sales or transactions carried out through such a broker or agent.

(2) The fact that a non-resident person executes sales or carries out transactions with other non-residents in circumstances which would make that person chargeable in pursuance of this Chapter in the name of a resident person shall not of itself make that person chargeable in respect of profits arising from those sales or transactions.

Cross References

To Section 1039

Section 5 Interpretation of Capital Gains Tax Acts.

Section 1040 Application of sections 1034 to 1039 for purposes of corporation tax.

1040 Application of sections 1034 to 1039 for purposes of corporation tax

[CTA76 s8(4)]

Without prejudice to the general application of income tax procedure to corporation tax, the provisions of this Chapter relating to the assessment and charge of income tax on persons not resident in the State, in so far as they are applicable to tax chargeable on a company, shall apply with any necessary modifications in relation to corporation tax chargeable on companies not resident in the State.

Cross References

From Section 1040

Section 1034 Assessment.

Section 1039 Restrictions on chargeability.

1041 Rents payable to non-residents

[FA69 s25]

(1) *Section 1034* shall not apply to—

(a) tax on profits or gains chargeable to tax under Case V of Schedule D, or

(b) tax on any of the profits or gains chargeable under Case IV of Schedule D which arise under the terms of a lease, but to a person other than the lessor, or which otherwise arise out of any disposition or contract such that if they arose to the person making it they would be chargeable under Case V of Schedule D,

where payment is made (whether in the State or elsewhere) directly to a person whose usual place of abode is outside the State; but *section 238* shall apply in relation to the payment as it applies to other payments, being annual payments charged with tax under Schedule D and not payable out of profits or gains brought into charge to tax.

(2) Where by virtue of *subsection (1)* the tax chargeable for any year of assessment on a person's profits or gains chargeable to tax under either or both of the Cases referred to in that subsection would but for this subsection be greater than the tax which would be chargeable on such profits or gains but for *subsection (1)*, then, on a claim in that behalf being made, relief shall be given from the excess, whether by repayment or otherwise.

Revenue Briefings

Tax Briefing

Tax Briefing December 2000 – Issue 42 pg 35 – Non-Resident Landlords – Taxation of Rental Income

Cross References

From Section 1041

Section 238 Annual payments not payable out of taxed income.

Section 1034 Assessment.

To Section 1041

Section 238 Annual payments not payable out of taxed income.

Section 390 Amount of assessment made under section 238 to be allowed as a loss for certain purposes.

CHAPTER 2

Capital Gains Tax

1042 Charging and assessment of persons not resident or ordinarily resident: modification of general rules

[CGTA75 s5(3); FA82 s33]

(1) Notwithstanding *section 28(2)*, *31* or *979*, any capital gains tax payable in respect of a chargeable gain which on a disposal accrues to a person not resident or ordinarily resident in the State at the time at which the disposal is made may be assessed and charged before the end of the year of assessment in which the chargeable gain accrues, and the tax so assessed and charged shall be payable at or before the expiration of a period of 3 months beginning with the time at which the disposal is made, or at the expiration of a period of 2 months beginning with the date of making the assessment, whichever is the later.

(2) In computing the amount of capital gains tax payable under *subsection (1)*, *section 31* shall apply with any necessary modifications as regards the deduction of any allowable losses which accrued to the person mentioned in *subsection (1)* before the date of making of the assessment mentioned in that subsection.

Cross References

From Section 1042

Section 28 Taxation of capital gains and rate of charge.
Section 31 Amount chargeable.
Section 979 Time for payment of capital gains tax assessed under sections 977(3) or 978(2) and (3).

To Section 1042

Section 954 Making of assessments.

1043 Application of sections 1034 and 1035 for purposes of capital gains tax

[CGTA75 s51(1) Sch4 and par2(2)]

[Without prejudice to *Part 41A*][1], *sections 1034* and *1035* shall apply, subject to any necessary modifications, to capital gains tax.

Amendments

[1] Substituted by FA12 sched4(part 2)(g).

Cross References

From Section 1043

Section 931 Making of assessments and application of income tax assessment provisions.
Section 1034 Assessment.
Section 1035 Profits from agencies, etc.

PART 46

Persons Chargeable in a Representative Capacity

CHAPTER 1

Income Tax and Corporation Tax

1044 Bodies of persons

[ITA67 s207]

(1) Subject to *section 21*, every body of persons shall be chargeable to income tax in the like manner as any person is chargeable under the Income Tax Acts.

(2) The treasurer (or other officer acting as such), auditor or receiver for the time being of any body of persons chargeable to income tax shall be answerable for doing all such acts as are required to be done under the Income Tax Acts for the purpose of the assessment of such body and for payment of the tax, and for the purpose of the assessment of the officers and persons in the employment of such body; but, in the case of a company, the person so answerable shall be the secretary of the company or other officer (by whatever name called) performing the duties of secretary.

(3) Every such officer may from time to time retain out of any money coming into his or her hands on behalf of the body so much of that money as is sufficient to pay the tax charged on the body, and shall be indemnified for all such payments made in pursuance of the Income Tax Acts.

Cross References

From Section 1044

Section 21 The charge to corporation tax and exclusion of income tax and capital gains tax.

To Section 1044

Section 882 Particulars to be supplied by new companies.
Section 1054 Penalties in the case of a secretary of a body of persons.
Section 1076 Supplementary provisions (Chapter 2).
Schedule 31 Consequential Amendments

1045 Trustees, guardians and committees

[ITA67 s208]

The trustee, guardian or committee of any incapacitated person having the direction, control or management of the property or concern of any such person, whether such person resides in the State or not, shall be assessable and chargeable to income tax in the like manner and to the like amount as that person would be assessed and charged if he or she were not an incapacitated person.

1046 Liability of trustees, etc

[ITA67 s209; CTA76 s8(4)]

(1) The person chargeable in respect of an incapacitated person or in whose name a non-resident person is chargeable shall be answerable for all matters required to be done under the Income Tax Acts for the purpose of assessment and payment of income tax.

(2) Any person charged under the Income Tax Acts in respect of any incapacitated or non-resident person may from time to time retain out of money coming into the first-mentioned person's hands on behalf of that incapacitated or non-resident person so much of that money as is sufficient to pay the tax charged, and shall be indemnified for all such payments made in pursuance of the Income Tax Acts.

(3) Without prejudice to the general application of income tax procedure to corporation tax, *subsections (1)* and *(2)*, in so far as they are applicable to tax chargeable on a company, shall apply with any necessary modifications in relation to corporation tax chargeable on companies not resident in the State.

Revenue Precedents

Where the trustees of a trust are resident in the State but the whole of the trust income is payable to a beneficiary with an absolute interest in the assets of the trust who is not resident in the State or divisible between two or more beneficiaries, none of whom is resident here, the liability is confined to income arising here, subject to any exemption on the basis that the beneficiary is resident in a treaty country. IT912023

1047 Liability of parents, guardians, executors and administrators

[(1) Where an individual chargeable to income tax dies, the executor or administrator of the deceased person shall be liable for—

(a) the tax charged on such deceased individual,

(b) the interest on late payment of tax in respect of which the deceased individual is liable, and

(c) any penalties in respect of which the deceased individual is liable,

and all such sums shall be a debt on the estate of the deceased individual and an executor or administrator may deduct all such payments out of the assets and effects of the person deceased.

(2) Where an individual chargeable to income tax is an infant, the parent or guardian of the infant shall be liable for the tax in default of payment by the infant and a parent or guardian who makes such payment shall be allowed all sums so paid in his or her accounts.][1]

Amendments

[1] Substituted by F(No.2)A08 sched5(part2)(1)(z). The enactments specified in Schedule 5 are amended or repealed to the extent and manner specified in that Schedule and, unless the contrary is stated, shall come into effect after 24 December 2008.

1048 Assessment of executors and administrators

[ITA67 s211(1) to (3); F(MP)A68 s4(3)(a) and s6(7); FA78 s11(1)]

(1) Where a person dies, [an assessment or an amended assessment, as the case may be, may be made for any year of assessment for which an assessment or an amended assessment could have been made][1] on the person immediately before his or her death, or could be made on the person if he or she were living, in respect of the profits or gains which arose or accrued to such person before his or her death, and the amount of the income tax on such profits or gains shall be a debt due from and payable out of the estate of such person, and the executor or administrator of such person shall be assessable and chargeable in respect of such tax.

(2) No assessment under this section shall be made later than 3 years after the expiration of the year of assessment in which the deceased person died in a case in which the grant of probate or letters of administration was made in that year, and

no such assessment shall be made later than 2 years after the expiration of the year of assessment in which such grant was made in any other case; but this subsection shall apply subject to the condition that where the executor or administrator—

(a) after the year of assessment in which the deceased person died, delivers an additional affidavit under [section 48 of the Capital Acquisitions Tax Consolidation Act 2003][2], or

(b) is liable to deliver an additional affidavit under that section, has been so notified by the Revenue Commissioners and did not deliver the additional affidavit in the year of assessment in which the deceased person died,

such assessment may be made at any time before the expiration of 2 years after the end of the year of assessment in which the additional affidavit was or is delivered.

(3) The executor or administrator of any such deceased person shall, when required to do so by a notice given to the executor or administrator by an inspector, prepare and deliver to the inspector a statement in writing signed by such executor or administrator and containing particulars, to the best of such executor's or administrator's judgment and belief, of the profits or gains which arose or accrued to such deceased person before his or her death and in respect of which such executor or administrator is assessable under this section, and the provisions of the Income Tax Acts relating to statements to be delivered by any person shall apply with any necessary modifications to statements to be delivered under this section.

Amendments

[1] Substituted by FA12 sched4(part 2)(g).

[2] Substituted by FA04 sched3(1)(ad). This section is deemed to have come into force and have taken effect as and from 21 February 2003.

Cross References

To Section 1048

Section 530N Assessment by Revenue officer.

Section 955 Amendment of and time limit for assessments.

Section 959 Miscellaneous (Part 41).

Section 1060 Proceedings against executor or administrator.

Section 1077D Proceedings against executor, administrator or estate.

1049 Receivers appointed by court

[ITA67 s212; CTA76 s147(1) and (2)]

(1) A receiver appointed by any court in the State which has the direction and control of any property in respect of which income tax or, as the case may be, corporation tax is charged in accordance with the Tax Acts shall be assessable and chargeable with income tax or, as the case may be, corporation tax in the like manner and to the like amount as would be assessed and charged if the property were not under the direction and control of the court.

(2) Every such receiver shall be answerable for doing all matters and things required to be done under the Tax Acts for the purpose of assessment and payment of income tax or, as the case may be, corporation tax.

1050 Protection for trustees, agents and receivers

[ITA67 s213]

(1) A trustee who has authorised the receipt of profits arising from trust property by or by the agent of the person entitled to such profits shall not, if—

(a) that person or agent actually received the profits under that authority, and

(b) the trustee makes a return as required by *section 890* of the name, address and profits of that person,

be required to do any other act for the purpose of the assessment of that person, unless the Revenue Commissioners require the testimony of the trustee pursuant to the Income Tax Acts.

(2) An agent or receiver of any person resident in the State, other than an incapacitated person, shall not, if that agent or receiver makes a return as required by *section 890* of the name, address and profits of that person, be required to do any other act for the purpose of the assessment of that person, unless the Revenue Commissioners require the testimony of the agent or receiver pursuant to the Income Tax Acts.

Cross References

From Section 1050

Section 890 Returns by persons in receipt of income belonging to others.

To Section 1050

Section 1051 Application of Chapter 1 for purposes of capital gains tax.

CHAPTER 2

Capital Gains Tax

1051 Application of Chapter 1 for purposes of capital gains tax

[CGTA75 s51(1) and Sch4 par2(2)]

Chapter 1 other than *section 1050* shall, subject to any necessary modifications, apply to capital gains tax.

Cross References

From Section 1051

Section 1050 Protection for trustees, agents and receivers.

To Section 1051

Section 959 Miscellaneous (Part 41).

PART 47

Penalties, Revenue Offences, Interest on Overdue Tax and Other Sanctions

CHAPTER 1

Income Tax and Corporation Tax Penalties

1052 Penalties for failure to make certain returns, etc

[ITA67 s70(4); s172(5) and s500; FA80 s57(2); FA82 s60; FA92 s248]

(1) Where any person—

(a) has been required, by notice or precept given under or for the purposes of any of the provisions specified in *column 1* or *2* of *Schedule 29*, to deliver any return, statement, declaration, list or other document, to furnish any particulars, to produce any document, or to make anything available for inspection, and that person fails to comply with the notice or [precept,][1]

[(aa) has delivered a return in the prescribed form for the purposes of any of the provisions specified in column 1 or 2 of *Schedule 29* and has failed to include on the prescribed form the details required by that form in relation to any exemption, allowance, deduction, credit or other relief the person is claiming (in this paragraph referred to as the "*specified details*") where the specified details are stated on the form to be details to which this paragraph refers; but this paragraph shall not apply unless, after the return has been delivered, it had come to the person's notice or had been brought to the person's attention that specified details had not been included on the form and the person failed to remedy matters without unreasonable delay, or][2]

(b) fails to do any act, to furnish any particulars or to deliver any account in accordance with any of the provisions specified in *column 3* of that Schedule,

that person shall, subject to *subsection (2)* and to *section 1054*, be liable to a penalty of [€3,000][3].

(2) Where the notice referred to in *subsection (1)* was given under or for the purposes of any of the provisions specified in *column 1* of *Schedule 29* and the failure continues after the end of the year of assessment following that during which the notice was given, the penalty mentioned in *subsection (1)* shall be [€4,000][4].

(3) *Subsections (1)* and *(2)* shall apply subject to *sections 877(5)(b)* and *897(5)*.

(4) In proceedings for the recovery of a penalty incurred [under this section, under section 1053 or under section 1077E][5]—

(a) a certificate signed by an officer of the Revenue Commissioners, or, in the case of such proceedings in relation to a return referred to in *section 879* or *880*, by an inspector, which certifies that he or she has examined his or her relevant records and that it appears from those records that a stated notice or precept was duly given to the defendant on a stated day shall be evidence until the contrary is proved that the defendant received that notice or precept in the ordinary course;

(b) a certificate signed by an officer of the Revenue Commissioners which certifies that he or she has examined his or her relevant records and that it appears from those records that during a stated period a stated notice or precept has not been complied with by the defendant shall be evidence until the contrary is proved that the defendant did not during that period comply with that notice or precept;

(c) in the case of such proceedings in relation to a return referred to in *section 879* or *880*, a certificate signed by an inspector which certifies that he or she has examined his or her relevant records and that it appears from those records that during a stated period a stated return was not received from the defendant shall be evidence until the contrary is proved that the defendant did not during that period deliver that return;

(d) a certificate signed by an officer of the Revenue Commissioners which certifies that he or she has examined his or her relevant records and that it appears from those records that during a stated period the defendant has failed to do a stated act, furnish stated particulars or deliver a stated account in accordance with any of the provisions specified in *column 3* of *Schedule 29* shall be evidence until the contrary is proved that the defendant did so fail;

(e) a certificate certifying as provided for in *paragraph (a)*, *(b)*, *(c)* or *(d)* and purporting to be signed by an officer of the Revenue Commissioners or, as the case may be, by an inspector may be tendered in evidence without proof and shall be deemed until the contrary is proved to have been signed by such officer or, as the case may be, such inspector.

Amendments

[1] Substituted by FA04 s86(2)(a). This section shall apply as respects any chargeable period commencing on or after 1 January 2004.

[2] Inserted by FA04 s86(2)(b). This section shall apply as respects any chargeable period commencing on or after 1 January 2004.

[3] Substituted by F(No.2)A08 sched5(part2)(1)(aa)(i). The enactments specified in Schedule 5 are amended or repealed to the extent and manner specified in that Schedule and, unless the contrary is stated, shall come into effect after 24 December 2008.

[4] Substituted by F(No.2)A08 sched5(part2)(1)(aa)(ii). The enactments specified in Schedule 5 are amended or repealed to the extent and manner specified in that Schedule and, unless the contrary is stated, shall come into effect after 24 December 2008.

[5] Substituted by F(No.2)A08 sched5(part2)(1)(aa)(iii). The enactments specified in Schedule 5 are amended or repealed to the extent and manner specified in that Schedule and, unless the contrary is stated, shall come into effect after 24 December 2008.

Case Law

Penalties imposed under section 152 are non-criminal in nature. McLoughlin & Tuite v The Revenue Commissioners and The Attorney General 1986 III ITR 387

In O'Callaghan v Clifford & Ors 1993 IV ITR 478 the Supreme Court concluded that the burden of proof in criminal matters is higher than in civil matters and while a certificate of non-compliance may be adequate in a civil matter, it may not be so in a criminal matter.

Cross References

From Section 1052

Section 877 Returns by persons chargeable.
Section 879 Returns of income.
Section 880 Partnership returns.
Section 897 Returns of employees' emoluments, etc.

Section 1054 Penalties in the case of a secretary of a body of persons.
Section 1077E Penalty for deliberately or carelessly making incorrect returns, etc.
Schedule 29 Provisions Referred to in Sections 1052, 1053 and 1054

To Section 1052

Section 264B Returns of special term accounts by relevant deposit takers.
Section 267E Returns of special term share accounts by credit unions.
Section 485FB Requirement to provide estimates and information.
Section 510 Approved profit sharing schemes: appropriated shares.
Section 530U Civil penalties.
Section 531 Payments to subcontractors in certain industries.
Section 531AJ Application of provisions relating to income tax.
Section 696E Returns (Chapter3).
Section 697LA Transactions between associated persons and between tonnage tax trade and other activities of same company.
Section 891A Returns of interest paid to non-residents.
Section 894 Returns of certain information by third parties.
Section 897A Returns by employers in relation to pension products.
Section 951 Obligation to make a return.
Section 1002 Deduction from payments due to defaulters of amounts due in relation to tax.
Section 1054 Penalties in the case of a secretary of a body of persons.
Section 1077 Penalties for failure to make returns, etc. and for deliberately or carelessly making incorrect returns.
Section 1078 Revenue offences.
Schedule 12 Employee Share Ownership Trusts
Schedule 12A Approved Savings-Related Share Option Schemes
Schedule 12C Approved Share Option Schemes
Schedule 29 Provisions Referred to in Sections 1052, 1053 and 1054
Schedule 32 Transitional Provisions

1053 Penalty for fraudulently or negligently making incorrect returns, etc

[ITA67 s501 and s502; F(MP)A68 s3(2) and Sch PtI; FA74 s86 and Sch2 PtI]

(1) Where any person fraudulently or negligently—

(a) delivers any incorrect return or statement of a kind mentioned in any of the provisions specified in *column 1* of *Schedule 29*,

(b) makes any incorrect return, statement or declaration in connection with any claim for any allowance, deduction or relief, or

(c) submits to the Revenue Commissioners, the Appeal Commissioners or an inspector any incorrect accounts in connection with the ascertainment of that person's liability to income tax,

that person shall, subject to *section 1054*, be liable to a penalty of—

(i) [€125][1], and

(ii) [...][2] the amount of the difference specified in *subsection (5)*.

[(1A) Where any person fails to comply with a requirement to deliver a return or statement of a kind mentioned in any of the provisions specified in column 1 of *Schedule 29*, by reason of fraud or neglect by that person, that person shall, subject to *section 1054*, be liable to a penalty of—

(a) €125, and

(b) [...][3] the amount of the difference specified in *subsection (5A)*][4]

(2) Where any person fraudulently or negligently furnishes, gives, produces or makes any incorrect return, information, certificate, document, record, statement, particulars, account or declaration of a kind mentioned in any of the provisions specified in *column 2* or *3* of *Schedule 29*, that person shall, subject to *section 1054*, be liable to a penalty of [€125][5] or, in the case of fraud, [€315][6].

(3) Where any return, statement, declaration or accounts mentioned in *subsection (1)* was or were made or submitted by a person, neither fraudulently nor negligently, and it comes to that person's notice (or, if the person has died, to the notice of his or her personal representatives) that it was or they were incorrect, then, unless the error is remedied without unreasonable delay, the return, statement, declaration or accounts shall be treated for the purposes of this section as having been negligently made or submitted by that person.

(4) Subject to *section 1060(2)*, proceedings for the recovery of any penalty under *subsection (1)* or *(2)* shall not be out of time because they are commenced after the time allowed by *section 1063*.

(5) The difference referred to in *subsection (1)(ii)* shall be the difference between—

(a) the amount of income tax payable for the relevant years of assessment by the person concerned (including any amount deducted at source and not repayable), and

(b) the amount which would have been the amount so payable if the return, statement, declaration or accounts as made or submitted by that person had been correct.

[(5A) The difference referred to in *subsection (1A)(b)* is the difference between—

(a) the amount of income tax paid by that person for the relevant years of assessment, and

(b) the amount of income tax which would have been payable for the relevant years of assessment if the return or statement had been delivered by that person and the return or statement had been correct.][7]

(6) The relevant years of assessment for the purposes of [*subsections (5)* and *(5A)*][8] shall be, in relation to anything delivered, made or submitted in any year of assessment, that year, the next year and any preceding year of assessment, and the references in that subsection to the amount of income tax payable shall not, in relation to anything done in connection with a partnership, include any tax not chargeable in the partnership name.

(7) For the purposes of this section, any accounts submitted on behalf of a person shall be deemed to have been submitted by the person unless that person proves that they were submitted without that person's consent or knowledge.

[(8) This section shall not apply in respect of any acts or omissions arising after the passing of the *Finance (No.2) Act 2008*.][9]

Amendments

[1, 5, 6] Substituted by FA01 sched5.

[2] Deleted by FA05 s141(1)(a)(i). This section applies to returns, statements, declarations, or accounts delivered, made or, as the case may be, submitted on or after 25 March 2005

[3] Deleted by FA05 s141(1)(a)(ii). This section applies to returns, statements, declarations, or accounts delivered, made or, as the case may be, submitted on or after 25 March 2005

[4] Inserted by FA02 s130(a)(i).

[7] Inserted by FA02 s130(a)(ii).

[8] Substituted by FA02 s130(a)(iii).

[9] Inserted by F(No.2)A08 sched5(part2)(1)(ab). The enactments specified in Schedule 5 are amended or repealed to the extent and manner specified in that Schedule and, unless the contrary is stated, shall come into effect after 24 December 2008.

Cross References

From Section 1053

Schedule
Section 1054 Penalties in the case of a secretary of a body of persons.
Section 1060 Proceedings against executor or administrator.
Section 1063 Time limit for recovery of fines and penalties.
Schedule 29 Provisions Referred to in Sections 1052, 1053 and 1054

To Section 1053

Section 1054 Penalties in the case of a secretary of a body of persons.
Section 1072 Penalties for fraudulently or negligently making incorrect returns, etc.
Section 1075 Penalties for failure to furnish certain information and for incorrect information.
Section 1077 Penalties for failure to make returns, etc. and for deliberately or carelessly making incorrect returns.
Schedule 29 Provisions Referred to in Sections 1052, 1053 and 1054

1054 Penalties in the case of a secretary of a body of persons

[(1) In this section, "secretary" includes persons mentioned in section 1044(2).

(2) Where the person mentioned in section 1052 is a body of persons the secretary shall be liable to—

(a) in a case where the notice was given under or for the purposes of any of the provisions specified in column 1 of Schedule 29 and the failure continues after the end of the year of assessment or accounting period following that during which the notice was given, a separate penalty of €2,000, and

(b) in any other case, a separate penalty of €1,000.

(3) Where the person mentioned in section 1053 or 1077E is a body of persons the secretary shall be liable to a separate penalty of €1,500 or, in the case of deliberate behaviour, €3,000.

(4) This section shall apply subject to sections 877(5)(*b*) and 897(5), but otherwise shall apply notwithstanding anything in the Income Tax Acts.][1]

Amendments

[1] Substituted by F(No.2)A08 sched5(part2)(1)(ac). The enactments specified in Schedule 5 are amended or repealed to the extent and manner specified in that Schedule and, unless the contrary is stated, shall come into effect after 24 December 2008.

Cross References

From Section 1054

Section 877 Returns by persons chargeable.
Section 897 Returns of employees' emoluments, etc.
Section 1044 Bodies of persons.
Section 1052 Penalties for failure to make certain returns, etc.
Section 1053 Penalty for fraudulently or negligently making incorrect returns, etc.
Section 1077E Penalty for deliberately or carelessly making incorrect returns, etc.

To Section 1054

Section 264B Returns of special term accounts by relevant deposit takers.
Section 267E Returns of special term share accounts by credit unions.
Section 510 Approved profit sharing schemes: appropriated shares.
Section 530U Civil penalties.
Section 891A Returns of interest paid to non-residents.
Section 894 Returns of certain information by third parties.
Section 897A Returns by employers in relation to pension products.
Section 951 Obligation to make a return.
Section 1002 Deduction from payments due to defaulters of amounts due in relation to tax.

Section 1052 Penalties for failure to make certain returns, etc.
Section 1053 Penalty for fraudulently or negligently making incorrect returns, etc.
Section 1077 Penalties for failure to make returns, etc. and for deliberately or carelessly making incorrect returns.
Schedule 12 Employee Share Ownership Trusts
Schedule 12A Approved Savings-Related Share Option Schemes
Schedule 12C Approved Share Option Schemes
Schedule 29 Provisions Referred to in Sections 1052, 1053 and 1054
Schedule 32 Transitional Provisions

1055 Penalty for assisting in making incorrect returns, etc

[ITA67 s505; FA74 s86 and Sch2 PtI; CTA76 s147(1) and (2)]

[Any person who deliberately assists in or induces the making or delivery for any purposes of income tax or corporation tax of any incorrect return, account, statement or declaration shall be liable to a penalty of €4,000.][1]

Amendments

[1] Substituted by F(No.2)A08 sched5(part2)(1)(ad). The enactments specified in Schedule 5 are amended or repealed to the extent and manner specified in that Schedule and, unless the contrary is stated, shall come into effect after 24 December 2008.

1056 Penalty for false statement made to obtain allowance

[ITA67 s516; CTA76 s147(1) and (2); WCTIPA93 s11]

(1) In this section, "*the specified difference*", in relation to a person, means the difference between—

(a) the amount of income tax or, as the case may be, corporation tax payable in relation to the person's or, as may be appropriate, another person's liability to income tax for a year of assessment or to corporation tax for an accounting period, as the case may be, and

(b) the amount which would have been the amount so payable if—

(i) any statement or representation referred to in *subsection (2)(a)* had not been false,

(ii) any account, return, list, declaration or statement referred to in *subsection (2)(b)(i)* had not been false or fraudulent, or

(iii) the full amount of income referred to in *subsection (2)(b)(ii)* had been disclosed.

(2) A person shall, without prejudice to any other penalty to which the person may be liable, be guilty of an offence under this section if—

(a) in relation to the person's liability to income tax for a year of assessment or to corporation tax for an accounting period, as the case may be, the person knowingly makes any false statement or false representation—

(i) in any return, statement or declaration made with reference to tax, or

(ii) for the purpose of obtaining any allowance, reduction, rebate or repayment of tax, or

(b) in relation to liability to income tax of any other person for a year of assessment or to liability to corporation tax of any other person for an accounting period, as the case may be, the person knowingly and wilfully aids, abets, assists, incites or induces that other person—

(i) to make or deliver a false or fraudulent account, return, list, declaration or statement with reference to property, profits or gains or to tax, or

(ii) unlawfully to avoid liability to tax by failing to disclose the full amount of that other person's income from all sources.

(3) A person guilty of an offence under this section shall be liable—

(a) on summary conviction where the amount of the specified difference is—

(i) less than [€1,520][1], to a fine not exceeding 25 per cent of the amount of the specified difference or, at the discretion of the court, to a term of imprisonment not exceeding 12 months or to both;

(ii) equal to or greater than [€1,520][2], to a fine not exceeding [€1,520][3] or, at the discretion of the court, to a term of imprisonment not exceeding 12 months or to both;

or

(b) on conviction on indictment where the amount of the specified difference is—

(i) less than [€6,345][4], to a fine not exceeding 25 per cent of the amount of the specified difference or, at the discretion of the court, to a term of imprisonment not exceeding 2 years or to both;

(ii) equal to or greater than [€6,345][5] but less than [€12,695][6], to a fine not exceeding 50 per cent of the amount of the specified difference or, at the discretion of the court, to a term of imprisonment not exceeding 3 years or to both;

(iii) equal to or greater than [€12,695][7] but less than [€31,740][8], to a fine not exceeding the amount of the specified difference or, at the discretion of the court, to a term of imprisonment not exceeding 4 years or to both;

(iv) equal to or greater than [€31,740][9] but less than [€126,970][10], to a fine not exceeding twice the amount of the specified difference or, at the discretion of the court, to a term of imprisonment not exceeding 8 years or to both;

(v) equal to or greater than [€126,970][11], to a fine not exceeding twice the amount of the specified difference and to a term of imprisonment not exceeding 8 years.

(4) *Subsections (4)* and *(6)* to *(8)* of *section 1078* shall, with any necessary modifications, apply for the purposes of this section as they apply for the purposes of that section.

(5) This section shall not apply to a declaration given under section 2 or 3 of the Waiver of Certain Tax, Interest and Penalties Act, 1993, by reason only of any false statement or false representation made in relation to subsection (3)(*a*)(iii) of section 2 of that Act or subsection (6)(*b*)(III) of section 3 of that Act, as the case may be.

Amendments

1, 2, 3, 4, 5, 6, 7, 8, 9, 10, 11 Substituted by FA01 sched5.

Cross References

From Section 1056

Section 1078 Revenue offences.

To Section 1056

Section 531J False statements.

Section 1064 Time for certain summary proceedings.

1057 Fine for obstruction of officers in execution of duties

[ITA67 s515; CTA76 s147(1) and (2)]

(1) Where any person (in this subsection referred to as "*the first-mentioned person*") or any person in the first-mentioned person's employ, obstructs, molests or hinders—

(a) an officer or any person employed in relation to any duty of income tax or corporation tax in the execution of his or her duty, or of any of the powers or authorities by law given to the officer or person, or

(b) any person acting in the aid of an officer or any person so employed,

the first-mentioned person shall for every such offence incur a fine of [€125][1].

(2) Without prejudice to any other mode of recovery, the fine imposed under this section may be proceeded for and recovered in the like manner and, in the case of summary proceedings, with the like power of appeal as any fine or penalty under any Act relating to the excise.

[(3) This section shall not apply in respect of any acts arising after the passing of the *Finance (No. 2) Act 2008*.][2]

Amendments

[1] Substituted by FA01 sched5.

[2] Inserted by F(No.2)A08 sched5(part2)(1)(ae). The enactments specified in Schedule 5 are amended or repealed to the extent and manner specified in that Schedule and, unless the contrary is stated, shall come into effect after 24 December 2008.

Cross References

To Section 1057

Section 911 Valuation of assets: power to inspect.

1058 Refusal to allow deduction of tax

[ITA67 s520; CTA76 s147(1) and (2); FA96 s132(1) and Sch5 PtI par10(5)]

(1) A person who refuses to allow a deduction of income tax or corporation tax authorised by the Tax Acts to be made out of any payment shall forfeit the sum of [€3,000][1].

(2) Every agreement for payment of interest, rent or other annual payment in full without allowing any such deduction shall be void.

Amendments

[1] Substituted by F(No.2)A08 sched5(part2)(1)(af). The enactments specified in Schedule 5 are amended or repealed to the extent and manner specified in that Schedule and, unless the contrary is stated, shall come into effect after 24 December 2008.

1059 Power to add penalties to assessments

[ITA67 s513; CTA76 s147(3) and (4)]

Where an increased rate of income tax or corporation tax is imposed as a penalty, or as part of or in addition to a penalty, the penalty and increased rate of tax may be added to the assessment and collected and levied in the like manner as any tax included in such assessment may be collected and levied.

1060 Proceedings against executor or administrator

[ITA67 s504; CTA76 s147(3) and (4); FA78 s11(2)]

(1) Where the person who has incurred any penalty has died, any proceedings under the Tax Acts which have been or could have been commenced against that person

may be continued or commenced against his or her executor or administrator, as the case may be, and any penalty awarded in proceedings so continued or commenced shall be a debt due from and payable out of his or her estate.

(2) Proceedings may not be commenced by virtue of *subsection (1)* against the executor or administrator of a person at a time when by virtue of *subsection (2)* of *section 1048* that executor or administrator is not assessable and chargeable under that section in respect of income tax on profits or gains which arose or accrued to the person before his or her death.

[(3) This section shall cease to have effect after the passing of the *Finance (No. 2) Act 2008*.][1]

Amendments

[1] Inserted by F(No.2)A08 sched5(part2)(1)(ag). The enactments specified in Schedule 5 are amended or repealed to the extent and manner specified in that Schedule and, unless the contrary is stated, shall come into effect after 24 December 2008.

Revenue Briefings

eBrief

eBrief No. 15/2008 – Penalties Involving Deceased Taxpayers and Personal Representatives

Cross References

From Section 1060

Section 1048 Assessment of executors and administrators.

To Section 1060

Section 1053 Penalty for fraudulently or negligently making incorrect returns, etc.

Section 1063 Time limit for recovery of fines and penalties.

1061 Recovery of penalties

[ITA67 s508; FA68 s6(6); CTA76 s147(3) and (4)]

(1) Without prejudice to any other mode of recovery of a penalty under the [preceding provisions of this Part, *Chapter 4* of *Part 38*][1] or under *section 305*, *783*, *789* or *886*, an officer of the Revenue Commissioners authorised by them for the purposes of this subsection may sue in his or her own name by civil proceedings [for the recovery of the penalty in any court of competent jurisdiction as a liquidated sum, and, where appropriate, section 94 of the Courts of Justice Act 1924 shall apply accordingly.][2]

(2) Where an officer who has commenced proceedings pursuant to this section, or who has continued the proceedings by virtue of this subsection, dies or otherwise ceases for any reason to be an officer authorised for the purposes of *subsection (1)*—

(a) the right of such officer to continue the proceedings shall cease and the right to continue them shall vest in such other officer so authorised as may be nominated by the Revenue Commissioners,

(b) where such other officer is nominated under *paragraph (a)*, he or she shall be entitled accordingly to be substituted as a party to the proceedings in the place of the first-mentioned officer, and

(c) where an officer is so substituted, he or she shall give notice in writing of the substitution to the defendant.

(3) In proceedings pursuant to this section, a certificate signed by a Revenue Commissioner certifying that—

(a) a person is an officer of the Revenue Commissioners, and

(b) he or she has been authorised by them for the purposes of *subsection (1)*,

shall be evidence of those facts until the contrary is proved.

(4) In proceedings pursuant to this section, a certificate signed by a Revenue Commissioner certifying that—
   (a) the plaintiff has ceased to be an officer of the Revenue Commissioners authorised by them for the purposes of *subsection (1)*,
   (b) another person is an officer of the Revenue Commissioners,
   (c) such other person has been authorised by them for the purposes of *subsection (1)*, and
   (d) he or she has been nominated by them in relation to the proceedings for the purposes of *subsection (2)*,

shall be evidence of those facts until the contrary is proved.

(5) In proceedings pursuant to this section, a certificate certifying the facts referred to in *subsection (3)* or *(4)* and purporting to be signed by a Revenue Commissioner may be tendered in evidence without proof and shall be deemed until the contrary is proved to have been so signed.

(6) Subject to this section, [the rules of court][3] for the time being applicable to civil proceedings shall apply to proceedings pursuant to this section.

[(7) This section shall not apply in respect of any acts or omissions arising after the passing of the *Finance (No.2) Act 2008*.][4]

Amendments

[1] Substituted by FA02 s130(c).

[2] Substituted by FA03 s162(1)(a). Applies as respects civil proceedings commenced on or after 28 March 2003

[3] Substituted by FA03 s162(1)(b). Applies as respects civil proceedings commenced on or after 28 March 2003

[4] Inserted by F(No.2)A08 sched5(part2)(1)(ah). The enactments specified in Schedule 5 are amended or repealed to the extent and manner specified in that Schedule and, unless the contrary is stated, shall come into effect after 24 December 2008.

Cross References

From Section 1061

Section 305 Income tax: manner of granting, and effect of, allowances made by means of discharge or repayment of tax.
Section 783 Interpretation and general (Chapter 2).
Section 789 Supplementary provisions (Chapter 3).
Section 876 Notice of liability to income tax.
Section 886 Obligation to keep certain records.
Section 899 Inspector's right to make enquiries.

To Section 1061

Section 731 Chargeable gains accruing to unit trusts.
Section 886A Retention and inspection of records in relation to claims by individuals.
Section 891B Returns of certain payments made by certain persons.
Section 898O Penalty for failure to make returns, etc.
Section 917EA Mandatory electronic filing and payment of tax.
Schedule 31 Consequential Amendments

1062 Proceedings where penalty recoverable cannot be definitely ascertained

[ITA67 s510; CTA76 s147(3) and (4)]

Notwithstanding that the amount of a penalty recoverable under the Tax Acts cannot be definitely ascertained by reason of the fact that the amount of income tax or, as the case may be, corporation tax by reference to which such penalty is to be calculated has not been finally ascertained, proceedings may be instituted for the recovery of such penalty and, if at the hearing of such proceedings the amount of such tax has not then been finally ascertained, the Court may, if it is of the opinion that such penalty is recoverable, adjourn such proceedings and shall not give any judgment or make any order for the payment of such penalty until the amount of such tax has been finally ascertained.

Cross References

To Section 1062

Schedule 31 Consequential Amendments

1063 Time limit for recovery of fines and penalties

[ITA67 s511; FA74 s86 and Sch2 PtI; CTA76 s147(3) and (4)]

Proceedings for the recovery of any fine or penalty incurred under the Tax Acts in relation to or in connection with income tax or corporation tax may, [subject to section 1060 or section 1077D][1], be begun at any time within 6 years after the date on which such fine or penalty was incurred.

Amendments

[1] Substituted by F(No.2)A08 sched5(part2)(1)(ai). The enactments specified in Schedule 5 are amended or repealed to the extent and manner specified in that Schedule and, unless the contrary is stated, shall come into effect after 24 December 2008.

Cross References

From Section 1063

Section 1060 Proceedings against executor or administrator.

Section 1077D Proceedings against executor, administrator or estate.

To Section 1063

Section 1053 Penalty for fraudulently or negligently making incorrect returns, etc.

Section 1077E Penalty for deliberately or carelessly making incorrect returns, etc.

Schedule 31 Consequential Amendments

1064 Time for certain summary proceedings

[ITA67 s517; FA79 s29; CTA76 s148]

Notwithstanding section 10(4) of the Petty Sessions (Ireland) Act, 1851, summary proceedings under *section 889*, *987* or *1056* may be instituted within 10 years from the date of the committing of the offence or incurring of the penalty, as the case may be.

Cross References

From Section 1064

Section 889 Returns of fees, commissions, etc. paid by certain persons.

Section 987 Penalties for breach of regulations.

Section 1056 Penalty for false statement made to obtain allowance.

To Section 1064

Schedule 31 Consequential Amendments

1065 Mitigation and application of fines and penalties

[ITA67 s512; CTA76 s147(3) and (4); WCTIPA93 s10]

[(1) The Revenue Commissioners may in their discretion—

(a) mitigate any penalty, and may also, after judgment, further mitigate any such penalty imposed under the Acts,

(b) stay or compound any proceedings for the recovery of any fine or penalty imposed under the Acts.][1]

(2) Notwithstanding *subsection (1)*—

(a) where a [...][2] penalty is mitigated or further mitigated, as the case may be, after judgment, the amount or amounts so mitigated shall, subject to *paragraph (b)*, not be greater than 50 per cent of the amount of the [...][3] penalty, and

(b) in relation to an individual, being an individual referred to in section 2(2) of the Waiver of Certain Tax, Interest and Penalties Act, 1993, or a person referred to in section 3(2) of that Act, who—

(i) fails to give a declaration required by section 2(3)(*a*) of that Act, or

(ii) gives a declaration referred to in *subparagraph (i)* or a declaration under section 3(6)(*b*) of that Act which is false or fails to comply with the requirements of subparagraph (iii) or (iv) of section 2(3)(*a*) of that Act or subparagraph (III) of section 3(6)(*b*) of that Act to the extent that any of those subparagraphs apply to that person,

no mitigation shall be allowed.

(3) Moneys arising from fines, penalties and forfeitures, and all costs, charges and expenses payable in respect of or in relation to such fines, penalties and forfeitures, shall be accounted for and paid to the Revenue Commissioners or as they direct.

[(4) In this section "*the Acts*" has the same meaning as in *section 1077A(1)*.][4]

Amendments

[1] Substituted by F(No.2)A13 s78(5)(a).

[2, 3] Deleted by F(No.2)A13 s78(5)(b).

[4] Inserted by F(No.2)A13 s78(5)(c).

Cross References

To Section 1065

Schedule 31 Consequential Amendments

1066 False evidence: punishment as for perjury

[ITA67 s518; CTA76 s147(1) and (2)]

If any person on any examination on oath, or in any affidavit or deposition authorised by the Tax Acts, wilfully and corruptly gives false evidence, or wilfully and corruptly swears any matter or thing which is false or untrue, that person shall on conviction be subject and liable to such punishment as persons convicted of perjury are subject and liable to.

Cross References

To Section 1066

Schedule 31 Consequential Amendments

1067 Admissibility of statements and documents in criminal and tax proceedings

[ITA67 s521; FA74 s86 and Sch2 PtI; CTA76 s147(1) and (2)]

(1) Statements made or documents produced by or on behalf of a person shall not be inadmissible in any proceedings mentioned in *subsection (2)* by reason only that it has been drawn to the person's attention that—

(a) in relation to income tax or, as the case may be, corporation tax, the Revenue Commissioners may accept pecuniary settlements instead of instituting proceedings, and

(b) although no undertaking can be given as to whether or not the Revenue Commissioners will accept such a settlement in the case of any particular person, it is the practice of the Revenue Commissioners to be influenced by the fact that a person has made a full confession of any fraud or default to which the person has been a party and has given full facilities for investigation,

and that the person was or may have been induced thereby to make the statements or produce the documents.

(2) The proceedings referred to in *subsection (1)* are—

(a) any criminal proceedings against the person in question for any form of fraud or wilful default in connection with or in relation to income tax or corporation tax, and

(b) any proceedings against the person in question for the recovery of any sum due from that person, whether by means of tax, fine, forfeiture or penalty, in connection with or in relation to income tax or corporation tax.

1068 Failure to act within required time

[ITA67 s507; CTA76 s147(1) and (2)]

[For the purposes of this Chapter, Chapter 3A and Chapter 3B of this Part, and Chapter 4 of Part 38][1], a person shall be deemed not to have failed to do anything required to be done within a limited time if the person did it within such further time, if any, as the Commissioners or officer concerned may have allowed and, where a person had a reasonable excuse for not doing anything required to be done, the person shall be deemed not to have failed to do it if the person did it without unreasonable delay after the excuse had ceased.

Amendments

[1] Substituted by F(No.2)A08 sched5(part2)(1)(aj). The enactments specified in Schedule 5 are amended or repealed to the extent and manner specified in that Schedule and, unless the contrary is stated, shall come into effect after 24 December 2008.

Cross References

From Section 1068

Section 876 Notice of liability to income tax.

Section 899 Inspector's right to make enquiries.

To Section 1068

Section 531 Payments to subcontractors in certain industries.

Schedule 31 Consequential Amendments

1069 Evidence of income

[ITA67 s506 and definition of "*assessment*" in ITA67 s509; F(MP)A68 s3(2) and Sch PtI; CTA76 s147(1) and (2); FA88 s21(2)]

[(1) In this section '*assessment*' includes an amended assessment.][1]

[(2) For the purposes of this Chapter, Chapter 3A and Chapter 3B of this Part, any assessment which can no longer be varied by the Appeal Commissioners on appeal or by the order of any court shall be sufficient evidence that—

(a) the income in respect of which income tax or, as the case may be, corporation tax, or

(b) the gain in respect of which capital gains tax,

is charged in the assessment arose or was received as stated in the assessment.][2]

Amendments

[1] Substituted by FA12 sched4(part 2)(e).

[2] Substituted by F(No.2)A08 sched5(part2)(1)(ak). The enactments specified in Schedule 5 are amended or repealed to the extent and manner specified in that Schedule and, unless the contrary is stated, shall come into effect after 24 December 2008.

Cross References

From Section 1069

Section 955 Amendment of and time limit for assessments.

To Section 1069

Section 531 Payments to subcontractors in certain industries.

1070 Saving for criminal proceedings

[ITA67 s514; CTA76 s147(1) and (2)]

The Tax Acts shall not affect any criminal proceedings for a felony or misdemeanour.

CHAPTER 2

Other Corporation Tax Penalties

1071 Penalties for failure to make certain returns

[CTA76 s143(7)(c) and (8)]

(1) Where any company has been required by notice served under *section 884* to deliver a return and the company fails to comply with the notice—

(a) the company shall be liable to a penalty of [€2,000][1] except in the case mentioned in *subsection (2)* and, if the failure continues after judgment has been given by the court before which proceedings for the penalty have been commenced, to a further penalty of [€60][2] for each day on which the failure so continues, and

(b) the secretary of the company shall be liable to a separate penalty of [€1,000][3] except in the case mentioned in *subsection (2)*.

(2) Where any failure mentioned in *subsection (1)* continues after the expiration of one year beginning with the date on which the notice was served, the first of the penalties mentioned in that subsection for which the company is liable shall be [€4,000][4], and the secretary of the company shall be liable to a separate penalty of [€2,000][5].

[(2A) (a) Where at any time not earlier than 3 months after the time at which a return is required to be delivered by a company in accordance with *section 884*, the company has failed to pay any penalty to which it is liable under *subsection (1)(a)* or *(2)* for failing to deliver the return, the secretary of the company shall, in addition to any penalty to which the secretary is liable under this section, be liable to pay such amount of any penalty to which the company is so liable as is not paid by the company.

(b) Where in accordance with *paragraph (a)* the secretary of a company pays any amount of a penalty to which the company is liable, the secretary shall be entitled to recover a sum equal to that amount from the company.][6]

(3) The reference in *subsection (1)* to the delivery of a return shall be deemed to include a reference to the doing of any of the things specified in *subparagraphs (i)* and *(ii)* of *paragraph (b)* of *section 884(9)*.

Amendments

[1] Substituted by F(No.2)A08 sched5(part2)(1)(al)(i). The enactments specified in Schedule 5 are amended or repealed to the extent and manner specified in that Schedule and, unless the contrary is stated, shall come into effect after 24 December 2008.

[2] Substituted by FA01 sched5.

[3] Substituted by F(No.2)A08 sched5(part2)(1)(al)(ii). The enactments specified in Schedule 5 are amended or repealed to the extent and manner specified in that Schedule and, unless the contrary is stated, shall come into effect after 24 December 2008.

[4] Substituted by F(No.2)A08 sched5(part2)(1)(al)(iii)(I). The enactments specified in Schedule 5 are amended or repealed to the extent and manner specified in that Schedule and, unless the contrary is stated, shall come into effect after 24 December 2008.

[5] Substituted by F(No.2)A08 sched5(part2)(1)(al)(iii)(II). The enactments specified in Schedule 5 are amended or repealed to the extent and manner specified in that Schedule and, unless the contrary is stated, shall come into effect after 24 December 2008.

[6] Inserted by FA99 s84(1)(a). This section shall apply as on and from the 1st day of March, 1999.

Cross References

From Section 1071

Section 884 Returns of profits.

To Section 1071

Section 182 Returns.

1072 Penalties for fraudulently or negligently making incorrect returns, etc

[CTA76 s143(9), (10) and (11)]

(1) Where a company fraudulently or negligently—

(a) delivers an incorrect return under *section 884*,

(b) makes any incorrect return, statement or declaration in connection with any claim for any allowance, deduction or relief in respect of corporation tax, or

(c) submits to an inspector, the Revenue Commissioners or the Appeal Commissioners any incorrect accounts in connection with the ascertainment of the company's liability to corporation tax,

the company shall be liable to a penalty of—

(i) [€630][1] or, in the case of fraud, [€1,265][2], and

(ii) the amount or, in the case of fraud, twice the amount of the difference specified in *subsection (2)*, and

the secretary of the company shall be liable to a separate penalty of [€125][3] or, in the case of fraud, [€250][4].

(2) The difference referred to in *subsection (1)* shall be the difference between—

(a) the amount of corporation tax payable by the company for the accounting period or accounting periods comprising the period to which the return, statement, declaration or accounts relate, and

(b) the amount which would have been the amount so payable if the return, statement, declaration or accounts had been correct.

[(2A) Where any company fails to comply with a requirement to deliver a return of a kind referred to in *section 884*, by reason of fraud or neglect by that company, that company shall be liable to a penalty of—

(a) €630 in the case of neglect or €1,265 in the case of fraud, and

(b) (i) the amount in the case of neglect, or

(ii) twice the amount in the case of fraud,

of the difference specified in *subsection (2B)*.

(2B) The difference referred to in *subsection (2A)(b)* is the difference between—

(a) the amount of corporation tax paid by the company for the accounting period or accounting periods comprising the period to which the return relates, and

(b) the amount of corporation tax which would have been payable for those periods if the return had been delivered by the company and the return had been correct.][5]

(3) *Subsection (3)* of *section 1053* shall apply for the purposes of this section as it applies for the purposes of *section 1053*.

[(4) This section shall not apply in respect of any acts or omissions arising after the passing of the *Finance (No.2) Act 2008*.][6]

Amendments

[1, 2, 3, 4] Substituted by FA01 sched5.

[5] Inserted by FA02 s131.

[6] Inserted by F(No.2)A08 sched5(part2)(1)(am). The enactments specified in Schedule 5 are amended or repealed to the extent and manner specified in that Schedule and, unless the contrary is stated, shall come into effect after 24 December 2008.

Cross References

From Section 1072

Section 884 Returns of profits.

Section 1053 Penalty for fraudulently or negligently making incorrect returns, etc.

1073 Penalties for failure to furnish particulars required to be supplied by new companies

[(1) Where a company fails to deliver a statement which it is required to deliver under *section 882*—

(a) the company shall be liable to a penalty of [€4,000][1] and, if the failure continues after judgement has been given by the court before which proceedings for the penalty have been commenced, to a further penalty of [€60][2] for each day on which the failure so continues, and

(b) the secretary of the company shall be liable to a separate penalty of [€3,000][3].

(2) (a) Where at any time not earlier than 3 months after the time at which a statement is required to be delivered by a company in accordance with *section 882*, the company has failed to pay any penalty to which it is liable under *subsection (1)(a)* for failing to deliver the statement, the secretary of the company shall, in addition to any penalty to which the secretary is liable under *subsection (1)(b)*, be liable to pay such amount of any penalty to which the company is so liable as is not paid by the company.

(b) Where in accordance with *paragraph (a)* the secretary of a company pays any amount of a penalty to which the company is liable, the secretary shall be entitled to recover a sum equal to that amount from the company.][4]

Amendments

[1] Substituted by F(No.2)A08 sched5(part2)(1)(an)(i). The enactments specified in Schedule 5 are amended or repealed to the extent and manner specified in that Schedule and, unless the contrary is stated, shall come into effect after 24 December 2008.

[2] Substituted by FA01 sched5.

[3] Substituted by F(No.2)A08 sched5(part2)(1)(an)(ii). The enactments specified in Schedule 5 are amended or repealed to the extent and manner specified in that Schedule and, unless the contrary is stated, shall come into effect after 24 December 2008.

[4] Substituted by FA99 s84(1)(b). This section shall apply as on and from the 1st day of March, 1999.

Cross References

From Section 1073

Section 882 Particulars to be supplied by new companies.

1074 Penalties for failure to give notice of liability to corporation tax

[CTA76 s142(2)]

Where a company fails to give a notice which it is required to give under *section 883*—

(a) the company shall be liable to a penalty of [€4,000][1] and, if the failure continues after judgment has been given by the court before which proceedings for the penalty have been commenced, to a further penalty of [€60][2] for each day on which the failure so continues, and

(b) the secretary of the company shall be liable to a separate penalty of [€3,000][3].

Amendments

[1] Substituted by F(No.2)A08 sched5(part2)(1)(ao)(i). The enactments specified in Schedule 5 are amended or repealed to the extent and manner specified in that Schedule and, unless the contrary is stated, shall come into effect after 24 December 2008.

[2] Substituted by FA01 sched5.

[3] Substituted by F(No.2)A08 sched5(part2)(1)(ao)(ii). The enactments specified in Schedule 5 are amended or repealed to the extent and manner specified in that Schedule and, unless the contrary is stated, shall come into effect after 24 December 2008.

Cross References

From Section 1074

Section 883 Notice of liability to corporation tax.

1075 Penalties for failure to furnish certain information and for incorrect information

[(1) Where any person has been required by notice given under or for the purposes of section 401 or 427 or Part 13 to furnish any information or particulars and that person fails to comply with the notice, that person shall be liable, subject to subsection (3), to a penalty of €3,000 and, if the failure continues after judgment has been given by the court before which proceedings for the penalty have been commenced, to a further penalty of €10 for each day on which the failure so continues.

(2) Where the person furnishes any incorrect information or particulars of a kind mentioned in section 239, 401 or 427 or Part 13, the person shall be liable, subject to subsection (4), to a penalty of €3,000.

(3) Where the person mentioned in subsection (1) is a company—

(a) the company shall be liable to a penalty of €4,000 and, if the failure continues after judgment has been given by the court before which proceedings for the penalty have been commenced, to a further penalty of €60 for each day on which the failure so continues, and

(b) the secretary of the company shall be liable to a separate penalty of €3,000.

(4) Where the person mentioned in subsection (2) is a company—

(a) the company shall be liable to a penalty of €4,000, and

(b) the secretary of the company shall be liable to a separate penalty of €3,000.

(5) Subsection (3) of section 1053 and subsection (9) of section 1077E shall apply for the purposes of this section as it applies for the purposes of section 1053 and of section 1077E.][1]

Amendments

[1] Substituted by F(No.2)A08 sched5(part2)(1)(ap). The enactments specified in Schedule 5 are amended or repealed to the extent and manner specified in that Schedule and, unless the contrary is stated, shall come into effect after 24 December 2008.

Cross References

From Section 1075

Section 239 Income tax on payments by resident companies.
Section 401 Change in ownership of company: disallowance of trading losses.
Section 427 Information as to arrangements for transferring relief, etc.
Section 1053 Penalty for fraudulently or negligently making incorrect returns, etc.
Section 1077E Penalty for deliberately or carelessly making incorrect returns, etc.

1076 Supplementary provisions (Chapter 2)

[CTA76 s154 and s147(3) and (4) (as it relates to application of ITA67 s172(5))]

[(1) In this Chapter, "*secretary*" includes—

(a) persons mentioned in *section 1044(2)* and, in the case of a company which is not resident in the State, the agent, manager, factor or other representative of the company, and

(b) in the case of a company the secretary (within the meaning of section 175 of the Companies Act, 1963) of which is not an individual resident in the State, an individual resident in the State who is a director of the company.][1]

(2) In proceedings for the recovery of a penalty incurred under the provisions of the Corporation Tax Acts—

(a) a certificate signed by an inspector which certifies that he or she has examined his or her relevant records and that it appears from those records that a stated notice was duly given to the defendant on a stated day shall be evidence until the contrary is proved that the defendant received that notice in the ordinary course;

(b) a certificate signed by an inspector which certifies that he or she has examined his or her relevant records and that it appears from those records that during a stated period a stated return was not received from the defendant shall be evidence until the contrary is proved that the defendant did not during that period deliver that return;

(c) a certificate certifying as provided for in *paragraph (a)* or *(b)* and purporting to be signed by an inspector may be tendered in evidence without proof and shall be deemed

Amendments

[1] Substituted by FA99 s84(1)(c). This section shall apply as on and from the 1st day of March, 1999.

Cross References

From Section 1076

Section 1044 Bodies of persons.

CHAPTER 3

Capital Gains Tax Penalties

1077 Penalties for failure to make returns, etc. and for deliberately or carelessly making incorrect returns

[(1) Without prejudice to the generality of section 913(1), Chapter 1 and Chapter 3B of this Part shall, subject to any necessary modifications, apply in relation to capital gains tax, and sections 1052, 1053, 1054 and 1077E, as applied by this section, shall for the purposes of the Capital Gains Tax Acts be construed as if in Schedule 29 there were included—

(a) in column 1, references to sections 914 to 917,

(b) in column 2, a reference to section 945, and

(c) in column 3, a reference to section 980.

(2) Where any person has been required by notice or precept given under the provisions of the Income Tax Acts as applied by section 913, or under section 914, 915, 916, 917 or 980, to do any act of a kind mentioned in any of those provisions or sections, and the person fails to comply with the notice or precept, or where any person deliberately or carelessly makes, delivers, furnishes or produces any incorrect return, statement, declaration, list, account, particulars or other document (or makes any false statement or false representation) under any of those provisions or sections, Chapter 1 and Chapter 3B of this Part shall apply to the person for the purposes of capital gains tax as it applies in the case of a like failure or act for the purposes of income tax.][1]

Amendments

[1] Substituted by F(No.2)A08 sched5(part2)(1)(aq). The enactments specified in Schedule 5 are amended or repealed to the extent and manner specified in that Schedule and, unless the contrary is stated, shall come into effect after 24 December 2008.

Cross References

From Section 1077

Section 913 Application of income tax provisions relating to returns, etc.
Section 914 Returns by issuing houses, stockbrokers, auctioneers, etc.
Section 915 Returns by nominee shareholders.
Section 916 Returns by party to a settlement.
Section 917 Returns relating to non-resident companies and trusts.
Section 945 Appeals against assessments.
Section 980 Deduction from consideration on disposal of certain assets.
Section 1052 Penalties for failure to make certain returns, etc.
Section 1053 Penalty for fraudulently or negligently making incorrect returns, etc.

Section 1054 Penalties in the case of a secretary of a body of persons.
Section 1077E Penalty for deliberately or carelessly making incorrect returns, etc.

To Section 1077

Section 959 Miscellaneous (Part 41).

CHAPTER 3A

Determination of Penalties and Recovery of Penalties

1077A Interpretation (Chapter 3A)

[In this Chapter—

"*the Acts*" means—

(a) the Tax Acts,

(b) the Capital Gains Tax Acts,

[(c) Parts 18A, 18B, 18C and 18D,][1]

(d) the Value-Added Tax Consolidation Act 2010, and the enactments amending or extending that Act,

(e) the Capital Acquisitions Tax Consolidation Act 2003, and the enactments amending or extending that Act,

(f) the Stamp Duties Consolidation Act 1999, and the enactments amending or extending that Act,

(g) the statutes relating to the duties of excise and to the management of those duties,

[(h) the Customs Acts,

(i) the Finance (Local Property Tax) Act 2012,][2]

and any instrument made thereunder and any instrument made under any other enactment relating to tax;

"*relevant court*" means the District Court, the Circuit Court or the High Court, as appropriate, by reference to the jurisdictional limits for civil matters laid down in the Courts of Justice Act 1924, as amended, and the Courts (Supplemental Provisions) Act 1961, as amended;

"*Revenue officer*" means an officer of the Revenue Commissioners,

"*tax*" means any tax, duty, levy or charge under the care and management of the Revenue Commissioners.][3]

Amendments

[1] Substituted by FA11 s3(1)(g). Applies for the year of assessment 2011 and each subsequent year of assessment.

[2] Substituted by F(No.2)A13 sched(1)(k). Deemed to have come into force and have taken effect on and from 1 January 2013.

[3] Inserted by F(No.2)A08 sched5(part1)(1). Has effect from 24 December 2008.

1077B Penalty notifications and determinations

[(1) Where—

(a) in the absence of any agreement between a person and a Revenue officer that the person is liable to a penalty under the Acts, or

(b) following the failure by a person to pay a penalty the person has agreed a liability to, a Revenue officer is of the opinion that the person is liable to a penalty under the Acts, then that officer shall give notice in writing to the person and such notice shall identify—

(i) the provisions of the Acts under which the penalty arises,

(ii) the circumstances in which that person is liable to the penalty, and

(iii) the amount of the penalty to which that person is liable,

and include such other details as the Revenue officer considers necessary.

(2) A Revenue officer may at any time amend an opinion that a person is liable to a penalty under the Acts and shall give due notice of such amended opinion in like manner to the notice referred to in subsection (1).

(3) Where a person to whom a notice issued under subsection (1) or (2) does not, within 30 days after the date of such a notice—

(a) agree in writing with the opinion or amended opinion contained in such notice, and

(b) make a payment to the Revenue Commissioners of the amount of the penalty specified in such a notice,

then a Revenue officer may make an application to a relevant court for that court to determine whether—

(i) any action, inaction, omission or failure of, or

(ii) any claim, submission or delivery by,

the person in respect of whom the Revenue officer made the application gives rise to a liability to a penalty under the Acts on that person.

(4) A copy of any application to a relevant court for a determination under subsection (3) shall be issued to the person to whom the application relates.

(5) This section applies in respect of any act or omission giving rise to a liability to a penalty under the Acts whether arising before, on or after the passing of the *Finance (No. 2) Act 2008* but shall not apply in respect of a penalty paid, or amounts paid in respect of a penalty, before the passing of that Act.][1]

Amendments

[1] Inserted by F(No.2)A08 sched5(part1)(1). The enactments specified in Schedule 5 are amended or repealed to the extent and manner specified in that Schedule and, unless the contrary is stated, shall come into effect after the passing of this Act.

Revenue Briefings

Tax Briefing

Tax Briefing December 2008 – Issue 70 – Finance (no.2) Bill 2008 – Notes on Some Aspects – Tax and Duty Civil Penalties

eBrief

Revenue eBrief No. 23/09 – New Penalties Regime – Finance (No.2) Act 2008

Revenue Information Notes

2010 Code of Practice for Revenue Audit

Code of Practice for Revenue Audit and other Compliance Interventions

Cross References

To Section 1077B

Section 817O Penalties.

Section 1086 Publication of names of tax defaulters.

1077C Recovery of penalties

[(1) Where a relevant court has made a determination that a person is liable to a penalty—

(a) that court shall also make an order as to the recovery of that penalty, and

(b) without prejudice to any other means of recovery, that penalty may be collected and recovered in like manner as an amount of tax.

(2) Where a person is liable to a penalty under the Acts, that penalty is due and payable from the date—

(a) it had been agreed in writing (or had been agreed in writing on that person's behalf) that the person is liable to that penalty,

(b) the Revenue Commissioners had agreed or undertaken to accept a specified sum of money in the circumstances mentioned in paragraph (*c*) or (*d*) of section 1086(2) from that [person][1], or

(c) a relevant court has determined that the person is liable to that penalty.

(3) This section applies in respect of any act or omission giving rise to a liability to a penalty under the Acts whether arising before, on or after the passing of the *Finance (No. 2) Act 2008*.][2]

Amendments

[1] Substituted by FA09 s30(2). This section is deemed to have come into force and have taken effect as on and from 24 December 2008.

[2] Inserted by F(No.2)A08 sched5(part1)(1). The enactments specified in Schedule 5 are amended or repealed to the extent and manner specified in that Schedule and, unless the contrary is stated, shall come into effect after 24 December 2008.

Revenue Briefings

Tax Briefing

Tax Briefing December 2008 – Issue 70 – Finance (no.2) Bill 2008 – Notes on Some Aspects – Tax and Duty Civil Penalties

eBrief

Revenue eBrief No. 23/09 – New Penalties Regime – Finance (No.2) Act 2008

Revenue Information Notes

2010 Code of Practice for Revenue Audit

Code of Practice for Revenue Audit and other Compliance Interventions

Cross References

From Section 1077C

Section 1086 Publication of names of tax defaulters.

To Section 1077C

Section 817O Penalties.

1077D Proceedings against executor, administrator or estate

[(1) Where before an individual's death—

(a) that individual had agreed in writing (or it had been agreed in writing on his or her behalf) that he or she was liable to a penalty under the Acts,

(b) that individual had agreed in writing with an opinion or amended opinion of a Revenue officer that he or she was liable to a penalty under the Acts (or such opinion or amended opinion had been agreed in writing on his or her behalf),

(c) the Revenue Commissioners had agreed or undertaken to accept a specified sum of money in the circumstances mentioned in paragraph (*c*) or (*d*) of section 1086(2) from that individual, or

(d) a relevant court has determined that the individual was liable to a penalty under the Acts,

then the penalty shall be due and payable and, subject to subsection (2), any proceedings for the recovery of such penalty under the Acts which have been, or could have been, instituted against that individual may be continued or instituted against his or her executor, administrator or estate, as the case may be, and any penalty awarded in proceedings so continued or instituted shall be a debt due from and payable out of his or her estate.

(2) Proceedings may not be instituted by virtue of subsection (1) against the executor or administrator of a person at a time when by virtue of subsection (2) of section 1048 that executor or administrator is not assessable and chargeable under that section in respect of tax on profits or gains which arose or accrued to the person before his or her death.][1]

Amendments

[1] Inserted by F(No.2)A08 sched5(part1)(1). The enactments specified in Schedule 5 are amended or repealed to the extent and manner specified in that Schedule and, unless the contrary is stated, shall come into effect after 24 December 2008.

Revenue Briefings

Tax Briefing

Tax Briefing December 2008 – Issue 70 – Finance (No.2) Bill 2008 – Notes on Some Aspects – Tax and Duty Civil Penalties

eBrief

Revenue eBrief No. 23/09 – New Penalties Regime – Finance (No.2) Act 2008

Revenue Information Notes

2010 Code of Practice for Revenue Audit

Code of Practice for Revenue Audit and other Compliance Interventions

Cross References

From Section 1077D

Section 1048 Assessment of executors and administrators.

Section 1086 Publication of names of tax defaulters.

To Section 1077D

Section 817O Penalties.

Section 1063 Time limit for recovery of fines and penalties.

Section 1077E Penalty for deliberately or carelessly making incorrect returns, etc.

CHAPTER 3B

Income Tax, Corporation Tax and Capital Gains Tax: Penalties for False Returns, etc.

1077E Penalty for deliberately or carelessly making incorrect returns, etc.

[(1) In this section—

['*the Acts*' means the Tax Acts, the Capital Gains Tax Acts, *Parts 18A*, *18B*, *18C*, *18D* of this Act and the *Finance (Local Property Tax) Act 2012*;][1]

"*carelessly*" means failure to take reasonable care;

"*liability to tax*" means a liability to the amount of the difference specified in *subsection (11)* or *(12)* arising from any matter referred to in *subsection (2)*, *(3)*, *(5)* or *(6)*;

"*period*" means a year of assessment or accounting period [or a return period, as defined in *section 530*][2], as the context requires;

"*prompted qualifying disclosure*", in relation to a person, means a qualifying disclosure that has been made to the Revenue Commissioners or to a Revenue officer in the period between—

(a) the date on which the person is notified by a Revenue officer of the date on which an investigation or inquiry into any matter occasioning a liability to tax of that person will start, and

(b) the date that the investigation or inquiry starts;

"*qualifying disclosure*", in relation to a person, means—

(a) in relation to a penalty referred to in *subsection (4)*, a disclosure that the Revenue Commissioners are satisfied is a disclosure of complete information in relation to, and full particulars of, all matters occasioning a liability to tax that gives rise to a penalty referred to in *subsection (4)*, and full particulars of all matters occasioning any liability to tax or duty that gives rise to a penalty referred to in section 116(4) of the Value-Added Tax Consolidation Act 2010, section 134A(2) of the Stamp Duties Consolidation Act 1999 and the application of *subsection (4)* to the Capital Acquisitions Tax Consolidation Act 2003, and

(b) in relation to a penalty referred to in *subsection (7)*, a disclosure that the Revenue Commissioners are satisfied is a disclosure of complete information in relation to, and full particulars of, all matters occasioning a liability to tax that gives rise to a penalty referred to in *subsection (7)* for the relevant period under whichever of the Acts the disclosure relates to,

made in writing to the Revenue Commissioners or to a Revenue officer and signed by or on behalf of that person and that is accompanied by—

(i) a declaration, to the best of that person's knowledge, information and belief, made in writing that all matters contained in the disclosure are correct and complete, and

(ii) a payment of either or both of the tax and duty payable in respect of any matter contained in the disclosure and the interest on late payment of that tax and duty.

"*Revenue officer*" means an officer of the Revenue Commissioners;

['*tax*' means any income tax, corporation tax, capital gains tax, [domicile levy,][3] income levy, parking levy [, universal social charge][4] or local property tax;][5]

"*unprompted qualifying disclosure*", in relation to a person, means a qualifying disclosure that the Revenue Commissioners are satisfied has been voluntarily furnished to them—

(a) before an investigation or inquiry had been started by them or by a Revenue officer into any matter occasioning a liability to tax of that person, or

(b) where the person is notified by a Revenue officer of the date on which an investigation or inquiry into any matter occasioning a liability to tax of that person will start, before that notification.

(2) Where any person—

(a) delivers any incorrect return or statement of a kind mentioned in any of the provisions specified in column 1 of Schedule 29 which contains a deliberate understatement of income, profits or gains or a deliberately false or overstated claim in connection with any allowance, deduction, relief or credit,

(b) makes any incorrect return, statement or declaration in connection with any claim for any allowance, deduction, relief or credit and does so deliberately, or

(c) submits to the Revenue Commissioners, the Appeal Commissioners or a Revenue officer any incorrect accounts which contain a deliberate understatement of income, profits or gains or a deliberate overstatement of any claim in connection with any allowance, deduction, relief or credit,

that person shall be liable to a penalty.

(3) Where any person deliberately fails to comply with a requirement to deliver a return or statement of a kind mentioned in any of the provisions specified in column 1 of Schedule 29, that person shall be liable to a penalty.

(4) The penalty referred to—

(a) in *subsection (2)*, shall be the amount specified in *subsection (11)*, and

(b) in *subsection (3)*, shall be the amount specified in *subsection (12)*,

reduced, where the person liable to the penalty cooperated fully with any investigation or inquiry started by the Revenue Commissioners or by a Revenue officer into any matter occasioning a liability to tax of that person, to—

(i) 75 per cent of that amount where *subparagraph (ii)* or *(iii)* does not apply,

(ii) 50 per cent of that amount where a prompted qualifying disclosure is made by that person, or

(iii) 10 per cent of that amount where an unprompted qualifying disclosure is made by that person.

(5) Where any person carelessly but not deliberately—

(a) delivers any incorrect return or statement of a kind mentioned in any of the provisions specified in column 1 of Schedule 29,

(b) makes any incorrect return, statement or declaration in connection with any claim for any allowance, deduction, relief or credit, or

(c) submits to the Revenue Commissioners, the Appeal Commissioners or a Revenue officer any incorrect accounts which contain an understatement of income, profits or gains or an overstatement of any claims in connection with any allowance, deduction, relief or credit,

that person shall be liable to a penalty.

(6) Where any person carelessly but not deliberately fails to comply with a requirement to deliver a return or statement of a kind mentioned in any of the provisions specified in column 1 of Schedule 29, that person shall be liable to a penalty.

(7) (a) The penalty referred to—

(i) in *subsection (5)* shall be the amount specified in *subsection (11)*, and

(ii) in *subsection (6)* shall be the amount specified in *subsection (12)*,

reduced to 40 per cent in cases where the excess referred to in *subparagraph (I)* of *paragraph (b)* applies and to 20 per cent in other cases.

(b) Where a person liable to a penalty cooperated fully with any investigation or inquiry started by the Revenue Commissioners or by a Revenue officer into any matter occasioning a liability to tax of that person, the penalty referred to—

(i) in *subsection (5)*, shall be the amount specified in *subsection (11)*, and

(ii) in *subsection (6)*, shall be the amount specified in *subsection (12)*,

reduced—

(I) where the difference referred to in *subsection (11)* or *subsection (12)*, as the case may be, exceeds 15 per cent of the amount referred to in *paragraph* (*b*) of *subsection (11)* or *paragraph* (*b*) of *subsection (12)*, to—

(A) 30 per cent of the difference referred to in *subsection (11)* or, as the case may be, *subsection (12)* (in clauses (B) and (C) referred to as "*that amount*") where clause (B) or (C) does not apply,

(B) 20 per cent of that amount where a prompted qualifying disclosure is made by that person, or

(C) 5 per cent of that amount where an unprompted qualifying disclosure is made by that person,

or

(II) where the difference referred to in *subsection (11)* or *subsection (12)*, as the case may be, does not exceed 15 per cent of the amount referred to in *paragraph* (*b*) of *subsection (11)* or *paragraph* (*b*) of *subsection (12)* to—

(A) 15 per cent of the difference referred to in *subsection (11)* or, as the case may be, *subsection (12)* (in clauses (B) and (C) referred to as "*that amount*") where clause (B) or (C) does not apply,

(B) 10 per cent of that amount where a prompted qualifying disclosure is made by that person, or

(C) 3 per cent of that amount where an unprompted qualifying disclosure is made by that person.

(8) Where any person deliberately or carelessly furnishes, gives, produces or makes any incorrect return, information, certificate, document, record, statement, particulars, account or declaration of a kind mentioned in any of the provisions specified in column 2 or 3 of *Schedule 29*, that person shall be liable to—

(a) a penalty of €3,000 where that person has acted carelessly, or

(b) a penalty of €5,000 where that person has acted deliberately.

(9) Where any return, statement, declaration or accounts mentioned in *subsection (2)* or *(5)* was or were made or submitted by a person, neither deliberately nor carelessly, and it comes to that person's notice that it was or they were incorrect, then, unless the error is remedied without unreasonable delay, the incorrect return, statement, declaration or accounts shall be treated for the purposes of this section as having been deliberately made or submitted by that person.

(10) Subject to section 1077D(2), proceedings or applications for the recovery of any penalty under this section shall not be out of time because they are commenced after the time allowed by *section 1063*.

(11) The amount referred to in *paragraph* (*a*) of *subsection (4)* and in *paragraph* (*a*)(*i*) of *subsection (7)* shall be the difference between—

(a) the amount of tax that would have been payable for the relevant periods by the person concerned (including any amount deducted at source and not repayable) if that tax had been computed in accordance with the incorrect or false return, statement, declaration or accounts as actually made or submitted by or on behalf of that person for those periods, and

(b) the amount of tax that would have been payable for the relevant periods by the person concerned (including any amount deducted at source and not repayable) if that tax had been computed in accordance with the true and correct return, statement, declaration or accounts that should have been made or submitted by or on behalf of that person for those periods,

and for the purposes of this subsection and of *subsection (12)* references in those subsections to tax payable shall be construed without regard to the definition of "*income tax payable*" in section 3.

(12) The amount referred to in *paragraph* (*b*) of *subsection (4)* and in [*paragraph* (*a*)(*ii*)][6] of *subsection (7)* shall be the difference between—

(a) the amount of tax paid by that person for the relevant periods before the start by the Revenue Commissioners or by any Revenue officer of any inquiry or investigation where the Revenue Commissioners had announced publicly that they had started an inquiry or investigation or where the Revenue Commissioners have, or a Revenue officer has, carried out an inquiry or investigation into any matter that would have been included in the return or statement if the return or statement had been delivered by that person and the return or statement had been correct, and

(b) the amount of tax which would have been payable for the relevant periods if the return or statement had been delivered by that person and the return or statement had been correct.

(13) Where a second qualifying disclosure is made by a person within 5 years of such person's first qualifying disclosure, then as regards matters pertaining to that second disclosure—

(a) in relation to *subsection (4)*—

(i) *paragraph (ii)* shall apply as if "75 per cent" were substituted for "50 per cent",

(ii) *paragraph (iii)* shall apply as if "55 per cent" were substituted for "10 per cent", and

(b) in relation to *subparagraph (I)* of *subsection (7)*(*b*)—

(i) clause (B) shall apply as if "30 per cent" were substituted for "20 per cent", and

(ii) clause (C) shall apply as if "20 per cent" were substituted for "5 per cent".

(14) Where a third or subsequent qualifying disclosure is made by a person within 5 years of such person's second qualifying disclosure, then as regards matters pertaining to that third or subsequent disclosure, as the case may be—

(a) the penalty referred to in *paragraphs* (*a*) and (*b*) of *subsection (4)* shall not be reduced, and

(b) the reduction referred to in *subparagraph (I)* of *subsection (7)*(*b*) shall not apply.

(15) A disclosure in relation to a person shall not be a qualifying disclosure where—

(a) before the disclosure is made, a Revenue officer had started an inquiry or investigation into any matter contained in that disclosure and had contacted or notified that person, or a person representing that person, in this regard, or

(b) matters contained in the disclosure are matters—

(i) that have become known, or are about to become known, to the Revenue Commissioners through their own investigations or through an investigation conducted by a statutory body or agency,

(ii) that are within the scope of an inquiry being carried out wholly or partly in public, or

(iii) to which the person who made the disclosure is linked, or about to be linked, publicly.

(16) The relevant period for the purposes of *subsections (11)* and *(12)* shall be, in relation to anything delivered, made or submitted in any period, that period, the next period and any preceding period, and the references in those subsections to the amount of tax payable shall not, in relation to anything done in connection with a partnership, include any tax not chargeable in the partnership name.

(17) For the purposes of this section, any returns or accounts submitted on behalf of a person shall be deemed to have been submitted by the person unless that person proves that they were submitted without that person's consent or knowledge.][7]

Amendments

[1] Substituted by F(LPT)A 12 s158 & sched(13)(a).

[2] Inserted by FA11 s20(1)(p). With effect from 1 January 2012 as per S.I. No. 660 of 2011.

[3] Inserted by FA14 s85(b).

[4] Inserted by F(No.2)A13 sched(1)(l). Has effect on and from 18 December 2013.

[5] Substituted by F(LPT)A 12 s158 & sched(13)(b).

[6] Substituted by FA12 sched6(1)(q). Has effect as on and from 31 March 2012.

[7] Inserted by F(No.2)A08 sched5(part1)(1). The enactments specified in Schedule 5 are amended or repealed to the extent and manner specified in that Schedule and, unless the contrary is stated, shall come into effect after 24 December 2008.

Revenue Briefings

Tax Briefing

Tax Briefing December 2008 – Issue 70 – Finance (No.2) Bill 2008 – Notes on Some Aspects – Tax and Duty Civil Penalties

eBrief

eBrief No. 23/2009 – New Penalties Regime – Finance (No.2) Act 2008
eBrief No. 51/2011 – Conditional Audit Settlement Offers
eBrief No. 68/2014 – Code of Practice for Revenue Audit and other Compliance Interventions

Revenue Information Notes

2010 Code of Practice for Revenue Audit
Code of Practice for Revenue Audit and other Compliance Interventions

Cross References

From Section 1077E

Section 3 Interpretation of Income Tax Acts.
Section 530 Interpretation (Chapter 2).
Section 1063 Time limit for recovery of fines and penalties.
Section 1077D Proceedings against executor, administrator or estate.

To Section 1077E

Section 530U Civil penalties.
Section 531 Payments to subcontractors in certain industries.
Section 1052 Penalties for failure to make certain returns, etc.
Section 1054 Penalties in the case of a secretary of a body of persons.
Section 1075 Penalties for failure to furnish certain information and for incorrect information.
Section 1077 Penalties for failure to make returns, etc. and for deliberately or carelessly making incorrect returns.
Section 1086 Publication of names of tax defaulters.
Schedule 29 Provisions Referred to in Sections 1052, 1053 and 1054
Schedule 32 Transitional Provisions

CHAPTER 4

Revenue Offences

1078 Revenue offences

[FA83 s94; FA86 s40(2); FA89 s18 and Sch1 par3(2); FA92 s243; FA96 s132(1) and (2) and Sch5 PtI par13(2) and PtII]

(1) In this Part—

"*the Acts*" means—

(a) the Customs Acts,

(b) the statutes relating to the duties of excise and to the management of those duties,

(c) the Tax Acts,

[(ca) Parts 18A, 18B, 18C and 18D,][1]

(d) the Capital Gains Tax Acts,

(e) the Value-Added Tax Consolidation Act 2010, and the enactments amending or extending that Act,

(f) the Capital Acquisitions Tax Consolidation Act 2003, and the enactments amending or extending that Act,

(g) the statutes relating to stamp duty and to the management of that duty, and

(h) Part VI of the Finance Act, 1983,

[(i) the *Finance (Local Property Tax) Act 2012*,][2]

[...][3]

and any instruments made thereunder and any instruments made under any other enactment and relating to tax;

"*authorised officer*" means an officer of the Revenue Commissioners authorised by them in writing to exercise any of the powers conferred by the Acts;

"*tax*" means any tax, duty, levy or charge under the care and management of the Revenue Commissioners.

[(1A) (a) In this subsection—

"*facilitating*" means aiding, abetting, assisting, inciting or inducing;

"fraudulent evasion of tax by a person" means the person—

(a) evading or attempting to evade any payment or deduction of tax required under the Acts to be paid by the person or, as the case may be, required under the Acts to be deducted from amounts due to the person, or

(b) claiming or obtaining, or attempting to claim or obtain, relief or exemption from, or payment or repayment of, any tax, being relief, exemption, payment or repayment, to which the person is not entitled under the Acts,

where, for those purposes, the person deceives, omits, conceals or uses any other dishonest means including—

(i) providing false, incomplete or misleading information, or

(ii) failing to furnish information,

to the Revenue Commissioners or to any other person.

(b) For the purposes of this subsection and *subsection (5)* a person (in this paragraph referred to as the "*first-mentioned person*") is reckless as to whether or not he or she is concerned in facilitating—

(i) the fraudulent evasion of tax by a person, being another person, or

(ii) the commission of an offence under *subsection (2)* by a person, being another person,

if the first-mentioned person disregards a substantial risk that he or she is so concerned, and for those purposes "*substantial risk*" means a risk of such a nature and degree that, having regard to all the circumstances and the extent of the information available to the first-mentioned person, its disregard by that person involves culpability of a high degree.

(c) A person shall, without prejudice to any other penalty to which the person may be liable, be guilty of an offence under this section if the person—

(i) is knowingly concerned in the fraudulent evasion of tax by the person or any other person,

(ii) is knowingly concerned in, or is reckless as to whether or not the person is concerned in, facilitating—

(I) the fraudulent evasion of tax, or

(II) the commission of an offence under *subsection (2)* (other than an offence under *paragraph (b)* of that subsection), by any other person, or

(iii) is knowingly concerned in the fraudulent evasion or attempted fraudulent evasion of any prohibition or restriction on importation for the time being in force, or the removal of any goods from the State, in contravention of any provision of the Acts.][4]

[(1B) A person is guilty of an offence under this section if he or she, with the intention to deceive—

(a) purports to be, or

(b) makes any statement, or otherwise acts in a manner, that would lead another person to believe that he or she is,

an officer of the Revenue Commissioners.][5]

(2) A person shall, without prejudice to any other penalty to which the person may be liable, be guilty of an offence under this section if the person—

(a) knowingly or wilfully delivers any incorrect return, statement or accounts or knowingly or wilfully furnishes any incorrect information in connection with any tax,

(b) knowingly aids, abets, assists, incites or induces another person to make or deliver knowingly or wilfully any incorrect return, statement or accounts in connection with any tax, [(ba) knowingly or wilfully possesses or uses, for the purpose of evading tax, a computer programme or electronic component which modifies, corrects, deletes, cancels, conceals or otherwise alters any record stored or preserved by means of any electronic device without preserving the original data and its subsequent modification, correction, cancellation, concealment or alteration,

(bb) provides or makes available, for the purpose of evading tax, a computer programme or electronic component which modifies, corrects, deletes, cancels, conceals or otherwise alters any record stored or preserved by means of any electronic device without preserving the original data and its subsequent modification, correction, cancellation, concealment or alteration,][6]

(c) claims or obtains relief or exemption from, or repayment of, any tax, being a relief, exemption or repayment to which, to the person's knowledge, the person is not entitled,

(d) knowingly or wilfully issues or produces any incorrect invoice, receipt, instrument or other document in connection with any tax,

[(dd) (i) fails to make any deduction of dividend withholding tax (within the meaning of Chapter 8A of Part 6) required to be made by the person under *section 172B(1)*,

(ii) fails, having made that deduction, to pay the sum deducted to the Collector-General within the time specified in that behalf in *section 172K(2)*,

(iii) fails to make any reduction required to be made by the person under *section 172B(2)*,

(iv) fails, having made that reduction, to pay to the Collector-General the amount referred to in *section 172B(2)(d)*, which amount is treated under that section as if it were a deduction of dividend withholding tax (within the meaning of Chapter 8A of Part 6), within the time specified in that behalf in *section 172K(2)*, or

(v) fails to pay to the Collector-General, within the time specified in that behalf in *section 172K(2)*, an amount referred to in *section 172B(3)(a)* which is required to be paid by the person to the Collector-General and which is treated under that section as if it were a deduction of dividend withholding tax (within the meaning of Chapter 8A of Part 6),][7]

(e) (i) fails to make any deduction required to be made by the person under *section 257(1)*,

(ii) fails, having made the deduction, to pay the sum deducted to the Collector-General within the time specified in that behalf in *section 258(3)*, or

(iii) fails to pay to the Collector-General an amount on account of appropriate tax (within the meaning of *Chapter 4* of *Part 8*) within the time specified in that behalf in *section 258(4)*,

[(f) fails to pay to the Collector-General appropriate tax (within the meaning of *section 739E*) within the time specified in that behalf in *section 739F*,][8]

[(fa) fails to comply with the requirement in *section 960S(4)*,][9]

(g) [fails without reasonable excuse] to comply with any provision of the Acts[10] requiring—

(i) the furnishing of a return of income, profits or gains, or of sources of income, profits or gains, for the purposes of any tax,

(ii) the furnishing of any other return, certificate, notification, particulars, or any statement or evidence, for the purposes of any tax,

(iii) the keeping or retention of books, records, accounts or other documents for the purposes of any tax, or

(iv) the production of books, records, accounts or other documents, when so requested, for the purposes of any tax,

(h) knowingly or wilfully, and within the time limits specified for their retention, destroys, defaces or conceals from an authorised officer—

(i) any documents, or

(ii) any other written or printed material in any form, including any information stored, maintained or preserved by means of any mechanical or electronic device, whether or not stored, maintained or preserved in a legible form, which a person is obliged by any provision of the Acts to keep, to issue or to produce for inspection,

[(hh) knowingly or wilfully falsifies, conceals, destroys or otherwise disposes of, or causes or permits the falsification, concealment, destruction or disposal of, any books, records or other documents—

(i) which the person has been given the opportunity to deliver, or as the case may be, to make available in accordance with *section 900(3)*, or

(ii) which the person has been required to deliver or, as the case may be, to make available in accordance with a notice served under *section 900, 902, 906A* or *907*, or an order made under *section 901, 902A* or *908*,][11]

(i) fails to remit any income tax payable pursuant to *Chapter 4* of *Part 42*, and the regulations under that Chapter, or value-added tax within the time specified in that behalf in relation to income tax or value-added tax, as the case may be, [by the Acts,][12]

[(ii) (i) fails to deduct tax required to be deducted by the person under [*Chapter 2* of *Part 18*][13], or

(ii) fails, having made that deduction, to pay the sum deducted to the Collector-General within the time specified in that behalf in [*Chapter 2* of *Part 18*][14],][15]

[(iii) (i) fails to deduct local property tax required to be deducted by the person under *Part 10* of the *Finance (Local Property Tax) Act 2012*, or

(ii) fails, having made that deduction, to remit the sum deducted to the Collector-General within the time specified in *Chapters 1, 2* or *3*, as the case may be, of *Part 10* of the *Finance (Local Property Tax) Act 2012*,][16]

(j) obstructs or interferes with any officer of the Revenue Commissioners, or any other person, in the exercise or performance of powers or duties under the Acts for the purposes of any tax.

(3) A person convicted of an offence under this section shall be liable—

(a) on summary conviction to a fine of [€5,000][17] which may be mitigated to not less than one fourth part of such fine or, at the discretion of the court, to imprisonment for a term not exceeding 12 months or to both the fine and the imprisonment, or

(b) on conviction on indictment, to a fine not exceeding [€126,970][18] or, at the discretion of the court, to imprisonment for a term not exceeding 5 years or to both the fine and the imprisonment.

[(3A) Where a person has been convicted of an offence referred to in *subparagraph (i)*, *(ii)* or *(iv)* of *subsection (2)(g)*, then, if an application is made, or caused to be made to the court in that regard, the court may make an order requiring the person concerned to comply with any provision of the Acts relating to the requirements specified in the said *subparagraph (i)*, *(ii)* or *(iv)*, as the case may be.][19]

[(3B) A person shall, without prejudice to any other penalty to which the person may be liable, be guilty of an offence under this section if the person fails or refuses to comply with an order referred to in *subsection (3A)* [within a period of 30 days commencing on the day the order is made][20].][21]

(4) Section 13 of the Criminal Procedure Act, 1967, shall apply in relation to an offence under this section as if, in place of the penalties specified in subsection (3) of that section, there were specified in that subsection the penalties provided for by *subsection (3)(a)*, and the reference in subsection (2)(*a*) of section 13 of the Criminal Procedure Act, 1967, to the penalties provided for in subsection (3) of that section shall be construed and apply accordingly.

(5) Where an offence under this section is committed by a body corporate and the offence is shown [to have been committed with the consent or connivance of or to be attributable to any recklessness (as provided for by *subsection (1A)(b)*) on the part of][22] any person who, when the offence was committed, was a director, manager, secretary or other officer of the body corporate, or a member of the committee of management or other controlling authority of the body corporate, that person shall also be deemed to be guilty of the offence and may be proceeded against and punished accordingly.

(6) In any proceedings under this section, a return or statement delivered to an inspector or other officer of the Revenue Commissioners under any provision of the Acts and purporting to be signed by any person shall be deemed until the contrary is proved to have been so delivered and to have been signed by that person.

(7) Notwithstanding any other enactment, proceedings in respect of an offence under this section may be instituted within 10 years from the date of the commission of the offence or incurring of the penalty, as the case may be.

(8) Section 1 of the Probation of Offenders Act, 1907, shall not apply in relation to offences under this section.

(9) [*Sections 530U*, *987(4)* and *1052(4)*][23], *subsections (3)* and *(7)* of *section 1053*, [subsections (9) and (17) of section 1077E][24], and *sections 1068* and *1069* [, and [sections 115(9) and 116(16) of the Value-Added Tax Consolidation Act 2010][25],][26] shall, with any necessary modifications, apply for the purposes of this section as they apply for the purposes of those sections, including, in the case of such of those sections as are applied by the Capital Gains Tax Acts, the Corporation Tax Acts, or Part VI of the Finance Act, 1983, the purposes of those sections as so applied.

[(10) Any summons, notice, order or other document relating to proceedings under this section, or relating to any appeal against a judgement pursuant to such proceedings, may be served by an officer of the Revenue Commissioners.][27]

Amendments

[1] Substituted by FA11 s3(1)(i). Applies for the year of assessment 2011 and each subsequent year of assessment.

[2] Inserted by F(LPT)A 12 s158 & sched(14)(a).

[3] Deleted by FA11 s3(1)(h). Applies for the year of assessment 2011 and each subsequent year of assessment.

[4] Inserted by FA05 s142(a).

[5] Inserted by FA07 s126.

[6] Inserted by FA11 s75.

[7] Inserted by FA99 s27(b).

[8] Substituted by FA05 s142(b)(i).

[9] Inserted by FA12 s126(2). Deemed to have come into force and takes effect on and from 1 January 2012.

[10] Substituted by FA02 s133(a).

[11] Inserted by FA99 s211(a).

[12] Substituted by FA05 s142(b)(ii).

[13] Substituted by FA11 s20(1)(q). With effect from 1 January 2011 as per S.I. No. 660 of 2011.

[14] Substituted by FA11 s20(1)(r). With effect from 1 January 2012 as per S.I. No. 660 of 2011.

[15] Inserted by FA05 s142(b)(iii).

[16] Inserted by F(LPT)A 12 s158 & sched(14)(b).

[17] Substituted by FA08 s138(1)(d). Applies as respects an offence committed on a day after 13 March 2008.

[18] Substituted by FA01 sched5.

[19] Inserted by FA99 s211(c).

[20] Inserted by F(No.2)A08 s92(k).

[21] Inserted by FA02 s133(b).

[22] Substituted by FA05 s142(c).

[23] Substituted by FA11 s20(1)(s). With effect from 1 January 2012 as per S.I. No. 660 of 2011.

[24] Inserted by F(No.2)A08 sched5(part2)(2)(ar)(i). The enactments specified in Schedule 5 are amended or repealed to the extent and manner specified in that Schedule and, unless the contrary is stated, shall come into effect after 24 December 2008.

[25] Substituted by FA10 sched(4)(1)(l). Has effect as on and from 3 April 2010.

[26] Substituted by F(No.2)A08 sched5(part2)(2)(ar)(ii). The enactments specified in Schedule 5 are amended or repealed to the extent and manner specified in that Schedule and, unless the contrary is stated, shall come into effect after 24 December 2008.

[27] Inserted by FA10 s155. Has effect as on and from 3 April 2010.

Revenue Briefings

Tax Briefing

Tax Briefing December 1999 – Issue 38 pg 10 – Criminal Proceedings

Revenue Information Notes

2010 Code of Practice for Revenue Audit
Code of Practice for Revenue Audit and other Compliance Interventions

Cross References

From Section 1078

Section 1 Interpretation of this Act.
Section 172B Dividend withholding tax on relevant distributions.
Section 172K Returns, payment and collection of dividend withholding tax.
Section 237 Annual payments payable wholly out of taxed income.
Section 256 Interpretation (Chapter 4).
Section 257 Deduction of tax from relevant interest.
Section 258 Returns and collection of appropriate tax.
Section 530U Civil penalties.
Section 739E Deduction of tax on the occurrence of a chargeable event.
Section 739F Returns and collection of appropriate tax.
Section 900 Power to call for production of books, information, etc.
Section 901 Application to High Court: production of books, information, etc.
Section 902 Information to be furnished by third party: request of an authorised officer.
Section 907 Application to Appeal Commissioners: information from financial institutions.
Section 908 Application to High Court seeking order requiring information: financial institutions.
Section 960 Date for payment of income tax other than under self assessment.
Section 983 Interpretation (Chapter 4).
Section 987 Penalties for breach of regulations.
Section 1052 Penalties for failure to make certain returns, etc.

To Section 1078

Section 530F Obligation on principals to deduct tax.
Section 896B Provision of information by Commission for Taxi Regulation.
Section 902 Information to be furnished by third party: request of an authorised officer.
Section 902A Application to High Court: information from third party.
Section 905 Inspection of documents and records.
Section 906A Information to be furnished by financial institutions.
Section 908A Revenue offence: power to obtain information from financial institutions.
Section 908B Application to High Court seeking order requiring information: associated institutions.
Section 908C Search warrants.
Section 908D Order to produce evidential material.
Section 912B Questioning of suspects in Garda Síochána custody in certain circumstances.
Section 1002 Deduction from payments due to defaulters of amounts due in relation to tax.
Section 1056 Penalty for false statement made to obtain allowance.
Section 1104 Short title and construction.
Schedule 31 Consequential Amendments

1078A Concealing facts disclosed by documents

[(1) Any person who—

(a) knows or suspects that an investigation by an officer of the Revenue Commissioners into an offence under the Acts or the Waiver of Certain Tax, Interest and Penalties Act 1993 is being, or is likely to be, carried out, and

(b) falsifies, conceals, destroys or otherwise disposes of material which the person knows or suspects is or would be relevant to the investigation or causes or permits its falsification, concealment, destruction or disposal,

is guilty of an offence.

(2) Where a person—

(a) falsifies, conceals, destroys or otherwise disposes of material, or

(b) causes or permits its falsification, concealment, destruction or disposal,

in such circumstances that it is reasonable to conclude that the person knew or suspected—

(i) that an investigation by an officer of the Revenue Commissioners into an offence under the Acts or the Waiver of Certain Tax, Interest and Penalties Act 1993 was being, or was likely to be, carried out, and

(ii) that the material was or would be relevant to the investigation, the person shall be taken, for the purposes of this section, to have so known or suspected, unless the court or the jury, as the case may be, is satisfied having regard to all the evidence that there is a reasonable doubt as to whether the person so knew or suspected.

(3) A person guilty of an offence under this section is liable—

(a) on summary conviction to a fine not exceeding [€5,000][1], or at the discretion of the court, to imprisonment for a term not exceeding 6 months or to both the fine and the imprisonment, or

(b) on conviction on indictment, to a fine not exceeding €127,000 or, at the discretion of the court, to imprisonment for a term not exceeding 5 years or to both the fine and the imprisonment.][2]

Amendments

[1] Substituted by FA08 s138(1)(e). Applies as respects an offence committed on a day after 13 March 2008.

[2] Inserted by FA03 s161.

1078B Presumptions

[(1) In this section—

"*return, statement or declaration*" means any return, statement or declaration which a person is required to make under the Acts or the Waiver of Certain Tax, Interest and Penalties Act 1993.

(2) The presumptions specified in this section apply in any proceedings, whether civil or criminal, under any provision of the Acts or the Waiver of Certain Tax, Interest and Penalties Act 1993.

(3) Where a document purports to have been created by a person it shall be presumed, unless the contrary is shown, that the document was created by that person and that any statement contained therein, unless the document expressly attributes its making to some other person, was made by that person.

(4) Where a document purports to have been created by a person and addressed and sent to a second person, it shall be presumed, unless the contrary is shown, that the document was created and sent by the first person and received by the second person and that any statement contained therein—

(a) unless the document expressly attributes its making to some other person, was made by the first person, and

(b) came to the notice of the second person.

(5) Where a document is retrieved from an electronic storage and retrieval system, it shall be presumed unless the contrary is shown, that the author of the document is the person who ordinarily uses that electronic storage and retrieval system in the course of his or her business.

(6) Where an authorised officer in the exercise of his or her powers under *subsection (2A)* of *section 905* [or subsection (3) of section 908C][1] has removed records (within the meaning of [*section 905* or *908C*, as the case may be][2]) from any place, gives evidence in proceedings that to the best of the authorised officer's knowledge and belief, the records are the property of any person, the records shall be presumed unless the contrary is proved, to be the property of that person.

(7) Where in accordance with *subsection (6)* records are presumed in proceedings to be the property of a person and the authorised officer gives evidence that, to the best of the authorised officer's knowledge and belief, the records are records which relate to any trade, profession, or, as the case may be, other activity, carried on by that person, the records shall be presumed unless the contrary is proved, to be records which relate to that trade, profession, or, as the case may be, other activity, carried on by that person.

(8) In proceedings, a certificate signed by an inspector or other officer of the Revenue Commissioners certifying that a return, statement or declaration to which the certificate refers is in the possession of the Revenue Commissioners in such circumstances as to lead the officer to conclude that, to the best of his or her knowledge and belief it was delivered to an inspector or other officer of the Revenue Commissioners, it shall be presumed unless the contrary is proved, to be evidence that the said return, statement, or declaration was so delivered.

(9) In proceedings, a certificate, certifying the fact or facts referred to in *subsection (8)* and purporting to be signed as specified in that subsection, may be tendered in evidence without proof and shall be deemed until the contrary is proved to

have been signed by a person holding, at the time of the signature, the office or position indicated in the certificate as the office or position of the person signing.

(10) References in this section to a document are references to a document in written, mechanical or electronic format and, for this purpose "*written*" includes any form of notation or code whether by hand or otherwise and regardless of the method by which, or the medium in or on which, the document concerned is recorded.][3]

Amendments

[1] Inserted by F(No.2)A08 sched6(1)(c). Has effect as on and from 24 December 2008.

[2] Substituted by FA12 sched6(1)(r). Has effect as on and from 31 March 2012.

[3] Inserted by FA03 s161.

Cross References

From Section 1078B

Section 905 Inspection of documents and records.

Section 908C Search warrants.

1078C Provision of information to juries

[(1) In a trial on indictment of an offence under the Acts or the Waiver of Certain Tax, Interest and Penalties Act 1993, the trial judge may order that copies of any or all of the following documents shall be given to the jury in any form that the judge considers appropriate:

(a) any document admitted in evidence at the trial,

(b) the transcript of the opening speeches of counsel,

(c) any charts, diagrams, graphics, schedules or agreed summaries of evidence produced at the trial,

(d) the transcript of the whole or any part of the evidence given at the trial,

(e) the transcript of the closing speeches of counsel,

(f) the transcript of the trial judge's charge to the jury,

(g) any other document that in the opinion of the trial judge would be of assistance to the jury in its deliberations including, where appropriate, an affidavit by an accountant or other suitably qualified person, summarising, in a form which is likely to be comprehended by the jury, any transactions by the accused or other persons which are relevant to the offence.

(2) If the prosecutor proposes to apply to the trial judge for an order that a document mentioned in *subsection (1)(g)* shall be given to the jury, the prosecutor shall give a copy of the document to the accused in advance of the trial and, on the hearing of the application, the trial judge shall take into account any representations made by or on behalf of the accused in relation to it.

(3) Where the trial judge has made an order that an affidavit by an accountant or other person mentioned in *subsection (1)(g)* shall be given to the jury, the accountant, or as the case may be, the other person so mentioned—

(a) shall be summoned by the prosecution to attend at the trial as an expert witness, and

(b) may be required by the trial judge, in an appropriate case, to give evidence in regard to any relevant procedures or principles within his or her area of expertise.][1]

Amendments

[1] Inserted by FA03 s161.

1079 Duties of relevant person in relation to certain revenue offences

[FA95 s172]

(1) In this section—

"*the Acts*" means—

(a) the Customs Acts,

(b) the statutes relating to the duties of excise and to the management of those duties,

(c) the Tax Acts,

[(ca) Parts 18A, 18B, 18C and 18D,][1]

(d) the Capital Gains Tax Acts,

(e) the Value-Added Tax Consolidation Act 2010, and the enactments amending or extending that Act,

(f) the Capital Acquisitions Tax Consolidation Act 2003, and the enactments amending or extending that Act,

(g) the statutes relating to stamp duty and to the management of that duty,

[(h) the *Finance (Local Property Tax) Act 2012*,][2]

and any instruments made thereunder and any instruments made under any other enactment and relating to tax;

"*appropriate officer*" means any officer nominated by the Revenue Commissioners to be an appropriate officer for the purposes of this section;

"*company*" means any body corporate;

"*relevant person*", in relation to a company and subject to *subsection (2)*, means a person who—

(a) (i) is an auditor to the company appointed in accordance with section 160 of the Companies Act, 1963 (as amended by the Companies Act, 1990), or

(ii) in the case of an industrial and provident society or a friendly society, is a public auditor to the society for the purposes of the Industrial and Provident Societies Acts, 1893 to 1978, and the Friendly Societies Acts, 1896 to 1977,

or

(b) with a view to reward, assists or advises the company in the preparation or delivery of any information, declaration, return, records, accounts or other document which he or she knows will be or is likely to be used for any purpose of tax;

"*relevant offence*" means an offence committed by a company which consists of the company—

(a) knowingly or wilfully delivering any incorrect return, statement or accounts or knowingly or wilfully furnishing or causing to be furnished any incorrect information in connection with any tax,

(b) knowingly or wilfully claiming or obtaining relief or exemption from, or repayment of, any tax, being a relief, exemption or repayment to which there is no entitlement,

(c) knowingly or wilfully issuing or producing any incorrect invoice, receipt, instrument or other document in connection with any tax, or

(d) knowingly or wilfully failing to comply with any provision of the Acts requiring the furnishing of a return of income, profits or gains, or of sources of income, profits or gains, for the purposes of any tax, but an offence under this paragraph committed by a company shall not be a relevant offence if the company has made a return of income, profits or gains to the Revenue Commissioners in respect of an accounting period falling wholly or partly in the period of 3 years preceding the accounting period in respect of which the offence was committed;

"*tax*" means any tax, duty, levy or charge under the care and management of the Revenue Commissioners.

(2) For the purposes of *paragraph (b)* of the definition of "*relevant person*", a person who but for this subsection would be treated as a relevant person in relation to a company shall not be so treated if the person assists or advises the company solely in the person's capacity as an employee of the company, and a person shall be treated as assisting or advising the company in that capacity where the person's income from assisting or advising the company consists solely of emoluments to which *Chapter 4* of *Part 42* applies.

(3) If, having regard solely to information obtained in the course of examining the accounts of a company, or in the course of assisting or advising a company in the preparation or delivery of any information, declaration, return, records, accounts or other document for the purposes of tax, as the case may be, a person who is a relevant person in relation to the company becomes aware that the company has committed, or is in the course of committing, one or more relevant offences, the person shall, if the offence or offences are material—

(a) communicate particulars of the offence or offences in writing to the company without undue delay and request the company to—

(i) take such action as is necessary for the purposes of rectifying the matter, or

(ii) notify an appropriate officer of the offence or offences,

not later than 6 months after the time of communication, and

(b) (i) unless it is established to the person's satisfaction that the necessary action has been taken or notification made, as the case may be, under *paragraph (a)*, cease to act as the auditor to the company or to assist or advise the company in such preparation or delivery as is specified in *paragraph (b)* of the definition of "*relevant person*", and

(ii) shall not so act, assist or advise before a time which is the earlier of—

(I) 3 years after the time at which the particulars were communicated under *paragraph (a)*, and

(II) the time at which it is established to the person's satisfaction that the necessary action has been taken or notification made, as the case may be, under *paragraph (a)*.

(4) Nothing in *paragraph (b)* of *subsection (3)* shall prevent a person from assisting or advising a company in preparing for, or conducting, legal proceedings, either civil or criminal, which are extant or pending at a time which is 6 months after the time of communication under *paragraph (a)* of that subsection.

(5) Where a person, being in relation to a company a relevant person within the meaning of *paragraph (a)* of the definition of "*relevant person*", ceases under this section to act as auditor to the company, then, the person shall deliver—

(a) a notice in writing to the company stating that he or she is so resigning, and
(b) a copy of the notice to an appropriate officer not later than 14 days after he or she has delivered the notice to the company.

(6) A person shall be guilty of an offence under this section if the person—
(a) fails to comply with *subsection (3)* or *(5)*, or
(b) knowingly or wilfully makes a communication under *subsection (3)* which is incorrect.

(7) Where a relevant person is convicted of an offence under this section, the person shall be liable—
(a) on summary conviction, to a fine of [€1,265][3] which may be mitigated to not less than one-fourth part of such fine, or
(b) on conviction on indictment, to a fine not exceeding [€6,345][4] or, at the discretion of the court, to imprisonment for a term not exceeding 2 years or to both the fine and the imprisonment.

(8) Section 13 of the Criminal Procedure Act, 1967, shall apply in relation to this section as if, in place of the penalties specified in subsection (3) of that section, there were specified in that subsection the penalties provided for by *subsection (7)(a)*, and the reference in subsection (2)(*a*) of section 13 of the Criminal Procedure Act, 1967, to the penalties provided for in subsection (3) of that section shall be construed and apply accordingly.

(9) Notwithstanding any other enactment, proceedings in respect of this section may be instituted within 6 years from the time at which a person is required under *subsection (3)* to communicate particulars of an offence or offences in writing to a company.

(10) It shall be a good defence in a prosecution for an offence under *subsection (6)(a)* in relation to a failure to comply with *subsection (3)* for an accused (being a person who is a relevant person in relation to a company) to show that he or she was in the ordinary scope of professional engagement assisting or advising the company in preparing for legal proceedings and would not have become aware that one or more relevant offences had been committed by the company if he or she had not been so assisting or advising.

(11) Where a person who is a relevant person takes any action required by *subsection (3)* or *(5)*, no duty to which the person may be subject shall be regarded as having been contravened and no liability or action shall lie against the person in any court for having taken such action.

(12) The Revenue Commissioners may nominate an officer to be an appropriate officer for the purposes of this section, and the name of an officer so nominated and the address to which copies of notices under *subsection (3)* or *(5)* shall be delivered shall be published in Iris Oifigiúil.

(13) This section shall apply as respects a relevant offence committed by a company in respect of tax which is—
(a) assessable by reference to accounting periods, for any accounting period beginning after the 30th day of June, 1995,
(b) assessable by reference to years of assessment, for the year 1995-96 and subsequent years of assessment,
(c) payable by reference to a taxable period, for a taxable period beginning after the 30th day of June, 1995,
(d) chargeable on gifts or inheritances taken on or after the 30th day of June, 1995,

(e) chargeable on instruments executed on or after the 30th day of June, 1995, or

(f) payable in any other case, on or after the 30th day of June, 1995.

Amendments

[1] Substituted by FA11 s3(1)(j). Applies for the year of assessment 2011 and each subsequent year of assessment.

[2] Inserted by F(LPT)A 12 s158 & sched(15).

[3, 4] Substituted by FA01 sched5.

Cross References

From Section 1079

Section 960 Date for payment of income tax other than under self assessment.

Section 983 Interpretation (Chapter 4).

To Section 1079

Section 1104 Short title and construction.

CHAPTER 5

Interest on Overdue Tax

1080 Interest on overdue income tax, corporation tax and capital gains tax

[(1) In this section—

"*chargeable period*" has the same meaning as in *section 321(2)*;

"*chargeable person*" has the same meaning as in [as it has for the purposes of *Part 41A*][1];

"*period of delay*", in relation to any tax due and payable, means the period during which that tax remains unpaid;

"*Table*" means the Table to *subsection (2)*;

"*tax*" means income tax, corporation tax or capital gains tax, as appropriate;

"*relevant period*", in relation to a period of delay which falls into more than one of the periods specified in *column (1)* of the Table, means any part of the period of delay which falls into, or is the same as, a period specified in that column.

(2) (a) Subject to this section and *section 1081*—

(i) as respects tax due and payable for a chargeable period beginning before 1 January 2005, any tax charged by any assessment to tax shall carry interest from the date when the tax becomes due and payable until payment, and

(ii) as respects tax due and payable for a chargeable period beginning on or after 1 January 2005, any tax due and payable by a chargeable person for a chargeable period shall carry interest from the date when the tax becomes due and payable until payment,

and the amount of that interest shall be determined in accordance with *paragraph (c)*.

[(b) Subject to this section and *section 1081*—

(i) any tax charged by any assessment to income tax, and

(ii) any tax contained in a statement sent in accordance with Regulation 37 of the Income Tax (Employments) (Consolidation) Regulations 2001 (S.I. No. 559 of 2001), shall, notwithstanding any appeal against such assessment or statement, carry interest from the date when, if there were no appeal against the assessment or statement, the tax would become due and payable under *section 960* until payment, and the amount of that interest shall be determined in accordance with *paragraph (c)*.][2]

(c) The interest to be carried by the tax referred to in *paragraph (a)* or *(b)*, as the case may be, shall be—

(i) where one of the periods specified in *column (1)* of the Table includes or is the same as the period of delay, the amount determined by the formula—

$$T \times D \times P$$

where—

T is the tax due and payable which remains unpaid,

D is the number of days (including part of a day) forming the period of delay, and

P is the appropriate percentage in *column (2)* of the Table opposite the period specified in *column (1)* of the Table within which the period of delay falls or which is the same as the period of delay,

and

(ii) where a continuous period formed by 2 or more of the periods specified in *column (1)* of the Table, but not (as in *subparagraph (i)*) only one such period, includes or is the same as the period of delay, the aggregate of the amounts due in respect of each relevant period which forms part of the period of delay, and the amount due in respect of each such relevant period shall be determined by the formula—

$$T \times D \times P$$

where—

T is the tax due and payable which remains unpaid,

D is the number of days (including part of a day) forming the relevant period, and

P is the appropriate percentage in *column (2)* of the Table opposite the period specified in *column (1)* of the Table into which the relevant period falls or which is the same as the relevant period.

[Table

(Period) (1)	(Percentage) (2)
From 6 April 1963 to 31 July 1971	0.0164%
From 1 August 1971 to 30 April 1975	0.0246%
From 1 May 1975 to 31 July 1978	0.0492%
From 1 August 1978 to 31 March 1998	0.0410%
From 1 April 1998 to 31 March 2005	0.0322%
From 1 April 2005 to 30 June 2009	0.0273%
From 1 July 2009 to the date of payment	0.0219%][3]

(3) The interest payable under this section—

(a) shall be payable without deduction of income tax and shall not be allowed as a deduction in computing any income, profits or losses for any of the purposes of the Tax Acts, and

(b) shall be deemed to be a debt due to the Minister for Finance for the benefit of the Central Fund and shall be payable to the Revenue Commissioners.

(4) Subject to *subsection (5)*—

(a) every enactment relating to the recovery of tax,

(b) every rule of court so relating,

(c) section 81 of the Bankruptcy Act 1988, and

(d) sections 98 and 285 of the Companies Act 1963,

shall apply to the recovery of any amount of interest payable on that tax as if that amount of interest were a part of that tax.

(5) In proceedings instituted by virtue of *subsection (4)*—

(a) a certificate signed by an officer of the Revenue Commissioners certifying that a stated amount of interest is due and payable by the person against whom the proceedings were instituted shall be evidence until the contrary is proven that that amount is so due and payable, and

(b) a certificate so certifying and purporting to be signed as specified in this subsection may be tendered in evidence without proof and shall be deemed until the contrary is proved to have been signed by an officer of the Revenue Commissioners.][4]

Amendments

[1] Substituted by FA12 sched4(part 2)(g).

[2] Substituted by FA11 s21(g). Deemed to have come into force and takes effect as on and from 1 January 2011.

[3] Substituted by FA09 s29(1)(h). Applies as respects any unpaid tax or duty, as the case may be, that has not been paid before 1 July 2009 regardless of whether that tax or duty became due and payable before, on or after that date.

[4] Substituted by FA05 s145(1). Shall apply to any unpaid income tax, corporation tax or capital gains tax, as the case may be, that has not been paid before 1 April 2005.

Cross References

From Section 1080

Section 321 Provisions of general application in relation to the making of allowances and charges.
Section 950 Interpretation (Part 41).
Section 960 Date for payment of income tax other than under self assessment.
Section 1081 Effect on interest of reliefs given by discharge or repayment.

To Section 1080

Section 128A Deferral of payment of tax under section 128.
Section 128B Payment of tax under section 128.
Section 172K Returns, payment and collection of dividend withholding tax.
Section 240 Provisions as to tax under section 239.
Section 258 Returns and collection of appropriate tax.
Section 487 Corporation tax: credit for bank levy.
Section 501 Claims.
Section 502 Assessments for withdrawing relief.
Section 531AJ Application of provisions relating to income tax.
Section 696F Collection and general provisions.
Section 730G Returns and collection of appropriate tax.

Section 739F Returns and collection of appropriate tax.
Section 787S Payment of tax due on chargeable excess.
Section 790AA Taxation of lump sums in excess of the tax free amount.
Section 848M Taxation of gains.
Section 921 Aggregation of assessments.
Section 933 Appeals against assessment.
Section 957 Appeals.
Section 958 Date for payment of tax.
Section 1022 Special provisions relating to tax on wife's income.
Section 1081 Effect on interest of reliefs given by discharge or repayment.
Section 1082 Interest on overdue income tax and corporation tax in cases of fraud or neglect.
Section 1083 Application of sections 1080 to 1082 for capital gains tax purposes.
Schedule 1 Supplementary Provisions Concerning the Extension of Charge to Tax to Profits and Income Derived from Activities Carried On and Employments Exercised on the Continental Shelf
Schedule 18 Accounting for and Payment of Tax Deducted from Relevant Payments and Undistributed Relevant Income

1081 Effect on interest of reliefs given by discharge or repayment

[(1) Subject to *subsection (2)*—

(a) where for any year of assessment or accounting period, as the case may be, relief from any tax referred to in *section 1080(2)* is given to any person by a discharge of any of that tax, such adjustment shall be made of the amount of interest payable under that section in relation to that tax, and such repayment shall be made of any amounts of interest previously paid under that section in relation to that tax, as are necessary to secure that the total sum, if any, paid or payable under that section in relation to that tax is the same as it would have been if the tax discharged had never been due and payable, and

(b) where relief from tax paid for any year of assessment or accounting period, as the case may be, is given to any person by repayment, that person shall be entitled to require that the amount repaid shall be treated for the purposes of this subsection to the extent possible as if it were a discharge of the tax charged on that person (whether alone or together with other persons) by any assessment for the same year or period; but the relief shall not be applied to any assessment made after the relief was given and shall not be applied to more than one assessment so as to reduce without extinguishing the amount of tax charged thereby.

(2) No relief, whether by discharge or repayment, shall be treated as affecting any tax charged by an assessment to—

(a) income tax or any income tax due and payable unless it is a relief from income tax,

(b) corporation tax or any corporation tax due and payable unless it is a relief from corporation tax, or

(c) capital gains tax or capital gains tax due and payable unless it is a relief from capital gains tax.][1]

Amendments

[1] Substituted by FA05 s145(1). Shall apply to any unpaid income tax, corporation tax or capital gains tax, as the case may be, that has not been paid before 1 April 2005.

Cross References

From Section 1081

Section 1080 Interest on overdue income tax, corporation tax and capital gains tax.

To Section 1081

Section 240 Provisions as to tax under section 239.
Section 501 Claims.
Section 921 Aggregation of assessments.
Section 1080 Interest on overdue income tax, corporation tax and capital gains tax.
Section 1082 Interest on overdue income tax and corporation tax in cases of fraud or neglect.

1082 Interest on overdue income tax and corporation tax in cases of fraud or neglect

[FA71 s20(1) to (4) and (6); FA74 s86 and Sch2 PtI; CTA76 s145(4); FA80 s14(2); FA82 s59]

[(1) In this section '*neglect*' has the same meaning as in *section 959AD*.][1]

(2) Where for any year of assessment or accounting period an assessment is made for the purpose of recovering an undercharge to income tax or corporation tax, as the case may be, attributable to the fraud or neglect of any person, the amount of the tax under-charged shall carry interest at the rate of 2 per cent for each month or part of a month from the date or dates on which the tax under-charged for that year or accounting period, as the case may be, would have been payable if it had been included in an assessment made—

(a) in the case of income tax, before the 1st day of October in that year, and

(b) in the case of corporation tax, on the expiration of 6 months from the end of that accounting period,

to the date of payment of the tax undercharged.

(3) Subject to *subsection (5)*, [*section 1080(2)*][2] shall not apply to tax carrying interest under this section.

(4) [*Subsections (3)* to *(5)* of *section 1080*][3] and, in the case of income tax, *section 1081* shall apply to interest chargeable under this section as they apply to interest chargeable under *section 1080*.

(5) Where an assessment of the kind referred to in *subsection (2)* is made—

(a) the inspector concerned shall give notice to the person assessed that the tax charged by the assessment will carry interest under this section,

(b) the person assessed may appeal against the assessment on the ground that interest should not be charged under this section, and the provisions of the Tax Acts relating to appeals against assessments shall apply with any necessary modifications in relation to the appeal as they apply in relation to those appeals, and

(c) if on the appeal it is determined that the tax charged by the assessment should not carry interest under this section, [*section 1080(2)*][4] shall apply to that tax.

[(6) This section shall not apply as respects any tax due and payable for a year of assessment or an accounting period beginning on or after 1 January 2005.][5]

Amendments

[1] Substituted by FA12 sched4(part 2)(f).

[2, 3, 4] Substituted by FA05 sched5.

[5] Inserted by FA05 s145(2). Applies and shall be deemed to have always applied from 1 January 2005.

Cross References

From Section 1082

Section 919 Assessments to corporation tax.
Section 924 Additional assessments.

Section 1080 Interest on overdue income tax, corporation tax and capital gains tax.
Section 1081 Effect on interest of reliefs given by discharge or repayment.

To Section 1082

Section 1083 Application of sections 1080 to 1082 for capital gains tax purposes.

1083 Application of sections 1080 to 1082 for capital gains tax purposes

[CGTA75 s51(1) and Sch4 par2(2)]

[Without prejudice to *Part 41A*][1] and [Chapters 1B and 1C of Part 42][2], *sections 1080* to *1082* shall, subject to any necessary modifications, apply to capital gains tax.[][3]

Amendments

[1] Substituted by FA12 sched4(part 2)(g).

[2] Substituted by F(No.2)A08 sched4(part2). Applies as respects any tax that becomes due and payable on or after 1 March 2009.

[3] Amended by FA05 s145(6)(b)(vii) as follows "The provisions of section 1083 of the Taxes Consolidation Act 1997 except in so far as they apply section 1082 of that Act to capital gains tax are repealed with effect from 1 April 2005 to the extent that they apply to interest chargeable or payable on capital gains tax that has not been paid before that date regardless of when that tax became due and payable."

Cross References

From Section 1083

Section 931 Making of assessments and application of income tax assessment provisions.
Section 1080 Interest on overdue income tax, corporation tax and capital gains tax.
Section 1082 Interest on overdue income tax and corporation tax in cases of fraud or neglect.

To Section 1083

Section 959 Miscellaneous (Part 41).

CHAPTER 6

Other Sanctions

1084 Surcharge for late returns

[FA86 s48; FA88 s16; FA90 s25(1); FA92 s245; FA95 s30(1)]

(1) (a) In this section—

"*chargeable person*", in relation to a year of assessment or an accounting period, means a person who is a chargeable person for the purposes of [*Part 41A*][1];

"*return of income*" means a return, statement, declaration or list which a person is required to deliver to the inspector by reason of a notice given by the inspector under any one or more of the specified provisions, and includes a return which a chargeable person is required to deliver under [*Chapter 3* of *Part 41A*][2];

"*specified return date for the chargeable period*" has the same meaning as in [*section 959A*][3];

"*specified provisions*" means *sections 877* to *881* and *884*, *paragraphs (a)* and *(d)* of *section 888(2)*, and *section 1023*;

"*tax*" means income tax, corporation tax or capital gains tax, as may be appropriate.

(b) For the purposes of this section—

[(i) (I) subject to clause (II), where a person deliberately delivers an incorrect return of income as set out in *section 1077E(2)* or carelessly delivers an incorrect return of income as set out in *section 1077E(5)* on or before the specified return date for the chargeable period, the person shall be deemed to have failed to deliver the return of income on or before that date unless the error in the return of income is remedied on or before that date,

(II) clause (I) shall not apply where a person—

(A) deliberately delivers an incorrect return of income as set out in *section 1077E(2)* or carelessly delivers an incorrect return of income as set out in *section 1077E(5)* on or before the specified return date for the chargeable period, and

(B) pays the full amount of any penalty referred to in either of the provisions referred to in subclause (A) to which the person is liable,][4]

[(ia) where a person who is a specified person in relation to the delivery of a specified return for the purposes of any regulations made under *section 917EA* delivers a return of income on or before the specified return date for the chargeable period but does so in a form other than that required by any such regulations the person shall be deemed to have delivered an incorrect return on or before the specified return date for the chargeable period and *subparagraph (ii)* shall apply accordingly,][5]

[(ib) where a person delivers a return of income for a chargeable period (within the meaning of *section 321(2)*) and fails to include on the prescribed form the details required by the form in relation to any exemption, allowance, deduction, credit or other relief the person is claiming (in this subparagraph referred to as the "*specified details*") and the specified details are stated on the form to be details to which this subparagraph refers, then, without prejudice to any other basis on which a person may be liable to the surcharge referred to in *subsection (2)*, the person shall be deemed to have failed to deliver the return of income on or before the specified return date for the chargeable period and to have delivered the return of income before the expiry of 2 months from that specified return date; but this subparagraph shall not apply unless, after the return has been delivered, it had come to the person's notice or had been brought to the person's attention that specified details had not been included on the form and the person failed to remedy matters without unreasonable delay,][6]

(ii) where a person delivers an incorrect return of income on or before the specified return date for the chargeable period but does so [neither deliberately nor carelessly][7] and it comes to the person's notice (or, if he or she has died, to the notice of his or her personal representatives) that it is incorrect, the person shall be deemed to have failed to deliver the return of income on or before the specified return date for the chargeable period unless the error in the return of income is remedied without unreasonable delay,

(iii) where a person delivers a return of income on or before the specified return date for the chargeable period but the inspector, by reason of being dissatisfied with any statement of profits or gains arising to the person from any trade or profession which is contained in the return of income, requires the person, by notice in writing served on the person under *section 900*, to do any thing, the person shall be deemed not to have delivered the return of income on or before the specified return date for the chargeable period unless the person does that thing within the time specified in the notice, and

(iv) references to such of the specified provisions as are applied, subject to any necessary modifications, in relation to capital gains tax by *section 913* shall be construed as including references to those provisions as so applied.

(2) (a) Subject to *paragraph (b)*, where in relation to a year of assessment or accounting period a chargeable person fails to deliver a return of income on or before the specified return date for the chargeable period, any amount of tax for that year of assessment or accounting period which apart from this section is or would be contained in an assessment to tax made or to be made on the chargeable person shall be increased by an amount (in this subsection referred to as "*the surcharge*") equal to—

(i) 5 per cent of that amount of tax, subject to a maximum increased amount of [€12,695][8], where the return of income is delivered before the expiry of 2 months from the specified return date for the chargeable period, and

(ii) 10 per cent of that amount of tax, subject to a maximum increased amount of [€63,485][9], where the return of income is not delivered before the expiry of 2 months from the specified return date for the chargeable period,

[and, except where the surcharge arises by virtue of *subparagraph (ib)* of *subsection (1)(b)*, if the tax contained in the assessment is not the amount of tax as so increased,][10] then, the provisions of the Tax Acts and the Capital Gains Tax Acts (apart from this section), including in particular those provisions relating to the collection and recovery of tax and the payment of interest on unpaid tax, shall apply as if the tax contained in the assessment to tax were the amount of tax as so increased.

(b) In determining the amount of the surcharge, the tax contained in the assessment to tax shall be deemed to be reduced by the aggregate of—

(i) any tax deducted by virtue of any of the provisions of the Tax Acts or the Capital Gains Tax Acts from any income, profits or chargeable gains charged in the assessment to tax in so far as that tax has not been repaid or is not repayable to the chargeable person and in so far as the tax so deducted may be set off against the tax [and][11] contained in the assessment to tax,

[…][12]

(iii) any other amounts which are set off in the assessment to tax against the tax contained in that assessment.

(3) In the case of a person—

(a) who is a director within the meaning of *section 116*, or

(b) [to whom *section 1017* or *1031C* applies and whose spouse or civil partner][13] is a director within the meaning of *section 116*,

subsection (2)(b)(i) shall not apply in respect of any tax deducted under *Chapter 4* of *Part 42* in determining the amount of a surcharge under this section.

(4) (a) Notwithstanding *subsections (1)* to *(3)*, the specified return date for the chargeable period, being a year of assessment (in *paragraph (b)* referred to as "*the first-mentioned year of assessment*") to which *section 66(1)* applies, shall be the date which is the specified return date for the year of assessment following that year.

(b) *Paragraph (a)* shall only apply if throughout the first-mentioned year of assessment the chargeable person or that [person's spouse or civil partner][14], not [being a spouse in relation to whom *section 1016* applies, or a civil partner in relation to whom *section 1031B* applies,][15] for that year of assessment, was not carrying on a trade or profession set up and commenced in a previous year of assessment.

[(5) This section shall apply in relation to an amount of [preliminary tax (within the meaning of *Part 41A*) paid under *Chapter 7* of that Part][16] as it applies to an amount of tax specified in an assessment.][17]

Amendments

[1, 2, 3, 16] Substituted by FA12 sched4(part 2)(g).

[4] Substituted by FA14 s94(1)(a). Applies in respect of returns of income (within the meaning of section 1084) delivered on or after 23 December 2014.

[5] Inserted by FA03 s164(1)(b). Has effect from such day as the Minister for Finance may appoint by order.

[6] Inserted by FA04 s86(3)(a). This section shall apply as respects any chargeable period commencing on or after 1 January 2004.

[7] Substituted by FA14 s94(1)(b). Applies in respect of returns of income (within the meaning of section 1084) delivered on or after 23 December 2014.

[8, 9] Substituted by FA01 sched5.

[10] Substituted by FA04 s86(3)(b). This section shall apply as respects any chargeable period commencing on or after 1 January 2004.

[11] Inserted by FA00 sched2(p).

[12] Deleted by FA00 sched2(i)(i)(II).

[13] Substituted by F(No.3)A11 sched1(251). Shall have effect from the passing of this Act 27 July 2011.

[14] Substituted by F(No.3)A11 sched1(252). Shall have effect from the passing of this Act 27 July 2011.

[15] Substituted by F(No.3)A11 sched1(253). Shall have effect from the passing of this Act 27 July 2011.

[17] Substituted by FA01 s78(2)(h). Applies as respects the year of assessment 2001 and subsequent years and as respects accounting periods of companies ending on or after 1 April 2001.

Revenue Briefings

Tax Briefing

Tax Briefing April 2005 – Issue 59 pg 20 – Share Option Cases – Late Filing Surcharge

Statements of Practice

Surcharge and other Penalties or Restrictions for Late Submission of Tax Returns – SP-GEN/1/93, and Directors SP – IT/1/93

Cross References

From Section 1084

Section 66 Special basis at commencement of trade or profession.

Section 116 Interpretation (Chapter 3).

Section 321 Provisions of general application in relation to the making of allowances and charges.
Section 877 Returns by persons chargeable.
Section 881 Returns by married persons.
Section 884 Returns of profits.
Section 888 Returns, etc. by lessors, lessees and agents.
Section 900 Power to call for production of books, information, etc.
Section 913 Application of income tax provisions relating to returns, etc.
Section 950 Interpretation (Part 41).
Section 951 Obligation to make a return.
Section 952 Obligation to pay preliminary tax.
Section 960 Date for payment of income tax other than under self assessment.
Section 983 Interpretation (Chapter 4).
Section 1016 Assessment as single persons.
Section 1017 Assessment of husband in respect of income of both spouses.
Section 1023 Application for separate assessments.

To Section 1084

Section 730H Interpretation and application.
Section 730I Returns on acquisition of foreign life policy.
Section 739E Deduction of tax on the occurrence of a chargeable event.
Section 747B Interpretation and application.
Section 747C Return on acquisition of material interest.
Section 895 Returns in relation to foreign accounts.
Section 896 Returns in relation to certain offshore products.
Section 1085 Corporation tax — late returns: restriction of certain claims for relief.
Schedule 31 Consequential Amendments

1085 Corporation tax — late returns: restriction of certain claims for relief

[FA92 s55(1) and (2); FA95 s66(1) and (2)]

(1) (a) In this section—

"*chargeable period*" means an accounting period of a company;

"*group relief*" has the meaning assigned to it by *section 411*;

"*return of income*" means a return which a company is required to deliver under [*Chapter 3* of *Part 41A*][1];

"*specified return date for the chargeable period*" has the same meaning as in [*section 959A*][2].

(b) *Subparagraphs (i)*, [*(ia)*, *(ib)*,][3] *(ii)* and *(iii)* of *paragraph (b)* of *subsection (1)* of *section 1084* shall apply for the purposes of this section as they apply for the purposes of that section.

(2) Notwithstanding any other provision of the Tax Acts, where in relation to a chargeable period a company fails to deliver a return of income for the chargeable period on or before the specified return date for the chargeable period, then, subject to *subsections (3)* and *(4)*, the following provisions shall apply:

(a) any claim in respect of the chargeable period under *section 308(4)*, *396(2)* [, *396A(3)*][4] or *399(2)* shall be so restricted that the amount by which the company's profits of that or any other chargeable period are to be reduced by virtue of the claim shall be 50 per cent of the amount it would have been if this section had not been enacted,

(b) the total amount of group relief which the company may claim in respect of the chargeable period shall not exceed 50 per cent of the company's profits of the chargeable period as reduced by any other relief from tax other than group relief, [(ba) the total amount of the relevant trading loss referred to in *subsection (2)* of *section 396B* for the chargeable period shall be treated for the purposes of that section as reduced by 50 per cent,][5]

(c) the total amount of the loss referred to in *subsection (1)* of *section 420* for the chargeable period and the total amount of the excess referred to in *subsection (2)*, *(3)* or *(6)* of that section for that period shall each be treated for the purposes of *Chapter 5* of *Part 12* as reduced by 50 per cent,

[(ca) the total amount of the loss or excess referred to in *subsection (3)* of *section 420A* for the chargeable period shall be treated for the purposes of *Chapter 5* of *Part 12* as reduced by 50 per cent,

(cb) the total amount of the relevant trading loss referred to in *subsection (2)* of *section 420B* for the chargeable period shall be treated for the purposes of *Chapter 5* of *Part 12* as reduced by 50 per cent,][6]

[…][7]

[(3) Subject to *subsection (4)*, any restriction or reduction imposed by *paragraph (a)*, *(b)*, *(ba)*, *(c)*, *(ca)* or *(cb)* of *subsection (2)* in respect of a chargeable period in the case of a company which fails to deliver a return of income on or before the specified return date for the chargeable period shall apply subject to a maximum restriction or reduction, as the case may be, of €158,715 in each case for the chargeable period.

(4) Where in relation to a chargeable period a company, having failed to deliver a return of income on or before the specified return date for the chargeable period, delivers that return before the expiry of 2 months from the specified return date for the chargeable period, *paragraphs (a)* to *(cb)* of *subsection (2)* shall apply as if the references in those paragraphs to "50 per cent" were references to "75 per cent" in the case of *paragraphs (a)* and *(b)* and "25 per cent" in the case of *paragraphs (ba)*, *(c)*, *(ca)* and *(cb)* subject to a maximum restriction or reduction, as the case may be, of €31,740.][8]

Amendments

[1, 2] Substituted by FA12 sched4(part 2)(g).

[3] Substituted by FA04 s86(4). This section shall apply as respects any chargeable period commencing on or after 1 January 2004.

[4] Inserted by FA03 s59(1)(e)(i).

[5] Inserted by FA03 s59(1)(e)(ii).

[6] Inserted by FA03 s59(1)(e)(iii).

[7] Deleted by FA03 s41(1)(p)(i). This section applies as respects accounting periods ending on or after 6 February 2003.

[8] Substituted by FA03 s41(1)(p)(ii). This section applies as respects accounting periods ending on or after 6 February 2003.

Cross References

From Section 1085

Section 308 Corporation tax: manner of granting, and effect of, allowances made by means of discharge or repayment of tax.

Section 381 Right to repayment of tax by reference to losses.

Section 396 Relief for trading losses other than terminal losses.

Section 396A Relief for relevant trading losses.

Section 396B Relief for certain trading losses on a value basis.

Section 399 Losses in transactions from which income would be chargeable under Case IV or V of Schedule D.

Section 410 Group payments.
Section 411 Surrender of relief between members of groups and consortia.
Section 420 Losses, etc. which may be surrendered by means of group relief.
Section 420A Group relief: relevant losses and charges.
Section 420B Group relief: Relief for certain losses on a value basis.
Section 950 Interpretation (Part 41).
Section 951 Obligation to make a return.
Section 1084 Surcharge for late returns.

1086 Publication of names of tax defaulters

[FA83 s23; FA92 s240(b); WCTIPA93 s3(7); FA97 s158]

(1) In this section—

"*the Acts*" means—

(a) the Tax Acts,

[(aa) Parts 18A, 18B, 18C and 18D,][1]

(b) the Capital Gains Tax Acts,

(c) the Value-Added Tax Consolidation Act 2010, and the enactments amending or extending that Act,

(d) the Capital Acquisitions Tax Consolidation Act 2003, and the enactments amending or extending that Act,

[(e) the Stamp Duties Consolidation Act, 1999, and the enactments amending or extending that Act][2]

(f) Part VI of the Finance Act, 1983,

[(g) the Customs Acts,

(h) the statutes relating to the duties of excise and to the management of those duties,][3]

[(i) the *Finance (Local Property Tax) Act 2012*,][4]

and any instruments made thereunder;

["*tax*" means any tax, duty, levy or charge under the care and management of the Revenue Commissioners.][5]

(2) The Revenue Commissioners shall, as respects each relevant period (being the period beginning on the 1st day of January, 1997, and ending on the 30th day of June, 1997, and each subsequent period of 3 months beginning with the period ending on the 30th day of September, 1997), compile a list of the names and addresses and the occupations or descriptions of every person—

(a) on whom a fine or other penalty was imposed [or determined][6] by a court under any of the Acts during that relevant period,

(b) on whom a fine or other penalty was otherwise imposed [or determined][7] by a court during that relevant period in respect of an act or omission by the person in relation to [tax,][8]

(c) in whose case the Revenue Commissioners, pursuant to an agreement made with the person in that relevant period, refrained from initiating proceedings for the recovery of any fine or penalty of the kind mentioned in *paragraphs (a)* and *(b)* and, in place of initiating such proceedings, accepted or undertook to accept a specified sum of money in settlement of any claim by the Revenue Commissioners in respect of any specified liability of the person under any of the Acts for—

(i) payment of any tax,

[(ii) except in the case of tax due by virtue of *paragraphs (g)* and *(h)* of the definition of "*the Acts*", payment of interest on that tax, and

(iii) a fine or other monetary penalty in respect of that tax including penalties in respect of the failure to deliver any return, statement, declaration, list or other document in connection with the tax, or][9]

[(d) in whose case the Revenue Commissioners, having initiated proceedings for the recovery of any fine or penalty of the kind mentioned in *paragraphs (a)* and *(b)*, and whether or not a fine or penalty of the kind mentioned in those paragraphs has been imposed [or determined][10] by a court, accepted or undertook to accept, in that relevant period, a specified sum of money in settlement of any claim by the Revenue Commissioners in respect of any specified liability of the person under any of the Acts for—

(i) payment of any tax,

[(ii) except in the case of tax due by virtue of *paragraphs (g)* and *(h)* of the definition of "*the Acts*", payment of interest on that tax, and

(iii) a fine or other monetary penalty in respect of that tax including penalties in respect of the failure to deliver any return, statement, declaration, list or other document in connection with the tax.][11]][12]

[(2A) For the purposes of *subsection (2)*, the reference to a specified sum in *paragraphs (c)* and *(d)* of that subsection includes a reference to a sum which is the full amount of the claim by the Revenue Commissioners in respect of the specified liability referred to in those paragraphs. Where the Revenue Commissioners accept or undertake to accept such a sum, being the full amount of their claim, then—

(a) they shall be deemed to have done so pursuant to an agreement, made with the person referred to in *paragraph (c)*, whereby they refrained from initiating proceedings for the recovery of any fine or penalty of the kind mentioned in *paragraphs (a)* and *(b)* of *subsection (2)*, and

(b) that agreement shall be deemed to have been made in the relevant period in which the Revenue Commissioners accepted or undertook to accept that full amount.][13]

[(2B) For the purposes of this section, where the Revenue Commissioners—

(a) accepted or undertook to accept a specified sum under *subsection (2)(c)*, or

(b) accepted or undertook to accept a specified sum under *subsection (2)(d)*,

and the person fails to pay the specified sum of money within the relevant period, the person shall nevertheless be included on the list referred to in *subsection (2)*.][14]

(3) Notwithstanding any obligation as to secrecy imposed on them by the Acts or the Official Secrets Act, 1963—

(a) the Revenue Commissioners shall, before the expiration of 3 months from the end of each relevant period, cause each such list referred to in *subsection (2)* in relation to that period to be published in Iris Oifigiúil, and

[(b) the Revenue Commissioners may, at any time after each such list referred to in *subsection (2)* has been published as provided for in *paragraph (a)*, cause any such list to be publicised or reproduced, or both, in whole or in part, in such manner, form or format as they consider appropriate.][15]

(4) [*Paragraphs (c)* and *(d)*][16] of *subsection (2)* shall not apply in relation to a person in whose case—

[(a) the Revenue Commissioners are satisfied that, before any investigation or inquiry had been started by them or by any of their officers into any matter occasioning a liability referred to in those paragraphs, the person had voluntarily furnished to them a qualifying disclosure (within the meaning of section 1077E, section 116 of the Value-Added Tax Consolidation Act 2010 or section 134A of the Stamp Duties Consolidation Act 1999, as the case may be) in relation to and full particulars of that matter,][17]

(b) section 72 of the Finance Act, 1988, or section 3 of the Waiver of Certain Tax, Interest and Penalties Act, 1993, [applied,][18]

(c) the specified sum referred to in [*Paragraph (c)* or *(d)*][19] of *subsection (2)* does not exceed [[€30,000][20], or][21].

[(d) the amount of fine or other penalty included in the specified sum referred to in *paragraph (c)* or *(d)*, as the case may be, of *subsection (2)* does not exceed 15 per cent of the amount of tax included in that specified sum.][22]

[(4A) (a) In this subsection—

"*the consumer price index number*" means the All Items Consumer Price Index Number compiled by the Central Statistics Office;

"*the consumer price index number relevant to a year*" means the consumer price index number at the mid-December before the commencement of that year expressed on the basis that the consumer price index at mid-December 2001 was 100;

"*the Minister*" means the Minister for Finance.

(b) The Minister shall, in the year 2010 and in every fifth year thereafter, by order provide, in accordance with *paragraph (c)*, an amount in lieu of the amount referred to in *subsection (4)(c)*, or where such an order has been made previously, in lieu of the amount specified in the last order so made.

(c) For the purposes of *paragraph (b)* the amount referred to in *subsection (4)(c)* or in the last previous order made under the said *paragraph (b)*, as the case may be, shall be adjusted by—

(i) multiplying that amount by the consumer price index number relevant to the year in which the adjustment is made and dividing the product by the consumer price index number relevant to the year in which the amount was previously provided for, and

(ii) rounding the resulting amount up to the next €1,000.

(d) An order made under this subsection shall specify that the amount provided for by the order—

(i) takes effect from a specified date, being 1 January in the year in which the order is made, and

(ii) does not apply to any case in which the specified liability referred to in *paragraphs (c)* and *(d)* of *subsection (2)* includes tax, the liability in respect of which arose before, or which relates to periods which commenced before, that specified date.][23]

[(4B) *Paragraphs (a)* and *(b)* of *subsection (2)* shall not apply in relation to a person in whose case—

(a) the amount of a penalty determined by a court does not exceed 15 per cent of, as appropriate—

(i) the amount of the difference referred to in *subsection (11)* or *(12)*, as the case may be, of *section 1077E*,

(ii) the amount of the difference referred to in *subsection (11)* or *(12)*, as the case may be, of section 116 of the Value-Added Tax Consolidation Act 2010, or

(iii) the amount of the difference referred to in *subsection (7), (8)* or *(9)*, as the case may be, of section 134A of the Stamp Duties Consolidation Act 1999,

(b) the aggregate of the—

(i) the tax due in respect of which the penalty is computed,

(ii) except in the case of tax due by virtue of *paragraphs* (*g*) and (*h*) of the definition of "*the Acts*", interest on that tax, and

(iii) the penalty determined by a court, does not exceed €30,000, or

(c) there has been a qualifying disclosure.][24]

(5) Any list referred to in *subsection (2)* shall specify in respect of each person named in the list such particulars as the Revenue Commissioners think fit—

(a) of the matter occasioning the fine or penalty of the kind referred to in *subsection (2)* imposed [or determined][25] on the person or, as the case may be, the liability of that kind to which the person was subject, […][26]

(b) of any interest, fine or other monetary penalty, and of any other penalty or sanction, to which that person was liable, or which was imposed [or determined][27] on that person by a court, and which was occasioned by the matter referred to in [*paragraph* (*a*), and][28].

[(c) of any amount of tax determined under the Acts, whether paid or not, by reference to which a penalty was determined by a court in accordance with *section 1077B*.][29]

[(5A) Without prejudice to the generality of *paragraph (a)* of *subsection (5)*, such particulars as are referred to in that paragraph may include—

(a) in a case to which *paragraph (a)* or *(b)* of *subsection (2)* applies, a description, in such summary form as the Revenue Commissioners may think fit, of the act, omission or offence (which may also include the circumstances in which the act or omission arose or the offence was committed) in respect of which the fine or penalty referred to in those paragraphs was imposed [or determined][30], and

(b) in a case to which *paragraph (c)* or *(d)* of *subsection (2)* applies, a description, in such summary form as the Revenue Commissioners may think fit, of the matter occasioning the specified liability (which may also include the circumstances in which that liability arose) in respect of which the Revenue Commissioners accepted, or undertook to accept, a settlement, in accordance with those paragraphs.][31]

Amendments

[1] Inserted by FA11 s3(1)(k). Applies for the year of assessment 2011 and each subsequent year of assessment.

[2] Substituted by FA02 s126(1)(a)(i)(I). This section applies as respects fines or other penalties, which are imposed by a court, on or after 25 March 2002

[3] Inserted by FA02 s126(1)(a)(i)(II). This section applies as respects fines or other penalties, which are imposed by a court, on or after 25 March 2002

[4] Inserted by F(LPT)A 12 s158 & sched(16).

[5] Substituted by FA02 s126(1)(a)(ii). This section applies as respects fines or other penalties, which are imposed by a court, on or after 25 March 2002

[6] Inserted by F(No.2)A08 sched5(part2)(1)(as)(i)(I). The enactments specified in Schedule 5 are amended or repealed to the extent and manner specified in that Schedule and, unless the contrary is stated, shall come into effect after 24 December 2008.

[7] Inserted by F(No.2)A08 sched5(part2)(1)(as)(i)(II). The enactments specified in Schedule 5 are amended or repealed to the extent and manner specified in that Schedule and, unless the contrary is stated, shall come into effect after 24 December 2008.

[8] Substituted by FA00 s162(1)(a)(i). Applies as respects fines or other penalties, which are imposed by a court, on or after 23 March 2000

[9] Substituted by FA02 s126(1)(b)(i). This section applies as respects fines or other penalties, which are imposed by a court, on or after 25 March 2002

[10] Inserted by F(No.2)A08 sched5(part2)(1)(as)(i)(III). The enactments specified in Schedule 5 are amended or repealed to the extent and manner specified in that Schedule and, unless the contrary is stated, shall come into effect after 24 December 2008.

[11] Substituted by FA02 s126(1)(b)(ii). This section applies as respects fines or other penalties, which are imposed by a court, on or after 25 March 2002

[12] Inserted by FA00 s162(1)(a)(ii). Applies as respects fines or other penalties, which are imposed by a court, on or after 23 March 2000

[13] Substituted by F(No.2)A08 sched5(part2)(1)(as)(ii). The enactments specified in Schedule 5 are amended or repealed to the extent and manner specified in that Schedule and, unless the contrary is stated, shall come into effect after 24 December 2008.

[14] Inserted by FA11 s76(a).

[15] Substituted by FA02 s126(1)(c). This section applies as respects specified sums, which the Revenue Commissioners accepted, or undertook to accept, in settlement of a specified liability, on or after 25 March 2002

[16] Substituted by FA00 s162(1)(c)(i). Applies as respects specified sums, which the Revenue Commissioners accepted, or undertook to accept, in settlement of a specified liability, on or after 23 March 2000

[17] Substituted by F(No.2)A08 sched5(part2)(1)(as)(iii). The enactments specified in Schedule 5 are amended or repealed to the extent and manner specified in that Schedule and, unless the contrary is stated, shall come into effect after 24 December 2008.

[18] Substituted by FA02 s126(1)(d)(ii). This section applies as respects specified sums, which the Revenue Commissioners accepted, or undertook to accept, in settlement of a specified liability, on or after 25 March 2002

[19] Substituted by FA00 s162(1)(c)(ii). Applies as respects specified sums, which the Revenue Commissioners accepted, or undertook to accept, in settlement of a specified liability, on or after 23 March 2000

[20] Substituted by FA05 s143(1)(a).

[21] Substituted by FA02 s126(1)(d)(iii). This section applies as respects specified sums, which the Revenue Commissioners accepted, or undertook to accept, in settlement of a specified liability, on or after 25 March 2002

[22] Inserted by FA02 s126(1)(d)(iv). This section applies as respects specified sums, which the Revenue Commissioners accepted, or undertook to accept, in settlement of a specified liability, on or after 25 March 2002

[23] Inserted by FA05 s143(1)(b).

[24] Inserted by F(No.2)A08 sched5(part2)(1)(as)(iv). The enactments specified in Schedule 5 are amended or repealed to the extent and manner specified in that Schedule and, unless the contrary is stated, shall come into effect after 24 December 2008.

[25] Inserted by F(No.2)A08 sched5(part2)(1)(as)(v)(I). The enactments specified in Schedule 5 are amended or repealed to the extent and manner specified in that Schedule and, unless the contrary is stated, shall come into effect after 24 December 2008.

[26] Deleted by FA11 s(76)(b).

[27] Inserted by F(No.2)A08 sched5(part2)(1)(as)(v)(II). The enactments specified in Schedule 5 are amended or repealed to the extent and manner specified in that Schedule and, unless the contrary is stated, shall come into effect after 24 December 2008.

[28] Substituted by FA11 s(76)(b).

[29] Inserted by FA11 s(76)(c).

[30] Inserted by F(No.2)A08 sched5(part2)(1)(as)(vi). The enactments specified in Schedule 5 are amended or repealed to the extent and manner specified in that Schedule and, unless the contrary is stated, shall come into effect after 24 December 2008.

[31] Inserted by FA00 s162(1)(d). Applies as respects specified sums, which the Revenue Commissioners accepted, or undertook to accept, in settlement of a specified liability, on or after 23 March 2000.

Note:

S.I. No. 643 of 2010 which cannot be consolidated reads as follows:

I, BRIAN LENIHAN, Minister for Finance, in exercise of the powers conferred on me by subsection (4A) (inserted by section 143 of the Finance Act 2005 (No. 5 of 2005)) of section 1086 of the Taxes Consolidation Act 1997 (No. 39 of 1997), hereby order, in accordance with paragraph (c) of that subsection, as follows:

1. This Order may be cited as the Taxes (Publication of Names of Tax Defaulters) Order 2010.

2. For the purposes of section 1086 of the Taxes Consolidation Act 1997 (No. 39 of 1997), the amount of €33,000 is specified as the amount in lieu of the amount of €30,000 referred to in subsection (4)(c) of that section.

3. The amount specified in paragraph 2—
   (a) takes effect from 1 January 2010, and
   (b) does not apply to any case in which the specified liability referred to in paragraphs (c) and (d) of section 1086(2) of the Taxes Consolidation Act 1997 includes tax, the liability in respect of which arose before, or which relates to periods which commenced before, 1 January 2010.

GIVEN under my Official Seal,
21 December 2010.
BRIAN LEHIHAN,
Minister for Finance.

Revenue Briefings

eBrief

eBrief No. 15/2008 – Penalties Involving Deceased Taxpayers and Personal Representatives
eBrief No. 68/2014 – Code of Practice for Revenue Audit and other Compliance Interventions

Revenue Information Notes

2010 Code of Practice for Revenue Audit
Code of Practice for Revenue Audit and other Compliance Interventions

Cross References

From Section 1086

Section 1077B Penalty notifications and determinations.
Section 1077E Penalty for deliberately or carelessly making incorrect returns, etc.

To Section 1086

Section 1077C Recovery of penalties.
Section 1077D Proceedings against executor, administrator or estate.
Section 1104 Short title and construction.

PART 48

Miscellaneous and Supplemental

1087 Charge and deduction of income tax not charged or deducted before passing of annual Act

[ITA67 s8 and s93(3); FA69 s 29; FA72 s12 and Sch3; CTA76 s140(1) and Sch2 PtI par2]

(1) Where in any year of assessment any payments have been made, before the passing of an Act increasing the rate of income tax for that year, on account of any interest, dividends or other annual profits or gains from which under the Tax Acts income tax is required to be deducted and tax has not been charged on or deducted from those payments, or has not been charged on or deducted from those payments at the increased rate of tax for that year—

(a) the amount not so charged or deducted shall be charged under Case IV of Schedule D in respect of those payments as profits or gains not charged by virtue of any other Schedule, and

(b) the agents entrusted with the payment of the interest, dividends or annual profits or gains shall furnish to the Revenue Commissioners a list containing—

(i) the names and addresses of the persons to whom payments have been made, and

(ii) the amount of those payments,

on a requisition made by the Revenue Commissioners in that behalf.

(2) Any person liable to pay any rent, interest or annuity, or to make any other annual payment, including a payment to which *section 104* applies (not being a payment of rent, interest or annuity)—

(a) shall be authorised—

(i) to make any deduction on account of income tax for any year of assessment which that person has failed to make before the passing of an Act increasing the rate of tax for that year, or

(ii) to make up any deficiency in any such deduction which has been so made,

on the occasion of the next payment of the rent, interest or annuity, or the making of the other annual payment, including a payment to which *section 104* applies (not being a payment of rent, interest or annuity), after the passing of the Act so increasing the rate of tax, in addition to any other deduction which that person may be by law authorised to make, and

(b) shall also be entitled, if there is no future payment from which the deduction may be made, to recover the sum which might have been deducted as if it were a debt due from the person as against whom the deduction could originally have been made if the Act increasing the rate of tax for the year had been in force.

(3) This section shall not apply to a payment which is a distribution within the meaning of *Chapter 2* of *Part 6*.

Cross References

From Section 1087

Section 104 Taxation of certain rents and other payments.

Section 129 Irish resident company distributions not generally chargeable to corporation tax.
Section 130 Matters to be treated as distributions.

1088 Restriction on deductions in computing profits

[ITA67 s535; FA74 s51]

(1) In determining the amount of profits or gains for the purpose of income tax—

(a) no deductions shall be made other than those expressly provided for by the Income Tax Acts, and

(b) no deduction shall be made on account of any annuity or other annual payment (other than interest) to be paid out of such profits or gains in regard that a proportionate part of the income tax is allowed to be deducted on making any such payment.

(2) In determining the amount of profits or gains from any property described in the Income Tax Acts or from any office or employment of profit, no deduction shall be made on account of diminution of capital employed, or of loss sustained, in any trade or in any profession or employment.

1089 Status of interest on certain unpaid taxes and duties

[FA73 s35; FA75 s27; FA76 s29]

(1) Interest payable under—

(a) [section 14 and subsections (3) and (4) of section 117 of the Stamp Duties Consolidation Act, 1999][1],

(b) section 114 of the Value-Added Tax Consolidation Act 2010, or

(c) [*section 530Q*, *531(9)* or *991*][2],

shall be payable without any deduction of income tax and shall not be allowed in computing any income, profits or losses for any of the purposes of the Income Tax Acts.

(2) Interest payable under section 18 of the Wealth Tax Act, 1975, or section 51 of the Capital Acquisitions Tax Consolidation Act 2003, shall not be allowed in computing any income, profits or losses for any of the purposes of the Tax Acts.

Amendments

[1] Substituted by SDCA99 sched4.

[2] Substituted by FA11 s20(1)(t). With effect from 1 January 2012 as per S.I. No. 660 of 2011.

Cross References

From Section 1089

Section 530Q Interest.
Section 531 Payments to subcontractors in certain industries.
Section 991 Interest.

1090 Income tax assessment to be conclusive of total income

[ITA67 s534]

Where an assessment has become final and conclusive for the purposes of income tax for any year of assessment, that assessment shall also be final and conclusive in estimating total income from all sources for the purposes of the Income Tax Acts, and no allowance or adjustment of liability, on the ground of diminution of income or loss, shall be taken into account in estimating such total income from all sources for such purposes unless that allowance or adjustment has been previously made on an application under the special provisions of the Income Tax Acts relating to that allowance or adjustment.

1091 Annexation of statements to interest warrants, etc

[ITA67 s458; CTA76 s140(1) and Sch2 PtI par25]

(1) In this section, "*company*" means a company within the meaning of the Companies Act, 1963, and a company created by letters patent or by or in pursuance of any statute.

(2) Every warrant, cheque or other order sent or delivered for the purpose of paying any interest which is not a distribution within the meaning of the Corporation Tax Acts by a company which is entitled to deduct income tax from such interest shall have annexed to it, or be accompanied by, a statement in writing showing—

(a) the gross amount which, after deduction of the income tax appropriate to such interest, corresponds to the net amount actually paid,

(b) the rate and amount of income tax appropriate to such gross amount, and

(c) the net amount actually paid.

[(3) Where a company fails to comply with any of the provisions of subsection (2), the company shall incur a penalty of €200 in respect of each failure, but the aggregate amount of the penalties imposed under this section on any company in respect of all such failures connected with any one distribution of dividends or interest shall not exceed €2,000.][1]

Amendments

[1] Substituted by F(No.2)A08 sched5(part2)(2)(at). The enactments specified in Schedule 5 are amended or repealed to the extent and manner specified in that Schedule and, unless the contrary is stated, shall come into effect after 24 December 2008.

1092 Disclosure of certain information to rating authorities, etc

[FA78 s47; FA80 s89]

(1) This section shall apply to any charge imposed on public moneys, being a charge for the purposes of relief (in this section referred to as "*the relief*") under the Rates on Agricultural Land (Relief) Acts, 1939 to 1980, and any subsequent enactment together with which those Acts may be cited.

(2) Where a charge to which this section applies is to be made, the Revenue Commissioners or any officer authorised by them for that purpose may, in connection with the establishment of title to the relief of a person (in this subsection referred to as "*the claimant*"), notwithstanding any obligation as to secrecy imposed on them under the Income Tax Acts or under any other enactment, disclose to any person specified in *column (1)* of the Table to this section information of the kind specified in *column (2)* of that Table, being information in respect of the claimant which is required by that person when considering the claimant's title to the relief.

(3) In the Table to this section, "*occupation*" has the same meaning as in *section 654*, and "*rating authority*" has the same meaning as in *section 898*.

TABLE

(1) Persons to whom information to be given	(2) Information to be given
The secretary or clerk, or a person acting as such, to a rating authority or any officer of the Minister for the Environment and Local Government authorised by that Minister for the purpose of this section.	Information relating to the occupation of land by the claimant and the rateable valuation of such land.

Cross References

From Section 1092

Section 654 Interpretation (Part 23).

Section 898 Returns of copies of rates and production of certain valuations.

1093 Disclosure of information to Ombudsman

[FA81 s52]

Any obligation to maintain secrecy or other restriction on the disclosure or production of information (including documents) obtained by or furnished to the Revenue Commissioners, or any person on their behalf, for taxation purposes, shall not apply to the disclosure or production of information (including documents) to the Ombudsman for the purposes of an examination or investigation by the Ombudsman under the Ombudsman Act, 1980, of any action (within the meaning of that Act) taken by or on behalf of the Revenue Commissioners, being such an action taken in the performance of administrative functions in respect of any tax or duty under the care and management of the Revenue Commissioners.

Cross References

To Section 1093

Section 1104 Short title and construction.

1093A Disclosure of certain information to Minister for Enterprise, Trade and Employment, etc

[(1) In this section—

"*Minister*" means the Minister for Enterprise, Trade and Employment;

"*specified body*" means the body dedicated to employment rights compliance to be established or established (both on an interim and a statutory basis) and referred to in sections 12.3 and 13.1 of Part Two of the publication entitled "Ten-Year Framework Social Partnership Agreement 2006–2015", published on behalf of the Department of the Taoiseach in June 2006 by the Stationery Office and known as "Towards 2016".

(2) Notwithstanding any obligation to maintain secrecy or any other restriction on the disclosure or production of information obtained by or furnished to the Revenue Commissioners, the Revenue Commissioners may transfer to the Minister or the specified body information held by them—

(a) in relation to the employers or the earned incomes of individuals, or

(b) which is contained in declarations made in accordance with Regulation 3 of the Income Tax (Relevant Contracts) Regulations 2000 (S. I. No. 71 of 2000),

and information of the type referred to in paragraph (a) held by the Minister or the specified body may be transferred by the Minister or the specified body, as the case may be, to the Revenue Commissioners.

(3) Information transferred by the Revenue Commissioners under subsection (2) to the Minister or the specified body may be used only by the Minister or the specified body, as the case may be, in the exercise of their powers and functions in relation to employment rights compliance and shall not be disclosed by the Minister or the specified body to any other person (other than to each other) for any other purpose whatsoever.][1]

Amendments

[1] Inserted by s38 of the Social Welfare and Pensions Act 2007.

1094 Tax clearance certificates in relation to certain licences

[FA92 s242; FA93 s140; FA97 s160(1)]

(1) In this section—

["*the Acts*" means—

(a) the Customs Acts,

(b) the statutes relating to the duties of excise and to the management of those duties,

(c) the Tax Acts,

[(ca) Parts 18A, 18B, 18C and 18D,][1]

(d) the Capital Gains Tax Acts,

[(e) the Value-Added Tax Acts, and any instruments made thereunder,

(f) the Finance (Local Property Tax) Act 2012;][2]][3]

[(g) the statutes relating to stamp duty and to the management of that duty,

(h) the Capital Acquisitions Tax Consolidation Act 2003, and the enactments amending or extending that Act,][4]

"*beneficial holder of a licence*" means the person who conducts the activities under the licence and, in relation to a licence issued under the Auctioneers and House Agents Act, 1947, includes the authorised individual referred to in section 8(4), or the nominated individual referred to in section 9(1), of that Act;

"*licence*" [means a licence, permit or authorisation][5], as the case may be, of the kind referred to in—

(a) the proviso (inserted by section 156 of the Finance Act, 1992) to section 49(1) of the Finance (1909-1910) Act, 1910,

(b) the further proviso (inserted by section 79(1) of the Finance Act, 1993) to section 49(1) of the Finance (1909-1910) Act, 1910,

(c) the proviso (inserted by section 79(2) of the Finance Act, 1993) to section 7(3) of the Betting Act, 1931,

(d) the proviso (inserted by section 79(3) of the Finance Act, 1993) to section 19 of the Gaming and Lotteries Act, 1956,

(e) the proviso (inserted by section 79(4)(*a*) of the Finance Act, 1993) to subsection (1) of section 8 of the Auctioneers and House Agents Act, 1947,

(f) the proviso (inserted by section 79(4)(*b*) of the Finance Act, 1993) to subsection (1) of section 9 of the Auctioneers and House Agents Act, 1947 (an auction permit under that section being deemed for the purposes of this section to be a licence),

(g) the proviso (inserted by section 79(4)(*c*) of the Finance Act, 1993) to subsection (1) of section 10 of the Auctioneers and House Agents Act, 1947,

[(h) *section 101* of the Finance Act, 1999[,][6][7]

(j) section 93, 116 or 144 of the Consumer Credit Act, 1995[,][8]

[(k) *subsection (2A)* (inserted by *section 106* of the Finance Act, 2000) of section 62 of the National Cultural Institutions Act, 1997[,][9]][10]

[(l) *subsection (1A)* (inserted by *section 172* of the Finance Act, 2001) of section 2 of the Intoxicating Liquor (National Concert Hall) Act, 1983[,][11]][12]

[(m) *subsection (3)* (inserted by the Finance Act, 2002) of section 122 of the Finance Act, [1992,][13]

(n) *subsection (1A)* (inserted by the Finance Act, 2002) of the Finance (1909-10) Act, [1910,][14]][15]

[(o) section 21 of the Intoxicating Liquor Act [2003, and][16]][17]

[(p) section 1 of the Intoxicating Liquor (National Conference Centre) Act 2010][18]

["*market value*", in relation to any property, means the price which such property might reasonably be expected to fetch on a sale in the open market on the date on which the property is to be valued;][19]

['*PPS number*' in relation to an individual, means the individual's personal public service number within the meaning of *section 262* of the Social Welfare Consolidation Act 2005;][20]

"*specified date*" means the date of commencement of a licence sought to be granted under any of the provisions referred to in [*paragraphs (a)* to [*(p)*][22]][22] of the definition of "*licence*" as specified for the purposes of a tax clearance certificate under *subsection (2)*;

"*tax clearance certificate*" shall be construed in accordance with *subsection (2)*.

['*tax clearance access number*' has the meaning given to it by *subsection (5)(b)*;][23]

['*tax reference number*', in relation to a person, means—

(a) in the case of an individual, the individual's PPS number, and

(b) in any other case—

(i) the reference number stated on any return of income form or notice of assessment issued to the person by a Revenue officer, or

(ii) the registration number assigned to that person under section 65 of the Value-Added Tax Consolidation Act 2010;][24]

(2) Subject to *subsection (3)*, the Collector-General shall, on an application to him or her by the person who will be the beneficial holder of a licence due to commence on a specified date, issue a certificate (in this section referred to as a "*tax clearance certificate*") for the purposes of the grant of a licence if—

(a) that person and, in respect of the period of that person's membership, any partnership of which that person is or was a partner,

(b) in a case where that person is a partnership, each partner,

(c) in a case where that person is a company, each person who is either the beneficial owner of, or able directly or indirectly to control, more than 50 per cent of the ordinary share capital of the company,

has or have complied with all the obligations imposed on that person or on them by the Acts in relation to—

(i) the payment or remittance of the taxes, interest and penalties required to be paid or remitted under the Acts, and

(ii) the delivery of returns.

[(2A) Compliance with the obligations imposed on a person referred to in *subsection (2)* may be reviewed from time to time by the Collector-General and a tax clearance certificate issued under *subsection (2)* may be rescinded by the Collector-General where those obligations are found at the time of any review not to be complied with.][25]

(3) Subject to *subsection (4)*, where a person (in this section referred to as "*the first-mentioned person*") will be the beneficial holder of a licence due to commence on a specified date and another person (in this section referred to as "*the second-mentioned person*") was the beneficial holder of the licence at any time during the year ending on that date, and—

(a) the second-mentioned person is a company connected (within the meaning of *section 10* as it applies for the purposes of the Tax Acts) with the first-mentioned person or would have been such a company but for the fact that the company has been wound up or dissolved without being wound up,

(b) the second-mentioned person is a company and the first-mentioned person is a partnership in which—

(i) a partner is or was able, or

(ii) where more than one partner is a shareholder, those partners together are or were able,

directly or indirectly, whether with or without a connected person or connected persons (within the meaning of *section 10* as it applies for the purposes of the Tax Acts), to control more than 50 per cent of the ordinary share capital of the company, or

(c) the second-mentioned person is a partnership and the first-mentioned person is a company in which—

(i) a partner is or was able, or

(ii) where more than one partner is a shareholder, those partners together are or were able,

directly or indirectly, whether with or without a connected person or connected persons (within the meaning of *section 10* as it applies for the purposes of the Tax Acts), to control more than 50 per cent of the ordinary share capital of the company,

then, a tax clearance certificate shall not be issued by the Collector-General under *subsection (2)* unless, in relation to the activities conducted under the licence, the second-mentioned person has complied with the second-mentioned person's obligations under the Acts as specified in *subsection (2)*.

[(3A) Where—

(a) the first-mentioned person will be the beneficial holder of a licence due to commence on a specified date on foot of a certificate granted or to be granted under *section 2(1)* (as amended by section 23 of the Intoxicating Liquor Act, 1960) of the Licensing (Ireland) Act, 1902,

(b) the second-mentioned person was the beneficial holder of the last licence issued prior to the specified date in respect of the premises for which the certificate referred to in *paragraph (a)* was granted, and

(c) the acquisition of the premises by the said first-mentioned person was for a consideration of less than market value at the date of such acquisition,

then, *subsection (3)* shall apply as if—

(i) the reference to the year ending on that date were a reference to 5 years ending on that date, and

(ii) the reference to the activities conducted under the licence was a reference to the activities conducted by the second-mentioned person under the last licence held by the said person prior to the specified date.][26]

(4) *Subsection (3)* shall not apply to a transfer of a licence effected before the 24th day of April, 1992, or to such transfer effected after that date where a contract for the sale or lease of the premises to which the licence relates was signed before that date.

[(5) (a) A person applying for a tax clearance certificate under this section shall apply to the Collector-General in such electronic format as the Revenue Commissioners require.

(b) A tax clearance certificate issued to a person under this section shall include a unique number (in this section referred to as the 'tax clearance access number') assigned by the Collector-General.

(c) A person to whom a tax clearance certificate is issued under this section shall provide the tax reference number and tax clearance access number to any person who is required to verify the validity of the tax clearance certificate using those numbers.

(d) Where a person who is required to verify the validity of a tax clearance certificate is provided with any person's tax reference number and tax clearance access number for the purpose of verifying the validity of the certificate, those numbers shall be used by the person for that purpose only and shall not be used by that person at any other time or for any other purpose.][27]

(6) Where an application for a tax clearance certificate under this section is refused [or rescinded][28] by the Collector-General, he or she shall as soon as is practicable communicate in writing such refusal [or rescission][29] and the grounds for such refusal [or rescission][30] to the person concerned.

(7) (a) Where an application under this section to the Collector-General for a tax clearance certificate is refused [or rescinded][31], the person aggrieved by the refusal [or rescission][32] may, by notice in writing given to the Collector-General within 30 days of the refusal [or rescission][33], apply to have such person's application heard and determined by the Appeal Commissioners; but no right of appeal shall exist by virtue of this section in relation to any amount of tax or interest due under the Acts.

(b) A notice under *paragraph (a)* shall be valid only if—

(i) that notice specifies—

(I) the matter or matters with which the person is aggrieved, and

(II) the grounds in detail of the person's appeal as respects each such matter,

and

(ii) any amount under the Acts which is due to be remitted or paid, and which is not in dispute, is duly remitted or paid.

(c) The Appeal Commissioners shall hear and determine an appeal made to them under this subsection as if it were an appeal against an assessment to income tax and, subject to *paragraph (d)*, the provisions of the Income Tax Acts relating to such an appeal (including the provisions relating to the rehearing of an appeal and to the statement of a case for the opinion of the High Court on a point of law) shall apply accordingly with any necessary modifications.

(d) On the hearing of an appeal made under this subsection, the Appeal Commissioners shall have regard to all matters to which the Collector-General is required to have regard under this section.

[(8) The following shall be in such electronic format as the Revenue Commissioners may make available for the time being for any such purpose:

(a) applications made for tax clearance certificates;

(b) the issue of tax clearance certificates by the Collector-General;

(c) the refusal or rescission of tax clearance certificates by the Collector-General;

(d) the verification of tax clearance certificates by persons who are required to verify such certificates.][34]

[…][35][36]

Amendments

[1] Inserted by FA11 s3(1)(l). Applies for the year of assessment 2011 and each subsequent year of assessment.

[2] Substituted by F(LPT)AA13 s15. Has effect as on and from 13 March 2013.

[3] Substituted by FA10 s156(a). Has effect as on and from 3 April 2010.

[4] Substituted by F(No.2)A13 sched(1)(m). Deemed to have come into force and have taken effect on and from 27 March 2013.

[5] Substituted by FA02 s127(a)(i)(I)(A). Applies with effect from 25 March 2002

[6, 8, 9, 11] Substituted by FA02 s127(a)(i)(I)(B). Applies with effect from 25 March 2002

[7] Substituted by FA99 s212(a)(i).

[10] Inserted by FA00 s163.

[12] Inserted by FA01 s234.

[13] Substituted by ILA03 s21(7)(a)(i).

[14] Substituted by IL (NCC) A10 s2(a)(i). Has effect as on and from 31 May 2010.

[15] Inserted by FA02 s127(a)(i)(I)(C). Applies with effect from 25 March 2002

[16] Substituted by IL (NCC) A10 s2(a)(ii). Has effect as on and from 31 May 2010.

[17] Inserted by ILA03 s21(7)(a)(i).

[18] Inserted by IL (NCC) A10 s2(a)(iii). Has effect as on and from 31 May 2010.

[19] Inserted by FA99 s212(a)(ii).

[20, 23, 24] Inserted by FA14 s95(1)(a)(i). Comes into operation on such day as the Minister for Finance may appoint by order.

[21] Substituted by IL (NCC) A10 s2(b). Has effect as on and from 31 May 2010.

[22] Substituted by ILA03 s21(7)(b).

[25] Inserted by FA14 s95(1)(a)(ii). Comes into operation on such day as the Minister for Finance may appoint by order.

[26] Inserted by FA99 s212(b).

[27] Substituted by FA14 s95(1)(a)(iii). Comes into operation on such day as the Minister for Finance may appoint by order.

[28] Inserted by FA14 s95(1)(a)(iv)(I). Comes into operation on such day as the Minister for Finance may appoint by order.

[29, 30] Inserted by FA14 s95(1)(a)(iv)(II). Comes into operation on such day as the Minister for Finance may appoint by order.

[31] Inserted by FA14 s95(1)(a)(v)(I). Comes into operation on such day as the Minister for Finance may appoint by order.

[32, 33] Inserted by FA14 s95(1)(a)(v)(II). Comes into operation on such day as the Minister for Finance may appoint by order.

[34] Substituted by FA14 s95(1)(a)(vi). Comes into operation on such day as the Minister for Finance may appoint by order.

[35] Deleted by FA14 s95(1)(a)(vii). Comes into operation on such day as the Minister for Finance may appoint by order.

[36] Inserted by FA02 s127(a)(iii). Applies with effect from 25 March 2002

Revenue Briefings

eBrief

eBrief No. 23/2013 – Local Property Tax and Tax Clearance Certificate Applications

eBrief No. 29/2013 – Licences and Tax Clearance

Tax Briefing

Tax Briefing April 2002 – Issue 47 pg 23 – Tax Clearance FA 2002

Revenue Information Notes

Revenue Guidelines for Tax Clearance – available on Revenue website www.revenue.ie

Cross References

From Section 1094

Section 10 Connected persons.
Section 101 Relief for amount not received.
Section 106 Tax treatment of receipts and outgoings on sale of premises.
Section 172 Application of Corporation Tax Acts.

To Section 1094

Section 847A Donations to certain sports bodies.
Section 980 Deduction from consideration on disposal of certain assets.
Section 1095 Tax clearance certificates: general scheme.
Section 1104 Short title and construction.
Schedule 31 Consequential Amendments

1095 Tax clearance certificates: general scheme

[(1) In this section—

["*the Acts*" means—

(a) the Customs Acts,

(b) the statutes relating to the duties of excise and to the management of those duties,

(c) the Tax Acts,

[(ca) Parts 18A, 18B, 18C and 18D,][1]

(d) the Capital Gains Tax Acts,

(e) the Value-Added Tax Acts,

[(f) the *Finance (Local Property Tax) Act 2012*,][2]

[(g) the statutes relating to stamp duty and to the management of that duty,

(h) the Capital Acquisitions Tax Consolidation Act 2003, and the enactments amending or extending that Act,][3]

and any instruments made thereunder;][4]

"*licence*" has the same meaning as in *section 1094*;

"*tax clearance certificate*" shall be construed in accordance with *subsection (3)*.

(2) The provisions of this section shall apply in relation to every application by a person to the Collector-General for a tax clearance certificate other than an application for such a certificate made—

(a) in relation to a licence, or

(b) pursuant to the requirements of—

(i) *section 847A* (inserted by the Finance Act, 2002),

(ii) the Standards in Public Office Act, 2001, or

(iii) Regulation 6 of the Criminal Justice (Legal Aid) (Tax Clearance Certificate) Regulations 1999 (S.I. No. 135 of 1999).

(3) Subject to this section, where a person who is in compliance with the obligations imposed on the person by the Acts in relation to—

(a) the payment or remittance of any taxes, interest or penalties required to be paid or remitted under the Acts, and

(b) the delivery of any returns to be made under the Acts,

applies to the Collector-General in that behalf the Collector-General shall issue to the person a certificate (in this section referred to as a "*tax clearance certificate*") stating that the person is in compliance with those obligations.

[(3A) Compliance with the obligations imposed on a person or persons referred to in *subsection (3)* may be reviewed from time to time by the Collector-General and a tax clearance certificate issued under *subsection (2)* may be rescinded by the Collector-General where those obligations are found at the time of review not to be complied with.][5]

(4) A tax clearance certificate shall not be issued to a person unless—

(a) that person and, in respect of the period of that person's membership, any partnership of which that person is or was a partner,

(b) in a case where that person is a partnership, each partner, and

(c) in a case where that person is a company, each person who is either the beneficial owner of, or able directly or indirectly to control, more than 50 per cent of the ordinary share capital of the company,

is in compliance with the obligations imposed on the person and each other person (including any partnership) by the Acts in relation to the matters specified in *paragraphs (a)* and *(b)* of *subsection (3)*.

(5) Where a person who applies for a tax clearance certificate in accordance with *subsection (3)* (in this section referred to as "*the first-mentioned person*") carries on a business activity which was previously carried on by, or was previously carried on

as part of a business activity by, another person (in this section referred to as "*the second-mentioned person*") and—

(a) the second-mentioned person is a company connected (within the meaning of *section 10* as it applies for the purposes of the Tax Acts) with the first-mentioned person or would have been such a company but for the fact that the company has been wound up or dissolved without being wound up,

(b) the second-mentioned person is a company and the first-mentioned person is a partnership in which—

(i) a partner is or was able, or

(ii) where more than one partner is a shareholder, those partners together are or were able,

directly or indirectly, whether with or without a connected person or connected persons (within the meaning of *section 10* as it applies for the purposes of the Tax Acts), to control more than 50 per cent of the ordinary share capital of the company, or

(c) the second-mentioned person is a partnership and the first-mentioned person is a company in which—

(i) a partner is or was able, or

(ii) where more than one partner is a shareholder, those partners together are or were able,

directly or indirectly, whether with or without a connected person or connected persons (within the meaning of *section 10* as it applies for the purposes of the Tax Acts), to control more than 50 per cent of the ordinary share capital of the company,

then, a tax clearance certificate shall not be issued by the Collector-General under *subsection (3)* to the first-mentioned person unless, in relation to that business activity, the second-mentioned person is in compliance with the obligations imposed on that person by the Acts in relation to the matters specified in *paragraphs (a)* and *(b)* of *subsection (3)*.

(6) *Subsections (5)* [to *(8)*][6] of *section 1094* shall apply to an application for a tax clearance certificate under this section as they apply to an application for a tax clearance certificate under that section.][7]

Amendments

[1] Inserted by FA11 s3(1)(m). Applies for the year of assessment 2011 and each subsequent year of assessment.

[2] Inserted by F(LPT)A 12 s158 & sched(17).

[3] Inserted by FA13 s94(b).

[4] Substituted by FA10 s156(b). Has effect as on and from 3 April 2010.

[5] Inserted by FA14 s95(1)(b)(i). Comes into operation on such day as the Minister for Finance may appoint by order.

[6] Substituted by FA14 s95(1)(b)(ii). Comes into operation on such day as the Minister for Finance may appoint by order.

[7] Substituted by FA02 s127(b). Applies with effect from 25 March 2002

Revenue Briefings

eBrief

eBrief No. 23/2013 – Local Property Tax and Tax Clearance Certificate Applications
eBrief No. 86/2014 – Tax Clearance Guidelines and Procedures Updated

Tax Briefing

Tax Briefing April 2002 – Issue 47 pg 23 – Tax Clearance FA 2002

Revenue Precedents

A Local Authority is not obliged to operate Tax Clearance when completing a compulsory purchase of land, since the Local Authority is not entering into a contract with the landowner. It is exercising its powers under a statutory scheme for land acquisition. This applies whether the price paid for the land has been agreed between the Local Authority and the land owner or has been fixed by arbitration. Where the Local Authority enters into a contract with a landowner for purchase of land it would be obliged to operate Tax Clearance, even though it could compulsorily acquire the land. IT922041

Individuals and companies need to produce a Tax Clearance Certificate in circumstances where rent in excess of £5,000 per annum is payable out of public funds. IT933508

The Tax Clearance requirements of Department of Finance Circular F49/13/87 apply to payments made by the Department of agriculture under the Forest Premium Scheme. IT953509

Cross References

From Section 1095

Section 847A Donations to certain sports bodies.

Section 1094 Tax clearance certificates in relation to certain licences.

To Section 1095

Section 477A Relief for energy efficient works.

Section 980 Deduction from consideration on disposal of certain assets.

Section 1104 Short title and construction.

1096 Assessment of Electricity Supply Board

[ITA67 s545(1)]

For the purpose of determining liability for assessment to and payment of income tax, the Electricity Supply Board is not and never was the State or a branch or department of the Government of the State.

1096A Construction of references to oaths, etc

[(1) Without prejudice to any express provision made elsewhere in those Acts in that behalf, references in the Tax Acts and the Capital Gains Tax Acts to an oath shall, in the case of persons for the time being allowed by law to affirm instead of swearing, be construed as including references to an affirmation, and references in those Acts to the administration, taking or swearing of an oath shall be construed accordingly.

(2) In *subsection (1)* "*law*" includes the Oaths Act, 1888, and, without prejudice to their application by virtue of any other provision of the Tax Acts or the Capital Gains Tax Acts, the Oaths Act, 1888, and every other enactment for the time being in force authorising an oath to be taken or an affirmation to be made in any particular manner, shall apply to an oath required to be taken or an affirmation required to be made by the Tax Acts or the Capital Gains Tax Acts.][1]

Amendments

[1] Inserted by FA99 s30.

1096B Evidence of computer stored records in court proceedings etc

[(1) In this section—

"*copy record*" means any copy of an original record or a copy of that copy made in accordance with either of the methods referred to in *subsection (2)* and accompanied by the certificate referred to in *subsection (4)*, which original record or copy of an original record is in the possession of the Revenue Commissioners;

"*original record*" means any document, record or record of an entry in a document or record or information stored by means of any storage equipment, whether or not in a legible form, made or stored by the Revenue Commissioners for the purposes of or in connection with tax, and which is in the possession of the Revenue Commissioners;

"*provable record*" means an original record or a copy record and, in the case of an original record or a copy record stored in any storage equipment, whether or not in a legible form, includes the production or reproduction of the record in a legible form;

"*storage equipment*" means any electronic, magnetic, mechanical, photographic, optical or other device used for storing information;

"*tax*" means any tax, duty, levy or charge under the care and management of the Revenue Commissioners.

(2) Where by reason of—

(a) the deterioration of,

(b) the inconvenience in storing, or

(c) the technical obsolescence in the manner of retaining or storing,

any original record or any copy record, the Revenue Commissioners may—

(i) make a legible copy of that record, or

(ii) store information concerning that record otherwise than in a legible form so that the information is capable of being used to make a legible copy of that record,

and, they may, thereupon destroy that original record or that copy record.

(3) The legible copy of—

(a) a record made, or

(b) the information concerning such record stored,

in accordance with *subsection (2)* shall be deemed to be an original record for the purposes of this section.

(4) In any proceedings a certificate signed by an officer of the Revenue Commissioners stating that a copy record has been made in accordance with the provisions of *subsection (2)* shall be evidence of the fact of the making of such a copy record and that it is a true copy, unless the contrary is shown.

(5) In any proceedings a document purporting to be a certificate signed by an officer of the Revenue Commissioners, referred to in *subsection (4)*, shall for the purposes of this section be deemed to be such a certificate and to be so signed unless the contrary is shown.

(6) A provable record shall be admissible in evidence in any proceedings and shall be evidence of any fact stated in it or event recorded by it unless the contrary is shown, or unless the court is not satisfied as to the reliability of the system used to make or compile—

(a) in the case of an original record, that record, and

(b) in the case of a copy record, the original on which it was based.

(7) In any proceedings a certificate signed by an officer of the Revenue Commissioners, stating that a full and detailed search has been made for a record of any event in every place where such records are kept and that no such record has been found,

shall be evidence that the event did not happen unless the contrary is shown or unless the court is not satisfied—

(a) as to the reliability of the system used to compile or make or keep such records,

(b) that, if the event had happened, a record would have been made of it, and

(c) that the system is such that the only reasonable explanation for the absence of such record is that the event did not happen.

(8) For the purposes of this section, and subject to the direction and control of the Revenue Commissioners, any power, function or duty conferred or imposed on them may be exercised or performed on their behalf by an officer of the Revenue Commissioners.][1]

Amendments

[1] Inserted by FA02 s135.

PART 49

Commencement, Repeals, Transitional Provisions, etc.

1097 Commencement

(1) Except where otherwise provided by or under this Act, this Act shall be deemed to have come into force—

(a) in relation to income tax, for the year 1997-98 and subsequent years of assessment,

(b) in relation to corporation tax, for accounting periods ending on or after the 6th day of April, 1997, and

(c) in relation to capital gains tax, for the year 1997-98 and subsequent years of assessment.

(2) So much of any provision of this Act as—

(a) authorises the making, variation or revocation of any order or regulation or other instrument,

(b) relates to the making of a return, the furnishing of a certificate or statement or the giving of any information, including any such provision which imposes a duty or obligation on—

(i) the Revenue Commissioners or on an inspector or other officer of the Revenue Commissioners, or

(ii) any other person,

(c) imposes a fine, forfeiture or penalty,

(d) (i) except where the tax concerned is all income tax for years of assessment before the year 1997-98, confers any power or imposes any duty or obligation the exercise or performance of which operates or may operate in relation to income tax for more than one year of assessment,

(ii) except where the tax concerned is all corporation tax for accounting periods ending before the 6th day of April, 1997, confers any power or imposes any duty or obligation the exercise or performance of which operates or may operate in relation to corporation tax for more than one accounting period, and

(iii) except where the tax concerned is all capital gains tax for years of assessment before the year 1997-98, confers any power or imposes any duty or obligation the exercise or performance of which operates or may operate in relation to capital gains tax for more than one year of assessment,

and

(e) relates to any tax or duty, other than income tax, corporation tax or capital gains tax,

shall be deemed to have come into force on the 6th day of April, 1997, in substitution for the corresponding provisions of the repealed enactments.

(3) For the purposes of *subsection (2)*, anything done under or in connection with the provisions of the repealed enactments which correspond to the provisions of this Act referred to in that subsection shall be deemed to have been done under or in connection with the provisions of this Act to which those provisions of

the repealed enactments correspond; but nothing in this subsection shall affect the operation of *subsections (3)* and *(4)* of *section 1102*.

(4) Notwithstanding *subsection (2)*, any provision of the repealed enactments which imposes a fine, forfeiture, penalty or punishment for any act or omission shall, in relation to any act or omission which took place or began before the 6th day of April, 1997, continue to apply in substitution for the provision of this Act to which it corresponds.

(5) If, and in so far as, by virtue of *subsection (2)*, a provision of this Act operates from the 6th day of April, 1997, in substitution for a provision of the repealed enactments, any order or regulation made or having effect as if made, and any thing done or having effect as if done, under the excluded provision before that date shall be treated as from that date as if it were an order or regulation made or a thing done under that provision of this Act.

Cross References

From Section 1097

Section 1102 Continuity and construction of certain references to old and new law.

To Section 1097

Section 1098 Repeals.

1098 Repeals

(1) The enactments mentioned in *column (2)* of *Schedule 30* (which in this Act are referred to as "*the repealed enactments*") are hereby repealed as on and from the 6th day of April, 1997, to the extent specified in *column (3)* of that Schedule.

(2) *Subsection (1)* shall come into force in accordance with *section 1097*, and accordingly, except where otherwise provided by that section, this Act shall not apply—

(a) to income tax for the year 1996-97 or any previous year of assessment,

(b) to corporation tax for accounting periods ending before the 6th day of April, 1997, and

(c) to capital gains tax for the year 1996-97 or any previous year of assessment,

and the repealed enactments shall continue to apply—

(i) to income tax for any year mentioned in *paragraph (a)*,

(ii) to corporation tax for any period mentioned in *paragraph (b)*, and

(iii) to capital gains tax for any year mentioned in *paragraph (c)*,

to the same extent that they would have applied if this Act had not been enacted.

Cross References

From Section 1098

Section 1097 Commencement.

Schedule 30 Repeals

To Section 1098

Section 1 Interpretation of this Act.

Schedule 30 Repeals

1099 Saving for enactments not repealed

This Act (other than *subsections (2)* to *(4)* of *section 1102*) shall apply subject to so much of any Act as contains provisions relating to or affecting income tax, corporation tax or capital gains tax as—

(a) is not repealed by this Act, and

(b) would have operated in relation to those taxes respectively if this Act had not been substituted for the repealed enactments.

Cross References

From Section 1099

Section 1102 Continuity and construction of certain references to old and new law.

1100 Consequential amendments to other enactments

Schedule 31, which provides for amendments to other enactments consequential on the passing of this Act, shall apply for the purposes of this Act.

Cross References

From Section 1100

Schedule 31 Consequential Amendments

To Section 1100

Schedule 31 Consequential Amendments

1101 Transitional provisions

Schedule 32, which contains transitional provisions, shall apply for the purposes of this Act.

Cross References

From Section 1101

Schedule 32 Transitional Provisions

To Section 1101

Schedule 32 Transitional Provisions

1102 Continuity and construction of certain references to old and new law

(1) The Revenue Commissioners shall have all the jurisdictions, powers and duties in relation to tax under this Act which they had before the passing of this Act.

(2) The continuity of the operation of the law relating to income tax, corporation tax and capital gains tax shall not be affected by the substitution of this Act for the repealed enactments.

(3) Any reference, whether express or implied, in any enactment or document (including this Act and any Act amended by this Act)—

(a) to any provision of this Act, or

(b) to things done or to be done under or for the purposes of any provision of this Act,

shall, if and in so far as the nature of the reference permits, be construed as including, in relation to the times, years or periods, circumstances or purposes in relation to which the corresponding provision in the repealed enactments applied or had applied, a reference to, or, as the case may be, to things done or to be done under or for the purposes of that corresponding provision.

(4) Any reference, whether express or implied, in any enactment or document (including the repealed enactments and enactments passed and documents made after the passing of this Act)—

(a) to any provision of the repealed enactments, or

(b) to things done or to be done under or for the purposes of any provision of the repealed enactments, shall, if and in so far as the nature of the reference permits, be construed as including, in relation to the times, years or periods, circumstances or purposes in relation to which the corresponding provision of this Act applies, a reference to, or as the case may be, to things done or deemed to be done or to be done under or for the purposes of that corresponding provision.

(5) Notwithstanding any other provision of this Act, no act, whether of commission or omission, which was committed or occurred before the 6th day of April, 1997, and was not an offence at the time of commission or omission, shall be an offence in the period from the 6th day of April, 1997, to the date of the passing of this Act.

Cross References

To Section 1102

Section 1097 Commencement.

Section 1099 Saving for enactments not repealed.

1103 Continuance of officers, instruments and documents

(1) All officers appointed under the repealed enactments and holding office immediately before the commencement of this Act shall continue in office as if appointed under this Act.

(2) All officers who immediately before the commencement of this Act stood authorised or nominated for the purposes of any provision of the repealed enactments shall be deemed to be authorised or nominated, as the case may be, for the purposes of the corresponding provision of this Act.

(3) All instruments, documents, authorisations and letters or notices of appointment made or issued under the repealed enactments and in force immediately before the commencement of this Act shall continue in force as if made or issued under this Act.

1104 Short title and construction

(1) This Act may be cited as the Taxes Consolidation Act, 1997.

(2) *Sections 7, 858, 859, 872(1), 905, 906, 910, 912, 1002, 1078, 1079* and *1093* (in so far as relating to Customs) shall be construed together with the Customs Acts and (in so far as relating to duties of excise) shall be construed together with the statutes which relate to the duties of excise and to the management of those duties.

(3) *Sections 7, 811, 858, 859, 872(1), 887, 905, 906, 910* and *912*, *subsections (2)* and *(3)* of [*section 959G*][1], and *sections 1001, 1002, 1006, 1078, 1079, 1086, 1093, 1094* and *1095* (in so far as relating to value-added tax) shall be construed together with the Value-Added Tax Consolidation Act 2010.

(4) *Sections 7, 8, 811, 858, 859, 872(1), 875, 905, 906, 910, 1002, 1078, 1079, 1086* and *1093* (in so far as relating to stamp duties) shall be construed together with the [Stamp Duties Consolidation Act 1999,][2] and the enactments amending or extending that Act.

(5) *Sections 7, 8, 811, 858, 859, 872(1), 887, 905, 906, 910, 912, 1002, 1003, 1006, 1078, 1079, 1086* and *1093* (in so far as relating to capital acquisitions tax) and *Part 34* (in so far as relating to capital acquisitions tax) shall be construed together with the Capital Acquisitions Tax Consolidation Act 2003, and the enactments amending or extending that Act.

(6) *Sections 7*, *811*, *859*, *872(1)*, *887*, *905*, *906*, *910*, *912*, *1006*, *1078*, *1086* and *1093* (in so far as they relate to Part VI of the Finance Act, 1983) shall be construed together with that Part and enactments amending or extending that Part.

Amendments

[1] Substituted by FA12 sched4(part 2)(g).

[2] Substituted by FA08 sched8(1)(t). Has effect as on and from 13 March 2008.

Cross References

From Section 1104

Section 7 Application to certain taxing statutes of Age of Majority Act, 1985.
Section 8 Construction of certain taxing statutes in accordance with Status of Children Act, 1987.
Section 811 Transactions to avoid liability to tax.
Section 818 Interpretation (Part 34).
Section 858 Evidence of authorisation.
Section 859 Anonymity of authorised officers in relation to certain matters.
Section 872 Use of information relating to other taxes and duties.
Section 875 Exemption of appraisements and valuations from stamp duty.
Section 887 Use of electronic data processing.
Section 905 Inspection of documents and records.
Section 906 Authorised officers and Garda Síochána.
Section 910 Power to obtain information from Minister of the Government.
Section 912 Computer documents and records.
Section 928 Transmission to Collector-General of particulars of sums to be collected.
Section 1001 Liability to tax, etc. of holder of fixed charge on book debts of company.
Section 1002 Deduction from payments due to defaulters of amounts due in relation to tax.
Section 1003 Payment of tax by means of donation of heritage items.
Section 1006 Poundage and certain other fees due to sheriffs or county registrars.
Section 1078 Revenue offences.
Section 1079 Duties of relevant person in relation to certain revenue offences.
Section 1086 Publication of names of tax defaulters.
Section 1093 Disclosure of information to Ombudsman.
Section 1094 Tax clearance certificates in relation to certain licences.
Section 1095 Tax clearance certificates: general scheme.

SCHEDULE 1

Supplementary Provisions Concerning the Extension of Charge to Tax to Profits and Income Derived from Activities Carried on and Employments Exercised on the Continental Shelf

Sections 13 and *567(4)*.

[FA73 Sch3 pars1, 3, 4, 5, 7 and 8; CTA76 s140(1) and Sch2 PtI par36(1) and (3) and s164 and Sch3 PtII]

Information

1. The holder of a licence granted under the Petroleum and Other Minerals Development Act, 1960, shall, if required to do so by a notice served on such holder by an inspector, give to the inspector within the time limited by the notice (which shall not be less than 30 days) such particulars as may be required by the notice of—

   (a) transactions in connection with activities authorised by the licence as a result of which any person is or might be liable to income tax by virtue of *section 13* or to corporation tax by virtue of that section as applied by *section 23*, and

   (b) emoluments paid or payable in respect of duties performed in an area in which those activities may be carried on under the licence and the persons to whom they were paid or are payable,

   and shall take reasonable steps to obtain the information necessary to enable such holder to comply with the notice.

Collection

2.

(1) Subject to the following provisions of this Schedule, where any income tax is assessed by virtue of *section 13*, or any corporation tax is assessed by virtue of that section as applied by *section 23*, on a person not resident in the State in respect of—

   (a) profits or gains from activities authorised, or carried on in connection with activities authorised, by a licence granted under the Petroleum and Other Minerals Development Act, 1960, or

   (b) profits or gains arising from exploration or exploitation rights connected with activities so authorised or carried on,

   and any of the tax remains unpaid later than 30 days after it has become due and payable, the Revenue Commissioners may serve a notice on the holder of the licence (in this paragraph referred to as "*the holder*") specifying particulars of the assessment, the amount of tax remaining unpaid and the date when it became payable, and requiring the holder to pay that amount, together with any interest due on that amount under *section 1080*, within 30 days of the service of the notice.

(2) Any amount of tax which the holder is required to pay by a notice under this paragraph may be recovered from the holder as if it were tax due and duly demanded from the holder, and the holder may recover any such amount paid by the holder from the person on whom the assessment was made as a simple contract debt in any court of competent jurisdiction.

3. *Paragraph 2* shall not apply to any assessment to income tax on emoluments from an office or employment referred to in *section 13(5)*.

4. *Paragraph 2* shall not apply if the profits or gains in respect of which the relevant assessment was made arose to the person on whom it was made in consequence of a contract made by the holder of the licence before the 16th day of May, 1973, unless that person is a person connected with the holder of the licence or the contract was varied on or after that date.

5. Where, on an application made by a person who will or might become liable to tax which if remaining unpaid could be recovered under *paragraph 2* from the holder of a licence, the Revenue Commissioners are satisfied that the applicant will comply with any obligations imposed on the applicant by the Tax Acts, they may issue a certificate to the holder of the licence exempting that holder from the application of that paragraph with respect to any tax payable by the applicant and, where such a certificate is issued, that paragraph shall not apply to any such tax which becomes due while the certificate is in force.

6. The Revenue Commissioners may, by notice in writing given to the holder of a certificate issued under *paragraph 5*, cancel the certificate from such date, not earlier than 30 days after the service of the notice, as may be specified in the notice.

Interpretation

[7. In this Schedule a reference to a licence granted under the Petroleum and Other Minerals Development Act, 1960, includes a reference to a lease granted under that Act.][1]

Amendments

[1] Inserted by FA01 s44(c).

Cross References

From Schedule 1

Section 13 Extension of charge to income tax to profits and income derived from activities carried on and employments exercised on the Continental Shelf.
Section 23 Application of section 13 for purposes of corporation tax.
Section 567 Nominees, bare trustees and agents.
Section 1080 Interest on overdue income tax, corporation tax and capital gains tax.

To Schedule 1

Section 13 Extension of charge to income tax to profits and income derived from activities carried on and employments exercised on the Continental Shelf.
Section 567 Nominees, bare trustees and agents.
Section 913 Application of income tax provisions relating to returns, etc.
Schedule 29 Provisions Referred to in Sections 1052, 1053 and 1054

SCHEDULE 2

Machinery for Assessment, Charge and Payment of Tax Under Schedule C and, in Certain Cases, Schedule D

Sections 33, 61 and *62.*

[ITA67 Sch1 PtsI and III to VI; F(MP)A68 s3(3) and Sch PtII, s3(4) and Sch PtIII and s3(5) and Sch PtIV; FA74 s11 and Sch1 PtII]

PART 1

Interpretation of Parts 2 to 4

1. *Section 32* shall apply for the interpretation of *Parts 2* to *4* of this Schedule as it applies for the interpretation of *Chapter 1* of *Part 3* of this Act, except that in *Part 4* of this Schedule "*dividends*" shall include all such interest, annuities or payments as are, within the meaning of *section 60*, dividends to which *Chapter 2* of *Part 4* of this Act applies.

[1A. In this Schedule—

'*chargeable person*' means any of the following:

(*a*) a person who is entrusted with the payment of any dividends which are payable to any persons in the State out of any public revenue;

(*b*) a person in the State who is entrusted with the payment of any dividends to which *Chapter 2* of *Part 4* applies;

(*c*) a banker or other person in the State who obtains payment of any dividends in such circumstances that the dividends are chargeable to income tax under *Schedule C* or, in the case of dividends to which *Chapter 2* of *Part 4* applies, under *Schedule D*;

(*d*) a banker in the State who sells or otherwise realises coupons in such manner that the proceeds of the sale or realisation are chargeable to income tax under *Schedule C* or, in the case of dividends to which *Chapter 2* of *Part 4* applies, under *Schedule D*;

(*e*) a dealer in coupons in the State who purchases coupons in such manner that the price paid on the purchase is chargeable to income tax under *Schedule C* or, in the case of dividends to which *Chapter 2* of *Part 4* applies, under *Schedule D*;

'*specified dividend income*' means—

(*a*) the amount of dividends which are payable to any person in the State out of any public revenue,

(*b*) the amount of dividends to which *Chapter 2* of *Part 4* applies,

(*c*) the amount of dividends received by a chargeable person in the State in such circumstances that the dividends are chargeable to income tax under *Schedule C* or, in the case of dividends to which *Chapter 2* of Part 4 applies, under *Schedule D*,

(*d*) the proceeds of sale or realisation of coupons where those proceeds are chargeable to income tax under *Schedule C* or, in the case of dividends to which *Chapter 2* of Part 4 applies, under *Schedule D*, or (*e*) the price paid on purchase of coupons where such price paid on purchase is chargeable to income tax under Schedule C or, in the case of dividends to which *Chapter 2* of *Part 4* applies, under *Schedule D*.][1]

PART 2

Public Revenue Dividends, etc., Payable to the Bank of Ireland, or Entrusted for Payment to the Bank of Ireland [Deleted]

[Deleted by FA12 s38(1)(e). With effect from 1 January 2013 per S.I. No. 561 of 2012.]

PART 3

Public Revenue Dividends Payable by Public Offices and Departments [Deleted]

[Deleted by FA12 s38(1)(e). With effect from 1 January 2013 per S.I. No. 561 of 2012.]

PART 4

[Public Revenue Dividends, Dividends to Which Chapter 2 of Part 4 Applies, Proceeds of Coupons and Price Paid on Purchase of Coupons

14. (1) Subject to *Chapter 2* of *Part 3*, every chargeable person shall, on making a payment of specified dividend income, deduct and retain a sum representing the amount of the income tax due on that income and pay that income tax on behalf of the person entitled to that income.

(2) The payment of the income tax by the chargeable person shall be deemed to be a payment of the income tax by the persons entitled to the specified dividend income and shall be allowed by those persons on the receipt of the residue of the dividends.

15. (1) Every chargeable person who makes a payment of specified dividend income shall make for each year of assessment within 20 days from the end of the year of assessment, a return to the Collector-General of that specified dividend income and of the income tax in relation to that specified dividend income.

(2) The income tax in relation to payments of specified dividend income which is required to be included in a return shall—

(*a*) be due at the time by which the return is to be made, and

(*b*) be paid by the chargeable person to the Collector-General,

and the income tax so due shall be payable by the chargeable person without the making of an assessment; but income tax which has become so due may be assessed on the chargeable person (whether or not it has been paid when the assessment is made) if that tax or any part of it is not paid on or before the due date.

(3) A return due under this Schedule shall be in a form prescribed by the Revenue Commissioners and shall include a declaration to the effect that the return is correct and complete.

16. (1) Where it appears to the inspector that there is any amount of income tax in relation to a payment of specified dividend income which should have been but was not included in a return or where the inspector is dissatisfied with any return, the inspector may make an assessment on the chargeable person to the best of his or her judgement. Any amount of income tax in relation to a payment of specified dividend income due under an assessment made by virtue of this subparagraph shall be treated for the purpose of interest on unpaid tax as having been payable at the time when it would have been payable if a correct return had been made.

(2) Any income tax assessed on a chargeable person under this Schedule shall be due within one month after the issue of the notice of assessment (unless that tax is due earlier under *paragraph 15*) subject to any appeal against the assessment, but no such appeal shall affect the date when any amount is due under *paragraph 15*.

(3) On the determination of an appeal against an assessment under this Chapter, any income tax overpaid shall be repaid.

17. Where any item has been incorrectly included in a return as income tax, the inspector may make such assessments, adjustments or set-offs as may in his or her judgement be required for securing that the resulting liabilities to tax, including interest on unpaid tax, whether of the chargeable person or any other person, are in so far as possible the same as they would have been if the item had not been so included.

18. (1) A chargeable person shall keep records to distinguish the separate accounts of each of the persons entitled to receive specified dividend income and such records shall include—

(*a*) the name and address of each such person,

(*b*) particulars of the amounts payable, and

(*c*) in the case of amounts payable out of any public revenue, particulars of the public revenue out of which each separate amount is payable.

(2) Records kept by a chargeable person in accordance with *subparagraph (1)* shall—

(*a*) be kept and retained by the chargeable person for a period of 6 years from the day on which the payment was made, and

(*b*) on being required by notice in writing given to the chargeable person by an inspector, be made available to the inspector within the time specified in the notice.

19. The provisions of *section 898N* shall apply with any necessary modifications as respects powers of an authorised officer as if a reference in that section to—

(*a*) books and records were a reference to books and records kept for the purposes of this Schedule,

(*b*) an authorised officer in that section were a reference to a Revenue officer as defined in *section 898B*, and

(*c*) a reference in that section to a paying agent were a reference to a chargeable person.

20. The provisions of the Income Tax Acts relating to—

(*a*) assessments to income tax,

(*b*) appeals against such assessments (including the rehearing of appeals and the statement of a case for the opinion of the High Court), and

(*c*) the collection and recovery of income tax,

shall, in so far as they are applicable, apply to the assessment, collection and recovery of income tax due under this Schedule.

21. (1) Any amount of income tax payable in accordance with this Schedule shall, without the making of an assessment, carry interest from the date when the amount becomes due and payable until payment for any day or part of a day during which the amount remains unpaid, at a rate of 0.0274 per cent.

(2) *Subsections (3)* to *(5)* of *section 1080* shall apply in relation to interest payable under *subparagraph (1)* as they apply in relation to interest payable under *section 1080*.

(3) In its application to any income tax charged by any assessment made in accordance with this Schedule, *section 1080* shall apply as if *subsection (2)(b)* of that section were deleted.

22. Where—

(*a*) income tax in respect of the proceeds of the sale or realisation of any coupon or in respect of the price paid on the purchase of any coupon has been accounted for under this Part by any banker or any dealer in coupons, and

(*b*) the Revenue Commissioners are satisfied that the dividends payable on the coupons in relation to which such proceeds or such price arises have been subsequently paid in such manner that income tax has been deducted from such dividends under any of the provisions of this Schedule,

then the income tax so deducted shall be repaid.][2]

PART 5

Relief from Obligation to Pay Tax on Certain Interest, Dividends and Other Annual Payments in the Case of Persons Entrusted with Payment

23. When any interest, dividends or other annual payments payable out of any public revenue other than that of the State, or in respect of the stocks, funds, shares or securities of any body of persons not resident in the State, are entrusted to any person in the State for payment to any person in the State, the Revenue Commissioners shall have power to relieve the person so entrusted with payment from the obligation to pay the income tax on such interest, dividends or other annual payments imposed on such person by *section 17* and *Chapter 1* of *Part 3*, or *Chapter 2* of *Part 4* and this Schedule.

24. When granting the relief referred to in *paragraph 23* the Revenue Commissioners shall have power to prescribe any conditions which may appear to them to be necessary to ensure the assessment and payment of any income tax assessable and payable in respect of such interest, dividends or other annual payments under the Income Tax Acts.

25. A letter signed by a Secretary or an Assistant Secretary of the Revenue Commissioners stating that the Revenue Commissioners have exercised all or

any of the powers conferred by this Part on them or the publication of a notice to that effect in Iris Oifigiúil shall be sufficient evidence that they have done so.

26. When, under the powers conferred on the Revenue Commissioners by this Part, the person entrusted with the payment of the interest, dividends or other annual payments is relieved from payment of the income tax on such interest, dividends or other annual payments, that tax shall be assessable and chargeable under the appropriate case of Schedule D on the person entitled to receive such interest, dividends or other annual payments and shall be payable by that person.

[…][3]

[28. Notwithstanding *paragraph 23*, when any interest, dividends or other annual payments payable out of any public revenue other than that of the State, or in respect of the stocks, funds, shares or securities of any body of persons not resident in the State, are entrusted to any person in the State for payment to an investment undertaking within the meaning of *section 739B* and the person so entrusted would, apart from this paragraph, have an obligation imposed by *section 17* and *Chapter 1* of *Part 3*, or *Chapter 2* of *Part 4* and this Schedule, to pay the income tax on such interest, dividends or other annual payments, that obligation shall not apply.][4]

Amendments

[1] Inserted by FA12 s38(1)(d). With effect from 1 January 2013 per S.I. No. 561 of 2012.

[2] Substituted by FA12 s38(1)(f). With effect from 1 January 2013 per S.I. No. 561 of 2012.

[3] Deleted by FA12 s38(1)(g). With effect from 1 January 2013 per S.I. No. 561 of 2012.

[4] Inserted by FA06 s46(1). Applies as respects any payments on or after the date of 31 March 2006

Cross References

From Schedule 2

Section 12 The charge to income tax.
Section 17 Schedule C.
Section 32 Interpretation (Chapter 1).
Section 33 Method of charge and payment.
Section 52 Persons chargeable.
Section 60 Interpretation (Chapter 2).
Section 61 Dividends entrusted for payment in the State.
Section 62 Dividends paid outside the State and proceeds of sale of dividend coupons.
Section 739B Interpretation and application.

To Schedule 2

Section 33 Method of charge and payment.
Section 61 Dividends entrusted for payment in the State.
Section 62 Dividends paid outside the State and proceeds of sale of dividend coupons.
Section 64 Interest on quoted Eurobonds.
Schedule 29 Provisions Referred to in Sections 1052, 1053 and 1054

SCHEDULE 2A

Dividend Withholding Tax

[*Section 172A.*

Interpretation

1. In this Schedule—

"*appropriate person*", in relation to a pension scheme, means—

(a) in the case of an exempt approved scheme (within the meaning of *section 774*), the administrator (within the meaning of *section 770*) of the scheme,

(b) in the case of a retirement annuity contract to which *section 784* or *785* applies, the person lawfully carrying on in the State the business of granting annuities on human life with whom the contract is made, and

(c) in the case of a trust scheme to which *section 784* or *785* applies, the trustees of the trust scheme;

"*beneficiary*", in relation to a trust, means any person (in this definition referred to as "*the first-mentioned person*") who, directly or indirectly, is beneficially entitled under the trust, or may, through the exercise of any power or powers conferred on any person or persons, reasonably expect to become so beneficially entitled, to income or capital or to have any income or capital applied for the first-mentioned person's benefit or to receive any other benefit;

"*settlor*", in relation to a trust, includes any person who has provided or undertaken to provide assets or income directly or indirectly for the purposes of the trust;

"*trust*" means any trust, disposition, settlement, covenant, agreement or arrangement established, made or entered into by one or more than one settlor, whereby—

(a) assets, which may or may not change from time to time in the course of the management of the trust, or

(b) income, the sources and nature of which may or may not also so change from time to time,

beneficially owned by the settlor or settlors are or is vested in a person or persons (in this Schedule referred to as the "*trustee*" or "*trustees*") to be—

(i) either or both held and managed for,

(ii) paid over to, or

(iii) applied for,

the benefit of any beneficiary or beneficiaries, but does not include a pension fund, charity or undertaking for collective investment in transferable securities which is established or regulated under the law of any relevant territory.

Currency of certain certificates

2. A certificate referred to in [*paragraph 8(f)*[...][1]][2] shall be treated as a current certificate for the period from the date of the issue of the certificate to the 31st day of December in the fifth year following the year in which the certificate was issued.

Currency of certain declarations

[2A. A declaration referred to in paragraph 9 shall be treated as a current declaration for the period from the date of the making of the declaration to the 31st day of December in the fifth year following the year in which the declaration was made.][3]

Declaration to be made by company resident in the State

3. The declaration referred to in *section 172C(2)(a)* shall be a declaration in writing to the relevant person in relation to the relevant distributions which—

(a) is made by the person (in this paragraph referred to as "*the declarer*") beneficially entitled to the relevant distributions in respect of which the declaration is made,

(b) is signed by the declarer,

(c) is made in such form as may be prescribed or authorised by the Revenue Commissioners,

(d) declares that, at the time when the declaration is made, the person beneficially entitled to the relevant distributions is a company resident in the State,

(e) contains the name and tax reference number of the company,

(f) contains an undertaking by the declarer that, if the person mentioned in *subparagraph (d)* ceases to be an excluded person, the declarer will, by notice in writing, advise the relevant person in relation to the relevant distributions accordingly, and

(g) contains such other information as the Revenue Commissioners may reasonably require for the purposes of *Chapter 8A* of *Part 6*.

Declaration to be made by pension scheme

4. The declaration referred to in *section 172C(2)(b)* shall be a declaration in writing to the relevant person in relation to the relevant distributions which—

(a) is made by the person (in this paragraph referred to as "*the declarer*") beneficially entitled to the relevant distributions in respect of which the declaration is made,

(b) is signed by the declarer,

(c) is made in such form as may be prescribed or authorised by the Revenue Commissioners,

(d) declares that, at the time when the declaration is made, the person beneficially entitled to the relevant distributions is a pension scheme,

(e) contains the name and tax reference number of the pension scheme,

(f) contains a certificate by the appropriate person in relation to the pension scheme that, to the best of that person's knowledge and belief, the declaration made in accordance with *subparagraph (d)* and the information furnished in accordance with *subparagraph (e)* are true and correct,

(g) contains an undertaking by the declarer that, if the person mentioned in *subparagraph (d)* ceases to be an excluded person, the declarer will, by notice in writing, advise the relevant person in relation to the relevant distributions accordingly, and

(h) contains such other information as the Revenue Commissioners may reasonably require for the purposes of *Chapter 8A* of *Part 6*.

Declaration to be made by qualifying fund manager or qualifying savings manager

[4A. The declaration referred to in *section 172C(2)(ba)(ii)* shall be a declaration in writing to the relevant person which—

(a) is made by the person (in this paragraph referred to as the "*declarer*") beneficially entitled to the relevant distribution in respect of which the declaration is made,

(b) is signed by the declarer,

(c) is made in such form as may be prescribed or authorised by the Revenue Commissioners,

(d) declares that, at the time the declaration is made, the person beneficially entitled to the relevant distribution is a person referred to in *section 172C(2)(ba)(i)*,

(e) contains the name and tax reference number of the person,

(f) contains a statement that, at the time when the declaration is made, the relevant distribution in respect of which the declaration is made will be applied as income of an approved retirement fund, an approved minimum retirement fund or, as the case may be, a special savings incentive account,

(g) contains an undertaking that, if the person mentioned in *paragraph (d)* ceases to be an excluded person, the declarer will, by notice in writing, advise the relevant person in relation to the relevant distribution accordingly, and

(h) contains such other information as the Revenue Commissioners may reasonably require for the purposes of *Chapter 8A* of *Part 6*.][4]

Declaration to be made by qualifying employee share ownership trust

5. The declaration referred to in *section 172C(2)(c)* shall be a declaration in writing to the relevant person in relation to the relevant distributions which—

(a) is made by the person (in this paragraph referred to as "*the declarer*") beneficially entitled to the relevant distributions in respect of which the declaration is made,

(b) is signed by the declarer,

(c) is made in such form as may be prescribed or authorised by the Revenue Commissioners,

(d) declares that, at the time when the declaration is made, the person beneficially entitled to the relevant distributions is a qualifying employee share ownership trust,

(e) contains the name and address of that person,

(f) contains a statement that at the time when the declaration is made the relevant distributions in respect of which the declaration is made will form part of the income of the qualifying employee share ownership trust and will be applied in accordance with the provisions of *paragraph 13* of *Schedule 12*,

(g) contains an undertaking by the declarer that, if the person mentioned in *subparagraph (d)* ceases to be an excluded person, the declarer will, by notice in writing, advise the relevant person in relation to the relevant distributions accordingly, and

(h) contains such other information as the Revenue Commissioners may reasonably require for the purposes of *Chapter 8A* of *Part 6*.

Declaration to be made by collective investment undertaking

6. The declaration referred to in *section 172C(2)(d)* shall be a declaration in writing to the relevant person in relation to the relevant distributions which—

(a) is made by the person (in this paragraph referred to as "*the declarer*") beneficially entitled to the relevant distributions in respect of which the declaration is made,

(b) is signed by the declarer,

(c) is made in such form as may be prescribed or authorised by the Revenue Commissioners,

(d) declares that, at the time when the declaration is made, the person beneficially entitled to the relevant distributions is a collective investment undertaking,

(e) contains the name and tax reference number of the collective investment undertaking,

(f) contains an undertaking by the declarer that, if the person mentioned in *subparagraph (d)* ceases to be an excluded person, the declarer will, by notice in writing, advise the relevant person in relation to the relevant distributions accordingly, and

(g) contains such other information as the Revenue Commissioners may reasonably require for the purposes of *Chapter 8A* of *Part 6*.

Declaration to be made by persons entitled to exemption from income tax under Schedule F

[6A. The declaration referred to in *section 172C(2)(da)(ii)* shall be a declaration in writing to the relevant person which—

(a) is made by the person (in this paragraph referred to as "*the declarer*") beneficially entitled to the relevant distributions in respect of which the declaration is made,

(b) is signed by the declarer,

(c) is made in such form as may be prescribed or authorised by the Revenue Commissioners,

(d) declares that, at the time when the declaration is made, the person beneficially entitled to the relevant distribution is a person referred to in *section 172C(2)(da)(i)*,

(e) contains the name and tax reference number of the person,

(f) contains an undertaking by the declarer that, if the person mentioned in *subparagraph (d)* ceases to be an excluded person, the declarer will, by notice in writing, advise the relevant person in relation to the relevant distributions accordingly, and

(g) contains such other information as the Revenue Commissioners may reasonably require for the purposes of *Chapter 8A* of *Part 6*.][5]

Declaration to be made by charity

7. The declaration referred to in *section 172C(2)(e)(ii)* shall be a declaration in writing to the relevant person in relation to the relevant distributions which—

(a) is made by the person (in this paragraph referred to as "*the declarer*") beneficially entitled to the relevant distributions in respect of which the declaration is made,

(b) is signed by the declarer,

(c) is made in such form as may be prescribed or authorised by the Revenue Commissioners,

(d) declares that, at the time when the declaration is made, the person beneficially entitled to the relevant distributions is a person referred to in *section 172C(2)(e)(i)*,

(e) contains the name and address of that person,

(f) contains a statement that at the time when the declaration is made the relevant distributions in respect of which the declaration is made will be applied to charitable purposes only and—

(i) form part of the income of a body of persons or trust treated by the Revenue Commissioners as a body or trust established for charitable purposes only, or

(ii) are, according to the rules or regulations established by statute, charter, decree, deed of trust or will, applicable to charitable purposes only and are so treated by the Revenue Commissioners,

(g) contains an undertaking by the declarer that, if the person mentioned in *subparagraph (d)* ceases to be an excluded person, the declarer will, by notice in writing, advise the relevant person in relation to the relevant distributions accordingly, and

(h) contains such other information as the Revenue Commissioners may reasonably require for the purposes of *Chapter 8A* of *Part 6*.

Declaration to be made by approved athletic or amateur sports body

[7A. The declaration referred to in *section 172C(2)(f)(ii)* shall be a declaration in writing to the relevant person which—

(a) is made by the person (in this paragraph referred to as "*the declarer*") beneficially entitled to the relevant distributions in respect of which the declaration is made,

(b) is signed by the declarer,

(c) is made in such form as may be prescribed or authorised by the Revenue Commissioners,

(d) declares that, at the time when the declaration is made, the person beneficially entitled to the relevant distribution is a person referred to in *section 172C(2)(f)(i)*,

(e) contains the name and address of the person,

(f) contains a statement that, at the time when the declaration is made, the relevant distributions in respect of which the declaration is made will be applied for the sole purpose of promoting athletic or amateur games or sports and are so treated by the Revenue Commissioners,

(g) contains an undertaking by the declarer that, if the person mentioned in *subparagraph (d)* ceases to be an excluded person, the declarer will, by notice in writing, advise the relevant person in relation to the relevant distributions accordingly, and

(h) contains such other information as the Revenue Commissioners may reasonably require for the purposes of *Chapter 8A* of *Part 6*.

Declaration to be made by designated stockbroker operating special portfolio investment account

7B. The declaration referred to in *section 172C(2)(g)(ii)* shall be a declaration in writing to the relevant person which—

(a) is made by the person (in this paragraph referred to as "*the declarer*") beneficially entitled to the relevant distributions in respect of which the declaration is made,

(b) is signed by the declarer,

(c) is made in such form as may be prescribed or authorised by the Revenue Commissioners,

(d) declares that, at the time when the declaration is made, the person beneficially entitled to the relevant distribution is a person referred to in *section 172C(2)(g)(i)*,

(e) contains the name and tax reference number of the person,

(f) contains a statement that, at the time when the declaration is made, the relevant distributions in respect of which the declaration is made will be applied as all or part of the relevant income or gains (within the meaning of *section 838*) of a special portfolio investment account and are so treated by the Revenue Commissioners,

(g) contains an undertaking by the declarer that, if the person mentioned in *subparagraph (d)* ceases to be an excluded person, the declarer will, by notice in writing, advise the relevant person in relation to the relevant distributions accordingly, and

(h) contains such other information as the Revenue Commissioners may reasonably require for the purposes of *Chapter 8A* of *Part 6*.][6]

Declaration to be made by qualifying non-resident person, not being a company

8. The declaration referred to in *section 172D(3) (a) (iii)* shall be a declaration in writing to the relevant person in relation to the relevant distributions which—

(a) is made by the person (in this paragraph referred to as "*the declarer*") beneficially entitled to the relevant distributions in respect of which the declaration is made,

(b) is signed by the declarer,

(c) is made in such form as may be prescribed or authorised by the Revenue Commissioners,

(d) declares that, at the time when the declaration is made, the person beneficially entitled to the relevant distributions is a qualifying non-resident person,

(e) contains the name and address of that person,

(f) is accompanied by a certificate given by the tax authority of the relevant territory in which the person is, by virtue of the law of that territory, resident for the purposes of tax certifying that the person is so resident in that territory,

(g) in the case where the relevant distributions (or amounts or other assets representing such distributions) are to be received by a trust, is accompanied by—

(i) a certificate signed by the trustee or trustees of the trust which shall show the name and address of—

(I) the settlor or settlors in relation to the trust, and

(II) the beneficiary or beneficiaries in relation to the trust,

and

[(ii) a notice in writing from the Revenue Commissioners stating that the Commissioners have noted the contents of the certificate referred to in clause (i),][7]

(h) contains an undertaking by the declarer that, if the person mentioned in *subparagraph (d)* ceases to be a qualifying non-resident person, the declarer will, by notice in writing, advise the relevant person in relation to the relevant distributions accordingly, and

(i) contains such other information as the Revenue Commissioners may reasonably require for the purposes of *Chapter 8A* of *Part 6*.

Declaration to be made by qualifying non-resident person, being a company

9. The declaration referred to in *section 172D(3)(b)* shall be a declaration in writing to the relevant person in relation to the relevant distributions which—

(a) is made by the person (in this paragraph referred to as "*the declarer*") beneficially entitled to the relevant distributions in respect of which the declaration is made,

(b) is signed by the declarer,

(c) is made in such form as may be prescribed or authorised by the Revenue Commissioners,

(d) declares that, at the time when the declaration is made, the person beneficially entitled to the relevant distributions is a company which is a qualifying non-resident person,

[(e) contains—

(i) the name and address of that company,

(ii) the name of the territory in which the company is resident for the purposes of tax,

(iii) in the case of a company within the meaning of *section 172D(3)(b)(ii)*, the name of the relevant territory or names of the relevant territories, as the case may be, in which the person or persons who control (within the meaning of *section 172D(4)(a)*), whether directly or indirectly, the company is or are resident for the purposes of tax by virtue of the law of that territory or the laws of those territories, and

(iv) in the case of a company within the meaning of *section 172D(3)(b)(iii)*, the name and address of a recognised stock exchange on which the principal class of the shares of the company or

(I) where the company is a 75 per cent subsidiary (within the meaning of *section 172D(5)*) of another company, of that other company, or

(II) where the company is wholly owned (within the meaning of *section 172D(6)*) by 2 or more companies, of each of those companies,

is substantially and regularly traded,][8]

[…][9]

[…][10]

(h) contains an undertaking by the declarer that, if the person mentioned in *subparagraph (d)* ceases to be a qualifying non-resident person, the declarer will, by notice in writing, advise the relevant person in relation to the relevant distributions accordingly, and

(i) contains such other information as the Revenue Commissioners may reasonably require for the purposes of *Chapter 8A* of *Part 6*.

Declaration to be made by a PRSA administrator

[10. The declaration referred to in *section 172C(2)(bb)* shall be a declaration in writing to the relevant person which—

(a) is made by the person (in this paragraph referred to as the "*declarer*") beneficially entitled to the relevant distribution in respect of which the declaration is made,

(b) is signed by the declarer,

(c) is made in such form as may be prescribed or authorised by the Revenue Commissioners,

(d) declares that, at the time when the declaration is made, the person beneficially entitled to the relevant distribution is a person referred to in *section 172C(2)(bb)*,

(e) contains the name and tax reference number of the person,

(f) contains a statement that, at the time when the declaration is made, the relevant distribution in respect of which the declaration is made will be applied as income of a PRSA,

(g) contains an undertaking by the declarer that, if the person mentioned in *subparagraph (d)* ceases to be an excluded person, the declarer will, by notice in writing, advise the relevant person in relation to the relevant distribution accordingly, and

(h) contains such other information as the Revenue Commissioners may reasonably require for the purposes of *Chapter 8A* of *Part 6*.

Declaration to be made by exempt unit trust

11. The declaration referred to in *section 172C(2)(db)* shall be a declaration in writing to the relevant person which—

(a) is made by the person (in this paragraph referred to as the "*declarer*") beneficially entitled to the relevant distributions in respect of which the declaration is made,

(b) is signed by the declarer,

(c) is made in such form as may be prescribed or authorised by the Revenue Commissioners,

(d) declares that, at the time when the declaration is made, the person beneficially entitled to the relevant distribution is a person referred to in *section 172C(2)(db)*,

(e) contains the name and tax reference number of the person,

(f) contains a statement that, at the time when the declaration is made, the relevant distribution in respect of which the declaration is made will be applied as income of an exempt unit trust to which *section 731(5)(a)* applies,

(g) contains an undertaking by the declarer that, if the person mentioned in *subparagraph (d)* ceases to be an excluded person, the declarer will, by notice in writing, advise the relevant person in relation to the relevant distribution accordingly, and

(h) contains such other information as the Revenue Commissioners may reasonably require for the purposes of *Chapter 8A* of *Part 6*.][11]][12]

Amendments

[1] Deleted by FA10 s33(1)(e). Has effect as on and from 3 April 2010.

[2] Substituted by FA00 s30(2)(a).

[3] Inserted by FA10 s33(1)(f). Has effect as on and from 3 April 2010.

[4] Inserted by FA01 s43(2)(a).

[5] Inserted by FA01 s43(2)(b).

[6] Inserted by FA00 s30(2)(b).

[7] Substituted by FA00 s30(2)(c).

[8] Substituted by FA10 s33(1)(g). Has effect as on and from 3 April 2010.

[9] Deleted by FA10 s33(1)(h). Has effect as on and from 3 April 2010.

[10] Deleted by FA00 s30(2)(d)(ii).

[11] Inserted by FA05 s47(2). This section shall apply as on and from 3 February 2005.

[12] Inserted by FA99 s27(c).

Cross References

From Schedule 2A

Section 20 Schedule F.
Section 129 Irish resident company distributions not generally chargeable to corporation tax.
Section 172C Exemption from dividend withholding tax for certain persons.
Section 172D Exemption from dividend withholding tax for certain non-resident persons.
Section 172E Qualifying intermediaries.
Section 731 Chargeable gains accruing to unit trusts.
Section 770 Interpretation and supplemental (Chapter 1).
Section 774 Certain approved schemes: exemptions and reliefs.
Section 784 Retirement annuities: relief for premiums.
Section 785 Approval of contracts for dependants or for life assurance.
Section 838 Special portfolio investment accounts.
Schedule 12 Employee Share Ownership Trusts

To Schedule 2A

Section 172A Interpretation.
Section 172B Dividend withholding tax on relevant distributions.
Section 172C Exemption from dividend withholding tax for certain persons.
Section 172D Exemption from dividend withholding tax for certain non-resident persons.
Section 172J Credit for, or repayment of, dividend withholding tax borne.
Section 172M Delegation of powers and functions of Revenue Commissioners.

SCHEDULE 2B

Investment Undertakings: Declarations

[*Section 739D*

Interpretation

1. In this Schedule—

"*appropriate person*", in relation to a pension scheme, means—

(a) in the case of an exempt approved scheme (within the meaning of *section 774*), the administrator (within the meaning of *section 770*) of the scheme,

(b) in the case of a retirement annuity contract to which *section 784* or *785* applies, the person lawfully carrying on in the State the business of granting annuities on human life with whom the contract is made, and

(c) in the case of a trust scheme to which *section 784* or *785* applies, the trustees of the trust scheme;

"*tax reference number*", in relation to a person, has the meaning assigned to it by *section 885* in relation to a specified person within the meaning of that section.

Declarations of pension schemes

2. The declaration referred to in *section 739D(6)(a)* is a declaration in writing to the investment undertaking which—

(a) is made by the person (in this paragraph referred to as the "*declarer*") entitled to the units in respect of which the declaration is made,

(b) is signed by the declarer,

(c) is made in such form as may be prescribed or authorised by the Revenue Commissioners,

(d) declares that, at the time when the declaration is made, the person entitled to the units is a pension scheme,

(e) contains the name and tax reference number of the pension scheme,

(f) contains a certificate by the appropriate person in relation to the pension scheme that, to the best of that person's knowledge and belief, the declaration made in accordance with *subparagraph (d)* and the information furnished in accordance with *subparagraph (e)* are true and correct, and

(g) contains such other information as the Revenue Commissioners may reasonably require for the purposes of *Chapter 1A* of *Part 27*.

Declaration of company carrying on life business

3. The declaration referred to in *section 739D(6)(b)* is a declaration in writing to the investment undertaking which—

(a) is made by the person (in this paragraph referred to as the "*declarer*") entitled to the units in respect of which the declaration is made,

(b) is signed by the declarer,

(c) is made in such form as may be prescribed or authorised by the Revenue Commissioners,

(d) declares that, at the time when the declaration is made, the person entitled to the units is a company carrying on life business within the meaning of *section 706*,

(e) contains the name and tax reference number of the company, and

(f) contains such other information as the Revenue Commissioners may reasonably require for the purposes of *Chapter 1A* of *Part 27*.

Declarations of investment undertakings

4. The declaration referred to in *section 739D(6)(c)* is a declaration in writing to the investment undertaking which—

(a) is made by the person (in this paragraph referred to as the "*declarer*") entitled to the units in respect of which the declaration is made,

(b) is signed by the declarer,

(c) is made in such form as may be prescribed or authorised by the Revenue Commissioners,

(d) declares that, at the time the declaration is made, the person entitled to the units is an investment undertaking,

(e) contains the name and tax reference number of the investment undertaking, and

(f) contains such other information as the Revenue Commissioners may reasonably require for the purposes of *Chapter 1A* of *Part 27*.

[4A. The declaration referred to in *section 739D(6)(cc)* is a declaration in writing to the investment undertaking which—

(a) is made by the person (in this paragraph referred to as the "*declarer*") who holds the units in respect of which the declaration is made,

(b) is signed by the declarer,

(c) is made in such form as may be prescribed or authorised by the Revenue Commissioners,

(d) declares that, at the time the declaration is made, the holder of the units is a general partner acting on behalf of the investment limited partnership,

(e) contains the name and tax reference number of the investment limited partnership, and

(f) contains such other information as the Revenue Commissioners may reasonably require for the purposes of Chapter 1A of Part 27.][1]

Declarations of special investment scheme

5. The declaration referred to in *section 739D(6)(d)* is a declaration in writing to the investment undertaking which—

(a) is made by the person (in this paragraph referred to as the "*declarer*") entitled to the units in respect of which the declaration is made,

(b) is signed by the declarer,

(c) is made in such form as may be prescribed or authorised by the Revenue Commissioners,

(d) declares that, at the time the declaration is made, the person entitled to the units is a special investment scheme,

(e) contains the name and tax reference number of the special investment scheme, and

(f) contains such other information as the Revenue Commissioners may reasonably require for the purposes of *Chapter 1A* of *Part 27*.

Declarations of unit trust

6. The declaration referred to in *section 739D(6)(e)* is a declaration in writing to the investment undertaking which—

(a) is made by the person (in this paragraph referred to as the "*declarer*") entitled to the units in respect of which the declaration is made,

(b) is signed by the declarer,

(c) is made in such form as may be prescribed or authorised by the Revenue Commissioners,

(d) declares that, at the time the declaration is made, the person entitled to the units is a unit trust to which *section 731(5)(a)* applies,

(e) contains the name and tax reference number of the unit trust, and

(f) contains such other information as the Revenue Commissioners may reasonably require for the purposes of *Chapter 1A* of *Part 27*.

Declaration of charity

7. The declaration referred to in *section 739D(6)(f)* is a declaration in writing to the investment undertaking which—

(a) is made by the person (in this paragraph referred to as the "*declarer*") entitled to the units in respect of which the undertaking is made,

(b) is signed by the declarer,

(c) is made in such form as may be prescribed or authorised by the Revenue Commissioners,

(d) declares that, at the time when the declaration is made, the person entitled to the units is a person referred to in *section 739D(6)(f)(i)*,

(e) contains the name and address of that person,

(f) contains a statement that at the time when the declaration is made the units in respect of which the declaration is made are held for charitable purposes only and—

(i) form part of the assets of a body of persons or trust treated by the Revenue Commissioners as a body or trust established for charitable purposes only, or

(ii) are, according to the rules or regulations established by statute, charter, decree, deed of trust or will, held for charitable purposes only and are so treated by the Revenue Commissioners,

(g) contains an undertaking by the declarer that if the person mentioned in *subparagraph (d)* ceases to be a person referred to in *section 739D(6)(f)(i)*, the declarer will notify the investment undertaking accordingly, and

(h) contains such other information as the Revenue Commissioners may reasonably require for the purposes of *Chapter 1A* of *Part 27*.

Declaration of qualifying management company and specified company

8. The declaration referred to in *section 739D(6)(g)* is a declaration in writing to the investment undertaking which—

(a) is made by a person (in this paragraph referred to as the "*declarer*") who is entitled to the units in respect of which the declaration is made,

(b) is signed by the declarer,

(c) is made in such form as may be prescribed or authorised by the Revenue Commissioners,

(d) declares that, at the time the declaration is made, the person entitled to the units is a qualifying management company or, as the case may be, a specified company,

(e) contains the name and tax reference number of the declarer, and

(f) contains such other information as the Revenue Commissioners may reasonably require for the purposes of *Chapter 1A* of *Part 27*.

Declaration of qualifying fund manager or qualifying savings manager

[9. The declaration referred to in *section 739D(6)(h)* is a declaration in writing to the investment undertaking which—

(a) is made by a qualifying fund manager or, as the case may be, a qualifying savings manager (in this paragraph referred to as the "*declarer*") in respect of the units which are assets in an approved retirement fund, an approved minimum retirement fund, or a special savings incentive account,

(b) is signed by the declarer,

(c) is made in such form as may be prescribed or authorised by the Revenue Commissioners,

(d) declares that, at the time the declaration is made, the units in respect of which the declaration is made—

(i) are assets of an approved retirement fund, an approved minimum retirement fund or, as the case may be, a special savings incentive account, and

(ii) are managed by the declarer for the individual who is beneficially entitled to the units,

(e) contains the name, address and tax reference number of the individual referred to in *paragraph (d)*,

(f) contains an undertaking by the declarer that if the units cease to be assets of the approved retirement fund, the approved minimum retirement fund or held in the special savings incentive account, including a case where the units are transferred to another such fund or account, the declarer will notify the investment undertaking accordingly, and

(g) contains such other information as the Revenue Commissioners may reasonably require for the purposes of *Chapter 1A* of *Part 27*.][2]

Declaration of PRSA Administrator

[9A. The declaration referred to in *section 739D(6)(i)* is a declaration in writing to the investment undertaking which—

(a) is made by a PRSA administrator (in this paragraph referred to as the "*declarer*") in respect of units which are assets in a PRSA,

(b) is signed by the declarer,

(c) is made in such form as may be prescribed or authorised by the Revenue Commissioners,

(d) declares that, at the time when the declaration is made, the units in respect of which the declaration is made—

(i) are assets of a PRSA, and

(ii) are managed by the declarer for the individual who is beneficially entitled to the units,

(e) contains the name, address and tax reference number of the individual referred to in *subparagraph (d)*,

(f) contains an undertaking by the declarer that if the units cease to be assets of the PRSA, including a case where the units are transferred to another PRSA, the declarer will notify the investment undertaking accordingly, and

(g) contains such other information as the Revenue Commissioners may reasonably require for the purposes of *Chapter 1A* of *Part 27*.][3]

Declaration of Credit Union

[9B. The declaration referred to in *section 739D(6)(j)* is a declaration in writing to the investment undertaking which—

(a) is made by the person (in this paragraph referred to as the "*declarer*") entitled to the units in respect of which the declaration is made,

(b) is signed by the declarer,

(c) is made in such form as may be prescribed or authorised by the Revenue Commissioners,

(d) contains the name and address of the declarer,

(e) declares that, at the time when the declaration is made the person entitled to the units is a credit union,

(f) contains such other information as the Revenue Commissioners may reasonably require for the purposes of *Chapter 1A* of *Part 27*.][4]

Declarations of non-resident on acquisition of units

10. The declaration referred to in *section 739(D)(7)(a)(i)* is a declaration in writing to the investment undertaking which—

(a) is made by a person (in this paragraph referred to as the "*declarer*") who is entitled to the units in respect of which the declaration is made,

(b) is made on or about the time when the units are applied for or acquired by the declarer,

(c) is signed by the declarer,

(d) is made in such form as may be prescribed or authorised by the Revenue Commissioners,

(e) declares that, at the time the declaration is made, the declarer is not resident in the State,

(f) contains the name and address of the declarer,

(g) contains an undertaking by the declarer that if the declarer becomes resident in the State, the declarer will notify the investment undertaking accordingly, and

(h) contains such other information as the Revenue Commissioners may reasonably require for the purposes of *Chapter 1A* of *Part 27*.

Declaration of non-corporate person

11. The declaration referred to in *section 739D(7)(a)(ii)* is a declaration in writing to the investment undertaking which—

(a) is made by the person (in this paragraph referred to as the "*declarer*") who is entitled to the units in respect of which the declaration is made,

(b) is signed by the declarer,

(c) is made in such form as may be prescribed or authorised by the Revenue Commissioners,

(d) declares that the declarer, at the time the declaration is made, is neither resident nor ordinarily resident in the State,

(e) contains the name and address of the declarer,

(f) contains an undertaking by the declarer that if the declarer becomes resident in the State, the declarer will notify the investment undertaking accordingly, and

(g) contains such other information as the Revenue Commissioners may reasonably require for the purposes of *Chapter 1A* of *Part 27*.

Declaration to Collector-General

12. The declaration referred to in *section 739D(8)(a)* is a declaration in writing to the Collector-General which—

(a) is made and signed by the investment undertaking,

(b) is made in such form as may be prescribed or authorised by the Revenue Commissioners,

(c) contains the name, address and tax reference number of the investment undertaking,

(d) declares that, to the best of the investment undertaking's knowledge and belief, no units in the investment undertaking were held on 1 April 2000 by a person who was resident in the State at that time, other than such persons whose names and addresses are set out on the schedule to the declaration, and

(e) contains a schedule which sets out the name and address of each person who on 1 April 2000 was a unit holder in the investment undertaking and who was on that date, resident in the State.

Declaration of intermediary

13. The declaration referred to in *section 739D(9)(a)* is a declaration in writing to the investment undertaking which—

(a) is made and signed by the intermediary,

(b) is made in such form as may be prescribed or authorised by the Revenue Commissioners,

(c) contains the name and address of the intermediary,

[(d) declares that—

(i) at the time of making the declaration, to the best of the intermediary's knowledge and belief, the person who has beneficial entitlement to each of the units in respect of which the declaration is made—

(I) is not resident in the State, where that person is a company, and

(II) where that person is not a company, the person is neither resident nor ordinarily resident in the State, and

(ii) unless the investment undertaking is notified in writing to the contrary, every subsequent application by the intermediary to acquire units in the investment undertaking or an investment undertaking associated with the first-mentioned investment undertaking, shall be on behalf of such a person,

(e) contains an undertaking that where the intermediary becomes aware at any time that the declaration made in accordance with *subparagraph (d)* is no longer correct, the intermediary will notify the investment undertaking in writing accordingly, and][5]

(f) contains such other information as the Revenue Commissioners may reasonably require for the purposes of *Chapter 1A* of *Part 27*.

Certain resident entities: declaration of intermediary

[14. The declaration referred to in *section 739D(9A)(a)* is a declaration in writing to the investment undertaking which—

(a) is made and signed by the intermediary,

(b) is made in such form as may be prescribed or authorised by the Revenue Commissioners,

(c) contains the name and address of the intermediary,

(d) declares that—

(i) at the time of making the declaration, to the best of the intermediary's knowledge and belief, the person who has beneficial entitlement to each of the units in respect of which the declaration is made is a person referred to in [*paragraphs (a)* to *(k)*][6] of *section 739D(6)*, and

(ii) unless the investment undertaking is notified in writing to the contrary, every subsequent application by the intermediary to acquire units in the investment undertaking or an investment undertaking associated with the first-mentioned investment undertaking, shall be on behalf of such a person,

(e) contains an undertaking that where the intermediary becomes aware at any time that the declaration made under *subparagraph (d)* is no longer correct, the intermediary will notify the investment undertaking in writing accordingly, and

(f) contains such other information as the Revenue Commissioners may reasonably require for the purposes of *Chapter 1A* of *Part 27*.][7]][8]

Amendments

[1] Inserted by FA13 s42(1)(g). Applies in respect of an investment limited partnership that has been granted an authorisation under section 8 of the Investment Limited Partnerships Act 1994 on or after 13 February 2013.

[2] Substituted by FA01 s75.

[3] Inserted by PAA02 s4(1)(f). With effect from 7 November 2002 per S.I. 502 of 2002.

[4] Inserted by FA03 s56(a).

[5] Substituted by FA02 s45(1)(a).

[6] Substituted by FA03 s56(b).

[7] Inserted by FA02 s45(1)(b).

[8] Inserted by FA00 s58(b).

Cross References

From Schedule 2B

Section 706 Interpretation and general (Part 26).
Section 731 Chargeable gains accruing to unit trusts.
Section 739 Taxation of unit holders in undertakings for collective investment.
Section 739D Gain arising on a chargeable event.
Section 770 Interpretation and supplemental (Chapter 1).
Section 774 Certain approved schemes: exemptions and reliefs.
Section 784 Retirement annuities: relief for premiums.
Section 785 Approval of contracts for dependants or for life assurance.
Section 885 Obligation to show tax reference number on receipts.

SCHEDULE 3

Reliefs in Respect of Income Tax Charged on Payments on Retirement, etc

Section 201.

[ITA67 Sch3; FA80 s10(2); FA90 s12; FA93 s8(b)]

PART 1

Interpretation and Preliminary

1.

(1) In this Schedule—

"*the relevant capital sum in relation to an office or employment*" means, subject to *subparagraph (2)*, the aggregate of—

(a) the amount of any lump sum (not chargeable to income tax) received,

(b) the amount equal to the value at the relevant date of any lump sum (not chargeable to income tax) receivable, and

(c) the amount equal to the value at the relevant date of any lump sum (not chargeable to income tax) which, on the exercise of an option or a right to commute, in whole or in part, a pension in favour of a lump sum, may be received in the future,

by the holder in respect of the office or employment in pursuance of any scheme or fund described in *section 778(1)*;

"*the standard capital superannuation benefit*", in relation to an office or employment, means a sum determined as follows:

(a) the average for one year of the holder's [taxable][1] emoluments of the office or employment for the last 3 years of his or her service before the relevant date (or for the whole period of his or her service if less than 3 years) shall be ascertained,

(b) one-fifteenth of the amount ascertained in accordance with *clause (a)* shall be multiplied by the whole number of complete years of the service of the holder in the office or employment, and

(c) an amount equal to the relevant capital sum in relation to the office or employment shall be deducted from the product determined in accordance with *clause (b)*.

(2) (a) The relevant capital sum in relation to an office or employment shall include the amount mentioned in *clause (c)* of the definition of "the relevant capital sum in relation to an office or employment" whether or not the option or right referred to in that clause is exercised.

(b) Where, under the conditions or terms of any scheme or fund described in *section 778(1)*, the holder of the office or employment is entitled to surrender irrevocably the option or right referred to in *clause (c)* of the definition of "the relevant capital sum in relation to an office or employment" and has done so at the relevant date, the relevant capital sum in relation to an office or employment shall not include the amount mentioned in that clause.

2. Any reference in this Schedule to a payment in respect of which income tax is chargeable under *section 123* is a reference to so much of that payment as is chargeable to tax after deduction of the relief applicable to that payment under *section 201(5)*.
3. Any reference in this Schedule to the amount of income tax to which a person is or would be chargeable is a reference to the amount of income tax to which the person is or would be chargeable either by assessment or by deduction.
4. Relief shall be allowed in accordance with this Schedule in respect of income tax chargeable by virtue of *section 123* where a claim is duly made in accordance with *section 201*.
5. A claimant shall not be entitled to relief under this Schedule in respect of any income the tax on which he or she is entitled to charge against any other person, or to deduct, retain or satisfy out of any payment which he or she is liable to make to any other person.

PART 2

Relief by Reduction of Sums Chargeable

6. In computing the charge to tax in respect of a payment chargeable to income tax under *section 123*, a sum equal to the amount (if any) by which the standard capital superannuation benefit for the office or employment in respect of which the payment is made exceeds the basic exemption shall be deducted from the payment.
7. Where income tax is chargeable under *section 123* in respect of 2 or more payments to which *paragraph 6* applies, being payments made to or in respect of the same person in respect of the same office or employment or in respect of different offices or employments held under the same employer or under associated employers, then—
   (a) *paragraph 6* shall apply as if those payments were a single payment of an amount equal to their aggregate amount and, where they are made in respect of different offices or employments, as if the standard capital superannuation benefit were an amount equal to the sum of the standard capital superannuation benefits for those offices or employments, and
   (b) where the payments are treated as income of different years of assessment, the relief to be granted under *paragraph 6* in respect of a payment chargeable for any year of assessment shall be the amount by which the relief computed in accordance with *subparagraph (a)* in respect of that payment and any payments chargeable for previous years of assessment exceeds the relief in respect of those payments chargeable for previous years of assessment,

   and, where the standard capital superannuation benefit for an office or employment in respect of which 2 or more of the payments are made is not the same in relation to each of those payments, it shall be treated for the purposes of this paragraph as equal to the higher or highest of those benefits.
8. In computing the charge to tax in respect of a payment chargeable to income tax under *section 123* in the case of a claimant, if the claimant has not [in the previous 10 years of assessmen][2] made a claim under *section 201* and the relevant capital sum (if any) in relation to the office or employment in respect of which

the payment is made does not exceed [€10,000][3], *subsection (5)* of *section 201* and *paragraph 6* shall apply to that payment as if each reference in that subsection and in that paragraph to the basic exemption were a reference to the basic exemption increased by the amount by which [€10,000][4] exceeds that relevant capital sum.

9. In computing the charge to tax in respect of a payment chargeable to income tax under *section 123*, being a payment made in respect of an office or employment in which the service of the holder includes foreign service, a sum which bears to the amount which would be chargeable to income tax apart from this paragraph the same proportion as the length of the foreign service bears to the length of the service before the relevant date shall be deducted from the payment (in addition to any deduction allowed under *paragraphs 6* to *8* of this Schedule).

[9A. *Paragraph 9* ceases to have effect for payments made [on or after the date of the passing of the Finance Act 2013][5].][6]

PART 3

Relief by Reduction of Tax

10. In the case of any payment in respect of which income tax is chargeable under *section 123*, relief shall be allowed by means of deduction from the tax chargeable by virtue of that section of an amount equal to the amount determined by the formula—

$$A - (P \times \frac{T}{I})$$

where—

A is the amount of income tax which apart from this paragraph would be chargeable in respect of the total income of the holder or past holder of the office or employment for the year of assessment of which the payment is treated as income after deducting from that amount of tax the amount of tax which would be so chargeable if the payment had not been made,

P is the amount of that payment after deducting any relief applicable to that payment under the preceding provisions of this Schedule,

T is the aggregate of the amounts of [income tax payable][7] in respect of the total income of the holder or past holder of the office or employment for the [3 years][8] of assessment preceding the year of assessment of which the payment is treated as income before taking account of any relief provided by *section 826*, and

I is the aggregate of the taxable incomes of the holder or past holder of the office or employment for the [3 years][9] of assessment preceding the year of assessment of which the payment is treated as income.

11. Where income tax is chargeable under *section 123* in respect of 2 or more payments to or in respect of the same person in respect of the same office or employment and is so chargeable for the same year of assessment, those payments shall be treated for the purposes of *paragraph 10* as a single payment of an amount equal to their aggregate amount.

12. Where income tax is chargeable under *section 123* in respect of 2 or more payments to or in respect of the same person in respect of different offices or

employments and is so chargeable for the same year of assessment, *paragraphs 10* and *11* shall apply as if those payments were made in respect of the same office or employment.

[13. (a) Notwithstanding *section 201*, *paragraph 10* shall cease to apply to any payment of €200,000 or more which is made on or after 1 January 2013 and which is chargeable to income tax under *section 123*.

(b) *Paragraphs 11* and *12* shall apply for the purposes of this paragraph.][10]

[14. Notwithstanding *section 201*, *paragraph 10* shall cease to apply to any payment which is made on or after 1 January 2014 and which is chargeable to income tax under *section 123*.][11]

Amendments

[1] Inserted by FA14 sched3(1)(g). Has effect on and from 23 December 2014.

[2] Substituted by FA02 s15(a). Applies as respects the year of assessment 2002 and subsequent years of assessment.

[3, 4] Substituted by FA02 s15(b). Applies as respects the year of assessment 2002 and subsequent years of assessment.

[5] Substituted by F(No.2)A13 s4(1)(a). Has effect as if it had come into operation on or after 27 March 2013.

[6] Inserted by FA13 s14(1)(e). Deemed to have come into force and takes effect on and from 1 January 2013.

[7] Substituted by FA01 sched1(1)(u). Applies as respects the year of assessment 2001 and subsequent years of assessment.

[8, 9] Substituted by FA05 s19(1)(b). Applies as respects the year of assessment 2005 and subsequent years of assessment.

[10] Inserted by FA13 s14(1)(f). Deemed to have come into force and takes effect on and from 1 January 2013.

[11] Inserted by F(No.2)A13 s4(1)(b). Comes into operation on 1 January 2014.

Revenue Briefings

Tax Briefing

Tax Briefing June 1996 – Issue 22 pg 14 – Redundancy Payments and Re-Engagement of Employee's
Tax Briefing October 1997 – Issue 28 pg 8 – Taxation Treatment of Redundancy / Termination Payments
Tax Briefing April 2002 – Issue 47 pg 10 – Finance Act 2002 – Ex-Gratia Payments
Tax Briefing December 2003 – Issue 54 – pg 10 – Redundancy payments
Tax Briefing November 2007 – Issue 67 – Lump Sum Payments & Top Slicing Relief

Revenue Information Notes

IT21 – Lump Sum Payments (Redundancy/Retirement)

Revenue Precedents

Calculation of SCSB where the employee has less than 3 years paid service in the immediate period, prior to the "relevant date". Employee may have been on career break, etc. To obtain the average under SCSB rules, one has to look at the emoluments of the employment for "the last 3 years of his service". The service in question is the service in the employment in respect of which the termination payment is being made. Where gaps in the service exist, it will be necessary to go back further than 36 months to determine the emoluments for the last 3 years of service. IT 94 1612

Cross References

From Schedule 3

Section 123 General tax treatment of payments on retirement or removal from office or employment.
Section 201 Exemptions and reliefs in respect of tax under section 123.
Section 778 Exceptions to charge to tax under section 777.
Section 826 Agreements for relief from double taxation.

To Schedule 3

Section 201 Exemptions and reliefs in respect of tax under section 123.

Section 202 Relief for agreed pay restructuring.

Cross References

From Schedule 4

Section 227 Certain income arising to specified non-commercial state-sponsored bodies.

To Schedule 4

Section 227 Certain income arising to specified non-commercial state-sponsored bodies.

SCHEDULE 4

Exemption of Specified Non-Commercial State Sponsored Bodies from Certain Tax Provisions

Section 227.

[FA94 Sch; S.I. No. 148 of 1997]

1. Agency for Personal Service Overseas.
2. Beaumont Hospital Board.
3. Blood Transfusion Service Board.
4. Board for Employment of the Blind.
5. An Bord Altranais.
6. An Bord Bia — The Irish Food Board.

[7. The National Tourism Development Authority.][1]

8. An Bord Glas.
9. An Bord Iascaigh Mhara.
10. Bord na Gaeilge.
11. Bord na Leabhar Gaeilge.
12. Bord na Radharcmhastóirí.
13. An Bord Pleanála.
14. Bord Scoláireachtaí Comalairte.
15. An Bord Tráchtála — The Irish Trade Board.
16. An Bord Uchtála.
17. Building Regulations Advisory Body.

[…][2]

[18A. The Courts Service.][3]

19. CERT Limited.
20. The Chester Beatty Library.
21. An Chomhairle Ealaíon.
22. An Chomhairle Leabharlanna.

[22A. An Chomhairle Oidhreachta - The Heritage Council.][4]

23. Coiste An Asgard.
24. Combat Poverty Agency.
25. Comhairle na Nimheanna.

[26. The Health Service Executive.][5]

[26A. Commission for Communications Regulation.][6]

27. Cork Hospitals Board.

[27A. A County Enterprise Board.][7]

[27B. The Credit Union Restructuring Board.][8]

28. Criminal Injuries Compensation Tribunal.
29. Dental Council.
30. Drug Treatment Centre Board.
31. Dublin Dental Hospital Board.
32. Dublin Institute for Advanced Studies.

[…][9]

34. Economic and Social Research Institute.
35. Employment Equality Agency.
36. Environmental Protection Agency — An Ghníomhaireacht um Chaomhnú Comhshaoil.
37. Eolas — The Irish Science and Technology Agency.
38. Federated Dublin Voluntary Hospitals.
39. Fire Services Council.

[39A. The Food Safety Authority of Ireland.][10]

40. An Foras Áiseanna Saothair.
41. Forbairt.
42. Forfás.
43. The Foyle Fisheries Commission.
44. Garda Síochána Appeal Board.
45. Garda Síochána Complaints Board.

[…][11]

47. Health Research Board — An Bord Taighde Sláinte.

[47A. The Health and Social Care Professionals Council.][12]

48. Higher Education Authority.

[…][13]

50. Hospitals Trust Board.
51. The Independent Radio and Television Commission — An Coimisiún um Raidio agus Teilifís Neamhspleách.
52. The Industrial Development Agency (Ireland).
53. The Industrial Development Authority.

[53A. The Institute of Public Health in Ireland Limited.][14]

[53AB. Inland Fisheries Ireland.][15]

54. Institiúid Teangeolaíochta Éireann.
55. Institute of Public Administration.

[55A. The Irish Auditing and Accounting Supervisory Authority.][16]

56. The Irish Film Board.
57. The Irish Medicines Board.

[57A. The Irish Sports Council.][17]

58. The Labour Relations Commission.
59. Law Reform Commission.
60. The Legal Aid Board.
61. Leopardstown Park Hospital Board.
62. Local Government Computer Services Board — An Bord Seirbhísí Ríomhaire Rialtais Aitiúil.
63. Local Government Staff Negotiations Board — An Bord Comhchaibidlí Foirne Rialtais Aitiúil.
64. The Marine Institute.
65. Medical Bureau of Road Safety — An Lia-Bhiúró um Shábháiltacht ar Bhóithre.
66. The Medical Council.
67. The National Authority for Occupational Safety and Health — An tÚdarás Náisiúnta um Shábháilteachta agus Sláinte Ceirde.

68. National Cancer Registry.
69. The National Concert Hall Company Limited — An Ceoláras Náisiúnta.
[69A. National Consultative Committee on Racism and Interculturalism.][18]
70. National Council for Educational Awards.
71. National Council for the Elderly.
72. The National Economic and Social Council.
73. The National Economic and Social Forum.
74. National Health Council.
[74A. The National Milk Agency.][19]
[74AB. National Qualifications Authority of Ireland.][20]
[…][21]
76. National Rehabilitation Board.
77. The National Roads Authority — An tÚdarás um Bóithre Náisiúnta.
78. National Safety Council — Comhairle Sábháiltacht Náisiúnta.
79. National Social Services Board.
[…][22]
[81A. Occupational Safety and Health Institute of Ireland.][23]
82. Office of the Data Protection Commissioner.
83. The Pensions Board.
[83A. The Personal Injuries Assessment Board.][24]
[83B. The Pharmaceutical Society of Ireland.][25]
84. Postgraduate Medical and Dental Board.
[84A. The Private Residential Tenancies Board.][26]
85. The Radiological Protection Institute of Ireland.
86. The Refugee Agency.
87. Rent Tribunal.
88. Royal Hospital Kilmainham Company.
89. Saint James's Hospital Board.
90. Saint Luke's and St Anne's Hospital Board.
91. Salmon Research Agency of Ireland Incorporated.
[91A. Science Foundation Ireland.][27]
[…][28]
[92A. The Sustainable Energy Authority of Ireland.][29]
[…][30]
96. Tallaght Hospital Board.
[96A. The Teaching Council.][31]
97. Teagasc.
98. Temple Bar Renewal Limited.
[98A. Tourism Ireland Limited.][32]
99. Údarás na Gaeltachta.

Amendments

[1] Substituted by FA06 s69(1)(c). This section is deemed to have come into force and have taken effect as on and from 28 May 2003.

[2, 9, 22, 30] Deleted by the Inland Fisheries Act 2010, Schedule 2, Part 13(1)(a).

[3] Inserted by FA06 s69(1)(a).

[4] Inserted by SI4301 2(a). The amendments effected by this Order shall - (a) as respects An Chomhairle Oidhreachta - The Heritage Council, be deemed to have come into operation on 10 July 1995, (b) as respects County Enterprise Boards, be deemed to have come into operation on 27 November 1995, and (c) as respects The National Milk Agency, be deemed to have come into operation on 30 December 1994.

[5] Substituted by FA06 s69(1)(d). This section is deemed to have come into force and have taken effect as on and from 1 January 2005.

[6] Inserted by FA08 s52(1). This section is deemed to have come into force and have taken effect as on and from 1 December 2002.

[7] Inserted by SI4301 2(b). The amendments effected by this Order shall - (a) as respects An Chomhairle Oidhreachta - The Heritage Council, be deemed to have come into operation on 10 July 1995, (b) as respects County Enterprise Boards, be deemed to have come into operation on 27 November 1995, and (c) as respects The National Milk Agency, be deemed to have come into operation on 30 December 1994.

[8] Inserted by FA14 s37(1)(a). Deemed to have come into force and have taken effect as on and from 1 January 2013.

[10] Inserted by FA12 s46(1)(a). Deemed to have come into force and have taken effect as on and from 1 January 1999.

[11, 13] Deleted by FA06 s69(1)(e).

[12] Inserted by FA14 s37(1)(b). Deemed to have come into force and have taken effect as on and from 20 March 2007.

[14] Inserted by F(No.2)A08 s40(1)(a). This section is deemed to have come into force and have taken effect on and from 1 October 2002.

[15] Inserted by the Inland Fisheries Act 2010 (Act 10 of 2010), Schedule 2, Part 13(1)(b).

[16] Inserted by FA06 s69(1)(b).

[17] Inserted by FA03 s64(a).

[18] Inserted by FA03 s64(b).

[19] Inserted by SI4301 2(c). The amendments effected by this Order shall - (a) as respects An Chomhairle Oidhreachta - The Heritage Council, be deemed to have come into operation on 10 July 1995, (b) as respects County Enterprise Boards, be deemed to have come into operation on 27 November 1995, and (c) as respects The National Milk Agency, be deemed to have come into operation on 30 December 1994.

[20] Inserted by FA03 s64(c).

[21] Deleted by SI4301 2(d). The amendments effected by this Order shall - (a) as respects An Chomhairle Oidhreachta - The Heritage Council, be deemed to have come into operation on 10 July 1995, (b) as respects County Enterprise Boards, be deemed to have come into operation on 27 November 1995, and (c) as respects The National Milk Agency, be deemed to have come into operation on 30 December 1994.

[23] Inserted by FA03 s64(d).

[24] Inserted by FA04 s40.

[25] Inserted by FA13 s36(2)(a). Deemed to have come into force and have taken effect as on and from 22 May 2007.

[26] Inserted by F(No.2)A08 s40(1)(b). This section is deemed to have come into force and have taken effect on and from 1 September 2004.

[27] Inserted by FA13 s36(2)(b). Deemed to have come into force and have taken effect as on and from 25 July 2003.

[28] Deleted by SA(SG)A14 s36.

[29] Inserted by FA12 s46(1)(b). Deemed to have come into force and have taken effect as on and from 1 May 2002.

[31] Inserted by F(No.2)A13 s37(1). Deemed to have come into force and have taken effect as on and from 28 March 2006.

[32] Inserted by FA03 s64(e).

Cross References

From Schedule 4

Section 227 Certain income arising to specified non-commercial state-sponsored bodies.

To Schedule 4

Section 227 Certain income arising to specified non-commercial state-sponsored bodies.

SCHEDULE 4A

[TABLE

(Class of Technology) (1)	(Description) (2)	(Minimum Amount) (3)
Motors and Drives	Electric motors and drives designed to achieve high levels of energy efficiency and that meet specified efficiency criteria.	€1,000
Lighting	Lighting equipment and systems designed to achieve high levels of energy efficiency and that meet specified efficiency criteria.	€3,000
Building Energy Management Systems	Building energy management systems designed to achieve high levels of energy efficiency and that meet specified efficiency criteria.	€5,000
Information and Communications Technology (ICT)	ICT equipment and systems designed to achieve high levels of energy efficiency and that meet specified efficiency criteria.	€1,000
Heating and Electricity Provision	Heating and electricity provision equipment and systems designed to achieve high levels of energy efficiency and that meet specified efficiency criteria.	€1,000
Process and Heating, Ventilation and Air-conditioning (HVAC) Control Systems	Process and heating, ventilation and airconditioning (HVAC) equipment and systems designed to achieve high levels of energy efficiency and that meet specified efficiency criteria.	€1,000
Electric and Alternative Fuel Vehicles	Electric and alternative fuel vehicles and equipment designed to achieve high levels of energy efficiency and that meet specified efficiency criteria.	€1,000
Refrigeration and Cooling Systems	Refrigerating and cooling equipment and systems designed to achieve high levels of energy efficiency and that meet specified efficiency criteria.	€1,000
Electro-mechanical Systems	Electro-mechanical equipment and systems designed to achieve high levels of energy efficiency and that meet specified efficiency criteria.	€1,000
Catering and Hospitality Equipment	Catering and hospitality equipment and systems designed to achieve high levels of energy efficiency and that meet specified efficiency criteria.][1]	€1,000

Amendments

[1] Substituted by FA14 s38(b). Comes into operation on 1 January 2015.

SCHEDULE 5

Description of Custom House Docks Area

Section 322.

[FA86 Sch4 PtsI and II]

Interpretation

1. In this Schedule—

"*thoroughfare*" includes any road, street, lane, place, quay, terrace, row, square, hill, parade, diamond, court, bridge, channel and river;

a reference to a line drawn along any thoroughfare is a reference to a line drawn along the centre of that thoroughfare;

a reference to a projection of any thoroughfare is a reference to a projection of a line drawn along the centre of that thoroughfare;

a reference to the point where any thoroughfare or projection of any thoroughfare intersects or joins any other thoroughfare or projection of a thoroughfare is a reference to the point where a line drawn along the centre of one thoroughfare or, in the case of a projection of a thoroughfare, along the projection, would be intersected or joined by a line drawn along the centre of the other thoroughfare or, in the case of another projection of a thoroughfare, along the other projection;

a reference to a point where any thoroughfare or projection of a thoroughfare intersects or joins a boundary is a reference to the point where a line drawn along the centre of such thoroughfare or, in the case of a projection of a thoroughfare, along the projection would intersect or join such boundary.

Description of Custom House Docks Area

2. That part of the county borough of Dublin bounded by a line commencing at the point (in this description referred to as "*the first-mentioned point*") where a line drawn along the westerly projection of the northern boundary of Custom House Quay would be intersected by a line drawn along Memorial Road, then continuing in a northerly direction along Memorial Road and Amiens Street to the point where it joins Sheriff Street Lower, then continuing, initially in an easterly direction, along Sheriff Street Lower and Commons Street to the point where it intersects the easterly projection of the northern boundary of Custom House Quay, and then continuing in a westerly direction along that projection and that boundary and the westerly projection of that boundary to the first-mentioned point.

Cross References

From Schedule 5

Section 322 Interpretation (Chapter 1).

To Schedule 5

Section 322 Interpretation (Chapter 1).

SCHEDULE 6

Description of Temple Bar Area

Section 330.

[FA91 Sch2]

Interpretation

1. In this Schedule—

"*thoroughfare*" includes any bridge, green, hill, river and street;

a reference to a line drawn along any thoroughfare is a reference to a line drawn along the centre of that thoroughfare;

a reference to a projection of any thoroughfare is a reference to a projection of a line drawn along the centre of that thoroughfare;

a reference to the point where any thoroughfare or projection of any thoroughfare intersects or joins any other thoroughfare is a reference to the point where a line drawn along the centre of one thoroughfare or, in the case of a projection of a thoroughfare, along the projection, would be intersected or joined by a line drawn along the centre of the other thoroughfare.

Description of Temple Bar Area

2. That part of the county borough of Dublin bounded by a line commencing at the point (in this description referred to as "*the first-mentioned point*") where the River Liffey is intersected by O'Connell Bridge, then continuing, initially in a southerly direction along O'Connell Bridge, Westmoreland Street, College Green, Dame Street, Cork Hill and Lord Edward Street to the point where it joins Fishamble Street, then continuing in a northerly direction along Fishamble Street and the northerly projection of that street to the point where it intersects the River Liffey, then continuing in an easterly direction along the River Liffey to the first-mentioned point.

Cross References

From Schedule 6

Section 330 Interpretation. (Chapter 2).

To Schedule 6

Section 330 Interpretation. (Chapter 2).

SCHEDULE 7

Description of Certain Enterprise Areas

Section 339.

[FA97 Sch10]

PART 1

Interpretation

In this Schedule

"*thoroughfare*" includes any canal, lane, motorway, railway line and road;

a reference to a line drawn along any thoroughfare is a reference to a line drawn along the centre of that thoroughfare;

a reference to the point where any thoroughfare intersects, joins or traverses any other thoroughfare is a reference to the point where a line drawn along the centre of one thoroughfare would be intersected, joined or traversed by a line drawn along the centre of the other thoroughfare;

a reference to a point where any thoroughfare is intersected by the projection of a boundary is a reference to the point where a line drawn along the centre of such thoroughfare would be intersected by the projection of such boundary.

PART 2

Description of Cherry Orchard/Gallanstown Enterprise Area

That part of the county borough of Dublin and the administrative county of South Dublin bounded by a line commencing at the point (in this description referred to as "*the first-mentioned point*") where the Grand Canal is traversed by the M50 motorway, then continuing in an easterly direction along the Grand Canal to the point where it is traversed by the unnamed road to the east of the Dublin Corporation Waterworks installation, then continuing in a north-westerly direction along that unnamed road for a distance of 250 metres, then continuing in a straight undefined line in a north-easterly direction to a point on the°° South Western Railway Line which is 950 metres east of the point where that railway line is traversed by the M50 motorway, then continuing in a westerly direction along that railway line to the point where it is traversed by the M50 motorway, then continuing in a south-easterly direction along that motorway to the first-mentioned point.

PART 3

Description of Finglas Enterprise Area

That part of the county borough of Dublin and the administrative county of Fingal bounded by a line commencing at the point (in this description referred to as "*the first-mentioned point*") where Jamestown Road is intersected by the western projection of the northern boundary of Poppintree Industrial Estate, then continuing in a northerly direction along Jamestown Road to the point where it joins St. Margaret's Road, then continuing in an easterly direction along St. Margaret's Road for a distance of 110 metres, then continuing in a straight undefined line due north to the point where it intersects the M50 motorway, then continuing in an easterly direction along the M50 motorway to the point where it is traversed by the unnamed road immediately to the west of the playing fields on the northern side of St. Margaret's Road, then continuing in a southerly direction along that unnamed road to the point where it joins St. Margaret's Road, then continuing in an easterly direction along St. Margaret's Road for a distance of 115 metres, then continuing in a straight undefined line in a southerly direction to the point where Balbutcher Lane is intersected by the eastern projection of the northern boundary of Poppintree Industrial Estate, then continuing in a westerly direction along the last-mentioned projection and boundary and the western projection of the last-mentioned boundary to the first-mentioned point.

PART 4

Description of Rosslare Harbour Enterprise Area

Ballygerry Area

That part of the administrative county of Wexford bounded by a line commencing at the point (in this description referred to as "*the first-mentioned point*"), where the N25 road intersects the Ballygerry Road at Kilrane then continuing initially in a northerly direction along Ballygerry Road to the point where it next joins the N25 road, then continuing initially in a southerly direction along the N25 road to the first-mentioned point.

Harbour Area

That part of the town of Rosslare Harbour in the administrative county of Wexford bounded by a line commencing at the point (in this description referred to as "*the first-mentioned point*") where the high-water mark joins the south-eastern end of the pier wall to the north-west of the premises known locally as the Old Customs Shed, then continuing in a north-westerly direction along that pier to the point where it intersects the eastern end of the new revetment, then continuing in a south-westerly direction along that revetment to the point which is a distance of 150 metres from the western end of that revetment, then continuing in a straight undefined line due south to the point where it intersects the railway track, then continuing in a north-easterly direction along the railway track to the point where it is intersected by the southern projection of the western boundary of the Old Customs Shed property, then continuing in a northerly direction along the last-mentioned projection and boundary to the point where it joins the north-western boundary of the Old Customs Shed property, then continuing in a north-easterly direction in a straight undefined line to the first-mentioned point.

Cross References

From Schedule 7

Section 339 Interpretation (Chapter 3).

To Schedule 7

Section 339 Interpretation (Chapter 3).

Section 345 Double rent allowance in respect of rent paid for certain business premises.

SCHEDULE 8

Description of Qualifying Resort Areas

Section 351.

[FA95 Sch3]

PART 1

Description of Qualifying Resort Areas of Clare Kilkee

1. That part of the District Electoral Division of Kilkee comprised in the Townlands of Kilkee Upper, Kilkee Lower and Dough.
2. That part of the District Electoral Division of Kilfearagh comprised in that part of the Townland of Ballyonan or Doonaghboy bounded by a line commencing at the point (in this description referred to as "*the first-mentioned point*") where the boundaries of the Townlands of Ballyonan or Doonaghboy, Kilkee Lower and Dough converge, then continuing in a south-westerly direction along the boundary of the Townlands of Kilkee Lower and Ballyonan or Doonaghboy for a distance of 568 yards to a point where it intersects a field measuring 1.829 acres, then continuing along the north-eastern boundary of that field to a point where it intersects Local Road (County Road 395), then continuing along the centre of that road in a south-westerly direction for a distance of 20 yards to a point where it intersects the northern projection of the north-eastern boundary of a field measuring 3.517 acres, then continuing along the north-eastern boundary of that field and of the adjoining field in a south-easterly direction, then continuing in that direction to the centre of the Kilkee/Loop Head Regional Road (R487), then continuing along the centre of that road in a southerly direction for 160 yards to a point where it intersects the westerly projection of the southern boundary of a field measuring 1.282 acres, then continuing in an easterly direction along the southern boundary of that field and adjoining fields to a point where it intersects with the eastern boundary of the Townland of Ballyonan or Doonaghboy, and then continuing, initially in a northerly direction, along that boundary to the first-mentioned point.
3. That part of the District Electoral Division of Kilfearagh comprised in that part of the Townland of Corbally bounded by a line commencing at the point (in this description referred to as "*the first-mentioned point*") being the most westerly point of the boundary between the Townlands of Corbally and Dough, then continuing along that boundary in an easterly direction for approximately 510 yards to a point where it intersects the south-eastern corner of a field measuring 2.020 acres, then continuing in a northerly direction along the eastern boundary of that field and of adjoining fields for a distance of 394 yards, then continuing in a generally westerly direction along the northern boundary of a field measuring 3.305 acres, then continuing in that direction to the cliff face of George's Head, and then continuing, initially in a southerly direction, along the high water mark to the first-mentioned point.

Lahinch

1. That part of the District Electoral Division of Ennistimon comprised in the Townlands of Lehinch and Dough.

2. That part of the District Electoral Division of Liscannor comprised in the Townland of Ballyellery.
3. That part of the District Electoral Division of Moy comprised in the Townland of Crag.

PART 2

Description of Qualifying Resort Areas of Cork

Clonakilty

1. The administrative area of the urban district of Clonakilty.
2. That part of the District Electoral Division of Ardfield comprised in the Townlands of Dunmore, Muckross, Lonagh, Drombeg and Pallas.
3. That part of the District Electoral Division of Clonakilty Rural comprised in the Townlands of Clogheen, Inchydoney Island, Gallanes, Tawnies Lower (Rural), Tawnies Upper (Rural), Desert (Rural), Youghalls (Rural) and Miles (Rural).

Youghal

1. The administrative area of the urban district of Youghal.
2. That part of the District Electoral Division of Youghal Rural comprised in the Townlands of Summerfield, Ballyvergan East, Ballyclamasy, Knocknacally, Pipersbog, Glanaradotia, Park Mountain, Muckridge Demense, Foxhole and Youghal Mudlands.
3. That part of the District Electoral Division of Clonpriest comprised in the Townlands of Clonard East and Redbarn.

PART 3

Description of Qualifying Resort Areas of Donegal

Bundoran

1. The administrative area of the urban district of Bundoran.
2. That part of the District Electoral Division of Bundoran Rural comprised in that part of the Townland of Magheracar which is situated west of the most westerly boundary of the administrative area of the urban district of Bundoran.
3. That part of the District Electoral Division of Bundoran Rural comprised in that part of the Townland of Finner bounded by a line commencing at the point (in this description referred to as "*the first-mentioned point*") where the eastern boundary of the administrative area of the urban district of Bundoran, on the southern side of the National Primary Road (N15), intersects with the centre of that National Primary Road, then continuing in an easterly direction along the centre of that road for a distance of 500 feet, then continuing in a north-westerly direction along the rear boundary to the east of Finner Avenue Housing Estate until the south-eastern corner of Tullan Strand is reached, then continuing in a westerly direction to the point where it joins the most north-easterly point of the boundary of the administrative area of the urban district of Bundoran, then

continuing in a southerly direction along the eastern boundary of the urban district to the point where it intersects the centre of the National Primary Road (N15), and then continuing in an easterly direction along the centre of that road to the first-mentioned point.

PART 4

Description of Qualifying Resort Areas of Galway

Salthill

1. That part of the County Borough of Galway bounded by a line commencing at the point (in this description referred to as "*the first-mentioned point*") where Threadneedle Road meets Salthill Road Upper, then continuing in a northerly direction along the centre of Threadneedle Road to its junction with the road from Seapoint Housing Estate, then continuing in an easterly direction along the southern edge of that estate road and in an easterly projection there-from to its intersection with a road named Rockbarton West, then continuing in an easterly direction along the centre of Revagh Road to its junction with Rockbarton Road, then continuing in a southerly direction along the centre of Rockbarton Road to its junction with Salthill Road Upper and then continuing in a westerly direction along Salthill Road Upper to the first-mentioned point.
2. That part of the County Borough of Galway bounded by a line commencing at the point (in this description referred to as "*the first-mentioned point*") where the Seapoint Promenade Road meets Salthill Road Upper, then continuing in a north-easterly direction along the centre of Salthill Road Upper to its junction with Salthill Road Lower, then continuing in an easterly direction along the centre of Grattan Road to its junction with Seapoint Promenade Road and then continuing in a south-westerly direction along the centre of Sea-point Promenade Road to the first-mentioned point.
3. That part of the County Borough of Galway bounded by a line commencing at the point (in this description referred to as "*the first-mentioned point*") where Dalysfort Road meets Salthill Road Upper, then continuing in an easterly direction along the centre of Salthill Road Upper to a point where it meets Monksfield, then continuing in a north-westerly direction along the centre of Monksfield to the rear of Number 212 Salthill Road Upper, then continuing in a westerly direction along the Commercial Zoning Boundary as set out in the Galway County Borough Development Plan, 1991, to a point at the rear of Western House where it adjoins Dalysfort Road and then continuing in a southerly direction to the first-mentioned point.
4. That part of the County Borough of Galway bounded by a line commencing at the point (in this description referred to as "*the first-mentioned point*") where Monksfield meets Salthill Road Upper, then continuing in a north-easterly direction along the centre of Salthill Road Upper to its junction with Salthill Road Lower, then continuing in a northerly direction along the centre of Salthill Road Lower to its junction with Devon Park Road, then continuing in a north-westerly direction along the centre of Devon Park Road to the rear of property known as Number 108 Lower Salthill Road, then continuing in a southerly direction along Devon Park along the rear boundaries of Numbers 108, 110, 112, 114,

116, 118, 120, 122, 124, 126, 128, 130, 132, 134, 136, 138, 140, 142, 144, 146 and 148 Lower Salthill Road to where it meets Lenaboy Park, then continuing along the Commercial Zoning Boundary, as set out in the Galway County Borough Development Plan, 1991, to the rear of Number 160 Upper Salthill Road, then continuing along the rear boundaries of Numbers 160, 162, 164, 166, 168 and 170 Upper Salthill Road, then continuing in a southerly direction to the side boundary of Number 178 Upper Salthill Road, then continuing in a westerly direction along the boundary of Number 178 Upper Salthill Road to its boundary with Lenaboy Gardens, then continuing in a southerly direction along the centre of Lenaboy Gardens to the north-western corner of the Sacre Coeur Hotel, then continuing in a southerly direction along the Commercial Zoning Boundary, as set out in the Galway Borough Development Plan, 1991, to its junction with Monksfield and then continuing in a south-easterly direction to the first-mentioned point.

5. That part of the County Borough of Galway bounded by a line commencing at the point (in this description referred to as "*the first-mentioned point*") where Lower Salthill Road meets Grattan Road, then continuing in an easterly direction along the centre of Grattan Road to its junction with Salthill Promenade Road, then continuing in a northerly direction along the boundary of the existing private car-park to the rear boundary of that car-park, then continuing in a westerly direction along the rear boundary of properties fronting onto Grattan Road as far as Salthill Road Lower and then continuing in a southerly direction along the centre of Salthill Road Lower to the first-mentioned point.

PART 5

Description of Qualifying Resort Areas of Kerry

Ballybunion

1. That part of the District Electoral Division of Killehenny comprised in the Townlands of Ballyeagh, Killehenny, Ballybunion, Dromin and Doon West.
2. That part of the District Electoral Division of Killehenny comprised in that part of the Townland of Gortnaskeha bounded by a line commencing at the point (in this description referred to as "*the first-mentioned point*") where the boundaries of the Townlands of Ballyeagh, Gortnaskeha and Ahimma converge, then continuing in an easterly direction along the boundary between the Townlands of Gortnaskeha and Ahimma to a point where it intersects with the centre of the Tralee/Ballybunion Regional Road (R551), then continuing in a north-westerly direction along the centre of that road for 1,192 metres to a point where the road would intersect with a line drawn along the westerly projection of the northern boundary of the existing ESB transformer site, then continuing in a north-easterly direction along the existing field boundary to the centre of the Listowel/Ballybunion Regional Road (R553), then continuing in a northerly direction to the centre of the Local Road (County Road 28), then continuing in a westerly direction along that road for 230 metres, then continuing in a northerly direction to a point where it intersects with the boundary between the Townlands of Dromin and Gortnaskeha, and then continuing in a southerly direction along the western boundary of the Townland of Gortnaskeha to the first-mentioned point.

3. That part of the District Electoral Division of Killehenny comprised in that part of the Townland of Doon East bounded by a line commencing at the point (in this description referred to as "*the first-mentioned point*") where the Ballybunion/ Beale Local Road (County Road 4) intersects the Ballybunion/Asdee Regional Road (R551), then continuing in a north-easterly direction along the centre of that Regional road for 250 metres, then continuing in a southerly direction along the rear boundary of the existing housing development to the boundary of the Townlands of Doon East and Doon West, then continuing in a westerly direction along that boundary to the centre of the Regional Road (R551), and then continuing in a northerly direction along the centre of that road to the first-mentioned point.

PART 6

Description of Qualifying Resort Areas of Louth

Clogherhead

That part of the District Electoral Division of Clogher comprised in the Townland of Clogher and that part of the Townland of Callys-town bounded on the west by the Termonfeckin/Annagassan Local Road (County Road 281) and on the north by the Dunleer/ Clogherhead Regional Road (R166).

PART 7

Description of Qualifying Resort Areas of Mayo

Achill

1. The District Electoral Divisions of Slievemore, Dooega, Achill and Corraun Achill.
2. That part of the District Electoral Division of Newport West comprised in the Townland of Mallanranny.

Westport

1. That part of the District Electoral Division of Westport Urban comprised in the Townlands of Ardmore, Cloonmonad, Cahernamart, Carrownalurgan, Knockranny, Westport Demesne (Urban District), Deerpark East, Carrowbeg and those parts of the Town-lands of Carrowbaun and Killaghoor contained within the administrative area of the urban district of Westport.
2. That part of the District Electoral Division of Westport Rural comprised in Roman Island and the Townland of Rossbeg.
3. That part of the District Electoral Division of Kilmeena comprised in that part of the Townland of Westport Demesne (Rural District) bounded by a line commencing at the point (in this description referred to as "*the first-mentioned point*") forming the most north-westerly point of the Townland of Westport Demesne (Urban District), then continuing in a westerly direction for 100 yards, then continuing in a northerly direction for 320 yards, then continuing in a south-easterly direction for 630 yards following the field boundary south of Kennedy's Wood as far as the administrative boundary of the urban district of Westport and

then continuing along that boundary initially in a south-westerly direction to the first-mentioned point.

PART 8

Description of Qualifying Resort Areas of Meath

Bettystown, Laytown and Mosney

1. That part of the District Electoral Division of Julianstown comprised in that part of the Townland of Mornington bounded on the north by a line commencing at the high water mark and continuing in a westerly direction along the northern boundary of Laytown/Bettystown Golf Links to a point where it intersects with the boundary of the Townland of Donacarney Great; and those parts of the Townlands of Betaghstown, Sevitsland, Ministown and Ninch which are situated to the east of the Dublin/Belfast railway line.
2. That part of the District Electoral Division of Julianstown comprised in the Townland of Mosney and that part of the Townland of Briarleas situated to the east of Local Road (County Road 438).

PART 9

Description of Qualifying Resort Areas of Sligo

Enniscrone

1. That part of the District Electoral Division of Kilglass comprised in the Townlands of Carrowhubbock North, Carrowhubbock South, Frankford, Kinard and Trotts.
2. That part of the District Electoral Division of Castleconnor West comprised in the Townlands of Bartragh, Carrowcardin, Muckduff and Scurmore.

PART 10

Description of Qualifying Resort Areas of Waterford

Tramore

1. That part of the District Electoral Division of Islandikane comprised in the Townlands of Westtown, Newtown and Cool-nagoppoge.
2. That part of the District Electoral Division of Tramore comprised in the Townlands of Ballycarnane, Monloum, Tramore East, Tramore West, Crobally Upper, Crobally Lower, Tramore Intake and including the land bounded on the west by the Townlands of Tramore West, Crobally Upper and Tramore Intake (part b), on the north by the Townlands of Ballinattin and Tramore Intake (part a), on the east by a line running in a south-easterly direction from Tramore

Intake (part a) along the centre of the embankment to the Townland of Tramore Burrow and continuing in that direction as far as the high water mark, and on the south by the high water mark.

PART 11

Description of Qualifying Resort Areas of Wexford

Courtown

1. That part of the District Electoral Division of Courtown comprised in the Townlands of Courtown and Ballinatray Lower.
2. That part of the District Electoral Division of Ardamine comprised in the Townlands of Ballinatray Upper, Seamount, Middletown, Parknacross and Glen (Richards).

PART 12

Description of Qualifying Resort Areas of Wicklow

Arklow

1. The administrative area of the urban district of Arklow.
2. That part of the District Electoral Division of Arklow Rural comprised in the Townlands of Clogga and Askintinny.
3. That part of the District Electoral Division of Kilbride comprised in the Townlands of Seabank and Johnstown South.

Cross References

From Schedule 8

Section 351 Interpretation (Chapter 4).

To Schedule 8

Section 351 Interpretation (Chapter 4).

SCHEDULE 8A

Description of Qualifying Rural Areas

[*Section 327L.*

PART 1

Description of Qualifying Rural Areas of Cavan

The District Electoral Divisions of Arvagh, Springfield, Killashandra, Milltown, Carrafin, Grilly, Kilconny, Belturbet Urban, Ardue, Carn, Bilberry, Diamond, Doogary, Lissanover, Ballymagauran, Ballyconnell, Bawnboy, Templeport, Benbrack, Pedara Vohers, Tircahan, Swanlinbar, Kinawley, Derrynananta, Dunmakeever, Dowra, Derrylahan, Tuam, Killinagh, Eskey, Teebane, Scrabby, Loughdawan, Bruce Hall, Drumcarban, Corr, Crossdoney and Killykeen.

PART 2

Description of Qualifying Rural Areas of Leitrim

The administrative county of Leitrim.

PART 3

Description of Qualifying Rural Areas of Longford

The administrative county of Longford.

PART 4

Description Of Qualifying Rural Areas of Roscommon

The District Electoral Divisions of Ballintober, Castleteheen, Carrowduff, Kilbride North, Lissonuffy, Killavackan, Termonbarry, Roosky, Kilglass North, Kilglass South, Bumlin, Cloonfinlough, Killukin (in Roscommon Rural District), Strokestown, Annaghmore, Tulsk, Coolougher, Ballinlough, Kiltullagh, Cloonfower, Artagh South, Artagh North, Ballaghaderreen, Edmondstown, Loughglinn, Buckill, Fairymount, Castlereagh, Frenchpark, Bellangare, Castleplunket, Baslick, Breedoge, Altagowlan, Lough Allen, Ballyfarnan, Keadue, Aghafin, Ballyformoyle, Crossna, Kilbryan, Boyle Rural, Boyle Urban, Tivannagh, Rushfield, Tumna North, Tumna South, Killukin (in Boyle No. 1 Rural District), Oakport, Rockingham, Danesfort, Cloonteem, Kilmore, Elia, Ballygarden, Aughrim East, Aughrim West, Creeve (in Boyle No. 1 Rural District), Creeve (in Roscommon Rural District), Elphin, Rossmore, Cloonyquinn, Ogulla,

Mantua, Lisgarve, Kilmacumsy, Kilcolagh, Estersnow, Croghan, Killummod, Cregga, Cloonygormican, Kilbride South, Kilgefin, Cloontuskert, Drumdaff and Kilteevan.

PART 5

Description of Qualifying Rural Areas of Sligo

The District Electoral Divisions of Ballintogher East, Ballynakill, Lisconny, Drumfin, Ballymote, Cloonoghill, Leitrim, Tobercurry, Kilturra, Cuilmore, Kilfree, Coolavin, Killaraght, Templevanny, Aghanagh, Kilmactranny, Ballynashee, Shancough, Drumcolumb, Riverstown, Lakeview, Bricklieve, Drumrat, Toomour, Kilshalvy, Killadoon, Streamstown, Cartron, Coolaney, Owenmore, Temple, Annagh, Carrickbannagher, Collooney and Ballintogher West.][1]

Amendments

[1] Inserted by FA98 s77(b).

Cross References

To Schedule 8A

Section 372AK Interpretation (Chapter 11).

SCHEDULE 8B

Description of Qualifying Mid-Shannon Areas

[*Section 372AW.*

PART 1

Description of Qualifying Mid-Shannon Areas of Clare

The District Electoral Divisions of Ayle, Ballynahinch, Boherglass, Caherhurley, Cappaghabaun, Carrowbaun, Cloonusker, Coolreagh, Corlea, Derrynagittagh, Drummaan, Fahymore, Feakle, Inishcaltra North, Inishcaltra South, Killaloe, Killokennedy, Killuran, Kilseily, Lackareagh, Loughea, Mountshannon, O'Briensbridge, Ogonnelloe and Scarriff.

PART 2

Description of Qualifying Mid-Shannon Areas of Galway

The District Electoral Divisions of Abbeygormacan, Abbeyville, Balinasloe Rural, Ballinasloe Urban, Ballyglass, Ballynagar, Bracklagh, Clonfert, Clontuskert, Coos, Derrew, Drumkeary, Drummin, Eyrecourt, Kellysgrove, Killimor (Portumna rural area), Kilmacshane, Kilmalinoge, Kilquain, Kiltormer, Kylemore, Laurencetown, Leitrim, Lismanny, Loughatorick, Marblehill, Meelick, Moat, Pallas, Portumna, Tiranascragh, Tynagh and Woodford.

PART 3

Description of Qualifying Mid-Shannon Areas of Offaly

The District Electoral Divisions of Ballycumber, Banagher, Birr Rural, Birr Urban, Broughal, Cloghan, Clonmacnoise, Derryad, Doon, Drumcullen, Eglish, Ferbane, Gallen, Hinds, Hunston, Killyon, Lumcloon, Lusmagh, Mounterin, Moyclare, Shannonbridge, Shannonharbour, Srah and Tinamuck.

PART 4

Description of Qualifying Mid-Shannon Areas of Roscommon

The District Electoral Divisions of Athleague East, Athleague West, Athlone West Rural, Ballydangan, Ballynamona, Castlesampson, Caltragh, Cams, Carnagh, Carrowreagh, Cloonburren, Cloonown, Crannagh, Creagh, Culliagh, Drumlosh, Dysart, Fuerty, Kilcar, Kiltoom, Lackan, Lecarrow, Lismaha, Moore, Mote, Rockhill, Roscommon Rural, Roscommon Urban, Scregg, Taghmaconnell, Thomastown and Turrock.

PART 5

Description of Qualifying Mid-Shannon Areas of Tipperary

The District Electoral Divisions of Aglishcloghane, Ardcrony, Ballina, Ballingarry (in Borrisokane rural area), Ballygibbon, Ballylusky, Ballymackey, Ballynaclogh, Birdhill, Borrisokane, Burgesbeg, Carrig, Carrigatogher, Castletown, Cloghprior, Clohaskin, Cloghjordan, Derrycastle, Finnoe, Graigue (in Borrisokane rural area), Greenhall, Kilbarron, Kilcomenty, Killoscully, Kilkeary, Kilmore, Kilnarath, Knigh, Lackagh, Lorrha East, Lorrha West, Mertonhall, Monsea, Nenagh East Urban, Nenagh Rural, Nenagh West Urban, Newport, Rathcabban, Redwood, Riverstown, Terryglass, Uskane and Youghalarra.

PART 6

Description of Qualifying Mid-Shannon Areas of Westmeath

The District Electoral Divisions of Athlone East Rural, Athlone East Urban, Athlone West Urban, Ardnagragh, Auburn, Ballymore, Bellanalack, Carn, Castledaly, Doonis, Drumraney, Glassan, Killinure, Moate, Mount Temple, Moydrum, Muckanagh, Noughaval, Templepatrick, Tubbrit, Umma and Winetown.][1]

Amendments

[1] Inserted by FA07 s29(1)(b). With effect from 1 June 2008 per S.I. 159 of 2008.

SCHEDULE 9

Change in Ownership of Company: Disallowance of Trading Losses

Sections 401 and 679(4).

[FA73 Sch5 PtI pars 1 to 7 and 9; FA97 s146(1) and Sch 9 PtI par5(3)]

Change in ownership of company

1. For the purposes of *sections 401* and *679(4)*, there shall be a change in the ownership of a company if—
   (a) a single person acquires more than 50 per cent of the ordinary share capital of a company,
   (b) 2 or more persons each acquire a holding of 5 per cent or more of the ordinary share capital of the company and those holdings together amount to more than 50 per cent of the ordinary share capital of the company, or
   (c) 2 or more persons each acquire a holding of the ordinary share capital of the company, and the holdings together amount to more than 50 per cent of the ordinary share capital of the company, but disregarding a holding of less than 5 per cent unless it is an addition to an existing holding and the 2 holdings together amount to 5 per cent or more of the ordinary share capital of the company.

2. In applying *paragraph 1*—
   (a) the circumstances at any 2 points in time with not more than 3 years between them may be compared, and a holder at the later time may be regarded as having acquired whatever such holder did not hold at the earlier time, irrespective of what such holder has acquired or disposed of between such 2 points in time;
   (b) so as to allow for any issue of shares or other reorganisation of capital, the comparison referred to in *subparagraph (a)* may be made in terms of percentage holdings of the total ordinary share capital at the respective times, so that a person whose percentage holding is greater at the later time may be regarded as having acquired a percentage holding equal to the increase;
   (c) in deciding for the purposes of *subparagraphs (b)* and *(c)* of *paragraph 1* whether any person has acquired a holding of at least 5 per cent or a holding which makes at least 5 per cent when added to an existing holding, acquisitions by, and holdings of, persons who are connected with each other shall be aggregated as if they were acquisitions by, and holdings of, one and the same person;
   (d) any acquisition of shares under the will or on the intestacy of a deceased person and any gift of shares, if it is shown that the gift is unsolicited and made without regard to *section 401* or *679(4)*, shall be disregarded.

3. Where persons, whether members of the company or not, possess extraordinary rights or powers under the articles of association or under any other document regulating the company and as a consequence ownership of ordinary share capital may not be an appropriate test of whether there has been a major change in the persons for whose benefit the losses or capital allowances may ultimately

enure, then, in considering whether there has been a change in ownership of the company for the purposes of *section 401* or *679(4)*, holdings of all kinds of share capital, including preference shares, or of any particular category of share capital, or voting power or any other special kind of power, may be taken into account instead of ordinary share capital.

4. Where *section 401* or *679(4)* has operated to restrict relief by reference to a change in ownership taking place at any time, no transaction or circumstance before that time shall be taken into account in determining whether there is any subsequent change in ownership.

Groups of companies

5. (1) For the purposes of *sections 401* and *679(4)*, a change in the ownership of a company shall be disregarded if—

(a) immediately before the change the company is a 75 per cent subsidiary of another company, and

(b) that other company continues after the change, despite a change in the direct ownership of the first-mentioned company, to own that first-mentioned company as a 75 per cent subsidiary.

(2) If there is a change in the ownership of a company which has a 75 per cent subsidiary, whether owned directly or indirectly, *section 401* or *679(4)*, as the case may be, shall apply as if there had also been a change in the ownership of that subsidiary unless the change in ownership of the first-mentioned company is to be disregarded under *subparagraph (1)*.

Provisions as to ownership

6. For the purposes of *sections 401* and *679(4)* and this Schedule—

(a) references to ownership shall be construed as references to beneficial ownership, and references to acquisition shall be construed accordingly,

(b) a company shall be deemed to be a 75 per cent subsidiary of another company if and so long as not less than 75 per cent of its ordinary share capital is owned by that other company, whether directly or through another company or other companies, or partly directly and partly through another company or other companies,

(c) the amount of ordinary share capital of one company owned by a second company through another company or other companies, or partly directly and partly through another company or other companies, shall be determined in accordance with *subsections (5)* to *(10)* of *section* 9, and

(d) "*share*" includes "*stock*".

Time of change in ownership

7.

(1) Where any acquisition of ordinary share capital or other property or rights taken into account in determining that there has been a change in ownership of a company—

(a) was made in pursuance of a contract of sale or option or other contract, or

(b) was made by a person holding such a contract,

the time when the change in ownership took place shall be determined as if the acquisition had been made when the contract was made with the holder or when the benefit of the contract was assigned to the holder so that, in the case of a person exercising an option to purchase shares, such person shall be regarded as having purchased the shares when such person acquired the option.

(2) *Subparagraph (1)* shall not apply where the contract was made before the 16th day of May, 1973.

Information

8. Any person in whose name any shares or securities of a company are registered shall, if required by notice in writing by an inspector given for the purposes of *section 401* or *679(4)*, state whether or not that person is the beneficial owner of those shares or securities or any of them and, if that person is not the beneficial owner of those shares or securities or any of them, that person shall furnish the name and address of the person or persons on whose behalf those shares or securities are registered in that person's name.

Cross References

From Schedule 9

Section 9 Subsidiaries.

Section 401 Change in ownership of company: disallowance of trading losses.

Section 679 Exploration expenditure.

To Schedule 9

Section 401 Change in ownership of company: disallowance of trading losses.

Section 674 Expenditure on abortive exploration.

Section 679 Exploration expenditure.

Section 694 Exploration expenditure incurred by certain companies.

Schedule 29 Provisions Referred to in Sections 1052, 1053 and 1054

SCHEDULE 10

Relief for Investment in Corporate Trades: Subsidiaries

[*Section 505*

[FA84 Sch2; FA87 s12(2); FA91 s15(2)]

Finance for Trade of Subsidiary

1. The shares issued by the qualifying company may, instead of or as well as being issued for the purpose mentioned in *section 489(1)(b)*, be issued for the purpose of raising money for a qualifying new venture being carried on by a subsidiary or which such a subsidiary intends to carry on and, where shares are so issued, *paragraph (a)* of the definition of "*relevant period*" in *section 488(1)* and *subsections (1)(c)*, *(5)*, *(6)* and *(8)* of *section 489* shall apply as if references to the company were or, as the case may be, included references to the subsidiary.

Individuals Qualifying for Relief

2. (1) In *subsections (2)*, *(4)* and *(6)* of *section 492*, references to a company (except in each subsection the first such reference) include references to a company which is during the relevant period a subsidiary of that company, whether it becomes a subsidiary before, during or after the year of assessment in respect of which the individual concerned claims relief and whether or not it is such a subsidiary while he or she is a partner, director or employee mentioned in *subsection (2)* of *section 492* or while he or she has or is entitled to acquire such capital or voting power or rights as are mentioned in *subsections (4)* and *(6)* of that section.

(2) Without prejudice to *section 492* as it applies in accordance with *subparagraph (1)*, an individual shall be treated as connected with a company if—

(a) he or she has at any time in the relevant period had control (within the meaning of *section 11*) of another company which has since that time and before the end of the relevant period become a subsidiary of the company, or

(b) he or she directly or indirectly possesses or is entitled to acquire any loan capital of a subsidiary of that company.

(3) *Subsections (5)* and *(9)* of *section 492* shall apply for the purposes of this paragraph.

Value Received

3. (1) In *sections 497(10)* and *499(5)*, references to the receipt of value from the company shall include references to the receipt of value from any company which during the relevant period is a subsidiary of the company, whether it becomes a subsidiary before or after the individual concerned receives any value from it, and references to the company in the other provisions of *section 497* and in *section 499(8)* shall be construed accordingly.

(2) In *section 499(1)*, references to the company (except the first such reference) shall include references to a company which during the relevant period is a subsidiary of the company, whether it becomes a subsidiary before or after the repayment, redemption, repurchase or payment referred to in that subsection.

Information

4. *Subsections (4)* and *(5)* of *section 503* apply in relation to any arrangements mentioned in *section 505(2)(c)* as they apply in relation to any arrangement mentioned in *section 500*.][1]

Amendments

[1] Substituted by FA11 s33(1)(b). Has effect in respect of shares issued on or after 25 November 2011.

Cross References

From Schedule 10

Section 11 Meaning of "control" in certain contexts.
Section 488 Interpretation (Part 16).
Section 489 The relief.
Section 492 Individuals qualifying for relief.
Section 497 Value received from company.
Section 499 Value received by persons other than claimants.
Section 500 Prevention of misuse.
Section 503 Information.
Section 505 Application to subsidiaries.

SCHEDULE 11

Profit Sharing Schemes

Section 510.

[FA82 Sch3; FA90 s136; FA95 s16; FA97 s50(c)]

PART 1

Interpretation

1. In this Schedule, "*control*" shall be construed in accordance with *section 432.*

2. For the purposes of this Schedule, a company shall be a member of a consortium owning another company if it is one of not more than 5 companies which between them beneficially own not less than 75 per cent of the other company's ordinary share capital and each of which beneficially owns not less than 5 per cent of that capital.

PART 2

Approval of Schemes

3.

(1) On the application of a body corporate (in this Schedule referred to as "*the company concerned*") which has established a profit sharing scheme which complies with *subparagraphs (3)* and *(4)*, the Revenue Commissioners shall, subject to *section 511*, approve of the scheme—

(a) if they are satisfied in accordance with *paragraph 4*, and

(b) unless it appears to them that there are features of the scheme which are neither essential nor reasonably incidental to the purpose of providing for employees and directors benefits in the nature of interests in shares.

(2) Where the company concerned has control of another company or companies, the scheme may be expressed to extend to all or any of the companies of which it has control, and in this Schedule a scheme which is expressed so to extend is referred to as a "*group scheme*" and, in relation to a group scheme, "*participating company*" means the company concerned or a company of which for the time being the company concerned has control and to which for the time being the scheme is expressed to extend.

(3) The scheme shall provide for the establishment of a body of persons resident in the State (in this Schedule referred to as "*the trustees*")—

(a) who, out of moneys paid to them by the company concerned or, in the case of a group scheme, by a participating company, are required by the scheme to acquire shares in respect of which the conditions in *Part 3* of this Schedule are fulfilled,

(b) who are under a duty to appropriate shares acquired by them to individuals who participate in the scheme, not being individuals ineligible by virtue of *Part 4* of this Schedule, and

(c) whose functions with respect to shares held by them are regulated by a trust which is constituted under the law of the State and the terms of which are embodied in an instrument which complies with *Part 5* of this Schedule.

[(4) The scheme shall provide that the total of the initial market values of the shares appropriated to any one participant in a year of assessment will not exceed [€12,700][1], or where *paragraph (b)* of *subsection (1)* of *section 515* applies, [€38,100][2].][3]

(5) An application under *subparagraph (1)* shall be made in writing and shall contain such particulars and be supported by such evidence as the Revenue Commissioners may require.

4.

(1) The Revenue Commissioners shall be satisfied that at any time every person who—

(a) (i) as respects a profit sharing scheme approved before the 10th day of May, 1997, is then a full-time employee or director of the company concerned or, in the case of a group scheme, of a participating company, or

(ii) as respects a profit sharing scheme approved on or after the 10th day of May, 1997, is then an employee or full-time director of the company concerned or, in the case of a group scheme, of a participating company,

(b) has been such an employee or director at all times during a qualifying period, not exceeding [3 years][4], ending at that time, and

(c) is chargeable to income tax in respect of his or her office or employment under Schedule E,

will then be eligible, subject to *Part 4* of this Schedule, to participate in the scheme on similar terms.

[(1A) (a) As respects a profit sharing scheme approved on or after the date of the passing of the *Finance Act, 1998*, the Revenue Commissioners must be satisfied—

(i) that there are no features of the scheme (other than any which are included to satisfy the requirements of *Chapter 1* of *Part 17* and this Schedule) which have or would have the effect of discouraging any description of employees or former employees who fulfil the conditions in *subparagraph (1)*[, having regard to subparagraph (1B),][5] from participating in the scheme, and

(ii) where the company concerned is a member of a group of companies, that the scheme does not and would not have the effect of conferring benefits wholly or mainly on directors of companies in the group or on those employees of companies in the group who are in receipt of higher or the highest levels of remuneration.

[(b) For the purposes of this subparagraph—

(i) "*a group of companies*" means a company and any other companies of which it has control or with which it is associated, and

(ii) a company shall be associated with another company where it could reasonably be considered that—

(I) both companies act in pursuit of a common purpose,

(II) any person or any group of persons or groups of persons having a reasonable commonality of identity have or had the means or power, either directly or indirectly, to determine the trading operations carried on or to be carried on by both companies, or

(III) both companies are under the control of any person or group of persons or groups of persons having a reasonable commonality of identity.][6]][7]

[(1B) As respects a scheme which has been established by a relevant company (within the meaning of *paragraph 1* of *Schedule 12*)—

(a) any reference in subparagraph (1)(*a*)(ii) to an employee or a full-time director shall be deemed to be a reference to an individual who was such an employee or a full-time director, as the case may be, of that relevant company or of a company within the relevant company's group (within the meaning of *paragraph 1(3A)* of *Schedule 12*) on the day the scheme was established, and

(b) for the purposes of satisfying the qualifying period requirement referred to in *subparagraph (1)(b)*, such periods in which an individual was or is an employee or a director of a company referred to in *subparagraphs (3)(b)* and (13) of *paragraph 11A* of *Schedule 12* shall also be taken into account.][8]

[(1C) (a) As respects a profit sharing scheme approved on or after 4 February 2010, the Revenue Commissioners shall be satisfied that there are no arrangements connected in any way, directly or indirectly, with the scheme, which make provision for a loan or loans to be made to some or all of the individuals eligible to participate in the scheme.

(b) For the purposes of this subparagraph—

"*arrangements*" include any scheme, agreement, undertaking, or understanding of any kind, whether or not it is, or it is intended to be legally enforceable;

"*loan*" includes any form of credit.][9]

(2) For the purposes of *subparagraph (1)*, the fact that the number of shares to be appropriated to the participants in a scheme varies by reference to the levels of their remuneration, the length of their service or similar factors shall not be regarded as meaning that the participants are not eligible to participate in the scheme on similar terms.

5.

(1) Where at any time after the Revenue Commissioners have approved of a scheme—

(a) a participant is in breach of any of his or her obligations under *paragraphs (a), (c)* and *(d)* of *section 511(4)*,

(b) there is, with respect to the operation of the scheme, any contravention of any provision of *Chapter 1* of *Part 17*, the scheme itself or the terms of the trust referred to in *paragraph 3(3)(c)*,

(c) any shares of a class of which shares have been appropriated to participants receive different treatment in any respect from the other shares of that class, being in particular different treatment in respect of—

(i) the dividend payable,

(ii) repayment,

(iii) the restrictions attaching to the shares, or

(iv) any offer of substituted or additional shares, securities or rights of any description in respect of the shares,

[...][10]

(d) the Revenue Commissioners cease to be satisfied in accordance with [*paragraph 4*, or][11]

[(e) where a person fails to provide information requested by the Revenue Commissioners under *section 510(7)* or information which is required to be delivered under *section 510(8)*][12]

then, the Revenue Commissioners may, subject to *subparagraph (3)*, withdraw the approval with effect from that time or from such later time as they may specify.

(2) Where at any time after the Revenue Commissioners have approved of a scheme an alteration is made in the scheme or the terms of the trust referred to in *paragraph 3(3)(c)*, the approval shall not have effect after the date of the alteration unless the Revenue Commissioners have approved of the alteration.

(3) It shall not be a ground for withdrawal of approval of a scheme that shares which have been newly issued receive, in respect of dividends payable with respect to a period beginning before the date on which the shares were issued, treatment less favourable than that accorded to shares issued before that date.

6.

(1) Where the company concerned is aggrieved by—

(a) the failure of the Revenue Commissioners to approve of a scheme,

(b) the failure of the Revenue Commissioners to approve of an alteration as mentioned in *paragraph 5(2)*, or

(c) the withdrawal of approval,

the company may, by notice in writing given to the Revenue Commissioners within 30 days from the date on which it is notified of their decision, make an application to have its claim for relief heard and determined by the Appeal Commissioners.

(2) Where an application is made under *subparagraph (1)*, the Appeal Commissioners shall hear and determine the claim in the like manner as an appeal made to them against an assessment, and the provisions of the Income Tax Acts relating to such an appeal (including the provisions relating to the rehearing of an appeal and to the statement of a case for the opinion of the High Court on a point of law) shall apply accordingly with any necessary modifications.

[...][13]

PART 3

Conditions as to the Shares

8. [[Subject to *paragraphs 8A* and *8B*,][14] the shares shall form part of the ordinary share capital of—][15]

(a) the company concerned,

(b) a company which has control of the company [concerned,][16]

(c) a company which either is or has control of a company which—

(i) is a member of a consortium owning either the company concerned or a company having control of that company, and

(ii) beneficially owns not less than 15 per cent of the ordinary share capital of the company [so owned, or][17]

[(d) a company which issued the shares to the trustees of an employee share ownership trust to which *section 519* applies, in an exchange to which *section 586* applies, which shares were transferred to the trustees of an approved scheme by the trustees of the employee share ownership trust.][18]

[8A Any reference in *subparagraph (d)* of *paragraph 8* to shares shall be construed as including a reference to shares which were issued to the trustees of the employee share ownership trust referred to in that subparagraph as a result of a reorganisation or reduction of share capital (in accordance with *section 584*) which occurred subsequent to the exchange referred to in that subparagraph and which shares represent—

(a) the shares issued in the exchange referred to in that subparagraph, or

(b) the specified securities issued in the exchange referred to in *paragraph (b)* of the definition of "*specified securities*" in *section 509(1)*.][19]

[8B.

(1) The shares shall not be shares—

(a) in a service company, or

(b) in a company that has control of a service company, where the company is under the control of a person or persons referred to in *subparagraph (2) (a)(i)* as it applies to a service company.

(2) For the purposes of this paragraph—

(a) a company is a service company if the business carried on by the company consists wholly or mainly of the provision of the services of persons employed by the company and the majority of those services are provided to—

(i) a person who has, or 2 or more persons who together have, control of the company,

(ii) a company associated with the company, or

(iii) a partnership associated with the company,

(b) a company is associated with another company where—

(i) both companies are under the control (within the meaning of *section 432*) of the same person or persons, or

(ii) it could reasonably be considered that—

(I) both companies act in pursuit of a common purpose,

(II) any person or any group of persons or groups of persons having a reasonable commonality of identity have or had the means or power, either directly or indirectly, to determine the trading operations carried on or to be carried on by both companies, or

(III) both companies are under the control of any person or group of persons or groups of persons having a reasonable commonality of identity,

(c) a partnership is associated with a company where the partnership and the company act in pursuit of a common purpose,

(d) a reference to a person includes a reference to a partnership, and

(e) where a partner, or a partner together with another person or persons, has control of a company, the partnership is to be treated as having control of that company.][20]

9. The shares shall be—

(a) shares of a class quoted on a recognised stock exchange,

(b) shares in a company not under the control of another company, or

(c) shares in a company under the control of a company (other than a company which is, or if resident in the State would be, a close company within the meaning of *section 430*) whose shares are quoted on a recognised stock exchange.

10.

(1) The shares shall be—

(a) fully paid up,

(b) not redeemable, and

(c) not subject to any restrictions other than restrictions which attach to all shares of the same class or, as respects a profit sharing scheme approved on or after the 10th day of May, 1997, a restriction authorised by *subparagraph (2)*.

(2) Subject to *subparagraphs (3)* and *(4)*, the shares may be subject to a restriction imposed by the company's articles of association—

(a) requiring all shares held by directors or employees of the company or of any other company of which it has control to be disposed of on ceasing to be so held, and

(b) requiring all shares acquired, in pursuance of rights or interests obtained by such directors or employees, by persons who are not, or have ceased to be, such directors or employees to be disposed of when they are acquired.

(3) A restriction is not authorised by *subparagraph (2)* unless—

(a) any disposal required by the restriction will be by means of sale for a consideration in money on terms specified in the articles of association, and

(b) the articles also contain general provisions by virtue of which any person disposing of shares of the same class (whether or not held or acquired as mentioned in *subparagraph (2)*) may be required to sell them on terms which are the same as those mentioned in [clause *(a)*][21].

(4) Nothing in *subparagraph (2)* authorises a restriction which would require a person, before the release date, to dispose of his or her beneficial interest in shares the ownership of which has not been transferred to him or her.

11. Except where the shares are in a company whose ordinary share capital, at the time of the acquisition of the shares by the trustees, consists of shares of one class only, the majority of the issued shares of the same class shall be held by persons other than—

(a) persons who acquired their shares—

(i) in pursuance of a right conferred on them or an opportunity afforded to them as a director or employee of the company concerned or any other company, and

(ii) not in pursuance of an offer to the public,

(b) trustees holding shares on behalf of persons who acquired their beneficial interests in the shares in pursuance of a right or opportunity mentioned in *subparagraph (a)*, and

(c) in a case where the shares are within *paragraph 9(c)* and are not within *paragraph 9(a)*, companies which have control of the company whose shares are in question or of which that company is an associated company within the meaning of *section 432*.

[11A

(1) Notwithstanding any other provision of this Schedule, in the case of specified securities, this Schedule shall, with any necessary modification, apply as if this paragraph were substituted for *paragraphs 8* to *11*.

(2) The specified securities shall be issued by—

(a) a company not under the control of another company, or

(b) a company under the control of a company (other than a company which is, or if resident in the State would be, a close company within the meaning of *section 430*) whose ordinary shares are quoted on a recognised stock exchange.

(3) The specified securities shall not be subject to any restrictions other than restrictions which attach to all specified securities of the same class, or a restriction authorised by *subparagraph (4)*.

(4) Subject to *subparagraphs (5)* and *(6)*, the specified securities may be subject to a restriction imposed by the company's articles of association—

(a) requiring all specified securities held by directors or employees of the company or of any other company of which it has control to be disposed of on ceasing to be so held, and

(b) requiring all specified securities acquired, in pursuance of rights or interests obtained by such directors or employees, by persons who are not, or have ceased to be, such directors or employees to be disposed of when they are acquired.

(5) A restriction is not authorised by *subparagraph (4)* unless—

(a) any disposal required by the restriction is to be by means of a sale for a consideration in money on terms specified in the articles of association, and

(b) the articles also contain general provisions by virtue of which any person disposing of specified securities of the same class (whether or not held or acquired as mentioned in *subparagraph (4)*) may be required to sell them on terms which are the same as those mentioned in clause (*a*).][22]

PART 4

Individuals Ineligible to Participate

12. An individual shall not be eligible to have shares appropriated to him or her under the scheme at any time unless he or she is at that time or was within the preceding 18 months a director or employee of the company concerned or, if the scheme is a group scheme, of a participating company.

[12A Notwithstanding *paragraph 12*, an individual shall be eligible to have shares appropriated to him or her under the scheme at any time if—

(a) the shares were transferred to the trustees of the scheme by the trustees of an employee share ownership trust to which *section 519* applies, and

(b) the individual is at that time, or was within the preceding 30 days, a beneficiary (within the meaning of *paragraph 11* [or *paragraph 11A*, as the case may be,][23] of *Schedule 12*) of that employee share ownership trust.][24]

13. An individual shall not be eligible to have shares appropriated to him or her under the scheme at any time in a year of assessment if in that year of assessment shares have been appropriated to him or her under another approved scheme established by the company concerned or by—

(a) a company which controls or is controlled by the company concerned or which is controlled by a company which also controls the company concerned, or

(b) a company which is a member of a consortium owning the company concerned or which is owned in part by the company concerned as a member of a consortium.

13A

[(1) Notwithstanding *paragraph 13*, an individual who has had shares appropriated to him or her in a year of assessment under an approved scheme established by a company ("the first-mentioned company") shall, subject to *subparagraph (2)*, be entitled to have shares appropriated to him or her in that year of assessment under an approved scheme established by another company ("the second-mentioned company") if, in that year of assessment, the second-mentioned company acquires control, or is part of a consortium that acquires ownership, of the first-mentioned company under a scheme of reconstruction or amalgamation (within the meaning of *section 587*).

(2) *Section 515* and *paragraph 3(4)* shall, subject to any necessary modification, apply as if the first-mentioned company and the second-mentioned company were the same company.

(3) This paragraph shall apply to an appropriation of shares made, on or after the date of the passing of the *Finance Act, 2000*, by the trustees of an approved scheme (within the meaning of *section 510(1)*).][25]

[13B.

(1) Nothing in paragraph 13 shall prevent shares being appropriated to an individual under an approved scheme established by a relevant company (within the meaning of *paragraph 1* of *Schedule 12*) and where, in a year of assessment, shares have been appropriated to an individual under such an approved scheme, *paragraph 13* shall apply as if those shares had not been appropriated to that individual in that year of assessment.

(2) *Section 515* and *paragraph 3(4)* shall, subject to any necessary modification, apply in respect of all shares appropriated to that individual in that year of assessment.][26]

14.

(1) An individual shall not be eligible to have shares appropriated to him or her under the scheme at any time if at that time he or she has, or at any time within the preceding 12 months had, a material interest in a close company which is—

(a) the company whose shares are to be appropriated, or

(b) a company which has control of that company or is a member of a consortium which owns that company.

(2) *Subparagraph (1)* shall apply in relation to a company which would be a close company but for *section 430(1)(a)* or *431*.

(3) (a) In this paragraph, "*close company*" has the meaning assigned to it by *section 430*.

(b) For the purpose of this paragraph—

(i) *subsection (3)* of *section 433* shall apply—

(I) in a case where the scheme in question is a group scheme, with the substitution of a reference to all participating companies for the first reference to the company in *paragraph (c)(ii)* of that subsection, and

(II) with the substitution of a reference to 15 per cent for the reference in that paragraph to 5 per cent, and

(ii) *section 437(2)* shall apply, with the substitution of a reference to 15 per cent for the reference in that section to 5 per cent, for the purpose of determining whether a person has or had a material interest in a company.

PART 5

Provisions as to the Trust Instrument

15. The trust instrument shall provide that, as soon as practicable after any shares have been appropriated to a participant, the trustees will give him or her notice in writing of the appropriation—

(a) specifying the number and description of those shares, and

(b) stating their initial market value.

16.

(1) The trust instrument shall contain a provision prohibiting the trustees from disposing of any shares, except as mentioned in *paragraphs (a)*, *(b)* or *(c)* of *section 511(6)*, during the period of retention (whether by transfer to the participant or otherwise).

(2) The trust instrument shall contain a provision prohibiting the trustees from disposing of any shares after the end of the period of retention and before the release date except—

(a) pursuant to a direction given by or on behalf of the participant or any person in whom the beneficial interest in the participant's shares is for the time being vested, and

(b) by a transaction which would not involve a breach of the participant's obligation under *paragraph (c)* or *(d)* of *section 511(4)*.

17. The trust instrument shall contain a provision requiring the trustees—

(a) subject to any direction referred to in *section 513(3)*, to pay over to the participant any money or money's worth received by them in respect of, or by reference to, any of the participant's shares, other than money consisting of a sum referred to in *section 511(4)(c)* or money's worth consisting of new shares within the meaning of *section 514*, and

(b) to deal only pursuant to a direction given by or on behalf of the participant (or any person referred to in *paragraph 16(2)(a)*) with any right conferred in respect of any of the participant's shares to be allotted other shares, securities or rights of any description.

18. The trust instrument shall impose an obligation on the trustees—

(a) to maintain such records as may be necessary to enable the trustees to carry out their obligations under *Chapter 1 of Part 17*, and

(b) where the participant becomes liable to income tax under Schedule E by reason of the occurrence of any event, to inform the participant of any facts relevant to determining that liability.

Amendments

[1,2] Substituted by FA01 sched5.

[3] Substituted by FA99 s69(1)(c)(i).

[4] Substituted by FA99 s69(1)(c)(ii). Shall apply as respects profit sharing schemes approved of on or after the date of 25 March 1999

[5] Inserted by FA01 s17(1)(b)(i)(I). Applies and has effect as respects a profit sharing scheme, or an employee share ownership trust, approved on or after 12 December 2000.

[6] Substituted by FA01 s16(a). Applies as respects profit sharing schemes approved on or after 30 March 2001

[7] Inserted by FA98 s36(1)(c).

[8] Inserted by FA01 s17(1)(b)(i)(II). Applies and has effect as respects a profit sharing scheme, or an employee share ownership trust, approved on or after 12 December 2000.

[9] Inserted by FA10 s19(1)(a). Deemed to have come into force and takes effect as on and from 1 January 2010.

[10] Deleted by F(No.2)A08 s9(1)(a)(i). Applies on and from 24 December 2008.

[11] Substituted by F(No.2)A08 s9(1)(a)(i). Applies on and from 24 December 2008.

[12] Inserted by F(No.2)A08 s9(1)(a)(ii). Applies on and from 24 December 2008.

[13] Deleted by FA02 s13(1)(d)(i). This section shall apply and have effect as on and from 16 April 2001.

[14] Substituted by FA10 s19(1)(b). Applies to an appropriation of 10 shares made by the trustees of an approved scheme (within the meaning of section 510(1)) on or after 4 February 2010.

[15] Substituted by FA02 s13(1)(d)(ii). This section shall apply and have effect as on and from 16 April 2001.

[16] Substituted by FA02 s13(1)(d)(iii). This section shall apply and have effect as on and from 16 April 2001.

[17] Substituted by FA02 s13(1)(d)(iv). This section shall apply and have effect as on and from 16 April 2001.

[18] Inserted by FA02 s13(1)(d)(v). This section shall apply and have effect as on and from 16 April 2001.

[19] Inserted by FA02 s13(1)(d)(vi). This section shall apply and have effect as on and from 16 April 2001.

[20] Inserted by FA10 s19(1)(b). Applies to an appropriation of 10 shares made by the trustees of an approved scheme (within the meaning of section 510(1)) on or after 4 February 2010.

[21] Substituted by FA02 s13(1)(d)(vii). This section shall apply and have effect as on and from 16 April 2001.

[22] Inserted by FA02 s13(1)(d)(viii). This section shall apply and have effect as on and from 16 April 2001.

[23] Inserted by FA01 s17(1)(b)(ii). Applies and has effect as respects a profit sharing scheme, or an employee share ownership trust, approved on or after 12 December 2000.

[24] Inserted by FA99 s69(1)(c)(iii). Shall apply as respects an appropriation of shares made by the trustees of an approved scheme on or after the date of 25 March 1999

[25] Inserted by FA00 s25.

[26] Inserted by FA01 s17(1)(b)(iii). Applies and has effect as respects a profit sharing scheme, or an employee share ownership trust, approved on or after 12 December 2000.

Revenue Briefings

eBrief

eBrief No. 17/2011 – Share-Based Remuneration – Finance Act 2011 Changes

Cross References

From Schedule 11

Section 430 Meaning of "close company".
Section 431 Certain companies with quoted shares not to be close companies.
Section 432 Meaning of "associated company" and "control".
Section 433 Meaning of "participator", "associate", "director" and "loan creditor".
Section 437 Interest paid to directors and directors' associates.
Section 509 Interpretation (Chapter 1).
Section 510 Approved profit sharing schemes: appropriated shares.
Section 511 The period of retention, release date and appropriate percentage.
Section 513 Capital receipts in respect of scheme shares.
Section 514 Company reconstructions, amalgamations, etc.
Section 515 Excess or unauthorised shares.
Section 519 Employee share ownership trusts.
Section 584 Reorganisation or reduction of share capital.
Section 586 Company amalgamations by exchange of shares.
Section 587 Company reconstructions and amalgamations.
Schedule 12 Employee Share Ownership Trusts

To Schedule 11

Section 130 Matters to be treated as distributions.
Section 509 Interpretation (Chapter 1).
Section 510 Approved profit sharing schemes: appropriated shares.
Section 511A Shares acquired from an employee share ownership trust.
Section 514 Company reconstructions, amalgamations, etc.
Section 515 Excess or unauthorised shares.
Section 518 Costs of establishing profit sharing schemes.
Section 519 Employee share ownership trusts.
Schedule 12 Employee Share Ownership Trusts

SCHEDULE 12

Employee Share Ownership Trusts

Section 519.

[FA97 Sch 3].

Interpretation

1.

(1) For the purposes of this Schedule—

"*ordinary share capital*" has the same meaning as in *section 2*;

["*relevant company*" means—

(a) a company into which a trustee savings bank has been reorganised under section 57 of the Trustee Savings Banks Act, 1989, [...][1]

(b) ICC Bank [plc,][2]][3]

[(c) ACC Bank plc, or

(d) a company which acquired control of the Irish National Petroleum Corporation Limited;][4]

"*securities*" means shares (including stock) and debentures.

(2) For the purposes of this Schedule, the question whether one company is controlled by another shall be construed in accordance with *section 432*.

[(3) For the purposes of this Schedule, a company falls within the founding company's group at a particular time if—

(a) it is the founding company, or

(b) at that time, it is controlled by the founding company and the trust concerned referred to in *paragraph 2(1)* is expressed to extend to it.][5]

[(3A) For the purposes of this Schedule a company falls within the relevant company's group at a particular time if—

(a) it is the relevant company, or

(b) at that time, it is controlled by the relevant company and the trust concerned referred to in *paragraph 2(1)* is expressed to extend to it.][6]

(4) (a) In this subparagraph—

["*associate*" has the meaning assigned to it by *subsection (3)* of *section 433*, subject to the reference to the employees in both places where it occurs in *subparagraph (ii)* of *paragraph (c)* of that subsection being construed as including a reference to former employees;][7]

"*control*" shall be construed in accordance with *section 432*.

(b) For the purposes of this Schedule, a person shall be treated as having a material interest in a company if the person, either on his or her own or with any one or more of his or her associates, or if any associate of his or her with or without any such other associates, is the beneficial owner of, or able directly or through the medium of other companies or by any other indirect means to control, more than 5 per cent of the ordinary share capital of the company.

(5) For the purposes of this Schedule, a trust shall be established when the deed under which it is established is executed.

Approval of Qualifying Trusts

[2.

(1) On the application of a body corporate (in this Schedule referred to as "the founding company") which has established an employee share ownership trust, the Revenue Commissioners shall approve of the trust as a qualifying employee share ownership trust if they are satisfied that the conditions in *paragraphs 6* to *18* are complied with in relation to the trust.

(2) (a) Where the founding company is a member of a group of companies, the Revenue Commissioners shall not approve of a trust under *subparagraph (1)* unless they are satisfied that the trust does not and would not have the effect of conferring benefits wholly or mainly on directors of companies in the group or on those employees of companies in the group who are in receipt of higher or the highest levels of remuneration.

[(b) For the purposes of this subparagraph—

(i) "*a group of companies*" means a company and any other companies of which it has control or with which it is associated, and

(ii) a company shall be associated with another company where it could reasonably be considered that—

(I) both companies act in pursuit of a common purpose,

(II) any person or any group of persons or groups of persons having a reasonable commonality of identity have or had the means or power, either directly or indirectly, to determine the trading operations carried on or to be carried on by both companies, or

(III) both companies are under the control of any person or group of persons or groups of persons having a reasonable commonality of identity.][8]][9]

3.

(1) Where at any time after the Revenue Commissioners have approved of a trust—

(a) there is with respect to the operation of the trust any contravention of the conditions in *paragraphs 6* to *18*, [...][10]

(b) any shares of a class of which shares have been acquired by the trustees receive different treatment in any respect from the other shares of that class, in particular, different treatment in respect of—

(i) the dividend payable,

(ii) repayment,

(iii) the restrictions attaching to the shares, or

(iv) any offer of substituted or additional shares, securities or rights of any description in respect of the shares, [or][11]

[(c) where a person fails to provide information requested by the Revenue Commissioners under paragraph 3(4) or information which is required to be delivered under paragraph 3(5),][12]

the Revenue Commissioners may, subject to *subparagraph (3)*, withdraw the approval with effect from that time or from such later time as they may specify.

(2) Where at any time after the Revenue Commissioners have approved of a trust an alteration is made to the terms of the trust, the approval shall not have

effect after the date of the alteration unless the Revenue Commissioners have approved of the alteration.

(3) It shall not be a ground for withdrawal of approval of a trust that shares which have been newly issued receive, in respect of dividends payable with respect to a period beginning before the date on which the shares were issued, treatment which is less favourable than that accorded to shares issued before that date.

(4) The Revenue Commissioners may by notice in writing require any person to furnish to them, within such time as they may direct which is not less than 30 days, such information as they think necessary to enable them to either or both—

(a) determine whether to approve of an employee share ownership trust or withdraw an approval already given, and

(b) determine the liability to tax of any beneficiary under an approved employee share ownership trust.

[(5) Without prejudice to subparagraph (4) the trustees of a trust shall as respects any year, prepare and deliver to the Revenue Commissioners on or before 31 March in the year following that year, a return in the prescribed form (within the meaning of [*Chapter 3* of *Part 41A*][13]) of such particulars relating to the trust for that year as may be required by the prescribed form and *sections 1052* and *1054* shall apply to a failure by the trustees to deliver a return in accordance with this subparagraph as they apply to a failure to deliver a return referred to in *section 1052*.][14]

4.

(1) Where the founding company is aggrieved by—

(a) the failure of the Revenue Commissioners to approve of an employee share ownership trust,

(b) the failure of the Revenue Commissioners to approve of an alteration as mentioned in *paragraph 3(2)*, or

(c) the withdrawal of approval,

the company may, by notice in writing given to the Revenue Commissioners within 30 days from the date on which it is notified of their decision, make an application to have its claim for relief heard and determined by the Appeal Commissioners.

(2) Where an application is made under *subparagraph (1)*, the Appeal Commissioners shall hear and determine the claim in the like manner as an appeal made to them against an assessment and the provisions of the Income Tax Acts relating to such an appeal (including the provisions relating to the rehearing of an appeal and to the statement of a case for the opinion of the High Court on a point of law) shall apply accordingly with any necessary modifications.

5. The Revenue Commissioners may nominate any of their officers, including an inspector, to perform any acts and discharge any functions authorised by this Schedule to be performed or discharged by them.

General

6.

(1) The trust shall be established under a deed (in this Schedule and in *section 519* referred to as "*the trust deed*").

(2) The trust shall be established by the founding company which at the time the trust is established is not controlled by another company.

[(3) Nothing in subparagraph (2) shall prohibit a company into which a trustee savings bank has been reorganised under *section 57* of the Trustee Savings Banks Act, 1989, from establishing the trust at a time when the company is controlled by another company.][15]

Trustees

7. The trust deed shall provide for the establishment of a body of trustees complying with *paragraph 8, 9* or *10*.

[7A Notwithstanding any other provision in this Schedule, in a case to which *paragraph 11A* applies, any reference in *paragraph 8, 9* or *10* to an employee or a director of a company shall be construed as a reference to an individual who—

(a) was an employee or a director, as the case may be, of the relevant company or of a company within the relevant company's group on the day the trust was established, and

(b) is, at the relevant time (within the meaning, as may be appropriate in the circumstances, of *paragraph 8, 9* or *10*), an employee or a director, as the case may be, of a company referred to in *paragraph 11A(3)(b)*.][16]

8.

(1) The trust deed shall—

(a) appoint the initial trustees;

(b) contain rules for the retirement and removal of trustees;

(c) contain rules for the appointment of replacement and additional trustees.

(2) The trust deed shall provide that at any time while the trust subsists (in this subparagraph referred to as "*the relevant time*")—

(a) the number of trustees shall not be less than 3;

(b) all the trustees shall be resident in the State;

(c) the trustees shall include one person who is a trust corporation, a solicitor, or a member of such other professional body as the Revenue Commissioners may from time to time allow for the purposes of this paragraph;

(d) the majority of the trustees shall be persons who are not and have never been directors of any company within the founding company's group at the relevant time;

(e) the majority of the trustees shall be representatives of the employees of the companies within the founding company's group at the relevant time, and who do not have and have never had a material interest in any such company;

(f) the trustees to whom *subparagraph (e)* relates shall, before being appointed as trustees, have been selected by a majority of the employees of the companies within the founding company's group at the time of the selection.

9.

(1) The trust deed shall—

(a) appoint the initial trustees;

(b) contain rules for the retirement and removal of trustees;

(c) contain rules for the appointment of replacement and additional trustees.

(2) The trust deed shall be so framed that at any time while the trust subsists the conditions in *subparagraph (3)* are fulfilled as regards the persons who are then trustees, and in that subparagraph "*the relevant time*" means that time.

(3) The conditions referred to in *subparagraph (2)* are that—

(a) the number of trustees is not less than 3;

(b) all the trustees are resident in the State;

(c) the trustees include at least one person who is a professional trustee and at least 2 persons who are non-professional trustees;

(d) at least half of the non-professional trustees were, before being appointed as trustees, selected in accordance with *subparagraph (6)* or *(7)*;

(e) all the trustees so selected are persons who are employees of companies within the founding company's group at the relevant time, and who do not have and have never had a material interest in any such company.

(4) For the purposes of this paragraph, a trustee shall be a professional trustee at a particular time if—

(a) the trustee is then a trust corporation, a solicitor, or a member of such other professional body as the Revenue Commissioners allow for the purposes of this subparagraph,

(b) the trustee is not then an employee or director of any company then within the founding company's group, and

(c) the trustee meets the requirements of *subparagraph (5)*,

and for the purposes of this paragraph a trustee shall be a non-professional trustee at a particular time if the trustee is not then a professional trustee for those purposes.

(5) A trustee shall meet the requirements of this subparagraph if—

(a) he or she was appointed as an initial trustee and, before being appointed as trustee, was selected only by the persons who later became the non-professional initial trustees, or

(b) he or she was appointed as a replacement or additional trustee and, before being appointed as trustee, was selected only by the persons who were the non-professional trustees at the time of the selection.

(6) Trustees shall be selected in accordance with this subparagraph if the process of selection is one under which—

(a) all the persons who are employees of the companies within the founding company's group at the time of the selection, and who do not have and have never had a material interest in any such company, are, in so far as is reasonably practicable, given the opportunity to stand for selection,

(b) all the employees of the companies within the founding company's group at the time of the selection are, in so far as is reasonably practicable, given the opportunity to vote, and

(c) persons gaining more votes are preferred to those gaining less.

(7) Trustees shall be selected in accordance with this subparagraph if they are selected by persons elected to represent the employees of the companies within the founding company's group at the time of the selection.

10.

(1) This paragraph shall apply where the trust deed provides that at any time while the trust subsists there shall be a single trustee.

(2) The trust deed shall—

(a) be so framed that at any time while the trust subsists the trustee is a company which at that time is resident in the State and controlled by the founding company;

(b) appoint the initial trustee;

(c) contain rules for the removal of any trustee and for the appointment of a replacement trustee.

(3) The trust deed shall be so framed that at any time while the trust subsists the company which is then the trustee is a company so constituted that the conditions in *subparagraph (4)* are then fulfilled as regards the persons who are then directors of the company, and in that subparagraph "*the relevant time*" means that time and "*the trust company*" means that company.

(4) The conditions referred to in *subparagraph (3)* are that—

(a) the number of directors is not less than 3;

(b) all the directors are resident in the State;

(c) the directors include at least one person who is a professional director and at least 2 persons who are non-professional directors;

(d) at least half of the non-professional directors were, before being appointed as directors, selected in accordance with *subparagraph (7)* or *(8)*;

(e) all the directors so selected are persons who are employees of companies within the founding company's group at the relevant time, and who do not have and have never had a material interest in any such company.

(5) For the purposes of this paragraph, a director shall be a professional director at a particular time if—

(a) the director is then a solicitor or a member of such other professional body as the Revenue Commissioners may at that time allow for the purposes of this subparagraph,

(b) the director is not then an employee of any company then within the founding company's group,

(c) the director is not then a director of any such company other than the trust company, and

(d) the director meets the requirements of *subparagraph (6)*,

and for the purposes of this paragraph a director shall be a non-professional director at a particular time if the director is not then a professional director for those purposes.

(6) A director shall meet the requirements of this subparagraph if—

(a) he or she was appointed as an initial director and, before being appointed as director, was selected only by the persons who later became the non-professional initial directors, or

(b) he or she was appointed as a replacement or additional director and, before being appointed as director, was selected only by the persons who were the non-professional directors at the time of the selection.

(7) Directors shall be selected in accordance with this subparagraph if the process of selection is one under which—

(a) all the persons who are employees of the companies within the founding company's group at the time of the selection, and who do not have and have never had a material interest in any such company, are, in so far as is reasonably practicable, given the opportunity to stand for selection,

(b) all the employees of the companies within the founding company's group at the time of the selection are, in so far as is reasonably practicable, given the opportunity to vote, and

(c) persons gaining more votes are preferred to those gaining less.

(8) Directors shall be selected in accordance with this subparagraph if they are selected by persons elected to represent the employees of the companies within the founding company's group at the time of the selection.

Beneficiaries

11. (1) The trust deed shall contain provision as to the beneficiaries under the trust in accordance with this paragraph.

[(2) The trust deed shall provide that a person is a beneficiary at a particular time (in this subparagraph referred to as "the relevant time") if—

(a) the person is at the relevant time an employee or director of a company within the founding company's group,

(b) at each given time in a qualifying period the person was such an employee or director of a company falling within the founding company's group at that given time,

(c) in the case of a director, at that given time the person worked as a director of the company concerned at the rate of at least 20 hours a week (disregarding such matters as holidays and sickness), and

(d) the person is chargeable to income tax in respect of his or her office or employment under Schedule E.

(2A) The trust deed may provide that a person is a beneficiary at a particular time if, but for *subparagraph (2)(d)*, he or she would be a beneficiary within the rule which is included in the deed and conforms with *subparagraph (2)*.][17]

[(2B) Subject to *subparagraph (2C)*, the trust deed may provide that a person is a beneficiary at a particular time (in this subparagraph referred to as "*the relevant time*") if—

(a) the person has at each given time in a qualifying period been an employee or director of a company within the founding company's group at that given time,

(b) the person was such an employee or director—

(i) on the date the trust was established or at some time within 9 months prior to that date, or

(ii) at any time in the period of 5 years beginning with such date,

(c) the person has ceased to be an employee or director of the company or the company has ceased to be within that group,

[(d) at each given time—

(i) in the case of an employee share ownership trust approved under paragraph 2 before the passing of the Finance Act, 2000, in the 5 year period referred to in clause (b), and

(ii) in the case of an employee share ownership trust approved under paragraph 2 on or after the passing of the Finance Act, 2000, in the 5 year period, or such lesser period as the Minister for Finance may by order prescribe, commencing on the date referred to in clause (*b*),

50 per cent, or such lesser percentage as the Minister for Finance may by order prescribe, of the securities retained by the trustees at that time were pledged by them as security for borrowings, and][18]

(e) at the relevant time a period of not more than [20 years][19] has elapsed since the trust was established.

(2C) The trust deed shall not contain a rule that conforms with *subparagraph (2B)* [or *(3)*][20] unless the rule is expressed as applying to every person within it.][21]

(3) The trust deed may provide that a person is a beneficiary at a particular time (in this subparagraph referred to as "*the relevant time*") if—

(a) the person has at each given time in a qualifying period been an employee or director of a company within the founding company's group at that given time,

(b) the person has ceased to be an employee or director of the company or the company has ceased to be within that group, and

[(c) (i) in a case where the founding company is the Electricity Supply Board and as respects securities acquired by the trustees of the trust on or before 31 December 2001, the person was an employee or a director, as the case may be, of a company within the founding company's group on 1 January 1998, and

(ii) in any other case, at the relevant time a period of not more than 18 months has elapsed since the person so ceased or the company so ceased, as the case may be.][22]

(4) The trust deed may provide for a person to be a beneficiary if the person is a charity and the circumstances are such that—

(a) there is no person who is a beneficiary within the rule which is included in the deed and conforms with *subparagraph (2)* or with any rule which is so included and conforms with [*subparagraphs (2A)*, *2B* and *(3)*][23], and

(b) the trust is in consequence being wound up.

(5) For the purposes of [*subparagraphs (2)* and *(2A)*][24], a qualifying period shall be a period—

(a) whose length is not more than [3 years][25],

(b) whose length is specified in the trust deed, and

(c) which ends with the relevant time (within the meaning of that subparagraph).

(6) For the purposes of [*subparagraphs (2B)* and *(3)*][26], a qualifying period shall be a period—

(a) whose length is equal to that of the period specified in the trust deed for the purposes of a rule which conforms with *subparagraph (2)*, and

(b) which ends when the person or company, as the case may be, ceased as mentioned in [*subparagraphs (2B)(c)* and *(3)(b)*][27].

(7) The trust deed shall not provide for a person to be a beneficiary unless the person is within the rule which is included in the deed and conforms with *subparagraph (2)* or any rule which is so included and conforms with [*subparagraph (2A)*, *(2B)*, *(3)* or *(4)*][28].

(8) The trust deed shall provide that, notwithstanding any other rule which is included in it, a person cannot be a beneficiary at a particular time (in this subparagraph referred to as "*the relevant time*") by virtue of a rule which conforms with if—

(a) at the relevant time the person has a material interest in the founding company, or

(b) at any time in the period of one year preceding the relevant time the person has had a material interest in that company.

(9) For the purposes of this paragraph, "*charity*" means any body of persons or trust established for charitable purposes only.

[(10) Where an order is proposed to be made under *subparagraph (2B)(d)*, a draft of the order shall be laid before Dáil Éireann, and the order shall not be made until a resolution approving of the draft has been passed by Dáil Éireann.][29]

[11A.

(1) Notwithstanding any other provision of this Schedule, in any case where a trust is established by a company which is a relevant company, this Schedule shall, with any necessary modification, apply as respects the beneficiaries under the trust as if this paragraph were substituted for *paragraph 11*.

(2) The trust deed shall contain provision as to the beneficiaries under the trust in accordance with this paragraph.

(3) The trust deed shall provide that a person is a beneficiary at a particular time (in this subparagraph referred to as the "*relevant time*") if—

(a) the person was an employee or a director of the relevant company or of a company within the relevant company's group on the day the trust was established by that relevant company,

(b) the person is at the relevant time an employee or a director of—

(i) a company (in this subparagraph referred to as the "*first-mentioned company*") which is, or was at any time since the day the trust was established, within the founding company's group,

(ii) a company within a group of companies (within the meaning of *paragraph 2(2)(b)*) which has acquired control of the first-mentioned company,

(iii) a company to which—

(I) an employee, or

(II) a director,

referred to in clause (*a*) has been transferred under either or both the European Communities (Safeguarding of Employees' Rights on Transfer of Undertaking) Regulations, 1980 and 2000 and the Central Bank Act, 1971, or

(iv) a company within a group of companies (within the meaning of *paragraph 2(2)(b)*), of which the company referred to in subclause (iii) is, or was at any time, a member,

(c) at each given time in a qualifying period the person was such an employee or a director of a company referred to in clause (*b*),

(d) in the case of a director, at that given time the person worked as a director of a company referred to in clause (*b*) or of a company within the relevant company's group at the rate of at least 20 hours a week (disregarding such matters as holidays and sickness), and

(e) the person is chargeable to income tax in respect of his or her office or employment under Schedule E.

(4) The trust deed may provide that a person is a beneficiary at a particular time if, but for *subparagraph (3)(e)*, he or she would be a beneficiary within the rule which is included in the deed and conforms with *subparagraph (3)*.

(5) Subject to *subparagraph (6)*, the trust deed may provide that a person is a beneficiary at a particular time (in this subparagraph referred to as the "*relevant time*") if—

(a) the person was an employee or a director of the relevant company or of a company within the relevant company's group on the day the trust was established by that relevant company, [or, in the case of a company referred to in clause (*d*) of the definition of "*relevant company*" in *paragraph 1(1)*, at some time within 9 months prior to that day,][30]

(b) the person has at each given time in a qualifying period been an employee or a director of a company referred to in *subparagraph (3)(b)* at that given time,

(c) the person has ceased to be an employee or a director of a company referred to in *subparagraph (3)(b)*,

(d) at each given time in the 5 year period, or such lesser period as the Minister for Finance may by order prescribe, commencing on the date the trust was established, 50 per cent or such lesser percentage as the Minister for Finance may by order prescribe, of the securities retained by the trustees at that time were pledged by them as security for borrowings, and

(e) at the relevant time a period of not more than [20 years][31] has elapsed since the trust was established.

(6) The trust deed may provide that a person is a beneficiary at a particular time (in this subparagraph referred to as the "*relevant time*") if—

(a) the person was an employee or a director of the relevant company or of a company within the relevant company's group on the day the trust was established by that relevant company, [or, in the case of a company referred to in clause (*d*) of the definition of "*relevant company*" in *paragraph 1(1)*, at some time within 9 months prior to that day,][32]

(b) the person has at each given time in a qualifying period been an employee or a director of a company referred to in *subparagraph (3)(b)* at that given time,

(c) the person has ceased to be an employee or a director of a company referred to in *subparagraph (3)(b)*, and

(d) at the relevant time a period of not more than 18 months has elapsed since the person so ceased.

(7) The trust deed shall not contain a rule that conforms with *subparagraph (5)* [or *(6)*][33] unless the rule is expressed as applying to every person within it.

(8) The trust deed may provide for a person to be a beneficiary if the person is a charity and the circumstances are such that—

(a) there is no person who is a beneficiary within the rule which is included in the deed and conforms with *subparagraph (3)* or with any rule which is so included and conforms with *subparagraph (4)*, *(5)* or *(6)*, and

(b) the trust is in consequence of being wound up.

(9) For the purposes of *subparagraph (3)*, a qualifying period shall be a period—

(a) whose length is not more than 3 years,

(b) whose length is specified in the trust deed, and

(c) which ends with the relevant time (within the meaning of that subparagraph).

(10) For the purposes of *subparagraphs (5)* and *(6)*, a qualifying period shall be a period—

(a) whose length is equal to that of the period specified in the trust deed for the purposes of a rule which conforms with *subparagraph (3)*, and

(b) which ends when the person ceased as mentioned in *subparagraph (5)(c)* or *(6)(c)*, as the case may be.

(11) The trust deed shall not provide for a person to be a beneficiary unless the person is within the rule which is included in the deed and conforms with *subparagraph (3)* or any rule which is so included and conforms with *subparagraph (4)*, *(5)*, *(6)* or *(8)*.

(12) The trust deed shall provide that, notwithstanding any other rule which is included in it, a person cannot be a beneficiary at a particular time (in this subparagraph referred to as the "*relevant time*") by virtue of a rule which conforms with *subparagraph (3)*, *(4)*, *(5)*, *(6)* or *(8)* if—

(a) at the relevant time the person has a material interest in a company referred to in *subparagraph (3)(b)*, or

(b) at any time in the period of one year preceding the relevant time the person has had a material interest in that company,

and for the purposes of this subparagraph any reference to a company shall, in a case to which clause (*a*) of the definition of relevant company applies, also include a reference to a trustee savings bank which has been reorganised into the relevant company concerned.

(13) For the purposes of satisfying the qualifying period requirement referred to in *subparagraphs (3)(c)*, *(5)(b)* and *(6)(b)* a person shall also be regarded as such an employee or a director for any period in which that person is an employee or a director of, in a case to which clause (*a*) of the definition of relevant company applies, a trustee savings bank which has been reorganised into that relevant company.

(14) For the purposes of this paragraph "*charity*" means any body of persons or trust established for charitable purposes only.

(15) Where an order is proposed to be made under *subparagraph (5)(d)*, a draft of the order shall be laid before Dáil Éireann and the order shall not be made until a resolution approving of the draft has been passed by Dáil Éireann.][34]

Trustees' functions

12.

(1) The trust deed shall contain provision as to the functions of the trustees.

(2) The functions of the trustees shall be so expressed that it is apparent that their general functions are—

(a) to receive sums from the founding company and other sums, by means of loan or otherwise;

(b) to acquire securities;

(c) to grant rights to acquire shares to persons who are beneficiaries under the terms of the trust deed;

(d) to transfer either or both securities and sums to persons who are beneficiaries under the terms of the trust deed;

[(da) to pay any sum or to transfer securities to the personal representatives of deceased persons who were beneficiaries under the terms of the trust deed;][35]

(e) to transfer securities to the trustees of profit sharing schemes approved under *Part 2* of *Schedule 11*;

(f) pending transfer, to retain the securities and to manage them, whether by exercising voting rights or otherwise.

Sums

13.

(1) The trust deed shall require that any sum received by the trustees—

(a) shall be expended within the expenditure period,

(b) may be expended only for one or more of the qualifying purposes, and

(c) shall, while it is retained by them, be kept as cash, or be kept in an account with a relevant deposit taker (within the meaning of *section 256*).

(2) For the purposes of *subparagraph (1)*, the expenditure period shall be the period of 9 months beginning on the day determined as follows—

(a) in a case where the sum is received from the founding company, or a company which is controlled by that company at the time the sum is received, the day following the end of the accounting period in which the sum is expended by the company from which it is received;

(b) in any other case, the day the sum is received.

(3) For the purposes of *subparagraph (1)*, each of the following shall be a qualifying purpose—

(a) the acquisition of shares in the founding company [or of securities to which *subparagraph (ii)* or *(iv)* of *paragraph (b)* of the definition of "*specified securities*" in *section 509(1)* applies][36];

(b) the repayment of sums borrowed;

(c) the payment of interest on sums borrowed;

(d) the payment of any sum to a person who is a beneficiary under the terms of the trust deed;

[(da) the payment of any sum to the personal representatives of a deceased person who was a beneficiary under the terms of the trust deed;][37]

(e) the meeting of expenses.

(4) The trust deed shall provide that, in ascertaining for the purposes of a relevant rule (being a provision which is included in the trust deed and conforms with *subparagraph (1)*) whether a particular sum has been expended, sums received earlier by the trustees shall be treated as expended before sums received by them later.

(5) The trust deed shall provide that, where the trustees pay sums to different beneficiaries at the same time, all the sums shall be paid on similar terms.

(6) For the purposes of *subparagraph (5)*, the fact that terms vary according to the levels of remuneration of beneficiaries, the length of their service or similar factors shall not be regarded as meaning that the terms are not similar.

Securities

14.

(1) Subject to *paragraph 15*, the trust deed shall provide that securities acquired by the trustees shall be shares in the founding company which—

(a) form part of the ordinary share capital of the company,

(b) are fully paid up,

(c) are not redeemable, and

(d) are not subject to any restrictions other than restrictions which attach to all shares of the same class or a restriction authorised by *subparagraph (2)*.

(2) Subject to *subparagraph (3)*, a restriction shall be authorised by this subparagraph if—

(a) it is imposed by the founding company's articles of association,

(b) it requires all shares held by directors or employees of the founding company, or of any other company which it controls for the time being, to be disposed of on ceasing to be so held, and

(c) it requires all shares acquired, in pursuance of rights or interests obtained by such directors or employees, by persons who are not, or have ceased to be, such directors or employees to be disposed of when they are acquired.

(3) A restriction shall not be authorised by *subparagraph (2)* unless—

(a) any disposal required by the restriction will be by means of sale for a consideration in money on terms specified in the articles of association, and

(b) the articles also contain general provisions by virtue of which any person disposing of shares of the same class (whether or not held or acquired as mentioned in *subparagraph (2)*) may be required to sell them on terms which are the same as those mentioned in *clause (a)*.

(4) The trust deed shall provide that shares in the founding company may not be acquired by the trustees at a price exceeding the price they might reasonably be expected to fetch on a sale in the open market.

[(5) The trust deed shall provide that shares in the founding company may not be acquired by the trustees at a time when that company is controlled by another company, other than where the founding company is a company into which a trustee savings bank has been reorganised under *section 57* of the Trustee Savings Banks Act, 1989.][38]

15. The trust deed may provide that the trustees may acquire securities other than shares in the founding company—

(a) if they are securities acquired by the trustees as a result of a reorganisation or reduction of share capital[…][39] (construing "*reorganisation or reduction of share capital*" […][40] in accordance with *section 584*), or

(b) if they are securities issued to the trustees in exchange in circumstances mentioned in *section 586*.

16.

(1) The trust deed shall provide that—

(a) where the trustees transfer securities to a beneficiary, they shall do so on qualifying terms;

(b) the trustees shall transfer securities before the expiry of 20 years beginning on the date on which they acquired them.

(2) For the purposes of *subparagraph (1)*, a transfer of securities shall be made on qualifying terms if—

(a) all the securities transferred at the same time are transferred on similar terms,

(b) securities have been offered to all the persons who are beneficiaries under the terms of the trust deed when the transfer is made, and

(c) securities are transferred to all such beneficiaries who have accepted.

(3) For the purposes of *subparagraph (2)*, the fact that terms vary according to the levels of remuneration of beneficiaries, the length of their service or similar factors shall not be regarded as meaning that the terms are not similar.

(4) The trust deed shall provide that, in ascertaining for the purposes of a relevant rule (being a provision which is included in the trust deed and conforms with *subparagraph (1)*) whether particular securities are transferred, securities acquired earlier by the trustees shall be treated as transferred by them before securities acquired by them later.

Other features

17. The trust deed shall not contain features which are not essential or reasonably incidental to the purpose of acquiring sums and securities, transferring sums and securities to employees and directors, and transferring securities to the trustees of profit sharing schemes approved under *Part 2* of *Schedule 11*.

18.

(1) The trust deed shall provide that for the purposes of the deed the trustees—

(a) acquire securities when they become entitled to them;

(b) transfer securities to another person when that other person becomes entitled to them;

(c) retain securities if they remain entitled to them.

(2) Where the trust deed provides for the matter set out in *paragraph 15*, the trust deed shall provide for the following exceptions to any rule which is included in it and conforms with *subparagraph (1)(a)*, namely—

(a) if the trustees become entitled to securities as a result of a reorganisation or reduction of share capital, they shall be treated as having acquired them when they became entitled to the original shares which those securities represent (construing "*reorganisation or reduction of share capital*" and "*original shares*" in accordance with *section 584*);

(b) if securities are issued to the trustees in exchange in circumstances mentioned in *section 586*, they shall be treated as having acquired them when they became entitled to the securities for which they are exchanged.

(3) The trust deed shall provide that—

(a) if the trustees agree to take a transfer of securities, for the purposes of the deed they become entitled to them when the agreement is made [or, if the agreement is subject to one or more specified conditions being satisfied, on that condition or those conditions being satisfied][41] and not on a later transfer made pursuant to the agreement;

(b) if the trustees agree to transfer securities to another person, for the purposes of the deed the other person becomes entitled to them when the agreement is made and not on a later transfer made pursuant to the agreement.

Amendments

[1] Deleted by FA02 s13(1)(e)(i)(I). This section shall apply and have effect as on and from 16 April 2001.

[2] Substituted by FA02 s13(1)(e)(i)(II). This section shall apply and have effect as on and from 16 April 2001.

[3] Inserted by FA01 s17(1)(c)(i)(I). Applies and has effect as respects a profit sharing scheme, or an employee share ownership trust, approved on or after 12 December 2000.

[4] Inserted by FA02 s13(1)(e)(i)(III). This section shall apply and have effect as on and from 16 April 2001.

[5] Substituted by FA98 s36(1)(d)(i)(I). Shall apply as respects employee share ownership trusts approved of under paragraph 2 on or after the date of 27 March 1998

[6] Inserted by FA01 s17(1)(c)(i)(II). Applies and has effect as respects a profit sharing scheme, or an employee share ownership trust, approved on or after 12 December 2000.

[7] Substituted by FA98 s36(1)(d)(i)(II). Shall apply as respects employee share ownership trusts approved of under paragraph 2 on or after the date of 27 March 1998

[8] Substituted by FA01 s16(b). Applies as respects employee share ownership trusts approved on or after 30 March 2001

[9] Substituted by FA98 s36(1)(d)(ii). Shall apply as respects employee share ownership trusts approved of under paragraph 2 on or after the date of 27 March 1998

[10] Deleted by F(No.2)A08 s9(1)(b)(i). Applies on and from 24 December 2008.

[11] Inserted by F(No.2)A08 s9(1)(b)(i). Applies on and from 24 December 2008.

[12] Inserted by F(No.2)A08 s9(1)(b)(ii). Applies on and from 24 December 2008.

[13] Substituted by FA12 sched4(part 2)(g).

[14] Inserted by FA08 s19(1)(b). Applies as on and from 1 January 2009.

[15] Inserted by TSBAA01 s3(a).

[16] Inserted by FA01 s17(1)(c)(ii). Applies and has effect as respects a profit sharing scheme, or an employee share ownership trust, approved on or after 12 December 2000.

[17] Substituted by FA98 s36(1)(d)(iii)(I). Shall apply as respects employee share ownership trusts approved of under paragraph 2 on or after the date of 27 March 1998

[18] Substituted by FA00 s26(a).

[19] Substituted by F(No.2)A13 s19(a). Comes into operation on 1 January 2014.

[20] Inserted by FA04 s15(a).

[21] Inserted by FA99 s69(1)(d)(i)(I). Shall apply as respects employee share ownership trusts approved on or after the date of 25 March 1999

[22] Substituted by FA04 s8.

[23] Substituted by FA99 s69(1)(d)(i)(II). Shall apply as respects employee share ownership trusts approved on or after the date of 25 March 1999

[24] Substituted by FA98 s36(1)(d)(iii)(III). Shall apply as respects employee share ownership trusts approved of under paragraph 2 on or after the date of 27 March 1998

[25] Substituted by FA99 s69(1)(d)(i)(III). Shall apply as respects employee share ownership trusts approved on or after the date of 25 March 1999

[26, 27] Substituted by FA99 s69(1)(d)(i)(IV). Shall apply as respects employee share ownership trusts approved on or after the date of 25 March 1999

[28] Substituted by FA99 s69(1)(d)(i)(V). Shall apply as respects employee share ownership trusts approved on or after the date of 25 March 1999

[29] Inserted by FA00 s26(b).

[30] Inserted by FA04 s15(b)(i).

[31] Substituted by F(No.2)A13 s19(b). Comes into operation on 1 January 2014.

[32] Inserted by FA04 s15(b)(ii).

[33] Inserted by FA04 s15(b)(iii).

[34] Inserted by FA01 s17(1)(c)(iii). Applies and has effect as respects a profit sharing scheme, or an employee share ownership trust, approved on or after 12 December 2000.

[35] Inserted by FA01 s13(b)(i).

[36] Inserted by FA02 s13(1)(e)(ii). This section shall apply and have effect as on and from 16 April 2001.

[37] Inserted by FA01 s13(b)(ii).

[38] Substituted by TSBAA01 s3(a).

[39] Deleted by FA02 s13(1)(e)(iii)(I). This section shall apply and have effect as on and from 16 April 2001.

[40] Deleted by FA02 s13(1)(e)(iii)(II). This section shall apply and have effect as on and from 16 April 2001.

[41] Inserted by FA99 s69(1)(d)(ii). Shall apply as respects employee share ownership trusts approved on or after the date of 25 March 1999

Cross References

From Schedule 12

Section 2 Interpretation of Tax Acts.
Section 57 Extension of charge to tax under Case III of Schedule D in certain circumstances.
Section 256 Interpretation (Chapter 4).
Section 432 Meaning of "associated company" and "control".
Section 433 Meaning of "participator", "associate", "director" and "loan creditor".
Section 509 Interpretation (Chapter 1).
Section 519 Employee share ownership trusts.
Section 584 Reorganisation or reduction of share capital.
Section 586 Company amalgamations by exchange of shares.
Section 951 Obligation to make a return.
Section 1052 Penalties for failure to make certain returns, etc.
Section 1054 Penalties in the case of a secretary of a body of persons.
Schedule 11 Profit Sharing Schemes

To Schedule 12

Section 130 Matters to be treated as distributions.
Section 172A Interpretation.
Section 509 Interpretation (Chapter 1).
Section 511A Shares acquired from an employee share ownership trust.
Section 519 Employee share ownership trusts.
Schedule 2A Dividend Withholding Tax
Schedule 11 Profit Sharing Schemes
Schedule 29 Provisions Referred to in Sections 1052, 1053 and 1054

SCHEDULE 12A

Approved Savings-Related Share Option Schemes

[*Section 519A*.

Interpretation

1.

(1) For the purposes of this Schedule—

"*approved*" in relation to a scheme, means approved under *paragraph 2*;

"*associated company*" has the same meaning as in *section 432*, except that, for the purposes of *paragraph 24*, *subsection (1)* of that section shall have effect with the omission of the words "or at any time within one year previously";

"*bonus date*" has the meaning assigned to it by *paragraph 18*;

"*control*" has the same meaning as in *section 432*;

"*full-time director*" has the same meaning as in *section 250*;

"*grantor*", in relation to a scheme, means the company which has established the scheme;

"*group scheme*" and, in relation to such a scheme, "*participating company*" have the meanings given by *subparagraphs (3)* and *(4)*, respectively, of *paragraph 2*;

"*market value*" shall be construed in accordance with *section 548*;

"*savings-related share option scheme*" means a scheme approved by the Revenue Commissioners in accordance with this Schedule and which approval has not been withdrawn;

"*scheme shares*" has the meaning assigned to it by *paragraph 10*;

"*shares*" includes [stock;][1]

["*specified age*" means an age that is not less than 60 years and not more than pensionable age (within the meaning of section 2 of the [Social Welfare Consolidation Act 2005][2]).][3]

(2) *Section 10* shall apply for the purposes of this Schedule.

(3) For the purposes of this Schedule, a company is a member of a consortium that owns another company if it is one of not more than 5 companies which between them beneficially own not less than 75 per cent of the other company's ordinary share capital and each of which beneficially owns not less than 5 per cent of that capital.

(4) For the purposes of this Schedule, the question whether one company is controlled by another shall be determined in accordance with *section 432*.

Approval of schemes

2.

(1) On the application of a body corporate (in this Schedule referred to as "*the grantor*") which has established a savings-related share option scheme, the Revenue Commissioners shall approve the scheme if they are satisfied that it fulfils the requirements of this Schedule.

(2) An application under *subparagraph (1)* shall be made in writing and contain such particulars and be supported by such evidence as the Revenue Commissioners may require.

(3) Where the grantor has control of another company or companies, the scheme may be expressed to extend to all or any of the companies of which it has control and in this Schedule a scheme which is expressed so to extend is referred to as a "*group scheme*".

(4) In relation to a group scheme, "*participating company*" means the grantor or any other company to which for the time being the scheme is expressed to extend.

[(5) The scheme shall indicate the specified age for the purposes of the scheme.][4]

3.

(1) The Revenue Commissioners shall not approve a scheme under this Schedule if it appears to them that it contains features which are neither essential nor reasonably incidental to the purpose of providing for employees and directors benefits in the nature of rights to acquire shares.

(2) The Revenue Commissioners shall be satisfied—

(a) that there are no features of the scheme other than any which are included to satisfy requirements of this Schedule which have or would have the effect of discouraging any description of employees who fulfil the conditions in *paragraph 9(1)* from actually participating in the scheme, and

(b) where the grantor is a member of a group of companies, that the scheme does not and would not have the effect of conferring benefits wholly or mainly on directors of companies in the group or on those employees of companies in the group who are in receipt of the higher or highest levels of remuneration.

[(3) For the purposes of *subparagaph (2)*—

(a) "*a group of companies*" means a company and any other companies of which it has control or with which it is associated, and

(b) a company shall be associated with another company where it could reasonably be considered that—

(i) both companies act in pursuit of a common purpose,

(ii) any person or any group of persons or groups of persons having a reasonable commonality of identity have or had the means or power, either directly or indirectly, to determine the trading operations carried on or to be carried on by both companies, or

(iii) both companies are under the control of any person or group of persons or groups of persons having a reasonable commonality of identity.][5]

4.

(1) If, at any time after the Revenue Commissioners have approved a scheme, any of the requirements of this Schedule cease to be satisfied or the grantor fails to provide information requested by the Revenue Commissioners under *paragraph 6*, the Revenue Commissioners may withdraw the approval with effect from that time or such later time as the Revenue Commissioners may specify but where rights obtained under a savings-related share option scheme before the withdrawal of approval from the scheme under this paragraph are exercised after the withdrawal, *section 519A(3)* shall apply in respect of the exercise as if the scheme were still approved.

(2) If an alteration is made in the scheme at any time after the Revenue Commissioners have approved the scheme, the approval shall not have effect after the date of the alteration unless the Revenue Commissioners have approved the alteration.

5. If the grantor is aggrieved by—

(a) the failure of the Revenue Commissioners to approve the scheme or to approve an alteration in the scheme,

(b) the withdrawal of approval, or

(c) the failure of the Revenue Commissioners to decide that a condition subject to which the approval has been given is satisfied,

it may, by notice in writing given to the Revenue Commissioners within 30 days from the date on which it is notified of the Revenue Commissioners' decision, require the matter to be determined by the Appeal Commissioners, and the Appeal Commissioners shall hear and determine the matter in like manner as an appeal made to them against an assessment and all the provisions of the Income Tax Acts relating to such an appeal (including the provisions relating to the rehearing of an appeal and to the statement of a case for the opinion of the High Court on a point of law) shall apply accordingly with any necessary modifications.

Information

6. The Revenue Commissioners may by notice in writing require any person to furnish them, within such time as the Revenue Commissioners may direct (not being less than 30 days), with such information as the Revenue Commissioners think necessary for the performance of their functions under this Schedule, and which the person to whom the notice is addressed has or can reasonably obtain, including in particular information—

(a) to enable the Revenue Commissioners to determine—

(i) whether to approve a scheme or withdraw an approval already given, or

(ii) the liability to tax, including capital gains tax, of any person who has participated in a scheme, and

(b) in relation to the administration of a scheme and any alteration of the terms of a scheme.

[6A. Without prejudice to paragraph 6 the trustees of an approved scheme shall as respects any year, prepare and deliver to the Revenue Commissioners on or before 31 March in the year following that year, a return in the prescribed form (within the meaning of [*Chapter 3* of *Part 41A*][6]) of such particulars relating to the approved scheme for that year as may be required by the prescribed form and *sections 1052* and *1054* shall apply to a failure by the trustees to deliver a return in accordance with this paragraph as they apply to a failure to deliver a return referred to in *section 1052*.][7]

7. The Revenue Commissioners may nominate any of their officers, including an inspector, to perform any acts and discharge any functions authorised by this Schedule to be performed or discharged by them.

Eligibility

8.

(1) The scheme shall not provide for any person to be eligible to participate in it, that is to say, to obtain and exercise rights under it at any time if at that time that person has, or has within the preceding 12 months had, a material interest in a close company which is—

(i) a company the shares of which may be acquired pursuant to the exercise of rights obtained under the scheme, or

(ii) a company which has control of such a company or is a member of a consortium which owns such a company.

(2) *Subparagraph (1)* shall apply in relation to a company which would be a close company but for *section 430(1)(a)* or *431*.

(3) (a) In this paragraph, "*close company*" has the meaning assigned to it by *section 430*.

(b) For the purpose of this paragraph—

(i) *subsection (3)* of *section 433* shall apply—

(I) in a case where the scheme in question is a group scheme, with the substitution of a reference to all participating companies for the first reference to the company in *paragraph (c)(ii)* of that subsection, and

(II) with the substitution of a reference to 15 per cent for the reference in that paragraph to 5 per cent, and

(ii) *section 437(2)* shall apply, with the substitution of a reference to 15 per cent for the reference in that section to 5 per cent, for the purpose of determining whether a person has or had a material interest in a company.

9.

(1) Subject to *paragraph 8*, every person who—

(a) is an employee or a full-time director of the grantor or, in the case of a group scheme, a participating company,

(b) has been such an employee or director at all times during a qualifying period not exceeding three years, and

(c) is chargeable to tax in respect of that person's office or employment under Schedule E,

shall be eligible to participate in the scheme, that is to say, to obtain and exercise rights under it, on similar terms.

(2) For the purposes of *subparagraph (1)*, the fact that the rights to be obtained by the persons participating in a scheme vary according to the levels of their remuneration, the length of their service or similar factors shall not be regarded as meaning that they are not eligible to participate in the scheme on similar terms.

(3) Except as provided by *paragraph 20* or pursuant to such a provision as is referred to in *paragraph 22(1)(e)* or *(f)*, a person shall not be eligible to participate in the scheme at any time unless he or she is at that time a director or employee of the grantor or, in the case of a group scheme, of a participating company.

Conditions as to the shares

10. The scheme shall provide for directors and employees to obtain rights to acquire shares (in this Schedule referred to as "*scheme shares*") which satisfy the requirements of *paragraphs 11* to *15*.

11. Scheme shares shall form part of the ordinary share capital of—

(a) the grantor,

(b) a company which has control of the grantor, or

(c) a company which either is, or has control of, a company which—

(i) is a member of a consortium which owns either the grantor or a company having control of the grantor, and

(ii) beneficially owns not less than 15 per cent of the ordinary share capital of the company so owned.

12. Scheme shares shall be—

(a) shares of a class quoted on a recognised stock exchange,

(b) shares in a company not under the control of another company, or

(c) shares in a company which is under the control of a company (other than a company which is, or if resident in the State would be, a close company within the meaning of *section 430*) whose shares are quoted on a recognised stock exchange.

13.

(1) Scheme shares shall be—

(a) fully paid up,

(b) not redeemable, and

(c) not subject to any restrictions other than restrictions which attach to all shares of the same class or a restriction authorised by *subparagraph (2)*.

(2) Subject to *subparagraph (3)*, the shares may be subject to a restriction imposed by the company's articles of association—

(a) requiring all shares held by directors or employees of the company or of any other company of which it has control to be disposed of on ceasing to be so held, and

(b) requiring all shares acquired, in pursuance of rights or interests obtained by such directors or employees, by persons who are not, or have ceased to be, such directors or employees to be disposed of when they are acquired.

(3) A restriction is not authorised by *subparagraph (2)* unless—

(a) any disposal required by the restriction will be by way of sale for a consideration in money on terms specified in the articles of association, and

(b) the articles also contain general provisions by virtue of which any person disposing of shares of the same class (whether or not held or acquired as mentioned in *subparagraph (2)*) may be required to sell them on terms which are the same as those mentioned in *paragraph (a)*.

14.

(1) In determining for the purposes of *paragraph 13(1)(c)* whether scheme shares which are or are to be acquired by any person are subject to any restrictions, there shall be regarded as a restriction attaching to the shares any contract, agreement, arrangement or condition by which such person's freedom to dispose of the shares or of any interest in them or of the proceeds of their sale or to exercise any right conferred by them is restricted or by which such a disposal or exercise may result in any disadvantage to that person or to a person connected with that person.

(2) *Subparagraph (1)* does not apply to so much of any contract, agreement, arrangement or condition as contains provisions similar in purpose and effect to any of the provisions of the Model Code set out in the Listing Rules of the Irish Stock Exchange.

15. Except where scheme shares are in a company whose ordinary share capital consists of shares of one class only, the majority of the issued shares of the same class shall be held by persons other than—

(a) persons who acquired their shares—

(i) in pursuance of a right conferred on them or an opportunity afforded to them as a director or employee of the grantor or any other company, and

(ii) not in pursuance of an offer to the public,

(b) trustees holding shares on behalf of persons who acquired their beneficial interests in the shares as mentioned in *subparagraph (a)*, and

(c) in a case where the shares fall within *paragraph 12(c)* and do not fall within *paragraph 12(a)*, companies which have control of the company whose shares are in question or of which that company is an associated company within the meaning of *section 432*.

Exchange provisions

16

(1) The scheme may provide that if any company ("*the acquiring company*")—

(a) obtains control of a company whose shares are scheme shares as a result of making a general offer—

(i) to acquire the whole of the issued ordinary share capital of the company which is made on a condition such that if it is satisfied the person making the offer will have control of the company, or

(ii) to acquire all the shares in the company which are of the same class as the scheme shares,

(b) obtains control of a company whose shares are scheme shares in pursuance of a compromise or arrangement sanctioned by the court under section 201 of the Companies Act, 1963, or

(c) becomes bound or entitled to acquire shares in a company, under section 204 of the Companies Act, 1963, whose shares are scheme shares,

any participant in the scheme may at any time within the appropriate period, by agreement with the acquiring company, release his or her rights under the scheme (in this paragraph referred to as "*the old rights*") in consideration of the grant to him or her of rights (in this paragraph referred to as "*the new rights*") which are equivalent to the old rights but relate to shares in a different company (whether the acquiring company itself or some other company falling within *subparagraph (b)* or *(c)* of *paragraph 11*).

(2) In *subparagraph (1)* "*the appropriate period*" means—

(a) in a case falling within clause *(a)* of that subparagraph, the period of six months beginning with the time when the person making the offer has obtained control of the company and any condition subject to which the offer is made is satisfied,

(b) in a case falling within clause *(b)* of that subparagraph, the period of six months beginning with the time when the court sanctions the compromise or arrangement, and

(c) in a case falling within clause *(c)* of that subparagraph, the period during which the acquiring company remains bound or entitled as mentioned in that clause.

(3) The new rights shall not be regarded for the purposes of this paragraph as equivalent to the old rights unless—

(a) the shares to which they relate satisfy the conditions specified, in relation to scheme shares, in *paragraphs 11* to *15*,

(b) the new rights will be exercisable in the same manner as the old rights and subject to the provisions of the scheme as it had effect immediately before the release of the old rights,

(c) the total market value, immediately before the release, of the shares which were subject to the participant's old rights is equal to the total market value, immediately after the grant, of the shares in respect of which the new rights are granted to the participant, and

(d) the total amount payable by the participant for the acquisition of shares in pursuance of the new rights is equal to the total amount that would have been payable for the acquisition of shares in pursuance of the old rights.

(4) Where any new rights are granted pursuant to a provision included in a scheme by virtue of this paragraph they shall be regarded—

(a) for the purposes of *section 519A* and this Schedule, and

(b) for the purposes of the subsequent application (by virtue of a condition complying with *subparagraph (3)(b)*) of the provisions of the scheme,

as having been granted at the time when the corresponding old rights were granted.

Exercise of rights

17. The scheme shall provide for the scheme shares to be paid for with moneys not exceeding the amount of repayments made and any interest paid to them under a certified contractual savings scheme within the meaning of *subsection (4)* of *section 519C.*

18. Subject to *paragraphs 19* to *22*, the rights obtained under the scheme must not be capable of being exercised before the bonus date, that is to say, the date on which repayments under the certified contractual savings scheme are due and for the purposes of this paragraph and *paragraph 17*—

(a) repayments under a certified contractual savings scheme may be taken as including or as not including a bonus,

(b) the time when repayments are due shall be, where repayments are taken as including the maximum bonus, the earliest date on which the maximum bonus is payable and, in any other case, the earliest date on which a bonus is payable under the scheme, and

(c) the question of what is to be taken as so included must be required to be determined at the time when rights under the scheme are obtained.

19. The scheme shall provide that if a person who has obtained rights under the scheme dies before the bonus date the rights must be exercised, if at all, within 12 months after the date of that person's death and if that person dies within 6 months after the bonus date the rights may be exercised within 12 months after the bonus date.

20. The scheme shall provide that if a person who has obtained rights under it ceases to hold the office or employment by virtue of which that person is eligible to participate in the scheme by reason of—

(a) injury or disability or on account of his or her being dismissed by reason of redundancy (within the meaning of the Redundancy Payments Acts, 1967 to 1991), or

(b) reaching [*the specified age*][8],

then the rights shall be exercised, if at all, within 6 months of that person so ceasing and, if that person so ceases for any other reason within 3 years of obtaining the rights, they may not be exercised at all except pursuant to such a provision of the scheme as is mentioned in *paragraph 22(1)(e)*; in relation to the case where that person so ceases, for any other reason, more than 3 years after obtaining the rights, the scheme shall either provide that the rights may not be exercised or that they must be exercised, if at all, within 6 months of that person so ceasing.

21. The scheme shall provide that where a person who has obtained rights under it continues to hold the office or employment by virtue of which that person is eligible to participate in the scheme after the date on which that person reaches [*the specified age*][9], that person may exercise the rights within 6 months of that date.

22.

(1) The scheme may provide that—

(a) if any person obtains control of a company whose shares are scheme shares as a result of making a general offer falling within clause (*a*)(i) or (*a*)(ii) of *paragraph 16(1)*, rights obtained under the scheme to acquire shares in the company may be exercised within 6 months of the time when the person making the offer has obtained control of the company and any condition subject to which the offer is made has been satisfied,

(b) if under *section 201* of the Companies Act, 1963, (compromise between company and its members or creditors) the court sanctions a compromise or arrangement proposed for the purposes of or in connection with a scheme for the reconstruction of a company whose shares are scheme shares or its amalgamation with any other company or companies, rights obtained under the share option scheme to acquire shares in the company may be exercised within 6 months of the court sanctioning the compromise or arrangement,

(c) if any person becomes bound or entitled, under *section 204* of the Companies Act, 1963, (power to acquire shares of shareholders dissenting from schemes or contract which has been approved by majority), to acquire shares in a company shares in which are scheme shares, rights obtained under the scheme to acquire shares in the company may be exercised at any time when that person remains so bound or entitled,

(d) if a company whose shares are scheme shares passes a resolution for voluntary winding up, rights obtained under a scheme to acquire shares in the company may be exercised within 6 months of the passing of the resolution,

(e) if a person ceases to hold an office or employment by virtue of which that person is eligible to participate in the scheme by reason only that—

(i) that office or employment is in a company of which the grantor ceases to have control, or

(ii) that office or employment relates to a business or part of a business which is transferred to a person who is neither an associated company of the grantor nor a company of which the grantor has control,

rights under the scheme held by that person may be exercised within 6 months of that person so ceasing, and

(f) if, at the bonus date, a person who has obtained rights under the scheme holds an office or employment in a company which is not a participating company but which is—

(i) an associated company of the grantor, or

(ii) a company of which the grantor has control,

those rights may be exercised within 6 months of that date.

(2) For the purposes of this paragraph a person shall be deemed to have obtained control of a company if that person and others acting in concert with that person have together obtained control of it.

23. Except as provided in *paragraph 19*, rights obtained by a person under the scheme shall not be capable—

(a) of being transferred by that person, or

(b) of being exercised later than 6 months after the bonus date.

24. No person shall be treated for the purposes of *paragraph 20* or *22(1)(e)* as ceasing to hold an office or employment by virtue of which that person is eligible to participate in the scheme until that person ceases to hold an office or employment in the grantor or in any associated company or company of which the grantor has control.

Acquisition of shares

25.

(1) The scheme shall provide for a person's contributions under the certified contractual savings scheme to be of such amount as to secure as nearly as may be repayment of an amount equal to that for which shares may be acquired in pursuance of rights obtained under the scheme, and for this purpose the amount of repayment under the certified contractual savings scheme shall be determined as mentioned in *paragraph 18*.

(2) The scheme shall not—

(a) permit the aggregate amount of a person's contributions under certified contractual savings schemes linked to savings-related share option schemes approved under this Schedule to exceed [€500][10] monthly, nor

(b) impose a minimum on the amount of a person's contributions which exceeds [€12][11] monthly.

[...][12]

Share price

26. The price at which scheme shares may be acquired by the exercise of a right obtained under the scheme—

(a) shall be stated at the time the right is obtained, and

(b) shall not be manifestly less than 75 per cent of the market value of shares of the same class at that time or, if the Revenue Commissioners and the grantor agree in writing, at such earlier time or times as may be provided in the agreement,

but the scheme may provide for such variation of the price as may be necessary to take account of any variation in the share capital of which the scheme shares form part.

Options etc.

27.

(1) For the purposes of *section 437(2)*, as applied by *paragraph 8(3)(b)(ii)* of this Schedule, a right to acquire shares (however arising) shall be taken to be a right to control them.

(2) Any reference in *subparagraph (3)* to the shares attributed to an individual is a reference to the shares which, in accordance with *section 437(2)* as applied by *paragraph 8(3)(b)(ii)* of this Schedule, fall to be brought into account in that individual's case to determine whether their number exceeds a particular percentage of the company's ordinary share capital.

(3) In any case where—

(a) the shares attributed to an individual consist of or include shares which that individual or any other person has a right to acquire, and

(b) the circumstances are such that, if that right were to be exercised, the shares acquired would be shares which were previously unissued and which the company is contractually bound to issue in the event of the exercise of the right;

then, in determining at any time prior to the exercise of that right whether the number of shares attributed to the individual exceeds a particular percentage of the ordinary share capital of the company, that ordinary share capital shall be taken to be increased by the number of unissued shares referred to in clause (*b*).][13]

Amendments

[1] Substituted by FA00 s51(b)(i)(I).

[2] Substituted by FA07 sched4(1)(ai). Shall have effect as on and from 1 January 2007.

[3] Inserted by FA00 s51(b)(i)(II).

[4] Inserted by FA00 s51(b)(ii).

[5] Substituted by FA01 s16(c). Applies as respects savings-related share option schemes approved on or after 30 March 2001

[6] Substituted by FA12 sched4(part 2)(g).

[7] Inserted by FA08 s19(1)(c). Applies as on and from 1 January 2009.

[8] Substituted by FA00 s51(b)(iii).

[9] Substituted by FA00 s51(b)(iv).

[10] Substituted by FA08 s13(1)(a). Applies as respects contributions made under certified contractual savings schemes entered into on or after 1 February 2008.

[11] Substituted by FA01 sched5.

[12] Deleted by FA08 s13(1)(b). Applies as on and from 1 February 2008.

[13] Inserted by FA99 s68(b).

Revenue Briefings

eBrief

eBrief No. 17/2011 – Share-Based Remuneration – Finance Act 2011 Changes

Revenue Information Notes

A Guide to Approved Savings Related Share Option Schemes

Cross References

From Schedule 12A

Section 10 Connected persons.

Section 201 Exemptions and reliefs in respect of tax under section 123.

Section 240 Provisions as to tax under section 239.

Section 250 Extension of relief under section 248 to certain individuals in relation to loans applied in acquiring interest in certain companies.

Section 430 Meaning of "close company".

Section 431 Certain companies with quoted shares not to be close companies.

Section 432 Meaning of "associated company" and "control".

Section 433 Meaning of "participator", "associate", "director" and "loan creditor".

Section 437 Interest paid to directors and directors' associates.

Section 519A Approved savings-related share option schemes.

Section 519C Interest, etc. under certified contractual savings schemes.

Section 548 Valuation of assets.

Section 951 Obligation to make a return.

Section 1052 Penalties for failure to make certain returns, etc.

Section 1054 Penalties in the case of a secretary of a body of persons.

To Schedule 12A

Section 519A Approved savings-related share option schemes.

Section 519B Costs of establishing savings-related share option schemes.

Section 519C Interest, etc. under certified contractual savings schemes.

Schedule 29 Provisions Referred to in Sections 1052, 1053 and 1054

SCHEDULE 12B

Certified Contractual Savings Schemes

[*Section 519C.*

1. This Schedule shall have effect for the purposes of *section 519C.*

Specifications by the Minister for Finance

2.

(1) The requirements which may be specified under *section 519C(4)(c)* are such requirements as the Minister for Finance thinks fit.

(2) In particular, the requirements may relate to—

(a) the descriptions of individuals who may enter into contracts under a scheme;

(b) the contributions to be paid by individuals;

(c) the sums to be paid or repaid to individuals.

3.

(1) Where a specification has been made under *section 519C(4)(c)*, the Minister for Finance may withdraw the specification and stipulate the date on which the withdrawal is to become effective and any certification made by the Revenue Commissioners by reference to such specification shall be deemed to have been withdrawn on the same date.

(2) No withdrawal under this paragraph shall affect—

(a) the operation of a certified contractual savings scheme before the stipulated date, or

(b) any contract under such a scheme entered into before that date.

(3) No withdrawal under this paragraph shall be effective unless the Revenue Commissioners—

(a) send a notice by post to each qualifying savings institution informing it of the withdrawal of both the specification and certification, and

(b) do so not less than 28 days before the stipulated date.

4.

(1) Where a specification has been made under *section 519C(4)(c)*, the Minister for Finance may vary the specification and stipulate the date on which the variation is to become effective and any certification made by the Revenue Commissioners by reference to the specification obtaining before the variation shall be deemed to have been withdrawn on the date the variation became effective.

(2) The Revenue Commissioners may at any time certify a scheme as fulfilling the requirements obtaining after the variation.

(3) No variation and withdrawal under this paragraph shall affect—

(a) the operation of a certified contractual savings scheme before the stipulated date, or

(b) any contract under such a scheme entered into before that date.

(4) No variation and withdrawal under this paragraph shall be effective unless the Revenue Commissioners—

(a) send a notice by post to each qualifying savings institution informing it of the variation of the specification and withdrawal of the certification, and

(b) do so not less than 28 days before the stipulated date.

Information

5. The Revenue Commissioners may by notice in writing require any person to furnish them, within such time as the Revenue Commissioners may direct (not being less than 30 days), with such information as the Revenue Commissioners think necessary for the performance of their functions under this Schedule, and which the person to whom the notice is addressed has or can reasonably obtain, including in particular information—
   (a) to enable the Revenue Commissioners to determine—
      (i) whether to certify a scheme or withdraw a certification already given, or
      (ii) the liability to tax, including capital gains tax, of any person who has participated in a scheme, and
   (b) in relation to the administration of a scheme and any alteration of the terms of a scheme.

6. The Revenue Commissioners may nominate any of their officers, including an inspector, to perform any acts and discharge any functions authorised by this Schedule to be performed or discharged by them.][1]

Amendments

[1] Inserted by FA99 s68(b).

Cross References

From Schedule 12B

Section 519C Interest, etc. under certified contractual savings schemes.

To Schedule 12B

Section 519C Interest, etc. under certified contractual savings schemes.

Schedule 29 Provisions Referred to in Sections 1052, 1053 and 1054

SCHEDULE 12C

Approved Share Option Schemes

[*Section 519D*

Interpretation

1.

(1) For the purposes of this Schedule—

"*approved*" in relation to a scheme, means approved under *paragraph 2*;

"*associated company*" has the same meaning as in *section 432*;

"*auditor*", in relation to a company, means the person or persons appointed as auditor of the company for the purposes of the Companies Acts, 1963 to 1999, or under the law of the territory in which the company is incorporated and which corresponds to those Acts;

"*control*" has the same meaning as in *section 432*;

"*full-time director*", in relation to a company, means a director who is required to devote substantially the whole of his or her time to the service of the company;

"*grantor*" has the meaning given by *paragraph 2(1)*;

"*group scheme*" has the meaning given by *paragraph 2(3)*;

"*key employee or director*", in relation to a company, means an employee or a full-time director of the company whose specialist skills, qualifications and relevant experience are vital to the future success of the company and is so certified to the Revenue Commissioners by the company;

"*market value*" shall be construed in accordance with *section 548*; "*participating company*", in relation to a group scheme, has the meaning given by *paragraph 2(4)*;

"*scheme shares*" has the meaning given by *paragraph 11*;

"*shares*" includes stock.

(2) *Section 10* shall apply for the purposes of this Schedule.

(3) *Subsection (3)* of *section 433* shall have effect in a case where the scheme is a group scheme, with the substitution of a reference to all the participating companies for the first reference to the company in *subparagraph (ii)* of *paragraph (c)* of that subsection.

(4) For the purposes of this Schedule—

(a) a company is a member of a consortium that owns another company if it is one of not more than 5 companies which between them beneficially own not less than 75 per cent of the other company's ordinary share capital and each of which beneficially owns not less than 5 per cent of that capital, and

(b) the question of whether one company is controlled by another shall be determined in accordance with *section 432*.

Approval of schemes

2.

(1) On the application of a body corporate (in this Schedule referred to as the "*grantor*") which has established a share option scheme, the Revenue Commissioners shall approve the scheme if they are satisfied that it fulfils the requirements of this Schedule.

(2) An application under *subparagraph (1)* shall be made in writing and contain such particulars and be supported by such evidence as the Revenue Commissioners may require.

(3) Where the grantor has control of another company or companies, the scheme may be expressed to extend to all or any of the companies of which it has control and in this Schedule a scheme which is expressed so to extend is referred to as a "*group scheme*".

(4) In relation to a group scheme, "*participating company*" means the grantor or any other company to which for the time being the scheme is expressed to extend.

3.

(1) The Revenue Commissioners shall not approve a scheme under this Schedule if it appears to them that it contains features which are neither essential nor reasonably incidental to the purpose of providing for employees' and full-time directors' benefits in the nature of rights to acquire shares.

(2) The Revenue Commissioners shall be satisfied—

(a) that there are no features of the scheme other than any which are included to satisfy requirements of this Schedule which have or would have the effect of discouraging any description of employees who fulfil the conditions in *paragraph 8(1)* from actually participating in the scheme, and

(b) where the grantor is a member of a group of companies, that the scheme does not and would not have the effect of conferring benefits wholly or mainly on directors of companies in the group or on those employees of companies in the group who are in receipt of the higher or highest levels of remuneration.

(3) For the purposes of *subparagraph (2)*, "*a group of companies*" means a company and any other companies of which it has control or with which it is associated.

(4) For the purposes of *subparagraph (3)*, a company shall be associated with another company where it could reasonably be considered that—

(a) both companies act in pursuit of a common purpose,

(b) any person or any group of persons or groups of persons having a reasonable commonality of identity have or had the means or power, either directly or indirectly, to determine the trading operations carried on or to be carried on by both companies, or

(c) both companies are under the control of any person or group of persons or groups of persons having a reasonable commonality of identity.

4.

(1) If, at any time after the Revenue Commissioners have approved a scheme, any of the requirements of this Schedule cease to be satisfied or the grantor fails to provide information requested by the Revenue Commissioners under *paragraph 20*, the Revenue Commissioners may withdraw the approval with effect from that time or such later time as the Revenue Commissioners may specify.

(2) If an alteration is made in the scheme at any time after the Revenue Commissioners have approved the scheme, the approval shall not have effect after the date of the alteration unless the Revenue Commissioners have approved the alteration.

5. If the grantor is aggrieved by—

(a) the failure of the Revenue Commissioners to approve the scheme or to approve an alteration in the scheme,

(b) the withdrawal of approval, or

(c) the failure of the Revenue Commissioners to decide that a condition subject to which the approval has been given is satisfied,

it may, by notice in writing given to the Revenue Commissioners within 30 days from the date on which it is notified of the Revenue Commissioners' decision, require the matter to be determined by the Appeal Commissioners, and the Appeal Commissioners shall hear and determine the matter in like manner as an appeal made to them against an assessment and all the provisions of the Income Tax Acts relating to such an appeal (including the provisions relating to the rehearing of an appeal and to the statement of a case for the opinion of the High Court on a point of law) shall apply accordingly with any necessary modifications.

6. The Revenue Commissioners may nominate any of their officers, including an inspector, to perform any acts and discharge any functions authorised by this Schedule to be performed or discharged by them.

Eligibility

7.

(1) The scheme shall not provide for any person to be eligible to participate in it, that is to say, to obtain and exercise rights under it—

(a) unless he or she is an employee or director of the grantor or, in the case of a group scheme, of a participating company, or

(b) at any time when he or she has, or has within the preceding 12 months had, a material interest in a close company within the meaning of *Chapter 1* of *Part 13*, which is—

(i) a company the shares of which may be acquired pursuant to the exercise of rights obtained under the scheme, or

(ii) a company which has control of such a company or is a member of a consortium which owns such a company.

(2) Notwithstanding *subparagraph 1(a)*, the scheme may provide that a person may exercise rights obtained under it despite having ceased to be an employee or a director.

8.

(1) The scheme shall provide that, at any time, every person who—

(a) is an employee or a full-time director of the grantor or, in the case of a group scheme, a participating company,

(b) has been such an employee or director at all times during a qualifying period not exceeding three years, and

(c) is chargeable to tax in respect of that person's office or employment under Schedule E,

shall be eligible to participate in the scheme, that is to say, to obtain and exercise rights under it.

(2) Subject to *paragraph 9* every person eligible to participate in the scheme shall do so on similar terms.

(3) For the purposes of *subparagraph (2)*, the fact that—

(a) the rights to be obtained by persons participating in a scheme vary or are different—

(i) in the year of assessment in which they commence to hold the office or employment by virtue of which they are entitled to participate in the scheme, or

(ii) according to the levels of their remuneration, the length of their service or similar factors,

or

(b) a person is not entitled to receive rights within a stated period of his or her normal retirement date,

shall not be regarded as meaning that they are not eligible to participate in the scheme on similar terms.

9.

(1) Subject to the conditions of this paragraph, the scheme may provide for an employee or a director, who is a key employee or director of the grantor or, in the case of a group scheme, a participating company, to obtain and exercise rights under it which do not satisfy the requirement of *paragraph 8* regarding participation in the scheme on similar terms.

(2) The conditions of this paragraph are that, in any year of assessment—

(a) the total number of shares in respect of which rights have been granted to key employees and directors in accordance with a rule of the scheme which conforms with this paragraph does not exceed 30 per cent of the total number of shares in respect of which rights have been granted to all employees and directors participating in the scheme whether in accordance with this paragraph or *paragraph 8*, and

(b) an individual who obtains rights for a year of assessment by virtue of this paragraph shall not also be entitled to obtain rights for that year in accordance with *paragraph 8*.

10. In determining for the purposes of *paragraph 7*—

(a) whether a company is a close company, *section 430(1)(a)* and *subsections (3)* to *(7)* of *section 431* shall be disregarded, and

(b) whether a person has or has had a material interest in a company, *sections 437(2)* and *433(3)(c)(ii)* shall have effect with the substitution for the references in those provisions to 5 per cent of references to 15 per cent.

Scheme shares

11. The scheme shall provide for directors and employees to obtain rights to acquire shares (in this Schedule referred to as "*scheme shares*") which satisfy the requirements of *paragraphs 12* to *16*.

12. Scheme shares shall form part of the ordinary share capital of—

(a) the grantor,

(b) a company which has control of the grantor, or

(c) a company which either is, or has control of, a company which—

(i) is a member of a consortium which owns either the grantor or a company having control of the grantor, and

(ii) beneficially owns not less than 15 per cent of the ordinary share capital of the company so owned.

13. Scheme shares shall be—

(a) shares of a class quoted on a recognised stock exchange,

(b) shares in a company which is not under the control of another company, or

(c) shares in a company which is under the control of a company (other than a company which is, or if resident in the State would be, a close company within the meaning of *section 430*) whose shares are quoted on a recognised stock exchange.

14.

(1) Scheme shares—

(a) shall be fully paid up,

(b) shall not be redeemable, and

(c) shall not be subject to any restrictions other than restrictions which attach to all shares of the same class or a restriction authorised by *subparagraph (2).*

(2) Subject to *subparagraph (3)*, the shares may be subject to a restriction imposed by the company's articles of association—

(a) requiring all shares held by directors or employees of the company or of any other company of which it has control to be disposed of on ceasing to be so held, and

(b) requiring all shares acquired, in pursuance of rights or interests obtained by such directors or employees, by persons who are not, or have ceased to be, such directors or employees to be disposed of when they are acquired.

(3) A restriction is not authorised by *subparagraph (2)* unless—

(a) any disposal required by the restriction will be by way of sale for a consideration in money on terms specified in the articles of association, and

(b) the articles also contain general provisions by virtue of which any person disposing of shares of the same class (whether or not held or acquired as mentioned in *subparagraph (2))* may be required to sell them on terms which are the same as those mentioned in clause *(a)*.

15.

(1) In determining for the purposes of *paragraph 14(1)(c)* whether scheme shares which are or are to be acquired by any person are subject to any restrictions, there shall be regarded as a restriction attaching to the shares any contract, agreement, arrangement or condition by which such person's freedom to dispose of the shares or of any interest in them or of the proceeds of their sale or to exercise any right conferred by them is restricted or by which such a disposal or exercise may result in any disadvantage to that person or to a person connected with that person.

(2) *Subparagraph (1)* does not apply to so much of any contract, agreement, arrangement or condition as contains provisions similar in purpose and effect to any of the provisions of the Model Rules set out in the Listing Rules of the Irish Stock Exchange.

16. Except where scheme shares are in a company whose ordinary share capital consists of shares of one class only, the majority of the issued shares of the same class shall be held by persons other than—

(a) persons who acquired their shares in pursuance of a right conferred on them or an opportunity afforded to them as a director or employee of the grantor or any other company and not in pursuance of an offer to the public,

(b) trustees holding shares on behalf of persons who acquired their beneficial interests in the shares as mentioned in subparagraph (*a*), and

(c) in a case where the shares fall within *subparagraph (c)* of *paragraph 13* but do not fall within *subparagraph (a)* of that paragraph, companies which have control of the company whose shares are in question or of which that company is an associated company.

Exchange provisions

17.

(1) The scheme may provide that if any company (in this paragraph referred to as "*the acquiring company*")—

(a) obtains control of a company whose shares are scheme shares as a result of making a general offer—

(i) to acquire the whole of the issued ordinary share capital of the company which is made on a condition such that if it is satisfied the person making the offer will have control of the company, or

(ii) to acquire all the shares in the company which are of the same class as the scheme shares,

(b) obtains control of a company whose shares are scheme shares in pursuance of a compromise or arrangement sanctioned by the court under section 201 of the Companies Act, 1963, or

(c) becomes bound or entitled to acquire shares, under section 204 of the Companies Act, 1963, in a company whose shares are scheme shares, any participant in the scheme may at any time within the appropriate period, by agreement with the acquiring company, release his or her rights under the scheme (in this paragraph referred to as "*the old rights*") in consideration of the grant to him or her of rights (in this paragraph referred to as "*the new rights*") which are equivalent to the old rights but relate to shares in a different company (whether the acquiring company itself or some other company falling within *subparagraph (b)* or *(c)* of *paragraph 12*).

(2) In *subparagraph (1)* "*the appropriate period*" means—

(a) in a case falling within clause (*a*) of that subparagraph, the period of 6 months beginning with the time when the person making the offer has obtained control of the company and any condition subject to which the offer is made is satisfied,

(b) in a case falling within clause (*b*) of that subparagraph, the period of 6 months beginning with the time when the court sanctions the compromise or arrangement, and

(c) in a case falling within clause (*c*) of that subparagraph, the period during which the acquiring company remains bound or entitled as mentioned in that clause.

(3) The new rights shall not be regarded for the purposes of this paragraph as equivalent to the old rights unless—

(a) the shares to which they relate satisfy the conditions specified, in relation to scheme shares, in *paragraphs 12* to *16*,

(b) the new rights will be exercisable in the same manner as the old rights and subject to the provisions of the scheme as it had effect immediately before the release of the old rights,

(c) the total market value, immediately before the release, of the shares which were subject to the participant's old rights is equal to the total market value, immediately after the grant, of the shares in respect of which the new rights are granted to the participant, and

(d) the total amount payable by the participant for the acquisition of shares in pursuance of the new rights is equal to the total amount that would have been payable for the acquisition of shares in pursuance of the old rights.

(4) Where any new rights are granted pursuant to a provision included in a scheme by virtue of this paragraph they shall be regarded—

(a) for the purposes of *section 519D* and this Schedule, and

(b) for the purposes of the subsequent application (by virtue of a condition complying with *subparagraph (3)(b)*) of the provisions of the scheme,

as having been granted at the time when the corresponding old rights were granted.

Transfer of rights

18.

(1) The scheme shall not permit any person obtaining rights under it to transfer any of them but may provide that if such a person dies before exercising them, they may be exercised after, but not later than one year after, the date of that person's death.

(2) Where the scheme contains the provision permitted by *subparagraph (1)* and any rights are exercised after the death of the person who obtained them, *subsection (3)* of *section 519D* shall apply with the omission of the reference to *subsection (4)* of that section.

Share price

19. The price at which scheme shares may be acquired by the exercise of a right obtained under the scheme shall be stated at the time the right is obtained and shall not be less than the market value of shares of the same class at that time or, if the Revenue Commissioners and the grantor agree in writing, at such earlier time or times as may be provided in the agreement, but the scheme may provide for such variation of the price so stated as may be necessary to take account of any variation in the share capital of which the scheme shares form part.

Information

20.

(1) The Revenue Commissioners may by notice in writing require any person to furnish them, within such time as the Revenue Commissioners may direct (not being less than 30 days), with such information as the Revenue Commissioners think necessary for the performance of their functions under this Schedule, and which the person to whom the notice is addressed has or can reasonably obtain, including in particular information—

(a) to enable the Revenue Commissioners to determine—

(i) whether to approve a scheme or withdraw an approval already given, or

(ii) the liability to tax, including capital gains tax, of any person who has participated in a scheme,

and

(b) in relation to the administration of a scheme and any alteration of the terms of a scheme.

(2) Notwithstanding the generality of *subparagraph (1)*, the Revenue Commissioners may request a certificate from the auditor of a grantor company certifying that, in his or her opinion—

(a) the terms of any rule or rules included in the scheme by virtue of either or both *paragraphs 8* and *9* are complied with in relation to a year of assessment, or

(b) as respects rights obtained under the scheme before it was approved under this Schedule, the conditions in *subsection (7)(b)* of *section 519D* are satisfied.

[20A. Without prejudice to paragraph 20 the trustees of an approved scheme shall as respects any year, prepare and deliver to the Revenue Commissioners on or before 31 March in the year following that year, a return in the prescribed form (within the meaning of [*Chapter 3* of *Part 41A*][1]) of such particulars relating to the approved scheme for that year as may be required by the prescribed form and *sections 1052* and *1054* shall apply to a failure by the trustees to deliver a return in accordance with this paragraph as they apply to a failure to deliver a return referred to in *section 1052*.][2]

Options etc.

21.

(1) For the purposes of *section 437(2)*, as applied by *paragraph 10(b)* of this Schedule, a right to acquire shares (however arising) shall be taken to be a right to control them.

(2) Any reference in *subparagraph (3)* to the shares attributed to an individual is a reference to the shares which, in accordance with *section 437(2)* as applied by *paragraph 10(b)* of this Schedule, fall to be brought into account in that individual's case to determine whether their number exceeds a particular percentage of the company's ordinary share capital.

(3) In any case where—

(a) the shares attributed to an individual consist of or include shares which that individual or any other person has a right to acquire, and

(b) the circumstances are such that, if that right were to be exercised, the shares acquired would be shares which were previously unissued and which the company is contractually bound to issue in the event of the exercise of the right,

then, in determining at any time prior to the exercise of that right whether the number of shares attributed to the individual exceeds a particular percentage of the ordinary share capital of the company, that ordinary share capital shall be taken to be increased by the number of unissued shares referred to in clause (*b*).][3]

Amendments

[1] Substituted by FA12 sched4(part 2)(g).

[2] Inserted by FA08 s19(1)(d). Applies as on and from 1 January 2009.

[3] Inserted by FA01 s15(b).

Revenue Briefings

eBrief

eBrief No. 17/2011 – Share-Based Remuneration – Finance Act 2011 Changes

Revenue Information Notes

A Guide to the New Approved Share Options Schemes

Cross References

From Schedule 12C

Section 10 Connected persons.
Section 430 Meaning of "close company".
Section 431 Certain companies with quoted shares not to be close companies.
Section 432 Meaning of "associated company" and "control".
Section 433 Meaning of "participator", "associate", "director" and "loan creditor".
Section 437 Interest paid to directors and directors' associates.
Section 519D Approved share option schemes.
Section 548 Valuation of assets.
Section 951 Obligation to make a return.
Section 1052 Penalties for failure to make certain returns, etc.
Section 1054 Penalties in the case of a secretary of a body of persons.

To Schedule 12C

Section 519D Approved share option schemes.
Schedule 29 Provisions Referred to in Sections 1052, 1053 and 1054

SCHEDULE 13

Accountable Persons for Purposes of Chapter 1 of Part 18

Section 521.

[FA92 Sch2; FA94 s11; FA96 s8]

1. A Minister of the Government.

[2. A local authority within the meaning of the Local Government Act 2001 (as amended by the *Local Government Reform Act* 2014).][1]

3. A body established under the Local Government Services (Corporate Bodies) Act, 1971.

[...][2]

[5. Primary Care Reimbursement Service.][3]

6. The Attorney General.

7. The Comptroller and Auditor General.

8. The Director of Public Prosecutions.

9. The Commissioner of Valuation.

10. The Chief Boundary Surveyor.

11. The Director of Ordnance Survey.

12. The Revenue Commissioners.

[13. Public Appointments Service.][4]

14. The Commissioners of Public Works in Ireland.

15. The Clerk of Dáil Éireann.

16. The Legal Aid Board.

[17. An education and training board.][5]

18. Teagasc.

19. A harbour authority.

[...][6]

21. Údarás na Gaeltachta.

22. The Industrial Development Agency (Ireland).

[...][7]

24. Shannon Free Airport Development Company Limited.

[25. The National Tourism Development Authority.][8]

26. An institution of higher education within the meaning of the Higher Education Authority Act, 1971.

[...][9]

28. The Radiological Protection Institute of Ireland.

29. A voluntary public or joint board hospital to which grants are paid by the Minister for Health and Children in the year 1988-89 or any subsequent year of assessment.

30. An authorised insurer within the meaning of *section 470*.

[...][10]

32. An Bord Pleanála.

[...][11]

[…][12]

[35. Dublin Airport Authority public limited company.][13]

[…][14]

37. Blood Transfusion Service Board.

38. An Bord Bia.

39. Bord na gCon.

40. Bord Gáis Éireann.

41. Bord Iascaigh Mhara.

[42. Bord na Móna plc.][15]

[…][16]

44. Coillte Teoranta.

[…][17]

46. Coras Iompair Éireann.

[…][18]

48. Electricity Supply Board.

49. Housing Finance Agency plc.

[…][19]

51. Irish National Petroleum Corporation Limited.

52. Irish National Stud Company Limited.

53. National Building Agency Limited.

54. National Concert Hall Company Limited.

55. The Marine Institute.

56. An Post National Lottery Company.

[…][20]

58. An Post.

59. Radio Telefís Éireann.

[…][21]

61. Royal Hospital Kilmainham Company.

62. The Environmental Protection Agency.

[…][22]

[…][23]

65. The Irish Aviation Authority.

[…][24]

68. The National Roads Authority.

69. Temple Bar Properties Limited.

70. The Irish Film Board.

[…][25]

[73. Pobal.][26]

74. The Commissioner of Irish Lights.

[…][27]

76. The Heritage Council.

77. The Higher Education Authority.

[...][28]

[79. Horse Racing Ireland.][29]

80. The Labour Relations Commission.

[...][30]

82. The Pensions Board.

[83. The Commission for Communications Regulation.][31]

84. The Law Reform Commission.

[...][32]

[...][33]

[...][34]

[...][35]

89. National Standards Authority of Ireland.

90. Enterprise Ireland.

91. Dublin Docklands Development Authority.

[92. A Referendum Commission established by order made under section 2(1) of the Referendum Act, 1998.][36]

93. The Office of the Ombudsman.

[94. The Standards in Public Office Commission.][37]

95. The Office of the Information Commissioner.][38]

[...][39]

[...][40]

99. Western Development Commission.

100. The Equality Authority.

101. Commissioners of Charitable Donations and Bequests for Ireland.

[102. Commission for Energy Regulation.][41]

103. A regional authority established by an order made under section 43(1) of the Local Government Act, 1991.][42]

[...][43]

[...][44]

105. Irish Sports Council.

[106. Údarás Uchtála na hÉireann.][45]

[...][46]

108. National Disability Authority.

109. Aquaculture Licences Appeals Board.

110. Office of the President.

[111. Director of the Equality Tribunal.][47]

[...][48]

[...][49]

[114. Competition Authority.][50]

115. Chief State Solicitor.

116. Central Statistics Office.

117. Commission to Inquire into Child Abuse.

[118. National Sports Campus Development Authority.][51]

[119. Digital Hub Development Agency.][52]][53]

[120. Citizens Information Board.][54]

[121. Human Rights Commission.

122. Pensions Ombudsman.

[…][55]

124. The Dublin Institute for Advanced Studies.

125. Pre-Hospital Emergency Care Council.

126. Sustainable Energy Ireland — The Sustainable Energy Authority of Ireland.

127. The Health Insurance Authority.

128. Commission for Aviation Regulation.

129. Railway Procurement Agency.

[…][56]

[…][57]

[…][58]

[…][59]

134. Mater and Children's Hospital Development Ltd.

135. The National Consultative Commission on Racism and Interculturalism.

[…][60]

137. The Marine Casualty Investigation Board.

138. National Treasury Management Agency as regards the performance of functions by it conferred on, or delegated to, it by or under Part 2 of the National Treasury Management Agency (Amendment) Act 2000. (State Claims Agency).

[…][61]][62]

[140. The Personal Injuries Assessment Board.][63]

[141. The National Council for Curriculum and Assessment.

142. The State Examinations Commission.][64]

[…][65]

[144. National Treatment Purchase Fund Board.

145. The Mental Health Commission.

[…][66]

[…][67]

148. Irish Medicines Board.

149. National Educational Welfare Board.

150. Oifig Choimisinéir na dTeangacha Oifigiúla.

151. The Health Service Executive.

152. Commission for Public Service Appointments.

[…][68]

[154. National Council for Special Education.

155. National Library of Ireland.

156. An Education Support Centre established under section 37 of the Education Act 1998.

[…][69]][70]

[158. The Road Safety Authority.
159. Grangegorman Development Agency.
160. The Railway Safety Commission.
161. The Teaching Council.
162. EirGrid.
[...][71]
164. Irish Auditing and Accounting Supervisory Authority.][72]
[...][73]
167. The Health Information and Quality Authority.
168. Teilifís na Gaeilge.
169. Food Safety Authority of Ireland.
[...][74]
171. Sea-Fisheries Protection Authority.
[...][75]
173. National Economic and Social Development Office.][76]
[174. The National Asset Management Agency or a company to which *section 616(1)(g)* relates.][77]
[174. Inland Fisheries Ireland.][78]
[175. National Transport Authority.
176. The Medical Council.
[177. Irish Bank Resolution Corporation Limited.][79]
[178. Central Bank of Ireland.][80]
179. Financial Services Ombudsman's Bureau.
180. Broadcasting Authority of Ireland.][81]
[181. Inland Fisheries Ireland.][82]
[182. National Consumer Agency.
183. The body known as the Credit Review Office established pursuant to guidelines issued under section 210 of the National Asset Management Agency Act 2009.
184. Health and Safety Authority.
185. Irish Takeover Panel.
186. The Pharmaceutical Society of Ireland.
187. Ombudsman for Children.][83]
[188. Health and Social Care Professional Council.][84]
[189. Qualifications and Quality Assurance Authority of Ireland.
190. Nursing and Midwifery Board of Ireland.
191. Garda Síochána Ombudsman Commission.][85]
[192. Credit Union Restructuring Board.][86]
[193. Child and Family Agency.
194. An tSeirbhís Oideachais Leanúnaigh agus Scileanna (SOLAS).
195. A regional assembly established by an order made under *section 43(1)* of the Local Government Act 1991.][87]

Amendments

[1] Substituted by LGRA14 sched2(part5).

[2, 67] Deleted by FA07 s13(1)(c). This section is deemed to have taken effect as and from 1 January 2007.

[3] Substituted by FA07 s13(1)(a). This section is deemed to have taken effect as and from 1 January 2005.

[4] Substituted by FA05 s15(2)(a). This section shall be deemed to have come into force and shall take effect as on and from 19 October 2004.

[5] Substituted by EATBA13 sched6(24).

[6, 14, 23, 40] Deleted by FA14 s8(1)(a). Applies as and from 23 December 2014.

[7, 18, 22] Deleted by FA99 s17(a).

[8] Substituted by FA04 s5(1)(a). This section shall be deemed to have come into force and shall take effect as on and from 28 May 2003.

[9] Deleted by FA04 s5(1)(b). Shall be deemed to have come into force and shall take effect as on and from 28 May 2003.

[10, 17, 20, 24, 25, 27, 28, 44, 49, 55, 56, 75] Deleted by FA10 s22(1)(a). Deemed to have come into force and takes effect as on and from 1 January 2010.

[11] Repealed by ACC BA01 s12(1) with effect from such date as the Minister of Finance may appoint by order.

[12, 30, 33, 46, 48, 69] Deleted by FA08 s12(1)(e). This section is deemed to have taken effect as and from 1 January 2008.

[13] Substituted by FA05 s15(2)(b). This section shall be deemed to have come into force and shall take effect as on and from 1 October 2004.

[15] Substituted by FA01 s14(b).

[16, 32] Deleted by FA00 s20(a).

[19] Repealed by ICC BA00 s7 and ICC BA00 (Sections 5 and 7) (Commencement) Order 2001 (S.I. 396/2001) with effect from 12 February 2001.

[21, 35] Deleted by FA01 s14(c).

[26] Substituted by FA10 s22(1)(b). Deemed to have come into force and takes effect as on and from 1 January 2010.

[29] Substituted by FA03 s10(2)(a). Applies with effect from 18 December 2001.

[31] Substituted by FA04 s5(1)(c). Shall be deemed to have come into force and shall take effect as on and from 1 December 2002.

[34] Deleted by FA05 s15(2)(c). This section shall be deemed to have come into force and shall take effect as on and from 1 January 2005.

[36] Substituted by FA00 s20(b).

[37] Substituted by FA04 s5(1)(d). Shall be deemed to have come into force and shall take effect as on and from 10 December 2001.

[38] Inserted by FA99 s17(b).

[39] Deleted by the Inland Fisheries Act 2010, Schedule 2, Part 13(2)(a).

[41] Substituted by FA10 s22(1)(c). Deemed to have come into force and takes effect as on and from 1 January 2010.

[42] Inserted by FA00 s20(c).

[43] Deleted by FA03 s10(2)(b).

[45] Substituted by AA10 s174(b). With effect from 1 November 2010 as per S.I. No. 511 of 2010.

[47] Substituted by FA08 s12(1)(a). This section is deemed to have taken effect as and from 19 July 2004.

[50] Substituted by FA08 s12(1)(b). This section is deemed to have taken effect as and from 1 October 1991.

[51] Substituted by FA07 s13(1)(b). This section is deemed to have taken effect as and from 1 January 2007.

[52] Substituted by FA10 s22(1)(d). Deemed to have come into force and takes effect as on and from 1 January 2010.

[53] Inserted by FA01 s14(d).

[54] Substituted by FA08 s12(1)(c). This section is deemed to have taken effect as and from 30 March 2007.

[57, 59, 71, 73] Deleted by FA13 s93(2)(a). Applies from 27 March 2013.

[58, 66] Deleted by FA11 s(18)(1)(a). Deemed to have come into force and takes effect as on and from 1 January 2011.

[60, 65, 68, 74] Deleted by FA12 s21(a). Deemed to have come into force and takes effect on and from 1 January 2012.

[61] Deleted by NTMA(A)A14 part4(11).

[62] Inserted by FA03 s10(2)(c). Applies with effect from 1 May 2003.

[63] Inserted by PIABA03 s85.

[64] Inserted by FA04 s5(1)(e). Comes into operation on 1 May 2004.

[70] Inserted by FA06 s10(1). This section comes into operation on 1 May 2006.

[72] Inserted by FA07 s13(1)(d). Applies as and from 1 May 2007.

[76] Inserted by FA08 s12(1)(f). This section takes effect as and from 1 May 2008.

[77] Inserted by the National Asset Management Agency Act 2009 Sched 3 part 10.

[78] Inserted by the Inland Fisheries Act 2010 (Act 10 of 2010), Schedule 2, Part 13(2)(b).

[79] Substituted by FA12 s21(b). Deemed to have come into force and takes effect on and from 1 January 2012.

[80] Substituted by FA12 s21(c). Deemed to have come into force and takes effect on and from 1 January 2012.

[81] Inserted by FA10 s22(1)(e). Applies as and from 1 May 2010.

[82] Inserted by FA11 s(18)(1)(c). Applies as and from 1 July 2010.

[83] Inserted by FA11 s(18)(1)(d). Applies as and from 1 May 2011.

[84] Inserted by FA12 s21(d). Deemed to have come into force and takes effect on and from 1 January 2012.

[85] Inserted by FA13 s93(2)(b). Applies as and from 1 May 2013.

[86] Inserted by F(No.2)A13 s17(2). Comes into operation on 1 January 2014.

[87] Inserted by FA14 s8(1)(b). Applies as and from 23 December 2014.

Cross References

From Schedule 13

Section 470 Relief for insurance against expenses of illness.
Section 520 Interpretation (Chapter 1).
Section 521 Accountable persons.

To Schedule 13

Section 521 Accountable persons.

SCHEDULE 14

Capital Gains Tax: Leases

Section 566.

[CGTA75 Sch3; CTA76 s140(2) and Sch2 PtII Par11]

Interpretation

1. In this Schedule, "*premium*" includes any like sum, whether payable to the intermediate or a superior lessor and, for the purposes of this Schedule, any sum (other than rent) paid on or in connection with the granting of a tenancy shall be presumed to have been paid by means of a premium except in so far as other sufficient consideration for the payment is shown to have been given.

Leases of land as wasting assets: restriction of allowable expenditure

2.

(1) A lease of land shall not be a wasting asset until its duration does not exceed 50 years.

(2) Where at the beginning of the period of ownership of a lease of land it is subject to a sub-lease not at a rent representing the full value of the land together with any buildings on the land, and the value of the lease at the end of the duration of the sub-lease, estimated as at the beginning of the period of ownership, exceeds the expenditure allowable under *section 552(1)(a)* in computing the gain accruing on a disposal of the lease, the lease shall not be a wasting asset until the end of the duration of the sub-lease.

(3) In the case of a wasting asset which is a lease of land, the rate at which expenditure is assumed to be written off shall, instead of being a uniform rate as provided by *section 560(3)*, be a rate fixed in accordance with the Table to this paragraph.

(4) Accordingly, for the purposes of the computation under *Chapter 2* of *Part 19* of the gain accruing on a disposal of a lease, and where—

(a) the percentage derived from the Table to this paragraph for the duration of the lease at the beginning of the period of ownership is P (1),

(b) the percentage so derived for the duration of the lease at the time when any item of expenditure attributable to the lease under *section 552(1)(b)* is first reflected in the nature of the lease is P (2), and

(c) the percentage so derived for the duration of the lease at the time of the disposal is P (3),

then—

(i) there shall be excluded from the expenditure attributable to the lease under *section 552(1)(a)* a fraction equal to—

$$\frac{P(1) - P(3)}{P(1)}$$

and

(ii) there shall be excluded from any item of expenditure attributable to the lease under *section 552(1)(b)* a fraction equal to—

$$\frac{P(2) - P(3)}{P(2)}$$

(5) This paragraph shall apply notwithstanding that the period of ownership of the lease is a period exceeding 50 years, and accordingly no expenditure shall be written off under this paragraph in respect of any period earlier than the time when the lease becomes a wasting asset.

(6) *Section 561* shall apply in relation to this paragraph as it applies in relation to *subsections (3)* to *(5)* of *section 560.*

(7) Where the duration of the lease is not an exact number of years, the percentage to be derived from the Table to this paragraph shall be the percentage for the whole number of years plus one-twelfth of the difference between that percentage and the percentage for the next higher number of years for each odd month, counting an odd 14 days or more as one month.

TABLE

Years	*Percentage*	*Years*	*Percentage*
50 (or more)	100.0	25	81.1
49	99.7	24	79.6
48	99.3	23	78.1
47	98.9	22	76.4
46	98.5	21	74.6
45	98.1	20	72.8
44	97.6	19	70.8
43	97.1	18	68.7
42	96.6	17	66.5
41	96.0	16	64.1
40	95.5	15	61.6
39	94.8	14	59.0
38	94.2	13	56.2
37	93.5	12	53.2
36	92.8	11	50.0
35	92.0	10	46.7
34	91.2	9	43.2
33	90.3	8	39.4
32	89.4	7	35.4
31	88.4	6	31.2
30	87.3	5	26.7
29	86.2	4	22.0
28	85.1	3	17.0
27	83.8	2	11.6
26	82.5	1	6.0
		0	0.0

Premiums for leases

3.

(1) Subject to this Schedule, where the payment of a premium is required under a lease of land or otherwise under the terms subject to which a lease of land is granted, there shall be a part disposal of the freehold or other asset out of which the lease is granted.

(2) In applying *section 557* to such a part disposal, the property which remains undisposed of shall include a right to any rent or other payments (other than a premium) payable under the lease, and that right shall be valued as at the time of the part disposal.

Payments during currency of lease treated as premium

4.

(1) Where under the terms subject to which a lease of land is granted a sum becomes payable by the lessee in place of the whole or part of the rent for any period or as consideration for the surrender of the lease, the lease shall be deemed for the purposes of this Schedule to have required the payment of a premium to the lessor (in addition to any other premium) of an amount equal to that sum for the period in relation to which the sum is payable.

(2) Where as consideration for the variation or waiver of any of the terms of a lease of land a sum becomes payable by the lessee otherwise than as rent, the lease shall be deemed for the purposes of this Schedule to have required the payment of a premium to the lessor (in addition to any other premium) of an amount equal to that sum for the period from the time when the variation or waiver takes effect to the time when it ceases to have effect.

(3) Where under *subparagraph (1)* or *(2)* a premium is deemed to have been received by the lessor otherwise than as consideration for the surrender of the lease, then—

(a) subject to *clause (b)*, both the lessor and the lessee shall be treated as if that premium were or were part of the consideration for the grant of the lease due at the time when the lease was granted, but

(b) if the lessor is a lessee under a lease the duration of which does not exceed 50 years, this Schedule shall apply as if—

(i) that premium had been given as consideration for the grant of the part of the sub-lease covered by the period in respect of which the premium is deemed to have been paid, and

(ii) that consideration were expenditure incurred by the sub-lessee and attributable to that part of the sub-lease under *section 552(1)(b)*.

(4) Where *subparagraph (3)(a)* applies, the gain accruing to the lessor on the disposal by means of the grant of the lease shall be recomputed and any necessary adjustments of capital gains tax shall be made accordingly, whether by means of assessment for the year in which the premium is deemed to have been received or by means of discharge or repayment of tax.

(5) Where under *subparagraph (1)* a premium is deemed to have been received as consideration for the surrender of a lease, that premium shall be regarded as consideration for a separate transaction consisting of the disposal by the lessor of the lessor's interest in the lease.

(6) *Subparagraph (2)* shall apply in relation to a transaction not at arm's length, and in particular in relation to a transaction entered into gratuitously, as if such sum had become payable by the tenant otherwise than as rent as might have been required of the tenant if the transaction had been at arm's length.

(7) *Subparagraph (4)* shall apply for the purposes of corporation tax as it applies for the purposes of capital gains tax.

Sub-leases out of short leases

5.

(1) This paragraph shall apply in relation to a lease which is a wasting asset.

(2) In the computation under *Chapter 2* of *Part 19* of the gain accruing on the part disposal of a lease by means of the grant of a sub-lease for a premium (in this paragraph referred to as "*the actual premium*"), the expenditure attributable to

the lease under *paragraphs (a)* and *(b)* of *section 552(1)* shall be apportioned in accordance with this paragraph, and *section 557* shall not apply.

(3) Out of each item of the expenditure attributable to the lease under *paragraphs (a)* and *(b)* of *section 552(1)* there shall be apportioned to the part disposal—

(a) if the amount of the actual premium is not less than the amount which would be obtainable by means of a premium for the sub-lease if the rent payable under the sub-lease were the same as the rent payable under the lease (in this paragraph referred to as "*the full premium*"), the amount (in this paragraph referred to as "*the allowable amount*") which under *paragraph 2(3)* is to be written off over the period which is the duration of the sub-lease, and

(b) if the amount of the actual premium is less than the full premium, such proportion of the allowable amount as is equal to the proportion which the actual premium bears to the full premium.

(4) Where the sub-lease is a sub-lease of only part of the land comprised in the lease, this paragraph shall apply only in relation to a proportion of the expenditure attributable to the lease under *paragraphs (a)* and *(b)* of *section 552(1)* which is the same as the proportion which the value of the land comprised in the sub-lease at the time when the sub-lease is granted bears to the value of that land and the other land comprised in the lease at that time, and the remainder of that expenditure shall be apportioned to the other land.

Exclusion of premiums taxed under Case V of Schedule D

6.

(1) Where by reference to any premium income tax has become chargeable under *section 98* on any amount, that amount shall be excluded from the consideration taken into account in the computation under *Chapter 2* of *Part 19* of a gain accruing on a disposal of the interest in respect of which income tax becomes so chargeable, except where in an apportionment under *section 557* the value of the consideration is taken into account in the aggregate of that value and the market value of the property which remains undisposed of.

(2) Where by reference to any premium in respect of a sub-lease granted out of a lease, being a lease the duration of which does not at the time of granting the lease exceed 50 years, income tax has become chargeable under *section 98* on any amount, that amount shall be deducted from any gain (as computed in accordance with the provisions of the Capital Gains Tax Acts apart from this subparagraph) accruing on the disposal for which the premium is consideration, but not so as to convert the gain into a loss or to increase any loss.

(3) (a) Subject to *clause (b)*, where income tax has become chargeable under *section 100* on any amount (in this subparagraph referred to as "*the relevant amount*"), the relevant amount shall be excluded from the consideration taken into account in the computation under *Chapter 2* of *Part 19* of a gain accruing on the disposal of the estate or interest in respect of which income tax becomes so chargeable, except where in an apportionment made under *section 557* the value of the consideration is taken into account in the aggregate of that value and the market value of the property which remains undisposed of.

(b) If the part or interest disposed of is the remainder of a lease or a sub-lease out of a lease the duration of which does not exceed 50 years, *clause (a)* shall not apply, but the relevant amount shall be deducted from any gain (as computed in accordance with the provisions of the Capital Gains Tax Acts apart from this subparagraph) accruing on the disposal, but not so as to convert the gain into a loss or to increase any loss.

(4) References in *subparagraphs (1)* and *(2)* to a premium include references to a premium deemed to have been received under *subsection (3)* or *(4)* of *section 98*.

(5) *Section 551* shall not be taken as authorising the exclusion of any amount from the consideration for a disposal of assets taken into account in the computation of the gain under *Chapter 2* of *Part 19* by reference to any amount chargeable to tax under *section 75* and *Chapter 8* of *Part 4*.

Disallowance of premium treated as rent under superior lease

7.

(1) Where under *section 103(2)* a person is to be treated as paying additional rent in consequence of having granted a sub-lease, the amount of any loss accruing to such person on the disposal by means of the grant of the sub-lease shall be reduced by the total amount of the rent which such person is thereby treated as paying over the term of the sub-lease (and without regard to whether relief is thereby effectively given over the term of the sub-lease), but not so as to convert the loss into a gain or to increase any gain.

(2) Nothing in *section 551* shall be taken as applying in relation to any amount on which tax is paid under *section 99*.

(3) Where any adjustment is made under *paragraph (b)* of *section 100(2)*, on a claim under that paragraph, any necessary adjustment shall be made to give effect to the consequences of the claim on the operation of this paragraph or *paragraph 6*.

Expenditure by lessee under terms of lease

8. If under *section 98(2)* income tax is chargeable on any amount as being a premium the payment of which is deemed to be required by the lease, the person so chargeable shall be treated for the purposes of the computation of any gain accruing to that person on the disposal by means of the grant of the lease, and on any subsequent disposal of the asset out of which the lease was granted, as having incurred at the time the lease was granted expenditure of that amount (in addition to any other expenditure) attributable to the asset under *section 552(1)(b)*.

Duration of leases

9.

(1) In ascertaining for the purposes of the Capital Gains Tax Acts the duration of a lease of land, the following provisions of this paragraph shall apply.

(2) Where the terms of the lease include provision for the determination of the lease by notice given by the lessor, the lease shall not be treated as granted for a term longer than one ending at the earliest date on which it could be determined by notice given by the lessor.

(3) Where any of the terms of the lease (whether relating to forfeiture or to any other matter) or any other circumstances render it unlikely that the lease will continue beyond a date falling before the expiration of the term of the lease, the lease shall not be treated as having been granted for a term longer than one ending on that date, and this subparagraph shall apply in particular where the lease provides for the rent to be increased after a given date, or for the lessee's

obligations to become in any other respect more onerous after a given date, but includes provision for the determination of the lease on that date by notice given by the lessee, and those provisions render it unlikely that the lease will continue beyond that date.

(4) Where the terms of the lease include provision for the extension of the lease beyond a given date by notice given by the lessee, this paragraph shall apply as if the term of the lease extended for as long as it could be extended by the lessee, but subject to any right of the lessor by notice to determine the lease.

(5) The duration of a lease shall be decided in relation to the grant or any disposal of the lease by reference to the facts which were known or ascertainable at the time when the lease was acquired or created.

Leases of property other than land

10.

(1) *Paragraphs 3* to *5* and *9* shall, subject to any necessary modifications, apply in relation to leases of property other than land as they apply to leases of land.

(2) In the case of a lease of a wasting asset which is movable property, the lease shall be assumed to terminate not later than the end of the life of the wasting asset.

Cross References

From Schedule 14

Section 52 Persons chargeable.
Section 75 Case V: basis of assessment.
Section 96 Interpretation (Chapter 8).
Section 98 Treatment of premiums, etc. as rent.
Section 99 Charge on assignment of lease granted at undervalue.
Section 100 Charge on sale of land with right to reconveyance.
Section 103 Deduction by reference to premiums, etc. paid in computation of profits for purposes of this Chapter.
Section 532 Assets.
Section 544 Interpretation and general (Chapter 2).
Section 551 Exclusion from consideration for disposals of sums chargeable to income tax.
Section 552 Acquisition, enhancement and disposal costs.
Section 557 Part disposals.
Section 560 Wasting assets.
Section 561 Wasting assets qualifying for capital allowances.
Section 566 Leases.

To Schedule 14

Section 5 Interpretation of Capital Gains Tax Acts.
Section 566 Leases.

SCHEDULE 15

List of Bodies for Purposes of Section 610

Section 610.

[CGTA75 s23; FA89 s33; FA91 s20(2) and s44; FA94 s32(5); FA95 s44(1) and (3); FA96 s39(1) and (6) and s64]

PART 1

1. An unregistered friendly society whose income is exempt from income tax under *section 211(1)*.
2. A registered friendly society whose income is exempt from income tax under *section 211(1)*.

[3. A registered trade union to the extent that the proceeds of the disposal giving rise to the […][1][gain or, if greater, the consideration for the disposal under the Capital Gains Tax Acts][2] have been, or will be, applied solely for the purposes of its registered trade union activities.][3]

[4. A local authority or a joint body within the meaning of the Local Government Act 2001 (as amended by the *Local Government Reform Act 2014*).][4]

5. A body established under the Local Government Services (Corporate Bodies) Act, 1971.
6. The Central Bank of Ireland.

[7. The Health Service Executive.][5]

[8. An education and training board.][6]

[9. Teagasc—The Agriculture and Food Development Authority.][7]

[10. The National Tourism Development Authority.][8]

11. The Dublin Regional Tourism Organisation Limited.

[12. Dublin Regional Tourism Authority Limited.

13. The South-East Regional Tourism Authority Limited.
14. South-West Regional Tourism Authority Limited.
15. The Western Regional Tourism Authority Limited.
16. The North-West Regional Tourism Authority Limited.
17. Midlands-East Regional Tourism Authority Limited.][9]
18. Tramore Fáilte Limited.
19. The National Treasury Management Agency.
20. Eolas—The Irish Science and Technology Agency.
21. Forbairt.
22. Forfás.
23. The Industrial Development Agency (Ireland).
24. The Industrial Development Authority.

[…][10]

26. Údarás na Gaeltachta.

27. [Horse Racing Ireland][11].

28. The company incorporated on the 1st day of December, 1994, as Irish Thoroughbred Marketing Limited.

29. The company incorporated on the 1st day of December, 1994, as Tote Ireland Limited.

30. A body designated under section 4(1) of the Securitisation (Proceeds of Certain Mortgages) Act, 1995.

31. The Dublin Docklands Development [Authority and any of its wholly-owned subsidiaries.][12]

[31A. The Dublin Institute of Technology in respect of any disposal made by it to the Grangegorman Development Agency.

31B. The Grangegorman Development Agency.][13]

32. The Interim Board established under the Milk (Regulation of Supply) (Establishment of Interim Board) Order, 1994 (S.I. No. 408 of 1994).

[33. National Rehabilitation Board.][14]

[33A. A Fund investment vehicle (within the meaning of *section 37* of the *National Treasury Management Agency (Amendment) Act 2014*) of which the Minister for Finance is the sole beneficial owner.][15]

[…][16]

[…][17]

[…][18]

[[…][19]

36. Tourism Ireland Limited.

[...][20]

38. Any body established by statute for the principal purpose of promoting games or sports and any company wholly owned by such a body, to the extent that the proceeds of the disposal giving rise to the […][21] [gain or, if greater, the consideration for the disposal under the Capital Gains Tax Acts][22] have been, or will be, applied for that purpose.][23]][24]

[39. The Courts Service.

40. The Irish Auditing and Accounting Supervisory Authority.][25]

[41. The Commission for Communications Regulation.

42. The Digital Hub Development Agency.][26]

[43. The National Asset Management Agency.][27]

[44. The Strategic Banking Corporation of Ireland or a subsidiary wholly owned by it or a subsidiary wholly owned by any such subsidiary.][28]

PART 2

1. The Dublin District Milk Board established under the Dublin District Milk Board Order, 1936 (S.R. & O., No. 254 of 1936).

2. The Cork District Milk Board established under the Cork District Milk Board Order, 1937 (S.R. & O., No. 91 of 1937).

3. The company incorporated on the 19th day of November, 1991, as Dairysan Limited.
4. The company incorporated on the 14th day of February, 1994, as Glenlee (Cork) Limited.

Amendments

[1, 21] Deleted by FA07 s54(1). Applies to disposals made on or after 1 February 2007.

[2, 22] Substituted by FA07 s54(1). Applies to disposals made on or after 1 February 2007.

[3] Substituted by FA06 s74(1)(a). This section applies as respects disposals made on or after 2 February 2006.

[4] Substituted by LGRA14 sched2(part 5).

[5] Substituted by FA05 s57(1)(a). This section is deemed to have applied as on and from 1 January 2005.

[6] Substituted by EATBA13 sched6(24).

[7] Substituted by FA12 s63(1)(a). Applies to disposals made on or after 8 February 2012.

[8] Substituted by FA06 sched2(1)(t). This section is deemed to have come into force and have taken effect as on and from 28 May 2003.

[9] Substituted by FA05 s57(1)(b). Applies as on and from 25 March 2005

[10] Deleted by SA(SG)A14 s36©.

[11] Substituted by HGRA01 s11(b).

[12] Substituted by FA01 s79(c). Applies as respects disposals made on or after 6 April 2001.

[13] Inserted by FA12 s63(1)(b). Applies to disposals made on or after 8 February 2012.

[14] Inserted by FA99 s93.

[15] Inserted by NTMA(A)A14 part4(12)(a).

[16] Deleted by NTMA(A)A14 part4(12)(b).

[17] Deleted by NTMA(A)A14 part4(12)(c).

[18] Deleted by NTMA(A)A14 part4(12)(d).

[19] Deleted by NTMA(A)A14 part4(12)(e).

[20] Deleted by FA12 s67(1)(b).

[23] Substituted by FA06 s74(1)(b). This section applies as respects disposals made on or after 2 February 2006.

[24] Inserted by FA03 s72(b).

[25] Inserted by FA06 s74(1)(c). This section applies as respects disposals made on or after 2 February 2006.

[26] Inserted by FA08 s56(1). As respects the Commission for Communications Regulation, subsection (1) is deemed to have applied as on and from 1 December 2002. (b) As respects the Digital Hub Development Agency, subsection (1) is deemed to have applied as on and from 1 January 2008.

[27] Inserted by the National Asset Management Agency Act 2009 Sched 3 part 10.

[28] Inserted by SBCoIA14 part7(1)(e). Does not apply in circumstances where the Minister does not hold all of the shares in the SBCI.

Cross References

From Schedule 15

Section 211 Friendly societies.
Section 235 Bodies established for promotion of athletic or amateur games or sports.
Section 610 Other bodies.

To Schedule 15

Section 610 Other bodies.
Section 980 Deduction from consideration on disposal of certain assets.

SCHEDULE 16

Building Societies: Change of Status

Section 703.

[FA90 Sch3]

Capital allowances

1.

(1) For the purposes of the allowances and charges provided for by *sections 307* and *308*, the trade of the society concerned shall not be treated as permanently discontinued and the trade of the successor company shall not be treated as a new trade set up and commenced by the successor company.

(2) There shall be made to or on the successor company in accordance with *sections 307* and *308* all such allowances and charges as would have been made to or on the society if the society had continued to carry on the trade, and the amount of any such allowance or charge shall be computed as if the successor company had been carrying on the trade since the society began to do so and as if everything done to or by the society had been done to or by the successor company.

(3) The conversion of the society into the successor company shall not be treated as giving rise to any such allowance or charge.

Financial assets

2.

(1) In this paragraph—

"*financial assets*" means assets held by the society in accordance with subsections (1) and (3) of section 39 of the Building Societies Act, 1989;

"*financial trading stock*" means such of the financial assets of the society as would constitute trading stock for the purposes of *section 89*.

(2) For the purposes of *section 89*, the financial trading stock of the society concerned shall be valued at an amount equal to its cost to the society.

(3) Where a society converts itself into the successor company, the vesting in the successor company of any financial assets, the profits or gains on the disposal of which would be chargeable to tax under Case I of Schedule D, shall be treated for the purposes of corporation tax as not constituting a disposal of those assets by the society; but, on the disposal of any of those assets by the successor company, the profits or gains accruing to the successor company shall be calculated (for the purposes of corporation tax) as if those assets had been acquired by the successor company at their cost to the society.

Capital gains: assets vested in the successor company, etc

3.

(1) For the purposes of capital gains tax and corporation tax on chargeable gains, the conversion of a society into the successor company shall not constitute—

(a) a disposal by the society of assets owned by it immediately before the conversion, or

(b) the acquisition at that time by the successor company of assets which immediately before the conversion were owned by the society.

(2) The Capital Gains Tax Acts, and the Corporation Tax Acts in so far as those Acts relate to chargeable gains, shall apply where a society has converted itself into the successor company as if the successor company had—

(a) acquired the assets which vested in the successor company on conversion at the same time and for the same consideration at which they were acquired by the society,

(b) been in existence as a company at all times since the society was incorporated,

(c) done all things done by the society relating to the acquisition and disposal of the assets which vested in the successor company on conversion, and

(d) done all other things done by the society before the conversion.

Capital gains: shares, and rights to shares, in successor company

4.

(1) In this paragraph—

"*free shares*", in relation to a member of the society, means any shares issued by the successor company to that member in connection with the conversion but for no new consideration;

"*member*", in relation to the society, means a person who is or has been a member of the society, in that capacity, and any reference to a member includes a reference to a member of any particular class or description;

"*new consideration*" means consideration other than—

(a) consideration provided directly or indirectly out of the assets of the society or the successor company, or

(b) consideration derived from a member's shares or other rights in the society or the successor company.

(2) Where in connection with the conversion there are conferred on members of the society concerned any rights—

(a) to acquire shares in the successor company in priority to other persons,

(b) to acquire shares in that company for consideration of an amount or value lower than the market value of the shares, or

(c) to free shares in that company,

any such rights so conferred on a member shall be regarded for the purposes of capital gains tax as an option (within the meaning of *section 540*) granted to and acquired by the member for no consideration and having no value at the time of that grant and acquisition.

(3) Where in connection with the conversion shares in the successor company are issued by that company to a member of the society concerned, those shares shall be regarded for the purposes of capital gains tax—

(a) as acquired by the member for a consideration of an amount or value equal to the amount or value of any new consideration given by the member for the shares or, if no new consideration is given, as acquired for no consideration, and

(b) as having at the time of their acquisition by the member a value equal to the amount or value of the new consideration so given or, if no new consideration is given, as having no value;

but this subparagraph is without prejudice to the application where appropriate of *subparagraph (2).*

(4) *Subparagraph (5)* shall apply in any case where—

(a) in connection with the conversion, shares in the successor company are issued by that company to trustees on terms which provide for the transfer of those shares to members of the society for no new consideration, and

(b) the circumstances are such that in the hands of the trustees the shares constitute settled property within the meaning of the Capital Gains Tax Acts.

(5) Where this subparagraph applies, then, for the purposes of capital gains tax—

(a) the shares shall be regarded as acquired by the trustees for no consideration,

(b) the interest of any member in the settled property constituted by the shares shall be regarded as acquired by that member for no consideration and as having no value at the time of its acquisition, and

(c) where on the occasion of a member becoming absolutely entitled as against the trustees to any of the settled property, both the trustees and the member shall be treated as if, on the member becoming so entitled, the shares in question had been disposed of and immediately reacquired by the trustees, in their capacity as trustees within *section 567(2)*, for a consideration of such an amount as would secure that on the disposal neither a gain nor a loss would accrue to the trustees and, accordingly, *section 576(1)* shall not apply in relation to that occasion.

(6) References in this paragraph to the case where a member becomes absolutely entitled to settled property as against the trustees shall be taken to include references to the case where the member would become so entitled but for being a minor or otherwise under a legal disability.

[(7) (a) In this section "*PPS Number*", in relation to an individual, means the individual's Personal Public Service Number within the meaning of section 262 of the Social Welfare Consolidation Act 2005.

(b) Where in connection with the conversion there is conferred on a member of the society a right to acquire shares in a successor company, or a right to a distribution of assets (including cash) of the society, the society shall, within 30 days of the registration of the society as a company or within such longer period as the Revenue Commissioners may on request allow, make a return to the Revenue Commissioners, in such electronic format as they require, which, in respect of each such member, specifies—

(i) the name of the member,

(ii) the address of the member,

(iii) subject to clause (*e*), the information referred to in clause (*c*),

(iv) the number of shares in the successor company which the member has a right to acquire,

(v) the amount of new consideration which the member is required to give to acquire those shares,

(vi) the value of any assets of the society to which the member has a right, and

(vii) such other information that the Revenue Commissioners advise the society that they require.

(c) A society proposing to convert into a company shall, in such manner as the Revenue Commissioners may specify, request from every member who is an individual that he or she furnish to the society—

(i) his or her PPS Number, or

(ii) where he or she does not have a PPS Number, confirmation to that effect,

on or before a specified date, which date shall be before the society converts into a company.

(d) An individual to whom clause (*c*) relates shall comply with the request in a manner so as to enable the society to have that information on or before the specified date.

(e) Where in making a return for the purposes of clause (*b*), the society as a company is unable to provide the information required by clause (*b*)(iii) in respect of an individual because he or she failed to furnish the information in accordance with clause (*c*), then the company shall, unless it can otherwise duly provide the information, state that it cannot provide the information so required.][1]

Amendments

[1] Inserted by FA06 s77.

Cross References

From Schedule 16

Section 89 Valuation of trading stock at discontinuance of trade.
Section 307 Corporation tax: allowances and charges in taxing a trade.
Section 308 Corporation tax: manner of granting, and effect of, allowances made by means of discharge or repayment of tax.
Section 540 Options and forfeited deposits.
Section 567 Nominees, bare trustees and agents.
Section 576 Person becoming absolutely entitled to settled property.
Section 703 Change of status of society.

To Schedule 16

Section 89 Valuation of trading stock at discontinuance of trade.
Section 703 Change of status of society.

SCHEDULE 17

Reorganisation into Companies of Trustee Savings Banks

Section 705.

[FA90 Sch4]

Interpretation

1. In this Schedule—

"*bank*" means either or both a trustee savings bank and a bank within the meaning of section 57(3)(*c*)(i) of the Trustee Savings Banks Act, 1989, as the context requires;

"*successor*" means the company to which any property, rights, liabilities and obligations are transferred in the course of a transfer;

"*transfer*" means the transfer by a trustee savings bank of all or part of its property and rights and all of its liabilities or obligations under an order made by the Minister for Finance under section 57 of the Trustee Savings Banks Act, 1989, authorising the reorganisation of one or more trustee savings banks into a company or the reorganisation of a company referred to in subsection (3)(*c*)(i) of that section into a company referred to in subsection (3)(*c*)(ii) of that section.

Capital allowances

2.

(1) This paragraph shall apply for the purposes of—

(a) allowances and charges provided for in *Part 9*, *section 670*, *Chapter 1* of *Part 29* and *sections 765* and *769*, or any other provision of the Tax Acts relating to the making of allowances or charges under or in accordance with that Part or Chapter or those sections, and

(b) allowances or charges provided for by *sections 307* and *308*.

(2) The transfer shall not be treated as giving rise to any allowance or charge provided for under *subparagraph (1)*.

(3) There shall be made to or on the successor in accordance with *sections 307* and *308* all such allowances and charges as would, if the bank had continued to carry on the trade, have been made to or on the bank, and the amount of any such allowance or charge shall be computed as if the successor had been carrying on the trade since the trustee savings bank began to do so and as if everything done to or by the bank had been done to or by the successor; but the successor shall not be entitled to any amount which would have been made to the trustee savings bank by virtue only of *section 304(4)*.

Trading losses

3. Notwithstanding any other provision of the Tax Acts—

(a) a company referred to in subsection (3)(*c*)(i) of section 57 of the Trustee Savings Banks Act, 1989, which becomes a company referred to in subsection (3)(*c*)(ii) of that section shall not be entitled to relief under *section 396(1)* in respect of any loss incurred by the company in a trade in any accounting period or part of an accounting period in which it was a company referred to in subsection (3)(*c*)(i) of section 57 of the Trustee Savings Banks Act, 1989, and

(b) a company referred to in subsection (3)(*c*)(ii) of section 57 of that Act shall not be entitled to relief under *section 396(1)* in respect of any loss incurred by a company referred to in subsection (3)(*c*)(i) of section 57 of that Act.

Financial assets

4.

(1) In this paragraph, "*financial trading stock*" means such of the assets of the bank as would constitute trading stock for the purposes of *section 89*.

(2) For the purposes of *section 89*, the financial trading stock of the bank concerned shall be valued at an amount equal to or treated for the purposes of *subparagraph (3)* as its cost to that bank.

(3) The acquisition in the course of a transfer by the successor of any assets, the profits or gains on the disposal of which by the bank would be chargeable to tax under Case I of Schedule D, shall be treated for the purposes of income tax and corporation tax as not constituting a disposal of those assets by that bank; but, on the disposal of any of those assets by the successor, the profits or gains accruing to the successor shall be calculated (for the purposes of corporation tax) as if those assets had been acquired by the successor at their cost to the bank.

Capital gains

5.

(1) This paragraph shall apply for the purposes of the Capital Gains Tax Acts, and of the Corporation Tax Acts in so far as those Acts relate to chargeable gains.

(2) The disposal of an asset by a bank to a company in the course of a transfer shall be deemed to be for a consideration of such amount as would secure that on the disposal neither a gain nor a loss would accrue to the bank.

(3) Where *subparagraph (2)* has applied in relation to the disposal of an asset by the bank, then, in relation to a subsequent disposal of the asset, the successor shall be treated as if the acquisition or provision of the asset by—

(a) the trustee savings bank, or

(b) if the asset was not acquired or provided by the trustee savings bank, the bank within the meaning of section 57(3)(*c*)(i) of the Trustee Savings Banks Act, 1989,

were the successor's acquisition or provision of the asset.

(4) Any allowable losses accruing at any time to a bank shall, on a transfer and in so far as they have not been allowed as a deduction from chargeable gains, be treated as allowable losses which accrued at that time to the successor.

(5) For the purposes of *section 597*, the bank and the successor shall be treated as if they were the same person.

(6) Where the liability in respect of any debt owed to a bank is transferred in the course of a transfer to a successor, the successor shall be treated as the original creditor for the purposes of *section 541*.

Cross References

From Schedule 17

Section 89 Valuation of trading stock at discontinuance of trade.

Section 304 Income tax: allowances and charges in taxing a trade, etc.

Section 307 Corporation tax: allowances and charges in taxing a trade.

Section 308 Corporation tax: manner of granting, and effect of, allowances made by means of discharge or repayment of tax.
Section 320 Other interpretation (Part 9).
Section 396 Relief for trading losses other than terminal losses.
Section 541 Debts.
Section 597 Replacement of business and other assets.
Section 670 Mine development allowance.
Section 705 Reorganisation of trustee savings banks into companies.
Section 754 Interpretation (Chapter 1).
Section 765 Allowances for capital expenditure on scientific research.
Section 769 Relief for training of local staff before commencement of trading.

To Schedule 17

Section 89 Valuation of trading stock at discontinuance of trade.
Section 704 Amalgamation of trustee savings banks.
Section 705 Reorganisation of trustee savings banks into companies.

SCHEDULE 17A

Accounting Standards

[*Section 76A.*

Interpretation

1. In this Schedule "*relevant accounting standards*" means—

(a) international accounting standards, […][1]

(b) as regards the matters covered by those published standards, Irish generally accepted accounting practice which is based on published standards—

(i) which are stated so as to embody, in whole or in part, international accounting standards, and

(ii) the application of which would produce results which are substantially the same as results produced by the application of international accounting [standards, or][2]

Transitional Measures (amounts receivable and deductible)

[(c) in relation to any accounting period beginning on or after 1 January 2015, Irish generally accepted accounting practice based on published standards to the extent that practice is based on the provisions of those published standards that are stated to embody international accounting standards.][3]

2.

(1) In this paragraph—

"*deductible amount*", in relation to a company, means the aggregate of the amounts of—

(a) so much of any amounts receivable by the company which falls to be taken into account as a trading receipt in computing the profits or gains for the purposes of Case I or II of Schedule D of the company for an accounting period computed in accordance with relevant accounting standards as was also taken into account as a trading receipt in computing such profits or gains of the company for any accounting period ending before the first accounting period in respect of which such profits or gains of the company were so computed, and

(b) so much of an expense incurred by the company, being an expense which would have been deductible in computing profits or gains for the purposes of Case I or II of Schedule D of the company if the expense had been incurred in an accounting period for which such profits or gains were computed in accordance with relevant accounting standards, as—

(i) was not deducted in computing the profits or gains for the purposes of Case I or II of Schedule D of the company for an accounting period ending before the first accounting period in respect of which such profits or gains of the company are computed in accordance with relevant accounting standards, and

(ii) is not deductible in computing the profits or gains for the purposes of Case I or II of Schedule D of the company for any accounting period for which such profits or gains of the company are so computed;

"*taxable amount*", in relation to a company, means the aggregate of the amounts of—

(a) so much of an amount receivable by the company, being an amount receivable which would have been taken into account as a trading receipt in computing the profits or gains for the purposes of Case I or II of Schedule D of the company if the amount had accrued in an accounting period for which such profits or gains were computed in accordance with relevant accounting standards, as is not so taken into account—

(i) for an accounting period for which such profits or gains of the company are computed in accordance with relevant accounting standards, or

(ii) for an accounting period ending before the first accounting period in respect of which such profits or gains are so computed,

and

(b) so much of an expense incurred by the company which is deductible in computing the profits or gains for the purposes of Case I or II of Schedule D of the company for an accounting period for which such profits or gains of the company are computed in accordance with relevant accounting standards as was deducted in computing such profits or gains of the company for any accounting period ending before the first accounting period of the company in respect of which such profits or gains were so computed.

(2) (a) An amount equal to the excess of the taxable amount in relation to a company over the deductible amount in relation to the company shall, subject to *subparagraph (4)*, be treated as a trading receipt of the company for the first accounting period of the company in respect of which profits or gains for the purposes of Case I or II of Schedule D of the company are computed in accordance with relevant accounting standards.

[(b) Notwithstanding clause (*a*), an amount (in this subparagraph referred to as the "*relevant amount*") which is treated under clause (*a*) as a trading receipt for an accounting period (in this clause referred to as the "*relevant accounting period*") shall not be taken into account in computing the profits or gains for the purposes of Case I or II of Schedule D of the company for that accounting period but instead, subject to clause (*c*), a part of the relevant amount shall be so taken into account for each accounting period falling wholly or partly into the period of 5 years beginning at the commencement of the relevant accounting period. The part of the relevant amount to be so taken into account for any such accounting period shall be such amount as bears to the relevant amount the same proportion as the length of the accounting period, or the part of the accounting period falling into the period of 5 years, bears to 5 years.

(c) Where any accounting period referred to in clause (*b*) is the last accounting period in which a company carried on a trade or profession, then such part of the relevant amount shall be taken into account for that accounting period as is required to ensure that the whole of that amount is accounted for.][4]

(3) (a) An amount equal to the excess of the deductible amount in relation to a company over the taxable amount in relation to the company shall, subject to *subparagraph (4)*, be treated as a deductible trading expense of the trade carried on by the company for the first accounting period of the company

in respect of which profits or gains for the purposes of Case I or II of Schedule D of the company are computed in accordance with relevant accounting standards.

[(b) Notwithstanding clause (*a*), an amount (in this subparagraph referred to as the "*relevant amount*") which is treated under clause (*a*) as a deductible trading expense for an accounting period (in this clause referred to as the "*relevant accounting period*") shall not be taken into account in computing the profits or gains for the purposes of Case I or II of Schedule D of the company for that accounting period but instead, subject to clause (*c*), a part of the relevant amount shall be so taken into account for each accounting period falling wholly or partly into the period of 5 years beginning at the commencement of the relevant accounting period. The part of the relevant amount to be so taken into account for any such accounting period shall be such amount as bears to the relevant amount the same proportion as the length of the accounting period, or the part of the accounting period falling into the period of 5 years, bears to 5 years.

(c) Where any accounting period referred to in clause (*b*) is the last accounting period in which a company carried on a trade or profession, then such part of the relevant amount shall be taken into account for that accounting period as is required to ensure that the whole of that amount is accounted for.][5]

(4) This paragraph does not apply as respects any amount taken into account under [*paragraph 3* or *4*][6].

Transitional Arrangements (bad debts)

3.

(1) In this paragraph—

"*current bad debts provision*", in relation to a period of account of a company, means so much of the aggregate value of debts at the end of the period of account as represents the extent to which they are estimated to be impaired in accordance with relevant accounting standards;

"*first relevant period of account*", in relation to a company, means the first period of account in respect of which the company prepares its accounts in accordance with relevant accounting standards;

"*opening bad debts provision*", in relation to a company, means so much of the aggregate value of debts at the beginning of the first relevant period of account of the company as represents the extent to which they are estimated to be impaired in accordance with those standards;

"*specific bad debts provision*", in relation to a company, means the aggregate of the amounts of doubtful debts which were respectively estimated to be bad at the end of the period of account immediately preceding the first relevant period of account of the company.

(2) This paragraph applies as respects a period of account in respect of which a company prepares its accounts in accordance with relevant accounting standards.

(3) Where, as respects any period of account for which a company prepares its accounts in accordance with relevant accounting standards, the amount of the opening bad debts provision exceeds the higher of—

(a) the current bad debts provision, or

(b) the specific bad debts provision,

the excess, reduced by any amount treated under this section as a trading expense for any earlier period of account or, if there is more than one such amount, by the aggregate of such amounts, shall be treated as a trading expense of the company's trade for the period of account.

[(4) A debt shall not be taken into account for the purposes of *paragraph 4* if it may be taken into account for the purposes of this paragraph.][7]

Transitional Measures (gains and losses in financial instruments)

4.

(1) In this paragraph—

"*changeover day*", in relation to a company, means the last day of the accounting period immediately preceding the first accounting period of the company in respect of which profits or gains for the purposes of Case I or II of Schedule D of the company are computed in accordance with relevant accounting standards which are, or include, relevant accounting standards in relation to profits or gains or losses on financial assets and financial liabilities;

"*deductible amount*", in relation to a company, means the aggregate of—

(a) so much of any amount of loss accruing on or before the changeover day on a financial asset or financial liability of the company, being a loss which had not been realised on or before that day and which would have been taken into account in computing profits or gains for the purposes of Case I or II of Schedule D of the company if it had accrued in an accounting period commencing after the changeover day, as, apart from this paragraph, would not be so taken into account for any accounting period of the company, and

(b) so much of any amount of profits or gains, accruing and not realised in a period or periods (in this clause referred to as the "first-mentioned period or periods") ending on or before the changeover day on a financial asset or financial liability of the company, which falls to be taken into account in computing the profits or gains for the purposes of Case I or II of Schedule D of the company for an accounting period or periods commencing before the changeover day as would, apart from this paragraph, be taken into account twice in computing profits or gains for the purposes of Case I or II of Schedule D of the company, by virtue of a profit, gain or loss, accruing in a period which includes the first-mentioned period or periods, being taken into account in computing profits or gains for the purposes of Case I or II of Schedule D of the company for an accounting period commencing after the changeover day;

"*taxable amount*", in relation to a company, means the aggregate of—

(a) so much of any amount of profits or gains accruing on or before the changeover day on a financial asset or financial liability of the company, being profits or gains which had not been realised on or before that day and which would have been taken into account in computing the profits or gains for the purposes of Case I or II of Schedule D of the company if they had accrued in an accounting period commencing after the changeover day, as apart from this paragraph, would not be so taken into account for any accounting period of the company, and

(b) so much of any amount of loss, accruing and not realised in a period or periods (in this clause referred to as the "first-mentioned period or periods") ending on or before the changeover day on a financial asset or financial liability of the company, which falls to be taken into account in computing the profits or gains for the purposes of Case I or II of Schedule D of the company for an accounting period or periods commencing before the changeover day as would, apart from this paragraph, be taken into account twice in computing profits or gains for the purposes of Case I or II of Schedule D of the company, by virtue of a profit, gain or loss, accruing in a period which includes the first-mentioned period or periods, being taken into account in computing profits or gains for the purposes of Case I or II of Schedule D of the company for an accounting period commencing after the changeover day.

(2) (a) An amount equal to the excess of the taxable amount in relation to a company over the deductible amount in relation to the company shall be treated as a trading receipt of the company for the first accounting period of the company commencing after the changeover day.

[(b) Notwithstanding clause (*a*), an amount (in this subparagraph referred to as the "*relevant amount*") which is treated under clause (*a*) as a trading receipt for an accounting period (in this clause referred to as the "*relevant accounting period*") shall not be taken into account in computing the profits or gains for the purposes of Case I or II of Schedule D of the company for that accounting period but instead, subject to clause (*c*), a part of the relevant amount shall be so taken into account for each accounting period falling wholly or partly into the period of 5 years beginning at the commencement of the relevant accounting period. The part of the relevant amount to be so taken into account for any such accounting period shall be such amount as bears to the relevant amount the same proportion as the length of the accounting period, or the part of the accounting period falling into the period of 5 years, bears to 5 years.

(c) Where any accounting period referred to in clause (*b*) is the last accounting period in which a company carried on a trade or profession, then such part of the relevant amount shall be taken into account for that accounting period as is required to ensure that the whole of that amount is accounted for.][8]

(3) (a) An amount equal to the excess of the deductible amount in relation to a company over the taxable amount in relation to the company shall be treated as a deductible trading expense of the trade carried on by the company for the first accounting period of the company commencing after the changeover day.

[(b) Notwithstanding clause (*a*), an amount (in this subparagraph referred to as the "*relevant amount*") which is treated under clause (*a*) as a deductible trading expense for an accounting period (in this clause referred to as the "*relevant accounting period*") shall not be taken into account in computing the profits or gains for the purposes of Case I or II of Schedule D of the company for that accounting period, but instead, subject to clause (*c*), a part of the relevant amount shall be so taken into account for each accounting period falling wholly or partly into the period of 5 years beginning at the commencement of the relevant accounting period. The part of the relevant amount to be so taken into account for any such accounting period shall be such amount as bears to the relevant amount the same proportion as the length of the accounting period, or the part of the accounting period falling into the period of 5 years, bears to 5 years.

(c) Where any accounting period referred to in clause (*b*) is the last accounting period in which a company carried on a trade or profession, then such part of the relevant amount shall be taken into account for that accounting period as is required to ensure that the whole of that amount is accounted for.][9]

(4) (a) *Subparagraph (5)* applies to a loss incurred by a company on the disposal at any relevant time of any financial asset or financial liability where, within a period beginning 4 weeks before and ending 4 weeks after that disposal, the company acquired a financial asset or financial liability of the same class providing substantially the same access to economic benefits and exposure to risk as would have been provided by the reacquisition of the asset or liability disposed of.

(b) In this paragraph "*relevant time*" means a time after 1 January 2005 which is in a period of 6 months ending on the changeover day.

[(5) A loss to which this subparagraph applies (in this subparagraph referred to as the "*relevant loss*"), which would otherwise be taken into account in computing profits or gains or losses of a company for the purposes of Case I or II of Schedule D for an accounting period (in this subparagraph referred to as the "*relevant accounting period*"), shall not be so taken into account but instead—

(a) (i) a part of the relevant loss shall be so taken into account for each accounting period falling wholly or partly into the period of 5 years beginning at the commencement of the relevant accounting period, and

(ii) the part of the relevant loss to be so taken into account for any such accounting period to which this clause applies shall be such amount as bears to the relevant loss the same proportion as the length of the accounting period, or the part of the accounting period falling into the period of 5 years, bears to 5 years,

and

(b) notwithstanding clause (*a*), where any accounting period referred to in that clause is the last accounting period in which a company carried on a trade or profession, then such part, of the amount referred to in that clause, shall be taken into account for that accounting period as is required to ensure that the whole of that amount is accounted for.][10]

[...][11]][12]

Amendments

[1] Deleted by FA14 s42(a). Comes into operation on 1 January 2015.

[2] Substituted by FA14 s42(b). Comes into operation on 1 January 2015.

[3] Inserted by FA14 s42(c). Comes into operation on 1 January 2015.

[4] Substituted by FA06 s61(1)(d)(i)(I). This section shall be deemed to have applied as respects any period of account beginning on or after 1 January 2005.

[5] Substituted by FA06 s61(1)(d)(i)(II). This section shall be deemed to have applied as respects any period of account beginning on or after 1 January 2005.

[6] Substituted by FA06 s61(1)(d)(i)(III). This section shall be deemed to have applied as respects any period of account beginning on or after 1 January 2005.

[7] Inserted by FA06 s61(1)(d)(ii). This section shall be deemed to have applied as respects any period of account beginning on or after 1 January 2005.

[8] Substituted by FA06 s61(1)(d)(iii)(I). This section shall be deemed to have applied as respects any period of account beginning on or after 1 January 2005.

[9] Substituted by FA06 s61(1)(d)(iii)(II). This section shall be deemed to have applied as respects any period of account beginning on or after 1 January 2005.

[10] Substituted by FA06 s61(1)(d)(iii)(III). This section shall be deemed to have applied as respects any period of account beginning on or after 1 January 2005.

[11] Deleted by FA08 s47(1)(b). This section has effect for any period of account beginning on or after 1 January 2005.

[12] Inserted by FA05 s48(1)(g). This section applies as respects any period of account beginning on or after 1 January 2005.

Cross References

To Schedule 17A

Section 76A Computation of profits or gains of a company – accounting standards.
Section 76B Treatment of unrealised gains and losses in certain cases.
Section 110 Securitisation.
Section 958 Date for payment of tax.

SCHEDULE 18

Accounting for and Payment of Tax Deducted from Relevant Payments and Undistributed Relevant Income

Section 734(5).

[FA89 Sch1 par1(1) to (7)(d) and (8) and par2; FA97 s146(2) and Sch7 PtII]

Time and manner of payment

1.

(1) Notwithstanding any other provision of the Acts, this paragraph shall apply for the purpose of regulating the time and manner in which tax deducted in accordance with *section 734(5)* shall be accounted for and paid.

(2) A collective investment undertaking which is not a specified collective investment undertaking shall, within 15 days from the 5th day of April each year, make a return to the Collector-General of all amounts from which it was required by *section 734(5)* to deduct tax in the year ending on that date and of the amount of appropriate tax which it was required to deduct from those amounts.

(3) The appropriate tax required to be included in a return shall be due and payable at the time by which the return is to be made and shall be paid by the collective investment undertaking to the Collector-General, and the appropriate tax so due shall be payable by the collective investment undertaking without the making of an assessment; but the appropriate tax which has become so due may be assessed on the collective investment undertaking (whether or not it has been paid when the assessment is made) if that tax or any part of it is not paid on or before the due date.

(4) Where it appears to the inspector that there is an amount of appropriate tax which ought to have been and has not been included in a return, or the inspector is dissatisfied with any return, he or she may make an assessment on the collective investment undertaking to the best of his or her judgment, and any amount of appropriate tax due under an assessment made by virtue of this subparagraph shall be treated for the purposes of interest on unpaid tax as having been payable at the time when it would have been payable if a correct return had been made.

(5) Where any item has been incorrectly included in a return, the inspector may make such assessments, adjustments or set-offs as may in his or her judgment be required for securing that the resulting liabilities to tax (including interest on unpaid tax) whether of the collective investment undertaking or any other person are, in so far as possible, the same as they would have been if the item had not been so included.

(6) (a) Any appropriate tax assessed on a collective investment undertaking under this Schedule shall be due within one month after the issue of the notice of assessment (unless that tax is due earlier under *subparagraph (3)*) subject to any appeal against the assessment, but no such appeal shall affect the date when any amount is due under *subparagraph (3)*.

(b) On the determination of an appeal against an assessment under this Schedule any appropriate tax overpaid shall be repaid.

(7) (a) The provisions of the Income Tax Acts relating to—

(i) assessments to income tax,

(ii) appeals against such assessments (including the rehearing of appeals and the statement of a case for the opinion of the High Court), and

(iii) the collection and recovery of income tax,

shall, with any necessary modifications, apply to the assessment, collection and recovery of appropriate tax.

(b) Any amount of appropriate tax payable in accordance with this Schedule without the making of an assessment shall carry interest at the rate of 1.25 per cent for each month or part of a month from the date when the amount becomes due and payable until payment.

(c) [*Subsections (3)* to *(5)* of *section 1080*][1] shall apply in relation to interest payable under *clause (b)* as they apply in relation to interest payable under *section 1080.*

(d) In its application to any appropriate tax charged by an assessment made in accordance with this Schedule, *section 1080* shall apply as if [*subsection (2)(b)*][2] of that section were deleted.

(8) Every return shall be in a form prescribed by the Revenue Commissioners and shall include a declaration to the effect that the return is correct and complete.

Statement to be given on making of relevant payment

2. Where a collective investment undertaking other than a specified collective investment undertaking makes a relevant payment from which appropriate tax is deductible in accordance with *section 734(5)*, or would be so deductible but for *paragraphs (i)* and *(ii)* of the definition of "*appropriate tax*" in *section 734(1)(a)*, it shall give to the unit holder to whom the relevant payment is made a statement showing—

(a) the amount of the relevant payment,

(b) the amount equal to the aggregate of the appropriate tax deducted from the relevant payment and any amount or amounts deducted pursuant to *paragraphs (i)* and *(ii)* of the definition of "*appropriate tax*" in *section 734(1)(a)* in determining the appropriate tax or, if by reason of those paragraphs there was no appropriate tax to deduct from the amount of the relevant payment, the aggregate of the amounts referred to in those paragraphs in so far as they refer to the relevant payment,

(c) the net amount of the relevant payment,

(d) the date of the relevant payment, and

(e) such other information in relation to the relevant payment as shall be necessary to enable the correct amount of tax, if any, payable by or repayable to the unit holder in respect of the relevant payment to be determined.

Amendments

[1, 2] Substituted by FA05 sched5.

Cross References

From Schedule 18

Section 734 Taxation of collective investment undertakings.

Section 1080 Interest on overdue income tax, corporation tax and capital gains tax.

To Schedule 18

Section 734 Taxation of collective investment undertakings.

Section 735 Certain unit trusts not to be collective investment undertakings.

Section 736 Option for non-application of section 735.

Section 737 Special investment schemes.

Schedule 29 Provisions Referred to in Sections 1052, 1053 and 1054

SCHEDULE 18A

Restriction on Set-off of Pre-entry Losses

[*Section 626A*

Application and construction of Schedule

1.

(1) This Schedule shall apply in the case of a company which is or has been a member of a group of companies (in this Schedule referred to as "*the relevant group*") in relation to any pre-entry losses of the company.

(2) In this Schedule "*pre-entry loss*", in relation to a company, means—

(a) an allowable loss that accrued to the company at a time before it became a member of the relevant group in so far as the loss has not been allowed as a deduction from chargeable gains accruing to the company prior to that time, or

(b) the pre-entry proportion of an allowable loss accruing to the company on the disposal of a pre-entry asset,

and for the purposes of this Schedule the pre-entry proportion of an allowable loss shall be calculated in accordance with *paragraph 2*.

(3) In this Schedule "*pre-entry asset*", in relation to a disposal means, subject to *subparagraph (4)*, an asset which was held [at the time immediately before the relevant event occurred in relation to it by a company which is or was]1 a member of the relevant group.

[(3A) (a) In this paragraph references to the relevant event occurring in relation to a company—

(i) in a case in which—

(I) the company was resident in the State at the time when it became a member of the relevant group, or

(II) the asset was a chargeable asset in relation to the company at that time,

are references to the company becoming a member of that group;

[(ia) in a case in which (whether or not *paragraph (a)*(i)(I) also applies)—

(I) the company is an SE or an SCE resident in the State, and

(II) the asset was transferred to—

(A) the SE as part of the process of its formation by the merger by acquisition of two or more companies in accordance with Articles 2(1) and 17(2)(*a*) or (*b*) of the SE Regulation (within the meaning of *section 630*), or

(B) the SCE as part of the process of its formation by merger in accordance with Article 2 of the SCE Regulation (within the meaning of *section 630*),

are references to the asset becoming a chargeable asset in relation to the SE or (as the case may be) the SCE or, if at the time of the formation of the SE or (as the case may be) the SCE the asset was a chargeable asset in relation to a company which ceased to exist as part of the process of the formation of the SE or (as the case may be) the SCE, to the asset becoming a chargeable asset in relation to that company;]2

(ii) in any other case, are references to whichever is the first of—

(I) the company becoming resident in the State, or

(II) the asset becoming a chargeable asset in relation to the company.

(b) For the purposes of *paragraph (a)*, an asset is a "*chargeable asset*" in relation to a company at any time if, were the asset to be disposed of by the company at that time [or, if the company is an SE or an SCE, by reason of the asset having been transferred to the SE or (as the case may be) the SCE on its formation][3], any gain accruing to the company would be a chargeable gain.][4]

(4) An asset is not a pre-entry asset in relation to a disposal where—

(a) the company which held the asset at the time [the relevant event occurred in relation to it][5] is not the company which makes the disposal, and

(b) since that time the asset has been disposed of otherwise than by a disposal to which *section 617* applies,

but, without prejudice to *subparagraph (8)*, where, on a disposal to which *section 617* does not apply, an asset would cease to be a pre-entry asset by virtue of this subparagraph and the company making the disposal retains any interest in or over the asset in question, that interest shall be a pre-entry asset for the purposes of this Schedule.

(5) References in this Schedule, in relation to a pre-entry asset, to the relevant time are references to the time when [the relevant event occurred in relation to the company by reference to which that asset is a pre-entry asset][6] and for the purposes of this Schedule—

(a) where [a relevant event has occurred in relation to a company][7] on more than one occasion, an asset is a pre-entry asset by reference to the company if the asset would be a pre-entry asset by reference to the company in respect of any one of those occasions, and

(b) references in the following provisions of this Schedule to the time when [a relevant event occurred in relation to a company][8], in relation to assets held on more than one such occasion as is mentioned in clause (a), are references to the later or latest of those occasions.

(6) Where—

(a) the principal company of a group of companies (in this paragraph referred to as "*the first group*") has at any time become a member of another group (in this paragraph referred to as "*the second group*") so that the two groups are treated as the same by virtue of *subsection (3)* [or *(3A)*][9] of *section 616*, and

(b) the second group, together in pursuance of the said *subsection (3)* with the first group, is the relevant group,

then, except where *subparagraph (7)* applies, the members of the first group shall be treated for the purposes of this Schedule as having become members of the relevant group at that time, and not by virtue of the said *subsection (3)* at the times when they became members of the first group.

(7) This subparagraph applies where—

(a) the persons who immediately before the time when the principal company of the first group became a member of the second group owned the shares comprised in the issued share capital of the principal company of the first group are the same as the persons who, immediately after that time, owned the shares comprised in the issued share capital of the principal company of the relevant group, and

(b) the company which is the principal company of the relevant group immediately after that time—

(i) was not the principal company of any group immediately before that time, and

(ii) immediately after that time had assets consisting entirely, or almost entirely, of shares comprised in the issued share capital of the principal company of the first group.

(8) For the purposes of this Schedule—

(a) an asset (in this subparagraph referred to as "*the first asset*") acquired or held by a company at any time and an asset (in this subparagraph referred to as "*the second asset*") held at a later time by the company (or by any company which is or has been a member of the same group of companies as the company) shall be treated as the same asset if the value of the second asset is derived in whole or in part from the first asset, and

(b) where—

(i) an asset is treated (whether by virtue of clause (a) or otherwise) as the same as an asset held by a company at a later time, and

(ii) the first asset would have been a pre-entry asset in relation to the company,

the second asset shall also be treated as a pre-entry asset in relation to the company,

and clause (a) shall apply in particular where the second asset is a freehold and the first asset is a leasehold the lessee of which acquires the reversion.

(9) In determining for the purposes of this Schedule whether an allowable loss accruing to a company on a disposal under *section 719* or *section 738(4)(a)* is a loss that accrued before the company became a member of the relevant group, the provisions of *section 720* or *section 738(4)(b)*, as the case may be, shall be disregarded.

Calculation of pre-entry loss by reference to market value

2.

(1) Where an allowable loss accrues on the disposal by a company of any pre-entry asset, the pre-entry proportion of that loss shall be whichever is the smaller of the amounts mentioned in *subparagraph (2)*.

(2) The amounts referred to in subparagraph (1) are—

(a) the amount of the allowable loss which would have accrued if the asset had been disposed of at the relevant time at its market value at that time, and

(b) the amount of the allowable loss accruing on the disposal mentioned in *subparagraph (1)*.

Gains from which pre-entry losses are to be deductible

3.

(1) Notwithstanding *section 78(2)* a pre-entry loss that accrued to a company on a disposal before the company became a member of the relevant group shall only be deductible from a chargeable gain accruing to the company where the gain is one accruing—

(a) on a disposal made by the company before the date (in this paragraph referred to as "*the entry date*") on which the company became a member of the relevant group and made in the same accounting period in which the entry date falls,

(b) on the disposal of an asset which was held by the company immediately before the entry date, or

(c) on the disposal of an asset which—

(i) was acquired by the company on or after the entry date from a person who was not a member of the relevant group at the time of the acquisition, and

(ii) since its acquisition from the person has not been used or held for any purposes other than those of a trade which was being carried on by the company at the time immediately before the entry date and which continued to be carried on by the company until the disposal.

(2) Notwithstanding *section 78(2)* the pre-entry proportion of an allowable loss accruing to a company on the disposal of a pre-entry asset shall only be deductible from a chargeable gain accruing to the company where—

(a) the gain is one accruing on a disposal made by the company before the entry date and made in the same accounting period in which the entry date falls and the company is the one (in this subparagraph referred to as "*the initial company*") by reference to which the asset on the disposal of which the loss accrues is a pre-entry asset,

(b) the pre-entry asset and the asset on the disposal of which the gain accrues were each held by the same company at a time immediately before the company became a member of the relevant group, or

(c) the gain is one accruing on the disposal of an asset which—

(i) was acquired by the initial company (whether before or after the initial company became a member of the relevant group) from a person who, at the time of the acquisition, was not a member of that group, and

(ii) since its acquisition from the person has not been used or held for any purposes other than those of a trade which was being carried on, immediately before the entry date, by the initial company and which continued to be carried on by the initial company until the disposal.

(3) Where 2 or more companies become members of the relevant group at the same time and those companies were all members of the same group of companies immediately before those companies became members of the relevant group, then—

(a) an asset shall be treated for the purposes of *subparagraph (1)(b)* as held, immediately before the company became a member of the relevant group, by the company to which the pre-entry loss in question accrued if the company is one of those companies and the asset was in fact so held by another of those companies,

(b) two or more assets shall be treated for the purposes of *subparagraph (2)(b)* as assets held by the same company immediately before the company became a member of the relevant group wherever they would be so treated if all those companies were treated as a single company, and

(c) the acquisition of an asset shall be treated for the purposes of *subparagraphs (1)(c)* and *(2)(c)* asan acquisition by the company to which the pre-entry loss in question accrued if the company is one of those companies and the asset was in fact acquired (whether before or after those companies became members of the relevant group) by another of those companies.

Change of a company's nature

4.

(1) Where—

(a) within any period of 3 years, a company becomes a member of a group of companies and there is (either earlier or later in that period, or at the same time) a major change in the nature or conduct of a trade carried on by the company, or

(b) at any time after the scale of the activities in a trade carried on by a company has become small or negligible, and before any considerable revival of the trade, the company becomes a member of a group of companies,

the trade carried on before the change mentioned in clause (*a*), or, as the case may be, the trade mentioned in clause (*b*), shall be disregarded for the purposes of *subparagraphs (1)(c)* and *(2)(c)* of *paragraph 3* in relation to any time before the company became a member of the group in question.

(2) In *subparagraph (1)* the reference to a major change in the nature or conduct of a trade includes a reference to—

(a) a major change in the type of property dealt in, or services or facilities provided, in the trade, or

(b) a major change in customers, markets or outlets of the trade,

and this paragraph shall apply even if the change is the result of a gradual process which began outside the period of 3 years mentioned in subparagraph (1)(*a*).

(3) Where the operation of this paragraph depends on circumstances or events at a time after the company becomes a member of a group of companies (but not more than 3 years after), an assessment to give effect to this paragraph shall not be out of time if made within 6 years from that time or the latest such time.

Companies changing groups on certain transfers of shares etc.

5. For the purposes of this Schedule, where—

(a) a company which is a member of a group of companies becomes at any time a member of another group of companies as the result of a disposal of shares in or other securities of the company or any other company, and

(b) that disposal is one on which, by virtue of any provision of the Tax Acts or the Capital Gains Tax Acts, neither a gain nor a loss would accrue,

this Schedule shall apply in relation to the losses that accrued to the company before that time and the assets held by the company at that time as if any time when the company was a member of the first group were included in the period during which the company is treated as having been a member of the second group.][10]

Amendments

[1] Substituted by FA01 s40(1)(a).

[2] Inserted by FA06 s60(f)(i).

[3] Inserted by FA06 s60(f)(ii).

[4] Inserted by FA01 s40(1)(b).

[5] Substituted by FA01 s40(1)(c).

[6] Substituted by FA01 s40(1)(d)(i).

[7] Substituted by FA01 s40(1)(d)(ii).

[8] Substituted by FA01 s40(1)(d)(iii).

[9] Inserted by FA06 s60(f)(iii).

[10] Inserted by FA99 s57(1). This section shall apply in respect of a company which becomes a member of a group of companies on or after the 1st day of March, 1999.

Cross References

From Schedule 18A

Section 78 Computation of companies' chargeable gains.
Section 616 Groups of companies: interpretation.
Section 617 Transfers of assets, other than trading stock, within group.
Section 630 Interpretation (Part 21).
Section 719 Deemed disposal and reacquisition of certain assets.
Section 720 Gains or losses arising by virtue of section 719.
Section 738 Undertakings for collective investment.

SCHEDULE 18B

Tonnage Tax

PART 1

Matters Relating to Election for Tonnage Tax

Method of making election

Method of making and giving effect to an election

[1.

(1) A tonnage tax election shall be made by notice to the Revenue Commissioners and shall be made by means of a form prescribed for that purpose by them.

(2) (a) The notice shall be supported by such information, particulars and documentation (in this paragraph referred to as "*information*") as the Revenue Commissioners may require for the purposes of this Part and the election shall not take effect until such information is provided to the satisfaction of the Revenue Commissioners.

(b) Without prejudice to the generality of this subparagraph, the information referred to in clause (*a*) may include information relating to the matters specified in *subparagraph (3).*

(3) (a) The information which may be requested from an applicant company by the Revenue Commissioners for the purposes of *subparagraph (2)* includes—

(i) documentation on legal status, memorandum and articles of association, and certificate of incorporation of the company,

(ii) business plans or similar documents of the company,

(iii) the name and address of each of the directors of the company,

(iv) the name and address of each of the beneficial shareholders of the company and the number and class of shares held by each,

(v) details of the qualifying ships owned or leased by the company,

(vi) particulars of how the strategic and commercial management of the qualifying ships is carried on by the company in the State,

(vii) in the case of a group election, particulars of all the companies in the group, their respective shareholdings, and the flow of funds between all of the companies in the group.

(b) For the purposes of this subparagraph, "*applicant company*" means a company that makes an election by notice to the Revenue Commissioners in accordance with *subparagraph (1).*][1]

When election may be made

2.

(1) A tonnage tax election may be made at any time before the end of the period (in this Schedule referred to as the "*initial period*") of 36 months beginning on the commencement date.

(2) After the end of the initial period a tonnage tax election may only be made in the circumstances specified in *subparagraphs (3)* and *(4)*.

(3) (a) An election may be made after the end of the initial period in respect of a single company that becomes a qualifying company and has not previously been a qualifying company at any time on or after the commencement date.

(b) Any election under this subparagraph shall be made before the end of the period of 36 months beginning with the day on which the company became a qualifying company.

(4) (a) An election may be made after the end of the initial period in respect of a group of companies that becomes a qualifying group of companies by virtue of a member of the group becoming a qualifying company, not previously having been a qualifying company, at any time on or after the commencement date.

(b) This subparagraph shall not apply if the group of companies-

(i) was previously a qualifying group at any time on or after the commencement date, or

(ii) is substantially the same as a group that was previously a qualifying group of companies at any such time.

(c) An election under this subparagraph shall be made before the end of the period of 36 months beginning with the day on which the group of companies became a qualifying group of companies.

(5) This paragraph shall not prevent an election being made under *Part 4*.

(6) The Minister for Finance may by order provide for further periods within which a tonnage tax election may be made, and any such order may provide for this Part of this Schedule to apply, with any necessary modifications, as appears to the Minister to be appropriate in relation to such further periods as it applies in relation to the initial period.

When election takes effect

3.

(1) Subject to this paragraph, a tonnage tax election shall have effect from the beginning of the accounting period in which it is made.

(2) A tonnage tax election shall not have effect in relation to an accounting period beginning before 1 January 2002, but where a tonnage tax election would have effect under *subparagraph (1)* for an accounting period beginning before 1 January 2002 the election shall have effect from the beginning of the accounting period following that in which it is made.

(3) The Revenue Commissioners may allow a tonnage tax election made before the end of the initial period to have effect from the beginning of an accounting period earlier than that in which it is made (but not one beginning before 1 January 2002).

(4) The Revenue Commissioners may allow a tonnage tax election made before the end of the initial period to have effect from the beginning of the accounting period following that in which it is made or, where the Revenue Commissioners determine that due to exceptional circumstances, unrelated to the avoidance or reduction of tax, it is commercially impracticable for the election to take effect, the beginning of the next following accounting period.

(5) In the case of a group election made in respect of a group of companies where the members have different accounting periods, *subparagraph (1)* or, if appropriate, *subparagraph (3)* or *(4)* shall apply in relation to each qualifying company by reference to that company's accounting periods.

(6) [A tonnage tax election][2] under *paragraph 2(3)* or (4) shall have effect from the time at which the company in question became a qualifying company.

Period for which election is in force

4.

(1) Subject to *subparagraphs (2)* and *(3)* and *paragraph 6(3)*, a tonnage tax election shall remain in force until it expires at the end of the period of 10 years beginning—

(a) in the case of a company election, with the first day on which the election has effect in relation to the company, and

(b) in the case of a group election, with the first day on which the election has effect in relation to any member of the group.

(2) A tonnage tax election shall cease to be in force—

(a) in the case of a company election, if the company ceases to be a qualifying company, and

(b) in the case of a group election, if the group of companies ceases to be a qualifying group.

(3) A tonnage tax election may also cease to be in force under *Part 4*.

Effect of election ceasing to be in force

5. A tonnage tax election that ceases to be in force shall cease to have effect in relation to any company.

Renewal election

6.

(1) At any time when a tonnage tax election is in force in respect of a single company or group of companies a further tonnage tax election (in *Part 24A* and this Schedule referred to as a "*renewal election*") may be made in respect of that company or group.

(2) *Section 697D* and *paragraphs 1, 4* and *5* shall apply in relation to a renewal election as they apply in relation to an original tonnage tax election.

(3) A renewal election supersedes the existing tonnage tax election.

PART 2

Matters Relating to Qualifying Ships

Company temporarily ceasing to operate qualifying ships

7.

(1) This paragraph shall apply where a company temporarily ceases to operate any qualifying ships.

(2) This paragraph shall not apply where a company continues to operate a ship that temporarily ceases to be a qualifying ship.

(3) If a company which temporarily ceases to operate any qualifying ships gives notice to the Revenue Commissioners stating—

(a) its intention to resume operating qualifying ships, and

(b) its wish to remain within tonnage tax,

the company shall be treated for the purposes of *Part 24A* and this Schedule as if it had continued to operate the qualifying ship or ships it operated immediately before the temporary cessation.

(4) The notice must be given on or before the specified return date for the chargeable period (within the meaning of [*Part 41A*][3]) of the company in which the temporary cessation begins.

(5) This paragraph shall cease to apply if and when the company—

(a) abandons its intention to resume operating qualifying ships, or

(b) again in fact operates a qualifying ship.

Meaning of operating a ship

8.

(1) Subject to this paragraph, a company is regarded for the purposes of *Part 24A* and this Schedule as operating any ship owned by, or chartered to, the company.

(2) (a) A company shall not be regarded as the operator of a ship where part only of the ship has been chartered to it.

(b) For the purpose of *subparagraph (a)*, a company shall not be taken as having part only of a ship chartered to it by reason only of the ship being chartered to it jointly with one or more other persons.

(3) Except as provided by *subparagraphs (4)* and *(5)*, a company shall not be regarded as the operator of a ship that has been chartered out by it on bareboat charter terms.

(4) (a) A company shall be regarded as operating a ship that has been chartered out by it on bareboat charter terms if the person to whom it is chartered is not a third party.

(b) For the purpose of *subparagraph (a)*, a "*third party*" means—

(i) in the case of a single company, any other person,

(ii) in the case of a member of a group of companies—

(I) any member of the group that is not a tonnage tax company (and does not become a tonnage tax company by virtue of the ship being chartered to it), or

(II) any person who is not a member of the group.

(5) A company shall not be regarded as ceasing to operate a ship that has been chartered out by it on bareboat charter terms if—

(a) the ship is chartered out because of short-term overcapacity, and

(b) the term of the charter does not exceed 3 years.

(6) A company shall be regarded as operating a qualifying ship for the purposes of the activity described in *paragraph (j)* of the definition of "*relevant shipping income*" in *section 697A* if that company has entered contractual arrangements in relation to the provision of ship management services for the qualifying ship for a stipulated period and the terms of those arrangements give the company—

(a) possession and control of the ship,

(b) control over the day to day management of the ship, including the right to appoint the master and crew and route planning,

(c) control over the technical management of the ship, including decisions on its repair and maintenance,

(d) control over the safety management of the ship, including ensuring that all necessary safety and survey certificates are current,

(e) control over the training of the officers and crew of the ship, and

(f) the management of the bunkering, victualling and provisioning of the ship,

and those terms are actually implemented for the period in which the company provides ship management services in respect of that ship.

Qualifying ship used as vessel of an excluded kind

9.

(1) A qualifying ship that begins to be used as a vessel of an excluded kind ceases to be a qualifying ship when it begins to be so used, but if—

(a) a company operates a ship throughout an accounting period of the company, and

(b) in that period the ship is used as a vessel of an excluded kind on not more than 30 days, that use shall be disregarded in determining whether the ship is a qualifying ship at any time during that period.

(2) In the case of an accounting period shorter than a year, the figure of 30 days in *subparagraph (1)* shall be proportionately reduced.

(3) If a company operates a ship during part only of an accounting period of the company, *subparagraph (1)* shall apply as if for 30 days, or the number of days substituted by *subparagraph (2)*, there were substituted the number of days that bear to the length of that part of the accounting period the same proportion that 30 days bears to a year.

PART 3

Capital Allowances, Balancing Charges and Related Matters

Plant and machinery used wholly for tonnage tax trade

10.

(1) (a) This subparagraph shall apply where, on a company's entry to tonnage tax, machinery or plant, in respect of which capital expenditure was incurred by the company before its entry into tonnage tax, is to be used wholly and exclusively for the purposes of the company's tonnage tax trade.

(b) Where this subparagraph applies—

(i) no balancing charge or balancing allowance shall be made under *section 288* as a result of the machinery or plant concerned being used for the purposes of the company's tonnage tax trade,

(ii) any allowance attributable to the machinery or plant referred to in *subparagraph (a)* which, but for this clause, would have been made to the company under *Part 9* or under any provision that is construed as one with that Part for any accounting period in which the company is a tonnage tax company shall not be made, and

(iii) *section 287* shall not apply as respects any accounting period during which the machinery or plant has been used wholly and exclusively for the purposes of a company's tonnage tax trade.

(2) (a) This subparagraph shall apply where the machinery or plant referred to in subparagraph (1)(*a*) begins to be used wholly or partly for purposes other than those of the company's tonnage tax trade.

(b) Where this subparagraph applies and the asset begins to be wholly used for purposes other than the company's tonnage tax trade—

(i) no balancing allowance shall be made on the company under *section 288(2)* for any period in which the company is subject to tonnage tax,

(ii) for the purposes of making a balancing charge under *section 288* on the happening of any of the events referred to in *subsection (1)* of that section—

(I) *section 296* shall not apply as respects any accounting period of a company in which the company is subject to tonnage tax,

(II) where the event occurs at a time when the company is subject to tonnage tax, the amount of the capital expenditure of the company still unallowed at the time of the event shall, notwithstanding *section 296*, be the amount of the capital expenditure of the company on the provision of the machinery or plant which was still unallowed at the time the company's election into tonnage tax had effect, and

(III) where the event occurs at a time when the company is subject to tonnage tax, the references in *section 288* to sale, insurance, salvage or compensation moneys and the reference in *section 289(3)(b)* to the open-market price of the machinery or plant shall be taken to be references to the least of—

(A) the actual cost to the company of the machinery or plant for the purpose of the trade carried on by the company,

(B) the price the machinery or plant would have fetched if sold in the open market at the time the company's election into tonnage tax had effect, and

(C) the sale, insurance, salvage or compensation moneys (within the meaning of *Part 9*) arising from the event or, where *paragraph (b)* of *section 289(3)* applies, the open-market price of the machinery or plant (within the meaning of that section) at the time of the event.

(c) Where this subparagraph applies and the asset begins to be partly used for purposes other than the company's tonnage tax trade—

(i) the machinery or plant shall be treated as 2 separate assets one in use wholly and exclusively for the purposes of the tonnage tax trade and the other in use wholly and exclusively for purposes other than the company's tonnage tax trade,

(ii) *subparagraph (2)(b)* shall apply in relation to the part of the asset treated by virtue of this subparagraph as in use wholly and exclusively for the purposes of the tonnage tax trade as it applies in relation to machinery or plant which begins to be used wholly for purposes other than the company's tonnage tax trade,

(iii) in determining the amount of any capital allowance or balancing charge, if any, to be made under *Part 9* or under any other provision to be construed as one with that Part in relation to the part of the asset treated by virtue of this subparagraph as in use wholly and exclusively for purposes other than the company's tonnage tax trade regard shall be had to all relevant circumstances and, in particular, to the extent of the use, if any, of the machinery or plant for the purposes of a trade, and there shall be made to or on the company, in respect of that trade, an allowance of such an amount or a balancing charge of such an amount, as may be just and reasonable.

Plant and machinery used partly for purposes of tonnage tax trade

11.

(1) This paragraph shall apply where, on a company's entry into tonnage tax, machinery or plant, in respect of which capital expenditure was incurred by the company before its entry into tonnage tax, is to be used partly for the purposes of the company's tonnage tax trade and partly for purposes other than the company's tonnage tax trade.

(2) Where this paragraph applies—

(a) the machinery or plant referred to in *subparagraph (1)* shall be treated as 2 separate assets one in use wholly and exclusively for the purposes of the tonnage tax trade and the other in use wholly and exclusively for the purposes of the other trade of the company,

(b) subject to clause (*c*), in determining the amount of—

(i) any capital allowance or balancing charge to be made in respect of that part of the asset treated as in use wholly and exclusively for purposes other than the company's tonnage tax trade under *Part 9* or under any provision which is to be construed as one with that Part, or

(ii) the amount of any balancing charge to be made for the purpose of the tonnage tax trade under *Part 9*, or under any provision which is to be construed as one with that Part, as applied by this Schedule,

regard shall be had to all relevant circumstances and, in particular, to the extent of the use of the machinery or plant for the purposes of a trade other than the tonnage tax trade, and there shall be made to or on the company, in respect of that trade, an allowance of such an amount, or, in respect of both the tonnage tax trade and the other trade, a balancing charge of such an amount, as may be just and reasonable, and

(c) *paragraph 10(1)(b)* and *paragraph 10(2)(b)* shall apply in relation to the part of the asset treated by virtue of this paragraph as in use wholly and exclusively for the purposes of the tonnage tax trade as they apply in relation to the machinery or plant referred to in *paragraph 10(1)(a)*.

Plant and machinery: new expenditure partly for tonnage tax purposes

12.

(1) This paragraph shall apply where a company subject to tonnage tax incurs capital expenditure on the provision of machinery or plant partly for the purposes of its tonnage tax trade and partly for the purposes of another trade carried on by the company.

(2) Where this paragraph applies the machinery or plant shall be treated as 2 separate assets one in use wholly and exclusively for the purposes of the tonnage tax trade and the other in use wholly and exclusively for the purposes of the other trade of the company and, in determining the amount of any capital allowance, or the amount of any charge to be made, under *Part 9* or under any provision which is to be construed as one with that Part in the case of that part of the asset treated as a separate asset for the purposes of the other trade of the company, regard shall be had to all relevant circumstances and, in particular, to the extent of the use of the machinery or plant for the purposes of the other trade, and there shall be made to or on the company, in respect of the other trade, an allowance of such an amount, or a charge of such an amount, as may be just and reasonable.

Plant and machinery: change of use of tonnage tax asset

13.

(1) This paragraph shall apply where, at a time when a company is subject to tonnage tax, machinery or plant acquired after the company became so subject and which is used wholly and exclusively for the purposes of the company's tonnage tax trade begins to be used wholly or partly for purposes of another trade.

(2) Where this paragraph applies—

(a) if the asset begins to be used wholly for purposes of another trade the provisions of *Part 9* shall apply as if capital expenditure had been incurred by the person carrying on the other trade on the provision of the plant or machinery for the purposes of that trade in that person's chargeable period (within the meaning of *Part 9*) in which the plant or machinery is brought into use for those purposes, and the amount of that expenditure shall be taken as the lesser of—

(i) the amount of the capital expenditure actually incurred by the person, and

(ii) the price which the machinery or plant would have fetched if sold on the open market on the date on which it was so brought into use, and

(b) if the asset begins to be used partly for purposes of another trade of the company and partly for the purposes of the tonnage tax trade—

(i) the machinery or plant shall be treated as 2 separate assets one in use wholly and exclusively for the purposes of the tonnage tax trade and the other in use wholly and exclusively for the purposes of the other trade of the company,

(ii) *Part 9* shall apply as if the company had incurred capital expenditure on the provision of that part of the asset treated as in use wholly and exclusively for the other trade of the company in the accounting period of the company in which that part of the asset is brought into use for those purposes, and

(iii) in determining the amount of any capital expenditure incurred on the provision of that part of the asset treated as in use as a separate asset for the purposes of the other trade of the company regard shall be had to all relevant circumstances as is just and reasonable.

Plant and machinery: change of use of non-tonnage tax asset

14.

(1) This paragraph shall apply where, at a time when a company is subject to tonnage tax, plant or machinery wholly and exclusively used for the purposes of another trade carried on by the company not being a tonnage tax trade begins to be used wholly or partly for the purposes of the company's tonnage tax trade.

(2) Where this paragraph applies and the asset begins to be wholly used for the purposes of the company's tonnage tax trade—

(a) no balancing allowance or balancing charge shall be made as a consequence of the change in use, and

(b) for the purposes of making a balancing charge under *section 288* on the happening subsequent to the change in use of any of the events referred to in *subsection (1)* of that section—

(i) *section 296* shall not apply as respects any accounting period of the company in which the asset is used wholly and exclusively for the purposes of the company's tonnage tax trade,

(ii) where the event occurs at a time when the asset is so used, the amount of the capital expenditure of the company still unallowed at the time of the event shall, notwithstanding *section 296*, be the amount of the capital expenditure of the company on the provision of the machinery or plant which was still unallowed at the time the asset began to be so used, and

(iii) where the event occurs at a time when the asset is so used, the references in *section 288* to sale, insurance, salvage or compensation moneys and the reference in *section 289(3)(b)* to the open-market value of the machinery or plant shall be taken to be references to the least of—

(I) the actual cost to the company of the machinery or plant for the purpose of the trade carried on by the company,

(II) the price the machinery or plant would have fetched if sold in the open market at the time the asset began to be so used, and

(III) the sale, insurance, salvage or compensation moneys (within the meaning of *Part 9*) arising on the event or, where paragraph (*b*) of *section 289(3)* applies, the open-market price of the machinery or plant (within the meaning of that section) at the time of the event.

(3) Where this paragraph applies and the asset begins to be partly used for the purposes of the company's tonnage tax trade—

(a) the machinery or plant referred to in *subparagraph (1)* shall be treated as 2 separate assets one in use wholly and exclusively for the purposes of the other trade of the company and the other in use wholly and exclusively for the purposes of the tonnage tax trade of the company,

(b) no balancing charge or balancing allowance shall be made in respect of the part treated as in use wholly and exclusively for the purposes of the tonnage tax trade as a consequence of the change in use,

(c) *subparagraph (2)(b)* shall apply in relation to the part of the asset treated by virtue of this subparagraph as in use wholly and exclusively for the purposes of the tonnage tax trade as it applies in relation to the machinery or plant wholly used for the purposes of the company's tonnage tax trade.

Plant and machinery: provisions relating to balancing charges

15.

(1) A balancing charge arising under *Part 9* as applied by this Schedule or under this Schedule shall—

(a) be treated as arising in connection with a trade carried on by the company other than the company's tonnage tax trade, and

(b) be made in taxing that trade.

(2) Subject to *paragraph 16* or *17*, the charge shall be given effect in the accounting period in which it arises.

(3) On the first occasion of the happening of an event which gives rise to a balancing charge (including such an event arising in respect of more than one asset on the same date) under *Part 9* as applied by this Schedule, or under this Schedule, on a tonnage tax company, the tonnage tax company shall by notice in writing to the Revenue Commissioners elect for relief against that charge under either *paragraph 16* or, if applicable, *paragraph 17* but not for relief under both, and any such election shall be irrevocable and be included in the company's return under [*Chapter 3* of *Part 41A*][4] for the accounting period in which the charge arises.

(4) Where a balancing charge arises on a tonnage tax company under *Part 9* as applied by this Schedule or under this Schedule subsequent to any charge on the company such as is referred to in *subparagraph (3)*, relief against that charge shall only be available under the paragraph for which the company elected for relief in accordance with that subparagraph.

(5) Relief under *paragraph 16* or *17* shall not be available to a company unless the company has made an election under *subparagraph (3)*.

Reduction in balancing charge by reference to time in tonnage tax

16. The amount of any balancing charge under *Part 9* as applied by this Schedule or under this Schedule shall be reduced by 20 per cent of the amount of the charge for each whole year in which the company on which the charge is to be made has been subject to tonnage tax calculated by reference to the time of the event giving rise to the charge.

Set-off of accrued losses against balancing charge

17. Where a balancing charge under *Part 9* as applied by this Schedule or under this Schedule arises in connection with the disposal of a qualifying ship, then the company may set off against any balancing charge so arising any losses (including any losses referable to capital allowances treated by virtue of *section 307* or *308* as trading expenses of the company) which accrued to the company before its entry to tonnage tax and which are attributable to—

(a) activities which under tonnage tax became part of the company's tonnage tax trade, or

(b) a source of income which under tonnage tax becomes relevant shipping income.

Deferment of balancing charge on re-investment

18.

(1) Where—

(a) a balancing charge under *Part 9* as applied by this Schedule arises in connection with the disposal of a qualifying ship, and

(b) within the period beginning on the date the company's election for tonnage tax takes effect and ending 5 years after the date of the event giving rise to the balancing charge, the company or another qualifying company which is a member of the same tonnage tax group as the company incurs capital expenditure on the provision of one or more other qualifying ships (in this paragraph referred to as the "*new asset*"),

then

(i) if the amount on which the charge would have been made, as reduced under *paragraph 16* or *17*, if applicable, is greater than the capital expenditure on providing the new asset, the balancing charge shall be made only on an amount equal to the difference, and

(ii) if the capital expenditure on providing the new asset is equal to or greater than the amount on which the charge would have been made, as reduced under *paragraph 16* or *17*, if applicable, the balancing charge shall not be made.

(2) Where an event referred to in *section 288(1)* occurs in relation to the new asset in the period in which the company which incurs the expenditure on the new asset is subject to tonnage tax then a balancing charge shall be made under this paragraph on that company.

(3) Subject to any reduction under *paragraph 16* or *17* and to any further application of this paragraph, the amount of the charge referred to in *subparagraph (2)* shall be—

(a) where *subparagraph (1)(i)* applies, the difference between the balancing charge which, but for *subparagraph (1)*, would have been made on the disposal referred to in *subparagraph (1)* and the actual charge made,

(b) where *subparagraph (1)(ii)* applies, the amount of the charge which, but for *subparagraph (1)*, would have been made on the disposal referred to in that subparagraph.

(4) *Section 290* shall not apply in relation to balancing charges to which this paragraph applies.

(5) For the purposes of *subparagraph (1)*, where machinery or plant is let to a tonnage tax company on the terms of that company being bound to maintain the machinery or plant and deliver it over in good condition at the end of the lease, and if the burden of the wear and tear on the machinery or plant will in fact fall directly on the company, then the capital expenditure on the provision of the machinery and plant shall be deemed to have been incurred by that company and the machinery and plant shall be deemed to belong to that company.

Exit: plant and machinery

19.

(1) Where a company leaves tonnage tax the amount of capital expenditure incurred on the provision of machinery or plant in respect of each asset used by the company for the purposes of its tonnage tax trade which asset was acquired at a time the company was subject to tonnage tax and held by the company at the time it leaves tonnage tax shall be deemed to be the lesser of—

(a) the capital expenditure actually incurred by the company on the provision of that machinery or plant for the purposes of the company's tonnage tax trade, and

(b) the price the machinery or plant would have fetched if sold in the open market at the date the company leaves tonnage tax.

(2) For the purposes of the making of allowances and charges under *Part 9* or any provision construed as one with that Part, the capital expenditure on the provision of the machinery or plant as determined in accordance with *subparagraph (1)* shall be deemed to have been incurred on the day immediately following the date the company leaves tonnage tax.

(3) (a) This subparagraph applies where a company—

(i) leaves tonnage tax having incurred expenditure on the provision of machinery or plant for the purposes of a trade carried on by the company before entry into tonnage tax,

(ii) has used that machinery or plant for the purposes of its tonnage tax trade,

(iii) has been denied allowances in respect of that machinery or plant by virtue of *section 697O* and the provisions of *paragraph 10(1)(b)*(ii) or *paragraph 11(2)(c)*, and

(iv) on leaving tonnage tax starts, recommences or continues to use that machinery or plant for the purposes of a trade carried on by it.

(b) Subject to clauses (*c*) and (*d*), where this subparagraph applies any allowance which, but for *section 697O* and *paragraph 10(1)(b)* or *11(2)(c)*, would have been made under *Part 9* or any provision construed as one with that Part to the company for any accounting period in which it was subject to tonnage tax shall, subject to compliance with that Part, be made instead for such accounting periods immediately after the company leaves tonnage tax as will ensure, subject to that Part, that all such allowances are made to the company in those accounting periods as would have been made to the company in respect of that machinery or plant if the company had never been subject to tonnage tax.

(c) No wear and tear allowance shall be made by virtue of this subparagraph in respect of any machinery or plant for any accounting period of a company if such allowance when added to the allowances in respect of that machinery or plant made to that company for any previous accounting period will make the aggregate amount of the allowances exceed the actual cost to that company of the machinery or plant, including in that actual cost any expenditure in the nature of capital expenditure on the machinery or plant by means of renewal, improvement or reinstatement.

(d) A wear and tear allowance in respect of any machinery or plant made by virtue of this subparagraph for any accounting period shall not exceed the amount appropriate to that machinery or plant as set out in *section 284(2)*.

Industrial buildings

20.

(1) Where any identifiable part of a building or structure is used for the purposes of a company's tonnage tax trade, that part is treated for the purposes of *Chapter 1* of *Part 9* as used otherwise than as an industrial building or structure.

(2) (a) This subparagraph applies where, in an accounting period during which a company is subject to tonnage tax, an event giving rise to a balancing charge occurs in relation to an industrial building or structure in respect of which capital expenditure was incurred by the company before its entry into tonnage tax.

(b) Where this subparagraph applies—

(i) the sale, insurance, salvage or compensation moneys to be brought into account in respect of any industrial building or structure shall be limited to the market value of the relevant interest when the company entered tonnage tax, and

(ii) the amount of any balancing charge under that Part shall, subject to *subparagraphs (3)* to *(5)* of *paragraph 15*, be reduced in accordance with *paragraph 16* or *17*, as appropriate.

(3) Where a company subject to tonnage tax disposes of the relevant interest in an industrial building or structure, *section 277* shall apply to determine the residue of expenditure in the hands of the person who acquires the relevant interest, as if—

(a) the company had not been subject to tonnage tax, and

(b) all writing-down allowances, and balancing allowances and charges, had been made as could have been made if the company had not been subject to tonnage tax.

(4) Where a company leaves tonnage tax the amount of capital expenditure qualifying for relief under *Chapter 1* of *Part 9* shall be determined as if—

(a) the company had never been subject to tonnage tax, and

(b) all such allowances and charges under that Part had been made as could have been made.

PART 4

Groups, Mergers and Related Matters

Company not to be treated as member of more than one group

21.

(1) Where a company is a member of both a tonnage tax group and a non-tonnage tax group which if a group election had been made would have been a tonnage tax group (in this paragraph referred to as a qualifying non-tonnage tax group), the company shall be treated as a member of the tonnage tax group and not of the qualifying non-tonnage tax group.

(2) Where a company is a member of 2 tonnage tax groups, the company shall be treated as a member of the group whose tonnage tax election was made first and not of the other tonnage tax group. In the case of group elections made

at the same time, the company shall choose which election it joins in and for the purposes of *Part 24A* and this Schedule the company shall be treated as a member of the group in respect of which that election is made and not of any other tonnage tax group.

Arrangements for dealing with group matters

22.

(1) The Revenue Commissioners may enter into arrangements with the qualifying companies in a group for one of those companies to deal on behalf of the group in relation to matters arising under *Part 24A* and this Schedule that may conveniently be dealt with on a group basis.

(2) Any such arrangements—

(a) may make provision in relation to cases where companies become or cease to be members of a group;

(b) may make provision for or in connection with the termination of the arrangements; and

(c) may make such supplementary, incidental, consequential or transitional provision as is necessary or expedient for the purposes of the arrangements.

(3) Any such arrangements shall not affect—

(a) any requirement under *Part 24A* and this Schedule that an election be made jointly by all the qualifying companies in the group; or

(b) any liability under *Part 24A*, this Schedule or any other provision of the Tax Acts of a company to which the arrangements relate.

Meaning of "*merger*" and "*demerger*"

23.

(1) In this Schedule—

"*merger*" means a transaction by which one or more companies become members of a group, and

"*demerger*" means a transaction by which one or more companies cease to be members of a group.

(2) References to a merger to which a group is a party include any merger affecting a member of the group.

Merger: between tonnage tax groups or companies

24.

(1) This paragraph shall apply where there is a merger—

(a) between 2 or more tonnage tax groups,

(b) between one or more tonnage tax groups and one or more tonnage tax companies, or

(c) between two or more tonnage tax companies.

(2) Where this paragraph applies the group resulting from the merger is a tonnage tax group as if a group election had been made.

(3) The deemed election referred to in *subparagraph (2)* continues in force, subject to the provisions of this Part, until whichever of the existing tonnage tax elections had the longest period left to run would have expired.

Merger: tonnage tax group/company and qualifying non-tonnage tax group/company

25.

(1) This paragraph shall apply where there is a merger between a tonnage tax group or company and a qualifying non-tonnage tax group or company.

(2) Where this paragraph applies the group resulting from the merger may elect that—

(a) it be treated as if a group election had been made which deemed election shall continue in force until the original election made by the tonnage tax group or company would have expired, or

(b) the tonnage tax election of the group or company ceases to be in force as from the date of the merger.

(3) Any election under *subparagraph (2)* shall be made jointly by all the qualifying companies in the group resulting from the merger and by way of notice in writing to the Revenue Commissioners within 12 months of the merger.

Merger: tonnage tax group or company and non-qualifying group or company

26.

(1) This paragraph shall apply where there is a merger between a tonnage tax group or company and a non-qualifying group or company.

(2) Where this subsection applies the group resulting from the merger is a tonnage tax group by virtue of the election of the tonnage tax group or company.

Merger: non-qualifying group or company and qualifying non-tonnage tax group or company

27.

(1) This paragraph shall apply where there is a merger between a non-qualifying group or company and a qualifying non-tonnage tax group or company.

(2) Where this paragraph applies, the group resulting from the merger may make a tonnage tax election having effect as from the date of the merger.

(3) Any such election shall be made jointly by all the qualifying companies in the group resulting from the merger, by notice in writing to the Revenue Commissioners, within 12 months of the merger.

Demerger: single company

28.

(1) This paragraph shall apply where a tonnage tax company ceases to be a member of a tonnage tax group and does not become a member of another group.

(2) Where this paragraph applies—

(a) the company in question remains a tonnage tax company as if a single company election had been made, and

(b) that deemed election continues in force, subject to the provisions of this Schedule, until the group election would have expired.

(3) If 2 or more members of the previous group remain, and any of them is a qualifying company, the group consisting of those companies shall be a tonnage tax group by virtue of the previous group election.

Demerger: group

29.

(1) This paragraph shall apply where a tonnage tax group splits into two or more groups.

(2) Where this paragraph applies each new group that contains a qualifying company that was a tonnage tax company before the demerger shall be a tonnage tax group as if a group election had been made.

(3) That deemed election continues in force, subject to the provisions of this Schedule, until the group election would have expired.

Duty to notify Revenue Commissioners of group changes

30.

(1) A tonnage tax company that becomes or ceases to be a member of a group, or of a particular group, shall give notice in writing to the Revenue Commissioners of that fact.

(2) The notice shall be given within the period of 12 months beginning with the date on which the company became or ceased to be a member of the group.

PART 5

Miscellaneous and Supplemental

Measurement of tonnage of ship

31.

(1) References in *Part 24A* and in this Schedule to the gross or net tonnage of a ship are to that tonnage as determined—

(a) in the case of a vessel of 24 metres in length or over, in accordance with the IMO International Convention on Tonnage Measurement of Ships 1969;

(b) in the case of a vessel under 24 metres in length, in accordance with tonnage regulations.

(2) A ship shall not be treated as a qualifying ship for the purposes of this Part and this Schedule unless there is in force—

(a) a valid International Tonnage Certificate (1969), or

(b) a valid certificate recording its tonnage as measured in accordance with tonnage regulations.

(3) In this paragraph "*tonnage regulations*" means regulations under section 91 of the Mercantile Marine Act, 1955 or the provisions of the law of a country or territory outside the State corresponding to those regulations.

Second or subsequent application of sections 697P and 697Q

32. Where *sections 697P* and *697Q* apply on a second or subsequent occasion on which a company ceases to be a tonnage tax company (whether or not those sections applied on any of the previous occasions)—

(a) the references to the company ceasing to be a tonnage tax company shall be read as references to the last occasion on which it did so, and

(b) the references to the period during which the company was a tonnage tax company do not include any period before its most recent entry into tonnage tax.

Appeals

33. Where in *Part 24A* and in this Schedule there is provision for the determination of any matter on a just and reasonable basis and it is not possible for the company concerned and [the appropriate inspector] to agree on what is just and reasonable in the circumstances then there shall be the right of appeal to the Appeal Commissioners in the like manner as an appeal would lie against an assessment to corporation tax and the provisions of the Tax Acts relating to appeals shall apply accordingly.

Delegation of powers and functions

34. The Revenue Commissioners may nominate any of their officers to perform any acts and discharge any functions authorised by *Part 24A* or this Schedule to be performed or discharged by the Revenue Commissioners.][6]

Amendments

[1] Substituted by FA06 s67(1)(f)(i). This section comes into operation on 1 July 2006.

[2] Substituted by FA06 s67(1)(f)(ii). This section come into operation on such day or days as the Minister for Finance may by order or orders appoint and different days may be appointed for different purposes or different provisions.

[3, 4] Substituted by FA12 sched4(part 2)(g).

[5] Substituted by FA12 sched5(1)(l).

[6] Inserted by FA02 s53(2). Per FA03 s62(2) with effect from 28 March 2003, the date of passing of FA03.

Cross References

From Schedule 18B

Section 268 Meaning of "industrial building or structure".
Section 277 Writing off of expenditure and meaning of "residue of expenditure".
Section 284 Wear and tear allowances.
Section 287 Wear and tear allowances deemed to have been made in certain cases.
Section 288 Balancing allowances and balancing charges.
Section 289 Calculation of balancing allowances and balancing charges in certain cases.
Section 290 Option in case of replacement.
Section 296 Balancing allowances and balancing charges: wear and tear allowances deemed to have been made in certain cases.
Section 307 Corporation tax: allowances and charges in taxing a trade.
Section 308 Corporation tax: manner of granting, and effect of, allowances made by means of discharge or repayment of tax.
Section 697A Interpretation (Part 24A).
Section 697D Election for tonnage tax.
Section 697O Capital allowances: general.
Section 697P Withdrawal of relief etc. on company leaving tonnage tax.
Section 697Q Ten year disqualification from re-entry into tonnage tax.
Section 950 Interpretation (Part 41).
Section 951 Obligation to make a return.

To Schedule 18B

Schedule 29 Provisions Referred to in Sections 1052, 1053 and 1054

SCHEDULE 19

Offshore Funds: Distributing Funds

Section 744.

[FA90 Sch5]

PART 1

The Distribution Test

Requirements as to distributions

1.

(1) For the purposes of *Chapter 2* of *Part 27*, an offshore fund pursues a full distribution policy with respect to an account period if—

(a) a distribution is made for the account period or for some other period which in whole or in part falls within that account period,

(b) subject to *Part 2* of this Schedule, the amount of the distribution which is paid to the holders of material and other interests in the fund—

(i) represents at least 85 per cent of the income of the fund for the period, and

(ii) is not less than 85 per cent of the fund's Irish equivalent profits for the period,

(c) the distribution is made during the account period or not more than 6 months after the expiry of that period, and

(d) the form of the distribution is such that, if any sum forming part of it were received in the State by a person resident in the State and did not form part of the profits of a trade, profession or vocation, that sum would be chargeable to tax under Case III of Schedule D,

and any reference in this subparagraph to a distribution made for an account period includes a reference to any 2 or more distributions so made or, in the case of *clause (b)*, the aggregate of those distributions.

(2) Subject to *subparagraph (3)*, with respect to any account period for which—

(a) there is no income of the fund, and

(b) there are no Irish equivalent profits of the fund,

the fund shall be treated as pursuing a full distribution policy notwithstanding that no distribution is made as mentioned in *subparagraph (1)*.

(3) For the purposes of *Chapter 2* of *Part 27*, an offshore fund shall be regarded as not pursuing a full distribution policy with respect to an account period for which the fund does not make up accounts.

(4) For the purposes of this paragraph—

(a) where a period for which an offshore fund makes up accounts includes the whole or part of 2 or more account periods of the fund, then, subject to *clause (c)*, income shown in those accounts shall be apportioned between those account periods on a time basis according to the number of days in each account period comprised in the period for which the accounts are made up,

(b) where a distribution is made for a period which includes the whole or part of 2 or more account periods of the fund, then, subject to *subparagraph (5)*, the distribution shall be apportioned between those account periods on a time basis according to the number of days in each account period which are comprised in the period for which the distribution is made,

(c) where a distribution is made out of specified income but is not made for a specified period, that income shall be attributed to the account period of the fund in which it in fact arose and the distribution shall be treated as made for that account period, and

(d) where a distribution is made neither for a specified period nor out of specified income, then, subject to *subparagraph (5)*, the distribution shall be treated as made for the last account period of the fund which ended before the distribution was made.

(5) Where but for this subparagraph the amount of a distribution made, or treated by virtue of *subparagraph (4)* as made, for an account period would exceed the income of that period, then, for the purposes of this paragraph—

(a) if the amount of the distribution was determined by apportionment under *subparagraph (4)(b)*, the excess shall be reapportioned, as may be just and reasonable, to any other account period which, in whole or in part, falls within the period for which the distribution was made or, if there is more than one such period, between those periods, and

(b) subject to *clause (a)*, the excess shall be treated as an additional distribution or series of additional distributions made for preceding account periods in respect of which the distributions or the aggregate distributions, as the case may be, would otherwise be less than the income of the period, applying the excess to later account periods before earlier ones until it is exhausted.

(6) In any case where—

(a) for a period which is or includes an account period an offshore fund is subject to any restriction as regards the making of distributions, being a restriction imposed by the law of any territory, and

(b) the fund is subject to that restriction by reason of an excess of losses over profits (applying the concept of "*profits*" and "*losses*" in the sense in which, and to the extent to which, they are relevant for the purposes of the law in question),

then, in determining for the purposes of *subparagraphs (1)* to *(5)* the amount of the fund's income for that account period, there shall be allowed as a deduction any amount which apart from this subparagraph would form part of the income of the fund for that account period and which may not be distributed by virtue of the restriction.

Funds operating equalisation arrangements

2.

(1) In the case of an offshore fund which throughout any account period operates equalisation arrangements, on any occasion in that period when there is a disposal to which this subparagraph applies, the fund shall be treated for the purposes of this Part of this Schedule as making a distribution of an amount equal to so much of the consideration for the disposal as, in accordance with this paragraph, represents income accrued to the date of the disposal.

(2) *Subparagraph (1)* shall apply to a disposal which—

(a) is a disposal of a material interest in the offshore fund concerned,

(b) is a disposal to which *Chapter 2* of *Part 27* applies (whether by virtue of *subsection (3)* of *section 742* or otherwise) or is one to which that Chapter would apply if *subsections (5)* and *(6)* of that section applied generally and not only for the purpose of determining whether, by virtue of *subsection (3)* of that section, there is a disposal to which that Chapter applies,

(c) is not a disposal with respect to which the conditions in *subsection (4)* of *section 742* are fulfilled, and

(d) is a disposal to the fund itself or to the persons concerned in the management of the fund (in this paragraph referred to as "*the managers of the fund*") in their capacity as such.

(3) On a disposal to which *subparagraph (1)* applies, the part of the consideration which represents income accrued to the date of the disposal shall be, subject to *subparagraph (4)* and *paragraph 4(4)*, the amount which would be credited to the equalisation account of the offshore fund concerned in respect of accrued income if on the date of the disposal the material interest disposed of were acquired by another person by means of initial purchase.

(4) Where, after the beginning of the period by reference to which the accrued income referred to in *subparagraph (3)* is calculated, the material interest disposed of by a disposal to which *subparagraph (1)* applies was acquired by means of initial purchase (whether or not by the person making the disposal), then—

(a) the amount which on that acquisition was credited to the equalisation account in respect of accrued income shall be deducted from the amount which in accordance with *subparagraph (3)* would represent income accrued to the date of the disposal, and

(b) if in that period there has been more than one such acquisition of that material interest by means of initial purchase, the deduction to be made under this subparagraph shall be the amount so credited to the equalisation account on the latest such acquisition before the disposal in question.

(5) Where by virtue of this paragraph an offshore fund is treated for the purposes of this Part of this Schedule as making a distribution on the occasion of a disposal, the distribution shall be treated for those purposes as—

(a) complying with *paragraph 1(1)(d)*,

(b) made out of the income of the fund for the account period in which the disposal occurs, and

(c) paid immediately before the disposal to the person who was then the holder of the interest disposed of.

(6) In any case where—

(a) a distribution in respect of an interest in an offshore fund is made to the managers of the fund,

(b) their holding of that interest is in their capacity as such, and

(c) at the time of the distribution the fund is operating equalisation arrangements,

then, the distribution shall not be taken into account for the purposes of *paragraph 1(1)* except to the extent that the distribution is properly referable to that part of the period for which the distribution is made during which that interest has been held by the managers of the fund in their capacity as such.

(7) *Subsection (2)* of *section 742* shall apply for the purposes of this paragraph as it applies for the purposes of that section.

Income taxable under Case III of Schedule D

3.

(1) *Subparagraph (2)* shall apply if any sums which form part of the income of an offshore fund within *paragraph (b)* or *(c)* of *section 743(1)* are of such a nature that—

(a) the holders of interests in the fund who are either companies resident in the State or individuals domiciled and resident in the State—

(i) are chargeable to tax under Case III of Schedule D in respect of such of those sums as are referable to their interests, or

(ii) if any of that income is derived from assets in the State, would be so chargeable had the assets been outside the State,

and

(b) the holders of interests, who are not such companies or individuals, would be chargeable as mentioned in *subclause (i)* or *(ii)* of *clause (a)* if they were resident in the State or, in the case of individuals, if they were domiciled and both resident and ordinarily resident in the State.

(2) To the extent that sums within *subparagraph (1)* do not actually form part of a distribution complying with *clauses (c)* and *(d)* of *paragraph 1(1)*, they shall be treated for the purposes of this Part of this Schedule—

(a) as a distribution complying with those clauses and made out of the income of which they form part, and

(b) as paid to the holders of the interests to which they are referable.

Commodity income

4.

(1) In this paragraph—

"*commodities*" means tangible assets (other than currency, securities, debts or other assets of a financial nature) dealt with on a commodity exchange in any part of the world;

"*dealing*", in relation to dealing in commodities, includes dealing by means of futures contracts and traded options.

(2) To the extent that the income of an offshore fund for any account period includes profits from dealing in commodities, 50 per cent of those profits shall be disregarded in determining for the purposes of *paragraphs 1(1)(b)* and *5*—

(a) the income of the fund for that period, and

(b) the fund's Irish equivalent profits for that period;

but in any account period in which an offshore fund incurs a loss in dealing in commodities the amount of that loss shall not be varied by virtue of this paragraph.

(3) Where the income of an offshore fund for any account period consists of profits from dealing in commodities and other income, then—

(a) in determining whether the condition in *paragraph 1(1)(b)* is fulfilled with respect to that account period, the expenditure of the fund shall be apportioned in such manner as is just and reasonable between the profits from dealing in commodities and the other income, and

(b) in determining whether and to what extent any expenditure is deductible under *section 83* in computing the fund's Irish equivalent profits for that period, so much of the business of the fund as does not consist of dealing in commodities shall be treated as a business carried on by a separate company.

(4) Where there is a disposal to which *paragraph 2(1)* applies, then, to the extent that any amount which was or would be credited to the equalisation account in respect of accrued income, as mentioned in *subparagraph (3)* or *(4)* of *paragraph 2*, represents profits from dealing in commodities, 50 per cent of that accrued income shall be disregarded in determining under those subparagraphs the part of the consideration for the disposal which represents income accrued to the date of the disposal.

Irish equivalent profits

5.

(1) In this paragraph, "*profits*" does not include chargeable gains.

(2) A reference in this Schedule to the Irish equivalent profits of an offshore fund for an account period shall be construed as a reference to the amount which, on the assumptions in *subparagraph (3)*, would be the total profits of the fund for that period on which, after allowing for any deductions available against those profits, corporation tax would be chargeable.

(3) The assumptions referred to in *subparagraph (2)* are that—

(a) the offshore fund is a company which in the account period is resident in the State,

(b) the account period is an accounting period of that company, and

(c) any dividends or distributions which by virtue of *section 129* should be disregarded in computing income for corporation tax purposes are nevertheless to be taken into account in that computation in the like manner as if they were dividends or distributions of a company resident outside the State.

(4) Without prejudice to any deductions available apart from this subparagraph, the deductions referred to in *subparagraph (2)* include—

(a) a deduction equal to any amount which by virtue of *paragraph 1(6)* is allowed as a deduction in determining the income of the fund for the account period in question,

(b) a deduction equal to any amount of Irish income tax paid by deduction or otherwise by, and not repaid to, the offshore fund in respect of the income of the account period, and

(c) a deduction equal to any amount of tax (paid under the law of a territory outside the State) taken into account as a deduction in determining the income of the fund for the account period in question but which, because it is referable to capital rather than income, is not to be taken into account by virtue of *section 71(1)* or *77(6)*;

but *section 2(4)* shall be disregarded for the purposes of *clause (b)*.

(5) For the avoidance of doubt it is hereby declared that, if any sums forming part of the offshore fund's income for any period have been received by the fund without any deduction of or charge to tax by virtue of *section 43, 49, 50* or *63*, the effect of the assumption in *subparagraph (3)(a)* is that those sums are to be taken into account in determining the total profits referred to in *subparagraph (2)*.

PART 2

Modifications of Conditions for Certification in Certain Cases

Exclusion of investments in distributing offshore funds

6.

(1) In this Part of this Schedule, an offshore fund within *subparagraph (2)(c)* is referred to as a "*qualifying fund*".

(2) In any case where—

(a) in an account period of an offshore fund (in this Part of this Schedule referred to as "*the primary fund*"), the assets of the fund consist of or include interests in another offshore fund,

(b) those interests (together with other interests which the primary fund may have) are such that, by virtue of *paragraph (a)* of *subsection (3)* of *section 744* or, if the other fund concerned is a company, *paragraph (b)* or *(c)* of that subsection, the primary fund could not apart from this paragraph be certified as a distributing fund in respect of the account period, and

(c) without regard to this paragraph, that other fund could be certified as a distributing fund in respect of its account period or, as the case may be, each of its account periods which comprises the whole or any part of the account period of the primary fund,

then, in determining whether in *section 744(3)* (other than *paragraph (d)*) anything prevents the primary fund being certified as mentioned in *clause (b)*, the interests of the primary fund in that other fund shall be disregarded except for the purposes of determining the total value of the assets of the primary fund.

(3) In a case within *subparagraph (2)*—

(a) *section 744(3)* (other than *paragraph (d)*) shall apply in relation to the primary fund with the modification in *paragraph 7* (in addition to that provided for by *subparagraph (2)*), and

(b) *Part 1* of this Schedule shall apply in relation to the primary fund with the modification in *paragraph 8*.

7. The modification referred to in *paragraph 6(3)(a)* is that in any case where—

(a) at any time in the account period referred to in *paragraph 6(2)*, the assets of the primary fund include an interest in an offshore fund or in any company (whether an offshore fund or not),

(b) that interest is to be taken into account in determining whether in *section 744(3)* (other than *paragraph (d)*) anything prevents the primary fund being certified as a distributing fund in respect of that account period, and

(c) at any time in that account period the assets of the qualifying fund include an interest in the offshore fund or company referred to in *clause (a)*,

then, for the purposes of the application in relation to the primary fund of *section 744(3)* (other than *paragraph (d)*), at any time when the assets of the qualifying fund include the interest referred to in *clause (c)*, the primary fund's share of that interest shall be treated as an additional asset of the primary fund.

8.

(1) The modification referred to in *paragraph 6(3)(b)* is that, in determining whether the condition in *paragraph 1(1)(b)(ii)* is fulfilled with respect to the account period of the primary fund referred to in *paragraph 6(2)*, the Irish equivalent profits of the primary fund for that account period shall be treated as increased by the primary fund's share of the excess income (if any) of the qualifying fund which is attributable to that account period.

(2) For the purposes of this paragraph, the excess income of the qualifying fund for any account period of that fund shall be the amount (if any) by which its Irish equivalent profits for that account period exceed the amount of the distributions made for that account period, as determined for the purposes of the application of *paragraph 1(1)* to the qualifying fund.

(3) Where an account period of the qualifying fund coincides with an account period of the primary fund, the excess income (if any) of the qualifying fund for that account period shall be the excess income which is attributable to that account period of the primary fund.

(4) In a case where *subparagraph (3)* does not apply, the excess income of the qualifying fund attributable to an account period of the primary fund shall be the appropriate fraction of the excess income (if any) of the qualifying fund for any of its account periods which comprises the whole or any part of the account period of the primary fund and, if there is more than one such account period of the qualifying fund, the aggregate of the excess income (if any) of each of them.

(5) For the purposes of *subparagraph (4)*, the appropriate fraction shall be determined by reference to the formula—

$$\frac{A}{B}$$

where—

A is the number of days in the account period of the primary fund which are also days in an account period of the qualifying fund, and

B is the number of days in that account period of the qualifying fund or, as the case may be, in each of those account periods of that fund which comprises the whole or any part of the account period of the primary fund.

9.

(1) The references in *paragraphs 7* and *8(1)* to the primary fund's share of—

(a) an interest forming part of the assets of the qualifying fund, or

(b) the excess income (within the meaning of *paragraph 8)* of the qualifying fund,

shall be construed as references to the fraction specified in *subparagraph (2)* of that interest or excess income.

(2) In relation to any account period of the primary fund, the fraction referred to in *subparagraph (1)* shall be determined by reference to the formula—

$$\frac{C}{D}$$

where—

C is the average value of the primary fund's holding of interests in the qualifying fund during that account period, and

D is the average value of all the interests of the qualifying fund held by any persons during that account period.

Offshore funds investing in trading companies

10.

(1) In this paragraph—

"*commodities*" has the same meaning as in *paragraph 4(1)*;

"*dealing*", in relation to commodities, currency, securities, debts or other assets of a financial nature, includes dealing by means of futures contracts and traded options;

"*trading company*" means a company whose business consists wholly of the carrying on of a trade or trades and does not to any extent consist of—

(a) dealing in commodities, currency, securities, debts or other assets of a financial nature, or

(b) banking or money-lending.

(2) In any case where the assets of an offshore fund for the time being include an interest in a trading company, *section 744(3)* shall apply subject to the modifications in *subparagraphs (3)* and *(4)*.

(3) In the application of *section 744(3)(b)* to so much of the assets of an offshore fund as for the time being consists of interests in a single trading company, "20 per cent" shall be substituted for "10 per cent".

(4) In the application of *section 730(3)(c)* to an offshore fund, for "more than 10 per cent", in so far as it would otherwise refer to the share capital of a trading company or to any class of such share capital, "50 per cent or more" shall be substituted.

Offshore funds with wholly-owned subsidiaries

11.

(1) In relation to an offshore fund which has a wholly-owned subsidiary which is a company, *section 744(3)* or *Part 1* of this Schedule shall apply subject to the modifications in *subparagraph (4)*.

(2) Subject to *subparagraph (3)*, for the purposes of this paragraph, a company shall be a wholly-owned subsidiary of an offshore fund if and so long as the whole of the issued share capital of the company is—

(a) in the case of an offshore fund within *section 743(1)(a)*, directly and beneficially owned by the fund,

(b) in the case of an offshore fund within *section 743(1)(b)*, directly owned by the trustees of the fund for the benefit of the fund, and

(c) in the case of an offshore fund within *section 743(1)(c)*, owned in a manner which as near as may be corresponds either to *clause (a)* or *(b)*.

(3) In the case of a company which has only one class of issued share capital, the reference in *subparagraph (2)* to the whole of the issued share capital shall be construed as a reference to at least 95 per cent of that share capital.

(4) The modifications referred to in *subparagraph (1)* are that for the purposes of *section 744(3)* and *Part 1* of this Schedule—

(a) the percentage of the receipts, expenditure, assets and liabilities of the subsidiary which is equal to the percentage of the issued share capital of the company concerned which is owned as mentioned in *subparagraph (2)* shall be regarded as the receipts, expenditure, assets and liabilities of the fund, and

(b) there shall be disregarded the interest of the fund in the subsidiary and any distributions or other payments made by the subsidiary to the fund or by the fund to the subsidiary.

Offshore funds with interests in dealing and management companies

12.

(1) *Section 744(3)(c)* shall not apply to so much of the assets of an offshore fund as consists of issued share capital of a company which is either—

(a) a wholly-owned subsidiary of the fund which is within *subparagraph (2)*, or

(b) a subsidiary management company of the fund (within the meaning of *subparagraph (3)*).

(2) A company which is a wholly-owned subsidiary of an offshore fund shall be one to which *subparagraph (1)(a)* applies if—

(a) the business of the company consists wholly of dealing in material interests in the offshore fund for the purposes of and in connection with the management and administration of the business of the fund, and

(b) the company is not entitled to any distribution in respect of any material interest for the time being held by the company,

and *paragraph 11(2)* shall apply to determine whether a company is for the purposes of this paragraph a wholly-owned subsidiary of an offshore fund.

(3) A company (being a company in which an offshore fund has an interest) shall be a subsidiary management company of the fund for the purposes of *subparagraph (1)(b)* if—

(a) the company carries on no business other than providing services within *subparagraph (4)* either for the fund alone or for the fund and for any other offshore fund which has an interest in the company, and

(b) the company's remuneration for the services it provides to the fund is not greater than it would be if it were determined at arm's length between the fund and a company in which the fund has no interest.

(4) The services referred to in *subparagraph (3)* are—

(a) holding property (being property of any description) occupied or used in connection with the management or administration of the fund, and

(b) providing administrative, management and advisory services to the fund.

(5) In determining in accordance with *subparagraph (3)* whether a company in which an offshore fund has an interest is a subsidiary management company of that fund—

(a) every business carried on by a wholly-owned subsidiary of the company shall be treated as carried on by the company,

(b) no account shall be taken of so much of the company's business as consists of holding its interests in a wholly-owned subsidiary, and

(c) any reference in *subparagraph (3)(b)* to the company shall be taken to include a reference to a wholly-owned subsidiary of the company.

(6) A reference in *subparagraph (5)* to a wholly-owned subsidiary of a company shall be construed as a reference to another company, the whole of the issued share capital of which is for the time being directly and beneficially owned by the first-mentioned company.

Disregarding of certain investments forming less than 5 per cent of a fund

13.

(1) In this paragraph, "*excess holding*" means any holding within *subparagraph (2)*.

(2) In any case where—

(a) in any account period of an offshore fund the assets of the fund include a holding of issued share capital (or any class of issued share capital) of a company, and

(b) that holding is such that by virtue of *section 744(3)(c)* the fund could not (apart from this paragraph) be certified as a distributing fund in respect of that account period,

then, if the condition in *subparagraph (3)* is fulfilled, that holding shall be disregarded for the purposes of *section 744(3)(c)*.

(3) The condition referred to in *subparagraph (2)* is that at no time in the account period in question does that portion of the fund which consists of—

(a) excess holdings, and

(b) interests in other offshore funds which are not qualifying funds,

exceed 5 per cent by value of all the assets of the fund.

Power of Revenue Commissioners to disregard certain breaches of conditions

14. Where in the case of any account period of an offshore fund it appears to the Revenue Commissioners that there has been a failure to comply with any of the conditions in *paragraphs (a)*, *(b)* and *(c)* of *section 744(3)* (as modified, where appropriate, by the preceding provisions of this Part of this Schedule) but they are satisfied that the failure—

(a) occurred inadvertently, and

(b) was remedied without unreasonable delay,

then, the Revenue Commissioners may disregard the failure for the purposes of determining whether to certify the fund as a distributing fund in respect of that account period.

PART 3

Certification Procedure

Application for certification

15.

(1) The Revenue Commissioners shall, in such manner as they consider appropriate, certify an offshore fund as a distributing fund in respect of an account period if—

(a) an application in respect of that period is made under this paragraph,

(b) the application is accompanied by the accounts of the fund for, or for a period which includes, the account period to which the application relates,

(c) such information as the Revenue Commissioners may reasonably require for the purpose of determining whether the fund should be so certified is furnished to the Revenue Commissioners, and

(d) the Revenue Commissioners are satisfied that nothing in *subsection (2)* or *(3)* of *section 744* prevents the fund being so certified.

(2) An application under this paragraph shall be made to the Revenue Commissioners by the fund or by a trustee or officer of the fund on behalf of the fund and may be so made before the expiry of the period of 6 months beginning at the end of the account period to which the application relates.

(3) In any case where on an application under this paragraph the Revenue Commissioners determine that the offshore fund concerned should not be certified as a distributing fund in respect of the account period to which the application relates, they shall give notice of that determination to the fund.

(4) Where at any time it appears to the Revenue Commissioners that—

(a) the accounts accompanying an application under this paragraph in respect of any account period of an offshore fund are not such, or

(b) any information furnished to them in connection with such an application is not such,

as to make full and accurate disclosure of all facts and considerations relevant to the application, the Revenue Commissioners shall give notice to the fund accordingly, specifying the period concerned.

(5) Where a notice is given by the Revenue Commissioners under *subparagraph (4)*, they shall be deemed never to have certified the offshore fund in respect of the account period in question.

Appeals

16.

(1) An appeal to the Appeal Commissioners—

(a) against a determination referred to in *paragraph 15(3)*, or

(b) against a notification under *paragraph 15(4)*,

may be made by the offshore fund or by a trustee or officer of the fund on behalf of the fund, and shall be so made by notice specifying the grounds of appeal and given to the Revenue Commissioners within 30 days of the date of the notice under *subparagraph (3)* or *(4)* of *paragraph 15* as the case may be.

(2) The Appeal Commissioners shall hear and determine an appeal under *subparagraph (1)* in accordance with the principles to be followed by the Revenue Commissioners in determining applications under *paragraph 15* and, subject to those principles, in the like manner as in the case of an appeal to the Appeal Commissioners against an assessment to income tax, and the provisions of the Income Tax Acts relating to such an appeal (including the provisions relating to the rehearing of an appeal and to the statement of a case for the opinion of the High Court on a point of law) shall apply accordingly with any necessary modifications.

(3) The jurisdiction of the Appeal Commissioners on an appeal under this paragraph shall include jurisdiction to review any decision of the Revenue Commissioners relevant to a ground of the appeal.

PART 4

Supplementary

Assessment: effect of non-certification

17. No appeal may be brought against an assessment to tax on the ground that an offshore fund should have been certified as a distributing fund in respect of an account period of the fund.

18.

(1) Without prejudice to *paragraph 17*, in any case where no application has been made under *paragraph 15* in respect of an account period of an offshore fund, any person liable to pay tax which that person would not be liable to pay if the offshore fund were certified as a distributing fund in respect of that period may by notice in writing require the Revenue Commissioners to take action under this paragraph for the purposes of determining whether the fund should be so certified.

(2) Subject to *subparagraphs (3)* and *(5)*, where the Revenue Commissioners receive a notice under *subparagraph (1)* they shall by notice, given in such manner as they consider appropriate in the circumstances, invite the offshore fund concerned to make an application under *paragraph 15* in respect of the period in question.

(3) Where *subparagraph (2)* applies, the Revenue Commissioners shall not be required to give notice under that subparagraph before the expiry of the account period to which the notice is to relate nor if an application under *paragraph 15* has already been made; but where notice is given under *subparagraph (2)*, an application under *paragraph 15* shall not be out of time under *paragraph 15(2)* if it is made within 90 days of the date of that notice.

(4) Where an offshore fund to which notice is given under *subparagraph (2)* does not make an application under *paragraph 15* in respect of the account period in question within the time allowed by *subparagraph (3)* or *paragraph 15(2)*, as the case may be, the Revenue Commissioners shall proceed to determine the question of certification in respect of that period as if such an application had been made.

(5) Where the Revenue Commissioners receive more than one notice under *subparagraph (1)* with respect to the same account period of the same offshore fund, their obligations under *subparagraphs (2)* and *(4)* shall be taken to be fulfilled with respect to each of those notices if they are fulfilled with respect to any of them.

(6) Notwithstanding anything in *subparagraph (5)*, for the purpose of a determination under *subparagraph (4)* with respect to an account period of an offshore fund, the Revenue Commissioners shall have regard to accounts and other information furnished by all persons who have given notice under *subparagraph (1)* with respect to that account period, and *paragraph 15* shall apply as if accounts and information so furnished had been furnished in compliance with *subparagraph (1)* of that paragraph.

(7) Without prejudice to *subparagraph (5)*, in any case where—

(a) at a time after the Revenue Commissioners have made a determination under *subparagraph (4)* that an offshore fund should not be certified as a distributing fund in respect of an account period, notice is given under *subparagraph (1)* with respect to that period, and

(b) the person giving that notice furnishes the Revenue Commissioners with accounts or information which had not been furnished to them at the time of the earlier determination, then, the Revenue Commissioners shall reconsider their previous determination in the light of the new accounts or information and, if they consider it appropriate, may determine to certify the fund accordingly.

(8) Where any person has given notice to the Revenue Commissioners under *subparagraph (1)* with respect to an account period of an offshore fund and no application has been made under *paragraph 15* with respect to that period, then—

(a) the Revenue Commissioners shall notify that person of their determination with respect to certification under *subparagraph (4)*, and

(b) *paragraph 16* shall not apply in relation to that determination.

Information as to decisions on certification etc.

19. Any obligation on the Revenue Commissioners to maintain secrecy or any other restriction upon the disclosure of information by them shall not preclude them from disclosing to any person appearing to them to have an interest in the matter—

(a) any determination of the Revenue Commissioners or (on appeal) the Appeal Commissioners as to whether an offshore fund should or should not be certified as a distributing fund in respect of any account period, or

(b) the content and effect of any notice given by the Revenue Commissioners under *paragraph 15(4)*.

20. The Revenue Commissioners may nominate any of their officers to perform any acts and discharge any functions authorised by this Schedule to be performed or discharged by the Revenue Commissioners, and references in this Schedule to the Revenue Commissioners shall, with any necessary modifications, be construed as including references to an officer so nominated.

Revenue Precedents

An offshore fund would qualify for certification as a distributing fund, notwithstanding the fact that no distribution is made and the fund has a nominal level of income, if the level of income does not exceed 1% of the average value of the funds assets held during the accounting period. 5067/95

Cross References

From Schedule 19

Section 2 Interpretation of Tax Acts.
Section 43 Certain securities issued by Minister for Finance.
Section 49 Exemption of certain securities.
Section 50 Securities of Irish local authorities issued abroad.
Section 63 Exemption of dividends of non-residents.
Section 71 Foreign securities and possessions.
Section 77 Miscellaneous special rules for computation of income.
Section 83 Expenses of management of investment companies.
Section 129 Irish resident company distributions not generally chargeable to corporation tax.
Section 730 Tax credit in respect of distributions.
Section 731 Chargeable gains accruing to unit trusts.
Section 742 Offshore funds operating equalisation arrangements.
Section 743 Material interest in offshore funds.
Section 744 Non-qualifying offshore funds.

To Schedule 19

Section 740 Interpretation (Chapter 2 and Schedules 19 and 20).
Section 742 Offshore funds operating equalisation arrangements.
Section 744 Non-qualifying offshore funds.
Schedule 20 Offshore Funds: Computation of Offshore Income Gains

SCHEDULE 20

Offshore Funds: Computation of Offshore Income Gains

Section 745.

[FA90 Sch6]

PART 1

Disposal of Interests in Non-Qualifying Funds

Interpretation

1. In this Part of this Schedule, "*material disposal*" means a disposal to which *Chapter 2* of *Part 27* applies otherwise than by virtue of *section 742.*

Calculation of unindexed gain

2\.

(1) Where there is a material disposal, there shall first be determined for the purposes of this Part of this Schedule the amount (if any) which in accordance with this paragraph is the unindexed gain accruing to the person making the disposal.

(2) Subject to *subsections (2)* to *(6)* of *section 741* and *paragraph 3*, the unindexed gain accruing on a material disposal shall be the amount which would be the gain on that disposal for the purposes of the Capital Gains Tax Acts if it were computed without regard to—

(a) any charge to income tax or corporation tax by virtue of *section 745*, and

(b) any adjustment (in this Part of this Schedule referred to as "*the indexation allowance*") made under *section 556(2)* to sums allowable as deductions in the computation of chargeable gains.

3\.

(1) Where the material disposal forms part of a transfer to which *section 600* applies, the unindexed gain accruing on the disposal shall be computed without regard to any deduction to be made under that section in computing a chargeable gain.

(2) Notwithstanding *sections 538* and *546*, where apart from this subparagraph the effect of any computation under the preceding provisions of this Part of this Schedule would be to produce a loss, the unindexed gain on the material disposal shall be treated as nil, and accordingly for the purposes of this Part of this Schedule no loss shall be treated as accruing on a material disposal.

Gains since the 6th day of April, 1990

4\.

(1) This paragraph shall apply where—

(a) the interest in the offshore fund which is disposed of by the person making a material disposal was acquired by that person before the 6th day of April, 1990, or

(b) that person is treated by virtue of any provision of *subparagraphs (3)* and *(4)* as having acquired the interest before that date.

(2) Where this paragraph applies, the amount which would have been the gain on the material disposal shall be determined for the purposes of this Part of this Schedule—

(a) on the assumption that on the 6th day of April, 1990, the interest was disposed of and immediately reacquired for a consideration equal to its market value at that time, and

(b) subject to that assumption, on the basis that the gain is computed in the like manner as the unindexed gain on the material disposal is determined under *paragraphs 2* and *3*,

and that amount is in *paragraph 5(2)* referred to as "the gain since the 6th day of April, 1990".

(3) Where the person making the material disposal acquired the interest disposed of—

(a) on or after the 6th day of April, 1990, and

(b) in such circumstances that by virtue of any enactment other than *section 556(4)* that person and the person (in this subparagraph and *subparagraph (4)* referred to as "*the previous owner*") from whom that person acquired the interest disposed of were to be treated for the purposes of the Capital Gains Tax Acts as if that person's acquisition were for a consideration of such an amount as would secure that, on the disposal under which that person acquired the interest disposed of, neither a gain or a loss accrued to the previous owner,

then, the previous owner's acquisition of the interest shall be treated as that person's acquisition of the interest.

(4) Where the previous owner acquired the interest disposed of—

(a) on or after the 6th day of April, 1990, and

(b) in circumstances similar to those referred to in *subparagraph (3)*,

then, the acquisition of the interest by the predecessor of the previous owner shall be treated for the purposes of this paragraph as the previous owner's acquisition, and so on back through previous acquisitions in similar circumstances until the first such acquisition before the 6th day of April, 1990, or, as the case may be, until an acquisition on a material disposal on or after that date.

The offshore income gain

5.

(1) Subject to *subparagraph (2)*, a material disposal shall give rise to an offshore income gain of an amount equal to the unindexed gain on that disposal.

(2) In any case where—

(a) *paragraph 4* applies, and

(b) the gain since the 6th day of April, 1990 (within the meaning of *paragraph 4(2)*) is less than the unindexed gain on the disposal,

the offshore income gain to which the disposal gives rise shall be an amount equal to the income gain since the 6th day of April, 1990 (within the meaning of that paragraph).

PART 2

Disposals Involving an Equalisation Element

6.

(1) Subject to *paragraph 7*, a disposal to which *Chapter 2* of *Part 27* applies by virtue of *section 742(3)* shall give rise to an offshore income gain of an amount equal to the equalisation element relevant to the asset disposed of.

(2) Subject to *subparagraphs (4)* to *(6)*, the equalisation element relevant to the asset disposed of by a disposal within *subparagraph (1)* shall be the amount which would be credited to the equalisation account of the offshore fund concerned in respect of accrued income if, on the date of the disposal, the asset disposed of were acquired by another person by means of initial purchase.

(3) In the following provisions of this Part of this Schedule, a disposal within *subparagraph (1)* is referred to as a "*disposal involving an equalisation element*".

(4) Where the asset disposed of by a disposal involving an equalisation element was acquired by the person making the disposal after the beginning of the period by reference to which the accrued income referred to in *subparagraph (2)* is calculated, the amount which apart from this subparagraph would be the equalisation element relevant to that asset shall be reduced by the following amount, that is—

(a) if that acquisition took place on or after the 6th day of April, 1990, the amount which on that acquisition was credited to the equalisation account of the offshore fund concerned in respect of accrued income or, as the case may be, would have been so credited if that acquisition had been an acquisition by means of initial purchase, and

(b) in any other case, the amount which would have been credited to that account in respect of accrued income if that acquisition had been an acquisition by means of initial purchase taking place on the 6th day of April, 1990.

(5) In any case where—

(a) the asset disposed of by a disposal involving an equalisation element was acquired by the person making the disposal at or before the beginning of the period by reference to which the accrued income referred to in *subparagraph (2)* is calculated, and

(b) that period began before the 6th day of April, 1990, and ends after that date,

the amount which apart from this subparagraph would be the equalisation element relevant to that asset shall be reduced by the amount which would have been credited to the equalisation account of the offshore fund concerned in respect of accrued income if the acquisition referred to in *clause (a)* had been an acquisition by means of initial purchase taking place on the 6th day of April, 1990.

(6) Where there is a disposal involving an equalisation element, then, to the extent that any amount which was or would be credited to the equalisation account of the offshore fund in respect of accrued income (as mentioned in *subparagraph (2)*, *(3)*, *(4)* or *(5)*) represents profits from dealing in commodities (within the meaning of *paragraph 4* of *Schedule 19*), 50 per cent of that accrued income shall be disregarded in determining under those subparagraphs the equalisation element relevant to the asset disposed of by that disposal.

7.

(1) For the purposes of this Part of this Schedule, the Part 1 gain (if any) on any disposal involving an equalisation element shall be determined in accordance with *paragraph 8*.

(2) Notwithstanding anything in *paragraph 6*—

(a) where there is no Part 1 gain on a disposal involving an equalisation element, that disposal shall not give rise to an offshore income gain, and

(b) where apart from this paragraph the offshore income gain on a disposal involving an equalisation element would exceed the Part 1 gain on that disposal, the offshore income gain to which that disposal gives rise shall be reduced to an amount equal to that Part 1 gain.

8.

(1) On a disposal involving an equalisation element, the Part 1 gain shall be the amount (if any) which, by virtue of *Part 1* of this Schedule (as modified by *subparagraphs (2)* and *(3)*), would be the offshore income gain on that disposal if it were a material disposal within the meaning of that Part.

(2) For the purposes only of the application of *Part 1* of this Schedule to determine the Part 1 gain (if any) on a disposal involving an equalisation element, *subsections (5)* and *(6)* of *section 742* shall apply as if in *subsection (5)* of that section "by virtue of *subsection (3)*" were deleted.

(3) Where a disposal involving an equalisation element is one which by virtue of any enactment other than *section 556(4)* is treated for the purposes of the Capital Gains Tax Acts as one on which neither a gain nor a loss accrues to the person making the disposal, then, for the purpose only of determining the Part 1 gain (if any) on the disposal, that enactment shall be deemed not to apply to such a disposal (but without prejudice to the application of that enactment to any earlier disposal).

Cross References

From Schedule 20

Section 1 Interpretation of this Act.
Section 538 Disposals where assets lost or destroyed or become of negligible value.
Section 546 Allowable losses.
Section 556 Adjustment of allowable expenditure by reference to consumer price index.
Section 600 Transfer of business to company.
Section 731 Chargeable gains accruing to unit trusts.
Section 741 Disposals of material interests in non-qualifying offshore funds.
Section 742 Offshore funds operating equalisation arrangements.
Section 745 Charge to income tax or corporation tax of offshore income gain.
Schedule 19 Offshore Funds: Distributing Funds

To Schedule 20

Section 740 Interpretation (Chapter 2 and Schedules 19 and 20).
Section 742 Offshore funds operating equalisation arrangements.
Section 745 Charge to income tax or corporation tax of offshore income gain.
Section 747 Deduction of offshore income gain in determining capital gain.

SCHEDULE 21

Purchase and Sale of Securities: Appropriate Amount in Respect of the Interest

Sections 749, 750 and 751.

[ITA67 Sch11; F(MP)A68 s3(2) and Sch PtI]

1. For the purposes of *section 749*, the appropriate amount in respect of the interest shall be the appropriate proportion of the net interest receivable by the first buyer.

2. For the purposes of *sections 750* and *751*, the appropriate amount in respect of the interest shall be the gross amount corresponding to the appropriate proportion of the net interest receivable by the first buyer.

3.

(1) For the purposes of *paragraphs 1* and *2*, the appropriate proportion shall be the proportion which—

(a) the period beginning on the first relevant date and ending on the day before the day on which the first buyer bought the securities,

bears to—

(b) the period beginning on the first relevant date and ending on the day before the second relevant date.

(2) In *subparagraph (1)*—

"*the first relevant date*" means—

(a) in a case where the securities have not been quoted in the official list of the Dublin Stock Exchange at a price excluding the value of the interest payment last payable before the interest receivable by the first buyer or, the securities having been so quoted, the date of the quotation was not the earliest date on which they could have been so quoted if an appropriate dealing in the securities had taken place, that earliest date, and

(b) in any other case, the date on which the securities have been first so quoted;

"*the second relevant date*" means—

(a) in a case where the securities have not been quoted in the official list of the Dublin Stock Exchange at a price excluding the value of the interest receivable by the first buyer or, the securities having been so quoted, the date of the quotation was not the earliest date on which they could have been so quoted if an appropriate dealing in the securities had taken place, that earliest date, and

(b) in any other case, the date on which the securities have been first so quoted.

(3) Where the interest receivable by the first buyer was the first interest payment payable in respect of the securities, *subparagraph (1)* shall apply with the substitution for the references to the first relevant date of references to the beginning of the period (in this subparagraph referred to as "*the relevant period*") for which the interest was payable; but where the capital amount of the securities was not fully paid at the beginning of the relevant period and one or more instalments of capital were paid during the relevant period, then—

(a) the interest shall be treated as divided into parts, calculated by reference to the amount of the interest attributable to the capital paid at or before the beginning of the relevant period and the amount of that interest attributable to each such instalment,

(b) treating each of those parts as interest payable for the relevant period or, where the part was calculated by reference to any such instalment, as interest payable for the part of the relevant period beginning with the payment of the instalment, the amount constituting the appropriate proportion of each part shall be calculated in accordance with the preceding provisions of this paragraph, and

(c) the appropriate proportion of the interest for the purposes of *paragraphs 1* and *2* shall be the proportion of the interest constituted by the sum of those amounts.

(4) In relation to securities not the subject of quotations in the official list of the Dublin Stock Exchange, *subparagraph (1)* shall apply with the substitution for the periods mentioned in that subparagraph of such periods as in the opinion of the Appeal Commissioners correspond with those in the case of the securities in question.

4. Where the securities are of a description such that the bargain price is increased, where interest is receivable by the buyer, by reference to gross interest accruing before the bargain date, *paragraphs 1* to *3* shall not apply; but for the purposes of *sections 749* to *751* the appropriate amount in respect of the interest shall be the amount of the increase in the bargain price.

Cross References

From Schedule 21

Section 749 Dealers in securities.
Section 750 Persons entitled to exemption.
Section 751 Traders other than dealers in securities.

To Schedule 21

Section 711 Chargeable gains of life business.
Section 737 Special investment schemes.
Section 738 Undertakings for collective investment.
Section 748 Interpretation and application (Chapter 1).
Section 749 Dealers in securities.
Section 750 Persons entitled to exemption.
Section 751 Traders other than dealers in securities.
Section 838 Special portfolio investment accounts.
Schedule 22 Dividends Regarded as Paid Out of Profits Accumulated Before Given Date

SCHEDULE 22

Dividends Regarded as Paid Out of Profits Accumulated Before Given Date

Sections 749 and *752*

[ITA67 Sch12; F(MP)A68 s3(2) and Sch PtI; CTA76 s140(1) and Sch2 PtI par28; FA79 s34]

1.

(1) Subject to *paragraph 2*, a dividend shall be regarded for the purposes of *section 752* and of this Schedule as paid wholly out of profits accumulated before a given date (in this Schedule referred to as "*the relevant date*") if—

(a) it is declared for a period falling wholly before the relevant date,

(b) there are no profits of the company arising in the period beginning on the relevant date and ending on the date on which the dividend is payable, or

(c) having regard to *paragraph 3*, no part is available for payment of the dividend out of such profits of the company as arose in the period beginning on the relevant date and ending on the date on which the dividend is payable.

(2) Subject to *paragraph 2*, where out of such profits of the company as arose in the period beginning on the relevant date and ending on the date on which the dividend is payable, some part is, having regard to *paragraph 3*, available for payment of the dividend but the total amount distributed in payment of the net dividend on all the shares of the class in question exceeds that part of the profits, the dividend shall be regarded for the purposes of *section 752* and of this Schedule as paid out of profits accumulated before the relevant date to an extent which is the same as the proportion which the excess bears to that total amount.

(3) For the purposes of this Schedule, a dividend which is declared for a period falling partly before and partly after the relevant date shall be regarded as consisting of 2 dividends respectively declared for the 2 parts of the period and of amounts proportionate to each such part.

2.

(1) Notwithstanding *paragraph 1*, a dividend shall not be regarded as paid to any extent out of profits accumulated before the relevant date if—

(a) it became payable within one year from that date, and

(b) in the opinion of the Appeal Commissioners the annual rate of dividend on the shares in question in that year—

(i) is not substantially greater than the annual rate of dividend on those shares in the period of 3 years ending on the relevant date, or

(ii) in a case where the shares in question were acquired in the ordinary course of a business of arranging public issues and placings of shares, represents a yield on the cost to the person receiving the dividend not substantially greater than the yield obtainable by investing in comparable shares the prices of which are quoted on stock exchanges in the State.

(2) For the purposes of *subparagraph (1)(b)*, the Appeal Commissioners shall have regard to—

(a) all dividends paid on the shares in the respective periods,

(b) any share issue made in those periods to holders of the shares, and

(c) in a case under *subparagraph (1)(b)(i)* where the shares were not in existence 3 years before the relevant date, the dividends paid on, and any share issue made to holders of, any shares surrendered in exchange for the first-mentioned shares or in right of which the first-mentioned shares were acquired,

and shall take such averages and make such adjustments as may appear to them to be required for a fair comparison.

3.

(1) The part of the profits of the company arising in the period beginning on the relevant date and ending on the date on which a dividend is payable which is available for payment of the dividend shall be determined in accordance with *subparagraphs* (2) to *(5)*.

(2) There shall be deducted from those profits such amount, whether fixed or proportionate to the amount of the profits, as in the opinion of the Appeal Commissioners ought justly and reasonably to be treated as set aside for payment of dividends on any other class of shares in the company, having regard to the respective rights attaching to the shares and on the assumption that the total amount available for distribution by means of net dividend on all the shares in the company over any period will be proportionately greater or less than the profits of the company arising in the period beginning on the relevant date and ending on the date on which the dividend mentioned in *subparagraph (1)* is payable, according as the first-mentioned period is longer or shorter than the second-mentioned period.

(3) In a case where, in the period beginning on the relevant date and ending on the date on which the dividend is payable, no previous dividend became payable on the shares of the class in question, the whole of the profits of the company arising in the period, less any deduction to be made under *subparagraph (2)*, shall be regarded as available for payment of the dividend.

(4) If any previous dividend became payable on the same shares in the period beginning on the relevant date and ending on the date on which the dividend is payable, there shall be determined in accordance with the preceding paragraphs the extent, if any, to which that previous dividend is to be regarded as paid out of profits accumulated before the relevant date, and the profits of the company arising in that period, less any deduction to be made under *subparagraph (2)*, shall be regarded as primarily available for payment of the net amount of that previous dividend in so far as it is not regarded as paid out of profits accumulated before the relevant date and only such balance, if any, as remains shall be regarded as available for payment of the later dividend.

(5) Where under *subparagraph (2)* the Appeal Commissioners are to determine what should be set aside for payment of dividends on shares of any class, and dividends on shares of that class have been treated under this Schedule as paid to any extent out of profits accumulated before the relevant date, the Appeal Commissioners may take that fact into account and reduce the amount to be so set aside accordingly.

4.

(1) For the purposes of this Schedule, the profits of a company arising in a given period (in this paragraph referred to as "*the specified period*") shall be determined in accordance with *subparagraphs (2)* and *(3)*.

(2) Those profits shall be the income of the company for the specified period diminished by—

(a) the income tax actually paid by the company for any year of assessment (not being a year of assessment after the year 1975–76) in the specified period, including any surtax borne by the company under section 530 of, and Schedule 16 to, the Income Tax Act, 1967,

(b) the corporation profits tax payable by the company for any accounting period in the specified period,

(c) the corporation tax (including corporation tax charged by virtue of *sections 440* and *441*) payable by the company for any accounting period in the specified period, and for this purpose the tax credit comprised in any franked investment income shall be treated as corporation tax payable by the company for the accounting period in which the distribution was received, and

(d) the capital gains tax payable by the company for any year of assessment (not being a year of assessment after the year 1975–76) in the specified period;

but where relief has been afforded to the company under section 360 of the Income Tax Act, 1967, or under *section 826* [...]1, references in this subparagraph to tax actually borne or to tax payable shall be construed as references to the tax which would have been borne or payable if that relief had not been given.

(3) In ascertaining for the purposes of this paragraph the amount of income tax, corporation profits tax and corporation tax by which the income of the company for the specified period is to be diminished, any tax on the amount to be deducted under *clause (g)* or *(h)* of *paragraph 5(3)* shall be disregarded.

5.

(1) For the purposes of this Schedule, the income of the company for a given period (in this paragraph referred to as "*the specified period*") shall be determined in accordance with *subparagraphs (2)* and *(3)*.

(2) There shall be computed the aggregate amount of—

(a) any profits or gains arising in the specified period from any trade carried on by the company computed in accordance with the provisions applicable to Case I of Schedule D,

(b) any income (including any franked investment income) arising in the specified period (computed in accordance with the Income Tax Acts or, in the case of franked investment income, in accordance with the Corporation Tax Acts), other than profits or gains arising from any trade referred to in *clause (a)*, and

(c) any capital profits arising in the specified period (whether or not chargeable to capital gains tax or corporation tax).

(3) There shall be deducted from the aggregate amount determined under *subparagraph (2)* the sum of the following amounts—

(a) any loss sustained by the company in the specified period in any trade referred to in *subparagraph (2)(a)* (computed in the same manner as profits or gains under the provisions applicable to Case I of Schedule D),

(b) any group relief given to the company in accordance with *Chapter 5* of *Part 12* for any accounting period in the specified period,

(c) any allowances for any year of assessment (not being a year of assessment after the year 1975–76) in the specified period in respect of any such trade under sections 241, 244(3) and 245, Chapter III of Part XIV, and Parts XV and XVI, of the Income Tax Act, 1967,

(d) any allowances in respect of any such trade under Chapter III of Part XIV of the Income Tax Act, 1967, which under section 14 of the Corporation Tax Act, 1976, were to be made in taxing the trade for the purposes of corporation tax for any accounting period in the specified period,

(e) any allowances in respect of any such trade under *Part 9*, *section 670*, *Chapter 1* of *Part 29* or *subsection (1)* or *(2)* of *section 765*, which under *section 307* are to be made in taxing the trade for the purpose of corporation tax for any accounting period in the specified period,

(f) (i) any payments made by the company in the specified period to which *section 237* or *238* applies, other than payments which are deductible in computing the profits or gains or losses of a trade carried on by the company,

(ii) any amount in respect of which repayment was made under section 496 of the Income Tax Act, 1967, for any year of assessment in the specified period, and

(iii) any charges on income which under *section 243(2)* are to be allowed as deductions against the total profits for any accounting period in the specified period,

(g) if the company is not engaged in carrying on a trade mentioned in *section 752(3)* and has received in the period—

(i) on or before the 5th day of April, 1976, a dividend which if the company had been engaged in such a trade would have been required by section 371(1) of the Income Tax Act, 1967, to be taken into account to any extent mentioned in that section, such amount as would, after deduction of income tax at the rate authorised by section 456 of that Act, be equal to the amount which would have been so required to be taken into account,

(ii) after the 5th day of April, 1976, a distribution within the meaning of *Chapter 2* of *Part 6* which if the company had been engaged in such a trade would have been required by *section 752(3)* to be taken into account to any extent mentioned in that section, an amount equal to so much of the distribution as would be so required to be taken into account increased by so much of the tax credit in respect of that distribution as bears to the amount of such tax credit the same proportion as the part of the distribution which would be so required to be taken into account bears to the distribution, and

(h) if the company is not engaged in carrying on a trade mentioned in *section 752(3)*, but were it so engaged any reduction under *section 749* would, or would but for *section 749(3)*, be made as respects the price paid by the company for securities (within the meaning of that section) bought by it in the period—

(i) on or before the 5th day of April, 1976, such amount as would, after deduction of income tax at the rate applicable to the payment, be equal to the amount of the reduction, or

(ii) after the 5th day of April, 1976, such amount as would be equal to an amount of gross interest corresponding to an amount of net interest equal to the amount of the reduction,

so however that where the securities are of the description specified in *paragraph 4* of *Schedule 21*, the amount shall be the amount of the reduction,

and the balance shall be the income of the company for the specified period.

6. Any reference in *paragraph 4* or *5* to an amount for a year of assessment in the period in question shall be taken as a reference to the full amount for any year of assessment falling wholly within that period and a proportionate part of the amount (on a time basis) for any year of assessment falling partly within that period, and the references in those paragraphs to an amount for an accounting period in that period shall be construed in a corresponding manner.

Amendments

[1] Deleted by FA98 sched3(11).

Cross References

From Schedule 22

Section 129 Irish resident company distributions not generally chargeable to corporation tax.
Section 130 Matters to be treated as distributions.
Section 237 Annual payments payable wholly out of taxed income.
Section 238 Annual payments not payable out of taxed income.
Section 243 Allowance of charges on income.
Section 307 Corporation tax: allowances and charges in taxing a trade.
Section 320 Other interpretation (Part 9).
Section 381 Right to repayment of tax by reference to losses.
Section 410 Group payments.
Section 440 Surcharge on undistributed investment and estate income.
Section 441 Surcharge on undistributed income of service companies.
Section 670 Mine development allowance.
Section 749 Dealers in securities.
Section 752 Purchases of shares by financial concerns and persons exempted from tax.
Section 754 Interpretation (Chapter 1).
Section 765 Allowances for capital expenditure on scientific research.
Section 826 Agreements for relief from double taxation.
Schedule 21 Purchase and Sale of Securities: Appropriate Amount in Respect of the Interest

To Schedule 22

Section 749 Dealers in securities.
Section 752 Purchases of shares by financial concerns and persons exempted from tax.

SCHEDULE 23

Occupational Pension Schemes

Section 770.

[FA72 Sch1 PtI pars1 to 3(3), 4 and 5 and PtVI pars 1 to 4; FA96 s132(1) and Sch5 PtI par6]

PART 1

General

Application for approval of a scheme

1. An application for the approval for the purposes of *Chapter 1* of *Part 30* (in this Schedule referred to as "*Chapter 1*") of any retirement benefits scheme shall be made in writing by the administrator of the scheme to the Revenue Commissioners [in such form and manner as they may specify][1] before the end of the first year of assessment for which approval is required, and shall be supported by—
   (a) a copy of the instrument or other document constituting the scheme,
   (b) a copy of the rules of the scheme and, except where the application is being made on the setting up of the scheme, a copy of the accounts of the scheme for the last year for which such accounts have been made up, and
   (c) such other information and particulars (including copies of any actuarial report or advice given to the administrator or employer in connection with the setting up of the scheme) as the Revenue Commissioners may consider relevant.

Information about payments under approved schemes

2. In the case of every approved scheme, the administrator of the scheme and every employer who pays contributions under the scheme shall, within 30 days from the date of the notice from the inspector requiring them so to do—
   (a) furnish to the inspector a return containing such particulars of contributions paid under the scheme as the notice may require;
   (b) prepare and deliver to the inspector a return containing particulars of all payments under the scheme, being—
      (i) payments by means of the return of contributions (including interest on contributions, if any),
      (ii) payments by means of the commutation of, or in place of, pensions or other lump sum payments, [...][2]
      (iii) other payments made to an [employer, and][3]
      [(iv) payments by means of pension, gratuity or other like benefits;][4]
   (c) furnish to the inspector a copy of the accounts of the scheme to the last date previous to the notice to which such accounts have been made up, together with such other information and particulars (including copies of any actuarial report or advice given to the administrator or employer in connection with the conduct of the scheme in the period to which the accounts relate) as the inspector considers relevant.

[2A Any such return, copy of accounts, information and particulars required to be provided under *paragraph 2* shall be in such form and manner as may be specified in the notice under that paragraph.][5]

Information to be provided in electronic format

[2B. In the case of an approved scheme in respect of which the administrator has to deliver annual scheme accounts to the Revenue Commissioners, the administrator shall deliver the accounts by such electronic means as are required or approved by the Commissioners.][6]

[Information to be provided in respect of pre-retirement access to additional voluntary contributions

2C. (1) An administrator (within the meaning of *section 782A(1)(a)*) shall, within 15 working days of the end of each quarter commencing with the quarter ending on 30 June 2013, deliver to the Revenue Commissioners, by such electronic means as are required or approved by the Commissioners, the following information in respect of amounts transferred under *section 782A* during the quarter—

(a) the number of transfers made,

(b) the aggregate value of the transfers made, and

(c) the tax deducted from the aggregate value of the transfers made.

(2) In this paragraph "*quarter*" means a period of 3 consecutive months ending on 31 March, 30 June, 30 September or 31 December.][7]

Information about schemes other than approved schemes or statutory schemes

3.

(1) This paragraph shall apply as respects a retirement benefits scheme which is neither an approved scheme nor a statutory scheme.

(2) It shall be the duty of every employer—

(a) if there subsists in relation to any of that employer's employees any such scheme, to deliver particulars of that scheme to the inspector within 3 months beginning on the date on which the scheme first comes into operation in relation to any of that employer's employees, and

(b) when required to do so by notice given by the inspector to furnish within the time limited by the notice such particulars as the inspector may require with regard to—

(i) any retirement benefits scheme relating to the employer, or

(ii) the employees of that employer to whom any such scheme relates.

(3) It shall be the duty of the administrator of any such scheme, when required to do so by notice given by the inspector, to furnish within the time limited by the notice such particulars as the inspector may require with regard to the scheme.

Responsibility of administrator of a scheme

4.

(1) Where the administrator of a retirement benefits scheme defaults, cannot be traced or dies, the employer shall be responsible in place of the administrator for the discharge of all duties imposed on the administrator under *Chapter 1* and this

Schedule and shall be liable for any tax due from the administrator in the capacity as administrator.

(2) No liability incurred under *Chapter 1* or this Schedule by the administrator of a scheme, or by an employer, shall be affected by the termination of the scheme or by its ceasing to be an approved scheme or an exempt approved scheme, or by the termination of the appointment of the person mentioned in [*section 772(2)(c)(ii)*.][8]

(3) References in this paragraph to the employer include, where the employer is resident outside the State, references to any factor, agent, receiver, branch or manager of the employer in the State.

Regulations

5.

(1) The Revenue Commissioners may make regulations generally for the purpose of carrying *Chapter 1* and this Schedule into effect.

(2) Every regulation made under this paragraph shall be laid before Dáil Éireann as soon as may be after it is made and, if a resolution annulling the regulation is passed by Dáil Éireann within the next 21 days on which Dáil Éireann has sat after the regulation is laid before it, the regulation shall be annulled accordingly, but without prejudice to the validity of anything previously done thereunder.

PART 2

Charge to Tax in Respect of Unauthorised and Certain Other Payments

6. This Part shall apply to any payment to or for the benefit of an employee, otherwise than in course of payment of a pension, being a payment made out of funds which are or have been held for the purposes of a scheme which is or has at any time been approved for the purposes of *Chapter 1*.

7. Where the payment—

(a) is not expressly authorised by the rules of the scheme, or

(b) is made at a time when the scheme is not approved for the purposes of *Chapter 1* and would not have been expressly authorised by the rules of the scheme when it was last so approved,

the employee (whether or not he or she is the recipient of the payment) shall be chargeable to tax on the amount of the payment under Schedule E for the year of assessment in which the payment is made.

8. Any payment chargeable to tax under this Part shall not be chargeable to tax under *section 780* or *781*.

9. References in this Part to any payment include references to any transfer of assets or other transfer of money's worth.

Amendments

[1] Inserted by FA05 s21(1)(f)(i). Applies as on and from 1 January 2005.

[2] Deleted by FA05 s21(1)(f)(ii)(I). Applies as on and from 1 January 2005.

[3] Substituted by FA05 s21(1)(f)(ii)(II). Applies as on and from 1 January 2005.

[4] Inserted by FA05 s21(1)(f)(ii)(III). Applies as on and from 1 January 2005.

[5] Inserted by FA05 s21(1)(f)(iii). Applies as on and from 1 January 2005.

[6] Inserted by FA10 s16(1)(c). Has effect as respects approved schemes whose accounting year ends on or after 1 January 2011.

[7] Inserted by FA13 s17(4)(a). Has effect from 27 March 2013.

[8] Substituted by FA05 s21(1)(f)(iv). Applies as on and from 1 January 2005.

Cross References

From Schedule 23

Section 770 Interpretation and supplemental (Chapter 1).
Section 772 Conditions for approval of schemes and discretionary approval.
Section 780 Charge to income tax on repayment of employees' contributions.
Section 781 Charge to income tax: commutation of entire pension.

To Schedule 23

Section 770 Interpretation and supplemental (Chapter 1).
Section 773 General Medical Services: scheme of superannuation.
Schedule 29 Provisions Referred to in Sections 1052, 1053 and 1054

SCHEDULE 23A

Specified Occupations and Professions

[*Section 787.*

Athlete

Badminton Player Boxer [Cricketer][1]

Cyclist

Footballer

Golfer

Jockey

Motor Racing Driver

Rugby Player

Squash Player

Swimmer

Tennis Player][2]

Amendments

[1] Inserted by FA12 s5(1). Applies for the year of assessment 2012 and subsequent year of assessment.

[2] Inserted by FA99 s19(1)(c). Shall apply as respects the year of assessment 1999–2000 and subsequent years.

Cross References

From Schedule 23A

Section 787 Nature and amount of relief for qualifying premiums.

To Schedule 23A

Section 480A Relief on retirement for certain income of certain sportspersons.

SCHEDULE 23B

Limit on Tax-Relieved Pension Funds

[*Part 30, Chapter 2C.*

Calculation of the uncrystallised pension rights of an individual on the specified date

1.

(1) For the purposes of *Chapter 2C* the amount of uncrystallised pension rights on the specified date in relation to an individual shall be the aggregate of the amounts of such rights on that date in respect of each of the relevant pension arrangements of which the individual is a member; but, where a benefit crystallisation event occurred in relation to the individual under a relevant pension arrangement on the specified date then it shall be deemed for the purposes of this paragraph to have occurred on the day following that date.

(2) Where a relevant pension arrangement referred to in *subparagraph (1)* is—

(a) a defined contribution arrangement, the individual's uncrystallised pension rights under that arrangement shall be so much of the aggregate of—

(i) the amount of any cash sums, and

(ii) the market value of any other assets,

held for the purposes of the arrangement on the specified date as represent the individual's rights under the arrangement,

(b) a defined benefit arrangement, the individual's uncrystallised pension rights under that arrangement shall be an amount equivalent to the amount determined by the formula—

$$(RVF \times AP) + LS$$

where—

RVF is the relevant valuation factor [on the specified date][1],

AP is the annual amount of the pension to which the individual would, on the valuation assumptions, be entitled under the arrangement on the specified date if, on that date, the individual acquired an actual rather than a prospective right to receive a pension in respect of the uncrystallised pension rights, and

LS is the amount of any lump sum to which the individual would, on the valuation assumptions, be entitled under the arrangement on the specified date (otherwise than by way of commutation of pension) if, on that date the individual acquired an actual rather than a prospective right to payment of a lump sum in respect of the rights.

(3) The valuation assumptions referred to in *subparagraph (2)(b)* are—

(a) if the individual has not reached such age, if any, as the individual is required to have reached under the relevant pension arrangement to avoid any reduction in the benefits on account of age, the assumption that the individual reached that age on the specified date, and

(b) the assumption that the individual's right to receive the benefits under the relevant pension arrangement had not been occasioned by incapacity of mind or body.

Occurrence of benefit crystallisation event

2. For the purposes of *Chapter 2C*, a benefit crystallisation event, in relation to an individual, under a relevant pension arrangement of which the individual is a member shall occur where—

(a) the individual becomes entitled under the relevant pension arrangement to any one or more of the following benefits—

(i) a pension,

(ii) an annuity,

(iii) a lump sum,

(b) the individual exercises an option in accordance with *section 772(3A)*, *784(2A)* or *787H(1)* for the transfer, on the date the annuity or, as the case may be, the pension would otherwise become payable, of an amount to any one or more of the following—

(i) the individual,

(ii) an approved retirement fund, or

(iii) an approved minimum retirement fund,

[(ba) the individual does not elect to exercise an option in accordance with *section 787H(1)* and instead retains the assets of the PRSA in that PRSA or any other PRSA,][2]

(c) a payment or transfer is made to an overseas arrangement by direction of the individual under the provisions of the Occupational Pension Schemes and Personal Retirement Savings Accounts (Overseas Transfer Payments) Regulations 2003 (S.I. No. 716 of 2003),

(d) the individual, having become entitled to a pension under a relevant pension arrangement on or after [7 December 2005][3], becomes entitled to the payment of that pension, other than in excepted circumstances, at an increased annual amount which exceeds by more than the permitted margin the annual amount at which it was payable on the day the individual became entitled to it.

Calculation of amount crystallised by a benefit crystallisation event

3. For the purposes of *Chapter 2C*, the amount crystallised by a benefit crystallisation event referred to in *paragraph 2* shall be—

[(a) subject to *subparagraph (aa)*, where the benefit crystallisation event is an event of the kind referred to in *paragraph 2(a)(i)*, an amount equivalent to the amount determined by the formula—

$$P \times A$$

where—

P is the amount of pension which would be payable to the individual, on the assumption that there is no commutation of part of the pension for a lump sum, in the period of 12 months beginning with the day on which the individual becomes entitled to it and on the assumption that there is no increase in the pension throughout that period, and

A is the relevant age-related factor,][4]

[(aa) where the benefit crystallisation event is an event of the kind referred to in *paragraph 2(a)(i)* and the administrator of the relevant pension arrangement is satisfied, based on information and records available to the administrator, that there is an accrued pension amount in respect of that event, an amount equivalent to the amount determined by the formula—

$$(APA \times B) + ((P - APA) \times A)$$

where 'P' and 'A' have the meanings given to them respectively in the formula in *subparagraph (a)* and where—

APA is the accrued pension amount, and

B is the relevant valuation factor on the specified date,

and the administrator shall keep and preserve for a period of 6 years after the date of the event such information and records as may be required for the purposes of demonstrating to the satisfaction of an officer of the Revenue Commissioners that there was an accrued pension amount in respect of the event,][5]

(b) where the benefit crystallisation event is an event of the kind referred to in *paragraph 2(a)(ii),* the aggregate of the amount of so much of the cash sums, and the market value of such of the other assets, representing the individual's rights under the relevant pension arrangement, as are applied to purchase the annuity,

(c) where the benefit crystallisation event is an event of the kind referred to in *paragraph 2(a)(iii)*, the amount of the lump sum paid to the individual,

(d) where the benefit crystallisation event is an event of a kind referred to in *paragraph 2(b)*, the aggregate of the amount of so much of the cash sums and the market value of such of the assets as are to be transferred following the exercise of an option referred to in that paragraph,

[(da) where the benefit crystallisation event is an event of a kind referred to in *paragraph 2(ba)*, the aggregate of the amount of so much of the cash sums and the market value of such of the assets as are retained in the PRSA or in any other PRSA,][6]

(e) where the benefit crystallisation event is an event of the kind referred to in *paragraph 2(c)*, the amount of the payment made, or as the case may be, the market value of the assets transferred, to an overseas arrangement in accordance with the provisions of the Occupational Pension Schemes and Personal Retirement Savings Accounts (Overseas Transfer Payments) Regulations 2003, and

(f) where the benefit crystallisation event is an event of the kind referred to in *paragraph 2(d)*, an amount equivalent to the amount determined by the formula—

$$[A \times IP]^7$$

where—

[A is the relevant age–related factor, and,][8]

IP is the amount (in this assignment of meaning referred to as the "*relevant amount*") by which the increased annual amount of the pension exceeds the annual amount at which it was payable on the day the individual became entitled to it, as increased by the permitted margin, but, if one or more benefit crystallisation events has or have previously occurred by reason of the individual having become entitled to payment of the pension at an increased annual amount, there shall be deducted from the relevant amount the amount crystallised by that event or the aggregate of the amounts crystallised by those events.

Amount of a standard fund threshold or personal fund threshold that is available at the date of a current event

4. For the purposes of *Chapter 2C*, the amount of the standard fund threshold or, as the case may be, personal fund threshold, for an individual, that is available at the date of the current event shall be determined as follows—

(a) if, prior to the current event, no benefit crystallisation event has occurred in relation to the individual on or after [7 December 2005][9], the whole of the standard or personal fund threshold,

(b) if, prior to the current event, one or more benefit crystallisation events have occurred in relation to the individual on or after [7 December 2005][10], and the previously used amount is equal to or greater than the amount of the individual's standard fund threshold or, as the case may be, personal fund threshold, none of the standard fund threshold or the personal fund threshold, and

(c) in any other case, so much of the individual's standard fund threshold or, as the case may be, personal fund threshold as is left after deducting the previously used amount.

Meaning of previously used amount

5.

(1) For the purposes of *paragraph 4* the previously used amount means—

(a) where one benefit crystallisation event has occurred in relation to the individual before the current event, the amount crystallised by the previous benefit crystallisation event adjusted in accordance with *subparagraph (2)*, or

(b) where 2 or more benefit crystallisation events have occurred before the current event, the aggregate of the amounts crystallised by each previous crystallisation event each of those amounts having been adjusted in accordance with *subparagraph (2)*.

[(2) The adjustment referred to in *subparagraph (1)* is the amount crystallised by the previous benefit crystallisation event multiplied by the higher of 1 and the number determined by the formula—

$$\frac{A}{B}$$

where—

A is the standard fund threshold or, as the case may be, the personal fund threshold at the date of the current event, and

B is the standard fund threshold or, as the case may be, the personal fund threshold at the date of the previous benefit crystallisation event,

and where an individual did not have a personal fund threshold at the date of the previous benefit crystallisation event, the standard fund threshold at that date shall be used for B in the formula.][11]][12]

[TABLE

Age	Relevant age–related factor
(1)	(2)
Up to and including 50	37
51	36
52	36
53	35
54	34
55	33
56	33
57	32
58	31
59	30
60	30
61	29
62	28
63	27
64	27
65	26
66	25
67	24
68	24
69	23
70 and over	22][13]

Amendments

[1] Inserted by F(No.2)A13 s18(3)(a). Has effect from 1 January 2014.

[2] Inserted by FA10 s16(1)(d). Has effect as on and from 4 February 2010.

[3] Substituted by FA11 s(19)(5)(a). Has effect as on and from 7 December 2010.

[4] Substituted by F(No.2)A13 s18(3)(b)(i). Has effect from 1 January 2014.

[5] Inserted by F(No.2)A13 s18(3)(b)(ii). Has effect from 1 January 2014.

[6] Inserted by FA10 s16(1)(e). Has effect as on and from 4 February 2010.

[7] Substituted by F(No.2)A13 s18(3)(b)(iii)(I). Has effect from 1 January 2014.

[8] Substituted by F(No.2)A13 s18(3)(b)(iii)(II). Has effect from 1 January 2014.

[9, 10] Substituted by FA11 s(19)(5)(b). Has effect as on and from 7 December 2010.

[11] Substituted by FA11 s(19)(5)(c). Has effect as on and from 7 December 2010.

[12] Inserted by FA06 s14(2). Has effect as on and from 7 December 2005.

[13] Inserted by F(No.2)A13 s18(3)(c). Has effect from 1 January 2014.

Cross References

From Schedule 23B

Section 772 Conditions for approval of schemes and discretionary approval.
Section 784 Retirement annuities: relief for premiums.
Section 787H Approved Retirement Fund option.

SCHEDULE 23C

Pre-Retirement Access to PRSA AVCs

[*Part 30, Chapter 1.*

Information to be provided in respect of pre-retirement access to additional voluntary PRSA contributions

1. An administrator (within the meaning of *section 782A(1)(a)*), who is a PRSA administrator (within the meaning of that provision), shall, within 15 working days of the end of each quarter commencing with the quarter ending on 30 June 2013, deliver to the Revenue Commissioners, by such electronic means as are required or approved by the Commissioners, the following information in respect of amounts transferred under *section 782A* during the quarter—
   (a) the number of transfers made,
   (b) the aggregate value of the transfers made, and
   (c) the tax deducted from the aggregate value of the transfers made.
2. In this Schedule "*quarter*" means a period of 3 consecutive months ending on 31 March, 30 June, 30 September or 31 December.][1]

Amendments

[1] Inserted by FA13 s17(4)(b). Has effect from 27 March 2013.

SCHEDULE 24

Relief from Income Tax and Corporation Tax by Means of Credit in Respect of Foreign Tax

Sections 826 and 833.

[ITA67 Sch10; F(MP)A68 s3(2) and Sch PtI; F(No.2)A70 s1(c); FA74 s86 and Sch2 PtI; CTA76 s23(2) to (4) and s166 and Sch4 PtsI and II; FA95 s60]

PART 1

Interpretation

[1.

(1) In this Schedule, except where the context otherwise requires—][1]

[*aggregate income for the tax year*" has the same meaning as in *section 531AL*;

"*aggregate of the tax value of the reduction*" means the income tax value of the amount by which all income for which credit is to be allowed for foreign tax is treated as reduced in accordance with *subparagraph (3)(c)* of *paragraph 7* ascertained by subtracting the income tax that is chargeable in respect of the year of assessment from the income tax that would be chargeable if all income for which credit is to be allowed for foreign tax had not been reduced in accordance with *subparagraph (3)(c)* of *paragraph 7*;][2]

"*arrangements*" means arrangements for the time being in force by virtue of [*section 826(1)*][3] [...][4];

["*the Irish taxes*" means income tax, income levy, universal social charge and corporation tax;][5]

["*EEA Agreement*" means the Agreement on the European Economic Area signed at Oporto on 2 May 1992, as adjusted by the Protocol signed at Brussels on 17 March 1993;

"*EEA State*" means a state which is a contracting party to the EEA Agreement;][6]

["*foreign tax*" means—

(a) in the case of any territory in relation to which arrangements have the force of law, any tax chargeable under the laws of that territory for which credit may be allowed under the arrangements, and

(b) in any other case, any tax chargeable in respect of which credit may be allowed by virtue of *subparagraph (3)* of *paragraph 9A*.][7]

["*relevant Member State*" means—

(a) a Member State of the European Communities, or

(b) not being such a Member State, an EEA State which is a territory with the government of which arrangements having the force of law by virtue of [*section 826(1)*][8] have been made;][9]

(2) Any reference in this Schedule to foreign tax shall be construed, in relation to credit to be allowed under any arrangements, as a reference only to tax chargeable under the laws of the territory in relation to which the arrangements are made.

General

2.

(1) Subject to this Schedule, where under the arrangements credit is to be allowed against any of the Irish taxes chargeable in respect of any income, the amount of the Irish taxes so chargeable shall be reduced by the amount of the credit.

(2) In the case of any income within the charge to corporation tax, the credit shall be applied in reducing the corporation tax chargeable in respect of that income.

[(2A) In the case of any income within the charge to income tax, the credit shall be applied first in reducing the income tax chargeable in respect of that income.][10]

(3) Nothing in this paragraph shall authorise the allowance of credit against any Irish tax against which credit is not allowable under the arrangements.

Requirements as to residence

3. [Subject to *paragraphs 9A, 9B* and *9C*, credit shall not be allowed][11] against income tax for any year of assessment or corporation tax for any accounting period unless the person in respect of whose income the tax is chargeable is resident in the State for that year or accounting period.

Limit on total credit — corporation tax

4.

(1) The amount of the credit to be allowed against corporation tax for foreign tax in respect of any income shall not exceed the corporation tax attributable to that income.

(2) For the purposes of this paragraph, the corporation tax attributable to any income or gain (in this subparagraph referred to as "*that income*" or "*that gain*", as the case may be) of a company shall, [subject to *subparagraphs (4)* and *(5)*][12], be the corporation tax attributable to so much (in this paragraph referred to as "*the relevant income*" or "*the relevant gain*", as the case may be) of the income or chargeable gains of the company computed in accordance with the Tax Acts and the Capital Gains Tax Acts, as is attributable to that income or that gain, as the case may be.

[(2A) For the purposes of *subparagraph (2)* [...],[13] where credit is to be allowed against corporation tax for [foreign tax in respect of any income of a company (in this subparagraph referred to as "*that income*"), being income (other than income from a trade carried on by the company through a branch or agency in a territory other than the State) which is taken into account][14] in computing the profits or gains of a trade carried on by the company in an accounting period, the relevant income shall be so much of the profits or gains of the trade for that accounting period as is determined by the formula—

$$P \times \frac{I}{R}$$

where—

P is the amount of the profits or gains of the trade for the accounting period before deducting any amount under *paragraph 7(3)(c)*,

I is the amount of that income for the accounting period before deducting any disbursements or expenses of the trade, and

R is the total amount receivable by the company in the carrying on of the trade in the accounting period.][15]

[...][16]

(4) Subject to *subparagraph (5)*, the amount of corporation tax attributable to the relevant income or gain shall be treated as equal to such proportion of the amount of that income or gain as corresponds to the rate of corporation tax payable by the company (before any credit for double taxation relief) on its income or chargeable gains for the accounting period in which the income arises or the gain accrues (in this paragraph referred to as "*the relevant accounting period*"); but, where the corporation tax payable by the company for the relevant accounting period on the relevant income or [gain—][17]

[(a) is charged at the rate specified in *section 21A*, the rate of corporation tax payable by the company on its income and chargeable gains for the relevant accounting period shall be the rate so specified,

[...][18]

(c) is to be computed in accordance with *section 713(3)* or *738(2)*, the rate of corporation tax payable by the company on its income and chargeable gains for the relevant accounting period shall be treated as the standard rate of income tax,

(d) is to be computed in accordance with *section 723(6)*, the rate of corporation tax payable by the company on its income and chargeable gains for the relevant accounting period shall be treated as 20 per cent,

(e) is reduced by virtue of *section 644B*, [by any fraction][19] the rate of corporation tax payable by the company on its income and chargeable gains for the relevant accounting period shall be treated as reduced by that fraction,][20]

for the purposes of computing the corporation tax attributable to that relevant income or gain, as the case may be.

(5) Where in the relevant accounting period there is any deduction to be made for charges on income, expenses of management or other amounts which can be deducted from or set off against or treated as reducing profits of more than one description—

(a) the company shall for the purposes of [this paragraph,][21] [*paragraphs 9D, 9DB* and *9DC*][22] [...][23] allocate every such deduction in such amounts and to such of its profits for that period as it thinks fit, and

(b) (i) the amount of the relevant income or gain shall be treated for the purposes of *subparagraph (4)*,

[…][24]

[(iv) the amount of income of a company treated for the purposes of *paragraph 9D* as referable to an amount of relevant interest (within the meaning of that paragraph) [shall be treated for the purposes of that paragraph][25],[...][26]][27]

[(v) the amount of income of a company treated for the purposes of *paragraph 9DB* as referable to an amount of relevant royalties (within the meaning of that paragraph) [shall be treated for the purposes of that paragraph][28],[and][29]][30]

[(vi) the amount of income of a company treated for the purposes of *paragraph 9DC* as referable to an amount of relevant leasing income (within the meaning of that paragraph) [shall be treated for the purposes of that paragraph][31],][32]

as reduced or, as the case may be, extinguished by so much (if any) of the deduction as is allocated to it.

[(6) (a) The provisions of subparagraph (5), in relation to the allocation of deductions, shall not apply to relevant trading charges on income.

(b) For the purposes of clause *(a)* "*relevant trading charges on income*" has the same meaning as in *section 243A*.][33]

Limit on total credit — income tax

5.

(1) The amount of the credit to be allowed against income tax for foreign tax in respect of any income shall not exceed the sum which would be produced by computing the amount of that income in accordance with the Income Tax Acts, and then charging it to income tax for the year of assessment for which the credit is to be allowed, but at a rate (in this paragraph referred to as "*the specified rate*") ascertained by dividing the income tax payable by that person for that year by the amount of the total income of that person for that year.

(2) For the purpose of determining the specified rate, the tax payable by any person for any year shall be computed without any reduction of that tax for any credit allowed or to be allowed under any arrangements having effect by virtue of [*section 826(1)*][34] but shall be deemed to be reduced by any tax which the person in question is entitled to charge against any other person, and the total income of any person shall be deemed to be reduced by the amount of any income the income tax on which that person is entitled to charge as against any other person.

(3) Where credit for foreign tax is to be allowed in respect of any income and any relief would but for this subparagraph be allowed in respect of that income under *section 830*, that relief shall not be allowed.

[(4) Where *Chapter 2A* of *Part 15* applies to a person for a tax year, the specified rate shall be ascertained by dividing the income tax payable by that person for that year in accordance with *section 485E* by the amount of the individual's adjusted income, within the meaning of *section 485C*, for that year.][35]

Limit on total credit — universal social charge

[5A.

(1) The amount of the credit to be allowed against universal social charge for foreign tax in respect of any income—

(a) shall not exceed the sum which would be produced by computing the amount of that income in accordance with *Part 18D*, and then charging it to universal social charge for the year of assessment for which the credit is to be allowed, but at a rate ascertained by dividing the universal social charge payable by that person for that year by the amount of the aggregate income for the tax year of that person, and

(b) shall be determined (subject to clause (a)) by the formula—

$$(FT - C) - TV$$

where—

FT is the foreign tax, including foreign tax not chargeable directly, in respect of the income,

C is the credit allowed against income tax for foreign tax in respect of the income, and

TV is the portion of the aggregate of the tax value of the reduction attributable to the income determined by the formula—

$$A \times \frac{B}{C}$$

where—

A is the aggregate of the tax value of the reduction,

B is the part of the foreign tax by which the income has been reduced in accordance with *subparagraph (3)(c)* of *paragraph 7*, and

C is the aggregate of the reductions by which all income for which credit is to be allowed for foreign tax has been reduced in accordance with *subparagraph (3)(c)* of *paragraph 7*.

(2) Subject to subparagraph (1), where an individual is assessed to tax in accordance with *section 1017* or *1031C* and each spouse or civil partner falls to be charged to universal social charge on his or her share of that income, the amount of the credit to be allowed against universal social charge in respect of each share of that income shall not exceed such part of the credit as bears to that credit the same proportion as the share of each spouse or civil partner in that income bears to that income.][36]

6. Without prejudice to *paragraph 5*, the total credit to be allowed to a person against income tax for any year of assessment shall not exceed the total income tax payable by the person in question for that year of assessment, less any tax which that person is entitled to charge against any other person.

Effect on computation of income of allowance of credit

7.

(1) Where credit for foreign tax is to be allowed against any of the Irish taxes in respect of any income, this paragraph shall apply in relation to the computation for the purposes of income tax or corporation tax of the amount of that income.

(2) Where the income tax or corporation tax payable depends on the amount received in the State, that amount shall be treated as increased by the amount of the credit allowable against income tax or corporation tax, as the case may be.

(3) Where *subparagraph (2)* does not apply—

(a) no deduction shall be made for foreign tax (whether in respect of the same or any other income), and

(b) where the income includes a dividend and under the arrangements foreign tax not chargeable directly or by deduction in respect of the dividend is to be taken into account in considering whether any, and if so what, credit is to be allowed against the Irish taxes in respect of the dividend, the amount of the income shall be treated as increased by the amount of the foreign tax not so chargeable which is to be taken into account in computing the amount of the credit, but

[(c) notwithstanding anything in clauses (a) and (b), where any part of the foreign tax in respect of the income (including any foreign tax which under clause (b) is to be treated as increasing the amount of the income) cannot be allowed as a credit against either income tax or corporation tax, the amount of the income shall be treated as reduced by that part of that foreign tax, but, for the purposes of corporation tax, the amount by which the income is treated as reduced by that part of the foreign tax shall not exceed the amount of income which would be the amount referred to in *paragraph 4* as "*the relevant income*", taking account of the provisions of *subparagraphs (2)* and *(2A)* of that paragraph.][37]

(4) In relation to the computation of the [total income or the adjusted income, as the case may be,][38] of a person for the purpose of determining the rate mentioned in *paragraph 5*, *subparagraphs (1)* to *(3)* shall apply subject to the following modifications:

(a) for the reference in *subparagraph (2)* to the amount of the credit allowable against income tax there shall be substituted a reference to the amount of the foreign tax in respect of the income (in the case of a dividend, foreign tax not chargeable directly or by deduction in respect of the dividend being disregarded), and

(b) *clauses (b)* and *(c)* of *subparagraph (3)* shall not apply,

and, subject to those modifications, shall apply in relation to all income in the case of which credit is to be allowed for foreign tax under any arrangements.

Effect on computation of income of allowance of credit against universal social charge

[7A.

(1) Where credit for foreign tax is to be allowed against any of the Irish taxes in respect of any income, this paragraph shall apply in relation to the computation for the purposes of universal social charge of the amount of that income.

(2) Where the universal social charge payable depends on the amount received in the State, that amount shall be treated as increased by the amount of the credit allowable against income tax.

(3) Where *subparagraph (2)* does not apply—

(a) no deduction shall be made for foreign tax (whether in respect of the same or any other income), and

(b) where the income includes a dividend and under the arrangements foreign tax not chargeable directly or by deduction in respect of the dividend is to be taken into account in considering whether any, and if so what, credit is to be allowed against the Irish taxes in respect of the dividend, the amount of the income shall be treated as increased by the amount of the foreign tax not so chargeable which is to be taken into account in computing the amount of the credit.

(4) In relation to the computation of the income of a person for the purposes of *paragraph 5A*, *subparagraphs (1)* to *(3)* shall apply in relation to all income in the case of which credit is to be allowed for foreign tax under any arrangements.][39]

Special provisions as to dividends

8.

(1) For the purposes of this paragraph, the relevant profits shall be—

(a) if the dividend is paid for a specified period, the profits of that period,

(b) if the dividend is not paid for a specified period but is paid out of specified profits, those profits, or

(c) if the dividend is paid neither for a specified period nor out of specified profits, the profits of the last period for which accounts of the body corporate were made up which ended before the dividend became payable;

but if, in a case within *clause (a)* or *(c)*, the total dividend exceeds the profits available for distribution of the period mentioned in *clause (a)* or *(c)*, as the case may be, the relevant profits shall be the profits of that period together with so much of the profits available for distribution of preceding periods (other than profits previously distributed or previously treated as relevant for the purposes of this paragraph) as is equal to the excess, and for this purpose the profits of the most recent preceding period shall first be taken into account, then the profits of the next most recent preceding period, and so on.

(2) Where, in the case of any dividend, foreign tax not chargeable directly or by deduction in respect of the dividend is under the arrangements to be taken into account in considering whether any, and if so what, credit is to be allowed against the Irish taxes in respect of the dividend, the foreign tax not so chargeable to be taken into account shall be that borne by the body corporate paying the dividend on the relevant profits in so far as it is properly attributable to the proportion of the relevant profits represented by the dividend.

9. Where—

(a) the arrangements provide, in relation to dividends of some classes but not in relation to dividends of other classes, that foreign tax not chargeable directly or by deduction in respect of dividends is to be taken into account in considering whether any, and if so what, credit is to be allowed against the Irish taxes in respect of the dividends, and

(b) a dividend is paid which is not of a class in relation to which the arrangements so provide,

then, if the dividend is paid to a company which controls, directly or indirectly, not less than 50 per cent of the voting power in the company paying the dividend, credit shall be allowed as if the dividend were a dividend of a class in relation to which the arrangements so provide.

PART 2

Unilateral Relief

[9A

(1) To the extent appearing from the following provisions of this paragraph, relief (in this paragraph referred to as "unilateral relief") from corporation tax in respect of profits represented by dividends shall be given in respect of tax payable under the law of any territory other than the State by allowing that tax as a credit against corporation tax, notwithstanding that there are not for the time being in force any arrangements providing for such relief.

(2) Unilateral relief shall be such relief as would fall to be given under this Schedule if arrangements with the government of the territory in question containing the provisions in *subparagraphs (3)* to *(5)* were in force, and a reference in this Schedule to credit under arrangements shall be construed as [including][40] a reference to unilateral relief.

(3) Subject to *Part 1* and to [*subparagraphs (3B)* and *(5)*][41], credit for tax paid under the law of a territory other than the State in relation to a relevant dividend paid by a company resident in the territory to a [company falling within *subparagraph (3A)*][42] shall be allowed against corporation tax attributable to the profits represented by the dividend.

[(3A) (a) A company falls within this subparagraph if—

(i) it is resident in the State, or

(ii) it is, by virtue of the law of a [relevant Member State][43] other than the State, resident for the purposes of tax in such a Member State and the dividend referred to in *subparagraph (3)* forms part of the profits of a branch or agency of the company in the State.

(b) For the purposes of *subparagraph (a)*(ii), "tax", in relation to a [relevant Member State][44] other than the State, means any tax imposed in the Member State which corresponds to corporation tax in the State.][45]

[(3B) Where a payment is made under the law of a territory other than the State to any person by reference to tax paid under the law of a territory other than the State in relation to a relevant dividend paid by a company, then the amount of the credit to be allowed under *subparagraph (3)* against corporation tax attributable to the profits represented by the dividend shall be reduced by an amount equal to the amount of the payment.][46]

(4) For the purposes of [*subparagraphs (3)* and *(3B)*][47]—

(a) "tax paid under the law of a territory other than the State in relation to a relevant dividend paid by a company" means—

(i) tax which is directly charged on the dividend, whether by charge to tax, deduction of tax at source or otherwise, and the whole of which tax neither the company nor the recipient would have borne if the dividend had not been paid, and

(ii) tax paid in respect of its profits under the law of the territory by the company paying the dividend in so far as that tax is properly attributable to the proportion of the profits represented by the dividend,

(b) "*relevant dividend*" means a dividend paid by a company resident in a territory other than the State to a [company falling within *subparagraph (3A)*][48] which either directly or indirectly owns, or is a subsidiary of a company which directly or indirectly owns, not less than [5 per cent][49] of the ordinary share capital of the company paying the dividend; for the purposes of this subparagraph one company is a subsidiary of another company if the other company owns, directly or indirectly, not less than 50 per cent of the ordinary share capital of the first company.

(5) Credit shall not be allowed by virtue of subparagraph (3)—

(a) for tax paid under the law of a territory where there are arrangements with the government of the territory [except[…][50] to the extent that credit may not be given for that tax under those arrangements][51],

(b) for any tax which is relevant foreign tax within the meaning of [...][52] *paragraph 9D*][53], or

(c) for any tax in respect of which credit may be allowed under *section 831*.

(6) Where—

(a) unilateral relief may be given in respect of a dividend, and

(b) it appears that the assessment to corporation tax made in respect of the dividends is not made in respect of the full amount thereof, or is incorrect having regard to the credit, if any, which falls to be given by way of unilateral relief,

any such assessment may be made or amended as is necessary to ensure that the total amount of the dividend is assessed, and the proper credit, if any, is given in respect thereof.

(7) In this Schedule in its application to unilateral relief, references to tax payable or paid under the law of a territory outside the State include only references to taxes which are charged on income or capital gains and which correspond to corporation tax and capital gains tax.

9B.

(1) Where a foreign company pays a dividend to [a company falling within *subparagraph (1A)* (in this paragraph referred to as the "*relevant company*")][54] and the foreign company is related to [*the relevant company*][55], then for the purpose of allowing credit under any arrangements against corporation tax in respect of the dividend, there shall, subject to Part 1, be taken into account as if it were tax payable under the law of the territory in which the foreign company is resident—

(a) any income tax or corporation tax payable in the State by the foreign company in respect of its profits, and

(b) any tax which, under the law of any other territory, is payable by the foreign company in respect of its profits.

[(1A) (a) A company falls within this subparagraph if—

(i) it is resident in the State, or

(ii) it is, by virtue of the law of a Member State of the European Communities other than the State, resident for the purposes of tax in such a Member State and the dividend referred to in *subparagraph (1)* forms part of the profits of a branch or agency of the company in the State.

(b) For the purposes of subparagraph (*a*)(ii), "tax", in relation to a [relevant Member State][56] other than the State, means any tax imposed in the Member State which corresponds to corporation tax in the State.][57]

(2) Where the foreign company has received a dividend from a third company and the third company is related to the foreign company and is connected with [*the relevant company*][58], then, subject to *subparagraph (4)*, [there shall be treated for the purposes of subparagraph (1) as tax paid by the foreign company in respect of its profits—][59]

[(a) any underlying tax payable by the third company, and

(b) any tax directly charged on the dividend which neither company would have borne had the dividend not been paid,][60]

[to the extent to which it would be taken into account][61] under this Schedule if the dividend had been paid by a foreign company to [a relevant company][62] and arrangements had provided for [underlying tax to be taken into account: and for this purpose there shall, subject to *Part 1*, be taken into account as if it were tax payable under the law of the territory in which the third company is resident—][63]

[(i) any income tax or corporation tax payable in the State by the foreign company in respect of its profits, and

(ii) any tax which, under the law of any other territory, is payable by the foreign company in respect of its profits.][64]

(3) Where the third company has received a dividend from a fourth company and the fourth company is related to the third company and is connected with [*the relevant company*][65], then, subject to *subparagraph (4)*, tax payable by the fourth company [or tax directly charged on the dividend][66] shall similarly be treated for the purposes of *subparagraph (2)* as tax paid by the third company, and so on for successive

companies each of which is related to the one before and is connected with the Irish company.

(4) *Subparagraphs (2)* and *(3)* are subject to the following limitations—

(a) no tax shall be taken into account in respect of a dividend paid by [*a relevant company*][67] except corporation tax payable in the State and any tax for which that company is entitled to credit under this Schedule, and

(b) no tax shall be taken into account in respect of a dividend paid by a foreign company to another such company unless it could have been taken into account under this Schedule had the other company been [*a relevant company*][68].

(5) (a) In this paragraph—

"*foreign company*" means a company resident outside the State;

[…][69]

"*underlying tax*", in relation to a dividend, means tax borne by the company paying the dividend on the relevant profits (within the meaning of *paragraph (8)*) in so far as it is properly attributable to the proportion of the relevant profits represented by the dividend.

(b) For the purposes of this paragraph—

(i) a company is related to another company if that other company—

(I) [controls][70] directly or indirectly, or

(II) is a subsidiary of a company which [controls][71] directly or indirectly,

not less than [5 per cent][72] of the ordinary [voting power][73] of the first-mentioned company,

(ii) one company is a subsidiary of another company if the other company owns, directly or indirectly, not less than 50 per cent of the ordinary share capital of the first-mentioned company, and

(iii) a company is connected with another company if that other company—

(I) [controls][74] directly or indirectly, or

(II) is a subsidiary of a company which [controls][75] directly or indirectly,

not less than [5 per cent][76] of the ordinary [voting power][77] of the first-mentioned company.][78]

[9C

(1) In this paragraph—

"*relevant company*" means a company which—

(a) is not resident in the State,

(b) is, by virtue of the law of a [relevant Member State][79] other than the State, resident for the purposes of tax in such a Member State, and

(c) carries on a trade in the State through a branch or agency,

and for the purposes of *subparagraph (b)* of this definition "tax", in relation to a [relevant Member State][80] other than the State, means any tax imposed in the Member State which corresponds to corporation tax in the State;

"*relevant tax*" means foreign tax paid in respect of the income or chargeable gains of a branch or agency in the State of a relevant company, other than such tax paid in a territory in which the company is liable to tax by reason of domicile, residence, place of management or other similar criterion.

(2) A relevant company shall, as respects an accounting period, be entitled to such relief under this Schedule in respect of relevant tax as would, if the branch or agency in the State had been a company resident in the State, have been given under any arrangements to that company resident in the State.][81]

[9D

(1) (a) In this paragraph—

"*relevant foreign tax*", in relation to interest receivable by a company, means tax—

(i) which under the laws of any foreign territory has been deducted from the amount of the interest,

(ii) which corresponds to income tax or corporation tax,

(iii) which has not been repaid to the company,

(iv) for which credit is not allowable under arrangements, and

(v) which, apart from this paragraph, is not treated under this Schedule as reducing the amount of income;

["*relevant interest*" means interest receivable by a company—

(a) which falls to be taken into account in computing the trading income of a trade carried on by the company, and

(b) from which relevant foreign tax is deducted.][82]

(b) For the purposes of this paragraph—

(i) the amount of corporation tax which apart from this paragraph would be payable by a company for an accounting period and which is attributable to an amount of relevant interest shall be an amount equal to—

(I) in so far as it is corporation tax charged on profits which under *section 26(3)* are apportioned to the financial year 2002, 16 per cent, and

(II) in so far as it is corporation tax charged on profits which under *section 26(3)* are apportioned to the financial year 2003 or any subsequent financial year, 12.5 per cent,

of the amount of the income of the company referable to the amount of the relevant interest [reduced by the relevant foreign tax][83], and

(ii) the amount of any income of a company referable to an amount of relevant interest in an accounting period [increased by the amount of the relevant foreign tax][84] shall, subject to *paragraph 4(5)*, be taken to be such sum as bears to the total amount of the trading income of the company for the accounting period the same proportion as the amount of relevant interest in the accounting period bears to the total amount receivable by the company in the course of the trade in the accounting period.

(2) Where, as respects an accounting period of a company, the trading income of a trade carried on by the company includes an amount of relevant interest, the

amount of corporation tax which, apart from this paragraph, would be payable by the company for the accounting period shall be reduced by so much of—

(a) in so far as it is corporation tax charged on profits which under *section 26(3)* are apportioned to the financial year 2002, 84 per cent, and

(b) in so far as it is corporation tax charged on profits which under *section 26(3)* are apportioned to the financial year 2003 or any subsequent financial year, 87.5 per cent,

of any relevant foreign tax borne by the company in respect of relevant interest in that period as does not exceed the corporation tax which would be so payable and which is attributable to the amount of the relevant interest.

[...][85]

Unilateral Relief (branch profits)

[9DA

(1) To the extent appearing from the following provisions of this paragraph, relief (in this paragraph referred to as "*unilateral relief*") from corporation tax in respect of profits of a company from a trade carried on by the company through a branch or agency in a territory other than the State shall be given in respect of tax payable under the law of any territory other than the State by allowing that tax as a credit against corporation tax, notwithstanding that there are not for the time being in force any arrangements providing for such relief.

(2) Unilateral relief shall be such relief as would fall to be given under this Schedule if arrangements with the government of the territory in question containing the provisions in *subparagraphs (3)* to *(5)* were in force, and a reference in this Schedule to credit under arrangements shall be construed as including a reference to unilateral relief.

(3) Subject to *Part 1* and to *subparagraph (5)*, credit for tax paid under the law of a territory other than the State and computed by reference to income of a company, being a company falling within *subparagraph (4)*, from a trade carried on by it through a branch or agency in that territory shall be allowed against corporation tax in the State computed by reference to that income.

(4) (a) A company falls within this subparagraph if—

(i) it is resident in the State, or

(ii) it is, by virtue of the law of a relevant Member State other than the State, resident for the purposes of tax in such a Member State and the income referred to in *subparagraph (3)* forms part of the income of a branch or agency of the company in the State.

(b) For the purposes of *subparagraph (a)(ii)*, "*tax*", in relation to a relevant Member State other than the State, means any tax imposed in the Member State which corresponds to corporation tax in the State.

(5) Credit shall not be allowed by virtue of *subparagraph (3)*—

(a) for tax paid under the law of a territory where there are arrangements with the government of the territory except to the extent that credit may not be given for that tax under those arrangements, or

(b) for any tax which is relevant foreign tax within the meaning of [...][86] paragraph 9D.

(6) Where—

(a) unilateral relief may be given in respect of any profits, and

(b) it appears that the assessment to corporation tax made in respect of the profits is not made in respect of the full amount thereof, or is incorrect having regard to the credit, if any, which falls to be given by way of unilateral relief,

then any such assessment may be made or amended as is necessary to ensure that the total amount of the profits is assessed, and the proper credit, if any, is given in respect thereof.

(7) In this Schedule in its application to unilateral relief, references to tax payable or paid under the law of a territory outside the State include only references to taxes which are charged on income or capital gains and which correspond to corporation tax and capital gains tax.][87]

Unilateral Relief (royalty income)

[9DB.

(1) (a) In this paragraph—

"*relevant foreign tax*", in relation to royalties receivable by a company, means tax—

(i) which under the laws of any foreign territory has been deducted from the amount of the royalty,

(ii) which corresponds to income tax or corporation tax,

(iii) which has not been repaid to the company,

(iv) for which credit is not allowable under arrangements, and

(v) which, apart from this paragraph, is not treated under this Schedule as reducing the amount of income;

"*relevant royalties*" means royalties receivable by a company—

(i) which fall to be taken into account in computing the trading income of a trade carried on by the company, and

(ii) from which relevant foreign tax is deducted;

"*royalties*" means payments of any kind as consideration for—

(i) the use of, or the right to use—

(I) any copyright of literary, artistic or scientific work, including cinematograph films and software,

(II) any patent, trade mark, design or model, plan, secret formula or process,

or

(ii) information concerning industrial, commercial or scientific experience.

(b) For the purposes of this paragraph—

(i) the amount of corporation tax which apart from this paragraph would be payable by a company for an accounting period and which is attributable to an amount of relevant royalties shall be an amount equal to 12.5 per cent of the amount by which the amount of the income of the company referable to the amount of the relevant royalties exceeds the relevant foreign tax, and

(ii) the amount of any income of a company referable to an amount of relevant royalties in an accounting period shall, subject to *paragraph 4(5)*, be taken to be such sum as bears to the total amount of the trading income of the company for the accounting period before deducting any relevant foreign tax the same proportion as the amount of relevant royalties in the accounting period bears to the total amount receivable by the company in the course of the trade in the accounting period.

(2) Where, as respects an accounting period of a company, the trading income of a trade carried on by the company includes an amount of relevant royalties, the amount of corporation tax which, apart from this paragraph, would be payable by the company for the accounting period shall be reduced by so much of 87.5 per cent of any relevant foreign tax borne by the company in respect of relevant royalties in that period as does not exceed the corporation tax which would be so payable and which is attributable to the amount of the relevant royalties.

[...][88]

[(4) Where as respects any relevant royalties received in an accounting period by a company, any part of the foreign tax cannot, due to an insufficiency of income, be treated as reducing income under *paragraph 7(3)(c)* or under *section 77(6B)*, then the amount which cannot be so treated shall, for the purposes of this paragraph, be unrelieved foreign tax.

(5) Where, as respects an accounting period, a company is in receipt of royalties from persons not resident in the State and such royalties are taken into account in computing the trading income of a trade carried on by the company, the company may—

(*a*) reduce the income (in this subparagraph referred to as '*royalty income*') referable to any such payments by any unrelieved foreign tax, and

(*b*) allocate such reductions in such amounts and to such of its royalty income for that accounting period as it sees fit.

(6) The aggregate amount of reductions under subparagraph (5) in an accounting period cannot exceed the aggregate of the unrelieved foreign tax in respect of all relevant royalties for that accounting period.][89]

[Unilateral Relief (leasing income)

9DC. (1) (*a*) In this paragraph—

'*leasing income*' means payments of any kind as consideration for the use of, or the right to use, industrial, commercial or scientific equipment;

'*relevant foreign tax*', in relation to leasing income receivable by a company, means tax—

(i) which under the laws of any foreign territory has been deducted from the amount of the lease payment,

(ii) which corresponds to income tax or corporation tax,

(iii) which has not been repaid to the company,

(iv) for which credit is not allowable under arrangements, and

(v) which, apart from this paragraph, is not treated under this Schedule as reducing the amount of income;

'*relevant leasing income*' means leasing income receivable by a company—

(i) which falls to be taken into account in computing the trading income of a trade carried on by the company, and

(ii) from which relevant foreign tax is deducted.

(*b*) For the purposes of this paragraph—

(i) the amount of corporation tax which apart from this paragraph would be payable by a company for an accounting period and which is attributable to an amount of relevant leasing income shall be an amount equal to 12.5 per cent of the amount by which the amount of the income of the company referable to the amount of the relevant leasing income exceeds the relevant foreign tax, and

(ii) the amount of any income of a company referable to an amount of relevant leasing income in an accounting period shall, subject to *paragraph 4(5)*, be taken to be such sum as bears to the total amount of the trading income of the company for the accounting period before deducting any relevant foreign tax the same proportion as the amount of relevant leasing income in the accounting period bears to the total amount receivable by the company in the course of the trade in the accounting period.

(2) Where, as respects an accounting period of a company, the trading income of a trade carried on by the company includes an amount of relevant leasing income, the amount of corporation tax which, apart from this paragraph, would be payable by the company for the accounting period shall be reduced by so much of 87.5 per cent of any relevant foreign tax borne by the company in respect of relevant leasing income in that period as does not exceed the corporation tax which would be so payable and which is attributable to the amount of the relevant leasing income.][90]

[(3) For the purposes of *subparagraph (4)*—

(a) as respects any leasing income included in trading income for an accounting period of a trade carried on by a company, and

(b) taking account of payments for the use of, or the right to use, specific equipment as a separate leasing income,

an amount shall be treated as unrelieved foreign tax, or unrelieved relevant foreign tax, of that accounting period in respect of that leasing income, being—

(i) in the case of foreign tax, which is deducted, or treated as so deducted by *subparagraph (4)*, from that leasing income, the sum of—

(I) so much of that tax as is neither allowed as a credit against corporation tax nor treated as reducing income under *paragraph 7(3)(c)*, and

(II) 87.5 per cent of the amount of foreign tax by which income is treated as reduced by virtue of *paragraph 7(3)(c)*,

and

(ii) in the case of relevant foreign tax, the amount by which 87.5 per cent of that relevant foreign tax, which is deducted, or treated as so deducted by *subparagraph (4)*, from that leasing income, exceeds the amount of corporation tax which is treated as attributable to that leasing income for the purposes of this paragraph.

(4) Where, taking account of payments for the use of, or the right to use, specific equipment as a separate leasing income, a company is in receipt of a leasing income for an accounting period (in this subparagraph referred to as "*the first-mentioned accounting period*") from which foreign tax or relevant foreign tax has been deducted, then for the purposes of the Corporation Tax Acts any unrelieved foreign tax, or unrelieved relevant foreign tax, of the accounting period immediately preceding the first-mentioned accounting period in respect of the same leasing income shall be treated as foreign tax or relevant foreign tax, as the case may be, deducted from such leasing income of the first-mentioned accounting period.][91]

[9E

(1) (a) In this paragraph—

"*foreign company*" means a company resident outside the State;

"*unrelieved foreign tax*" has the meaning assigned to it in *subparagraph (2)*.

"*unrelieved foreign tax in respect of specified dividends*" has the meaning assigned to it in subparagraph (3).

(b) For the purposes of this paragraph—

(i) a dividend is a relevant dividend if it is received by a company (in this clause referred to as the "*receiving company*") from a company which is not resident in the State (in this clause referred to as the "*paying company*") and the paying company is related to the receiving company (within the meaning of *paragraph 9B(5)(b)*), and

(ii) the aggregate amount of corporation tax payable by a company for an accounting period in respect of any dividends received by the company in the accounting period from foreign companies means so much of the corporation tax that, apart from this paragraph, would be payable by the company for that accounting period as would not have been payable had those dividends not been received by the company.

(2) (a) Where, as respects a relevant dividend received in an accounting period by a company and which is charged to corporation tax in accordance with *section 21A*, any part of the foreign tax cannot, apart from this paragraph, be allowed as a credit against any of the Irish taxes and, accordingly, the amount of income representing the dividend is treated under *paragraph 7(3)(c)* as reduced by that part of the foreign tax, then an amount determined by the formula—

$$\frac{100 - R}{100} \times D$$

where—

R is the rate per cent specified in *section 21A(3)*, and

D is the amount of the part of the foreign tax by which the income is to be treated under *paragraph 7(3)(c)* as reduced, shall be treated for the purposes of clause (*b*) as unrelieved foreign tax of that accounting period.

(b) The aggregate amount of corporation tax payable by a company for an accounting period in respect of relevant dividends received by the company in that accounting period from foreign companies shall be reduced by the unrelieved foreign tax of that accounting period.

(c) Where the unrelieved foreign tax in relation to an accounting period of a company exceeds the aggregate amount of corporation tax payable by the company for the accounting period in respect of relevant dividends received by the company in that accounting period from foreign companies, the excess shall be carried forward and treated as unrelieved foreign tax of the next succeeding accounting period, and so on for succeeding accounting periods.

(3) (a) In this subparagraph "*specified dividend*" means a relevant dividend which is not charged to corporation tax in accordance with *section 21A*.

(b) Where, as respects a specified dividend received in an accounting period by a company, any part of the foreign tax cannot, apart from this paragraph, be allowed as a credit against any of the Irish taxes and, accordingly, the amount of income representing the dividend is treated under *paragraph 7(3)(c)* as reduced by that part of the foreign tax, then an amount determined by the formula—

$$\frac{100 - R}{100} \times D$$

where—

R is the rate per cent specified in *section 21*, and

D is the amount of the part of the foreign tax by which the income is to be treated under *paragraph 7(3)(c)* as reduced,

shall be treated for the purposes of clause (*c*) as unrelieved foreign tax in respect of specified dividends of that accounting period.

(c) The aggregate amount of corporation tax payable by a company for an accounting period in respect of specified dividends received by the company in that accounting period from foreign companies shall be reduced by the unrelieved foreign tax in respect of specified dividends of that accounting period.

(d) Where the unrelieved foreign tax in respect of specified dividends in relation to an accounting period of a company exceeds the aggregate amount of corporation tax payable by the company for the accounting period in respect of specified dividends received by the company in that accounting period from foreign companies, the excess shall be carried forward and treated as unrelieved foreign tax in respect of specified dividends of the next succeeding accounting period, and so on for succeeding accounting periods.][92]

[9F

(1) (a) In this paragraph—

the "aggregate amount of corporation tax payable by a company for an accounting period in respect of relevant interest of the company for the accounting period from foreign companies" means so much of the corporation tax which, apart from this paragraph, would be payable by the company for that accounting period as would not have been payable had the interest not been chargeable to tax;

"*foreign company*" means a company resident outside the State;

"*foreign tax*", in relation to interest receivable by a company, means tax which—

(i) under the laws of any foreign territory has been deducted from the amount of the interest,

(ii) corresponds to income or corporation tax,

(iii) has not been repaid to the company;

"*unrelieved foreign tax*" has the meaning assigned to it in *subparagraph (2)*.

(b) For the purposes of this paragraph—

(i) interest which is receivable by a company (in this clause referred to as the "*receiving company*") from a company is relevant interest if—

(I) the interest falls to be taken into account in computing the trading income of a trade carried on by the receiving company,

(II) the interest arises from a source within a territory in regard to which arrangements have the force of law, and

(III) one of those companies is the 25 per cent subsidiary of the other or both companies are 25 per cent subsidiaries of a third company,

(ii) subject to subclause (iii), a company shall be deemed to be a 25 per cent subsidiary of another company if and so long as not less then 25 per cent of its ordinary share capital would be treated as owned directly or indirectly by that other company if *section 9* (other than *subsection (1)* of that section) were to apply for the purposes of this paragraph,

(iii) a company (in this subclause referred to as a "*subsidiary company*") shall not be deemed to be a 25 per cent subsidiary of another company (in this subclause referred to as the "*parent company*") at any time if the percentage—

(I) of any profits, which are available for distribution to equity holders, of the subsidiary company at such time to which the parent company is beneficially entitled at such time, or

(II) of any assets, which are available for distribution to equity holders on a winding up, of the subsidiary company at such time to which the parent company would be beneficially entitled at such time on a winding up of the subsidiary company,

is less than 25 per cent of such profits or assets (as the case may be) of the subsidiary company at such time, and *sections 413*, *414*, *415* and *418* shall, with any necessary modifications but without regards to *section 411(1)(c)* in so far as it relates to those sections, apply to the determination of the percentage of those profits or assets (as the case may be) to which a company is beneficially entitled as they apply to the determination for the purposes of *Chapter 5* of *Part 12* of the percentage of any such profits or assets to which a company is so entitled.

[(c) (i) In this clause "*arrangements*" means arrangements made with the government of a territory which on completion of the procedures set out in *section 826(1)* will have the force of law.

(ii) A territory not otherwise within *subparagraph (1)(b)(i)(II)* shall for the purposes of this paragraph be so treated if it is a territory with the government of which arrangements have been made.][93]

(2) Where, as respects any relevant interest received in an accounting period by a company, any part of the foreign tax cannot, apart from this paragraph, be allowed as a credit against corporation tax and, accordingly, the amount of income representing the interest is treated under *paragraph 7(3)(c)* as reduced by that part of the foreign tax, then an amount determined by the formula—

$$\frac{100 - R}{100} \times D$$

where—

R is the rate per cent specified in *section 21(1)*, and

D is the amount of the part of the foreign tax by which the income is to be treated under *paragraph 7(3)(c)* as reduced,

shall be treated for the purposes of *subparagraph (3)* as unrelieved foreign tax of that accounting period.

(3) The aggregate amount of corporation tax payable by a company for an accounting period in respect of relevant interest of the company for the accounting period from foreign companies shall be reduced by the unrelieved foreign tax of that accounting period.][94]

[9FA

(1) In this paragraph—

"aggregate amount of corporation tax payable by a company for an accounting period in respect of foreign branch income of the company for the accounting period" means so much of the corporation tax which, apart from this paragraph, would be payable by the company for that accounting period as would not have been payable had the foreign branch income been disregarded for the purposes of tax;

"*foreign branch*", in relation to a company, means a branch or agency of the company in a territory other than the State through which the company carries on a trade in that territory;

"*foreign branch income*", in relation to a company, means so much of the income of the company as is attributable to a foreign branch;

"*foreign tax*", in relation to foreign branch income of a company, means tax which—

(a) is paid under the laws of the territory in which the foreign branch is situated on income attributable to that branch, and

(b) corresponds to corporation tax.

(2) Where, as respects any foreign branch income of a company for an accounting period, any part of the foreign tax cannot, apart from this paragraph, be allowed as a credit against corporation tax and, accordingly, the amount of the income is treated under *paragraph 7(3)(c)* as reduced by that part of the foreign tax, then an amount equal to the aggregate of—

(a) where income that is chargeable to tax at the rate specified in *section 21(1)* for the accounting period is treated under *paragraph 7(3)(c)* as reduced, an amount determined by the formula—

$$\frac{100 - R}{100} \times D$$

where—

R is the rate per cent specified in *section 21(1)*, and

D is the amount by which that income is so treated as reduced,

and

(b) where income that is chargeable to tax at the rate specified in *section 21A(3)* for the accounting period is treated under *paragraph 7(3)(c)* as reduced, an amount determined by the formula—

$$\frac{100 - R}{100} \times D$$

where—

R is the rate per cent specified in *section 21A(3)*, and

D is the amount by which that income is so treated as reduced,

shall be treated for the purposes of [*subparagraphs (3)* and *(4)*][95] as unrelieved foreign tax of that accounting period.

(3) The aggregate amount of corporation tax payable by a company for an accounting period in respect of foreign branch income of the company for the accounting period shall be reduced by the unrelieved foreign tax of that accounting period.

[(4) Where the unrelieved foreign tax of an accounting period of a company exceeds the aggregate amount of corporation tax payable by the company for the accounting period in respect of foreign branch income of the company for that accounting period, the excess shall be carried forward and treated as unrelieved foreign tax of the next succeeding accounting period, and so on for succeeding accounting periods.][96]

Unilateral Relief (capital gains)

9FB

(1) To the extent appearing from the following provisions of this paragraph, relief (in this paragraph referred to as "*unilateral relief*") from capital gains tax (including corporation tax in respect of chargeable gains) in respect of chargeable gains accruing to a person on the disposal of an asset (in this paragraph referred to as a "*specified asset*") which is located in a territory other than the State shall be given in respect of tax payable under the law of any specified territory by allowing that tax as a credit against capital gains tax (or as the case may be corporation tax

in respect of chargeable gains), notwithstanding that there are not for the time being in force any arrangements providing for such relief.

(2) Unilateral relief shall be such relief as would fall to be given under this Schedule if arrangements with the government of the specified territory in question contained the provisions in *subparagraphs (3)* and *(4)*, and a reference in this Schedule to credit under arrangements shall be construed as including a reference to unilateral relief.

(3) Subject to *Part 1* and to *subparagraph (5)*, credit for tax paid under the law of a specified territory and computed by reference to a capital gain of a person from the disposal by the person of a specified asset, shall be allowed against capital gains tax (or as the case may be corporation tax in respect of chargeable gains) in the State computed by reference to that capital gain.

(4) Credit shall not be allowed by virtue of *subparagraph (3)* for tax paid under the law of a specified territory to the extent that credit may be given for that tax under—

(a) arrangements with the government of the territory, or

(b) any other provision of this Schedule.

(5) Where—

(a) unilateral relief may be given in respect of any chargeable gain, and

(b) it appears that any assessment made in respect of the chargeable gain is not made in respect of the full amount thereof, or is incorrect having regard to the credit, if any, which falls to be given by way of unilateral relief,

then any such assessment may be made or amended as is necessary to ensure that the total amount of the chargeable gain is assessed, and the proper credit, if any, is given in respect thereof.

(6) In this Schedule in its application to unilateral relief, references to tax payable or paid under the law of a territory outside the State include only references to taxes which are charged on capital gains and which correspond to income tax, corporation tax or capital gains tax.

(7) In this paragraph "*specified territory*" means any of the following territories with the government of which arrangements have been made, that is to say, the Kingdom of Belgium, Cyprus, the Republic of France, the Federal Republic of Germany, the Italian Republic, Japan, the Grand Duchy of Luxembourg, the Kingdom of the Netherlands, Pakistan or Zambia.][97]

Dividends paid by companies that are taxed as a group under the law of a territory outside the State

[9G

(1) This paragraph applies in any case where—

(a) under the law of a territory outside the State, tax is payable by a company (in this paragraph referred to as the "*responsible company*") resident in that territory in respect of the aggregate profits, or aggregate profits and aggregate gains, of that company and one or more other companies (in this paragraph referred to as the "*consolidated companies*"), taken together as a single taxable entity, and

(b) a dividend is paid—

(i) by any one of the consolidated companies (in this paragraph referred to as the "*paying company*") to a company that is not one of the consolidated companies (in this paragraph referred to as the "*recipient company*"), or

(ii) by a company that is not one of the consolidated companies (in this paragraph referred to as the "*third company*") to any one of the consolidated companies.

(2) (a) Where this paragraph applies, then for the purposes of allowing credit under this Schedule for foreign tax in respect of profits attributable to dividends this Schedule shall apply with any necessary modifications as if—

(i) the consolidated companies, taken together, were a single company (in this paragraph referred to as the "*single company*"),

(ii) any dividend paid by any of the consolidated companies to a recipient company was paid by the single company,

(iii) any dividend paid by a third company to any one of the consolidated companies was paid to the single company,

(iv) the single company is related to the recipient company if the paying company is related to the recipient company,

(v) the third company is related to the single company if the third company is related to that one of the consolidated companies to which it paid the dividend, and

(vi) the single company is resident in the territory in which the responsible company is resident,

so that the relevant profits for the purposes of *paragraph 8* is a single aggregate figure in respect of the single company and the foreign tax paid by the responsible company is foreign tax paid by the single company.

(b) For the purposes of this paragraph—

(i) a single company that is treated as paying a dividend shall be treated as connected with a relevant company (within the meaning given to it in *paragraph 9B)* in relation to the dividend if the company that paid the dividend is connected with that relevant company,

(ii) a relevant dividend (within the meaning given to it in *paragraph 9A*) paid by any one of the consolidated companies to a recipient company will be treated as a relevant dividend paid by the single company to that recipient company,

(iii) references in *paragraph 8* to "*body corporate*" shall include references to a single company within the meaning of this paragraph.][98]

Dividends paid out of transferred profits

[9H

(1) This paragraph applies in any case where—

(a) under the law of a territory outside the State, tax is paid by a company (in this paragraph referred to as the "*first company*") resident outside the State in respect of any of its profits,

(b) some or all of those profits become profits of another company (in this paragraph referred to as the "*second company*") resident outside the State otherwise than by virtue of the payment of a dividend to the second company, and

(c) the second company pays a dividend out of those profits to another company, wherever resident.

(2) Where this paragraph applies, then for the purposes of allowing credit under this Schedule for foreign tax in respect of profits of the first company attributable to any dividends paid—

(a) by any company (whether or not the second company) resident outside the State,

(b) to a company resident in the State,

this Schedule shall apply with any necessary modifications as if the second company had paid the tax paid by the first company in respect of those profits of the first company which have become profits of the second company in accordance with subparagraph (1)(*b*).

(3) Subparagraphs (1) and (2) are subject to the following limitations—

(a) the credit against corporation tax allowable to a company resident in the State shall not exceed the amount which would have been allowable to that company had those profits become profits of the second company by virtue of the payment of a dividend by the first company to the second company, and

(b) no tax shall be taken into account in respect of profits referred to in subparagraph (1) where such profits become the profits of the second company by virtue of a scheme or arrangement the purpose or one of the main purposes of which is the avoidance of tax.][99]

Dividends: additional credit

[91.

(1) In this paragraph—

"*excluded dividend*" means a dividend, or any part of a dividend, paid by a source company to a relevant company, in so far as it is paid out of so much, if any, of the relevant profits of a source company, as—

(a) has not been subject to tax, and

(b) has been received, from a company which is connected with the relevant company and is not resident in a relevant Member State—

(i) directly by means of a dividend or other distribution of profits, being profits which have not been subject to tax, or

(ii) indirectly, from the profits mentioned in subclause (i), by the payment of dividends, or the making of other distributions, by one or more companies, without the income or profits represented by any of those dividends or distributions having been subject to tax;

"*relevant company*", in relation to a dividend, means a company that—

(a) is resident in the State, or

(b) is, by virtue of the law of a relevant Member State other than the State, resident for the purposes of tax in such a Member State and the dividend forms part of the profits of a branch or agency in the State;

"*relevant dividend*" means so much of a dividend as is neither—

(a) an excluded dividend, nor

(b) a dividend which, by virtue of *section 21B(4)(c)*, is not to be taken into account in computing income for corporation tax;

"*source company*" means a company which—

(a) is not resident in the State, and

(b) is, by virtue of the law of a relevant Member State other than the State, resident for the purposes of tax in such a Member State;

"*tax*", except in the case of corporation tax in the State, means—

(a) tax imposed in a country other than the State, which corresponds to such corporation tax, and

(b) tax, corresponding to income tax in the State, which is imposed in a country other than the State by deduction from dividends or other distributions of profits,

but [...][100] any tax charged by reference to a dividend or other distribution of profits such that most of the value of that dividend or distribution is exempted from that charge to tax shall be excluded from the meaning of "*tax*".

(2) For the purposes of this paragraph, the relevant profits of a source company in relation to a dividend shall be—

(a) if the dividend is paid for a specified period, the profits of that period,

(b) if the dividend is not paid for a specified period but is paid out of specified profits, those profits, or

(c) if the dividend is paid neither for a specified period nor out of specified profits, the profits of the last period for which accounts of the body corporate were made up which ended before the dividend became payable,

but if, in a case within clause (a) or (c), the total dividend exceeds the profits available for distribution of the period mentioned in clause (a) or (c), as the case may be, the relevant profits shall be the profits of that period together with so much of the profits available for distribution of preceding periods (other than profits previously distributed or previously treated as relevant for the purposes of this subparagraph) as is equal to the excess, and for this purpose the profits of the most recent preceding period shall first be taken into account, then the profits of the next most recent preceding period, and so on.

(3) Where a source company pays a relevant dividend to a relevant company then, for the purpose of allowing credit against corporation tax for foreign tax in respect of that dividend, there shall, subject to *paragraph 4*, and *subparagraph (5)*, be taken into account, as if it were tax payable in respect of that dividend under the law of the territory in which a source company is resident, an amount (referred to in this paragraph as "*additional foreign credit*") determined in accordance with *subparagraph (4)*.

(4) The additional foreign credit referred to in *subparagraph (3)* in respect of a relevant dividend shall be—

(a) where the relevant dividend is subject to corporation tax at the rate specified in *section 21(1)*, an amount determined by the formula—

$$(A \times B) - C$$

where—

A is the amount of the relevant dividend brought into charge to corporation tax in the State,

B is the lower of—

(i) the rate per cent specified in *section 21(1)*, or

(ii) the rate per cent of tax, which corresponds, in the relevant Member State in which the source company is resident for the purposes of tax, to corporation tax in the State, applicable to the relevant profits in relation to the relevant dividend,

and

C is the amount of the credit for tax against corporation tax attributable to the relevant dividend which, apart from this paragraph, would be allowable under this Schedule,

or

(b) where the relevant dividend is [subject to corporation tax at the rate specified in *section 21A(3)(a)*][101], the amount determined by the formula—

$$(A \times B) - C$$

where—

A is the amount of the relevant dividend brought into charge to corporation tax in the State,

B is the lower of—

(i) 25 per cent, or

(ii) the rate per cent of tax, which corresponds, in the relevant Member State in which the source company is resident for the purposes of tax, to corporation tax in the State, applicable to the relevant profits in relation to the relevant dividend,

and

C is the amount of the credit for tax against corporation tax attributable to the relevant dividend which, apart from this paragraph, would be allowable under this Schedule.

[(4A) (a) Where the relevant profits in relation to the relevant dividend referred to in *clause (a)* or *(b)* of *subparagraph (4)* have not been subject to tax, which corresponds to corporation tax in the State, but are attributable to profits of a company which have been subject to such tax, then, for the purposes of *subparagraph (4)*, the rate per cent of tax, which is referred to in *clause (a)* or *(b)* of that subparagraph as applicable to the relevant profits in relation to the relevant dividend, shall be deemed to be the rate per cent of tax, which corresponds to corporation tax in the State, applicable to those profits of that company which have been subject to such tax.

(b) For the purposes of *clause (a)* and *subparagraphs (3)* and *(4)*—

(i) each part, if any, of a relevant dividend mentioned in *clause (a)* or *(b)* of *subparagraph (4)*, being—

(I) an amount (referred to in this subclause as the "*directly taxed amount*"), which is so much of the relevant dividend as does not exceed the relevant profits in relation to the relevant dividend which have been subject to tax, which corresponds to corporation tax in the State, or

(II) so much of the excess of the relevant profits in relation to the relevant dividend over the directly taxed amount as is attributable to profits of a company which have been subject to tax, which corresponds to corporation tax in the State,

shall be treated as a separate relevant dividend, and

(ii) the aggregate value of the parts of the relevant dividend so treated under *subclause (i)* shall not exceed the value of that relevant dividend.

(c) For the purposes of this subparagraph—

(i) profits of a company are attributable to the profits of another company if they have been received directly or indirectly by the payment of dividends or the making of distributions by one or more companies directly or indirectly from the profits of that other company, and

(ii) relevant profits in relation to a relevant dividend shall not be attributable to the same profits of a company more than once.

(d) For the purposes of *clause (c)(ii)*, any profits of a company, other than relevant profits in relation to a relevant dividend, and any profits of any other company to which they are attributable shall be deemed to be the same profits.][102]

(5) The provisions of *paragraph 9E* shall not apply to 40 any additional foreign credit calculated in accordance with this paragraph.

(6) This paragraph shall not apply to dividends paid in any case where *paragraph 9H* applies.][103]

PART 3

Miscellaneous

10. Credit shall not be allowed under the arrangements against the Irish taxes chargeable in respect of any income of any person if the person in question elects that credit shall not be allowed in respect of that income.

11. Where under the arrangements relief may be given either in the State or in the territory in relation to which the arrangements are made in respect of any income, and it appears that the assessment to income tax or to corporation tax made in respect of the income is not made in respect of the full amount of that income or is incorrect having regard to the credit, if any, which is to be given under the arrangements, [that assessment may be amended to ensure that the total amount of the income is assessed and the proper credit, if any, is given in respect of that income, and where the income is entrusted to any person in the State for payment, an assessment to income tax may be made or amended on the recipient of the income under Case IV of Schedule D.][104]

12.

(1) In this paragraph—

"*the relevant year of assessment*", in relation to credit for foreign tax in respect of any income, means the year of assessment for which that income is to be charged to income tax or would be so charged if any income tax were chargeable in respect of that income;

"*the relevant accounting period*", in relation to credit for foreign tax in respect of any income, means the accounting period for which that income is to be charged to corporation tax or would be so charged if any corporation tax were chargeable in respect of that income.

(2) Subject to *paragraph 13*, any claim for an allowance by means of credit for foreign tax in respect of any income shall be made in writing to the inspector not later than 6 years from the end of the relevant year of assessment or the relevant accounting period, as the case may be, and, if the inspector objects to any such claim, it shall be heard and determined by the Appeal Commissioners as if it were an appeal to the Appeal Commissioners against an assessment to income tax and the provisions of the Income Tax Acts relating to the rehearing of an appeal and to the statement of a case for the opinion of the High Court on a point of law shall, with the necessary modifications, apply accordingly.

13. Where the amount of any credit given under the arrangements is rendered excessive or insufficient by reason of any adjustment of the amount of any tax payable either in the State or in the territory in relation to which the arrangements are made, nothing in the Tax Acts limiting the time for the making of assessments or claims for relief shall apply to any assessment or claim to which the adjustment gives rise, being an assessment or claim made not later than 6 years from the time when all such assessments, adjustments and other determinations have been made, as are material in determining whether any, and if so what, credit is to be given.

[14. The provisions of this Schedule shall apply for income levy as they apply for universal social charge with any necessary modifications.][105]

Amendments

[1] Inserted by FA98 s60(a). Applies as respects accounting periods ending on or after the 1st day of April, 1998.

[2] Inserted by FA13 s26(1)(a). Has effect as if they had come into operation for the year of assessment (within the meaning of section 2) 2011 and each subsequent year of assessment.

[3] Substituted by FA07 sched2(1)(ah)(i)(I). Has effect as on and from 2 April 2007.

[4] Deleted by FA98 sched3(12).

[5] Substituted by FA11 s3(1)(n). Applies for the year of assessment 2011 and each subsequent year of assessment.

[6] Inserted by FA02 s38(a)(i).

[7] Substituted by FA98 s60(b). Applies as respects accounting periods ending on or after the 1st day of April, 1998.

[8] Substituted by FA07 sched2(1)(ah)(i)(II). Has effect as on and from 2 April 2007.

[9] Inserted by FA02 s38(a)(ii).

[10] Inserted by FA13 s26(1)(b). Has effect as if they had come into operation for the year of assessment (within the meaning of section 2) 2011 and each subsequent year of assessment.

---

[11] Substituted by FA01 s41(1)(a). This section applies as respects accounting periods ending on or after 15 February 2001.

[12] Substituted by FA12 sched1(26)(a).

[13] Deleted by FA12 sched1(26)(b).

[14] Substituted by FA08 s49(1)(a). Applies as on and from 31 January 2008. Shall be deemed to have applied as respects any company as on and from 1 January 2006, if an election in writing is made by the company to the Revenue Commissioners to that effect.

[15] Inserted by FA06 s63(a).

[16] Deleted by FA12 sched1(26)(c).

[17, 20] Substituted by FA00 s71(1)(a). This section shall apply as respects accounting periods ending on or after 1 January 2000.

[18] Deleted by FA12 sched1(26)(d).

[19] Inserted by FA01 s41(1)(b). This section applies as respects accounting periods ending on or after 15 February 2001.

[21] Substituted by FA02 s57(a)(i).

[22] Substituted by FA12 s52(1)(a). Applies in respect of leasing income (within the meaning of paragraph 9DC(1)(a) (inserted by subsection (1)) of Schedule 24) received on or after 1 January 2012.

[23] Deleted by FA12 sched1(26)(e).

[24] Deleted by FA12 sched1(26)(f).

[25] Inserted by FA13 sched2(1)(l)(i). Has effect on and from 27 March 2013.

[26] Deleted by FA12 s52(1)(b). Applies in respect of leasing income (within the meaning of paragraph 9DC(1)(a) (inserted by subsection (1)) of Schedule 24) received on or after 1 January 2012.

[27] Inserted by FA02 s57(a)(ii)(III).

[28] Inserted by FA13 sched2(1)(l)(ii). Has effect on and from 27 March 2013.

[29, 32] Inserted by FA12 s52(1)(b). Applies in respect of leasing income (within the meaning of paragraph 9DC(1)(a) (inserted by subsection (1)) of Schedule 24) received on or after 1 January 2012.

[30] Inserted by FA10 s46(1)(c). This section applies in respect of royalties received on or after 1 January 2010.

[31] Inserted by FA13 sched2(1)(l)(iii). Has effect on and from 27 March 2013.

[33] Inserted by FA11 s35(1). Shall have effect for an accounting period of a company for which the return under section 951 for the purposes of corporation tax is made by the company on or after 7 December 2010, and for any other accounting period, in relation to any claim to repayment of, or reduction of liability to, corporation tax for that accounting period where such claim is made on or after 7 December 2010.

[34] Substituted by FA07 sched2(1)(ah)(ii). Has effect as on and from 2 April 2007.

[35] Inserted by F(No.2)A13 s28(1)(a). Applies as respects any relief, deduction, credit in relation to tax or, as the case may be, a reduction in the amount of tax payable, details of which fall to be included in particulars on a return, required to be delivered under section 951, which was delivered on or after 31 January 2008.

[36] Inserted by FA13 s26(1)(c). Has effect as if they had come into operation for the year of assessment (within the meaning of section 2) 2011 and each subsequent year of assessment.

[37] Substituted by F(No.2)A13 s28(1)(b)(i). Applies as respects accounting periods beginning on or after 1 January 2014.

[38] Substituted by F(No.2)A13 s28(1)(b)(ii). Applies as respects any relief, deduction, credit in relation to tax or, as the case may be, a reduction in the amount of tax payable, details of which fall to be included in particulars on a return, required to be delivered under section 951, which was delivered on or after 31 January 2008.

[39] Inserted by FA13 s26(1)(e). Has effect as if they had come into operation for the year of assessment (within the meaning of section 2) 2011 and each subsequent year of assessment.

[40] Inserted by FA99 s81(b)(i).

[41] Substituted by FA10 s41(2)(a). This section applies to income and dividends received on or after 4 February 2010.

[42] Substituted by FA01 s41(1)(c)(i). This section applies as respects accounting periods ending on or after 15 February 2001.

[43] Substituted by FA02 s38(b)(i).

[44] Substituted by FA02 s38(b)(ii).

[45] Inserted by FA01 s41(1)(c)(ii). This section applies as respects accounting periods ending on or after 15 February 2001.

[46] Inserted by FA10 s41(2)(b). This section applies to income and dividends received on or after 4 February 2010.

[47] Substituted by FA10 s41(2)(c). This section applies to income and dividends received on or after 4 February 2010.

[48] Substituted by FA01 s41(1)(c)(iii). This section applies as respects accounting periods ending on or after 15 February 2001.

[49] Substituted by FA04 s31(1)(a)(i). This section comes into operation on such day or days as the Minister for Finance by order appoints, either generally or with reference to any particular purpose or provision, and different days may be so appointed for different purposes or different provisions.

[50] Deleted by FA04 s31(1)(a)(ii). This section comes into operation on such day or days as the Minister for Finance by order appoints, either generally or with reference to any particular purpose or provision, and different days may be so appointed for different purposes or different provisions.

[51] Inserted by FA99 s81(b)(ii).

[52] Deleted by FA12 sched1(26)(g).

[53] Substituted by FA02 s57(b).

[54, 55] Substituted by FA01 s41(1)(d)(i). This section applies as respects accounting periods ending on or after 15 February 2001.

[56] Substituted by FA02 s38(c)(ii).

[57] Inserted by FA01 s41(1)(d)(ii). This section applies as respects accounting periods ending on or after 15 February 2001.

[58, 65] Substituted by FA01 s41(1)(d)(iii). This section applies as respects accounting periods ending on or after 15 February 2001.

[59, 60, 61] Substituted by FA00 s71(1)(b)(i). This section shall be deemed to have applied as respects accounting periods ending on or after 1 April 1998.

[62] Substituted by FA06 s63(b).

[63, 64] Substituted by FA04 s31(1)(b)(i). This section comes into operation on such day or days as the Minister for Finance by order appoints, either generally or with reference to any particular purpose or provision, and different days may be so appointed for different purposes or different provisions.

[66] Inserted by FA00 s71(1)(b)(ii). This section shall be deemed to have applied as respects accounting periods ending on or after 1 April 1998.

[67, 68] Substituted by FA01 s41(1)(d)(iv). This section applies as respects accounting periods ending on or after 15 February 2001.

[69] Deleted by FA01 s41(1)(d)(v). This section applies as respects accounting periods ending on or after 15 February 2001.

[70, 71, 74, 75] Substituted by FA99 s81(c)(i).

[72] Substituted by FA04 s31(1)(b)(ii)(I). This section comes into operation on such day or days as the Minister for Finance by order appoints, either generally or with reference to any particular purpose or provision, and different days may be so appointed for different purposes or different provisions.

[73, 77] Substituted by FA99 s81(c)(ii).

[76] Substituted by FA04 s31(1)(b)(ii)(II). This section comes into operation on such day or days as the Minister for Finance by order appoints, either generally or with reference to any particular purpose or provision, and different days may be so appointed for different purposes or different provisions.

[78] Inserted by FA98 s60(c). Applies as respects accounting periods ending on or after the 1st day of April, 1998.

[79, 80] Substituted by FA02 s38(d).

[81] Inserted by FA01 s41(1)(e). This section applies as respects accounting periods ending on or after 15 February 2001.

[82] Substituted by FA03 s60(2)(a). Applies as respects accounting periods ending on or after 6 February.

[83] Inserted by FA03 s60(2)(b)(i). Applies as respects accounting periods ending on or after 6 February.

[84] Inserted by FA03 s60(2)(b)(ii). Applies as respects accounting periods ending on or after 6 February.

[85] Deleted by FA12 sched1(26)(h).

[86] Deleted by FA12 sched1(26)(i).

[87] Inserted by FA07 s36(1)(b)(i).

[88] Deleted by FA12 sched1(26)(j).

[89] Inserted by FA12 s49(1). Applies as respects relevant royalties (within the meaning of paragraph 9DB(1)(a) of Schedule 24) received on or after 1 January 2012.

[90] Inserted by FA12 s52(1)(c). Applies in respect of leasing income (within the meaning of paragraph 9DC(1)(a) (inserted by subsection (1)) of Schedule 24) received on or after 1 January 2012.

[91] Inserted by F(No.2)A13 s28(1)(c). Apply as respects accounting periods beginning on or after 1 January 2014.

[92] Substituted by FA08 s43(1)(f). This section shall be deemed to have applied as respects a dividend received on or after 1 January 2007.

[93] Inserted by F(No.2)A08 s33(h). This section is deemed to have come into force and takes effect as on and from 1 January 2009.

[94] Inserted by FA06 s63(c).

[95] Substituted by FA10 s47(1)(a). Applies as respects accounting periods ending on or after 1 January 2010.

[96] Inserted by FA10 s47(1)(b). Applies as respects accounting periods ending on or after 1 January 2010.

[97] Inserted by FA07 s36(1)(b)(ii).

[98] Inserted by FA06 s63(d).

[99] Inserted by FA08 s49(1)(b). Applies to dividends paid on or after 31 January 2008.

[100] Deleted by F(No.2)A13 40(1)(a). Has effect as respects dividends paid on or after 18 December 2013.

[101] Substituted by F(No.2)A13 40(1)(b). Has effect as respects dividends paid on or after 18 December 2013.

[102] Inserted by F(No.2)A13 40(1)(c). Has effect as respects dividends paid on or after 18 December 2013.

[103] Inserted by FA13 s26(1)(f). Applies to dividends paid on or after 1 January 2013.

[104] Substituted by FA12 sched4(part 2)(g).

[105] Inserted by FA13 s26(1)(g). Has effect as if it had come into operation for the years of assessment (within the meaning of section 2) 2009 and 2010.

Revenue Briefings

Tax Briefing

Tax Briefing June 1998 – Issue 32 pg 15 -Double tax relief, foreign effective rates

Tax Briefing April 2004 – Issue 55 pg 6 – Credit for Foreign Tax

Tax Briefing July 2007 – Issue 66 – Finance Act 2007 – Double tax relief
Tax Briefing November 2007 – Issue 67 – Foreign Effective Rates (with effect from 1 January 2007)
Tax Briefing November 2007 – Issue 67 – Double tax relief – Legal and General Case and Related Issues

Statements of Practice

SP-CT: Foreign Branch Double Taxation Relief

Cross References

From Schedule 24

Section 1 Interpretation of this Act.
Section 9 Subsidiaries.
Section 21 The charge to corporation tax and exclusion of income tax and capital gains tax.
Section 21A Higher rate of corporation tax.
Section 26 General scheme of corporation tax.
Section 243A Restriction of relevant charges on income.
Section 381 Right to repayment of tax by reference to losses.
Section 410 Group payments.
Section 411 Surrender of relief between members of groups and consortia.
Section 413 Profits or assets available for distribution.
Section 414 Meaning of "the profit distribution".
Section 415 Meaning of "the notional winding up".
Section 418 Beneficial percentage.
Section 442 Interpretation (Part 14).
Section 448 Relief from corporation tax.
Section 449 Credit for foreign tax not otherwise credited.
Section 450 Double taxation relief.
Section 644B Relief from corporation tax in respect of income from dealing in residential development land.
Section 713 Investment income reserved for policyholders.
Section 723 Special investment policies.
Section 738 Undertakings for collective investment.
Section 826 Agreements for relief from double taxation.
Section 830 Relief to certain companies liable to foreign tax.
Section 831 Implementation of Council Directive No. 90/435/EEC concerning the common system of taxation applicable in the case of parent companies and subsidiaries of different Member States.
Section 833 Convention with United States of America.

To Schedule 24

Section 29A Temporary non-residents.
Section 247 Relief to companies on loans applied in acquiring interest in other companies.
Section 267J Credit for foreign tax.
Section 449 Credit for foreign tax not otherwise credited.
Section 450 Double taxation relief.
Section 697M Exclusion of reliefs, deductions and set-offs.
Section 749 Dealers in securities.
Section 826 Agreements for relief from double taxation.
Section 826A Unilateral relief from double taxation.
Section 827 Application to corporation tax of arrangements made in relation to corporation profits tax under old law.
Section 828 Capital gains tax: double taxation relief.
Section 829 Treatment for double taxation relief purposes of foreign tax incentive reliefs.
Section 830 Relief to certain companies liable to foreign tax.
Section 831 Implementation of Council Directive No. 90/435/EEC concerning the common system of taxation applicable in the case of parent companies and subsidiaries of different Member States.

SCHEDULE 24A

Arrangements Made by the Government with the Government of any Territory Outside the State in Relation to Affording Relief from Double Taxation and Exchanging Information in Relation to Tax

PART 1

Arrangements in Relation to Affording Relief from Double Taxation in Respect of the Taxes Referred to in Section 826(1), Made by the Government and Specified in Orders Made by the Government

[1. The Double Taxation Relief (Taxes on Income and Capital) (Australia) Order 1983 (S.I. No. 406 of 1983).

[1A. The Double Taxation Relief (Taxes on Income) (Republic of Albania) Order 2011 (S.I. No. 16 of 2011).][1]

[1AA. The Double Taxation Relief (Taxes on Income and on Capital) (Republic of Armenia) Order 2012 (S.I. No. 21 of 2012).][2]

[2. The Double Taxation Relief (Taxes on Income) (Republic of Austria) Order 1967 (S.I. No. 250 of 1967), the Double Taxation Relief (Taxes on Income and Capital Gains) (Republic of Austria) Order 1988 (S.I. No. 29 of 1988) and the Double Taxation Relief (Taxes on Income and Capital Gains) (Republic of Austria) Order 2011 (S.I. No. 30 of 2011).][3]

[2A. The Double Taxation Relief (Taxes on Income and Capital Gains) (Kingdom of Bahrain) Order 2010 (S.I. No. 24 of 2010).

2B. The Double Taxation Relief (Taxes on Income and on Capital) (Republic of Belarus) Order 2010 (S.I. No. 25 of 2010).][4]

[3. The Double Taxation Relief (Taxes on Income) (Kingdom of Belgium) Order 1973 (S.I. No. 66 of 1973) and the Double Taxation Relief (Taxes on Income) (Kingdom of Belgium) Order 2014 (S.I. No. 466 of 2014).][5]

[3A. The Double Taxation Relief (Taxes on Income and Capital Gains) (Bosnia and Herzegovina) Order 2010 (S.I. No. 17 of 2010).][6]

[3B. The Double Taxation Relief (Taxes on Income) (Botswana) Order 2014 (S.I. No. 467 of 2014).][7]

4. The Double Taxation Relief (Taxes on Income and Capital Gains) (The Republic of Bulgaria) Order 2000 (S.I. No. 372 of 2000).

5. The Double Taxation Relief (Taxes on Income and Capital Gains) (Government of Canada) Order 2004 (S.I. No. 773 of 2004).

[5A. The Double Taxation Relief (Taxes on Income and Capital Gains) (Republic of Chile) Order 2005 (S.I. No. 815 of 2005).][8]

6. The Double Taxation Relief (Taxes on Income) (People's Republic of China) Order 2000 (S.I. No. 373 of 2000).

7. The Double Taxation Relief (Taxes on Income and Capital Gains) (Republic of Croatia) Order 2002 (S.I. No. 574 of 2002).

8. The Double Taxation Relief (Taxes on Income) (Cyprus) Order 1970 (S.I. No. 79 of 1970).

9. The Double Taxation Relief (Taxes on Income and Capital) (Czech Republic) Order 1995 (S.I. No. 321 of 1995).

[10. The Double Taxation Relief (Taxes on Income) (Kingdom of Denmark) Order 1993 (S.I. No. 286 of 1993) and the Double Taxation Relief (Taxes on Income) (Kingdom of Denmark) Order 2014 (S.I. No. 468 of 2014).][9]

10. The Double Taxation Relief (Taxes on Income) (Kingdom of Denmark) Order 1993 (S.I. No. 286 of 1993).

[10A. The Double Taxation Relief (Taxes on Income and Capital Gains) (Arab Republic of Egypt) Order 2013 (S.I. No. 27 of 2013).][10]

11. The Double Taxation Relief (Taxes on Income and Capital Gains) (Republic of Estonia) Order 1998 (S.I. No. 496 of 1998).

12. The Double Taxation Relief (Taxes on Income and Capital Gains) (Republic of Finland) Order 1993 (S.I. No. 289 of 1993).

13. The Double Taxation Relief (Taxes on Income) (Republic of France) Order 1970 (S.I. No. 162 of 1970).

[13A. The Double Taxation Relief (Taxes on Income) (Georgia) Order 2010 (S.I. No. 18 of 2010).][11]

[14. The Double Taxation Relief (Taxes on Income and Capital and Gewerbesteuer (Trade Tax)) (Federal Republic of Germany) Order 1962 (S.I. No. 212 of 1962) and the Double Taxation Relief (Taxes on Income and on Capital) (Federal Republic of Germany) Order 2011 (S.I. No. 31 of 2011).][12]

[14A. The Double Taxation Relief (Taxes on Income and on Capital) (Federal Republic of Germany) Order 2012 (S.I. No. 22 of 2012).][13]

15. The Double Taxation Relief (Taxes on Income and Capital Gains) (Government of the Hellenic Republic) Order 2004 (S.I. No. 774 of 2004).

[15A. The Double Taxation Relief (Taxes on Income) (Hong Kong Special Administrative Region) Order 2011 (S.I. No. 17 of 2011).][14]

16. The Double Taxation Relief (Taxes on Income) (Republic of Hungary) Order 1995 (S.I. No. 301 of 1995).

17. The Double Taxation Relief (Taxes on Income and on Capital) (Republic of Iceland) Order 2004 (S.I. No. 775 of 2004).

18. The Double Taxation Relief (Taxes on Income and Capital Gains) (Republic of India) Order 2001 (S.I. No. 521 of 2001).

19. The Double Taxation Relief (Taxes on Income) (Italy) Order 1973 (S.I. No. 64 of 1973).

20. The Double Taxation Relief (Taxes on Income) (State of Israel) Order 1995 (S.I. No. 323 of 1995).

21. The Double Taxation Relief (Taxes on Income) (Japan) Order 1974 (S.I. No. 259 of 1974).

22. The Double Taxation Relief (Taxes on Income and Capital Gains) (Republic of Korea) Order 1991 (S.I. No. 290 of 1991).

[22A. The Double Taxation Relief (Taxes on Income) (State of Kuwait) Order 2011 (S.I. No. 21 of 2011).][15]

23. The Double Taxation Relief (Taxes on Income and Capital Gains) (Republic of Latvia) Order 1997 (S.I. No. 504 of 1997).

24. The Double Taxation Relief (Taxes on Income and Capital Gains) (Republic of Lithuania) Order 1997 (S.I. No. 503 of 1997).

[25. The Double Taxation Relief (Taxes on Income and on Capital) (Grand Duchy of Luxembourg) Order 1973 (S.I. No. 65 of 1973) and the Double Taxation Relief (Taxes on Income and on Capital) (Grand Duchy of Luxembourg) Order 2014 (S.I. No. 469 of 2014).][16]

[25A. The Double Taxation Relief (Taxes on Income) (Republic of Macedonia) Order 2008 (S.I. No. 463 of 2008).][17]

[26. The Double Taxation Relief (Taxes on Income) (Malaysia) Order 1998 (S.I. No. 495 of 1998) and the Double Taxation Relief (Taxes on Income) (Malaysia) Order 2011 (S.I. No. 32 of 2011).][18]

[26A. The Double Taxation Relief (Taxes on Income) (Malta) Order 2008 (S. I. No. 502 of 2008).][19]

27. The Double Taxation Relief (Taxes on Income and Capital Gains) (The United Mexican States) Order 1998 (S.I. No. 497 of 1998).

[27A. The Double Taxation Relief (Taxes on Income) (Republic of Moldova) Order 2010 (S.I. No. 19 of 2010).][20]

[27B. The Double Taxation Relief (Taxes on Income) (Montenegro) Order 2011 (S.I. No. 18 of 2011).

27C. The Double Taxation Relief (Taxes on Income) (Kingdom of Morocco) Order 2011 (S.I. No. 19 of 2011).][21]

28. The Double Taxation Relief (Taxes on Income and Capital) (Kingdom of the Netherlands) Order 1970 (S.I. No. 22 of 1970).

29. The Double Taxation Relief (Taxes on Income and Capital Gains) (New Zealand) Order 1988 (S.I. No. 30 of 1988).

30. The Double Taxation Relief (Taxes on Income and on Capital) (Kingdom of Norway) Order 2001 (S.I. No. 520 of 2001).

31. The Double Taxation Relief (Taxes on Income) (Pakistan) Order 1974 (S.I. No. 260 of 1974).

[31A. The Double Taxation Relief (Taxes on Income and Capital Gains) (Republic of Panama) Order 2012 (S.I. No. 25 of 2012)][22].

32. The Double Taxation Relief (Taxes on Income) (Republic of Poland) Order 1995 (S.I. No. 322 of 1995).

33. The Double Taxation Relief (Taxes on Income) (Portuguese Republic) Order 1994 (S.I. No. 102 of 1994) and the Double Taxation Relief (Taxes on Income) (Portuguese Republic) Order 2005 (S.I. No. 816 of 2005).

[33A. The Double Taxation Relief (Taxes on Income and Capital Gains) (State of Qatar) Order 2013 (S.I. No. 28 of 2013).][23]

34. The Double Taxation Relief (Taxes on Income and Capital Gains) (Romania) Order 1999 (S.I. No. 427 of 1999).

35. The Double Taxation Relief (Taxes on Income) (Russian Federation) Order 1994 (S.I. No. 428 of 1994).

[35AA. The Double Taxation Relief (Taxes on Income) (Kingdom of Saudi Arabia) Order 2012 (S.I. No. 26 of 2012).][24]

[35A. The Double Taxation Relief (Taxes on Income) (Republic of Serbia) Order 2010 (S.I. No. 20 of 2010).][25]

[35B. The Double Taxation Relief (Taxes on Income) (Republic of Singapore) Order 2011 (S.I. No. 34 of 2011).][26]

36. The Double Taxation Relief (Taxes on Income and Capital Gains) (The Slovak Republic) Order 1999 (S.I. No. 426 of 1999).

37. The Double Taxation Relief (Taxes on Income and Capital Gains) (Republic of Slovenia) Order 2002 (S.I. No. 573 of 2002).

[38. The Double Taxation Relief (Taxes on Income and Capital Gains) (Republic of South Africa) Order 1997 (S.I. No. 478 of 1997) and the Double Taxation Relief (Taxes on Income and Capital Gains) (Republic of South Africa) Order 2011 (S.I. No. 33 of 2011).][27]

39. The Double Taxation Relief (Taxes on Income and Capital Gains) (Kingdom of Spain) Order 1994 (S.I. No. 308 of 1994).

40. The Double Taxation Relief (Taxes on Income and Capital Gains) (Sweden) Order 1987 (S.I. No. 348 of 1987) and the Double Taxation Relief (Taxes on Income and Capital Gains) (Sweden) Order 1993 (S.I. No. 398 of 1993).

[41. The Double Taxation Relief (Taxes on Income and Capital) (Swiss Confederation) Order 1967 (S.I. No. 240 of 1967), the Double Taxation Relief (Taxes on Income and Capital) (Swiss Confederation) Order 1984 (S.I. No. 76 of 1984) and the Double Taxation Relief (Taxes on Income and on Capital) (Swiss Confederation) Order 2013 (S.I. No. 30 of 2013).][28]

[41A. The Double Taxation Relief (Taxes on Income and Capital Gains) (Republic of Turkey) Order 2008 (S. I. No. 501 of 2008).][29]

[41AA. The Double Taxation Relief (Taxes on Income and Capital Gains) (Ukraine) Order 2013 (S.I. No. 397 of 2013).][30]

[41AB. The Double Taxation Relief (Taxes on Income and Capital Gains) (Kingdom of Thailand) Order 2014 (S.I. No. 465 of 2014).][31]

[41B. The Double Taxation Relief (Taxes on Income and Capital Gains) (United Arab Emirates) Order 2011 (S.I. No. 20 of 2011).][32]

42. The Double Taxation Relief (Taxes on Income and Capital Gains) (United Kingdom) Order 1976 (S.I. No. 319 of 1976), the Double Taxation Relief (Taxes on Income and Capital Gains) (United Kingdom) Order 1995 (S.I. No. 209 of 1995) and the Double Taxation Relief (Taxes on Income and Capital Gains) (United Kingdom of Great Britain and Northern Ireland) Order 1998 (S.I. No. 494 of 1998).

43. The Double Taxation Relief (Taxes on Income and Capital Gains) (United States of America) Order 1997 (S.I. No. 477 of 1997) and the Double Taxation Relief (Taxes on Income and Capital Gains) (United States of America) Order 1999 (S.I. No. 425 of 1999).

[43AA. The Double Taxation Relief (Taxes on Income and on Property) (Republic of Uzbekistan) Order 2013 (S.I. No. 31 of 2013).][33]

[43A. The Double Taxation Relief (Taxes on Income)(Socialist Republic of Vietnam) Order 2008 (S.I. No. 453 of 2008).][34]

44. The Double Taxation Relief (Taxes on Income) (Republic of Zambia) Order 1973 (S.I. No. 130 of 1973).

45. The Double Taxation Relief (Taxes on Income) (Adjustment of Profits of Associated Enterprises) (European Community) Order 1994 (S.I. No. 88 of 1994)

as amended by the Double Taxation Relief (Taxes on Income) (Adjustment of Profits of Associated Enterprises) (European Communities) Order 2004 (S.I. No. 40 of 2004), the Double Taxation Relief (Taxes on Income) (Adjustment of Profits of Associated Enterprises) (Republic of Austria, Republic of Finland and Kingdom of Sweden) Order 2004 (S.I. No. 41 of 2004) and the Double Taxation Relief (Taxes on Income) (Adjustment of Profits of Associated Enterprises) (Accession States) Order 2006 (S.I. No. 112 of 2006).

PART 2

Arrangements, Pursuant to Section 826(1A) in Relation to Affording Relief from Double Taxation of Air Transport Undertakings and their Employees, Made by the Government and Specified in Orders Made by the Government

Double Taxation Relief (Air Transport Undertakings and their Employees) (Union of Soviet Socialist Republics) Order 1987 (S.I. No. 349 of 1987).

PART 3

Arrangements, Pursuant to Section 826(1B) in Relation to Exchange of Information Relating to Tax and in Relation to Other Matters Relating to Tax

[1. The Exchange of Information Relating to Taxes (Anguilla) Order 2010 (S.I. No. 21 of 2010).

[1A. The Exchange of Information Relating to Tax Matters (Antigua and Barbuda) Order 2011 (S.I. No. 22 of 2011).

1B. The Exchange of Information Relating to Tax Matters (Belize) Order 2011 (S.I. No. 23 of 2011).][35]

2. The Exchange of Information Relating to Taxes (Bermuda) Order 2010 (S.I. No. 22 of 2010).

[2A. The Exchange of Information Relating to Taxes (British Virgin Islands) Order 2011 (S.I. No. 24 of 2011).][36]

3. The Agreement Concerning Information on Tax Matters (Cayman Islands) Order 2010 (S.I. No. 23 of 2010).

[3A. The Exchange of Information Relating to Tax Matters (Cook Islands) Order 2011 (S.I. No. 25 of 2011).][37]

[3B. The Exchange of Information Relating to Taxes and Tax Matters (Dominica) Order 2013 (S.I. No. 398 of 2013).][38]

4. The Exchange of Information Relating to Taxes (Gibraltar) Order 2010 (S.I. No. 26 of 2010).

[4A. The Exchange of Information Relating to Tax Matters (Grenada) Order 2012 (S.I. No. 23 of 2012).][39]

5. The Exchange of Information Relating to Tax Matters and Double Taxation Relief (Taxes on Income) (Guernsey) Order 2010 (S.I. No. 27 of 2010).][40]

[6. The Exchange of Information relating to Tax Matters and Double Taxation Relief (Taxes on Income)(Isle of Man) Order 2008 (S.I. No. 459 of 2008).][41]

[7. The Exchange of Information Relating to Tax Matters and Double Taxation Relief (Taxes on Income) (Jersey) Order 2010 (S.I. No. 28 of 2010).

8. The Exchange of Information Relating to Taxes (Liechtenstein) Order 2010 (S.I. No. 29 of 2010).

[8A. The Exchange of Information Relating to Tax Matters (Republic of the Marshall Islands) Order 2011 (S.I. No. 26 of 2011).

[8AA. The Exchange of Information Relating to Tax Matters (Montserrat) Order 2013 (S.I. No. 82 of 2013).][42]

8B. The Exchange of Information Relating to Tax Matters (Saint Lucia) Order 2011 (S.I. No. 27 of 2011).

8C. The Exchange of Information Relating to Tax Matters (Saint Vincent and the Grenadines) Order 2011 (S.I. No. 28 of 2011).

8D. The Exchange of Information Relating to Tax Matters (Samoa) Order 2011 (S.I. No. 29 of 2011).][43]

[8E. The Exchange of Information Relating to Taxes (San Marino) Order 2013 (S.I. No. 29 of 2013).][44]

9. The Exchange of Information Relating to Taxes (Turks and Caicos Islands) Order 2010 (S.I. No. 30 of 2010).][45][46]

[9A. The Agreement to Improve Tax Compliance and Provide for Reporting and Exchange of Information concerning Tax Matters (United States of America) Order 2013 (S.I. No. 33 of 2013).][47]

[10. The Exchange of Information Relating to Tax Matters (Republic of Vanuatu) Order 2012 (S.I. No. 24 of 2012).][48]

PART 4

Orders Pursuant to Section 826(1C) in Relation to the Recovery of Tax and in Relation to Other Matters Relating to Tax

[The Mutual Assistance in Tax Matters Order 2013 (S.I. No. 34 of 2013).][49]

Amendments

[1] Inserted by FA11 s80(1)(a). Applies as on and from 6 February 2011.

[2] Inserted by FA12 s137(1)(a)(i). Applies on and from 31 March 2012.

[3] Substituted by FA11 s80(1)(b). Applies as on and from 6 February 2011.

[4] Inserted by FA10 s158(1)(a)(i). Has effect as on and from 3 April 2010.

[5] Substituted by FA14 s96(a).

[6] Inserted by FA10 s158(1)(a)(ii). Has effect as on and from 3 April 2010.

[7] Inserted by FA14 s96(b).

[8] Inserted by FA08 sched8(1)(u). Has effect as on and from 13 March 2008.

[9] Substituted by FA14 s96(c).

[10] Inserted by FA13 s104(1)(a). Applies on and from 27 March 2013.

[11] Inserted by FA10 s158(1)(a)(iii). Has effect as on and from 3 April 2010.

[12] Substituted by FA11 s80(1)(c). Applies as on and from 6 February 2011.

[13] Inserted by FA12 s137(1)(a)(ii). Applies on and from 31 March 2012.

[14] Inserted by FA11 s80(1)(d). Applies as on and from 6 February 2011.

[15] Inserted by FA11 s80(1)(e). Applies as on and from 6 February 2011.

[16] Substituted by FA14 s96(d).

[17] Inserted by F(No.2)A08 sched6(1)(d)(i)(I). Has effect as on and from 24 December 2008.

[18] Substituted by FA11 s80(1)(f). Applies as on and from 6 February 2011.

[19] Inserted by F(No.2)A08 sched6(1)(d)(i)(II). Has effect as on and from 24 December 2008.

[20] Inserted by FA10 s158(1)(a)(iv). Has effect as on and from 3 April 2010.

[21] Inserted by FA11 s80(1)(g). Applies as on and from 6 February 2011.

[22] Inserted by FA12 s137(1)(a)(iii). Applies on and from 31 March 2012.

[23] Inserted by FA13 s104(1)(b). Applies on and from 27 March 2013.

[24] Inserted by FA12 s137(1)(a)(iv). Applies on and from 31 March 2012.

[25] Inserted by FA10 s158(1)(a)(v). Has effect as on and from 3 April 2010.

[26] Inserted by FA11 s80(1)(h). Applies as on and from 6 February 2011.

[27] Substituted by FA11 s80(1)(i). Applies as on and from 6 February 2011.

[28] Substituted by FA13 s104(1)(c). Applies on and from 27 March 2013.

[29] Inserted by FA14 s96(e).

[30] Inserted by F(No.2)A08 sched6(1)(d)(i)(III). Has effect as on and from 24 December 2008.

[31] Inserted by F(No.2)A13 s83(a).

[32] Inserted by FA11 s80(1)(j). Applies as on and from 6 February 2011.

[33] Inserted by FA13 s104(1)(d). Applies on and from 27 March 2013.

[34] Inserted by F(No.2)A08 sched6(1)(d)(i)(IV). Has effect as on and from 24 December 2008.

[35] Inserted by FA11 s80(1)(k). Applies as on and from 6 February 2011.

[36] Inserted by FA11 s80(1)(l). Applies as on and from 6 February 2011.

[37] Inserted by FA11 s80(1)(m). Applies as on and from 6 February 2011.

[38] Inserted by F(No.2)A13 s83(b)(i).

[39] Inserted by FA12 s137(1)(b)(i). Applies on and from 31 March 2012.

[40] Inserted by FA10 s158(1)(b)(ii). Has effect as on and from 3 April 2010.

[41] Substituted by FA10 s158(1)(b)(i). Has effect as on and from 3 April 2010.

[42] Inserted by F(No.2)A13 s83(b)(ii).

[43] Inserted by FA11 s80(1)(n). Applies as on and from 6 February 2011.

[44] Inserted by FA13 s104(1)(e). Applies on and from 27 March 2013.

[45] Inserted by FA10 s158(1)(b)(iii). Has effect as on and from 3 April 2010.

[46] Inserted by FA07 s35(1)(b). Has effect as on and from the date of passing of this Act. FA07 2 April 2007

[47] Inserted by FA13 s104(1)(f). Applies on and from 27 March 2013.

[48] Inserted by FA12 s137(1)(b)(ii). Applies on and from 31 March 2012.

[49] Inserted by FA13 s104(1)(g). Applies on and from 27 March 2013.

Cross References

From Schedule 24A

Section 826 Agreements for relief from double taxation.

SCHEDULE 25

Convention Between the Government of Ireland and the Government of the United States of America for the Avoidance of Double Taxation and the Prevention of Fiscal Evasion with Respect to Taxes on Income [Deleted]

Deleted by FA98 sched3(13).

SCHEDULE 25A

Exemption from Tax in the Case of Gains on Certain Disposals of Shares

[*Section 626B*

Section 626C

Effect of earlier no-gain/no-loss transfer

1.

(1) For the purposes of this paragraph shares are "derived" from other shares only where—

(a) one holding of shares is treated by virtue of *section 584* as the same asset as another, or

(b) there is a sequence of 2 or more of the occurrences mentioned in *paragraph (a)*.

(2) The period for which a company has held shares is treated as extended by any earlier period during which the shares concerned, or shares from which they are derived, were held—

(a) by a company from which the shares concerned were transferred to the company on a no-gain/no-loss transfer, or

(b) by a company from which the shares concerned, or shares from which they are derived, were transferred on a previous no-gain/no-loss transfer—

(i) to a company within clause (*a*), or

(ii) to another company within this clause.

(3) For the purposes of *subparagraph (2)* a "no-gain/no-loss transfer" means a disposal and corresponding acquisition that, by virtue of the Capital Gains Tax Acts, are deemed to be for a consideration such that no gain or loss accrues to the person making the disposal.

(4) Where *subparagraph (2)* applies to extend the period for which a company (in this paragraph referred to as the "*first-mentioned company*") is treated as having held any shares, the first-mentioned company shall be treated for the purposes of *section 626B(2)(a)* as having had at any time the same entitlement—

(a) to shares, and

(b) to any rights enjoyed by virtue of holding shares,

as the company (in this paragraph referred to as the "*other company*") that at that time held the shares concerned or, as the case may be, the shares from which they are derived.

(5) The shares and rights to be attributed to the first-mentioned company include any holding or entitlement attributed to the other company under *section 626B(1)(b)(ii)*.

Effect of deemed disposal and reacquisition

2.

(1) In this paragraph—

"deemed disposal and reacquisition" means a disposal and immediate reacquisition treated as taking place under the Capital Gains Tax Acts;

"*derived*" has the same meaning as in *paragraph 1*.

(2) A company is not regarded as having held shares throughout a period if, at any time during that period, there is a deemed disposal and reacquisition of—

(a) the shares concerned, or

(b) shares from which those shares are derived.

Effect of repurchase agreement

3.

(1) In this paragraph a "*repurchase agreement*" means an agreement under which—

(a) a person (in this paragraph referred to as the "*original owner*") transfers shares to another person (in this paragraph referred to as the "*interim holder*") under an agreement to sell them, and

(b) the original owner or a person connected with him is required to buy them back either—

(i) in pursuance of an obligation to do so imposed by that agreement or by any related agreement, or

(ii) in consequence of the exercise of an option acquired under that agreement or any related agreement,

and for the purposes of *paragraph (b)* agreements are related if they are entered into in pursuance of the same arrangements (regardless of the date on which either agreement is entered into).

(2) Any reference in this paragraph to the period of a repurchase agreement is a reference to the period beginning with the transfer of the shares by the original owner to the interim holder and ending with the repurchase of the shares in pursuance of the agreement.

(3) This paragraph applies where a company that holds shares in another company transfers the shares under a repurchase agreement.

(4) In determining whether the conditions in *paragraph (a)* of *section 626B(2)* are satisfied but subject to *subparagraph (5)*—

(a) the original owner shall be treated as continuing to hold the shares transferred and accordingly as retaining entitlement to any rights attached to them, and

(b) the interim holder shall be treated as not holding the shares transferred and as not becoming entitled to any such rights, during the period of the repurchase agreement.

(5) If at any time before the end of the period of the repurchase agreement the original owner, or another member of the same group as the original owner, becomes the holder—

(a) of any of the shares transferred, or

(b) of any shares directly or indirectly representing any of the shares transferred,

subparagraph (4) does not apply after that time in relation to those shares or, as the case may be, in relation to the shares represented by those shares; and for the purposes of this subparagraph "*group*" means a company which has one or more 51 per cent subsidiaries together with those subsidiaries.

Effect of stock lending arrangements

4.

(1) In this paragraph a "*stock lending arrangement*" means arrangements between two persons (in this paragraph referred to as the "*borrower*" and the "*lender*") under which—

(a) the lender transfers shares to the borrower otherwise than by way of sale, and

(b) a requirement is imposed on the borrower to transfer those shares back to the lender otherwise than by way of sale.

(2) Any reference in this paragraph to the period of a stock lending arrangement is a reference to the period beginning with the transfer of the shares by the lender to the borrower and ending—

(a) with the transfer of the shares back to the lender in pursuance of the arrangement, or

(b) when it becomes apparent that the requirement for the borrower to make a transfer back to the lender will not be complied with.

(3) This paragraph applies where a company that holds shares in another company transfers the shares under a stock lending arrangement.

(4) In determining whether the conditions in *paragraph (a)* of *section 626B(2)* are satisfied but subject to *subparagraph (5)*—

(a) the lender shall be treated as continuing to hold the shares transferred and accordingly as retaining entitlement to any rights attached to them, and

(b) the borrower shall be treated for those purposes as not holding the shares transferred and as not becoming entitled to any such rights,

during the period of the stock lending arrangement.

(5) (a) If at any time before the end of the period of the stock lending arrangement the lender, or another member of the same group as the lender, becomes the holder—

(i) of any of the shares transferred, or

(ii) of any shares directly or indirectly representing any of the shares transferred,

subparagraph (4) does not apply after that time in relation to those shares or, as the case may be, in relation to the shares represented by those shares.

(b) For the purposes of this subparagraph "*group*" means a company which has one or more 51 per cent subsidiaries together with those subsidiaries.

Effect in relation to investee company of earlier company reconstruction etc.

5.

(1) In this paragraph "original shares" and "new holding" shall be construed in accordance with *sections 584*, *586* and *587*.

(2) This paragraph applies where shares in one company (in this paragraph referred to as the "*first company*")—

(a) are exchanged (or deemed to be exchanged) for shares in another company (in this paragraph referred to as the "*second company*"), or

(b) are deemed to be exchanged by virtue of *section 587* for shares in the first company and shares in the second company,

in circumstances such that, under *section 584* as that section applies by virtue of *section 586* or *587*, the original shares and the new holding are treated as the same asset.

(3) Where the second company—

(a) is an investee company, and is accordingly the company by reference to which the shareholding requirement under *section 626B(2)(a)* falls to be met, or

(b) is a company by reference to which, by virtue of this paragraph, that requirement may be met,

that requirement may instead be met, in relation to times before the exchange, or deemed exchange, by reference to the first company.

(4) If in any case that requirement can be met by virtue of this paragraph, it shall be treated as met.

Negligible value

6. A claim under *section 538(2)* may not be made in relation to shares held by a company if by virtue of *section 626B* any loss accruing to the company on a disposal of the shares at the time of the claim, or at any earlier time at or after which the value of the shares becomes negligible, would not be an allowable loss.

Degrouping: time when deemed sale and reacquisition treated as taking place

7. Where—

(a) a company, as a result of ceasing at any time (in this paragraph referred to as the "*time of degrouping*") to be a member of a group, is treated by *section 623(4)* as having sold and immediately reacquired an asset, and

(b) if the company owning the asset at the time of degrouping had disposed of it immediately before that time, any gain accruing on the disposal would by virtue of *section 626B* not have been a chargeable gain,

then *section 623(4)* shall have effect as if it provided for the deemed sale and reacquisition to be treated as taking place immediately before the time of degrouping.

Appropriations to trading stock

8.

(1) Where—

(a) an asset acquired by a company otherwise than as trading stock of a trade carried on by it is appropriated by the company for the purposes of the trade as trading stock (whether on the commencement of the trade or otherwise), and

(b) if the company had then sold the asset for its market value, a chargeable gain or allowable loss would have accrued to the company but for the provisions of *section 626B*,

then the company shall be treated for the purposes of the Capital Gains Tax Acts as if it had thereby disposed of the asset for its market value.

(2) *Section 618* applies in relation to this paragraph as it applies in relation to *section 596*.][1]

Amendments

[1] Inserted by FA04 s42(1)(b). This section comes into operation on such day as the Minister for Finance may appoint by order.

Revenue Briefings

Tax Briefing

Tax Briefing April 2004 – Issue 55 pg 8 – Finance Act 2004 – Capital Gains Tax

Cross References

From Schedule 25A

Section 538 Disposals where assets lost or destroyed or become of negligible value.
Section 584 Reorganisation or reduction of share capital.
Section 586 Company amalgamations by exchange of shares.
Section 587 Company reconstructions and amalgamations.
Section 596 Appropriations to and from stock in trade.
Section 618 Transfers of trading stock within group.
Section 623 Company ceasing to be member of group.
Section 626B Exemption from tax in the case of gains on disposals of shares.

SCHEDULE 25B

List of Specified Reliefs and Method of Determining Amount of Specified Relief Used in a Tax Year

[*Section 485C*.

Reference Number (1)	Specified Relief (2)	Amount of Specified Relief used in a Tax Year (3)
1.	*Section 140* (exemption of distributions out of income from stallion fees, stud greyhounds, and occupation of woodlands).	So much of any distribution made out of exempt profits (within the meaning of *section 140*) as is received by the individual in the tax year.
2.	*Section 141* (exemption of distributions out of patent royalty income).	So much of any distribution made out of disregarded income (within the meaning of *section 141*) or treated as a distribution made out of disregarded income as is received by the individual in the tax year and to which distribution *section 141(3)(a)(i)* applies for that year.
3.	*Section 142* (exemption of distributions out of profits of certain mining operations).	So much of any distribution made out of exempted income (within the meaning of *section 142*) as is received by the individual in the tax year.

Reference Number (1)	Specified Relief (2)	Amount of Specified Relief used in a Tax Year (3)
4.	*section 143* (exemption of distributions out of profits of certain mining operations).	So much of any distribution made out of relieved income (within the meaning of *section 143*) as is received by the individual in the tax year.
5.	*section 195* (exemption of certain earnings of writers, composers and artists).	So much of any profits or gains arising to the individual for the tax year from the publication, production or sale, as the case may be, of— (a) a work or works in relation to which the Revenue Commissioners have made a determination under clause (I) or (II) of *subsection (2)(a)(ii)* of *section 195*, or (b) a work of the individual in the same category as that work.
6.	*Section 231* (exemption of profits or gains from stallion fees).	So much of any profits or gains arising for the tax year— (a) to the owner of a stallion, which is ordinarily kept on land in the State, from the sale of services of mares within the State by the stallion, or (b) to the part-owner of such a stallion from the sale of such services or of rights to such services, or
		(c) to the part-owner of a stallion, which is ordinarily kept on land outside the State, from the sale of services of mares by the stallion or of rights to such services, where the part-owner carries on in the State a trade which consists of or includes bloodstock breeding and it is shown to the satisfaction of the inspector, or on appeal to the satisfaction of the Appeal Commissioners, that the part-ownership of the stallion was acquired and is held primarily for the purposes of the service by the stallion of mares owned or partly-owned by the part-owner of the stallion in the course of that trade.
7.	*Section 232* (exemption of profits from occupation of woodlands).	So much of any profits or gains arising to the individual for the tax year from the occupation (within the meaning of *section 232*) of woodlands (within the meaning of that section) managed on a commercial basis and with a view to the realisation of profits.
8	*Section 233* (exemption of profits from stud greyhound service fees).	So much of any profits or gains arising for the tax year— (a) to the owner of a stud greyhound, which is ordinarily kept in the State, from the sale of services of greyhound bitches within the State by the stud greyhound, or (b) to the part-owner of such a stud greyhound from the sale of such services or of rights to such services, or

Reference Number (1)	Specified Relief (2)	Amount of Specified Relief used in a Tax Year (3)
		(c) to the part-owner of a stud greyhound, which is ordinarily kept outside the State, from the sale of services of greyhound bitches by the stud greyhound or of rights to such services, where the part-owner carries on in the State a trade which consists of or includes greyhound breeding and it is shown to the satisfaction of the inspector, or on appeal to the satisfaction of the Appeal Commissioners, that the part-ownership of the stud greyhound was acquired and is held primarily for the purposes of the service by the stud greyhound of greyhound bitches owned or partly-owned by the part-owner of the stud greyhound in the course of that trade.
9.	*Section 234* (exemption of certain income from patent royalties).	So much of any income from a qualifying patent (within the meaning of *section 234*) arising to the individual for the tax year that the individual is entitled to have disregarded for the purposes of the Income Tax Acts in accordance with *section 234(2)(a)*.
10.	*Section 248* (relief for interest paid on loans used to acquire an interest in a company).	The amount of any payment of interest by the individual in the tax year, being interest eligible for relief under *section 248* for the tax year in which the interest is paid, which is deducted from or set off against the income of the individual for that year.
11.	*Section 248* (relief for interest paid on loans used to acquire an interest in a company) as extended by *section 250* (extension of relief under *section 248* to certain individuals in relation to loans applied in acquiring interest in certain companies).	The amount of any payment of interest by the individual in the tax year, being interest eligible for relief under *section 248* as extended by *section 250* for the tax year in which the interest is paid, which is deducted from or set off against the income of the individual for that year.
12.	*Section 253* (relief for interest paid on loans used to acquire an interest in a partnership).	The amount of any payment of interest by the individual in the tax year, being interest eligible for relief under *section 253* for the tax year in which the interest is paid, which is deducted from or set off against the income of the individual for that year.
13.	*Section 272* (writing-down allowances).	An amount equal to— (a) the aggregate amount of writing-down allowances (within the meaning of *section 272*) made to the individual for the tax year under *section 272*, including any such allowances or part of any such allowances made to the individual for a previous tax year and carried forward from that previous year in accordance with *Part 9*, in respect of the following buildings or structures:

Reference Number (1)	Specified Relief (2)	Amount of Specified Relief used in a Tax Year (3)
		(i) an industrial building or structure within the meaning of— (I) *section 268(1)(d)*, (II) *section 268(1)(g)*, (III) *section 268(1)(i)*, (IV) *section 268(1)(j)*, (V) *section 268(1)(k)*, (VI) *section 268(1)(l)* (inserted by the Finance Act 2006), [(VII) *section 268(1)(m)* (inserted by the Finance Act 2008),][1] [(VIII) *section 268(1)(n)* (inserted by the Finance Act 2013),][2] (ii) a building or structure which is deemed to be a building or structure in use for the purposes of the trade of hotel-keeping by virtue of *section 268(3)*, [(iii) a building or structure which is deemed to be a building or structure in use for the purposes of a trade referred to in *section 268(1)(g)* by virtue of *section 268(3B)*, but there shall not be included in the aggregate any allowance referred to in *section 272(3)(c)(iii)*,][3] or (b) where full effect has not been given in respect of the aggregate for that tax year, the part of that aggregate in respect of which full effect has been given for that tax year in accordance with *section 278* and *section 304* or *305*, as the case may be, or any of those sections as applied or modified by any other provision of the Tax Acts.
14.	*Section 273* (acceleration of writing-down allowances in respect of certain expenditure on certain industrial buildings or structures).	An amount equal to— (a) the aggregate amount of writing-down allowances (within the meaning of *section 272*) as increased under *section 273* made to the individual for the tax year under *section 272* as modified by *section 273*, including any such increased allowances or part of any such increased allowances made to the individual for a previous tax year and carried forward from that previous year in accordance with *Part 9*, or (b) where full effect has not been given in respect of that aggregate for that tax year, the part of the aggregate in respect of which full effect has been given for that tax year in accordance with *section 278* and *section 304* or *305*, as the case may be, or any of those sections as applied or modified by any other provision of the Tax Acts.

Reference Number (1)	Specified Relief (2)	Amount of Specified Relief used in a Tax Year (3)
15.	*Section 274* (balancing allowances and balancing charges).	An amount equal to— (a) the aggregate amount of balancing allowances (within the meaning of *section 274*) made to the individual for the tax year under *section 274*, including any such allowances or part of any such allowances made to the individual for a previous tax year and carried forward from that previous year in accordance with *Part 9*, in respect of the following buildings or structures: (i) an industrial building or structure within the meaning of— (I) *section 268(1)(d)*, (II) *section 268(1)(g)*, (III) *section 268(1)(i)*, (IV) *section 268(1)(j)*, (V) *section 268(1)(k)*, (VI) *section 268(1)(l)* (inserted by the Finance Act 2006), [(VII) *section 268(1)(m)* (inserted by the Finance Act 2008),][4] [(VIII) *section 268(1)(n)* (inserted by the Finance Act 2013),][5] (ii) a building or structure which is deemed to be a building or structure in use for the purposes of the trade of hotel-keeping by virtue of *section 268(3)*, (iii) a building or structure which is deemed to be a building or structure in use for the purposes of a trade referred to in *section 268(1)(g)* by virtue of *section 268(3B)*,
		(iv) a building or structure in respect of which an allowance under *section 272* as increased under *section 273* was made, but there shall not be included in the aggregate any balancing allowance made in respect of a building or structure to which *section 272(3)(c)(iii)* applies, or (b) where full effect has not been given in respect of the aggregate for that year, the part of that aggregate in respect of which full effect has been given for that tax year in accordance with *section 278* and *section 304* or *305*, as the case may be, or any of those sections as applied or modified by any other provision of the tax Acts.
15A	*Section 304(4)* (income tax: allowances and charges in taxing a trade, etc.).	An amount equal to— (a) as respects the tax year 2007, the amount determined in accordance with *paragraph 1* of *Schedule 25C* as referable to specified reliefs less any part of that amount (in this provision referred to as the "*surplus*") for which effect cannot be given in that tax year, and

Reference Number (1)	Specified Relief (2)	Amount of Specified Relief used in a Tax Year (3)
		(b) as respects any subsequent tax year, the surplus or that part of the surplus for which effect is given in that subsequent tax year.
15B	*Section 305(1)* (income tax: manner of granting, and effect of, allowances made by means of discharge or repayment of tax).	An amount equal to— (a) as respects the tax year 2007, the amount determined in accordance with *paragraph 3* of *Schedule 25C* as referable to specified reliefs less any part of that amount (in this provision referred to as the "*surplus*") for which effect cannot be given in that tax year, and (b) as respects any subsequent tax year, the surplus or that part of the surplus for which effect is given in that subsequent tax year.][6]
[15C	*Section 284* (wear and tear allowances) subject to *section 485C(1B)*.	An amount equal to the amount of weaand tear allowances (within the meaning of *section 284*) made to an individual in relation to specified plant and machinery for the tax year under *section 284*, or deemed to have been made to an individual under *section 287*, whether by virtue of *section 298* or otherwise, including any such allowances or part of any such allowance made to the individual in a previous tax year and carried forward from that previous tax year in accordance with *Part 9*.
15D	*Section 288* (balancing allowances and balancing charges) subject to *section 485C(1B)*.	An amount equal to the amount of the balancing allowance (within the meaning of *section 288*) made to an individual for the tax year under *section 288* in relation to specified plant and machinery.][7]
16.	*Section 323* (capital allowances in relation to the construction of certain commercial premises).	An amount equal to— (a) the aggregate amount of allowances (including balancing allowances) made to the individual for the tax year under *Chapter 1* of *Part 9* as that Chapter is applied by *section 323*, including any such allowances or part of any such allowances made to the individual for a previous tax year and carried forward from that previous year in accordance with *Part 9*, or (b) where full effect has not been given in respect of that aggregate for that tax year, the part of that aggregate to which full effect has been given for that tax year in accordance with *section 278* and *section 304* or *305*, as the case may be, or any of those sections as applied or modified by any other provision of the Tax Acts.
17.	*Section 324* (double rent allowance in respect of rent paid for certain business premises).	Where any further deduction is given to the individual for the tax year under *section 324(2)*, the amount by which that deduction reduces the amount of the individual's profits or gains to be charged to tax under Case I or Case II of Schedule D.

Reference Number (1)	Specified Relief (2)	Amount of Specified Relief used in a Tax Year (3)
18.	*Section 331* (accelerated capital allowances in relation to construction or refurbishment of certain industrial buildings or structures).	An amount equal to— (a) the aggregate amount of allowances (including balancing allowances) made to the individual for the tax year under *Chapter 1* of *Part 9* as that Chapter is applied by *section 331*, including any such allowances or part of any such allowances made to the individual for a previous tax year and carried forward from that previous year in accordance with *Part 9*, or (b) where full effect has not been given in respect of that aggregate for that tax year, the part of that aggregate to which full effect has been given for that tax year in accordance with *section 278* and *section 304* or *305*, as the case may be, or any of those sections as applied or modified by any other provision of the Tax Acts.
19.	*Section 332* (capital allowances in relation to construction or refurbishment of certain commercial premises).	An amount equal to— (a) the aggregate amount of allowances (including balancing allowances) made to the individual for the tax year under *Chapter 1* of *Part 9* as that Chapter is applied by *section 332*, including any such allowances or part of any such allowances made to the individual for a previous tax year and carried forward from that previous year in accordance with *Part 9*, or (b) where full effect has not been given in respect of that aggregate for that tax year, the part of that aggregate to which full effect has been given for that tax year in accordance with *section 278* and *section 304* or *305*, as the case may be, or any of those sections as applied or modified by any other provision of the Tax Acts.
20.	*Section 333* (double rent allowance in respect of rent paid for certain business premises).	Where any further deduction is given to the individual for the tax year under *section 333(2)*, the amount by which that deduction reduces the amount of the individual's profits or gains to be charged to tax under Case I or Case II of Schedule D.
21.	*Section 341* (accelerated capital allowances in relation to construction or refurbishment of certain industrial buildings or structures).	An amount equal to— (a) the aggregate amount of allowances (including balancing allowances) made to the individual for the tax year under *Chapter 1* of *Part 9* as that Chapter is applied by *section 341*, including any such allowances or part of any such allowances made to the individual for a previous tax year and carried forward from that previous year in accordance with *Part 9*, or (b) where full effect has not been given in respect of that aggregate for that tax year, the part of that aggregate to which full effect has been given for that tax year in accordance with *section 278* and *section 304* or *305*, as the case may be, or any of those sections as applied or modified by any other provision of the Tax Acts.

Reference Number (1)	Specified Relief (2)	Amount of Specified Relief used in a Tax Year (3)
22.	*Section 342* (capital allowances in relation to construction or refurbishment of certain commercial premises).	An amount equal to— (a) the aggregate amount of allowances (including balancing allowances) made to the individual for the tax year under *Chapter 1* of *Part 9* as that Chapter is applied by *section 342*, including any such allowances or part of any such allowances made to the individual for a previous tax year and carried forward from that previous year in accordance with *Part 9*, or (b) where full effect has not been given in respect of that aggregate for that tax year, the part of that aggregate to which full effect has been given for that tax year in accordance with *section 278* and *section 304* or *305*, as the case may be, or any of those sections as applied or modified by any other provision of the Tax Acts.
23.	*Section 343* (capital allowances in relation to construction or refurbishment of certain buildings or structures in enterprise areas).	An amount equal to— (a) the aggregate amount of allowances (including balancing allowances) made to the individual for the tax year under *Chapter 1* of *Part 9* as that Chapter is applied by *section 343*, including any such allowances or part of any such allowances made to the individual for a previous tax year and carried forward from that previous year in accordance with *Part 9*, or (b) where full effect has not been given in respect of that aggregate for that tax year, the part of that aggregate to which full effect has been given for that tax year in accordance with *section 278* and *section 304* or *305*, as the case may be, or any of those sections as applied or modified by any other provision of the Tax Acts.
24.	*Section 344* (capital allowances in relation to construction or refurbishment of certain multi-storey car parks).	An amount equal to— (a) the aggregate amount of allowances (including balancing allowances) made to the individual for the tax year under *Chapter 1* of *Part 9* as that Chapter is applied by *section 344*, including any such allowances or part of any such allowances made to the individual for a previous tax year and carried forward from that previous year in accordance with *Part 9*, or (b) where full effect has not been given in respect of that aggregate for that tax year, the part of that aggregate to which full effect has been given for that tax year in accordance with *section 278* and *section 304* or *305*, as the case may be, or any of those sections as applied or modified by any other provision of the Tax Acts.

Reference Number (1)	Specified Relief (2)	Amount of Specified Relief used in a Tax Year (3)
25.	*Section 345* (double rent allowance in respect of rent paid for certain business premises).	Where any further deduction is given to the individual for the tax year under *section 345(3)*, the amount by which that deduction reduces the amount of the individual's profits or gains to be charged to tax under Case I or Case II of Schedule D.
26.	*Section 352* (accelerated capital allowances in relation to construction or refurbishment of certain industrial buildings or structures).	An amount equal to— (a) the aggregate amount of allowances (including balancing allowances) made to the individual for the tax year under *Chapter 1* of *Part 9* as that Chapter is applied by *section 352*, including any such allowances or part of any such allowances made to the individual for a previous tax year and carried forward from that previous year in accordance with *Part 9*, or (b) where full effect has not been given in respect of that aggregate for that tax year, the part of that aggregate to which full effect has been given for that tax year in accordance with *section 278* and *section 304* or *305*, as the case may be, or any of those sections as applied or modified by any other provision of the Tax Acts.
27.	*Section 353* (capital allowances in relation to construction or refurbishment of certain commercial premises).	An amount equal to— (a) the aggregate amount of allowances (including balancing allowances) made to the individual for the tax year under *Chapter 1* of *Part 9* as that Chapter is applied by *section 353*, including any such allowances or part of any such allowances made to the individual for a previous tax year and carried forward from that previous year in accordance with *Part 9*, or (b) where full effect has not been given in respect of that aggregate for that tax year, the part of that aggregate to which full effect has been given for that tax year in accordance with *section 278* and *section 304* or *305*, as the case may be, or any of those sections as applied or modified by any other provision of the Tax Acts.
28.	*Section 354* (double rent allowance in respect of rent paid for certain business premises).	Where any further deduction is given to the individual for the tax year under *section 354(3)*, the amount by which that deduction reduces the amount of the individual's profits or gains to be charged to tax under Case I or Case II of Schedule D.

Reference Number (1)	Specified Relief (2)	Amount of Specified Relief used in a Tax Year (3)
29.	*Section 372C* (accelerated capital allowances in relation to construction or refurbishment of certain industrial buildings or structures).	An amount equal to— (a) the aggregate amount of allowances (including balancing allowances) made to the individual for the tax year under *Chapter 1* of *Part 9* as that Chapter is applied by *Section 372C*, including any such allowances or part of any such allowances made to the individual for a previous tax year and carried forward from that previous year in accordance with *Part 9*, or (b) where full effect has not been given in respect of that aggregate for that tax year, the part of that aggregate to which full effect has been given for that tax year in accordance with *section 278* and *section 304* or *305*, as the case may be, or any of those sections as applied or modified by any other provision of the Tax Acts.
30.	*Section 372D* (capital allowances in relation to construction or refurbishment of certain commercial premises).	An amount equal to— (a) the aggregate amount of allowances (including balancing allowances) made to the individual for the tax year under *Chapter 1* of *Part 9* as that Chapter is applied by *Section 372D*, including any such allowances or part of any such allowances made to the individual for a previous tax year and carried forward from that previous year in accordance with *Part 9*, or (b) where full effect has not been given in respect of that aggregate for that tax year, the part of that aggregate to which full effect has been given for that tax year in accordance with *section 278* and *section 304* or *305*, as the case may be, or any of those sections as applied or modified by any other provision of the Tax Acts.
31.	*Section 372M* (accelerated capital allowances in relation to construction or refurbishment of certain industrial buildings or structures).	An amount equal to— (a) the aggregate amount of allowances (including balancing allowances) made to the individual for the tax year under *Chapter 1* of *Part 9* as that Chapter is applied by *Section 372M*, including any such allowances or part of any such allowances made to the individual for a previous tax year and carried forward from that previous year in accordance with *Part 9*, or (b) where full effect has not been given in respect of that aggregate for that tax year, the part of that aggregate to which full effect has been given for that tax year in accordance with *section 278* and *section 304* or *305*, as the case may be, or any of those sections as applied or modified by any other provision of the Tax Acts.

Reference Number (1)	Specified Relief (2)	Amount of Specified Relief used in a Tax Year (3)
32.	*Section 372N* (capital allowances in relation to construction or refurbishment of certain commercial premises).	An amount equal to— (a) the aggregate amount of allowances (including balancing allowances) made to the individual for the tax year under *Chapter 1* of *Part 9* as that Chapter is applied by *Section 372N*, including any such allowances or part of any such allowances made to the individual for a previous tax year and carried forward from that previous year in accordance with *Part 9*, or (b) where full effect has not been given in respect of that aggregate for that tax year, the part of that aggregate to which full effect has been given for that tax year in accordance with *section 278* and *section 304* or *305*, as the case may be, or any of those sections as applied or modified by any other provision of the Tax Acts.
33.	*Section 372V* (capital allowances in relation to construction or refurbishment of certain park and ride facilities).	An amount equal to— (a) the aggregate amount of allowances (including balancing allowances) made to the individual for the tax year under *Chapter 1* of *Part 9* as that Chapter is applied by *section 372V*, including any such allowances or part of any such allowances made to the individual for a previous tax year and carried forward from that previous year in accordance with *Part 9*, or (b) where full effect has not been given in respect of that aggregate for that tax year, the part of that aggregate to which full effect has been given for that tax year in accordance with *section 278* and *section 304* or *305*, as the case may be, or any of those sections as applied or modified by any other provision of the Tax Acts.
34.	*Section 372W* (capital allowances in relation to construction or refurbishment of certain commercial premises).	An amount equal to— (a) the aggregate amount of allowances (including balancing allowances) made to the individual for the tax year under *Chapter 1* of *Part 9* as that Chapter is applied by *section 372W*, including any such allowances or part of any such allowances made to the individual for a previous tax year and carried forward from that previous year in accordance with *Part 9*, or (b) where full effect has not been given in respect of that aggregate for that tax year, the part of that aggregate to which full effect has been given for that tax year in accordance with *section 278* and *section 304* or *305*, as the case may be, or any of those sections as applied or modified by any other provision of the Tax Acts.

Reference Number (1)	Specified Relief (2)	Amount of Specified Relief used in a Tax Year (3)
35.	*Section 372AC* (accelerated capital allowances in relation to construction or refurbishment of certain industrial buildings or structures).	An amount equal to— (a) the aggregate amount of allowances (including balancing allowances) made to the individual for the tax year under *Chapter 1* of *Part 9* as that Chapter is applied by *section 372AC*, including any such allowances or part of any such allowances made to the individual for a previous tax year and carried forward from that previous year in accordance with *Part 9*, or (b) where full effect has not been given in respect of that aggregate for that tax year, the part of that aggregate to which full effect has been given for that tax year in accordance with *section 278* and *section 304* or *305*, as the case may be, or any of those sections as applied or modified by any other provision of the Tax Acts.
36.	*Section 372AD* (capital allowances in relation to construction or refurbishment of certain commercial premises).	An amount equal to— (a) the aggregate amount of allowances (including balancing allowances) made to the individual for the tax year under *Chapter 1* of *Part 9* as that Chapter is applied by *section 372AD*, including any such allowances or part of any such allowances made to the individual for a previous tax year and carried forward from that previous year in accordance with *Part 9*, or (b) where full effect has not been given in respect of that aggregate for that tax year, the part of that aggregate to which full effect has been given for that tax year in accordance with *section 278* and *section 304* or *305*, as the case may be, or any of those sections as applied or modified by any other provision of the Tax Acts.
36A.	*Section 372AX* (accelerated capital allowances in relation to the construction or refurbishment of certain registered holiday camps).	An amount equal to— (a) the aggregate amount of allowances (including balancing allowances) made to the individual for the tax year under *Chapter 1* of *Part 9* as that Chapter is applied by *Section 372AX*, including any such allowances or part of any such allowances made to the individual for a previous tax year and carried forward from that previous year in accordance with *Part 9*, or (b) where full effect has not been given in respect of that aggregate for that tax year, the part of that aggregate to which full effect has been given for that tax year in accordance with *section 278* and *section 304* or *305*, as the case may be, or any of those sections as applied or modified by any other provision of the Tax Acts.

Reference Number (1)	Specified Relief (2)	Amount of Specified Relief used in a Tax Year (3)
36B.	*Section 372AY* (capital allowances in relation to the construction or refurbishment of certain tourism infrastructure facilities).	An amount equal to— (a) the aggregate amount of allowances (including balancing allowances) made to the individual for the tax year under *Chapter 1* of *Part 9* as that Chapter is applied by *section 372AY*, including any such allowances or part of any such allowances made to the individual for a previous tax year and carried forward from that previous year in accordance with *Part 9*, or (b) where full effect has not been given in respect of that aggregate for that tax year, the part of that aggregate to which full effect has been given for that tax year in accordance with *section 278* and *section 304* or *305*, as the case may be, or any of those sections as applied or modified by any other provision of the Tax Acts.][8]
37.	*Section 372AP* (relief for lessors).	An amount equal to the lesser of— (a) the aggregate of the amounts the individual deducts in the tax year under *section 372AP* in computing for the purpose of *section 97(1)* the amount of a surplus or deficiency in respect of the rent from each qualifying premises (within the meaning of *section 372AM*) and each special qualifying premises (within the meaning of that section), and (b) the aggregate of the gross amount of each rent received by the individual plus the individual's total receipts from easements for the tax year less the deductions authorised by *section 97(2)* to which the individual is entitled for the tax year, other than any deduction authorised by *section 372AP*, but where both amounts are the same, the amount shall be the amount given under *paragraph (a)*.
38.	*Section 372AU(1)* (saver for relief due, and for clawback of relief given under, old schemes).	An amount equal to the lesser of— (a) the aggregate of the amounts the individual deducts in the tax year by virtue of the provisions of *section 372AU(1)* in computing for the purpose of *section 97(1)* the amount of a surplus or deficiency in respect of the rent from each premises, and [(b the amount determined by the formula— $(G + E) — (D + R)$ where— G is the aggregate of the gross amount of each rent received by the individual for the tax year, E is the individual's total receipts from easements for the tax year,

Reference Number (1)	Specified Relief (2)	Amount of Specified Relief used in a Tax Year (3)
		D is the total amount of deductions authorised by *section 97(2)* to which the individual is entitled for the tax year apart from any deduction authorised by *section 372AP* or *section 372AU*, and R is the amount determined under this Schedule as the amount of specified relief in respect of *section 372AP*, but the amount so determined shall not exceed the amount determined by the formula— $$(G + E) — D$$ where G, E and D have the same meanings as they have in the first formula in this paragraph,][9] but where both amounts are the same, the amount shall be the amount given under paragraph (a).
[38A.][10]	[*Section 372AAC* (capital allowances in relation to conversion or refurbishment of certain commercial premises)][11]	[An amount equal to— (a) the aggregate amount of allowances (including balancing allowances) made to the individual under *Chapter 1* of *Part 9* as that Chapter is applied by *section 372AAC*, including any such allowance or part of any allowances made to the individual for a previous tax year and carried forward from that previous tax year in accordance with *Part 9*, or (b) where full effect has not been given in respect of that aggregate for that tax year, the part of that aggregate to which full effect has been given for that tax year in accordance with *section 278* and *section 304* or *305*, as the case may be, or any of those sections as applied or modified by any other provision of the Tax Acts.][12]
39.	*Section 381* (right to repayment of tax by reference to losses).	To the extent that any loss or any part of a loss sustained by the individual in the tax year is referable to a further deduction given to the individual under *section 324*, *333*, *345*, *354* or *paragraph 13* of *Schedule 32*, the amount of the loss or any portion of the loss that is so referable in respect of which relief is given to the individual for the tax year under *section 381* less any amount of such loss as is carried forward under *section 382*.
40.	*Section 381* (right to repayment of tax by reference to losses) as extended by *section 392* (option to treat capital allowances as creating or augmenting a loss).	To the extent that any loss or any part of a loss sustained by the individual in the tax year is referable to capital allowances, being allowances which are specified reliefs, made to the individual for the tax year, the amount of the loss or any portion of the loss that is so referable in respect of which relief is given to the individual for the tax year under *section 381* less any amount of such loss as is carried forward under *section 382*.

Reference Number (1)	Specified Relief (2)	Amount of Specified Relief used in a Tax Year (3)
41.	*Section 382* (right to carry forward losses to future years).	To the extent that any loss or any part of a loss is referable to [a specified relief][13], made to the individual for any previous tax year, the amount of the loss or any portion of the loss that is so referable which is carried forward to the tax year under *section 382* and in respect of which the individual is given relief under that section for the tax year less any part of that loss for which relief cannot be given under that section for that year.
42.	*Section 383* (relief under Case IV for losses).	To the extent that any loss or any part of a loss is referable to a specified relief to which the individual is or was entitled to for a tax year, the amount of the loss or any portion of the loss that is so referable in respect of which the individual is given relief under *section 383* for that year.
43.	*Section 384* (relief under Case V for losses).	[To the extent that the excess referred to in *section 384* is referable to a specified relief, the amount of the excess or any portion of the excess that is so referable in respect of which the individual is given relief under that section for the tax year less any part of that excess for which relief cannot be given under that section for that year.][14]
44.	*Section 385* (terminal loss).	To the extent that a terminal loss (within the meaning of *section 385*) or any part of such a loss is referable to a specified relief, the amount of the loss or any portion of the loss that is so referable in respect of which the individual is given relief under *section 385* for the tax year.
45.	*Section 481* (relief for investment in films).	The amount of a relevant deduction (within the meaning of *section 481*) that is deducted from the individual's total income for the tax year under *section 481*, including any amount of relief carried forward under that section to that year and deducted from the individual's total income for that year.
46.	*Section 482* (relief for expenditure on significant buildings and gardens).	The amount of qualifying expenditure (within the meaning of *section 482*) incurred by the individual in the tax year for which relief is given for the tax year under *section 381*, including any amounts in respect of which relief is given in that year by virtue of *section 482(3)*.
47.	*Section 485F* (carry-forward of excess relief).	The total amount deducted from the individual's total income for the tax year under *section 485F* in respect of all amounts of excess relief carried forward by the individual to that year under that section.

Reference Number (1)	Specified Relief (2)	Amount of Specified Relief used in a Tax Year (3)
[47A.][15]	[*Section 489(2)(a)* (Employment and Investment Incentive Scheme).][16]	[The total amount deducted from the individual's total income for the tax year under section 489(2)(*a*) (as inserted by the *Finance Act 2011*)in respect of any amount subscribed for eligible shares by the individual in the tax year, including any amount deducted from the individual's total income for that year by virtue of any amount of relief carried forward to that year under *subsection (3)* or *(4)* of [*section 490*, where the subscription for eligible shares is made on or before 15 October 2013 or on or after 1 January 2017][17].][18]
48.	*Section 489(3)* (BES relief).	The total amount deducted from the individual's total income for the tax year under *section 489(3)* in respect of any amount subscribed for eligible shares by the individual in the tax year, including any amount of relief carried forward under *section 490(3)* to that year and deducted from the individual's total income for that year.
[48A.][19]	[*Section 823A* (deduction for income earned in certain foreign states)][20].	[An amount equal to the total amount deducted from the individual's total income for the tax year under section 823A.][21]
49.	*Section 843* (capital allowances for buildings used for third level educational purposes).	An amount equal to— (a) the aggregate amount of allowances (including balancing allowances) made to the individual for the tax year under *Chapter 1* of *Part 9* as that Chapter is applied by *section 843*, including any such allowances or part of any such allowances made to the individual for a previous tax year and carried forward from that previous year in accordance with *Part 9*, or (b) where full effect has not been given in respect of that aggregate for that tax year, the part of that aggregate to which full effect has been given for that tax year in accordance with *section 278* and *section 304* or *305*, as the case may be, or any of those sections as applied or modified by any other provision of the Tax Acts.
50.	*Section 843A* (capital allowances for buildings used for certain childcare purposes).	An amount equal to— (a) the aggregate amount of allowances (including balancing allowances) made to the individual for the tax year under *Chapter 1* of *Part 9* as that Chapter is applied by *Section 843A*, including any such allowances or part of any such allowances made to the individual for a previous tax year and carried forward from that previous year in accordance with *Part 9*, or (b) where full effect has not been given in respect of that aggregate for that tax year, the part of that aggregate to which full effect has been given for that tax year in accordance with *section 278* and *section 304* or *305*, as the case may be, or any of those sections as applied or modified by any other provision of the Tax Acts.

Reference Number (1)	Specified Relief (2)	Amount of Specified Relief used in a Tax Year (3)
51.	*Section 847A* (donations to certain sports bodies).	The amount of a relevant donation (within the meaning of *Section 847A*) made by an individual in a relevant year of assessment (within the meaning of that section) which is [deducted from or set off against any income of the individual][22] in the tax year.
[…][23]	[…][24]	[…][25]
53.	*Paragraph 11* (Urban Renewal Scheme, 1986— capital allowances in relation to certain commercial premises in designated areas other than the Customs House Docks Area) of *Schedule 32*.	An amount equal to— (a) the aggregate amount of allowances (including balancing allowances) made to the individual for the tax year under *Chapter 1* of *Part 9* as applied by virtue of *paragraph 11* of *Schedule 32*, including any such allowances or part of any such allowances made to the individual for a previous tax year and carried forward from that previous year in accordance with *Part 9*, or (b) where full effect has not been given in respect of that aggregate for that tax year, the part of that aggregate to which full effect has been given for that tax year in accordance with *section 278* and *section 304* or *305*, as the case may be, or any of those sections as applied or modified by any other provision of the Tax Acts.
54.	*Paragraph 13* (Urban Renewal Scheme, 1986— double rent allowance in relation to certain premises in designated areas other than the Customs House Docks Area) of *Schedule 32*.	Where any further deduction is given to the individual for the tax year by virtue of *paragraph 13* of *Schedule 32*, the amount by which that deduction reduces the amount of the individual's profits or gains to be charged to tax under Case I or Case II of Schedule D.][26]

Amendments

[1] Inserted by FA08 s26(1)(d)(i). This section comes into operation on such day or days as the Minister for Finance may by order or orders appoint and different days may be appointed for different purposes or different provisions.

[2] Inserted by FA13 s31(1)(m). Comes into operation on such day or days as the Minister for Finance may by order or orders appoint and different days may be appointed for different purposes or for different provisions.

[3] Substituted by FA07 s18(2)(a). Applies for the year of assessment 2007 and subsequent years of assessment.

[4] Inserted by FA08 s26(1)(d)(ii). This section comes into operation on such day or days as the Minister for Finance may by order or orders appoint and different days may be appointed for different purposes or different provisions.

[5] Inserted by FA13 s31(1)(n). Comes into operation on such day or days as the Minister for Finance may by order or orders appoint and different days may be appointed for different purposes or for different provisions.

[6] Inserted by FA07 s18(2)(b). Applies for the year of assessment 2007 and subsequent years of assessment.

[7] Inserted by F(No.2)A13 s16(a)(ii). Comes into operation on 1 January 2014.

[8] Inserted by FA07 s29(1)(c). With effect from 1 June 2008 per S.I. No. 159 of 2008.

[9] Substituted by FA07 s18(2)(c). Applies for the year of assessment 2007 and subsequent years of assessment.

[10, 11, 12] Inserted by FA13 s30(1)(d). Comes into operation on such day as the Minister for Finance may by order appoint.

[13] Substituted by FA07 s18(2)(d). Applies for the year of assessment 2007 and subsequent years of assessment.

[14] Substituted by FA07 s18(2)(e). Applies for the year of assessment 2007 and subsequent years of assessment.

[15, 16, 18] Inserted by FA11 s33(1)(c). Has effect in respect of shares issued on or after 25 November 2011.

[17] Substituted by F(No.2)A13 s16(a)(i). Comes into operation on 1 January 2014.

[19, 20, 21] Inserted by FA12 s12(1)(b). Applies as respects the years of assessment 2012, 2013 and 2014.

[22] Substituted by FA07 s18(2)(f). Applies for the year of assessment 2007 and subsequent years of assessment.

[23, 24, 25] Deleted by FA13 s19(2). Applies as respects a relevant donation (within the meaning of section 848A) made on or after 1 January 2013.

[26] Inserted by FA06 s17(2). Applies for the year of assessment 2007 and subsequent years of assessment.

Revenue Briefings

eBrief

eBrief No. 61/10 – High Income Individuals' Restriction

Revenue Information Notes

High Income Individuals Restriction – Tax Year 2010 Onwards – Guidance Documents

Cross References

From Schedule 25B

Section 97 Computational rules and allowable deductions.

Section 140 Distributions out of profits or gains from stallion fees, stud greyhound services fees and occupation of certain woodlands.

Section 141 Distributions out of income from patent royalties.

Section 142 Distributions out of profits of certain mines.

Section 143 Distributions out of profits from coal, gypsum and anhydrite mining operations.

Section 195 Exemption of certain earnings of writers, composers and artists.

Section 231 Profits or gains from stallion fees.

Section 232 Profits from occupation of certain woodlands.

Section 233 Stud greyhound service fees.

Section 234 Certain income derived from patent royalties.

Section 248 Relief to individuals on loans applied in acquiring interest in companies.

Section 250 Extension of relief under section 248 to certain individuals in relation to loans applied in acquiring interest in certain companies.

Section 253 Relief to individuals on loans applied in acquiring interest in partnerships.

Section 268 Meaning of "industrial building or structure".

Section 272 Writing-down allowances.

Section 273 Acceleration of writing-down allowances in respect of certain expenditure on certain industrial buildings or structures.

Section 274 Balancing allowances and balancing charges.

Section 278 Manner of making allowances and charges.

Section 304 Income tax: allowances and charges in taxing a trade, etc.

Section 305 Income tax: manner of granting, and effect of, allowances made by means of discharge or repayment of tax.

Section 323 Capital allowances in relation to construction of certain commercial premises.

Section 324 Double rent allowance in respect of rent paid for certain business premises.

Section 331 Accelerated capital allowances in relation to construction or refurbishment of certain industrial buildings or structures.

Section 332 Capital allowances in relation to construction or refurbishment of certain commercial premises.

Section 333 Double rent allowance in respect of rent paid for certain business premises.

Section 341 Accelerated capital allowances in relation to construction or refurbishment of certain industrial buildings or structures.

Section 342 Capital allowances in relation to construction or refurbishment of certain commercial premises.

Section 343 Capital allowances in relation to construction or refurbishment of certain buildings or structures in enterprise areas.
Section 344 Capital allowances in relation to construction or refurbishment of certain multi-storey car parks.
Section 345 Double rent allowance in respect of rent paid for certain business premises.
Section 352 Accelerated capital allowances in relation to construction or refurbishment of certain industrial buildings or structures.
Section 353 Capital allowances in relation to construction or refurbishment of certain commercial premises.
Section 354 Double rent allowance in respect of rent paid for certain business premises.
Section 372C Accelerated capital allowances in relation to construction or refurbishment of certain industrial buildings or structures.
Section 372D Capital allowances in relation to construction or refurbishment of certain commercial premises.
Section 372M Accelerated capital allowances in relation to construction or refurbishment of certain industrial buildings or structures.
Section 372N Capital allowances in relation to construction or refurbishment of certain commercial buildings or structures.
Section 372V Capital allowances in relation to construction or refurbishment of certain park and ride facilities.
Section 372W Capital allowances in relation to construction or refurbishment of certain commercial premises.
Section 372AC Accelerated capital allowances in relation to construction or refurbishment of certain industrial buildings or structures.
Section 372AD Capital allowances in relation to construction or refurbishment of certain commercial premises.
Section 372AM Grant of certain certificates and guidelines, qualifying and special qualifying premises.
Section 372AP Relief for lessors.
Section 372AU Saver for relief due, and for clawback of relief given under, old schemes.
Section 372AX Accelerated capital allowances in relation to the construction or refurbishment of certain registered holiday camps.
Section 372AY Capital allowances in relation to the construction or refurbishment of certain tourism infrastructure facilities.
Section 381 Right to repayment of tax by reference to losses.
Section 382 Right to carry forward losses to future years.
Section 383 Relief under Case IV for losses.
Section 384 Relief under Case V for losses.
Section 385 Terminal loss.
Section 392 Option to treat capital allowances as creating or augmenting a loss.
Section 481 Relief for investment in films.
Section 482 Relief for expenditure on significant buildings and gardens.
Section 485F Carry forward of excess relief.
Section 489 The relief.
Section 490 Limits on the relief.
Section 843 Capital allowances for buildings used for third level educational purposes.
Section 843A Capital allowances for buildings used for certain childcare purposes.
Section 847A Donations to certain sports bodies.
Section 848A Donations to approved bodies.
Schedule 32 Transitional Provisions

To Schedule 25B
Section 485C Interpretation (Chapter 2A).

SCHEDULE 25C

Determination of Amount of Relief to be Treated as Referable to Specified Reliefs as Respects Relief Carried Forward from Tax Year 2006 to Tax Year 2007

[*Section 485C.*

Determination of amount of capital allowances carried forward under section 304 which are referable to specified reliefs

1.

(1) Where, in relation to any trade or profession carried on by an individual, any allowances or part of any such allowances made under *Part 9*, including that Part as applied by any other provision of the Tax Acts, for the tax year 2006 to the individual in taxing the individual's trade or profession—

(a) are, in accordance with *section 304(4)*, added to the amount of the allowances to be made to the individual under that Part for the tax year 2007, or

(b) if there are no such allowances in 2007, are, in accordance with that section, deemed to be the allowances under that Part for that year,

then, the amount so added or so deemed (referred to in *subparagraph (2)* as the "relief forward") which is to be treated as referable to specified reliefs shall be determined for the tax year 2007 in accordance with *subparagraph (2)*.

(2) The amount referred to in *subparagraph (1)* is an amount determined in accordance with the formula—

$$RF \times \frac{SR}{TR}$$

where—

RF is the relief forward,

SR is the aggregate of the amounts of the allowances made to the individual under *Chapter 1* of *Part 9* (being allowances made in respect of a specified relief or specified reliefs) in taxing the trade or profession of the individual in respect of the tax year 2006 and each of the 3 preceding tax years, other than any such allowances or part of such allowances which—

(a) were added to the allowances to be made for any of those years by *section 304(4)*, or

(b) were deemed to be the allowances for any of those years by that section,

and

TR is the aggregate of the amounts of the allowances made to the individual under *Part 9*, including that Part as applied by any other provision of the Tax Acts, in taxing the trade or profession of the individual in respect of the tax year 2006 and each of the 3 preceding tax years, other than any such allowances or part of such allowances which—

(a) were added to the allowances to be made for any of those years by *section 304(4)*, or

(b) [...][1] were deemed to be the allowances for any of those years by that section.

Determination of amount of losses carried forward under section 382 which are referable to specified reliefs

2.

(1) Where, in relation to any trade or profession carried on by an individual, a loss is carried forward from the tax year 2006 to the tax year 2007 in accordance with *section 382*, then the amount of the loss so carried forward (in *subparagraph (2)* referred to as the "relief forward") to be treated as referable to specified reliefs shall, for the purposes of Schedule 25B, be determined for the tax year 2007 in accordance with *subparagraph (2)*.

(2) The amount referred to in *subparagraph (1)* is the amount determined in accordance with the formula—

$$RF \times \frac{SR}{TR}$$

where—

RF is the amount of the relief forward,

SR is the sum of—

$$(DR + SA)$$

where—

DR is the aggregate of the amounts of the further deductions the individual was entitled to under *sections 324*, *333*, *345*, *354* and *paragraph 13* of *Schedule 32* in respect of the trade or profession for the tax year 2006 and the 3 preceding tax years, but the amount in respect of each year to be included in the aggregate shall not exceed an amount determined by the formula—

$$(L - CA)$$

where—

L is the amount of the loss for that year in respect of which the individual was entitled to make a claim under *section 381* in respect of that trade or profession, and

CA is the amount of any claim made in that year by the individual in respect of that trade or profession by virtue of the provisions of *Chapter 2* of *Part 12*,

and

SA is the aggregate of the amounts of the allowances made to the individual under *Chapter 1* of *Part 9*, including that Chapter as applied by any other provision of the Tax Acts, (being allowances made in respect of a specified relief or specified reliefs) in taxing the trade or profession of the individual in respect of the tax year 2006 and each of the 3 preceding tax years, other than any such allowances or part of such allowances which—

(a) were added to the allowances to be made for any of those years by *section 304(4)*, or

(b) were deemed to be the allowances for any of those years by that section,

but the allowances made to the individual in respect of any year shall only be included in the aggregate if a claim was made in respect of those allowances for that year by virtue of the provisions of *Chapter 2* of *Part 12*,

TR is the sum of—

$$(TL + TA)$$

where—

TL is the aggregate of the amounts of losses eligible for relief under *section 381* in respect of that trade or profession for the tax year 2006 and each of the 3 preceding tax years less the amount of any claim made in any of those years by the individual in respect of that trade or profession by virtue of the provisions of *Chapter 2* of *Part 12*, and

TA is the aggregate of the amounts of the allowances made to the individual under Part *9*, including that Part as applied by any other provision of the Tax Acts, in taxing the trade or profession of the individual in respect of the tax year 2006 and each of the 3 preceding tax years, other than any such allowances or part of such allowances which—

(a) were added to the allowances to be made for any of those years by *section 304(4)*, or

(b) [...][2] were deemed to be the allowances for any of those years by that section,

but the allowances made to the individual in respect of any year shall only be included in the aggregate if a claim was made in respect of those allowances for that year by virtue of the provisions of *Chapter 2* of *Part 12*.

Determination of the amount of capital allowances made in charging income under Case V of Schedule D and carried forward under section 305 that is referable to specified reliefs

3.

(1) Where—

(a) the balance of any allowances or part of such allowances made under *Chapter 1* of *Part 9*, including that Chapter as applied by any other provision of the Tax Acts, for the tax year 2006 to an individual in charging income under Case V of Schedule D, or

(b) if an election is made in accordance with *section 305(1)(b)* in respect of those allowances or part of those allowances, the balance of the excess in respect of that year referred to in *section 305(1)(b)(ii)*,

is, in accordance with *section 305(1)*, available for deduction from or set off against the individual's income chargeable under Case V of Schedule D for the tax year 2007, then the amount of the balance or, as the case may be, the amount of the balance of the excess (in *subparagraph (2)* referred to as the "relief forward") which is to be treated as referable to specified reliefs shall be determined for the tax year 2007 in accordance with *subparagraph (2)*.

(2) The amount referred to in *subparagraph (1)* is an amount determined in accordance with the formula—

$$RF \times \frac{SR}{TR}$$

where—

RF is the amount of the relief forward,

SR is the aggregate of the amounts of the allowances (being allowances made in respect of a specified relief or specified reliefs) made to the individual under *Chapter 1* of *Part 9*, including that Chapter as applied by any other provision of the Tax Acts, in charging the individual's income for the tax year 2006 and each of the 3 preceding tax years under Case V of Schedule D, and

TR is the aggregate of the amounts of the allowances made to the individual under *Chapter 1* of *Part 9*, including that Chapter as applied by any other provision of the Tax Acts, in charging the individual's income for the tax year 2006 and each of the 3 preceding tax years under Case V of Schedule D.

Determination of the amount of the excess carried forward under section 384 which is referable to specified reliefs

4.

(1) Where, in accordance with *section 384*, an excess such as is referred to in that section is carried forward from the tax year 2006 to the tax year 2007 and is available to be deducted from or set off against the amount of the individual's profits or gains chargeable to tax under Case V of Schedule D, then the amount of the excess so carried forward (in *subparagraph (2)* referred to as the "relief forward") which is to be treated as referable to specified reliefs shall, for the purposes of Schedule 25B, be determined for the tax year 2007 in accordance with *subparagraph (2)*.

(2) The amount referred to in *subparagraph (1)* is an amount determined in accordance with the formula—

$$RF \times \frac{SR}{TR}$$

where—

RF is the amount of the relief forward,

SR is the aggregate of the amounts of the deductions the individual was entitled to deduct under *sections 372AP* and *372AU*, for the tax year 2006 and each of the 3 preceding tax years, and

TR is the aggregate of the amounts of the deductions the individual was entitled to deduct under *section 97(2)*, including deductions authorised under that section by virtue of *sections 372AP* and *372AU*, for the tax year 2006 and each of the 3 preceding tax years.

Right to seek a different apportionment basis

5.

(1) If an individual is not satisfied with the determination of any amount under *paragraphs 1* to *4* he or she may apply by notice in writing to the Revenue Commissioners for the amount to be replaced by an amount determined by reference to such longer or shorter continuous period before the tax year 2006, but always including that tax year, that in the opinion of the individual gives a more just and reasonable result.

(2) Where an application is made under *subparagraph (1)*, the Revenue Commissioners shall issue a determination in writing to the individual either accepting the amount or amounts on the basis proposed by the individual, setting out an amount which is just and reasonable determined by reference to some other time period or confirming the amount determined under *paragraphs 1* to *4*.

(3) If an individual is not satisfied with the determination of the Revenue Commissioners under *subparagraph (2)*, he or she may by notice in writing given to the Revenue Commissioners within 30 days of the receipt of the determination under *subparagraph (2)*appeal to the Appeal Commissioners.

(4) The Appeal Commissioners shall hear and determine an appeal made to them under *subparagraph (3)* as if it were an appeal against an assessment to income tax and the provisions of the Income Tax Acts relating to such appeals and to the rehearing of an appeal and to the statement of a case for the opinion of the High Court on a point of law shall apply accordingly with any necessary modifications.

(5) In considering an application under *subparagraph (1)* or an appeal under *subparagraph (3)* neither the Revenue Commissioners nor the Appeal Commissioners shall have any regard to an application or appeal that—

(a) requires specified reliefs to have been given effect to before reliefs that are not specified reliefs, unless a provision of the Tax Acts authorises such priority, or

(b) subject to *subparagraphs (1)* to *(4)*, requires that an amount be determined otherwise than is provided for by this Schedule.

(6) Where an amount determined under *paragraph 1*, *2*, *3* or *4* is replaced by an amount determined in accordance with this paragraph (in this paragraph referred to as the "new amount"), the new amount shall be deemed to be the amount determined under *paragraph 1*, *2*, *3* or *4*, as the case may be.][3]

Amendments

[1] Deleted by FA08 sched8(1)(v)(i). Has effect as on and from 13 March 2008.

[2] Deleted by FA08 sched8(1)(v)(ii). Has effect as on and from 13 March 2008.

[3] Inserted by FA07 s18(3). Applies for the year of assessment 2007 and subsequent years of assessment.

Cross References

From Schedule 25C

Section 97 Computational rules and allowable deductions.
Section 268 Meaning of "industrial building or structure".
Section 304 Income tax: allowances and charges in taxing a trade, etc.
Section 305 Income tax: manner of granting, and effect of, allowances made by means of discharge or repayment of tax.
Section 324 Double rent allowance in respect of rent paid for certain business premises.
Section 333 Double rent allowance in respect of rent paid for certain business premises.
Section 345 Double rent allowance in respect of rent paid for certain business premises.
Section 354 Double rent allowance in respect of rent paid for certain business premises.
Section 372AP Relief for lessors.
Section 372AU Saver for relief due, and for clawback of relief given under, old schemes.
Section 381 Right to repayment of tax by reference to losses.
Section 382 Right to carry forward losses to future years.
Section 384 Relief under Case V for losses.
Section 391 Interpretation (Chapter 2).
Schedule 32 Transitional Provisions

To Schedule 25C

Section 485C Interpretation (Chapter 2A).

SCHEDULE 26

Replacement of Harbour Authorities by Port Companies

Section 842.

[FA97 Sch5]

Interpretation

1. In this Schedule—

"*relevant port company*" means a company formed pursuant to section 7 or 87 of the Harbours Act, 1996;

"*relevant transfer*" means—

(a) the vesting in a relevant port company of assets in accordance with section 96 of the Harbours Act, 1996, and

(b) the transfer to a relevant port company of rights and liabilities in accordance with section 97 of that Act.

Capital allowances

2.

(1) This paragraph shall apply for the purposes of—

(a) allowances and charges provided for in *Part 9*, *section 670*, *Chapter 1* of *Part 29* and *sections 765* and *769*, or any other provision of the Tax Acts relating to the making of allowances or charges under or in accordance with that Part or Chapter or those sections, and

(b) allowances or charges provided for by *sections 307* and *308*.

(2) The relevant transfer shall not be treated as giving rise to any allowance or charge under any of the provisions referred to in *subparagraph (1)*.

(3) There shall be made to or on the relevant port company in accordance with *sections 307* and *308* all such allowances and charges in respect of an asset acquired by it in the course of a relevant transfer as would have been made if—

(a) allowances in relation to the asset made to the person from whom the asset was acquired had been made to the relevant port company, and

(b) everything done to or by that person in relation to the asset had been done to or by the relevant port company.

Capital gains

3.

(1) This paragraph shall apply for the purposes of the Capital Gains Tax Acts, and of the Corporation Tax Acts in so far as those Acts relate to chargeable gains.

(2) The disposal of an asset by a person in the course of a relevant transfer shall be deemed to be for a consideration of such amount as would secure that on the disposal neither a gain nor a loss would accrue to the person.

(3) Where *subparagraph (2)* has applied in relation to a disposal of an asset, then, in relation to any subsequent disposal of the asset by the relevant port company, the relevant port company shall be treated as if the acquisition or provision of the asset by the person from whom it was acquired by the relevant port company was that company's acquisition or provision of the asset.

(4) For the purposes of *section 597*, the relevant port company and the person from whom an asset was acquired in the course of a relevant transfer shall be treated as if they were the same person.

Cross References

From Schedule 26

Section 307 Corporation tax: allowances and charges in taxing a trade.
Section 308 Corporation tax: manner of granting, and effect of, allowances made by means of discharge or repayment of tax.
Section 320 Other interpretation (Part 9).
Section 597 Replacement of business and other assets.
Section 670 Mine development allowance.
Section 754 Interpretation (Chapter 1).
Section 765 Allowances for capital expenditure on scientific research.
Section 769 Relief for training of local staff before commencement of trading.
Section 842 Replacement of harbour authorities by port companies.

To Schedule 26

Section 842 Replacement of harbour authorities by port companies.

SCHEDULE 26A

Donations to Approved Bodies, etc.

[*Section 848A*.

PART 1

List of Approved Bodies for the Purposes of Section 848A

1. A body approved for education in the arts in accordance with *Part 2*.
2. A body approved as an eligible charity in accordance with *Part 3*.
3. An institution of higher education within the meaning of section 1 of the Higher Education Authority Act, 1971, or any body established [...][1] for the sole purpose of raising funds for such an institution.
4. An institution in the State in receipt of public funding which provides courses to which a scheme approved by the Minister for Education and Science under the Local Authorities (Higher Education Grants) Acts, 1968 to 1992, applies or any body established [...][2] for the sole purpose of raising funds for such an institution.

[5. An institute of higher education [...][3] which provides courses which are validated by the Qualifications and Quality Assurance Authority of Ireland under the *Qualifications and Quality Assurance (Education and Training) Act 2012*.][4]

6. An institution or other body [...][5] which provides primary education up to the end of sixth standard, based on a programme prescribed or approved by the Minister for Education and Science.
7. An institution or other body [...][6] which provides post-primary education up to the level of either or both the Junior Certificate and the Leaving Certificate based on a programme prescribed or approved by the Minister for Education and Science.

[...][7]

17. A body to which *section 209* applies which is a body for the promotion of the observance of the Universal Declaration of Human Rights or the implementation of the European Convention for the Protection of Human Rights and Fundamental Freedoms or both the promotion of the observance of that Declaration and the implementation of that Convention.

[…][8]

[…][9]

[…][10]

PART 2

Approval of a Body for Education in the Arts

1. In this Part—

["*approved body*" means any body or institution which may be approved of by the Minister for Finance and which—

(a) provides any course one of the conditions of entry to which is related to the results of the Leaving Certificate Examination, a matriculation examination of a recognised university in the State or an equivalent examination held outside the State, or

(b) (i) is established on a permanent basis solely for the advancement of one or more approved subjects,

(ii) contributes to the advancement of that subject or those subjects on a national or regional basis, and

(iii) is prohibited by its constitution from distributing to its members any of its assets or profits;][11]

"*approved subject*" means—

(a) the practice of architecture,

(b) the practice of art and design,

(c) the practice of music and musical composition,

(d) the practice of theatre arts,

(e) the practice of film arts, or

(f) any other subject approved of for the purpose of this Part by the Minister for Finance.

2. (a) The Minister for Finance may, by notice in writing given to the body or institution, as the case may be, withdraw the approval of any body or institution for the purposes of this Part, and on the giving of the notice the body or institution shall cease to be an approved body from the day after the date of the notice referred to in subparagraph (*b*).

(b) Where the Minister for Finance withdraws the approval of any body or institution for the purposes of this Part, notice of its withdrawal shall be published as soon as may be in *Iris Oifigiúil*.

PART 3

Approval of Body as Eligible Charity

1. In this Part—

"*authorisation*" shall be construed in accordance with *paragraph 3*;

"*eligible charity*" means any body [...][12] that is the holder of an authorisation that is in force.

2. Subject to *paragraph 3*, the Revenue Commissioners may, on application to them by a body [...][13], and on the furnishing of the body to the Revenue Commissioners of such information as they may reasonably require for the purpose of their functions under this Part, issue to the body a document (in this Part referred to as "*an authorisation*") stating that the body is an eligible charity for the purposes of this Part.

3. An authorisation shall not be issued to a body unless it shows to the satisfaction of the Revenue Commissioners that—

(a) it is a body of persons or a trust established for charitable purposes only,

(b) the income of the body is applied for charitable purposes only,

[(c) before the date of the making of the application concerned under paragraph 2—

(i) it has been granted exemption from tax for the purposes of *section 207* for a period of not less than 2 years, or

(ii) it received a notice of determination from the Revenue Commissioners in accordance with *section 208A* at least 2 years before that date,][14]

(d) it provides such other information to the Revenue Commissioners as they may require for the purposes of their functions under this Part, and

(e) it complies with such conditions, if any, as the Minister for Social, Community and Family Affairs may, from time to time, specify for the purposes of this Part.

4. An eligible charity shall publish such information in such manner as the Minister for Finance may reasonably require, including audited accounts of the charity comprising—

(a) an income and expenditure account or a profit and loss account, as appropriate, for its most recent accounting period, and

(b) a balance sheet as at the last day of that period.

5. Notwithstanding any obligations as to secrecy or other restriction upon disclosure of information imposed by or under any statute or otherwise, the Revenue Commissioners may make available to any person the name and address of an eligible charity.

6. Subject to *paragraph 7*, an authorisation shall have effect for such period, not exceeding 5 years, as the Revenue Commissioners may determine and specify therein.

7. Where the Revenue Commissioners are satisfied that an eligible charity has ceased to comply with *paragraph 3* or *4*, they shall, by notice in writing served by registered post on the charity, withdraw the authorisation of the charity and the withdrawal shall apply and have effect from such date [...][15] as is specified therein

[, which date shall not be earlier than the date on which the charity has ceased to so comply][16].

[8. Information to be furnished to the Revenue Commissioners or published as required by the Minister for Finance for the purposes of this Part shall be furnished or published in an official language of the State.][17]][18]

Amendments

[1, 2, 5, 6, 7, 8] Deleted by FA07 s27(1)(a)(i). Applies as on and from 1 February 2007.

[3] Deleted by FA14 sched3(1)(h). Deemed to have come into operation on and from 5 November 2012.

[4] Substituted by Qualifications and Quality Assurance (Education and Training) Act 2012 sched3(11).

[9] Deleted by FA10 s24(b). Deemed to have come into force and takes effect as on and from 1 January 2010.

[10] Deleted by FA08 s34(1). Applies as on and from 31 January 2008.

[11] Substituted by FA07 s27(1)(b). Applies as on and from 1 February 2007.

[12] Deleted by FA10 s24(c)(i). Deemed to have come into force and takes effect as on and from 1 January 2010.

[13] Deleted by FA10 s24(c)(ii). Deemed to have come into force and takes effect as on and from 1 January 2010.

[14] Substituted by FA10 s24(d). Deemed to have come into force and takes effect as on and from 1 January 2010.

[15] Deleted by FA14 s18(1)(b)(i). Has effect from 1 January 2015 as respects an authorisation issued, whether before, on or after that date, under paragraph 2 of Part 3 of Schedule 26A.

[16] Inserted by FA14 s18(1)(b)(ii). Has effect from 1 January 2015 as respects an authorisation issued, whether before, on or after that date, under paragraph 2 of Part 3 of Schedule 26A.

[17] Inserted by FA10 s24(e). Deemed to have come into force and takes effect as on and from 1 January 2010.

[18] Inserted by FA01 s45(4).

Cross References

From Schedule 26A

Section 207 Rents of properties belonging to hospitals and other charities.

Section 208A Overseas charities.

Section 209 Bodies for the promotion of Universal Declaration of Human Rights and the implementation of European Convention for the Protection of Human Rights and Fundamental Freedoms.

Section 848A Donations to approved bodies.

SCHEDULE 27

Forms of Declarations to be Made by Certain Persons

Sections 855, 857, 867 and *942.*

[ITA67 Sch17; F(MP)A68 s3(4) and Sch Pt III]

PART 1

Form of Declaration to be Made by Appeal Commissioners Acting in Respect of Tax Under Schedule D

"I, A.B., do solemnly declare, that I will truly, faithfully, impartially and honestly, according to the best of my skill and knowledge, execute the powers and authorities vested in me by the Acts relating to income tax, and that I will exercise the powers entrusted to me by the said Acts in such manner only as shall appear to me necessary for the due execution of the same; and that I will judge and determine upon all matters and things which shall be brought before me under the said Acts without favour, affection, or malice; and that I will not disclose any particular contained in any schedule, statement, return or other document delivered with respect to any tax charged under the provisions relating to Schedule D of the said Acts, or any evidence or answer given by any person who shall be examined, or shall make affidavit or deposition, respecting the same, in pursuance of the said Acts, except to such persons only as shall act in the execution of the said Acts, and where it shall be necessary to disclose the same to them for the purposes of the said Acts, or to the Revenue Commissioners, or in order to, or in the course of, a prosecution for perjury committed in such examination, affidavit or deposition."

Form of declaration to be made by inspectors

"I, A.B., do solemnly declare, that in the execution [of the Tax Acts and the Capital Gains Tax Acts][1] I will examine and revise all statements, returns, schedules and declarations delivered within my district, and, in objecting to the same, I will act according to the best of my information and knowledge; and that I will conduct myself without favour, affection, or malice, and that I will exercise the powers entrusted to me by the said Acts in such manner only as shall appear to me to be necessary for the due execution of the same, or as I shall be directed by the Revenue Commissioners; and that I will not disclose any particular contained in any statement, return, schedule or other document, with respect to any tax charged under the provisions [...][2] of the said Acts, or any evidence or answer given by any person who shall be examined, or shall make affidavit or deposition, respecting the same, in pursuance of the said Acts, except to such persons only as shall act in the execution of the said Acts, and where it shall be necessary to disclose the same to them for the purposes of the said Acts, or to the Revenue Commissioners, or in order to, or in the course of, a prosecution for perjury committed in such examination, affidavit or deposition."

Form of declaration to be made by persons appointed under section 854 or section 855 as assessors

[...][3]

Form of declaration to be made by the Collector-General and officers for receiving tax

"I, A.B., do solemnly declare, that in the execution [of the Tax Acts and the Capital Gains Tax Acts][4], I will not disclose any assessment, or the amount of any sum paid or to be paid by any person, under the said Acts, or the books of assessment which shall be delivered to me in the execution of the said Acts, with respect to any tax charged under the provisions [...][5] of the said Acts, except to such persons only as shall act in the execution of the said Acts, and where it shall be necessary to disclose the same to them for the purposes of the said Acts, or to the Revenue Commissioners, or in order to, or in the course of, a prosecution for perjury committed in relation to the said tax."

Form of declaration to be made by the Clerk to the Appeal Commissioners

"I, A.B., do solemnly declare, that I will diligently and faithfully execute the office of a clerk according to the Acts relating to income tax, to the best of my knowledge and judgment; and that I will not disclose any particular contained in any statement, return, declaration, schedule or other document, with respect to the tax charged under the provisions relating to Schedule D of the said Acts, or any evidence or answer given by any person who shall be examined, or shall make affidavit or deposition, respecting the same, except to such persons only as shall act in the execution of the said Acts, and where I shall be directed so to do by the said Acts, or by the commissioners under whom I act, or by the Revenue Commissioners, or in order to, and in the course of, a prosecution for perjury committed in such examination, affidavit or deposition."

[...][6]

Amendments

[1] Substituted by FA12 sched5(3)(a)(i). Applies as respects a person appointed after 31 March 2012.

[2] Deleted by FA12 sched5(3)(a)(ii). Applies as respects a person appointed after 31 March 2012.

[3] Deleted by FA12 sched5(3)(b).

[4] Substituted by FA12 sched5(3)(c)(i). Applies as respects a person appointed after 31 March 2012.

[5] Deleted by FA12 sched5(3)(c)(ii). Applies as respects a person appointed after 31 March 2012.

[6] Deleted by FA12 sched5(4).

Cross References

From Schedule 27

Section 854 Appointment of persons for purposes of assessment of certain public offices.
Section 855 Declaration to be made by Commissioners.
Section 857 Declarations on taking office.
Section 867 Amendment of statutory forms.
Section 942 Appeals to Circuit Court.

To Schedule 27

Section 855 Declaration to be made by Commissioners.
Section 857 Declarations on taking office.
Section 867 Amendment of statutory forms.
Section 942 Appeals to Circuit Court.

SCHEDULE 28

Statements, Lists and Declarations

Sections 458, 866 and 867.

[ITA67 Sch18 pars II to IX; FA69 s33(1) and Sch4 PtI; FA90 s20(1); FA97 s146(2) and Sch9 PtII]

1. BY OR FOR EVERY PERSON CARRYING ON ANY TRADE OR EXERCISING ANY PROFESSION TO BE CHARGED UNDER SCHEDULE D.

   The amount of the profits or gains thereof arising within the year of assessment.

2. BY EVERY PERSON ENTITLED TO PROFITS OF AN UNCERTAIN VALUE NOT BEFORE STATED, OR ANY INTEREST, ANNUITY, ANNUAL PAYMENT, DISCOUNT OR DIVIDEND, TO BE CHARGED UNDER SCHEDULE D.

   The full amount of the profits or gains arising therefrom within the year of assessment.

3. BY EVERY PERSON ENTITLED TO OR RECEIVING INCOME FROM SECURITIES OR POSSESSIONS OUT OF THE STATE TO BE CHARGED UNDER SCHEDULE D.

(1) The full amount arising within the year of assessment, and the amount of every deduction or allowance claimed in respect thereof, together with the particulars of such deduction and the grounds for claiming such allowance; or

(2) In the case of any such person who satisfies the Revenue Commissioners that he or she is not domiciled in the State, or that being a citizen of Ireland he or she is not ordinarily resident in the State, or in the case of income arising from such securities and possessions aforesaid which form part of the investments of the foreign life assurance fund of an assurance company the full amount of the actual sums received in the State from remittances payable in the State or from property imported, or from money or value arising from property not imported, or from money or value so received on credit or on account in respect of such remittances, property, money or value brought into the State in the year of assessment without any deduction or abatement.

4. BY EVERY PERSON ENTITLED TO ANY ANNUAL PROFITS OR GAINS NOT FALLING UNDER ANY OF THE FOREGOING RULES, AND NOT CHARGED BY ANY OF THE OTHER SCHEDULES, TO BE CHARGED UNDER SCHEDULE D.

The full amount thereof received annually, or according to the average directed to be taken by the inspector on a statement of the nature of such profits or gains and the grounds on which the amount has been computed, and the average taken, to the best of the knowledge and belief of such person.

5. STATEMENT OF PROFITS OF ANY PUBLIC OFFICE, OR EMPLOYMENT OF PROFIT, TO BE CHARGED UNDER SCHEDULE E.

The amount of the salary, fees, wages, perquisites and profits of the year of assessment.

6. GENERAL DECLARATION BY EACH PERSON RETURNING A STATEMENT OF PROFITS OR GAINS TO BE CHARGED UNDER SCHEDULES D OR E

Declaring the truth thereof, and that the same is fully stated on every description of property, or profits or gains, included in the Act relating to the said tax, and appertaining to such person, estimated to the best of such person's judgment and belief, according to the provisions of the Income Tax Acts.

7. LISTS AND DECLARATIONS FOR FACILITATING THE EXECUTION OF THE INCOME TAX ACTS IN RELATION TO THE TAX CHARGEABLE ON OTHERS.

First. List containing the name and place of residence of every person in any service or employ, and the payments made to every such person in respect of the service or employment.

Second. List to be delivered by every person chargeable on behalf of another person, and by any person whomsoever who, in whatever capacity, is in receipt of any money or value, or of profits or gains, of or belonging to any other person, describing that other person for whom the person acts, and stating that other person's name and address, and the amount of such money, value, profit or gains, and declaring whether that other person is of full age, or [a married woman living with her husband, or a civil partner living with his or her civil partner, or a married woman whose husband is not accountable for the payment of tax charged on her, or a civil partner whose civil partner is not accountable for the payment of tax charged on his or her civil partner,]1 or is resident in the State, or is an incapacitated person. The person delivering such list shall also deliver a list containing the names and addresses of any other person or persons acting jointly with such person.

Third. Declaration on whom the tax is chargeable in respect of any such money, value, profits or gains.

Fourth. List containing the proper description of every body of persons, or trust for which any person is answerable under the Income Tax Acts and where any such person is answerable under the Income Tax Acts for the tax to be charged in respect of the property or profits or gains of other persons, that person shall deliver such lists as aforesaid, together with the required statements of such profits or gains.

8. LISTS, DECLARATIONS, AND STATEMENTS TO BE DELIVERED IN ORDER TO OBTAIN ANY ALLOWANCE OR DEDUCTION.

First. Declaration of the amount of value of property or profits or gains returned, or for which the claimant has been, or is liable to be, assessed.

Second. Declaration of the amount of rents, interests, annuities, or other annual payments, in respect of which the claimant is liable to allow the tax, with the names of the respective persons by whom such payments are to be made, distinguishing the amount of each payment.

Third. Declaration of the amount of interest, annuities, or other annual payments to be made out of the property or profits or gains assessed on the claimant, distinguishing each source.

Fourth. Statement of the amount of income derived according to the 3 preceding declarations.

Fifth. Statement of any tax which the claimant may be entitled to deduct, retain or charge against any other person.

Amendments

[1] Substituted by F(No.3)A11 sched1(254). Shall have effect from 27 July 2011.

Cross References

From Schedule 28

Section 458 Deductions allowed in ascertaining taxable income and provisions relating to reductions in tax.

Section 866 Rules as to delivery of statements.

Section 867 Amendment of statutory forms.

To Schedule 28

Section 188 Age exemption and associated marginal relief.

Section 234 Certain income derived from patent royalties.

Section 458 Deductions allowed in ascertaining taxable income and provisions relating to reductions in tax.

Section 664 Relief for certain income from leasing of farm land.

Section 866 Rules as to delivery of statements.

Section 867 Amendment of statutory forms.

Section 1020 Special provisions relating to year of marriage.

Section 1025 Maintenance in case of separated spouses.

Schedule 32 Transitional Provisions

SCHEDULE 29

Provisions Referred to in *Sections 1052, 1054* and *1077E*

Section 1052, 1053 and 1054.

[ITA67 Sch15; F(MP)A68 s5(2); FA72 s13(4) and Sch1 PtIII par3; FA73 s33(7) and Sch 3 par2 and s39 and Sch5 par10; FA74 s59(6) and s73(5); FA75 s22(2) and Sch2 PtII; FA76 s11(4); FA81 s29(4); FA82 s4(8), s5(2)(b) and s51(8); FA83 s20(5), s21(3), and s22(3); FA84 s24(9) and s29(6); FA85 s19(4); FA86 s9(11)(b) and s40(1); FA88 s10(12) and s73(7)(a); FA89 s18(5)(b), s19(4) and Sch 1 par3(1); FA91 s68(4); FA92 s226(7); WCTIPA93 s12; FA95 s7(9)(b) and s236(7); FA97 s13(2)]

Column 1	Column 2	Column 3
section 121	[…][7]	section 123(6)
[section 172K(1)	[…][8]	[section 128C(15)
section 172L(2)][1]		section 128D(8)
[*section 244A* and Regulations under that section][2]		section128E(9)][9]
[*section 470* and Regulations under that section][3]		
[*section 470A* and Regulations under that section][4]		
[*section 470B* and Regulations under that section][5]		
section 473 or Regulations under that section	section 183	section 238(3)
	[…][10]	section 257(1)
	[section 264B	[section 267B][13]
	section 267E][11]	[section 473A][14]
		[section 477B][15]
		[section 481(2F)][16]
[*section 531AF*][6]	[*section 503(3)* and *(4)* (as substituted by *section 33* of the Finance Act 2011)	[*section 503(1)* and *(2)* (as substituted by *section 33* of the Finance Act 2011)
	section 505(3) and *(4)* (before the coming into operation of *section 33* of the Finance Act 2011)][12]	*section 505(1)* and *(2)* (before the coming into operation of section 33 of the Finance Act 2011)][20]
[Chapter 2 of Part 18 and regulations made under that Chapter][17]	section 510(7)	[section 510(8)][21]
[section 730FA(2)][18]	section 645	[Chapter 2 of Part 18 and regulations made under that Chapter][22]
[section 730G(2)		
section 739F(2)][19]		
section 877	section 804(4)	
section 878	section 808	section 734(5)
		[section 784A(8)][23]
section 879(2)	section 812(4)	section 876
section 880	section 815	section 885
[*Chapter 3* of *Part 41A*][24]	section 881	[section 896][26]
[*section 986* and Regulations under that section][25]		[section 896A][27]

Column 1	Column 2	Column 3
paragraphs (a)(iii)(I) and (c) of *subsection (2)* and paragraphs (*a*)(i) and (b)(i) of *subsection (4)* of section 1002	section 888 section 890 section 891 [section 891A][28] section 892	[*section 897B*][29] section 904 section 972 Schedule 2, paragraph 14 [Schedule 12, paragraph 3(5); Schedule 12A, paragraph 6A; Schedule 12C, paragraph 20A;][30] Schedule 23, paragraph 3(2)(*a*)
section 1023	[…][31]	Waiver of Certain Tax, Interest and Penalties Act, 1993, sections 2(3)(*a*) and 3(6)(*b*)
Waiver of Certain Tax, Interest and Penalties Act, 1993, sections 2(3)(*a*) and 3(6)(*b*)	section 894(3) [section 896][32] section 897 section 898 section 900 section 909 section 935 section 947 Schedule 1, paragraph 1 Schedule 9, paragraph 8 [*Schedule 12, paragraph 3(4)* *Schedule 12A, paragraph 6* *Schedule 12B*, paragraph 5 *Schedule 12C, paragraph 20.*][33] Schedule 18, paragraph 1(2) [Schedule 18B, paragraph 30][34] Schedule 23, paragraphs 2, 3(2)(*b*) and 3(3)	

Amendments

[1] Inserted by FA02 s128(a)(i).

[2] Inserted by FA01 s23(2). Applies as respects the year of assessment 2002 and subsequent years of assessment.

[3] Inserted by FA01 s19(3).

[4] Inserted by FA01 s20(c).

[5] Inserted by the Health Insurance (Miscellaneous Provisions) Act 2009 sec 25

[6] Inserted by FA14 s85(c).

[7] Deleted by FA00 s27(c)(i).

[8, 10] Deleted by FA02 s128(b).

[9] Inserted by F(No.2)A08 s11(a). This section is deemed to have come into force and takes effect as on and from 1 January 2009.

[11] Inserted by FA01 s57(1)(c)(i). With effect from 1 January 2002 as per S.I. No. 596 of 2001.

[12] Substituted by FA12 sched6(1)(s)(i). Has effect on and from 1 January 2012.

[13] Inserted by FA01 s57(1)(c)(ii). With effect from 1 January 2002 as per S.I. No. 596 of 2001.

[14] Inserted by F(No.2)A13 s14(b). Comes into operation on 1 January 2014.

[15] Inserted by F(No.2)A13 s5(b). Comes into operation on 1 January 2014.

[16] Inserted by FA12 sched6(1)(s)(ii). Has effect on and from 1 January 2012.

[17, 22] Substituted by FA11 s20(1)(u). With effect from 1 January 2012 as per S.I. No. 660 of 2011.

[18] Inserted by FA02 s40(4). Applies as on and from 5 December 2001.

[19] Inserted by FA00 s72.

[20] Substituted by FA12 sched6(1)(s)(iii). Has effect on and from 1 January 2012.

[21] Inserted by FA08 s19(1)(e)(i). Applies as on and from 1 January 2009.

[23] Inserted by FA03 s14(1)(g). Has effect as on and from 28 March 2003.

[24] Substituted by FA12 sched4(part 2)(g).

[25] Inserted by FA99 s41(a).

[26] Substituted by FA05 sched6(1)(p)(ii). Applies as on and from 25 March 2005.

[27] Inserted by F(No.2)A08 s11(b). This section is deemed to have come into force and takes effect as on and from 1 January 2009.

[28] Inserted by FA99 s41(b).

[29] Inserted by FA10 s18(1)(b). Has effect as on and from 3 April 2010.

[30] Inserted by FA08 s19(1)(e)(ii). Applies as on and from 1 January 2009.

[31] Deleted by FA05 sched6(1)(p)(i)(I). Applies as on and from 25 March 2005.

[32] Inserted by FA05 sched6(1)(p)(i)(II). Applies as on and from 25 March 2005.

[33] Inserted by FA01 s15(c).

[34] Inserted by FA02 s53(4). Per FA03 s62(2) with effect from 28 March 2003.

Cross References

From Schedule 29

Section 121 Benefit of use of car.
Section 123 General tax treatment of payments on retirement or removal from office or employment.
Section 172K Returns, payment and collection of dividend withholding tax.
Section 172L Reporting of distributions made under stapled stock arrangements.
Section 183 Information.
Section 238 Annual payments not payable out of taxed income.
Section 244A Application of section 244 (relief for interest paid on certain home loans) of Principal Act.
Section 257 Deduction of tax from relevant interest.
Section 264B Returns of special term accounts by relevant deposit takers.
Section 267B Election to open a special share account or a special term share account.
Section 267E Returns of special term share accounts by credit unions.
Section 470 Relief for insurance against expenses of illness.
Section 470A Relief for premiums under qualifying long-term care policies.
Section 470B Age-related relief for health insurance premiums.
Section 473 Allowance for rent paid by certain tenants.
Section 477 Relief for service charges.
Section 505 Application to subsidiaries.
Section 510 Approved profit sharing schemes: appropriated shares.
Section 645 Power to obtain information.
Section 730FA Assessment of appropriate tax where tax not deducted under section 730F.
Section 730G Returns and collection of appropriate tax.
Section 734 Taxation of collective investment undertakings.
Section 739F Returns and collection of appropriate tax.

Section 784A Approved retirement fund.
Section 804 Adjustments and information.
Section 808 Power to obtain information.
Section 812 Taxation of income deemed to arise from transfers of right to receive interest from securities.
Section 815 Taxation of income deemed to arise on certain sales of securities.
Section 876 Notice of liability to income tax.
Section 877 Returns by persons chargeable.
Section 878 Persons acting for incapacitated persons and non-residents.
Section 879 Returns of income.
Section 880 Partnership returns.
Section 881 Returns by married persons.
Section 885 Obligation to show tax reference number on receipts.
Section 888 Returns, etc. by lessors, lessees and agents.
Section 890 Returns by persons in receipt of income belonging to others.
Section 891 Returns of interest paid or credited without deduction of tax.
Section 891A Returns of interest paid to non-residents.
Section 892 Returns by nominee holders of securities.
Section 894 Returns of certain information by third parties.
Section 896 Returns in relation to certain offshore products.
Section 896A Returns in relation to settlements and trustees.
Section 897 Returns of employees' emoluments, etc.
Section 897B Returns of information in respect of awards of shares to directors and employees.
Section 898 Returns of copies of rates and production of certain valuations.
Section 900 Power to call for production of books, information, etc.
Section 904 Power of inspection: tax deduction from payments to certain subcontractors.
Section 909 Power to require return of property.
Section 935 Power to issue precepts.
Section 947 Appeals against determination under sections 98 to 100.
Section 951 Obligation to make a return.
Section 972 Duty of employer as to income tax payable by employees.
Section 986 Regulations.
Section 1002 Deduction from payments due to defaulters of amounts due in relation to tax.
Section 1023 Application for separate assessments.
Section 1052 Penalties for failure to make certain returns, etc.
Section 1053 Penalty for fraudulently or negligently making incorrect returns, etc.
Section 1054 Penalties in the case of a secretary of a body of persons.
Section 1077E Penalty for deliberately or carelessly making incorrect returns, etc.
Schedule 1 Supplementary Provisions Concerning the Extension of Charge to Tax to Profits and Income Derived from Activities Carried On and Employments Exercised on the Continental Shelf
Schedule 2 Machinery for Assessment, Charge and Payment of Tax under Schedule C and, in Certain Cases, Schedule D
Schedule 9 Change in Ownership of Company: Disallowance of Trading Losses
Schedule 12 Employee Share Ownership Trusts
Schedule 12A Approved Savings-Related Share Option Schemes
Schedule 12B Certified Contractual Savings Schemes
Schedule 12C Approved Share Option Schemes
Schedule 18 Accounting for and Payment of Tax Deducted from Relevant Payments and Undistributed Relevant Income
Schedule 18B Tonnage Tax
Schedule 23 Occupational Pension Schemes

To Schedule 29

Section 805 Surcharge on certain income of trustees.
Section 1052 Penalties for failure to make certain returns, etc.
Section 1053 Penalty for fraudulently or negligently making incorrect returns, etc.
Schedule 32 Transitional Provisions

SCHEDULE 30

Repeals

Section 1098.

Number and year (1)	Short title (2)	Extent of repeal (3)
No. 11 of 1928.	Finance Act, 1928.	Section 34(2).
No. 6 of 1967.	Income Tax Act, 1967.	The whole Act, in so far as it is unrepealed.
No. 7 of 1967.	Income Tax (Amendment) Act, 1967.	The whole Act, in so far as it is unrepealed.
No. 17 of 1967.	Finance Act, 1967.	Part I, in so far as it is unrepealed. Section 25, in so far as it relates to income tax. Section 27(2) and (6). Third Schedule, Part I, in so far as it relates to income tax.
No. 7 of 1968.	Finance (Miscellaneous Provisions) Act, 1968.	Parts I and IV, in so far as they are unrepealed. Sections 25 to 27. Section 29(2). Schedule, Parts I to IV.
No. 33 of 1968.	Finance Act, 1968.	Part I, in so far as it is unrepealed. Sections 37 to 39. Section 48(2) and (5).
No. 37 of 1968.	Finance (No. 2) Act, 1968.	Sections 8 and 11(4), in so far as they are unrepealed.
No. 21 of 1969.	Finance Act, 1969.	Parts I and II, in so far as they are unrepealed. Section 63, in so far as it is unrepealed. Sections 64 and 65(1). Section 67(2) and (7). Fourth Schedule, Part I. Fifth Schedule, Part I.
No. 14 of 1970.	Finance Act, 1970.	Part I, in so far as it is unrepealed. Sections 57 to 59. Section 62(2) and (7).
No. 25 of 1970.	Finance (No. 2) Act, 1970.	Section 1. Section 8(2) and (5).
No. 23 of 1971.	Finance Act, 1971.	Part I, in so far as it is unrepealed. Section 55(2) and (6).
No. 19 of 1972.	Finance Act, 1972.	Part I, in so far as it is unrepealed. Section 42. Section 43, in so far as it is unrepealed. Section 46, in so far as it relates to income tax. Section 48(2) and (5). First Schedule, in so far as it is unrepealed. Third Schedule, in so far as it relates to income tax. Fourth Schedule, in so far as it relates to income tax.
No. 19 of 1973.	Finance Act, 1973.	Part I, in so far as it is unrepealed. Section 92, except in so far as it relates to death duties and stamp duty. Section 98(2) and (6). Third Schedule. Fifth Schedule.

Number and year (1)	Short title (2)	Extent of repeal (3)
No. 17 of 1974.	Finance (Taxation of Profits of Certain Mines) Act, 1974.	The whole Act, in so far as it is unrepealed.
No. 27 of 1974.	Finance Act, 1974.	Part I, in so far as it is unrepealed. Section 86. Section 88(2) and (5). First Schedule. Second Schedule.
No. 6 of 1975.	Finance Act, 1975.	Part I, in so far as it is unrepealed. Section 57(2) and (5). First Schedule. Second Schedule.
No. 19 of 1975.	Finance (No. 2) Act, 1975.	Sections 1 and 4(2).
No. 20 of 1975.	Capital Gains Tax Act, 1975.	The whole Act, in so far as it is unrepealed.
No. 7 of 1976.	Corporation Tax Act, 1976.	The whole Act, in so far as it is unrepealed.
No. 16 of 1976.	Finance Act, 1976.	Part I, in so far as it is unrepealed. Section 81(1) and (3)(*a*). Section 83(2) and (6). First Schedule. Fifth Schedule, Part I.
No. 18 of 1977.	Finance Act, 1977.	Part I, in so far as it is unrepealed. Section 53. Section 54, in so far as it relates to income tax, corporation tax and capital gains tax. Section 56(2) and (7). First Schedule. Second Schedule, in so far as it relates to income tax, corporation tax and capital gains tax.
No. 21 of 1978.	Finance Act, 1978.	Part I, in so far as it is unrepealed. Section 46, in so far as it relates to income tax, corporation tax and capital gains tax. Sections 47, 52(1) and 54(2) and (8). First Schedule. Second Schedule. Fourth Schedule, Part I.
No. 33 of 1978.	Capital Gains Tax (Amendment) Act, 1978.	The whole Act, in so far as it is unrepealed.
No. 11 of 1979.	Finance Act, 1979.	Part I, in so far as it is unrepealed. Section 59(2) and (6). First Schedule. Second Schedule.
No. 14 of 1980.	Finance Act, 1980.	Part I, in so far as it is unrepealed. Sections 89 and 96(2) and (7). First Schedule.
No. 16 of 1981.	Finance Act, 1981.	Part I, in so far as it is unrepealed. Sections 52 and 54(2) and (7). First Schedule.
No. 14 of 1982.	Finance Act, 1982.	Part I, in so far as it is unrepealed. Sections 105(2) and (7). First Schedule. Second Schedule.

Number and year (1)	Short title (2)	Extent of repeal (3)
		Third Schedule.
No. 15 of 1983.	Finance Act, 1983.	Part I, in so far as it is unrepealed. Part V. Section 120, in so far as it relates to income tax, corporation tax and capital gains tax. Section 122(2) and (6). Fourth Schedule, in so far as it relates to income tax, corporation tax and capital gains tax.
No. 9 of 1984.	Finance Act, 1984.	Part I, in so far as it is unrepealed. Section 116(2) and (7). First Schedule. Second Schedule.
No. 10 of 1985.	Finance Act, 1985.	Part I. Sections 69 and 71(2) and (7). First Schedule.
No. 13 of 1986.	Finance Act, 1986.	Part I, in so far as it is unrepealed. Sections 112 to 116. Sections 118(2), (7) (in so far as it relates to income tax, corporation tax and capital gains tax) and (8). First Schedule. Second Schedule. Third Schedule. Fourth Schedule.
No. 34 of 1986.	Income Tax (Amendment) Act, 1986.	The whole Act.
No. 10 of 1987.	Finance Act, 1987.	Part I. Sections 52 and 55(2) and (7).
No. 12 of 1988.	Finance Act, 1988.	Part I, in so far as it is unrepealed. Sections 70 to 74. Sections 77(2), (7) (except in so far as it relates to the Local Loans Fund) and (8). First Schedule. Second Schedule. Third Schedule.
No. 6 of 1989.	Judicial Separation and Family Law Reform Act, 1989.	Section 26.
No. 10 of 1989.	Finance Act, 1989.	Part I, in so far as it is unrepealed. Sections 86 to 89. Sections 95, 98 and 100(2), (7) (except in so far as it relates to capital acquisitions tax) and (8). First Schedule.
No. 10 of 1990.	Finance Act, 1990.	Part I. Sections 131, 136, 137, 138 and 140(2) and (8). First Schedule. Second Schedule. Third Schedule. Fourth Schedule. Fifth Schedule.

Number and year (1)	Short title (2)	Extent of repeal (3)
		Sixth Schedule.
No. 13 of 1991.	Finance Act, 1991.	Part I, in so far as it is unrepealed. Sections 126, 128, 130 and 132(2) and (8). First Schedule. Second Schedule.
No. 3 of 1992.	Oireachtas (Allowances to Members) and Ministerial and Parliamentary Offices Act, 1992.	Section 4.
No. 9 of 1992.	Finance Act, 1992.	Part I, in so far as it is unrepealed. Part VII, except section 248 in so far as it relates to residential property tax. Section 254(2), (8) (except in so far as it relates to residential property tax) and (9). First Schedule. Second Schedule.
No. 28 of 1992.	Finance (No. 2) Act, 1992.	Part I. Section 30(2).
No. 13 of 1993.	Finance Act, 1993.	Part I, in so far as it is unrepealed. Sections 140 and 143(2) and (8). First Schedule.
No. 24 of 1993.	Waiver of Certain Tax, Interest and Penalties Act, 1993.	Sections 10 to 13.
No. 13 of 1994.	Finance Act, 1994.	Part I, in so far as it is unrepealed. Part VII, Chapter I. Section 161, except in so far as it relates to stamp duty. Sections 162, 163(2), 164 and 166(2) and (8). First Schedule. Second Schedule.
No. 8 of 1995.	Finance Act, 1995.	Part I, in so far as it is unrepealed. Part VII, Chapter I. Sections 172 to 177. Section 179(2), (8) and (9). First Schedule. Second Schedule. Third Schedule. Fourth Schedule.
No. 26 of 1995.	Family Law Act, 1995.	Section 37.
No. 9 of 1996.	Finance Act, 1996.	Part I, in so far as it is unrepealed. Part VI. Sections 139 and 143(2), (7) and (8). First Schedule. Fifth Schedule.
No. 25 of 1996.	Disclosure of Certain Information for Taxation and Other Purposes Act, 1996.	Sections 5, 6, 10, 11 and 12.
No. 31 of 1996.	Criminal Assets Bureau Act, 1996.	Sections 23 and 24(1) and (2).

Number and year (1)	Short title (2)	Extent of repeal (3)
No. 33 of 1996.	Family Law (Divorce) Act, 1996.	Section 31.
No. 22 of 1997.	Finance Act, 1997.	Parts I and VII. Sections 157, 158, 159, 160(1) and 166(2), (8) and (9). First Schedule. Second Schedule. Third Schedule. Fourth Schedule. Fifth Schedule. Sixth Schedule. Ninth Schedule. Tenth Schedule.

Cross References

From Schedule 30

Section 160 Set-off of advance corporation tax.

Section 1098 Repeals.

To Schedule 30

Section 1098 Repeals.

SCHEDULE 31

Consequential Amendments

Section 1100.

In the enactments specified in *Column (1)* of the following Table for the words set out or referred to in *Column (2)* there shall be substituted the words set out in the corresponding entry in *Column (3)*.

Enactment amended (1)	Words to be replaced (2)	Words to be substituted (3)
The Stamp Act, 1891:		
section 13(1), in the definition of "*Appeal Commissioners*"	section 156 of the Income Tax Act, 1967	section 850 of the Taxes Consolidation Act, 1997
section 13(4)	Part XXVI (Appeals) of the Income Tax Act, 1967	Chapter 1 of Part 40 (Appeals) of the Taxes Consolidation Act, 1997
The Finance (1909-10) Act, 1910:		
section 49, in the first proviso to subsection (1)	section 242 of the Finance Act, 1992	section 1094 of the Taxes Consolidation Act, 1997
section 49, in the second proviso to subsection (1)	section 242 (as amended by the Finance Act, 1993) of the Finance Act, 1992	section 1094 of the Taxes Consolidation Act, 1997
section 49, in paragraph (*a*) of subsection (1A)	section 242 of the Finance Act, 1992	section 1094 of the Taxes Consolidation Act, 1997
	subsection (6) of the said section 242	subsection (7) of that section

Enactment amended (1)	Words to be replaced (2)	Words to be substituted (3)
The Betting Act, 1931, the proviso to section 7 (3)	section 242 (as amended) by the Finance Act, 1993) of the Finance Act, 1992	section 1094 of the Taxes Consolidation Act, 1997
The Auctioneers and House Agents Act, 1947:		
section 8, in the proviso to subsection (1)	section 242 (as amended by the Finance Act, 1993) of the Finance Act, 1992	section 1094 of the Taxes Consolidation Act, 1997
section 9, in the proviso to subsection (1)	section 242 (as amended by the Finance Act, 1993) of the Finance Act, 1992	section 1094 of the Taxes Consolidation Act, 1997
section 10, in the proviso to subsection (1)	section 242 (as amended by the Finance Act, 1993) of the Finance Act, 1992	section 1094 of the Taxes Consolidation Act, 1997
The Finance Act, 1952, section 19(2)	section 156 of the Corporation Tax Act, 1976	section 9 of the Taxes Consolidation Act, 1997
The Gaming and Lotteries Act, 1956, the proviso to section 19	section 242 (as amended by the Finance Act, 1993) of the Finance Act, 1992	section 1094 of the Taxes Consolidation Act, 1997
The Civil Service Commissioners Act, 1956, section 27(3)	section 156(1) of the Income Tax Act, 1967	section 850(1) of the Taxes Consolidation Act, 1997
The Income Tax (Purchased Life Annuities) Regulations, 1959 (S.I. No. 152 of 1959):		
Regulation 2, in the definition of "*the principal section*"	section 22 of the Finance Act, 1959	section 788 of the Taxes Consolidation Act, 1997
Regulation 5	subsection (3) subsection (4)	subsection (5) subsection (6)
Regulation 7	Subsection (3) of section 5 of the Finance Act, 1929 (No. 32 of 1929), as amended by section 3 of the Finance Act, 1958 (No. 25 of 1958)	Subsection (3) of section 933 of the Taxes Consolidation Act, 1997
Regulation 9	Sections 149 and 196 of the Income Tax Act, 1918	Sections 941 and 942 of the Taxes Consolidation Act, 1997
Regulation 17	Rule 17 of the General Rules	Section 1023 of the Taxes Consolidation Act, 1997
The Income Tax (Employments) Regulations, 1960 (S.I. No. 28 of 1960):		
Regulation 2, in paragraph (1)	"*the Act*" means the Finance (No. 2) Act, 1959 (No. 42 of 1959)	"*the Act*" means the Taxes Consolidation Act, 1997
Regulation 2, paragraph (1), in the definition of "*emoluments*"	Part II of the Act	Chapter 4 of Part 42 of the Act
Regulation 36, in paragraph (2)	Section 7 of the Finance Act, 1923 (No. 21 of 1923), as applied by section 11 of the Act	Section 962 of the Act, as applied by section 993 of the Act
Regulation 36, in paragraph (3)	Section 11 of the Finance Act, 1924 (No. 27 of 1924), as applied by section 11 of the Act	Section 963 of the Act, as applied by section 993 of the Act

Enactment amended (1)	Words to be replaced (2)	Words to be substituted (3)
Regulation 59	section 222 or 223 of the Income Tax Act, 1967 (No. 6 of 1967) or by virtue of section 16, 17 or 25 of the Finance Act, 1972 (No. 19 of 1972)	section 774 or 776 of the Act
Regulation 60	Chapter IV of Part V of the Income Tax Act, 1967	Chapter 4 of Part 42 of the Act
The Income Tax (Construction Contracts) Regulations, 1971 (S.I. No. 1 of 1971):		
Regulation 2, in the definition of "*certified sub-contractor*"	subsection (9)*(a)* of the principal section	*subsection (13)(a)* of section 531 of the Act
Regulation 2, in the definition of "*principal*"	the principal section	section 530 of the Act
	subsection (2) of that section	section 531 of the Act
Regulation 2	"*principal section*" means section 17 (inserted by the Finance Act, 1976 (No. 16 of 1976)) of the Finance Act, 1970 (No. 14 of 1970);	"*the Act*" means the Taxes Consolidation Act, 1997;
Regulation 2, in the definition of "*relevant contract*"	the principal section	section 530 of the Act
Regulation 2, in the definition of "*repayment period*"	subsection (4) of the principal section	subsection (5) of section 531 of the Act
Regulation 2, in the definition of "*sub-contractor*"	subsection (2) of the principal section	subsection (1) of section 531 of the Act
Regulation 2, in the definition of "*sub-contractor's certificate*"	subsection (7) of the principal section	subsection (11) of section 531 of the Act
Regulation 4	subsection (8)*(a)* of the principal section	subsection (12)*(a)* of section 531 of the Act
Regulation 4A, in paragraph (1)	subsection (8)*(a)* of the principal section	subsection (12)*(a)* of section 531 of the Act
Regulation 4A, in paragraph (2)(c)	section 103(5) of the Corporation Tax Act, 1976	section 433(4) of the Act
	subsection (1) of the principal section	subsection (1) of section 530 of the Act
Regulation 4B, in paragraph (4)	subsection (8)*(a)* of the principal section	subsection (12)*(a)* of section 531 of the Act
Regulation 4C, in paragraph (2)*(a)*(ii)	subsection (7) of the principal section	subsection (11) of section 531 of the Act
Regulation 4C, in paragraph (2)*(b)*	subsection (5)*(a)*(i) of the principal section	subsection (6)*(a)*(i) of section 531 of the Act
Regulation 4C, in paragraph (2)*(c)*	the principal section	section 530 of the Act
Regulation 4C, in paragraph (2)*(d)*	subsection (7) of the principal section	subsection (11) of section 531 of the Act
Regulation 6, in paragraph (3)	subsection (8) of the principal section	subsection (12) of section 531 of the Act
Regulation 8, in paragraph (1)	subsection (2) of the principal section	subsection (1) of section 531 of the Act

Enactment amended (1)	Words to be replaced (2)	Words to be substituted (3)
Regulation 10, in paragraph (1)	the principal section	section 531 of the Act
Regulation 11, in paragraph (1)	the principal section	section 531 of the Act
	sections 480, 485, 486, 488 and 491 of the Income Tax Act, 1967	sections 962, 963, 966 and 998 of the Act
Regulation 12, in paragraph (1)	the principal section	section 531 of the Act
Regulation 13, in paragraph (1)	subsection (2) of the principal section	subsection (1) of section 531 of the Act
Regulation 13, in paragraph (3)	subsection (4)(*c*)(ii) of the principal section	subsection (5)(*c*)(ii) of section 531 of the Act
Regulation 14	Chapter IV of Part V of the Income Tax Act, 1967	Chapter 4 of Part 42 of the Act
Regulation 19, in paragraph (1)	subsection (8)(*a*) of the principal section	subsection (12)(*a*) of section 531 of the Act
Regulation 20	subsection (9)(*a*) of the principal section	subsection (13)(*a*) of section 531 of the Act
	the said subsection (9)(*a*)	subsection (13)(*a*) of section 531 of the Act
Regulation 21, in paragraph (3)	Chapter III of Part IV of the Income Tax Act, 1967 (No. 6 of 1967)	Part 43 of the Act
The Finance Act, 1969, section 49(2B)(*c*)	section 94 of the Finance Act, 1983	section 1078 of the Taxes Consolidation Act, 1997
The Value-Added Tax Act, 1972:		
section 1, in the definition of "*Appeal Commissioners*"	section 156 of the Income Tax Act, 1967	section 850 of the Taxes Consolidation Act, 1997
section 1, in the definition of "*Collector-General*"	section 162 of the Income Tax Act, 1967	section 851 of the Taxes Consolidation Act, 1997
section 1, in the definition of "*inspector of taxes*"	section 161 of the Income Tax Act, 1967	section 852 of the Taxes Consolidation Act, 1997
section 1, in the definition of "*secretary*"	section 207(2) of the Income Tax Act, 1967	section 1044(2) of the Taxes Consolidation Act, 1997
section 1(2)(*bb*)	section 73 of the Finance Act, 1988	section 1002 of the Taxes Consolidation Act, 1997
section 1(2)(*c*)(i)	Chapter III of Part I of the Finance Act, 1987	Chapter 1 of Part 18 of the Taxes Consolidation Act, 1997
section 1(2)(*c*)(ii)	section 17 of the Finance Act, 1970	Chapter 2 of Part 18 of the Taxes Consolidation Act, 1997
section 18(1)(*a*)(ii*a*)	section 94 (as amended by section 243 of the Finance Act, 1992) of the Finance Act, 1983	section 1078 of the Taxes Consolidation Act, 1997
section 24(1)(*b*)	sections 480, 485, 486, 487, 488 and 491 of the Income Tax Act, 1967	sections 962, 963, 964(1), 966, 967 and 998 of the Taxes Consolidation Act, 1997
section 24(5)	under section 485 of the Income Tax Act, 1967	under section 962 of the Taxes Consolidation Act, 1997
	section 485	section 962
section 27(11)	section 94 (as amended by section 243 of the Finance Act, 1992) of the Finance Act, 1983	section 1078 of the Taxes Consolidation Act, 1997
section 31	section 512 of the Income Tax Act, 1967	section 1065 of the Taxes Consolidation Act, 1997

Enactment amended (1)	Words to be replaced (2)	Words to be substituted (3)
First Schedule, in paragraph (i)(*g*)	section 18 of the Finance Act, 1989	section 734 of the Taxes Consolidation Act, 1997
The Imposition of Duties (No. 21) (Excise Duties) Order, 1975 (S.I. No. 307 of 1975), the proviso to paragraph 12 (12)	section 242 (as amended by the Finance Act, 1993) of the Finance Act, 1992	section 1094 of the Taxes Consolidation Act, 1997
The Capital Acquisitions Tax Act, 1976:		
section 16(2), in the definition of "*private company*"	section 95 of the Corporation Tax Act, 1976	section 431 of the Taxes Consolidation Act, 1997
	subsection (1)	subsection (3)
	subsection (4)	subsection (6)
section 52(1), in the definition of "*Appeal Commissioners*"	section 156 of the Income Tax Act, 1967	section 850 of the Taxes Consolidation Act, 1997
section 58(2)(*b*)	section 142 of the Income Tax Act, 1967	section 466 of the Taxes Consolidation Act, 1997
section 63(9)	sections 128(4), 507, 508, 510, 511, 512, 517 and 518 of the Income Tax Act, 1967	sections 987(4), 1061, 1062, 1063, 1064, 1065, 1066 and 1068 of the Taxes Consolidation Act, 1997
Second Schedule, Part I, paragraph 9, in the definition of "*investment income*"	section 2 of the Income Tax Act, 1967	section 3 of the Taxes Consolidation Act, 1997
The Value-Added Tax Regulations, 1979 (S.I. No. 63 of 1979):		
Regulation 15, in paragraph (2)	Section 485 of the Income Tax Act, 1967	Section 962 of the Taxes Consolidation Act, 1997
	the words from "modifications in subsection (1)" to the end of the paragraph	modification in subsection (1), namely, the words "any sum which may be levied on that person in respect of income tax" shall be construed as referring to value-added tax payable by the person concerned
Regulation 15, in paragraph (3)	Section 486 of the Income Tax Act, 1967	Section 963 of the Taxes Consolidation Act, 1997
Regulation 15, in paragraph (3)(*a*)	income tax or sur-tax	income tax
Regulation 15, in paragraph (3)(*b*)	the Collector or other officer of the Revenue Commissioners, duly authorised to collect the said tax	the Collector-General or other officer of the Revenue Commissioners duly authorised to collect the tax
	the Collector or other officer under this section	the Collector-General or other officer under this section
Regulation 15, in paragraph (4)	Section 487 of the Income Tax Act, 1967	Section 964(1) of the Taxes Consolidation Act, 1997
Regulation 15, in paragraph (5)	Section 488 of the Income Tax Act, 1967	Section 966 of the Taxes Consolidation Act, 1997
Regulation 15, in paragraph (5)(*a*)	income tax or sur-tax	income tax
Regulation 15, in paragraph (5)(*b*)	references to an inspector and to the Collector	references to an inspector and to the Collector-General

Enactment amended (1)	Words to be replaced (2)	Words to be substituted (3)
Regulation 15, in paragraph (6)	Section 491 of the Income Tax Act, 1967 income tax or sur tax	Section 998 of the Taxes Consolidation Act, 1997 income tax
The Health Contributions Act, 1979:		
section 1, in the definition of "*the Collector-General*"	section 162 of the Income Tax Act, 1967	section 851 of the Taxes Consolidation Act, 1997
section 1, in the definition of "*emoluments*"	Chapter IV of Part V *of the* Income Tax Act, 1967, but without regard to section 192 of that Act	Chapter 4 of Part 42 of the Taxes Consolidation Act, 1997, but without regard to section 1015 of that Act
section 7A	section 3 of the Finance Act, 1983	section 1025 of the Taxes Consolidation Act, 1997
The Health Contribution Regulations, 1979 (S.I. No. 107 of 1979):		
Regulation 3, in the definition of "*the Collector*"	section 162 of the Income Tax Act, 1967 (No. 6 of 1967)	section 851 of the Taxes Consolidation Act, 1997
Regulation 3, in the definition of "*excepted farmer*"	"an individual to whom section 16 applies" within the meaning of Chapter II of Part I of the Finance Act, 1974 (No. 27 of 1974), if paragraphs (*b*) and (*d*) of section 16(1), and section 16(2), of that Act did not apply	"an individual to whom subsection (1) applies" within the meaning of section 657 of the Taxes Consolidation Act, 1997, if paragraphs (*b*) and (*d*) of the definition of "an individual to whom subsection (1) applies" in subsection (1) of that section of that Act and subsection (2) of that section of that Act did not apply
Regulation 3, in the definition of "*farm land occupied by the individual*"	section 13(1) of the Finance Act, 1974	section 654 of the Taxes Consolidation Act, 1997
Regulation 4	Chapter IV of Part V of the Income Tax Act, 1967, applies but without regard to Chapter I of Part IX of that Act	Chapter 4 of Part 42 of the Taxes Consolidation Act, 1997, applies but without regard to sections 1015 to 1024 of that Act
Regulation 6	Chapter I (inserted by the Finance Act, 1980) (No. 14 of 1980) of Part IX of the Income Tax Act, 1967 (No. 6 of 1987)	sections 1015 to 1024 of the Taxes Consolidation Act, 1997
	section 33 of the Finance Act, 1975 (No. 6 of 1975)	the definition of "*capital allowance*" in section 2(1) of the Taxes Consolidation Act, 1997
The Youth Employment Agency Act, 1981:		
section 1 (1), in the definition of "*the Collector-General*"	section 162 of the Income Tax Act, 1967	section 851 of the Taxes Consolidation Act, 1997
section 1 (1), in the definition of "*emoluments*"	Chapter IV of Part V of the Income Tax Act, 1967 (but without regard to Chapter I (inserted by the Finance Act, 1980) of Part IX of that Act)	Chapter 4 of Part 42 of the Taxes Consolidation Act, 1997 (but without regard to sections 1015 to 1024 of that Act)

Enactment amended (1)	Words to be replaced (2)	Words to be substituted (3)
section 18A	section 3 of the Finance Act, 1983	section 1025 of the Taxes Consolidation Act, 1997
The Youth Employment Levy Regulations 1982, (S.I. No. 84 of 1982):		
Regulation 3, in the definition of "*the Collector*"	section 162 of the Income Tax Act, 1967 (No. 6 of 1967)	section 851 of the Taxes Consolidation Act, 1997
Regulation 3, in the definition of "*excepted farmer*"	an individual to whom section 16 applies within the meaning of Chapter II of Part I of the Finance Act, 1974 (No. 27 of 1974), if paragraph (*b*) and (*d*) of subsection (1) and subsection (2) of section 16 of that Act did not apply	an individual to whom subsection (1) applies within the meaning of section 657 of the Taxes Consolidation Act, 1997, if paragraphs (*b*) and (*d*) of the definition of "an individual to whom subsection (1) applies" in subsection (1) of that section of that Act and subsection (2) of that section of that Act did not apply
Regulation 3, in the definition of "*farm land occupied by the individual*"	section 13(1) of the Finance Act, 1974	section 654 of the Taxes Consolidation Act, 1997
Regulation 6	Chapter I (inserted by the Finance Act, 1980 (No. 14 of 1980)) of Part IX of the Income Tax Act, 1967 (No. 6 of 1967)	sections 1015 to 1024 of the Taxes Consolidation Act, 1997
	section 33 of the Finance Act, 1975 (No. 6 of 1975)	the definition of "*capital allowance*" in section 2(1) of the Taxes Consolidation Act, 1997
Regulation 16	section 195 of the Income Tax Act, 1967	section 1018 of the Taxes Consolidation Act, 1997
The Income Tax (Rent Relief) Regulations, 1982 (S.I. No. 318 of 1982):		
Regulation 2	Chapter IV of Part IV of the Income Tax Act, 1967 (No. 6 of 1967)	Chapter 8 of Part 4 of the Taxes Consolidation Act, 1997
	section 142A (inserted by section 5 of the Finance Act, 1982 (No. 14 of 1982)) of the Income Tax Act, 1967	section 473 of the Taxes Consolidation Act, 1997
Regulation 3	subsection (5)(a)(i)	subsection (6)(a)(i)
Regulation 5	section 6 of the Finance Act, 1968 (No. 33 of 1968), and section 34 of the Finance Act, 1976 (No. 16 of 1976)	sections 886 and 905
The Finance Act, 1984, section 108(1)(*b*)(ii)	subsection (9) of section 235 of the Income Tax Act, 1967	subsection (1) of section 783 of the Taxes Consolidation Act, 1997
	section 235A	section 785
The Finance Act, 1986:		
section 94(1)(*a*), in the definition of "*Corporation Tax Acts*"	section 155(1) of the Corporation Tax Act, 1976	section 1 of the Taxes Consolidation Act, 1997

Enactment amended (1)	Words to be replaced (2)	Words to be substituted (3)
section 94(1)(*a*), in the definition of "*relevant interest*"	section 84(2)(*d*) of the Corporation Tax Act, 1976	section 130(2)(*d*) of the Taxes Consolidation Act, 1997
The Health Contributions (Amendment) Regulations, 1988 (S.I. No. 51 of 1988), Regulation 3, in paragraph (2)	section 195 of the Income Tax Act, 1967	section 1018 of the Taxes Consolidation Act, 1997
The Finance Act, 1989, the proviso to section 45(3)(b)	section 242 (as amended by the Finance Act, 1993) of the Finance Act, 1992	section 1094 of the Taxes Consolidation Act, 1997
The Finance Act, 1990:		
section 112(5)	section 94 of the Finance Act, 1983	section 1078 of the Taxes Consolidation Act, 1997
section 129(1)	subsection (9) of section 235 of the Income Tax Act, 1967	subsection (1) of section 783 of the Taxes Consolidation Act, 1997
The Finance Act, 1991:		
section 108(1)	section 485 of the Income Tax Act, 1967	section 962 of the Taxes Consolidation Act, 1997
section 109(1)	Sections 128(4), 507, 508, 510, 511, 512, 517 and 518 of the Income Tax Act, 1967	Sections 987(4), 1061, 1062, 1063, 1064, 1065, 1066 and 1068 of the Taxes Consolidation Act, 1997
	Income Tax Act, 1967	Taxes Consolidation Act, 1997
section 129(1), in the definition of "*the Collector*"	section 162 of the Income Tax Act, 1967	section 851 of the Taxes Consolidation Act, 1997
section 129(3)	Section 187 of the Income Tax Act, 1967	Section 928(1) and 964(2) of the Taxes Consolidation Act, 1997
The Finance Act, 1992: section 206(*a*), (*aa*) and (*c*)(ii)	section 18 of the Finance Act, 1989	section 734 of the Taxes Consolidation Act, 1997
section 206(*b*)	subsection (5A) (inserted by section 34 of the Finance Act, 1977) of section 31 of the Capital Gains Tax Act, 1975	subsection (6) of section 731 of the Taxes Consolidation Act, 1997
section 207(2)	section 18 of the Finance Act, 1989	section 734 of the Taxes Consolidation Act, 1997
The Finance Act, 1993:		
section 106(2)(*b*)	section 31 of the Finance Act, 1991	section 110 of the Taxes Consolidation Act, 1997
section 109(1), in the definition of "*dependent relative*"	subsection (9A) (inserted by the Finance Act, 1979) of section 25 of the Capital Gains Tax Act, 1975	subsection (11) of section 604 of the Taxes Consolidation Act, 1997
section 112(*a*)(i)(A)	section 235(9) of the Income Tax Act, 1967	section 783(1) of the Taxes Consolidation Act, 1997
section 112(*a*)(i)(B)	section 235 or section 235A	section 784 or section 785
section 112(*a*)(iii)	section 236 of the Income Tax Act, 1967	section 787 of the Taxes Consolidation Act, 1997
section 112(*d*), proviso (i)	subsection (1A) of section 142 of the Income Tax Act, 1967	subsection (1) of section 466 of the Taxes Consolidation Act, 1997
section 133(1)	section 36 of the Finance Act, 1988	section 451 of the Taxes Consolidation Act, 1997

Enactment amended (1)	Words to be replaced (2)	Words to be substituted (3)
The Social Welfare (Consolidation) Act, 1993:		
section 2, in the definition of "*Collector-General*"	section 162 of the Income Tax Act, 1967	section 851 of the Taxes Consolidation Act, 1997
section 2, in the definition of "*reckonable emoluments*"	*Chapter IV of Part V of the* Income Tax Act, 1967	Chapter 4 of Part 42 of themTaxes Consolidation Act, 1997
section 2, in the definition of "*reckonable income*"	section 2 or section 18 of the Finance Act, 1969	section 195, 231 or 232 of the Taxes Consolidation Act, 1997
	Chapter 1 (inserted by the Finance Act, 1980) of Part IX of the Income Tax Act, 1967	Chapter 1 of Part 44 of the Taxes Consolidation Act, 1997
section 2, in the definition of "*reckonable income*"	section 33 of the Finance Act, 1975	the definition of "*capital allowance*" in section 2(1) of the Taxes Consolidation Act, 1997
section 18(1)(*b*)	section 48(1) of the Finance Act, 1986	section 1084(1) of the Taxes Consolidation Act, 1997
section 20(5)	section 195 of the Income Tax Act, 1967	section 1018 of the Taxes Consolidation Act, 1997
section 212(5)	section 17 (as amended by section 28 of the Finance Act, 1992) of the Finance Act, 1970	Chapter 2 of Part 18 of the Taxes Consolidation Act, 1997
First Schedule, Part III, paragraph 3(*a*)	section 33 of the Finance Act, 1975	the definition of "*capital allowance*" in section 2(1) of the Taxes Consolidation Act, 1997
First Schedule, Part III, paragraph 4	Chapter II or III of Part IV of the Income Tax Act, 1967	Chapter 3 of Part 4, or Part 43, of the Taxes Consolidation Act, 1997
First Schedule, Part III, paragraph 6	Chapter II or III of Part IV of the Income Tax Act, 1967	Chapter 3 of Part 4, or Part 43, of the Taxes Consolidation Act, 1997
The Industrial Training (Apprenticeship Levy) Act, 1994, section 1(1)	section 162 of the Income Tax Act, 1967	section 851 of the Taxes Consolidation Act, 1997
The Casual Trading Act, 1995, section 4(2A)	section 161 of the Income Tax Act, 1967	section 852 of the Taxes Consolidation Act, 1997
The Finance Act, 1995:		
section 103	section 156 of the Income Tax Act, 1967	section 850 of the Taxes Consolidation Act, 1997
section 105(3)	Part XXVI (as amended) other than sections 429 and 430 and (in so far as it relates to those sections) section 431, of the Income Tax Act, 1967	Part 40, other than sections 942, 943 and (in so far as it relates to those sections) 944 of the Taxes Consolidation Act, 1997
The Consumer Credit Act, 1995:		
section 93(10)(d)	section 242 (as amended by the Finance Act, 1997) of the Finance Act, 1992	section 1094 of the Taxes Consolidation Act, 1997
section 93(10A)(a)(i)	section 242 of the Finance Act, 1992	section 1094 of the Taxes Consolidation Act, 1997
section 93(10A)(a)(ii)	section 242	section 1094
section 116(9)(d)	section 242 (as amended by the Finance Act, 1997) of the Finance Act, 1992	section 1094 of the Taxes Consolidation Act, 1997
section 116(9A)(a)(i)	section 242 of the Finance Act, 1992	section 1094 of the Taxes Consolidation Act, 1997

Enactment amended (1)	Words to be replaced (2)	Words to be substituted (3)
section 116(9A)(a)(ii)	section 242	section 1094
section 144(9)(d)	section 242 (as amended by the Finance Act, 1997) of the Finance Act, 1992	section 1094 of the Taxes Consolidation Act, 1997
section 144(9A)(a)(i)	section 242 of the Finance Act, 1992	section 1094 of the Taxes Consolidation Act, 1997
section 144(9A)(a)(ii)	section 242	section 1094
The Finance Act, 1996, section 108(4)	section 94(2)(*d*) of the Finance Act, 1983	section 1078(2)(*d*) of the Taxes Consolidation Act, 1997
The Social Welfare (Consolidated Contributions and Insurability) Regulations, 1996 (S.I. No. 312 of 1996):		
Regulation 3, in the definition of "*inspector of taxes*"	section 161 of the Act of 1967	section 852 of the Act of 1997
Regulation 3, in the definition of "*reckonable earnings*"	Chapter IV of Part V of the Act of 1967	Chapter 4 of Part 42 of the Act of 1997
	section 192 of that Act	section 1015 of that Act
	the Act of 1967 (other than Chapter IV of Part V)	the Act of 1997 (other than Chapter 4 of Part 42)
	section 192 of that Act	section 1015 of that Act
Regulation 3, in the definition of "*reckonable income*"	the Act of 1967	the Act of 1997
	Chapter 11 of Part I of the Finance Act, 1972 (No. 19 of 1972)	Chapter 1 of Part 30
Regulation 3, the definition of "*the Act of 1967*"	"the Act of 1967" means the Income Tax Act, 1967 (No. 6 of 1967);	"*the Act of 1997*" means the Taxes Consolidation Act, 1997;
Regulation 10, in paragraph (1)	section 129 of the Act of 1967	section 991 of the Act of 1997
Regulation 27	section 8(1) of the Finance Act, 1979 (No. 11 of 1979)	section 125 of the Act of 1997

Cross References

From Schedule 31

Section 1 Interpretation of this Act.
Section 2 Interpretation of Tax Acts.
Section 3 Interpretation of Income Tax Acts.
Section 7 Application to certain taxing statutes of Age of Majority Act, 1985.
Section 9 Subsidiaries.
Section 16 Income tax charged by deduction.
Section 52 Persons chargeable.
Section 65 Cases I and II: basis of assessment.
Section 96 Interpretation (Chapter 8).
Section 110 Securitisation.
Section 130 Matters to be treated as distributions.
Section 195 Exemption of certain earnings of writers, composers and artists.
Section 231 Profits or gains from stallion fees.
Section 232 Profits from occupation of certain woodlands.
Section 431 Certain companies with quoted shares not to be close companies.
Section 451 Treatment of income and gains of certain trading operations carried on in Custom House Docks Area from investments held outside the State.

Section 466 Dependent relative tax credit.
Section 473 Allowance for rent paid by certain tenants.
Section 520 Interpretation (Chapter 1).
Section 530 Interpretation (Chapter 2).
Section 604 Disposals of principal private residence.
Section 654 Interpretation (Part 23).
Section 657 Averaging of farm profits.
Section 731 Chargeable gains accruing to unit trusts.
Section 734 Taxation of collective investment undertakings.
Section 770 Interpretation and supplemental (Chapter 1).
Section 774 Certain approved schemes: exemptions and reliefs.
Section 776 Certain statutory schemes: exemptions and reliefs.
Section 783 Interpretation and general (Chapter 2).
Section 784 Retirement annuities: relief for premiums.
Section 785 Approval of contracts for dependants or for life assurance.
Section 787 Nature and amount of relief for qualifying premiums.
Section 788 Capital element in certain purchased annuities.
Section 850 Appeal Commissioners.
Section 851 Collector-General.
Section 852 Inspectors of taxes.
Section 886 Obligation to keep certain records.
Section 905 Inspection of documents and records.
Section 928 Transmission to Collector-General of particulars of sums to be collected.
Section 932 Prohibition on alteration of assessment except on appeal.
Section 933 Appeals against assessment.
Section 942 Appeals to Circuit Court.
Section 943 Extension of section 941.
Section 944 Communication of decision of Appeal Commissioners.
Section 960 Date for payment of income tax other than under self assessment.
Section 962 Recovery by sheriff or county registrar.
Section 963 Power of Collector-General and authorised officer to sue in Circuit Court or District Court.
Section 964 Continuance of pending proceedings.
Section 966 High Court proceedings.
Section 967 Evidence of electronic transmission of particulars of income tax to be collected in proceedings for recovery of tax.
Section 983 Interpretation (Chapter 4).
Section 987 Penalties for breach of regulations.
Section 993 Recovery of tax.
Section 998 Recovery of moneys due.
Section 1002 Deduction from payments due to defaulters of amounts due in relation to tax.
Section 1007 Interpretation (Part 43).
Section 1015 Interpretation (Chapter 1).
Section 1018 Election for assessment under section 1017.
Section 1023 Application for separate assessments.
Section 1024 Method of apportioning reliefs and charging tax in cases of separate assessments.
Section 1025 Maintenance in case of separated spouses.
Section 1044 Bodies of persons.
Section 1061 Recovery of penalties.
Section 1062 Proceedings where penalty recoverable cannot be definitely ascertained.
Section 1063 Time limit for recovery of fines and penalties.
Section 1064 Time for certain summary proceedings.
Section 1065 Mitigation and application of fines and penalties.
Section 1066 False evidence: punishment as for perjury.
Section 1068 Failure to act within required time.
Section 1078 Revenue offences.
Section 1084 Surcharge for late returns.
Section 1094 Tax clearance certificates in relation to certain licences.
Section 1100 Consequential amendments to other enactments.

To Schedule 31

Section 1100 Consequential amendments to other enactments.

SCHEDULE 32

Transitional Provisions

Section 1101.

[ITA67 s472(1)]

Stock of local authorities

1.

(1) Any stock under section 87 of the Local Government Act, 1946, issued on or after the 13th day of July, 1955, shall be deemed to be securities issued under the authority of the Minister for Finance under *section 36*, and that section shall apply accordingly.

(2) *Section 49* shall apply as if in *subsection (1)* of that section "or *paragraph 1* of Schedule *32*" were inserted after "or *41*".

Income tax: exemption from tax of income from certain scholarships

[ITA67 s353; FA97 s11(2)]

2. Where a payment of income is made before the 6th day of April, 1998, in respect of a scholarship awarded before the 26th day of March, 1997, *section 193* shall apply as if—

(a) in *subsection (1)* of that section the definitions of "*relevant body*" and "*relevant scholarship*" and *paragraph (b)* were deleted, and

(b) *subsections (3)* and *(4)* of that section were deleted.

Corporation tax: exemption from tax of profits of Custom House Docks Development Authority

[FA88 s42; FA97 s49(4)]

3.

(1) Notwithstanding any provision of the Corporation Tax Acts, profits arising to the Custom House Docks Development Authority in any accounting period ending on or after the 17th day of November, 1986, shall be exempt from corporation tax.

(2) *Subparagraph (1)* shall be repealed with effect from the 1st day of May, 1997.

Meaning of "*relevant distributions*" for the purposes of section 147 in relation to distributions made before 6th April, 1989

[FA80 s45(1) and (2)]

[...][1]

Distributions out of certain income of manufacturing companies — provisions relating to relief for certain losses and capital allowances carried forward from 1975–76

[FA80 s47; FA88 s32(3) and Sch2 PtII pars1(c) and (d); FA95 s54(2) and Sch4 PtII pars2(1)(a) and (b); FA97 s59(2) and Sch6 PtII par2]

[...][2]

[...][3]

Approved share option schemes
[FA86 s10(1) and (2)(a) and (b); FA92 s12]

7.

(1) This paragraph shall apply where on or after the 6th day of April, 1986, an individual obtains a right to acquire shares in a body corporate—

(a) by reason of his or her office or employment as a director or employee of that or any other body corporate, and

(b) in accordance with the provisions of a scheme approved under the Second Schedule to the Finance Act, 1986;

but neither this paragraph nor that Schedule shall apply in relation to such a right obtained on or after the 29th day of January, 1992.

(2) Where the individual exercises the right in accordance with the provisions of the scheme referred to in *subparagraph (1)(b)* at a time when it is approved under the Second Schedule to the Finance Act, 1986—

(a) income tax shall not be chargeable under *section 128* in respect of any gain realised by the exercise of the right, and

(b) if but for this clause *section 547* would apply, that section shall not apply in calculating the consideration for the acquisition of the shares by the individual or for any corresponding disposal of them to the individual.

(3) (a) This paragraph shall apply notwithstanding that the Second Schedule to the Finance Act, 1986, is not re-enacted by this Act, and accordingly this Act shall apply with any modifications necessary to give effect to this paragraph.

(b) Without prejudice to the generality of *clause (a)*, [*sections 1052, 1054* and *1077E*][4] shall apply for the purposes of that clause as if in *Schedule 29* there were included in *Column 2* a reference to paragraph 14 of the Second Schedule to the Finance Act, 1986.

Interest on certain loans: relief from corporation tax
[CTA76 s177]

8.

(1) For the purposes of this paragraph, "*permanent loan*" means a loan of a permanent character made under an agreement entered into before the 27th day of November, 1975, and which under the agreement is—

(a) secured by mortgage or debenture or otherwise on the assets or income of a company, and

(b) if subject to repayment, is subject to repayment at not less than 3 months' notice;

but a loan shall not be regarded as a permanent loan for the purposes of this paragraph if under the terms of the loan agreement the rate of interest or other conditions of the loan may be altered during the currency of the loan.

(2) Where for the purposes of corporation tax the income of a company for an accounting period includes interest payable in respect of a permanent loan, the company shall be entitled on a due claim to have its liability to corporation tax for the accounting period reduced as provided by *subparagraph (3)*.

(3) The reduction referred to in *subparagraph (2)* shall be determined in accordance with *subparagraph (4)* (apart from *clause (c)*) of *paragraph 18* as if the interest were a relevant deficiency within the meaning of *subparagraph (1)* of that paragraph.

(4) Where in computing the reduction provided for by *subparagraph (3)* the appropriate amount as determined in accordance with *paragraph 18(4)(a)(ii)* is the company's income for the accounting period, the excess of such interest as is mentioned in *subparagraph (2)* for the accounting period over that income shall for the purposes of this paragraph be aggregated with the amount of any such interest for the next accounting period and relief shall be allowed for that period in respect of the aggregated amount and, if that aggregated amount exceeds the income for that period, the excess shall be carried forward to the accounting period succeeding that period and so on.

(5) A claim under this paragraph shall be made to the inspector within 2 years from the end of the accounting period.

Allowance for certain capital expenditure on construction of multi-storey car-parks

[FA81 s25; FA86 s51(2); FA88 s49]

9.

(1) In this paragraph—

"*multi-storey car-park*" means a building or structure consisting of 3 or more storeys wholly in use for the purpose of providing, for members of the public generally without preference for any particular class of person, on payment of an appropriate charge, parking space for mechanically propelled vehicles;

"*relevant expenditure*" means capital expenditure incurred on or after the 29th day of January, 1981, and before the 1st day of April, 1991, on the construction of a multi-storey car-park.

(2) The provisions of the Tax Acts (other than *section 273*) relating to the making of allowances or charges in respect of capital expenditure on the construction of an industrial building or structure shall apply to relevant expenditure as if it were expenditure incurred on the construction of a building or structure in respect of which an allowance is to be made for the purposes of income tax or corporation tax, as the case may be, under *Part 9* by reason of its use for a purpose specified in *section 268(1)(a)*.

Allowance for certain capital expenditure on roads, bridges, etc

[FA81 s26; FA84 s39; FA89 s17]

10.

(1) In this paragraph—

"*chargeable period*" and "*chargeable period or its basis period*" have the same meanings as in *section 321(2)*;

"*qualifying period*" means the period commencing on the 29th day of January, 1981, and ending on the 31st day of March, 1989, or, in the case of a relevant agreement entered into on or after the 6th day of April, 1987, ending on the 31st day of March, 1992;

"*relevant agreement*" means an agreement between a road authority and another person under section 9 of the Local Government (Toll Roads) Act, 1979, by virtue of which that other person incurs relevant expenditure;

"*relevant expenditure*" means capital expenditure incurred by a person during the qualifying period by virtue of a relevant agreement including, in the case of a relevant agreement entered into on or after the 6th day of April, 1987, interest on money borrowed to meet such capital expenditure, but does not include any expenditure in respect of which any person is entitled to a deduction, relief or allowance under any provision of the Tax Acts other than this paragraph;

"*relevant income*" means income which arises to a person by virtue of a relevant agreement;

"*road authority*" has the meaning assigned to it by the Local Government (Toll Roads) Act, 1979.

(2) Where in the case of a relevant agreement entered into before the 6th day of April, 1987, a person, having made a claim in that behalf, proves as respects a chargeable period that relevant income was receivable by such person in that chargeable period or its basis period and that such person has incurred relevant expenditure, then, such person shall, subject to *subparagraph (4)*, be entitled, for the purpose only of ascertaining the amount (if any) of relevant income on which such person is to be charged to tax for the chargeable period, to an allowance equal to 50 per cent of the relevant expenditure; but the aggregate amount of all allowances made to that person under this subparagraph in relation to any relevant expenditure shall not exceed an amount equal to 50 per cent of that expenditure.

(3) Where a person, having made a claim in that behalf, proves as respects a chargeable period that relevant income was receivable and relevant expenditure was incurred by such person in the chargeable period or its basis period by virtue of the relevant agreement (being a relevant agreement entered into on or after the 6th day of April, 1987) giving rise to the relevant income, such person shall, subject to *subparagraph (4)*, be entitled, for the purpose only of ascertaining the amount (if any) of that relevant income on which such person is to be charged to tax—

(a) to an allowance equal to 50 per cent of the relevant expenditure for that chargeable period, and

(b) to an allowance equal to 10 per cent of the relevant expenditure for each of the next 5 chargeable periods in which that relevant income is receivable by such person;

and, for the purposes of this subparagraph, all relevant expenditure so incurred before the chargeable period in which relevant income is first receivable shall be deemed to have been incurred on the first day of that chargeable period.

(4) Where an allowance to which a person is entitled under this paragraph cannot be given full effect for any chargeable period by reason of a want or deficiency of relevant income, then (so long as the person has relevant income), the amount unallowed shall be carried forward to the succeeding chargeable period and the amount so carried forward shall be treated for the purposes of this paragraph, including any further application of this subparagraph, as the amount of a corresponding allowance for that period.

(5) An appeal to the Appeal Commissioners shall lie on any question arising under this paragraph in the like manner as an appeal would lie against an assessment to income tax or corporation tax, and the provisions of the Tax Acts relating to appeals shall apply accordingly.

Urban Renewal Scheme, 1986 — capital allowances in relation to certain commercial premises in designated areas other than the Custom House Docks Area

[FA86 s42]

11. Where but for the repeal by this Act of the repealed enactments an allowance or charge would be made to or on a person for any chargeable period under Chapter II of Part XV, or Chapter I of Part XVI, of the Income Tax Act, 1967 (including any such allowance as increased under section 25 of the Finance Act, 1978), by virtue of section 42 of the Finance Act, 1986 (in so far as that section applied to areas other than the Custom House Docks Area within the meaning section 41 of that Act), then, notwithstanding that that section as it so applied is not re-enacted by this Act, that allowance or charge shall be made to or on the person under this Act, and accordingly this Act shall apply with any modifications necessary to give effect to this paragraph.

Urban Renewal Scheme, 1986 — allowances to owner-occupiers in relation to certain residential premises in designated areas other than the Custom House Docks Area

[FA86 s44]

12. Where but for the repeal by this Act of the repealed enactments a person would, in the computation of his or her total income for any year of assessment, be entitled to a deduction under section 44 of the Finance Act, 1986 (in so far as that section applied to areas other than the Custom House Docks Area within the meaning of section 41 of that Act), then, notwithstanding that that section as it so applied is not re-enacted by this Act, the person shall be entitled to that deduction for that year of assessment under this Act, and accordingly this Act shall apply with any modifications necessary to give effect to this paragraph.

Urban Renewal Scheme, 1986 — double rent allowance in relation to certain premises in designated areas other than the Custom House Docks Area

[FA86 s45]

13. Where but for the repeal by this Act of the repealed enactments a further deduction on account of rent in respect of any premises would be made to a person under section 45 of the Finance Act, 1986 (in so far as that section applied to areas other than the Custom House Docks Area within the meaning of section 41 of that Act), in the computation of the amount of the profits or gains of the person's trade or profession, then, notwithstanding that that section as it so applied is not re-enacted by this Act, that further deduction shall be made to the person under this Act, and accordingly this Act shall apply with any modifications necessary to give effect to this paragraph.

Rented residential accommodation — deduction for expenditure incurred on construction, conversion or refurbishment in areas other than the Custom House Docks Area

[FA81 s23 and s24; FA85 s21 and s22; FA91 s56, s57 and s58]

14. Where, in computing the amount of a surplus or deficiency in respect of rent from any premises in any area other than the Custom House Docks Area (within

the meaning of section 41 of the Finance Act, 1986), a person would, but for the repeal by this Act of the repealed enactments—

(a) be entitled to a deduction, or

(b) be deemed to have received an amount as rent,

under—

(i) section 23 of the Finance Act, 1981,

(ii) section 23 of the Finance Act, 1981, as applied by virtue of section 24 of that Act or section 22 of the Finance Act, 1985, or

(iii) section 23 of the Finance Act, 1981, as applied by section 21 of the Finance Act, 1985,

in so far as those sections applied to areas other than the Custom House Docks Area (within the meaning of section 41 of the Finance Act, 1986), then, notwithstanding that those sections as they so applied are not re-enacted by this Act, the person shall be entitled to that deduction or be deemed to have received that amount as rent, as the case may be, under this Act, and accordingly this Act shall apply with any modifications necessary to give effect to this paragraph.

Loss relief, etc

15. The substitution of this Act for the corresponding enactments repealed by this Act shall not alter the effect of any provision enacted before this Act (whether or not there is a corresponding provision in this Act) in so far as it determines whether and to what extent—

(a) losses or expenditure incurred in, or an excess of deficiencies over surpluses in, or other amounts referable to, a year of assessment or accounting period earlier than a year of assessment or accounting period to which this Act applies may be taken into account for any tax purposes in a year of assessment or accounting period to which this Act applies, or

(b) losses or expenditure incurred in, or an excess of deficiencies over surpluses in, or other amounts referable to, a year of assessment or accounting period to which this Act applies may be taken into account for any tax purposes in a year of assessment or accounting period earlier than a year of assessment or accounting period to which this Act applies.

Relief in respect of unrelieved losses and capital allowances carried forward from the year 1975–76

[CTA76 s182 (apart from clauses (b) and (c) of proviso to (3)); FA80 s47(1); FA97 s59 and Sch6 PtI par2(1) and (3)]

16.

(1) In this paragraph—

"*relevant amount*", in relation to a company, means the aggregate of the following amounts—

(a) such part of a loss, including any amount to be treated as a loss under section 316 of the Income Tax Act, 1967, incurred by the company in a trade before the date on which the company comes within the charge to corporation tax in respect of the trade and which, but for the Corporation Tax Act, 1976, could have been carried forward to the year 1976–77 under section 309 of the Income Tax Act, 1967, and

(b) such part of any capital allowance to which the company which carries on the trade was entitled in charging the profits or gains of the trade for years before the year 1976-77 and to which effect has not been given by means of relief before that year;

"*relevant corporation tax*", in relation to an accounting period, means the corporation tax (other than an amount which by virtue of *sections 239*, *241*, *440* and *441* is to be treated as corporation tax of an accounting period) which, apart from this paragraph, *paragraph 18* and *section 448*, would be chargeable for the accounting period exclusive of the corporation tax chargeable on the part of the company's profits attributable to chargeable gains for that period, and that part shall be taken to be the amount brought into the company's profits for that period for the purposes of corporation tax in respect of chargeable gains before any deduction for charges on income, expenses of management or other amounts which can be deducted from or set against or treated as reducing profits of more than one description.

(2) Relief, as provided in *subparagraph (3)*, shall be allowed in respect of a relevant amount against corporation tax payable by the company and such relief shall be given as far as possible from the tax payable for the first accounting period for which the company is within the charge to corporation tax in respect of the trade and, in so far as it cannot be so given, from the tax payable for the next accounting period and so on.

(3) The relief for an accounting period shall be an amount calculated by applying to that part of the relevant amount in respect of which relief from tax has not been allowed a rate equal to—

[(a) as respects accounting periods beginning on or after the 1st day of January, 1998, and ending before the 1st day of January, 1999, 17 per cent,

(b) as respects accounting periods beginning on or after the 1st day of January, 1999, and ending before the 1st day of January, 2000, 13 per cent,

(c) as respects accounting periods beginning on or after the 1st day of January, 2000, and ending before the 1st day of January, 2001, 9 per cent,

(d) as respects accounting periods beginning on or after the 1st day of January, 2001, and ending before the 1st day of January, 2002, 5 per cent, and

(e) as respects accounting periods beginning on or after the 1st day of January, 2002, and ending before the 1st day of January, 2003, 1 per cent;][5]

but—

(i) the amount to which that rate is applied shall not exceed the amount of income from the trade included in chargeable profits for the accounting period reduced by the amount, if any, included in charges on income paid by the company in the accounting period in respect of payments made wholly and exclusively for the purposes of the trade, and

(ii) where the corporation tax payable by the company for an accounting period is reduced by virtue of a claim under *section 448(2)*, the relief to be given under this paragraph for the accounting period shall be reduced in the same proportion as the corporation tax payable by the company for the accounting period in so far as it is attributable to the income from the trade is so reduced; and the corporation tax attributable to the income from the trade shall be an amount equal to the same proportion of the relevant corporation tax for the accounting period as the income from the trade for the accounting period bears to the total income brought into charge to corporation tax.

(4) Relief under this paragraph shall not be allowed against corporation tax payable by a company which by virtue of agreements between the Government and the Government of the United Kingdom in respect of double income tax was entitled to exemption from income tax for the year 1975-76 in respect of income arising in the State.

[(5) Relief shall not be allowed under this paragraph against corporation tax payable by a company in respect of accounting periods beginning on or after the 1st day of January, 2003.

(6) For the purposes of this paragraph, where an accounting period begins before the 1st day of January of a financial year and ends on or after that day, it shall be divided into two parts, one part beginning on the day on which the accounting period begins and ending on the 31st day of December of the preceding financial year, and another part beginning on the 1st day of January of the financial year and ending on the day on which the accounting period ends, and both parts shall be treated as if they were separate accounting periods.][6]

Relief in respect of losses or deficiencies within Case IV or V of Schedule D

[CTA76 s183]

17.

(1) Where—

(a) a company was entitled to relief under section 89 or 310 of the Income Tax Act, 1967, or would have been entitled to relief under section 310 of that Act if section 237(5) of that Act had not been enacted, for the year 1975-76 or an earlier year of assessment in respect of a loss within Case IV of Schedule D or a deficiency or an excess of deficiencies within Case V of Schedule D, with the addition of any associated capital allowances in each case, and

(b) because of an insufficiency of income of the description concerned, relief could not be fully granted to the company under those sections for any of those years of assessment,

then, the unrelieved amount of loss, deficiency or excess of deficiencies (with the addition of any unrelieved associated capital allowances), as the case may be, shall be treated as if it were a loss in a trade carried on by a company and, if the company so requires, may be relieved under *paragraph 16* against income of the same description of the company within the charge to corporation tax as if that income were income of the same trade, and that paragraph shall apply accordingly with any necessary modifications.

(2) Notwithstanding *subparagraph (1)*—

(a) a loss within Case IV of Schedule D, with the addition of any associated capital allowances, shall be relieved under this paragraph only against income of the company chargeable to corporation tax under Case IV of Schedule D,

(b) a deficiency or an excess of deficiencies within Case V of Schedule D, with the addition of any associated capital allowances, shall be relieved only against income of the company chargeable to corporation tax under Case V of Schedule D, and

(c) so much of any deficiency or so much of any amount treated as a loss as, under section 62 of the Finance Act, 1974, could not have been carried forward or set against profits or gains for income tax purposes if that tax had continued shall be treated as not being a deficiency or loss for the purposes of this paragraph.

Relief in respect of corporation profits tax losses

[CTA76 s174(3)-proviso and s184 (apart from clauses (i), (ii) and (iii) of proviso to (3)); FA80 s48(1); FA97 s59 and Sch6 PtI par2]

18.

(1) In this paragraph, "*relevant deficiency*", in relation to a company, means, subject to *subparagraph (2)*, the aggregate of the following amounts—

(a) the total of the amounts which under section 25 of the Finance Act, 1964, could (on the assumption that for corporation profits tax purposes an accounting period of the company ended on the 5th day of April, 1976, and a new accounting period commenced on the 6th day of April, 1976, and the enactments in relation to corporation profits tax mentioned in the Third Schedule to the Corporation Tax Act, 1976, had not been repealed) have been deducted from or set off against profits of the company's business in an accounting period commencing on the 6th day of April, 1976, and

(b) the total of the amounts by which under subsections (1) and (3) of section 181 of the Corporation Tax Act, 1976, losses and allowances in respect of capital expenditure were reduced for the purposes of corporation tax;

but any loss or any excess of deficiencies over surpluses which if such loss or excess were a profit or an excess of surpluses over deficiencies would be chargeable to corporation tax on the company for the accounting period shall not be taken into account for the purposes of *clause (a)*.

(2) Where for any accounting period an election was made under section 174(3) of the Corporation Tax Act, 1976, all amounts which under section 25 of the Finance Act, 1964, could be deducted from or set off against profits of the company's trade or business for that accounting period, computed without regard to section 174(3) of the Corporation Tax Acts, 1976, shall be deemed to have been so deducted or set off and shall not be included in the computation of any relevant deficiency for the purposes of this paragraph.

(3) (a) Subject to *clause (b)*, relief as provided in *subparagraph (4)* shall be allowed in respect of a relevant deficiency against corporation tax payable by the company and such relief shall be given as far as possible from the tax payable for the first accounting period for which the company is within the charge to corporation tax and, in so far as it cannot be so given, from the tax payable for the next accounting period and so on.

(b) Relief shall not be allowed against corporation tax payable for any accounting period against the profits of which (if the Corporation Tax Act, 1976, had not been enacted and if the enactments in relation to corporation profits tax referred to in the Third Schedule of that Act had not been repealed) a loss incurred before the 6th day of April, 1976, could not be set off under section 25 of the Finance Act, 1964.

(4) (a) For the purposes of this subparagraph—

(i) the income of a company for an accounting period shall be taken to be the amount of its profits for that period on which corporation tax falls finally to be borne exclusive of the part of the profits attributable to chargeable gains, and that part shall be taken to be the amount brought into the company's profits for that period for the purposes of corporation tax in respect of chargeable gains before any deduction for charges on income, expenses of management or other amounts which can be deducted from or set against or treated as reducing profits of more than one description, and

(ii) the appropriate amount shall be the smaller of the amount of the relevant deficiency in respect of which relief has not been allowed and the amount of the company's income for the accounting period.

[(b) Subject to *clause (c)*, relief for an accounting period shall be an amount determined by the formula—

$$(A - B) - (C - D)$$

where—

A is the amount of corporation tax which, apart from *paragraph 16*, this paragraph and *section 448*, is chargeable for the accounting period,

[B is an amount determined by applying a rate equal to—

(a) as respects accounting periods beginning on or after the 1st day of January, 1998, and ending before the 1st day of January, 1999, 17 per cent,

(b) as respects accounting periods beginning on or after the 1st day of January, 1999, and ending before the 1st day of January, 2000, 13 per cent,

(c) as respects accounting periods beginning on or after the 1st day of January, 2000, and ending before the 1st day of January, 2001, 9 per cent,

(d) as respects accounting periods beginning on or after the 1st day of January, 2001, and ending before the 1st day of January, 2002, 5 per cent, and

(e) as respects accounting periods beginning on or after the 1st day of January, 2002, and ending before the 1st day of January, 2003, 1 per cent, to the amount of the company's income for the accounting period,][7]

C is the amount of corporation tax which, apart from *paragraph 16*, this paragraph and *section 448*, would be chargeable for the accounting period if the amount of the company's income for the accounting period were reduced by the appropriate amount, and

[D is an amount determined by applying a rate equal to—

(a) as respects accounting periods beginning on or after the 1st day of January, 1998, and ending before the 1st day of January, 1999, 17 per cent,

(b) as respects accounting periods beginning on or after the 1st day of January, 1999, and ending before the 1st day of January, 2000, 13 per cent,

(c) as respects accounting periods beginning on or after the 1st day of January, 2000, and ending before the 1st day of January, 2001, 9 per cent,

(d) as respects accounting periods beginning on or after the 1st day of January, 2001, and ending before the 1st day of January, 2002, 5 per cent, and

(e) as respects accounting periods beginning on or after the 1st day of January, 2002, and ending before the 1st day of January, 2003, 1 per cent,

to the amount of the company's income for the accounting period as reduced by the appropriate amount.][8]][9]

[(bb) Subject to clause *(c)*, relief for any accounting period beginning on or after the 1st day of January, 2003, shall be an amount determined by the formula—

$$A - B$$

where—

A is the amount of corporation tax which, apart from this paragraph and *section 448*, is chargeable for the accounting period, and

B is the amount of corporation tax which, apart from this paragraph and *section 448*, would be chargeable for the accounting period if the amount of the company's income for the accounting period were reduced by the appropriate amount.][10]

(c) [Notwithstanding clauses *(b)* and *(bb)*][11], where the corporation tax payable by a company for an accounting period is reduced by virtue of a claim under *section 448(2)*, the amount of relief to be allowed under the preceding provisions of this paragraph shall be reduced in the same proportion which the amount by which the corporation tax referable to the income from the sale of goods (within the meaning of *section 448*) for that accounting period is so reduced bears to the relevant corporation tax, and for the purposes of this clause "*relevant corporation tax*" has the same meaning as in *paragraph 16*.

(5) (a) *Subparagraphs (3)* and *(4)* shall not apply to a company which by virtue of agreements between the Government and the Government of the United Kingdom in respect of double income tax was entitled to exemption from income tax for the year 1975-76 in respect of income arising in the State; but in such a case the relevant deficiency shall, subject to *clause (b)*, be set off against income coming within the charge to corporation tax for the accounting period commencing on the 6th day of April, 1976, and, in so far as the relevant deficiency cannot be so set off, it shall be set off against income coming within the charge to corporation tax for the next accounting period and so on.

(b) A relevant deficiency shall not be set off under *clause (a)* against income arising in any accounting period against the profits of which (if the Corporation Tax Act, 1976, had not been enacted and if the enactments in relation to corporation profits tax mentioned in the Third Schedule to that Act had not been repealed) a loss incurred before the 6th day of April, 1976, could not be set off under section 25 of the Finance Act, 1964.

[(6)

[(a) *Subparagraph (6)* of *paragraph 16* shall apply for the purposes of this paragraph as it applies for the purposes of that paragraph.][12]

(i) where an accounting period begins before the 1st day of April, 1997, and ends on or after that day, it shall be divided into one part beginning on the day on which the accounting period begins and ending on the 31st day of March, 1997, and another part beginning on the 1st day of April, 1997, and ending on the day on which the accounting period ends, and both parts shall be treated as if they were separate accounting periods, and

(ii) where an accounting period, including a period treated under *subclause (i)* as an accounting period, begins before the 1st day of January, 1998, and ends on or after that day, it shall be divided into one part beginning on the day on which the accounting period begins and ending on the 31st day of December, 1997, and another part beginning on the 1st day of January, 1998, and ending on the day on which the accounting period ends, and both parts shall be treated as if they were separate accounting periods.][13]

(b) Where under *clause (a)* a part of an accounting period is treated as a separate accounting period, the corporation tax charged for the part which is so treated shall, in so far as it is affected by the rate of corporation tax which is taken to have been charged, be taken for the purposes of this paragraph to be the corporation tax which would have been charged if that part were a separate accounting period.

Capital gains tax losses accruing before 6th April, 1976

[CTA76 s175]

19. Any losses of a company allowable against chargeable gains for the purposes of capital gains tax in respect of the year of assessment 1974-75 or 1975-76, in so far as they cannot be allowed against chargeable gains for the purposes of that tax, shall be treated for the purposes of corporation tax as if they were allowable losses accruing to the company while within the charge to corporation tax.

Income tax: relief for expenditure on certain buildings in certain areas

[FA89 s4(1) to (6); FA93 s31]

20.

(1) Where a person is immediately before the commencement of this Act, entitled to have a deduction made from his or her total income under section 4 of the Finance Act, 1989, he or she shall not cease to be so entitled by reason only of the repeal by this Act of that section, notwithstanding that that section is not re-enacted by this Act, and accordingly this Act shall apply with any modifications necessary to give effect to any such entitlements.

(2) Notwithstanding the repeal by this Act of section 4 of the Finance Act, 1989, relief given under that section, whether before or after the passing of this Act,

may be withdrawn in accordance with subsection (4) of that section where the circumstances set out in that subsection apply; and accordingly this Act shall apply with any modifications necessary to give effect to such withdrawal.

Income tax: relief for income accumulated under trusts

[ITA67 s154; FA73 s5]

21.

(1) Where—

(a) in pursuance of any will or settlement any income arising from any fund is accumulated for the benefit of any person contingently on that person attaining a specified age or marrying, and

(b) the aggregate amount (in this paragraph referred to as "*the aggregate yearly income*") in any year of assessment of—

(i) that income,

(ii) the income from any other fund subject to the like trusts for accumulation, and

(iii) the total income of that person from all sources,

is of such an amount only as would entitle an individual either to total exemption from income tax or to relief from income tax,

then, that person shall, on making a claim for the purpose within 6 years after the end of the year of assessment in which the contingency happens, be entitled, on proof of the claim in the manner prescribed by *subsections (3)* and *(4)* of *section 459* and *paragraph 8* of *Schedule 28*, to have repaid to him or her on account of the income tax which has been paid in respect of the income during the period of accumulation a sum equal to the aggregate amount of relief to which he or she would have been entitled if his or her total income from all sources for each of the several years of that period had been equal to the aggregate yearly income for that year; but in calculating that sum a deduction shall be made in respect of any relief already received.

(2) For the purposes of *subparagraph (1)*, no account shall be taken of any income tax paid in respect of income for a year of assessment beginning after the year 1972-73 or of any relief to which a person would have been entitled for such a year of assessment in the circumstances mentioned in *subparagraph (1)*.

Relief for investment in films in respect of certain sums

[FA96 s31(2)(a), (3) and (4); FA97 s30(2)]

22.

(1) Where an allowable investor company has in the period of 12 months ending on the 22nd day of January, 1997, made a relevant investment, the reference in *section 481(4)* to [€10,157,904.63][14] shall, in respect of that period, be construed as a reference to [€7,618,428.47][15] or, where the company has in that period paid a sum of money to which *subparagraph (2)* applies, as a reference to [€7,618,428.47][16] less the amount or, if there are more amounts than one, the aggregate of such amounts of such sums of money.

(2) The amendments effected to section 35 of the Finance Act, 1987, by section 31(1) of the Finance Act, 1996, shall not apply as respects a sum of money paid on or after the 23rd day of January, 1996, and on or before the 31st day of March, 1996,

where the sum of money is paid in respect of shares in a qualifying company, and—

(a) the Minister for Arts, Culture and the Gaeltacht had received before the 23rd day of January, 1996, an application in writing to give a certificate to the company stating, in relation to a film to be produced by the company, that the film is a qualifying film, and

(b) a certificate given by the Minister to the company after the 23rd day of January, 1996, includes a statement that the Minister had received that application before that date.

(3) Where a sum of money is a sum of money—

(a) to which the amendments effected to section 35 of the Finance Act, 1987, by section 31(1) of the Finance Act, 1996, do not apply by virtue of *subparagraph (2)*, or

(b) which is paid before the 23rd day of January, 1996,

the provisions of section 35 of the Finance Act, 1987, which were in force immediately before the 23rd day of January, 1996, (in this paragraph referred to as "*the former provisions*") shall, subject to *subparagraph (4)*, continue to apply to that sum of money.

(4) Where the sum of money referred to in *subparagraph (3)* is a sum of money paid on or after the 6th day of April, 1995, or is a sum of money to which *subparagraph (2)* applies, and the sum of money is used for the purpose of enabling the qualifying company to produce a qualifying film in respect of which an application (to give a certificate under subsection (1A) of the former provisions) had not been received by the Minister before the 23rd day of January, 1996, the former provisions shall apply as if—

(i) subsection (2) of the former provisions was amended by the substitution for "a deduction of the amount of that investment" of "a deduction of an amount equal to 80 per cent of that investment", and

(ii) subsection (3A) of the former provisions was amended by the substitution for "a deduction of the amount of that investment" of "a deduction of an amount equal to 80 per cent of that investment".

(5) *Subparagraphs (2)* to *(4)* shall apply notwithstanding that the former provisions are not re-enacted by this Act and shall be construed together with the former provisions, and accordingly this Act shall apply with any modifications necessary to give effect to those subparagraphs.

(6) As respects a relevant investment made before the 26th day of March, 1997, *section 481* shall apply as if in *subsection (4)(b)(i)* of that section the reference to [€3,809,214.24][17] were a reference to [€2,539,476.16][18].

(7) As respects the 12 months period ending on the 22nd day of January, 1996, *section 481* shall apply as if in *subsection (4)(b)(ii)* of that section the reference to [€3,809,214.24][19] were a reference to [€2,539,476.16][20].

(8) In relation to a film in respect of which the Minister has received an application before the 26th day of March, 1997, to enable the Minister to consider whether a certificate should be given under *subsection (2)* of *section 481*, that subsection shall apply as if *paragraph (c)(ii)(II)* of that subsection were deleted.

Farming: application of section 658 in relation to expenditure incurred before 27th January, 1994

[FA74 s22(2); FA77 s14; FA82 s16; FA88 s52(1)(a); FA89 s15; FA90 s77; FA91 s25(a)]

23.

(1) *Section 658* shall apply—

(a) as respects capital expenditure incurred before the 27th day of January, 1994, as if the following subsections were substituted for *subsection (2)* of that section:

"(2) (a) Where a person to whom this section applies incurs, for the purpose of a trade of farming land occupied by such person, any capital expenditure on the construction of farm buildings (excluding a building or part of a building used as a dwelling), fences, roadways, holding yards, drains or land reclamation or other works, there shall, subject to *paragraph (b)*, be made to such person during a writing-down period of 10 years beginning with the chargeable period related to that expenditure, writing-down allowances (in this section referred to as "farm buildings allowances") in respect of that expenditure, and such allowances shall be made in taxing the trade.

(b) The farm buildings allowance to be granted for any chargeable period shall, subject to paragraphs (c) and (d), be increased by such amount as is specified in the claim for the allowance by the person to whom the allowance is to be made and, in relation to a case in which this paragraph has applied, any reference in the Tax Acts to a farm buildings allowance made under this section shall be construed as a reference to that allowance as increased under this paragraph.

(c) The maximum farm buildings allowance to be made under this section by means of an allowance increased under *paragraph (b)*—

(i) in relation to capital expenditure incurred before the 1st day of April, 1989, shall not for any chargeable period exceed 30 per cent of that capital expenditure,

(ii) in relation to capital expenditure incurred on or after the 1st day of April, 1989, and before the 1st day of April, 1991, whether claimed in one chargeable period or more than one such period, shall not in the aggregate exceed 50 per cent of that capital expenditure, and

(iii) in relation to capital expenditure incurred on or after the 1st day of April, 1991, and before the 1st day of April, 1992, whether claimed in one chargeable period or more than one such period, shall not in the aggregate exceed 25 per cent of that capital expenditure.

(d) Notwithstanding *paragraph (c)(iii)*, the maximum farm buildings allowances to be made under this section by means of an allowance increased under *paragraph (b)* in relation to capital expenditure incurred—

(i) on or after the 1st day of April, 1991, and before the 1st day of April, 1993,

(ii) for the purposes of the control of farmyard pollution, and

(iii) on works in respect of which grant-aid has been paid under—

(I) the programme, as amended, known as "the Farm Improvement Programme" implemented by the Minister for Agriculture and Food pursuant to Council Regulation (EEC) No. 797/85 of 12 March 1985*, or

* O.J. No. L 93 of 30.3.1985, p.1.

(II) the scheme known as "the Scheme of Investment Aid for the Control of Farmyard Pollution" implemented by the Minister for Agriculture and Food pursuant to an operational programme under Council Regulation (EEC) No. 2052/88 of 24 June 1988*,

* O.J. No. L 185 of 15.7.1988, p.9.

whether claimed for one chargeable period or more than one such period, shall not in the aggregate exceed 50 per cent of that capital expenditure.

(e) The reference in *paragraph (a)* to roadways, holding yards, drains or land reclamation shall apply only as respects expenditure incurred on or after the 1st day of April, 1989.

(2A) (a) For the purposes of this subsection, the first relevant year of assessment in relation to expenditure incurred by any person is—

(i) the year of assessment in the basis period for which that person incurs the expenditure, or

(ii) the year of assessment in the basis period for which (if that person's profits or gains from farming for that year of assessment had been chargeable to tax under Case I of Schedule D) that person incurred the expenditure.

(b) Where any capital expenditure referred to in *subsection (2) (a)* was incurred by a person on or after the 6th day of April, 1971, and before the 6th day of April, 1974, a farm buildings allowance shall for the purposes of this section be deemed—

(i) to have been made to that person, and

(ii) to have been made in charging the profits or gains of the trade for the first relevant year of assessment and for each subsequent year of assessment before the year 1974–75;

but where that expenditure was incurred in the year 1973–74, a farm buildings allowance shall for the purposes of this section be deemed to have been made in charging the profits or gains of the trade for that year of assessment.

(2B) Notwithstanding any other provision of this section other than *subsection (2)(d)*, no farm buildings allowance made in relation to capital expenditure incurred on or after the 1st day of April, 1992, shall be increased under this section.",

and

(b) as respects expenditure incurred before the 6th day of May, 1993, as if the following subsection were substituted for *subsection (13)* of that section:

"(13) Expenditure shall not be regarded for the purposes of this section as having been incurred by a person in so far as it has been met directly or indirectly by the State, by any board established by statute or by any public or local authority."

(2) (a) This subparagraph shall apply to expenditure incurred on the construction of fences, roadways, holding yards or drains or on land reclamation.

(b) Where on or after the 6th day of April, 1977, and before the 1st day of April, 1989, a person to whom *section 658* applies incurs capital expenditure to which this subparagraph applies, being expenditure in respect of which the person is entitled to claim an allowance under that section, the allowance to be granted for the chargeable period related to the expenditure or any subsequent chargeable period shall be increased by such amount as is specified by the person to whom the allowance is to be made in making the person's claim for the allowance, and in relation to a case in which this subsection has applied, any reference in the Tax Acts to a farm buildings allowance made under *section 658* shall be construed as a reference to that allowance as increased under this subparagraph.

Transitional provisions arising from amendments made to the system of taxation of life assurance companies by Finance Act, 1993

[FA93 s12(2)(b)]

24. Notwithstanding *section 713*, where chargeable gains and allowable losses accrued on disposals deemed by virtue of *section 46A* of the Corporation Tax Act, 1976, as applied by section 12(2)(*a*) of the Finance Act, 1993, to have been made by a life assurance company for the accounting period ended on the 31st day of December, 1992, the amount of any fraction of the difference between the aggregate of such chargeable gains and the aggregate of such allowable losses treated by virtue of *section 720* (being the re-enactment of *section 46B* of the Corporation Tax Act, 1976) as a chargeable gain of any accounting period ending on or after the 6th day of April, 1997, shall be deducted from the amount of the unrelieved profits (within the meaning of *section 713*) of that accounting period for the purposes of computing the relief due under *section 713*.

Disposals in the year 1993-94 of units in certain unit trusts

[CGTA75 s31(5); FA94 s64(2)]

25. Where throughout the year of assessment 1993-94 all the assets of a unit trust were assets, whether mentioned in section 19 of the Capital Gains Tax Act, 1975, or in any other provision of that Act, or of any other enactment relating to capital gains tax, to which section 19 of the Capital Gains Tax Act, 1975, applied, the units in the unit trust shall for that year be deemed not to be chargeable assets for the purposes of the Capital Gains Tax Acts.

Application of section 774(6) in certain circumstances

[FA72 s16(4); CTA76 s140(1) and Sch2 PtI par 31]

26. In the case of any employer for a chargeable period, being—

(i) where the chargeable period is an accounting period of a company, an accounting period ending on or before the 21st day of April, 1997, and

(ii) where the chargeable period is a year of assessment, any year of assessment the employer's basis period for which ends on a day after that date,

section 774 shall apply as if the following subsection were substituted for subsection (6) of that section:

"(6) (a) Any sum paid by an employer by means of contributions under the scheme shall—

(i) in the case of income tax, for the purposes of Case I or II of Schedule D, be allowed to be deducted as an expense incurred in the year in which the sum is paid, and

(ii) in the case of corporation tax, for the purposes of Case I or II of Schedule D and the provisions of *sections 83* and *707(4)* relating to expenses of management, be allowed to be deducted as an expense or expense of management incurred in the accounting period in which the sum is paid.

(b) The amount of an employer's contributions which may be deducted under *paragraph (a)* shall not exceed the amount contributed by the employer under the scheme in respect of employees in a trade or undertaking in respect of the profits of which the employer is assessable to income tax or corporation tax, as the case may be.

(c) A sum not paid by means of an ordinary annual contribution shall for the purposes of this subsection be treated, as the Revenue Commissioners may direct, either as an expense incurred in the year or the accounting period, as the case may be, in which the sum is paid, or as an expense to be spread over such period of years as the Revenue Commissioners think proper.".

Settlements: application of section 792 for the year of assessment 1997-98 in relation to certain dispositions to certain individuals residing with, and sharing normal household expenses with, the disponer

[FA95 s13(3)]

27.

(1) Where—

(a) the conditions set out in *subparagraph (3)* are satisfied, and

(b) the Revenue Commissioners are satisfied that the application of the amendments to section 439 of the Income Tax Act, 1967, effected by subsections (1) and (2) of section 13 of the Finance Act, 1995, which subsections are re-enacted in *subsections (1)* and *(2)* of *section 792*, would give rise to hardship,

then, those amendments shall not, to the extent that the Revenue Commissioners consider just, apply before the [6th day of April, 2000]21, in respect of a disposition, to which *clause (a)* of *subparagraph (2)* applies, by a person (in this paragraph referred to as "*the disponer*"), in so far as, by virtue or in consequence of such disposition, income is payable in a year of assessment to or for the benefit of an individual to whom *clause (b)* of *subparagraph (2)* applies, and accordingly, notwithstanding that section 439 of the Income Tax Act, 1967, as it stood before its amendment by subsections (1) and (2) of section 13 the Finance Act, 1995, is not re-enacted by this Act, this Act shall apply with any modifications necessary to give effect to this paragraph.

(2) (a) This clause shall apply to—

(i) a disposition made before the 6th day of April, 1993, or

(ii) a disposition made on or after the 6th day of April, 1993, to immediately replace a disposition made before that date which has ceased to be effective and only to the extent that the amount payable to or for the benefit of an individual to whom *clause (b)* applies under such later disposition does not exceed the amount payable to or for the benefit of that individual under the earlier disposition.

(b) This clause shall apply to an individual who is not a child of the disponer and who, for the whole of the year of assessment, is resident with, and shares the normal household expenses with, the disponer.

(3) The conditions referred to in *subparagraph (1)* are:

(a) the making of the disposition referred to in *subparagraph (2)(a)(i)* shall have been notified to the Revenue Commissioners before the 8th day of February, 1995,

(b) a child, to whom *subparagraph (4)* applies, of the disponer or of the individual to whom *clause (b)* of *subparagraph (2)* applies or of both of them is resident with them for the whole or substantially the whole of the year of assessment, and

(c) the child to whom *clause (b)* relates is wholly or mainly maintained by the disponer and the individual jointly at their own expense.

(4) A child to whom this subparagraph applies shall be a child who for a year of assessment—

(i) is under the age of 16 years, or

(ii) if over the age of 16 years at the commencement of the year of assessment, is receiving full-time instruction at any university, college, school or other educational establishment.

Construction of certain references to Ministers of the Government

28.

(1) Subject to *subparagraphs (2)* and *(3)*, a reference in this Act to a Minister of the Government mentioned in *column (1)* of the Table to this paragraph shall, in

respect of the period from the commencement of this Act to the date mentioned in *column (3)* of that Table opposite that mention in *column (1)*, be construed as a reference to the Minister of the Government mentioned in *column 2)* of that Table opposite that mention in *column (1)*.

(2) A reference in *Chapter 1* of *Part 24* to the Minister for the Marine and Natural Resources shall—

(a) in respect of the period from the commencement of this Act to the 11th day of July, 1997, be construed as a reference to the Minister for Transport, Energy and Communications, and

(b) in respect of the period from the 12th day of July, 1997, to the 14th day of July, 1997, be construed as a reference to the Minister for Public Enterprise.

(3) A reference in *Chapter 2* of *Part 24* to the Minister for the Marine and Natural Resources shall—

(a) in respect of the period from the commencement of this Act to the 11th day of July, 1997, be construed as a reference to the Minister for Transport, Energy and Communications, and

(b) in respect of the period from the 12th day of July, 1997, to the 30th day of September, 1997, be construed as a reference to the Minister for Public Enterprise.

TABLE

(1)	(2)	(3)
Minister for Justice, Equality and Law Reform	Minister for Justice	8th July, 1997
Minister for Health and Children	Minister for Health	11th July, 1997
Minister for Social, Community and Family Afairs	Minister for Social Welfare	11th July, 1997
Minister for Arts, Heritage, Gaeltacht and the Islands	Minister for Arts, Culture and the Gaeltacht	11th July, 1997
Minister for Enterprise, Trade and Employment	Minister for Enterprise and Employment	11th July, 1997
Minister for Tourism, Sport and Recreation	Minister for Tourism and Trade	11th July, 1997
Minister for Agriculture and Food	Minister for Agriculture, Food and Forestry	11th July, 1997
Minister for the Marine and Natural Resources	Minister for the Marine	11th July, 1997
Minister for Public Enterprise	Minister for Transport, Energy and Communications	11th July, 1997
Minister for the Environment and Local Government	Minister for the Environment	21st July, 1997
Minister for Education and Science	Minister for Education	30th September, 1997

Construction of certain references to Government Departments

29. A reference in this Act to a Government Department mentioned in *column (1)* of the Table to this paragraph shall, in respect of the period from the commencement of this Act to the date mentioned in *column (3)* of that Table opposite that mention in *column (1)*, be construed as a reference to the Government Department mentioned in *column (2)* of that Table opposite that mention in *column (1)*.

TABLE

(1)	(2)	(3)
Department of Agriculture and Food	Department of Agriculture, Food and Forestry	11th July, 1997
Department of the Environment and Local Government	Department of the Environment	21st July, 1997

Construction of reference to Secretary General of Department of Finance

30. A reference in this Act to the Secretary General of the Department of Finance shall, in respect of the period from the commencement of this Act to the 31st day of August, 1997, be construed as a reference to the Secretary of the Department of Finance.

Construction of certain references to educational institutions

31. A reference in this Act to an educational institution mentioned in *column (1)* of the Table to this paragraph shall, in respect of the period from the commencement of this Act to the date mentioned in *column (3)* of that Table opposite that mention in *column (1)*, be construed as a reference to the educational institution mentioned in *column (2)* of that Table opposite that mention in *column (1)*.

TABLE

(1)	(2)	(3)
National University of Ireland, Dublin	University College, Dublin	15th June, 1997
National University of Ireland, Cork	University College, Cork	15th June, 1997

Amendments

[1] Deleted by FA00 sched2.

[2] Deleted by FA99 sched1(2)(b). Paragraph 5 shall be deleted with effect from the 6th day of April, 1999.

[3] Deleted by FA99 sched1(2)(d). Paragraph 6 shall be deleted with effect from the 6th day of April, 1999.

[4] Substituted by F(No.2)A08 sched5(part2)(1)(av). The enactments specified in Schedule 5 are amended or repealed to the extent and manner specified in that Schedule and, unless the contrary is stated, shall come into effect after 24 December 2008.

[5] Substituted by FA99 sched1(2)(e)(i).

[6] Substituted by FA99 sched1(2)(e)(ii).

[7] Substituted by FA99 sched1(2)(f)(i)(I).

[8] Substituted by FA99 sched1(2)(f)(i)(II).

[9] Substituted by FA98 sched6(4)(d)(i).

[10] Inserted by FA99 sched1(2)(f)(i)(III).

[11] Substituted by FA99 sched1(2)(f)(i)(IV).

[12] Substituted by FA99 sched1(2)(f)(ii).

[13] Substituted by FA98 sched6(4)(d)(ii).

[14, 15, 16, 17, 18, 19, 20] Substituted by FA01 sched5.

[21] Substituted by FA98 s7.

Revenue Precedents

Whether development of a carpark & shopping area is within meaning of Schedule 32 paragraph 9? Only where a separate contract is negotiated exclusively for carpark facilities would Revenue consider to be within meaning of Schedule 32 paragraph 9.

Cross References

From Schedule 32

Section 36 Government securities.
Section 46A
Section 46B
Section 49 Exemption of certain securities.
Section 83 Expenses of management of investment companies.
Section 128 Tax treatment of directors of companies and employees granted rights to acquire shares or other assets.
Section 147 Distributions.
Section 193 Income from scholarships.
Section 239 Income tax on payments by resident companies.
Section 241 Income tax on payments by non-resident companies.
Section 268 Meaning of "industrial building or structure".
Section 273 Acceleration of writing-down allowances in respect of certain expenditure on certain industrial buildings or structures.
Section 320 Other interpretation (Part 9).
Section 321 Provisions of general application in relation to the making of allowances and charges.
Section 440 Surcharge on undistributed investment and estate income.
Section 441 Surcharge on undistributed income of service companies.
Section 448 Relief from corporation tax.
Section 459 General provisions relating to allowances, deductions and reliefs.
Section 481 Relief for investment in films.
Section 547 Disposals and acquisitions treated as made at market value.
Section 658 Farming: allowances for capital expenditure on construction of buildings and other works.
Section 670 Mine development allowance.
Section 684 Interpretation (Chapter 2).
Section 707 Management expenses.
Section 713 Investment income reserved for policyholders.
Section 720 Gains or losses arising by virtue of section 719.
Section 774 Certain approved schemes: exemptions and reliefs.
Section 792 Income under dispositions for short periods.
Section 1052 Penalties for failure to make certain returns, etc.
Section 1054 Penalties in the case of a secretary of a body of persons.
Section 1077E Penalty for deliberately or carelessly making incorrect returns, etc.
Section 1101 Transitional provisions.
Schedule 28 Statements, Lists and Declarations
Schedule 29 Provisions Referred to in Sections 1052, 1053 and 1054
Schedule 32 Transitional Provisions
Schedule 41

To Schedule 32

Section 144 Distributions out of profits from trading within Shannon Airport.
Section 193 Income from scholarships.
Section 401 Change in ownership of company: disallowance of trading losses.
Section 448 Relief from corporation tax.
Section 458 Deductions allowed in ascertaining taxable income and provisions relating to reductions in tax.
Section 481 Relief for investment in films.
Section 485C Interpretation (Chapter 2A).
Section 658 Farming: allowances for capital expenditure on construction of buildings and other works.
Section 674 Expenditure on abortive exploration.
Section 675 Exploration expenditure incurred by certain bodies corporate.
Section 676 Expenditure incurred by person not engaged in trade of mining.
Section 711 Chargeable gains of life business.
Section 713 Investment income reserved for policyholders.
Section 739 Taxation of unit holders in undertakings for collective investment.
Section 774 Certain approved schemes: exemptions and reliefs.
Section 791 Income under revocable dispositions.

Section 792 Income under dispositions for short periods.
Section 797 Recovery of tax from trustee and payment to trustee of excess tax recoupment.
Section 1013 Limited partnerships.
Section 1024 Method of apportioning reliefs and charging tax in cases of separate assessments.
Section 1101 Transitional provisions.
Schedule 25B List of Specified Reliefs and Method of Determining Amount of Specified Relief Used in a Tax Year
Schedule 25C Determination of Amount of Relief to be Treated as Referable to Specified Reliefs as Respects Relief Carried Forward from Tax Year 2006 to Tax Year 2007
Schedule 32 Transitional Provisions

SCHEDULE 33

Specific Anti-Avoidance Provisions for the Purposes of Part 33

[The following sections shall be specific anti-avoidance provisions for the purposes of Part 33:

Section 381B
Section 381C
Section 546A
Section 590
Section 806
Section 807A
Section 811B
Section 812
Section 813
Section 814
Section 815
Section 816
Section 817
Section 817A
Section 817B
Section 817C][1]

Amendments

[1] Inserted by FA14 s87(1)(d). Comes into effect as and from 23 October 2014.

TABLE OF CASES

ABBREVIATIONS

ITR = Irish Tax Reports
IR = Irish Reports
KB = King's Bench
QB = Queen's Bench
STC = Simon's Tax Cases
SpC = UK Special Commissioner
TC = Official Tax Case Reports
WLR = Weekly Law Reports

All references to sections or schedules in Taxes Consolidation Act 1997

Case	**Case Reference**	**Section**
A & B v WJ Davies (Inspector of Taxes)	1942 II ITR 60	s941
Aberdeen Construction Group Ltd v IRC	1978 STC 127	s541
Able (UK) Ltd v Revenue & Customs Commissioners	2007 STC 1738	s18, s65
Action Aid v Revenue Commissioners	1997 V ITR 392	s792
Albert Harding and others v O'Cahill	1990 IV ITR 233	s123
Algemene Maatschappij voor Investering en Dienstverlening NV v Belgian State	2003 STC 356	s412
Allchin v Corporation of South Shields	25 TC 445	s237
Allen v Farquharson Bros & Co	1932 17 TC 59	s81
Allen v IRC	1995 STC 945	s112
Alliance & Dublin Consumers Gas Co v McWilliams	1927 I ITR 207	s65
American Thread Co v Joyce	1913 6 TC 163	s23A
Attwood (HMIT) v Anduff Car Wash Ltd	1997 STC 1167	s284
AW Chapman Ltd v Hennessy	1982 STC 214	s429
Ayerst v C & K (Construction) Ltd	1975 STC 1	s9
Bairead v Carr	1993 IV ITR 505	s943
Bank of Ireland Finance Ltd v Revenue Commissioners	1989 IV ITR 217	s537, s980
Barclays Mercantile Industrial v Melluish	1990 STC 314	s312
Barnett v Brabyn	1996 STC 716	s112
Batey v Wakefield	1981 STC 326	s604
Beatty's Exors v IRC	TC 574	s806
Bedford (Collector General) v H	1968 II ITR 588	s996
Begg MacBrearty v Stilwell (Trustee of the Croke Settlement)	1996 STC 413	s576
Beirne v St Vincent de Paul Society, Wexford	1932 1 ITR 388	s208
Bennett v Revenue & Customs Commissioners	2007 SpC 576	s114
Benson v Yard Arm Club	1979 STC 266	s284
Bentley v Pike	1981 STC 360	s552
Berry v Warnett	1980 STC 504	s796
Bestway (Holdings) Ltd v Luff (HM Inspector of Taxes)	1998 STC 357	s268
Bird v Martland	1982 STC 603	s112
Birmingham District Cattle By-Products Co Ltd v IRC	1919 12 TC 92	s66

Case	Case Reference	Section
Bolands Ltd v Davis	1 ITC 91	s396
Bond v Pickford	1983 STC 517	s567
Booth v Mirror Group of Newspapers plc	1992 STC 615	s983
Boothe v Ellard	1980 I WLR 1443	s567
Bourne & Hollingsworth Ltd v Ogden	1929 14 TC 349	s81
Bourne v Auto School of motoring (Norwich)	42 TC 217	s373
Brennan v Deanby Investment Co	2001 STC 536	s438
Brightwater Selection [Ireland] Ltd v Minister for Social and Family Affairs	2011 IEHC 510	s18, s112
British Basic Slag Ltd's Application	1963 WLR 727	s427
British Railways Board v Franklin	1993 STC 487	s985
Brosnan v Leeside Nurseries Ltd	1997 V ITR 21	s443
Brown v Bullock	40 TC 1	s114
Browne & Ors v The Revenue Commissioners & Ors	1991 IV ITR 323	s121
Bullivant Holdings v IRC	1998 STC 905	s547
Bullock v Unit Construction Co Ltd	1959 38 TC 712	s23A
Burnham (Inspector of Taxes) v Westminster Press Ltd	1982 STC 669	s603
Burt & Co v CIR	1919 KB 650	s441
Cadbury Schweppes Plc & Another v Inland Revenue Commissioners	2006 STC 1908	s446
Cairns v MacDiarmid	56 TC 556	s246
California Copper Syndicate v Harris	1904 5 TC 159	s18, s65
Carlisle & Silloth Golf Club v Smith	1913 6 TC 198	s18, s65
Carroll Industries plc (Formerly PJ Carroll & Co Ltd) and PJ Carroll & Co Limited v S Ó'Culacháin (Inspector of Taxes)	1988 IV ITR 135	s18
Carstairs (HMIT) v Sykes	2000 STC 1103	s823
Carver v Duncan	1985 STC 356	s805
Carvill v IRC	2002 STC 1167	s806
Casey v Monteagle estate Co v Davis	1962 3 ITC 313	s82
Cassell v Crutchfiled	1995 STC 663	s933
Cecil v CIR	1919 TLR 164	s441
Cenlon Finance Co Ltd v Ellwood	40 TC 176	s924
Chetwode v IRC	1977 STC 64	s806
Chetwode v IRC	1974 STC 474	s807
Christopher Barker & Sons v CIR	1919 KB 222	s441
CHW (Huddersfield) Ltd v CIR	41 TC 92	s441
CIR v Challenge Corporation	1986 STC 548	s811
CIR v Duncan Hay	8 TC 686	s246
CIR v Maxse	1919 12 TC 41	s441
CIR v North and Ingram	1918 KB 705	s441
CIR v Shroder	1983 STC 480	s806
CIR v Tyre Investment Trust Ltd	1924 12 TC 646	s82
CIR v Wattie and anor	1998 STC 1160	s18

Case	Case Reference	Section
Clarke(HMIT) v British Telecom Pension Scheme Trustees and others	2000 STC 222	s774
Collins v Fraser	46 TC 143	s232
Colquhoun v Brooks	1889 2 TC 490	s18
Colquhoun v R&C Commrs	2010 UKUT (TCC) 431	s123
Compagnie de Saint-Gobain, Zweignierderlassung Deutschland and Finanzamt Aachen-Onenstadt	2000 STC 855	s826
Connolly v McNamara	3 ITC 341	s112
Cook (HM Inspector of Taxes) v Billings & Ors	2001 STC 61	s493
Cook v Medway Housing Society Ltd	1997 STC 90	s82
Cooke v Beach Caravans Ltd	1974 STC 402	s284
Copeman v Coleman	1939 22 TC 594	s796
Corinthian Securities Ltd v Cato	46 TC 93	s246
Couch v Caton's Administrators	1996 STC 201	s552
Criminal Assets Bureau v D (K)	2002 VI ITR 445	s933
Criminal Assets Bureau v Hutch	1999 VI ITR 125	s955
Criminal Assets Bureau v P McS	2001 VI ITR 421	s933
Criminal Assets Bureau v PS	High Court 2004	s954
Criminal Assets Bureau v Sean and Rosaleen Hunt (nee) Maher	2003 VI ITR 559	s933
Cronin (Inspector of Taxes) v Cork and County Property Company Ltd	1986 III ITR 198	s18
Cronin (Inspector of Taxes) v Strand Dairy Ltd	1985 III ITR 441	s443
Cronin (Inspector of Taxes) v Youghal Carpets (Yarns) Limited	1985 III ITR 229	s411
Currie v CIR	1921 TC 245	s441
Cyril Lord Carpets v Schofiled	42 TC 637	s317
D Ua Clothasaignh (Inspector of Taxes) v Patrick McCann	1947 II ITR 75	s461
D'Ambrumenil v IRC	1940 TC 440	s791
Davenport v Chilver	1983 STC 426	s535
Davenport v Hasslacher	1997 STC 254	s598
Davies v Braithwaite	1931 18 TC 198	s112, s441
Davies v Superioress, Mater Misericordiae Hospital, Dublin	1933 1 ITR 387	s208
Davis v Powell	1977 STC 32	s535
Dawsongroup Ltd v R & C Commrs	2010 EWHC 1061 (Ch)	s83
de Beers Consolidated Mines v Unit Construction Co Ltd	1906 5 TC 198	s23A
Deutsche Morgan Grenfell Group plc v Attorney General	2005 STC 329	s865
Dillen v Kearns	1993 IV ITR 547	s540
Director of Public Prosecutions v Downes	1987 III ITR 641	s986
Dixon v Fitches Garage	1975 STC 480	s284
Dolan (Inspector of Taxes) v "K" National School Teacher	1943 I ITR 656	s112
Donovan (Inspector of Taxes) v CG Crofts	1926 I ITR 115	s461
Doyle v Davison	40 TC 140	s118
DPP v George Redmond	3 IR 390	s951

Case	Case Reference	Section
Dreyfus Foundation Inc v IRC	1955 36 TC 126	s207
DTE Financial Services Ltd v Wilson	1999 STC 1061	s811
Dunnes Stores (Oakville) Ltd v McCronin (Inspector of Taxes)	1988 IV ITR 68	s284
Durant v CIR	1921 TC 245	s441
Eagles v Levy	19 TC 23	s114
Earlspring Properties v Guest	1995 STC 479	s438
Edwards v Clinch	1980 STC 438	s19, s112
EG v MacSamhrain	1957 II ITR 352	s792, s794
Egyptian Delta Land and Investment Co Ltd v Todd	1928 14 TC 119	s23A
Elliss v BP Northern Ireland Refinery Ltd; Elliss v BP Tyne Tanker Co Ltd	1987 STC 52	s307
EMI Group Electronics v Coldicott	1997 STC 1372	s112, s123
Emms v Revenue and Customs Commissioners	2008 STC (SCD) 618	s114
English Crown Spelter Co Ltd v Baker	1908 5 TC 327	s81
Erichsen v Last	1881 4 TC 422	s18
Ex parte the debtor v IRC	1992 STC 751	s869
Fall v Hitchen	1972 49 TC 433	s112
Falmer Jeans Ltd v Rodin	1990 STC 270	s400
Farmer v Bankers Trust International Ltd	1990 STC 564	s429
Fawcett v Special Commissioners & Lancaster Farmer's Auction Mart Co Ltd	1995 STC 61	s890
FCT v Peabody	94 ATC 4663	s811
Fennessy (Inspector of Taxes) v John McConellogue	1995 V ITR 129	s461
Fielder v Vedlynn	1992 STC 553	s563
Figael Ltd v Minister Fox	1992 STC 83	s985
First Nationwide v Commissioners for HMRC	2010 UKFTT 24 TC	s130
FKP Konzertproduktionen GmBH v Finanzamt Hamburg-Eimsbuttell	C290/04	s826
Fletcher (Inspector of Taxes) v Thompson and anor	2002 STC 1149	s499
Floor v Davis	1979 STC 379	s543
Flynn v Noone Ltd	1953 II ITR 222	s98
Fragmap Developments v Cooper	44 TC 366	s82
Frampton and Another v IRC	1985 STC 186	s567
Francis Griffin v Minister for Social, Community and Family Affairs	2001 VI ITR 371	s1007
Fuge v Mc Clelland	36 TC 571	s112
Gaines-Cooper v R&C Commrs	2011 UKSC 47	s819, s820
Garner v Pounds	1999 STC 18	s540
Gascoines Group Ltd v Inspector of Taxes	2004 STC 844	s432
George Humphries & Co v Cook	19 TC 191	s400
Girobank plc v Clarke (HM Inspector of Taxes)	1998 STC 182	s268
Girvan v Orange Personal Communications Services	1985 STC 567	s70
Glaxo Group v IRC	1996 STC 191	s934

Case	Case Reference	Section
Glenboig Union Fireclay Company Ltd	1921 12 TC 427	s535
Goodbrand v Loffland Bros North Sea	1998 STC 930	s563
Goodwin v Curtis	1998 STC 475	s604
Gordon & Blair Ltd v IRC	1962 40 TC 358	s67, s396
Gormley v EMI Records	1998 ILRM 124	s195
Goslings & Sharpe v Blake	2 TC 450	s246
Gower Chemicals Ltd v Revenue and Customs Commissioners	2008 STC 1242	s865
Graham v Green	1925 TC 309	s441
Grant v Watton	1999 STC 330	s438
Gray v Seymour Garden Centre	1995 STC 706	s284
Great Western Railway v Bater	1922 8 TC 231	s19, s112
Greenfields v Bains	1992 STC 746	s438
Guinness & Mahon Limited v Browne (Inspector of Taxes)	1985 III ITR 373	s18
Gurney v Richards	1989 STC 682	s373
Hall v Lorimer	1994 STC 23	s112
Hammond Lane Metal Co Ltd v O'Culachain	1989 IV ITR 197	s924
Harmel v Wright	1974 49 TC 149	s71
Harper v R&C Commrs	2009 TC 00317	s538
Harris v Quigley & Irwin	2005 VI ITR 839	s934, s941, s942
Harvey v Williams	1995 STC 329	s122
Hayes v Duggan	1929 I ITR 195	s58
Healy v Breathnach	1986 III ITR 496	s195
Hearne v O'Cionna	1988 IV ITR 113	s983
Henry Denny & Sons v Minister for Social Welfare	1997 V ITR 283	s112
Herbet Smith v Honour	1999 STC 173	s81
Herdman v IRC	1969 45 TC 394	s806
HF Kelly (Inspector of Taxes) v H	II ITR 460	s114
HH v MJ Forbes (Inspector of Taxes)	1974 II ITR 614	s18, s65
Hibernian Insurance Company Ltd v MacUimis	2000 V ITR 495	s81, s82
Hillyer v Leeke	1976 STC 490	s114
Hood Barrs v IRC	1945 TC 385	s796
Horner v Hasted	1995 STC 766	s1007
Horner v Madden	1995 STC 802	s879
Howell and Anor v Trippier (Inspector of Taxes)	2004 STC 1245	s805
Howth Estate Co v Davis	1934 21 TC 74	s82
Hughes v Smyth (Sister Mary Bernard)	1932 I ITR 411	s791
Hurley v Taylor (Inspector of Taxes)	1998 STC 202	s941
Hussey v M.J. Gleeson & Co Ltd	1993 IV ITR 533	s443
Imperial Chemical Industries plc v Colmer (Inspector of Taxes)	1999 STC 1089	s411
In Commercial Union Assurance Co plc v Shaw (HM Inspector of Taxes)	1999 STC 109	s396

Case	Case Reference	Section
Incorporated Council of Law Reporting for England and Wales v AG	3 All ER 1029	s207
Inspector of Taxes v Arida Ltd	1996 IV ITR 401	s942
IRC v Botnar	1999 STC 711	s806
IRC v Buchanan	37 TC 365	s433
IRC v Carron Co	45 TC 18	s81
IRC v Fraser	24 TC 498	s18
IRC v John Lewis Properties plc	2001 STC 1118	s18, s75
IRC v Lebus' Executors	1946 27 TC 136	s1007
IRC v Livingston	11 TC 538	s18
IRC v Luke	40 TC 630	s118
IRC v Mardon	1956 TC 565	s802
IRC v Old Bushmills Distillery Co Ltd	1928 12 TC 1148	s18, s65
IRC v Pratt	1982 STC 756	s806
IRC v Scott Adamson	17 TC 679	s382
IRC v Scottish and Newcastle Breweries Limited	1982 STC 296	s284
IRC v St Luke's Hostel Trustee	1930 TC 682	s792
IRC v Trustees of the Sema Group Pension Scheme	2002 STC 276	s811
Irish Agricultural Machinery Ltd v S O'Culachain (Inspector of Taxes)	1989 III ITR 611	s443
IT Comrs v Pemsel	1891 3 TC 53	s207
J Bibby & Sons Ltd v CIR	29 TC 167	s433
Jacques v Revenue & Customs Commissioners (No 2)	2007 STC 166	s900
Jaggers v Ellis	1996 SpC 98	s232
Jarrold (HM Inspector of Taxes) v John Good & Sons Limited	1962 40 TC 681	s284
Jarrold v Boustead	41 TC 701	s112
JB O'C v PCD and Anor	1984 III ITR 153	s908
Jeffs v Ringtons Ltd	1985 STC 809	s81
Jenkinson (HM Inspector of Taxes) v Freedland	1961 39 TC 636	s18
Johnson v IRC	1996 STI 270	s905
Johnson v Walden	1996 STC 124	s933
Joint v Bracken Developments Ltd	1994 STC 300	s438
Kealy v O'Mara	1942 1 ITR 642	s81
Kelly (Inspector of Taxes) v Cobb Straffan Ireland Ltd	1993 IV ITR 526	s443
Kelsall v Investment Chartwork Ltd	1994 STC 33	s774
Kennedy v Hearne and Ors	1988 III ITR 590	s989
Kennerley v Revenue & Customs Commissioner	2007 SpC 578	s889, s933
Keogh v Criminal Assets Bureau, Revenue Commissioners	2003 VI ITR 635	s933
Kevin McGarry (Inspector of Taxes) v Harding (Lord Edward St.) Properties Ltd	2004 IEHC 131	s268
Kidson v MacDonald & Another	1974 STC 54	s567
King v United Kingdom (No 3)	2005 STC 438	s942
Kinsella v The Revenue Commissioners	2007 ITR 151	s828

Case	Case Reference	Section
Kirby v Hughes	1993 STC 77	s18
Kirby v Thorn EMI plc	1987 STC 621	s532
Kirkshell Timber Ltd v Revenue & Customs Commissioners	2006 SpC 559	s983
Kirkwood v Evans	2002 STC 231	s114
Kneen v Martin	19 TC 33	s71
Koenigsberger v Mellor	1995 STC 547	s783
Kofoed v Skatteministeriet – Case C 321/05	2008 STC 1202	s631
Lang v Rice	1984 STC 172	s535
Latilla v IRC	1943 TC 107	s806
Laylock v Freeman Hardy & Wlillis Ltd	22 TC 288	s400
Lee v IRC	1941 TC 207	s806
Leedale v Lewis	1982 STC 169	s579
Lion v Inspector of Taxes	1997 SpC 115	s623
Lloyds UDT Finance Ltd v Chartered Finance Trust Holdings plc and Others	2002 STC 956	s377
Loffland Bros North Sea Inc v Goodbrand	1977 STC 102	s552
Loss v CIR	1945 ER 683	s441
Lyon v Pettigrew	1985 STC 369	s542
M Cronin (Inspector of Taxes) v Lunham Brothers Ltd	1985 III ITR 363	s66, s401
M Deighan v E Hearne and Others	1986 III ITR 533	s459, s870, s933
Mac Giolla Mhaith (Inspector of Taxes) v Cronin & Associates Ltd	1984 III ITR 211	s441
Mac Mathuna v Ireland and the Attorney General	1994 SC	s461
Macken v Revenue Commissioners	1962 IR 302	s1007
MacKeown (Inspector of Taxes) v Patrick J Ros	1927 I ITR 214	s19
Maco Door & Window Hardware (UK) Ltd v Revenue and Customs Commissioners	2008 STC 2594	s268
Madeley and another v Revenue and Customs Commissioner	2006 SpC 547	s114
Madigan & Madigan v AG	1984 III ITR 127	s806
Mairs v Haughey	1992 STC 495	s118
Makins v Elson	1977 STC 46	s604
Mallalieu v Drummond	1983 STC 665	s81
Market Investigations v Minister of Social Security	1969 2 QB 173	s112
Marks & Spencer plc v Halsey	C-446/03	s411, s420
Marren v Ingles	1980 STC 500	s532
Marson v Marriage	1980 STC 177	s563
Martin v Lowry	1926 11 TC 297	s18
McCausland v Ministry of Commerce	1956 NIRC 36	s443
McDermott v Loy	TL 118 (HC July 1982)	s112
McGarry v Limerick Gas Co	1 ITR 375	s81
McGuckian v CIR	1997 STC 908	s806
McGurrin v The Champion Publications Ltd	1993 IV ITR 466	S443, s448

Case	Case Reference	Section
McKinney (HMIT) v Hagan Caravans Manufacturing Ltd	1997 STC 1023	s317
McLoughlin & Tuite v The Revenue Commissioners and The Attorney General	1986 III ITR 387	s1052
McLoughlin v Director of Public Prosecutions	1986 III ITR 467	s112
McManus v Griffiths	1997 STC 1089	s18
McMenamin v Diggles	1991 STC 419	s19
Melbarien Enterprises v Revenue Commissioners	1985 III ITR 290	s851
Mellor v Gurney	1994 STC 1025	s941
Menolly Homes Limited v The Appeal Commissioners & Anor	2010 IEHC 49	s933, s934
Metal products Ltd (in receivership) v Hearn	1988 High Court	s851
Mhic Mhathuna v Ireland	1995 ILRM 69	s462, s465
Michael Daly v The Revenue Commissioners, Ireland and the Attorney General	1995 V ITR 213	s520
Ministere des Finances v Weidert and Paulas	2004 C-242/03	s495
Monro v Revenue & Customs Commissioners	2008 STC 1815	s865
Mooney v McSweeney	1997 V ITR 163	s541
Morgan v Tate & Lyle Ltd	1954 35 TC 367	s81
Muir v CIR	1966 TC 367	s941
Murgatroyd v Evans Jackson	1966 43 TC 581	s81
Murnaghan Bros v J O Maoldhomhnaigh (Inspector of Taxes)	1990 IV ITR 304	s18
Murphy (Inspector of Tax) v Asahi Synthetic Fibres (Ireland) Ltd	1986 IR 777	s826
Murphy V Dataproducts (Dublin) Ltd	1988 IV ITR 12	s25
Murphy v The Attorney General	1980 V ITR 613	s1015
N Cohan's Executors v IRC	12 TC 602	s18, s65
NAP Holdings UK Ltd v Whittles	1994 STC 979	s584
National Westminister Bank plc v IRC	1994 STC 580	s489
Naval Colliery Co Ltd v IRC	1928 12 TC 1017	s81
Navan Carpets Ltd v O'Culachain	III ITR 403	s382
Neenan Travel Limited v Minister for Social and Family Affairs	2011 IEHC 458	s18, s112
Noddy Subsidiary Rights Co. Ltd	1966 43 TC 458	s18
Norman v Golder	1944 25 TC 293	s81
Nuclear Electric plc v Bradley	1979 STC 750	s18
O'Brien v Benson's Hosiery (Holdings) Ltd	1979 STC 735	s532
O'Connor v Coady	2004 IESC 54	s542
O'Callaghan v Clifford & Ors	1993 IV ITR 478	S864, s1052
O'Cleirigh (Inspector of Taxes) v Jacobs International Ltd	1985 III ITR 165	s18, s65
O'Coindealbhain v Mooney	1988 IV ITR 45	s112
O'Connaill (Inspector of Taxes) v Waterford Glass	1983 III ITR 65	s268
O'Culachain v Hunter Advertising Ltd	1988 IV ITR 35	s442, s443
O'Culachain v McMullan Bros	1995 V ITR 200	s284
O'Dwyer v Irish Exporters and Importers Ltd (in liquidation)	1942 I ITR 629	s941
O'Laochdha v Johnson & Johnson Ireland Ltd	1991 IV ITR 361	s443

Case	Case Reference	Section
O'Rourke v The Appeal Commissioners	2010 IEHC 264	s933, s942, s955
O'Srianain v Lakeview Ltd	1984 III ITR 219	s942
O'Sullivan v O'Connor	1947 II ITR 61	s71
Ogden v Medway Cinemas	1934 18 TC 691	s81
Ogilive v Kitton	1908 5 TC 338	s18
Oram v Johnson	1980 STC 222	s552
Orange v The Revenue Commissioners	1994 V ITR 70	s1002
P O'Muircheasa v Bailey Wastepaper Ltd	2003 VI ITR 579	s443
Palmer v Moloney and anor	1999 STC 890	s598
Pandion Haliaetus Limited Ospreycare Ltd, Osprey Systems Design Ltd v The Revenue Commissioners	1987 III ITR 670	s852
Patrick J O'Connell (Inspector of Taxes) v Tara Mines	2002 VI ITR 523	s444
Patrick J O'Connell (Inspector of Taxes) v Fyffes Banana Processing Ltd	2000 VI ITR 131	s443
Patrick Monahan (Drogheda) Limited v O'Connell (Inspector of Taxes)	1987 III ITR 661	s268
Pattison v Marine Midland Ltd	1984 STC 10	s79
Pegler v Abell	1975 STC 23	s783
Pepper v Hart	1993 1 AL ER 42	s119
Petch v Gurney	1994 STC 689	s941
Pharmaceutical Society of Ireland v Revenue Commissioners	1938 1 ITR 542	s207
Pilkington v IRC	1982 STC 103	s424
Pobjoy Mint Ltd v Lane	1984 STC 327	s401
Pook v Owen	45 TC 571	s114
Pritchard v Arundale	1971 47 TC 680	s112, s123
Property Loan and Investment Company Ltd v Revenue Commissioners	1945 II ITR 25	s65
Prudential plc & Anor, R (on the application of) v Special Commissioner of Income Tax & Anor	2013 UKSC 1	s817H
Purchase v Tesco Stores Ltd	1984 STC 304	s401
Pyrah v Annis	37 TC 163	s81
Quigley v Burke	1995 V ITR 265	s886, s900
R (on the application of Cook) v General Commissioners of Income Tax & Another	2007 STC 499	s956
R v Dimsey and Allen	1999 STC 846	s806
R v Inland Revenue Commissioners, ex parte Commerzbank AG	1993 STC 605	s411
R v IR Commissioners ex parte Newfields Developments Ltd	2000 STC 52	s432
R v IRC (ex parte Roux Waterside Inn Ltd)	1997 STC 781	s772
R v IRC ex parte Ulster Bank Ltd	1997 STC 832	s900
R v IRC, ex parte Caglar	1995 STC 741	s933
R v IRC, ex parte Unilever plc	1996 STC 681	s396
Rahinstown Estates Co v M Hughes (Inspector of Taxes)	1976 III ITR 517	s441
Ramsden v IRC	1957 TC 619	s806
Ransom v Higgs	1974 STC 539	s18

Case	Case Reference	Section
Ready Mixed Concrete (SE) Ltd v Minister of Pensions and National Insurance	1968 2 QB 497	s112
Reed v Nova Securities	1985 STC 724	s18
Revenue and Customs Commissioners v Decadt	2008 STC 1103	s114
Revenue Commissioners v HI	1984 III ITR 242	s792
Revenue Commissioners v O'Flynn Construction & Ors	2011 IESC 47	s811
Revenue Commissioners v ORMG	1982 III ITR 28	s806
Revenue Commissioners v Sisters of Charity of the Incarnate Word	1998 VI ITR 7	s207
Revenue Commissioners v Wen-Plast (Research & Development) Ltd	2007 IEHC 66	s141, s234
Richart v Bass Holdings Ltd	1993 STC 122	s933
Ricketts v Colquhoun	10 TC 118	s114
Rigby v Jayatilaka (HM Inspector of Taxes)	2000 STC 179	s956
Rigby v Samson (HM Inspector of Taxes)	1997 STC 524	s382
Roche v Kelly	1968 IR 100	s112
Rolls Royce Motors Ltd v Bamford	1976 STC 162	s67, s400
Saatchi & Saatchi Advertising Ltd v McGarry (Inspector of Taxes)	1996 V ITR 376	s442, s448
Sainsbury plc v O'Connor (Inspector of Taxes)	1991 STC 318	s412, s417
San Paulo (Brazilian) Railway Company v Carter	1896 3 TC 407	s18
Sarsfield (HM Inspector of Taxes) v Dixons Group plc and related appeals	1998 STC 938	s268
Schutdenfrei v Hilton	1998 STC 404	s933
Seldon v Croom-Johnson	1932 TC 740	s441
Shadford v Fairweather	1966 43 TC 291	s18
Shepherd v Law Land plc	1990 STC 795	s424
Shepherd v Revenue & Customs Commissioners	2006 SpC 484	s819
Shilton v Wilmshurst	1991 STC 88	s112
Shortt v McIlgorm	26 TC 262	s114
Shove (Inspector of Taxes) v Lingfield Park 1991 Ltd	2004 STC 805	s284
Smith Barry v Cordy	28 TC 250	s18
Sokoya v Revenue & Customs Commissioners	2008 STC 51	s899
Southern v Aldwych Property Trust Ltd	1940 23 TC 707	s82
Southern v Borax Consolidated	1940 23 TC 597	s81
Spa Estates v O'hArgain	1975 HC	s18
Spectros International plc v Madden	1997 STC 114	s547
Sports Club and others v Inspector of Taxes	2000 STC 443	s112
Steele v EVC	1996 STC 785	s10
Stephen Court Ltd v Browne	1983 V ITR 680	s97
Stephens v T Pittas Ltd	1983 STC 576	s122, s438
Stokes v Costain Property Investments Ltd	1984 STC 204	s317
Sugar Distributors Ltd	1996 ILRM 339	s443
Sutherland & Partners' v Barnes	1993 STC 399	s941

Case	Case Reference	Section
Swedish Central Railway Co Ltd v Thompson	1925 9 TC 342	s23A
Tanfield v Carr	1999 STC (SCD) 213	s65
Tapemaze Ltd v Melluish (HM Inspector of Taxes)	2000 STC 189	s18, s65
Tapper v Eyre	43 TC 720	s373
Tarmac Roadstone Holdings Ltd v Williams	1996 SpC 409	s541
Taylor v Bratherton	2004 SpC 448	s900
Taylor v Taylor	1937 3 All ER 571	s237
Templeton V Jacobs	1996 STC 991	s118
Tenbry Investments Ltd v Peugeot Motor Co Ltd	1992 STC 791	s238
Tennant v Smith	1892 3 TC 158	s112
Tesco plc v Crimmin	1997 STC 981	s621
Teward v IRC	2001 STC 36	s112
Texaco (Ireland) Ltd v Murphy	1992 IV ITR 91	s763
The City of Limerick VEC v Lucy Carr and the Revenue Commissioners	2001 High Court	s997
The Executors and Trustees of AC Ferguson (deceased) v Donovan (Inspector of Taxes)	1927 I ITR 183	s1034
The State v Michael Smidic (Appeal Commissioners)	1938 I ITR 571	s933
The Trustees of the Ward Union Hunt Races v Hughes	1937 I ITR 538	s215
Thomas v R Evans & Co Ltd	11 TC 790	s81
Thomas v Reynolds	1988 STC 135	s284
Thompson (HMIT) v Hart	2000 STC 381	s489
Tierney v An Post	2000 1 IR 536	s112
Tod v South Essex Motors	1988 STC 392	s933
Training Consultant v Revenue & Customs Commissioners	2007 STC SCD	s826
Trustees of Omega Group Pension Scheme v IRC	2001 STC 121	s811
Turvey v Dentons Ltd	1952 2 ALL ER 1025	s237
Unit Corporation Ltd v IRC	34 TC 269	s23A
Van den Berghs Limited v Clark (H.M. Inspector of Taxes)	1935 19 TC 390	s18
Varty v Lyons	1976 STC 508	s604
Venables and others v Hornby	2004 STC 84	s770
Vestey V IRC	1980 STC 10	s806
Vestey's Executors v IRC	31 TC 1	s806
Vibroplant v Holland (H. M. Inspector of Taxes)	1981 54 TC 548	s268
W Ltd v Wilson	1974 II ITR 627	s924
Wain v Cameron	1995 STC 555	s18
Walker (HMIT) v Centaur Clothes Group	2000 STC 324	s27
Walker v Joint Credit Card Co	1982 STC 427	s81
Walsh v National Irish Bank	2013 IESC 2	s908
Warren v Warren	1895 72 LT 628	s237
Wase v Bourke	1996 STC 18	s598
Watney Combe Reid & Co Ltd v Pike	1982 STC 733	s81
Watson Bros v Lothian	1902 4 TC 441	s69

Case	Case Reference	Section
Wayte (Holdings) Ltd (in receivership) Alex Burns v Edward N Hearne	1986 III ITR 553	s26, s919
Wicks v Firth	1984 56 TC 318	s118, s193
Wild v Cannavan (HMIT)	1997 STC 966	s493
Wilkins v Rogerson	39 TC 44	s112
Williams v Bullivant	1983 STC 107	s538
Williams v Todd	1988 STC 676	s122
Willingale v Islington Green Investment Co	48 TC 547	s433
Willis v Peeters Picture Frames Ltd	1983 STC 453	s401
Willoughby v IRC	1997 STC 995	s806
Wing v O'Connell	1 ITC 170	s112
Wisdom v Chamberlain (H.M. Inspector of Taxes)	1969 45 TC 92	s18
Wood Preservation Ltd v Prior	45 TC 112	s411
Xi Software Ltd v Laing (Inspector of Taxes)	2004 SpC 450	s438
Young Austen v Dunstan	1989 STC 69	s584
Young v Pearce	1996 STC 73	s5
Zim Properties Ltd v Proctor	1985 STC 90	s532

SUBJECT INDEX

Taxes Consolidation Act 1997

ABBREVIATIONS
CGT = Capital Gains Tax
CT = Corporation Tax
DIRT = Deposit Interest Retention Tax
DWT = Dividend Withholding Tax
IT = Income Tax

D

G

H

M

S

V

Y